CANADIAN ALMANAC & DIRECTORY

RÉPERTOIRE ET ALMANACH CANADIEN

2017

Additional Publications

For more detailed information or to place an order, see the back of the book.

CANADIAN WHO'S WHO 2017

Approx. 1,400 pages, 8 3/8 x 10 7/8, Hardcover
December 2016
ISBN 978-1-68217-212-4
ISSN 0068-9963
Published for over 100 years, this authoritative annual publication offers access to over 10,000 notable Canadians in all walks of life, including details such as date and place of birth, education, family details, career information, memberships, creative works, honours, languages, and awards, together with full addresses. Included are outstanding Canadians from business, academia, politics, sports, the arts and sciences, and more, selected because of the positions they hold in Canadian society, or because of the contributions they have made to Canada.

FINANCIAL POST DIRECTORY OF DIRECTORS 2017
Répertoire des administrateurs

1,363 pages, 5 7/8 x 9, Hardcover
70th Edition, September 2016
ISBN 978-1-68217-396-1
ISSN 0071-5042
Published biennially and annually since 1931, this comprehensive resource offers readers access to approximately 16,300 executive contacts from Canada's top 1,400 corporations. The directory provides a definitive list of directorships and offices held by noteworthy Canadian business people, as well as details on prominent Canadian companies (both public and private), including company name, contact information and the names of executive officers and directors. Includes all-new front matter and three indexes.

GOVERNMENTS CANADA SUMMER/FALL 2016
Gouvernements du Canada

1,476 pages, 8 ½ x 11, Softcover
Summer/Fall 2016
ISBN 978-1-61925-967-6
ISSN 1493-3918
Governments Canada provides a solution to finding the departments and people that you are searching for within our federal and provincial political system.

FINANCIAL SERVICES CANADA 2016-2017
Services financiers au Canada

1,608 pages, 8 ½ x 11, Softcover
19th edition, May 2016
ISBN 978-1-61925-959-1
ISSN 1484-2408
This directory of Canadian financial institutions and organizations includes banks and depository institutions, non-depository institutions, investment management firms, financial planners, insurance companies, accountants, major law firms, government and regulatory agencies, and associations. Fully indexed.

ASSOCIATIONS CANADA 2016
Associations du Canada

2,192 pages, 8 ½ x 11, Softcover
37th edition, February 2016
ISBN 978-1-61925-957-7
ISSN 1186-9798
Over 20,000 entries profile Canadian and international organizations active in Canada. Over 2,000 subject classifications index activities, professions and interests served by associations. Includes listings of NGOs, institutes, coalitions, social agencies, federations, foundations, trade unions, fraternal orders, political parties. Fully indexed by subject, geographic location, electronic addresses, executive name, acronym, mailing list availability, conferences and publications.

CANADIAN ENVIRONMENTAL RESOURCE GUIDE 2016-2017
Guide des ressources environnementales canadiennes

880 pages, 8 ½ x 11, Softcover
21st Edition, July 2016
ISBN 978-1-61925-955-3
ISSN 1920-2725
Canada's most complete national listing of environmental organizations, product and service companies and governmental bodies, all indexed and categorized for quick and easy reference. Also included is the Environmental Industry Update, with recent events, maps, rankings, statistics, and trade shows and conferences. The online version features even more content, including associations, special libraries, law firms, and federal/provincial government information.

LIBRARIES CANADA 2016-2017
Bibliothèques Canada

880 pages, 8 ½ x 11, Softcover
31st edition, August 2016
ISBN 978-1-61925-961-4
ISSN 1920-2849
Libraries Canada offers comprehensive information on Canadian libraries, resource centres, business information centres, professional associations, regional library systems, archives, library schools, government libraries, and library technical programs.

HEALTH GUIDE CANADA 2015-2016
Guide canadien de la santé

1,002 pages, 8 ½ x 11, Softcover
2nd edition, June 2015
ISBN: 978-1-61925-677-4
ISSN: 2368-4232
Health Guide Canada contains thousands of ways to deal with the many aspects of chronic or mental health disorders. It includes associations, government agencies, libraries and resource centres, educational facilities, hospitals and publications.

MAJOR CANADIAN CITIES: COMPARED & RANKED
Comparaison et classement des principales villes canadiennes

816 pages, 8 ½ x 11, Softcover
1st edition, November 2013
ISBN 978-1-61925-260-8
Major Canadian Cities: Compared & Ranked provides an in-depth comparison and analysis of the 50 most populated cities in Canada. Following the city chapters are ranking tables that compare the demographics, economics, education, religion and infrastructure of the cities listed.

CANADIAN ALMANAC & DIRECTORY

RÉPERTOIRE ET ALMANACH CANADIEN

2017

170th YEAR

Grey House Publishing Canada

PUBLISHER:	Leslie Mackenzie
GENERAL MANAGER:	Bryon Moore
MANAGING EDITOR:	Stuart Paterson
ASSOCIATE EDITORS:	Elysia Cheung, Daniella D'souza, Laura Lamanna, Vennesa Weedmark

Grey House Publishing

EDITORIAL DIRECTOR:	Laura Mars
MARKETING DIRECTOR:	Jessica Moody
PRODUCTION MANAGER & COMPOSITION:	Kristen Thatcher
CONTRIBUTOR:	Maj. (Ret.) Richard K. Malott, C.D.*, F.R.P.S.C., F.R.P.S.L., F.C.A.S., A.H.F. (British & Commonwealth Honours)

Grey House Publishing Canada
555 Richmond Street West, Suite 512
Toronto, ON M5V 3B1
866-433-4739
FAX 416-644-1904
www.greyhouse.ca
e-mail: info@greyhouse.ca

Printed in Canada by Webcom, Inc.

170th edition published 2016
ISBN: 978-1-61925-953-9
ISSN: 0068-8193
Cataloguing in Publication data is available from Library and Archives Canada

PRIME MINISTER · PREMIER MINISTRE

Canadian Almanac & Directory 2017 Edition

It is with great pleasure that I extend my warmest greetings to the readers of the Canadian Almanac Directory 2017 Edition on its 170th anniversary.

Since its establishment in 1847, the Canadian Almanac & Directory has provided Canadians and readers alike with a comprehensive look into Canada. From national statistics to economic and business summaries, this vital information serves as a valuable resource to all.

I would like to congratulate and thank everyone at Grey House Publishing for all of your success and hard work. I wish you well with all future endeavours.

Please accept my best wishes and warmest regards!

Ottawa
2016

PRIME MINISTER · PREMIER MINISTRE

Édition 2017 du Répertoire et almanach canadien

C'est avec grand plaisir que je souhaite la plus cordiale des bienvenues aux lecteurs de l'édition 2017 du Répertoire et almanach canadien à l'occasion de son 170e anniversaire.

Depuis sa création, en 1847, le Répertoire et almanach canadien offre aux Canadiens et à l'ensemble des lecteurs l'occasion de jeter un regard approfondi sur le Canada. Qu'il s'agisse de statistiques nationales ou de résumés économiques et commerciaux, ces renseignements d'une importance cruciale constituent une précieuse ressource pour tous.

J'aimerais féliciter le personnel de Grey House Publishing de leur réussite et de leur travail acharné. Je vous souhaite bonne chance dans tous vos projets.

Je vous prie d'accepter mes meilleurs vœux et mes sincères salutations!

Ottawa
2016

Introduction

First published 170 years ago as *Canadian Mercantile Almanac for 1847*, the *Canadian Almanac & Directory* is now published by Grey House Publishing Canada. The 2017 edition of this significant work includes over 50,000 entries covering hundreds of topics, making this the number one reference for collected facts and figures about Canada.

The *Almanac* continues to be widely used by business professionals, government officials, information specialists, researchers, publishers, and anyone needing current, accessible information on all topics relevant to those who live and work in Canada. This latest edition provides the most comprehensive picture of Canada, from physical attributes to economic and business summaries to leisure and recreation. It combines textual material, charts, colour photographs and directory listings. This 2017 edition includes hundreds more listings and thousands more details than its predecessor. The comprehensiveness and currency of data is unparalleled.

Each of the 17 sections in the *Almanac* includes a detailed Table of Contents, outlining hundreds of subcategories. A *Topical Table of Contents* on the following pages and a comprehensive *Entry Name Index* at the end of the work make navigation of the massive amount of material quick and easy.

Section 1: Almanac comprises 10 major categories, including History, Vital Statistics, Geography, Science, Awards & Honours, Economics and more. Readers will find articles, colour maps and photographs, charts and tables for a fact-filled snapshot of Canada. This resource section, invaluable for residents, politicians, and the business community, includes a detailed Table of Contents for easy access.

DIRECTORY SECTIONS

Section 2: Arts & Culture begins the **Directory Listings** and includes nine categories: Aquaria, Art Galleries, Botanical Gardens, Museums, National Parks, Observatories, Performing Arts, Science Centres and Zoos. Categories are arranged by province and city. All listings include address, phone, fax, website, email, key executives and a brief description.

Section 3: Associations lists thousands of associations and organizations arranged in 142 topics from Aboriginal Peoples to Youth. Each listing includes valuable descriptions and current contact information. An Association Name Index precedes the listings.

Section 4: Broadcasting begins with Canada's Major Broadcasting Companies, then lists, by Province, all Radio and Television Stations, as well as Cable Companies and Specialty Broadcasters.

Section 5: Business & Finance combines Accounting, Banking, Insurance, and Canada's Major Companies and Stock Exchanges. It includes a separate section for Major Accounting Firms with company descriptions, as well as an Insurance Class Index.

Section 6: Education is arranged by Province, and includes Government Agencies, Districts, Specialized and Independent Schools, University and Technical facilities, many with valuable descriptions.

Section 7: Federal/Provincial Government begins with a Quick Reference Guide to help you find your way around government agencies. The Guide is followed by Federal and Provincial listings, plus information on The Royal Family and Diplomatic and Consular Representatives in Canada and abroad.

Section 8: Municipal Government details all County and Municipal Districts and segregated Major Municipalities. All profiles include date of incorporation, square miles, and population figures. Also included are District Maps and descriptions for all Provinces.

Section 9: Judicial Government provides thorough coverage for Courts in Canada, including Federal and Provincial. Listings are categorized by type of Court and City within each Province, and include presiding judges.

Section 10: Hospitals and Health Care Facilities is an overview of available facilities by Province. Government agencies, hospitals, community health centres, retirement care and mental health facilities, are all arranged alphabetically by city for easy access.

Originairement publié sous le nom « Canadian Mercantile Almanac for 1847 » il y a 170 ans, le *Répertoire et Almanach Canadien* est maintenant publié par Grey House Publishing Canada. L'édition 2017 comprend plus de 50 000 entrées couvrant des centaines de sujets, faisant de ce répertoire l'*Almanach* le plus complet jamais publié sur les faits et données concernant le Canada.

Le *Répertoire et Almanach Canadien* continu d'être largement consulté par les éditeurs, les gens d'affaires, les bureaux gouvernementaux, les spécialistes de l'information, les chercheurs et par tous ceux qui ont besoin d'une information à jour et facilement accessible sur tous les sujets imaginables concernant le travail et la vie au Canada. La présente édition brosse le tableau le mieux documenté qui soit du Canada en un seul volume, comprenant ses attributs physiques et économiques en passant par les activités commerciales, les divertissements et les loisirs qu'on y pratique. Il constitue un amalgame exceptionnel de textes, de chartes, de photographies couleur et de listes de répertoire. Cette édition comprend un plus grand nombre de données, de profils détaillés et des quantités de mises à jour.

Chaque section de l'ouvrage, qui en compte 17, comprend une table des matières détaillée qui définit des centaines de sous-catégories. Une table des matières par sujet sur les pages suivantes et un index nominatif exhaustif à la fin de l'ouvrage simplifient la consultation de la quantité impressionnante d'information offerte et la rendent plus rapide.

Section 1 : Almanach est composée de 10 catégories principales, notamment Histoire, Statistiques essentielles, Géographie, Sciences, Prix et distinctions, Économie. Il contient plus d'articles, de cartes et de photographies couleur, de chartes et de tableaux qui offrent un portrait juste et à jour des faits et données importants sur le Canada. Elle constitue une source unique de renseignements pour tous les citoyens, les politiciens et les communautés d'affaires. Les tables des matières détaillées de chacune des catégories rendent maintenant la consultation plus facile.

RÉPERTOIRES

Section 2 : Arts et Culture comprend neuf matières principales, des galeries d'art aux parcs zoologiques. Les renseignements y sont regroupés par province et par ville. Chaque entrée comprend des données d'identification, dont l'adresse, numéros de téléphone et télécopieur, site Internet, courriel, cadres, ainsi qu'une brève description.

Section 3 : Associations énumère des milliers d'associations et d'organismes classés selon 142 sujets, de l'agriculture aux voyages. Chaque entrée comprend des données d'identification, dont celles de contacts. Un index par nom au début des catégories facilite la recherche.

Section 4 : Radiodiffusion et télédiffusion présente une liste des principales sociétés de radiodiffusion et télédiffusion au pays suivie des listes, par province, des stations de radio et de télévision ainsi que des entreprises de distribution par câble et des émetteurs spécialisés.

Section 5 : Affaires et finance comprend de l'information sur les cabinets comptables, les banques, les compagnies d'assurances, les plus grandes sociétés canadiennes et les bourses. Elle comprend une section distincte pour les principaux cabinets comptables, y compris des descriptions d'entreprise et un index des catégories d'assurance.

Section 6 : Éducation est divisée par province et donne des renseignements sur les agences gouvernementales, les commissions scolaires, les écoles privées et spécialisées, les institutions universitaires, collégiales et techniques. Vous y trouverez également plusieurs autres renseignements d'intérêts en matière d'éducation.

Section 7 : Gouvernement fédéral/provincial commence par un Guide de références rapide qui vous aidera à trouver votre chemin parmi la multitude d'agences gouvernementales répertoriées, suivi de leurs listes au niveau du pays et des provinces. Cette section comprend également les plus récents résultats d'élection. Vous y trouverez de plus de l'information sur la Famille royale ainsi que les représentants diplomatiques et consulaires au Canada et à l'étranger.

Section 8 : Gouvernement municipal fournit de l'information sur les comtés, les municipalités régionales de comté et les principales villes canadiennes. Chaque profil a été revu pour y incorporer la date d'incorporation, la superficie

Section 11: Law Firms includes a separate section of Major Law Firms with descriptions and Senior Partners. Following the Majors are law firms arranged by Province.

Section 12: Libraries begins with Canada's main Library/Archive and Government Departments for Libraries. Provincial listings follow, with Regional Systems listed first, then Public Libraries and Archives.

Section 13: Publishing includes Publishers—Book, Magazine, Newspapers—and Newspapers by Province. Magazine listings are arranged in six major categories, preceded by a Magazine Name Index for easy searching. Details include frequency and circulation figures.

Section 14: Religion starts off with broad information on religious groups, then lists Associations, arranged alphabetically by 37 denominations.

Section 15: Sports provides information on a variety of sports categories, including associations, and detailed League and Team listings for Baseball, Basketball, Football, Hockey, Lacrosse and Soccer. You'll also find the major sports venues in Canada, from stadiums to racetracks.

Section 16: Transportation offers comprehensive listings for major transportation modes, plus industry Associations, Government Agencies and Airport and Port Authorities.

Section 17: Utilities includes Associations, Government Agencies and Provincial Utility Companies.

Entry Name Index

The *Canadian Almanac & Directory 2017* is also available as part of **Grey House Publishing's Canada's Information Resource Centre (CIRC)** at www.greyhouse.ca where subscribers have full access to this rich database. Trial subscriptions to CIRC are available by calling 866-433-4739.

We acknowledge the valuable contributions of those individuals and organizations that have responded to our information gathering process. Their help and responses to our phone calls, faxes and questionnaires are greatly appreciated.

Every effort has been made to assure the accuracy of the information included in this edition of the *Canadian Almanac & Directory*. Do not hesitate to contact the editorial office in Toronto with comments, or if revisions are necessary.

et la population approximative. Comprend également des plans des secteurs ainsi que des descriptions pour toutes les provinces.

Section 9 : Gouvernement - Juridique adresse la liste de tous les tribunaux judiciaires au Canada, tant fédéraux que provinciaux. Les renseignements y sont regroupés par genre de tribunal et par ville, au niveau de chaque province. On y trouve également le nom des juges actuellement en fonction.

Section 10 : Hôpitaux et soins de santé donne une vue d'ensemble des établissements de santé par province. Pour simplifier la consultation, les agences gouvernementales, les hôpitaux, les centres de santé communautaire, les centres de santé mentale et les établissements de soins de longues durées pour personnes âgées sont regroupés par ville, en ordre alphabétique.

Section 11 : Bureaux d'avocats inclue une sous-section détaillant les principaux cabinets d'avocats au Canada et donnant une brève description de ceux-ci et de leurs principaux associés. Vient ensuite, la liste des bureaux d'avocats regroupés par province.

Section 12 : Bibliothèque présente en premier lieu les principales bibliothèques au Canada et les bibliothèques gouvernementales et d'archives. On y trouve ensuite des renseignements sur les bibliothèques, par province, où sont décrits les systèmes régionaux, suivis des principales bibliothèques publiques et d'archives.

Section 13 : Édition fournit de l'information, détaillé par province, sur les éditeurs des livres, magazines et journaux, ainsi que les quotidiens et autres journaux. La nomenclature des magazines est présentée en six catégories précédées d'un index par nom pour faciliter la recherche. Plusieurs données ont été ajoutées dont celles concernant la fréquence de publication et le tirage.

Section 14 : Religion fournit une vaste quantité d'informations sur les groupements religieux, suivie de celles sur les 37 principales confessions.

Section 15 : Sports fournit des principales informations beaucoup des associations et des catégories de sports et des données sur les ligues et équipes de baseball, basketball, football, hockey, lacrosse et soccer. Vous y trouverez aussi des renseignements sur les majeures installations sportives du Canada comprenant les stades et les pistes de course.

Section 16 : Transport comprend des renseignements complets sur les principaux moyens de transport ainsi que les associations du secteur, les organismes gouvernementaux et les autorités aéroportuaires et portuaires.

Section 17 : Services publics regroupe sous un même chapitre les associations, les agences gouvernementales et les entreprises oeuvrant dans les services publics de chaque province.

Index nominatif

Le *Répertoire et almanach canadien 2017* fait partie des vaste données électroniques du **Centre de documentation du Canada (CDC) de Grey House Publishing Canada** (www.greyhouse.ca) auquel les abonnés peuvent avoir accès de leur ordinateur personnel. Vous pouvez obtenir un abonnement d'essai aux données du CDC en composant le 866 433-4739.

Nous tenons à souligner la précieuse contribution des personnes et des organismes qui ont collaboré tout au long de l'année à notre procédé de cueillette d'information; votre aide, vos réponses à notre questionnaire dans les délais impartis, nos appels téléphoniques et nos envois par télécopieur sont grandement appréciés.

Nous avons mis tous les efforts pour nous assurer de l'exactitude de l'information contenue dans cette édition du *Répertoire et almanach canadien*. N'hésitez pas à communiquer avec le bureau de la rédaction pour faire part de vos commentaires ou si des modifications s'avèrent nécessaires.

Table of Contents

Table des matières

Topical Table of Contents

Table des Matières par Sujets

Science

Services publics

Sports

Tourisme

Transport

SECTION 1

ALMANAC

History

History of Canada

Over the past 400 years, Canada has evolved from a sparsely populated trading post to the tenth-richest sovereign power in the world. It stands alone as the only country to separate from its colonial power through peaceful means.

The political boundary of what is now known as Canada recorded thousands of years of history before European colonization, but was one of the last places on Earth to host human habitation. While modern *Homo sapiens* emerged from the eastern region of Africa 200,000 years ago, most scientists agree that it took another 175,000 years for humans to find their way across the ice bridge that once joined Alaska and Eastern Siberia. The land that now constitutes Canada has seen the longest period of human habitation in the New World: from the original migration 25,000 years ago came all the indigenous cultures of North and South America including the Arctic Inuit, Blackfoot, Cree, Algonquin, Dene, and Iroquois League of Five Nations. Estimates put the number of native peoples in the United States and Canada before European contact at about two million.

Columbus may have been given credit for the "discovery" of America in 1492, but proof exists that Vikings voyaged to Greenland and further west as early as 982 A.D. Archeological evidence points to Norse settlements in Newfoundland at L'Anse aux Meadows dating back to approximately 1000 A.D., making Canada the actual site of the European discovery of North America. The Vikings, however, were not concerned with permanent colonization, only Canadian natural resources. By the time Christopher Columbus arrived, the Norse settlements had been abandoned.

With Christopher Columbus came the European fervour of colonizing the New World. Seeking a way to circumvent the long land trade routes to Asian goods by crossing the Atlantic to what he thought was India, Columbus inadvertently began the Age of Discovery. European powers established colonies, seeking spice, gold, slaves, and new crops, as well as the promotion of Christianity among the native peoples. The earlier colonies, mostly Spanish and Portuguese, were concentrated in South America, Central America, and the Caribbean. England and France, however, turned their attention north. John Cabot, an Italian-born English explorer, is credited as being the first European explorer after the Vikings to set foot in North America. Although this exploration occurred only five years after Columbus's discoveries, it was not until 1605 that permanent settlements were established. Many explorers, including Henry Hudson, still attempted to find the Northwest Passage, a reputed waterway through the New World to Asia. The reasons for this 100-year gap have more to do with European affairs than those of the New World.

Two events slowed the colonization of North America: religious unrest and war in Europe. In 1517, Martin Luther distributed his list of 95 grievances against the Catholic Church by means of a new invention, the printing press. Thus began the Protestant Reformation. This schism was to have far-reaching consequences across all of European history, but in the short term, it created rancorous religious strife. Most of Europe turned inward to deal with unrest and religious crisis. Escalating political conflicts enveloped most of Western Europe for decades, drawing resources away from colonization efforts. The French Wars of Religion, the Italian Wars, and popular uprisings combined with new religious uprisings to turn the attention of Europe away from the New World for more than a century.

France looked to North America as the best possible source of wealth and power and as a relief from war debt. When French explorer Jacques Cartier sailed up the St. Lawrence River in 1534, he claimed the territory for France, and gave it the name it still bears today: Canada. Once fur traders arrived in Eastern Canada in the 1500s, France monopolized the fur trade. While the French made an effort to establish friendly trading relations with the native population, the Iroquois in particular proved openly hostile. Conflicts with local tribes soon convinced the crown that if traders were to make a profit in Canada, a permanent military and civilian presence was essential. King Henry IV sent his royal "hydrographer," Samuel de Champlain to map the region.

In 1605, after exploring the coast of North America as far south as Cape Cod, Champlain established the first permanent French settlement at Port Royal, and in 1608 he founded Quebec City. New France, as it was then called, grew slowly, mainly due to disinterest from the mainland and war with the Iroquois. The settlers survived attacks from native peoples through their alliance with the Algonquin, Montagnais, and Huron peoples. These alliances not only secured their survival, but greatly increased France's control of the fur trade. Europeans had little experience in the thick wilderness of the area, an expertise that the native peoples supplied.

Once again religious tensions in Europe interfered with Canada's settlement and growth. By the mid-seventeenth century, while England's American and Caribbean colonies grew self-sufficient, New France remained underpopulated. The struggling colony drained France's resources. The French crown decided to take action by creating land incentives for emigrants to New France. Only one caveat stood in the way: all settlers must be Roman Catholic, or convert to Roman Catholicism before leaving Europe. This change of policy, undertaken at the urging of the fanatical Catholic Cardinal Richelieu, closest advisor to King Louis XIII, created friction. Previously, French Protestants, especially the persecuted sect known as Huguenots, had fled to New France to escape religious persecution. Cardinal Richelieu's new edict would have a lasting impact on the religious and political makeup of modern Canada.

In the late seventeenth century, English and French colonies in the New World began to take a stronger foothold. Both nations finally saw a large-scale financial return on their investments, but a war in Europe again infringed on Canada's nascent growth. New France, already in the middle of brutal intertribal warfare with the Algonquins, conflicted with the Iroquois confederacy opposing them. With the War of the Grand Alliance in 1688, which pitted France against almost all of continental Europe, the Iroquois began to receive English weapons as part of government policy. This escalation by the English heightened the already bloody warfare. English armies and their Iroquois allies captured Port Royal, but were turned back from Quebec City, due mainly to a decimation of forces by disease. The war eventually petered out, and a peace was signed in 1697. The Iroquois, however, continued the fight without British help, and eventually suffered a series of major defeats, forcing them to sue for peace four years later.

New France, and thereby Canada, seemed securely in the mother country's domain following the end of the War of the Grand Alliance. However, France's control of the region was not to last. Queen Anne's War, which began only a year after the French peace with the Iroquois, lead England to claim Nova Scotia and Newfoundland, as well as the rights to the land surrounding Hudson Bay. Fighting broke out again three decades later in 1744, in a battle known as King George's War, but neither side was able to enlarge their colonial positions.

By 1754 the long-standing animosity between the English and French seeped into the New World, culminating in the Seven Years War, known in the Americas as the French and Indian War. The causes of the conflict were threefold. The lucrative fur trade, rich fishing grounds, ample lumber, and mineral deposits all promised great wealth to whoever controlled Canada. Secondly, the fiercely anti-Catholic British felt that the Protestant French were heretics, a feeling that was reciprocated by the French. Thirdly, possession of colonies overseas could be used as diplomatic bargaining chips should the war in Europe go badly.

The Seven Years War was the first worldwide war, fought on five continents: North America, South America, Africa, Europe and Asia. More than a million died, and the war resulted in a complete change in the power structure of the New World. Britain gained all of France's colonial possessions in North America, and Canada became a British colony. However, 150 years of French colonization didn't disappear overnight. Even today, French-English relations in Canada can be contentious.

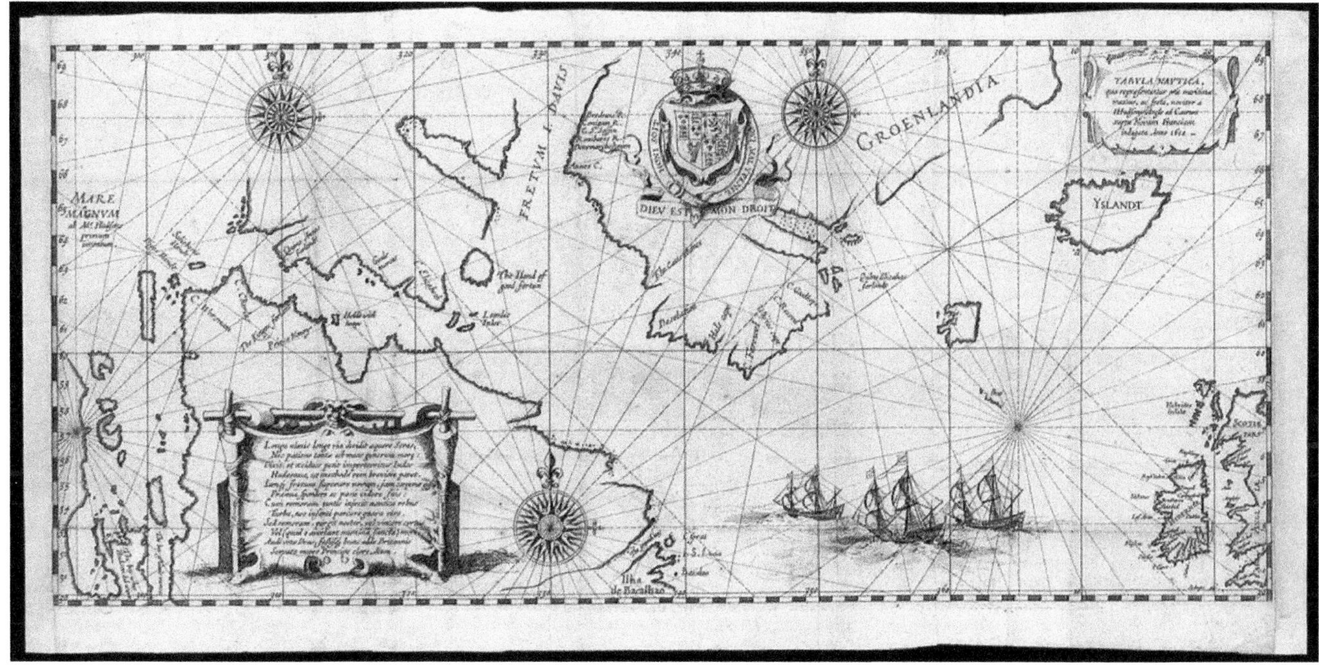

Henry Hudson arrived in Arctic waters in 1610 determined to find the Northwest Passage. He explored Hudson Bay and the mouth of the Bay. His crew mutinied and abandoned him in 1611 and returned to Europe. This map by Dutch cartographer Gerritsz is based on Hudson's discoveries.

Champlain's Map 1632

The British, upon taking control of Canada in 1764, left intact the religious and economic systems already in place, to the relief of the Catholic French colonists. The Quebec Act of 1774 allowed a separate system of French law to continue in Quebec. The British now controlled the entire eastern half of North America, from the eastern seaboard to the Mississippi River. However, George III's mistreatment of the American colonies would soon cause a shift in the balance of power in the New World.

As a base for the British forces, a refuge for fleeing Americans loyal to the British crown, and a source of militia for both the British and American armies, Canada played a large role in the American Revolution. The American army originally attempted to convince Canada to join their revolution but Canadians had just finished rebuilding after the Seven Years War and most did not want no take part in another feud. On June 27, 1775, American troops attacked Quebec and Montreal was taken without a fight. The attack on Quebec City was eventually defeated and in 1776, the American troops evacuated Montreal.

When America gained independence from Britain in 1783, citizens loyal to the British Empire were exiled. Over 35,000 of these loyalists flooded into Nova Scotia. This massive influx prompted the British government to divide Nova Scotia, creating the new colony of New Brunswick. Soon, the loyalists in Quebec were also making demands for their own colony, while the French Canadians were equally determined to have their own elected assembly. In 1791, Quebec was divided into Upper Canada and Lower Canada in order to meet the distinct needs of the English loyalists and the French Canadians.

Tensions between Britain and America remained high in the proceeding decades, and once again a conflict erupted that ensnared Canada. The United States declared war on Britain in 1812 over the arming and supplying of hostile Native American tribes and the forced conscription of American sailors into the British Navy. Canada became one of the primary battlegrounds in this conflict, with the United States planning to seize Canada and use it as leverage against the British. America expected support from the people of Canada, who they assumed were unhappy under English colonial rule. However, many Canadians at that time were children of British loyalists who fled America and saw the United States as invaders and occupiers.

The American army suffered a loss early in the war when they were soundly defeated by General Isaac Brock and his force of Indian allies and local military men at the Battle of Queenston Heights. But the American army did go on to occupy and loot many cities, including York (now Toronto) and Newark (now Niagara-on-the-Lake), eventually controlling much of present day Ontario and Quebec. Ultimately, the American army was driven back, and although the war ended with no real victor, the fact that an attempted American takeover had been thwarted gave Canadians confidence and stimulated national pride.

While Canadians rejected the idea of American invaders on their soil, the political example of the United States resonated throughout the country. Rebellions broke out against the British in 1837. Canadians, angry over the unfair distribution of wealth derived from Canada's natural resources, balked against not being represented in the British government. Based on the opinion of the British that friction between the French and English people was causing conflict in Canada, all of the Canadian colonies were merged together into the United Province of Canada in 1840. In 1849 the United States and the British Empire agreed that the 49th north parallel would be the boundary between the two nations, and the British extended Canada to the western seaboard, encompassing British Columbia.

Canadian independence had been debated in Britain and in Canada almost since the American Revolution. Some advocated violent revolution and total Canadian independence. Others wanted a slower, more gradual autonomy. On July 1st, 1867, the British parliament passed the British North America Act, which established The Dominion of Canada as a separate and self-governing colony. While it was not completely severed from England, especially in matters of foreign policy, domestically, Canada was allowed free reign.

During the next decades, Canada continued to expand westward. With the purchase of two huge northern territories, The North-Western Territory and Rupert's Land, from the Hudson Bay Company, the country more than doubled its size. The sections of Canada west of Ontario housed a large population of French-speaking, Catholic Métis, the children of indigenous people and white settlers. After the sale of Rupert's Land, many settlers from Ontario flooded into the region hoping to claim land. The Métis became worried that this influx of mostly English Protestant settlers would threaten their rights to language, religion and land. The Métis leader Louis Riel organized the Red River Resistance in 1869 in order to ensure that these rights were guaranteed. The revolt led to the creation of Manitoba, a province with strong laws protecting the Métis, French-speaking people and Catholics. By 1905, the founding provinces of Upper and Lower Canada, New Brunswick, and Nova Scotia were soon joined by British Columbia, Saskatchewan, Prince Edward Island, and Alberta.

The construction of a transcontinental railroad, completed in 1885, spurred Canada's expansion. While the railroad enabled additional settlers to move west into the new provinces, it also pushed the Native people aside. Again rebellion flared, resulting in more bloodshed. The sentiment that the Canadian government didn't heed the concerns of French-speaking Catholic citizens caused a political crisis resulting in the resignation of prime minister Mackenzie Bowell in 1896, when the government tried to ban French as an official language of Manitoba, contrary to the laws of the province.

Both Canada and the United States shared a period of western expansion in the late nineteenth century, based on the prominence of the railroad, the promise of free land and the discovery of mineral deposits. These factors, joined with a large influx of European immigrants, led to Canada becoming the fastest-growing economy in the world between 1896 and 1911. During that time, the Canadian government created the Yukon Territory, a land mass about the size of Germany, Austria and Switzerland combined, then populated by only 8,500 people.

On the verge of the twentieth century, Canada faced the first serious conflict with its colonial power. When Britain entered the Boer War in 1899, most English-speaking Canadians supported bringing South Africa into the fold of the British Empire. French Canadians, however, had little interest in British imperialism, seeing themselves as a separate concern, only nominally part of the Empire. As a compromise, volunteers were allowed to serve in the Boer War, but the Canadian Army stayed uninvolved. The view of French Canada as a separate entity, exacerbated by rebellion and anti-French laws of the past decades, would continue to play out in Canadian politics in years to come.

Arctic regions 1953

Although many French Canadians wanted out from under the British Empire's yoke, the country was still obligated to fall in line with British foreign policy. With the assassination of Archduke Ferdinand on June 28, 1914, Canada was swept into the chaotic system of alliances that created World War I. When Britain declared war on the central powers on August 4th, Canadian troops were called into action. Like most of the allied powers, internal disputes were put aside and support for the war remained high, even among French Canadians. After suffering more than 200,000 dead and wounded casualties out of a population of seven million, support for the war began to wane. By the time the government attempted to introduce conscription in 1917, many Canadians, especially in French Canada, were fiercely anti-war. Despite the popular sentiment, World War I greatly increased the sense of Canadian nationalism and identity, fed by the country's significant role in the largest war mankind had ever known. Massive Canadian casualties in what many Canadians saw as a "British" war also created additional animosity towards the Empire.

World War I radically changed Canada's political landscape. Soldiers returned home from the horrors of the conflict with altered political ideologies. Socialism, communism, trade unionism and other left-wing progressive movements gained traction in the years immediately after the war, as the influx of soldiers returning home caused high unemployment and wage cuts. The Winnipeg General Strike of 1919, the largest of a wave of strikes that swept the country, was violently crushed by police, killing one man and wounding 30. When women's suffrage was enacted nationwide in 1918, the ruling Conservative Party collapsed, partly because of their actions during the strike. The Liberal Party, upon assuming control of the government, enacted many of the original strike committee's demands, including the right to form unions without government permission. Progressive and socialist parties formed in subsequent years, including the Progressive Party of Canada and the Cooperative Commonwealth Federation.

In 1931, the British Parliament passed the Statute of Westminster, establishing all the colonies and dominions of the British Empire, including Canada, Australia, New Zealand, and Ireland as separate legislative entities. This act allowed these countries to write their own constitutions and removed the power of the British Government to legislate in these areas, effectively making them independent, while still being contained in a worldwide British Commonwealth.

When the American Stock Market crashed on Black Tuesday in 1929 kicking off the Great Depression, the Canadian economy soon felt the effects. By 1933, the Canadian gross national product had dropped 40 percent. Manufacturing and farming suffered the most, with the price of wheat, Canada's main export, cut in half. At its worst point in 1933, 30 percent of Canadians were out of work. Newfoundland, deciding that Canadian government policy was the cause of the economic difficulty, voted to leave the Canadian federation and rejoin the British Empire.

When both the Liberal and Conservative parties were unable to produce any solutions to the crisis, many Canadians began to turn to third parties, such as the socialist Cooperative Commonwealth Federation and the Social Credit Party of Canada. After the Conservative government of R.B. Bennett put unemployed men into work camps to offset the great cost of supporting a huge welfare system, the Workers' Unity League put together a massive protest called the "On to Ottawa Trek" in order to call for improved conditions and benefits. Bennett's attempt to repress the Trek resulted in the Regina Riot, and contributed to his defeat in the 1935 election. The new Liberal government did away with the camps and instituted social programs to help lessen the effects of the Depression, but Canada was still severely affected. Almost one-fifth of the population was surviving on government payouts and social support systems. Even after a resurgent boom in Canada's economy, brought on by World War II, these systems remained in place, and continued to evolve.

World War II officially began on September 1, 1939. Canada did not immediately enter the war upon the British declaration as it had in World War I. With its growing independence from England, Canada decided to declare war on its own nine days later. While the Japanese and Nazi onslaught was still in full effect, Canadian supplies and war material were instrumental in keeping Britain from succumbing to German invasion. Once the Allies were in a position to counterattack, Canadian troops were deployed all over the world, and served valiantly in some of the major battles, including the invasion of Sicily and Italy in 1943, the allied landing at Normandy in 1944, the liberation of the Netherlands, and the drive across France and Germany to end the war. However, Canada endured its own share of loss. A predominantly Canadian raid, at Dieppe, France, resulted in more than 3,000 dead, wounded or captured and German U-boats, which prowled Canadian waters, sank many supply ships. In the end, Canada suffered a total of 42,000 casualties.

When the Japanese bombed Pearl Harbor on December 7, 1941, the 22,000 Japanese Canadians then living in British Columbia took the brunt of the resulting pain and anger. The anti-Asian sentiment in the province was further fueled when thousands of Canadians were killed or captured in the Japanese invasion of Hong Kong. In 1942, all people of Japanese descent were sent to internment camps, and after the war, all Japanese

Canadians were deported from British Columbia. It was not until 1949 that they became free to live anywhere in Canada. Japanese Canadians were finally compensated in 1988 for the wrongs that they had suffered during the war.

At the close of World War II, Canada and the United States alone benefited from never having seen fighting on their home soil. Each country was, therefore, in a unique economic position. Due to a revitalized manufacturing sector, the discovery of oil in Alberta, and as the main trading partner to the economic superpower on their southern border, the Canadian economy exploded. This newfound wealth was put into a radical new program of social support. Based upon the centralized welfare state of the late 1930s and early 1940s, as well as many of the policies of the socialist Cooperative Commonwealth Federation, Canadians enjoyed hospital insurance, old-age pensions, veterans' pensions, and family allowance. These progressive social policies convinced Newfoundland to rejoin Canada in a 1949 referendum.

Canada cemented its position in the Cold War with its founding membership in NATO in 1949. The country's fortunes were firmly rooted with the United States. Canada participated in the Korean War, and Canadian troops were stationed in West Germany, on the border of the communist Eastern Bloc. Canada's voting record in the United Nations was not always aligned with the United States, but there is no question that Canada was an American ally pitted against the Soviet Union.

Canada's treatment of its Native peoples has a sad history. As far back as the late 1800s, when the buffalo were hunted almost to extinction and the expansion of the railroad brought more settlers to native territories, First Nations people were treated as second-class citizens. Starvation, assimilation and a crushed rebellion largely put an end to the native resistance movement, but it gained strength again after World War II. Decolonialization and a newfound spirit of democracy was being put forth by the Western powers in their opposition to Soviet tyranny, yet most First Nations people could not vote as late as 1950. In order to vote, First Nations people had to gain suffrage by renouncing their status as "Indians." It was not until 1960 (1969 in Quebec) that all First Nations people were allowed to vote freely.

As Canada entered the 1960s, the government faced growing radicalism and organization among its populace. Quebec nationalism had been growing ever since the British took Canada from the French in 1764. French Canadians saw themselves as a separate nation, and frequently found themselves disagreeing with the policies of the Canadian government. The more radical French Canadian factions felt they were being oppressed, and that their language and culture were under attack. Inspired by revolutions around the world, nationalist and left-wing terrorism began to rise, Canada was not unaffected. The Front de Libération du Québec (FLQ), committed more than 200 bombings, and killed five people in pursuit of an independent Quebec. While violence was rejected by a majority of the population, a genuine desire for independence fueled Québécois protests. When Pierre Elliott Trudeau was elected prime minister in 1968, he declared martial law in Quebec, arresting most members of the FLQ.

While the crisis in Quebec worsened throughout the 1970s, the United States became involved in one of the most controversial conflicts in modern history: the war in Indochina. The Vietnam War resulted in over 1,500,000 dead, and radicalized an entire generation. Canada was no exception. Young people throughout the country protested against what they saw as American imperialism. The Canadian government refused to participate in the war, and granted citizenship to as many as 125,000 American draft dodgers over the course of the conflict. This led to serious friction between the governments of Canada and the US. To this day Vietnam and Canada have a close relationship, and hundreds of thousands of Vietnamese have immigrated to Canada's west coast. The period of the Vietnam War also saw the rise of the New Democratic Party (NDP), the successor to the socialist Cooperative Commonwealth Federation. Since its beginning in 1962, the NDP has altered the balance of Canadian politics, regularly receiving between 10 and 20 percent of the national vote, and often having the ability to form a majority coalition by grouping itself with the winning party. In the 2011 federal election, the NDP had its best result, winning 30 percent of the vote and the role of official opposition for the first time. It has fought for the continuation of Canada's welfare state, a humanitarian foreign policy, and native rights.

Young people across Canada became increasingly involved in politics as a result of the Vietnam War, and this new political awareness allowed the question of Quebec sovereignty to be addressed. The Parti Québécois was formed in 1968 and elected to govern Quebec in 1976, making French the official language of the province in 1977. Finally, the party made good on its biggest promise and introduced a referendum to decide Quebec's fate. The actual referendum simply said that Quebec would "negotiate a new agreement with the rest of Canada, based on the equality of nations; this agreement would enable Quebec to acquire the exclusive power to make its laws, levy its taxes and establish relations abroad - in other words, sovereignty." The fact that the referendum did not advocate full independence, in combination with a full-out public relations assault from the federal government, doomed the referendum.

While Canada became a sovereign entity in 1867, and had its independence increased in 1931, it was not technically a separate nation. Canada could not make amendments to its own constitution and the power of Canada to act directly against the wishes of the British government was in question. In 1982, Trudeau finally sealed Canada's status as its own unique nation by signing the Canada Act and the Charter of Rights and Freedoms. Although still a member of the British Commonwealth, Canada was now free from control by the British parliament.

With Canada's complete independence from Britain, the question of trade with the United States became central to the Canadian economy. The Canada-United States Free Trade Agreement drafted in 1988 set the model for the subsequent North American Free Trade Agreement and Central American Free Trade Agreement. The criticism of the agreement, as well as later free trade agreements, was that by eliminating trade barriers, Canadian consumers and labour unions would be at the mercy of more powerful US corporations. The agreement was a decisive issue in the 1988 elections, with the Liberal Party and NDP in opposition, and the ruling Progressive Conservatives attempting to pass it. A 57 percent majority voted against the Progressive Conservatives, but because they received the most votes for one single party, they were rewarded with the most seats in parliament, and passed the free trade agreement.

The Parti Québécois, after failing in its referendum of 1980, had formed a national party, the Bloc Québécois, and doggedly pursued its agenda of an independent Quebec. A second referendum, called in 1995, created an even bigger debate than the referendum of 1980, with massive media campaigns on both sides of the issue. When the vote finally came up, it failed by a slim 54,000 votes, but the issue illustrated a true divide in Quebec. Considering that 86,000 ballots were thrown out as invalid, the question of Quebec independence failed by a razor-thin margin, and the probability of it arising again in the future is still possible.

In 1990, in a small town called Oka, west of Montreal, a First Nations revolt led to the intervention of the Canadian Army and three deaths. While this was far from the first violent conflict between First Nations people and the Canadian government, it has marked a new era of militant native resistance. With more than one million people of Aboriginal descent living in Canada, many native organizations have called for more indigenous control over resources in their lands, resulting in violent conflicts between First Nations people and corporations attempting to mine, fish, or harvest lumber. One effect of these protests was the creation of a new territory, Nunavut, in the far north of Canada in 1999. While the population is less than 35,000, more than 85 percent of its inhabitants claim Inuit status, and the territory has adopted many laws securing their rights and claims to land and resources.

After the crashing of airplanes into the World Trade Center in New York on September 11, 2001, Canada entered the Afghanistan war as part of the International Security Assistance Force in a response to Islamist extremists and stayed to stabilize the country until 2011.

As climate change became more and more a concern, Canada entered into the Kyoto Protocol agreement, an international agreement intended to help reduce greenhouse gases, in 2005. It exited the agreement in 2011, under Stephen Harper, with emissions far over the target rates.

Today, Canada continues to deal with its internal relations with French-speaking Canadians and First Nations peoples. As a unified country, it also faces other issues such as participation in peacekeeping missions, drug decriminalization, immigration and control over Arctic seaways.

Histoire du Canada

Au cours des 400 dernières années, le Canada est passé de simple poste de traite peu peuplé au dixième état souverain le plus riche au monde. Il s'agit de plus du seul pays à s'être séparé pacifiquement de sa puissance coloniale.

Malgré que le grand territoire composant aujourd'hui le Canada avait déjà une histoire vieille de plusieurs millénaires au début de la colonisation européenne, il a néanmoins été un des derniers endroits au monde à accueillir des populations humaines. Alors que l'*Homo Sapiens* moderne aurait émergé dans l'est de l'Afrique il y a 200 000 ans, la majorité des scientifiques conviennent qu'il aura fallu 175 000 années de plus pour que les hommes traversent le pont de glace reliant jadis l'Alaska et l'est de la Sibérie. Sur ce nouveau continent, c'est l'espace que délimitent les frontières canadiennes actuelles qui est habité depuis le plus longtemps; la migration originale qui a eu lieu il y a 25 000 ans est la source des cultures indigènes d'Amérique du Nord et du Sud, incluant les Inuits de l'Arctique, les Pieds-Noirs, les Cris, les Algonquins, les Dénés et la Ligue iroquoise des Cinq-Nations. On estime à environ deux millions le nombre d'Autochtones vivant aux États-Unis et au Canada avant l'arrivée des Européens dans le Nouveau Monde.

Christophe Colomb est peut-être celui à qui l'on attribue la « découverte » de l'Amérique en 1492, mais l'on sait aujourd'hui avec certitudes que les Vikings ont atteint et dépassé le Groenland en 982 apr. J.-C. Des traces archéologiques qui dateraient d'environ 1000 ans indiquent la présence à cette époque de peuples norois à L'Anse aux Meadows, à Terre-Neuve, ce qui ferait du Canada le véritable lieu de découverte de l'Amérique du Nord par les Européens. Les Vikings ne visaient pas toutefois à établir une colonisation permanente, mais étaient plutôt intéressés aux ressources naturelles du Canada. Quand Christophe Colomb foula le sol américain pour la première fois, les installations qui y avaient été construites par les peuples norois étaient abandonnées depuis longtemps déjà.

Le voyage de Christophe Colomb déclencha en Europe une course à la colonisation du Nouveau Monde. En traversant l'Atlantique vers ce qu'il croyait être l'Inde pour trouver une voie alternative aux longues routes de commerce terrestres menant à l'Asie et à ses produits, Christophe Colomb donna sans le vouloir le coup d'envoi à l'Ère des grandes découvertes. Les puissances européennes établirent des colonies à la recherche d'épices, d'or, d'esclaves et de nouvelles cultures, ainsi que pour convertir les peuples autochtones au christianisme. Les premières colonies, principalement espagnoles et portugaises, étaient concentrées en Amérique du Sud, en Amérique Centrale et dans les Caraïbes. L'Angleterre et la France ont plutôt tourné leurs efforts vers le Nord. Jean Cabot, un explorateur anglais d'origine italienne, est considéré comme le premier explorateur européen à avoir mis le pied en Amérique du Nord après les Vikings. Bien que cette exploration eut lieu seulement cinq années après les découvertes de Christophe Colomb, il faudra attendre jusqu'en 1605 pour que des installations permanentes soient établies. À cette époque, beaucoup d'explorateurs, dont Henry Hudson, tentaient encore de trouver le passage du Nord-Ouest, la fameuse voie navigable qui devait relier le Nouveau Monde à l'Asie. Si plus de cent ans se sont écoulés avant ces premières installations permanentes, c'est davantage en raison d'événements se déroulant en Europe que de facteurs attribuables au Nouveau Monde.

Deux événements sont venus ralentir la colonisation de l'Amérique du Nord : l'agitation religieuse et la guerre en Europe. En 1517, Martin Luther diffusa sa liste de 95 griefs contre l'Église catholique en utilisant une invention toute nouvelle, la presse à imprimer. Ainsi débuta la réforme protestante. Ce schisme détournera de façon importante le cours de l'Histoire en Europe, mais à court terme, il suscita surtout un conflit religieux tumultueux. Presque toute l'Europe connut un repli sur soi pour faire face à cette agitation ainsi qu'à cette crise religieuse. Des conflits politiques croissants secouèrent la majeure partie de l'Europe de l'Ouest durant des décennies, accaparant les ressources qui auraient dû être attribuées aux efforts de colonisation. Les guerres de religion en France, les guerres en Italie et les révoltes populaires combinées aux soulèvements religieux ont détourné l'attention de l'Europe du Nouveau Monde pendant plus d'un siècle.

La France voyait l'Amérique du Nord comme la meilleure source de richesse et de puissance possible et souhaitait, en exploitant ces contrées, arriver à alléger ses dettes de guerre. Quand l'explorateur français Jacques Cartier navigua sur le fleuve Saint-Laurent en 1534, il revendiqua le territoire au nom de la France et lui donna le nom qu'il porte encore aujourd'hui : le Canada. Après que les commerçants de fourrure se furent implantés dans l'Est du Canada, la France monopolisa le commerce de la fourrure. Bien que les Français tentèrent d'établir des relations commerciales amicales avec les peuples autochtones, certains d'entre eux, dont les Iroquois, se révélèrent particulièrement hostiles. Les conflits avec les tribus locales ont rapidement fait de convaincre la Couronne que pour assurer la rentabilité du commerce au Canada, une présence militaire et civile permanente était essentielle. Le roi Henri IV dépêcha donc sur place son « hydrographe » Samuel de Champlain pour cartographier la région.

En 1605, après avoir exploré la côte de l'Amérique du Nord jusqu'à Cape Cod, Champlain établira un premier peuplement français à Port-Royal et fondera ensuite la ville de Québec en 1608. La Nouvelle-France, comme on l'appelait à l'époque, se développa lentement, principalement en raison du manque d'intérêt de la mère patrie et de la guerre avec les Iroquois. Les colons survécurent aux attaques des Autochtones grâce à leurs alliances avec les Algonquins, les Montagnais et les Hurons. En plus de garantir la survie des colons, ces alliances permirent à la France d'affermir son contrôle du commerce des fourrures. Les Européens n'avaient aucune notion du milieu sauvage de la région, connaissances que les Autochtones leur procureront.

Une fois de plus, des tensions religieuses en Europe vinrent interférer avec le développement des établissements au Canada. Vers le milieu du dix-septième siècle, alors que les colonies anglaises en Amérique et dans les Caraïbes devenaient autosuffisantes, la Nouvelle-France demeurait sous-peuplée. Cette colonie éprouvait des difficultés et épuisait les ressources de la France. La monarchie française décida de prendre les choses en mains en offrant des primes à ceux qui décideraient d'émigrer en Nouvelle-France. Une seule condition s'imposait : tous les colons en partance devaient être catholiques ou se convertir au catholicisme avant de quitter l'Europe. Ce changement de politique, imposé à la demande du fervent cardinal Richelieu, le conseiller le plus proche du roi Louis XIII, créera de nombreuses frictions. Auparavant, les protestants français, particulièrement la secte persécutée connue sous le nom de Huguenots, s'exilaient souvent en Nouvelle-France pour fuir les persécutions religieuses. Ce nouveau décret du cardinal Richelieu aura un effet durable sur la composition politique et religieuse du Canada moderne.

Vers la fin du dix-septième siècle, les assises des colonies anglaises et françaises du Nouveau Monde commençaient enfin à gagner en solidité. Les deux nations avaient remporté leur mise et leurs colonies dégageaient un bon profit, mais une guerre en Europe devait venir gêner une fois de plus la croissance balbutiante du Canada. La Nouvelle-France, déjà au cœur d'une brutale guerre intertribale avec les Algonquins, entra en conflit avec la confédération iroquoise qui s'opposait à elle. Avec la guerre de Neuf Ans, qui débuta en 1688 et vit la France entrer en conflit avec presque tout le reste de l'Europe, les Iroquois commencèrent à recevoir des armes de la part des Anglais, en accord aux politiques de leur gouvernement. Cette escalade de violence des Anglais envenima cette guerre déjà sanglante. L'armée anglaise et ses alliés iroquois capturèrent Port-Royal, mais furent repoussés de Québec, principalement en raison des maladies qui décimaient les forces. La guerre finit par s'essouffler sur le Continent, et un traité de paix fut signé en 1697. Les Iroquois continueront cependant à se battre sans les Britanniques, mais subiront finalement d'importantes défaites qui les forceront à établir la paix quatre ans plus tard.

La Nouvelle-France (et le Canada par le fait même) semblait bien acquise à la mère patrie à la suite de la conclusion de la guerre de Neuf Ans. Toutefois, le contrôle de la région par la France ne durera pas longtemps. La guerre de Succession d'Espagne, qui commencera un an seulement après la signature du traité de paix entre la France et les Iroquois, permettra à l'Angleterre de prendre possession de la Nouvelle-Écosse et de Terre-Neuve, ainsi que des droits sur la région entourant la baie d'Hudson. Un nouveau conflit, nommé la guerre du roi George, débutera trois décennies plus tard, soit en 1744, mais aucun des deux belligérants ne réussira à élargir alors ses positions coloniales.

En 1754, l'animosité de longue date entre les Anglais et les Français gagnera le Nouveau Monde, avec comme point culminant la guerre de Sept Ans, appelée aussi en Amérique guerre franco-indienne. Trois causes principales étaient à la base de ce conflit. D'abord, le lucratif commerce de la fourrure, l'abondance des poissons, la richesse des forêts et les gisements de minerais étaient tous des sources de fortune pour quiconque contrôlerait le Canada. Ensuite, les Anglais, anticatholiques invétérés, croyaient que les Français étaient des hérétiques, un sentiment qui était d'ailleurs réciproque! Enfin, le contrôle des colonies outre-mer pourrait servir comme monnaie d'échange diplomatique si la guerre en Europe devait se détériorer.

La guerre de Sept Ans fut la première guerre à l'échelle mondiale et qui fit rage sur cinq continents : l'Amérique du Nord, l'Amérique du Sud, l'Afrique, l'Europe et l'Asie. Plus d'un million de personnes perdront la vie et la conclusion de cette guerre changera totalement le partage du pouvoir dans le Nouveau Monde. La Grande-Bretagne obtiendra le contrôle de toutes les colonies françaises en Amérique du Nord, faisant ainsi du Canada une colonie britannique. Toutefois, 150 années de colonisation française ne pouvaient disparaître du jour au lendemain. Encore aujourd'hui, les relations entre Anglais et Français au Canada connaissent leurs tensions et contrariétés.

Les Britanniques, suite à leur prise de contrôle du Canada en 1764, ne touchèrent pas aux systèmes religieux et économiques en place, au grand soulagement des colons catholiques français. L'Acte de Québec de 1774 permit qu'un système indépendant de lois françaises continue au Québec. Les Britanniques contrôlaient maintenant complètement la portion est de l'Amérique du Nord, depuis la rive est du fleuve Mississippi jusqu'à la côte Atlantique. Le mauvais traitement réservé aux colonies américaines par George III viendrait cependant bientôt modifier de nouveau l'équilibre du pouvoir dans le Nouveau Monde.

À titre de base pour les forces britanniques, de refuge pour les Américains loyaux à la monarchie britannique qui étaient en fuite et de source de milice pour les armées britanniques et américaines, le Canada joua un rôle important dans la guerre de l'Indépendance américaine. L'armée américaine tenta à l'origine de convaincre le Canada de prendre part à sa révolution, mais les Canadiens se relevaient à peine de la guerre de Sept Ans, et la majorité d'entre eux ne voulaient pas d'un autre conflit. Le 27 juin 1775, les troupes américaines attaquèrent Québec. Montréal fut pris sans résistance, mais l'attaque sur la ville de Québec se solda par une défaite, et en 1776, les troupes américaines évacuèrent Montréal.

Lorsque l'Amérique gagna son indépendance de la Grande-Bretagne en 1783, les citoyens loyaux à l'Empire britannique durent s'exiler. Plus de 35 000 d'entre eux se rendirent en Nouvelle-Écosse. Cet important mouvement de masse força le gouvernement britannique à diviser la Nouvelle-Écosse, créant ainsi la nouvelle colonie du Nouveau-Brunswick. Peu de temps après, les loyalistes établis au Québec commencèrent à présenter des demandes pour obtenir leur propre colonie, alors que les Canadiens français étaient aussi déterminés à avoir leur propre assemblée d'élus. En 1791, le Québec fut divisé en deux parties, le Haut-Canada et le Bas-Canada, afin de répondre aux exigences des loyalistes anglais et des Canadiens français.

Au cours des décennies qui suivirent, les tensions entre la Grande-Bretagne et l'Amérique demeurèrent vives, et encore une fois, un conflit déchira le Canada. Les États-Unis déclarèrent la guerre à la Grande-Bretagne en 1812 en raison de l'approvisionnement en armes des tribus amérindiennes hostiles et du service militaire obligatoire des marins américains à la marine britannique. Le Canada fut un des champs de bataille principaux de ce conflit puisque les États-Unis avaient planifié s'emparer du Canada et l'utiliser comme monnaie d'échange pour négocier avec les Britanniques. Les Américains s'attendaient à gagner le soutien des Canadiens qu'ils croyaient malheureux sous le contrôle colonial des Anglais. Toutefois, beaucoup de Canadiens, descendants de loyalistes britanniques qui avaient fui l'Amérique, percevaient les États-Unis comme des envahisseurs et des occupants.

L'armée américaine subit une défaite tôt dans le conflit lorsqu'elle fut battue par le général Isaac Brock et ses forces d'alliés indiens et de militaires locaux lors de la bataille de Queenston Heights. L'armée américaine en arriva quand même occuper et à piller un grand nombre de villes, incluant York (aujourd'hui Toronto) et Newark (aujourd'hui Niagra-on-the-Lake), jusqu'à contrôler à un certain moment presque tout le territoire correspondant à l'Ontario et au Québec d'aujourd'hui, mais en fin de compte, l'armée américaine fut repoussée, et bien que la guerre finit sans réel vainqueur, le fait qu'une prise de contrôle américaine fut empêchée donna aux Canadiens un regain de confiance et devint source de fierté nationale.

Même si les Canadiens rejetaient l'idée d'un envahisseur américain sur leur sol, l'exemple politique des États-Unis laissait sa marque à travers le pays. Des rébellions éclatèrent contre les Britanniques en 1837. Les Canadiens, insatisfaits de la distribution inéquitable des richesses tirées des ressources naturelles du Canada, s'insurgeaient de ne pas être représentés au sein du gouvernement britannique. Puisque les Britanniques considéraient que les frictions entre les Français et les Anglais étaient la source des conflits qu'ils vivaient avec le Canada, toutes les colonies canadiennes furent réunies en 1840 sous le nom de la Province du Canada, aussi appelée le Canada-Uni. En 1849, les États-Unis et l'Empire britannique se mirent d'accord pour que le 49e parallèle nord serve de frontière entre les deux nations, et les Britanniques étendirent le Canada jusqu'au au littoral ouest, annexant ainsi la Colombie-Britannique.

C'est pratiquement depuis la guerre d'Indépendance américaine que l'indépendance du Canada fait l'objet de débats en Grande-Bretagne comme au Canada. Certains prônaient une révolution violente et une indépendance canadienne totale. D'autres désiraient suivre un processus vers l'autonomie plus lent et graduel. Le 1er juillet 1867, le Parlement britannique édicta l'Acte de l'Amérique du Nord britannique, qui établit le Dominion du Canada comme une colonie distincte et dotée d'un gouvernement autonome. Sans être complètement détaché de l'Angleterre, particulièrement en ce qui a trait à la politique étrangère, sur le plan de la politique intérieure, le Canada gagnait pleine liberté et souveraineté.

Au cours des décennies suivantes, le Canada continua son expansion vers l'Ouest. Grâce à l'achat de deux énormes territoires au nord, les Territoires du Nord-Ouest et la Terre de Rupert, acquis de la Compagnie de la Baie d'Hudson, le pays doubla pratiquement sa superficie. Beaucoup de francophones et de Métis catholiques, les enfants d'Autochtones et de pionniers, vivaient à l'ouest de l'Ontario. Après la vente de la Terre de Rupert, plusieurs colons ontariens affluèrent dans cette région en espérant réclamer ces terres. Les Métis se mirent à craindre que cette arrivée massive de protestants anglais mette en péril leurs droits linguistiques, religieux et territoriaux. Le chef Métis Louis Riel organisa la Rébellion de la rivière Rouge en 1869 dans le but de garantir la protection de ces droits. Cette révolte mena à la création du Manitoba, une province qui mit en place des lois rigoureuses protégeant les Métis, les francophones et les catholiques. En 1905, la Colombie-Britannique, la Saskatchewan, l'Île-du-Prince-Édouard et l'Alberta furent coup sur coup jointes aux provinces fondatrices du Haut et du Bas-Canada, au Nouveau-Brunswick et à la Nouvelle-Écosse.

La construction d'un chemin de fer transcontinental, complété en 1885, stimula l'expansion du Canada. Ce chemin de fer incita de nouveaux colons à déménager dans l'Ouest pour s'établir dans les nouvelles provinces, mais ces nouveaux arrivants voulurent chasser les Autochtones de leurs terres, ce qui, une fois de plus, fit éclater des rébellions qui finirent en bains de sang. Le sentiment que le gouvernement canadien n'écoutait pas les préoccupations des catholiques francophones engendra une crise politique qui entraîna la démission du premier ministre Mackenzie Bowell en 1896 lorsque le gouvernement tenta de retirer au français son statut de langue officielle au Manitoba, ce qui allait à l'encontre des lois de la province.

Le Canada et les États-Unis connurent une période d'expansion vers l'ouest à la fin du dix-neuvième siècle grâce au développement du chemin de fer, à l'attrait qu'exerçaient ses contrées vierges et à la découverte de gisements de minerais. Ces facteurs, additionnés de l'arrivée massive d'immigrants en provenance d'Europe, permirent au Canada d'être le pays présentant la croissance économique la plus forte entre 1896 et 1911. Durant cette période, le gouvernement canadien créa le Yukon, un territoire dont la superficie se compare à celle de l'Allemagne, l'Autriche et la Suisse combinées, et dont la population se chiffrait à seulement 8 500 habitants à ce moment.

À l'aube du vingtième siècle, le Canada connut son premier conflit d'importance avec sa puissance coloniale. Lorsque la Grande-Bretagne entra dans la Guerre des Boers en 1889, la majorité des Anglo-canadiens appuyaient l'annexion de l'Afrique du Sud à l'Empire britannique. Les Canadiens français, toutefois, ne s'intéressaient pas vraiment à l'impérialisme britannique, car ils se considéraient comme un cas à part et considéraient qu'ils faisaient partie de l'Empire britannique uniquement pour la forme. En guise de compromis, tous ceux se portant volontaires purent servir dans la Guerre des Boers, mais l'Armée canadienne comme telle ne s'impliqua pas dans ce conflit. Cette vision du Canada français comme une entité à part, vision exacerbée par les rébellions et par les lois anti-françaises des décennies précédentes, continuera de se manifester dans la politique du Canada des années à venir.

Bien qu'un grand nombre de Canadiens français désirait se départir du joug de l'Empire britannique, le pays devait tout de même se plier à la politique étrangère britannique. Avec l'assassinat de l'Archiduc Ferdinand le 28 juin 1914, le Canada fut pris dans le chaotique système d'alliances que suscita la Première Guerre mondiale. Lorsque la Grande-Bretagne déclara la guerre aux puissances centrales le 4 août, les troupes canadiennes furent appelées en renfort. Comme pour la majorité des puissances alliées, les disputes internes furent temporairement mises de côté, et l'appui à la guerre demeura massif, même chez les Canadiens français. Après plus de 200 000 morts et blessés de guerre, sur une population de 7 millions d'habitants, l'effort de guerre commença à s'essouffler. Au moment où le gouvernement tenta d'introduire le service obligatoire en 1917, beaucoup de Canadiens, et principalement des Canadiens français, s'opposèrent farouchement à la guerre. Malgré l'opinion populaire, la Première Guerre mondiale contribua à alimenter le sentiment de nationalisme et d'identité canadienne, surtout grâce au rôle important que joua le Canada dans la guerre la plus importante de l'histoire de l'humanité. Les très nombreuses victimes canadiennes occasionnées par ce conflit que plusieurs considéraient comme une guerre

« britannique » vint aussi augmenter le ressentiment accumulé envers l'Empire.

La Première Guerre mondiale changea radicalement le visage politique du Canada. Après les horreurs vécues pendant ce conflit, les soldats rentrèrent chez eux avec de nouvelles idéologies politiques. Le socialisme, le communisme, le syndicalisme et d'autres courants progressistes de gauche gagnèrent en popularité dans les années suivant la guerre, tandis que le retour massif des soldats faisait augmenter le taux de chômage et diminuer les salaires. La grève générale de Winnipeg de 1919, la plus importante d'une série de grèves qui paralysèrent le pays, fut brutalement mise fin par la police, au prix d'un mort et de 30 blessés. Lorsque le Canada accorda le droit de vote aux femmes en 1918, le Parti conservateur en place s'effondra, en partie en raison de ses actions durant la grève. Le Parti libéral, en prenant le contrôle du gouvernement, acquiesça à une bonne partie des demandes originales du comité de grève, incluant le droit de former des syndicats sans la permission du gouvernement. Des partis progressistes et socialistes se formèrent les années suivantes, incluant le Parti progressiste du Canada et la Fédération du Commonwealth coopératif.

En 1931, le Parlement britannique promulgua le Statut de Westminster, qui donna le statut d'entité législative indépendante à toutes les colonies et à tous les dominions de l'Empire britannique, incluant le Canada, l'Australie, la Nouvelle-Zélande et l'Irlande. Cet acte permit à ces pays de rédiger leur propre constitution et supprima le pouvoir législatif qu'avait le gouvernement britannique dans ces régions, assurant ainsi l'indépendance de celles-ci tout en les incluant dans un Commonwealth britannique à l'échelle mondiale.

Lorsque le marché boursier américain connut son krach lors du mardi noir de 1929, événement qui marqua le début de la Grande dépression, l'économie canadienne ne tarda pas à en ressentir les effets. En 1933, le produit national brut canadien connut une baisse de 40 %. Les secteurs manufacturiers et agricoles furent le plus durement touchés, et le prix de blé, le principal produit d'exportation du Canada, chuta de moitié. Au creux de la vague, 30 % des Canadiens étaient sans emploi. Terre-Neuve, affirmant que les politiques du gouvernement canadien étaient la cause de ce creux économique, vota de quitter la Fédération canadienne pour rejoindre l'Empire britannique.

Après que les partis Libéral et Conservateur se soient montrés incapables de trouver des solutions à cette crise, beaucoup de Canadiens se tournèrent vers d'autres partis, comme la Fédération du Commonwealth coopératif et le Parti Crédit Social du Canada. Après que le gouvernement conservateur de R. B. Bennet ait placé des chômeurs dans des camps de travail pour pallier au coût élevé du système d'aide sociale, la Ligue d'unité ouvrière (LUO) organisa une importante manifestation appelée la « Marche sur Ottawa » dans le but d'obtenir des améliorations aux conditions et avantages dans les camps. La tentative de Bennett pour arrêter cette marche provoquera l'émeute de Regina et contribua en fin de compte à sa défaite aux élections de 1935. Le nouveau gouvernement libéral élimina les camps et institua des programmes sociaux pour diminuer les effets de la Dépression, mais ceci n'empêcha pas le Canada d'être fortement touché par cette dernière. Environ un cinquième de la population dépendait des allocations du gouvernement et du soutien des programmes sociaux. Même après le boom de l'économie canadienne causé par la Seconde Guerre mondiale, ces programmes restèrent en place et continuèrent d'évoluer.

La Seconde Guerre mondiale débuta le 1er septembre 1939. Puisque le Canada était de plus en plus indépendant de l'Angleterre, le pays n'entra pas en guerre immédiatement après la déclaration de la Grande-Bretagne comme il l'avait fait lors de la Première Guerre mondiale, mais décida plutôt de déclarer d'elle-même la guerre neuf jours plus tard. Alors que le massacre japonais et nazi était toujours à son comble, le ravitaillement et le matériel de guerre des Canadiens s'avérèrent d'une importance capitale pour permettre à la Grande-Bretagne de résister à l'invasion allemande. Une fois que les Alliés furent en position de contre-attaquer, les troupes canadiennes furent déployées partout dans le monde, et servirent vaillamment dans plusieurs batailles importantes, incluant l'invasion de la Sicile et de l'Italie en 1943, le débarquement allié en Normandie en 1944, la libération des Pays-Bas et la traversée de la France et de l'Allemagne pour mettre fin à la guerre. Un raid majoritairement canadien à Dieppe en France se solda par 3 000 morts, blessés et captifs, et les sous-marins allemands qui infestaient les eaux canadiennes coulèrent un grand nombre de navires de ravitaillement. En tout et partout, la Seconde Guerre mondiale entraînera la mort de 42 000 canadiens.

Lorsque les Japonais bombardèrent Pearl Harbor le 7 décembre 1941, les 22 000 Canadiens d'origine japonaise vivant alors en Colombie-Britannique durent composer avec les conséquences de la douleur et de la colère qui s'ensuivirent. Le sentiment anti-asiatique dans la province fut davantage attisé lorsque des milliers de Canadiens furent tués ou capturés durant l'invasion de Hong Kong par les Japonais. En 1942, toutes les personnes de descendance japonaise furent envoyées dans des camps d'internement, et après la fin de la guerre, tous les Canadiens d'origine japonaise furent déportés de la Colombie-Britannique. Ce n'est qu'en 1949 qu'ils furent libres de vivre n'importe où au Canada. En 1988, les Canadiens d'origine japonaise furent finalement indemnisés pour le tort qu'ils ont dû subir durant la guerre.

À la conclusion de la Seconde Guerre mondiale, le Canada et les États-Unis étaient les deux seuls pays à n'avoir pas eu de combats liés à cette guerre sur leur territoire. Cela permit à ces deux pays de profiter d'un contexte économique unique. Grâce à un secteur manufacturier en pleine relance, à la découverte de pétrole en Alberta et à sa position de partenaire commercial principal de la superpuissance économique juste au sud de la frontière, le Canada vit son économie exploser. Cette nouvelle prospérité favorisa la création d'un programme d'aide sociale radicalement amélioré. Grâce à l'aide sociale centralisée de la fin des années 1930 et du début des années 1940 ainsi qu'aux nombreuses politiques sociales de la Fédération du Commonwealth coopératif, les Canadiens profiteront de l'assurance-hospitalisation, d'un régime de pensions et des allocations familiales. Ces politiques sociales progressistes convainquirent Terre-Neuve de rejoindre le Canada suite à un référendum en 1949.

Le Canada consolida sa position lors de la Guerre froide grâce à son statut de membre fondateur de l'OTAN en 1949. L'économie du pays était directement liée à celle des États-Unis. Le Canada participa à la guerre de Corée, et ses troupes furent postées en Allemagne de l'Ouest, à la frontière du bloc communiste. Le vote canadien aux Nations Unies ne fut pas toujours identique à celui des États-Unis, mais il n'y avait aucun doute que le Canada était un allié des Américains dans sa guerre contre l'Union soviétique.

Le traitement que le Canada réserva à ses peuples autochtones au fil du temps présente une histoire peu reluisante. Si l'on recule à la fin des années 1800, lorsque le bison fut chassé au point d'être presque totalement exterminé et que les chemins de fer amenèrent davantage de colons dans les territoires autochtones, les membres des Premières nations furent traités comme des citoyens de second ordre. La famine, l'assimilation et une rébellion avortée mirent fin à la résistance autochtone, mais celle-ci reprit vigueur après la Seconde Guerre mondiale. La décolonisation et un esprit de démocratie renouvelé étaient mis de l'avant par les puissances occidentales dans leur lutte contre la tyrannie soviétique, mais la majorité des Premières nations n'obtinrent quand même le droit de vote qu'à la fin des années 1950. Pour pouvoir voter, les gens des Premières nations devaient renoncer à leur statut « d'Indien ». Ce n'est qu'en 1960 (1969 au Québec) que les gens des Premières nations obtinrent le droit de voter librement.

Au début des années 1960, le gouvernement canadien dut faire face à une croissance marquée du radicalisme et d'organisations populaires. Le mouvement nationaliste québécois n'avait cessé de prendre de l'ampleur depuis que les Britanniques avaient pris le contrôle du Canada aux dépens des Français en 1764. Les Canadiens français se considéraient comme une nation distincte, et étaient souvent en désaccord avec les politiques gouvernementales canadiennes. Les factions canadiennes-françaises les plus radicales avaient le sentiment d'être opprimées, et que leur langue et leur culture étaient menacées. Inspirés par les révolutions se déroulant partout dans le monde, les groupes de gauche nationalistes ou terroristes se multiplièrent, et le Canada ne fut pas épargné. Le Front de Libération du Québec commit plus de 200 attentats à la bombe, tuant ainsi cinq personnes dans sa quête d'un Québec indépendant. Bien que les actes de violence furent majoritairement condamnés par la population, un profond désir d'indépendance alimentait les protestations des Québécois. Lorsque Pierre Elliott Trudeau fut élu Premier ministre en 1968, il mit le Québec sous la loi martiale et procéda à l'arrestation de plusieurs membres du FLQ.

Pendant que la crise au Québec s'aggravait durant les années 1970, les États-Unis s'engagèrent dans un des conflits les plus controversés de l'histoire moderne : la guerre en Indochine. La guerre du Vietnam entraîna la mort de 1 500 000 personnes et radicalisa une génération entière. Le Canada ne fit pas exception. Les jeunes de tout le pays protestèrent contre ce qu'ils considéraient être l'impérialisme américain. Le gouvernement canadien refusa de participer à cette guerre, et accorda la citoyenneté à plus de 125 000 Américains réfractaires tout au long du conflit. Ceci mena à d'importantes frictions entre les gouvernements canadien et américain. Aujourd'hui encore, le Vietnam et le Canada jouissent d'une relation privilégiée, et des centaines de milliers de Vietnamiens ont immigré sur la côte Ouest du Canada. La guerre du Vietnam coïncida aussi avec l'ascension du Nouveau Parti Démocratique, le successeur de la Fédération du Commonwealth coopératif. Depuis ses débuts en 1962, le NPD changea le visage de la politique canadienne en obtenant régulièrement entre 10 et 20 % des votes et en formant une coalition majoritaire avec le parti vainqueur. Lors des élections fédérales de 2011, le NPD a obtenu son meilleur résultat à ce jour, en récoltant 30 % des voix et le rôle de l'opposition officielle pour la première fois. Il a combattu pour la sauvegarde du programme d'aide sociale du Canada, pour une politique étrangère humanitaire ainsi que pour les droits des Autochtones.

Les jeunes de tous les coins du Canada devinrent de plus en plus impliqués en politique après la guerre du Vietnam, et ce nouvel intérêt marqué pour la politique permit d'aborder la question de la souveraineté du Québec. Le Parti québécois fut formé en 1968, remporta les élections au Québec en 1976 et fit du français la langue officielle de la province en 1977. Finalement, le parti tint sa promesse et instaura un référendum pour décider de l'avenir du Québec. Ce référendum stipulait simplement que le Québec « négocierait une nouvelle entente avec le reste du Canada, entente fondée sur l'égalité des peuples, en vertu de laquelle le Québec aurait obtenu le pouvoir exclusif de faire ses lois, autrement dit, la souveraineté ». Le fait que le référendum ne garantissait pas une indépendance complète, combiné à un assaut du service des relations publiques du gouvernement, fit échouer le référendum.

Bien que le Canada devint une entité souveraine en 1867, et que son indépendance s'est accrue en 1931, techniquement, le pays n'était pas encore tout à fait une nation souveraine. Le Canada n'était pas en mesure d'apporter des amendements à sa propre constitution, et la capacité du Canada d'agir à l'encontre des désirs du gouvernement britannique était encore mise en doute. En 1982, Trudeau confirma le statut de nation souveraine du Canada en signant la loi constitutionnelle et la Charte canadienne des droits et libertés. Bien qu'il était encore membre du Commonwealth britannique, le Canada n'était plus sous le contrôle du parlement britannique.

Suite à l'indépendance complète du Canada par rapport à la Grande-Bretagne, la question du commerce avec les États-Unis devint la principale préoccupation de l'économie canadienne. L'Accord de libre-échange Canada-États-Unis rédigé en 1988 devint un modèle pour l'Accord de libre-échange nord-américain et l'Accord de libre-échange de l'Amérique centrale. Cet accord, de même que les accords de libre-échange subséquents, fut critiqué, car on considérait qu'éliminer les barrières commerciales ferait en sorte que les consommateurs canadiens seraient à la merci des puissantes corporations américaines. Cet accord fut au centre des élections de 1988 : le Parti libéral et le NPD s'y opposaient, alors que les progressistes conservateurs tentaient de le faire passer. Une majorité de 57 % vota contre les progressistes conservateurs, mais puisqu'ils reçurent néanmoins le plus grand nombre de votes pour un unique parti, ils obtinrent une majorité de sièges au parlement et conclurent l'accord de libre-échange.

Le Parti Québécois, suite à l'échec du référendum de 1980, forma un parti politique canadien, le Bloc Québécois, et poursuivit avec acharnement son échéancier pour un Québec indépendant. Un deuxième référendum, en 1995, occasionna un débat encore plus virulent que celui du référendum de 1980, avec des campagnes médiatiques massives de part et d'autres des deux camps. Le jour du scrutin, le référendum échoua par une mince marge de 54 000 votes, un résultat qui mit au jour la division du Québec sur cette question. Considérant que 86 000 bulletins avaient été rejetés comme invalides, le résultat sur la question de l'indépendance du Québec a été si près de la ligne décisive qu'il ne serait pas surprenant qu'un autre referendum ait lieu dans le futur.

En 1990, une révolte amérindienne dans une petite ville baptisée Oka, à l'ouest de Montréal, a mené à l'intervention de l'armée canadienne. Trois personnes moururent au cours de cette crise. Bien qu'il y ait précédemment eu de nombreux conflits violents entre les membres des Premières nations et le gouvernement du Canada, la situation à Oka marqua le début d'une nouvelle ère de résistance active des Autochtones. Comme le Canada compte plus d'un million d'habitants de descendance amérindienne, de nombreuses organisations autochtones ont réclamé un meilleur contrôle des ressources sur leurs terres, ce qui a causé des conflits violents entre les membres des Premières nations et les sociétés exploitant les ressources minières, maritimes ou forestières sur leurs territoires. L'une des conséquences de ces manifestations fut la création d'un nouveau territoire, le Nunavut en 1999, dans les régions de l'extrême nord du pays. Bien que ce territoire compte moins de 35 000 habitants, près de 85 % de sa population y possède le statut d'Inuit, et le territoire a été en mesure d'adopter de nombreuses lois assurant les droits des Inuits et donnant corps à leurs revendications concernant le territoire et ses ressources.

Après l'écrasement des avions d'al-Qaida dans les tours du World Trade Center à New York, le 11 septembre 2001, le Canada s'est engagé dans le conflit en Afghanistan en tant qu'élément de la Force d'assistance à la sécurité internationale en réaction aux extrémistes islamistes; il est resté au pays jusqu'en 2011 afin de l'aider à se stabiliser.

Alors que la question des changements climatiques devenait de plus en plus une source d'inquiétude, le Canada adhère, en 2005, au Protocole de Kyoto, une entente internationale dont l'objectif est de réduire l'émission de gaz à effet de serre. Il s'est retiré de l'entente en 2011, sous la gouverne de Stephen Harper, alors que les émissions excédaient de beaucoup les taux cibles.

Aujourd'hui, le Canada doit continuer à gérer ses relations avec le Québec et les membres des Premières nations tout en faisant face à d'autres enjeux, comme la dépénalisation des drogues, l'immigration, sa participation aux missions de maintien de la paix et le contrôle des bras de mer de l'Arctique.

National Anthem: O Canada

From "Chapter 5, Statutes of Canada 1980; proclaimed July 1, 1980." Composed by Calixa Lavallée; French lyrics written by Judge Adolphe-Basile Routhier; English lyrics written by Robert Stanley Weir (with some changes incorporated in 1967).

O Canada! Our home and native land!
True patriot love in all thy sons command.
With glowing hearts we see thee rise,
The True North strong and free!
From far and wide, O Canada, We stand on guard for thee.
God keep our land glorious and free!
O Canada, we stand on guard for thee.
O Canada, we stand on guard for thee.

O Canada! Terre de nos aïeux!
Ton front est ceint de fleurons glorieux!
Car ton bras sait porter l'épée, Il sait porter la croix!
Ton histoire est une épopée Des plus brillants exploits.
Et ta valeur, de foi trempée,
Protégera nos foyers et nos droits,
Protégera nos foyers et nos droits.

Note: Private Member's Bill C-210 passed in the House of Commons on June 15, 2016, which changed the second line "in all thy sons command" to "in all of us command," thereby making it gender-neutral.

Emblems of Canada

The Beaver
Recognized as a symbol of Canada's sovereignty. Official status as an emblem of Canada as of May 24, 1975.
Maple Tree
Arboreal emblem of Canada, proclaimed April 25, 1996.
Official Colours
Red and white, as proclaimed in 1921.
Official Sports
Hockey (winter); Lacrosse (summer).

Full-colour images of Canadian and provincial flags, coats of arms, floral emblems, and selected honours start on page A-14.

Fathers of Confederation

Three conferences helped to pave the way for Confederation - those held at Charlottetown (September, 1864), Québec City (October, 1864) and London (December, 1866). As all the delegates who were at the Charlottetown conferences were also in attendance at Québec, the following list includes the names of all those who attended one or more of the three conferences. *Hewitt Bernard was John A. Macdonald's private secretary. He served as secretary of both the Québec and London conferences.

DELEGATES TO THE CONFEDERATION CONFERENCES, 1864-1866

LEGEND:
Charlottetown, 1 September, 1864 - C
Québec, 10 October, 1864 - Q
London, 4 December, 1866 - L

CANADA

John A. Macdonald	C Q L
George E. Cartier	C Q L
Alexander T. Galt	C Q L
William McDougall	C Q L
Hector L. Langevin	C Q L
George Brown	C Q
Thomas D'Arcy McGee	C Q
Alexander Campbell	C Q
Sir Etienne P. Taché	Q
Oliver Mowat	Q
J.C. Chapais	Q
James Cockburn	Q
W.P. Howland	L
*Hewitt Bernard	

NOVA SCOTIA

Charles Tupper	C Q L
William A. Henry	C Q L
Jonathan McCully	C Q L
Adams G. Archibald	C Q L
Robert B. Dickey	Q
J.W. Ritchie	L

NEW BRUNSWICK

Samuel L. Tilley	C Q L
J.M. Johnson	C Q L
William H. Steeves	C Q
E.B. Chandler	C Q
John Hamilton Gray	C Q
Peter Mitchell	Q L
Charles Fisher	Q L
R.D. Wilmot	L

PRINCE EDWARD ISLAND

John Hamilton Gray	C Q
Edward Palmer	C Q
William H. Pope	C Q
A.A. Macdonald	C Q
George Coles	C Q
T.H. Haviland	Q
Edward Whelan	Q

NEWFOUNDLAND

F.B.T. Carter	Q
Ambrose Shea	Q

PARTICIPANTS TO THE FIRST MINISTERS' CONSTITUTIONAL CONFERENCE ON PATRIATION OF THE CONSTITUTION (Held in Ottawa from September 2 to 5, 1981)

- The Right Honourable Pierre Elliott Trudeau, P.C., Q.C., M.P., Prime Minister of Canada;
- The Honourable William G. Davis, Q.C., Premier of Ontario;
- The Honourable René Lévesque, Premier of Québec; The Honourable John M. Buchanan, Q.C., Premier of Nova Scotia;
- The Honourable Richard B. Hatfield, Premier of New Brunswick;
- The Honourable Sterling R. Lyon, Q.C., Premier of Manitoba;
- The Honourable W.R. Bennett, Premier of British Columbia;
- The Honourable J. Angus MacLean, P.C., D.F.C., C.D., Premier of Prince Edward Island; The Honourable Allan Blakeney, Q.C., Premier of Saskatchewan; The Honourable Peter Lougheed, Q.C., Premier of Alberta;
- The Honourable Brian Peckford, Premier of Newfoundland.

Timeline of Canadian History

- 12000 BC Migration of natives across the Bering land bridge
- 2000 BC Inuit arrive in North America
- 1000 Leif Erickson lands on Baffin Island
- 1497 John Cabot reaches Newfoundland
- 1524-1528 Giovanni da Verrazano's voyages; New France named
- 1534-1541 Jacque Cartier explores North America
- 1604 Attempt to settle Acadia by Sieur de Monts and Samuel de Champlain
- 1608 Champlain founds Quebec
- 1610 Henry Hudson's European discovery of Hudson Bay
- 1611 Port-Royal established
- 1621 Nova Scotia granted to Sir William Alexander
- 1627 Company of New France established
- 1628 Kirke brothers raid New France
- 1632 Quebec returned to the French
- 1640s Huron decimated by Iroquois raids and disease
- 1642 Montreal established by Paul de Chomedey de Maisonneuve and Jeanne Mance
- 1663 France regains control of New France
- 1670 Charles II forms the Hudson Bay Company. Fur trade attracts settlers to the Great Lakes area.
- 1689-1697 King William's War
- 1702-1713 Queen Anne's War
- 1713 Treaty of Utrecht cedes Newfoundland and Acadia to Britain; Louisbourg established
- 1744-1748 King George's War
- 1749 Halifax established
- 1755-1762 Acadian deportation
- 1756-1763 Seven Years' War leads to Conquest
- 1759 Quebec City falls to the British
- 1763 Treaty of Paris cedes most of North America to British; Royal Proclamation reformulates British North America
- 1774 Quebec Act extends Quebec's territory and grants limited rights to French
- 1770s-1780s Loyalists arrive in British North America
- 1783 Treaty of Paris; United States victorious in Revolutionary War
- 1784 New Brunswick established by Loyalists
- 1791 Constitutional Act (Canada Act) creates Upper and Lower Canada
- 1793 Alexander Mackenzie crosses the continent and reaches the Pacific Ocean
- 1812 Selkirk grant in Red River (Assiniboia)
- 1812-1814 War of 1812
- 1817 Rush-Bagot Agreement
- 1818 Convention of 1818 creates boundary with the United States at forty-ninth parallel
- 1821 Hudson's Bay Company and North West Company merge
- 1829 Welland Canal opened
- 1832 Rideau Canal completed
- 1837-1838 Rebellions in Lower and Upper Canada
- 1839 Durham's Report; 'Aroostook War'
- 1841 Act of Union creates Canada East and Canada West
- 1846 Oregon Boundary settlement
- 1848-1855 Responsible government established in British North American colonies
- 1849 Annexation Manifesto
- 1854-1866 Reciprocity Treaty with United States
- 1858 British Columbia Colony formed
- 1864 September: Charlottetown Conference; October: Quebec City Conference
- 1867 July 1: Dominion of Canada formed
- 1869-1870 Red River Resistance
- 1870 Manitoba Act
- 1871 British Columbia enters Confederation
- 1872 Dominion Lands Act
- 1873 Prince Edward Island enters Confederation; Supreme Court created
- 1878 National Policy introduced
- 1880 Canada acquires Arctic islands from Britain
- 1885 North-West Rebellion; Canadian Pacific Railway completed
- 1888 Jesuits' Estates Act
- 1890-1897 Manitoba schools controversy
- 1899-1902 South African War (Boer War)
- 1903 Alaska Boundary award
- 1905 Saskatchewan and Alberta join Confederation
- 1909 Boundary Waters Treaty establishes International Joint Commission
- 1910 Naval Service Act creates Canadian navy
- 1911 Reciprocity Agreement with United States rejected
- 1914-1918 World War I
- 1914 War Measures Act passed
- 1917 Battle of Vimy Ridge; Halifax explosion; conscription; Union government formed
- 1917-1920s Canadian National Railway created
- 1918 Women's suffrage for federal elections
- 1919 Winnipeg General Strike
- 1921 Agnes Macphail elected, Canada's first female member of Parliament
- 1923 Halibut Treaty with United States
- 1925-1926 King-Byng controversy

- 1929 U.S. stock market crashes. Drought hits prairies.
- 1931 Statute of Westminster
- 1932 Unemployment Relief Camps organized; Canadian Broadcasting Corporation formed
- 1932-1933 Co-operative Commonwealth Federation established
- 1935 Richard Bedford Bennett's 'New Deal'; On-to-Ottawa Trek
- 1939-1945 World War II (Canada enters war in September 1939)
- 1940 Rowell-Sirois Report on Dominion-Provincial Relations; Ogdensburg Agreement with United States
- 1941 Hyde Park Agreement with United States; Canada declares war on Japan
- 1942 Conscription pledge plebiscite; Dieppe raid
- 1942-1947 Japanese-Canadian relocation
- 1944 Normandy invasion; PC 1003 grants workers the right to collective bargaining
- 1945 Canada joins United Nations as charter member
- 1949 Newfoundland enters Confederation; North Atlantic Treaty Organization (NATO) formed
- 1950-1953 Korean War
- 1951 Massey Commission reports
- 1952 Vincent Massey becomes First Canadian-born governor general
- 1956 Suez Crisis and UN peacekeeping forces organized
- 1957 Hospital Insurance Plan; North American Air Defense Agreement (NORAD) formed
- 1959 St. Lawrence Seaway opens
- 1960s 'Quiet Revolution' in Quebec
- 1961 New Democratic Party (NDP) formed
- 1962 Cuban missile crisis strains Canadian-American relations
- 1965 Canada Assistance Act; Medicare; Canada Pension Plan
- 1967 Expo in Montreal
- 1969 Manhattan incident; Official Languages Act
- 1970 October Crisis
- 1971 National Action Committee on the Status of Women (NAC)
- 1973 Foreign Investment Review Agency (FIRA) created
- 1975 Petro-Can formed; James Bay Agreement between Quebec government, Cree, and Inuit
- 1976 Parti Québécois (PQ) elected in Quebec
- 1977 Bill 101, Charter of the French Language, passed in Quebec
- 1980 National Energy Program; Quebec Referendum on Sovereignty-Association; Canada joins Organization of American States (OAS)
- 1982 Constitution Act passed, including Charter of Rights and Freedoms; Assembly of First Nations formed; Canada agrees to UN Convention on the Law of the Sea
- 1987 Meech Lake Accord; Reform party formed
- 1988 Bill 178 passed in Quebec
- 1989 Free trade agreement with United States implemented
- 1990 Gulf War fought with Canada's participation; Mohawk tensions in Quebec
- 1992 Charlottetown Accord
- 1993 North American Free Trade Agreement (NAFTA) created with United States and Mexico; Bloc Québécois forms official opposition in Canadian Parliament
- 1995 Second Quebec Referendum
- 1997 Canada signs Kyoto Protocol
- 1999 Nunavut, a self-governing territory, established
- 2000 Canadian Alliance formed
- 2001 Canada sends military forces to Afghanistan
- 2003 Conservative Party of Canada (CPC) formed
- 2005 Civil Marriages Act legalizes same-sex marriage
- 2006 Indian Residential Schools Settlement Agreement
- 2008 Economic Recession
- 2010 Vancouver Winter Olympics
- 2014 Formal end to Canada's operations in Afghanistan
- 2015 Canada helps establish the Trans-Pacific Partnership (TPP) trade agreement
- 2016 Federal government launches National Inquiry into Missing and Murdered Indigenous Women and Girls

Chronologie de l'histoire du Canada

- 12 000 av. J.-C. Des peuples en migration traversent le pont continental de Béring
- 2000 av. J.-C. Arrivée des Inuits en Amérique du Nord
- 1000 apr. J.-C. Leif Erickson débarque sur l'Île de Baffin
- 1497 Jean Cabot atteint Terre-Neuve
- 1524-1528 Voyages de Giovanni da Verrazano; la Nouvelle-France obtient son nom
- 1534-1541 Jacques Cartier explore l'Amérique du Nord
- 1604 Le Sieur de Monts et Samuel de Champlain tentent de s'établir en Acadie.
- 1608 Champlain fonde la ville de Québec
- 1610 Découverte européenne de la Baie d'Hudson par Henry Hudson
- 1611 Fondation de Port-Royal
- 1621 La Nouvelle-Écosse est donnée à Sir William Alexander
- 1627 Création de la Compagnie de la Nouvelle-France
- 1628 Les frères Kirke assiègent la Nouvelle-France
- 1632 Québec est remis à la France
- 1640 Les Hurons sont décimés par des attaques d'Iroquois et la maladie
- 1642 Fondation de Montréal par Paul de Chomedey de Maisonneuve et Jeanne Mance
- 1663 La France reprend le contrôle de la Nouvelle-France
- 1670 Le roi Charles II forme la Compagnie de la Baie d'Hudson. Le commerce des fourrures attire des colons vers la région des Grands Lacs.
- 1689-1697 Guerre du roi Guillaume (Guerre de Neuf ans)
- 1770-1780 Arrivée des Loyalistes en Amérique du Nord britannique
- 1702-1713 Guerre de la reine Anne (Deuxième guerre intercoloniale)
- 1713 Traité d'Utrecht cède Terre-Neuve et l'Acadie à l'Angleterre; fondation de Louisbourg
- 1744-1748 Guerre du roi George (Troisième guerre intercoloniale)
- 1749 Fondation de Halifax
- 1755-1762 Déportation des Acadiens
- 1756-1763 La Guerre de Sept ans mène à la conquête de la Nouvelle-France par les Britanniques
- 1759 Chute de la ville de Québec aux mains des Britanniques
- 1763 Le Traité de Paris cède la plus grande partie de l'Amérique du Nord aux Britanniques; la Proclamation royale réorganise l'Amérique du Nord britannique
- 1774 L'Acte de Québec recule les limites du territoire québécois et cède des droits limités aux Français
- 1783 Traité de Paris; les États-Unis remportent la Guerre d'indépendance
- 1784 Les Loyalistes fondent le Nouveau-Brunswick
- 1791 L'Acte constitutionnel créé le Haut et le Bas-Canada
- 1793 Alexander Mackenzie traverse le continent et atteint l'océan Pacifique
- 1812 Selkirk fonde un établissement sur la Rivière Rouge (Assiniboia)
- 1812-1814 Guerre de 1812
- 1817 Accord de Rush-Bagot
- 1818 La Convention de 1818 définit la frontière avec les États-Unis au 49e parallèle
- 1821 Fusion de la Compagnie de la Baie d'Hudson et de la North West
- 1829 Ouverture du Canal Welland
- 1832 Achèvement du Canal Rideau
- 1837-1838 Rébellions des patriotes dans le Bas et le Haut-Canada
- 1839 Rapport Durham; Guerre d'Aroostook
- 1846 Règlement de la frontière de l'Oregon
- 1848-1855 Établissement d'un gouvernement responsable dans les colonies d'Amérique du Nord britannique
- 1849 Manifeste annexionniste
- 1854-1866 Traité de réciprocité avec les États-Unis
- 1858 Création de la colonie de la Colombie-Britannique
- 1864 septembre : Conférence de Charlottetown; octobre : Conférence de la ville de Québec
- 1867, 1er juillet Création de la Confédération
- 1869-1870 Résistance à Rivière Rouge
- 1870 Acte du Manitoba
- 1871 La Colombie-Britannique intègre la Confédération
- 1872 Acte concernant les terres de la Puissance (*Loi des terres fédérales*)
- 1873 L'Île-du-Prince-Édouard intègre la Confédération; création de la Cour Suprême
- 1878 Introduction d'une Politique nationale
- 1880 Le Canada fait l'acquisition des îles arctiques auprès de l'Angleterre
- 1885 Soulèvement des Métis du Nord-Ouest; le chemin de fer du Canadien Pacifique est complété
- 1888 Règlement final des biens des Jésuites
- 1890-1897 Controverse concernant les écoles du Manitoba (abolition des écoles séparées)
- 1899-1902 Guerre d'Afrique du Sud (Guerre des Boers)
- 1905 La Saskatchewan et l'Alberta intègrent la Confédération
- 1909 Le Traité des eaux limitrophes créé la Commission mixte internationale
- 1910 La *Loi du service naval* établit la Marine canadienne
- 1911 Rejet de l'Accord de réciprocité avec les États-Unis
- 1914-1918 Première Guerre mondiale
- 1914 Adoption de la *Loi sur les mesures de guerre*
- 1917 Bataille de Vimy; explosion à Halifax; conscription; formation d'un gouvernement national
- 1917 aux années 1920 Création du chemin de fer du Canadien National
- 1918 Le droit de vote est accordé aux femmes pour les élections fédérales
- 1919 Grève générale à Winnipeg
- 1921 Élection d'Agnes Macphail, la première députée au Parlement du Canada
- 1923 Signature du Traité du flétan avec les États-Unis
- 1925-1926 Affaire King-Byng
- 1929 Aux États-Unis, le marché s'effondre. La sécheresse fait rage dans les Prairies
- 1931 Statut de Westminster
- 1932 Création de camps de secours pour les chômeurs; fondation de la Canadian Broadcasting Corporation
- 1932-1933 Fondation de la Fédération du Commonwealth coopératif (devenu Nouveau Parti démocratique)

- 1935 *New Deal* (Nouvelle Donne) de Richard Bedford Bennett; marche sur Ottawa
- 1939-1945 Deuxième Guerre mondiale (le Canada entre en guerre en septembre 1939)
- 1940 Publication du Rapport Rowell-Sirois sur les relations fédérales-provinciales; Accord d'Ogdensburg avec les États-Unis
- 1941 Hyde Park Agreement avec les États-Unis; le Canada déclare la guerre au Japon
- 1942 Plébicite concernant l'engagement à la guerre; raid de Dieppe
- 1942-1947 Déplacement forcé des Canadiens d'origine japonaise
- 1944 Débarquement de Normandie; le C.P. 1003 accorde aux travailleurs le droit à la négociation collective
- 1945 Le Canada intègre les Nations Unies en tant que membre fondateur
- 1949 Terre-Neuve entre dans la Confédération; création de l'Organisation du traité de l'Atlantique Nord (OTAN)
- 1950-1953 Guerre de Corée
- 1951 Publication des rapports de la Commission Massey
- 1952 Vincent Massey devient le premier gouverneur général né au Canada
- 1956 Crise de Suez et organisation des forces de maintien de la paix des Nations Unies
- 1957 Régime d'assurance-hospitalisation; formation de l'Accord de la défense aérienne de l'Amérique du Nord (NORAD)
- 1959 Ouverture des voies maritimes du St-Laurent
- Années 1960 Révolution tranquille au Québec
- 1961 Formation du Nouveau Parti démocratique (NPD)
- 1962 La crise des missiles cubains met à rude épreuve les relations canado-américaines
- 1965 *Loi sur l'aide sociale*; assurance-maladie; régime de retraite du Canada
- 1967 L'Expo 67 bat son plein à Montréal
- 1969 Épisode du Manhattan; *Loi sur les langues officielles*
- 1970 Crise d'octobre
- 1971 Comité d'action national sur le statut de la femme
- 1973 Création de l'Agence d'examen de l'investissement étranger (AEIE)
- 1975 Fondation de Pétro-Canada; Accord de la Baie James entre le gouvernement du Québec, les Cris et les Inuits
- 1976 Élection du Parti Québécois (PQ) au Québec
- 1977 Adoption du projet de loi 101, Charte de la langue française au Québec
- 1980 Programme énergétique national; référendum québécois sur la souveraineté-association; le Canada se joint à l'organisation des États américains (OÉA)
- 1982 Adoption de la Loi constitutionnelle, y compris la Charte des droits et libertés; fondation de l'Assemblée des Premières Nations; le Canada adhère à la Convention des Nations Unies sur le droit de la mer.
- 1987 Accord du Lac Meech; fondation du Parti réformiste du Canada (Reform Party)
- 1988 Adoption du projet de loi 178 au Québec
- 1989 Entrée en vigueur de l'accord de libre-échange entre le Canada et les États-Unis
- 1990 Participation du Canada à la Guerre du Golfe; Crise d'Oka au Québec
- 1992 Accord de Charlottetown
- 1993 Création de l'Accord de libre-échange nord-américain (ALÉNA) avec les États-Unis et le Mexique; le Bloc québécois constitue l'opposition officielle au Parlement canadien
- 1995 Deuxième référendum au Québec
- 1997 Le Canada signe le Protocole de Kyoto
- 1999 Création du Nunavut en tant que territoire autonome
- 2000 Formation de l'Alliance canadienne
- 2001 Le Canada envoie des forces armées en Afghanistan
- 2003 Formation du Parti conservateur du Canada (PCC)
- 2005 La *Loi sur le mariage civil* légalise le mariage des couples du même sexe
- 2006 Accord de règlement sur l'adjudication des pensionnats indiens
- 2008 Récession
- 2010 Jeux olympiques d'hiver à Vancouver
- 2014 Fin officielle de la présence du Canada en Afghanistan
- 2015 Le Canada aide à mettre en place l'entente du Partenariat transpacifique (PTP)
- 2016 Le gouvernement fédéral a lancé l'Enquête nationale sur les femmes et les filles autochtones disparues et assassinées

THE ROYAL ARMS OF CANADA BY PROCLAMATION OF KING GEORGE V IN 1921

The Royal Arms of Canada were established by proclamation of King George V on 21 November, 1921. On the advice of the Prime Minister of Canada, Her Majesty the Queen approved, on 12 July, 1994, that the arms be augmented with a ribbon bearing the motto of the Order of Canada, DESIDERANTES MELIOREM PATRIAM - "They desire a better country".

This coat of arms was developed by a special committee appointed by Order in Council and is substantially based on a version of the Royal Arms of the United Kingdom, featuring the historic arms of England and Scotland. To this were added the old arms of Royal France and the historic emblem of Ireland, the harp of Tara, thus honouring many of the founding European peoples of modern Canada. To mark these arms as Canadian, the three red maple leaves on a field of white were added.

The supporters, and the crest, above the helmet, are also versions of elements of the Royal Arms of the United Kingdom, including the lion of England and unicorn of Scotland. The lion holds the Union Jack and the unicorn, the banner of Royal France. The crowned lion holding the maple leaf, which is the The Royal Crest of Canada, has, since 1981, also been the official symbol of the Governor General of Canada, the Sovereign's representative.

At the base of the Royal Arms are the floral emblems of the founding nations of Canada, the English Rose, the Scottish Thistle, the French Lily and the Irish Shamrock.

The motto - A MARI USQUE AD MARE - "From sea to sea" - is an extract from the Latin version of verse 8 of the 72nd Psalm - "He shall have dominion also from sea to sea, and from the river unto the ends of the earth."

THE NATIONAL FLAG

The National Flag of Canada, otherwise known as the Canadian Flag, was approved by Parliament and proclaimed by Her Majesty Queen Elizabeth II to be in force as of February 15, 1965. It is described as a red flag of the proportions two by length and one by width, containing in its centre a white square the width of the flag, bearing a single red maple leaf. Red and white are the official colours of Canada, as approved by the proclamation of King George V appointing Arms for Canada in 1921. The Flag is flown on land at all federal government buildings, airports, and military bases within and outside Canada, and may appropriately be flown or displayed by individuals and organizations. The Flag is the proper national colours for all Canadian ships and boats; and it is the flag flown on Canadian Naval vessels.

The Flag is flown daily from sunrise to sunset. However, it is not contrary to etiquette to have the Flag flying at night. No flag, banner or pennant should be flown or displayed above the Canadian Flag. Flags flown together should be approximately the same size and flown from separate staffs at the same height. When flown on a speaker's platform, it should be to the right of the speaker. When used in the body of an auditorium; it should be to the right of the audience. When two or more than three flags are flown together, the Flag should be on the left as seen by spectators in front of the flags. When three flags are flown together, the Canadian Flag should occupy the central position.

A complete set of rules for flying the Canadian Flag can be obtained from the Department of Canadian Heritage.

THE ROYAL UNION FLAG

The Royal Union Flag, generally known as the Union Jack, was approved by Parliament on December 18, 1964 for continued use in Canada as a symbol of Canada's membership in the Commonwealth of Nations and of her allegiance to the Crown. It will, where physical arrangements make it possible, be flown along with the National Flag at federal buildings, airports, and military bases and establishments within Canada on the date of the official observance of the Queen's birthday, the Anniversary of the Statute of Westminster (December 11th), Commonwealth Day (second Monday in March), and on the occasions of Royal visits and certain Commonwealth gatherings in Canada.

QUEEN'S PERSONAL CANADIAN FLAG

In 1962, Her Majesty The Queen adopted a personal flag specifically for use in Canada. The design comprises the Arms of Canada with The Queen's own device in the centre. The device - the initial "E" surmounted by the St. Edward's Crown within a chaplet of roses - is gold on a blue background.

When the Queen is in Canada, this flag is flown, day and night, at any building in which She is in residence. Generally, the flag is also flown behind the saluting base when She conducts troop inspections, on all vehicles in which She travels, and on Her Majesty's Canadian ships (HMCS) when the Queen is aboard.

FLAG OF THE GOVERNOR GENERAL

The Governor General's standard is a blue flag with the crest of the Arms of Canada in its centre. A symbol of the Sovereignty of Canada, the crest is made of a gold lion passant imperially crowned, on a wreath of the official colours of Canada, holding in its right paw a red maple leaf. The standard was approved by Her Majesty The Queen on February 23, 1981. The Governor General's personal standard flies whenever the incumbent is in residence, and takes precedence over all other flags in Canada, except The Queen's.

CANADIAN ARMED FORCES BADGE

The Canadian Armed Forces Badge was sanctioned by Her Majesty Queen Elizabeth II in May 1967. The description is as follows:

Within a wreath of 10 stylized maple leaves Red, a cartouche medium Blue edge Gold, charged with a foul anchor Gold, surmounted by Crusader's Swords in Saltire Silver and blue, pommelled and hilted Gold; and in front an eagle volant affront head to the sinister Gold, the whole ensigned with a Royal Crown proper.

The Canadian Forces Badge replaces the badges of the Royal Canadian Navy, the Canadian Army, and the Royal Canadian Air Force.

ALBERTA

The Arms of the Province of Alberta were granted by Royal Warrant on May 30, 1907. On July 30th, 1980, the Arms were augmented as follows: Crest: Upon a Helm with a Wreath Argent and Gules a Beaver couchant upholding on its back the Royal Crown both proper; Supporters: On the dexter side a Lion Or armed and langued Gules and on the sinister side a Pronghorn Antelope (Antilocapra americana) proper; the Compartment comprising a grassy mount with the Floral Emblem of the said Province of Alberta the Wild Rose (Rosa acicularis) growing therefrom proper; Motto: FORTIS ET LIBER (Strong and Free) to be borne and used together with the Arms upon Seals, Shields, Banners, Flags or otherwise according to the Laws of Arms.

In 1958, the Government of Alberta authorized the design and use of an official flag. A flag bearing the Armorial Ensign on a royal ultramarine blue background was adopted and the Flag Act proclaimed June 1st 1968. Proportions of the flag are two by length and one by width with the Armorial Ensign seven-elevenths of the width of the flag carried in the centre. The flag may be used by citizens of the Province and others in a manner befitting its dignity and importance but no other banner or flag that includes the Armorial Ensign may be assumed or used.

Floral Emblem: Wild Rose (Rosa Acicularis). Chosen in the Floral Emblem Act of 1930.

Provincial Bird: Great horned owl (budo virginianus). Adopted May 3, 1977.

BRITISH COLUMBIA

The shield of British Columbia was granted by Royal Warrant on March 31, 1906. On October 15th, 1987, the shield was augmented by Her Majesty Queen Elizabeth II. The crest and supporters have become part of the provincial Arms through usage. The heraldic description is as follows: Crest: Upon a Helm with a Wreath Argent and Gules the Royal Crest of general purpose of Our Royal Predecessor Queen Victoria differenced for Us and Our Successors in right of British Columbia with the Lion thereof garlanded about the neck with the Provincial Flower that is to say the Pacific Dogwood (Cornus nuttallii) with leaves all proper Mantled Gules doubled Argent; Supporters: On the dexter side a Wapiti Stag (Cervus canadensis) proper and on the sinister side a Bighorn Sheep Ram (Oviscanadensis) Argent armed and unguled Or; Compartment: Beneath the Shield a Scroll entwined with Pacific Dogwood flowers slipped and leaved proper inscribed with the Motto assigned by the said Warrant of Our Royal Predecessor King Edward VII that is to say SPLENDOR SINE OCCASU, (splendour without diminishment).

The flag of British Columbia was authorized by an Order-in-Council of June 27, 1960. The Union Jack symbolizes the province's origins as a British colony, and the crown at its centre represents the sovereign power linking the nations of the Commonwealth. The sun sets over the Pacific Ocean. The original design of the flag was located in 1960 by Hon. W.A.C. Bennett at the College of Arms in London.

Floral emblem: Pacific Dogwood (Cornus Nuttallii, Audubon). Adopted under the Floral Emblem Act, 1956.

Provincial Bird: Steller's jay. Adopted November 19, 1987.

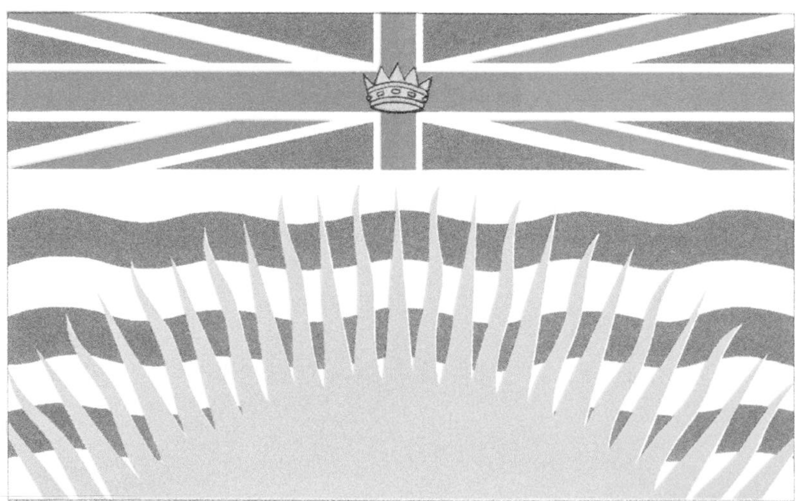

MANITOBA

The Arms of the Province of Manitoba were granted by Royal Warrant on May 10, 1905, augmented by warrant of the Governor General on October 23, 1992. The description is as follows: above the familiar shield of 1905 is a helmet and mantling; above the helmet is the Crest, including the beaver holding a prairie crocus, the province's floral emblem. On the beaver's back is the royal crown. The left supporter is a unicorn wearing a collar bearing a decorative frieze of maple leaves, the collar representing Manitoba's position as Canada's "keystone" province. Hanging from the collar is a wheel of a Red River cart. The right supporter is a white horse, and its collar of bead and bone honours First Peoples. The supporters and the shield rest on a compartment representing the province's rivers and lakes, grain fields and forests, composed of the provincial tree, the white spruce, and seven prairie crocuses. At the base is a Latin translation of the phrase "Glorious and Free."

The flag of the Province of Manitoba was adopted under The Provincial Flag Act, assented to May 11, 1965, and proclaimed into force on May 12, 1966. It incorporates parts of the Royal Armorial Ensigns, namely the Union and Red Ensign; the badge in the fly of the flag is the shield of the arms of the province.

Description: A flag of the proportions two by length and one by width with the Union Jack occupying the upper quarter next the staff and with the shield of the armorial bearings of the province centered in the half farthest from the staff.

Floral Emblem: Pasque Flower, known locally as Prairie Crocus (Anemone Patens). Adopted 1906.

Provincial Bird: Great gray owl. Adopted July 16, 1987.

NEW BRUNSWICK

The Arms of New Brunswick were granted by Royal Warrant on May 26, 1868. The motto SPEM REDUXIT (hope restored) was added by Order-in-Council in 1966. The description is as follows: The upper third of the shield is red and features a gold lion, symbolizing New Brunswick's ties to Britain. The lion is also found in the arms of the Duchy of Brunswick in Germany, the ancestral home of King George III. The lower part of the shield displays an ancient galley with oars in action. It could be interpreted as a reference to the importance of both shipbuilding and seafaring to New Brunswick in those days. It is also based on the design of the province's original great seal which featured a sailing ship on water. The shield is supported by two white-tailed deer wearing collars of Indian wampum. From one is suspended the Royal Union Flag (the Union Jack), from the other the fleur-de-lis to indicate the province's British and French background. The crest consists of an Atlantic Salmon leaping from a coronet of gold maple leaves and bearing St. Edward's Crown on its back. The base, or compartment, is a grassy mound with fiddleheads as well as purple violets, the provincial floral emblem. The motto "Spem Reduxit" is taken from the first great seal of the province and means "Hope restored.".

The flag of New Brunswick, adopted by Proclamation on February 24, 1965, is based on the Arms of the province. The chief and charge occupy the upper one-third of the flag, and the remainder of the armorial bearings occupy the lower two-thirds. The proportion is four by length and two and one half by width.

Floral Emblem: Purple Violet (Viola Cuculata). Adopted by Order-in-Council, December 1, 1936, at the request of the New Brunswick Women's Institute.

Provincial Bird: Black-capped chickadee. Adopted August 1983.

NEWFOUNDLAND & LABRADOR

The Arms of Newfoundland were granted by Royal Letters Patent dated January 1, 1637, by King Charles I. The heraldic description is as follows: Gules, a Cross Argent, in the first and fourth quarters a Lion passant guardant crowned Or, in the second and third quarters an Unicorn passant Argent armed and crined Or, gorged with a Coronet and a Chain affixed thereto reflexed of the last. Crest: on a wreath Or and Gules a Moose passant proper. Supporters: two Savages of the clime armed and apparelled according to their guise when they go to war. The motto reads QUAERITE PRIMEREGNUM DEI (seek ye first the kingdom of God).

The official flag of Newfoundland, adopted in 1980, has primary colours of Red, Gold and Blue, against a White background. The Blue section on the left represents Newfoundland's Commonwealth heritage and the Red and Gold section on the right represents the hopes for the future with the arrow pointing the way. The two triangles represent the mainland and island parts of the province.

Floral Emblem: Purple Pitcher Plant (Sarracenia Purpurea). Adopted June 1954.

Provincial Bird: Atlantic puffin. Adopted 1992.

NORTHWEST TERRITORIES

The Arms of the Northwest Territories were approved by Her Majesty Queen Elizabeth II on February 24, 1956. The crest consists of two gold narwhals guarding a compass rose, symbolic of the magnetic north pole. The white upper third of the shield represents the polar ice pack and is crossed by a wavy blue line portraying the Northwest Passage. The tree line is reflected by a diagonal line separating the red and green segments of the lower portion of the shield: the green symbolizing the forested areas south of the tree line, and the red standing for the barren lands north of it. The important bases of northern wealth, minerals and fur, are represented by gold billets in the green portion and the mask of a white fox in the red.

The official flag of the Northwest Territories was adopted by the Territorial Council on January 1, 1969. Blue panels at either side of the flag represent the lakes and waters of the Territories. The white centre panel, equal in width to the two blue panels combined, symbolizes the ice and snow of the North. In the centre of the white portion is the shield from the Arms of the Territories.

Floral Emblem: Mountain Avens (Dryas Integrifolia). Adopted by the Council on June 7, 1957.

Territorial Bird: Gyrfalcon. Adopted June 1990.

NOVA SCOTIA

The Arms of the Province of Nova Scotia were granted to the Royal Province in 1625 by King Charles I. The complete Armorial Achievement includes the Arms, surmounted by a royal helm with a blue and silver scroll or mantling representing the Royal cloak. Above is the crest of heraldic symbols: two joined hands, one armoured and the other bare, supporting a spray of laurel for peace and thistle for Scotland. On the left is the mythical royal unicorn and on the right a 17th century representation of the North American Indian. The motto reads MUNIT HAEC ET ALTERA VINCIT (one defends and the other conquers). Entwined with the thistle of Scotland at the base is the mayflower, added in 1929, as the floral emblem of Nova Scotia.

The flag of the Province of Nova Scotia is a blue St. Andrew's Cross on a white field, with the Royal Arms of Scotland mounted thereon. The width of the flag is three-quarters of the length.

The flag was originally authorized by Charles I in 1625. In 1929, on petition of Nova Scotia, a Royal Warrant of King George V was issued, revoking the modern Arms and ordering that the original Arms granted by Charles I be borne upon (seals) shields, banners, and otherwise according to the laws of Arms.

Floral Emblem: Trailing Arbutus, also known as Mayflower (Epigaea Repens). Adopted April 1901.

Provincial Bird: Osprey. Adopted Spring, 1994.

NUNAVUT

The dominant colours blue and gold are the ones preferred by the Nunavut Implementation Commissioners to symbolize the riches of the land, sea and sky.

Red is a reference to Canada. In the base of the shield, the inuksuk symbolizes the stone monuments which guide the people on the land and mark sacred and other special places. The qulliq, or Inuit stone lamp, represents light and the warmth of family and the community. Above, the concave arc of five gold circles refers to the life-giving properties of the sun arching above and below the horizon, the unique part of the Nunavut year. The star is the Niqirtsuituq, the North Star and the traditional guide for navigation and more broadly, forever remains unchanged as the leadership of the elders in the community.

In the crest, the iglu represents the traditional life of the people and the means of survival. It also symbolizes the assembled members of the Legislature meeting together for the good of Nunavut; with the Royal Crown symbolizing public government for all the people of Nunavut and the equivalent status of Nunavut with other territories and provinces in Canadian Confederation. The tuktu (caribou) and qilalugaq tugaalik (narwhal) refer to land and sea animals which are part of the rich natural heritage of Nunavut and provide sustenance for people. The compartment at the base is composed of land and sea and features three important species of Arctic wild flowers.

Floral Emblem: Purple Saxifrage (Saxifraga oppositifolia). Adopted May 1, 2000.

Territorial Bird: Rock Ptarmigan.

ONTARIO

The Arms of the Province of Ontario were granted by Royal Warrants on May 26, 1868 (shield), and February 27, 1909 (crest and supporters). The heraldic description is as follows: Vert, a Sprig of three leaves of Maple slipped Or on a Chief Argent the Cross of St. George. Crest: upon a wreath Vert and Or a Bear passant Sable. The supporters are on the dexter side, a Moose, and on the sinister side a Canadian Deer, both proper. The motto reads: UT INCEPIT FIDELIS SIC PERMANET (loyal in the beginning, so it remained).

The flag of the Province of Ontario was adopted under the Flag Act of May 21, 1965. It incorporates parts of the Royal Armorial Ensigns, namely the Union and Red Ensign; the badge in the fly of the flag is the shield of the Arms of the province. The flag is of the proportions two by length and one by width, with the Union Jack occupying the upper quarter next the staff and the shield of the armorial hearings of the province centered in the half farthest from the staff.

Floral Emblem: White Trillium (Trillium Grandiflorum). Adopted March 25, 1937.

Provincial Bird: Common loon. Adopted June 23, 1994.

PRINCE EDWARD ISLAND

The Arms of the Province of Prince Edward Island were granted by Royal Warrant, May 30, 1905. The heraldic description is as follows: Argent on an Island Vert, to the sinister an Oak Tree fructed, to the dexter thereof three Oak saplings sprouting all proper, on a Chief Gules a Lion passant guardant Or. The motto reads: PARVA SUB INGENTI (the small under the protection of the great).

The flag of the Province of Prince Edward Island was authorized by an Act of the Legislative Assembly, March 24, 1964. The design of the flag is that part of the Arms contained within the shield, but is of rectangular shape, with a fringe of alternating red and white. The chief and charge of the Arms occupies the upper one-third of the flag, and the remainder of the Arms occupies the lower two-thirds. The proportions of the flag are six, four and one-quarter in relation to the fly, the hoist and the depth of the fringe.

Floral Emblem: Lady's Slipper (Cypripedium Acaule). Designated as the province's floral emblem by the Legislative Assembly in 1947. A more precise botanical name was included in an amendment to the Floral Emblem Act in 1965.

Provincial Bird: Blue Jay (cyanocitta cristata) was designated as avian emblem by the Provincial Emblems Acts, May 13, 1977.

QUÉBEC

The Arms of the Province of Québec were granted by Queen Victoria, May 26, 1868, and revised by a Provincial Order-in-Council on December 9, 1939. The heraldic description is as follows: Tierced in fess: Azure, three Fleurs-de-lis Or; Gules, a Lion passant guardant Or armed and langued Azure; Or, a Sugar Maple sprig with three leaves Vert veined Or. Surmounted with the Royal Crown. Below the shield a scroll Argent, surrounded by a bordure Azure, inscribed with the motto JE ME SOUVIENS (I remember) Azure.

The official flag of the Province of Québec was adopted by a Provincial Order-in-Council of January 21, 1948. It is a white cross on a sky blue ground, with the fleur-de-lis in an upright position on the blue ground in each of the four quarters. The proportion is six units wide by four units deep.

Floral Emblem: Iris Versicolor. Adopted November 5, 1999.

Provincial Bird: Snowy owl. Adopted December 17, 1987.

SASKATCHEWAN

The complete armorial bearings of the Province of Saskatchewan were granted by Royal Warrant on September 16, 1986, through augmentation of the original shield of arms granted by King Edward VII on August 25, 1906. The heraldic description is as follows: Shield: Vert three Garbs in fesse Or, on a Chief of the last a Lion passant guardant Gules. Crest: Upon a Helm with a Wreath Argent and Gules a Beaver upholding with its back Our Royal Crown and holding in the dexter fore-claws a Western Red Lily (Lilium philadelphicumandinum) slipped all proper Mantled Gules doubled Argent. Supporters: On the dexter side a Lion Or gorged with a Collar of Prairie Indian beadwork proper and dependent therefrom a six-pointed Mullet faceted Argent fimbriated and garnished Or charged with a Maple Leaf Gules and on the sinister side a White tailed deer (Odocoileus virginianus) proper gorged with a like Collar and dependent therefrom a like Mullet charged with a Western Red Lily slipped and leaved proper. Motto: Beneath the Shield a Scroll entwined with Western Red Lilies slipped and leaved proper inscribed with the motto MULTIS E GENTIBUS VIRES (From many peoples strength).

The official flag was dedicated on September 22, 1969, and features the Arms of the province in the upper quarter nearest the staff, with the Western Red Lily, in the half farthest from the staff. The upper green portion represents forests, while the gold symbolizes prairie wheat fields. The basic design was adopted from the prize-winning entry of Anthony Drake of Hodgeville from a province-wide flag design competition.

Floral Emblem: Western Red Lily (Lilium philadelphicum var. andinum). Adopted April 8, 1941.

Provincial Bird: Prairie sharp-tailed grouse. Adopted March 30, 1945.

YUKON

The Arms of the Yukon, granted by Queen Elizabeth II on February 24, 1956, have the following explanation: The wavy white and blue vertical stripe represents the Yukon River and refers also to the rivers and creeks where gold was discovered. The red spire-like forms represent the mountainous country, and the gold discs the mineral resources. The St. George's Cross is in reference to the early explorers and fur traders from Great Britain, and the roundel in vair in the centre of the cross is a symbol for the fur trade. The crest displays a Malamute dog, an animal which has played an important part in the early history of the Yukon.

The Yukon flag, designed by Lynn Lambert, a Haines Junction student, was adopted by Council in 1967. It is divided into thirds: green for forests, white for snow, and blue for water.

The flag consists of three vertical panels, the centre panel being one and one-half times the width of each of the other two panels. The panel adjacent to the mast is coloured green, the centre panel is coloured white and has the Yukon Crest disposed above a symbolic representation of the floral emblem of the territory, epilobium angustifolium, (fireweed), and the panel on the fly is coloured blue. The stem and leaves of the floral emblem are coloured green, and the flowers thereof are coloured red. The Yukon Crest is coloured red and blue, with the Malamute dog coloured black.

Floral Emblem: Fireweed (Epilobium Angustifolium). Adopted November 16, 1957.

Territorial Bird: Common raven. Adopted October 28, 1985.

SYMBOLS OF CANADA

Provinces and Territories	Floral Emblem	Tree	Bird
Alberta	Wild Rose	Lodgepole Pine	Great Horned Owl
British Columbia	Pacific Dogwood	Western Red Cedar	Stellar's Jay
Manitoba	Prairie Crocus	White Spruce	Great Gray Owl
New Brunswick	Purple Violet	Balsam Fir	Black-capped Chickadee
Newfoundland & Labrador	Purple Pitcher Plant	Black Spruce	Atlantic Puffin
Northwest Territories	Mountain Avens	Tamarack Larch	Gyrfalcon
Nova Scotia	Mayflower	Red Spruce	Osprey
Nunavut	Purple Saxifrage		Rock Ptarmigan
Ontario	White Trillium	Eastern White Pine	Loon
Prince Edward Island	Lady's Slipper	Red Oak	Blue Jay
Quebec	Iris Versicolor	Yellow Birch	Snowy Owl
Saskatchewan	Western Red Lily	Paper Birch	Sharp-tailed Grouse
Yukon	Fireweed	Subalpine Fir	Common Raven

Vital Statistics

POPULATION COUNTS, FOR CANADA, PROVINCES AND TERRITORIES, 2011 AND 2006 CENSUSES

Geographic name	Population, 2011	Population, 2006	Population, % change	Population density per kilometre, 2011
Canada	33,476,688	31,612,897	5.9	3.7
Newfoundland and Labrador	514,536	505,469	1.8	1.4
Prince Edward Island	140,204	135,851	3.2	24.7
Nova Scotia	921,727	913,462	0.9	17.4
New Brunswick	751,171	729,997	2.9	10.5
Quebec	7,903,001	7,546,131	4.7	5.8
Ontario	12,851,821	12,160,282	5.7	14.1
Manitoba	1,208,268	1,148,401	5.2	2.2
Saskatchewan	1,033,381	968,157	6.7	1.8
Alberta	3,645,257	3,290,350	10.8	5.7
British Columbia	4,400,057	4,113,487	7	4.8
Yukon	33,897	30,372	11.6	0.1
Northwest Territories	41,462	41,464	0	0.0
Nunavut	31,906	29,474	8.3	0.0

Source: Adapted from the Statistics Canada publication *Population and Dwelling Count Highlight Tables, 2011 Census*. Catalogue no. 98-310-XWE2011002. Accessed August 8, 2016.

POPULATION BY SEX AND AGE GROUP, BY PROVINCE AND TERRITORY (NUMBER, BOTH SEXES)

	2011				2015			
	All ages	0 to 14	15 to 64	65 and older	All ages	0 to 14	15 to 64	65 and older
Canada	33,476,690	5,607,345	22,924,290	4,945,060	35,851,774	5,749,396	24,321,452	5,780,926
Newfoundland and Labrador	514,535	76,630	355,805	82,105	527,756	75,630	354,857	97,269
Prince Edward Island	140,205	23,055	94,360	22,785	146,447	23,252	96,015	27,180
Nova Scotia	921,725	138,215	630,140	153,370	943,002	132,378	632,458	178,166
New Brunswick	751,175	113,575	513,960	123,635	753,871	109,058	501,669	143,144
Quebec	7,903,000	1,258,620	5,386,690	1,257,685	8,263,600	1,279,011	5,532,074	1,452,515
Ontario	12,851,820	2,180,770	8,792,725	1,878,325	13,792,052	2,192,984	9,387,916	2,211,152
Manitoba	1,208,270	231,165	804,655	172,450	1,293,378	240,788	860,673	191,917
Saskatchewan	1,033,380	197,860	681,815	153,710	1,133,637	215,882	751,861	165,894
Alberta	3,645,260	684,790	2,554,745	405,725	4,196,457	770,867	2,938,423	487,167
British Columbia	4,400,055	677,360	3,033,975	688,720	4,683,139	682,294	3,182,781	818,064
Yukon	33,895	5,865	24,945	3,095	37,428	6,334	27,015	4,079
Northwest Territories	41,460	9,010	30,055	2,395	44,088	9,443	31,626	3,019
Nunavut	31,905	10,425	20,420	1,060	36,919	11,475	24,084	1,360

Source: Adapted from the Statistics Canada publications *Age and Sex Highlight Tables, 2011 Census* (Catalogue no. 98-311-XWE-2011002) and *Annual Demographic Estimates: Canada, Provinces and Territories, 2014* (Catalogue no. 91-215-X). Accessed August 8, 2016.

POPULATION OF CENSUS METROPOLITAN AREAS (2006, 2011)

Geographic name	Total (2011 counts)	Total (2006 counts)	Total (2006 to 2011 % change)
Canada	33,476,690	31,612,895	5.9
St. John's (N.L.)	196,965	181,110	8.8
Halifax (N.S.)	390,325	372,860	4.7
Saint John (N.B.)	127,765	122,390	4.4
Fredericton (N.B.)	94,270	86,225	9.3
Québec (Que.)	765,705	719,155	6.5
Trois-Rivières (Que.)	151,775	144,840	4.8
Montréal (Que.)	3,824,220	3,635,570	5.2
Ottawa - Gatineau (Ont.)	1,236,320	1,133,635	9.1
Kingston (Ont.)	159,560	152,355	4.7
Peterborough (Ont.)	118,975	116,570	2.1
Toronto (Ont.)	5,583,065	5,113,150	9.2
Hamilton (Ont.)	721,050	692,910	4.1
Guelph (Ont.)	141,100	133,700	5.5
London (Ont.)	474,790	457,720	3.7
Windsor (Ont.)	319,245	323,340	-1.3
Barrie (Ont.)	187,015	177,060	5.6
Thunder Bay (Ont.)	121,595	122,905	-1.1
Winnipeg (Man.)	730,015	694,665	5.1
Regina (Sask.)	210,560	194,970	8
Saskatoon (Sask.)	260,600	233,930	11.4
Calgary (Alta.)	1,214,840	1,079,310	12.6
Edmonton (Alta.)	1,159,870	1,034,945	12.1
Kelowna (B.C.)	179,840	162,275	10.8
Vancouver (B.C.)	2,313,325	2,116,580	9.3
Victoria (B.C.)	344,615	330,085	4.4

Source: Statistics Canada. 2012. Age Population by broad age groups and sex, 2011 counts for both sexes, for Canada and census metropolitan areas and census agglomerations. Age and Sex Highlight Tables, 2011 Census. Statistics Canada Catalogue no. 98-311-XWE2011002. Ottawa. Released May 29, 2012.

POPULATION OF CANADA, PROJECTIONS, 2017-2063

IN THOUSANDS

Year	Projection Scenario						
	L: low-growth	M1: medium-growth, 1991/1992 to 2010/2011 trends	M2: medium-growth, 1991/1992 to 1999/2000 trends	M3: medium-growth, 1999/2000 to 2002/2003 trends	M4: medium-growth, 2004/2005 to 2007/2008 trends	M5: medium-growth, 2009/2010 to 2010/2011 trends	H: high-growth
2017	36,258.3	36,584.9	36,584.3	36,585.4	36,585.8	36,584.9	36,842.6
2018	36,505.0	36,939.9	36,939.0	36,940.7	36,941.2	36,939.8	37,302.9
2019	36,737.5	37,293.8	37,292.5	37,294.9	37,295.8	37,293.6	37,779.4
2020	36,957.4	37,646.5	37,644.6	37,647.9	37,649.2	37,646.1	38,272.3
2021	37,164.3	37,997.5	37,995.1	37,999.4	38,001.1	37,996.9	38,781.7
2022	37,357.3	38,346.6	38,343.6	38,349.0	38,351.2	38,345.7	39,307.8
2023	37,537.7	38,694.9	38,691.4	38,697.8	38,700.7	38,693.7	39,842.2
2024	37,711.7	39,041.5	39,037.3	39,044.9	39,048.4	39,039.9	40,378.1
2025	37,879.0	39,385.8	39,380.9	39,389.7	39,394.0	39,383.6	40,914.8
2026	38,039.2	39,727.1	39,721.5	39,731.5	39,736.7	39,724.3	41,451.4
2027	38,191.8	40,064.9	40,058.7	40,069.9	40,076.0	40,061.4	41,987.3
2028	38,336.5	40,398.7	40,391.7	40,404.3	40,411.3	40,394.5	42,521.9
2029	38,473.2	40,728.1	40,720.4	40,734.3	40,742.4	40,723.0	43,054.6
2030	38,601.7	41,052.8	41,044.3	41,059.6	41,068.8	41,046.7	43,585.0
2031	38,721.9	41,372.6	41,363.3	41,380.1	41,390.5	41,365.5	44,112.9
2032	38,834.1	41,687.5	41,677.4	41,695.7	41,707.5	41,679.4	44,638.3
2033	38,938.5	41,997.8	41,986.7	42,006.7	42,019.9	41,988.5	45,163.6
2034	39,035.3	42,303.6	42,291.5	42,313.3	42,328.1	42,293.1	45,689.2
2035	39,124.9	42,605.3	42,592.2	42,615.9	42,632.3	42,593.6	46,215.6
2036	39,207.6	42,903.4	42,889.1	42,914.8	42,932.9	42,890.4	46,743.3
2037	39,283.9	43,198.1	43,182.6	43,210.5	43,230.5	43,183.9	47,272.9
2038	39,353.9	43,490.1	43,473.3	43,503.4	43,525.4	43,474.4	47,804.9
2039	39,418.2	43,779.6	43,761.4	43,794.0	43,818.1	43,762.5	48,339.9
2040	39,476.9	44,067.1	44,047.4	44,082.6	44,109.0	44,048.5	48,878.4
2041	39,530.3	44,352.9	44,331.6	44,369.5	44,398.3	44,332.8	49,421.2
2042	39,578.6	44,637.4	44,614.5	44,655.2	44,686.5	44,615.7	49,968.7
2043	39,622.0	44,920.8	44,896.1	44,939.9	44,973.9	44,897.5	50,521.5
2044	39,660.8	45,203.6	45,177.0	45,224.0	45,260.8	45,178.5	51,080.2
2045	39,695.1	45,485.9	45,457.4	45,507.7	45,547.5	45,459.0	51,645.3
2046	39,725.2	45,768.1	45,737.6	45,791.3	45,834.3	45,739.4	52,217.6
2047	39,751.3	46,050.6	46,017.9	46,075.3	46,121.6	46,019.9	52,797.5
2048	39,773.8	46,333.7	46,298.7	46,360.0	46,409.7	46,301.0	53,385.5
2049	39,793.1	46,617.8	46,580.5	46,645.7	46,699.2	46,583.0	53,982.4
2050	39,809.5	46,903.4	46,863.6	46,933.0	46,990.4	46,866.4	54,588.5
2051	39,823.5	47,191.0	47,148.5	47,222.2	47,283.7	47,151.6	55,204.5
2052	39,835.7	47,481.0	47,435.8	47,514.0	47,579.8	47,439.2	55,830.7
2053	39,846.7	47,773.9	47,725.9	47,808.8	47,879.0	47,729.6	56,467.6
2054	39,857.1	48,070.4	48,019.5	48,107.1	48,182.1	48,023.5	57,115.7
2055	39,867.5	48,370.9	48,316.9	48,409.5	48,489.4	48,321.2	57,775.4
2056	39,878.5	48,675.9	48,618.8	48,716.5	48,801.5	48,623.4	58,447.3
2057	39,890.4	48,985.8	48,925.5	49,028.4	49,118.8	48,930.4	59,131.5
2058	39,903.8	49,300.9	49,237.2	49,345.6	49,441.5	49,242.4	59,828.4
2059	39,918.7	49,621.2	49,554.0	49,668.1	49,769.8	49,559.5	60,538.1
2060	39,935.3	49,946.8	49,875.9	49,995.8	50,103.5	49,881.8	61,260.4
2061	39,953.4	50,277.4	50,202.8	50,328.6	50,442.6	50,209.0	61,995.4
2062	39,973.1	50,612.9	50,534.4	50,666.4	50,786.9	50,541.0	62,742.9
2063	39,994.0	50,952.9	50,870.4	51,008.8	51,136.1	50,877.5	63,502.8

Source: Statistics Canada. Table 052-0005 - Projected population, by projection scenario, sex and age group as of July 1, Canada, provinces and territories, annual (persons) (accessed: August 8, 2016).

People | 2.1 World Development Indicators: Population dynamics

	Population			Average annual population growth %		Population age composition			Dependency ratio		Crude death rate	Crude birth rate
						Ages 0-14	Ages 15-64	Ages 65+	young	old		
	millions					%	%	%	% of working-age population	% of working-age population	per 1,000 people	per 1,000 people
	2000	2015	2025	2000-15	2015-25	2015	2015	2015	2015	2015	2014	2014
Afghanistan	19.7	32.5	40.2	3.3	2.1	44	53	2	82	5	8	34
Albania	3.1	2.9	3.0	-0.4	0.2	19	69	12	27	18	7	13
Algeria	31.2	39.7	45.9	1.6	1.5	29	66	6	44	9	5	24
American Samoa	0.1	0.1	0.1	-0.2	0.3	..	..	..	..	..	..	..
Andorra	0.1	0.1	0.1	0.5	-0.1	..	..	..	..	..	..	..
Angola	15.1	25.0	34.0	3.4	3.1	48	50	2	95	5	14	45
Antigua and Barbuda	0.1	0.1	0.1	1.1	1.0	24	69	7	35	10	6	16
Argentina	37.1	43.4	47.5	1.1	0.9	25	64	11	39	17	8	18
Armenia	3.1	3.0	3.0	-0.1	0.0	18	71	11	26	15	9	13
Aruba	0.1	0.1	0.1	0.9	0.2	18	69	12	26	18	9	10
Australia	19.2	23.8	26.8	1.4	1.2	19	66	15	28	23	7	13
Austria	8.0	8.6	8.8	0.5	0.2	14	67	19	21	28	9	10
Azerbaijan	8.0	9.7	10.4	1.2	0.8	22	72	6	30	8	6	18
Bahamas, The	0.3	0.4	0.4	1.8	1.0	21	71	8	30	12	6	15
Bahrain	0.7	1.4	1.6	4.8	1.3	21	76	2	28	3	2	15
Bangladesh	131.3	161.0	179.1	1.4	1.1	29	66	5	45	8	5	20
Barbados	0.3	0.3	0.3	0.3	0.2	19	66	14	29	21	11	12
Belarus	10.0	9.5	9.2	-0.3	-0.3	16	70	14	23	20	13	13
Belgium	10.3	11.3	11.8	0.6	0.4	17	65	18	26	28	9	11
Belize	0.2	0.4	0.4	2.5	1.9	32	64	4	51	6	6	23
Benin	6.9	10.9	13.9	3.0	2.5	42	55	3	77	5	9	36
Bermuda	0.1	0.1	..	0.4	..	..	..	..	..	..	8	11
Bhutan	0.6	0.8	0.9	2.1	1.0	27	68	5	39	7	6	18
Bolivia	8.3	10.7	12.4	1.7	1.4	32	61	6	53	11	7	24
Bosnia and Herzegovina	3.8	3.8	3.7	0.0	-0.3	13	71	15	19	22	11	9
Botswana	1.7	2.3	2.6	1.8	1.6	32	64	4	50	6	7	25
Brazil	175.8	207.8	223.0	1.1	0.7	23	69	8	33	11	6	15
Brunei Darussalam	0.3	0.4	0.5	1.6	1.2	23	72	4	32	6	3	16
Bulgaria	8.2	7.2	6.6	-0.9	-0.8	14	66	20	21	30	15	9
Burkina Faso	11.6	18.1	23.9	3.0	2.8	46	52	2	88	5	10	40
Burundi	6.8	11.2	15.2	3.3	3.1	45	53	2	85	5	11	44
Cabo Verde	0.4	0.5	0.6	1.1	1.2	30	66	5	45	7	5	21
Cambodia	12.2	15.6	17.9	1.6	1.4	32	64	4	49	6	6	24
Cameroon	15.9	23.3	29.5	2.5	2.4	43	54	3	78	6	11	37
Canada	30.8	35.9	38.9	1.0	0.8	16	68	16	24	24	7	11
Cayman Islands	0.0	0.1	0.1	2.4	1.3	..	..	..	..	..	..	..
Central African Republic	3.7	4.9	5.9	1.8	1.9	39	57	4	68	7	15	34
Chad	8.3	14.0	19.1	3.5	3.1	48	50	2	96	5	14	45
Channel Islands	0.1	0.2	0.2	0.6	0.4	15	68	17	22	25	9	9
Chile	15.2	17.9	19.6	1.1	0.9	20	69	11	29	16	5	13
China	1,262.6	1,371.2	1,409.0	0.5	0.3	17	73	10	24	13	7	12
Hong Kong SAR, China	6.7	7.3	7.8	0.6	0.6	12	73	15	16	21	6	9
Macao SAR, China	0.4	0.6	0.7	2.1	1.4	13	78	9	17	12	5	12
Colombia	40.4	48.2	51.9	1.2	0.7	24	69	7	35	10	6	16
Comoros	0.5	0.8	1.0	2.4	2.2	40	57	3	71	5	8	34
Congo, Dem. Rep.	48.0	77.3	104.5	3.2	3.0	46	51	3	90	6	10	42
Congo, Rep.	3.1	4.6	6.0	2.6	2.6	43	54	4	79	7	9	37
Costa Rica	3.9	4.8	5.2	1.4	0.9	22	69	9	32	13	5	15
Cote d'Ivoire	16.5	22.7	28.7	2.1	2.4	42	54	3	78	6	14	37
Croatia	4.4	4.2	4.1	-0.3	-0.4	15	66	19	23	29	12	9
Cuba	11.1	11.4	11.3	0.2	-0.1	16	70	14	23	20	8	10
Curacao	0.1	0.2	0.2	1.1	0.7	19	66	15	29	22	9	13
Cyprus	0.9	1.2	1.3	1.4	0.8	17	71	13	23	18	7	11
Czech Republic	10.3	10.6	10.6	0.2	0.0	15	67	18	22	27	10	10
Denmark	5.3	5.7	5.9	0.4	0.4	17	64	19	26	30	9	10
Djibouti	0.7	0.9	1.0	1.4	1.2	33	63	4	52	7	9	25
Dominica	0.1	0.1	0.1	0.3	0.4	..	..	..	..	..	..	..
Dominican Republic	8.6	10.5	11.6	1.4	1.0	30	63	7	47	10	6	21
Ecuador	12.6	16.1	18.5	1.6	1.4	29	64	7	45	10	5	21

People | 2.1 World Development Indicators: Population dynamics

	Population			Average annual population growth %		Population age composition			Dependency ratio		Crude death rate	Crude birth rate
						Ages 0-14	Ages 15-64	Ages 65+	young	old		
	millions					%	%	%	% of working-age population	% of working-age population	per 1,000 people	per 1,000 people
	2000	2015	2025	2000-15	2015-25	2015	2015	2015	2015	2015	2014	2014
Egypt, Arab Rep.	68.3	91.5	108.9	1.9	1.7	33	62	5	54	8	6	28
El Salvador	5.8	6.1	6.3	0.4	0.3	27	65	8	42	13	7	17
Equatorial Guinea	0.5	0.8	1.1	3.1	2.7	39	58	3	68	5	11	35
Eritrea	3.5	..	..	..	..	..	..	..	..	..	7	34
Estonia	1.4	1.3	1.3	-0.4	-0.3	16	65	19	25	29	12	10
Ethiopia	66.4	99.4	125.0	2.7	2.3	41	55	3	75	6	7	32
Faroe Islands	0.0	0.0	0.0	0.2	0.2	..	..	..	..	..	8	13
Fiji	0.8	0.9	0.9	0.6	0.4	29	65	6	44	9	7	20
Finland	5.2	5.5	5.6	0.4	0.3	16	63	20	26	32	10	11
France	60.9	66.8	69.3	0.6	0.4	18	62	19	30	31	8	12
French Polynesia	0.2	0.3	0.3	1.2	0.7	22	70	8	31	11	6	16
Gabon	1.2	1.7	2.1	2.2	2.0	37	58	5	64	9	9	30
Gambia, The	1.2	2.0	2.7	3.2	3.0	46	52	2	90	4	9	42
Georgia	4.4	3.7	3.6	-1.2	-0.2	17	69	14	25	20	12	14
Germany	82.2	81.4	80.4	-0.1	-0.1	13	66	21	20	32	11	9
Ghana	18.8	27.4	33.7	2.5	2.1	39	58	3	67	6	9	33
Greece	10.8	10.8	10.5	0.0	-0.3	15	64	21	23	33	11	9
Greenland	0.1	0.1	..	0.0	..	..	..	..	..	..	8	14
Grenada	0.1	0.1	0.1	0.3	0.4	26	66	7	40	11	7	19
Guam	0.2	0.2	0.2	0.6	1.2	25	66	9	39	13	5	17
Guatemala	11.7	16.3	19.7	2.2	1.9	37	59	5	63	8	5	27
Guinea	8.8	12.6	16.2	2.4	2.5	43	54	3	78	6	10	37
Guinea-Bissau	1.3	1.8	2.3	2.3	2.2	41	56	3	73	6	12	37
Guyana	0.7	0.8	0.8	0.2	0.5	29	66	5	44	8	8	19
Haiti	8.5	10.7	12.0	1.5	1.1	34	62	5	55	8	9	25
Honduras	6.2	8.1	9.2	1.7	1.3	32	63	5	50	8	5	21
Hungary	10.2	9.8	9.5	-0.2	-0.4	15	68	18	22	26	13	10
Iceland	0.3	0.3	0.4	1.1	0.7	20	66	14	31	21	6	13
India	1,053.5	1,311.1	1,461.6	1.5	1.1	29	66	6	44	9	7	20
Indonesia	211.5	257.6	284.5	1.3	1.0	28	67	5	41	8	7	20
Iran, Islamic Rep.	65.9	79.1	86.5	1.2	0.9	24	71	5	33	7	5	18
Iraq	23.6	36.4	47.8	2.9	2.7	41	56	3	73	5	5	35
Ireland	3.8	4.6	5.0	1.3	0.8	22	65	13	33	20	6	14
Isle of Man	0.1	0.1	0.1	0.9	0.7	..	..	..	..	..	..	..
Israel	6.3	8.4	9.7	1.9	1.5	28	61	11	46	18	5	21
Italy	56.9	60.8	60.3	0.4	-0.1	14	64	22	21	35	10	8
Jamaica	2.6	2.7	2.8	0.3	0.3	24	67	9	35	14	6	14
Japan	126.8	127.0	122.7	0.0	-0.3	13	61	26	21	43	10	8
Jordan	4.8	7.6	8.5	3.1	1.2	36	61	4	59	6	4	27
Kazakhstan	14.9	17.5	19.3	1.1	1.0	27	67	7	40	10	8	23
Kenya	31.1	46.1	58.6	2.6	2.4	42	55	3	76	5	8	35
Kiribati	0.1	0.1	0.1	1.9	1.6	35	61	4	57	6	7	29
Korea, Dem. People's Rep.	22.8	25.2	26.3	0.6	0.4	21	69	10	31	14	9	14
Korea, Rep.	47.0	50.6	52.2	0.5	0.3	14	73	13	19	18	5	9
Kosovo	1.7	1.8	2.0	0.4	1.1	26	68	7	38	10	7	17
Kuwait	1.9	3.9	4.7	4.7	1.8	22	76	2	29	3	3	20
Kyrgyz Republic	4.9	6.0	6.8	1.3	1.3	31	64	4	49	7	6	28
Lao PDR	5.3	6.8	8.0	1.6	1.6	35	61	4	57	6	7	27
Latvia	2.4	2.0	1.9	-1.2	-0.5	15	66	19	23	29	14	11
Lebanon	3.2	5.9	5.4	3.9	-0.8	24	68	8	35	12	5	15
Lesotho	1.9	2.1	2.4	0.9	1.1	36	60	4	60	7	15	29
Liberia	2.9	4.5	5.7	3.0	2.4	42	55	3	77	6	9	35
Libya	5.3	6.3	7.1	1.1	1.2	30	66	5	45	7	5	21
Liechtenstein	0.0	0.0	0.0	0.8	0.6	..	..	..	..	..	7	10
Lithuania	3.5	2.9	2.8	-1.2	-0.5	15	67	19	22	28	14	10
Luxembourg	0.4	0.6	0.6	1.8	1.2	16	70	14	24	20	7	11
Macedonia, FYR	2.0	2.1	2.1	0.2	0.1	17	71	12	24	17	9	11
Madagascar	15.7	24.2	31.7	2.9	2.7	42	55	3	75	5	7	34
Malawi	11.2	17.2	23.1	2.9	3.0	45	51	3	88	7	8	39
Malaysia	23.4	30.3	34.3	1.7	1.2	25	69	6	36	9	5	17
Maldives	0.3	0.4	0.5	2.4	1.3	27	68	5	41	7	4	21

People | 2.1 World Development Indicators: Population dynamics

	Population			Average annual population growth %		Population age composition			Dependency ratio		Crude death rate	Crude birth rate
						Ages 0-14	Ages 15-64	Ages 65+	young	old		
	millions					%	%	%	% of working-age population	% of working-age population	per 1,000 people	per 1,000 people
	2000	2015	2025	2000-15	2015-25	2015	2015	2015	2015	2015	2014	2014
Mali	11.0	17.6	23.7	3.1	3.0	48	50	3	95	5	10	44
Malta	0.4	0.4	0.4	0.8	0.2	14	66	19	22	29	8	10
Marshall Islands	0.1	0.1	0.1	0.1	0.2	..	..	..	..	..	..	..
Mauritania	2.7	4.1	5.1	2.7	2.3	40	57	3	70	6	8	33
Mauritius	1.2	1.3	1.3	0.4	0.2	19	71	10	27	13	8	11
Mexico	102.8	127.0	141.9	1.4	1.1	28	66	6	42	10	5	19
Micronesia, Fed. Sts.	0.1	0.1	0.1	-0.2	0.7	34	62	4	55	7	6	24
Moldova	3.6	3.6	3.4	-0.2	-0.3	16	74	10	21	13	11	11
Monaco	0.0	0.0	0.0	1.1	0.3	..	..	..	..	..	..	..
Mongolia	2.4	3.0	3.4	1.4	1.3	28	68	4	42	6	6	24
Montenegro	0.6	0.6	0.6	0.2	-0.1	19	68	14	28	20	10	12
Morocco	29.0	34.4	38.3	1.1	1.1	27	67	6	41	9	6	21
Mozambique	18.3	28.0	36.5	2.8	2.6	45	51	3	88	7	11	39
Myanmar	47.7	53.9	58.4	0.8	0.8	28	67	5	41	8	8	18
Namibia	1.9	2.5	3.0	1.7	2.0	37	60	4	61	6	7	30
Nepal	23.7	28.5	31.8	1.2	1.1	33	62	6	53	9	6	21
Netherlands	15.9	16.9	17.4	0.4	0.3	17	65	18	25	28	8	10
New Caledonia	0.2	0.3	0.3	1.6	1.1	22	68	10	33	15	5	17
New Zealand	3.9	4.6	5.0	1.2	0.8	20	65	15	31	23	7	13
Nicaragua	5.0	6.1	6.7	1.3	1.0	30	65	5	46	8	5	20
Niger	11.2	19.9	29.6	3.8	4.0	50	47	3	107	5	9	49
Nigeria	122.9	182.2	233.6	2.6	2.5	44	53	3	83	5	13	40
Northern Mariana Islands	0.1	0.1	0.1	-1.4	0.2	..	..	..	..	..	..	..
Norway	4.5	5.2	5.7	1.0	0.9	18	66	16	27	25	8	12
Oman	2.2	4.5	5.1	4.6	1.2	21	77	3	27	3	3	20
Pakistan	138.3	188.9	227.2	2.1	1.8	35	60	4	58	7	7	29
Palau	0.0	0.0	0.0	0.7	1.2	..	..	..	..	..	..	..
Panama	3.0	3.9	4.5	1.7	1.4	27	65	8	42	12	5	19
Papua New Guinea	5.4	7.6	9.2	2.3	1.9	37	60	3	62	5	8	29
Paraguay	5.3	6.6	7.5	1.5	1.2	30	64	6	47	9	6	21
Peru	25.9	31.4	35.2	1.3	1.1	28	65	7	43	10	6	20
Philippines	77.9	100.7	116.2	1.7	1.4	32	63	5	50	7	7	24
Poland	38.3	38.0	37.3	0.0	-0.2	15	70	16	21	22	10	10
Portugal	10.3	10.3	10.0	0.0	-0.3	14	65	21	22	32	10	8
Puerto Rico	3.8	3.5	3.5	-0.6	-0.1	19	67	14	28	22	8	10
Qatar	0.6	2.2	2.6	8.8	1.7	16	83	1	19	1	1	12
Romania	22.4	19.8	18.6	-0.8	-0.6	16	67	17	23	26	13	9
Russian Federation	146.6	144.1	141.9	-0.1	-0.2	17	70	13	24	19	13	13
Rwanda	8.0	11.6	14.4	2.5	2.1	41	56	3	73	5	7	32
Samoa	0.2	0.2	0.2	0.7	0.6	37	57	5	65	9	5	26
San Marino	0.0	0.0	0.0	1.0	0.4	..	..	..	..	..	8	9
Sao Tome and Principe	0.1	0.2	0.2	2.2	2.0	43	54	3	79	6	7	34
Saudi Arabia	21.4	31.5	36.8	2.6	1.6	29	69	3	42	4	3	20
Senegal	9.9	15.1	20.0	2.9	2.8	44	53	3	82	6	6	38
Serbia	7.5	7.1	6.8	-0.4	-0.4	16	67	17	24	26	14	9
Seychelles	0.1	0.1	0.1	0.9	0.3	23	70	7	34	10	8	17
Sierra Leone	4.1	6.5	7.9	3.1	2.0	42	55	3	77	5	14	36
Singapore	4.0	5.5	6.1	2.1	1.0	16	73	12	21	16	5	10
Sint Maarten (Dutch part)	0.0	0.0	..	1.6	..	..	..	..	..	..	..	..
Slovak Republic	5.4	5.4	5.4	0.0	0.0	15	71	14	21	19	10	10
Slovenia	2.0	2.1	2.1	0.2	0.0	15	67	18	22	27	9	10
Solomon Islands	0.4	0.6	0.7	2.3	1.8	39	57	3	69	6	6	30
Somalia	7.4	10.8	14.3	2.5	2.8	47	50	3	93	6	12	44
South Africa	44.0	55.0	62.0	1.5	1.2	29	66	5	44	8	12	21
South Sudan	6.7	12.3	16.0	4.1	2.6	42	54	3	77	6	12	37
Spain	40.3	46.4	46.4	0.9	0.0	15	66	19	22	28	9	9
Sri Lanka	18.7	21.0	21.7	0.8	0.3	25	66	9	37	14	7	16
St. Kitts and Nevis	0.0	0.1	0.1	1.3	0.9	..	..	..	..	..	..	..
St. Lucia	0.2	0.2	0.2	1.1	0.6	23	68	9	34	13	7	15

People | 2.1 World Development Indicators: Population dynamics

	Population			Average annual population growth %		Population age composition			Dependency ratio		Crude death rate	Crude birth rate
						Ages 0-14	Ages 15-64	Ages 65+	young	old		
	millions					%	%	%	% of working-age population	% of working-age population	per 1,000 people	per 1,000 people
	2000	2015	2025	2000-15	2015-25	2015	2015	2015	2015	2015	2014	2014
St. Martin (French part)	0.0	0.0	..	0.7	..	..	..	..	..	..	4	16
St. Vincent and the Grenadines	0.1	0.1	0.1	0.1	0.2	25	68	7	36	11	7	16
Sudan	28.1	40.2	50.7	2.4	2.3	41	56	3	72	6	8	33
Suriname	0.5	0.5	0.6	0.8	0.7	27	66	7	40	10	7	18
Swaziland	1.1	1.3	1.4	1.3	1.1	37	59	4	63	6	14	30
Sweden	8.9	9.8	10.5	0.7	0.7	17	63	20	28	32	9	12
Switzerland	7.2	8.3	8.9	1.0	0.7	15	67	18	22	27	8	10
Syrian Arab Republic	16.4	18.5	25.6	0.8	3.2	37	59	4	63	7	6	23
Tajikistan	6.2	8.5	10.3	2.1	1.9	35	62	3	56	5	6	31
Tanzania	34.0	53.5	72.0	3.0	3.0	45	52	3	88	6	7	39
Thailand	62.7	68.0	68.6	0.5	0.1	18	72	10	25	15	8	11
Timor-Leste	0.8	1.2	1.5	2.6	2.0	42	52	6	82	11	7	38
Togo	4.9	7.3	9.4	2.7	2.5	42	55	3	77	5	9	36
Tonga	0.1	0.1	0.1	0.5	0.8	37	57	6	64	10	6	25
Trinidad and Tobago	1.3	1.4	1.4	0.5	0.1	21	70	9	30	13	9	14
Tunisia	9.6	11.1	12.2	1.0	0.9	23	69	8	34	11	6	19
Turkey	63.2	78.7	84.9	1.5	0.8	26	67	8	38	11	6	17
Turkmenistan	4.5	5.4	6.0	1.2	1.0	28	68	4	42	6	8	21
Turks and Caicos Islands	0.0	0.0	0.0	4.0	1.3	..	..	..	..	..	..	..
Tuvalu	0.0	0.0	0.0	0.3	0.1	..	..	..	..	..	..	..
Uganda	23.8	39.0	53.5	3.3	3.2	48	49	2	97	5	10	43
Ukraine	49.2	45.2	42.8	-0.6	-0.6	15	70	15	21	22	15	11
United Arab Emirates	3.1	9.2	10.4	7.3	1.3	14	85	1	16	1	2	11
United Kingdom	58.9	65.1	68.9	0.7	0.6	18	64	18	28	28	9	12
United States	282.2	321.4	344.7	0.9	0.7	19	66	15	29	22	8	13
Uruguay	3.3	3.4	3.6	0.2	0.3	21	64	14	33	23	9	14
Uzbekistan	24.7	31.3	34.8	1.6	1.1	29	67	5	43	7	5	23
Vanuatu	0.2	0.3	0.3	2.4	2.0	37	59	4	62	7	5	26
Venezuela, RB	24.5	31.1	35.0	1.6	1.2	28	66	6	43	10	6	20
Vietnam	77.6	91.7	100.2	1.1	0.9	23	70	7	33	10	6	17
Virgin Islands (U.S.)	0.1	0.1	0.1	-0.3	0.0	20	62	18	33	28	8	11
West Bank and Gaza	2.9	4.4	5.7	2.8	2.5	40	57	3	71	5	4	33
Yemen, Rep.	17.8	26.8	33.2	2.7	2.1	40	57	3	71	5	7	32
Zambia	10.6	16.2	21.9	2.8	3.0	46	51	3	90	6	9	40
Zimbabwe	12.5	15.6	19.4	1.5	2.2	42	55	3	75	5	10	35
World	6,115.4	7,346.6	8,139.3	1.2	1.0	26	66	8	40	13	8	19
East Asia & Pacific	2,045.7	2,279.2	2,386.3	0.7	0.5	20	71	10	28	14	7	14
Europe & Central Asia	862.0	907.9	922.8	0.3	0.2	18	67	16	27	23	10	12
Latin America & Caribbean	525.9	633.0	694.0	1.2	0.9	26	67	8	39	11	6	17
Middle East & North Africa	315.1	424.1	497.4	2.0	1.6	30	65	5	46	7	5	24
North America	313.0	357.3	383.6	0.9	0.7	19	66	15	28	22	8	12
South Asia	1,386.0	1,744.2	1,962.8	1.5	1.2	30	65	5	46	8	7	21
Sub-Saharan Africa	667.7	1,001.0	1,292.4	2.7	2.6	43	54	3	80	6	10	37
Low income	423.7	638.3	823.9	2.7	2.6	43	54	3	79	6	9	36
Lower middle income	2,312.5	2,927.4	3,346.0	1.6	1.3	31	64	5	48	8	8	23
Upper middle income	2,267.4	2,550.3	2,688.2	0.8	0.5	21	71	9	29	13	7	15
High income	1,074.9	1,187.2	1,233.7	0.7	0.4	17	66	17	25	26	8	11

Most Recent Value (MRV) if data for the specified year or full period are not available; or growth rate is calculated for less than the full period.

Source: The World Bank.

BIRTHS, ESTIMATES, BY PROVINCE AND TERRITORY

	2010/2011	2011/2012	2012/2013	2013/2014	2014/2015
			number		
Canada	**376,951**	**377,897**	**382,980**	**386,044**	**388,729**
Newfoundland and Labrador	4,775	4,552	4,533	4,484	4,409
Prince Edward Island	1,428	1,426	1,431	1,429	1,428
Nova Scotia	8,818	8,727	8,687	8,613	8,588
New Brunswick	7,140	7,028	6,933	6,827	6,715
Quebec	88,611	88,311	89,000	88,250	86,950
Ontario	139,448	139,658	141,248	142,970	144,395
Manitoba	15,614	15,702	15,979	16,248	16,540
Saskatchewan	14,438	14,498	14,951	15,345	15,676
Alberta	50,853	52,230	54,054	56,078	57,677
British Columbia	43,908	43,774	44,153	43,781	44,323
Yukon	404	440	445	439	443
Northwest Territories	676	692	697	695	687
Nunavut	838	859	869	885	898

Notes:
Period from July 1 to June 30.
The numbers for births are final up to 2011/2012, updated for 2012/2013 and 2013/2014 and preliminary for 2014/2015.
Preliminary and updated estimates of births were produced by Demography Division, Statistics Canada. Final data were produced by Health Statistics Division, Statistics Canada. However, the final estimates included in this table may differ from the data released by the Health Statistics Division, due to distribution of unknown province.

Source: Adapted from Statistics Canada, CANSIM, table 051-0004 and Catalogue no. 91-215-X.
Last modified: September 29, 2015. Accessed August 8, 2016.

LIFE EXPECTANCY

	1941	1960 to 1962	1985 to 1987	2007 to 2009
		years		
Females				
At birth	66.3	74.2	79.7	83.3
At 65	14.1	16.1	19.1	21.6
Males				
At birth	63.0	68.4	73.0	78.8
At 65	12.8	13.5	14.9	18.5

Source: Statistics Canada, CANSIM table 102-0512.
Last modified May 31, 2012. Accessed August 8, 2016.

RANKING, NUMBER AND PERCENTAGE OF DEATH FOR THE 10 LEADING CAUSES OF DEATH, CANADA, 2000, 2011 AND 2012

Cause of death	2000			2011			2012		
	rank	number	percent	rank	number	percent	rank	number	percent
All causes of death	...	**218,062**	**100**	...	**243,511**	**100**	...	**246,596**	**100**
Total, ten leading causes of death	...	**175,149**	**80.3**	...	**182,795**	**75**	...	**184,869**	**75**
Malignant neoplasms (cancer)	1	62,672	28.7	1	72,736	29.9	1	74,361	29.9
Diseases of heart	2	55,070	25.3	2	47,911	19.7	2	48,681	19.7
Cerebrovascular diseases (stroke)	3	15,576	7.1	3	13,332	5.5	3	13,174	5.3
Accidents	5	8,589	3.9	5	10,961	4.5	4	11,290	4.6
Chronic lower respiratory diseases	4	9,813	4.5	4	11,243	4.6	5	11,130	4.5
Diabetes mellitus (diabetes)	6	6,714	3.1	6	7,255	3	6	6,993	2.8
Alzheimer's disease	7	5,007	2.3	7	6,377	2.6	7	6,293	2.6
Influenza and pneumonia	8	4,966	2.3	8	5,787	2.4	8	5,694	2.3
Intentional self-harm (suicide)	9	3,606	1.7	9	3,896	1.6	9	3,926	1.6
Nephritis, nephrotic syndrome and nephrosis (kidney disease)	10	3,136	1.4	10	3,297	1.4	10	3,327	1.3
All other causes	...	42,913	19.7	...	60,716	25	...	61,727	25

... not applicable

Note: The order of the causes of death in this table is based on the ranking of the 10 leading causes of death in 2012.
Source: Adapted from Vital statistics: Death database, CANSIM Table 102-0561. Accessed August 9, 2016.

IMMIGRANTS TO CANADA, BY CLASS, 1992 - 2012

Year	Economic	Family	Protected Persons	Others [1]	Total
1992	95,796	101,112	52,345	5,544	254,797
1993	105,653	112,647	30,600	7,751	256,651
1994	102,309	94,193	20,435	7,455	224,392
1995	106,626	77,386	28,093	761	212,866
1996	125,370	68,359	28,478	3,866	226,073
1997	128,350	59,979	24,308	3,400	216,037
1998	97,912	50,896	22,843	2,547	174,198
1999	109,249	55,274	24,397	1,031	189,951
2000	136,287	60,616	30,092	460	227,455
2001	155,718	66,795	27,919	207	250,639
2002	137,863	62,292	25,114	3,780	229,049
2003	121,047	65,120	25,983	9,199	221,349
2004	133,748	62,269	32,687	7,121	235,825
2005	156,312	63,367	35,776	6,786	262,241
2006	138,251	70,517	32,499	10,375	251,642
2007	131,245	66,242	27,954	11,313	236,754
2008	149,071	65,580	21,860	10,736	247,247
2009	153,491	65,208	22,850	10,623	252,172
2010	186,918	60,230	24,697	8,846	280,691
2011	156,118	56,451	27,873	8,305	248,747
2012	161,000	69,000	27,000	8,000	265,000
		%			
1992	37.6	39.7	20.5	2.2	100.0
1993	41.2	43.9	11.9	3.0	100.0
1994	45.6	42.0	9.1	3.3	100.0
1995	50.1	36.4	13.2	0.4	100.0
1996	55.5	30.2	12.6	1.7	100.0
1997	59.4	27.8	11.3	1.6	100.0
1998	56.2	29.2	13.1	1.5	100.0
1999	57.5	29.1	12.8	0.5	100.0
2000	59.9	26.6	13.2	0.2	100.0
2001	62.1	26.6	11.1	0.1	100.0
2002	60.2	27.2	11.0	1.7	100.0
2003	54.7	29.4	11.7	4.2	100.0
2004	56.7	26.4	13.9	3.0	100.0
2005	59.6	24.2	13.6	2.6	100.0
2006	54.9	28.0	12.9	4.1	100.0
2007	55.4	28.0	11.8	4.8	100.0
2008	60.3	26.5	8.8	4.3	100.0
2009	60.9	25.9	9.1	4.2	100.0
2010	66.6	21.5	8.8	3.2	100.0
2011	62.8	22.7	11.2	3.3	100.0
2012	60.8	26.0	10.1	3.0	100.0

[1] Includes deferred removal order class, post-determination refugee claimant class, temporary resident permit holders, humanitarian and compassionate/public policy cases and unknowns.

Note: Data available as of November 2012.

Note: 2012 figures are greatest planned number of immigrants, rather than observed.

Sources: Citizenship and Immigration Canada, *Annual Report to Parliament on Immigration*, 2009 to 2012.

Source: Adapted from the Statistics Canada publication Report on the demographic situation in Canada, Catalogue 91-209-X, http://www.statcan.gc.ca/pub/91-209-x/91-209-x2014001-eng.htm

NET MIGRATION FOR PROVINCES AND TERRITORIES, 1997-2015

	NL	PEI	NS	NB	QC	ON	MB	SK	AB	BC	YT	NWT	NU
1997-1998	-9,490	-416	-2,569	-3,192	-16,958	9,231	-5,276	-1,940	43,089	-10,029	-1,024	-1,316	-110
1998-1999	-5,695	193	201	-1,244	-13,065	16,706	-2,113	-4,333	25,191	-14,484	-747	-555	-55
1999-2000	-4,263	104	-270	-1,183	-12,146	22,369	-3,456	-7,947	22,674	-14,610	-691	-651	70
2000-2001	-4,493	165	-2,077	-1,530	-9,442	18,623	-4,323	-8,410	20,457	-8,286	-572	-160	48
2001-2002	-3,352	62	-898	-1,218	-4,350	5,354	-4,344	-8,820	26,235	-8,556	-221	84	24
2002-2003	-1,683	165	510	-843	-1,829	637	-2,875	-5,141	11,903	-1,037	149	242	-198
2003-2004	-2,027	144	-772	-760	-822	-6,935	-2,565	-4,521	10,606	7,865	27	-105	-135
2004-2005	-3,710	-139	-3,041	-2,074	-4,963	-11,172	-7,227	-9,515	34,423	8,214	53	-668	-181
2005-2006	-4,342	-639	-3,024	-3,487	-9,411	-17,501	-7,881	-7,083	45,795	8,800	-73	-954	-200
2006-2007	-4,067	-849	-4,126	-2,632	-12,865	-20,047	-5,500	1,549	33,809	15,005	101	-221	-157
2007-2008	-528	-291	-1,794	-908	-11,682	-14,750	-3,703	4,171	15,317	14,643	235	-420	-290
2008-2009	1,877	-536	-751	-237	-7,419	-15,601	-3,111	2,983	13,184	9,995	228	-577	-35
2009-2010	1,558	60	612	571	-3,258	-4,662	-2,412	2,153	-3,271	8,728	325	-351	-53
2010-2011	30	-210	-41	-158	-4,763	-4,007	-3,517	545	8,443	3,421	363	-179	73
2011-2012	545	-618	-2,866	-1,806	-6,915	-10,611	-4,212	1,878	27,652	-2,711	313	-496	-153
2012-2013	495	-901	-3,517	-3,290	-10,431	-13,901	-5,006	392	38,598	-1,868	-94	-482	5
2013-2014	234	-941	-2,571	-3,517	-14,312	-14,564	-6,851	-1,839	35,382	9,475	51	-488	-59
2014-2015	-1,398	-1,243	-1,286	-2,800	-14,656	-8,763	-7,759	-3,200	28,921	12,413	90	-452	133

Source: Statistics Canada. *Table 051-0004 - Components of population growth, Canada, provinces and territories, annual (persons),* CANSIM. Accessed August 9, 2016.

MOTHER TONGUE

2011 CENSUS (TOP 25)

Language	Total Responses
English	18,858,980
French	7,054,975
Panjabi (Punjabi)	430,705
Chinese, n.o.s.	425,210
Spanish	410,670
German	409,200
Italian	407,485
Cantonese	372,460
Arabic	327,870
Tagalog (Pilipino, Filipino)	327,445
Manadarin	248,705
Portuguese	211,335
Polish	191,645
Urdu	172,800
Persian (Farsi)	170,045
Vietnamese	144,880
Korean	137,925
Tamil	131,265
Ukranian	111,540
Dutch	110,490
Greek	108,925
Gujarati	91,450
Hindi	90,545
Romanian	90,300
Cree, n.o.s.	77,900

Adapted from the Statistics Canada publication 2011 Census,

Catalogue 98-316-XWE, Released October 24, 2012. http://www12.statcan.gc.ca/census-recensement /2011/dp-pd/prof/index.cfm?Lang=E.

INDIVIDUALS USING THE INTERNET FROM ANY LOCATION, 2010-2012

	Internet use (%)	
	2010	**2012**
Canada	**80**	**83**
Newfoundland and Labrador	73	77
Prince Edward Island	75	80
Nova Scotia	79	79
New Brunswick	70	77
Quebec	76	81
Ontario	81	84
Manitoba	79	83
Saskatchewan	80	82
Alberta	84	85
British Columbia	86	87

Source: Adapted from Statistics Canada's Survey of Household Survey, 2012, table 2 and CANSIM table 358-0167, 358-0171.

POSTSECONDARY ENROLMENTS, BY INSTITUTION TYPE AND CLASSIFICATION OF INSTRUCTIONAL PROGRAMS, PRIMARY GROUPING

Classification of Instructional Programs, Primary Grouping (CIP_PG)	2007-2008	2008-2009	2009-2010	2010-2011	2011-2012	2012-2013	2013-2014
Total, instructional programs	1,717,692	1,747,740	1,905,231	1,961,475	2,000,274	2,023,158	2,048,019
University enrolment	1,072,902	1,113,507	1,201,062	1,235,916	1,261,911	1,283,241	1,300,440
College enrolment	644,790	634,233	704,169	725,559	739,363	739,917	747,576
Personal improvement and leisure [0]	9,981	12,105	22,317	25,143	26,358	24,882	24,672
Education [1]	87,837	88,851	97,152	99,147	98,535	96,258	96,441
Visual and performing arts and communications technologies [2]	73,176	74,712	80,202	82,467	83,250	82,869	82,674
Humanities [3]	296,349	295,368	333,066	333,954	334,665	319,758	323,973
Social and behavioural sciences and law [4]	227,622	230,493	241,584	252,132	262,383	272,895	278,991
Business, management and public administration [5]	312,756	323,475	345,864	351,900	359,775	367,311	374,427
Physical and life sciences and technologies [6]	109,728	112,104	116,253	119,208	123,234	128,028	131,439
Mathematics, computer and information sciences [7]	50,352	50,709	52,344	53,325	54,978	58,221	61,782
Architecture, engineering and related technologies [8]	155,274	160,416	177,189	184,347	190,347	198,885	207,294
Agriculture, natural resources and conservation [9]	24,123	24,714	26,205	27,747	28,779	29,706	30,399
Health and related fields[10]	183,693	190,878	209,640	222,849	229,284	237,453	243,804
Personal, protective and transportation services [11]	29,628	30,816	40,173	41,826	41,874	42,417	42,171
Other instructional programs [12]	157,167	153,099	163,242	167,430	166,809	164,472	149,958

Source: Statistics Canada. *Table 477-0019 - Postsecondary enrolments, by registration status, Pan-Canadian Standard Classification of Education (PCSCE), Classification of Instructional Programs, Primary Grouping (CIP_PG), sex and immigration status, annual (number).* CANSIM. Accessed August 9, 2016.

SELECTED INCIDENT-BASED CRIME STATISTICS, BY DETAILED VIOLATIONS

Violations	Statistics	2011	2012	2013	2014	2015
Total, all violations	Actual incidents	2,275,917	2,244,458	2,098,776	2,052,925	2,111,021
	Rate per 100,000 population	6,627.06	6,458.48	5,970.19	5,775.78	5,888.19
Homicide [110][17, 24]	Actual incidents	598	543	512	521	604
	Rate per 100,000 population	1.74	1.56	1.46	1.47	1.68
Total other violations causing death [120]	Actual incidents	76	102	141	108	88
	Rate per 100,000 population	0.22	0.29	0.40	0.30	0.25
Attempted murder [1210]	Actual incidents	665	665	636	630	774
	Rate per 100,000 population	1.94	1.91	1.81	1.77	2.16
Sexual assault, level 3, aggravated [1310]	Actual incidents	149	124	133	116	104
	Rate per 100,000 population	0.43	0.36	0.38	0.33	0.29
Sexual assault, level 2, weapon or bodily harm [1320]	Actual incidents	400	372	368	332	377
	Rate per 100,000 population	1.16	1.07	1.05	0.93	1.05
Sexual assault, level 1 [1330]	Actual incidents	21,311	21,374	20,695	20,183	20,881
	Rate per 100,000 population	62.05	61.5	58.87	56.78	58.24
Total sexual violations against children [130][26, 70, 73]	Actual incidents	3,804	3,953	4,174	4,534	4,532
	Rate per 100,000 population	11.08	11.37	11.87	12.76	12.64
Assault, level 3, aggravated [1410]	Actual incidents	3,526	3,532	3,241	3,273	3,286
	Rate per 100,000 population	10.27	10.16	9.22	9.21	9.17
Assault, level 2, weapon or bodily harm [1420]	Actual incidents	50,431	49,807	46,019	45,096	47,119
	Rate per 100,000 population	146.85	143.32	130.91	126.87	131.43
Assault, level 1 [1430]	Actual incidents	173,099	170,291	158,259	153,832	156,688
	Rate per 100,000 population	504.03	489.99	449.65	432.80	437.04
Total assaults against a peace officer [135][25, 35]	Actual incidents	11,424	10,776	9,826	9,557	9,835
	Rate per 100,000 population	33.26	31.01	27.65	26.89	27.43
Total other assaults [140]	Actual incidents	2,986	2,906	2,639	2,148	2,140
	Rate per 100,000 population	8.69	8.36	7.51	6.04	5.97
Total firearms, use of, discharge, pointing [150]	Actual incidents	1,944	2,057	1,892	1,862	2,295
	Rate per 100,000 population	5.66	5.92	5.38	5.24	6.40
Total robbery [160][18]	Actual incidents	29,790	27,748	23,249	20,932	20,080
	Rate per 100,000 population	86.74	79.85	66.13	58.89	61.59
Total forcible confinement or kidnapping [510][34]	Actual incidents	3,780	3,637	3,231	3,290	3,555
	Rate per 100,000 population	11.01	10.47	9.19	9.26	9.92
Total abduction [170]	Actual incidents	404	393	375	388	386
	Rate per 100,000 population	1.18	1.13	1.07	1.09	1.08
Extortion [1620]	Actual incidents	1,527	1,730	2,310	2,727	3,057
	Rate per 100,000 population	4.45	4.98	6.57	7.67	8.53
Criminal harassment [1625][36]	Actual incidents	21,752	22,280	21,546	19,640	20,001
	Rate per 100,000 population	63.34	64.11	61.29	55.26	55.79
Total other violent violations [180]	Actual incidents	4,636	4,665	4,649	4,507	4,980
	Rate per 100,000 population	13.5	13.42	13.22	12.68	13.89
Total breaking and entering [210]	Actual incidents	181,250	176,250	156,470	152,167	159,338
	Rate per 100,000 population	527.77	507.16	445.10	428.11	444.44
Total possession of stolen property [211][42, 46]	Actual incidents	21,349	16,956	16,407	16,840	19,106
	Rate per 100,000 population	62.16	48.79	46.67	47.38	53.29
Total trafficking in stolen property [212][42, 43, 46]	Actual incidents	311	494	576	577	692
	Rate per 100,000 population	0.91	1.42	1.64	1.62	1.93
Total theft of motor vehicle [220][46]	Actual incidents	82,460	78,068	72,512	74,010	78,849
	Rate per 100,000 population	240.11	224.63	206.27	208.22	219.93
Total theft over $5,000 (non-motor vehicle) [230]	Actual incidents	15,095	15,436	14,336	14,249	15,573
	Rate per 100,000 population	43.95	44.42	40.78	40.09	43.44
Total theft under $5,000 (non-motor vehicle) [240]	Actual incidents	500,496	499,484	472,226	472,912	488,540
	Rate per 100,000 population	1,457.35	1,437.28	1,343.30	1,330.51	1,362.67
Fraud [2160][30]	Actual incidents	77,741	78,661	79,744	81,179	94,396

	Rate per 100,000 population	226.37	226.35	226.84	228.39	263.30
Identity theft [2165][30, 56]	Actual incidents	1,411	1,854	2,112	2,149	2,497
	Rate per 100,000 population	4.11	5.33	6.01	6.05	6.96
Identity fraud [2166][30]	Actual incidents	8,022	8,953	9,523	10,761	11,704
	Rate per 100,000 population	23.36	25.76	27.09	30.28	32.65
Total mischief [250][63]	Actual incidents	315,724	306,124	273,569	264,887	274,725
	Rate per 100,000 population	919.33	880.82	778.20	745.24	766.28
Arson [2110]	Actual incidents	10,401	11,096	8,915	8,528	8,791
	Rate per 100,000 population	30.29	31.93	25.36	23.99	24.52
Counterfeiting [3420][19]	Actual incidents	622	440	630	586	669
	Rate per 100,000 population	1.81	1.27	1.79	1.65	1.87
Total weapons violations [310]	Actual incidents	14,003	13,992	13,733	13,930	14,560
	Rate per 100,000 population	40.77	40.26	39.06	39.19	40.61
Child pornography [3455][27, 50, 52, 57, 69, 70, 76]	Actual incidents	1,958	2,177	2,818	3,894	4,310
	Rate per 100,000 population	5.7	6.26	8.02	10.96	12.02
Total prostitution [320][64]	Actual incidents	2,452	2,102	2,046	1,046	171
	Rate per 100,000 population	7.14	6.05	5.82	2.94	0.48
Total other violations [340]	Actual incidents	31,294	31,538	29,451	28,998	29,381
	Rate per 100,000 population	91.12	90.75	83.78	81.58	81.95
Impaired operation, causing death [9210]	Actual incidents	128	137	106	119	115
	Rate per 100,000 population	0.37	0.39	0.3	0.33	0.32
Impaired operation (drugs), causing death [9215]	Actual incidents	2	4	6	11	7
	Rate per 100,000 population	0.01	0.01	0.02	0.03	0.02
Driving while prohibited [9320]	Actual incidents	7,199	6,693	6,782	7,108	6,897
	Rate per 100,000 population	20.96	19.26	19.29	20.00	19.24

Footnotes:

17. Homicide data are extracted from the homicide survey database. For further information, refer to: http://www.statcan.gc.ca/imdb-bmdi/3315-eng.htm.

18. Robbery counts have been revised for the years 1998 to 2007. This change has resulted in an increase of approximately 12% annually in the number of reported robbery incidents for this time period. Use caution when comparing these data with prior years.

19. Counterfeiting counts have been revised for the years 1998 to 2007. This change has resulted in a significant decrease in counterfeiting incidents over this time period. Use with caution when comparing these data with prior years.

24. In general, the Uniform Crime Reporting Survey (UCR) counts any adult and youth charged for the year in which the charge was laid. The homicide totals, which come from The Homicide Survey, count any adult or youth charged with a homicide that occurred in the reference year, regardless of when the charge was laid.

25. Any reference to Police Officer has been changed to read Peace Officer, as per the Canadian Criminal Code. Peace officer refers to any person employed for the preservation and maintenance of the public peace or for the service or execution of civil process. Examples of a Peace Officer are a mayor, warden, police officer, or bailiff constable. Please see the Canadian Criminal Code for a complete list of designates.

27. In 2002, legislative changes were made to include the use of the Internet for the purpose of committing child pornography offences. As such, the percent change in this offence is calculated from 2003 to 2009.

30. In January 2010, the Uniform Crime Reporting Survey (UCR) was modified to create new violation codes for identity fraud and identity theft. Prior to 2010, those offences would have been coded as fraud.

34. Historically police services have reported kidnapping and forcible confinement under a single combined violation code. In 2008 the Incident-based Uniform Crime Reporting Survey (UCR2) introduced separate codes for these violations which police services utilize as their Records Management Systems are updated to allow them. As a result, comparison with previous years should be done with caution.

35. In 2009, legislation was introduced to create the offences of assault with a weapon or causing bodily harm to a peace officer (level 2) and aggravated assault to a peace officer (level 3). The introduction of these new codes into the UCR Survey created a system anomaly which resulted in some non-peace officer assaults being coded as peace officer assaults in 2010. Comparisons to 2010 should be made with caution.

42. In April 2011, legislation came into effect making it an offence to traffic in property obtained by crime, including possession with intent to traffic property obtained by crime. In addition to creating new Uniform Crime Reporting Survey (UCR) violation codes to capture these offences, the existing UCR violation code pertaining to possession of stolen property was modified. The UCR now separates possession of stolen property into possession of stolen property under $5,000 and possession of stolen property over $5,000 in order to be more in line with the Criminal Code of Canada. As a result of this change, a number of incidents of possession of stolen property under $5,000 are now being reported as secondary offences when they occur in conjunction with more serious offences, leading to a decrease in the number of possession of stolen property incidents reported in 2011.

43. In April 2011, legislation came into effect making it an offence to traffic in property obtained by crime, including possession with intent to traffic property obtained by crime. The Uniform Crime Reporting Survey (UCR) introduced two new violations codes to collect this information. They are Trafficking in Stolen Goods over $5,000 (incl. possession with intent to traffic) and Trafficking in Stolen Goods under $5,000 (incl. possession with intent to traffic).

46. Detailed information of this category is available upon request.

50. In 2012, it was discovered that the Montreal Police Service had been incorrectly applying the agreed upon definition for reporting child pornography incidents to the Uniform Crime Reporting Survey (UCR). As such, the number of violations has been revised for the years 2008 to 2011.

52. Ottawa numbers also include child pornography incidents reported by the National Child Exploitation Coordination Centre of the Royal Canadian Mounted Police (RCMP) which is located in the City of Ottawa. The Centre responds to internet-facilitated sexual abuse cases nationally. Therefore, while the incidents are detected by the RCMP Centre located in Ottawa and appear in Ottawa's crime statistics, the incidents themselves or the offenders are not limited to the city of Ottawa.

56. In 2013, it was discovered that an error in Quebec's provincial reporting system had incorrectly resulted in a number of thefts being coded as identity thefts in Montreal. As such, the number of incidents of identity theft has been revised for the years 2010 to 2012.

57. Due to the complexity of these incidents, the data likely reflect the number of active or closed investigations for the year rather than the total number of incidents reported to police.

63. In 2014, legislation was introduced to create the offence of Mischief to war memorials (Bill C-217). The offence of mischief in relation to cultural property was also introduced as a result of this legislation. Police services are able to utilise these codes as their Records Management Systems are updated to allow them. As a result, these data may be under-counted and should therefore be interpreted with caution.

64. Bill C-36 came into effect in December 2014. The new legislation targets "the exploitation that is inherent in prostitution and the risks of violence posed to those who engage in it" (Criminal Code Chapter 25, preamble). New violations classified as "Commodification of sexual activity" under "violations against the person" include: the purchasing of sexual services or communicating for that purpose, receiving a material benefit deriving from the purchase of sexual services, procuring of persons for the purpose of prostitution, and advertising sexual

services offered for sale. In addition, a number of other offences related to prostitution continue to be considered non-violent offences and are classified under "Other Criminal Code offences". These include communicating to provide sexual services for consideration, and; stopping or impeding traffic for the purpose of offering, providing or obtaining sexual services for consideration. At the same time, the survey was amended to classify the violations codes of Parent or guardian procuring sexual activity, and Householder permitting prohibited sexual activity under "violations against the person". The following violations officially expired on December 05, 2014: bawdy house, living off the avails of prostitution of a person under 18, procuring, obtains/communicates with a person under 18 for purpose of sex, and other prostitution. Police services are able to utilize these codes as their Records Management Systems are updated to allow it. As a result, these data should be interpreted with caution.
69. Historically, police service reported all child pornography offences under a single combined violation code, of which the majority of the offences were possessing child pornography. In early 2016, the Uniform Crime Reporting Survey (UCR) was modified to allow police to report making and distributing child pornography from other child pornography offences (i.e., possession and accessing child pornography). Since police services are able to utilize these codes as their Records Management Systems are updated to allow them, a few were reported in 2015. As a result, these data should therefore be interpreted with caution.
70. Coming into effect on July 17th, 2015, Bill C-26 increased the maximum penalties for certain sexual offences against children, including failure to comply with orders and probation conditions relating to sexual offences against children. In the Uniform Crime Reporting Survey (UCR), the most serious violation is partially determined by the maximum penalty. As such, changes in maximum penalty may affect the most serious violation in an incident reported by police. Police services are able to utilize these amendments as their Records Management Systems are updated to allow them.
73. Includes Criminal Code violations that specifically concern offences involving child and youth victims. These include sexual interference, invitation to sexual touching, sexual exploitation, making sexually explicit material available to children for the purpose of facilitating sexual offences against children/youth, luring a child via a computer/agreement or arrangement, and, as of December 2014, the offences of parent or guardian procuring sexual activity (Criminal Code, s. 170), and householder permitting prohibited sexual activity (Criminal Code, s. 171). Incidents of child pornography are not included in the category of sexual violations against children. Excludes incidents of sexual assault levels 1, 2 and 3 against children and youth which are counted within those three violation categories. Other sexual offences not involving assault or sexual violations against children are included with "other violent offences".
76. The increase in incidents of child pornography between 2014 and 2015 can be in part attributed to a proactive project initiated by the British Columbia Integrated Child Exploitation Unit which recorded Internet Protocol (IP) addresses that were in possession of, and possibly sharing child pornography. As the initiative focused on Victoria in 2015, notable increases in these offences were reported by this jurisdiction.

Source: Statistics Canada. *Table 252-0051 - Incident-based crime statistics, by detailed violations, annual (number unless otherwise noted),* CANSIM. Accessed August 9, 2016.

Geography

Reproduced with the permission of Natural Resources Canada, 2016.

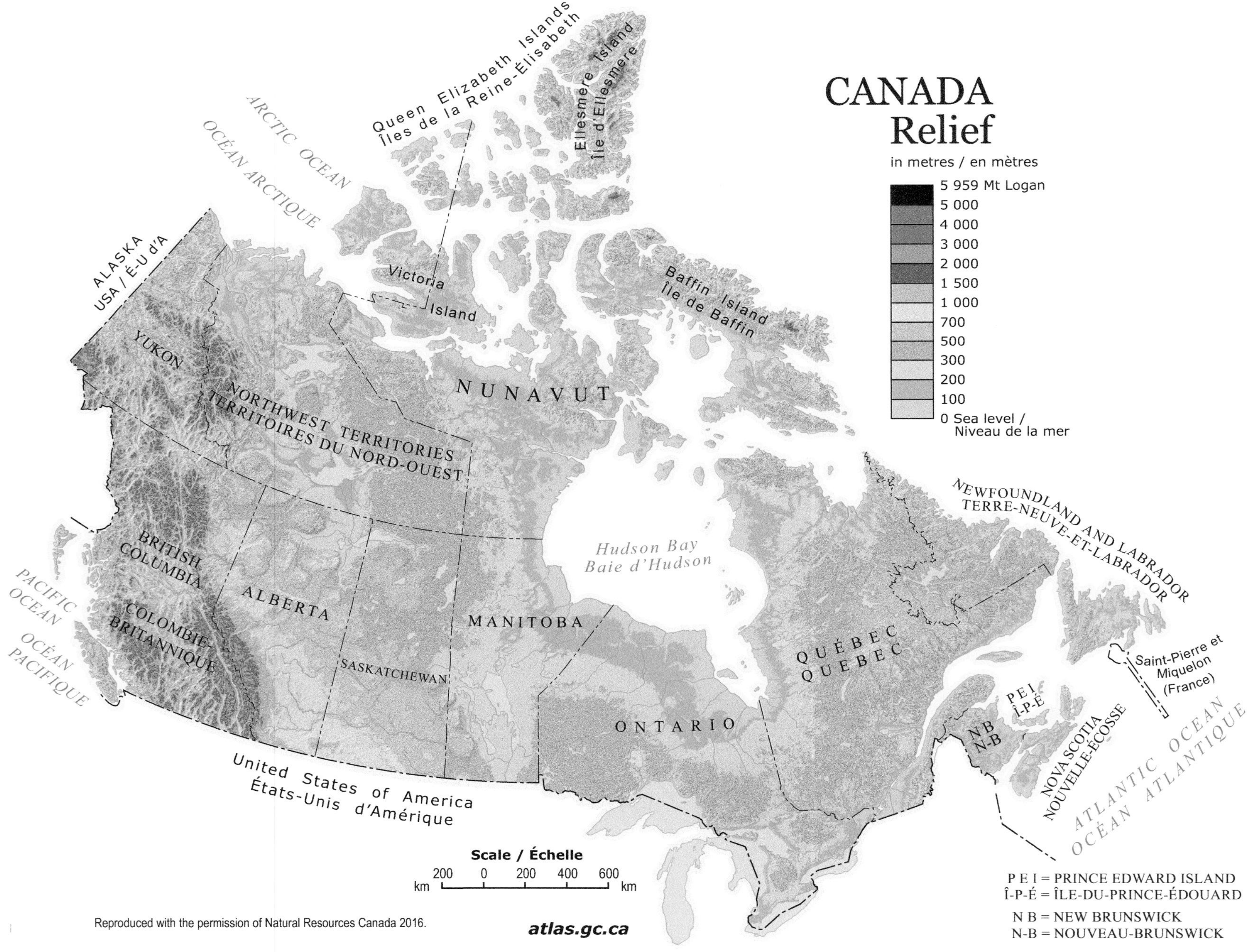
CANADA
Relief
in metres / en mètres
5 959 Mt Logan
5 000
4 000
3 000
2 000
1 500
1 000
700
500
300
200
100
0 Sea level / Niveau de la mer
ARCTIC OCEAN
OCÉAN ARCTIQUE
Queen Elizabeth Islands
Îles de la Reine-Élisabeth
Ellesmere Island
Île d'Ellesmere
Victoria Island
Baffin Island
Île de Baffin
ALASKA
USA / É-U d'A
YUKON
NORTHWEST TERRITORIES
TERRITOIRES DU NORD-OUEST
NUNAVUT
Hudson Bay
Baie d'Hudson
BRITISH COLUMBIA
COLOMBIE-BRITANNIQUE
ALBERTA
SASKATCHEWAN
MANITOBA
ONTARIO
QUÉBEC
QUEBEC
NEWFOUNDLAND AND LABRADOR
TERRE-NEUVE-ET-LABRADOR
Saint-Pierre et Miquelon (France)
PEI
Î-P-É
NB
N-B
NOVA SCOTIA
NOUVELLE-ÉCOSSE
ATLANTIC OCEAN
OCÉAN ATLANTIQUE
PACIFIC OCEAN
OCÉAN PACIFIQUE
United States of America
États-Unis d'Amérique
Scale / Échelle
km 200 0 200 400 600 km
P E I = PRINCE EDWARD ISLAND
Î-P-É = ÎLE-DU-PRINCE-ÉDOUARD
N B = NEW BRUNSWICK
N-B = NOUVEAU-BRUNSWICK
atlas.gc.ca

Reproduced with the permission of Natural Resources Canada 2016.

Pacific Rim National Park Reserve, BC
© Parks Canada / Scott Munn

Spirit Island in Maligne Lake, Jasper, AB
© Parks Canada / Ryan Bray

Danielson Provincial Park, SK
Courtesy of Tourism Saskatchewan / Kevin Hogarth Photography

Pisew Falls, Mystery Lake, MB
Courtesy of Travel Manitoba

Rideau Canal, Ottawa, ON

Courtesy of Ontario Tourism Marketing Partnership Corp., 2016

Marché Bonsecours, Montréal, QC

© TQ / P. Flemming

Three Sisters Rock Formation, Bay of Fundy, NS
Courtesy of Tourism Nova Scotia

Botwood, NL
Courtesy of Newfoundland and Labrador Tourism

Two Rivers Inlet, Cape Enrage, NB
Courtesy of Tourism New Brunswick

Charlottetown, PE
Courtesy of www.DiscoverCharlottetown.com

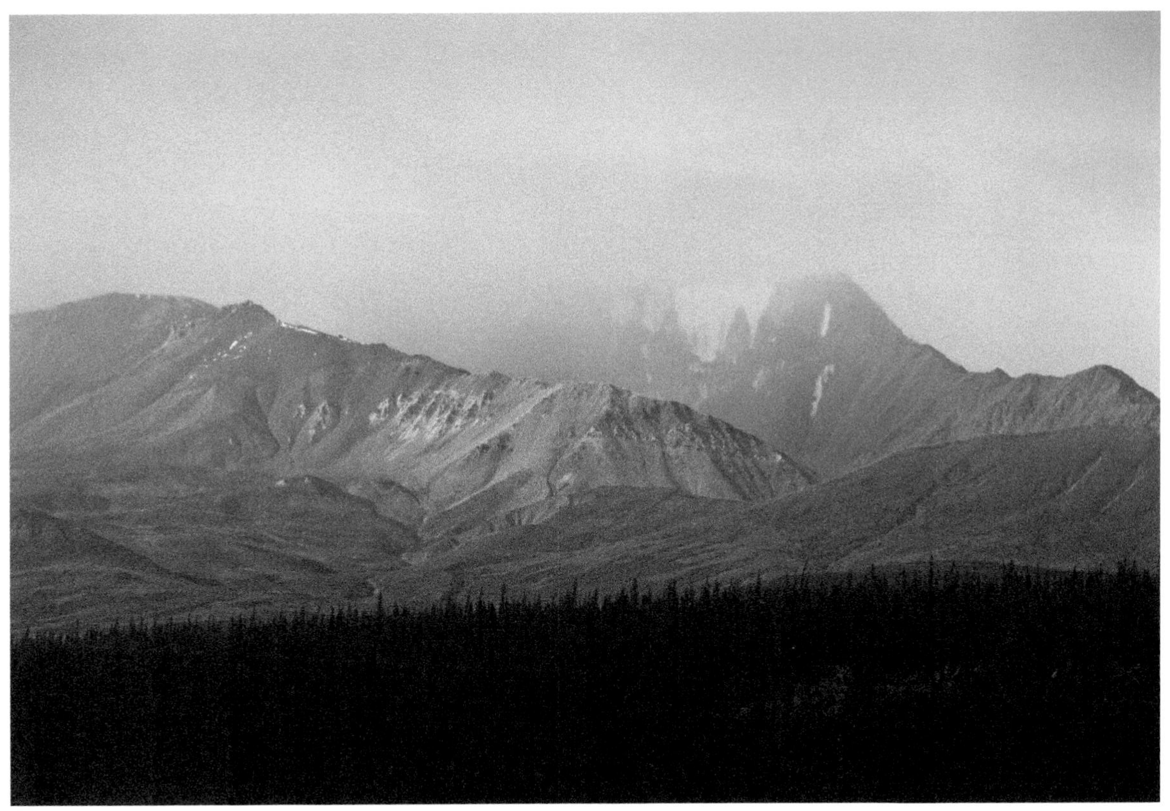

Kluane National Park Reserve, YT
© Parks Canada / Fritz Mueller

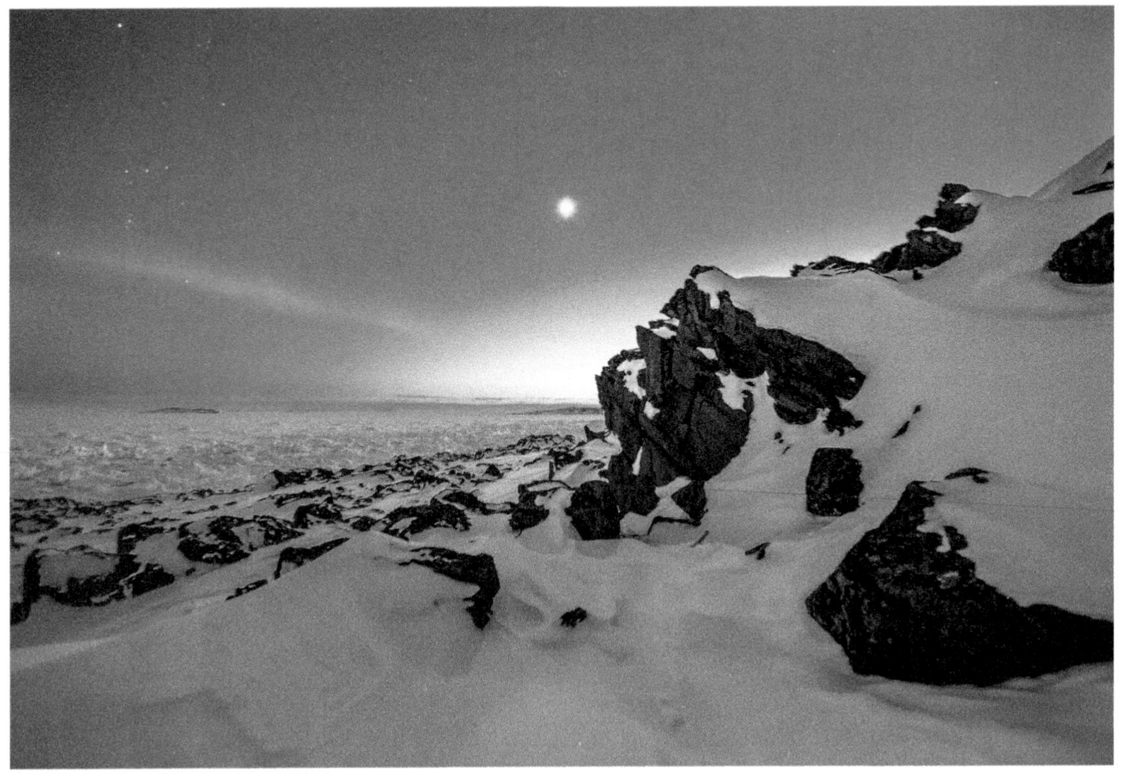

Rotary Park, Iqaluit, NU
Courtesy of www.NunavutImages.com

Fort Simpson, NT
Courtesy of Shawna McLeod

LAND AND FRESHWATER AREAS
(IN SQUARE KILOMETRES)

Provinces and Territories	Land	Water	Total Area	Percentage of Canadian Total
Newfoundland and Labrador	373,872	31,340	405,212	4.1
Prince Edward Island	5,660	Not Available	5,660	0.1
Nova Scotia	53,338	1,946	55,284	0.6
New Brunswick	71,450	1,458	72,908	0.7
Quebec	1,365,128	176,928	1,542,056	15.4
Ontario	917,741	158,654	1,076,395	10.8
Manitoba	553,556	94,241	647,797	6.5
Saskatchewan	591,670	59,366	651,036	6.5
Alberta	642,317	19,531	661,848	6.6
British Columbia	925,186	19,549	944,735	9.5
Yukon Territory	474,391	8,052	482,443	4.8
Northwest Territories	1,183,085	163,021	1,346,106	13.5
Nunavut	1,936,113	157,077	2,093,190	21.0
Canada	9,093,507	891,163	9,984,670	100

LARGEST LAKES WHOLLY OR PARTIALLY IN CANADA

Name	Provinces and Territories	Area (square kilometres)
Superior	Ontario (and United States)	82,101 (total); 28,748 in Canada
Huron	Ontario (and United States)	59,569 (total); 36,000 in Canada
Great Bear	Northwest Territories	30,764
Great Slave	Northwest Territories	27,048
Erie	Ontario (and United States)	25,666 (total); 12,768 in Canada
Winnipeg	Manitoba	23,760
Ontario	Ontario (and United States)	19,554 (total); 10,334 in Canada

LONGEST RIVERS IN CANADA

Rank	Name (at outflow)	Length (kilometres)	Outflow	Component Parts
1	Mackenzie	4,241	Beaufort Sea	Mackenzie - Slave - Peace - Findlay
2	Yukon	3,185 (1,143 kilometres in Canada)	Bering Sea	Yukon
3	St. Lawrence	3,058 (small part wholly in U.S.)	Gulf of St. Lawrence	St. Lawrence - Niagara - Detroit - St. Clair - St. Marys - St. Louis
4	Nelson	2,575	Hudson Bay	Nelson - Saskatchewan - South Saskatchewan - Bow
5	Columbia	2,000 (801 kilometres in Canada)	Pacific Ocean	Columbia
6	Churchill	1,609	Hudson Bay	Churchill [of Manitoba and Saskatchewan]
7	Fraser	1,370	Pacific Ocean	Fraser
8	North Saskatchewan	1,287	Saskatchewan River	North Saskatchewan
9	Ottawa	1,271	St. Lawrence River	Ottawa
10	Athabasca	1,231	Slave River	Athabasca
11	Liard	1,115	Mackenzie River	Liard
12	Assiniboine	1,070	Red River (part of Nelson River drainage basin)	Assiniboine

LARGEST ISLANDS OF CANADA

Rank	Name	Provinces and Territories	Area (square kilometres)
1	Baffin (5th largest in the world)	Nunavut	507,451
2	Victoria	Nunavut and Northwest Territories	217,291
3	Ellesmere	Nunavut	196,236
4	Island of Newfoundland	Newfoundland and Labrador	108,860
5	Banks	Northwest Territories	70,028
6	Devon	Nunavut	55,247
7	Axel Heiberg	Nunavut	43,178
8	Melville	Northwest Territories and Nunavut	42,149
9	Southampton	Nunavut	41,214
10	Prince of Wales	Nunavut	33,339
11	Vancouver	British Columbia	31,285

Reproduced with the permission of Natural Resources Canada 2016.

SELECTED WATERFALLS IN CANADA

Name of Waterfall	Vertical Drop (metres)	Location
Della Falls	440	Della Lake, BC
Takakkaw Falls	254	Daly Glacier, BC
Hunlen Falls	253	Atnarko River, BC
Panther Falls	183	Nigel Creek, AB
Helmcken Falls	137	Murtle River, BC
Bridal Veil Falls	122	Bridal Creek, BC
Virginia Falls	90	South Nahanni River, NT
Chute Montmorency	84	Rivière Montmorency, QC
Twin Falls	80	Yoho National Park, BC
Chute Ouiatchouan	79	Rivière Ouiatchouan, QC
Brandywine Falls	61	Brandywine Creek, BC
Niagara Falls (American Falls)	59	(Niagara River, USA)
Niagara Falls (Horseshoe Falls)	57	Niagara River, ON
Wilberforce Falls	49	Hood River, NU
Dog Falls	47	Kaministiquia River, ON
Kakabeka Falls	47	Kaministiquia River, ON
Chute de Shawinigan	46	Rivière Saint-Maurice, QC
Grand Falls	43	Exploits River, NL
Parry Falls	40	Lockhart River, NT
Wawaitin Falls	38	Mattagami River, ON
Elizabeth Falls	34	Fond du Lac River, SK
Aubrey Falls	33	Mississagi River, ON
Alexandra Falls	32	Hay River, NT
Thomas Falls	31	Unknown River, NL
Marengo Falls	30	Marengo Creek, NT
Barrow Falls	27	Barrow River, NU
Pigeon Falls	27	Pigeon River, ON
Scott Falls	27	Unknown River, NL
Tyrrell Falls	26	Lockhart River, NT
High Falls	24	Onaping River, ON
Schist Falls	24	Pukaskwa River, ON
Smoky Falls	24	Mattagami River, ON
Christopher Falls	23	Opasatika River, ON
Chute du Calcaire	22	Rivière Caniapiscau, QC
Chute au Granite	21	Rivière Caniapiscau, QC
Partridge Falls	21	Pigeon River, ON
Steephill Falls	21	Magpie River, ON
Louise Falls	20	Hay River, NT
Muhigan Falls	19	Muhigan River, MB
Big Beaver Falls	18	Kapuskasing River, ON
Chutes aux Schistes	18	Rivière Caniapiscau, QC
Twin Falls	18	Abitibi River, ON
Lady Evelyn Falls	17	Kakisa River, NT
Muskrat Falls	15	Churchill River, NL
Taskinigup Falls	15	Burntwood River, MB
Kazan Falls	14	Kazan River, NU
Rideau Falls	12	Rideau River, ON

Reproduced with the permission of Natural Resources Canada 2016.

HIGHEST POINTS BY PROVINCE AND TERRITORY

Provinces and Territories	Name of Highest Point	Height (metres)
British Columbia	Fairweather Mountain (on Alaska-British Columbia border)	4,663
Alberta	Mount Columbia (on Alberta-British Columbia border)	3,747
Saskatchewan	Cypress Hills	1,392
Manitoba	Baldy Mountain	832
Ontario	Ishpatina Ridge	693
Quebec	Mont D'Iberville (on Quebec-Newfoundland and Labrador boundary; known as Mount Caubvick in Newfoundland and Labrador)	1,652
New Brunswick	Mount Carleton	817
Nova Scotia	White Hill	532
Prince Edward Island	Unnamed hill at 46 degrees 20 minutes North, 63 degrees 25 minutes West	142
Newfoundland and Labrador	Mount Caubvick (on Newfoundland and Labrador-Quebec boundary; known as Mont D'Iberville in Quebec)	1,652
Yukon Territory	Mount Logan (highest point in Canada)	5,959
Northwest Territories	Unnamed peak at 61 degrees 52 minutes North, 127 degrees 42 minutes West	2,773
Nunavut	Barbeau Peak (on Ellesmere Island)	2,616

AVERAGE TEMPERATURE AND PRECIPITATION

	Average daily temperature		Average precipitation
	January	July	Annual
	°C		mm
St. John's	-4.5	15.8	1534.2
Charlottetown	-7.7	18.7	1158.2
Halifax	-5.9	18.8	1396.2
Fredericton	-9.4	19.3	1077.7
Quebec	-12.8	19.3	1189.7
Ottawa	-10.2	21.2	919.5
Toronto	-5.5	21.5	785.9
Winnipeg	-16.4	19.7	521.1
Regina	-14.7	18.9	389.7
Edmonton	-12.1	16.2	446.1
Victoria	4.6	16.9	882.9
Whitehorse	-15.2	14.3	262.3
Yellowknife	-25.6	17	288.6
Iqaluit	-26.9	8.2	403.7

Source: Environment and Climate Change Canada, *Canadian Climate Normals & Averages 1981-2010.*

KILOMETRES

MILES

	BANFF	BRANDON	CALGARY	CHARLOTTETOWN	CHICOUTIMI	CORNER BROOK	DAWSON CREEK	EDMONTON	FLIN FLON	FORT SMITH	FREDERICTON	GANDER	GASPÉ	HALIFAX	HAMILTON	JASPER	KENORA	LETHBRIDGE	LONDON	MONCTON	MONTRÉAL	NIAGARA FALLS	NORTH BAY	OTTAWA	PORT AUX BASQUES	PRINCE ALBERT	PRINCE GEORGE	PRINCE RUPERT	QUÉBEC	REGINA	RIVIÈRE-DU-LOUP	ROUYN	SAINT JOHN	ST. JOHN'S	SASKATOON	SAULT STE. MARIE	SEPT-ÎLES	SHERBROOKE	SUMMERSIDE	SYDNEY	THE PAS	THUNDER BAY	TORONTO	VANCOUVER	VICTORIA	WHITEHORSE	WINDSOR	WINNIPEG	YARMOUTH	YELLOWKNIFE
BANFF	•	782	80	3147	2702	3484	633	266	846	1094	2924	3725	2997	3225	2256	178	1037	216	2327	3047	2406	2299	2059	2288	3356	567	393	853	2574	555	2687	1960	2990	3932	465	1794	2980	2503	3131	3356	920	1354	2214	577	618	1562	2457	910	3055	1205
BRANDON	1259	•	702	2392	1920	2714	1082	715	451	1543	2142	2943	2215	2447	1474	944	255	622	1545	2292	1624	1517	1277	1506	2574	454	1159	1619	1792	227	1905	1178	2208	3152	387	1012	2198	1721	2349	2574	357	572	1432	1359	1400	2011	1677	128	2273	1654
CALGARY	129	1130	•	3055	2622	3404	553	186	766	1011	2832	3633	2917	3133	2176	258	957	136	2247	2955	2326	2219	1979	2208	3264	487	473	933	2494	475	2607	1880	2898	3842	385	1714	2900	2423	3051	3264	840	1274	2134	657	698	1482	2377	830	2963	1125
CHARLOTTETOWN	5065	3850	4917	•	552	368	3442	3075	2787	3903	223	597	516	144	1143	3304	2105	3014	1184	100	736	1147	1083	854	228	2814	3519	3979	587	2587	460	1136	192	804	2747	1348	531	706	39	228	2749	1788	1071	3719	3760	4371	1303	2232	257	4014
CHICOUTIMI	4348	3090	4220	888	•	901	3002	2635	2347	3463	329	1130	402	544	673	2864	1665	2542	744	452	296	716	643	414	761	2374	3079	3539	128	2147	92	696	383	1357	2307	908	385	261	536	761	2277	1348	631	3279	3320	3931	858	1792	460	3574
CORNER BROOK	5607	4368	5478	592	1450	•	3791	3424	3136	4252	572	229	865	402	1462	3653	2454	3336	1534	449	1085	1500	1432	1203	140	3163	3868	4328	936	2936	809	1485	541	436	3096	1697	911	1055	407	140	3071	2137	1420	4068	4109	4720	1652	2581	566	4363
DAWSON CREEK	1019	1741	890	5539	4831	6101	•	367	1020	640	3224	4020	3297	3525	2556	467	1337	689	2627	3342	2706	2599	2359	2588	3651	741	252	712	2874	855	2987	2260	3290	4227	695	2094	3280	2803	3426	3651	1013	1654	2514	747	788	929	2731	1210	3343	751
EDMONTON	428	1151	299	4949	4241	5510	591	•	653	828	2857	3653	2930	3158	2189	299	970	322	2260	2975	2339	2232	1992	2221	3284	374	444	904	2507	488	2620	1893	2923	3860	328	1727	2913	2436	3059	3284	646	1287	2147	773	814	1296	2364	843	2988	939
FLIN FLON	1362	668	1233	4485	3777	5047	1642	1051	•	1481	2569	3365	2642	2870	1901	882	682	862	1972	2687	2051	1944	1704	1933	2996	279	1097	1557	2219	467	2332	1605	2635	3572	381	1439	2625	2148	2771	2996	94	999	1859	1423	1464	1949	2086	555	2700	1592
FORT SMITH	1761	2483	1627	6281	5573	6843	1030	1333	2383	•	3685	4480	3758	3986	3017	995	1798	1150	3083	3803	3167	3055	2820	3049	4112	1202	892	1352	3335	1316	3448	2721	3751	4692	1156	2555	3741	3264	3887	4112	1474	2115	2975	1387	1428	1569	3192	1671	3816	443
FREDERICTON	4706	3447	4558	359	529	921	5189	4598	4134	5930	•	801	435	215	895	3086	1887	2764	966	123	518	938	865	636	432	2596	3301	3761	364	2369	237	918	66	1008	2529	1130	481	483	207	432	2499	1570	853	3501	3542	4153	1080	2014	131	3796
GANDER	5995	4736	5847	961	1819	369	6470	5879	5415	7210	1289	•	1094	631	1691	3882	2683	3560	1762	678	1314	1734	1661	1432	369	3392	4097	4557	1165	3165	1038	1714	770	207	3325	1926	1140	1284	636	369	3300	2366	1649	4297	4338	4949	1881	2810	795	4592
GASPÉ	4823	3565	4694	830	647	1392	5306	4715	4252	6048	700	1761	•	587	968	3159	1960	2837	1039	416	591	1011	938	709	725	2669	3374	3834	437	2442	310	991	501	1301	2602	1203	299	556	500	725	2572	1643	926	3574	3615	4226	1153	2087	566	3869
HALIFAX	5190	3938	5042	232	875	647	5673	5082	4619	6415	346	1015	945	•	1196	3387	2188	3065	1267	171	819	1239	1166	937	262	2897	3602	4062	567	2670	452	1219	149	838	2830	1431	628	698	188	262	2800	1871	1154	3802	3843	4454	1381	2315	217	4097
HAMILTON	3631	2372	3502	1839	1083	2353	4114	3523	3059	4855	1440	2721	1558	1925	•	2418	1219	2096	84	1013	377	43	250	290	1322	1928	2633	3093	545	1701	658	431	961	1898	1861	462	951	474	1097	1322	1831	902	42	2833	2874	3485	198	1346	1026	3128
JASPER	286	1519	415	5317	4609	5879	752	369	1419	1601	4966	6247	5084	5451	3891	•	1199	394	2489	3204	2568	2461	2221	2450	3513	603	215	675	2736	717	2849	2122	3152	4089	557	1956	3142	2665	3288	3513	875	1516	2376	544	585	1396	2635	1072	3217	1106
KENORA	1669	410	1510	3388	2680	3949	2152	1561	1098	2894	3037	4318	3154	3521	1962	1930	•	877	1290	2005	1369	1262	1022	1251	2314	709	1414	1874	1537	482	1650	923	1953	2890	642	757	1943	1466	2089	2314	612	317	1177	1614	1655	2266	1404	127	2018	1909
LETHBRIDGE	384	1001	219	4851	4091	5369	1109	518	1387	1851	4448	5729	4566	4933	3373	634	1411	•	2167	2882	2246	2139	1899	2128	3191	623	609	1069	2414	395	2527	1800	2830	2767	412	1626	2820	2343	2966	3191	768	1194	2054	710	751	1618	2297	750	2902	1261
LONDON	3745	2486	3616	1905	1197	2469	4228	3637	3174	4962	1555	2836	1672	2039	135	4006	2076	3487	•	1084	448	126	321	361	1393	2009	2704	3164	616	1772	729	502	1032	1969	1932	533	1022	545	1166	1393	1902	973	113	2904	2945	3548	126	1417	1097	3199
MONCTON	4904	3689	4756	161	727	723	5378	4788	4324	6120	198	1091	669	275	1630	5156	3227	4638	1745	•	636	1056	983	754	309	2714	3419	3879	487	2487	360	1036	92	885	2647	1248	462	606	84	309	2649	1688	971	3619	3660	4271	1203	2132	157	3914
MONTRÉAL	3872	2614	3743	1184	476	1746	4355	3764	3301	5097	834	2115	951	1318	607	4133	2203	3615	721	1024	•	420	347	118	945	2078	2783	3243	168	1851	281	400	584	1521	2011	612	574	97	720	945	1981	1052	335	2983	3024	3635	562	1496	649	3278
NIAGARA FALLS	3700	2441	3571	1846	1152	2414	4183	3592	3129	4917	1510	2791	1627	1994	69	3961	2031	3442	203	1699	676	•	293	333	1365	1971	2676	3136	588	1744	701	474	1004	1941	1904	505	983	517	1140	1365	1874	945	85	2876	2917	3528	241	1389	1069	3171
NORTH BAY	3314	2055	3185	1743	1035	2305	3796	3206	2742	4538	1392	2673	1510	1876	402	3574	1645	3056	517	1582	558	472	•	229	1292	1731	2436	2896	515	1504	628	181	931	1868	1664	265	921	444	1067	1292	1634	705	208	2636	2677	3280	435	1149	996	2931
OTTAWA	3682	2424	3553	1374	666	1936	4165	3574	3111	4907	1024	2305	1141	1508	467	3943	2013	3425	581	1213	190	536	369	•	1063	1960	2665	3125	286	1733	399	343	702	1639	1893	494	692	215	838	1063	1863	934	248	2865	2906	3517	475	1378	767	3160
PORT AUX BASQUES	5401	4142	5253	367	1225	225	5876	5285	4822	6618	695	594	1167	422	2128	5654	3724	5135	2242	497	1521	2197	2079	1711	•	3023	3728	4188	796	2796	669	1345	401	576	2956	1557	771	915	267	129	2931	1997	1280	3928	3969	4580	1512	2441	426	4223
PRINCE ALBERT	912	731	784	4529	3821	5090	1193	602	449	1934	4178	5459	4295	4662	3103	970	1141	1003	3233	4368	3344	3172	2786	3154	4865	•	818	1278	2246	227	2359	1632	2662	3599	102	1466	2652	2175	2798	3023	272	1026	1896	1144	1185	1670	2082	582	2727	1313
PRINCE GEORGE	632	1865	761	5663	4955	6225	406	715	1765	1436	5312	6593	5430	5797	4237	346	2276	980	4352	5502	4479	4307	3920	4289	6000	1316	•	460	2951	932	3064	2337	3367	4304	772	2163	3357	2880	3503	3728	1090	1731	2591	495	536	1181	2850	1287	3432	1003
PRINCE RUPERT	1373	2606	1502	6404	5695	6965	1146	1455	2506	2176	6053	7334	6170	6537	4978	1086	3016	1720	5092	6243	5219	5047	4661	5029	6740	2057	740	•	3411	1392	3524	2797	3827	4764	1232	2623	3817	3340	3963	4188	1550	2191	3051	955	996	1641	3310	1747	3892	1463
QUÉBEC	4142	2884	4014	945	206	1506	4625	4035	3571	5367	586	1875	703	912	877	4403	2474	3885	991	784	270	946	829	460	1281	3615	4749	5489	•	2019	127	568	418	1372	2179	780	406	133	571	796	2149	1220	503	3151	3192	3803	730	1664	495	3446
REGINA	893	365	764	4163	3455	4725	1376	785	752	2118	3813	5094	3930	4297	2737	1154	776	636	2852	4002	2979	2807	2420	2789	4500	365	1500	2240	3249	•	2132	1405	2435	3372	160	1231	2425	1948	2571	2796	373	799	1659	1132	1173	1784	1902	355	2507	1427
RIVIÈRE-DU-LOUP	4324	3066	4196	740	148	1302	4807	4216	3753	5549	381	1670	499	727	1059	4585	2655	4067	1173	579	452	1128	1011	642	1077	3796	4931	5671	204	3431	•	681	303	1245	2292	893	231	246	444	669	2262	1333	616	3264	3305	3916	843	1777	368	3559
ROUYN	3154	1896	3026	1828	1120	2390	3637	3046	2583	4379	1477	2758	1595	1962	694	3415	1485	2897	808	1667	644	763	291	552	2165	2626	3761	4501	914	2261	1096	•	984	1921	1565	446	974	497	1120	1345	1535	606	389	2537	2578	3189	616	1050	1049	2832
SAINT JOHN	4812	3553	4664	309	616	871	5295	4704	4241	6037	106	1239	806	240	1547	5073	3143	4554	1661	148	940	1616	1498	1130	645	4284	5419	6159	673	3919	488	1584	•	977	2595	1196	547	537	176	401	2565	1636	919	3567	3608	4219	1146	2080	65	3862
ST. JOHN'S	6328	5073	6183	1294	2184	702	6803	6212	5749	7551	1622	333	2094	1349	3055	6581	4651	4453	3169	1424	2448	3124	3006	2638	927	5792	6927	7667	2208	5427	2004	3092	1572	•	3532	2133	1347	1491	843	576	3507	2573	1856	4504	4545	5156	2088	3017	1012	4799
SASKATOON	748	623	620	4421	3713	4983	1118	528	613	1860	4070	5351	4188	4554	2995	896	1033	663	3109	4260	3236	3064	2678	3046	4757	164	1242	1983	3507	257	3689	2519	4176	5684	•	1391	2585	2108	2731	2956	346	959	1819	1042	1083	1624	2036	515	2660	1267
SAULT STE. MARIE	2887	1629	2758	2169	1461	2731	3370	2779	2360	4112	1819	3100	1936	2303	744	3148	1218	2617	858	2008	985	813	426	795	2506	2359	3481	4221	1255	1981	1437	718	1925	3422	2239	•	1186	709	1332	1557	1369	440	420	2363	2404	3015	647	884	1261	2666
SEPT-ÎLES	4796	3537	4667	855	620	1466	5279	4688	4225	6021	774	1835	481	1011	1530	5057	3127	4538	1645	744	924	1582	1482	1114	1241	4268	5403	6143	653	3903	372	1568	880	2168	4160	1909	•	539	515	771	2555	1626	909	3557	3598	4209	1136	2070	612	3852
SHERBROOKE	4028	2770	3899	1136	420	1698	4511	3920	3457	5253	777	2066	895	1123	763	4289	2359	3771	877	975	156	832	715	346	1473	3500	4635	5375	214	3135	396	800	864	2400	3392	1141	867	•	690	915	2078	1149	432	3080	3121	3732	659	1593	614	3375
SUMMERSIDE	5039	3780	4910	63	863	655	5514	4923	4459	6256	333	1024	805	303	1765	5292	3362	4773	1876	135	1159	1835	1717	1349	430	4503	5638	6378	919	4138	715	1802	283	1357	4395	2144	829	1110	•	267	2706	1772	1053	3703	3744	4355	1287	2216	241	3998
SYDNEY	5401	4142	5253	367	1225	225	5876	5285	4822	6618	695	594	1167	422	2128	5654	3724	5135	2242	497	1521	2197	2079	1711	207	4865	6000	6740	1281	4500	1077	2165	645	927	4757	2506	1241	1473	430	•	2931	1997	1280	3928	3969	4580	1512	2441	426	4223
THE PAS	1481	575	1352	4424	3664	4942	1630	1040	151	2372	4022	5311	4139	4506	2947	1408	985	1236	3061	4263	3188	3016	2630	2998	4717	438	1754	2494	3458	600	3640	2470	4128	5644	557	2203	4112	3344	4355	4717	•	929	1789	1388	1429	1942	2008	485	2630	1585
THUNDER BAY	2179	921	2050	2878	2169	3439	2662	2071	1608	3404	2527	3808	2644	3011	1452	2440	510	1922	1566	2717	1693	1521	1135	1503	3214	1651	2786	3526	1963	1286	2145	975	2633	4141	1543	708	2617	1849	2852	3214	1495	•	860	1931	1972	2583	1087	444	741	2226
TORONTO	3563	2305	3434	1724	1015	2285	4046	3455	2992	4788	1373	2654	1490	1857	68	3824	1894	3306	182	1563	539	137	335	399	2060	3051	4170	4910	810	2670	991	626	1479	2987	2927	676	1463	695	1695	2060	2879	1384	•	2791	2832	3435	227	1304	984	3086
VANCOUVER	929	2187	1057	5985	5277	6547	1202	1244	2290	2232	5634	6915	5752	6119	4559	875	2597	1143	4674	5824	4801	4628	4242	4611	6322	1841	797	1537	5071	1822	5253	4083	5741	7248	1677	3803	5724	4957	5959	6322	2234	3108	4492	•	41	1676	3034	1487	3632	1498
VICTORIA	995	2253	1123	6051	5343	6613	1268	1310	2356	2298	5700	6981	5818	6185	4625	941	2663	1209	4740	5890	4867	4694	4308	4677	6387	1907	863	1603	5137	1818	5319	4149	5807	7314	1743	3869	5790	5023	6025	6387	2300	3174	4558	66	•	1717	3053	1528	3673	1539
WHITEHORSE	2514	3236	2385	7034	6326	7596	1495	2086	3137	2525	6684	7965	6801	7168	5609	2247	3647	2604	5710	6874	5850	5678	5279	5660	7371	2688	1901	2641	6120	2871	6302	5132	6790	8298	2614	4852	6774	6006	7009	7371	3125	4157	5528	2697	2763	•	3660	2190	4284	1680
WIINDSOR	3954	2699	3825	2097	1381	2659	4395	3804	3357	5137	1738	3027	1856	2223	319	4241	2260	3697	203	1936	904	388	700	764	2433	3351	4587	5327	1175	3061	1357	991	1844	3360	3277	1041	1828	1061	2071	2433	3232	1749	365	4883	4913	5890	•	1547	1211	3303
WINNIPEG	1465	206	1336	3592	2884	4154	1947	1357	893	2689	3241	4522	3359	3726	2166	1725	204	1207	2280	3431	2408	2235	1849	2218	3928	937	2071	2812	2678	571	2860	1690	3347	4855	829	1423	3331	2564	3566	3928	781	715	2099	2393	2459	3524	2490	•	2145	1782
YARMOUTH	4917	3658	4768	414	740	911	5380	4809	4345	6141	211	1279	911	349	1651	5177	3248	4670	1765	253	1044	1720	1603	1234	686	4389	5523	6264	797	4035	592	1688	105	1629	4281	2029	985	988	388	686	4233	1193	1584	5845	5911	6894	1949	3452	•	3927
YELLOWKNIFE	1939	2662	1811	6460	5752	7022	1209	1511	2562	713	6109	7390	6227	6593	5034	1780	3072	2029	5148	6299	5275	5103	4717	5086	6796	2113	1614	2354	5546	2297	5728	4558	6215	7723	2039	4291	6199	5432	6418	6796	2551	3582	4966	2411	2477	2704	5316	2868	6320	•

Source: National Atlas Service, Natural Resources Canada

Science

Astronomical Calculations

ASTRONOMY IN CANADA

Astronomical research in Canada is carried out in universities, supported by the Natural Sciences and Engineering Research Council (NSERC) of Canada, and by the Canada Foundation for Innovation (CFI), and also in the National Research Council (NRC) — specifically by the Herzberg Institute of Astrophysics (HIA), which operates the following observatories: The Dominion Astrophysical Observatory (DAO) at Victoria, with optical telescopes of 1.8m and 1.2m aperture; and the Dominion Radio Astrophysical Observatory (DRAO) near Penticton, which has a 26m paraboloid and a 7-element array of 9m antennae. The National Research Council also maintains Canada's Time Service in its Institute of National Measurement Standards. The Canadian Astronomy Data Centre (CADC) is housed within HIA.

A number of Canadian universities offer graduate education in astronomy: Victoria, British Columbia (Vancouver), Alberta (Edmonton), Calgary, Saskatchewan (Saskatoon), Manitoba (Winnipeg), Western Ontario (London), Waterloo, McMaster (Hamilton), York (Toronto), Toronto, Queen's (Kingston), Montréal, McGill (Montréal), Laval (Québec), and St. Mary's (Halifax). Most of these have some local facilities for observational and theoretical studies, and all of them have access to national facilities in Canada and elsewhere. Among the major observatories operated by Canadian universities are: a 1.8m infrared telescope opened in 1987 by the University of Calgary; a 1.2m telescope at the University of Western Ontario; a 0.6m telescope now located in, and shared with, Argentina with access through the University of Toronto; and a 1.5m telescope at the Mont Mégantic Observatory operated by the University of Montréal, and Laval University. There is also a Canadian Institute for Theoretical Astrophysics hosted by the University of Toronto. Canadian astronomers established the Association of Canadian Universities for Research in Astronomy (ACURA) to co-ordinate universities' participation in astronomy, especially in the development of large-scale facilities.

Through the National Research Council, Canadian astronomers also have access to excellent international facilities. One of these is the 3.6m Canada-France-Hawaii optical telescope atop Mauna Kea on the island of Hawaii, at an elevation of nearly 4200m. This telescope is shared, both as to cost and operation, by Canada, France, and the state of Hawaii. Canadian astronomers also share (with the Netherlands and the UK) in the operation of the James Clerk Maxwell telescope, a sophisticated millimetre-wave radio telescope at the same site. Canada also is a partner, along with several other countries, in the twin Gemini 8m telescopes, which are in operation in Hawaii and in Chile. Balloon-borne telescopes, Canada's first astronomical satellite MOST (Microvariability and Oscillations of STars), and participation in other space astronomy missions are funded through the Canadian Space Agency, and Canada is a partner in the James Webb Space Telescope, the planned successor to the Hubble Space Telescope. Canada is also a partner in the North American Program in Radio Astronomy, including the Atacama Large Millimetre Array, under contruction high in the Atacama Desert in Chile.

Astronomical education and outreach are carried out in a wide variety of settings. In the formal education system, astronomy is part of the elementary and secondary school science curriculum in most provinces, and is taught in most universities, most commonly in the form of introductory astronomy courses for non-majors. Canada's planetariums, science centres, and public observatories play a major role in communicating the nature and excitement of astronomy, as do science journalists, and the many professional and amateur astronomers who give public lectures, and organize open houses and star parties.

OBSERVATORIES

Observatories are open to the public as follows:

Burke-Gaffney Observatory: St. Mary's University, Halifax NS B3H 3C3 - 902-420-5633; Info line: 902-496-8257; Fax: 902-496-8218; Email: bgo@ap.smu.ca; URL: www.ap.smu.ca/pr/bgo

Free public tours are held, weather permitting, on the 1st and 3rd Saturday of each month, except from June through September when they are held every Saturday. Tours begin at 7pm between November 1 and March 30 and at either 9pm or 10pm (depending on when it gets dark) between April 1 and October 31. On clear evenings, the 40-cm telescope is used to view the planets, the Moon, or other interesting celestial objects.

There will be no tour on cloudy or rainy nights. The decision to hold or cancel a tour is usually made by 6pm on Saturday. Always call the information line after 6pm to find out if the tour is on or off.

Groups wishing special tours can be accommodated on Monday evenings by reservation.

Canada Science & Technology Museum, Helen Sawyer Hogg Observatory: 2421 Lancaster Rd., Ottawa ON K1G 5A3 - 613-991-3044; Email: cts@technomuses.ca; URL: cstmuseum.techno-science.ca

38-cm refractor (from the former Dominion Observatory). See website for details and special programs.

Canada-France-Hawaii Telescope: CFHT Corporation, #65, 1238 Mamalahoa Hwy., Kamuela HI, 96743 - 808-885-7944; Fax: 808-885-7288; E-mail: info@cfht.hawaii.edu; URL: www.cfht.hawaii.edu

By appointment only.

Climenhaga Observatory: Dept. of Physics & Astronomy, University of Victoria, PO Box 1700, Station CSC, Victoria BC V8W 2Y2 - 250-721-7700; Fax: 250-721-7715; URL: astrowww.phys.uvic.ca/events

Daytime tours are open from the beginning of April until the end of July. The tour includes an entertaining educational presentation, a look through the big, fully automated telescope in the Climenhaga Observatory and weather permitting, an opportunity to search for sunspots using the smaller telescopes on the roof. The tours are free but space is limited. Interested parties are encouraged to book in advance.

Night time viewing sessions are open on Wednesdays from 8 p.m. (or sunset) until 10 p.m. (Oct. - April), and 9 p.m. (or sunset) until 10 p.m. (May - Aug.).

Gordon MacMillan Southam Observatory: H.R. MacMillan Space Centre, 1100 Chestnut St., Vancouver BC V6J 3J9 - 604-738-7827; Fax: 604-736-5665; E-mail: info@spacecentre.ca; URL: www.spacecentre.ca/gms

Open Friday and Saturday starting at 8:00 p.m. To confirm observatory openings, please call 604-738-2855. Admission is by donation.

Hume Cronyn Memorial Observatory: Dept. of Physics & Astronomy, University of Western Ontario, London ON N6A 3K7 - 519-661-2111, ext. 83283; URL: physics.uwo.ca/community/cronyn/index.html

Public Nights run monthly from October through April, and weekly May through August (Saturday evenings, 8:30 p.m.-11:00 p.m.). No reservations needed. Private Exploring the Stars program available through a booking system.

National Research Council Canada, Dominion Astrophysical Observatory: 5071 West Saanich Rd., Victoria BC V9E 2E7 - 250-363-0001; Fax: 250-363-0045; E-mail: NRC.NSIHerzbergAstroInfoISN.CNRC@nrc-cnrc.gc.ca; URL: www.nrc-cnrc.gc.ca/eng/solutions/facilities/dao.html

Both DOA telescopes are available to qualified researchers through a quarterly peer-reviewed process. The general public should contact the observatory directly.

National Research Council Canada, Dominion Radio Astrophysical Observatory: 717 White Lake Road, PO Box 248, Penticton BC V2A 6J9 - 250-493-2300; Fax: 250-497-2355; E-mail: NRC.DRAO-OFR.CNRC@nrc-cnrc.gc.ca; URL: www.nrc-cnrc.gc.ca/eng/solutions/facilities/drao.html

Both DOA telescopes are available to qualified researchers through a quarterly peer-reviewed process. The general public should contact the observatory directly. A visitor centre is located on-site at the Dominion Radio Astrophysical Observatory.

Observatoire Astronomique Du Mont Mégantic: 189 route du Parc, Notre-Dame-des-Bois QC J0B 2E0 - 819-888-2645; E-mail: parc.mont-megantic@sepaq.com; URL: omm.craq-astro.ca

The observatory hosts "Festival d'Astronomie Populaire du mont Mégantic" on the weekends in July. For other times of the year, visits including interactive exhibitions, high definition multimedia show, and tours of the observatories can be arranged through AstroLab du Mont Mégantic. See website for details on dates & times.

Rothney Astrophysical Observatory: Dept. of Physics & Astronomy, University of Calgary, 2500 University Dr. NW, Calgary AB T2N 1N4 - 403-931-2366; E-mail: rao@phas.ucalgary.ca; URL: www.ucalgary.ca/rao

Day and evening programs are available for school groups, which involve a grade appropriate presentation, tour of the observatory and skyviewing. Free drop-in visits to the Interpretive Centre, private tours and school group tours are also available. See website for details.

Telus World of Science - RASC Observatory: 11211 - 142 St., Edmonton AB T5M 4A1 - 780-451-3344; Email: info@twose.ca; URL: telusworldofscienceedmonton.ca/rasc-observatory

Summer hours (July to Labour Day weekend) 1:00 p.m. - 5:00 p.m. and 6:30 p.m. - 10 p.m. 7 days a week. Fall/Winter/Spring hours (After Labour Day to the following summer) Saturdays, Sundays & holidays 1:00 p.m. - 4:00 p.m., and Fridays, Saturdays & Sundays 7:00 p.m. - 10:00 p.m. Open weather permitting.

University of Alberta Observatory: Dept. of Physics, University of Alberta, Edmonton AB T6G 2E1 - 780-492-5286; Email: stars@ualberta.ca; URL: www.ualberta.ca/physics/outreach/department-of-physics-astronomical-observatory

Open to the public Thursday nights from September through April (closed for final exams and winter holidays), weather permitting. School groups, youth groups and other groups can book a private visit free of charge. See website for exact hours and details.

University of Saskatchewan Observatory: Dept. of Physics & Engineering Physics, University of Saskatchewan, 116 Science Place, Saskatoon SK S7N 5E2 - 306-966-6396; Email: phys_engphys@usask.ca; URL: physics.usask.ca/observatory

Saturday evening programs year round; times vary. Tours for school and community groups are arranged for Friday evenings (October - March). Special tours may be arranged during the summer months.

University of Toronto, St. George Campus Observatory: Dept. of Astronomy & Astrophysics, University of Toronto, 50 St. George Street, Toronto ON M5S 3H4 - Email: tours@astro.utoronto.ca; URL: www.astro.utoronto.ca/astrotours

Free tours are offered on the first Thursday of every month (excluding January). Tours start at 8 p.m. during winter months and 9 p.m. during summer months. Extra public tours may also be arranged. See website for details.

York University Observatory: 4700 Keele St., Toronto ON M3J 1P3 - 416-736-2100, ext. 77773 (voice mail); Email: observe@yorku.ca; pdelaney@yorku.ca; URL: observatory.info.yorku.ca

The observatory is open for online viewing Monday nights and public (in-person) viewing on Wednesday nights at the following times: October - March 7:30 p.m. - 9:30 p.m., and April - September 9:00 p.m. - 11:00 p.m. See website for further details.

PLANETARY FACT SHEET - METRIC

	MERCURY	VENUS	EARTH	MOON	MARS	JUPITER	SATURN	URANUS	NEPTUNE	PLUTO
Mass (1024kg)	0.33	4.87	5.97	0.073	0.642	1898	568	86.8	102	0.0146
Diameter (km)	4879	12,104	12,756	3475	6792	142,984	120,536	51,118	49,528	2370
Density (kg/m3)	5427	5243	5514	3340	3933	1326	687	1271	1638	2095
Gravity (m/s2)	3.7	8.9	9.8	1.6	3.7	23.1	9	8.7	11	0.7
Escape Velocity (km/s)	4.3	10.4	11.2	2.4	5	59.5	35.5	21.3	23.5	1.3
Rotation Period (hours)	1407.6	-5832.5	23.9	655.7	24.6	9.9	10.7	-17.2	16.1	-153.3
Length of Day (hours)	4222.6	2802	24	708.7	24.7	9.9	10.7	17.2	16.1	153.3
Distance from Sun (106 km)	57.9	108.2	149.6	0.384*	227.9	778.6	1433.5	2872.5	4495.1	5906.4
Perihelion (106 km)	46	107.5	147.1	0.363*	206.6	740.5	1352.6	2741.3	4444.5	4436.8
Aphelion (106 km)	69.8	108.9	152.1	0.406*	249.2	816.6	1514.5	3003.6	4545.7	7375.9
Orbital Period (days)	88	224.7	365.2	27.3	687	4331	10,747	30,589	59,800	90,560
Orbital Velocity (km/s)	47.4	35	29.8	1	24.1	13.1	9.7	6.8	5.4	4.7
Orbital Inclination (degrees)	7	3.4	0	5.1	1.9	1.3	2.5	0.8	1.8	17.2
Orbital Eccentricity	0.205	0.007	0.017	0.055	0.094	0.049	0.057	0.046	0.011	0.244
Axial Tilt (degrees)	0.01	177.4	23.4	6.7	25.2	3.1	26.7	97.8	28.3	122.5
Mean Temperature (C)	167	464	15	-20	-65	-110	-140	-195	-200	-225
Surface Pressure (bars)	0	92	1	0	0.01	Unknown*	Unknown*	Unknown*	Unknown*	0
Number of Moons	0	0	1	0	2	67	62	27	14	5
Ring System?	No	No	No	No	No	Yes	Yes	Yes	Yes	No
Global Magnetic Field?	Yes	No	Yes	No	No	Yes	Yes	Yes	Yes	Unknown
	MERCURY	VENUS	EARTH	MOON	MARS	JUPITER	SATURN	URANUS	NEPTUNE	PLUTO

Source: NSSDC/NASA

PLANETARIUMS

A selection of planetaria with URL, phone number & related information:

ASTROLab du parc national du Mont-Mégantic: 189 route du Parc, Notre-Dame-des-Bois, QC J0B 2E0 - 819-888-2941; Toll Free: 1-800-665-6527; URL: www.astrolab-parc-national-mont-megantic.org

Cosmic Rhythms multimedia show; on-site lodging.

Doran Planetarium: Laurentian University, 935 Ramsey Lake Rd., Sudbury ON P3E 2C6 - URL: laurentian.ca/planetarium

Largest planetarium in northern Ontario. Shows are available for students, as well as presentations, media lectures and special shows.

The Lockhart Planetarium: University of Manitoba, 500 Dysart Rd., Winnipeg MB R3T 2M8 - 204-474-9785; URL: www.physics.umanitoba.ca/planetarium

Dome seats 60; open year-round for public groups.

MacMillan Planetarium: H.R. MacMillan Space Centre, 1100 Chestnut St., Vancouver BC V6J 3J9. - 604-738-7827, Fax: 604-736-5665; URL: www.spacecentre.ca

Special laser shows in summer, numerous programs for school groups of all ages, teacher packages online.

Manitoba Museum Planetarium: 190 Rupert Ave., Winnipeg MB R3B 0N2 - 204-956-2830; Fax: 204-942-3679; Email: info@manitobamuseum.ca; URL: manitobamuseum.ca/main/visit/planetarium

First opened in 1968, this planetarium now offers shows featuring pre-recorded sequences and live presenters.

Ontario Science Centre Planetarium: 770 Don Mills Road, North York ON M3C 1T3 - 416-696-1000; URL: www.ontariosciencecentre.ca/Tour/Live-Planetarium-Show

Toronto's only public permanent planetarium. See website for details.

Planétarium Rio Tinto Alcan Montréal: 4801, av Pierre-De Coubertin, Montréal QC H1V 3V4 - 514-868-3000; URL: espacepourlavie.ca/planetarium

Programs, activity sheets, classroom kits, advanced workshop for teachers & educators.

Royal Ontario Museum Travelling Planetarium: Travelling Programs, Learning Department, Royal Ontario Museum, 100 Queens Park, Toronto ON M5S 2C6 - 416-586-5681; Fax: 416-586-5832; E-mail: outreach@rom.on.ca; URL: www.rom.on.ca

Portable Starlab domes (standard or large) available for any location in Ontario.

Science North: 100 Ramsey Lake Road, Sudbury ON P3E 5S9 - 705-522-3701 or toll-free 1-800-461-4898; Fax: 705-522-4954; E-mail: contactus@sciencenorth.ca; URL: sciencenorth.ca/science-north/planetarium

Digital planetarium with feature films about astronomy and other space topics.

Telus Spark: 220 St. George's Dr. NE, Calgary AB T2E 5T2 - 403-817-6800; E-mail: info@sparkscience.ca; URL: www.sparkscience.ca/visit/movies-and-planetarium-shows

The Planetarium dome offers several programs and multimedia shows.

CALENDAR OF ASTRONOMICAL EVENTS, 2017

Date	GMT (h:m)	Event
02-Jan	9:20	Venus 1.9°S of Moon
02	18:14	Moon at Descending Node
03	6:47	Mars 0.2°S of Moon: Occn.
03	14	Quadrantid Meteor Shower
04	15	Earth at Perihelion: 0.98331 AU
05	19:47	FIRST QUARTER MOON
09	09	Mercury 6.7° of Saturn
10	6:07	Moon at Perigee: 363242 km
12	11:34	FULL MOON
12	13	Venus at Greatest Elong: 47.1°E
15	10:44	Moon at Ascending Node
19	5:26	Jupiter 2.7°S of Moon
19	10	Mercury at Greatest Elong: 24.1°W
19	22:14	LAST QUARTER MOON
22	00:14	Moon at Apogee: 404913 km
24	10:37	Saturn 3.6°S of Moon
26	00:46	Mercury 3.7°S of Moon
28	00:07	NEW MOON
29	22:21	Moon at Descending Node
31	14:34	Venus 4.1°N of Moon
01-Feb	1:09	Mars 2.3°N of Moon
04	4:19	FIRST QUARTER MOON
06	13:59	Moon at Perigee: 368817 km
07	14	Mercury at Aphelion
11	00:33	FULL MOON
11	00:44	Pen. Lunar Eclipse; mag=0.988
11	19:49	Moon at Ascending Node
15	14:55	Jupiter 2.7°S of Moon
18	19:33	LAST QUARTER MOON
18	21	Jupiter at Aphelion
18	21:14	Moon at Apogee: 404376 km
20	16	Venus at Perihelion
20	23:44	Saturn 3.6°S of Moon
26	6:28	Moon at Descending Node
26	14:53	Annular Solar Eclipse; mag=0.992
26	14:58	NEW MOON
01-Mar	18:58	Mars 4.3°N of Moon
02	02	Neptune in Conjunction with Sun
03	7:24	Moon at Perigee: 369065 km
05	11:32	FIRST QUARTER MOON
07	00	Mercury at Superior Conjunction
11	4:17	Moon at Ascending Node
12	14:54	FULL MOON
14	20:04	Jupiter 2.5°S of Moon
18	17:25	Moon at Apogee: 404651 km
20	10:29	Vernal Equinox
20	10:49	Saturn 3.4°S of Moon
20	15:58	LAST QUARTER MOON
23	14	Mercury at Perihelion
25	11	Venus at Inferior Conjunction
25	15:41	Moon at Descending Node
01-Jul	00:51	FIRST QUARTER MOON
01	7:28	Jupiter 2.7°S of Moon
03	20	Earth at Aphelion: 1.01668 AU
06	4:27	Moon at Apogee: 405934 km
07	3:34	Saturn 3.2°S of Moon
09	4:07	FULL MOON
12	5:17	Moon at Descending Node
16	19:26	LAST QUARTER MOON
20	11:13	Venus 2.7°N of Moon
21	17:09	Moon at Perigee: 361238 km
23	9:46	NEW MOON
25	00:46	Moon at Ascending Node
25	8:49	Mercury 0.9°S of Moon: Occn.
27	00	Mars in Conjunction with Sun
28	03	Delta-Aquarid Meteor Shower
28	20:15	Jupiter 3.1°S of Moon
30	04	Mercury at Greatest Elong: 27.2°E
30	15:23	FIRST QUARTER MOON
02-Aug	13	Mercury at Aphelion
02	17:55	Moon at Apogee: 405026 km
03	7:31	Saturn 3.5°S of Moon
07	18:11	FULL MOON
07	18:20	Partial Lunar Eclipse; mag=0.246
08	10:56	Moon at Descending Node
12	19	Perseid Meteor Shower
15	1:15	LAST QUARTER MOON
18	13:14	Moon at Perigee: 366129 km
19	4:45	Venus 2.2°N of Moon
21	10:34	Moon at Ascending Node
21	18:26	Total Solar Eclipse; mag=1.031
21	18:30	NEW MOON
25	13:00	Jupiter 3.5°S of Moon
26	21	Mercury at Inferior Conjunction
29	8:13	FIRST QUARTER MOON
30	11:25	Moon at Apogee: 404307 km
30	14:23	Saturn 3.6°S of Moon
04-Sep	18:41	Moon at Descending Node
05	00	Mercury 3.2° of Mars
05	04	Neptune at Opposition
06	7:03	FULL MOON
12	10	Mercury at Greatest Elong: 17.9°W
13	6:25	LAST QUARTER MOON
13	16:04	Moon at Perigee: 369856 km
15	12	Mercury at Perihelion
16	18	Mercury 0.1° of Mars
17	18:28	Moon at Ascending Node
18	00:56	Venus 0.5°N of Moon: Occn.
18	23:22	Mercury 0.0°N of Moon: Occn.
20	5:30	NEW MOON
22	7:51	Jupiter 3.7°S of Moon
22	20:02	Autumnal Equinox

28	2:57	NEW MOON
30	12:39	Moon at Perigee: 363855 km
30	13:03	Mars 5.5°N of Moon
01-Apr	10	Mercury at Greatest Elong: 19.0°E
03	18:39	FIRST QUARTER MOON
07	9:14	Moon at Ascending Node
07	21	Jupiter at Opposition
10	21:20	Jupiter 2.2°S of Moon
11	6:08	FULL MOON
14	6	Uranus in Conjunction with Sun
15	10:05	Moon at Apogee: 405478 km
16	18:39	Saturn 3.2°S of Moon
19	9:57	LAST QUARTER MOON
20	06	Mercury at Inferior Conjunction
21	22:30	Moon at Descending Node
22	12	Lyrid Meteor Shower
23	17:59	Venus 5.2°N of Moon
26	12:16	NEW MOON
27	16:18	Moon at Perigee: 359325 km
03-May	2:47	FIRST QUARTER MOON
04	10:42	Moon at Ascending Node
05	01	Eta-Aquarid Meteor Shower
07	21:24	Jupiter 2.1°S of Moon
10	21:43	FULL MOON
12	19:51	Moon at Apogee: 406212 km
13	23:07	Saturn 3.1°S of Moon
17	23	Mercury at Greatest Elong: 25.8°W
19	00:33	LAST QUARTER MOON
19	1:30	Moon at Descending Node
22	12:32	Venus 2.4°N of Moon
24	1:20	Mercury 1.6°N of Moon
25	19:44	NEW MOON
26	1:23	Moon at Perigee: 357210 km
31	11:56	Moon at Ascending Node
01-Jun	12:42	FIRST QUARTER MOON
03	11	Venus at Greatest Elong: 45.9°W
03	23:57	Jupiter 2.3°S of Moon
08	22:21	Moon at Apogee: 406402 km
09	13:10	FULL MOON
10	1:25	Saturn 3.1°S of Moon
13	00	Venus at Aphelion
15	2:40	Moon at Descending Node
15	09	Saturn at Opposition
17	11:33	LAST QUARTER MOON
19	13	Mercury at Perihelion
20	21:13	Venus 2.4°N of Moon
21	4:25	Summer Solstice
21	14	Mercury at Superior Conjunction
23	10:49	Moon at Perigee: 357938 km
24	2:31	NEW MOON
27	16:26	Moon at Ascending Node

Note: Add one hour to the times listed if Daylight Savings Time is in effect.
Source: Planetary dates courtesy of Fred Espenak, AstroPixels.com, accessed August 9, 2016.

27	00:09	Saturn 3.5°S of Moon
27	6:49	Moon at Apogee: 404342 km
28	2:54	FIRST QUARTER MOON
02-Oct	2:05	Moon at Descending Node
03	09	Venus at Perihelion
05	18:40	FULL MOON
08	00	Mars at Aphelion
08	21	Mercury at Superior Conjunction
09	5:51	Moon at Perigee: 366868 km
12	12:25	LAST QUARTER MOON
14	22:10	Moon at Ascending Node
17	10:04	Mars 1.8°S of Moon
18	00:21	Venus 2.0°S of Moon
19	17	Uranus at Opposition
19	19:12	NEW MOON
21	11	Orionid Meteor Shower
24	11:54	Saturn 3.3°S of Moon
25	2:25	Moon at Apogee: 405151 km
26	18	Jupiter in Conjunction with Sun
27	22:22	FIRST QUARTER MOON
29	6:41	Moon at Descending Node
04-Nov	5:23	FULL MOON
05	11	S Taurid Meteor Shower
06	00:09	Moon at Perigee: 361438 km
10	20:37	LAST QUARTER MOON
10	22:40	Moon at Ascending Node
12	11	N Taurid Meteor Shower
15	00:40	Mars 3.2°S of Moon
17	17	Leonid Meteor Shower
18	11:42	NEW MOON
21	00:34	Saturn 3.0°S of Moon
21	18:52	Moon at Apogee: 406132 km
24	00	Mercury at Greatest Elong: 22.0°E
25	8:22	Moon at Descending Node
26	17:03	FIRST QUARTER MOON
03-Dec	15:47	FULL MOON
04	8:42	Moon at Perigee: 357496 km
07	00	Mercury 1.3° of Saturn
08	00:39	Moon at Ascending Node
10	7:51	LAST QUARTER MOON
12	12	Mercury at Perihelion
13	02	Mercury at Inferior Conjunction
13	16:27	Mars 4.2°S of Moon
14	06	Geminid Meteor Shower
14	14:26	Jupiter 4.2°S of Moon
18	6:31	NEW MOON
19	1:27	Moon at Apogee: 406605 km
21	16:29	Winter Solstice
21	20	Saturn in Conjunction with Sun
22	10:04	Moon at Descending Node
22	15	Ursid Meteor Shower
26	9:20	FIRST QUARTER MOON

METEOR SHOWER CALENDAR, 2017

Shower	Activity	Peak Night	Radiant	ZHR	Velocity	Parent Object
Quadrantids	Jan. 1 – Jan. 10	Jan. 3-4	15:18 +49.5°	120	26 miles/sec (medium - 42.2km/sec)	2003 EH (Asteroid)
Lyrids	Apr. 16 – Apr. 25	Apr. 22-23	18:04 +34°	18	30 miles/sec (medium - 48.4km/sec)	C/1861 G1 (Thatcher)
Eta Aquariids	Apr. 19 – May 26	May 6-7	22:32 -1°	55	42 miles/sec (swift - 66.9km/sec)	1P/Halley
Delta Aquariids	July 21 – Aug. 23	July 28-29	22:40 -16.4°	16	26 miles/sec (medium - 42km/sec)	96P/Machholz?
Alpha Capricornids	July 11 – Aug. 10	July 27-28	20:28 -10.2°	5	15 miles/sec (slow - 24km/sec)	169P/NEAT
Perseids	July 13 – Aug. 26	Aug. 11-12	03:12 +57.6°	100	37 miles/sec (swift - 60km/sec)	109P/Swift-Tuttle
Orionids	Oct. 4 – Nov. 14	Oct. 21-22	06:20 +15.5°	25	41 miles/sec (swift - 67km/sec)	1P/Halley
Southern Taurids	Sept. 7 – Nov 19	Oct. 9-10	02:08 +8.7°	5	17 miles/sec (slow - 28km/sec)	2P/Encke
Northern Taurids	Oct. 19 – Dec. 10	Nov. 11-12	03:52 +22.7°	5	18 miles/sec (medium - 30km/sec)	2P/Encke
Leonids	Nov. 5 – Nov. 30	Nov. 17-18	10:08 +21.6°	15	44 miles/sec (swift - 71km/sec)	55P/Tempel-Tuttle
Geminids	Dec. 4 – Dec. 16	Dec. 13-14	07:28 +32.2°	120	22 miles/sec (medium - 35km/sec)	3200 Phaethon (asteroid)
Ursids	Dec. 17 – Dec. 23	Dec. 21-22	14:28 +74.8°	10	20 miles/sec (medium - 32km/sec)	8P/Tuttle

Source: American Meteor Society.

Telus World of Science - Edmonton: 11211 - 142 St., Edmonton AB T5M 4A1 - 780-451-3344; URL: telusworldofscienceedmonton.ca/educators/outreach/mobile-planetarium

Mobile planetarium available. Gift shop, IMAX theatre, science programs & computer lab; observatory operated by RASC volunteers.

University of Toronto: Dept. Of Astronomy & Astrophysics, University of Toronto, 50 St. George Street, Toronto ON M5S 3H4 - Email: tours@astro.utoronto.ca; URL: www.astro.utoronto.ca

AstroTours program consists of a talk, planetarium shows and telescope observing. Tours start at 8 p.m. during winter months and 9 p.m. during summer months. Extra public tours may be also arranged. See website for details.

W.J. McCallion Planetarium: Dept. of Physics & Astronomy, McMaster University, 1280 Main St. West, Hamilton ON L8S 4M1 - 905-525-9140, ext. 27777; Fax: 905-546-1252; Email: planetarium@physics.mcmaster.ca; URL: www.physics.mcmaster.ca/planetarium

Planetarium has long history of support from RASC Hamilton Centre; first in Ontario open to the public. Public shows are Wednesdays (subject to change on occasion). See website for details.

Winnipeg Planetarium: The Manitoba Museum, 190 Rupert Ave., Winnipeg MB R3B 0N2 - 204-956-2830; E-mail: info@manitobamuseum.ca; URL: manitobamuseum.ca/main/visit/planetarium

Science centre, museum & planetarium in one site; mobile planetarium.

Many of Canada's professional astronomers, & most of Canada's enthusiastic amateur astronomers are members of the Royal Astronomical Society of Canada (see index) which has 29 Centres across Canada. An extensive list of astronomy clubs in Canada has been published online by SkyNews and can be found at www.skynews.ca/resources/astronomy-clubs. Many of these clubs have programs for the general public.

ECLIPSES AND TRANSITS IN 2017

In 2017, there will be four eclipses, two solar, and two lunar.

1. A **penumbral eclipse** of the Moon on February 11.

2. An **annular eclipse** of the Sun on February 26, not visible from North America.

3. A **partial eclipse** of the Moon on August 7, not visible from North America.

4. A **total eclipse** of the Sun on August 21.

Source: NASA, eclipse.gsfc.nasa.gov/eclipse.html, September 13, 2016.

METEORS, METEORITES, AND METEOR SHOWERS

A *meteor* or "shooting star" appears momentarily in the sky when a particle from beyond the earth enters the earth's atmosphere at a high velocity. Most visible meteors are caused by particles smaller than a grape or marble, and these small particles are completely vaporized in the atmosphere at a height of about 80 km. A spectacular meteor, known as a *fire-ball*, is caused by a larger body which may fall to the earth's surface in one or more pieces. Particles seen thus to fall, or subsequently found by analysis to be of this nature, are called meteorites.

Meteorites may be divided into two main classes—the irons, which are almost pure nickel-iron, and the stones. Any freshly-fallen meteorite is characterized by a dark, smooth crust caused by the fusion of the outer part.

Meteors may be observed on any clear, moonless night at an average rate of about five an hour. At times *meteor showers* occur, when meteors are seen with much greater frequency and appear to radiate from a particular part of the sky which is called the *radiant*. This is an effect of perspective, the radiant being the vanishing point of the parallel tracks of the meteors. Meteor showers usually repeat themselves annually, and in some cases have been associated with the orbits of comets. When the earth passes through or near the orbit of a comet it can intercept the small particles (meteoroids) which cause meteors. A calendar is provided above showing the principal meteor showers for the northern hemisphere, and the dates on which they should occur in the coming year.

The study of meteors and meteorites adds to our knowledge of the nature and origin of the solar system and also to our knowledge of the earth's outer atmosphere.

MAPS OF THE NIGHT SKY

The maps on the next six pages cover the northern sky. Stars are shown down to a magnitude of 5, i.e. those which are readily apparent to the unaided eye on a reasonably dark night.

The maps are designed for 44°N latitude, but are useful for latitudes several degrees north or south of this. They show the hemisphere of sky visible to an observer at various times of the year. Because the aspect of the night sky changes continuously with both longitude and time, while time zones change discontinuously with both longitude and time of year, it is not possible to state simply when, in general, a particular observer will find that his or her sky fits exactly one of the twelve maps. The month indicated above each map is the time of year when the map will match the sky at 11 pm or 12 am. On any particular night, successive maps will represent the sky as it appears every two hours. For example, at 2 am on a March night, the April map should be used. Just after dinner on a January night, the October map will be appropriate. The centre of each map is the zenith, the point directly overhead; the circumference is the horizon. To identify the stars, hold the map in front of you so that the part of the horizon which you are facing (west, for instance) is downward. (The four letters around the periphery of each map indicate compass directions.)

On the maps, stars forming the usual constellation patterns are linked by straight lines, constellation names being given in upper case letters. The names in lower case are those of first magnitude stars and Polaris, which is near the north celestial pole. Small clusters of dots indicate the positions of bright star clusters, nebulae or galaxies. Although a few of these are just visible to the naked eye, and most can be located in binoculars, a telesope is needed for good views of these objects. A dashed line appears on each of the twelve maps, which is the celestial equator. Coloured dots, each named, show the location of visual planets.

The twelve star charts on the following pages were prepared by Dirk Matussek and are copyright of AstroViewer, 2016.

Sky Map

Toronto - Jan. 15, 2017 11:00 PM EST

© Dirk Matussek, www.astroviewer.com

Sky Map

Toronto - Feb. 15, 2017 11:00 PM EST

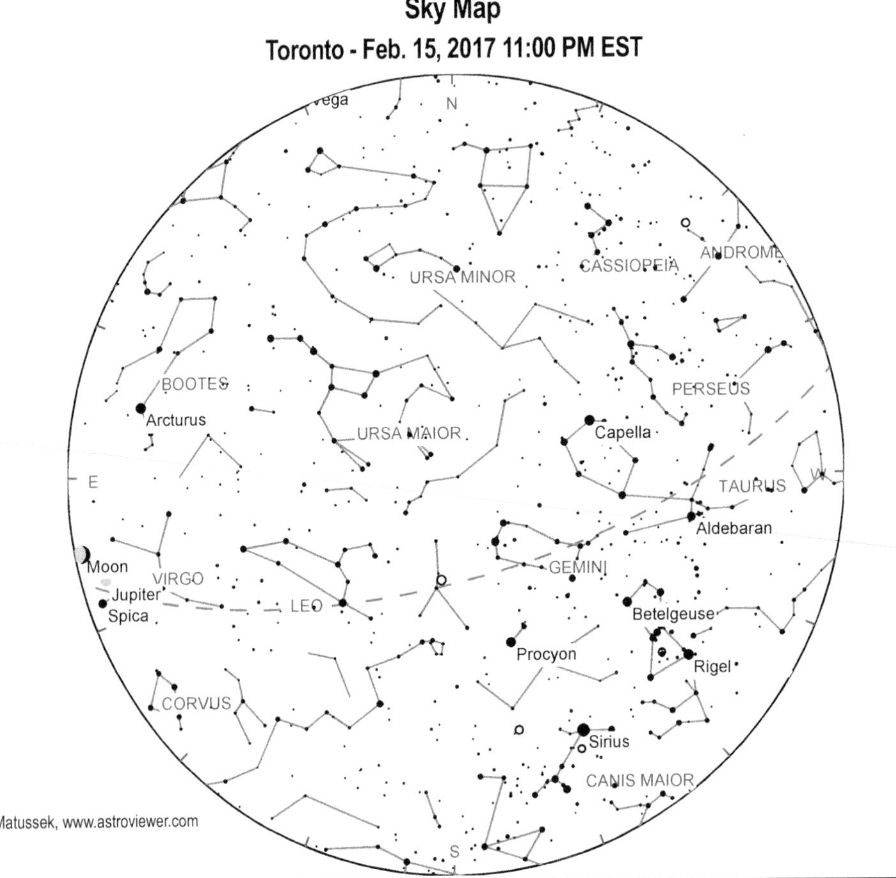

© Dirk Matussek, www.astroviewer.com

Sky Map

Toronto - Mar. 15, 2017 11:00 PM EST

N
Vega
ANDRO
CASSIOPEIA
URSA MINOR
PERSEUS
Capella
BOOTES
URSA MAIOR
TAURUS
E
Arcturus
W
Aldebaran
GEMINI
Moon
Betelgeuse
VIRGO
LEO
Jupiter
Spica
Procyon
Rigel
CORVUS
Sirius
CANIS M
S

Sky Map

Toronto - Apr. 15, 2017 11:00 PM EST

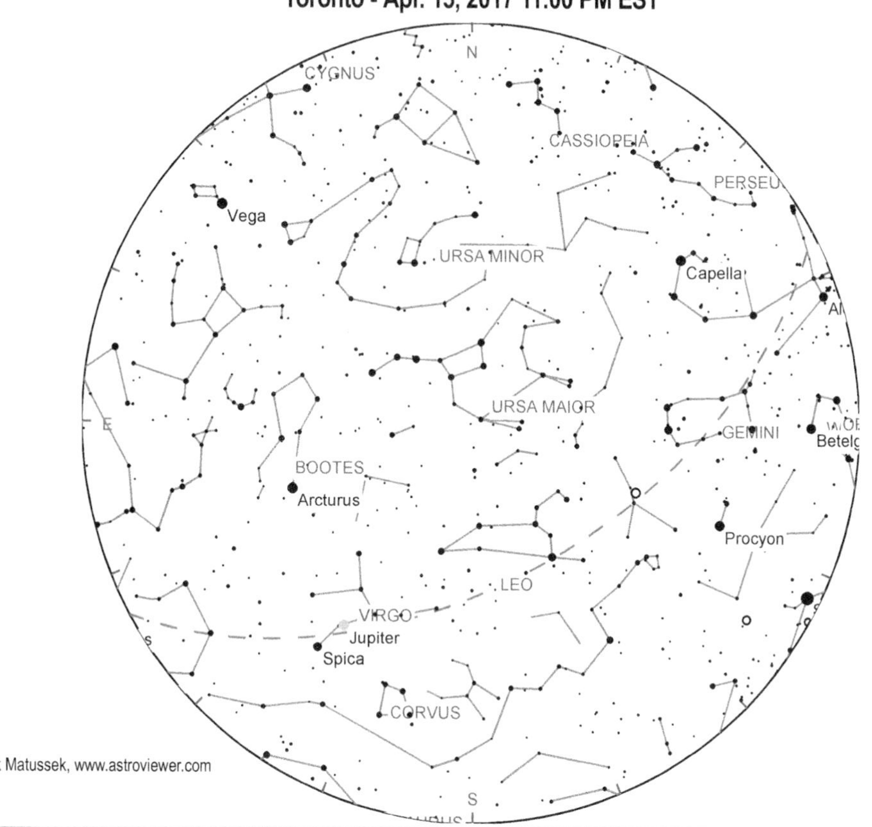

Sky Map

Toronto - May 15, 2017 11:00 PM EST

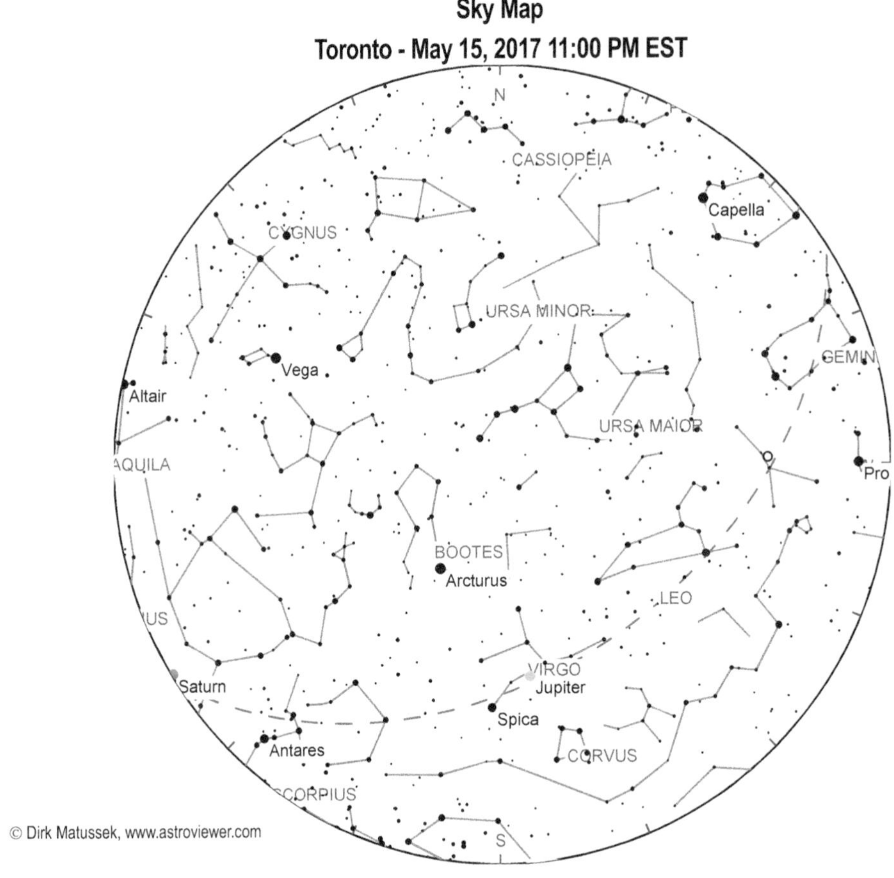

Sky Map

Toronto - June 15, 2017 11:00 PM EST

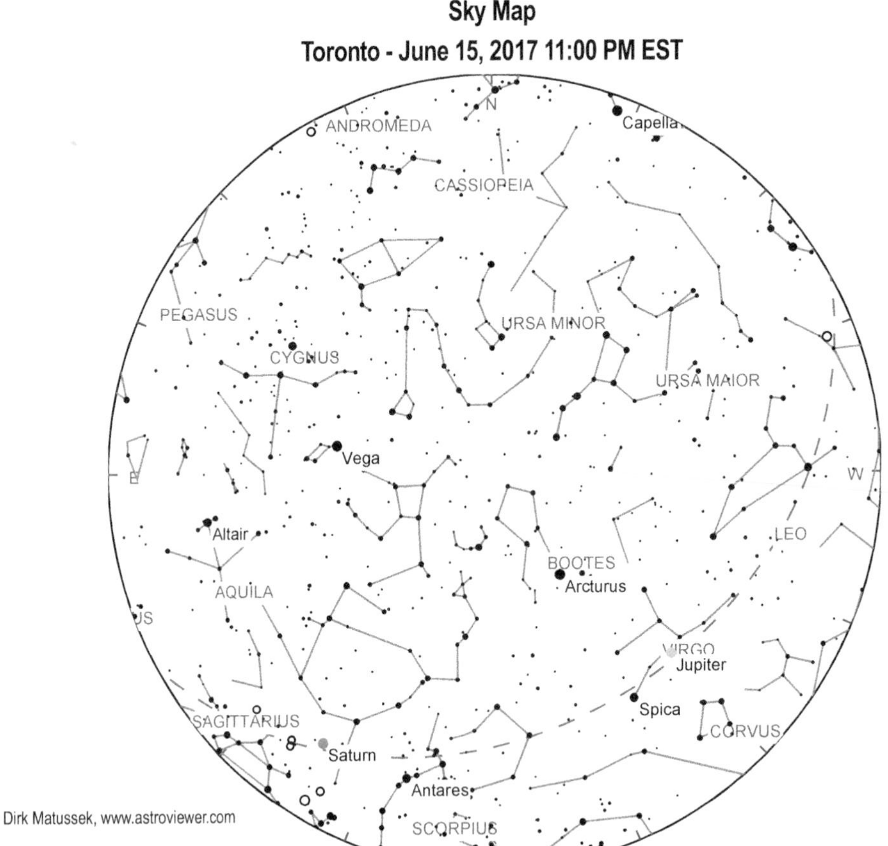

Sky Map

Toronto - July 15, 2017 11:00 PM EST

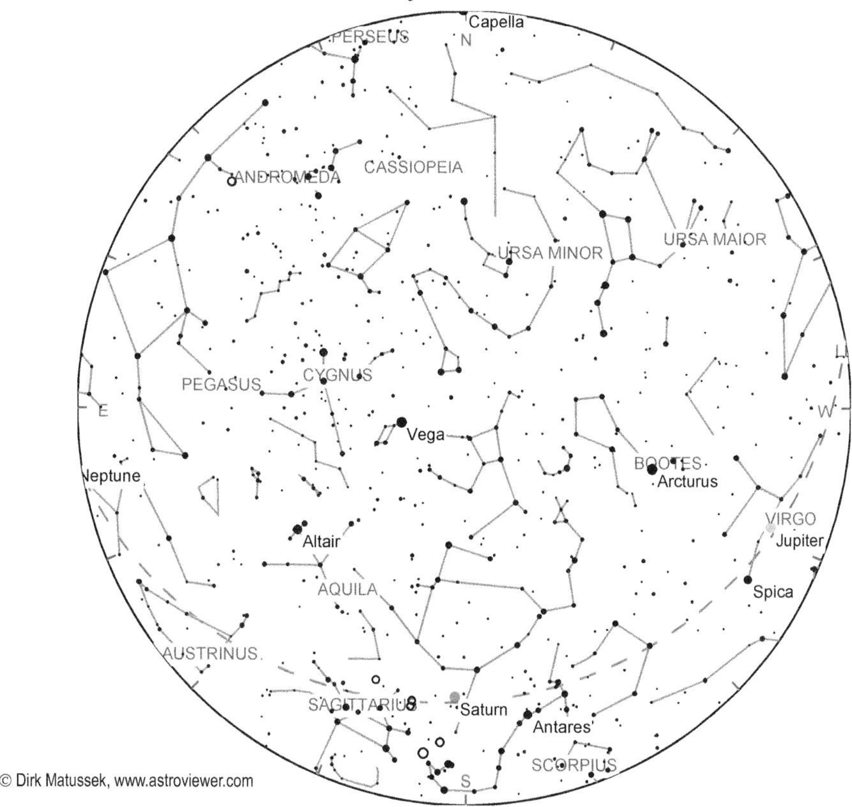

Sky Map

Toronto - Aug. 15, 2017 11:00 PM EST

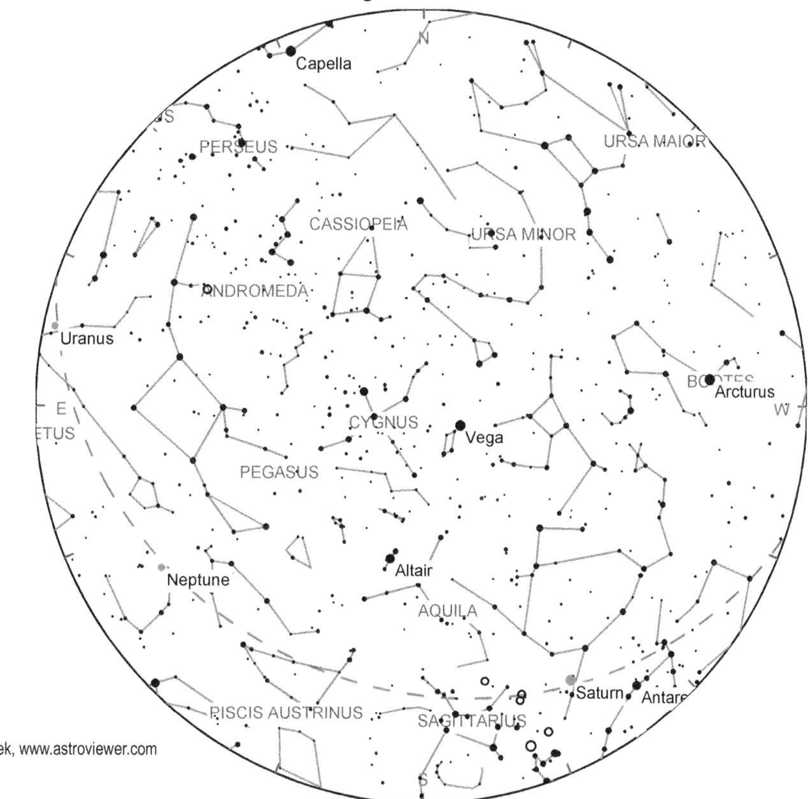

Sky Map

Toronto - Sept. 15, 2017 11:00 PM EST

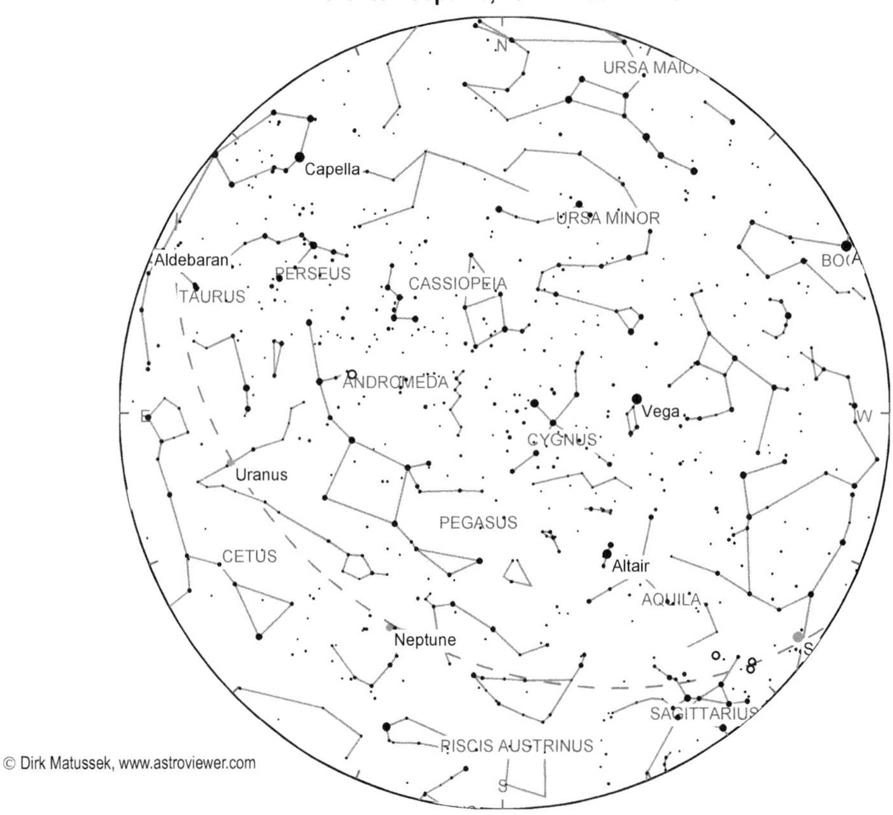

Sky Map

Toronto - Oct. 15, 2017 11:00 PM EST

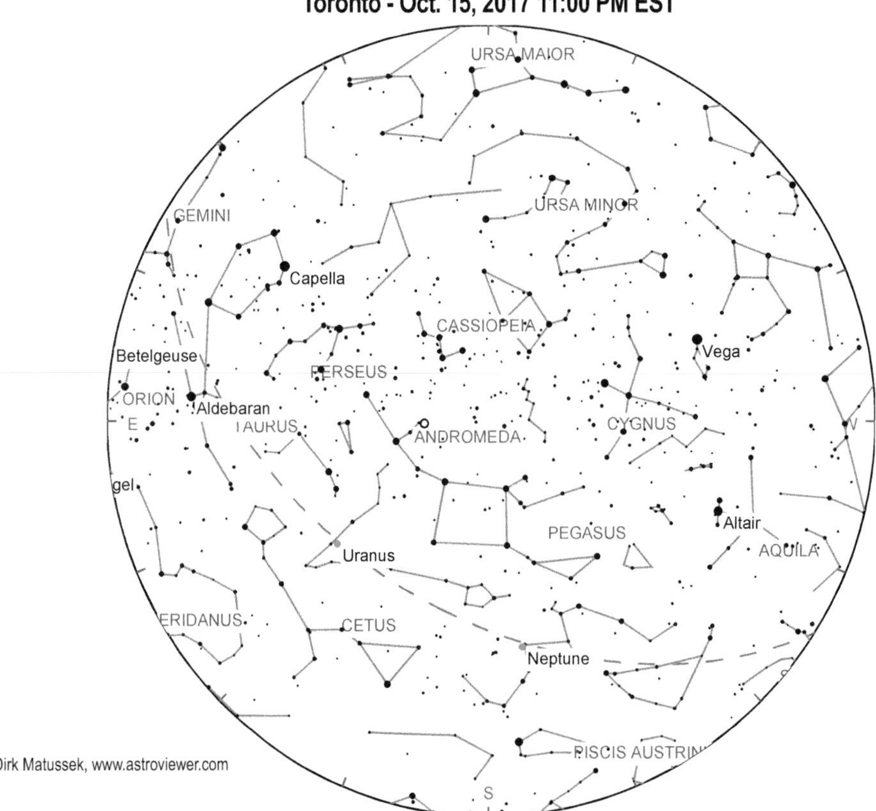

Sky Map
Toronto - Nov. 15, 2017 11:00 PM EST

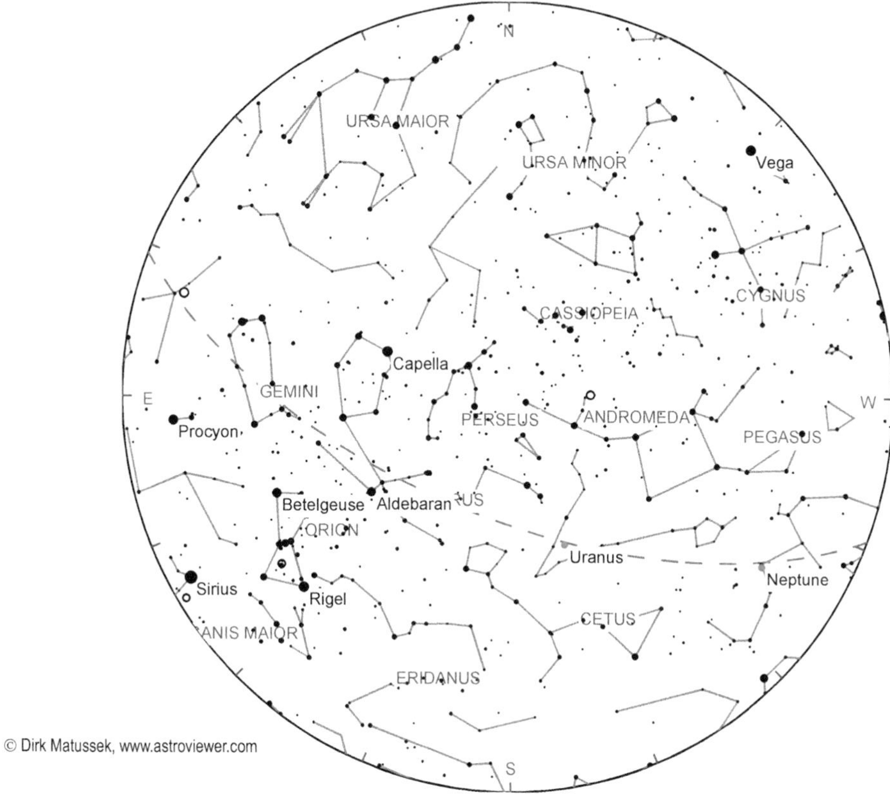

Sky Map
Toronto - Dec. 15, 2017 11:00 PM EST

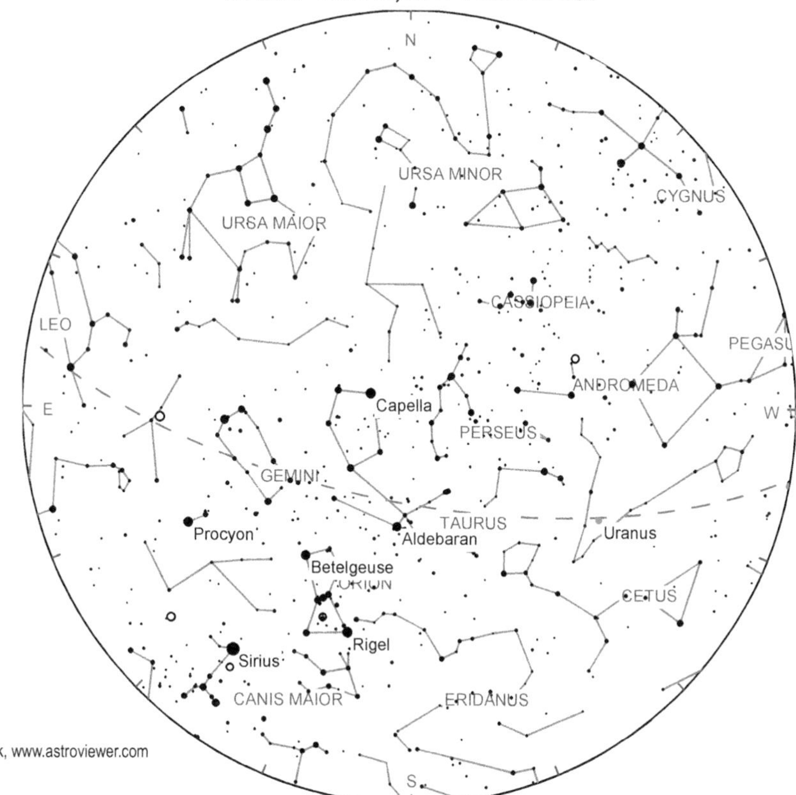

AZIMUTHS OF THE POINTS OF RISING AND SETTING OF THE SUN FOR LATITUDES 43°N TO 52°N

IN DEGREES EAST OF NORTH FOR RISING AND WEST OF NORTH FOR SETTING

			43°N	44°N	45°N	46°N	47°N	48°N	49°N	50°N	51°N	52°N
Jan. 2	and	Dec. 11	122	123	124	124	125	126	127	127	128	129
Jan. 10	and	Dec. 3	121	121	122	123	123	124	125	126	127	127
Jan. 16	and	Nov. 27	119	120	120	121	122	122	123	124	125	126
Jan. 21	and	Nov. 22	118	118	119	120	120	121	121	122	123	124
Jan. 25	and	Nov. 17	116	117	117	118	119	119	120	120	121	122
Jan. 29	and	Nov. 14	115	115	116	116	117	118	118	119	119	120
Feb. 2	and	Nov. 10	114	114	114	115	115	116	116	117	118	118
Feb. 5	and	Nov. 6	112	113	113	113	114	114	115	115	116	116
Feb. 9	and	Nov. 3	111	111	111	112	112	113	113	114	114	115
Feb. 12	and	Oct. 31	109	110	110	110	111	111	112	112	113	113
Feb. 15	and	Oct. 28	108	108	109	109	109	110	110	110	111	111
Feb. 18	and	Oct. 25	107	107	107	107	108	108	108	109	109	110
Feb. 20	and	Oct. 22	105	105	106	106	106	106	107	107	108	108
Feb. 23	and	Oct. 19	104	104	104	104	105	105	105	106	106	106
Feb. 26	and	Oct. 17	102	103	103	103	103	104	104	104	104	105
Mar. 1	and	Oct. 14	101	101	101	102	102	102	102	102	103	103
Mar. 3	and	Oct. 11	100	100	100	100	100	100	101	101	101	101
Mar. 6	and	Oct. 9	98	98	98	99	99	99	99	99	100	100
Mar. 8	and	Oct. 6	97	97	97	97	97	97	98	98	98	98
Mar. 11	and	Oct. 4	95	96	96	96	96	96	96	96	96	96
Mar. 13	and	Oct. 1	94	94	94	94	94	94	95	95	95	95
Mar. 16	and	Sept. 28	93	93	93	93	93	93	93	93	93	93
Mar. 18	and	Sept. 26	91	91	91	91	91	92	92	92	92	92
Mar. 21	and	Sept. 23	90	90	90	90	90	90	90	90	90	90
Mar. 23	and	Sept. 21	89	89	89	89	89	88	88	88	88	88
Mar. 26	and	Sept. 18	87	87	87	87	87	87	87	87	87	87
Mar. 28	and	Sept. 16	86	86	86	86	86	86	85	85	85	85
Mar. 31	and	Sept. 13	85	84	84	84	84	84	84	84	84	84
Apr. 3	and	Sept. 10	83	83	83	83	83	83	82	82	82	82
Apr. 5	and	Sept. 8	82	82	82	81	81	81	81	81	80	80
Apr. 8	and	Sept. 5	80	80	80	80	80	80	79	79	79	79
Apr. 11	and	Sept. 2	79	79	79	78	78	78	78	78	77	77
Apr. 13	and	Aug. 30	78	77	77	77	77	76	76	76	76	75
Apr. 16	and	Aug. 28	76	76	76	76	75	75	75	74	74	74
Apr. 19	and	Aug. 25	75	75	74	74	74	73	73	73	72	72
Apr. 22	and	Aug. 22	73	73	73	73	72	72	72	71	71	70
Apr. 25	and	Aug. 19	72	72	71	71	71	70	70	70	69	69
Apr. 28	and	Aug. 16	71	70	70	70	69	69	68	68	67	67
May 1	and	Aug. 12	69	69	69	68	68	67	67	66	66	65
May 5	and	Aug. 9	68	67	67	67	66	66	65	65	64	63
May 8	and	Aug. 5	66	66	66	65	65	64	64	63	62	62
May 12	and	Aug. 2	65	65	64	64	63	62	62	61	61	60
May 16	and	July 28	64	63	63	62	61	61	60	60	59	58
May 21	and	June 24	62	62	61	60	60	59	59	58	57	56
May 26	and	June 19	61	60	60	59	58	58	57	56	55	54
June 1	and	July 12	59	59	58	57	57	56	55	54	53	53
June 10	and	July 3	58	57	56	56	55	54	53	53	52	51

Astronomical Data, U.S. Naval Observatory

LUNAR PHASES FOR 2017

UNIVERSAL TIME

New Moon	First Quarter	Full Moon	Last Quarter
--	2017 Jan 05 19:47	2017 Jan 12 11:34	2017 Jan 19 22:13
2017 Jan 28 00:07	2017 Feb 04 04:19	2017 Feb 11 00:33	2017 Feb 18 19:33
2017 Feb 26 14:58	2017 Mar 05 11:32	2017 Mar 12 14:54	2017 Mar 20 15:58
2017 Mar 28 02:57	2017 Apr 03 18:39	2017 Apr 11 06:08	2017 Apr 19 09:57
2017 Apr 26 12:16	2017 May 03 02:47	2017 May 10 21:42	2017 May 19 00:33
2017 May 25 19:44	2017 Jun 01 12:42	2017 Jun 09 13:10	2017 Jun 17 11:33
2017 Jun 24 02:31	2017 Jul 01 00:51	2017 Jul 09 04:07	2017 Jul 16 19:26
2017 Jul 23 09:46	2017 Jul 30 15:23	2017 Aug 07 18:11	2017 Aug 15 01:15
2017 Aug 21 18:30	2017 Aug 29 08:13	2017 Sep 06 07:03	2017 Sep 13 06:25
2017 Sep 20 05:30	2017 Sep 28 02:53	2017 Oct 05 18:40	2017 Oct 12 12:25
2017 Oct 19 19:12	2017 Oct 27 22:22	2017 Nov 04 05:23	2017 Nov 10 20:36
2017 Nov 18 11:42	2017 Nov 26 17:03	2017 Dec 03 15:47	2017 Dec 10 07:51
2017 Dec 18 06:30	2017 Dec 26 09:20	--	--

Source: Astronomical Applications Department of the U.S. Naval Observatory, http://aa.usno.navy.mil/data/docs/MoonPhase.php

AZIMUTH OF THE SUN AT RISING AND SETTING

Only twice a year, namely about March 21 and September 23, does the sun rise and set more or less exactly in the east and west respectively. It is of interest and sometimes of value to know the position of Sunrise and Sunset at other times. The table above tabulates these in degrees east of north and west of north for Sunrise and Sunset respectively for a selection of latitudes and dates. For latitudes and dates other than those tabulated take simple proportions. See table on previous page.

REFERENCES

The tables and charts in the Canadian Almanac are intended for simple astronomical observations. To make more extensive observations the following are recommended: *The Observer's Handbook* (obtainable from the Royal Astronomical Society of Canada, #203, 4920 Dundas St. West, Toronto, ON M9A 1B7); *Astronomical Phenomena* (obtainable from the U.S. Government Bookstore, URL: bookstore.gpo.gov).

SUGGESTIONS FOR FURTHER READING

There are many excellent astronomy books and materials. Here are some; the books are ones with a Canadian flavour.

Astronomical Society of the Pacific, 390 Ashton Ave., San Francisco CA USA 94112; URL: www.astrosociety.org. Excellent source of astronomical teaching resources, and other useful material; catalogue available. Also publish a free quarterly teachers' newsletter (available on-line).

Astronomy, PO Box 1612, Waukesha WI USA 53187; URL: www.astronomy.com. Popular non-technical monthly magazine for general astronomy readers.

The Backyard Astronomer's Guide, by Terence Dickinson & Alan Dyer. 3rd edition, Firefly Books, 2010. The best guide to equipment & techniques.

The Beginner's Observing Guide, by Leo Enright. Royal Astronomical Society of Canada, #203, 4920 Dundas St. West, Toronto, ON M9A 1B7. A simple but serious introduction to the night sky. (6th edition)

The Cold Light of Dawn, by Richard Jarrell. University of Toronto Press, 1988. An authoritative and comprehensive history of Canadian astronomy.

Exploring the Night Sky, by Terence Dickinson. Camden House Publishing, 1987. An award-winning guide, especially for young people.

Looking Up, by Peter Broughton. Dundurn Press, 1993. A history of the Royal Astronomical Society of Canada, illustrated.

Nightwatch, by Terence Dickinson. Firefly Books, (4th revised edition, 2006). Excellent introduction to the night sky.

Sky Atlas 2000.0, by Wil Tirion. Sky Publishing. A popular sky atlas for amateur astronomers.

Sky & Telescope, PO Box 420235, Palm Coast, FL USA 32142-0235; URL: skyandtelescope.com. A popular monthly magazine for amateur astronomers.

SkyNews, PO Box 10, Yarker, ON K0K 3N0; URL: www.skynews.ca. General astronomy from a Canadian perspective.

SkyWays, by Mary Lou Whitehorne. Royal Astronomical Society of Canada, 2003 (also available in French). A guide for Canadian schoolteachers.

Summer Stargazing, by Terence Dickinson. Firefly Books, 1996. A practical, user-friendly guide.

The Universe and Beyond, by Terence Dickinson, 5th Edition, Firefly Books, 2010. Excellent general book on Astronomy.

The Universe at your Fingertips, and More Universe at Your Fingertips, edited by Andrew Fraknoi et al. Astronomical Society of the Pacific, 390 Ashton Avenue, San Francisco CA USA 94112. An excellent collection of teaching activities & resources.

The Universe on a T-Shirt, by Dan Falk, Arcade Publishing, 2005 (paperback). An excellent short introduction to our understanding of the universe.

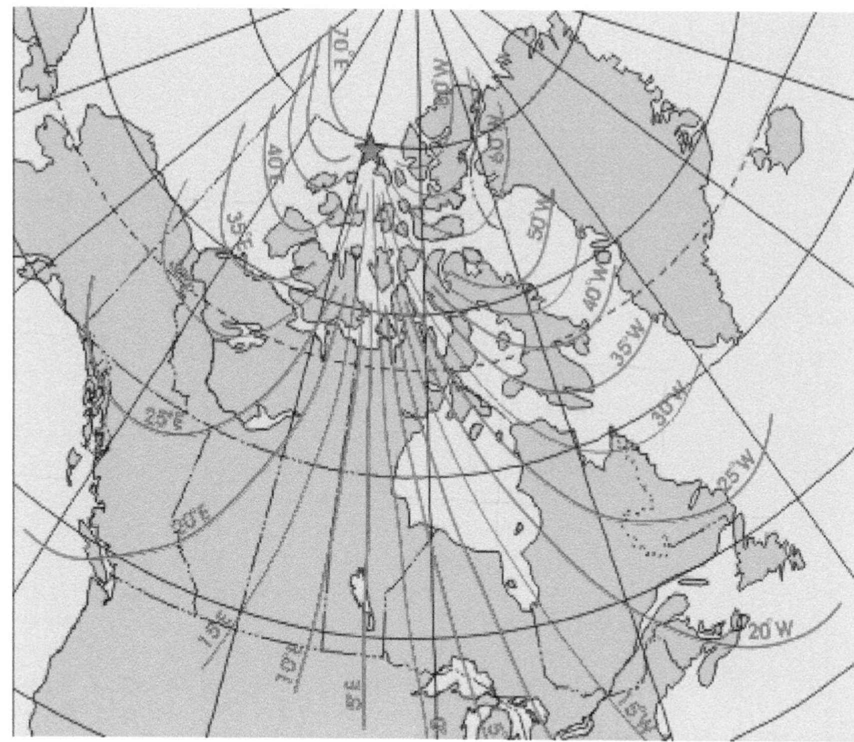

Reproduced with the permission of Natural Resources Canada 2016, courtesy of RETScreen International.

CANADIAN ASTRONOMY WEBSITES

Most astronomical institutions and many of the branches of the Royal Astronomical Society of Canada have websites. They can be accessed from the following key sites:

- Canadian Astronomical Society: www.casca.ca
- Canadian Astronomy Data Centre: www.cadc-ccda.hia-iha.nrc-cnrc.gc.ca
- Canadian Space Agency: www.asc-csa.gc.ca
- Department of Astronomy and Astrophysics, University of Toronto: www.astro.utoronto.ca/home.html
- Environment Canada - Astronomy: weather.gc.ca/astro
- Herzberg Institute of Astrophysics: www.nrc-cnrc.gc.ca/eng/rd/nsi
- Royal Astronomical Society of Canada: www.rasc.ca. Local branches of the RASC can be accessed through this site.

CHART OF MAGNETIC DECLINATION

A compass needle, even when unaffected by extraneous magnetic fields, does not in general point due north. The amount and direction by which its direction differs from true north is called magnetic declination or variation. The declination varies with the position of the observer and also varies slowly with time. The above chart gives the values of declination over Canada as of 2000. The chart is © Natural Resources Canada, and was kindly provided by Dr. Larry Newitt, National Geomagnetism Program, Geological Survey of Canada, Natural Resources Canada.

Example: What is the direction of the compass needle at the southern tip of Lake Manitoba?

That location is on the 5° east line; the declination is 5° east; the compass needle points 5° east of the true north.

For more information, see: http://geomag.nrcan.gc.ca; on the page http://geomag.nrcan.gc.ca/apps/mdcal-eng.php, you can do an online calculation of the magnetic declination for any place at any time.

NOTES ON THE ASTRONOMICAL TABLES

The purpose of the following notes is to explain the tables on pages A-66 to A-73 and to illustrate how they may be used for places other than those specified.

These tables give Standard Times of Sunrise and Sunset for Ottawa, Toronto, Winnipeg and Vancouver. When Daylight Saving Time is in effect, of course, one hour must be added to the listed times. The calculations are for the upper limb (edge) of the sun and for the astronomical (sea) horizon. Accordingly, the actual observation of Sunrise or Sunset will differ from the tabulated value if the observer is below or above the level of her visible horizon at the point of Sunrise or Sunset.

The listed times of Moonrise and Moonset have been calculated for places at the stated latitudes and for longitude 5 hours west.

To obtain the approximate times of Sunrise, Sunset, Moonrise and Moonset for other Canadian cities and towns proceed as indicated in the table on page A-74. The errors for Sunrise and Sunset by this approximate method will seldom exceed 10 minutes in winter and summer or 4 minutes in spring and fall, and for Moonrise and Moonset they will seldom exceed 15 minutes.

The tables have been calculated using the U.S.Naval Observatory website: aa.usno.navy.mil.

Rise & Set for the Sun 2017
Ottawa

	Jan		Feb		March		Apr		May		June		July		Aug		Sept		Oct		Nov		Dec	
Day	Rise	Set	Rise	Set	Rise	Set	Rise	Set	Rise	Set	Rise	Set	Rise	Set	Rise	Set	Rise	Set	Rise	Set	Rise	Set	Rise	Set
	hm	hm	hm	hm	hm	hm	hm	hm	hm	hm	hm	hm	hm	hm	hm	hm	hm	hm	hm	hm	hm	hm	hm	hm
1	743	1631	723	1710	641	1750	543	1831	451	1910	418	1944	418	1955	447	1930	525	1840	601	1743	643	1650	722	1621
2	743	1632	722	1712	639	1752	541	1833	449	1911	417	1945	419	1955	448	1929	526	1838	603	1741	644	1648	724	1621
3	743	1633	721	1713	637	1753	539	1834	448	1912	417	1946	420	1954	450	1928	527	1836	604	1739	645	1647	725	1621
4	743	1634	720	1714	635	1754	537	1835	446	1913	416	1947	420	1954	451	1926	528	1834	605	1737	647	1646	726	1620
5	742	1635	718	1716	633	1756	535	1836	445	1915	416	1947	421	1954	452	1925	529	1832	606	1735	648	1644	727	1620
6	742	1636	717	1717	632	1757	533	1838	444	1916	415	1948	422	1953	453	1923	531	1831	608	1733	650	1643	728	1620
7	742	1637	716	1719	630	1758	532	1839	442	1917	415	1949	422	1953	454	1922	532	1829	609	1731	651	1642	729	1620
8	742	1638	714	1720	628	1800	530	1840	441	1918	415	1949	423	1952	456	1920	533	1827	610	1730	652	1640	730	1620
9	741	1639	713	1722	626	1801	528	1842	440	1920	415	1950	424	1952	457	1919	534	1825	611	1728	654	1639	731	1620
10	741	1640	711	1723	624	1802	526	1843	438	1921	414	1951	425	1951	458	1917	536	1823	613	1726	655	1638	732	1620
11	741	1641	710	1725	622	1804	524	1844	437	1922	414	1951	426	1951	459	1916	537	1821	614	1724	656	1637	733	1620
12	740	1643	708	1726	621	1805	522	1845	436	1923	414	1952	426	1950	500	1914	538	1819	615	1722	658	1636	734	1620
13	740	1644	707	1728	619	1806	521	1847	435	1924	414	1952	427	1949	502	1913	539	1817	617	1720	659	1635	734	1620
14	739	1645	705	1729	617	1808	519	1848	433	1926	414	1953	428	1949	503	1911	540	1815	618	1719	701	1634	735	1620
15	739	1646	704	1730	615	1809	517	1849	432	1927	414	1953	429	1948	504	1910	542	1813	619	1717	702	1632	736	1620
16	738	1648	702	1732	613	1810	515	1851	431	1928	414	1953	430	1947	505	1908	543	1811	621	1715	703	1631	737	1621
17	737	1649	701	1733	611	1812	514	1852	430	1929	414	1954	431	1946	506	1906	544	1809	622	1713	705	1631	737	1621
18	737	1650	659	1735	609	1813	512	1853	429	1930	414	1954	432	1945	508	1905	545	1808	623	1712	706	1630	738	1621
19	736	1652	658	1736	607	1814	510	1854	428	1931	414	1954	433	1945	509	1903	546	1806	625	1710	707	1629	739	1622
20	735	1653	656	1738	605	1816	508	1856	427	1932	414	1955	434	1944	510	1901	548	1804	626	1708	709	1628	739	1622
21	734	1654	654	1739	604	1817	507	1857	426	1933	414	1955	435	1943	511	1900	549	1802	627	1707	710	1627	740	1623
22	734	1656	653	1740	602	1818	505	1858	425	1935	415	1955	436	1942	512	1858	550	1800	629	1705	711	1626	740	1623
23	733	1657	651	1742	600	1820	503	1900	424	1936	415	1955	437	1941	514	1856	551	1758	630	1703	713	1626	741	1624
24	732	1659	649	1743	558	1821	502	1901	423	1937	415	1955	438	1940	515	1854	553	1756	631	1702	714	1625	741	1624
25	731	1700	648	1745	556	1822	500	1902	422	1938	416	1955	439	1939	516	1853	554	1754	633	1700	715	1624	741	1625
26	730	1701	646	1746	554	1823	459	1903	422	1939	416	1955	441	1938	517	1851	555	1752	634	1659	716	1624	742	1626
27	729	1703	644	1747	552	1825	457	1905	421	1940	416	1955	442	1936	519	1849	556	1750	636	1657	718	1623	742	1626
28	728	1704	642	1749	550	1826	455	1906	420	1941	417	1955	443	1935	520	1847	558	1748	637	1656	719	1623	742	1627
29	727	1706			548	1827	454	1907	420	1942	417	1955	444	1934	521	1845	559	1746	638	1654	720	1622	742	1628
30	726	1707			546	1829	452	1908	419	1942	418	1955	445	1933	522	1844	600	1745	640	1653	721	1622	742	1629
31	724	1709			545	1830			418	1943			446	1931	523	1842			641	1651			743	1630

Note: Blank space in the table indicates that a rising or setting did not occur during that 24-hour interval

Note: Daylight Savings Time is not implemented in this table. When Daylight Savings Time is in use, add one hour to the times listed in the table.

Location: W075 42, N45 25

Zone: 5h West of Greenwich

Astronomical Applications Dept.

Washington, DC 20392-5420

Rise & Set for the Moon 2017
Ottawa

	Jan		Feb		March		Apr		May		June		July		Aug		Sept		Oct		Nov		Dec	
Day	Rise	Set	Rise	Set	Rise	Set	Rise	Set	Rise	Set	Rise	Set	Rise	Set	Rise	Set	Rise	Set	Rise	Set	Rise	Set	Rise	Set
	hm	hm	hm	hm	hm	hm	hm	hm	hm	hm	hm	hm	hm	hm	hm	hm	hm	hm	hm	hm	hm	hm	hm	hm
1	942	2012	952	2234	826	2134	858		939		1151	40	1251	8	1439	4	1558	41	1553	115	1555	317	1527	427
2	1015	2118	1024	2344	859	2246	950	4	1044	45	1256	110	1352	35	1535	39	1641	133	1626	217	1625	427	1607	542
3	1047	2225	1057		935	2357	1047	105	1150	128	1358	137	1451	103	1628	117	1720	230	1657	322	1659	540	1653	658
4	1117	2333	1134	55	1016		1148	159	1256	204	1459	204	1550	132	1718	200	1755	330	1727	430	1736	655	1748	811
5	1148		1216	205	1102	106	1253	246	1400	236	1559	231	1647	203	1804	249	1828	434	1758	540	1819	811	1851	918
6	1220	43	1305	313	1154	211	1358	326	1503	305	1659	258	1743	239	1845	343	1858	540	1829	651	1908	924	2000	1015
7	1255	154	1400	417	1253	309	1503	400	1605	332	1757	328	1835	319	1922	441	1928	648	1904	804	2006	1031	2111	1103
8	1335	307	1502	515	1355	401	1608	431	1706	359	1854	402	1923	405	1956	543	1958	757	1942	917	2109	1131	2222	1143
9	1421	419	1608	606	1501	446	1711	500	1806	426	1948	439	2007	455	2027	647	2030	907	2027	1029	2216	1222	2331	1217
10	1514	528	1716	649	1607	524	1813	528	1905	455	2038	521	2046	550	2056	752	2105	1018	2118	1137	2325	1305		1247
11	1615	632	1824	727	1714	559	1914	555	2003	526	2125	608	2121	649	2126	859	2144	1129	2215	1240		1342	37	1315
12	1721	728	1930	800	1819	629	2014	623	2059	601	2206	700	2153	751	2156	1007	2230	1238	2318	1335	33	1413	142	1342
13	1829	816	2034	830	1922	658	2113	653	2152	640	2244	756	2223	855	2228	1116	2322	1344		1422	140	1442	245	1409
14	1937	856	2137	858	2024	726	2210	726	2240	724	2318	856	2252	1000	2304	1226		1443	25	1503	245	1509	347	1437
15	2044	931	2238	926	2125	754	2304	802	2325	812	2349	958	2321	1107	2345	1337	22	1536	133	1538	349	1536	447	1507
16	2149	1002	2338	954	2224	823	2356	843		906		1103	2352	1215		1446	127	1622	241	1609	452	1604	547	1541
17	2252	1031		1023	2322	854		929	5	1004	19	1209		1326	33	1551	235	1702	348	1638	554	1633	644	1620
18	2352	1058	36	1055		928	43	1019	42	1105	48	1318	26	1438	129	1650	345	1736	454	1705	655	1705	738	1703
19		1125	133	1131	18	1006	126	1115	115	1209	119	1429	105	1550	233	1742	454	1807	559	1733	754	1741	827	1751
20	52	1153	228	1211	111	1049	206	1215	146	1316	152	1543	150	1700	341	1826	602	1836	702	1802	850	1821	912	1843
21	150	1224	321	1257	202	1137	242	1319	217	1425	229	1658	243	1805	452	1905	708	1904	804	1832	942	1906	952	1940
22	248	1257	410	1348	248	1231	315	1427	248	1538	312	1812	344	1903	603	1938	812	1933	904	1906	1029	1956	1027	2039
23	344	1335	455	1445	331	1330	347	1537	320	1652	402	1921	452	1952	712	2009	915	2002	1002	1944	1112	2050	1059	2140
24	439	1417	537	1547	409	1433	419	1649	356	1809	501	2024	603	2034	819	2037	1016	2034	1056	2026	1150	2148	1128	2242
25	530	1506	615	1653	445	1540	452	1804	438	1925	607	2117	715	2109	924	2105	1115	2110	1146	2113	1224	2248	1156	2347
26	618	1600	649	1801	519	1650	527	1921	525	2037	716	2202	825	2141	1028	2134	1211	2149	1232	2204	1256	2351	1223	
27	702	1659	722	1911	551	1802	605	2037	620	2142	827	2239	932	2210	1129	2204	1303	2233	1313	2300	1325		1252	53
28	742	1803	754	2022	623	1915	649	2149	722	2239	936	2312	1037	2237	1228	2237	1352	2322	1350		1353	56	1322	203
29	817	1908			657	2030	740	2256	829	2326	1043	2341	1140	2305	1325	2314	1436		1424	0	1422	203	1358	315
30	850	2016			733	2144	837	2355	937		1148		1241	2334	1420	2355	1516	16	1455	103	1453	314	1439	429
31	922	2124			813	2256			1045	6			1341		1511				1525	208			1528	543

Note: Blank space in the table indicates that a rising or setting did not occur during that 24-hour interval

Note: Daylight Savings Time is not implemented in this table. When Daylight Savings Time is in use, add one hour to the times listed in the table.

Location: W075 42, N45 25

Zone: 5h West of Greenwich

Astronomical Applications Dept.

U. S. Naval Observatory

Washington, DC 20392-5420

Rise & Set for the Sun for 2017
Toronto

	Jan.		Feb.		Mar.		Apr.		May		June		July		Aug.		Sept.		Oct.		Nov.		Dec.	
Day	Rise	Set	Rise	Set	Rise	Set	Rise	Set	Rise	Set	Rise	Set	Rise	Set	Rise	Set	Rise	Set	Rise	Set	Rise	Set	Rise	Set
1	751	1652	734	1729	654	1807	559	1845	510	1920	439	1953	440	2003	507	1940	542	1853	616	1758	654	1708	732	1642
2	751	1653	733	1731	652	1808	557	1846	508	1922	438	1953	441	2003	508	1939	543	1851	617	1756	655	1707	733	1642
3	751	1654	732	1732	650	1809	555	1847	507	1923	438	1954	441	2002	509	1938	544	1849	618	1755	656	1705	734	1641
4	751	1655	730	1733	649	1811	554	1848	506	1924	438	1955	442	2002	510	1936	545	1847	619	1753	658	1704	735	1641
5	751	1656	729	1735	647	1812	552	1850	504	1925	437	1956	443	2002	511	1935	546	1846	620	1751	659	1703	736	1641
6	751	1657	728	1736	645	1813	550	1851	503	1926	437	1956	443	2002	512	1934	547	1844	621	1749	700	1702	737	1641
7	751	1658	727	1737	644	1814	548	1852	502	1927	437	1957	444	2001	514	1932	548	1842	623	1748	702	1701	738	1641
8	751	1659	726	1739	642	1816	547	1853	500	1929	436	1958	445	2001	515	1931	549	1840	624	1746	703	1659	739	1641
9	750	1700	724	1740	640	1817	545	1854	459	1930	436	1958	445	2000	516	1930	551	1838	625	1744	704	1658	740	1641
10	750	1701	723	1742	638	1818	543	1856	458	1931	436	1959	446	2000	517	1928	552	1837	626	1742	706	1657	741	1641
11	750	1702	721	1743	637	1819	541	1857	457	1932	436	1959	447	1959	518	1927	553	1835	627	1741	707	1656	741	1641
12	749	1703	720	1744	635	1821	540	1858	456	1933	436	2000	448	1959	519	1925	554	1833	629	1739	708	1655	742	1641
13	749	1704	719	1746	633	1822	538	1859	455	1934	436	2000	449	1958	520	1924	555	1831	630	1737	710	1654	743	1641
14	749	1706	717	1747	631	1823	536	1900	453	1935	436	2001	449	1957	521	1922	556	1829	631	1736	711	1653	744	1641
15	748	1707	716	1748	629	1824	535	1901	452	1936	436	2001	450	1957	523	1921	557	1827	632	1734	712	1652	745	1641
16	747	1708	714	1750	628	1825	533	1903	451	1937	436	2002	451	1956	524	1919	558	1826	633	1732	713	1651	745	1642
17	747	1709	713	1751	626	1827	531	1904	450	1939	436	2002	452	1955	525	1918	600	1824	635	1731	715	1650	746	1642
18	746	1711	711	1752	624	1828	530	1905	449	1940	436	2002	453	1954	526	1916	601	1822	636	1729	716	1649	747	1642
19	746	1712	710	1754	622	1829	528	1906	448	1941	436	2002	454	1954	527	1915	602	1820	637	1727	717	1649	747	1643
20	745	1713	708	1755	620	1830	526	1907	447	1942	436	2003	455	1953	528	1913	603	1818	638	1726	719	1648	748	1643
21	744	1714	707	1756	619	1832	525	1909	447	1943	436	2003	456	1952	529	1911	604	1816	640	1724	720	1647	748	1644
22	743	1716	705	1758	617	1833	523	1910	446	1944	436	2003	457	1951	530	1910	605	1815	641	1723	721	1646	749	1644
23	743	1717	704	1759	615	1834	522	1911	445	1945	437	2003	458	1950	532	1908	606	1813	642	1721	722	1646	749	1645
24	742	1718	702	1800	613	1835	520	1912	444	1946	437	2003	459	1949	533	1906	607	1811	644	1720	723	1645	750	1646
25	741	1720	700	1802	611	1836	519	1913	443	1947	437	2003	500	1948	534	1905	609	1809	645	1718	725	1645	750	1646
26	740	1721	659	1803	610	1838	517	1915	443	1948	438	2003	501	1947	535	1903	610	1807	646	1717	726	1644	750	1647
27	739	1722	657	1804	608	1839	515	1916	442	1948	438	2003	502	1946	536	1901	611	1805	647	1715	727	1644	751	1648
28	738	1724	655	1805	606	1840	514	1917	441	1949	439	2003	503	1945	537	1900	612	1804	649	1714	728	1643	751	1648
29	737	1725			604	1841	513	1918	441	1950	439	2003	504	1944	538	1858	613	1802	650	1712	729	1643	751	1649
30	736	1726			602	1842	511	1919	440	1951	440	2003	505	1943	539	1856	614	1800	651	1711	730	1642	751	1650
31	735	1728			601	1844			439	1952			506	1941	541	1854			653	1709			751	1651

Note: Blank space in the table indicates that a rising or setting did not occur during that 24-hour interval

Note: Daylight Savings Time is not implemented in this table. When Daylight Savings Time is in use, add one hour to the times listed in the table.

Location: W079 25, N43 40

Zone: 5h West of Greenwich

Astronomical Applications Dept.

U. S. Naval Observatory

Washington, DC 20392-5420

Rise & Set for the Moon for 2017
Toronto

Day	Jan. Rise	Jan. Set	Feb. Rise	Feb. Set	Mar. Rise	Mar. Set	Apr. Rise	Apr. Set	May Rise	May Set	June Rise	June Set	July Rise	July Set	Aug. Rise	Aug. Set	Sept. Rise	Sept. Set	Oct. Rise	Oct. Set	Nov. Rise	Nov. Set	Dec. Rise	Dec. Set
	hm	hm	hm	hm	hm	hm	hm	hm	hm	hm	hm	hm	hm	hm	hm	hm	hm	hm	hm	hm	hm	hm	hm	hm
1	953	2031	1008	2249	842	2148	918		959	5	1209	52	1305	24	1450	23	1608	102	1604	135	1610	333	1545	440
2	1028	2135	1040	2358	916	2259	1010	14	1104	56	1312	123	1405	52	1546	58	1652	154	1638	236	1642	442	1626	554
3	1101	2241	1115		954		1107	116	1209	139	1413	152	1504	120	1639	137	1731	250	1711	340	1716	554	1714	709
4	1132	2348	1153	108	1035	9	1209	210	1314	216	1513	220	1602	150	1728	221	1807	350	1742	447	1755	708	1809	821
5	1204		1236	217	1122	117	1312	257	1417	249	1613	247	1658	223	1814	310	1841	453	1813	555	1839	822	1912	928
6	1237	57	1325	324	1215	221	1417	337	1519	319	1711	316	1753	259	1856	403	1912	558	1846	705	1929	934	2020	1025
7	1313	207	1421	428	1313	319	1521	413	1620	347	1808	347	1845	340	1934	501	1943	704	1922	817	2027	1042	2131	1114
8	1354	319	1522	526	1416	411	1624	445	1720	415	1904	421	1933	425	2008	602	2014	812	2002	929	2130	1141	2240	1155
9	1441	430	1628	617	1520	457	1726	515	1819	443	1958	459	2017	516	2040	705	2047	921	2047	1040	2236	1233	2348	1230
10	1535	538	1735	701	1626	536	1827	543	1917	513	2048	542	2057	611	2111	809	2123	1031	2138	1148	2344	1316		1301
11	1636	642	1842	739	1731	611	1927	611	2014	545	2135	629	2133	709	2141	915	2204	1140	2236	1250		1354	54	1330
12	1741	738	1947	813	1835	643	2027	641	2109	621	2217	721	2206	810	2212	1022	2250	1249	2339	1345	51	1427	157	1358
13	1849	827	2050	844	1937	713	2124	711	2202	700	2255	816	2237	913	2246	1130	2343	1354		1433	157	1456	259	1426
14	1956	908	2152	914	2038	742	2221	745	2251	744	2330	915	2307	1017	2323	1239		1454	45	1514	301	1525	400	1455
15	2102	944	2252	942	2138	811	2315	822	2335	833		1017	2337	1122		1348	42	1547	152	1550	404	1553	459	1526
16	2205	1016	2351	1011	2237	841		903		926	2	1120		1230	5	1456	147	1633	259	1622	506	1621	558	1601
17	2307	1046		1042	2334	912	6	949	16	1023	33	1225	9	1339	54	1601	255	1714	405	1652	607	1652	654	1640
18		1114	48	1114		947	53	1040	53	1124	103	1333	44	1450	150	1700	403	1749	509	1721	706	1725	747	1724
19	7	1142	144	1151	29	1026	137	1135	127	1227	135	1443	124	1601	253	1753	511	1821	613	1750	804	1801	837	1812
20	105	1211	239	1232	122	1109	217	1235	200	1333	209	1556	210	1711	401	1838	618	1851	715	1820	900	1842	922	1904
21	203	1242	331	1317	212	1158	254	1338	231	1441	247	1709	304	1815	511	1917	723	1921	816	1851	952	1927	1002	2000
22	259	1316	420	1409	258	1251	328	1444	303	1552	331	1823	405	1913	621	1952	826	1950	915	1926	1039	2017	1038	2058
23	355	1355	506	1505	341	1349	401	1553	337	1706	423	1932	513	2003	729	2023	928	2021	1012	2004	1122	2111	1111	2158
24	449	1438	548	1607	421	1452	434	1705	415	1821	522	2034	623	2046	835	2053	1028	2053	1106	2047	1201	2207	1141	2300
25	541	1527	627	1711	458	1558	508	1818	457	1936	627	2128	733	2122	939	2122	1126	2129	1156	2134	1236	2307	1210	
26	629	1621	702	1818	532	1707	544	1933	545	2048	736	2213	842	2155	1041	2151	1221	2209	1242	2225	1308		1238	3
27	713	1719	736	1927	606	1817	624	2048	641	2153	846	2252	948	2225	1141	2223	1313	2254	1324	2321	1338	9	1308	108
28	753	1822	809	2037	639	1930	709	2200	743	2249	954	2325	1052	2253	1240	2256	1402	2343	1401		1408	112	1340	216
29	830	1927			714	2043	800	2307	849	2337	1100	2355	1154	2322	1336	2334	1447		1436	20	1438	219	1416	327
30	904	2033			751	2156	858		957		1204		1254	2352	1430		1527	37	1508	121	1510	328	1459	440
31	936	2140			832	2307			1104	17			1353		1521	15			1539	226			1549	553

Note: Blank space in the table indicates that a rising or setting did not occur during that 24-hour interval

Note: Daylight Savings Time is not implemented in this table. When Daylight Savings Time is in use, add one hour to the times listed in the table.

Location: W079 25, N43 40

Zone: 5h West of Greenwich

Astronomical Applications Dept.

U. S. Naval Observatory

Washington, DC 20392-5420

Rise & Set for the Sun for 2017
Winnipeg

	Jan		Feb		Mar		Apr		May		June		July		Aug		Sept		Oct		Nov		Dec	
Day	Rise	Set	Rise	Set	Rise	Set	Rise	Set	Rise	Set	Rise	Set	Rise	Set	Rise	Set	Rise	Set	Rise	Set	Rise	Set	Rise	Set
	h m	h m	h m	h m	h m	h m	h m	h m	h m	h m	h m	h m	h m	h m	h m	h m	h m	h m	h m	h m	h m	h m	h m	h m
1	827	1639	801	1724	711	1812	605	1901	505	1948	425	2029	425	2040	459	2010	544	1912	629	1806	719	1705	805	1630
2	826	1640	800	1726	709	1813	603	1903	503	1949	424	2030	425	2040	500	2008	546	1910	631	1804	720	1704	807	1630
3	826	1641	758	1727	707	1815	600	1904	501	1951	424	2031	426	2040	502	2007	547	1907	632	1802	722	1702	808	1629
4	826	1642	757	1729	705	1817	558	1906	500	1952	423	2032	427	2039	503	2005	549	1905	634	1800	724	1700	809	1629
5	826	1643	755	1731	703	1818	556	1907	458	1954	422	2033	428	2039	505	2004	550	1903	635	1758	725	1659	810	1628
6	826	1644	754	1733	701	1820	554	1909	456	1955	422	2033	428	2038	506	2002	552	1901	637	1756	727	1657	812	1628
7	825	1645	752	1734	659	1821	552	1910	455	1957	421	2034	429	2038	508	2000	553	1859	638	1754	729	1656	813	1628
8	825	1647	750	1736	657	1823	550	1912	453	1958	421	2035	430	2037	509	1959	555	1857	640	1751	730	1654	814	1628
9	824	1648	749	1738	654	1825	548	1914	452	2000	421	2036	431	2036	510	1957	556	1854	642	1749	732	1653	815	1627
10	824	1649	747	1739	652	1826	546	1915	450	2001	420	2036	432	2036	512	1955	558	1852	643	1747	734	1651	816	1627
11	823	1651	745	1741	650	1828	544	1917	449	2002	420	2037	433	2035	513	1953	559	1850	645	1745	735	1650	817	1627
12	823	1652	744	1743	648	1829	542	1918	447	2004	420	2038	434	2034	515	1951	601	1848	646	1743	737	1648	818	1627
13	822	1654	742	1745	646	1831	539	1920	446	2005	420	2038	435	2033	516	1950	602	1846	648	1741	738	1647	819	1627
14	821	1655	740	1746	644	1833	537	1921	444	2007	420	2039	436	2032	518	1948	604	1844	649	1739	740	1646	819	1627
15	820	1656	738	1748	642	1834	535	1923	443	2008	420	2039	437	2032	519	1946	605	1841	651	1737	742	1645	820	1628
16	820	1658	736	1750	639	1836	533	1924	441	2010	420	2040	438	2031	521	1944	607	1839	653	1735	743	1643	821	1628
17	819	1659	735	1751	637	1837	531	1926	440	2011	420	2040	440	2030	522	1942	608	1837	654	1733	745	1642	822	1628
18	818	1701	733	1753	635	1839	529	1928	439	2012	420	2040	441	2029	524	1940	610	1835	656	1731	746	1641	822	1628
19	817	1703	731	1755	633	1841	527	1929	438	2014	420	2041	442	2027	525	1938	611	1833	657	1729	748	1640	823	1629
20	816	1704	729	1757	631	1842	525	1931	436	2015	420	2041	443	2026	527	1936	613	1830	659	1727	750	1639	824	1629
21	815	1706	727	1758	629	1844	523	1932	435	2016	420	2041	444	2025	528	1934	614	1828	701	1725	751	1638	824	1630
22	814	1707	725	1800	626	1845	521	1934	434	2017	420	2041	446	2024	530	1932	616	1826	702	1723	753	1637	825	1630
23	813	1709	723	1802	624	1847	520	1935	433	2019	421	2041	447	2023	531	1930	617	1824	704	1721	754	1636	825	1631
24	812	1711	721	1803	622	1849	518	1937	432	2020	421	2041	448	2021	533	1928	619	1822	705	1719	756	1635	825	1632
25	811	1712	719	1805	620	1850	516	1938	431	2021	421	2041	449	2020	534	1926	620	1819	707	1718	757	1634	826	1632
26	809	1714	717	1807	618	1852	514	1940	430	2022	422	2041	451	2019	536	1924	622	1817	709	1716	759	1633	826	1633
27	808	1716	715	1808	616	1853	512	1942	429	2023	422	2041	452	2017	537	1922	623	1815	710	1714	800	1633	826	1634
28	807	1717	713	1810	613	1855	510	1943	428	2025	423	2041	453	2016	539	1920	625	1813	712	1712	801	1632	826	1635
29	805	1719			611	1856	508	1945	427	2026	423	2041	455	2015	540	1918	626	1811	714	1710	803	1631	827	1635
30	804	1721			609	1858	507	1946	426	2027	424	2041	456	2013	541	1916	628	1808	715	1709	804	1631	827	1636
31	803	1722			607	1859			426	2028			458	2012	543	1914			717	1707			827	1637

Note: Blank space in the table indicates that a rising or setting did not occur during that 24-hour interval

Note: Daylight Savings Time is not implemented in this table. When Daylight Savings Time is in use, add one hour to the times listed in the table.

Location: W097 10, N49 53

Zone: 6h West of Greenwich

Astronomical Applications Dept.

U. S. Naval Observatory

Washington, DC 20392-5420

Rise & Set for the Moon for 2017
Winnipeg

	Jan		Feb		Mar		Apr		May		June		July		Aug		Sept		Oct		Nov		Dec	
Day	Rise	Set	Rise	Set	Rise	Set	Rise	Set	Rise	Set	Rise	Set	Rise	Set	Rise	Set	Rise	Set	Rise	Set	Rise	Set	Rise	Set
	h m	h m	h m	h m	h m	h m	h m	h m	h m	h m	h m	h m	h m	h m	h m	h m	h m	h m	h m	h m	h m	h m	h m	h m
1	1020	2033	1019	2307	851	2209	914		954	39	1216	114	1323	35	1521	21	1642	54	1631	132	1622	345	1547	504
2	1051	2141	1048		921	2324	1004	48	1101	127	1323	141	1427	59	1618	54	1724	147	1702	237	1650	459	1624	623
3	1119	2251	1118	20	954		1101	150	1210	207	1428	205	1529	123	1713	131	1800	245	1730	345	1720	616	1708	742
4	1146		1152	134	1033	38	1204	243	1318	240	1533	229	1630	150	1803	213	1833	349	1757	456	1754	735	1802	857
5	1214	3	1232	247	1117	149	1311	327	1426	309	1636	253	1730	219	1847	302	1902	455	1824	610	1834	853	1905	1003
6	1243	116	1320	357	1209	255	1419	404	1532	335	1738	318	1826	253	1927	358	1929	605	1852	725	1922	1009	2015	1059
7	1315	231	1415	502	1307	353	1527	436	1636	359	1838	346	1919	332	2001	458	1956	716	1923	841	2019	1117	2129	1144
8	1352	347	1517	559	1412	443	1634	504	1740	423	1937	417	2007	418	2032	602	2023	828	1959	958	2123	1216	2243	1221
9	1437	502	1625	648	1520	526	1740	529	1843	448	2032	453	2049	509	2100	709	2052	942	2041	1112	2233	1305	2355	1252
10	1529	612	1736	728	1629	602	1845	554	1945	514	2123	534	2127	606	2126	818	2124	1056	2131	1222	2344	1345		1318
11	1630	716	1847	803	1738	633	1949	618	2045	543	2208	621	2159	707	2152	928	2201	1210	2229	1325		1418	105	1343
12	1737	811	1956	833	1846	700	2052	644	2142	616	2249	714	2228	812	2219	1040	2244	1322	2334	1419	55	1446	213	1406
13	1848	856	2103	900	1953	726	2153	711	2236	653	2324	812	2255	918	2248	1152	2336	1428		1504	205	1512	319	1430
14	1959	934	2209	925	2058	751	2252	742	2325	737	2355	915	2321	1027	2322	1306		1528	43	1541	314	1536	424	1456
15	2109	1006	2313	950	2201	816	2348	817		826		1020	2347	1137		1419	36	1619	154	1613	421	1600	527	1524
16	2216	1034		1015	2303	842		856	8	921	23	1127		1249	1	1530	143	1703	305	1641	527	1625	629	1556
17	2322	1059	15	1042		911	40	942	46	1021	50	1237	15	1403	48	1636	254	1739	415	1706	632	1651	728	1633
18		1124	116	1112	3	943	127	1034	120	1124	116	1350	46	1518	143	1735	406	1810	524	1731	736	1721	823	1715
19	25	1148	215	1146	101	1020	209	1131	151	1232	143	1505	122	1633	248	1824	519	1838	632	1756	837	1755	912	1804
20	128	1213	311	1225	155	1102	246	1234	219	1342	213	1622	205	1745	358	1906	630	1904	738	1822	934	1834	956	1857
21	229	1241	405	1311	246	1151	319	1341	247	1455	247	1740	257	1850	512	1941	739	1929	843	1850	1027	1919	1034	1956
22	329	1313	454	1403	331	1246	350	1451	314	1611	328	1856	359	1947	626	2011	847	1954	946	1921	1114	2009	1106	2057
23	427	1349	538	1501	412	1347	419	1605	344	1730	417	2007	508	2033	739	2038	952	2021	1045	1957	1155	2105	1135	2201
24	523	1431	617	1605	448	1453	447	1721	416	1850	515	2108	622	2112	849	2103	1056	2051	1141	2039	1231	2205	1202	2307
25	614	1520	652	1714	521	1603	516	1840	455	2008	622	2159	736	2144	957	2128	1157	2124	1231	2126	1303	2308	1226	
26	702	1615	724	1826	552	1716	548	2000	540	2122	733	2241	849	2212	1103	2154	1255	2202	1316	2218	1331		1251	15
27	744	1716	753	1939	621	1832	624	2119	634	2227	847	2315	1000	2238	1207	2222	1348	2246	1356	2316	1357	14	1316	125
28	821	1822	822	2054	650	1949	705	2234	737	2322	959	2344	1108	2302	1309	2253	1436	2336	1430		1423	122	1344	238
29	854	1931			720	2107	754	2341	845		1109		1214	2327	1408	2328	1519		1501	19	1448	233	1416	354
30	924	2042			753	2224	851		956	7	1217	10	1318	2353	1504		1558	31	1529	124	1516	347	1455	511
31	952	2154			830	2339			1106	43			1420		1556	8			1556	233			1542	628

Note: Blank space in the table indicates that a rising or setting did not occur during that 24-hour interval

Note: Daylight Savings Time is not implemented in this table. When Daylight Savings Time is in use, add one hour to the times listed in the table.

Location: W097 10, N49 53

Zone: 6h West of Greenwich

Astronomical Applications Dept.

U. S. Naval Observatory

Washington, DC 20392-5420

Rise & Set for the Sun for 2017
Vancouver

	Jan		Feb		Mar		Apr		May		June		July		Aug		Sept		Oct		Nov		Dec	
Day	Rise	Set	Rise	Set	Rise	Set	Rise	Set	Rise	Set	Rise	Set	Rise	Set	Rise	Set	Rise	Set	Rise	Set	Rise	Set	Rise	Set
	h m	h m	h m	h m	h m	h m	h m	h m	h m	h m	h m	h m	h m	h m	h m	h m	h m	h m	h m	h m	h m	h m	h m	h m
1	808	1625	743	1710	654	1756	549	1844	450	1930	412	2010	412	2021	445	1952	529	1854	613	1750	701	1651	747	1616
2	808	1626	742	1711	652	1758	547	1846	449	1931	411	2011	412	2021	447	1950	531	1852	614	1748	703	1649	748	1616
3	807	1627	740	1713	650	1759	545	1847	447	1933	410	2012	413	2020	448	1949	532	1850	616	1746	704	1647	749	1616
4	807	1629	739	1715	648	1801	543	1849	445	1934	410	2013	414	2020	449	1947	534	1848	617	1744	706	1646	750	1615
5	807	1630	737	1716	646	1803	541	1851	444	1936	409	2013	414	2020	451	1945	535	1846	619	1742	708	1644	752	1615
6	807	1631	736	1718	644	1804	539	1852	442	1937	409	2014	415	2019	452	1944	536	1844	620	1740	709	1643	753	1615
7	806	1632	734	1720	642	1806	536	1854	441	1939	408	2015	416	2018	453	1942	538	1842	622	1738	711	1641	754	1614
8	806	1633	733	1722	640	1807	534	1855	439	1940	408	2016	417	2018	455	1940	539	1840	623	1736	712	1640	755	1614
9	805	1635	731	1723	638	1809	532	1857	437	1941	408	2016	418	2017	456	1939	541	1838	625	1734	714	1638	756	1614
10	805	1636	729	1725	636	1811	530	1858	436	1943	407	2017	419	2017	458	1937	542	1835	626	1732	716	1637	757	1614
11	804	1637	728	1727	634	1812	528	1900	434	1944	407	2018	420	2016	459	1935	544	1833	628	1730	717	1636	758	1614
12	804	1639	726	1728	631	1814	526	1901	433	1946	407	2018	421	2015	501	1933	545	1831	629	1728	719	1634	759	1614
13	803	1640	724	1730	629	1815	524	1903	432	1947	407	2019	422	2014	502	1932	547	1829	631	1725	720	1633	800	1614
14	803	1641	722	1732	627	1817	522	1904	430	1948	407	2019	423	2013	503	1930	548	1827	633	1723	722	1632	801	1614
15	802	1643	721	1733	625	1818	520	1906	429	1950	407	2020	424	2013	505	1928	549	1825	634	1722	723	1630	801	1614
16	801	1644	719	1735	623	1820	518	1907	428	1951	406	2020	425	2012	506	1926	551	1823	636	1720	725	1629	802	1615
17	800	1646	717	1737	621	1821	516	1909	426	1952	407	2021	426	2011	508	1924	552	1820	637	1718	727	1628	803	1615
18	759	1647	715	1738	619	1823	514	1910	425	1954	407	2021	427	2010	509	1922	554	1818	639	1716	728	1627	803	1615
19	758	1649	713	1740	617	1825	512	1912	424	1955	407	2021	428	2009	511	1920	555	1816	640	1714	730	1626	804	1616
20	758	1650	712	1742	614	1826	510	1913	423	1956	407	2022	430	2007	512	1919	557	1814	642	1712	731	1625	805	1616
21	757	1652	710	1743	612	1828	508	1915	422	1958	407	2022	431	2006	513	1917	558	1812	643	1710	733	1624	805	1617
22	755	1654	708	1745	610	1829	507	1916	420	1959	407	2022	432	2005	515	1915	600	1810	645	1708	734	1623	806	1617
23	754	1655	706	1747	608	1831	505	1918	419	2000	408	2022	433	2004	516	1913	601	1807	647	1706	736	1622	806	1618
24	753	1657	704	1748	606	1832	503	1919	418	2001	408	2022	435	2003	518	1911	603	1805	648	1704	737	1621	806	1618
25	752	1658	702	1750	604	1834	501	1921	417	2002	408	2022	436	2001	519	1909	604	1803	650	1703	739	1620	807	1619
26	751	1700	700	1751	602	1835	459	1922	416	2004	409	2022	437	2000	521	1907	605	1801	651	1701	740	1620	807	1620
27	750	1702	658	1753	600	1837	457	1924	415	2005	409	2022	438	1959	522	1905	607	1759	653	1659	741	1619	807	1620
28	749	1703	656	1755	557	1838	456	1925	415	2006	410	2022	440	1957	524	1903	608	1757	655	1657	743	1618	807	1621
29	747	1705			555	1840	454	1927	414	2007	410	2022	441	1956	525	1901	610	1755	656	1656	744	1618	808	1622
30	746	1706			553	1841	452	1928	413	2008	411	2021	442	1955	526	1859	611	1752	658	1654	745	1617	808	1623
31	745	1708			551	1843			412	2009			444	1953	528	1857			659	1652			808	1624

Note: Blank space in the table indicates that a rising or setting did not occur during that 24-hour interval

Note: Daylight Savings Time is not implemented in this table. When Daylight Savings Time is in use, add one hour to the times listed in the table.

Location: W123 08, N49 15

Zone: 8h West of Greenwich

Astronomical Applications Dept.

U. S. Naval Observatory

Washington, DC 20392-5420

Rise & Set for the Moon for 2017
Vancouver

Day	Jan Rise	Jan Set	Feb Rise	Feb Set	Mar Rise	Mar Set	Apr Rise	Apr Set	May Rise	May Set	June Rise	June Set	July Rise	July Set	Aug Rise	Aug Set	Sept Rise	Sept Set	Oct Rise	Oct Set	Nov Rise	Nov Set	Dec Rise	Dec Set
	h m	h m	h m	h m	h m	h m	h m	h m	h m	h m	h m	h m	h m	h m	h m	h m	h m	h m	h m	h m	h m	h m	h m	h m
1	1004	2023	1005	2255	837	2157	903		945	25	1205	59	1311	20	1507	9	1627	44	1616	122	1608	334	1535	453
2	1035	2131	1034		908	2312	954	35	1052	112	1312	126	1414	45	1604	42	1708	137	1646	227	1636	448	1612	611
3	1104	2241	1105	9	942		1052	136	1200	152	1417	151	1516	110	1658	120	1745	236	1715	335	1707	605	1658	730
4	1132	2352	1141	122	1021	26	1155	228	1308	225	1520	215	1617	137	1747	203	1817	339	1742	446	1742	723	1752	843
5	1200		1221	234	1106	136	1301	312	1415	254	1623	239	1716	207	1832	252	1847	445	1810	559	1823	841	1856	949
6	1230	105	1309	344	1159	241	1409	349	1520	320	1724	305	1812	242	1911	348	1915	554	1839	714	1912	955	2007	1044
7	1303	220	1405	448	1258	339	1516	420	1625	345	1825	333	1904	322	1946	448	1942	705	1911	830	2010	1103	2120	1129
8	1341	335	1508	544	1402	428	1623	449	1728	409	1923	405	1952	407	2017	552	2009	817	1948	946	2114	1201	2233	1206
9	1426	449	1616	633	1510	511	1729	515	1830	434	2017	442	2034	459	2045	659	2039	930	2031	1059	2224	1250	2345	1237
10	1519	559	1726	713	1619	547	1833	540	1932	501	2108	524	2111	556	2112	807	2111	1044	2121	1209	2335	1329		1304
11	1620	702	1836	748	1728	618	1937	605	2031	531	2153	611	2144	657	2138	917	2149	1157	2220	1311		1403	54	1328
12	1728	756	1945	818	1835	646	2039	631	2128	604	2233	705	2213	802	2206	1028	2234	1308	2324	1404	45	1431	201	1352
13	1838	841	2052	845	1941	712	2140	659	2221	643	2308	803	2240	908	2236	1140	2326	1415		1448	155	1457	307	1417
14	1949	919	2157	911	2046	737	2238	730	2309	726	2340	905	2307	1016	2310	1253		1514	33	1526	303	1522	411	1443
15	2058	951	2300	936	2149	803	2333	805	2353	816		1010	2333	1126	2350	1406	27	1605	144	1558	409	1546	514	1512
16	2205	1019		1002	2250	829		846		911	8	1117		1238		1517	134	1648	255	1626	515	1611	615	1544
17	2310	1045	2	1029	2350	859	25	932	31	1011	35	1226	2	1351	37	1622	244	1724	404	1652	619	1639	713	1622
18		1109	102	1100		932	111	1024	105	1115	102	1338	33	1506	134	1720	357	1755	513	1717	722	1709	808	1705
19	13	1134	201	1134	47	1009	153	1121	136	1222	130	1453	110	1620	239	1809	508	1823	620	1742	823	1744	857	1754
20	115	1200	257	1214	141	1052	230	1224	204	1331	200	1610	154	1732	349	1851	619	1850	726	1809	920	1823	940	1848
21	216	1229	350	1300	230	1141	304	1331	232	1444	235	1728	247	1836	503	1926	728	1915	830	1837	1012	1909	1018	1946
22	315	1301	439	1353	316	1236	335	1441	300	1600	317	1843	350	1932	616	1956	835	1941	932	1910	1059	1959	1051	2047
23	413	1338	522	1452	357	1337	404	1554	330	1718	407	1953	459	2018	728	2023	940	2009	1031	1946	1140	2055	1120	2151
24	508	1420	602	1556	433	1443	433	1710	404	1838	506	2054	613	2056	838	2049	1043	2039	1126	2028	1216	2155	1146	2257
25	600	1510	637	1704	506	1553	503	1829	443	1956	613	2144	727	2129	945	2115	1143	2113	1216	2116	1247	2258	1211	
26	646	1605	709	1815	537	1706	535	1948	530	2109	725	2226	839	2157	1051	2141	1240	2151	1301	2209	1316		1236	4
27	728	1707	739	1928	606	1821	612	2106	625	2213	838	2300	949	2223	1154	2209	1333	2236	1340	2307	1342	3	1302	114
28	805	1812	808	2043	636	1938	655	2220	728	2307	949	2329	1057	2248	1255	2241	1421	2326	1415		1408	111	1331	226
29	838	1921			707	2055	744	2327	836	2352	1059	2356	1202	2313	1354	2316	1504		1446	9	1434	222	1404	342
30	909	2031			741	2212	841		946		1206		1305	2340	1449	2357	1542	21	1514	114	1503	336	1444	459
31	937	2143			819	2326			1057	28			1407		1541				1541	223			1532	615

Note: Blank space in the table indicates that a rising or setting did not occur during that 24-hour interval

Note: Daylight Savings Time is not implemented in this table. When Daylight Savings Time is in use, add one hour to the times listed in the table.

Location: W123 08, N49 15

Zone: 8h West of Greenwich

Astronomical Applications Dept.

U. S. Naval Observatory

Washington, DC 20392-5420

TABLE FOR FINDING APPROXIMATE STANDARD TIME OF SUNRISE, SUNSET, MOONRISE, MOONSET, FOR CANADIAN CITIES AND TOWNS

PLACE	Time Zone	FOR SUNRISE OR SUNSET Take value for	and apply correction	FOR MOONRISE OR MOONSET Take value for	and apply correction
Brandon	C	Winnipeg	+11*m*	50°	+40*m*
Brantford	E	Toronto	+ 4	45	+21
Calgary	M	Winnipeg	+ 8	50	+36
Charlottetown	A	Ottawa	+10	45	+13
Cornwall	E	Ottawa	- 4	45	- 1
Edmonton	M	Winnipeg	+ 6	50	+34
Fredericton	A	Ottawa	+24	45	+27
Gander	N	Vancouver	- 4	50	+ 8
Glace Bay	A	Ottawa	- 3	45	0
Goose Bay	A	Winnipeg	-26	50	- 2
Granby	E	Ottawa	-12	45	- 9
Guelph	E	Toronto	+ 3	45	+21
Halifax	A	Ottawa	+11	45	+14
Hamilton	E	Toronto	+ 2	45	+21
Hull	E	Ottawa	0	45	+ 3
Kapuskasing	E	Vancouver	+17	50	+30
Kingston	E	Toronto	-12	45	+ 6
Kitchener	E	Toronto	+ 4	45	+22
London	E	Toronto	+ 8	45	+25
Medicine Hat	M	Winnipeg	- 4	50	+22
Moncton	A	Ottawa	+16	45	+19
Montréal	E	Ottawa	- 9	45	- 6
Moosonee	E	Winnipeg	- 6	50	+23
Moose Jaw	C	Winnipeg	+34	50	+62
Niagara Falls	E	Toronto	- 1	45	+16
North Bay	E	Ottawa	+14	45	+18
Ottawa	E	Ottawa	0	45	+ 3
Owen Sound	E	Ottawa	+21	45	+24
Penticton	P	Vancouver	-14	50	- 2
Peterborough	E	Toronto	- 4	45	+13
Prince Albert	C	Winnipeg	+36	50	+64
Prince Rupert	P	Winnipeg	+12	50	+40
Québec	E	Ottawa	-18	45	-15
Regina	C	Winnipeg	+30	50	+58
St. Catharines	E	Toronto	0	45	+17
St. Hyacinthe	E	Ottawa	-11	45	- 8
Saint John, NB	A	Ottawa	+22	45	+24
St. John's, NL	N	Vancouver	-11	50	+ 1
Sarnia	E	Toronto	+12	45	+30
Saskatoon	C	Winnipeg	+38	50	+66
Sault Ste. Marie	E	Ottawa	+34	45	+37
Shawinigan	E	Ottawa	-12	45	- 9
Sherbrooke	E	Ottawa	-14	45	-12
Stratford	E	Toronto	+ 6	45	+24
Sudbury	E	Ottawa	+21	45	+24
Sydney	A	Ottawa	- 2	45	+ 1
The Pas	C	Winnipeg	+16	50	+44
Trois-Rivières	E	Ottawa	-12	45	- 9
Thunder Bay	E	Vancouver	+44	50	+57
Timmins	E	Vancouver	+13	50	+25
Toronto	E	Toronto	0	45	+18
Trail	P	Vancouver	-22	50	-10
Truro	A	Ottawa	+10	45	+13
Vancouver	P	Vancouver	0	50	+12
Victoria	P	Vancouver	+2	50	+14
Windsor	E	Toronto	+14	45	+32
Winnipeg	C	Winnipeg	0	50	+28

PROMINENT CANADIAN SCIENTISTS

John F. Allen

Working with Pyotr Leonidovich Kapitsa and Don Misener, Allen discovered the superfluid phase of matter in 1937 at the Royal Society Mond Laboratory in Cambridge, England. A state achieved by a few liquids, such as helium, at extreme temperature where they become able to flow without friction, superfluids are used in high-precision devices, such as gyroscopes, which allow the measurement of some theoretically predicted gravitational effects. Allen along with Harry Jones also discovered the "fountain effect," in which superfluid helium flows up a tube and shoots into the air upon being exposed to a small heat source (the heat source in the original experiment was a flashlight that they were using to look at the apparatus). Allen was born in Winnipeg in 1908 and was professor of physics at St Andrews University, Scotland, from 1947 to 1978, and then emeritus professor until his death in 2001.

Sidney Altman

Born in 1939 in Montreal, the molecular biologist received a Nobel Prize in Chemistry in 1989 for his work with Thomas R. Cech on the catalytic properties of RNA. Their discovery, that ribonucleic acid in living cells is not only a molecule of heredity but also can function as a biocatalyst, affects fundamental aspects of the molecular basis of life. Virtually all chemical reactions taking place in a living cell require catalysts. Such biocatalysts are called enzymes and are determined by hereditary genes. Until the findings of Altman and Cech became known, all enzymes were considered to be proteins. The discovery of catalytic RNA will provide a new tool for gene technology, with potential to create defenses against viral infections. Altman is currently the Sterling Professor of Molecular, Cellular, and Developmental Biology and Professor of Chemistry at Yale University.

Frederick G. Banting

A doctor of orthopedic medicine and a decorated World War I veteran, Banting received a Nobel Prize in Medicine in 1923 for his discovery of insulin, a hormone that controls the metabolism of sugar. Early in his medical career, Banting became interested in diabetes, caused by a lack of insulin secreted by the pancreas. Before Banting's work, attempts to supply the missing insulin by feeding patients with fresh pancreas, or extracts of it, had failed. While working with his assistant Charles Best, Banting discovered how to extract insulin from the pancreas before it destroyed itself, thus birthing the first treatment for diabetes sufferers. The Banting and Best Diabetes Centre at the University of Toronto continues the work of the two doctors. The cause of diabetes remains a mystery. Banting was killed in an airplane disaster in 1941 in Newfoundland.

Arthur S. Goss/Library and Archives Canada/PA-123481

Alexander Graham Bell

A Naturalized U.S. citizen, Bell proved himself a Canadian at heart. While he spent winters in the U.S., Bell spent his summers on scientific research in his home in Baddeck, Cape Breton Island. His work with hearing & speech in 1875 birthed his idea of the telephone, which he developed & patented in1876. Bell experimented with the first long distance telephone call between Brantford & Paris, ON, in addition to other scientific experiments on the genetics of sheep breeding, his Silver Draft aircraft, & his hydrofoil speed boat, among others. Bell died of diabetes in 1922, and his grave lies on the summit of Cape Breton's Beinn Bhreagh Mountain overlooking the Bras D'or Lakes of Nova Scotia.

Moffett Studio/Library and Archives Canada/C-017335

Williard S. Boyle

Boyle's family moved from Nova Scotia to Québec when he was a child. Boyle was homeschooled by his mother until secondary school when he enrolled in Lower Canada College, a Montreal private school. Upon graduation, Boyle joined the Royal Canadian Navy to fight in World War II; however, he became sea-sick & transferred to the Fleet Air Arm of the navy where he completed pilot training. He earned his doctorate in Physics from McGill University in 1950.

Three years later, Boyle joined Bell Laboratories where he contributed to the branch of Solid State Physics or Condensed Matter Physics. His inventions & innovations include the first continuously operating ruby laser & semiconductor lasers. Boyle went on to receive various awards, including his addition into the Science & Engineering Hall of Fame in 2005. In 2009, he received the Nobel Prize in Physics for co-inventing the Charge Coupled Device (CCD), a circuit used in many camcorders & digital cameras as imaging devices & which revolutionized astronomy when used in large telescopes. In 2010, he was recognized as a Companion of the Order of Canada for his lifetime achievements.

Boyle passed away in Wallace, Nova Scotia, in May 2011.

Bertram Brockhouse

Brockhouse was born in 1918 to homesteaders in Alberta and attended a one-room schoolhouse in Vancouver. During the Depression, the impoverished Brockhouses moved to Chicago, where, to help out with family finances, Brockhouse learned how to repair radios, and became involved in the socialist democratic movement. During World War II, he served six years in the Royal Canadian Navy repairing submarine-tracking equipment. At the war's end he attended the University of British Columbia, where he studied physics and mathematics, and received a PhD from the University of Toronto in the budding field of nuclear physics. In 1994 Brockhouse and Clifford G. Shull received a Nobel Prize in Physics for their contributions to the development of neutron scattering techniques for studies of condensed matter. Neutron scattering techniques are used in widely differing areas such as the study of the new ceramic superconductors, catalytic exhaust cleaning, elastic properties of polymers and virus structure.

Brockhouse passed away in Hamilton, Ontario, in October 2003.

Elizabeth Cannon

Born in Charlottetown, PEI, Cannon went to work for Nortech Surveys in Calgary where she utilized her BSc in Geomatics Engineering from the University of Calgary. During the halcyon days of the Global Positioning System (GPS) when it was largely used only by the US military, Cannon worked with the seismic surveying & geomatics company to develop new GPS methodologies. She returned to the University of Calgary to further her study in Geomatics, the science of production & management of spatial information, and won the 1988 Institute of Nagivation (ION) in a student paper competition.

She received her PhD in Geomatics Engineering and has since become a President and Vice-Chancellor of the University of Calgary. Currently, she researches the use of the GPS with aircraft positioning and altitude, precision farming, and improvements in precise positioning. She received the Calgary YWCA Women of Distinction Award in 1993, was named one of Canada's Top 40 Under 40 in 1998 and is a Fellow of the Canadian Academy of Engineering and the Royal Society of Canada. She is currently President & Vice-Chancellor of the University of Calgary.

John Herbert Chapman

For nearly two decades, Chapman served as scientist, superintendent and deputy chief superintendent in the Ottawa-based Defense Research Telecommunications Establishment, and then as assistant deputy minister for research in the Canadian Department of Communications. In 1966, a government study group appointed Chapman chairman; his report resulted in the redirection of the Canadian space program from scientific to application satellites. He also cooperated with NASA and the European Space Agency to design, develop and establish the Hermes Communications Technology Satellite. These initiatives shaped the Canadian space program. He passed away in Vancouver, B.C., in 1979, the same year he received a posthumous McNaughton Award to add to a list of awards he earned throughout his life.

H.S.M. Coxeter

Coxeter was born and educated in England. Shortly after finishing his doctoral studies at Cambridge University, he spent two years as a research visitor at Princeton University. In 1936 he joined the Faculty of the University of Toronto, where he remained as a mathematics professor until his death in 2003. Coxeter's work was mainly in geometry. In particular he made contributions of major importance in the theory of non-euclidean geometry, group theory, combinatorics, and polytopes or complicated geometric shapes of any number of dimensions that cannot be constructed in the real world but can be described mathematically and can sometimes be drawn. Much of Coxeter's time was devoted to group theory, or ways of measuring symmetry. This concerns the geometry of, for instance, kaleidoscopes and reflections in different planes, now known as Coxeter groups. Coxeter met the artist M.C. Escher, the master of depicting impossible reality, in 1954 and the two became lifelong friends. Coxeter also influenced Buckminster Fuller who used Coxeter's mathematical concepts of symmetry in his architecture. He attributed his long and productive life to vegetarianism and physical fitness.

J.C. Fields

John Charles Fields was born in Hamilton, Ontario, then Upper Canada, in 1863. He graduated with a degree in mathematics from the University of Toronto and was awarded a PhD from Johns Hopkins University in 1887. Dissatisfied with the state of mathematics in North America, Fields left for Europe, where he met the greatest mathematicians of the time, and changed his mathematical interests to algebraic functions. Fields worked tirelessly to raise the stature of mathematics within academic and public circles. He successfully lobbied the Ontario Legislature for an annual research grant of $75,000 for the university and helped establish the National Research Council of Canada, and the Ontario Research Foundation. Fields is best known for establishing what is now known as the Fields Medal, the premier award in mathematics, often called the Nobel Prize in Mathematics. It is awarded every four years to two to four mathematicians, under the age of 40, who have made important contributions to the field.

Sir Sandford Fleming

Fleming was born in Scotland in 1827, and at the age of 17, he emigrated to Ontario, where he was employed as a surveyor and map maker. In 1851 Fleming designed Canada's first postage stamp, which would do much to publicize the beaver as a distinctly Canadian emblem. In 1855 he became the chief engineer of the Northern Railway of Canada, where he instituted the construction of iron bridges instead of wood for safety reasons. Over the next few years he led a team of surveyors and engineers to investigate the first coast-to-coast railway line. Fleming was present in 1885 when the last spike was driven in Craigellachie, British Columbia. After missing a train in 1876 in Ireland because the printed schedule listed p.m. instead of a.m., he proposed Universal Time, a single 24-hour clock for the entire world, located in Greenwich, England, the center of the Earth and not linked to any surface meridian. He urged that standard time zones be used locally, but they were to be subordinate to his single world time. By 1929 all of the major countries of the world had accepted time zones. Fleming was knighted by Queen Victoria In 1897.

Library and Archives Canada, Acc. No. 1951-566-1

John Kenneth Galbraith

The economist's first major book, published in 1952, was American Capitalism: The Concept of Countervailing Power. In it he argued that giant firms had replaced small ones to the point where the competitive model no longer applied to much of the American economy. But, he argued, the muscle of large firms was offset by the power of large unions, so that consumers were protected by competing centres of power.

In his best-selling 1958 book The Affluent Society, Galbraith contrasted the affluence of the private sector with the squalor of the public sector. Galbraith's main argument is that as society becomes relatively more affluent, so private business must "create" consumer wants through advertising, and while this generates artificial affluence through the production of commercial goods and services, the "public sector" becomes neglected as a result. He proposed significant investment in parks, transportation, education, and other public amenities - what we now call infrastructure - to ameliorate these differences and postpone depression and revolution indefinitely.

Although born in Canada, Galbraith spent most of his life in the United States, namely as a professor at Harvard University. He was active in politics, serving four US presidents and was the US Ambassador to India under Kennedy. He was awarded the Order of Canada in 1997 and two Presidential Medals of Freedom. He died in 2006 at the age of 97.

Birutė Galdikas

Galdikas was born in 1946 in Germany en route to Canada from Lithuania. She grew up in Toronto where she frequented High Park, a home to the wild animals she spent hours observing. She moved to California to complete her undergraduate, Masters & PhD in Anthropology in UCLA & since then has received the PETA Humanitarian Award in 1990, the United Nations Global 500 Award in 1993 and many others. She co-founded and heads the Orangutan Foundation International and is recognized as the world's foremost authority on orangutans and the apes' anthropological connection with humans.

Galdikas is currently a Professor of Anthropology at Simon Fraser University and splits her time between her three homes in Deep Cove, BC; Los Angeles, CA; & Borneo.

William Francis Giauque

Born to American parents on the Canadian side of Niagara Falls, Giauque began his career at the Hooker Electro-Chemical Company in Niagara Falls, NY, as a chemical engineer. Soon after, he received a Ph.D. degree in chemistry with a minor in physics from the University of California, where he became a professor of chemistry in 1934. His principal objective was to demonstrate through a variety of accurate tests that the third law of thermodynamics is a basic natural law. In 1927 he proposed a new method of achieving extremely low temperatures using a process called adiabatic demagnetization. By 1933 he had a working apparatus that obtained a temperature within one-tenth of a degree of absolute zero. In the course of his low-temperature studies of oxygen, Giauque discovered with Herrick L. Johnston the oxygen isotopes of mass 17 and 18 in the Earth's atmosphere. He received the Nobel Prize in Chemistry in 1949.

James Gosling

The father of Java programming language was born in 1955 near Calgary, where he attended university. He received his PhD in Computer Science from Carnegie Mellon University. While at the college he built a multi-processor version of Unix, as well as several compilers and computer mail systems.

From 1984 to 2010, Gosling served Sun Microsystems as Vice President and Fellow. After spending six months at Google, Gosling moved to Liquid Robotics in August 2011, where he is chief software architect in the creation of robots that can explore the bottom of the ocean.

In February 2007, he was named an officer of the Order of Canada.

Gerhard Herzberg

Physicist Herzberg was born in Hamburg, Germany in 1904 but was forced to flee Nazi Germany in 1935, when he settled at the University of Saskatchewan. Herzberg's main contributions have enriched the fields of atomic and molecular spectroscopy for which he won a Nobel Prize in Chemistry in 1971. He and his associates determined the makeup of a large number of diatomic and polyatomic molecules, including the structures of many free radicals difficult to determine in any other way. Herzberg has also applied spectroscopic studies to the identification of certain molecules in planetary atmospheres, in comets, and in interstellar space. Herzberg was elected a Fellow of the Royal Society of Canada in 1939 and of the Royal Society of London in 1951. Herzberg died in 1999.

David Hubel

Hubel, along with Torsten Wiesel, greatly expanded the scientific knowledge of sensory processing, describing how signals from the eye are processed by the brain to generate edge detectors, motion detectors, stereoscopic depth detectors and color detectors, the building blocks of the visual scene. These studies opened the door for the understanding and treatment of childhood cataracts and strabismus. For their work the team was awarded the 1981 Nobel Prize in Physiology or Medicine. Hubel was born to American parents in Windsor, but spent his formative years in Montreal. He died in 2013, in Lincoln, Mass.

Harold Elford Johns

Johns was born in China but grew up in Ontario, where he earned his MA and PhD from the University of Toronto. He was a biophysicist and professor who helped develop the Medical Biophysics Department of the University of Toronto. He invented the cobalt bomb, a nuclear device that birthed the cobalt-60 therapy, which treats cancers located deep within the body that otherwise cannot be reached by other therapies. It has since saved more than 7 million cancer patients. Johns received the 1973 Gairdner International Award and the 1985 W.B. Lewis Award from the Canadian Nuclear Society.

Cecilia Krieger

Krieger was born in Poland but emigrated from Vienna to Toronto in 1920 to escape the persecution of Jews in Europe. Krieger taught at the University of Toronto for three decades after becoming the first woman to earn a Doctorate in Mathematics in Canada in 1930. In honour of Krieger & another woman mathematician, Evelyn Nelson, the Canadian Mathematical Society awarded the CMS Krieger-Nelson Prize Lectureship for Distinguished Research by Women.

Fernand Labrie

Labrie earned his M.D. in 1962 and Ph.D. in endocrinology in 1966 from the University of Laval. He left his Québec home to study in England with two-time Nobel Prize winner in medicine, Frederick Sanger, and returned in 1969 to found the Laboratory of Molecular Endocrinology at his alma mater. Labrie discovered that castrating hormones from the testes by adding a hormone called GNrH in prostate cancer patients eliminates the need for surgical castration. Next, he discovered that blocking male hormones from the adrenal glands prevents cancer from spreading, thus prolonging life of prostate cancer patients. Labrie also developed medication to prevent the binding of estrogens in the breast and uterus once he discovered that adding estrogen in women was linked to uterine and breast cancer.

Labrie resides in Québec and works as Director of the Laboratory of Molecular Endocrinology, and CEO and CSO of EndoCeutics, a private pharmaceutical company. Among other awards, He was appointed Fellow of the Royal Society of Canada in 1979 and Officer of the Order of Canada in 1981, and earned the Queen's Golden Jubilee Medal in 2002 and King Faisal International Prize in 2007.

Rudolph Marcus

Born in Montreal in 1923, Marcus received the 1992 Nobel Prize in Chemistry for his theory of electron transfer. The Marcus theory, named after him, provides a thermodynamic and kinetic framework for describing one electron outer-sphere electron transfer. The Marcus theory describes, and makes predictions concerning, such widely differing phenomena as the fixation of light energy by green plants, photochemical production of fuel, chemiluminescence (cold light), the conductivity of electrically conducting polymers, corrosion, the methodology of electrochemical synthesis and analysis, and more.

Marcus developed his theory for what is perhaps the simplest chemical elementary process, the transfer of an electron between two molecules. No chemical bonds are broken in such a reaction, but changes take place in the molecular structure of the reacting molecules and their nearest neighbors. This molecular change enables the electrons to jump between the molecules. He is currently a professor at Caltech and is a member of the International Academy of Quantum Molecular Science.

Sir William Osler

Osler, often dubbed the father of modern medicine, grew up in Ontario, the son of an Anglican minister. After two years at the Toronto School of Medicine, Osler obtained his medical degree in 1872 from McGill University. Upon his death, Osler willed his library to the Montreal university where it forms the nucleus of McGill's Osler Library of the History of Medicine, which opened in 1929. Osler's greatest contribution to medicine was to insist that students learned from seeing and talking to patients and the establishment of the medical residency program. In 1889, Osler accepted the position of Physician-in-Chief at the recently founded Johns Hopkins Hospital in Baltimore where he refined the residency program. He died, at the age of 70, in 1919, during the Spanish influenza epidemic.

Wilder Penfield

The American-born Canadian neurosurgeon studied at Princeton before becoming a Rhodes Scholar at Oxford University where he studied neuropathology, the scientific study of diseases of the nervous system. With his colleague, Herbert Jasper, he invented what is now called the Montreal procedure for treating patients with severe epilepsy by destroying nerve cells in the brain where the seizures originated. Before operating, he stimulated the brain with electrical probes while the patients were conscious on the operating table and observed their responses. In this way he could more accurately target the areas of the brain responsible, reducing the side-effects of the surgery. His technique enabled him to map the sensory and motor parts of the brain, thus showing their connection to the various limbs and organs of the body. After studying epilepsy in New York, Penfield moved to Montreal where he taught at at McGill University and the Royal Victoria hospital, becoming the city's first neurosurgeon. He eventually became the director of the Montreal Neurological Institute and the associated Montreal Neurological Hospital, which was established with funding from the Rockefeller Foundation. In 1967 he was made a Companion of the Order of Canada. In 1994 he was inducted into the Canadian Medical Hall of Fame.

John Polanyi

After completing his undergraduate education at Manchester University, Polanyi moved to Canada in 1952 at the age of 23 to work for the for the National Research Council of Canada before moving to the University of Toronto, where he remains to this day. In 1986 Polanyi shared a Nobel Prize in Chemistry with Dudley R. Herschbach and Yuan T. Lee for their research in reaction dynamics, offering much more understanding into how energy disposal in chemical reactions takes place. Polanyi developed the method of infrared chemiluminescence, in which the extremely weak infrared emission from a newly formed molecule is measured and analyzed.

Arthur Schawlow

Schawlow grew up in Canada in a deeply religious family and studied at the University of Toronto. After World War II, he studied at Columbia University, spent a decade at Bell Labs, then left to become a professor at Stanford, where he remained as professor emeritus until his retirement in 1996. While at Stanford, he teamed up with Robert Hofstadter, who, like Schawlow, had an autistic child, to help each other find solutions to the condition. Later Schawlow spearheaded an institution to care for people with autism in Paradise, CA, named the Arthur Schawlow Center. Although his research focused on optics, in particular, lasers and their use in spectroscopy, he also pursued investigations in the areas of superconductivity and nuclear resonance. He and Nicolaas Bloembergen shared the 1981 Nobel Prize in Physics by using lasers to study the interactions of electromagnetic radiation with matter.

Myron Scholes

The 1997 winner of the Nobel Memorial Prize in Economics began his early years in Timmins. After the family moved to Hamilton, Scholes attended McMaster University and earned an MBA and PhD from the University of Chicago. He eventually put his name to the Black-Scholes model, which provides the fundamental conceptual framework for valuing options, such as calls or puts, and has become the standard in financial markets globally. All did not go well for Scholes, however. In 2005, Scholes was implicated in the case of Long-Term Capital Holdings v. United States, where he attempted to invest funds from his company, Long-Term Capital Holdings, in an illegal tax shelter in order to avoid having to pay taxes on profits from company investments. It was found that Scholes and his partners were not eligible for US$106 million in tax deductions they had claimed. They were fined more than US$40 million by the IRS. Scholes is now the Chief Investment Strategist at Janus Capital Group. He was awarded the 2011 CME Group Fred Arditti Innovation Award for his co-creation of the Black-Scholes options pricing model.

Michael Smith

Born in 1932 in Blackpool, England, Smith attended the University of Manchester and soon after receiving his PhD accepted a fellowship in Vancouver to work on the synthesis of biologically important organo-phosphates. The 1992 Nobel Prize winner in chemistry didn't keep the money he was granted from the award. He gave half of it to researchers working on the genetics of schizophrenia and shared the other half between Science World BC and the Society for Canadian Women in Science and Technology. Smith could afford to be generous. He had made a small fortune in 1988 when he sold his share of Zymogenetics Incorporated, a Seattle-based biotechnology company that he co-founded in 1981.

Andrew Michael Spence

For his work on the dynamics of information flows and market development, Spence and his colleagues George A. Akerlof and Joseph E. Stiglitz, received the 2001 Nobel Memorial Prize in Economics. In his Job-Market Signaling model, employees convey their respective skills to employers by acquiring a certain degree of education, which is costly to them. Employers will pay higher wages to more educated employees, because they know that the proportion of employees with high abilities is higher among the educated ones, as it is less costly for them to acquire education than it is for employees with low abilities. For the model to work, it is not even necessary for education to have any intrinsic value if it can convey information about the sender (employee) to the recipient (employer) and if the signal is costly. Spence is currently a professor at the NYU Stern School of Business. He grew up in Canada, during and after the war, before leaving for college in the United States.

Henry Taube

For his work on the mechanisms of electron transfer reactions, especially in metal complexes, Taube won the 1983 Nobel Prize in Chemistry. Born in Saskatchewan, Taube has published more than 350 articles and a book as a result of his research. A member of the Stanford University faculty since 1962, Taube was "one of the most creative contemporary workers in inorganic chemistry," according to the Nobel committee who rewarded him for his insights into how electrons are transferred from one molecule to another during chemical reactions. Taube maintained a lifelong interest in oxidation-reduction or redox reactions, in which electrons are lost and gained during a chemical reaction. He died in 2005 at the age of 89 at his home on the Stanford campus.

Richard E. Taylor

Born in 1929 in Medicine Hat, Alberta, Taylor received the 1990 Nobel Prize in Physics for his pioneering investigations concerning deep inelastic scattering of electrons on protons and bound neutrons, which have been of essential importance for the development of the quark model in particle physics. He shared the prize with Jerome Friedman and Henry Kendall. Taylor received his undergraduate degree from the University of Alberta and his PhD from Stanford, where he is a professor emeritus.

William Vickrey

Vickrey was born in Victoria, British Columbia, in 1914. His elementary and secondary education was in Europe and the United States, with graduation from Phillips Andover Academy in 1931. He received a B.S. in mathematics from Yale in 1935, followed by graduate work in economics at Columbia University from 1935 to 1937. A conscientious objector during World War II, he spent part of his alternate service designing a new inheritance tax for Puerto Rico. In 1946 he began his teaching career at Columbia University as a lecturer in economics. An essential part of Vickrey's research focused on the properties of different types of auctions, and how they can best be designed to generate economic efficiency. His work provided the basis for a field of research which has also been extended to practical applications such as auctions of treasury bonds and band spectrum licenses. He received the 1996 Nobel Prize in Economics for his endeavors, and passed away just three days later.

John Tuzo Wilson

The Ottawa-born geologist achieved world-wide acclaim for his contributions to study of plate tectonics. Plate tectonics is the idea that the rigid outer layers of the Earth are broken up into numerous pieces that move independently over the weaker soft zone of the upper mantle. Wilson maintained that the Hawaiian Islands were created as a tectonic plate, extending across much of the Pacific Ocean, shifted slowly over a fixed hotspot, spawning a long series of volcanoes. He also conceived of the transform fault, a major plate boundary where two plates move past each other horizontally, such as the San Andreas Fault. The Wilson cycle of seabed expansion and contraction bears his name. He died in 1993 in Toronto.

CANADA'S ENERGY SOURCES

Canada is endowed with an abundant variety of energy resources. It ranks among top countries in the world for production of oil, natural gas, uranium and coal. Most of the country's energy is derived from hydrocarbons-coal, natural gas, and oil. These are used both as direct fuels and in the production of electricity. The only significant non-hydrocarbon energy sources are hydroelectricity and nuclear power. Canadians are the second-highest per capita consumers of energy in the world, doubling Japan and most of Europe. How will Canada cope with future energy needs and consumption?

Oil and Gas

Canada faces the same oil industry challenges as the rest of the world: recent crude oil prices have been high and volatile, and geopolitical uncertainty continues to be a threat to supply around the globe. The impact of severe weather on refining and production has resulted in higher crude oil and gasoline prices. Based on Canada's production rate, they have 10 years or less of proven reserves. This does not mean that Canada will run out of oil in 10 years. It means this is the size of its resource based on the oil pools today, production rates, and the portion that is recoverable using existing technology.

Canadian oil sands—a mixture of sand or clay, water, and extremely heavy crude oil—are estimated to contain 1.7 trillion barrels of oil, and based on today's technology, it's believed that 178 billion barrels can be recovered. To put this in perspective, the size of the recoverable resources ranks second only to Saudi Arabia. The oil sands currently account for approximately one-third of the 3.3 million barrels of oil produced per day in Canada. Conventional oil production in the Western Canada Sedimentary Basin peaked in 1973, but it still accounts for a significant portion of oil supply. There is call to slow the pace of oil sands development in order to allow for better understanding and assessment of the risks to the environment. This could mean temporarily halting further approvals of projects.

Natural Gas

There has been an ongoing trend on the part of large energy consumers and the general public toward increased use of natural gas as the fuel of choice. This has been particularly noteworthy in the electricity generation industry. Canadian production of natural gas has probably already peaked, and will gradually decline as wells mature and become exhausted faster than new discoveries are made. In 2007, Canadian Liquefied Natural Gas production declined, but those deficiencies were offset by higher US imports. Drilling activity was weaker than it had been at the same time in each of the past three years. Annual increases in drilling activity and connection of new gas wells are necessary to maintain stable Canadian gas deliverability, because the productivity of new gas wells in the Western Canada Sedimentary Basin has lessened. In 2006, natural gas prices fell below the fuel oil range and competed with coal in the power generation market.

With North American natural gas supply expected to lag future increases in demand, imports of LNG from offshore sources are viewed as the largest source of additional natural gas to the continent. Over 40 import terminal projects have been proposed for North America and development of significant LNG trade could have implications for North American natural gas supply, demand and prices.

Canada will continue to research and develop gas hydrates, a form of natural gas found in the molecular structure of ice, in Northern provinces and offshore on both coasts. Canadian resource estimates are impressive: 1,500 to 28,000 trillion cubic feet of gas in place contained in hydrates, with 311 trillion cubic feet in the Beaufort/Mackenzie Delta region. Both the Pacific and Atlantic margins have confirmed gas hydrates deposits. If there was a system available to transport these deposits, hydrates would be as economical as gas. However, costs are not competitive with conventional gas at this time. Additional testing and modeling is required to ensure results. Plans are to have a full scale production test in about five years and first production by 2020.

Compressed natural gas seems to be a viable transportation option for stranded natural gas offshore Newfoundland. Development still has a number of hurdles to overcome, including safety issues for the delivery to Boston or New York harbours.

Electricity and Coal

The size of Canada's coal resource dwarfs all other energy forms, even the oil sands. Based on current production rates, Canada has a 1,000-year reserve of coal. Currently about 60 percent of Canada's electricity comes from hydro projects, 18 percent from coal combustion, 13 percent from nuclear, 5 percent from natural gas, and the balance from oil and renewables. Coal-based generation became unpopular during the 1980s and 1990s because of its carbon emissions. Canada must develop ways to use coal in a manner that is environmentally acceptable. Until a few years ago, there were two ways to address the challenge of greenhouse gas management: to produce and use energy more efficiently or, to rely increasingly on low-carbon and carbon-free fuels. Unfortunately, energy efficiency and the use of alternative energy may not be enough to stabilize global concentrations of carbon dioxide. Carbon sequestration offers a third option that could, in tandem with the continued development of clean coal generation technologies, prove affordable, effective and environmentally safe.

Canadian metallurgical coal (coal consumed in making steel) is experiencing a comeback in Alberta and British Columbia, and opportunities for Canadian metallurgical coal are driven by demand in China, India and Brazil. Canadian steam coal (all non-metallurgical coal) production remains consistent with some export growth. Ontario became the first province in Canada to eliminate coal as a source of electrical power, after shutting down the last of its plants in 2014. Steam coal production remains strong in Alberta, Saskatchewan and Nova Scotia.

A number of provinces have introduced or are in the process of introducing plans to address electricity needs by way of new generation and transmission projects. For example, British Columbia Transmission Corp. introduced a $3.2-billion 10-year transmission plan, Alberta Electric System Operator began a $3.5 billion 10-year transmission plan, Saskatchewan agreed to address its aging fleet of coal-fired generators with Carbon Capture and Storage technology, and the Ontario Power Authority moved on its Power System Plan.

Nuclear Energy

Ontario dominates Canada's nuclear industry, containing most of the country's nuclear power generating capacity. Ontario has 20 reactors, providing about half of the province's electricity. New Brunswick has one reactor, and Quebec did as well, until it was shut down in 2012. Overall, nuclear power provides about 15.5 percent of Canada's electricity. The cost of nuclear power generation has been dropping over the last decade. This is because declining fuel (including enrichment), operating and maintenance costs, while the plant concerned has been paid for, or at least is being paid off. In general the construction costs of nuclear power plants are significantly higher than for coal- or gas-fired plants because of the need to use special materials, and to incorporate sophisticated safety features and back-up control equipment. These contribute much of the nuclear generation cost, but once the plant is built the cost variables are minor. Canada's nuclear plants, however, are quickly reaching the end of their operating lifespans and are entering the long and costly decommissioning phase.

Canada is one of the world's largest producers of uranium with about one third of world production coming from Saskatchewan mines. The country exports uranium and radioisotopes for medical and industrial purposes. These exports are subject to stringent nuclear non-proliferation policies.

Canada's used reactor fuel is now stored on an interim basis at licensed facilities located where the waste is produced. Like many other countries with nuclear power programs, Canada has yet to decide what to do with this used fuel over the long term. On site storage options are expected to perform well over the near term; however, existing reactor sites were not chosen for their suitability as permanent storage sites. Furthermore, the communities hosting the nuclear reactors have a reasonable expectation that used nuclear fuel will eventually be moved.

Alternative and Renewable Energy

Canadian energy development strategies traditionally focused on low-cost electric power, crude oil, and accessible energy resources. These strategies led to a strong energy industry that has contributed to Canadian prosperity. But today, the world's appetite for cheap energy is counterbalanced by climate change concerns and greenhouse gas emission restrictions. Canada has the potential to become a global leader in renewable energy given its abundant renewable energy resources such as solar, wind, earth, wave, water, tide and biomass. With its large forest and agricultural land base relative to its population, Canada is uniquely positioned to be a world leader in the production and use of biofuels derived from lignocellulose (forestry) biomass. However, renewable energy sources account for less than one percent of the total energy supply today. Utilization of these alternate sources will expand, but they will not become more than small, specialized niche contributors to Canada's energy supply for the foreseeable future.

A study by the Pembina Institute, a sustainable-energy think tank, concluded that smart, targeted investments in a diverse array of energy efficiency and renewable energy solutions over the next 20 years will achieve major cuts in greenhouse gas emissions, accelerate the closure of highly-polluting coal plants and avoid the need for new nuclear investments.

PERPETUAL CALENDAR
(Table for Determining the Weekday of a Given Date)

In the YEAR table, locate the first two figures of the given year (lower left) and the last two figures (upper right) and take the number at the intersection.
With that number, enter the MONTH table, and take the number at the intersection with the given month. Note the special columns for January and February in the case of a bissextile (leap) year.
With that number, enter the DAY OF THE MONTH table. The weekday is found at the intersection with the given day of the month.

Example: 1970 March 7

YEAR											
					00	01	02	03	—	04	05
					06	07	—	08	09	10	11
					—	12	13	14	15	—	16
					17	18	19	—	20	21	22
					23	—	24	25	26	27	—
					28	29	30	31	—	32	33
					34	35	—	36	37	38	39
					—	40	41	42	43	—	44
					45	46	47	—	48	49	50
					51	—	52	53	54	55	—
					56	57	58	59	—	60	61
					62	63	—	64	65	66	67
					—	68	69	70	71	—	72
					73	74	75	—	76	77	78
					79	—	80	81	82	83	—
					84	85	86	87	—	88	89
					90	91	—	92	93	94	95
					—	96	97	98	99		
0	7	14	17	21	6	0	1	2	3	4	5
1	8	15 *J*			5	6	0	1	2	3	4
2	9		18	22	4	5	6	0	1	2	3
3	10				3	4	5	6	0	1	2
4	11	15 *G*	19	23	2	3	4	5	6	0	1
5	12	16	20	24	1	2	3	4	5	6	0
6	13				0	1	2	3	4	5	6

J: until 1582 October 4 inclusively (Julian Calendar)
G: from 1582 October 15 onwards (Gregorian Calendar)
Example: In the first table, we find 5 at the intersection of 19 and 70.

MONTH	May	Feb. (*B*) Aug.	Feb. March Nov.	June	Sept. Dec.	Jan. (*B*) April July	Jan. Oct.
1	2	3	4	5	6	0	1
2	3	4	5	6	0	1	2
3	4	5	6	0	1	2	3
4	5	6	0	1	2	3	4
5	6	0	1	2	3	4	5
6	0	1	2	3	4	5	6
0	1	2	3	4	5	6	0

(*B*) = Bissextile (leap) year
Example: In the second table, we find 1 at the intersection of 5 and March.

DAY OF MONTH	1 8 15 22 29	2 9 16 23 30	3 10 17 24 31	4 11 18 25	5 12 19 26	6 13 20 27	7 14 21 28
1	Sun.	Mon.	Tue.	Wed.	Thur.	Fri.	Sat.
2	Mon.	Tue.	Wed.	Thur.	Fri.	Sat.	Sun.
3	Tue.	Wed.	Thur.	Fri.	Sat.	Sun.	Mon.
4	Wed.	Thur.	Fri.	Sat.	Sun.	Mon.	Tue.
5	Thur.	Fri.	Sat.	Sun.	Mon.	Tue.	Wed.
6	Fri.	Sat.	Sun.	Mon.	Tue.	Wed.	Thu.
0	Sat.	Sun.	Mon.	Tue.	Wed.	Thu.	Fri.

Example: In the third table, we find *Saturday* at the intersection of 1 and 7.

FIXED AND MOVABLE FESTIVALS AND ANNIVERSARIES

(Gregorian Calendar)	2017			2018			2019			2020			2021		
JANUARY begins on	Sun.			Mon.			Tue.			Wed			Fri.		
New Year's Day	Su	Jan.	1	Mo	Jan.	1	Tu	Jan.	1	We	Jan.	1	Fr	Jan.	1
Circumcision	Su	Jan.	1	Mo	Jan.	1	Tu	Jan.	1	We	Jan.	1	Fr	Jan.	1
Gantan-sai (Shinto New Year)	Su	Jan.	1	Mo	Jan.	1	Tu	Jan.	1	We	Jan.	1	Fr	Jan.	1
Mary Mother of God	Su	Jan.	1	Mo	Jan.	1	Tu	Jan.	1	We	Jan.	1	Fr	Jan.	1
Twelfth Night	Th	Jan.	5	Fr	Jan.	5	Sa	Jan.	5	Su	Jan.	5	Tu	Jan.	5
Epiphany	Fr	Jan.	6	Sa	Jan.	6	Su	Jan.	6	Mo	Jan.	6	We	Jan.	6
Maghi	Fr	Jan.	13	Sa	Jan.	13	Su	Jan.	13	Mo	Jan.	13	We	Jan.	13
New Year's Day (Orthodox)	Sa	Jan.	14	Su	Jan.	14	Mo	Jan.	14	Tu	Jan.	14	Th	Jan.	14
Lunar New Year	Sa	Jan.	28	Fr	Feb.	16	Tu	Feb.	5	We	Feb.	5	Fr	Feb.	12
FEBRUARY begins on	Wed.			Thu.			Fri.			Sat.			Mon.		
Tu B'shvat	Sa	Feb.	11	We	Jan.	31	Su	Feb.	10	Tu	Jan.	28	Th	Jan.	28
St. Valentine's Day	Tu	Feb.	14	We	Feb.	14	Th	Feb.	14	Fr	Feb.	14	Su	Feb.	14
Nirvana	We	Feb	15	Th	Feb.	15	Fr	Feb.	15	Sa	Feb.	15	Mo	Feb.	15
MARCH begins on	Wed.			Thu.			Fri.			Sun.			Mon.		
Ash Wednesday	We	Mar.	1	We	Feb.	14	We	Mar.	6	We	Feb.	26	We	Feb.	17
St. David	We	Mar.	1	Th	Mar.	1	Fr	Mar.	1	Su	Mar.	1	Mo	Mar.	1
World Day of Prayer	Fr	Mar.	3	Fr	Mar.	2	Fr	Mar.	1	Fr	Mar.	6	Fr	Mar.	5
First Sunday of Lent	Su	Mar.	5	Su	Feb.	18	Su	Mar.	10	Su	Mar.	1	Su	Feb.	21
Purim	Su	Mar.	12	Su	Mar.	11	Th	Mar.	21	Tu	Mar.	10	Fr	Feb.	26
Daylight Savings Time begins**	Su	Mar.	12	Su	Mar.	11	Su	Mar.	10	Su	Mar.	8	Su	Mar.	14
St. Patrick's Day	Fr	Mar.	17	Sa	Mar.	17	Su	Mar.	17	Tu	Mar.	17	We	Mar.	17
St. Joseph's Day	Su	Mar.	19	Mo	Mar.	19	Tu	Mar.	19	Th	Mar.	19	Fr	Mar.	19
Naw Ruz (Baha'i New Year)	Tu	Mar.	21	We	Mar.	21	Th	Mar.	21	Sa	Mar.	21	Su	Mar.	21
Norouz (Persian/Zoroastrian)	Tu	Mar.	21	We	Mar.	21	Th	Mar.	21	Sa	Mar.	21	Su	Mar.	21
Annunciation	Sa	Mar.	25	Su	Mar.	25	Mo	Mar.	25	We	Mar.	25	Th	Mar.	25
Hindu New Year***	Tu	Mar.	28	Su	Mar.	18	Sa	Apr.	6	We	Mar.	25	Tu	Apr.	13
Khordad Sal (Birth of Prophet Zarathushtra)	Tu	Mar.	28	We	Mar.	28	Th	Mar.	28	Sa	Mar.	28	Fr	Mar.	26
APRIL begins on	Sat.			Sun.			Mon.			Wed.			Thu.		
Palm Sunday (Orthodox Christian)	Su	Apr.	2	Su	Apr.	1	Su	Apr.	21	Su	Apr.	12	Su	Apr.	25
Palm Sunday (Christian)	Su	Apr.	9	Su	Mar.	25	Su	Apr.	14	Su	Apr.	5	Su	Mar.	28
First Day of Passover (Pesach)	Tu	Apr.	11	Sa	Mar.	31	Sa	Apr.	20	Th	Apr.	9	Su	Mar.	28
Baisakhi	Fr	Apr.	14	Sa	Apr.	14	Su	Apr.	14	Tu	Apr.	14	We	Apr.	14
Good Friday	Fr	Apr.	14	Fr	Mar.	30	Fr	Apr.	19	Fr	Apr.	10	Fr	Apr.	2
Easter Sunday	Su	Apr.	16	Su	Apr.	1	Su	Apr.	21	Su	Apr.	12	Su	Apr.	4
First Day of Ridvan	Fr	Apr.	21	Sa	Apr.	21	Su	Apr.	21	Tu	Apr.	21	Fr	Apr.	16
St. George's Day	Su	Apr.	23	Mo	Apr.	23	Tu	Apr.	23	Th	Apr.	23	Fr	Apr.	23
Yom HaSho'ah	Su	Apr.	23	Th	Apr.	12	Th	May	2	Tu	Apr.	21	Th	Apr.	8
St. James the Great Day	Su	Apr.	30	Mo	Apr.	30	Tu	Apr.	30	Th	Apr.	30	Fr	Apr.	30
MAY begins on	Mon.			Tue.			Wed.			Fri.			Sat.		
Buddha Day (Visakha Puja)	We	May	10	Su	Apr.	29	Sa	May	18	Th	May	7	We	May	26
Mother's Day	Su	May	14	Su	May	13	Su	May	12	Su	May	10	Su	May	9
Rogation Sunday	Su	May	21	Su	May	6	Su	May	26	Su	May	17	Su	May	9
Victoria Day	Mo	May	22	Mo	May	21	Mo	May	20	Mo	May	18	Mo	May	24
Ascension Thursday	Th	May	25	Th	May	10	Th	May	30	Th	May	21	Th	May	13
First Day of Ramadan*	Sa	May	27	We	May	16	Mo	May	6	Fr	Apr.	24	Tu	Apr.	13
Ascension Sunday	Su	May	28	Su	May	13	Su	June	2	Su	May	24	Su	May	16
Ascension of Baha'u'llah	Mo	May	29	Tu	May	29	We	May	29	Fr	May	29	Sa	May	29
Pentecost (Shavuoth)	Tu	May	30	Sa	May	19	Sa	June	8	Th	May	28	Mo	May	17
JUNE begins on	Thu.			Fri.			Sat.			Mon.			Tue.		
Pentecost (Whit Sunday)	Su	June	4	Su	May	20	Su	June	9	Su	May	31	Su	May	23
Trinity Sunday	Su	June	11	Su	May	27	Su	June	16	Su	June	7	Su	May	30
Corpus Christi (Thursday)	Th	June	15	Th	May	31	Th	June	20	Th	June	11	Th	June	3
Corpus Christi (Sunday)	Su	June	18	Su	June	3	Su	June	23	Su	June	14	Su	June	6
Father's Day	Su	June	18	Su	June	17	Su	June	16	Su	June	21	Su	June	20
National Aboriginal Day	We	June	21	Th	June	21	Fr	June	21	Su	June	21	Mo	June	21
Sacred Heart of Jesus	Fr	June	23	Fr	June	8	Fr	June	28	Fr	June	19	Fr	June	11
St-Jean-Baptiste Day	Sa	June	24	Su	June	24	Mo	June	24	We	June	24	Th	June	24
Eid al Fitr (Ramadan ends)	Mo	June	26	Fr	June	15	We	June	5	Fr	June	5	Fr	May	14
Feast of St. Peter and St. Paul	Th	June	29	Fr	June	29	Sa	June	29	Mo	June	29	Tu	June	29
JULY begins on	Sat.			Sun.			Mon.			Wed.			Thu.		
Canada Day	Sa	July	1	Su	July	1	Mo	July	1	We	July	1	Th	July	1
Martyrdom of the Bab	Su	July	9	Mo	July	9	Tu	July	9	Th	July	9	Fr	July	9
St. Benedict Day	Tu	July	11	We	July	11	Th	July	11	Sa	July	11	Su	July	11
Pioneer Day	Mo	July	24	Tu	July	24	We	July	24	Fr	July	24	Sa	July	24
AUGUST begins on	Tue.			Wed.			Thu.			Sat.			Sun.		
Lammas	Tu	Aug.	1	We	Aug.	1	Th	Aug.	1	Sa	Aug.	1	Su	Aug.	1
Tisha B'Av	Tu	Aug.	1	Su	July	22	Sa	Aug.	10	Th	July	30	We	Aug.	18
Transfiguration	Su	Aug.	6	Mo	Aug.	6	Tu	Aug.	6	Th	Aug.	6	Fr	Aug.	6
Assumption	Tu	Aug.	15	We	Aug.	15	Th	Aug.	15	Sa	Aug.	15	Su	Aug.	15
SEPTEMBER begins on	Fri.			Sat.			Sun.			Tue.			Wed.		
Labour Day	Mo	Sept.	4	Mo	Sept.	3	Mo	Sept.	2	Mo	Sept.	7	Mo	Sept.	6
Hebrew New Year (Rosh Hashanah)	Th	Sept.	21	Mo	Sept.	10	Mo	Sept.	30	Sa	Sept.	19	Tu	Sept.	7
Islamic New Year	Th	Sept.	21	We	Sept.	12	Su	Sept.	1	Th	Aug.	20	Tu	Aug.	10
Feast of St. Michael & all Angels	Fr	Sept.	29	Sa	Sept.	29	Su	Sept.	29	Tu	Sept.	29	We	Sept.	29
Day of Atonement (Yom Kippur)	Sa	Sept.	30	We	Sept.	19	We	Oct.	9	Mo	Sept.	28	Mo	Sept.	13
OCTOBER begins on	Sun.			Mon.			Tue.			Thu.			Fr.		
St. Francis Day	We	Oct.	4	Th	Oct.	4	Fr	Oct.	4	Su	Oct.	4	Mo	Oct.	4

First Day of Feast of Tabernacles (Sukkoth)	Th	Oct.	5	Mo	Sept.	24	Mo	Oct.	14	Sa	Oct.	3	Tu	Sept.	21
Thanksgiving	Mo	Oct.	9	Mo	Oct.	8	Mo	Oct.	14	Mo	Oct.	12	Mo	Oct.	11
Shemini Atzeret	Th	Oct.	12	Mo	Oct.	1	Mo	Oct.	21	Sa	Oct.	10	Tu	Sept.	28
Simchat Torah	Fr	Oct.	13	Tu	Oct.	2	Tu	Oct.	22	Su	Oct.	11	We	Sept.	29
Diwali	Th	Oct.	19	We	Nov.	7	Su	Oct.	27	Sa	Nov.	14	Th	Nov.	4
Birth of the B'ab	Fr	Oct.	20	Sa	Oct.	20	Su	Oct.	20	Tu	Oct.	20	We	Oct.	20
Milvian Bridge Day	Sa	Oct.	28	Su	Oct.	28	Mo	Oct.	28	We	Oct.	28	Th	Oct.	28
Reformation Day	Su	Oct.	29	Su	Oct.	28	Tu	Oct.	29	Su	Oct.	25	Su	Oct.	31
All Hallows Eve	Tu	Oct.	31	We	Oct.	31	Th	Oct.	31	Sa	Oct.	31	Su	Oct.	31
NOVEMBER begins on	Wed.			Thu.			Fri.			Sun.			Mon.		
All Saints' Day	We	Nov.	1	Th	Nov.	1	Fr	Nov.	1	Su	Nov.	1	Mo	Nov.	1
All Souls' Day	Th	Nov.	2	Fr	Nov.	2	Sa	Nov.	2	Mo	Nov.	2	Tu	Nov.	2
Daylight Savings Time ends**	Su	Nov.	5	Su	Nov.	4	Su	Nov.	3	Su	Nov.	1	Su	Nov.	7
Remembrance Day	Sa	Nov.	11	Su	Nov.	11	Mo	Nov.	11	We	Nov.	11	Th	Nov.	11
Birth of Baha'u'llah	Su	Nov.	12	Mo	Nov.	12	Tu	Nov.	12	Th	Nov.	12	Fr	Nov.	12
Day of Covenant	Su	Nov.	26	Mo	Nov.	26	Tu	Nov.	26	Th	Nov.	26	Fr.	Nov.	26
St. Andrew's Day	Th	Nov.	30	Fr	Nov.	30	Sa	Nov.	30	Mo	Nov.	30	Tu	Nov.	30
DECEMBER begins on	Fri.			Sat.			Sun.			Tue.			Wed.		
Mawlid an Nabi	Fr	Dec.	1	We	Nov.	21	Su	Nov.	10	Th	Oct.	29	Mo	Oct.	18
First Sunday in Advent	Su	Dec.	3	Su	Dec.	2	Su	Dec.	1	Su	Nov.	29	Su	Nov.	28
Bodhi Day	Fr	Dec.	8	Sa	Dec.	8	Su	Dec	8	Tu	Dec.	8	We	Dec.	8
Feast Day (Our Lady of Guadalupe)	Tu	Dec.	12	We	Dec.	12	Th	Dec.	12	Sa	Dec.	12	Su	Dec.	12
First Day in Hanukkah	We	Dec.	13	Mo	Dec.	3	Mo	Dec.	23	Fr	Dec.	11	Mo	Nov.	29
Christmas Day	Mo	Dec.	25	Tu	Dec.	25	We	Dec.	25	Fr	Dec.	25	Sa	Dec.	25
Kwanzaa begins on	Tu	Dec.	26	We	Dec.	26	Th	Dec.	26	Sa	Dec.	26	Su	Dec.	26
Zarathosht Diso (Death of Prophet Zarathushtra)	Tu	Dec.	26	We	Dec.	26	Th	Dec.	26	Sa	Dec.	26	Su	Dec.	26
Last Day of Year	Sun.			Mon.			Tue.			Thur.			Fri.		

*These are tabular dates; the festival begins at sunset on the day before. According to Islamic custom, the date is actually set by the direct observation of the new crescent moon. **Alberta, British Columbia, Manitoba, New Brunswick, Newfoundland, Northwest Territories, Nova Scotia, Nunavut, Ontario, Prince Edward Island, Quebec and Yukon start Daylight Saving Time on the second Sunday in March and return to standard time on the first Sunday in November. Newfoundland, Nunavut and Yukon start Daylight Saving Time on the first Sunday in April and return to standard time on the last Sunday in October. Saskatchewan doesn't observe Daylight Saving Time. *** Different branches of Hinduism celebrate the new year at different times Jewish holidays begin at sunset the previous evening.

STANDARD HOLIDAYS in Canada include the following: New Year's Day, Good Friday, Victoria Day, Canada Day, Labour Day, Thanksgiving Day, Remembrance Day, Christmas Day, Boxing Day and any other day so proclaimed by the Governor General of Canada, or the Lieutenants Governor of the Provinces. Additionally, Provincial Holidays include: ALBERTA: Alberta Family Day (3rd Monday in February), Heritage Day (1st Monday in August); British Columbia Day (1st Monday in August); MANITOBA: Louis Riel Day (3rd Monday in February), Civic Holiday (1st Monday in August); NEW BRUNSWICK: New Brunswick Day (1st Monday in August); NEWFOUNDLAND: Regatta Day/Civic Holiday (by municipal orders); following celebrated on nearest Monday: St. Patrick's Day (Mar. 17), St. George's Day (Apr. 23), Discovery Day (June 24), Orangemen's Day (July 12); NORTHWEST TERRITORIES: National Aboriginal Day (June 21), Civic Holiday (1st Monday in August); NOVA SCOTIA: Natal Day (1st Monday in August, varies in Halifax); NUNAVUT: Nunavut Day (July 9), 1st Monday in August (1st Monday in August); ONTARIO: Family Day (3rd Monday in February); PRINCE EDWARD ISLAND: Natal Day (by proclamation, usually 1st Monday in August); QUEBEC: National Day (Fête nationale du Québec) (June 24); SASKATCHEWAN: Family Day (3rd Monday in February), Civic Holiday (1st Monday in August); YUKON: Discovery Day (3rd Monday in August)

THE CALENDAR

The calendar is a method of identifying the passage of time and thereby regulating our civil life and religious observances.

Days, months and years are based on astronomical periods. The day is the time it takes the earth to make one revolution on its axis, the month is associated with the period of orbiting of the moon around the earth, while the year has to do with the orbiting of the earth around the sun.

Many religious ideas and observances have been connected with the changes of the moon, and in ancient times the calendar took account of the moon rather than the seasons. From new moon to new moon is 29.530 days, and from one spring equinox to the next is 365.24219 days. Since the two are incommensurable, the modern calendar disregards the moon, except insofar as our months are roughly equal to a lunation.

The Week

The division of the week is found only among Aryan nations and in nations and regions into which they have penetrated. The day is, for convenience, divided into 24 equal parts and is the period of a single rotation of the earth upon its own axis.

A solar or astronomical day commences at midnight, and is divided into two equal portions of 12 hours each - those before noon being termed (A.M.) those after noon (P.M.).

The Chinese week consists of 5 days, which are named after iron, wood, water, feathers and earth; they divide the day into 12 parts of 2 hours each.

The Anglo-Saxons named the days of the week after the following deities: Sunday, the Sun; Monday, the Moon; Tuesday, Tuesco (God of War); Wednesday, Woden (God of Storms); Thursday, Thor (God of Thunder); Friday, Freya (Goddess of Love); Saturday, Saturn (God of Time).

The word *week* is from Wikon (German); it means change, succession.

The Julian Calendar

When Julius Caesar came to power, the Roman Calendar was hopelessly confused. With the advice of the Alexandrian astronomer Sosigenes, Julius Caesar established the Julian Calendar. The length of the year was taken as 365 1/4 days, and in order to account for the 1/4 day, an extra day was added every fourth year. From 45 B.C. each month has had its present number of days. In the old Roman Calendar which was based on the moon an extra month was inserted to straighten out the difference between 12 lunations 354.37 days, and 355 days, which they called a year. This was inserted when necessary after February 23rd. In the Julian Calendar the extra day was added by repeating the sixth day before the Kalends (1st) of March, whence comes our word bissextile for leap year.

No very significant change was made until the reform by Pope Gregory XIII in A.D. 1582.

The Julian Calendar is known as the "Old Style" whereas the calendar as improved by Pope Gregory is known as the "New Style". The difference between the two is now 13 days.

The Gregorian Calendar

Because the Solar Year is 11 minutes, 12 seconds less than the Julian Year of 365 1/4 days, it followed in course of years that the Julian Calendar became inaccurate by several days, and in 1582 this difference amounted to 10 days. Pope Gregory XIII, at the suggestion of Aloysius Lilus, an astronomer of Naples, determined to rectify this, and devised the Calendar now known as the Gregorian Calendar. He dropped or cancelled these 10 days—October 5th being called October 15th—and made centurial years leap years only once in 4 centuries; so that whilst 1700, 1800 and 1900 were to be ordinary years, 2000 would be a leap year. This modification brought the Gregorian year into such close exactitude with the solar year that there is only a difference of 26 seconds, which amounts to a day in 3,323 years. This is the "New Style". The Gregorian Calendar was adopted in Italy, France, Spain, Portugal and Poland in 1582, by most of the German Roman Catholic states, Holland and Flanders in 1583, Hungary in 1587. The adoption in Switzerland began in 1584 and was not completed till 1812. The German and Dutch Protestant states generally, along with Denmark, adopted it in 1700, British dominions in 1752, Sweden in 1753, Japan in 1873, China in 1912, Bulgaria in 1915, Soviet Russia in 1918, Yugoslavia in 1919, Romania and Greece in 1924, Turkey in 1927. The rules for Easter have not, however, been adopted by those oriental churches that are not subject to the Papacy.

The difference between the two "Styles" will remain 13 days until A.D. 2100.

The Jewish Calendar

The Jewish Calendar from the institution of the Mosaic Law downward was a lunar one, consisting of 12 months. The cycles of religious feasts commencing with the Passover depended not only on the month but on the moon; the 14th of the month of Abid or Nisan was coincident with the full moon; and the new moons themselves were the occasions of regular festivals; the commencement of the month was generally determined by observations of the new moon, but 12 lunar months would make but 354 1/2 days, the years would be short 12 days of the true year and it was necessary that an additional month, Veader, be inserted about every third year.

The modern Jewish Calendar is based on fixed rules and not on observation. A common year may contain 353, 354 or 355 days and the leap year 383, 384 or 385 days. The intercalary month always contains 30 days and is inserted before the month Adar, the name and place of which it takes, Adar itself called second Adar or Veadar. Tishri 1 is the Jewish New Year and it cannot be a Sunday, Wednesday or Friday. Tishri 1 is not necessarily the day of new moon but is governed by a mean new moon which is calculated from the value of a mean lunation. It is complicated as compared with the Gregorian Calendar. The intercalary month is introduced seven times in every 19 years.

The identification of the Jewish months with our own cannot be effected with precision on account of the variations existing between the lunar and solar month.

The Muslim Calendar

The Muslim Calendar is called also the calendar of Hegira (i.e. Migration) and is attributed to the primary migration of Mohammed, the Prophet of Islam, on July 16, 622 A.D. from Mecca, his native city in the land of Hejaz, Arabia, to the city of Medina in the north of the same land. In Medina the Prophet and Founder of the Islamic Faith died and was buried.

Each year consists of 12 lunar months and, since no intercalation is made, the months go round the seasons in between 32 and 33 years.

Far Eastern Calendars

The ancient Chinese calendar is a lunar calendar, divided into 12 months of either 29 or 30 days. It is synchronized with the solar calendar by the addition of extra months as required. The four-day Chinese New Year (Hsin Nien) begins at the first new moon over China after the sun enters Aquarius, and may fall between January 21 and February 19. The calendar runs on a 60-year cycle, and each year has both a number and a name: 2016 (Monkey), 2017 (Rooster), 2018 (Dog), 2019 (Pig) and 2020 (Rat). The three-day Vietnamese New Year (Tet) and the three-to-four-day Korean festival Suhl are set by the same new moon. The Japanese calendar uses the Gregorian date of new year, but with a different epoch.

The Hindu Calendar

The Hindu calendar contains both lunar and solar elements, and is therefore complex. Each lunar month is divided into two halves: the dark half (full moon to new moon) and the bright half (new moon to full moon). For some Hindus (primarily South Indian), the lunar month begins on the day following the new moon; for others (primarily North Indian), it begins on the day following the full moon. Likewise, the calculation of the date of New Year varies. There are some holidays which are set by the solar calendar, as well as several which are set by the lunar calendar.

The Indian Calendar

Various religious groups in India have their own calendars (see The Muslim Calendar, and The Hindu Calendar, above). The Indian civil calendar sets the New Year on March 22 in a common year, and on March 21 in a leap year. The years are reckoned according to the native Saka historical era.

The Zoroastrian Calendar

The Zoroastrian calendar is solar, and consists of 12 months of 30 days; five additional days called "gatha" bring the total days in a year to 365. The calculation of the date of the New Year varies among the various Zoroastrian groups.

The Baha'í Calendar

The Baha'í calendar is astronomically fixed, commencing at the vernal equinox. The calendar is solar, and consists of 19 months of 19 days, with the addition of four or five days to bring the total to 365 or 366.

US Civil Calendar 2017

New Year's Day	Sun. Jan. 1
Martin Luther King Day	Mon. Jan. 16
Presidents' Day	Mon. Feb. 20
Memorial Day	Mon. May 29
Independence Day	Tues. July 4
Labor Day	Mon. Sept. 4
Columbus Day	Mon. Oct. 9
Veterans' Day	Sat. Nov. 11
Thanksgiving Day	Thu. Nov. 23

United Kingdom Civil Calendar 2017

St. David (Wales)	Wed. Mar. 1
Commonwealth Day	Mon. Mar. 13
St. Patrick (Ireland)	Fri. Mar. 17
Birthday of Queen Elizabeth II	Fri. Apr. 21
St. George (England)	Sun. Apr. 23
May Day	Mon. May 1
Remembrance Sunday	Sun. Nov. 12
St. Andrew (Scotland)	Thu. Nov. 30

For Canadian holidays and festivals, please see page A-79.

THE SEASONS 2017

Eastern Standard Time
- Spring begins March 20th 6 h 29 m
- Summer begins June 21st 0 h 24 m
- Autumn begins Sept. 22nd 16 h 02 m
- Winter begins Dec. 21st 11 h 28 m

Eastern Standard Time applies in Ontario and Québec. Newfoundland time is 1 1/2 hours later than Eastern Standard time; in the Maritime Provinces, on Atlantic time, time is 1 hour later; in Manitoba and Saskatchewan, on Central time, time is 1 hour earlier; in Alberta and the western half of Saskatchewan, on Mountain time, time is 2 hours earlier; in B.C., on Pacific time, time is 3 hours earlier.

EPOCHS 2017

- Julian Period (year of) 6730.
- January 1, 2017, of the Julian Calendar corresponds to Jan. 14, 2017, of the Gregorian Calendar.
- The year 7526 of the Byzantine era begins Thurs., Sep. 14, 2017.
- The year 5778 of the Hebrew era begins at sunset on Thurs., Sept. 20, 2017.
- The New Year of the Chinese (ding you) era begins on Sat., Jan. 28, 2017.
- The year 2770 of the Roman era (ab urbe condita) begins on Sat., Jan. 14, 2017.
- The year 2766 of the Nabonassar (Babylonian) era begins on Wed., April 19, 2017.
- The year 2677 of the Japanese era begins on Sun., Jan. 1, 2017.
- The year 2329 of the Grecian (Seleucidae) era begins on Thurs., Sep. 14, 2017 (or on Sat., Oct. 14, 2017).
- The year 1939 of the Indian (Saka) era begins on Wed., Mar. 22, 2017.
- The year 1734 of the Diocletian (Coptic) era begins on Mon., Sept. 11, 2017.
- The year 1439 of the Islamic era (Hegira) begins at sunset on Thurs., Sept. 21, 2017.
- The 65th year of the reign of Queen Elizabeth II begins on Mon., Feb. 6, 2017.
- The 150th year of the Dominion of Canada begins Sat., July 1, 2017.
- The 241st year of the Independence of the United States of America begins Tues., July 4, 2017.

STANDARD TIME

Owing to the great breadth of Canada the difference in solar time in various parts of the country is adjusted by the creation of Standard Time Zones, one hour in width, fixed between arbitrary lines running approximately north and south, 15° of longitude apart, the time observed in each zone being an exact, except for Newfoundland, number of hours slow from Greenwich. Example: When it is 8 a.m. by Pacific Time it is 12 noon by Atlantic Time and 4 p.m. at Greenwich.

There are six zones divided as follows, reckoning from Greenwich:
- *Newfoundland Standard Time:* Newfoundland, excluding most of Labrador, 3 1/2 hours slow.
- *Atlantic Standard Time/60th Meridian Time:* most of Labrador, New Brunswick, Nova Scotia, Prince Edward

Island, and those parts of Québec and Northwest Territories east of the 63rd Meridian, 4 hours slow.

- *Eastern Standard Time/75th Meridian Time:* Québec west of the 63rd Meridian and Ontario as far west as the 90th Meridian; Northwest Territories between the 68th and 85th Meridian, 5 hours slow.
- *Central Standard Time/90th Meridian Time:* Ontario west of the 90th Meridian, Manitoba, Saskatchewan and Northwest Territories between the 85th and 102nd Meridian, 6 hours slow.
- *Mountain Standard Time/105th Meridian Time:* Throughout Alberta and in Northwest Territories west of the 102nd Meridian, 7 hours slow.
- *Pacific Standard Time/120th Meridian Time:* Throughout most of British Columbia and in the Yukon, 8 hours slow.

Railways and airways make up their schedules according to Standard Time in winter and Daylight Saving Time in summer. Solar time around the globe varies four minutes with each degree of longitude.

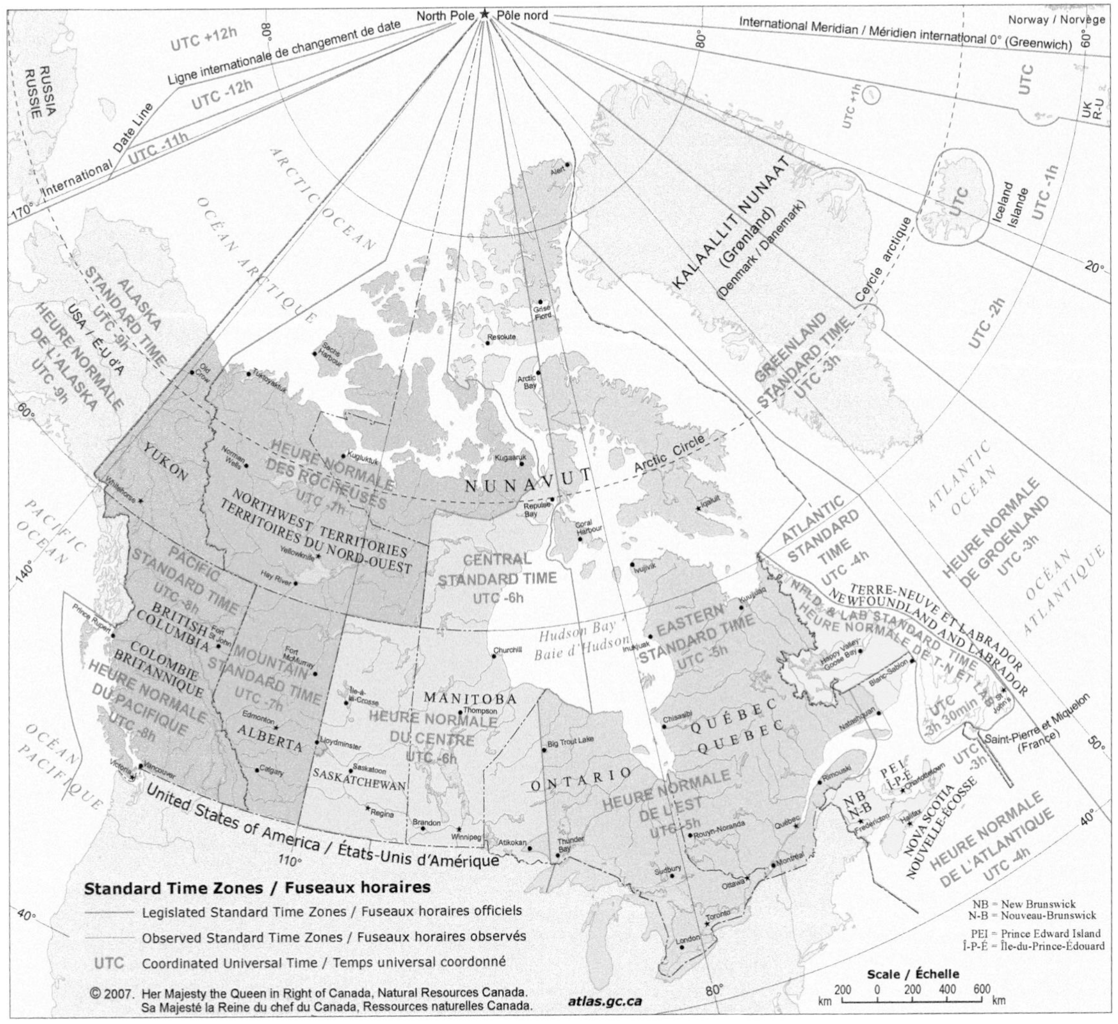

Reproduced with the permission of Natural Resources Canada 2016.

WORLD MAP OF TIME ZONES

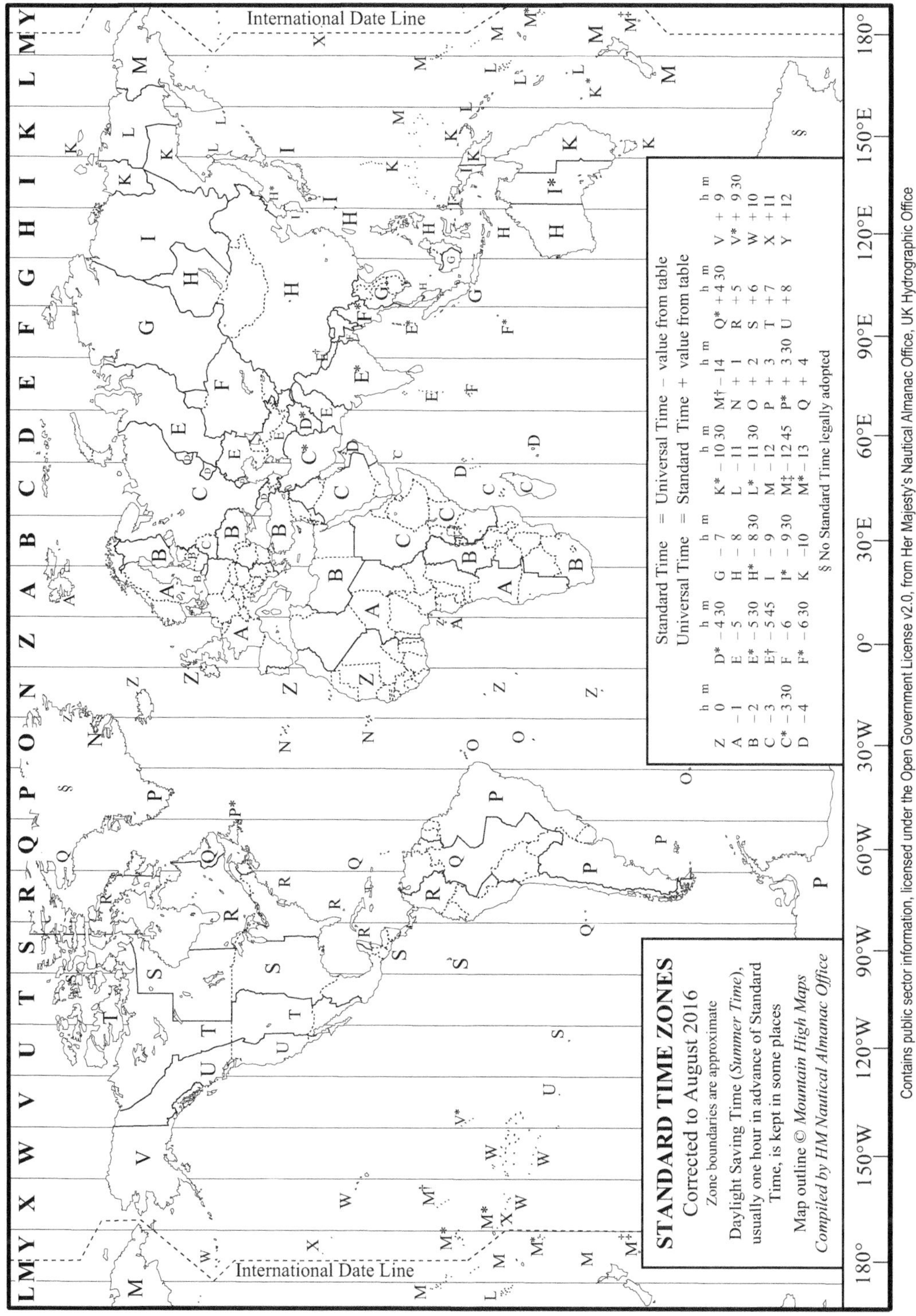

Economics & Finance

Canada's Economy

Since World War II, the growth of Canada's manufacturing, mining and service sectors has transformed the economy of the world's second-largest nation from a largely rural model into one that is primarily industrial and urban. This transformation has been so progressive that Canada has long enjoyed top-level economic status within the G-7, the international grouping of seven leading industrial countries that also includes the United States, the United Kingdom, France, Germany, Italy and Japan.

The 1989 U.S.-Canada Free Trade Agreement and the 1994 North American Free Trade Agreement (which also includes Mexico) spurred a dramatic increase in trade and economic integration of the North American continent. Given its significant natural resources, skilled labor force and modern plants, Canada has benefited tremendously from the free-trade initiatives. Currently, some 75.8 percent of Canadian exports are absorbed by Canada's principal trading partner, making it the largest foreign supplier of energy, including oil, gas, uranium and electric power, to the U.S.

In general, Canada's overall economy is steady. After the recession, the economy returned to growth in the third quarter of 2009. Canada is the only G-7 country to have nearly recouped the loss incurred in the recession. The government succeeded in returning to a budgetary surplus by 2015. Canada posted a 7 percent unemployment rate in August 2016, staying basically consistent with the year prior.

However, like any other allied country from World War II, Canada is now seeing the baby-boom generation pass into retirement, causing the working-age proportion of its population to diminish. As well, there is continuing public debate regarding the rising cost of Canada's world-famous and well-regarded, publicly funded healthcare system.

In the last few decades, Canada's economic model has moved away from being natural-resource dependant to being service-based. While the production of goods remains significant, accounting for a third of the national economy, three out of four citizens are currently employed in service industries. Maintaining the transportation and storage of goods, along with servicing restaurants, shops, entertainment, healthcare, education, defense and government now occupies more Canadians than the actual manufacturing of materials. Canada's gross domestic product, being the balance between consumers' expenditures and income, has shown healthy progress, illustrating a growing demand for big-ticket items including houses, cars, furniture and electronics.

In 2007, the Canadian dollar had reached a 31-year high against the American dollar, achieving one-to-one parity with its neighbour's currency. Later that same year, Bloomberg reported that the dollar was approaching $1.10 U.S., the currency's all-time high since the information-service company began monitoring it in February 1971 (the Bank of Canada only let the currency float in 1970). The Canadian dollar continues to be strong, starying near parity with the U.S., although by July 2015 the dollar sank to $0.76 U.S. — the lowest level since September 2004 — largely due to weaking oil prices. This trend continued into following year, with the dollar hovering around $0.76 U.S. by September 2016.

In May 2012, the Royal Canadian Mint halted production of the one-cent piece, with distribution of the penny ending in February 2013. Canadian consumer outlets no longer return pennies with change.

As a major international oil exporter, Canada has benefited from soaring crude prices, although the recent downturn in oil prices, which began in the summer of 2014, has had a major impact on the oil industry, including the loss of 35,000 energy industry jobs in Alberta alone by October 2015. In September 2015, Goldman Sachs downgraded its oil forecast, predicting that prices could reach as low as $20 per barrel. Oil sands production was projected in 2008 to expand to reach close to 3.4 million barrels per day by 2017. In 2014, the Alberta Energy Regulator reported that oil sands production reached 2.3 million barrels per day.

The country has profited from the export of nickel, copper, aluminum and zinc, commodities that all sit at or near record highs. Though mineral prices declined from 2012 to 2013, minerals and metals continue to be a major contributor to Canada's economy. With commodities and goods-producing industries accounting for approximately 30 percent of Canada's exports, the loonie is finally being viewed around the world as a commodity-based currency and has been bid up accordingly.

Following the recession in 2008, the American housing market saw a decline in lumber prices, hurting British Columbia's forestry industry. However, strong domestic housing starts have boosted the overall production of lumber and other timber products, increasing forestry exports despite U.S. softwood lumber tariffs. The United States is the largest importer of Canadian lumber and, in terms of quantity, accounted for 64.6% of Canada's lumber exports in 2012. US housing starts rose 28.2% in 2012, while housing starts in Canada were back to a level much closer to their peak of the past decade

In May 2003, the discovery of Bovine Spongiform Encephalopathy (BSE), commonly known as mad-cow disease, in one cow from Alberta caused severe harm to Canada's beef-export market. Compounded by the advent of Severe Acute Respiratory Syndrome (SARS) in the late summer of that same year, Canada's growth forecast dampened from 3.4 percent to 2.3 percent, but the current outlook is improving. In September 2007, the U.S. Department of Agriculture (USDA) agreed to expand cattle trade with Canada, additionally urging beef-importing nations to eliminate unnecessary barriers erected after the mad-cow scare. More trade with the United States will help export-dependent Canadian ranchers recover from trade bans. The impact of the stronger Canadian dollar will also result in higher beef-processing costs relative to competitors in the U.S., which could offset more gains.

Canada's commercial ocean fisheries have experienced overall production decline, due in part to the 2003 closure of northern cod fishing grounds. The volume of production has been adversely affected by an average rate of 4 percent a year as a result of dwindling resources and problems caused by over-exploitation of some major species. West Coast over-fishing has led to a reduction in the size of the salmon fleet, as well as extensive government intervention in the fishing industry on both coasts. Meanwhile aquaculture, or fish farming, continues to thrive. In particular, Eastern Canada boasts extensive operations, growing predominantly Atlantic salmon and mussels. Other key species include bay and sea scallops, brook trout, oysters, bay quahogs, sea urchins, arctic char, haddock and bar clams, and significant progress has been made in the development of new species such as halibut, sturgeon, abalone and cod. That said, almost every province and territory in Canada, including the Yukon, runs commercial freshwater aquaculture operations, mostly raising rainbow and brook trout. Ontario and Québec are the dominant producers of freshwater fish in Canada, followed by Saskatchewan, Alberta and New Brunswick. As the Canadian freshwater aquaculture industry is young, it is also ideally poised for growth.

Always historically strong, the Canadian stock market has continued to thrive. The Toronto Stock Exchange (TSX) is the country's largest and the world's eighth largest by market capitalization. In addition, the TSX Group is the international leader in the oil and gas sector, boasting more oil and gas sector listings on the Toronto Stock Exchange and TSX Venture Exchange than any other exchange in the world (in 2016, 253 oil and gas companies were listed, with a quoted market value of over $270 billion). Oil and gas companies continue to raise equity on Canadian exchanges with over $7 billion raised in 2016.

Sourcing from China continues to offer an economically viable solution for Canadian companies. This option to reduce costs while growing wealth in major Chinese cities creates vast new opportunities for Canadian firms, particularly exporters of services. With a small domestic market, the steady expansion of multilateral trade is critical to the structure of the country's economy and the continued prosperity of its citizens. The rapid and ongoing industrialization of China has boosted the world price of Canadian oil, gas, mineral, metal and farm-product exports. Canadian exports to China in 2015 accounted for 3.8 percent of our total, slightly down from 4.4 percent in 2013. However, Canadian sales to Japan have lagged. In 1996, Japan received 4.1 percent of Canada's exports, but only 1.8 percent in 2015.

Since the early 1990s, the focus of Canadian monetary policy on low, stable and predictable inflation has helped to both anchor inflation expectations and reduce the ups and downs in economic activity. Canadians have been able to make spending, saving and investment decisions with greater certainty, knowing that their central bank will hold the line on future inflation and that the economy will be more stable. Low interest rates and greater confidence about the future have encouraged Canadian firms to undertake important restructuring initiatives, stepping up to meet the challenges of sweeping worldwide technological change and intensely competitive global markets.

GROSS DOMESTIC PRODUCT RANKING TABLE

		Economy	$US dollars (millions)
USA	1	United States	17,946,996
CHN	2	China	10,866,444
JPN	3	Japan	4,123,258
DEU	4	Germany	3,355,772
GBR	5	United Kingdom	2,848,755
FRA	6	France	2,421,682
IND	7	India	2,073,543
ITA	8	Italy	1,814,763
BRA	9	Brazil	1,774,725
CAN	10	Canada	1,550,537
KOR	11	Korea, Rep.	1,377,873
AUS	12	Australia	1,339,539
RUS	13	Russian Federation	1,326,015*
ESP	14	Spain	1,199,057
MEX	15	Mexico	1,144,331
IDN	16	Indonesia	861,934
NLD	17	Netherlands	752,547
TUR	18	Turkey	718,221
CHE	19	Switzerland	664,738
SAU	20	Saudi Arabia	646,002

*Based on data from official statistics of Ukraine and Russian Federation; by relying on these data, the World Bank does not intend to make any judgment on the legal or other status of the territories concerned or to prejudice the final determination of the parties' claims.

Source: World Development Indicators, The World Bank. "Gross domestic product ranking table." 2016. http://data.worldbank.org/data-catalog/GDP-ranking-table.

YEARLY AVERAGE OF EXCHANGE RATES

Country Pays	Present Value in CAN Currency						
	2015	2014	2013	2012	2011	2010	2009
United States (dollar)	1.27871080	1.10446640	1.0299148	0.99958008	0.9890692	1.02993904	1.14197729
European (euro)	1.4182	1.4671	1.3681	1.285	1.3767	1.3661	1.5855
China (renminbi/yuan)	0.2034	0.1793	0.1675	0.1584	0.1531	0.1521	0.1672
United Kingdom (British pounds)	1.95398400	1.81903120	1.6112656	1.58399402	1.58607	1.59177012	1.78035578
Switzerland (franc)	1.3286	1.2078	1.1117	1.0662	1.1187	0.9896	1.0505
Hong Kong (dollar)	0.164940	0.142425	0.132779	0.128861	0.127055	0.132572	0.147321
Japan (yen)	0.01056	0.01046	0.01057	0.01254	0.01242	0.01176	0.0122
Australia (dollar)	0.9604	0.9963	0.9966	1.0353	1.0206	0.947	0.8969
New Zealand (dollar)	0.8933	0.9170	0.8448	0.8098	0.7824	0.743	0.7193
Mexico (peso)	0.08063	0.08304	0.08073	0.07602	0.07976	0.08157	0.08448
South Korea (won)	0.001129	0.001049	0.000941	0.000887	0.000893	0.000891	0.000895
Taiwan (new dollar)	0.04025	0.03644	0.0347	0.0338	0.03365	0.03269	0.03453

Note: All Bank of Canada exchange rates are indicative rates only, obtained from averages of transaction prices and price quotes from financial institutions.

Source: Bank of Canada

PRINCIPAL TRADING PARTNERS IN 2015

Imports ($ millions)		Exports ($ millions)	
United States	363,054.4	United States	397,061.7
China	38,910.2	China	21,463.1
Mexico	18,369.2	United Kingdom	16,608.7
Germany	14,970.9	Japan	10,126.1
Japan	10,905.9	Mexico	7,920.9
United Kingdom	8,634.9	India	4,497.0
South Korea	6,157.0	South Korea	4,220.6
Italy	5,424.6	Hong Kong	4,059.8
Switzerland	5,313.0	Germany	3,897.3
France	4,555.9	Netherlands	3,721.9
Other Countries	71,469.1	Other Countries	51,727.7
All Countries	547,765.1	All Countries	525,304.8

Source: Adapted from Statistics Canada, "Imports, exports and trade balance of goods on a balance-of-payments basis, by country or country grouping." http://www.statcan.gc.ca/tables-tableaux/sum-som/l01/cst01/gblec02a-eng.htm. Accessed Aug. 19, 2016.

IMPORTS AND EXPORTS FOR CANADA, 2015

	EXPORTS ($)	IMPORTS ($)
Afghanistan	13,907,807	3,014,773
Albania	36,291,558	8,339,623
Algeria	599,030,294	951,263,476
American Samoa	5,246,383	522,355
Andorra	238,892	274,329
Angola	69,644,886	664,770,927
Anguilla	1,404,698	226,265
Antarctica	5,600,088	222,524
Antigua and Barbuda	10,630,913	465,603
Argentina	310,275,651	1,869,683,316
Armenia	12,702,873	142,761,893
Aruba	9,599,584	54,182,431
Australia	1,890,310,131	1,680,023,851
Austria	328,671,447	1,791,012,223
Azerbaijan	14,271,774	446,749,420
Bahamas	73,507,980	35,716,402
Bahrain	45,698,059	43,361,485
Bangladesh	904,062,220	1,481,201,222
Barbados	71,775,269	11,297,192
Belarus (formerly Byelorussia)	7,379,098	35,300,492
Belgium	3,124,938,854	2,178,468,408
Belize	10,140,398	3,714,542
Benin	34,871,378	18,102
Bermuda	42,102,406	1,799,567
Bhutan	316,754	340,229
Bolivia	28,492,161	191,045,791
Bonaire, Sint Eustatius & Saba	2,086,494	337
Bosnia-Hercegovina	2,544,834	22,336,598
Botswana	708,044,857	1,986,350
Bouvet Island	--	6,379
Brazil	2,250,194,235	3,743,000,240
British Indian Ocean Territories	18,617	22,085
British Virgin Islands	12,787,976	1,520,375
Brunei Darussalam	2,907,678	4,385,305
Bulgaria	86,339,693	128,870,456
Burkina Faso	35,972,983	36,376,487
Burundi	478,997	518,782
Cambodia (Kampuchea)	26,375,087	1,030,816,085
Cameroon	72,912,888	7,020,158
Cape Verde	2,194,598	91,034
Cayman Islands	9,817,068	593,629
Central African Republic	1,657,360	373,468
Chad	10,318,275	203,880
Chile	790,308,350	1,853,167,089
China	20,221,443,377	65,649,625,851
Christmas Island	1,227,929	26,769
Cocos (Keeling) Islands	25,310	28,780
Colombia	782,805,567	828,980,185
Comoros	583,864	100,932
Congo (formerly Brazzaville)	28,234,722	18,159,052
Congo (formerly Zaire)	27,107,812	71,203,187
Cook Islands	638,752	112,259
Costa Rica	162,703,862	503,227,514
Côte-d'Ivoire	67,875,478	303,650,281
Croatia	51,364,108	53,608,071
Cuba	494,974,232	520,149,832
Curacao	16,186,426	5,332,529
Cyprus	8,024,656	3,911,591
Czech Republic	192,002,330	583,231,259
Denmark	341,633,980	1,019,265,606
Djibouti	1,748,671	11,868
Dominica	4,888,790	727,317
Dominican Republic	177,225,788	1,021,849,689
East Timor	100,127	2,848,500
Ecuador	328,316,814	316,987,810
Egypt	428,007,059	741,173,120
El Salvador	59,829,156	108,762,061
Equatorial Guinea	3,947,238	20,739
Eritrea	449,624	19,416,734
Estonia	23,007,388	107,497,012
Ethiopia	33,102,518	24,438,455
Faeroe Islands	590,862	13,770,801
Falkland Islands	31,350	886,186
Fiji	24,934,363	6,118,374
Finland	640,307,241	971,011,281
France (incl. Monaco, French Antilles)	3,136,326,854	6,804,284,159
French Polynesia	11,150,068	1,146,525
French Southern Territories	42,194	1,100
Gabon	32,089,600	17,953,867
Gambia	841,819	158,459
Georgia	15,474,272	100,661,193
Germany	3,612,491,190	17,341,053,415
Ghana	215,514,582	49,798,410
Gibraltar	314,057	18,876
Greece	113,198,135	228,571,591
Greenland	22,221,079	552,333
Grenada	6,116,267	2,210,991
Guam	2,004,500	256,170
Guatemala	121,001,262	626,093,028
Guinea	14,331,349	58,617,562
Guinea-Bissau	32,180	3,167
Guyana	25,640,902	271,554,930
Haiti	55,337,906	38,489,634
Heard and McDonald Island	433,389	19,614
High Seas	--	--
Honduras	39,993,760	336,851,072
Hong Kong	3,913,904,328	323,165,097
Hungary	94,468,498	611,555,485
Iceland	88,125,907	98,119,672
India	4,321,240,180	3,935,333,343
Indonesia	1,815,455,325	1,671,557,508
Iran	99,024,429	26,961,377
Iraq	180,226,343	252,539
Ireland	601,462,529	1,678,021,496
Israel	342,222,301	1,208,240,821
Italy (incl. Vatican City State)	2,276,903,508	7,371,786,069
Jamaica	114,176,303	240,484,042
Japan	9,772,033,354	14,775,893,698
Jordan	89,743,709	77,180,154
Kazakhstan	117,160,827	522,545,938
Kenya	93,052,368	30,825,521
Kiribati	99,014	30,710
Korea, North	--	184,096
Korea, South	4,027,326,078	7,876,616,980
Kuwait	176,632,638	15,641,114
Kyrgyzstan	14,789,012	248,794
Laos	5,795,868	23,753,410
Latvia	29,337,377	43,565,975
Lebanon	114,125,034	28,023,969
Lesotho	1,451,111	7,044,842
Liberia	10,592,277	40,600,503
Libya	28,994,501	14,221,220
Lithuania	51,866,689	235,319,850
Luxembourg	205,409,661	184,553,757
Macau (Macao)	58,457,824	6,048,944
Macedonia	5,758,772	13,016,370
Madagascar	23,281,618	79,893,260
Malawi	15,373,641	3,104,323
Malaysia	790,051,150	2,637,997,027
Maldives	19,184,204	1,092,635
Mali	20,581,959	884,630
Malta	949,231,853	56,071,139
Mauritania	7,112,446	223,387
Mauritius	9,446,628	24,291,577
Mexico	6,593,781,721	31,196,973,429
Moldova	1,656,854	9,929,624
Mongolia	8,752,568	2,809,552
Montenegro	1,857,409	677,390
Montserrat	247,862	233,245
Morocco	306,247,919	410,878,842
Mozambique	44,434,536	905,705
Myanmar (Burma)	23,796,475	27,473,141
Namibia	7,813,090	127,806,050
Nauru	23,905	351,485
Nepal	22,556,602	14,235,226
Netherlands	3,555,601,983	3,434,140,702
Netherlands Antilles	--	--
New Caledonia	60,607,776	654,559
New Zealand	474,848,519	682,656,035
Nicaragua	44,063,749	139,283,225
Niger	5,892,385	1,873,014
Nigeria	1,873,014	1,041,297,780
Niue	94,512	225,356
Norfolk Island	352,102	37,096
Norway	1,868,437,461	1,697,833,574
Oman (formerly Muscat and Oman)	153,951,384	51,722,689
Pakistan	693,117,778	350,973,088
Panama	138,281,523	10,988,129
Papua New Guinea	31,323,858	3,231,060
Paraguay	20,467,666	12,708,467
Peru	858,284,266	3,260,128,260
Philippines	751,425,165	1,419,187,779
Pitcairn Island	--	19,432
Poland	445,393,611	1,762,883,760
Portugal	186,253,586	619,296,362
Qatar	177,770,965	49,374,584
Re-Imports (Canada)	--	3,962,148,517
Romania	85,439,657	269,584,115
Russia	600,415,824	1,038,166,685
Rwanda	31,420,394	1,150,961
Saint Helena	65,212	163,025
Saint Kitts and Nevis	7,228,331	4,068,098
Saint Lucia	11,264,513	242,237
Saint Pierre-Miquelon	19,860,578	2,170,173
Saint Vincent and the Grenadines	12,122,406	109,689
Samoa (Western)	369,191	47,067
Sao Tomé-Principe	--	20,328
Saudi Arabia	1,195,574,265	1,995,112,831
Senegal	34,178,767	8,389,829
Serbia	17,076,342	78,867,030
Seychelles	10,576,006	4,663,773
Sierra Leone	9,069,609	2,825,515
Singapore	1,506,816,947	954,005,283
Sint Maarten	8,486,371	24,310
Slovakia	23,493,312	384,803,459
Slovenia	26,245,300	143,708,823
Solomon Islands	1,432,554	270,015
Somalia	1,411,009	313,203
South Africa	621,155,725	880,127,107
South Sudan	2,520,637	421
Spain	1,130,714,765	2,346,792,248
Sri Lanka	315,625,719	333,837,513
Sudan	118,454,310	30,781,096
Suriname	84,646,886	123,567,956
Swaziland	2,960,277	1,891,373
Sweden	480,945,885	1,865,454,228
Switzerland	1,186,211,359	4,527,771,899
Syria	3,471,618	917,755
Taiwan	1,461,532,832	5,457,482,180
Tajikistan	14,725,143	41,740
Tanzania	51,566,040	12,397,548
Thailand	889,777,058	3,112,891,341
Togo	18,456,956	24,600,794
Tonga	1,064,835	9,777
Trinidad and Tobago	305,641,197	343,210,498
Tunisia	127,109,388	85,245,767
Turkey	1,126,689,216	1,293,618,447
Turkmenistan	6,711,585	2,073,018
Turks and Caicos Islands	4,057,272	842,951
U.S. Minor Outlying Islands	17,643,304	4,865,482
Uganda	27,283,447	9,395,314
Ukraine	210,490,530	67,546,371
United Arab Emirates	2,025,288,512	141,447,634
United Kingdom	15,951,684,203	9,195,347,572
United States	402,173,104,887	285,199,792,741
Uruguay	82,509,389	92,855,612
Uzbekistan	13,995,763	375,713
Vanuatu (New Hebrides)	673,614	40,074
Venezuela	634,806,453	107,216,575
Vietnam	656,603,513	4,089,027,391
Wallis and Futuna Islands	43,178	32,045
Western Sahara	--	36,559
Yemen	6,522,989	291,702
Zambia (Zambi)	41,483,027	2,939,355
Zimbabwe	5,539,840	2,243,478
TOTAL	524,048,602,092	535,604,499,072

Data Source: Statistics Canada & US Census Bureau

Source: "Trade Data Online", retrieved on: http://www.ic.gc.ca. Last accessed Aug. 22, 2016. Trade data is subject to revision. Reproduced with the permission of the Minister of Innovation, Science & Economic Development Canada, 2016.

RETAIL TRADE, TOTAL SALES AND E-COMMERCE SALES, BY NORTH AMERICAN INDUSTRY CLASSIFICATION SYSTEM (NAICS)

North American Industry Classification System (NAICS)	Sales	2011	2012
Retail trade [44-45]	Total sales (x 1,000)	488,269,411	502,646,254
	E-commerce sales (x 1,000)	6,629,585	7,707,540
	E-commerce as percentage of total sales (percent)	1.4	1.5
	Distribution of E-commerce (percent)	100	100
Motor vehicle and parts dealers [441]	Total sales (x 1,000)	104,635,557	109,094,842
	E-commerce sales (x 1,000)	2,422,757	2,681,411
	E-commerce as percentage of total sales (percent)	2.3	2.5
	Distribution of E-commerce (percent)	36.5	34.8
Furniture and home furnishings stores [442]	Total sales (x 1,000)	15,507,172	15,587,914
	E-commerce sales (x 1,000)	86,416	97,951
	E-commerce as percentage of total sales (percent)	x	0.6
	Distribution of E-commerce (percent)	1.3	1.3
Electronics and appliance stores [443]	Total sales (x 1,000)	16,517,330	15,874,013
	E-commerce sales (x 1,000)	472,048	543,078
	E-commerce as percentage of total sales (percent)	2.9	3.4
	Distribution of E-commerce (percent)	7.1	7
Building material and garden equipment and supplies dealers [444]	Total sales (x 1,000)	28,298,806	29,062,857
	E-commerce sales (x 1,000)	101,663	103,014
	E-commerce as percentage of total sales (percent)	0.4	0.4
	Distribution of E-commerce (percent)	1.5	x
Food and beverage stores [445]	Total sales (x 1,000)	107,062,050	109,075,969
	E-commerce sales (x 1,000)	x	x
	E-commerce as percentage of total sales (percent)	x	x
	Distribution of E-commerce (percent)	x	x
Health and personal care stores [446]	Total sales (x 1,000)	35,727,104	37,068,254
	E-commerce sales (x 1,000)	48,092	64,110
	E-commerce as percentage of total sales (percent)	0.1	0.2
	Distribution of E-commerce (percent)	0.7	0.8
Gasoline stations [447]	Total sales (x 1,000)	57,932,738	60,237,754
	E-commerce sales (x 1,000)	x	x
	E-commerce as percentage of total sales (percent)	x	x
	Distribution of E-commerce (percent)	x	x
Clothing and clothing accessories stores [448]	Total sales (x 1,000)	26,597,314	27,610,682
	E-commerce sales (x 1,000)	267,998	341,354
	E-commerce as percentage of total sales (percent)	1	1.2
	Distribution of E-commerce (percent)	4	4.4
Sporting goods, hobby, book and music stores [451]	Total sales (x 1,000)	11,241,457	11,231,237
	E-commerce sales (x 1,000)	178,830	196,608
	E-commerce as percentage of total sales (percent)	1.6	1.8
	Distribution of E-commerce (percent)	2.7	2.6
General merchandise stores [452]	Total sales (x 1,000)	56,831,685	58,657,513
	E-commerce sales (x 1,000)	55,214	97,097
	E-commerce as percentage of total sales (percent)	0.1	0.2
	Distribution of E-commerce (percent)	0.8	1.3
Miscellaneous store retailers [453]	Total sales (x 1,000)	11,957,979	12,269,576
	E-commerce sales (x 1,000)	256,323	270,266
	E-commerce as percentage of total sales (percent)	2.1	2.2
	Distribution of E-commerce (percent)	3.9	3.5
Non-store retailers [454]	Total sales (x 1,000)	15,960,219	16,875,643
	E-commerce sales (x 1,000)	2,657,801	3,192,441

	E-commerce as percentage of total sales (percent)	16.7	18.9
	Distribution of E-commerce (percent)	40.1	41.4
Electronic shopping and mail-order houses [45411]	Total sales (x 1,000)	4,418,866	4,814,150
	E-commerce sales (x 1,000)	2,556,888	3,131,871
	E-commerce as percentage of total sales (percent)	57.9	65.1
	Distribution of E-commerce (percent)	38.6	40.6

Symbol legend:
X Suppressed to meet the confidentiality requirements of the Statistics Act

Footnotes:
1. The estimates are based on data from the 2011 Annual Retail Trade Survey and on the 2007 North American Industry Classification System (NAICS).
2. Figures may not add up to total due to rounding.

Source: Statistics Canada. *Table 080-0026 - Retail trade, total sales and e-commerce sales, by North American Industry Classification System (NAICS), annual (dollars unless otherwise noted),* CANSIM (database). (accessed: 2016-08-23)

SUPPLY AND DISPOSITION OF REFINED PETROLEUM PRODUCTS
MONTHLY (CUBIC METRES)

Supply and disposition	2016				
	January	February	March	April	May
Net production [34]	9,723,834	8,620,435	9,556,649	9,200,440	8,181,453
Opening Inventory	8,280,459	8,305,590	8,013,270	8,112,916	7,768,076
Closing Inventory	8,305,590	8,031,917	8,113,023	7,777,438	6,708,781
Imports	1,224,976	990,979	808,179	926,106	1,245,998
Exports	2,659,459	2,164,932	2,303,664	2,166,850	2,009,845
Inter-provincial transfers in	2,129,986	2,028,825	2,102,816	1,835,857	1,863,168
Inter-provincial transfers out	2,129,986	2,028,825	2,102,816	1,835,857	1,863,168
Domestic sales[30]	8,630,652	8,032,064	8,438,805	8,301,074	8,911,315

Total refined petroleum products

Notes:
30. Sales by reporting companies, exclusive of exports and sales to other reporting companies, and adjusted for exports and imports by non-reporting companies.
34. Refinery production less inter-product transfers, less the portion of inter-product transfers transferred to petro-chemical feedstocks.

Source: Statistics Canada. *Table 134-0004 - Supply and disposition of refined petroleum products, monthly (cubic metres),* CANSIM (database). (accessed: 2016-09-01)

MANUFACTURING SALES BY SUBSECTOR

ANNUAL ($ MILLIONS)

North American Industry Classification System (NAICS)	2011	2012	2013	2014	2015
Manufacturing [31-33]	568,282.2	585,335.7	587,886.3	619,084.8	609,499.5
Food manufacturing [311]	84,377.1	84,511	86,484.4	92,973.1	95,697.8
Beverage and tobacco product manufacturing [312]	11,095.8	11,623.2	11,694.3	11,991.1	12,456.3
Textile mills [313]	1,588.7	1,502.9	1,361	1,449.5	1,550.9
Textile product mills [314]	1,658.6	1,639.9	1,497.4	1,671.6	1,616.6
Clothing manufacturing [315]	2,818.3	2,642.8	2,366	2,558.7	2,389.8
Leather and allied product manufacturing [316]	381.4	359.5	406.7	420.1	440.6
Paper manufacturing [322]	25,792.2	24,047.5	23,640.1	25,057.7	26,867.9
Printing and related support activities [323]	8,836.2	8,923.9	9,076.7	8,911.3	9,005.6
Petroleum and coal product manufacturing [324]	79,169.7	85,111.2	82,519	83,104.3	59,335.7
Chemical manufacturing [325]	46,428.9	45,074.4	47,622.2	49,781.8	48,566.8
Plastics and rubber products manufacturing [326]	23,879.3	24,229.1	25,225	26,463.4	27,953
Wood product manufacturing [321]	18,300.7	20,095.7	23,762.7	24,990	26,011.8
Non-metallic mineral product manufacturing [327]	12,817.7	12,728.4	12,226.2	13,090.3	12,941.3
Primary metal manufacturing [331]	47,958.9	45,949.9	43,527.8	47,921.6	44,738.6
Fabricated metal product manufacturing [332]	32,521.4	34,749.3	33,474.5	34,581.4	34,448.6
Machinery manufacturing [333]	33,151.8	34,792.5	34,932.4	35,703.9	34,742.5
Computer and electronic product manufacturing [334]	15,173	13,487.1	12,410.2	12,825.3	13,688
Electrical equipment, appliance and component manufacturing [335]	9,732.4	10,024.8	10,235.1	10,096	9,962.7
Transportation equipment manufacturing [336]	91,211.2	103,226.5	102,940	112,936.2	122,964.9
Furniture and related product manufacturing [337]	10,062.9	10,040.3	10,593.3	11,049.6	11,620.5
Miscellaneous manufacturing [339]	11,326.1	10,575.7	11,872.6	11,507.8	12,497.5

Note: North American Industry Classification System (NAICS).
Source: Statistics Canada, CANSIM, table 304-0014. Statistics Canada. "Manufacturing sales, by subsector." Last modified Aug. 16, 2016. http://www.statcan.gc.ca/tables-tableaux/sum-som/l01/cst01/manuf11-eng.htm. Accessed Aug. 26, 2016.

GROWTH STATISTICS: FINANCIAL, CONSOLIDATED GOVERNMENT
QUARTERLY (DOLLARS X 1,000,000)

		Revenue	Total expenditure	Net worth	Net financial worth
2001	Q1	118,671	120,807	-237,719	-738,319
	Q2	124,744	114,478	-260,603	-710,619
	Q3	116,944	115,207	-328,007	-724,972
	Q4	116,693	119,940	-322,456	-730,708
2002	Q1	114,647	124,393	-300,001	-728,618
	Q2	120,717	116,262	-306,924	-739,325
	Q3	120,994	118,850	-325,058	-762,801
	Q4	123,614	122,674	-301,255	-763,801
2003	Q1	123,222	130,307	-268,261	-761,668
	Q2	124,358	123,401	-307,060	-773,053
	Q3	128,231	124,516	-278,800	-746,628
	Q4	128,566	127,134	-271,982	-739,964
2004	Q1	129,416	134,779	-259,452	-752,346
	Q2	132,592	127,505	-219,447	-731,919
	Q3	136,096	128,427	-194,093	-730,315
	Q4	135,618	132,023	-200,903	-726,138
2005	Q1	138,495	138,464	-188,418	-719,138
	Q2	142,186	134,541	-179,648	-726,077
	Q3	143,799	135,414	-116,453	-704,363
	Q4	145,993	139,186	-71,597	-695,322
2006	Q1	148,559	147,681	-64,819	-682,487
	Q2	151,566	141,569	-32,853	-669,469
	Q3	151,916	142,655	-1,030	-669,469
	Q4	154,768	146,694	-44,959	-658,916
2007	Q1	155,883	152,225	-6,846	-646,859
	Q2	162,444	149,513	31,804	-617,588
	Q3	159,565	151,447	87,618	-617,967
	Q4	159,399	154,515	63,073	-635,277
2008	Q1	166,485	164,757	98,937	-649,539
	Q2	162,882	157,700	239,669	-649,539
	Q3	162,340	155,805	315,941	-657,013
	Q4	154,890	164,262	-15,563	-692,835
2009	Q1	159,198	171,549	-102,013	-715,786
	Q2	152,711	166,079	-38,496	-710,504
	Q3	153,076	169,419	19,915	-735,748
	Q4	157,314	175,238	-6,834	-756,738
2010	Q1	162,156	181,941	34,673	-762,520
	Q2	161,925	174,149	-14,647	-792,571
	Q3	155,984	178,215	-6,000	-813,489
	Q4	159,489	183,161	-22,296	-830,822
2011	Q1	169,979	189,953	24,675	-827,064
	Q2	171,807	180,322	11,703	-864,952
	Q3	167,902	182,348	-32,944	-917,423
	Q4	170,239	184,948	-39,882	-937,795
2012	Q1	179,062	192,055	-91,926	-936,371
	Q2	176,278	182,114	-139,908	-977,968
	Q3	172,810	184,949	-59,377	-961,958
	Q4	174,557	188,686	-150,378	-977,748
2013	Q1	182,465	195,579	-87,504	-958,348
	Q2	182,036	185,787	-94,503	-939,019
	Q3	181,603	189,322	8,627	-926,226
	Q4	182,711	192,634	-51,033	-921,453
2014	Q1	195,303	194,717	24,966	-920,717
	Q2	189,750	184,579	-8,036	-929,698
	Q3	187,580	192,915	83,074	-925,354
	Q4	187,215	196,502	-61,302	-954,263
2015	Q1	197,114	201,161	-129,488	-991,211
	Q2	194,859	195,544	23,841	-946,088
	Q3	189,590	201,249	-102,248	-953,316
	Q4	194,558	203,295	-138,093	-966,886
2016	Q1	199,635	207,787	-159,419	-976,690

Consolidated Government includes federal government, provincial and territorial government, local government, Canada Pension Plan (CPP) and Quebec Pension Plan (QPP).

Source: Statistics Canada. *Table 385-0032 - Government finance statistics, statement of government operations and balance sheet, quarterly (dollars)*, CANSIM (database). (accessed: 2016-08-26)

GROWTH STATISTICS: FINANCIAL BALANCE OF INTERNATIONAL PAYMENTS

$ MILLIONS

Year	Canadian Direct Investment Abroad (All Countries, $000,000)							Foreign Direct Investment in Canada (All Countries, $000,000)						
	All Industries	Wood and paper	Energy and metallic minerals	Machinery and Transportation Equipment	Finance and Insurance	Services and Retailing	Other Industries	All Industries	Wood and paper	Energy and metallic minerals	Machinery and Transportation Equipment	Finance and Insurance	Services and Retailing	Other Industries
1995	-15,732	-1,171	-5,669	-431	-817	-1,321	-6,322	12,703	647	-441	1,802	1,086	2,032	7,577
1996	-17,858	782	-9,125	-1,230	-3,813	-2,317	-2,155	13,137	15	3,249	729	2,443	2,659	4,040
1997	-31,937	-1,130	-8,728	-2,046	-8,320	-3,859	-7,853	15,958	282	3,566	2,304	4,054	1,606	4,146
1998	-50,957	-440	-4,915	-2,988	-13,287	-7,718	-21,610	33,828	2,847	9,104	2,185	5,931	2,796	10,965
1999	-25,625	-258	-5,964	-1,999	-11,809	-1,237	-4,357	36,762	2,280	4,362	1,447	12,633	3,033	13,008
2000	-66,352	82	-9,982	-12,532	-7,278	-3,033	-33,610	99,198	4,286	13,492	13,717	4,122	1,804	61,776
2001	-55,800	-2,469	-10,740	-5,161	-27,838	-3,566	-6,027	42,844	442	23,940	4,640	3,598	529	9,694
2002	-42,015	-555	-8,665	-3,913	-26,669	-1,592	-621	34,769	889	16,207	6,131	1,599	3,722	6,220
2003	-32,118	-647	-14,379	-2,670	-8,764	-971	-4,686	10,483	-45	2,782	-1,227	4,229	958	3,785
2004	-56,395	1,330	-16,118	-5,473	-24,627	-8,672	-2,835	-579	-1,010	3,392	-2,470	-6,212	1,569	4,151
2005	-33,370	-352	-11,133	234	-23,377	-1,532	2,789	31,132	62	22,157	-4,297	4,734	3,538	4,938
2006	-52,423	-2,498	-6,745	667	-34,098	-5,643	-4,104	68,395	850	45,166	5,477	-4,046	4,258	16,690
2007	-62,003	-1,177	-16,306	-120	-33,633	-1,198	-9,570	123,148	3,241	69,236	7,060	22,758	7,985	12,869
2008	-85,143	-437	-21,263	1,064	-53,212	-2,382	-8,913	61,010	-1,392	38,120	-1,619	6,938	4,995	13,969
2009	-47,627	-692	-3,815	-477	-29,176	-1,100	-12,368	24,469	-473	11,464	1,523	3,459	2,861	5,634
2010	-39,749	-2,852	-7,273	311	-26,891	-2,848	-196	24,119	662	11,627	255	5,217	2,875	3,483
2011	-49,050	-869	-8,027	-742	-26,466	-5,489	-7,457	40,503	289	22,133	4,305	2,104	1,984	9,688

Source: Statistics Canada. Table 376-0014 - Balance of international payments, flows of Canadian direct investment abroad and foreign direct investment in Canada, by industry and type of transactions, annual (dollars), (accessed: 2016-08-31).

GROWTH STATISTICS: MAJOR CANADIAN AIRLINES

ANNUAL SUM (DATA IN THOUSANDS)

	Passengers	Passenger-kilometres	Kilograms of goods	Goods tonne-kilometres (tonne-kilometres)	Hours flown	Turbo fuel consumed (litres)
1996	23,164	57,015,549	405,975	1,882,803	785	3,349,814
1997	24,363	62,479,410	449,828	2,058,953	826	3,631,436
1998	24,571	64,426,065	431,150	2,340,594	843	3,855,178
1999	24,047	65,711,146	451,801	2,016,503	904	3,571,445
2000	24,480	68,516,738	407,876	1,934,683	921	3,871,274
2001	23,414	67,018,521	361,834	1,725,325	856	3,678,966
2002	23,430	69,254,337	355,493	1,800,415	806	3,453,486
2003	20,042	59,508,960	298,990	1,419,988	703	2,999,282
2004	28,159	76,122,855	297,246	1,478,716	926	3,660,671
2005	32,091	83,909,440	268,947	1,378,548	981	3,855,953
2006	33,439	88,323,198	265,470	1,425,103	1,010	3,980,077
2007	35,568	93,363,940	242,511	1,301,260	1,078	4,137,528
2008	37,494	96,677,633	218,944	1,260,823	1,119	4,178,965
2009	36,244	93,336,414	195,068	1,169,416	1,077	3,893,014
2010	38,837	102,682,704	253,098	1,510,325	1,155	4,328,366
2011	40,318	107,976,582	249,575	1,519,268	1,215	4,540,715
2012	42,184	112,077,394	254,972	1,593,304	1,239	4,647,021
2013	42,685	114,140,255	251,229	1,594,734	1,243	4,699,769
2014	45,144	123,149,380	274,846	1,731,107	1,274	4,907,146
2015	68,122	171,276,306	..	..	1,985	6,485,495

.. : data no longer published.

Notes:

1. As of January 2004, major airline data include both WestJet and Air Canada.
2. As of April 2014, Air Canada data include Air Canada rouge.
3. As of January 2015, the major airlines include all Canadian Level I air carriers, which are comprised of Air Canada (including Air Canada rouge), Air Transat, Jazz, Porter, Sunwing and WestJet.

Source: Statistics Canada. *Table 401-0001 - Operating and financial statistics of major Canadian airlines, annual,* CANSIM (database). (accessed: 2016-08-31)

GROWTH STATISTICS: AGRICULTURE
FARM CASH RECEIPTS, ANNUAL (% CHANGE)

	2011	2012	2013	2014	2015
	% change				
Total farm cash receipts	**12**	**8.3**	**2.7**	**4.8**	**2.7**
Total crops	**15.8**	**14.2**	**5.1**	**-3**	**5.2**
Wheat, excluding durum[1]	42.5	20.1	22.5	-8.1	5.1
Wheat, excluding durum, marketing board payments[1]	-1.3	-2.9	-60.1	-86.2	-97
Durum wheat[1]	32.6	63.9	36	8.2	-2.4
Durum wheat, marketing board payments[1]	-24.2	12.9	24.5	-50.7	-86.2
Oats	32.5	-1.3	1.1	-14	11.4
Barley[1]	23.1	24.2	38.5	-27.2	-10.8
Barley, Canada wheat board payments[1]	-17.6	-22.2	1.6	-81.1	-81.1
Deferments	-70.7	-18.1	5.4	19.9	-14.9
Liquidations	-9.1	70.7	16.4	-7.1	-18.1
Flaxseed	-27.7	34.1	23.2	14.3	-9.2
Canola	38.2	7.3	-11	0.6	8.5
Soybeans	1.4	48.9	6.9	-7.7	4.3
Corn	33.5	17.7	-4.8	-15.8	-5.7
Potatoes	5.4	-2.1	2.5	1.7	-1.1
Greenhouse vegetables	4.8	-3.4	18.6	-0.9	2.9
Field vegetables	3.2	6.7	9.3	6.2	6.5
Total tree fruits[2]	-0.1	9.7	17.8	1.1	-2.4
Apples[2]	-4.3	6.9	21.4	2.2	-6.8
Total small fruits[3]	18.7	11.8	-8.1	12.8	1.3
Blueberries[3]	37.7	18.8	-22.7	41.6	-0.8
Strawberries[3]	5.2	-1.1	-1.9	3.6	14.4
Grapes[3]	10.2	13	6.7	-24.8	4.5
Total floriculture, nursery and sod	-1.4	-0.1	1.6	2.2	4.2
Floriculture	-2.5	0.1	5	2.7	3.6
Nursery	0.3	-3.3	-4.2	1.7	4.4
Sod	-0.3	11.2	-1.3	0.2	7.4
Tobacco	6	1	7.1	5.1	-23.4
Mustard seed	-13.6	4.5	48.9	-16.2	2.3
Lentils	-8.1	-7	37.2	26.2	110.1
Canary seed	31.5	-28.7	16.9	0.9	-25.1
Dry beans	-19.9	45.1	-10.4	16.2	3.3
Dry peas	44.7	2.7	8.5	-11.4	5
Chick peas	0.7	-31	4	-30.4	102.5
Forage and grass seed	17.8	13.4	-2.9	-11.7	51.2
Hay and clover	-10.4	10.3	12.7	11.1	17.4
Maple products	16.6	-10.2	34.3	-6.9	-5.5

Forest products	-17.8	3	6.1	1.7	2.2
Ginseng	-38.1	112.1	18.6	40.3	-0.2
Christmas trees	-7	-2.3	6.3	16.6	21.6
Miscellaneous crops[4]	7.9	13	7.1	-8.7	-9
Total livestock	**7.6**	**2.7**	**3.2**	**19.3**	**-0.2**
Cattle and Calves	1.9	3.9	4.5	44.4	7
Hogs	16.9	-2.2	5.5	25.2	-17
Sheep and Lambs	11.5	-12.1	-13.7	32.4	16.4
Dairy products	5.3	1.8	-0.4	3.1	-0.8
Hens and chicken	14.9	5	3.6	-3	0.7
Turkeys	9.8	6.9	5	-1.9	2
Total eggs	11.4	9.1	5.7	0.5	5.5
Honey	7.6	13	7.5	9.1	13.8
Furs	8.9	39.1	14.1	-53.1	40.6
Hatcheries (chicks and poults)	8	6.6	2	5.8	3.7
Miscellaneous livestock[5]	3.5	3.1	3.7	21.8	0.2
Total payments	**10.9**	**-2.1**	**-21.1**	**-21.8**	**1.2**
Crop insurance	13.2	-7.2	-12.2	-27.2	42.4
AgriInvest	29.4	6.5	-7.4	-23.3	-16.2
AgriStability	-11.2	-2	-28.7	-16.3	-31.7
Private hail insurance	4.4	74.3	-35.1	45.9	-31.8
Provincial stabilization payments	118.4	9.8	-33.5	-47.6	-31.1
Net income stabilization account payments	-14.1	-11.9	-15.9	..	..
Other payments[6]	-15.1	-39.6	-27.6	-20.9	16.8

.. : not available for a specific reference period.

Note: Figures may not add to totals because of rounding.

1. Beginning with the 2012/2013 crop year, the former Canadian Wheat Board (CWB) payments to producers are included in the respective crop receipts.
2. The category total tree fruits comprises receipts from the sale of numerous tree fruits. Apples is one of the components of total tree fruits.
3. The category total small fruits comprises receipts from the sale of numerous small fruits. Blueberries, strawberries and grapes are the major sub-components of total small fruits.
4. Miscellaneous crops includes all crops not elsewhere specified.
5. Miscellaneous livestock includes all livestock not elsewhere specified.
6. Generally, these are programs to deal with unusual climatic and/or economic conditions in the agriculture sector.

Source: Statistics Canada, CANSIM, table 002-0001 and Catalogue no. 21-011-X. Last modified: 2016-05-25.

CONSUMER PRICE INDEX, CANADA
MONTHLY, 2002=100

	2006	2007	2008	2009	2010	2011	2012	2013	2014	2015	2016
Products and product groups[15]	**Jan.**	**Jan.**	**Jan.**	**Jan.**	**Jan.**	**Jan.**	**Jan.**	**Jan.**	**Jan.**	**Jan.**	**Jan.**
All-items	108.2	109.4	111.8	113	115.1	117.8	120.7	121.3	123.1	124.3	126.8
Food[17]	108.4	110.9	112.4	120.6	122.3	124.9	130.2	131.6	133	139.1	144.6
Shelter[18]	111.8	114.8	119.2	123.1	121.8	124.5	127.1	127.8	130.5	133.1	134.6
Household operations, furnishings and equipment	102.3	102.4	103.3	105.7	107.9	109.6	112.2	113.5	114.7	118	120
Clothing and footwear	94.2	94.2	92.2	91.8	90.1	87.9	89.3	87.9	89.2	91.1	90.8
Transportation	114.7	113.3	117.6	108.8	117.2	122.8	127.4	126.7	129.2	122.4	125.1
Gasoline	136.9	126.4	152.8	116.9	144.8	163.6	174.7	171.6	179.5	131.3	134.1
Health and personal care	105	106.3	107.5	110.4	113.8	115.8	118.1	118.5	118.3	120	121.5
Recreation, education and reading	99.1	99.2	99.6	99.7	101.1	102.7	102.6	103.7	104.7	105.6	107.9
Alcoholic beverages and tobacco products	120	124.2	126.4	129.2	131.1	135.2	136.3	138.9	140.9	149.9	154.5
Bank of Canada's core index[23]	106.2	108.6	110.1	112.2	114.4	116	118.4	119.6	121.3	124	126.5
All-items excluding food and energy[25]	105.8	107.6	109	110.3	111.6	113.4	115.2	115.9	117.3	119.5	121.6
All-items excluding energy[25]	106.3	108.2	109.6	112.1	113.6	115.5	117.9	118.7	120.1	122.9	125.6
Energy[25]	132.7	125.2	139	123.8	133.9	146	155.5	152.8	160.2	139.5	139
Goods[27]	107.3	106.3	107.3	106.2	108.4	110.5	113.6	112.9	114.2	114	116.6
Services[28]	109.2	112.5	116.2	119.7	121.8	125	127.8	129.6	131.9	134.7	137

Footnotes:

15. The goods and services that make up the Consumer Price Index (CPI) are organized according to a hierarchical structure with the "all-items CPI" as the top level. Eight major components of goods and services make up the "all-items CPI". They are: "food", "shelter", "household operations, furnishings and equipment", "clothing and footwear", "transportation", "health and personal care", "recreation, education and reading", and "alcoholic beverages and tobacco products". These eight components are broken down into a varying number of sub-groups which are in turn broken down into other sub-groups. Indents are used to identify the components that make up each level of aggregation. For example, the eight major components appear with one indent relative to the "all-items CPI" to show that they are combined to obtain the "all-items CPI". NOTE: Some items are recombined outside the main structure of the CPI to obtain special aggregates such as "all-items excluding food and energy", "energy", "goods", "services", or "fresh fruit and vegetables". They are listed after the components of the main structure of the CPI following the last major component entitled "alcoholic beverages and tobacco products".

17. Food includes non-alcoholic beverages.

18. Part of the increase first recorded in the shelter index for Yellowknife for December 2004 inadvertently reflected rent increases that actually occurred earlier. As a result, the change in the shelter index was overstated in December 2004, and was understated in the previous two years. The shelter index series for Yellowknife has been corrected from December 2002. In addition, the Yellowknife All-items Consumer Price Index (CPI) and some Yellowknife special aggregate index series have also changed. Data for Canada and all other provinces and territories were not affected.

23. The Bank of Canada's core index excludes eight of the Consumer Price Index's most volatile components (fruit, fruit preparations and nuts; vegetables and vegetable preparations; mortgage interest cost; natural gas; fuel oil and other fuels; gasoline; inter-city transportation; and tobacco products and smokers' supplies) as well as the effects of changes in indirect taxes on the remaining components. For additional information on the core index, please consult the Bank of Canada website:http://www.bankofcanada.ca/rates/indicators/key-variables/inflation-control-target/. Starting with the October 2006 Consumer Price Index, Statistics Canada produces and disseminates the core index as defined by the Bank of Canada.

25. The special aggregate "energy" includes: "electricity", "natural gas", "fuel oil and other fuels", "gasoline", and "fuel, parts and accessories for recreational vehicles".

27. Goods are physical or tangible commodities usually classified according to their life span into non-durable goods, semi-durable goods and durable goods. Non-durable goods are those goods that can be used up entirely in less than a year, assuming normal usage. For example, fresh food products, disposable cameras and gasoline are non-durable goods. Semi-durable goods are those goods that may last less than 12 months or greater than 12 months depending on the purpose to which they are put. For example, clothing, footwear and household textiles are semi-durable goods. Durable goods are those goods which may be used repeatedly or continuously over more than a year, assuming normal usage. For example, cars, audio and video equipment and furniture are durable goods.

28. A service in the Consumer Price Index (CPI) is characterized by valuable work performed by an individual or organization on behalf of a consumer, for example, car tune-ups, haircuts and city public transportation. Transactions classified as a service may include the cost of goods by their nature. Examples include food in restaurant food services and materials in clothing repair services.

Source: Statistics Canada. *Table 326-0020 - Consumer Price Index, monthly (2002=100 unless otherwise noted),* CANSIM (database). (accessed: 2016-09-01)

NEW HOUSING PRICE INDEX

	2011	2012	2013	2014	2015
	2007=100				
Canada	**105.5**	**108**	**109.9**	**111.6**	**113.1**
House only	105.6	108.4	110.6	112.6	114.2
Land only	104.9	106.7	107.9	108.9	110.3
Metropolitan areas (house and land)					
St. John's (N.L.)	146.9	147.2	149.8	151.1	151.5
Charlottetown (P.E.I)	102.4	102.7	103.2	102	102.2
Halifax (N.S.)	112	114.4	117.3	117.7	118.6
Saint John, Moncton, and Fredericton (N.B.)	108.1	108	108.3	108.2	108
Québec (Que.)	117.9	121.4	122.7	122.9	122.6
Montréal (Que.)	113.9	115.5	116.6	117.1	117.4
Ottawa–Gatineau (Ont./Que.)	112.8	115.7	116.1	114.8	113.7
Toronto and Oshawa (Ont.)	111	116.7	119.6	122.1	126
Hamilton (Ont.)	104.2	105.8	108.4	111.3	115
St. Catharines–Niagara (Ont.)	104	106.1	109.4	112	113.1
London (Ont.)	108.3	109.7	111.6	113.8	115.6
Kitchener-Cambridge-Waterloo (Ont.)	107.4	110.5	111.3	112.2	114.1
Windsor (Ont.)	96.6	98.6	99.5	101.1	101.3
Greater Sudbury / Grand Sudbury and Thunder Bay (Ont.)	105.7	107.1	108.1	108.5	108.8
Winnipeg (Man.)	124.1	129.3	135.6	137.8	139.3
Regina (Sask.)	147.3	153.8	158.2	159.8	157.7
Saskatoon (Sask.)	116.2	118.8	120.5	123.4	122.9
Calgary (Alta.)	95.5	97.1	102.2	109.4	110.5
Edmonton (Alta.)	89.9	90.7	91.1	91.2	91.6
Vancouver (B.C.)	98.7	98.2	97.1	96	96.9
Victoria (B.C.)	88.1	85.7	84.6	83.7	82.7

Source: Statistics Canada, CANSIM, table 327-0046 and Catalogue no. 62-007-X. Last modified: 2016-08-11.

SURVEY OF HOUSEHOLD SPENDING (SHS), 2012-2014

Household expenditures, summary-level categories	2012	2013	2014
	Annual (dollars)		
Total expenditure	75,695	79,098	80,728
Total current consumption	56,330	58,576	59,057
Food expenditures	7,760	7,934	8,109
Food purchased from stores	5,564	5,718	5,880
Food purchased from restaurants	2,195	2,216	2,229
Shelter	15,807	16,361	17,160
Principal accommodation	14,364	14,891	15,471
Rented living quarters	3,521	3,234	3,589
Owned living quarters	8,536	9,278	9,332
Water, fuel and electricity for principal accommodation	2,307	2,380	2,551
Other accommodation	1,444	1,470	1,689
Household operations	4,122	4,344	4,393
Communications	1,851	1,997	2,096
Household furnishings and equipment	2,165	1,974	2,067
Household furnishings	978	854	925
Household equipment	1,055	986	1,015
Household appliances	485	450	461
Clothing and accessories	3,461	3,551	3,503
Transportation	11,202	12,044	11,891
Private transportation	10,076	10,832	10,717
Public transportation	1,126	1,212	1,175
Health care	2,303	2,475	2,251
Direct health care costs to household	1,594	1,730	1,558
Health insurance premiums	709	745	..
Personal care	1,194	1,226	1,207
Recreation	3,808	3,930	3,843
Recreation equipment and related services	920	981	827
Home entertainment equipment and services	334	298	253
Recreation services	1,848	1,956	2,064
Recreational vehicles and associated services	706	695	698
Education	1,410	1,518	1,502
Reading materials and other printed matter	213	183	144
Tobacco products and alcoholic beverages	1,244	1,352	1,222
Games of chance	202	162	156
Miscellaneous expenditures	1,440	1,521	1,608
Income taxes	13,240	14,038	14,867
Personal insurance payments and pension contributions	4,284	4,570	4,871
Gifts of money, support payments and charitable contributions	1,840	1,914	1,934

.. : data no longer provided.

Footnotes:

1. Children are defined as never-married sons, daughters, or foster children of the reference person and may be of any age.
3. For more information about survey methodology, data quality, variable definitions and data products, see the Survey of Household Spending User Guide (catalogue number 62F0026MIE) available free on the Statistics Canada website: http://www5.statcan.gc.ca/bsolc/olc-cel/olc-cel?catno=62F0026M&chropg=1&lang=eng, Household expenditures research papers series.
4. For 2012, household expenditure data were also collected in the three territories. The data are available on CANSIM table 203-0030. However, caution should be used when comparing provincial and territorial data since the collection method was different in the territories.
5. Expenditures for registration fees for automobiles, vans and trucks and public and private insurance premiums have been combined for the provinces of Manitoba (starting in 2010), Saskatchewan and British Columbia (starting in 2013). In these provinces, it can be difficult to make a clear distinction between registration fees and public and private insurance premiums.
6. The Survey of Household Spending uses survey weights which take into account population projections from the 2011 Census.
7. To ensure data quality, suppression of expenditure estimates is based on the coefficient of variation (CV). Expenditures that have a CV greater than or equal to 35% are suppressed as they are too unreliable to be published.
8. Starting in 2014, expenditure estimates for provincial health insurance premiums are included with income taxes. These estimates are calculated using information from personal income tax data (T1). Previously, provincial health insurance premiums were included with health care expenditures.
9. Expenditures for registration fees and licences for recreational vehicles and insurance premiums for recreational vehicles have been combined for Manitoba (starting in 2012). In this province, it can be difficult to make a clear distinction between registration fees and insurance premiums.

Source: Statistics Canada. *Table 203-0023 - Survey of household spending (SHS), household spending, by household type, annual (dollars),* CANSIM (database). (accessed: 2016-09-01)

AVERAGE FEMALE AND MALE INCOME, AND FEMALE-TO-MALE INCOME RATIO

ANNUAL, 2014 CONSTANT DOLLARS

	Average income, females (dollars)	Average income, males (dollars)	Female-to-male average income ratio (percent)
1994	26,500[A]	43,800[A]	60.5
1995	27,300[A]	43,300[A]	63
1996	26,600[A]	43,700[A]	60.8
1997	26,400[A]	44,100[A]	59.8
1998	27,400[A]	45,600[A]	60
1999	28,300[A]	46,800[A]	60.4
2000	28,800[A]	48,100[A]	59.8
2001	29,500[A]	48,600[A]	60.6
2002	29,700[A]	48,400[A]	61.3
2003	29,600[A]	48,200[A]	61.4
2004	30,000[A]	49,100[A]	61
2005	30,800[A]	48,900[A]	62.9
2006	31,600[A]	48,600[A]	65
2007	32,700[A]	49,800[A]	65.6
2008	32,800[A]	50,600[A]	64.8
2009	33,900[A]	49,200[A]	68.9
2010	33,700[A]	46,600[A]	72.3
2011	33,700[A]	50,000[A]	67.4
2012	34,300[A]	51,000[A]	67.2
2013	35,000[A]	51,700[A]	67.6
2014	35,000[A]	52,400[A]	66.7

Footnotes:

1. Source: Income Statistics Division, Statistics Canada
2. Data quality indicators are based on the coefficient of variation (CV) and number of observations. Quality indicators indicate the following: A - Excellent (CV between 0% and 2%); B - Very good (CV between 2% and 4%); C - Good (CV between 4% and 8%); D - Acceptable (CV between 8% and 16%); E - Use with caution (1976 to 1992: CV greater than or equal to 16%; 1993 and subsequent years: CV between 16% and 33.3%).
3. Estimates are based on data from the following surveys: the Survey of Consumer Finances (SCF) from 1976 to 1992, a combination of the SCF and the Survey of Labour and Income Dynamics (SLID) from 1993 to 1997, the SLID from 1998 to 2011 and the Canadian Income Survey (CIS) beginning in 2012. For more information, see Statistics Canada, 2015, "Revisions to 2006 to 2011 income data", Income Research Paper Series, Cat. no. 75F0002MIE - No. 003. Also, two previous revisions of income data are described in Cotton, Cathy, 2000, "Bridging Two Surveys: An Integrated Series of Income Data from SCF and SLID 1989-1997", Statistics Canada, Cat. No. 75F0002MIE - No. 002, and Lathe, Heather, 2005, "Survey of Labour and Income Dynamics: 2003 Historical Revision", Statistics Canada, Cat. No. 75F0002MIE - No. 009.

Source: Adapted from Statistics Canada. *Table 206-0052 - Income of individuals by age group, sex and income source, Canada, provinces and selected census metropolitan areas, annual (number unless otherwise noted),* CANSIM (database). (accessed: 2016-09-01).

AVERAGE AFTER-TAX INCOME, 2004-2014

ECONOMIC FAMILIES & PERSONS NOT IN AN ECONOMIC FAMILY, 2014 CONSTANT DOLLARS

	2004	2005	2006	2007	2008	2009	2010	2011	2012	2013	2014
Canada	60,000[A]	60,800[A]	62,000[A]	64,100[A]	65,100[A]	65,200[A]	65,100[A]	65,100[A]	66,500[A]	67,600[A]	68,000[A]
Newfoundland and Labrador	48,600[A]	50,500[A]	52,500[A]	56,100[A]	57,500[A]	58,500[A]	60,300[A]	62,000[A]	63,600[A]	66,400[A]	66,400[A]
Prince Edward Island	51,100[A]	51,600[A]	52,900[A]	53,400[A]	55,000[A]	56,200[A]	56,500[A]	57,400[A]	56,600[A]	59,400[A]	59,200[A]
Nova Scotia	51,000[A]	52,700[A]	53,300[A]	54,300[A]	53,700[A]	55,700[A]	54,900[A]	56,100[A]	56,800[A]	58,500[A]	58,000[A]
New Brunswick	50,700[A]	50,300[A]	51,400[A]	53,500[A]	54,000[A]	55,800[A]	55,700[A]	57,100[A]	56,900[A]	57,000[A]	57,200[A]
Quebec	52,500[A]	52,000[A]	53,700[A]	55,000[A]	55,100[A]	56,000[A]	55,600[A]	56,500[A]	57,300[A]	57,800[A]	58,100[A]
Ontario	67,400[A]	67,700[A]	67,100[A]	68,800[A]	69,700[A]	69,300[A]	69,900[A]	68,600[A]	70,000[A]	70,700[A]	71,100[A]
Manitoba	54,000[A]	54,900[A]	56,600[A]	60,100[A]	62,100[A]	61,800[A]	61,800[A]	61,100[A]	61,900[A]	63,800[A]	64,500[A]
Saskatchewan	52,300[A]	54,600[A]	57,500[A]	60,900[A]	63,300[A]	66,000[A]	65,100[A]	68,300[A]	68,700[A]	70,100[A]	73,200[B]
Alberta	66,100[A]	68,800[A]	74,000[A]	77,500[A]	78,900[A]	79,300[A]	78,700[A]	79,700[A]	83,300[A]	85,100[A]	85,700[A]
British Columbia	57,700[A]	60,000[A]	61,400[A]	64,200[A]	66,700[A]	65,100[A]	64,200[A]	64,000[A]	65,100[A]	67,100[A]	66,500[A]

Footnotes:

1. Source: Income Statistics Division, Statistics Canada
2. Data quality indicators are based on the coefficient of variation (CV) and number of observations. Quality indicators indicate the following: A - Excellent (CV between 0% and 2%); B - Very good (CV between 2% and 4%); C - Good (CV between 4% and 8%); D - Acceptable (CV between 8% and 16%); E - Use with caution (1976 to 1992: CV greater than or equal to 16%; 1993 and subsequent years: CV between 16% and 33.3%).
3. Estimates are based on data from the following surveys: the Survey of Consumer Finances (SCF) from 1976 to 1992, a combination of the SCF and the Survey of Labour and Income Dynamics (SLID) from 1993 to 1997, the SLID from 1998 to 2011 and the Canadian Income Survey (CIS) beginning in 2012. For more information, see Statistics Canada, 2015, "Revisions to 2006 to 2011 income data", Income Research Paper Series, Cat. no. 75F0002MIE - No. 003. Also, two previous revisions of income data are described in Cotton, Cathy, 2000, "Bridging Two Surveys: An Integrated Series of Income Data from SCF and SLID 1989-1997", Statistics Canada, Cat. No. 75F0002MIE - No. 002, and Lathe, Heather, 2005, "Survey of Labour and Income Dynamics: 2003 Historical Revision", Statistics Canada, Cat. No. 75F0002MIE - No. 009.
4. The concept of income covers income received while a resident of Canada or as relevant for income tax purposes in Canada. Market income is the sum of earnings (from employment and net self-employment), net investment income, private retirement income, and the items under other income. It is also called income before taxes and transfers. Total income refers to income from all sources including government transfers and before deduction of federal and provincial income taxes. It may also be called income before tax (but after transfers). After-tax income is total income less income tax. It may also be called income after tax.

12. Estimates from the Survey of Consumer Finances include income data for persons aged 15 years and over. Estimates from the Survey of Labour and Income Dynamics and the Canadian Income Survey include income data for persons aged 16 years and over.

Source: Statistics Canada. *Table 206-0011 - Market income, government transfers, total income, income tax and after-tax income, by economic family type, Canada, provinces and selected census metropolitan areas (CMAs), annual,* CANSIM (database). (accessed: 2016-09-01)

CURRENT AND FORTHCOMING MINIMUM HOURLY WAGE RATES FOR EXPERIENCED ADULT WORKERS IN CANADA

Jurisdiction	Effective Date	Wage Rate	Note
Federal[1]	18-Dec-1996	$7.50	The minimum wage rate applicable in regard to employees under federal jurisdiction is the general adult minimum rate of the province or territory where the employee is usually employed
Alberta	01-Oct-2015	$11.20	
Alberta	01-Oct-2016	$12.20	
British Columbia	15-Sep-2015	$10.45	
British Columbia	15-Sep-2016	$10.85	
British Columbia	15-Sep-2017	$11.25	
Manitoba	01-Oct-2015	$11.00	
New Brunswick	01-Apr-2016	$10.65	
Newfoundland and Labrador	01-Oct-2015	$10.50	
Northwest Territories	01-Jun-2015	$12.50	
Nova Scotia	01-Apr-2016	$10.70	On April 1 of each year, this rate is adjusted by the percentage change in the projected annual Consumer Price Index for Canada in the preceding calendar year, rounded to the nearest $0.05.
Nunavut	01-Apr-2016	$13.00	
Ontario	01-Oct-2015	$11.25	
Ontario	01-Oct-2016	$11.40	
Prince Edward Island	01-Jun-2016	$10.75	
Prince Edward Island	01-Oct-2016	$11.00	
Quebec	01-May-2016	$10.75	
Saskatchewan	01-Oct-2015	$10.50	
Saskatchewan	01-Oct-2016	$10.72	On October 1 of each year, this rate increases based on the average of the percentage change in the Consumer Price Index and the percentage change in average hourly wage for Saskatchewan during the previous year. Minimum wage increases are subject to Cabinet approval.
Yukon	01-Apr-2016	$11.07	On April 1 of each year, this rate increases by an amount corresponding to the annual increase for the preceding year in the Consumer Price Index for the city of Whitehorse.

Note: In most jurisdictions, these rates also apply to young workers. More information is available on special rates for young workers under "Current And Forthcoming Minimum Wage Rates in Canada for Young Workers and Specific Occupations".

1. The federal jurisdiction includes labour market sectors coming under federal authority by virtue of the Constitution, such as international and interprovincial transportation, telecommunication and banking.
2. There is a special minimum wage rate for inexperienced employees. See "Current and Forthcoming Minimum Wage Rates in Canada for Young Workers and Specific Occupations".

Source: Title: Current And Forthcoming Minimum Hourly Wage Rates For Experienced Adult Workers. URL: http://srv116.services.gc.ca/dimt-wid/sm-mw/rpt1.aspx?lang=eng. Employment and Social Development Canada, 2016. Reproduced with the permission of the Minister of Employment and Social Development Canada, 2016.

LABOUR FORCE SURVEY ESTIMATES (LFS)

ANNUAL AVERAGE (PERSONS UNLESS OTHERWISE NOTED)

Labour force characteristics	Population (x 1,000)[2]	Labour force (x 1,000)[3]	Employment (x 1,000)[4]	Employment full-time (x 1,000)[5]	Employment part-time (x 1,000)[6]	Unemployment (x 1,000)[7]	Unemployment rate (rate)[8]	Participation rate (rate)[9]	Employment rate (rate)[10]
1996	22,959.50	14,847.90	13,418.80	10,865.30	2,553.40	1,429.20	9.6	64.7	58.5
1997	23,246.70	15,074.90	13,704.70	11,091.60	2,613.10	1,370.20	9.1	64.8	59.0
1998	23,515.70	15,316.20	14,047.50	11,404.60	2,642.90	1,268.60	8.3	65.1	59.7
1999	23,781.50	15,586.00	14,407.50	11,758.40	2,649.20	1,178.50	7.6	65.5	60.6
2000	24,089.70	15,849.30	14,765.70	12,090.60	2,675.00	1,083.70	6.8	65.8	61.3
2001	24,419.40	16,102.00	14,938.20	12,224.80	2,713.40	1,163.80	7.2	65.9	61.2
2002	24,768.60	16,555.80	15,285.90	12,428.40	2,857.50	1,269.90	7.7	66.8	61.7
2003	25,079.90	16,938.70	15,654.70	12,689.20	2,965.50	1,284.00	7.6	67.5	62.4
2004	25,408.10	17,149.00	15,921.80	12,968.20	2,953.50	1,227.20	7.2	67.5	62.7
2005	25,754.70	17,294.30	16,126.70	13,152.70	2,974.00	1,167.60	6.8	67.2	62.6
2006	26,115.50	17,505.80	16,401.50	13,415.20	2,986.30	1,104.30	6.3	67.0	62.8
2007	26,461.70	17,851.90	16,775.00	13,696.40	3,078.60	1,077.00	6.0	67.5	63.4
2008	26,824.40	18,117.60	17,003.90	13,851.10	3,153.00	1,113.80	6.2	67.5	63.4
2009	27,202.50	18,255.70	16,731.90	13,503.30	3,228.60	1,523.80	8.4	67.1	61.5
2010	27,573.60	18,449.70	16,969.60	13,647.10	3,322.40	1,480.10	8.0	66.9	61.5
2011	27,913.30	18,621.70	17,223.80	13,898.20	3,325.60	1,397.90	7.5	66.7	61.7
2012	28,283.30	18,820.40	17,444.30	14,128.60	3,315.70	1,376.20	7.3	66.5	61.7
2013	28,647.20	19,036.50	17,685.40	14,321.30	3,365.20	1,350.00	7.1	66.4	61.8
2014	28,980.60	19,118.70	17,796.90	14,367.10	3,429.80	1,321.80	6.9	66.0	61.4
2015	29,279.80	19,280.30	17,949.30	14,558.70	3,390.50	1,331.10	6.9	65.8	61.3

Footnotes:

1. Fluctuations in economic time series are caused by seasonal, cyclical and irregular movements. A seasonally adjusted series is one from which seasonal movements have been eliminated. Seasonal movements are defined as those which are caused by regular annual events such as climate, holidays, vacation periods and cycles related to crops, production and retail sales associated with Christmas and Easter. It should be noted that the seasonally adjusted series contain irregular as well as longer-term cyclical fluctuations. The seasonal adjustment program is a complicated computer program which differentiates between these seasonal, cyclical and irregular movements in a series over a number of years and, on the basis of past movements, estimates appropriate seasonal factors for current data. On an annual basis, the historic series of seasonally adjusted data are revised in light of the most recent information on changes in seasonality.
2. Number of persons of working age, 15 years of age and over. Estimates in thousands, rounded to the nearest hundred.
3. Number of civilian, non-institutionalized persons 15 years of age and over who, during the reference week, were employed or unemployed. Estimates in thousands, rounded to the nearest hundred.
4. Number of persons who, during the reference week, worked for pay or profit, or performed unpaid family work or had a job but were not at work due to own illness or disability, personal or family responsibilities, labour dispute, vacation, or other reason. Those persons on layoff and persons without work but who had a job to start at a definite date in the future are not considered employed. Estimates in thousands, rounded to the nearest hundred.
5. Full-time employment consists of persons who usually work 30 hours or more per week at their main or only job. Estimates in thousands, rounded to the nearest hundred.
6. Part-time employment consists of persons who usually work less than 30 hours per week at their main or only job. Estimates in thousands, rounded to the nearest hundred.
7. Number of persons who, during the reference week, were without work, had actively looked for work in the past four weeks, and were available for work. Those persons on layoff or who had a new job to start in four weeks or less are considered unemployed. Estimates in thousands, rounded to the nearest hundred.
8. The unemployment rate is the number of unemployed persons expressed as a percentage of the labour force. The unemployment rate for a particular group (age, sex and marital status) is the number unemployed in that group expressed as a percentage of the labour force for that group. Estimates are percentages, rounded to the nearest tenth.
9. The participation rate is the number of labour force participants expressed as a percentage of the population 15 years of age and over. The participation rate for a particular group (age, sex and marital status) is the number of labour force participants in that group expressed as a percentage of the population for that group. Estimates are percentages, rounded to the nearest tenth.
10. The employment rate (formerly the employment/population ratio) is the number of persons employed expressed as a percentage of the population 15 years of age and over. The employment rate for a particular group (age, sex and marital status) is the number employed in that group expressed as a percentage of the population for that group. Estimates are percentages, rounded to the nearest tenth.

Source: Statistics Canada. *Table 282-0087 - Labour force survey estimates (LFS), by sex and age group, seasonally adjusted and unadjusted, annual (persons unless otherwise noted),* CANSIM (database). (accessed: 2016-09-02)

LABOUR FORCE SURVEY ESTIMATES (LFS), BY NATIONAL OCCUPATIONAL CLASSIFICATION FOR STATISTICS (NOC-S) AND SEX

ANNUAL (PERSONS X 1,000)

National Occupational Classification for Statistics (NOC-S)[7]	2011	2012	2013	2014	2015
Total, all occupations[10]	17,221	17,438	17,691.1	17,802.2	17,946.6
Management occupations [A]	1,481.6	1,516.5	1,458.7	1,422.7	1,443.6
Senior management occupations [A0]	76.9	65	65.8	57	45.6
Other management occupations [A1-A3]	1,404.7	1,451.5	1,392.9	1,365.7	1,398
Business, finance and administrative occupations [B]	3,090.6	3,065.7	3,102	3,088.8	3,096.9
Professional occupations in business and finance [B0]	570.6	597.9	588.5	591.4	625.5
Financial, secretarial and administrative occupations [B1-B3]	827.7	818.2	889.6	892.9	879.6
Clerical occupations, including supervisors [B4-B5]	1,692.2	1,649.6	1,623.9	1,604.5	1,591.8
Natural and applied sciences and related occupations [C]	1,237.5	1,265.8	1,306.9	1,352.8	1,405.2
Health occupations [D]	1,156.8	1,185.3	1,208.2	1,222.3	1,275.7
Professional occupations in health, nurse supervisors and registered nurses [D0-D1]	525.1	549.1	582.3	565.8	605.5
Technical, assisting and related occupations in health [D2-D3]	631.7	636.2	625.9	656.5	670.2
Occupations in social science, education, government service and religion [E]	1,548.8	1,591.4	1,641.6	1,648.9	1,720.8
Occupations in social science, government service and religion [E0, E2]	876.9	891.1	932.7	944.6	982.7
Teachers and professors [E1, E130][12]	671.9	700.3	708.8	704.3	738
Occupations in art, culture, recreation and sport [F]	560.9	544.2	579.4	600.5	593.9
Sales and service occupations [G][11]	4,209.8	4,270.5	4,354.9	4,428.6	4,413.4
Wholesale, technical, insurance, real estate sales specialists, and retail, wholesale and grain buyers [G1]	552.9	550.5	560.2	561.2	595.5
Retail salespersons, sales clerks, cashiers, including retail trade supervisors [G011, G2-G3]	1,074.2	1,078.7	1,116.3	1,135.3	1,111
Chefs and cooks, and occupations in food and beverage service, including supervisors [G012, G4-G5]	562.4	576.6	601.8	616.3	609.4
Occupation in protective services [G6]	257.2	256	246.6	255.7	270.3
Childcare and home support workers [G8]	206.8	224.1	230.4	232	224.5
Sales and service occupations n.e.c., including occupations in travel and accommodation, attendants in recreation and sport as well as supervisors [G013-G016, G7, G9]	1,556.3	1,584.6	1,599.7	1,628	1,602.7
Trades, transport and equipment operators and related occupations [H]	2,599.4	2,668	2,672	2,668.8	2,674.4
Contractors and supervisors in trades and transportation [H0]	273.4	289.4	297.5	300	321.2
Construction trades [H1]	400.1	395.2	397.3	405.8	398
Other trades occupations [H2-H5]	916.2	946.6	917.1	926.5	916.2
Transport and equipment operators [H6-H7]	653.8	661.9	675.8	683.2	675
Trades helpers, construction, and transportation labourers and related occupations [H8]	355.9	374.9	384.2	353.3	364
Occupations unique to primary industry [I]	533.6	536.2	562	560.1	524.8
Occupations unique to processing, manufacturing and utilities [J]	802	794.4	805.5	808.8	798
Machine operators and assemblers in manufacturing, including supervisors [J0-J2]	643.7	634.7	655.5	656.4	650
Labourers in processing, manufacturing and utilities [J3]	158.2	159.7	150	152.4	148

Footnotes:

2. Number of persons who, during the reference week, worked for pay or profit, or performed unpaid family work or had a job but were not at work due to own illness or disability, personal or family responsibilities, labour dispute, vacation, or other reason. Those persons on layoff and persons without work but who had a job to start at a definite date in the future are not considered employed. Estimates in thousands, rounded to the nearest hundred.
7. Occupation estimates are based on the 2006 National Occupational Classification - Statistics (NOC-S). Occupation refers to the kind of work persons 15 years of age and over were doing during the reference week, as determined by the kind of work reported and the description of the most important duties of the job. If the individual did not have a job during the reference week, the data relate to the previous job, if that job was held in the past year. Those unemployed persons who have never worked before, and those persons who last worked more than 1 year ago make up the "unclassified" category in this table.
10. This combines the National Occupational Classification for Statistics (NOC-S) codes A011 to J319.
11. This combines the National Occupational Classification for Statistics (NOC-S) codes G011 to G983.
12. Labour Force Survey (LFS) National Occupational Classification - Statistics (NOC-S) code exception: Add group E130 - Elementary/Secondary Teacher - not elsewhere classified (nec). On occasion it is impossible to determine the type or level of school reported in the industry field. This special code was adopted as a solution.

Source: Statistics Canada. *Table 282-0010 - Labour force survey estimates (LFS), by National Occupational Classification for Statistics (NOC-S) and sex, annual (persons unless otherwise noted),* CANSIM (database). (accessed: 2016-09-02)

UNEMPLOYMENT RATES IN CANADA, ANNUAL

Geography	2008	2009	2010	2011	2012	2013	2014	2015
Canada	**6.1**	**8.3**	**8.1**	**7.5**	**7.3**	**7.1**	**6.9**	**6.9**
Newfoundland & Labrador	13.3	15.5	14.7	12.6	12.3	11.6	11.9	12.8
Prince Edward Island	10.9	11.9	11.4	11	11.2	11.6	10.6	10.4
Nova Scotia	7.6	9.2	9.6	9	9.1	9.1	9	8.6
New Brunswick	8.5	8.7	9.2	9.5	10.2	10.3	9.9	9.8
Quebec	7.2	8.6	8	7.9	7.7	7.6	7.7	7.6
Ontario	6.6	9.1	8.7	7.9	7.9	7.6	7.3	6.8
Manitoba	4.2	5.2	5.4	5.5	5.3	5.4	5.4	5.6
Saskatchewan	4	4.9	5.2	4.9	4.7	4.1	3.8	5
Alberta	3.6	6.5	6.6	5.4	4.6	4.6	4.7	6
British Columbia	4.6	7.7	7.6	7.5	6.8	6.6	6.1	6.2

Note: The unemployment rate is the number of unemployed persons expressed as a percentage of the labour force. The unemployment rate for a particular group (age, sex, marital status) is the number of unemployed in that group expressed as a percentage of the labour force for that group. Estimates are percentages, rounded to the nearest tenth.

Source: Statistics Canada. *Table 282-0004 - Labour force survey estimates (LFS), by educational attainment, sex and age group, annual (persons unless otherwise noted),* CANSIM (database). (accessed: 2016-09-02)

TOP 15 COUNTRIES VISITED BY CANADIANS, 2014

ONE OR MORE NIGHTS

Country visited	Visits (thousands)	Nights (thousands)	Spending in country (C$ millions)
United States	23,009	233,341	21,195
Mexico	1,900	25,979	2,262
United Kingdom	1,125	13,692	1,353
France	1,019	12,355	1,334
Cuba	844	8,882	780
Dominican Republic	528	6,086	562
Italy	468	5,021	572
Germany	467	4,397	420
China	367	7,526	758
Spain	332	3,846	360
Netherlands	275	2,040	221
Republic of Ireland	271	3,345	332
Hong Kong	236	3,068	284
Bahamas	227	2,153	196
Australia	210	5,179	516

Source: Statistics Canada. *Table 427-0007 - Travel by Canadians to foreign countries, top 15 countries visited, annual,* CANSIM (database). (accessed: 2016-09-02)

TOURISM DEMAND IN CANADA
QUARTERLY (DOLLARS X 1,000,000)

Expenditures	2015				2016
	Q1	Q2	Q3	Q4	Q1
Tourism expenditures	19,937	20,092	20,289	20,342	20,574
Total tourism commodities	16,759	16,912	17,099	17,149	17,376
Transportation	8,160	8,247	8,384	8,415	8,562
Passenger air transport	4,748	4,840	4,944	4,986	5,075
Passenger rail transport	65	66	67	64	64
Interurban bus transport	237	237	235	234	232
Vehicle rental	412	417	422	423	428
Vehicle repairs and parts	382	384	380	385	391
Vehicle fuel	2,169	2,155	2,189	2,177	2,224
Other transportation	147	148	147	146	148
Accommodation	2,877	2,906	2,922	2,922	2,969
Food and beverage services	2,729	2,765	2,777	2,780	2,781
Other tourism commodities	2,993	2,994	3,016	3,032	3,064
Recreation and entertainment	1,169	1,190	1,201	1,213	1,225
Travel agency services	977	987	993	989	984
Pre-trip expenditures	788	757	762	770	794
Convention fees	59	60	60	60	61
Total other commodities	3	1783	1803	1903	1933

Note: Current dollar, seasonally adjusted series are no longer updated.

Source: Statistics Canada. *Table 387-0001 - Tourism demand in Canada, quarterly (dollars),* CANSIM (database). (accessed: 2016-09-02)

Exhibitions, Shows & Events

The following list includes Consumer & Trade Shows, Public Events, Conferences & Festivals arranged by category of interest. The addresses given are the addresses of associations/sponsors. Focus is on events of an ongoing annual or biennial nature. The lists are not complete but are fairly representative of shows held throughout Canada. Users are cautioned that dates or venues may vary.

ABORIGINAL *See* MULTICULTURAL

AGRICULTURE *See* FARM BUSINESS/AGRICULTURE

AIR SHOWS/AVIATION

15 Wing Armed Forces Day, 15 Wing, PO Box 5000, Moose Jaw, SK S6H 7Z8 - 306-694-2222; Fax: 306-694-2880; Email: 15wingpao@forces.gc.ca; URL: www.airforce.forces.gc.ca/en/15wing - Static displays, plus ground & aerial demonstrations - Aug., Moose Jaw SK

19 Wing Comox Armed Forces Day & Airshow, 19 Wing, CFB Comox, PO Box 1000, Stn. Forces, Lazo BC V0R 2K0 - 250-339-8211; Fax (Media Information): 250-339-8120;Celebrates Canadian Forces Day. Biennial - July or Aug.

Abbotsford International Airshow, Abbotsford International Airshow Society, 1464 Tower St., Abbotsford, BC V2T 6H5 - 604-852-8511; Fax: 604-852-6093; Tollfree: 1-855-852-8511 Email: info@abbotsfordairshow.com; URL: www.abbotsfordairshow.com - Large static display. Six hour flying show - Aug., Abbotsford International Airport, BC

Atlantic Canada International Airshow, Nova Scotia International Air Show Association (NSIASA), 166 Ingram Dr., Fall River, NS B2T 1A4 - 902-465-2725; Fax: 902-484-3222; Tollfree: 1-855-465-2725; URL: www.airshowatlantic.ca - Executive Director, Colin Stephenson, Email: colin@airshowatlantic.ca - Aerial displays, including military & civilian aircraft. Ground displays - Aug.

Borden Canadian Forces Day & Airshow, CFSTG/Base Borden Public Affairs Officer, Canadian Forces Base Borden, PO Box 1000 Stn. Main, Borden, ON L0M 1C0 - 705-424-1200; URL: www.bordenairshow.ca - Military & civilian air demonstration & acrobatic teams. Ground displays - June, Canadian Forces Base Borden, Borden, ON

Canada Remembers Airshow, Herzberg Park Saskatoon, SK - 306-222-9901; URL: www.canadaremembersourheroes.com - Volunteer Director, Brian Swidrovich, Email: b.swid@sasktel.net - Annual. Parade of Veterans. Active & static displays - Aug

Canadian International Airshow, Press Bldg., Exhibition Place, 210 Princes' Blvd., Toronto, ON M6K 3C3 - 416-263-3650; Fax: 416-263-3654 ; Email: info@cias.org; URL: www.cias.org - Annually, three days of the Labour Day Weekend. Best viewed from Canadian National Exhibition grounds - Sept., Over Lake Ontario, Toronto, ON

Festival of Flight, Festival of Flight Staff, Parks, Recreation & Tourism, Town of Gander, 100 Elizabeth Dr., Gander, NL A1V 1G7 - 709-256-4195; Fax: 709-256-4195 URL: www.gandercanada.com - A celebration of Gander's aviation history - 1st Mon. in Aug.

Lethbridge International Airshow, Lethbridge International Airshow Association, PO Box 1351, Stn. Main, Lethbridge, AB T1J 4K1 - 403-380-4245; Fax: 403-380-4998; URL: lethbridgeairshow.ca - July, Lethbridge International Airport, AB

Yukon Sourdough Rendezvous Airshow, Yukon Sourdough Rendezvous Society, PO Box 33210, Whitehorse YT Y1A 6L3 - 867-667-2148; Email: info@yukonrendezvous.com; URL: www.yukonrendezvous.com - Vice-President, Public Relations, Lee Stevens - Annual. Aerial & static displays - Feb., Whitehorse Airport, Whitehorse, YT

ANTIQUES

The Toronto Toy & Doll Collectors' Show, PO Box 217, Grimsby, ON L3M 4G3 - 905-945-2775; Email: info@antiquetoys.ca; URL: www.antiquetoys.ca - Contact, Doug Jarvis - Annual antique & collectible childhood memorabilia - Nov., Mississauga, ON

APPAREL *See* FASHION

ARCHITECTURE *See* CONSTRUCTION

ART/ARTS

***See Also* First Night; Crafts; Music; Events**

Art Toronto, Informa Canada, #100, 10 Alcorn Ave., Toronto ON M4V 3A9 - 416-512-3807; Email: events@informacanada.com; URL: www.arttoronto.ca - Oct.

The Artist Project, Informa Canada, #100, 10 Alcorn Ave., Toronto ON M4V 3A9 - 416-960-9030; Email: info@theartistproject.com; URL: www.theartistproject.com - Show Director, Claire Taylor, Email: claire@theartistproject.com

Banff Summer Arts Festival, The Banff Centre, PO Box 1020, Banff AB T1L 1H5 - 403-762-6100; Fax: 403-762-6444; Tollfree: 1-800-565-9989; Email: communications@banffcentre.ca; URL: www.banffcentre.ca - President, Janice Price

Bard on the Beach Shakespeare Festival, #201, 162 West - 1st. Ave., Vancouver, BC V5Y 0H6 - 604-737-0625; Box Office: 604-739-0559; Fax: 604-737-0425; Email: info@bardonthebeach.org; URL: www.bardonthebeach.org - Artistic Director, Christopher Gaze; Managing Director, Claire Sakaki - June - Sept., Vanier Park waterfront, Vancouver, BC

Blyth Festival, 423 Queen St., PO Box 10, Blyth, ON N0M 1H0 - 519-523-9300; Fax: 519-523-9804; Tollfree: 1-877-862-5984; Email: info@blythfestival.com; URL: www.blythfestival.com - Artistic Director, Gil Garratt, Email:ggarratt@blythfestival.com - June - Sept., Blyth Memorial Community Hall, Blyth, ON

Charlottetown Festival, Confederation Centre of the Arts, 145 Richmond St., Charlottetown PE C1A 1J1 - 902-628-1864; Fax: 902-566-4648; Email: info@confederationcentre.com; URL: www.charlottetownfestival.com - CEO, Jessie Inman - Annual - Musical & dramatic entertainment - June - Sept.

Edmonton International Fringe Theatre Festival, 10330 - 84 Ave., Edmonton AB T6E 2G9 - 780-448-9000; Box Office: 780-409-1910; Fax: 780-431-1893; Email: fta@fringetheatre.ca; URL: fringetheatre.ca - Acting Executive Director, Adam Mitchell, Email: adam.mitchell@fringetheatre.ca - Aug.

Electric Eclectics, 202 Scotch Mountain Rd., RR#2, Meaford ON N0H 2S0 - 519-378-9899; Email: info@electric-eclectics.com; URL: www.electric-eclectics.com - Contact, Laura Kikauka - Three day art festival in Meaford, ON

Festival Antigonish, Bauer Theatre, St. Francis Xavier University, PO Box 5000, Antigonish NS B2G 2W5 - 902-867-3333; Tollfree: 1-800-563-7529; URL: www.festivalantigonish.com - Artistic Producer Ed Thomason - July - Sept., Bauer Theatre, Antigonish, NS

Lunenburg Summer Festival of Crafts, Lunenburg Community Centre Arena, 21 Green St., Lunenburg NS B0J 2C0 - 902-634-851; Contact, Robert Black, Email: rsblack@ns.sympatico.ca - Annual - Features over 100 Nova Scotian crafters - July

Manitoba Holiday Festival of the Arts, Viscount Cultural Centre, PO Box 147, Neepawa, MB R0J 1H0 - 204-476-3232; URL: neepawavcc.ca - Annual. Programs for children, youth, & adults - July, Neepawa, MB

Nova Scotia Folk Art Festival, PO Box 1773, Lunenurg, NS B0J 2C0; 902-634-3498; Email: mail@nsfolkartfestival.com; URL: www.nsfolkartfestival.com - Annual. Juried event, featuring an exhibition, workshops, speaker's corner, & sale of work by Nova Scotia folk artists - Aug., Lunenburg Memorial Arena, Lunenburg, NS

Open Ears Festival of Music & Sound, PO Box 26011, Stn. College, 250 King St. West, Kitchener, ON N2G 1B0; Email: info@openears.ca; URL: www.openears.ca - Musical performances, music in alternative venues, sound poetry, sound installations, & conference activity - June, Kitchener, ON

Ottawa Fringe Theatre, Ottawa Fringe Festival, #100, 2 Daly Ave., Ottawa ON K1N 6E2 - 613-232-6162; Email: info@ottawafringe.com; URL: www.ottawafringe.com

PotashCorp Fringe Theatre Festival, 25th Street Theatre Centre Inc., #217, 220 - 20th St. West, Saskatoon, SK S7M 0W9 - 306-664-2239; Fax: 306-955-5852; URL: www.25thstreettheatre.org - Annual - July / Aug., 6 venues, Saskatoon, SK

Scotiabank Nuit Blanche Toronto, City of Toronto Special Events, Toronto City Hall, West Tower, 100 Queen St. West, 6th Fl., Toronto ON M5H 2N2 - Email: scotiabanknuitblanche@toronto.ca; URL: www.scotiabanknuitblanche.ca

Shakespeare by the Sea, 5799 Charles St., Halifax NS B3K 1K7 - 902-422-0295; Email: info@shakespearebythesea.ca; URL: www.shakespearebythesea.ca

Shakespeare by the Sea Festival, c/o 14 Scott St., St. John's NL A1C 2P7 - 709-691-7287; Email: info@shakespearebytheseafestival.com; URL: shakespearebytheseafestival.com

Shakespeare in High Park, The Canadian Stage Company, 26 Berkeley St., Toronto, ON M5A 2W3 - 416-367-8243; Box Office: 416-368-3110; Fax: 416-367-1768; Email: boxoffice@canstage.com; URL: www.canadianstage.com - Artistic Director & General Manager, Matthew Jocelyn - June-Aug., High Park, Toronto, ON

Shakespeare on the Saskatchewan Festival, 205A Pacific Ave., Saskatoon SK S7K 1N9 - 306-653-2300; URL: www.shakespeareonthesaskatchewan.com - Artistic Producer, Will Brooks - July/Aug.

Shaw Festival, PO Box 774, Niagara-on-the-Lake, ON L0S 1J0 - 905-468-2153 ; Fax: 905-468-5438; Tollfree: 1-800-657-1106; URL: www.shawfest.com - Artistic Director, Jackie Maxwell - Theatre festival with an emphasis on the work of George Bernard Shaw

Stratford Festival, PO Box 520 , Stratford ON N5A 6V2 - 519-273-1600; Tollfree: 1-800-567-1600; URL: www.stratfordfestival.ca - Artistic Director, Antoni Cimolino - Theatre festival with an emphasis on the work of William Shakespeare

Summerworks, #423, 401 Richmond St. West, Toronto ON M5V 3A8 - 416-628-8216; URL: www.summerworks.ca - Artistic and Managing Director, Laura Nanni, Email: laura@summerworks.ca - Aug.

Toronto Fringe Festival, #204, 668 Richmond St. West, Toronto, ON M6J 1C5 - 416-966-1062; Email: general@fringetoronto.com; URL: fringetoronto.com; Executive Director, Kelly Straughan; July

Toronto International Art Show, Informa Canada, #100, 10 Alcorn Ave., Toronto ON M4V 3A9 - 416-960-9030; Email: info@arttoronto.ca; URL: arttoronto.ca - Director, Susannah Rosenstock, Email: susannah@arttoronto.ca

Toronto Outdoor Art Exhibition, #264, 401 Richmond St. West, Toronto, ON M5V 3A8 - 416-408-2754; Email:info@torontooutdoorart.org; URL: www.torontooutdoorart.org - Executive Director, Anahita Azrahimi, Email: anahita@torontooutdoorart.org - Canada's largest oudoor art exhibition, held annually. Award program for participating artists - July, Nathan Phillips Square, Toronto ON

Vancouver Fringe Festival, PO Box 203, 1398 Cartwright St., Vancouver BC V6H 3R8 - 604-257-0350; Email: administration@vancouverfringe.com; URL: www.vancouverfringe.com - Executive Director, David Jordan - Annual - Sept.

Winnipeg Fringe Theatre Festival, Manitoba Theatre Centre, 174 Market Ave., Winnipeg MB R3B 0P8 - 204-943-7464; Email: info@winnipegfringe.com; URL: www.winnipegfringe.com - Annual, July

World Stage, Harbourfront Centre, 235 Queens Quay West, Toronto ON M5J 2G8 - 416-973-4600; Email: info@harbourfrontcentre.com; URL: www.harbourfrontcentre.com/worldstage - CEO, Marah Braye - International theatre festival - Harbourfront Centre, Toronto ON

AUTOMOTIVE

Atlantic Truck Show, Master Promotions Ltd., PO Box 565, 48 Broad St., Saint John, NB E2L 3Z8 - 506-658-0018; Fax: 506-658-0750; Tollfree: 1-888-454-7469; Email: info@mpltd.ca; URL: www.atlantictruckshow.com - Annual - Show Manager, Mark Cusack, June - Coliseum, Moncton, NB

Edmonton Motor Show, Edmonton Expo Centre, Hall C, #C104, 7515 - 118 Ave., Edmonton, AB T5B 4X5 - 780-423-2401; Fax: 780-423-2413; URL: www.edmontonmotorshow.com - Show Manager, Eleasha Naso - Annual consumer show - Edmonton Expo Centre

ExpoCam, Newcom Média Québec inc., #100, 6450, rue Notre Dame ouest, Montréal, QC H4C 1V4 - 416-614-5817; Tollfree: 1-877-682-7469; URL: www.expocam.ca - Show Manager, Joan Wilson, Email: joanw@newcom.ca - Biennial trade & consumer show - April.

Grand Prix of Canada, #100, 2170, av Pierre-Dupuy, Montreal, QC H3C 3R4 - 514-350-4731; Fax: 514-350-0007; URL: www.circuitgillesvilleneuve.ca - Annual international auto racing event - June - Gilles-Villeneuve Circuit, Montréal QC

Halifax RV Show, Master Promotions Ltd., PO Box 565, 48 Broad St., Saint John, NB E2L 3Z8 - 506-658-0018; Fax: 506-658-0750; Tollfree: 1-888-454-7469; Email: info@mpltd.ca; URL: www.masterpromotions.ca - Annual consumer show - Show Manager, Scott Sprague - Jan., Halifax NS

Hamilton RV Expo, Continuum Productions Inc., 3488 Trelawny Circle, Mississauga ON L5N 6N7 - 905-824-1060; Fax:

905-824-9923; Email: info@continuumevents.ca; URL: www.continuumevents.ca - Jan.

Honda Indy Toronto, #300A, 370 Queens Quay West, Toronto, ON M5V 3J3 - 416-588-7223; Tollfree: 1-877-503-6869; URL: www.hondaindytoronto.com - Annual - July, Toronto ON

Manitoba RV Show, Recreation Vehicle Dealers Association of Manitoba, 31A Eric St., Winnipeg, MB R2M 5J2 - 204-456-1916; Email: showmanager@manitobarvshow.com; URL: www.manitobarvshow.com - Show Manager, Dave Amey - Annual consumer show - March, Winnipeg, MB

Moncton RV Show, Master Promotions Ltd., PO Box 565, 48 Broad St., Saint John, NB E2L 3Z8 - 506-658-0018; Fax: 506-658-0750; Tollfree: 1-888-454-7469; Email: info@mpltd.ca; URL: www.masterpromotions.ca - Annual consumer show - Show Manager, Scott Sprague, Feb., Moncton, NB

Montréal International Auto Show, 1001, Pl. Jean-Paul-Riopelle, Montréal, QC H2Z 1H5 - 514-331-6571; Fax: 514-331-2045; Email: communications@ccqm.qc.ca; URL: www.montrealautoshow.com - Event Manager, Julie Lachance - Annual consumer show. New cars, light trucks, accessories - Jan. - Palais des Congrès, Montréal QC

Motorama Custom Car & Motorsports Expo, The International Centre, 6900 Airport Rd., Mississauga ON L4V 1E8 - 416-962-7223; Email: info@motoramashow.com; URL: www.motoramashow.com; Annual consumer show - March

Motorcycle & Powersport Atlantic, North Atlantic Fish & Workboat Show, Master Promotions Ltd., PO Box 565, 48 Broad St., Saint John, NB E2L 3Z8 - 506-658-0018; Fax: 506-658-0750; Tollfree: 1-888-454-7469; Email: info@mpltd.ca; URL: www.masterpromotions.ca - March - Halifax NS

North American International Motorcycle Supershow, PO Box 551, Willow Beach ON L0E 1S0 - Fax: 1-888-680-7469; Tollfree: 1-888-661-7469; Email: info@motorcyclesupershow.ca; URL: www.motorcyclesupershow.ca - Senior Show and Sales Manager, Mike BLakoe, Email: mblakoe@bellnet.ca, Jan., International Centre, Toronto, ON

RV Exposition & Sale, Recreation Vehicle Dealers Association of Alberta, 10561 - 172 St. NW, Edmonton AB T5S 1P1 - Tollfree: 1-888-858-8787; Email: rvda@rvda-alberta.org; URL: www.rvda-alberta.org - Annual consumer show held in Calgary, Edmonton & Red Deer - Feb.

Salon de la Moto de Montréal, Power Sport Services, #238, 3700, rue Saint-Patrick, Montréal QC H4E 1A1 - 514-375-1974; Fax: 514-221-3725; URL: www.montrealmotorcycleshow.ca - Director, Bianca Kennedy, Email: bekennedy@powersportservices.ca - Annual consumer show - Feb/March

Toronto Fall Classic Car Auction, Collector Car Productions, Inc., PO Box 1120, 186 Talbot St. West, Blenheim, ON N0P 1A0 - 416-923-7500; Fax: 905-248-3353; Email: info@ccpauctions.com; URL: www.collectorcarproductions.com - Annual consumer show. Vintage cars, sale of parts & accessories - Oct./Nov. - International Centre, Mississauga, ON

Toronto International Motorcycle Springshow, Bar Hodgson Productions Inc., 8780 Baldwin St., Ashburn ON L0B 1A0 - 905-655-5403; Fax: 905-655-3812; URL: motorcyclespringshow.com - President, Bar Hodgson, March - International Centre, Toronto ON

Toronto Spring Classic Car Auction, Collector Car Productions, Inc., PO Box 1120, 186 Talbot St. West, Blenheim, ON N0P 1A0 - 416-923-7500; Fax: 905-248-3353; Email: info@ccpauctions.com; URL: www.collectorcarproductions.com - Annual consumer show. Vintage cars, sale of parts & accessories - April - International Centre, Mississauga, ON

Vancouver Island RV Show & Sale, Recreation Vehicle Dealers Association of British Columbia, #195B, 1151 - 10th Ave. SW, Salmon Arm, BC VIE 1T3 - 778-489-5057; Fax: 778-489-5097; Email: info@rvda.bc.ca; URL: www.rvda.bc.ca - Annual consumer show - April, Vancouver, BC

BLUEGRASS *See* MUSIC

BOATING

Boat, Fishing & Outdoor Shows, Continuum Productions Inc., 3488 Trelawny Circle, Mississauga, ON L5N 6N7 - 905-824-1060; Fax: 905-824-9923; URL: www.ontarioboatshows.com - President, Continuum Productions Inc. - Consumer show - Feb., London ON & March, Hamilton ON

Halifax International Boat Show, North Atlantic Fish & Workboat Show, Master Promotions Ltd., PO Box 565, 48 Broad St., Saint John, NB E2L 3Z8 - 506-658-0018; Fax: 506-658-0750; Tollfree: 1-888-454-7469; Email: info@mpltd.ca; URL: www.masterpromotions.ca - Feb.

Kingston Boat & Recreation Show & Sale, c/o 20/20 Show Productions Inc., PO Box 400, Belle River ON N0R 1A0 - 226-363-0550; Fax: 226-363-0455; URL: ontariotradeshows.com - President, Stuart Galloway, Email: stuart@exposition.com

Moncton Boat Show, Master Promotions Ltd., PO Box 565, 48 Broad St., Saint John NB E2L 3Z8 - 506-658-0018; Fax: 506-658-0750; Tollfree: 1-888-454-7469; Email: info@mpltd.ca; URL: www.masterpromotions.ca - Annual consumer show - Show Manager, Scott Sprague, March - Moncton Coliseum, Moncton, NB

Muskoka In Water Boat & Cottage Show, CanNorth Shows Inc., Phone: 647-344-6700; Toll-Free: 1-855-723-1156; URL: www.muskokashows.com

Niagara Regional RV & Boat Show, c/o 20/20 Show Productions Inc., PO Box 400, Belle River, Ontario N0R 1A0- 226-363-0550; Fax: 226-363-0455; URL: ontariotradeshows.com - Contact, Stuart Galloway, Email: stuart@exposition.com

Sudbury Sportsman Show, DAC Marketing Ltd., PO Box 2837, Stn A, Sudbury ON P3A 5J3 - 705-929-7469; Email: dacsudbury@gmail.com; URL: www.dacshows.com, April, Sudbury, ON

Toronto International Boat Show, Canadian Boat Shows, #8, 14 McEwan Dr. West, Bolton, ON L7E 1H1 - 905-951-0009; Fax: 905-951-0018; URL: www.torontoboatshow.com - Jan. - Enercare Centre, Exhibition Place, Toronto, ON

Victoria Boat & Fishing Show, Canwest Productions Inc., #218, 7710 – 5 St. SE, Calgary, AB T2H 2L9 - 403-242-0859; Fax: 403-246-3856; Tollfree: 1-800-626-1538; URL: www.victoriaboatshow.com - Show Director, Kevin Blackburn, Email: kevin@canwestproductions.com - Annual consumer show - Feb. - Pearkes Recreation Centre, Victoria BC

Victoria Classic Boat Festival, c/o Maritime Museum of British Columbia, 634 Humboldt St., Victoria, BC V8W 1A4 - Phone: 250-385-4222; URL: www.classicboatfestival.ca - Acting Chair, Stasi Manser - Annually, Labour Day weekend, Victoria BC

Windsor Boat, RV & Recreation Show, c/o 20/20 Show Productions Inc., PO Box 400, Belle River ON N0R 1A0 - 226-363-0550; Fax: 226-363-0455; URL: ontariotradeshows.com - Contact, Stuart Galloway, Email: stuart@exposition.com

BOOKS

International Festival of Authors, 235 Queen's Quay West, Toronto, ON M5J 2G8 - 416-973-4760; Fax: 416-954- 4323; Email: info@ifoa.org; URL: ifoa.org - Director, Geoffrey E. Taylor - Interviews & readings by novelists, poets, playwrights & biographers - Oct. - Harbourfront Centre, Toronto, ON

Montréal Book Fair/Salon du livre de Montréal, #430, 300, rue du Saint-Sacrement, Montréal, QC H2Y 1X4 - 514-845-2365; Fax: 514-845-7119; Email: slm.info@videotron.ca; URL: www.salondulivredemontreal.com - Directrice Générale, Francine Bois - Annual consumer show - Nov., Montréal QC

Salon international du Livre de Québec, 26, rue Saint-Pierre, Québec, QC G1K 8A3 - 418-692-0010; Fax: 418-692-0029; URL: www.silq.ca - Président-directeur général, Philippe Sauvageau - Annual consumer show - avril, Québec, QC

The Word on the Street, The Word on the Street Canada, National Office, 147 Liberty St., Toronto, ON M6K 3G3 - 416-658-3144; URL: www.thewordonthestreet.ca - National Coordinator, Helena Aalto, Email: helena.aalto@rogers.com - Annual celebration of literacy & the printed word; held in Toronto, Halifax, Lethbridge, Saskatoon & Kitchenerr - Sept.

BRIDAL

Canada's Bridal Show, #10, 136 Winges Rd., Woodbridge, ON L4L 6C4 - 905-264-7000; Fax: 905-264-7300; Email: info@canadasbridalshow.com; URL: www.canadasbridalshow.com - Annual consumer show. Bridal fashion shows, gifts, florists, photography, entertainment, travel - Jan. & Sept., Metro Toronto Convention Centre, Toronto, ON

National Bridal Show, c/o Metroland Media, #6, 3715 Laird Rd., Mississauga, ON L5L 0A3 - Fax: 905-281-5656; Fax: 905-281-5630; URL: nationalbridalshow.com - Show Manager, Marti Milks, Email: marti.milks@sympatico.ca - Annually, Feb. & Sept.

The Total Wedding Show, Ten Star Productions Inc., #10, 136 Winges Rd., Woodbridge ON L4L 6C4 - 905-264-7000; Fax: 905-264-7300; Email: info@totalweddingshow. com; URL: www.totalweddingshow.com - Annual consumer show - Jan. - International Centre, Mississauga, ON

Vancouver Island Bridal Exhibition, 3319 Savannah Pl., Nanaimo BC V9T 6R9 - 250-244-8449; Fax: 1-877-325-3299; Tollfree: 1-888-501-9696; Email: bridalexhibition@ieginc.ca; URL: www.bridalexhibition.ca

Wedding Wishes Formal Fair, Thunder Bay Chamber of Commerce, #102, 200 Syndicate Ave. South, Thunder Bay, ON P7E 1C9 - 807-624-2626; Fax: 807-622-7752; Email: chamber@tbchamber.ca; URL: www.tbchamber.ca - Show Manager, Nancy Milani, Email: nancy@tbchamber.ca - Annual consumer show - Nov., Thunder Bay, ON

BUSINESS

Business Event Expo, Ignite Magazine, #317, 6-1500 Upper Middle Rd. West, Oakville ON L6M 0C2 - 905-582-8988; Email: info@ignitemag.ca; URL: ignitemag.ca - April - Metro Toronto Convention Centre, Toronto, ON

Business Expo, Greater Nanaimo Chamber of Commerce, 2133 Bowen Rd., Nanaimo BC V9S 1H8 - 250-756-1191; Fax: 250-756-1584; Email: info@nanaimochamber. bc.ca; URL: www.nanaimochamber.bc.ca - CEO, Kim Smythe, Oct. - Vancouver Island Conference Centre

CDW Canada Business Technology Expo, #300, 20 Carlson Ct., Toronto, ON M9W 7K6; 647-288-5700; URL: www.cdw.ca - June

Franchise Expos, c/o National Event Management Inc., #102, 260 Town Centre Blvd., Markham ON L3R 8H8 - 905-477-2677; Fax: 905-477-7872; Tollfree: 1-800-891-4859; Email: info@nationalevent.com; URL: www.franchiseshowinfo.com

Orillia & Lake Country Business Expo, 705-329-1084; URL: www.orilliabusinessexpo.ca - Chair Ken Forbes, Email: ken@orilliatrim.com - Oct. - Best Western Plus Mariposa Conference Centre

SOHO SME Business Expo, SOHO Business Group, #1, 1680 Lloyd Ave., North Vancouver, BC V7P 2N6; 604-929-8250; Tollfree: 1-800-290-7646; URL: sohosme.soho.ca - Sept./Oct. - Held in Vancouver, BC, Calgary, AB and Toronto, ON

Traders Forum Show, #200, 96 Bradwick Dr., Concord, ON L4K 1K8; 905-760-7694; Fax: 905-738-3557; Email: info@tradersforum.ca; URL: www.tradersforum.ca - Trade show for the discount & mass merchandise industry - Aug./Sept. - Held in Toronto, ON, Edmonton, AB, Halifax, NS & Montreal, QC

CARS *See* AUTOMOTIVE

CHEMISTRY

Canadian Society of Clinical Chemists Conference, CSCC Head Office, #310, 4 Cataraqui St., Kingston ON K7K 1Z7 - 613-531-8899; Tollfree Fax: 1-866-303-0626; Email: office@cscc.ca; URL: www.cscc.ca - June

CHILDREN

Calgary International Children's Festival, 205 - 8th Ave. SE, Calgary AB T2G 0K9 - 403-294-7414; URL: calgarykidsfest.ca - Festival Operations Manager, Brian Beaulieu, Email: bbeaulieu@calgarykidsfest.ca - Annual - May, Calgary, AB

International Children's Festival of the Arts, St. Albert Place, 5 St. Anne St., St. Albert, AB T8N 3Z9 - 780-459-1542; Email: boxoffice@st-albert.net; URL: www.childfest.com - Cultural Services Director, Kelly Jerrott, Email: kjerrott@stalbert.ca - Annual - May - The Arden Theatre, St. Albert, AB

Mom, Pop & Tots Fair, Family Productions Inc., 4634 - 90A Ave., 2nd Fl., Edmonton AB T6B 2P9 - 780-490-0215 ; Fax: 780-450-3757; Email: info@edmontonshows.com; URL: mpt.edmontonshows.com

PotashCorp Children's Festival of Saskatchewan, Delta Bessborough Hotel, #706, 601 Spadina Cres. East, 7th Fl., Saskatoon, SK S7K 3G8 - 306-664-3378; Fax: 306-664-2344; Email: gmchildfest@gmail.com; URL: www.potashcorpchildrensfestival.com - Annually, June. Four-day international festival of the performing arts for children

Winnipeg International Children's Festival, #201, 1 Forks Market Rd.., Winnipeg MB R3C 4L9 - 204-958- 4730; Fax: 204-943-7915; Tollfree: 1-800-527-1515; Email: kidsfest@kidsfest.ca; URL: www.kidsfest.ca - Executive Producer, Neal Rempel - Annual - June, Winnipeg, MB

CHRISTMAS CRAFTS *See* CRAFTS

COMMUNICATIONS

Canadian CommTech Show & Seminars, Dazzle Me Productions, 25 Forest Rd., Grimsby, ON L3M 2J4; 905-309-1914; Fax: 289-235-9867; Tollfree: 1-855-215-1334;

Email: info@commtechshow.com; www.commtechshow.com - Annual, May

COMPUTERS

Western Canada Information Security Conference, ISACA Winnipeg Chapter, 375 York Ave., Winnipeg, MB R3C 3J3 - 204-926-1745; URL: www.wcisc.ca - Annual conference - May - Winnipeg Convention Centre, Winnipeg, MB

CONSTRUCTION & BUILDING PRODUCTS

Atlantic Building Materials Show, Atlantic Building Supply Dealers Association, 70 Englehart St., Dieppe NB E1A 8H3 - 506-858-0700; Fax: 506-859-0064; Email: absda@nbnet.nb.ca; URL: www.absda.ca - Annual trade show - Feb.

Buildex, Informa Canada, #510, 1185 West Georgia St., Vancover BC V6E 4E6 - 1-877-739-2112; URL: www.buildexcalgary.com - Show Director, Paul Maryschak, Email: paul.maryschak@informa.com

The Buildings Show, Informa Canada, #100, 10 Alcorn Ave., Toronto ON M4V 3A9 - 416-512-3807; Email: events@informacanada.com; URL: www.thebuildingsshow.com - Late Nov./early Dec. - Toronto ON

Construct Canada, Informa Canada, #100, 10 Alcorn Ave., Toronto ON M4V 3A9 - 416-512-0203; Email: events@informacanada.com; URL: www.constructcanada.com - Annual trade show. Products, technologies & systems for the design & construction of all building types - Dec. - Metro Toronto Convention Centre, Toronto ON

Contech Expos, Informa Canada, #100, 10 Alcorn Ave., Toronto ON M4V 3A9 - 416-512-3807; Email: events@informacanada.com; URL: www.contech.qc.ca/en/tradeshows - Mauricie, Saguenay, Montréal, Québec

HomeBuilder & Renovator Expo, Informa Canada, #100, 10 Alcorn Ave., Toronto ON M4V 3A9 - 416-512-0203; Email: events@informacanada.com; URL: www.homebuilderexpo.ca - Annual trade show - Dec. - Metro Toronto Convention Centre, Toronto ON

National Heavy Equipment Show, @Body Texh Exhibit = North Atlantic Fish & Workboat Show, Master Promotions Ltd., PO Box 565, 48 Broad St., Saint John, NB E2L 3Z8 - 506-658-0018; Fax: 506-658-0750; Tollfree: 1-888-454-7469; Email: info@mpltd.ca; URL: www.masterpromotions.ca - April

World of Concrete Pavilion, Informa Canada, #100, 10 Alcorn Ave., Toronto ON M4V 3A9 - 416-512-3807; Email: events@informacanada.com; URL: www.worldofconcretepavilion.com - Late Nov./early Dec. - Toronto ON

CRAFTS

Art Market, Art Market Productions, 565 Tralee Cres., Tsawwassen, BC V4M 3R9 - Fax: 778-434-3156; Tollfree: 1-877-929-9933; URL: www.artmarketcraftsale.com - Show Manager, Nichole Windblad - Annual consumer show; art & craft sale - Nov., Calgary AB

Atlantic Craft Trade Show, Nova Scotia Business Inc.,Box 3, #15, 1574 Argyle St., Halifax NS B3J 2B3 - 902-492-2773; Fax: 902-429-9059; Email: acts@craftalliance.ca; URL: www.actshow.ca - Director, Bernard Burton - Annual trade show. Juried craft & giftware products

Bazaart, MacKenzie Art Gallery, 3475 Albert St., Regina SK S4S 6X6 - 306-584-4250; Fax: 306-569-8191; Email: info@mackenzieartgallery.ca; URL: www.mackenzieartgallery.sk.ca - Juried outdoor art show & sale; complete range of crafts - June

Beaches Arts & Crafts Show, Signatures Shows Ltd., 113 Murray St., Ottawa ON K1N 5M5 - 613-241-5777; Fax: 613-241-5678; Tollfree: 1-888-773-4444; Email: info@signatures.ca; URL: www.beachesartsandcraftsshow.com - Annual consumer show - June, Toronto, ON

Butterdome Craft Show, Signatures Shows Ltd., 113 Murray St., Ottawa ON K1N 5M5 - 613-241-5777; Fax: 613-241-5678; Tollfree: 1-888-773-4444; Email: info@signatures.ca; URL: www.butterdome.ca - Spring & Fall - Edmonton

By Hand, Signatures Shows Ltd., 113 Murray St., Ottawa ON K1N 5M5 - 613-241-5777; Fax: 613-241-5678; Tollfree: 1-888-773-4444; Email: info@signatures.ca; URL: www.byhand.ca

Christmas at the Forum Crafts Festival, DMS Enterprises, Ltd., PO Box 51064, Halifax NS B3M 4R8; Tollfree: 1-866-995-7469; Tollfree Fax: 1-877-524-4336; Email: dmstradeshows@gmail.com; URL: www.christmasattheforum.com - Coordinator, Chris Banks - Annual consumer show - Nov., Halifax NS

Creativ Festival, CanNorth Shows Inc., Phone: 647-344-6700; Toll-Free: 1-855-723-1156; URL: csnf.com - Oct. - Toronto ON

Creative Stitches & Crafting Alive, CanNorth Shows Inc., Phone: 647-344-6700; Toll-Free: 1-855-723-1156; URL: creativestitchesshow.com - Annual consumer show in Calgary & Edmonton - Sept.

Fall Into Christmas Craft Show, Signatures Shows Ltd., 113 Murray St., Ottawa ON K1N 5M5 - 613-241-5777; Fax: 613-241-5678; Tollfree: 1-888-773-4444; Email: info@signatures.ca; URL: www.fallintochristmas.com - Oct. - Medicine Hat AB, Lethbridge AB

Festival of Crafts, Signatures Shows Ltd., 113 Murray St., Ottawa ON K1N 5M5 - 613-241-5777; Fax: 613-241-5678; Tollfree: 1-888-773-4444; Email: info@signatures.ca; URL: www.festivalofcrafts.ca - Dec. - Calgary AB

Indie Handmade, Signatures Shows Ltd., 113 Murray St., Ottawa ON K1N 5M5 - 613-241-5777; Fax: 613-241-5678; Tollfree: 1-888-773-4444; Email: info@signatures.ca; URL: www.indiehandmade.ca - April. & Nov. - St. Albert AB

One of a Kind Christmas Canadian Craft Show & Sale, Informa Canada, #100, 10 Alcorn Ave., Toronto ON M4V 3A9 - 416-960-3680; Fax: 416-923-5624; URL: www.oneofakindshow.com - Show Director, Patti Stewart, Email: patti@oneofakindshow.com - Annual consumer show - Nov./Dec. - Enercare Centre, Exhibition Place, Toronto ON

One of a Kind Springtime Canadian Craft Show & Sale, Informa Canada, #100, 10 Alcorn Ave., Toronto ON M4V 3A9 - 416-960-3680; Fax: 416-923-5624; URL: www.oneofakindshow.com - Show Director, Patti Stewart, Email: patti@oneofakindshow.com - Annual consumer show - March - Enercare Centre, Exhibition Place, Toronto ON

Originals Christmas Craft Show & Sale, Signatures Shows Ltd., 113 Murray St., Ottawa ON K1N 5M5 - 613-241-5777; Fax: 613-241-5678; Tollfree: 1-888-773-4444; URL: www.originalsshow.ca, Dec.

Our Best to You, Signatures Shows Ltd., 113 Murray St., Ottawa ON K1N 5M5 - 613-241-5777; Fax: 613-241-5678; Tollfree: 1-888-773-4444; Email: info@signatures.ca; URL: www.ourbesttoyou.ca - Red Deer AB, Oct. & Regina SK, Nov.

Pine Tree Potters' Guild Spring Potters Sale, PO Box 28586, Aurora ON L4G 6S6 - 905-727-1278; www.pinetreepotters.ca/sales.html - Dec.

Saskatchewan Handcraft Festival, Saskatchewan Craft Council, 813 Broadway Ave., Saskatoon SK S7N 1B5 - 306-653-3616; Email: saskcraftcouncil@sasktel.net; URL: www.saskcraftcouncil.org - Executive Director, Carmen Milenkovic - July, Battleford SK

Signatures Ottawa, Signatures Shows Ltd., 113 Murray St., Ottawa ON K1N 5M5 - 613-241-5777; Fax: 613-241-5678; Tollfree: 1-888-773-4444; Email: info@signatures.ca; URL: www.signaturesottawa.ca - Annual consumer show - Nov., Ottawa ON

Signatures Winnipeg, Signatures Shows Ltd., 113 Murray St., Ottawa ON K1N 5M5 - Fax: 613-241-5678; Tollfree: 1-800-773-4444; Email: info@signatures.ca; URL: www.signatureswinnipeg.ca - Annual consumer show - Nov., Winnipeg MB

Sundog Arts & Entertainment Faire, PO Box 7183, Saskatoon SK S7K 4J1 - 306-384-7364; Fax: 306-384-7364; Email: sundoghandcraftfaire@sasktel.net; www.sundoghandcraftfaire.com - Coordinator, Diane Boyko - Juried three-day craft market plus continuous stage acts & gourmet food court. Annually, first weekend of Dec.

Touch of Talent Craft Sale, Signatures Shows Ltd., 113 Murray St., Ottawa ON K1N 5M5 - 613-241-5777; Fax: 613-241-5678; Tollfree: 1-888-773-4444; Email: info@signatures.ca; URL: www.touchoftalent.ca - Sept. - Sherwood Park AB

Victoria Park Arts & Crafts Fair, PO Box 1394, Moncton NB E1C 8T6 - 506-386-1200; Fax: 506-857-0279; Email: hotrides1@hotmail.com; URL: www.victoriapark-crafts.com - Annually - Aug.

WinterGreen Fine Craft Market, Saskatchewan Craft Council, 813 Broadway Ave., Saskatoon SK S7N 1B5 - 306-653-3616; Fax: 306-244-2711; Tollfree: 1-866-653-3616; Email: saskcraftcouncil@sasktel.net; URL: www.saskcraftcouncil.org - Executive Director, Carmen Milenkovic - Annual. Threeday Christmas craft market - Nov., Regina SK

DANCE *See* MUSIC

DECORATING *See* HOME SHOWS

ELECTRICAL/ELECTRONICS

Electrical Showcase, Electrical Association of Manitoba, #104, 1780 Wellington Ave., Winnipeg MB R3H 1B3 - 204-783-4125; Fax: 204-783-4216; URL: www.eamanitoba.ca - Executive Director, Gord Macpherson - Triennial trade show - April

Eptech, Electronic Products & Technology, 80 Valleybrook Dr., Toronto ON M3B 2S9 - 416-442-5600; Fax: 416-510-5134; Email: info@ept.ca; URL: www.ept.ca - Trade show held in various locations. Electronic components, systems

MEET (Mechanical Electical Electronic Technology), Master Promotions Ltd., PO Box 565, Saint John NB E2L 3Z8 - 506-658-0018; Fax: 506-658-0750; Tollfree: 1-888- 454-7469; Email: info@masterpromotions.ca; URL: www.masterpromotions.ca - Biennial

ENVIRONMENT

Canadian National Drinking Water Conference, Canadian Water & Wastewater Association, #11, 1010 Polytek Rd., Ottawa ON K1J 9H9 - 613-747-0524; Fax: 613-747-0523; Email: admin@cwwa.ca; URL: www.cwwa.ca - Executive Director, Robert Haller, Email: rhaller@cwwa.ca - Biennial - April, 2008, Québec QC

ETHNIC *See* MULTICULTURAL

EVENTS

***See Also* specific categories for events such as Winter Carnivals, Music Festivals, Rodeos, Exhibitions, etc.**

Ashkenaz: A Festival of New Yiddish Culture, #303, 455 Spadina Ave., Toronto ON M5S 2G8 - 416-979-9901; URL: www.ashkenaz.ca - Managing Director, Samantha Parnes, Email: sam@ashkenaz.ca - Biennial; Aug./Sept.

Billy Barker Days, PO Box 4441, Quesnel BC V2J 3J4 - 250-992-1234; Fax: 250-992-5083; Email: office@billybarkerdays.ca; URL: www.billybarkerdays.ca, July

Creston Valley Blossom Festival, PO Box 329, Creston BC V0B 1G0 - 250-428-4284; Fax: 250-428-9411; Email: info@blossomfestival.ca; URL: www.blossomfestival.ca - May, long weekend

The Canadian Tulip Festival, Canadian Tulip Festival, #203, 1525 Princess Patricia Way, Ottawa, ON K1S 5J3, Tollfree: 1-800-668-8547; Email: info@tulipfestival.ca; URL: www.tulipfestival.ca - May

The Canadian Gaming Summit, MediaEDGE Communications, #1000, 5255 Yonge St., Toronto ON M2N 6P4 - 416-512-8186; Fax: 416-512-8344; Tollfree: 1-866-216-0860; URL: canadiangamingsummit.com - Director, Show Operations, Gillian Fedchak, Email: gillianf@mediaedge.ca

Canmore Highland Games, Three Sisters Scottish Festival Society, PO Box 8102, Canmore AB T1W 2T8 - 403-678-9454; Fax: 403-678-3385; Email: info@canmorehighlandgames.ca; URL: www.canmorehighlandgames.ca - Annually, Labour Day Sunday - Sept., Canmore AB

Calgary Baby & Tot Show, Can West Productions Inc., #218, 7710 – 5th St. SE, Calgary, AB T2H 2L9 - Fax: 403-246 -3856; Tollfree: 1-800-626-1538; Email: info@canwestshows.com; URL: www.canwestproductions.com - Oct. - Calgary AB

Calgary Tattoo & Arts Festival, Can West Productions Inc., #218, 7710 – 5th St. SE, Calgary, AB T2H 2L9 - Fax: 403-246 -3856; Tollfree: 1-800-626-1538; Email: info@canwestshows.com; URL: www.canwestproductions.com - Oct. - Calgary AB

Chocolate Fest, Chocolate Festival, 9 Mark St., St. Stephen NB E3L 1G4 - 506-465-5616; Fax: 506-465- 5610; Email: info@chocolate-fest.ca; URL: www.chocolate-fest.ca

The Christmas Show, c/o Premier Publications & Shows, #2, 5046 Mainway, Burlington ON L7L 5Z1 - 905-842-6591, Tollfree: 1-800-693-7986; URL: thechristmasshow.ca - Event Manager, Jackie Fenton, Email: jackiefenton@metroland.com

Discovery Days Festival, PO Box 389, Dawson YT Y0B 1G0 - 867-993-5575; Fax: 867-993- 6415; Email: kva@dawson.net; URL: www.dawsoncity.ca - Aug.

The Gentlemen's Expo, Metro Toronto Convention Centre, 222 Bremner Blvd., Toronto ON M5V 3L9; URL: www.gentlemensexpo.com

Feast of St. Louis, Fortress of Louisbourg Volunteer Association, 259 Park Service Rd., Louisbourg NS B1C 2L2 - 902-733-3548; Fax: 902-733-3046; Email: info@fortressoflouisbourg.ca - Eighteenth-century celebrations in honour of St. Louis - August, Louisbourg NS

Festival des peches et de aquaculture du Nouveau Brunswick, #200, 1 av Hotel de Ville, Shippagan NB E8S 1M1 - 506-336-8726; Email: festivalshippagan@gmail.com; URL: www.festival.shippagan.com

Holiday Gift Market, c/o Premier Publications & Shows, 3145 Wolfedale Rd., Mississauga ON L5C 3A9 - Fax:

905-277-9917; URL: holidaygiftmarket.ca - Event Specialist, Filomena Feltmante, Email: ffeltmante@metrolandwest.com
Icelandic Festival of Manitoba, #107, 94 - 1st Ave., Gimli MB R0C 1B0 - 204-642-7417; Fax: 204-642-9382; Email: info@icelandicfestival.com; URL: www.icelandicfestival.com, Aug., Gimli MB
Just for Laughs Festival, 2101, boul Saint-Laurent, Montréal QC H2X 2T5 - 514-845-3155; Fax: 514-845-4140; Tollfree: 1-888-244-3155; Email: info@hahaha.com; URL: www.hahaha.com, July
Kitchener-Waterloo Oktoberfest, 17 Benton St., PO Box 1053, Kitchener ON N2G 4G1 - 519-570-4267; Fax: 519-742-3072; Tollfree: 1-888-294-4267; Email: info@oktoberfest.ca; URL: www.oktoberfest.ca - Executive Director, Dave MacNeil - Annually, October. Bavarian festival: foods, entertainment, parades
Labrador Straits Bakeapple Folk Festival, PO Box 112, Forteau NL A0K 2P0 - 709-931-2042 - Annually, Aug.
Manitoba Sunflower Festival, PO Box 1630, Altona MB R0G 0B0 - 204-324-9005; Fax: 204-324-1550; URL: www.altona.ca/msf - Annual, last weekend of July
Mom, Pop & Tots Fair, Family Productons Inc., 4634 - 90A Ave., 2nd Fl., Edmonton AB T6B 2P9 - 780-490-0215; Fax: 780-450-3757; Email: info@edmontonshows.com; URL: edmontonshows.com - March - Edmonton Expo Centre, Edmonton AB
Northern Manitoba Trappers Festival, Inc., PO Box 475, The Pas MB R9A 1K6 - 204-623-2912; Fax: 204-623- 1974; URL: trappersfestival.ca - Annually, Feb.; world championship sled dog race
Northwest Territorial Days, c/o Battlefords Agricultural Society, PO Box 668, North Battleford SK S9A 2Y9 - 306-445-2024; Fax: 306-445-3352; URL: www.agsociety.com - Aug.
Penticton Peach Festival, PO Box 21003, Cherry Lane Postal Outlet, #165, 2111 Main St., Penticton BC V2A 8K8 - 250-487-9709; Email: peach-festival@hotmail.com; URL: www.peachfest.com - Aug.
Peterborough MusicFest, Del Crary Park, Peterborough ON - URL: www.ptbomusicfest.ca- General Manager, Tracey Randall - June to Aug. every Wednesday & Saturday evening
Pictou Lobster Carnival, PO Box 1480, Pictou NS B0K 1H0 - 902-485-5150; URL: pictoulobstercarnival.ca - Annual - July
The Project Management Conference, Informa Canada, #100, 10 Alcorn Ave, Toronto ON M4V 3A9 - 416-512-3865; URL: www.thepmconference.com; Registration Manager, Gillian Wright, Email: gillian.wright@informacanada.com
Québec City Summer Festival, #150, 683, rue Saint-Joseph est, Québec QC G1K 3C1 - 418-523-4540; Fax: 418-523- 0194; Tollfree: 1-888-992-5200; Email: infofestival@ infofestival.com; URL: www.infofestival.com - Entertainment in the streets & parks of Old Québec, July
Royal Nova Scotia International Tattoo, 1586 Queen St., Halifax NS B3J 2V1 - 902-420-1114; Fax: 902-423-6629; Tollfree: 1-800-563-1114; Email: info@nstattoo.ca; URL: www.nstattoo.ca - Ian Fraser - Annually, June/July
Royal St. John's Regatta, PO Box 214, St. John's NL A1C 5J2 - 709-576-8012; Fax: 709-576-3315; Email: events@stjohnsregatta.com - North America's oldest continuing sporting event - Aug., St. John's NL
Sam Steele Days, PO Box 115, Cranbrook BC V1C 4H6 - 250-426-4161; Fax: 250-426-3873; URL: www.samsteeledays.org, June
Scotiabank CHIN Picnic, 622 College St., Toronto, ON M6G 1B6 - 416-531-7838 - June-July
Shediac Lobster Festival, 231A Belliveau Ave., Shediac NB E4P 1H4 - 506-532-1122; Fax: 506-532-7986; Tollfree: 1-888-707-1755; URL: www.shediaclobsterfestival.ca - Annually, first week of July
Spur Festival, #710, 170 Bloor St. West, Toronto ON M5S 1T9 - 416-531-1483 ; Fax 416-944-8915; Email: info@spurfestival.ca; URL: spurfestival.ca - Festival Director, Helen Walsh, Email: h.walsh@spurfestival.ca - An event during which current events are discussed & art is showcased
Steamwhistle Annual Oktoberfest, Steamwhistle Brewing, 255 Bremner Blvd., Toronto ON M5V 3N9 - 416-362-2337; Tollfree: 1-866-240-2337; Email: info@steamwhistle.ca; URL: www.steamwhistle.ca
Steinbach Pioneer Days, c/o Mennonite Heritage Village, 231, PTH 12 North, Steinbach MB R0A 2A0 - 204/326- 9661; URL: www.steinbach.ca
Summerside Lobster Festival, City Hall, 275 Fitzroy St., Summerside PE C1N 1H9 - 902-432-1279; URL: summersidelobsterfest.com, July
Threshermen's Show & Seniors' Festival, PO Box 98, Yorkton SK S3N 2V6 - 306-783-8361; Fax: 306-782- 1027; Email: yorkton@wdm.ca; URL: www.wdm.ca - Annually, Aug.
Toronto Storytelling Festival, The Storytellers School of Toronto, Artscape Wychwood Barns, Studio #173, 601 Christie St., Toronto ON M6G 4C7 - 416-656-2445; Fax: 416-656-8510; Email: admin@storytellingtoronto.org; URL: www.torontostorytellingfestival.ca - Director, Dan Yashinsky - Held annually, April
Trinity-Conception Fall Fair, c/o Town of Grace Harbour, PO Box 310, Harbour Grace NL A0A 2M0 - 709-596-3631; Fax: 709-596-1991 - CAO/Town Clerk, Michael Saccary - Annually, Sept.
Welland Rose Festival, 30 East Main St., Welland ON L3B 3W3 - 905-732-7673; Email: info@wellandrosefestival.on.ca; URL: www.wellandrosefestival.on.ca - President, Allen Bunyan - Annually, June. Rose show, lobsterfest, sporting events, juried art show, seniors' events, day in the park, day-on-the-island, craft show, fishing derby, children's events, grand parade
World's Invitational Class A Gold Panning Championships, Taylor Gold Panning Society, District of Taylor, PO Box 300, Taylor BC V0C 2K0 - 250-789-3004; Fax: 250-789-9076; URL: www.districtoftaylor.com - Annually, Aug. long weekend
Yukon Gold-Panning Championships, Klondike Visitors Association, PO Box 389, Dawson YT Y0B 1G0 - 867-993-5575; Fax: 867-993-6415; Email: kva@dawson.net; URL: www.dawsoncity.org - On Canada Day - July, Dawson City YT
Yukon River Bathtub Race, Yukon Sourdough Rendezvous Society, PO Box 33210 Whitehorse, Yukon Y1A 6S1- 867-667-2148; Email: info@yukonrendezvous.com; URL: www.yukonrendezvous.com - Longest & hardest bathtub race. Two days, 486 miles, Yukon River - Aug.
Yukon Sourdough Rendezvous, Yukon Sourdough Rendezvous Society, PO Box 33210 Whitehorse, Yukon Y1A 6S1- 867-667-2148; Email: info@yukonrendezvous.com; URL: www.yukonrendezvous.com - Annually - Celebrates the gold rush times. Mad trapper, flour packing, tug-a-truck contests, fiddle show, lip sync & queen contests - Feb.

EXHIBITIONS

***See Also* Farm Business/Agriculture, Rodeos**

Canadian Association of Fairs & Exhibitions Annual Convention, PO Box 21053 (WEPO), Brandon ON R7B 3W8 - 613-233-0012; Tollfree: 1-800-663-1714; Email: info@canadian-fairs.ca; URL: www.canadian-fairs.ca
Canadian Lakehead Exhibition, 425 Northern Ave., Thunder Bay ON P7C 2V7 - 807-622-6473; Fax: 807-623-5540; Email: clex@tbaytel.net; URL: www.cle.on.ca - Annually, Aug.
Canadian National Exhibition, Canadian National Exhibition Association, Exhibition Place, 210 Princes' Blvd., Toronto, ON M6K 3C3 - 416-263-3330; Fax: 416-263-3838; Email: info@theex.com; URL: www.theex.com - Annual public show
Comox Valley Exhibition, #201, 580 Duncan Ave., Courtenay BC V9N 2M7 - 250-338-8177; Fax: 250-338-4244; Email: mvokey@frex.ca; URL: www.cvex.ca
New Brunswick Provincial Exhibition, PO Box 235, Stn A, Fredericton NB E3B 4Y9 - 506-458-8819; Fax: 506-458-9294; Email: frex@frex.ca; URL: www.frex.ca - Annual, Sept.
Great Northern Exhibition, PO Box 523, Stayner ON L0M 1S0 - 705-444-0308; Fax: 705-446-1972; Email: greatnorthernexhibition@gmail.com; URL: www.greatnorthernex.com - Agricultural Society President, Maureen McLeod, Email: pres@greatnorthernex.com
Home Town Fair, Hometown Fair, c/o Moose Jaw Exhibition Co. Ltd., 250 Thatcher Dr. East, Moose Jaw SK S6J 1L7 - 306-692-2723; Fax: 306-692-2762; URL: www.moosejawex.ca - Annually - June
Interior Provincial Exhibition, Interior Provincial Exhibition & Stampede, PO Box 490, Armstrong BC V0E 1B0 - 250-546-9406; Fax: 250-546-6181; Email: info@armstrongipe.com; URL: www.armstrongipe.com - General Manager, Ted Fitchett - Annual consumer agricultural fair & show, Aug.-Sept. - Aug.
K-Days, 7515 - 118 Ave. NW, Edmonton AB T5B 4X5 - 780-471-7210; Fax: 780-471-8112; Toll-Free: 1-888-800-7275; URL: www.k-days.com - Annual consumer show
Lindsay Central Exhibition, 354 Angeline St. South, Lindsay ON K9V 4R2 - 705-324-5551; Email: info@lindsayex.com; URL: www.lindsayex.com - Annual consumer agricultural fair & show - Sept.
Markham Agricultural Fair, 10801 McCowan Rd., Markham ON L3P 3J3 - 905-642-3247; Fax: 905-640- 8458; Tollfree: 1-800-450-3557; Email: office@markhamfair.ca; URL: www.markhamfair.ca - Annual consumer show - Sept./Oct.
Medicine Hat Exhibition & Stampede, 2055 - 21st Ave. SE, PO Box 1298, Medicine Hat AB T1A 7N1 - 403-527- 1234; Fax: 403-529-6553; Email: mhstampede@mhstampede. com; URL: www.mhstampede.com - Annual consumer show - July
Miramichi Agricultural Exhibition, PO Box 422, 24 Church St., Miramichi City NB E1N 3A8 - 506-773-5133; Fax: 506-773-6173; Email: ask_me@ex-one.com; URL: www.ex-one.com - CEO, John Trevors, Email: ceo@ex-one.com
Niagara Regional Exhibition, 1100 Niagara St. North, Welland ON L3C 1M6 - 905-735-6413; Fax: 905-735- 2317; Email: nfo@niagararegionalexhibition.com; URL: www.niagararegionalexhibition.com - Annual consumer agricultural fair & show, Sept. - Sept.
Nova Scotia Provincial Exhibition, 73 Ryland Ave., Truro, NS B2N 2V5 - 902-893-9222; Fax: 902-897-0069; Email: nspe@eastlink.ca; URL: www.nspe.ca - General Manager, Joe Nicholson - August, Bible Hill NS
Pacific National Exhibition, 2901 East Hastings St., Stn Hastings Park, Vancouver BC V5K 5J1 - 604-253- 2311; Fax: 604-251-7753; Email: info@pne.ca; URL: www.pne.ca - President & CEO, Michael McDaniel - Annual event; agricultural competitions, parade
Paris Fall Fair, PO Box 124, Paris ON N3L 3E7 - 519-442-2823; Fax: 519-442-5121; Email: info@parisfairgrounds.com; URL: www.parisfair.com - Annual Labour Day weekend consumer show
Prince Albert Exhibition, Prince Albert Exhibition Association, PO Box 1538, Prince Albert SK S6V 5T1 - 306-764-1711; Fax: 306-764-5246; Email: paex@sasktel.net; URL: www.paexhibition.com - President, Brennin Jack - Annual
Queen City Ex, Regina Exhibition Park, PO Box 167, 1700 Elphinstone St., Regina SK S4P 2Z6 - 306-781-9200; Fax: 306/565-3443; Email: info@evrazplace.com; URL: www.thequeencityex.com - July
Red River Exhibition, Red River Exhibition Association, Red River Exhibition Park, 3977 Portage Ave., Winnipeg MB R3K 2E8 - 204-888-6990; Fax: 204-888-6992; URL: www.redriverex.com - Manitoba's largest fair & single-site entertainment event. Annually, 10 days, last two weeks in June
Saint John Ex, PO Box 284, Saint John NB E2L 3Y2 - 506-633-2020; Fax: 506-636-6958; URL: www.exhibitionparksj.com - Annual - Aug.
Saltscapes East Coast Expo, #209, 30 Damascus Rd., Bedford NS B4A 0C1 - 902-464-7258; Fax: 902-464-3755; Tollfree: 1-877-311-5877; URL: www.saltscapes.com
Threshermen's Reunion & Stampede, Central Canada's Fiddle Festival, PO Box 10, Austin MB R0H 0C0 - 204-637-2354; Fax: 204-637-2395; Email: agmuseum@mymts.net; URL: www.ag-museum.mb.ca - Annual
Western Nova Scotia Exhibition, PO Box 425, Yarmouth NS B5A 4B3 - 902-742-8222; President, Mark Firth - Six-day agricultural fair & talent competition - July or Aug., Yarmouth NS

FARM BUSINESS/AGRICULTURE

***See Also* Exhibitions, Rodeos**

Atlantic Agricultural Fall Fair, 200 Prospect Rd., Goodwood, NS B3T 1P2 - 902-876-1811; URL: www.atlanticfair.ca - Annual consumer exhibition, Oct., over the Thanksgiving weekend
CAAR Convention, Canadian Association of Agri-Retailers, #628, 70 Arthur St, Winnipeg MB R3B 1G7 - 204-989-9300; Fax: 204-989-9306; Tollfree: 1-800-463-9323; Email: info@caar.org; URL: www.caar.org
Canada's Farm Progress Show, PO Box 167, Regina SK S4P 2Z6 - 306-781-9200; Fax: 306-565-3443; Email: info@evrazplace.com; URL: www.myfarmshow.com - Annual consumer & trade show - June - Regina Exhibition Park, Regina SK
Canadian National Hereford Show, c/o Canadian Hereford Association, 5160 Skyline Way NE, Calgary AB T2E 6V1 - 403-275-2662; Fax: 403-295-1333; URL: www.hereford.ca, Nov., Regina SK
Canadian Western Agribition, c/o Public Relations Office, Canadian Western Agribition, PO Box 3535, Regina SK S4P 3J8 - 306-565-0565; Fax: 306-757-9963; Email: cwaquestions@agribition. com; URL: www.agribition.com - CEO, Chris Lane - Annually, Nov.
Chatham-Kent Farm Show, c/o 20/20 Show Productions Inc., PO Box 400, Belle River ON N0R 1A0 - 226-363-0550; Fax: 226-363-0455; URL: ontariotradeshows.com - Contact, Stuart Galloway, Email: stuart@exposition.com
Farmfair International, PO Box 1480, Edmonton AB T5J 2N5 - 780-471-7210; Fax: 780-471- 8112; Tollfree: 1-888-800-7275; URL: www.farmfairinternational.com - Annually, Nov.
London Farm Show, Western Fair Association, 316 Rectory St., PO Box 7550, London ON N5Y 5P8 - 519-438- 7203; Tollfree: 1-800-619-4629; Email: contact@westernfairdistrict.com; URL: www.westernfairdistrict.com - Annual consumer show
Norfolk County Fair & Horse Show, Norfolk County Agricultural Society, 172 South Dr., Simcoe ON N3Y 1G6 - 519-426-7280;

Fax: 519-426-7286; URL: www.norfolkcountyfair.com - Annual consumer show

Nova Scotia 4-H Show, c/o NS Dept. of Agriculture, 60 Research Dr., Bible Hill NS B6L 2R2 - 902-843-3990; Fax: 902-843-3989; URL: novascotia4h.ca - Annual consumer show, Oct.

Ontario Fruit & Vegetable Convention, #135, 104-155 Main St East, Grimsby ON L3M 1P2 - 905-945-5363; Fax: 905-945-5386; URL: www.ofvc.ca - Manager, Ross Parker, Email: ross@ofvc.ca

Grand Falls Regional Potato Festival, #200, 131 Pleasant St., Grand Falls NB E3Z 1G6 - 506-475-7777 - June

Royal Agricultural Winter Fair, Royal Agricultural Winter Fair Association, The Coliseum, National Trade Centre, Exhibition Place, Toronto ON M6K 3C3 - 416-263-3400; Fax: 416-263-3488; Email: info@royalfair.org; URL: www.royalfair.org - Annual consumer show. World's largest agricultural fair & equestrian event - Nov., Toronto ON

Salon de l'Agriculture, 4770, rue Martineau, Saint-Hyacinthe QC J2R 1V1 - 450-771-1226; Fax: 450-771- 6073; Email: info@salonagr.qc.ca; URL: www.salondelagriculture.com - Annual trade show. Agricultural products - Jan., St-Hyacinthe QC

Western Fair, Western Fair Association, 316 Rectory St., PO Box 7550, London ON N5Y 5P8 - 519-438-7203; Tollfree: 1-800-619-4629; Email: contact@westernfairdistrict.com; URL: www.westernfairdistrict.com - CEO, Hugh Mitchell - Annual consumer show

FASHION

Luggage, Leathergoods, Handbags & Accessories, PO Box 144, Station A, Toronto, ON M9C 4V2 - Fax: 519-624-6408; Tollfree: 1-866-872-2420 ; Email: info@llha.ca; URL: www.llha.ca - Show Manager, Tammy Mang, Email: tammy@llha.ca - Annual trade show - Sept. - International Centre, Mississauga ON

FESTIVALS *See* EVENTS

FILM & VIDEO FESTIVALS & SPECIAL EVENTS

Alberta Film & Television Awards, Alberta Media Production Industries Association, #200, 7316 - 101 Ave., Edmonton AB T6A 0J2 - 780-944-0707; Fax: 780-426- 3057; URL: www.ampia.org - Executive Director, Bill Evans, Email: bevans@ampia.org - April.

Buffer Festival, Toronto ON; URL: bufferfestival.com; Email: support@bufferfestival.com - YouTube film festival

Le Carrousel international du film de Rimouski, #204, 133, rue Julien-Réhel, Rimouski QC G5L 9B1 - 418-722-0103; Fax: 418-724-9504; Email: info@carrousel.qc.ca; URL: www.cifr.club - Films for children. Competition, workshops - Sept., Rimouski QC

Cinéfest - The Sudbury International Film Festival, #103, 40 Larch St., Sudbury ON P3E 5M7 - 705-688-1234; Email: cinefest@cinefest.com; URL: www.cinefest.com -Full-length feature festival with over 100 Canadian & international films, animations, shorts, Midnight Madness, documentary & children's film series - Sept., Sudbury ON

Festival du cinéma international en Abitibi-Témiscamingue, 215, av Mercier, Rouyn-Noranda QC J9X 5W8 - 819/762-6212; Fax: 819-762-6212; Email: info@festivalcinema. ca; URL: www.festivalcinema.ca - Features, mediumlength & short films. Competition; regional jury award for short or medium-length film; people's choice award for feature & animation - Oct., Rouyn-Noranda QC

Festival du film étudiant canadien/Canadian Student Film Festival, 1432, rue de Bleury, Montréal QC H3A 2J1 - 514-848-3883; Fax: 514-848-3886; Email: info@ffm-montreal.org; URL: www.ffm-montreal.org - Films & videos by Canadian students. Film competition - Aug., Montréal QC

Festival du nouveau cinéma de Montréal, 3805, boul Saint-Laurent, Montréal QC H2W 1X9 - 514-282-0004; Fax: 514-282-6664; Email: info@nouveaucinema.ca; URL: www.nouveaucinema.ca - Executive Director, Nicolas Girard Deltruc - New trends in new cinema, video & new media; non-competitive; people's choice award

Festival Vues d'Afrique, Vues d'Afrique, #3100,100, rue Sherbrooke est, Montréal, QC H2X 1C3 - 514-284-3322; Fax: 514-845-0631; URL: www.vuesdafrique.org - Films by & about African & Creole peoples - April, Montréal QC

Film Studies Association of Canada Conference, Film Studies Association of Canada, c/o Ryerson University, Sociology - JOR 306, 350 Victoria St., Toronto ON M5B 2K3; URL: www.filmstudies.ca; Email: membership@filmstudies.ca - President, Darrell Varga - May/June annually, held at a different university each year

Flicks: Saskatchewan International Youth Film Festival, #707, 601 Spadina Cres. East, Saskatoon, SK S7K 3G8 - 306-956-3456 - Annually in March, three day international film festival for children

Images Festival of Independent Film & Video, #309, 401 Richmond St. West, Toronto ON M5V 3A8 - 416-971-8405; Fax: 416-971-7412; URL: www.imagesfestival.com - Executive Director, Heather Keung - Annual. Independent films & videos. Workshops - April, Toronto ON

Les Rendez-vous du cinéma québécois, 1680, rue Ontario est, Montréal QC H2L 1S7 - 514-526-9635; Fax: 514-526-1955; Email: info@quebeccinema.ca; URL: www.quebeccinema.ca - Directrice générale, Ségolène Roedere - Restrospective of recent Québec productions - Feb., Montréal QC

Montréal World Film Festival, 1432, rue de Bleury, Montréal QC H3A 2J1 - 514-848-3883; Fax: 514-848-3886; Email: info@ffm-montreal.org; URL: www.ffm-montreal.org - Features, mediumlength & short films. Competition, symposium, markets - Aug., Montréal QC

Ottawa International Animation Festival, #120, 2 Daly Ave., Ottawa ON K1N 6E2 - 613-232-8769; Fax: 613-232-6315; Email: info@animationfestival.ca; URL: www.animationfestival.ca - Annual. Animation films & videos. Television animation conference. Workshops & panels - Sept., Ottawa ON

St. John's Women's Film & Video Festival, PO Box 984, Stn. C, St. John's NL A1C 5M3 - 709-754-3141; Fax: 709-754-0049; Email: info@womensfilmfestival.com; URL: www.womensfilmfestival.com - Women's films & videos. Workshops & panels - Oct., St. John's NL

Toronto International Film Festival, Toronto International Film Festival Group, TIFF Bell Lightbox, Reitman Square, 350 King Street West, Toronto ON M5V 3X5 - 416-934-3200; URL: tiff.net - Features & theatrical shorts. Competition. Awards for excellence in Canadian production. People's choice & film critics awards. Symposium, workshops, sales office - Sept., Toronto ON

Toronto Jewish Film Festival, 19 Madison Ave., Toronto ON M5R 2S2 - 416-324-9121; Fax: 416-324-9415; Email: tjff@tjff.ca; URL: tjff.com - Executive Director, Debbie Werner

Vancouver International Film Festival, Vancouver International Film Centre, 1181 Seymour St., Vancouver BC V6B 3M7 - 604-685-0260; Fax: 604-688-8221; Email: info@viff.org; URL: www.viff.org - Features medium-length & short films. Competition; juried awards for best western Canadian feature film, best young western Canadian director of a short film, best documentary feature & best film by a new director from Pacific Asia; people's choice award for most popular international film & for most popular Canadian film. - Sept., Vancouver

FISHING/AQUACULTURE

Adams River Sockeye Salmon Run, PO Box 24034, Scotch Creek BC V0E 3L0 - Email: info@salmonsociety.com; URL: www.salmonsociety.com - Oct.

Eastern Canadian Fisheries Exposition, Master Promotions Ltd., PO Box 565, Saint John NB E2L 3Z8 - 506-658- 0018; Fax: 506-658-0750; Tollfree: 1-888-454-7469; Email: info@mpltd.ca; URL: www.easterncanadianfisheriesexpo.ca - Annual commercial fishing show - Show Manager, Shawn Murphy; Email: smurphy@mpltd.ca Feb - Mariner's Centre, Yarmouth NS

Fish Canada/Workboat Canada, Master Promotions Ltd., PO Box 565, Saint John NB E2L 3Z8 - 506/658- 0018; Fax: 506-658-0750; Tollfree: 1-888-454-7469; Email: info@mpltd.ca; URL: www.masterpromotions.ca - Biennial commercial fishing/boat show - Nov., Vancouver BC

Flin Flon Trout Festival, PO Box 751, Flin Flon MB R8A 1N6 - 204-687-5160, June, Flin Flon MB

Nipawin Pike Festival, PO Box 2134, Nipawin SK S0E 1E0 - 306-862-9866; Fax: 306-862-3076; URL: www.nipawin.com/fishing-pikefestival.html

North Atlantic Fish & Workboat Show, Master Promotions Ltd., PO Box 565, 48 Broad St., Saint John, NB E2L 3Z8 - 506-658-0018; Fax: 506-658-0750; Tollfree: 1-888-454-7469; Email: info@mpltd.ca; URL: www.masterpromotions.ca - Nov.

Salmon Festival, PO Box 100, Campbellton NB E3N 3G1 - 506-789-2700; Fax: 506-759-7403; Tollfree: 1-888- 813-4433; Email: campbellton.salmonfestival@gmail.com; URL: salmon-festival.com - June

FLOWERS/LANDSCAPING/GARDENING

Canada Blooms, 7856 Fifth Line South, Milton, ON L9T 2X8; 416-447-8655; Fax: 416-447-1567; Tollfree: 1-800-730-1020; Email: info@canadablooms.com; URL: www.canadablooms.com - March

Hamilton & Burlington Rose Society Show, Royal Botanical Gardens, 680 Plains Rd. West, Burlington ON L7T 4H4 - 905-527-1158; Fax: 905-577-0375; URL: www.gardenmaking.com/hamilton-burlington-rose-society - June

Orchid Show, Royal Botanical Gardens, 680 Plains Rd. West, Burlington ON L7T 4H4 - 905-527- 1158; Fax: 905-577-0375; URL: www.osrbg.ca - March

FOOD & BEVERAGE

***See Also* Hospitality Industry**

Canada's Gluten Free Market, c/o Premier Publications & Shows, 3145 Wolfdale Rd., Mississauga ON K5C 3A9 - 905-293-0710; Fax: 905-277-9917; URL: www.canadasglutenfreemarket.com - Show Manager, Christy Jacobs; Email: cjacobs@metroland.com

Canadian Health Food Association Conferences, #302, 235 Yorkland Blvd., Toronto, ON M2J 4Y8 - 905-479-6939; Fax: 905-497-3214; Tollfree: 1-800-661-4510, fax 1-888-2927; Email: info@chfa.ca; URL: www.chfa.ca - Organic & natural products; homeopathy, food supplements & herbs - West, East & Québec conferences - April, Oct. & Feb.

Gluten Free Expo, Vancouver BC - 604-430-2090; Email: info@glutenfreeexpo.ca; URL: www.glutenfreeexpo.ca

Gourmet Food & Wine Expo, c/o Sun Media, 365 Bloor St. East, 3rd Fl., Toronto ON M4W 3L4 - URL: www.foodandwineexpo.ca - Show Manager, Paul McNair, Email: pmcnair@postmedia.com - Consumer show - Nov. - Metro Toronto Convention Centre, Toronto ON

La Grande Dégustation de Montréal, c/o Association Québécoise des Agences de Vins, Bières et Spiritueux Inc. (AQAVBS), 905, av de Lorimier, Montréal QC K2J 3V9; URL: www.lagrandedegustation.com

Ottawa Wine & Food Festival - 613-523-6356 - URL: www.ottawawineandfoodfestival.com - Annual trade & consumer show - Oct./Nov.

SIAL Canada & SET Canada, #901, 2120, rue Sherbrooke Est, Montréal, QC H2K 1C3; 514-289-9669; Fax: 514-289-1034; Tollfree: 1-866-281-7425; URL: www.sialcanada.com - International Food & Beverage Tradeshow/National Food Equipment & Technology Tradeshow - April

Toronto Food & Drink Market, Premier Publications & Shows, 3145 Wolfdale Rd., Mississauga ON K5C 3A9 - 289-293-0710; Fax: 905-277-9917; URL: www.tofoodanddrinkmarket.com - Show Manager, Christy Jacobs; Email: cjacobs@metroland.com - Annual consumer festival - April - Enercare Centre, Exhibition Place, Toronto, ON

Toronto Garlic Festival, PO Box 82861 RPO Cabbagetown, 467 Parliament St., Toronto ON M5A 3Y2 - 416-888-7829; URL: www.torontogarlicfestival.ca - Festival Director, Peter McClusky, Email: peterm@TorontoGarlicFestival.ca

Veg Expo, Vancouver BC - Email: info@vegexpo.ca; URL: www.vegexpo.ca

FOREST INDUSTRY

Canada North Resources Expo, @Body Texh Exhibit = North Atlantic Fish & Workboat Show, Master Promotions Ltd., PO Box 565, 48 Broad St., Saint John, NB E2L 3Z8 - 506-658-0018; Fax: 506-658-0750; Tollfree: 1-888-454-7469; Email: info@mpltd.ca; URL: www.masterpromotions.ca - May - Prince George BC

DEMO International, Master Promotions Ltd., PO Box 565, Saint John NB E2L 3Z8 - 506-658-0018; Fax: 506-658- 0750; Tollfree: 1-888-454-7469; Email: info@mpltd.ca; URL: www.demointernational.com - Active demonstrations of all types of industrial woodlands equipment. Harvesting, silviculture, transportation & handling - Sept.

InterSaw, Master Promotions Ltd., PO Box 565, Saint John NB E2L 3Z8 - 506-658-0018; Fax: 506-658-0750; Tollfree: 1-888-454-7469; Email: info@mpltd.ca; URL: www.masterpromotions.ca - Biennial show - Show Manager, Shawn Murphy, May - Centre de foires, Québec QC

FURNITURE *See* HOME SHOWS

GARDENING *See* FLOWERS

GIFTS & JEWELLERY

Alberta Gift Fair, 42 Voyager Ct. South, Toronto, ON M9W 5M7 - 416-679-0170; URL: www.cangift.org - Annual trade show. Giftware, stationery, kitchenware, luggage & leathergoods, pottery, china, glass, jewellery - Feb. & Aug.

Expo Prestige, Corporation des bijoutiers du Québec, 868, rue Brisette, Sainte-Julie QC J3E 2B1 - 514-485-3333; Fax:

450-649-8984; Email: info@cbq.qc.ca; URL: www.cbq.qc.ca - août - Palais des Congrès, Montréal QC

Québec Gift Fair/Salon du Cadeau du Québec - 42 Voyager Ct. South, Toronto, ON M9W 5M7- 416-679-0170; URL: www.cangift.org - Annual trade show. Giftware, stationery, kitchenware, luggage & leathergoods, pottery, china, glass, jewellery - March

Toronto Gift Fair, 42 Voyager Ct. South, Toronto, ON M9W 5M7 - 416-679-0170; URL: www.cangift.org - Annual trade show. Giftware, stationery, kitchenware, luggage & leathergoods, pottery, china, glass, jewellery - Jan., Toronto, ON

Vancouver Gift Expo, Smart Shows Inc., PNE Forum Building 2901 East Hastings St., Vancouver, BC V5K 5J1; 604-767-0400; Tollfree Fax: 1-888-395-0474; Email: smartshows@shaw.ca; URL: www.vancouvergiftexpo.com - Owner, Smart Shows Inc., Cameron Dix - Annual trade show. Giftwares, housewares, luggage & leathergoods, jewellery. Jan. & Aug.

GRAPHIC ARTS

Print World, #8, 1606 Sedlescomb Dr., Mississauga ON L4X 1M6 - 905-625-7070; Fax: 905-625- 4856; Tollfree: 1-800-331-7408; URL: www.printworldshow.com - Biennial trade show - Nov. - Enercare Centre, Exhibition Place, Toronto ON

HAIRDRESSING

Allied Beauty Show, Allied Beauty Association, #26-27, 145 Traders Blvd. East, Mississauga ON L4Z 3L3 - Fax: 905-568-1581; Toll-Free: 800-268-6644; Email: info@abacanada.com; URL: www.abacanada.com - Held in various locations

HEALTH & WELLNESS

Activate Ottawa Health & Fitness Expo, Ottawa Convention & Event Centre, 200 Coventry Rd., Ottawa ON K1K 4S3; 613-822-7488; Email: info@activateexpo.ca; URL: www.activateexpo.ca

BMO Vancouver Marathon Health, Sports & Lifestyle Expo, 1288 Vernon Dr., Vancouver BC V6A 4C9 - 604-872-2928; Fax: 604-872-2928; Email: info@bmovanmarathon.ca; URL: www.bmovanmarathon.ca - April/May - Vancouver Convention Centre

Burlington Wholistic Wellness Expo, Burlington ON; Email: info@wholisticwellnesscommunities.com; URL: www.burlingtonwholisticwellnessexpo.com

Ottawa Health & Wellness Expo, Shenkman Arts Centre, 245 Centrum Blvd., Ottawa ON K1E 3W8 - 613-837-2883; Email: OttawaHealthandWellnessExpo@gmail.com; URL: www.orleanswellnessexpo.com

Scotiabank Toronto Waterfront Marathon Running, Health & Fitness Expo, 264 The Esplanade, Toronto ON M5A 4J6 - 416-944-2765; Fax: 416-944-8527; URL: www.torontowaterfrontmarathon.com/en/expo.htm

Total Health Show, Total Health Events Inc., #1901, 355 St. Clair Ave. West, Toronto ON M5P 1N5 - 416-924-9800; Fax: 416-924-6404; Tollfree; 1-877-389-0996; Email: info@totalhealthshow.com; URL: www.totalhealthshow.com - April - Metro Toronto Convention Centre

Whole Life Expo, 356 Dupont St., Toronto ON M5R 1V9 - 416-515-1330; Email: info@wholelifeexpo.ca; URL: www.wholelifecanada.com - Nov. - Metro Toronto Convention Centre, Toronto ON

HEATING, PLUMBING & AIR CONDITIONING

***See Also* Hardware**

CMPX Show, 25 Bradgate Rd. Toronto, ON M3B 1J6; 416-444-5225; Tollfree: 1-800-282-0003; Email: cmpx@salshow.com; URL: www.cmpxshow.com - Annual trade show - March - Metro Toronto Convention Centre, Toronto, ON

HOBBIES

***See Also* Crafts**

Gem, Mineral & Fossil Show, Calgary Rock & Lapidary Club, Calgary AB T3E 5E3 - URL: www.crlc.ca - Annual

National Postage Stamp & Coin Show, c/o Canadian Coin News and Canadian Stamp News, International Centre, 6900 Airport Rd., Mississauga ON L4V 1E8; URL: www.stampandcoinshow.com

Sportcard & Memorabilia Expo, 10 Wynnview Crt., Toronto ON M1N 3K3; Toll-Free: 888-466-7116; E-mail: sales@sportcardexpo.ca; URL: www.sportcardexpo.com

Toronto Gem & Mineral Show, 130 Don Mills Rd., Toronto ON M3C 1W6; Email: torontogemshow@gmail.com; URL: www.torontogemshow.com - April

HOME ENTERTAINMENT *See* ELECTRICAL/ELECTRONICS

HOME SHOWS

Atlantic National Home Show, Master Promotions Ltd., PO Box 565, Saint John NB E2L 3Z8 - 506-658-0018; Fax: 506-658-0750; Tollfree: 1-888-454-7469; Email: info@mpltd.ca; URL: www.atlanticnationalhomeshow.ca - Annual consumer show - March, Saint John NB

BC Home + Garden Show, Marketplace Events, LLC, #212, 1847 West Broadway, Vancouver BC V6J 1Y6; 604-639-2288 Fax: 604-639-2289; Tollfree: 1-800-633-8332; URL: www.bchomeandgardenshow.com - Annual consumer show - Show Manager, Tyson Kidd, Email: tysonk@mpeshows.com - Feb.

Burlington Lifestyle Home Shows, Jenkins Show Productions, ON - 905-827-4632; Fax: 905-827-4632; Tollfree: 1-800-465-1073; URL: www.jenkinsshow.com - President, Dave Jenkins, Email: dave@jenkinsshowproductions.com - Annual consumer show - April & Sept., Burlington ON

Calgary Home + Design Show, Marketplace Events, LLC, Macleod Place II, #602, 5940 Macleod Trail SW, Calgary, AB T2H 2G4; 403-253-1177; Fax: 403-253-7878; Tollfree: 1-866-941-0673; URL: www.calgaryhds.com - Annual consumer show - Show Manager, Teri Salazar, Email: teris@mpeshows.com - Sept. - BMO Centre, Calgary AB

Canadian Spa & Pool Conference & Expo, Pool & Hot Tub Council of Canada, 5 MacDougall Dr., Brampton, ON L6S 3P3 - 905-458-7242; Fax: 905-458-7037; Tollfree: 1-800-879-7066; Email: office@poolcouncil. ca; URL: www.poolandspaexpo.ca - Annual trade & consumer show - Dec. - Toronto Congress Centre, Toronto ON

Chatham-Kent Home & Garden Shows, c/o 20/20 Show Productions Inc., PO Box 400, Belle River, Ontario N0R 1A0- 226-363-0550; Fax: 226-363-0455; URL: ontariotradeshows.com - Contact, Stuart Galloway, Email: stuart@exposition.com - Annual - April

Colchester County Home Show, Master Promotions Ltd., PO Box 565, Saint John NB E2L 3Z8 - 506-658-0018; Fax: 506-658-0750; Tollfree: 1-888-454-7469; Email: info@mpltd.ca; URL: www.masterpromotions.ca - Show Manager, Scott Sprague - Annual consumer show - April

Edmonton Fall Home Show, Marketplace Events LLC, Macleod Place II, #602, 5940 Macleod Trail SW, Calgary AB T2H 2G4; 403-253-1177; Fax: 403-253-7878; Tollfree: 1-866-941-0673; URL: www.edmontonhomeandgarden.com - Annual consumer show - Oct. - Edmonton Expo Centre, Edmonton, AB

Edmonton Home & Garden Show, Marketplace Events LLC, Macleod Place II, #602, 5940 Macleod Trail SW, Calgary AB T2H 2G4; 403-253-1177; Fax: 403-253-7878; Tollfree: 1-866-941-0673; URL: www.edmontonhomeandgarden.com - Annual consumer show - March - Edmonton Expo Centre, Edmonton, AB

Edmonton Renovation Show, Marketplace Events LLC, Macleod Place II, #602, 5940 Macleod Trail SW Calgary, AB T2H 2G4 - 403-253-1177; Fax: 403-253-7878; Tollfree: 1-866-941-0673; URL: www.edmontonrenovationshow.com - Annual consumer show - January

Expo-Habitat de St-Hyacinthe, DBC Communications inc., 655, av Sainte-Anne, Saint-Hyacinthe, QC, J2S 5G4 - 450-773-3976; Fax: 450-773-3115; URL: www.expo-habitatst-hyacinthe.com - Personne ressource, Patrick Desrosiers - Annual consumer show. Home construction & renovation products & services - April - Pavillion de Pionnieres, St-Hyacinthe QC

Fredericton Home Show, Master Promotions Ltd., PO Box 565, Saint John NB E2L 3Z8 - 506-658-0018; Fax: 506-658-0750; Tollfree: 1-888-454-7469; Email: info@mpltd.ca; URL: www.masterpromotions.ca - Annual consumer show - March - Capital Exhibit Centre, Fredericton NB

Great West Home & Leisure Show, Medicine Hat & District Chamber of Commerce, 413 - 6th Ave. SE, Medicine Hat AB T1A 2S7 - 403-527-5214; Fax: 403-527-5182; Email: info@medicinehatchamber.com; URL: www.medicinehatchamber. com - Consumer show - March - Cypress Centre, Stampede Park, Medicine Hat AB

GTA Home & Reno Show, Building Industry & Land Development Association, #100, 20 Upjohn Rd., Toronto, ON M3B 2V9 - 416-644-5408; URL: www.gtahomeandrenoshow.com - Annual consumer show - Feb. - The International Centre, Mississauga, ON

Hamilton RE/MAX Spring Home & Garden Show, Continuum Productions Inc., 3488 Trelawny Circle, Mississauga ON L5N 6N7 - 905-824-1060; Fax: 905-824-9923; Email: info@continuumevents.ca; URL: www.continuumevents.ca - April

IIDEXCanada, Informa Canada, #100, 10 Alcorn Ave., Toronto ON M4V 3A9 - 416-944-3350; Fax: 416-921-2707 Email: news@iidexcanada.com; URL: www.iidexcanada.com - Vice President, IIDEXCanada, Tracy Bowie, Email: tbowie@iidexcanada.com

Interior Design Show, Informa Canada, #100, 10 Alcorn Ave., Toronto ON M4V 3A9 - 416-599-3222; Fax: 416-944-9261; Email: info@interiordesignshow.com; URL: www.interiordesignshow.com

Kingston Home & Garden Show, c/o 20/20 Show Productions Inc., PO Box 400, Belle River ON N0R 1A0 - 226-363-0550; Fax: 226-363-0455; URL: ontariotradeshows.com - Contact, Stuart Galloway, Email: stuart@exposition.com

London Spring Home & Garden Show, London Show Productions, 2326 Fanshawe Park Rd. East, London ON N5X 4A2 - 519-455-5888; Fax: 519-455-7780; URL: londonhomeandgardenshow.com - Consumer show - April, London ON

Miramichi Home Show, Master Promotions Ltd., PO Box 565, Saint John NB E2L 3Z8 - 506-658-0018; Fax: 506-658-0750; Tollfree: 1-888-454-7469; Email: info@mpltd.ca; URL: www.masterpromotions.ca - Annual consumer show - April - Miramichi Civic Centre, Miramichi NB

Montréal National Home Show, Expo Media, #210, 370, rue Guy, Montréal, QC H3J 1S6 - 514-527-9221; Fax: 514-527-8449; URL: salonnationalhabitation.com

National Home Show, Building Industry & Land Development Association, #100, 20 Upjohn Rd., Toronto, ON M3B 2V9 - 416-263-3200; URL: www.nationalhomeshow.com - Senior Exhibit Sales Consultant, Kelly Haney, Email: khaney@bildgta.ca - Annual consumer show - April - Enercare Centre, Exhibition Place, Toronto ON

Niagara Lifestyle Home Show, Jenkins Show Productions, ON - 905-827-4632; Fax: 905-827-8139; Tollfree: 1-800-465-1073; Email: info@jenkinsshow.com; URL: www.jenkinsshow.com - President, Dave Jenkins - Annual consumer show - April - Garden City/Rex Stimers Arena, St Catharines

Niagara Regional Home Show, c/o 20/20 Show Productions Inc., PO Box 400, Belle River, Ontario N0R 1A0- 226-363-0550; Fax: 226-363-0455; URL: ontariotradeshows.com - Contact, Stuart Galloway, Email: stuart@exposition.com - March

Nova Scotia Fall Ideal Home Show, Master Promotions Ltd., PO Box 565, Saint John NB E2L 3Z8 - 506-658- 0018; Fax: 506-658-0750; Tollfree: 1-888-454-7469; Email: info@mpltd.ca; URL: www.masterpromotions.ca - Annual consumer show - Oct., Halifax NS

Nova Scotia Spring Ideal Home Show, Master Promotions Ltd., PO Box 565, Saint John NB E2L 3Z8 - 506-658- 0018; Fax: 506-658-0750; Tollfree: 1-888-454-7469; Email: info@mpltd.ca; URL: www.masterpromotions.ca - Annual consumer show - April, Halifax NS

Oakville Lifestyle Home Show, Jenkins Show Productions, ON - 905-827-4632; Fax: 905-827-8139; Tollfree: 1-800-465-1073; URL: www.jenkinsshow.com - President, Dave Jenkins, Email: dave@jenkinsshowproductions.com - Annual consumer show - April

Ottawa Home & Garden Show, Marketplace Events LLC, #210, 370, rue Guy, Montréal, QC H3J 1S6 - 613-667-0509; Fax: 514-527-8449; URL: www.ottawahomeshow.com - Annual consumer show. March

PEI Provincial Home Show, Master Promotions Ltd., PO Box 565, Saint John NB E2L 3Z8 - 506-658-0018; Fax: 506-658-0750; Tollfree: 1-888-454-7469; Email: info@mpltd.ca; URL: www.masterpromotions.ca - Annual consumer show - March, Charlottetown PE

Red Deer Home Show, Canadian Homebuilders' Association Central Alberta, #200, 6700 - 76 St., Red Deer AB T4P 4G6 - 403-346-5321; Fax: 403-342-1301; Email: info@chbacentralalberta.ca; URL: www.reddeerhomeshow.ca - Annual, Feb./March

Sudbury Home Show, Sudbury & District Homebuilders' Association, 1942 Regent St., Unit C, Sudbury ON P3E 5V5 - 705-671-6099; Fax: 705-671-9590; URL: sudburyhomebuilders.com, March, Sudbury ON

Sunshine Home & Garden Show, Medicine Hat & District Chamber of Commerce, 413 - 6th Ave. SE, Medicine Hat AB T1A 2S7 - 403-527-5214; Fax: 403-527-5182; Email: info@medicinehatchamber.com; URL: www.medicinehatchamber.com - Annual consumer show - Nov.

Toronto Fall Home Show, Building Industry & Land Development Association, #100, 20 Upjohn Rd., Toronto, ON M3B 2V9 - 416-644-5408; URL: www.fallhomeshow.com - Oct.

Vancouver Home & Design Show, Marketplace Events, LLC, #212, 1847 West Broadway, Vancouver BC V6J 1Y6 - 604-639-2288, Fax: 604-639-2289; Tollfree: 1-800-633-8332;

URL: www.vancouverhomeanddesignshow.com - Annual consumer show - Show Manager, Tyson Kidd, Email: tysonk@mpeshows.com, Oct.

Win-Door, Shield Associates Ltd., 25 Bradgate Rd., Toronto ON M3B 1J6 - 416-444-5225; Fax: 416-444-8268; Toll-Free: 1-800-282-0003; URL: www.windoorshow.com - Trade, Windows & doors show, new products & technologies - Nov.

Windsor Home & Garden Show, c/o 20/20 Show Productions Inc., PO Box 400, Belle River, ON N0R 1A0 - 226-363-0550; Fax: 226-363-0455; Email: stuart@exposition.com; URL: ontariotradeshows.com - Stuart Galloway - Annual - Feb. - University of Windsor, Windsor ON

Winnipeg Renovation Show, Marketplace Events LLC, #212, 1847 West Broadway, Vancouver BC V6J 1Y6 - 604-639-2288; Fax: 604-639-2289; Tollfree: 1-800-633-8332; URL: www.winnipegrenovationshow.com - Show Manager, Jenn Tait, Email: jennt@mpeshows.com - Annual consumer show

HORSES

Arabian & Half-Arabian Championship Horse Show, Canadian Nationals, Arabian Horse Association, Keystone Centre, #1, 1175 - 18th St., Brandon, MB R7A 7C5 - 204-726-3500; Fax: 204-727-5552; Tollfree: 877-610-6015; URL: www.arabianhorses.org/CNL - Annual - Aug.

Masters Show Jumping Tournament, Spruce Meadows, 18011 Spruce Meadows Way SW, Calgary AB T2J 5G5 - 403-974-4200; Fax: 403-974-4270; Email: information@sprucemeadows.com; URL: www.sprucemeadows.com - Annual tournament. Includes consumer/trade show Equi-Fair, & the Festival of Nations - Sept.

North American Tournament, 18011 Spruce Meadows Way SW, Calgary AB T2J 5G5 - 403-974-4200; Fax: 403-974-4270; Email: information@sprucemeadows.com; URL: www.sprucemeadows.com - Showcased through Sun Life Financials at Fort Meadows - June

HORTICULTURE *See* FLOWERS

HOSPITALITY INDUSTRY (HOTEL, MOTEL, RESTAURANT)

***See Also* Food & Beverage**

ApEx, Canadian Restaurant & Foodservices Association, MediaEdge Communications Inc., #1000, 5 Communications Inc., #1000, 5255 Yonge St., Toronto, ON M2N 6P4 - 416-512-8186 ext. 227; Fax: 416-512-8344; Tollfree: 1-866-216-0860; URL: www.albertafoodserviceexpo.ca - Manager, Show Operations, Rachel Leslie, Email: rachell@mediaedge.ca

Restaurants Canada Show, Restaurants Canada, 1155 Queen St. West Toronto, ON M6J 1J4 - 416-923- 8416; Tollfree: 1-800-387-5649; Email: info@restaurantscanada.org; URL: restaurantshow.ca - Annual trade show

Grocery Innovations Canada, Canadian Federation of Independent Grocers, #401, 105 Gordon Baker Rd., Toronto ON M2H 3P8 - 416-492-2311; Fax: 416-492-2347 ; Tollfree: 1-800-661-2344; Email: info@cfig.ca; URL: www.cfig.ca - Annual trade show - Oct

Grocery & Specialty Food West, Canadian Federation of Independent Grocers, #401, 105 Gordon Baker Rd., Toronto ON M2H 3P8 - 416-492-2311; Fax: 416-492-2347; Tollfree: 1-800-661-2344; Email: info@cfig.ca; URL: www.cfig.ca - Annual trade show - March - Vancouver Convention Centre, Vancouver BC

INDUSTRIAL

Advanced Manufacturing Canada, Society of Manufacturing Engineers, #312, 7100 Woodbine Ave., Markham, ON L3R 5J2 - Tollfree: 1-888-322-7333; Email: canadasales@sme.org; URL: www.advancedmfg.ca - Trade show - Nov.

FABTECH Canada, Society of Manufacturing Engineers, #312, 7100 Woodbine Ave., Markham, ON, L3R 5J2 - 905-752-4415; Fax: 905-479-0113; Tollfree: 888.322.7333; URL: www.fabtechcanada.com - March - Toronto Congress Centre, Toronto, ON

Montreal Manufacturing Technology Show, Society of Manufacturing Engineers, #312, 7100 Woodbine Ave., Markham, ON, L3R 5J2 - Tollfree: 1-888-322-7333; URL: www.mmts.ca - Biennial trade show - Place Bonaventure, Montréal, QC

Salon industriel Abitibi-Témiscamingue, Les Promotions André Pageau Inc., 1627, boul Bastien, Québec QC G2K 1H1 - 418-623-3383; Fax: 418-623-5033; Tollfree: 1-800-387- 3383; Email: info@promoapageau.com; URL: www.promoapageau.com - Président, André Pageau, May, Rouyn-Noranda QC

Salon industriel Bas-St-Laurent, Les Promotions André Pageau Inc., 1627, boul Bastien, Québec QC G2K 1H1 - 418-623-3383; Fax: 418-623-5033; Tollfree: 1-800-387- 3383; Email: info@promoapageau.com; URL: www.promoapageau.com - Président, André Pageau, April, Rimouski QC

Salon industriel Centre-du-Québec, Les Promotions André Pageau Inc., 1627, boul Bastien, Québec QC G2K 1H1 - 418-623-3383; Fax: 418-623-5033; Tollfree: 1-800-387- 3383; Email: info@promoapageau.com; URL: www.promoapageau.com - Président, André Pageau, April Drummondville QC

Salon industriel de L'Estrie, Les Promotions André Pageau Inc., 1627, boul Bastien, Québec QC G2K 1H1 - 418-623-3383; Fax: 418-623-5033; Tollfree: 1-800-387- 3383; Email: info@promoapageau.com; URL: www.promoapageau.com - Président, André Pageau, Sept., St-Hyacinthe QC

Salon Industriel de Québec, Les Promotions André Pageau Inc., 1627, boul Bastien, Québec QC G2K 1H1 - 418-623-3383; Fax: 418-623-5033; Tollfree: 1-800-387- 3383; Email: info@promoapageau.com; URL: www.promoapageau.com - Président, André Pageau - Biennial trade show - Oct., Québec QC

Salon Industriel du SAGLAC, Les Promotions André Pageau Inc., 1627, boul Bastien, Québec QC G2K 1H1 - 418-623-3383; Fax: 418-623-5033; Tollfree: 1-800-387-3383; Email: info@promoapageau. com; URL: www.promoapageau.com - Président, André Pageau - Biennial - May, Chicoutimi QC

Western Manufacturing Technology Show - Edmonton, Society of Manufacturing Engineers, #312, 7100 Woodbine Ave., Markham, ON, L3R 5J2 - 905-752-4415; Fax: 905-479-0113; Tollfree: 1-888-322-7333; Email: infocanada@sme.org; URL: wmts.ca - Trade show - June, Edmonton AB

JEWELLERY *See* GIFTS

LANDSCAPING *See* FLOWERS

LEGAL

Canadian Association of Law Libraries Annual General Meeting, c/o National Office, #200, 411 Richmond St. East, Toronto, ON M5A 3S5 - 647-346-8723; Email: office@callacbd.ca; URL: www.callacbd.ca/Conference - Annual - May

CBA Legal Conference, Canadian Bar Association, #500, 865 Carling Ave., Ottawa, ON K1S 5S8 - 613-237-2925; 613-237-1988; Fax: 613-237-0185; Tollfree: 1-800-267-8860; Email: pd@cba.org; URL: www.cbalegalconference.org - Senior Director, Meetings, Stephanie Lockhart, Email: slockhart@cba.org - Aug.

Construction & Infrastructure Law Conference, Canadian Bar Association, #500, 865 Carling Ave., Ottawa, ON K1S 5S8 - 613/237-2925; 613-237-1988; Fax: 613-237-0185; Tollfree: 1-800-267-8860; Email: pd@cba.org; URL: www.cbalegalconference.org - Senior Director, Meetings, Stephanie Lockhart, Email: slockhart@cba.org - April

LEISURE *See* SPORTS & RECREATION

LGBTQ

Edmonton Pride Festival, Edmonton Pride Festival Society - 10820 - 119 St., Edmonton AB T5H 3P2 - URL: www.edmontonpride.ca

Fête arc-en-ciel de Québec, l'Alliance Arc-en-ciel de Québec, #3, 435, rue du Roi, Québec, QC G1K 2X1 - 418-809-3383 - URL: arcencielquebec.ca - Directrice générale, Louis Filip, Email: dg@arcencielquebec.ca

Halifax Pride, Halifax Pride Committee, PO Box 47027, Halifax NS B3K5Y2 - Email: info@halifaxpride.com; URL: halifaxpride.com

Inside Out LGBT Film Festival - #219, 401 Richmond St. West, Toronto ON M5V 3A8 - 416-977-6847; Fax: 416-977-8025; URL: www.insideout.ca - Festival featuring films by gay, lesbian, bisexual & trans people - Toronto & Ottawa

Ottawa Capital Pride, #310, 176 Gloucester St., Ottawa ON K2P 0A6 - Email: info@ottawacapitalpride.ca; URL: ottawacapitalpride.ca

OUTformation Fair, Pride Niagara, PO Box 4020, St Catharines ON L2R 3B0 - Email: info@prideniagara.com; URL: prideniagara.com

Pride Calgary, PO Box 1205, Stn. M, Calgary AB T2P 2K9 - Fax: 1-877-404-8074; URL: pridecalgary.ca

Pride Festival, Vancouver Pride Society - #304, 1080 Howe St., Vancouver BC V6Z 2T1 - 604-687-0955; Fax: 604-687-0965; Email: info@vancouverpride.ca; URL: vancouverpride.ca - A celebration of LGBTQ culture & accpetance

Pride Montréal, 260, rue Sainte-Catherine Est, Montréal QC H2X 1L4 - 514-903-6193; Fax: 514-666-0189; Email: info@fiertemontrealpride.com; URL: www.fiertemontrealpride.com - President, Éric Pineault

Pride Niagara, PO Box 4020, St Catharines ON L2R 3B0 - Email: info@prideniagara.com; URL: prideniagara.com

Pride Toronto, 55 Berkeley St.., Toronto ON M5A 2W5 - 416-927-7433; Email: office@pridetoronto.com; URL: www.pridetoronto.com - Celebration of LGBT culture & acceptance - June - Toronto

Pride Winnipeg, PO Box 2101, Stn. Main, Winnipeg MB R3C 3R4 - URL: www.pridewinnipeg.com

Saskatoon Pride, Saskatoon Diversity Network, 320 - 21 St. West, Saskatoon SK S7M 4E6; Email: info@saskatoonpride.ca; URL: saskatoonpride.ca

Victoria Pride, Victoria Pride Society, PO Box 8607, Stn. Main, Victoria BC V8W 3S2 - Email: info@victoriapridesociety.org; URL: victoriapridesociety.org

Whistler Pride & Ski Festival, Alpenglow Productions, 4005 Whistler Way, Whistler BC V0N 1B4 - Tollfree: 1-866-787-1966; URL: gaywhistler.com

LOGISTICS

Cargo Logistics Canada Expo & Conference, Informa Canada Vancouver Office, #510, 1185 West Georgia St., Vancouver BC V6E 4E6; Tollfree: 1-877-739-2112; Email: info@cargologisticscanada.com; URL: www.cargologisticscanada.com

MACHINERY & MANUFACTURING

***See Also* Industrial**

Atlantic Heavy Equipment Show, Master Promotions Ltd., PO Box 565, Saint John NB E2L 3Z8 - 506-658-0018; Fax: 506-658-0750; Tollfree: 1-888-454-7469; Email: info@mpltd.ca; URL: www.masterpromotions.ca - Biennial - April - Coliseum, Moncton NB

Canadian Manufacturing Technology Show, Society of Manufacturing Engineers, #312, 7100 Woodbine Ave., Markham, ON, L3R 5J2 - Tollfree: 1-888-322-7333; URL: cmts.ca - Customer Service Contact, Chris Raso, Email: craso@sme.org - Biennial trade show - Sept., Toronto ON

National Heavy Equipment Show, Master Promotions Ltd., PO Box 565, Saint John NB E2L 3Z8 - 506-658-0018; Fax: 506-658-0750; Tollfree: 1-888-454-7469; Email: info@mpltd.ca; URL: www.nhes.ca - Biennial - March - International Centre, Toronto ON

MAGAZINES

Publishing World, #8, 1606 Sedlescomb Dr., Mississauga ON L4X 1M6 - 905-625-7070; Fax: 905-625- 4856; Tollfree: 1-800-331-7408 - URL: www.printworldshow.com/publishing; Annual conference & trade show for publishing professionals - Nov., Toronto ON

MARKETING *See* ADVERTISING

MATERIALS HANDLING *See* LOGISTICS

MEDICAL

Canadian Neurological Sciences Federation Congress, Intertask Conferences, 275 Bay St., Ottawa ON K1R 5Z5; Email: info@intertaskconferences.com - URL: congress.cnsfederation.org

COS Annual Meeting & Exhibition, Canadian Ophthalmological Society, #110, 2733 Lancaster Rd., Ottawa ON K1B 0A9 - 613-729-6779; Fax: 613-729-7209; Email: cos@cos-sco.ca; URL: www.cos-sco.ca - Executive Director, Jennifer Brunet-Colvey, June

MayFest, Ontario Association of the Deaf, 2395 Bayview Ave., Toronto ON M2L 1A2 - 416-413-9191; Fax: 416-413-4822; TTY: 416-513-1893; Email:office@deafontario.ca; URL: wwww.deafontario.ca - Latest innovations & access for deaf, deafened & hard of hearing people - May, Toronto ON

MINING & MINERALS

CIM Conference & Exhibition, Canadian Institute of Mining, Metallurgy & Petroleum, #1250, 3400, boul de Maisonneuve ouest, Montréal QC H3Z 3C1 - 514-939-2710; Fax: 514-939-2714; Email: cim@cim.org; URL: convention.cim.org - Annual consumers show. Mining industry, equipment & services - April-May

Mines & Minerals Symposia, Ontario Prospectors Association, c/o Gary Clark, 1000 Alloy Dr., Thunder Bay, ON P7B 6A5 -

807-622-3284 - URL: www.ontarioprospectors.com - Annual trade shows & seminars related to regional associations

MOTORCYCLES *See* AUTOMOTIVE

MULTICULTURAL

Canada's National Ukrainian Festival, 1550 Main St. South, PO Box 368, Dauphin MB R7N 2V2 - 204-622-4600; Fax: 204-622-4606; Tollfree: 1-877-474-2683; Email: cnuf@mymts.nett; URL: www.cnuf.ca - Annual. Three days of song, dance, music, costume, cuisine, culture - Aug.

Le Festival de l'Escaouette, a/s La Société Saint-Pierre, PO Box 430, Cheticamp NS B0E 1H0 - 902-224-2612; Fax: 902-224-1579; URL: www.cheticamp.ca - Annually. Acadian folklore, traditions, culture - Aug.

Foire Brayonne, 95 Victoria St., Edmundston NB E3V 3K8 - 506-739-6608; Fax: 506-739-9578; Email: info@foirebrayonne.com; URL: www.foirebrayonne.com - July/Aug. Brayon heritage festival

Folklorama - Canada's Cultural Celebration, 183 Kennedy St., Winnipeg MB R3C 1S6 - 204-982-6210; Fax: 204-943-1956; Tollfree: 1-800-665-0234; Email: info@folklorama.ca; URL: www.folklorama.ca - Executive Director, Debra Zoerb, Email: zoerbd@folklorama.ca - Annual. Fourteen days. More than forty ethnic pavilions - Aug.

Manitoba Highland Gathering, PO Box 59, Selkirk MB R1A 2B1 - 204-794-6587; URL: www.manitobahighlandgathering.org - Annual - July

Mosaic A Festival of Cultures, Regina Multicultural Council, 2054 Broad St., Regina SK, S4P 1Y3 - 306-757-5990; Fax: 306-352-1977; Email: admin.rmc@sasktel.net; URL: www.reginamulticulturalcouncil.ca - Annual. End of May/early June. Twenty ethno-cultural pavilions

Saskatoon Folkfest, 127B Ave. D North, Saskatoon, SK S7L 1M5 - 306-931-0100; Fax: 306-665-3421; Email: info@saskatoonfolkfest.com; URL: www.saskatoonfolkfest.com - Annual. Three days. Twenty or more ethnic pavilions - Aug.

Vesna Festival, PO Box 1592, Saskatoon SK S7K 3R3 - URL: www.vesnafestival.com - Annual Spring celebration. Two days of entertainment, dancing, cultural demonstrations & displays. The World's Largest Ukrainian Cabaret - May

MUSIC

Beaches International Jazz Festival, 1998 Queen St. East, Toronto ON M4L 1G8 - 416-698-2152; Fax: 416-698- 2064; URL: www.beachesjazz.com - Executive Producer, Lido Chilelli, July, Toronto ON

Big Valley Jamboree, 4238 -37th St., Camrose AB T4V 4L6 - 780-672-0224; Fax: 780-672-9530; Tollfree: 1-888-404-1234; Email: bvj@bigvalleyjamboree. com; URL: www.bigvalleyjamboree.com - Country music - Aug.

Brandon Folk, Music & Arts Festival, PO Box 22091, Brandon MB R7A 6Y9 - Email: brandonfolkfestival@gmail.com; URL: brandonfolkfestival.ca - Music Director, Jody Weger - Annually, last weekend in July

Canada Dance Festival, Canada Dance Festival Society, PO Box 1376, Stn B, Ottawa ON K1P 5R4 - 613-947-7000, ext.576; Fax: 613-943-1399; Email: cdffdc@nac-cna.ca; URL: www.canadadance.ca - Producing Director, Jason Dubois, Email: jason@canadadance.ca - Biennial - June

Dawson City Music Festival, PO Box 456, Dawson YT Y0B 1G0 - 867-993-5584; Fax: 867-993-5510; Email: info@dcmf.com; URL: www.dcmf.com - Annually, second last weekend in July

Downtown Oakville Jazz Festival,Downtown Oakville BIA, 146 Lakeshore Rd. East, Oakville ON L6J 1H4 - 905-844-4520; Fax: 905-844-1154; Email: info@oakvilledowntown.com; URL: www.oakvillejazz.com, Aug., Oakville ON

Edgefest, Edge 102, Corus Quay, 25 Dockside Dr., Toronto ON M5A 0B5 - 416-479-7000; URL: www.edge.ca, July

Edmonton International Jazz Festival, Edmonton Jazz Festival Society, 10046 - 116 St., Edmonton, AB, T5K 1V6 - 780-990-0222; Fax: 780-990-0212; Email: info@edmontonjazz.com; URL: www.edmontonjazz.com - Annual - June

Elora Festival & Singers, 136 Metcalfe St., Elora ON N0B 1S0 - 519/846-0331; Fax: 519/846-5947; Tollfree: 1-800-265-8977; Email: info@elorafestival. com; URL: www.elorafestival.com - July - Aug. Choral & contemporary Canadian & international music

Festival de Lanaudière, 1500, boul Base-de-Roc, Joliette QC J6E 3Z1 - 450-759-7636; Fax: 450-759-3082; Email: festival@lanaudiere.org; URL: www.lanaudiere.org - Annually June-Aug.; biggest mostly classical festival in Canada

Festival International de Jazz de Montréal, 400, boul Maisonneuve ouest, 9e étage, Montréal QC H3A 1L4 - 514-523-3378; Fax: 514-525-8033; Tollfree: 1-888-515-0515; URL: www.montrealjazzfest.com - Annual. Over 2,000 musicians & 450 shows - July, Montréal QC

Le Festival International du Domaine Forget, Le Festival International de Domaine Forget, 5, rang Saint-Antoine, Saint-Irénée QC G0T 1V0 - 418-452-8111; Fax: 418-452-3503; Tollfree: 1-888-336-7438; Email: info@domaineforget. com; URL: www.domaineforget.com - June-Aug.

Festival International Nuits d'Afrique de Montréal, 4374, boul St-Laurent, 1e ,tage, Montréal QC H2W 1Z5 - 514-499-9239, 9520; Fax: 514-499-9215; Email: info@festivalnuitsdafrique.com; URL: www.festivalnuitsdafrique.com, juil.

Festival of the Sound, 42 James St., PO Box 750, Parry Sound ON P2A 2Z1 - Tollfree: 1-866-364-0061; Email: info@festivalofthesound.ca; URL: www.festivalofthesound.ca - July-Aug.

Folk on the Rocks, PO Box 326, Yellowknife NT X1A 2N3 - 867-920-7806; Fax: 867-873-6535; URL: folkontherocks.com - Annual. Two days. Inuit, Dene, other northern & southern folk groups - July

Guelph Jazz Festival, #301, 6 Dublin St. South, Guelph ON N1H 4L5 - 519-763-4952; Email: info@guelphjazzfestival.com; URL: www.guelphjazzfestival.com, Sept., Guelph ON

Halifax Jazz Festival, JazzEast, PO Box 33043, Halifax NS B3L 4T6 - 902-492-2225; Fax: 902-425-7946 - Email: info@halifaxjazzfestival.ca; URL: halifaxjazzfestival.ca - Executive Director, Heather Gibson, Email: heather@halifaxjazzfestival.ca - July

Harvest Jazz & Blues Festival, 81 Regent St., Fredericton NB E3B 3W3 - 506-454-2583; Fax: 506-457-1815; Tollfree: 1-888-622-5837; Email: info@harvestjazzandblues. com; URL: www.harvestjazzandblues.com; Managing Director: Vanessa Paesani, Email: vanessa@harvestjazzandblues.com - Sept.

Hillside Festival, 341 Woolwich St., Guelph, ON N1H 3W4 - 519-763-6396; Fax: 519-763-9514; Email: info@hillsidefestival.ca; URL: www.hillsidefestival.ca

International Festival of Baroque Music, International Baroque Music Festival, #2, 28, rue de l'Hôpital, Lameque NB E8T 1C3 - 506-344-3261; Fax: 506-344-3266; Email: baroque@lameque.ca; URL: www.festivalbaroque.com - Early music festival with five productions, last week of July (Northeastern New Brunswick, on Lameque Island)

Kiwanis Music Festival of Greater Toronto, #A, 1422 Bayview Ave., Toronto, ON M4G 3A7 - 416-487-5885; Fax: 416-487-5784; Email: kiwanismusic@bellnet.ca; URL: kiwanismusictoronto.org - General Manager, Pam Allen, Email: pam@kiwanismusictoronto.org - Feb., Toronto, ON

L'OFF Festival de Jazz, L'OFF Festival de Jazz de Montréal, #305, 1097, rue St-Alexandre, Montréal QC H2J 1P8 - 514-524-0831; Email: info@lofffestivaldejazz.com; URL: www.lofffestivaldejazz.com

Mariposa Folk Festival, Mariposa Folk Foundation, 10 Peter St. South, PO Box 383, Orillia ON L3V 6J8 - 705-326-3655; Fax: 705-326-5963; URL: www.mariposafolk.com

Maritime Fiddle Festival, #600, 73 Tacoma Dr., Dartmouth NS B2W 3Y6 - Email: info@maritimefiddlefestival.ca; URL: maritimefiddlefestival.ca - July

Markham Jazz Festival, #281, 4261 A-145, Hwy.#7, Unionville ON L3R 9W6 - 905-471-5299; Fax: 905-471-7764; URL: www.markhamjazzfestival.com, Aug., Markham ON

Miramichi Folksong Festival, PO Box 13, Miramichi NB E1V 3M2 - 506-623-2150; Fax: 506-623-2261; URL: www.miramichifolksongfestival.com - Aug.

Moose Jaw Band & Choral Festival, PO Box 883, Moose Jaw SK S6H 4P5 - 306-693-7078; URL: www.mjbandfestival.com - 3,000 musicians, evening concerts. Annual - May, Moose Jaw SK

Newfoundland & Labrador Folk Festival, #206, 223 Duckworth St., St. John's NL A1C 6N1 - 709-576-8508; Fax: 709-757-8500; Tollfree: 1-866-576-8508; Email: office@nlfolk.com; URL: nlfolk.com - Contact, Erin McArthur - Traditional Newfoundland & Labrador music & dance - Aug.

Nova Scotia Bluegrass Oldtime Music Festival, The Downeast Bluegrass & Oldtime Music Society, PO Box 1275, Greenwood NS B0P 1N0 - Tollfree: 1-844-442-2656; Email: info@nsbluegrass.com; URL: www.nsbluegrass.com - Annually, last weekend in July

Nova Scotia Kiwanis Music Festival, PO Box 107, 5657 Spring Garden Rd., Halifax NS B3J 3R4 - 902-423-6147; URL: hfxmusicfest.com - Adjudicated music festival & closing concert - Feb., Halifax NS

Orford Festival, 3165, Parc Orford Rd., Orford QC J1X 7A2 - 819-843-9871; Fax: 819-843-7274; Tollfree: 1-800-567-6155; URL: www.arts-orford.org - June-Aug.

Ottawa Bluesfest, 450 Churchill Ave. North, Ottawa ON K1Z 5E2 - 613-247-1188; Fax: 613-247-2220; Tollfree: 1-866-258-3748; URL: ottawabluesfest.ca - Executive Director, Mark Monahan - Annual blues music & gospel festival - July

Ottawa Folk Festival (CityFolk), 450 Churchill Ave. North, Ottawa ON K1Z 5E2 - 613-230-8234; Fax: 613-247-2220; URL: cityfolkfestival.com - Sept.

Ottawa International Chamber Music Festival, Ottawa Chamber Music Society, #201, 4 Florence St., Ottawa ON K2P 0W7 - 613-234-8008; Fax: 613-234-7692; Email: info@chamberfest.com; URL: www.chamberfest.com, July-Aug.

Ottawa Jazz Festival, #602, 294 Albert St., Ottawa ON K1P 6E6 - 613-241-2633; Tollfree: 1-888-226-4495; URL: ottawajazzfestival.com - Executive Director, Catherine O'Grady, Email: director@ottawajazzfestival.com - June-July

Pembroke Old Time Fiddle & Step Dancing Championships, PO Box 1329, Deep River ON K0J 1P0 - 613-584-3962; URL: bright-ideas-software.com/pembrokefiddle - Labour Day weekend, annually

Regina Folk Festival, #101, 1855 Scarth St., PO Box 1203, Regina SK S4P 3B4 - 306-757-0308; Email: info@reginafolkfestival.com; URL: www.reginafolkfestival.com - Artistic Director, Sandra Butel - Annual three day folk-based music festival - Aug.

Scotia Festival of Music, 6181 Lady Hammond Rd., Halifax NS B3K 2R9 - 902-429-9467; Fax: 902-425-6785; Email: admin@scotiafestival.ns.ca; URL: www.scotiafestival.ns.ca - Artistic & Managing Director, Christopher Wilcox - Annually, May. Chamber music

Shelburne Heritage Music Festival, PO Box 27, Shelburne ON L9V 3L8 - URL: www.heritagemusicfestival.com; Manager, Canadian Open Fiddle Championship, Bill Waite, Email: bill.waite@mdacorporation.com - Aug.

Stan Rogers Folk Festival, PO Box 46, Canso NS B0H 1H0 - Fax: 902-366-2978; Tollfree: 1-888-554-7826; URL: www.stanfest.com

Summerfolk Music & Crafts Festival, Georgian Bay Folk Society, PO Box 521, Owen Sound ON N4K 5R1 - 519-371-2995; Fax: 51-371-2973; Email: gbfs@bmts.com; URL: summerfolk.org - General Manager/Festival Coordinator, Roxane Davidson

Symphony Under the Sky, Edmonton Symphony Orchestra, 9720 - 102 Ave., Edmonton AB T5J 4B2 - 780-428-1108; Tollfree: 1-800-563-5081; Email: info@winspearcentre.com; URL: www.edmontonsymphony.com - Executive Director, Annemarie Petrov - Aug.-Sept.

Toronto Jazz Festival, Toronto Downtown Jazz Society, 82 Bleecker St., Toronto ON M4X 1L8 - 416-928- 2033; Fax: 416-928-0533; URL: www.torontojazz.com - Annual - June

Vancouver Folk Music Festival, #230, 275 East 1st Ave., Vancouver BC V5T 1A7 - 604-602-9798; Fax: 604-602-9790; URL: www.thefestival.bc.ca - Artistic Director, Linda Tanaka - Annual festival - July, Vancouver BC

Vancouver International Jazz Festival, Vancouver International Jazz Festival/Coastal Jazz & Blues Society, 295 West 7th Ave., Vancouver BC V5Y 1L9 - 604-872- 5200; Fax: 604-872-5250; Tollfree: 1-888-438-5200; Email: cjbs@coastaljazz.ca; URL: www.coastaljazz.ca - June-July

Vancouver Island Chamber Music Festival, Nanaimo Conservatory of Music, 375 Selby St., Nanaimo BC V9R 2R4 - 250-754-4611; Fax: 250-716-7274; Tollfree: 877-754-4611; www.vancouverislandchambermusic.blogspot.ca - April

Vancouver Island MusicFest, PO Box 3788, Courtenay BC V9N 7P2 - 250-871-8463; Email: info@islandmusicfest.com; URL: www.islandmusicfest.com - Artistic Director, Doug Cox, July

Victoria International JazzFest, Victoria Jazz Society, Harbour Towers Hotel, #202, 345 Quebec St., 2nd Fl., Victoria, BC V8V 1W4 - 250-388-4423; Fax: 250-388-4407; Email: info@jazzvictoria.ca; URL: jazzvictoria.ca

Victoriaville International Festival of New Music, 82, rue Notre-Dame est, CP 460, Victoriaville QC G6P 6T3 - 819-752-7912; Fax: 819-758-4370; Email: info@fimav.qc.ca; URL: www.fimav.qc.ca - 25 concerts in 5 days, musicians from 12 different countries - May

Winnipeg Folk Festival, #203, 211 Bannatyne Ave., Winnipeg MB R3B 3P2 - 204-231-0096; Fax: 204-231- 0076; Email: info@winnipegfolkfestival.ca; URL: www.winnipegfolkfestival.ca - Annually, July

Winnipeg Jazz Festival, #007, 100 Arthur St., Winnipeg MB R3B 1H3 - 204-989-4656; Email: info@jazzwinnipeg.com; URL: jazzwinnipeg.com, June

OKTOBERFESTS *See* EVENTS

PACKAGING

PACKEX Montréal, UBM Canon, #100, 2901 - #100, 2901 - 28 St., Santa Monica CA, USA, 90405 - 310-445-4200; Fax: 310-996-9499 packexmontreal.com - Biennial trade show - Nov. - Palais des congrès de Montréal, Montréal, QC

PACKEX Toronto, UBM Canon, #100, 2901 - #100, 2901 - 28 St., Santa Monica CA, USA, 90405 - 310-445-4200; Fax: 310-996-9499; URL: packextoronto.packagingdigest.com - Biennial trade show - June - Toronto Congress Centre, Toronto ON

PARENTS *See* CHILDREN

PETROLEUM

Atlantic Canada Petroleum Show, dmg events (Canada) Inc., #302, 1333 – 8 St. SW, Calgary AB T2R 1M6; 403-209-3555; Fax: 403-245-8649; Tollfree: 1-888-799-2545; URL: atlanticcanadapetroleumshow.com - Event Director, Nick Samain, Email: nicksamain@dmgevents.com - Annual event in June

Global Petroleum Show, dmg events (Canada) Inc., #302, 1333 – 8 St. SW, Calgary AB T2R 1M6 - 403-209-3555; Fax: 403-245- 8649; Tollfree: 1-888-799-2545; URL: globalpetroleumshow.com - Event Director, Bruce Carew, Email: brucecarew@dmgevents.com - Biennial trade show - Petroleum & natural gas products, services & technology

PETS

Calgary Pet Expo, CanNorth Shows Inc., 821 Bay St., Gravenhurst ON P1P 1G7 - Tollfree: 855-723-1156; URL: www.calgarypetexpo.com - Show Manager, Breanne Blackburn, Email: breanna@cannorthshows.com - Annual consumer trade show - April

Edmonton Pet Expo, Family Productions Inc., 4634 - 90A Ave., 2nd Fl., Edmonton AB T6B 2P9 - 780-490-0215; Fax: 780-450-3757; Email: info@edmontonshows.com; URL: www.petexpo.ca

Exposition Canine, Club Canin de l'Estrie - URL: www.clubcanindelestrie.com - Annual - All breed dog exhibition - Sept.

Salon national des animaux de compagnie (SNAC), C.P. 28530, CSP Verdun, Verdun, QC H4G 3L7 - 514-766-6293; Fax: 514-766-0410; URL: www.snac.ca - Annual exhibition for all types of pets - Québec, Montréal & Sherbrooke - Oct., Nov. & April

Vancouver Pet Lover Show, PO Box 178, #800, 15355 - 24th Ave., Vancouver BC V4A 2H9 - 604-535-7584; Fax: 604-535-1463; Email: petlovershow@shaw.ca; URL: www.petlovershow.ca - Show Manager, Nanette Jacques, Email: njacques@shaw.ca - Annual consumer trade show - Feb./March

PLASTICS & RUBBER

Expoplast, UBM Canon, #100, 2901 - #100, 2901 - 28 St., Santa Monica CA, USA, 90405 - 310-445-4200; Email: UBMCanonConferences@ubm.com; URL: www.admmontreal.com/en/expoplast - Nov., Palais des congrès, Montreal

PLAST-EX, UBM Canon, #100, 2901 - #100, 2901 - 28 St., Santa Monica CA, USA, 90405 - 310-445-4200; Email: UBMCanonConferences@ubm.com; URL: www.plastex.plasticstoday.com - Triennial international trade show: plastics machinery, raw materials suppliers, mold makers, processors, fabricators, auxiliary equipment - May - Toronto Congress Centre, Toronto ON

POPULAR CULTURE

Calgary Comic & Entertainment Expo, BMO Centre, Stampede Park, 20 Roundup Way SE, Calgary AB T2G 2W1 - URL: www.calgaryexpo.com

Comiccon de Québec, 1,000,000 COMIX, 1418 Pierce St., Montréal QC H3H 2S2 - 514-989-9587; URL: www.comicconquebec.com - Oct. - Centre des congrès, Québec

East Coast Comic Expo, 99 Wynwood Dr., Moncton NB E1A 6X4 - URL: www.eastcoastcomicexpo.com

Edmonton Comic & Entertainment Expo, Edmonton Expo Centre, 7515 - 118 Ave. NW, Edmonton AB T5B 4X5 - Email: info@EdmontonExpo.com; URL: edmontonexpo.com

Fan Expo, Informa Canada, #100, 10 Alcorn Ave., Toronto ON M4V 3A9 - Fax: 416-927-8032; Email: info@fanexpohq.com; URL: fanexpocanada.com - Show Director, Andrew Moyes

Fan Expo Vancouver, Informa Canada, #100, 10 Alcorn Ave., Toronto ON M4V 3A9 - Email: info@fanexpohq.com; URL: www.fanexpovancouver.com - Show Director, Andrew Moyes

Montréal Comiccon, 1,000,000 COMIX, 1418 Pierce St., Montréal QC H3H 2S2 - 514-989-9587; URL: www.montrealcomiccon.com - Sept. - Palais des congrès, Montréal

Ottawa Comiccon, 1,000,000 COMIX, 1418 Pierce St., Montréal QC H3H 2S2 - 514-989-9587; URL: www.ottawacomiccon.com

Ottawa Pop Expo, 1,000,000 COMIX, 1418 Pierce St., Montréal QC H3H 2S2 - 514-989-9587; URL: www.ottawapopexpo.ca - Nov. - Centre EY, Ottawa ON

Revolution Gaming Expo, Fredericton Convention Centre, 670 Queen St., Fredericton NB E3B 1C2 - Email: info@revolutiongamingexpo.com; URL: www.revolutiongamingexpo.com

Saskatoon Comic & Entertainment Expo, Prairieland Park, 503 Ruth St W, Saskatoon, SK S7J 0S6 - Email: info@saskexpo.com; URL: saskexpo.com

Toronto ComiCon, Informa Canada, #100, 10 Alcorn Ave., Toronto ON M4V 3A9 - Fax: 416-927-8032; Email: info@fanexpohq.com; URL: www.comicontoronto.com - Show Director, Andrew Moyes

Unplugged Expo, c/o Join Team Unplugged, #102, 40 Wynford Dr., Toronto ON M3C 1J5 - 647-998-9537; Email: info@unpluggedexpo.com; URL: unpluggedexpo.com - Sept.

Vancouver Retro Gaming Expo, Anvil Centre, 777 Columbia St., New Westminster BC V3M 1B6 - 604-515-3830; Email: vancouvergamingexpo@gmail.com; URL: www.vancouvergamingexpo.com

PSYCHIC PHENOMENA

Psychic Fairs, First Star Enterprises; Email: firstar@me.com; URL: www.fspsychicfairs.com - Annual consumer shows - GTA, Kitchener, Niagara, Peterborough, Toronto

Psychic Expos, Vision Quest Inc.; Email: info@psychicexpos.com; URL: www.psychicexpos.com - Annual consumer shows - Brantford, Belleville, Guelph, Hamilton, London

REAL ESTATE

Global Property Market Conference, Informa Canada, #100, 10 Alcorn Ave., Toronto ON M4V 3A9 - 416-512-3807; Email: events@informacanada.com; URL: www.realestateforums.com

Informa Canada Real Estate Forums, #100, 10 Alcorn Ave., Toronto ON M4V 3A9 - 416-512-3807; Email: events@informacanada.com; URL: www.realestateforums.com - Held annually in Calgary, Edmonton, Montréal, Ottawa, Saskatchewan, Toronto, Vancouver & Halifax

Informa Canada Real Estate Strategy & Leasing Conferences, #100, 10 Alcorn Ave., Toronto ON M4V 3A9 - 416-512-3807; Email: events@informacanada.com; URL: www.realestateforums.com - Held annually in Montréal & Vancouver

Land & Development Conference, Informa Canada, #100, 10 Alcorn Ave., Toronto ON M4V 3A9 - 416-512-3807; Email: events@informacanada.com; URL: www.realestateforums.com

Leadership Conference, The Ontario Real Estate Association, 99 Duncan Mill Rd., Toronto, ON M3B 1Z2; 416-445-9910; Fax: 416-445-2644; Tollfree: 1-800-265-6732; Email: info@orea.ca; URL: www.orea.com - Annual trade show - March

PM Expo, Property Management Exposition & Conference, Informa Canada, #100, 10 Alcorn Ave., Toronto ON M4V 3A9 - 416/960-9030; Email: events@informacanada.com ; URL: www.pmexpo.com - Annual - Dec. - Metro Toronto Convention Centre, South Building, Toronto, ON

Québec Apartment Investment Conference, Informa Canada, #100, 10 Alcorn Ave., Toronto ON M4V 3A9 - 416-512-3807; Email: events@informacanada.com; URL: www.realestateforums.com/qaic - Feb. - Montréal QC

RECREATIONAL VEHICLES *See* AUTOMOTIVE

RODEOS

***See Also* Exhibitions, Farm Business/Agriculture**

Calgary Exhibition & Stampede, PO Box 1060, Stn M, Calgary AB T2P 2K8 - 403-261-0101; Fax: 403-265-7197; Tollfree: 1-800-661-1260; Email: info@calgarystampede.com; URL: www.calgarystampede.com - Annual city-wide festival; agricultural exhibits

CCA Finals Rodeo, Canadian Cowboys Association, PO Box 1027, Regina, SK S4P 3B2 - 306-931-2700; Fax: 306-931-2701; Email: canadiancowboys@sasktel.net; URL: canadiancowboys.ca - Annually, Oct. Four days

Maple Creek Cowtown Pro-Rodeo, PO Box 428, Maple Creek SK S0N 1N0 - 306-661-8184; URL: www.maplecreek.ca - Contact, Slim Needham, Phone: 306-661-8595 - Annually, June

Williams Lake Stampede, Williams Lake Stampede Association, PO Box 4076, Williams Lake BC V2G 2V2 - 250-392-6585; Fax: 250-398-7701; Tollfree: 1-800- 717-6336; Email: info@williamslakestampede.com; URL: www.williamslakestampede.com - July

RVS *See* AUTOMOTIVE; SPORTS & RECREATION

SEWING *See* CRAFTS

SEX

The Everything to Do with Sex Show, SX Marketing Inc., #203, 2700 Steeles Ave. West, Concord, ON L4K 3C8 - 905-738-8884 ; Fax: 905-738-7848; Tollfree: 1-866-929-7399; URL: toronto.everythingtodowithsex.com - Annual Trade Show - Toronto, Montréal, Halifax

Taboo Naughty but Nice Sex Show, Can West Productions, #218, 7710 – 5th St. SE, Calgary, AB T2H 2L9 - Fax: 403-246 -3856; Tollfree: 1-800-626-1538; Email: tickets@canwestshows.com; URL: www.canwestproductions.com - Annual Trade Show - Calgary, Edmonton, Vancouver, Regina, Red Deer

SPORTS & RECREATION

***See Also* Boating; Automotive, for combined auto/RV shows**

24 Hours of Adrenalin, Twenty4 Sports Inc., #301, 1321 Blanshard St., Victoria BC V8W 0B6 - Email: info@twenty4sports.com; URL: www.24hoursofadrenalin.com - Team & solo mountain biking events that take place in Alberta, Ontario & BC in June, July & Aug.

Atlantic Outdoor Sports & RV Show, Darwin Event Group, PO Box 667, #16, 60 Morse Lane, Berwick NS B0P 1E0 - 902-679-7177; Fax: 902-678-4436; Email: info@darwineventgroup.com; URL: www.sportsandrvshow.com - Annual consumer show. Trailer & motor homes, 4x4s, tent trailers, boats, motors, hunting, fishing & camping, tourism & sporting goods - March, Halifax NS

Calgary Boat & Sportsmen's Show, Canadian National Sportsmen's Shows (1989) Ltd., #502, 5920 Macleod Trail SW, Calgary, AB T2H 0K2 - 403-245-9008; Fax: 403-245-5100; Tollfree: 1-866-704-4412; URL: www.calgaryboatandsportshow.ca - Annual consumer show - Feb. - BMO Centre, Stampede Park, Calgary, AB

Canadian Power Toboggan Championships, PO Box 22, Beausejour MB R0E 0C0 - 204-268-2049; Fax: 204-268-4209; URL: www.cptcracing.com - Annual - March

Calgary Snow Show, Can West Productions Inc., #218, 7710 – 5th St. SE, Calgary, AB T2H 2L9 - Fax: 403-246 -3856; Tollfree: 1-800-626-1538; Email: info@canwestshows.com; URL: www.canwestproductions.com - Nov.

Edmonton Boat & Sportsmen's Show, Canadian National Sportsmen's Shows (1989) Ltd., #502, 5920 Macleod Trail SW, Calgary, AB T2H 0K2 - 403-245-9008; Fax: 403-245-5100; Tollfree: 1-866-704-4412; URL: www.edmontonboatandsportshow.ca - Annual consumer show - March - Edmonton Expo Centre, Northlands, Edmonton, AB

Edmonton Ski & Snowboard Show, Family Productions Inc., 4634 - 90A Ave., 2nd Fl., Edmonton AB T6B 2P9 - 780-490-0215 ; Fax: 780-450-3757; Email: info@edmontonshows.com; URL: powderfest.com

Ironman Canada Triathlon Championship, 416 Westminster Ave. West, Penticton BC V2A 1K5 - 250-490-8787; Fax: 250-490-8788; Email: canada@ironman.com; URL: www.ironman.ca - Annual four-day trade expo staged as part of the events prior to the Ironman race - Aug.

London Boat Fishing & Outdoor Show, Western Fair District, 316 Rectory St., London ON N5W 3V9 - 519-438-7203; Tollfree: 800-619-4629; URL: www.westernfairdistrict.com/events/london-boat-fishing-outdoor-show - Annual consumer show - Feb.

Ottawa Boat Show, Canadian National Sportsmen's Shows (1989) Ltd., 30 Village Centre Pl., Mississauga, ON L4Z 1V9 - 905-361-2677; Fax: 905-361-2678; Tollfree: 1-888-695-2677 URL: www.ottawaboatandsportshow.ca - Show Manager, Meagan Sheehan, Email: meagan@sportshows.ca - Annual consumer show - Feb. - Ernst & Young Centre, Ottawa, ON

The Outdoor Adventure Show, c/o National Event Management Inc., #102, 260 Town Centre Blvd., Markham ON L3R 8H8 - 905-477-2677; Fax: 905-477-7872; Tollfree: 1-800-891-4859; Email: info@nationalevent.com; URL: outdooradventureshow.ca

Salon Camping, Plein Air, Chasse et Pêche de Montréal/Montréal Sportsmen's Show, Canadian National Sportsmen's Shows (1989) Ltd., #330, 8150 boul

Métropolitain est, Montréal QC H1K 1A1 - 514-866-5409; Fax: 514-866-4092; URL: www.salonexpertchassemontreal.ca - Annual consumer show: camping, fishing, hunting, RVs, tourism

Salon Camping, Plein Air, Chasse et Pêche de Québec/Québec City Sportsmen's Show, Canadian National Sportsmen's Shows (1989) Ltd., #330, 8150 boul Métropolitain est, Montréal QC H1K 1A1 - 418-622-8118; Fax: 514-866-4092; URL: www.salonexpertchassequebec.ca - Annual consumer show: camping, fishing, hunting, RVs, tourism

Toronto International Bicycle Show, #1801, 1 Yonge St., Toronto ON M5E 1W7 - 416-363-1292; Fax: 416-369-0515; URL: www.bicycleshowtoronto.com - Marketing & Sales Manager, Josie Graziosi, Email: josie@telsec.net - Annual consumer show, March; Annual blowout sale, Oct. - Toronto ON

Toronto International Snowmobile, ATV & Powersports Show, Marketer Shows Inc., PO Box 551, 27083 Kennedy Rd. , Willow Beach, ON L0E 1S0 - 905-898-8585; Fax: 905-898-8071; Tollfree: 1-888-661-7469; Email: info@torontosnowmobileatvshow.com; URL: www.torontosnowmobileatvshow.com - Senior Show & Sales Manager, Mike Blakoe, Email: mblakoe@bellnet.ca - Annual consumer show, March - Toronto International Centre, Toronto ON

Toronto Snow Show, Canadian National Sportsmen's Shows (1989) Ltd., 30 Village Centre Pl., Mississauga, ON L4Z 1V9 - 905-361-2677; Fax: 905-361-2679; Tollfree: 1-888-695-2677; URL: www.torontoskishow.ca - Annual consumer show - Show Manager, Sajid Rahman, Email: saj@sportshows.ca - Oct. - International Centre, Mississauga ON

Toronto Sportsmen's Show, Canadian National Sportsmen's Shows (1989) Ltd., 30 Village Centre Pl., Mississauga, ON L4Z 1V9 - 905-361-2677; Fax: 905-361-2679; Tollfree: 1-888-695-2677; URL: www.torontosportshow.ca - Annual consumer show - Show Manager, Jennifer Allaby, Email: allaby@sportshows.ca - March - International Centre, Mississauga ON

The Toronto Star Golf & Travel Show, Premier Publications & Shows, #2, 5046 Mainway, Burlington ON L7L 5Z1 - Fax: 905-842-6843; Tollfree: 1-800-693-7986; URL: www.torontogolfshow.com - General Manager, Lars Melander, Email: lmelander@metroland.com - Annual consumer show - Late Feb./Early March

Vancouver Bike Show, c/o National Event Management Inc., #102, 260 Town Centre Blvd., Markham ON L3R 8H8 - 905-477-2677; Fax: 905-477-7872; Tollfree: 1-800-891-4859; Email: info@nationalevent.com; URL: vancouverbikeshow.com - Show Manager, Seamus McGrath, Email: bikeshow@nationalevent.com

STAMPEDES *See* RODEOS

THEATRE *See* ARTS

TOYS & GAMES

Brantford Model Train Show and Sale, Ontario Collector Shows, PO Box 705, Simcoe ON N3Y 4T2 - 519-426-8875; URL: www.collectorshows.ca

Kitchener Model Train Show & Sale, Ontario Collector Shows, PO Box 705, Simcoe ON N3Y 4T2 - 519-426-8875; URL: www.collectorshows.ca

Lindsay & District Model Railroaders Model Railway Show, PO Box 452, Lindsay, ON K9V 4S5 - Email: allaboard@ldmr.org; URL: www.ldmr.org

North American International Toy Fair, Canadian Toy Association, PO Box 218, #2219, 160 Tycos Dr., Toronto, ON M6B 1W8; 416-596-0671; Fax: 416-596-1808; Email: info@cdntoyassn.com; URL: www.cdntoyassn.com; Show Manager, Michael Dargavel, Phone: 416-596-0671, ext. 225 - Annual trade show - Jan. - International Centre, Mississauga, ON

Toronto Toy & Nostalgia Auction, Toronto Show Promotions, c/o Doug Jarvis, PO Box 217, Grimsby ON L3M 4G3; 905-945-2775; Email: info@antiquetoys.ca; URL: antiquetoys.ca - Annual consumer shows/auction - May

Woodstock Model Train Show & Sale, Ontario Collector Shows, PO Box 705, Simcoe ON N3Y 4T2 - 519-426-8875; URL: www.collectorshows.ca

TRANSPORTATION

***See Also* Automotive**

Ontario Transportation Expo Conference & Trade Show, 3401 Wolfedale Rd., Mississauga ON L5C 1V8 - 416-695-9965 Ext. 6; Fax: 416-695-9977; URL: www.ote.ca - Annual conference & trade show. Safety, fuel economy, buses & accessories, computers

Transit Trade Show, Canadian Urban Transit Association, #1401, 55 York St., Toronto, ON M5J 1R - 416-365-9800; Fax: 416-365-1295; URL: www.cutaactu.ca - Annual transit industry event, held in conjunction with the CUTA Fall Conference - Nov.

TRAVEL & TOURISM

IncentiveWorks Trade Show, Meetings & Incentive Travel, 80 Valleybrook Dr., Toronto ON M3B 2S9 - 416-510-5231; URL: www.incentiveworksshow.com - Show Manager, Robin Paisley, Email: robin@newcom.ca - Annual trade show & conference - Aug.

The Ottawa Travel & Vacation Show, Player Expositions Inc., 255 Clemow Ave., Ottawa ON K1S 2B5 - 613-567-6408; Fax: 613-567-2718; URL: www.travelandvacationshow.ca - Annual consumer & trade show - April - Ottawa Convention Centre, Ottawa ON

The Outfitters & Travel Expo, Canadian National Sportsmen's Shows (1989) Ltd., 30 Village Centre Pl., Mississauga, ON L4Z 1V9 - 905-361-2677; Fax: 905-361-2679; Tollfree: 1-888-695-2677; URL: www.torontosportshow.ca - Annual - Part of the Toronto Sportsmen's Show - Feb. - Enercare Centre, Exhibition Place, Toronto, ON

Salon international tourisme voyages, Expo Media, #210, 370, rue Guy, Montréal, QC H3J 1S6 - 514-527-9221; Email: info@expomediainc.com; URL: salontourismevoyages.com

Toronto's Ultimate Travel Show, c/o Premier Publications, #2, 5046 Mainway, Burlington ON L7L 5Z1 - Fax: 905-842-6843; Tollfree: 1-800-693-7986; URL: totravelshow.com

Travel Expo, URL: www.travelexpo.ca - Annual

TRUCKS *See* AUTOMOTIVE

TVS, STEREOS *See* ELECTRICAL/ELECTRONICS

VIDEO *See* COMMUNICATIONS

UNIVERSITY/COLLEGE

Maclean's Student Life Expo, Pumped Inc., #9, 20 Amber St., Markham ON L3R 5P4 - 905-415-3643 - Email: info@pumped.ca; URL: studentlifeexpo.com

Study & Go Abroad Fairs, 1484 Doran Rd., North Vancouver, BC V7K 1N2 - 604-986-7704; Fax: 604-986-3047; Email: info@studyandgoabroad.com; URL: www.studyandgoabroad.com - Annual. Vancouver, Edmonton, Calgary, Ottawa, Toronto & Halifax

WINTER CARNIVALS

Banff/Lake Louise Winterstart Festival, PO Box 1298, Banff AB T1L 1B3 - 403-762-8421; Fax: 403-762-8163; URL: www.banfflakelouise.com, Nov/Dec.

Carnaval de Québec/Québec Winter Carnival, Carnaval de Québec, 205, boul des Cèdres, Québec QC G1L 1N8 - 418-626-3716; Tollfree: 1-866-422-7628; URL: www.carnaval.qc.ca - Directrice générale, Mélanie Raymond, Courriel: melanie.raymond@carnaval.qc.ca - 14, major winter event

Conception Bay South Winterfest, Town of Conception Bay South, PO Box 14040, Stn. Manuels, 11 Remembrance Sq., Conception Bay South NL A1W 3J1 - 709-834-6500, Fax: 709-834-8337; URL: www.conceptionbaysouth.ca - Feb.

Corner Brook Winter Carnival, PO Box 886, Corner Brook NL A2H 6H6 - 709-632-5343; Fax: 709-632-5344; URL: www.cornerbrookwintercarnival.ca - Annually, 10 days - Feb.

Elliot Lake Winterfest, Lester B. Pearson Civic Centre, Hwy.#108, Elliot Lake ON P5A 2T1 - 705-848-2084; Fax: 705-848-7121; URL: www.cityofelliotlake.com - Feb.

Fête des Neiges, Parc Jean-Drapeau, 1, circuit Gilles-Villeneuve, Montréal QC H3C 1A9 - 514-872-6120; Email: clientele@parcjeandrapeau.com; URL: www.parcjeandrapeau.com - 6 day major winter event. Sports, cultural, ice sculptures - Jan.

Hamilton Winterfest, Tourism Hamilton, 28 James St. North, 2nd Fl., Hamilton ON L8P 4Y5 - 905-546-2666; Fax: 905-546-2667; URL: www.hamiltonwinterfest.ca - Feb.

Jasper in January, Tourism Jasper, PO Box 568, Jasper, AB T0E 1E0 - URL: www.jasperinjanuary.travel - Jan.

Kapuskasing Winter Carnival, 88 Riverside Dr., Kapuskasing ON P5N 1B3 - 705-335-2341; URL: kapuskasing.ca - Feb. & March

Kirkland Lake Winter Carnival, Kirkland Lake Festivals Committee, PO Box 277, Kirkland Lake ON P2N 3H7 - Email: klfestivals@hotmail.com; URL: www.klfestivals.com - March

Mount Pearl Frosty Festival, PO Box 898, Mount Pearl, NL A1N 3C8 - 709-748-6480; Fax: 709-748-6499; Email: frostyfestival@live.com; URL: www.frostyfestival.ca - Feb.

Prince Albert Winter Festival, Email: info@pawinterfestival.com; URL: www.pawinterfestival.com - Feb.

Riverview Winter Carnival, 30 Honour House Court, Riverview NB E1B 3Y9 - 506-387-2020; URL: www.townofriverview.ca - Feb.

Vernon Winter Carnival, 3401 - 35th Ave., Vernon BC V1T 2T5 - 250-545-2236; Fax: 250-545-0006; URL: www.vernonwintercarnival.com - Feb.

Winterlude, National Capital Commission, #202, 40 Elgin St., Ottawa ON K1P 1C7 - 613-239-5000; Tollfree: 1-800-465-1867; Email: info@pch.gc.ca; URL: www.pch.gc.ca/winterlude - Major winter festival, first three weekends of February. Skating on Rideau Canal, international ice & snow sculpture competitions, musical & figure skating shows, North America's largest winter playground for kids, various sporting & social events, fireworks, stage performances & buskers - Feb.

Winterlude, PO Box 439, Grand Falls-Windsor NL A2A 2J8 - 709-489-0407; URL: grandfallswindsor.com - Director of Parks and Recreation, Keith Antle, Email: kantle@townofgfw.com - Feb.

WOMEN

Calgary Woman's Show, The Calgary Woman's Show Ltd., #218, 7710 - 5th St. SE, Calgary, AB T2H 2L9 - 403-242-0859; Fax: 403-246-3856; Email: calgarywomansshow@canwestproductions.com; URL: www.calgarywomansshow.com - Show Director, Terra Connors, Email: terra@canwestproductions.com - Semi-annual consumer show in April & Oct.; Products & services.

Edmonton Woman's Show, Family Productions Inc., 4634 - 90A Ave., 2nd Fl., Edmonton AB T6B 2P9 - 780-490-0215 ; Fax: 780-450-3757; URL: womanshow.com

National Women's Show, National Event Management Inc., #102, 260 Town Centre Blvd., Markham, ON L3R 8H8 - 905-477-2677; Fax: 905-477-7872; Tollfree: 1-800-891-4859; Email: info@nationalevent.com; URL: www.nationalwomenshow.com - Annual - Toronto, Ottawa, Montréal & Québec

Women's Lifestyle Show, The Bayley Group, PO Box 39, 72924 Airport Line, Hensall, ON N0M 1X0 - 519-263-5050; Fax: 519-263-2936; Email: womenrock@bayleygroup.com; URL: womenslifestyle.ca - Annual - March - London Convention Centre, London, ON

WOOD/WOODWORKING

Hamilton Woodworking Show, Canadian Warplane Heritage Museum, 9280 Airport Rd., Hamilton, Ontario L0R 1W0 - 905-779-0422; www.woodshows.com - Annual - Jan.

Salon Bois ouvré de l'est du Canada, Master Promotions Inc., PO Box 565, 48 Broad St., Saint John NB E2L 3Z8 - 506-658-0018; Fax: 506-658-0750; Tollfree: 1-888-454-7469; Email: info@mpltd.ca; URL: www.masterpromotions.ca - Sept., Montréal QC

Woodworking, Machinery & Supply Expo (WMS), ON - Tollfree: 1-800-343-2016; URL: www.woodworkingnetwork.com/events-contests/wms - Annual - International Centre, Mississauga, ON

Awards & Honours

Canadian Awards

(Including Scholarships, Grants, Bursaries)

Awards are listed under the following categories:

ADVERTISING & PUBLIC RELATIONS

The Advertising & Design Club of Canada

#205, 344 Bloor St. West, Toronto ON M5S 3A7
416/423-4113; Fax: 416/423-3362
Email: info@theadcc.ca; URL: www.theadcc.ca

The Advertising & Design Club of Canada Awards
Main categories of awards are: Advertising Broadcast & Print, Graphic Design, Editorial Design and Interactive Media; winners receive gold, silver or merit awards. The four new major awards are: Agency of the Year, Design Studio of the Year; Interactive Agency of the Year; and Production Company of the Year.

Association of Canadian Advertisers Inc. / Association canadienne des annonceurs

#1103, 95 St. Clair Ave. West, Toronto ON M4V 1N6
416/964-3805; Fax: 416/964-0771; Toll Free: 1-800-565-0109
Email: rlund@ACAweb.ca; URL: www.aca-online.com

ACA Gold Medal
Established in 1941 to encourage high standards of personal achievement in advertising - for introducing new concepts or techniques, for significantly improving existing practices, or for enhancing the stature of advertising

Canadian Marketing Association / Association canadienne du marketing

#607, One Concorde Gate, Toronto ON M3C 3N6
416/391-2362; Fax: 416/441-4062
Email: info@the-cma.org; URL: www.the-cma.org

CMA Awards
Celebrating the art and science of marketing, CMA has restructured its judging breakdown to be based equally on Strategy, Creativity and Results. Entries can be submitted under type of business, type of program or specialty, representing particular innovative solutions. CMA also offers Student Awards to post-secondary students enrolled in direct marketing, marketing or business programs.

Institute of Communication Agencies / Institut des communications

#3002, 2300 Yonge St., Toronto ON M4P 1E4
416/482-1396; Fax: 416/482-1856
Email: ica@icacanada.ca; URL: icacanada.ca; cassies.ca

CASSIES Awards
Established 1993; CASSIES (Canadian Advertising Success Stories) are open to all channels of marketing communications. Eligible submissions must show impressive business results and convincingly prove their success was a result of the advertising.

Marketing Magazine

1 Mount Pleasant Rd., 7th floor Toronto ON M4Y 2Y5
416/764-2000; Fax: 416/764-1519
URL: www.marketingmag.ca

The Marketing Awards
Annual advertising awards offering 40 Gold Awards in the following categories: television/cinema, radio, magazine, newspaper, transit, business press, direct mail, outdoor, point-of-purchase/interior store design, multimedia campaign, non-traditional & public service. Silver Awards, Bronze Awards, & Certificates of Excellence are also awarded. Entries must have run in the previous year & must have been conceived & created by people working in English in the Canadian advertising business. New categories were added in 2011 that include social media, brand content, and experiemental and event marketing.

AGRICULTURE & FARMING

Canadian Society of Animal Science / Société canadienne de science animale

c/o Agriculture & Agri-Food Canada Research Station, PO Box 90, Lennoxville QC J1M 1Z3
819/565-9171; Fax: 819/564-5507
Email: info@csas.net; URL: www.csas.net
CSAS offers five prestigious awards:

Award for Excellence in Nutrition and Meat Sciences

Award for Technical Innovation in Enhancing Production of Safe Affordable Food

Animal Indutries Award in Extension & Public Service

Fellowship Award
Awarded to members who have made an outstanding contribution in any field of animal contribution

Young Scientist Award

International Development Research Centre / Centre de recherches pour le développement international

PO Box 8500, Ottawa ON K1G 3H9
613/236-6163; Fax: 613/238-7230
Email: info@idrc.ca; URL: www.idrc.ca
IDRC offers many competitions and awards for developing-country researchers, institutions, and Canadian researchers. Some awards include:

Bentley Cropping Systems Fellowship

Doctoral Research Awards

IDRC International Fellowships

IDRC Research Awards

Provincial Exhibition of Manitoba

#115 - 10th St., Brandon MB R7A 4E7
204/726-3590; Fax: 204/725-0202; Toll Free: 1-877-729-0001
Email: info@brandonfairs.com; URL: www.brandonfairs.com

Royal Manitoba Winter Fair Awards
Prizes given in various categories for best of show for agricultural products, animals & crops; several equestrian events offer prizes for best in competition

Royal Agricultural Winter Fair Association / Foire agricole royale d'hiver

The Ricoh Coliseum, Enercare Centre
Exhibition Place, Toronto ON M6K 3C3
416/263-3400; Fax: 416/263-3488
Email: info@royalfair.org; URL: www.royalfair.org

Agricultural Awards
Grand Champion is the highest honour in the following categories: dairy, beef, sheep, goats, swine, market livestock, field crops, vegetables, honey & maple, poultry, jams/jellies/pickles, dairy products, square dancing, fiddling, fleece wool, rabbits, & eight youth activities

Breeding Horse Awards
17 sections award prizes in this category

Performance Horse Awards
35 divisions & classes offer prizes; Leading International Rider is the highest honour in the horse show

BROADCASTING & FILM

Academy of Canadian Cinema & Television / Académie canadienne du cinéma et de la télévision

172 King St. East, Toronto ON M5A 1J3
416/366-2227; Fax: 416/366-8454; Toll Free: 1-800-644-5194
Email: info@academy.ca; URL: www.academy.ca

Canadian Screen Awards
The Canadian Screen Awards began in 2013 as the result of a merger between the Academy's previous Gemini Awards and Genie Awards. These new awards honour achievement in the fields of Canadian television, film production and digital media.

Alberta Media Production Industries Association

5305 Allard Way, 3rd Fl., Edmonton AB T6H 5X8
780/944-0707; Fax: 780/426-3057
URL: www.ampia.org

Alberta Film & Television Awards
Awarded annually, the "Rosie Awards", are presented to producers and craftpeople, who reside in Alberta, in recognition of their outstanding film & television works. Awards are given in 22 class categories (ie. Best Documentary, Best Drama, Best Movie, Best Musical etc.) and 22 craft categories (ie. Best Director; Best Screenwriter, Cinematography etc.)

David Billington Award
Awarded to a special individual in recognition of their incomparable dedication and contribution to the growth of Alberta's film and television industry.

Banff World Media Festival

c/o Achilles Media Ltd., 21 St. Clair Ave. East, Toronto ON M4T 1L9
416/921-3171
Email: info@achillesmedia.com; URL: www.bwtvf.com

Banff Rockie Awards
Annual television and digital content awards in the categories of: Kids & Animation, Factual Entertainment, Interactive Media, Drama; and Entertainment. Also a grand prize winner, two special jury awards & best HDTV program.

Canadian Association of Broadcasters / Association canadienne des radiodiffuseurs

#770-45 O'Connor St., Ottawa ON K1P 1A4
613/233-4035; Fax: 613/233-6961
Email: cab@cab-acr.ca; URL: www.cab-acr.ca

Jim Allard Broadcast Journalism Scholarship
Established 1983; awarded annually to an aspiring broadcaster enrolled in a broadcast journalism program at a Canadian college or university, who best combines academic achievement with natural talent
$2,500

Ruth Hancock Memorial Scholarships
Award established jointly in 1975 by the association, the Broadcast Executives Society & Canadian Association of Broadcast Representatives; presented annually to three Canadian students enrolled in recognized communications courses
$1,500 (x3)

Canadian Ethnic Media Association

24 Tarlton Rd., Toronto ON M5P 2M4
416/764-3081; Fax: 416/764-3245
URL: www.canadianethnicmedia.com

CEMA Awards
Up to nine plaques are offered annually to jounalists in print, radio, television & innovation; awards are given to journalists for excellence in their field; competition is open to all journalists, in any language, whether or not they are members of the Club; a single award is also given to writers of a published work of fact, fiction or poetry in book form.

Canadian Media Production Association

601 Bank St., 2nd Fl., Ottawa ON KIS 3T4
613/233-1444; Fax: 613/233-0073; Toll Free: 1-800-656-7440
Email: ottawa@cmpa.ca; URL: www.cmpa.ca

Feature Film Producer's Award
Awarded to an independent producer of a Canadian feature being screened at the Toronto International Film Festival.

Canadian Society of Cinematographers

#131, 3007 Kingston Rd., Toronto ON M1M 1P1
416/266-0591; Fax: 416/266-3996
Email: admin@csc.ca; URL: www.csc.ca/default_home.asp

Canadian Society of Cinematography Awards
18 Awards given annually for various genres and contributions.

Hot Docs Canadian International Documentary Festival

#333, 110 Spadina Ave., Toronto ON M5V 2K4
416/203-2155; Fax: 416-203-0446
Email: info@hotdocs.ca; URL: www.hotdocs.ca

Hot Docs Awards
The Hot Docs Awards include 15 awards in eight categories that recognize outstanding work in documentary film.

Media Communications Association International - Toronto Chapter

PO Box 5822, Stn A, Toronto ON M5W 1P2
416/910-4776
Email: execdirect@mca-i.org; URL: www.mca-i.org

The Board of Directors Award
This award recognizes and honours members who have demonstrated outstanding service to the Association on a regional or national level. Candidates are nominated by the Board of Directors.

The Chuck Webb Award
This award recognizes and honours individuals who have demonstrated the highest level of involvement in, dedication and commmitment to the Association without regard for personal profit of gain. Candidates are nominated by the Board of Directors.

G. Warren Scholarship Award
Presented annually, this $500 scholarship program was developed in memory of G. Warren. The only requirement is that the student will be returning for at least one more term of school

The President's Award
This prestigious recognition is not given annually, but allows the President to recognize individuals who have been of particular significance during his or her term.

Shining Star Award
This award was developed to recognize the special volunteers who give freely of their time and talents to the Association. The International Shining Star award recognizes chapter leaders who standout above all other member with their significant contributions to the chapter. The Chapter Shining Star recognizes chapter members who have gone above and beyond for the chapter.

Toronto International Film Festival Group
2 Carlton St., Suite 1600., Toronto ON M5B 1J3
416/967-7371; Fax: 416/967-9477
Email: customerrelations@tiffg.ca; URL: www.tiffg.ca

Best Canadian Feature Film

Best Canadian First Feature Film

Excellence in Canadian Production

FIPRESCI Prize
Selected by an international FIPRESCI jury, awarded to a feature film by an emerging filmmaker having its world premiere at the festival

NETPAC Award
Awarded by the Network for the Promotion of Asian Cinema to spotlight exceptional Asian feature films & promising new talent

People's Choice Award
Awarded to the best film of the festival, as voted by festival audiences

People's Choice Documentary Award

People's Choice Midnight Madness Award

Short Cuts Award for Best Canadian Film

Short Cuts Award for Best Film

BUSINESS & TRADE

Bennett Jones LLP
4500 Bankers Hall East, 855 - 2 St. SW, Calgary, AB T2P 4K7
403/298-3100; Fax: 403/265-7219
URL: www.bennettjones.com

Canada's Outstanding CEO of the Year
Sponsored by Bennett Jones LLP, this annual award takes into consideration the candidate's leadership, innovation, business achievements, corporate performance, social responsibility, sense of vision & global competitiveness

Business Development Bank of Canada (BDC)
5, Place Ville-Marie, Suite 400, Montréal QC H3B 5E7
Fax: 1-877-329-9232; Toll Free: 1-877-232-2269
Email: yea@bdc.ca; URL: www.bdc.ca

BDC Mentorship Award

BDC Entrepreneurial Resiliency Award

Entrepreneurship Champion Awards

The Caldwell Partners
165 Avenue Rd., Toronto ON M5R 3S4
416/920-7702; Fax: 416/922-8646
Email: leaders@caldwell.ca; URL: www.caldwell.ca

Canada's Outstanding CEO of the Year

Canada's Top 40 Under 40
Established & managed by The Caldwell Partners, celebrates Canadian leaders who have demonstrated remarkable success before the age of 40.

Chartered Professional Accountants Canada
277 Wellington St. West, Toronto, ON M5V 3H2
416/977-3222; Fax: 416/977-8585; Toll-Free: 1-800-268-3793
Email: member.services@cpacanada.ca; URL: www.cpacanada.ca

Award of Excellence in Public Sector Financial Management: Financial Leadership (CFO)

Awards of Excellence in Public Sector Financial Management: Innovation

Award of Excellence in Public Sector Financial Management: Lifetime Achievement

The Conference Board of Canada
255 Smyth Rd., Ottawa ON K1H 8M7
613/526-3280; Fax: 613/526-4857; Toll Free: 1-866-711-2262
Email: infoserv@conferenceboard.ca; URL: www.conferenceboard.ca

Global Best Awards
Awarded to celebrate outstanding business, education, and community organization partnerships; categories include: Building Learning Communities; Developing Skills for the Future Workforce; Enabling Economic Development through Enterprise and Livelihoods; and Promoting Health and Well-being of Children in Education

The Honorary Associate Award
Awarded to individuals who have served both their organization and their country with distinction during their working career.

Ernst & Young
Ernst & Young Tower, TD Centre, 222 Bay St., PO Box 251, Toronto ON M5K 1J7
416/943-3785; Fax: 416/943-2207; Toll Free: 1-888-946-3694
Email: linda.moss@ca.ey.com; URL: www.eoy.ca

Ernst & Young Entrepreneur of the Year Award
Best entrepreneurs in 5 regions nationwide (Pacific Canada, The Prairies, Ontario, Québec, Atlantic Canada); other awards include Master Entrepreneur, Emerging Entrepreneur, Turnaround Entrepreneur, Young Entrepreneur, Supporter of Entrepreneurship. Awarded annually

The National Trust for Canada / Fiducie nationale du Canada
190 Bronson Ave., Ottawa, ON K1R 6H4
613/237-1066; Fax: 613/237-5987
Email: nationaltrust@nationaltrustcanada.ca; URL: www.nationaltrustcanada.ca

Ecclesiastical Insurance Cornerstone Awards
Recognizes excellence in the regeneration of heritage buildings and sites.

Gabrielle Léger Award for Lifetime Achievement
Founded in 1978, this annual award is Canada's premier hounour fo individual achievement in heritage conservation

Lieutenant Governor's Award for Heritage Conservation
Established in 1979, honours outstanding achievement in heritage conservation at the provincial/territorial level.

The Prince of Wales Prize for Municipal Heritage Leadership
Established in 1999, The Prince of Wales agreed to lend his title to this annual award in recognition of the government of a municipality, which has demonstrated a strong and sustained commitment to the conservation of its historic places.

Prix du XXe siècle
This award is presented jointly by the National Trust for Canada and the Royal Architectural Institute of Canada to raise awareness about nationally significant 20th century architecture in Canada.

Excellence Canada
#402, 154 University Ave.
416/251-7600; Fax: 416/251-9131; Toll Free: 1-800-263-9648
Email: info@excellence.ca; URL: www.excellence.ca

Canada Awards for Excellence
Previously called the Canada Awards for Business Excellence & established by the Government of Canada in 1984, the awards recognize outstanding continuous achievement in seven key areas: Leadership, Customer Focus, Planning for Improvement, People Focus, Process Optimization, Supplier Focus & Organizational Performance

Skills/Compétences Canada
#205, 260, boul Saint Raymond, Gatineau QC J9A 3G7
819/771-7545; Fax: 819/771-5575; Toll Free: 1-877-754-5226
Email: skillscanada@skillscanada.com; URL: www.skillscanada.com

Canadian Skills Competition
Awarded annually; is an olympic-style skills competition in over 40 skilled trades, technology & leadership contests, representing 6 industry sectors, designed to test skills required in technology & trade occupations; allows students access to newest technologies & communicate with industry experts who serve as mentors Students compete at the local, regional & provincial levels to win the right to represent their province at the national level
Gold, silver & bronze medals

Transportation Association of Canada
2323 St. Laurent Blvd., Ottawa, ON K1G 4J8
613/736-1350; Fax: 613/736-1395
Email: secretariat@tac-atc.ca; URL: www.tac-atc.ca

Member Recognition Awards
Awarded to recognize member contributions; categories include: 25-Year Membership, Honorary Life Membership

Technical Excellence Awards
Awarded to recognize the technical excellence of member endeavours; categories include: Educational Achievement, Environmental Achievement, Road Safety Engineering, Sustainable Urban Transportation

Volunteer Recognition Awards
Awarded to recognize volunteer contributions; categories include: Distinguished Service, Award for Service, Award of Merit, Retiring Committee Chair

University of Alberta
School of Business, 3-23 Business Bldg.
Edmonton AB T6G 2R6
780/492-7676; Fax: 780/492-3325
URL: www.business.ualberta.ca

Canadian Business Leader Award
Annual award recognizes distinguished professional achievements & contributions to the community

CITIZENSHIP & BRAVERY

Alberta Order of Excellence
Executive Secretary, Alberta Order of Excellence Council
c/o Policy Coordination Office
Executive Council
1201 Legislature Annex
9718 - 107 Street., Edmonton AB T5K 1E4
780/427-7243; Fax: 780/427-0305
Email: aoe@gov.ab.ca; URL: www.lieutenantgovernor.ab.ca/aoe/

Alberta Order of Excellence
Established in 1979, the award recognizes those persons who have rendered service of the greatest distinction & of singular excellence for or on behalf of Albertans.

Bridgestone Canada Inc.
#400, 5770 Hurontario St., Mississauga ON L5R 3G5
905/890-1990; Fax: 905/890-1991; Toll Free: 1-800-267-1318
URL: www.truckhero.ca

National Truck Hero Award
Established 1956; presented jointly with the Ontario Trucking Association; endorsed by the Canada Safety Council, the Traffic Injury Research Foundation & the trucking industry; designed to promote highway safety by focusing public attention on acts of bravery performed by professional Canadian truck drivers in the course of their daily work

The Canadian Council of the Blind / Le Conseil canadien des aveugles
#401, 396 Cooper St., Ottawa ON K2P 2H7
613/567-0311; Fax: 613/567-2728; Toll Free: 1-877-304-0968
Email: ccb@ccbnational.net; URL: ccbnational.net

Bursaries
Established at the Paul Menton Centre at Carleton University in Ottawa; eligible blind and vision impaired students across Canada.

Canadian Decorations for Bravery
c/o The Chancellory, Rideau Hall, One Sussex Drive
Ottawa ON K1A 0A1
613/991-0895; Fax: 613/991-1681; Toll Free: 1-800-465-6890
URL: www.gg.ca/document.aspx?id=73

Canadian Decorations for Bravery
Presented by the Governor General, Bravery decorations recognize people who have risked their lives to save or protect others; Three levels - the Cross of Valour, the Star of Courage & the Medal of Bravery - reflect the varying degrees of risk involved in any act of bravery

The Duke of Edinburgh's Award
#450, 207 Queen's Quay West, PO Box 124
Toronto ON M5J 1A7
416/203-0674; Fax: 416/203-0676
Email: sanderson@dukeofed.org; URL: www.dukeofed.org

Young Canadians Challenge
Established in Canada in 1963 with His Royal Highness Prince Philip as Patron, the award recognizes personal achievement in a voluntary program of activities by young people in the age range of 14-25.
Open to all Canadian youth; young people participate independently or through youth groups, clubs, schools, etc.; program is operated throughout Canada, with divisional offices located in each of the ten provinces.
Award is in the form of a pin & an inscribed certificate representing Gold, Silver, & Bronze levels; Gold awards are presented by Her Excellency The Governor General of Canada, or a member of the Royal Family, at national awards ceremonies

Indspire
PO Box 5, #100, 50 Generations Dr., Six Nations of the Grand River, Ohsweken, ON NOA 1M0
519/445-3021; Fax: 866/433-3159

Indspire Awards
The Indspire Awards recognize Indigenous professionals & youth who demonstrate outstanding career achievement. These awards serve to promote self-esteem and pride for Indigenous communities

Ontario Ministry of Citizenship, Immigration & International Trade
Ontario Honours & Awards
400 University Ave. West, 6th Fl., Toronto ON M7A 2R9
416/327-2422; Fax: 416/314-4965; Toll Free: 1-800-267-7329
URL: www.citizenship.gov.on.ca/english/citizenship/honoursandawards.shtml

June Callwood Outstanding Achievement Award
Created in 2007 to commemorate the life of June Callwood CC, O.Ont, LL.D, a Canadian journalist whose life was marked by a strong concern for social justice, especially on issues affecting children and women. This annual award is given to 20 individual volunteers, volunteer groups, businesses and other organizations in recognition of their outstanding contributions to their communities ad the province.

Lieutenant Governor's Community Volunteer Award for Students
This award honours one graduating student from each of Ontario's post secondary schools who not only completed the number of volunteer hours required to graduate, but have gone above and byond.

The Lincoln M. Alexander Award
Recognizes young people who have demonstrated exemplary leadership in eliminating racial discrimination; 3 student awards & 1 community award are offered yearly

The Ontario Medal for Firefighter Bravery
Established 1976 to recognize acts of superlative courage & bravery performed in the line of duty by members of Ontario's firefighting forces

The Ontario Medal for Good Citizenship
Established 1973 to recognize people who, through exceptional long-term efforts have made outstanding contributions to the well being of their communities

The Ontario Medal for Police Bravery
Established 1975 to recognize acts of superlative courage & bravery performed in the line of duty by members of Ontario's police forces

The Ontario Medal for Young Volunteers
Recognizes the outstanding achievements of 10 young volunteers, 15-24 who have made a difference to their communities

The Order of Ontario
Established 1986 to recognize those men & women who have rendered service of the greatest distinction & of singular excellence in all fields of endeavour benefiting society in Ontario & elsewhere

Order of British Columbia
Honours & Awards Secretariat, PO Box 9422, Stn Prov Govt, Victoria BC V8W 9V1
250/387-1616; Fax: 250/356-2814
Email: protocol@gov.bc.ca; URL: www.protocol.gov.bc.ca

Order of British Columbia
Established in 1989 to recognize individuals who have served with the greatest distinction & excelled in any field of endeavour benefiting the people of British Columbia or elsewhere.

Order of Manitoba
The Office of the Lieutenant Governor of Manitoba, Legislative Bldg., #235, 450 Broadway, Winnipeg, MB R3C 0V8
204/945-2753
Email: ltgov@leg.gov.mb.ca; URL: manitobalg.ca/awards/order-of-manitoba

Order of Manitoba
Established in 1999 to recognize individuals who demonstrate excellence and achievement in any field of endeavour benefitting in an outstanding manner the social, cultural or economic well-being of the province and its residents.

Order of New Brunswick / Ordre du Nouveau-Brunswick
Intergovernmental & International Relations,
Office of Protocol
#274, 670 King St., PO Box 6000, Fredericton NB E3B 5H1
506/453-2671; Fax: 506/453-2995
URL: www2.gnb.ca/content/gnb/en/corporate/promo/order_of_new_brunswick.html

Order of New Brunswick
Established in December, 2000 to recognize individuals who have demonstrated excellence & achievement & who have made outstanding contributions to the social, cultural or economic well-being of New Brunswick & its residents. Maximum of 10 recipients annually

Order of Newfoundland & Labrador
The Order of Newfoundland and Labrador, Director of Protocol, Government of Newfoundland and Labrador
P.O. Box 8700, St. John's, NL A1B 4J6
709/729-3670; Fax: 709/729-6878; Email: onl@gov.nl.ca; URL: www.exec.gov.nl.ca/onl

Order of Newfoundland and Labrador
The Order recognizes individuals who demonstrate excellence and achievement in any field benefitting in an exceptional manner theprovince and its residents. The first investiture occurred in 2004.

Order of the Northwest Territories
Legislative Assembly of the Northwest Territories
P.O. Box 1320, 4570 - 48th St., Yellowknife, NT X1A 2L9
867/669-2200
URL: www.assembly.gov.nt.ca/node/298113

Order of the Northwest Territories
Established in 2013, the Order is the highest honour awarded to residents of the territory. It recognizes individuals who have excelled in any field of endeavour benefitting the people of the Northwest Territories or elsewhere.

Order of Nova Scotia
Protocol Office
P.O. Box 1617, Halifax, NS B3J 2Y3
902/424/4463; Fax: 902/424-4309
URL: novascotia.ca/iga/order.asp

Order of Nova Scotia
The Order was established in 2001, and encourages excellence by recognizing citizens of Nova Scotia for ourstanding contributions or achievements.

Order of Nunavut
The Legislative Assembly of Nunavut
P.O. Box 1200, 926 Federal Rd., Iqaluit, NU X0A 0H0
867/975-5000; Fax: 867/975-5190; Toll Free: 1-877-334-7266
Email: leginfo@assembly.nu.ca; URL: www.assembly.nu.ca/order-nunavut

Order of Nunavut
Established in 2010, the Orer honours individuals who have provided an outstanding contribution to the cultural, social or economic well-being of the territory.

Order of Prince Edward Island
Legislative Assembly, Province House, PO Box 2000, Charlottetown PE C1A 7N8
902/368-5970; Fax: 902/368-5175
Email: chmackay@gov.pe.ca; URL: www.assembly.pe.ca

Order of Prince Edward Island
Highest provincial honour that can be bestowed on a resident of the province; it is awarded in public recognition of individual Islanders whose efforts & accomplishments have been exemplary An enameled medallion, which incorporates the Provincial emblem against a blue background worn with a ribbon of rust, green & white. Recipients receive a stylized lapel pin & miniature medal, an official certificate & are entitled to use O.P.E.I. after their names

The Saskatchewan Order of Merit
Saskatchewan Honours & Awards Program
Office of Protocol & Honours
#1530 - 1855 Victoria Ave., Regina SK S4P 3T2
306/787-8965; Fax: 306/787-1269; Toll Free: 1-877-427-5505
Email: honours@gr.gov.sk.ca; URL: www.saskatchewan.ca/government/heritage-honours-and-awards/saskatchewan-order-of-merit

The Saskatchewan Order of Merit
This is a prestigious recognizes of excellence, achievement and contributions to the social, cultural and economic well-being of the province and its residence.

Secrétariat de l'Ordre national du Québec
Ministère du Conseil exécutif, #3.221, 875, Grande Allée Est, Québec QC G1R 4Y8
418/643-8895; Fax: 418/646-4307
Email: ordre-national@mce.gouv.qc.ca; URL: www.mce.gouv.qc.ca/secretariats/secretariat_ordre_national.htm

Ordre national du Québec
L'Ordre national du Québec est la plus haute distinction décernée par le gouvernement du Québec. Il a été institué par la Loi sur l'Ordre national du Québec (L.R.Q., c. 0-7.01) sanctionnée le 20 juin 1984 par le Parlement de Québec. L'Ordre national du Québec est composé de personnes à qui le gouvernement a conféré le titre de Grand Officier (G.O.) ou d'Officier (O.Q.) ou de Chevalier de l'Ordre national du Québec (C.Q.). La loi prévoit qu'une nomination puisse être faite à titre posthume. Elle accorde aussi au premier ministre du Québec le privilège exclusif de procéder à des nominations étrangères

Société Saint-Jean-Baptiste de Montréal
82, rue Sherbrooke Ouest, Montréal QC H2X 1X3
514/843-8851; Fax: 514/844-6369
Email: mbeaulieu@ssjb.com; URL: www.ssjb.com

Prix Bene Merenti De Patria
Créée en 1923, cette médaille souligne les mérites d'un compatriote ayant rendu des services exceptionnels à la patrie. La maquette est l'oeuvre d'un artiste qui a préparé les chars allégoriques de nos grands défilés pendant de nombreuses années
Médaille d'argent

Prix Chomedey-de-Maisonneuve
Créé en 1983; décerné à une personnalité dont les réalisations contribuent au rayonnement de Montréal

Prix Patriote de l'année
Décerné à une personnalité qui s'est distinguée dans la défense des intérêts du Québec et de la démocratie des peuples, en mémoire des Patriotes des années 1830; créé en 1975

Prix Séraphin-Marion
Créé en 1984; décerné à une personnalité qui défend les droits de la francophonie hors-Québec

St. John Ambulance / Ambulance Saint-Jean
#400, 1900 City Park Dr., Ottawa ON K1J 1A3
613/236-7461; Fax: 613/236-2425
Email: nhq@sja.ca; URL: www.sja.ca

Life-saving Awards of the Order of St. John
Instituted in 1874, recognizes those who risk their lives in unselfish acts of bravery & heroism when saving or attempting to save a life.

United Nations Association in Canada / Association canadienne pour les Nations-Unies
#300, 309 Cooper St., Ottawa ON K2P 0G5
613/232-5751; Fax: 613/563-2455
Email: info@unac.org; URL: www.unac.org

Pearson Peace Medal
Awarded to a Canadian who has contributed significantly to humanitarian causes

CULTURE, VISUAL ARTS & ARCHITECTURE

The Canada Council for the Arts / Conseil des Arts du Canada
350 Albert St., PO Box 1047, Ottawa ON K1P 5V8
613/566-4414; Fax: 613/566-4390; Toll Free: 1-800-263-5588
Email: info@canadacouncil.ca; URL: www.canadacouncil.ca

Bernard Diamant Prize
Awarded in addition to the regular grant to an outstanding Canadian classical singer under 35

Burt Award for First Nations, Métis and Inuit Literature
Awarded annually to English-language Young Adult literary works written by First Nations, Métis or Inuit authors; first prize is valued at $12,000, second prize is valued at $8,000 and third prize is valued at $5,000

Coburn Fellowships
Awarded in alternating years to Canadian and Israeli students; Fellowships are intended to cover travel expenses, tuition and accomodation at the University of Tel Aviv or Hebrew University of Jerusalem (for Canadian students) and the University of Toronto (for Israeli students)

Duke & Duchess of York Prize in Photography
Endowed by the Government of Canada in 1986 on the occasion of Prince Andrew's marriage; $8,000 prize awarded annually to the best candidate in the competition for the Grants to Professional Artists in visual arts; prize is given in addition to the arts grant received

Governor General's Medals in Architecture
Awarded every two years; recognizes excellence in the art of architecture in completed projects; Canada Council adminsters the jurying of the awards & contributes $20,000 to the Royal Architectural Institute of Canada towards the publication of a book/catalogue on the winning projects

Governor-General's Awards for Visual & Media Arts
Six $15,000 prizes awarded annually for distinguished career achievement in visual & media arts, plus one $15,0000 prize for distinguished contributions to the visual & media arts through voluntarism, philanthropy, board governance or community outreach activities.

Eckhardt-Gramatté National Music Competition
Provides $9,000 towards the cost of administrating the competition; First Prize consists of a national concert tour and $5,000; Second Prize is valued at $3,000; Third Prize at $2,000. Competition alternates annually between piano, voice and strings and is administered by a separate organization at Brandon University.

Jacqueline Lemieux Prize
Valued at $6,000 and awarded to the most deserving applicants in the Dance Sections's Grants Program.

J.B.C. Watkins Award
A bequest from the estate of the late John B.C . Watkins, provides special fellowships of $5,000 to Canadian artists in any field, who are graduates of a Canadian university or post-secondary art institution or training school. Preference is given to those who wish to carry out their post-graduate studies in Denmark, Norway, Sweden or Iceland, but applications are accepted for studies in any country other than Canada. Post-graduate schools include post-secondary institutions or training schools, whether or not these are degree-granting institutions; fellowships are normally awarded in music, visual arts (architecture only), theatre & media arts

Jean-Marie Beaudet Award
Awarded annually to a youn Canadian orchestra conductor; valued at $1,000

John G. Diefenbaker Award
Valued at $95,000 and awarded annually to a distinguished German researcher in the social sciences and humanities; the award is funded by an endowment from the Government of Canada

John Hirsch Prize
Awarded to new and developing theatre directors who demonstrate potential for future excellence; one prize each for French and English theatre is awarded every two years. Candidates must be nominated by fellow theatre professionals

John Hobday Awards in Arts Management
Two awards, valued at $10,000 each, are presented each year and alllow recipients to enhance their own professional development by taking part in a program, seminar or workshop. The competition is open to both established and mid-career arts managers

Joseph S. Stauffer Prizes
Each year the Canada Council designates up to three Canadians who have been awarded an arts grant in the fields of music, visual arts or literature as winners; the prizes, which provide an additional $5,000 each, honour the memory of the benefactor whose bequest to the Canada Council enables it to "encourage young Canadians of outstanding promise or potential"

Jules- Léger Prize for New Chamber Music
Administered by the Canadian Music Centre and funded by the Canada Council for the Arts, this award encourages Canadian composers to write for chamber music groups. CBC Radio Two and Espace musique de Radio-Canada broadcast the winning work. The value of the prize is $8,500

Killam Prizes
The Killam Program offers awards to Canadian scholars working in the humanities, social and health sciences, natural sciences and engineering. Five prizes of $100,000 are awarded each year in recognition of outstanding achievements in these fields

Killam Research Fellowship
The Killam Program offers awards to Canadian scholars working in the humanities, social and health sciences, natural sciences and engineering. Fellowships are valued at $70,000

Molson Prizes
Two prizes of $50,000 each are awarded annually to distinguished individuals, one in the social sciences/humanities and one in the arts

Michael Measures Prize
Awarded to honour promising young performers of classical music; one student (between the ages of 16 and 22) is selected annually from students of the National Youth Orchestra who has successfully completed the NYO summer training program. Prize is valued at up to $25,000

Peter Dwyer Scholarships
A total of $20,000 is awarded annually to the two most promising students at the National Ballet School ($10,000) and the National Theatre School ($10,000). The schools choose their respective recipients

Prix de Rome in Architecture
Established 1987; designed to recognize the work of a Canadians actively engaged in the field of contemporary architecture whose career is well under way & whose personal work shows exceptional talent. Winner is chosen by a peer asessment committee convened by the Canada Council for the Arts

Prix de Rome for Emerging Practitioners
Valued at $34,000 and awarded to a recent graduate of one of Canada's ten accredited schools of architecture who demonstrates potential in architectural design. The recipient also has the opportunity to expand his or her skills with an internship at an internationally acclaimed architectural firm anywhere in the world

Prix Joan Lowndes
Awarded annually to an independent curator or critic in recognition of achievement and excellence in critical or curatorial writing on contemporary Canadian visual art

Robert Fleming Prize
Awarded annually to the outstanding candidate in the Grants to Professional Musicians competition; value of the award is $2,000

Ronald J. Thom Award for Early Design Achievement
$10,000 awarded every two years to a Canadian in the early stages of his/her career in architecture who must demonstrate both outstanding creative talent & exceptional potential in architectural design.

Saidye Bronfman Awards
Funded by the Samuel & Saidye Bronfman Family Foundation, $25,000 prize is awarded annually to an exceptional craftsperson for excellence in the fine crafts; in addition to the cash award, works by the recipient are acquired by the Canadian Museum of Civilization.

Victor Martyn Lynch-Staunton Awards
Each year the Canada Council designates several Canadian artists who have been awarded grants in music & visual arts as holders of Victor Martyn Lynch-Staunton Awards; this designation is made to honour the memory of the benefactor whose bequest to the Council enables it to increase the number of grants available to senior or established artists; the awards provide each recipient with $4,000 in addition to the arts grant, which is also provided by the income from this bequest

Virginia Parker Prize
Valued at $25,000 and awarded to a young performer of classical music who is under 32 years of age and who demonstrates outstanding talent and musicianship

Walter Carsen Prize for Excellence in the Performing Arts
Awarded annually on a four year cycle (dance, theatre, dance, and music) and valued at up to $50,000, this prize recognizes the highest level of artistic excellence and career achievement by Canadian artists

York Wilson Endowment Awards
$30,000 awarded annually; enables Canadian art museums & public art galleries to purchase original works by living, contemporary Canadian painters & sculptors; awarded through a Canada Council for the Arts competition, to an eligible Canadian institution to allow it to purchase an original artwork that would significantly enhance its collection of contemporaray Canadian painting or sculpture. Winner is chosen by a peer assessment committee of Canadian curators of contemporary art or other appropriate peers

Canadian Conference of the Arts / Conférence canadienne des arts
#804, 130 Albert St., Ottawa ON K1P 5G4
613/238-3561; Fax: 613/238-4849
Email: info@ccarts.ca; URL: www.ccarts.ca

Diplôme d'honneur
Established in 1954; presented annually to Canadians who have contributed outstanding service to the arts; recipients have included Vincent Massey, Wilfrid Pelletier, Maureen Forrester, Floyd Chalmers, Gabrielle Roy, Glenn Gould, Alfred Pellan, Bill Reid, Antonine Maillet

Keith Kelly Award for Cultural Leadership
Presented annually to a Canadian who has made a significant contribution to the arts through policy development and/or advocacy

Canadian Historical Association / Société historique du Canada
395 Wellington St., Ottawa ON K1A 0N3
613/233-7885; Fax: 613/567-3110
Email: cha-shc@lac-bac.bc.ca; URL: www.cha-shc.ca

Albert B. Corey Prize
Established 1966 & jointly sponsored by the CHA & the American Historical Association; awarded every two years to the best book dealing with the history of Canadian-American relations or the history of both countries
$1,000

Canadian Aboriginal History Prizes
Awarded to the best book on Aboriginal history

CCWH-CCHF Book Prize in Women's and Gender History
Awarded every two years to the best book published in the field of women's and gender history, in either English or French

CHA Journal Prize
Awarded annually for the best essay published each year in the Journal of the Canadian Historical Association

CHA Student Prize
Valued at $250 and awarded to the best article published in a peer-reviewed journal by a PhD or MA-level student, in either English or French

Clio Prizes
Awarded annually to meritorious publications or for exceptional contributions by individuals or organizations to regional history

Eugene A. Forsey Prize
Awarded to the best thesis on labour history

François-Xavier Garneau Medal
Awarded every five years to honour an outstanding Canadian contribution to historical research

Hilda Neatby Prizes
Recognizes the best articles of the year on women's history; one awarded for English-language article and another for French-language article

John Bullen Prize
Awarded to an outstanding PhD thesis on a historical topic submitted in a Canadian university

Neil Sutherland Article Prize
Awarded biennially to an outstanding work on children's and youth history

Political History Prizes
Awarded in three categories: Best Book, Best Article (French) and Best Article (English)

Public History Prize
Awarded in conjunction with the Canadian Committee on Public History; awarded to the best project in public history

Sir. John A. Macdonald Prize
Valued at $5,000 and awarded annually to the best scholarly book in Canadian History; presented at the yearly Governor General Awards for Excellence in Teaching Canadian History event at Rideau Hall in Ottawa. Sponsored by Manulife since 2010

The Wallace K. Ferguson Prize
Established 1979; awarded annually for outstanding work in a field of history other than Canadian
$1,000

The City of Toronto

Chief Administrator's Office, City Hall, 100 Queen St. West, 11th Fl., East Tower, Toronto ON M5H 2N2
416/392-8592; Fax: 416/696-3645

Toronto Book Awards
Awarded annually to recognize books of literary/artistic merit that are evocative of Toronto; Winning author is awarded $10,000 and finalists are awarded $1,000

Fondation Émile-Nelligan

261, rue Bloomfield, Outremont QC H2V 3R6
514/278-4657; Fax: 514/271-6369
Email: info@fondation-nelligan.org; URL: www.fondation-nelligan.org

Prix Émile-Nelligan
Ce prix annuel date de 1979, année de la création de la Fontation Émile-Nelligan. C'est un prix de poésie décerné à des poètes de 35 ans ou moins, pour un recueil publié au cours de l'année.
7 500$

Prix Gilles-Corbeil
Le prix Gilles-Corbeil est un prix de littérature. C'est un prix triennal et is al été décerné pour la première fois en 1990.
100 000$

Prix Ozias-Leduc
Prix triennal en arts visuels (peinture, sculpture, gravure, installations, 'land art'). Décerné à un artiste citoyen du Canada né au Québec ou à un artiste citoyen du Canada ayant sa résidence principale au Québec depuis au moins dix ans
25 000$

Prix Serge-Garant
Le prix Serge-Garant est un prix de compostiion musicale. C'est un prix triennal qui a été décerné pour le première fois en 1991.
25 000$

The Gershon Iskowitz Foundation

#302, 862 Richmond St. West, Toronto ON M6J 1C9
416/351-0216; Fax: 416/351-0217

Gershon Iskowitz Prize
$25,000 to recognize achievements in visual art

Ontario Arts Council / Conseil des arts de l'Ontario

121 Bloor St. East, 7th Fl., Toronto ON M4W 3M5
416/961-1660; Fax: 416/961-7796; Toll Free: 1-800-387-0058
Email: info@arts.on.ca; URL: www.arts.on.ca
The Ontario Arts Council provides a variety of Funds and Scholarships for different studies and careers in the arts. For more information visit their website.

Québec Ministère de la culture et des communications

225, Grande Allée est, Québec QC G1R 5G5
418/380-2300; Fax: 418/080-2364
Email: DC@mcc.gouv.qc.ca; URL: www.mcc.gouv.qc.ca

Les Prix du Québec:

Prix Albert-Tessier

Prix Athanse-David

Prix Ernest-Cormier

Prix d'excellence en architecture
Ce prix souligne, depuis 1978, la contribution essentielle des architectes québecois au cadre bâti. Les prix accordés par l'Order des architectres du Québec permettent d'identifier et de valoriser les meilleures réalisations architecturales au Québec et ailleurs dans le monde.

Prix Georges-Émile-Lapalme

Prix Gérard-Morisset

Prix Guy-Mauffette

Prix Paul-Émile-Borduas
Accordée à un artisan ou un artiste pour l'ensemble de son oeuvre dans le domaine des arts visuels, des métiers d'art, de l'architecture et du design

Royal Architectural Institute of Canada / Institut royal d'architecture du Canada

#330, 55 Murray St., Ottawa ON K1N 5M3
613/241-3600; Fax: 613/241-5750
Email: info@raic.org; URL: www.raic.org

Architectural Firm Award
Awarded to recognize excellence from Canadian architectural firms

Awards of Excellence
These awards are bestowed every two years, recognizing the greatest achievement in several different categories.

Emerging Architectural Practice Award
Awarded to honour excellence and promise from an emerging architectural practice in Canada

National Urban Design Awards
Presented in conjunction with the the Canadian Institute of Planners and the Canadian Society of Landscape Architects, as well as with cooperation from Canadian municipalities; the award recognizes individuals, organizations, firms and other projects that contribute to the quality of Canadian city life

RAIC Gold Medal
Established 1930; this medal is awarded annually in recognition of an individual whose personal work has demonstrated exceptional excellence in the design and practice of architecture; and/or, whose work related to architecture, has demonstrated exceptional excellence in research or education.

Student Medal
Awarded annually to a student graduating from a professional degree program in each accredited University's School of Architecture in Canada who has achieved the highest level of academic excellence

Young Architect Award
Awarded to honour excellence among young architects in Canada

The Royal Society of Canada / La Société royale du Canada

170 Waller St., Ottawa ON K1N 9B9
613/991-6990; Fax: 613/991-6996
Email: info@rsc.ca; URL: www.rsc.ca

Alice Wilson Award
Established in 1991; awarded annually to three women of oustanding academic qualifications studying the Arts and Humanities, Social Sciences or Science, who are entering a career in research at the post-doctoral level

Centenary Medal
Established 1982; awarded at irregular intervals in recognition of outstanding contributions to the object of the society & to recognize links to international organizations

Innis-Gérin Medal
Established in 1966 and awarded biennially to honour a sustained and distinguished contribution to literature of the social sciences

The J.B. Tyrrell Historical Medal
Established 1927; awarded at least every two years for outstanding work in the history of Canada

Konrad Adenauer Research Award
Established in 1988 and awarded annually to a Canadian scholar in the social sciences or humanities; the recipient is invited to carry out a research project of her or his choice in Germany. The award is worth €50,000

Pierre Chauveau Medal
Established in 1951 to and awarded biennially to honour a distinguished and significant contribution to knowledge in the humanities in subjects other than Canadian literature and Canadian history

Sir John William Dawson Medal
Established 1985; awarded biennially for important & sustained contributions by one individual in at least two different fields in the general areas of interest of the Society or in a broad domain that transcends the usual disciplinary boundaries

Ursula Franklin Award in Gender Studies
Established in 1999 and awarded biennially to a Canadian scholar who has made significant contributions in the humanities and social sciences relating to gender issues

Sobey Art Foundation

c/o Art Gallery of Nova Scotia
1723 Hollis Street, PO Box 2262, Halifax NS B3J 3C8
902/424.5169;
Email: fillmose@gov.ns.ca URL: www.sobeyartaward.ca

Sobey Art Award
Awarded every year to an artist 39 years old or younger who has shown their work in a public or commercial art gallery in Canada in the past 18 monthe.
$50 000

Social Sciences & Humanities Research Council of Canada

350 Albert St., PO Box 1610, Ottawa ON K1P 6G4
613/992-0691; Fax: 613/992-1787
Email: info@sshrc.ca; URL: www.sshrc.ca
The Social Sciences & Humanities Research Council of Canada offers various funding opportunities under the three categories: Talent, Insight and Connection. Funding is available for Master's and Doctoral students, Postdoctoral researchers, and particularly for research by and with Aboriginal peoples. For more information, visit the Council's website

Société Saint-Jean-Baptiste de Montréal

82, rue Sherbrooke Ouest, Montréal QC H2X 1X3
514/843-8851; Fax: 514/844-6369
Email: mbeaulieu@ssjb.com; URL: www.ssjb.com

Médaille Bene Merenti de Patria
Décerné pour honorer un service exceptionnel au Canada

Prix André-Guérin
Créé en 1990; Décerné pour l'excellence dans le cinéma

Prix Calixa-Lavallée
Décerné à une personnalité qui s'illustre dans le domaine de la musique

Prix Esdras-Minville
Créé en 1978; décerné à une personnalité canadienne-française qui s'illustre dans le domaine des sciences humaines

Prix Hélène-Pedneault
Rend hommage à une femme qui contribue de manière exceptionnelle à l'avancement de la société québécoise

Prix Léon-Lortie
Décerné pour l'excellence en sciences

Prix Louis Philippe-Hébert
Décerné pour l'excellence dans les beaux-arts

Prix Maurice-Richard
Attribué pour célébrer l'excellence sportive

Prix Olivar-Asselin
Décerné pour l'excellence en journalisme

Prix Victor-Morin
Créé en 1962; décerné à une personnalité canadienne-française qui s'illustre dans le domaine des arts de la scène

Toronto Arts Council Foundation

141 Bathurst St., Toronto ON M5V 2R2
416/392-6800; Fax: 416/392-6920
Email: mail@torontoartscouncil.org; URL: www.torontoartscouncil.org

Arts for Youth Award
Established in 2007 and awarded annually, the award celebrates an individual, organization or collective that has shown outstanding commitment to engaging Toronto's youth through the arts; winner receives $15,000 and finalists receive $2,000

Emerging Artist Award
Established in 2006 and awarded annually to celebrate the accomplishments and future potential of an emerging Toronto artist; award winner receives a $10,00 cash prize, while finalists receive $1,000

Margo Bindhardt and Rita Davies Award
$10,000 cash prize presented every second year to Toronto artist or administrator whose leadership & vision, whether through their creative work or cultural activism, have had a significant impact on the arts in Toronto & for whom the cash prize will make a difference

Muriel Sherrin Award
$10,000 cash prize presented to an artist or creator who has made a contribution to the cultural life ot Toronto through outstanding achievement in music. The recipient will also have participated in international initiatives, including touring, study abroad & artist exchanges. Awarded every second year

Roy Thomson Hall Award
Awarded annually and valued at $10,000; award is presented to an individual, ensemble or organization to honour outstanding contributions (creative, performative, administrative, philanthropic) to Toronto's musical life

Toronto Arts and Business Award
Presented annually in conjunction with the Toronto Star; presented to a local business that has sponsored the arts for the first time

William Kilbourn Award for the Celebration of Toronto's Cultural Life
$5,000 cash prize presented to an individual performer, teacher, administrator or creator in any arts discipline, including architecture & design, whose work is a celebration of life through the arts in Toronto. Awarded every second year

Ville de Montréal
Service du développement culturel
5650, d'Iberville, 4e étage, Montréal QC H2G 3E4
514/872-1156
URL: www.ville.montreal.qc.ca/culture/culture.htm

Prix François-Houdé
La Ville de Montréal, en collaboration avec le Conseil des métiers d'art du Québec décerne annuellement ce Prix afin de promouvoir l'excellence de la nouvelle création montréalaise en métiers d'art et de favoriser la diffusion d'oeuvres des jeunes artisans créateurs. Bourse de 3000$ et 2 500$ pour organiser une exposition

Prix Louis-Comtois
La Ville de Montréal, en collaboration avec l'Association des galeries d'art contemporain, décerne annuellement ce Prix qui vient apppuyer et promouvoir le travail d'un artiste en mi-carrière qui s'est distingué dans le domaine de l'art contemporain à Montréal depuis les 15 dernières années. Bourse 5000$ et 2 500$ pour organiser une exposition solo

Prix Pierre-Ayot
La Ville de Montréal, en collaboration avec l'Association des galeries d'art contemporain, décerne annuellement ce Prix qui souligne la facture exceptionnelle et l'apport original de la production des jeunes artistes en peinture, en estampe, en dessin, en illustration, en photographie ou tout autre médium. Bourse 3000$ et 2 500$ pour organiser une exposition solo

EDUCATIONAL

Alberta Scholarship Programs
PO Box 28000, Stn Main, Edmonton AB T5J 4R4
780/427-8640; Fax: 780/427-1288
Email: scholarships@gov.ab.ca; URL: www.studentaid.alberta.ca/scholarships/alberta-scholarships

Alberta Scholarships Program
Scholarships & awards are available in various fields of study

BC Ministry of Advanced Education
PO Box 9173, Stn Prov Govt, Victoria BC V8W 9H7
250/387-6100; Fax: 250/356-9455; Toll Free: 1-800-561-1818
URL: www.bcsap.bc.ca

Irving K. Barber Scholarship
Up to 150 scholarships worth $5,000 annually; open to students who have completed two years at a BC community college, university college or institute & must transfer to a public degree-granting institution in BC in order to complete their degrees

Lieutenant Governor's Silver Medal Award
Established in 1994 in a partnership with the University of Victoria; awarded for outstanding work by a graduate student in a Master's program

Black Business & Professional Association
180 Elm St., Toronto, ON M5T 3M4
416/504-4097; Fax: 416/504-7343
Email: information@bbpa.org; URL: www.bbpa.org

Harry Jerome Awards and Scholarship Fund
Scholarships celebrates excellence in achievement in the Black community. Award recipients are selected from among Canada-wide nominees recommended by business and professional colleagues, teachers, relatives and friends.
Five $2,000 annual awards

Canadian Association of University Business Officers / Association canadienne du personnel administratif universitaire
#320, 350 Albert St., Ottawa ON K1R 1B1
613/230-6760; Fax: 613/563-7739
Email: cworkman@caubo.ca; URL: www.caubo.ca

CAUBO Quality & Productivity Awards
Designed to recognize, reward & share university achievements in improving the quality & reducing the cost of higher education programs & services; National & Regional categories
Awards evaluated on portability, originality, quality impact, productivity impact, & involvement
National: first prize $10,000; second prize $5,000; third prize $3,000

Canadian Mathematical Society / Société mathématique du Canada
#109, 577 King Edward St., Ottawa ON K1N 6N5
613/562-5702; Fax: 613/565-1539
Email: office@cms.math.ca; URL: www.cms.math.ca

Sun Life Financial Canadian Mathematical Olympiad
Annual mathematics competition established to provide an opportunity for students to perform well on the Canadian Open Mathematics Challenge & to complete on a national basis. Fifteen cash prizes

Canadian Sociology & Anthropology Association / Société canadienne de sociologie et d'anthropologie
Université Concordia University SB-323
1455, De Maisonneuve Ouest, Montréal QC H3G 1M8
514/848-8780; Fax: 514/848-8780
Email: info@csaa.ca; URL: www.csaa.ca

John Porter Award
Recognizes outstanding published scholarly contributions within the "John Porter Tradition" to the advancement of sociological and/or anthropological knowledge in Canada
Outstanding Contribution Award
Given to recognize the work of eminent sociologists & anthropologists

Best Student Paper Award
Recognizes the best paper among those received for adjudication, written by a graduate student

CIDA Awards Program
Canadian Bureau for International Education
#1550, 220 Laurier Ave. West, Ottawa ON K1P 5Z9
613/237-4820; Fax: 613/237-1073
Email: info@cbie.ca; URL: www.cbie.ca

CBIE Excellence Awards Program
Consists of ten awards that honour excellence in the field of international education

Foundation for Educational Exchange Between Canada & the United States of America
#2015, 350 Albert St., Ottawa ON K1R 1A4
613/688-5540; Fax: 613/237-2029
Email: info@fulbright.ca; URL: www.fulbright.ca

Canada-US Fulbright Program
To expand research, teaching & study opportunities for Canadian & American faculty & students engaged in the study of Canada, the United States & the relationship between the two countries; based on academic excellence & the merit of the applicant's proposed project, awards given annually for study in a number of different fields including conservation, ecology, environmental management, resource analysis & environmental policy. Applicants must relocate from the U.S. to Canada, or Canada to the U.S.
$15,000 US for graduate students; $25,000 US for faculty

International Development Research Centre / Centre de recherches pour le développement international
250 Albert St., Ottawa ON K1G 3H9
613/236-6163; Fax: 613/238-7230
Email: info@idrc.ca; URL: www.idrc.ca

Canadian Window on International Development Awards
Award offered for doctoral research that explores the relationship between Canadian aid, trade, immigration & diplomatic policy, & international development & the alleviation of global policy
Applicants must hold Canadian citizenship or permanent residency status; be registered at a Canadian university; be conducting the proposed research for a doctoral dissertation & have completed course work & passed comprehensive examinations by the time of the award tenure
$20,000 per year - Centre Training & Awards Unit, 613/236-6163 ext 2098; Fax: 613/563-0815; Email: cta@idrc.ca

IDRC Research Awards
Awards offered annually to Canadians, permanent residents of Canada, and citizens of developing countries pursuing or having completed master's or doctoral studies at a recognized university.

The Japan Foundation, Toronto / Kokosai Koryu Kikin Toronto Nihon Bunka Centre
#213, 131 Bloor St. West, Toronto ON M5S 1R1
416/966-1600; Fax: 416/966-9773
Email: info@jftor.org; URL: www.japanfoundationcanada.org

The Japan Foundation Fellowships
Scholars, researchers, artists & other professionals are provided an opportunity to conduct research or pursue projects in Japan. Term of award is from two to 14 months, depending on category; annual application deadline is Dec. 1 for funding year beginning the following April 1

The Japan Foundation Scholarships & Programs
The Foundation offers a wide range of programs in more than 180 countries, including the following: exchange of persons (fellowships); support for Japanese-language instruction; support for Japanese studies; support for arts-related exchange; support for media exchange

Loran Scholars Foundation
#502 - 460 Richmond Street West St., Toronto ON M5V 1Y1
416/646-2120; Fax: 416/646-0846; Toll Free: 1-866-544-2673
Email: info@loranscholar.ca; URL: www.loranscholar.ca

Finalist Award
Given to every finalist who is selected for & attends, National Selections
$3,000 awarded to outstanding students from across the country as one-time entrance awards to be used at any accredited Canadian university

Loran Award
Up to $10,000 per year plus a tuition stipend, for up to four years of full-time undergraduate study at any one of the participating Canadian universities

Provincial Award
One-time entrance award tenable at any accredited university in Canada at which the recipient gains admission & enrolls in a full-time program of study
$2,000

Indspire
PO Box 5, #100, 50 Generations Dr., Six Nations of the Grand River, Ohsweken, ON NOA 1M0
519/445-3021; Fax: 866/433-3159

Indspire Bursaries and Scholarships
Designed to assist First Nation, Inuit and Métis students obtain post-secondary education

Northern Enterprise Fund Inc.
PO Box 220, Beauval SK S0M 0G0
306/288-2258; Fax: 306/288-4667; Toll Free: 1-800-864-3022
Email: info@nefi.ca; URL: www.nefi.ca

Northern Spirit Scholarship Program
To promote entrepreneurial spirit in Northern Saskatchewan by providing scholarships to students enrolled in courses related to business or based on occupational shortages in the north
Ten $2,500 scholarships are awarded to full-time students who are permanent northern residents of the Northern Administration District; priority will be given to applicants showing intention of returning to, or remaining in the north; with an academic record of 70% average in most recent year completed

Ontario Council on Graduate Studies / Conseil ontarien des études supérieures
#1100, 180 Dundas St. West, Toronto ON M5G 1Z8
416/979-2165; Fax: 416/595-7392
Email: kpanesar@cou.on.ca; URL: ocgs.cou.on.ca

John Charles Polanyi Prizes
In honour of the achievement of John Charles Polanyi, co-recipient of the 1986 Nobel Prize in Chemistry, the Government of Ontario has established a fund to provide annually up to five prizes to persons continuing to post-doctoral studies at an Ontario university; prizes available in the areas of Physics, Chemistry, Physiology or Medicine, Literature & Economic Science
$15,000

Universities Canada/Universités Canada
#600, 350 Albert St., Ottawa ON K1R 1B1
613/563-1236; Fax: 613/563-9745
Email: awards@aucc.ca; URL: www.univcan.ca

Bayer CropScience Scholarship for Future Leaders in Agriculture
Up to 5 scholarships available; $5,000.

C.D. Howe Scholarship Endowment Fund National Engineering Scholarship
(One male, one female) for students who have completed the first year of an engineering program
Two $7,500 scholarships

C.D. Howe Scholarship Fund Thunder Bay/Port Arthur Scholarship Program
Scholarships open to all disciplines but students must be residents of Thunder Bay or the former federal constituency of Port Arthur
Two $5,500

Conocophillips Canada Centennial Scholarship
Scholarship program encourages individuals with academic excellence and demonstrated leadership.
Three scholarships of up to $10,000 per year for a maximum of 2 consecutive years

Fessenden-Trott Scholarship
Scholarships open to all disciplines; restricted to Ontario in 2005
Four $9,000

Frank Knox Memorial Fellowship Program
Awards, plus tuition fees & health insurance for Canadian citizens or permanent residents who have graduated from a AUCC member institution before Sept. 2005 & wish to study at Harvard in the following disciplines: arts & sciences (including engineering), business administration, design, divinity studies, education, law, public administration, medicine, dental medicine & public health; applications for students currently studying in the US will not be considered
Up to three US$18,500

Horatio Alger Canada Scholarship Program
All disciplines are eligible.
Eighty scholarships are available at $5,000; 5 national entrepreneurial scholarships valued at $10,000

L'Oréal Canada For Women in Science Research Excellence Fellowships
Two post-doctoral fellowships; $20,000

Mattinson Scholarship Program for Students with Disabilities
For undergraduate study, all disciplines
$2,000

Multiple Sclerosis Society of Canada Scholarship Programs
Three Follow the Leader Scholarships ($25,000 per school year, up to four years) and two John Helou Scholarships ($6,250 per school year, up to four years) are available for students directly affected by MS or an allied disease

Nexen Oil Sands Scholarship
$2,500 for degrees, diplomas or certificates; $750 for apprenticeships

Queen Elizabeth II Silver Jubilee Endowment Fund for Study in a Second Official Language Award Program
Scholarships open to all disciplines, except translations, for students studying in their second language
Three $7,000 (plus travel costs)

TD Scholarships for Community Leadership
All disciplines, undergraduate degrees
20 renewable scholarships for $7,500 living stipend, plus all tuition & compulsory fees, plus summer employment

Vale Manitoba Operations Scholarship
Up to 3 scholarships available; $5,000 for Bachelor degree program and $2,500 for diploma program.

Yukon Government
PO Box 2703, Whitehorse YT Y1A 2C6
867/667-5811; Fax: 867/393-6339
Email: information@gov.yk.ca

Yukon Excellence Awards
Awarded to encourage academic achievement in a Yukon secondary school; students are eligible to receive up to $3,000 for 10 awards ($300 per award) to offset post-secondary education/training costs

ENVIRONMENTAL

Alberta Emerald Foundation
c/o McLennan Ross LLP, #400, 12220 Stony Plain Rd., Edmonton AB T5N 3Y4
780/413-9629; Fax: 780/482-9100; Toll Free: 1-800-219-8329
Email: info@emeraldfoundation.ca; URL: emeraldfoundation.ca/

Emerald Awards
Awarded to Albertans who have made a significant contribution to the protection or enhancement of the environment
Nominations are open to individual, not-for-profit organizations, business & industry, communities & government, educational institutions & volunteer organizations excelling in environmental achievements

Alberta Environmental & Sustainable Resource Development
Fish & Wildlife Division
Information Centre, Main Floor, 9920 - 108 St. Edmonton AB T5K 2M4
780/944-0313; Fax: 780/427-4407; Email: ESRD.Info-Centre@gov.ab.ca; URL: srd.alberta.ca

Order of the Bighorn
Fish & wildlife conservation awards presented every other year, to individuals, organizations & corporations for their outstanding contributions to fish & wildlife conservation in Alberta - Program Manager, Dave England

Atlantic Salmon Federation / Fédération du saumon atlantique
15 Rankine Mill Road, Chamcook NB E5B 3A9
506/529-1033; Fax: 506/529-4438; Toll Free: 1-800-565-5666
Email: tiffinic@nb.aibn.com; URL: www.asf.ca

Lee Wulff Conservation Award
Presented annually to an individual who has made noteworthy, long-term contributions to Atlantic salmon conservation.

Olin Fellowship
Fellowships offered annually to individuals seeking to improve their knowledge or skills in fields dealing with current problems in biology, management, or conservation of Atlantic salmon & its habitat; the fellowship may be applied toward a wide range of endeavours such as salmon management, graduate study, & research.
Applicants need not be enrolled in a degree program, but must be legal residents of the US or Canada
$1,000-$3,000
ASF member in good standing

T.B. "Happy" Fraser Award
Presented annually to an individual who has made outstanding long-term contributions to Atlantic salmon conservation in Canada. The award reflects efforts on a regional or national level

Canadian Land Reclamation Association / Association canadienne de réhabilitation des sites dégradés
PO Box 61047, RPO Kensington, Calgary AB T2N 4S6
403/289-9435; Fax: 403/289-9435
Email: clra@telusplanet.net; URL: www.clra.ca

Dr. Edward M. Watkin Award
Presented annually to an association member in recognition of outstanding contribution to the field of reclamation, through research, field work, teaching or innovation, or distinguished service to the association through active participation & leadership

The Noranda Land Reclamation Award
Presented annually by the association on behalf of Noranda Mines Inc. in recognition of superior research or field work in reclamation; not restricted to members

Canadian Wildlife Federation / Fédération canadienne de la faune
350 Michael Cowpland Dr., Kanata ON K2M 2W1
613/599-9594; Fax: 613/599-4428; Toll Free: 1-800-563-9453
Email: info@cwf-fcf.org; URL: www.cwf-fcf.org

Canadian Conservation Achievement Awards Program:

Doug Clarke Memorial Award
Presented to a CWF affiliate for the most outstanding conservation project completed during the previous year by the affiliate, its clubs, or its members

Past Presidents' Canadian Legislator Award
Presented annually to an elected legislator in recognition of a meaningful contribution to wildlife conservation in Canada

Robert Bateman Award
Awarded to recognize an individual or group who has furthered the awareness of and/or the appreciation for Canada's wildlife through artistic expression; artistic expression can include: painting, sculpture, photography, choreography, writing, song

Roderick Haig-Brown Memorial Award
Awarded annually to an individual who has made a significant contribution to furthering the sport of angling &/or conservation & wise use of Canada's recreational fisheries resources

Roland Michener Conservation Award
A trophy is given annually in recognition of an individual's outstanding achievement in the field of conservation in Canada

Stan Hodgkiss Outdoorsperson of the Year Award
Presented annually to an outdoorsperson who has demonstrated an active commitment to conservation in Canada

WILD Educator of the Year Award
Established in 2015 and awarded to any WILD Education instructor who utilizes CWF's education programming to provide innovative experiences for youth that focus on wildlife and conservation

Youth Conservation Award
Awarded to a Canadian youth and/or youth group that has participated in a wildlife conservation project or activity

Youth Mentor Award
Awarded to any individual or group who has made significant contributions in creating or presenting programs that are dedicated toward youth and focus on introducing the importance of conservation, wildlife or habitat

International Development Research Centre / Centre de recherches pour le développement international
250 Albert St., Ottawa ON K1P 6M1
613/236-6163; Fax: 613/238-7230
Email: info@idrc.ca; URL: www.idrc.ca
Applicants must hold Canadian citizenship or permanent residency status; be registered at a Canadian university; research proposal is for a doctoral thesis; provide evidence of affiliation with an institution or organization in the region in which the research will take place; have completed course work & passed comprehensive examinations by the time of award tenure
Maximum of $20,000 per year - Centre Training & Awards Unit, 613/236-6163 ext 2098; Fax: 613/563-0815; Email: cta@irdc.ca

Newfoundland & Labrador Department of Environment & Conservation
Confederation Bldg., West Block, 4th Fl., PO Box 8700, St. John's NL A1B 4J6
709/729-2664; Fax: 709/729-6639
Email: envcinquires@gov.nl.ca; URL: www.env.gov.nl.ca/env/env_edu/awards.html

The Newfoundland & Labrador Environmental Awards Program
Established in partnership with the Newfoundland & Labrador Women's Institutes Multi-Materials Stewardship Board & the Dept. of Environment to create public awareness for the proactive environmental actions being taken by Newfoundlanders & Labradorians; the object is to demonstrate the contributions people are making to create a healthier environment & through their efforts, encourage others to do the same; awards are given in seven categories: individual, citizen's group or organization, educator, youth, school, business, & municipal

Recycling Council of Ontario / Conseil du recyclage de l'Ontario
#407 - 215 Spadina Av., Toronto ON M5T 2C7
416/657-2797; Fax: 416/960-8053
Email: rco@rco.on.ca; URL: www.rco.on.ca

RCO Awards
A series of awards for outstanding achievement in recycling: includes 3Rs initiatives in commercial, industrial & institutional settings; Outstanding Municipal, Non-profit Organization, Recycling Program Operator; Outstanding School Program, & Media Contribution Award

Royal Canadian Geographical Society
#200, 1155 Lola St., Ottawa ON K1K 4C1
613/745-4629; Fax: 613/744-0947
URL: www.rcgs.org

3M Environmental Innovation Award
Established in 2009 in partnership with 3M Canada to recognize outstanding individuals in business, academia, government or community organizations whose innovation and contributions to the environment are affecting positive change in Canada/for Canadians

University of Toronto School of the Environment
University of Toronto, #1021, 33 Wilcocks St.
Toronto ON M5S 3E8
416/978-3475; Fax: 416/978-3884
URL: www.environment.utoronto.ca

Alan H. Weatherley Graduate Fellowship in Environmental Leadership

Alexander B. Leman Memorial Award

Arthur and Sonia Labatt Fellowships

Beatrice and Arthur Minden Graduate Research Fellowship at the School of the Environment

Eric David Baker Krause Graduate Fellowship

George Burwash Langford Award

The GreenSaver Alastair Fairweather Memorial Award in the Environment

John R. Brown Award

Sperrin Chant Award

HEALTH & MEDICAL

Action Canada for Sexual Health & Rights / Fédération canadienne pour la santé sexuelle
251 Bank St., 2nd Fl., Ottawa ON K2P 1X3
613/241-4474
Email: info@sexualhealthandrights.ca; URL: www.sexualhealthandrights.ca

The Helen & Fred Bentley Awards for Excellence of Achievement
Recognizes the achievements of Action Canada Associate Organizations.

Canadian Association of Medical Radiation Technologists / Association canadienne des technologues en radiation médicale
#500, 1095 Carling Ave., Ottawa ON K1Y 4P6
613/234-0012; Fax: 613/234-1097; Toll Free: 1-800-463-9729
Email: lgoulet@camrt.ca; URL: www.camrt.ca

CAMRT Awards
Administers awards for students & registered technologists including: Dr. M. Mallett Student Award, Dr. Petrie Memorial Award, George Reason Memorial Award, E.I. Hood Award, CAMRT Student Achievement Award, Philips Award, CR/PACS Technology Award

Canadian Association on Gerontology / Action Canada pour la santé et les droits sexuels
#106 - 222 College St., Toronto ON M5T 3J1
416/978-7977; Fax: 416/978-4771
Email: contact@cagacg.ca; URL: www.cagacg.ca

CAG Award for Contribution to Gerontology
To recognize an individual who has recently made an outstanding contribution to the field of aging
Certificate

Canadian Institutes of Health Research
160 Elgin St., 9th Floor; Address Locator 4809A, Ottawa ON K1A 0W9
613/941-2672; Fax: 613/954-1800; Toll Free: 1-888-603-4178
Email: info@cihr-irsc.gc.ca; URL: www.cihr-irsc.gc.ca

Michael Smith Prize in Health Research
A medal plus $100,000 research grant per year for five years awarded annually to an outstanding Canadian researcher who has demonstrated innovation, creativity & dedication to health research

Canadian Nurses Association / Association des infirmières et infirmiers du Canada
50 Driveway, Ottawa ON K2P 1E2
613/237-2133; Fax: 613/237-3520; Toll Free: 1-800-361-8404
Email: info@cna-aiic.ca; URL: www.cna-aiic.ca

Jeanne Mance Awards
Established in 1971, this award is named after one of Canada's most inspirational nurses. Awarded every other year, Nurses nominated for this have have made significant and innovative contributions to the health of Canadians.

Order of Merit Awards
Established in 2008 and awarded to recognize excellence in clinical nursing practice, nursing administration, nursing education, nursing research and nursing policy

Canadian Orthopaedic Foundation / Fondation orthopédique du Canada
PO Box 1036, Toronto, ON M5K 1P2
416/410-2341; Toll Free: 1-800-461-3639
Email: mailbox@canorth.org; URL: www.whenithurtstomove.org

J. Edouard Samson Award
Medal & $15,000 awarded for outstanding orthopaedic research by a young investigator; paper presented at the annual meeting of the Canadian Orthopaedic Research Society

Canadian Society for Medical Laboratory Science / Société canadienne de science de laboratoire médical
PO Box 2830, Stn LCD 1, Hamilton ON L8N 3N8
905/528-8642; Fax: 905/528-4968; Toll Free: 1-800-263-8277
Email: michellee@csmls.org; URL: www.csmls.org

E.V. Booth Scholarship Award
Awarded to certified medical laboratory technologists who are enrolled in studies leading to a degree in medical laboratory science
Two awards of $500

Canadian Veterinary Medical Association / Association canadienne des médecins vétérinaires
339 Booth St., Ottawa ON K1R 7K1
613/236-1162; Fax: 613/236-9681; Toll Free: 1-800-567-2862
Email: admin@cvma-acmv.org; URL: www.canadianveterinarians.net; www.veterinairesaucanada.net

CVMA Humane Award
Established 1986 to encourage care & well-being of animals; awarded to an individual (veterinarian or non-veterinarian) whose work is judged to have contributed significantly to the welfare & well-being of animals; $1,000 & a plaque awarded

Intervet/Schering-Plough Veterinary Award
Established 1985 to enhance progress in large animal medicine & surgery; award made to a veterinarian whose work in large animal practice, clinical research or basic sciences is judged to have contributed significantly to the advancement of large animal medicine, surgery & theriogenology, including herd health management; $1,000 & a plaque awarded

Merck Veterinary Award
Established in 1985 and sponsored by Merck Animal Health; presented to a CVMA member whose work in food and animal production practice, research or science has contributed significantly to the advancement of food animal medicine. Award consists of a plaque and a cash prize of $1,000

Small Animal Practitioner Award
Established 1987 to encourage progress in the field of small animal medicine & surgery; awarded to a veterinarian whose work in small animal practice, clinical research or basic sciences is judged to have contributed significantly to the advancement of small animal medicine, surgery, or the management of small animal practice, including the advancement of the public's knowledge of the responsibilities of pet ownership; $1,000 & a plaque awarded

Catholic Health Association of Canada / Association catholique canadienne de la santé
1247 Kilborn Pl., Ottawa ON K1H 6K9
613/731-7148; Fax: 613/731-7797
Email: info@chac.ca; URL: www.chac.ca

Performance Citation Award
Established 1981; awarded annually to an individual who makes an outstanding contribution to health care in a Christian context, who exhibits exemplary leadership of a national effort at building the Christian community & unselfish dedication to others

College of Family Physicians of Canada / Collège des médecins de famille du Canada
2630 Skymark Ave., Mississauga ON L4W 5A4
905/629-0900; Fax: 905/629-0893; Toll Free: 800/387-6197
Email: info@cfpc.ca; URL: www.cfpc.ca

Awards of Excellence
Awarded to recognize CFPC members who have made an outstanding contribution in a specific area, in one of the following areas: patient care, community service, health care institutions/hospitals, teaching or research

Family Physician of the Year/Reg Perkins Award
Awarded to physicians who have been in family practice for a minimum of 15 years & members of the college for at least 10 years, & who have made outstanding contributions to family medicine, to their communities & to the college

Family Medicine Researcher of the Year Award
Sponsored by the CFPC'S Research & Education Foundation, this award recognizes a Family Medicine researcher who has been a pivotal force in the definition, development and dissemination of concepts central to the discipline of family medicine.

Epilepsy Canada / Épilepsie Canada
#336, 2255B Queen St. East, Toronto ON M4E 1G3
Toll Free: 1-877-734-0873
Email: epilepsy@epilepsy.ca; URL: www.epilepsy.ca

Epilepsy Canada Research Fellowships
To develop expertise in clinical or basic epilepsy research & to enhance the quality of care for epilepsy patients in Canada; awarded annually to a Ph.D. or M.D. for clinical research at a Canadian institution; designed as a training program & not intended for those holding faculty appointments

The Royal College of Physicians & Surgeons of Canada / Le Collège royal des médecins et chirurgiens du Canada
774 Echo Dr., Ottawa ON K1S 5N8
613/730-8177; Fax: 613/730-8830; Toll Free: 1-800-668-3740
Email: feedback@royalcollege.ca; URL: www.royalcollege.ca

The Office of Fellowship Affairs administers an annual competition for five Fellowship grants, three Awards that recognize original research, and three faculty development projects.

The Royal Society of Canada / La Société royale du Canada
170 Waller St., Ottawa ON K1N 9B9
613/991-6990; Fax: 613/991-6996
Email: info@rsc.ca; URL: www.rsc.ca

Jason A. Hannah Medal
Established 1976; awarded annually for an important publication in the history of medicine
$1,500 & a bronze medal

The McLaughlin Medal
Awarded annually for important research of sustained excellence in any branch of medical science
$2,500 & a medal

JOURNALISM

Atlantic Journalism Awards
46 Swanton Dr., Dartmouth NS B3W 2C5
902/425-2727; Fax: 902/462-1892
Email: office@ajas.ca; URL: ajas.ca

Atlantic Journalism Awards
Originally a program of the University of King's College School of Journalism established in 1981, is now a non-profit organization to recognize excellence & achievement in work by Atlantic Canadian journalists; covers work in English or French; 23 award categories featuring work published or broadcast in the news media of Atlantic Canada.
Winners in individual categories will receive framed certificate presented at the Awards dinner.

Canadian Association of Journalists / L'Association canadienne des journalistes
c/o Algonquin College, #B224, 1385 Woodroffe Ave., Ottawa ON K2G 1V8
613/526-8061; Fax: 613/521-3904
Email: canadianjour@magma.ca; URL: www.caj.ca

The CAJ Awards Program
Awards presented for excellence in Canadian journalism with a focus on investigative work, also includes the Don McGillivray award for Best Investigative Report

Canadian Business Media Association
Email: staff@cbmassociation.com; URL: www.cbmassociation.wordpress.com

Canadian Business Media Awards in Memory of Kenneth R. Wilson
Recognize excellence in writing & graphic design (17 categories) in specialized business/professional publications; open to all business publications, regardless of CBP membership, that are published in English &/or French; all awards, except the Harvey Southam Editorial Career Award, require an entry fee - krwawards@cbp.ca

Canadian Newspaper Association / Association canadienne des journaux
#200, 890 Yonge St., Toronto ON M4W 3P4
416/923-3567; Fax: 416/923-7206
Email: info@cna-acj.ca; URL: www.cna-acj.ca

National Newspaper Awards/Concours canadien de journalisme
Awards are presented annually in early spring in 16 categories: Spot News Reporting, Enterprise Reporting, Special Project, Layout & Design, Critical Writing, Sports Writing, Feature Writing, Cartooning, Columns, Business Reporting, International Reporting, Spot News Photography, Feature Photography, Sports Photography, Editorial Writing, Local Reporting.
Eligible are those employed by or freelance for daily newspapers or wire services in French or English; awards are governed by an independent board of governors consisting of newspaper & public representatives.
Winners receive $2,500 plus certificates; two runners-up in each category receive citations of merit & $250

Canadian Science Writers' Association / Association canadienne des rédacteurs scientifiques
PO Box 75, Stn A, Toronto ON M5W 1A2
Toll Free: 1-800-796-8595
Email: office@sciencewriters.ca; URL: www.sciencewriters.ca

Herb Lampert Science in Society Emerging Journalist Award

Science in Society Journalism Awards
Open to Canadian journalists in all media for work appearing in the previous calendar year; 14 categories include newspapers, magazines, trade publications, radio, television, children's books & general books; awards total $14,000

National Magazine Awards Foundation / Fondation nationale des prix du magazine canadien
#700, 425 Adelaide St. West, Toronto ON M5V 3C1
416/828-9011; Fax: 416/504-0437
Email: staff@magazine-awards.com; URL: www.magazine-awards.com

National Magazine Awards
Awards are presented annually in 26 categories including Personal Journalism, Arts & Entertainment, Humour, Business, Science, Health & Medicine, Sports & Recreation, Fiction, Poetry, Travel, Magazine Illustration, Photojournalism, Art Direction, Magazine Covers, & Photography; all above awards go to individual magazine writers, photographers, illustrators, or art directors; Magazine of the Year recognizes continual overall excellence, The President's Medal is awarded to an article from the text categories & offers a prize of $3,000; The Foundation Award for Outstanding Achievement was introduced in 1990 & recognizes an individual's innovation & creativity through career-long contributions to the magazine industry
Awards are gold or silver scrolls with $1,500 & $500 cash prizes respectively; President's Medal $3,000

Ontario Newspaper Awards
Email: info@onawards.ca; URL: www.onawards.ca
Celebrated annually and available in a variety of journalism categories such as: Novice Reporting; Sports Writing; Sports Photography, Humour Writing.

Société Saint-Jean-Baptiste de Montréal
82, rue Sherbrooke Ouest, Montréal QC H2X 1X3
514/843-8851; Fax: 514/844-6369
Email: mbeaulieu@ssjb.com; URL: www.ssjb.com

Prix Olivar-Asselin
Established 1955; $1,500 & a medal awarded annually to a French Canadian in recognition of outstanding achievement in journalism in serving the higher interests of the French Canadian people

LEGAL, GOVERNMENTAL, PUBLIC ADMINISTRATION

Alberta Justice & Solicitor General
Bowker Bldg., 9833-109 Street NW, Edmonton, AB T5K 2E8
780/427-3441
URL: www.solgps.alberta.ca

Community Justice Awards
Awards highlight the activities & accomplishments of special Albertans who prove that preventing crime is everyone's responsibility; awards are presented to an individual, for youth leadership, business, community program or organization & police member for efforts beyond regular duties

Canadian Society of Association Executives / Société canadienne des directeurs d'association
#1100, 10 King St. East, Toronto ON M5C 1C3
416/363-3555; Fax: 416/363-3630; Toll Free: 1-800-461-3608
Email: csae@csae.com; URL: www.csae.com

Pinnacle Award
Recognizes the association executive who has demonstrated exceptional & outstanding leadership qualities within their organization, has contributed to other voluntary organizations & the community at large, to CSAE at local & national levels

Institute of Public Administration of Canada / Institut d'administration publique du Canada
#401, 1075 Bay St., Toronto ON M5S 2B1
416/924-8787; Fax: 416/924-4992
URL: www.ipac.ca

IPAC Award for Innovative Management
Awarded in recognition of outstanding organizational achievement in the public sector

Vanier Medal
A gold medal is awarded annually as a mark of distinction & exceptional achievement to a person who has shown outstanding leadership in public administration in Canada

Justice Canada
Legal Studies for Aboriginal People Program, Department of Justice Canada, Programs Branch, 284 Wellington St., 6th Fl., Ottawa ON K1A 0H8
613/941-0388; Fax: 613/941-2269; Toll Free: 1-888-606-5111
Email: LSAP@justice.gc.ca; URL: www.justice.gc.ca/eng/fund-fina/acf-fca/lsap-aeda.html

Legal Studies for Aboriginal People Program
A scholarship program to encourage Métis & Non-Status Indians to enter the legal profession by providing financial assistance through a pre-law orientation course & an annual scholarship program for a maximum of 3 years
Open to Aboriginal People (Métis & Non-Status Indians)

The Professional Institute of the Public Service of Canada / Institut professionnel de la fonction publique du Canada
250 Tremblay Rd., Ottawa ON K1G 3J8
613/228-6310; Fax: 613/228-9048; Toll Free: 1-800-267-0446
URL: www.pipsc.ca

Gold Medal Awards
Established 1937; the gold medals are presented biennially. Those eligible are scientific, professional, or technical workers or groups of workers employed by the federal, provincial, or municipal government services of Canada who have made a contribution of outstanding importance to national or world well-being in either pure or applied science or in some field outside pure or applied science

LITERARY ARTS, BOOKS & LIBRARIES

Book Publishers Association of Alberta
10523 - 100 Ave., Edmonton AB T5J 0A8
780/424-5060; Fax: 780/424-7943
Email: info@planet.eon.net; URL: www.bookpublishers.ab.ca

Alberta Book Awards
To recognize outstanding achievements in Alberta publishing; nine awards are given - Alberta Publisher of the Year, Alberta Trade Book of the Year, Alberta Book Design Award, Alberta Book Cover Design Award, Alberta Educational Book of the Year, Alberta Childrens' Book of the Year, Alberta Book Illustration Award, Alberta Scholarly Book, Alberta Emerging Publisher of the Year.
Stone carvings by Brian Clark are presented & kept by the winner in the award year & exchanged for plaques the following year.

Alberta Book Publishing Achievement Award
Established to recognize long-standing contributions made to Alberta book publishing.

Lois Hole Award for Editorial Excellence
Established in honour of Lois Hole's dedication to books, libraries, literacy and respect for editors.

British Columbia Historical Federation
PO Box 5254, Stn B, Victoria BC V8R 6N4
604/277-2627; Fax: 604/277-2657
Email: info@bchistory.ca; URL: www.bchistory.ca

W. Kaye Lamb Essay Scholarships
Awarded for essays written by students at BC colleges or universities on a topic related to BC history

Writing Awards
Established 1983; Honours outstanding contributions by individuals and groups through historical writing, best article and best website

The Canada Council for the Arts / Conseil des Arts du Canada
350 Albert St., PO Box 1047, Ottawa ON K1P 5V8
613/566-4414; Fax: 613/566-4390; Toll Free: 1-800-263-5588
Email: info@canadacouncil.ca; URL: www.canadacouncil.ca

Canada-Japan Literary Awards
Valued at $10,000 each and awarded biennially to both an English language writer & a French language writer; awards are designed to encourage Canadian authors to explore and celebrate Japan, Japanese themes or Japanese-Canadian relations

Governor-General's Literary Awards
Seven $25,000 prizes awarded annually for the best books in seven categories; the publisher of each winning book receives $3,000 to support promotional activities

Canadian Association of Children's Librarians
c/o Canadian Library Association, 328 Frank St., Ottawa ON K2P 0X8
613/232-9625; Fax: 613/563-9895
Email: info@cla.ca; URL: www.cla.ca/divisions/capl/cacl.htm

Amelia Frances Howard-Gibbon Illustrators Medal
Established 1971; a silver medal awarded annually for outstanding illustrations in a children's book published in Canada; the illustrator must be a Canadian or a Canadian resident - Brenda Shield

Book of the Year for Children Medal
A silver medal awarded annually for the outstanding children's book published during the calendar year; book must have been written by a Canadian or a resident of Canada - Brenda Shield

Canadian Authors Association
320 South Shores Rd., PO Box 419, Campbellford ON K0L 1L0
705/653-0323; Fax: 705/653-0593; Toll Free: 1-866-216-6222
Email: admin@canauthors.org; URL: www.canauthors.org

CAA Award for Fiction
$1,000

CAA Award for Poetry
$2,000 & a silver medal

CAA Emerging Writer Award
$500

CAA Award for Canadian History
$1,000

The Canadian Children's Book Centre
#101, 40 Orchard View Blvd., Toronto ON M4R 1B9
416/975-0010; Fax: 416/975-8970
Email: info@bookcentre.ca; URL: www.bookcentre.ca

The Geoffrey Bilson Award for Historical Fiction
Rewards excellence in outstanding work of historical fiction for young people by a Canadian author, published in previous calendar year; judges are: a writer, bookseller, children's books specialist, historian, librarian
$1,000

The Norma Fleck Award for Non-Fiction
Rewards excellence in outstanding work of non-fiction for young people by a Canadian author, published in previous calendar year; jury members include a teacher, a librarian, a reviewer & a bookseller
$10,000

Canadian Historical Association / Société historique du Canada
395 Wellington St., Ottawa ON K1A 0N3
613/233-7885; Fax: 613/567-3110
Email: cha-shc@lac-bac.gc.ca; URL: www.cha-shc.ca
10 Awards available for outstanding nonfiction publications in the field of history.
Prizes also available for High School and University levels as well as Research Work and Popular Work.

CBC Literary Prizes/Prix Littéraires Radio-Canada
CBC Radio, PO Box 6000, Montréal QC H3C 3A8
Toll Free: 1-877-888-6788
URL: www.cbc.ca/books/literaryprizes

CBC Literary Awards/Prix Littéraires Radio-Canada
The only literary competition that celebrates original, unpublished works, in Canada's two official languages. Prizes are available in three categories: short story, poetry and creative nonfiction. Winning entries are published in Air Canada's enRoute magazine.

The Crime Writers of Canada
3007 Kingston Rd., PO Box 113, Toronto ON M1M 1P1
416/597-9938
Email: info@crimewriterscanada.com; URL: www.crimewriterscanada.com

The Arthur Ellis Awards
Established 1984; awarded annually in the following categories: best crime novel (by a previously published novelist), best crime non-fiction, best first crime novel (by a previously unpublished novelist), best crime short story, best juvenile crime book, & best crime writing in French

Donner Canadian Foundation
c/o Meisner Publicity & Promotion, 394A King St. East, Toronto ON M5A 1K9
416/368-8253; 368-3763; Fax: 416/363-1448
Email: meisnerpublicity@sympatico.ca; URL: www.donnerbookprize.com

The Donner Prize
Award of $50,000 for the best book on Canadian public policy; five runners-up prizes of $7,500 each

Fondation Les Forges
1497, rue Laviolette, CP 335, Trois-Rivières QC G9A 5G4
819/379-9813; Fax: 819/376-0774
Email: info@fiptr.com; URL: www.fiptr.com

Grand Prix du Festival International de la Poésie
Le Festival International de la Poésie remet une bourse de 5 000 $ au lauréat lors de l'ouverture officielle du festival; le candidat doit: être de citoyenneté canadienne et avoir déjà publié trois ouvrages de poésie chez un éditeur reconnu

Prix Félix-Antoine-Savard de poésie
Décerné annuellement lors des cérémonies d'ouverture du Festival International de la Poésie; vise à honorer, tout en les respectant, la mémoire, l'esprit et l'oeuvre poétique de cet écrivain; une bourse de 250$ y est rattachée et le contenant de 100 feuilles de papier Saint-Gilles sont remis à St-Joseph-de-la-Rive, le jour de l'Action de Grâce

Prix Félix-Leclerc de poésie
Créé en octobre 1997, à l'occasion du 10e anniversaire de la mort du poète; décerné tous les 2 ans lors des cérémonies d'ouverture du Festival International de la Poésie; prix de 1000$

Prix Piché de poésie
Les bourses sont offertes par le Festival International de la Poésie; 1er prix, 2 000 $, 2e prix, 500 $; le candidat doit être de citoyenneté canadienne et n'avoir jamais publié d'ouvrage de poésie chez un éditeur reconnu

The Griffin Trust for Excellence in Poetry
6610 Edwards Blvd., Mississauga ON L5T 2V6
905/565-5993
Email: info@griffinpoetryprize.com; URL: www.griffinpoetryprize.com

The Griffin Prize
Established in 2000, two prizes of $65,000 each awarded annually for collections of poetry published in English during the preceding year; one will go to a living Canadian poet; the other to a living poet or translator from any other country which may include Canada

International Board on Books for Young People - Canadian Section / Union internationale pour les livres de jeunesse
c/o Canadian Children's Book Centre, #101, 40 Orchard View Blvd., Toronto ON M4R 1B9
416/975-0010; Fax: 416/975-8970
Email: info@ibby-canada.org; URL: www.ibby-canada.org

Claude Aubry Award
Awarded biennially for distinguished contributions to Canadian children's literature by a librarian, teacher, author, illustrator, publisher, bookseller, or editor

Elizabeth Mrazik-Cleaver Picture Book Award
Awarded for distinguished Canadian picture book illustration; submissions to Children's Literature Service, National Library of Canada, 395 Wellington St., Ottawa, ON K1A 0N4
$1,000

Frances E. Russell Grant
Awarded to initiate & encourage research in children's literature in Canada
$1,000

The League of Canadian Poets
#608, 920 Yonge St., Toronto ON M4W 3C7
416/504-1657; Fax: 416/504-0096
Email: info@poets.ca; URL: www.poets.ca

Gerald Lampert Memorial Award
Established 1979; awarded annually for excellence in a first book of poetry, written by a Canadian citizen or landed immigrant, & published in the preceding year
$1,000

Jessamy Stursberg Poetry Prize
Awarded to young poets in Canada from grades 7-12; first place prize is $400, second place prize is $350 and third place prize is $300

Pat Lowther Memorial Award
$1,000 awarded annually for excellence in a book of poetry, written by a Canadian female citizen or landed immigrant, & published in the preceding year

Raymond Souster Award
Awarded to a book of poetry by a League of Canadian Poets member published in the preceding year

Sheri-D Wilson Award for Spoken Word
$1,000

The Lionel Gelber Prize
c/o Prize Administrator, Munk Centre for International Studies, University of Toronto, 1 Devonshire Pl., Toronto ON M5S 3K7
416/946-8901; Fax: 416/946-9815
Email: gelberprize.munk@utoronto.ca; URL: munkschool.utoronto.ca/gelber

The Lionel Gelber Prize
This $15,000 prize is the largest of its kind in the world; a legacy of Lionel Gelber, international writer who died in 1989 & who was much acclaimed for his service to Canada; the prize is "designed to stimulate authors of any nationality who write about international relations, & to encourage the audience for these books to grow"
Books published in English or English translation, must be copyrighted in the year in which the prize is awarded; books must be published or distributed in Canada; submissions by publishers only

Literary Translators' Association of Canada / Association des traducteurs et traductrices littéraires du Canada
Concordia University LB 631, 1455, boul de Maisonneuve ouest, Montréal QC H3G 1M8
514/848-2424, ext. 8702; Fax: 514/848-4514
Email: info@attlc-ltac.org; URL: www.attlc-ltac.org

Glassco Translation Prize
Awarded annually for a translator's first work in book-length literary translation into French or English, published in Canada during the previous calendar year
$1,000 & one year's membership in the association

Manitoba Writers' Guild Inc.
#206, 100 Arthur St., Winnipeg MB R3B 1H3
204/942-6134; Fax: 204/942-5754; Toll Free: 1-888-637-5802
Email: info@mbwriter.mb.ca; URL: www.mbwriter.mb.ca

Manitoba Book Awards:

Alexander Kennedy Isbister Award for Non-Fiction
Presented to the Manitoba writer whose book is judged the best book of adult non-fiction written in English
$3,500

Beatrice Mosionier Aboriginal Writer of the Year Award
Awarded to an Aboriginal writer for excellence in writing and support and encouragement for Aboriginal writing in Manitoba
$1,500

Carol Shields City of Winnipeg Award
To honour books that evoke the special caracter of & contribute to the appreciation & understanding of the City of Winnipeg
$5,000

Eileen McTavish Sykes Award for Best First Book
Awarded annually to a Manitoba author whose first professionally published book is deemed the best written
Must have been written in the previous year
$1,500

John Hirsch Award for Most Promising Manitoba Writer
Awarded annually to the most promising Manitoba writer working in poetry, fiction, creative non-fiction or drama
$2,500

Manuela Dias Book Design and Illustration Awards
For the best overall design in Manitoba book publishing in two categories: book design & best illustration

Margaret Laurence Award for Fiction
Presented to the Manitoba writer whose book is judged the best book of adult fiction written in English
$3,500

Mary Scorer Award for Best Book by a Manitoba Publisher
Awarded to the best book published by a Manitoba publisher & written for the trade, bookstore, educational, academic or scholarly market
$1,000

McNally Robinson Book for Young People Awards
Awarded annually to the writer whose young person's book is judged the best written by a Manitoba author; two categories: children's & young adult
$2,500

McNally Robinson Book of the Year
To the Manitoba author judged to have written the best book in the calendar year
$5,000

Le Prix littéraire Rue des Chambeault
Biennial award presented to the author whose published book or play is judged to be the best French language work by a Manitoba author
$3,500

McClelland & Stewart
c/o McClelland & Stewart Ltd., #900 - 481 University Ave., Toronto ON M5G 2E9
416/598-1114; Fax: 416/598-7764
Email: journeyprize@mcclelland.com; URL: www.mcclelland.com/jpa

The Writers' Trust of Canada/McClelland & Stewart Journey Prize
$10,000 awarded annually to a new & developing writer of distinction for a short story published in a Canadian literary journal. The shortlisted stories are selected from journal submissions & published annually by McClelland & Stewart as The Journey Prize Anthology. M&S presents its own award of $2,000 to the literary journal that originally published the winning story.
Only submissions from Canadian literary journals are accepted. Stories must have had original publication in the nominating journal during the previous year.

The Municipal Chapter of Toronto IODE
#205, 40 St. Clair Ave. East, Toronto ON M4T 1M9
Phone: 416/925-5078; Fax: 416/925-5127
Email: iodetoronto@bellnet.ca

IODE Book Award
Established in 1975; an inscribed scroll & not less than $1,000 awarded annually to the author or illustrator of the best children's book written or illustrated by a Canadian resident in Toronto or surrounding area & published by a Canadian publisher within the preceding 12 months

The National Chapter of Canada IODE
#254, 40 Orchard View Blvd., Toronto ON M4R 1B9
416/487-4416; Fax: 416/487-4417; Toll Free: 1-866-827-7428
Email: iodecanada@bellnet.ca

The National Chapter of Canada IODE Violet Downey Book Award
Awarded annually for the best English-language book, containing at least 500 words of text, preferably with Canadian content, in any category suitable for children aged 13 & under
$3,000

Nova Scotia Library Association
c/o Nova Scotia Provincial Library, 3770 Kempt Rd., Halifax NS B3K 4X8
902/742-2486; Fax: 902/742-6920
Email: mlandry@nsme.library.ns.ca; URL: www.nsla.ns.ca

Ann Connor Brimer Award
Awarded to the author of fiction or non-fiction books published in Canada currently in print & intended for children up to the age of 15; writer must be residing in Atlantic Canada
$2,000 - Heather Mackenzie, Halifax Regional Library, 5381 Spring Garden Rd., Halifax NS B3J 1E9; Email: mahm1@nsh.library.ns.ca

Norman Horrocks Award for Library Leadership
Honours leadership in the Nova Scotia Library community & is awarded for distinguished contributions to the promotion & development of library service in Nova Scotia - Trudy Amirault, Western Counties Regional Library, 405 Main St., Yarmouth NS B5A 1G3, Email: tamiraul@nsy.library.ns.ca

Ontario Arts Council / Conseil des arts de l'Ontario
151 Bloor St. West, 5th Fl., Toronto ON M5S 1T6
416/961-1660; Fax: 416/961-7796; Toll Free: 1-800-387-0058
Email: info@arts.on.ca; URL: www.arts.on.ca

Ruth and Sylvia Schwartz Children's Book Award
Two awards presented annually; $6,000 for best picture book & $6,000 for best young adult/middle reader book; in conjunction with the Canadian Booksellers Association

Ontario Library Association
50 Wellington St. East, Suite 201, Toronto, ON M5E 1C8
416/363-3388; Fax: 416/941-9581
Email: info@accessola.com; URL: www.accessola.com

Blue Spruce™ Award Program
The Blue Spruce Award™ is a provincial primary reading program which brings recently published Canadian children's picture books to Ontario children ages 4 to 7 in kindergarten through to grade two. Award given out in May every year.

The Evergreen™ Award Program
The Evergreen Award™ is OLA's newest addition to the Forest of Reading®. It was introduced at Super Conference 2005 for adults of any age. It gives adult library patrons the opportunity to vote for a work of Canadian fiction or non-fiction that they have liked the most.

Red Maple™ Award Program
The Red Maple Award™ reading program is offered for the enjoyment of students in Grades 7 and 8. The program, like the Association's Silver Birch Awards™ reading program, gives students who have read a minimum number of nominated titles the opportunity to vote with a large group of their peers for the nominated title that they feel should win the Red Maple Award™ each year.

Silver Birch® Fiction, Non-Fiction And Express Award Program
The Silver Birch Award® is given by Grade 3, 4, 5 and 6 students in a spectacular ceremony held annually in May before fifteen hundred of their peers. The children choose winners in Fiction, Non-Fiction and Express when they cast their ballots on the province-wide Voting Day earlier in the same month. It is the most democratic and unbiased process possible when the children make their choice. The program is administered by the Ontario Library Association and run by teacher-librarians and teachers in schools and by children's librarians in public libraries. But the choice belongs to the children. And, in their tens of thousands, they know what they are doing.

White Pine™ Award Program
The White Pine Award™ reading program offers high school-aged teens at all grade levels the opportunity to read the best of Canada's recent young adult fiction titles. All of these 10 books for Young Adults on this list are accessible and will allow all readers to be successful participants/voters. As in all of the independent reading programs, a reader only needs to read 5 books out of a list of 10 to qualify to vote. Based on student voting across the province, the most popular book is then selected and author is honoured with the White Pine Award™.

Ontario Media Development Corporation
c/o OMDC, North Tower, #501, 175 Bloor St. East, Toronto ON M4W 3R8
416/314-6858; Fax: 416/314-6876
Email: mail@omdc.on.ca; URL: www.omdc.on.ca

Trillium Book Award for Poetry
Awarded in both English & French
$10,000

Trillium Book Award/Prix Trillium
Awarded annually to an Ontario author of a book of excellence; the winning book must have been published within the preceding 12 months; books in English or French in any genre are eligible; winner receives $20,000 & the publisher receives $2,500

PEI Council of the Arts
115 Richmond St., Charlottetown PE C1A 1A7
902/368-4410; Fax: 902/368-4418; Toll Free: 1-888-734-2784
Email: info@peiartscouncil.com; URL: www.peiartscouncil.com

Island Literary Awards
Established in 1987 in recognition of Island writers in six categories: Short Story, Poetry, Children's Literature, Feature Article, Creative Writing for Children, Playwriting; an additional award is made "for distinguished contribution to the literary arts"
$500, $200 & $100

Periodical Marketers of Canada
South Tower, #1007, 175 Bloor St. East, Toronto ON M4W 3R8
416/968-7311; Fax: 416/968-6281; URL: www.periodical.ca

Aboriginal Literature Award
$5,000

PriceWaterhouseCoopers
Royal Trust Tower, #3000, 77 King St. West,
Toronto ON M5K 1G8
416/869-1130; Fax: 416/941-8345
URL: www.pwcglobal.com/ca/eng/about/events/nbba.html

National Business Book Award
Established 1985; annual prize of $30,000 awarded to author of book containing key material on business in Canada - Mary Ann Freedman

Prism International
Creative Writing Program, UBC, Buch. E462 - 1866 Main Mall, Vancouver BC V6T 1Z1
604/822-2514; Fax: 604/822-3616
Email: prism@interchange.ubc.ca; URL: prism.arts.ubc.ca

Creative Non-Fiction Contest
$1,500; $600 runner-up; $400 second runner-up

Jacob Zilber Prize for Short Fiction
$1,500; $600 runner-up; $400 second runner-up

Pacific Spirit Poetry Prize
$1,500; $600 runner-up; $400 second runner-up

Prix Aurora Awards
#501, 88 Bruce St., Kitchener ON N2B 1Y8
Email: prix.aurora.awards@gmail.com; URL: www.prixaurorawards.ca

Prix Aurora Awards
Awards presented annually for the best in Canadian Science Fiction & Fantasy; 10 categories: six professional awards (three English & three French), three fan awards & the artistic achievement award

Québec Ministère de la culture et des communications
225, Grande Allée est, Québec QC G1R 5G5
418/380-2300; Fax: 418/080-2364
Email: prixduquebec@mcc.gouv.qc.ca; URL: www.prixduquebec.gouv.qc.ca

Les Prix du Québec
Founded in 1977, these awards are given annually by the Government of Quebec to individuals for cultural and scientific achievements. There are six awards in the cultural field.

Québec Ministère des Relations internationales
225, Grande Allée Est, bloc C, 2e étage, Québec QC G1R 5G5
418/380-2335; Fax: 418/380-2340
URL: www.prix-qwb-litteraturejeunesse.org

Prix Québec Wallonie-Bruxelles de littérature de jeunesse
Créé en 1978; vise à encourager le développement de la littérature de jeunesse de langue fran‡aise et à faire la promotion des lauréats. Décerné conjointement par le ministère des Relations internationales et ministère de la Culture et des Communications

Québec Writers' Federation / Fédération des Écrivaines et Écrivains du Québec
1200 Atwater av., Montréal QC H3Z 1X4
514/933-0878; Fax: 514/933-0878
Email: info@qwf.org; URL: www.qwf.org

QWF Prizes
Established 1988; awards five annual prizes of $2,000 each to honour literary excellence: The A.M. Klein poetry prize, The Hugh MacLennan fiction prize, Mavis Gallant prize for non-fiction, The McAuslan First Book Award & Translation award Books can be submitted for prizes in five categories by publishers or authors; four copies, accompanied by entry form & $10 registration fee per submission; authors must have lived in Québec three of the past five years

The Royal Society of Canada / La Société royale du Canada
170 Waller St., Ottawa ON K1N 9B9
613/991-6990; Fax: 613/991-6996
Email: info@rsc.ca; URL: www.rsc.ca

Lorne Pierce Medal
Established in 1926 and awarded biennially to creative or critical literature written in either English or French

Salon International du livre de Québec
26, rue Saint-Pierre, Québec QC G1K 8A3
418/692-0010; Fax: 418/692-0029
Email: info@prixdeslibraires.qc.ca; URL: prixdeslibraires.qc.ca

Prix des libraires du Québec
Ce prix fut créé en 1994 par l'Association des libraires du Québec et le Salon international du livre de Québec; il souligne l'excellence d'un roman québécois par sa qualité d'écriture et son originalité; une bourse de 2 000 $ est offerte en 2005 par le Conseil des Arts et des Lettres du Québec

Saskatchewan Book Awards
#205B, 2314 - 11th Ave., Regina SK S4P 0K1
306/569-1585; Fax: 306/569-4187
Email: director@bookawards.sk.ca; URL: www.bookawards.sk.ca

City of Regina Book Awards

City of Saskatoon and Public Library Saskatoon Book Award

Fiction Award

Ministry of Parks, Culture and Sport Publishing Award

O'Reilly Insurance and the Co-operators First Book Award

Rasmussen, Rasmussen & Charowsky Aboriginal Peoples' Writing Award

Regina Public Library Aboriginal Peoples' Publishing Award

Saskatchewan Arts Board Poetry Award

SaskEnergy Children's Literature Award

University of Regina Arts and Luther College Award for Scholarly Writing

University of Regina Book of the Year Award

University of Regina Faculty of Education and Campion College Award for Publishing in Education

University of Saskatchewan Non-Fiction Award

Saskatchewan Library Association
#15, 2010 - 7th Ave., Regina SK S4R 1C2
306/780-9413; Fax: 306/780-9447
Email: slaexdir@sasktel.net; URL: www.lib.sk.ca/sla/

The Mary Donaldson Award of Merit
Awarded for excellence to a student studying at a library education institution in Saskatchewan

The SLA Frances Morrison Award
Awarded for outstanding service to libraries

Saskatchewan Writers Guild Inc.
#205, 2314 - 11th Ave., Regina SK S4P 0K1
306/757-6310; Fax: 306/565-8554; Toll Free: 1-800-667-6788
Email: swg@sasktel.net; URL: www.skwriter.com

City of Regina Writing Award
To a Regina writer to reward merit & enable a writer to work on a specific writing project; funded by the City of Regina Arts Commission & administered by the SWG
$4,000

The Scotiabank Giller Prize
c/o Michelle Kadarusman, 543 Logan Ave., Toronto ON M4K 3B6
416/934-0755
Email: info@scotiabankgillerprize.ca; URL: www.scotiabankgillerprize.ca

The Giller Prize
$100,000 award to the author of the best Canadian novel or collection of short stories published in English. $10,000 is awarded to each of the short-listed authors.

Société Saint-Jean-Baptiste de Montréal
82, rue Sherbrooke ouest, Montréal QC H2X 1X3
514/843-8851; Fax: 514/844-6369
Email: mbeaulieu@ssjb.com; URL: www.ssjb.com

Prix Ludger-Duvernay
Le prix a été crée en 1944 afin de signaler les mérites d'un compatriote dont la compétence et le rayonnement dans le domaine intellectuel et littéraire servent les intérêts supérieurs de la nation québécoise; le prix est de 3 000 $, accompagne une médaille, et est attribué à tous les trois ans

Stephen Leacock Association Inc.
PO Box 854, Orillia ON L3V 6K8
705/835-7061; Fax: 705/835-7062
Email: info@leacock.ca; URL: www.leacock.ca

Stephen Leacock Memorial Medal
Established 1946 to encourage the writing & publishing of humorous works in Canada; given annually for the best Canadian book of humour published in the preceding year
Winner receives the medal & a cash award of $10,000 donated by TD Canada Trust

The Order of Mariposa
Awarded occasionally to someone who has contributed significantly to humour in Canada, in other than the written word

University of British Columbia
President's Office, 6328 Memorial Rd., Vancouver BC V6T 1Z2
604/822-4439; Fax: 604/822-6906
Email: jflick@interchange.ubc.ca

Medal for Canadian Biography
Established 1952; awarded annually for the best biography written either about or by a Canadian & published in the preceding year - Jane Flick

Ville de Montréal
Service du développement culturel
5650, d'Iberville, 4e étage, Montréal QC H2G 3E4
514/872-1156
URL: ville.montreal.qc.ca/culture/grand-prix-du-livre-de-montreal

Grand Prix du livre de Montréal
Le prix est offert par la Ville de Montréal à l'auteur ou aux co-auteurs d'un ouvrage de langue française ou anglaise, pour la facture exceptionnelle et l'apport original de cette publication; le prix consiste en une bourse de 15 000 $, ount admissibles un auteur ou un éditeur qui habite sur le territoire de la Ville de Montréal

West Coast Book Prize Society
#901, 207 West Hastings St., Vancouver BC V6B 1H7
604/687-2405; Fax: 604/669-3701
Email: info@bcbookprizes.ca; URL: www.bcbookprizes.ca

BC Book Prizes:
Established 1985; awards of $2,000 presented to winners in each of six categories; the book may have been published anywhere in the world; $25 fee per entry

The Bill Duthie Booksellers' Choice Prize
Awarded for the best book in terms of public appeal, initiative, design, production & content; the book must have been published in BC

The Christie Harris Illustrated Children's Literature Prize
Prize shared by author and illustrator

Dorothy Livesay Poetry Prize
Awarded to the author of the best work of poetry; the writer must have lived in BC for three of the preceding five years

The Ethel Wilson Fiction Prize
Awarded to the author of the best work of fiction; the writer must have lived in BC for three of the preceding five years

The Hubert Evans Non-Fiction Prize
Awarded to the author of the best original non-fiction literary work (philosophy, belles lettres, biography, history, etc.); the writer must have lived in BC for three of the preceding five years

Lieutenant Governor's Award of Literary Excellence

Roderick Haig-Brown Regional Prize
Awarded to the author of the book that contributes most to the enjoyment & understanding of BC; the book may deal with any aspect of the province & should epitomize the BC experience

The Sheila A. Egoff Children's Prize
Awarded to the author of the best book for young people aged 16 & under; the author or illustrator must have lived in BC for three of the preceding five years

Writers Guild of Alberta
11759 Groat Rd., Edmonton AB T5M 3K6
780/422-8174; Fax: 780/422-2663; Toll Free: 1-800-665-5354
Email: mail@writersguild.ab.ca; URL: www.writersguild.ab.ca

Alberta Literary Awards
Awarded to recognize outstanding Alberta writing

City of Calgary W.O. Mitchell Book Prize
Awarded in conjunction with the City of Calgary to honour literary achievement by Calgary authors; award is worth $5,000

Golden Pen Award
Awarded to acknowledge the lifetime achievements of outstanding Alberta writers

Robert Kroetsch City of Edmonton Book Prize
Entries must deal with some aspect of the city of Edmonton or be written by an Edmonton author; award is worth $10,000

Sharon Drummond Chapbook Prize

Writers' Federation of Nova Scotia
1113 Marginal Rd., Halifax NS B3H 4P7
902/423-8116; 902/422-0881
Email: talk@writers.ns.ca; URL: www.writers.ns.ca

Evelyn Richardson Non-Fiction Award
Award was established in 1978 to recognize outstanding work in non-fiction by a Nova Scotian writer (native or resident)
$2,000

J.M. Abraham Poetry Award (Atlantic Poetry Prize)
$2,000

Thomas H. Raddall Atlantic Fiction Award
Honours the best fiction writing by an Atlantic Canadian writer
$10,000

The Writers' Trust of Canada
#200, 90 Richmond St. East, Toronto ON M5C 1P1
416/504-8222; Fax: 416/504-9090
Email: info@writerstrust.com; URL: www.writerstrust.com

The Engel/Findley Award
Established 1986; awarded annually to a female Canadian writer, for a body of work & in hope of future contributions
$25,000

Dayne Ogilvie Prize for LGBT Emerging Writers
$4,000; $250 for finalists

Hilary Weston Writers' Trust Non-Fiction Prize
Awarded annually to the author of the work of non-fiction published in the previous year that, in the opinion of the judges, shows the best literary merit
$60,000

Latner Writers' Trust Poetry Prize
$25,000

Matt Cohen Award
For a lifetime of distinguished work by a Canadian writer, working in either poetry or prose, writing in either French or English who has dedicated their life to writing as a primary pursuit
$20,000

McClelland & Stewart Journey Prize
Awarded annually to a new & developing writer
$10,000

RBC Bronwen Wallace Memorial Award
Awarded annually to a Canadian writer under the age of 35 who is not yet published in book form; award alternates each year between poetry & short fiction
$5,000

Rogers Writers' Trust Fiction Prize
Annually to the author of the work of fiction published in the previous year that in the opinion of the judges, shows the best literary merit
$25,000

Shaughnessy Cohen Award for Political Writing
Awarded to a non-fiction book of outstanding literary merit that enlarges our understanding of contemporary Canadian political & social issues
$25,000

Vicky Metcalf Award for Literature for Young People
Awarded annually to an author of children's literature, either fiction, non-fiction, picture books or poetry, not for a single book, but for a body of work, unless, in the opinion of the jury, there is no author worthy of the award that year
$20,000

The Writers' Union of Canada
#200, 90 Richmond St. East, Toronto ON M5C 1P1
416/703-8982; Fax: 416/504-9090
Email: info@writersunion.ca; URL: www.writersunion.ca

Danuta Gleed Literary Award
Awarded to a Canadian writer for the best first collection of published short stories in the English language
$10,000

Freedom to Read Award

Graeme Gibson Award

Short Prose Competition for Developing Writers
$2,500

PERFORMING ARTS

Alberta Scholarship Programs
PO Box 28000, Stn Main, Edmonton AB T5J 4R4
780/427-8640; Fax: 780/427-1288
Email: scholarships@gov.ab.ca; URL: studentaid.alberta.ca/scholarships/alberta-scholarships

Arts Graduate Scholarships
Five awards of $5,000 at graduate level for study in music, drama, dance & the visual arts & up to $50,000 is available to assist Alberta artists to further their training through non-academic short-term courses & internship or apprenticeship programs

Association québécoise de l'industrie du disque, du spectacle et de la vidéo
6420, rue Saint-Denis, Montréal QC H2S 2R7
514/842-5147; Fax: 514/842-7762
Email: info@adisq.com; URL: www.adisq.com

Félix Awards
The event honours the best musical achievement produced in Québec during the past year

The Banff Centre
PO Box 1020, Banff AB T1L 1H5
403/762-6180; Fax: 403/762-6345
Email: arts_info@banffcentre.ca; URL: www.banffcentre.ca

The Clifford E. Lee Choreography Award
Established 1978; awarded annually in recognition of outstanding Canadian choreography & jointly sponsored by the Banff Centre & the Edmonton-based Clifford E. Lee Foundation. Winner receives a $5,000 cash prize & a commission to mount a new work for premiere at the Banff Festival of the Arts - George Ross.

The Canada Council for the Arts / Conseil des Arts du Canada
350 Albert St., PO Box 1047, Ottawa ON K1P 5V8
613/566-4414; Fax: 613/566-4390; Toll Free: 1-800-263-5588
Email: info@canadacouncil.ca; URL: www.canadacouncil.ca

Bernard Diamant Prize
Offers professional Canadian classical singers under 35 an opportunity to pursue their career through further studies. $5,000 awarded in addition to the regular grant to an outstanding young classical singer in the annual competition for Grants to Professional Musicians

Canada Council for the Arts Grand Prize for the CBC Young Composers Competition
$10,000 grand prize awarded every two years to the winner of the CBC Young Composers Competition

Canada Council for the Arts/CBC First Prizes for the CBC Radio National Young Performers Competition
Every two years; two first prizes of $15,000 is awarded to the winners of each of the two categories

Canada Council Musical Instrument Bank
Created in 1987 as a means of acquiring exceptional instruments to be loaned to established Canadian musicians or gifted young musicians who are about to embark on an international solo career, following a national jured competition; collection includes the 1827 McConnel Nicolaus Gagliano cello & the 1717 Windsor-Weinstein Stradivarius violin

Eckhardt-Gramatté National Music Competition
Provides assistance in the amount of $9,000 towards the cost of administering the competiton

Healey Willan Prize
$5,000 awarded every two years to the Canadian amateur choir that gives the best performance in terms of musicianship, technique & program in the CBC National Radio Competition for Amateur Choirs

Jacqueline Lemieux Prize
$6,000 awarded annually to the most talented Canadian candidate in the Grants to Dance Professionals competition

Japan-Canada Fund
Supports performance, exhibitions, distribution networks, etc. of Japanese performing artists, media artists, visual artists through established, professional Canadian presenters, as well as for the translations of Canadian & Japanese literary works

Jean-Marie Beaudet Award in Orchestra Conducting
$1,000 awarded annually to a young Canadian conductor, is adjudicated by a committee of music professionals convened by the Canada Council

John Hirsh Prize
$6,000 awarded to a new & developing theatre director who has demonstrated great potential for future excellence & exciting artistic vision; awarded every two years, one in each of the Anglophone & Francophone theatre communites; nominations are made by the professional theatre community & the winners are chosen by a peer assessment committee for the Canada Council Grants to Theatre Artists program

Jules Léger Prize for New Chamber Music
Established in 1978; annual $7,500 prize designed to encourage Canadian composers to write for chamber music groups & to foster the performance of Canadian chamber music by these groups; the Canadian Music Centre administers the award, the Canada Council funds the award & selects the assessment committee of musicians to study the submitted scores; the CBC Radio Two & La Chaîne culturelle de Radio-Canada broadcasts the winning work on the English- & French-language stereo networks

Peter Dwyer Scholarships
Annual scholarships totalling $20,000 awarded to the most promising Canadian students at the National Ballet School & the National Theatre School; each school is awarded $10,000 & chooses the winner on behalf of the Canada Council

Robert Fleming Prizes
The annual $2,000 prize in memory of Robert Fleming is intended to encourage the career development of young composers & is awarded to the most talented Canadian music composer in the competition for Canada Council Grants to Professional Musicians in classical music

Sylva Gelber Foundation Award
Established 1981; $15,000 awarded annually to the most talented Canadian artist under the age of 30 in the "Grants to Musicians" competition for performers in classical music

Virginia Parker Award
Approximately $25,000 awarded annually to a young Canadian classical musician, instrumentalist, or conductor who has received at least one Canada Council grant awarded by a peer assessment committee; the prize is intended to assist a young performer in furthering his/her career

Walter Carsen Prize for Excellence in the Performing Arts
Awarded annually, $50,000 prize recognizes the highest level of artistic excellence & distinguished career in the performing arts; awarded to a Canadian artist who is actively performing or who has spent the major part of his/her career in Canada in dance, theatre, or music - in creation or interpretation; prize will be presented on a four-year cycle - dance, theatre, dance, music

Canadian Academy of Recording Arts & Sciences / Académie canadienne des arts et des sciences de l'enregistrement
345 Adelaide Street West, 2nd Floor, Toronto ON M5V 1R5
416/485-3135, ext.227; Fax: 416/485-4978; Toll Free: 1-888-440-5866
Email: info@carasonline.ca; URL: www.carasonline.ca; junoawards.ca

Juno Awards
Annual awards for: Canadian Hall of Fame Award, Allan Waters Humanitarian Award, Walt Grealis Special Achievement Award, Juno Fan Choice (presented by TD), Single of the Year, International Album of the Year, Album of the Year (sponsored by Music Canada), Francophone Album of the Year, Artist of the Year, Group of the Year, Breakthrough Artist of the Year (sponsored by FACTOR, the Government of Canada, Radio Starmaker Fund and Canada's Private Radio Broadcasters), Breakthrough Group of the Year (sponsored by FACTOR, the Government of Canada, Radio Starmaker Fund and Canada's Private Radio Broadcasters), Instrumental Album of the Year, Songwriter of the Year, Country Album of the Year, Adult Alternative Album of the Year, Alternative Album of the Year (sponsored by Long & McQuade), Rap Recording of the Year, Pop Album of the Year (sponsored by TD), Rock Album of the Year, Vocal Jazz Album of the Year, Jazz Album of the Year: Solo, Jazz Album of the Year: Group, Children's Album of the Year, Classical Album of the Year: Solo or Chamber Ensemble, Classical Album of the Year: Large Ensemble or Soloist(s) with Large Ensemble Accompaniment, Classical Album of the Year: Vocal or Choral Performance, Classical Composition of the Year, Dance Recording of the Year, Also: R&B/Soul Recording of the Year, Reggae Recording of the Year, Contemporary Roots Album of the Year, Traditional Roots Album of the Year, Aboriginal Album of the Year (sponsored by Aboriginal Peoples Television Network), Blues Album of the Year, Contemporary Christian/Gospel Album of the Year, World Music Album of the Year (sponsored by Canada Council for the Arts), Jack Richardson Producer of the Year, Recording Engineer of the Year (sponsored by the Ontario Institute of Audio Recording Technology), Recording Package of the Year, Video of the Year (sponsored by MuchFACT, exclusively funded by Bell Media), Electronic Album of the Year, Heavy Metal Album of the Year, Adult Contemporary Album of the Year

Canadian Broadcasting Corporation
CBC Radio Music, PO Box 500, Stn A, Toronto ON M5W 1E6
416/205-3311; Fax: 416/205-6040
URL: www.radio.cbc.ca

National Radio Competition for Amateur Choirs
Established 1975; awarded biennially; prizes offered in following categories: Children's, Youth, Large, Adult Mixed Chamber, Adult Equal Voice, Church, Traditional & Ethno-Cultural, & Contemporary Choral Music.
Eight first prizes of $3,000 each; eight 2nd prizes of $2,000 each; $1,000 for best performance of a Canadian work.

National Radio Competition for Young Composers
Established 1973; competition sponsored every two years by CBC & the Canada Council; entrants must be Canadian citizens or landed immigrants, 30 years of age or under, & must not be employees of the CBC.
Up to 10 prizes are given: three 1st prizes of $5,000 each; three 2nd prizes of $4,000 each; three 3rd prizes; a $5,000 Grand Prize; a performance of the winning works is given on CBC English & French radio networks.

National Radio Competition for Young Performers
Established 1960; competition sponsored every two years by CBC/Radio-Canada & the Canada Council for the Arts; entrants must be Canadian citizens or landed immigrants, 30 years of age or under (32 for singers); categories rotate among strings, piano, voice, winds & brass; finals of competiton heard live on CBC Radio Two & La Chaîne culturelle.
First prize $15,000; 2nd prize $10,000; 3rd prize $5,000; prizes also include recital & concert engagements across Canada.

Canadian Country Music Association / Association de la musique country canadienne
#203, 626 King St. West, Toronto ON M5V 1M7
416/947-1331; Fax: 416/947-5924
Email: country@ccma.org; URL: www.ccma.org

Music Awards
Awards in 10 categories are presented annually to outstanding performers; 35 citations honour individuals & organizations which, have made a significant contribution to country music

Canadian Theatre Critics Association / Association des critiques de théâtre du Canada
#700, 250 Dundas St. West, Toronto ON M5T 2Z5
416/782-0966; Fax: 416/782-0366
Email: aruprech@ccs.carleton.ca; URL: www.canadiantheatrecritics.ca

The Herbett Whittaker/CTCA Award for Distinguished Contribution to Canadian Theatre
Presented annually to Canadian citizen or permanent resident working in any theatrical discipline who has demonstrated distinguished contribution in playwriting, performance, direction or design; named after Herbert Whittaker Founding Chairman of the Canadian Theatre Critics Assoc.

Nathan Cohen Award for Excellence in Critical Writing
Two awards presented annually: one for reviews of up 1,000 words and one for longer critical pieces

Council for Business & the Arts in Canada / Conseil pour le monde des affaires et des arts du Canada
#903, 165 University Ave., Toronto ON M5H 3B8
416/869-3016; Fax: 416/869-0435
Email: info@businessforarts.org; URL: www.businessforarts.org

Edmund C. Bovey Award
To recognize individual members of the business community who contribute leadership, time, money & expertise to the arts
A sculpture to the winner & $20,000 distributed to the arts in a way specified by the winner.

Globe and Mail Business for the Arts Awards
These awards honour businesses in the categories of Best Arts/Entrepreneur Partnership, Most Effective Corporate Program, Most Innovative Marketing Sponsorship and The First Dance Award.

Dance Ontario Association / Association Ontario Danse
Case Goods Bldg., #304, 55 Mill St., Toronto ON M5A 3C4
416/204-1083; Fax: 416/204-1085
Email: contact@danceontario.ca; URL: www.danceontario.ca

Dance Ontario Award
Recognizes a lifetime commitment to dance

Dancer Transition Resource Centre / Centre de ressources et transition pour danseurs
The Lynda Hamilton Centre, #500, 250 The Esplanade, Toronto ON M5A 1J2
416/595-5655; Fax: 416/595-0009; Toll Free: 1-800-667-0851
Email: nationaloffice@dtrc.ca; URL: www.dtrc.ca

Anne M. Delicaet Bursary
To help fund tuition, books &/or supplies for applicant in their third year of full-time retraining/grants received from the DTRC
Award amount is discretionary

David Pitblado Memorial Award
Awarded to a former modern dance artist who requires a second year to complete or continue a proposed course of study

Dr. Stanley E. Greben Award
Awarded to a dancer for a second year of full-time study in a health related field

Erik Bruhn Memorial Award
Awarded to a dancer in transition who requires a second year to complete or continue a proposed course of study

Karen Kain Award
Given to a dancer entering a second or subsequent year of full-time retraining
Award is discretionary

Lynda Hamilton Award
Awarded annually to a dancer in transition who has completed two years of study & requires a third to complete or continue the proposed course of study
$18,000 subsistence & $4,000 for tuition & supplies

Peter F. Bronfman Memorial Award
It is earmarked for a second or third year of retraining & subsistence & may be only awarded for the full amount
$18,000 subsistence & $4,000 for tuition & supplies

Zella Wolofsky/Doug Wright Bursary
Awarded to a dancer with a degree from a recognized university & who is in second or subsequent year of professional program or doing graduate studies or second degree
$2,000 for any purpose

East Coast Music Association / Association de la musique de la côte est
#5, 6029 Cunard St., Halifax, NS B3K 1E5
902/423-6770; Fax: 888-519-0346; Toll-Free: 800-513-4953
Email: ecma@ecma.com; URL: www.ecma.com

East Coast Music Awards
Annual awards in the following categories: Album of the Year, Song of the Year, Aboriginal Recording of the Year, Blues Recording of the Year, Children's Recording of the Year, Classical Composition of the Year, Classical Recording of the Year, Country Recording of the Year, Electronic Recording of the Year, Folk Recording of the Year, Francophone Recording of the Year, Gospel Recording of the Year, Group Recording of the Year, Jazz Recording of the Year, Loud Recording of the Year, Pop Recording of the Year, Producer of the Year, R&B/Soul Recording of the Year, Rap/Hip-Hop Recording of the Year, Rising Star Recording of the Year, Rock Recording of the Year, Roots/Traditional Group Recording of the Year, Roots/Traditional Solo Recording of the Year, Solo Recording of the Year, Songwriter of the Year, Traditional Instrumental Recording of the Year, World Recording of the Year, Fans' Choice Entertainer of the Year, Fans' Choice Video of the Year, Event of the Year, Graphic/Media Artist of the Year, Live Sound Engineer of the Year, Management/Manager of the Year, Media Outlet of the Year, Media Person of the Year, Music Merchant of the Year, Studio of the Year, Studio Engineer of the Year, Venue of the Year, Video of the Year

Elinore & Lou Siminovitch Prize in Theatre
c/o BMO Financial Group, 55 Bloor St. West, 4th Fl., Toronto ON M4W 3N5
(416) 9927-2771
Email: andrew.soren@bmo.com; URL: www.siminovitchprize.com

Elinore & Lou Siminovitch Prize
Awarded annually; honours a director, playwright, or designer who in mid-career has made a significant contribution through a body of work to the theatre in Canada; direction, playwriting & design will be honoured on a three year cycle.
$100,000; the winner will receive an immediate cash prize of $75,000, in addition the honoured artist will be invited to designate $25,000 to a protegé of his/her choice who is involved in direction, playwriting or design in theatre in Canada or to an institution (theatre or educational facility) that contributes to better & more successful theatre in Canada

Fondation Émile-Nelligan
261, rue Bloomfield, Outremont QC H2V 3R6
514/278-4657; Fax: 514/278-1943
Email: info@fondation-nelligan.org; URL: www.fondation-nelligan.org

Prix Serge-Garant
Prix triennal de composition musicale décerné à un compositeur citoyen du Canada né au Québec ou à un compositeur citoyen du Canada ayant sa résidence principale au Québec depuis au moins dix ans
25 000$

Governor General's Performing Arts Awards Foundation
#113, 24 York St., Ottawa ON K1N 1K2

613/241-5297; Fax: 613/241-4677
URL: www.bce.ca/ggawards

Governor General's Performing Arts Awards
Established in 1992; honours six performing artists for their lifetime achievement & contribution to the cultural enrichment of Canada; each recipient is awarded $15,000 & a commemorative medal

Ramon John Hnatyshyn Award for Voluntarism in the Performing Arts
Recognizes outstanding service to the performing arts; the recipient is presented with a specially commissioned artwork by Canadian glass artist Naoko Takenouchi

Ontario Arts Council / Conseil des arts de l'Ontario
151 Bloor St. West, 5th Fl., Toronto ON M5S 1T6
416/969-7422; Fax: 416/961-7796;
Toll Free: 1-800-387-0058 ext. 7422
Email: mwarren@arts.on.ca; URL: www.arts.on.ca

Colleen Peterson Songwriting Award
Established in 2003, in honour of Colleen Peterson's contribution to Canadian folk and country music. This annual award was designed to support and promote the work of an emerging professional singer/songwriter in the genres of roots, traditional, folk and country music
$1,000

Heinz Unger Award
Awarded every two years; Established 1968 & awarded biennially to honour the memory of the York Concert Society music director; administered by the Music Office of the Ontario Arts Council in cooperation with the Association of Canadian Orchestras

John Adaskin Memorial Fund
Established in memorial of the Canadian Music Centre's first executive secretary; supports a project that encourages the promotion & development of Canadian music in the school system

John Hirsch Director's Award
Established by a bequest to the Ontario Arts Council from the late John Hirsch; presented every three years to a promising theatre director in Ontario
$5,000

Leslie Bell Scholarship for Choral Conducting
Established 1973; awarded biennially in competition; the purpose of the award is to help young emerging choral conductors in Ontario further their studies in the choral music field either in Canada or abroad; competition organized by the Ontario Choral Federation

Pauline McGibbon Award
Annual award alternates between designers, directors & production crafts persons
$7,000

Premier's Award for Excellence in the Arts
Established in 2006, the Government of Ontario created this award to recognize outstanding achievement in the professional arts by an individual and a group.
$120,000 total award value; divided into categories

Tim Sims Encouragement Fund Award
Established in 1995; to be awarded annually to a promising young comedic performer or troupe

The Vida Peene Fund
Provides assistance to projects which benefit the orchestra community as a whole

Québec Ministère de la culture et des communications
Direction générale du secrétariat et des sociétés d'Etat
225, Grande Allée est, Québec QC G1R 5G5
418/380-2358 ext. 7220; Fax: 418/080-2364
Email: claude.janelle@mcc.gouv.qc.ca; URL: www.prixduquebec.gouv.qc.ca

Prix Denise-Pelletier
Prix réservé aux domaines de la chanson, de la musique, de l'art lyrique, du théâtre et de la danse

Québec Ministère des Relations internationales
Édifice Hector-Fabre, 525, boul René-Lévesque est, Québec QC G1R 5R9
418/649-2300; Fax: 418/649-2656
URL: www.mri.gouv.qc.ca

Prix Rapsat-Lelièvre du disque de chanson
Initialement connu sous le nom Prix Québec/Wallonie-Bruxelles du disque de chanson; vise à encourager le développement et la promotion de la langue française, à stimuler la production et la diffusion de disques francophones

Société Saint-Jean-Baptiste de Montréal
82, rue Sherbrooke ouest, Montréal QC H2X 1X3
514/843-8851; Fax: 514/844-6369
Email: mbeaulieu@ssjb.com; URL: www.ssjb.com

Prix Calixa-Lavallée
Established 1959; $1,500 & a medal awarded annually to a French Canadian in recognition of outstanding achievement in music in serving the higher interests of the French Canadian people

Toronto Alliance for the Performing Arts
#210, 215 Spadina Ave., Toronto ON M5T 2C7
416/536-6468; Fax: 416/536-3463; Toll Free: 1-800-541-0499
URL: www.tapa.ca

Dora Mavor Moore Awards
Established 1979; celebrating excellence in Toronto theatre, 33 awards in large, medium & small theatre divisions, Theatre for Young Audiences & New Choreography

Western Canadian Music Alliance
#637, 776 Corydon Ave., Winnipeg MB R3M 0Y1
204/943-8485; Fax: 204/453-1594
Email: info@wcmw.ca; URL: www.wcmw.ca

Western Canadian Music Awards
Annual Awards in the following categories: Aboriginal Recording of the Year, Blues Recording of the Year, Children's Recording of the Year, Classical Composition of the Year, Classical Recording of the Year, Country Recording of the Year, Electronic/Dance Recording of the Year, Francophone Recording of the Year, Independent Album of the Year, Instrumental Recording of the Year, Jazz Recording of the Year, Metal/Hard Music Recording of the Year, Pop Recording of the Year, Urban Recording of the Year, Rap/Hip-Hop Recording of the Year, Rock Recording of the Year, Roots Recording of the Year - Duo/Group, Roots Recording of the Year - Solo, Songwriter(s) of the Year, World Recording of the Year

Western Canadian Music Industry Awards
Annual awards in the following categories: Agency of the Year, Producer of the Year, Engineer of the Year, Manager of the Year, Talent Buyer of the Year, Live Music Venue of the Year, Independent Record Label, Best Album Design, Video of the Year

PUBLIC AFFAIRS

B'nai Brith Canada
15 Hove St., Toronto ON M3H 4Y8
416/633-6224; Fax: 416/630-2159
Email: bnb@bnaibrith.ca; URL: www.bnaibrith.ca

Award of Merit & Humanitarian Awards
Established 1981; presented annually at gala events in major communities across Canada
Selection of honourees based on outstanding achievement in their chosen fields as well as personal commitment to the overall betterment of Canadian society

Canadian Association on Gerontology / Association canadienne de gérontologie
#106, 222 College St., Toronto ON M5T 3J1
416/978-7977; Fax: 416/978-4771
Email: contact@cagacg.ca; URL: www.cagacg.ca

The CAG Donald Menzies Bursary
To support post-baccalaureate students registered in a program of study focused on aging or the aged
$1,500

The CAG Margery Boyce Bursary
To support post-baccalaureate students who have made a significant contribution to their community through volunteer activities with or on behalf of seniors & who are registered in a program of study focused on aging or the aged
$500

Canadian Council of Professional Engineers / Conseil canadien des ingénieurs
#1100, 180 Elgin St., Ottawa ON K2P 2K3
613/232-2474; Fax: 613/230-5759
Email: info@engineerscanada.ca; URL: www.engineerscanada.ca

Meritorious Service Award for Community Service
Awarded for exemplary voluntary contribution to a community organization or humanitarian endeavour

The Canadian Council of the Blind / Le Conseil canadien des aveugles
#401, 396 Cooper St., Ottawa ON K2P 2H7
613/567-0311; Fax: 613/567-2728; Toll Free: 1-877-304-0968
Email: ccb@ccbnational.net; URL: ccbnational.net

Award of Merit
Established 1952; presented to a Canadian, blind or sighted, who has rendered outstanding work for the blind
A gold medal & clasp, a specially printed & bound citation & honorary life membership in the CCB

The City of Toronto
Diversity Management and Community Engagement, Strategic and Corporate Policy/Healthy City Office, Manager's Office, City Hall, 100 Queen St. West, 11th Fl., East Tower, Toronto ON M5H 2N2
416/392-8592; Fax: 416/696-3645
Email: diversity@toronto.ca; URL: www.toronto.ca/civicawards

Aboriginal Affairs Award
Est. 2003, given to a person(s) or organization whose volunteer efforts have made or are making a significant or ongoing contribution to the well-being & advancement of the Aboriginal community in Toronto

Access Award for Disability Issues
Established 1982; honours people or organizations that have made or are making a significant or ongoing contribution, beyond legislated requirements, to the well-being & advancement of people with disabilities; the award honours those who are sensitive to the access needs of persons with disabilities when planning structures or programs (this could include consideration of access requirements in the design of new or renovated buildings, a job creation campaign, a transportation system, recreational program, etc.)

Constance E. Hamilton Award on the Status of Women
This award commemorates the Privy Council of Great Britain granting women status as persons in 1929; award is named after the first woman member of City Council; recipients are persons who have made a significant contribution to securing equitable treatment for Toronto women

Pride Award for Lesbian Gay Bisexual Transgender Transsexual Two Spirited Issues
Est. 2003, the Pride Award honours individuals &/or organizations that have made or are making a significant or ongoing contribution to the well-being & advancement of these communities in Toronto

William P. Hubbard Race Relations Award
Named for Toronto's first visible minority Member of Council & Acting Mayor, this award honours persons with outstanding achievement & commitment to this field in Toronto; award was presented for the first time in 1990

Ethics in Action Awards
Kenneth C. Rowe Management Bldg., 6100 University Ave., Halifax, NS B3H 4R2
902/494-4129
Email: ethicsinaction@dal.ca; URL: ethicsinaction.ca/award

Ethics in Action Awards
Awards recognize businesses & individuals in business, whose actions & decisions have made a positive impact on our communities

Ontario Ministry of Citizenship & Immigration
Ontario Honours & Awards
Secretariat Ministry of Citizenship and Immigration, 400 University Ave., 4th Fl., Toronto ON M7A 2R9
416/314-7526; Fax: 416/314-7743
Email: ontariohonoursandawards@ontario.ca; URL: www.citizenship.gov.on.ca/english/honours

Ontario Senior Achievement Awards
Presented annually to Ontario residents who have made a significant contribution to their communities after reaching 65 years of age; nominations may be made by any individual or organization

Status of Women Canada
Ottawa ON K1P 1H9
613/995-7835; Fax: 613/943-2386
URL: www.swc-cfc.gc.ca

Governor General's Award in Commemoration of Persons Case
Established 1979 to celebrate the 50th anniversary of the "Persons Case" which resulted in women being declared eligible for appointment to the Senate; annual awards recognize contributions by individuals toward promoting the equality of women in Canada

SCIENTIFIC, ENGINEERING, TECHNICAL

The Canada Council for the Arts / Conseil des Arts du Canada

350 Albert St., PO Box 1047, Ottawa ON K1P 5V8
613/566-4414; Fax: 613/566-4390; Toll Free: 1-800-263-5588
Email: info@canadacouncil.ca; URL: www.canadacouncil.ca

Killam Prizes
Up to five prizes of $100,000 each are given annually to eminent Canadian scholars in recognition of a distinguished career achievement in the natural sciences, health sciences, engineering, social sciences & humanities. Candidates must be nominated by three experts in their field. Chosen by Killam Selection

Killam Research Fellowships
Fellowships offered on a competitive basis to support specific research projects by distinguished Canadian researchers in any of the following broad fields: humanities, social sciences, natural sciences, health sciences, engineering & studies linking any of the disciplines within these broad fields; provide release time to individual scholars, normally full professors in Canadian universitites, who wish to pursue individual research; provides two years of teaching replacement to a maximum of $53,000 per year, plus the cost of fringe benefits of the Fellow, based on actual salary for the year before the tenure of the award; application must be made by individuals, not by institutions, universities or organizations

Canadian Aeronautics & Space Institute / Institut aéronautique et spatial du Canada

#104, 350 Terry Fox Drive., Kanata ON K2K 2W5
613/591-8787; Fax: 613/591-7291
Email: casi@casi.ca; URL: www.casi.ca

C.D. Howe Award
Established 1966; a silver plaque presented annually for achievement in the fields of planning, policy making & overall leadership in Canadian aeronautics & space activities

McCurdy Award
Established 1954; a silver medal & trophy presented annually for outstanding achievement in art, science & engineering relating to aeronautics & space

Romeo Vachon Award
Established 1969; bronze plaque awarded annually for outstanding contribution of a practical nature to the art, science, & engineering of aeronautics & space in Canada

Trans-Canada (McKee) Trophy
Canada's oldest aviation award established 1927; presented annually except when no qualified recipient is nominated for outstanding achievement in the field of air operations

Canadian Institute of Forestry / Institut forestier du Canada

#504, 151 Slater St., Ottawa ON K1P 5H3
613/234-2242; Fax: 613/234-6181
Email: cif@cif-ifc.org; URL: www.cif-ifc.org

Canadian Forest Management Group Achievement Award
Established 1998; to recognize outstanding achievement by teams in groups of Natural Resource managers, researchers and NGO groups in forest resources related activities in Canada.

Canadian Forestry Achievement Award
Established 1966 & presented annually in recognition of superior accomplishments in forestry research &/or in recognition of outstanding administrative leadership in management, education, research & affairs of professional & scientific societies

Canadian Forestry Scientific Achievement Award
Established 1980; presented annually in recognition of superior accomplishments in scientific forestry

International Forestry Achievement Award
Established 1980; presented in recognition of outstanding achievement in international forestry

James M. Kitz Award
Awarded to a person who has made outstanding contributions to the practice of forestry, including: superior personal accomplishments; outstanding leadership in education, management research or professional association work; promotion of forestry to various audiences
Open to anyone involved in forestry

Canadian Institute of Mining, Metallurgy & Petroleum / Institut canadien des mines, de la métallurgie et du pétrole

#855, 3400, boul de Maisonneuve ouest, Montréal QC H3Z 3B8
514/939-2710; Fax: 514/939-2714
Email: cim@cim.org; URL: www.cim.org

CIM Awards
The institute administers 24 awards recognizing achievement in mining, metallurgy & petroleum industries

The Chemical Institute of Canada / Institut de chimie du Canada

#550, 130 Slater St., Ottawa ON K1P 6E2
613/232-6252; Fax: 613/232-5862; Toll Free: 1-888-542-2242
Email: info@cheminst.ca; URL: www.cheminst.ca

Chemical Institute of Canada Awards
The institute administers several awards & scholarships in chemistry, chemical engineering, & macromolecular science or engineering

E.W.R. Steacie Memorial Fund / Fondation E.W.R. Steacie

100 Sussex Dr., Ottawa ON K1A 0R6
613/993-1212; Fax: 613/954-5242
Email: PrixSteaciePrize.SIMS@nrc-cnrc.gc.ca; URL: www.steacieprize.ca/index_e.html

The Steacie Prize
Canada's most prestigious award for young scientists & engineers; named to honour the memory of Edgar William Richard Steacie, a physical chemist & former President of the National Research Council of Canada; established 1963; awarded annually to a young scientist or engineer up to 40 years of age for outstanding scientific work in a Canadian context; winner receives a certificate & $10,000

The Engineering Institute of Canada / Institut canadien des ingénieurs

1295 Hwy. 2 East, Kingston ON K7L 4V1
613/547-5989; Fax: 613/547-0195
Email: jplant1@cogeco.ca; URL: www.eic-ici.ca

The Sir John Kennedy Medal
Established in 1927 in commemoration of the great services rendered in the field of engineering by Sir John Kennedy, a past president of the EIC; medal is awarded every two years by the council in recognition of outstanding merit in the profession or of noteworthy contributions to the science of engineering or to the benefit of the institute

Engineers Canada / Ingénieurs Canada

#300, 55 Metcalfe St., Ottawa ON K1P 6L9
613/232-2474; Fax: 613/230-5759; Toll-Free: 877-408-9273
Email: info@engineerscanada.ca; URL: www.engineerscanada.ca

Award for the Support of Women in the Engineering Profession

Gold Medal Award and Gold Medal Student Award
Awarded for exceptional individual achievement & distinction in a field of engineering

Medal for Distinction in Engineering Education
Awarded for exemplary contribution to engineering teaching at a Canadian University

Meritorious Service Awards
Two categories: Professional Service and Community Service

National Award for an Engineering Project or Achievement
Awarded for outstanding engineering projects by a team in which Canadian engineers were part of

The Young Engineer Achievement Award
Awarded for outstanding contribution in a field of engineering by an engineer 35 years of age or younger

Ernest C. Manning Awards Foundation

#421 - 7th Ave. SW, 38th floor, Calgary AB T2P 4K9
403/645-8277; Fax: 403/645-8320
Email: manning@encana.com; URL: www.manningawards.ca

The Manning Awards
Given annually to Canadian innovators who have conceived & developed new concepts, procedures, processes or products of benefit to Canada; awards may be in any area of activity.
One $100,000 Principal Award; one $25,000 Award of Distinction; two $10,000 Innovation prizes, & four $4,000 Young Canadian Innovation Awards.

Natural Sciences & Engineering Research Council of Canada / Conseil de recherches en sciences naturelles et en génie

350 Albert St., Ottawa ON K1A 1H5
613/995-5992; Fax: 613/992-5337
URL: www.nserc-crsng.gc.ca

The E.W.R. Steacie Memorial Fellowships
Awarded to enhance the career development of outstanding & highly promising scientists & engineers who are staff members of Canadian universities; successful fellows are relieved of any teaching & administrative duties, enabling them to devote all their time & energy to research; up to four fellowships are awarded annually for a one or two-year period; fellowships are held at a Canadian university or affiliated research institution
Set at $90,000 to be paid to the university by NSERC to cover the cost of replacing the Steacie Fellow's teaching & administrative responsibilities.

Gerhard Herzberg Gold Medal for Science & Engineering
Awarded annually to an individual who has made outstanding & sustained contributions to Canadian research in natural sciences & engineering; the gold medal will be awarded for any activity of exceptional importance & impact that leads to the enhancement of the research enterprise in Canada - such activities may include contributions to knowledge, the application of existing knowledge, to the novel solution of practical problems, the promotion or management of research activity, the leadership in the transfer of knowledge.
The accomplishments for which the award is given must have been carried out in Canada & achieved over a substantial period of time; persons from any sector (academic, business & industry, or government) are eligible; current members of council are not eligible; awardee's performance in relation to the cited achievement must demonstrate an unusually high degree of ability & the application of such qualities as expertise, creativity, imagination, leadership, perseverance & dedication.

Prix Galien Canada

#240, 1100 av des Canadiens-de-Montréal, Montréal QC H3B 2S2
514/216-2513
Email: info@prix-galien-canada.com; URL: eng.prix-galien-canada.com

Prix Galien - Innovative Product Award
Awarded to a company that has developed & marketed a drug that has made the most significant contribution to the well-being of the general public, in terms of efficacy, safety & innovation

Prix Galien - Research Awards
Awarded to a scientist who is known for his/her contribution to pharmaceutical research in Canada

Québec Ministère du Développement économique, de l'Innovation et de l'Exportation

710, place D'Youville, 3e étage, Québec QC G1R 4Y4
418/691-5950; Fax: 418/644-0118
URL: www.economie.gouv.qc.ca

Prix Armand-Frappier
Décerné pour la création ou le développement d'institutions de recherche, ou pour l'administration et la promotion de recherche

Prix Lionel-Boulet
Décerné au chercheur qui s'est distingué par ses inventions, ses innovations scientifiques et technologiques, son leadership dans le développement scientifique et sa contribution à la croissance économique du Québec

Prix Marie-Victorin
Décerné aux chercheurs de sciences exactes et naturelles, les sciences de l'ingénierie et technologiques ainsi que les sciences agricoles

Prix Wilder-Penfield
Décerné aux scientifiques dont l'objet de recherche appartient au domaine biomédical

Royal Astronomical Society of Canada / Société royale d'astronomie du Canada

136 Dupont St., Toronto ON M5R 1V2
416/924-7973; Fax: 416/924-2911; Toll Free: 1-888-924-7272
Email: nationaloffice100000@rasc.ca; URL: www.rasc.ca

Chant Medal
Established 1940 in appreciation of the great work of the late Prof. C.A. Chant in furthering the interests of astronomy in Canada; silver medal is awarded no more than once a year to an amateur astronomer resident in Canada on the basis of the value of the work which he/she has carried out in astronomy & closely allied fields of original investigation

Ken Chilton Prize
Established 1977; plaque awarded annually to an amateur astronomer resident in Canada, in recognition of a significant piece of work carried out or published during the year

The Plaskett Medal
Presented jointly with CASCA for an outstanding doctoral thesis

Qilak Award
Awarded to recognize Canadian individuals or teams that have made an outstanding contribution to either the public understanding or the informal education of astronomy in Canada

Simon Newcomb Award
Established 1978; trophy awarded annually for the best article on astronomy, astrophysics or space sciences submitted by a member of the society during the year

The Royal Canadian Geographical Society / Société géographique royale du Canada

39 McArthur Ave., Vanier ON K1L 8L7
613/745-4629; Fax: 613/744-0947; Toll Free: 1-800-267-0824
Email: rcgs@rcgs.org; URL: www.rcgs.org

The Gold Medal
Established 1972; to recognize a particular achievement of one or more individuals in the field of geography, or a significant national or international event - Coordinator, Society Programs, Carolyn Milano

The Massey Medal
Established 1959; awarded annually for outstanding personal achievement in the exploration, development, or description of the geography of Canada

The Royal Society of Canada / La Société royale du Canada

170 Waller St., Ottawa ON K1N 9B9
613/991-6990; Fax: 613/991-6996
Email: info@rsc.ca; URL: www.rsc.ca

A.G. Huntsman Award
Established in 1980; awarded annually to honour a marine scientist of any nationality who has had a significant influence on the course of marine science and marine scientific thought

Bancroft Award
Established 1968; awarded every two years for publication, instruction & research in the earth sciences that have conspicuously contributed to public understanding & appreciation of the subject
$2,500 & a presentation scroll - Geneviève Gouin, Awards Coordinator, 613/991-5760

The Flavelle Medal
Established 1924; awarded every two years (since 1966) for an outstanding contribution to biological science during the preceding 10 years or for significant additions to a previous outstanding contribution to biological science

The Henry Marshall Tory Medal
Established 1941; awarded every two years (since 1947) for outstanding research in a branch of astronomy, chemistry, mathematics, physics, or an allied science

John L. Synge Award
Established 1986; awarded at irregular intervals for outstanding research in any of the branches of mathematics
$2,500 & a diploma

The McNeil Medal

Miroslaw Romanowski Medal
Established in 1994 and awarded annually to honour significant contributions to the resolution of scientific aspects of environmental problems; award also includes an annual lecture series for the recipient
Awarded to encourage communication of science to students & the public
$1,500 bursary & a medal

Rutherford Memorial Medals: Chemistry & Physics
Established 1980; awarded annually for outstanding research, one in chemistry, one in physics
Two medals & $2,500 each

Sir John William Dawson Medal
For important contributions of knowledge in multiple domains of interest to the RSC

Willet G. Miller Medal
Established 1943; awarded every two years for outstanding research in any branch of the earth sciences

Société Saint-Jean-Baptiste de Montréal

82, rue Sherbrooke ouest, Montréal QC H2X 1X3
514/843-8851; Fax: 514/844-6369
Email: mbeaulieu@ssjb.com; URL: www.ssjb.com

Prix Léon-Lortie
Established 1987; awarded for achievement in the area of pure & applied sciences

Society of Chemical Industry - Canadian Section

#550, 130 Slater St., Ottawa ON K1P 6E2
Email: communications@soci.org; URL: www.soci.org

Canada Medal Award
Established 1939; awarded every two years for outstanding services in the Canadian chemical industry; recipient delivers an address at a meeting of the society

International Award
Established 1976; award is presented in recognition of outstanding service in the chemical industry in the international sphere, preferably to Canadians or persons who have contributed measurably to the Canadian chemical scene

Julia Levy Award
Presented to recognize the successful commercialization of innovation in Canada in the field of Biomedical Science and Engineering

Kalev Pugi Award
Presented to an individual or team for specific research and development projects (performed in the previous 10-15 years) that exemplify creativity, good experimental design and/or good project management

Le Sueur Memorial Award
Established 1955 to commemorate Ernest A. Le Sueur; award is presented in recognition of outstanding innovation in the Canadian chemical industry

Purvis Memorial Award
Awarded for the development and implementation of strategies that have strengthened the field of chemisty.

SPORTS & RECREATION

Canadian Association for the Advancement of Women & Sport & Physical Activity / Association canadienne pour l'avancement des femmes du sport et de l'activité physique

#N202, 801 King Edward Ave., Ottawa ON K1N 6N5
613/562-5667; Fax: 613/562-5668
Email: caaws@caaws.ca; URL: www.caaws.ca

Breakthrough Awards
Presented annually to outstanding nominees who have used innovative ideas & alternative approaches to encourage & enable more girls & women to participate/lead/coach in sport & physical activity - Karin Lofstrom

WISE Fund
Jointly with Sport Canada; 10 grants annually, valuaed at $1,000 each.

Canadian Curling Association / Association canadienne de curling

1660 Vimont Ct., Cumberland ON K4A 4J4
613/834-2076; Fax: 613/834-0716; Toll Free: 1-800-550-2875
Email: info@curling.ca; URL: www.curling.ca

Award of Achievement
Commemorative plaque presented in recognition of individuals who have contributed significantly to any aspect of Canadian curling operations

Ray Kingsmith Award
Awarded to an individual who parallels the level of involvement & commitment exemplified by Ray Kingsmith

Volunteer of the Year Award
Based on contributions from the previous curling season; national volunteer of the year receives an all-expense paid weekend trip to Nokia Brier or Scott Tournament of Hearts, where they will be recognized during a playoff game

Ontario Ministry of Tourism, Culture & Sport

Hearst Block, 9th Fl., 900 Bay St., Toronto ON M7A 2E1
416/326-9326; Fax: 416/314-7854; Toll-Free: 888-997-9015
URL: www.mtc.gov.on.ca/en/sport/sport/awards.shtml

Ontario Sports Awards
Awards for Athlete of the Year (Male & Female), Coach of the Year (Male & Female), Athlete with a Disability of the Year (Male & Female), Team of the Year, Special Achievement Award for Volunteers, Corporate Sport Citation

Physical Health and Education Canada/Éducation physique et santé Canada

#301, 2197 Riverside Dr., Ottawa ON K1H 7X3
613/523-1348; Fax: 613/523-1206; Toll Free: 1-800-663-8708
Email:info@phecanada.ca; URL: www.phecanada.ca

R. Tait McKenzie Award of Honour
Instituted at the Montreal Convention in 1948, this is the most prestigious award presented by CAHPERD; named after the distinguished Canadian physician, sculptor & physical educator, Dr. Robert Tait McKenzie; candidate shall have performed distinguished, meritorious service as a recognized leader regionally & nationally in his/her field

Société Saint-Jean-Baptiste de Montréal

82, rue Sherbrooke ouest, Montréal QC H2X 1X3
514/843-8851; Fax: 514/844-6369
Email: mbeaulieu@ssjb.com; URL: www.ssjb.com

Prix Maurice-Richard
Established 1979; $1,500 & a medal awarded annually to a French Canadian in recognition of outstanding achievement in sports & athletics in serving the higher interests of the French Canadian people

Swimming/Natation Canada

#B140, 2445 St. Laurent Blvd., Ottawa ON K1G 6C3
613/260-1348; Fax: 613/260-0804
Email: natloffice@swimming.ca; URL: www.swimming.ca

Victor Davis Memorial Award
Annual awards from the Victor Davis Memorial Fund assist young Canadian swimmers to continue their training, education & pursuit of excellence at the international level of competition; recipients are determined by the Victor Davis Memorial Fund Awards Committee

Canadian Honours System

For some years after Confederation, awards were made of a few hereditary honours and some knighthoods and companionships in orders of chivalry, and this policy continued until the end of the First World War.

From 1919 until 1933 no titular honours were granted. There was a brief revival of the defunct honours policy during the Conservative administration of R.B. Bennett, and several distinctions were awarded from 1934 to 1935, but the prohibition was reinstated with the return of the Liberals to office in 1935. Consequently, at the outset of the Second World War, Canadians in the armed services were not entitled to receive awards in the order of chivalry for which other Commonwealth personnel were eligible. A parliamentary committee appointed in 1943 recommended that the ban on nontitular honours be lifted, clearing the way for members of the military and civilians to receive recognition for wartime services.

The hundredth anniversary of Confederation, July 1st, 1967, was the occasion on which the Order of Canada was created as the first component of a distinctly Canadian honours system. More information concerning Orders, Decorations and Medals (as well as various Governor General's awards) may be obtained by writing to: Public Information Directorate, Government House, 1 Sussex Dr., Ottawa ON K1A 0A1.

HERALDRY

Coats-of-arms, flags, badges and other heraldic devices are marks of honour and symbols of identity, authority and, in some cases, sovereignty. Each is granted by the Crown under an exercise of the Sovereign's prerogative to create heraldic honours.

Until June 4, 1988, Canadian corporations and individuals wishing to bear lawful arms petitioned the Sovereign's traditional heraldic officers in London and Edinburgh. On that date, by Royal Letters Patent, the Queen transferred the exercise of her heraldic prerogative, as Queen of Canada, to the Governor General who now heads a new office, the Canadian Heraldic Authority. With the act, heraldry, which has a long history in Canada, has been fully repatriated.

These vice-regal responsibilities are administered by Canadian officers of arms appointed by commission under the Governor General's privy seal: the Herald Chancellor (the Secretary to the Governor General), the Deputy Herald Chancellor (the Deputy Secretary, Chancellery) and the Chief Herald of Canada (Director, Heraldry). He is assisted by three officers of arms: Saint-Laurent, Athabaska, and Fraser heralds, and one officer of arms extraordinary, Dauphin Herald.

New heraldic emblems are granted, and existing ones registered, by the Chief Herald upon receipt of an enabling Warrant from the Herald Chancellor or the Deputy Herald Chancellor acting on behalf of the Governor General. Grants and registrations are made by Letters Patent, documents that set out the Governor General's heraldic responsibilities, describe the emblem granted, and feature a representation of the Governor General's personal arms. To ensure a lasting record, the newly granted and registered emblems are entered in Canada's national armorial, the Public Register of Arms, Flags and Badges of Canada.

Since the Authority was created, hundreds of petitions have been received from every part of the country, most for new grants of arms.

Canadian Honours List

ORDER OF CANADA

As mentioned above, the Order of Canada was created July 1, 1967. Her Majesty The Queen is Sovereign of the Order of Canada and the Governor General is, by virtue of that office, Chancellor and Principal Companion. He/She is assisted in the administration of the Order by an Advisory Council which comprises of:

a) the Chief Justice of Canada (Chair)
b) the Clerk of the Privy Council
c) the Deputy Minister, Canadian Heritage
d) the Chair of the Canada Council
e) the President of the Royal Society of Canada
f) the Chair of the Board of the Association of Universities and Colleges of Canada
g) not more than five other members, when considered appropriate by the Governor General, can be appointed for three-year terms.

The Secretary to the Governor General is, by his/her office, Secretary General of the Order.

The Order of Canada is designed to honour Canadian citizens for outstanding achievement and service to the country or to humanity at large and also for distinguished service in particular localities and fields of activity. The Order comprises three levels of membership: Companion, Officer, and Member. Up to 15 Companions may be appointed annually, but the total number of living Companions may not exceed 165. Up to 64 Officers and 136 Members may be appointed annually with no over-all limit.

The Order includes no titles of honour and confers no special privileges, hereditary or otherwise. Awards are made solely on the basis of merit. Members of the Order are entitled to place after their names the letters "C.C." for Companions, "O.C." for Officers, and "C.M." for Members.

Any person or organization may make nominations for appointment to the Order by writing to the Chancellery, Rideau Hall, Ottawa. The Advisory Council submits to the Governor General lists of those nominees who, in the opinion of the Council, are of greatest merit. Appointments to the Order are made by the Sovereign of the Order on the recommendation of the Governor General as Chancellor of the Order, under an instrument sealed with the Seal of the Order.

Non-Canadians whom the Government desires to honour may be accorded honourary membership in the Order.

Companions of the Order of Canada/
Compagnons de l'Ordre du Canada (C.C.)
(Invested September 23, 2016)
Brenda Andrews, C.C., Toronto, Ont.

(Announced June 30, 2016)
Barbara Sherwood Lollar, C.C., Toronto, Ont.

(Invested May 13, 2016)
Arthur B. McDonald, C.C., Kingston, Ont.
**This is a promotion within the Order.*
Janet Rossant, C.C., Toronto, Ont.

(Invested February 12, 2016)
The Honourable Robert Keith Rae, P.C., C.C., O.Ont., Toronto, Ont.
**This is a promotion within the Order.*

(Announced December 30, 2015)
Brenda Andrews, C.C., Toronto, Ont.
The Honourable Lloyd Axworthy, P.C., C.C., O.M., Winnipeg, Man.
**This is a promotion within the Order.*
Atom Egoyan, C.C., Toronto, Ont.
**This is a promotion within the Order.*
Angela Hewitt, C.C., O.B.E., London, U.K. & Ottawa, Ont.
**This is a promotion within the Order.*
Margaret MacMillan, C.C., Oxford, U.K. & Ottawa, Ont.
**This is a promotion within the Order.*
Arthur B. McDonald, C.C., Kingston, Ont.
**This is a promotion within the Order.*

Officers of the Order of Canada/
Officiers de l'Ordre du Canada (O.C.)
(Invested September 23, 2016)
Nassif Ghoussoub, O.C., Vancouver, B.C.
Guy Latraverse, O.C., C.Q.,Montréal, Que.
Brian Levitt, O.C., Westmount, Que.
John H. McCall MacBain, O.C., Niagara Falls, Ont. and Geneva, Switzerland
Richard H. McLaren, O.C., London, Ont.
Daniel Poliquin, O.C., Ottawa, Ont.
**This is a promotion within the Order.*
James Thomas Rutka, O.C., O.Ont., Toronto, Ont.
Frances Alice Shepherd, O.C., Toronto, Ont.
Jennifer Stoddart, O.C., Montréal, Que.

(Announced June 30, 2016)
Kenneth Armson, O.C., Toronto, Ont.
Yvon Charest, O.C., Québec, Que.
Gregory Charles, O.C., Westmount, Que.
John Richard English, O.C., Kitchener and Toronto, Ont.
**This is a promotion within the Order.*
Eduardo L. Franco, O.C., Montréal, Que.
Jacques Godbout, O.C., C.Q., Montréal, Que.
Serge Godin, O.C., O.Q., Montréal, Que.
**This is a promotion within the Order.*
Robert Arthur Gordon, O.C., O.Ont., Toronto, Ont.
Philippe Gros, O.C., Montréal, Que.
Piers Guy Paton Handling, O.C., O.Ont., Toronto, Ont.
Roberta L. Jamieson, O.C., Ohsweken, Ont.
**This is a promotion within the Order.*
Nathalie Lambert, O.C., Anjou, Que.
Andres Lozano, O.C., Toronto, Ont.
John McCall MacBain, O.C., Niagara Falls, Ont. and Geneva, Switzerland
John McGarry, O.C., Kingston, Ont.
Rene Theophile Nuytten, O.C., O.B.C., Vancouver, B.C.
Dennis O'Connor, O.C., Toronto. Ont.
Sophie May Pierre, O.C., O.B.C., Cranbrook, B.C.
Thomas Quinn, O.C., Beaconsfield, Que.
Noralou Roos, O.C., Winnipeg, Man.
**This is a promotion within the Order.*
Abraham Anghik Ruben, O.C., Salt Spring Island, B.C.
Tsun-Kong Sham, O.C., London, Ont.
Dorothy Shaw, O.C., Vancouver, B.C.
Anthony von Mandl, O.C., O.B.C., Vancouver, B.C.
The Honourable Warren Winkler, O.C., O.Ont., Toronto, Ont.
Ronald J. Wonnacott, O.C., London, Ont.

(Invested May 13, 2016)
Daniel J. Drucker, O.C., Toronto, Ont.
Paul D.N. Hebert, O.C., Puslinch, Ont.
Stephen Nash, O.C., O.B.C., Victoria, B.C. and Manhattan Beach, CA, U.S.A.
Stephen J. Toope, O.C., Toronto, Ont.

(Invested February 12, 2016)
Mary Gospodarowicz Evans, O.C., Toronto, Ont.
Magella Gros-Louis, O.C., O.Q., Wendake, Que.
Norman Emilio Marcon, O.C., Toronto, Ont.
Julio Montaner, O.C., O.B.C., Vancouver, B.C.
Linda F. Nazar, O.C., Waterloo, Ont.
The Honourable Louise Otis, O.C., O.Q., Montréal, Que.
Donald John Taylor, O.C., Calgary, Alta.
**This is a promotion within the Order.*

(Invested November 18, 2015)
Mark Carney, O.C., London, U.K. and Ottawa, Ont.
Harvey Max Chochinov, O.C., O.M., Winnipeg, Man.
James Gordon Cuddy, O.C., Toronto, Ont.
Judson Graham Day, O.C., O.N.S., C.D., Hantsport, N.S.
Gerald Hunter Finley, O.C., Mark Cross, Crowborough, U.K. and Montréal, Que.
Catherine Frazee, O.C., Canning, N.S.
Colonel Chris Austin Hadfield, O.C., O.Ont., M.S.C., C.D. (Ret'd), Sarnia, Ont.
James Gregory Keelor, O.C., Toronto, Ont.
Mark Lautens, o.c., Toronto, Ont.
Wendy Levinson, O.C., Toronto, Ont.
The Honourable Allen Linden, O.C., Toronto, Ont.
James Rodger Miller, O.C., S.O.M., Saskatoon, Sask.

Members of the Order of Canada/
Membres de l'Ordre du Canada (O.C.)
(Invested September 23, 2016)
George Baird, C.M., Toronto, Ont.
Baidar Bakht, C.M., Scarborough, Ont.
Bernard Bélanger, C.M., La Pocatière, Que.
Richard Fredrick Bradshaw, C.M., Vancouver, B.C.
Laura Brandon, C.M., Ottawa, Ont.
Donald C. Brinton, C.M., West Vancouver. B.C.
Sophie Brochu, C.M., Bromont, Que.
Rudy Buttignol, C.M., Vancouver. B.C.
Robert Campbell, C.M., Sackville, N.B.
Robert Cecil Cole, C.M., St. John's, N.L.
Wade Davis, C.M., Bowen Island, B.C.
Lisa de Wilde, C.M., Toronto, Ont.
Elaine Dobbin, C.M., Portugal Cove–St. Philip's, N.L.
Diane Dufresne, C.M., C.Q., Montréal, Que.
Margaret Fountain, C.M., Halifax, N.S.
Meric Gertler, C.M., Toronto, Ont.
David Roy Gillespie, C.M., Chilliwack, B.C.
Ned Goodman, C.M., Toronto, Ont.
Yolande Grisé, C.M., Vancouver, B.C.
Odette Heyn, C.M., Winnipeg, Man.
Lawrence Hill, C.M., Hamilton, Ont.
Marie-Nicole Lemieux, C.M., C.Q., Terrebonne, Que.
Pierre H. Lessard, C.M., Montréal, Que.
Peter S. Li, C.M., Richmond, B.C.
Sidney B. Linden, C.M., O. Ont., Toronto, Ont.
Christine Magee, C.M., Oakville, Ont.
Don McKellar, C.M., Toronto, Ont.
Marie-José Nadeau, C.M., Montréal, Que.
Niels Ole Nielsen, C.M., Spruce Grove, Alta.
Erna Paris, C.M., Toronto, Ont.
Placide Poulin, C.M., Sainte-Marie-de-Beauce, Que.
Heather Maxine Reisman, C.M., Toronto, Ont.
Fran Rider, C.M., Etobicoke, Ont.
Faye Thomson, C.M., Winnipeg, Man.
Douglas Ward, C.M., Ottawa, Ont.
Frederic Wien, C.M., Halifax, N.S.

(Announced June 30, 2016)
Joseph Georges Arsenault, C.M., O.P.E.I., Charlottetown, P.E.I.
Salah John Bachir, C.M., Toronto, Ont.
Isabel Bassett, C.M., O.Ont., Toronto, Ont.
Gerald Batist, C.M., Montréal, Que.
Geoffrey Battersby, C.M., Revelstoke, B.C.
Françoise Baylis, C.M., Halifax, N.S.
Gregory S. Belton, C.M., C.V.O., Toronto, Ont.
Johanne Berry, C.M.
Timothy Borlase, C.M., O.N.L., Pointe-du-Chêne, N.B. and Happy Valley-Goose Bay, N.L.
Richard Fredrick Bradshaw, C.M., Vancouver, B.C.
Peter Bregg, C.M., Toronto, Ont.
Donald C. Brinton, C.M., West Vancouver, B.C.
Michael Budman, C.M., Toronto, Ont.
Cassie Campbell, C.M., Calgary, Alta.
Mariette Carrier-Fraser, c.m., Ottawa, Ont.
The Honourable Sharon Carstairs, P.C., C.M., Ottawa, Ont. and Winnipeg, Man.
Neena L. Chappell, C.M., Victoria, B.C.
Zita Cobb, C.M., Joe Batt's Arm, N.L. and Ottawa, Ont.
Mary Cornish, C.M., Toronto, Ont.
L. Mark Cullen, C.M., Stouffville, Ont.
Madeleine Delaney-Leblanc, C.M., Shediac, N.B.
Patricia Demers, C.M., Edmonton, Alta.
Serge Denoncourt, C.M., Montréal, Que.
Charlotte Diamond, C.M., Richmond, B.C.
Rupert James Duchesne, C.M., Toronto, Ont.
Michael Eskin, C.M., Winnipeg, Man.
Carole Anne Estabrooks, C.M., Edmonton, Alta.
Yvon Ethier, C.M., Terrebonne, Que.
Gerald Richard Fagan, C.M., O.Ont., London, Ont.
Linda Marie Fedigan, C.M., Calgary, Alta.
Marie Esther Fortier, C.M., Ottawa, Ont.
Stephen Gaetz, C.M., Toronto, Ont.
Ned Goodman, C.M., Toronto, Ont.
Don Green, C.M., Toronto, Ont.
Paul John Perry Guloien, C.M., Edmonton, Alta.
Barbara Hannigan, C.M., Waverley, N.S. and Amsterdam, Netherlands
Gregory Hanson, C.M., Winnipeg, Man.
Susan Johnson, C.M., Ottawa, Ont.
Diane Juster, C.M., Montréal, Que.
Eli Kassner, C.M., Toronto, Ont.
Hassan Khosrowshahi, C.M., O.B.C., Vancouver, B.C.
Michael Charles Klein, C.M., Roberts Creek, B.C.
Laurier Lacroix, C.M., Montréal, Que.
Mark Levine, C.M., Hamilton, Ont.
Shar Levine, C.M., Vancouver, B.C.
Sidney B. Linden, C.M., O.Ont., Toronto, Ont.
Gail Dexter Lord, C.M., Toronto, Ont.
Steve Lurie, C.M., Toronto, Ont.
Bruce MacKinnon, C.M., O.N.S., Halifax, N.S.
Harriet MacMillan, C.M., Hamilton, Ont.
Joe Mancini, C.M., Kitchener, Ont.
Stephanie Mancini, C.M., Kitchener, Ont.
Roger L. Martin, C.M., Toronto, Ont.
Don McKellar, C.M., Toronto, Ont.
Linda E. McKnight, C.M., Toronto, Ont.
Emily Molnar, C.M., Vancouver, B.C.
Terrence Montague, C.M., C.D., Edmonton, Alta.
Richard Ian Guy Morrison, C.M., Ottawa, Ont.
The Honourable Graydon Nicholas, C.M., O.N.B., Fredericton, N.B.
Niels Ole Nielsen, C.M., Spruce Grove, Alta.
Shane O'Dea, C.M., O.N.L., St. John's, N.L.
Robert Pace, C.M., Halifax, N.S.

ORDER OF CANADA

Companions of the Order of Canada

Members of the Order of Canada

Officers of the Order of Canada

ORDER OF MILITARY MERIT

Officers of the Order of Military Merit

Commanders of the Order of Military Merit

Members of the Order of Military Merit

Eric L. Peterson, C.M., Heriot Bay, B.C.
Michel Picher, C.M., Ottawa, Ont.
Deborah Poff, C.M., Ottawa, Ont.
Andrew M. Pringle, C.M., Toronto, Ont.
Dani Reiss, C.M., Toronto, Ont.
Howard Warren Rundle, C.M., London, Ont.
Robert J. Sawyer, C.M., Toronto, Ont.
Kathryn Shields, C.M., O.B.C., Victoria, B.C.
Ilkay Silk C.M., Fredericton, N.B.
Jean Swanson, C.M., Vancouver, B.C.
Kathleen Patricia Taylor, C.M., Toronto, Ont.
Richard Tremblay, C.M., C.Q., St-Jean-sur-Richelieu, Que.
Louis Vachon, C.M., Montréal, Que.
Geraldine Van Bibber, C.M., Whitehorse, Y.T.
David Vaver, C.M., Toronto, Ont.
James W. St. G. Walker, C.M., Waterloo, Ont.
Michael A. Walker, C.M., Vancouver, B.C.
Howard Wetston, C.M., Toronto, Ont.
Catharine Whiteside, C.M., Toronto, Ont.
Marie Wilson, C.M., Yellowknife, N.W.T.
James G. Wright, C.M., Toronto, Ont. and Oxford, U.K.
Glenda Yeates, C.M., Ottawa, Ont.

(Invested May 13, 2016)
William A. Black, C.M., Halifax, N.S.
Denise Bombardier, C.M., C.Q., Montréal, Que.
Nathalie Bondil, C.M., C.Q., Montréal, Que.
Beverley Boys, C.M., Surrey, B.C.
Blake Brooker, C.M., Calgary, Alta.
Peter Calamai, C.M., Ottawa, Ont.
Bruce D. Campbell, C.M., Winnipeg, Man.
Pat Capponi, C.M., O.Ont., Toronto, Ont.
Susan M.W. Cartwright, C.M., Ottawa, Ont.
Wayne Suk Wing Chiu, C.M., Calgary, Alta.
John V. Cross, C.M., S.O.M., Saskatoon, Sask.
Conrad Charles Daellenbach, C.., Toronto, Ont.
Linda Gaboriau, C.M., Montréal, Que.
Graham Greene, C.M., Stratford, Ont.
Kathryn Jane Nightingale Hannah, C.M., Calgary, Alta.

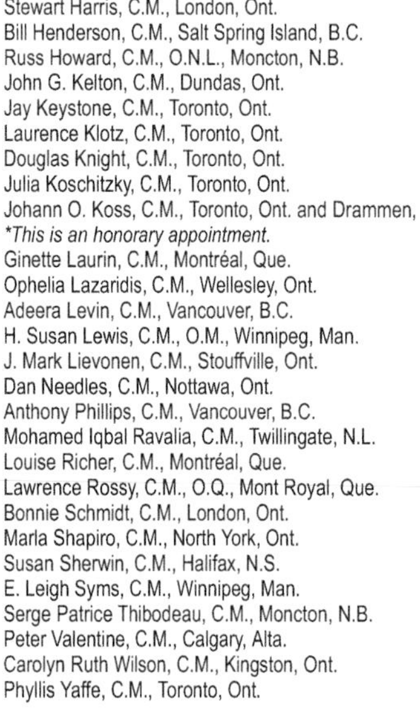

Stewart Harris, C.M., London, Ont.
Bill Henderson, C.M., Salt Spring Island, B.C.
Russ Howard, C.M., O.N.L., Moncton, N.B.
John G. Kelton, C.M., Dundas, Ont.
Jay Keystone, C.M., Toronto, Ont.
Laurence Klotz, C.M., Toronto, Ont.
Douglas Knight, C.M., Toronto, Ont.
Julia Koschitzky, C.M., Toronto, Ont.
Johann O. Koss, C.M., Toronto, Ont. and Drammen, Norway
**This is an honorary appointment.*
Ginette Laurin, C.M., Montréal, Que.
Ophelia Lazaridis, C.M., Wellesley, Ont.
Adeera Levin, C.M., Vancouver, B.C.
H. Susan Lewis, C.M., O.M., Winnipeg, Man.
J. Mark Lievonen, C.M., Stouffville, Ont.
Dan Needles, C.M., Nottawa, Ont.
Anthony Phillips, C.M., Vancouver, B.C.
Mohamed Iqbal Ravalia, C.M., Twillingate, N.L.
Louise Richer, C.M., Montréal, Que.
Lawrence Rossy, C.M., O.Q., Mont Royal, Que.
Bonnie Schmidt, C.M., London, Ont.
Marla Shapiro, C.M., North York, Ont.
Susan Sherwin, C.M., Halifax, N.S.
E. Leigh Syms, C.M., Winnipeg, Man.
Serge Patrice Thibodeau, C.M., Moncton, N.B.
Peter Valentine, C.M., Calgary, Alta.
Carolyn Ruth Wilson, C.M., Kingston, Ont.
Phyllis Yaffe, C.M., Toronto, Ont.

(Invested February 12, 2016)
Ida Albo C.M., Winnipeg, Man.
Aubie Angel, C.M., Toronto, Ont.
Pierre Bergeron, C.M., Gatineau, Que.
Denis Brott, C.M., Saint-Sauvuer, Que.
Christina Stuart Cameron, C.M., Ottawa, Ont.
Martin Chernin, C.M., Sydney, N.S.
A. Gordon Craig, C.M., Toronto, Ont.
John W. Crichton, C.M., Manotick, Ont.
Rollande Desbois, C.M., C.Q., Montréal, Que.

James F. Dinning, C.M., Calgary, Alta.
Madeleine Dion Stout, C.M., Tsawwassen, B.C.
Ivan Kenneth Eyre, C.M., O.M., Winnipeg, Man.
Michèle Fortin, C.M., Montréal, Que.
Douglas Edgar Fregin, C.M., Waterloo, Ont.
James K. Gordon, C.M., Sudbury, Ont.
Ted Grant, C.M., Victoria, B.C.
John Grew, C.M., Montréal, Que.
Carolyn Hansson, C.M., Waterloo, Ont.
Thomas Jon Harle, C.M., C.D., Ottawa, Ont.
Frank Hasenfratz, C.M., Guelph, Ont.
Leah Hollins, C.M., Victoria, B.C.
Sandra Irving, C.M., Saint John, N.B.
Major Tetsuo Theodore Itani, C.M., O.M.M., C.D. (Ret'd), Ottawa, Ont.
Jean-Marc Lalonde, C.M., Rockland, Ont.
Judy Loman, C.M., Toronto, Ont.
John G. McAvity, C.M., Ottawa, Ont.
Lynn McDonald, C.M., Toronto, Ont.
John Morden, C.M., Toronto, Ont.
Ervin Podgorsak, C.M., Montréal, Que.

Vivian Morris Rakoff, C.M., Toronto, Ont.
Garry Rempel, C.M., Waterloo, Ont.
Mary Rozsa de Coquet, C.M., Calgary, Alta.
Sandra Scarth, C.M., Brentwood Bay, B.C.
Barbara Kristina Schmidt, C.M., Philadelphia, Pennsylvania, U.S.A. and Burlington, Ont.
François Schubert, C.M., Montréal, Que.
P. Kim Sturgess, C.M., Montréal, Que.
Don Tapscott, C.M., Toronto, Ont.
Lorraine Vaillancourt, C.M., Montréal, Que.
Helen Vari, C.M., Toronto, Ont.
Martin Yaffe, C.M., Toronto, Ont.

(Invested November 18, 2015)
The Honourable Jacob Austin, P.C., C.M., O.B.C., Vancouver, B.C.

CANADIAN BRAVERY DECORATIONS

Star of Courage

Cross of Valor

Medal of Bravery

MERITORIOUS SERVICE DECORATIONS

Meritorious Service Cross
Obverse (Military Version)

Meritorious Service Medal
Reverse (Civil Version)

Kenneth MacClure Baird, C.M., Ottawa, Ont.
Mitchell A. Baran, C.M. *(deceased)*, London, Ont.
Daniel Bertolino, C.M., Montréal, Que.
Josiane Boulad-Ayoub, C.M., Montréal, Que.
Wendy Marion Cecil, C.M., Toronto, Ont.
Jagannath Prasad Das, C.M., Toronto, Ont.
Michael DeGagné, C.M., O.Ont., North Bay, Ont.
Edgar J. Dosman, C.M., Toronto, Ont.
Marcia "Kappy" Flanders, C.M., M.S.M., Montréal, Que.
Brenda Louise Gallie, C.M., O.Ont., Toronto, Ont.
Christophe Guy, C.M., O.Q., Montréal, Que.
Mel Hoppenheim, C.M., Montréal, Que.
Monique Jérôme-Forget, C.M., O.Q., Montréal, Que.
Patrick Johnston, C.M., Roslin, Ont.
Donna Soble Kaufman, C.M., Toronto, Ont.
Guy Gavriel Kay, C.M., Toronto, Ont.
Arthur Alexander Kube, C.M., Surrey, B.C.
Grégoire Legendre, C.M., Québec, Que.
Jens Lindemann, C.M., Pacific Palisades, California, U.S.A., and Edmonton, Alta.
Michel Louvain, C.M., C.Q., Montréal, Que.

Keith MacLellan, C.M., Bristol, Que.
Thomas J. Marrie, C.M., Halifax, N.S.
The Honourable Michael A. Meighen, C.M., Toronto, Ont.
Fiona Nelson, C.M., Toronto, Ont.
Cal Nichols, C.M., Edmonton, Alta.
Charles E. Pascal, C.M., Toronto, Ont.
Hubert Sacy, C.M., C.Q., Montréal, Que.
H. Olav Slaymaker, C.M., Vancouver, B.C.
Morley Torgov, C.M., Toronto, Ont.
Barbara Turnbull, C.M. *(deceased)*, Toronto, Ont.
V. Prem Watsta, C.M., Toronto, Ont.
H. Bruce Williams, C.M., Montréal, Que.

ORDER OF MILITARY MERIT

The Order of Military Merit was created on July 1, 1972 to recognize meritorious service and devotion to duty by members of the Canadian Forces. The Order has three grades of membership: Commander (C.M.M.), Officer (O.M.M.) and Member (M.M.M.). The annual number of appointments is limited to one-tenth of one percent of the number of persons in the Canadian Forces in the preceding year.

Commanders of the Order of Military Merit/ Commandeurs de l'Ordre du mérite militaire (C.M.M.) (Invested June 3, 2016)

Lieutenant-General Michael John Hood, C.M.M., C.D., Ottawa, Ont.
Rear-Admiral John Frederick Newton, C.M.M., M.S.M., C.D., Halifax, N.S.
Lieutenant-General Christine Theresa Whitecross, C.M.M., M.S.M., C.D., Ottawa, Ont.

(Invested November 10, 2015)

Major-General Dean James Milner, C.M.M., M.S.C., C.D., Kingston, Ont.
**This is a promotion within the Order.*
Major-General Pierre St-Amand, C.M.M., C.D., Colorado Springs, Colorado, U.S.A.
**This is a promotion within the Order.*

Officers of the the Order of Military Merit/ Officiers de l'Ordre du mérite militaire (O.M.M.) (Invested June 3, 2016)

Lieutenant-Colonel Roy Armstrong, O.M.M., C.D., Ottawa, Ont.
Colonel Marie Annabelle Jennie Carignan, O.M.M., M.S.M., C.D., Richelain, Que.
Colonel Peter Samson Dawe, O.M.M., M.S.M., C.D., Petawawa, Ont.
Brigadier-General Luis Alberto Botelho de Sousa, O.M.M., C.D., Montréal, Que.
Lieutenant-Colonel George Heber Gillam, O.M.M., C.D., Ottawa, Ont.
Captain(N) Joseph Jeannot Hervé Richard Jean, O.M.M., C.D., Ottawa, Ont.
Major John Allison Lewis, O.M.M., C.D., Astra, Ont.
Colonel David William Lowthian, O.M.M., M.S.M., C.D., Astra, Ont.
Brigadier-General Joseph Paul Alain Pelletier, O.M.M., M.S.M., C.D., Florida, U.S.A.
Brigadier-General Neville Edward Russell, O.M.M., C.D., Ottawa, Ont.
Colonel Michel-Henri St-Louis, O.M.M., M.S.M., C.D., Ottawa, Ont.
Lieutenant-Commander John Aubrey Williston, O.M.M., M.S.M., C.D., Ottawa, Ont.

(Invested November 10, 2015)

Lieutenant-Colonel Joseph Michel Steve Boivin, O.M.M., M.S.M., C.D., Ottawa, Ont.
Colonel Joseph Serge Steve Dany Fortin, O.M.M., C.D., Courcelette, Que.
Lieutenant-Colonel Steven Leslie Hart, O.M.M., C.D., Oromocto, N.B.
Lieutenant-Colonel Mark Bradley Larsen, O.M.M., C.D., Winnipeg, Man.
Major Rickey Maxwell Lewis, O.M.M., C.D., Victoria, B.C.
Colonel Marie Céline Danielle Savard, O.M.M., M.S.M., C.D., Ottawa, Ont.
Colonel David Ross Weger, O.M.M., C.D., Ottawa, Ont.
Colonel Terrence Leroy Wood, O.M.M., C.D., Ottawa, Ont.

Members of the Order of Military Merit/ Membres de l'Ordre du mérite militaire (M.M.M.) (Invested June 3, 2016)

Chief Petty Officer 1st Class David Ronald Arsenault, M.M.M., C.D., Québec, Que.
Chief Warrant Officer Robert Joseph Beaudry, M.M.M., C.D., Oromocto, N.B.

Warrant Officer David Timothee Bérubé, M.M.M., M.M.V., C.D., Oromocto, N.B.
Chief Warrant Officer Mario Paul Bizier, M.M.M., C.D., Ottawa, Ont.
Chief Petty Officer 2nd Class Colin Philip Bond, M.M.M., C.D., Halifax, N.S.
Chief Warrant Officer Joseph Jacques Boucher, M.M.M., C.D., Kingston, Ont.
Master Warrant Officer Todd Barry Buchanan, M.M.M., M.S.M., C.D., Shilo, Man.
Major Marie Françoise Lucie Burelle, M.M.M., C.D., Montréal, Que.
Chief Petty Officer 1st Class Norman William Cawthra, M.M.M., C.D., Victoria, B.C.
Chief Warrant Officer Edward Joseph John Curtis, M.M.M., C.D., Oromocto, N.B.
Chief Warrant Officer Mary Elizabeth Demetruk, M.M.M., C.D., Toronto, Ont.
Captain Joseph Robert Alain Deslauriers, M.M.M., C.D., Montréal, Que.
Master Warrant Officer Dana Robert Eagles, M.M.M., C.D., Burton, N.B.
Major Erica Leigh Fleck, M.M.M., C.D., Halifax, N.S.
Master Warrant Officer Michael Fuentespina, M.M.M., C.D., Winnipeg, Man.
Ranger Donald Upton Gourlay, M.M.M., C.D., Edmonton, Alta.
Chief Warrant Officer John Henry Graham, M.M.M., M.S.M., C.D., Ottawa, Ont.
Chief Petty Officer 2nd Class Stephen Harold Haughn, M.M.M., C.D., Ottawa, Ont.
Captain Carl Homer, M.M.M., C.D., Kingston, Ont.
Warrant Officer Kimberlee Jones, M.M.M., C.D., Ottawa, Ont.
Chief Warrant Officer Joseph Réal Luc Lacombe, M.M.M., C.D., Courcelette, Q.C.
Master Warrant Officer William Edward Lang, M.M.M., C.D., Petawawa, Ont.
Major Line Michele Leboeuf, M.M.M., C.D., Ottawa, Ont.
Master Warrant Officer Grant Clarence Lewis, M.M.M., C.D., Astra, Ont.
Petty Officer 1st Class Marie Stephanie Dawn MacKay, M.M.M., C.D., Halifax, N.S.
Warrant Officer Joseph James William Lorne McAdam, M.M.M., C.D., Montréal, Que.
Master Warrant Officer Patrick William Moran, M.M.M., C.D., Hornell Heights, Ont.
Lieutenant Karen Deborah Mullen, M.M.M., C.D., Ottawa, Ont.
Master Warrant Officer Thomas Kincaid Neill, M.M.M., C.D., Oromocto, N.B.
Warrant Officer Robert Harold John Peldjak, M.M.M., C.D., Hornell Heights, Ont.
Chief Warrant Officer Joseph Gerald Donald Pelletier, M.M.M., C.D., Québec, Que.
Major Jaime Phillips, M.M.M., C.D., Oromocto, N.B.
Warrant Officer Claude Pierre Provost, M.M.M., C.D., Ottawa, Ont.
Master Warrant Officer Wallace Rideout, M.M.M., C.D., Kingston, Ont.
Warrant Officer Stuart John Dalton Russelle, M.M.M., C.D., Petawawa, Ont.
Chief Warrant Officer Jeffrey Harold Saunders, M.M.M., C.D., Ottawa, Ont.
Master Warrant Officer Keith Alan Sexstone, M.M.M., C.D., Ottawa, Ont.
Ranger Stanley Robert Stephens, M.M.M., C.D., English River, Ont.
Chief Warrant Officer Robert Peter Michael Talach, M.M.M., C.D., London, Ont.
Petty Officer 2nd Class Jody Patrick Waterfield, M.M.M., C.D., Halifax, N.S.

(Invested November 10, 2015)
Master Warrant Officer Ian Ronald Jude Bennett, M.M.M., C.D., Petawawa, Ont.
Warrant Officer David Carman Bibby, M.M.M., C.D., Edmonton, Alta.
Master Warrant Officer Marnie Davis, M.M.M., C.D., Edmonton, Alta.
Warrant Officer Stephen Michael Dawe, M.M.M., C.D., Edmonton, Alta.
Master Warrant Officer Paul André Christian Doucet, M.M.M., C.D., Ottawa, Ont.
Chief Petty Officer 1st Class Paul Andrew Fenton, M.M.M., C.D., Victoria, B.C.
Sergeant Timothy Ferguson, M.M.M., C.D., Ottawa, Ont.
Master Warrant Officer Joseph Lucien Steve Fréchette, M.M.M., C.D., Alouette, Q.C.
Chief Warrant Officer Joseph Gérard Marc Gabanna, M.M.M., C.D., Montréal, Que.
Master Warrant Officer Clermont Gagné, M.M.M., C.D., Alouette, Que.
Chief Warrant Officer Joseph Dominic Stéphane Gaudreau, M.M.M., C.D., Courcelette, Que.
Master Warrant Officer David Edward Hepditch, M.M.M., C.D., Shearwater, N.S.
Chief Petty Officer 2nd Class Cyrus Jawahar John, M.M.M., C.D., Halifax, N.S.
Chief Petty Officer 1st Class Ian Mark Kelly, M.M.M., C.D., Victoria, B.C.
Captain Joseph Ghislain Levesque, M.M.M., C.D., Montréal, Que.
Captain Malcolm Alastair McMurachy, M.M.M., C.D., Borden, Ont.
Master Warrant Officer John Robert McNabb, M.M.M., M.S.C., C.D., Kentville, N.S.
Private Thomas Nickel, M.M.M., C.D., Victoria, B.C.
Master Warrant Officer Joseph Gilles Alain Oligny, M.M.M., C.D., Richelain, Que.
Warrant Officer Kimberly Christine Pyke, M.M.M., C.D., Kingston, Ont.
Chief Warrant Officer Eric John Rolfe, M.M.M., M.S.M., C.D., Burton, N.B.
Warrant Officer Scott Vernon Russell, M.M.M., C.D., Petawawa, Ont.
Master Warrant Officer David George Shultz, M.M.M., S.M.V., C.D., Edmonton, Alta.
Petty Officer 2nd Class Philip Wade Smith, M.M.M., C.D., Victoria, B.C.
Chief Petty Officer 2nd Class Eric Wilfred Stone, M.M.M., C.D., Halifax, N.S.
Warrant Officer Jason Tomlinson, M.M.M., C.D., Oromocto, N.B.
Chief Warrant Officer Martin Woods, M.M.M., C.D., Calgary, Alta.
Major Darcy James Wright, M.M.M., C.D., Edmonton, Alta.
Chief Petty Officer 2nd Class Kelly Allan Yerama, M.M.M., C.D., Victoria, B.C.

ORDER OF MERIT OF THE POLICE FORCES

In October 2000, Her Majesty The Queen approved the creation of the Order as a means of recognizing conspicuous merit and exceptional service by members and employees of the Canadian police forces whose contributions extend beyond protection of the community. There are three levels of membership - Commander, Officer and Member - that reflect long-term, outstanding service in varying degrees of responsibility. Each level has corresponding nominal letters: C.O.M., O.O.M. and M.O.M.

Commander of the Order of Merit of the Police Forces/ Commandeur de l'Ordre du mérite des corps policiers (C.O.M.)

(Invested September 16, 2016)
Commissioner J. Vincent N. Hawkes, C.O.M., Orillia, Ont.
**This is a promotion within the Order.*

Officers of the the Order of Merit of the Police Forces/ Officiers de l'Ordre du mérite des corps policiers (O.O.M.)

(Invested September 16, 2016)
Deputy Commissioner Bradley Blair, O.O.M., Ont.
**This is a promotion within the Order.*
Deputy Commissioner Craig Steven MacMillan, O.O.M., Ont.
**This is a promotion within the Order.*
Chief Douglas A. Palson, O.O.M., Ont.
Chief Superintendent Jennifer Anne Strachan, O.O.M., Ont.

Members of the the Order of Merit of the Police Forces/ Membres de l'Ordre du mérite des corps policiers (M.O.M.)

(Invested September 16, 2016)
Chief Superintendent Rosemary Abbruzzese, M.O.M., Ont.
Chief Terry Ray Armstrong, M.O.M., Ont.
Superintendent Paul A. Beesley, M.O.M., Ont.
Daniel J. Bowman, M.O.M., Ont.
Sergeant Howard James Burns, M.O.M., Prairies & Northern Territories
Corps Sergeant Major Darren C. Campbell, M.O.M., Ont.
Inspector Lawrence Cope, M.O.M., B.C.
Superintendent Joseph Bernard Serge Côté, M.O.M., Ont.
Chief Stephen E. Covey, M.O.M., Que.
Chief Superintendent David Thomas Critchley, M.O.M., B.C.
Sergeant Robert C. Daly, M.O.M., B.C.
Superintendent Kari Dart, M.O.M., Ont.
Director Denis Desroches, M.O.M., Que.
Chief Shawn Devine, M.O.M., Ont.
Susan C. Double, M.O.M., Ont.
Deputy Chief Nishan J. Duraiappah, M.O.M., Ont.
Inspector Stuart K. Eley, M.O.M., Ont.
Deputy Chief Timothy Farquharson, M.O.M., Ont.
Inspector Patrick S. Flanagan, M.O.M., Ont.
Staff Sergeant Douglas Frank Gambicourt, M.O.M., B.C.
Chief Constable Ralph Leonard Goerke, M.O.M., B.C.
Superintendent Nancy Goodes-Ritchie, M.O.M., Ont.
Superintendent James Ian Hardy, M.O.M., Prairies & Northern Territories
Chief Constable Wayne Douglas Holland, M.O.M., B.C.
Staff Sergeant Douglas James Houston, M.O.M., Prairies & Northern Territories
Staff Sergeant Wilfred E. Hurren, M.O.M., Ont.
Deputy Chief David Jarvis, M.O.M., Ont.
Inspector Edmund P. Kodis, M.O.M., Ont.
Deputy Director Bernard Lamothe, M.O.M., Que.
Chief Bryan M. Larkin, M.O.M., Ont.
Staff Sergeant Robert Ellwood Lemon, M.O.M., B.C.
Inspector David J. Lucas, M.O.M., Ont.
Sergeant Stephen MacDonald, M.O.M., Ont.
Superintendent Mandip Singh Mann, M.O.M., B.C.
Constable David Marchand, M.O.M., B.C.
Superintendent Glenn Arnold Martindale, M.O.M., Ont.
Sergeant David Bruce Muirhead, M.O.M., Ont.
Corporal Jacques M. A. Neri, M.O.M., Prairies & Northern Territories
Staff Superintendent Randall Patrick, M.O.M., Ont.
Inspector Jamie Alan David Pearce, M.O.M., B.C.
Sergeant Denis Perrier, M.O.M., Que.
Chief Superintendent Richard A. J. Philbin, M.O.M., Ont.
Chief Inspector Pierre Pinel, M.O.M., Que.
Chief Darryl J. Pinnell, M.O.M., Ont.
Sergeant Clifford T. Priest, M.O.M., Ont.
Deputy Chief Constable Satwinder Rai, M.O.M., B.C.
Staff Sergeant Brian John Reed, M.O.M., Ont.
Inspector Daniel W. Ritchie, M.O.M., B.C.
Staff Sergeant Thomas Robb, M.O.M., Ont.
Superintendent John Alfred Robin, M.O.M., Ont.
Inspector David B. Saunders, M.O.M., Ont.
Commander David Shane, M.O.M., Que.
Lisa Shipley, M.O.M., Ont.
Superintendent Konrad Lionel Shourie, M.O.M., Ont.
Sergeant Marty Roy Singleton, M.O.M., Ont.
Superintendent Guy Warwick Slater, M.O.M., Prairies & Northern Territories
Superintendent Hilton Basil Smee, M.O.M., B.C.
Superintendent Wayne Alexander Sutherland, M.O.M., B.C.
Sergeant Robert Montgomery Tan, M.O.M., Ont.
Inspector Karl Thomas, M.O.M., Ont.
Chief Superintendent Sandra Anne Thomas, M.O.M., Ont.
Deputy Chief Paul VandeGraaf, M.O.M., Ont.
Staff Sergeant Lauren Weare, M.O.M., B.C.
Sergeant William Michael James Whalen, M.O.M., B.C.
Constable Andrew Preston Wilder, M.O.M., Ont.
Superintendent Peter C. Yuen, M.O.M., Ont.

(Invested October 1, 2015)
Assistant Commissioner Brenda Butterworth-Carr, M.O.M., Regina, Sask.
Staff Sergeant John W. Goodman, M.O.M., Waterloo, Ont.
Assistant Commissioner Gilles Moreau, M.O.M., Ottawa, Ont.
Deputy Chief John B. Pare, M.O.M., London, Ont.
Chief Paul E. Pedersen, M.O.M., Sudbury, Ont.
Assistant Commissioner Dale Sheehan, M.O.M., Ottawa, Ont.
Assistant Commissioner Stephen White, M.O.M., London, Ont.

MILITARY VALOUR DECORATIONS/DÉCORATIONS DE LA VAILLANCE MILITAIRE

Military Valour Decorations are national honours awarded to recognize acts of valour, self-sacrifice or devotion to duty in the presence of the enemy. The decorations were approved by Her Majesty Queen Elizabeth II in 1993. They consist of the Victoria Cross, the Star of Military Valour and the Medal of Military Valour.

Victoria Cross/La Croix de Victoria (C.V.)

None awarded since last edition.

Star of Military Valour/Étoile de la vaillance militaire (É.V.M.)

None awarded since last edition.

Medal of Military Valour/ Médaille de la vaillance militaire (M.V.M)

None awarded since last edition.

CANADIAN BRAVERY DECORATIONS/DÉCORATIONS CANADIENNES POUR ACTES DE BRAVOURE

The Decorations for Bravery, consisting of the Cross of Valour, the Star of Courage, and the Medal of Bravery, were instituted and created on May 10, 1972. They may be awarded to Canadian citizens or to non-Canadians who have performed an act of bravery in Canada, or outside Canada if the act was in Canada's interest. The Decorations for Bravery may be awarded posthumously.

The Cross of Valour is awarded for acts of the most conspicuous courage in circumstances of extreme peril. The Star of Courage is awarded for acts of conspicuous courage in circumstances of great peril. The Medal of Bravery is awarded for acts of bravery in hazardous circumstances.

Cross of Valour/Croix de Valeur (C.V.)
None awarded since last edition.

Star of Courage/Étoile du courage (S.C.)
(Awarded February 8, 2016)
Constable Curtis Barrett, S.C., Chelsea, Que.
Corporal Dany Daigle, S.C., Ottawa, Ont.
Constable Martin Fraser, S.C., Gatineau, Que.
Constable Louis Létourneau, S.C., Gatineau, Que.
Sergeant Richard Rozon, S.C., Gatineau, Que.
Constable Samearn Son, S.C., Ottawa, Ont.
Sergeant-at-Arms Kevin Vickers, O.N.B., S.C., Miramichi, N.B. and Dublin, Ireland

Medal of Bravery/Médaille de la bravoure (M.B.)
(Awarded July 13, 2016)
Rorey Dee Chamberlain, M.B., Saint-George, N.B.
Jason Ronald Comeau, M.B., Moncton, N.B.

(Awarded March 4, 2016)
Thomas Charles Blair, M.B., Kamloops, B.C.
Guy Hawk, M.B.., Agassiz, B.C.
Michael Robert Henderson, M.B., Nelson, B.C.
Kevin Laverne Hiebert, M.N., Kelowna, B.C.
Constable Kevin Johnson, M.B., Golden, B.C.
Wilbert Kent, M.B., Kamloops, B.C.
Corporal Michael Edward Loerke M.B. (Retired), Lake Country, B.C.
Jason McMillan, M.B., Vancouver, B.C.
Anthony Norman, M.B., Victoria, B.C.
Marc Overacker, M.B., Athabasca, Alta.
Deputy Fire Chief Brent Ian Penner, M.B., Lake Country, B.C.
Maurice Poirier, M.B., Calgary, Alta.
Robert Reid, M.B., Kamloops, B.C.
Cindy Leigh Rogers, M.B., Kelowna, B.C.
Randolph Schwindt, M.B., Vancouver, B.C.
Jordan Smith, M.B., Edmonton, Alta.
Donald Alan St. Pierre, M.B., Blind Bay, B.C.
Constable Carl Russell Stene, M.B., Lake Country, B.C.
Stephen VanderVelden, M.B., Lacombe, Alta.
Leading Air Cadet Shannon Young, M.B., Kamloops, B.C.

(Awarded February 8, 2016)
Constable Michelle Bergeron, M.B., Ottawa, Ont.
Constable Gary Bubelis, M.B., Spencerville, Ont.
Constable Somoza Célestin, M.B., Ottawa, Ont.
Corporal Maxim Malo, M.B., Gatineau, Que.
Constable Sylvie Marcoux, M.B., Embrun, Ont.
Constable Michel Palmer, M.B., Rockland, Ont.
Constable Patrick Ruest, M.B., Embrun, Ont.
Constable Charles Thom, M.B., Ottawa, Ont.
Constable Herbert Waye, M.B., Oxford Mills, Ont.

MERITORIOUS SERVICE DECORATIONS/DÉCORATIONS POUR SERVICE MÉRITOIRE

Approved by Her Majesty the Queen on July 10, 1991, the Meritorious Service Decorations were created to honour Canadians & foreigners (military) for commendable actions performed on or after June 11, 1984.

The Meritorious Service Cross (Military Division) is awarded for the performance of a military deed or a military activity in an outstandingly professional manner or of a rare high standard that brings considerable benefit or great honour to the Canadian Forces.

The Meritorious Service Medal (Military Division) is awarded for the performance of a military deed or a military activity in a highly professional manner or of a very high standard that brings benefit or honour to the Canadian Forces.

Meritorious Service Cross/M.S.C. (Military)/
La Croix du service méritoire (militaire)
(Awarded May 13, 2016)
Admiral William E. Gortney, M.S.C. (United States Navy), Cornwall-on-Hudson, New York, U.S.A.

(Awarded October 1, 2015)
Sergeant Terrence Gregory Grandy, M.S.C., C.D., Grand Bank, Nfld.

Meritorious Service Medal M.S.M. (Military)/
La Médaille du service méritoire (militaire)
(Awarded July 13, 2016)
Honorary Captain(N) Fred George, O.N.S., M.S.M., Bedford, N.S.

(Awarded March 4, 2016)
Second Lieutenant Robert Archie Alliston, M.S.M., C.D., Surrey, B.C.
Commander Jason Robert Boyd, M.S.M., C.D., Regina, S.K.
Sergeant Brian Harding, M.S.M., Québec, Que.
Master Corporal Jordan Irvine, M.S.M., C.D., White Rock, B.C.
Sergeant Russell Scott Short, M.S.M., C.D., Lazo, B.C.

Meritorious Service Cross M.S.C. (Civil)/
La Croix du service méritoire (civile)
(Awarded July 13, 2016)
Paul A. Young, M.S.C., Sydney, N.s.

(Awarded June 23, 2016)
Michael Andrew Burns, M.S.C., Toronto, Ont.
Chief Superintendent Craig J. Callens, O.O.M, M.S.C., Vancouver, B.C.
Jacques Corcos, M.S.C., Montréal, Que.
Paul Dubé, M.S.C., Edmonton, Alta.
Edwina Jarvis Eddy, M.S.C., Ottawa, Ont.
Andréanne Emard, M.S.C., The Hague, Netherlands
Shaun Francis, M.S.C., Toronto, Ont.
Mike Frastacky, M.S.C.*(posthumous)*, Vancouver, B.C.
Sergeant Cristopher Gastaldo, M.S.C., Ottawa, Ont.
Superintendent James R.D. Gresham, M.O.M., M.S.C., Vancouver, B.C.
Janet Longmore, M.S.C., Chelsea, Que.
Jean-Claude Mahé, M.S.C., Montréal, Que.
Corporal Benoit J. S. Maure, M.S.C., Ottawa, Ont.
Sergeant Major Alan Daniel McCambridge, M.S.C., Yellowknife, N.W.T.
Inspector Trent Rolfe, M.O.M., M.S.C., Vancouver, B.C.
James Drewry Stewart, M.S.C.*(posthumous)*, Toronto, Ont.
Hannah Taylor, M.S.C., Winnipeg, Man.

(Awarded March 4, 2016)
Colin Balfour Glassco, A.O.E., M.S.C., Calgary, Alta.
Morgan Wienberg, M.S.C., Les Cayes, Haiti and Whitehorse, Y.T.
George Bittman, M.S.M. (posthumous), Calgary, Alta.
J. Murray McCann, M.S.M., Calgary, Alta.
Lembi Buchanan, M.S.M., Victoria, B.C.
Lieutenant-Colonel Sydney E. Burrows, A.F.C., M.S.M., C.D. (Retired)
Daniel Claypool, M.S.M., Devon, A.B.
Erin Gravelle, M.S.M., Vancouver, B.C.
Sharon Hapton, M.S.M., Calgary, Alta.
David Lemon, M.S.M., Vancouver, B.C.
David McGuire, M.S.M., New Westminster, B.C.
Lauren Woolstencroft, M.S.M., Vancouver, B.C.

(Awarded December 8, 2015)
Jean-François Archambault, M.S.C., Candiac, Que.
Leena Tatiggaq Evic, M.S.C., Iqaluit, NU
Robert Allston Fowler, M.S.C., Toronto, Ont.
Mylène Paquette, M.S.C., Montréal, Que.
Raymond Zahab, M.S.C. Chelsea, Que.

Meritorious Service Medal M.S.M. (Civil)/
La Médaille du service méritoire (civile)
(Awarded July 13, 2016)
Sandra Clark, M.S.M., St. John's, N.L.
Peter James Cowan, M.S.M., Halifax, N.S.
Geoff Eaton, M.S.M., St. John's, N.L.
J.A. Heffernan, M.S.M., St. John's, N.L.
Philip D. Hiscock, M.S.M., St. John's, N.L.
Robert Hollet, M.S.M., St. John's, N.L.
Jessie Lynn Jollymore, M.S.M., Halifax, N.S.
Anthony Kelly, M.S.M., Halifax, N.S.
Major James Gerald Lynch, M.S.M., C.D. (Retired), St. John's, N.L.
Laurie Mallery, M.S.M., Halifax, N.S.
Roderick Allister McCulloch, M.S.M., Halifax, N.S.
Penny Walsh McGuire, M.S.M., Charlottetown, P.E.I.
Paige Alison Moorhouse, M.S.M., Halifax, N.S.
Harold J. Paddock, M.S.M., St. John's, N.L.
Michael Parkhill, O.Ont., M.S.M., Halifax, N.S.
Byron Alexander Samson, M.S.M., Halifax, N.S.
John Alexander Seymour, M.S.M., Halifax, N.S.
Maike van Niekerk, M.S.M., Corner Brook, N.L.
Gerald Walsh, M.S.M., Halifax, N.S.
Paul J. York, M.S.M., Halifax, N.S.

(Awarded June 23, 2016)
Tammy Aristilde, M.S.M., Kingston, Ont.
Martin A.E. Bergmann, M.S.M.*(posthumous)*, Winnipeg, Man.
Alexandre Bilodeau, M.S.M., Montréal, Que.
Esther Bryan, M.S.M., Williamstown, Ont.
Gavin Buchan, M.S.M., Ottawa, Ont.
Anthony G. Clark, M.S.M.*(posthumous)*, Guelph, Ont.
Geneviève Dechêne, M.S.M., Montréal, Que.
Ivan X. de Souza, M.S.M., Etobicoke, Ont.
Armand Calixte Doucet, M.S.M., Moncton, N.B.
Lee Durdon, M.S.M., Brantford, Ont.
Elizabeth Elliott, M.S.M.*(posthumous)*, Vancouver, B.C.
Angela Elster, M.S.M., Westport, Ont.
Nicolino Frate, M.S.M., Montréal, Que.
Lisa Gluthero, M.S.M., Chelsea, Que.
Zabeen Hirji, M.S.M., Toronto, Ont.
Deborah Kerr, M.S.M., Caledonia, Ont.
Allan H. Kristofferson, M.S.M., Gimli, Man.
Pierre Legault, M.S.M., Dorval, Que.
Barbara Ruth Marian, M.S.M., Colborne, Ont.
Deborah Maskens, M.S.M., Guelph, Ont.
René L. Matthey, M.S.M.*(posthumous)*, Ottawa, Ont.
Brian McKeever, M.S.M., Canmore, Alta.
Robin McKeever, M.S.M., Canmore, Alta.
Wyatt McWilliams, M.S.M., Navan, Ont.
Vincent Charles Pawis, O.Ont., M.S.M., Nobel, Ont.
Ben Peterson, M.S.M., Caledonia, Ont.
Félix Saint-Denis, M.S.M., Ottawa, Ont.
Alexanger George Salki, M.S.M., Winnipeg, Man.
Mary Suzanne Saunders-Matthey, M.S.M.*(posthumous)*, Ottawa, Ont.
Ellen Schwartz, M.S.M., Toronto, Ont.
Jeffrey Schwartz, M.S.M., Toronto, Ont.
Alexandra Sicotte-Lévesque, M.S.M., Montréal, Que. and Brooklyn, New York
Michael Stainton, M.S.M., Elie, Man.
Mike Stevens, M.S.M., Sarnia, Ont.
Anne-Marie Zajdlik, O.Ont., M.S.M., Rockwood, Ont.

(Awarded December 8, 2015)
Sergeant Samuel Ernest Anderson, M.S.M., Winnipeg, Man.
Frank George Hans Baillie, M.S.M., Burlington, Ont.
Marc Balevi, M.S.M., Hudson, Que.
Catherine P. Baylis, M.S.M., Prince George, B.C.
Jessie M. Bowden, M.S.M., Timberlea, N.S.
Bonnie Buxton, M.S.M., Toronto, Ont.
Hélène Sage Josée Campbell, M.S.M., Ottawa, Ont.
James Casey, M.S.M., Charlottetown, P.E.I.
Frédéric G. Cassir, M.S.M., Beaconsfield, Que.
Hubert Chrétien, M.S.M., Gatineau, Que.
Mark Cohon, M.S.M., Toronto, Ont.
Sergeant John Allen Comeau, M.S.M.
Andrew Cottrell, M.S.M., Toronto, Ont.
Superintendent Stephen Covey, M.S.M.
Melissa Emblin, M.S.M., Montréal, Que.
Robert Fetherstonhaugh, M.S.M., Dorval, Que.
Allison A. Fisher, M.S.M., Ottawa, Ont.
L. Jean Fournier, M.S.M., Trois-Rivières, Que.
Sergeant James J. Giczi, M.S.M., Whitehorse, Y.T.
Joé Juneau, M.S.M., Saint-Raymond, Que.
Gregory M. Lagacé, M.S.M., Ottawa, Ont.
Jenna Brianne Lambert, M.S.M., Kingston, Ont.
Kenneth Randal MacLeod, M.S.M., Moncton, N.B.
Paul Nguyen, M.S.M., Toronto, Ont.
Marie-Élaine Patenaude, M.S.M., Montréal, Que.
Sergeant David A. Patterson, M.S.M.
Luca Patuelli, M.S.M., Montréal, Que.
Brian Philcox, M.S.M., Toronto, Ont.
Owen Maxwell Rees, M.S.M., Toronto, Ont.
Véronique Rivest, M.S.M., Gatineau, Que.
Louise Russo, M.S.M., Toronto, Ont.
Tom Sampson, M.S.M., Chestermere, Alta.
Kimberley D. Sutherland, M.S.M., Regina, Sask.
Lloyd Allan Swick, M.S.M., Ottawa, Ont.
Jowi Taylor, M.S.M., Toronto, Ont.
Rebecca Veevee, M.S.M., Iqaluit, NU and Saint-Étienne-de-Lauzon, Que.
Grégoire Charles Webber, M.S.M., Ottawa, Ont.
Ruslana A. Wrzesnewskyj, M.S.M., Toronto, Ont.

GENERAL SERVICE AWARDS

Rather than creating a new honour for each new Canadian Forces operation as it arises, in July of 2004, Her Majesty the Queen approved the creation of the following:

The General Campaign Star (G.C.S.) recognizes military service in a theatre of operations in the presence of an armed enemy.

The General Service Medal (G.S.M.) acknowledges civilian and military service in direct support of operations in the presence of an armed enemy.

General Campaign Star/Étoile de campagne générale (G.C.S.)
None awarded since last edition.

General Service Medal/Médaille du service général (G.S.M.)
None awarded since last edition.

British & Commonwealth Honours

In earlier times Canadians could receive hereditary titles, knighthoods and other such honours under the British system of honours, and this is still the case with Canadians who pursue careers in the United Kingdom. Furthermore, the Canadian military system of decorations was based on the British system and many Canadians hold British honours as a result of service in Canadian, British or other Commonwealth forces. While Canada has developed its own honours system, honours are still from time to time granted by the Sovereign to Canadians for, among other things, service to the Commonwealth.

VICTORIA CROSS (V.C.)

The Victoria Cross was founded by Queen Victoria at the close of the Crimean War in 1856, but made retroactive to 1854. It is described as a Maltese cross, made of gun metal, with a Royal Crest in the centre and underneath it an escroll bearing the inscription "For Valour". It is awarded, irrespective of rank, to members of any branch of Her Majesty's services, either in the British Forces or those of any Commonwealth realm, dominion, colony or dependency, the Mercantile Marine, nurses or staffs of hospitals, or to civilians of either sex while serving in either regular or temporary capacity during naval, military, or air force operations. It is awarded only "for most conspicuous bravery or some daring or pre-eminent act of valour or self-sacrifice or extreme devotion to duty in the presence of the enemy." For additional conduct of similar bravery, a Bar is added. The ribbon was formerly red for the Army and blue for the Navy, but it is now red (a dull crimson) for all services. Since June 17th, 1943, the financial responsibility for a stipend to Canadian recipients has been assumed by the Canadian Government. Ninety-six V.C.s have been awarded to Canadians or to foreigners serving in Canadian forces. There are no living Canadian recipients of the Victoria Cross.

GEORGE CROSS (G.C.)

King George VI instituted the George Cross for civilians and members of the services alike, male or female, who performed "acts of the greatest heroism or of the most conspicuous courage in circumstances of extreme danger." This decoration - the second highest Commonwealth award for bravery - is a plain silver cross bearing in the centre a representation of Saint George slaying the dragon and the words: "For Gallantry". The ribbon is garter blue. Eleven Canadians, and a Bermudian serving in the Canadian Forces, have won the G.C. Not all were members of the armed forces. There are no living Canadian recipients of the George Cross.

ALBERT MEDAL (A.M.)

Ernest Alfred Wooding, A.M., R.C.N.V.R. Queen Elizabeth II requested that all living Albert Medal recipients convert their Albert Medal to a George Cross. For some reason Mr. Wooding did not convert his Albert Medal.

ROYAL HONOURS (COMMONWEALTH)

The Order of Baronets, the lowest Hereditary rank, was instituted in 1611; a Baronet is designated "Sir John Smith, Baronet." The abbreviation Bt. is used in Court Circulars and has been generally adopted in lieu of "Bart." Taking precedence to Baronets are members of The Most Honourable Privy Council, who are addressed "Right Honourable."

The Most Noble Order of the Garter, instituted 1349. - K.G.

The Most Ancient and Most Noble Order of the Thistle, instituted 1687. - K.T.

The Most Honourable Order of the Bath, instituted in 1399, and revived in 1725, is divided into three classes - Knights Grand Cross, G.C.B.; Knights Commanders, K.C.B.; and Companions, C.B.

The Order of Merit, O.M., carries no title.

The Most Distinguished Order of St. Michael and St. George, instituted in 1818, has three classes - Knights Grand Cross, G.C.M.G.; Knights Commanders, K.C.M.G.; Companions, C.M.G.

The Most Eminent Order of the Indian Empire instituted 1877, has three classes - Knights Grand Commanders, G.C.I.E.; Knights Commanders, K.C.I.E.; Companions, C.I.E. (This Order has not been conferred since 1947.)

The Royal Victorian Order, instituted in 1896, has five classes - Knights Grand Cross, G.C.V.O.; Knights Commanders, K.C.V.O.; Commanders, C.V.O., Lieutenants, L.V.O.; Members 4th and 5th classes - M.V.O. Ribbon, blue with red and white edges.

The Most Excellent Order of the British Empire, instituted in 1917, has five classes - Knights (or Dames) Grand Cross, G.B.E.; Knights Commanders, K.B.E.; Dames Commanders, D.B.E.; Commanders, C.B.E.; Officers, O.B.E.; and Members, M.B.E. Ribbon (Military) rose pink, pearl grey edging, vertical pearl stripe in centre; (Civil) rose pink, pearl grey edging, and no central vertical stripe.

Knights Bachelors are gentlemen unconnected with any order who have received the honour of Knighthood, and are entitled to the prefix "Sir". They rank immediately after Knights Commanders of the British Empire.

The Companions of Honour, C.H., instituted in 1917 rank immediately after Knights (Dames) Grand Cross of the Order of the British Empire. Membership is limited and carries no title.

In all Orders of Knighthood the Knights Grand Cross and the Knights Commanders have the prefix "Sir" with the initials of their class following the name. Companions and Members bear no title, but have the letters C.B., C.M.G., L.V.O., M.V.O., as the case may be, attached to their names.

The Garter, the Thistle, The Order of Merit and the Royal Victorian Order are all in the personal bestowal of the Sovereign. Appointments to the other Orders are made by Her Majesty on recommendation of the Prime Ministers of Commonwealth countries who wish to secure such appointments. Premiers of individual Australian states may also make recommendations.

MARQUESS

The Most Hon. the Marquess of Exeter, Michael Anthony Cecil, 8th Marquess

The Most Hon. the Marquess of Ely, Charles John Tottenham, 9th Marquess

EARLS

The Right Hon. the Earl Grey, Philip Kent Grey, 7th Earl

The Right Hon. the Earl of Orkney, Peter St. John, 9th Earl

The Right Hon. the Earl Winterton, Donald David Turnour, 8th Earl

VISCOUNTS

The Right Hon. the Viscount Charlemont, John Dodd Caulfield, 15th Viscount

The Right Hon. the Viscount Galway, L.Cdr. George Rupert Monckton, R.C.N. (Ret'd), 12th Viscount

The Right Hon. the Viscount Hardings, Thomas Henry de Montarville Hardings, 8th Viscount

OLD CANADIAN TITLE

The title of Baron de Longueuil existed prior to the Treaty of Paris (1763), and was duly recognized by Queen Victoria pursuant to that treaty.

BARONS

The Right Hon. the Lord Beaverbrook, Maxwell William Henry Aitken, 3rd Baron and 3rd Baronet

The Right Hon. the Lord Brain, Michael Cottrell Brain, 3rd Baron

The Right Hon. the Lord Cullen of Ashbourne, Edmund Willoughby Marsham Cokayne, 3rd Baron

The Right Hon. the Lord Lucas of Chilworth, Simon William Lucas, 3rd Baron

The Right Hon. the Lord Martonmere, John Stephen Robinson, 2nd Baron

The Right Hon. the Lord Morris, Thomas Anthony Salmon Morris, 4th Baron

The Right Hon. the Lord Rodney, John George Brydges Rodney, 11th Baron and 11th Baronet

The Right Hon. the Lord Sanford, James John Mowbray Edmonton Sanford, 3rd Baron

The Right Hon. the Lord Shaughnessy, Charles George Patrick Shaughnessy, 5th Baron

The Right Hon. the Lord Strathcona and Mount Royal, Hon. Col. Donald Euan Palmer Howard, 4th Baron

The Right Hon. the Lord Thomson of Fleet David Kenneth Roy Thomson, 3rd Baron

The Right Hon. the Lord Wasserman, Jordon Joshua Wasserman, Life Baron.

BARONETS

Sir Richard Aylmer (16th Bt.)
Sir Christopher Hilaro Barlow (7th Bt.)
Sir James Barlow (4th Bt.)
Sir Benjamin Barrington (8th Bt.)
Sir James Bates (7th Bt)
Sir John Irving Bell, (1st Bt.)
Sir Alexander Boyd (3rd Bt.)
Sir Theodore Brinckman (6th Bt.)
Sir James Brunton (4th Bt.)
Sir Peter Burbidge (6th Bt.)
Sir Richard Butler (4th Bt.)
Sir Robert Cave-Brown-Cave (16th Bt.)
Sir Bruce Chaytor (9th Bt.)
Sir Peter Chetwynd (10th Bt.)
Sir John Davis (3rd Bt.)
Sir David Hart Dyke (10th Bt.)
The Revd. Sir Christopher Gibson, Bt., C.P. (4th Bt.)
Sir James Grant-Suttie (9th Bt.)
Sir Philip Grotrian (3rd Bt.)
Sir Charles Gunning C.D., (8th Bt.)
Sir Wayne King (8th Bt,)
Sir Charles Knowles (7th Bt.)
Sir Colpoys Johnson (8th Bt.)
Sir Peter Lambert (10th Bt.)
Sir Richard Latham (3rd Bt.)
Sir John Leeds (9th Bt.)
Sir Ian McGregor (8th Bt.)
Sir Roderick McQuhae MacKenzie (12th Bt.)
Sir Allan Morris (11th Bt.)
Sir Christopher Oakes (3rd Bt.)
Sir Mathew Philipson-Stow (6th Bt.)
Sir James Piers (11 Bt.)
Sir Francis Price, Bt. (7th Bt.)
Sir Christopher Robinson (8th Bt.)
Sir John James Michael Laud Robinson (11th Bt.)
Sir Julian Rose (5th Bt.)
Sir James Rugge-Price (10th Bt.)
Sir John Samuel (5th Bt.)
Sir Adrian Sharp (4th Bt.)
Sir Stephen Simeon (9th Bt.)
The Rev. Sir Michael Stonhouse (19th Bt.)
Sir Adrian Stott (4th Bt.)
Sir John Stracey (9th Bt.)
Sir Philip Stuart (9th Bt.)
Sir Richard Sullivan (9th Bt.)
Sir Allen Synge (9th Bt.)
Sir Rodney Touche (2nd Bt.)
Sir Charles Hibbert Tupper (6th Bt.)
Sir Gerald Walsham (6th Bt.)
Sir Ralph Wedgwood (4th Bt.)
Sir Christopher Wells, M.D. (3rd Bt.)
Sir Donald Williams (10th Bt.)

Knight Grand Cross of the Most Honourable Order of the Bath (G.C.B.)

Air Chief Marshal Sir David Evans, G.C.B., C.B.E.

The Order of Merit (O.M.)

The Right Honourable Jean Chrétien, PC, OM, CC.

Knight Grand Cross or Dame Grand Cross of the Most Excellent Order of the British Empire (G.B.E.)

Member of the Order of the Companions of Honour (C.H.)

General John de Chastelaine, C.C., C.M.M., C.H., C.D.

Knight Commander of the Most Distinguished Order of St. Michael and St. George (K.C.M.G.)

Knight Commander of the Royal Victorian Order (K.C.V.O.)

Sir Conrad Swan, K.C.V.O.

Knight Commander of the Most Excellent Order of the British Empire (K.B.E.)

Knight Commander or Dame Commander of the Most Excellent Order of the British Empire (K.B.E. or D.B.E.)

Dame Clara Furse, D.B.E.

KNIGHT BACHELOR

Sir George Bain
Sir Graham Day
Sir John Reginald Gorman, C.V.O., C.B.E., M.C
Sir Terence Matthews, O.B.E.
Sir Christopher Ondaatje, C.B.E.
Sir Neil Shaw

Companion of the Most Honourable Order of the Bath (C.B.)

Air Vice-Marshal George Brookes, C.B., O.B.E.

Companion of the Most Distinguished Order of St. Michael and St. George (C.M.G.)

Laurent Robert Beaudoin, C.M.G.
H.J. Carmichael, C.M.G.
Edmond Cloutier, C.M.G., B.A., L.Ph.
Donovan Bartley Finn, C.M.G., M.Sc., Ph.D., F.R.S.C., F.C.I.C.
George H. McIvor, C.M.G.
Hector Brown McKinnon, C.C., C.M.G.
William Andrew O'Neil, C.M.G.
Alexander Ross, C.M.G.
Joseph Emile St. Laurent, C.M.G.
Ivor Otterbein Smith, C.M.G., O.B.E.

Companion of the Most Eminent Order of the Indian Empire (C.I.E.)

Maj. Frederick Wernham Gerrard, C.I.E.
Capt. John Ryland, C.I.E., R.C.N.
Maj. Frederick Augustus Berrill Sheppard, C.I.E., O.B.E.

Commander of the Royal Victorian Order (C.V.O.)

Leopold Henry Amyot, C.V.O.

Dr. Michael Jackson, C.V.O., C.D.
The Hon. David C. Lam, C.V.O., C.M., K.St.J., O.B.C., B.A.(Econ.), M.B.A., L.L.D., D.Mil.Sc., D.H.L., D.H.
Veronica Jane Langton, C.V.O.
Judith A. LaRocque, C.V.O.
Kevin Stewart MacLeod, C.V.O.
Cdr. G.J. Manson, C.V.O., C.D., R.C.N.
John Crosbie Perlin, C.V.O.
Peter Michael Pitfield, C.V.O., P.C., Q.C.
L.Cdr. Lawrence James Wallace, C.V.O., O.C., O.B.C., R.C.N.V.R.
The Honourable Hilary Mary Weston, C.M., C.V.O., O.On.t

Commander of the Order of the British Empire (C.B.E.)
William Eric Adams, C.B.E.
James Pomeroy Anderson, C.B.E.
George Herbert Bowler, C.B.E.
Garrett Brownrigg, C.B.E.
John Burke, C.B.E.
Alfred Charpentier, C.B.E.
Howard Brown Chase, C.B.E.
Brig. Frederick Graham Coleman, C.B.E.
Air Commodore Barbara Cooper, C.B.E., R.A.F.
Conrad Trelawny Fitz-Gerald, C.B.E., M.D.
Charles Gavsie, C.B.E., Q.C.
Gerald Godsoe, C.B.E., Q.C.
Joseph Ernest Gregoire, C.B.E.
Frank Sydney Grisdale, C.B.E.
Raymond Gushue, O.C., C.B.E., Q.C.
Wallace Bruce Haughan, C.B.E.
Brig. Robert James Henderson, C.B.E.
Harold Ferguson Hodgson, C.B.E.
Sandra Horley, C.B.E.
Capt. Francis Deschamps Howie, C.B.E., D.S.O., R.N.
Alexander George Irvine, C.B.E.
Lester Millman Keachie, C.B.E., Q.C.
Capt. Thomas Douglas Kelly, C.B.E., R.C.N.R.
Allan Collingwood Travers Lewis, C.B.E., Q.C.
Col. Edward Raymond Lewis, C.B.E.
Wilfrid Bennett Lewis, C.O., C.B.E., Ph.D
Gordon Clapp Lindsay, C.B.E.
John Struthers McNeil, C.B.E.
E.J. Mackie, C.B.E.
Raymond Charles Manning, C.B.E.
Walter Melvill Marshall, C.B.E.
James Matson, C.B.E.
Colin Matthews, C.B.E.
Ronald Henry Moray Mavor, C.B.E.
Air Vice-Marshal Walter Alyn Orr, C.B.E., C.D., R.C.A.F.
Luke William Pearsall, C.B.E.
Cyril Horace Frederick Pierrepont, C.B.E., E.D.
James Joseph Alexander Ross, C.B.E., C.D.
T.H. Savage, C.B.E.
Lynn Seymour, C.B.E.
Air Vice-Marshal Douglas McCully Smith, C.B.E., C.D.
Brig. Gerald Lucian Morgan Smith, C.B.E., C.D.
George Spence, C.B.E., LL.D.
William Leonard O'Brien Stallard, C.B.E.
Basil Otto Stevenson, C.B.E.
Air Cdre. Stanley Gibson Tackaberry, C.B.E.
Kenneth Wiffin Taylor, O.C., C.B.E.
George Gamlin Thomas, C.B.E.
Lyman Trumbull, C.B.E.
Henry Wrong, C.B.E.

IMPERIAL SERVICE ORDER (I.S.0.)
George Clayton Anderson
Robert Albert Andison
Arthur Barnstead
Avila Bedard
Peter Cooligan
Henri Fortier
Frank Henry French
Arthur Leigh Jolliffe
Edward Jost
Louis MacMillan
Walter Clifton Ronson
David John Scott
Ivan Vallee

ROYAL VICTORIAN CHAIN
Bestows no precedence; currently not held by anyone.

QUEEN ELIZABETH II'S DIAMOND JUBILEE MEDAL
**The Diamond Jubilee Medal program closed on February 28, 2013.*

Order of Precedence for Orders, Decorations and Medals

The following is the approved order of prededence as of April 2, 1998. The asterisk indicates honours added since that date.

SEQUENCE 1
1. The sequence for wearing the insignia of Canadian orders, decorations and medals, and the post-nominal letters associated with such orders, decorations and medals are the following:
Victoria Cross (V.C.)
Cross of Valour (C.V.)

NATIONAL ORDERS
Companion of the Order of Canada (C.C.)
Officer of the Order of Canada (O.C.)
Member of the Order of Canada (C.M.)
Commander of the Order of Military Merit (C.M.M.)
*Commander of the Order of Merit of the Police Forces (C.O.M.)
Commander of the Royal Victorian Order (C.V.O.)
Officer of the Order of Military Merit (O.M.M.)
*Officer of the Order of Merit of the Police Forces (O.O.M.)
Lieutenant of the Royal Victorian Order (L.V.O.)
Member of the Order of Military Merit (M.M.M.)
*Member of the Order of Merit of the Police Forces (M.O.M.)
Member of the Royal Victorian Order (M.V.O.)
The Most Venerable Order of the Hospital of St. John of Jerusalem (all grades) (post-nominal letters only for internal use by the Order of St. John)

PROVINCIAL ORDERS
*Ordre national du Québec (G.O.Q., O.Q., C.Q.)
Saskatchewan Order of Merit (S.O.M.)
Order of Ontario (O.Ont.)
Order of British Columbia (O.B.C.)
Alberta Order of Excellence (A.O.E.)
Order of Prince Edward Island (O.P.E.I.)
Order of Manitoba (O.M.)
Order of New Brunswick (O.N.B.)
Order of Nova Scotia (O.N.S.)
Order of Newfoundland & Labrador (O.N.L.)

DECORATIONS
Star of Military Valour (S.M.V.)
Star of Courage (S.C.)
Meritorious Service Cross (M.S.C.)
Medal of Military Valour (M.M.V.)
Medal of Bravery (M.B.)
Meritorious Service Medal (M.S.M.)
Royal Victorian Medal (R.V.M.)

MEDALS
*Sacrifice Medal (S.M.)

WAR AND OPERATIONAL SERVICE MEDALS
Korea Medal
Canadian Volunteer Service Medal for Korea
Gulf and Kuwait Medal
Somalia Medal
*South-West Asia Service Medal
*General Campaign Star
*General Service Medal
*Operational Service Medal

SPECIAL SERVICE MEDALS (S.S.M.)
S.S.M. with bars for:
Pakistan (1989-1990)
Alert
Humanitas
NATO/OTAN
Peace/Paix
*Ranger
*Expedition
*Canadian Peacekeeping Service Medal (C.P.S.M.)

UNITED NATIONS MEDALS
Service (Korea) (1950-1954)
Emergency Force (Egypt/Sinai) (1956-67)
Truce Supervision Organization in Palestine (1948-) and Observer Group in Lebanon (1958)
Military Observation Group in India and Pakistan (1948-)
Operation in Congo (1960-64)
Temporary Executive Authority in West New Guinea (1962-63)
Yemen Observation Mission (1963-64)
Force in Cyprus (1964-)
India/Pakistan Observation Misison (1965-66)
Emergency Force Middle East (1973-79)
Disengagement Observation Force Golan Heights (1974-)
Interim Force in Lebanon (1978-)
Military Observation Group in Iran/Iraq (1988-91)
Transition Assistance Group (Namibia) (1989-90)
Observer Group in Central America (1989-92)
Iraq/Kuwait Observer Mission (1991-)
Angola Verification Mission (1988-97)
Mission for the Referendum in Western Sahara (1991-)
Observer Mission in El Salvador (1991-95)
Protection Force (Yugoslavia) (1992-95)
Advance Mission in Cambodia (1991-92)
Transitional Authority in Cambodia (1992-93)
Operation in Somalia (1992-93)
Operation in Mozambique (1992-94)
Observation Mission in Uganda/Rwanda (1993-94)
Assistance Mission in Rwanda (1993-96)
Mission in Haïti (1993-)
Verification of Human Rights and Compliance with the Comprehensive Agreement on Human Rights in Guatemala (1997-98)
*Mission in the Central African Republic (1998-2000)
*Preventive Deployment Force (Macedonia) (1995- 99)
*Mission in Bosnia and Herzegovina (1995-)
*Mission of Observers in Prevlaka (Croatia) (1996-)
*Interim Administration Mission in Kosovo (1999-)
*Observer Mission in Sierra Leone (1999-)
*Mission in East Timor and Transitional Administration in East Timor (1999-)
*Mission in the Democratic Republic of the Congo (1999-)
*Mission in Ethiopia and Eritrea (2000-)
*Stabilization Mission in Haiti (2004-)
*Operation in Côte D'Ivoire (2004-)
*Mission in Sudan (2005-)
*Integrated Mission in Timor-Leste (2006-)
*Hybrid Mission with the African Union in Darfur (2007-)
*Mission in the Republic of South Sudan
Special Service (1995-)
*Headquarters

NATO MEDALS
*North Atlantic Treaty Organization (NATO) Medal for the Former Yugoslavia (1992-2002)
*NATO Medal for Kosovo (1999-)
*NATO Medal for the Former Yugoslav Republic of Macedonia (2001-02)
*Article 5 NATO Medal for Operation "Eagle Assist" (2001-02)
*Article 5 NATO Medal for Operation "Active Endeavour" (2001-)
*Non-Article 5 NATO Medal for Operations in the Balkans (2003-)
*Non-Article 5 NATO Medal for the NATO Training Mission in Iraq (2004-)
*Non-Article 5 NATO Medal for NATO Logistical Support to the African Union Mission in Sudan (2005-)
*Non-Article 5 NATO Medal for service on operations and activities approved by the North Atlantic Council in relation to Africa (2008-)
*Non-Article 5 NATO Medal for Service on NATO Operation "Unified Protector - Libya" (2011-)

INTERNATIONAL MISSION MEDALS
International Commission for Supervision and Control (Indo-China) (1954-74)
International Commission for Control and Supervision (Vietnam) (1973)
Multinational Force and Observers (Sinai) (1982-)
European Community Monitor Mission (Yugoslavia) (1991-)
*International Force East Timor (1999-)
*European Security and Defence Policy Service Medal

COMMEMORATIVE MEDALS
Canadian Centennial Medal (1967)
Queen Elizabeth II's Silver Jubilee Medal (1977)
125th Anniversary of the Confederation of Canada Medal (1992)
*Queen Elizabeth II's Golden Jubilee Medal (2002)
*Queen Elizabeth II's Diamond Jubilee Medal (2012)

LONG SERVICE AND GOOD CONDUCT MEDALS
R.C.M.P. Long Service Medal
Canadian Forces Decoration (C.D.)

EXEMPLARY SERVICE MEDALS
Police Exemplary Service Medal
Corrections Exemplary Service Medal
Fire Services Exemplary Service Medal
Canadian Coast Guard Exemplary Service Medal
Emergency Medical Services Exemplary Service Medal
*Peace Officer Exemplary Service Medal

SPECIAL MEDAL
Queen's Medal for Champion Shot

OTHER DECORATIONS AND MEDALS
Ontario Medal for Good Citizenship (O.M.C.)
Ontario Medal for Police Bravery

Ontario Medal for Firefighters Bravery
Saskatchewan Volunteer Medal (S.V.M.)
Ontario Provincial Police Long Service and Good Conduct Medal
Service Medal of the Most Venerable Order of the Hospital of St. John of Jerusalem
Commissionaire Long Service Medal
*Newfoundland and Labrador Bravery Award
*Newfoundland and Labrador Volunteer Service Medal
*British Columbia Fire Services Long Service and Bravery Medals
*Commemorative Medal for the Centennial of Saskatchewan
*Alberta Centennial Medal

2. The Bar to the Special Service Medal is worn centred on the ribbon. If there is more than one Bar, they are spaced evenly on the ribbon with the most recent uppermost.

3. Commonwealth orders, decorations and medals, the award of which is approved by the Government of Canada, are worn after Canadian orders, decorations and medals listed in Section 1, the precedence in each category being set by the date of appointment or award.

4. Foreign orders, decorations and medals, the award of which is approved by the Government of Canada, are worn after those referred to in Sections 1 and 3, the precedence in each category being set by the date of appointment or award.

5. Notwithstanding Sections 1, 3 and 4, a person who, **prior to 1 June, 1972,** was a member of a British Order or the recipient of a British decoration or medal referred to in this section, may wear the insignia of the decoration or medal together with the insignia of any Canadian order, decoration or medal that the person is entitled to wear, the proper sequence being the following:
Victoria Cross (V.C.)
George Cross (G.C.)
Cross of Valour (C.V.)
Order of Merit (O.M.)
Order of the Companions of Honour (C.H.)
Companion of the Order of Canada (C.C.)
Officer of the Order of Canada (O.C.)
Member of the Order of Canada (C.M.)
Commander of the Order of Military Merit (C.M.M.)
*Commander of the Order of Merit of the Police Forces (C.O.M.)
Companion of the Order of the Bath (C.B.)
Companion of the Order of St. Michael and St. George (C.M.G.)
Commander of the Royal Victorian Order (C.V.O.)
Commander of the Order of the British Empire (C.B.E.)
Distinguished Service Order (D.S.O.)
Officer of the Order of Military Merit (O.M.M.)
*Officer of the Order of Merit of the Police Force (O.O.M.)
Lieutenant of the Royal Victorian Order (L.V.O.)
Officer of the Order of the British Empire (O.B.E.)
Imperial Service Order (I.S.O.)
Member of the Order of Military Merit (M.M.M.)
*Member of the Order of the Police Forces (M.O.M.)
Member of the Royal Victorian Order (M.V.O.)
Member of the Order of the British Empire (M.B.E.)
Member of the Royal Red Cross (R.R.C.)
Distinguished Service Cross (D.S.C.)
Military Cross (M.C.)
Distinguished Flying Cross (D.F.C.)
Air Force Cross (A.F.C.)
Star of Military Valour (S.M.V.)
Star of Courage (S.C.)
Meritorious Service Cross (M.S.C.)
Medal of Military Valour (M.M.V.)
Medal of Bravery (M.B.)
Meritorious Service Medal (M.S.M.)
Associate of the Royal Red Cross (A.R.R.C.)
The Most Venerable Order of St. John of Jerusalem (all grades) (post-nominal letters only for internal use by the Order of St. John)
Provincial Orders (order of precedence as set out in Section 1)
Distinguished Conduct Medal (D.C.M.)
Conspicuous Gallantry Medal (C.G.M.)
George Medal (G.M.)
Distinguished Service Medal (D.S.M.)
Military Medal (M.M.)
Distinguished Flying Medal (D.F.M.)
Air Force Medal (A.F.M.)
Queen's Gallantry Medal (Q.G.M.)
Royal Victorian Medal (R.V.M.)
British Empire Medal (B.E.M.)

WAR AND OPERATIONAL SERVICE MEDALS

Africa General Service Medal (1902-1956)
India General Service Medal (1908-1935)
Naval General Service Medal (1915-1962)
India General Service Medal (1936-39)
General Service Medal - Army and Air Force (1918- 1962)
General Service Medal (1962-)
1914 Star
1914-15 Star
British War Medal (1914-18)
Mercantile Marine War Medal (1914-18)
Victory Medal (1914-18)
Territorial Force War Medal (1914-19)
1939-45 Star
Atlantic Star
Air Crew Europe Star
Africa Star
Pacific Star
Burma Star
Italy Star
France and Germany Star
Defence Medal
Canadian Volunteer Service Medal
Newfoundland Second World War Volunteer Service Medal (see Section 6)
War Medal (1939-45)
Korea Medal
Canadian Volunteer Service Medal for Korea
Gulf and Kuwait Medal Somalia Medal
*South-West Asia Service Medal
*General Campaign Medal
*General Service Medal

SPECIAL SERVICE MEDALS

(The order of precedence is as set out for Special Service Medals in Section 1.)

UNITED NATIONS MEDALS

(The order of precedence is as set out for United Nations Medals in Section 1.)

INTERNATIONAL COMMISSION AND ORGANIZATION MEDALS

(The order of precedence is as set out for International Commission and Organization Medals in Section 1.)

POLAR AND VOLUNTEER MEDALS

(The order of precedence is by order of date awarded.)

COMMEMORATIVE MEDALS

King George V's Silver Jubilee Medal (1935)
King George VI's Coronation Medal (1937)
Queen Elizabeth II's Coronation Medal (1953)
Canadian Centennial Medal (1967)
Queen Elizabeth II's Silver Jubilee Medal (1977)
125th Anniversary of the Confederation of Canada Medal (1992)
*Queen Elizabeth II's Golden Jubilee Medal (2002)
*Queen Elizabeth II's Diamond Jubilee Medal (2012)

LONG SERVICE AND GOOD CONDUCT MEDALS

Army Long Service and Good Conduct Medal
Naval Long Service and Good Conduct Medal
Air Force Long Service and Good Conduct Medal
RCMP Long Service Medal
Canadian Forces Decoration (C.D.)
Volunteer Officer's Decoration (V.D.)
Volunteer Long Service Medal
Colonial Auxiliary Forces Officer's Decoration (V.D.)
Colonial Auxiliary Forces Long Service Medal
Efficiency Decoration (E.D.)
Efficiency Medal
Naval Volunteer Reserve Decoration (V.R.D.)
Naval Volunteer Reserve Long Service and Good Conduct Medal
Air Efficiency Award Canadian Forces Decoration (C.D.)

EXEMPLARY SERVICE MEDALS

(The order of precedence is as set out for Exemplary Service Medals in Section 1.)

SPECIAL MEDAL

Queen's Medal for Champion Shot

OTHER DECORATIONS AND MEDALS

(The order of precedence is as set out for Other Decorations and Medals in Section 1.)

6. The Newfoundland Volunteer War Service Medal has the same precedence as the Canadian Volunteer Service Medal.

7. The insignia of orders, decorations and medals not listed above, as well as foreign awards, the award of which has not been approved by the Government of Canada, shall not be mounted or worn in conjunction with orders, decorations and medals listed above.

8. The insignia of orders, decorations and medals shall not be worn by anyone other than the recipient of the orders, decorations or medals.

NOTE: Policy regarding the wearing on non-authorized awards Only the insignia of orders, decorations and medals officially awarded under the authority of the Crown or that the wearing of which has been authorized by the Crown may be worn. Only the actual recipient of an honour can wear its insignia; no family member or any person other than the original recipient may wear the insignia of an order, decoration or medal. Insignia that are purchased or otherwise acquired may be used for display purpose only and cannot be worn on the person in any form or manner.

Abbreviations Indicating Honours and Decorations

A.F.C. - Air Force Cross. Ribbon, wide diagonal stripes of white and red.
A.F.M. - Air Force Medal. Ribbon, narrow diagonal stripes of white and red.
A.M. - Albert Medal, gold (Sea). Ribbon, nine alternate narrow stripes of blue and white.
Albert Medal, gold (Land). Ribbon, nine alternate narrow stripes of red and white.
Albert Medal, bronze (Sea). Ribbon, blue ground with two wide stripes of white.
Albert Medal, bronze (Land). Ribbon, red ground with two wide stripes of white.
B.E.M. - British Empire Medal.
Bt. - Baronet
C.B. - Companion of the Most Honourable Order of the Bath.
C.B.E. - Commander of the Order of the British Empire.
C.C. - Companion of the Order of Canada.
C.D. - Canadian Forces Decoration.
C.G.M. - Conspicuous Gallantry Medal; Navy and Air Force. It carries a cash grant. The Navy Medal ribbon is white with dark blue edges; the Air Force ribbon is light blue with dark blue edges.
C.H. - Member of the Order of the Companions of Honour.
C.I.E. - Companion of the Most Eminent Order of the Indian Empire.
C.M. - Member of the Order of Canada.
C.M.G. - Companion of the Most Distinguished Order of St. Michael and St. George.
C.M.M. - Commander of the Order of Military Merit.
C.P.S.M. - Canadian Peacekeeping Service Medal.
C.S.I. - Companion of the Most Exalted Order of the Star of India.
C.V. - Cross of Valour.
C.V.O. - Commander of the Royal Victorian Order.
D.C.M. - Distinguished Conduct Medal. Ribbon, red ground, dark blue stripe in centre.
D.F.C. - Distinguished Flying Cross. Ribbon, wide diagonal stripes of violet and white.
D.F.M. - Distinguished Flying Medal. Ribbon, narrow diagonal stripes of white and violet.
D.S.C. - Distinguished Service Cross. Ribbon, three broad bands, dark blue, white, dark blue.
D.S.M. - Distinguished Service Medal.
D.S.O. - Companion of the Distinguished Service Order. Instituted 1886. Ribbon, dark red with dark blue stripe at each end.
E.D. - Canadian Efficiency Decoration for Officers of Military Auxiliary Forces.
E.M. - Edward Medal. Posthumous award.
E.M. - Efficiency Medal.
G.B.E. - Knight Grand Cross or Dame Grand Cross of the Most Excellent Order of the British Empire.
G.C. - George Cross.
G.C.B. - Knight Grand Cross of the Most Honourable Order of the Bath.
G.C.I.E. - Knight Grand Commander of the Most Eminent Order of the Indian Empire.
G.C.M.G. - Knight Grand Cross of the Most Distinguished Order of St. Michael and St. George.
G.C.S.I. - Knight Grand Commander of the Most Exalted Order of the Star of India.
G.C.V.O. - Knight Grand Cross of the Royal Victorian Order.
G.M. - George Medal.
I.S.M. - Imperial Service Medal.
I.S.O. - Companion of the Imperial Service Order. Instituted 1902.
K.B.E. - Knight Commander of the Most Excellent Order of the British Empire.
K.C.B. - Knight Commander of the Most Honourable Order of the Bath.
K.C.I.E. - Knight Commander of the Most Eminent Order of the Indian Empire.

K.C.M.G. - Knight Commander of the Most Distinguished Order of St. Michael and St. George.
K.C.S.I. - Knight Commander of the Most Exalted Order of the Star of India.
K.C.V.O. - Knight Commander of the Royal Victorian Order.
K.G. - Knight of the Most Noble Order of the Garter.
K.P. - Knight of the Most Illustrious Order of St. Patrick.
Kt. - Knight Bachelor.
K.T. - Knight of the Most Ancient and Most Noble Order of the Thistle.
L.V.O. - Lieutenant of the Royal Victorian Order.
M.B. - Medal of Bravery.
M.B.E. - Member of the Order of the British Empire.
M.C. - Military Cross. Instituted 1915. Ribbon, white with broad band of blue in centre.
M. du C. - Canada Medal.
M.M. - Military Medal.
M.M.M. - Member of the Order of Military Merit.
M.V.O. - Member of the Royal Victorian Order.
M.S.C. - Meritorous Service Cross.
M.S.M. - Meritorious Service Medal.
O.B.E. - Officer of the Order of the British Empire.
O.C. - Officer of the Order of Canada.
O.M. - Member of the Order of Merit.
O.M.M. - Officer of the Order of Military Merit.
P.C. - Privy Counsellor.
R.R.C. - Royal Red Cross. Instituted 1883. Ribbon, dark blue with narrow band of dark red at each end.
R.V.M. - Royal Victorian Medal.
S.C. - Star of Courage.
S.S.M. - Special Service Medal
U.E. - Unity of Empire. Descendants of United Empire Loyalists.
V.C. - Victoria Cross.
V.D. - Auxiliary Forces (Volunteer) Officers' Decoration.
V.R.D. - Naval Volunteer Reserve Decoration.

Canada's Walk of Fame

Since 1998, Canada's Walk of Fame has helped to celebrate the great depth of talent found in Canadian culture. Here is a list of the inductees honoured by the Walk of Fame, by year.

	2016	2015	2014
	Jeanne Beker Corey Hart Deepa Mehta Jason Priestley Darryl Sittler Al Waxman	Michael Bublé Wendy Crewson Don Cherry & Ron MacLean Lorne Greene Lawrence Hill Silken Laumann	Louise Arbour CC GOQ The Band Jeff Healey Rachel McAdams Ryan Reynolds Hayley Wickenheiser
2013	**2012**	**2011**	**2010**
Bob Ezrin Terry Fox Victor Garber Craig Kielburger Marc Kielburger Oscar Peterson Christine Sinclair Alan Thicke	Team Canada 1972 Randy Bachman Phil Hartman Russ Jackson Sarah McLachlan Sonia Rodriguez	Dr. Roberta Bondar Burton Cummings Daniel Nestor Sandra Oh Russell Peters Mordecai Richler	David Clayton-Thomas Nelly Furtado Doug Henning Clara Hughes Eric McCormack Farley Mowat Sarah Polley
2009	**2008**	**2007**	**2006**
Blue Rodeo Raymond Burr Dan and Dean Caten Kim Cattrall Tom Cochrane Howie Mandel Robert Munsch Chantal Petitclerc	Frances Bay James Cameron Kids in the Hall k.d. lang Steve Nash Douglas Shearer Norma Shearer Daria Werbowy	Johnny Bower Rick Hansen Jill Hennessy Nickelback Catherine O'Hara Gordon Pinsent Lloyd Robertson	Pamela Anderson Jann Arden Crazy Canucks Brendan Fraser Robert Goulet Eugene Levy Paul Shaffer Alex Trebek
2005	**2004**	**2003**	**2002**
Paul Anka George Chuvalo Michael Cohl Pierre Cossette Rex Harrington Daniel Lanois Alanis Morissette Kiefer Sutherland Fay Wray	Denys Arcand Jim Carrey Shirley Douglas John Kay Diana Krall Mario Lemieux Louis B. Mayer Mack Sennett Helen Shaver Jack L. Warner	Scotty Bowman Toller Cranston Jim Elder Linda Evangelista Lynn Johnston Lorne Michaels Mike Myers Luc Plamondon Robbie Robertson David Steinberg Shania Twain	Dan Aykroyd Cirque du Soleil Alex Colville Timothy Findley David Foster Wayne Gretzky Monty Hall Ronnie Hawkins Arthur Hiller Guy Lombardo SCTV The Tragically Hip
2001	**2000**	**1999**	**1998**
Kenojuak Ashevak Margaret Atwood Jean Béliveau Alexander Graham Bell Kurt Browning Ferguson Jenkins Harry Winston Jerome Robert Lepage Leslie Nielsen Walter Ostanek Ivan Reitman Teresa Stratas Veronica Tennant The Guess Who	Maureen Forrester Michael J. Fox Evelyn Hart Gordie Howe William Hutt Joni Mitchell Ginette Reno Jean-Paul Riopelle Royal Canadian Air Farce William Shatner Martin Short Donald Sutherland Neil Young	Juliette Cavazzi David Cronenberg Hume Cronyn Céline Dion Nancy Greene Lou Jacobi Mary Pickford Maurice Richard Rush Buffy Sainte-Marie Wayne and Shuster	Bryan Adams Pierre Berton John Candy Glenn Gould Norman Jewison Karen Kain Gordon Lightfoot Rich Little Anne Murray Bobby Orr Christopher Plummer Barbara Ann Scott Jacques Villeneuve

Government

Table of Precedence for Canada

1. The Governor General of Canada or the Administrator of the Government of Canada. (Notes 1, 1.1, 2 & 2.1).
2. The Prime Minister of Canada. (Note 3).
3. The Chief Justice of Canada. (Note 4).
4. The Speaker of the Senate.
5. The Speaker of the House of Commons.
6. Ambassadors, High Commissioners, Ministers Plenipotentiary. (Note 5).
7. Members of the Canadian Ministry:
   a. Members of the Cabinet; and
   b. Ministers of State; with relative precedence within sub-categories (a) and (b) governed by the date of their appointment to the Queen's Privy Council for Canada.
8. The Leader of the Opposition. (Subject to Note 3).
9. The Lieutenant Governor of Ontario;
   The Lieutenant Governor of Québec;
   The Lieutenant Governor of Nova Scotia;
   The Lieutenant Governor of New Brunswick;
   The Lieutenant Governor of Manitoba;
   The Lieutenant Governor of British Columbia;
   The Lieutenant Governor of Prince Edward Island;
   The Lieutenant Governor of Saskatchewan;
   The Lieutenant Governor of Alberta;
   The Lieutenant Governor of Newfoundland & Labrador (Note 6).
10. Members of the Queen's Privy Council for Canada, not of the Canadian Ministry, in accordance with the date of their appointment to the Privy Council but with precedence given to those who bear the honorary title "Right Honourable" in accordance with the date of receiving the honorary title.
11. Premiers of the Provinces of Canada in the same order as Lieutenant Governors. (Note 6).
12. The Commissioner of the Northwest Territories; The Commissioner of the Yukon Territory; The Commissioner of Nunavut
13. Premiers of the Territories of Canada in the same order as Commissioners. (Note 7).
14. Representatives of faith communities. (Note 8).
15. Puisne Judges of the Supreme Court of Canada.
16. The Chief Justice and the Associate Chief Justice of the Federal Court of Canada.
17. (a) Chief Justices of the highest court of each Province and Territory; and
    (b) Chief Justices and Associate Chief Justices of the other superior courts of the Provinces and Territories; with precedence within sub-categories (a) and (b) governed by the date of appointment as Chief Justice.
18. (a) Judges of the Federal Court of Canada.
    (b) Puisne Judges of the superior courts of the Provinces and Territories.
    (c) the Chief Judge of the Tax Court of Canada;
    (d) the Associate Chief Judge of the Tax Court of Canada; and
    (e) Judges of the Tax Court of Canada; with precedence within each sub-category governed by date of appointment.
19. Senators of Canada.
20. Members of the House of Commons.
21. Consuls General of countries without diplomatic representation.
22. Clerk of the Privy Council and Secretary to Cabinet.
23. The Chief of the Defence Staff and the Commissioner of the Royal Canadian Mounted Police. (Note 9).
24. Speakers of Legislative Assemblies, within their Provinces and Territory.
25. Members of the Executive Councils, within their Province and Territory.
26. Judges of Provincial and Territorial Courts, within their Province and Territory.
27. Members of Legislative Assemblies, within their Province and Territory.
28. Chairperson of the Canadian Association of Former Parliamentarians.

NOTES

1. The presence of the Sovereign in Canada does not impair or supersede the authority of the Governor General to perform the functions delegated to him under the Letters Patent constituting the office of the Governor General. The Governor General, under all circumstances, should be accorded precedence immediately after the Sovereign.

1.1. In the absence of the Governor General of Canada and the Administrator of the Government of Canada, precedence to be given immediately after the Prime Minister of Canada to the Lieutenant Governor of the province in which the ceremony or occasion takes place.

2. Precedence to be given immediately after the Chief Justice of Canada to former Governors General, with relative precedence among them governed by the date of their leaving office.

2.1 Precedence to be given immediately after the former Governors General to surviving spouses of deceased former Governors General (applicable only where the spouse was married to the Governor General during the latter's term of office), with relative precedence among them governed by the dates on which the deceased former Governor General left office.

3. Precedence to be given immediately after the surviving spouses of deceased former Governors General referred to in Note 2.1 to former Prime Ministers, with relative precedence among them governed by the dates of their first assumption of office.

4. Precedence to be given immediately after former Prime Ministers to former Chief Justices of Canada, with relative precedence among them governed by the dates of their appointment as Chief Justice of Canada.

5. Precedence among Ambassadors and High Commissioners, who rank equally, to be determined by the date of the presentation of their credentials. Precedence to be given to Chargés d'Affaires immediately after Ministers Plenipotentiary.

6. This provision does not apply to such ceremonies and occasions which are of a provincial nature.

7. This provision does not apply to such ceremonies and occasions which are of a territorial nature.

8. The religious dignitaries will be senior Canadian representatives of faith communities having a significant presence in a relevant jurisdiction. The relevant precedence of the representatives of faith communities is to be governed by the date of their assumption in their present office, their representatives being given the same relative precedence.

9. This precedence to be given to the Chief of the Defence Staff and the Commissioner of the R.C.M.P. on occasions when they have official functions to perform, otherwise they are to have equal precedence with Deputy Ministers, with their relative position to be determined according to the respective dates of their appointments to office. The relative precedence of Deputy Ministers and other high officials of the public service of Canada is to be determined from time to time by the Minister of Canadian Heritage in consultation with the Prime Minister.

Courtesy of the Department of Canadian Heritage.

http://canada.pch.gc.ca/eng/1452187406834. Reproduced with the permission of the Minister of Canadian Heritage, 2016.

Table of Titles to Be Used in Canada

1. The Governor General of Canada to be styled "Right Honourable" for life and to be styled "His Excellency" and his wife "Her Excellency", or "Her Excellency" and her husband "His Excellency", as the case may be, while in office.
2. The Lieutenant Governor of a Province to be styled "Honourable" for life and to be styled "His Honour" and his wife "Her Honour", or "Her Honour" and her husband "His Honour", as the case may be, while in office.
3. The Prime Minister of Canada to be styled "Right Honourable" for life.
4. The Chief Justice of Canada to be styled "Right Honourable" for life.
5. Privy Councillors of Canada to be styled "Honourable" for life.
6. Senators of Canada to be styled "Honourable" for life.
7. The Speaker of the House of Commons to be styled "Honourable" while in office.
8. The Commissioner of a Territory to be styled "Honourable" while in office.
9. Puisne judges of the Supreme Court of Canada and judges of the Federal Court and of the Tax Court of Canada as well as the judges of the under mentioned Courts in the Provinces and Territories to be styled "Honourable" while in office:

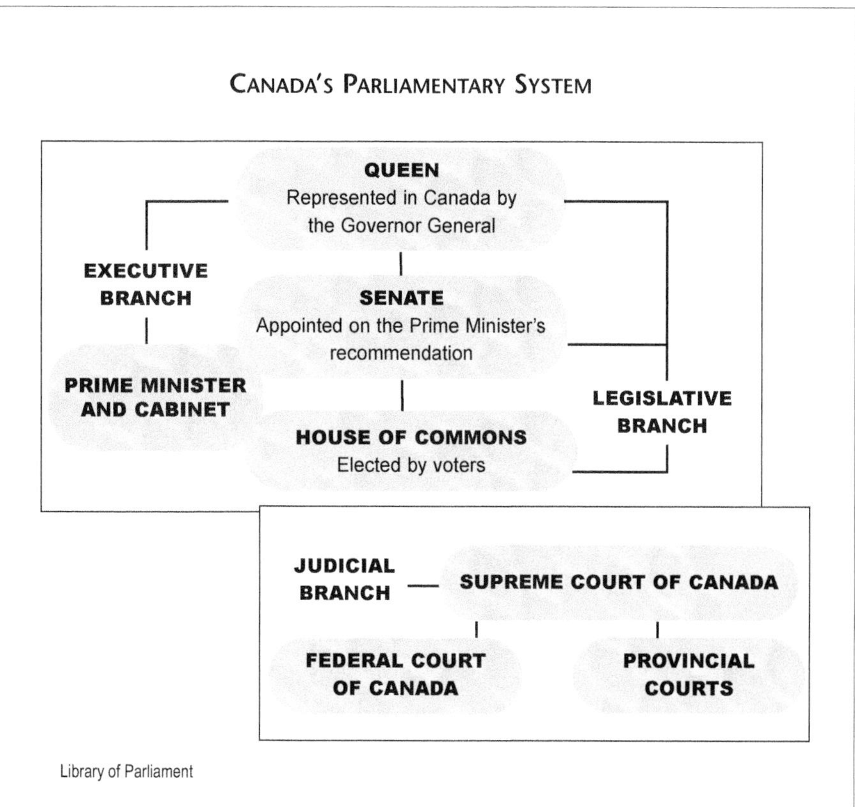

Parliament as a legislative body functions as an instrument of government within a broader structure that includes the Executive Branch and the Judicial Branch. In the Westminster-based model of parliamentary government, the Executive, comprised of the Prime Minister and the Cabinet, is incorporated into Parliament, while retaining a separate sphere of authority and autonomy. The Judiciary, consisting of the Supreme Court and all the other courts of the land, is the third branch of government that is also independent of either Parliament or the Executive.

Ontario - Court of Appeal and the Ontario Court of Justice (General Division)
Québec - The Court of Appeal and the Superior Court of Québec
Nova Scotia - The Court of Appeal and the Supreme Court of Nova Scotia
New Brunswick - The Court of Appeal and the Court of Queen's Bench of New Brunswick
Manitoba - The Court of Appeal and the Court of Queen's Bench of Manitoba
British Columbia - The Court of Appeal and the Supreme Court of British Columbia
Prince Edward Island - The Supreme Court of Prince Edward Island
Saskatchewan - The Court of Appeal and the Court of Queen's Bench of Saskatchewan
Alberta - The Court of Appeal and the Court of Queen's Bench of Alberta
Newfoundland - The Supreme Court of Newfoundland
Northwest Territories - The Supreme Court of Northwest Territories
Yukon Territory - The Supreme Court of Yukon
Nunavut Territory - The Nunavut Court of Justice

10. Presidents and Speakers of the Legislative Assemblies of the Provinces and Territories to be styled "Honourable" while in office.
11. Members of the Executive Councils of the Provinces and Territories to be styled "Honourable" while in office.
12. Judges of Provincial and Territorial Courts (appointed by the Provincial and Territorial Governments) to be styled "Honourable" while in office.
13. The following are eligible to be granted permission by the Governor General, in the name of Her Majesty The Queen, to retain the title of "Honourable" after they have ceased to hold office: (a) Speakers of the House of Commons; (b) Commissioners of Territories; (c) Judges designated in item 9.
14. The title "Right Honourable" is granted for life to the following eminent Canadian: The Right Honourable Donald F. Mazankowski

Courtesy of the Department of Canadian Heritage.

http://canada.pch.gc.ca/eng/1452187406810. Reproduced with the permission of the Minister of Canadian Heritage, 2016.

GOVERNORS GENERAL OF CANADA SINCE CONFEDERATION

(WITH INSTALLATION DATE)

The Viscount Monck,
G.C.M.G.
July 1, 1867

Lord Lisgar,
G.C.M.G.
February 2, 1869

The Earl of Dufferin,
K.P., G.C.B., G.C.S.I., G.C.M.G., G.C.I.E
June 25, 1872

The Marquess of Lorne,
K.T., G.C.M.G., G.C.V.O.
November 25, 1878

The Marquess of Lansdowne,
K.G., G.C.S.I., G.C.M.G., G.C.I.E.
October 23, 1883

Lord Stanley of Preston,
K.G., G.C.B., G.C.V.O.
June 11, 1888

The Earl of Aberdeen,
K.T., G.C.M.G., G.C.V.O.
September 18, 1893

The Earl of Minto,
K.G., G.C.S.I., G.C.M.G., G.C.I.E.
November 12, 1898

The Earl Grey,
G.C.B., G.C.M.G., G.C.V.O.
December 10, 1904

H.R.H. the Duke of Connaught & Strathearn,
K.G., K.T., K.P., G.M.B., G.C.S.I., G.C.M.G., G.C.I.E., G.C.V.O., G.B.E., T.D.
October 13, 1911

The Duke of Devonshire,
K.G., G.C.M.G., G.C.V.O., T.D.
November 11, 1916

General Lord Byng of Vimy,
G.C.B., G.C.M.G., M.V.O.
August 11, 1921

The Viscount Willingdon of Ratton,
G.C.S.I., G.C.M.G., G.C.I.E., G.B.E.
October 2, 1926

The Earl of Bessborough,
G.C.M.G.
April 4, 1931

Lord Tweedsmuir of Elsfield, P.C., G.C.M.G., G.C.V.O., C.H.
Nov. 2, 1935

Major-General the Earl of Athlone, K.G., P.C., G.C.B., G.C.M.G., G.C.V.O., D.S.O.
June 21, 1940

Field Marshal the Rt. Hon. Viscount Alexander of Tunis, K.G., P.C., G.C.B., O.M., G.C.M.G., C.S.I., D.S.O., M.C., D.C.
April 12, 1946

The Rt. Hon. Vincent Massey, P.C., C.C., C.H., C.D.
Feb. 28, 1952

Major-General the Rt. Hon. Georges-P. Vanier, P.C., D.S.O., M.C., C.D.
Sept. 15, 1959

The Rt. Hon. Roland Michener, P.C., C.C., C.M.M., O.Ont., C.D., Q.C.
Apr. 17, 1967

The Rt. Hon. Jules Léger P.C., C.C., C.M.M., C.D.
Jan. 14, 1974

The Rt. Hon. Edward Richard Schreyer, P.C., C.C., C.M.M., O.M., C.D.
Jan. 22, 1979

The Rt. Hon. Jeanne Sauvé, P.C., C.C., C.M.M., C.D.
May 14, 1984

Photo Credit: Yousuf Karsh. Reproduced with the permission of the Estate.

The Rt. Hon. Ramon John Hnatyshyn, P.C., C.C., C.M.M., C.D., Q.C.
Jan. 29, 1990

Photo Credit: Yousuf Karsh. Reproduced with the permission of the Estate.

The Rt. Hon. Roméo LeBlanc, P.C., C.C., C.M.M., O.N.B., C.D.
Feb. 8, 1995

Photo Credit: © House of Commons, 1980

The Rt. Hon. Adrienne Clarkson, P.C., C.C., C.M.M., C.O.M., C.D.
Oct. 7, 1999

Photo Credit: Andrew MacNaughtan
© Her Majesty The Queen in Right of Canada
represented by the
Office of the Secretary to the Governor General
(OSGG), 1999.
Reproduced with permission of the OSGG, 2016.

The Rt. Hon. Michaëlle Jean, P.C., C.C., C.M.M., C.O.M., C.D.
Sept. 27, 2005

Photo Credit: Sgt Eric Jolin, Rideau Hall
© Her Majesty The Queen in Right of Canada
represented by the
Office of the Secretary to the Governor General
(OSGG), 2006.
Reproduced with permission of the OSGG, 2016.

His Excellency the Rt. Hon. David Johnston, C.C., C.M.M., C.O.M., C.D.
Oct. 1, 2010

Photo Credit: Sgt Serge Gouin, Rideau Hall
© Her Majesty The Queen in Right of Canada
represented by the
Office of the Secretary to the Governor General
(OSGG), 2010.
Reproduced with permission of the OSGG, 2016.

CANADIAN PRIME MINISTERS

(WITH PARTY AFFILIATION AND TIME IN OFFICE)

Rt. Hon. Sir John A. Macdonald (Conservative)
July 1, 1867 to Nov. 5, 1873
Oct. 17, 1878 to June 6, 1891
Photo credit: William James Topley/Library and Archives Canada/PA-027013

Hon. Alexander MacKenzie (Liberal)
Nov. 7, 1873 to Oct. 16, 1878
Photo credit: William James Topley/Library and Archives Canada/PA-026308

Hon. Sir John J. Abbott (Conservative)
June 16, 1891 to Nov. 24, 1892
Photo credit: William James Topley/Library and Archives Canada/PA-033933

Rt. Hon. Sir John S. D. Thompson (Conservative)
Dec. 5, 1892 to Dec. 12, 1894
Photo Credit: Library and Archives Canada/C-000698

Hon. Sir Mackenzie Bowell (Conservative)
Dec. 21, 1894 to April 27, 1896
Photo Credit: William James Topley/Library and Archives Canada/PA-027159

Rt. Hon. Sir Charles Tupper (Conservative)
May 1, 1896 to July 8, 1896
Photo Credit: Library and Archives Canada/PA-027743

Rt. Hon. Sir Wilrid Laurier (Liberal)
July 11, 1896 to Oct. 6, 1911
Photo Credit: William James Topley/Library and Archives Canada/C-001971

Rt. Hon. Sir Robert L. Borden
Oct. 10, 1911 to Oct. 12, 1917
(Conservative Administration)
Oct. 12, 1917 to July 10, 1920
(Unionist Administration)
Photo Credit: William James Topley/Library and Archives Canada/PA-028128

Rt. Hon. Arthur Meighen
July 10, 1920 to Dec. 29, 1921
(Unionist "National Liberal and Conservative Party")
June 29, 1926 to Sept. 25, 1926
(Conservative)
Photo Credit: William James Topley/Library and Archives Canada/PA-026987

Rt. Hon. William Lyon Mackenzie King (Liberal)
Dec. 29, 1921 to June 28, 1926
Sept. 25, 1926 to Aug. 6, 1930
Oct. 23, 1935 to Nov. 15, 1948
Photo Credit: Library and Archives Canada/C-027645

Rt. Hon. Richard Bedford Bennett (Conservative) (Became Viscount Bennett, 1941)
Aug. 7, 1930 to Oct. 23, 1935
Photo Credit: Library and Archives Canada/C-000687

Rt. Hon. Louis Stephen St. Laurent (Liberal)
Nov. 15, 1948 to June 21, 1957
Photo Credit: Library and Archives Canada/C-010461

Rt. Hon. John G. Diefenbaker (Progressive Conservative)
June 21, 1957 to April 22, 1963
© Estate of Paul Horsdal
Source: Library and Archives Canada/Credit: Paul Horsdal/The Montreal Star Fonds/PA-130070

Rt. Hon. Lester Bowles Pearson (Liberal)
April 22, 1963 to April 20, 1968
Photo Credit: Ashley and Crippen Studio/Library and Archives Canada/PA-126393

Rt. Hon. Pierre Elliott Trudeau (Liberal)
April 20, 1968 to June 4, 1979
Mar. 3, 1980 to June 30, 1984
© Library and Archives Canada. Reproduced with the permission of Library and Archives Canada.
Photo Credit: Duncan Cameron/Office of the Prime Minister Collection/Library and Archives Canada/C-046600

Rt. Hon. Charles Joseph Clark (Progressive Conservative)
June 4, 1979 to Mar. 3, 1980
Photo Credit: © House of Commons, Ottawa

Rt. Hon. John Napier Turner (Liberal)
June 30, 1984 to Sept. 17, 1984
Photo Credit: With permission of the Liberal Party of Canada

Rt. Hon. Martin Brian Mulroney (Progressive Conservative)
Sept 17, 1984 to June 25, 1993
Photo Credit: Yousuf Karsh. Reproduced with the permission of the Estate.
Library and Archives Canada/Yousuf Karsh Collection/Archival Source PA-164231

Rt. Hon. Kim Campbell (Progressive Conservative)
June 25, 1993 to Nov. 4, 1993
Photo Credit: Denise Grant
Courtesy of the
Office of the Rt. Hon. Kim Campbell

Rt. Hon. Jean Chrétien (Liberal)
Nov. 4, 1993 to Dec. 11, 2003
Photo Credit: With permission of the Liberal Party of Canada

Rt. Hon. Paul Edgar Philippe Martin (Liberal)
Dec. 12, 2003 to Feb. 6, 2006
Photo Credit: With permission of the Liberal Party of Canada

Rt. Hon. Stephen Joseph Harper (Conservative)
Feb. 6, 2006 to Nov. 3, 2015
Photo Credit: Jason Ransom
Photo provided by the Privy Council Office
© Her Majesty the Queen in Right of Canada, 2016

Rt. Hon. Justin Pierre James Trudeau (Liberal)
Nov. 4, 2015 to --
Photo Credit: Adam Scotti
Photo provided by the Office of the Prime Minister
© Her Majesty the Queen in Right of Canada, 2016

PORTRAITS OF PRIME MINISTERS IN THE HOUSE OF COMMONS

Reproduced with the permission of the Curator, House of Commons

Rt. Hon. Sir John Alexander Macdonald
Credit: Henry Sandham
Library and Archives Canada C-025743

Hon. Alexander Mackenzie
Credit: John Wycliffe Lowes Forster
Library and Archives Canada C-116811

Hon. Sir John J. Abbott
Credit: Muli Tang
House of Commons Collection

Rt. Hon. Sir John Thompson
Credit: John Wycliffe Lowes Forster
Library and Archives Canada C-116812

Hon. Sir Mackenzie Bowell
Credit: Joanne Tod
House of Commons Collection

Rt. Hon. Sir Charles Tupper
Credit: Victor A. Long
Library and Archives Canada C-116813

Rt. Hon. Sir Wilfrid Laurier
Credit: John Wentworth Russell
Library and Archives Canada C-116814

Rt. Hon. Sir Robert Borden
Credit: Kenneth Keith Forbes
Library and Archives Canada C-116815

Rt. Hon. Arthur Meighen
Credit: George Ernest Fosbery
Library and Archives Canada C-116816

Rt. Hon. William Lyon Mackenzie King
Credit: Frank O. Salisbury
Library and Archives Canada C-116818

Rt. Hon. Richard Bedford Bennett
Credit: Kenneth Keith Forbes
Library and Archives Canada C-116817

Rt. Hon. Louis St. Laurent
Credit: Audrey Watts McNaughton
Library and Archives Canada C-116819

Rt. Hon. John G. Diefenbaker
Credit: Arthur Edward Cleeve Horne
Library and Archives Canada C-116820

Rt. Hon. Lester Bowles Pearson
Credit: Hugh Seaforth MacKenzie
Library and Archives Canada C-116821

Rt. Hon. Pierre Elliott Trudeau
Credit: Myfanwy Pavelic
House of Commons Collection

Rt. Hon. Charles Joseph Clark
Credit: Patrick Douglass Cox
House of Commons Collection

Rt. Hon. John Napier Turner
Credit: Brenda Bury
House of Commons Collection

Rt. Hon. Brian Mulroney
Credit: Igor Babailov
House of Commons Collection

Rt. Hon. Kim Campbell
Credit: David Goatley
Courtesy of the Office of the Rt. Hon. Kim Campbell

Rt. Hon. Jean Chrétien
Credit: Christian Nicholson
House of Commons Collection

Rt. Hon. Paul Martin
Credit: Paul Wyse
House of Commons Collection

Regulations & Abbreviations

Styles of Address

Styles of Address courtesy of the Department of Canadian Heritage.

The Royal Family/La Famille Royale

THE QUEEN:
Her Majesty The Queen, Buckingham Palace, London SW1A 1AA United Kingdom
Salutation - Your Majesty:
Final Salutation - I remain Your Majesty's faithful and devoted servant,
In Conversation - "Your Majesty" first then "Ma'am"
Note: The Queen's full title is "Her Majesty Queen Elizabeth II, Queen of Canada" Normally one refers to "Her Majesty The Queen" or "The Queen"

LA REINE:
Sa Majesté la Reine, Palais de Buckingham, Londres SW1A 1AA Royaume-Uni
Appel - Majesté,
Salutation - Je prie Votre Majesté d'agréer l'expression de ma très haute considération.
Conversation - «Majesté»
Remarques: Le titre complet de la Reine est le suivant: «Sa Majesté la reine Ellizabeth II, Reine du Canada» On parle normalement de «Sa Majesté» ou de «la Reine»

THE PRINCE OF WALES:
His Royal Highness The Prince of Wales, Clarence House, London SW1A 1BA United Kingdom
Salutation - Your Royal Highness:
Final Salutation - Yours very truly,
In Conversation - "Your Royal Highness" first then "Sir"
Note: Should never be referred to as: "Charles, Prince of Wales" or "Prince Charles".

LE PRINCE DE GALLES:
Son Altesse Royale le prince de Galles, Clarence House, Londres SW1A 1BA Royaume-Uni
Appel - Altesse Royale,
Saluation - Je prie Votre Altesse Royal d'agréer l'expression de ma très haute considération.
Conversation - «Altesse Royale»
Remarques: Il ne faut jamais dire: «Charles, prince de Galles» ou «le prince Charles»

Government/Gouvernement

GOVERNOR GENERAL OF CANADA:
His/Her Excellency the Right Honourable (full name), C.C., C.M.M., C.O.M., C.D., Governor General of Canada, Rideau Hall, 1 Sussex Dr., Ottawa ON K1A 0A1
Salutation - Excellency:
Final Salutation - Yours truly,
In Conversation - "Your Excellency" or "Excellency" first then "Sir" or "Madam"
Note: The Governor General may have other postnominal letters, such as P.C., Q.C.

GOVERNEUR GÉNÉRAL DU CANADA:
(homme) Son Excellence le très honorable (prénom et nom), C.C., C.M.M., C.O.M., C.D., Gouverneur général du Canada, Rideau Hall, 1, promenade Sussex, Ottawa ON K1A 0A1
(femme) Son Excellence la très honorable (prénom et nom), C.C., C.M.M., C.O.M., C.D., Gouverneure générale du Canada, Rideau Hall, 1, promenade Sussex, Ottawa ON K1A 0A1
Appel - (homme) Excellence,
(femme) Excellence,
Saluation - (homme) Je vous prie d'agréer, Monsieur le Gouverneur général, l'expression de ma très haute considération.
(femme) Je vous prie d'agréer, Madame la Gouverneure générale, l'hommage de mon profond respect.
Conversation - On commence par «Excellence». On poursuit avec «Monsieur» ou «Madame».
Remarques: D'autres initiales peuvent suivre le nom du gouverneur général, comme C.P. et C.R.

LIEUTENANT GOVERNOR OF A PROVINCE:
His/Her Honour the Honourable (full name) Lieutenant Governor of (Province), Address
Salutation - Your Honour or My dear Lieutenant Governor:
Final Salutation - Yours sincerely,
In Conversation - "Your Honour" first then "Sir" or "Madam" or "Mr./Mrs./Ms./Miss (name)"
Note: The Lieutenant Governor of a province has the title "Honourable" for life; the courtesy title "His/ Her Honour" is used only while in office.

LIEUTENANT-GOUVERNEUR
(homme) Son Honneur l'honorable (prénom et nom) Lieutenant-gouverneur de (province), Adresse
(femme) Son Honneur l'honorable (prénom et nom) Lieutenante-gouverneure de (province), Adresse
Appel - (homme) Monsieur le Lieutenant-Gouverneur,
(femme) Madame la Lieutenante-Gouverneure,
Salutation - (homme) Je vous prie d'agréer, Monsieur le Lieutenant-Gouverneur, l'expression de ma haute considération.
(femme) Je vous prie d'agréer, Madame la Lieutenante-Gouverneure, l'hommage de mes respectueux hommages.
Conversation - On commence par «Votre Honneur». On poursuit avec «Monsieur» ou «Madame»
Remarques: Le titre «honorable» est accordé à vie au lieutenant-gouverneur; le titre de courtoisie «Son Honneur» n'est utilisé que pendant la durée du mandat.

THE PRIME MINISTER OF CANADA:
The Right Honourable (full name), P.C., M.P., Prime Minister of Canada, Langevin Block, Ottawa, ON K1A 0A2
Salutation - Dear Prime Minister, or Prime Minister:
Final Salutation - Yours sincerely,
In Conversation - "Prime Minister" first then "Mr./ Mrs./Ms./Miss (name)"
Note: The term "Mr. Prime Minister" should not be used. The Prime Minister may have other post-nominal letters, such as Q.C.

PREMIER MINISTRE DU CANADA
(homme) Le très honorable (prénom et nom), C.P., député Premier Ministre du Canada, Édifice Langevin, Ottawa ON K1A 0A2
(femme) La très honorable (prénom et nom), C.P., députée Première Ministre du Canada, Édifice Langevin, Ottawa ON K1A 0A2
Appel - (homme) Monsieur le Premier Ministre,
(femme) Madame la Première Ministre,
Salutation -
(homme) Je vous prie d'agréer, Monsieur le Premier Ministre, l'expression de ma très haute considération.
(femme) Je vous prie d'agréer, Madame la Première Ministre, l'hommage de mon profond respect.
Conversation - (homme) On commence par «Monsieur le Premier Ministre». On poursuit avec «Monsieur»
(femme) On commence par «Madame la Première Ministre». On pousuit avec «Madame»
Remarques: D'autres initiales peuvent suivre le nom, comme C.R.

THE PREMIER OF A PROVINCE OF CANADA:
The Honourable (full name), M.L.A. or (M.P.P., M.N.A., or M.H.A.), Premier of (Province), Address
Salutation - Dear Premier:
Final Salutation - Yours sincerely,
In Conversation - "Premier" first then "Mr./Mrs./Ms./ Miss (name)"
Note: The title "Honourable" is used only while in office, unless he/she is a member of the Privy Council. The term "Mr./Madam Premier" should not be used.

LE PREMIER MINISTRE D'UNE PROVINCE
(homme) L'honorable (prénom et nom) M.A.L ou (M.A.N., M.P.P. ou M.C.A) Premier Ministre de (province), Adresse
(femme) L'honorable (prénom et nom) M.A.L ou (M.A.N., M.P.P. ou M.C.A) Première Ministre de (province), Adresse
Appel - (homme) Monsieur le Premier Ministre,
(femme) Madame la Première Ministre,
Salutation - (homme) Je vous prie d'agréer, Monsieur le Premier Ministre, l'expression de ma haute considération.
(femme) Je vous prie d'agréer, Madame la Première Ministre, l'hommage de mon profond respect.
Conversation - On commence par «Monsieur le Premier Ministre». On poursuit avec «Monsieur»
(femme) On commence par «Madame la Première Ministre». On poursuit avec «Madame»
Remarques: Les premiers ministres ne conservent pas le titre «honorable» après la fin de leur mandat, à moins qu'ils ne soient membres du Conseil privé.

COMMISSIONER OF A TERRITORY:
The Honourable (full name), Commissioner of (Territory), Address
Salutation - Commissioner (name):
Final Salutation - Yours sincerely,
In Conversation - "Sir" or "Madam" or "Mr./Mrs./ Ms./Miss (name)"
Note: The Commissioner of a territory has the title "Honourable" only while in office.

COMMISSAIRE DU TERRITOIRE
(homme/femme) L'honorable (prénom et nom) Commissaire du (territoire), Adresse
Appel - (homme) Monsieur le Commissaire,
(femme) Madame la Commissaire,
Salutation - Je vous prie d'agréer, Monsieur le Commissaire, l'expression de ma haute considération.
(femme) Je vous prie d'agréer, Madame la Commissaire, l'expression de mes respectueux hommages.
Conversation - (homme) «Monsieur»
(femme) «Madame»
Remarques: Le titre «honorable» n'est utilisé que pendant la durée de ses fonctions.

PREMIER OF A TERRITORY:
The Honourable (full name), M.L.A., Premier of (Territory), Address
Salutation - Dear Mr./Mrs./Ms./Miss (name):
Final Salutation - Yours sincerely,
In Conversation - "Mr./Mrs./Ms./Miss (name)"
Note: The title "Honourable" is used only while in office, unless he/she is a member of the Privy Council. The term "Mr./Madam Premier" should not be used.

LE PREMIER MINISTRE D'UN TERRITOIRE
(homme) L'honorable (prénom et nom), M.A.L. Premier ministre du (territoire), Adresse
(femme) L'honorable (prénom et nom), M.A.L. Première Ministre du (territoire), Adresse
Appel - (homme) Monsieur le Premier Ministre,
(femme) Madame la Première Ministre,
Salutation - (homme) Je vous prie d'agréer, Monsieur le Premier Ministre, l'expression de ma haute consideration.
(femme) Je vous prie d'agréer, Madame la Première Ministre, l'hommage de mon profond respect.
Conversation - On commence par «Monsieur le Premier Ministre». On poursuit avec «Monsieur»
(femme) On commence par «Madame la Première Ministre». On poursuit avec «Madame»
Remarques: Les premiers ministres ne conservent pas le titre «honorable» après la fin de leur mandat, à moins qu'ils ne soient membres du Conseil privé.

CABINET MINISTERS:
Member of the House of Commons: The Honourable (full name), P.C., M.P., Minister of ________, House of Commons, Ottawa ON K1A 0A6
Salutation - Dear Minister: or Dear Colleague: (between colleagues)
Final Salutation - Yours sincerely,
In Conversation - "Minister" first then "Mr./Mrs./ Ms./Miss (name)"
For a Senator: Senator the Honourable (full name), P.C., Minister of ________, The Senate, Ottawa, ON K1A 0A4
Salutation - Dear Minister: or Dear Colleague: (between colleagues)
Final Salutation - Yours sincerely,
In Conversation - "Minister" first then "Mr./Mrs./ Ms./Miss (name)"

CONSEIL DES MINISTRES DU CANADA
(homme) L'honorable (prénom et nom), C.P. député Ministre de ________, Chambre de communes, Ottawa ON K1A 0A6
(femme) L'honorable (prénom et nom), C.P. députée Ministre de ________, Chambre de communes, Ottawa ON K1A 0A6
Appel - (homme) Monsieur le Ministre, ou Cher collègue, (Entre collègues)
(femme) Madame la Ministre, ou Chère collègue, (Entre collègues)
Salutation - (homme) Je vous prie d'agréer, Monsieur le Ministre, l'expression de ma considération respectueuse.
(femme) Je vous prie d'agréer, Madame la Ministre, l'hommage de mon profond respect.
Conversation - (homme) On commence par «Monsieur le Ministre». On poursuit avec «Monsieur»
(femme) On commence par «Madame la Ministre». On poursuit avec «Madame»
Remarques: Les ministres fédéraux sont membres du Conseil privé de la Reine pour le Canada et conservent le titre «honorable» à vie. On place les initiales C.P. après leur nom.

MINISTERS OF STATE:
The Honourable (full name), P.C., M.P., Minister of State (Portfolio), House of Commons, Ottawa, ON K1A 0A6
Salutation - Dear Minister of State: or Dear Colleague: (between colleagues)
Final Salutation - Yours sincerely,
In Conversation - "Minister of State" first then "Mr./ Mrs./Ms./Miss (name)"
Note: Members of the Ministry are members of the Queen's Privy Council for Canada and retain the title "Honourable" for life, using the initials P.C. after their name. The term "Mr. Min-

ister" or "Madame Minister" should not be used. The term "Mr. Minister of State" or "Madame Minister of State" should not be used.

MINISTRE D'ÉTAT

(homme) L'honorable (prénom et nom), C.P. député Ministre d'État (Portefeuille), Chambre des communes, Ottawa ON K1A 0A6

(femme) L'honorable (prénom et nom), C.P. députée Ministre d'État (Portefeuille), Chambre des communes, Ottawa ON K1A 0A6

Appel - (homme) Monsieur le Ministre d'État, ou Cher collègue, (Entre collègues)

(femme) Madame la Ministre d'État, ou Chère collègue, (Entre collègues)

Salutation - (homme) Je vous prie d'agréer, Monsieur le Ministre d'État, l'expression de ma considération respectueuse. Ou Je vous prie, cher collègue, de recevoir mes cordiales salutations. (Entre collègues)

(femme) Je vous prie d'agréer, Madame la Ministre d'État, l'hommage de mon profond respect. Ou Je vous prie, chère collègue, de recevoir mes cordiales salutations. (Entre collègues)

Conversation - (homme) On commence par «Monsieur le Ministre d'État». On poursuit avec «Monsieur»

(femme) On commence par «Ministre la Secrétaire d'État». On poursuit avec «Madame»

Remarques: Les ministres d'État sont membres du Conseil privé de la Reine pour le Canada et conservent le titre «honorable» à vie. On place les initiales C.P. aprés leur nom.

SPEAKER OF THE SENATE:

The Honourable (full name), Senator, Speaker of the Senate, The Senate, Ottawa, ON K1A 0A4

Salutation - Dear Mr./Madam Speaker:

Final Salutation - Yours sincerely,

In Conversation - "Mr. Speaker" or "Madam Speaker"

Note: A senator who is a member of the Canadian Privy Council is addressed as "Senator the Honourable (name), P.C. " After a Senator retires, he/she retains the title "Honourable" but the salutation is "Dear Sir/ Madam" or "Dear Mr./Mrs./Ms./Miss (name)"

PRÉSIDENT OU PRÉSIDENTE DU SÉNAT

(homme) L'honorable (prénom et nom), sénateur Président du Sénat, Le Sénat, Ottawa ON K1A 0A4

(femme) L'honorable (prénom et nom), sénatrice Présidente du Sénat, Le Sénat, Ottawa ON K1A 0A4

Appel - (homme) Monsieur le Président,

(femme) Madame la Présidente,

Salutation - (homme) Je vous prie d'agréer, Monsieur le Président, l'expression de ma haute considération.

(femme) Je vous prie d'agréer, Madame la Présidente, l'hommage de mon profond respect.

Conversation - (homme) «Monsieur le Président»

(femme) «Madame la Présidente»

Remarques: Dans le cas d'un sénateur ou d'une sénatrice qui est membre du Conseil privé, la formule d'appel à utiliser est «L'honorable (nom), C.P., sénateur(trice)». Après leur retraite, les sénateurs conservent le titre «honorable» mais la formule d'appel devient: «Monsieur/Madame».

SPEAKER OF THE HOUSE OF COMMONS:

The Honourable (full name), M.P., Speaker of the House of Commons, House of Commons, Ottawa, ON K1A 0A6

Salutation - Dear Mr./Madam Speaker:

Final Salutation - Yours sincerely,

In Conversation - "Mr. Speaker" or "Madam Speaker"

PRÉSIDENT OU PRÉSIDENTE DE LA CHAMBRE DES COMMUNES

(homme) L'honorable (prénom et nom) député Président de la Chambre des communes, Chambre des communes, Ottawa ON K1A 0A6

(femme) L'honorable (prénom et nom) députée Présidente de la Chambre des communes, Chambre des communes, Ottawa ON K1A 0A6

Appel - (homme) Monsieur le Président,

(femme) Madame la Présidente,

Salutation - (homme) Je vous prie d'agréer, Monsieur le Président, l'expression de ma haute considération.

(femme) Je vous prie d'agréer, Madame la Présidente, l'hommage de mon profond respect.

Conversation - (homme) «Monsieur le Président»

(femme) «Madame la Présidente»

SENATORS:

The Honourable (full name), Senator, The Senate, Ottawa, ON K1A 0A4

Salutation - Dear Senator (name):

Final Salutation - Yours sincerely,

In Conversation - "Senator (name)"

Note: A senator who is a member of the Queen's Privy Council is addressed as "Senator the Honourable (full name), P.C." After a Senator retires, he/she retains the title "Honourable" for life but the salutation is "Dear Sir/Madam" or "Dear Mr./Mrs./Ms./Miss (name)".

SÉNATEURS:

(homme) L'honorable (prénom et nom) sénateur, Le Sénat, Ottawa ON K1A 0A4

(femme) L'honorable (prénom et nom) sénatrice, Le Sénat, Ottawa ON K1A 0A4

Appel - (homme) Monsieur le Sénateur,

(femme) Madame la Sénatrice,

Salutation - (homme) Je vous prie d'agréer, Monsieur le Sénateur, l'expression de mes meilleurs sentiments.

(femme) Je vous prie d'agréer, Madame la Sénatrice, mes hommages respectueux.

Conversation - (homme) «Monsieur le Sénateur». On poursuit avec «Monsieur»

(femme) «Madame la Sénatrice». On poursuit avec «Madame»

Remarques: Après leur retraite, les sénateurs conservent le titre «honorable», mais la formule d'appel devient: «Monsieur» ou «Madame».

MEMBERS OF THE HOUSE OF COMMONS:

Mr. John Smith, M.P. or The Honourable John Smith, P.C., M.P., House of Commons, Ottawa, ON K1A 0A6

Salutation - Dear Mr./Mrs./Ms./Miss (name):

Final Salutation - Yours sincerely,

In Conversation - "Mr./Mrs./Ms./Miss (name)"

Note: The members of the House of Commons who are members of the Queen's Privy Council retain the title "Honourable" for life and use the initials "P.C." after their name. M.P.: Member of the House of Commons P.C., M.P.: Member of the Privy Council and Member of the House of Commons

DÉPUTÉS FÉDÉRAUX

(homme) Monsieur (prénom et nom), député ou L'honorable (prénom et nom), C.P., député Chambre des communes, Ottawa ON K1A 0A6

(femme) Madame (prénom et nom), députée ou L'honorable (prénom et nom), C.P., députée Chambre des communes, Ottawa ON K1A 0A6

Appel - (homme) Monsieur le Député,

(femme) Madame la Députée,

Salutation - (homme) Je vous prie d'agréer, Monsieur le Député, l'expression de mes meilleurs sentiments.

(femme) Je vous prie d'agréer, Madame la Députée, mes respectueux hommages.

Conversation - (homme) On commence par «Monsieur le Député». On poursuit avec «Monsieur»

(femme) On commence par «Madame la Députée». On poursuit avec «Madame»

Remarques: Les députés qui sont membres du Conseil privé de la Reine pour le Canada ont le «honorable» à vie et portent les initiales «C.P.» après leur nom.

MEMBER OF THE PROVINCIAL/TERRITORIAL CABINET:

The Honourable (full name), M.L.A. or (M.P.P., M.N.A. or M.H.A.), Minister of ________, Address

Salutation - Dear Minister: or Dear Colleague: (between colleagues)

Final Salutation - Yours sincerely,

In Conversation - "Minister" first then "Mr./Mrs./ Ms./Miss (name)"

Note: A provincial/territorial cabinet minister does not retain the title "Honourable" after tenure of office unless he/she is a member of the Privy Council. M.L.A.: all provinces/territories except for: Ontario (M.P.P.); Québec (M.N.A.); Newfoundland (M.H.A.). The term "Mr./Madam Minister" should not be used.

MINISTRES PROVINCIAUX/TERRITORIAUX

(homme/femme) L'honorable (prénom et nom), M.A.L. ou (M.A.N., M.P.P. ou M.C.A.) Ministre de ________, Adresse

Appel - (homme) Monsieur le Ministre, ou Cher collègue, (Entre collègues)

(femme) Madame la Ministre, ou Chère collègue, (Entre collègues)

Salutation - (homme) Je vous prie d'agréer, Monsieur le Ministre, l'expression de ma considération respectueuse. Ou Je vous prie, cher collègue, de recevoir mes cordiales salutations. (Entre collègues)

(femme) Je vous prie d'agréer, Madame la Ministre, l'expression de ma considération respectueuse. Ou Je vous prie, chère collègue, de recevoir mes cordiales salutations. (Entre collègues)

Conversation - (homme) On commence par «Monsieur le Ministre». On poursuit avec «Monsieur»

(femme) On commence par «Madame la Ministre». On poursuit avec «Madame»

Remarques: Les ministres provinciaux/territoriaux ne conservent pas le titre «honorable» après la fin de leur mandat à moins qu'ils ne soient membres du Conseil privè. M.A.L.: toutes les provinces et les territoires, sauf: - l'Ontario (M.P.P.) - le Québec (M.A.N.) - Terre- Neuve (M.C.A.)

MEMBER OF A PROVINCIAL/TERRITORIAL LEGISLATIVE ASSEMBLY:

Mr. John Smith, M.L.A. or (M.P.P., M.N.A., or M.H.A.), Address

Salutation - Dear Mr./Mrs./Ms./Miss (name),

Final Salutation - Yours sincerely,

In Conversation - "Mr./Mrs./Ms./Miss (name)"

Note: Members of the Queen's Privy Council retain the title "Honourable" for life and use the initials "P.C." after their name. M.L.A.: all provinces/territories except for: Ontario (M.P.P.); Quebec (M.N.A.); Newfoundland (M.H.A.) P.C., M.L.A.: Member of the Privy Council and Member of the Legislative Assembly

DÉPUTÉS PROVINCIAUX/TERRITORIAUX

(homme) Monsieur (prénom et nom), M.A.L. ou (M.P.P., M.A.N. ou M.C.A.), Adresse

(femme) Madame (prénom et nom), M.A.L. ou (M.P.P., M.A.N. ou M.C.A.), Adresse

Appel - (homme) Monsieur le Député,

(femme) Madame la Députee,

Salutation - (homme) Je vous prie d'agréer, Monsieur le Député, l'expression de mes meilleurs sentiments.

(femme) Je vous prie d'agréer, Madame la Députée, mes respectueux hommages.

Conversation - (homme) «Monsieur»

(femme) «Madame»

Remarques: Les membres du Conseil privé de la Reine conservent le titre «honorable» à vie et placent les initiales C.P. après leur nom. M.A.L.: toutes les provinces et les territoires sauf: - l'Ontario (M.P.P.) - le Québec (M.A.N.), Terre-Neuve (M.C.A.) C.P., M.A.L.: Membre du Conseil privé et membre de l'Assemblée législative.

MAYOR OF A CITY OR TOWN:

His/Her Worship (full name), Mayor of (name), Address

Salutation - Dear Sir/Madam: or Dear Mr./Madam Mayor:

Final Salutation - Yours sincerely,

In Conversation - "Your Worship" first then "Mayor (name)"

MAIRE/MAIRESSE

(homme) Son Honneur monsieur (prénom et nom), Maire de (Ville), Adresse

(femme) Son Honneur madame (prénom et nom), Mairesse de (Ville), Adresse Appel - Monsieur le Maire,

(femme) Madame la Mairesse,

Salutation - (homme) Je vous prie d'agréer, Monsieur le Maire, l'expression de mes meilleurs sentiments.

(femme) Je vous prie d'agréer, Madame la Mairesse, mes hommages respectueux.

Conversation - (homme) On commence par «Votre Honneur». On poursuit avec «Monsieur le Maire»

(femme) On commence par «Votre Honneur». On poursuit avec «Madame la Mairesse»

JUDGES/JUGES

CHIEF JUSTICE: The Right Honourable (full name), P.C., Chief Justice of Canada, Supreme Court of Canada, Ottawa, ON K1A 0J1

Salutation - Dear Chief Justice:

Final Salutation - Yours sincerely,

In Conversation - "Mr./Madam Chief Justice" first then "Sir/Madam" or "Mr./Mrs./Ms./Miss (name)"

JUGE EN CHEF DU CANADA

(homme) Le très honorable (prenom et nom), C.P. Juge en chef du Canada, Cour suprême du Canada, Ottawa ON K1A 0J1

(femme) La très honorable (prenom et nom), C.P. Juge en chef du Canada, Cour suprême du Canada, Ottawa ON K1A 0J1

Appel - (homme) Monsieur le Juge en chef,

(femme) Madame la Juge en chef,

Salutation - (homme) Je vous prie d'agréer, Monsieur le Juge en chef, l'expression de ma très haute considération.

(femme) Je vous prie d'agréer, Madame la Juge en chef, l'hommage de mon profond respect.

Conversation - (homme) On commence par «Monsieur le Juge en chef». On poursuit avec «Monsieur»

(femme) On commence par «Madame la Juge en chef». On poursuit avec «Madame»

JUDGES OF SUPERIOR COURTS:

Supreme Court of Canada & Federal Court of Canada: The Honourable (full name), Judge of the ________ Court of Canada, Address.

Salutation - Dear Mr./Madam Justice (name):

Final Salutation - Yours sincerely,

In Conversation - "Mr./Madam Justice"

Appeal Court, Superior Court, Court of the Queen's Bench: The Honourable (full name), Judge of ________, Address

Salutation - Dear Mr./Madam Justice (name):

Final Salutation - Yours sincerely,

In Conversation - "Mr./Madam Justice (name)"

JUGES DES COURS SUPÉRIEURES

Cour suprême, Cour fédérale et Cour de l'impôt: L'honorable (prénom et nom), Titre, Adresse
Appel - (homme) Monsieur le Juge,
(femme) Madame la Juge,
Salutation - (homme) Je vous prie d'agréer, Monsieur le Juge, l'expression de ma haute considération.
(femme) Je vous prie d'agréer, Madame la Juge l'hommage de mon profond respect.
Conversation - (homme) ‹‹Monsieur le Juge››
(femme) ‹‹Madame la Juge››
Cour d'appel, Cour supérieure, Cour du Banc de la Reine, L'honorable (prénom et nom) Juge de ________, Adresse
Appel - (homme) Monsieur le Juge,
(femme) Madame la Juge,
Salutation - (homme) Je vous prie d'agréer, Monsieur le Juge, l'expression de ma haute considération.
(femme) Je vous prie d'agréer, Madame la Juge, l'hommage de mon profond respect.
Conversation - (homme) ‹‹Monsieur le Juge››
(femme) ‹‹Madame la Juge››

JUDGES OF THE TAX COURT:

The Honourable (full name), Judge of the Tax Court of Canada, Address
Salutation - Dear Chief Judge/Judge (name):
Final Salutation - Yours sincerely,
In Conversation - "Chief Judge/Judge (name)"
Remarques: En français, voir ci-dessus.

CHIEF JUDGES/JUDGES OF PROVINCIAL/TERRITORIAL COURTS:

The Honourable (full name), Provincial/Territorial Court of ________ , Address
Salutation - Dear Chief Judge/Judge (name):
Final Salutation - Yours sincerely,
In Conversation - "Judge (name)"
Note: The titles to be used in Canada now recognize the title "Honourable" for provincially/territorially appointed judges. The courtesy title "His/Her Honour" is no longer appropriate given an official title has been granted.

JUGES EN CHEF/JUGES DES COURS PROVINCIALES/ TERRITORIALES

L'honorable (prénom et nom), Cour provinciale de ________, Adresse
Appel - (homme) Monsieur le Juge en chef/le Juge,
(femme) Madame la Juge en chef/la Juge,
Salutation -
(homme) Je vous prie d'agréer, Monsieur le Juge en chef/le Juge, l'expression de mon profond respect.
(femme) Je vous prie d'agréer, Madame la Juge en chef//la Juge, l'hommage de mon profond respect.
Conversation - (homme) ‹‹Monsieur le Juge en chef/ le Juge››
(femme) ‹‹Madame la Juge en chef/la Juge››
Remarques: Le tableau des titres pour le Canada reconnaît le titre ‹‹honorable›› aux juges des cours provinciales/ territoriales; le titre de courtoisie ‹‹Son Honneur›› n'est plus de mise maintenant qu'un titre officiel est utilisé.

Religion

Anglican Church of Canada/ Église anglicane du Canada

PRIMATE:

The Most Reverend (full name), Primate of the Anglican Church of Canada, Address
Salutation - Dear Archbishop (name):
Final Salutation - Yours sincerely,
In Conversation - "Archbishop"

PRIMAT:

Le révérendissime (prénom et nom), Primate de l'Église anglicane du Canada, Adresse
Appel - Monsieur le Primat,
Salutation - Je vous prie d'agréer, Monsieur le Primat, l'expression de mes sentiments les plus respectueux.
Conversation - ‹‹Monsieur l'Archevêque››

ARCHBISHOP:

The Most Reverend (full name), D.D., Archbishop of (name of Diocese), Address
Salutation - Dear Archbishop (name):
Final Salutation - Yours very truly,
In Conversation - "Archbishop"

ARCHEVÊQUE:

Le révérendissime (prénom et nom), Archevêque de (nom du diocèse), Adresse
Appel - Monsieur l'Archevêque,
Salutation - Je vous prie d'agréer, Monsieur l'Archevêque, l'expression de mes sentiments les plus respectueux.
Conversation - ‹‹Monsieur l'Archevêque››

BISHOP:

The Right Reverend (full name), Bishop of (name of Diocese), Address
Salutation - Dear Bishop (name):
Final Salutation - Yours very truly,
In Conversation - "Bishop (name)" or "Bishop"

ÉVÊQUE:

(homme) Le très révérend (prénom et nom), Évêque de (nom du diocèse), Adresse
(femme) La très révérende (prénom et nom), Évêque de (nom du diocèse), Adresse
Appel - (homme) Monsieur l'Évêque,
(femme) Madame l'Évêque,
Salutation - (homme) Je vous prie d'agréer, Monsieur l'Évêque, l'expression de mes sentiments les plus respectueux.
(femme) Je vous prie d'agréer, Madame l'Évêque, l'hommage de mon profond respect.
Conversation - (homme) ‹‹Monsieur l'Évêque››
(femme) ‹‹Madame l'Évêque››

DEAN:

The Very Reverend (full name), Dean of (name of Cathedral), Address
Salutation - Dear Dean (name):
Final Salutation - Yours sincerely,
In Conversation - "Dean (name)" or "Mr./Mrs./Ms./ Miss (name)"

DOYEN:

(homme) Le très révérend (prénom et nom), Doyen de (nom de la cathédrale), Adresse
(femme) La très révérende (prénom et nom), Doyenne de (nom de la cathédrale), Adresse
Appel - (homme) Monsieur le Doyen,
(femme) Madame la Doyenne,
Salutation - (homme) Je vous prie d'agréer, Monsieur le Doyen, l'expression de mes sentiments les plus respectueux.
(femme) Je vous prie d'agréer, Madame la Doyenne, l'hommage de mon profond respect.
Conversation - (homme) ‹‹Monsieur le Doyen›› ou ‹‹Monsieur››
(femme) ‹‹Madame la Doyenne›› ou ‹‹Madame››

ARCHDEACON:

The Venerable (full name), Archdeacon, Address
Salutation - Dear Archdeacon (name):
Final Salutation - Yours sincerely,
In Conversation - "Archdeacon (name)"

ARCHIDIACRE:

(homme) Le vénérable (prénom et nom), Archidiacre, Adresse
(femme) La vénérable (prénom et nom), Archidiacre, Adresse
Appel - (homme) Monsieur l'Archidiacre,
(femme) Madame l'Archidiacre,
Salutation - (homme) Je vous prie d'agréer, Monsieur l'Archidacre, l'expression de mes sentiments les plus respectueux.
(femme) Je vous prie d'agréer, Madame l'Archidacre, l'hommage de mon profond respect.
Conversation - (homme) ‹‹Monsieur l'Archidiacre››
(femme) ‹‹Madame l'Archidiacre››

CANON:

The Reverend Canon (full name), Address
Salutation - Dear Canon (name):
Final Salutation - Yours sincerely,
In Conversation - "Canon (name)"

CHANOINE:

(homme) Le chanoine, (prénom et nom), Adresse
(femme) La chanoinesse, (prénom et nom), Adresse
Appel - (homme) Monsieur le Chanoine,
(femme) Madame la Chanoinesse,
Salutation - (homme) Je vous prie d'agréer, Monsieur le Chanoine, l'expression de mes sentiments les plus respectueux.
(femme) Je vous prie d'agréer, Madame La Chanoinesse, l'hommage de mon profond respect.
Conversation - (homme) ‹‹Monsieur le Chanoine››
(femme) ‹‹Madame la Chanoinesse››

PRIEST:

The Reverend (full name), Address
Salutation - Dear Father (name) or Dear Mr. (name): or Dear Mrs./Ms./Miss (name)
Final Salutation - Yours sincerely,
In Conversation - "Father" or "Father (name) or "Mrs./Ms./Miss (name)"

Note: "Reverend" is an adjective which is never used without the full name.

PRÊTRE:

(homme) Le révérend père (prénom et nom), Adresse
(femme) La révérende (prénom et nom), Adresse
Appel - (homme) Monsieur le Curé, Monsieur l'Abbé,
(femme) Madame,
Salutation - (homme) Je vous prie d'agréer, Monsieur le Curé, l'expression de mes sentiments respectueux.
(femme) Je vous prie d'agréer, Madame, l'expression de mes sentiments respectueux.
Conversation - (homme) ‹‹Monsieur le Curé/Monsieur l'Abbé››
(femme) ‹‹ Madame)››

RELIGIOUS:

(man) The Reverend Father (full name), Address
(woman) Reverend Mother (full name)/ Reverend Sister (full name)
Salutation - Dear Father (name):
Dear Reverend Mother:/ Dear Reverend Sister:
Final Salutation - Yours sincerely,
In Conversation - "Reverend Father", (woman) Reverend Mother (full name)/Reverend Sister (full name)

RELIGIEUX/RELIGIEUSE:

(homme) Le révérend père (prénom et nom), Adresse
(femme) La révérende mère/ soeur (prénom et nom), Adresse
Appel - (homme) Révérend père/Mon père,
(femme) Révérende mère/Ma soeur
Salutation - (homme) Je vous prie d'agréer, Révérend père/Mon père, l'expression de mes sentiments les plus respectueux.
(femme) Je vous prie d'agréer, Révérende mère/ Ma soeur, l'hommage de mon profond respect.
Conversation - (homme) ‹‹Révérend père/Mon père››
(femme) ‹‹Révérende mère/Ma soeur››

Roman Catholic Church/Église catholique romaine

THE POPE:

His Holiness Francis, Address
Salutation - Your Holiness:
Final Salutation - I have the honour to remain Your Holiness's obedient servant,
In Conversation - "Your Holiness"

LE PAPE:

Sa Sainteté le pape François, Adresse
Appel - Très Saint-Père,
Salutation - Je vous prie d'agréer, Très Saint-Père, l'expression de mon profond respect et de ma très haute considération.
Conversation - ‹‹Votre Sainteté›› ou ‹‹Très Saint- Père››

CARDINAL:

His Eminence John Cardinal Smith, Address
Salutation - Your Eminence: or Dear Cardinal (name):
Final Salutation - Yours very truly,
In Conversation - "Your Eminence"

CARDINAL:

Son Éminence le cardinal (prénom et nom), Adresse
Appel - Monsieur le Cardinal,
Salutation - Je vous prie d'agréer, Monsieur le Cardinal, l'expression de mon profond respect.
Conversation - ‹‹Éminence››

ARCHBISHOP/BISHOP:

The Most Reverend (full name), Archbishop/Bishop of (name of Diocese). Address
Salutation - Dear Archbishop/Bishop (name):
Final Salutation - Yours very truly,
In Conversation - "Archbishop/Bishop"
Note: The Holy See accorded the courtesy title "His Excellency" to Roman Catholic Archbishops and Bishops; that title is not recognized by Canadian civil authorities.

ARCHEVÊQUE/ÉVÊQUE:

Monseigneur (prénom et nom), Archevêque ou Évêque de (nom du diocèse), Adresse
Appel - Monseigneur,
Salutation - Je vous prie d'agréer, Monseigneur , l'expression de mes sentiments les plus respectueux.
Conversation - ‹‹Monseigneur››
Remarques: Le titre ‹‹Son Excellence›› est utilisé par le Saint-Siège pour les archevêques et évêques catholiques; il n'est toutefois pas reconnu par les autorités civiles canadiennes.

ABBOT:

The Right Reverend (full name), Abbot of (name of ________), Address
Salutation - Right Reverend Father: or Dear Abbott (name):
Final Salutation - Yours sincerely,

In Conversation - "Father Abbott"

ABBÉ:

Le révérend père (prénom et nom), Adresse Appel - Monsieur l'Abbé,
Salutation - Je vous prie d'agréer, Monsieur l'Abbé, l'expression de mes sentiments les plus respectueux.
Conversation - ‹‹Monsieur l'Abbé››

CANON:

The Very Reverend (full name), Address
Salutation - Dear Canon (name):
Final Salutation - Yours sincerely,
In Conversation - "Canon (name)"

CHANOINE:

Le chanoine (prénom et nom), Adresse Appel - Monsieur le Chanoine,
Salutation - Je vous prie d'agréer, Monsieur le Chanoine, l'expression de mes sentiments respectueux.
Conversation - ‹‹Monsieur le Chanoine››

PRIEST

The Reverend (full name), Address
Salutation - Dear Father:
Final Salutation - Yours sincerely,
In Conversation - "Father" or "Father (name)"
Note: "Reverend" is an adjective which is never used without the full name.

PRÊTRE:

Le révérend père (prénom et nom), Adresse
Appel - Monsieur le Curé/l'Abbé,
Salutation - Je vous prie d'agréer, Monsieur le Curé, l'expression de mes sentiments respectueux.
Conversation - ‹‹Monsieur le Curé/l'Abbé››

SULPICIAN:

Mr. (full name), Address
Salutation - Dear Mr. (name):
Final Salutation - Yours truly,
In Conversation - "Mr. (name)"

SULPICIEN:

Monsieur (prénom et nom), Adresse
Appel - Monsieur,
Salutation - Je vous prie d'agréer, Monsieur, l'expression de mes sentiments respectueux.
Conversation - ‹‹Monsieur››

RELIGIOUS:

(man) The Reverend Father (full name), Address
(woman) Reverend Mother (full name)/ Reverend Sister (full name)
Salutation - Dear Father (name):, Dear Reverend Mother:/ Dear Reverend Sister
Final Salutation - Yours sincerely,
In Conversation - "Reverend Father", (woman) Reverend Mother (full name)/ Reverend Sister (full name)

RELIGIEUX/RELIGIEUSE:

(homme) Le révérend père (prénom et nom), Adresse
(femme) La révérende mère/soeur (prénom et nom), Adresse
Appel - (homme) Révérend père/Mon père,
(femme) Révérende mère/Ma soeur,
Salutation - (homme) Je vous prie d'agréer, Révérend père/Mon père, l'expression de mes sentiments respectueux.
(femme) Je vous prie d'agréer, Révérende mère/Ma soeur, l'hommage de mon profond respect.
Conversation - (homme) ‹‹Révérend père ou Mon père››
(femme) ‹‹Révérende mère/Ma soeur››

Other Religious Denominations/ Autres dénominations:

MODERATOR:

(United Church of Canada and Presbyterian Church in Canada)
A present ordained Moderator: The Right Reverend (full name), Moderator of (name of Church), Address
Salutation - Dear Mr./Mrs./Ms./Miss (name):
Final Salutation - Yours sincerely,
In Conversation - "Mr./Mrs./Ms./Miss (name)"
A past ordained Moderator: The Very Reverend (full name), Moderator of (name of Church), Address
Salutation - Dear Mr./Mrs./Ms./Miss (name):
Final Salutation - Yours sincerely,
In Conversation - "Mr./Mrs./Ms./Miss (name)"

MODÉRATEURS:

(Église unie du Canada et Église presbytérienne au Canada)
(homme) Le très révérend (prénom et nom), Modérateur de (nom de l'Église), Adresse
(femme) La très révérende (prénom et nom), Modératrice de (nom de l'Église), Adresse
Appel - (homme) Monsieur le Modérateur,
(femme) Madame la Modératrice,
Salutation - (homme) Je vous prie d'agréer, Monsieur le Modérateur, l'expression de mes sentiments respectueux.
(femme) Je vous prie d'agréer, Madame la Modératrice, l'hommage de mon profond respect.
Conversation - (homme) ‹‹Monsieur le Modérateur››
(femme) ‹‹Madame la Modératrice››

MINISTER:

The Reverend (full name), Address
Salutation - Dear Mr./Mrs./Ms./Miss (name):
Final Salutation - Yours sincerely,
In Conversation - "Mr./Mrs./Ms./Miss (name)"
Note: "Reverend" is an adjective which is never used without the full name.

MINISTRE:

(homme) Le révérend (prénom et nom), Adresse
(femme) La révérende (prénom et nom), Adresse
Appel - (homme) Monsieur le Pasteur,
(femme) Madame,
Salutation - (homme) Je vous prie d'agréer, Monsieur le Pasteur, l'expression de mes sentiments respectueux.
(femme) Je vous prie d'agréer, Madame, l'hommage de mon profond respect.
Conversation - (homme) ‹‹Monsieur le Pasteur››
(femme) ‹‹Madame››

RABBI:

Rabbi (full name), Address
Salutation - Dear Rabbi (name):
Final Salutation - Yours sincerely,
In Conversation - "Rabbi (name)"

RABBIN:

Le rabbin (prénom et nom), Adresse Appel - Monsieur le Rabbin,
Salutation - Je vous prie d'agréer, Monsieur le Rabbin, l'expression de mes sentiments respectueux.
Conversation - ‹‹Monsieur le Rabbin››

Diplomatic/Diplomates

AMBASSADORS/HIGH COMMISSIONERS of foreign countries in Canada:

His/Her Excellency (full name), Ambassador of Canada to ________ /High Commissioner for ________ , Address
Salutation - Dear Ambassador/High Commissioner:
Final Salutation - Yours sincerely,
In Conversation - "Your Excellency" or "Excellency"
Note: British High Commissioner and not High Commissioner for Britain

AMBASSADEURS/HAUTS-COMMISSAIRES de pays étrangers au Canada:

(homme) Son Excellence monsieur (prénom et nom), Ambassadeur de ________/Haut-Commissaire de ________, Adresse
(femme) Son Excellence madame (prénom et nom), Ambassadrice de ________/Haute-Commissaire de ________, Adresse
Appel - (homme) Monsieur/l'Ambassadeur/le Haut - Commissaire,
(femme) Madame l'Ambassadrice/la Haute-Commissaire,
Salutation - (homme) Je vous prie d'agréer, Monsieur l'Ambassadeur/le Haut-Commissaire, l'expression de ma haute considération.
(femme) Je vous prie d'agréer, Madame l'Ambassadrice/ la Haute-Commissaire, l'expression de mes respectueux hommages.
Conversation - ‹‹Excellence››

CANADIAN AMBASSADORS/HIGH COMMISSIONERS abroad:

Mr./Mrs. (full name), Ambassador of Canada to ________ /High Commissioner for Canada to ________ , Address
Salutation - Dear Ambassador/High Commissioner:
Final Salutation - Yours sincerely,
In Conversation - "Mr./Madam Ambassador/High Commissioner"

AMBASSADEURS DU CANADA/HAUTS-COMMISSAIRES à l'étranger

(homme) Monsieur (prénom et nom) Ambassadeur du Canada/Haute-commissaire du Canada au ________, Adresse
(femme) Madame (prénom et nom) l'Ambassadrice du Canada/Haute-commissaire du Canada au ________, Adresse
Appel - (homme) Monsieur l'Ambassadeur/le Haut-Commissaire,
(femme) Madame l'Ambassadrice/la Haute-Commissaire,
Salutation - (homme) Je vous prie d'agréer, Monsieur l'Ambassadeur/le Haut-commissaire, l'expression de ma haute considération.
(femme) Je vous prie d'agréer, Madame l'Ambassadrice/ la Haute-commissaire, l'expression de mes respectueux hommages.
Conversation - (homme) ‹‹Monsieur l'Ambassadeur/ le Haut-Commissaire››
(femme) ‹‹Madame l'Ambassadrice/la Haut-Commissaire››
Remarques: Si un ambassadeur du Canada ou un haut-commissaire du Canada se trouve au Canada ou à l'étranger, la formule à employer est simplement ‹‹Ambassadeur›› ou ‹‹Haut-commissaire››. Le titre ‹‹Excellence›› n'est pas accordé par un citoyen canadien à un ambassadeur du Canada ou à un haut-commissaire du Canada, mais par le gouvernement et les citoyens du pays auprès duquel l'ambassadeur ou le haut-commissaire est accédité.

Armed Forces/Forces Armeés

OFFICER RANK:

Brigadier General/Major General/Lieutenant General/General (full name), Address
Salutation - Dear General:
Final Salutation - Yours sincerely,
In Conversation - "General (name)"
Colonel (full name), Address
Salutation - Dear Colonel:
Final Salutation - Yours sincerely,
In Conversation - "Colonel (name)"
Lieutenant Colonel (full name), Address
Salutation - Lieutenant Colonel:
Final Salutation - Yours sincerely,
In Conversation - "Lieutenant Colonel (name)"
Major (full name), Address
Salutation - Dear Major:
Final Salutation - Yours sincerely,
In Conversation - "Major (name)"
Captain (full name), Address
Salutation - Dear Captain:
Final Salutation - Yours sincerely,
In Conversation - "Captain (name)"
Lieutenant (full name), Address
Salutation - Dear Lieutenant:
Final Salutation - Yours sincerely,
In Conversation - "Lieutenant (name)"

AVEC GRADE:

(homme) Le brigadier-général/major-général/lieutenant- général (prénom et nom), Adresse
(femme) La brigadière-générale/majore-générale/lieutenante-générale (prénom et nom), Adresse
Appel - (homme) Général,
(femme) Générale,
Salutation - (homme) Je vous prie d'agréer, Général, l'expression de mes meilleurs sentiments.
(femme) Je vous prie d'agréer, Générale, l'expression de mes hommages respectueux.
Conversation - (homme) ‹‹Général››
(femme) ‹‹Générale››
(homme) Le colonel (prénom et nom), Adresse
(femme) La colonelle (prénom et nom), Adresse
Appel - (homme) Colonel,
(femme) Colonelle,
Salutation - (homme) Je vous prie d'agréer, Colonel, l'expression de mes meilleurs sentiments.
(femme) Je vous prie d'agréer, Colonelle, l'expression de mes hommages respectueux.
Conversation - (homme) ‹‹Colonel››
(femme) ‹‹Colonelle››
(homme) La lieutenant-colonel, (prénom et nom), Adresse
(femme) La lieutenante-colonelle, (prénom et nom), Adresse
Appel - (homme) Lieutenant-Colonel,
(femme) Lieutenante-Colonelle,
Salutation - (homme) Je vous prie d'agréer, Lieutenant- Colonel, l'expression de mes meilleurs sentiments.
(femme) Je vous prie d'agréer, Lieutenante-Colonelle, l'expression de mes meilleurs hommages respectueux.
Conversation - (homme) ‹‹Lieutenant-Colonel››
(femme) ‹‹Lieutenante-Colonelle››
(homme) Le major (prénom et nom), Adresse
(femme) La majore (prénom et nom), Adresse
Appel - (homme) Major,
(femme) Majore,
Salutation - (homme) Je vous prie d'agréer, Major, l'expression de mes meilleurs sentiments.
(femme) Je vous prie d'agréer, Majore, l'expression de mes hommages respectueux.
Conversation - (homme) ‹‹Major››
(femme) ‹‹Majore››
(homme) Le capitaine (prénom et nom), Adresse

(femme) La capitaine (prénom et nom), Adresse
Appel - Capitaine,
Salutation - (homme) Je vous prie d'agréer, Capitaine, l'expression de mes meilleurs sentiments.
(femme) Je vous prie d'agréer, Capitaine, l'expression de mes hommages respectueux.
Conversation - ‹‹Capitaine››
(homme) Le lieutenant (prénom et nom), Adresse
(femme) La lieutenante (prénom et nom), Adresse
Appel - (homme) Lieutenant,
(femme) Lieutenante,
Salutation - (homme) Je vous prie d'agréer, Lieutenant, l'expression de mes meilleurs sentiments.
(femme) Je vous prie d'agréer, Lieutenante, l'expression de mes hommages respectueux.
Conversation - (homme) ‹‹Lieutenant››
(femme) ‹‹Lieutenante››

NCO and other ranks:
Chief Warrant Officer (full name)
Salutation - Dear Chief Warrant (name)
Final Salutation - Yours sincerely,
In Conversation - "Mr./Mrs./Ms./Miss (name)"
Master Warrant Officer (full name)
Salutation - Dear Master Warrant (name):
Final Salutation - Yours sincerely,
In Conversation - "Mr./Mrs./Ms./Miss (name)"
Warrant Officer (full name)
Salutation - Dear Warrant (name):
Final Salutation - Yours sincerely,
In Conversation - "Mr./Mrs./Ms./Miss (name)"
Sergeant (full name)
Salutation - Dear Sergeant (name):
Final Salutation - Yours sincerely,
In Conversation - "Mr./Mrs./Ms./Miss (name)"
Corporal (full name)
Salutation - Dear Corporal (name):
Final Salutation - Yours sincerely,
In Conversation - "Mr./Mrs./Ms./Miss (name)"
Private (full name)
Salutation - Dear Private (name):
Final Salutation - Yours sincerely,
In Conversation - "Mr./Mrs./Ms./Miss (name)"

SOUS OFFICIERS ET AUTRES GRADES:
(homme) L'adjudant-chef (prénom et nom)
(femme) L'adjudante-chef (prénom et nom)
Appel - (homme) Adjudant-chef,
(femme) Adjudante-chef,
Salutation - (homme) Je vous prie d'agréer, Adjudant-chef, l'expression de mes meilleurs sentiments.
(femme) Je vous prie d'agréer, Adjudante-chef, l'expression de mes hommages respectueux.
Conversation - Le qualificatif du grade ‹‹Monsieur/ Madame/Mademoiselle››
(homme) L'adjudant-maître (prénom et nom)
(femme) L'adjudante-maîtresse (prénom et nom)
Appel - (homme) Adjudant-maître,
(femme) Adjudante-maîtresse,
Salutation - (homme) Je vous prie d'agréer, Adjudant-maître, l'expression de mes meilleurs hommages respectueux.
(femme) Je vous prie d'agréer, Adjudantemaîtresse, l'expression de mes hommages respectueux.
Conversation - Le qualificatif du grade ‹‹Monsieur/ Madame/Mademoiselle››
(homme) L'adjudant (prénom et nom)
(femme) L'adjudante (prénom et nom)
Appel - (homme) Adjudant,
(femme) Adjudante,
Salutation - (homme) Je vous prie d'agréer, Adjudant, l'expression de mes meilleurs sentiments.
(femme) Je vous prie d'agréer, Adjudante, l'expression de mes hommages respectueux.
Conversation - Le qualificatif du grade ‹‹Monsieur/ Madame/Mademoiselle››
(homme) Le sergent (prénom et nom)
(femme) La sergente (prénom et nom)
Appel - (homme) Sergent,
(femme) Sergente,
Salutation - (homme) Je vous prie d'agréer, Sergent, l'expression de mes meilleurs sentiments.
(femme) Je vous prie d'agréer, Sergente, l'expression de mes hommages respectueux.
Conversation - Le qualificatif du grade ‹‹Monsieur/ Madame/Mademoiselle››
(homme) Le caporal (prénom et nom)
(femme) La caporale (prénom et nom)
Appel - (homme) Caporal,
(femme) Caporale,
Salutation - (homme) Je vous prie d'agréer, Caporal, l'expression de mes meilleurs sentiments.
(femme) Je vous prie d'agréer, Caporale, l'expression de mes hommages respectueux.
Conversation - Le qualificatif du grade ‹‹Monsieur/ Madame/Mademoiselle››
(homme) Le soldat (prénom et nom)
(femme) La soldate (prénom et nom)
Appel - Monsieur/Madame/Mademoiselle,
Salutation - (homme) Je vous prie d'agréer, Monsieur, l'expression de mes meilleurs sentiments.
(femme) Je vous prie d'agréer, Madame/Mademoiselle, l'expression de mes hommages respectueux.
Conversation - Le qualificatif du grade ‹‹Monsieur/ Madame/Mademoiselle››

Foreign Dignitaries/Les Dignitaires Étrangers

AN EMPEROR:
His Imperial Majesty Akihito, Emperor of Japan, Address
Salutation - Your dignified Majesty:
Final Salutation - I have the honour to remain, Your Imperial Majesty's obedient servant,
In Conversation - "Your Majesty" first then "Sire"

EMPEREUR:
Sa Majesté Impériale (Nom) ________, Empereur du ________, Adresse Appel - Votre Majesté Impériale,
Salutation - Je prie Votre Majesté Impériale d'agréer l'hommage de mon profond respect et de ma très haute considération.
Conversation - On commence par ‹‹Majesté››. On poursuit avec ‹‹Sire››

A KING:
His Majesty Juan Carlos, King of Spain, Address
Salutation - Your Majesty/Sire:
Final Salutation - I have the honour to remain, Your Majesty's obedient servant,
In Conversation - "Your Majesty" first then "Sire"

UN ROI:
Sa Majesté (Nom) ________, Roi de ________, Adresse Appel - Majesté/Sire,
Salutation - Je prie Votre Majesté d'agréer l'hommage de mon profond respect et de ma très haute considération.
Conversation - On commence par ‹‹Majesté››. On poursuit avec ‹‹Sire››

A QUEEN:
Her Majesty Queen Sophia, Queen of Spain, Address
Salutation - Your Majesty/Madame:
Final Salutation - I have the honour to remain, Your Majesty's obedient servant,
In Conversation - "Your Majesty" first then "Ma'am"

UNE REINE:
Sa Majesté la reine (Nom) ________, Reine de ________, Adresse Appel - Majesté/Madame,
Salutation - Je vous prie d'agréer Madame, l'hommage de mon profond respect et de ma très haute considération.
Conversation - On commence par ‹‹Majesté››. On poursuit avec ‹‹Madame››

A PRESIDENT OF A REPUBLIC:
His/Her Excellency (full name), President of the Republic of (name), Address
Salutation - Excellency:
Final Salutation - Yours sincerely
In Conversation - "Excellency" first then "President" or "Sir/Madam"

UN PRÉSIDENT DE RÉPUBLIQUE:
(homme) Son Excellence monsieur (prénom et nom) Président de la République (nom), Adresse
(femme) Son Excellence madame (prénom et nom) Présidente de la République (nom), Adresse
Appel - (homme) Monsieur le Président,
(femme) Madame la Présidente,
Salutation - (homme) Je vous prie d'agréer Monsieur le Président, l'expression de ma très haute considération.
(femme) Je vous prie d'agréer Madame la Présidente, l'hommage de mon profond respect.
Conversation - (homme) On commence par ‹‹Excellence››. On poursuit avec ‹‹Monsieur le Président›› ou ‹‹Monsieur››
(femme) On commence par ‹‹Excellence››. On poursuit avec ‹‹Madame la Présidente›› ou ‹‹Madame››

THE PRESIDENT OF THE UNITED STATES:
His Excellency the Honourable (full name), President of the United States, The White House, Washington, D.C.
Salutation - Dear Mr. President:
Final Salutation - Yours sincerely,
In Conversation - "Mr. President" or "Excellency" first then "Sir"

PRÉSIDENT DES ÉTATS-UNIS D'AMÉRIQUE:
Son Excellence l'honorable (prénom et nom) Président de États-Unis d'Amérique, The White House, Washington D.C.
Appel - Monsieur le Président,
Salutation - Je vous prie d'agréer Monsieur le Président, l'expression de ma très haute considération.
Conversation - On commence par ‹‹Monsieur le Président›› ou ‹‹Excellence››

A PRIME MINISTER:
His/Her Excellency (full name), Prime Minister of (name), Address
Salutation - Dear Prime Minister:
Final Salutation - Yours sincerely,
In Conversation - "Prime Minister" or "Excellency" first then "Sir/Madam" or "Mr./Mrs./Ms./Miss (name)"

PREMIER MINISTRE:
(homme) Son Excellence monsieur (prénom et nom) Premier Ministre de ________, Adresse
(femme) Son Excellence madame (prénom et nom) Première Ministre de ________, Adresse
Appel - (homme) Monsieur le Premier Ministre,
(femme) Madame la Première Ministre,
Salutation - (homme) Je vous prie d'agréer Monsieur le Premier Ministre, l'expression de ma haute considération.
(femme) Je vous prie d'agréer Madame la Première Ministre, l'hommage de mon profond respect.
Conversation - (homme) On commence par ‹‹Monsieur le Premier Ministre›› ou ‹‹Excellence››. On poursuit par ‹‹Monsieur››
(femme) On commence par ‹‹Madame la Première Ministre›› ou ‹‹Excellence››. On poursuit par ‹‹Madame››

Others/Autres

LAWYERS/NOTARIES:
Mr./Mrs./Ms./Miss (full name) or Mr./Mrs./Ms./Miss, Q.C.
Salutation - Dear Mr./Mrs./Ms./Miss (name):
Final Salutation - Yours sincerely,
In Conversation - "Mr./Mrs./Ms./Miss (name)"

AVOCATS/NOTAIRES:
Me (prénom et nom) Appel - Maître,
Salutation - Je vous prie d'agréer, Maître, l'expression de mes meilleurs sentiments.
Conversation - ‹‹Maître››

AIDE-DE-CAMP:
Military: (according to rank; See Armed Forces) Civilian (according to their title), Mr./Mrs./Ms./Miss (full name)
Salutation - Dear Mr./Mrs./Ms./Miss (name):
Final Salutation - Yours sincerely,
In Conversation - "Mr./Mrs./Ms./Miss (name)"
Note: Post nominals "A. de C." have been authorized for Aides-de-camps to the Governor General and Lieutenant Governors.
Militaire: (selon le grade; voir la rubrique ‹‹Forces armées››) Civil (selon le titre), Monsieur/Madame/Mademoiselle (prénom et nom) Appel - Monsieur/Madame/Mademoiselle,
Salutation - Je vous prie d'agréer, Monsieur/Madame/ Mademoiselle, l'expression de mes sentiments les meilleurs.
Conversation - ‹‹Monsieur/Madame/Mademoiselle›› Remarque: Les initiales ‹‹A. de C.›› sont autorisées pour les aides de camp du Governeur général et des lieutenants-gouverneurs.

NATIVE CITIZENS/AUTOCHTONES:

Indian Chiefs:
Chief (full name), Chief of (name), Address
Salutation - Chief (name):
Final Salutation - Yours sincerely,
In Conversation - "Chief (name)"

Chefs indiens:
Chef (prénom et nom), Chef de (nom), Adresse Appel - Chef,
Salutation - Je vous prie d'agréer, Chef, l'expression de mes sentiments les meilleurs.
Conversation - ‹‹Chef››

Band Councillors:
Mr./Mrs./Ms./Miss (full name):
Salutation - Mr./Mrs./Ms./Miss (name):
Final Salutation - Yours sincerely,
In Conversation - "Mr./Mrs./Ms./Miss (name)"

Conseillers de bandes:
Monsieur/Madame/Mademoiselle (prénom et nom), Adresse Appel - Monsieur/Madame/Mademoiselle,
Salutation - Je vous prie d'agréer, Monsieur/Madame/ Mademoiselle, l'expression de mes sentiments les meilleurs.
Conversation - ‹‹Monsieur/Madame/Mademoiselle››

Abbreviations

Indicating Academic, Ecclesiastical and other Degrees, membership in Societies and Institutions, military ranks, etc., appearing in the Canadian Almanac and Directory.

AACCA .... Associate of Association of Certified Accountants & Corporate Accountants (British)
AACI .... Accredited Appraiser Canadian Institute
AAE .... Associate of Accountants' & Executives' Corp. of Canada
AAGO .... — of the American Guild of Organists
AASA............... — of the Alberta Society of Artists
AB .... Bachelor of Arts, American (Artium Baccalaureus)
AC .... "Advanced Certification" Canadian Association of Medical Radiation Technologists
ACA................ Associate of Institute of Chartered Accountants (Eng.)
ACAM .... Associate Certified Administrative Manager
ACCO .... — of Canadian College of Organists
AccSCRP............ — of Canadian Public Relations Society Inc.
ACD................ Archaeologiae Christianae Doctor
ACGI .... Associate of the City & Guilds of London Institute
ACIC .... — of Canadian Institute of Chemistry
ACInstM............. — of the Institute of Marketing
ACIS .... — of Chartered Institute of Secretaries (British)
ACSM .... — of Cambourne School of Mines
Adm. .... Admiral
Adm. A. Pl.Fin......... Administrateur agréé en planification financière
AFC................ Accredited Financial Counsellor
AFRAS (AFRAeS) ..... Fellow of the Royal Aeronautical Society
Ag de l'U (Paris)....... Honorary Professor of University of Paris (Agrégé de l'Université Paris)
Ag. de Phil. .... Professor of Philosophy (Agrégé en Philosophie Louvain)
AGSM .... Associate of the Guildhall School of Music (British)
AIC................. — of the Institute of Chemistry (British)
AICB .... Associate of the Institute of Canadian Bankers
AIIC .... — of the Insurance Institute of Canada
AKC................ — of King's College (London)
ALCM............... — of London (Canada) Conservatory of Music
ALS .... Commissioned Alberta Land Surveyor
AM................. Master of Arts (Artium Magister)
AMEIC.............. Associate Member of the Engineering Institute of Canada
AMICE.............. — Member of the Institution of Civil Engineers (British)
AMIEE .... — Member of the Institute of Electrical Engineers
AMIMechE........... — Member of the Institution of Mechanical Engineers (British)
A.Mus............... — of Music
APA .... — Member of the Institute of Accredited Public Accountants (British)
APHA............... — Member of the Public Health Association (British)
APR................ Accredited Member of the Canadian Public Relations Society
ARA................ Associate of the Royal Academy (honorary)
ARCD............... — of the Royal College of Dancing
ARCM .... — of the Royal College of Music
ARCO .... — of the Royal College of Organists (Canadian)
ARCS (A.R.C.Sc.) ..... — of the Royal College of Science
ARCT............... — of the Royal Conservatory of Music of Toronto
ARCVS .... — of the Royal College of Veterinary Surgeons
ARDIO.............. — of Registered Interior Designers of Ontario
ARDS............... — of the Royal Drawing Society (London, Eng.)
ARIBA .... — of the Royal Institute of British Architects
ARIC .... — of the Royal Institute of Chemistry
ARSH............... — of the Royal Society of Health
ARSM .... — of the Royal School of Mines
ARSM .... — of the Royal School of Music
AScT .... Applied Science Technologist
Assoc. Inst. M.M....... Associate of the Institute of Mining and Metallurgy (British)
ATCL .... — of Trinity College, London (Eng.)
ATCM............... — of the Toronto Conservatory of Music
A.Th. .... — in Theology
BA .... Bachelor of Arts
BAA................ — of Applied Arts
B.Acc. .... — of Accountancy
B.Adm. (B.Admin.)..... — of Administration
B.Adm.Pub. .... — Baccalauréat spécialisé en administration publique
BAeE (BAeroE) .... Bachelor of Aeronautical Engineering
BAI................. — of Engineering (U. of Dublin)
BALS .... — of Arts in Library Science
BAO................ — of Obstetrics
B.Arch............... — in Architecture
BAS (B.A.Sc.) .... — of Applied Science
BASM............... — of Arts, Master of Science
B.A.Theo............. — of Arts in Theology
BBA................ — of Business Administration
BCD .... Bachelier en Chirurgie Dentale
BCE .... Bachelor of Civil Engineering
B.Ch. (ChB).......... — in Surgery (British)
BChE............... — in Chemical Engineering (American)
BCL .... — of Civil Law (or Canon Law)
B.Com. (B. Comm.) .... — of Commerce
B.Comp.Sc. .... — of Computer Science
BD .... — of Divinity
BDC .... Bachelier en droit canonique
B.Des. .... Bachelor of Design
BDS................ — of Dental Surgery (British)
BE (B.Eng.) .... — of Engineering
B.Ed. (BEAD)......... — of Education
BEDS............... — of Environmental Design Studies
BEE .... — of Electrical Engineering (American)
B. en Ph. .... Bachelier en Philosophie
B. en Sc. Com......... — en Science Commerciale
BES .... Bachelor of Environmental Sciences (or Studies)
B ès A .... Bachelier ès Arts
B ès L............... — ès Lettres
B. ès Sc. .... — ès Science
B. ès Sc. App. .... — ès Science Appliquée
BF .... Bachelor of Forestry (American)
BFA .... — of Fine Arts
B.Gen. .... Brigadier-General
BHE (B.H.Ec.) .... Bachelor of Home Economics
B.H.Sc............... — of Household Science
BJ .... — of Journalism
BJC .... — in Canon Law
BL .... — in Literature (or of Laws)
BLA .... — of Landscape Architecture
B.Litt................ — of Literature (American & British)
BLS .... — of Library Science
BM................. — of Medicine
B.Mus............... — of Music
BMV .... Bachelier en Médecine Vetérinaire
BN .... Bachelor of Nursing
B.N.Sc............... — of Nursing Science
B. Paed. (Péd.) .... — of Pedagogy
BPA .... — of Public Administration
BPE .... — of Physical Education
B.Ph. (B.Phil.) .... — of Philosophy
BPHE............... — of Physical & Health Education
B.Ps. .... Baccalauréat en Psychologie
Br. .... Brother
BS .... Bachelor of Science (or of Surgery) (American)
BSA .... — of Science in Agriculture (or in Accounting, or in Administration)
B.Sc. .... — of Science
BScA .... Bachelier ès science appliquées
BScB .... — en Bibliothéconomie
B.Sc.(CE) .... Bachelor of Science in Civil Engineering
B.Sc.Com............ — of Commercial Science
B.Sc.Dom............ Baccalauréat en Sciences Domestiques
BScF (BSF) .... Bachelor of Science in Forestry
BScFE .... — of Science in Forestry Engineering
BScH .... Bachelier en Sciences Hospitalières
BScN .... Bachelor of Science in Nursing
B.Sc.(Nurs.) .... — of Science in Nursing
B.Sc.(Occ.Ther.) ...... — of Science in Occupational Therapy
B.Sc.(OT)............ — of Science in Occupational Therapy
B.Sc.Phm.(BSP) ...... — of Science in Pharmacy
B.Sc.Soc............. — of Social Science
BSCE............... — of Science in Civil Engineering
B.S.Ed............... — of Science in Education
BSEE............... — of Science in Electrical Engineering
BSN .... — of Science in Nursing
BSS .... — of Social Sciences
BSW................ — of Social Work (or Welfare)
B.Tech............... — of Technology
B.Th. .... — of Theology
BTS .... — of Technological Science (Edinburgh)
B.V.Sc............... — of Veterinary Science
CA .... Chartered Accountant
C. Adm., F.P. .... Chartered Administrator in Financial Planning
CAAP .... Certified Advertising Agency Practitioner
CAE .... — Association Executive
CAE/c.a.é. .... Chartered Account Executive
CAM .... Certified Administrative Manager
CAP .... Certificat d'Aptitude Pedagogique
Capt. (or Capt.(N)) .... Captain (or Captain (Naval))
CBE .... Commander, Order of the British Empire
CBV .... Chartered Business Valuator
CC................. Chartered Cartographer

CC .... Companion, Order of Canada
CD .... Canadian Forces Decoration
Cdr. .... Commander
CE .... Civil Engineer
CEA .... Certified Environmental Administrator
CEA .... Certified Environmental Auditor
CEBS .... Certified Employee Benefit Specialist
Cer.E. .... Ceramic Engineer
Cert. Bus. Admin. ..... Doctor of Applied Science Diploma Business Administration
CES .... Certificat d'Études Secondaires (La Sorbonne)
CFA .... Chartered Financial Analyst
CFP .... Chartered Financial Planner
CGA .... Certified General Accountant
CHA .... Certified Housing Administrator
Chan. .... Chanoine (Canon)
Ch.E. .... Chartered Executive
CHE .... Certified Health Executive
Chem. Ing. .... Ingénieur Chimiste Diplomé (Swiss Fed. Inst. Technology)
CHFC .... Chartered Financial Consultant
CIF .... Canadian Institute of Forestry
CIM .... Certificate in Management
CIM .... Certified Industrial Manager
CIM .... Certified Investment Manager
CIS&P .... Canadian Inst. of Surveying & Photogrammetry
CLA .... Canadian Library Association
CLS .... Canada Land Surveyor
CLU .... Chartered Life Underwriter
CM .... Master in Medicine (British)
CM .... Member, Order of Canada
CMA .... Certified Management Accountant (or Canadian Medical Association or Canadian Management Association)
CMC .... Certified Management Consultant
CmdO .... Commissioned Officer
Cmdre. .... Commodore
CMM .... Certified Municipal Manager (Ontario)
CMM .... Commander, Order of Military Merit
COM .... Commander of the Order of Merit (Police Forces)
Col. .... Colonel
CPA .... Chartered Professional Accountant (formerly Certified Public Accountant)
CPC................ — Personnel Consultant
CPM .... Certificate in Personnel Management
CPPMA .... — in Public Personnel Management Association
CPPO .... Certified Public Purchasing Officer
CPP................ — Professional Purchaser
CR (c.r.) .... Conseiller de la Reine (Queen's Counsel)
CRA .... Canadian Residential Appraiser
CSC .... Canadian Securities Course
CSR .... Chartered Stenographic Reporter
CTC .... Certified Travel Counsellor
C.Tech.............. — Technician
CWO .... Chief Warrant Officer
DA .... Doctor of Arts (honorary)
DA .... — of Archaeology (Laval)
D.Arch.............. — of Architecture
D.A.Sc.............. — in Applied Sciences
DC .... — of Chiropractic
DCD .... Docteur en Chirurgie Dentale
D.Ch................ Doctor of Surgery (British)
DChE............... — of Chemical Engineering (American)
DCL .... — of Civil Law (or Canon Law)
DD .... — of Divinity
DDC .... Doctorat Droit Canonique
D. de l'Un. .... — Docteur de l'Université
DDS .... Doctor of Dental Surgery (British)
DDT .... — of Drugless Therapy
D.Ed. .... — of Education
D.Eng. .... — of Engineering
D. en Méd. Vet. .... Docteur en Médecine Vetérinaire
D. en Ph. .... — en Philosophie
D ès L .... — ès Lettres (Doctor of Letters)
D. ès Sc. App. .... Doctor of Applied Science
DF .... — of Forestry (American)
DFA .... — of Fine Arts (often honorary)
D.F.Sc.............. — of Financial Science (Laval)
DIC .... Diploma of Membership of Imperial College of Science & Technology (British)
Dip. Bact............. — in Bacteriology
Dip d'É .... Diplome d'Études
Dip de l'U (P) .... Diploma of the U. of Paris
Dip. d'É. Sup. or DipES .. Diplome d'Études Supérieures, Paris
Dip. Ing. .... Diploma in Engineering
Dipl. Bus. Admin. ..... Diploma Business Administration
D.Jour .... Doctor of Journalism
D. Lit. (D. Litt.) .... — of Letters (or Literature)
DLO .... Diploma in Laryngology & Otology
DLS .... Dominion Land Surveyor (or Doctor of Library Science)
DM .... Doctorat Médecine
DMD .... Doctor of Dental Medicine
D.Ms................ — in Missionology
D.Mus. .... Doctorat en Musique
DMR (D or T) .... Diploma in Medical Radiology (Royal Coll. of Surgeons, London)
DMT................ — in Tropical Medicine
DMT & H (Eng.)....... — in Tropical Medicine & Hygiene
D.N.S (D.N.Sc.) .... Doctor of Nursing Science
DO .... — of Osteopathy
Doct.Arch. .... — of Christian Archaeology (Pontifical Institute, Rome)
D.Paed. (Péd.)........ — of Paedagogy
DPE .... Diploma in Physical Education
D.Ph. (D.Phil. or PhD) . . Doctor of Philosophy
D.P.Ec............... — of Political Economy
DPH................ — (or Diploma) in Public Health
D.Ps. (D.Psy.) .... — of Psychologie
D.P.Sc............... — of Political Science
D.Psych. .... — (or Diploma) in Psychiatry
DPT .... — of Physio-Therapy
Dr. .... Doctor
DR .... Doctor of Radiology
Dr.Com.Sc. .... — of Commercial Science
Dr de l'U (P).......... — of the U. of Paris
Dr. ès Lettres .... — of Letters (History of Literature)
Dr. jur. .... — of Law (Dr. Juris)
Dr. rer. pol............ — of Political Economy (Dr. Rerum Politicarum) (Docteur des Sciences Politiques)
DSA (DScA) .... Docteur ès science appliqués
D.Sc. .... Doctor of Science
D.Sc.Mil. .... — of Military Science
DSL .... — of Sacred Letters
D.Sc.Com............ — of Commercial Science
D.Sc.Fin. .... — of Financial Science
D.Sc.Nat............. — in Natural Science
D.Sc.Soc............. — of Social Science
D.Th. .... — of Theology
DVM (DMV).......... — of Veterinary Medicine
D.V.Sc............... — of Veterinary Science
E.C.E. .... Early Childhood Educator
EdD .... Doctor of Education
EdM .... Master of Education (Harvard)
EE .... Electrical Engineer
EM .... Mining Engineer
ETCM .... Graduate of Eastern Townships Conservatory of Music
FAAO .... Fellow of the American Academy of Optometry
F.A.A.O.Dip. .... Diplomatic Fellow of the American Academy of Optometry
FACD .... Fellow of the American College of Dentists
FACO............... — of the American College of Organists
FACP .... — of the American College of Physicians
FACR............... — of the American College of Radiology
FACS .... — of the American College of Surgeons
FAE .... — of the Accountants' & Executives' Corp. of Canada
FAGS............... — of the American Geographical Society
FAIA................ — of the American Institute of Actuaries
.... — of the American Institute of Architects
FAIA .... Association of International Accountants
FAOU .... Fellow of the American Ornithologists Union
FAPHA.............. — of the American Public Health Association
FAPS .... — of the American Physical Society
FAS .... — of the Actuarial Society
FBA .... — of the British Academy (honorary)
FBOA............... — of British Association of Optometrists
FCA .... — of the Institute of Chartered Accountants (British)
FCAM............... — of the Certified Administrative Manager
FCBA............... — of Canadian Bankers' Association
FCCA............... — of the Association of Certified Accountants
FCCO............... — of the Canadian College of Organists
FCCT............... — of the Canadian College of Teachers
FCCUI .... — of the Canadian Credit Union Institute
FCGI .... — of the City & Guilds of London Institute
FCI................. — of the Canadian Credit Institute
FCIC .... — of the Chemical Institute of Canada
FCII .... — of the Chartered Insurance Institute (British)
FCIS................ — of the Chartered Institute of Secretaries (British)

FCOG .... — of the College of Obstetricians & Gynaecologists (British)
FCAMRT .... — of Canadian Association of Medical Radiation Technologists
FCIA................ — of the Canadian Institute of Actuaries
FCMA............... — of the Society of Management Accountants of Canada
FCSI................ — of the Canadian Securities Institute
FCTC............... — of the Canadian Institute of Travel Counsellors
FCUIC .... — of the Credit Union Institute of Canada
FE .... Forest Engineer
FEIC .... Fellow of the Engineering Institute of Canada
FFA .... — of the Faculty of Actuaries (Scotland)
FFR .... — of the Faculty of Radiologists (British)
FGS................ — of the Geological Society (British)
FGSA............... — of the Geological Society of America
FIA................. — of the Institute of Actuaries (British)
FIC................. — of the Institute of Chemistry
FICB................ — of the Institute of Canadian Bankers
FICE................ — of the Institution of Civil Engineers
FIEE................ — of the Institution of Electrical Engineers
FIIC .... — of the Insurance Institute of Canada
FIL................. — of the Institute of Linguists (British)
FLA .... — of the Library Association (England)
FMA .... Financial Management Advisor
FMSA............... — of the Mineralogical Society of America
Fr. .... Father
FRAI .... Fellow of the Royal Anthropological Institute
FRAIC .... — of the Royal Architectural Institute of Canada
FRAM............... — of the Royal Academy of Music
FRAS............... — of the Royal Astronomical Society
FRCCO .... — of the Royal Canadian College of Organists
FRCM .... — of the Royal College of Music
FRCO............... — of the Royal College of Organists
FRCOG .... — of the Royal College of Obstetricians & Gynaecologists
FRCP............... — of the Royal College of Physicians of London
FRCP(C) .... — of the Royal College of Physicians of Canada
FRCP(E) .... — of the Royal College of Physicians of Edinburgh
FRCP(I) .... — of the Royal College of Physicians of Ireland
FRCP(Glas).......... — of the Royal College of Physicians of Glasgow
FRCS............... — of the Royal College of Surgeons of England
FRCS(C) .... — of the Royal College of Surgeons of Canada
FRCS(E) .... — of the Royal College of Surgeons of Edinburgh
FRCS(I) .... — of the Royal College of Surgeons of Ireland
FRCS(Glas).......... — of the Royal College of Surgeons of Glasgow
FRGS............... — of the Royal Geographical Society
FRHistS............. — of the Royal Historical Society
FRHortS............. — of the Royal Horticultural Society
FRIBA .... — of the Royal Institute of British Architects
FRIC .... — of the Royal Institute of Chemistry
FRICS .... — of the Royal Institution of Chartered Surveyors
FRMCM .... — of Royal Manchester College of Music
FRMS (FRMetS) ...... — of the Royal Meteorological Society
FRS................ — of the Royal Society (honorary)
FRSA............... — of the Royal Society of Arts
FRSC............... — of the Royal Society of Canada
FRSE............... — of the Royal Society of Edinburgh
FRSH............... — of the Royal Society of Health
FRSL............... — of the Royal Society of Literature
FSA................ — of the Society of Actuaries (or of Antiquaries) (honorary)
FSMAC .... — of the Society of Management Accountants of Canada
FSS................ — of the Royal Statistical Society
FTCL............... — of Trinity College of Music (London)
FZS................ — of the Zoological Society (British)
Gen. .... General
GJ .... Graduate Jeweller
HARCVS .... Honorary Associate of Royal College of Veterinary Surgeons
IA .... Investment Advisor
IC .... Investment Counsellor
IngETP .... Diplome de l'École Spéciale des Travaux Publiques
JCB .... Bachelor of Canon Law
JCD .... Doctor of Canon Law (or of Civil Law)
JCL .... Licentiate in Canon Law (Juris Canonici Licentiatus)
JD .... Doctor of Jurisprudence
JDS .... — of Jurisdical Science
Jr. .... Junior
JUL .... Licentiate of Law in Utroque (both Civil & Canon Law)
JurM .... Master of Jurisprudence
Jur. utr. Dr. .... Juris utriusque doctor, Equiv. to LL.D.
LAB .... Licentiate of the Assoc. Bd. of Royal Schools of Music (London, Eng.)
L.Cdr. .... Lieutenant-Commander
LCL .... Licentiate in Canon Law
LCMI .... — of the Cost & Management Institute
L.Col. .... Lieutenant-Colonel
LDC .... Licencié ès Droit Canonique
LDS .... Licentiate in Dental Surgery (British)
L ès L .... Licencié ès Lettres
L. ès Sc.............. — ès Sciences
L.Gen. .... Lieutenant-General
LGSM .... Licentiate of the Guildhall School of Music & Drama (London, Eng.)
LittD .... Doctor of Letters (or Literature)
LittL .... Licence ès Lettres
Litt.M. .... Master of Letters (or Literature)
LJC .... Licentiatus Juris Canonici
LL .... License in Civil Law
LLB .... Bachelor of Laws (Legum Baccalaureus)
LLD .... Doctor of Laws (usually honorary)
LLL .... Licence en droit
LLM .... Master of Law
L. Mus. .... Licentiate in Music
LMUS............... — in Music of the Univ. of Saskatchewan
L Mus TCL........... — in General Musicianship of Trinity College, London
L.Péd. .... Licence en Pédagogie
L.Ph. .... — en Philosophie
L.Psych. .... Licencié en Psychologie
LRAM .... Licentiate of the Royal Academy of Music (London)
LRCM............... — of the Royal College of Music (London)
LRCP............... — of the Royal College of Physicians
LRCS............... — of the Royal College of Surgeons
LRCT............... — of the Royal Conservatory of Toronto
LRE .... — in Religious Education
LRSM............... — of the Royal Schools of Music (London)
LS .... Land Surveyor
LSA .... Licentiate in Agricultural Science
L.Sc.Com. .... — in Commercial Science
LScO .... Licence en optométrie
L.S.Sc. .... Licentiate in Sacred Scriptures
L.Sc.Soc. .... Licence in Social Science
LST .... Licentiate in Sacred Theology
Lt. (or Lt(N)) .... Lieutenant (or Lieutenant (Naval))
LTCL .... Licentiate of Trinity College of Music (London)
LTCM............... — of the Toronto Conservatory of Music
L.Th .... Licentiate in Theology
M. .... Monsieur
MA .... Master of Arts
M.Acc. .... — of Accountancy
MACF .... Membre de l'Académie canadiennefrançaise
MAeE .... Master of Aeronautical Engineering
MAIEE.............. Member of American Institute of Electrical Engineers
MAIME.............. — of American Institute of Mining Engineers
Maj. .... Major
MALS .... Master of Arts in Library Science
MAP .... Maîtrise en administration publique
M.Arch. .... Master of Architecture
MAS................ — of Archival Studies
M.A.Sc. (MAS)........ — of Applied Science
MASCE .... Member of the American Society of Civil Engineers
MASME .... — of the American Society of Mechanical Engineers
MAust IM .... — of the Australian Institute of Mining & Metallurgy
MB .... Bachelor of Medicine (British)
MBA .... Master in Business Administration
MCE................ — of Civil Engineering
M.Ch. (ChM) .... — of Surgery (British)
MChE............... — of Chemical Engineering (American)
MCI .... Member of the Credit Institute
MCIC .... — of the Chemical Institute of Canada
MCIF .... — of the Canadian Institute of Forestry
MCIM............... — of the Canadian Institute of Mining
MCIMM .... — of the Canadian Institute of Mining & Metallurgy
MCInstM .... — of the Canadian Institute of Marketing
MCL .... Master of Civil Law
M.Com. .... — of Commerce
M.Comp. .... — of Canon Law
M.Comp.Sc........... — of Computer Science
MD .... Doctor of Medicine
MDC .... Master of Canon Law
MDCM .... Doctor of Medicine & Master of Surgery
M.Des. .... Master of Design
M.Div................ — of Divinity
MDS................ — of Dental Surgery (British)
MDV .... Doctor of Veterinary Medicine
Me .... Maître
ME .... Master of Mechanical Engineering

M.Ed. (M.A.Ed.) .... — of Education
MEDS .... — of Environmental Design Studies
MEE .... — of Electrical Engineering (American)
MEIC .... Member of the Engineering Institute of Canada
M.Eng. .... Master of Engineering
MF .... — of Forestry
MFA .... — of Fine Arts
M.Gen. .... Major-General
Mgr. .... Monsignor (or Manager or Monseigneur)
MHA .... Master of Health (or Hospital) Administration
MHE (M.H.Ec.) .... — of Home Economics
MICE .... Member of the Institution of Civil Engineers (British)
MICIA .... — of Industrial, Commercial & Institutional Accountants
MIEE .... — of the Institution of Electrical Engineers (British)
MIMM .... — of the Institute of Mining & Metallurgy (British)
MINA .... — of the Institute of Naval Architects
MIRE .... — of the Institute of Radio Engineers
M.I.St. .... Master of Information Studies
MJ .... — of Journalism
M.Litt. .... — of Letters (or Literature)
MLIS .... — of Library & Information Science
MLS .... — of Library Science (or Licentiate in Medieval Studies)
MM (M.Mus.) .... — of Music
MMM .... Member, Order of Military Merit
MOM .... Member of the Order of Merit (Police Forces)
MN (M.Nurs.) .... Master of Nursing
MP .... — of Planning
MP .... Member of Parliament
MPE .... Master of Physical Education
M.Ph. (M.Phil.) .... — of Philosophy
MPM .... — of Pest Management
MPP .... Member of Provincial Parliament
M.Ps. (M.Psy.) .... Master of Psychology
MRAIC .... Member of the Royal Architectural Institute of Canada
MRCOG .... — of the Royal College of Obstetricians & Gynaecologists
MRCP .... — of the Royal College of Physicians
MRCP(E) .... — of the Royal College of Physicians of Edinburgh
MRCP(I) .... — of the Royal College of Physicians of Ireland
MRCP(Glas) .... — of the Royal College of Physicians of Glasgow
MRCS .... — of the Royal College of Surgeons
MRCS(E) .... — of the Royal College of Surgeons of Edinburgh
MRCVS .... — of the Royal College of Veterinary Surgeons
MRM .... Master of Resource Management
MRSC .... Member of the Royal Society of Canada
MRSH .... — of the Royal Society of Health
MRST .... — of the Royal Society of Teachers
MS .... Master of Surgery (British)
MSA .... — of Science in Agriculture
M.Sc. .... — of Science
MScA .... — of Applied Science
MSCE .... — of Science in Civil Engineering
MScF .... — of Science in Forestry
M.Sc.(Med.) .... — of Science in Medicine
MScN (MSN) .... — of Science in Nursing
M.Sc.Phm. .... — of Science in Pharmacy
M.Sc.Soc. .... — in Social Sciences
M.S.Ed. .... — of Science in Education
M.S.Litt. .... — of Sacred Letters
MSPE .... McGill School of Physical Education
MSRC .... Membre Société Royale du Canada
MSS .... Master of Social Science
MSW .... — of Social Work
MTCI .... Member of Trust Companies Institute
M.U.Dr. .... Medecinae Universae Doctor (Prague) (Dentistry & Medicine)
MUP .... Master of Planning
MURP .... — of Urban & Rural Planning
Mus. Bac. (Mus.B.) .... Bachelor of Music
Mus. Doc. (Mus.D.) .... Doctor of Music
Mus. G. Paed. .... Musicae Graduatus Paedagogus (Graduate Teacher in Music)
MusM .... Master of Music
MV .... Médecin Vétérinaire
M.V.Sc. .... Master of Veterinary Science
NDA .... National Diploma in Agriculture (Royal Ag. Soc. of Engineering)
NDD .... National Diploma in Dairying (Scotland)
NP .... Notary Public
OA .... Officier d'Académie (France)
OC .... Order of Canada
OD .... Doctor of Optometry
OIP .... Officier de l'Instruction Publique
OLS .... Ontario Land Surveyor
OMM .... Officer, Order of Military Merit
OOM .... Officer of the Order of Merit (Police Forces)
OSA .... Ontario Society of Artists
PC .... Privy Councillor
PD .... Doctor of Parapsychology
PE .... Professional Engineer
P.Eng. .... Registered Professional Engineer
PFC .... Planificateur Financier Certifié
PFP .... Personal Financial Planner
PhB .... Bachelor of Philosophy
PhC .... Philosopher of Chiropractic
PhD .... Doctor of Philosophy
PhTD .... Physical Therapy Doctor
PhL .... Licentiate in Philosophy
PLS .... Professional Legal Secretary
P.Mgr. .... — Manager
PP .... — Purchaser
PPB .... — Public Buyer
Prof. .... Professor
PTIC .... Patent & Trade Mark Institute of Canada
QAA .... Qualified Administrative Assistant
QC .... Queen's Counsel
QLS .... Québec Land Surveyor
RA .... Royal Academy (honorary)
R.Adm. .... Rear-Admiral
RAM .... Royal Academy of Music (Budapest)
RAS .... Royal Aeronautical Society
RBA .... Royal Society of British Artists
RCA .... Royal Canadian Academy of Arts
RCAM .... Royal College & Academy of Music (Budapest)
RCM .... Royal Conservatory of Music (Leipzig)
RE .... Royal Engineers
REBC .... Registered Employee Benefits Consultant
Rev. .... Reverend
RFP .... Registered Financial Planner
RHU .... Registered Health Underwriter
RMS .... Royal Society of Miniature Painters
RMT .... Registered Music Teacher
RN .... — Nurse
ROI .... Royal Institute of Oil Painters
RP .... Member of the Royal Society of Portrait Painters
RP .... Révérend Père (Reverend Father)
RPA .... Registered Professional Accountant
R.P.Bio. .... — Professional Biologist
R.P.Dt. .... — Professional Dietitian
RPF .... — Professional Forester
RRL .... — Record Librarian
RSH .... Royal Society of Health
RSW .... Registered Specification Writer
RT .... — Technician of the Cdn. Association of Medical Radiation Technologists
SC .... Senior Counsel (Eire) equivalent of Q.C.
ScD .... Doctorat ès Sciences
ScL .... Licence ès Sciences
Sc Soc B .... Bachelier Science Sociale
Sc Soc D .... Doctor of Social Science
Sc Soc L .... License in Social Science
SFC .... Specialist in Financial Counselling
SJ .... Society of Jesus
SLS .... Saskatchewan Land Surveyor
S.Lt. .... Sub-Lieutenant
SM .... Master of Science
Sr. .... Senior
Sr. .... Sister
SSB .... Bachelier en Science Sacrée
SSC .... Sculptors' Society of Canada
SSL .... Licentiate in Sacred Scripture
STB (SThB) .... Bachelor of Sacred Theology
STD (SThD) .... Doctor of Sacred Theology
STL (SThL) .... Sacrae Theologiae Licentiatus (Licentiate in Sacred Theology)
STM .... Master of Sacred Theology
TCL .... Trinity College, London
TMMG .... Teacher, Massage & Medical Gymnastics
ThD .... Doctor of Theology
V.Adm. .... Vice-Admiral
VG .... Vicar-General
VS .... Veterinary Surgeon

Business & Shipping Abbreviations

As shipping terms vary in different countries, insurance or shipping agents should be consulted.

a/c .... Account
Ad val. .... Ad valorem
avoir .... Avoirdupois
bbl. .... Barrel
B/L. .... Bill of Lading
b.m. .... Board Measure
B.O. .... Buyer's Option
B/P. .... Bills Payable
B/R. .... Bills Receivable
B/S. .... Bill of Sale
c. .... Hundred
C or Cent. ..... Centigrade
cf. .... Compare
C. and F. ...... Cost & Freight
Cie .... Compagnie
c.i.f. .... Cost insurance & freight
C.L. .... Car Load (of freight)
Co. .... Company
C.O.D. .... Cash on Delivery
C. of F. .... Cost of Freight
Cr. .... Credit
C.W.O. .... Cash with Order
Cwt. .... Hundredweight
D/A. .... Documents Attached, also Deposit Account
Dis. (Disct.) .... Discount
Dl. (or Tl.) ...... Double (or triple) first class
D.O.A. .... Deliver Documents on Acceptance of Draft
D.O.P. .... Deliver Documents on Payment of Draft
Dr. .... Debit
D.V. .... God willing (Deo volente)
e.g. .... For example (exempli gratia)
E.&O.E. .... Errors & omissions excepted
Est. Wt. .... Estimated Weight
et seq. .... And the following (et sequens)
Ex. Div. .... Without Dividend
Ex-Warehouse .. Purchaser pays carriage charges & assumes risks from seller's warehouse
F. .... Fahrenheit
F.a.a. .... Free of Average (marine insurance)
F.A.S. .... Free Alongside (Seller assumes risks & delivers goods to alongside of steamer free of carriage charges)
F.O.B. .... Free on Board (Purchaser pays carriage charges & assumes risks from point specified)
F.P.A. .... Free of Particular Average (Insured can recover only for a total loss, subject to other conditions of the contract)
Franco. .... Pre-paid free of expense to point specified
G.A. .... General Average (All owners of cargo & vessel share in any loss arising from expense incurred to preserve ship & contents from greater loss)
gm. .... Grammes
gr. .... Grain; grains, or gross
ibid. .... In the same place (ibidem)
i.e. .... That is (id est)
Inc. .... Incorporated
Int. .... Interest
K.D. .... Knocked down
lb. (libra) .... Pound
L/C. .... Letter of Credit
L.C.L. .... Less than Car Load (of freight)
Limited; Ltd. .... Limited Liability (Shareholders are "limited" in liability to the amount of their subscribed stock in certain companies)
L.P. .... List Price
M. .... Thousand (Mille)
MS., MSS. ..... Manuscript(s)
N.E.S. (N.O.P.) .. Not Otherwise Provided For (Customs)
N.O.S. .... Not Otherwise Specified
N.S.F. .... Not Sufficient Funds (re cheques)
Nstd. .... Nested
O.K. .... Correct
op. cit. .... In the work quoted (opere citato)
O.R. .... At Owner's Risk
O.R.B. .... At Owner's Risk of Breakage
oz. .... Ounce
P.A. .... Particular Average (As used in Marine Insurance, means damage to the goods caused by perils insured against & named in the contract. This form is often written with a Franchise Clause, & means there will be no claim unless the loss exceeds the percentage named)
P/A. .... Power of Attorney
P & D. .... Pick Up & Deliver
pp. .... Pages
Pro forma ...... As a Matter of Form
P.S. .... Postscript
q.v. .... Which see (quod vide)
R.R. .... Rural Route (Postal delivery)
S.B. .... Shipping Bill
s.s. .... Steamship
s/o .... Ship's Option, weight or measurement
S.U. .... Set Up (meaning article is complete)
T.B.L. .... Through Bill of Lading
Tare .... Weight of Container (Deducting tare from "gross weight" gives "net weight")
Ton .... 2,000 (short ton) or 2,240 (long ton) lbs. avoirdupois. A cubic ton in marine freight = 40 cubic feet
Ton wt/M. ...... Ton, weight or measurement (ship's option)
vide .... See
viz .... Namely; to wit (videlicet)

Border Services, Customs Regulations for Canadians Returning from Abroad

Note: The Canada Border Services Agency (CBSA) operates as an agency under the Public Safety portfolio, and its mission is to ensure the security and prosperity of Canada by managing the access of people and goods to and from Canada. With a workforce of approximately 13,000 public servants, the Canada Border Services Agency (CBSA) provides services at 1,200 points across Canada and 39 locations abroad. At over 100 land border crossings and 13 international airports, it operates on a 24/7 basis. It administers more than 90 acts and regulations on behalf of other Government of Canada departments and agencies, and international agreements.

It integrates several key functions previously spread among three organizations: the Customs program from the Canada Customs Revenue Agency, the Intelligence, Interdiction and Enforcement program from Citizenship and Immigration Canada, and the Import Inspection at Ports of Entry program from the Canadian Food Inspection Agency.

If you have information about suspicious cross-border activity, please call the CBSA Border Watch tollfree line at 1-888-502-9060.

Canadians returning to Canada may bring any amount of goods into the country subject to duties and any provincial or territorial assessments, with the exception of restricted items. This applies even if you do not qualify for a personal exemption. The term duty can include Goods and Services. Duties represent duty, excise taxes and the Goods & Services Tax (GST) or Harmonized Sales Tax (HST). In addition to duties, provincial and territorial taxes (PST) are assessed if an agreement has been signed between the federal government and a province or territory whereby the federal government collects the PST, levies and fees on their behalf.

Goods included in personal exemptions must be for personal or household use, souvenirs or gifts. Goods brought in for commercial use, or on behalf of another person do not qualify and are subject to full duties.

On your return to Canada, you must declare to the Canada Border Services Agency (CBSA) all goods acquired (purchases, gifts, awards, prizes, and purchases made at Canadian or foreign duty-free shops and still in your possession) and repairs or modifications you made to your vehicle, vessel or aircraft while outside Canada.

Personal Exemptions

To qualify for personal exemptions you must be:

- Canadian resident returning from a trip abroad;
- former resident of Canada returning to live in Canada; or
- temporary resident of Canada.

Children and infants qualify for personal exemptions as long as the goods are for the use of the child or infant. The parent or guardian makes the customs declaration for the child.

Personal exemptions are applicable after the following minimum absences:

1. After an absence of 24 hours but less than 48 hours: up to a value of $200 (Canadian) in total (with the exception of tobacco products and alcoholic beverages) any number of times a year. If the value of the goods exceeds $200, you pay duties and PST on the full value (exemption cannot be claimed). The goods must accompany you on your return to Canada.

2. After an absence of 48 hours but less than seven days: up to $800 (Canadian) in total any number of times in a year. The goods must accompany you on your return to Canada.

3. After an absence of seven days or more: up to $800 (Canadian) any number of times in a year. You may have to make a written declaration. Goods you claim under this exemption may follow you by mail or other means, with the exception of alcoholic beverages and tobacco products. You require a Form E24, Personal Exemption Customs Declaration, which is to be completed at the time of arrival and can be obtained from a customs officer. To claim your goods when they arrive, present your copy of the E24 to the CBSA for clearance. Goods must be claimed within 40 days of their arrival in Canada; duties and taxes are then payable, along with a Canada Post Corporation processing fee. You may pay the duties and then apply to the CBSA for a refund (if the personal exemption applies) or refuse delivery; following a review that determines if the goods are eligible for free importation, the goods will be released to you without an assessment.

Persons residing outside Canada for part of the year are considered to be residents of Canada and are entitled to the above personal exemptions.

Exemptions cannot be transferred to another person or combined with another person's personal exemption. You cannot combine a 24-hour ($200) or 48-hour ($800) or the seven-day ($800) exemption when claiming an exemption, nor can you carry over an unused portion of an exemption for another period of absence.

Tobacco & Alcohol

Tobacco products and alcoholic beverages must accompany you in your hand or checked luggage and may be included in the 48-hour ($800) or the seven-day ($800) exemptions, but not in the 24-hour ($200) exemption. You must meet the age requirements set by the province or territory where you enter Canada. In addition the following conditions apply:

1. You may bring in up to 200 cigarettes, 50 cigars or cigarillos, 200 tobacco sticks **and** 200 grams of manufactured tobacco. Duties must be paid on anything above this allowance, plus any applicable provincial or territorial limits or assessments.

If you include cigarettes, tobacco sticks, or manufactured tobacco in your personal allowance, only a partial exemption will apply. You will have to pay a special duty on these products **unless** they are marked "DUTY-PAID CANADA — DROIT ACQUITTÉ." You will find Canadian-made products sold at a duty-free shop marked this way. You can speed up your clearance by having your tobacco products available for inspection when you arrive.

2. You may include up to 1.5 litres of wine, or 1.14 litres (40 ounces) of liquor, or a total of 1.14 litres (40 ounces), or 24 x 335 ml (12-ounce) cans or bottles (8.5 litres) of beer or ale. Wine coolers are classified as wine; beer coolers are classified as beer. Beer or wine that contains 0.5% alcohol by volume or less is not classified as an alcoholic beverage, so no quantity limits apply. You may bring in more than this allowance of alcohol anywhere in Canada (with the exception of the Northwest Territories and Nunavut) as long as the quantities are within the limits set by the province or territory. If bringing in more than the free allowance, you must pay customs and provincial/territorial assessments. For more information, check with the appropriate provincial/ territorial liquor control agency prior to leaving Canada.

Gifts

While abroad, you may send gifts duty- and tax-free to recipients in Canada. To qualify, the gift must be valued at $60 CAN or less and cannot be an alcoholic beverage, tobacco product, or advertising material. Gifts in excess of $60 CAN require duty payment by the recipient on the excess amount. Gifts that accompany you on your return to Canada must be included in your personal exemption, while gifts you send from abroad are not included. Some conditions apply - for additional information, contact the CBSA Border Information Service (BIS) at one of the numbers listed at the end of this section.

Prizes & Awards

In most cases, you pay regular duties on prizes or awards received outside Canada. Contact the BIS line for more information.

Paying Duties

Duties may be paid by cash or travellers' cheques. Personal cheques are also acceptable (for amounts of $2,500 or less and with proper identification); VISA, American Express and MasterCard are accepted at most border services locations and Debit Cards at many locations.

For information on duty rates for particular items, contact the BIS line.

NAFTA Special Duty Rate

Goods qualify for a lower U.S. duty rate under NAFTA if they are:
- for personal use
- marked as made in the U.S., Canada or Mexico
- not marked or labelled to indicate they were made anywhere other than in the U.S., Canada or Mexico

If you do not qualify for a personal exemption, or if you exceed your exemption limit, you will have to pay GST or HST over and above applicable duties or taxes on the portion not eligible under your exemption. The rates vary according to the goods, their country of origin, and the country from which you are importing them.

For information on goods eligible for the special duty rate under NAFTA, contact your nearest CBSA office and ask for a copy of Memorandum D11-4-13, Rules of Origin for Casual Goods Under Free Trade Agreements.

Regular Duty Rates

If you do not qualify for a personal exemption, or you exceed your exemption limit, you will pay GST or HST over and above all duties, taxes, and assessments that apply on the portion not eligible under your exemption. The rates vary according to the goods, their country of origin, and the country from which you are importing them. You may also have to pay provincial sales tax if you live in a province where we have an agreement to collect the tax and you return from your trip through your province.

World Trade Organization (WTO) Agreement

The duty on a wide range of products originating in non-NAFTA countries has been eliminated or will be reduced to zero within the next few years. NAFTA goods also qualify for the WTO rate, so if the rate on the goods you are importing is lower under WTO than under NAFTA, the lower rate will automatically be applied.

Value for Duty/Foreign Sales Tax

Value for duty is the amount used to calculate duty and is generally the price you paid for the item. Foreign sales tax is included in the price and forms part of the value of the item.

Some foreign governments will refund sales tax to you if you export the items you bought. If this is the case, you do not include the amount of the foreign sales tax that was or will be refunded to you.

Declaration

When returning to Canada by commercial aircraft, a Canada Border Services Agency (CBSA) declaration card is distributed for completion before arrival. The cards are also used at some locations for people arriving by train, vessel or bus. If arriving by a private vehicle (e.g., automobile), you must make an oral declaration unless you are claiming goods that preceded or will follow your arrival in Canada as part of your $800 exemption. If this is the case, ask the border services officer for Form E24, Personal Exemption Customs Declaration. You will need your copy of this form to claim your goods. Otherwise, you may have to pay regular duty on them.

CBSA officers are legally entitled to examine luggage; you are responsible for opening, unpacking and repacking the luggage. Retain receipts of purchases and repairs made to verify length of stay and value of goods or repairs. Failure to declare or a false declaration may result in the seizure of goods. Penalties range from 25% to 80% of the value of the seized goods. Vehicles used to transport unlawfully imported goods may also be seized, with a penalty imposed before the vehicle can be returned. Commodities such as alcohol and tobacco are seized and not returned.

Currency and Monetary Instruments

If you are importing or exporting monetary instruments equal to or greater than CAN$10,000 (or its equivalent in a foreign currency), whether in cash or other monetary instruments, you must report it to the CBSA when you arrive or before you leave Canada. For more information, ask for a copy of the publication called "Crossing the Border with $10,000 or More?" or select "Publications" on the CBSA Web site at www.cbsa-asfc.gc.ca.

Restrictions

Firearms: Contact the Canadian Firearms Program at: 506-624-6626, Toll-Free Phone: 1-800-731-4000, Fax: 613-993-0260, Email: cfp-pcaf@rcmp-grc.gc.ca; URL: www.rcmp-grc.gc.ca/cfp-pcaf.

Replica firearms are designed or intended to resemble a firearm with near precision. They are classified as prohibited devices and you cannot import them into Canada.

Mace or pepper spray that is used for the purpose of injuring, immobilizing or otherwise incapacitating any person is considered a prohibited weapon. You cannot import it into Canada. Aerosol or similar dispensers that contain substances capable of repelling or subduing animals are not considered weapons if the label of the container specifically indicates that they are for use against animals.

Explosives, fireworks, certain types of ammunition: You require written authorization and permits. Contact Chief Inspector of Explosives Regulatory Division, Natural Resources Canada, 580 Booth St., 10th Fl., Ottawa ON K1A 0G1, 613-948-5200, Fax: 613-948-5195, Email: ERDmms@nrcan.gc.ca.

Vehicles: Vehicles must meet the requirements of the CBSA, Transport Canada and the Canadian Food Inspection Agency before they can be imported. Transport Canada defines a vehicle as any vehicle that is capable of being driven or drawn on roads, by any means other than muscular power exclusively, but does not run exclusively on rails. It considers trailers such as recreational, camping, boat, horse and stock trailers as vehicles, as well as woodchippers, generators and any other equipment mounted on rims and tires.

CBSA import restrictions apply to most used or second- hand vehicles that are not manufactured in the current year. Transport Canada requirements apply to vehicles that are less than fifteen years old. All imported vehicles less than fifteen years old must comply with Canadian federal safety and emission standards. The person importing the vehicle is responsible for ensuring it meets the Canadian safety standards.

If you have acquired a vehicle from the United States, you must contact the Transport Canada's Registrar of Imported Vehicle (RIV) before you import your vehicle, to ensure that it is admissible for importation and can be modified to meet the Canadian standards after you import it.

Registrar of Imported Vehicles: Telephone: 1-888-848-8240 (toll free in Canada, the United States and Mexico); 416-626-6812 (from all other countries), Fax: 1-888-346-8235, Website: www.riv.ca.

Import restrictions apply to most used or secondhand cars, generally from countries other than the United States. Under NAFTA, restrictions do not apply to vehicles imported from the U.S., however, not all vehicles that are manufactured for sale in the U.S. can be imported because they do not meet the Transport Canada requirements; special duty rates, as outlined above, apply. Excise tax and GST continue to apply in the usual way. Under NAFTA, customs restrictions continued to apply to vehicles imported from Mexico until 2009, after which time you are able to import vehicles ten years or older. The age restriction will drop every second year until the restriction is dropped altogether in 2019.

In most instances, Canadian residents are not allowed to import vehicles into Canada that have been purchased or obtained in countries other than the United States. If you have acquired a vehicle from a country other than the United States, before importing it, contact: Transport Canada, Motor Vehicle Safety, Place de Ville, Tower C, 330 Sparks St., Ottawa ON K1A 0N5, 800-333-0371 (toll free from Canada and the U.S.), Email: mvs-sa@tc.gc.ca, Website: www.tc.gc.ca.

Your vehicle may be subject to provincial or territorial sales tax; contact your provincial or territorial department of motor vehicles for information. In addition, you may need to meet some requirements in the country which the vehicle is being exported.

Import Controls: Importations of certain goods are controlled. You may need a permit to import, even for personal and household use. For information, visit: Export & Import Controls, Foreign Affairs, Trade & Development, Website: www.international.gc.ca/controls-controles.

Meat, dairy products, wheat, barley, and their products: Complex requirements and restrictions exist; importation of certain meat and dairy products from certain U.S. states is allowed. All meat and meat products have to be identified as products of the United States. Limits exist for amounts or dollar value in certain foodstuffs you can import for personal use; if above those limits, duty ranges from 150 to 300% and you may also require an agricultural inspection certificate. For more information, contact the CBSA BIS line.

Agricultural products: Restrictions exist on live animals and animal products, meat and poultry products, dairy products, egg and egg products, honey and fresh fruits and vegetables, seeds and grains, animal feeds, plant and plant products, forestry products, soil and fertilizers, pest control products, biological products. For information on these products, refer to the Automated Import Reference System (AIRS) on the CFIA Website at www.inspection.gc.ca or call the CBSA BIS line.

Cultural property: Antiquities or cultural objects of significance in the country of origin cannot be imported into Canada. For information, contact Secretariat to the Canadian Cultural Property Export Review Board, Canadian Heritage, 25 Eddy St., 9th Fl., Gatineau, QC K1A 0M5, 819-997-7761, Fax: 613-997-7757, Email: PCH.secretariatdelacommission-reviewboardsecretariat.PCH@canada.ca.

Endangered species: Canada has signed an international agreement restricting the sale, trade or movement of endangered animals, birds, reptiles, fish, insects and certain forms of plant life; the restrictions also apply to their parts or products made from their parts. Before you bring back any of these products, you should contact CITES Administrator, Canadian Wildlife Service, Environment & Climate Change Canada, Ottawa ON K1A 0H3, 1-800-668-6767 (toll-free number in Canada), 819-938-4119 (local calls and from all other countries).

Appeals

If you disagree with the amount of duty and taxes that you had to pay, please ask to speak with the superintendent on duty. A consultation can often resolve the issue quickly and without cost. If you are still not satisfied, CBSA officers can tell you how to make a formal appeal. If you do not declare goods, or if you falsely declare them,the CBSA can seize the goods. This means that you may lose the goods permanently, or that you may have to pay a penalty to get them back.

If you do not declare tobacco products and alcoholic beverages at the time of importation, they will be permanently seized.

Depending on the type of goods and the circumstances involved, the CBSA may impose a penalty that ranges from 25% to 80% of the value of the seized goods.

In addition, the *Customs Act* provides CBSA officers with the authority to seize all vehicles that were used unlawfully to import goods. When this happens, a penalty will be imposed, which you will have to pay before the vehicle is returned.

If goods have been seized and you disagree with the action taken, you must notify the CBSA in writing within 90 days of the seizure date of your intention to appeal. You should send your appeal to the CBSA Office where the seizure took place. You can find more information about this process on the front of your seizure receipt form.

In addition to the activities mentioned above, designated CBSA officers may arrest for a criminal offence under the *Criminal Code* or any other Act of Parliament. This includes the offences of impaired driving, outstanding arrest warrants, stolen property, and abductions/kidnappings. If you are arrested, you may be compelled to attend court in Canada. You should note that all persons arrested in Canada are protected by, and will be treated in accordance with, the *Canadian Charter of Rights and Freedoms*.

A record of infractions is kept in the CBSA computer system. If you have an infraction record, you may have to undergo a more detailed examination on future trips.

Precautions

Carry proper identification.

Traveling with Children

Border services officers are on alert for children who need protection. Children under the age of 18 are classified as minors and are subject to the same entry requirements as any other visitor to Canada.

Border officers will conduct a more detailed examination of minors entering Canada without proper identification or those traveling in the company of adults other than their parents or legal guardian(s). This additional scrutiny helps ensure the safety of the children.

Minors traveling alone must have proof of citizenship and a letter from both parents detailing the length of stay, providing the parents' telephone number and authorizing the person waiting for them to take care of them while they are in Canada.

If you are traveling with minors, you must carry proper identification for each child such as a birth certificate, passport, citizenship card, permanent resident card or Certificate of Indian Status.

If you are a parent traveling alone with your child, it is recommended that you have a letter of authorization from your spouse. If you are divorced or separated, you should carry with you copies of the legal custody agreements for your children. If you are traveling with minors and you are not their parent/guardian, you should have written permission from the parent/guardian authorizing the trip. The letter should include addresses and telephone numbers of where the parents or guardian can be reached and identify a person who can confirm that the children are not being abducted or taken against their will. Some travellers have the consent letter notarized to further support its authenticity.

If you are traveling with a group of vehicles, make sure you arrive at the border in the same vehicle as your children, to avoid any confusion.

Identification of Articles for Temporary Exportation

CBSA offices offer a free identification program for valuables; a list of your valuables (excluding jewellery) and their serial numbers on a wallet-sized form will show border services officers that the items were previously purchased in Canada or that you lawfully imported them prior to your current time abroad. In the case of jewellery, carry an appraisal of the item(s) from a gemmologist, jeweller or insurance agent, together with a signed and dated photograph and a written declaration that the items in the photograph are those described in the appraisal report. If previously imported, carry a copy of the customs receipt.

If you take any item outside Canada and modify it, it is considered to be a new item and its full value will need to be declared. Similarly, under Canadian law, any repairs or modifications to a vehicle that increase its value, improve its condition or modify it while abroad may require that you pay duties on its full value on your return to Canada. This does not apply to incidental repairs to keep the car in operational condition while abroad, although you may be required to pay duties on the repairs and parts. A special provision is available that waives duties payable in such cases. Contact the CBSA for information.

Additional Information

If you have any other questions, contact the Border Information Service (BIS) line. This is a 24-hour telephone service that automatically answers all incoming calls and provides general border services information. If you call during regular business hours (8:00 a.m. to 4:00 p.m. local time, Monday to Friday, except holidays), you can speak directly to an agent by pressing "0" at any time.

Calls inside Canada:

English Enquiries: 1-800-461-9999 (toll-free in Canada)
French Enquiries: 1-800-959-2036 (toll-free in Canada)

TTY: 866-335-3237

Out-of-Canada callers can reach BIS by calling:

Western

English: . . . . . . 204-983-3500 (long-distance charges will apply)

Eastern

English: . . . . . . 506-636-5064 (long-distance charges will apply)

Website: www.cbsa-asfc.gc.ca

Election Regulations

According to the Canada Elections Act, and subject to certain exceptions, the general rule as to the franchise of electors at a federal election is that every person is qualified as an elector if such person

(a) is of the full age of 18 years on election day;

(b) is a Canadian citizen.

Among persons disqualified are certain officials charged with administering the elections, and, individuals who have lost their right to vote for a specified period for the commission of an election-related offence.

Writs for an election (general or by-election) are issued at least 36 days before the date fixed for election day.

Similar qualifications apply in the Provinces and Territories, although for provincial and territorial elections there is usually a residence requirement of either six or twelve months before the date of the issue of the writ of election. The age requirement is 18 years.

To contact election officers see "Elections" under the Government Quick Reference Guide in Section 7.

Elections Canada - 613-993-2975; Toll Free in Canada and the U.S.: 1-800-463-6868; Toll Free in Mexico: 001-800-514-6868; TTY: 1-800-361-8935; Fax: 1-888-524-1444; URL: www.elections.ca.

Liquor Regulations

For Liquor Control Board contact information, see "Liquor Control" in the Government Quick Reference Guide, in Section 7.

Alberta

- Ensure integrity, transparency, disclosure, public consultation & accountability in Alberta's gaming & liquor industries;
- Administer the Alberta Lottery Fund with full public disclosure & continue to support communities & charitable organizations;
- License, regulate & monitor liquor & gaming activities, as well as certain aspects of tobacco sales;
- Implement & account for specific lottery fund programs administered by Alberta Gaming;
- Develop & communicate provincial gaming & liquor policy

Alberta Gaming & Liquor Commission, 50 Corriveau Ave., St. Albert AB T8N 3T5 - 780-447-8600; Toll Free: 1-800-272-8876; Fax: 780-447-8989; URL: www.aglc.ca

British Columbia

The Liquor Control & Licensing Branch is responsible for issuing licences to:

- pubs, bars, lounges, stadiums, nightclubs & restaurants to sell liquor by the glass, & cold beer & wine stores to sell liquor by the bottle
- breweries, distilleries & wineries to manufacture liquor, &
- UBrews/UVins to sell their customers the ingredients, equipment & advice they need to make their own beer, wine cider or coolers

In addition, the branch:

- regulates both Serving It Right: The Responsible Beverage Service Program & Special Occasion Licences for the events such as community celebrations, weddings or banquets
- educates those who hold liquor licences (called licensees) about the laws & rules that may affect them inspects licensed establishments, &
- takes enforcement action when licensees do not follow the *Liquor Control & Licensing Act*, Regulations, &/or the specific terms & conditions of their licences

British Columbia Liquor Control & Licensing Branch, PO Box 9292, Stn Prov Govt, Victoria BC V8W 9J8; street address: 3350 Douglas St., Victoria BC V8Z 3L1, 250-952-5787; Fax: 250-952-7066; Toll Free: 1-866-209-2111; Email: lclb.lclb@gov.bc.ca; URL: www.pssg.gov.bc.ca/lclb

Manitoba

The Liquor and Gaming Authority of Manitoba is the regulator for liquor and gaming in the province, as of 2014. The LGA was created as a result of a merger between the Manitoba Liquor Control Commission and the Manitoba Gaming Control Commission.

Persons over the age of 18 years and who are not otherwise prohibited may purchase and consume spirits, wine and beer in premises licensed by Manitoba Liquor & Lotteries - a Crown corporation that distributes and sells liquor. Further, those persons may purchase from an MBLL liquor mart, liquor vendor or specialty wine store for consumption in a residence.

Beer may also be purchased from beer vendor depots located in most hotels throughout the province.

Parents dining with their children may purchase alcoholic beverages for the latter, for consumption with meals, only in licensed restaurants, dining rooms, cocktail lounges or cabarets.

Beverage rooms and cocktail rooms must be vacated within 30 minutes after the hour at which sale of liquor must cease.

Manitoba Liquor & Lotteries, 1555 Buffalo Place, PO Box 1023, Winnipeg MB R3C 2X1 - 204-957-2500; Toll-Free: 1-800-265-3912; Fax: 204-284-3500; URL: www.liquormarts.ca; www.mbll.ca

New Brunswick

Intoxicating liquor is sold in sealed packages at Liquor Stores and agency stores. Where a permit and/or a license has been obtained, liquor may be sold by the glass in dining rooms, restaurants, taverns, cabarets, lounges, beverage rooms, and clubs. Age of majority is 19.

New Brunswick Liquor Corp., PO Box 20787, 170 Wilsey Rd., Fredericton NB E3B 5B8 - 506-452-6826; Fax: 506-462-2024; URL: www.anbl.com

Newfoundland & Labrador

The importation, manufacture, and sale of alcoholic beverages through Retail Liquor outlets is the responsibility of the Newfoundland Liquor Corp.

The Newfoundland Liquor Corporation is also responsible for the issuing of all licenses, including those to manufacture and to sell packaged beer, and enforcement of regulations including, but not limited, to the following:

- All liquor sold upon licensed premises shall be consumed thereon.
- All liquor served in licensed premises shall be dispensed from the original container in which the liquor is purchased from or under the authority of the Liquor Corp.
- The drinking age in Newfoundland is 19 years.

Nfld. Liquor Corp., PO Box 8750, Stn A, 90 Kenmount Rd., St. John's NL A1B 3V1 - 709-724-1100; Fax: 709-754-0321; Email: info@nlliquor.com; URL: www.nlliquor.com

Northwest Territories

The *Northwest Territories Act*, Chapter 331 of the Revised Statutes of Canada, 1952, authorizes the Commissioner in Council of the Northwest Territories to make acts respecting intoxicants.

The Liquor Licensing Board, established under Part I of the *Liquor Act*, controls the conduct of licensees and operation of licensed premises; grants, renews and transfers licenses and, after a hearing, may cancel or suspend licenses. There are presently twelve types of licenses issued by the Board. Part I also provides for plebiscites to be held concerning new liquor license applications and also concerning restriction or prohibition in a community.

Part II of the *Liquor Act* establishes a Liquor Commission. The Minister responsible for this Part may designate his powers to the Liquor Commission to operate liquor stores and to purchase, sell and distribute liquor in the Northwest Territories. Through agency agreements, private contractors operate retail liquor stores on behalf of the Liquor Commission in Fort Simpson, Fort Smith, Hay River, Inuvik, Yellowknife, Norman Wells and liquor warehouses in Hay River and Yellowknife.

Northwest Territories Liquor Commission, #201, 31 Capital Dr., Hay River NT X0E 1G2 - 867-874-8700; Fax: 867-874-8720; URL: www.fin.gov.nt.ca/services/liquor

Nova Scotia

- All liquor is sold through Government Stores.
- Generally local option vote applies.
- Eating establishment liquor licenses, lounges, clubs and cabarets serve spirits, draught beer, bottled beer and wine.
- The legal minimum drinking age is 19 years.

Nova Scotia Liquor Corporation, Bayers Lake Business Park, 93 Chain Lake Dr., Halifax NS B3S 1A3 - 1-800-567-5874; URL: www.mynslc.com

Nunavut

Nunavut Liquor Management is a Branch of the Department of Finance within the Government of Nunavut. Nunavut Liquor Management has two sections, referred to as the Nunavut Liquor Commission and the Nunavut Liquor Licensing Board.

The Nunavut Liquor Commission is responsible for, as first receiver, the purchasing, storage and distribution of alcohol products within the Nunavut Territory.

The Nunavut Liquor Licensing Board deals with the issuance of liquor licenses, liquor permits, inspection and enforcement under the *Nunavut Liquor Act*.

Communities in Nunavut are empowered and are enabled to establish their own liquor controls through the *Nunavut Liquor Act*. They are prohibited, restricted (variety) and unrestricted (only Liquor Act applies). The age of majority in Nunavut is 19.

Nunavut Liquor Commission, Bag 002, Rankin Inlet, NU X0C 0G0 - 867-645-8478; 867-645-3327; URL: www.gov.nu.ca/finance/information/nunavut-liquor-commission

Nunavut Liquor Licensing Board, Executive Secretary, PO Box 1269, Iqaluit, NU X0A 0H0 - 867-975-6533; 867-975-6367; Email: nllb@gov.nu.ca; URL: www.nllb.ca

Ontario

In accordance with the provisions of the *Liquor Control Act* of Ontario, the Liquor Control Board buys wine, spirits and beer from all over the world for distribution and sale to Ontario consumers and licensed establishments. To provide this service, the LCBO operates five major regional storage and distribution centres which supply more than 650 retail liquor stores.

In the interests of consumer protection, the LCBO also regularly tests all alcoholic beverages sold in Ontario. This "quality control" testing ensures that all products carried by LCBO stores, Ontario winery stores and Brewers Retail outlets comply with the standards required under the Federal *Food & Drug Act* and Regulations.

In 2016, the LCBO introduced an online shopping option.

The Alcohol and Gaming Commission of Ontario (AGCO) is a Provincial agency that was established on February 23, 1998 after legislation was tabled to merge the Liquor Licence Board of Ontario (LLBO) with the Gaming Control Commission (GCC). The AGCO is responsible for administering the *Liquor Licence Act*, the *Gaming Control Act*, 1992, and the *Wine Content Act*. The AGCO conducts hearings as required: to determine the eligibility for liquor licences or gaming registration; to determine the eligibility for, or the revocation of liquor licences in public interest cases; and, in disciplinary cases involving liquor licensees or gaming registrants.

Liquor-related responsibilities include: licensing of public places which serve beverage alcohol for on-premises consumption; licensing of Ontario liquor manufacturers and the sales representatives of foreign manufacturers; promoting moderation and the responsible use of beverage alcohol.

Gaming-related responsibilities include: regulating charitable and casino gambling in Ontario; ensuring that games of chance are conducted fairly in compliance with the *Gaming Control Act*, regulations, and the terms and conditions that are imposed with charity gaming licences; ensuring that the people and the companies involved in casino and charitable gaming satisfy high standards of honesty, integrity and financial responsibility; registering commercial suppliers and gaming assistants of charitable gaming events and administering the issuance of charity gaming licences in partnership with municipalities.

Liquor Control Board of Ontario, #1100, 1 Yonge St., Toronto, ON M5E 1E5 - 416-365-5900; Toll-Free: 1-800-668-5226; TTY: 1-800-361-3291; URL: www.lcbo.com

Alcohol and Gaming Commission of Ontario, #200-300, 90 Sheppard Ave. E., Toronto ON M2N 0A4; Enquiries: 416-326-8700, or 1-800-522-2876 (toll-free in Ontario); Fax: 416-326-5555; Email: customer.service@agco.ca; URL: www.agco.on.ca

Prince Edward Island

Beverage alcohol sealed packages may be purchased at Commission Stores throughout the Province by any person 19 or older who is not otherwise disqualified.

Spirits by the glass, and beer and wine by the open bottle or glass, may be purchased in dining rooms, lounges, clubs and military canteens licensed by the Commission.

Prince Edward Island Liquor Control Commission, 3 Garfield St., PO Box 967, Charlottetown, PE C1A 7M4 - 902-368-5710; Fax: 902-368-5735; URL: liquorpei.com

Québec

Spirits and wines are sold by Québec Liquor Corporation (Société des alcools du Québec) stores only.

Spirits, beer and wine may be sold to the public by restaurants, bars and clubs under permit for consumption on the premises. Taverns may sell beer and cider. Pubs may sell beer, draught wine and cider.

A licensed grocery store may sell beer and certain designated wines and the product must not be consumed on the premises.

Persons under the age of 18 years old cannot be admitted into bars, pubs and taverns and at no time may alcoholic beverages be sold to them in other establishments.

Société des Alcools du Québec, 905 av De Lorimier, Montréal QC H2K 3V9 - 514-254-2020, or 1-866-873-2020; Email: info@saq.com; URL: www.saq.com

Saskatchewan

The Saskatchewan Liquor & Gaming Authority, a Treasury Board Crown corporation, regulates liquor and gaming activities and conducts and manages gaming in the Saskatchewan Indian Gaming Authority Casinos and the Video Lottery Terminals throughout the province. It is responsible for the control, sale and distribution of liquor in the province, and also licenses and regulates bingos, raffles, casinos, and breakopen tickets.

The minimum drinking age is 19.

Saskatchewan Liquor & Gaming Authority, PO Box 5054, 2500 Victoria Ave., Regina SK S4P 3M3 -306-787-5563; Toll-Free: 1-800-667-7565; www.saskliquor.com; www.slga.gov.sk.ca

Yukon Territory

The *Yukon Act*, Chapter Y-2 of the Revised Statutes of Canada, 1970, authorizes the Commissioner in Executive Council, Yukon Territory, to make acts respecting intoxicants.

By virtue of Chapter 105 cited as the *Liquor Act*, established the laws governing the importation, distributing, licensing and retailing of alcoholic beverages in Yukon.

The formation of the Yukon Liquor Corporation by means of amendments to the *Liquor Act* came into force on April 1st, 1977. The separation as a Corporate entity resulted in increased responsibility and full accountability in all areas except major government policy.

The five members of the Board of Directors are appointed by the Commissioner in executive council to hold office at pleasure.

The President and Chief Executive Officer of the Corporation, is charged with the general direction, supervision and control of the Corporation and the administration of the Act.

Yukon Liquor Corp., 9031 Quartz Road, Whitehorse YT Y1A 4P9 - 867-667-5245; Fax: 867-393-6306; Toll-free: 1-800-661-0408, ext. 5245; Email: yukon.liquor@gov.yk.ca; URL: www.ylc.yk.ca

Legal Age of Consent to Sexual Activity

Age of Consent, under the *Tackling Violent Crime Act, 2008*:

Raises the age at which youths can consent to non-exploitative sexual activity from 14 to 16 years of age;

Maintains the existing age of protection of 18 years for exploitative sexual activity (i.e. sexual activity involving prostitution, pornography, or a relationship of trust, authority or dependency or that is otherwise exploitative); and

Includes a close-in-age exception which permits 14- and 15-year old youths to engage in consensual, non-exploitative sexual activity with a partner who is less than five years older. An exception also exists for 12- and 13-year old youths, whereby persons of those ages can consent to non-exploitative sexual activity with another young person who is less than two years older.

Marriage Regulations

Divorce Act in Canada

Divorce grounds in Canada, under the *Divorce Act, 1985:*

Breakdown of marriage, established by:

- Spouses intentionally living separate and apart at least one year with the idea that the marriage is over, or

Since the marriage, either spouse has:

- Committed adultery, or
- Treated the other spouse with physical or mental cruelty rendering continued cohabitation intolerable.

Alberta

Marriageable age:

- Without parental consent: 18 years
- With parental consent: 16 years
- No one younger than 16 years of age may marry

Blood Test: not required

Waiting Period: None. Marriage Licence is valid immediately & is valid for 3 months (from date of issuance).

Licence fee: $50 + agent

Civic Marriage ceremony fee: uncapped

British Columbia

Marriageable age:

- Without parental consent: 19 years
- With parental consent: 16 to 18 years
- A court order of consent: under 16 years

Blood test: not required

Waiting period for licence: none

Marriage Licence: $100

Civil Marriage Ceremony: $75

Manitoba

Marriageable age:

- Without parental consent: 18 years
- With parental consent: 16 years (Persons under 16 years of age can be married only with the consent of a judge of the Family Court.)

Blood test: not required

Waiting period for licence: none

Waiting period after issuance of licence: 24 hours (This may be waived in exceptional circumstances by person performing ceremony.)

Licence fee: $100. Licence valid for 3 months (from date of issuance).

New Brunswick

Marriageable age:

- Without parental consent: 18 years
- With parental consent: under 18 years
- Under 16 years: a declaration of a Judge of the Court of Queen's Bench that the proposed marriage may take place is necessary.

Blood test: not required

Waiting period for licence: none

Licence fee: $115. Licence valid for 3 months (from date of issuance).

Newfoundland & Labrador

Marriageable age:

- Greater than or equal to 19 years: without parental consent
- Greater than or equal to 18 years: without parental consent in certain circumstances
- Greater than or equal to 16 years and less than 19 years: with the applicable parental, guardian or Director of Child Welfare consent (Consent may be dispensed within exceptional cases.)
- Less than 16 years: where by reason of pregnancy a judge issues a licence

Blood test: not required

Licence fee: $100. Licence valid for 30 days (from date of issuance).

Northwest Territories

Marriageable age:

- Without parental consent: 19 years
- Under the age of 19 years and declares via statutory declaration that:
    - (a) that no person has lawful custody of the minor; or
    - (b) that any person who has lawful custody of the minor not a resident of the Territories & that the minor has been a resident of the Territories for not less than 12 months immediately preceding the date of the declaration; or
    - (c) that any person who has lawful custody of the minor is unable to consent by reason of disability; or
    - (d) that the minor has, for not less than six months immediately preceding the date of the declaration, withdrawn from the charge of the persons who have lawful custody of the minor & that the minor has not returned to such charge
- With parental consent: 15 years, or under 15 years & pregnant

Blood test: not required

Waiting period for licence: none

Licence fee: $60

Nova Scotia

Marriageable age:

- Without parental consent: 19 years or over
- With parental consent, or if a widow, widower, or divorcee: 16 years
- With court order: under 16 years

Blood test: not required

Waiting period for licence: 5 days

Licence fee: $132.70

Nunavut

Marriageable age:

- Without parental consent: 19 years
- At least 18 years of age

Blood test: not required

Waiting period for licence: none

Licence fee: $25

Ontario

Marriageable age:

- Without parental consent: 18 years
- With parental consent: 16 years

Blood test: not required

Waiting period after issuance of licence: none

Licence fee: $125-$140

Fee for solemnization of marriage by judge or justice of the peace: $75
Purchased marriage licence must be used within 3 months.

Prince Edward Island

Marriageable age:
- Without parental consent: 18 years
- With parental consent: under 18 years

Other requirements: birth certificates and Social Insurance Numbers; in the case of a widow or widower, death certificate; in the case of a divorced person, certified copy of the Decree Absolute or Certificate of Divorce
Waiting period for licence: none
Licence fee: $100. License valid for 3 months from date of issuance.

Québec

Marriageable age:
- Minimum age: 16 years (ref.: art. 373, Code Civil du Québec)
- Moreover, a minor (under 18 years of age) must have the authorization of his or her parent(s) or tutor to get married.

Blood test: not required
Waiting period for licence: none
Fee for civil marriage: $268

Saskatchewan

Marriageable age:
- Without parental consent: 18 years
- With parental consent: 16 to 17 years
- With parental and court consent: under 16 years

Blood test: not required
Licence fee: $60

Yukon Territory

Marriageable age:
- Without parental consent: 19 years (In the case of an 18 year old person who has lived apart from his parents/guardians for at least 6 months & received no financial aid from them during that time, no consent is needed.)
- With parental consent: under 19 years.
- With a Supreme Court Order: between the ages of 15 to 19 years

A certificate of divorce or death must be produced if previously married
Blood test: not required
Waiting period for licence: none
Waiting period after issuance of licence: 24 hours
Licence fee: $20. Licence valid for 3 months (from date of issuance).

Postal Information

Services and rates quoted are subject to change. For complete and up-to-date information you may: consult a local Canada Post retail outlet; call 1-800-267-1177, TTY 1-800-267-2797; or refer to the Canada Post website at www.canadapost.ca. For refunds, or to make a claim, call 1-888-550-6333. For Postal Code information (fees apply) call 1-900-565-2633 (English) or 1-900-565-2634 (French).

Communications Services

LETTERMAIL™ SERVICE RATES FOR DELIVERY IN CANADA

Includes letters, postcards, greeting cards and business correspondence.

Standard Lettermail™ service:

Up to 30 g	$1.00
Over 30 g to 50 g	$1.20

*Medium Lettermail™ has been discontinued as of 2014.

Other Lettermail™ Incl. Non-Standard & Oversize:

Up to 100 g	$1.80
Over 100 g to 200 g	$2.95
Over 200 g to 300 g	$4.10
Over 300 g to 400 g	$4.70
Over 400 g to 500 g	$5.05

For cards and postcards, the maximum dimensions are 245 mm (length) x 156 mm (width). Oversize Letter Rates apply to all letters with any dimension greater than 140 mm (length) x 90 mm (width) x 0.18 mm (thickness), but not greater than 380 mm (length) x 270 mm (width) x 20 mm (thickness). Maximum weight for Standard and Medium Lettermail™ service is 50 g and for Other Lettermail™ service is 500g. Items with any dimension exceeding the maximum dimension for Oversize Lettermail™ mailpieces or exceeding 500g must be paid at parcel rates. Incentive Rates are available under sales agreements for customers whose mailing meets volume and mail preparation requirements. For details, please contact a Canada Post representative. Canada Post is committed to consistently deliver Lettermail™ mailpieces as follows: two business days within the same metropolitan area/community; three business days within the same province; four business days between provinces (some exceptions apply).

Distribution Services

PRIORITY™ SERVICE

Priority™ service is an overnight domestic courier service providing next business day noon delivery of your items for local and regional destinations and next business day noon to three day delivery nationally between major Canadian centres. This service comes with an on-time delivery guarantee, an acceptance scan, delivery confirmation, free insurance up to $100 and a no-charge signature-on-delivery option. Prepaid envelopes are available in two sizes and prepaid labels are available to business customers in 4 weight increments. For item delivery status or product information, customers can call 1-888-550-6333 or visit the website at www.canadapost.ca.

XPRESSPOST™ SERVICE

Xpresspost™ service is an affordable, simple to use delivery service for packages and documents which provides an on-time service guarantee and confirmation of delivery. Positioned right in the middle between Priority™ and Regular Post services in terms of price, service and features, Xpresspost™ service offers next business day locally and regionally, and two days nationally between most major urban centres. Customers can verify delivery of their items or obtain product information by calling 1-888-550-6333, or by accessing the Internet.

EXPEDITED PARCEL™ SERVICE

Expedited Parcel™ service is the fastest ground service providing next business day local, 1-3 business day regional and 2-7 business day national delivery and a no-charge delivery confirmation/guarantee option. A full range of prepaid labels are also available to business customers.

REGULAR PARCEL™ SERVICE

Regular Parcel™ service is the most economical, domestic, ground parcel service. Service is 2 business days local, 3-5 business days regional and 4-9 business days national between most major urban centres.

ADVICE OF RECEIPT (USA/INTERNATIONAL ONLY)

The Advice of Receipt (AR) service provides mailers with the actual signature of the addressee. An Advice of Receipt card is purchased at the time of mailing. The addressee's signature is obtained on the AR card and returned to the sender, thus providing the mailer with a Delivery Confirmation.

To international and USA destinations, AR can be used only with Registered Mail and only at the time of mailing, for a fee of $1.80.

AIR STAGE SERVICE (LESS THAN 5 ITEMS)

Canada Post services many communities where the only access to the community is by air. These communities are called Air Stage Offices.

The casual mailer who sends the occasional letter and parcel to these isolated communities pays the normal rate outlined in the various rate charts for Lettermail™, Parcel Post, Xpresspost™ & Priority™ services.

Any customer (individual or business) who ships more than 5 parcels or more than 20 kg of parcels on any day or more than 20 parcels or more than 80 kg of parcels in any month is considered an Air Stage Service Shipper and must pay Air Stage Freight Service rates. These shippers must also sign an agreement with Canada Post in order to use this service. An infrequent mailer who meets the volume or weight criteria can use the Air Stage Freight Service rates providing the goods shipped are not for resale. There are various rate levels based on the type of goods shipped.

Air Stage Freight Service rates apply whether the mailer is a business or an individual. Appropriate Regular Post zoned parcel rates apply for all other shippers, and appropriate Priority™ or Xpresspost™ service rates apply.

CANADIAN FORCES MAIL SERVICE

Canadian Forces Mail is mail sent to or by Canadian Forces personnel, their dependents and the civilians attached to the Canadian Forces served through the Canadian Forces Post Office (CFPO) or the Fleet Mail Office (FMO).

The rate charged for domestic mail is applicable for mail sent to Canadian Forces personnel providing it is sent through a CFPO or an FMO.

All parcels must include an International Customs Declaration form (CP72) and are subject to customs inspection in the country of destination. Oversize parcels and parcels over 20 kg are not acceptable.

COLLECT ON DELIVERY (COD)

COD is a service for domestic mail for which an amount due to the sender, up to $1,000 where the amount to be collected is in cash and $5,000 where the amount to be collected is by bank draft or certified cheque, is collected from the addressee before delivery and returned to the mailer. It is a service available to consumer and business mailers. COD is available for parcels only or items mailed at parcel rates. The amount collected from the addressee can include:

1. Amount representing the value of the item.
2. Service charge in the case of repairs.
3. Sales tax.
4. Postage.
5. COD fee & special service fees.

COD cannot be used to collect on items not ordered or requested by the addressee or to collect money owing on previous accounts. Insurance is available up to $5,000. Items sent COD must abide by Canada Post mail preparation requirements. The amount of the COD collected from the addressee will be forwarded to the sender by Postal Money Order when payment is made by cash or by cheque drawn up by the addressee payable to the sender. The sender must pay the COD fee of $7.25 plus shipping fees.

DEFICIENT POSTAGE FEE

Unpaid or shortpaid mail is mail for which the postage or fees have not been paid or have been partially paid. Lettermail™ and Parcelmail items are returned to the sender for the collection of the postage.

When there is no return address on the item, the item is forwarded to the addressee for the collection of the postage plus an administrative charge. All postage due charges must be paid before delivery.

DO NOT FORWARD SERVICE

Do Not Forward is a service for Lettermail™ items, mailed in Canada for delivery in Canada. If mail cannot be delivered as addressed because the addressee has a Mail Forwarding service in place, it will be returned to the sender rather than forwarded to the addressee.

FRANKED MAIL

Canada Post provides free mailing privileges to the following:

1. Governor General or Secretary to the Governor General;
2. Speaker or Clerk of the Senate or House of Commons;
3. Parliamentary Librarian or Associate Parliamentary Librarian;
4. Members of the Senate;
5. Members of the House of Commons.
6. Conflict of Interest and Ethics Commissioner or Senate Ethics Officer
7. Director of the Parliamentary Protective Service

In addition, anyone mailing an item to the above in Canada receives free postage. As a general rule, only Lettermail™ items, Publications Mail™ items and addressed Admail™ mailpieces are acceptable. Parcels and add-on services are not acceptable as part of this service. As long as the letters M.P. appear on the mailing, it can be sent free of postage.

FLEXDELIVERY™

This service is provided for customers who shop online. It allows customers to have their purchases shipped to a post office of their chosing, rather than a home address. The service is free of charge, but customers must sign up online.

COLLECTION OF THE GST

The Goods & Service Tax (GST) is a value added consumption tax instituted by the Federal Government. By law, businesses must charge 5% on most goods and services provided.

Most postal services and products are subject to the GST, such as stamps, Advance Purchase Products, all add-on options (e.g., Insurance, Trace Mail, COD), optional Postal Box rentals, and postage meter fill-ups.

There are certain items sold by Canada Post that are not taxable such as Postal Money Orders, the fee on a Money Order and the exchange on a Money Order. Provincial governments are exempt from paying the GST.

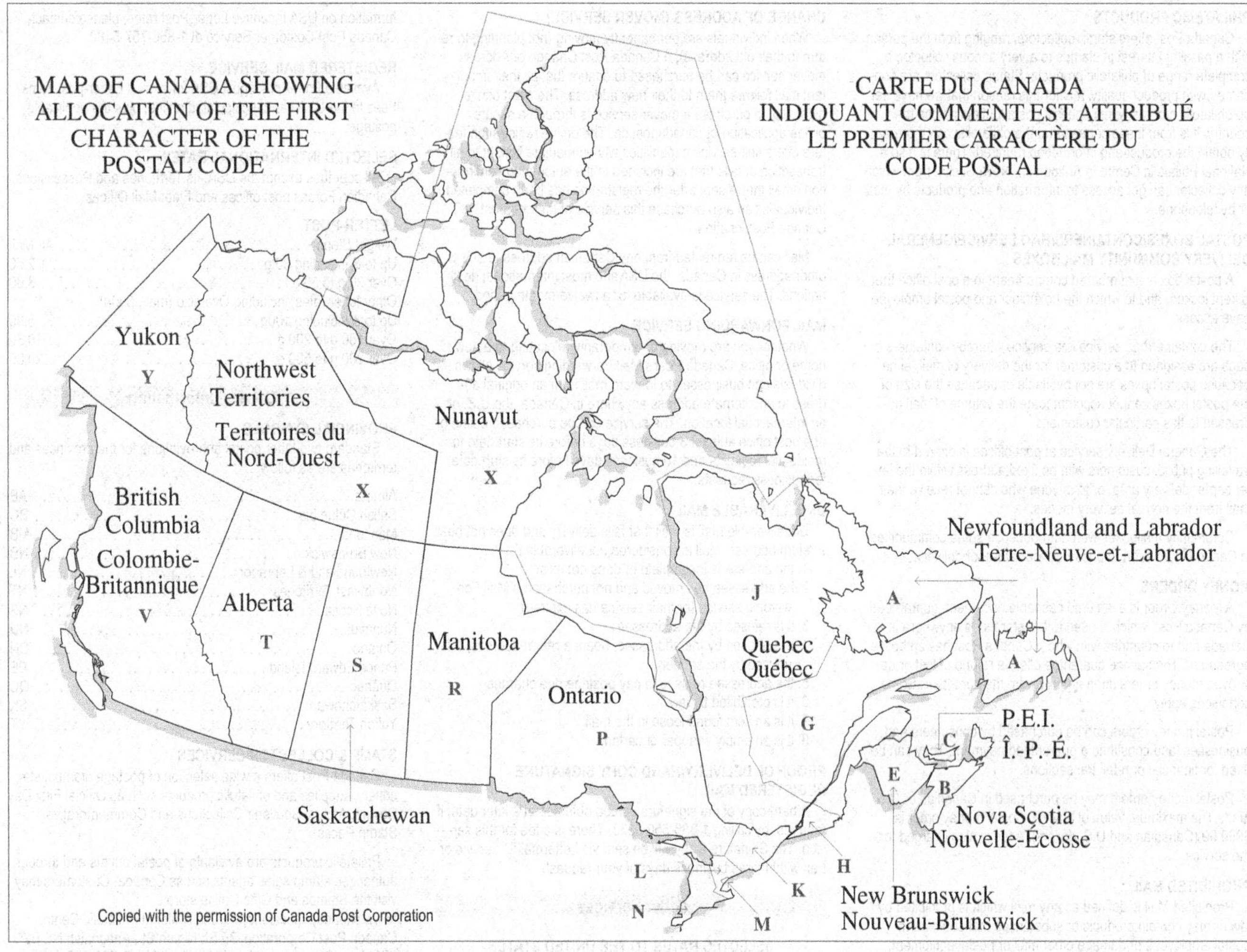

Copied with the permission of Canada Post Corporation

Mail addressed to foreign destinations requiring total shipping charges of $5 or more (single item or a cumulative purchase) and products ordered from and shipped directly by Canada Post to a foreign destination, such as Philatelic and Retail products, are not subject to the GST. The 5% tax is calculated on the total taxable purchased and rounded up or down to the nearest cent.

HOLD MAIL

Canada Post's Hold Mail service securely stores your mail whenyou are away from your home or business. Delivery resumes the day following the service's end date. The service can be purchased online in a few easy steps or at a post office.

The Hold Mail service's set-up fee includes two weeks of service for residential purchases, and one week of service for commercial purchases. Service can be extended in weekly increments with applicable fees.

MIGRATORY GAME BIRD HUNTING PERMITS

Prior to and during the migratory game bird hunting season, hunting permits can be purchased from a postal outlet. The rules, regulations and fees pertaining to these permits are provided to the outlets by the Federal body (Environment & Climate Change Canada) responsible for these permits.

INSURANCE

Insurance is available from Canada Post to provide compensation for the loss or damage of mailable items if the requirements are met. Coverage for up to $100 is included for Registered Mail™ services; however, Canada Post shall have no liability for loss or damage of Registered Mail™ items containing:

1. Bank notes, travellers' cheques & coins;
2. Stocks, bonds, coupons, & other securities negotiable by bearer;
3. Lottery tickets;
4. Jewellery;
5. Manufactured & non-manufactured precious metals, precious stones, gold bullion & gold dust;
6. Canceled or uncanceled postage stamps.

Additional coverage is available, for a fee, for domestic Registered Mail™ items up to $5,000.

To USA destinations, coverage for up to $60 is included for Registered Mail™ services, with the same exceptions as above.

KEY SERVICE™ SERVICES

Hotel, motel and automobile keys can be mailed without postage at any postal outlet in Canada for delivery in Canada if the keys have a tag clearly showing the complete address of the addressee. They can also be dropped in a street letter box.

LIBRARY BOOKS

Available to Public Libraries, University Libraries, and Libraries maintained by non-profit organizations for use by the general public in Canada to mail library books to their Canadian patrons. This service is for library materials such as books, magazines, records, CDs, CD-ROMs, audiocassettes, videocassettes, DVDs and other audiovisual materials, as well as other similar library materials. The library completes a "Library Materials Service Application" form and be authorized by the Canadian Urban Libraries Council (CULC) to use this service. The maximum weight per shipment is 5 kg.

Rates are based on a per item cost plus weight and destination. Postage paid by the library at the time of mailing covers both the outgoing and the return postage.

LITERATURE FOR THE BLIND

Literature for the Blind is a service available free of charge from Canada Post allowing blind persons and recognized institutions for the blind to mail free of postage specific items used by blind persons.

Admissible items in Canada include items impressed in Braille or similar raised type, plates for printing literature for the blind, tapes, records and CDs posted by the blind in Canada for delivery in Canada and recording tapes, records, CDs and special writing paper intended solely for the use of the blind-when mailed by or addressed to a recognized institution for the blind.

The maximum weight in Canada is 7 kg. Add on services such as Registered (500 g), and Advice of Receipt (USA/International only), which should be endorsed "Braille Free" can be applied to Literature for the Blind at no charge.

This service is also available to the USA and to international destinations at no charge. The maximum weight is 7 kg. International Literature for the Blind items must bear a label or the words "CÉCOGRAMMES" or "CÉCOGRAMMES (LITERATURE FOR THE BLIND)" in the upper right-hand corner on the address side of the item (by means of marking, printing or labelling). All other forms of labelling must be approved by Canada Post.

MAILING LISTS

Some Canadians may object to receiving Addressed Admail™ mailpieces and would like their name removed from all mailing lists. Canadians are advised to contact the sender of the Addressed Admail™ mailpiece to request that his or her name be removed from their mailing list.

If any recipient of this type of mail wishes to have all Addressed Admail™ mailpieces stopped, the customer should write to the following addresses asking them to have their members delete his or her name from their mailing lists.

In Canada:
Canadian Marketing Association
Do Not Mail Service
#607, 1 Concorde Gate, Toronto ON M3C 3N6
416-391-2362; Fax: 416-441-4062; E-mail: info@the-cma.org;
URL: www.the-cma.org/consumers/do-not-mail

In the United States:
Direct Marketing Association
DMAchoice™ Mail Preference Service
1615 L St., Washington DC 20036, USA.
212-768-7277, ext. 1888; URL: www.dmachoice.org

PHILATELIC PRODUCTS

Canada Post offers stamp collectors, ranging from the person with a passing interest in stamps to a very serious collector, a complete range of philatelic products. Stamp collectors are concerned with product quality. It is for this reason that we have set up philatelic centres within specific postal outlets across the country. It is from these centres that the philatelist can more easily obtain the product and information required. There is also a National Philatelic Centre in Antigonish, Nova Scotia, from which any collector can get access to information and products by mail or by telephone.

POSTAL BOXES/CONTAINERS/BAG SERVICE/GENERAL DELIVERY/COMMUNITY MAILBOXES

A postal box is a numbered compartment in a post office that is kept locked, and to which the boxholder and postal employee have access.

The container/bag service is a service whereby containers or bags are assigned to a customer for the delivery of mail, either because postal boxes are not available or because the size of the postal boxes cannot accommodate the volume of mail addressed to this particular customer.

The General Delivery service at post offices is offered to the travelling public, customers with no fixed address within the letter carrier delivery area, or to anyone who cannot receive their mail from the normal delivery modes.

Community mailboxes were introduced in some communities in Canada in an effort to phase out door-to-door delivery.

MONEY ORDERS

A Money Order is a secured cashable document, guaranteed by Canada Post, which is used to transfer funds anywhere in Canada and to countries with whom Canada Post has an active agreement. The service guarantee offers a refund of lost or destroyed money orders upon enquiry from the purchaser. Some conditions apply.

Postal money orders can be purchased by consumers and businesses, and constitute a guaranteed payment. They can be used for financial or retail transactions.

Postal money orders may be purchased in Canadian or U.S funds.The maximum value of a single postal money order is $999.99 (Canadian and U.S. dollars). A fee is also charged for the service.

PROHIBITED MAIL

Prohibited Mail is defined as any mail which is prohibited by law or may contain products or substances that could harm postal employees or damage other mail or postal equipment. The mail service cannot be used for criminal activities or for the transportation of dangerous goods. Animals and plants are generally not acceptable except under certain well-defined conditions in Canada. Prohibitions and restrictions on mail sent to the USA and to international destinations exists and are wide-ranging.

CANADA POST MOVER AND REDIRECTION SERVICES

Canada Post provides a secure and affordable mail redirection service that allows all individuals across Canada to have their mail forwarded to their new home or a temporary address. All individuals with residential requests must allow at least 3 business days before services start, and 10 business days for commercial requests.

CHANGE OF ADDRESS (MOVER SERVICE)

When individuals are permanently moving (not planning to return to their old address), a Canada Post Change of Address mover service can be purchased to ensure that all their important mail follows them to their new address. The most convenient way to purchase a mover service is through a secure online application at canadapost.ca. The online registration feature offers self-service capabilities with immediate insight to all transaction details that are included in the automated confirmation email that is sent after the registration has been completed. Individuals can also purchase this service at their nearest Canada Post location.

Mail can be redirected from any Canadian address to any other address in Canada, the USAand most international destinations. The service is available for a twelve-month period.

MAIL FORWARDING SERVICE

Whether you are moving or temporarily relocating to a new home or office, Canada Post's Mail Forwarding service allows individuals and businesses to forward mail from an original address to an alternate address anywhere in Canada, the U.S. or an international location. The service can be purchased online or at a post office at least 3 business days before its start date for residential requests and 10 business days before its start date for business requests.

UNDELIVERABLE MAIL

Undeliverable Mail is mail that fails delivery and does not bear a return address. Mail is considered undeliverable if:

1. the address is incomplete or does not exist
2. the addressee has moved and not purchased a Mail Forwarding service (or their service has expired)
3. it is refused by the addressee
4. it is refused by the addressee, bears a return address, & is refused by the sender
5. the addressee refuses to pay postage due charges
6. it is prohibited by law
7. it is an item found loose in the mail
8. it is an empty wrapper or carton.

PROOF OF DELIVERY/HARD COPY SIGNATURE - REGISTERED MAIL

A hard copy of the signature can be obtained at a later date, if required, by calling 1-888-550-6333. There is a fee for this service. The Signature Copy will be sent via Lettermail™ service or Fax within three business days of your request.

Other Services

SELECTED RATES TO THE UNITED STATES (its Territories & Possessions):

LETTER-POST

Weight Steps:	
Up to & including 30 g	$ 1.20
Over 30 g to 50 g	1.80
Oversize letter rates (max. 500g)	
Up to & including 100 g	2.95
100 g to 200 g	5.15
Over 200 g to 500 g	10.30

Letter-post cannot be more than 245 mm (width) x 150 mm (length) x 5 mm (thickness).

USA Incentive Letterpost offers Canadian mailers postage savings linked to volume, and quality of mail preparation. For information on USA Incentive Letter-Post rates, please contact Canada Post Customer Service at 1-866-757-5480.

REGISTERED MAIL SERVICE

Available from Xpresspost USA for airmail Letter-post items. Fees to the USA can be calculated online, plus the applicable postage.

SELECTED INTERNATIONAL RATES

All countries except the USA, its Territories and Possessions, Canadian Forces post offices and Fleet Mail Offices.

LETTER-POST

Weight Steps	Air Mail
Up to & including 30 g	$ 2.50
Over 30 g to 50 g	3.60
Other letter rates, including Oversize (max. 500g)	
Up to & including 100g	5.90
Over 100 g to 200 g	10.30
Over 200 g to 500 g	20.60

General Information

PROVINCIAL SYMBOLS

Standard two-letter postal abbreviations for the provinces and territories are as follows:

Alberta	AB
British Columbia	BC
Manitoba	MB
New Brunswick	NB
Newfoundland & Labrador	NL
Northwest Territories	NT
Nova Scotia	NS
Nunavut	NU
Ontario	ON
Prince Edward Island	PE
Québec	QC
Saskatchewan	SK
Yukon Territory	YT

STAMP & COLLECTOR SERVICES

Canada Post offers a wide selection of postage stamps, stationery, supplies and philatelic products such as Official First Day Covers, Annual Souvenir Collections and Commemorative Stamp Packs.

Philatelic products are available at postal outlets and through authorized stamp sales agents across Canada. Customers may visit the Stamps and Gifts Online store (www.canadapost.ca/shop) or the National Philatelic Centre, Canada Post Corporation, 75 St. Ninian St., Antigonish NS B2G 2R8; from Canada and the USA call toll-free 1-800-565-4362, and from other countries call 902-863-6550.

CUSTOMER SERVICE

Further information on Canada Post's products and services can be obtained through your local postal outlets, postal directory, your local customer service representative, or by calling one of the following numbers:

Toll Free (Canada) (8 a.m. to 6 p.m. local time)	1-800-267-1177
Outside of Canada	416-979-8822
Hearing Impaired with TTY-Teletyping	1-800-267-2797

Customers may also contact Canada Post via the Internet: www.canadapost.ca or mail: Canada Post Corporation, 2701 Riverside Dr., Ottawa ON K1A 0B1.

Weights & Measures

THE INTERNATIONAL SYSTEM OF UNITS (SI) (BASE & DERIVED UNITS)

With the permission of the Canadian Standards Association (operating as CSA Group), material is reproduced from CSA Group withdrawn standard **Z234.1-00 (R2011) - Metric Practice Guide,** which is copyrighted by CSA Group, 178 Rexdale Blvd., Toronto, ON, M9W 1R3. This material is not the complete and official position of CSA Group on the referenced subject, which is represented solely by the standard in its entirety. While use of the material has been authorized, CSA Group is not responsible for the manner in which the data is presented, nor for any interpretations thereof. For more information or to purchase codes or standards from CSA Group, please visit http://shop.csa.ca/ or call 1-800-463-6727.

SI BASE UNITS

The International System of Units includes two classes of units: seven base units, and derived units. The base units are seven precisely defined units used internationally for transactions, teaching and scientific research.

Quantity	Unit name	Unit symbol
length	metre	m
mass	kilogram	kg
time	second	s
electric current	ampere	A
thermodynamic temperature	kelvin	K
amount of substance	mole	mol
luminous intensity	candela	cd

SI PREFIXES

SI Prefixes and their symbols given in this table are used to form names and symbols of decimal multiples or sub-multiples of SI units.

Prefix	Symbol	Multiplying factor	
yotta	Y		10^{24}
zetta	Z		10^{21}
exa	E		10^{18}
peta	P		10^{15}
tera	T		10^{12}
giga	G		10^{9}
mega	M		10^{6}
kilo	k	1000	10^{3}
hecto	h	100	10^{2}
deca	da	10	10^{1}
deci	d	0.1	10^{-1}
centi	c	0.01	10^{-2}
milli	m	0.001	10^{-3}
micro	µ		10^{-6}
nano	n		10^{-9}
pico	p		10^{-12}
femto	f		10^{-15}
atto	a		10^{-18}
zepto	z		10^{-21}
yocto	y		10^{-24}

SI DERIVED UNITS WITH SPECIAL NAMES

Name	Symbol	Typical formula	In base units	Quantity
becquerel	Bq	s^{-1}	s^{-1}	activity (referred to a radionuclide)
coulomb	C	$s \cdot A$	$s \cdot A$	quantity of electricity, electric charge
degree Celsius	°C	K	K	Celsius temperature *
farad	F	C/V	$m^{-2} \cdot kg^{-1} \cdot s^{4} \cdot A^{2}$	capacitance
gray	Gy	J/kg	$m^{2} \cdot s^{-2}$	absorbed dose, kerma, specific energy (imparted)
henry	H	Wb/A	$m^{2} \cdot kg \cdot s^{-2} \cdot A^{-2}$	inductance
hertz	Hz	s^{-1}	s^{-1}	frequency
joule	J	$N \cdot m$	$m^{2} \cdot kg \cdot s^{-2}$	energy, work, quantity of heat
katal	kat	mol/s^{-1}	mol/s^{-1}	catalytic activity
lumen	lm	$cd \cdot sr$	Cd	luminous flux
lux	lx	lm/m^{2}	$m^{-2} \cdot cd$	illuminance
newton	N	$m \cdot kg/s^{2}$	$m \cdot kg \cdot s^{-2}$	force
ohm	Ω	V/A	$m^{2} \cdot kg \cdot s^{-3} \cdot A^{-2}$	electric resistance
pascal	Pa	N/m^{2}	$m^{-1} \cdot kg \cdot s^{-2}$	pressure, stress
radian	rad	m/m	$m \cdot m^{-1} = 1$	plane angle
siemens	S	A/V	$m^{-2} \cdot kg^{-1} \cdot s^{3} \cdot A^{2}$	electric conductance
sievert	Sv	J/kg	$m^{2} \cdot s^{-2}$	dose equivalent, dose equivalent index
steradian	sr	m^{2}/m^{2}	$m^{2} \cdot m^{-2} = 1$	solid angle
tesla	T	Wb/m^{2}	$kg \cdot s^{-2} \cdot A^{-1}$	magnetic flux density
volt	V	W/A	$m^{2} \cdot kg \cdot s^{-3} \cdot A^{-1}$	electric potential, potential difference, electromotive force
watt	W	J/s	$m^{2} \cdot kg \cdot s^{-3}$	power, radiant flux
weber	Wb	$V \cdot s$	$m^{2} \cdot kg \cdot s^{-2} \cdot A^{-1}$	magnetic flux

*Celsius temperature scale (once called centigrade, a name abandoned in 1948 to avoid confusion with "centigrad", associated with the centesimal system of angular measurement) is the commonly used scale, except for certain scientific and technological purposes where the thermodynamic temperature scale is preferred. Note the use of upper case C for Celsius.

EXAMPLES OF SI DERIVED UNITS WITHOUT SPECIAL NAMES

Unit Name	Typical formula	In base units	Typical quantity
ampere per metre	A/m	$A \cdot m^{-1}$	magnetic field strength
ampere per square metre	A/m^2	$A \cdot m^{-2}$	current density
candela per square metre	cd/m^2	$cd \cdot m^{-2}$	luminance
coulomb per cubic metre	C/m^3	$m^{-3} \cdot s \cdot A$	electric charge density
coulomb per kilogram	C/kg	$A \cdot s \cdot kg^{-1}$	exposure (X or γ rays)
coulomb per square metre	C/m^2	$m^{-2} \cdot s \cdot A$	electric flux density
cubic metre	m^3	m^3	volume
cubic metre per kilogram	m^3/kg	$m^3 \cdot kg^{-1}$	specific volume
farad per metre	F/m	$m^{-3} \cdot kg^{-1} \cdot s^4 \cdot A^2$	permittivity
gray per second	Gy/s	$m^2 \cdot s^{-3}$	absorbed dose rate
henry per metre	H/m	$m \cdot kg \cdot s^{-2} \cdot A^{-2}$	permeability
joule per cubic metre	J/m^3	$m^{-1} \cdot kg \cdot s^{-2}$	energy density
joule per kelvin	J/K	$m^2 \cdot kg \cdot s^{-2} \cdot K^{-1}$	heat capacity, entropy
joule per kilogram	J/kg	$m^2 \cdot s^{-2}$	specific energy
joule per kilogram kelvin	$J/(kg \cdot K)$	$m^2 \cdot s^{-2} \cdot K^{-1}$	specific heat capacity
joule per mole	J/mol	$m^2 \cdot kg \cdot s^{-2} \cdot mol^{-1}$	molar energy
joule per mole kelvin	$J/(mol \cdot K)$	$m^2 \cdot kg \cdot s^{-2} \cdot K^{-1} \cdot mol^{-1}$	molar entropy
kilogram per cubic metre	kg/m^3	$kg \cdot m^{-3}$	density
metre per second	m/s	$m \cdot s^{-1}$	linear speed
metre per second squared	m/s^2	m/s^2	linear acceleration
mole per cubic metre	mol/m^3	$mol \cdot m^{-3}$	concentration
newton metre	$N \cdot m$	$m^2 \cdot kg \cdot s^{-2}$	moment of force
newton per metre	N/m	$kg \cdot s^{-2}$	surface tension
pascal second	$Pa \cdot s$	$m^{-1} \cdot kg \cdot s^{-1}$	viscosity
radian per second	rad/s	s^{-1}	angular velocity
radian per second squared	rad/s^2	s^{-2}	angular acceleration
reciprocal metre	m^{-1}	m^{-1}	wavenumber
square metre	m^2	m^2	area
square metre per second	m^2/s	$m^2 \cdot s^{-1}$	kinematic viscosity
volt per metre	V/m	$m \cdot kg \cdot s^{-3} \cdot A^{-1}$	electric field strength
watt per metre kelvin	$W/(m \cdot K)$	$m \cdot kg \cdot s^{-3} \cdot K^{-1}$	thermal conductivity
watt per square metre	W/m^2	$kg \cdot s^{-3}$	heat flux density
watt per steradian	W/sr	$m^2 \cdot kg \cdot s^{-3}$	radiant intensity

UNITS THAT ARE USED WITH THE SI

Quantity	Unit name	Unit symbol	Definition (Note 1)	See Note
time	minute	min	1 min = **60** s	2
	hour	h	1 h = **3600** s	2
	day	d	1 d = **86 400** s	2
	year	a	See conversion table	2
plane angle	degree	°	1 ° = (π/**180**) rad	3
	minute	′	1 ′ = (π/**10 800**) rad	3
	second	″	1 ″ = (π/**648 000**) rad	3
	revolution	r	1 r = **2** π rad	3
length	nautical mile	M	1 nautical mile = **1852** m	5
speed	knot	kn	1 nautical mile per hour 1 kn = (**1852/3600**) m/s	6
area	hectare	ha	1 ha = **1** hm^2 = **10 000** m^2	7
volume	litre	L	1 L = **1** dm^3	
mass	metric ton or tone	t	1 t = **1000** kg = **1** Mg	8
linear density	tex	tex	1 tex = **1 x 10^{-6}** kg/m	9
pressure	millibar	mbar	1 mbar = **100** Pa	10
energy	electronvolt	eV	*	11
mass of an atom	unified atomic mass unit	u	*	12
length	astronomical unit	ua		13
	parsec	pc	*	14

*The values for these units must be obtained by experiment and are therefore not known exactly.

1. Conversion factors that are exact are shown in boldface type throughout this Table.
2. These symbols are used only in the sense of duration of time and not for expressing the time of day. See also CSA Standard CAN/CSA-Z234.4.
3. As an exception to Clause 4.6.2, no space is left between these symbols and the last digit of a numerical value. The unit "degree", with its decimal subdivisions, is used when the unit "radian" is not suitable.
4. The designations revolution per minute (r/min) and revolution per second (r/s) are widely used in connection with rotating machinery.
5. The nautical mile is a special unit employed for marine and aerial navigation to express distances. There is no universally recognized symbol for the nautical mile; M has been recommended by the International Hydrographic Organization. The conventional value given above was adopted by the First International Extraordinary Hydrographic Conference, Monaco, 1929, under the name "International nautical mile".
6. There is no universally recognized symbol for the knot; kn has been recommended by the International Hydrographic Organization.
7. Because of the need for a unit of similar magnitude to the acre, the hectare will continue to be recognized as a unit for use in surveying and agriculture.
8. Care must be taken in the interpretation of the word "tonne" when it occurs in French text of Canadian origin, where the meaning may be a "ton of 2000 pounds".
9. The tex is used only in the textile industry.
10. Pressure and stress should be expressed in pascals. The millibar may continue to be used, but only for international meteorological work. One millibar is equal to one hectopascal.
11. One electronvolt is the kinetic energy acquired by an electron in passing through a potential difference of 1 V in vacuum; 1 eV . 0.160 217 733 aJ.
12. The unified atomic mass unit is equal to the fraction 1/12 of the mass of an atom of the nuclide 12C; 1 u . 1.660 540 2 yg.
13. The astronomical unit of distance is the length of the radius of the unperturbed circular orbit of a body of negligible mass moving around the sun with a sidereal angular velocity of 0.017 202 098 950 radian per day of 86 400 ephemeris seconds. In the system of astronomical constants of the International Astronomical Union, the value adopted for it is 1 ua = 149.597 870 Gm.
14. 1 parsec (pc) is the distance at which 1 astronomical unit subtends an angle of 1 second of arc; thus 1 pc . 206 265 ua . 30.857 Pm.

CONVERSION OF UNITS TO THE INTERNATIONAL SYSTEM OF UNITS

Area

1 acre	= 0.404 685 6 ha
1 arpent (French measure)	= 0.341 889 4 ha
1 circular mil	= 506.707 5 μm^2
1 hectare	= **1** hm^2
1 legal subdivision (40 acres)	= 0.161 874 2 km^2
1 perch (French measure)	= 34.188 94 m^2
1 rood (1210 square yards)	= 0.101 171 4 ha
1 section (1 mile square, 640 acres)	= 2.589 988 km^2
1 square foot	= **929.030 4** cm^2
1 square foot (French measure)	= 1 055.214 cm^2
1 square inch	= **645.16** mm^2
1 square mile	= 2.589 988 km^2
1 square rod	= 25.292 85 m^2
1 square yard	= 0.836 127 4 m^2

Energy

1 British thermal unit (Btu) (International Table)*	= 1.055 056 kJ
1 British thermal unit (Btu) (mean)*	= 1.055 87 kJ
1 British thermal unit (Btu) (thermochemical)*	= 1.054 35 kJ
1 British thermal unit (Btu) (39°F)*†	= 1.059 67 kJ
1 British thermal unit (Btu) (59°F, 15 °C)*	= 1.054 80 kJ
1 British thermal unit (Btu) (60.5°F)*	= 1.054 615 kJ
1 Calorie (dietetic)	= 4.185 5 kJ
1 calorie (International Table)	= **4.186 8** J
1 calorie (thermochemical)	= **4.184** J
1 calorie (15 °C)†§	= 4.185 5 J
1 electronvolt	= 0.160 217 7 aJ
1 erg	= **0.1** μJ
1 foot poundal	= 42.140 11 mJ
1 foot pound-force	= 1.355 818 J
1 horsepower hour	= 2.684 520 MJ
1 kilowatt hour	= **3.6** MJ
1 quad	= 1.055 EJ
1 therm	= 105.506 MJ
1 ton (nuclear equivalent of TNT)	= 4.2 GJ
1 watt hour	= **3.6** kJ
1 watt second	= **1** J

Force

1 dyne	= **10 μN**
1 kilogram-force	= **9.806 65** N
1 kilopond	= **9.806 65** N
1 kip (thousand pounds force)	= 4.448 222 kN
1 ounce-force	= 0.278 013 9 N
1 poundal	= 0.138 255 0 N
1 pound-force	= 4.448 222 N
1 ton-force	= 8.896 443 kN
1 ton-force (UK)	= 9.964 016 kN

Length

1 ångström	= **0.1** nm
1 arpent (French measure)	= 58.471 31 m
1 astronomical unit	= 149.597 870 Gm
1 chain (66 feet)	= **20.116 8** m
1 ell (45 inches)	= **1.143** m
1 fathom	= **1.828 8** m
1 fermi	= **1** fm
1 foot	= **0.304 8** m
1 foot (French measure)	= **0.324 840 6** m
1 foot (US survey, limited usage)	= 0.304 800 6 m
1 furlong	= **0.201 168** km
1 inch	= **25.4** mm
1 league (International nautical)	= **5.556** km
1 league (UK nautical)	= **5.559 552** km
1 league (US)	= **4.828 032** km
1 light year	= 9.460 528 Pm
1 link (1/100 chain)	= **0.201 168** m
1 microinch	= **25.4** nm
1 micron	= **1** μm
1 mil (0.001 inch)	= **25.4** μm
1 mile	= **1.609 344** km
1 mile (International nautical)	= **1.852** km
1 mile (UK nautical)	= **1.853 184** km
1 parsec	= 30.856 78 Pm
1 perch	= **5.029 2** m
1 perch (French measure)	= **5.847 130 8** m
1 pica (printer's)	= 4.217 518 mm
1 point (Didot)	= 0.375 972 9 mm
1 point (paper or card thickness)	= **25.4** μm
1 point (pica)	= 0.351 459 8 mm
1 pole	= **5.029 2** m
1 rod	= **5.029 2** m
1 X unit	= 100.2 fm
1 yard	= **0.914 4** m

Mass

1 carat	= **200** mg
1 cental (100 lb)	= **45.359 237** kg
1 coal tub (100 lb, Newfoundland)	= **45.359 237** kg
1 drachm (apothecary)	= 3.887 935 g
1 dram (troy or apothecary, US)	= 3.887 935 g
1 dram (avoirdupois)	= 1.771 845 g
1 gamma	= **1** μg
1 grain	= **64.798 91** mg
1 hundredweight (100 lb)	= **45.359 237** kg

1 hundredweight (long) (112 lb, UK)	= 50.802 35 kg
1 metric carat	= **200** mg
1 ounce (avoirdupois)	= 28.349 523 g
1 ounce (troy or apothecary)	= **31.103 476 8** g
1 pennyweight	= 1.555 174 g
1 pound (avoirdupois)	= **0.453 592 37** kg
1 pound (troy or apothecary)	= **373.241 721 6** g
1 quarter (28 lb, UK)	= 12.700 58 kg
1 scruple (apothecary, 20 grains)	= 1.295 978 g
1 slug	= 14.593 90 kg
1 stone (14 lb, UK)	= 6.350 293 kg
1 ton (long, 2240 lb, UK)	= **1.016 046 908 8** Mg
1 ton (short, 2000 lb)	= **0.907 184 74** Mg
1 unified atomic mass	= 1.660 540 yg

Power - General

1 Btu (IT) per hour	= 0.293 071 1 W
1 Btu (thermochemical) per hour	= 0.292 875 1 W
1 Btu (thermochemical) per minute	= 17.572 50 W
1 Btu (thermochemical) per second	= 1.054 350 kW
1 foot pound-force per hour	= 0.376 616 1 mW
1 foot pound-force per minute	= 22.596 97 mW
1 foot pound-force per second	= 1.355 818 W
1 horsepower (boiler)	= 9.809 50 kW
1 horsepower (electric)	= **746** W
1 horsepower (metric, *cheval vapeur*)	= **735.498 75** W
1 horsepower (water)	= 746.043 W
1 horsepower (550 ft·lbf/s)	= 745.699 9 W
1 ton of refrigeration (12 000 Btu/h)	= 3514 W

Pressure or Stress (Force per Unit Area)

1 atmosphere, standard (= 760 torr)	= **101.325** kPa
1 atmosphere, technical (= 1 kgf/cm^2)	= **98.066 5** kPa
1 bar	= **100** kPa
1 foot of water (39.2°F, 4 °C)	= 2.988 98 kPa
1 inch of mercury (0 °C)	= 3.386 39 kPa
1 inch of mercury (60°F)	= 3.376 85 kPa
1 inch of mercury (68°F, 20 °C)	= 3.374 11 kPa
1 inch of water (conventional)	= 249.088 9 Pa
1 inch of water (39.2°F, 4 °C)	= 249.082 Pa
1 inch of water (60°F)	= 248.843 Pa
1 inch of water (68°F, 20 °C)	= 248.641 Pa
1 ksi (1000 lbf/in2)	= 6.894 757 MPa
1 mm mercury (0 °C)	= 133.322 4 Pa
1 poundal per square foot	= 1.488 164 Pa
1 pound-force per square foot	= 47.880 26 Pa
1 pound-force per square inch (psi)	= 6.894 757 kPa
1 ton-force per square inch	= 13.789 514 MPa
1 ton-force (UK) per square inch	= 15.444 3 MPa
1 torr	= 133.322 4 Pa

Temperature – Scales

Celsius temperature	= temperature in kelvins **– 273.15**
Fahrenheit temperature	= **1.8** (Celsius temperature) **+ 32**
Fahrenheit temperature	= **1.8** (temperature in kelvins) **– 459.67**
Rankine temperature	= **1.8** (temperature in kelvins)

Time

1 day	= **86.4** ks
1 day (sidereal)	= 86.164 09 ks
1 hour	= **3.6** ks
1 hour (sidereal)	= 3.590 17 ks
1 minute	= **60** s
1 minute (sidereal)	= 59.836 17 s
1 second (sidereal)	= 0.997 269 6 s
1 Svedberg unit	= **0.1** ps
1 year (365 days)	= **31.536** Ms
1 year (sidereal)	= 31.558 150 Ms
1 year (tropical)	= 31.556 930 Ms
year 1900, tropical, January day 0, hour 12 (ephemeris)	= 31.556 926 Ms

Velocity (Speed)

1 foot per hour	= 84.666 67 µm/s
	= **304.8** mm/h
1 foot per minute	= **5.08** mm/s
	= **304.8** mm/min
1 foot per second	= **304.8** mm/s
1 inch per minute	= **25.4** mm/min
1 inch per second	= **25.4** mm/s
1 knot (International)	= **1.852** km/h
	= 0.514 444 4 m/s
1 knot (UK)	= **1.853 184** km/h
1 mile per hour	= **0.447 04** m/s
	= **1.609 344** km/h
1 mile per minute	= **26.822 4** m/s

Volume - General

1 acre foot	= 1233.482 m^3
1 barrel (oil, 42 US gallons)	= 0.158 987 3 m^3
1 barrel (US dry, 7056 in^3)	= 0.115 627 1 m^3
1 barrel (US dry, cranberries, 5826 in^3)	= 95.471 03 dm^3
1 barrel (UK, 36 gallons)	= 0.163 659 2 m^3
1 board foot*	= 2.359 737 dm^3
1 bushel	= 36.368 72 dm^3
1 bushel (US dry, 2150.42 in^3)	= 35.239 07 dm^3
1 cord (128 ft^3)†	= 3.624 556 m^3
1 cubic foot	= 28.316 85 dm^3
1 cubic inch	= **16.387 064** cm^3
1 cubic yard	= 0.764 554 9 m^3
1 cunit (100 ft^3 solid wood)	= 2.831 685 m^3
1 cup‡	= **250** cm^3
1 demiard	= 0.284 130 6 dm^3
1 drop (1/100 teaspoon)‡	= **0.05** cm^3
1 fluid dram	= 3.551 633 cm^3
1 fluid dram (US measure)	= 3.696 691 cm^3
1 fluid ounce	= 28.413 062 cm^3
1 fluid ounce (US)	= 29.573 53 cm^3
1 gallon§	= **4.546 09** dm^3
1 gallon (US)	= **3.785 411 784** dm^3
1 gill	= 0.142 065 dm^3
1 herring barrel	= 145.474 9 dm^3
1 herring tub	= **72.737 44** dm^3
1 hogshead	= 245.488 9 dm^3
1 lambda	= **1** mm^3
1 minim	= 59.193 9 mm^3
1 minim (US)	= 61.611 52 mm^3
1 peck	= 9.092 180 dm^3
1 peck (US dry)	= 8.809 768 dm^3
1 Petrograd standard (165 ft3, sawn timber)	= 4.672 280 m^3
1 pint	= 0.568 261 2 dm^3
1 pint (US dry)	= 0.550 610 5 dm^3
1 pint (US liquid)	= 0.473 176 5 dm^3
1 quart	= 1.136 522 dm^3
1 quart (US dry)	= 1.101 221 dm^3
1 quart (US liquid)	= 0.946 352 9 dm^3
1 salt cart	= 490.977 7 dm^3
1 salt tub	= **81.829 62** dm^3
1 sand barrel	= **81.829 62** dm^3
1 tablespoon‡	= **15** cm^3
1 teaspoon‡	= **5** cm^3
1 ton (register)	= 2.831 685 m^3

Measures Having Former Household Usage

1 cup (8 fluid ounces)	= 227 cm^3
1 cup (US, 8 US fluid ounces)	= 237 cm^3
1 cup (UK, 10 fluid ounces)	= 284 cm^3
1 tablespoon (1/2 fluid ounce)	= 14.21 cm^3
1 tablespoon (UK, 5/8 fluid ounce)	= 17.8 cm^3
1 tablespoon (US, 1/2 US fluid ounce)	= 14.8 cm^3
1 teaspoon (1/6 fluid ounce)	= 4.74 cm^3
1 teaspoon (UK, 5/24 fluid ounce)	= 5.92 cm^3
1 teaspoon (US, 1/6 US fluid ounce)	= 4.93 cm^3

Note that 1 cm^3 = 1 mL.

Notes

Energy

*To convert from British thermal units (Btu) to the SI requires knowledge of which Btu is used, in order that the correct factor may be applied. The Btu is defined as the energy required to heat 1 lb of water through 1°F; however, because the specific heat of water varies with temperature, it is necessary to identify the particular Btu. This is done by specifying the midpoint of the range used, eg, the Btu (60.5°F) was determined over the range 60–61°F. The value for the Btu (60.5°F), 1.054 615 kJ, is the value that has been adopted for use in the Canadian petroleum and natural gas industry. The value recognized by ISO is 1.0545 kJ.

†Based on CIPM value.

‡Based on US National Bureau of Standards value.

§The values for the 15 °C calorie have been determined experimentally. The value generally used in North America, 4.1858 J, was determined at the US National Bureau of Standards in 1939. There is another value, 4.1855 J, which is a weighted average of several data; this value was adopted by CIPM in March 1950.

For further details, refer to CIPM, P.-V. 2e série, tome 22, Annexe 1, "Table 1950 des valeurs les plus précises que l'on peut tirer des expériences faites sur la chaleur spécifique de l'eau entre 0° et 100 °C".

Volume – General

*The board foot is nominally 1 × 12 × 12 = 144 in^3. However, the actual volume of wood is about 2/3 of the nominal quantity.

†This applies to stacked wood, comprising wood, bark, and airspace, to a total volume of 128 ft^3.

‡Rational metric values.

§Also referred to as the "imperial gallon".

SECTION 2
ARTS & CULTURE

Many of the following categories are also represented in Section 3: Associations.

Art Galleries

National Art Gallery

National Gallery of Canada (NGC) / Musée des beaux-arts du Canada (MBAC)
PO Box 427 A, 380 Sussex Dr.
Ottawa, ON K1N 9N4
Tel: 613-990-1985; *Fax:* 613-990-8075
Toll-Free: 800-319-2787
info@gallery.ca
www.gallery.ca
Social Media: www.instagram.com/ngc_mbac
twitter.com/gallerydotca
www.facebook.com/nationalgallerycanada
Other contact information: TDD: 613-990-0777
The permanent collection of the National Gallery comprises paintings, sculpture, prints & drawings, photographs, film & video art from the Canadian, European, American & Asian schools, including the collection of the former Canadian Museum of Contemporary Photography. Special exhibitions as well as permanent installations of the gallery's collections are on display. The gallery also sends its exhibitions on tour across the country & participates in international exhibitions. Online showcases are also available for select material.
Michael J. Tims, Chair, Board of Trustees
Marc Mayer, Director & Chief Executive Officer
Paul Lang, Chief Curator & Deputy Director, Collections, Research & Education
Julie Peckham, Deputy Director & Chief Financial Officer, Administration & Finance
Yves Théoret, Director, Exhibitions & Outreach
Jean-François Bilodeau, Deputy Director, Advancement & Public Engagement
Stephen Gritt, Director, Conservation & Technical Research
Sylvie Sarault, Director, Human Resources
Matthew Symonds, Director/Ministerial Liaison, Corporate Secretariat
J. Drouin-Brisebois, Curator, Contemporary Art
K. Atanassova, Curator, Canadian Art
G. Hill, Curator, Indigenous Art
A. Thomas, Curator, Photographs

Alberta

Provincial Art Gallery

Art Gallery of Alberta (AGA)
2 Sir Winston Churchill Sq.
Edmonton, AB T5J 2C1
Tel: 780-422-6223; *Fax:* 780-426-3105
info@youraga.ca
www.youraga.ca
Social Media: www.youtube.com/user/ArtGalleryAlberta
twitter.com/yourAGA
www.facebook.com/artgalleryofalberta
Year Founded: 1924 Collections include: Canadian & international contemporary & historical paintings, sculpture, photography, video & graphic art. Research fields: Western Canadian art, historical & contemporary art; painting; sculpture; photography; graphics. Activities: Guided tours; lectures; films; gallery talks; art rental & sales gallery; studio art classes for children & adults; program workshops & seminars
Darcy Trufyn, Chair
Catherine Crowston, Executive Director & Chief Curator
Rochelle Ball, Registrar
Oksana Gowin, Director, Marketing & Communications

Local Art Galleries

***Banff:* Canada House Gallery**
201 Bear St.
Banff, AB T1L 1B5
Toll-Free: 800-419-1298
info@canadahouse.com
canadahouse.com
Social Media: instagram.com/ch_gallery
twitter.com/ch_gallery
www.facebook.com/CanadaHouseGallery
Year Founded: 1974 Paintings & sculptures by Canadian & Inuit artists.
Barbara Pelham, Owner

***Banff:* Mountain Galleries at the Fairmount Fairmont Banff Springs**
PO Box 898, 405 Spray Ave.
Banff, AB T1L 1J4
Tel: 403-760-2382*Toll-Free:* 888-310-9726
banff@mountaingalleries.com
www.mountaingalleries.com
Social Media: www.youtube.com/mountaingalleries
twitter.com/MntGalleries
www.facebook.com/pages/Mountain-Galleries/198382838938
Year Founded: 1992 Exhibits work by Canadian artists
Aimee Woo, Co-Director

***Banff:* Walter Phillips Gallery (WPG)**
The Banff Centre, Banff National Park, PO Box 1020 14, 107 Tunnel Mountain Dr.
Banff, AB T1L 1H5
Tel: 403-762-6281; *Fax:* 403-762-6659
walter_phillipsgallery@banffcentre.ca
www.banffcentre.ca/WPG
Social Media: www.youtube.com/thebanffcentre
twitter.com/thebanffcentre
www.facebook.com/242702459137814
Year Founded: 1976 Contemporary, national & international fine arts; open year round
Janice Price, President & CEO
Jen Mizuik, Director, Jen_Mizuik@banffcentre.ca

***Brocket:* Oldman River Cultural Centre**
PO Box 70
Brocket, AB T0K 0H0
Tel: 403-965-3939
Aboriginal history

***Calgary:* Contemporary Calgary City Hall Location**
#104, 800 MacLeod Trail SE
Calgary, AB T2P 2M5
Tel: 403-262-1737

***Calgary:* Contemporary Calgary**
117 - 8th Ave. SW
City Hall Location, #104, 800 Macleod Trail SE, Calgary, AB, T2P 2M5
Calgary, AB T2P 1B4
Tel: 403-770-1350
info@contemporarycalgary.com
www.contemporarycalgary.com
Social Media: www.youtube.com/user/artgalleryofcalgary
twitter.com/C_Calgary
www.fac ebook.com/contemporary.yyc
Non-profit public gallery, exhibiting works by contemporary Canadian artists; travelling exhibitions & education programs

***Calgary:* Endeavour Arts Gallery**
#200, 1209 - 1 St. SW
Calgary, AB T2R 0V3
Tel: 403-532-7800
info@endeavorarts.com
www.endeavorarts.com
Social Media: plus.google.com/107972692568536773652
twitter.com/endeavorarts
www.fac ebook.com/endeavorarts
Year Founded: 2010

***Calgary:* Esker Foundation Contemporary Art Gallery**
#444, 1011 - 9 Ave. SE
Calgary, AB T2G 0H7
Tel: 403-930-2490
info@eskerfoundation.com
eskerfoundation.com
Social Media: instagram.com/eskerfoundation
twitter.com/eskercalgary
www.facebook.co m/pages/Esker-Foundation/355772491162964
Year Founded: 2012 Contemporary work by international artists.
Naomi Potter, Director/Curator

***Calgary:* Gainsborough Galleries**
441 - 5 Ave. SW
Calgary, AB T2P 2V1
Tel: 403-262-3715; *Fax:* 403-262-3743
Toll-Free: 866-425-5373
art@gainsboroughgalleries.com
www.gainsboroughgallerie s.com
twitter.com/GainsboroughG
www.facebook.com/gainsboroughgalleries
Year Founded: 1923 Representational & impressionistic work by Canadian & international artists.

***Calgary:* Gerry Thomas Art Gallery**
302 - 11 Ave. SW
Calgary, AB T2R 1J3
Tel: 403-265-1630
info@gerrythomasgallery.com
www.gerrythomasgallery.com
www.facebook.com/gerry.thomas.gallery
Gerry Thomas, Owner

***Calgary:* Gibson Fine Art**
628 - 11 Ave. SW
Calgary, AB T2R 0E2
Tel: 403-244-2000; *Fax:* 403-244-2036
info@gibsonfineart.ca
www.gibsonfineart.ca
twitter.com/GibsonFineArt
www.facebook.com/Gibsonfineart
Year Founded: 1970 Work by new & established artists, with over 50% of the collection coming from Albertan artists.

***Calgary:* Illingworth Kerr Gallery (IKG)**
Alberta College of Art + Design, 1407 - 14 Ave. NW
Calgary, AB T2N 4R3
Tel: 403-284-7680; *Fax:* 403-289-6682
www.acad.ca/ikg.html
Year Founded: 1958 Contemporary art exhibitions, publications, lectures, screenings & related events
Wayne Baerwaldt, Director/Curator, 403-284-7632, wayne.baerwaldt@acad.ca
Alexandra McIntosh, Assistant Curator, 403-284-7633, alexandra.mcintosh@acad.ca
Ann Thrale, Head Technician, ann.thrale@acad.ca

***Calgary:* Latitude Art Gallery**
#102A, 708 - 11 Ave. SW
Calgary, AB T2R 0E1
Tel: 403-262-9598
info@latitudeartgallery.com
www.latitudeartgallery.com
twitter.com/LatitudeArtYYC
www.facebook.com /LatitudeArtGallery
Year Founded: 2007 Contemporary Canadian artwork

***Calgary:* Leighton Art Centre**
Box 9, Site 31, RR#8
Calgary, AB T2J 2T9
Tel: 403-931-3153; *Fax:* 403-931-3673
info@leightoncentre.org
www.leightoncentre.org
www.facebook.com/pages/
Leighton-Art-Centre/537513416268691
Year Founded: 1974 A.C. Leighton's paintings, as well as those by other prominent Alberta artists; programs for children & adults; open year round
Sally Greg, Chair
Mary Dean, Managing Director, maryd@leightoncentre.org
Chad Pratch, Director, Education Centre, chadp@leightoncentre.org

***Calgary:* Loch Gallery Calgary**
1516 - 4 St. SW
Calgary, AB T2R 0Y4
Tel: 403-209-8542
www.lochgallery.com
Year Founded: 2006 Work by Canadian & European artists both contemporary & historical.
Ian Loch, Manager

***Calgary:* Marion Nicoll Gallery (MNG)**
Alberta College of Art + Design, 1407 - 14th Ave. NW
Calgary, AB T2N 4R3
Tel: 403-283-7655
mng.acadsa@acad.ca
www.acad.ca/mng.html
Social Media: marionnicollgallery.wordpress.com
Student-run gallery for students attending the Alberta College of Art & Design.

***Calgary:* Planet Art Gallery**
1451 - 14 St. SW
Calgary, AB T3C 1C8
Tel: 403-619-0976
planetartinc@gmail.com
www.planetartgallery.ca
Social Media: www.linkedin.com/profile/view?id=95105962
twitter.com/janplanetart
www .facebook.com/planetartgallery
Year Founded: 2010
Janice Mather, Owner

***Calgary:* Stephen Lowe Art Gallery**
Bow Valley Square III, #251, 255 - 5 Ave. SW
Calgary, AB T2P 3G6
Tel: 403-261-1602; *Fax:* 403-261-2981
contact@stephenloweartgallery.ca
www.stephenloweartgallery.ca
Year Founded: 1970 Contemporary art

***Calgary:* Stride Gallery**
1006 MacLeod Trail SE
Calgary, AB T2G 2M7
Tel: 403-262-8507; *Fax:* 403-269-5220
info@stride.ab.ca
www.stride.ab.ca
www.facebook.com/pages/Stride-Galle ry/149046095161193
Year Founded: 1985
Larissa Tiggelers, Gallery Director, director@stride.ab.ca

***Calgary:* Wallace Galleries**
500 - 5 Ave. SW
Calgary, AB T2P 3L5
Tel: 403-262-8050; *Fax:* 403-264-7112
Toll-Free: 877-962-8050
info@wallacegalleries.com
www.wallacegalleries.com
t witter.com/WallaceGallery
www.facebook.com/164627393594465
Year Founded: 1986 Exhibits visual artwork by artists in all stages of their careers.
Heidi Hubner, Contact, heidi@wallacegalleries.com

***Calgary:* Webster Galleries Inc.**
812 - 11 Ave. SW
Calgary, AB T2R 0E5
Tel: 403-263-6500; *Fax:* 403-263-6501
info@webstergalleries.com
www.webstergalleries.com
Year Founded: 1979 Canadian artwork
John Webster, Owner
Lorraine Webster, Owner

***Camrose:* Candler Art Gallery**
5002 - 50 St.
Camrose, AB T4V 1R2
Tel: 780-672-8401 *Toll-Free:* 888-672-8401
candler@syban.net
www.candlerartgallery.com
Year Founded: 1978

***Cochrane:* Rustica Gallery**
PO Box 1267, 123 - 2 Ave. West, Bay #1
Cochrane, AB T4C 1B3
Tel: 403-851-5181; *Fax:* 403-241-0263
info@rusticagallery.com
www.rusticaartgallery.com

***Edmonton:* The Daffodil Gallery**
10412 - 124 St.
Edmonton, AB T5N 1R5
Tel: 780-760-1278
info@daffodilgallery.ca
www.daffodilgallery.ca
Social Media: www.pinterest.com/daffodilgallery
twitter.com/DaffodilGallery
www.face book.com/DaffodilGallery
Year Founded: 2011
Karen Bishop, Owner, karenbishop@daffodilgallery.ca
Rick Rogers, Owner, rickrogers@daffodilgallery.ca

***Edmonton:* Front Gallery**
12312 Jasper Ave. NW
Edmonton, AB T5N 3K6
Tel: 780-488-2952; *Fax:* 780-452-6240
info@thefrontgallery.com
thefrontgallery.com
twitter.com/thefrontgalle ry
Also provides picture framing services.

***Edmonton:* Latitude 53**
10248 - 106 St.
Edmonton, AB T5J 1H5
Tel: 780-423-5353; *Fax:* 780-424-9117
info@latitude53.org
www.latitude53.org
twitter.com/Latitude53
www.fa cebook.com/Latitude53
Other contact information: Administration E-mail: admin@latitude53.org
Year Founded: 1973 Contemporary artistic projects, experimental cultural development; performance art; literary projects; interdisciplinary art
Jessie Beier, President, board@latitude53.org
Todd Janes, Executive Director, todd.janes@latitude53.org

***Edmonton:* University of Alberta Fine Arts Building Gallery**
Fine Arts Building, University of Alberta, 112 St. & 89 Ave.
Edmonton, AB T6G 2C9
Tel: 780-492-2081
www.artdesign.ualberta.ca/en/FAB_Gallery
www.facebook.com/FABgallery
Work by students, faculty, staff & professional artists.
Blair Brennan, Contact, bbrennan@gpu.srv.ualberta.ca

***Edmonton:* West End Gallery**
12308 Jasper Ave. NW
Edmonton, AB T5N 3K5
Tel: 780-488-4892 *Toll-Free:* 855-488-4892
art@westendgalleryltd.com
www.westendgalleryltd.com
twitter.com/westen dgallery
www.facebook.com/pages/West-End-Gallery/185219480017
Year Founded: 1975 Fine art gallery representing Canadian paintings & sculpture; the largest representation of glass artists in Canada

***Victoria:* West End Gallery**
Victoria Location
1203 Broad St.
Victoria, BC V8W 2A4
Tel: 250-388-0009 *Toll-Free:* 877-388-0009
Year Founded: 1994

***Grande Prairie:* The Art Gallery of Grande Prairie**
#103, 9839 - 103 Ave.
Grande Prairie, AB T8V 6M7
Tel: 780-532-8111; *Fax:* 780-539-9522
info@prariegallery.com
aggp.ca
www.facebook.com/pages/Prairie-Art-Gall ery/11799376302
Public art gallery. The gallery's collection currently stands at approximately 600 works of art, almost exclusively created in Alberta in the midto late 20th Century.
Melanie Jenner, Manager, Marketing & Visitor Service, melanie@prairiegallery.com

***Jasper:* Mountain Galleries at the Fairmount Fairmont Jasper Park Lodge**
PO Box 1651, 1 Old Londge Rd.
Jasper, AB T0E 1E0
Tel: 780-852-5378 *Toll-Free:* 888-310-9726
jasper@mountaingalleries.com
www.mountaingalleries.com
Social Media: www.pinterest.com/mntgalleries
twitter.com/MntGalleries
www.facebook.com/mountaingalleries

***Lethbridge:* Southern Alberta Art Gallery (SAAG)**
601 - 3 Ave. South
Lethbridge, AB T1J 0H4
Tel: 403-327-8770; *Fax:* 403-328-3913
info@saag.ca
www.saag.ca
twitter.com/THESAAG
www.facebook.com/southe rnalbertaartgallery
Fosters the work of contemporary visual artists who challenge the boundaries of their discipline & advance their work in a larger public realm
Ryan Doherty, Director/Curator, rdoherty@saag.ca

***Lethbridge:* University of Lethbridge Art Gallery**
W600, Centre for the Arts, 4401 University Dr.
Lethbridge, AB T1K 3M4
Tel: 403-329-2666; *Fax:* 403-382-7115
www.uleth.ca/artgallery
Social Media: vimeo.com/ulethartgallery
twitter.com/ulethartgallery
www.facebook.com /201495055897
Features rotating exhibits from the University of Lethbridge art collection
Josephine Mills, Director & Curator, josephine.mills@uleth.ca

***Okotoks:* Okotoks Art Gallery (OAG)**
Station Cultural Centre, 53 North Railway St.
Okotoks, AB T1S 1K1
Tel: 403-938-3204
culture@okotoks.ca
www.okotoks.ca
Year Founded: 1981 The art gallery serves the Town of Okotoks & the Foothills region, promoting art & visual culture. Summer hours: M-F 10:00-5:00, Sa, Su 12:00-5:00; Fall & Winter hours: Tu-Sa 10:00-5:00

***St Albert:* Art Gallery of St. Albert (AGSA)**
19 Perron St.
St Albert, AB T8N 1E5
Tel: 780-460-4310; *Fax:* 780-460-9537
ahfgallery@artsheritage.ca
artgalleryofstalbert.ca
Social Media: pinterest.com/artgallerysa
twitter.com/artgallerystalb
www.facebook.co m/ArtsAndHeritageStAlbert
Hours of operation: Tu, W, F, Sa 1:00-5:00, Th 10:00-8:00.
Jenny Willson-McGrath, Exhibition Curator & Interim Director, jennyw@artsheritage.ca

British Columbia

Provincial Art Gallery

Vancouver Art Gallery
750 Hornby St.
Vancouver, BC V6Z 2H7
Tel: 604-662-4700; *Fax:* 604-682-1086
customerservice@vanartgallery.bc.ca
www.vanartgallery.bc.ca
Social Media: www.youtube.com/user/VanArtGallery
twitter.com/VanArtGallery
www.faceb ook.com/VancouverArtGallery
Other contact information: Info Line: 604-662-4719
Largest gallery in western Canada; presents major exhibitions from contemporary art to historical masters; founded in 1931, has over 7,800 works in its collection, 41,400 sq. ft. of exhibition space & is located in the former provincial courthouse in downtown Vancouver; collection includes acclaimed Canadian artists such as Douglas Coupland, Janet Cardiff & George Bures Miller
Bruce Wright, Chair
Kathleen Bartels, Director
Paul Larocque, Associate Director

Local Art Galleries

***Abbotsford:* Kariton Art Gallery**
2387 Ware St.
Abbotsford, BC V2S 3C6
Tel: 604-852-9358
abbotsfordartscouncil.com
www.facebook.com/AbbotsfordArtsCouncil
Year Founded: 1995 Work by local artists. Operated by the Abbotsford Arts Council
Charles Wiebe, President, Abbotsford Arts Council

***Agassiz:* Ruby Creek Art Gallery**
58611 Lougheed Hwy., RR#2
Agassiz, BC V0M 1A2
Tel: 604-796-0740; *Fax:* 604-796-9289
info@rubycreekartgallery.com
rubycreekartgallery.com
Social Media: www.youtube.com/channel/UCe9ozb70hgRy2vWRaTj40uQ
twitter.com/RubyCreekArt
www.facebook.com/RubyCreekArtGallery
Northwest First Nations artwork

***Brackendale:* Brackendale Art Gallery Theatre Teahouse**
PO Box 100, 41950 Government Rd.
Brackendale, BC V0N 1H0
Tel: 604-898-3333; *Fax:* 604-898-3333
www.brackendaleartgallery.com
www.facebook.com/139533814492
The gallery also serves food, holds concerts, presents theatre productions, hosts workshops with artists, & more. Hours of operation: Sa, Su, & holidays 12:00-10:00.

***Burnaby:* Burnaby Art Gallery**
6344 Deer Lake Ave.
Burnaby, BC V5G 2J3
Tel: 604-297-4422; *Fax:* 604-205-7339
gallery@burnaby.ca
www.burnabyartgallery.ca
Social Media: burnabyartgallery.tumblr.com
twitter.com/BurnabyArtGall
www.facebook.c om/BurnabyArtGallery
Services include educational programs for children, adults & seniors; community projects & exhibitions in libraries & recreational centres; school programs support the exhibitions & take works of art into the schools
Ellen van Eijnsbergen, Director/Curator

Burnaby: **The Simon Fraser University Gallery**
AQ 3004, Burnaby Campus, Simon Fraser University, 8888 University Dr.
Burnaby, BC V5A 1S6
Tel: 778-782-4266
gallery@sfu.ca
www.sfu.ca/gallery
twitter.com/SFU_Ga llery
www.facebook.com/SFU.Gallery
Year Founded: 1970 Hosts six or seven exhibitions a year, both historical & contemporary, covering the full range of media; serves the SFU community directly by providing an occasional platform for student, staff & faculty work to be shown; The Gallery also administers the Teck Gallery at the SFU Vancouver Campus, a small space used to show work that deals with social & environmental issues
Melanie O'Brian, Director, melanie_obrian@sfu.ca
Mandy Ginson, Coordinator

Campbell River: **Campbell River Art Gallery**
Parent: **Campbell River & District Public Art Gallery**
Tyee Plaza, 1235 Shopper's Row
Campbell River, BC V9W 2C7
Tel: 250-287-2261
contact@crartgallery.ca
www.crartgallery.ca
www.facebook.com/290415662283
Contemporary work from both local & visiting artists; classes, lectures & workshops throughout the year; open Tu-Sa 12:00-5:00; May-Sept. M-Sa 10:00-5:00
Kris Anderson, Executive Director, director@crartgallery.ca
Liz Larsen Stoneberger, Curator, curator@crartgallery.ca

Castlegar: **Kootenay Gallery of Art, History & Science**
120 Heritage Way
Castlegar, BC V1N 4M5
Tel: 250-365-3337
kootenaygallery@telus.net
www.kootenaygallery.com
Exhibits on art, history & science, from international to local sources; offers workshops, performances, lectures & classes; gift shop. Hours: Mar-Nov: Tu-Sa 10:00-5:00; Dec: M-Su 10:00-5:00.
Audrey Maxwell-Polovnikof, Chair
Valentine Field, Executive Director

Courtenay: **Comox Valley Art Gallery**
580 Duncan Ave.
Courtenay, BC V9N 2M7
Tel: 250-338-6211; *Fax:* 250-338-6287
contact@comoxvalleyartgallery.com
www.comoxvalleyartgallery.com
Social Media: www.youtube.com/user/CVArtGallery
twitter.com/C_V_A_G
www.facebook.com /184055261880
The Comox Valley Art Gallery features contemporary art by regional, national, & international artists. Open Th-Sa 10:00-5:00.
Lee White, President
Glen Sanford, Executive Director, director@comoxvalleyartgallery.com
Angela Somerset, Curator, curator@comoxvalleyartgallery.com

Dawson Creek: **Dawson Creek Art Gallery**
Parent: **South Peace Arts Society**
#101, 816 Alaska Ave.
Dawson Creek, BC V1G 4T6
Tel: 250-782-2601; *Fax:* 250-782-8801
artadmin@dcartgallery.ca
www.dcartgallery.ca
www.facebook.com/DawsonCr eekArtGallery
Managed by the South Peace Art Society. Open year round
Kit Fast, Curator, curator@dcartgallery.ca

Gibsons: **Gibsons Public Art Gallery (GPAG)**
PO Box 1576
Located at 431 Marine Dr., Gibsons, BC
Gibsons, BC V0N 1V0
Tel: 604-886-0531
gpag@dccnet.com
gibsonspublicartgallery.ca
Social Media: instagram.com/gpagart
twitter.com/GPAGart
www.facebook.com/316757548359391
Year Founded: 2003
Jeannie Harlow, President

Golden: **Kicking Horse Culture: Art Gallery of Golden (AGOG)**
PO Box 228
Located at 516 - 9th Ave. North, Golden, BC
Golden, BC V0A 1A0
Tel: 250-344-6186
info@kickinghorseculture.ca
kickinghorseculture.ca/art-gallery-of-golden
Social Media: www.youtube.com/user/khcgdac
twitter.com/goldenculture
Open M-Sa 10:00-6:00.
Bill Usher, Executive Director, director@kickinghorseculture.ca

Grand Forks: **Grand Forks & District Art & Heritage Centre**
PO Box 2140, 524 Central Ave.
Grand Forks, BC V0H 1H0
Tel: 250-442-2211; *Fax:* 250-442-0099
communications@g2gf.ca
www.gallery2grandforks.ca
Historical & contemporary works by established & emerging regional, national & international artists
Steve Hollet, Co-President
Ted Fogg, Director/Curator, curator@g2gf.ca
Marlene Wollenberg, Co-President

Hope: **John Weaver Sculpture Museum**
PO Box 1723, 19225 Silverhope Rd.
Hope, BC V0X 1L0
Tel: 604-869-5312; *Fax:* 604-869-5117
johnweaver@johnweaverfinearts.com
www.johnweaverfinearts.com
Year Founded: 1977 John Weaver's work of bronzes based on historical, anthropological, & charity-work themes can be viewed by those wishing to learn about bronze sculpture & by those who wish to be commissioners of work; collection of over 60 years of work

Kamloops: **Kamloops Art Gallery**
#101, 465 Victoria St.
Kamloops, BC V2C 2A9
Tel: 250-377-2400; *Fax:* 250-828-0662
kamloopsartgallery@kag.bc.ca
www.kag.bc.ca
twitter.com/artsinkamloops
www.facebook.com/KamloopsArtsGallery
Year Founded: 1978 Changing exhibits of contemporary & historical art; permanent collection of Canadian art. Hours: M-W, F-Sa 10:00-5:00. Th 10:00-9:00.
Jaimie Drew, President
Jann L.M. Bailey, Executive Director, jlmb@kag.bc.ca
Charo Neville, Curator, cneville@kag.bc.ca

Kaslo: **Langham Cultural Centre**
Parent: **The Langham Cultural Society**
PO Box 1000
Location: 447 A Ave., Kaslo, BC
Kaslo, BC V0G 1M0
Tel: 250-353-2661; *Fax:* 250-353-2671
langham@netidea.com
www.thelangham.ca
www.facebook.com/thelangham
Year Founded: 1975 Art exhibits; theatre; music; workshops; The Japanese Canadian Museum. Open Th-Su 1:00-4:00
Maggie Tchir, Executive Director

Kelowna: **Alternator Centre for Contemporary Art**
#103, 421 Cawston Ave.
Kelowna, BC V1Y 6Z1
Tel: 250-868-2298
info@alternatorgallery.com
alternatorcentre.com
twitter.com/alternatortweet
www.facebook.com/page s/Kelowna-BC/Alternator/341781252998
Year Founded: 1989 Work by emerging local & national artists.
Lorna McParland, Artistic & Administrative Director, dir@alternatorgallery.com

Kelowna: **Kelowna Art Gallery**
1315 Water St.
Kelowna, BC V1Y 9R3
Tel: 250-762-2226; *Fax:* 250-762-9875
info@kelownaartgallery.com
www.kelownaartgallery.com
Social Media: www.youtube.com/user/KelownaArt
twitter.com/kelownaart
www.facebook.com/KelownaArtGallery
Year Founded: 1976 Historical & contemporary fine art; extensive education programs; open year round
Marla O'Brien, President
Nataley Nagy, Executive Director, nataley@kelownaartgallery.com
Liz Wylie, Curator, liz@kelownaartgallery.com

Kelowna: **Sopa Fine Arts**
2934 South Pandosy St.
Kelowna, BC V1Y 1V9
Tel: 250-763-5088
info@sopafinearts.com
www.sopafinearts.com
twitter.com/SopaFineArts
www.facebook.com/1066249 62755286
Year Founded: 2005 Contemporary art with an emphasis on abstract work.

Kelowna: **Tutt Street Gallery**
#9, 3045 Tutt St.
Kelowna, BC V1Y 2H4
Tel: 250-861-4992; *Fax:* 250-861-4992
info@tuttartgalleries.com
www.tuttartgalleries.ca
www.facebook.com/Tut tStreetGallery
Canadian oil & acrylic paintings
Martina Kral, Owner

Koksilah: **Hill's Native Art Duncan**
5209 Trans-Canada Hwy.
Koksilah, BC V0R 2C0
Tel: 250-746-6731*Toll-Free:* 866-685-5422
www.hills.ca
First Nations artwork

Ladysmith: **Ladysmith Waterfront Arts Centre Gallery**
PO Box 2370
Located at 610 Oyster Bay Dr., Ladysmith, BC
Ladysmith, BC V9G 1B8
Tel: 250-245-1252
info@ladysmithwaterfrontgallery.com
www.ladysmithwater frontgallery.com
Social Media: www.linkedin.com/company/ladysmith-waterfront-arts-centre-gallery
www.fa cebook.com/ladysmithwaterfrontgallery
Year Founded: 2007 Artwork from residents of Vancouver Island & the Gulf Islands.
Kathy Holmes, President, admin@ladysmithwaterfrontgallery.com

Lake Country: **Lake Country Art Gallery**
10356A Bottom Wood Lake Rd .
Lake Country, BC V4V 1T9
Tel: 250-766-1299
lakecountryartgallery@shaw.ca
www.lakecountryartgallery.ca
Social Media: instagram.com/lakecountryartgallery
twitter.com/LakeCountryArtG
www.fa cebook.com/Lakecountryartgallery
Year Founded: 2010
Petrina McNeill, Gallery Manager
Katie Brennan, Gallery Curator

Maple Ridge: **Maple Ridge Art Gallery Society**
11944 Haney Pl.
Maple Ridge, BC V2X 6G1
Tel: 604-476-2787; *Fax:* 604-476-2187
info@mract.org
www.theactmapleridge.org
twitter.com/mapleridgeact
ww w.facebook.com/mapleridgeact
Exhibition of local, amateur & professional artists; art rental program for patrons
Lindy Sisson, Executive Director

Nakusp: **Bonnington Arts Centre**
619A - 4 St. NW
Nakusp, BC V0G 1R0
Tel: 250-265-3731
Located in Nakusp Elementary School. Open Sept.-June.

Nanaimo: **Hill's Native Art Nanaimo**
76 Bastion St.
Nanaimo, BC V9R 3A1
Tel: 250-755-7873*Toll-Free:* 866-685-5422
www.hills.ca
First Nations artwork

***Nanaimo:* Nanaimo Art Gallery**
Vancouver Island University, Nanaimo Campus, #330, 900 - 5th St.
150 Commercial St., Nanaimo, BC, V9R 5G6
Nanaimo, BC V9R 5S5
Tel: 250-740-6350
www.nanaimogallery.ca
Social Media: www.youtube.com/user/nanaimoartgallery
twitter.com/NanaimoArt
www.facebook.com/pages/Nanaimo-Art-Gallery/127280883976484
Celebrating art on the west coast; art central & sales program; gift shop full of elegant & eclectic gifts; inspiring & thought provoking exhibitions
Deborah Giunio-Zorkin, President
Jesse Birch, Interim Executive/Artistic Director
Justin McGrail, Curator
Chris Kuderle, Administrative Director

***New Westminster:* Amelia Douglas Gallery**
Douglas College, 700 Royal Ave., 4th Fl. North
New Westminster, BC V3M 5Z5
Tel: 604-527-5723
artsevents@douglascollege.ca
www.douglascollege.ca
www.facebook.com/AmeliaDouglasGallery
Year Founded: 1992 A non-profit organization run by members of the Arts Exhibition Committee at Douglas College; mandate is to feature new & established BC artists & to enhance the educational offerings of the College
Krista Eide, Arts Events Officer

***North Vancouver:* Gordon Smith Gallery of Canadian Art**
2121 Lonsdale Ave.
North Vancouver, BC V7M 2K6
Tel: 604-998-8563
info@smithfoundation.ca
www.gordonsmithgallery.ca
twitter.com/GSmithGallery
www.facebook.com/G ordon.Smith.Gallery
Year Founded: 1990 Exhibits work by Canadian artists

***North Vancouver:* Presentation House Museum Galleries**
333 Chesterfield Ave.
North Vancouver, BC V7M 3G9
Tel: 604-986-1351; *Fax:* 604-986-5380
info@presentationhousegallery.org
presentationhousegallery.org
twitter .com/PHOUSEGALLERY
www.facebook.com/presentation.gallery
Year Founded: 1976 Celebrates & preserves North Vancouver's social, industrial & cultural history. Operated by the British Columbia Photography & Media Arts Society. Hours: W-Su 12:00-5:00
Paula Palyga, President
Reid Shier, Director/Curator, rshier@presentationhousegallery.org
Helga Pakasaar, Curator, hpakasaar@presentationhousegallery.org

***North Vancouver:* Seymour Art Gallery**
4360 Gallant Ave.
North Vancouver, BC V7G 1L2
Tel: 604-924-1378; *Fax:* 604-924-3786
info@seymourartgallery.com
seymourartgallery.com
twitter.com/seymourga llery
www.facebook.com/373276142313
Open year round
Alan Bell, President
Hilary Letwin, Interim Curator
Marina Van Den Berg, Gallery Administrator

***Oliver:* Oliver Art Gallery (OAG)**
6046 Main St.
Oliver, BC V0H 1T0
Tel: 778-439-3320
office@oliverartgallery.ca
www.oliverartgallery.ca
twitter.com/olivergallery
www.facebook.com/oli verartgallery
Year Founded: 2011 Exhibits work by artists in South Okanagan

***Osoyoos:* Osoyoos Art Gallery**
8713 Main St.
Osoyoos, BC V0H 1V0
Tel: 250-495-2800
osoyoosartgallery@gmail.com
www.osoyoosarts.com/artgallery.html
Open year round
Patrick Turner, President, Osoyoos & District Arts Council Bd. of Dir., 250-495-2895, pkturner@telus.net
Diane Hughes, Acting Director, 250-495-5050

***Penticton:* Penticton Art Gallery**
199 Marina Way
Penticton, BC V2A 1H3
Tel: 250-493-2928; *Fax:* 250-493-3992
info@pentictonartgallery.com
www.pentictonartgallery.com
Year Founded: 1972 The Penticton Art Gallery offers in-house & touring exhibitions from local, regional & national sources.
Nicholas Vincent, President
Paul Crawford, Director/Curator, curator@pentictonartgallery.com

***Port Alberni:* Rollin Art Centre**
3061 - 8th Ave.
Port Alberni, BC V9Y 2K5
Tel: 250-724-3412
communityarts@shawcable.com
www.portalberniarts.com/rollin-art-centre
www.facebook.com/CommunityArts CouncilOfTheAlberniValley
Fine arts gallery, gift shop, classroom & gardens.
Melissa Martin, Arts Administrator

***Prince George:* Two Rivers Gallery**
***Parent:* Prince George Regional Art Gallery Association**
Prince George Art Gallery Association, 725 Civic Plaza
Prince George, BC V2L 5T1
Tel: 250-614-7800; *Fax:* 250-563-3211
www.tworiversartgallery.com
Social Media: www.youtube.com/user/TwoRiversGalleryBC
twitter.com/tworiversart
www.f acebook.com/tworiversart
Year Founded: 1949 The Two Rivers Gallery is a centre for visual art in Prince George & the central interior of British Columbia, Canada. It seeks to encourage lifelong learning through the arts, create an environment for artistic & cultural expression, & provide opportunities through participation & exhibition.
Peter L. Thompson, Managing Director, peter@tworiversgallery.ca
George Harris, Curator, george@tworiversgallery.ca

***Qualicum Beach:* The Old School House Arts Centre (TOSH)**
122 Fern Rd. West
Qualicum Beach, BC V9K 1T2
Tel: 250-752-6133
qbtosh@shaw.ca
www.theoldschoolhouse.org
Twelve resident artists; 3 exhibition galleries; concert series; classrooms; gift shop
Corinne James, Executive Director

***Quesnel:* Quesnel Art Gallery**
500 North Star Rd.
Quesnel, BC V2J 5P6
Tel: 250-991-4014
quesnelartgallery@gmail.com
www.quesnelartgallery.com
www.facebook.com/pages/Quesnel-Art-Gallery/125213850878875

***Richmond:* Richmond Art Gallery**
7700 Minoru Gate
Richmond, BC V6Y 1R9
Tel: 604-247-8300; *Fax:* 604-247-8368
gallery@richmond.ca
www.richmondartgallery.org
Social Media: www.youtube.com/user/RichmondArtGallery
www.facebook.com/RichmondArtGall eryBC
Year Founded: 1980 Presents a diverse program of exhibitions, workshops, lectures & special events, as well as outreach programs which focus on contemporary art & art issues
Marc Lindy, President
Rachel Rosenfield Lafo, Director
Nan Capogna, Curator

***Salt Spring Island:* Blue Horse Folk Art Gallery**
175 North View Dr.
Salt Spring Island, BC V8K 1A9
Tel: 250-537-0754
bluehorsefolkart@gmail.com
www.bluehorse.ca
www.facebook.com/BlueHorseFolkArt
Year Founded: 1994 Wooden animal carvings by Paul Burke & raku vases & lamps by Anna Gustafson.
Paul Burke, Owner/Artist
Anna Gustafson, Owner/Artist

***Salt Spring Island:* Gallery 8**
Grace Point Square, #3104, 115 Fulford Ganges Rd.
Salt Spring Island, BC V8K 2T9
Tel: 250-537-8822; *Fax:* 250-537-8822
Toll-Free: 866-537-8822
art@gallery8saltspring.com
www.artgallery8.com
www.f acebook.com/pages/Gallery-8/213336578738365
Work by local & national contemporary artists

***Sidney:* Peninsula Gallery**
#100, 2506 Beacon Ave.
Sidney, BC V8L 1Y2
Tel: 250-655-1282*Toll-Free:* 877-787-1896
info@pengal.com
www.pengal.com
Year Founded: 1986

***Smithers:* Smithers Art Gallery**
PO Box 122
Located at #1, 1425 Main St., Smithers, BC
Smithers, BC V0J 2N0
Tel: 250-847-3898
info@smithersart.org
smithersart.org
Social Media: www.youtube.com/user/SmithersArtGallery
www.facebook.com/smithersartgallery
Year Founded: 1971 Public gallery, admission by donation; monthly exhibition rotation; workshops & artcamps for young & old, all artisan levels & mediums; call for a current listing
Susan Smith, President, president@smithersart.org
Caroline Bastable, Gallery Manager

***Surrey:* Arnold Mikelson Mind & Matter Gallery**
13743 - 16 Ave.
Surrey, BC V4A 1P7
Tel: 604-536-6460
www.mindandmatterart.com
twitter.com/MikelsonGallery
www.facebook.com/129219007093865
Year Founded: 1966 Wood sculptures of the late Arnold Mikelson
Mary Mikelson, Owner/Director, mary@mindandmatterart.com

***Surrey:* Surrey Art Gallery**
Surrey Arts Centre, 13750 - 88 Ave.
Surrey, BC V3W 3L1
Tel: 604-501-5566; *Fax:* 604-501-5581
artgallery@surrey.ca
www.arts.surrey.ca
www.facebook.com/pages/Surrey-Art-Gallery/141848319171587
Year Founded: 1975 Promotes contemporary BC & Canadian artists; exhibitions & public programs encourage community appreciation of contemporary visual art; open year round
Liane Davison, Manager, Visual & Community Art, ljdavison@surrey.ca
Jordan Strom, Curator, Exhibitions & Collections, ljdavison@surrey.ca

***Terrace:* Terrace Art Gallery**
Terrace Public Library, 4610 Park Ave.
Terrace, BC V8G 1V6
Tel: 250-638-8884; *Fax:* 250-638-8884
coordinator@terraceartgallery.com
www.terraceartgallery.com
www.facebo ok.com/TerraceArtGallery
Year Founded: 1981

***Vancouver:* AHVA Gallery**
Audain Art Centre, University of British Columbia, #1001, 6398 University Blvd.
Vancouver, BC V6T 1Z4
Tel: 604-822-4563
gallery.ahva.ubc.ca
Features student & faculty artwork.

***Vancouver:* Art Works**
225 Smithe St.
Vancouver, BC V6B 4X7
Tel: 604-688-3301; *Fax:* 604-683-4552
Toll-Free: 800-663-0341
info@artworksbc.com
artworksbc.com
www.facebook.com/ ArtWorksGallery

Vancouver: Artspeak Gallery
233 Carrall St.
Vancouver, BC V6B 2J2
Tel: 604-688-0051
info@artspeak.ca
artspeak.ca
Social Media: ieartspeakgallerysociety.tumblr.com
twitter.com/artspeakgallery
www.fa cebook.com/ArtspeakGallery
Year Founded: 1986 A non-profit artist-run centre for contemporary art & writing.

Vancouver: Bau-Xi Gallery
3045 Granville St.
Vancouver, BC V6H 3J9
Tel: 604-733-7011
info@bau-xi.com
Www.bau-xi.com
twitter.com/BauXiGallery
Year Founded: 1965
Riko Nakasone, Director
Tien Huang, Director
Tien Huang, Director

Vancouver: Bill Reid Gallery of Northwest Coast Art
639 Hornby St.
Vancouver, BC V6C 2G3
Tel: 604-682-3455; *Fax:* 604-682-3310
info@billreidgallery.ca
www.billreidgallery.ca
Social Media: www.flickr.com/photos/billreidgallery
twitter.com/billreidgallery
www. facebook.com/122773297776639
Year Founded: 2008 Contemporary work by Aboriginal artists of the Northwest Coast.

Vancouver: Centre A
PO Box 88363 Chinatown
Located at 229 East Georgia St., Vancouver, BC
Vancouver, BC V6A 4A6
Tel: 604-683-8326; *Fax:* 604-683-8632
info@centrea.org
centrea.org
Social Media: instagram.com/centre_a
twitter.com/centrea
www.facebook.com/CentreAGal lery
Year Founded: 1999 Contemporary Asian visual art
Tyler Russell, Executive Director/Curator

Vancouver: Chali-Rosso Art Gallery
2250 Granville St.
Vancouver, BC V6H 4H7
Tel: 604-733-3594
gallery@chalirosso.com
www.chalirosso.com
Social Media:
www.youtube.com/channel/UC3XkC7HTtnBg5VKKuQKJDXw
twitter.com/chalirosso
www.facebook.com/chalirosso
Year Founded: 2005 Graphic works of surrealist artists
Susanna Stern, Contact

Vancouver: Charles H. Scott Gallery
Emily Carr University of Art + Design, 1399 Johnston St., Granville Island
Vancouver, BC V6H 3R9
Tel: 604-844-3809; *Fax:* 604-844-3801
scottgal@ecuad.ca
chscott.ecuad.ca
Social Media: instagram.com/chs_gallery
twitter.com/CharlesHScott
www.facebook.com/C harles.H.Scott.Gallery
Year Founded: 1980 A public art gallery specializing in contemporary art. Open seven days a week.
Cate Rimmer, Curator

Vancouver: Circle Craft Gallery
Net Loft Granville Island, #1, 1666 Johnston St.
Vancouver, BC V6H 3S2
Tel: 604-669-8021; *Fax:* 604-669-8585
info@circlecraft.net
www.circlecraft.net
Social Media: www.flickr.com/photos/circle_craft_coop
twitter.com/circlecraft
www.fa cebook.com/CircleCraft
Year Founded: 1973 Features over 200 works of BC artists
Kathryn Youngs, Co-op Manager & Director, Store, kathryn@circlecraft.net
Paul Yard, Show Producer, market@circlecraft.net

Vancouver: Coastal Peoples Fine Arts Gallery
1024 Mainland St.
Vancouver, BC V6B 2T4
Tel: 604-685-9298; *Fax:* 604-684-9248
Toll-Free: 888-686-9298
coastalpeoples@telus.net
www.coastalpeoples.com
Year Founded: 1996 Exhibits work by Northwest Coast First Nations & Inuit.
Astrid Heyerdahl, Contact

Vancouver: Contemporary Art Gallery (CAG)
555 Nelson St.
Vancouver, BC V6B 6R5
Tel: 604-681-2700; *Fax:* 604-683-2710
contact@contemporaryartgallery.ca
www.contemporaryartgallery.ca
Social Media: www.youtube.com/user/TheCAGchannel
twitter.com/CAGVancouver
www.facebook.com/114252503695
Year Founded: 1971 Promotes knowledge & understanding of contemporary visual art through: exhibitions that address current issues in contemporary art; educational programs in the form of artist & curator talks, student tours, high school projects, public symposia; publications; visiting artist/curator programs; information & resource services; The City of Vancouver Art Collection of 3,000 works of art
Ross Hill, President
Nigel Prince, Executive Director
Jenifer Papararo, Curator

Vancouver: Equinox Gallery
525 Great Northern Way
Vancouver, BC V5T 1E1
Tel: 604-736-2405
info@equinoxgallery.com
www.equinoxgallery.com
twitter.com/equinoxgallery
Year Founded: 1972

Vancouver: Gallery Gachet
88 East Cordova St.
Vancouver, BC V6A 1K3
Tel: 604-687-2468; *Fax:* 604-687-1196
contact@gachet.org
gachet.org
Social Media: www.flickr.com/photos/gallerygachet
twitter.com/gallerygachet
Gallery Gachet is an artist-run public gallery in Vancouver's Downtown Eastside. Open W-Su 12:00-6:00.
Kristin Lantz, Programming Coordinator, programming@gachet.org

Vancouver: grunt gallery
#116, 350 East 2nd Ave.
Vancouver, BC V5T 4R8
Tel: 604-875-9516
grunt@telus.net
grunt.ca
Social Media: www.youtube.com/user/gruntgallery1
twitter.com/gruntgallery
www.facebo ok.com/gruntgallery
Year Founded: 1984 Artist-run centre furthering contemporary art through exhibitions, performances, artist talks, publications, & other projects. Open Wed. - Sat., 12-6
Glenn Alteen, Program Director, glenn@grunt.ca
Meagan Kus, Operations Director, meagan@grunt.ca
Karlene Harvey, Director, Communications, karlene@grunt.ca

Vancouver: Heffel Gallery Limited
2247 Granville St.
Vancouver, BC V6H 3G1
Tel: 604-732-6505; *Fax:* 604-732-4245
Toll-Free: 800-528-9608
mail@heffel.com
www.heffel.com
Social Media: www.youtube.com/user/HeffelAuctions
twitter.com/heffelauction
Fine art auction house.
David K.J. Heffel, President, david@heffel.com
Robert C.S. Heffel, Vice-President, robert@heffel.com

Vancouver: Hill's Native Art Vancouver
165 Water St.
Vancouver, BC V6B 1A7
Tel: 604-685-4249; *Fax:* 604-682-4197
Toll-Free: 866-685-5422
www.hills.ca
www.facebook.com/HillsNativeArt
First Nations artwork

Vancouver: Howe Street Gallery of Fine Art
555 Howe St.
Vancouver, BC V6C 2C2
Tel: 604-681-5777
555@howestreetgallery.com
www.howestreetgallery.com
Social Media: ca.linkedin.com/in/howestreetgallery
twitter.com/HoweGallery
www.faceb ook.com/163428913868
Year Founded: 1996

Vancouver: Ian Tan Gallery
2202 Granville St.
Vancouver, BC V6H 4H7
Tel: 604-738-1077
info@iantangallery.com
www.iantangallery.com
Social Media: iantangallery.tumblr.com
twitter.com/iantangallery
www.facebook.com/iantangallery
Year Founded: 1999 Exhibits contemporary work by Canadian artists, with an emphasis on west coast art.

Vancouver: Jacana Contemporary Art Gallery
2435A Granville St.
Vancouver, BC V6H 3G5
Tel: 604-879-9306
contact@jacanagallery.com
www.jacanagallery.com
twitter.com/jacanaart
www.facebook.com/jacanaart gallery
Year Founded: 2000 Work by Canadian & international artists with a focus on contemporary Asian work.

Vancouver: Kurbatoff Gallery
2435 Granville St.
Vancouver, BC V6H 3G5
Tel: 406-736-5444
art@kurbatoffgallery.com
kurbatoffgallery.com
www.facebook.com/pages/Kurbatoff-Gallery/2470161753 41630
Year Founded: 2002 Canadian works from emerging & established artists.

Vancouver: Marion Scott Gallery/Kardosh Projects
2423 Granville St.
Vancouver, BC V6B 1B6
Tel: 604-685-1934
art@marionscottgallery.com
www.marionscottgallery.com
www.facebook.com/141219279227412
Established in 1975, & one of the leading galleries dealing with Canadian Inuit art
Judy Kardosh, Director, judy@marionscottgallery.com
Robert Kardosh, Director/Curator, robert@marionscottgallery.com

Vancouver: Morris & Helen Belkin Art Gallery
University of British Columbia, 1825 Main Mall
Vancouver, BC V6T 1Z2
Tel: 604-822-2759; *Fax:* 604-822-6689
belkin.gallery@ubc.ca
belkin.ubc.ca
Social Media: www.youtube.com/user/belkinartgallery
www.facebook.com/BelkinArtGallery
Year Founded: 1948 Specializes in exhibiting contemporary work by national & international artists; programming includes exhibitions, artists' talks, publications & collaborative projects with other galleries/organizations; masters program in Critical Curatorial Studies; archival collections focus on Vancouver Canadian avant garde in 1960s-70s
Scott Watson, Director/Professor, Art History, Visual Art & Theory, scott.watson@ubc.ca
Shelly Rosenblum, Curator, krisztina.laszlo@ubc.ca

Vancouver: RendezVous Art Gallery
323 Howe St.
Vancouver, BC V6C 3N2
Tel: 604-687-7466
info@rendezvousartgallery.com
www.rendezvousartgallery.com
Social Media:
www.linkedin.com/company/rendez-vous-art-gallery
www.facebook.com/pages/
RendezVous-Art-Gallery/131690716852102
Year Founded: 2011 Work by Canadian artists.

Vancouver: Rennie Collection at Wing Sang Building
51 East Pender St.
Vancouver, BC V6A 1S9
renniecollection.org

Exhibits work of 200 artists.
Bob Rennie, Principal

Vancouver: Stewart Stephenson Modern Art Gallery
1300 Robson St.
Vancouver, BC V6E 1C5
Toll-Free: 877-278-7100
info@stewartstephenson.com
www.stewartstephenson.com
Social Media: pinterest.com/modernartco
twitter.com/ModernArtCo
www.facebook.com/Ste wartStephensonModernArtGallery
Year Founded: 2011
Stewart Stephenson, Owner

Vancouver: Trench Contemporary Art Gallery
#102, 148 Alexander St.
Vancouver, BC V6A 1B5
Tel: 604-681-2577 *Toll-Free:* 877-681-2577
info@trenchgallery.com
trenchgallery.com
twitter.com/TrenchGallery
w ww.facebook.com/TrenchGallery
Year Founded: 2010
Craig Sibley, Owner/Director

Vancouver: VIVO Media Arts Centre
1965 Main St.
Vancouver, BC V5T 3C1
Tel: 604-872-8337; *Fax:* 604-876-1185
info@vivomediaarts.com
vivomediaarts.com
twitter.com/VIVOMediaArts
w ww.facebook.com/vivomediaarts
Year Founded: 1973 VIVO is vancouver's oldest media arts access centre, specializing in video production, exhibition, & distribution. Open Tu-Sa 11:00-6:00, & M by appointment.
Crista Dahl, Co-Chair
Marina Roy, Co-Chair
Emma Hendrix, General Manager

Vancouver: Western Front
303 East 8th Ave.
Vancouver, BC V5T 1S1
Tel: 604-876-9343; *Fax:* 604-876-4099
front.bc.ca
twitter.com/western_front
www.facebook.com/164127636934501
Year Founded: 1973 An artist-run centre dedicated to contemporary art & new music. The centre is open Tu-Sa 12:00-5:00.

Vancouver: Wickaninnish Gallery
The Net Loft, #14, 1166 Johnston St.
Vancouver, BC V6H 3S2
Tel: 604-681-1057; *Fax:* 604-331-1066
wickgallery@gmail.com
www.wickaninnishgallery.com
Year Founded: 1987 Native-owned art gallery & boutique
Patricia Rivard, Owner

Vernon: Vernon Public Art Gallery (VPAG)
3228 - 31st Ave.
Vernon, BC V1T 2H3
Tel: 250-545-3173
info@vernonpublicartgallery.com
www.vernonpublicartgallery.com
Social Media: www.youtube.com/user/artgalleryvernon
twitter.com/VernonAGallery
www.f acebook.com/92358973285
Year Founded: 1945 Community programming; local, regional, national & international exhibitions; gift shop; art & video rentals; group tours
Andrew Powell, President
Dauna Kennedy-Grant, Executive Director, dauna@vernonpublicartgallery.com
Lobos Culen, Curator, curator@vernonpublicartgallery.com

Victoria: Alcheringa Gallery
665 Fort St.
Victoria, BC V8W 1G6
Tel: 250-383-8224; *Fax:* 250-383-9399
alcheringa@islandnet.com
www.alcheringa-gallery.com
www.facebook.com/p ages/Alcheringa-Gallery/249334011694
Work by Aboriginal artists from the Northwest Coast of Canada, Papua New Guinea & Australia.
Elaine Monds, Director & Founder

Victoria: Art Gallery of Greater Victoria (AGGV)
1040 Moss St.
Victoria, BC V8V 4P1
Tel: 250-384-4171; *Fax:* 250-361-3995
info@aggv.ca
aggv.ca
Social Media: www.youtube.com/user/ArtGalleryVictoriaBC
twitter.com/artgalleryvic
ww w.facebook.com/artgalleryvictoria
Year Founded: 1951 Canadiana 1860 to present; work of Emily Carr; extensive collection of Asian art
John Tupper, Director, jtupper@aggv.ca

Victoria: The Avenue Gallery
2184 Oak Bay Ave.
Victoria, BC V8R 1G3
Tel: 250-598-2184 *Toll-Free:* 844-598-2184
info@theavenuegallery.com
theavenuegallery.com
twitter.com/galleryaven ue
www.facebook.com/pages/The-Avenue-Gallery/2113669355630 40
Year Founded: 2002 Exhibits paintings, sculptures, glass art & jewellery.
Heather Wheeler, Owner

Victoria: Hill's Native Art Victoria
1008 Government St.
Victoria, BC V8W 1X7
Tel: 250-385-3911; *Fax:* 250-385-5371
Toll-Free: 866-685-5422
www.hills.ca
First Nations artwork

Victoria: Open Space
510 Fort St., 2nd Fl.
Victoria, BC V8W 1E6
Tel: 250-383-8833
openspace@openspace.ca
www.openspace.ca
Social Media: www.flickr.com/groups/79807275@N00
www.facebook.com/openspace.victoria
Year Founded: 1972 An artist-run centre dedicated to exploring the boundaries of contemporary art & media in all forms. Hours of Operation: Tu-Sa 12:00-5:00.
Robert Randall, Chair
Helen Merzolf, Executive Director, director@openspace.ca
Doug Jarvis, Guest Curator, program.coordinator@openspace.ca

Victoria: Red Art Gallery
2249 Oak Bay Ave.
Victoria, BC V8R 1G4
Tel: 250-881-0462
redartgallery.ca
www.facebook.com/pages/Red-Art-Gallery/158074164265760
Year Founded: 2010
Marion Evamy, Co-owner, me@redartgallery.ca
Bobb Hamilton, Co-owner, bobb@redartgallery.ca

Victoria: Maltwood Prints & Drawings Gallery
Parent: University of Victoria Art Collections
McPherson Library, University of Victoria, PO Box 1800
Victoria, BC V8W 3H5
Tel: 250-472-5619
curator@uvic.ca
uvac.uvic.ca
Social Media: www.flickr.com/people/maltwood
Named after the collection of fine, decorative & applied arts of English sculptress & antiquarian Katherine Emma Maltwood, F.R.S.A. (1878-1961); over 6,000 items representing the work of contemporary Western Canadian artists

Victoria: University of Victoria Art Collections Legacy Art Gallery
630 Yates St.
Victoria, BC V8W 1K9
Tel: 250-721-6562; *Fax:* 250-721-6607
legacy@uvic.ca
uvac.uvic.ca
twitter.com/UVICGalleries
www.facebook.c om/uvac.legacygallery
Now the University of Victoria's main gallery space; showcasing the Michael C. Williams Collection, as well as other holdings of the university
Mary Jo Hughes, Director, artgallerydirector@uvic.ca
Caroline Riedel, Curator, curator@uvic.ca

Victoria: Victoria Emerging Art Gallery (VEAG)
1016 Fort St.
Victoria, BC V8V 3K4
Tel: 778-430-5585
info@victoriaemergingart.com
www.victoriaemergingart.com
Social Media: veag.tumblr.com
twitter.com/TAGARTVEAG
www.facebook.com/174173005952018
Year Founded: 2010
Ellen Manning, Director

Victoria: Xchanges Gallery & Studios
#6E, 2333 Government St.
Victoria, BC V8T 4P4
Tel: 250-382-0442
www.xchangesgallery.org
www.facebook.com/Xchanges.Gallery
Year Founded: 1967

Wells: Island Mountain Gallery
PO Box 65
Wells, BC V0K 2R0
Tel: 250-994-3466; *Fax:* 250-994-3433
Toll-Free: 800-442-2787
info@imarts.com
www.imarts.com
twitter.com/ima_arts
www.facebook.com/pages/Island-Mountain-Arts/282969084068
Year Founded: 1977 Provides visual, literary & performing arts instruction; presents contemporary art exhibitions; concert venue in summer; also holds workshops
Yael Wand, President
Julie Fowler, Executive Director, media@imarts.com

West Vancouver: Ferry Building Gallery
1414 Argyle Ave.
West Vancouver, BC V7T 1C2
Tel: 604-925-7290
gallery@westvancouver.ca
ferrybuildinggallery.com
www.facebook.com/ferrybuildinggallery
Year Founded: 1989 Work by new & established artists who are former & current residents of the North Shore area.
Ruth Payne, Coordinator, Visual Arts, 604-925-7266

Whistler: Adele Campbell Fine Art Gallery
#109, 4090 Whistler Way
Whistler, BC V0N 1B4
Tel: 604-938-0887
art@adelecampbell.com
www.adelecampbell.com
Social Media: instagram.com/adelecampbellart
twitter.com/Whistlerart
www.facebook.co m/222490657791094
Year Founded: 1993 Exhibits work by emerging & established Canadian artists.
Elizabeth Harris, Curator

Whistler: Mountain Galleries at the Fairmount Fairmont Chateau Whistler
4599 Chateau Blvd.
Whistler, BC V0N 1B4
Tel: 604-935-1862 *Toll-Free:* 888-310-9726
whistler@mountaingalleries.com
www.mountaingalleries.com
Social Media: instagram.com/mountaingalleries
twitter.com/MntGalleries
www.facebook.com/mountaingalleries
Elizabeth Peacock, Co-Director

Whistler: Whistle Village Art Gallery
#110, 4293 Mountain Sq.
Whistler, BC V0N 1B4
Tel: 604-938-3001; *Fax:* 604-938-3113
info@whistlerart.com
www.whistlerart.com
www.facebook.com/248419491849 863
Year Founded: 1992

Williams Lake: Station House Gallery & Gift Shop
1 Mackenzie Ave. North
Williams Lake, BC V2G 1N4
Tel: 250-392-6113; *Fax:* 250-392-6184
manager@stationhousegallery.com
www.stationhousegallery.com
www.facebo ok.com/stationhousegallery
Year Founded: 1981 Monthly exhibitions; gift shop
Kathryn Steen, President
Diane Toop, Gallery Manager

Manitoba

Provincial Art Gallery

The Winnipeg Art Gallery (WAG)
300 Memorial Blvd.
Winnipeg, MB R3C 1V1
Tel: 204-786-6641; *Fax:* 204-788-4998
inquiries@wag.mb.ca
wag.ca
Social Media: www.youtube.com/winnipegartgallery1
twitter.com/wag_ca
www.facebook.co m/wag.ca
Other contact information: Info Line: 204-789-1760
Year Founded: 1912 The WAG is Western Canada's oldest civic art gallery. With over 23,000 works in its collection, the WAG features 9 galleries of contemporary & historical works (fine arts, decorative arts & photography) by Manitoban, Canadian & international artists. A highlight is the Gort Collection of Northern Gothic & Renaissance paintings & altar panels.
Stephen Borys, Director & CEO, Director-CEO@wag.ca
Seema Hollenberg, Head of Curatorial, shollenberg@wag.ca

Local Art Galleries

***Brandon:* The Art Gallery of Southwestern Manitoba (AGSM) / Le Musé D'art du Sud-ouest du Manitoba**
#2, 710 Rosser Ave.
Brandon, MB R7A 0K9
Tel: 204-727-1036; *Fax:* 204-726-8139
info@agsm.ca
www.agsm.ca
Social Media: instagram.com/meetartagsm
twitter.com/TheAGSM
www.facebook.com/groups/ artgalleryswm
Year Founded: 1907 Contemporary Manitoban art; approximately 16 exhibitions a year; open year round
Murray Whitehead, Chair
Jennifer Woodbury, Executive Director, director@agsm.ca
Natalia Lebedinskaia, Curator, Contemporary Art, curator@agsm.ca

***Flin Flon:* Northern Visual Arts Centre**
177 Green St.
Flin Flon, MB R8A 0G5
Tel: 204-686-4237
norvacentre@gmail.com
www.norvacentre.com
twitter.com/NorvaCentre
www.facebook.com/pages/Nor va-Centre/130941357110936
Year Founded: 2010 Gallery specializing in a variety of art forms, includign pottery & painting. Visitors can watch artists at work.

***Winnipeg:* aceartinc.**
290 McDermot Ave., 2nd Fl.
Winnipeg, MB R3B 0T2
Tel: 204-944-9763
gallery@aceart.org
www.aceart.org
Social Media: instagram.com/aceartinc
twitter.com/aceartinc
aceartinc. is an artist-run centre dedicated to the development, exhibition & dissemination of contemporary art by cultural producers; dedicated to cultural diversity
Helga Jakobson, President
Hannah G., Co-Director, hannah_g@aceart.org
Jamie Wright, Co-Director, jamie@aceart.org

***Winnipeg:* Birchwood Art Gallery**
#7, 1170 Taylor Ave.
Winnipeg, MB R3M 3Z4
Tel: 204-888-5840*Toll-Free:* 800-822-5840
info@birchwoodartgallery.com
www.birchwoodartgallery.com
www.facebook. com/birchwoodartgallerywpg
Year Founded: 1993

***Winnipeg:* Centre culturel franco-manitobain (CCFM)**
340, boul Provencher
Winnipeg, MB R2H 0G7
Tel: 204-233-8972; *Fax:* 204-233-3324
communication@ccfm.mb.ca
www.ccfm.mb.ca
twitter.com/CCFManitobain
ww w.facebook.com/CCFManitobain
Year Founded: 1974 Le Centre culturel franco-manitobain a un rôle de premier plan comme maison de la culture et carrefour de la vie culturelle et artistique en français à Winnipeg et au Manitoba/The Centre culturel franco-manitobain is the focal point of French cultural life in Winnipeg & Manitoba
Sylviane Lanthier, Directrice générale, slanthier@ccfm.mb.ca

***Winnipeg:* Loch Gallery Winnipeg**
306 St. Mary's Rd.
Winnipeg, MB R2H 1J8
Tel: 204-235-1033
www.lochgallery.com
Year Founded: 1972 Work by Canadian & European artists both contemporary & historical.
Alison Loch, Manager

***Winnipeg:* Pavilion Gallery Museum**
Assiniboine Park, 55 Pavilion Cres.
Winnipeg, MB R3P 2N6
Tel: 204-927-6000
info@assiniboinepark.ca
www.assiniboinepark.ca/attractions/pavilion-gallery-museum.php
Year Founded: 1998 The gallery museum features a large collection of works by Ivan Eyre, Clarence Tillenius, & Walter J. Phillips, all renowned Manitoba artists. Open May-Sept.

***Winnipeg:* Plug In ICA Gallery**
#1, 460 Portage Ave.
Winnipeg, MB R3C 0E8
Tel: 204-942-1043; *Fax:* 204-944-8663
info@plugin.org
www.plugin.org
Social Media: plug-in-ica.tumblr.com
twitter.com/pluginica
www.facebook.com/80299913 276
Heather Laser, Acting Director

***Winnipeg:* School of Art Gallery**
ARTlab, School of Art, University of Manitoba, #255, 180 Dafoe Rd.
Winnipeg, MB R3T 2N2
Tel: 204-474-9322
gallery@umanitoba.ca
umanitoba.ca/schools/art
Year Founded: 1965 The gallery exhibits & collects contemporary & historical art, & includes the FitzGerald Study Collection, featuring papers, drawings & watercolours of L.L. Fitzgerald. Open year round.
Mary Reid, Gallery Director/Curator, mary.reid@ad.umanitoba.ca

***Winnipeg:* University of Winnipeg Fine Art Collection & Gallery 1C03**
515 Portage Ave.
Winnipeg, MB R3B 2E9
Tel: 204-786-9253; *Fax:* 204-774-4134
www.uwinnipeg.ca/index/artgallery-index
Social Media: gallery1c03.blogspot.ca
twitter.com/1c03
www.facebook.com/23472162878
Year Founded: 1986 19th & 20th century paintings, drawings, prints, photographs & sculptures; open year round
Jennifer Gibson, Director/Curator, 204-786-9253, j.gibson@uwinnipeg.ca

***Winnipeg:* Urban Shaman: Contemporary Aboriginal Art (US)**
#203, 290 McDermot Ave.
Winnipeg, MB R3B 0T2
Tel: 204-942-2674; *Fax:* 204-942-2674
info@urbanshaman.org
urbanshaman.org
Year Founded: 1996 Exhibits contemporary work by First Nations, Métis & Inuit artists.
Diana Warren, Gallery Director, daina@urbanshaman.org

New Brunswick

Provincial Art Gallery

Owens Art Gallery
Mount Allison University, 61 York St.
Sackville, NB E4L 1E1
Tel: 506-364-2574; *Fax:* 506-364-2575
owens@mta.ca
www.mta.ca/owens
www.facebook.com/pages/Owens-Art-Gallery /118900188982
Year Founded: 1895 Permanent collection of over 2500 works, dating from the 18th century; 30 exhibitions yearly
Gemey Kelly, Director/Curator, gkelly@mta.ca

Local Art Galleries

***Campbellton:* Galerie Restigouche Gallery**
39 Andrew St.
Campbellton, NB E3N 3H1
Tel: 506-753-5750; *Fax:* 506-759-9601
www.grg.nb.ca
Year Founded: 1975

***Edmundston:* Galerie Colline**
195, boul Hébert
Edmundston, NB E3V 2S8
Tél: 506-737-5282; *Téléc:* 506-727-5373
galerie@umce.ca
www.umoncton.ca/umce/galerie_colline
www.facebook.com/galerie.colline
Fondée en: 1968 Trente ans d'expositions d'artistes amateurs et professionnels qui ont aidé à l'appréciation de l'art dans notre milieu.
Louise Bourque, Présidente

***Fredericton:* Beaverbrook Art Gallery / La galerie d'art Beaverbrook**
PO Box 605, 703 Queen St.
Fredericton, NB E3B 5A6
Tel: 506-458-8545; *Fax:* 506-459-7450
emailbag@beaverbrookartgallery.org
www.beaverbrookartgallery.org
Social Media: beaverbrookartgallery.wordpress.com
twitter.com/BeaverbrookAG
www.facebook.com/BeaverbrookArtGallery
Other contact information: Alternate Phones: 506-458-0970; 506-458-2028
Year Founded: 1959 Atlantic Canadian art & historical British art; open year round
Terry Graff, Director & CEO; Chief Curator O.C., 506-458-2030, tgraff@beaverbrookartgallery.org

***Fredericton:* Connexion ARC**
Charlotte Street Arts Centre, 732 Charlotte St.
Fredericton, NB E3B 1M7
Tel: 506-454-1433
connex@nbnet.nb.ca
connexionarc.org
www.facebook.com /pages/Gallery-Connexion/101926419859581
Artist-run centre, non-profit & non commercial; gallery exists for the purpose of exhibiting, supporting, & promoting the development & understanding of all forms of contemporary art practice of local, national & international significance
Brendan Doyle, President
John Edward Cushnie, Executive Director

***Fredericton:* Gallery 78**
796 Queen St.
Fredericton, NB E3B 1C6
Tel: 506-454-5192; *Fax:* 506-443-0199
Toll-Free: 888-883-8322
art@gallery78.com
www.gallery78.com
Social Media: www.pinterest.com/gallery78
twitter.com/Gallery78
www.facebook.com/Gallery78.ca
Year Founded: 1976 Exhibits visual art, with a focus on work by Atlantic Canadians, & a special emphasis on artists from New Brunswick.
Inge Pataki, Director

***Fredericton:* New Brunswick Art Bank**
PO Box 6000, 670 King St., 4th Fl.
Fredericton, NB E3B 5H1
Tel: 506-453-3115; *Fax:* 506-453-2416
thctpcinfo@gnb.ca
www2.gnb.ca
Year Founded: 1968 The Art Bank has over 700 works of art by 250 New Brunswick artists in its collection. The art is accessible to the public through the Bank's loans program, & the Bank purchases art biannually through its acquisitions program. The exhibition program allows the work to be displayed publicly both in New Brunswick & elsewhere.

***Fredericton:* UNB Art Centre**
Memorial Hall, University of New Brunswick, PO Box 4400, 9 Bailey Dr.
Fredericton, NB E3B 5A3
Tel: 506-453-4623; *Fax:* 506-453-5012
artcntr@unb.ca
www.unb.ca/cel/programs/creative/exhibition/index.html
Historical & contemporary exhibitions; interpretive programs; Atlantic art collection
Marie Maltais, Director

***Moncton:* Atelier IMAGO**
Centre Culturel Aberdeen, #17, rue 140 Botsford
Moncton, NB E1C 4X5
Tel: 506-388-1431
atelierestampeimago@gmail.com
www.atelierimago.com
Year Founded: 1986 Artist-run not-for-profit printmaking studio

1 Jennifer Bélanger, Directrice et technicienne

***Moncton:* Galerie d'art Louise-et-Reuben-Cohen**
Campus de Moncton, Université de Moncton, 18, av Antonine-Maillet
Emplacement: Pavillon Clément-Cormier, Centre universitaire de Moncton, #118, 405, av de l'Université, Moncton, NB
Moncton, NB E1A 3E9
Tél: 506-858-4088
galrc@umoncton.ca
www.umoncton.ca/umcm-ga
Fondée en: 1964 La Galerie a pour mission encourager la créativité des artistes acadiens/acadiennes, et collectioner et documenter les oeuvres d'art; centre de documentation; programmation.
Nisk Imbeault, Directeur-conservateur, 506-858-4687

***Moncton:* Galerie Georges-Goguen SRC**
Radio-Canada Acadie, CP 950, 250, av Université
Moncton, NB E1C 8N8
Tél: 506-382-8326
ghg@nbnet.nb.ca
www.radio-canada.ca/acadie
Promeut les travaux des artistes de l'Atlantique

***Moncton:* Galerie Sans Nom Coop Ltée (GSN)**
Centre Culturel Aberdeen, #13 & 16, 140 rue Botsford
Moncton, NB E1C 4X5
Tél: 506-854-5381; *Téléc:* 506-857-2064
info@galeriesansnom.org
galeriesansnom.org
twitter.com/GalerieSansNom
www.facebook.com/123436297725404
Fondée en: 1977 Galerie Sans Nom (GSN) est à but non lucratif, centre géré par des artistes engagés dans la promotion, la production et l'exposition d'art contemporain. GSN est un lieu d'expression créative de la communauté artistique et agissant comme un moyen de communication essentiel, fournit une impulsion à l'innovation et la créativité.
Léo Goguen, Président
Amanda Dawn Christie, Directrice, direction@galeriesansnom.org

***Saint John:* Saint John Arts Centre (SJAC)**
20 Peel Plaza
Saint John, NB E2L 3G6
Tel: 506-633-4870; *Fax:* 506-674-1040
sjac@saintjohnartscentre.com
www.saintjohnartscentre.com
twitter.com/S JArtsCentre
www.facebook.com/114375408575288
First municipally funded art gallery in Atlantic Canada; features monthly exhibitions of local & regional art works
Andrew Kierstead, Executive Director, a.kierstead@saintjohnartscentre.com

***St Andrews:* Sunbury Shores Arts & Nature Centre**
139 Water St.
St Andrews, NB E5B 1A7
Tel: 506-529-3386
info@sunburyshores.org
www.sunburyshores.org
www.facebook.com/sunburyshores
Year Founded: 1964 Provides facilities for the study, practice & appreciation of the art, crafts & environmental sciences; stresses the aesthetic appreciation of nature & the importance of its use
James Steel, Executive Director

Newfoundland & Labrador

Provincial Art Gallery

The Rooms Provincial Art Gallery
The Rooms Corporation of Newfoundland & Labrador, PO Box 1800 C, 9 Bonaventure Ave.
St. John's, NL A1C 5P9
Tel: 709-757-8040; *Fax:* 709-757-8041
artgallery@therooms.ca
www.therooms.ca
Regularly changing exhibitions of all media, chiefly contemporary Canadian, with some international, historic Canadian & Newfoundland folk art & traditional crafts; permanent collection of contemporary Canadian art in many media, with strong holdings of Newfoundland work; art slide library. Extensive public programming & special projects with emphasis on collaboration with professional artists.

Local Art Galleries

***Corner Brook:* Sir Wilfred Grenfell College Art Gallery (SWGC)**
Fine Arts Bldg., Memorial University of Newfoundland, University Dr.
Corner Brook, NL A2H 6P9
Tel: 709-637-6209
www2.swgc.ca/artgallery
www.facebook.com/GrenfellArtGallery
Contemporary art

***St. John's:* Eastern Edge Art Gallery**
PO Box 2641 C
Located at 72 Harbour Dr., St. John's, NL
St. John's, NL A1C 6K1
Tel: 709-739-1882; *Fax:* 709-739-1866
easternedgegallery@gmail.com
www.easternedge.ca
twitter.com/easternedg e
www.facebook.com/groups/2661000728
Year Founded: 1984 Not-for-profit, artist-run centre dedicated to exhibiting contemporary art in diverse media; exhibitions include work by Newfoundland artists & artists from the rest of Canada
Jen McVeigh, Chair
Mary MacDonald, Director

***Tors Cove:* Five Island Art Gallery**
7 Cove Rd.
Tors Cove, NL AOA 4AO
Tel: 709-334-3645*Toll-Free:* 866-876-3645
fiveislandgallery@nf.aibn.com
www.fiveisland.ca
Social Media: www.youtube.com/user/fiveislandgallery
www.facebook.com/pages/Five-Islan d-Art-Gallery/166705803371245
Work by local artists including paintings, sculptures & rugs.

***Twillingate:* Ted Stuckless Fine Arts & Driftwood Gallery**
124 Main St.
Twillingate, NL A0G 4M0
Tel: 709-884-5239; *Fax:* 709-884-1213
info@tedstuckless.com
www.tedstuckless.com
www.facebook.com/TedStuckle ss

Northwest Territories

Territorial Art Gallery

Gallery of the Midnight Sun
5005 Bryson Dr.
Yellowknife, NT X1A 2A3
Tel: 867-873-8064; *Fax:* 867-873-8065
galleryofthemidnightsun.com
www.facebook.com/508366822519344
Year Founded: 1998 NWT's largest selection of Inuit & Dene arts & crafts

Nova Scotia

Provincial Art Galleries

Art Gallery of Nova Scotia Halifax (AGNS)
PO Box 2262
Located at 1723 Hollis St., Halifax, NS
Halifax, NS B3J 3C8
Tel: 902-424-5280; *Fax:* 902-424-7359
info.desk@novascotia.ca
www.artgalleryofnovascotia.ca
twitter.com/ArtG alleryNS
www.facebook.com/ArtGalleryNS
Year Founded: 1908 Housed in 1868 heritage building. The Gallery has over 13,000 peices in its permanent collection.
Lisa Bugden, Interim CEO, Director_AGNS@gov.ns.ca
Sarah Fillmore, Chief Curator, sarah.fillmore@novascotia.ca

Art Gallery of Nova Scotia Yarmouth (AGNS)
PO Box 246
Yarmouth, NS B5A 4B2
Tel: 902-749-2248; *Fax:* 902-749-2255
agnsyarmouth@gov.ns.ca
www.artgalleryofnovascotia.ca/visit-yarmouth
tw itter.com/ArtGalleryNS
www.facebook.com/89366582597
Year Founded: 2006
Angela Collier, Gallery Coordinator, collieal@gov.ns.ca

Local Art Galleries

***Antigonish:* St. Francis Xavier Art Gallery**
Bloomfield Centre 103
Antigonish, NS B2G 2W5
Tel: 902-867-2303; *Fax:* 902-867-5115
gallery@stfx.ca
sites.stfx.ca/artgallery
www.facebook.com/StfxArtGalle ry
Year Founded: 1976 Exhibits work by Nova Scotia artists
Bruce Campbell, Contact, bcampbel@stfx.ca

***Chéticamp:* Les Trois Pignon**
c/o La Société St-Pierre, CP 430
Situé à 15584, Cabot Trail, Chéticamp, Nouvelle-Écosse
Chéticamp, NS B0E 1H0
Tél: 902-224-2642; *Téléc:* 902-224-1579
lestroispignons@ns.sympatico.ca
www.lestroispignons.com
twitter.com/Le sTroisPignons
www.facebook.com/249801311699866
Fondée en: 1947 Les tapisseries du Dr. Elizabeth LeFort ainsi que d'autres tapis historiques de la région; le musée d'antiquité à Marguerite Gallant est attaché sur la Galerie aussi que centre généalogique
Lisette Aucoin-Bourgeois, Directrice générale, lisettebourgeois@ns.sympatico.ca

***Halifax:* Centre for Art Tapes**
2238 Maitland St.
Halifax, NS B3K 2Z9
Tel: 902-422-6822
info@cfat.ca
cfat.ca
twitter.com/CentreforArtTap
www.facebook.com/centre4arttapes
Year Founded: 1979 An artist-run centre that facilitates & supports emerging, intermediate & established artists working with electronic media, such as video, audio & new media; strives to provide production facilities, ongoing programming & training to a diverse membership whose creative abilities contribute to social & artistic goals
Laura Carmichael, Co-Chair
Daniel Pink, Co-Chair
Keith McPhail, Director, keith@cfat.ca
Annalise Prodor, Coordinator, Communications & Program, annalise@cfat.ca

***Halifax:* Dalhousie Art Gallery (DAG)**
6101 University Ave.
Halifax, NS B3H 1W8
Tel: 902-494-2403; *Fax:* 902-423-0591
art.gallery@dal.ca
artgallery.dal.ca
twitter.com/DalArtGallery
www.f acebook.com/197088913670695
Year Founded: 1953 The Dalhousie Art Gallery is a public art gallery, an academic support unit within the educational & research context of Dalhousie University, & a cultural resource for the whole community.
Peter Dykuis, Director/Curator, peter.dykhuis@dal.ca

***Halifax:* Eye Level Gallery**
#101, 5663 Cornwallis St.
Halifax, NS B3K 1B6
Tel: 902-425-6412
www.eyelevelgallery.ca
twitter.com/EyeLevelGallery
www.facebook.com/EYELEVEL.arc
Year Founded: 1974 Not-for-profit organization dedicated to presenting, developing, & promoting contemporary art. Open Tu-F 12:00-5:00, or at random times when the lights are on.
Andrew Rabyniuk, Chair
Katie Belcher, Executive Director, director@eyelevelgallery.ca

***Halifax:* Gallery Page & Strange**
1869 Granville St.
Halifax, NS B3J 1Y1
Tel: 902-422-8995
info@pageandstrange.com
www.pageandstrange.com
www.facebook.com/GalleryPageAndStrange

***Halifax:* MSVU Art Gallery, Mount Saint Vincent University**
166 Bedford Hwy.
Halifax, NS B3M 2J6
Tel: 902-457-6160; *Fax:* 902-457-2447
art.gallery@msvu.ca
msvuart.ca
twitter.com/msvuartgallery
www.facebook.com/pages/MSVU-Art-Gallery/177537538924695
Year Founded: 1971 Open daily except Mondays; exhibition program emphasizes women as cultural subjects & producers, new Nova Scotia artists, & themes relevant to the university's academic programs; admission free
Ingrid Jenkner, Director, director@msvuart.ca
David Dahms, Gallery Technician, david.dahms@msvuart.ca
Susan Wolf, Program Coordinator, 902-457-6291, susan.wolf@msvu.ca

***Halifax:* Nova Scotia Centre for Craft & Design & Maray E. Black Gallery (NSCCD)**
#104, 1061 & 1096 Marginal Rd.
Halifax, NS B3H 4P7
Tel: 902-424-2522; *Fax:* 902-492-2526
info@craft-design.ns.ca
www.craft-design.ns.ca
Social Media: www.youtube.com/user/NSCentreforCraft
twitter.com/NSCraftStudios
www.facebook.com/NSCentreforCraftandDesign
Year Founded: 1991 Develops & promotes crafts & design in Nova Scotia; includes the Mary E. Black Gallery, a craft showroom, an info. centre, & 5 studios; open year round
Susan Charles, Director, director@craft-design.ns.ca
Laurie Murchison, Chair, lb.murchison@hotmail.com
Lori Burke, Executive Director, lori@capebretoncraft.com

***Sydney:* Cape Breton Centre for Craft & Design (CBCC&D)**
PO Box 1686
Located at 322 Charlotte St., Sydney, NS
Sydney, NS B1P 6T7
Tel: 902-539-7491; *Fax:* 902-539-4807
info@capebretoncraft.com
www.capebretoncraft.com
Social Media: www.youtube.com/user/capebretoncraft
twitter.com/CapeBretonCraft
www.facebook.com/capebretoncentreforcraftanddesign
Offers educational arts programs, as well as exhibitions, special events & a gallery.

***Halifax:* Nova Scotia College of Art & Design Anna Leonowens Gallery**
1891 Granville St.
Mailing address: 5163 Duke St., Halifax, NS, B3J 3J6
Halifax, NS B3J 3L7
Tel: 902-494-8223
annaleonowens@nscad.ca
nscad.ca/en/home/galleriesevents/galleries
www.facebook.com/AnnaLeonowen sGallery
Year Founded: 1968 Work primarily by students of the school.
Melanie Colosimo, Exhibitions Coordinator

***Halifax:* Nova Scotia College of Art & Design Port Loggia Gallery**
1107 Marginal Rd.
Mailing address: 5163 Duke St., Halifax, NS, B3J 3J6
Halifax, NS B3H 4P8
Tel: 902-494-8223
nscad.ca/en/home/galleriesevents/galleries
Work by undergraduate & graduate students.
Melanie Colosimo, Exhibitions Coordinator

***Halifax:* Saint Mary's University Art Gallery**
923 Robie St.
Location: Loyola Building, 5865 Gorsebrook Ave., 1st Fl., Halifax, NS B3H 1G3
Halifax, NS B3H 3C3
Tel: 902-420-5445
gallery@smu.ca
www.smu.ca/campus-life/art-gallery.html
www.facebook.com/SMUartgallery
Year Founded: 1971 Contemporary visual arts by artists within & outside the region; lectures, publications & performing arts program; permanent collection of over 1,800 works
Robin Metcalfe, Director/Curator, robin.metcalfe@smu.ca

***Lunenburg:* Lunenburg Art Gallery (LAG)**
PO Box 1418
Located at 79-81 Pelham St., Lunenburg, NS
Lunenburg, NS B0J 2C0
Tel: 902-640-4044; *Fax:* 902-640-3035
lag@eastlink.ca
www.lunenburgartgallery.com
twitter.com/art_lag
www. facebook.com/LunenburgArtGallery
Year Founded: 1972 The gallery promotes the works of local, provincial & international artists, sponsors workshops & raises funds; houses the Meldrum collection by the late Earl Bailly; month-long solo exhibitions & ongoing Members Gallery; open seasonally: Mar.-Oct., Tu-Sa 10:00-5:00 & Su 1:00-5:00.
Helen Dalton, President
Diana Dines, Treasurer
Garry Woodcock, Contact, Planning & Exhibition

***Pictou:* Hector Exhibit Centre & Archives**
PO Box 1210
Located at 86 Haliburton Rd., Pictou, NS
Pictou, NS B0K 1H0
Tel: 902-485-4563
pcghs@gov.ns.ca
www.mccullochcentre.ca
twitter.com/HectorCentre
www.facebook.com/23415 2123269050
Year Founded: 1973 Genealogical & historical archives for Pictou County - census records, cemetery records, shipping lists, newspapers, etc.; local historical, cultural, genealogical & craft exhibits

***Sydney:* Cape Breton University Art Gallery**
PO Box 5300, 1250 Grand Lake Rd.
Sydney, NS B1P 6L2
Tel: 902-563-1342
www.cbu.ca/art-gallery
First & only full-time public art gallery on Cape Breton Island; acquires & presents art with emphasis on contemporary Canadian works & the artistic traditions of Cape Breton Island; offers educational & research facilities; a major cultural resource within the educational & research context of the university
Laura Schneider, Director/Curator, laura_schneider@cbu.ca
John Matthews, Technician, Gallery & Collections, john_mathews@cbu.ca

***Wolfville:* Acadia University Art Gallery**
10 Highland Ave.
Wolfville, NS B4P 2R6
Tel: 902-585-1373
artgallery@acadiau.ca
gallery.acadiau.ca
www.facebook.com/95064121286
Year Founded: 1978 The University Gallery serves both as a public gallery & as a teaching facility within Acadia's Faculty of Arts. Its purpose in the community & on the campus is to enrich visual experience through showcasing original works of historical or contemporary importance. The Gallery looks after Acadia's collection of art.
Laurie Dalton, Director/Curator

Ontario

Provincial Art Galleries

Art Gallery of Hamilton (AGH)
123 King St. West
Hamilton, ON L8P 4S8
Tel: 905-527-6610; *Fax:* 905-577-6940
info@artgalleryofhamilton.com
www.artgalleryofhamilton.com
Social Media: instagram.com/at_theagh
twitter.com/TheAGH
www.facebook.com/artgalleryofhamilton
Collection of 8,000 art objects; holds one of Canada's most comprehensive collections of Canadian historical, modernist & contemporary art; British, American & European works
Shelley Falconer, President & CEO, shelley@artgalleryofhamilton.com

Art Gallery of Ontario (AGO) / Musée des beaux-arts de l'Ontario
317 Dundas St. West
Toronto, ON M5T 1G4
Tel: 416-979-6648 *Toll-Free:* 877-225-4246
www.ago.net
Social Media: www.youtube.com/user/ArtGalleryofOntario
twitter.com/agotoronto
www.facebook.com/AGOToronto
Other contact information: Donations: 416-979-6619
Year Founded: 1918 The AGO, located in the heart of Toronto, has an expansive art collection that includes European Old Masters, Group of Seven, & Canadian & international contemporary works — plus the world's largest public collection of sculptures by Henry Moore.
Maxine Granovsky Gluskin, President, Board of Trustees
Stephan Jost, Director & Chief Executive Officer
Stephanie Smith, Chief Curator

Art Gallery of Windsor (AGW)
401 Riverside Dr. West
Windsor, ON N9A 7J1
Tel: 519-977-0013; *Fax:* 519-977-0776
www.agw.ca
twitter.com/A_G_W
www.facebook.com/198 575240184786
Year Founded: 1943 One of the larger, non-government run galleries in Ontario; focus is on Canadian art in an international context; permanent collection of 2,500 paintings & sculptures; resource centre & gift shop. Hours: W-Su 11:00-5:00
Peter Wasylyk, President
Catharine M. Mastin, Director, cmastin@agw.ca
Srimoyee Mitra, Curator, Contemporary Art, smitra@agw.ca

Government of Ontario Art Collection
c/o The Archives of Ontario, 134 Ian Macdonald Boul.
Toronto, ON M7A 2C5
Tel: 416-327-1600; *Fax:* 416-327-1999
Toll-Free: 800-668-9933
reference@ontario.ca
www.archives.gov.on.ca/en/goac/in dex.aspx
The Government of Ontario's art collection is spread throughout ministry & government offices around Toronto, although many of the works are featured in the Legislative Building. In all, the collection comprises around 2,500 pieces.

McMichael Canadian Art Collection
10365 Islington Ave.
Kleinburg, ON L0J 1C0
Tel: 905-893-1121; *Fax:* 905-893-0692
Toll-Free: 888-213-1121
info@mcmichael.com
www.mcmichael.com
Social Media: www.youtube.com/mcmichaelgallery
twitter.com/mcacgallery
www.facebook.com/206491259365240
Year Founded: 1965 The collection features works of art created by First Nations & Inuit artists, the artists of the Group of Seven & their contemporaries, & other artists who have contributed to the development of Canadian art. Comprehensive education program at kindergarten, elementary & secondary school levels; guided group tours by appt.; extension program & temporary exhibition program. Programs are also available for adults. Museum is open Monday to Sunday 10am to 5pm.
Victoria Dickenson, Executive Director/CEO FCMA, PhD
Upkar Arora, Chair

Local Art Galleries

***Ajax:* Cultural Expressions Art Gallery**
62 Old Kingston Rd.
Ajax, ON L1T 2Z7
Tel: 905-427-2412
culturalexpressions@sympatico.ca
www.culturalexpressions.ca
Work by emerging Canadian visual artists.

***Amherstburg:* Gibson Gallery**
140 Richmond St.
Amherstburg, ON N9V 1G4
Tel: 519-736-2826
office@gibsonartgallery.com
www.gibsonartgallery.com
Year Founded: 1975 Exhibits work of local artist, photographers & stitchers & offers art classes.

***Aurora:* Aurora Cultural Centre**
22 Church St.
Aurora, ON L4G 1G4
Tel: 905-713-1818
info@auroraculturalcentre.ca
www.claringtonmuseums.com
www.facebook.com/pages/Aurora-Cultural-Centre/189279284457640
Year Founded: 2010 The centre exhibits visual artwork, holds concerts & provides art classes for the Aurora community.
Laura Schembri, Executive Director, lauraschembri@auroraculturalcentre.ca

***Bancroft:* The Art Gallery of Bancroft (AGB)**
PO Box 398
Located at 10 Flint Ave., Bancroft, ON
Bancroft, ON K0L 1C0
Tel: 613-332-1542
info@artgallerybancroft.ca
www.artgallerybancroft.ca
www.facebook.com/pages/Art-Gallery-of-Bancroft/136404233116851
Local & other Ontario artists; gift shop for area artists only; open year round

***Barrie:* MacLaren Art Centre**
37 Mulcaster St.
Barrie, ON L4M 3M2
Tel: 705-721-9696
maclaren@maclarenart.com
www.maclarenart.com
twitter.com/MacLarenArt
www.facebook.com/127102583 989513
Year Founded: 1986 Open Tu-F 10:00-5:00, Sa 10:00-4:00
Carolyn Bell Farrell, Executive Director

***Bloomfield:* OENO Gallery**
2274 County Road #1
Bloomfield, ON K0K 1G0
Tel: 613-393-2216; *Fax:* 613-393-2215
info@oenogallery.com
www.oenogallery.com
twitter.com/OenoGallery
www .facebook.com/29363322998
Year Founded: 2004 Artwork by senior Canadian painters

***Bowmanville:* Visual Arts Centre of Clarington (VAC)**
PO Box 52
Located at 143 Simpson Ave., Bowmanville, ON
Bowmanville, ON L1C 3K8
Tel: 905-623-5831; *Fax:* 905-623-0276
visual@vac.ca
www.vac.ca
Social Media: ca.linkedin.com/in/visualarts
twitter.com/c_vac
www.facebook.com/visua lartscentre.clarington
Year Founded: 1974 A non-profit visual arts gallery
James Campbell, Executive Director & Curator

***Bracebridge:* Chapel Gallery**
c/o Muskoka Arts & Crafts Inc., PO Box 376
Located at 15 King St., Bracebridge, ON
Bracebridge, ON P1L 1T7
Tel: 705-645-5501; *Fax:* 705-645-0385
info@muskokaartsandcrafts.com
www.muskokaartsandcrafts.com/Chapel_Gallery/chapel_gallery.htm
Year Founded: 1989 Hours: Tu-Sa 10:00-1:00, 2:00-5:00
Mary-Ruth Newell, President
Elene J. Freer, Executive Director

***Bracebridge:* Ziska Gallery Muskoka**
1012 Baldwin Rd.
Bracebridge, ON P1L 1W8
Tel: 705-645-2587
The beauty of nature in paintings & sculpture; open June to Oct.

***Brampton:* Beaux-Arts Brampton**
#70, 74 Main St. North
Brampton, ON L6V 1N7
Tel: 905-454-5677*Toll-Free:* 866-339-7779
beauxart1@bellnet.ca
beaux-artsbrampton.com
www.facebook.com/BeauxArts Brampton

***Brampton:* Peel Art Gallery, Museum & Archives (PAMA)**
Peel Heritage Complex, 9 Wellington St. East
Brampton, ON L6W 1Y1
Tel: 905-791-4055; *Fax:* 905-451-4931
InfoPAMA@peelregion.ca
pama.peelregion.ca
Social Media: www.flickr.com/photos/peelheritage
www.facebook.com/visitPAMA
Year Founded: 1968 Located within a cluster of 19th century buildings; features the works of local artists in Peel & contemporary art from across Canada; collection of over 1,500 works consists of contemporary & historic Canadian works with a special emphasis on artists from Peel.
Gerrie Loveys, Acting Curator

***Brantford:* Glenhyrst Art Gallery of Brant**
20 Ava Rd.
Brantford, ON N3T 5G9
Tel: 519-756-5932; *Fax:* 519-756-5910
info@glenhyrstartgallery.ca
www.glenhyrst.ca
twitter.com/Glenhyrst
w ww.facebook.com/376509061505
Year Founded: 1986 Permanent collection comprises contemporary works on paper & paintings by Robert Reginald Whale & his descendants; offers a rotating schedule of art exhibitions, an art rental & sales showroom, giftshop & a variety of classes & programmes
Adam Szabluk, President, board@glenhyrst.ca
Bryce Kanbara, Curator

***Bright's Grove:* Gallery in the Grove**
PO Box 339
Located at 2618 Hamilton Rd., Bright's Grove, ON
Bright's Grove, ON N0N 1C0
Tel: 519-869-4643
info@galleryinthegrove.com
www.galleryinthegrove.com
www.facebook.com/178962708813607
Year Founded: 1980 The gallery is housed on the second floor of the historic Faethorne House, circa 1875. Open M-Th 11:00-5:00, Sa 11:00-3:00.
Terri Jackson, Chair
Sheila Brown, Contact, Exhibition Planning

***Brockville:* Marianne van Silfhout Gallery**
Brockville Campus, St. Lawrence College, 2288 Parkedale Ave.
Brockville, ON K6V 5X3
Tel: 613-345-0660
gallery@sl.on.ca
www.stlawrencecollege.ca
Christina Chrysler, Gallery Curator, 613-345-0660

***Burlington:* Art Gallery of Burlington (AGB)**
1333 Lakeshore Rd.
Burlington, ON L7S 1A9
Tel: 905-632-7796; *Fax:* 905-632-0278
info@artgalleryofburlington.com
artgalleryofburlington.com
Social Media: www.linkedin.com/company/burlington-art-centre
twitter.com/ArtGallBurl
www.facebook.com/ArtGallBurl
Year Founded: 1978 Exhibitions of regional & nationally recognized Canadian artists; a permanent collection of contemporary Canadian ceramic art & a gallery shop, art rental & sales & studios; open daily
Ian D. Ross, President & CEO MFA, iross@artgalleryofburlington.com
Jonathan Smith, Curator, Permanent Collection, jsmith@artgalleryofburlington.com

***Caledon:* Yaneff.com**
18949 Centreville Creek Rd.
Caledon, ON L7K 2M2
Tel: 905-584-9398*Toll-Free:* 888-304-7843
posters@yaneff.com
www.yaneff.com
www.facebook.com/207960699224765
Year Founded: 1975 Specializes in rare, 19th-century, 20th century & modern posters online
Greg Yaneff, Director/Curator

***Cambridge:* Idea Exchange**
Queen's Square, 1 North Square
Cambridge, ON N1S 2K6
Tel: 519-621-0460; *Fax:* 519-621-2080
socialmedia@ideaexchange.org
ideaexchange.org
twitter.com/IdeaXchng
www.facebook.com/pages/Idea-Exchange/161803547206997
Exhibitions offered at 3 locations within Cambridge (as well as Hespeler & Clemens Mill libraries) reflect a range of local & international developments in contemporary & historical visual arts & architecture; collection of contemporary Canadian fibre art; studio courses for all ages; concerts
Mary Misner, Gallery Director, mmisner@ideaexchange.org
Iga Janik, Curator, ijanik@ideaexchange.org
Esther E. Shipman, Curator, Architecture & Design

***Cambridge:* Design at Riverside**
7 Melville St. South
Cambridge, ON N1S 2H4
Tel: 519-621-0460

***Cambridge:* Idea Exchange Preston Branch**
435 King St. East
Cambridge, ON N3H 3N1
Tel: 519-653-3632

***Chatham:* Thames Art Gallery (TAG)**
Chatham Cultural Centre, 75 William St. North
Chatham, ON N7M 4L4
Tel: 519-354-8338*Toll-Free:* 800-714-7497
ckartgallery@chatham-kent.ca
www.chatham-kent.ca/ThamesArtGallery
twit ter.com/TAG_CK
www.facebook.com/tagck
Year Founded: 1975 Historical & contemporary artwork by local, national & international artists; hosts 12-15 exhibitions a year; guided tours available with advanced bookings; art lectures & workshops for children & adults; open daily 1-5; admission by donation
Carl L. Lavoy, Curator

***Cobourg:* Art Gallery of Northumberland**
Victoria Hall, 55 King St. West, 3rd Fl.
Cobourg, ON K9A 2M2
Tel: 905-372-0333; *Fax:* 905-372-1587
director@artgalleryofnorthumberland.com
www.artgalleryofnorthumberland.c om
twitter.com/ArtGofN
www.facebook.com/ArtGalleryOfNorthumberland
Year Founded: 1960 Maintains a permanent collection of more than 600 works of art; changing exhibitions are displayed throughout the year; lectures; education trips; workshops & special events
Bob Fudge, President
Fraces Clancy, Interim Director

***Port Hope:* Art Gallery of Northumberland Port Hope**
8 Queen St.
Port Hope, ON L1A 2Y7
Tel: 905-885-2115
director@artgalleryofnorthumberland.com
Year Founded: 2000

***Colborne:* Colborne Art Gallery**
PO Box 903
Located at 51 King St. East, Colborne, ON
Colborne, ON K0K 1S0
Tel: 905-355-1798
info@thecolborneartgallery.ca
www.thecolborneartgallery.ca
www.facebook.com/pages/Colborne-Art-Gallery/159525184113252
Year Founded: 1997

***Cornwall:* The Art Gallery Cornwall**
168 Pitt St.
Cornwall, ON K6J 3P4
Tel: 613-938-7387
info@tagcornwall.ca
www.tagcornwall.ca
Social Media: www.youtube.com/user/TAGcornwall
twitter.com/TAGcornwall
www.facebook. com/tagcornwall
Year Founded: 1982 Promotes and stimulates interest in and the study of the visual arts; advances knowledge and appreciation of the visual arts; provides improved opportunities for Canadian artistic talent; advances the development of the visualarts in Canada.
Carilyne Hébert, President, carilyne_hebert@hotmail.com

***Curve Lake Indian Reserve:* Whetung Ojibwa Centre**
875 County Rd. 22
Curve Lake Indian Reserve, ON K0L 1R0
Tel: 705-657-3661; *Fax:* 705-657-3412
www.whetung.com
www.facebook.com/WhetungOjibwaCentre
Year Founded: 1966 Craft centre & art gallery; authentic works by Indian artists from across Canada.
Michael Whetung, Owner, mwhetung@whetung.com

***Dundas:* The Carnegie Gallery**
Andrew Carnegie Library, 10 King St. West
Dundas, ON L9H 1T7
Tel: 905-627-4265
carnegie@carnegiegallery.org
www.carnegiegallery.org
twitter.com/carnegiegallery
www.facebook.com/c arnegiegallery
Year Founded: 1980
Barbara Patterson, Administrator

***Durham:* Durham Art Gallery**
PO Box 1021
Located at 251 George St. East, Durham, ON
Durham, ON N0G 1R0
Tel: 519-369-3692
info@durhamart.on.ca
www.durhamart.on.ca
www.facebook.com/Durham.Art.Gallery
The gallery features 6 exhibits by established artists & 6 exhibits from emerging arts from Durham & surrounding areas per year. They also are involved with festivals, lectures & performances.
Ilse Gassinger, Director, igassinger@durhamart.on.ca

***Fergus:* Wellington Artists' Gallery & Art Centre**
6142 Wellington Rd. 29, RR#4
Fergus, ON N1M 2W5
Tel: 519-843-6303
www.wellingtonartistsgallery.ca
www.facebook.com/214303928584209
Year Founded: 2007

***Fort Erie:* Mewinzha Archaeology Gallery**
***Parent:* Fort Erie Museum Services**
100 Queen St.
Fort Erie, ON L2A 3S6
Tel: 905-894-5322
www.museum.forterie.ca
Native tools, weapons & contemporary artwork; a joint project between the Buffalo-Fort Erie Public Bridge Authority, the Town of Fort Erie, Fort Erie Museum Services & the Fort Erie Native Friendship Centre

***Golderich:* Elizabeth's Art Gallery**
54 Courthouse Sq.
Golderich, ON N7A 1M5
Tel: 519-524-4080
artinfo@elizabeths.ca
www.elizabeths.ca
Social Media:
www.youtube.com/channel/UCrqecqTVVgWTFVQne9pYo0g
twitter.com/ArtAwhile
www.facebook.com/203810526308209
Year Founded: 1992
Elizabeth Van den Broeck, Owner

***Grimsby:* Grimsby Public Art Gallery**
18 Carnegie Lane
Grimsby, ON L3M 1Y1
Tel: 905-945-3246; *Fax:* 905-945-1789
gpag@grimsby.ca
www.grimsby.ca/residents/cultural-facilities/art-gallery
Social Media: grimsbypublicartgallery.tumblr.com
twitter.com/thegpag
www.facebook.com/129646767112893
Year Founded: 1975 Permanent collection of 1,000+ works; contemporary exhibitions & programmes year round

***Guelph:* Macdonald Stewart Art Centre (MSAC)**
358 Gordon St.
Guelph, ON N1G 1Y1
Tel: 519-837-0010; *Fax:* 519-767-2661
info@msac.ca
www.msac.ca
Social Media:
ca.linkedin.com/pub/msac-macdonald-stewart-art-centre/22/2b5/443
twitter .com/MSAC
www.facebook.com/10806818998
Year Founded: 1980 Permanent collection of over 4,000 works; contemporary Inuit drawings & the Donald Forster Sculpture Park
Dawn Owen, Acting Director/Curator, dowen@msac.ca

***Haileybury:* Temiskaming Art Gallery / Galerie d'Art du Temaiskaming**
PO Box 1090
Located at 325 Farr Dr., Haileybury, ON
Haileybury, ON P0J 1K0
Tel: 705-672-3706
temiskamingartgallery@ntl.sympatico.ca
www.temiskaming artgallery.ca
twitter.com/TemisArtGallery
Public gallery; open year round
Lydia Alexander, President
Maureen Steward, Executive Director/Curator

***Haliburton:* Ethel Curry Gallery**
PO Box 242
Located at 94 Maple Ave., Haliburton, ON
Haliburton, ON K0M 1S0
Tel: 705-457-9687
www.theethelcurrygallery.com
Work that is inspired by nature by Ontario artists
Wayne Hooks, Contact, wayne@theethelcurrygallery.com

***Haliburton:* Rails End Gallery & Arts Centre**
PO Box 912
Located at 23 York St., Haliburton, ON
Haliburton, ON K0M 1S0
Tel: 705-457-2330
info@railsendgallery.com
www.railsendgallery.com
twitter.com/RailsEnd
www.facebook.com/railsend
Year Founded: 1980 Open year round

***Hamilton:* Design Annex**
***Parent:* Art Gallery of Hamilton**
118 James St. North
Hamilton, ON L8R 2K7
Tel: 902-667-6620; *Fax:* 905-667-6621
annex@artgalleryofhamilton.com
www.artgalleryofhamilton.com/da_index.php
Exhibition space; art & design store; rental space; live performances.

***Hamilton:* McMaster Museum of Art (MMA)**
Alvin A. Lee Building, McMaster University, 1280 Main St. West
Hamilton, ON L8S 4L6
Tel: 905-525-9140; *Fax:* 905-527-4548
museum@mcmaster.ca
museum.mcmaster.ca
Social Media: www.youtube.com/McMasterMuseum
twitter.com/macmuseum
www.facebook.com/ mcmastermuseum
Year Founded: 1967 Historical, modern & contemporary art.
Carol Podedworny, Director & Chief Curator, podedwo@mcmaster.ca

***Hamilton:* Nathaniel Hughson Art Gallery**
27 John St. North
Hamilton, ON L8R 1H1
Tel: 905-923-1192
info@nathanielhughsongallery.com
nathanielhughsongallery.com
twitter.com/NHGonJohn
www.facebook.com/Nat hanielHughsonGallery
Year Founded: 2012 Artwork by established Ontario artists
Jocelyn McKeown, Contact, jm@nathanielhughsongallery.com

***Huntsville:* Eclipse Art Gallery**
1235 Deerhurst Dr.
Huntsville, ON P1H 2E8
Tel: 705-789-8803
info@eclipsegallery.ca
www.eclipseartgallery.ca
twitter.com/EclipseArt
www.facebook.com/eclip seartgallery.kriekaard
Exhibits work by emerging & established Canadian artists.

***Ingersoll:* Ingersoll Creative Arts Centre**
PO Box 384
Located at 125 Centennial Lane, Ingersoll, ON
Ingersoll, ON N5C 3V3
Tel: 519-485-4691
creative.arts@on.aibn.com
creativeartscentre.com
www.facebook.com/304505136251524
Year Founded: 1972 The centre aims to provide members of the community with the opportunity for creative expression & development, specifically in the following areas: fine arts, pottery, quilting, rug hooking, & fibre arts. The centre also hosts exhibitions & a gallery. Office hours: M-F 9:00-12:00 & 1:00-4:00; Gallery hours: F-Su 2:00-4:00.
Heather MacIntosh, Contact

***Jordan Village:* Jordan Art Gallery**
3836 Main St.
Jordan Village, ON L0R 1S0
Tel: 905-562-6680
info@jordanartgallery.com
www.jordanartgallery.com
www.facebook.com/JordanArtGallery
Year Founded: 2001

***Kanata:* Kanata Civic Art Gallery**
2500 Campeau Dr.
Kanata, ON K2K 2W3
Tel: 613-580-2424
info@kanatagallery.ca
www.kanatagallery.ca
twitter.com/kanatagallery
www.facebook.com/Kanata Gallery

***Kingston:* Agnes Etherington Art Centre (AEAC) / Centre d'art Agnes Etherington**
Queen's University, 36 University Ave.
Kingston, ON K7L 3N6
Tel: 613-533-2190; *Fax:* 613-533-6765
aeac@queensu.ca
www.aeac.ca
twitter.com/aeartcentre
www.facebook.com /aeartcentre
Other contact information: Shop E-mail: artgall@queensu.ca
Year Founded: 1957 Contemporary & historical art collections & exhibitions; gallery shop, art rental & sales gallery, facility rentals; open year round
Jan Allen, Director, jan.allen@queensu.ca
Alicia Boutilier, Curator, Canadian Historical Art, alicia.boutilier@queensu.ca
David de Witt, Curator, European Art, david.dewitt@queensu.ca

***Kingston:* Modern Fuel Artist-Run Centre**
21 Queen St.
Kingston, ON K7K 1A1
Tel: 613-548-4883
info@modernfuel.org
www.modernfuel.org
twitter.com/modernfuelarc
www.facebook.com/ModernFu el
Year Founded: 1977 Exhibits visual, time-based & interdisciplinary art.
Phoebe Cohoe, President

***Kitchener:* Homer Watson House & Gallery**
1754 Old Mill Rd.
Kitchener, ON N2P 1H7
Tel: 519-748-4377; *Fax:* 519-748-6808
development@homerwatson.on.ca
www.homerwatson.on.ca
twitter.com/HomerW atson
www.facebook.com/HomerRWatson
Year Founded: 1980 Hours: Tu-Su 12:00-4:30
Faith Hieblinger, Executive Director

***Kitchener:* Kitchener-Waterloo Art Gallery (KWAG)**
101 Queen St. North
Kitchener, ON N2H 6P7
Tel: 519-579-5860; *Fax:* 519-578-0740
mail@kwag.on.ca
www.kwag.ca
Social Media: www.youtube.com/user/kwagadmin
twitter.com/kwartgallery
www.facebook.c om/kwartgallerypage
Year Founded: 1956 Open year round; Monday - Wednesday, Friday: 9:30-5:00; Thursday: 9:30-9:00; Saturday: 10:00-5:00; Sunday 1:00-5:00.
Shirley Madill, Exective Director

***Leamington:* Leamington Art Centre (LAC)**
72 Talbot St. West
Leamington, ON N8H 1M4
Tel: 519-326-2711
info@leamingtonartscentre.com
www.leamingtonartscentre.com
Social Media:
ca.linkedin.com/pub/leamington-arts-centre/65/602/716/
twitter.com/leami ngton_arts
www.facebook.com/leamingtonartscentre
Year Founded: 1971 The Leamington Arts Centre, run by the South Essex Arts Association, is a charitable, not-for-profit organization. Its purpose is to serve the community through arts & culture. The Leamington Arts Centre includes a main gallery, which exhibits the work of local artists. Heinz Memorabilia explains the history of the Heinz Co.. The Centre also features the Marine Heritage Interpretive Centre, Signature Gifts, & several educational programs throughout the year for both adults & children.
Mike Thibodeau, Chair
Chad Riley, Gallery Director M.F.A., director@leamingtonartscentre.com

***Lindsay:* The Lindsay Gallery**
190 Kent St. West, 2nd Fl.
Lindsay, ON K9V 2Y6
Tel: 705-324-1780; *Fax:* 705-324-9349
art@thelindsaygallery.com
www.thelindsaygallery.com
www.facebook.com/l indsay.artgallery
Year Founded: 1976 Not-for-profit gallery offering regular exhibitions, art classes & a boutique

London: Art Gallery of Lambeth
2454 Main St.
London, ON N6P 1R2
Tel: 519-652-5556
info@artgalleryoflambeth.com
www.artgalleryoflambeth.com
Social Media: www.youtube.com/user/artgalleryoflambeth
twitter.com/AGL39
www.faceboo k.com/ArtGalleryOfLambeth
Year Founded: 2010 Work by local artists, as well as events & educational programming.
Vivian Tserotas, Curator
Brenda Colley, Curator

London: The Innuit Gallery
201 Queens Ave.
London, ON N6A 1J1
Tel: 519-672-7770; Fax: 519-672-7770
Toll-Free: 866-589-9990
art@innuitgallery.com
www.innuitgallery.com
twitter. com/innuitgallery
www.facebook.com/theinnuitgallery
Year Founded: 1983 Contemporary Inuit art, including prints, paintings, drawings, sculpture, & jewellery
Howard Isaacs, Founder
Janet Evans, Partner

London: McIntosh Gallery
1151 Richmond St.
London, ON N6A 3K7
Tel: 519-661-3181
mcintoshgallery@uwo.ca
www.mcintoshgallery.ca
twitter.com/McIntoshGallery
www.facebook.com/Mc IntoshGallery
Year Founded: 1942 Exhibitions featuring local, national, & international artists working in various media; exhibitions change every 6 weeks & are accompanied by art-related videos, films & lectures; art collection & gallery's records, some artist archives & periodical library available as resources to students for research purposes; open 6 days/week
James Patten, Director/Chief Curator, jpatten2@uwo.ca
Catherine Elliot Shaw, Curator, celliots@uwo.ca
Brian Lambert, Collections Manager, blamber3@uwo.ca

London: Michael Gibson Gallery
157 Carling St.
London, ON N6A 1H5
Tel: 519-439-0451; Fax: 519-439-2842
Toll-Free: 866-644-2766
www.gibsongallery.com
twitter.com/gibsongallery
www. facebook.com/262411200478508
Year Founded: 1984 Contemporary Canadian & international art

Minden: Agnes Jamieson Gallery
Minden Hills Cultural Centre, PO Box 648, #174, 176 Bobcaygeon Rd. North
Minden, ON K0M 2K0
Tel: 705-286-3763
gallery@mindenhills.ca
mindenhills.ca/art-gallery
Year Founded: 1981 The collection mostly consists of work by Andre Lapine.
Laurie Carmount, Curator

Mississauga: Art Gallery of Mississauga (AGM)
300 City Centre Dr.
Mississauga, ON L5B 3C1
Tel: 905-896-5088
agm.connect@mississauga.ca
www.artgalleryofmississauga.com
Social Media: artgalleryofmississauga.wordpress.com
twitter.com/artgallerymiss
www.f acebook.com/ArtGalleryofMississauga
A public art gallery providing state of the art exhibitions by local, national & international artists; exhibits change every 7 weeks; admission is free; open M-F 9:00-5:00, Sa-Su 12:00-4:00
Michael Douglas, President
Stuart Keeler, Director/Curator, stuart.keeler@mississauga.ca

Mississauga: Blackwood Gallery
Kaneff Centre, University of Toronto Mississauga, 3359 Mississauga Rd. North
Mississauga, ON L5L 1C6
Tel: 905-828-3789
blackwood.gallery@utoronto.ca
www.blackwoodgallery.ca
twitter.com/the_Blackwood
www.facebook.com/Bla ckwoodGallery
Year Founded: 1992 Presents exhibitions of contemporary art in all media. Hours: M, Tu, Th, F 12:00-5:00; W 12:00-9:00; Sa-Su 12:00-3:00.
Christine Shaw, Director & Curator, christine.shaw@utoronto.ca
Juliana Zalucky, Exhibition Coordinator, j.zalucky@utoronto.ca

Mississauga: Harbour Gallery
1697 Lakeshore Rd. West
Mississauga, ON L5J 1J4
Tel: 905-822-5495
inforequest@harbourgallery.com
www.harbourgallery.com
Rotating collection of over 30 accredited Canadian artists in a variety of mediums.

Mississauga: Visual Arts Mississauga
4170 Riverwood Park Lane
Mississauga, ON L5C 2S7
Tel: 905-277-4313
info@visualartsmississauga.com
www.visualartsmississauga.com
Social Media: instagram.com/visualartsmississauga
twitter.com/VisualArtsMiss
www.fac ebook.com/pages/Visual-Arts-Mississauga/125990340768419
Visual Arts Mississauga offers art exhibition space, as well as classes, workshops & art camps.

Niagara Falls: Niagara Falls Art Gallery
8058 Oakwood Dr.
Niagara Falls, ON L2E 6S5
Tel: 905-356-1514; Fax: 905-356-3039
info@niagarafallsartgallery.ca
www.niagarafallsartgallery.ca
Year Founded: 1979 Houses the William Kurelek Art Collection as well as the John Burtniak Niagara Collection.
Debra Attenborough, Executive Director, deb@niagarafallsartgallery.ca

North Bay: W.K.P. Kennedy Gallery
150 Main St. East
North Bay, ON P1B 1A8
Tel: 705-474-1944
info@kennedygallery.org
www.kennedygallery.org
A changing program of historical & contemporary visual art; free
Alex Maeve Campbell, Gallery Officer

North Bay: White Water Gallery (WWG)
PO Box 1491
Located at 122 Main St. East, North Bay, ON
North Bay, ON P1B 8K6
Tel: 705-476-2444
info@whitewatergallery.com
whitewatergallery.com
twitter.com/wwgnorthbay
www.facebook.com/whitewa ter.gallery
Year Founded: 1974 Artist-run centre for contemporary art
Clayton Windatt, Programming Director & Executive Director, programming@whitewatergallery.com

Oakville: In2art Gallery
#2, 350 Lakeshore Rd. East
Oakville, ON L6J 1J6
Tel: 905-582-6739
info@in2artgallery.com
www.in2artgallery.com
Social Media: pinterest.com/in2artoakville
twitter.com/In2artOakville
www.facebook.c om/pages/In2artgallerycom/112348635458464

Oakville: Oakville Galleries
1306 Lakeshore Rd. East
Oakville, ON L6J 1L6
Tel: 905-844-4402; Fax: 905-844-7968
info@oakvillegalleries.com
www.oakvillegalleries.com
twitter.com/Oakvl leGalleries
www.facebook.com/OakvilleGalleries
Year Founded: 1974 Contemporary art gallery with 2 exhibition spaces: Oakville Galleries at Centennial Square, 120 Navy St. & Oakville Galleries in Gairloch Gardens, 1306 Lakeshore Rd. East
Matthew Hyland, Director, matthew@oakvillegalleries.com
Marnie Fleming, Curator, Contemporary Art, marnie@oakvillegalleries.com

Ohsweken: Two Turtle Iroquois Fine Art Gallery
c/o Arnold Jacobs, RR#1
Location: Middleport Plaza, Hwy. 54, Middleport, ON
Ohsweken, ON N0A 1M0
Tel: 519-751-2774
twoturtleartgallery@live.ca
www.twoturtle.ca
Year Founded: 1985 Showcasing the art of the Hodenosaunee & Arnold Jacobs.
Arnold Aron Jacobs, Owner

Orillia: Orillia Museum of Art & History (OMAH)
30 Peter St. South
Orillia, ON L3V 5A9
Tel: 705-326-2159
info@orilliamuseum.org
www.orilliamuseum.org
twitter.com/OrilliaMuseum
www.facebook.com/orill iamuseum
Year Founded: 1999 Public art gallery & museum; gift shop; open Tu-Su.
Ninette Gyorody, Executive Director

Orillia: Zephyr Art Gallery
11 Peter St. South
Orillia, ON L3V 5A8
Tel: 705-326-0480
zephyrgallery@yahoo.ca
www.zephyrartgallery.ca
twitter.com/zephyrgallery
www.facebook.com/pag es/Zephyr-Art-Gallery/40388653574
Year Founded: 2000
Paul Baxter, Contact, Operations & Events

Oshawa: The Robert McLaughlin Gallery (RMG)
Civic Centre, 72 Queen St.
Oshawa, ON L1H 3Z3
Tel: 905-576-3000
communications@rmg.on.ca
www.rmg.on.ca
Social Media: www.youtube.com/RMGOshawa
twitter.com/theRMG
www.facebook.com/TheRMG
Year Founded: 1967 Permanent exhibitions include masterpieces of Canadian Art: Emily Carr, members of the Group of Seven, Painters Eleven
Gabrielle Peacock, CEO, gpeacock@rmg.on.ca
Christine Castle, President
Linda Jansma, Senior Curator, ljansma@rmg.on.ca

Ottawa: Artists' Centre d'Artistes Ottawa Inc.
51B Young St.
Ottawa, ON K1S 3H6
Tel: 613-230-2799
office@g101.ca
www.g101.ca
Year Founded: 1979 A non-profit artist operated centre dedicated to the professional presentation & circulation of visual & media arts; solo & curated group exhibitions by local Canadian & international contemporary artists
Laura Margita, Director/Curator, director@g101.ca

Ottawa: Carleton University Art Gallery (CUAG)
Carleton University, St. Patrick's Bldg., 1125 Colonel By Dr.
Ottawa, ON K1S 5B6
Tel: 613-520-2120; Fax: 613-520-4409
cuag.carleton.ca
Social Media: www.youtube.com/user/CUArtGallery
twitter.com/CUArtGallery
www.faceboo k.com/carleton.university.art.gallery
Year Founded: 1992 27,000 works in contemporary Canadian art; European prints & drawings from the 16th to 19th centuries; Inuit prints & sculpture.
Sandra Dyck, Director, sandra.dyck@carleton.ca

Ottawa: Exposure Gallery
Thyme & Again, 1255 Wellington St. West, 2nd Fl.
Ottawa, ON K1Y 3A6
Tel: 604-722-0093
spaoatexposure@gmail.com
www.exposuregallery.info
www.facebook.com/ExposureGallery
Year Founded: 2009 Gallery specializing in fine art photography, located in the second floor studio of Thyme & Again catering & food shop. From 2011 onward the gallery will feature guest curators on a changing basis.

***Ottawa:* Heffel Gallery Ottawa**
451 Daly Ave.
Ottawa, ON K1N 6H6
Tel: 613-230-6505; *Fax:* 613-230-8884
Toll-Free: 866-747-6505
ottawa@heffel.com
www.heffel.com
Fine art auction house, headquartered in Vancouver, BC.
Andrew J.H. Gibbs, Ottawa Representative, andrew@heffel.com

***Ottawa:* Koyman Galleries**
1771 St. Laurent Blvd.
Ottawa, ON K1G 3V4
Tel: 613-526-1562; *Fax:* 613-521-8056
Toll-Free: 877-526-1562
information@koymangalleries.com
www.koymangalleries.co m
Social Media: www.youtube.com/koymangalleries
twitter.com/KoymanGalleries
www.facebook.com/KoymanGalleries
Year Founded: 1965 Work by established & up and coming Canadian artists

***Ottawa:* Orange Art Gallery**
290 City Centre Ave.
Ottawa, ON K1R 7R7
Tel: 613-761-1500
orangeartgallery@bellnet.ca
www.orangeartgallery.ca
www.facebook.com/pages/Orange-Art-Gallery/289138834525530
Year Founded: 2010 Contemporary work from artists in the Ottawa & surrounding areas.
Ingrid Hollander, Owner

***Ottawa:* Ottawa Art Gallery (OAG) / La Galerie d'art d'Ottawa**
Arts Court, 2 Daly Ave.
Ottawa, ON K1N 6E2
Tel: 613-233-8699; *Fax:* 613-569-7660
info@ottawaartgallery.ca
www.ottawaartgallery.ca
twitter.com/OttawaArt G
www.facebook.com/ottawaartgallery
Year Founded: 1988 The galerie's programs include exhibits, lectures, tours & publications.
Alexandra Badzak, Director & CEO, abadzak@ottawaartgallery.ca

***Owen Sound:* Tom Thomson Art Gallery (TTAG)**
840 - 1st Ave. West
Owen Sound, ON N4K 4K4
Tel: 519-376-1932; *Fax:* 519-376-3037
ttag@tomthomson.org
tomthomson.org
Social Media: www.youtube.com/user/TomThomsonArtGallery
twitter.com/TheTomThomson
ww w.facebook.com/331381710714
Year Founded: 1967 Public art gallery featuring an extensive collection of Canadian art, historical & contemporary, with a focus on Thomson & the Group of Seven; full range of educational activities including lectures, workshops, & tours; gallery shop
Virginia Eichhorn, Director/Curator, veichhorn@tomthomson.org

***Peterborough:* Art Gallery of Peterborough**
250 Crescent St.
Peterborough, ON K9J 2G1
Tel: 705-743-9179; *Fax:* 705-743-8168
Toll-Free: 855-738-3755
www.agp.on.ca
www.facebook.com/139384686142024
Year Founded: 1979 Public art gallery with changing exhibitions
Peter Frood, President
Celeste Scopelites, Director, cscopelites@peterborough.ca
Fynn Leitch, Curator

***Peterborough:* Artspace**
PO Box 1748, #3, 378 Aylmer St. North
Peterborough, ON K9J 7X6
Tel: 705-748-3883
gallery@artspace-arc.org
www.artspace-arc.org
Social Media: artspaceptbo.tumblr.com; vimeo.com/artspacearc
www.facebook.com/ARTSPACEptbo
Year Founded: 1974 Committed to supporting the growth & development of contemporary artists & related-art practices; dedicated to artistic freedom & exploration
Fynn Leitch, Director, fynn@artspace-arc.org

***Queenston:* RiverBrink Art Museum**
PO Box 266
Located at 116 Queenston St., Queenston, ON
Queenston, ON L0S 1J0
Tel: 905-262-4510
riverbrink.org
twitter.com/RiverBrinkArt
www.facebook.com/riverbrink.artmuseum
Year Founded: 1981 Open Victoria Day - Thanksgiving
Denis Greenall, President
David Aurandt, Director/Curator, director@riverbrink.org
Debra Antoncic, Associate Curator, curator@riverbrink.org

***St Catharines:* Rodman Hall Art Centre**
109 St. Paul Cres.
St Catharines, ON L2S 1M3
Tel: 905-684-2925; *Fax:* 905-682-4733
rodmanhall@brocku.ca
www.brocku.ca/rodman-hall
Social Media: www.flickr.com/photos/rodmanhall
twitter.com/RodmanHall
www.facebook.c om/286652891904
Collection of about 1000 works of art, contemporary & historical, majority by Canadian artists; closed Mon.
Peter Partridge, Chair
Stuart Reid, Director/Curator, stuart.reid@brocku.ca
Marcie Bronson, Curator, Art/Registrar, mbronson2@brocku.ca

***St Catharines:* TAG Art Gallery**
214 King St.
St Catharines, ON L2R 3J9
Tel: 905-682-5072 *Toll-Free:* 877-682-5072
info@tagartgallery.ca
www.tagartgallery.ca
Social Media: instagram.com/tag_artgallery
twitter.com/TAG_ArtGallery
www.facebook.c om/pages/TAG-Art-Gallery/194823673869376
Tom Goldspink, Founder

***St Thomas:* St Thomas-Elgin Public Art Centre**
301 Talbot St.
St Thomas, ON N5P 1B5
Tel: 519-631-4040
info@stepac.ca
www.stepac.ca
twitter.com/STEPACDOTCA
www.facebook.com/111283576116
Year Founded: 1970 Promotion of visual arts by a permanent collection of over 800 artworks, exhibitions by current artists, & a variety of art education programs; volunteers & new members welcome; facility rental available; open Tu- Su.
Pat Johnson, President
Laura Woermke, Executive Director/Curator, lwoermke@stepac.ca
Sherri Howard, Education Coordinator/Events Coordinator, showard@stepac.ca

***Sarnia:* Judith & Norman Alix Art Gallery**
147 Lochiel St.
Sarnia, ON N7T 0B4
Tel: 519-336-8127; *Fax:* 519-336-8128
www.jnaag.ca
twitter.com/GalleryLambton
www.facebook.com/gallery.lambt on
Year Founded: 1961 Exhibitions of contemporary art, featuring some of the best artists working in Ontario today, many with national & international reputations; collection contains paintings by the Group of Seven, & others, which are important to Canadian art history & are considered national treasures; wide range of changing exhibitions; tours for adults & school groups; education services; artist talks; film; pub
Lisa Daniels, Curator/Director, lisa.daniels@county-lambton.on.ca

***Sault Ste Marie:* Art Gallery of Algoma**
10 East St.
Sault Ste Marie, ON P6A 3C3
Tel: 705-949-9067; *Fax:* 705-949-6261
galleryinfo@artgalleryofalgoma.com
www.artgalleryofalgoma.com
Social Media: www.youtube.com/channel/UCgO-xHc5pCq_we0swCkRwAg
twitter.com/ArtAlgoma
www.facebook.com/pages/Art-Gallery-of-Algoma/263847760317149
Year Founded: 1975 Dedicated to cultivating & advancing the awareness of visual arts in Sault Ste Marie & the district of Algoma; open year round
Heather-Ann Mendes, Chair, hamendes@saultlawyers.com
Jasmina Jovanovic, Director, jasmina@artgalleryofalgoma.com

***Simcoe:* Norfolk Arts Centre**
Lynnwood Historic Site, 21 Lynnwood Ave.
Simcoe, ON N3Y 2v7
Tel: 519-428-0540
norfolkartscentre@norfolkcounty.ca
www.norfolkartscentre.ca
twitter.com/NorfolkArts
www.facebook.com/Norf olkArtsCentre
Norfolk county's only arts centre, located in downtown Simcoe; programming includes exhibitions, kids studio, adult art workshops, Lynnwood's Film Simcoe, annual drive-thru art gallery exhibition
Deirdre Chisholm, Curator/Director

***Southampton:* Southampton Art Gallery**
201 High St.
Southampton, ON N0H 2L0
Tel: 519-797-5068 *Toll-Free:* 800-806-8838
info@southamptonart.com
www.southamptonart.com
Year Founded: 1999 Exhibits handmade work by local artists
April Patry, Director

***Stouffville:* The Latcham Gallery**
6240 Main St.
Stouffville, ON L4A 7Z4
Tel: 905-640-8954; *Fax:* 905-640-6246
info@latchamgallery.ca
www.latchamgallery.ca
Social Media: www.youtube.com/user/latchamgallery
www.facebook.com/pages/The-Latcham-G allery/103279314716
Year Founded: 1979 Public art gallery
Roz Pritchard, Director
Chai Duncan, Curator

***Stratford:* Gallery Stratford**
54 Romeo St. South
Stratford, ON N5A 4S9
Tel: 519-271-5271; *Fax:* 519-271-1642
info@gallerystratford.on.ca
www.gallerystratford.on.ca
Social Media: www.linkedin.com/company/gallery-stratford
twitter.com/GalleryStrtfrd
www.facebook.com/pages/Gallery-Stratford/2804 1706502
Year Founded: 1967 A non-profit, public art gallery open year round; contemporary, historical, local, national & international artists are highlighted annually in the heritage building; offers educational programs, workshops & fundraisers
Matthew Rees, President
Aidan Ware, Director & Curator, aware@gallerystratford.on.ca

***Sudbury:* Art Gallery of Sudbury / Galerie d'art de Sudbury**
251 John St.
Sudbury, ON P3E 1P9
Tel: 705-675-4871; *Fax:* 705-674-3065
gallery@artsudbury.org
www.artsudbury.org
twitter.com/ArtSudbury
www .facebook.com/artsudbury
Year Founded: 1967 Historical & contemporary Canadian art; hours: Tu-Sa 10:00-5:00, Su 12:00-5:00
Karen Tait-Peacock, Director, ktait@artsudbury.org

***Sutton:* Georgina Arts Centre & Gallery**
PO Box 1455
Located at 149 High St., Sutton, ON
Sutton, ON L0E 1R0
Tel: 905-722-9587
gac@gacag.com
www.gacag.com
www.facebook.com/GACAG
Heather Fullerton, Executive Director

***Thornhill:* Gallery M**
7039 Yonge St.
Thornhill, ON L3T 2A6
Tel: 905-597-7837
info@gallerym.ca
gallerym.ca
Year Founded: 2013 Contemporary art gallery, with a focus on unconventional pieces.
Janet Park, Director

***Thunder Bay:* Ahnisnabae Art Gallery**
269 Red River Rd.
Thunder Bay, ON P7B 1A9
Tel: 807-577-2656; *Fax:* 807-577-2656
www.ahnisnabae-art.com
Year Founded: 1997 First Nations artwork
Louise Thomas, Owner, louisethomas@ahnisnabae-art.com

Thunder Bay: Thunder Bay Art Gallery
PO Box 10193, 1080 Keewatin St.
Thunder Bay, ON P7B 6T7
Tel: 807-577-6427; *Fax:* 807-577-3781
info@theag.ca
www.theag.ca
www.facebook.com/pages/Thunder-Bay-Art-Gallery/129041813492
Year Founded: 1976 Collection & exhibition of contemporary First Nations art, regional & international exhibits
Sharon Godwin, Director, segodwin@theag.ca
Nadia Kurd, Curator, curator@theag.ca
Heidi Uhlig, President

Toronto: Angell Gallery
12 Ossington Ave.
Toronto, ON M6J 2Y7
Tel: 416-530-0444
info@angellgallery.com
www.angellgallery.com
www.facebook.com/pages/Angell-Gallery/256380025273
Year Founded: 1996 W-Sa 12:00-5:00
Jamie Angell, Director/Owner
Joey Chiu, Gallery Manager

Toronto: Annex Art Centre
1075 Bathurst St.
Toronto, ON M5R 3G8
Tel: 416-433-8373
annexartcentre@gmail.com
annexartcentre.com
Social Media: instagram.com/annexartcentre
www.facebook.com/AnnexArtCentre
Art gallery & teaching studio located in Toronto's Annex, offering visual art & drama for kids, teens, & adults.

Toronto: Art Dialogue Gallery
#501, 900 Yonge St.
Toronto, ON M4W 3P5
Tel: 416-928-5904
Provides educated information & guidance in acquiring fine art; exhibitions & consultations for the display of artwork; lectures on various topics of contemporary art
Luciana Benzi, Director

Toronto: Art Gallery of York University (AGYU)
Accolade East Bldg., 4700 Keele St.
Toronto, ON M3J 1P3
Tel: 416-736-5169
agyu@yorku.ca
theagyuisoutthere.org/everywhere
Devoted to the presentation of innovative contemporary art; aims to situate Canadian art within an international context & to introduce Canadian audiences to important artists working abroad
Philip Monk, Director, pmonk@yorku.ca
Emelie Chhangur, Assistant Director/Curator, emelie@yorku.ca

Toronto: The Art Gallery, Neilson Park Creative Centre
56 Neilson Dr.
Toronto, ON M9C 1V7
Tel: 416-622-5294; *Fax:* 416-622-0892
info@neilsonparkcreativecentre.com
www.neilsonparkcreativecentre.com
w ww.facebook.com/122065277825690
Provides a community focus for creative visual arts; variety of exhibitions with strong emphasis on local & contemporary artists
Kathleen Haushalter, President
Cathy Frank, Manager, Gallery

Toronto: Art Metropole
1490 Dundas St. West
Toronto, ON M6K 1T5
Tel: 416-703-4400; *Fax:* 416-703-4404
info@artmetropole.com
www.artmetropole.com
Social Media: artmetropole.blogspot.ca
twitter.com/ArtMetropole
www.facebook.com/354 88411573
Year Founded: 1974 Specializes in contemporary art in multiple formats; offers artists' products for sale on premises & through web site as well as publishes, promotes, exhibits & distributes artists' products in various formats
Corinn Gerber, Director, corinn@artmetropole.com

Toronto: Art Yard
30 Abell St.
Toronto, ON M6J 0A9
Tel: 416-659-3077
Www.artyard.ca
Social Media: www.pinterest.com/artyard0253
twitter.com/ArtYard_Gallery
Www.facebook .com/artyardgallery
A concept gallery that features work by new & mid-career local artists.
Natasza Cieplik, Gallery Director

Toronto: AWOL Gallery
#76-78 Ossington Ave.
Toronto, ON M6J 2Y7
Tel: 416-535-5637; *Fax:* 416-535-0787
awol@awolgallery.com
www.awolgallery.com
twitter.com/AWOLGallery
Year Founded: 1999
Nurit Basin, Co-Founder

Toronto: Baffin Inuit Art Gallery
120 Portland St.
Toronto, ON M5V 2N5
Tel: 416-931-3540*Toll-Free:* 877-326-9700
info@baffininuitart.com
www.baffininuitart.com
Year Founded: 1987 Preserves & exhibits art created by First Nations from Cape Dorset on Baffin Island.
Darrell Brown, President, dbrown@bezpalabrown.com
Lyudmila Bezpala-Brown, Gallery Director, mila@bezpalabrown.com

Toronto: Bezpala Brown Gallery
17 Church St.
Toronto, ON M5E 1M2
Tel: 416-907-6875
info@bezpalabrown.com
www.bezpalabrown.com
twitter.com/bezpalabrown
www.facebook.com/1453664 15531583
Year Founded: 2010 The gallery exhibits Canadian & Eastern European art.

Toronto: The Bluffs Gallery
***Parent:* Scarborough Arts**
Scarborough Arts, 1859 Kingston Rd.
Toronto, ON M1N 1T3
Tel: 416-698-7322; *Fax:* 416-698-7972
info@scarborougharts.com
www.scarborougharts.com
Social Media: www.youtube.com/scarborougharts
twitter.com/scararts
www.facebook.com/ scarborougharts
Year Founded: 1979 The Bluffs Gallery is dedicated to the exhibition & sale of artwork by Scarborough Arts members. The Gallery offers solo & group exhibitions of all arts media, special events, workshops, & city-wide programs to promote the arts. Open Monday - Saturday; Closed on long weekends.
Daniel Broome, Chair
Jen Fabico, Program Director, programs@scarborougharts.com

Toronto: Canadian Fine Arts (CFA)
577 Mount Pleasant Rd.
Toronto, ON M4S 2M5
Tel: 416-544-8806
canadianfinearts@rogers.com
canadianfinearts.com
twitter.com/PaintingSales
www.facebook.com/pages/ CFA-Gallery/221698531249646
Year Founded: 2000 Artwork by Canadian masters

Toronto: Cedar Ridge Creative Centre
225 Confederation Dr.
Toronto, ON M1G 1B2
Tel: 416-396-4026
crcc@toronto.ca
www.toronto.ca/culture/cedar_ridge/index.htm
www.facebook.com/cedarridge creativecentre
Year Founded: 1912 An arts hub housed in a 1912 mansion. Art exhibitions are featured in the ground floor gallery from Sept.-June.

Toronto: Christopher Cutts Gallery
21 Morrow Ave.
Toronto, ON M6R 2H9
Tel: 416-532-5566; *Fax:* 416-532-7272
info@cuttsgallery.com
www.cuttsgallery.com
Year Founded: 1986 The gallery exhibits art by well known Canadian & international artists.
Christopher Cutts, Director

Toronto: Communication Art Gallery
209 Harbord St.
Toronto, ON M5S 1H6
Tel: 416-588-2011
contact@communicationgallery.net
www.communicationgallery.net
twitter.com/CommunicateART
www.facebook.c om/Communicationartgallery
Year Founded: 2010

Toronto: Corkin Gallery
7 Tank House Lane
Toronto, ON M5A 3C4
Tel: 416-979-1980
info@corkingallery.com
www.corkingallery.com
Social Media: instagram.com/corkin_gallery
twitter.com/corkingallery
www.facebook.co m/corkingallery
Year Founded: 1978 Eclectic works by contemporary artists in all media
Jane Corkin, Owner

Toronto: Creative Spirit Art Centre (CSAC)
999 Dovercourt Rd.
Toronto, ON M6H 2X7
Tel: 416-588-8801; *Fax:* 416-588-8966
csac@creativespirit.on.ca
creativespirit.on.ca
Social Media: instagram.com/CSACDovercourt
twitter.com/ACreativeSpirit
www.facebook. com/299210340430
Year Founded: 1992 Arts & Disabilities - Public Art Gallery/Studio, resource and information centre. Monthly exhibitions - Special area of collection of Art Brut, Outsider Art, Folk Art - Integrated exhibitions of Art produced by Artists with disabilities and Artists without disabilities.
Ellen Anderson, Director

Toronto: de luca fine art gallery (DFLA)
217 Avenue Rd.
Toronto, ON M5R 2J3
Tel: 416-537-4699
info@delucafineart.com
www.delucafineart.com
twitter.com/delucafineart
www.facebook.com/pages /de-luca-fine-art/152695608225013
Year Founded: 2004
Corrado De Luca, Director, corrado@delucafineart.com

Toronto: DISH GALLERY + STUDIO
#112, 15 Case Goods Lane
Toronto, ON M5A 3C4
Tel: 416-700-3474
www.dishgalleryandstudio.com
www.facebook.com/pages/DISH-GALLERY-Studio/274760405892264
Year Founded: 2006 The gallery exhibits handmade sculptures & pottery
Susan Card, Contact, susan.l.card@gmail.com

Toronto: Doris McCarthy Gallery (DMG)
University of Toronto Scarborough, 1265 Military Trail
Toronto, ON M1C 1A4
Tel: 416-287-7007
dmg@utsc.utoronto.ca
www.utsc.utoronto.ca/~dmg
twitter.com/DMG_UTSC
www.facebook.com/DorisM cCarthyGallery
Year Founded: 2004 The gallery seeks to display works in all media forms by contemporary Canadian & international artists. Open W-F 10:00-4:00, Sa 12:00-5:00.
Ann MacDonald, Director/Curator, amacdonald@utsc.utoronto.ca

Toronto: Edward Day Gallery
#200, 952 Queen St. West
Toronto, ON M6J 1G8
Tel: 416-921-6540
info@edwarddaygallery.com
www.edwarddaygallery.com
Social Media: www.youtube.com/user/EdwardDayGallery
twitter.com/marysuerankin
www.facebook.com/pages/Edward-Day-Gallery/187160541302483
Year Founded: 1992 The gallery houses contemporary art from Canadian & international artists.
Mary Sue Rankin, Director/Owner

***Toronto:* Eric Arthur Gallery**
John H. Daniels Faculty of Architecture, University of Toronto, 230 College St., Main Fl.
Toronto, ON M5T 1R2
www.daniels.utoronto.ca
Year Founded: 2001 Architecture, landscape & urban design exhibits.

***Toronto:* The Eskimo Art Gallery**
#220, 8 Case Goods Lane
Toronto, ON M5A 3C4
Tel: 416-366-3000*Toll-Free:* 888-238-5442
info@eskimoart.com
www.eskimoart.com
www.facebook.com/pages/Eskimo-Art-Gallery-Inuit-Art/187820091804
Year Founded: 1981 Contemporary Inuit art

***Toronto:* Etobicoke Civic Centre Art Gallery**
399 The West Mall
Toronto, ON M9C 2Y2
Tel: 416-394-8628; *Fax:* 416-394-2455
eccartgallery@toronto.ca
www.toronto.ca
The gallery hosts monthly exhibits & juried art shows.

***Toronto:* Feheley Fine Arts**
65 George St.
Toronto, ON M5A 4L8
Tel: 416-323-1373; *Fax:* 647-361-7667
Toll-Free: 877-904-9114
gallery@feheleyfinearts.com
www.feheleyfinearts.com
Social Media: www.youtube.com/user/FeheleyFineArts/feed
twitter.com/FeheleyFineArts
www.facebook.com/FeheleyFineArts
Year Founded: 1961 The gallery exhibits Inuit artwork

***Toronto:* Gabor Mezei Studio**
587 Markham St.
Toronto, ON M6G 2L7
Tel: 416-534-9800
gallerygabor@gmail.com
www.gallerygabor.com
www.facebook.com/GalleryGaborArtforYourWalls
Other contact information: Mobile: 647-857-0914
Year Founded: 1977 Small art gallery showing mainly the owner's work & a small selection of Canadian & international artists; approximately four exhibitions per year; by appt.
Gabor P. Mezei, Director/Curator

***Toronto:* LE Gallery (GAS)**
1183 Dundas St. West
Toronto, ON M6J 1X3
Tel: 416-532-8467
info@le-gallery.ca
le-gallery.ca
www.facebook.com/LE.gallery
Year Founded: 2003 Contemporary art gallery for new & mid-career artists
Wil Kucey, Director

***Toronto:* Gallery Arcturus**
80 Gerrard St. East
Toronto, ON M5B 1G6
Tel: 416-977-1077; *Fax:* 416-977-1066
ob-art@arcturus.ca
www.arcturus.ca
Social Media: www.youtube.com/user/GalleryArcturus
twitter.com/GalleryArcturus
www.f acebook.com/pages/Gallery-Arcturus/752363494784993
Other contact information: Alternate E-mail: info@arcturus.ca
Contemporary art gallery.
Eron Boyd, Gallery Manager
Cathy Stilo, Curator
Deborah Harris, Artist-in-Residence

***Toronto:* Gallery at Next**
#102B, 219 Dufferin St.
Toronto, ON M6K 3J1
Tel: 416-646-0460
galleryatnext.ca
Social Media: instagram.com/galleryatnext
twitter.com/GalleryatNext
www.facebook.com /artatnext
Contemporary art gallery
Alexandre Legault, Co-Owner
Jonathan Girard, Co-Owner

***Toronto:* Gallery Catalyst**
Toronto, ON
Tel: 647-297-3482
info@gallerycatalyst.com
gallerycatalyst.ca
Social Media: www.youtube.com/gallerycatalyst
twitter.com/GalleryCatalyst
www.facebo ok.com/GalleryCatalyst
Year Founded: 2013 Contemporary art gallery

***Toronto:* Gallery on Wade**
#302, 87 Wade Ave.
Toronto, ON M6H 1P5
Tel: 647-494-9633
info@galleryonwade.com
www.galleryonwade.com
Social Media: pinterest.com/galleryonwade
twitter.com/GalleryonWade
www.facebook.com /pages/Gallery-on-Wade/438339906272813
Hosts art viewing events.

***Toronto:* Gallery TPW**
1256 Dundas St. West
Toronto, ON M6J 1X5
Tel: 416-645-1066; *Fax:* 416-645-1681
info@gallerytp.ca
gallerytpw.ca
twitter.com/GalleryTPW
www.facebook. com/GalleryTPW.Toronto
Year Founded: 1977 Contemporary photography by Canadian & international artists.
Gary Hall, Executive Director, gary@gallerytpw.ca
Kim Simon, Curator, kim@gallerytpw.ca

***Toronto:* Gerrard Art Space (GAS)**
1390 Gerrard St. East
Toronto, ON M4L 1Z4
Tel: 416-778-0923
gerrardartspace@gmail.com
gerrardartspace.com

***Toronto:* Glendon Gallery / Galerie Glendon**
Glendon Hall, Glendon College, York University, 2275 Bayview Ave.
Toronto, ON M4N 3M6
Tel: 416-487-6721
artculture@glendon.yorku.ca
www.glendon.yorku.ca/gallery
www.facebook.com/pages/Galerie-Glendon-Gallery/85509681583
University-affiliated public art gallery that focuses on contemporary Canadian art of merit with an added interest in francophone artistic expression; literature in French & English; guided tours & lectures
Martine Rheault, Coordinator, Cultural & Artistic Affairs
Marc Audette, Gallery Curator

***Toronto:* Heffel Gallery Inc.**
13 Hazelton Ave.
Toronto, ON M5R 2E1
Tel: 416-961-6505; *Fax:* 416-961-4245
Toll-Free: 866-961-6505
mail@heffel.com
www.heffel.com
Year Founded: 2002 Fine art auction house, headquartered in Vancouver, BC.
David K.J. Heffel, President, david@heffel.com
Judith Scolnick, Director, Toronto Office, judith@heffel.com

***Toronto:* InterAccess Electronic Media Arts Centre (I/A)**
9 Ossington Ave.
Toronto, ON M6J 2Y8
Tel: 416-532-0597
info@interaccess.org
www.interaccess.org
Social Media: www.youtube.com/user/interaccessTO
twitter.com/InterAccessTO
www.faceb ook.com/InterAccessTO
Year Founded: 1983 New media exhibitions.
Laura Berazadi, Executive Director, laura.berazadi@interaccess.org

***Toronto:* Joseph D. Carrier Art Gallery**
Columbus Centre, 901 Lawrence Ave. West
Toronto, ON M6A 1C3
Tel: 416-789-7011; *Fax:* 416-789-3951
www.villacharities.com/carrier
Year Founded: 1987 Third largest public art gallery in Toronto; features contemporary photography, painting, sculpture, & design.

***Toronto:* The Justina M. Barnicke Gallery**
Hart House, University of Toronto, 7 Hart House Circle
Toronto, ON M5S 3H3
Tel: 416-978-8398; *Fax:* 416-978-8387
jmb.gallery@utoronto.ca
www.jmbgallery.ca
www.facebook.com/justinambar nickegallery
Year Founded: 1982 Each year, 8-10 exhibitions are mounted featuring contemporary Canadian artists as well as historical exhibitions
Barbara Fischer, Executive Director/Chief Curator, barbara.fischer@utoronto.ca
Wanda Nanibush, Curator-in-Residence, wnanibush@gmail.com

***Toronto:* Knight Galleries International**
472 Coldstream Ave.
Toronto, ON M5N 1Y5
Tel: 416-923-0836
www.knightgall.com
The galleries specialize in contemporary international prints & paintings, as well as South African contemporary artwork & beadwork. There are two locations: Toronto, Canada, & Johannesburg, South Africa.
Julian Liknaitzky, President, 416-566-9027, julian@knightgalleries.net
Natalie Knight, Contact, The Art Source, Johannesburg, South Africa, 011-485-3606, Fax: 011-485-3614, nknight@icon.co.za

***Toronto:* Koffler Gallery/Koffler Centre of the Arts**
Artscape Youngplace, #104-105, 180 Shaw St.
Toronto, ON M6J 2W5
Tel: 647-925-0643
info@kofflerarts.org
kofflerarts.org
Social Media: www.youtube.com/user/KofflerArts
twitter.com/KofflerArts
www.facebook.com/KofflerArts
Year Founded: 1977 The Koffler Gallery maintains a year-round exhibition program of contemporary art; programming emphasizes new work by mid-career & more senior Canadian artists, & within this context, work of special interest to the Jewish community
Tiana Koffler Boyman, Chair
Mona Filip, Curator/Director, Koffler Gallery, mfilip@kofflerarts.org
Cathy Jonasson, Executive Director, cjonasson@kofflerarts.org

***Toronto:* KUMF Gallery**
#204, 2118A Bloor St. West
Toronto, ON M6S 1M8
Tel: 416-766-6802
info@kumfgallery.com
kumfgallery.com
www.facebook.co m/kumfartgallery
Year Founded: 1975 Exhibits work of by artists of Ukranian descent.
Taissa Matiashek-Ruzycky, President

***Toronto:* Le Labo**
568 Richmond St. West
Toronto, ON M5V 1Y9
Tel: 647-352-4411
info@lelabo.ca
www.lelabo.ca
Social Media: instagram.com/le_labo_artmedia
twitter.com/Le_Laboratoire_
www.faceboo k.com/lelabotoronto
Year Founded: 2004 Le Labo is a Toronto-based organization that produces & hosts French media arts projects.
Clelia Farrugia, Executive Director

***Toronto:* Larry Wayne Richards Project Gallery**
John H. Daniels Faculty of Architecture, University of Toronto, 230 College St., Main Fl.
Toronto, ON M5T 1R2
www.daniels.utoronto.ca
Year Founded: 2001 Ongoing & recently completed student projects.

***Toronto:* Liss Gallery**
140 Yorkville Ave.
Toronto, ON M5R 1C2
Tel: 416-787-9872; *Fax:* 416-787-6843
info@lissgallery.com
www.lissgallery.com
twitter.com/LissGallery
www .facebook.com/LissGallery
Year Founded: 1983 Contemporary art gallery houses paintings, photographs, sculptures & prints
Brian Liss, Consultant

Toronto: Loch Gallery Toronto
16 Hazelton Ave.
Toronto, ON M5R 2E2
Tel: 416-964-9050
www.lochgallery.com
Year Founded: 2003 Work by Canadian & European artists both contemporary & historical.
Alan Loch, Manager

Toronto: The Market Gallery
South St. Lawrence Market, 95 Front St. East, 2nd Fl.
Toronto, ON M5E 1C2
Tel: 416-392-7604; _Fax:_ 416-392-0572
marketgallery@toronto.ca
www.toronto.ca
www.facebook.com/TorontoMarket Gallery
Year Founded: 1979 A focus on the art & history of Toronto

Toronto: Mercer Union, A Centre for Contemporary Visual Art
1286 Bloor St. West
Toronto, ON M6H 1N9
Tel: 416-536-1519; _Fax:_ 416-536-2955
office@mercerunion.org
www.mercerunion.org
www.facebook.com/1238236576 40991
Year Founded: 1979 An artist-run centre dedicated to the existence of contemporary art; provides a forum for the production & exhibition of Canadian & international conceptually & aesthetically engaging art & related cultural practices; pursues primary concerns through critical activities that include exhibitions, lectures, screenings, performances, publications, events & special projects; non-profit, charitable organization.
York Lethbridge, Director, Operations & Development, york@mercerunion.org
Georgina Jackson, Director, Exhibitions & Publications, georgina@mercerunion.org

Toronto: MJG Gallery
1028 Queen St. East
Toronto, ON M4M 1K4
Tel: 416-923-4031
www.facebook.com/238062092892271
Year Founded: 2011 Artwork by Toronto artists
Mark Gleberzon, Owner

Toronto: Museum of Contemporary Canadian Art (MOCCA)
952 Queen St. West
Toronto, ON M6J 1G8
Tel: 416-395-0067
info@mocca.ca
www.mocca.ca
Social Media: www.youtube.com/moccatoronto
twitter.com/MOCCA_TO
www.facebook.com/MOC CA.Toronto
Year Founded: 1999 Contemporary Canadian artists' works, including traditional & new media; six exhibitions a year showcase established & emerging artists from across Canada; exhibition based programming; open Tue.-Sun., 11-6; free admission; groups & tours by appt.
Julia Ouellette, Chair
David Liss, Artistic Director/Curator

Toronto: Museum of Inuit Art (MIA)
207 Queen's Quay West
Toronto, ON M5J 1A7
Tel: 416-640-1571
contact@miamuseum.ca
miamuseum.ca
Social Media: www.youtube.com/user/miamuseum
twitter.com/miamuseum
www.facebook.com/museumofinuitart
The only museum in Canada dedicated to art made by Inuit within the country.
Brittany Holliss, Manager, Operations
Lauren Williams, Manager, Collections

Toronto: Navillus Gallery
110 Davenport Rd.
Toronto, ON M5R 3R3
Tel: 416-921-6467
inquire@navillusgallery.com
www.navillusgallery.com
Social Media: navillusgallery.tumblr.com
twitter.com/navillusgallery
www.facebook.co m/navillusgallery
Year Founded: 2011 Artwork by established & emerging artists
Katie Robertson, Gallery Manager, krobertson@navillusgallery.com

Toronto: Norman Felix Gallery
445 Adelaide St. West
Toronto, ON M5V 1T1
Tel: 416-366-6676; _Fax:_ 416-366-6686
art@normanfelix.com
www.normanfelix.com
twitter.com/normanfelixart
w ww.facebook.com/normanfelixgallery
Year Founded: 2006 Contemporary visual work by new & established artists.

Toronto: Odon Wagner Contemporary
198 Davenport Rd.
Toronto, ON M5R 1J2
Tel: 416-962-0438; _Fax:_ 416-962-1581
Toll-Free: 800-551-2465
info@odonwagnergallery.com
www.odonwagnergallery.com/o wc_home.php
Social Media: odonwagnercontemporary.tumblr.com
twitter.com/owgallery
www.facebook.com/odonwagnergallery
Year Founded: 1969 Specializes in paintings, sculpture, & prints by Canadian & international artists.
Odon Wagner, Contact, odon@odonwagnergallery.com

Toronto: Odon Wagner Gallery
196 Davenport Rd.
Toronto, ON M5R 1J2
Tel: 416-962-0438; _Fax:_ 416-962-1581
Toll-Free: 800-551-2465
info@odonwagnergallery.com
www.odonwagnergallery.com/o wg_home.php
Social Media: odonwagnercontemporary.tumblr.com
twitter.com/owgallery
www.facebook.com/odonwagnergallery
Year Founded: 1969 Fine art gallery featuring masterpieces of past & present; sale & purchase of quality paintings, restoration, appraisal, consultation & framing services
Odon Wagner, Director, odon@odonwagnergallery.com

Toronto: Olga Korper Gallery Inc.
17 Morrow Ave.
Toronto, ON M6R 2H9
Tel: 416-538-8220; _Fax:_ 416-538-8772
info@olgakorpergallery.com
www.olgakorpergallery.com
www.facebook.com/pages/Olga-Korper-Gallery/142055022532758
Year Founded: 1973 The gallery exists to exhibit & promote Canadian & international contemporary art
Shelli Cassidy-McIntosh, Executive Director
Olga Korper, Director
Sasha Korper, Director

Toronto: Onsite [at] OCAD University
230 Richmond St. West
Toronto, ON M5V 3E5
Tel: 416-977-6006
onsite@ocadu.ca
www.ocadu.ca/onsite
twitter.com/ONSI TEatOCADU
www.facebook.com/OnsiteOCADU
Year Founded: 2007 Professional gallary at OCAD U, exhibits work by national & international artists
Lisa Smith, Acting Curator

Toronto: Open Studio
#104, 401 Richmond St. West
Toronto, ON M5V 3A8
Tel: 416-504-8238; _Fax:_ 416-504-8238
www.openstudio.on.ca
Social Media: www.youtube.com/user/OpenStudioTO
twitter.com/openstudioTO
www.faceboo k.com/OpenStudioPrintmakingCentre
An artist-run centre that seeks to produce, preserve & promote contemporary printmaking practice.
Jennifer Bhogal, Executive Director

Toronto: Pentimento Fine Art Gallery
1164 Queen St. East
Toronto, ON M4M 1L4
Tel: 416-406-6772
www.pentimento.ca
www.facebook.com/209919509047567
Year Founded: 2006

Toronto: The Power Plant Contemporary Art Gallery at Harbourfront Centre
231 Queens Quay West
Toronto, ON M5J 2G8
Tel: 416-973-4949
info@thepowerplant.org
www.thepowerplant.org
Social Media: vimeo.com/thepowerplant
twitter.com/ThePowerPlantTO
www.facebook.com/ThePowerPlantContemporaryAr tGallery
Year Founded: 1987 Exclusively promotes Canadian contemporary art through exhibitions, publications & public programming.
Margaret McNee, President
Gaëtane Verna, Director

Toronto: Project Gallery
1109 Queen St. East
Toronto, ON M4M 1K7
Tel: 416-890-5051
info@projectgallerytoronto.com
projectgallerytoronto.com
Social Media: instagram.com/projectgallerytoronto
twitter.com/ProjectGalleryT
www.fa cebook.com/Projectgallerytoronto
Year Founded: 2013 Contemporary art gallery
Devan Patel, Co-Founder
Callen Schaub, Co-Founder
Alex Buchanan, Co-Founder

Toronto: Propeller Centre for the Visual Arts
984 Queen St. West
Toronto, ON M6J 1H1
Tel: 416-504-7142
propellerctr.com
www.facebook.com/PropellerTO
Year Founded: 1997

Toronto: p|m Gallery
1518 Dundas St. West
Toronto, ON M6K 1T9
Tel: 416-937-3862
pmgallery.ca
twitter.com/pmgallery1518
Year Founded: 2004
Powell MacDougall, Founder

Toronto: Ryerson Image Centre (RIC)
33 Gould St.
Toronto, ON M5B 2K3
Tel: 416-979-5164
ric@ryerson.ca
www.ryerson.ca/ric
Social Media: www.vimeo.com/user4159523
twitter.com/RICgallery
www.facebook.com/ryersonimagecentre
Year Founded: 2012 Contemporary Canadian & international artwork.
Paul Roth, Director, paul.roth@ryerson.ca

Toronto: A Space Gallery
#110, 401 Richmond St. West
Toronto, ON M5V 3A8
Tel: 416-979-9633; _Fax:_ 416-979-9683
info@aspacegallery.org
www.aspacegallery.org
www.facebook.com/pages/A- Space-Gallery/130666663707397
Year Founded: 1971 A Space has a thirty year history of multi-disciplinary artist-run activity. The organizations' mandate encompasses the investigation, presentation & interpretation of contemporary art forms, different disciplines & theories. A Space maintains a politically engaged issue oriented programming that is inclusive of a wide range of media, disciplines & views.
Rebecca McGowan, Executive Director
Vicky Moufwad-Paul, Artistic Director

Toronto: Stephen Bulger Gallery
1026 Queen St. West
Toronto, ON M6J 1H6
Tel: 416-504-0575; _Fax:_ 416-504-8929
info@bulgergallery.com
www.bulgergallery.com
www.facebook.com/BulgerGa llery
Year Founded: 1994 Exhibits photographs from Canada & international countries
Stephen Bulger, President

***Toronto:* Susan Hobbs Gallery**
137 Tecumseth St.
Toronto, ON M6J 2H2
Tel: 416-504-3699; *Fax:* 416-504-8064
info@susanhobbs.com
www.susanhobbs.com
www.facebook.com/48701573223
Year Founded: 1993 Exhibition & sales of contemporary Canadian art; artists represented include Ian Carr-Harris, Magdalen Celestino, Robin Collyer, Max Dean, Brian Groombridge, Scott Lyall, Arnaud Maggs, Liz Magor, Sandra Meigs, Colette Whiten, Robert Wiens, Shirley Wiitasalo, & Kevin Yates

***Toronto:* TD Bank Inuit Art Collection**
79 Wellington St. West
Toronto, ON M5K 1A2
Tel: 416-982-8473
art.td.com
Year Founded: 1987 Open daily.

***Toronto:* Telephone Booth Gallery**
3148 Dundas St. West
Toronto, ON M6P 2A1
Tel: 647-270-7903
www.telephoneboothgallery.ca
twitter.com/TBoothGallery
www.facebook.com/pages/Telephone-Booth-Gallery/138897496155128
Year Founded: 2010 Contemporary Canadian & international art
Sharlene Rankin, Gallery Director, sharlene@telephoneboothgallery.ca

***Toronto:* Thompson Landry Gallery Stone Distillery**
32 Distillery Lane
Toronto, ON M5A 3C4
Tel: 416-364-4955*Toll-Free:* 416-364-4866
info@thompsonlandry.com
www.thompsonlandry.com
twitter.com/ThompsonLan dry
www.facebook.com/128159643919824
Year Founded: 2006 Work by Québec artists

***Toronto:* Thompson Landry Gallery The Cooperage**
6 Trinity St.
Toronto, ON M5A 3C4
Tel: 416-364-4955*Toll-Free:* 416-364-4866
info@thompsonlandry.com
www.thompsonlandry.com
Year Founded: 2009 Work by Québec artists

***Toronto:* Toronto Free Gallery (TFG)**
1277 Bloor St. West
Toronto, ON M4E 2J8
Tel: 416-913-0461
torontofreegallery.org
www.facebook.com/pages/Toronto-Free-Gallery/124361940976535
Year Founded: 2004 Art that revolves around the subjects of social justice, cultural, sustainability & environmental.
Heather Haynes, Founder & Executive Director, heather@torontofreegallery.org

***Toronto:* Twist Gallery**
1100 Queen St. West
Toronto, ON M6J 1H9
Tel: 416-588-2222
info@twistgallery.ca
www.twistgallery.ca
Social Media: pinterest.com/TwistGallery
twitter.com/TwistGallery
www.facebook.com/TwistGallery
Year Founded: 2010
Nadia Kakridonis, Director, nadia@twistgallery.ca

***Toronto:* University of Toronto Art Centre**
University College, 15 King's College Circle
Toronto, ON M5S 3H7
Tel: 416-978-1838
www.utac.utoronto.ca
twitter.com/utac
www.facebook.com/UofTArtCentre
Year Founded: 1996 Housing galleries with selections from university collections as well as a schedule of changing exhibitions
Diana Bennett, Chair
Barbara Fischer, Director/Chief Curator, 416-978-2453, barbara.fischer@utoronto.ca
Heather Darling Pigat, Collections Manager, 416-946-7090, heather.pigat@utoronto.ca

***Toronto:* Urban Gallery**
400 Queen St. East
Toronto, ON M5A 1T3
Tel: 647-270-7903
urbangalleryart1@gmail.com
urbangallery.ca
Social Media: www.pinterest.com/urbangallery400
www.facebook.com/pages/Urban-Gallery/3 29901097131926
Year Founded: 2012

***Toronto:* V Tape**
#452, 401 Richmond St. West
Toronto, ON M5V 3A8
Tel: 416-351-1317; *Fax:* 416-351-1509
info@vtape.org
www.vtape.org
V Tape houses a collection of Canadian video art projects with over 3,500 tapes & other works.

***Toronto:* Wellington Street Art Gallery**
270 Wellington St. West
Toronto, ON M5V 3P5
Tel: 647-352-3463
wellington.street.art.gallery@gmail.com
www.wellingtonstreetartgallery.c a
www.facebook.com/111931708886789
Year Founded: 2011 Canadian contemporary & abstract art.

***Toronto:* York Quay Gallery**
Harbourfront Centre, 235 Queens Quay West
Toronto, ON M5J 2G8
Tel: 416-973-4600; *Fax:* 416-973-6055
info@harbourfrontcentre.com
www.harbourfrontcentre.com
Contemporary art at Toronto's Harbourfront Centre.

***Toronto:* YYZ Artists' Outlet**
#140, 401 Richmond St. West
Toronto, ON M5V 3A8
Tel: 416-598-4546; *Fax:* 416-598-2282
yyz@yyzartistsoutlet.org
www.yyzartistsoutlet.org
twitter.com/YYZ_YYZB OOKS
www.facebook.com/yyzartistsoutlet
Year Founded: 1979 YYZ is dedicated to the support of work by contemporary artists working in all media, & to the provision of a venue for the exhibition of this work through on-going programs in both visual & time-based arts - video, film & performance.
Darryl Bank, Chair, bod@yyzartistsoutlet.org
Ana Barajas, Director, abarajas@yyzartistsoutlet.org

***Unionville:* Varley Art Gallery of Markham & McKay Art Centre**
216 Main St.
Unionville, ON L3R 2H1
Tel: 905-477-7000; *Fax:* 905-477-6629
varley@markham.ca
www.varleygallery.ca
twitter.com/VarleyGallery
www .facebook.com/VarleyGallery
Named after Frederick Varley, a member of the Group of Seven; both the Varley & McKay offer exhibition space to regional & national artists; supported by the Varley-McKay Art Foundation of Markham.
Niamh O'Laoghaire, Director, nolaoghaire@markham.ca
Anik Glaude, Curator, aglaude@markham.ca

***Waterloo:* Canadian Clay & Glass Gallery / Galerie Canadienne de la Céramique et du Verre**
25 Caroline St. North
Waterloo, ON N2L 2Y5
Tel: 519-746-1882; *Fax:* 519-746-6396
info@canadianclayandglass.ca
www.canadianclayandglass.ca
twitter.com/c dnclayandglass
www.facebook.com/190913524282373
Exhibits contemporary artworks executed in clay, glass, stained glass & enamel for public education & enjoyment
Jan D'Ailly, Chair
William D. Poole, Executive Director, director@canadianclayandglass.ca
Christian Bernard Singer, Curator, christian@canadianclayandglass.ca

***Waterloo:* Robert Langen Art Gallery (RLAG)**
Wilfrid Laurier University, 75 University Ave. West
Waterloo, ON N2L 3C5
Tel: 519-884-0710
www.wlu.ca/rlag
www.facebook.com/RobertLangenArtGallery
Year Founded: 1989 The University's visual arts centre; provides knowledge, stewardship, appreciation & enjoyment of Canadian art & culture to members of the Laurier community & the community at large
Suzanne Luke, Curator, 519-884-0710, sluke@wlu.ca

***Waterloo:* University of Waterloo Art Gallery (UWAG)**
University of Waterloo, 200 University Ave. West.
Located at East Campus Hall, #1239, 263 Phillip St., Waterloo, ON
Waterloo, ON N2L 3G1
Tel: 519-888-4567
uwag.uwaterloo.ca
Social Media: www.flickr.com/photos/56851697@N04
www.facebook.com/uwag.waterloo
Year Founded: 1964 Produces exhibitions of contemporary Canadian art in all media; holds a collection of contemporary Canadian art since 1960; open Tue. - Sat. during academic year at two sites: Modern Languages Building & the main gallery in East Campus Hall
Ivan Jurakic, Director/Curator, ijurakic@uwaterloo.ca

***Whitby:* The Station Gallery**
1450 Henry St.
Whitby, ON L1N 0A8
Tel: 905-668-4185; *Fax:* 905-668-1934
art@whitbystationgallery.com
www.whitbystationgallery.com
Social Media: www.linkedin.com/company/885487
twitter.com/stationgallery
www.facebook.com/stationgallery
Year Founded: 1970 The gallery's Permanent Collection exceeds 300 original prints, paintings, sculpture, & mixed media works.
James Ritchie, Chair
Donna Raetsen-Kemp, CEO, raetsen-kempd@whitbystationgallery.com
Olexander Wlasenko, Curator, wlasenkoo@whitbystationgallery.com

***Windsor:* Artcite Inc.**
109 University Ave. West
Windsor, ON N9A 5P4
Tel: 519-977-6564; *Fax:* 519-977-6564
info@artcite.ca
www.artcite.ca
Social Media: www.flickr.com/photos/artcite
twitter.com/artcite
www.facebook.com/Art citeInc
Year Founded: 1982 Artcite is Windsor's only artist-run centre exclusively dedicated to presenting contemporary & experimental art forms. The gallery is open W-Sa 12:00-5:00, or by appointment; the office is open Tu-Sa 12:00-5:00.
Christine Burchnall, Administrative Coordinator, xtine@artcite.ca
Bernard Helling, Artistic Coordinator

***Woodstock:* Woodstock Art Gallery (WAG)**
PO Box 1536
Located at 449 Dundas St., Woodstock, ON
Woodstock, ON N4S 0A7
Tel: 519-539-2382; *Fax:* 519-539-2564
waginfo@cityofwoodstock.ca
www.woodstockartgallery.ca
Year Founded: 1967 Features contemporary & historical exhibitions; wide range of classes & workshops for adults & children; focuses on local painter Florence Carlyle through an extensive permanent collection & family artifacts
Sheila Perry, Director/Curator, sperry@cityofwoodstock.ca

Prince Edward Island

Provincial Art Gallery

Confederation Centre of the Arts / Le Musée d'Art du Centre de la Confédération
145 Richmond St.
130 Queen Street, Charlottetown, PE
Charlottetown, PE C1A 1J1
Tel: 902-628-1864; *Fax:* 902-566-4648
info@confederationcentre.com
www.confederationcentre.com
Social Media: www.youtube.com/confedcentre
twitter.com/confedboxoffice
www.facebook.com/ccoagallery
Year Founded: 1964 Critical inquiry into 200 years of Canadian art; 28 annual exhibitions; 15,000 work collection
Jessie Inman, Chief Executive Officer

Local Art Gallery

Charlottetown: Pilar Shephard Art Gallery
82 Great George St.
Charlottetown, PE C1A 4K4
Tel: 902-892-1953; Fax: 902-892-6137
www.pilarshephard.com
Year Founded: 1992 Contemporary artwork
Pilar Shephard, Owner

Québec

Provincial Art Galleries

Musée d'art contemporain de Montréal (MACM)
185, rue Ste-Catherine ouest
Montréal, QC H2X 3X5
Tél: 514-847-6226; Téléc: 514-847-6292
www.macm.org
Médias sociaux: www.youtube.com/macmvideos
twitter.com/macmtl
www.facebook.com/macMontréal
Fondée en: 1964 Possède une collection de plus de 6000 oeuvres datant de 1939 par des artistes du Québec, du Canada et du monde entier; un centre de référence spécialisé est disponible pour la recherche; divers spectacles, conférences et programmes éducatifs sont offerts par le musée tout au long de l'année; restaurant, boutique et librairie.
Alexandre Taillefer, Président
John Zeppetelli, Directeur général et conservateur en chef

Musée des beaux-arts de Montréal (MBAM) / Montréal Museum of Fine Arts (MMFA)
CP 3000 H
Située à 1380, rue Sherbrooke Ouest, Montréal, QC, H3G 1J5
Montréal, QC H3G 2T9
Tél: 514-285-2000
Ligne sans frais: 800-899-6873
www.mbam.qc.ca
Médias sociaux: www.instagram.com/mbamtl
twitter.com/mbamtl
www.facebook.com/mbamtl
Fondée en: 1860 Le musée abrite une collection encyclopédique qui comprend l'art canadien, art contemporain, art européen, arts décoratifs, cultures antiques et archéologie méditerranéenne; depuis 2007, le musée a reçut la collection de l'ancien Musée Marc-Aurèle Fortin; l'accès à la collection permanente est gratuite
Nathalie Bondil, Directrice/Conservatrice en chef, L'art européens
Hilliard T. Goldfarb, Conservateur en chef adjoint, Maîtres anciens

Musée national des beaux-arts du Québec
Parc des Champs-de-Bataille
Québec, QC G1R 5H3
Tél: 418-643-2150
Ligne sans frais: 866-220-2150
info@mnba.qc.ca
www.mnba.qc.ca
Médias sociaux: www.youtube.com/mnbaqorg
twitter.com/mnbaq
www.facebook.com/mnbaq
Fondée en: 1933 Le musée, situé sur les plaines d'Abraham, abrite des collections d'art de la 17e, 18e, et 19e siècles, en plus d'une collection d'art contemporain. Diverses expositions temporaires sont également organisées. Ouvert toute l'année, le musée propose également une bibliothèque, une librairie, et un service éducatif.
Line Ouellet, Directrice et conservatrice en chef

Local Art Galleries

Alma: Langage Plus
CP 518
Situé à 555, rue collard ouest, Alma, QC
Alma, QC G8B 5W1
Tél: 418-668-6635; Téléc: 418-668-3263
info@langageplus.com
www.langageplus.com
fr-fr.facebook.com/LangagePlu s
Fondée en: 1979
Claude Girard, Président
Jocelyne Fortin, Directrice, direction@langageplus.com

Amos: Centre d'exposition d'Amos
222, 1e av est
Amos, QC J9T 1H3
Tél: 819-732-6070; Téléc: 819-732-3242
exposition@ville.amos.qc.ca
www.ville.amos.qc.ca/fr/citoyen/centre_expos ition
L'art actuel et traditionnel; les sciences et l'histoire
Marianne Trudel, Directrice

Aylmer: Centre d'exposition l'Imagier
9, rue Front
Aylmer, QC J9H 4W8
Tél: 819-684-1445; Téléc: 819-684-4058
info@limagier.qc.ca
www.limagier.qc.ca
www.facebook.com/Imagier
Marianne Breton, Directrice

Baie-Saint-Paul: Musée d'art contemporain de Baie-Saint-Paul
23, rue Ambroise-Fafand
Baie-Saint-Paul, QC G3Z 2J2
Tél: 418-435-3681; Téléc: 418-435-6269
info@macbsp.com
www.macbsp.com
Médias sociaux: www.youtube.com/user/MACBaieStPaul
fr-ca.facebook.com/MACBSP
Fondée en: 1992 Le musée est consacré à la présentation de l'art contemporain au Québec.
Mathieu Simard, Président
Jacques Saint-Gelais Tremblay, Directeur général, j.s.tremblay@macbsp.com

Beaconsfield: Chase Art Gallery / Galerie d'art Chase
450 Beaconsfield Blvd.
Beaconsfield, QC H9W 4B9
Tel: 514-426-3700; Fax: 514-426-2820
info@chaseart.ca
chaseartgallery.com
twitter.com/ChaseArtGallery
www .facebook.com/chaseartgallery
Year Founded: 1991

Bromont: Galerie Artêria / Artêria Gallery
625, rue Shefford
Bromont, QC J2L 1C2
Tel: 450-919-3133; Fax: 450-919-1250
www.arteriagallery.com
twitter.com/Arteriagallery
www.facebook.com/pag es/Artêria-Art-Gallery/189111521104083
Year Founded: 2005 Illustration visuelle contemporaine par des artistes nouveaux et établis

Carleton-sur-Mer: Centre d'Artistes Vaste et Vague
774, boul Perron
Carleton-sur-Mer, QC G0C 1J0
Tél: 418-364-3123; Téléc: 418-364-6822
communication@vasteetvague.ca
www.vasteetvague.ca
Médias sociaux: www.youtube.com/user/Vasteetvague
twitter.com/vasteetvague
www.faceboo k.com/vasteetvague
Fondée en: 1990 Centre de production et de diffusion en art actuel et contemporain Expositions, résidences d'artiste, atelier de production, production d'événements majeurs (Symposium)
Caroline Barriault, Présidente
Guylaine Langlois, Directrice générale

Chicoutimi: Espace Virtuel
534, rue Jacques-Cartier est
Chicoutimi, QC G7H 1Z6
Tél: 418-698-3873; Téléc: 418-543-6730
information@centrebang.ca
www.centrebang.ca
www.facebook.com/centreban g
Fondée en: 1958
Sébastien Harvey, Directeur général, direction@centrebang.ca

Drummondville: Maison des arts Desjardins Drummondville
175, rue Ringuet
Drummondville, QC J2C 2P7
Tél: 819-477-5412
Ligne sans frais: 800-265-5412
billetterie@artsdrummondville.com
www.artsdrummondville.com
Médias sociaux: www.youtube.com/drspectacles
twitter.com/artsdrummond
www.facebook.com/maisondesarts
Fondée en: 2011 Ouverte toute l'année
Roland Janelle, Directeur, rjanelle@artsdrummondville.com

Gatineau: AXENÉO7
80, rue Hanson
Gatineau, QC J8Y 3M5
Tél: 819-771-2122; Téléc: 819-771-0696
axeneo7@axeneo7.qc.ca
www.axeneo7.qc.ca
twitter.com/axeneo7
www.face book.com/AXENEO7
Fondée en: 1983
Véronique Guitard, Directrice par intérim, direction@axeneo7.qc.ca

Gatineau: Centre d'exposition Art-Image et espace Odyssée Maison de la Culture de Gatineau
855, boul de la Gappe
Gatineau, QC J8T 8H9
Tél: 819-243-2325; Téléc: 819-243-2527
artimage@gatineau.ca
www.gatineau.ca/artimage
fr-ca.facebook.com/artim ageespaceodyssee
Fondée en: 1992 Pour améliorer la communication entre les domaines artistiques et le grand public
Marie Hélène Giguère, Coordonnatrice des espaces d'exposition

Gatineau: Galerie Montcalm
Maison du Citoyen, 25, rue Laurier, 1er étage
Gatineau, QC J8X 3Y9
Tél: 819-595-7488
galeriemontcalm1@gatineau.ca
www.gatineau.ca
www.facebook.com/galerie.montcalm
Fondée en: 1980 La galerie accueille 6 expositions par an d'art visuel local et international.

Jonquière: Centre national d'exposition (CNE)
CP 605, 4160, rue du Vieux Pont
Jonquière, QC G7X 7W4
Tél: 418-546-2177; Téléc: 418-546-2180
info@centrenationalexposition.com
www.centrenationalexposition.com
Présente des expositions d'ouvres d'artistes professionnels et plusieurs expositions itinérantes; démontre la richesse des collections du Québec et d'autres musées canadiens et internationaux; visites guidées, ateliers, démonstrations et trousses éducatives disponibles.

Kamouraska: Centre d'art de Kamouraska
111, av Morel
Kamouraska, QC G0L 1M0
Tél: 418-492-9458
info@kamouraska.org
www.kamouraska.org
twitter.com/c_art_k
www.facebook.com/centre.dart.de .kamouraska
Fondée en: 1988 Le centre accueille des expositions, ainsi que des ateliers et des conférences.

Laval: Salle Alfred Pellan, Maison des arts de Laval
1395, boul de la Concorde ouest
Laval, QC H7N 5W1
Tél: 450-662-4440; Téléc: 450-662-4428
sallealfredpellan@ville.laval.qc.ca
www.ville.laval.qc.ca
www.facebook .com/maisondesartsdelaval
Arts visuels à caractère contemporain

Lennoxville: Foreman Art Gallery of Bishop's University / Galerie d'art Foreman de l'Université Bishop's
Bishop's University, 2600 College St.
Lennoxville, QC J1M 1Z7
Tel: 819-822-9600; Fax: 819-822-9703
gallery@ubishops.ca
www.foreman.ubishops.ca
twitter.com/ForemanArtGal
www.facebook.com/foremanartgallery
Other contact information: Alternate URL: artlab.ubishops.ca
Year Founded: 1998 To serve as a forum for the presentation & examination of the visual arts through the programming of contemporary & historical exhibitions as well as lecture series , workshops & films; open Tu-Sa 12:00-5:00, evenings when Centennial Theatre open; admission free
Vicky Chainey Gagnon, Director/Curator, vicky.chaineygagnon@ubishops.ca

Longueuil: **Plein sud, centre d'exposition en art actuel à Longueuil**
#D-0626, 150, rue de Gentilly Est
Longueuil, QC J4H 4A9
Tél: 450-679-2966; *Téléc:* 450-679-4480
plein-sud@plein-sud.org
www.plein-sud.org
www.facebook.com/PleinSudcen treexposition
Fondée en: 1985 Diffuse la production d'artistes professionnels dont les recherches s'inscrivent en art actuel; présente des expositions temporaires et offre des activités qui visent à familiariser le public avec les différentes avenues proposées par cet art
Bruno Grenier, Président et trésorier
Hélène Poirier, Directrice générale et artistique, hpoirier@plein-sud.org

Matane: **Galerie d'art de Matane**
#101, 520, av Saint-Jérôme
Matane, QC G4W 3B5
Tél: 418-566-6687; *Téléc:* 418-562-6675
gartm@globetrotter.qc.ca
Présenter environ 8 expositions d'artistiques du Québec, du Canada et de l'étranger

Mont-Laurier: **Centre d'exposition Mont-Laurier**
CP 334, 385, rue Du Pont
Mont-Laurier, QC J9L 3N7
Tél: 819-623-2441
ceml@lino.sympatico.ca
www.expomontlaurier.ca
fr-ca.facebook.com/472445632795269
Fondée en: 1977 Le Centre d'exposition de Mont-Laurier est une institution muséale dont la mission est la diffusion, l'éducation et l'action culturelle en arts visuels et en patrimoine
Nicolas Orreindy, Directeur

Montréal: **Artothèque**
5720, rue St-André
Montréal, QC H2S 2K1
Tél: 514-278-8181; *Téléc:* 514-278-3044
info@artotheque.ca
www.artotheque.ca
Médias sociaux: www.youtube.com/user/Artothequeca
twitter.com/artotheque
www.facebook. com/artotheque.quisemporte

Montréal: **La Centrale (Galerie Powerhouse)**
4296, boul Saint-Laurent
Montréal, QC H2W 1Z3
Tél: 514-871-0268
galerie@lacentrale.org
www.lacentrale.org
twitter.com/lacentralemtl
www.facebook.com/25308401 1386087
Fondée en: 1973 Centre d'artistes autogéré qui se consacre à la présentation de l'art contemporain des femmes
Virginie Jourdain, Coordonnatrice des expositions
Jen Leigh Fisher, Coordonnatrice artistique, programmation@lacentrale.org
Diane St-Antoine, Coordonnatrice administration, administration@lacentrale.org

Montréal: **Centre international d'art contemporain de Montréal (CIAC)**
CP 42105 Roy
Montréal, QC H2W 2T3
Tél: 514-288-0811
ciac@ciac.ca
www.ciac.ca
www.facebook.com/ciacMontréal
Centre international d'art contemporain de Montréal est un bureau pour l'art contemporain, la production d'expositions de la Biennale de Montréal, un magazine d'art électronique, publications, et événements.
Marie Perrault, Directrice générale et artistique C.M., marie.perrault@ciac.ca

Montréal: **Galerie de l'UQAM**
Université du Québec à Montréal, #J-R120, 1400, rue Berri, Pavillon Judith-Jasmin
Montréal, QC H3C 3P8
Tél: 514-987-6150; *Téléc:* 514-987-6897
galerie@uqam.ca
www.galerie.uqam.ca
twitter.com/galeriedeluqam
www.f acebook.com/galerie.uqam
Fondée en: 1975 La collection comprend surtout du travail contemporain d'artistes québécois. Heures: Ma-S 12h-18h. L'entrée est gratuite.
Louise Déry, Directrice, dery.louise@uqam.ca

Montréal: **Galerie Heffel Québec Ltée**
1840, rue Sherbrooke Ouest
Montréal, QC H3H 1E4
Tél: 514-939-6505; *Téléc:* 514-939-1100
Ligne sans frais: 866-939-6505
mail@heffel.com
www.heffel.com
Beaux-arts maison de vente aux enchères, dont le siège est à Vancouver, en Colombie-Britannique.
1 Tania Poggione, Directrice, tania@heffel.com

Montréal: **Galerie Visual Voice / Visual Voice Art Gallery**
Édifice Belgo, #421, 373, rue Ste-Catherine Ouest
Montréal, QC H3B 1A2
Tel: 514-878-3663
info@visualvoicegallery.com
www.visualvoicegallery.com
Social Media: www.flickr.com/photos/visualvoicegallery
twitter.com/VisualVoiceMtl
ww w.facebook.com/visualvoicegallery
Year Founded: 2007 Oeuvres d'artistes contemporains

Montréal: **Guilde canadienne des métiers d'art / Canadian Guild of Crafts**
1460-B, rue Sherbrooke ouest
Montréal, QC H3G 1K4
Tél: 514-849-6091; *Téléc:* 514-849-7351
Ligne sans frais: 866-477-6091
info@canadianguild.com
www.guildecanadiennedesmetiersdart.com
www.facebook.com/197720636923063
Sculptures et artefacts d'art inuit et de l'art des Premières Nations; produits de métiers d'art canadien; gravures
Michelle Joannette, Directrice

Montréal: **Han Art**
4209 rue Ste-Catherine West
Montréal, QC H3Z 1P6
Tel: 514-876-9278; *Fax:* 514-876-1566
info@hanartgallery.com
www.hanartgallery.com
Year Founded: 1995
Andrew Lui, Art Director

Montréal: **Leonard & Bina Ellen Art Gallery / Galerie Leonard et Bina Ellen**
Concordia University, #LB-165, 1455 boul de Maisonneuve ouest
Montréal, QC H3G 1M8
Tel: 514-848-2424; *Fax:* 514-848-4751
ellen.artgallery@concordia.ca
ellengallery.concordia.ca
twitter.com/el lengallery
www.facebook.com/ellengallery
Year Founded: 1966 Committed to researching, collecting & interpreting Canadian art; programming centres on exhibitions that help advance knowledge in the visual arts; in keeping with Concordia's academic mission, the Gallery is committed to the enhancement of the University's educational programmes & cultural environment
Michèle Thériault, Director, michele.theriault@concordia.ca

Montréal: **Musée des maîtres et artisans du Québec (MMAQ)**
615, av Sainte-Croix
Montréal, QC H4L 3X6
Tél: 514-747-7367; *Téléc:* 514-747-8892
accueil@mmaq.qc.ca
www.mmaq.qc.ca
Médias sociaux: www.youtube.com/user/MuseeMAQ
twitter.com/museemaq
www.facebook.com/74 228420780
Fondée en: 1977 Chefs d'oeuvres de grands maîtres et pièces exceptionnelles d'artisans anonymes présentent un panorama de la culture traditionnelle québécoise dans une église néo-gothique de 1867
Pierre Wilson, Directeur-conservateur, 514-747-7367, p.wilson@mmaq.qc.ca
Manon Dubé, Adjointe Administrateur, 514-747-7367, m.dube@mmaq.qc.ca

Montréal: **OBORO**
#301, 4001, rue Berri
Montréal, QC H2L 4H2
Tél: 514-844-3250; *Téléc:* 514-847-0330
oboro@oboro.net
www.oboro.net
www.facebook.com/366480043419

Fondée en: 1984 Art, des pratiques contemporaines et des nouveaux médias
Bernard Bilodeau, Codirecteur général et directeur administratif
Claudine Hubert, Codirectrice générale et directrice artistique

Montréal: **Segal Centre for Performing Arts**
5170, ch de la Côte-Ste-Catherine
Montréal, QC H3W 1M7
Tel: 514-739-2301; *Fax:* 514-739-9340
www.segalcentre.org
Social Media: www.youtube.com/user/SegalCentre
twitter.com/segalcentre
www.facebook. com/segalcentre
A performing arts centre, staging productions involving theatre, music, dance and cinema. The Segal Centre for the Performing Arts also holds workshops involving these categories.
Joel Segal, President
Elliot Lifson, Vice-President
Lisa Rubin, Artistic & Executive Director
Barry Taggart, Director, Finance & Operations
Michael Blumenstein, Secretary
Michael Etinson, Treasurer

Montréal: **Yves Laroche Galerie d'Art**
6355, boul Saint-Laurent
Montréal, QC H2S 3C3
Tel: 514-393-1999
info@yveslaroche.com
www.yveslaroche.com
twitter.com/ylgallery
www.facebook.com/72285833284
Year Founded: 1991 Exhibits work of underground graffiti, tattoo, comic, pop, illustration & surrealist artists.

Mont-Saint-Hilaire: **Musée des beaux-arts de Mont-Saint-Hilaire**
150, rue du Centre-Civique
Mont-Saint-Hilaire, QC J3H 5Z5
Tél: 450-536-3033; *Téléc:* 450-536-3032
www.mbamsh.qc.ca
www.facebook.com/171755132131
Fondée en: 1995 Favorise le travail d'artistes locaux Ozias Leduc, Paul-Émile Borduas et Jordi Benet; des ouvres d'artistes contemporains
Marie-Andrée Leclerc, Directrice générale, maleclerc@mbamsh.qc.ca

Pointe-Claire: **La Galerie d'art Stewart Hall Art Gallery**
Centre culturel de Pointe-Claire Stewart Hall, 176, ch Bord-du-Lac
Pointe-Claire, QC H9S 4J7
Tél: 514-630-1254; *Téléc:* 514-630-1285
www.ville.pointe-claire.qc.ca
Fondée en: 1963 Open year round; exhibitions from local, national & international sources; paintings, photographs, sculptures, graphics & theme exhibitions; free admission; wheelchair access
Joyce Millar, Directrice/Conservatrice, millarj@ville.pointe-claire.qc.ca

Pointe-Claire: **Viva Vida Art Gallery / Galerie d'Art Viva Vida**
#278, 2 Lakeshore Rd.
Pointe-Claire, QC H9S 4K9
Tel: 514-694-1110
info@vivavidaartgallery.com
www.vivavidaartgallery.com
www.facebook.com/118827194843807
Year Founded: 2009
Nedia El Khouri, Owner

Québec: **VU centre de diffusion et de production de la photographie**
523, Saint-Vallier est
Québec, QC G1K 3P9
Tél: 418-640-2558; *Téléc:* 418-640-2586
info@vuphoto.org
www.vuphoto.org
www.facebook.com/pages/VU-PHOTO/18771 4927147
Fondée en: 1981 VU se consacre à la promotion et au développement de la photographie d'auteur. Son mandat vise principalement le soutien aux activités de recherche et de création en photographie à travers des expositions, des résidences d'artistes, des publications et des événements spéciaux. VU offre un accès privilégié à une vaste gamme d'équipements de production en photographie argentique et numérique
Rodrigue Bélanger, Président
Pascale Bureau, Directrice générale, direction@vuphoto.org

***Rimouski:* Galerie Coup d'Oeuil**
CP 710
22, rue Sainte-Marie, Rimouski, QC
Rimouski, QC G5L 7C7
Tél: 418-724-3235; *Téléc:* 418-724-3139

***Rouyn-Noranda:* Centre d'exposition de Rouyn-Noranda inc. (CERN)**
#154, 201, av Dallaire
Rouyn-Noranda, QC J9X 4T5
Tél: 819-762-6600; *Téléc:* 819-762-9425
info.cern@rouyn-noranda.ca
www.cern.ca
www.facebook.com/centredexposit ion.rouynnoranda
Noël Neveu, Président
Jean-Jacques Lachapelle, Directeur général, direction.cern@rouyn-noranda.ca

***Sainte-Hénédine:* Centre d'art Révérend Louis-Napoléon-Fiset**
109, rue Principale
Sainte-Hénédine, QC G0S 2R0
Tél: 418-935-7022
carlnf@videotron.ca
Autre numéros: **Tél.: 418-935-3543**
Sculptures sur bois; scènes d'époque; orfèverie; broderie; hangar à dîme

***Saint-Hyacinthe:* Expression, Centre d'exposition de Saint-Hyacinthe**
495, rue Saint-Simon
Saint-Hyacinthe, QC J2S 5C3
Tél: 450-773-4209; *Téléc:* 450-773-5270
expression@expression.qc.ca
www.expression.qc.ca
www.facebook.com/Expr essionCentreDExpositionDeSaintHyacinthe
Fondée en: 1985 Une institution muséale dont la mission est de promouvoir et de diffuser l'art contemporain et actuel. Depuis 1985, Expression présente au public, dans une salle magnifique et spacieuse, des expositions réputées pour leur qualité artistique. A ces expositions, s'ajoutent un service d'animation, des conférences et des publications. De plus, Expression insère ponctuellement des activités satellites
Marcel Blouin, Direction générale et artistique

***Saint-Jean-Port-Joli:* Maison-musée Médard-Bourgault**
322, av de Gaspé ouest
Saint-Jean-Port-Joli, QC G0R 3G0
Tél: 418-598-3880
mmbcontact@gmail.com
medardbourgault.org
Fondée en: 1980 Le musée est la maison de l'artiste Médard Bourgault. La maison affiche son ouvre et possessions et est ouvert au public pendant l'été.

***Saint-Léonard:* Galerie Port-Maurice**
8420, boul Lacordaire
Saint-Léonard, QC H1R 3G5
Tél: 514-328-8500
Fondée en: 1979 Crée en 1979; sensibilise la population aux différents courants contemporains d'arts visuels

***La Sarre:* Centre d'art Rotary**
195, rue Principale
La Sarre, QC J9Z 1Y3
Tél: 819-333-2294; *Téléc:* 819-333-2296
www.ville.lasarre.qc.ca/culture
www.facebook.com/centredartrotary.lasarr e
Le centre d'art abrite les ouvres d'artistes locaux et internationaux. Il offre également des programmes d'éducation artistique.
Véronique Trudel, Responsable du Centre d'art Rotary, vtrudel@ville.lasarre.qc.ca

***Shawinigan:* Centre d'exposition Léo-Ayotte**
c/o Corporation culturelle de Shawinigan, 2100, boul Des Hêtres
Shawinigan, QC G9N 8R8
Tél: 819-539-1888; *Téléc:* 819-539-2400
corporationculturelle@shawinigan.ca
www.cultureshawinigan.ca/CentreExpos ition.aspx
Le centre accueille des expositions et offre des programmes d'éducation artistique
Louise Martin, Directrice générale et artistique, lmartin@shawinigan.ca
Clémence Bélanger, Muséologue, cbelanger@shawinigan.ca
Isabelle Gingras, Responsable des programmes éducatifs, igingras@shawinigan.ca

***Sherbrooke:* Galerie d'art du Centre culturel de l'Université de Sherbrooke**
2500, boul de l'Université
Sherbrooke, QC J1K 2R1
Tél: 819-820-1000
galerie@ushebrooke.ca
www.centrecultureludes.ca
fr-ca.facebook.com/328711283927317
Fondée en: 1964 Abrite l'art contemporain
Suzanne Pressé, Coordonnatrice

***Sherbrooke:* Musée des beaux-arts de Sherbrooke**
241, rue Dufferin
Sherbrooke, QC J1H 4M3
Tél: 819-821-2115; *Téléc:* 819-821-4003
mbas@mbas.qc.ca
mbas.qc.ca
Médias sociaux: instagram.com/mbasherbrooke
twitter.com/MBASherbrooke
www.facebook.com /148126951901795
Fondée en: 1982 Plusieurs expositions temporaires ainsi que la collection du Musée, notamment les oeuvres de Frederick Simpson Coburn et la collection Luc LaRochelle
Cécile Gèlinas, Directrice, cgelinas@mbas.qc.ca

***St-Georges:* Centre d'Art de St-Georges**
Centre culturel Marie-Fitzbach, 250, 18e rue ouest
St-Georges, QC G5Y 4S9
Tél: 418-226-2238
Fondée en: 1992

***Trois-Rivières:* Galerie d'art du Parc et Manoir de Tonnancour**
CP 871, 864, rue des Ursulines
Trois-Rivières, QC G9A 5J9
Tél: 819-374-2355
www.galeriedartduparc.qc.ca
www.facebook.com/galeriedartduparc
Dessins, peintures, sculptures, timbres, photos, vidéos et expositions techniques mixtes; exposition permanente sur l'histoire du Manoir de Tonnancour.

***Valcourt:* Centre culturel Yvonne L. Bombardier**
1002, av J.-A.-Bombardier
Valcourt, QC J0E 2L0
Tél: 450-532-2250
ccylb@fjab.qc.ca
www.centreculturelbombardier.com
www.facebook.com/CentreCulturelBombardi er
Le centre culturel abrite les arts visuels, ainsi que d'une bibliothèque et diverses activités artistiques

***Val-d'Or:* Centre d'exposition de Val-d'Or (CEVD)**
600, 7e rue
Val-d'Or, QC J9P 3P3
Tél: 819-825-0942; *Téléc:* 819-825-3062
expovd@ville.valdor.qc.ca
www.expovd.ca
www.facebook.com/centredexposi tiondevaldor
Fondée en: 1978 Le centre expose des peintures, sculptures, photographies, vidéos d'artistes locaux. Il accueille également des activités éducatives, des ateliers et des conférences.
Ginette Vézina, Présidente
Carmelle Adam, Directrice, carmelle.adam@ville.valdor.qc.ca

***Verdun:* Centre culturel de Verdun**
5955, rue Bannantyne
Verdun, QC H4H 1H6
Tél: 514-765-7170
Year Founded: 1967

Saskatchewan

Provincial Art Gallery

MacKenzie Art Gallery (MAG)
3475 Albert St.
Regina, SK S4S 6X6
Tel: 306-584-4250; *Fax:* 306-569-8191
info@mackenzieartgallery.ca
www.mackenzieartgallery.sk.ca
Social Media: www.youtube.com/atthemag
twitter.com/AtTheMAG
www.facebook.com/MacKenzieArtGallery
Year Founded: 1953 Historical & contemporary Canadian, American & European works; special emphasis on western Canadian art; works on paper, contemporary photography, major touring exhibits; facilities include learning centre, studios, theatre, gift shop; sculpture court; outdoor sculpture garden; open daily year round
Anthony Kiendl, Executive Director & CEO, anthony.kiendl@mackenzieartgallery.ca
Timothy Long, Head Curator, timothy.long@mackenzieartgallery.ca

Local Art Galleries

***Assiniboia:* Shurniak Art Gallery**
PO Box 1178
Located at 122 - 3 Ave. West, Assiniboia, SK
Assiniboia, SK S0H 0B0
Tel: 306-642-5292; *Fax:* 306-642-4541
info@shurniakartgallery.com
shurniakartgallery.com
Year Founded: 2005 Canadian & international artwork as well as a library of art books

***North Battleford:* Allen Sapp Gallery**
PO Box 460, 1 Railway Ave. East
North Battleford, SK S9A 2Y6
Tel: 306-445-1760; *Fax:* 306-445-1694
sapp@accesscomm.ca
www.allensapp.com
Social Media: www.youtube.com/user/ASGallery
www.facebook.com/AllenSappGallery
Year Founded: 1989 Cree art & interpretive centre; open year round
Leah Garven, Curator/Manager

***North Battleford:* The Chapel Gallery**
PO Box 460
Located at 891 - 99th St., North Battleford, SK
North Battleford, SK S9A 2Y6
Tel: 306-445-1757; *Fax:* 306-445-1009
sapp@accesscomm.ca
www.chapelgallery.ca
Exhibition of local to international artists, permanent collection of the city of North Battleford
Lea Garven, Curator/Manager of Galleries

***Prince Albert:* Grace Campbell Gallery**
John M. Cuelenaere Public Library, 125 - 12 St. East
Prince Albert, SK S6V 1B7
Tel: 306-763-8496; *Fax:* 306-763-3816
library@jmcpl.ca
www.jmcpl.ca/grace-campbell-gallery
Year Founded: 1973 Local, provincial & national exhibitions; no permanent collection

***Prince Albert:* Mann Art Gallery**
142 - 12th St. West
Prince Albert, SK S6V 3B5
Tel: 306-763-7080; *Fax:* 306-763-7838
info@mannartgallery.ca
mannartgallery.ca
www.facebook.com/mann.artgall ery
The gallery specializes in contemporary art, & seeks to promote artistic creation & appreciation in the region.
Griffith Aaron Baker, Director/Curator, curator@mannartgallery.ca

***Regina:* Art Gallery of Regina**
Neil Balkwill Civic Arts Centre, PO Box 1790
Located at 2420 Elphinstone St., Regina, SK
Regina, SK S4P 3C8
Tel: 306-522-5940; *Fax:* 306-522-5944
agr@sasktel.net
www.artgalleryofregina.ca
www.facebook.com/22839986056 2366
Year Founded: 1974 The gallery focuses on contemporary art, especially works by Saskatchewan artists.
Karen Schoonover, Director/Curator

***Regina:* Assiniboia Gallery**
2266 Smith St.
Regina, SK S4P 2P4
Tel: 306-522-0997 *Toll-Free:* 866-378-0997
info@assiniboia.com
www.assiniboia.com
Social Media: instagram.com/assiniboiaart
twitter.com/ArtYouCanBuy
www.facebook.com/ pages/Assiniboia-Gallery/76039978390
Year Founded: 1977 Houses visual work by emerging & established artists.
Mary Weimer, Owner
Jeremy Weimer, Owner

***Regina:* Dunlop Art Gallery**
Regina Public Library, PO Box 2311
Located at 2311 - 12 Ave., Regina, SK
Regina, SK S4P 3Z5
Tel: 306-777-6040; *Fax:* 306-949-7264
www.dunlopartgallery.org

Year Founded: 1964 Permanent art collection of contemporary & historical significance by Saskatchewan artists; open year round
Jennifer Matotek, Director/Curator, jmatotek@reginalibrary.ca
Wendy Peart, Curator, Education & Community Outreach, wpeart@reginalibrary.ca

***Regina:* Sherwood Village Branch Gallery**
6121 Rochdale Blvd.
Regina, SK S4X 2R1
Tel: 306-777-6040; *Fax:* 306-949-7264
Open year round; closed Sundays July & Aug.

***Regina:* McIntyre Gallery**
2347 McIntyre St.
Regina, SK S4P 2S3
Tel: 306-757-4323
mcintyre.gallery@sasktel.net
Year Founded: 1985 Contemporary Saskatchewan art; open year round
Louise Durnford, Director/Owner

***Regina:* Slate Fine Art Gallary**
2878 Halifax St.
Regina, SK S4P 1T7
Tel: 306-775-0300
slate@sasktel.net
slategallery.ca
www.facebook.com/1 41311352710080
Year Founded: 2013 Houses visual work by emerging & established artists.
Kimberly Fyfe, Contact
Gina Fafard, Contact

***Saskatoon:* A.K.A. Gallery**
424 - 20th St. West
Saskatoon, SK S7M 0X4
Tel: 306-652-0044
info@akagallery.org
www.akagallery.org
twitter.com/aka_artist_run
www.facebook.com/akaarti strun
Year Founded: 1971 Artist-run centre; membership open to all
Tarin Hughes, Executive Director, director@akaartistrun.com

***Saskatoon:* The Gallery/art placement inc.**
228 - 3 Ave. South
Saskatoon, SK S7K 1L9
Tel: 306-664-3385; *Fax:* 306-933-3252
gallery@artplacement.com
www.artplacement.com
Year Founded: 1978 Work by mid-career & experienced artists from Saskatchewan.

***Saskatoon:* Gordon Snelgrove Art Gallery**
Room 191 Murray Bldg., University of Saskatchewan, 3 Campus Dr.
Saskatoon, SK S7N 5A4
Tel: 306-966-4208; *Fax:* 306-966-4266
www.usask.ca/snelgrove
Social Media: vimeo.com/gordonsnelgrove/albums
twitter.com/gordonsnelgrove
www.faceb ook.com/groups/gordonsnelgrove
The gallery, managed by the Univ. of Sask. department of Art & Art History, supports program & course instruction, student shows & exhibitions, & community outreach.
Marcus Miller, Director, marcus.miller@usask.ca

***Saskatoon:* St. Thomas More Art Gallery**
St. Thomas More College, 1437 College Dr.
Saskatoon, SK S7N 0W6
Tel: 306-966-8900; *Fax:* 306-966-8904
Toll-Free: 800-667-2019
www.stmcollege.ca
Social Media: www.youtube.com/stm1936
twitter.com/stm1936
www.facebook.com/stmcolleg e
Year Founded: 1964 Located on the 2nd floor of the College, next to the Library. Exhibitions from Sept. through April, featuring local & regional artists with a university level studio background or extensive formal training. Submissions accepted year round.
Linda Stark, Curator, lstark@stmcollege.ca

***Saskatoon:* U of S Art Galleries**
University of Saskatchewan, #12, College Bldg., 107 Administration Pl.
Saskatoon, SK S7N 5A2
Tel: 306-966-4571; *Fax:* 306-978-8340
kag.cag@usask.ca
www.art.usask.ca
Social Media: kagcag.tumblr.com
www.facebook.com/kenderdine.gallery
Year Founded: 1991 This central office administers the following university galleries: The University of Saskatchewan Permanent Art Collection (UAC); The Kenderdine Art Gallery (KAG); & The College Art Galleries 1 & 2 (CAG). Office open M-F 8:30-4:30; Kenderdine Art Gallery open Tu-F 11:30-4:00; College Art Gallery open Tu-Sa 11:00-4:00.
Kent Archer, Director/Curator, kent.archer@usask.ca
Leah Taylor, Associate Curator, leah.taylor@usask.ca
Blair Barbeau, Gallery Technician, blair.barbeau@usask.ca

***Swift Current:* Art Gallery of Swift Current (AGSC)**
411 Hebert St. East
Swift Current, SK S9H 1M5
Tel: 306-778-2736; *Fax:* 306-773-8769
www.artgalleryofswiftcurrent.org
www.facebook.com/ArtGalleryofSwiftCurre nt
Year Founded: 1974 Non-profit public art gallery & national standard art museum offering exhibitions of provincial, national & international artwork; provides access to & education in visual art culture for Southwest Saskatchewan
Kim Houghtaling, Director/Curator, k.houghtaling@swiftcurrent.ca

***Watrous:* Gallery on 3rd**
PO Box 63
Located at 102 - 3rd Ave. East
Watrous, SK S0K 4T0
Tel: 306-261-1728
The gallery features local artists, as well as traveling art shows. Open year-round, W-Sa 1:00-4:00.
Bryce Erickson, Contact, bryceerickson@me.com
Lynnette Wall, Contact, 306-946-3451

***Weyburn:* Allie Griffin Art Gallery (AGAG)**
45 Bison Ave.
Weyburn, SK S4H 0H9
Tel: 306-848-3922; *Fax:* 306-848-3271
weyburnartscouncil@weyburn.ca
www.weyburnartscouncil.ca
Year Founded: 1964 Features touring exhibitions from the Mendel Art Gallery, the Mackenzie Art Gallery, the Saskatchewan Craft Council, the Saskatchewan Arts Board through OSAC, and many locally curated shows. The exhibitions feature the work of well-known as well as emerging Saskatchewan artists.
Alice Neufeld, Arts Director
Ron Ror, Curator

***Weyburn:* Signal Hill Arts Centre (SHAC)**
424 - 10 Ave. South
Weyburn, SK S4H 2A1
Tel: 306-848-3278; *Fax:* 306-848-3271
www.weyburn.ca
Year Founded: 1985 The Signal Hill Arts Centre is located in a five storey multi-purpose civic heritage facility, which also houses a pottery studio, gallery, gift shop, kitchen, dance studio, an office, & meeting rooms.
Alice Neufeld, Arts Director

***Yorkton:* Godfrey Dean Art Gallery**
Yorkton Arts Council, 49 Smith St. East
Yorkton, SK S3N 0H4
Tel: 306-786-2992; *Fax:* 306-782-2767
gdag@sasktel.net
www.deangallery.ca
twitter.com/deangallery
www.face book.com/GodfreyDeanArtGallery
Year Founded: 1981 Devoted to the exhibition of visual art that reflects contemporary issues relevant to the Yorkton region; classes & special events programming.
Donald Stein, Executive Director

Yukon Territory

Territorial Art Gallery

Yukon Arts Centre (YAC)
PO Box 16
Located at 300 College Dr., Whitehorse, YT
Whitehorse, YT Y1A 5X9
Tel: 867-667-8575; *Fax:* 867-393-6300
info@yac.ca
yukonartscentre.com
twitter.com/YukonArtsCentre
www.face book.com/YukonArtsCentre
Year Founded: 1992 Yukon Arts Centre is the territory's premier venue for performing &d visual arts. The Gallery hosts 10-14 contemporary art exhibitions per year. Emphasis is to showcase work of professional Yukon artists & to bring exhibitions of national importance to the Yukon. The Theatre is a 428-seat proscenium theatre.
Wendy Tayler, Chair
Al Cushing, Chief Executive Officer, ceo@yac.ca
Mary Bradshaw, Curator, mary.bradshaw@yac.ca
Eric Epstein, Artistic Director, ad@yac.ca

Local Art Gallery

***Pelly Crossing:* Big Jonathan House**
PO Box 40
Pelly Crossing, YT Y0B 1P0
Tel: 867-537-3150; *Fax:* 867-537-3902
www.facebook.com/253593068031724
Big Jonathan House is a cultural centre for the Selkirk First Nations people, featuring works by local artists, as well as locally made clothing, baskets, & traditional items. A video presentaion called "Fort Selkirk: Voices of the People" reveals the history of the region & its people. Open May-Sept., daily 9:00-7:00.

Aquaria

British Columbia

Local Aquaria

***Sidney:* Shaw Ocean Discovery Centre**
Port Sidney Marina, 9811 Seaport Pl.
Sidney, BC V8L 4X3
Tel: 250-665-7511; *Fax:* 778-426-0715
info@oceandiscovery.ca
www.oceandiscovery.ca
twitter.com/oceandiscover y
www.facebook.com/oceandiscovery
Year Founded: 2009 Dedicated to marine education, awareness & stewardship; open year round
Nancy Barbour, Chair
Alison Barratt, Executive Director

***Vancouver:* Vancouver Aquarium**
PO Box 3232
Located at: Aquaquest Reception, 845 Avison Way, Vancouver, BC V6G 3E2
Vancouver, BC V6B 3X8
Tel: 604-659-3400; *Fax:* 604-659-3515
Toll-Free: 800-931-1186
visitorexperience@vanaqua.org
www.vanaqua.org
Social Media: www.youtube.com/user/VancouverAquarium
twitter.com/vancouveraqua
www.facebook.com/vanaqua
Other contact information: Info Line: 604-659-3474
Year Founded: 1956 The largest aquarium in Canada & one of the five largest in North America; a self-sufficient, non-profit organization, the Aquarium is internationally recognized for display & interpretation excellence & was the first facility to incorporate professional Naturalists into the galleries to complement interpretive graphics; research projects extend world wide & it is internationally recognized for its success
Brian Hanna, Chair
Dr. John Nightingale, President & CEO Ph.D.

New Brunswick

Local Aquaria

***St Andrews:* Huntsman Marine Science Centre**
1 Lower Campus Rd.
St Andrews, NB E5B 2L7
Tel: 506-529-1200; *Fax:* 506-529-1212
huntsman@huntsmanmarine.ca
www.huntsmanmarine.ca
Social Media: huntsmaneducation.blogspot.ca
www.facebook.com/HuntsmanMarineScienceCent re
Year Founded: 1969 Public aquarium/museum with local flora & fauna, & the Atlantic Reference Centre which houses a zoological & botanical museum reference collection; research & teaching in marine sciences & coastal biology; marine education courses for elementary, high school & university groups; aquaculture research & development facilities
Jarney Smith, Executive Director, jsmith@huntsmanmarine.ca

***Shippagan:* Aquarium et Centre marin du Nouveau-Brunswick (ACM)**
100, rue de l'Aquarium
Shippagan, NB E8S 1H9
Tél: 506-336-3013; *Téléc:* 506-336-3057
info@aquariumnb.ca
aquariumnb.ca
www.facebook.com/116268635055142
Aquarium publique qui expose un nombre impressionnant d'espèces de poissons qui vivent dans les eaux du golfe St-Laurent ainsi que dans les lacs et rivières de l'est du Canada. L'Attraction vedette est une famille de phoque communs;

présentation audio-visuelle; bassin touchez-y; ouvert de mai à sept.; acceptons réservations de groups hors saison

Newfoundland & Labrador

Local Aquarium

St. John's: The Suncor Energy Fluvarium
5 Nagle's Pl.
St. John's, NL A1B 2Z2
Tel: 709-754-3474; Fax: 709-754-5947
info@fluvarium.ca
www.fluvarium.ca
Social Media: www.flickr.com/photos/fluvarium
twitter.com/Fluvarium
www.facebook.com /Fluvarium
Other contact information: Alternate Phone: 709-722-3825
Year Founded: 1989 Delivers an environmental education program to over 10,000 school children annually; houses interactive fresh water exhibits & nine underwater viewing windows into Nagle's Hill Brook
Dan Helmbold, General Manager

Ontario

Local Aquaria

Niagara Falls: Marineland of Canada Inc.
c/o Marineland, Marketing/Group Sales Dept., 8375 Stanley Ave.
Location: 7657 Portage Rd., Niagara Falls, ON
Niagara Falls, ON L2G 0C8
Tel: 905-356-9565; Fax: 905-356-6305
marketing@marineland.ca
www.marinelandcanada.com
twitter.com/Marinelan dCan
www.facebook.com/MarinelandofCanada
Interactive marina & amusement park; facility for animal & marine mammal care, where guests can learn about animals through a mix of entertainment & education. Contains the largest whale habitat in the world. Open May - Oct.
John Holer, President/Owner

Toronto: Ripley's Aquarium of Canada
288 Bremner Blvd.
Toronto, ON M5J 3A6
Tel: 647-351-3474
TGServices@ripleysaquariumofcanada.com
www.ripleyaquar iums.com/canada/
Social Media: instagram.com/RipleysAquaCA
twitter.com/RipleysAquaCA
www.facebook.com/RipleysAquariumCanada
Year Founded: 2013 Ripley's Aquarium of Canada is a 12,500 square-metre (135,000 square-feet) attraction with more than 5.7 million litres (1.5 million gallons) of water depicting marine and freshwater habitats from around the world. There are more than 13,500 underwater creatures, including a 2.84 million litre (750,000 gallon) Shark Lagoon. The aquarium also offers an extensive Education and Conservation program.

Prince Edward Island

Local Aquarium

Stanley Bridge: Stanley Bridge Marine Aquarium & Manor of Birds
Rte. 6
Stanley Bridge, PE C0A 1E0
Tel: 902-886-3355
www.kata.pe.ca/attract/marine/marine.htm
The aquarium features live fish, the World of Butterflies display, & over 700 mounted birds. Also featured are the histories of Malpeque oysters, Irish moss, & shellfish industries. Carr's Oyster Bar & Restaurant is located on-site.

Québec

Local Aquaria

Les Escoumins: Marine Environment Discovery Centre
41, rue des Pilotes
Les Escoumins, QC G0T 1K0
Tel: 418-233-4414
www.pc.gc.ca/saguenay
Other contact information: Off-Season Phone: 418-235-4703
Marine interpretation site featuring live collections & an amphitheatre; located in Saguenay-St. Lawrence Marine Park.

Sainte-Anne-des-Monts: Exploramer, la mer à découvrir / Exploramer: Discovering the Sea
1, rue du Quai
Sainte-Anne-des-Monts, QC G4V 2B6
Tél: 418-763-2500; Téléc: 418-763-5528
info@exploramer.qc.ca
www.exploramer.qc.ca
Médias sociaux: www.youtube.com/user/Exploramer
twitter.com/Exploramer
www.facebook.co m/Exploramer
Fondée en: 1995
Gilles Thériault, Président
Sandra Gauthier, Directrice générale, sandra.gauthier@exploramer.qc.ca

Sainte-Flavie: Parc de la rivière Mitis (CISA)
900, route de la Mer
Sainte-Flavie, QC G0J 2L0
Tél: 418-775-2969
info@parcmitis.com
www.parcmitis.com
Le Parc de la rivière Mitis est situé à Saint-Flavie et se veut un site écotouriste qui améne les gens à porter un nouveau regard sur l'interprétation et la préservation du patrimonie naturel et culturel. Ouvert mi-juin - sept.

Sainte-Foy: Aquarium du Québec
1675, av des Hôtels
Sainte-Foy, QC G1W 4S3
Tél: 418-659-5264; Téléc: 418-646-9238
Ligne sans frais: 866-659-5264
aquarium@sepaq.com
www.sepaq.com/ct/paq
Médias sociaux: instagram.com/aquariumduqc
twitter.com/AquariumduQC
www.facebook.com/aquariumduQuébec
Fondée en: 1959 Un parc de 16 hectares englobant les aspects de l'écosystème du nord et la vie marine. Observer et d'interagir avec plus de 10.000 échantillons frais et d'eau salée poissons, les reptiles, les amphibiens, les invertébrés, ainsi que des mammifères marins tels que les morses de l'Atlantique et du Pacifique, les phoques et les ours polaires. Horaire d'hiver: tous les jours 10 h à 16 h; horaire d'été: tous les jours 9 h à 17 h.

Saskatchewan

Local Aquarium

Fort Qu'appelle: Fish Culture Station
PO Box 190
Fort Qu'appelle, SK S0G 1S0
Tel: 306-332-3200
fish.culture@gov.sk.ca

Botanical Gardens

Alberta

Local Botanical Gardens

Brooks: Golden Prairie Arboretum
Alberta Agriculture & Rural Development, 301 Horticulture Station Rd. East
Brooks, AB T1R 1E6
Tel: 403-362-1350; Fax: 403-362-1306
Collection of deciduous trees & shrubs
Shelley Barkley, Contact, shelley.barkley@gov.ab.ca

Calgary: University of Calgary Herbarium
Dept. of Biological Sciences, 2500 University Dr. NW
Calgary, AB T2N 1N4
Tel: 403-220-7465; Fax: 403-289-9311
www.ucalgary.ca/herbarium
Vascular plants
Dr. C.C. Chinnappa, Director, cchinna@ucalgary.ca
Dr. Jana Vamosi, Director, Online Herbarium, jvamosi@ucalgary.ca

Edmonton: Devonian Botanic Garden
University of Alberta, 1A University Campus NW
Edmonton, AB T6G 2E1
Tel: 780-987-3054
www.devonian.ualberta.ca
twitter.com/DevonianGarden
www.facebook.com/DevonianBotanicGarden
Year Founded: 1953 80 acres of cultivated gardens & 110 acres of natural area; native & alpine plants, ecological reserves, Kurimoto Japanese Garden & Orchid House & a Butterly House; picnic area, patio cafe & gift shop; open May-Oct.
Lee Foote, Director, lee.foote@ualberta.ca
Ruby Swanson, Managing Director, ruby.swanson@ualberta.ca
Rene Belland, Curator/DataSystems Manager, Plant Herbarium, rbelland@ualberta.ca

Edmonton: Muttart Conservatory
9626 - 96A St.
Edmonton, AB T6C 4L8
Tel: 780-442-5311
muttartquestions@edmonton.ca
www.edmonton.ca/muttart
www.facebook.com/muttart.conservatory1
Four pyramids house flora of different world climatic zones, including arid, temperate, & tropical; Show Pyramid features 6 different floral shows per year; species orchid greenhouse; outdoor trail gardens in summer; in Edmonton, call 311 to reach the Conservatory

Edmonton: University of Alberta Vascular Plant Herbarium (ALTA)
Dept. of Biological Sciences, University of Alberta, B-414, Biological Sciences Building
Edmonton, AB T6G 2E1
Tel: 780-492-8611
biology.museums.ualberta.ca/VascularPlantHerbarium.aspx
Year Founded: 1912 Houses prairie, arctic & alpine plants.
Jocelyn Hall, Curator, jocelyn.hall@ualberta.ca
Dorothy Fabijan, Assistant Curator, 780-492-5523, dorothy.fabijan@ualberta.ca

Lethbridge: Nikka Yuko Japanese Garden
c/o Lethbridge & District Japanese Garden Society, PO Box 751
Located at 9 Ave. South & Mayor Magrath Dr., Lethbridge, AB
Lethbridge, AB T1J 3Z6
Tel: 403-328-3511; Fax: 403-328-0511
info@nikkayuko.com
www.nikkayuko.com
twitter.com/NikkaYuko
www.faceb ook.com/123765594310823
Year Founded: 1967 The Nikka Yuko Japanese Garden is a mature four acre garden providing a quiet, serene place for the appreciation of nature & discovery of inner peace. Includes dry rock garden, mountain & waterfall, streams & bridges, ponds and islands, flat prarie garden.
John Harding, President

Trochu: Trochu Arboretum & Gardens
c/o Trochu Arboretum Society, PO Box 803
Trochu, AB T0M 2C0
Tel: 403-588-8600
www.town.trochu.ab.ca/trochu-arboretum-gardens
Year Founded: 1989

British Columbia

Local Botanical Gardens

Burnaby: Simon Fraser University Arboretum
Dept. of Biological Sciences, Simon Fraser University, 8888 University Dr.
Burnaby, BC V5A 1S6
Tel: 778-782-4475; Fax: 778-782-3496
biscrec@sfu.ca
www.biology.sfu.ca
Elizabeth Elle, Department Chair, Dept. of Biological Sciences, biscchr@sfu.ca

Kimberley: Cominco Gardens
290 Rossland Blvd.
Kimberley, BC V1A 2R6
Tel: 250-427-5160

North Vancouver: Park & Tilford Gardens
Park & Tilford Centre, 333 Brookbank Ave.
North Vancouver, BC V7J 3S8
www.parkandtilford.ca
8 themed public gardens; free admission; open dawn to dusk

Vancouver: Bloedel Conservatory
4600 Cambie St.
Vancouver, BC V5Y 2M4
Tel: 604-257-8584
vancouver.ca/parks-recreation-culture/bloedel-conservatory.aspx
Year Founded: 1969 Canada's largest single-structure tropical conservatory featuring over 500 species in simulated rain-forest, subtropic & desert environments; also features free-flying tropical birds & a Japanese Koi fish collection

***Vancouver:* Dr. Sun Yat-Sen Classical Chinese Garden**
578 Carrall St.
Vancouver, BC V6B 5K2
Tel: 604-662-3207; *Fax:* 604-682-4008
communications@vancouverchinesegarden.com
vancouverchinesegarden.com
Social Media: www.youtube.com/user/vanchinesegarden
twitter.com/vangarden
www.facebook.com/vancouverchinesegarden
Year Founded: 1986 The first authentic, full-scale, classical Chinese garden built outside China; museum, garden & cultural attraction
Jeannette Hlavach, President
Kathy Gibler, Executive Director, director@vancouverchinesegarden.com

***Vancouver:* Nitobe Memorial Garden**
c/o UBC Botanical Garden & Centre for Plant Research, 6804 Southwest Marine Dr.
Vancouver, BC V6T 1Z4
Tel: 604-822-6038; *Fax:* 604-822-2016
garden.nitobe@ubc.ca
www.botanicalgarden.ubc.ca/nitobe
Authentic Japanese tea & stroll garden; cherry blossoms; Japanese Irises, Japanese Maples; Koi; lanterns & much more

***Vancouver:* UBC Botanical Garden**
University of British Columbia, 6804 Southwest Marine Dr.
Vancouver, BC V6T 1Z4
Tel: 604-822-3928; *Fax:* 604-822-2016
garden.info@ubc.ca
www.botanicalgarden.ubc.ca
twitter.com/UBCgarden
www.facebook.com/UBCgarden
Living museum of plants in 110 acres of BC coastal native forest; over 10,000 assorted trees, shrubs, flowers; divided into various components
Patrick Lewis, Director, Garden, patrick.lewis@ubc.ca
Douglas Justice, Associate Director, Horticulture & Collections, douglas.justice@ubc.ca

***Vancouver:* VanDusen Botanical Garden**
5251 Oak St.
Vancouver, BC V6M 4H1
Tel: 604-257-8666; *Fax:* 604-257-8679
VanDusenAdmin@vancouver.ca
www.vandusengarden.org
Social Media: www.flickr.com/photos/vandusenbotanicalgarden
www.facebook.com/210746535 227
Other contact information: 24-Hour Information Line: 604-257-8335
22-hectare garden comprised of over 255,000 plants. Open year-round.
Howard Normann, Interim Garden Director, howard.normann@vancouver.ca

***Victoria:* The Butchart Gardens Ltd.**
PO Box 4010
Location: 800 Benvenuto Ave., Brentwood Bay, BC V8M 1J8
Victoria, BC V8X 3X4
Tel: 250-652-4422; *Fax:* 250-652-7751
Toll-Free: 866-652-4422
email@butchartgardens.com
www.butchartgardens.com
Social Media: www.youtube.com/thebutchartgardens
twitter.com/butchartgardens
www.facebook.com/butchartgardens
Other contact information: General Information Phone: 250-652-5256
Year Founded: 1904 55 acres of manicured gardens on a 130 acre private estate; open year-round
Dale Ryan, Director, Public Relations

***Victoria:* Government House Gardens**
***Parent:* Friends of the Government House Gardens Society**
1401 Rockland Ave.
Victoria, BC V8S 1V9
Tel: 250-387-2080; *Fax:* 250-387-2078
ghinfo@gov.bc.ca
www.ltgov.bc.ca/gardens/individ-gardens/default.html
Other contact information: Alt. URL: www.fghgs.ca
The gardens are open to the public, & walking tours for groups are offered through the Friends of the Government House Gardens Society. There are nearly thirty individual gardens at the site.

***Victoria:* Horticultural Center of the Pacific**
505 Quayle Rd.
Victoria, BC V6E 2J7
Tel: 250-479-6162; *Fax:* 250-479-6047
events@hcp.ca
hcp.ca
Social Media: www.youtube.com/hcpacific
twitter.com/hcpacific
www.facebook.com/HCPacific
Year Founded: 1979 A nonprofit organization founded in 1979 as The Horticultural Center of the Pacific or HCP, it manages 103 acres to demonstrate sound gardening practices using the diversity of plants that can be grown in this area, to preserve natural plant & animal habitat, & to provide a unique environment for preparing students for careers in horticulture. It relies on public funding, on local businesses, & on its own fundraising activities to support these activities.

***Victoria:* Royal Roads Botanical Garden**
c/o Royal Roads University, 2005 Sooke Rd.
Victoria, BC V9B 5Y2
Tel: 250-391-2511; *Fax:* 250-391-2500
Toll-Free: 800-788-8028
www.hatleypark.ca
Native coastal forest & formal gardens

Manitoba

Local Botanical Gardens

***Boissevain:* International Peace Garden**
PO Box 419
Boissevain, MB R0K 0E0
Tel: 204-534-2510*Toll-Free:* 888-432-6733
peaceweb@srt.com
www.peacegarden.com
www.facebook.com/128773100471418
2300-acre park located on the North Dakota & Manitoba boarders; tribute to peace & friendship between the people of Canada & the United States of America; maintains extensive gardens containing a wide variety of shrubs, perennials, & annual plants; souvenir shop, interpretative centre, picnic sites, hiking trails, International music camp, Royal Canadian Legion sports camp, & 9/11 Memorial Site.
Doug Hevenor, CEO, dhevenor@peacegarden.com

***Leaf Rapids:* Leaf Rapids National Exhibition Centre**
Town Centre Complex, PO Box 220
Leaf Rapids, MB R0B 1W0
Tel: 204-473-8682; *Fax:* 204-473-2707
The Exhibition Centre features traveling displays and local and regional artists exhibits. Each year, two to four live performances are offered for youth and adults.

***Morden:* Morden Arboretum**
Morden Research Centre, Agriculture & Agri-Food Canada, PO Box 3001, 100 - 101, Rte. 100
Morden, MB R6M 1Y5
Tel: 204-822-4471; *Fax:* 204-983-4604
A federal government research centre; variety of programs including breeding & development of trees, shrubs, roses & herbaceous perennials; improvement & agronomic research programs carried out on linseed flax, field peas & dry edible beans

***Winnipeg:* Assiniboine Park**
55 Pavilion Cres.
Winnipeg, MB R3P 2N6
Tel: 204-927-6000; *Fax:* 204-927-7200
Toll-Free: 877-927-6006
info@assiniboinepark.ca
www.assiniboinepark.ca
Social Media: www.youtube.com/user/AssiniboinePark
twitter.com/assiniboinepark
www.facebook.com/assiniboineparkzoo
Includes Assiniboine Park Zoo, Assiniboine Park Conservatory, Leo Mol Sculpture Garden, Pavillion Art Gallery, English & Formal Gardens, Assiniboine Forest Natural Area
Hartley Richardson, Chair
Margaret Redmond, President & CEO

***Winnipeg:* Living Prairie Museum Interpretive Centre**
2795 Ness Ave.
Winnipeg, MB R3J 3S4
Tel: 204-832-0167
www.winnipeg.ca/publicworks/naturalist/livingprairie
38-hectare preserve of original tall grass; interpretive centre; open May - Jun on Sundays; July - Aug open daily

New Brunswick

Local Botanical Gardens

***Edmunston:* New Brunswick Botanical Garden (NBBG) / Jardin botanique du Nouveau-Brunswick**
PO Box 1629, 15 Main St.
Edmunston, NB E7B 1A3
Tel: 506-737-4444
info@jardinNBgarden.com
jardinnbgarden.com
Social Media: www.youtube.com/user/JardinBotaniqueNB
twitter.com/jardinNBgarden
www. facebook.com/jardinNBgarden
Year Founded: 1993 7 hectares; over 50,000 plants.
Jean Aucoin, Director

***Fredericton:* Fredericton Bontanic Garden**
c/o Fredericton Botanic Garden Association, PO Box 57 A
Located in Odell Park, 10 Cameron Ct., Fredericton, NB, E3B 4Y2
Fredericton, NB E3B 4Y2
Tel: 506-452-9269
fbga@nb.aibn.com
frederictonbotanicgarden.com
www.facebook.com/FrederictonBotanicGarden
Year Founded: 1990
Wendy Bourque, President, Fredericton Botanic Garden Association

***Saint Andrews:* Kingsbrae Garden**
220 King St.
Saint Andrews, NB E5B 1Y8
Tel: 506-529-3335; *Fax:* 506-529-4875
Toll-Free: 866-566-8687
kingsbraegarden.com
Social Media: www.flickr.com/photos/kingsbraegarden
twitter.com/KingsbraeGarden
www. facebook.com/Kingsbrae.Garden
The gardens total 20 acres, and are home to over 4,000 different plants.
John Flemer, Founder
Lucinda Flemer, Founder

Newfoundland & Labrador

Local Botanical Garden

***St. John's:* The Memorial University of Newfoundland Botanical Garden**
Memorial University of Newfoundland
St. John's, NL A1C 5S7
Tel: 709-737-8590; *Fax:* 709-864-8596
bgprograms@mun.ca
www.mun.ca/botgarden
www.facebook.com/pages/MUN-Botanical-Garden-Inc/280608787849
Year Founded: 1977 The Memorial University of Newfoundland Botanical Garden maintains cultivated gardens and natural habitats for public display and is a centre for botanical, horticultural and environmental research and education.
Liz Klose, Director, garden@mun.ca

Nova Scotia

Local Botanical Gardens

***Annapolis Royal:* Annapolis Royal Historic Gardens**
PO Box 278
Located at 441 St. George St., Annapolis Royal, NS, B0S 1A0
Annapolis Royal, NS B0S 1A0
Tel: 902-532-7018; *Fax:* 902-532-7445
admin@historicgardens.com
www.historicgardens.com
Social Media: www.youtube.com/historicgardens
twitter.com/Historicgardens
www.facebebo ok.com/historic.gardens.7
Theme gardens, collections & displays reflect historical periods - Open May - Oct.
Trish Fry, Manager

***Halifax:* Halifax Public Gardens**
PO Box 13, 5665 Spring Garden Rd.
Halifax, NS B3J 3S9
info@halifaxpublicgardens.ca
www.halifaxpublicgardens.ca
Social Media: www.flickr.com/groups/halifaxpublicgardens
twitter.com/HfxPublicGarden
www.facebook.com/128749280505802
Year Founded: 1867 Formal Victorian Garden, located at Summer St. & Spring Garden Rd.

***Wolfville:* E.C. Smith Herbarium**
K.C. Irving Environmental Science Centre, Acadia University, 32 University Ave.
Wolfville, NS B4P 2P8
Tel: 902-585-1710
herbarium.acadiau.ca
The herbarium contains over 200,000 specimens, & is the first herbarium in Canada to have a digital database containing of images of the collection.
Rodger Evans, Director, rodger.evans@acadiau.ca
Ruth Newell, Curator, 902-585-1335, ruth.newell@acadiau.ca

***Wolfville:* Harriet Irving Botanical Gardens**
Acadia University, 32 University Ave.
Wolfville, NS B4P 2R6
botanicalgardens.acadiau.ca
Peter A, Romkey, Executive Director, 902-585-1757, peter.romkey@acadiau.ca

Ontario

Local Botanical Gardens

***Burlington:* Centre for Canadian Historical Horticultural Studies (CCHHS)**
c/o Royal Botanical Gardens, 680 Plains Rd. West
Burlington, ON L7T 4H4
Tel: 905-527-1158; *Fax:* 905-577-0375
info@rbg.ca
Alex Henderson, Curator, Collections & Horticulturist

***Burlington:* Royal Botanical Gardens (RBG)**
680 Plains Rd. West
Burlington, ON L7T 4H4
Tel: 905-527-1158; *Fax:* 905-577-0375
Toll-Free: 800-694-4769
info@rbg.ca
www.rbg.ca
Social Media: www.youtube.com/user/royalbotanicalgarden
twitter.com/RBGCanada
www.fa cebook.com/RoyalBotanicalGardens
Year Founded: 1939 A living museum which serves local, regional & global communities while developing & promoting public understanding of the relationship between the plant world, humanity & the rest of nature. 1,100 hectares of land: 120 cultivated hectares, while the rest remains a managed natural area including marshlands & walking trails.
Mark Runciman, CEO, mrunciman@rbg.ca

***Guelph:* The Arboretum**
University of Guelph
Guelph, ON N1G 2W1
Tel: 519-824-4120; *Fax:* 519-763-9598
arbor@uoguelph.ca
www.uoguelph.ca/arboretum
Social Media: www.flickr.com/photos/52649814@N05
twitter.com/ArborUofG
www.facebook. com/226671253176
Year Founded: 1970 Environmental education & research activities; plant collections; formal gardens; recreational workshops; dinner theatre; meeting & banquet facilities
Prof. Shelley Hunt, Director, shunt@uoguelph.ca
Ric Jordan, Manager, rjordan@uoguelph.ca

***Kingsville:* Colasanti's Tropical Gardens**
1550 Rd. 3 East
Kingsville, ON N9Y 2E5
Tel: 519-326-3287; *Fax:* 519-322-2302
tropical@colasanti.com
www.colasanti.com
Social Media: instagram.com/colasanti_farms
twitter.com/colasantifarms
www.facebook. com/332835756894703
Year Founded: 1941 Colasanti's Tropical Gardens features over 3.5 acres of tropical greenhouses. It is open 363 days each year. Attractions include exotic plants, animals, indoor miniature golf, children's rides, an indoor playground, an arcade, a restaurant, plus home decor & collectables.

***London:* Sherwood Fox Arboretum**
University of Western Ontario, Richmond St. North
London, ON N6A 5B7
Tel: 519-661-2111; *Fax:* 519-661-3935
arboretum@uwo.ca
www.uwo.ca/biology/arboretum
Year Founded: 1981 The arboretum includes the trees planted on the campus of the university
Sandra K. Mackin, Technical Assistant

***Niagara Falls:* Niagara Parks Botanical Gardens & School of Horticulture**
PO Box 150
Niagara Falls, ON L2E 6T2
Tel: 905-356-8554
schoolofhorticulture@niagaraparks.com
www.niagaraparks .com/school-of-horticulture
Includes the Niagara Parks Butterfly Conservatory

***North Bay:* North Bay Heritage Gardeners Nipissing Botanical Gardens**
***Parent:* Heritage North Bay**
100 Ferguson St.
North Bay, ON P1B 1W8
Tel: 705-472-4006
gardener.executive@heritagenorthbay.com
gardeners.heritagenorthbay.ca
The Nipissing Botanical Gardens is a committee of the Heritage Gardeners, whose mission is to identify, preserve, & create green space in the City of North Bay. Please see the Heritage Gardeners' website for a detailed map of heritage gardens around the city.
Monica McLaren, Coordinator

***Oshawa:* Oshawa Valley Botanical Gardens (OVBG)**
50 Centre St. South
Oshawa, ON L1H 3Z7
Tel: 905-436-3311
ovbg@oshawa.ca
www.oshawa.ca/tourism/ovbg/default.asp
Year Founded: 2001

***Ottawa:* Central Experimental Farm**
c/o CEF Information, Agriculture & Agri-Food Canada, K.W. Neatly Bldg., #1103, 960 Carling Ave.
Ottawa, ON K1A 0C6
Tel: 613-759-1982; *Fax:* 613-759-6901
cef-fec@agr.gc.ca
www.agr.gc.ca/eng/about-us/offices-and-locations/central-experimental-farm
The farm is a National Historic Site of Canada.

***Ridgetown:* J.J. Neilson Arboretum**
Ridgetown Campus, University of Guelph, 120 Main St. East
Ridgetown, ON N0P 2C0
Tel: 519-674-1500
www.ridgetownc.uoguelph.ca/aboutus/arboretum.cfm
Year Founded: 1986 Includes upwards of 500 taxa., including Carolinian trees & shrubs, & collections of Viburnum & Dogwood, along with perennial & annual displays, & theme landscape areas. Free admission; open every day; staff available M-F 8:30-4:30.

***St Catharines:* Walker Botanical Garden**
Rodman Hall Art Centre, Brock University, 109 St. Paul Cres.
St Catharines, ON L2M 1M3
Tel: 905-684-2925; *Fax:* 905-682-4733
www.brocku.ca/rodman-hall
Year Founded: 1988
Stuart Reid, Director/Curator, stuart.reid@brocku.ca

***Sault Ste Marie:* Great Lakes Forestry Centre Arboretum (GLFC)**
Canadian Forest Service, 1219 Queen St. East
Sault Ste Marie, ON P6A 2E5
Tel: 705-949-9461; *Fax:* 705-541-5700
cfs.nrcan.gc.ca/centres/read/glfc
Two hectares of natural land & forest featuring a wide array of trees collected & labelled by species.

***Thunder Bay:* Centennial Botanical Conservatory**
c/o City Parks Division, 111 Syndicate Ave. South
Thunder Bay, ON P7E 6S4
Tel: 807-622-7036; *Fax:* 807-622-7602
www.thunderbay.ca/parks
Year Founded: 1967 Four seasonal flower displays; cactus & tropical displays year round; open year round, 1-4 pm daily; free admission

***Thunder Bay:* Soroptimist International Friendship Garden**
Parks Division, Victoriaville Civic Centre, 111 Syndicate Ave. South
Thunder Bay, ON P7E 6S4
Tel: 807-625-2941; *Fax:* 807-625-3258
www.thunderbay.ca/parks
www.facebook.com/111021215615503
Soroptimist International Friendship Garden was created by Canadians of varied ethnic origins as a centennial gift to Canada & the community. Individual gardens have been planned, designed, constructed, & financed by the respective groups; Each group has created a garden typical of their culture & homeland.

***Toronto:* Allan Gardens Conservatory**
19 Horticultural Ave.
Toronto, ON M5A 2P2
Tel: 416-392-7288
www.facebook.com/pages/Allan-Gardens-Conservatory/253727411341921
Year Founded: 1879 Permanent plant collection of tropical & sub-tropical plants; seasonal plant displays; open daily 10-5

***Toronto:* Edwards Gardens**
777 Lawrence Ave. East
Toronto, ON M3C 1P2
www.toronto.ca/parks
Edwards Gardens is a former Estate garden turned public park, featuring a wide variety of plants & flowers, as well as rock gardens, a greenhouse, wooden arch bridges, a waterwheel, fountains, & walking trails. The Toronto Botanical Gardens (TBG) is also housed here.

***Toronto:* Humber Arboretum & Centre for Urban Ecology**
205 Humber College Blvd.
Toronto, ON M9W 5L7
Tel: 416-675-6622; *Fax:* 416-675-2755
arboretum@humber.ca
www.humberarboretum.on.ca
twitter.com/HumberArb
www.facebook.com/HumberArb
Other contact information: Centre for Urban Ecology Phone: 416-675-5009
Year Founded: 1977 100 hectares of ornamental gardens & green space on the west branch of the Humber River; also on-site is the educational Centre for Urban Ecology

***Toronto:* Toronto Botanical Gardens (TBG)**
777 Lawrence Ave. East
Toronto, ON M3C 1P2
Tel: 416-397-1340; *Fax:* 416-397-1354
info@torontobotanicalgarden.ca
torontobotanicalgarden.ca
Social Media: www.youtube.com/user/tobotanical
twitter.com/TBG_Canada
www.facebook.com/TorontoBotanicalGarden
Other contact information: Reception: 416-397-1341
Year Founded: 1964 Located within the Edwards Gardens public park, the Toronto Botanical Gardens features 17 themed gardens on four acres of land. The TBG offers garden tours, day camps, field trips, a horticultural library, rental facilities, gift shop, & seasonal café.
Mary Fisher, President/Co-Chair
Harry Jongerden, Executive Director, 416-397-1346, director@torontobotanicalgarden.ca
Paul Zammit, Nancy Eaton Director, Horticulture, 416-397-1358, horticulture@torontobotanicalgarden.ca
Sandra Pella, Head Gardener, 416-397-1316, gardener@torontobotanicalgarden.ca

***Toronto:* Toronto Sculpture Garden**
115 King St. East
Toronto, ON M5C 1G6
Tel: 416-515-9658
info@torontosculpturegarden.com
www.torontosculpturegarden.com
Year Founded: 1981 Semi-annual exhibitions of contemporary sculpture in a park.
Louis L. Odette, Founder
Rina Greer, Director

***Wilsonville:* Whistling Gardens Ltd.**
698 Concession 3
Wilsonville, ON N0E 1Z0
Tel: 519-443-5773; *Fax:* 519-443-4141
info@whistlinggardens.ca
www.whistlinggardens.ca
twitter.com/Whistling G
www.facebook.com/pages/Whistling-Gardens/133949146691279
Year Founded: 2012 The gardens total 20 acres, and are home to over 4,000 different plants.
Darren Heimbecker, Founder

***Windsor:* Fogolar Furlan Botanic Garden**
Fogolar Furlan Windsor, 1800 North Service Rd.
Windsor, ON N8W 1Y3
Tel: 519-966-2230; *Fax:* 519-966-2237
info@fogolar.com
www.fogolar.com

***Windsor:* Jackson Park Queen Elizabeth II Garden**
c/o Parks & Forestry Dept., 2450 McDougall St.
Location: 125 Tecumseh Road East, Windsor, ON
Windsor, ON N8X 3N6
Tel: 519-253-2300; *Fax:* 519-255-7990
parkrec@city.windsor.on.ca
www.citywindsor.ca
More than 10,000 plants, formal gardens, fountains, & sports park.

Prince Edward Island

Local Botanical Garden

***Malpeque:* Malpeque Gardens**
PO Box 7617, Kensington RR#1
Malpeque, PE C0B 1M0
Open June 15 - Aug. 15

Québec

Local Botanical Gardens

***Grand-Métis:* Jardin de Métis / Reford Gardens**
200, rte 132
Grand-Métis, QC G0J 1Z0
Tél: 418-775-2222; *Téléc:* 418-775-6201
info@jardinsdemetis.com
www.jardinsmetis.com
twitter.com/jardinsdemeti s
www.facebook.com/JardinsdeMetis
3,000 espèces; plantes indigènes et exotiques.
Alexander Redford, Directeur,
alexander.reford@jardinsdemetis.com
Brigitte Bourdages, Agente de secrétariat,
brigitte.bourdages@jardinsdemetis.com

***Montréal:* Jardin botanique de Montréal / Montréal Botanical Garden**
4101, rue Sherbrooke est
Montréal, QC H1X 2B2
Tél: 514-872-1400
espacepourlavie.ca/jardin-botanique
Médias sociaux: www.youtube.com/Espacepourlavie
twitter.com/espacepourlavie
www.facebo ok.com/Espacepourlavie
Collection de 22000 espèces de plantes et variétés, 10 serres d'exposition et 30 jardins thématiques du monde entier; insectarium; couvre 75 hectares
René Pronovost, Directeur

***Québec:* Jardin botanique Roger-Van den Hende**
Pavillon de L'Envirotron, Université Laval, #1227, 2480, boul Hochelaga
Québec, QC G1V 0A6
Tél: 418-656-2046; *Téléc:* 418-656-3515
jardin@fsaa.ulaval.ca
www.jardin.ulaval.ca
www.facebook.com/JardinBota nique.Québec
Fondée en: 1978 Plus de 4000 espèces et cultivars qui sont disposées dans l'ordre de la famille botanique. Ouvert de mai à octobre; entrée libre.
Hélène Corriveau, Responsable agronomique,
Helene.Corriveau@fsaa.ulaval.ca

***Sainte-Anne-de-Bellevue:* Morgan Arboretum**
Macdonald Campus, McGill University, PO Box 186, 21111 Lakeshore Rd.
Located at Macdonald Campus, McGill University, 150 chemin des Pins, Sainte-Anne-de-Bellevue, QC, H9X 3V9
Sainte-Anne-de-Bellevue, QC H9X 3V9
Tel: 514-398-7811; *Fax:* 514-398-7959
morgan.arboretum@mcgill.ca
www.morganarboretum.org
www.facebook.com/pa ges/Morgan-Arboretum/310991045821
Year Founded: 1945 Situated at the western tip of the island of Montréal; trees grow in forests, experimental plantations & ornamental collections

Saskatchewan

Local Botanical Gardens

***Estevan:* Shand Greenhouse**
PO Box 280
Estevan, SK S4A 2A3
Fax: 306-634-6682
Toll-Free: 866-778-7337
greenhouse@saskpower.com
www.saskpower.com/shandgreenhouse
Greenhouse, shade houses, nursery, display area; uses by-products of energy generation from the Shand Power Station; open year round

***Indian Head:* Agri-Environment Services Branch Agroforestry Development Centre (AESB)**
PO Box 940
Indian Head, SK S0G 2K0
Tel: 306-695-2284
agroforestry@agr.gc.ca
www.agr.ca/pfra/shelterbelt.htm
The AESB administers the Prairie Shelterbelt Program out of the Agroforestry Development Centre, supplying farmers with tree & shrub seedlings as well as technical services.

***Saskatoon:* Patterson Garden Arboretum**
Dept. of Plant Sciences, University of Saskatchewan, 51 Campus Dr.
Located on Preston Ave. North, Saskatoon, SK, S7N 2W4
Saskatoon, SK S7N 5A8
Tel: 306-966-5855; *Fax:* 306-966-5015
patterson-arboretum.usask.ca
Year Founded: 1966 Patterson Garden Arboretum is one of the last remaining Prairie Regional Trials for Woody Ornamentals sites, dedicated to Dr. Cecil Patterson in 1969.
Alan Weninger, Arborist, 306-978-8316,
alan.weninger@usask.ca
Jackie Bantle, Manager, 306-966-5864, jackie.bantle@usask.ca

***Saskatoon:* W.P. Fraser Herbarium Saskatchewan (SASK)**
Agriculture Building, University of Saskatchewan, #3C77
Agriculture Bldg., 51 Campus Dr.
Saskatoon, SK S7N 5A8
Tel: 306-966-4968
sask.herbarium@usask.ca
www.herbarium.usask.ca
Year Founded: 1961 The herbarium houses 180,000 specimens, the largest collection in Saskatchewan. Open by permission only.
Dr. J. Hugo Cota-Sánchez, Curator/Associate Professor,
hugo.cota@usask.ca

Museums

National Museums

Bank of Canada Museum / Musée de la Banque du Canada
234 Laurier Ave. West
Ottawa, ON K1A 0G9
Tel: 613-782-8914
museum@bankofcanada.ca
www.bankofcanadamuseum.ca
twitter.com/BoCMuseum
The most complete collection of Canadian notes & coins in the world, plus representative collections of world coins & paper money, including whales' teeth, glass pearls, elephant-hair bracelets, shells & copper axes.

Canada Agriculture & Food Museum / Musée de l'agriculture du Canada
PO Box 9724 T
Located at 901 Prince of Wales Dr., Ottawa, ON, K2C 3K1
Ottawa, ON K1G 5A3
Tel: 613-991-3044; *Fax:* 613-993-7923
Toll-Free: 866-442-4416
cts@techno-science.ca
www.agriculture.technomuses.ca
Social Media: www.youtube.com/user/cagmweb
twitter.com/AgMuseum
www.facebook.com/AgM useum
Other contact information: TTY: 613-991-9207; Phone, Media: 613-949-5732
The Canada Agriculture & Food Museum is a demonstration farm & research station, which features animal barns, the Dominion Arboretum, ornamental gardens, & special exhibitions. It is part of the Canada Science & Technology Museums Corporation.
Alex Benay, President & CEO, Canada Science & Technology Museums Corporation

Canada Aviation & Space Museum / Musée de l'aviation et de l'espace du Canada
PO Box 9724 T
Ottawa, ON K1G 5A3
Tel: 613-991-3044; *Fax:* 613-990-3655
Toll-Free: 800-463-2038
cts@technomuses.ca
www.aviation.technomuses.ca
Social Media: www.youtube.com/user/CanadaAviationMuseum
twitter.com/avspacemuseum
www.facebook.com/AvSpaceMuseum
Year Founded: 1960 As a component of the Canada Science & Technology Museums Corporation, the Canada Aviation & Space Museum collects, preserves, & displays aviation-related objects, from the pioneer era, through war & peace & to the present time.
Alex Benay, President & CEO, Canada Science & Technology Museums Corporation
Stephen Quick, Director General, Canada Aviation & Space Museum

Canada Science & Technology Museum Corporation (CSTMC/SMSTC) / Société du Musée des Sciences et de la technologie du Canada
PO Box 9724 T
Ottawa, ON K1G 5A3
Tel: 613-991-3044; *Fax:* 613-993-7923
Toll-Free: 866-442-4416
cts@techno-science.ca
techno-science.ca
Social Media: www.youtube.com/cstmweb
twitter.com/SciTechMuseum
www.facebook.com/SciTechMuseum
Exhibits at the Canada Science & Technology Museum include astronomy, space, marine & land transportation, communications, computer technology, & domestic technology. The library of the Canada Science & Technology Museum contains material about the history & development of science & technology, with an emphasis upon Canada. Part of the Canadian Science & Technology Museums Corporation.
Gary Polonsky, Chair, Canada Science & Technology Museums Corporation
Alex Benay, President & CEO, Canada Science & Technology Museums Corporation

Canadian Museum of History / Musée canadien de l'histoire
100 Laurier St.
Gatineau, QC K1A 0M8
Tel: 819-776-7000*Toll-Free:* 800-555-5621
www.civilization.ca
Social Media: www.youtube.com/user/CanMusCiv
twitter.com/CanMusHistory
www.facebook. com/museumofcivilization
Other contact information: TTY: 819-776-7003
Year Founded: 1989 Conducts research in Canadian studies & collects, preserves & displays objects which reflect Canada's cultural heritage. Its activities extend across the country through field research programs, publications & loans to various groups & institutions. Visitors can see permanent & changing exhibitions, public programs & film & theatre programs. The museum is also affiliated with the Canadian War Museum.
Mark O'Neill, President & CEO, mark.oneill@historymuseum.ca

Canadian Museum of Immigration at Pier 21 (CIMP 21)
1055 Marginal Rd.
Halifax, NS B3H 4P7
Tel: 902-425-7770; *Fax:* 902-423-4045
Toll-Free: 855-526-4721
info@pier21.ca
www.pier21.ca
Social Media: www.youtube.com/Pier21Museum
twitter.com/pier21
www.facebook.com/21041 2625764977
Year Founded: 2009 The Canadian Museum of Immigration at Pier 21 details the country's immigration history through personal stories, with an emphasis on the Pier 21 site. Pier 21 was the gateway for around one million immigrants between 1928 & 1971, as well as for soldiers departing Canada during WWII. The museum is Atlantic Canada's only National Museum.
Tung Chan, Chair, Board of Trustees
Marie Chapman, Chief Executive Officer, 902-425-7770,
mchapman@pier21.ca
Tanya Bouchard, Chief Curator, 902-425-7770,
tbouchard@pier21.ca
Cailin MacDonald, Manager, Communications,
cmacdonald@pier21.ca

Canadian Museum of Nature / Musée canadien de la nature
PO Box 3443 D
Located at 240 McLeod St., Ottawa, ON
Ottawa, ON K1P 6P4
Tel: 613-566-4700; *Fax:* 613-364-4021
Toll-Free: 800-263-4433
www.nature.ca
Social Media: www.youtube.com/user/canadanaturemuseum
twitter.com/MuseumofNature
www .facebook.com/canadianmuseumofnature
Other contact information: TTY: 613-566-4770; 1-866-600-8801
The natural sciences & natural history museum features specimens, such as fossils, horned dinosaurs, fish, freshwater

mussels, tropical beetles, animals, lichens, plants, & minerals from Canada & around the world.
Meg Beckel, President & CEO
Michel Houle, Vice-President & CFO
Ailsa Barry, Vice-President, Experience & Engagement
Mark S. Graham, Vice-President, Research & Collections Services
Jennifer Doubt, Curator, Botany
Jean-Marc Gagnon, Curator, Invertebrates
Kamal Khidas, Curator, Vertebrates
Kieran Shepherd, Curator, Palaeobiology

Canadian War Museum (CWM) / Musée canadien de la guerre
1 Vimy Place
Ottawa, ON K1A 0M8
Tel: 819-776-7000*Toll-Free:* 800-555-5621
www.warmuseum.ca
Social Media: www.youtube.com/user/CanWarMus
twitter.com/CanWarMuseum
www.facebook.com/warmuseum
Other contact information: TTY: 800-555-5621
Affiliated museum of the Canadian Museum of Civilization Corporation; war art; uniforms & accoutrements; medals; weapons & small arms; archives; the Hartland Molson library; vast collection of military vehicles & artillery
Stephen Quick, Director General & Vice President, Canadian War Museum; Canadian Museum of History, 819-776-8523, stephen.quick@warmuseum.ca
Yasmine Mingay, Director, Public Affairs, 819-776-8608, yasmine.mingay@warmuseum.ca

Hockey Hall of Fame (HHOF) / Le Temple de la Renommée du Hockey
Brookfield Place, 30 Yonge St.
Toronto, ON M5E 1X8
Tel: 416-360-7765; *Fax:* 416-360-1501
info@hhof.com
www.hhof.com
Social Media: www.youtube.com/user/HockeyHallFame
twitter.com/HockeyHallFame
www.fac ebook.com/10405440140
Year Founded: 1961 The museum holds artifacts, memorabilia, films & photos, displayed in multi-media exhibits, all on a hockey theme. Also on site is the D.K. (Doc) Seaman Hockey Resource Centre, which stores a vast archive. The museum offers a variety of educational programs, & visitors can enjoy interactive games. This is the home of the Stanley Cup.
Jeff Denomme, President & Chief Executive Officer, jdenomme@hhof.com
Phil Pritchard, Vice President & Curator, Resource Centre, ppritchard@hhof.com

Alberta

Provincial Museums

Glenbow Museum, Art Gallery, Library & Archives
130 - 9 Ave. SE
Calgary, AB T2G 0P3
Tel: 403-268-4100; *Fax:* 403-265-9769
info@glenbow.org
www.glenbow.org
Social Media: instagram.com/glenbowmuseum
twitter.com/glenbowmuseum
www.facebook.com /pages/Glenbow-Museum/10480470627
Glenbow documents the settlement of western Canada with exhibits tracing the lives & traditions of native peoples, the development of the railway, ranching, farming & growing up in the West. A large art gallery highlights historical & contemporary art from Glenbow's own collections as well as from national & international collections. Hours are Tu-Sa 9:00-5:00, Su 12:00-5:00.
Jacqueline Eliasson, President

The Military Museums of Calgary (TMM)
4520 Crowchild Trail SW
Calgary, AB T2T 5J4
Tel: 403-410-2340; *Fax:* 403-410-2359
www.themilitarymuseums.ca
twitter.com/tmm_yyc
www.facebook.com/The-Mil itary-Museums
Other contact information: General info: 403-410-2322
Year Founded: 1986 The Military Museums features the following museums, houses under one roof: Air Force Museum of Alberta; Army Museum of Alberta; Lord Strathcona's Horse (Royal Canadians) Museum; Princess Patricia's Canadian Light Infantry Museum & Archives; The Calgary Highlanders Regimental Museum & Archives; The King's Own Calgary Regiment (Royal Canadian Armoured Corps) Museum; & The University of Calgary Military Museums Library & Archives. The Military Museums also contains art & exhibit space, an Education Centre for students, & an Archival Reading Room.
Jody Marchuk, Operations Manager, 403-410-2340, ops@themilitarymuseums.ca
Rory M. Cory, Senior Curator/Director, Collections, 403-410-2340, seniorcurator@themilitarymuseums.ca

Royal Alberta Museum
12845 - 102 Ave.
Edmonton, AB T5N 0M6
Tel: 780-453-9100
www.royalalbertamuseum.ca
Social Media: www.youtube.com/user/royalalbertamuseum
twitter.com/RoyalAlberta
www.facebook.com/RoyalAlbertaMuseum
Major collections & exhibits of Alberta's natural & human history, including habitat groups, geology, palaeontology, archaeology, & western Canadian history & the Syncrude Gallery of Aboriginal Culture; feature exhibitions, museum shop, café, films, lectures, live demonstrations & cultural performances; special programs for schools & other groups; & discovery room.
A new museum building is currently being built, & will include heritage features such as nine mosaic murals from Edmonton's former main post office building. The museum will close its current location at the end of 2015, with the new building scheduled to open in 2017 or 2018.
Chris Robinson, Executive Director
Sean Moir, Curator, Collections Management, 780-453-9184
Jayne Custance, Director, Business Operations, 780-453-9130
Tom Thurston, Director, Capital Development, 780-638-1367
Elizabeth Whitney, Marketing Officer, 780-453-9111

Royal Tyrrell Museum
PO Box 7500
Drumheller, AB T0J 0Y0
Tel: 403-823-7707; *Fax:* 403-823-7131
Toll-Free: 888-440-4240
tyrrell.info@gov.ab.ca
www.tyrrellmuseum.com
Social Media: www.youtube.com/user/RoyalTyrrellMuseum
twitter.com/royaltyrrell
www.facebook.com/tyrrellmuseum
Year Founded: 1985 Located in Midland Provincial Park, on Hwy #838 in Drumheller, the Royal Tyrrell Museum is situated in one of the richest fossil localities in the world. The Museum is dedicated exclusively to palaeontology & showcases Alberta's abundant, diverse fossil record, featuring more than 800 fossils & 35 dinosaur skeletons on display. Other highlights include dioramas, interactive exhibits, computer stations & mini-theatre, special events & programming, gift shop & cafeteria.
Andrew Neuman, Executive Director M.Sc.

Local Museums

***Airdrie:* Nose Creek Valley Museum**
1701 Main St. SW
Airdrie, AB T4B 1C5
Tel: 403-948-6685
ncvm@telus.net
www.nosecreekvalleymuseum.com
www.facebook.com/127280337296152
Nose Creek Valley Museum offers the history of Airdrie & the surrounding region. Visitors will learn about the geology & natural history of the area, the First Nations & pioneers, farming, antique automobiles, & military history. A Canadian Pacific caboose is also on display. The museum is open year-round.
Laurie Harvey, Curator

***Alberta Beach:* Alberta Beach & District Museum**
PO Box 68
Located at 5000 - 47 Ave., Alberta Beach, AB
Alberta Beach, AB T0E 0A0
Tel: 780-924-2140; *Fax:* 780-924-2053
abmuseum@xplornet.ca
www.albertabeachmuseum.com
History of the Lac Ste Anne area; open every day July & Aug., except Tuesdays

***Alix:* Alix Wagon Wheel Museum**
PO Box 245
Located at 4912 - 50th St., Alix, AB
Alix, AB T0C 0B0
Tel: 403-747-2584
alixwagonwheelmusuem@live.ca
alixwagonwheelmuseum.wordpress.com
Local history and artifacts; souvenir shop. Open year round, but by appointment from Oct. through May.
Donna Peterson, Contact

***Alliance:* Alliance & District Museum**
***Parent:* Alliance & District Museum Society**
PO Box 101
Alliance, AB T0B 0A0
Tel: 780-879-2333
Local history; pioneer & farming artifacts; early log cabin & blacksmith shop on-site; doll collection; Norman Johnston room.

***Andrew:* Andrew & District Local History Museum**
5313 - 50 Ave.
Andrew, AB T0B 0C0
Local artifacts & records; open year round

***Banff:* Banff Park Museum National Historic Site**
PO Box 900
91 Banff Ave, Banff, AB, T1L 1K2
Banff, AB T1L 1K2
Tel: 403-762-1558; *Fax:* 403-762-1565
banff.vrc@pc.gc.ca
www.pc.gc.ca/lhn-nhs/ab/banff/index_e.asp
Year Founded: 1903 The Banff Park Museum is a natural history museum, showcasing a collection of 5,000 specimens. The park also features an outdoor activities for children.

***Banff:* Buffalo Nations Luxton Museum**
PO Box 850
Located at 1 Birch Ave., Banff, AB
Banff, AB T1L 1A8
Tel: 403-762-2388
buffalonations@telus.net
buffalonationsmuseum.com
twitter.com/buffalonations
www.facebook.com/B uffaloNationsLuxtonMuseum
Year Founded: 1952 The Buffalo Nations Luxton Museum depicts the cultures & traditions of the First Nations people of the Plains. Artifacts date back over 100 years.

***Banff:* Luxton Historic Home**
***Parent:* Eleanor Luxton Historical Foundation**
PO Box 1480
Located at 206 Beaver St., Banff, AB
Banff, AB T1L 1B4
Tel: 403-762-2105
luxton@webarmour.ca
www.luxtonfoundation.org
The house was once owned by one of Banff's prominent pioneer families, the Luxtons. Now the museum holds a collection featuring native artifacts, antiques, costumes, & unique international items. Open F-Su & holiday mondays May-Sept. 11:00-3:00.

***Banff:* Whyte Museum of the Canadian Rockies**
PO Box 160, 111 Bear St.
Banff, AB T1L 1A3
Tel: 403-762-2291; *Fax:* 403-762-8919
info@whyte.org
www.whyte.org
Other contact information: Phone, Archives: 403-762-2291, ext. 335; E-mail: archives@whyte.org
Visitors to the Whyte Museum discover the history, art, & social & cultural past of the Canadian Rockies. Guided tours are provided of the heritage gallery, the art gallery, heritage homes, the Luxton home & garden, & historic Banff. The Archives & Library, located at the museum, collects books, journals, maps, newspaper clippings, microforms, textual records, photographs, & audio-visual materials related to the Canadian Rockies.
Brett Oland, CEO, Whyte Foundation
Anne Ewen, Curator, Art & Heritage
Craig Richards, Curator, Photography
Elizabeth Kundert-Cameron, Manager, Library & Reference Service
Jennifer Rutkair, Head Archivist

***Barrhead:* Barrhead Centennial Museum & Visitor Information Center**
5629 - 49th St.
Barrhead, AB T7N 1K9
Tel: 780-674-5203
Year Founded: 1967 The Barrhead Centennial Museum is operated by the Barrhead & District Historical Society. Exhibits at the Barrhead Centennial Museum & Visitor Information Center include Barrhead settlers' furniture, pioneer farm equipment, & tools. The complete local newspaper is also available at the museum, plus a large collection of African artifacts. The museum is open from the Victoria Day weekend in May to the Labour Day weekend in September.

***Beaverlodge:* South Peace Centennial Museum**
PO Box 493
Beaverlodge, AB T0H 0C0
Tel: 780-354-8869
www.spcm.ca
Other contact information: off season: 780-354-2779
Year Founded: 1967 Pioneer equipment & buildings; open mid-May - Sept. 1
Lois Dueck, President

***Bellevue:* Bellevue Underground Mine**
***Parent:* Crowsnest Pass Ecomuseum Trust Society**
PO Box 519
Bellevue, AB T0K 0E0
Tel: 403-564-4700; *Fax:* 403-564-4711
info@bellevuemine.org
www.bellevueundergroundmine.org
twitter.com/Bell evueMine
Guided tours through a mine originally used from 1903-1961. Open May-Sept., daily 10:00-6:30 & Oct.-Apr., M-F 9:00-5:00

***Bentley:* Bentley Museum**
PO Box 620
Located at 4929 - 51st Ave., Bentley, AB
Bentley, AB T0C 0J0
Tel: 403-748-2455; *Fax:* 403-748-4537
bentleymuseum@shaw.ca
The museum depicts the lives of early settlers through exhibits housed in a 1924 farmhouse & separate agricultural buildings. Summer Hours: M-W & Sa 9:00-5:00, Su 2:00-5:00. Winter Hours: Open W morning, or by request.

***Big Valley:* Big Valley Creation Science Museum (BVCSM)**
PO Box 340
Big Valley, AB T0J 0G0
Tel: 403-876-2100
info@bvcsm.com
www.bvcsm.com
Year Founded: 2008 The museum seeks to "refute the lie of evolution" through its exhibits, which include fossils & a large model of Noah's ark.

***Big Valley:* Big Valley Museum**
PO Box 342
Located at 57 Railway Ave. South, Big Valley, AB
Big Valley, AB T0J 0G0
Tel: 403-741-5522
bvhistoricsociety@gmail.com
bvhistoricsociety.wix.com/bvhs
The museum includes a number of sites: a garage featuring artifacts & antique vehicles & machinery; St. Edmund's Church; former Alberta Wheat Pool grain elevator; two antique railway baggage cars featuring thousands of artifacts; & a section of the CNR station, featuring local memorabilia. Open May-Sept., 10:00-6:00; open by request the rest of the year.

***Bowden:* Bowden Pioneer Museum**
***Parent:* Bowden Historical Society**
PO Box 576
Located at 2201 - 19 Ave., Bowden, AB
Bowden, AB T0M 0K0
Tel: 403-224-2122
2201@shawbiz.ca
www.bowdenpioneermuseum.com
Year Founded: 1967 Goverened by the Bowden Historical Society, the Bowden Pioneer Museum is located in the old Bowden curling rink. The museum contains the following artifacts & exhibits: The Bob Hoare Photography Exhibit; The Eastern Star Exhibit; The Irene M. Wood Avon Collection, The Women of Aspenland Lives & Works; a hardware & general store display; military artifacts; geological collections, decorative arts, such as musical instruments; fine arts of First Nations & European origins; & human hisotry artifacts, such as religious objects, household items, & sports equipment. The museum also conducts research services. It is open from the long weekend in May to September.
Syd Cannings, President

***Breton:* Breton & District Historical Museum**
Breton Elementary School, 4711 - 52st St.
Breton, AB T0C 0P0
Tel: 780-696-2551
bretonmuse@yahoo.com
www.village.breton.ab.ca/history.html
Year Founded: 1989 The museum focuses on the history of black prisoners who emigrated to Canada during the early 1900s, becomming prisoners as they established their own community in central Alberta.
Allan Goddard, Contact

***Brooks:* Brooks & District Museum & Historical Society**
568 Sutherland Dr. East
Brooks, AB T1R 1C7
Tel: 403-362-5073; *Fax:* 403-362-5085
museum@xplornet.com
www.brooksmuseum.ca
Year Founded: 1974 Local history; open May-Sept., daily 9:00-5:00; weekly March-May.

***Brownvale:* Brownvale North Peace Agricultural Museum**
PO Box 186
Brownvale, AB T0H 0L0
Tel: 780-597-3934; *Fax:* 780-597-3950
The Brownvale North Peace Agricultural Museum features artifacts such as historic farm machinery, horse-powered equipment, & construction equipment. The museum is open during July & August.

***Calgary:* Aero Space Museum of Calgary**
4629 McCall Way NE
Calgary, AB T2E 8A5
Tel: 403-250-3752; *Fax:* 403-250-8399
info@asmac.ab.ca
www.asmac.ab.ca
twitter.com/aero_museum
www.faceboo k.com/AeroMuseum
Year Founded: 1985 With over 20 historical aircrafts on display, guests can explore Canadian achievements in aviation & space. Aircraft engines, extensive aviation library & interactive exhibits; educational programs & tours; gift shop; meeting/function room rentals. Open year round.
Anne Lindsay, Executive Director

***Calgary:* Air Force Museum of Alberta (AFMA)**
***Parent:* The Military Museums of Calgary**
4520 Crowchild Trail SW
Calgary, AB T2T 5J4
Tel: 403-410-2340; *Fax:* 403-410-2359
moradmin@telusplanet.net
www.themilitarymuseums.ca/gallery-airforce
The Air Force Museum of Alberta tells the story of Canada's Air Force through artifacts, models, interactive displays, & films.
Alison Mercer, Curator, 403-410-2340, alison@themilitarymuseums.ca

***Calgary:* Army Museum of Alberta (AMA)**
***Parent:* The Military Museums of Calgary**
4520 Crowchild Trail SW
Calgary, AB T2T 5J4
Tel: 403-410-2340; *Fax:* 403-410-2359
moradmin@telusplanet.net
www.themilitarymuseums.ca/gallery-army
The Army Museum of Alberta exhibits the province's army heritage from 1885 to the present. A major exhibit is The Fall of '44, which commemorates the efforts of Canadian troops during the last years of the Second World War.
Rory M. Cory, Senior Curator, seniorcurator@themilitarymuseums.ca

***Calgary:* Brooks Aqueduct National & Provincial Historic Site**
c/o Alberta Historic Sites & Museum, #2410, 801 - 6 Ave. SW
Calgary, AB T2P 3W2
Tel: 403-362-4451
www.history.alberta.ca/brooksaqueduct
The Brooks Aqueduct is located 8 km southeast of Brooks, Alberta. The structure was completed in 1914 by the irrigation division of the Canadian Pacific Railway. It has been preserved by the Government of Alberta, Environment Canada, the Prairie Farm Rehabilitation Administration, & the Eastern Irrigation District. The interpretive center at the aqueduct is open from May 15th to Labour Day, 10:00-5:00.
Rick Green, Facility Supervisor

***Calgary:* Calgary Chinese Cultural Centre**
197 - 1st St. SW
Calgary, AB T2P 4M4
Tel: 403-262-5071; *Fax:* 403-232-6387
info@culturalcentre.ca
www.culturalcentre.ca
Year Founded: 1992 The Calgary Chinese Cultural Centre promotes Chinese heritage, history & culture, as well as cultural diversity.
Jake Louie, Chair
Malcolm Chow, Vice-Chair
Tony Wong, Secretary
Leonard Chow-Wah, Treasurer

***Calgary:* The Calgary Highlanders Museum & Archives**
***Parent:* The Military Museums of Calgary**
4520 Crowchild Trail SW
Calgary, AB T2T 5J4
Tel: 403-410-2340; *Fax:* 403-410-2359
museum@calgaryhighlanders.com
www.calgaryhighlanders.com
A history & recollection of the Calgary Highlanders.
Captain Peter Boyle, Curator CD, AdeC
Sergeant Dennis Russell, Curator CD
Mike Henry, Archivist

***Calgary:* Canada's Sports Hall of Fame (CSHOF) / Panthéon des Sports Canadiens**
169 Canada Olympic Rd. SW
Calgary, AB T3B 6B7
Tel: 403-776-1040
info@cshof.ca
www.sportshall.ca
twitter.com/CANsportshall
www.facebook.com/CANsportshall
Year Founded: 1955 Canada's Sports Hall of Fame tells the stories of Canadian amateur & professional athletes, as well as sport builders, who have made outstanding achievements thoughout sports history.
Colin MacDonald, Chair M.A., B.B.A.
Mario Siciliano, President & CEO, msiciliano@cshof.ca
Janice Smith, Director, Exhibits & Programs, jsmith@cshof.ca

***Calgary:* Fort Calgary**
***Parent:* Fort Calgary Preservation Society**
PO Box 2100 M
Located at 750 - 9 Ave. SE, Calgary, AB
Calgary, AB T2P 2M5
Tel: 403-290-1875; *Fax:* 403-265-6534
info@fortcalgary.com
www.fortcalgary.com
Social Media: instagram.com/fortcalgary
twitter.com/fortcalgary
www.facebook.com/for tcalgary
40-acre park; interpretive centre; 1875 fort reconstruction project; guided tours; open year round
Sara Jane Gruetzner, President & CEO

***Calgary:* The Grain Academy**
Plus 15, BMO Centre, 20 Roundup Way SE
Calgary, AB T2G 2W1
Tel: 403-263-4594
grainacademy@nucleus.com
www.grainacademymuseum.com
Year Founded: 1981 Grain elevator; grain transportation exhibit

***Calgary:* Heritage Park Historical Village**
1900 Heritage Dr. SW
Calgary, AB T2V 2X3
Tel: 403-268-8500; *Fax:* 403-268-8501
info@heritagepark.ab.ca
www.heritagepark.ca
twitter.com/HeritageParkYY C
www.facebook.com/177397676028
Year Founded: 1964 Billed as a living history museum, the expansive site offers a wide range of exhibits and activities, most notably the exploration of a village of historical, "old west" buildings replete with antiques, artifacts and costumed guides. Gasoline Alley Museum focuses on the history of the automobile. There is a steam train, antique midway and Haskayne Mercantile Block of shops. Open May - Sept.
Ms Alida Visbach, President/CEO

***Calgary:* The King's Own Calgary Regiment (RCAC) Museum**
***Parent:* The Military Museums of Calgary**
4520 Crowchild Trail SW
Calgary, AB T2T 5J4
Tel: 403-410-2340; *Fax:* 403-410-2359
www.kingsown.ca
Depicts the history of the four regiments of Calgary; art gallery; open all year. Artifacts & pictures of regimental "family tree"; permanent displays of the 50th Battalion C.E.F. which deature The Deadly Sniper; Cpl. Henry Norwest; M.M. Vimy; Pte. John George Pattison V.C.; non-permanent active militial Dieppel The Prisoner of War Room; Sicily, Italy, including the Kingsmill Bridge & the Battle of Cassino. Special film & military documentaties in the Amoco Theatre.
Al Judson, Curator/Archivist, 403-410-2340, archivist.kocr@gmail.com

***Calgary:* Lord Strathcona's Horse (Royal Canadians) Regimental Museum**
***Parent:* The Military Museums of Calgary**
4520 Crowchild Trail SW
Calgary, AB T2T 5J4
Tel: 403-410-2340; *Fax:* 403-410-2359
museum@strathconas.ca
www.strathconas.ca/strathcona-museum
www.faceboo k.com/Strathconas
Year Founded: 1990 Museum relates the history of the Regiment from 1900 to present. The collection holds many artifacts yet undisplayed. The Archives store photographs, records, documents & diaries and research is conducted for personal & professional institutions. Open year round.
Warrant Officer D.E. (Ted) MacLeod, Curator, 403-410-2340, museum@strathconas.ca
Sgt. Todd Gibberson, Collections Manager, 403-410-2340, archives@strathconas.ca

***Calgary:* Lougheed House**
***Parent:* Lougheed House Conservation Society**
707 - 13th Ave. SW
Calgary, AB T2R 0K8
Tel: 403-244-6333; *Fax:* 403-244-6354
info@lougheedhouse.com
www.lougheedhouse.com
Social Media: lougheedhouse.blogspot.ca
twitter.com/lougheedhouse
www.facebook.com/1 05991712783670
Lougheed House was built in 1891 & was originally known was Beaulieu, & is a National Historic Site. Visitors can tour the building, eat lunch in the on-site restaurant, & visit the gift shop. The house is open W-F 11:00-4:00, Sa & Su 10:00-4:00.
Kirstin Evenden, Executive Director, kirstinevenden@lougheedhouse.com
Cassandra Cummings, Curator, cassandra@lougheedhouse.com
Cathy Olson, General Manager, cathyolson@lougheedhouse.com

***Calgary:* Naval Museum of Alberta (NMA)**
***Parent:* The Military Museums of Calgary**
4520 Crowchild Trail SW
Calgary, AB T2T 5J4
Tel: 403-410-2340; *Fax:* 403-410-2359
moradmin@telusplanet.net
www.themilitarymuseums.ca/gallery-navy
Year Founded: 1988 Collection includes one each of the 3 naval aircraft (fighter planes) used by RCN; naval armament including guns, torpedos, anti-submarine equipment, clothing etc.
Bruce Connolly, Curator, bruce@themilitarymuseums.ca

***Calgary:* The Nickle Arts Museum**
Taylor Family Digital Library, The University of Calgary, 410 University Ct. N.W.
Calgary, AB T2N 1N4
Tel: 403-210-6201
nickle@ucalgary.ca
nickle.ucalgary.ca
twitter.com/nicklegalleries
www.facebook.com/113752 113969
Founded in 1979 through a donation from Sam Nickle & a Province of Alberta grant; champions contemporary Canadian art, numismatics & Oriental carpets; changing exhibitions & programs.
Christine Sowiak, Chief Curator, cfsowiak@ucalgary.ca

***Calgary:* Princess Patricia's Canadian Light Infantry Regimental Museum & Archives (PPCLI)**
***Parent:* The Military Museums of Calgary**
4520 Crowchild Trail S.W.
Calgary, AB T2T 5J4
Tel: 403-410-2340; *Fax:* 403-410-2360
ppcli.museumgm@gmail.com
www.ppcli.com
www.facebook.com/ppcli
Princess Patricia's Canadian Light Infantry Regimental Museum & Archives collects & preserves items that cover the dates from 1914, when Princess Patricia's Canadian Light Infantry was founded, to the present day. The Infantry is known for its service in both World Wars, Korea, & Afghanistan, & during other operations for the United Nations & NATO. Holdings include war journals, photographs, training manuals, cartographic materials, & audio-visual resources, especially related to the Princess Patricia's Canadian Light Infantry, & to the Canadian Army in general. The museum is open year-round.
Capt. Dave Peabody, General Manager, 403-410-2340

***Calgary:* Tsuu T'ina Culture Museum**
3700 Anderson Rd. SW
Calgary, AB T2W 3C4
Tel: 403-238-2677
Year Founded: 1983 Located on Sarcee (Tsuu T'ina) Reserve, the museum features artifacts such as headdresses from around 1938 & a model tipi.

***Calgary:* Ukrainian Museum of Canada (UMC) Calgary Collection**
St. Vladimir's Ukrainian Orthodox Cultural Centre, 404 Meredith Rd. NE
Calgary, AB T2E 5A6
Tel: 403-264-3437
www.stvlads.com/museum.html
Open Tues. 10:00-2:30, or by appointment.

***Calgary:* University of Calgary, Museum of Zoology**
Biological Sciences Bldg., 507 Campus Dr. N.W.
Calgary, AB T2N 1N4
Tel: 403-220-5261; *Fax:* 403-289-9311
bio.ucalgary.ca/research/zoology_museum
Teaching museum used for zoology & ecology courses; also services the Archaeology, Geology, & Art departments, as well as Inglewood Bird Sanctuary & the Alberta Science Centre.
Warren Fitch, Curator, fitch@ucalgary.ca

***Calgary:* Youthlink Calgary: Calgary Police Service Interpretive Centre**
#594, 5111 - 47th St. NE
Calgary, AB T3J 3R2
Tel: 403-206-4566; *Fax:* 403-974-0508
info@youthlinkcalgary.com
www.youthlinkcalgary.com
Social Media: www.youtube.com/youthlinkcgy
twitter.com/YouthLinkCGY
www.facebook.com /YouthLinkCGY
Interactive exhibits & programs educate youth about life, crime, & law enforcement.
Tara Robinson, Executive Director, tara.robinson@calgarypolice.ca
Noreen Barros, Manager, Museum & Operations Manager, nbarros@calgarypolice.ca

***Calgary:* YouthLink Calgary: The Calgary Police Interpretive Centre**
5111 - 47th St. NE
Location: 316 - 7th Ave. SE, 2nd Fl., Calgary, AB
Calgary, AB T3J 3R2
Tel: 403-428-4566
info@youthlinkcalgary.com
www.youthlinkcalgary.com
Social Media: www.youtube.com/youthlinkcgy
twitter.com/YouthLinkCGY
www.facebook.com /YouthLinkCGY
Year Founded: 1995 The purpose of YouthLink is to education young people about the role of police in society, & the consequences of crime, through exhibits & programs.
Tara Robinson, Executive Director, tara.robinson@calgarypolice.ca

***Camrose:* Camrose & District Centennial Museum**
PO Box 1622
Camrose, AB T4V 1X6
Tel: 780-672-3298
info@camrosemuseum.ca
www.camrosemuseum.ca
Year Founded: 1967 Buildings on the museum grounds include a pioneer home, The Likeness School, the St. Dunstan's Church, a firehall, the local newspaper building, a blacksmith shop, the Mona Sparling Building, the Oldtimers Hut, & the R.C.M.P. Machine Building. The musuem is open from Victoria Day weekend to Labour Day weekend. Appointments may be arranged at other times of the year.

***Canmore:* Canmore Museum & Geoscience Centre**
Civic Centre, PO Box 8849, 902B - 7th Ave.
Canmore, AB T1W 3K1
Tel: 403-678-2462; *Fax:* 403-678-2216
www.cmags.org
twitter.com/Canmoremuseum
www.facebook.com/canmoremuseum
The Canmore Museum & Geoscience Centre features historical artifacts, geological collections, & information about the heritage of Canmore & the surrounding mountainous area. The museum also operates the 1893 North West Mounted Police Barracks, which is situated on 609 Main Street.
Andrew Holder, President
Debbie Carrico, Director
Lynne Huras, Manager, Collections

***Cardston:* C.O. Card Pioneer Home & Museum**
337 Main St.
Cardston, AB T0K 0K0
Tel: 403-653-3366
C.O. Card Home & Museum is a Provincial Historic Site. It features the log cabin built by Charles Ora Card, who was the founder of Cardston. The museum is open during July & August. During the off season, appointments may be arranged.

***Cardston:* Courthouse Museum**
89 - 3rd Ave. West
Cardston, AB T0K 0K0
www.cardstonhistoricalsociety.org
The Courthouse is a Provincial Historic Site, which was constructed in 1907 from local sandstone. Court artifacts are on display, including the witness stand, judge's bench, & orginal jail cells. The musuem is open during July & August. During the off season, appointments may be arranged.

***Cardston:* Remington Carriage Museum**
PO Box 1649
Cardston, AB T0K 0K0
Tel: 403-653-5139; *Fax:* 403-653-5160
remingtoncarriagemuseum@gov.ab.ca
www.history.alberta.ca/remington/defau lt.aspx
www.facebook.com/RemingtonCarriageMuseum1
Year Founded: 1993 The Remington Carriage Museum features the largest collection of horse-drawn vehicles in North America, such as carriages, sleighs, & wagons. The facility also contains a working stable, a carriage factory, & a restoration shop. Educational programs are offered. The museum is open year-round.

***Caroline:* Caroline Wheels of Time Museum**
***Parent:* Community Historical Society of Caroline**
PO Box 535
Caroline, AB T0M 0M0
Tel: 403-722-3884
wheels3884@gmail.com
www.carolinemuseum.ca
Year Founded: 1991 The museum operates five historic buildings, including a country store, a school, & a trapper's cabin. Open May-Sept., 12:00-6:00

***Carstairs:* Roulston Museum**
***Parent:* Carstairs & District Historical Society**
PO Box 1067, 1138 Nanton St.
Carstairs, AB T0M 0N0
Tel: 403-337-3710
info@roulstonmuseum.ca
carstairsroulstonmuseum.ca
Year Founded: 1988 Main collection housed in the hall of Knox Presbyterian Church (1901), a registered historic site; church records; pictures & artifacts of local life from early settlement to present; McCaig House (1901); archives; new library research room; new farm implement display building
Betty Ayers, Curator
Robert Disney, President

***Castor:* Castor & District Museum**
PO Box 864
Located at 5101 - 49 Ave., Castor, AB
Castor, AB T0C 0X0
Tel: 403-882-3271
Year Founded: 1978 Local history, including a 1910 Alberta Pacific Grain Elevator & collection of restored railcars. Open March-Nov., Th, Sa & Su 2:00-4:00.

***Cereal:* Cereal Prairie Pioneer Museum**
PO Box 131
Cereal, AB T0J 0N0
Museum of artifacts from Pioneer days; pictures, papers & cards of the period; museum was once old CN Railway Station with living quarters; yard includes old jail house & restoration of old Cereal Town Office

***Claresholm:* Appaloosa Horse Club of Canada Museum & Archives**
***Parent:* ApHCC Museum & Archive Society**
PO Box 940
Located at 4189 - 3rd St. SE, Claresholm, AB
Claresholm, AB T0L 0T0
Tel: 403-625-3326; *Fax:* 403-625-2274
registry@appaloosa.ca
www.appaloosa.ca/museum.html
History of the Appaloosa horse
Donna Wyatt, Museum Liaison, dmwyatt@live.com

***Claresholm:* Claresholm Museum**
5115 - 2nd St. East
Claresholm, AB T0L 0T0
Tel: 403-625-1742
museum@townofclaresholm.com
www.claresholmmuseum.com
twitter.com/claresholmuseum
Other contact information: Information Centre, Phone: 403-625-3131
Year Founded: 1969 Local history museum in the old Sandstone Railway Station; Claresholm was home to Louise C. McKinney, a social activist for the cause of women's welfare and legal status, and the first woman parliamentarian in the British Empire; open daily May-Sept; admission by donation

***Cochrane:* Cochrane Ranche Historic Site**
PO Box 1522
Cochrane, AB T0L 0W0
Tel: 403-932-2902
Located off Hwy #22, north of downtown Cochrane, The Cochrane Ranche is Alberta's first large-scale livestock ranch, comprising approx. 136 acres; open May 15 - Labour Day; hiking & picnic areas open year round

***Cold Lake:* Cold Lake Air Force Museum**
PO Box 5770 Forces
Cold Lake, AB T9M 2C6
Tel: 780-594-3546
clafm@telus.net
www.facebook.com/pages/Cold-Lake-Museums/343764180120

***Coleman:* Crowsnest Museum**
***Parent:* Crowsnest Historical Society**
PO Box 306, 7701 - 18 Ave.
Coleman, AB T0K 0M0
Tel: 403-563-5434; *Fax:* 403-753-0782
cnmuseum@shaw.ca
www.crowsnestmuseum.ca
Year Founded: 1985 Over 25,000 artifacts on display interpreting the history of the Crowsnest Pass & its people; themed galleries include pioneers, underground mining, general store/blacksmith shop, Legends of Prohibition, Gushul Studio. Veterans' exhibit, wildlife diorama; open year round

***Crowsnest Pass:* The Frank Slide Interpretive Centre (FSIC)**
PO Box 959 Blairmore
Crowsnest Pass, AB T0K 0E0
Tel: 403-562-7388; *Fax:* 403-562-8635
frankslideinfo@gov.ab.ca
www.history.alberta.ca/frankslide/
www.facebo ok.com/454421064610400
Other contact information: In Alberta, toll free 310-0000
Site of the 1903 rockslide avalanche; visual presentation "In the Mountain's Shadow" shown daily; open year-round.

***Crowsnest Pass:* Leitch Collieries Provincial Historic Site**
c/o Frank Slide Interpretive Centre, PO Box 959 Blairmore
Crowsnest Pass, AB T0K 0E0
Tel: 403-562-7388; *Fax:* 403-562-8635
frankslideinfo@gov.ab.ca
www.history.alberta.ca/leitch/default.aspx
Other contact information: May-Sept. Phone: 403-564-4211
Ruin of coal mining operation; staffed May 15 - Labour Day; located off Hwy. #3 in Crowsnest Pass, AB.

***Czar:* Prairie Panorama Museum**
PO Box 5
Czar, AB T0B 0Z0
Tel: 780-857-2012
Displays many historical artifacts; includes a school section

***DeBolt:* DeBolt & District Pioneer Museum**
Hubert Memorial Park, PO Box 298
DeBolt, AB T0H 1B0
Tel: 780-957-3957; *Fax:* 780-957-2934
deboltmuseum@gmail.com
www.facebook.com/197729256911960
Year Founded: 1975 The museum comprises 8 heritage buildings with displays: in Hubert Memorial Park on Virginia Ave., in the community church & Legion Hall; collections include the Bickell Fossil Collection. Open summer.
Fran Moore, Curator

***Delburne:* Anthony Henday Museum**
2517 - 20 St.
Delburne, AB T0M 0V0
Tel: 403-749-2711
ahenday@xplornet.com
Other contact information: Alternate Phone: 403-749-2186
Housed in the former CNR train station; water tank tower, caboose, machine shed & pioneer cabin replica on site; depicts history of Delburne & district with emphasis on agriculture, households & coal mining. Open June M-F, 9:00-5:00. From July to Labour Day open daily 9:00-5:00.

***Dewberry:* Dewberry Valley Museum**
PO Box 30
Dewberry, AB T0B 1G0
Tel: 403-847-3053
dewberry@hmsinet.ca
www.villageofdewberry.ca/museum.html
Year Founded: 1974 History of the Dewberry Valley area, including prehistoric, fur trade, Riel Rebellion, & pioneer artifacts; also features a pioneer log cabin.
Phillip Porter, Curator

***Didsbury:* Didsbury & District Museum**
***Parent:* Didsbury & District Historical Society**
PO Box 1175, 2110 - 21st Ave.
Didsbury, AB T0M 0W0
Tel: 403-335-9295
ddhs@telusplanet.net
www.didsburymuseum.com
Year Founded: 1978 1906 building; local history; open year round; Tue.-Wed. 1-4:30; Sat. 1-5

***Donalda:* Donalda & District Museum**
PO Box 179
Donalda, AB T0B 1H0
Tel: 403-883-2100
info@donaldamuseum.com
www.donaldamuseum.com
www.facebook.com/donaldamuseum
Over 850 lamps; Whitford Collection of Métis artifacts from the late 1800s; native tools; artifacts; open year round
Kash Clouson, Manager

***Drayton Valley:* Drayton Valley & District Historical Society**
PO Box 5099, 6009 - 43rd Ave.
Drayton Valley, AB T7A 1R3
Tel: 780-542-4908
www.draytonvalley.ca/museum
Local history; open Wed. & Sat. 1-4
Charlie Miner, Contact

***Drumheller:* Homestead Antique Museum**
PO Box 3154
Located at 901 North Dinosaur Trail, Drumheller, AB
Drumheller, AB T0J 0Y1
Tel: 403-823-2600; *Fax:* 403-823-5411
hamuseum@telus.net
Year Founded: 1965 Situated in the Canadian Badlands, the Homestead Pioneer Museum presents exhibits from the Drumheller Valley, including farm machinery & tools, vehicles, & a 1919 house. The museum is open from mid May to mid October.

***East Coulee:* Atlas Coal Mine National Historic Site**
PO Box 521, 110 Century Ave.
East Coulee, AB T0J 1B0
Tel: 403-822-2220; *Fax:* 403-822-2225
info@atlascoalmine.ab.ca
www.atlascoalmine.ab.ca
Social Media: www.youtube.com/user/atlascoalmine
www.facebook.com/184631621585939
Year Founded: 1989 Located in the Canadian Badlands, the Atlas Coal Mine National Historic Site offers tours & educational programs. Visitors can go underground, explore the last wooden tipple in Canada, see the blacksmith shop, & ride an authentic mine locomotive. The site is open from the beginning of May to mid-October.

***East Coulee:* East Coulee School Museum (ECSM)**
PO Box 514
Located at 359 - 2nd Ave. East, Coulee, AB
East Coulee, AB T0J 1B0
Tel: 403-822-3970
www.ecsmuseum.ca
www.facebook.com/ecspringfest
Open year round

***Edmonston:* Father Lacombe Chapel - Provincial Historic Site / La Chapelle du Père Lacombe**
c/o Alberta Culture & Tourism, 8820 - 112 St.
Edmonston, AB T6G 2P8
Tel: 780-431-2321; *Fax:* 780-427-0808
father.lacombe@gov.ab.ca
www.history.alberta.ca/fatherlacombe
www.face book.com/121418196030
Other contact information: Winter phone: 403-728-3929
Year Founded: 1983 Alberta's oldest building; Located on St. Vital Ave., St. Albert; open May 15 - Labour Day
Olga Fowler, Contact, olga.fowler@gov.ab.ca

***Edmonton:* Alberta Aviation Museum**
11410 Kingsway Ave.
Edmonton, AB T5G 0X4
Tel: 780-451-1175; *Fax:* 780-451-1607
aama@live.ca
www.albertaaviationmuseum.com
www.facebook.com/7372851530 9
Tells & interprets the story of aviation & its importance to Edmonton & Northern Alberta; displays & exhibits allow visitors to embrace the spirit of those involved in early aviation endeavours that helped Edmonton establish its title as "Gateway to the North"; flight simulators, aircraft restoration area, activities for children, guided tours, special events; space rentals, with theatre projection & sound system; wireless Internet available; open year-round.

***Edmonton:* Alberta Railway Museum**
24215 - 34th St.
Edmonton, AB T5Y 6B4
Tel: 780-472-6229; *Fax:* 780-968-0167
www.albertarailwaymuseum.com
twitter.com/abrailwaymuseum
www.facebook. com/AlbertaRailwayMuseum
Year Founded: 1968 The Alberta Railway Museum features over sixty railway cars & locomotives, interpretive displays, a Morse telegraph demonstration, tours, & train rides on selected long weekends. The museum is open on weekends only from Victoria Day (the long weekend in May) to Labour Day (the long weekend in September).
Herb Dixon, President

***Edmonton:* Calgary & Edmonton (1891) Railway Museum**
***Parent:* Junior League of Edmonton**
10447 - 86th Ave.
Edmonton, AB T6E 2M4
Tel: 780-433-9739
admin@jledmonton.org
a62312.wix.com/canderailwaymuseum
www.twitter.com/TheCandEStation
www. facebook.com/CandERailwayStation
Year Founded: 1982 Visitors to the Calgary & Edmonton (1891) Railway Museum can see a replica railway station, which served the area from 1891 to 1907. Train & station artifacts are on display, including a working telegraph service. The museum is open from June to August. At other times, appointments may be arranged.

***Edmonton:* College & Association of Registered Nurses of Alberta (CARNA) Museum & Archives**
CARNA Provincial Office, 11620 - 168 St.
Edmonton, AB T5M 4A6
Tel: 780-451-0043; *Fax:* 780-452-3276
Toll-Free: 800-252-9392
carna@nurses.ab.ca
www.nurses.ab.ca/Carna/index.aspx?W ebStructureID=2690
The museum & archives are available for research purposes; permanent & temporary exhibits are maintained; collection includes a lamp used by Florence Nightingale during the Crimean War; databases can be searched online; open M-F 8:30-4:30.

***Edmonton:* College & Association of Registered Nurses Of Alberta Museum & Archives**
11620 - 168 St.
Edmonton, AB T5M 4A6
Tel: 780-451-0043; *Fax:* 780-452-3276
Toll-Free: 800-252-9392
carna@nurses.ab.ca
www.nurses.ab.ca
Items related to the founding & development of the AARN (now known as CARNA), as well as the early history of professional nursing in Alberta; Collection includes caps, pins, uniforms, yearbooks, original diplomas, & photographs from early days of nurses' education in Alberta to present; Scrapbooks, uniforms, & military medals (WWI & WWII) from the Nursing Sisters Association; Records of various nursing interest groups

***Edmonton:* Edmonton Power Historical Foundation Museum (EPHF)**
PO Box 31121 Namao
Located at 49507-49517 Range Rd. 260, Calmar, AB
Edmonton, AB T5Z 2P3
Tel: 780-471-4285
www.ephf.ca/museum
Social Media:
www.youtube.com/channel/UChvlzsR_U5DVnxGtxZqLHAw

The museum seeks to relate Alberta's electrical power industry to the general public, including hands-on activities & games for kids. The website also features a Online Museum with pictures & descriptions of items from the physical collection. Open once in May, twice in July & once in September; open to groups by appointment.

Edmonton: Edmonton Public Schools Archives & Museum
McKay Avenue School, 10425 - 99 Ave. NW
Edmonton, AB T5K 0E5
Tel: 780-422-1970; *Fax:* 780-426-0192
archivesmuseum@epsb.ca
archivesmuseum.epsb.ca
Social Media: www.flickr.com/photos/133877484@N08
twitter.com/EPSB_McKay
Located in historic McKay Ave. School, site of the first session of the Alberta Legislature; 1905 restored brick building & features the restored 1906 legislative Chamber; holdings include Edmonton Public School Board District #7 & individual school records from 1885 to present
Cindy Davis, Manager

Edmonton: Edmonton Radial Railway Society
Strathcona Streetcar Barn, PO Box 76057 Southgate
Edmonton, AB T6H 5Y7
Tel: 780-437-7721
info@edmonton-radial-railway.ab.ca
edmonton-radial-railway.ab.ca
twitter.com/yegstreetcar
www.facebook.co m/edmontonstreetcar
Other contact information: Park Line: 780-496-1464
Vintage 3 km streetcar ride from Strathcona to downtown Edmonton along former CPR right of way & across the High Level Bridge; restored streetcar rides for visitors to Fort Edmonton Park

Edmonton: Fort Edmonton Park
c/o City of Edmonton Community Services, PO Box 2359
Edmonton, AB T5J 2R7
Tel: 780-442-5311
info@fortedmontonpark.ca
www.fortedmontonpark.ca
twitter.com/fortedpark
www.facebook.com/forted montonpark
Canada's largest living history park; a complete 1846 fur-trading fort & 1885, 1905 & 1920 costumed interpreters; steam train & street car; giftshops & restaurants; fully operational hotel on site
Douglas O. Goss, Chair Q.C.

Edmonton: John Janzen Nature Centre
PO Box 2359
Location: 7000 - 143 St., Edmonton, AB
Edmonton, AB T5J 2R7
Tel: 780-442-5311
attractions@edmonton.ca
www.edmonton.ca
www.facebook.com/JohnJanzenNatureCentre
Year Founded: 1976 Nature appreciation programming.

Edmonton: John Walter Museum
9180 Walterdale Hill NW
Edmonton, AB T6E 2V3
Tel: 780-496-4855; *Fax:* 780-496-6813
attractions@edmonton.ca
www.edmonton.ca/johnwalter
The museum consists of houses from 1874, 1886, & 1901. A variety of group programs are available. John Walter Museum is open from mid March to mid December.

Edmonton: The Loyal Edmonton Regiment Military Museum
Prince of Wales Armouries, #118, 10440 - 108 Ave.
Edmonton, AB T5H 3Z9
Tel: 780-421-9943; *Fax:* 780-421-9943
info@lermuseum.org
www.lermuseum.org
www.facebook.com/203117963074315
Military museum focusing on history of The Loyal Edmonton Regiment & other military service branches from Northern Alberta
Kathleen Haggarty, Collections Manager

Edmonton: Rutherford House Provincial Historic Site
11153 Saskatchewan Dr.
Edmonton, AB T6G 2S1
Tel: 780-427-3995; *Fax:* 780-427-4288
Rutherford.House@gov.ab.ca
www.history.alberta.ca/rutherford
Home of Alberta's first premier; gift shop, tea room, tours & special events; open year round

Edmonton: Stephansson House Provincial Historic Site
c/o Albert Culture, 8820 - 112 St.
Edmonton, AB T6G 2P8
Tel: 780-431-2321; *Fax:* 780-427-0808
stephansson.house@gov.ab.ca
www.history.alberta.ca/stephansson
Other contact information: Summer Phone: 403-728-3929; Fax: 403-728-3928
Icelandic poet's pioneer home; open May 15 - Labour Day; located 7 km. north of Markerville off Hwy. 592 or 781
Olga Fowler, Contact, olga.fowler@gov.ab.ca

Edmonton: The Telephone Historical Centre (THC)
PO Box 188 Main
Located at 10440 - 108 Ave. NW, Edmonton, AB
Edmonton, AB T5J 2J1
Tel: 780-433-1010; *Fax:* 780-426-1876
thc3@telus.net
www.telephonehistoricalcentre.com
www.facebook.com/1496 52501779810
Year Founded: 1987 Open year-round; Canada's largest independent telephone museum

Edmonton: Ukrainian Canadian Archives & Museum of Alberta (UCAMA)
9543 - 110 Ave. NW
Edmonton, AB T5H 1H3
Tel: 780-424-7580; *Fax:* 780-420-0562
ucama@shaw.ca
www.ucama.ca
www.facebook.com/ucama.museum
Year Founded: 1972 The Ukrainian Canadian Archives & Museum of Alberta is dedicated to preserving Ukrainian-Canadian history & culture. Collections include Ukrainian-Canadian military memorabilia such as uniforms, textiles made by Ukrainian pioneers in Alberta, as well as ecclesiastical artifacts. The museum is open year-round, from Tuesday to Friday.
Paul Teterenko, President
Nestor Makuch, Vice-President
Barry Newton, Secretary

Edmonton: Ukrainian Catholic Women's League of Canada Arts & Crafts Museum (UCWLC)
10825 - 97th St.
Edmonton, AB T5H 2M4
Tel: 780-424-7505
www.ucwlc.ca
Open by appt.
Sophie Manulak, UCWLC National President, 204-633-8783, sophie46@mymts.net

Edmonton: Ukrainian Cultural Heritage Village
8820 - 112 St. NW
Edmonton, AB T6G 2P8
Tel: 780-662-3640; *Fax:* 780-662-3273
uchv@gov.ab.ca
www.ukrainianvillage.ca
www.facebook.com/ukrainianvilla ge.ca
The provincial historic site presents Ukrainian settlement in east central Alberta between 1892 & 1930. The Ukrainian Cultural Heritage Village has over 30 historic buildings for visitors to explore, including a grain elevator, a budei (a sod hut), & three churches of Eastern Byzantine Rite. The village is open from the May long weekend to Labour Day. School groups may book a tour at other times of the year.
Arnold Grandt, Director, 780-662-3855, Arnold.Grandt@gov.ab.ca
Becky Dahl, Curator, 780-662-3855, Becky.Dahl@gov.ab.ca
Christina Mandrusiak, Contact, Special Events, 780-662-3855, Christina.Mandrusiak@gov.ab.ca
Pamela Trischuk, Head, Education & Interpretation Services, 780-662-3855, Pamela.Trischuk@gov.ab.ca
Radomir Bilash, Senior Historian, 780-431-2354, Radomir.Bilash@gov.ab.ca
Bruce McGregor, Coordinator, Historic Farm Program, 780-662-3855, Bruce.McGregor@gov.ab.ca

Edmonton: Ukrainian Museum of Canada (UMC) Alberta Branch
St. John's Cultural Centre, 10611 - 110 Ave. NW
Edmonton, AB T5H 1H7
Tel: 780-441-1062
info@umcalberta.org
www.umcalberta.org
Open year round.

Edmonton: University of Alberta Dental Museum
Edmonton, AB T6G 2N8
Tel: 780-492-3427
Collection of antique dental instruments & furniture; natural history collection of animal skulls & fossil hominid models. Although the collection still exists, the museum is currently inactive, as the School of Dentistry moved to a location that could not accommodate the collection.
Dr. Loren Kline, Curator, lkline@ualberta.ca

Edmonton: University of Alberta Museum of Paleontology
Department of Earth & Atmospheric Science
University of Alberta - B-01 Earth Sciences Building
Edmonton, AB T6G 2E3
Tel: 780-492-3265; *Fax:* 780-492-2030
eas.inquiries@ualberta.ca
easweb.eas.ualberta.ca/page/Paleontology_Museu m
twitter.com/UofA_EAS
www.facebook.com/UofAEarthandAtmosphericScience sDepartment
The museum presents the history of life over the course of geological time, starting with PreCambrian stromatolites & ending with Pleistocene megafauna; open during business hours Mon.-Thu.

Edmonton: University of Alberta Museum of Zoology (UAMZ)
#Z1011, Biological Sciences Bldg., University of Alberta
Edmonton, AB T6G 2E9
Tel: 780-492-4622
www.biology.ualberta.ca/uamz.hp/uamz.html
Open year round
Cindy Paszkowski, Curator, Amphibian, Reptile and Ornithology Collections, cindy.paszkowski@ualberta.ca

Edmonton: University of Alberta Museums
c/o Museums & Collections Services, University of Alberta, Ring House #1
Edmonton, AB T6G 2E1
Tel: 780-492-5834; *Fax:* 780-492-6185
museums@ualberta.ca
www.museums.ualberta.ca
twitter.com/UAlbertaMuseum s
www.facebook.com/ualbertamuseums
Museum services & expertise are provided to more than 35 teaching & research collections at the University; human history, fine art, natural & applied science collections, public programs, educational outreach & other community service programs offered
Janine Andrews, Executive Director, 780-492-0783, janine.andrews@ualberta.ca
Frannie Blondheim, Associate Director, 780-492-2642, frannie.blondheim@ualberta.ca
Jim Corrigan, Curator, Univ. of Alberta Art Collection, jim.corrigan@ualberta.ca

Edmonton: Victoria School Archives & Museum
10210 - 108 Ave.
Edmonton, AB T5H 1A8
Tel: 780-492-8715
Year Founded: 1995 Artifacts that relate to the school from 1903 to present; student & teacher records from 1911; books, playbills, posters, uniforms, photos, sweaters; the museum's collection is temporarily in storage while staff search for a new home.

Edson: Galloway Station Museum & Travel Centre
223 - 55 St.
Edson, AB T7E 1L5
Tel: 780-723-5696
manager@gallowaystationmuseum.com
gallowaystationmuseum.com
Forestry; coal mining; railway
Jim Gomuwka, President, gomjb@telus.net

Edson: Red Brick Arts Centre & Museum
4818 - 7 Ave.
Edson, AB T7E 1K8
Tel: 780-723-3582
echored@telus.net
www.redbrickartscentre.com
www.facebook.com/RedBrickArtsCentre
Year Founded: 1987 Art gallery, theatre, school room museum, dance studio & gift shop

Etzikom: Etzikom Museum & Historic Windmill Centre
PO Box 585
Etzikom, AB T0K 0W0
Tel: 403-666-3737; *Fax:* 403-666-2002
Canadian national historic windmill centre; open May long weekend - Sept. long weekend Mon-Sat 10-5, Sun. 12-6

Fairview: **RCMP Centennial Celebration Museum**
PO Box 326
Fairview, AB T0H 1L0
Tel: 780-835-2847
Original barracks; also 2nd museum on a 10-acre site; open summer

Forestburg: **Forestburg & District Museum**
Parent: **Forestburg Historical Society**
PO Box 46
Forestburg, AB T0B 1N0
Housed in former Masonic Hall; displays relevant to the area; open by appt.

Fort Chipewyan: **Fort Chipewyan Bicentennial Museum**
PO Box 203, 109 Mackenzie Ave.
Fort Chipewyan, AB T0P 1B0
Tel: 780-697-3844; *Fax:* 780-697-2389
fortchipmuseum@telus.net
www.woodbuffalo.ab.ca
Year Founded: 1991 The museum is a replica of the Hudson's Bay Store; local artifacts & archives; library reference collection; classes

Fort MacLeod: **The Fort Museum**
219 Jerry Potts Blvd.
Fort MacLeod, AB T0L 0Z0
Tel: 403-553-4703; *Fax:* 403-553-3451
Toll-Free: 866-273-6841
info@nwmpmuseum.com
www.nwmpmuseum.com
Social Media: www.flickr.com/photos/63129174@N04
twitter.com/thefortmuseum
www.faceb ook.com/106507912770906
Tells the story of the arrival of the NWMP into Western Canada, & the Natives & Pioneers of that time

Fort MacLeod: **Head-Smashed-In Buffalo Jump**
PO Box 1977
Fort MacLeod, AB T0L 0Z0
Tel: 403-553-2731; *Fax:* 403-553-3141
info.hsibj@gov.ab.ca
www.head-smashed-in.com
Other contact information: Toll free in Alberta: 310-0000
Year Founded: 1987 Designated a UNESCO World Heritage Site in 1981, this jump is a testimony to the hunting customs of native peoples, particularly the Blackfoot, for thousands of years. The Interpretive Centre, blending into a sandstone cliff, explores the lives of the Blackfoot peoples from the geography of the region to the family life and ceremonies. Open year round.

Fort McMurray: **Fort McMurray Oil Sands Discovery Centre**
515 MacKenzie Blvd.
Fort McMurray, AB T9H 4X3
Tel: 780-743-7167; *Fax:* 780-791-0710
osdc@gov.ab.ca
history.alberta.ca/oilsands
Open year round

Fort McMurray: **Heritage Park**
Parent: **Fort McMurray Historical Society**
1 Tolen Dr.
Fort McMurray, AB T9H 1G7
Tel: 780-791-7575; *Fax:* 780-791-5180
heritage@fortmcmurrayhistory.com
www.fortmcmurrayhistory.com
twitter.c om/McMurrayHistory
www.facebook.com/260650299824
Year Founded: 1974 The park is a village of 17 historic buildings, including a trapper's cabin & a Catholic Mission, designed to celebratethe history of Ft. McMurray & the region. On site are 2 railway cars. Exhibits cover the logging, fishing & trapping industries. There is an extensive archive of photographs & historical documents.
Roseann Davidson, Executive Director, 780-791-7575

Fort Saskatchewan: **Fort Saskatchewan Museum & Historic Site**
10006 - 100 Ave.
Fort Saskatchewan, AB T8L 0J3
Tel: 780-998-1783; *Fax:* 780-998-1783
museum@fortsask.ca
www.fortsask.ca
Year Founded: 1970

Girouxville: **Musée Girouxville Museum**
5015 - 50 St.
Girouxville, AB T0H 1S0
Tel: 780-323-4252; *Fax:* 780-323-4110
girouxvl@telusplanet.net
Year Founded: 1969 Located in the heart of Girouxville, museum offers visitors a glimpse back into a time when pioneers first settled in the Smoky River Region; more than 6,000 pieces on display; collections includes: Religion, Native history, Natural history, Pioneer life, Hunting & Trapping, Transportation, Fur trade, Domestic history, Communications, Agriculture, Photography, Education, Geology & Palaeontology

Grande Prairie: **Grande Prairie Museum**
10329 - 101 Ave.
Grande Prairie, AB T8V 6V3
Tel: 780-830-7030
info@grandeprairiemuseum.org
www.cityofgp.com
twitter.com/GPMuseum
www.facebook.com/GPMuseum
Dinosaur bones; arrowheads; wildlife exhibits; pioneer artifacts; heritage village; archives; open daily, closed on holidays

Grande Prairie: **The Heritage Discovery Centre (HDC)**
Centre 2000, 11330 - 106 St., Lower Level
Grande Prairie, AB T8V 7X9
Tel: 780-532-5790; *Fax:* 780-532-8039
www.culture.cityofgp.com
Located at Centre 2000 in the Tourist Information Bldg.; includes a main exhibit gallery, a Rotary Learning Theatre, & the Kin Gallery. Also includes dinosaur exhibit, survivor games, mini-theatres, and hands-on display. Open M - F 8:30 - 4:30 and Sa - Su 10:00 - 4:30.
Kathy Pfau, Contact, 780-532-5790, kpfau@cityofgp.com

Grouard: **Native Cultural Arts Museum**
62 Mission St.
Grouard, AB T0G 1C0
Tel: 780-751-3306; *Fax:* 780-751-3308
Toll-Free: 866-652-3456
www.northernlakescollege.ca/content.aspx?id=2472
Year Founded: 1976 Cultural & arts collections of the Woodland Cree & Métis People of northern Alberta. Summer hours: July-Aug., M-Sa 10:00-4:00; Winter hours: Sept.-May, Tu-Th 10:00-4:00; closed in Jan. May-June by appointment only.

Hanna: **Hanna Museum & Pioneer Village**
Parent: **Hanna & District Historical Society**
502 Pioneer Trail
Hanna, AB T0J 1P0
Tel: 403-854-4244; *Fax:* 403-854-3381
www.hanna.ca
Historic buildings at the pioneer village include a ranch house, a one room schoolhouse, a store, a church, a hospital, a dental office, & a power mill. Archives are also available for research. The museum & pioneer village is open from June to August, & in May & September by appointment.

High Prairie: **High Prairie & District Museum & Historical Society**
PO Box 1442
Located at 5301 - 49 St., High Prairie, AB
High Prairie, AB T0G 1E0
Tel: 780-523-2601; *Fax:* 780-523-2633
www.facebook.com/284591171565755
Year Founded: 1967 The museum preserves the history of High Prairie & surrounding area by conserving artifacts used by homesteaders from the early 1900s. Stories of the settlers are also archived. Programs offered to children include butter-making, bread-making and sewing lessons. Open year round, with summer & winter hrs.

High River: **Museum of the Highwood**
PO Box 5334
High River, AB T1V 1M5
Tel: 403-652-7156
info@museumofthehighwood.com
www.museumofthehighwood.com
twitter.com/MuseumHighwood
www.facebook.co m/151479634900011
The museum, located inside a former CPR station, is home to thousands of photographs of High River area; open year round, M - Su.

Hinton: **Alberta Forest Service Museum**
1176 Switzer Dr.
Hinton, AB T7V 1V3
Tel: 780-865-8200; *Fax:* 780-865-8266
Established to preserve a history of forestry in the province of Alberta; displays reflect work performed by the early rangers & provide an appreciation of their accomplishments achieved without benefit of modern transportation, tools & technology; "compact disk" guided tour; ranger headquarters cabin built in 1922; open daily; weekends by appt

Holden: **Holden Historical Society Museum**
PO Box 32
Located at 4920 - 50 Holden Ave., Holden, AB
Holden, AB T0B 2C0
Tel: 780-688-3593; *Fax:* 780-688-3928
holdenmuseum@gmail.com
The collection is of the local farming community with objects pertaining to pioneer life. Open Wed., Fri., & Sun. in summer, 2-4

Iddesleigh: **Rainy Hills Historical Society Pioneer Exhibits (RHHS)**
Parent: **Rainy Hills Historical Society**
PO Box 107
Iddesleigh, AB T0J 1T0
Tel: 403-898-2443
Community museum exhibiting homestead items including furnishings, clothing, farm equipment & photographs; also features a blacksmith shop, school room, general store, an old-time kitchen & the original Iddesleigh Alberta Wheat Post Office building

Innisfail: **Innisfail & District Historical Village**
Parent: **Innisfail & District Historical Society**
PO Box 6042
Innisfail, AB T4G 1S7
Tel: 403-227-2906; *Fax:* 403-227-2901
idhs@telus.net
www.innisfailhistory.ca
Year Founded: 1970 Promote the preservation, interpretation, enjoyment of the history of Innisfail & District; village is made up of seventeen buildings on two acres of land; farm machinary and picnic area.

Irvine: **Prairie Memories Museum**
PO Box 215
Irvine, AB T0J 1V0
Tel: 403-834-3923; *Fax:* 403-834-3923
Local history; open June 30 - Sept.

Islay: **Morrison Museum of the Country School**
PO Box 4
Islay, AB T0B 2J0
Tel: 780-744-2271
Contains a collection of the artifacts to be found in a western Canadian country school of the 1930s & 1940s
Shirley Ronaghan, Contact, 780-744-2271
Mary Ternoster, Contact, 780-744-2260

Jasper: **Jasper Yellowhead Museum & Archives (JYHS)**
PO Box 42, 400 Bonhomme St.
Jasper, AB T0E 1E0
Tel: 780-852-3013
manager@jaspermuseum.org
www.jaspermuseum.org
twitter.com/jaspermuseum
www.facebook.com/1235617 47657136
Year Founded: 1963 The Jasper Yellowhead Museum & Archives collects, preserves, & exhibits artifacts & documents related to the human history of Jasper National Park & the Yellowhead corridor. Displays in the historical gallery tell the story of the fur trade, the railway, & early tourism. The area has been designated as part of a World Heritage Site. The Jasper Yellowhead Museum & Archives is open year-round. Visits to the archives are by appointment only. Open daily from Jun - Sept. and Th - Su from Oct - May.

Kingman: **Kingman Regional School Museum & Tea House**
PO Box 97
Located at 222 Main St., Kingman, AB
Kingman, AB T0B 2M0
Tel: 780-672-8220
Other contact information: Alternate Phone: 780-672-6969
Country school building from 1938.

Leduc: **Dr. Woods House Museum**
4801 - 49 Ave.
Leduc, AB T9E 6L6
Tel: 780-986-1517
woodsmuseum@telus.net
www.woodsmuseum.com
Restored 1920s house with attached garage & medical wing

***Lethbridge:* Fort Whoop-Up National Historic Site**
PO Box 1074
Located at 200 Indian Battle Park Rd., Lethbridge, AB T1J 5B3
Lethbridge, AB T1J 4A2
Tel: 403-329-0444; *Fax:* 403-329-0645
info@fortwhoopup.ca
www.fortwhoopup.ca
twitter.com/FortWhoopUp
www.f acebook.com/WhoopUp
Located in Indian Battle Park, west end of 3rd Ave. As an Interpretive Centre, "the Fort" has been reconstructed & interpreted to be the norotirious whiskey fort: as such is has electronic displays, historical sights & sounds to pay tribute to & commentorate the legacy of the NMMP, Aboriginal People, & pioneers that shaped Western Canada. Open year round.

***Lethbridge:* Galt Historic Railway Park**
c/o Great Canadian Plains Railway Society, PO Box 1013
Located at 65032 Range Rd. 19-4C, Stirling, AB, T0K 2E0
Lethbridge, AB T1J 4A2
Tel: 403-756-2220
gcprs@telus.net
galtrailway.com
www.facebook.com/103478453113008
Year Founded: 1998 Exhibits include a variety of items related to rail travel in the late 1800s.
Ray Oldenburger, President, 403-756-3313

***Lethbridge:* Sir Alexander Galt Museum & Archives**
910 - 4 Ave. South
Located at 502 - 1 St. South, Lethbridge, AB
Lethbridge, AB T1J 0P6
Tel: 403-320-3898; *Fax:* 403-329-4958
Toll-Free: 866-320-3898
info@galtmuseum.com
www.galtmuseum.com
Social Media: www.flickr.com/photos/galtmuseum
twitter.com/GaltMuseum
www.facebook.com/GaltMuseum
Other contact information: Recorded information: 403-320-4258
Year Founded: 1967 The human history of Lethbridge & southern Alberta in 5 galleries & an outdoor courtyard; free admission
Wendy Aitkens, Curator, 403-320-3907, wendy.aitkins@galtmuseum.com
Susan Burrows-Johnson, CEO/Exective Director, 403-329-7300, susan.burrowsjohnson@galtmuseum.com

***Longview:* Bar U Ranch National Historic Site of Canada**
PO Box 168
Longview, AB T0L 1H0
Tel: 403-395-2212; *Fax:* 403-395-2331
Toll-Free: 888-773-8888
baru.info@pc.gc.ca
www.pc.gc.ca/lhn-nhs/ab/baru/index_ e.asp
With 35 buildings & structures, the Bar U Ranch commemorates the history of ranching in Canada. The Ranch is open from late May to the end of September. Visits can be arranged during the off season.

***Lougheed:* Iron Creek Museum**
PO Box 312
Lougheed, AB T0B 2V0
Tel: 780-386-2337
Two one-room schoolhouses; church; blacksmith & shoe repair shop; log hall housing artifacts & farm machinery: located at 49 St. & 51 Ave., Lougheed, AB.

***Magrath:* Magrath Museum**
37 North 1st St. West
Magrath, AB T0K 1J0
Tel: 403-758-6618
magrathmuseum@gmail.com
www.magrathmuseum.org
Social Media: www.youtube.com/user/magrathmuseum
twitter.com/MagrathMuseum
www.faceb ook.com/146547325418743
Local history & pioneer artifacts; open May-Aug., M-F 9:00-5:30.

***Mallaig:* Mallaig & District Museum**
PO Box 211
Mallaig, AB T0A 2K0
Tel: 780-726-2614; *Fax:* 780-635-3757
mallaigmuseum@hotmail.com
The museum's exhibits are housed in a replica 1920 log schoolhouse & a 1931 church. Open Tu-F 10:00-4:00.

***Manning:* Battle River Pioneer Museum**
PO Box 574
Manning, AB T0H 2M0
Tel: 780-836-2180; *Fax:* 780-836-2180
www.manning.govoffice.com
Other contact information: Alternate Phone: 780-836-2374
Artifacts from pioneer life; 1,500 year-old arrowhead; albino moose; open May-Sept., daily 1:00-6:00; open 10:00 am in July & Aug.

***Markerville:* Historic Markerville Creamery**
***Parent:* Stephan G. Stephansson Icelandic Society**
114 Creamery Way
Markerville, AB T0M 1M0
Tel: 403-728-3006; *Fax:* 403-728-3225
Toll-Free: 877-728-3007
admin@historicmarkerville.com
www.historicmarkerville. com
twitter.com/Markerville
www.facebook.com/Historic.Markerville
Creamery museum restored to 1930s profiles Icelandic settlement of central Alberta; "Kaffistofa" features Icelandic menu

***Medicine Hat:* Esplanade Arts & Heritage Centre**
401 - 1st St. SE
Medicine Hat, AB T1A 8W2
Tel: 403-502-8580; *Fax:* 403-502-8589
esplanade@medicinthat.ca
www.esplanade.ca
Social Media: pinterest.com/esplanadeag
twitter.com/Esplanade
www.facebook.com/MedHa tEsplanade
Museum: Permanent Gallery featuring the history of Medicine Hat & area using pieces from vast collection, including pioneer home funishings, Victorian period artifacts, archaeological artifacts, military, sporting & Native artifacts, business & industry equipment, clothing & more; Archives: database of manuscripts, extensive black & white photographic collection, genealogical information & more.

***Medicine Hat:* Medicine Hat Clay Industries National Historic District**
713 Medalta Ave. SE
Medicine Hat, AB T1A 3K9
Tel: 403-529-1070
info@medalta.org
www.medalta.org
twitter.com/medalta
www.facebook.com/112945865394219
The 150-acre Historic Clay District preserves the history of the region's pottery industry. With working, circular kilns and original factory, it is living museum. The Medalta International Artists in Residence (MIAIR) program hosts contemporary ceramic artists. An interactive clay area and education programs are available for children.

***Millet:* Millet & District Museum & Archives**
PO Box 178
Located at 5120 - 50 St., Millet, AB
Millet, AB T0C 1Z0
Tel: 780-387-5558
info@milletmuseum.ca
www.milletmuseum.ca
twitter.com/MilletMuseum
www.facebook.com/22109293 1274232
Year Founded: 1985 Exhibits incude archives on local history, home settings from 1900-1950 and portraits of over 200 local veterans of World Wars I, II. Building also houses the Millet Visitor Information Centre; open year round.
Tracey Leavitt, Executive Director/Curator

***Mirror:* Mirror & District Museum**
PO Box 246, 4910 - 53 St.
Mirror, AB T0B 3C0
Tel: 403-788-3828
mmuseum@telus.net
Settler & railway artifacts are presented at the Mirror & District Museum. The museum is open from mid June to the beginning of September. Appointments may be arranged at other times.

***Morinville:* Musée Morinville Museum**
PO Box 3252, 10010 - 101 St.
Morinville, AB T8R 1S2
Tel: 780-572-5585; *Fax:* 780-572-5586
morinvillemuseum@shaw.ca
museemorinvillemuseum.com
Local history; designated a Provincial Historic Site; open W-Sa 12:00-5:00.
Sheila Houle, President
Donna Garrett, Museum Attendant

***Mundare:* Basilian Fathers Museum**
PO Box 386, 5335 Sawchuk St.
Mundare, AB T0B 3H0
Tel: 780-764-3887; *Fax:* 780-764-3825
www.basilianmuseum.ca
Ukrainian culture & religion

***Nanton:* Bomber Command Museum of Canada**
PO Box 1051
Nanton, AB T0L 1R0
Tel: 403-646-2270; *Fax:* 403-646-2214
office@bombercommandmuseum.ca
www.bombercommandmuseum.ca
twitter.com/B CMofCanada
www.facebook.com/101722206538665
Other contact information: Library & Archives: library@bombercommandmuseum.ca
Year Founded: 1986 The Bomber Command Museum of Canada honours persons associated with Bomber Command during World War II. It also commemorates the operations of the British Commonwealth Air Training Plan. School & group visits may be organized by contacting the following e-mail address: visitorservices@bombercommandmuseum.ca.
Bob Evans, Curator, curator@bombercommandmuseum.ca
Robert Pedersen, President

***Nobleford:* Nobleford Area Museum**
PO Box 505
Located at 225 Milnes St., Nobleford, AB
Nobleford, AB T0L 1S0
Tel: 403-824-3909
www.facebook.com/157129377662576
Year Founded: 1989 The museum replicates the manufacturing process of the Noble Blade, invented by Charles Noble. Open July & Aug., M-Sa 10:00-4:00, or by appointment.

***Okotoks:* Okotoks Museum & Archives (OMA)**
Heritage House, 49 North Railway St.
Okotoks, AB T1S 1K1
Tel: 403-938-8969; *Fax:* 403-938-8963
culture@okotoks.ca
www.okotoks.ca
Year Founded: 2000 Local history; the online archives allows users to search the Archive's photographic collection. Summer hours: M-Sa 10:00-5:00, Su & holidays 12:00-5:00.

***Olds:* Mountain View Museum & Archives**
***Parent:* Olds Historical Society**
PO Box 3882
Olds, AB T4H 1P6
Tel: 403-556-8464
mountainviewmuseum@gmail.com
www.oldsmuseum.ca
Social Media: vimeo.com/user21328675
twitter.com/mvmuseum_olds
www.facebook.com/Mountain-View-Museum-Olds-646167382075285
Year Founded: 1972 The Olds Historical Society preserves artifacts, textual documents, & photographs, which depict the history & heritage of Olds & its surrounding area. Items are displayed & research services are available at the Mountain View Museum & Archives, which is located in the 1920 Olds AGT building. The museum is open from Monday to Friday. Guided tours & educational programs are offered.
Chantal Marchildon, Program Director

***Onoway:* Onoway Museum**
***Parent:* Onoway & District Historical Guild**
c/o Onoway & District Historical Guild, PO Box 1368
Located at 4708 Lac Ste Anne Trail North, Onoway, AB, T0E 1V0
Onoway, AB T0E 1V0
Tel: 780-967-1015
info3@onowaymuseum.ca
www.onowaymuseum.ca
www.facebook.com/OnowayMuseum
Other contact information: Appointment Phone: 780-967-5263
Year Founded: 2007 Housed in an old schoolhouse, the museum presents artifacts of local Onoway life from the communtiy's early years. Opening hours: May - Aug. Tu-Sa 10:00-3:00 or by appointment.

***Oyen:* Crossroads Museum**
312 - 1st Ave. East
Oyen, AB T0J 2J0
Tel: 403-664-2330
OyenMuseum@outlook.com
oyencrossroadsmuseum.weebly.com
www.facebook.com/OyenMuseum
Buildings include a period house (1918); cook car; blacksmith shop; tractor & truck building; a 120x40 Quonset; 1912 schoolhouse; former community hall; "teepee" type building

containing archaelogical artifacts; season May-Aug., 9:00-12:00 & 1:00-5:00.

Paradise Valley: Climb Thru Time Museum
Paradise Valley, AB

Tel: 780-745-2412
www.facebook.com/ClimbThruTimeMuseum
Other contact information: Alternate Phone: 780-745-2150
The museum is located inside the Paradise Valley grain elevator, & features objects & art portraying agricultural life in Western Canada.

Patricia: Dinosaur Provincial Park
PO Box 60
Patricia, AB T0J 2K0

Tel: 403-378-4342
albertaparks.ca/dinosaur.aspx
www.facebook.com/AlbertaParksDinosaur
Year Founded: 1955 Some of the most extensive dinosaur fossil fields in the world are found here; the area's badlands & cottonwood river habitat are the other significant features that resulted in the park's designation as a UNESCO World Heritage Site in 1979; also includes the Royal Tyrrell Museum of Palaeontology Field Station, located within the park.
Donna Martin, Contact, donna.martin@gov.ab.ca

Peace River: Peace River Museum, Archives, & Mackenzie Centre
10302 - 99 St.
Peace River, AB T8S 1K1

Tel: 780-624-4261; *Fax:* 780-624-2470
museum@peaceriver.net
www.peaceriver.ca/visitors/museum
Social Media: peacerivermuseum.blogspot.ca
Displays include: Sir Alexander Mackenzie, fur trade, town of Peace River
Laura Gloor, Director & Curator

Picture Butte: Prairie Acres Museum
PO Box 768
Located at 3A St. South, Secondary Hwy. 843, Picture Butte, AB
Picture Butte, AB T0K 1V0

Tel: 403-329-1201
The museum's collection includes antique automobiles, machinery, tractors, combines, & small antique items.

Pincher Creek: Heritage Acres Farm Museum
PO Box 2496
Pincher Creek, AB T0K 1W0

Tel: 403-627-2082
heritageacres.org
Year Founded: 1988 The museum seeks to preserve & promote the agricultural history of Southern Alberta from 1880-1960. In its collection it has a grain elevator, antique cars, Doukhobor barn, church, model railway, log house, general store, sawmill, & school. Open May-Sept., 9:00-5:00.

Pincher Creek: Kootenai Brown Pioneer Village
PO Box 1226, 1037 Bev McLachlin Dr.
Pincher Creek, AB T0K 1W0

Tel: 403-627-3684
mail.kbpv@gmail.com
www.kootenaibrown.org
Year Founded: 1966 Open year round

Plamondon: Plamondon & District Museum
c/o Emilie Chevigny, PO Box 119
Plamondon, AB T0A 2T0

Tel: 780-798-3765
Operated by the Plamondon & District Museum Society, the Plamondon & District Museum features local cultural artifacts from early pioneers. The museum is open from June to August.
Emilie Chevigny, Contact, emiliechevigny@hotmail.com

Ponoka: Fort Ostell Museum
Parent: **Fort Ostell Museum Society**
5320 - 54 St.
Ponoka, AB T4J 1L8

Tel: 403-783-5224
fom01@telus.net
www.fortostellmuseum.com
www.facebook.com/163429217054156
Year Founded: 1967 Open May 24-Sept. 4, winter special occasions or by appt.
Sandy Allsopp, Manager

Raymond: Raymond Pioneer Museum
Parent: **Raymond & District Historical Society**
10 Broadway North
Raymond, AB T0K 2S0

Tel: 403-752-4799
raymondhistory.ca
www.facebook.com/RaymondHistory
Other contact information: After-hours Phone: 403-752-0060
Year Founded: 1989 The museum's collection details the founding of the town of Raymond, mostly through photographs & text.

Red Deer: Alberta Sports Hall of Fame & Museum (ASHFM)
102 - 4200 Hwy. 2
Red Deer, AB T4N 1E3

Tel: 403-341-8614; *Fax:* 403-341-8619
info@ashfm.ca
www.albertasportshalloffame.com
twitter.com/ASHFM1
www .facebook.com/ashfm.ca
Year Founded: 1957 To preserve artifacts & archival material that are significant in Alberta's sporting history; 7 Honoured Members are inducted into the Sports Hall of Fame each year, plus 3 award recipients; interactive multisport virtual game system & a curriculum based education program; theatre; boardroom rental.
Donna Hately, Managing Director

Red Deer: Kerry Wood Nature Centre
6300 - 45 Ave.
Red Deer, AB T4N 3M4

Tel: 403-346-2010; *Fax:* 403-347-2550
general@waskasoopark.ca
www.waskasoopark.ca
Social Media: www.youtube.com/user/NatureCentre
twitter.com/naturecentre
Year Founded: 1986 Central Alberta's year-round home of entertaining & informative nature activities & exhibits; gateway to Gaetz Lakes Sanctuary; features art gallery, bookshop, A/V theatre, meeting rooms, children's Discovery Room & exhibits; extensive programs, courses, field trips for all ages; open daily except Christmas; admission by donation
Jim Robertson, Executive Director, jim.robertson@waskasoopark.ca

Red Deer: Norwegian Laft Hus Society & Museum
4402 - 47th Ave.
Red Deer, AB T4N 6T4

Tel: 403-347-2055
norwegianlafthus@gmail.com
www.norwegianlafthussociety.ca
Social Media: instagram.com/lafthus
twitter.com/Laft_Hus
www.facebook.com/lafthus
Norwegian-style log house with a sod roof, located in downtown Red Deer. Open year-round; Winter hours: W 9:00-3:00; Summer hours: Tu-Sa 10:00-4:00, Su 12:00-4:00.

Red Deer: Red Deer Museum & Art Gallery
4525 - 47A Ave.
Red Deer, AB T4N 6Z6

Tel: 403-309-8405; *Fax:* 403-342-6644
museum@reddeer.ca
www.reddeermuseum.com
twitter.com/RedDeerMuseum
ww w.facebook.com/RedDeerMuseumandArtGallery
Year Founded: 1978 The Red Deer Museum & Art Gallery tells the story of the people, history, & culture of central Alberta, through its collections, exhibitions, & programs. The museum's more than 85,000 objects include clothing & First Nations & Inuit art. A library on the site houses artifact books, catalogues, & other printed material.
Lorna Johnson, Executive Director BFA, M.ED, lorna.johnson@reddeer.ca
Valerie Miller, Coordinator, Collections, valerie.miller@reddeer.ca

Red Deer: Sunnybrook Farm Museum
4701 - 30th St.
Red Deer, AB T4N 5H7

Tel: 403-340-3511; *Fax:* 403-340-3574
sbfs@shaw.ca
www.sunnybrookfarmmuseum.ca
twitter.com/SunnybrookFarmM
www.facebook.com/108012702586571
The museum celebrates the early days of farming in Alberta, as the farm itself dates back to the turn of the century. Summer hours: May-Sept., daily 10:00-4:00; off-season hours: M-F 1:00-4:00, or by appointment.
Ian Warwick, Executive Director, 403-340-3511, sbfs@shaw.ca
Baukje Groothof, Coordinator, Interpretive Program

Redcliff: Redcliff Historical & Museum Society
2 - 3rd St. NE
Redcliff, AB T0J 2P0

Tel: 403-548-6260
redcliff.museum@gmail.com
www.facebook.com/209102239185210
Exhibits showing the commercial & recreational aspect of Redcliff citizens; extensive drug store, domestic, school, toy & organizational exhibits; history of past industries with manufactured artifacts; weekly newpaper on microfilm 1910-1939; open May-Aug., Tue.-Sat., Sun., Oct.-Apr. by appt.

Rimbey: PasKaPoo Historic Park & Smithson International Truck Museum
Parent: **Rimbey Historical Society**
PO Box 813
Located at 5620 - 51st St., Rimbey, AB
Rimbey, AB T0C 2J0

Tel: 403-843-2004
paskapoo@telus.net
www.paskapoopark.com
Year Founded: 1990 The park offers two museum buildings & ten historic buildings; included in the park is the Truck Museum, which features 19 refurbished International trucks, as well as farm machinery, a police car, an ambulance, vintage photographs, & more.

Rochfort: Lac Ste-Anne Historical Society Pioneer Museum
Rochfort, AB

Tel: 780-785-2816

Rocky Mountain House: Nordegg Heritage Museum/Brazeau Collieries Mine Site
Parent: **Nordegg Historical Society**
c/o Nordegg Historical Society, PO Box 550
Rocky Mountain House, AB T4T 1A4

Tel: 403-845-4444
administrator@nordegghistoricalsociety.org
www.nordegghistoricalsociety. org
Other contact information: Museum Phone: 403-721-2625
The museum holds artifacts pertaining to local history & coal mining at the Brazeau Collieries. The mine site, which is a both a Provincial & National Historic Site, is open for guided tours. The museum is open May-Sept., daily 9:00-5:00; the mine tour season is May-Sept.; site tours are held at 10:00 am, & technical tours are held at 1:00 pm, July-Aug.
Tom Clark, President
Rick Emmons, Director, Planning
Amanda Rodriguez, Coordinator, Heritage

Rocky Mountain House: Rocky Mountain House National Historic Site of Canada
Comp. 6, Site 127, RR#4
Rocky Mountain House, AB T4T 2A4

Tel: 403-845-2412; *Fax:* 403-845-5320
rocky.info@pc.gc.ca
www.pc.gc.ca/rockymountainhouse
Site of four fur trading posts dating back to 1799; Commemorates the fur trade & the role of Native peoples in the fur trade & western exploration (David Thompson); Over 500 acres; Hiking trails, displays, herd of bisons; Exhibits; 3/4 size playfort; Eight trailside listening stations; Heritage demonstrations & presentations; Open Victoria Day weekend - Labour Day

Rosebud: Rosebud Centennial & District Museum
Parent: **Rosebud Historical Society**
PO Box 601
Rosebud, AB T0J 2T0

Tel: 403-677-2601
rosebud.museum@gmail.com
www.rosebud.ca/museum_home.htm
Year Founded: 1967 A collection of pioneer tools, etc. that have been donated to the museum; open year round
George Comstock, President

Rowley: Yesteryear Artifacts Museum
Rowley, AB

Tel: 403-368-3757
Other contact information: Alternate Phone: 403-772-3901; 403-368-2355 (Tour Info)
Early settlers artifacts housed in original buildings

St Albert: Little White School
2 Madonna Dr.
St Albert, AB T8N 2M2

Tel: 780-459-4404
museum@artsheritage.ca
museeheritage.ca
Call ahead to book a visit.

***St Albert:* Musée Heritage Museum**
***Parent:* Arts & Heritage St. Albert**
St. Albert Place, 5 St. Anne St.
St Albert, AB T8N 3Z9
Tel: 780-459-1528; *Fax:* 780-459-1232
museum@artsheritage.ca
museeheritage.ca
Social Media: museeheritagemuseum.blogspot.ca
twitter.com/artsandheritage
www.facebo ok.com/ArtsAndHeritageStAlbert
The museum presents the history of St. Albert through various exhibits & programs, in an effort to preserve the community's history. It also manages St. Albert's Heritage Sites: Little White School, St. Albert Grain Elevator Park, & River Lot 24. Hours of operation: Tu-Sa 10:00-5:00, Su 1:00-5:00.
Shari Strachan, Director, sharis@artsandheritage.ca
Joanne White, Curator, joannew@artsheritage.ca
Vinothaan Vipulanantharajah, Archivist, vinov@artsandheritage.ca

***St Albert:* Musée Héritage Museum & Archives**
St. Albert Place, 5 St. Anne St.
St Albert, AB T8N 3Z9
Tel: 780-459-1528; *Fax:* 780-459-1234
museum@artsheritage.ca
museeheritage.ca
Social Media:
www.youtube.com/channel/UCa3LaEOwZPzvBBLTtACkt2g
twitter.com/artsandheri tage
www.facebook.com/ArtsAndHeritageStAlbert
History of St. Albert & surrounding area
Shari Strachan, Director, sharis@artsandheritage.ca
Joanne White, Curator, 780-459-1528, curatormhm@artsandheritage.ca
Vinothaan Vipulanantharajah, Archivist, 780-459-1528, vinov@artsheritage.ca

***St Albert:* St. Albert Grain Elevator Park**
4 Meadowview Dr.
St Albert, AB T8N 2R9
Tel: 780-419-7354
museum@artsheritage.ca
museeheritage.ca
Open May-Sept., W-Su 10:00-5:00.

***St Paul:* Fort George & Buckingham House Provincial Historic Site (FGBH)**
Provincial Bldg., #318, 5025 - 49th Ave.
St Paul, AB T0A 3A4
Tel: 780-645-6256; *Fax:* 780-645-4760
fort.george@gov.ab.ca
www.history.alberta.ca/fortgeorge/default.aspx
Other contact information: Summer Phone: 780-724-2611
Archaeological remains of 2 fur trade forts; interpretive centre & gift shop; open May 15 - Labour Day; located 13 km SE of Elk Point on Hwy. 646

***St Paul:* Musée St. Paul Museum**
PO Box 639
Situé à 5409 - 50 Ave, St. Paul, AB
St Paul, AB T0A 3A0
Tel: 780-645-5562; *Fax:* 780-645-5959
stpaulmuseum.ca
Relever l'histoire de la communauté de Saint-Paul; expositions; cours d'histoire aux élèves; projets spécials.

***St Paul:* Musée St. Paul Museum**
PO Box 410
Located at 5409 - 50th Ave., St Paul, AB
St Paul, AB T0A 3A0
Tel: 780-645-5562
www.town.stpaul.ab.ca
The museum is located on the same site as People's Museum of St. Paul & District.

***St Paul:* People's Museum of St. Paul & District**
***Parent:* Peoples Museum Society of St. Paul & District**
PO Box 410
Located at 5409 - 50th Ave., St Paul, AB
St Paul, AB T0A 3A0
Tel: 780-645-5562; *Fax:* 780-645-5273
www.town.stpaul.ab.ca
Local agricultural history; part of the same complex as Musée St. Paul Museum.

***St Paul:* Victoria Settlement Provincial Historic Site**
Provincial Bldg., #318, 5025 - 49th Ave.
St Paul, AB T0A 3A4
Tel: 403-645-6256; *Fax:* 403-645-4760
www.history.alberta.ca/victoria
www.facebook.com/Vic.Settlement
Other contact information: Summer Phone/Fax: 780-656-2333
Located 10 km south of Smoky Lake on Hwy. 855, 6 km east along Victoria Trail; Hudson Bay Company post & settlement; open May 15-Labour Day
Ross Stromberg, Contact, ross.stromberg@gov.ab.ca

***Seba Beach:* Seba Beach Heritage Museum**
104 - 1st St. North
Seba Beach, AB T0E 2B0
Tel: 780-797-3863
sebamuseum@shaw.ca
sebabeachmuseum.ca
www.facebook.com/sebaheritage
Summer resort themed artifacts, such as regatta trophies & photographs; historical material related to Seba Beach.
Sandy Drummond, Curator

***Sedgewick:* Sedgewick Archives, Gallery & Museum**
PO Box 508, 4813 - 47 St.
Sedgewick, AB T0B 4C0
Tel: 780-384-3741
www.sedgewick.ca
Year Founded: 1989 Clothing, jewelry, books, photographs, tools; open Tues-Fri, 1:30-4:30; located in the historic Bank of Montréal building on Main St. in Sedgewick

***Sherwood Park:* Strathcona County Museum & Archives**
913 Ash St.
Sherwood Park, AB T8A 2G3
Tel: 780-467-8189
www.strathconacountymuseum.ca
Social Media: www.youtube.com/user/strathconacountymuse
twitter.com/strathcomuseum
w ww.facebook.com/StrathconaCountyMuseumArchives
Year Founded: 1997 Local history; open year round
Monroe Kinloch, President

***Siksika:* Siksika Nation Museum**
PO Box 1730
Siksika, AB T0J 3W0
Tel: 403-734-5361; *Fax:* 403-264-9659

***Spirit River:* Spirit River & District Museum**
***Parent:* Spirit River Settlement Historical Society**
PO Box 221
Located at 4403 - 48th St., Spirit River, AB
Spirit River, AB T0H 3G0
Tel: 780-864-2180; *Fax:* 780-864-2199
contact@spiritrivermuseum.com
Local history; open May-Sept., M-Su 10:00-5:00; Oct.-Apr., M-F 10:00-4:00

***Spruce View:* Danish Canadian National Museum & Gardens**
PO Box 92
Located at 35544 Range Rd. 31, Red Deer County, AB
Spruce View, AB T0M 1V0
Tel: 403-728-0019; *Fax:* 403-728-0020
Toll-Free: 888-443-4114
manager@danishcanadians.com
www.danishcanadians.com
twitter.com/danishcanadians
www.facebook.com/DanishCanadianNationalMuseu m
Year Founded: 2002 The museum's exhibits celebrate the contribution of Danish immigrants to Canada. The grounds also offer paths, hiking trails, picnic spots, & a man-made lake. Open May-June, W-Su 10:00-5:30, July-Sept., M-Su 10:00-5:30.

***Spruce View:* Dickson Store Museum**
PO Box 146
Location: 1928 - 2nd Ave., Dickson, AB
Spruce View, AB T0M 1V0
Tel: 403-728-3355; *Fax:* 403-728-3351
dicksonstoremuseum@gmail.com
www.dicksonstoremuseum.com
Social Media: dicksonstoremuseum.blogspot.ca
www.facebook.com/dicksonstoremuseum1
Year Founded: 1991 A general store circa the 1930s, staffed by costumed interpreters who recreate the store's operations for visitors. Open May-Sept., M-Sa 10:00-5:30, Su 12:30-5:30

***Stettler:* Stettler Town & Country Museum**
6302 - 44th Ave.
Stettler, AB T0C 2L0
Tel: 403-742-4534
stcmuse@telus.net
stettlermuseum.com
A village replica housing artifacts from the local & surrounding areas; includes a courthouse, schools, church, CN station, pioneer homes & barns, agricultural items as well as a local sports museum; also an original Estonian Grist mill & log cabin of the early twenties constructed by early Estonian pioneers; situated on 10 acres in SW Stettler; open daily May-Sept. or by appt.

***Stony Plain:* Multicultural Heritage Centre**
PO Box 2188, 5411 - 51 St.
Stony Plain, AB T7Z 1X7
Tel: 780-963-2777; *Fax:* 780-963-0233
info@multicentre.org
multicentre.org
twitter.com/MultiCentre
www.fac ebook.com/143010392428737
The Heritage Centre includes restored buildings including a 1925 high school, a settler's cabin, & a homestead's kitchen. This living history museum offers entertainment & weekend demos. Open M-Su 9:00-4:00.
Judy Unterschultz, Executive Director, judyu@multicentre.org

***Stony Plain:* Stony Plain & Parkland Pioneer Museum Society**
5120 - 41 Ave.
Stony Plain, AB T7Z 1L5
Tel: 780-963-1234; *Fax:* 780-968-5564
info@pioneermuseum.ca
www.pioneermuseum.ca
Year Founded: 1992 Open year round.

***Strome:* Sodbuster Archives Museum**
5029 - 50th St.
Strome, AB T0B 4H0
Tel: 780-376-3688
museumsa@telus.net
www.villageofstrome.com/museum
Shows the development of the West & of the Strome & district community from 1900 to the 1950s

***Sundre:* Sundre & District Pioneer Village Museum**
211 - 1st Ave. SW
Sundre, AB T0M 1X0
Tel: 403-638-3233
info@sundremuseum.com
www.sundremuseum.com
twitter.com/sundremuseum
www.facebook.com/2133717 28691126
Year Founded: 1968 Home to artifacts that represent the history of the Sundre community; wildlife museum is adjacent; open year long.

***Taber:* Taber Irrigation Impact Museum**
4702 - 50 St.
Taber, AB T1G 2B6
Tel: 403-223-5708; *Fax:* 403-223-0529
www.facebook.com/569300306428531
Open year-round, closed in Aug.

***Thorhild:* Thorhild Museum**
***Parent:* Thorhild & District Historical Society**
c/o Thorhild & District Municipal Library, PO Box 658
Thorhild, AB T0A 3A0
Tel: 780-398-3502; *Fax:* 780-398-3504
www.thorhildlibrary.ab.ca/Museum
Local history; housed in the town library; open year-round.

***Three Hills:* Kneehill Historical Museum**
PO Box 653
Located at 1301 - 2nd St. North, Three Hills, AB
Three Hills, AB T0M 2A0
Tel: 403-443-2092; *Fax:* 403-443-7941
khsmuseum@gmail.com
www.unlockthepast.ca/places/Kneehill-Historical-Muse um_8285
Local history; collection housed in three historic buildings; open May-Sept., M-Sa 9:00-4:30, Su 1:00-4:30.

***Tofield:* Beaverhill Lake Nature Centre & Tofield Museum**
PO Box 30, 5020 - 48th Ave.
Tofield, AB T0B 4J0
Tel: 780-662-3269; *Fax:* 780-662-3929
Year Founded: 1985 The Beaverhill Lake Nature Centre presents information about Beaverhill Lake & its wildlife. The lake is a federally recognized bird sanctuary. Located in the Beaverhill Lake Nature Centre facility is the Tofield Museum. The

museum features the history of the community since 1882. The Tofield Museum is open from mid-April to Labour Day. Appointments may be arranged at other times of the year.

***Trochu:* Trochu & District Museum**
***Parent:* Trochu & District Historical Society**
PO Box 538, 315 Arena Ave.
Trochu, AB T0M 2C0
Tel: 403-442-2220
trochumuseum@gmail.com
www.town.trochu.ab.ca/culture-tourism/trochu-museum
Displays on the early pioneers including a kitchen, blacksmith shop, general store, schools, coal mining & an extensive collection of WW I & II pictures & uniforms; open May to Aug.
Bill Cunningham, President, willcunningham@persona.ca

***Two Hills:* Two Hills & District Historical Museum**
PO Box 566
Located at 5910 - 51 St., Two Hills, AB
Two Hills, AB T0B 4K0
Tel: 403-657-2461
Houses 4,000 artifacts pertaining to the area; collection of steamers, automobiles, farm equipment, farm tools, early household artifacts, buildings, railways caboose, etc.

***Valhalla Centre:* Melsness Mercantile Café & Museum**
***Parent:* Valhalla Heritage Society**
PO Box 52
Valhalla Centre, AB T0H 3M0
Tel: 780-356-3535
vhs@gpnet.ca
www.valhallaheritagesociety.ca
Provincial historic site; museum displays, deli café, gift shop

***Vegreville:* Vegreville Regional Museum**
PO Box 328
Vegreville, AB T9C 1R3
Tel: 780-632-7650
museum@digitalweb.net
www.vegreville.com/visiting/what-to-see-and-do/regional-museum
Located on the site of the solonetzic soils research station of Agriculture Canada, The Vegreville Regional Museum depicts the history of Vegreville & its agricultural & business development. A special collection is The Right Honourable Donald Mazankowski, P.C. Collection. Mazankowski was the former Deputy Prime Minister of Canada. The regional museum also houses the Vegreville & District Sports Hall of Fame. The museum is open year-round.

***Vermilion:* Vermilion Heritage Museum**
5310 - 50 Ave.
Vermilion, AB T9X 1L1
Tel: 780-853-6211
History of Vermilion, AB; located in the forme S.R.P. Cooper School.

***Viking:* Viking Historical Museum**
PO Box 270, 5108 - 61st Ave.
Viking, AB T0B 4N0
Tel: 780-336-3066
Displays various facets of pioneer life; includes 1907 school, 1903 log store, 1938 church & 1919 farm house; open summer; May 15 - Thanksgiving
Mike Lawes, President, 780-336-3173, mikekyla@rivnet.ca

***Vulcan:* Vulcan & District Museum**
***Parent:* Vulcan & District Historical Society**
232 Centre St.
Vulcan, AB T0L 2B0
Tel: 403-485-2768
www.vdhs.vulcancountyhistory.com
The museum's collection emphasizes agriculture, communications, medical history & education. Open July & Aug., Tu-Sa 10:00-12:00, 12:45-4:30. Off season by appointment.

***Wainwright:* Wainwright & District Museum**
***Parent:* Battle River Historical Society**
PO Box 2994, 1001 - 1st Ave.
Wainwright, AB T9W 1S9
Tel: 780-842-3115; *Fax:* 780-842-3115
wainwrightmuseum@gmail.com
Year Founded: 1984 Open year round

***Wainwright:* Wainwright Rail Park**
***Parent:* Wainwright Railway Preservation Society**
c/o Wainwright Railway Preservation Society, PO Box 2972
Wainwright, AB T9W 1S8
Tel: 780-842-3138
info@railpark.org
www.railpark.org
www.facebook.com/ 131026620265329
Year Founded: 1995 The Society collects & preserves items relating to Canadian National Railways in the Wainwright area. The park is open May-Sept., 10:00-4:00.

***Wanham:* Grizzly Bear Prairie Museum**
4405 - 50 St.
Wanham, AB T0H 3P0
Tel: 780-694-2484
Other contact information: Alternate Phone: 780-993-7664
Several buildings including 1920s log house, Presbyterian church & storage building; displays of agricultural machinery & artifacts used by the pioneers of the area; forestry tower; forestry cabin containing schoolroom, toolroom & pioneer kitchen displays; 1920 era hiproof barn; CNR rail display: building to store two handcars; two handcars; various tools related to work on CNR

***Warner:* Devil's Coulee Dinosaur Heritage Museum**
PO Box 156
Warner, AB T0K 2L0
Tel: 403-642-2118; *Fax:* 403-642-3660
dinoegg@telusplanet.net
www.devilscoulee.com
Dinosaur eggs; local fossils; local history

***Westlock:* Canadian Tractor Museum**
***Parent:* Westlock & District Tractor Museum Foundation**
PO Box 5414, 9704 - 96 Ave.
Westlock, AB T7P 2P5
Tel: 780-349-3353
canadiantractormuseum@telus.net
www.canadiantractormuseum.ca
www.facebook.com/732971786755110
Year Founded: 1999 The museum features over 200 restored antique tractors, as well as steam engines.

***Westlock:* Westlock Pioneer Museum**
***Parent:* Westlock & District Historical Society**
c/o Westlock & District Historical Society, PO Box 5806
Located at 10216-100 St., Westlock, AB
Westlock, AB T7P 2P6
Tel: 780-349-4849*Toll-Free:* 866-349-4445
info@westlock.ca
westlockmuseum.com
Social Media: www.youtube.com/user/westlockmusem/videos
www.facebook.com/1375256362730 05
Other contact information: Off-Season Phone: 780-349-4444; Alt. E-mail: westlockmuseum@yahoo.ca
Year Founded: 1962 Local history; open May-Sept.; off-season by appointment.

***Wetaskiwin:* Alberta Central Railway Museum**
RR#2
Wetaskiwin, AB T9A 1W9
Tel: 780-352-2257; *Fax:* 780-352-1606
acrm@xplornet.com
www.abcentralrailway.com
Year Founded: 1981 Collection of early heavy weight cars from the passenger era, as well as fright equipment, cabooses, freight cars, and a snowplow. They also house the second oldest standing grain elevator in Alberta built by the Alberta Grain Company in 1906. Located southeast of Westaskiwin. Open from Victoria Day until Labour Day.

***Wetaskiwin:* Canada's Aviation Hall of Fame (CAHF) / Panthéon de l'Aviation du Canada**
PO Box 6090
Wetaskiwin, AB T9A 2G1
Tel: 780-312-2084; *Fax:* 780-361-1239
Toll-Free: 800-661-4726
cahf2@telus.net
www.cahf.ca
Social Media: www.youtube.com/user/cahf1973
www.facebook.com/7078424647
Year Founded: 1973 Canada's Aviation Hall of Fame collects, preserves, & exhibits material related to individuals & organizations that have made outstanding contributions to aviation & aerospace in Canada. Open Tu-Th, 9:00-4:00.
Tom Appleton, Chair
Brian Fowler, Chair, Operations
Dawn Gayle, Administrator

***Wetaskiwin:* Reynolds-Alberta Museum**
PO Box 6360
Located at 6426 - 40 Ave., Westaskiwin, AB
Wetaskiwin, AB T9A 2G1
Tel: 780-312-2065; *Fax:* 780-361-1239
Toll-Free: 800-661-4726
reynoldsalbertamuseum@gov.ab.ca
www.history.alberta.ca /reynolds
Social Media: www.youtube.com/user/ReynoldsABMuseum
twitter.com/friendsofram
www.facebook.com/pages/Reynolds-Alberta-Museum/7542224425
Year Founded: 1992 The museum houses more than 5,000 artifacts, around 100 of which are on display. The collections are organized by the following themes: Transportation, Aviation, Agriculture, & Industry. The core collection of 1,500 items was donated by the late Stan Reynolds between 1982 & 1986, & continued to donate items until his death in 2012.
Noel Ratch, Director, Noel.ratch@gov.ab.ca

***Wetaskiwin:* Wetaskiwin & District Heritage Museum**
5007 - 50th Ave.
Wetaskiwin, AB T9A 0S3
Tel: 780-352-0227; *Fax:* 780-352-0226
wdhm@persona.ca
www.wetaskiwinmuseum.com
twitter.com/HeritageMuseum1
www.facebook.com/156610574404392
Year Founded: 1986 The Wetaskiwin & District Heritage Museum presents the history of Westaskiwin, Alberta & the surrounding area, from dinosaur fossils, to First Nations' history, to the war years. Visitors can also learn about life on a Hutterite colony. A resource library is part of the museum. The museum is open year-round.
Kathy Lund, President
Karen Aberle, Executive Director & Chief Curator

British Columbia

Provincial Museums

Museum of Anthropology
University of British Columbia, 6393 Northwest Marine Dr.
Vancouver, BC V6T 1Z2
Tel: 604-827-5932
info@moa.ubc.ca
www.moa.ubc.ca
Social Media: www.instagram.com/moa_ubc
twitter.com/MOA_UBC
www.facebook.com/MOAUBC
Other contact information: 24-Hour Phone: 604-822-5087
Art & objects from around the world, with emphasis on First Nations cultures of the Northwest Coast; displayed in architect Arthur Erickson's award-winning building overlooking Howe Sound
Anthony Shelton, Director, anthony.shelton@ubc.ca

Museum of Vancouver (MOV)
1100 Chestnut St.
Vancouver, BC V6J 3J9
Tel: 604-736-4431
guestservices@museumofvancouver.ca
www.museumofvancouver.ca
Social Media: www.youtube.com/user/MuseumofVancouver
twitter.com/museumofvan
www.fac ebook.com/MuseumofVancouver
Year Founded: 1994 The Museum of Vancouver offers permanent displays, exhibitions, & educational programs about the human, cultural, & natural history of the city of Vancouver & the surrounding area. The Local History Lab & the Archaeology Education Centre contribute to the museum's school programs. The museum is open year-round.
Nancy Noble, Chief Executive Officer

The Royal BC Museum Corporation
675 Belleville St.
Victoria, BC V8W 9W2
Tel: 250-356-7226*Toll-Free:* 888-447-7977
reception@royalbcmuseum.bc.ca
www.royalbcmuseum.bc.ca
Social Media: www.instagram.com/royalbcmuseum
twitter.com/RoyalBCMuseum
www.facebook.com/RoyalBCMuseum
Year Founded: 1886 The RBCM specializes in the natural & human history of British Columbia.
Jack Lohman, Chief Executive Officer, Collections

Local Museums

108 Mile Ranch: 108 Mile House Heritage Site & Museum
100 Mile & District Historical Society, PO Box 225, Hwy. 97
108 Mile Ranch, BC V0K 2Z0
Tel: 250-791-5288; *Fax:* 250-791-1947
historical@bcinternet.net
www.historical.bc.ca
Original 105 Mile Roadhouse along the Cariboo Gold Rush Trail, 10 other historical buildings including the largest log barn in Canada (c.1908); also mill equipment display

108 Mile Ranch: 108 Mile Ranch Heritage Site
Parent: 100 Mile & District Historical Society
PO Box 225
108 Mile Ranch, BC V0K 2Z0
historical@bcinternet.net
www.historical.bc.ca/main.html
The 108 Mile Ranch Heritage Site comprises 11 historical buildings dating from the Gold Rush era; largest log barn in Canada; open May long weekend to Labour Day

Abbotsford: Fraser Valley Antique Farm Machinery Association
Abbotsford, BC
Tel: 604-746-4880
2011website@pioneercorner.com
pioneercorner.com
To collect & restore to working condition antique farm & household machinery; displays annually at Agrifair; maintains the Pioneer Barn, where visitors welcome to building any time of year except December; call for appt.
Ed Steinke, President
Jerry Gosling, Treasurer, 604-864-2916

Abbotsford: Matsqui-Sumas-Abbotsford Museum - Trethewey House
Parent: MSA Museum Society
2313 Ware St.
Abbotsford, BC V2S 3C6
Tel: 604-853-0313; *Fax:* 866-373-2771
info@msamuseum.ca
www.msamuseum.ca
Social Media: www.flickr.com/photos/msamuseum
twitter.com/MSAMuseum
Trethewey House was built in 1920 by B.C. timber baron, J.O. Trethewey & has been restored to period style, incuding its gardens and grounds. Also on site are the Playhouse & the Carriage House with the museum offices. Exhibits include an extensive collection of historical photographs of the region, in addition to an array of artifacts from local home life & businesses, particularly the lumber industry. Tours are available.
Yvonne Hayden, President, MSA Museum Society
Dorothy van der Ree, Executive Director

Agassiz: Agassiz-Harrison Museum & Visitor Information Centre
PO Box 313
Located at 7011 Pioneer Ave., Agassiz, BC
Agassiz, BC V0M 1A0
Tel: 604-796-3545
agassizharrisonmuseum@shawbiz.ca
www.agassizharrisonmuseum.org
twitter.com/AgassizMuseum
www.facebook.c om/110299242344218
Year Founded: 1986 The museum presents local & Canadian Pacific Railway history, & is housed in a CPR station, circa 1893. Hours of operation: M-Sa 10:00-4:00, Su 1:00-4:00; May-Oct. M-F 8:30-4:00.
Joan Vogstad, President
Judy Pickard, Museum Staff Contact, jpickard.ahmuseum@shawbiz.ca

Alert Bay: Alert Bay Public Library & Museum
PO Box 440, 118 Fir St.
Alert Bay, BC V0N 1A0
Tel: 250-974-5721; *Fax:* 250-974-5026
abplb@island.net
alertbay.bc.libraries.coop
Ethnographic material; artifacts related to the fishing industry, local history; gift shop
Joyce Wilby, Managing Librarian & Archivist

Alert Bay: U'mista Cultural Centre
Parent: U'mista Cultural Society
c/o U'mista Cultural Society, PO Box 253
Located at 1 Front St., Alert Bay, BC
Alert Bay, BC V0N 1A0
Tel: 250-974-5403; *Fax:* 250-974-5499
Toll-Free: 800-690-8222
info@umista.org
www.umista.org
Year Founded: 1980 Kwakwaka'wakw masks depicting the Potlatch ceremony; traditional & contemporary arts & crafts

Armstrong: Armstrong Spallumcheen Museum & Arts Society (ASMAS)
PO Box 308
Located at 3415 Pleasant Valley Rd., Armstrong, BC
Armstrong, BC V0E 1B0
Tel: 250-546-8318
www.asmas.ca
Year Founded: 1974 The Armstrong Spallumcheen Museum & Arts Society features a museum, archives, & an art gallery. Visitors are educated about the history of the local region. Genealogy & art workshops are conducted.
Sherry MacFarlane, Administrator

Ashcroft: Ashcroft Museum & Archives
PO Box 129
Ashcroft, BC V0K 1A0
Tel: 250-453-9232; *Fax:* 250-453-9664
admin@ashcroftbc.ca
www.ashcroftbc.ca
Year Founded: 1935 History of the Southern Cariboo region, & the farming & ranching communities of Hat Creek Valley. Open 5 days a week, Apr.-Nov.; open 7 days a week July & Aug. Admission by donation. Located at the corner of Brink & Fourth streets in Ashcroft.

Atlin: Atlin Historical Museum
PO Box 111
Atlin, BC V0W 1A0
Tel: 250-651-7522
First Nations artifacts; gold mining artifacts; photo collections. Open May 15 - Labour Day; closed on Mondays.

Bamfield: Bamfield Community Museum & Archive
Parent: Bamfield Community School Association
240 Nuthatch Rd.
Bamfield, BC V0R 1B0
Tel: 250-728-1220; *Fax:* 250-728-1220
bcsa.ct@gmail.com
bamfieldcommunity.ca
Local history; collection built from community donations; open M-F 9:00-4:30.

Barkerville: Barkerville Historic Town
Parent: Barkerville Heritage Trust
PO Box 19
Barkerville, BC V0K 1B0
Tel: 250-994-3332; *Fax:* 250-994-3435
Toll-Free: 888-994-3332
barkerville@barkerville.ca
www.barkerville.ca
twitte r.com/BarkervilleBC
www.facebook.com/barkervillebc
Other contact information: Info Email: barkerville@gems8.gov.bc.ca
Year Founded: 1862 Restored Cariboo Gold Rush town; Blessing's Grave; Richfield Court House; open year round; peak season from early May to late Sept.
John Massier, Chair
Judy Campbell, CEO

Barriere: North Thompson Museum
Parent: Barriere & District Heritage Society
PO Box 228
Located at 352 Lilley Rd., Barriere, BC
Barriere, BC V0E 1E0
Tel: 250-672-5583; *Fax:* 250-672-9501
Year Founded: 1987 Local history; open seasonally.
Shirley Kristensen, Vice-President

Bella Coola: Bella Coola Valley Museum (BCVM)
PO Box 726, 269 Hwy. 20
Bella Coola, BC V0T 1C0
Tel: 250-799-5767
info@bellacoolamuseum.ca
www.bellacoolamuseum.ca
Other contact information: Phone, Archives: 250-982-2130
Year Founded: 1963 Owned & operated by the Bella Coola Valley Museum Society, the Bella Coola Valley Museum depicts the human history of the Bella Coola Valley. Exhibits present the history of the area from European contact to 1955. The museum's historic building is open from June to September. School presentations can be arranged at other times of the year. The British Columbia Central Coast Archives is open year-round, from Tuesday to Thursday.

Bowen Island: Bowen Island Museum & Archives
PO Box 97
Located at 1014 Miller Rd., Bowen Island, BC
Bowen Island, BC V0N 1G0
Tel: 604-947-2655
bihistorians@telus.net
bowenhistory.ca
twitter.com/BowenMuseum
www.facebook.com/bowen.Island. Museum.Archives
Year Founded: 1967 Local history displayed through two exhibits & the archival collection. Open daily in the summer, 10:00-4:00, Sept.-Apr. Su-W 11:00-3:00.
Cathy Bayly, Curator, curator@bowenislandmuseum.ca

Bralorne: Bralorne Pioneer Museum
PO Box 40
Located at 400 Hawkes Ave., Bralorne, BC
Bralorne, BC V0K 1P0
Tel: 250-238-2349
bralornepioneermuseum@gmail.com
Year Founded: 1977 Bralorne Pioneer Museum depicts the history of a community which is known as the home of the Bralorne Mine, a productive gold mine during the gold mining era. Mining artifacts are part of the museum's collection, as well as general historical information about the local Bridge River Valley area. The museum is situated in the industrial education shop of the Bralorne High School. It is open during the summer & on weekends.

Britannia Beach: Britannia Mine Museum (BCMM)
PO Box 188
Britannia Beach, BC V0N 1J0
Tel: 604-896-2233; *Fax:* 604-896-2260
Toll-Free: 800-896-4044
company.store@bcmm.ca
www.britanniaminemuseum.ca
Social Media: www.youtube.com/BritanniaMineMuseum
twitter.com/britanniamine
www.facebook.com/BritanniaMineMuseum
Year Founded: 1971 Governed by the Britannia Beach Historical Society, the British Columbia Museum of Mining preserves the material & social history of mining in British Columbia.
Kirsten Clausen, Executive Director
Diane Mitchell, Curator, Education & Collections, dmitchell@bcmm.ca
Carol Watts, Director, Operations, cwatts@bcmm.ca
Katherine Flett, Director, Marketing, 604-924-5542, katherine@blueskycommunications.ca

Burnaby: Burnaby Village Museum & Carousel
6501 Deer Lake Ave.
Burnaby, BC V5G 3T6
Tel: 604-297-4565; *Fax:* 604-297-4557
bvm@burnaby.ca
www.burnabyvillagemuseum.ca
twitter.com/bbyvillage
ww w.facebook.com/BurnabyVillageMuseum
Other contact information: Phone, Schools: 604-297-4558; Phone, Rentals: 604-297-4552
Year Founded: 1971 The Burnaby Village Museum consists of heritage & replica buildings from the 1920s, such as a blacksmith shop, a general store, a print shop, a farmhouse, a restored interurban tram & a carousel.

Burnaby: Canadiana Costume Society of British Columbia & Western Canada
6501 Deer Lake Ave.
Burnaby, BC V5G 3T6
www.facebook.com/203038403236068
Year Founded: 1976 The Canadiana Costume Society of British Columbia & Western Canada collects, conserves, researches, & displays British Columbia's costume heritage. The collection dates from the late 1700s to the 1980s. The Society's members create displays & provide lectures.

Burnaby: Nikkei National Museum & Cultural Centre (NNMCC)
6688 Southoaks Cres.
Burnaby, BC V5E 4M7
Tel: 604-777-7000
info@nikkeiplace.org
centre.nikkeiplace.org
Social Media: www.youtube.com/user/nikkeimuse
twitter.com/nikkeimuse
www.facebook.co m/NNMCC
Year Founded: 2000 The complex houses a Japanese-Canadian cultural centre, the museum, a community centre, & a

Japanese-Canadian garden. Centre hours: Tu-F 10:00-9:30, Sa 9:00-5:00, Su 10:00-5:00; Museum hours: Tu-Sa 11:00-5:00.
Mitsuo Hayashi, Chair
Cathy Makihara, President
Roger Lemire, Executive Director, rlemire@nikkeiplace.org
Beth Carter, Director/Curator, bcarter@nikkeiplace.org

***Burnaby:* Simon Fraser University Museum of Archaeology & Ethnology**
Simon Fraser University, 8888 University Dr.
Burnaby, BC V5A 1S6
Tel: 778-782-3325; *Fax:* 778-782-5666
www.sfu.museum
Major emphasis on the Pacific Northwest coast; open year round
Dr. Barbara J. Winter, Curator, bwinter@sfu.ca

***Burns Lake:* Lakes District Museum Society**
PO Box 266
Burns Lake, BC V0J 1E0
Tel: 250-692-7450
Year Founded: 1978 Artifacts, archival records, & historical reference material relation to the Lakes District of northwestern B.C., including Burns Lake, Palling, Francois Lake, Babine Lake, Ootsa Lake, & Tweedsmuir Provinvial Park. Includes interviews with early settlers (& descendants) in the Lakes District.

***Cache Creek:* Historic Hat Creek Ranch**
PO Box 878
Cache Creek, BC V0K 1H0
Tel: 250-457-9722; *Fax:* 250-457-9311
Toll-Free: 800-782-0922
contact@hatcreekranch.com
www.hatcreekranch.com
Social Media: plus.google.com/112771217543072452676
twitter.com/hatcreekranch
www.facebook.com/hatcreekranch
Year Founded: 1984 Offering a blend of cultures, on site are an 1860 roadhouse with gold rush era artifacts and a traditional kekuli, or pit house, used as a winter home by people of the Shuswap Nation. Costumed guides explain the life of area's history & culture and visitors can experience firsthand a stagecoach ride. Other activities include gold panning and archery. There are a gift shop, food services, as well as cabins & campground facilities. Open daily, May to Sept.

***Campbell River:* Campbell River Maritime Heritage Centre**
***Parent:* Maritime Heritage Society**
PO Box 483
Located at 621 Island Hwy., Campbell River, BC
Campbell River, BC V9W 5C1
Tel: 250-286-3161; *Fax:* 250-286-3162
info@maritimeheritagecentre.ca
www.maritimeheritagecentre.ca
www.faceb ook.com/221432144123
Year Founded: 1998 The Maritime Heritage Centre seeks to educate visitors about the mhistory of the Campbell River area, & to preserve marine documents & artifacts. Open M-Su 10:00-4:00.
Marv Everett, President
Trish Whiteside, Operations Manager

***Campbell River:* Haig-Brown Heritage House**
***Parent:* Museum at Campbell River**
2250 Campbell River Rd.
Campbell River, BC V9W 4N7
Tel: 250-286-6646; *Fax:* 250-286-0109
haig.brown@crmuseum.ca
www.haig-brown.bc.ca
Social Media: haig-brownhouse.blogspot.ca
Operated by the Museum at Campbell River, the Haig-Brown House is a historic building that offers bed & breakfast accomodation, & can be rented for private functions.

***Campbell River:* Museum at Campbell River (CRMuseum)**
PO Box 70 A
Located at 470 Island Hwy and 5th Ave., Campbell River, BC
Campbell River, BC V9W 4Z9
Tel: 250-287-3103; *Fax:* 250-286-0109
general.inquiries@crmuseum.ca
www.crmuseum.ca
twitter.com/CRMuseum
w ww.facebook.com/100483307218
Year Founded: 1958 Exhibits include First Nations ceremonial masks & regalia, coastal logging, fishing history & settler development; archives & research centre; gift shop; open year-round.
Sandra Parrish, Executive Director, sandra.parrish@crmuseum.ca
Megan Purcell, Manager, Collections, megan.purcell@crmuseum.ca
Beth Boyce, Curator & Manager, Education, beth.boyce@crmuseum.ca

***Castlegar:* Castlegar & District Heritage Society**
400 - 13th Ave.
Castlegar, BC V1N 1G2
Tel: 250-365-6440
www.stationmuseum.ca
The Society operates the CPR Museum, housed in a 99 year old station, & Zuckerberg Island park; newspaper archives; gift shop featuring local artisans; special events & programming.

***Celista:* Shuswap Lake Provincial Park Nature House**
4120 Squilax-Anglemont Rd.
Celista, BC V0E 1M6
Tel: 250-955-0861
shuswaplakepark@gmail.com
shuswaplakepark.com
Natural history

***Chase:* Chase & District Museum & Archives Society**
1042 Shuswap Ave.
Chase, BC V0E 1M0
Tel: 250-679-8847
info@chasemuseum.ca
www.chasemuseum.ca
www.facebook.com/125651564125503
Year Founded: 1984 Housed in the Blessed Sacrament Catholic Church, built in 1910.

***Chemainus:* Chemainus Valley Museum**
***Parent:* Chemainus Valley Historical Society**
c/o Chemainus Valley Historical Society, PO Box 172, 9799 Water Wheel Cres.
Chemainus, BC V0R 1K0
Tel: 250-246-2445
cvhs@telus.net
www.chemainusvalleymuseum.ca
Local history; Hours of operation: daily 9:00-4:00.

***Chetwynd:* Little Prairie Heritage Museum**
***Parent:* Little Prairie Heritage Society**
PO Box 1777
Chetwynd, BC V0C 1J0
Tel: 250-788-3358
Open July & Aug.

***Chilliwack:* Canadian Military Education Centre Museum**
PO Box 2123 Main, 45540 Petawawa Rd.
Chilliwack, BC V2R 1A5
www.cmedcentre.org
The CMEC is a Non Profit Museum Society. They are a member of the Organization Of Military Museums and a recognized Military Museum by the DND. Operated by a group of volunteers, the museum functions by public donations and the support of the City of Chilliwack.
Dan Jahn, Contact, 604-467-1988, danjahn@cmedcentre.org

***Chilliwack:* Chilliwack Museum & Archives**
45820 Spadina Ave.
Chilliwack, BC V2P 1T3
Tel: 604-795-5210; *Fax:* 604-795-5291
info@chilliwackmuseum.ca
www.chilliwackmuseum.ca
Social Media: www.youtube.com/user/ChilliwackMuseum
twitter.com/Chwkmusandarch
www.f acebook.com/ChilliwackMuseumArchive
Year Founded: 1958 The Archives are located at 9291 Corbould St. in Chilliwack, phone 604-795-9255; newspapers, photographs, books, DVDs, maps relating to the flood history of Chilliwack; special exhibits; programming; gift shop; open year round. Hours: M-F 9:00-4:30
Deborah Hudson, Director, deborah@chilliwackmuseum.ca
Brenda Paterson, Museum Educator

***Clinton:* Clinton Museum**
***Parent:* South Cariboo Historical Museum Society**
PO Box 217
Located at 1419 Cariboo Hwy., Clinton, BC
Clinton, BC V0K 1K0
Tel: 250-459-2442; *Fax:* 250-459-0058
clintonmuseum@telus.net
Other contact information: Clinton Village Office Phone: 250-459-2261
Year Founded: 1956 Open daily June - Sept.

***Comox:* Comox Archives & Museum Society**
1729 Comox Ave.
Comox, BC V9M 3M2
Tel: 250-339-2885
info@comoxmuseum.ca
www.comoxmuseum.ca
Local history; open Tu-Sa 10:00-4:00, Su 1:00-4:00.
Pam Moughton, Chair

***Comox:* Filberg Heritage Lodge & Park**
***Parent:* Filberg Heritage Lodge & Park Association**
c/o Filberg Heritage Lodge & Park Association, 61 Filberg Rd.
Comox, BC V9M 2S7
Tel: 250-339-2715
info@filberg.com
filberg.com
www.facebook.com/FHLPA
The park features nine acres of landscaped grounds, on which sit a number of heritage buildings. Former Comox Logging Company President Robert Filberg once owned the land.
Mo MacKendrick, Chair
Eden Lindsay-Bodie, Administrator

***Coquitlam:* Mackin House Museum**
***Parent:* Coquitlam Heritage Society**
1116 Brunette Ave.
Coquitlam, BC V3K 1G3
Tel: 604-516-6151
info@coquitlamheritage.ca
www.coquitlamheritage.ca
www.facebook.com/mackin.house
An historic house that serves as a museum, tourist information stop, & administrative offices for the Coquitlam Heritage Society. Open year-round, M-F 11:00-5:00, Sa 12:00-4:00.
Hazel Postma, Chair, postmah@douglas.bc.ca
Jill Cook, Executive Director, jcook@coquitlamheritage.ca
Sandra Martins, Manager, smartins@coquitlamheritage.ca

***Courtenay:* Courtenay & District Museum & Palaeontology Centre**
207 - 4th St.
Courtenay, BC V9N 1G7
Tel: 250-334-0686; *Fax:* 250-338-0619
museum@island.net
www.courtenaymuseum.ca
Social Media: www.youtube.com/user/courtenaymuseum
twitter.com/courtenaymuseum
www.f acebook.com/103653546358656
Other contact information: Alt. E-mails: info@courtenaymusuem.ca; archives@island.net
Year Founded: 1961 Natural history of the Comox Valley region, including marine fossils; includes archives; open year round.
Deborah Griffiths, Executive Director

***Cowichan Bay:* Cowichan Bay Maritime Centre**
***Parent:* Cowichan Wooden Boat Society**
PO Box 22
Located at 1761 Cowichan Bay Rd., Cowichan Bay, BC
Cowichan Bay, BC V0R 1NO
Tel: 250-746-4955
cwbs@classicboats.org
www.classicboats.org
Exhibits housed in unique pods designed to reflect the surrounding landspace & reveal the rich maritime history of Cowichan Bay; offers classic wooden boat building programs & undertakes restoration projects; open daily
Chris Banner, President

***Cranbrook:* Aasland Museum Taxidermy**
3700 Collinson Rd.
Cranbrook, BC V1C 7B8
Tel: 250-426-3566
Small natural history museum displaying mounted birds & animals for the public; admission free; a lecture accompanies the visit if prior arrangements are made; school groups, handicapped, adult groups & individual visitors welcome; Mon.-Sat.

***Cranbrook:* Canadian Museum of Rail Travel**
PO Box 400
Located at 57 Van Horne St. South, Cranbrook, BC
Cranbrook, BC V1C 4H9
Tel: 250-489-3918; *Fax:* 250-489-5744
mail@trainsdeluxe.com
www.trainsdeluxe.com
The Canadian Museum of Rail Travel depicts the story of rail travel in Canada, through the collection, restoration & display of historic rail equipment from various eras. The museum features a large historic railcar collection. Other sights at the museum include the Royal Alexandra Hall, which was the former cafe from the Canadian Pacific Railway's 1906 Royal Alexandra Hotel

in Winnipeg, an 1898 railway freight shed & a wooden railway water tower.
Garry W. Anderson, Executive Director
Brian Dees, Office Manager

Creston: Creston & District Museum
219 Devon St.
Creston, BC V0B 1G3
Tel: 250-428-9262
mail@creston.museum.bc.ca
www.creston.museum.bc.ca
twitter.com/CrestonMuseum
www.facebook.com/Cr estonMuseum
Year Founded: 1982 Guided tours, permanent & temporary exhibits; open spring, summer, fall; in winter by appt.
Ian Currie, President

Crofton: Old Crofton School Museum Society
PO Box 49
Located at 1507 Joan St., Crofton, BC
Crofton, BC V0R 1R0
Tel: 250-246-9731; Fax: 250-246-2456
History of old schools, Crofton & area; open June-Sept.

Cumberland: Cumberland Museum & Archives
PO Box 258, 2680 Dunsmuir Ave.
Cumberland, BC V0R 1S0
Tel: 250-336-2445
info@cumberland.museum.bc.ca
www.cumberlandmuseum.ca
www.facebook.com/cumberlandbc.museum
Year Founded: 1981 Open year round

Dawson Creek: Dawson Creek Station Museum
Parent: South Peace Historical Society
900 Alaska Ave.
Dawson Creek, BC V1G 4T6
Tel: 250-782-9595
info@tourismdawsoncreek.com
Two galleries, the Northern Alberta Railway & the Natural History Gallery. Open year round

Dawson Creek: Walter Wright Pioneer Village & Sudeten Hall
1901 Alaska Hwy.
Dawson Creek, BC V1G 1P7
Tel: 250-782-2590
www.mile0park.ca/#!pioneer-village
www.facebook.com/362278520475336
The Walter Wright Pioneer Village presents life in Dawson Creek, before the construction of the Alaska Highway. Historic buildings include the Pouce Coupe School, the W.O. Harper General Store, & the St. Paul's Anglican Church. The Sudeten Hall honours Germany's Sudeten people who arrived in the area in 1939. Located in Mile 0 Park.

Delta: Delta Museum & Archives
4858 Delta St.
Delta, BC V4K 2T8
Tel: 604-946-9322; Fax: 604-946-5791
info@deltamuseum.ca
www.deltamuseum.ca
www.facebook.com/DeltaMuseumAnd ArchivesSociety
Year Founded: 1969 1912 heritage building; archives; exhibitions on pioneer homelife, village life, farming, fishing, duck decoys, First Nations archeology, basketry
Gabrielle Martin, Executive Director, gmartin@deltamuseum.ca
Darryl MacKenzie, Curator, dmackenzie@deltamuseum.ca
Robert McLelland, Archivist

Denman Island: Denman Island Museum
PO Box 28, 1111 Northwest Rd.
Denman Island, BC V0R 1T0
Tel: 250-335-3196
www.denmanisland.com/denman/museum.htm
Collection houses Northwest Coast artifacts from the Salish; natural history specimens; European settlement items; photographs & maps; administered by the Denman Island Seniors & Museum Society.
Christine Oliver, President

Duncan: British Columbia Forest Discovery Centre
2892 Drinkwater Rd.
Duncan, BC V9L 6C2
Tel: 250-715-1113
info.bcfdc@shawlink.ca
www.discoveryforest.com
twitter.com/forestmuseum
www.facebook.com/1122 91022115893
Year Founded: 1965 The BC Forest Discovery Centre is a 100-acre, open air museum, which features forest & marsh trails, logging artifacts, & heritage buildings.
Chris Gale, General Manager, cgale.bcfdc@shaw.ca
Jenna Kiesman, Curator/Coordinator, Education Programs, jkiesman.bcfdc@shaw.ca

Duncan: Cowichan Valley Museum
PO Box 1014
Location: 130 Canada Ave., Duncan, BC
Duncan, BC V9L 3Y2
Tel: 250-746-6612; Fax: 250-746-6612
www.cowichanvalleymuseum.bc.ca
Local history museum; includes archives; open year round

Duncan: Fairbridge Chapel Heritage Society
4791 Fairbridge Dr.
Duncan, BC V9L 6N9
Tel: 250-746-7519
fairbridgechapel.com
Year Founded: 1987 The Society protects & maintains the Fairbridge Chapel, a provincial heritage site, & provides guided tours on request.
Ron Smith, Secretary-Treasurer, rgwsmiths@hotmail.com

Enderby: Enderby & District Museum Society
PO Box 367, 901 George St.
Enderby, BC V0E 1V0
Tel: 250-838-7170
enderbymuseum@gmail.com
www.enderbymuseum.ca
www.twitter.com/enderbymuseum
www.facebook.com/en derbymuseum
Year Founded: 1973 Hours: Tu-Sa 10:00am-4:00pm
Naomi Fournier, Curator/Administrator

Fernie: Fernie & District Historical Society Museum
PO Box 1527
Located at 491 Victoria Ave., Fernie, BC
Fernie, BC V0B 1M0
Tel: 250-423-7016
www.ferniemuseum.com
Year Founded: 1979 Coal mining history museum; local history & early families research

Fort Langley: British Columbia Farm Museum
PO Box 279
Fort Langley, BC V1M 2R6
Tel: 604-888-2273
info@bcfma.com
www.bcfma.com
twitter.com/FarmBC
www.facebook.com/bcfma
British Columbia Farm Machinery & Agricultural Museum Association presents the history of farming in British Columbia. Displays include horse drawn carriages & wagons, steam, gas & diesel powered grinders & tractors, an 1890s sawmill, a blacksmith shop & British Columbia's first crop duster, the Tiger Moth airplane. The museum is open seven days a week from April 1st to Thanksgiving Day.

Fort Langley: Fort Langley National Historic Site of Canada (FLNHSC) / Lieu historique national du Canada Fort-Langley
PO Box 129, 23433 Mavis Ave.
Fort Langley, BC V1M 2R5
Tel: 604-513-4777; Fax: 604-513-4798
fort.langley@pc.gc.ca
www.pc.gc.ca/lhn-nhs/bc/langley.aspx
www.faceboo k.com/FortLangleyNHS
Birthplace of British Columbia; 19th century Hudson's Bay Co. trading post; Open year round

Fort Langley: Langley Centennial Museum & National Exhibition Centre
PO Box 800
Located at 9135 King St., Fort Langley, BC
Fort Langley, BC V1M 2S2
Tel: 604-532-3536
museum@tol.ca
www.langleymuseum.org
Art, history & science exhibits; open year round
Peter Tulumello, Manager, Cultural Services, ptulumello@tol.ca

Fort Nelson: Fort Nelson Heritage Museum
PO Box 716
Fort Nelson, BC V0C 1R0
Tel: 250-774-3536
info@fortnelsonmuseum.ca
www.fortnelsonmuseum.ca
Artifacts related to the construction of the Alaska Highway; open mid-May - mid-Sept.

Fort St. James: Fort St. James National Historic Site of Canada
PO Box 1148
Fort St. James, BC V0J 1P0
Tel: 250-996-7191; Fax: 250-996-8566
stjames@pc.gc.ca
www.pc.gc.ca/lhn-nhs/bc/stjames/index.aspx
The Fort St James National Historic Site offers a large collection of original wooden buildings representing the fur trade in Canada. The following buildings are located at the site: Fur WareHouse (1888-1889); Fish Cache (1889); Men's House (1884); Trade Store & Office (1884); Murray House (1883-1884); Dairy (1884); & Wharf & Tramway (1894-1914). The Historic Site is open daily from 9:00 to 5:00, from the long weekend in May to the end of September.
Bob Grill, Site Manager, bob.grill@pc.gc.ca

Fort St John: Fort St. John-North Peace Museum
9323 - 100 St.
Fort St John, BC V1J 4N4
Tel: 250-787-0430
fsjnpmuseum@fsjmail.com
www.fsjmuseum.com
www.facebook.com/102713059806910
Hours: Open year round, M-Sa 9:00-5:00
Heather Longworth, Curator/Manager

Fort Steele: Fort Steele Heritage Town
9851 Hwy. 93/95
Fort Steele, BC V0B 1N0
Tel: 250-417-6000; Fax: 250-489-2624
info@FortSteele.bc.ca
fortsteele.ca
twitter.com/fortsteele
www.faceb ook.com/fortsteeleheritagetown
Year Founded: 1961 Restored 1890s mining boom town of the East Kootenay; open year round with varying program levels each season, call for details
Brad Froggatt, Manager, Heritage Services, Brad.Froggatt@FortSteele.bc.ca

Fraser Lake: Fraser Lake Museum
PO Box 430, 30 Carrier Cres.
Fraser Lake, BC V0J 1S0
Tel: 250-699-8844
www.fraserlake.ca
Open summer

Gabriola Island: Gabriola Museum
Parent: Gabriola Historical & Museum Society
PO Box 213
Located at 505 South Rd., Gabriola Island, BC
Gabriola Island, BC V0R 1X0
Tel: 250-247-9987
info@gabriolamuseum.org
www.gabriolamuseum.org
Year Founded: 1996 Through its museum, the Historical Society presents the history of the island through displays, exhibits, lectures, presentations, & tours.
Diane Cornish, President
Janet Stobbs, Director/Archivist

Gibsons: Sunshine Coast Museum & Archives (SCMA)
PO Box 766, 716 Winn Rd.
Gibsons, BC V0N 1V0
Tel: 604-886-8232
scm_a@dccnet.com
www.sunshinecoastmuseum.ca
Collection of historical documents & artifacts pertaining to the Sunshine Coast of BC; open year round; closed Sun. & Mon.

Golden: Golden & District Museum
PO Box 992, 1302 - 11 Ave. South
Golden, BC V0A 1H0
Tel: 250-344-5169; Fax: 250-344-5169
museum.golden@gmail.com
www.goldenbcmuseum.com
www.facebook.com/150197 378373720
Year Founded: 1974 Open May-Sept.

Grand Forks: Boundary Museum
6145 Reservoir Rd.
Grand Forks, BC V0H 1H0
Tel: 250-442-3737
boundarymuse@shaw.ca
www.boundarymuseum.com
Year Founded: 1958 The Boundary Museum is situated in a former schoolhouse, which was built in 1929 by the Christian Communities of Universal Brotherhood Doukhobors. The grounds of the restored schoolhouse feature a fruit drying facility & a bread oven which were also built by the society.

Cher Wyers, Manager

***Grand Forks:* Mountain View Doukhobor Museum**
PO Box 1235
Located at 3655 Hardy Mountain Rd., Grand Forks, BC
Grand Forks, BC V0H 1H0
Tel: 250-442-8855

***Granisle:* Granisle Museum & Information Centre**
PO Box 128
Granisle, BC V0J 1W0
Tel: 250-697-2428; *Fax:* 250-697-2568
infocentre@villageofgranisle.ca
The log house museum contains artifacts from pioneer days & earlier.

***Greenville:* Nisga'a Museum**
PO Box 300
Located at 810 Highway Dr., Greenville, BC
Greenville, BC V0J 1X0
Tel: 250-633-3050
nisgaamuseum@nisgaa.net
nisgaamuseum.ca
Year Founded: 2011 Artifacts that represent the Nisga'a society & culture.

***Greenwood:* Greenwood Museum & Visitor Centre**
PO Box 399, 214 South Copper Ave.
Greenwood, BC V0H 1J0
Tel: 250-445-6355; *Fax:* 250-445-6355
www.greenwoodmuseum.com
Year Founded: 1967 Mining, forestry, ranching & the internment of Japanese Canadians; Greenwood was an internment camp during WWII

***Groundbirch:* Bruce Groner Museum**
PO Box 124
Groundbirch, BC V0C 1T0
Open summer

***Harrison Mills:* Kilby Historic Site**
PO Box 55
Located at 215 Kilby Rd., Harrison Mills, BC V0M 1L0
Harrison Mills, BC V0M 1L0
Tel: 604-796-9576; *Fax:* 604-796-9592
info@kilby.ca
kilby.ca
Social Media: www.youtube.com/user/kilbyhistoricsite
twitter.com/kilbys
www.facebook .com/KilbyHistoricSite
Year Founded: 1972 Open daily May-Sept. 11-5, then seasonal hours

***Hazelton:* 'Ksan Historical Village & Museum**
PO Box 440
Hazelton, BC V0J 1Y0
Tel: 250-842-5544; *Fax:* 250-842-6533
Toll-Free: 877-842-5518
ksan@ksan.org
www.ksan.org
Year Founded: 1960 Replica Gitxkan Indian Village; museum has approx. 600 items on display, including ceremonial artifacts, hunting and fishing tools, masks and shaman's regalia; open year round

***Hazelton:* Hazelton Pioneer Museum & Archives**
PO Box 323, 4255 Government St.
Hazelton, BC V0J 1Y0
Tel: 250-842-5961; *Fax:* 250-842-2176
hazlib@bulkley.net
hazelton.bclibrary.ca/services
The museum is located in the Hazelton District Public Library, & houses artifacts pertaining to local history.

***Hope:* Hope Museum**
919 Water Ave.
Hope, BC V0X 1L0
Tel: 604-869-7322; *Fax:* 604-869-2160
Toll-Free: 866-467-3842
vc@hope.bc.ca
Open summer; off-season tours by request. Located in the Hope Visitor Centre.
Inge Wilson, Manager

***Horsefly:* Jack Lynn Memorial Museum**
PO Box 11
Located on Boswell St., Horsefly, BC
Horsefly, BC V0L 1L0
Tel: 250-620-3304
Open daily July to Aug. anually; Sept. to June by appointment only; small museum run by volunteers; features artifacts, photos & paper archives, all relating to Horsefly

***Hudson's Hope:* Hudson's Hope Museum & Historical Society**
PO Box 98
Located at 9510 Beattie Dr., Hudson's Hope, BC
Hudson's Hope, BC V0C 1V0
Tel: 250-783-5735; *Fax:* 250-783-5770
hhmuseum@gmail.com
www.hudsonshopemuseum.com
twitter.com/hhmuseum
ww w.facebook.com/124162084280248
Other contact information: Alt. E-mail: hhmuseum@pris.ca
Hudson's Bay Company store of 1942; archives; fossil collection; Aboriginal display; North West & Hudson's Bay Company artifacts; North West Mounted Police, trapping, coal mining, gold mining, pioneer, logging & World War memorabilia & photographic history of W.A.C. Bennett dam

***Invermere:* Windermere Valley Museum & Archives**
PO Box 2315, 222 - 6th Ave.
Invermere, BC V0A 1K0
Tel: 250-342-9769
wvmuseum@shaw.ca
www.windermerevalleymuseum.ca
Open M-Su 10:00-4:00 during summer hours; open Tu 12:00-4:00 during spring & fall hours

***Kamloops:* Kamloops Museum & Archives**
207 Seymour St.
Kamloops, BC V2C 2E7
Tel: 250-828-3576; *Fax:* 250-828-3760
museum@kamloops.ca
www.kamloops.ca/museum
www.facebook.com/kamloopsmus eum
Open year round

***Kamloops:* Rocky Mountain Rangers Museum & Archives**
PO Box 3250
Located in the J.R. Vicars Armoury at 1221 McGill Rd., Kamloops, BC
Kamloops, BC V2C 6K7
Tel: 250-372-2717; *Fax:* 250-374-1063

***Kamloops:* Secwepemc Museum & Heritage Park (SCES)**
***Parent:* Secwepemc Cultural Education Society**
355 Yellowhead Hwy.
Kamloops, BC V2H 1H1
Tel: 250-828-9749; *Fax:* 250-372-8833
www.secwepemc.org/museum
Museum is located on 12 acres & exhibits artifacts, photographs & histories of the Secwepemc people; displays include canoes, hunting & fishing objects, clothing, games; the Heritage Park complements the Museum with outdoor displays & reconstructed winter pit houses. lean-tos, smoke house & traditional plant foods; trails, gardens; giftshop (seasonal); museum open year round
Daniel Saul, Museum Manager, dsaul@kib.ca

***Kaslo:* Kaslo Village Hall**
PO Box 576
Located at 312 - 4th St., Kaslo, BC
Kaslo, BC V0G 1M0
Tel: 250-353-2311; *Fax:* 250-353-7767
www.kaslo.ca
One of only two wooden municipal buildings left in Canada still used as a seat of government; designated National Historic Site; open Mon. - Fri.
Neil Smith, CAO, cao@kaslo.ca

***Kaslo:* S.S. Moyie National Historic Site**
***Parent:* Kootenay Lake Historical Society**
PO Box 537
Kaslo, BC V0G 1M0
Tel: 250-353-2525; *Fax:* 250-353-2525
www.klhs.bc.ca
Moored in the town of Kaslo, this is the oldest intact passenger sternwheeler in the world; gift shop; operated by the Kootenay Lake Historical Society; open daily mid-May to mid-Oct.
Bill Yeo, President

***Kelowna:* Benvoulin Heritage Park & Benvoulin Heritage Church**
***Parent:* Central Okanagan Heritage Society**
c/o Central Okanagan Heritage Society, 1060 Cameron Ave.
Located at 2279 Benvoulin Rd., Kelowna, BC
Kelowna, BC V1Y 8V3
Tel: 250-861-7188
cohs@telus.net
www.okheritagesociety.com
The Benvoulin Church was built in 1892 in the Gothic Revival style. The pioneer church was restored by the Central Okanagan Heritage Society, which owns & operates Benvoulin Heritage Park.
Janice Henry, Executive Director, Central Okanagan Heritage Society

***Kelowna:* British Columbia Orchard Industry Museum**
***Parent:* Kelowna Museums**
1304 Ellis St.
Kelowna, BC V1Y 1Z8
Tel: 778-478-0347
www.kelownamuseums.ca/museums/the-bc-orchard-industry-mu seum
Year Founded: 1989 The BC Orchard Industry Museum is located in the historic, restored Laurel Packinghouse. The museum features exhibits about the Okanagan Valley's orchard industry, including picking, processeing, packing, preserving, & marketing. The BC Wine Museum & VQA Wine Shop is also at this location. The museum is open year round.

***Kelowna:* British Columbia Wine Museum & VQA Wine Shop**
***Parent:* Kelowna Museums**
1304 Ellis St.
Kelowna, BC V1Y 1Z8
Tel: 250-868-0441
www.kelownamuseums.ca/museums/the-bc-wine-museum-vqa-wine-shop
The museum aims to bring Okanagan wine heritage, as well as the broader history of BC wine, to the public. The VQA Wine Shop carries wine from over 90 BC wineries. The museum & shop are at the same location as the British Columbia Orchard Industry Museum. Open year round.

***Kelowna:* Central Okanagan Heritage Society**
1060 Cameron Ave.
Kelowna, BC V1Y 8V3
Tel: 250-861-7188
cohs@telus.net
www.okheritagesociety.com
www.facebook.com/OkHeritageSociety
Year Founded: 1982 The Society promotes & participates in the preservation of the Central Okanagan region's natural, cultural & horticultural heritage; operates the Guisachan Heritage Park, the Benvoulin Heritage Park & Brent's Grist Mill Park.
Janice Henry, Executive Director

***Kelowna:* Central Okanagan Sports Hall of Fame & Museum**
***Parent:* Kelowna Museums**
c/o Kelowna Museums, 470 Queensway Ave.
Kelowna, BC V1Y 6S7
Tel: 250-763-2417
www.kelownamuseums.ca/museums/the-central-okanagan-sport s-hall-of-fame
Located at the Capri Mall on Gordon Drive. Open year round.

***Kelowna:* Father Pandosy Mission**
3685 Benvoulin Rd.
Kelowna, BC V1W 4M7
Tel: 250-860-8369
www.okanaganhistoricalsociety.org/pandosy_mission.html
Oblate Mission, 1859
Tracy Satin, President, Okanagan Historical Society, okheritagehistory@gmail.com

***Kelowna:* Kelowna Museums Okanagan Heritage Museum**
***Parent:* Kelowna Museums Society**
470 Queensway Ave.
Kelowna, BC V1Y 6S7
Tel: 250-763-2417
www.kelownamuseum.ca
Social Media: www.youtube.com/user/KelownaMuseums
twitter.com/kelownamuseums
www.fac ebook.com/pages/KelownaMuseums/260810793981037
Open Tue.-Sat. 10-5; admission by donation; this location also houses the Kelowna Public Archives.
Linda Digby, Executive Director, ldigby@kelownamuseums.ca
Debbie Rehm, Manager, Administraition & Operations, drehm@kelownamuseums.ca
Tara Hurley, Community Archivist, thurley@kelownamuseums.ca

***Kelowna:* Okanagan Military Museum**
***Parent:* Kelowna Museums**
1424 Ellis St.
Kelowna, BC V1Y 2A5
Tel: 250-763-9292
www.kelownamuseums.ca/museums/the-okanagan-military-museum
Other contact information: Alt. URL: www.okmilmuseum.ca
The museum is dedicated to preserving the military heritage of Okanagan Valley residents. The collection includes small arms, uniforms, insignia, badges, & equipment. Open year round.
Keith Boehmer, Manager, Operations,
KBoehmer@KelownaMuseums.ca

***Keremeos:* Keremeos Museum**
***Parent:* South Similkameen Museum Society**
PO Box 135, 604 - 6th Ave.
Keremeos, BC V0X 1N0
Tel: 250-499-9204
info@keremeosmuseum.ca
www.keremeosmuseum.ca
Year Founded: 1972 Restored gaol-house with B.C. provincial police displays, pioneer artifacts
John Armstrong, President
Francis Peck, Appointed Historian

***Keremeos:* The Old Grist Mill & Gardens at Keremeos**
2691 Upper Bench Rd., SS#4
Keremeos, BC V0X 1N4
Tel: 250-499-2888
info@oldgristmill.ca
www.oldgristmill.ca
twitter.com/old_grist_mill
www.facebook.com/oldgri stmill
Designated British Columbia Heritage Site; open May - Oct & by appt.

***Kimberley:* Kimberley Heritage Musuem**
105 Spokane St.
Kimberley, BC V1A 2E5
Tel: 250-427-7510
kdhs@shawbiz.ca
kimberleyheritagemuseum.blogspot.ca
www.facebook.com/263618083650062
Year Founded: 1980 Early Kimberley History; Sullivan Mine display; open year round; admission by donation; archives available for research, by request, at a nominal fee
Marie Stang, Curator

***Kitimat:* Kitimat Museum & Archives**
293 City Centre
Kitimat, BC V8C 1T6
Tel: 250-632-8950; *Fax:* 250-632-7429
info@kitimatmuseum.ca
www.kitimatmuseum.ca
www.facebook.com/pages/Kitimat-Museum-Archives/161440070544293
Year Founded: 1968 Natural history; homesteader & Haida histories; Kemano-Kitimat Project history; temporary exhibitions; giftshop. Hours: June-Aug. M-Sa 10:00-5:00; Sept.-May M-F 10:00-4:00, Sa 12:00-4:00
Louise Avery, Curator, 250-632-8951,
lavery@kitimatmuseum.ca

***Kitwanga:* Meanskinisht Museum**
PO Box 183
Kitwanga, BC V0J 2A0
Tel: 250-849-5732
Houses the history & remnants of ancient village of Gitlusec, Meanskinisht village & Cedarvale; also looks after the graveyard (private); open by appt.
Mary G. Dalen, Director

***Lake Cowichan:* Kaatza Station Museum & Archives**
PO Box 135
Lake Cowichan, BC V0R 2G0
Tel: 250-749-6142
kaatzamuseum@shaw.ca
www.kaatzamuseum.ca
Open year round
Barbara Simkins, Curator/Manager

***Langley:* Canadian Museum of Flight (CMF)**
Hangar 3, Langley Airport, 5333 - 216th St.
Langley, BC V2Y 2N3
Tel: 604-532-0035; *Fax:* 604-532-0056
info@canadianflight.org
www.canadianflight.org
Social Media: www.youtube.com/user/CanadianFlight
twitter.com/CanadianFlight
www.fac ebook.com/CanadianMuseumOfFlight
Year Founded: 1977 The Canadian Museum of Flight restores, preserves, & displays Canada's aviation heritage. The museum & restoration site features more than twenty-five aircraft, such as a World War II Handley Page Hampden & a T-33 Silver Star. The Millennium Kids Room is a "hands-on" facility for young visitors.
Bruce Bakker, President
Mike Sattler, General Manager

***Lazo:* Comox Air Force Museum (CAFM)**
PO Box 1000 Forces, 19 Wing Comox
Located at 19 Wing Military Row, Comox, BC, V0R 2K0
Lazo, BC V0R 2K0
Tel: 250-339-8162; *Fax:* 250-339-8162
cafm.info@gmail.com
comoxairforcemuseum.ca
Social Media: www.youtube.com/user/WatchCAFM
www.facebook.com/ComoxAirForceMuseum
Year Founded: 1987 History of CFB Comox & West Coast aviation
Capt. Lynn Barley, Director

***Lillooet:* Lillooet District Historical Society & Museum**
PO Box 441
Lillooet, BC V0K 1V0
Tel: 250-256-4308; *Fax:* 250-256-0043
lillmuseum@cablelan.net
www.lillooetbc.com
www.facebook.com/1254371874 88516
Open May-Oct., Tue.-Sat., 10-4; daily July & Aug. 9-5

***Lytton:* Lytton Museum & Archives**
PO Box 640, 420 Fraser St.
Lytton, BC V0K 1Z0
Tel: 250-455-2254; *Fax:* 250-455-2142
curator@lyttonmuseum.ca
www.botaniecreek.com/museum
Year Founded: 1995 Built by the Canadian National Railway as a residence in 1942, the museum is filled with local artifacts and archives, including pieces formally used at the C.N. station.
Dorothy V. Dodge, Curator

***Mackenzie:* Mackenzie & District Museum**
***Parent:* Mackenzie & District Museum Society**
Ernie Bodin Centre, PO Box 340, 86 Centennial Dr.
Mackenzie, BC V0J 2C0
Tel: 250-997-3021
museum@mackbc.com
www.mackenziemuseum.ca
www.facebook.com/mackenziemuseum
Other contact information: Virtual Museum:
www.settlerseffects.ca
Year Founded: 1991

***Maple Ridge:* Haney House Museum**
***Parent:* Maple Ridge Historical Society**
11612 - 224th St.
Maple Ridge, BC V2X 5Z7
Tel: 604-463-1377
www.mapleridgemuseum.org
Year Founded: 1981 Haney House was the residence of pioneer Thomas Haney, who came to Maple Ridge, British Columbia in 1876. Guided tours are available year-round.

***Maple Ridge:* Maple Ridge Museum & Archives**
***Parent:* Maple Ridge Historical Society**
22520 - 116th Ave.
Maple Ridge, BC V2X 0S4
Tel: 604-463-5311
www.mapleridgemuseum.org
www.facebook.com/106860626035721
Year Founded: 1984 Open year round
Val Patenaude, Director
Allison White, Curator

***Mayne Island:* Mayne Island Museum**
Comp. 4, Site 1, RR#1
Location: 431 Fernhill Rd., Mayne Island, BC V0N 2J0
Mayne Island, BC V0N 2J0
Tel: 250-539-5286

***McBride:* Valley Museum & Archives**
PO Box 775, 241 Dominion St.
McBride, BC V0J 2E0
Tel: 250-569-2749
www.mcbridemuseum.ca
Other contact information: Virtual Museum:
www.settlerseffects.ca
Displays within McBride & District Public Library

***Merritt:* Nicola Valley Museum & Archives**
PO Box 1262, 1675 Tutill Court
Merritt, BC V1K 1B8
Tel: 250-378-4145; *Fax:* 250-378-4145
nvma@uniserve.com
www.nicolavalleymuseum.org
www.facebook.com/12329292 3631
Year Founded: 1976 The museum houses an extensive collection of artifacts & photographs of various aspects of Nicola Valley's history, including churches, the general hospital, rail travel & other transportation, Craigmont mine history, Judge Henry Castillou, ranching & mining displays; James Teit Gallery & First Nations displays; Merritt Model Railway club display; the Archives preserves the James Teit First Nations reference material, early newspapers, mining reports, cemetery information, early maps & hundreds of photopgraphs. Open year round.
Barbara Watson, Office Manager

***Midway:* Kettle River Museum**
***Parent:* Kettle River Museum Society**
907 Hwy. 3
Midway, BC V0H 1M0
Tel: 250-449-2614
kettlerivermuseum@shaw.ca
www.facebook.com/pages/Kettle-River-Museum/224641084317690
Year Founded: 1976 Mile of Kettle Valley Railway; restored 1900s CPR Station; B.C. Provincial Police display

***Mission:* Fraser River Heritage Park**
PO Box 3341
Mission, BC V2V 4J5
Tel: 604-826-0277; *Fax:* 604-826-0333
mhaadmin@telus.net
www.heritagepark-mission.ca
www.facebook.com/Fraser RiverHeritagePark
Original site of St. Mary's Mission & Indian Residential School, founded in 1861; park features foundations of mission

***Mission:* Mission District Historical Society & Museum**
33201 - 2nd Ave.
Mission, BC V2V 1J9
Tel: 604-826-1011
info@missionmuseum.com
www.missionmuseum.com
www.facebook.com/missionmuseum
Year Founded: 1972 Permanent exhibits include Sto:lo First Nations display, the history of settlement with pioneers, rails, rivers, and items from business and home life, notably period 1920s rooms. Also featured are items from Mission's old Chinatown. Museum is housed in a 1907 B.C. Mills, prefabricated, Canadian Bank of Commerce Bldg. Gift shop offers books on Mission's history. There is a selection of school tours.
Hazel Godley, Manager

***Mission:* Xá:ytem Longhouse Interpretive Centre**
***Parent:* Sto:lo Heritage Trust Society**
c/o Sto:lo Heritage Trust Society, 35087 Lougheed Hwy.
Mission, BC V2V 6T1
Tel: 604-820-9725; *Fax:* 604-820-9735
On the coast of British Columbia, Xá:ytem has been an important Salish spiritual site. Today, Xá:ytem is a National Historic Site, where visitors discover a traditional Salish cedar longhouse & two pit houses. The site is open year-round.

***Naksup:* Arrow Lakes Historical Society**
PO Box 819
Located at 92 - 7th Ave., Nakusp, AB
Nakusp, BC V0G 1R0
Tel: 250-265-0110
alhs1234@telus.net
alhs-archives.com
Other contact information: Appointment Phone: 250-265-3323
The society stores archival material for the Arrow Lakes & Trout Lake regions.

***Nanaimo:* The Bastion**
c/o Nanaimo Museum, 100 Museum Way
Nanaimo, BC V9R 5J8
Tel: 250-753-1821
www.nanaimomuseum.ca
Year Founded: 1853 1853 Hudson's Bay Co. log fortification; located on the Pioneer Waterfront Plaza (Front St. & Bastion St.), across from the Coast Bastion Hotel.

***Nanaimo:* Museum of Natural History**
Building 370, Vancouver Island University, Nanaimo Campus, 900 - 5th St.
Nanaimo, BC V9R 5S5
Tel: 250-753-3245
www.viu.ca/museum
www.facebook.com/240014161924
Year Founded: 1976 The museum supports student, faculty, & external research. It is open in the summer by appointment only.
Wendy Simms, Contact, Wendy.Simms@viu.ca

***Nanaimo:* Nanaimo District Museum (NDM)**
100 Museum Way
Nanaimo, BC V9R 5J8
Tel: 250-753-1821
www.nanaimomuseum.ca
www.facebook.com/NanaimoMuseum
Open year round
Debbie Trueman, General Manager, debbie@nanaimomuseum.ca

***Nanaimo:* Vancouver Island Military Museum**
***Parent:* Vancouver Island Military Museum Society**
100 Cameron Rd.
Nanaimo, BC V9R 0C8
Tel: 250-753-3814
oic@vimms.ca
www.vimms.ca
Year Founded: 1986 The museum is entirely staffed by volunteers, & seeks to collect, conserve, & display artifacts related to the Canadian armed forces.

***Naramata:* Naramata Heritage Museum**
PO Box 95, 224 Robinson Ave.
Naramata, BC V0H 1N0
Tel: 250-496-5572
contact@naramatamuseum.com
naramatamuseum.com
Year Founded: 1997 Local history; 3 permanent displays

***Nelson:* Touchstones Nelson: Museum of Art & History**
502 Vernon St.
Nelson, BC V1L 4E7
Tel: 250-352-9813
info@touchstonesnelson.ca
www.touchstonesnelson.ca
Social Media: www.flickr.com/photos/touchstonesnelson
www.facebook.com/62908084663
Year Founded: 1955 The museum displays the history & culture of Nelson, British Columbia. Archives & an art gallery are also part of the museum. It is open year round.
Leah Best, Executive Director, director@touchstonesnelson.ca
Laura Fortier, Collections Manager & Archivist, collections@touchstonesnelson.ca
Jessica Demers, Curator, exhibitions@touchstonesnelson.ca
Rod Taylor, Curator, rod@touchstonesnelson.ca
Alex Dudley, Visitor Services Manager, shop@touchstonesnelson.ca
Linda Sawchyn, Executive Assistant / Volunteer and Membership Coordinator, linda@touchstonesnelson.ca

***New Denver:* Sandon Historical Society Museum & Visitors' Centre**
***Parent:* Sandon Historical Society**
PO Box 52
New Denver, BC V0G 1S0
Tel: 250-358-7920
www.sandonmuseum.ca
Historic museum & archives of Sandon & area; heritage photographs, artifacts, guided tours
Dan Nicholson, President, 250-358-7215

***New Denver:* Silvery Slocan Historical Museum**
***Parent:* Silvery Slocan Historical Society**
PO Box 301
Located at 202 - 6 Ave., New Denver, BC
New Denver, BC V0G 1S0
Tel: 250-358-2201; *Fax:* 250-358-7251
Cultural & economic history of the Slocan Lake area; open July & Aug.

***New Westminster:* Canadian Lacrosse Hall of Fame**
***Parent:* Canadian Lacrosse Association**
PO Box 308
65 East 6th Ave., New Westminister, BC V3L 4G6
New Westminster, BC V3L 4Y6
info@canadianlacrossehalloffame.com
www.canadianlacrossehalloffame.com
twitter.com/CanLaxHall
www.facebook .com/136016359899545
Year Founded: 1965 Inductees to the Canadian Lacrosse Hall of Fame are featured in the following categories: builders, box players, field players, veteran players, & teams.

***New Westminster:* New Westminster Museum & Archives**
777 Columbia St.
New Westminster, BC V3M 1B6
Tel: 604-527-4640
museum@newwestcity.ca
www.nwpr.bc.ca
www.facebook.co m/NWMuseumandArchives
Year Founded: 1950 The New Westminster Museum, with more than 30,000 items in its collection, depicts the history of British Columbia's first capital. The New Westminster Archives, which contains 13,000 archival items, preserves the documentary heritage of the city from its time as a Royal Engineers' settlement camp. Irving House is an 1865 colonial period house. Guided tours are given of the home.

***New Westminster:* The Royal Westminster Regiment Historical Society & Museum**
The Armoury, 530 Queens Ave.
New Westminster, BC V3L 1K3
Tel: 604-526-5116
museum@royal-westies-assn.ca
www.royal-westies-assn.ca/museum.html
Permanent collection of military artifacts & memorabilia from the experience of The Royal Westminster Regiment & its antecedents; open every Tue. & Thurs.
Brig. Gen. Herb E. Hamm, Contact C.D., (Ret'd)

***New Westminster:* Samson V Maritime Museum**
880 Quayside Dr.
New Westminster, BC V3M 6T8
Tel: 604-527-4640
museum@newwestcity.ca
www.newwestpcr.ca
A restored sternwheel snagpuller, moored on the Fraser River at the Westminster Quay Market; history of the vessel, educational programming

***North Vancouver:* Deep Cove Heritage Society**
4360 Gallant Rd.
North Vancouver, BC V7G 1L2
Tel: 604-929-5744
info@deepcoveheritage.com
deepcoveheritage.com
www.facebook.com/deepcoveheritage
Year Founded: 1985 The Society provides archival documents on Deep Cove's history, as well as an organized walking tour of the area, highlighting many historical sites that helped shape the community.

***North Vancouver:* Lynn Canyon Ecology Centre**
3663 Park Rd.
North Vancouver, BC V7J 3G3
Tel: 604-990-3755
ecocentre@dnv.org
www.dnv.org/ecology
twitter.com/ecologycentre
www.facebook.com/1301270 93705007
Open year round

***North Vancouver:* North Vancouver Museum & Archives (NVMA)**
Community History Centre, 3203 Institute Rd.
North Vancouver, BC V7K 3E5
Tel: 604-990-3700; *Fax:* 604-987-5688
nvmac@dnv.org
www.northvanmuseum.ca
twitter.com/NorthVanMuseum
www.f acebook.com/NorthVancouverMuseumArchives
Celebrates & preserves North Vancouver's social, industrial & cultural history; WWII shipbuilding; P.G.E. Railway; logging; Archives Reading Room & Archives Collection
Nancy L. Kirkpatrick, Director, kirkpatrickn@dnv.org

***North Vancouver:* Pacific Great Eastern (PGE) Railway Station**
107 Carrie Cates Ct.
North Vancouver, BC V7M 3J4
www.facebook.com/800217229990484
Restored station building with railway exhibits

***Okanagan:* Lake Country Museum**
11255 Okanagan Centre Rd. West
Okanagan, BC V4V 2J7
Tel: 250-766-0111
lcmuseum@shaw.ca
www.lakecountrymuseum.com
Social Media: www.youtube.com/channel/UCaLQH3PBcsHp5srS6l8e2pA
www.facebook.com/lakeco untrymuseum
Year Founded: 1985 Open year round
Dr. Duane Thomson, President, duane.thomson@shaw.ca
Shannon Jorgenson, Manager, slgca@shaw.ca
Dan Bruce, Curator, caballero@shaw.ca
Laura Neame, Archivist, lauraneame@gmail.com

***Okanagan Falls:* Okanagan Falls Heritage House & Museum**
Okanagan Falls Heritage & Museum Society, PO Box 323
Located at 1145 Main St., Okanagan Falls, BC
Okanagan Falls, BC V0H 1R0
Tel: 250-497-7047
www3.telus.net/okmuseum
The Bassett House is a prefabricated house. Ordered from the T. Eaton & Company catalogue, the house was shipped by rail from the east, and then by sternwheeler, & horse-drawn wagon to Okanagan Falls. The pioneer Bassett family lived in the home from 1909.

***Oliver:* Oliver & District Heritage Society Museum & Archives**
PO Box 847
Museum: 474 School Ave., Oliver, BC; Archives: 430 Fairview Rd., Oliver, BC
Oliver, BC V0H 1T0
Tel: 250-498-4027; *Fax:* 250-498-4027
info@oliverheritage.ca
www.oliverheritage.ca
Year Founded: 1980 Local history; Museum open Th-Sa 10:00-4:00 from June-Aug. Archives open W-F 10:00-4:00 from June-Aug.
Pamela Woolner, Community Heritage Manager, pwoolner@oliverheritage.ca

***Osoyoos:* Nk'Mip Desert Cultural Centre**
1000 Rancher Creek Rd.
Osoyoos, BC V0H 1V6
Tel: 250-495-7901; *Fax:* 250-495-7912
Toll-Free: 888-495-8555
marketing@oib.ca
www.nkmipdesert.com
Social Media: www.flickr.com/photos/nkmipdesert
twitter.com/NkmipDesert
www.facebook.com/NkmipDCC
The centre houses indoor & outdoor cultural & nature exhibits, & provides guided desert trail walks by interpreters.
Charlotte Stringam, Manager, cstringam@oib.ca

***Osoyoos:* Osoyoos & District Museum & Archives**
***Parent:* Osoyoos Museum Society**
PO Box 791, 19 Park Pl.
Osoyoos, BC V0H 1V0
Tel: 250-495-2582
info@osoyoosmuseum.ca
osoyoosmuseum.ca
Year Founded: 1963 Local history; open Sept.-May, Tu-F 11:00-3:00; June, Tu-Sa 11:00-3:00; July & Aug., M-Sa 10:00-4:00.
Mat Hassen, President
Kara Burton, Manager, 250-689-2353

***Osoyoos:* Osoyoos Desert Society & Osoyoos Desert Centre**
PO Box 123
Osoyoos, BC V0H 1V0
Tel: 250-495-2470*Toll-Free:* 877-899-0897
mail@desert.org
www.desert.org
Year Founded: 1991 The Osoyoos Desert Society operates the Osoyoos Desert Centre, which is an interpetive centre with hands-on exhibits & a 1.5 km elevated wooden walkway that allows visitors to explore the desert, either with a guided or self-guided tour. The Desert Centre is open annually from April through October.
Denise Eastlick, Executive Director

***Parksville:* Parksville Museum & Archives**
1245 East Island Hwy.
Parksville, BC V9P 2E5
Tel: 250-248-6966
www.parksvillemuseum.ca
Social Media: www.pinterest.com/parksvillepast
twitter.com/ParksvillePast
www.facebo ok.com/parksvillemuseum
Operated by the Parksville & District Historical Society. Open mid-May - Sept. 30.
Nikki Gervais, Curator

***Pemberton:* Pemberton & District Museum & Archives Society**
PO Box 267
Located at 7455 Prospect St., Pemberton, BC
Pemberton, BC V0N 2L0
Tel: 604-894-5504
www.pembertonmuseum.org
www.facebook.com/163218437085511
Year Founded: 1982 Three heritage buildings decorated with artifacts depicting local history dating back to 1850s
George Henry, President
Niki Madigan, Curator

***Penticton:* Penticton Museum**
785 Main St.
Penticton, BC V2A 5E3
Tel: 250-490-2451; *Fax:* 250-490-2442
www.pentictonmuseum.com
Social Media: www.youtube.com/user/OkanaganSteamfest
www.facebook.com/108559494129
Year Founded: 1954 The museum is open Tu-Sa 10:00-5:00; the archives are open Wed-F 1:00-4:00.
Peter Ord, Manager/Curator
Jeanne Boyle, Museum Assistant

***Penticton:* S.S. Sicamous Inland Marine Museum**
***Parent:* Historic Okanagan Lake Steamships**
1099 Lakeshore Dr. West
Penticton, BC V2A 7B3
Tel: 250-492-0403; *Fax:* 250-490-0492
Toll-Free: 866-492-0403
info@sssicamous.ca
sssicamous.ca
twitter.com/sssicam ous
www.facebook.com/sssicamous
Year Founded: 1998 The 1914 steamship that houses the museum is a Provincial Heritage site. The museum is in the process of restoring another steamship, the S.S. Naramata. Hours of Operation: June-Aug, daily 10:00-8:00.

***Pitt Meadows:* Pitt Meadows Museum & Archives**
12294 Harris Rd.
Pitt Meadows, BC V3Y 2E9
Tel: 604-465-4322
pittmeadowsmuseum@telus.net
www.pittmeadowsmuseum.com
Social Media: www.flickr.com/photos/pittmeadowsmuseum
twitter.com/PittMeadowsmuse
ww w.facebook.com/pittmeadowsmuseum
Year Founded: 1997 Located in an 1885 general store, which was later used as a post office & a residence, the Pitt Meadows Museum relates the pioneer & agricultural history of the Pitt Meadows community. An archives is also situated at the museum. The Hoffmann & Son machine shop & ditching business was donated to the Pitt Meadows Heritage & Museum Society. Hoffmann & Son Ltd. had been in business since the 1920s. The museum is open year-round.

***Port Alberni:* Alberni Valley Museum**
4255 Wallace St.
Port Alberni, BC V9Y 3Y6
Tel: 250-723-2181
info@alberniheritage.com
www.alberniheritage.com
www.facebook.com/143084405755239
Year Founded: 1971 History & culture of Alberni Valley & West Coast of Vancouver Island; exhibits include aboriginal artifacts, particularly the Nuu chah Nulth basketry; clothing and textiles; household implements and tools; agricultural equipment; local memorabilia; and 17,000 historic photographs available for research purposes or reproduction on request. Open year round

***Port Alberni:* McLean Mill National Historic Site**
***Parent:* Alberni District Museum & Historical Society**
5633 Smith Rd.
Port Alberni, BC V9Y 7L5
Tel: 250-723-1376*Toll-Free:* 855-866-1376
info@alberniheritage.com
www.alberniheritage.com/mclean-mill/welcome-mcl ean-steam-sawmill
www.facebook.com/106253281318
Year Founded: 1989 Operated by R.B. McLean & his three sons from 1926 to 1965, the site commemorates the history of logging & saw milling in British Columbia. As well as the steam sawmill, typical remote coastal lumber camp buildings are being restored. A resident troupe of interpretive actors called the Tin Pants Theatre Company perform original stage shows & offer guided tours. There is also a cafe & gift shop.

***Port Clements:* Port Clements Museum**
PO Box 417
Located at 45 Bayview Dr., Port Clements, BC
Port Clements, BC V0T 1R0
Tel: 250-557-4576
www.portclementsmuseum.org
www.facebook.com/175359227203
Year Founded: 1987 The Port Clements Museum contains artifacts of pioneer life on the Queen Charlotte Islands, including information & photographs about the logging, farming, fishing, & mining industries. The museum grounds display early machinery from the logging industry.

***Port Coquitlam:* Port Coquitlam Heritage & Cultural Society**
#2100, 2253 Leigh Square
Port Coquitlam, BC V3C 3B8
Tel: 604-927-8403
info@pocoheritage.org
www.pocoheritage.org
www.facebook.com/168106719902719
Year Founded: 1988 Members of the Society create exhibits & displays at the Display Centre, Port Coquitlam City Hal, & the Terry Fox Library, showcasing their collection of photographs, collectables, antiques, maps, & First Nations artifacts. The Society opened a Heritage Centre in 2013.
Brian Hubbard, President, president@pocoheritage.org

***Port Edward:* North Pacific Cannery Historic Site & Museum**
1889 Skeena Dr.
Port Edward, BC V0V 1G0
Tel: 250-628-3538; *Fax:* 250-628-3540
info@northpacificcannery.ca
www.northpacificcannery.ca
twitter.com/NPC _NHS
www.facebook.com/NorthPacificCannery
Year Founded: 1889 National historic site; oldest & most complete cannery village in BC; guided tours, gift shop, café; open May-Sept.
Stephanie Puleo, Operations Manager, manager@northpacificcannery.ca

***Port Hardy:* Port Hardy Museum & Archives**
***Parent:* Port Hardy Heritage Society**
c/o Port Hardy Heritage Society, PO Box 2126
Located at 7110 Market St., Port Hardy, BC
Port Hardy, BC V0N 2P0
Tel: 250-949-8143
info@porthardymuseum.com
porthardymuseum.com
The Port Hardy Museum & Archives houses geological & First Nations displays, as well as exhibits of settlers' history. The story of the fishing & logging industries in Port Hardy, Port Alice, Cape Scott, & Quatsino is also depicted at the museum. The museum is open year-round.

***Port McNeill:* Port McNeill Museum**
351 Shelley Cres.
Port McNeill, BC V0N 2R0
Tel: 250-956-9898
Hornsby steam tractor located at Seven Hills Golf Course

***Port Moody:* Port Moody Station Museum**
2734 Murray St.
Port Moody, BC V3H 1X2
Tel: 604-939-1648
info@portmoodymuseum.org
www.portmoodymuseum.org
Social Media: www.flickr.com/photos/55316408@N00
twitter.com/pmmuseum
www.facebook.c om/169200448399
Year Founded: 1983 Exhibits & programs about the heritage of Port Moody & the surrounding area are presented at the Port Moody Station Museum. The museum is located in the Port Moody Station, which was built by the Canadian Pacific Railway Company in 1905. The Port Moody Heritage Society is the owner & operator of the museum.
Jim Millar, Executive Director, jim@portmoodymuseum.org
Deb Naso, Bookkeeper

***Pouce Coupe:* Pouce Coupe Museum**
PO Box 293
Located at 5006 - 49 Ave., Pouce Coupe, BC
Pouce Coupe, BC V0C 2C0
Tel: 250-786-5555; *Fax:* 250-786-5555
admin@poucecoupe.ca
www.poucecoupe.ca/content/museum
www.facebook.com/pages/Village-of-Pouce-Coupe/298206710267806
Other contact information: Winter Phone: 250-786-5794
Year Founded: 1932 Pioneer artifacts & archives
Joe Tremblay, President

***Powell River:* Powell River Historical Museum & Archives**
PO Box 42
Located at 4798 Marine Ave., Powell River, BC
Powell River, BC V8A 4Z5
Tel: 604-485-2222; *Fax:* 604-485-2327
museum@powellrivermuseum.ca
www.powellrivermuseum.ca
www.facebook.com/ PRHMuseum
Open year-round, exhibits at the Powell River Historical Museum & Archives include the local First Nation culture, logging at the Powell River Mill, & the war years.
Lee Coulter, President
Teedie Kagume, Collections Manager
Frances Cudworth, Bookkeeper

***Powell River:* Townsite Heritage Society of Powell River**
6211 Walnut St.
Powell River, BC V8A 4K2
Tel: 604-483-3901; *Fax:* 604-483-3991
thetownsite@shaw.ca
www.powellrivertownsite.com
Year Founded: 1992 The Society seeks to preserve local history through education, by providing workshops, restoration projects, guided tours, as well as hosting a research centre.
Linda Nailer, Coordinator

***Prince George:* The Exploration Place at the Fraser-Fort George Regional Museum (FFGRM)**
PO Box 1779
Located at 333 Becott Pl., Prince George, BC, V2N 4V7
Prince George, BC V2L 4V7
Tel: 250-562-1612; *Fax:* 250-562-6395
Toll-Free: 866-562-1612
info@theexplorationplace.com
www.theexplorationplace.c om
Social Media: instagram.com/theexplorationplace
twitter.com/ExplorationPG
www.facebook.com/TheExplorationPlace
Children's gallery; hands-on Explorations Gallery of Science & Natural History; History Hall of regional development; photo archives; motion simulator ride; Nature Exchange; Sports Hall of Fame Gallery with interactive sports machine
Tracy Calogheros, CEO, tracy.calogheros@theexplorationplace.com

***Prince George:* Huble Homestead/Giscome Portage Heritage Society**
#202, 1685 - 3rd Ave.
Prince George, BC V2L 3G5
Tel: 250-564-7033; *Fax:* 250-564-7040
admin@hublehomestead.ca
www.hublehomestead.ca
www.facebook.com/hubleho mestead
Year Founded: 1984 A living heritage site with over one dozen historic buildings

***Prince George:* The Railway & Forestry Museum, Prince George & Region**
850 River Rd.
Prince George, BC V2L 5S8
Tel: 250-563-7351
trains@pgrfm.bc.ca
www.pgrfm.bc.ca
twitter.com/pgrai lmuseum
www.facebook.com/railwayandforestrymuseum
1913 100-tonne steam wrecking crane; wooden 1903 Ruissell snowplow; open daily during the summer, Tu - Sa from Sept. to mid-May.

***Prince Rupert:* Kwinitsa Station Railway Museum**
PO Box 669
Prince Rupert, BC V8J 3S1
Tel: 250-624-3207; *Fax:* 250-627-8009
www.museumofnorthernbc.com
Depicts the life of early station agents & linemen who worked the Grand Trunk Railway at the turn of the 20th century; located at the Prince Rupert waterfront next to Rotary Waterfront Park; June - Aug.

***Prince Rupert:* Museum of Northern British Columbia**
PO Box 669
Located at 100 - 1st Ave. West, Prince Rupert, BC
Prince Rupert, BC V8J 3S1
Tel: 250-624-3207; *Fax:* 250-627-8009
www.museumofnorthernbc.com
Exhibits artifacts depicting 12,000 years of human & natural history of the Northwest Coast of BC

***Prince Rupert:* Prince Rupert Fire Museum Society**
200 - 1st Ave. West
Prince Rupert, BC V8J 1A8
Tel: 250-624-2211; *Fax:* 250-624-3407
shirts@citytel.net
www.princerupertlibrary.ca/fire
Firefighting in Prince Rupert since 1908; restored 1925 fire engine; old fire alarm system

***Princeton:* Princeton & District Museum & Archives Society**
PO Box 281
Located at 167 Vermilion Ave., Princeton, BC
Princeton, BC V0X 1W0
Tel: 250-295-7588
princetonmuseum@gmail.com
www.princetonmuseum.org
twitter.com/PrincetonMuseum
www.facebook.com/p rincetonmuseum
Year Founded: 1958 The museum's collection features fossils & mining artifacts, as well as Aboriginal, Chinese, & pioneer items. Archives collected include records of Princeton & surrounding area organizations, land assessment rolls, court information, photographs, historical newspapers, postcards, posters, & personal papers.
Robin Lowe-Irwin, Operations Manager, 250-295-7588

***Qualicum Beach:* Qualicum Beach Museumum**
***Parent:* Qualicum Beach Historical & Museum Society**
587 Beach Rd.
Qualicum Beach, BC V9K 1K7
Tel: 250-752-5533; *Fax:* 250-752-0111
qbmuseum@shaw.ca
www.qbmuseum.ca
www.facebook.com/pages/Qualicum-Beach -Museum/411367768880517
Year Founded: 1984 Local history
Wendy Maurer, President

***Quathiaski Cove:* Nuyumbalees Cultural Centre**
***Parent:* Nuyumbalees Society**
PO Box 8
Located at 34 Weway Rd. Quathiaski Cove, BC, V0P 1N0
Quathiaski Cove, BC V0P 1N0
Tel: 250-285-3733; *Fax:* 250-285-3753
info@nuyumbalees.com
www.museumatcapemudge.com
twitter.com/Nuyumbalees
www.facebook.com/132765133452990
Year Founded: 1979 Potlatch collection of Kwakwaka'wakw (Kwagiulth) ceremonial artifacts
Jodi Simkin, Executive Director, executivedirector@nuyumbalees.com

***Queen Charlotte:* Gitwangak Battle Hill National Historic Site**
c/o Gwaii Haanas Field Unit, Parks Canada, PO Box 37
Queen Charlotte, BC V0T 1S0
Tel: 250-559-8818; *Fax:* 250-559-8366
gwaii.haanas@pc.gc.ca
www.pc.gc.ca/eng/lhn-nhs/bc/gitwangak/index.aspx
Other contact information: TTY: 250-559-8139
Commemorates the culture of the Tsimshian people & their history; located near an important native trade route between the Skeena & Nass Rivers; Battle Hill features archaeological evidence from the 1750-1835 period

***Quesnel:* Cottonwood House Historic Site**
241 Kinchant St.
Location: 4460 Barkerville Hwy., Quesnel, BC V2J 6T8
Quesnel, BC V2J 2R3
Tel: 250-992-2071; *Fax:* 250-992-6830
cottonwoodhouse@sd28.bc.ca
cottonwoodhouse.ca
twitter.com/cottonwoodh
www.facebook.com/cottonwood.house
Year Founded: 1963 A Provincial Historic Site that trains secondary & post-secondary students in the areas of tourism & agriculture. The house is open to the public, & visitors can explore the site, farm, & nearby trail system, as well as stay overnight in one of the site's cabin accommodations. Open May-Sept., daily 7:00-4:00.
Bill Edwards, Manager, Operations, edwardsb404@hotmail.com

***Quesnel:* Quesnel & District Museum & Archives (QDMA)**
705 Carson Ave.
Quesnel, BC V2J 2B6
Tel: 250-992-9580
www.quesnelmuseum.ca
Year Founded: 1963 Artifacts & archival items include Chinese artifacts, pioneer items, medical instruments, World War II letters from service men & women, & photographs from Quesnel & the surrounding area. Quesnel & District Museum & Archives is open year-round.
Elizabeth Hunter, Manager, Museum & Heritage, ehunter@quesnel.ca

***Revelstoke:* Revelstoke Court House**
1123 - 2nd St. West
Revelstoke, BC V0E 2S0
Tel: 250-837-6981; *Fax:* 250-837-4669
Courthouse built in 1913; no tours & no collections

***Revelstoke:* Revelstoke Firefighters Museum**
227 West 4th St.
Revelstoke, BC V0E 2S0
Tel: 250-837-4892; *Fax:* 250-837-4171
The museum exhibits artifacts depicting the history of firefighting in Revelstoke.

***Revelstoke:* Revelstoke Museum & Archives**
PO Box 1908
Located at 315 - 1 St. West, Revelstoke, BC
Revelstoke, BC V0E 2S0
Tel: 250-837-3067; *Fax:* 250-837-3094
info@revelstokemuseum.ca
www.revelstokemuseum.ca
Social Media: revelstokemuseum.blogspot.ca
twitter.com/revmuseum
www.facebook.com/14 4528853796
Year Founded: 1962 The Revelstoke Museum & Archives is situated in Revelstoke's former post office & customs building, where the history of Revelstoke & the surrounding district is presented. The museum organizes exhibits, programs, heritage walks, & cemetery tours. The archives, consisting of photographs, newspapers, assessment rolls, & records of local businesses & organizations, are housed on the second floor of the building. There, visitors will find a microform reader/printer to facilitate their research. Hours: M-Sa 10:00-5:00

***Revelstoke:* Revelstoke Railway Museum (RRM)**
***Parent:* The Revelstoke Heritage Railway Society**
PO Box 3018
Located at 719 Track St. West, Revelstoke, BC
Revelstoke, BC V0E 2S0
Tel: 250-837-6060; *Fax:* 250-837-3732
Toll-Free: 877-837-6060
railway@telus.net
www.railwaymuseum.com
www.facebook .com/123173327744215
Other contact information: E-mail, Gift Shop: giftshop.railway@telus.net
Visitors to the Revelstoke Railway Museum will learn about the challenges of building the Canadian Pacific Railway through British Columbia. Displays include survey & railway tools, CPR china & silverware, a locomotive, a car, a CPR telegraph service office, & a CPR weight scale shack. The museum also collects & organizes photographic archives. The museum is open year-round.

***Revelstoke:* Rogers Pass National Historic Site**
Mount Revelstoke & Glacier National Parks, PO Box 350
Revelstoke, BC V0E 2S0
Tel: 250-837-7500; *Fax:* 250-837-7536
Toll-Free: 866-787-6221
revglacier.reception@pc.gc.ca
www.pc.gc.ca/eng/lhn-nhs /bc/rogers/index.aspx
Natural & human history of Mount Revelstoke & Glacier National Park

***Revelstoke:* Three Valley Gap Heritage Ghost Town & Railway Round House**
PO Box 860
Revelstoke, BC V0E 2S0
Tel: 250-837-2109; *Fax:* 250-837-5220
Toll-Free: 888-667-2109
hello@3valley.com
www.3valleyroundhouse.com
Guided tours of historic town of late 1800s; open mid April - mid Oct.

***Richmond:* 12 (Vancouver) Service Battalion Museum**
The Sherman Armoury, 5500 No. 4 Rd.
Richmond, BC V6X 3L5
Tel: 604-238-2320; *Fax:* 604-238-2302
12svcbnmuseum.org
Year Founded: 1990 An accredited Canadian Forces museum; military artifacts, with particular emphasis on the 12 Service Battalion & it's predecessor corps; small reference library of military-related materials; open Tue. - Fri. by appointment.

***Richmond:* Britannia Heritage Shipyard**
***Parent:* Britannia Heritage Shipyard Society**
Britannia Heritage Shipyard Site Office, 5180 Westwater Dr.
Richmond, BC V7E 6P3
Tel: 604-718-8050; *Fax:* 604-718-8040
britannia@richmond.ca
www.britannia-hss.ca
Britannia Heritage Shipyard is a National Historic Site, which depicts Canada's west coast marine history. It is an example of a village which served the fishing industry. Many buildings date back to 1885. The Britannia Heritage Shipyard Society works to preserve the history of commercial boat building in Steveston. The shipyard is open from the beginning of May to the end of September. From Oct. to Apr., the shipyard is open on weekends.

***Richmond:* Gulf of Georgia Cannery National Historic Site**
***Parent:* Gulf of Georgia Cannery Society**
12138 - 4th Ave.
Richmond, BC V7E 3J1
Tel: 604-664-9009
gog.info@pc.gc.ca
www.gulfofgeorgiacannery.com
Social Media: www.flickr.com/groups/gulfofgeorgiacannery
twitter.com/gogcannery
www. facebook.com/GulfofGeorgiaCannery
Year Founded: 1986 History of the west coast fishing industry.
Rebecca Clarke, Executive Director, rebecca.clarke@pc.gc.ca

***Richmond:* Richmond Museum**
7700 Minoru Gate
Richmond, BC V6Y 1R9
Tel: 604-247-8300; *Fax:* 604-247-8341
museum@richmond.ca
www.richmond.ca
www.facebook.com/143214483190
The mission of the Richmond Musuem is to collect, research, document, preserve, exhibit, & interpret items of significance to the history of the community.
Connie Baxter, Supervisor, Museum & Heritage Services
Rebecca Forrest, Curator, Collections
Emily Ooi, Coordinator, Educational Programs

***Richmond:* Steveston Museum**
3811 Moncton St.
Richmond, BC V7C 3A0
Tel: 604-718-8439
www.steveston.bc.ca/online/museum.html
Year Founded: 1976 Housed in a 1905 bank building, currently a post office; summer music series on the museum grounds; music & craft programs; museum tours; walking tours of Steveston Village.

***Rose Prairie:* Doig River First Nation Cultural Centre**
c/o Band Office, Indian Reserve 206, PO Box 56
Rose Prairie, BC V0C 2H0
Tel: 250-827-3776; *Fax:* 250-827-3778
Year Founded: 2003 The centre houses a museum, administrative space, gathering space, health care offices, a gym, & rodeo grounds.

Rossland: Rossland Historical Museum
Parent: Rossland Museum & Archives Association
c/o Rossland Museum & Archives Association, PO Box 26, 11 Hwy. 3B
Rossland, BC V0G 1Y0
Tel: 250-362-7722 Toll-Free: 888-448-7444
rosslandmuseum@netidea.com
www.rosslandmuseum.ca
Local pioneer & mining history; Western Canada Ski Hall of Fame; underground mine tour; open daily mid-May - mid-Sept.; in winter by appt.
Joyce Austin, Manager

Saanichton: Log Cabin Museum & Archives
Parent: Saanich Pioneer Society
c/o Saanich Pioneer Society, 7910 Polo Park Cres.
Saanichton, BC V8M 2J4
Tel: 250-658-8347
info@saanichpioneersociety.org
www.saanichpioneersociety.org
Artifacts & archives from the early days of the Saanich Peninsula pioneer families; operates in the log cabin built for this purpose in 1933

Saanichton: Saanich Historical Artifacts Society (SHAS)
7321 Lochside Dr.
Saanichton, BC V8M 1W4
Tel: 250-652-5522
shas@shas.ca
shas.ca
Collects & preserves artifacts from Saanich's rural past, including household & industrial objects, working steam engines, tractors & other agricultural machinery; chapel, schoolhouse & other buildings on site; trails & picnic area; open year round

Salmo: Salmo Museum
100 - 4th St.
Salmo, BC V0G 1Z0
Tel: 250-357-2200; Fax: 250-357-2596
salmomus@telus.net
www.salmovillage.ca
Administered by the Salmo Arts & Museum Society; local histories, photographs, mining/logging/farming artifacts; household objects & clothing; tours; educational programming; annual Heritage Tea & annual Dinner Evening; admission by donation; open May-Sept.

Salmon Arm: R.J. Haney Heritage Village & Museum (SAM)
Parent: Salmon Arm Museum & Heritage Association
PO Box 1642, 751 Hwy. 97B NE
Salmon Arm, BC V1E 4P7
Tel: 250-832-5243; Fax: 250-832-5291
info@salmonarmmuseum.org
www.salmonarmmuseum.org
twitter.com/HaneyHeri tage
www.facebook.com/Haneyheritage
Other contact information: Archives phone: 250-832-5289; E-mail: archives@salmonarmmuseum.org
40-acre parcel of land with a municipally designated heritage home; 10 relocated, replicated & restored buildings from the village depict thematic displays on the history of Salmon Arm; 2-km nature trail; majority of collection housed in Salmon Arm Museum; Ernie Doe Archives Room also on site, with 111 linear feet of records dating from turn of 20th century; Museum open May-June & Sept.-Oct. W-Su, 10-5, July-Aug. M-Su 10-5. Archives open all year round, W & Th, 10-4.
Susan Mackie, General Manager
Deborah Chapman, Curator

Sechelt: Téms Swíya Museum
PO Box 740
Located at 5555 Hwy. 101, Sechelt, BC
Sechelt, BC V0N 3A0
Tel: 604-885-2273; Fax: 604-885-3490

Shawnigan Lake: Shawnigan Lake Museum
PO Box 331
Located at 1775 Shawnigan-Mill Bay Rd., Shawnigan Lake, BC
Shawnigan Lake, BC V0R 2W0
Tel: 250-743-8675
shawniganlakemuseum@shaw.ca
www.shawniganlakemuseum.com
twitter.com/shawniganmuseum
www.facebook.c om/145218715433
Year Founded: 1977 Local history, featuring information on the Kinsol Trestle, the Esquimalt-Nanaimo railway, & artist E.J. Hughes.

Lori Treloar, Curator

Sicamous: Sicamous & District Museum & Historical Society
PO Box 944
Sicamous, BC V0E 2V0
Tel: 250-836-4456
Museum & archives; collects, preserves, records, exhibits & promotes information, of artifacts & archival, historical & cultural value associated with the Columbia Shuswap Regional District Electoral Area E; open July & Aug.; located in Finlayson Park

Sidney: A.N.A.F. Vets Sidney No. 302 Museum Unit
9831 - 4th St.
Sidney, BC V8L 3S3
Tel: 250-656-3777; Fax: 250-656-6410
www.unit302.ca
Other contact information: Office Phone: 250-656-2051
Military artifacts

Sidney: British Columbia Aviation Museum
1910 Norseman Rd.
Sidney, BC V8L 5V5
Tel: 250-655-3300; Fax: 250-655-1611
inquiries@bcam.net
www.bcam.net
Located beside Victoria International Airport, the British Columbia Aviation Museum preserves & displays aircraft & aviation artifacts, with an emphasis on the history of aviation in British Columbia. Aircraft on display include the Avro Anson MK II, the Eastman E2 Sea Rover, & the Bristol Bolingbroke MK IV. The museum is open year-round.

Sidney: Sidney Museum & Archives
Parent: Society of Saanich Peninsula Museums
2423 Beacon Ave., L3
Archives located at 2440 Sidney Ave, Sidney, BC, V8L 1Y7
Sidney, BC V8L 1X5
Tel: 250-655-6355
info@sidneymuseum.ca
www.sidneymuseum.ca
twitter.com/sidneymuseum
www.facebook.com/SidneyMu seumArchives
Year Founded: 1971 The museum's collection features over 6,000 items related to the history of Sidney & North Saanich. Museum open daily 10:00-4:00; archives open M-Sa 10:00-3:00.
Peter Wainwright, President
Peter Graham, Executive Director

Silverton: Silverton Outdoor Mining Exhibit
PO Box 69
Silverton, BC V0G 1S0
Tel: 250-358-2485; Fax: 250-358-2485
Scott Marsden, Director, museum@haidagwaii.net
Nika Collison, Curator, nika@skidegate.ca

Skidegate: Haida Gwaii Museum at Kaay Llnagaay
Parent: Haida Heritage Centre at Kaay Llnagaay
PO Box 1373
Skidegate, BC V0T 1S1
Tel: 250-559-4643
haidagwaiimuseum@skidegate.ca
www.haidagwaiimuseum.ca
History collections of the Queen Charlotte Islands; open year round

Skidegate: Haida Heritage Centre at Kaay Llnagaay
Second Beach Rd.
Skidegate, BC V0T 1S1
Tel: 250-559-7885; Fax: 250-559-7886
info@haidaheritagecentre.com
www.haidaheritagecentre.com
Michaela McGuire, Contact

Smithers: Adams Igloo Wildlife Museum
Hwy. 16 West
Smithers, BC V0J 2N2
Tel: 250-847-3188
Display of area wildlife, including bear & cougar.

Smithers: Bulkley Valley Museum
PO Box 2615, 1425 Main St.
Smithers, BC V0J 2N0
Tel: 250-847-5322
www.bvmuseum.com
Year Founded: 1976 The Bulkley Valley Museum's collection showcases the social & technological development of the Bulkley Valley. Exhibits include the Bulkley Valley First Nations, the Grand Trunk Pacific Railway in Smithers, & the forestry & mining industries in the area. The museum, operated under the Bulkley Valley Historical & Museum Society, is open year-round.

Sooke: Sooke Region Museum, Gallery, Historic Cottage & Lighthouse
PO Box 774
Located at 2070 Phillips Rd., Sooke, BC
Sooke, BC V9Z 1H7
Tel: 250-642-6351; Fax: 250-642-7089
Toll-Free: 866-888-4748
info@sookeregionmuseum.com
www.sookeregionmuseum.com
twitter.com/SookeRegionMuse
www.facebook.com/118482471530145
Extensive archive and significant collection of photographs from Sooke's past. Artifacts include a restored steam engine yarder, blacksmith shop, and a rotating lighthouse light.
Lee Boyko, Executive Director

Squamish: West Coast Railway Heritage Park
Parent: West Coast Railway Association
39645 Government Rd.
Squamish, BC V8B 0B6
Tel: 604-898-9336 Toll-Free: 800-722-1233
info@wcra.org
www.wcra.org
Social Media: www.youtube.com/WCRailway
twitter.com/WCRailway
www.facebook.com/wcrhp
Other contact information: E-mail, Archives: archives@wcra.org
The mission of the West Coast Railway Association is the collection & preservation of British Columbia's railway heritage. Visitors to the West Coast Railway Heritage Park have the opportunity to view authentic railway equipment, including seventy locomotives & cars. The site also features the 1914 Pacific Great Eastern carshop & a railway station, built to 1915 Pacific Great Eastern plans. The heritage park is open year-round.

Stewart: Stewart Historical Museum
PO Box 402, 703 Brightwell St.
Stewart, BC V0T 1W0
Tel: 250-636-2229
stewartbcmuseum@gmail.com
www.stewartmuseum.ca

Summerland: Kettle Valley Steam Railway (KVSR)
Parent: Kettle Valley Railway Society
PO Box 1288
Located at 18404 Bathville Rd., Summerland, BC
Summerland, BC V0H 1Z0
Tel: 250-494-8422 Toll-Free: 877-494-8424
reservation@kettlevalleyrail.org
www.kettlevalleyrail.org
www.facebook .com/194424890596120
The Kettle Valley Steam Railway operates on ten miles preserved historic land, & visitors can ride in a passenger coach or open-air car. Please see the website for schedule details.
Doug Clayton, President

Summerland: Summerland Museum & Heritage Society
PO Box 1491
Located at 9521 Wharton St., Summerland, BC
Summerland, BC V0H 1Z0
Tel: 250-494-9395; Fax: 250-494-9326
info@summerlandmuseum.org
www.summerlandmuseum.org
www.facebook.com/su mmerlandmuseum
Collections & displays devoted to Summerland's history.
Ruth ten Veen, Registrar, ruth@summerlandmuseum.org

Surrey: Historic Stewart Farmhouse
13723 Crescent Rd.
Surrey, BC V4P 1J4
Tel: 604-592-6956; Fax: 604-591-4789
www.surrey.ca/culture-recreation/2875.aspx
twitter.com/StewartFarm1
This restored Victorian farmhouse was originally built in 1894 and features a parlor, dining room and kitchen with working wood-burning stove. Also on site are a circa-1900 pole barn which used to house 6 draft horses and other animals, as well as a fully loaded hay wagon. A team of staff and volunteers tend the heritage gardens of period flowers, vegetables and herbs, and to the orchards with trees of apple, pear and plum. Tours and school programs are also available.

Surrey: Surrey Museum
17710 - 56A Ave.
Surrey, BC V3S 5H8
Tel: 604-592-6956; Fax: 604-592-6957
www.surrey.ca
twitter.com/ASurreyMuseum
City Museum; Local history collections; Textile studio; open Tuesdays to Saturdays; admission free

Tahsis: **Tahsis Heritage Museum**
c/o Village of Tahsis Municipal Office, PO Box 219
Tahsis, BC V0P 1X0
Tel: 250-934-6344
reception@villageoftahsis.com
www.villageoftahsis.com/history-heritage.php
Year Founded: 2000 Local history; open seasonally, or by appointment in the off-season.

Telkwa: **Telkwa Museum**
PO Box 595
Telkwa, BC V0J 2X0
Tel: 250-846-9656
Open from June - Aug.
Doug Boersema, Contact, dboersema@bulkley.net

Terrace: **Heritage Park Museum**
PO Box 512
Located at 4702 Kerby Ave., Terrace, BC
Terrace, BC V8G 4B5
Tel: 250-635-4546; *Fax:* 250-635-4536
curator@heritageparkmuseum.com
heritageparkmuseum.com
Contains historic log buildings, depicting the history of the pioneers in the region; guided tours offered; open May - Aug.
Kelsey Wiebe, Curator

Trail: **Trail Museum**
Parent: **Trail Historical Society**
PO Box 405, 1051 Victoria St.
Trail, BC V1R 4L7
Tel: 250-364-0829; *Fax:* 250-364-0830
history@trail.ca
www.trailhistory.com
Open June - Aug., or by appointment.

Valemount: **Valemount Museum & Archives**
Parent: **Valemount Historic Society**
PO Box 850
Located at 1090 Main St., Valemount, BC
Valemount, BC V0E 2Z0
Tel: 250-566-4177; *Fax:* 250-566-4244
administrator@valemountmuseum.ca
www.valemountmuseum.ca
www.facebook.c om/ValemountMuseum
Year Founded: 1992 The Valemount Museum & Archives is housed in the original train station, where visitors learn about the history of the community. Exhibits include information about trapping, the railroad, early settlers, & the Japanese internment camps. The museum is open from May to September.

Van Anda: **Texada Island Historical Society, Museum & Archives**
PO Box 53
Van Anda, BC V0N 3K0
Tel: 604-486-7109
info@texadaheritagesociety.com
www.texadaheritagesociety.com
Local history; open July-Sept., Th-Su 11:00-3:00; open rest of the year W 10:00-12:00.
Ken Barton, President
Peter Stiles, Corresponding Secretary/Treasurer
Doug Paton, Curator, 604-486-7109

Vancouver: **15th Field Artillery Regiment Museum & Archives Society**
Bessborough Armoury, 2025 West 11th Ave.
Vancouver, BC V6J 2C7
Tel: 604-666-4370; *Fax:* 604-666-4083
Equipment of artillery units from Vancouver area; open year round

Vancouver: **Beaty Biodiversity Museum**
University of British Columbia, 2212 Main Mall
Vancouver, BC V6T 1Z4
Tel: 604-827-4955; *Fax:* 604-822-0686
info@beatymuseum.ubc.ca
www.beatymuseum.ubc.ca
Social Media: www.youtube.com/user/beatymuseum
twitter.com/beatymuseum
www.facebook. com/BeatyMuseum
Year Founded: 2010 The museum is divided into six different collections: Cowan Tetrapod Collection, The Herbarium, Spencer Entomological Collection, The Fish Museum, Marine Invertebrate Collection, & Fossil Collection.
Eric B. Taylor, Director, etaylor@zoology.ubc.ca
Mairin Kerr, Coordinator, Marketing, Communication & Events, mairin.kerr@ubc.ca
Evan Hilchey, Administrative Manager, evan.hilchey@ubc.ca

Vancouver: **British Columbia Golf Museum & Hall of Fame**
Parent: **BC Golf House Society**
University Golf Club, 2545 Blanca St.
Vancouver, BC V6R 4N1
Tel: 604-222-4653
office@bcgolfhouse.com
www.bcgolfhouse.com
twitter.com/BCGolfHouse
www.facebook.com/BCGolfHou se
Year Founded: 1986 The BC Golf Museum & Hall of Fame collects, preserves, & displays the history of golf & golfers in British Columbia. A collection of golf clubs dates back to 1790. The reference library houses a collection of over 5,000 books, plus player biographies & tournament records. The museum is open year round.

Vancouver: **British Columbia Medical Association Medical Museum**
c/o British Columbia Medical Association Archives Department, #115, 1665 West Broadway
Vancouver, BC V6J 5A4
museum@bcma.bc.ca
www.bcmamedicalmuseum.org
Year Founded: 1962 The BCMA Medical Museum holdings include instruments & other equipment used by physicians in British Columbia throughout the past 150 years.

Vancouver: **British Columbia Sports Hall of Fame & Museum**
Gate A, BC Place Stadium, 777 Pacific Blvd. South
Vancouver, BC V6B 4Y8
Tel: 604-687-5520; *Fax:* 604-687-5510
sportsinfo@bcsportshalloffame.com
www.bcsportshalloffame.com
Social Media: www.youtube.com/user/BCSportsHallofFame
twitter.com/BCSportsHall
www.facebook.com/bcsportshall
Year Founded: 1966 The BC Sports Hall of Fame & Museum contains interactive displays about British Columbia's world-class athletes. In addition to its history galleries, the Hall of Fame & Museum features galleries devoted to Terry Fox & Rick Hansen, a Greg Moore gallery, & a participation gallery.
Allison Mailer, Executive Director, allison.mailer@bcsportshalloffame.com
Jason Beck, Curator, jason.beck@bcsportshalloffame.com

Vancouver: **Cowan Vertebrate Museum**
Parent: **Beaty Biodiversity Museum**
Beaty Biodiversity Museum, Univ. of British Columbia, 2212 Main Mall
Vancouver, BC V6T 1Z4
Tel: 604-822-4665
vertmus@zoology.ubc.ca
www.zoology.ubc.ca/~vertmus
Natural history collection with bird, mammal & herpetological specimens; part of the Beaty Biodiversity Museum; open year round, by appt.
Dr. Darren Irwin, Director

Vancouver: **Deeley Motorcycle Exhibition**
1875 Boundary Rd.
Vancouver, BC V5M 3Y7
Tel: 604-293-2221
info@deeleymotorcycleexhibition.ca
www.deeleymotorcycleexhibition.ca
twitter.com/DeeleyMuseum
www.faceboo k.com/deeleymotorcycleexhibition
Display of over 250 classic & antique motorcycles; open year round M-F, 10:00-4:00.
Naomi Deildal, Manager

Vancouver: **Jewish Museum & Archives of British Columbia**
Peretz Centre for Secular Jewish Culture, 6184 Ash St.
Vancouver, BC V5Z 3G9
Tel: 604-257-5199
info@jewishmuseum.ca
www.jewishmuseum.ca
Social Media: www.flickr.com/photos/jewishmuseum
twitter.com/JMA_BC
www.facebook.com /JewishBC
Other contact information: Alt. URL: www.peretz-centre.org
Year Founded: 1971 The museum's administrative offices are located at the Peretz Centre, & are open to researchers & volunteers by appointment only. Museum exhibits & displays are located in various venues throughout the year; please see the website for current listings. The museum also has a virtual component accessible through their website.
Perry Seidelman, President
Marcy Babins, Administrator
Jennifer Yuhasz, Archivist, archives@jewishmuseum.ca

Vancouver: **Old Hastings Mill Store Museum**
1575 Alma Rd.
Vancouver, BC V6R 3P3
Tel: 604-734-1212
www.hastings-mill-museum.ca
www.facebook.com/OldHastingsMillStoreMuseum
Year Founded: 1919 Considered the oldest building in Vancouver; owned by The Native Daughters of British Columbia Post No. 1; houses artifacts pertaining to the pioneers of the city & Native peoples; open June 15 - Sept. 15, Tu-Su 1-4; weekends in winter months, closed Dec. & Jan.

Vancouver: **The Pacific Museum of the Earth**
Earth, Ocean & Atmospheric Sciences, University of British Columbia, 6339 Stores Rd.
Vancouver, BC V6T 1Z4
pme@eos.ubc.ca
www.eos.ubc.ca/resources/museum
Social Media: plus.google.com/110390493423212082809
twitter.com/UBCPME
www.facebook.com/PacificMuseumoftheEarth
Year Founded: 1925 Includes mounted dinosaur, insects in amber, wide variety of fossils & minerals
Kirsten Hodge, Curator

Vancouver: **Roedde House Museum**
Parent: **Roedde House Preservation Society**
1415 Barclay St.
Vancouver, BC V6G 1J6
Tel: 604-684-7040
info@roeddehouse.org
www.roeddehouse.org
Social Media: www.youtube.com/user/roeddehouse
twitter.com/RoeddeHouse
www.facebook. com/RoeddeHouseMuseum
Year Founded: 1990 Roedde House is a late-Victorian home, built in 1893. Today, the house reflects the life of an immigrant, middle class family around 1900. The museum provides guided tours & educational & cultural programs. Hours: Seasonal hours may vary, contact for details. Open for Tea & Tour Su 1:00-4:00. Regular hours Tu - Sa 11:00 - 4:00
Anthony Norfolk, President, anorfolk@uniserve.com
Matthew Thiesen, Vice President
Susan Erb, Secretary, dserb@shaw.ca
Josh Philipchalk, Treasurer, nikhilaprakash@hotmail.com
Sheila Giffen, Museum Manager, 604-684-7040, info@roeddehouse.org

Vancouver: **St. Roch National Historic Site**
c/o Vancouver Maritime Museum, 1095 Ogden Ave.
Vancouver, BC V6J 1A3
Tel: 604-257-8300; *Fax:* 604-737-2621
info@vancouvermaritimemuseum.com
vancouvermaritimemuseum.com/permanent-e xhibit/st-roch
Social Media: www.flickr.com/photos/84985836@N03
twitter.com/vanmaritime
www.faceboo k.com/vanmaritime
Arctic patrol vessel & 1944 RCMP memorabilia; part of the Vancouver Maritime Museum
Simon Robinson, Executive Director, director@vancouvermaritimemuseum.com

Vancouver: **Seaforth Highlanders Regimental Museum**
Seaforth Armoury, 1650 Burrard St.
Vancouver, BC V6J 3G4
Tel: 604-225-2520
seaforthhighlanders.ca/organization/seaforth-museum
Social Media: www.youtube.com/SeaforthsofCanada
twitter.com/seaforth100
www.facebook .com/172606082834734
Year Founded: 1972 Artifacts pertaining to the Seaforth Highlanders of Canada & affiliated regiments
Jim Purdy, Curator, Seaforth.curator@gmail.com

Vancouver: **Ukrainian Museum of Canada (UMC) British Columbia Branch**
Parent: **Ukrainian Women's Association of Canada**
154 East 10th Ave.
Vancouver, BC V5T 1Z4
Tel: 604-876-4747

Vancouver: Vancouver Holocaust Education Centre (VHEC)
Parent: Vancouver Holocaust Centre Society
#50, 950 - 41st Ave. West
Vancouver, BC V5Z 2N7
Tel: 604-264-0499; Fax: 604-264-0497
info@vhec.org
www.vhec.org
twitter.com/VHolocaustCntr
www.facebook.c om/140874547755
Other contact information: Library: library@vhec.org
Year Founded: 1994 The Vancouver Holocaust Education Centre is a teaching museum which provides Holocaust based anti-racism education. It aims to promote human rights, genocide awareness, & social justice. The causes & consequences of discrimination, racism, & antisemitism are explored. The centre includes a museum collection, archives, a library, & a resource centre. The education centre is also engaged in a survivor testimony project. School programs & outreach speakers are available. Exhibits are not recommended for children under the age of ten. The education centre is open year-round.
Nina Krieger, Executive Director
Adara Goldberg, Education Director
Shannon LaBelle, Librarian
Elizabeth Shaffer, Archivist
Gisi Levitt, Coordinator, Suvivivor Services

Vancouver: Vancouver Maritime Museum (VMM)
1905 Ogden Ave.
Vancouver, BC V6J 1A3
Tel: 604-257-8300; Fax: 604-737-2621
info@vancouvermaritimemuseum.com
www.vancouvermaritimemuseum.com
Social Media: www.flickr.com/photos/84985836@N03
twitter.com/vanmaritime
www.facebook.com/vanmaritime
Year Founded: 1959 Includes National Historic Site St. Roch, RCMP Schooner. Closed Mondays.
Ken Burton, Executive Director, 604-257-8301, director@vancouvermaritimemuseum.com
Duncan MacLeod, Curator MA, 604-257-8307, collections@vancouvermaritimemuseum.com

Vancouver: Vancouver Naval Museum & Heritage Society
PO Box 91399 West
Located at 1200 Stanley Park Dr., Vancouver, BC
Vancouver, BC V7V 3P1
Tel: 604-913-3363
Depicts the history of the Royal Canadian Navy since its inception: uniforms, medals & decorations, 3D artifacts, pictorial displays, including naval library & archives

Vancouver: Vancouver Police Museum
Parent: Vancouver Police Historical Society
240 East Cordova St.
Vancouver, BC V6A 1L3
Tel: 604-665-3346
info@vancouverpolicemuseum.ca
www.vancouverpolicemuseum.ca
Social Media: instagram.com/policemuseum
twitter.com/policemuseum
www.facebook.com/P oliceMuseum
Year Founded: 1986 Located in the historic City Morgue & Coroner's Court in Vancouver, the Vancouver Police Museum presents a collection of artifacts, papers, photographs, & published materials related to the history of the Vancouver Police Department. The museum is open year-round.
Kristin Hardie, Curator

Vanderhoof: Vanderhoof Community Museum & O.K. Cafe
Parent: Nechako Valley Historical Society
PO Box 1515
Located at 478 - 1 St. West, Vanderhoof, BC
Vanderhoof, BC V0J 3A0
Tel: 250-567-2991; Fax: 250-567-2331
www.vanderhoofchamber.com
Other contact information: Cafe Phone: 250-567-5262
1920's heritage village & community museum with restaurant café serving old-fashioned food
Chelsea Thorne, Curator, curator@vanderhoofmuseum.ca

Vavenby: Michif Métis Museum
Parent: Michif Historical & Cultural Preservation Society
c/o Michif Historical & Cultural Preservation Society, PO Box 126
Vavenby, BC V0E 3A0
Tel: 250-676-0096; Fax: 250-676-0069
metismuseum@yahoo.ca
www.michifmetismuseum.org
The museum seeks to preserve Michif Métis culture; it is the only museum in British Columbia of its kind.
Dale R. Haggerty, President/Curator

Vernon: Greater Vernon Museum & Archives
3009 - 32 Ave.
Vernon, BC V1T 2L8
Tel: 250-542-3142; Fax: 250-542-5358
mail@vernonmuseum.ca
www.vernonmuseum.ca
www.facebook.com/vernonmuseum
Open year round
Ron Candy, Director & Curator, rcandy@vernonmuseum.ca
Barbara Bell, Archivist, archives@vernonmuseum.ca

Vernon: O'Keefe Ranch
PO Box 955, 9380 Hwy. 97
Vernon, BC V1T 6M8
Tel: 250-542-7868
info@okeeferanch.ca
www.okeeferanch.ca
twitter.com/okeeferanchca
www.facebook.com/Historic OkeefeRanch
Year Founded: 1867 Founded in 1867, the O'Keefe Ranch operated when thousands of cattle grazed in the Okanagan, Thompson, & Cariboo regions. Today, Historic O'Keefe Ranch depicts the story of early ranching in British Columbia. The ranch offers an informative & entertaining school program. Each summer the ranch hosts a Cowboy Festival.
Glen Taylor, Manager, manager@okeeferanch.ca

Victoria: Canadian Forces Base Esquimalt Naval & Military Museum
Canadian Forces Base Esquimalt, PO Box 17000 Forces
Victoria, BC V9A 7N2
Tel: 250-363-4312; Fax: 250-363-4252
info@navalandmilitarymuseum.org
www.navalandmilitarymuseum.org
Other contact information: Alternate Phone: 250-363-5655
The CFB Esquimalt Naval & Military Museum collects, preserves, & displays the history of naval presence on the Canadian west coast. In addition, the history of the military on southern Vancouver Island is also depicted. The musuem features an archive & research library. Reproductions of photographs in the archive are available.

Victoria: The Canadian Scottish Regiment (Princess Mary's) Regimental Museum
Bay Street Armoury, 715 Bay St.
Victoria, BC V8T 1R1
Tel: 250-363-8753; Fax: 250-363-3593
cscotrmuseum@shaw.ca
www.canadianscottishregiment.ca
Year Founded: 1980 Items of historical significance to the regiment; located in the Bay Street Armoury, a National Historic Site built in 1915

Victoria: Craigdarroch Castle
1050 Joan Cres.
Victoria, BC V8S 3L5
Tel: 250-592-5323; Fax: 250-592-1099
info@thecastle.ca
www.thecastle.ca
twitter.com/craigdarrochc
www.fac ebook.com/craigdarrochcastle
Historic house museum, built in 1890 by Robert Dunsmuir, a wealthy coal baron; 39 rooms, 87 stairs to tower, Victorian era furnishings, woodwork, stained glass
John Hughes, Executive Director
Bruce Davies, Curator

Victoria: Craigflower Manor & Schoolhouse National Historic Sites of Canada
Parent: The Land Conservancy
110 Island Hwy.
Victoria, BC V9B 1M5
Tel: 250-356-1432; Fax: 250-356-2842
The farm & schoolhouse are part of a Hudson's Bay Company complex built in 1853.

Victoria: Emily Carr House
207 Government St.
Victoria, BC V8V 2K8
Tel: 250-383-5843
info@emilycarr.com
www.emilycarr.com
twitter.com/Emi lyCarrHouse
www.facebook.com/164231946928850
Birthplace of Emily Carr; People's Gallery; open May-Oct. & Dec. or by appointment
Jan Ross, Curator

Victoria: Fort Rodd Hill & Fisgard Lighthouse National Historic Sites
603 Fort Rodd Hill Rd.
Victoria, BC V9C 2W8
Tel: 250-478-5849; Fax: 250-478-2816
fort.rodd@pc.gc.ca
www.fortroddhill.com
Turn of the century coastal defence gun batteries & first permanent lighthouse (1860) on Canada's west coast; open daily year-round, except Christmas

Victoria: Hatley Park National Historic Site Hatley Park Museum
2005 Sooke Rd.
Victoria, BC V9B 5Y2
Tel: 250-391-2666; Fax: 250-391-2620
Toll-Free: 866-241-0674
info@hatleypark.ca
www.hatleypark.ca
Year Founded: 1999 The museum is located in the basement of Hatley Castle & features two rooms of artifacts, photos, replicas & reconstructions, & local history.
Bonnie Nelson, Director, Campus Services

Victoria: Helmcken House
Parent: Royal BC Museum Corp.
Royal BC Museum, 675 Belleville St.
Victoria, BC V8W 9W2
Tel: 250-356-7226Toll-Free: 888-447-7977
reception@royalbcmuseum.bc.ca
www.royalbcmuseum.bc.ca
Social Media: www.flickr.com/photos/36463010@N05
twitter.com/RoyalBCMuseum
www.faceb ook.com/RoyalBCMuseum
Home of Dr. John Sebastian Helmcken built in 1852; medical & domestic collections; managed by the Royal BC Museum

Victoria: Lt. General Ashton Armoury Museum
724 Vanalman Ave.
Victoria, BC V8Z 3B5
Tel: 250-363-8346; Fax: 250-363-8326
Army service support

Victoria: Maritime Museum of British Columbia (MMBC)
28 Bastion Sq.
Victoria, BC V8W 1H9
Tel: 250-385-4222; Fax: 250-382-2869
info@mmbc.bc.ca
www.mmbc.bc.ca
Social Media: www.youtube.com/user/maritimemuseumvic
twitter.com/MaritimeMusBC
www.f acebook.com/maritimemuseumofbc
Year Founded: 1954 This extensive museum of 3 floors covers the history of marine navigation on the BC coast from First Nation cultures through to European explorers & territorial tussles. Interactive displays include a mock-up of a ship's deck complete with climbable crow's nest & ratlines. The 2nd floor offers model ships for viewing, while the 3rd floor houses a library. Open all year, with winter & summer hours.
Anissa Paulsen, Curator/Collections Manager, apaulsen@mmbc.bc.ca
Jillan Valpy, Volunteer Coordinator, jvalpy@mmbc.bc.ca

Victoria: Metchosin School Museum
Parent: Metchosin Museum Society
4475 Happy Valley Rd.
Victoria, BC V9C 3Z3
metchosinmuseum.ca
Year Founded: 1972 School, household & agricultural exhibits/archives pertaining to the School and the area; operated by a society of volunteers; open April-Oct.

Victoria: Museum & Archives of 5 (BC) Regiment, Royal Canadian Artillery
The Armoury, #305, 715 Bay St.
Victoria, BC V8T 1R1
Tel: 250-363-8270
www.5thartilleryregiment.ca

Year Founded: 1996 The Museum & Archives of 5 (BC) Regiment depicts the history of coast artillery & associated units. Displays date from 1861 to the present. Examples of artifacts include a rifled muzzle loading gun & a vintage cannon. An archives & reference library are also available for research. The museum is open year-round on Tuesday nights. For visits outside regular hours, please call 250-363-8270 or 250-363-3626.

***Victoria:* Point Ellice House & Gardens**
***Parent:* Point Ellice House Preservation Society**
2616 Pleasant St.
Victoria, BC V8T 4V3
Tel: 250-380-6506
ellicehouse@gmail.com
www.pointellicehouse.ca
twitter.com/ElliceHouse
www.facebook.com/Point ElliceHouse
Point Ellice House was owned by Magistrate & Gold Commissioner Peter O'Reilly, starting in 1867. The home & garden are open from May to September.

***Victoria:* St. Ann's Academy National Historic Site**
PO Box 9188, 835 Humboldt St.
Victoria, BC V8V 9V1
Tel: 250-953-8829
stanns.academy@gov.bc.ca
www.stannsacademy.com
The restored 1920s-era building services as office space for BC's Ministry of Advanced Education, as well as housing an Interpretive Centre for visitors. Winter hours: Sept.-May, Th-Su 1:00-4:00; Summer hours: May-Sept., daily 10:00-4:00.

***Victoria:* Victoria Police Historical Society**
850 Caledonia Ave.
Victoria, BC V8T 5J8
Tel: 250-995-7654
History of the Victoria police, est. 1858; exhibits include 1921 "Commerce" Patrol Wagon, 1938 UL Harley Davidson motorcycle & sidecar, 1940 Dodge police car

***Wells:* Wells Museum**
***Parent:* Wells Historical Society**
PO Box 244
Wells, BC V0K 2R0
Tel: 250-994-3422
museum@wellsbc.come
www.wellsmuseum.ca
Wells Museum is located within the Island Mountain Mine office, which was built during the 1930s when Wells was established as a company town for the Cariboo Gold-Quartz Mine. The museum features displays about the mining history in the area. It is open from May to September. The museum's website, Mining the Motherlode, features a digital collection of historical information & photographs.

***West Vancouver:* West Vancouver Museum**
680 - 17th St.
West Vancouver, BC V7V 3T2
Tel: 604-925-7295
www.westvancouvermuseum.ca
www.facebook.com/westvanmuseum
The West Vancouver Museum offers exhibitions & educational programs to increase awareness of the history, culture, & art of the West Vancouver region & the country. The museum is open year-round.
Darrin Morrison, Curator, 604-925-7296, dmorrison@westvancouver.ca
Carol Howie, Coordinator, Collections, 604-925-7294, chowie@westvancouver.ca
Isaac Vanderhorst, Coordinator, Education, 604-925-7297, ivanderhorst@westvancouver.ca

***Westbank:* Westbank Museum**
2376 Dobbin Rd.
Westbank, BC V4T 2H9
Tel: 250-768-0110
info@westbankmuseum.com
www.westbankmuseum.com
twitter.com/WestbankHistory
www.facebook.com/31 9972028046683
Year Founded: 1978 Local history; also houses the West Kelowna Visitor Centre; open M-Su 9:00-6:00.
Anastasia Fox, Coordinator
Carmen Clark, Executive Director

***Whistler:* Whistler Museum & Archives**
4333 Main St.
Whistler, BC V0N 1B4
Tel: 604-932-2019; *Fax:* 604-932-2077
info@whistlermuseum.org
www.whistlermuseum.org
Social Media: instagram.com/whistlermuseum
twitter.com/WhistlerMuseum
www.facebook.c om/WhistlerMuseum
Year Founded: 1987 The museum celebrates the history of the Whistler community. Open daily 11:00-5:00.
Sarah Drewery, Curator & Executive Director

***White Rock:* White Rock Museum & Archives**
14970 Marine Dr.
White Rock, BC V4B 1C4
Tel: 604-541-2221; *Fax:* 604-541-2223
whiterockmuseum@telus.net
www.whiterock.museum.bc.ca
www.facebook.com/ whiterockmuseumandarchives
Located in the White Rock Train Station; collections include artifacts relating to the history & families of White Rock, documentation relating to the civic, political & business life of the community, objects relating to the Great Northern Railway & rail history of the area, and natural history objects of the locality.
Marilena Fluckiger, President
Sharon Oldaker, Executive Director, whiterockoffice@telus.net
Hugh Ellenwood, Archives Manager, whiterockarchives@telus.net

***Williams Lake:* Museum of the Cariboo-Chilcotin**
113 North 4th Ave.
Williams Lake, BC V2G 2C8
Tel: 250-392-7404; *Fax:* 250-392-7404
mccwl@uniserve.com
cowboy-museum.com
Displays focusing on the ranching & rodeo history of the Cariboo Chilcotin area; home of the BC Cowboy Hall of Fame; Shuswap First Nation, Chinese & Chilcotin materials; open June-Aug., Mon.-Sat. 10-4; Sept.-May, Tues.-Sat. 11-4

***Yale:* Historic Yale Museum**
***Parent:* Yale & District Historical Society**
PO Box 74
Located at 31187 Douglas St., Yale, BC
Yale, BC V0K 2S0
Tel: 604-863-2324
info@historicyale.ca
historicyale.ca
www.facebook.co m/pages/Yale-Historic-Site/193966850649397
First Nations; Gold Rush; Railway Era

***Ymir:* Ymir Arts & Museum Society**
7306 - 3 Ave.
Ymir, BC V0G 2K0
Tel: 250-357-9262
ymirartsandmuseumsociety@hotmail.com
www.ymirbc.com/ya ms
The Ymir Arts & Museum Society preserves the Ymir Schoolhouse, where arts & culture in Ymir are promoted. Located in the West Kootenays of British Columbia, Ymir was an active mining town in the late 1800s.
Robyn Balaski, Contact, rainspirit13@hotmail.com

Manitoba

Provincial Museum

The Manitoba Museum / Le Musée du Manitoba
190 Rupert Ave.
Winnipeg, MB R3B 0N2
Tel: 204-956-2830; *Fax:* 204-942-3679
info@manitobamuseum.ca
www.manitobamuseum.ca
twitter.com/ManitobaMuseu m
www.facebook.com/ManitobaMuseum
Nine permanent galleries & Alloway Hall which houses temporary & travelling exhibitions. Permanent galleries are: Orientation, Earth History, Grasslands, Urban (a section of Winnipeg, reconstructed as it might have been in 1920), Nonsuch (a replica of the 17th-century Ketch), Arctic-Subarctic & Boreal Forest. The Hudson's Bay Company Gallery reflects the legacy of the Company & the drama & history of Canada's fur trade. The Parklands/mixed woods Gallery represents the most natural & culturally diverse region of the province. The Planetarium provides programs for the general public & school groups in the 287-seat Star Theatre, including feature presentations on astronomy, science facts/science fiction, as well as present day space programs & technology. The Science Gallery allows visitors to test various scientific principles through 100 hands-on exhibits.
Claudette Leclerc, Chief Executive Officer, leclerc@manitobamuseum.ca
Adèle Hempel, Director, Research, Collections & Exhibits, ahempel@manitobamuseum.ca
Debra Fehr, Director, Marketing, Sales & Programs, dfehr@manitobamuseum.ca
David Thompson, Director CA, CMC, CMA, Finance & Operations
Mike Jensen, Supervisor, Science Gallery & Planetarium Programs, mjensen@manitobamuseum.ca

Local Museums

***Alonsa:* Alex Robertson Museum**
PO Box 161
Located at 6 Church Ave., Alonsa, MB, R0H 0H0
Alonsa, MB R0H 0A0
Tel: 204-767-2101
Antique guns; pioneer tools & artifacts; 1939 fire engine; open year round

***Angusville:* Angusville & District Museum**
235 Main St.
Angusville, MB R0J 0A0
Local history. Located inside the former rural municipality building.

***Anola:* Anola & District Museum**
PO Box 153
Anola, MB R0E 0A0
Tel: 204-866-2922
Open May - Sept., Sun. or by appt.

***Arborg:* Arborg & District Multicultural Heritage Village**
PO Box 4007
Arborg, MB R0C 0A0
Tel: 204-376-5653
admhv4007@gmail.com
www.arborgheritagevillage.ca
www.facebook.com/228744913909942
Year Founded: 1999 A working museum & interpretive centre specializing in the multicultural history of rural life in the pre-1930s Interlake region. Structures from the former Winnipeg Beach Ukrainian Homestead are now housed here.
Barb Wachal, Association Contact

***Ashern:* Ashern Pioneer Museum**
PO Box 642
Located at 36 - 1st St. South, Ashern, MB
Ashern, MB R0C 0E0
Tel: 204-768-3051; *Fax:* 204-768-3051
Other contact information: Phone, appointments: 204-768-2394
The Ashern Museum features the following restored buildings: St Michael's Anglican Church, the CNR station, the Ashern Post Office, the Hoffman Log House, the Darwin School House, & Ashern's first Rural Municipality of Siglunes Office. Artifacts include a threshing machine, tractor, bailer, & plow. The museum is open from May to September. At other times, tours can be arranged.

***Austin:* Manitoba Agricultural Museum**
PO Box 10
Austin, MB R0H 0C0
Tel: 204-637-2354; *Fax:* 204-637-2395
www.ag-museum.mb.ca
twitter.com/manitobaag
www.facebook.com/mbagmuseum
Year Founded: 1953 Located 3 km south of Hwys. 1 & 34, the site boasts Canada's largest collection of vintage agricultural equipment from 1900 on. There is also a pioneer village with over 20 buildings from log cabins to mills & mansions. The Manitoba Amateur Radio Museum is also housed on site. Events include the annual Thresherman's Reunion & Stampede last week in July. Open daily 9:00-5:00, May 12 - Oct. 5.

***Austin:* Manitoba Amateur Radio Museum Inc. (MARM)**
PO Box 10
Austin, MB R0H 0C0
Tel: 204-637-2354
info@ag-museum.mb.ca
www.marminc.ca
Located on the grounds of the Manitoba Agricultural Museum, Hwy. #34 in Austin; Canada's only amateur radio museum; home of amateur radio station VE4ARM/VE4MTR.
Dave Snydal, Curator & Secretary-Treasurer, 204-728-2463, dsnydal@mts.net

***Beausejour:* Pioneer Village Museum**
***Parent:* Broken Beau Historical Society**
PO Box 310
Located at 7th St. & Park Ave., Beauséjour, MB
Beausejour, MB R0E 0C0

Tel: 204-265-3345
PioneerVillageMuseum@gmail.com
www.pioneervillagemuseum.com

Year Founded: 1967 Open July & Aug.

***Belmont:* Belmont & District Museum**
PO Box 69, 202 - 5th St.
Belmont, MB R0K 0C0

Tel: 204-528-3300
Other contact information: Phone, Off-season: 204-537-2405; 204-537-2474; 204-537-2604

The Belmont & District Museum features a CNR caboose, plus displays of medical equipment, sports memorabilia, military uniforms, & printing equipment for the Belmont News. The museum is open during July & August, & by appointment at other times of the year.

***Belmont:* Evergreen Firearms Museum Inc.**
PO Box 57
Belmont, MB R0K 0C0

Tel: 204-537-2647

Military & non-military historical firearms; open year round

***Binscarth:* Binscarth & District Gordon Orr Memorial Museum**
PO Box 239, 162 - 2nd Ave.
Binscarth, MB R0J 0G0

Tel: 204-532-2217; *Fax:* 204-532-2153
vilbins@mts.net
www.binscarthmb.com

The Binscarth & District Gordon Orr Memorial Museum contains displays such as Native artifacts, a chapel, a general store, a school room, & large agricultural machinery. The museum is open during July & Aug.

***Birtle:* Birdtail Country Museum**
PO Box 508
Located at 738 Main St., Birtle, MB
Birtle, MB R0M 0C0

Tel: 204-842-3363

The Birdtail Country Museum is housed in the former Union Bank Building in Birtle. It contains a variety of objects from pioneer days in the Birtle area. The museum also holds local newspapers on microfilm. Birdtail Country Museum is open from mid-May to the end of August.

***Boissevain:* Beckoning Hills Museum**
PO Box 389, 425 Mill Rd. South
Boissevain, MB R0K 0E0

Tel: 204-534-6544
bhmuseum@mts.net
www.boissevain.ca/visitors/beckoninghills.htm
Other contact information: Alt. Phones: 204-534-6813; 204-534-8506

The Beckoning Hills Museum presents historical displays from Boissevain & the surrounding area. Exhibits include pioneer household items, agricultural tools & implements, native artifacts, & military items. The museum is open from June until September. Appointments can be arranged at other times of the year.

***Boissevain:* Irvin Goodon International Wildlife Museum**
PO Box 368
Located at 298 Mountain St., Boissevain, MB
Boissevain, MB R0K 0E0

Tel: 204-534-6662
turtlemountain@mymts.net
www.boissevain.ca/goodonmuseum

The museum features over 300 mounted animals in natural scenes, with full descriptions of each creature. Open in the summer, Su-Sa 11:00-7:00.

***Boissevain:* Moncur Gallery**
PO Box 1241, Civic Centre
Boissevain, MB R0K 0E0

Tel: 204-534-6478; *Fax:* 204-534-3710
info@moncurgallery.org
www.moncurgallery.org

Year Founded: 1984 Gallery showcases an extensive collection of ancient artifacts portraying the earliest history of the Turtle Mountain and surrounding prairie area in southwestern Manitoba. Exhibits include lifestyle artifacts of nomadic peoples which predate the written record, such as ceremonial items, food preparation utensils & tools. Open Tue.-Sat., 10:00-5:00.
Shannon Moncur, Chair
Phyllis Hallett, Secretary

***Brandon:* Chapman Museum**
PO Box 43, RR#2
Brandon, MB R7A 5Y2

Year Founded: 1967 Village-type museum setting with 16 historic buildings, among them the Roseville Church, Harrow School, Pendennis Rail Station, Robinville School, & various shops; guided tours; special needs facilities & wheelchair access; picnic area; open during the summer, free admission or donations appreciated.

***Brandon:* Commonwealth Air Training Plan Museum**
PO Box 3, Group 520, RR#5
Brandon, MB R7A 5Y5

Tel: 204-727-2444; *Fax:* 204-725-2334
airmuseum@inetlink.ca
www.airmuseum.ca

Canada's only air museum dedicated to those who trained & fought for the British Commmonwealth during WWII; artifacts include photographs, uniforms & clothing, personal papers, logbooks, station magazines, tools, equipment, trade badges, & medals; display of training aircraft
Stephen Hayter, Executive Director

***Brandon:* Daly House Museum & Steve Magnacca Research Centre**
122 - 18 St.
Brandon, MB R7A 5A4

Tel: 204-727-1722; *Fax:* 204-727-1722
dalymuseum@wcgwave.ca
www.dalyhousemuseum.ca
twitter.com/DalyHouseMuse um

Period home of the 1880s; 1903 grocery store; 1892 council chambers; open daily in the summer; Tue.-Sun. winter
Eileen Trott, Curator

***Brandon:* Manitoba Agricultural Hall of Fame**
1129 Queens Ave.
Brandon, MB R7A 1L9

Tel: 204-728-3736; *Fax:* 204-726-6260
info@manitobaaghalloffame.com
www.manitobaaghalloffame.com

Recognizing those who improved agricultural & rural living; plaques are at the Keystone Centre in Brandon (1175 - 18th St.); open daily
Bill Anderson, President
Patricia Bailey, Executive Director

***Brandon:* XII Manitoba Dragoons/26 Field Regiment Museum**
Brandon Armoury, 1116 Victoria Ave.
Brandon, MB R7A 1B2

Tel: 204-725-4579; *Fax:* 204-725-1766
26fdregCurator@wcgwave.ca
www.12mbdragoons.com
www.facebook.com/369782 049790739

Year Founded: 1979 The museum has a wide range of military memorabilia and artifacts on display, including photos, uniforms and equipment; small research library; archival materials; regimental button collection; open Tuesdays throughout the year
Mr. Ed McArthur, Curator, 204-726-3498, 26fdregCurator@wcgwave.ca
Gord Sim, Researcher, 204-727-7691

***Carberry:* Carberry Plains Museum**
PO Box 1072
Located at 520 - 4 Ave., Carberry Plains, MB
Carberry, MB R0K 0H0

Tel: 204-834-6609
www.townofcarberry.ca

The Carberry Plains Museum reflects early prairie life, through its collections from former residents, including a First World War pilot & Ernest Thompson Seton, a well-known naturalist. The museum is open during July & August. Appointments may be made during June & September.

***Carberry:* The Seton Centre**
PO Box 508
Located at 116 Main St., Carberry, MB
Carberry, MB R0K 0H0

Tel: 204-834-2509
etseton@mts.net
www.thesetoncentre.ca
www.facebook.com/TheSetonCentre

Materials by & about Ernest Thompson Seton, 1860-1946; open June - Sept. long weekend
Cheryl Orr-Hood, Chair, 204-834-2056

***Carberry:* Spruce Woods Provincial Heritage Park**
c/o Manitoba Conservation, PO Box 900
Carberry, MB R0K 0H0

Tel: 204-834-8800
www.manitobaparks.com

Northwest Co. fur-trading artifacts

***Carman:* Dufferin Historical Museum**
PO Box 1646
Carman, MB R0G 0J0

Tel: 204-745-3597
info@dufferinhistoricalmuseum.ca
www.dufferinhistoricalmuseum.ca

An early 20th century home. Open Mid-June - Sept.
Trish Aubin, President, 204-745-6790

***Carman:* Heaman's Antique Autorama**
PO Box 105
Carman, MB R0G 0J0

Tel: 204-745-2981

Canadian & American automobiles dating back to 1902

***Cartwright:* Heritage Village Museums**
***Parent:* Cartwright/Roblin Historical Society**
PO Box 9
Cartwright, MB R0K 0L0

Tel: 204-529-2363
www.cartwrightroblin.ca/node/97

This is a collection of historic buildings representing village life in pioneer days. The Blacksmith Museum is a fully restored, functional smithy. Todds Shoe Repairs has authentic cobbling equipment. Badger Creek Museum conserves artifacts of rural family life. There are also a schoolhouse, post office and telephone office.

***CFB Shilo:* The RCA Museum; Canada's National Artillery Museum / Le Musée national de l'Artillerie du Canada; Le Musée de l'ARC**
N-118, Patricia Road
Box 5000, Station Main, CFB Shilo, MB, R0K 2A0
CFB Shilo, MB R0K 2A0

Tel: 204-765-3000
RCAMuseum@intern.mil.ca
www.rcamuseum.com
twitter.com/TheRCAMuseum
www.facebook.com/1460996254 88939

Three permanent galleries, one temporary exhibits gallery; archives; library; kit shop; 109 major pieces of equipment; largest collection of Canadian military-pattern vehicles; open year round. Winter hours: M - F 10:00 - 5:00. Summer hours: M - Su 10:00 - 5:00.

***Churchill:* Eskimo Museum**
PO Box 10
Located at 242 Laverendrye Ave., Churchill, MB
Churchill, MB R0B 0E0

Tel: 204-675-2030; *Fax:* 204-675-2140

Open Mon.-Sat., year-round
Lorraine Brandson, Curator

***Churchill:* Manitoba North National Historic Sites**
PO Box 127
Churchill, MB R0B 0E0

Tel: 204-675-8863; *Fax:* 204-675-2026
mannorth.nhs@pc.gc.ca
www.pc.gc.ca/eng/lhn-nhs/mb/prince/index.aspx

Guided tours are offered to Prince of Wales Fort, Cape Merry Battery, Sloop Cove & York Factory by contacting the Parks Canada Visitor Centre in Churchill which houses exhibits introducing the history of the Hudson's Bay Company and the fur trade of the 1700s. Open year round.

***Cranberry Portage:* Cranberry Portage Heritage Museum Corp.**
PO Box 310
Cranberry Portage, MB R0B 0H0

cphmuseum@gmail.com
www.cpmuseum.ca

Year Founded: 2001 Local history.
Richard Gibbons, President, r.cgibbons@mymts.net
Mary-Ann Playford, Curator
Rene Grenier, Building Acquisition & Preservation Officer, louisegrenier1@gmail.com

***Crystal City:* Crystal City Community Printing Museum**
PO Box 302
Located at 218 Broadway St. South, Crystal City, MB
Crystal City, MB R0K 0N0

Tel: 204-873-2095

Newspaper print shop started by Thomas Greenway (7th premier of Manitoba) in 1881; tours on request
Jim Martin, Contact
Mike Webber, Contact, 204-873-2374
Bill Sandercock, Contact, 204-873-2659

Darlingford: **Darlingford School Heritage Museum**
c/o Darlingford School Heritage Fund, PO Box 67
Located at 197 Bradburn St., Darlingford, MB R0G 0L0
Darlingford, MB R0G 0L0
Tel: 204-822-6882
School built in 1910; open by appointment

Dauphin: **Cross of Freedom Inc.**
PO Box 183
Trembowla Rd, Valley River, MB R0L 2B0
Dauphin, MB R7N 2V1
Tel: 204-638-9641
The history & culture of Ukrainian pioneers; Cross of Freedom site of first Ukrainian Catholic Divine Liturgy & first Ukrainian Catholic Church St. Michael's, the oldest such church in Canada & dedicated as an Heritage site building in 2000; monuments include a large granite cross, bronze bust of Rev. Nestor Dmytriw, a grotto & monument of the first Ukrainian Catholic Bishop in Canada, Bishop Nyky
Kay Slobodzian, Contact

Dauphin: **Dauphin Rail Museum**
101 - 1st Ave. NW
Dauphin, MB R7N 1G8
Tel: 204-638-5495 *Toll-Free:* 877-566-5669
dauphinrailmuseum@dauphin.ca
tourismdauphin.ca/to-do/attractions-and-activities/dauphin-rail-museum
The museum is housed in a CNR railway station circa 1912, & features artifacts, pictures, & archival material about the history of rail travel in Dauphin.

Dauphin: **Fort Dauphin Museum**
PO Box 181
Located at 140 Jackson St., Dauphin, MB
Dauphin, MB R7N 2V1
Tel: 204-638-6630; *Fax:* 204-629-2327
fortdphn@mymts.net
fortdauphinmuseum.wordpress.com
twitter.com/FortDau phin
www.facebook.com/pages/Fort-Dauphin-Museum/225124957503412
Fur trade history, pioneer history, local history, the Parkland Archaeological Laboratory; open mid-May - early Sept & by appt. Oct - Apr.

Dauphin: **Trembowla Cross of Freedom Museum**
121 - 7th Ave. SE
Dauphin, MB R7N 2E3
Tel: 204-638-9641; *Fax:* 204-638-5746
Other contact information: Alternate Phone: 204-638-9047
History of early Ukrainian settlement in the Dauphin area. Open June-Aug., or by appointment.

Dufresne: **Aunt Margaret's Museum of Childhood Inc.**
Trans-Canada Hwy.
Dufresne, MB R0A 0J0
Tel: 204-422-8426
Aunt Margaret's Museum of Childhood includes a collection of antique furniture & artifacts.

Dugald: **Cook's Creek Heritage Museum**
Group 2, Box 10, RR#2
Dugald, MB R0E 0K0
Tel: 204-444-4448; *Fax:* 204-444-4224
info@cchm.ca
www.cchm.ca
www.facebook.com/pages/CCHM/124965140914084
Other contact information: Off-Season Contact Liz: 204-444-3247
Year Founded: 1968 Open daily, except Wed., May-Aug. 11-5

Elgin: **Elgin & District Historical Museum Inc.**
PO Box 102
Located at 131 Main St., Elgin, MB
Elgin, MB R0K 0T0
Tel: 204-769-2147; *Fax:* 204-769-2002
Year Founded: 1995 Local history; open by appointment only.

Elkhorn: **Manitoba Antique Automobile Museum**
PO Box 477
Elkhorn, MB R0M 0N0
Tel: 204-845-2161; *Fax:* 204-845-2312
www.mbautomuseum.com
www.facebook.com/ManitobaAntiqueAutomoblieMuseum
Year Founded: 1961 Donated to the community by local farmer, Isaac "Ike" Clarkson, the collection began with a hand-restored 1909 Hupmobile to a sizeable array of vintage automobiles. The site also includes exhibits of agricultural machinery and household articles. Open May - Sept., 9:00-6:00.

Eriksdale: **Eriksdale Museum**
PO Box 71
Eriksdale, MB R0C 0W0
Tel: 204-739-5322; *Fax:* 204-739-2140
www.eriksdale.com/profile
Other contact information: Alt. Phone: 204-739-2140
Open mid-May - Sept., excluding Thurs. & Sun.

Ethelbert: **Ethelbert & District Museum**
35 Railway Ave. North
Ethelbert, MB R0L 0T0
Tel: 204-742-8860
ethelbertmuseum@gmail.com
ethelbertmuseum.googlepages.com
Other contact information: Alternate Phones: 204-742-3761; 204-742-3376; 204-742-3672
The museum's collections pertain to the pioneer history of the area, featuring a kitchen, sewing room, nursery, bedroom, & school room. Open July & Aug., all other times by appointment only.

Flin Flon: **Flin Flon Station Museum**
CN Building, PO Box 160, Highway 10
Flin Flon, MB R8A 1M6
Tel: 204-687-2946
www.cityofflinflon.ca
Household artifacts from the late 1920s; mining; open Victoria Day - Labour Day

Foxwarren: **Foxwarren Historical Society Inc.**
PO Box 85
Foxwarren, MB R0J 0R0
Tel: 204-847-2185
foxmuseum@mts.net
Local history.

Gardenton: **Ukrainian Museum & Village Society**
PO Box 88
Gardenton, MB R0A 0M0
Tel: 204-425-3501
Clothing, icons & many articles from the early settlers; an exhibit of churches & photos of early pioneer life; clay thatched roof house & a one-room school; picnic facilities; tours & meals upon request

Gilbert Plains: **Gilbert Plains & District Historical Society Inc.**
PO Box 662
Gilbert Plains, MB R0L 0X0
Tel: 204-548-2326
rmofgilbertplains@mts.net
www.gilbertplains.com
10 log buildings; Negrych Pioneer Homestead; Ukrainian artifacts; open July & Aug.

Gimli: **New Iceland Heritage Museum**
The Waterfront Centre, #108, 94 - 1st Ave.
Gimli, MB R0C 1B1
Tel: 204-642-4001; *Fax:* 204-642-9382
nihm@mts.net
www.nihm.ca
www.facebook.com/263641135716
Year Founded: 1974 The New Iceland Heritage Museum preserves & interprets the history of New Iceland & Lake Winnipeg & its fishing industry.
Tammy Axelsson, Executive Director

Gladstone: **Gladstone District Museum Inc.**
PO Box 651, #49, 6th St.
Gladstone, MB R0J 0T0
Tel: 204-385-2551
www.gladstone.ca
www.facebook.com/gladstonemuseum
Other contact information: Alt. Phone: 204-385-2979
Local pioneer artifacts; open Tues.-Sun.

Glenboro: **Burrough of the Gleann Museum**
Parent: **Glenboro Community Development Corporation**
PO Box 385
Located at 235 Broadway St., Glenboro, MB
Glenboro, MB R0K 0X0
Tel: 204-827-2105; *Fax:* 204-827-2444
glenboro.com/visiting/museum
Other contact information: Alt Phone: 204-827-2444
Antiques & memorabilia related to the history of Glenboro.
Ernestine Sepke, Contact

Grandview: **The Watson Crossley Community Museum**
405 Railway Ave. North
Grandview, MB R0L 0Y0
Tel: 204-546-2748; *Fax:* 204-546-3368
Year Founded: 1973 Facility includes museum display of local area pioneer artifacts, shedded display of antique farm machinery, tractors & automobiles; also included is a pioneer homestead building (1896), pioneer house (1918), rural one-room schoolhouse & a pioneer Ukrainian Orthodox church; open June-Sept. & year round by appt.

Haines Junction: **Da Ku (Our House)**
PO Box 5310
Located at 280 Alaksa Hwy., Haines Junction, YT
Haines Junction, MB Y0B 1L0
Tel: 867-634-3300; *Fax:* 867-634-2162
daku@cafn.ca
www.cafn.ca/centre.html
The centre is owned & operated by the Champagne & Aishihik First Nations, & features cultural displays, heritage resource centre, classroom space, language lab, & more.
Diane Strand, Director, dstrand@cafn.ca

Hamiota: **Hamiota Pioneer Club Museum**
PO Box 279
Located at Hamiota Municipal Park, 7th St. South, east side, Hamiota, MB
Hamiota, MB R0M 0T0
Tel: 204-764-2552
www.hamiota.com/hc_museum.html
Open by appointment & for special events.
Ken Smith, Contact

Hartney: **Hart-Cam Museum**
PO Box 399
Located at 310 Poplar St., Harney, MB
Hartney, MB R0M 0X0
Tel: 204-858-2127
hartney@mts.net
www.hartney.ca
Year Founded: 1999 Artifacts from Aboriginal to post-settlement times
Pat Phillips, Contact
Eleanor Vandusen, Contact, 204-858-2064

Headingly: **Headingley Heritage Centre, Jim's Vintage Garages**
5353 Portage Ave.
Headingly, MB R4H 1J9
Tel: 204-889-3132; *Fax:* 204-831-0816
www.rmofheadingley.ca
Year Founded: 2005 The museum's collection features automotive & petroleum industry memorabilia collected & donated to the Rural Municipality of Headingley by a couple of long-time residents. Hours of Operation: May-Sept., M-Sa 10:00-5:00, Su 12:00-5:00; Sept.-Apr. by appointment.

Inglis: **Inglis Grain Elevators National Historic Site**
Parent: **Inglis Area Heritage Committee**
PO Box 81
Inglis, MB R0J 0X0
Tel: 204-564-2243; *Fax:* 204-564-2617
iahc@mts.net
www.inglisele vators.com
The site represents the development of Canada's grain industry from 1900-1930. Open summer, M-Sa 10:00-6:00, Su 12:00-6:00; off-season, F-Sa 10:00-6:00, Su 12:00-6:00.

Inglis: **St. Elijah Pioneer Museum**
Inglis, MB R0J 0X0
Tel: 204-564-2228
info@stelijahpioneermuseum.ca
www.stelijahpioneermuseum.ca
twitter.com/stelijahmuseum
www.facebook.c om/133664709977119
Year Founded: 1979 Designated provincial historic site

Killarney: **J.A.V. David Museum**
PO Box 584
Located at 414 William St., Killarney, MB
Killarney, MB R0K 1G0
Tel: 204-523-7325
Museum of artifacts, clothing & memorabilia associated with Killarney & area history

Lac du Bonnet: **Lac du Bonnet & District Historical Society**
PO Box 658
Lac du Bonnet, MB R0E 1A0
Tel: 204-345-2726
ldbhistorical.ca

Year Founded: 1988 Preserves the history of Lac du Bonnet.
Leon Clegg, President, leon.clegg@gmail.com

Ladywood: Atelier Ladywood Museum
PO Box 14, RR#3
Ladywood, MB R0E 0C0
Year Founded: 1991 Atelier Ladywood Museum features the former H. Gabel's General Store, with items from the 1930s to the 1950s.

Lundar: Lundar Museum Society
PO Box 265
Lundar, MB R0C 1Y0
Tel: 204-762-5689
Open mid-June - Sept.; located at Railway & Main St.

Lynn Lake: Lynn Lake Mining Town Museum
PO Box 100, 460 Cobalt Pl.
Lynn Lake, MB R0B 0W0
Tel: 204-356-8302
Open May 24 - Aug. 31
Neil Campbell, Contact

McCreary: Satterthwaite Log Cabin
PO Box 251
McCreary, MB R0J 1B0
Tel: 204-835-2341; *Fax:* 204-835-2658
A restored 1800s log cabin that shows pioneer building methods, & offers visitors a recreated pioneer garden, memorial plaques, & a rest area.

Melita: Antler River Historical Society Museum
71 Ash St.
Melita, MB R0M 1L0
Tel: 204-522-3103
Other contact information: Alternate Phones: 204-522-3438; 204-522-3825
Year Founded: 1972 Local history

Miami: Miami Museum
PO Box 153
Located at 3rd St. & Kerby Ave., Miami, MB
Miami, MB R0G 1H0
Tel: 204-435-2305; *Fax:* 204-435-2534
Fossils; souvenirs of WWI & WWII; wedding dresses from 1896-1900

Miniota: Miniota Municipal Museum Inc.
PO Box 189
Located at 110 Steuart Ave., Miniota, MB
Miniota, MB R0M 1M0
Tel: 204-567-3690; *Fax:* 204-567-3807
Open May - Oct.; pioneer & Aboriginal artifacts

Minnedosa: Minnedosa Heritage Museum
100 Heritage Park Cres.
Minnedosa, MB R0J 1E0
Tel: 204-867-3542
minnedosamuseum@gmail.com
www.minnedosa.com
Other contact information: Off-Season Phone: 204-867-2027
Local history includes Cadurcis House, Hunterville Church, Havelock School, McManus Trappers' Cabin, Munro Blacksmith Shop, Minnedosa Power House, Hopkins Log Barn & operating windmill & waterwheel; museum open July 1st - Sept. long weekend; group tours by appt.

Moosehorn: Moosehorn Heritage Museum Inc.
PO Box 28
Located in the Station Building, at Railway Ave. & 1st St. North, Moosehorn, MB
Moosehorn, MB R0C 2E0
Local pioneer history; radar equipment

Morden: Canadian Fossil Discovery Centre (CFDC)
111B Gilmour St.
Morden, MB R6M 1N9
Tel: 204-822-3406; *Fax:* 204-272-3303
info@discoverfossils.com
www.discoverfossils.com
Social Media: www.youtube.com/cdnfossildiscovery
twitter.com/discoverfossils
www.fac ebook.com/bruce.mosasaur
Housing an extensive collection of marine reptile fossils, the galleries of the Canadian Fossil Discovery Centre interpret life in the Western Interior Seaway during the cretaceous period. The museum is open year round.
Peter Cantelon, Executive Director, peter@discoverfossils.com

Morden: Manitoba Baseball Hall of Fame (MBHOF)
111C Gilmour St.
Morden, MB R6M 1M9
Tel: 204-822-4634; *Fax:* 204-822-1483
mbbbhof@mts.net
www.mbhof.ca
Year Founded: 1997 The Hall of Fame also includes a museum where visitors can explore the history of baseball in Manitoba. Open daily 8:00-9:00.
Morris Mott, Chair, 204-726-5167
Joe Wiwchar, Administrative Manager, Museum, 204-822-5682

Morris: Morris & District Centennial Museum Inc.
350 Main St. South
Morris, MB R0G 1K0
Tel: 204-746-2169
mormus@mts.net
Exhibits artifacts which depict pioneer life in the Red River Valley

Neepawa: Beautiful Plains Museum
91 Hamilton St. West
Neepawa, MB R0J 1H0
Tel: 204-476-3896
www.neepawa.ca
Other contact information: Virtual Museum:
www.neepawa.ca/museum/front.htm
Year Founded: 1976 The Beautiful Plains Museum features the following attractions: a military room; costume rooms; a medical hall; jewellery & general store displays; a post office exhibit; a local history room; office equipment; farm & home tools; information about local lodges; sports memorabilia; information about the local Ukranian Polish culture; & a chapel room, which depicts the history of religious settlement in the Neepawa area. The museum is house in the CNR station, which was built in 1902. Neepawa's Beautiful Plains Museum is open from Victoria Day to Labour Day.

Neepawa: The Margaret Laurence Home
312 First Ave.
Neepawa, MB R0J 1H0
Tel: 204-476-3612
Year Founded: 1987 Birthplace of Margaret Laurence; includes research area, meeting room & modern artwork; open daily in summer, other times by appt.

Notre Dame de Lourdes: Pioneers & Chanoinesses Museum / Musée des Pionniers et des Chanoinessess
PO Box 186
Located at 55 Rogers St., Notre-Dame-de-Lourdes, MB
Notre Dame de Lourdes, MB R0G 1M0
Tel: 204-248-2687
museend@mts.net
The first pioneers in Notre Dame de Lourdes arrived from Québec in 1880, & soon after pioneers came from France & Switzerland. The Chanoinesses Regulieres des Cinq-Plaies du Sauveur came to Notre Dame de Lourdes from Lyon, France in 1895. The Pioneers & Chanoinesses Museum houses artifacts of the pioneers & Chanoinesses in the community. The museum is open year round.

Nutimik Lake: Whiteshell Natural History Museum
Whiteshell Provincial Park, PR 307
P.O. Box 130, Rennie, MB, R0E 1R0
Nutimik Lake, MB R0E 1Y0
Tel: 204-369-3157
ParkInterpretation@gov.mb.ca
www.gov.mb.ca/conservation/parks/act_interp/centres/wnhm
Other contact information: Museum (summer only): 204-248-2846
Year Founded: 1960 Located in the Whiteshell Provincial Park, the natural history museum contains informative displays about the wildlife in the park, the boreal forest, sturgeon & the Winnipeg River, petroforms, & the Aborignal people. The Whiteshell Natural History Museum, located in a log building at Nutimik Lake, is open from the long weekend in May to the long weekend in September.

The Pas: Charlebois Heritage Museum
76 - 1st St. West
The Pas, MB R9A 1K4
Tel: 204-623-6152
archives@keepas.ca
www.facebook.com/869511819743970
History & information about Bishop Charlebois, housed in a chapel built in 1897.

The Pas: The Sam Waller Museum
PO Box 185, 306 Fischer Ave.
The Pas, MB R9A 1K4
Tel: 204-623-3802; *Fax:* 204-623-5506
samwallermuseum@mts.net
www.samwallermuseum.ca
Permanent collection comprises some 70,000 items of natural history specimens, historical artifacts, books & other library materials, photographs & negatives, fine art objects, & archival resources of the Town of The Pas; temporary exhibits; special events & programming. Open daily 1:00 - 5:00. Jul - Aug 10:00 - 5:00.
Sharain Jones, Director
Joanna Munholland, Curator and Archivist

Pilot Mound: Marringhurst Pioneer Park Museum
RR#2
Pilot Mound, MB R0G 1P0
Tel: 204-825-2334
Schoolhouse with original furnishings; open year round

Pilot Mound: Pilot Mound Museum
Pilot Mound Millennium Complex, 213 Lorne Ave.
Pilot Mound, MB R0G 1P0
Pioneer household & agricultural items; natural history artifacts; open year round

Plum Coulee: Plum Coulee & District Museum
277 Main Ave.
Plum Coulee, MB R0G 1R0
Tel: 204-829-3419; *Fax:* 204-829-3436
pcoulee@mts.net
www.townofplumcoulee.com/tourism
Artifacts & photographs portray the Ukrainian, Mennonite, Jewish, & Ukrainian pioneer history of Plum Coulee & the surrounding area. The Plum Coulee & District Museum is open during the summer, or by appointment.

Portage la Prairie: The Fort-La-Reine Museum & Pioneer Village
PO Box 744, 2652 Saskatchewan Ave. East
Portage la Prairie, MB R1N 3C2
Tel: 204-857-3259; *Fax:* 204-239-4917
www.fortlareinemuseum.ca
Social Media: fort-la-reine.tumblr.com
twitter.com/fortlareine
www.facebook.com/1295 53080390522
Year Founded: 1967 Depicts native & pioneer life in the 1800s & includes a fort, trading post, village store, country church, schoolhouse, print shop, fire hall, stable, trapper's cabin & several heritage homes; also includes a railway display of a caboose, 1882 official private railcar of Sir William Van Horne, several maintenance railroad vehicles & railway crossing; Muskateer Aircraft & Allis Chalmers Museum.
Tracey Turner, Executive Director/Curator, manager@fortlareinemuseum.ca

Rapid City: Rapid City Museum
PO Box 271
Located on 4th Ave., Rapid City, MB
Rapid City, MB R0K 1W0
Tel: 204-826-2732
racimus@live.ca
www.rapidcitymb.ca/museum
Cundy watch display; Frederick Philip Grove display; old school building; old Rapid City Reporter building with press & back copies; open July & Aug., other times by appt.

Reston: Reston & District Museum
PO Box 280
Located at 102 - 9 St., Reston, MB
Reston, MB R0M 1X0
Tel: 204-877-3641
Local artifacts & archival material

Riverton: Hecla Island Heritage Home Museum
c/o Manitoba Conservation
Riverton, MB R0C 2R0
Tel: 204-279-2056
gov.mb.ca/conservation/parks/act_interp/centres/hecla-heritage.html
Depiction of the life of an Icelandic family, 1920-1940s; located in Hecla Village, off PTH 8.

La Riviere: Archibald Historical Museum
PO Box 97
La Riviere, MB R0G 1A0
Tel: 204-242-2825
www.rmofpembina.com/museum.htm
Other contact information: Alternate Phones: 204-242-2554; 204-242-2235

1878 log house furnished as it was during Nellie McClung's residency plus large frame home (furnished) where she lived, had the first of her family & wrote her first books; also La Rivière C.P.R. Station & more; open mid-May - Labour Day, closed Wed. & Thu. unless by appt.

RM of Blanshard: The Clack Family Heritage Museum
RM of Blanshard, MB R0K 1X0
Tel: 204-328-5240
riversdaly.ca/attractions
Other contact information: Alt. Phone: 204-764-2726
Antique cars, tractors, trucks & farm implements; Victorian china & clothing; railway, RCMP military & native artifacts; open June-Sept.; guided tours available.
Vernon J. "Tim" Clack, Contact

Roblin: Keystone Pioneers Museum Inc.
PO Box 10
Roblin, MB R0L 1P0
Tel: 204-937-2979
keystonemuseum@gmail.com
kpmroblinmb.webs.com
www.facebook.com/189524247747064
Agricultural equipment & artifacts; Elaschuk House; Makaroff Church; Sawmill
Richard Wileman, President, 204-773-6634
Marilyn Simpson, Secretary, 204-937-4914
Donna Poyser, Treasurer, 204-937-8764

Roland: Roland 4-H Museum
72 - 3rd St.
Roland, MB R0G 1T0
Tel: 204-343-2061
info@roland4hmuseum.ca
www.roland4hmuseum.ca
History of the 4-H club in Roland, MB. Open July & Aug., M-F 1:00-4:00.

Rossburn: Rossburn Museum
c/o Town of Rossburn, PO Box 70, 43 Main St. North
Rossburn, MB R0J 1V0
Tel: 204-859-2762; *Fax:* 204-859-2022
town.rsb@mts.net
www.town.rossburn.mb.ca
The Rossburn Museum features rooms representing a pioneer kitchen, a classroom, a hospital room, a print shop, & a hairdressing salon. The museum also displays a miniature Ukrainian village, plus Ukrainian artifacts.

St Andrews: Lower Fort Garry National Historic Site of Canada
5925 Hwy. 9
St Andrews, MB R1A 4A8
Tel: 204-785-6050; *Fax:* 204-482-5887
Toll-Free: 888-773-8888
lfg.info@pc.gc.ca
pc.gc.ca/garry
twitter.com/lowerft garrynhs
www.facebook.com/lowerfortgarrynhs
Other contact information: TTY: 866-787-6221
1830s stone Hudson's Bay Co. fort; costumed interpreters, visitor centre, gift store, restaurant; open May 15 - Labour Day, daily from 9-5

St Andrews: Riel House National Historic Site of Canada / Parc historique national du Canada de la Maison-Riel
c/o Lower Fort Garry National Historic Site, 5925 Hwy 9
Located at 330 River Rd., Winnipeg, MB
St Andrews, MB R1A 4A8
Tel: 204-785-6050; *Fax:* 204-482-5887
riel.info@pc.gc.ca
www.pc.gc.ca/lhn-nhs/mb/riel/contact.aspx
Other contact information: TTY: 1-866-787-6221
Riel family home, depicts life of Métis family in St. Vital during the 1880s; open daily mid-May - Labour Day

Saint-Boniface: La Maison Gabrielle-Roy
CP 133, 375, rue Deschambault
Saint-Boniface, MB R2H 3B4
Tél: 204-231-3853; *Téléc:* 204-231-3910
info@maisongabrielleroy.mb.ca
www.maisongabrielleroy.mb.ca
www.faceboo k.com/LaMaisonGabrielleRoy
Fondée en: 2003 Honore le travail de Gabrielle Ray.
Laurent Gimenez, Président
Lucienne Châteauneuf, Directrice générale

Saint-Boniface: Le Musée de Saint-Boniface Museum
494, av Taché
Saint-Boniface, MB R2H 2B2
Tel: 204-237-4500; *Fax:* 204-986-7964
info@msbm.mb.ca
msbm.mb.ca
Social Media: www.youtube.com/user/StBonifaceMuseum
twitter.com/msbm_mb_ca
www.faceb ook.com/msbm.mb.ca
Year Founded: 1967 Logé dans l'ancien couvent des Soeurs Grises, le musée a pour mission d'effectuer des recherches sur des objets reliés au patrimoine canadien-français et métis de l'Ouest canadien; préservation et interprétation; expositions thématiques; plus de 30 000 objets historiques et ethnologiques dans la collection; programmation; boutique.
Dr. Philippe R. Mailhot, Directeur, pmailhot@msbm.mb.ca
Pierrette Boily, Conservatrice, pboily@msbm.mb.ca

St Claude: Manitoba Dairy Museum
***Parent:* St. Claude Historical Society**
164 Jobin Ave.
St Claude, MB R0G 1Z0
Tel: 204-379-2156
shstclaude@gmail.com
Artifacts from settlers, many of whom came from France; variety of dairy artifacts

Sainte-Anne-des-chênes: Musée Pointe des Chênes
208, av Centrale
Sainte-Anne-des-chênes, MB R5H 1C9
Tél: 204-422-5639; *Téléc:* 204-422-5514
Situé dans un parc à côté de la Villa Youville; vieux musée présente des objets de pionniers de la région

Sainte-Anne-des-Chênes: Site Historique Monseigneur Taché / Monseigneur Taché Historic Site
CP 97, Grp. 20, RR#2
Situé à 98, rue Saltel, Sainte-Geneviève, MB
Sainte-Anne-des-Chênes, MB R5H 1R2
Tél: 204-853-7509; *Téléc:* 204-422-8508
info@sitetache.ca
www.sitetache.ca
Fondée en: 1989
Diane Dornez-Laxdal, Présidente

St Joseph: Musée St-Joseph Museum Inc.
PO Box 34
St Joseph, MB R0G 2C0
Tel: 204-737-2244
museestjoseph@gmail.com
museestjoseph.ca
Social Media:
www.youtube.com/channel/UC_z6SB6v_1rAf_r6Djm60mA
www.facebook.com/MuseeS tJosephMuseum
Year Founded: 1977 Domestic & agricultural artifacts; the oldest timber house in southern Manitoba; antique tractors.

Saint-Pierre-Jolys: Musée de St-Pierre-Jolys / St-Pierre-Jolys Museum
CP 321, 432 rue Joubert
Saint-Pierre-Jolys, MB R0A 1V0
Tél: 204-433-7002
museestpierrejolys@live.ca
www.museestpierrejolys.ca
www.facebook.com/MuseeDeStPierreJolysMuseum
Autre numéros: **Alt. Phone: 204-792-6149**
Le musée est un ancien couvent et sert à se rappeler le patrimoine et les contributions des religieuses au développement du village de Saint-Pierre-Jolys; on retrouve aussi la Maison Goulet, et un cabane à sucre.

Sandy Lake: Ukrainian Cultural Heritage Museum
Railway Ave.
Sandy Lake, MB R0J 1X0
Tel: 204-585-2636
1899 Ukrainian settlement; traditional Ukrainian arts & crafts; open June - Sept. & by appt.

Selkirk: Marine Museum of Manitoba (Selkirk) Inc.
PO Box 7, 490 Eveline St.
Selkirk, MB R1A 2B1
Tel: 204-482-7761
marinemuseum@mymts.net
www.marinemuseum.ca
www.facebook.com/286895044784
Year Founded: 1973 The museum gathers and restores marine vessels related to Manitoba's Lake Winnipeg and the Red River from about 1850 to the present. Storehouses of artifacts and records are located aboard historic vessels, including the S.S. Keenora and the C.G.S. Bradbury. Open May - Sept.; school/group tours available.

Selkirk: St. Andrews' Rectory National Historic Site
374 River Rd.
Selkirk, MB R1A 2Y1
Tel: 204-785-6050; *Fax:* 204-482-5887
Toll-Free: 888-773-8888
lfg.info@pc.gc.ca
www.pc.gc.ca/lhn-nhs/mb/standrews/in dex.aspx
Other contact information: TTY: 1-866-787-6221
Collection of panels & antiques; open May - Sept.

Shoal Lake: Clegg Carriage Museum
c/o Prairie Mountain Regional Museums Collection Inc., PO Box 568
Shoal Lake, MB R0J 1Z0
Tel: 204-759-2245; *Fax:* 204-759-2245
Located 3 miles south of Hwy #24 in Arrow River; collection of 90 completely restored horse-drawn vehicles, including a WW1 ambulance, a covered wagon, peddlar's wagon & hearse

Shoal Lake: Prairie Mountain Regional Museums Collection Inc.
PO Box 568
Shoal Lake, MB R0J 1Z0
Tel: 204-759-2245; *Fax:* 204-759-2484
www.facebook.com/388979924562556
Local history.

Shoal Lake: Shoal Lake Police & Pioneer Museum
PO Box 233
Located at 201 - 1 Ave., Lakeview Park, Shoal Lake, MB
Shoal Lake, MB R0J 1Z0
Tel: 204-759-2429; *Fax:* 204-759-2704
Other contact information: Summer phone: 204-759-3326
A replica of an 1875 NWMP building; it houses a collection of North West Mounted Police & Royal Canadian Mounted Police displays; official Museum for the Mounted Police in Manitoba; open June-Sept. by summer staff, other times by appt.; school talks & presentations available

Snowflake: Star Mound School Museum
General Delivery
Snowflake, MB R0G 2K0
Tel: 204-876-4749
One-room country school c. 1886

Souris: Hillcrest Museum
26 Crescent Ave. East
Souris, MB R0K 2C0
Tel: 204-483-2008
www.sourismanitoba.com/hillcrest-museum.html
Year Founded: 1967 Includes agricultural museum & CPR caboose; open May - Sept.; collection of over 5000 butterflies on display

Souris: The Plum - 1883 Souris Heritage Church Museum & Tea Room
***Parent:* Souris & District Heritage Club Inc.**
PO Box 548
Located at 142 - 1st St. South, Souris, MB
Souris, MB R0K 2C0
Tel: 204-483-3643
sourisheritage@mymts.net
www.esouris.com/theplum
Other contact information: Off-Season Phone: 204-483-2643
Housed in St. Luke's Anglican Church, circa 1883, the museum's collection focuses on local art & history. Open July-Sept., 11:00-7:00.
Averill Whitfield, Contact

Sprague: Sprague & District Historical Museum
PO Box 60
Sprague, MB R0A 1Z0
Tel: 204-437-2342; *Fax:* 204-437-2032
Local & military history.

Steinbach: Mennonite Heritage Village (Canada) Inc.
231 Provincial Trunk Hwy. 12 North
Steinbach, MB R5G 1T8
Tel: 204-326-9661; *Fax:* 204-326-5046
Toll-Free: 866-280-8741
info@mhv.ca
www.mennoniteheritagevillage.com
twitter .com/MHVSteinbach
www.facebook.com/MHVSteinbach
Includes J.J. Reimer Historical Library & Archives; historical village with traditional housebarns, semlin, blacksmith shop, printery, general store, operating windmill, farm fields, exhibition gallery; livery barn restaurant serving ethnic Mennonite food; library; gift shop; special events throughout the summer;

educational programming; online bookstore on the website. Open May through September.
Barry Dyck, Executive Director, barryd@mhv.ca
Andrea Dyck, Curator, andread@mhv.ca
Anne Toews, Program Director, annet@mhv.ca

St-Malo: Le Musée Pionnier St Malo
CP 328
St-Malo, MB R0A 1T0
Tél: 204-347-5767
Représentation de la vie des premiers colons

Stonewall: Stonewall Quarry Park
PO Box 250
Located at 166 Main St., Stonewall, MB
Stonewall, MB R0C 2Z0
Tel: 204-467-7980; *Fax:* 204-467-7985
stoneqp@stonewall.ca
stonewallquarrypark.ca
www.facebook.com/269886949 741047
Exhibits pertain to the limestone quarries & their role in the development of the community of Stonewall

Strathclair: The Strathclair Museum Association
PO Box 383, 33 Main St.
Strathclair, MB R0J 2C0
Tel: 204-720-6041
info@strathclairmuseum.com
strathclairmuseum.com
Year Founded: 1972 In a restored CPR station and residence, the museum contains material relating to the district, which includes geneaology and information on Lord Elphinstone; replica blacksmith shop and machine shed; Open July & August or by appt.

Swan River: Swan Valley Historical Museum & Archives
PO Box 2078
Located at 10 Hwy. North, Swan River, MB
Swan River, MB R0L 1Z0
Tel: 204-734-3585
Year Founded: 1972 History of Swan River Valley, Ice Age to settlement; open mid-May - mid-Sept.; archives open by appt. Tues. 9-2, summer

Teulon: Teulon & District Museum
c/o Mary Revel, PO Box 197
Located at Green Acres Park, Hwy 7, Teulon, MB
Teulon, MB R0C 3B0
Tel: 204-886-2216
www.teulon.ca/TeulonandDistrictMuseum.htm
Site includes a log house, a caboose, two schoolhouses, a small church, a large machine shed, old shoe shop, outside bake oven & the Dr. Hunter Home, 1918 Ford car, doll house with over 300 dolls; open June - Sept., Tues. to Sun., or by appt.

Thompson: Heritage North Museum
162 Princeton Dr.
Thompson, MB R8N 2A4
Tel: 204-677-2216; *Fax:* 204-677-8953
hnmuseum@mts.net
www.heritagenorthmuseum.ca
Year Founded: 1990 The museum preserves the heritage & history of Thompson & area, where in 1956 nickel was discovered. One of the log buildings displays a taxidermy array of animals native to the region, hides, furs and fossils, while the other building focuses on the mining industry. There is a gift shop.
Tanna Teneycke, Executive Director
Charlene Teneycke, Assistant Manager
Sandy Thompson, Museum Assistant

Treherne: Treherne Museum
183 Vanzile St.
Treherne, MB R0G 2V0
Tel: 204-723-2621
trehernemuseum@gmail.com
www.treherne.ca
Year Founded: 1978 A period house museum, furnished by items from the early 20th century.

Virden: Currahee Military Museum
PO Box 729, River Valley Road North
Virden, MB R0M 2C0
Tel: 204-748-1461
Open by appt. only year round.
John Hipwell, President, john@wolverinesupplies.com

Virden: River Valley School Museum
PO Box 2048
Virden, MB R0M 2C0
Tel: 204-748-3920
Country school furnishings & library 1896-1955

Virden: Virden Pioneer Home Museum Inc.
PO Box 2001
Located at 390 King St., Virden, MB
Virden, MB R0M 2C0
Tel: 204-748-1659; *Fax:* 204-748-2501
virden_pioneer_home@mts.net
virden.cimnet.ca/cim/187C1_4T421T3T168.dhtm
Open summer daily

Wabowden: Wabowden Historical Museum
PO Box 219
Located at 2 Fleming Dr., Wabowden, MB
Wabowden, MB R0B 1S0
The Wabowden Historical Museum preserves & displays artifacts from Wabowden & the surrounding region, such as mining, logging, fishing, & trapping items. The museum is open from Canada Day until the Labour Day weekend.

Wasagaming: Riding Mountain Historical Society & Pinewood Museum
PO Box 578
Located at 154 Wasagaming Dr., Wasagaming, MB R0J 2H0
Wasagaming, MB R0J 1N0
Tel: 204-848-2810
Records & preserves the history of humans in the Riding Mountain National Park; open daily 2-5pm in July & Aug.

Wasagaming: Riding Mountain National Park (RMNPC) / Parc national du Canada du Mont-Riding
133 Wasagaming Dr.
Wasagaming, MB R0J 2H0
Tel: 204-848-7275; *Fax:* 204-848-2596
rmnp.info@pc.gc.ca
www.pc.gc.ca/ridingmountain
twitter.com/RidingNP
www.facebook.com/RidingNP
Other contact information: TTY: 1-866-787-6221; Friends of RMNP: 204-848-4037
The Riding Mountain National Park of Canada covers 3,000 km2 of the Manitoba prairie & escarpment. The park provides a variety of school & interpretation programs. The Visitor Centre is open from mid May to mid October.
Marjorie Huculak, Partnering and Engagement Officer, 204-848-7256, marjorie.huculak@pc.gc.ca

Waskada: Waskada Museum
c/o Village of Waskada, PO Box 27, 43 Railway Ave.
Waskada, MB R0M 2E0
Tel: 204-673-2503
waskadamuseum@mail.com
www.waskada.org/visitors/museum
Other contact information: Appointments: 204-673-2557
Year Founded: 1970 The Waskada Museum features the following buildings: the 1914 Anglican Church, the 1906 Union (Royal) Bank, a 1927 blacksmith shop, the 1896 Menota country school, a vehicle display building, & a display building. The museum is open during July & August.

Wawanesa: Sipiweske Museum
102 - 4th St.
Wawanesa, MB R0K 2G0
Tel: 204-824-2289; *Fax:* 204-824-2244
wacomcon@mts.net
Memorabilia from pioneers, Nellie McClung, Native people & 1903 insurance company; open July-Aug.; by appointment other times

Whitemouth: Whitemouth Municipal Museum
Henderson Ave. & 1st St.
Whitemouth, MB R0E 2G0
Tel: 204-348-2708
www.facebook.com/WhitemouthMunicipalMuseum
Year Founded: 1975 Museum depicting the different ways of life in the area - farming, railway, forestry, trapping, peat moss plants, hydro, AECL, fishing, brickyard, flour mill; artifacts housed in six buildings & two pole sheds; cairn honouring Dr. Charlotte Ross (The Iron Rose), first female to practice medicine in Manitoba; turn of the century house; 1905 Anglican Church; CPR Caboose; seasonal hours.

Winkler: Pembina Threshermen's Museum Inc.
PO Box 1103
Winkler, MB R6W 4B2
Tel: 204-325-7497; *Fax:* 204-331-3733
info@threshermensmuseum.com
www.threshermensmuseum.com
www.facebook.co m/505837972767511
Year Founded: 1968 The Pembina Threshermen's Museum preserves the area's agricultural & Mennonite heritage. The grounds of the museum feature several heritage buildings, such as the 1909 Pomeroy School, the 1905-1906 Morden CPR Sation, an 1885 log house, plus a sawmill, windmill, blacksmith shop, barbershop, & post office. The museum is open from the beginning of May to the end of September.

Winnipeg: Air Force Heritage Museum & Air Park / Le Musée du patrimoine de la force aérienne et du parc aérien
PO Box 17000 Forces
Located in Bldg. 25 Air Force Way, Winnipeg, MB
Winnipeg, MB R3J 3Y5
Tel: 204-833-2500; *Fax:* 204-833-2512
The museum, located in the Billy Bishop building, is part of a complex that consists of an outdoor air park showcasing 14 aircraft. The air park is open year round. Museum is open daily Mon-Fri throughout the summer from 8:00-4:00 by appointment. Guided tours, with services in English and French; wheelchair accessible; food service and restrooms. Located on Air Force Way, north off Ness Ave. on Sharp Blvd.

Winnipeg: Anthropology Museum
University of Winnipeg, 515 Portage Ave.
Winnipeg, MB R3B 2E9
Tel: 204-786-9282; *Fax:* 204-771-4134
www.uwinnipeg.ca/index/anthropology-museum
Items in the collection fall under the categories of Archaeology, Cultural Anthropology & Ethnography, & Biological Anthropology.
Val McKinley, Curator, v.mckinley@uwinnipeg.ca

Winnipeg: Canadian Museum for Human Rights (CMHR)
85 Israel Asper Way
Winnipeg, MB R3C 0L5
Tel: 204-289-2000; *Fax:* 204-289-2001
Toll-Free: 877-877-6037
info@humanrights.ca
humanrights.ca
Social Media: www.youtube.com/humanrightsmuseum
twitter.com/cmhr_news
www.facebook.com/canadianmuseumforhumanrights
Other contact information: TTY: 204-289-2050
Year Founded: 2014
John Young, President & Chief Executive Officer, john.young@humanrights.ca

Winnipeg: Costume Museum of Canada
#301, 250 McDermot Ave.
Winnipeg, MB R3B 0s5
Tel: 204-989-0072
costumemuseumcanada@gmail.com
www.costumemuseumcanada.com
www.facebook.com/94897456640
Over 35,000 artifacts spanning over 400 years; collection of costumes, textiles & related accessories. The museum is currently closed, but seeking support to continue their efforts.
Maralyn MacKay Hussain, President

Winnipeg: The Ed Leith Cretaceous Menagerie
Dept. of Geological Sciences, University of Manitoba, Wallace Bldg., 125 Dysart Rd.
Winnipeg, MB R3T 2N2
Tel: 204-474-9371
umanitoba.ca/geoscience/cretaceousmenagerie
The Menagerie displays four complete skeletal replicas of creatures from the Cretaceous Period. Open M-F 8:30-4:30.

Winnipeg: The Fire Fighters Museum of Winnipeg
56 Maple St.
Winnipeg, MB R3B 0Y8
Tel: 204-942-4817; *Fax:* 204-885-1306
firemuseum@gatewest.net
www.winnipegfiremuseum.ca
The museum's collections cover every aspect of Winnipeg's fire service. Call the museum for their hours of operation.

Winnipeg: Fort Garry Horse Regimental Museum & Archives Inc.
c/o McGregor Armoury, 551 Machray Ave.
Winnipeg, MB R2W 1A8
Tel: 204-586-6298; *Fax:* 204-582-0370
www.fortgarryhorse.ca
Depicts the history of the Fort Garry Horse from 1912 to present; open Mon. evenings 7:30-10:30; other times by appt.

Winnipeg: FortWhyte Alive
1961 McCreary Rd.
Winnipeg, MB R3P 2K9
Tel: 204-989-8355; *Fax:* 204-895-4700
info@fortwhyte.org
www.fortwhyte.org
twitter.com/fortwhytealive
www. facebook.com/FortWhyteAlive

Year Founded: 1966 74 hectares of lakes, marshes aspen parkland for environmental education; exhibit building

Winnipeg: Historical Museum of St. James-Assiniboia
Parent: Historical Museum Association of St. James-Assiniboia
3180 Portage Ave.
Winnipeg, MB R3K 0Y5
Tel: 204-888-8706
Open year round

Winnipeg: Ivan Franko Museum
200 McGregor St.
Winnipeg, MB R2W 5L6
Tel: 204-589-4397; *Fax:* 204-589-3404
History of Ivan Franko, Ukrainian poet, novelist, & social activist & Ukrainian pintings; ceramics, woodcarving, glassware, embroidery, & weaving; open year-round.

Winnipeg: J.B. Wallis Museum of Entomology
Dept. of Entomology, University of Manitoba
Winnipeg, MB R3T 2N2
Tel: 204-474-9257; *Fax:* 204-474-7628
head_entomo@umanitoba.ca
umanitoba.ca/faculties/afs/entomology/jbwallis.html
250,000 species of insects
Dr. Rob Currie, Department Head Ph.D., rob_currie@umanitoba.ca

Winnipeg: Jewish Heritage Centre of Western Canada Inc.
Asper Jewish Community Campus, #C140, 123 Doncaster St.
Winnipeg, MB R3N 2B2
Tel: 204-477-7460
jewishheritage@jhcwc.org
www.jhcwc.org
www.facebook.com/JewishHeritageCentre
The centre includes a library, archive collections, a Holocaust resource & education centre, artifact exhibitions, & seasonal visiting exhibits. Open M-Th 9:00-4:00.

Winnipeg: Manitoba Children's Museum
45 Forks Market Rd.
Winnipeg, MB R3C 4T6
Tel: 204-924-4000; *Fax:* 204-956-2122
general@childrensmuseum.com
www.childrensmuseum.com
Social Media: pinterest.com/mcminwinnipeg
twitter.com/mcminwinnipeg
Year Founded: 1983 Catering to children, the site includes such hands-on exhibits as a 1950s train station with CNR diesel locomotive. Open daily, year round.
Sara Hancheruk, Executive Director

Winnipeg: Manitoba Crafts Museum & Library (MCML)
#1B, 183 Kennedy St.
Winnipeg, MB R3C 1S6
Tel: 204-487-6117; *Fax:* 204-487-6117
info@mcml.ca
www.mcml.ca
Social Media: pinterest.com/mcraftsml
www.facebook.com/258347936251
Year Founded: 1986 The museum's collection focuses on the development of Canadian, and particularly Manitoban, crafts since the 1920s. The library houses about 2,500 titles pertaining to crafts, including scrapbooks and design patterns. Open year round
Stephanie Cooper, Co-President, president@mcml.ca
Amanda Harding, Co-President, president@mcml.ca
Andrea Reichert, Curator, curator@mcml.ca

Winnipeg: Manitoba Electrical Museum & Education Centre
PO Box 815, 680 Harrow St.
Winnipeg, MB R3C 2P4
Tel: 204-477-7905
www.hydro.mb.ca/about_us/electrical_museum.shtml
Year Founded: 1971 The museum explores the history of electricity in Manitoba from the 1800s. Exhibits include archival photographs, documents & electrical artifacts, including vintage household appliances & an electric streetcar. In the lower level is an interactive section with Hazard Hamlet where, children can learn about potentially hazardous situations if electricity is not used properly.

Winnipeg: Manitoba Military Aviation Museum
Bldg. 66, Canadian Forces Base 17 Wing Winnipeg, 715 Wuhiri Rd.
Winnipeg, MB R3J 3Y5
Tel: 204-833-2500
www.manitobamilitaryaviationmuseum.com
The museum is dedicated to preserving Manitoba aviation heritage through its collection & exhibits. Open Tu-F, 1:00-5:00.
Lt. Donna Riguidel, Heritage Officer
Rob Iwacha, 17 Wing Heritage Assistant
Norman Malayney, Resident Miltary Aviation Historian

Winnipeg: Manitoba Sports Hall of Fame & Museum Inc. (MSHOF)
Parent: Sport Manitoba
Sport for Life Centre, 145 Pacific Ave.
Winnipeg, MB R3B 2Z6
Tel: 204-925-5736; *Fax:* 204-925-5916
halloffame@sportmanitoba.ca
www.halloffame.mb.ca
Social Media: www.youtube.com/user/sportmanitoba
twitter.com/SportManitoba
www.faceb ook.com/sportmb
Year Founded: 1993 The museum aims to honour those people who have contributed significantly to Manitoba's rich sports history. The exhibits use various memorabilia and photos to cover such sports as athletics, basketball, baseball/softball, curling, football, golf, hockey, and the Winter Olympics.
Rick D. Brownlee, Sport Heritage Manager
Andrea Reichert, Collections Manager, andrea.reichert@sportmanitoba.ca

Winnipeg: Naval Museum of Manitoba
HMCS Chippawa Bldg., 1 Navy Way
Winnipeg, MB R3C 4J7
Tel: 204-943-7745; *Fax:* 204-947-9533
curator@naval-museum.mb.ca
naval-museum.mb.ca
The museum honours Manitoba's contributions to the Canadian Navy. Open to visitors on Wednesdays from 9:00 to 3:00; also open Sundays 1:00 to 4:00 in the summer.

Winnipeg: Ogniwo Polish Museum Society Inc.
1417 Main St.
Winnipeg, MB R2W 3V3
Tel: 204-586-5070
info@polishmuseum.com
www.polishmuseum.com
twitter.com/Ogniwo
www.facebook.com/1204092847117 55
Year Founded: 1985 Artifacts related to Polish immigrants in Canada; open year round

Winnipeg: Queen's Own Cameron Highlanders of Canada Regimental Museum Inc.
Minto Armoury, #230, 969 St. Matthew's Ave.
Winnipeg, MB R3G 0J7
Tel: 204-786-4330
thequeensowncameronhighlandersofcanada.net
Regimental dress, equipment & archives from 1910 to present

Winnipeg: Robert B. Ferguson Museum of Mineralogy
Dept. of Geological Sciences, University of Manitoba, Wallace Bldg., 125 Dysart Rd.
Winnipeg, MB R3T 2N2
Tel: 204-474-9371; *Fax:* 204-474-7623
www.umanitoba.ca
Year Founded: 1971 The museum's collection includes mineral specimins & research papers.

Winnipeg: Ross House Museum
Joe Zuken Heritage Park, 140 Meade St. North
Winnipeg, MB R2W 3K5
Tel: 204-943-3958
rosshouse@mhs.mb.ca
www.mhs.mb.ca
twitter.com/RossHo useMuseum
www.facebook.com/groups/107918235910933
Other contact information: Fall/Winter Phone: 204-947-0559
Ross House was the first post office in western Canada. It is now a museum, owned by the City of Winnipeg & operated by the Manitoba Historical Society. The museum depicts the operation of early postal service & the life of the Ross family around 1850. Ross House is open from the beginning of June to the end of August. Schools & large groups may arrange appointments at other times of the year.
Victor Sawelo, Museum Manager

Winnipeg: Royal Aviation Museum of Western Canada / Musée de l'aviation de l'ouest du Canada
Hangar T-2, 958 Ferry Rd.
Winnipeg, MB R3H 0Y8
Tel: 204-786-5503; *Fax:* 204-775-4761
Info@RoyalAviationMuseum.com
www.wcam.mb.ca
twitter.com/historyoflight
The Western Canada Aviation Museum's recovery & restoration department works to prepare aircraft for display. The museum features sights such as Canada's first helicopter, bushplanes, historic military jets, & commercial aircraft. The museum also contains an aviation reference library, with collections of books, magazines, manuals, photographs, drawings, & audio-visual materials. The library is open to the public by appointment. The museum is open year-round.

Winnipeg: Royal Canadian Mint - Winnipeg Facility
520 Lagimodière Blvd.
Winnipeg, MB R2J 3E7
Tel: 204-983-6429; *Fax:* 204-255-5203
Toll-Free: 877-974-6468
info@rcmint.ca
www.mint.ca
Social Media: www.youtube.com/user/canadianmint
twitter.com/CanadianMint
www.faceboo k.com/RoyalCanadianMint
Tours of the mint available year round; call for reservations. Winter hours: Tu - Sa 9:00 - 4:00. Summer hours: M - Su 9:00 - 4:00.

Winnipeg: Royal Winnipeg Rifles Regimental Museum
Minto Armoury, #109, 969 St. Matthews Ave.
Winnipeg, MB R3G 0J7
Tel: 204-786-4300
www.royalwinnipegrifles.com
Year Founded: 1970 Collects & preserves the history of the Regiment, & also houses displays relevant to the Winnipeg Light Infantry & the Winnipeg Grenadiers; military artifacts & memorabilia, pictures, books & other documents; open Tu 3:00 - 9:00. Tours can be arranged by appointment
Gerry Woodman, Operations Manager, 204-895-2588, gerrywoodman@live.ca

Winnipeg: St. Norbert Provincial Heritage Park
PO Box 30, 200 Saulteaux Cres.
Location: 40 Turnbull Dr., St. Norbert, Winnipeg, MB
Winnipeg, MB R3J 3W3
Tel: 204-945-4236
www.gov.mb.ca/conservation/parks/popular_parks/central/norbert_info.html
Other contact information: Off season: 204-945-7665
Illustrates how a natural landscape used for hunting, fishing & camping by Aboriginal peoples evolved into a French-speaking Métis settlement, then a French-Canadian agricultural community of the pre-World War I period; guided tours of restored Turenne & Bohémier houses; open daily May long weekend to Labour Day weekend.

Winnipeg: St. Vital Museum
Parent: St. Vital Historical Society Inc.
600 St. Mary's Rd.
Winnipeg, MB R2M 3L5
Tel: 204-255-2864
info@svhs.ca
www.svhs.ca
Social Media: www.youtube.com/user/stvitalmuseum
twitter.com/SVHistoricalSoc
www.fac ebook.com/stvitalmuseum
Year Founded: 2008 Educational centre, bringing "the history of St. Vital" to the community by way of shows & displays; museum holds artifacts
Bob Holliday, President
John Dempster, Resident Historian

Winnipeg: St. Volodymyr Ukrainian Catholic Museum
Parent: Ukrainian Catholic Archeparchy of Winnipeg
233 Scotia St.
Winnipeg, MB R2V 1V7
Tel: 204-338-7801; *Fax:* 204-339-4006
museum@escape.ca
archeparchy.ca
Year Founded: 1967 Religious & cultural collection pertaining to the life of the church in Canada.

***Winnipeg:* Sandilands Forest Centre**
***Parent:* Manitoba Forestry Association**
c/o Manitoba Forestry Association, 900 Corydon Ave.
Winnipeg, MB R3M 0Y4
Tel: 204-453-3182; *Fax:* 204-477-5765
sandilands.mfa@gmail.com
www.thinktrees.org/Sandilands_Forest_Discovery_Centre.aspx
www.facebook.com/229261507091158
Year Founded: 1957 The Centre is sited on 122 hectares of land granted to the Manitoba Forestry Association, & is located near Hadashville, just south of the Trans Canada Highway, east of Winnipeg; information on biodiversity, forest ecology, sustainable management of forest resources, fire prevention & management; nature trails, museum, fire tower & picnic area; educational programming; commemorative tree planting
Dr. Christina McDonald, President, Manitoba Forestry Association
Patricia Pohrebniuk, Executive Director, Manitoba Forestry Association

***Winnipeg:* Seven Oaks House Museum**
50 Mac St.
Winnipeg, MB R2V 4Z9
Tel: 204-339-7429
sohmuseum@gmail.com
www.mhs.mb.ca/docs/sites/sevenoakshousemuseum
www.facebook.com/SevenOaks HouseMuseum
Year Founded: 1958 Seven Oaks House is a log residence, which was built between 1851 & 1853. It has been restored to reflect life during the Red River settlement in the 19th century. The museum is open from mid-May to Labour Day.

***Winnipeg:* Stewart Hay Memorial Museum**
Duff Roblin Bldg., Dept. of Zoology, University of Manitoba
Winnipeg, MB R3T 2N2
Tel: 204-474-9245; *Fax:* 204-474-7588
Mounted & study specimens of mammals, birds, fish, reptiles, amphibians, crustaceans, mollusks & other invertebrates; casts of fossils; open year round

***Winnipeg:* Transcona Historical Museum**
141 Regent Ave. West
Winnipeg, MB R2C 1R1
Tel: 204-222-0423; *Fax:* 204-222-0208
info@transconamuseum.mb.ca
www.transconamuseum.mb.ca
Social Media: www.youtube.com/user/TransconaMuseum
www.facebook.com/transconamuseum
Archives, photographs, rare books, reference files, natural history (including an 8,000 specimen lepidoptera collection), First Nations cultural artifacts (3,500 items), Euro-Canadian cultural artifacts & a clothing & textile collection
Alanna Horejda, Curator

***Winnipeg:* Ukrainian Cultural & Educational Centre**
184 Alexander Ave. East
Winnipeg, MB R3B 0L6
Tel: 204-942-0218
ucec@mymts.net
www.ukrainianwinnipeg.ca/oseredok
Library & historical & archival collections dealing with the history of Ukrainians in Canada & the history of Ukraine; open Tues. - Sat. year round

***Winnipeg:* Ukrainian Museum of Canada (UMC) Manitoba Branch**
1175 Main St.
Winnipeg, MB R2W 3S4
Tel: 204-582-1018
www.htuomc.org/museum.html
Year Founded: 1950 Open July - Aug., or by appointment the rest of the year.

***Winnipeg:* University of Winnipeg Geography Museum**
515 Portage Ave.
Winnipeg, MB R3B 2E9
Tel: 204-786-9485; *Fax:* 204-774-4134
geography@uwinnipeg.ca
geograph.uwinnipeg.ca/facilities.htm
Teaching & reference collection of rocks, minerals & fossils, with a Manitoba focus; open year round
Kim Monson, Curator, k.monson@uwinnipeg.ca

***Winnipeg:* UVAN Historical Museum & Archives**
#203, 456 Main St.
Winnipeg, MB R3B 1B6
Tel: 204-942-5861
Historical, ethnological & archival material

***Winnipeg:* Winnipeg Police Museum**
***Parent:* Winnipeg Police Museum & Historical Society Inc.**
Winnipeg Police Headquarters, 245 Smith St.
PO Box 1680, Winnipeg, MB R3C 2Z7
Winnipeg, MB R3C 1K1
Tel: 204-986-3976
wps-museum@winnipeg.ca
www.winnipeg.ca/police/Museum
Year Founded: 1974 The Winnipeg Police Museum exhibits items related to the Winnipeg Police Force, which formed in 1874. Objects on display include early handcuffs,& identification cameras, & a jail cell which was built in 1911. There are also exhibits surrounding the 1919 Winnipeg General Strike & Earle "The Strangler" Nelson. Located at the Winnipeg Police Academy, the Winnipeg Police Museum is open daily. Conducted group tours can be arranged.

***Winnipeg:* Winnipeg Railway Museum**
PO Box 48, 123 Main St.
Winnipeg, MB R3C 1A3
Tel: 204-942-4632
wpgrail@mts.net
www.wpgrailwaymuseum.com
The museum contains artifacts, trains, & train-related vehicles & equipment. Open year-round, M & Th 9:00-12:00.

***Winnipegosis:* Medd House Museum**
***Parent:* Winnipegosis Historical Society Inc.**
c/o Winnipegosis Historical Society Inc., PO Box 336
324 - 2 St., Winnipegosis, MB
Winnipegosis, MB R0L 2G0
Tel: 204-656-4318
winnipegosismuseum@yahoo.ca
www.winnipegosis.org
Other contact information: Alternate Phone: 204-656-4273
Historic house once owned by a local Winnipegosis doctor, Dr. Medd.

***Winnipegosis:* Winnipegosis Museum**
***Parent:* Winnipegosis Historical Society Inc.**
c/o Winnipegosis Historical Society Inc., PO Box 336
Winnipegosis, MB R0L 2G0
Tel: 204-656-4273
winnipegosismuseum@yahoo.ca
www.winnipegosis.org
Housed in former CNR Railway Station (c.1897); 65-foot freighter, the "Myrtle M"; artifacts; CNR historical material; War Memorial items; native handiwork

***Woodlands:* Woodlands Pioneer Museum**
PO Box 206
Woodlands, MB R0C 3H0
Tel: 204-383-5691
Other contact information: Alternate Phones: 204-383-5919; 204-383-5589
Post office; municipal office; doctor's office; church; school; log house; located off Hwy 6; open July-Aug.

New Brunswick

Provincial Museums

Kings Landing Historical Settlement / Village historique de Kings Landing
5904 Rte. 102
Prince William, NB E6K 0A5
Tel: 506-363-4999; *Fax:* 506-363-4989
info.kingslanding@gnb.ca
kingslanding.nb.ca
twitter.com/KLTeamster
w ww.facebook.com/KingsLandingHistory
Year Founded: 1974 Historical settlement on the St. John River with more than 100 costumed interpreters depicting rural life from 1790-1910; 65,000 artifacts; open June - Oct.

Musée Acadien (MAUM)
c/o Pavillon Léopold-Taillon, Campus de Moncton, Université de Moncton, 18, av Antonine-Maillet
Situé à Pavillon Clément-Cormier, Université de Moncton, #134, 405, av de l'Université, Moncton, NB E1A 3E9
Moncton, NB E1A 3E9
Tél: 506-858-4088; *Téléc:* 506-858-4043
maum@umoncton.ca
www.umoncton.ca/umcm-maum
Fondée en: 1886 Le plus ancien musée acadien au monde est fondé par le père Camille Lefebvre. La collection dépasse 35,000 objets et photographies et représente tous les aspects de la vie acadienne. Exposition permanente; expositions temporaires; expositions virtuelles.
Jeanne-Mance Cormier, Conservatrice
Bernard LeBlanc, Conservateur
Nicole LeBlanc, Secrétaire administrative

New Brunswick Museum (NBM/MNB) / Musée du Nouveau-Brunswick
277 Douglas Ave.
Exhibitions Centre located at Market Square, Saint John, NB, E2L 4Z6
Saint John, NB E2K 1E5
Tel: 506-643-2300; *Fax:* 506-643-2360
Toll-Free: 888-268-9595
NBM-MNB@nbm-mnb.ca
www.nbm-mnb.ca
Social Media: instagram.com/nbm_mnb
twitter.com/nbmmnb
www.facebook.com/nbmmnb
Year Founded: 1934 Collections at the provincial museum of New Brunswick include human history, marine & technology, prints, fine & decorative arts, botany, zoology, & geology; A full range of exhibitions & programs are offered daily; Closed Christmas Day, Good Friday, Easter Sunday & Easter Monday.
Jane Fullerton, CEO, 506-643-2351
Felicity Osepchook, Head, Archives & Research Library, 506-643-2324

Local Museums

***Aulac:* Fort Beauséjour National Historic Site**
111 Fort Beauséjour Rd.
Aulac, NB E4L 2W5
Tel: 506-364-5080; *Fax:* 506-536-4399
fort.beausejour@pc.gc.ca
www.pc.gc.ca/lhn-nhs/nb/beausejour/index_E.asp
twitter.com/nhsnb
Year Founded: 1751 Built in 1751 by the French; star-shaped fort overlooking the Bay of Fundy. Features such activites as kite flying, bird watching and scavenger hunts.

***Bartibog Bridge:* MacDonald Farm Historic Site**
600 Rte. 11
Bartibog Bridge, NB E1V 7G1
Tel: 506-778-6085
info@macdonaldfarm.ca
www.macdonaldfarm.ca
www.facebook.com/441360032574933
Year Founded: 1970 Constructed by Scottish settler, Lt. Col. Alexander MacDonald of Bartibog, between 1815 & 1820 in Georgian style, the site includes a barn, 4 outbuildings, as well as a wharf & boat house. Costumed guides demonstrate cooking, crafts & care of animals. The site is operated by the Highland Society of New Brunswick.

***Bathurst:* Musee de la Guerre / Memorial War Museum**
Légion Royale Canadienne, Herman J.Good V.C. Branche 18, 575, av St-Peter
Bathurst, NB E2A 2Y5
Tél: 506-546-3135

***Bathurst:* Nepisiquit Centennial Museum & Cultural Centre**
***Parent:* Bathurst Heritage Trust Commission Inc.**
360 Douglas Ave.
Bathurst, NB E2A 4S6
Tel: 506-546-9449; *Fax:* 506-545-7050
bhtc@nb.aibn.com
bathurstheritage.ca
www.facebook.com/BathurstHeritage MuseeBathurst
Year Founded: 2003 The Centre houses the Bathurst Heritage Museum, Nepisiquit Genealogy/Archives, & Multicultural Association of the Chaleur Region.

***Bayfield:* Cape Jourimain Nature Centre Inc.**
5039 Rte. 16
Bayfield, NB E4M 3Z8
Tel: 506-538-2220; *Fax:* 506-538-2226
Toll-Free: 866-538-2220
www.capejourimain.ca
Year Founded: 2001 The Centre contains a lighthouse (c.1870), observation tower, exhibit hall & art gallery.
Bill Prescott, Chair
Joy Banks, Administrative Assistant & General Contact

***Boiestown:* Central New Brunswick Woodmen's Museum Inc.**
6342 Rte. 8
Boiestown, NB E6A 1Z5
Tel: 506-369-7214; *Fax:* 506-369-9081
woodmen@nb.aibn.com
www.woodmensmuseum.com
www.facebook.com/WoodmensMu seum
Year Founded: 1979 Sixteen exhibit buildings; depicts life of Central New Brunswick lumberjack & culture of Miramichi people

Bernice Price, Executive Director

Bouctouche: Musée de Kent Inc.
150, ch du Couvent
Bouctouche, NB E4S 3C1
Tél: 506-743-5005
admin@museedekent.ca
www.museedekent.ca
Fondée en: 1978 Formerly known as the Convent of the Immaculate Conception boarding school, c.1880.
Pierre Cormier, President

Caraquet: Éco-Musée de l'huître / Oyster Museum
675, boul Saint-Pierre ouest
Caraquet, NB E1W 1A2
Tel: 506-727-3226
rmne.ca/eco-musee-huitre

Caraquet: Musée Acadien de Caraquet / Acadian Museum of Caraquet
15, boul St-Pierre est
Caraquet, NB E1W 1B6
Tél: 506-726-2682; *Téléc:* 506-726-2660
museecaraquet.ca
Fondée en: 1963 Favorise l'histoire et la culture des Acadiens de la Péninsule acadienne en utilisant sa propre collection ainsi que d'autres collections et archives régionales

Caraquet: Village Historique Acadien
PO Box 5626
Adresse civique: 14311, Rte. 11, Rivière-du-Nord, NB E8N 2V6
Caraquet, NB E1W 1B7
Tel: 506-726-2600*Toll-Free:* 877-721-2200
vha@gnb.ca
www.vhanb.ca
www.facebook.com/villagehistoriqueacadien
Gabriel LeBreton, Directeur général par intérim, gabriel.lebreton@gnb.ca
Philippe Basque, Historien et conservateur en chef, philippe.basque@gnb.ca

Clair: Société historique de Clair Inc.
724, rue Principale
Clair, NB E7A 2H4
Tel: 506-992-3637
sochclair@nb.aibn.com
Museum & historic site guided tours; Beaux-arts, Historie humaine; visites guidées; summer hours: M - Su 9:30 - 6:00; off season hours by appointment

Connors: Pioneer Historical Connors Museum
3614 Rte. 205
Connors, NB E7A 1S3
Tel: 506-992-2500; *Fax:* 506-992-2500
Items used in general store; blacksmith shop; Victorian mansion

Dalhousie: Musée Restigouche Regional Museum
115 George St.
Dalhousie, NB E8C 1R6
Tel: 506-684-7490; *Fax:* 506-684-7490
gurrm@nbnet.nb.ca
Year Founded: 1967 Local history museum, archives, gallery

Doaktown: Atlantic Salmon Museum
263 Main St.
Doaktown, NB E9C 1A9
Tel: 506-365-7787
museum@nbnet.nb.ca
www.atlanticsalmonmuseum.com
www.facebook.com/AtlanticSalmonMuseum
Year Founded: 1982 Through interpretive displays & the an aquarium, the Atlantic Salmon Museum shows the history of the life of the Atlantic salmon, as well as the cultural & economic value of the Atlantic salmon to the Miramichi River & New Brunswick. Conservation is also emphasized. The museum is open from June to October. Appointments for rentals can be made during other times.

Doaktown: Doak House Historic Site
386 Main St.
Doaktown, NB E9C 1E4
Tel: 506-365-2026
museum@nbnet.nb.ca
www.facebook.com/DoakHistoricSite
Open end of June - early Sept.

Dorchester: Westmorland Historical Society Inc. Dorchester Heritage Properties Committee
#5, 3497 Cape Rd.
Dorchester, NB E4K 2X2
Tel: 506-379-6633
keillorhouse@nb.aibn.com
www.keillorhousemuseum.com
Operating: The Keillor House (Westmorland Centennial Museum, c. 1813), 506-379-6633; open June - Sept. or by appt.; Bell Inn (c.1811), 506-379-2580; open Apr. - Oct.; St. James Presbyterian Church Museum, 506-379-6633; Beachkirk Collection (c. 1884); open June - Sept. or by appt.; The Maritime Penetentiary Museum, 506-379-6633; open June - Sept.

Edmundston: Musée historique du Madawaska
c/o Campus d'Edmundston, Université de Moncton, 165, boul Hébert
Edmundston, NB E3V 2S8
Tel: 506-737-5282; *Fax:* 506-737-5373
musee@umce.ca
www.umoncton.ca/umce/node/89
twitter.com/UMCE_UMoncton
www.facebook.com/UdeMEdmundston
Christian Michaud, Responsable, 506-737-5050

Florenceville-Bristol: Shogomoc Historical Railway Site
19 Station Rd.
Location: 9189 Main St., Florenceville-Bristol, NB E7L 2G4
Florenceville-Bristol, NB E7L 3J8
Tel: 506-392-8226; *Fax:* 506-392-5211
tourism@florencevillebristol.ca
www.florencevillebristol.ca/html/shogomo c.html
Other contact information: Off-season Phone: 506-392-6763, ext. 202
Restored 1914 CPR railway station featuring three renovated train cars; open May-Aug., Mon.-Sat.

Fredericton: 'School Days' Museum
PO Box 752
Fredericton, NB E3B 5R6
Tel: 506-459-3738; *Fax:* 506-459-3738
sdmuseum@nb.sympatico.ca
museum.nbta.ca
NB's educational heritage from 19th century; located in Justice Bldg. ANNEX, off Queen St.; artifacts pertaining to NB schools & teacher training
Harry Palmer, President, hspalmer@nb.sympatico.ca

Fredericton: Brydone Jack Observatory Museum
University of New Brunswick, PO Box 4400
Fredericton, NB E3B 5A3
Tel: 506-453-4723
The first astronomical observatory in Canada, built in 1851. The building is now a National Historic Site & a museum on the campus of the University of New Brunswick. It houses tools & equipment used by Dr. William Brydone Jack, who was a professor of mathematics, natural philosophy, & astronomy.

Fredericton: Fredericton Region Museum / Musée de la région de Fredericton
***Parent:* York Sunbury Historical Society**
PO Box 1312 A
Located at 571 Queen St., Fredericton, NB
Fredericton, NB E3B 5C8
Tel: 506-455-6041; *Fax:* 506-458-8741
info@frederictonregionmuseum.com
www.frederictonregionmuseum.com
Social Media: www.youtube.com/user/ysmuseum
twitter.com/FredMuseum
www.facebook.com/ FrederictonRegionMuseum
Ruth Murgatroyd, Executive Director

Fredericton: Guard House & Soldiers' Barracks
c/o Fredericton Tourism, PO Box 130, 11 Carleton St.
Fredericton, NB E3B 4Y7
Tel: 506-460-2041; *Fax:* 506-460-2474
Toll-Free: 888-888-4768
www.tourismfredericton.ca
Historic military buildings 1828-1866

Fredericton: Mary's Point Shorebird Reserve & Interpretive Centre
c/o Nature NB, #110, 924 Prospect St.
Location: 419 Mary's Point Rd., Harvey, NB E4H 2M9
Fredericton, NB E3B 2T9
Tel: 506-459-4209; *Fax:* 506-459-4209
maryspt@nbnet.nb.ca
www.naturenb.ca/maryspoint.html
www.facebook.com/n aturenb
Other contact information: Nature NB E-mail: nbfn@nb.aibn.com
Year Founded: 1992 Located in the Shepody National Wildlife Area & administered by both Nature NB & Environment Canada's Canadian Wildlife Service, these wetlands protect large numbers of shorebird species. The Interpretation Centre educates the public on the shorebirds' habitats & their hemispheric migrations over the Bay of Fundy region.

Fredericton: New Brunswick Sports Hall of Fame Inc. / Temple de la renommée sportive du Nouveau-Brunswick
PO Box 6000, 503 Queen St.
Fredericton, NB E3B 5H1
Tel: 506-453-3747
nbsportshalloffame@gnb.ca
www.nbsportshalloffame.nb.ca
twitter.com/NBSHF
www.facebook.com/NBSpor tsHallofFame
Open year round, hours vary; recognizes, collects, preserves, exhibits & promotes New Brunswick's sports heroes & sports heritage.

Fredericton: Old Government House
PO Box 6000
Located at 51 Woodstock Rd., Fredericton, NB E3B 9L8
Fredericton, NB E3B 5H1
Tel: 506-453-2505
www.gnb.ca/lg/ogh/index-e.asp
Constructed from 1826 to 1828, Government House was the residence of New Brunswick's Governors & Lieutenant-Governors. Government House also served as a school for hearing impaired students, a military barracks during World War I, a hospital for returning soldiers, & an RCMP headquarters. The House has been open to the public since 1999, featuring restored rooms, exhibits, & bilingual tours during the summer. Government House still contains the Lieutenant-Governor's office & residence.

Fredericton: Sheriff Andrews House
PO Box 6000
Location: 63 King St., St Andrews, NB E5B 1X6
Fredericton, NB E3B 5H1
Tel: 506-529-5080; *Fax:* 506-453-2416
www.townofstandrews.ca
Guided tours are offered through this 19th century home.
Guy Tremblay, Manager, Museum Services, Government of New Brunswick, Guy.Tremblay@gnb.ca

Fredericton: Wulastook Museums Inc.
PO Box 700
Located at 108 Queen St., Fredericton, NB
Fredericton, NB E3B 5B4
Tel: 506-451-7777; *Fax:* 506-451-1029

Fredericton Junction: Currie House
110 Currie Lane
Fredericton Junction, NB E0G 1T0
Tel: 506-368-2818
www.facebook.com/CurrieHouseMuseum
Museum with displays of antiques and artifacts, history of area and local families. Large picnic area, nature trails through woods and by river.

Gagetown: Queens County Heritage
69 Front St.
Gagetown, NB E5M 1A4
Tel: 506-488-2483; *Fax:* 504-488-2483
info@queenscountyheritage.com
www.queenscountyheritage.com
twitter.com /QCHeritage
www.facebook.com/QCHeritage
The Tilley House was the home of Sir Leonard Tilley, a Father of Confederation. The museum within it contains furnishings of the Loyalist & Victorian periods, plus historical exhibits. It is open from mid-June to mid-Sept.

Grand Falls: Grand Falls Museum / Musée de Grand-Sault
68 Madawaska Rd.
Grand Falls, NB E3Y 1C6
Tel: 506-473-5265
Local artifacts; Extensive collection of church records, genealogies, etc.; Open mid-June to end of Aug. or by appt.

Grand Manan: Grand Manan Art Gallery Inc.
PO Box 2 Castalia, 21 Cedar St.
Grand Manan, NB E5G 2C3
Tel: 506-662-2662
gmag2121@gmail.com
www.grandmananartgallery.ca
www.facebook.com/260096487401938
Artwork by local & visiting artists with a connection to Grand Manan Island; open daily June-Sept.

***Grand Manan:* Grand Manan Museum**
1141 Rte. 776
Grand Manan, NB E5G 4E9
Tel: 506-662-3524; *Fax:* 506-662-3009
gmadmin@grandmananmuseum.ca
www.grandmananmuseum.ca
twitter.com/GMMuse um
www.facebook.com/pages/Grand-Manan-Museum/11481146193 8351
Open June - Sept.; in winter by appt.

***Grand Manan:* Swallowtail Lightstation**
***Parent:* Swallowtail Keepers Society**
50 Lighthouse Rd.
Grand Manan, NB E5G 2A2
Tel: 506-662-8316 *Toll-Free:* 888-525-1655
www.tourismnewbrunswick.ca/Products/S/Swallowtail-Lightstatio n.aspx
Social Media: swallowtailkeepers.blogspot.ca
The Lightstation was established in 1860, renovated in 1980 & is still active today. It is one of the few remaining wooden lighthouses in Canada.
Patti Davidson, Contact

***Grand-Anse:* Musée des Papes**
184, rue Acadie
Grand-Anse, NB E8N 1A6
Tél: 506-732-3003; *Téléc:* 506-732-5491
museedespapes@gmail.com
museedespapes.snappages.com
www.facebook.com/1 90968550939951
Fondée en: 1985 Concerne l'évolution du christianisme aux présentes congrégations religieuses; Ouvert de mi-Juin à fin Août

***Hampton:* Kings County Museum**
***Parent:* Kings County Historical & Archival Society Inc.**
27 Centennial Rd.
Hampton, NB E5N 6N3
Tel: 506-832-6009
kingscm@nbnet.nb.ca
www.kingscountymuseum.com
www.facebook.com/pages/Kings-County-Museum/434 926949879214
Year Founded: 1968 Artifacts include textiles, clothing, china, guns, glassware, military, royalty, art & archival material

***Harvey, Albert County:* Old Bank Museum**
***Parent:* Albert County Heritage Trust**
c/o Albert County Heritage Trust, 435 Mary's Point Rd.
Located at 5985 Rte. 114, Riverside-Albert, NB E4H 4B8
Harvey, Albert County, NB E4H 2M9
Tel: 506-882-2015
Other contact information: Off-Season Phone: 506-882-2100
Historic bank building now a museum & information centre

***Hillsborough:* Hon. William Henry Steeves House**
40 Mill St.
Hillsborough, NB E4H 2Z8
Tel: 506-734-3102
steevesmuseum@nb.aibn.com
www.steeveshousemuseum.ca
Social Media: instagram.com/SteevesHouseMuseum
www.facebook.com/249068845106673
Year Founded: 1971 Operated by Heritage Hillsborough Inc.; birthplace of William Henry Steeves, a Father of Confederation; open every day July 1 to Labour Day

***Hillsborough:* New Brunswick Railway Museum**
2847 Main St.
Hillsborough, NB E4H 2X7
Tel: 506-734-3195
nbrailway@nb.aibn.com
www.nbrm.ca
Year Founded: 1984 Dedicated to preserving the history of train travel in New Brunswick, the museum has on site an extensive collection of full-sized railway cars. This is the province's only operating railway museum, with excursion trains 4 days a week along the Petitcodiac River & southeastern New Brunswick. Displays of equipment & artifacts highlight the local & area railway history. There is a gift shop. Open daily, June - Sept.

***Hopewell Cape:* Albert County Museum**
***Parent:* Albert County Historical Society Inc.**
3940 Rte. 114
Hopewell Cape, NB E4H 3J8
Tel: 506-734-2003; *Fax:* 506-734-3291
albertcountymuseum@nb.aibn.com
www.albertcountymuseum.ca
twitter.com/A lbertCoMuseum
www.facebook.com/albertcountymuseum
The museum is located in the UNESCO Fundy Biosphere Reserve. Visitors can experience early life in Albert County & the Shepody Bay region by visiting the original Shire Town buildings, circa 1845. The site also features the former County Jail complete with cells, displays & collections relating to the early history of the area, & the County Courthouse. The museum also has a 20-seat theatre that shows a documentary film on R.B. Bennett, Canada's 11th Prime Minister. Displays include shipbuilding & farming. Other features include a gift shop, meeting rooms & a research resources room.
Donald Alward, Manager & Curator

***Kingston:* John Fisher Memorial Museum**
***Parent:* Kingston Peninsula Heritage Inc.**
874 Rte. 845
Kingston, NB E5N 1V3
Tel: 506-763-2101
jfmmuseum@nb.aibn.com
www.kingstonnb.ca/JFMM
Located in the basement of Macdonald Consolidated School. Open June-Aug.

***McAdam:* McAdam Railway Station**
***Parent:* McAdam Historical Restoration Commission**
146 Saunders Rd.
McAdam, NB E6J 1L2
Tel: 506-784-2293
villageofmcadam@nb.aibn.com
www.mcadamstation.ca
www.facebook.com/391194767611207
The McAdam Railway Station (c.1900) is both a national & provincial historic site, as well as a heritage railway station. The museum offers guided tours, catered meals, conference facilities & a visitors centre.

***Memramcook:* Monument Lefebvre National Historic Site / Lieu historique national du Monument-Lefebvre**
***Parent:* Société du Monument-Lefebvre**
480, rue Centrale
Memramcook, NB E4K 3S6
Tel: 506-758-9808; *Fax:* 506-758-9813
monument@nbnet.nb.ca
www.pc.gc.ca/lhn-nhs/nb/lefebvre/index_e.asp
twit ter.com/nhsnb
Other contact information: Alt. URL: www.monumentlefebvre.ca
Year Founded: 1982 Located in the Monument LeFebvre building, in cooperation with Parks Canada, the centre focuses on the survival of the Acadian people from 1755 to present. Shows are performed in the theatre. There is a gift shop with a variety of Acadian products. Guided tours are offered.
Claude Boudreau, Executive Director

***Memramcook:* Société historique de la Vallée de Memramcook inc.**
612, rue Centrale
Memramcook, NB E4K 3S7
Tél: 506-758-0087; *Téléc:* 506-758-0087
shvm@shvm.ca
shvm.ca
Anita Boudreau, Présidente

***Minto:* Minto Museum & Information Centre**
187 Main St.
Minto, NB E4B 3N4
Tel: 506-327-3383
Open July 1 - Sept. 1

***Minto:* New Brunswick Internment Camp Heritage Museum**
#1, 420 Pleasant Dr.
Minto, NB E4B 2T3
Tel: 506-327-3573; *Fax:* 506-328-6008
nbinternmentcampmuseum.ca
Artifacts & model of the Ripples Internment Camp
Ed Caissie, Project Coordinator, 506-450-9666, edmuseum62@hotmail.com

***Miramichi:* Beaubears Island Interpretive Centre & Museum**
***Parent:* Friends of Beaubears Island Inc.**
35 St. Patrick's Dr.
Miramichi, NB E1N 4P6
Tel: 506-622-8526
info@beaubearsisland.ca
www.beaubearsisland.com
twitter.com/beaubearsisland
www.facebook.com/b eaubearsisland
The interpretive centre is a living museum with actors portraying shipbuilders, fur traders & the Marquis Charles Deschamps de Boishebert. The Friends of Beaubears Island oversee the Boishébert National Historic Site of Canada & the Beaubears Island Shipbuilding National Historic Site of Canada & J.Leonard O'Brien Memorial.

***Miramichi:* Rankin House Museum**
2224 Wellington St.
Miramichi, NB E1V 6N3
Tel: 506-773-3448
1837; example of mansions built by the early lumber & shipping barons; unique collection of historic items; tourist information centre; open July & Aug.

***Miramichi:* St. Michael's Museum**
PO Box 368, 10 Howard St.
Miramichi, NB E1N 3A7
Tel: 506-778-5152
mmuseum@nbnet.nb.ca
saintmichaelsmuseum.com
Miramichi history & extensive civil & church records for most denominations; geneology; tours in June-Aug.

***Miramichi:* W.S. Loggie Cultural Centre**
222 Wellington St.
Miramichi, NB E1N 1M9
Tel: 506-773-7645

***Moncton:* Free Meeting House**
***Parent:* Moncton Museum**
20 Mountain Rd.
Moncton, NB E1C 2J8
Tel: 506-856-4383; *Fax:* 506-389-5904
info@resurgo.ca
resurgo.ca

***Moncton:* Lutz Mountain Heritage Museum**
Lutz Mountain Heritage Foundation, 3143 Mountain Rd.
Moncton, NB E1G 2X1
Tel: 506-384-7719
lutzmtnheritage@rogers.com
www.lutzmtnheritage.ca
Year Founded: 1975 Operates a heritage museum & genealogical research facility; open mid-June to mid-Sept., Mon.-Sat., other times by appointment.

***Moncton:* Moncton Museum / Musée de Moncton**
20 Mountain Rd.
Moncton, NB E1C 2J8
Tel: 506-856-4383; *Fax:* 506-856-4355
info@resurgo.ca
resurgo.ca
Year Founded: 1974 The permanent exhibits showcase Moncton's history from the time of the Micmacs to the period preceding the Deportation of Acadians, when agriculture was Moncton's primary economic engine, to the golden shipbuilding years & the railway era. There are also temporary & travelling exhibits. A research library & educational programs are offered. Open year round. The museum also operates the Free Meeting House & Thomas Williams House.

***Moncton:* Thomas Williams House**
***Parent:* Moncton Museum**
103 Park St.
Moncton, NB E1C 2B2
Tel: 506-856-4383; *Fax:* 506-857-0590
info.museum@moncton.ca
www.moncton.ca
Other contact information: Summer Phone: 506-857-0590

***New Denmark:* New Denmark Memorial Museum**
***Parent:* New Denmark Historical Society**
6 Main Rd.
New Denmark, NB E0J 1T0
Tel: 506-553-6725
New Denmark Memorial Museum honours the Danish immigrants who settled in the New Denmark area of New Brunswick in 1872. It is the oldest Danish settlement in Canada. Exhibits include books, china, & farm machinery. The museum is open from mid June to the beginning of September.

***Oromocto:* Canadian Military Engineers Museum**
Canadian Forces School of Military Engineering, CFB / ASG Gagetown, #J-10, Mitchell Bldg.
Oromocto, NB E2V 4J5
Tel: 506-422-2000; *Fax:* 506-422-1220
cmemuseum@forces.gc.ca (Museum Staff)
www.cmemuseum.ca
Other contact information: E-mail, Research Inquiries: cme.research@sympatico.ca
Year Founded: 1957 Displays at the Canadian Military Engineers Museum date back before the 1800s, with drawings, plans, & photographs of forts built by engineers, such as the Citadel in

Nova Scotia. Displays also depict trench life during World War I. Weapons & uniforms from World War II, artifacts from the Korean War, & a United Nations display are also part of the museum. A research library houses photographs, reference books, training manuals, & personal diaries. The museum is open year round.
Col. John Tattersall, Chair
Maj. Joe Gale, Museum Executive Officer
CWO Blaine Thurston, Vice-President, History & Heritage
Sgt John Wilt, Curator & Treasurer

***Oromocto:* Fort Hughes Military Blockhouse**
62 Miramichi Rd.
Oromocto, NB E2V 1S2
Tel: 506-357-4400; *Fax:* 506-357-2266
recreation@oromocto.ca
www.oromocto.ca
Located in Sir Douglas Hazen Park, 1 Wharf Rd., Oromocto, NB.

***Oromocto:* New Brunswick Military History Museum (NBMHM) / Museum Musée d'histoire militaire du nouveau brunswick**
Bldg. A-5, PO Box 17000 Forces
Oromocto, NB E2V 4J5
Tel: 506-422-1304
info@nbmilitaryhistorymuseum.ca
nbmilitaryhistorymuseum.ca
Year Founded: 1973 The museum presents exhibits about the Canadian Army, the Royal Canadian Navy, & the Royal Canadian Air Force, from 1800-1968, & the Canadian Armed Forces from 1968 to the present. Since 2010 the museum has expanded its mandate to include pre-1800 New Brunswick military history.

***Paquetville:* Salon de la renommée de Paquetville et village natal d'Edith Butler**
1094, rue du Parc
Paquetville, NB E8R 1J4
Tel: 506-764-2500
rmne.ca/salon-de-la-renommee-de-paquetville-et-village-natal-d-edith-butle r

***Petitcodiac:* Maritime Motorsports Hall of Fame**
5 Hooper Lane
Petitcodiac, NB E4Z 0B4
Tel: 506-756-2110
maritimemotorsports@gmail.com
www.maritimemotorsporthalloffame.com
twitter.com/MMHallOfFame
www.face book.com/185591104855616
Other contact information: Alt. E-mail: admin@mmhf.ca
Year Founded: 2009 The Hall also features a museum showcasing the heritage of maritime motorsports. Open Mon.-Sat., Sun. by appointment until June.
Ernest McLean, President
Winona McLean, Managing Director

***Petitcodiac:* Petitcodiac War Museum**
2 Smith St.
Location: Legion Building, 8 Kay St., Petitcodiac, NB E4Z 4K6
Petitcodiac, NB E4Z 4W1
Tel: 506-756-7461
wrmuseum@nb.aibn.com
www.villageofpetitcodiac.com
The museum commemorates soliders from Petitcodiac who served in WWI, WWII, the Korean War & on peace keeping missions.

***Petit-Rocher:* New Brunswick Mining & Mineral Interpretation Centre (CIMMNB) / Centre d'interprétation des mines & minerais du Nouveau-Brunswick**
397, rue Principale
Petit-Rocher, NB E8J 1L9
Tel: 506-542-2672
petit-rocher@nb.aibn.com
The Mining & Mineral Interpretation Centre features exhibitions about the mining heritage of New Brunswick, plus a simulation of an underground descent.

***Plaster Rock:* Plaster Rock Museum & Information Centre**
159 Main St.
Plaster Rock, NB E7G 2H2
Tel: 506-356-6077
Plaster Rock Museum & Information Centre features exhibits about the community's past, including the lumbering & farming activities in Plaster Rock & the surrounding region.

***Rexton:* Bonar Law Common**
31 Bonar Law Ave., #A
Rexton, NB E4W 1V6
Tel: 506-523-7615*Toll-Free:* 877-731-7007
bonarlawcommon@nb.aibn.com
www.bonarlawcommon.com
Social Media: www.youtube.com/BonarLawCommons
www.facebook.com/bonar.common
Other contact information: Off-season Phone: 506-523-6921
Birthplace of the Right Honourable Andrew Bonar Law (1858-1923), who was the only Prime Minister of Britain who was born outside the British Isles. Also located in the Common is the Richibucto River Historical Society Museum.

***Rexton:* Richibucto River Historical Society Museum (RRHS)**
***Parent:* Richibucto River Historical Society**
Bonar Law Common, 31 Bonar Law Ave., #B
Rexton, NB E4W 1V6
Tel: 506-523-7615*Toll-Free:* 877-731-7007
bonarlawcommon@nb.aibn.com
www.bonarlawcommon.com/RRHS.html
Social Media: www.youtube.com/BonarLawCommons
www.facebook.com/bonar.common
Other contact information: Off-season Phone: 506-523-6921
The museum documents local Rexton history.

***Sackville:* Boultenhouse Heritage Centre**
***Parent:* Tantramar Heritage Trust, Inc.**
PO Box 3554, 29 Queen's Rd.
Sackville, NB E4L 4G4
Tel: 506-536-2541; *Fax:* 506-536-2537
tantramarheritage@nb.aibn.com
heritage.tantramar.com/THTBoultenhouse.htm l
Former home of shipwright Christopher Boultenhouse, c.1842; site also houses the Tantramar Heritage Trust office.

***Sackville:* Campbell Carriage Factory Museum**
***Parent:* Tantramar Heritage Trust, Inc.**
PO Box 3554, 29B Queens Rd.
Location: 19 Church St., Sackville, NB E4L 1J6
Sackville, NB E4L 4G4
Tel: 506-536-3079; *Fax:* 506-536-2537
tantramarheritage@nb.aibn.com
heritage.tantramar.com/THTCampbell.html
Other contact information: Off-season phone: 506-536-2541
19th century industrial site featuring a carriage factory & blacksmith shop.

***Sackville:* Struts Gallery & Faucet Media Arts Centre**
7 Lorne St.
Sackville, NB E4L 3Z6
Tel: 506-536-1211
info@strutsgallery.ca
www.strutsgallery.ca
www.facebook.com/133378256676635
Year Founded: 1982 An artist-run centre dedicated to presenting regional & national contemporary artist-initiated activities
Rebecca Blankert, President
Amanda Fauteux, Program Co-coordinator
Elliott Hearte, Media Arts Co-coordinator, faucet@strutsgallery.ca

***Saint John:* Barbour's General Store**
***Parent:* G.E. Barbour Inc.**
10 Market Sq.
Saint John, NB E2L 4Z6
www.facebook.com/208036962572426
Year Founded: 1967 Artifacts housed at Barbour's General Store include authentic grocery items, pharmaceutical items, cooking utensils, china, farm implements, & yard goods. The restored nineteenth-century country general stored is open from mid-June to mid-September.

***Saint John:* Hayward Fine China Museum**
85 Princess St.
Saint John, NB E2L 1K5
Tel: 506-653-9066; *Fax:* 506-658-1201
Toll-Free: 888-653-9066
www.haywardandwarwick.com
The museum details the history of the Hayward & Warwick family-owned china company.

***Saint John:* Loyalist House Museum**
120 Union St.
Saint John, NB E2L 1A3
Tel: 506-652-3590
info@loyalisthouse.com
www.loyalisthouse.com
Year Founded: 1960 Operated by the New Brunswick Historical Society as a national historic site, Loyalist House was built in 1817 by David Daniel Merritt, a United Empire Loyalist from Rye, NY. The house remains very much as it was built & still displays its original furniture: piano-organ, swooning divans, 'yoke-back' chairs, four-poster bed, etc. This buiding is one of the few surviving buildings of the Great Saint John Fire in 1877.

***Saint John:* Saint Croix Island International Historic Site / Lieu historique international de l'Ile-Sainte-Croix**
Carleton Martello Tower, 454 Whipple St.
Saint John, NB E2M 2R3
Tel: 506-636-4011; *Fax:* 506-636-4574
info.martello@pc.gc.ca
www.pc.gc.ca/eng/lhn-nhs/nb/stcroix/index.aspx
twitter.com/nhsnb
Other contact information: TTY: 506-887-6015
Year Founded: 1984 Located on Rte. 127 Bayside, with a view of Saint Croix Island; site of Pierre Dugua's first attempt to found a settlement in North America; viewing deck & self-guided interpretive trail; picnic area. The site is also a U.S. National Monument (www.nps.gov/sacr).

***Saint John:* Saint John Firefighters Museum**
24 Sydney St.
Saint John, NB E2L 2L3
Tel: 506-633-1840
The museum is the site of the No. 2 Engine house, built in 1840; a collection of firefighting artifacts & photographs; includes an entire room dedicated to the Great Saint John Fire of 1877, an authentic hand pump, a 1956 LaFrance Fire Engine, a Junior Firefighters play room & much more.

***Saint John:* Saint John Jewish Historical Museum**
91 Leinster St.
Saint John, NB E2L 1J2
Tel: 506-633-1833; *Fax:* 506-642-9926
sjjhm@nbnet.nb.ca
jewishmuseumsj.com
www.facebook.com/118753971549220
Year Founded: 1986 Housed in the same building with the Shaarei Zedek Synagogue, the museum collects, displays & preserves articles related specifically to the Saint John Jewish community; provides a research facility for genealogists, historians & religious scholars; 7 display areas; Jewish education outreach kits, membership program
Katherine Biggs-Craft, Curator

***Saint John:* Saint John Sports Hall of Fame**
Leisure Services, 171 Adelaide St.
Saint John, NB E2K 1W9
Tel: 506-658-2908
www.saintjohn.ca
Located in Harbour Station

***Saint John:* St. Andrews Blockhouse National Historic Site**
454 Whipple St.
Saint John, NB E2M 2R3
Tel: 506-529-4270; *Fax:* 506-636-4574
fundy.info@pc.gc.ca
www.pc.gc.ca/lhn-nhs/nb/standrews/index.aspx
Other contact information: Off-season Tel: 506-636-4011
Blockhouse built for border defence during the War of 1812; contains elements of the oldest blockhouse in New Brunswick; located at 23 Joe's Point Rd., St. Andrews NB E5B 2J7

***St Andrews:* Atlantic Reference Centre (ARC)**
1 Lower Campus Rd.
St Andrews, NB E5B 2L7
Tel: 506-529-1203; *Fax:* 506-529-1212
arc@sta.dfo.ca
www.mar.dfo-mpo.gc.ca/e0011886
The ARC acts as a museum, biodiversity centre, laboratory & provider of scientific services. It is a joint project between Department of Fisheries & Oceans, St. Andrews Biological Station & the Huntsman Marine Science Centre (HMSC).

***St Andrews:* Ross Memorial Museum / Musée mémorial Ross**
188 Montague St.
St Andrews, NB E5B 1J2
Tel: 506-529-5124; *Fax:* 506-529-5183
rossmuse@nb.aibn.com
www.rossmemorialmuseum.ca
Year Founded: 1824 Decorative arts museum in one of St. Andrews' finest early houses; open daily from Jun. - Sept.

***Saint-Jacques:* Antique Automobile Museum**
35 Main St.
Saint-Jacques, NB E7B 1V6
Tel: 506-737-2637
Open June-Sept.

***St Martins:* Quaco Museum & Library**
***Parent:* Quaco Historical & Library Society**
236 Main St.
St Martins, NB E5R 1B8
Tel: 506-833-4740; *Fax:* 506-833-2008
www.quaco.ca
Year Founded: 1978 Displays the history & heritage of the Quaco-St. Martins area with a specific focus on the shipbuilding heritage of the region; archives available for historical/genealogical research; the Carson Memorial Library, located behind the museum, is a volunteer-run public reading/lending library; gift shop. Museum & archives open June-Sept., other times by apppointment. Library is open Wednesdays & Saturdays throughout the year.
Jacqueline Bartlett, President, president@quaco.ca
Eric Bartlett, Manager, ericb@nb.aibn.com
Elizabeth Thibodeau, Librarian, 506-833-2553, librarian@quaco.ca

***St Stephen:* Charlotte County Museum Inc.**
443 Milltown Blvd.
St Stephen, NB E3L 1J9
Tel: 506-466-3295
www.town.ststephen.nb.ca
Year Founded: 1977 Exhibits on 3 floors of the 1864 James Murchie Home; collection includes china, including early Chinese porcelain dating to the 17th century; hand-crafted articles, quilts, samplers; costumes; early tools & furniture; theme rooms portray area from the late 18th - early 20th century. The museum has a satellite location at 127 Milltown Blvd., St Stephen, NB, which includes displays of lumbering & shipbuilding, past industries, 19th & 20th century gowns, kitchen artifacts, school room, & tool shed.

***St Stephen:* The Chocolate Museum**
73 Milltown Blvd.
St Stephen, NB E3L 1G5
Tel: 506-466-7848; *Fax:* 506-466-7701
chocolate.museum@nb.aibn.com
www.chocolatemuseum.ca
www.facebook.com/t hechocolatemuseum
Year Founded: 1999 History of local candy maker Ganong Bros. Limited

***Shippagan:* Societé historique Nicolas-Denys (SHND)**
218, boul J.D. Gauthier
Shippagan, NB E8S 1P6
Tél: 506-336-3461; *Téléc:* 506-336-3603
shnd@umoncton.ca
www.umoncton.ca/umcs-bibliotheque/node/6
www.facebook .com/187957724571999
Fondée en: 1969 Heures d'ouvertures et les différentes coordonnées comment nous joindre pour le centre de documentation: mardi au jeudi de 9 h 00 à 12 h et de 13 h à 16 h, mercredi soir de 19 à 21 h.
Philippe Basque, Président
Nathalie M. Lanteigne, Responsable

***St-Isidore:* St-Isidore Museum Inc. / Musée de Saint Isidore Inc.**
3942, boul des Fondateurs
St-Isidore, NB E8M 1C2
Tel: 506-358-6003
villasti@nb.aibn.com
Exhibits depict agricultural & forestry background of the region; open in July & Aug., Thu.-Sun.

***Sussex:* 8th Hussars Regimental Museum**
***Parent:* 8th Canadian Hussars Association**
#3, 66 Broad St.
Sussex, NB E4E 5S2
Tel: 506-433-5226
info.8thhussars@yahoo.ca
8chassociation.com/Museum.html
Other contact information: Alt. E-mail: hussarssussex@nb.aibn.com
The museum, located in the historical Sussex train station, houses 16 displays, including those about the Boer War, WWI & WWII.
Tom McLaughlan, President, 8th Canadian Hussars Association, 506-471-4251, mclaughlan.tj@forces.gc.ca
Borden McLellan, Curator, 506-832-4228, mclelbol@nb.sympatico.ca

***Sussex:* Agricultural Museum of New Brunswick**
28 Perry St.
Sussex, NB E4E 2N7
Tel: 506-433-6799
info@agriculturalmuseumofnb.com
www.agriculturalmuseumofnb.com
www.facebook.com/469958723016450
Year Founded: 1986 The museum houses agricultural equipment, military memorabilia, and furniture & housewares. Open mid-June - mid-Sept.

***Tabusintac:* Tabusintac Centennial Memorial Library & Museum**
4490 Rte. 11
Tabusintac, NB E9H 1J3
Tel: 506-779-1918
www.tabusintac.ca/library_museum.html
Other contact information: Alternate Phone: 506-779-8045
Houses historical artifacts & memorabilia from the Tabusintac area; also features a craft shop

***Tracadie-Sheila:* Musée Historique de Tracadie Inc.**
#399, 222, rue du Couvent
Tracadie-Sheila, NB E1X 1E1
Tél: 506-393-6366; *Téléc:* 506-395-6355
museehis@nb.sympatico.ca
www.musee-tracadie.com
Fondée en: 1968 Lèpre dans le 19ème siècle; aussi l'histoire de Tracadie, des objets datant de plusieurs siècles avant l'arrivée des colons blancs, des articles relatifs à la vie des Acadiens. L-V 9h-17h; Sa, D 12h-17h

***Welshpool:* Roosevelt Campobello International Park / Parc international Roosevelt de Campobello**
459 Rte. 774
Welshpool, NB E5E 1A4
Tel: 506-752-2922; *Fax:* 506-752-6000
Toll-Free: 877-851-6663
info@fdr.net
www.fdr.net
Social Media: www.youtube.com/user/RooseveltCampobello
twitter.com/FDRCampobello
www .facebook.com/Roosevelt.Campobello
The Roosevelt Campobello International Park, located on Campobello Island in New Brunswick's Bay of Fundy, features the 34-room summer residence of Franklin D. Roosevelt & his wife Eleanor. Guided tours are given of the home. The park also contains the Edmund S. Muskie Visitor Center, where visitors learn the story of the former president of the United States, through displays & a film. The Roosevelt Cottage & Visitor Centre are open from mid May to mid October. The park is open year-round, & is administered by a commission of six members & six alternates, with equal representation from both Canada & the United States.

***Woodstock:* Old Carleton County Court House**
***Parent:* Carleton County Historical Society**
c/o Carleton County Historical Society, 128 Connell St.
Woodstock, NB E7M 1L5
Tel: 506-328-9706
cchs@nb.aibn.com
www.cchs-nb.ca
Year Founded: 1986 The Carleton County Historical Society restored the Old County Court House which was built in 1833. The court house originally served as the County seat of justice & was also the meeting place for the first County Council in New Brunswick. Guided tours are available during the summer & by appointment at other times.
John Thompson, President

Newfoundland & Labrador

Provincial Museum

The Rooms
PO Box 1800 C, 9 Bonaventure Ave.
St. John's, NL A1C 5P9
Tel: 709-757-8000; *Fax:* 709-757-8017
information@therooms.ca
www.therooms.ca
Social Media:
www.youtube.com/channel/UC4Orp6_CWbIZuYUZVVi2i5g
twitter.com/TheRooms_NL
www.facebook.com/TheRoomsNL
Other contact information: Archives: 709-757-8030; Museum: 709-757-8020; Gallery: 709-757-8040
The Rooms consists of the Newfoundland & Labrador Provincial Archives, Art Gallery, & Museum. The Archives collects records of the Government of Newfoundland & Labrador, as well as records from private sources which have value to the history of the province. Permanent exhibits at the museum depict Newfoundland & Labrador's early people, as well as Fort Townsend, the home of British soldiers &, since 1870, the Royal Newfoundland Constabulary. One level of the museum is dedicated to the birds of Newfoundland & Labrador. The Rooms Provincial Art Gallery presents more than 7,000 historical & contemporary works.
Tom Foran, Chair, Board of Directors

Local Museums

***L'Anse Au Loup:* Labrador Straits Museum**
PO Box 281
L'Anse Au Loup, NL A0K 3L0
Tel: 709-927-5600
labstraitsmuseum@gmail.com
www.labradorstraitsmuseum.ca
Hunting & fishing collections, household communication & religious items

***Baie Verte:* Baie Verte Peninsula Miners' Museum**
319 Rte. 410
Baie Verte, NL A0K 1B0
Tel: 709-532-8090; *Fax:* 709-532-4166
baievertepeda@nf.aibn.com
Year Founded: 1975 The Miners' Museum presents a replica of life & work during the mining years (1860 - 1864 & 1901-1915) on the Baie Verte Peninsula.

***Bonavista:* Bonavista Historical Society Museum**
Building 2, Ryan Premises, PO Box 295
Bonavista, NL A0C 1B0
Tel: 709-468-2920; *Fax:* 709-468-2495
Year Founded: 1969 The Bonavista Historical Society Museum is situated in the restored turn-of-the-century Ryan Retail Store at the Ryan Premises National Historic Site. The collection reflects local life in the late 19th century in one of Newfoundland's inshore fishing communities. The musuem also holds a collection of medical artifacts from the early twentieth century. Bonavista Museum is open from mid-June to mid-October.

***Botwood:* Botwood Heritage Centre**
PO Box 490
Botwood, NL A0H 1E0
Tel: 709-257-4612; *Fax:* 709-257-3330
botwoodheritage@hotmail.com
town.botwood.nl.ca
The Botwood Heritage Centre depicts the time of the Beothuk, the European exploration era in the Exploits Valley, & the early railway & shipping period of Abitibi.

***Burin:* Burin Heritage House**
33 Seaview Dr.
Burin, NL A0E 1E0
Tel: 709-891-2355; *Fax:* 709-891-2358
burinheritagemuseums@nf.aibn.com
www.townofburin.com
The Burin Heritage House features artifacts related to the history of Burin, including the fishery & the tidal wave. The museum is open from mid May to the beginning of October.

***Carbonear:* Baccalieu Trail Heritage Corporation (BTHC)**
PO Box 249
Carbonear, NL A1Y 1B6
Tel: 709-596-1906; *Fax:* 709-596-2121
contact@baccalieudigs.ca
www.baccalieudigs.ca
Year Founded: 1993 The corporation preserves, protects, & promotes the heritage of the Baccalieu Trail Region, which consists of approximately seventy communities along 240 km of coastline on Newfoundland & Labrador's Avalon Peninsula.

***Carbonear:* Carbonear C.N. Railway Station**
PO Box 999, 223 Water St.
Carbonear, NL A1Y 1C5
Tel: 709-596-0714; *Fax:* 709-596-5021
www.carbonear.ca
The Carbonear Railway Station is one of Newfoundland & Labrador's Resgistered Heritage Structures. Built around 1917, the building exemplifies a station during the one hundred year era of the Newfoundland railroad. Operated by the Carbonear Heritage Society, the station contains railway artifacts, exhibits about the history of Carbonear, genealogical information, & a tourist information centre. The Carbonear C.N. Railway Station is open from June to September. Appointments may be arranged during the off season.

***Cow Head:* Dr. Henry N. Payne Community Museum**
Conservation & Heritage Inc., 143 Main St.
Cow Head, NL A0K 2A0
Tel: 709-243-2023
cowheadheritage@gmail.com
www.facebook.com/149833015034340
Restored theme home; artifacts tell story of Dr. Henry N. Payne & cultural heritage of area; gift shop. Located at the northern tip of Gros Morne National Park.

Cupids: **Cupids Legacy Centre**
PO Box 210, 368 Seaforest Dr.
Cupids, NL A0A 2B0
Tel: 709-528-1610
info@cupidslegacycentre.ca
www.cupidslegacycentre.ca
twitter.com/CupidsLegacy
www.facebook.com/22 6983024085013
Year Founded: 2010 Built to commemorate the 400th anniversary of the first English settlement in Canada. Open seasonally, seven days a week.
Linda Kane, Curator

Deer Lake: **Roy Whalen Heritage Museum**
44 Trans Canada Hwy.
Deer Lake, NL A8A 2E4
Tel: 709-635-4440; *Fax:* 709-635-5103
www.town.deerlake.nf.ca
www.facebook.com/Valley.Crafts.Roy.Whalen.Museum
Year Founded: 1988 The museum preserves the local history with displays related to logging, agriculture and the settlers' lives in the Humber Valley. Open May-Dec.

Durrell: **Durrell Museum & Crafts**
PO Box 83
Durrell, NL A0G 1Y0
Tel: 709-884-2780
Other contact information: Alternate Phone: 709-884-5537
Open end of May - end of Sept.; mounted polar bear exhibit & crafts
Lloyd Bulgin, President, lebulgin@hotmail.com

Ferryland: **Historic Ferryland Museum**
PO Box 7
Ferryland, NL A0A 2H0
Tel: 709-432-2155
Located in the old Courthouse; exhibits depicting community life & Ferryland's role in colonization of North America; open mid-June - Labour Day

Flatrock: **Flat Rock Museum**
c/o Town Council of Flatrock, 663 Windgap Rd.
Flatrock, NL A1K 1C7
Tel: 709-437-6312; *Fax:* 709-437-6311
www.townofflatrock.com/museum
Open July - Sept. or by appt.

Fogo: **Bleak House Museum**
#32, 36 North Shore Rd.
Fogo, NL A0G 2B0
Tel: 709-266-2487; *Fax:* 709-266-1323
recreation@townoffogoisland.ca
Other contact information: Alternative Phone: 709-266-2237
Year Founded: 1988 Bleak House was built around 1816 for the Slade family, who were involved in the Fogo Island fish trade. The home was restored & made into a museum. The home features items that belonged to owners of the home, plus artifacts that depict the history of Fogo. Bleak House Museum is open from July to September.

Forteau: **Point Amour Lighthouse Provincial Historic Site**
c/o Labrador Straits Historical Development Corporation, PO Box 112
Forteau, NL A0K 2P0
Tel: 709-927-5825; *Fax:* 709-656-3150
Toll-Free: 800-563-6353
lshdc@labradorstraits.net
www.pointamourlighthouse.ca
www.facebook.com/ProvincialHistoricSites.NL
Other contact information: Alt. Phone: 709-931-2013; Alt. URL: www.ourlabrador.ca
Consisting of several buildings, the Point Amour Light station dates back to the 1850s. The Provincial Historic Site in Newfoundland & Labrador has been restored, & now features displays that depict the maritime history of the Labrador Straits. An interpretive trail at the site takes visitors to the site of the HMS Raleigh & HMS Lily shipwrecks. The site is open from mid May to the beginning of October.
Bonnie Goudie, Executive Director
Kim Shipp, Contact, kimshipp@gov.nl.ca

Gander: **North Atlantic Aviation Museum**
Parent: **North Atlantic Aviation Museum Association**
135 Trans Canada Hwy.
Gander, NL A1V 1P6
Tel: 709-256-2923; *Fax:* 709-256-8561
info@northatlanticaviationmuseum.com
www.northatlanticaviationmuseum.com
twitter.com/NAAMGANDER
www.facebook.com/NAAMGander
Year Founded: 1986 The North Atlantic Aviation Museum depicts important aviation moments over the North Atlantic, from the war years to commercial flying. The focus is upon Gander's involvement in aviation history. The Museum features six aircraft.
Bob Briggs, President
Carl Squires, Vice-President
Jonathan Waterman, Secretary
Sandra Seaward, Executive Director

Grand Bank: **Provincial Seamen's Museum (PSM)**
Parent: **The Rooms**
PO Box 1109
Located at 54 Marine Dr., Grand Bank, NL
Grand Bank, NL A0E 1W0
Tel: 709-832-1484; *Fax:* 709-757-8023
psminfo@therooms.ca
Artifacts pertaining to the banks fishery

Grand Falls-Windsor: **Logger's Life Provincial Museum**
c/o Provincial Bldg., Cromer Ave.
Grand Falls-Windsor, NL A2A 1W9
Tel: 709-486-0492
mmpminfo@therooms.ca
www.therooms.ca/museum/loggers_life_museum.asp
Other contact information: Off-Season Phone: 709-757-8023
Logging exhibit is a replica of 1920s logging camp; displays tools & clothing representative of that era; located west of Grand Falls-Windsor on Trans Canada Hwy.

Grand Falls-Windsor: **Mary March Provincial Museum**
c/o Provincial Building, Cromer Ave.
Location: 24 St. Catherine St, Grand Falls-Windsor, NL
Grand Falls-Windsor, NL A2A 1W9
Tel: 709-292-4522
www.therooms.ca/mmpm
Year Founded: 1988 From the European name of one of the last Beothuks, the aboriginal people of the island of Newfoundland, the Mary March Museum traces the Aboriginal, European, natural & geological history of the Central Newfoundland Region. Open daily 9am-4:45pm, May-Oct. It is part of The Rooms Regional Museums network.

Happy Valley-Goose Bay: **Northern Lights Military Museum**
Northern Lights Bldg., 170 Hamilton River Rd.
Happy Valley-Goose Bay, NL A0P 1E0
Tel: 709-896-5939

Harbour Grace: **Conception Bay Museum**
PO Box 298
Harbour Grace, NL A0A 2M0
Tel: 709-596-5465; *Fax:* 709-596-5465
cbm@nf.aibn.com
Open June - Aug; off season by appt.

Hopedale: **Moravian Mission Museum**
Parent: **Agvituk Historical Society**
PO Box 12
Hopedale, NL A0P 1G0
Tel: 709-933-3777; *Fax:* 709-933-3746
Moravian Mission House; archaeology artifacts from 1500-2000 years ago; items related to Labrador Inuit; European medical supplies & furniture

Lewisporte: **By The Bay Museum & Craft Shop**
235 Main Rd.
Lewisporte, NL A0G 3A0
Tel: 709-535-1911
bythebayshop@bellaliant.com
www.facebook.com/lporteHeritageCentre
Year Founded: 1872 Exhibits at the Bye The Bay Museum show the history of Lewisporte & its surrounding region, including Beothuk artifacts, the shipbuilding & logging industries & World War I & World War II. Owned & operated by the Lewisporte Area Development Association, the museum is open from the end of May to the end of August.

Marystown: **Marystown Heritage Museum Corporation**
PO Box 688
Marystown, NL A0E 2M0
Tel: 709-279-1462
The museum exhibits include everyday articles from the town's historic past, from squid jiggers to priests. Open daily mid-June - Aug.; Jan.-May, Sept.-Dec. Mon.-Fri 9-5

Moreton's Harbour: **Moreton's Harbour Community Museum**
6A Main Rd.
Moreton's Harbour, NL A0G 3H0
Tel: 709-684-2353
Other contact information: Alt. Phone: 709-684-2351
Operated by the Moreton's Harbour Women's Institute, the Moreton's Harbour Community Museum is situated in a house which was built in 1916. The museum features various artifacts, including agricultural implements & equipment used during the inshore fishery. Archives include census records, diaries, & school minute books. The community museum is open from mid June to the beginning of September. Tours may be arranged during the off season.

Mount Pearl: **Admiralty House Communications Museum**
3 Centennial St.
Located at 365 Old Placentia Rd. Mount Pearl, NL
Mount Pearl, NL A1N 1G4
Tel: 709-748-1124
admiraltyhouse@mountpearl.ca
www.admiraltymuseum.ca
www.facebook.com/AdmiraltyHouse
The museum is housed inside a building that serves as a H.M. Wireless Station for the British Royal Navy during WWI. Exhibits focus on local hisotyr as well as wireless communication history.

Musgrave Harbour: **Fisherman's Museum**
PO Box 159
Musgrave Harbour, NL A0G 3J0
Tel: 709-655-2589; *Fax:* 709-655-2064
bantinghti@nf.aibn.com
www.musgraveharbour.com/museum.html
Year Founded: 1910 Ship models, engines, photographs, accounts of local shipwrecks. Open from the third week of June until labour day weekend.
Mitzi Abbott, Contact

Newtown: **Barbour Living Heritage Village**
PO Box 135
Newtown, NL A0G 3L0
Tel: 709-536-3220; *Fax:* 709-536-3150
barboursite@nf.aibn.com
www.barbour-site.com
www.facebook.com/34990249 8362983
An historic fishing village, featuring a schoolhouse, sealing interpretation centre, fisherman's stage, theatre, & art gallery. The historic Greenspond Court House is located nearby; the court house is owned by Cape Freels Heritage Trust Inc. and can be contacted at 709-536-3220.

North West River: **Labrador Heritage Museum**
Parent: **Labrador Heritage Society**
c/o Labrador Heritage Society, PO Box 99
North West River, NL A0P 1M0
Tel: 709-497-8858; *Fax:* 709-497-8228
info@labradorheritagemuseum.ca
www.labradorheritagemuseum.ca
Other contact information: Craft Shop Phone: 709-497-8282
Exhibit includes arifacts & infomation about the Hudson Bay Company store, trapping, exploration of Labrador & the International Grenfell Association in North West River

Old Perlican: **Howard House of Artifacts**
PO Box 100
Old Perlican, NL A0A 3G0
Tel: 709-587-2022
Located 3 miles from Old Perlican on Shore Line country road at Daniel's Cove; artifacts represent the 1890s & 1900 to 1945; collection of Newfoundland homemade furniture of the 1930s; open daily

Placentia: **O'Reilly House Museum**
Parent: **Placentia Area Historical Society**
c/o Placentia Area Historical Society, PO Box 233
Located at 48 Orcan Dr., Placentia, NL
Placentia, NL A0B 2Y0
Tel: 709-227-5568
www.placentiahistory.ca
Year Founded: 1989 Built in 1902 as a residence for magistrate, William O'Reilly, O'Reilly House is now a museum operated by the Placentia Area Historical Society. The Victorian home displays many items from Placemtia' past. The museum is open from the beginning of June to mid October.
Tom O'Keefe, President, 709-227-0322, tokeefe@personainternet.com

***Placentia Bay:* Castle Hill National Historic Site of Canada**
PO Box 10 Jerseyside
Off season address: PO Box 1268, St. John's, NL, A1C 5M9
Placentia Bay, NL A0B 2G0
Tel: 709-227-2401; *Fax:* 709-227-2452
castle.hill@pc.gc.ca
www.pc.gc.ca/eng/lhn-nhs/nl/castlehill/index.aspx
17th & 18th century remains of French & English fortifications; picnic areas & hiking trails; special events & programming; Visitor Centre with gift shop.

***Placentia Bay:* St. Bartholomew's Church**
c/o Mt. Arlington Hts.
Placentia Bay, NL A0B 2J0
Tel: 709-228-2583
Church built in 1930 by parishoners

***Port au Choix:* Port au Choix National Historic Park Site**
PO Box 140
Port au Choix, NL A0K 4C0
Tel: 709-861-3522; *Fax:* 709-861-3827
pac-historic-site@pc.gc.ca
www.pc.gc.ca/lhn-nhs/nl/portauchoix/index.asp x
Commemorates area's rich aboriginal history dating back 5400 years; visitors can view artifacts & exhibits on the four prehistoric cultures that occupied area; walking trails, archaeological sites, lighthouse & fossils

***Port au Port:* Our Lady of Mercy Museum**
PO Box 330
Located at 103 Main St., Port-au-Port West, NL
Port au Port, NL A0N 1T0
Tel: 709-648-2632
Former rectory now holds artifacts from the Bay St. George area; open May - Sept.

***Port aux Basques:* Gulf Museum**
c/o South West Coast Historical Society, PO Box 1299
Located at 118 Main St., Port Aux Basques, NL
Port aux Basques, NL A0M 1C0
Tel: 709-695-7604
Nautical items & the astrolabe (dated 1628): an instrument used by early navigators to determine latitude. The Society operates a refurbished train site facility consisting of a railway station & nine rail cars.

***Port aux Basques:* Port aux Basques Railway Heritage Centre**
PO Box 1299
Port aux Basques, NL A0M 1C0
Tel: 709-695-7560
www.portauxbasques.ca/tourism/railway_heritage_center.php
Other contact information: Alt. Phone: 709-695-7604
The Port aux Basques Railway Heritage Centre depicts the significance of the railway to Newfoundland's history. In the late 1890s, Port aux Basques became the western terminus of the Newfoundland Railway, where the railway schedule connected with steamers. Open from June to October, the heritage centre features the train station & various rail cars.

***Port de Grave:* Fishermen's Museum, Porter House & School**
Port de Grave, NL A0A 3J0
Tel: 709-786-3912
hermanporter@personainternet.com
Year Founded: 1979 Museum contains artifacts depicting life & times of Newfoundland fishermen; Porter House is a traditional fisherman's house restored to early 1900s; Hibbs' Hole Schoolhouse, a restored one-room school

***Port Union:* Port Union Museum**
PO Box 98
Port Union, NL A0C 2J0
Tel: 709-469-2728
Other contact information: Alternate Phone: 709-469-2159
Includes estate of the late Sir Wm. F. Coaker, founder of Port Union & Sir Wm. F. Coaker Memorial Cemetery; open mid June - Sept.; small admission fees apply

***Pouch Cove:* Pouch Cove Museum**
Town Hall, PO Box 59, 660 Main Rd.
Pouch Cove, NL A0A 3L0
Tel: 709-335-2848; *Fax:* 709-335-2840
pouchcove.ca
Open year round
Barbara Tilley, Town Manager, info@pouchcove.ca

***Red Bay:* Red Bay National Historic Site of Canada**
PO Box 103
Off season mailing address: Red Bay National Historic Site, Gros Morne National Park, PO Box 130, Rocky Harbor, NL A0K 4N0
Red Bay, NL A0K 4K0
Tel: 709-920-2142; *Fax:* 709-920-2144
redbay.info@pc.gc.ca
www.pc.gc.ca/lhn-nhs/nl/redbay/natcul/basque.aspx
During the 16th century, Basque merchants & ship owners from France & Spain planned seasonal expeditions to the south coast of Labrador & the north shore of Québec to hunt whales. The port they used most often was called Butus, which is now Red Bay. Red Bay is now a National Historic Site with a Visitor Centre. The Visitor Centre features discoveries from a marine archaeology project in the Red Bay area. Visitors learn about Labrador's 16th century history, through displays of original artifacts recovered from archaeological excavations, plus reproductions. The site is open from June to October.

***Rocky Harbour:* Gros Morne National Park Visitor Reception Centre**
PO Box 130
Rocky Harbour, NL A0K 4N0
Tel: 709-458-2417; *Fax:* 709-458-2059
grosmorner.info@pc.gc.ca
www.pc.gc.ca/eng/pn-np/nl/grosmorne/index.aspx
Other contact information: TTY: 709-772-4564
Gros Morne was declared a UNSESCO World Heritage site in 1987. GM discovery centre looks at the forces of nature. The centre looks at geology, plant & animal life, marine story & human history. It is located on the south side of Bonne Bay, one hour from Deer Airport & the Trans Canada Highway.

***St Anthony:* Grenfell Historic Properties**
PO Box 93
Located at 4 Maravel Rd., St. Anthony, NL
St Anthony, NL A0K 4S0
Tel: 709-454-4010; *Fax:* 709-454-4047
info@grenfell-properties.com
www.grenfell-properties.com
Year Founded: 1998 Dr. Wilfred Grenfell's former home restored circa 1920. Seasonal Hours: M-F 9:00-6:00pm; Off-Season Hours: M-F 9:00-5:00

***St. John's:* Anglican Cathedral of St. John the Baptist Museum & Archives**
PO Box 23112
St. John's, NL A1B 4J9
Tel: 709-726-5677; *Fax:* 709-726-2053
angcathedral@nf.aibn.com
www.stjohnsanglicancathedral.org
Pictures, artifacts, records, documents & books related to the history of the Cathedral & Parish; established in 1699, the parish is the oldest non-Roman Catholic religious foundation in Canada; Cathedral building is one of the finest examples of English neo-Gothic architecture in North America. The Church is located at 16 Church Hill, St. John's, NL.

***St. John's:* Beothuk Interpretation Centre Provincial Historic Site**
Provincial Historic Sites, Dept. of Tourism, Culture & Recreation, PO Box 8700
St. John's, NL A1B 4J6
Tel: 709-729-0592; *Fax:* 709-729-7989
Toll-Free: 800-563-6353
info@seethesites.ca
www.seethesites.ca/the-sites/beoth uk-interpretation-centre.aspx
Year Founded: 1981 The Beothuk site at Boyd's Cove dates back to the late 17th & early 18th centuries. The site features the archaeological remains of Beothuk life, including their house pits. Visitors can learn about these extinct people at the interpretive centre, where several artifacts from the site are displayed & on the interpretive trail. The centre is open from mid June to mid October.
Kim Shipp, Historic Sites Officer

***St. John's:* Cape Bonavista Lighthouse Provincial Historic Site**
Provincial Historic Sites, Dept. of Tourism, Culture & Recreation, PO Box 8700
St. John's, NL A1B 4J6
Tel: 709-729-0592; *Fax:* 709-729-7989
Toll-Free: 800-563-6353
info@seethesites.ca
www.seethesites.ca/the-sites/cape- bonavista-lighthouse.aspx
Year Founded: 1970 The Cape Bonavista Lighthouse was built in 1843. The site features guided tours & a walking trail. The lighthouse is open from mid May to the beginning of October.
Kim Shipp, Historic Sites Officer

***St. John's:* Cape Spear National Historic Site of Canada / Lieu historique national du Canada du Cap-Spear**
PO Box 1268
St. John's, NL A1C 5M9
Tel: 709-772-5367; *Fax:* 709-772-6302
cape.spear@pc.gc.ca
www.pc.gc.ca/eng/lhn-nhs/nl/spear/index.aspx
Located at most easterly point in North America, the Cape Spear lighthouse is the oldest in Newfoundland & Labrador. The lighthouse has been restored to reflect 1839. Visitors can view displays about the history of lighthouses & lightkeeping. The grounds are open year round, & the lighthouse, Visitor Interpretation Centre & the Heritage Gift Shop are open from mid May to mid October.

***St. John's:* Commissariat House Provincial Historic Site**
Provincial Historic Sites, Dept. of Tourism, Culture & Recreation, PO Box 8700
St. John's, NL A1B 4J6
Tel: 709-729-0592; *Fax:* 709-729-7989
Toll-Free: 800-563-6353
info@seethesites.ca
www.seethesites.ca/the-sites/the-c ommissariat.aspx
Year Founded: 1818 This building, one of the oldest buildings in Newfoundland, was built especially for the Commissariat to supply the city's garrison and has been restored back to the 1830's era complete with traditionally dressed maids and clerks to help answer questions.
Kim Shipp, Historic Sites Officer

***St. John's:* Heart's Content Cable Station Provincial Historic Site, Heart's Content NF**
Provincial Historic Sites, Dept. of Tourism, Culture & Recreation, PO Box 8700
St. John's, NL A1B 4J6
Tel: 709-729-0592; *Fax:* 709-729-7989
Toll-Free: 800-563-6353
info@seethesites.ca
www.seethesites.ca/the-sites/heart 's-content-cable-station.aspx
www.facebook.com/ProvincialHistoricSites.N L
Year Founded: 1974 Located on Hwy. 80, this cable station marks the first successful transatlantic telegraph cable landing in 1866. Displays focus on the history of cable, with equipment and instrumentation on exhibit. Open May-Oct., 10:00-5:30 daily.
Kim Shipp, Historic Sites Officer

***St. John's:* Hiscock House Provincial Historic Site**
Provincial Historic Sites, Dept. of Tourism, Culture & Recreation, PO Box 8700
St. John's, NL A1B 4J6
Tel: 709-729-0592; *Fax:* 709-729-7989
Toll-Free: 800-563-6353
info@seethesites.ca
www.seethesites.ca/the-sites/trini ty-historic-sites/hiscock-house.aspx
www.facebook.com/ProvincialHistoric Sites.NL
Year Founded: 1982 Owned solely by the Hiscock family until it was reborn as a museum, the house has been restored to its 1910 style. Located on Church St., it is open late spring to early autumn, 10:00-5:30 daily.
Kim Shipp, Historic Sites Officer

***St. John's:* James J. O'Mara Pharmacy Museum**
***Parent:* Newfoundland & Labrador Pharmacy Board**
Apothecary Hall, 488 Water St.
St. John's, NL A1E 1B3
Tel: 709-753-5877; *Fax:* 709-753-8615
inforx@nlpb.ca
www.nlpb.ca/museum.html
Drug store c. 1895; open end-June - end-Aug. or by appt.

***St. John's:* Mockbeggar Plantation Provincial Historic Site**
Provincial Historic Sites, Dept. of Tourism, Culture & Recreation, PO Box 8700
St. John's, NL A1B 4J6
Tel: 709-729-0592; *Fax:* 709-729-7989
Toll-Free: 800-563-6353
info@seethesites.ca
www.seethesites.ca/the-sites/mockb eggar-plantation.aspx
www.facebook.com/ProvincialHistoricSites.NL
Year Founded: 1990 Built in the 1870s, the museum was the home of Newfoundland statesman, Senator F. Gordon Bradley & is restored to that 1939 period. Other buildings include a carpenter shop, fish store & cod-liver oil factory from the 18 century. The museum is located on Roper St., Bonavista, NL, A0C 1B0.
Kim Shipp, Historic Sites Officer

***St. John's:* Quidi Vidi Battery Provincial Historic Site**
PO Box 8700
St. John's, NL A1B 4J6
Tel: 709-729-2977
rnchs.ca/tattoo/qvb2.html
The Quidi Vidi Battery was built by the French in the 1700s. It was later taken over by the British, who rebuilt the guardhouse. The site is now restored to the era of 1812, when it was used to ward off a possible American attack. The Quidi Vidi Battery is located on Cuckhold's Cove Road in Quidi Vidi Village, Newfoundland & Labrador. Tours are available from guides dressed in period costumes, from late June until September.

***St. John's:* Royal Newfoundland Constabulary Historical Society Archives & Museum**
PO Box 7247
Located on Parade St., in the RNC Headquarters at Fort Townshend.
St. John's, NL A1E 3Y4
Tel: 709-729-8000; *Fax:* 709-729-8214
www.rnchs.ca
Collects & preserves early police records; 48+ audio tapes of oral history interviews, as well as 10,000+ photographs; researchers may contact the office of the Chief of Police, indicating their area of interest, to arrange for access to the archives; photocopying available upon request, subjet to copyright protocols; open year round

***St. John's:* The Royal St. John's Regatta Museum**
PO Box 214
St. John's, NL A1C 5J2
Tel: 709-576-8921; *Fax:* 709-576-3315
general@stjohnsregatta.com
www.stjohnsregatta.org
Social Media: www.youtube.com/user/regattacommittee
twitter.com/StJohnsRegatta
www.f acebook.com/royalstjohnsregatta
The long history of rowing competition in St. John's, dating back to the early 1800s, is depicted at the Regatta Museum, through photographs, trophies, & other memorabilia. Please contact the Regatta Museum to arrange an appointment to visit.
Paul Rogers, President
Chris Neary, Vice-President

***St. John's:* St. Thomas' Church Museum**
8 Military Rd.
St. John's, NL A1C 2C4
Tel: 709-576-6632; *Fax:* 709-737-0472
office@st-thomaschurch.com
www.st-thomaschurch.com
Museum located in the basement; church c. 1836

***St. John's:* Signal Hill National Historic Site of Canada / Lieu historique national du Canada de Signal Hill**
PO Box 1268
St. John's, NL A1C 5M9
Tel: 709-772-5367; *Fax:* 709-772-6302
signal.hill@pc.gc.ca
www.pc.gc.ca/lhn-nhs/nl/signalhill/index.aspx
In 1901, Signal Hill was the reception point of the first transatlantic wireless signal. From the 18th century to World War II, Signal Hill was also the site of harbour defence for St. John's, Newfoundland. Today, visitors can tour the Visitor Interpretation Centre & visit Cabot Tower to view the Marconi exhibit. The site is open year-round.

***St Lawrence:* St. Lawrence Miner's Memorial Museum**
PO Box 1992
St Lawrence, NL A0E 2V0
Tel: 709-873-2222; *Fax:* 709-873-3352
Open daily in summer

***St Lunaire-Griquet:* L'Anse aux Meadows National Historic Site**
PO Box 70
St Lunaire-Griquet, NL A0K 2X0
Tel: 709-623-2608; *Fax:* 709-623-2028
viking.lam@pc.gc.ca
www.pc.gc.ca/eng/lhn-nhs/nl/meadows/index.aspx
UNESCO World Heritage Site depicting first authenticated European presence in North America; the focal point are the reconstructions of three Norse buildings of this archaeological site. There are also exhibits the Viking lifestyle, artifacts, & the archaeological discovery of the site. Visitor centre open mid-June - early Oct.

***Salvage:* Salvage Fishermens' Museum**
General Delivery
Salvage, NL A0G 3X0
Tel: 709-677-2414
The museum building, a home once owned by the Lane family, dates from 1860 & is the oldest dwelling in the area; collection of fishing & domestic artifacts relates to the history & cultural life of Salvage, from the late 19th c. to the present; open daily, mid-June to Labour Day; wheelchair accessible; archive; gift shop

***Springdale:* Harvey Grant Heritage Centre**
50 Main St.
Springdale, NL A0J 1T0
Tel: 709-637-3439; *Fax:* 709-673-4969
Artifacts from 1940s, 50s & 60s, related to life of Harvey Grant; open July & Aug.

***Torbay:* Torbay Museum**
1288 Torbay Rd.
Torbay, NL A1K 1K4
Tel: 709-437-6532
www.torbay.ca/torbaymuseum
www.facebook.com/TorbayMuseum
Year Founded: 1988 Over 500 artifacts dating from early 1800s; the collection is dedicated to produce a display of historical artifacts for public viewing, and the preservation and promotion of the heritage of Torbay. Open M-F 9:00-4:00, Tu, Th 6:30-8:30 in summer; Tu, Th 6:30-8:30 off season; otherwise by appt.
Contessa Small, Curator, csmall@torbay.ca

***Trepassey:* Trepassey Area Museum**
PO Box 63
Trepassey, NL A0A 4B0
Tel: 709-436-2044
Open July & Aug.

***Trinity:* Cooperage**
***Parent:* Trinity Historical Society**
PO Box 8
Trinity, NL A0C 2S0
Tel: 709-464-3599; *Fax:* 709-464-3599
info@trinityhistoricalsociety.com
www.trinityhistoricalsociety.com/coope rage.htm
www.facebook.com/193216850915
Year Founded: 2008 Functional living history museum where a working cooper demonstrates the 17th century craft; built in 2007 from an artists rendering of an actual cooperage from that era

***Trinity:* Court House, Gaol & General Building**
***Parent:* Trinity Historical Society**
PO Box 8
Trinity, NL A0C 2S0
Tel: 709-464-3599; *Fax:* 709-464-3599
info@trinityhistoricalsociety.com
www.trinityhistoricalsociety.com/court _house_gaol.htm
www.facebook.com/193216850915
Year Founded: 2010 The building is c.1903, & originally housed a court house, jail, customs house, magistrate's office, post & telegraph office & residence.

***Trinity:* Fort Point Military Site**
***Parent:* Trinity Historical Society**
PO Box 8
Trinity, NL A0C 2S0
Tel: 709-464-3599; *Fax:* 709-464-3599
info@trinityhistoricalsociety.com
www.trinityhistoricalsociety.com/fort_ point.htm
www.facebook.com/193216850915
Year Founded: 2010 The site details the history of the fort, c.1746, which was captured by the French in 1762, then rebuilt by the British in 1780, during the American Revolution. Other local history is also explored, such as the salt cod trade, lighthouse keepers & shipwrecks. The site is open daily from mid-May to mid-October.

***Trinity:* Green Family Forge**
***Parent:* Trinity Historical Society**
PO Box 8
Trinity, NL A0C 2S0
Tel: 709-464-3599; *Fax:* 709-464-3599
info@trinityhistoricalsociety.com
www.trinityhistoricalsociety.com/green _family_forge.htm
www.facebook.com/193216850915
Year Founded: 1991 Smithy c.1895-1900; still functional today; open daily mid-May to mid-Oct.

***Trinity:* Lester-Garland Premises Provincial Historic Site**
***Parent:* Trinity Historical Society**
PO Box 8
Trinity, NL A0C 2S0
Tel: 709-464-3599; *Fax:* 709-464-3599
info@trinityhistoricalsociety.com
www.trinityhistoricalsociety.com/trini ty_museum.htm
www.facebook.com/193216850915
Mercantile bldg. including counting house restored to 1820 & retail shop restored to 1910; located on West St., Trinity following Rtes. 230 or 239; open daily June - Sept.

***Trinity:* Trinity Interpretation Centre**
PO Box 6
Trinity, NL A0C 2S0
Tel: 709-464-2042; *Fax:* 709-464-2349
Toll-Free: 800-563-6353
trinity@nf.aibn.com
www.townoftrinity.com
Exhibits on the commercial & social history of Trinity; open June - Sept.
Gerry Osmond, Manager, Provincial Historic Sites, 709-729-7212, gerryosmond@gov.nl.ca
Joan Kane, Site Supervisor

***Trinity:* Trinity Museum**
***Parent:* Trinity Historical Society**
PO Box 8
Trinity, NL A0C 2S0
Tel: 709-464-3599; *Fax:* 709-464-3599
info@trinityhistoricalsociety.com
www.trinityhistoricalsociety.com
www .facebook.com/193216850915
Year Founded: 1967 The artifacts of Trinity Museum are displayed in a salt box style house, which was built in the 1880s. The collection reflects the history of Trinity, & includes fishing, boat building, commercial, & domestic items. The site also features a fire engine shed, which displays an 1811 fire pump. The museum is open from mid June to mid October, & by appointment at other times during the year.

***Twillingate:* Twillingate Museum & Craft Shop**
PO Box 369
Twillingate, NL A0G 4M0
Tel: 709-884-2825
info@tmacs.ca
www.tmacs.ca
Year Founded: 1973 Twillingate Museum is located in the former Anglican Church Rectory, which was built around 1900. Furnishings in the museum reflect the Victorian era. Examples of exhibits include Inuit, Dorset, & Beothuk First Nations artifacts. Archives include photographs, family histories, & cemetery data. The museum is open from May to October.
Linda Blondin, Contact

***Wesleyville:* Bonavista North Museum & Gallery**
PO Box 257
Wesleyville, NL A0G 4R0
Tel: 709-536-2110; *Fax:* 709-536-3039
museum@nf.aibn.com
www.bonavistanorth.blogspot.com
twitter.com/Bonavis taNorth
www.facebook.com/368789463136218
The Bonavista North Museum & Gallery contains photographs, artifacts, & artwork from the local area. The museum is open daily from the beginning of July to the end of August. Appointments can be arranged during the off season.

Northwest Territories

Territorial Museum

Prince of Wales Northern Heritage Centre (PWNHC)
c/o Government of NWT, PO Box 1320
Yellowknife, NT X1A 2L9
Tel: 867-873-7551; *Fax:* 867-873-0205
pwnhc@gov.nt.ca
www.pwnhc.ca
twitter.com/nrthrnheritage
www.facebook .com/pwnhc
Year Founded: 1979 Located on the shores of Frame Lake, the Prince of Wales Northern Heritage Centre is open year-round. Visitors to the centre will discover various exhibits about the people, places, & natural history of the Northwest Territories.
Sarah Carr-Locke, Director, 867-873-7551, sarah_carr-locke@gov.nt.ca
Joanne Bird, Curator of Collections, 867-873-7668, joanne_bird@gov.nt.ca
Rosalie Scott, Conservator, 867-873-7664, rosalie_scott@gov.nt.ca
Ian Moir, Territorial Archivist, 867-873-7177, ian_moir@gov.nt.ca

Local Museums

***Colville Lake:* Colville Lake Museum & Gallery**
PO Box 54
Colville Lake, NT X0E 1L0
Tel: 867-709-2500
Museum housing ethnographic artifacts, art gallery & archives; discovery centre; guided tours; gift shop; part of Colville Lake Lodge, a log cabin facility in a Dene community

***Fort Good Hope:* Dene Museum & Archives**
General Delivery
Fort Good Hope, NT X0E 0H0
Tel: 403-598-2331
The museum's collection includes photographs of area elders & residents, oral history tapes, written materials (including transcripts of tapes), & printed material.

***Fort Smith:* Northern Life Museum & Cultural Centre (NLMCC)**
PO Box 420
Fort Smith, NT X0E 0P0
Tel: 867-872-2859; *Fax:* 867-872-5808
admin@NLMCC.ca
www.nlmcc.ca
twitter.com/NorthernLifeMus
www.facebook .com/NLMCC
Year Founded: 1972 Collection, preservation & presentation of NWT culture & history; open year round
Mathieu Doucet, Executive Director

***Hay River:* Hay River Heritage Centre**
39 Lakeshore Dr.
Location: 101 St., Hay River, NT X0E 0R9
Hay River, NT X0E 0R9
Tel: 867-874-3872
The museum has collections in human history, natural sciences, the arts, & an archive of photos, maps, prints & drawings, & manuscripts.

***Holman:* Holman Museum**
PO Box 162
Holman, NT X0E 0S0
Tel: 867-396-3804; *Fax:* 867-396-3054
The museum's collection features Inuit artifacts from the Holman area.

***Norman Wells:* Norman Wells Historical Centre**
***Parent:* Norman Wells Historical Society**
PO Box 145
Norman Wells, NT X0E 0V0
Tel: 867-587-2415; *Fax:* 867-587-2469
canol.trail@theedge.nw.ca
www.normanwellsmuseum.com
Year Founded: 1989 Dene cultural artifacts; geological history; WWI & Canol Project interpretation; Great Bear Lake & MacKenzie River explorers; local archives
Sarah Colbeck, Manager/Curator

Nova Scotia

Provincial Museums

Fisheries Museum of the Atlantic
Lunenburg Waterfront, PO Box 1363, 68 Bluenose Dr.
Lunenburg, NS B0J 2C0
Tel: 902-634-4794; *Fax:* 902-634-8990
Toll-Free: 866-579-4909
fma@gov.ns.ca
fisheriesmuseum.novascotia.ca
twitter. com/FisheriesMuseum
www.facebook.com/FisheriesMuseumoftheAtlantic
Part of the Nova Scotia Museum; features historic buildings with 3 floors of exhibits & activities: Millenium Aquarium; Bluenose Memorabilia; Fishermen's Memorial Room; August Gales 1926-1927; Bank Fishery Gallery; Rum Running; life in fishing communities; Hall of Inshore Fisheries; fisherman's store; Marine Engine Room, whales, boat shop; schooner Theresa E. Connor; side trawler Cape Sable; part of the Nova Scotia Museum. Summer hours: M - Su 9:30 - 5:30. Winter hours: M - F 9:30 - 4:00.
Angela Saunders, General Manager

Maritime Museum of the Atlantic / Musée Maritime d'Atlantique
1675 Lower Water St.
Halifax, NS B3J 1S3
Tel: 902-429-7490
maritimemuseum.novascotia.ca
twitter.com/ns_mma
www.facebook.com/maritimemuseum
Year Founded: 1982 Marine history branch of the Nova Scotia Museum; on waterfront; marine artifacts, memorabilia from the Titanic, Halifax explosion exhibit, restored ship chandlery, extensive small craft collection; library & gift shop; Vessel CSS Acadia at museum wharf; open year-round
Kim Reinhardt, General Manager, 902-424-6440, reinhaka@gov.ns.ca
Richard MacMichael, Coordinator, Visitor Services & Interpretive Programming, 902-424-8897, MACMICRS@gov.ns.ca

Nova Scotia Museum (NSM)
NS Communities, Culture & Heritage, 1747 Summer St.
Halifax, NS B3H 3A6
Tel: 902-424-7353; *Fax:* 902-424-0560
museum.novascotia.ca
twitter.com/ns_museum
www.facebook.com/novascotia museum
The Nova Scotia Museum family includes 27 museums across the province, including Museum of Natural History, Halifax; Maritime Museum of the Atlantic, Halifax; Haliburton House, Windsor; Uniacke Estate Museum Park, Mount Uniacke; Prescott House, Starr's Point; Lawrence House, Maitland; Balmoral Grist Mill, Balmoral; Sutherland Steam Mill, Denmark; Fisherman's Life Museum, Jeddore; & Shand House, Windsor.
Rhonda Walker, Executive Director

Local Museums

***Amherst:* Cumberland County Museum & Archives**
150 Church St.
Amherst, NS B4H 3C4
Tel: 902-667-2561
www.cumberlandcountymuseum.com
Year Founded: 1973 Exhibits & archives on the natural, social & industrial heritage of Cumberland County; located in the 1838 heritage home of Robert Barry Dickey, a Father of Confederation; the archives houses genealogical & other material; fine art collection by County artists; well maintained gardens surround the museum. Open year round.
Natasha Richard, Manager/Curator

***Amherst:* Nova Scotia Highlanders Regimental Museum**
Col. James Layton Ralson Armoury, 36 Acadia St.
Amherst, NS B4H 3L6
Tel: 902-661-6797; *Fax:* 902-667-6551
nshmuseum@eastlink.ca
nshighlanders.fav.cc
Exhibits military artifacts such as uniforms, badges & vehicles.
C.W.O. (Ret'd) Ray Coulson, Curator C.D.

***Annapolis Royal:* Fort Anne National Historic Site / Lieu historique national du Fort-Anne**
PO Box 9
Annapolis Royal, NS B0S 1A0
Tel: 902-532-2397; *Fax:* 902-532-2232
information@pc.gc.ca
www.pc.gc.ca/eng/lhn-nhs/ns/fortanne/index.aspx
Other contact information: Off-Season Phone: 902-532-2321
Year Founded: 1917 French & English period fortifications, 1629-1854; exhibits; open daily 9:00 - 5:30, July and August. Hours are Tu - Sa 9:00 - 5:30 during June and September.

***Annapolis Royal:* Fort Edward National Historic Site / Lieu historique national du Fort Édouard**
PO Box 9
Annapolis Royal, NS B0S 1A0
Tel: 902-532-2321; *Fax:* 902-532-2232
information@pc.gc.ca
www.pc.gc.ca/lhn-nhs/ns/edward/index.aspx
twitter .com/ParksCanada_NS
Built in 1750 by Major Charles Lawrence, this Fort protected the route from Halifax to the Annapolis Valley & remains one of Nova Scotia's oldest buildings. The site is located at 67 Fort Edward St., Windsor, NS B0N 2T0.

***Annapolis Royal:* North Hills Museum**
***Parent:* Annapolis Heritage Society**
PO Box 503
Located at 5065 Granville Rd., Granville Ferry, NS
Annapolis Royal, NS B0S 1A1
Tel: 902-532-2168
northhills.novascotia.ca
Late 18th-century farmhouse which serves as the setting for the collection of Georgian furniture, ceramics, glass, silver & paintings of former owner Robert Patterson. Part of the Nova Scotia Museum.

***Annapolis Royal:* O'Dell House Museum**
***Parent:* Annapolis Heritage Society**
PO Box 503, 136 Saint George St.
Annapolis Royal, NS B0S 1A0
Tel: 902-532-7754; *Fax:* 902-532-0700
historic@ns.aliantzinc.ca
www.annapolisheritagesociety.com/museums/odell .html
Social Media: www.annapolisroyalheritage.blogspot.com
twitter.com/odellmuseum
The museum is housed in a stagecoach inn & tavern from around 1869. O'Dell House is the former home of Nova Scotia Pony Express rider, Corey O'Dell & his family. Among the displays are items from Annapolis Royal's ship-building & sea-faring history. The Annapolis Heritage Society's Genealogy Centre's Archives & Collections Centre is also located at O'Dell House Museum. The Centre contains local histories, vital statistics for Annapolis & Digby counties, deeds, & church, cemetery, & probate records.
Jane DeWolfe, Chair, Annapolis Heritage Society

***Annapolis Royal:* Port-Royal National Historic Site of Canada / Lieu historique national de Port-Royal**
PO Box 9
Location: 53 Historic Lane, Port Royal, NS B0S 1K0
Annapolis Royal, NS B0S 1A0
Tel: 902-532-2898; *Fax:* 902-532-2232
information@pc.gc.ca
www.pc.gc.ca/lhn-nhs/ns/portroyal/index.aspx
Other contact information: Off-season Phone: 902-532-2321 (mid-Oct. to mid-May)
The national historic site on the coast of Nova Scotia is a reconstruction of early 17th-century buildings. The buildings represent a French colony from the era. The site features costumed interpreters & demonstrations to reflect life in one of the earliest settlements in North America.

***Annapolis Royal:* Sinclair Inn Museum**
***Parent:* Annapolis Heritage Society**
230 St. George St.
Annapolis Royal, NS B0S 1A0
Tel: 902-532-0996
www.annapolisheritagesociety.com/museums/sinclair.html
Other contact information: Off-season Phone: 902-532-7754
Built in the early 1700s, this National Historic Site is the earliest surviving Acadian building in Canada.

***Antigonish:* Antigonish Heritage Museum**
20 East Main St.
Antigonish, NS B2G 2E9
Tel: 902-863-6160
antheritage@parl.ns.ca
www.parl.ns.ca/aheritage
www.facebook.com/AntigonishHeritageMuseum
Open year round
Jocelyn Gillis, Curator

***Arichat:* Lenoir Forge Museum**
PO Box 223
Located at 708 Veteran's Memorial Dr., Arichat, NS
Arichat, NS B0E 1A0
Tel: 902-226-9364; *Fax:* 902-226-1919
Community museum; local artifacts; local artisan blacksmith

***Baddeck:* Alexander Graham Bell National Historic Site of Canada / Lieu historique national Alexander-Graham-Bell du Canada**
PO Box 159, 559 Chebucto Street
Baddeck, NS B0E 1B0
Tel: 902-295-2069; *Fax:* 902-295-3496
information@pc.gc.ca
www.pc.gc.ca/lhn-nhs/ns/grahambell/index.aspx
twi tter.com/ParksCanada_NS
www.facebook.com/AGBNHS
Presents Dr. Bell's life & work, with emphasis on his accomplishments in Baddeck; open year round; Nov. 1 - Apr. 30 site visits by arrangement. The site is located on Chebucto St. (Rte 205), on the eastern edge of Baddeck.

***Baddeck:* Canso Islands National Historic Site / Iles-Canso Lieux historiques**
PO Box 159
Location: 1465 Union Street, Canso, NS
Baddeck, NS B0E 1B0
Tel: 902-295-2069; *Fax:* 902-295-3496
information@pc.gc.ca
www.pc.gc.ca/eng/lhn-nhs/ns/canso/index.aspx
www. facebook.com/cansoislands
Other contact information: Summer Phone: 902-366-3136
The Canso Islands were a fishing base for the French during the 16th & 17th centuries. The British used the fishing port during the first half of the 18th century. The Islands were the scene of

several battles between the French & English & the Mi'kmaq. In 1744, the Canso settlement was destroyed by the French. The visitor centre & interpretive trail are open from June 1st to September 15th.

Baddeck: Marconi National Historic Site of Canada / Lieu historique national Marconi du Canada
c/o Alexander Graham Bell National Historic Site, PO Box 159
Location: 15 Timmerman St., Table Head, Glace Bay, NS
Baddeck, NS B0E 1B0
Tel: 902-295-2069; *Fax:* 902-295-3496
information@pc.gc.ca
www.pc.gc.ca/lhn-nhs/ns/marconi.aspx
www.facebook .com/MarconiNHS
Other contact information: Summer Phone: 902-842-2530
The site marks where Guglielmo Marconi initiated the age of global communications in 1902 by transmitting the first wireless message across the Atlantic Ocean. Visitors can see the Wireless Hall of Fame and walk to the original transmission station. Open June 1 - Sept.

Barrington: Barrington Woolen Mill Museum
***Parent:* Cape Sable Historical Society**
2368 Hwy. 3
Barrington, NS B0W 1E0
Tel: 902-637-2185
woolenmill.novascotia.ca
Year Founded: 1968 A preserved wool mill from the 1800s; part of the Nova Scotia Museum; open June-Sept.

Barrington: Cape Sable Historical Society Centre
PO Box 67
Located at the Old Courthouse, 2401 Hwy. 3, Barrington, NS
Barrington, NS B0W 1E0
Tel: 902-637-2185
barmuseumcomplex@eastlink.ca
www.capesablehistoricalsociety.com
Year Founded: 1937 The Cape Sable Historical Society illustrates the history of Shelburne & Yarmouth Counties by collecting historical documents, genealogical records, & other items, & preserving historical sites. The Cape Sable Historical Society Centre is open year round.

Barrington: Old Meeting House Museum
***Parent:* Cape Sable Historical Society**
2408 Hwy. 3
Barrington, NS B0W 1E0
Tel: 902-637-2185
museum.gov.ns.ca/omh
A preserved New England-style meeting house c.1765; part of the Nova Scotia Museum; open June-Sept.

Bedford: Atlantic Canada Aviation Museum (ACAM) / Musée D'aviation des provinces Atlantique
***See:* Location: 20 Sky Blvd, Goffs, NS B2T 1K3**
PO Box 44006, 1658 Bedford Hwy.
Bedford, NS B4A 3X5
Tel: 902-873-3773
info@atlanticcanadaaviation.com
www.atlanticcanadaaviation.com
Social Media: atlanticcanadaaviationmuseum.wordpress.com
www.facebook.com/ACAMMuseum
Other contact information: Off season phone: 902-446-7606
Year Founded: 1977 The Atlantic Canada Aviation Museum preserves the aviation heritage of Atlantic Canada. The aircraft collection includes the Bell 47-J-2 Ranger Helicopter, the CF-5A Freedom Fighter, a Harvard Mk II, & a CF-104 Starfighter. The museum is open from mid-May to mid-October. At other times, tours can be arranged.
Michael White, Public Affairs Officer, 902-446-7606

Bedford: Scott Manor House
***Parent:* Fort Sackville Foundation**
15 Fort Sackville Rd.
Bedford, NS B4A 2G6
Tel: 902-832-2336
scott.manor@ns.sympatico.ca
www.scottmanorhouse.ca
The house dates from 1749 & was still a private residence until 1992. The former Fort Sackville is located nearby, & the Manor House contains artifacts excavated from that site.

Berwick: Apple Capital Interpretive Centre
***Parent:* Apple Capital Museum Society**
PO Box 730, 173 Commercial St.
Berwick, NS B0P 1E0
Tel: 902-538-9229; *Fax:* 902-538-9229
www.acmuseum.ednet.ns.ca
Other contact information: Off-season: 902-538-4016
Artifacts & information relating to the apple industry of Berwick & District

Bridgetown: James House Museum
PO Box 645, 12 Queen St.
Bridgetown, NS B0S 1C0
Tel: 902-665-4530
www.jameshousemuseum.com
Social Media: www.instagram.com/bridgetownahs
twitter.com/bridgetownahs
www.facebook.com/jameshousemuseum1835
Other contact information: Genealogy contact: 902-825-1287
Year Founded: 1979 James House was built in 1835 by Richard James, a member of the British Army who served in England & India. The house was donated to the Bridgetown & Area Historical Society. It became a Provincial Heritage Building, & now operates as the museum for the town of Bridgetown. James House features the Memorial Military Museum, which is sponsored by the Royal Canadian Legion, Branch 33. The museum is open from June to August daily or by appointment from September to May.

Bridgewater: DesBrisay Museum & Exhibition Centre
c/o 60 Pleasant St.
Located at 130 Jubilee Rd., Bridgewater, NS
Bridgewater, NS B4V 3X9
Tel: 902-543-4033; *Fax:* 902-543-4713
museum@bridgewater.ca
www.desbrisaymuseum.ca
Social Media: www.youtube.com/desbrisaybridgewater
www.facebook.com/pages/DesBrisay-Museum/190907454254694
Year Founded: 1902 Home of famed porcupine quill-decorated cradle; parkland & trails; open year round.
Barbara Thompson, Director, bthompson@bridgewater.ca
Linda Bedford, Curator, lbedford@bridgewater.ca

Bridgewater: Wile Carding Mill Museum
c/o DesBrisay Museum, 60 Pleasant St.
Located at 242 Victoria Rd., Bridgewater, NS
Bridgewater, NS B4V 3X9
Tel: 902-543-8233; *Fax:* 902-543-4713
wilecardingmill@bridgewater.ca
cardingmill.novascotia.ca
www.facebook. com/447062668657408
Year Founded: 1974 Last surviving plant of a 19th-century water-powered industrial park; part of Nova Scotia Museum & DesBrisay Museum; open June 1 - Sept. 30.

Canso: Whitman House Museum & Tourist Bureau
***Parent:* Canso Historical Society**
c/o Canso Historical Society, PO Box 128, 1297 Union St.
Canso, NS B0H 1H0
Tel: 902-366-2170; *Fax:* 902-366-3093
tgis@atcon.com
whitmania.com/whitmanhousemuseum.htm
Year Founded: 1975 Whitman House was built in 1885. The first resident was C.H. Whitman, a Baptist minister. The operation of the Whitman House Museum is now overseen by the Canso Historical Society. Exhibits at the Whitman House Museum depict the history of the town of Canso & eastern Guysborough County, & Canso Harbour. The museum is open from June 1st to September 30th. At other times of the year, appointments may be arranged.
Martha Kavanaugh, Curator, 902-366-2170
Joseph Walsh, Society Chairperson, 902-366-2329

Centreville: Charles Macdonald Concrete House Museum
19 Saxon St.
Centreville, NS B0P 1J0
Tel: 902-678-3177
info@concretehouse.ca
www.concretehouse.ca
House originally belonging to Nova Scotian artist Charles Macdonald, now converted into a museum, art gallery & sculpture garden

Cherry Brook: Black Cultural Centre for Nova Scotia (BCC)
10 Cherry Brook Rd
Cherry Brook, NS B2Z 1A8
Tel: 902-434-6223; *Fax:* 902-434-2306
Toll-Free: 800-465-0767
contact@bccns.com
www.bccns.com
Social Media: www.youtube.com/user/bccnsvideo
twitter.com/BCC_NS
www.facebook.com/18 8265867860941
Year Founded: 1983 Programs at the cultural education centre have include guided tours, music, plays, workshops, & lectures. Winter hours: by appointment. Summer hours: Tu - F 10:00 - 4:00, Sa - M 12:00 - 3:00.

Russell Grosse, Executive Director
Rielle Williams, Cultural Tour Developer

Chester: Chester Train Station
***Parent:* Chester Municipal Heritage Society**
PO Box 628, 133 Central St.
Chester, NS B0J 1J0
Tel: 902-275-3842
www.chesterbound.com/heritage.htm
www.facebook.com/180126828677505
The site contains a visitor information centre, Train Station Gallery, Forman Hawboldt exhibit & Explore Oak Island display. Oak Island is an island on the south shore of Nova Scotia featuring the so-called "Money Pit," which has been the site of treasure hunting for over 200 years.
Carol Nauss, Chair, Chester Municipal Heritage Society
Danny Hennigar, Contact, Oak Island

Chester: Lordly Estate Municipal Museum
***Parent:* Chester Municipal Heritage Society**
PO Box 628, 133 Central St.
Chester, NS B0J 1J0
Tel: 902-275-3842
chester-municipal-heritage-society.ca
Social Media: www.youtube.com/user/lordlymuseum
www.facebook.com/180126828677505
Other contact information: After-hours Phone: 902-275-3826
The Georgian house is c.1806, & was the first municipal building of Municipality of the District of Chester. Chester Municipal Heritage Society also operates the Chester Train Station.
Roberta Harrington, Contact

Church Point: Musée Église Sainte-Marie Museum
PO Box 28, 1713 Hwy. 1
Church Point, NS B0W 1M0
Tel: 902-769-2378; *Fax:* 902-769-0048
www.museeeglisesaintemariemuseum.ca
Largest wooden church in North America; open June - Oct.

Clark's Harbour: Archelaus Smith Museum & Historical Society
PO Box 190
Located at 915 Hwy 330, Cape Sable Island, NS
Clark's Harbour, NS B0W 1P0
Tel: 902-745-2642
www.archelaus.org
Portrays the history of Cape Sable Island including fishing techniques & gear, the Cape Island boat, shipwrecks, lives of sea captains, items from old kitchens, paintings by local artists, geneological & other historical records. The collection illustrates the background & growth of a pre-Loyalist fishing community
Blanche O'Connell, President,
blancherossoconnell@hotmail.com

Clementsport: Old St. Edward's Anglican Loyalist Church Museum
PO Box 171
Located at 34 Old Post Rd., Clementsport, NS
Clementsport, NS B0S 1E0
Tel: 902-638-8554
Original Loyalist, Old St. Edward's Anglican Church & Cemetery consecrated 1797; managed by volunteers.

Cole Harbour: Cole Harbour Heritage Farm Museum
471 Poplar Dr.
Cole Harbour, NS B2W 4L2
Tel: 902-434-0222
farm.museum@ns.aliantzinc.ca
www.coleharbourfarmmuseum.ca
www.facebook.com/ColeHarbourHeritageFarmMus eum
Operated by the Cole Harbour Rural Heritage Society; open daily from May 15 - Oct. 15, or by appt.
Elizabeth Corser, Volunteer

Dartmouth: Dartmouth Heritage Museum
***Parent:* Dartmouth Heritage Museum Society**
26 Newcastle St.
Dartmouth, NS B2Y 3M5
Tel: 902-464-2300; *Fax:* 902-464-8210
www.dartmouthheritagemuseum.ns.ca
www.facebook.com/205574426126756
Local history museum focusing on social history & arts & crafts
Bonnie Elliott, Executive Director, 902-464-2916,
elliottb@bellaliant.com
Crystal Martin, Curator, 902-464-2916, martinc@bellaliant.com

***Debert:* Debert Military Museum**
***Parent:* Debert Military History Society (DMHS)**
PO Box 154
Located at 35 Acadia Ave., Debert, NS
Debert, NS B0M 1G0
Tel: 902-662-2860
debert.museum@ns.sympatico.ca
debertmilitaryhistorysociety.weebly.com
Military exhibits
Susan Taylor, President, 902-662-3875

***Digby:* Admiral Digby Museum**
PO Box 1644, 95 Montague Row
Digby, NS B0V 1A0
Tel: 902-245-6322
admuseum@ns.sympatico.ca
admiraldigbymuseum.ca
Other contact information: Geneology E-mail: adgen1@ns.aliantzinc.ca
Museum is housed in a Georgian-style home & is named for Rear Admiral Robert Digby. On display are period rooms, furnishings & artifacts relating to the history of Digby; costumes; Marine Room with charts, ship models, & navigational equipment; photographs; online gift shop; online archives which include family registers & other items of interest to genealogical & historical researchers. Open mid-June - mid-Oct.; two days a week in winter
Gail Hersey, President

***Dingwall:* North Highlands Community Museum & Culture Centre**
29243 Cabot Trail
Located at 29263 The Cabot Trail, Cape North, Cape Breton, NS, B0C 1G0
Dingwall, NS B0C 1G0
Tel: 902-383-2579
nhco2579@gmail.com
www.northhighlandsmuseum.ca
Social Media: www.youtube.com/user/nhcmuseum
twitter.com/NHCmuseum
www.facebook.com/ northhighlandscommunitymuseum
The history & culture of northern Cape Breton Island is celebrated at the North Highlands Community Museum & Culture Centre, through artifacts & documents. The collection includes maritime artifacts, such as shipwreck booty, schoolroom materials, doctor's instruments, & farming tools.
Ron Nickel, Co-Chair
Ken Murray, Co-Chair
Meghan Dudley, Manager

***East Lake Ainslie:* MacDonald House Museum**
***Parent:* Lake Ainslie Historical Society**
3458 Hwy. 395
East Lake Ainslie, NS B0E 3M0
Tel: 902-258-3317
lahistorical@seasidehighspeed.com
www.seasidehighspeed.com/~p.maclean
The site contains the MacDonald House Museum, Glenmore School & Display Barn

***Englishtown:* Great Hall of The Clans, Highland Pioneers Museum**
***Parent:* The Gaelic College**
PO Box 80, 51779 Cabot Trail
Englishtown, NS B0C 1H0
Tel: 902-295-3411; *Fax:* 902-295-2912
info@gaeliccollege.edu
www.gaeliccollege.edu
Social Media: www.youtube.com/user/gaeliccollege
twitter.com/GaelicCollege
www.faceb ook.com/gaeliccollege
Open daily June - Sept.

***Glace Bay:* Cape Breton Miners' Museum**
PO Box 310, 17 Museum St.
Glace Bay, NS B1A 5T8
Tel: 902-849-4522
www.minersmuseum.com
twitter.com/CBMinersMuseum
www.facebook.com/CapeBretonMinersMuseumGB
The Cape Breton Miners' Museum tells the story of the area's history of coal mining. Visitors may tour the Ocean Deeps Colliery, which is a coal mine situated beneath the museum building. Exhibits include coal mining equipment. Research inquiries will be responded to by museum staff. The museum also features the Men of the Deeps Theatre.

***Glace Bay:* Glace Bay Heritage Museum (GBHM)**
***Parent:* Glace Bay Heritage Museum Society**
14 McKeen St.
Glace Bay, NS B1A 5B9
Tel: 902-842-5345
gbhms@seaside.ns.ca
home.seaside.ns.ca/~gbhms/info.html
Located in Glace Bay's Old Town Hall; local history; open Fall, Winter & Spring Tues., Thurs. & Sat.; July & Aug. Tues.-Sat.; closed Jan. & Feb.

***Grand Pre:* Grand-Pré National Historic Site of Canada**
2205 Grand-Pré Rd.
Grand Pre, NS B0P 1M0
Tel: 902-542-3631
info@visitgrandpre.ca
www.grand-pre.com
www.facebook.com/DestinationGrandPre
Year Founded: 1997 Bilingual guides interpret history of the Acadians; open daily May 1 - Oct. 30; entrance fee
Victor Tétrault, Executive Director

***Greenwood:* Greenwood Military Aviation Museum (GMAM)**
PO Box 786
Greenwood, NS B0P 1N0
Tel: 902-765-1494; *Fax:* 902-765-1261
dndwingmuseum@bellaliant.com
gmam.ca
twitter.com/gmamuseum
www.faceb ook.com/GMAM.CA
Year Founded: 1995 Recording the history of RAF/RCAF/CF station 1942 to present
Robert Johnson, General Manager, 902-765-1492, Fax: 902-765-1261, robert.johnson9@forces.gc.ca
Bryan Nelson, Curator, 902-765-1492, Fax: 902-765-1261, dndwingmuseum@bellaliant.com

***Guysborough:* Old Court House Museum & Information Centre**
***Parent:* Guysborough Historical Society**
c/o Guysborough Historical Society, PO Box 232
Location: 106 Church St., Guysborough, NS, B0H 1N0
Guysborough, NS B0H 1N0
Tel: 902-533-4008
guysborough.historical@ns.sympatico.ca
www.guysborough historicalsociety.ca
Open June - Oct.
Sandra Grant, Curator

***Halifax:* Africville National Historic Site**
***Parent:* Africville Genealogy Society**
Halifax, NS
www.africville.ca
www.facebook.com/africville
Accessible year round
Irvine Carvery, President, Africville Genealogy Society, irvine@africville.ca

***Halifax:* Army Museum**
Cavalier Bldg., Halifax Citadel National Historic Site, PO Box 9080 A
Halifax, NS B3K 5M7
Tel: 902-422-5979; *Fax:* 902-426-4228
armymuseum@ns.aliantzinc.ca
www.pc.gc.ca/lhn-nhs/ns/halifax/visit/visit1 1.aspx
Year Founded: 1953 The Army Museum preserves & promotes the military heritage of Atlantic Canada. Displays, including uniforms, decorations, weapons, & firearms, are related to the British, Canadian Regular Force, & Militia. The museum is open from May to Oct.

***Halifax:* Fisherman's Life Museum**
Jeddore, Oyster Pond, 58 Navy Pool Loop
Halifax, NS B0J 1W0
Tel: 902-889-2053
museum.gov.ns.ca/flm
The home used to belong to a fishing family, c.1900; part of the Nova Scotia Museum; open daily June 1 - Oct. 15
Martha Monk, Site Manager, monkma@gov.ns.ca

***Halifax:* Halifax Citadel National Historic Site of Canada**
PO Box 9080 A
Halifax, NS B3K 5M7
Tel: 902-426-5080; *Fax:* 902-426-4228
halifax.citadel@pc.gc.ca
www.pc.gc.ca/eng/lhn-nhs/ns/halifax/index.aspx
twitter.com/ParksCanada_NS
www.facebook.com/ParksCanada
The Citadel was completed in 1856 & was the fourth in a series of British forts on the site. Now the Citadel serves as a national landmark commemorating Halifax's role as a key naval station in the British Empire. The historic site features a living history program with the 78th Highlanders & the precision of the Royal Artillery.

***Halifax:* HMCS Sackville**
PO Box 99000 Forces
Halifax, NS B3K 5X5
Tel: 902-429-2132; *Fax:* 902-427-1346
canadasnavalmemorial.ca
Social Media: vimeo.com/user7544880
twitter.com/HMCSSACKVILLE1
www.facebook.com/254372034574664
Other contact information: Winter Phone: 902-427-2837
Year Founded: 1985 Canada's Naval Memorial; WWII corvette museum; open summer, downtown Halifax, open winter, HMCS Dockyard
Commodore (Ret'd) Bruce Belliveau, Chair, chair@canadasnavalmemorial.ca
LCdr. (Ret'd) Jim Reddy, Director/Commanding Officer, co@canadasnavalmemorial.ca
Doug Thomas, Executive Director, execdir@canadasnavalmemorial.ca

***Halifax:* The Khyber Centre for the Arts / Le Khybre**
***Parent:* Khyber Arts Society**
1588 Barrington St.
Halifax, NS B3J 1Z6
Tel: 902-422-9668
info@khyber.ca
www.khyber.ca
twitter.com/KhyberArts
www.facebook.com/95203450869
Year Founded: 1995 Apart from art exhibitions, the Khyber offers concerts, an educational program for kids, lectures, & fund-raising events
Daniel Joyce, Artistic Director, director@khyber.ca

***Halifax:* Maritime Command Museum / Musée du Commandement Maritime**
Admiralty House, PO Box 99000 Forces
Located at the Canadian Forces Base Halifax (Stadacona) on Gottingen St. in Halifax
Halifax, NS B3K 5X5
Tel: 902-721-8250; *Fax:* 902-721-8541
marcommuseum@forces.gc.ca
psphalifax.ca/marcommuseum
Year Founded: 1974 Of the Dept. of National Defence's 55 museums, this is the largest. Housed within 30 rooms of Admiralty House, a Georgian mansion, are displays representing facets of the Canadian Military. The collection consists of a research library, uniforms, model ships, medals, badges, ships' bells and other memorabilia associated with naval life. Open year round

***Halifax:* Museum of Natural History (MNH)**
1747 Summer St.
Halifax, NS B3H 3A6
Tel: 902-424-7353; *Fax:* 902-424-0747
museum.gov.ns.ca/mnhnew
twitter.com/MNH_Naturalists
www.facebook.com/m nhnovascotia
Other contact information: Collections, Fax: 902-424-0560
Part of the Nova Scotia Museum, the Museum of Natural history features galleries on archeology, geology, mammals, aquatic life & more. It also has a collection of live animals native to Nova Scotia, including 90-year-old Gus the Tortoise, who originally comes from Florida.
Calum Ewing, Director, Nova Scotia Museum, 902-424-7715
John Kemp, Manager, Museum of Natural History, 902-424-6515
Jeff Gray, Curator, Marketing & Communications, 902-424-6511, grayjr@gov.ns.ca

***Halifax:* Nova Scotia Sport Hall of Fame (NSSHF)**
#446, 1800 Argyle St.
Halifax, NS B3J 3N8
Tel: 902-421-1266; *Fax:* 902-425-1148
sporthalloffame@eastlink.ca
www.novascotiasporthalloffame.com
Social Media: www.linkedin.com/company/nova-scotia-sport-hall-of-fame
twitter.com/NSSH F
www.facebook.com/116064731766960
The Hall of Fame honours Nova Scotians who have made an impact on sports during the past 100 years. Inductees are addeed to the Hall of Fame each year, during The Hall of Fame Induction Night.
Bill Robinson, Chief Executive Officer, bill@nsshf.com

Shane Mailman, Manager, Programs & Facility, shane@nsshf.com
Karolyn Sevcik, Manager, Administration & Special Events, karolyn@nsshf.com

Halifax: Prince of Wales Tower National Historic Site of Canada
c/o Halifax Citadel National Historic Site, PO Box 9080 A
Halifax, NS B3K 5M7
Tel: 902-426-5080; *Fax:* 902-426-4228
halifax.citadel@pc.gc.ca
www.pc.gc.ca/lhn-nhs/ns/prince/index.aspx
The Prince of Wales Tower was built in 1796 & 1797. Its purpose was to protect the British from French attack. Over 200 years later, visitors will discover exhibits which show the tower's history. The Tower is open from the beginning of July to the end of August.

Halifax: Thomas McCulloch Museum
Biology Dept., Life Science Centre, Dalhousie University, 1355 Oxford St.
Halifax, NS B3H 4J1
Tel: 902-494-3515; *Fax:* 902-494-3736
Year Founded: 1883 Collection of mounted birds, artifacts, Lorenzen ceramic mushrooms, shells & insects; marine & freshwater aquaria; occasional temporary exhibits; open weekdays; free admission

Halifax: York Redoubt National Historic Site of Canada
c/o Halifax Citadel National Historic Site, PO Box 9080 A
Halifax, NS B3K 5M7
Tel: 902-426-5080; *Fax:* 902-426-4228
halifax.citadel@pc.gc.ca
www.pc.gc.ca/lhn-nhs/ns/york/index.aspx
York Redoubt was established in 1793 to defend the Halifax Harbour. Today, it is a National Historic Site of Canada, which is part of the Halifax Defence Complex. The site is open year-round.

Hants County: East Hants Historical Museum
6971, Rte. 215, Lower Selma
P.O. Box 121, Maitland, NS, B0N 1T0
Hants County, NS B0N 1C0
Tel: 902-261-2293
hantshistorical@gmail.com
ehhs.weebly.com
www.facebook.com/241534932553607
Year Founded: 1981 Small museum containing historical Nova Scotian artifacts with local connections, historical documents, military records & cemetary records
Nancy Doane, Committee Co-Chair, East Hants Historical Society, 902-632-2504, f.wallace@ns.sympatico.ca
Doug Lynch, Committee Co-Chair, 902-261-2293, dglynch8@gmail.com
Olive Terris, Treasurer

Hantsport: Churchill House & Marine Memorial Room
c/o Hantsport & Area Historical Society, PO Box 525
Location: 30 William St., Hantsport, NS B0P 1P0
Hantsport, NS B0P 1P0
Tel: 902-684-3461
hantsportareahistoricalsociety@gmail.com
nsgna.ednet.ns.ca/hantsport/Chu rchillHouse.html
Located at 6 Main St., Hantsport; open daily July - Sept., or by appt.; classic Victorian architecture; documents local shipbuilding history

La Have: Fort Point Museum
Parent: Lunenburg County Historical Society
c/o Lunenburg County Historical Society, PO Box 99
La Have, NS B0R 1C0
Tel: 902-688-1632
lchsftpt@gmail.com
www.fortpointmuseum.com
Social Media: fortpointmuseum.wordpress.com
twitter.com/fortpointmuseum
www.facebook .com/fort.point.5
Year Founded: 1974 On National Historic Site of Fort Ste. Marie de Grâce, 1632

La Have: LaHave Islands Marine Museum
PO Box 69
Located at 100 LaHave Islands Rd., LaHave, NS
La Have, NS B0R 1C0
www.lahaveislandsmarinemuseum.ca
Historical treasures from a community that derived its life & livelihood from the sea
Douglas Berrigan, President
Kathy Sullivan, Curator

Inverness: Inverness Miners Museum
Parent: Inverness Historical Society
PO Box 598
Located at 62 Lower Railway St., Inverness, NS
Inverness, NS B0E 1N0
Tel: 902-258-3291
www.inverness-ns.ca/inverness-miners-museum.html
Exhibits work that illustrates mining history.
Terry MacDonald, Curator, 902-258-2877

Iona: Highland Village Museum / An Clachan Gàidhealach
4119 Hwy. 223
Iona, NS B2C 1A3
Tel: 902-725-2272; *Fax:* 902-725-2227
Toll-Free: 866-442-3542
highlandvillage@gov.ns.ca
highlandvillage.novascotia.c a
twitter.com/highlandv
www.facebook.com/highlandvillagemusuem
Year Founded: 1959 The museum's mission is to collect & preserve the Gaelic heritage of Nova Scotia, with a focus on advancing the language. Included on site are: interpretation centre & museum, carding mill, 1880-1900 frame house, schoolhouse, forge, country store, barn, frame house (1830-1875), log cabin, stone (black) house, outdoor performance centre. There is also an extensive database of genealogical information. The museum is open June - Oct., 9:30-5:30 daily. Part of the Nova Scotia Museum.
Rodney Chaisson, Director, rodney.chaisson@novascotia.ca

Kentville: Blair House Museum
c/o N.S. Fruit Growers' Association, Kentville Agricultural Centre, 32 Main St.
Kentville, NS B4N 1J5
Tel: 902-678-1093; *Fax:* 902-678-1567
www.nsapples.com/museumb.htm
Year Founded: 1981 The Blair House Museum was opened by the Nova Scotia Fruit Growers' Association. The purpose of the museum is the preservation & presentation of the history of the apple growing industry. The Agriculture Canada wing of the museum displays past & present research conducted at the station. The museum is located in a 1911 building, which was the residence of the research station's first superintendent, Dr. William Saxby Blair.
Dela Erith, Executive Director, Nova Scotia Fruit Growers' Association, derith@nsapples.com
Marjo Balknap, Services Coordinator, mbelknap@nsapples.com
Teresa Rooney, Bookkeeper, trooney@nsapples.com

Kentville: Kings County Museum
Parent: Kings Historical Society
37 Cornwalllis St.
Kentville, NS B4N 2E2
Tel: 902-678-6237; *Fax:* 902-678-2764
museum@okcm.ca
www.okcm.ca
www.facebook.com/kingscountymuseum
Year Founded: 1980 Cultural & natural history of Kings County; Parks Canada commemorative exhibit to the New England Planters; genealogy & community history archives
Bria Stokesbury, Curator, curator@okcm.ca

Lake Charlotte: Memory Lane Heritage Village
Parent: Lake Charlotte Area Heritage Society
5435 Clam Harbour Rd.
Lake Charlotte, NS B0J 1Y0
Tel: 902-845-1937 *Toll-Free:* 877-287-0697
info@heritagevillage.ca
heritagevillage.ca
twitter.com/MemoryLane_News
www.facebook.com/heritagevillage
Living history village including 16 buildings, meant to show visitors what life in rural Nova Scotia during the 1940s would have been like
Thea Wilson-Hammond, Executive Director, admin@heritagevillage.ca

Liverpool: Hank Snow Home Town Museum
PO Box 1419, 17 Hank Snow Dr.
Liverpool, NS B0T 1K0
Tel: 902-354-4675; *Fax:* 902-354-5199
Toll-Free: 888-450-5525
info@hanksnow.com
www.hanksnow.com
twitter.com/HankS nowMuseum
www.facebook.com/198142203553851
Year Founded: 1996 A tribute to Hank Snow, legendary country/folk singer from "down east," the displays include a plethora of photos and memorabilia, from his guitar strings to his iconic toupées to his yellow 1947 Cadillac. The centre also houses the Nova Scotia Country Music Hall of Fame.
Kelly Inglis, Manager, 902-354-4675, info@hanksnow.com

Liverpool: Milton Blacksmith Shop Museum
PO Box 10
Liverpool, NS B0T 1K0
Tel: 902-354-5663
Managed by the Milton Heritage Society, the museum is a 1903 smithy, complete with forge, ox sling & original workbenches, as well as a wide array of tools of the trade; also large display of photographs of historical Milton, NS

Liverpool: Perkins House Museum
PO Box 1078
105 Main St., Liverpool, NS
Liverpool, NS B0T 1K0
Tel: 902-354-4058
perkinshouse.novascotia.ca
Connecticut style cottage built by merchant & diarist Simeon Perkins in 1766; Part of the Nova Scotia Museum; open June - Oct. 15

Liverpool: Queens County Museum
PO Box 1078, 109 Main St.
Liverpool, NS B0T 1K0
Tel: 902-354-4058; *Fax:* 902-354-2050
www.queenscountymuseum.com
www.facebook.com/205294966183248
Year Founded: 1980 The Queens County Museum depicts the cultural history of Nova Scotia's Queens County. The south shore of the province has a strong history related to the Mi'kmaq culture, fishing, & the forest. Programs are available for schools & the public.
Linda Rafuse, Director, rafusela@gov.ns.ca

Lockeport: Little School Museum
PO Box 189
Located at 29 & 37 Locke St., Lockeport, NS
Lockeport, NS B0T 1L0
Tel: 902-656-2850; *Fax:* 902-656-2935
townoflockeport@ns.sympatico.ca
www.lockeport.ns.ca
Replica of a former school room & a marine room; historical artifacts of local area

Louisbourg: Fortress of Louisbourg National Historic Site / Forteresse-de-Louisbourg, Lieu historique national
259 Park Service Rd.
Louisbourg, NS B1C 2L2
Tel: 902-733-3552; *Fax:* 902-733-2362
louisbourg.info@pc.gc.ca
www.pc.gc.ca/eng/lhn-nhs/ns/louisbourg/index.as px
twitter.com/ParksCanada_NS
www.facebook.com/FortressOfLouisbourgNHS

Louisbourg: Sydney & Louisburg Railway Museum
7330 Main St.
Louisbourg, NS B1C 1P5
Tel: 902-733-2720; *Fax:* 902-733-2214
Year Founded: 1972 Exhibits include railroad artifacts, models, photographs & other documentation; paintings; rolling stock, model railroad, souvenirs; open June 1 - Oct. 15; tourist information centre

Lower Sackville: Fultz House Museum
Parent: Fultz Corner Restoration Society
PO Box 124, 33 Sackville Dr.
Lower Sackville, NS B4C 2S8
Tel: 902-865-3794; *Fax:* 902-865-6940
fultz.house@ns.sympatico.ca
www.fultzhouse.ca
www.facebook.com/7782627 6228
Year Founded: 1982 1860s home which belonged to the Fultz family of Sackville, NS; contains many artifacts & photographs from the Sackville area; blacksmith shop & cooperage shop from 1800s

Lower Wedgeport: Wedgeport Sport Tuna Fishing Museum & Interpretive Centre / Musée de la pêche sportive au thon et Centre d'interprétati
Parent: L'Association du musée de Wedgeport
PO Box 488
Lower Wedgeport, NS B0W 2B0
Tel: 902-663-4345; *Fax:* 902-663-2075
www.wedgeporttunamuseum.com
Year Founded: 1996 The museum preserves artifacts, photos, literature & archives from Wedgeport's tuna sport-fishing history.
Clinton Saulnier, President

***Lower West Pubnico:* Le Village historique acadien de la Nouvelle-Écosse / Historic Acadian Village of Nova Scotia**
CP 70
Lower West Pubnico, NS B0W 2C0
Tél: 902-762-2530; *Téléc:* 902-762-2543
Ligne sans frais: 888-381-8999
villagehistorique@ns.aliantzinc.ca
levillage.novascotia.ca
Fondée en: 1999 Un village historique vivant dédié à la préservation et mettre en valeur la façon de vie des Acadiens d'autrefois; partie de la musée de la Nouvelle-Écosse; ouvert juin à octobre.
Roger W. d'Entremont, Directeur général, roger@ns.aliantzinc.ca

***Lunenburg:* Knaut-Rhuland House**
***Parent:* Lunenburg Heritage Society**
PO Box 674, 125 Pelham St.
Lunenburg, NS B0J 2C0
Tel: 902-634-3498
lunenburgheritagesociety@hotmail.com
lunenburgheritage society.ca/museum
twitter.com/lunenburghs
www.facebook.com/lunenburg.h eritage.9
Living history museum depicting the early history of Lunenburg; designated Canadian National Historic Site, & Heritage Property of both Nova Scotia & the Town of Lunenburg

***Mabou:* An Drochaid**
***Parent:* Mabou Gaelic & Historical Society**
PO Box 175
Located at 11513 Hwy 19, Malbou, NS
Mabou, NS B0E 1X0
Tel: 902-945-2311
Housed in an old general store; a centre for arts & crafts, genealogical & historical records, & research.
Rodney MacDonald, Contact

***Mahone Bay:* Mahone Bay Settlers Museum**
PO Box 583
Located at 578 Main St., Mahone Bay, NS, B0J 2E0
Mahone Bay, NS B0J 2E0
Tel: 902-624-6263
info@settlersmuseum.ns.ca
www.settlersmuseum.ns.ca
twitter.com/SettlersMuseum
www.facebook.com/6 0254904029
Year Founded: 1979 Community Museum which provides vistors with a local history of the area; Open June to Sept.
Michael J. O'Connor, Chair
Haylee Alderson, Museum Manager
Wilma Stewart-White, Volunteer Curator

***Main-à-Dieu:* Coastal Discovery Centre**
2886 Louis-Main-à-Dieu Rd.
Main-à-Dieu, NS B1C 1X5
Tel: 902-733-2258; *Fax:* 902-733-2653
reception@coastaldiscoverycentre.ca
coastaldiscoverycentre.ca
The Coastal Discovery Centre contains the Main-à-Dieu Fishermen's Museum, as well as a number of nature areas, including a boardwalk, Main-à-Dieu beach & Moque's Head Trail.

***Maitland:* Lawrence House Museum**
***Parent:* Nova Scotia Museum**
8660 Hwy. 215, RR #1
Maitland, NS B0N 1T0
Tel: 902-261-2628
lawrencehouse.novascotia.ca
c.1865 home of William D. Lawrence, shipwright; part of the Nova Scotia Museum; open June 1 - Oct. 4

***Malagash:* Malagash Salt Miners' Museum**
1926 North Shore Rd.
Malagash, NS B0K 1E0
Tel: 902-257-2407
malagash_museum@live.ca
Details the history of Canada's first salt mine, which operated from 1918-1959.
Tammy Rafuse, Curator, 902-257-2142, tammy.rafuse@ns.sympatico.ca

***Maplewood:* Parkdale-Maplewood Community Museum**
3005 Barss Corner Rd., RR#1
Maplewood, NS B0R 1A0
Tel: 902-644-2893
p-mcm@hotmail.com.ca
parkdale.ednet.ns.ca
www.facebook.com/94020106181
Founded by Thomas I. Spidell, a missionary-salesman for the New & Latter House of Israel
Alice Rafuse, Chair
Donna Arenburg, Curator

***Middleton:* Annapolis Valley Macdonald Museum**
***Parent:* Annapolis Valley Historical Society**
PO Box 925
Middleton, NS B0S 1P0
Tel: 902-825-6116; *Fax:* 902-825-0531
macdonald.museum@ns.sympatico.ca
www.macdonaldmuseum.ca
Features antique clocks and pocket watches; Art Gallery featuring local artists; historical artifacts, household items, tools; recreated classroom and general store; sports heritage wall of fame; gift shop.

***Millbrook:* Glooscap Heritage Centre & Mi'kmaw Museum**
65 Treaty Hall
Millbrook, NS B6L 1W3
Tel: 902-843-3493; *Fax:* 902-893-2269
info@glooscapheritagecentre.com
www.glooscapheritagecentre.com
Social Media: www.youtube.com/user/GlooscapHeritage
twitter.com/GlooscapCentre
www.facebook.com/glooscapheritagecentre
The museum is dedicated to preserving the heritage of the Mi'kmaw people through programs & exhibits, & features a 40-foot statue of the legendary Glooscap.

***Minudie:* Amos Seaman School Museum**
***Parent:* The Minudie Heritage Association**
5558 Barronsfield Rd.
Minudie, NS B0L 1G0
Tel: 902-251-2289; *Fax:* 902-251-2422
minudieheritage@gmail.com
Photographs & documents relating to Amos "King" Seaman, who was a merchant & industrialist in the 18th century; museum housed in a one-room schoolhouse; walking tour of the area available

***Mount Uniacke:* Uniacke Estate Museum Park**
***Parent:* Nova Scotia Museum**
758 Hwy. 1
Mount Uniacke, NS B0N 1Z0
Tel: 902-866-0032; *Fax:* 902-866-2560
uniacke.novascotia.ca
Part of the Nova Scotia Museum; features a country mansion from 1816; open June 1 - Oct. 4
Winfried Viebahn, Site Manager, VIEBAHWI@gov.ns.ca

***Musquodoboit Harbour:* Musquodoboit Railway Museum**
***Parent:* Nova Scotia Railway Heritage Society (NSRHS)**
7895 Main St.
Musquodoboit Harbour, NS B0J 2L0
Tel: 902-889-2689
www.novascotiarailwayheritage.com/musquodoboit.htm
Open June 1 - Sept. 1.

***New Glasgow:* Carmichael Stewart House**
86 Temperance St.
New Glasgow, NS B2H 3A7
Tel: 902-752-5583
carmich@eastlink.ca
www.parl.ns.ca/csmuseum
Year Founded: 1965 Operated by the Pictou County Historical Society, the Carmichael Stewart House Museum is a late Victorian home which contains collections such as photographs, clothing, & Trenton Glassware. The museum is open during the summer.
Lynn MacLean, President

***New Glasgow:* Carmichael Stewart House Museum**
***Parent:* Pictou County Historical Society**
86 Temperance St.
New Glasgow, NS B2H 3A7
Tel: 902-752-5583
carmich@eastlink.ca
www.parl.ns.ca/csmuseum
www.facebook.com/224779827547853
Year Founded: 1965 Exhibits items belonging to the Carmichael Stewart family, as well as historical pieces from the area.
Lynn MacLean, President

***New Ross:* Ross Farm Museum**
4568 Hwy 12
New Ross, NS B0J 2M0
Tel: 902-689-2210; *Fax:* 902-689-2264
Toll-Free: 877-689-2210
rossfarm@gov.ns.ca
rossfarm.novascotia.ca
twitter.co m/RossFarmMuseum
www.facebook.com/RossFarmMuseum
Year Founded: 1969 Ross family farm 1817; part of the Nova Scotia Museum
Lisa Wolfe, Director, wolfelm@gov.ns.ca

***North East Margaree:* Margaree Salmon Museum**
60 East Big Intervale Rd.
North East Margaree, NS B0E 2H0
Tel: 902-248-2848
margareesalmonmuseum@yahoo.ca
www.margareens.com/margaree_salmon.html
Year Founded: 1965 Exhibits relate to salmon angling on the Margaree River. Located in a former schoolhouse; includes collections of fishing tackle, photos & memorabilia of famous anglers. Open June-Oct.
Frances Hart, Curator

***North Sydney:* North Sydney Historical Museum**
***Parent:* North Sydney Historical Society**
PO Box 163
North Sydney, NS B2A 3M3
Tel: 902-794-2524
nsydmuseum@ns.sympatico.ca
northsydneymuseum.ca
Year Founded: 1985 Local history; exhibit themes include fire fighting, communications, politics, immigration, military & transportation

***Orangedale:* Orangedale Railway Museum**
***Parent:* Orangedale Station Association**
1428 Orangedale Rd.
Orangedale, NS B0E 2K0
Tel: 902-756-3384; *Fax:* 902-756-2547
orangedale.station@gmail.com
www.novascotiarailwayheritage.com/orangedal e.htm
Open June - Sept.; railway station built in 1911
Jay Underwood, President, jp.underwood@ns.sympatico.ca

***Parrsboro:* Fundy Geological Museum**
162 Two Island Rd.
Parrsboro, NS B0M 1S0
Tel: 902-254-3814; *Fax:* 902-254-3666
Toll-Free: 866-856-9466
fundygeo@gov.ns.ca
museum.gov.ns.ca/fgm
www.facebook .com/120369588016683
Features exhibits on rocks, minerals, dinosaurs & glaciers; part of the Nova Scotia Museum; Open year-round
Karen Dickinson, Chair
Kenneth Adams, Director/Curator, adamskd@gov.ns.ca

***Parrsboro:* Ottawa House By-the-Sea Museum**
PO Box 98, 1155 Whitehall Rd.
Parrsboro, NS B0M 1S0
Tel: 902-254-2376
ottawa.house@ns.sympatico.ca
www.ottawahousemuseum.ca
Housed in a building over 200 years old that once belonged to Sir Charles Tupper, who was Premier of Nova Scotia in the 1870s, a Father of Confederation & Prime Minister of Canada. The museum's collection contains photographs, artifacts, documents & furnishings from many of the building's owners.
Susan Clarke, Facility Manager

***Pictou:* McCulloch House Museum**
100 Haliburton Rd.
Pictou, NS B0K 1H0
Tel: 902-485-4563
mccullochhouse.novascotia.ca
Year Founded: 1972 Administered by the Pictou County Genealogy & Heritage Society, & part of the Nova Scotia Museum, the museum was built in 1805 as home to Rev. Dr. McCulloch, the founder of Pictou Academy & first president of Dalhousie University. The exhibits reflect the life & times of the Scottish immigrants & their influence on today's Nova Scotia.

***Pictou:* Northumberland Fisheries Museum & Pictou Lobster Hatchery (NFMHA)**
PO Box 1489
Pictou, NS B0K 1H0
Tel: 902-485-4972; *Fax:* 902-485-6586
nfm-business@ns.aliantzinc.ca
www.northumberlandfisheriesmuseum.com
tw itter.com/lobsterhatchery
www.facebook.com/131163863589998
Year Founded: 1978 Located in the historic C.N. Station; fishing artifacts from the late 1800s to present day; original fisherman's Bunkhouse; The "Silver Bullet"; photographs; boat models; fishing tools; artifacts on lobster processing; shell fish/live fish displays; sea heritage education for schools & seniors; education is based on fact & scientific data from Northumberland Strait area; local research conducted on fishing & sea heritage; recent additions to the museum include a lobster hatchery & lighthouse museum & research centre.
Michelle Davey, Business & Operations Manager, 902-485-4972, nfm-business@ns.aliantzinc.ca

***Port Grenville:* Age of Sail Heritage Museum**
***Parent:* Greville Bay Shipbuilding Museum Society**
8334 Hwy. 209
Port Grenville, NS B0M 1T0
Tel: 902-348-2030
gbsmsageofsail@yahoo.com
www.ageofsailmuseum.ca
www.facebook.com/123382484377107
Local history from communities along the Minas Channel, with an emphasis on shipbuilding & lumbering. Open May - Oct.
Oralee O'Byrne, Curator, 902-254-2079

***Port Hastings:* Port Hastings Museum & Archives**
24 Rte. 19
Port Hastings, NS B9A 1M1
Tel: 902-625-1295
office@porthastingsmuseum.ca
www.porthastingsmuseum.ca
Located in 100-year-old Cape Breton house; displays include pioneer artifacts, photographic displays & exhibits on construction of causeway; genealogical records available
Bob MacEachern, President

***Port Hood:* Chestico Museum & Historical Society**
PO Box 144, 8095 Rte. 19
Port Hood, NS B0E 2W0
Tel: 902-787-2244
chesticoplace.com
twitter.com/chesticomuseum
www.facebook.com/106197469418363
Year Founded: 1986 Located in Harbourview, the museum houses artifacts from the local community; house histories, historical events, people of the Port Hood area; gift shop; tea room; special programming.
Susan Mallette, Director

***Pubnico-Ouest:* Musée des Acadiens des Pubnicos et Centre de recherche**
CP 92
Pubnico-Ouest, NS B0W 3S0
Tél: 902-762-3380; *Téléc:* 902-762-0726
musee.acadien@ns.sympatico.ca
www.museeacadien.ca
www.facebook.com/101 935276541461
Le Musée: #898, autoroute 335; consacré au patrimoine des Acadiens/Acadiennes de Pubnico-Ouest; articles de maison; documents; photographies; archives; potager traditionnel; boutique de souvenirs.
Elaine Surette, Président

***Riverport:* Ovens Natural Park & Museum**
PO Box 38
Located at 326 Ovens Rd., Riverport, NS
Riverport, NS B0J 2W0
Tel: 902-766-4621
info@ovenspark.com
www.ovenspark.com
Social Media: ovenspark.tumblr.com
www.facebook.com/ovensnaturalpark
Year Founded: 1987 Located on the Atlantic coast of Nova Scotia, Ovens Natural Park is a reserve of coastal forest, featuring the sea caves or "Ovens". The area became known internationally during th 1861 gold rush. The Gold Rush Museum contains artifacts from that era.

***St Peters:* Nicolas Denys Museum**
PO Box 204, 46 Denys St.
St Peters, NS B0E 3B0
Tel: 902-535-2379
www.facebook.com/NicolasDenysMuseum
Year Founded: 1967 Micmac, Acadien, Scottish & Irish artifacts
Judy Madden, Curator, judy_madden80@hotmail.ca

***Shag Harbour:* Chapel Hill Museum**
PO Box 46, 5492 Hwy #3
Shag Harbour, NS B0W 3B0
Tel: 902-723-1313
chapelhillns@gmail.com
www.chapelhillmuseumns.com
Located in a former Baptist Church; features various displays related to local area including tools for ship-building, genealogical research materials, various fishing exhibits; able to view 4 local lighthouses from observation tower; open June 1 - Sept. 15 daily; rest of the year by appt.
Douglas Shand, President, Chapel Hill Historical Society, 902-723-2949, shawimm@ns.sympatico.ca
Veronica Hopkins, Vice President/Treasurer, Chapel Hill Historical Society, vhopkins@ns.sympatico.ca

***Shag Harbour:* Shag Harbour Incident Society Museum**
PO Box 53
Shag Harbour, NS B0W 3B0
Tel: 902-723-0174
shagharbour@gmail.com
cuun.i2ce.com/misc/shagHarbourMuseum
Year Founded: 2007 The museum displays memorabilia, TV programs, & other material related to the documented 1967 crash of a UFO in the Gulf of Maine, near Shag Harbour. The museum also details local history unrelated to the crash. Open M-F 10:00-5:00, Sa 12:00-5:00, Su 1:00-5:00; also open by appointment.
Cindy Nickerson, Chair

***Shearwater:* Shearwater Aviation Museum**
PO Box 5000 Main, 12 Wing
Located at 34 Bonaventure St., Dartmouth, NS
Shearwater, NS B0J 3A0
Tel: 902-720-1083; *Fax:* 902-720-2037
info@shearwateraviationmuseum.ns.ca
www.shearwateraviationmuseum.ns.ca
twitter.com/YAWmuseum
www.facebook.com/shearwateraviationmuseum
Year Founded: 1978 Maritime military aviation artifacts.

***Sheet Harbour:* MacPhee House Community Museum**
PO Box 239
Sheet Harbour, NS B0J 3B0
Tel: 902-885-2092
macpheehouse@gmail.com
www.sheetharbour.ca
www.facebook.com/macpheehouse
The museum is located in a house that's over 100 years old. In its history it has served as a private home, post office, grocery store & rooming house.

***Shelburne:* The Dory Shop Museum**
***Parent:* Shelburne Historical Society**
PO Box 39
Located at 11 Dock St., Shelburne, NS
Shelburne, NS B0T 1W0
Tel: 902-875-3219; *Fax:* 902-875-4141
doryshop.novascotia.ca
Restored dory factory, est. 1880; part of the Nova Scotia Museum; open June 1 - Oct. 15; dories still built to order

***Shelburne:* Ross-Thomson House & Store Museum**
***Parent:* Shelburne Historical Society**
PO Box 39
Shelburne, NS B0T 1W0
Tel: 902-875-3219; *Fax:* 902-875-4141
shelburne.museum@ns.sympatico.ca
www.historicshelburne.com/rth.htm
www .facebook.com/364893103570881
Located on Charlotte St. in Shelburne; 1785 Loyalist house & garden; 18th-century store & chandlery; 19th-century military artifacts; operated by the Shelburne Historical Society & part of the Nova Scotia Museum; open June 1 - Oct. 15

***Shelburne:* Shelburne County Museum**
***Parent:* Shelburne Historical Society**
PO Box 39, 20 Dock St.
Shelburne, NS B0T 1W0
Tel: 902-875-3219; *Fax:* 902-875-4141
shelburne.museum@ns.sympatico.ca
www.historicshelburne.com/scm.htm
www .facebook.com/364893103570881
Cultural & economic history of Shelburne from 1783; genealogy information; open year round

***Sherbrooke:* St. Mary's River Association Education & Interpretive Centre**
PO Box 179, 8404 #7 Hwy.
Sherbrooke, NS B0J 3C0
Tel: 902-522-2099; *Fax:* 902-522-2241
stmarysriver@ns.sympatico.ca
www.stmarysriverassociation.com/eandicentre .html
Year Founded: 2001 Artifacts & educational information relating to salmon fishing on the St. Mary's river; open daily

***Sherbrooke:* Sherbrooke Village**
***Parent:* Historic Sherbrooke Village Development Society**
42 Main St.
Sherbrooke, NS B0J 3C0
Tel: 902-522-2400; *Fax:* 902-522-2974
Toll-Free: 888-743-7845
svillage@gov.ns.ca
sherbrookevillage.novascotia.ca
Social Media: www.youtube.com/user/sherbrookevillage
twitter.com/Sherbrooke_NS
www.facebook.com/114818421893386
Historic village with 25 original buildings; part of the Nova Scotia Museum; open June 1 - Oct. 4.
Michelle MacArthur, Chair
Mark Sajatovich, Executive Director, sajatomc@gov.ns.ca

***Smith's Cove:* Old Temperance Hall Museum**
590 Hwy. 1
Smith's Cove, NS B0S 1S0
Tel: 902-245-4665
smithscovemuseum@gmail.com
Exhibits of the 19th and 20th century pertaining to the local community including the earliest inhabitants, the Mi'kmaq; history of the Sons of Temperance.

***Springhill:* The Anne Murray Centre**
PO Box 610, 36 Main St.
Springhill, NS B0M 1X0
Tel: 902-597-8614; *Fax:* 902-597-2001
amcentre@eastlink.ca
www.annemurraycentre.com
twitter.com/AnneMurrayCe ntr
www.facebook.com/amcentre
Year Founded: 1989 Pays tribute to the achievements of singer Anne Murray, who was born in Springhill, Nova Scotia; open May - Oct., otherwise by appt. or by chance.

***Springhill:* Springhill Miner's Museum**
145 Black River Rd.
Springhill, NS B0M 1X0
Tel: 902-597-3449
springhillminersmuseum@hotmail.com
www.town.springhill.ns.ca/Attractions.html
www.facebook.com/189786421079 587
Tours of the Springhill coal mine, famous in song & legend; gift shop & picnic area.

***Starr's Point:* Prescott House**
1633 Starr's Point Rd.
Starr's Point, NS B0P 1T0
Tel: 902-542-3984
prescotthouse.novascotia.ca
c.1814 Georgian house, open June 1 - Oct. 4; museum shop; bus tours welcome; part of the Nova Scotia Museum
Diana Baldwin, Contact, baldwidj@gov.ns.ca

***Stellarton:* Museum of Industry**
147 North Foord St.
Stellarton, NS B0K 1S0
Tel: 902-755-5425; *Fax:* 902-755-7045
industry@gov.ns.ca
museumofindustry.novascotia.ca
Atlantic Canada's largest museum; chronicles the impact of industrialization on the people, economy & landscape of Nova Scotia; features Canada's oldest steam locomotives, an historic model railway layout, a belt-driven working machine shop & a collection of Nova Scotia's Trenton glass. Part of the Nova Scotia Museum.
Debra McNabb, Director
Erika Smith, Curator, Collections
Andrew Phillips, Curator, Education & Public Programming

***Sydney:* Cape Breton Centre for Heritage & Science**
225 George St.
Sydney, NS B1P 1J5
Tel: 902-539-1572
oldsydneysociety@ns.aliantzinc.ca
www.oldsydney.com/cape-breton-centre-for-heritage-science
twitter.com/Ol dSydney
www.facebook.com/OldSydneySociety

The Lyceum was built in 1904 by the Roman Catholic diocese. The Opera House contained a 900 seat theatre, as well as a library, gymnasium, billiards room, & clubrooms. Today, the Lyceum houses the Cape Breton Centre for Heritage & Science. The Old Sydney Society provides tours of the Colonial Town of Old Sydney, which was first the home to Mi'Kmaq people, then Basque fishermen, Loyalists, & later immigrating Scots. In the Cape Breton Centre for Heritage & Science, visitors will discover the natural & social histories of Cape Breton County. The museum is open year round.

Sydney: Cossit House Museum
Parent: **Old Sydney Society**
c/o Cape Breton Centre for Heritage & Science, 225 George St.
Location: 75 Charlotte St., Sydney, Cape Breton, NS
Sydney, NS B1P 4P4
Tel: 902-539-7973
cossithouse.novascotia.ca
One of the oldest buildings on Cape Breton Island, c.1787; part of the Nova Scotia Museum.

Sydney: Jost House Musuem
54 Charlotte St.
Sydney, NS B1P 6T7
Tel: 902-539-0366; *Fax:* 902-539-7998
www.facebook.com/230720683606240
Local history; ground floor depicts Victorian era living; third floor features an apothecary & a marine room

Sydney: Whitney Pier Historical Museum
Parent: **Whitney Pier Historical Society**
88 Mount Pleasant St.
Sydney, NS B1N 2G1
Tel: 902-564-9819; *Fax:* 902-564-1115
wphs@syd.eastlink.ca
whitneypiermuseum.org
Year Founded: 1988 The museum seeks to capture the diversity of the Whitney Pier community through its exhibits
Simon Gillis, Vice-President, 902-564-4248
Sandra Dunn, Treasurer, 902-562-8454

Sydney Mines: Sydney Mines Heritage Museum, Cape Breton Fossil Centre & Sydney Mines Sports Museum
Parent: **Sydney Mines Heritage Society**
159 Legatto St.
Sydney Mines, NS B1V 5S6
Tel: 902-544-0992
smheritage@ns.aliantzinc.ca
sydneyminesheritage.ca
The Heritage Museum is located in the historic Sydney Mines Train Station & contains local artifacts, including photographs, pottery & memorabilia. The Cape Breton Fossil Centre showcases fossils, mostly of plants, that come from the Sydney Coalfields. The Sports Museum contains photographs & memorabilia relating to Sydney Mines' sporting history.

Tatamagouche: Anna Swan Museum
PO Box 402, 39 Creamery Sq.
Tatamagouche, NS B0K 1V0
Tel: 902-657-3449
info@tatamagoucheheritagecentre.ca
tatamagoucheheritagecentre.ca/anna-swan.html
The museum features items from the life of Nova Scotia giantess Anna Swan.

Tatamagouche: Balmoral Grist Mill
RR#4
Located at 544 Peter Macdonald Rd., Balmoral Mills, NS
Tatamagouche, NS B0K 1V0
Tel: 902-657-3016; *Fax:* 902-657-2606
balmoralgristmill.novascotia.ca
Located at 660 Matheson Brook Rd. in Balmoral Mills, the 1874 three-storey grist mill is still operational. The grist mill is part of the Nova Scotia Museum, & is open from June 1st to October 15th.
Darrell Burke, Site Manager, burked@gov.ns.ca

Tatamagouche: Margaret Fawcett Norrie Heritage Centre at Creamery Square
39 Creamery Rd.
Tatamagouche, NS B0K 1V0
Tel: 902-657-3500; *Fax:* 902-657-0240
info@tatamagoucheheritagecentre.ca
www.tatamagoucheheritagecentre.ca
t witter.com/tataheritage
www.facebook.com/129652823882556
Other contact information: Alt. E-mail: cs.heritage@ns.aliantzinc.ca
The Heritage Centre contains the following: Creamery Museum, Sunrise Trail Museum, Anna Swan Museum & the Brule Fossil Museum.

Tatamagouche: Sutherland Steam Mill Museum
Parent: **Nova Scotia Museum**
c/o Balmoral Grist Mill, RR#4
Location: 3169 Denmark Station Rd., Denmark, NS
Tatamagouche, NS B0K 1V0
Tel: 902-657-3365; *Fax:* 902-657-2606
sutherlandsteammill.novascotia.ca
Part of the Nova Scotia Museum; open June 1 - Oct. 15
Darrell Burke, Site Manager, 902-657-3017, burked@gov.ns.ca

Truro: Colchester Historeum
Parent: **Colchester Historical Society**
PO Box 412
Located at 20 Young St., Truro, NS
Truro, NS B2N 5C5
Tel: 902-895-6284; *Fax:* 902-895-9530
colchesterhistoreum.ca
twitter.com/Col_Historeum
www.facebook.com/colc hesterhistoreum
Other contact information: Archives Phone: 902-895-9530
Year Founded: 1976 Museum & archive devoted to preserving the history of Colchester County; open year round.
Jordan LeBlanc, Curator
Nan Harvey, Archivist

Truro: The Little White Schoolhouse
PO Box 1252
Located at 20 Arthur St., Truro, NS
Truro, NS B2N 5N2
Tel: 902-895-5170
littlewhiteschoolhousemuseum@bellaliant.com
littlewhiteschool.ca
www.f acebook.com/465855396834380
Year Founded: 1982 Original Riverton School; commemorates schoolhouses in Nova Scotia from Confederation to the 1950s; contains books & artifacts from the era of one-room schoolhouse; requests for research on the graduates of the Provincial Normal School & College & in old copies of the NS Journal of Education, accepted; open early June - Aug. & by appt.

Tupperville: Tupperville School Museum
2663 Hwy. 201
Tupperville, NS B0S 1C0
Tel: 902-665-2579; *Fax:* 902-665-4875
tuppervillemuseum@gmail.com
Year Founded: 1972 Open daily mid-May - mid-Sept.

Wallace: Wallace & Area Museum
Parent: **Wallace & Area Museum Society**
PO Box 179
Located at 13440 Rte. 6, Wallace, NS
Wallace, NS B0K 1Y0
Tel: 902-257-2191; *Fax:* 902-257-2191
wallacemuseum@ns.aliantzinc.ca
www.wallaceandareamuseum.com
www.facebo ok.com/120610681314312
Year Founded: 1983 The museum collect, preserves, & displays the history of Wallace & the surrounding region. Artifacts include nineteenth century marine charts & maps, the United Empire Loyalist grant, pre-Confederation letters, & items about shipbuilding in Wallace & the Wallace sandstone quarries. Open year round.
Doris Purdy, President
Warren Hebb, Vice-President
David Dewar, Curator
Doug Perry, Secretary

Waverley: Waverley Heritage Museum
2463 Rocky Lake Dr.
Waverley, NS B2R 1S1
Tel: 902-861-1463
waverleyheritagemuseum@gmail.com
Local history

West Bay: Marble Mountain Library & Museum
RR#1
West Bay, NS B0E 3K0
Tel: 902-756-2638

West Chezzetcook: Acadian House Museum
Parent: **L'Acadie de Chezzetcook**
Site 12, Box 18, RR#2
Located at 79 Hill Rd., West Chezzetcook, NS
West Chezzetcook, NS B0J 1N0
Tel: 902-827-5992
acadiedechezzetcook@gmail.com
Local Acadian history.

Windsor: Haliburton House Museum
Parent: **Nova Scotia Museum**
414 Clifton Ave.
Windsor, NS B0N 2T0
Tel: 902-798-2915
haliburtonhouse.novascotia.ca
www.facebook.com/HaliburtonShandHouseMuseums
Year Founded: 1940 Former home of author Thomas Chandler Haliburton, who lived there from 1837-1856; part of the Nova Scotia Museum; open June 1-Oct. 4

Windsor: Shand House Museum
389 Avon St.
Windsor, NS B0N 2T0
Tel: 902-798-8213; *Fax:* 902-798-5619
shandhouse.novascotia.ca
www.facebook.com/HaliburtonShandHouseMuseums
Historic family home c.1890; part of the Nova Scotia Museum; open June 1 - Oct. 15

Windsor: West Hants Historical Society Museum
PO Box 2335, 281 King St.
Windsor, NS B0N 2T0
Tel: 902-798-4706
whhs@ns.aliantzinc.ca
westhantshistoricalsociety.ca
www.facebook.com/141349919273121
Artifacts related to the history of Hants County in Nova Scotia are collected & preserved by the West Hants Historical Society & displayed at its museum. Visitors will find information about the Mi'kmaq, the Acadians, the Loyalists, the Great Windsor Fire of 1897, & the local shipbuilding industry. The society also operates a genealogy department. The museum is open five days a week from mid June to the end of August, & one day a week from September to June. Summer tours are available of the Fort Edward Blockhouse. Appointments may be arranged for times when the museum is closed.

Wolfville: Randall House Museum
Parent: **Wolfville Historical Society**
259 Main St.
Wolfville, NS B4P 1C6
Tel: 902-542-9775
randallhouse@live.ca
www.wolfvillehs.ednet.ns.ca
The Randall House is an historic farmhouse, from around 1800, which is owned & operated by the Wolfville Historical Society. The Randall House Museum reflects life in Wolfville & the surrounding area during the 18th & 19th centuries. On display are furniture, clothing, china, & a collection of Victorian greeting cards. A library is located in The Randall House for persons researching local history & genealogy.
Anthony J. Harding, President
Heather Watts, Archivist, 902-542-0307

Yarmouth: Firefighters' Museum of Nova Scotia
Nova Scotia Museum Complex, 451 Main St.
Yarmouth, NS B5A 1G9
Tel: 902-742-5525
museum.gov.ns.ca/fm
Artifacts date to the early 1800s; part of the Nova Scotia Museum; open year round
David Darby, Curator

Yarmouth: Yarmouth County Museum & Archives
Parent: **Yarmouth County Historical Society**
22 Collins St.
Yarmouth, NS B5A 3C8
Tel: 902-742-5539; *Fax:* 902-749-1120
ycmuseum@eastlink.ca
yarmouthcountymuseum.ca
www.facebook.com/92402018 979
Year Founded: 1969 Also operates the Pelton-Fuller House in Yarmouth, the historic summer home of A.C. Fuller, the Fuller Brush Man & the Killam Brothers' shipping office, the oldest in Canada, during the summer months
Nadine Gates, Director/Curator
Ingrid Deon, Assistant Director, ycm.asst.dir@eastlink.ca
Lisette Gaudet, Archivist, ycarchives@eastlink.ca

Nunavut

Local Museums

Baker Lake: Inuit Heritage Centre
PO Box 149
Baker Lake, NU X0C 0A0
Tel: 867-793-2598; *Fax:* 867-793-2315
blheritage@netkaster.ca
www.bakerlakearts.com
Year Founded: 1998 The Centre's goal is to preserve, protect & promote Inuit culture through a collection of Inuit artifacts & a

teaching room where elders can record oral histories & teach youth about traditional ways of life.

***Cambridge Bay:* Kitikmeot Heritage Society (KHS)**
PO Box 2160, 20 Omingmak St.
Cambridge Bay, NU X0B 0C0
Tel: 867-983-3009; *Fax:* 867-983-3397
heritage@qiniq.com
www.kitikmeotheritage.ca
Located in the May Hakongak Community Library & Cultural Centre, the KHS strives to preserve the history, culture & language of the people of the Kitikmeot region. The collection includes oral histories as told by elders & archeological artifacts.
Kim Crockatt, President, kimcr@netkaster.ca
Renee Krucas, Executive Director
Darren Keith, Senior Researcher, dkeith@cgocable.ca

***Iqaluit:* Nunatta Sunakkutaangit Museum**
PO Box 1900
Located in Bldg. 212, Iqualuit, NU
Iqaluit, NU X0A 0H0
Tel: 867-979-5537; *Fax:* 867-979-4533
museum@nunanet.com
Founded in 1969; housed in a historic Hudson Bay Company warehouse building; collections focus on Inuit culture & history from the Baffin region, including historical & archeological artifacts, tools, clothing, & equipment as well as arts & crafts; also maintains a collection of archival photographs, publications & documents for exhibition & research purposes; open year-round

***Pangnirtung:* Sipalaseequtt Museum Society**
Angmarlik Visitor Centre, PO Box 227
Pangnirtung, NU X0A 0R0
Tel: 867-473-8737
Inuit artifacts; whaling history in Cumberland Sound Baffin Island; Elders' meetings; craft production; tours

***Sanikiluaq:* Najuqsivik Community Museum**
General Delivery
Sanikiluaq, NU X0A 0W0
Tel: 867-266-8400; *Fax:* 867-266-8843
www.najuqsivik.com
The museum provides hands-on cultural activities during limited hours in July & Aug. The museum is operated by the Najuqsivik Society, which also operates a daycare, custom frameshop, polar bear rug business, archaeological & lost wax casting business, fishskin doll production business, coffee mug artwork business, garment screening business, an upholstery shop, a community access program, & a TV station & radio station.

Ontario

Provincial Museum

Royal Ontario Museum (ROM)
Visitor Services Department, 100 Queen's Park Ave.
Toronto, ON M5S 2C6
Tel: 416-586-8000
info@rom.on.ca
www.rom.on.ca
Social Media: www.youtube.com/user/RoyalOntarioMuseum
twitter.com/ROMtoronto
www.fac ebook.com/royalontariomuseum
Year Founded: 1912 The Royal Ontario Museum (ROM) is Canada's largest museum, an internationally renowned facility & popular public attraction. Created in 1912, the ROM has an unusually broad dual mandate of collecting & preserving in the areas of natural history & human cultures, & communicating its research to the world. Today, the ROM holds in excess of 6 million objects in its collections, which include galleries of art, archaeology & science.
Mark Engstrom, Deputy Director, Collections & Research
Nick Bobrow, Deputy Director; Chief Financial Officer; Secretary, Operations
Chen Shen, Vice President, World Cultures

Local Museums

***Ailsa Craig:* Donald Hughes Annex Museum**
***Parent:* North Middlesex Historical Society**
169 George St.
Ailsa Craig, ON N0M 1A0
Tel: 519-517-0105
northmiddlesexhs@gmail.com
www.ailsacraigmuseum.ca
Local history.

***Algonquin Highlands:* Stanhope Heritage Discovery Museum**
1123 North Shore Rd.
Algonquin Highlands, ON K0M 1J1
Tel: 705-489-2379
info@stanhopemuseum.on.ca
www.stanhopemuseum.on.ca
www.facebook.com/pages/Stanhope-Museum/23440667 2514
Year Founded: 1996 Local history
Betty Moffat, Chair, 705-489-3021

***Alliston:* Museum on the Boyne**
10 Wellingston St. East
Located at 250 Fletcher Cres., Alliston, ON
Alliston, ON L9R 1A1
Tel: 705-435-3900; *Fax:* 705-434-3006
boynemuseum@newtecumseth.ca
www.motb.ca
Community museum displaying household, agricultural & industrial artifacts from 1840's to present; site features 1850's log cabin, 1860 English barn & 1915 fair building

***Almonte:* Mississippi Valley Textile Museum (MVTM)**
PO Box 784, 3 Rosamond St. East
Almonte, ON K0A 1A0
Tel: 613-256-3754
mvtm.ca
twitter.com/MVTextileMuseum
www.facebook.com /MVTextileMuseum
Year Founded: 1985 Museum is a National Historic Site; located in the annex of the former Rosamond Woolen Company constructed in 1867; houses information on the early mills & their owners, displays of period offices, artifacts & machinery related to the beginnings of the textile industry, and a gift shop.
Michael Rikley-Lancaster, Executive Director & Curator, curator@mvtm.ca

***Almonte:* North Lanark Regional Museum**
***Parent:* North Lanark Historical Society**
PO Box 218
Located at 647 River Rd., Appleton, ON, K0A 1A0
Almonte, ON K0A 1A0
Tel: 613-257-8503
appletonmuseum@hotmail.com
northlanarkregionalmuseum.com
Year Founded: 1971 Small regional museum; open May 22nd to Thanksgiving, W-Su, 10-4; admission $2
Doreen Wilson, Manager, 613-256-2866

***Ameliasburg:* Ameliasburgh Historical Museum**
517 County Rd. 19
Ameliasburg, ON K0K 1A0
Tel: 613-968-9678
amelmuseum@pecounty.on.ca
pecounty.on.ca/government/community_development/museums/ameliasburgh.php
Year Founded: 1968 Household items, quilts, crafts, agricultural machinery & tools & a 1910 Goldie Corlis engine with an 18-foot flywheel in a village setting; lots of events during season; tea room.
Jennifer Lyons, Head Curator, Museums of Prince Edward County, 613-476-3833, Fax: 613-471-2050, museums@pecounty.on.ca
Janice Hubbs, Site Curator

***Ameliasburg:* Quinte Educational Museum & Archives, Inc.**
PO Box 14, 13 Coleman St.
Ameliasburg, ON K0K 1A0
Tel: 613-966-5501
info@qema1978.com
www.qema1978.com
The history of education in Prince Edward County & Ontario is preserved at the Quinte Educational Museum & Archives, through educational artifacts & archival material.
Lynda Sommer, President, lyndasommer@qema1978.com

***Amherstburg:* Amherstburg Freedom Museum**
277 King St.
Amherstburg, ON N9V 2C7
Tel: 519-736-5433
www.amherstburgfreedom.org
www.facebook.com/AmherstburgFreedom
The Museum allows visitors to experience Black history through the Taylor Log Cabin, a home of escaped slaves from the United States, the Nazrey African Methodist Episcopal Church & a Cultural Centre.
Terran Fader, Curator & Administrator

***Amherstburg:* Fort Malden National Historic Site of Canada (FMNHS) / Lieu historique national du Canada du Fort-Malden**
PO Box 38, 100 Laird Ave.
Amherstburg, ON N9V 2Z2
Tel: 519-736-5416; *Fax:* 519-736-6603
ont.fort-malden@pc.gc.ca
www.parkscanada.gc.ca/malden
twitter.com/Park sCan_SWOnt
www.facebook.com/FortMaldenNHS
Year Founded: 1796 Riverfront site includes original earthworks, a restored soldier's barrack & a museum

***Amherstburg:* Park House Museum**
Kings Navy Yard, 214 Dalhousie St.
Amherstburg, ON N9V 1W4
Tel: 519-736-2511; *Fax:* 519-736-2511
parkhousemuseum.com
Built during the 1790s by a family of Loyalists, Park House is an example of Pièce sur Pièce log construction. The Park House Museum is open year-round to display items of historical significance to the town of Amherstburg & the surrounding area. During the summer, tinsmithing is demonstrated in the pensioner's cottage.
Stephanie Pouget, Curator, curator@parkhousemuseum.com

***Ancaster:* Dundas Valley Trail Centre**
c/o Hamilton Conservation Authority, PO Box 81067
Ancaster, ON L9G 4X1
Tel: 905-627-1233; *Fax:* 905-648-4622
dvalley@conservationhamilton.ca
www.conservationhamilton.ca/dundas-valle y
Social Media: www.youtube.com/user/HamiltonConservation
twitter.com/Hamilton_CA
www.facebook.com/HamiltonConservation
Centre is a replica of an 1800-era train station; displays/exhibits on the Niagara Escarpment, local cultural heritage & trail etiquette governing the valley's extensive, multi-use trail network; bird watching, cycling or historical tours
Carissa Bishop, Superintendent, Dundas Valley Conservation Area, Carissa.Bishop@conservationhamilton.ca
Karen Laur, Contact, Trail Centre

***Ancaster:* Fieldcote Memorial Park & Museum**
64 Sulphur Springs Rd.
Ancaster, ON L9G 1L8
Tel: 905-648-8144; *Fax:* 905-648-4857
fieldcote@hamilton.ca
www.hamilton.ca
Collection, preservation & exhibition of local history; landscaped gardens & walking trails

***Ancaster:* Griffin House National Historic Site**
733 Mineral Springs Rd.
Ancaster, ON L9H 1A1
Tel: 905-648-8144; *Fax:* 905-546-2338
griffinhouse@hamilton.ca
www.hamilton.ca
The house commemorates the determination of black men & women who journeyed to Canada via the Underground Railroad. Open July-Sept., Su 1:00-4:00.

***Ancaster:* Hermitage Gatehouse Museum**
PO Box 7099
Ancaster, ON L9G 3L3
Tel: 905-627-1233
nature@conservationhamilton.ca
www.conservationhamilton.ca
Displays various artifacts from the family that formerly owned Hermitage Gatehouse as well as items that are relevant to the area.

***Ancaster:* Ingledale**
c/o Hamilton Region Conservation Authority, PO Box 7099
Located at Fifty Point Conservation Area, Stoney Creek, ON
Ancaster, ON L9G 3L3
Tel: 905-643-2103
c. 1812 home of Inglehart family

***Ancaster:* Valens Log Cabin Museum**
PO Box 7099
Located at 1691 Regional Road 97, RR#6, Cambridge, ON
Ancaster, ON L9G 3L3
Tel: 905-659-7715
C. 1836 restored homestead.

***Appin:* Ekfrid Community Museum**
48 Wellington St.
Appin, ON N0L 1A0
Tel: 519-287-2015
Located in the former Appin Post Office & Orange Hall; artifacts from late 1800s; open May-Aug., weekends & by request

***Arnprior:* Arnprior & District Museum / Musée d'Arnprior et Région**
35 Madawaska St.
Arnprior, ON K7S 1R6

Tel: 613-623-4902
www.arnpriormuseum.org
Social Media: www.youtube.com/user/ArnpriorMuseum
www.facebook.com/220198278002242

Located in the former post office, which was built in 1896, the Arnprior & District Museum features local artifacts & photograpsh, a 1928 fire engine, a lumbering exhibit, & an early 19th century canon. The museum is open Monday to Saturday.
Janet Carlile, Curator, jcarlile@arnprior.ca

***Astra:* National Air Force Museum of Canada**
8Wing/CFB Trenton, PO Box 1000
Located at 220 RCAF Rd., Trenton, ON K0K 2W0
Astra, ON K0K 3W0

Tel: 613-965-7223*Toll-Free:* 866-701-7223
publicrelations@airforcemuseum.ca
airforcemuseum.ca
twitter.com/nafmca nada
www.facebook.com/120719991296340

Year Founded: 1984 Social history museum dedicated to the airmen & airwomen who served in Canada's Air Force; features daily viewing of the on-going restoration of the world's only fully restored Halifax bomber aircraft; an Air Park displays 14 aircraft, 21 commemorative cairns & 5,600 "Ad Astra" granite stones; a large collection of artifacts; & a specialty gift shop; open daily May 1 - Sept. 30 W-Su
Chris Colton, Executive Director, director@airforcemuseum.ca
Kevin Windsor, Curator, curator@airforcemuseum.ca

***Atikokan:* Atikokan Centennial Museum & Historical Park**
PO Box 849
Off season: P.O. Box 1330, Atikokan, ON, P0T 1C0
Atikokan, ON P0T 1C0

Tel: 807-597-6585; *Fax:* 807-597-6585
acmuseum@bellnet.ca
www.facebook.com/27862016983

Restored logging engine & train; mining & logging exhibits; Steep Rock & Caland Iron Ore Mines; local archival & art collections
Lois Fenton, Museum Curator

***Aurora:* Aurora Historical Society & Hillary House, National Historic Site**
15372 Yonge St.
Aurora, ON L4G 1N8

Tel: 905-727-8991
aurorahs.com
www.facebook.com/HillaryHouseNHS

Year Founded: 1963 Heritage artifacts held by the Aurora Historical Society date back over 200 years. The collections are related to the history of Aurora & to Hillary House. Hillary House, the Koffler Museum of Medicine, contains a significant collection of medical instruments.
Erika Mazanik, Curator

***Aurora:* Hillary House, the Koffler Museum of Medicine**
***Parent:* Aurora Historical Society**
15372 Yonge St.
Aurora, ON L4G 1N8

Tel: 905-727-8991
www.hillaryhouse.ca
www.facebook.com/HillaryHouseNHS

Built in 1862, the house was home to 3 generations of medical doctors & their families, covering the evolution of medicine from the era of leeches & bleeding to the discovery of penicillin. Exhibits include: medicial instruments, books, papers, household furnishings & equipment dating from the early 19th century. The museum is a National Historic Site. Open May - Aug., 9:30-4:30 daily; Sept. - Apr. by appointment only.

***Aylmer:* Aylmer-Malahide Museum & Archives (AMMA)**
14 East St.
Aylmer, ON N5H 1W2

Tel: 519-773-9723
aylmermuseum@amtelecom.net
www.amtelecom.net/~aylmermuseum
twitter.com/AylmerMuseum
www.facebook. com/AylmerMalahideMuseumArchives

The Aylmer & District Museum Association preserves & promotes the history of Aylmer & Malahide. The museum is open from the beginning of March to the end of November.

***Aylmer:* Gay Lea Dairy Heritage Museum**
***Parent:* Gay Lea Foods Co-operative Limited**
48075 Jamestown Line, RR#2
Aylmer, ON N5H 2R2

Toll-Free: 887-732-955
museum@gayleafoods.com
www.dairyheritagemuseum.ca
twitter.com/DairyMuseum

Artifacts that dairy farmers would have used previous to the development of modern technology.

***Aylmer:* Ontario Police College Museum**
PO Box 1190, 10716 Hacienda Rd.
Aylmer, ON N5H 2T2

Tel: 519-773-5361; *Fax:* 519-773-5762

Year Founded: 1962 Small display of police related items including speed measuring devices, breath collection & testing equipment, handcuffs & batons, police uniforms & hats, First Nations Police display, Forensics Investigative display

***Azilda:* Rayside-Balfour Museum**
Azilda Public Library, 120 Ste-Agnes St.
Azilda, ON P0M 1B0

Tel: 705-688-3955; *Fax:* 705-983-4119
www.sudburymuseums.ca

The museum houses artifacts related to the agricultural history of the area. Open Sept-June, M 10:00-2:00, Tu-Th 3:00-8:00, Sa 10:00-2:00.

***Baden:* Castle Kilbride National Historic Site**
60 Snyder's Rd. West
Baden, ON N3A 1A1

Tel: 519-634-8444; *Fax:* 519-634-5035
Toll-Free: 800-469-5576
castle.kilbride@wilmot.ca
www.castlekilbride.ca
www. facebook.com/pages/Castle-Kilbride/223242424376794

Year Founded: 1994 A restored 1877 mansion originally built by industrialist James Livingston, now a National Historic Site. Open Tu-F 10:00-4:00, Sa-Su 1:00-4:00.

***Baden:* Wilmot Heritage Fire Brigades**
10 Bell Dr.
Baden, ON N3A 4J8

Tel: 519-634-8153
www.wilmotfiremuseum.com

Year Founded: 1996 Local & national firefighting artifacts

***Bala:* Bala's Museum, with Memories of Lucy Maud Montgomery**
PO Box 14
Located at 1024 Maple Ave., Muskoka, ON
Bala, ON P0C 1A0

Tel: 705-762-5876*Toll-Free:* 888-579-7739
balamus@muskoka.com
bala.net/museum
www.facebook.com/BalasMuseumWithMemoriesOfLucyMaudMontgomery

Year Founded: 1992 The museum's collection features items related to Lucy Maud Montgomery. Spring hours: May-June, Sa 11:00-4:00; Summer hours: June-Sept., Tu-Sa 11:00-4:00; Fall hours: Sept.-Oct., Sa 11:00-4:00.

***Bancroft:* Bancroft Mineral Museum**
8 Hastings Heritage Way
Bancroft, ON K0L 1C0

Tel: 613-332-1513; *Fax:* 613-332-2119
Toll-Free: 888-443-9999

The Bancroft Mineral Museum is a natural science museum which features mineral specimens collected from the local area. The museum is open year-round.

***Bancroft:* North Hastings Heritage Museum**
PO Box 239
Located at 26B Station St., Bancroft, ON
Bancroft, ON K0L 1C0

Tel: 613-332-1884
nhastingshertiage@bellnet.ca
www.town.bancroft.on.ca/index.php/visiting/north-hastings-heritage-museum

Log house built in 1859; documents of North Hastings area

***Barrie:* Grey & Simcoe Foresters Regimental Museum**
c/o Barrie Armoury, 37 Parkside Dr.
Location: 36 Mulcaster St., Barrie, ON L4M 3M1
Barrie, ON L4N 1W8

Tel: 705-737-5559
gsfmus@csolve.net
thegreyandsimcoeforesters.org

Grey & Simcoe Foresters Regiment artifacts on display include: period uniforms, medals, field gear, & official recognitions & documentation.
Peter Litster, Curator

***Bath:* Bath Museum of Loyalist County**
The Old Town Hall, 434 Main St.
Bath, ON K0H 1G0

Tel: 613-352-7716
bathmuseum1861@hotmail.com.ca
www.bathmuseum.ca

Year Founded: 1936 Local history, including aboriginal artifacts; open May-Sept., W-Su 10:00-4:00.

***Bath:* United Empire Loyalist Heritage Centre & Park**
***Parent:* Bay of Quinte Br., United Empire Loyalist Association of Canada**
54 Adolphustown Park Rd.
Bath, ON K0H 1G0

Tel: 613-373-2196*Toll-Free:* 877-384-1784
library@uel.ca
www.uel.ca

The United Empire Loyalist Heritage Centre houses the H.C. Burleigh Archives, a library & museum. The Heritage Centre is owned & operated by the Bay of Quinte Branch of the United Empire Loyalist Association of Canada. It is open from April to October, & by appointment at other times of the year.
Brian Tackaberry, Bay of Quinte Branch Vice-President, United Empire Loyalist Association, 1784@uel.ca

***Beachville:* Beachville District Museum**
PO Box 220
Located at 584371 Beachville Rd., Beachville, ON
Beachville, ON N0J 1A0

Tel: 519-423-6497; *Fax:* 519-423-6935
bmchin@execulink.com
www.beachvilledistrictmuseum.ca

Year Founded: 1992 The Beachville District Museum features artifacts, such as Mastadon bones found on the O.J. Bond farm. The history of limestone quarries is also depicted at the museum, since the area is home to the largest open face quarries in Canada. A baseball display is featured because Beachville is the place where the first recorded baseball game in North America took place. The museum is open year round.

***Beaverton:* Beaver River Museum**
PO Box 314, 284 Simcoe St.
Beaverton, ON L0K 1A0

Tel: 705-426-9641
bte.hist.soc@bellnet.ca
www.btehs.com

The Beaver River Museum consists of the Old Stone Jail, a settlers' log cabin (c.1850), & a brick house (c.1900). The museum is open during weekends in May, June, & September, & daily, except on Tuesdays, in July & August.
Jane Veale, Curator
Ken Alsop, Archivist

***Belleville:* Belleville Public Library & John M. Parrott Art Gallery**
254 Pinnacle St.
Belleville, ON K8N 3B1

Tel: 613-968-6731; *Fax:* 613-968-6841
Toll-Free: 866-979-5877
gallery@bellevillelibrary.com
bellevillelibrary.com/jo hnmparrottartgallerys9.php
twitter.com/BellevillePL
www.facebook.com/2 19197338115817

Year Founded: 1973 The gallery is located on the third floor of the public library. The gallery is open Tu, W & F 9:30-5:00, Th 9:30-8:00 & Sa 9:30-5:30.
Susan Holland, Curator

***Belleville:* Belleville Scout-Guide Museum**
350 Dundas St. West
Belleville, ON K8P 1B2

Tel: 613-966-2740
www3.sympatico.ca/pandj
Social Media: www.youtube.com/user/ScoutsAgonquinte
www.facebook.com/231236203598422

Year Founded: 1975 Scout & guide memorabilia; 25,000 items; open by appointment only
Paul Deryaw, Curator, pandj@sympatico.ca
David Bentley, Historian & Archivist

***Belleville:* Glanmore National Historic Site**
257 Bridge St. East
Belleville, ON K8N 1P4

Tel: 613-962-2329; *Fax:* 613-962-6340
glanmore.ca
twitter.com/glanmorenhs
www.facebook.com/GlanmoreNHS

The restored Victoria home of the Phillips-Burrows-Faulkner families; original & period furnishings displayed in principal rooms; paintings & decorative art from the Couldery Collection on permanent exhibit; lamps from the Paul Lamp Collection, as well as other exhibits; special exhibits/events held throughout the year
Rona Rustige, Curator

Belleville: Hastings & Prince Edward Regiment Military Museum
The Armoury, 187 Pinnacle St.
Belleville, ON K8N 3A5
Tel: 613-966-2125; *Fax:* 613-966-2110
www.theregiment.ca/hpmuseum.html
Open year round.

Blind River: Timber Village Museum
PO Box 628, 180 Leacock St.
Blind River, ON P0R 1B0
Tel: 705-356-7544
www.blindriver.com
Other contact information: Year round: 705-356-2251
Year Founded: 1967 Provides guest with a sense of what a lumberjack's life was like at the turn of the last century; displays include axes, saws, logging tools & a portable forge; art gallery which exhibits works of contemporary local artists & artisans; workshops, children's educational programmes; lumberjack dinner, 1st Sat. in Oct.; open year round.

Bobcaygeon: The Boyd Museum
PO Box 1221
Located at 21 Canal St. East, Bobcaygeon, ON
Bobcaygeon, ON K0M 1A0
Tel: 705-738-9482; *Fax:* 705-738-0918
info@theboydmuseum.com
www.theboydmuseum.com
The museum shows, through artifacts & archival material, how the Boyd family helped develop the Bobcaygeon & Kawartha Lakes region. Open May, June & Sept., Sa 11:00-3:00, Su 1:00-3:00; July & Aug., W-Su 10:00-4:00.

Bobcaygeon: Kawartha Settlers' Village
PO Box 755
Located at 85 Dunn St., Bobcaygeon, ON, K0M 1A0
Bobcaygeon, ON K0M 1A0
Tel: 705-738-6163
info@settlersvillage.org
settlersvillage.org
twitter.com/KSVillage
www.facebook.com/kawartha.se ttlersvillage
Twelve historic homes & buildings collected on former Kawartha farm; regional arts & heritage centre offering courses in the Arts
Al Ingram, President
Maureen Lytle, General Manager, maureen.lytle@settlersvillage.org

Borden: Base Borden Military Museum
Canadian Forces Base Borden, 27 Ram St.
Borden, ON L0M 1C0
Tel: 705-423-3531; *Fax:* 705-423-3623
www.cg.cfpsa.ca
The Base Borden Military Museum consists of several buildings & a memorial park. It features the history of CFB Borden, with a collection of armoured vehicles, artillery pieces, trucks, & aircraft from World War I, World War II, & the present. As the birthplace of the Canadian Air Force, Base Borden also displays the Avro 504 K aircraft, a Tiger Moth, a Silver Star, & a Tutor aircraft.

Bothwell: Fairfield Museum
14878 Longwoods Rd., RR#5
Bothwell, ON N0P 1C0
Tel: 519-692-4397
fairfield.museum@sympatico.ca
www.friendsoffairfieldmuseum.ca
Site of Moravian Delaware mission, est. 1792, destroyed 1813 by US soldiers; artifacts from burnt village
Chris Aldred, Curator, 519-692-4397

Bowmanville: Bowmanville Museum
Parent: Clarington Museums & Archives
37 Silver St.
Bowmanville, ON L1C 3C4
Tel: 905-623-2734
www.claringtonmuseums.com

Bowmanville: Clarington Museums & Archives
Municipality of Clarington, 62 Temperance St.
Bowmanville, ON L1C 3A8
Tel: 905-623-2734
info@claringtonmuseums.com
www.claringtonmuseums.com
Social Media: claringtonmuseumsandarchives.blogspot.ca
twitter.com/ClarMuseum
www.fa cebook.com/110074875701103
Comprised of Bowmanville Museum, Clarke Museum, Sarah Jane Williams Heritage Centre; depicts the early urban & rural roots of the Municipality of Clarington; special collections including Dominion Pianos & Organs; one of the largest doll collections in Canada
Michael Adams, Executive Director, madams@claringtonmuseums.com

Bowmanville: Sarah Jane Williams Heritage Centre
Parent: Clarington Museums & Archives
62 Temperance St.
Bowmanville, ON L1C 3A8
Tel: 905-623-2734; *Fax:* 905-623-5684
www.claringtonmuseums.com
Houses the majority of the Clarington Museums & Archives' collection.

Bracebridge: Muskoka Rails Museum
53 Covered Bridge Trail
Location: Maple Orchard Farms, 14 Gray Road, Bracebridge, ON P1L 1P8.
Bracebridge, ON P1L 1Y2
Tel: 705-646-9711
www.muskokarailsmuseum.com
Dedicated to showcasing the history of Canadian rail travel, with an emphasis on the Muskoka area. Guided historical tours of the area are available.
David Powley, Contact

Bracebridge: Woodchester Villa
100 Taylor Ct.
Located at 15 King St., Bracebridge, ON, P1L 1T7
Bracebridge, ON P1L 1R6
Tel: 705-645-5264; *Fax:* 705-645-7525
www.octagonalhouse.com
Woodchester Villa is an octagonal house museum, which dates back to 1882. The house is designated as a historic site, under the Ontario Heritage Act. Woodchester Villa is open from Canada Day to Labour Day.

Brampton: Lorne Scots Regimental Museum
2 Chapel St.
Brampton, ON L6W 2H1
Tel: 519-833-9008
www.lornesmuseum.ca
Other contact information: Alternate URL: www.lornescots.ca/museum.php
Maj. (Ret'd) Richard E. Ruggle, Chair, shepherd@kw.igs.net
Maj. (Ret'd) Tom Graham, Curator, tom069@sympatico.ca

Brantford: Bell Homestead National Historic Site
94 Tutela Heights Rd.
Brantford, ON N3T 1A1
Tel: 519-756-6220; *Fax:* 519-759-5975
bellhomestead@brantford.ca
www.bellhomestead.ca
www.facebook.com/BellH omestead
Displays at the Bell Homestead National Historic Site depict the 1870 to 1881 household of Alexander Graham Bell, the invention of the telephone, & the origins of Canadian telephone operations.
Brian Wood, Curator

Brantford: Brant Museum & Archives
Parent: Brant Historical Society
c/o Brant Historical Society, 57 Charlotte St.
Brantford, ON N3T 2W6
Tel: 519-752-2483; *Fax:* 519-752-1931
information@brantmuseums.ca
www.brantmuseum.ca
Social Media: www.youtube.com/user/branthistorical
twitter.com/branthistorical
www.f acebook.com/BrantHistoricalSociety
Operated by the Brant Historical Society, the Brant Museum & Archives collects, preserves, researches, & exhibits items related to the founding, settlement, & diversity of Brant County & the surrounding area. Researchers will discover items such as photographs, diaries, letters, & maps in the archive collection. Open year round.
Chelsea Carss, Curator

Brantford: Canadian Military Heritage Museum
347 Greenwich St.
Location: 347 Greenwich St., Brantford, ON N3S 7V1
Brantford, ON N3S 7X4
Tel: 519-759-1313
cmhm@execulink.com
www.cmhmhq.ca
A privately owned & operated museum displaying artifacts from Canada's military history. Hours of Operation: March & Apr., F-Su 10:00-4:00; May-Sept., Tu-Su 10:00-4:00; Oct. & Nov., F-Su 10:00-4:00.
Richard Shaver, Chair

Brantford: Myrtleville House Museum
Parent: Brant Historical Society
34 Myrtleville Dr.
Brantford, ON N3V 1C2
Tel: 519-752-3216
information@brantmuseums.ca
www.brantmuseums.ca
One of the oldest homes in Brant County (1837); the museum also promotes interactive learning & provide hands-on activities to aid students in explore the heritage of the county. Open year-round M-F 9:00-4:00, Sa-Su 1:00-4:00 in July and August.

Brantford: Personal Computer Museum
13 Alma St.
Brantford, ON N3R 2G1
Tel: 519-753-8825
www.pcmuseum.ca
twitter.com/vintagepc
www.facebook.com/personalcomputermuseum
Year Founded: 2005 Exhibits early personal computers as well as software & related magazines & books.
Syd Bolton, Contact, sbolton@bfree.on.ca

Brantford: Woodland Cultural Centre
PO Box 1506, 184 Mohawk St.
Brantford, ON N3T 5V6
Tel: 519-759-2650; *Fax:* 519-759-8912
www.woodland-centre.on.ca
Social Media: www.youtube.com/user/woodlandcc1972
twitter.com/woodlandcc
www.faceboo k.com/WoodlandCulturalCentre
Year Founded: 1972 Houses a First Nations art gallery as well as a museum whose collection includes historical documents, furniture & visual art.

Brighton: Presqu'ile Provincial Park
328 Presqu'ile Pkwy.
Brighton, ON K0K 1H0
Tel: 613-475-4324
www.ontarioparks.com/english/pres.html
Social Media: www.pinterest.com/ontarioparks/presqu-ile/
One of Ontario's oldest provincial parks (1922); displays & programs of early history of the area; working lighthouse

Brighton: Proctor House Museum
Parent: Save Our Heritage Organization
PO Box 578, 96 Young St.
Brighton, ON K0K 1H0
Tel: 613-475-2144
info@proctorhousemuseum.ca
proctorhousemuseum.ca
Living museum: 1860s gentleman's home, completely furnished; open daily July & August for tours; or by appt. The Brighton Barn Theatre is housed in the Proctor-Simpson Barn adjacent to the property.

Brockville: Brockville Museum
5 Henry St.
Brockville, ON K6V 6M4
Tel: 613-342-4397; *Fax:* 613-342-7345
museum@brockville.com
www.brockvillemuseum.com
www.facebook.com/586855 381324643
Year Founded: 1981 The Brockville Museum is committed to preserving and promoting the history of Brockville through quality exhibits and education programs.
Natalie Wood, Director/Curator

Brockville: Fulford Place
Parent: Ontario Heritage Trust
287 King St. East
Brockville, ON K6V 1E3
Tel: 613-498-3003; *Fax:* 613-498-1050
fulford@heritagetrust.on.ca
www.heritagetrust.on.ca/Fulford-Place/Home.a spx
Year Founded: 1993 Historic Edwardian mansion which seasonally holds art exhibits.
Pamela Brooks, Coordinator, Eastern Ontario Museum Sites

***Brooke-Alvinston:* A.W. Campbell House Museum**
8477 Shiloh Line
Brooke-Alvinston, ON N0N 1A0
Tel: 519-245-3710
www.scrca.on.ca
www.facebook.com/196653253699385
Other contact information: In-season phone: 519-847-5357
The museum is located in the A.W. Campbell Conservation Area, R.R.#2 Alvinston, ON, off Nauvoo Rd. A typical 1890s southwestern Ontario rural home comprises the museum, & the conservation area also includes a campground & walking trails.
Brian McDougall, General Manager, St. Clair Conservation, bmcdougall@scrca.on.ca

***Bruce Mines:* Bruce Mines Museum**
Hwy. 17
Bruce Mines, ON P0R 1C0
Tel: 705-206-9642
bmd.historicalsociety@gmail.com
www.facebook.com/522714371178738
Year Founded: 1961 Situated in a church built in 1894, the Bruce Mines Museum features pioneer items such as an 1876 slot machine, a Victorian doll house, & a Yakaboo canoe.

***Burlington:* Ireland House at Oakridge Farm**
2168 Guelph Line
Burlington, ON L7P 5A8
Tel: 905-332-9888; *Fax:* 905-332-1714
Toll-Free: 800-374-2099
www.museumsofburlington.com/ireland-house
Home of Joseph Ireland, built between 1835 & 1837; open year round
Barbara Teatero, Director, Museums

***Burlington:* Joseph Brant Museum**
1240 North Shore Blvd. East
Burlington, ON L7S 1C5
Tel: 905-634-3556; *Fax:* 905-634-4498
Toll-Free: 888-748-5386
www.museumsofburlington.com/joseph-brant
Social Media: vimeo.com/museumsofburlington
twitter.com/BurlingtonMuse
www.facebook.com/pages/Museums-of-Burlington/14389272142
Year Founded: 1942 The museum is a replica of the original 1800 home of Mohawk, Captain Joseph Brant, "Thayendanegea"; exhibits relating to indigeneous culture, with emphasis on the Iroquois; history of Burlington; historical costume exhibit, one of Ontario's finest collection of Victorian clothing & accessories; open year round.
Barbara Teatero, Director of Museums

***Burlington:* Spruce Lane Farm House**
Bronte Provincial Park, 1219 Burloak Dr.
Burlington, ON L7R 3X5
Tel: 905-827-6911
www.brontecreek.org
Social Media: pinterest.com/brontecreekpp
twitter.com/brontecreekpp
www.facebook.com/203544433021485
A living history museum located in Bronte Provincial Park.
Sheila Wiebe, Contact, sheila.wiebe@ontario.ca

***Caledonia:* Edinburgh Square Heritage & Cultural Centre**
PO Box 2056
Located at 80 Caithness St. East, Caledonia, ON
Caledonia, ON N3W 2G6
Tel: 905-765-3134; *Fax:* 905-765-3009
esquare.centre@haldimandcounty.on.ca
www.haldimandcounty.on.ca
Artifacts relating to Town of Haldimand, from pioneer times to 1970s; open year round
Anne Unyi, Curator

***Callander:* Callander Bay Heritage Museum**
PO Box 100, 107 Lansdowne St.
Callander, ON P0H 1H0
Tel: 705-752-2282; *Fax:* 705-752-3116
museum@callander.ca
www.mycallander.ca/museum
www.facebook.com/4031686 0327
The Callander Bay Heritage Museum was the home & office of Dr. Allan R. Dafoe from 1914 to 1943. Dr. Dafoe was the doctor for the Dionne Quintuplets. The museum contains exhibits about the doctor & the quintuplets. The Alex Dufrense Gallery features the work of local artists. The museum also houses local genealogical sources & historical records for research.
Carol Pretty, Curator, cpretty@callander.ca

***Cambridge:* Cambridge Sports Hall of Fame**
#444, 425 Hespeler Rd.
Cambridge, ON N1R 6J2
Tel: 519-653-7071
cambridgesportshalloffame.ca
Year Founded: 1997 The Hall of Fame seeks to celebrate the sporting history of Cambridge through text, images, & memorabilia, as well as annually inducting athletes, teams & builders.
Gary Hedges, Chair, gr.hedges@sympatico.ca
Jim Cox, Contact, Displays & Memorabilia, mjcox11@rogers.com
Bob Howison, Contact, jbhowison@aol.com

***Cambridge:* The Fashion History Museum**
64 Grand Ave. South
Cambridge, ON N1S 2L8
Tel: 519-267-2091
info@FashionHistoryMuseum.com
www.fashionhistorymuseum.com
Year Founded: 2004 The museum's collection features over 8,000 garments & accessories, from the 1660s to the present. The museum currently lacks a permanent home, but creates travelling exhibitions & engages in research.
Catherine Vernon, Chair
Jonathan Walford, Curator & Co-Founder, curator@fashionhistorymuseum.com
Kenn Norman, Director & Co-Founder, ceo@fashionhistorymuseum.com

***Campbellford:* Campbellford-Seymour Heritage Centre**
Campbellford-Seymour Heritage Society, PO Box 1294, 113 Front St. North
Campbellford, ON K0L 1L0
Tel: 705-653-2634
csheritage@persona.ca
www.csheritage.org
Year Founded: 1989 The Campbellford-Seymour Heritage Centre is the home of the Campbellford-Seymour Heritage Society. The Society preserves & communicates the history of Campbellford / Seymour, maintains local archives, & assists with genealogical research.
Anne Linton, Secretary
Ian McCulloch, President

***Cannington:* Cannington Historical Museum**
c/o Cannington & Area Historical Society, PO Box 196, 21 Laidlaw St. South
Cannington, ON L0E 1E0
Tel: 705-432-3136
canningtonhistoricalsociety@hotmail.ca
www.canningtonh istoricalsociety.ca
Located in Cannington's MacLeod Park on Peace Street, the Cannington Historical Museum features the following buildings: log homes (circa 1827 & 1857), an 1871 Canadian Northern Railway station, a 1929 Canadian National Railway caboose, the 1934 Derryville (LOL) Hall, & a driving shed. The museum is open from Victoria Day to Labour Day, or by appointment.
Ted Foster, President

***Capreol:* Northern Ontario Railroad Museum & Heritage Centre (NORMHC)**
36 Bloor St.
Capreol, ON P0M 1H0
Tel: 705-858-5050; *Fax:* 705-858-4539
info@normhc.ca
www.normhc.ca
www.facebook.com/normhc67
Year Founded: 1993 Lumber, mining & railroad exhibits.
Wendy Paul, President

***Carleton Pl.:* Mill of Kintail Conservation Area**
***Parent:* Mississippi Valley Conservation**
10970 Hwy. 7
Location: 2854 Ramsay Concession 8, Mississippi Mills, ON K0A 1A0
Carleton Pl., ON K7C 3P1
Tel: 613-259-3610
info@mvc.on.ca
www.mvc.on.ca/conservation-areas/mill-of-kintail
twitter.com/MVC5
www. facebook.com/17441971925O747
Kintail Museum, housed in a heritage grist mill, is a collection & a conservation site on the Indian River in Lanark County. The museum showcases the life & works of Robert Tait McKenzie as the mill was his summer home & sculpture studio; the museum showcases the largest collection of McKenzie's sculptures & memorabilia in Canada.

***Carleton Place:* Carleton Place & Beckwith Heritage Museum & Gardens**
***Parent:* C.P. & Beckwith Historical Society**
267 Edmund St.
Carleton Place, ON K7C 3E8
Tel: 613-253-7013
cpbheritagemuseum@bellnet.ca
cpbheritagemuseum.com
www.facebook.com/173158069407762
Local history of Carleton Place & Beckwith Township
Jennifer Irwin, Manager

***Carp:* Diefenbunker, Canada's Cold War Museum / Musée canadien de la Guerre froide**
PO Box 466, 3911 Carp Rd.
Carp, ON K0A 1L0
Tel: 613-839-0007*Toll-Free:* 800-409-1965
www.diefenbunker.ca
Social Media: pinterest.com/diefenbunker;
www.youtube.com/TheDiefenbunker
twitter.com/Diefenbunker
www.facebook. com/diefenbunker
Other contact information: Wordpress: diefenbunker.wordpress.com
Year Founded: 1994 The museum is housed in a once-secret Cold War-era bunker meant to shelter members of the government in the event of a nuclear attack. The bunker is now a National Historic Site of Canada. The museum seeks to preserve the history of Canada's involvement in the Cold War, & to create interest in the Cold War in general. Open daily 11:00-4:00.
Sylvie Morel, President
Henriette Riegel, Executive Director, director@diefenbunker.ca

***Cayuga:* Haldimand County Museum & Archives**
PO Box 38
Located at 8 Echo St., Cayuga, ON
Cayuga, ON N0A 1E0
Tel: 905-772-5880; *Fax:* 905-772-1725
museum.archives@haldimandcounty.on.ca
www.haldimandcounty.on.ca
twitte r.com/visithaldimand
www.facebook.com/128909910457566
Temporary & permanent exhibits; 1835 log cabin on site; regional & genealogical archives
Karen E. Richardson, Curator

***Cayuga:* Ruthven Park**
PO Box 610
Located at 243 Haldimand Hwy #54, Cayuga, ON, N0A 1E0
Cayuga, ON N0A 1E0
Fax: 905-772-0561
Toll-Free: 877-705-7275
info@ruthvenpark.ca
ruthvenparknationalhistoricsite.com
Social Media:
www.youtube.com/channel/UCmA7uT-L6BB1a6t3rGFmDFg
twitter.com/search/RuthvenPark_NHS
www.facebook.com/184655724898271
A national historic site representing Canadian landscapes & houses one of the three Haldimand Bird Observatory Banding Stations. Former home of the Thompson family.

***Chapleau:* Chapleau Centennial Museum**
PO Box 129
Located at 94 Monk St., Chapleau, ON
Chapleau, ON P0M 1K0
Tel: 705-864-1122; *Fax:* 705-864-2138
www.chapleau.ca/en/visit/museumsteamengine.asp
Year Founded: 1967 Located in Centennial Park, on Monk St. in Chapleau; tourist information centre; mineral collection, mounted animals, material related to Chapleau & area; archives; educational programming; bilingual services; special needs facilities; picnic area; open May 15 - Oct. 15

***Chatham:* Chatham Railroad Museum**
PO Box 434, 2 McLean St.
Chatham, ON N7M 5K5
Tel: 519-352-3097
crms@mnsi.net
www.chathamrailroadmuseum.ca
www.facebook.com/195849387130379
Located in a CN baggage car built in 1955; contains early railroad equipment, several model trains & other memorabilia; open May through Labour Day, with group tours available all year round

***Chatham:* Chatham-Kent Black Historical Society**
177 King St. East
Chatham, ON N7M 3N1
Tel: 519-352-3565
info@ckblackhistoricalsociety.org
www.ckblackhistoricalsociety.org
Year Founded: 1992 The society offers guided tours of heritage sites around the Essex & Kent areas of Southern Ontario, as well as a Heritage Room featuring displays & archival material.
Blair Newby, Executive Director

***Chatham:* Chatham-Kent Museum**
***Parent:* The Cultural Centre**
Chatham Cultural Centre, 75 William St. North
Chatham, ON N7M 4L4
Tel: 519-360-1998; *Fax:* 519-354-4170
Toll-Free: 800-714-7497
ckcccmuseum@chatham-kent.ca
www.chatham-kent.ca
twit ter.com/culturalcentre1
www.facebook.com/231501020233902
Local history museum & archives; features a retrospective of Chatham-Kent during first half of 20th century; special exhibitions gallery with changing displays throughout year; open daily
Stephanie Saunders, Curator

***Chatham:* Milner Heritage House**
59 William St. North
Chatham, ON N7M 4L4
Tel: 519-360-1998; *Fax:* 519-354-4170
ckcccmuseum@chatham-kent.ca
www.chatham-kent.ca/milnerheritagehouse
ww w.facebook.com/231501020233902
Year Founded: 1943 Museum depicts the turn-of-the-century lifestyle of Robert Milner,a successful, local industrialist and carriage maker; also features award-winning artwork by Robert's wife Emma; second floor features the Rev. Sandys bird collection & the MacPhail exotic animal collection; affiliated with the Chatham-Kent Museum (The Cultural Centre)
Stephanie Saunders, Curator

***Cheltenham:* The Great War Flying Museum**
c/o Brampton Flying Club, PO Box 27, 13691 McLaughlin Rd., RR#1
Cheltenham, ON L7C 3L7
Tel: 905-838-4936
info@greatwarflyingmuseum.com
www.greatwarflyingmuseum.com
Social Media: www.youtube.com/TheGWFM
www.facebook.com/186888438015885
Volunteer group builds, maintains & flies WWI replica fighter aircraft; artifacts from WWI; located at the Brampton Airport
Nat McHaffie, Curator

***Chesterville:* Chesterville & District Historical Society Heritage Centre**
PO Box 693
Located at 14 Victoria St., Chesterville, ON
Chesterville, ON K0C 1H0
Tel: 613-448-9130
www.northdundas.com/tourism/chesterville-heritage-centre
Year Founded: 1984 The centre is housed in an 1867 building, & features a collection of artifacts on local history.
Carol Goddard, President
Alec J. Ball, Vice-President, 613-821-3934
Margot Dixon, Secretary, 613-984-2880

***Clinton:* School on Wheels Railcar Museum**
PO Box 488
Located at 76 Victoria Terrace, Clinton, ON
Clinton, ON N0M 1L0
Tel: 519-482-3997
cnrschoolonwheelsgmail.com
www.schoolcar.ca
www.facebook.com/151143751653755
Year Founded: 1982 A former railway school that both children & adults attended in Northern Ontario between 1926 & 1965.

***Cloyne:* Cloyne Pioneer Museum & Archives**
***Parent:* The Cloyne & District Historical Society**
PO Box 228
Located at Hwy. 41, Cloyne, ON
Cloyne, ON K0H 1K0
Tel: 613-336-8011
pioneerinfo@mazinaw.on.ca
pioneer.mazinaw.on.ca
Artifacts from the pioneer days of the area including tools, clothing, kitchen and other households effects, glass bottles, flat irons, a rolling pin made from a block of solid maple, photos and old catalogues; genealogical archive. Located across from the Post Office in Cloyne. Summer Hours: M-Su 10:00-4:00

***Cobalt:* The Bunker Military Museum**
PO Box 848
Located at 24 Prospect Ave., Cobalt, ON
Cobalt, ON P0J 1C0
Tel: 705-679-5191; *Fax:* 705-679-5050
bunkermilitarymuseum@gmail.com
www.bunkermilitarymuseum.ca
www.faceboo k.com/bunkermilitarymuseum
Year Founded: 1990 The museum consists of the private military memorabilia collection of Cobalt resident Jim Jones, & is housed in the Bilsky Block, in Cobalt.

***Cobalt:* Cobalt Mining Museum**
PO Box 215
Located at 24 Silver St., Cobalt, ON
Cobalt, ON P0J 1C0
Tel: 705-679-8301; *Fax:* 705-679-8301
cnomchin@ntl.sympatico.ca
Year Founded: 1953 The museum preserves the world's largest collection of native silver ore, mining & prospecting equipment & artifacts, & fluorescent rock; other displays highlight the early cultural & social life of Cobalt; unique, handcrafted silver jewelry available in the gift shop; underground tours of the Colonial Adit can be arranged. Open all year.

***Cobourg:* Marie Dressler House**
212 King St. West
Cobourg, ON K9A 2N1
www.mariedressler.ca
Local history & birthplace of actress Marie Dressler.

***Cobourg:* Sifton-Cook Heritage Centre (SCHC)**
***Parent:* Cobourg Museum Foundation (CMF)**
c/o Cobourg Museum Foundation, Victoria Hall, 55 King St. West
Cobourg, ON K9A 2M2
Tel: 905-373-7222
info@cobourgmuseum.ca
northumberlandheritage.ca
Social Media: pinterest.com/CobourgMuseum
twitter.com/CobourgMuseum
www.facebook.com/153555487994142
Year Founded: 1999 The centre is housed in an old barracks building; the site also includes an 1860s workman's cottage.
Joan Chalovich, Chair

***Cochrane:* Cochrane Railway & Pioneer Museum**
PO Box 490
Cochrane, ON P0L 1C0
Tel: 705-272-4361; *Fax:* 705-272-6068
Located across from the train station in Cochrane; railway artifacts & memorabilia, photographs, displays

***Coldwater:* Coldwater Canadiana Heritage Museum**
PO Box 125, 1474 Woodrow Rd.
Coldwater, ON L0K 1E0
Tel: 705-955-1930
www.coldwatermuseum.com
www.facebook.com/581207571912813
1840s log house & other buildings; open May - Oct.
Wayne Scott, Director/Curator

***Collingwood:* Bygone Days Heritage Village**
879 - 6th St.
Collingwood, ON L9Y 3Y9
Tel: 705-441-3130
www.bygonedays.ca
www.facebook.com/696149730432954
Year Founded: 1965 The village features 30 buildings that date from the mid-1800s, as well as costumed interpreters who walk about the village. Open June-Oct., weekends 10:00-5:00.
Adara Bull, Contact, adarabull@yahoo.ca

***Collingwood:* The Collingwood Museum**
PO Box 556, 45 St. Paul St.
Collingwood, ON L9Y 4B2
Tel: 705-445-4811
www.collingwood.ca/museum
www.facebook.com/collingwoodmuseum
Located in the "Station"; large collection relating to history of Collingwood & area; exhibits showcasing shipping & shipbuilding & early history; archival materials & special events & activities throughout the year
Susan Warner, Supervisor, Station & Museum, swarner@collingwood.ca

***Comber:* Comber & District Historical Society Museum**
10405 Hwy. 77
Comber, ON N0P 1J0
Tel: 519-687-3400
combermuseum1.wix.com/comber-museum
www.facebook.com/2 90834654327344
Pioneer articles & agricultural items; admission by donation; open Thu.-Mon.
Mark McKinlay, Contact, markmckinlay@xplornet.com

***Combermere:* Madonna House Pioneer Museum**
Madonna House Apostolate, 2888 Dafoe Rd., RR#2
Combermere, ON K0J 1L0
Tel: 613-756-3713; *Fax:* 613-756-0211
combermere@madonnahouse.org
www.madonnahouse.org
Social Media: www.youtube.com/MadonnaHouseCanada
twitter.com/madonnahouse
www.facebo ok.com/MadonnaHouse
Year Founded: 1967 History of early settlers in the area; located in century-old barn
Fr. David May, Director General
Mark Schlingerman, Director General
Susanne Stubbs, Director General

***Commanda:* Commanda Museum**
4077 Hwy. 522
Commanda, ON P0H 1J0
Tel: 705-729-1384
www.commandamuseum.ca
Complete with original shelves, counter & floor from the 1870s; features artifacts from 1870s - 1930s as well as a gift shops which features work from the region; tea room; open daily mid-June - mid-Oct.

***Copper Cliff:* Copper Cliff Museum**
26 Balsam St.
Copper Cliff, ON P0M 1N0
Tel: 705-674-4455
curator@greatersudbury.ca
www.sudburymuseums.ca
Year Founded: 1901 Located in 1890 log house; contains artifacts pertaining to the lifestyle of residents of a mining community; photographs & documents leading back to establishment of Copper Cliff

***Cornwall:* Cornwall Community Museum**
160 Water St. West
Cornwall, ON K6H 5T5
Tel: 613-936-0280
cornwallcommunitymuseum@gmail.com
cornwallcommunitymuseum.wordpress.com
twitter.com/CornwallCMuseum
www. facebook.com/CornwallCommunityMuseum
Loyalist & local history archives, local domestic manufacturing; open year round, W-Su
Ian Bowering, Curator, 613-936-0842, ian10@bellnet.ca

***Cornwall:* Cornwall Community Museum in the Wood House**
***Parent:* Stormont, Dundas & Glengarry Historical Society**
PO Box 773
Cornwall, ON K6H 5T5
Tel: 613-963-0280
sdg_historicalsociety@bellnet.ca
www.facebook.com/190680844279914
Local history
Jeffrey Crooke, President, 613-537-2075
Ian Bowering, Curator, 613-936-0842

***Cornwall:* Stormont, Dundas & Glengarry Highlanders Regimental Museum**
505 - 4th St. East
Cornwall, ON K6H 2J7
Tel: 613-936-9124; *Fax:* 613-993-8147
Open year round.

***Cornwall Island:* Ronathahon:ni Cultural Centre**
RR#3
Cornwall Island, ON K6H 5R7
Tel: 613-932-9452; *Fax:* 613-932-0092
Iroquois, Cree & Ojibwa artifacts

***Cumberland:* Cumberland Heritage Village Museum**
2940 Old Montréal Rd.
Cumberland, ON K4C 1E6
Tel: 613-833-3059
cumberlandmuseum@ottawa.ca
www.ottawa.ca/museums
www.facebook.com/cumberlandmuseum

Representation of a rural village in the Lower Ottawa Valley, with artifacts related to period of 1880-1935; open year round

Deep River: Canadian Clock Museum
PO Box 1684
Located at 60 James St., Deep River, ON
Deep River, ON K0J 1P0
Tel: 613-584-9687
enquiries@canclockmuseum.ca
www.canclockmuseum.ca
Year Founded: 2000 Clock seller & manufacturer history.

Delhi: Delhi Ontario Tobacco Museum & Heritage Centre
200 Talbot Rd.
Delhi, ON N4B 2A2
Tel: 519-582-0278; *Fax:* 519-582-0122
delhi.museum@norfolkcounty.ca
www.delhimuseum.ca
www.facebook.com/2208 43701442455
Year Founded: 1979 Tobacco-related machinery; a ginseng exhibit; multicultural exhibits & street scene depicting five historic buildings at turn of the 20th century; a large pavilion complete with barbecues is available in Quance Park nearby

Delta: The Old Stone Mill, National Historic Site (DMS)
Parent: The Delta Mill Society
PO Box 172
Located at 46 King St., Delta, ON
Delta, ON K0E 1G0
Tel: 613-928-2584
info@deltamill.org
www.deltamill.org
www.facebook.co m/DeltaMill
Stone mill c. 1810. Part of the Family of National Historic Sites;the oldest surviving automatic stone grist mill in Ontario; showcases milling technology and 1800s industrial heritage; artifacts include buhr millstones, 48 inch Swain turbines, roller mills.

Dorset: Dorset Heritage Museum
PO Box 111
Located at 1040 Main St., Dorset, ON
Dorset, ON P0A 1E0
Tel: 705-766-0323
dhm@muskoka.com
www.dorsetheritagemuseum.ca
Local history; open May-July, Sa & Su 10:00-4:00; July-Oct. W-Sa 10:00-4:00.
Kerry Lock, Chair

Dresden: Uncle Tom's Cabin Historic Site (UTCHS)
29251 Uncle Tom's Rd.
Dresden, ON N0P 1M0
Tel: 519-683-2978; *Fax:* 519-683-1256
utchs@heritagetrust.on.ca
www.heritagetrust.on.ca/Uncle-Tom-s-Cabin-Historic-Site/home.aspx
www.facebook.com/208228612579633
Uncle Tom's Cabin educates visitors about fugitive slaves in the Dresden area. The site focuses on the life of the Reverend Josiah Henson, a slave who escaped with his family to Upper Canada via the Underground Railroad. The grounds feature the following attractions: the Josiah Henson Interpretive Centre, the North Star Theatre, the Underground Railroad Freedom Gallery, the Harris House, a smokehouse, a sawmill, the Josiah Henson House, a pioneer church, & the Henson Family Cemetery. Open from mid May to the end of October. At other times of the year, groups of twenty or more may make an appointment.

Drumbo: Drumbo & District Museum
Parent: Drumbo & District Heritage Society
42 Centre St.
Drumbo, ON N0J 1G0
Tel: 519-463-5233
DDHS1995Drumbo@yahoo.ca
ddhs1995.wordpress.com
Year Founded: 2012 Local history.

Dryden: Dryden & District Museum
15 Van Horne Ave.
Dryden, ON P8N 2A5
Tel: 807-223-4671; *Fax:* 807-223-7354
lgardner@dryden.ca
www.dryden.ca/city_services/museum
www.facebook.com /42558327650
First Nations & pioneer artifacts; minerals; archival material
Leah Gardner, Curator, lgardner@dryden.ca

Dundas: Dundas Museum & Archives
Parent: Dundas Historical Society Museum
139 Park St. West
Dundas, ON L9H 1X8
Tel: 905-627-7412; *Fax:* 905-627-4872
mail@dundasmuseum.ca
www.dundasmuseum.ca
twitter.com/DundasMuseum
ww w.facebook.com/DundasMuseum
Celebrates & preserves the story of the Dundas community; museum features true to life displays, & a diversified collection of exhibits reflecting the varied occupations & activities of those who have contributed to the development of the community
Kevin Puddister, Curator, kpuddister@dundasmuseum.ca

Dunvegan: The Glengarry Pioneer Museum (GPM)
1645 County Rd. 30, RR#1
Dunvegan, ON K0C 1J0
Tel: 613-527-5230
info@glengarrypioneermuseum.ca
www.glengarrypioneermuseum.ca
www.facebook.com/171844766199518
1840 log inn; miniature cheese factory; 1869 municipal hall; carriage shed & log barn; blacksmith shop

Ear Falls: Ear Falls District Museum
PO Box 309
Ear Falls, ON P0V 1T0
Tel: 807-222-3624
Dedicated to the history of exploration, transportation, & the settlement of the area

Egmondville: The Van Egmond House
80 Kippen Rd.
Egmondville, ON N0K 1W0
Tel: 519-523-4411
Restored & furnished Georgian county-manor house dating to the mid-19th century with antiques indicitive of the time; founded by Constant Van Egmond.

Elgin: Jones Falls Defensible Lockmaster's House & Blacksmith Shop
PO Box 10
Located at Rideau Canal, 182 Lock Rd., Elgin, ON
Elgin, ON K0G 1E0
Tel: 613-507-3185
Lockmaster's house c. 1841; blacksmith shop produces hardware c. 1843

Elgin: Lockmaster's House Museum
PO Box 162
Elgin, ON K0G 1E0
Tel: 613-359-5022; *Fax:* 613-359-6376
www.rideau-info.com/lockhouse/museum.html
Year Founded: 1982 Local history

Elk Lake: Elk Lake Heritage Museum
c/o Corporation of Township of James, 575 Main St.
Elk Lake, ON P0J 1G0
Tel: 705-678-2237
History of area, in particular, mining, lumbering, agriculture

Elliot Lake: Elliot Lake Nuclear & Mining Museum
Lester B. Pearson Civic Centre, Hwy. 108
Elliot Lake, ON P5A 2T1
Tel: 705-848-2287
Mining heritage; northern home of the Canadian Mining Hall of Fame; Dr. Franc Joubin Mineral Collection; open Sept. - June, Mon.-Fri.; July - Aug., daily

Emeryville: Maidstone Bicentennial Museum
Parent: Maidstone & District Historical Society
1093 Puce Rd., RR#3
Emeryville, ON N8M 2X7
Tel: 519-727-3766
stonegbb@cogeco.ca
Year Founded: 1984 Contains artifacts from the former Maidstone Township; the New Heritage Gardens feature native plants, trees, & shrubs.

Emo: Rainy River District Women's Institute Museum
PO Box 511
Located at 21 Tyrell St., Emo, ON
Emo, ON P0W 1E0
Tel: 807-482-2007; *Fax:* 807-482-2556
Small pioneer museum; open mid May - Oct.; other times by appointment

Englehart: Englehart & Area Historical Museum
67 - 6th Ave.
Englehart, ON P0J 1H0
Tel: 705-544-2400
englehartandareamuseum@ntl.sympatico.ca
www.englehart.ca
Exhibits show how settlement along the Temiskaming & Northern Ontario railway created town of Englehart & brought homesteaders to the claybelt's rural communites, 1900-1950; open May 1 - Dec. 1 & exhibition room

Essex: Essex Railway Station
Parent: Heritage Essex Inc.
87 Station St.
Essex, ON N8M 2C5
Tel: 519-776-9800; *Fax:* 519-776-7241
heritageessex@bellnet.ca
www.essexrailwaystation.ca
A restored stone railway station from 1887. Also on site are a heritage gardens area, & two antique railcars.

Exeter: Arkona Lions Museum & Information Centre
Parent: Ausable Bayfield Conservation
c/o Ausable Bayfield Conservation Authority, 71108 Morrison Line, RR#3
Exeter, ON N0M 1S5
Tel: 519-235-2610; *Fax:* 519-235-1963
Toll-Free: 888-286-2610
www.abca.on.ca
Social Media: www.youtube.com/user/TheAusable
twitter.com/LandWaterNews
www.facebook .com/163006113762184
Arkona Lions Museum & Information Centre features local First Nations artifacts, Devonian era fossils, minerals, & semi-precious stone.
Brian Horner, General Manager, bhorner@abca.on.ca

Fenelon Falls: Fenelon Falls Museum
PO Box 179, 50 Oak St.
Fenelon Falls, ON K0M 1N0
Tel: 705-887-1044
curator@maryboro.ca
www.maryboro.ca
Open daily June 15 - Labour Day; weekends only May 20-June 15 & Labour Day to Thanksgiving
Ali Scott, Curator

Fenelon Falls: Horseless Carriage Museum
1427 County Rd. 8
Fenelon Falls, ON K0M 1N0
Tel: 705-738-9576
info@horselesscarriage.net
www.horselesscarriage.net
Social Media: www.youtube.com/user/lauracbennett
The museum is privately owned & operated, & specializes in early transportation & mechanical antiquities. Please call for an appointment.

Fergus: Wellington County Museum & Archives
0536 Wellington Rd. 18
Fergus, ON N1M 2W3
Tel: 519-846-0916; *Fax:* 519-846-9630
Toll-Free: 800-663-0750
www.wellington.ca/en/museum.asp
Other contact information: Museum: 519-846-0916, ext. 5221
The Wellington County Museum reflects the history of Wellington County people. The museum is housed in the former House of Industry & Refuge, which was built in 1877. Permanent exhibits include a World War I military exhibit, a pioneer log cabin, a 1920s kitchen, & textiles. The archives feature historical & genealogical records which date back to the first settlement in Wellington County. The Couling Collection consists of architectural information.
Susan Dunlop, Curator
Karen Wagner, Archivist
Patty Whan, Conservator

Flesherton: South Grey Museum & Historical Library
PO Box 299, 40 Sydenham St.
Flesherton, ON N0C 1E0
Tel: 519-924-2843
museum@greyhighlands.ca
www.southgreymuseum.ca
www.facebook.com/240275574222
Open Tues. - Sat. end of June - Labour Day, or by appt; Open Thurs. - Sat. Labour Day - June.
Kate Russell, Curator/Manager, 519-924-2843

***Forest:* Forest-Lambton Museum**
8 Main St. North
Forest, ON N0N 1J0
Tel: 519-786-3239
museum.forest@gmail.com
www.facebook.com/240210859331349
Local artifacts including doll collection; flax industry; early telephone equipment; Grand Truck Railroad; First Nation's Artifacts; pictures & documents from the 1800s

***Foresters Falls:* Ross Museum**
***Parent:* Whitewater Historical Society**
2022 Foresters Falls Rd.
Foresters Falls, ON K0J 1V0
Tel: 613-646-2622
info@rossmuseum.ca
www.rossmuseum.ca
Year Founded: 1995 Local history

***Fort Erie:* Fort Erie Railroad Museum**
***Parent:* Fort Erie Museum Services**
400 Central Ave.
Fort Erie, ON L2A 3T6
Tel: 905-894-5322
www.museum.forterie.ca/railroad.html
Located on Central Ave.; includes Steam engine #6218, caboose & 2 train stations; open daily Victoria Day - Labour Day; open weekends until Thanksgiving
Jane Davies, Curator BA

***Fort Erie:* Old Fort Erie**
350 Lakeshore Rd.
Fort Erie, ON L2A 1B5
Tel: 905-871-0540
www.niagaraparks.com/old-fort-erie
Collection of military equipment housed in a reconstructed fort. Open May-Oct.

***Fort Frances:* Fort Frances Museum & Cultural Centre**
259 Scott St.
Fort Frances, ON P9A 1G8
Tel: 807-274-7891
ffmuseum@fort-frances.com
www.fort-frances.com/museum
www.facebook.com/FortFrancesMuseum
The community museum is housed in an 1898 schoolhouse. The exhibits of the Fort Frances Museum & Cultural Centre reflect the development of Fort Frances & the Rainy River District from pre-contact to present day.
Sherry George, Contact

***Frankville:* Maple Sugar House & Museum**
41 Leacock Rd., RR#1
Frankville, ON K0E 1H0
Tel: 613-275-2893 *Toll-Free:* 877-440-7887
mail@gibbonsmaple.com
www.rideau-info.com/gibbons
The House produces & sells maple syrup, maple sugar, maple butter & other maple products. As well, there displays from the past and present of maple syrup making equipment. Tours are offered.

***Gananoque:* Arthur Child Heritage Museum of the Thousand Islands**
***Parent:* Historic Thousand Islands Village Foundation**
125 Water St.
Gananoque, ON K7G 3E3
Tel: 613-382-2535; *Fax:* 613-382-2912
Toll-Free: 877-217-7391
ivillage@cogeco.net
www.1000islandsheritagemuseum.com
twitter.com/GanHeritage
www.facebook.com/ArthurChildHeritageMuseum
Year Founded: 1995 The museum building was once the main station for the Thousand Islands Railway; now it is the centrepiece of the Historic Thousand Islands Village complex. Open daily 10:00-6:00.
Linda Mainse, Executive Director

***Georgetown:* Halton Hills Sports Museum & Resource Centre (HHSM)**
Gordon Alcott Heritage Hall, Mold-Masters SportsPlex, 221 Guelph St.
Georgetown, ON L7G 4A8
Tel: 905-875-7901
www.hhsm.ca
www.facebook.com/groups/215339958504378
Year Founded: 2009 The museum commemorates the history of sports in the communities of Halton Hills.
Finn Poulstrup, Chair, fpoulstrup@johnsonassociates.ca

***Gloucester:* Gloucester Museum & Historical Society**
4550B Bank St.
Gloucester, ON K1T 3W6
Tel: 613-822-2076
www.gloucesterhistory.com
Domestic ware; agricultural implements; Gloucester History Society archives; City of Gloucester archives

***Goderich:* Huron County Museum & Historic Gaol**
110 North St.
Goderich, ON N7A 2T8
Tel: 519-524-2686; *Fax:* 519-524-1922
www.huroncounty.ca/museum
Social Media: instagram.com/huroncountymuseum
twitter.com/hcmuseum
www.facebook.com/ huroncountymuseum
Year Founded: 1951 Local history including transportation, military, agriculture & furniture

***Gore Bay:* Gore Bay Museum**
12 Dawson St.
Gore Bay, ON P0P 1H0
Tel: 705-282-2040 *Toll-Free:* 887-732-955
Artifacts that early settlers of the area would have used. Housed in a former jail.

***Gore Bay:* Western Manitoulin Island Historical Society Museum**
PO Box 298
Located at 150 Water St., Gore Bay, ON
Gore Bay, ON P0P 1H0
Tel: 705-282-2420
Canadian 19th century artifacts, including historical & documentary art; open Mar.-Nov.

***Gormley:* Whitchurch-Stouffville Museum & Community Centre**
14732 Woodbine Ave.
Gormley, ON L0H 1G0
Tel: 905-727-8954; *Fax:* 905-727-1282
Toll-Free: 888-290-0337
www.townofws.ca/en/explore/museum.asp
Year Founded: 1971 The museum is located in the hamlet of Vandorf & includes the Bogarttown Schoolhouse, a restored 1850 log cabin, the Brown House, barn, & the Vandorf Public School; special events & programming, tours, craft workshops, & research material. Open year round.

***Gowganda:* Gowganda & Area Museum**
General Delivery
Gowganda, ON P0J 1J0
Tel: 705-624-3171
Silver mining displays; log cabin; research library & resource centre; open mid-May - mid-Sept.

***Grafton:* Barnum House Museum**
PO Box 161, 10568 Country Rd. 2
Grafton, ON K0K 2G0
Tel: 905-349-2656
barnum@heritagetrust.on.ca
www.heritagetrust.on.ca
Owned by the Ontario Heritage Trust, Barnum House was built in 1819. The home is an example of Neo-Classical architecture. The decor of Barnum House reflects an Upper Canada home between 1820 & 1840. Barnum House Museum is open from June to Labour Day.

***Grand Bend:* Lambton Heritage Museum**
10035 Museum Rd., RR#2
Grand Bend, ON N0M 1T0
Tel: 519-243-2600; *Fax:* 519-243-2646
heritage.museum@county-lambton.on.ca
www.lclmg.org
www.facebook.com/la mbtonheritagemuseum
Year Founded: 1978 Eight buildings on a 30 acre site; extensive collection of pressed glass & Currier & Ives prints; features history of Sarnia-Lambton area including large collection of agricultural implements

***Gravenhurst:* Bethune Memorial House National Historic Site**
235 John St. North
Gravenhurst, ON P1P 1G4
Tel: 705-687-4261; *Fax:* 705-687-4935
ont-bethune@pch.gc.ca
www.pc.gc.ca/bethune
At the Bethune Memorial House National Historic Site, the life & achievements of Dr. Henry Norman Bethune are commemorated. The house is his birthplace. Dr. Bethune is recognized for his time in China, where he served as a surgeon & a teacher. The site is open from June 1st to October 31st. At other times, group tours may be arranged by phone.

***Gravenhurst:* Muskoka Boat & Heritage Centre**
275 Steamship Bay Rd.
Gravenhurst, ON P1P 1Z9
Tel: 705-687-2115
realmuskoka.com
Social Media: www.youtube.com/user/muskokasteamships
twitter.com/RMSSegwun
www.faceb ook.com/MuskokaSteamships
The Muskoka Boat & Heritage Centre presents the history of boat-building, Muskoka's steamship era, & life on the water in Muskoka. At the site is a large in water collection of antique boats. The RMS Segwun is the oldest operating steamship in North America. The Muskoka Boat & Heritage Centre is open year-round.

***Grimsby:* Grimsby Museum**
PO Box 244, 6 Murray St.
Grimsby, ON L3M 4G5
Tel: 905-945-5292; *Fax:* 905-945-0715
www.grimsby.ca/residents/cultural-facilities/museum
twitter.com/GrimsbyM useum
www.facebook.com/GriMuseum
Year Founded: 1984 Owned & operated by the Town of Grimsby, the museum interprets the history of Grimsby from prehistoric times. The Gallery of the Forty explores the settlement of the United Empire Loyalists in 1787. The Grimsby museum provides educational programs, as well as local history & genealogical information. It is open year-round.
Janet Cannon, Director & Curator

***Guelph:* C.A.V. Barker Museum of Canadian Veterinary History**
Ontario Veterinary College, University of Guelph, 50 Stone Rd.
Guelph, ON N1G 2W1
Tel: 519-823-8800; *Fax:* 519-837-3230
www.ovc.uoguelph.ca/history
The museum details the history of the Ontario Veterinary College, as well as Canadian veterinary medicine in general, & holds more than 10,000 items in its collection. The museum is open by appointment only.

***Guelph:* Guelph Civic Museum**
52 Norfolk St.
Guelph, ON N1H 4H8
Tel: 519-836-1221
guelphmuseums.ca
twitter.com/guelphmuseums
www.facebook.com/guelphmuseums
Year Founded: 1967 The museum is housed in a c. 1850 limestone building and features over 30,000 artifacts and 4,000 photos relating to the istory of Guelph and area; special events and programming for children.
Tammy Adkin, Manager, Tammy.Adkin@guelph.ca
Bev Dietrich, Curator, 519-822-1260, bev.dietrich@guelph.ca

***Guelph:* Hammond Museum of Radio**
595 Southgate Rd.
Guelph, ON N1G 3W6
Tel: 519-822-2441
curator@HammondMuseumOfRadio.org
www.hammondmuseumofradio.org
Year Founded: 1982 The museum's collection includes hundreds of radios; open M-F 9:00-5:00, & weekends by request.
Nori Irwin-Hahn, Curator, curator@hammondmuseumofradio.org

***Guelph:* McCrae House**
108 Water St.
Guelph, ON N1G 1A6
Tel: 519-836-1482
museum@guelph.ca
guelphmuseums.ca
twitter.com/guelph museums
www.facebook.com/109822192370415
Year Founded: 1968 The house, built in 1858, is the 1872 birthplace of John McCrae, author of "In Flanders Fields", & a National Historic Site. Exhibitions interpret McCrae's life & times, & an award-winning historic garden is maintained by volunteers. Activities include garden teas, the Poppy Push, Teddy Bear Picnic & Canada Day celebration.
Bev Dietrich, Curator, 519-822-1260, bev.dietrich@guelph.ca

Haileybury: **Haileybury Heritage Museum**
PO Box 911
Located at 575 Main St., Haileybury, ON
Haileybury, ON P0J 1K0
Tel: 705-672-1922; *Fax:* 705-672-2551
hhmuseum@hotmail.ca
www.alexand.ca
Haileybury Heritage Museum is focused on one of Canada's ten worst natural disasters, the Great Fire of 1922 which destroyed 90 percent of the Town of Haileybury & communities in 18 surrounding townships in South Temiskaming; features a restored 1904 Toronto Railway Company streetcar (used as housing after the '22 fire); a 1922 Ruggles Fire Pumper; & the tugboat M.V. Beauchene.

Haliburton: **Haliburton Highlands Museum**
66 Museum Rd.
Haliburton, ON K0M 1S0
Tel: 705-457-2760
info@haliburtonhighlandsmuseum.com
haliburtonhighlandsmuseum.com
twitter.com/HH_Museum
www.facebook.com/4 98191436905810
Year Founded: 1968 Local domestic, lumbering & agricultural history. Open year round. Hours: Summer: Tu-Su 10:00-5:00; Spring/Fall: Tu-Sa 10:00-5:00; Winter: Currently being reviewed.
Kate Butler, Director
Stephen Hill, Curator

Halton Hills: **Canadian Motorsport Hall of Fame & Museum (CMHF)**
Parent: **Canadian Motorsport Heritage Foundation**
8220 - 5th Line
Halton Hills, ON L7G 4S6
Tel: 905-876-2454
archives@cmhf.ca
www.cmhf.ca
Social Media: www.youtube.com/user/canadianmhf
twitter.com/CMHF2014
www.facebook.com /CanadianMotorsportHallOfFame
Year Founded: 1993 The CMHF seeks to honour & recognize the Canadians who have made a contribution to the area of motorsports. The CMHF is currently looking for a new location.
Dr. Hugh Scully, President/Chair
Sid Priddle, General Manager, sgwpriddle@gmail.com

Hamilton: **Canadian Football Hall of Fame & Museum**
58 Jackson St. West
Hamilton, ON L8P 1L4
Tel: 905-528-7566; *Fax:* 905-528-9781
info@cfhof.ca
www.cfhof.ca
Social Media: www.youtube.com/user/CFHOFandM
twitter.com/CFHOF
www.facebook.com/CFHO FandM
Year Founded: 1962 The Canadian Football Hall of Fame & Museum features exhibits which depict the history of the game at all levels. A special section is dedicated to the Hall of Famers.
Mark DeNobile, Executive Director, mark@cfhof.ca
Dave Marler, Chair
Christopher Alfred, Curator, chris@cfhof.ca

Hamilton: **Dundurn Castle**
610 York Blvd.
Hamilton, ON L8R 3H1
Tel: 905-546-2872; *Fax:* 905-546-2875
dundurn@hamilton.ca
www.dundurncastle.com
Restored home of Sir Allan MacNab, one of Canada's first premiers; depiction of mid-19th century life in over 40 rooms; open year round

Hamilton: **Hamilton & Scourge National Historic Site**
c/o Hamilton Military Museum, 610 York Blvd.
Hamilton, ON L9H 5Z9
Tel: 905-546-2872; *Fax:* 905-546-2875
military@hamilton.ca
www.hamilton-scourge.hamilton.ca
Research files on the Hamilton & Scourge, armed merchant schooners from the War of 1812, which capsized & lie in water off Port Dalhousie.
Michael McAllister, Curator

Hamilton: **Hamilton Children's Museum**
1072 Main St. East
Hamilton, ON L8M 1N6
Tel: 905-546-4848; *Fax:* 905-546-4851
childrensmuseum@hamilton.ca
www.hamilton.ca/CultureandRecreation/Arts_Cu lture_And_Museums
Year Founded: 1978 This is an interactive, hands-on learning centre that offers children the opportunity to explore a wide variety of themes from the natural sciences and arts. Closed on Mondays.

Hamilton: **Hamilton Military Museum / Le musée militaire de Hamilton**
610 York Blvd.
Hamilton, ON L8R 3H1
Tel: 905-546-2872; *Fax:* 905-546-2875
military@hamilton.ca
www.hamilton.ca
Uniforms, weapons & lifestyle from War of 1812, Rebellion of 1837-38, the Victorian era, Boer War, & WWI; open year round

Hamilton: **Hamilton Museum of Mental Health Care**
Level 2 Atrium, St. Joseph's Healthcare Hamilton, West 5th Campus, 100 West 5th St.
Hamilton, ON L9C 0E3
Tel: 905-522-1155 *Toll-Free:* 887-732-955
museumpc@stjoes.ca
www.stjoes.ca
Artifacts that showcase mental health care practices from the early years of the hospital.
Katrina Peredun, Museum Coordinator, kperedun@stjoes.ca

Hamilton: **Hamilton Museum of Steam & Technology**
900 Woodward Ave.
Hamilton, ON L8H 7N2
Tel: 905-546-4797
steammuseum@hamilton.ca
www.hamilton.ca
Housed in a 19th century public works building. The facility is a Civil & Power Engineering Landmark & a National Historic Site. It contains two steam engines that pumped water to Hamilton more than 140 years ago. Open year-round.

Hamilton: **Hamilton Psychiatric Hospital Museum**
c/o St. Joseph's Healthcare Hamilton, 100 West 5th St.
Hamilton, ON L8N 3K7
Tel: 905-388-2511
museumpc@stjoes.ca
www.stjosham.on.ca
Other contact information: Alt. Phone: 905-522-1155 ext. 35512
With a variety of artifacts & photographs, the museum preserves the history of psychiatric care & treatment in Ontario with an emphasis on events at the Hamilton Psychiatric Hospital & in the regions it serves.
Katrina Peredun, Museum Coordinator, kperedun@stjoes.ca

Hamilton: **HMCS Haida National Historic Site of Canada**
57 Discovery Dr.
Location: Pier 9, 658 Catharine St. North, Hamilton, ON
Hamilton, ON L8L 8K4
Tel: 905-526-6742; *Fax:* 905-526-9734
haida.Info@pc.gc.ca
www.pc.gc.ca/lhn-nhs/on/haida.aspx
Commissioned in 1943 & dubbed "the fightingest ship in the Royal Canadian Navy," HMCS Haida saw service in WWII & the Korean War. Canada's most famous warship & the last of the Tribal Class destroyers left in the world is berthed at Hamilton.

Hamilton: **Royal Hamilton Light Infantry Heritage Museum**
John Weir Foote VC Armoury, 200 James St. North
Hamilton, ON L8R 2L1
Tel: 905-528-2945
museumcurator@rhli.ca
www.rhli.ca/museum/museum.html
Military artifacts from 1830 to present, with specific reference to the Royal Hamilton Light Infantry; library
Stan Overy, Curator, 905-573-2002, museumcurator@rhli.ca

Hamilton: **Whitehern Historic House & Garden**
41 Jackson St. West
Hamilton, ON L8P 1L3
Tel: 905-546-2018; *Fax:* 905-546-4933
whitehern@hamilton.ca
www.whitehern.ca/whitehern.php
Former home of the McQuesten family from 1852 - 1968; period rooms feature original furnishings

Hamilton: **Workers Arts & Heritage Centre (WA&HC)**
51 Stuart St.
Hamilton, ON L8L 1B5
Tel: 905-522-3003
wahc@wahc-museum.ca
www.wahc-museum.ca
twitter.com/WAHC
www.facebook.com/WorkersArtsandHer itageCentre
Year Founded: 1991 Located at Hamilton's former Custom House, which was built in 1860, the Workers Arts & Heritage Centre celebrates the history & culture of all working people in Canada. Exhibits include the labour movement in the Hamilton area, a history of office work, & the history of life on the shop floor, which explores Canada's early industrial days to the rise of automation in the workplace. The museum is open year-round.
Florencia Berinstein, Executive Director, florencia@wahc-museum.ca
Katherine Roy, Coordinator, Development, katherine@wahc-museum.ca
Brian Kelly, Coordinator, Facilities, brian@wahc-museum.ca
Andrew Lochhead, Coordinator, Program, andrew@wahc-museum.ca

Harrow: **John R. Park Homestead**
915 County Rd. 50 East, RR#1
Harrow, ON N0R 1G0
Tel: 519-738-2029
jrph@erca.org
erca.org/conservation-areas-events/conservation-areas/john-r-p ark-homestea d
twitter.com/essexregionca
Living history museum; open year round

Hornell Heights: **Canadian Forces Museum of Aerospace Defence**
Canadian Forces Base North Bay, 22 Wing
Hornell Heights, ON P0H 1P0
Tel: 705-494-2011
aerospace.defence@live.ca
www.aerospacedefence.ca

Huntsville: **Muskoka Heritage Place**
88 Brunel Rd.
Huntsville, ON P1H 1R1
Tel: 705-789-7576; *Fax:* 705-789-6169
Toll-Free: 888-696-4255
www.muskokaheritageplace.org
Other contact information: TTY: 705-789-1768
Muskoka Heritage Place contains the following: Muskoka Museum, Muskoka Pioneer Village & the Portage Flyer Train.
Ron Gostlin, Manager, 705-789-7576
Sarah McIntosh, Collections Coordinator, 705-789-7576

Ignace: **Ignace Heritage Centre**
PO Box 480
Located at 36 Main St., Ignace, ON
Ignace, ON P0T 1T0
Tel: 807-934-2280; *Fax:* 807-934-6452
www.olsn.ca/ignace
www.facebook.com/218910864872499
Local artifacts; located in the Ignace Public Library

Ingersoll: **Ingersoll Cheese & Agricultural Museum**
c/o Town of Ingersoll, 130 Oxford St., 2nd Fl.
Located at 290 Harris St., Hwy. 119, Ingersoll, ON
Ingersoll, ON N5C 2V5
Tel: 519-485-5510
curator@ingersoll.ca
www.ingersoll.ca
Located in Centennial Park; 6 buildings including cheese factory museum, blacksmith shop; barn; community museum featuring spectacular woodcarved scene "pathway of the giants" & Ingersoll Sports Hall of Fame houses Harold Wilson's Miss Canada IV Speedboat; open daily July - Aug.; open weekends through May & June to Thanksgiving
Scott Gillies, Curator

Ingersoll: **Oxford County Museum School**
PO Box 232
School Location: Centennial Park, 290 Harris St., Ingersoll, ON
Ingersoll, ON N5C 3K5
Tel: 519-926-0206
info@museumschool.ca
www.museumschool.ca
Now located in the Ingersoll Cheese & Agricultural Museum, in a replica rural schoolhouse; collection & archives located at the Ingersoll Town Hall

Iron Bridge: **Iron Bridge Historical Museum**
PO Box 460
Located at 1 James St., Iron Bridge, ON
Iron Bridge, ON P0R 1H0
Year Founded: 1974 Pioneer artifacts

Iroquois: **Carman House Museum**
PO Box 249
Iroquois, ON K0E 1K0
Tel: 613-652-4422; *Fax:* 613-652-4636
Other contact information: Phone, Summertime: 613-652-4808

Carman House is a United Empire Loyalist home, which was built in 1815. It is a living history museum, which reflects life in 1835. The museum is open from late June to Labour Day.

Iroquois Falls: Iroquois Falls Pioneer Museum
PO Box 448
Located at 245 Devonshire Ave., Iroquois Falls, ON
Iroquois Falls, ON P0K 1E0
Tel: 705-258-3730; *Fax:* 705-258-3730
www.facebook.com/557678680916361
Year Founded: 1970 The Garden Town of the North is home of the Shay Train Engine, the workhorse of the logging industry. The Iroquois Falls Pioneer Museum offers many displays, including the history of a company which became the world's largest producer of pulp & paper, the general store, a telephone exhibit, a hands-on display for children, the 1916 fire, a replica of a tug boat, & the Iroquois Hotel, which was built by the company.

Jordan: Ball's Falls Centre for Conservation
3292 - 6th Ave.
Jordan, ON L0R 1S0
Tel: 905-562-5235; *Fax:* 905-788-1121
info@ballsfalls.ca
www.ballsfalls.ca
Social Media: www.youtube.com/user/ballsfallsca
twitter.com/BallsFallsCA
www.faceboo k.com/209357529103582
Other contact information: Wordpress: ballsfalls.wordpress.com
Year Founded: 2008 The Ball's Falls Centre for Conservation offers information about the Niagara Peninsula's history, the natural history of the Twenty Valley & its watershed, & the Niagara Escarpment Biosphere Reserve. Historical homes, a mill, & a church are available for touring.

Jordan: Jordan Historical Museum
3800 Main St.
Jordan, ON L0R 1S0
Tel: 905-563-2799
museum@lincoln.ca
www.lincoln.ca/content/jordan-historical-museum
Local history.
Helen Booth, Director

Kagawong: Old Mill Heritage Centre & Post Office Museum
PO Box 34
Kagawong, ON P0P 1J0
Tel: 705-282-1442
oldmillheritage@billingstwp.ca
www.manitoulintourism.com/museumsgalleries/
Local history
Rick Nelson, Curator

Kakabeka Falls: Hymers Museum
RR#1
Kakabeka Falls, ON P0T 1W0
Tel: 807-577-4787
www.facebook.com/HymersMuseum
Local history
Linda Turk, Contact, lindat@tbaytel.net

Kapuskasing: Ron Morel Memorial Museum
88 Riverside Dr.
Kapuskasing, ON P5N 1B3
Tel: 705-337-4274; *Fax:* 705-337-1741
mci390.wix.com/ron-morel-museum
Museum is housed in two railway cars & a caboose headed by steam locomotive 5107; changing seasonal exhibits & permanent displays; one railway car is devoted to trains & railway history, with a large working HO-gauge model; the Heritage Caravan with its clay sculptures depict Northern Ontario history; open daily from early June to Labour Day
Julie Latimer, Curator, 705-337-4474

Kars: Swords & Ploughshares Museum
7500 Reeve Craig Rd. North, RR#1
Kars, ON K0A 2E0
Tel: 613-489-3447; *Fax:* 613-489-1166
swords@calnan.com
www.calnan.com/swords
Military artifacts, 1914-present; agricultural machinery & implements, 1840-1940; open May - Oct. & by appt.

Kenora: Lake of the Woods Museum
PO Box 497
Located at 300 Main St. South, Kenora, ON
Kenora, ON P9N 3X5
Tel: 807-467-2105; *Fax:* 807-467-2109
museum@kmts.ca
www.lakeofthewoodsmuseum.ca
www.facebook.com/LakeOfTheW oodsMuseum
Year Founded: 1964 Collection of more than 20,000 articles; displays feature native & pioneer artifacts, natural history, minerals, textiles, pictorial & archival material illustrating the history of the Lake of the Woods & surrounding area
Jan Lindstrom, Chair
Lori Nelson, Director

Keswick: Georgina Military Museum (GMM)
26061 Woodbine Ave., RR#2
Keswick, ON L4P 3E9
Tel: 905-989-9900
frontdesk@georginamilitarymuseum.ca
www.georginamilita rymuseum.ca
www.facebook.com/georginamilitarymuseum
Year Founded: 2007 The museum is dedicated to teaching the public about the involvement of Canadians in wartime conflicts throughout history. Open Sa & Su 10:00-4:00.
John Cannon, President/Secretary
Phil Craig, Curator/Co-Founder

Keswick: Georgina Pioneer Village & Archives
Parent: **Georgina Historical Society**
26557 Civic Centre Rd., RR#2
Keswick, ON L4P 3G1
Tel: 905-476-4301; *Fax:* 905-476-7492
curator@georgina.ca
www.georginapioneervillage.ca
Social Media: www.flickr.com/photos/georginapioneervillage
twitter.com/GeorginaHistory
www.facebook.com/353678207978112
Year Founded: 1974 Late 19th century historic village; interpreters & demonstrators; special exhibitions, events, tours, workshops & genealogical archives; open June-Sept., Th-Su, 10:00-5:00 or by appt.
Melissa D. Matt, Cultural Services Representative

Killarney: Killarney Centennial Museum
29 Commissioners St.
Killarney, ON P0M 2A0
Tel: 705-287-2424; *Fax:* 705-287-2660
www.municipality.killarney.on.ca
Year Founded: 1967 The museum preserves historical artifacts from the time of the fur trade to the present; collection includes household items, objects from local commercial fishing, logging, mining & tourism industries, & photographs. Located at 29 Commissioners St. in Killarney. Open 6 days per week from late June to early September.

King City: King Township Museum
2920 King Rd.
King City, ON L7B 1L6
Tel: 905-833-2331
kingmuseum@king.ca
www.king.ca
www.facebook.com/KingTownshipMuseum
Year Founded: 1982 Housed in the Old Kinghorn School SS #23; administered by the King Township Historical Society.

Kingston: Bellevue House National Historic Site (BHNHS)
35 Centre St.
Kingston, ON K7L 4E5
Tel: 613-545-8666; *Fax:* 613-545-8721
bellevue.house@pc.gc.ca
www.pc.gc.ca/lhn-nhs/on/bellevue/index_e.asp
Built in the early 1840s, Bellevue House was the home of Sir John A. Macdonald. The site is closed from November to March, but groups may make reservations.

Kingston: Canada's Penitentiary Museum (CPM) / Musée pénitentiaire du Canada
PO Box 1174
Located at 555 King St. West, Kingston, ON
Kingston, ON K7L 4Y8
Tel: 613-530-3122; *Fax:* 613-536-4815
fpm@cogeco.net
www.penitentiarymuseum.ca
twitter.com/CSCmuseum
www.f acebook.com/381003918638580
To preserve & interpret the past & contemporary experiences of the people & places associated with the history of corrections in Canada
Dave St. Onge, Curator

Kingston: Cataraqui Archaeological Research Foundation / Kingston Archaeological Centre (CARF)
611 Princess St.
Kingston, ON K7L 1E1
Tel: 613-542-3483
www.carf.info/archaeological-centre
twitter.com/carfki ngston
www.facebook.com/Kingstonarchaeologicalcentre
Year Founded: 1986 The Foundation was established to oversee the excavation of Fort Frontenac, & to collect and preserve artifacts from the site. It is now involved in numerous archaeological projects at sites in Eastern Ontario, & operates the Kingston Archaeological Centre; educational programming & research collection. Open Mon to Fri, 9:30-4:00.
Kip Parker, Executive Director
Ashley Mendes, Curator

Kingston: City of Kingston Fire Department Museum
271 Brock St.
Kingston, ON K7L 1S5
Antique firefighting equipment, photographs & models

Kingston: Fort Henry
1 Fort Henry Dr.
Kingston, ON K7K 5G8
Tel: 613-542-7388*Toll-Free:* 800-437-2233
getaway@parks.on.ca
www.forthenry.com
twitter.com/FortHenry
www.face book.com/forthenry1832
The Citadel of Upper Canada, brought to life by the Fort Henry Guard; restaurant; gift stores; children's muster parades; festivals, events, historic dining
Darren Dalgleish, General Manager & CEO, St. Lawrence Parks Commission

Kingston: Frontenac County Schools Museum (FCSM)
PO Box 2146, 414 Regent St.
Kingston, ON K7L 5J9
Tel: 613-544-9113
fcschoolsmuseum@gmail.com
www.fcsmuseum.com
www.facebook.com/SchoolsMuseum
This community museum & archives has a geographical focus on Frontenac County & the City of Kingston, with a heritage schoolroom (1900-1920), a late 19th- & 20th-century archival collection & public elementary school records. Public programming includes costumed interpretive tours, educational programs & research assistance.

Kingston: Kingston Mills Blockhouse
573 Kingston Mills Rd.
Kingston, ON K7L 4V3
Tel: 613-283-5170
1840s animated militia barracks

Kingston: Kingston Scout Museum (KSM)
PO Box 2259, 640 MacDonnell St.
Kingston, ON K7M 5J9
Tel: 613-329-3456
www.kingstonscoutmuseum.ca
Social Media: blog.kingstonscoutmuseum.ca
Scouting memorabilia; open by appointment only.
Linda Bates, Co-Chair, linda@kingstonscoutmuseum.ca
Stephen Reid, Co-Chair, stephen@kingstonscoutmuseum.ca

Kingston: MacLachlan Woodworking Museum
2993 Hwy. 2 East
Kingston, ON K7L 4V1
Tel: 613-542-0543
woodworkingmuseum.ca
twitter.com/maclachlanwood
www.facebook.com/maclachlanwood
Year Founded: 1967 Exhibits include tools & lifestyles of 19th century tradespeople; hands-on workshops, educational programs & demonstrations are offered. The gift shop stocks handmade wooden kitchenware, linen, toys & wooden ornaments.
Tom Riddolls, Curator, triddolls@cityofkingston.ca

Kingston: Marine Museum of the Great Lakes at Kingston
55 Ontario St.
Kingston, ON K7L 2Y2
Tel: 613-542-2261; *Fax:* 613-542-0043
marmus@marmuseum.ca
www.marmuseum.ca
twitter.com/MMGLK
Year Founded: 1976 The museum showcases an original pumping station & steam engines built in 1891. Exhibits include

the history of boat building, as well as Kingston's maritime history on the Great Lakes. An Eco Gallery focuses on environmental issues related to the Great Lakes. At dock is the Alexander Henry, a icebreaking ship built in 1959.
Doug Cowie, Museum Manager, manager@marmuseum.ca
Sandrena Raymond, Curator, curator@marmuseum.ca

Kingston: Military Communications & Electronics Museum
PO Box 17000 Forces
Located at CFB Kingston, 95 Craftsman Blvd, Hwy. 2, Kingston, ON
Kingston, ON K7K 7B4
Tel: 613-541-4675; *Fax:* 613-540-8111
www.c-and-e-museum.org
Year Founded: 1963 Preserves & interprets the Communications & Electronics Branch military history; provides group & individual tours; responds to research requests & is available to provide expert artifact appraisals; supports community activities with mobile displays & temporary loans of artifacts
Maj. (Ret'd) Mike DeNoble, Director, Museum Operations, 613-541-4211, denoble.mp@forces.gc.ca
Annette Gillis, Curator, Artifacts & Research Inquiries, 613-541-5130, gillis.ae@forces.gc.ca

Kingston: Miller Museum of Mineralogy & Geology
Miller Hall, Queen's University, 36 Union St.
Kingston, ON K7L 3N6
Tel: 613-533-6767; *Fax:* 613-533-6592
geol.queensu.ca/museum
Year Founded: 1931 Collection of rocks, minerals & fossils from around the world; education tour programs available by request

Kingston: Murney Tower Museum
***Parent:* Kingston Historical Society**
c/o Kingston Historical Society, PO Box 54
Located at King St. & Barrie St., Kingston, ON
Kingston, ON K7L 4V6
Tel: 613-572-5181
kingstonhs@gmail.com
www.kingstonhistoricalsociety.ca/Murney_Tower.html
Tower, built in 1846, now houses military, agricultural, Aboriginal & early settlers' artifacts; open summer
Peter Gower, President, Kingston Historical Society
Graeme Watson, Chair, Murney Tower Committee

Kingston: Museum of Health Care at Kingston
Ann Baillie Bldg. National Historic Site, 32 George St.
Kingston, ON K7L 2V7
Tel: 613-548-2419
info@museumofhealthcare.ca
www.museumofhealthcare.ca
Social Media: www.youtube.com/user/MuseumOfHealthCare
twitter.com/MuseumofHealth
www .facebook.com/9025182465
Year Founded: 1991 The museum, located in an early 1900s residence for student nurses, tells the story of the evolution of health care in Canada. Open May-Aug., Tu-Su 10:00-4:00.
Hugh Gorwill, Chair & President
Dr. James Low, Executive Director Emeritus, lowj@kgh.kari.net
Maxime Chouinard, Curator, chouinam@kgh.kari.net
Jenny Stepa, Museum Manager & Program Director, brownj8@kgh.kari.net

Kingston: Original Hockey Hall of Fame & Museum
PO Box 82
Located at the Invista Centre, 1350 Gardiners Rd., 2nd Fl., Kingston, ON
Kingston, ON K7L 4V6
Tel: 613-583-1718
info@originalhockeyhalloffame.com
www.originalhockeyhalloffame.com
twitter.com/ihhof43
www.facebook.com/ 207141552735961
Year Founded: 1943 Home to 10,000 sq. feet of hockey memories; open mid-June - Labour Day, daily 10-3; off-season group tours by appt.
Mark Potter, President, mpotter1@cogeco.ca
Larry Paquette, Vice-President, ihhof@kos.net

Kingston: Princess of Wales' Own Regiment Military Museum
The Armouries, 100 Montréal St.
Kingston, ON K7K 3E8
Tel: 613-532-1027
pwormuseum@hotmail.com
pwormuseum.ca
Year Founded: 1969 Open year round.
Stuart MacDonald, Curator

Kingston: Pump House Steam Museum
23 Ontario St.
Kingston, ON K7L 2Y2
Tel: 613-544-7867
steammuseum.ca
twitter.com/PumpMuseum
www.facebook.com/pumphousemuseum
Former pumping station with artifacts relating to steam power; operating steam & pump engines
Gordon Robinson, Curator, grobinson2@cityofkingston.ca

Kingston: The Royal Military College Museum / Le musée du Collège militaire royal du Canada
PO Box 17000 Forces
Kingston, ON K7K 7B4
Tel: 613-541-6000; *Fax:* 613-542-3565
www.rmc.ca/cam/mus
Year Founded: 1962 Housed in the Fort Frederick Martello Tower on the College grounds; holdings relate to the history of the College, the achievements of its ex-cadets & to the history of the Royal Navy Dockyard which once occupied the site; amongst the Museum's possessions is the Douglas Arms Collection; open daily last Sat. in June - Labour Day
Lena Beliveau, Curator

Kingsville: Canadian Transportation Museum & Heritage Village (CTMHV)
6155 Arner Townline
Kingsville, ON N9Y 2E5
Tel: 519-776-6909; *Fax:* 519-776-8321
info@ctmhv.com
www.ctmhv.com
Year Founded: 1954 Located on County Road #23 in Kingsville, Ontario, the Canadian Transportation Museum collects, restores, & exhibits modes of transportation from the mid 1800s to 1992. Examples of displays include horse drawn carts, fire trucks, & Ford Model Ts. The Heritage Village contains buildings, such as a one room schoolhouse, a train station, a log home, & a general store.

Kingsville: Jack Miner Bird Sanctuary & Museum
360 Rd. 3 West
Kingsville, ON N9Y 2E5
Tel: 519-733-4034
www.jackminer.com
twitter.com/JM_Sanctuary
www.facebook.com/JackMinerMigratoryBirdSanctuar y
Year Founded: 1904 Known as "Wild Goose Jack," Jack Miner founded the bird sanctuary in 1904 & stipulated that admission would remain free. In addition to the sanctuary & grounds, the museum holdings include memorabilia, wildlife prints, medals, manuscripts & newspaper clippings, books, a bust of Jack Miner & letter from friend Henry Ford, & baseball bats from Ty Cobb.
Mary E. Baruth, Executive Director

Kingsville: Kingsville Historical Park
145 Division Rd. South
Kingsville, ON N9Y 1P5
Tel: 519-733-2803
khpi@mnsi.net
khpi.mnsi.net
Year Founded: 2000 A military museum that exhibits artifacts from the United Empire Loyalists & Essex County citizens regarding their contribution to various wars.

Kingsville: The Windsor Wood Carving Museum
Elford United Church, 6155 Arner Town Line, County Rd. 23
Kingsville, ON N9Y 2E5
Tel: 519-776-7056
woodcarvingmuseum@gmail.com
www.windsorwoodcarvingmuseum.ca
Year Founded: 1996 Located in Windsor's Central Library, the museum holds a collection of wood carvings from around the world.

Kirby: Clarke Museum
***Parent:* Clarington Museums & Archives**
7086 Old Kirby School Rd.
Kirby, ON L0B 1M0
Tel: 905-983-9243
info@claringtonmuseums.com
www.claringtonmuseums.com
Exhibits pioneer life in the Clarke township.

Kirkland Lake: Museum of Northern History at the Sir Harry Oakes Chateau
2 Chateau Dr.
Kirkland Lake, ON P2N 3M7
Tel: 705-568-8800
museum@tkl.ca
www.museumkl.com
Social Media: instagram.com/mnhchateau
twitter.com/MNHChateau
www.facebook.com/pages /Museum-of-Northern-History/113034976406
Year Founded: 1967 The Chateau, built by Sir Henry Oakes and has been preserved as a museum exhibit and is also a space to preserve northern history.

Kitchener: Doon Heritage Village
***Parent:* Waterloo Region Museum**
10 Huron Rd.
Kitchener, ON N2P 2R7
Tel: 519-748-1914; *Fax:* 519-748-0009
WaterlooRegionMuseum@regionofwaterloo.ca
www.waterlooregionmuseum.com
Social Media: www.youtube.com/user/WaterlooRegionMuseum
twitter.com/WRegionMuseum
www.facebook.com/WaterlooRegionMuseum
Other contact information: TTY: 519-575-4608
Turn of the century living history village; open daily May - Dec.
Thomas A. Reitz, Curator/Manager, 519-748-1914, TReitz@regionofwaterloo.ca

Kitchener: Joseph Schneider Haus Museum
466 Queen St. South
Kitchener, ON N2P 2R7
Tel: 519-742-7752; *Fax:* 519-742-0089
jsh@regionofwaterloo.ca
www.regionofwaterloo.ca/en/discoveringtheregion/ josephschneiderhaus.asp
www.facebook.com/163934690313150
Other contact information: TTY: 519-575-4608
Year Founded: 1981 Traces back to the Schneider family, one of the first group of Pennsylvania German Mennonites in the area

Kitchener: THEMUSEUM
10 King St. West
Kitchener, ON N2G 1A3
Tel: 519-749-9387; *Fax:* 519-749-8612
info@THEMUSEUM.ca
www.themuseum.ca
Social Media: www.youtube.com/THEMUSEUMtv
twitter.com/THEMUSEUM
www.facebook.com/pag es/THEMUSEUM/118612191529752
Year Founded: 2003 Interactive cultural museum.
Laurel McKellar, Director, Programs & Exhibitions

Kitchener: Waterloo Region Museum
10 Huron Rd.
Kitchener, ON N2P 2R7
Tel: 519-748-1914; *Fax:* 519-748-0009
WaterlooRegionMuseum@regionofwaterloo.ca
www.waterlooregionmuseum.com
Social Media: www.youtube.com/user/WaterlooRegionMuseum
twitter.com/WRegionMuseum
www.facebook.com/WaterlooRegionMuseum
Other contact information: TTY: 519-575-4608
Local history
Tom Reitz, Manager & Curator, TReitz@regionofwaterloo.ca

Kitchener: Woodside National Historic Site of Canada / Lieu historique national de Woodside
528 Wellington St. North
Kitchener, ON N2H 5L5
Tel: 519-571-5684; *Fax:* 519-571-5686
Toll-Free: 888-773-8888
ont-woodside@pc.gc.ca
www.pc.gc.ca/lhn-nhs/on/woodside /index.aspx
Woodside National Historic Site was the childhood home of Canada's longest-serving Prime Minister, William Lyon Mackenzie King. Today, the house is restored to the Victorian era of the 1890s. The site is open from mid May to late December. Groups may reserve tours during the off season.

Komoka: Komoka Railway Museum Inc.
PO Box 22
Located at 133 Queen St., Komoka, ON
Komoka, ON N0L 1R0
Tel: 519-657-1912
station-master@komokarailmuseum.ca
www.komokarailmuseum.ca
Year Founded: 1978 Restored railroad station; site includes 1913 Shay logging locomotive, 1939 CN baggage car, 1972 caboose & a collection of CN maintenance jiggers

***Lakefield:* Christ Church Community Museum**
c/o St. John the Baptist Anglican Church, PO Box 217
Lakefield, ON K0L 2H0
Tel: 705-652-8302
stjohnslakefield.ca
History of Lakefield, & the Strickland family; The Bill Twist Collection; display of old toys, dolls & doll furniture, cards; open 1:00-4:00 daily

***Lanark:* Lanark & District Museum**
c/o The Corporation of the Township of Lanark Highlands, PO Box 340, 75 George St.
Located at 80 George St., Lanark, ON
Lanark, ON K0G 1K0
Tel: 613-259-2575
lanarkanddistrictmuseum@gmail.com
www.lanarkcountymuseums.ca
twitter.com/LandDMuseum
www.facebook.com/La narkDistrictMuseum
Other contact information: Alt. URL: lanarkanddistrictmuseum.blogspot.ca
Year Founded: 1977 Open weekends, mid-May to mid-Oct.

***Latchford:* House of Memories**
PO Box 82
Latchford, ON P0J 1N0
Tel: 705-676-2417
Year Founded: 1967 Local artifacts from 1900-1940; WWI & WWII items; natural history exhibits

***Leamington:* Point Pelee National Park of Canada, Visitor Centre, DeLaurier Historical House, & Trail / Parc national du Canada de la Pointe-Pelée**
407 Monarch Lane, RR#1
Leamington, ON N8H 3V4
Tel: 519-322-2365; *Fax:* 519-322-1277
Toll-Free: 888-773-8888
pelee.info@pc.gc.ca
www.pc.gc.ca./pelee
Social Media: www.youtube.com/user/ParksCanadaAgency
twitter.com/PointPeleeNP
www.facebook.com/ParksCanada
Other contact information: TTY: 1-866-787-6221
Located at the southern tip of Canada, Point Pelee National Park features the DeLaurier Historical House. The homestead & barn depict the park's human & cultural heritage. The Visitor Centre houses exhibits, a children's discovery room, & theatre programs about the area's natural & cultural heritage.

***Limehouse:* Canadian Military Studies Museum**
RR#1
Limehouse, ON L0P 1H0
Tel: 905-877-6522
The Canadian Military Studies Museum features artifacts from the mid-17th century, the Boer War, World War I, & World War II, to the Korean & Vietnam Wars.

***Lindsay:* Olde Gaol Museum**
***Parent:* Victoria County Historical Society**
50 Victoria Ave. North
Lindsay, ON K9V 4G3
Tel: 705-324-3404
info@oldegaolmuseum.ca
www.oldegaolmuseum.cam
Social Media: www.linkedin.com/company/olde-gaol-museum
www.facebook.com/OldeGaolMuseu m.VCHS
The Lindsay Jail, built in 1863, was historically known as the County Gaol. The Victoria County Historical Society collects, preserves, & exhibits the history of the County of Victoria.

***Little Current:* Centennial Museum of Sheguiandah**
10862 Hwy. 6
Little Current, ON P0P 1K0
Tel: 705-368-2367
museum@townofnemi.on.ca
www.manitoulin-island.com/museums/centennial_museum.html
Year Founded: 1967 Pioneer culture & history on Manitoulin Island. Fall hours: Tu - Sa 9:00 - 4:30. Summer hours: M - W, F - Su 9:00 - 4:30; Th 9:00 - 8:00.
Heidi Ferguson, Curator

***London:* Banting House National Historic Site**
***Parent:* Canadian Diabetes Association**
442 Adelaide St. North
London, ON N6B 3H8
Tel: 519-673-1752; *Fax:* 519-660-8992
banting@diabetes.ca
www.diabetes.ca/about-us/who/banting-house
twitter .com/BantingHouse
www.facebook.com/BantingHouseNHS
Other contact information: Alt URL: bantinghousenhsc.wordpress.com
Year Founded: 1984 The hosue where Dr. F.G. Banting, the co-discoverer of insulin, once lived. Open Tu-Sa 12:00-4:00.
Grant Maltman, Curator, grant.maltman@diabetes.ca

***London:* Canadian Medical Hall of Fame**
#202, 267 Dundas St.
London, ON N6A 1H2
Tel: 519-488-2003; *Fax:* 519-488-2999
cmhf@cdnmedhall.org
www.cdnmedhall.org
Social Media: www.youtube.com/user/cdnmedhall
twitter.com/CdnMedHallFame
www.faceboo k.com/cdnmedhall
Year Founded: 2003 The Hall features a portrait gallery, featured exhibits, a wall fo quotations, a stamp display refelcting the history of Canadian health care, & a media theatre. Open M-F 8:30-4:30, Sa 10:00-5:00, Su 10:00-5:00 (May-Sept. only).
Stewart Hamilton, Chair
Lissa Foster, Executive Director, lfoster@cdnmedhall.org

***London:* Eldon House**
481 Ridout St. North
London, ON N6A 5H4
Tel: 519-661-5169
info@eldonhouse.ca
www.eldonhouse.ca
www.facebook.co m/EldonHouseHeritageMuseum
Year Founded: 1961 House of the Harris family from 1834-1959
Maureen Spencer Golovchenko, Chair
Tara Whittmann, Curator, wittmann@eldonhouse.ca

***London:* Fanshawe Pioneer Village (FPV)**
2609 Fanshawe Park Rd. East
London, ON N5X 4A1
Tel: 519-457-1296
info@fanshawepioneervillage.ca
www.fanshawepioneervillage.ca
Costumed interpreters demonstrate life in mid-1800s to early 1900s rural Ontario crossroads community
Sheila Johnson, Executive Director, sjohnson@fanshawepioneervillage.ca
Shanna Dunlop, Curator, sdunlop@fanshawepioneervillage.ca

***London:* First Hussars Museum**
"A" Block, Wolseley Barracks, 701 Oxford St. East
London, ON N5Y 4T7
1hmuseum@sympatico.ca
www.firsthussars.ca/museum.html
Social Media: www.youtube.com/user/firsthussarstv
twitter.com/1stHussars
www.facebook.com/groups/2374582807
Follows the history of the 1st Hussars from 1856 until today; includes material on the Boer War, the Great War & WWII; located at 1 Dundas St., London, ON.
Alastair Neely, Curator

***London:* Forest City Gallery (FCG)**
258 Richmond St.
London, ON N6B 2H7
Tel: 519-434-5875
info@forestcitygallery.com
www.forestcitygallery.com
Social Media: www.youtube.com/user/forestcitygallery
twitter.com/ForestCityGlry
www. facebook.com/forestcitygallery
Other contact information: Blog: www.fcgintern.blogspot.ca
Year Founded: 1973 An artist-run centre dedicated to showcasing national & international artists working in visual/media arts, performance, literature, & music. Open W-Sa 12:00-5:00.
Benjamin Robinson, President
Jenna Faye Powell, Director, director@forestcitygallery.com

***London:* Grosvenor Lodge**
***Parent:* Heritage London Foundation**
1017 Western Rd.
London, ON N6G 1G5
Tel: 519-645-2845; *Fax:* 519-645-0981
info@grosvenorlodge.com
www.grosvenorlodge.com
www.facebook.com/grosve norlodge
Year Founded: 1981 1853 estate; operates as London Regional Resource Centre for Heritage & the Environment, administered by the Heritage London Foundation; resources available on heritage & environmental issues; venue for meetings, seminars & social events; library & display areas open to public; open M-F 9:00-4:00

***London:* Guy Lombardo Music Centre**
205 Wonderland Rd. South
London, ON N6K 3T3
Tel: 519-473-9003
www.guylombardomusic.com/museum.html
Memorabilia relating to bandleader & his band, the Royal Canadians, including original recordings & videotapes; open June-Aug., W-Su, 11-7; Sept. 12:30-4:30 or by appt.
Doug Flood, Director, 519-652-3417, seventyeights@aol.com

***London:* Jet Aircraft Museum (JAM)**
#2, 2465 Aviation Lane
London, ON N5V 3Z9
Tel: 519-453-7000
info@jetaircraftmuseum.ca
www.jetaircraftmuseum.ca
Social Media: www.youtube.com/user/JetAircraftMuseum
twitter.com/_JAM_News
www.faceb ook.com/JetAircraftMuseum
Year Founded: 2009 Modern Royal Canadian Air Force history.
Rick Hammond, President

***London:* London Regional Children's Museum**
21 Wharncliffe Rd. South
London, ON N6J 4G5
Tel: 519-434-5726
info@londonchildrensmuseum.ca
www.londonchildrensmuseum.ca
Social Media: www.youtube.com/user/LdnChildrensMuseum
twitter.com/children_museum
ww w.facebook.com/LondonChildrensMuseum
Year Founded: 1975 Hands-on, interactive museum; features ten themed galleries, school programs, outreach programs, day camps, workshops, birthday parties & membership programs
Natalie Spoozak, President
Amanda Conlon, Executive Director, amanda@londonchildrensmuseum.ca

***London:* Museum London**
421 Ridout St. North
London, ON N6A 5H4
Tel: 519-661-0333; *Fax:* 519-661-2559
www.museumlondon.ca
Social Media: plus.google.com/u/0/109986306694279488979
twitter.com/MuseumLondon
www .facebook.com/MuseumLondon
Operates Eldon House; exhibits include family life, historical & contemporary art & historical artifacts from the London area from 1834 to 1960
Brian Meehan, Executive Director
Cydna Mercer, Head of Administration
Melanie Townsend, Head of Exhibitions & Collections

***London:* Museum of Ontario Archaeology & Iroquoian Village Site (MOA)**
Lawson-Jury Bldg., University of Western Ontario, 1600 Attawandaron Rd.
London, ON N6G 3M6
Tel: 519-473-1360; *Fax:* 519-850-2363
info@archaeologymuseum.ca
www.archaeologymuseum.ca
twitter.com/MuseOnt Arch
www.facebook.com/ArchaeologyMuseum
Year Founded: 1981 Archaeological & ethnographical collection; prehistoric archaeological Iroquois village site; museum open year round with reduced hours in fall & winter
Maria Ferraro, President
Joan Kanigan, Executive Director, director@archaeologymuseum.ca

***London:* The Royal Canadian Regiment Museum**
Wolseley Barracks, 701 Oxford St. East
London, ON N5Y 4T7
Tel: 519-660-5275
info@thercrmuseum.ca
www.thercrmuseum.ca
twitter.com/RCRMuseum
www.facebook.com/RCRMuseum
To serve as a training medium to teach regimental history; to preserve regimental history through the collection of documents, pictures, books & artifacts with emphasis on the RCR; to serve as a place of military interest for the public & Canadian Forces personnel; to provide research facilities for the study of Canadian military history.
Georgiana Stanciu, Curator

London: Secrets of Radar Museum
PO Box 24033
London, ON N6H 5C4
Tel: 519-691-5922
info@secretsofradar.com
secretsofradar.com
www.facebook.com/SecretsofRadar
Year Founded: 2001 Exhibits artifacts that were used by radar mechanics, operators, teachers, trainers, physicists & researchers during WWII.

London: Spirit of Flight Aviation Museum
Parent: 427 Wing Association
2155 Crumlin Side Rd.
London, ON N5V 3Z9
Tel: 519-455-0430
info@427wing.com
www.427wing.com/museum
Aviation history
Michael Adams, Executive Director & Curator, michaeladamstv@gmail.com

Lucan: Donnelly Homestead
34937 Roman Line, RR#3
Lucan, ON N0M 2J0
Tel: 519-227-1244
www.quadro.net/~donnelly
Historical on-site tours given on the original Donnelly property by current owner; artifacts & photographs; tours preferably by appt., year-round; private residence
J. Robert Salts, Owner, rsalts@quadro.net

Lucan: Lucan Area Heritage & Donnelly Museum
PO Box 427
Located at 171 Main St., Lucan, ON
Lucan, ON N0M 2J0
Tel: 519-227-0756
lucanheritage@donnellymuseum.com
www.donnellymuseum.com
twitter.com/LucanHeritage
www.facebook.com/luca ndonnellymuseum
Year Founded: 1995 Local history

Madoc: O'Hara Mill Homestead & Conservation Area
PO Box 56, 638 Mill Rd.
Madoc, ON K0K 2K0
Tel: 613-473-2084
info@ohara-mill.org
www.ohara-mill.org
www.facebook.com/OHaraMillHomesteadAndConservationAre a
Year Founded: 1965 Attractions include O'Hara House, a log house, a saw mill, & a one room log schoolhouse. O'Hara House is restored to represent the Victorian era around 1840. The saw mill is a rare working English Gate or Reciprocating Frame saw mill. Grounds are open daily all year. Buildings are open from mid-May to October.

Magnetawan: Magnetawan Historical Museum
PO Box 70, Hwy. 520
Magnetawan, ON P0A 1P0
Tel: 705-387-3308
www.magnetawan.com
Other contact information: Alternate Phone: 705-387-3357
Restored plant & turbine that supplied first electricity for village; log cabin; located at Biddy St. at the Magnetawan Locks.

Manitowaning: Assiginack Museum & Heritage Park
125 Arthur St.
Manitowaning, ON P0P 1N0
Tel: 705-859-3905
assiginackinfo@amtelecom.net
The Assiginack Museum & Heritage Park is a community & marine museum. Artifacts are from the mid-1800s to the mid-1900s. Visitors can see a pioneer home & school, a 19th century grist mill, plus the Great Lakes steamship, S.S. Norisle, which was built in 1946. The museum is open from June to October.
Jeanette Allen, Curator

Manotick: Watson's Mill
PO Box 145, 5525 Dickinson St.
Manotick, ON K4M 1A3
Tel: 613-692-6455
manager@watsonsmill.com
www.watsonsmill.com
twitter.com/watsonsmill
www.facebook.com/WatsonsMi llManotick
Year Founded: 1860 Operated by Watson's Mill Manotick Incorporated; 19th century working gristmill, built 1860; gift shop; tours; picnic area; live interpretation, gossip tours
Karlis Adamsons, President, Board of Directors

Marathon: Marathon District Museum
PO Box 728
Located at 25 Stevens Ave., Marathon, ON
Marathon, ON P0T 2E0
Tel: 807-229-8175
marathonmuseum@gmail.com
marathondistrictmuseum.weebly.com
Local history

Markham: Markham Museum & Historic Village
9350 Hwy. 48
Markham, ON L3P 3J3
Tel: 905-294-4576; Fax: 905-294-4590
museuminfo@markham.ca
www.markham.ca/wps/portal/Markham/RecreationCultur e/MarkhamMuseum
Buildings, vehicles, furnishing & agricultural & industrial equipment that relate to Markham Township's history, from native presence to the 20th century; open year round

Markham: York Region District School Board Museum & Archives
21 Renfrew Dr.
Markham, ON L3R 8H3
Tel: 905-470-6119
heritage.schoolhouse@yrdsb.edu.on.ca
www.yrdsb.edu.on. ca/page.cfm?id=BLRCH0001
The museum & archives collect & preserve material related to the development of education in what is now known as York Region. Open year-round with reduced hours in the summer.
Janet Emonson, Curator, jan.emonson@yrdsb.edu.on.ca

Marten River: Marten River Provincial Park Logging Museum
c/o Marten River Provincial Park, 2860 Hwy. 11 North
Marten River, ON P0H 1T0
Tel: 705-892-2200
ontarioparks.com/english/mart.html
Social Media: pinterest.com/ontarioparks/marten-river/
Artifacts for early logging era in Northern Ontario

Massey: Massey Area Museum (MAM)
150 Sable St.
Massey, ON P0P 1P0
Tel: 705-865-2266
info@masseyareamuseum.com
www.masseyareamuseum.com
www.facebook.com/121143151263273
Year Founded: 1967 The Massey Area Museum is housed in the original Bretzlaff General Store, which was built in 1909. The museum details logging history, as well as Aboriginal, Fort LaCloche, mining, farming, & early settler history. Model rooms, a chapel, a general store, & Massey's first horse-drawn fire engine are featured at the museum. There is also an historical & genealogical research centre, which includes records of the Township of Sables-Spanish River's ten cemeteries.

Matheson: Thelma Miles Historical Museum
374 Hough Rd.
Matheson, ON P0K 1N0
Tel: 705-273-2325
History of the communities of Val Gagné, Shillington, Wavel, Ramore, Holtyre & Matheson from 1900-1945

Mattawa: Mattawa & District Museum
285 - 1st St.
Mattawa, ON P0H 1V0
Tel: 705-744-5495
mattawamuseum@on.aibn.com
mattawamuseum.com
Year Founded: 1976 Open daily July - Aug.; weekends in May, June, Sept., Oct.

Mattawa: Voyageur Heritage Centre
Samuel de Champlain Provincial Park, PO Box 147
Mattawa, ON P0H 1V0
Tel: 705-744-2276
www.ontarioparks.com/park/samueldechamplain
The Voyageur Heritage Centre tells the story of the Mattawa River & the lives of the voyageurs. The centre features one of the largest reproduced birch bark canoes.

Maxville: Glengarry Sports Hall of Fame
35 Fair St.
Maxville, ON K0C 1A0
Tel: 613-527-1044
glenhalloffame@bellnet.ca
www.glengarrysports.com
www.facebook.com/121512007937959
Year Founded: 1978
William Hinse-MacCulloch, Curator

Meaford: Meaford Museum
111 Bayfield St.
Meaford, ON N4L 1N4
Tel: 519-538-5974; Fax: 519-538-5974
meafordmuseum@meaford.ca
www.meafordmuseum.ca
Year Founded: 1961 The Meaford Museum aims to collect, educate, display, conserve and feature the history of the former Town of Meaford and the surrounding area, from early settlements to the present. Hours: Open hours vary. Check website or call for details.
Jody Seeley, Services Coordinator, jseeley@meaford.ca

Meldrum Bay: Mississagi Strait Lighthouse Museum
Meldrum Bay, ON
info@themississagilighthouse.com
www.themississagilighthouse.com
www.facebook.com/pages/Mississagi-Lighth ouse/116354762988
Lighthouse built in 1873, includes artifacts related to seafaring & fishing; keeper's house features 19th-century furnishings; open mid-May - Sept. Lighthouse staff request to be contacted by email during the summer. Located at the western tip of Manitoulin Island, near the village of Meldrum Bay.
Mary Eadie, Manager

Meldrum Bay: The Net Shed Museum
Water St.
Meldrum Bay, ON
Tel: 705-283-3324
www.facebook.com/517808374965274
Open June & Aug.; artifacts of pioneer fishing, lumbering & farming; display of nursing in WWII

Merrickville: The Blockhouse Museum
Parent: Merrickville & District Historical Society
PO Box 294
Merrickville, ON K0G 1N0
Tel: 613-269-4034
info@merrickvillehistory.org
www.merrickvillehistory.org/museum.html
Built as a defence for the Rideau Canal built in 1830. Contains local pioneer artifacts.

Middleville: Middleville & District Museum
2130 Concession Rd. 6D
Middleville, ON K0G 1K0
Tel: 613-259-0229; Fax: 613-259-5462
middlevillemuseum@gmail.com
www.middlevillemuseum.blogspot.ca
www.face book.com/186945718019189
Year Founded: 1974 Local pioneer artifacts including items for the maple syrup, cheese & lumbering industries; open May 24-Thanksgiving

Midland: Huronia Museum
PO Box 638
Located at 549 Little Lake Park, Midland, ON
Midland, ON L4R 4P4
Tel: 705-526-2844; Fax: 705-527-6622
info@huroniamuseum.com
www.huroniamuseum.com
Social Media: www.flickr.com/photos/huroniamuseum
twitter.com/HuroniaMuseum
www.face book.com/huroniamuseum
Recreated Huron Village represents one of hundreds that existed in the Georgian Bay area, representing a unique & sophisticated society which lasted nearly 1,000 years; Canada's first recreated Native village; extensive exhibits on regional history, art gallery, archives & Mundys Bay Store; a large selection of native & historical books
Gary French, Chair

Midland: Martyrs' Shrine
PO Box 7, 16163 Hwy. 12 West
Midland, ON L4R 4K6
Tel: 705-526-3788 Toll-Free: 855-526-3788
info@martyrs-shrine.com
www.martyrs-shrine.com
twitter.com/martyrsshri ne1
www.facebook.com/204667312903160
Year Founded: 1926 Built in 1926 in tribute to the Jesuit missionaries who laboured among the Huron, 1625-50, & to the eight who were martyred, the interior of this church with its wooden walls & canoe-like ceiling celebrates the melding of historical cultures. Open daily, Victoria Day weekend through Thanksgiving weekend; tours & talks given on request.
Fr. Bernie Carroll, Director

***Midland:* Sainte-Marie among the Hurons / Sainte-Marie-au-Pays-des-Hurons**
16164 Hwy. 12 East
Midland, ON L4R 4K8
Tel: 705-526-7838; *Fax:* 705-526-9193
www.saintemarieamongthehurons.on.ca
Other contact information: TTY: 705-528-7697
During the 17th century, Sainte-Marie served as the fortress & headquarters for the French Jesuit mission to the Huron nation. Based upon archaeological & historical research, Sainte-Marie was recreated on its original site. Special programs & courses are offered about the first European community in Ontario. The site is open from the end of April to the end of October.
Will Baird, General Manager, Huronia Historical Parks

***Milford:* Mariners Park Museum**
2065 County Rd. 13
Milford, ON K0K 2P0
Tel: 613-476-8392
marinersmuseum@pecounty.on.ca
pecounty.on.ca/government/community_development/museums/mariners.php
www .facebook.com/museumspec
Year Founded: 1967 Indoor & outdoor exhibits distinguish the site, with displays of various artifacts from marine activity in the area, including treasures from diving expeditions, as well as pieces related to local fishing, ship building, ice harvesting & rum running days. The False Duck Lighthouse has become a memorial to the County's sailors.
Jennifer Lyons, Head Curator, Museums of Prince Edward County, 613-476-3833, museums@pecounty.on.ca
Diane Denyes-Wenn, Site Curator, 613-476-8392

***Miller Lake:* Cabot Head Lightstation Museum & Visitor Centre**
806 Cabot Head Rd.
Miller Lake, ON N0H 1Z0
Tel: 519-795-7780
www.cabothead.ca
www.facebook.com/CabotHead
Local history.

***Milton:* Country Heritage Park**
PO Box 38, 8560 Tremaine Rd.
Milton, ON L9T 2Y3
Toll-Free: 888-681-2497
www.countryheritagepark.com
Social Media: pinterest.com/countryherpark
twitter.com/countryherpark
www.facebook.c om/CountryHeritagePark
Display of machinery & tools related to all aspects of agricultural industry in Ontario

***Milton:* Halton County Radial Railway (HCRR)**
c/o Ontario Electric Railway Historical Association Inc., PO Box 578
Location: 13629 Guelph Line, Milton, ON
Milton, ON L9T 5A2
Tel: 519-856-9802; *Fax:* 519-856-1399
streetcar@hcry.org
www.hcry.org
twitter.com/streetcarmuseum
Operating streetcar & electric railway museum

***Milton:* Halton Region Museum**
Kelso Conservation Area, 5181 Kelso Rd., RR#3
Milton, ON L9T 2X7
Tel: 905-875-2200; *Fax:* 905-876-4322
Toll-Free: 866-442-5866
museum@halton.ca
www.halton.ca/museum
www.facebook.c om/HaltonRegionMuseum
Year Founded: 1962 Focusing on Halton's natural & cultural heritage, the main exhibits are located in Alexander Barn & in the Visitor Centre on the main floor. Both Heritage & Environmental Programmes are offered. The Reference Library stores various regional, historical records available for research purposes. Open year round.

***Milton:* Waldie Blacksmith Shop**
16 James St.
Milton, ON L9T 2P4
Tel: 905-875-4156
miltonhistoricalsociety@bellnet.ca
www.miltonhistoricalsociety.ca
Social Media: miltonhistoricalsociety.wordpress.com
twitter.com/miltonsoldiers
www.f acebook.com/184811598254298
Administered by the Milton Historical Society; open mid-March to Dec., Wed & Sat.
Jan Mowbray, President, Milton Historical Society

***Mindemoya:* Central Manitoulin Historical Society Pioneer Museum**
PO Box 320
Mindemoya, ON P0P 1S0
Tel: 705-377-4383
www.centralmanitoulin.ca
Other contact information: Alt Phone: 705-377-4045
The museum features a log cabin, workshop & blacksmith shop, frame barn, farm equipment, & reinactments of pioneer life. Open July & Aug., M-F 1:00-4:00, or by appointment.
Ted Taylor, President, 705-377-5649, tedeve@amtelecom.net
Pat Costigan, Acting Curator, 705-377-6640, patriciawilliamson39@gmail.com
Norma Hughson, Acting Curator, 705-368-3416, nlhughson@manitoulin.net

***Minden:* Minden Hills Museum**
Minden Hills Cultural Centre, 174-176 Bobcaygeon Rd.
Minden, ON K0M 2K0
Tel: 705-286-3454
museum@mindenhills.ca
mindenhills.ca/community-centre
Year Founded: 1984 Local history & pioneer village.

***Minesing:* Simcoe County Museum**
1151 Hwy. 26
Minesing, ON L0L 1Y2
Tel: 705-728-3721; *Fax:* 705-728-9130
museum@simcoe.ca
museum.simcoe.ca
Social Media: www.youtube.com/countyofsimcoe
twitter.com/simcoecountymus
www.faceboo k.com/simcoecountymuseum
Year Founded: 1928 Local history, including a replica of Barrie's main street from th turn of the 20th century. Open daily, 9:00-4:30 Monday to Saturday & 1:00-4:30 Sunday.

***Mississauga:* Benares Historic House & Visitor Centre**
1507 Clarkson Rd. North
Mississauga, ON L5J 2W8
Tel: 905-822-2347
www.mississauga.ca/portal/discover/benareshistorichouse
Year Founded: 1995 Owned & operated by the City of Mississauga, Community Services Department, the Benares Historic House is a Georgian style home, which was built in 1857. The home has been restored to reflect the early 20th century & displays original artifacts from the Harris family & home. The Benares House is believed to be the inspiration for Mazo de la Roche's Jalna novels.

***Mississauga:* Bradley House Museum**
1620 Orr Rd.
Mississauga, ON L5J 4T2
Tel: 905-615-4860
www.mississauga.ca/portal/discover/bradleymuseum
Year Founded: 1967 The Bradley Museum is owned & operated by the City of Mississauga, Community Services Department. The museum grounds feature an early 19th century home known as The Anchorage, a farmhouse which was built in 1830, & a log cabin. The farmhouse was owned by the Bradleys, who were a United Empire Loyalist couple. The museum is open year round.

***Mississauga:* Lithuanian Museum/Archives of Canada (LMAC)**
***Parent:* Lithuanian Canadian Community**
2185 Stavebank Rd.
Mississauga, ON L5C 1T3
Tel: 416-533-3292
info@klb.org
www.klb.org/muziejusEN.html
Year Founded: 1989 To collect, display, organize & preserve documents, photographs, fine art, textiles, memorabilia, souvenirs of community events, uniforms, medals, coins, maps, flags, videos, audio tapes & rare books or periodicals which pertain to Lithuania & Lithuanian Canadians; small lending library

***Mississauga:* Old Britannia Schoolhouse**
Friends of the Schoolhouse, 5576 Hurontario St.
Mississauga, ON L5R 1B3
Tel: 905-890-1010
chair@britanniaschoolhousefriends.org
www.britanniasch oolhousefriends.org
The building is a one-room schoolhouse built in 1852. Today, modern school children are given the chance to role-play what it would have been like to attend the school in the 1800s. The building is open to visitors on the second Sunday of each months, & the space is also available for special functions.

***Mooretown:* Moore Museum**
94 Moore Line
Mooretown, ON N0N 1M0
Tel: 519-867-2020
www.mooremuseum.ca
Year Founded: 1975 Open year round; Jan. - Feb. by appt.
Laurie Mason, Curator

***Morpeth:* Rondeau Provincial Park Visitor Centre**
RR#1 (Hwy. 15)
Morpeth, ON N0P 1X0
Tel: 519-674-1750
rondeau@ontario.ca
www.rondeauprovincialpark.ca
www.facebook.com/pantsgloydi
Other contact information: Alternate URL: ontarioparks.com/english/rond.html
Herbarium, egg, mammal, insect, archaeological, photographic & bird collection; contact the Visitor Centre at 519-674-1768
Anne Ondrovcik, President, Friends of Rondeau

***Morrisburg:* Upper Canada Village**
13740 County Rd. 2
Morrisburg, ON K0C 1X0
Tel: 613-543-4328*Toll-Free:* 800-437-2233
getaway@parks.on.ca
www.uppercanadavillage.com
twitter.com/UpperCanada Vill
www.facebook.com/100502250000481
Upper Canada Village features more than forty heritage buildings. The village depicts daily life in the 1860s, through demonstrations, talks, & hands-on activities. The site also has a library & research facility. Upper Canada Village is open from mid May to mid October.

***Mount Brydges:* Ska-Nah-Doht Iroquoian Village & Museum**
8348 Longwoods Rd.
Located at 8449 Irish Dr., R.R. #1, Mount Brydes, ON, N0L 1W0
Mount Brydges, ON N0L 1W0
Tel: 519-264-2420; *Fax:* 519-264-1562
info@ltvca.ca
www.lowerthames-conservation.on.ca
Year Founded: 1973 This recreated Iroquoian village of 1,000 years ago has 18 outdoor exhibits including a palisade with maze & longhouses; museum in resource centre; displays on nature & conservation; trails, wetland boardwalks & picnic areas.There are hands on exhibits and an archaeological collection.

***Mount Hope:* Canadian Warplane Heritage Museum (CWHM)**
9280 Airport Rd.
Mount Hope, ON L0R 1W0
Tel: 905-679-4183; *Fax:* 905-679-4186
Toll-Free: 877-347-3359
museum@warplane.com
www.warplane.com
Social Media: www.youtube.com/user/CWHMuseum
twitter.com/CWHM
www.facebook.com/CanadianWarplaneHeritageMuseum
Year Founded: 1971 The museum is dedicated to the acquisition & preservation of aircraft flown by Canadians from WWII to the present, & the collection of related aviation artifacts & memorabilia; library & archival resources; meeting room & hangar rental; special events & programming; group tours available. Open daily 9-5, year round.
David G. Rohrer, President & Chief Executive Officer, 905-679-4183
Erin Napier, Curator, 905-679-4183, erin@warplane.com

***Mulmur:* Dufferin County Museum & Archives (DCMA)**
936029 Airport Rd.
Mulmur, ON L9V 0L3
Tel: 705-435-1881; *Fax:* 705-435-9876
Toll-Free: 877-941-7787
info@dufferinmuseum.com
www.dufferinmuseum.com
twitt er.com/DufferinMuseum
www.facebook.com/DufferinCountyMuseum
Two log structures; CPR flagging station; historic church; changing exhibits; archives
Sarah Robinson, Curator, srobinson@dufferinmuseum.com

***Napanee:* Allan Macpherson House**
180 Elizabeth St.
Napanee, ON K7R 1B5
Tel: 613-354-3027
www.macphersonhouse.ca
www.facebook.com/200934956626534

Year Founded: 1967 1826 mansion of Allan Macpherson, one of Napanee's leading citizens; reflects the taste, public & private activities of an entrepreneurial Scottish immigrant. Open May-Dec. School programs; bridal party rentals; children's summer activity days; annual whiskey tasting.

***Napanee:* Lennox & Addington County Museum & Archives**
97 Thomas St. East
Napanee, ON K7R 4B9
Tel: 613-354-3027
nmuseum@lennox-addington.on.ca
www.lennox-addington.on.ca
Other contact information: Archives E-mail: archives@lennox-addington.on.ca
Located in former County jail (1864); genealogy & historical research centre, county's origins, Loyalist settlement & development from 1784 to present, displays & extensive archives; open year round
Jane Foster, Manager, jfoster@lennox-addington.on.ca
Shelley Respondek, Archivist, srespondek@lennox-addington.on.ca

***Napanee:* Old Hay Bay Church**
2365 South Shore Rd.
Napanee, ON K7R 3K7
Tel: 613-373-2261
A National Historic Site, Old Hay Bay Church was erected in 1792. Located at 2365 South Shore Road in Adolphustown, Ontario, the church is the oldest Methodist building in Canada.

***Nepean:* Nepean Museum Inc. / Musée de Nepean**
16 Rowley Ave.
Nepean, ON K2G 1L9
Tel: 613-580-9638; *Fax:* 613-723-7936
museums@ottawa.ca
www.nepeanmuseum.ca
twitter.com/NepeanMuseum
www.f acebook.com/NepeanMuseum
Year Founded: 1983 Housed in the first Nepean Library, the museum displays historical objects related to Nepean's past & present. Nepean Museum contains two meeting rooms.

***New Liskeard:* Little Claybelt Homesteaders Museum**
PO Box 1718, 883356 Hwy. 65
New Liskeard, ON P0J 1P0
Tel: 705-647-9575
claybeltmuseum.ca
Year Founded: 1974 Displays of geological origin of Little Claybelt, pioneer activities, historical documents, artifacts & agricultural implements, pioneer family histories

***Newmarket:* Elman W. Campbell Museum**
134 Main St. South
Newmarket, ON L3Y 3Y7
Tel: 905-953-5314; *Fax:* 905-898-2083
Exhibits trace the development of Newmarket from the time of the first settlers. Open Tues.-Sat.

***Niagara Falls:* Battle Ground Hotel Museum**
6137 Lundy's Lane
Niagara Falls, ON L2G 1T4
Tel: 905-358-5082
niagarafallsmuseums.ca/visit/battle-ground-hotel-museum.aspx
The museum is located on the site of the Lundy's Lane Battlefield, is housed in a restored 1850s tavern, & showcases artifacts related to the War of 1812. Open May-Aug., F-Su 11:00-5:00.

***Niagara Falls:* Daredevil Gallery**
6170 Fallsview Blvd.
Niagara Falls, ON L2G 7T8
Tel: 905-358-3611; *Fax:* 905-358-3613
Toll-Free: 866-405-4629
info@imaxniagara.com
imaxniagara.com/daredevil-exhibit
Only collection of original daredevil barrels found in Niagara Falls

***Niagara Falls:* Guinness World Records Museum**
4943 Clifton Hill
Niagara Falls, ON L2G 3N5
Tel: 905-356-2266
www.guinnessniagarafalls.com
Displays of human achievements; models of the extraordinary; computer databanks & videos; open year round

***Niagara Falls:* Louis Tussaud's Waxworks**
4983 Clifton Hill
Niagara Falls, ON L2G 3N4
Tel: 905-374-6601
www.ripleys.com/niagarafalls/wax
Year Founded: 1953 Museum displays wax models of famous & infamous people, such as artists, musicians, celebrities, politicians & religious & historical figures. Open year-round.

***Niagara Falls:* Movieland Wax Museum of the Stars**
4848 Clifton Hill
Niagara Falls, ON L2G 3N4
Tel: 905-358-3061
www.cliftonhill.com/attractions/movieland-wax-museum-stars
Open year round

***Niagara Falls:* Niagara Falls History Museum**
5810 Ferry St.
Niagara Falls, ON L2G 1S9
Tel: 905-358-5082
nfhmuseum@niagarafalls.ca
www.niagarafallsmuseum.ca
Social Media: plus.google.com/NiagarafallsmuseumsCanada
twitter.com/nfmuseums
www.fa cebook.com/nfmuseums
Year Founded: 1961 The 1874 museum was originally located on Drummond Rd., the site of the Battle of Lundy's Lane, July 25, 1814, but was moved to its present site in 1970. Exhibits include a significant collection of War of 1812 artifacts, as well as historic prints of Niagara Falls. The Museum also houses a variety of artifacts relating to all aspects of the founding & development of the City of Niagara Falls.
Clark Bernat, Manager

***Niagara Falls:* Niagara Military Museum**
5049 Victoria Ave.
Niagara Falls, ON L2E 4E2
Tel: 905-358-1949
niamilmuseum@gmail.com
www.facebook.com/Niagara.Military.Museum.the.armoury
Year Founded: 2012 Military artifacts & local history.

***Niagara Falls:* Niagara Scouting Museum**
4377 Fourth Ave.
Niagara Falls, ON L2E 4N1
Tel: 905-354-6864
wj55.org/Museum.php
Collection contains scouting badges, uniform, items from the 8th World Jamboree in 1955 & other items; open by appointment only.
Tony Roberts, Curator, tandi@mergetel.com

***Niagara Falls:* Ripley's Believe It or Not! Museum**
4960 Clifton Hill
Niagara Falls, ON L2G 3N4
Tel: 905-356-2238
nfalls@ripleys.com
ripleysniagara.com
Social Media: ripleysniagara.tumblr.com
twitter.com/ripleysniagara
Year Founded: 1963 Ripley's Believe It or Not! in Niagara Falls presents strange & bizarre exhibits. The museum is open year-round.

***Niagara Falls:* Willoughby Historical Museum**
9935 Niagara Pkwy.
Niagara Falls, ON L2E 6S6
Tel: 905-295-4036; *Fax:* 905-295-4036
niagarafallsmuseums.ca/visit/willoughby-historical-museum.aspx
The Willoughby Historical Museum collects, preserves, interprets, & displays items related to Ontario's former Township of Willoughby, the Village of Chippawa, & the surrounding region. Examples of artifacts include household objects, school materials, toys, telephones, & a functioning magneto switchboard. The museum is open year-round. Tours & research can be arranged by phoning the museum.

***Niagara-on-the-Lake:* Laura Secord Homestead**
29 Queenston St.
Niagara-on-the-Lake, ON L0S 1L0
Tel: 905-262-4851
www.niagaraparks.com/heritage-trail/laura-secord-homestead.html
www.face book.com/FriendsofLauraSecord
Open May-Sept.
Caroline McCormick, President, Friends of Laura Secord

***Niagara-on-the-Lake:* McFarland House**
15927 Niagara Pkwy.
Niagara-on-the-Lake, ON L0S 1J0
Tel: 905-468-3322
mcfarland@niagaraparks.com
www.niagaraparks.com/niagara-falls-attractions/mcfarland-house.html
Year Founded: 1959 Built in 1800 & home to John McFarland & his family for 150 years, the house served as a hospital for both the British & American wounded during the War of 1812. Restored by the Niagara Parks Commission in period style, there are also traditional grounds & the McFarland Tea Garden to enjoy refreshments. Nature trails can be accessed from the park.

***Niagara-on-the-Lake:* Niagara Apothecary**
5 Queen St.
Niagara-on-the-Lake, ON L0S 1J0
Tel: 905-468-3845*Toll-Free:* 800-220-1921
niagaraapothecary@ocpinfo.com
www.niagaraapothecary.ca
The Niagara Apothecary depicts an 1869 pharmacy. Artifacts include the Harvey bottles & jars, which were imported from Britain around 1830, mortars & pestles, a 19th century leech jar, & an early cash register.

***Niagara-on-the-Lake:* Niagara Fire Museum**
2 Anderson Lane
Niagara-on-the-Lake, ON L0S 1J0
Tel: 905-468-7279
Fire-fighting equipment dating back 140 years. Not open to the public.

***Niagara-on-the-Lake:* Niagara Historical Society & Museum**
PO Box 208, 43 Castlereagh St.
Niagara-on-the-Lake, ON L0S 1J0
Tel: 905-468-3912; *Fax:* 905-468-1728
contact@niagarahistorical.museum
www.niagarahistorical.museum
Year Founded: 1895 Ontario's first purpose-built museum; artifacts from Niagara's social & military history
Sarah Kaufman, Managing Director

***Nipigon:* Nipigon Museum**
40 Front St.
Nipigon, ON P0T 2J0
Tel: 807-887-0356
nipigonmuseumtheblog.blogspot.ca
www.facebook.com/128774150545422
Artifacts relating to local lumbering & fur trading; rocks & minerals; bottles
Betty Brill, Curator

***Nipissing:* Nipissing Township Museum**
General Delivery
Location: Hwy. 654, Nipissing, ON P0H 1W0
Nipissing, ON P0H 1W0
Tel: 705-724-2938
www.nipissingtownship.com
Housed in a former Anglican church built in late 1800s of logs; displays mostly of tools, clothing & photos pertaining to the families who first settled in the area
Tracy Butler, Curator

***North Bay:* Dionne Quints Museum**
c/o North Bay & District Chamber of Commerce, 1375 Seymour St.
North Bay, ON P1B 9V6
Tel: 705-472-8480; *Fax:* 705-472-8027
Toll-Free: 888-249-8998
museum@northbaychamber.com
www.northbaychamber.com/tou rism/museum
The Quints Museum is a not for profit institution dedicated to the Dionne Quintuplets; artifacts from the Quints's early days and their growing up years; baby buggies, baby dresses, books, newspaper and magazine articles, artisitic reproductions, postcards. Located at Hwys 11 and 17 at Seymour Street in North Bay.
Kimberly Lyon, Director

***North Bay:* Discovery North Bay Museum**
***Parent:* Heritage North Bay**
100 Ferguson St.
North Bay, ON P1B 1W8
Tel: 705-476-2323
www.discoverynorthbay.com
twitter.com/discoverynbay
www.facebook.com/pages/Discovery-North-Bay-Museum/73440203927
10,000 domestic & business objects related to settling & development of local region; open year round

Naomi Rupke, Director/Curator, naomi.rupke@heritagenorthbay.com

North Buxton: Buxton National Historic Site & Museum
21975 A.D. Shadd Rd.
North Buxton, ON N0P 1Y0

Tel: 519-352-4799
buxton@ciaccess.com
www.buxtonmuseum.com
www.facebook.com/168126086579515

Year Founded: 1967 The site is a memorial to the Elgin Settlement, which was the last stop on the Underground Railroad for many fugitives of the American system of slavery in the pre-Civil War years. The Raleigh (Buxton) Schoolhouse of 1861 & a settlement cabin from 1854 are now part of the museum. The museum preserves the artifacts of the original settlers of the Elgin Settlement & their descendants.
Shannon Prince, Curator

Norwich: The Norwich & District Museum & Archives
***Parent:* Norwich & District Historical Society**
89 Stover St. North
Norwich, ON N0J 1P0

Tel: 519-863-3101; *Fax:* 519-863-3638
norwichdhs@execulink.com
www.norwichdhs.ca
twitter.com/norwichdhs
www.facebook.com/archives@norwichdhs.ca
Other contact information: Archives e-mail: archives@norwichdhs.ca

1889 Quaker meeting house; archives & genealogical library; blacksmith shop; CN station; restored Lossing house; dairy & agricultural barns; windmill & stump; Quaker school house

Oakville: Canadian Golf Hall of Fame & Museum (CGHF)
Glen Abbey Golf Club, 1333 Dorval Dr.
Oakville, ON L6M 4X7

Tel: 905-849-9700
cghf@golfcanada.ca
www.rcga.org/cghf

Year Founded: 1971 Located at Glen Abbey, the Canadian Golf Hall of Fame & Museum tells the history of golf in Canada. The Hall of Fame honours amateur & professional golfers & builders of the sport, who have made extraordinary contributions to the game of golf in Canada. The archives & library collects photographs & documents, as well as golf publications about the game, golf courses & golfers. Staff are available to assist with research. The museum also arranges travelling exhibitions. The Canadian Golf Hall of Fame & Museum is open year round.
Karen Hewson, Managing Director, Membership & Heritage Services, khewson@golfcanada.ca
Meggan Gardner, Curator, mgardner@golfcanada.ca

Oakville: Oakville Museum at Erchless Estate
8 Navy St.
Oakville, ON L6J 2Y5

Tel: 905-338-4400
oakvillemuseum@oakville.ca
www.oakville.ca/museum
twitter.com/oakville_museum
www.facebook.com/oakvillemuseum

The Oakville Museum at Erchless Estate features the following historical buildings: Erchless Estate (c. 1858), The Custom House & Toronto Bank (c. 1856), & The Old Post Office (c. 1835). The Thomas Museum is operated by the Oakville Historical Society.
Bill Nesbitt, Museum Supervisor
Carolyn Cross, Curator, Collections
Susan Crane, Learning and Community Development Officer, Learning & Community Development

Odessa: Historic Babcock Mill
100 Bridge St.
Odessa, ON K0H 2H0

Tel: 613-386-7363
www.loyalisttownship.ca

Restored, fully operational water-powered 1856 mill

Ohsweken: Chiefswood National Historic Site
PO Box 640
Located at 1037 Hwy. 54, Ohsweken, ON N0A 1M0
Ohsweken, ON N0A 1M0

Tel: 519-752-5005; *Fax:* 519-758-0768
chiefswood@sixnations.ca
www.chiefswood.com
Social Media: www.youtube.com/user/Chiefswood
twitter.com/epaulinejohnson
www.facebook.com/epauline.johnson

The site is the location of the Chiefswood Museum, birthplace & childhood home of poet Emily Pauline Johnson (Tekahionwake); educational programming; tours; gift shop; "The Homing Bee" newsletter. Open Tues. through Sun., 10:00-3:00, May-Oct. Open by appointment Oct.-May.

Oil Springs: Oil Museum of Canada
PO Box 16, 2423 Kelly Rd.
Oil Springs, ON N0N 1P0

Tel: 519-834-2840; *Fax:* 519-834-2840
oil.museum@county-lambton.on.ca
www.lambtonmuseums.ca/oil
www.facebook .com/OilMuseumofCanada

Situated in Oil Springs, Ontario, The Oil Museum of Canada preserves the site of the first commercial oil well in North America. Visitors learn the story of Canadian oil pioneers, through petroleum industry artifacts, working exhibits & photographs. Visitors can also see original oil wells, which continue to produce oil.

Orillia: OPP Museum / Musée de l'OPP
777 Memorial Ave.
Orillia, ON L3V 7V3

Tel: 705-329-6889; *Fax:* 705-329-6618
opp.museum@ontario.ca
www.opp.ca/museum

Exhibits artifacts used throughout the history of the Ontario Provincial Police.
Chris Johnstone, Acting Curator, christine.johnstone@ontario.ca

Orillia: Stephen Leacock Museum
PO Box 625
Located at 50 Museum Dr., Orillia, ON
Orillia, ON L3V 6K5

Tel: 705-329-1908; *Fax:* 705-326-5578
admin@leacockmuseum.com
www.leacockmuseum.com
www.facebook.com/1040441 92964809

The home of Canadian author Stephen Leacock.
Jenny Martynyshyn, Administrative Coordinator, 705-329-1908

Oshawa: Canadian Automotive Museum
99 Simcoe St. South
Oshawa, ON L1G 4G7

Tel: 905-576-1222; *Fax:* 905-576-1223
camuseum@bellnet.ca
www.oshawa.ca/tourism/can_mus.asp

Year Founded: 1961 The Canadian Automotive Museum depicts the history & future plans of the Canadian automotive industry. More than sixty vehicles, dating from 1898 to 1981 are on display. Items related to the era of the vehicles are also displayed.

Oshawa: Ontario Regiment (RCAC) Museum
Col. R.S. McLaughlin Armoury, 53 Simcoe St. North
Location: South Field, Oshawa Municipal Airport, 1000 Stevenson Rd. North, Oshawa, ON L1J 5P5
Oshawa, ON L1G 4R9

Tel: 905-728-6199
info@ontrmuseum.ca
www.ontrmuseum.ca
www.facebook.co m/Ontario.Regiment.Museum

Operational military vehicles
David Mountenay, President, president@ontrmuseum.ca
Earl Wotten, Curator, president@ontrmuseum.ca

Oshawa: Oshawa Community Museum & Archives (OCMA)
***Parent:* Oshawa Historical Society**
Guy House, 1450 Simcoe St. South
Oshawa, ON L1H 8S8

Tel: 905-436-7624
info@oshawamuseum.org
www.oshawamuseum.org
twitter.com/oshawamuseum
www.facebook.com/OshawaM useum

Henry House c. 1849; Robinson House c. 1846; Guy House c. 1835; Drive Shed
Merle Cole, President, Oshawa Historical Society
Melissa Cole, Curator

Oshawa: Parkwood National Historic Site, The R.S. McLaughlin Estate
270 Simcoe St. North
Oshawa, ON L1G 4T5

Tel: 905-433-4311
info@parkwoodestate.com
www.parkwoodestate.com
Social Media: www.youtube.com/user/ParkwoodEstate
twitter.com/ParkwoodEstate
www.fac ebook.com/194658330590548

Year Founded: 1989 Built between 1915 & 1917, Parkwood was the grand estate of R. Samuel McLaughlin, who was the founder of General Motors of Canada. The McLaughlin family lived at the home from 1917 to 1972. Today, it is furnished to reflect the 1920s & 1930s. The National Historic Site is open year-round.
Nancy Shaw, President
Diana Kirk, Vice-President
William Smith, Comptroller

Oshawa: Slovak Canadian Heritage Museum (SCHM)
485 Ritson Rd.
Oshawa, ON L1G 5R3

info@schm.ca
www.schm.ca

Artifacts relating to Slovak culture in the context of Canadian society
Margaret Dvorsky, President, president@schm.ca

Ottawa: The Billings Estate National Historical Site / Lieu historique national du domaine Billings
2100 Cabot St.
Ottawa, ON K1H 6K1

Tel: 613-247-4830; *Fax:* 613-247-4832
museums@ottawa.ca
www.ottawa.ca/museums
www.facebook.com/billingsestat e

Home & property of Braddish & Lamira Billings, two of Ottawa's earliest settlers, c. 1828; exhibits highlight 5 generations of family & community history
Brahm Lewandowski, Museum Administrator

Ottawa: Bytown Museum / Musée Bytown
PO Box 523 B
Located at 1 Canal Lane, Ottawa, ON
Ottawa, ON K1P 5P6

Tel: 613-234-4570; *Fax:* 613-234-4846
info@bytownmuseum.ca
www.bytownmuseum.com
www.facebook.com/bytown

Bytown Museum is situated in the oldest stone building in Ottawa, which was a treasury & storehouse during the construction of the Rideau Canal. Within the museum, the history of Bytown & the nation's capital is traced. The museum is open from the beginning of April to the end of November, & during March Break. From December to March, the museum is open by appointment only.
Tom Caldwell, President
Robin Etherington, Executive Director, robinetherington@bytownmuseum.ca

Ottawa: Cameron Highlanders of Ottawa Regimental Museum
Cartier Sq. Drill Hall, 2 Queen Elizabeth Dr.
Ottawa, ON K1A 0K2

Tel: 613-990-3507
chofoassociation@sympatico.ca
www.camerons.ca

The Regimental Museum contains memorabilia of the Cameron Highlanders of Ottawa. It is open one evening each week.

Ottawa: The Canadian Museum of Scouting
1345 Baseline Rd.
Ottawa, ON K2C 0A7

Tel: 613-224-5131 *Toll-Free:* 888-855-3336
museum@scouts.ca
www.scouts.ca
twitter.com/scoutscanada
www.facebook .com/scoutscanada

Year Founded: 1907 Scouting artifacts & historical memorobilia (Canada/UK/World); Open by appointment only
Gord Kelly, Contact

Ottawa: Fairfields Heritage House
3080 Richmond Rd.
Ottawa, ON K2B 7J5

Tel: 613-726-2652
www.nepeanmuseum.ca/content/fairfields

19th century gothic revival farmhouse.
Emily Greenlaw, Contact, emily.greenlaw@ottawa.ca

Ottawa: Governor General's Foot Guards Regimental Museum
Drill Hall, Cartier Sq., 2 Queen Elizabeth Dr.
Ottawa, ON K1A 0K2

Tel: 613-233-6979
footguards.ca

Regimental museum; brief history of regiment from 1872 to present by way of artifacts
Martin J. Lane, Curator CD, martinlane@rogers.com

Ottawa: J.H. Naismith Museum & Hall of Fame
c/o Dr. James Naismith Foundation, 2729 Draper Ave.
Ottawa, ON K2H 7A1
Tel: 613-256-3610
info@naismithmuseum.com
www.naismithmuseum.com
Artifacts related to life of Dr. James Naismith, originator of game of basketball; Canadian Basketball Hall of Fame exhibits & archives

Ottawa: Laurier House National Historic Site
335 Laurier Ave. East
Ottawa, ON K1N 6R4
Tel: 613-992-8142; *Fax:* 613-947-4851
Toll-Free: 888-773-8888
laurier-house@pc.gc.ca
www.pc.gc.ca/lhn-nhs/on/laurier /index.aspx
Residence of Sir Wilfrid Laurier & the Right Honourtable William Lyon MacKenzie King, built in 1878

Ottawa: Muséoparc Vanier Museopark
300, av des Pères, 2e étage
Ottawa, ON K1L 7L5
Tel: 613-580-2424; *Fax:* 613-580-2897
info@museoparc.ca
www.museoparc.ca
Social Media: www.youtube.com/museoparcvanier
twitter.com/museoparc
www.facebook.com /MuseoparcVanier
Year Founded: 2006 Dedicated to preserving the heritage of the French-speaking community in Ottawa
Rachel Crête, Executive Director, directrice@museoparc.ca
Janik Aubin-Robert, Curator, projet@museoparc.ca

Ottawa: Pinhey's Point Historic Site
2100 Cabot St.
Location: 270 Pinhey's Point Rd., Dunrobin, ON K0A 1T0
Ottawa, ON K1H 6K1
Tel: 613-832-4347
museums@ottawa.ca
www.ottawa.ca/museums
Former home of Hamnett Kirkes Pinhey, a British settler & prominent individual in Upper Canada. Open May - September.

Ottawa: Skate Canada Hall of Fame & Museum
865 Shefford Rd.
Ottawa, ON K1J 1H9
Tel: 613-747-1007; *Fax:* 613-748-5718
Toll-Free: 888-747-2372
skatecanada@skatecanada.ca
www.skatecanada.ca
Year Founded: 1990 Photographs, videos, trophies & other materials significant to figure skating in Canada. Collection is available by appointment.

Ottawa: Workers' History Museum (WHM) / Musée de l'histoire ouvrière
PO Box 4461 E
Located at 251 Bank St., 2nd Fl., Ottawa, ON
Ottawa, ON K1S 5B4
Tel: 613-566-3448
info@workershistorymuseum.ca
workershistorymuseum.ca
Social Media: www.youtube.com/user/WorkersHistoryMuseum
twitter.com/workershistory
w ww.facebook.com/WHM.MHO
Year Founded: 2011 Labour history in the National Capital Region.
Robert Hatfield, President

Owen Sound: Billy Bishop Home & Museum
948 - 3rd Ave. West
Owen Sound, ON N4K 4P6
Tel: 519-371-0031
info@billybishop.org
www.billybishop.org
twitter.com/osmuseums
www.facebook.com/BillyBishop HomeMuseum
Year Founded: 1987 The museum, housed in the former home of Air Marshal William Avery Bishop, serves to preserve Canada's aviation history. Hours of Operation: Regular, Tu-F 11:00-5:00, Sa & Su 12:00-5:00; May-Oct., M-Sa 10:00-5:00, Su 12:00-5:00; Holidays 12:00-4:00.
Virginia Eichhorn, Director & Chief Curator, veichhorn@tomthomson.org

Owen Sound: Grey Roots Museum & Archives
102599 Grey Rd. 18, RR#4
Owen Sound, ON N4K 5N6
Tel: 519-376-3690; *Fax:* 519-376-4654
Toll-Free: 877-473-9766
info@greyroots.com
www.greyroots.com
twitter.com/gre yrootsmuseum
www.facebook.com/grey.roots
Year Founded: 1955 Collects, preserves, restores, documents, interprets & displays the material culture of Grey County & the city of Owen Sound, c. 1815 - present; research, interpretive programs, tours; gift shop
Petal Furness, Manager, 519-376-3690, petal.furness@greyroots.com

Paris: Paris Museum
51 William St. West
Paris, ON N3L 2M2
Tel: 519-442-9295
info@parishistoricalsociety.ca
www.parishistoricalsociety.ca
twitter.com/TheParisMuseum
www.facebook. com/TheParisMuseum
Local history
Mary Gladwin, President, Paris Museum & Historical Society

Parry Sound: West Parry Sound District Museum (WPSDM)
17 George St.
Parry Sound, ON P2A 2X4
Tel: 705-746-5365; *Fax:* 705-746-8775
info@museumontowerhill.com
museumontowerhill.com
www.facebook.com/TheM useumonTowerHill
Year Founded: 1983 Situated in Tower Hill Park, the West Parry Sound District Museum displays items related to the First Nations, settlement, logging, shipping, agriculture, recreation, & natural history. The museum is open year-round.
Nadine Hammond, Curator/Manager

Pelee Island: Pelee Island Heritage Centre
1073 West Shore Rd.
Pelee Island, ON N0R 1M0
Tel: 519-724-2291
peleeislandhc@gmail.com
www.peleeislandmuseum.ca
twitter.com/Pelee_Heritage
www.facebook.com/P eleeIslandHeritageCentre
Rare Flora & fauna exhibits; early navigation displays; local shipwreck information

Pembroke: 42nd Field Regiment (Lanark and Renfrew Scottish) RCA Regimental Museum
177 Victoria St.
Pembroke, ON K8A 4K2
Tel: 613-588-6166
Free admission; open year round, by appointment only.

Pembroke: Champlain Trail Museum & Pioneer Village
1032 Pembroke St. East
Pembroke, ON K8A 6Z2
Tel: 613-735-0517; *Fax:* 613-629-5067
pembrokemuseum@nrtco.net
www.champlaintrailmuseum.com
Economic, political & social history of upper Ottawa Valley & Renfrew County; archival & genealogical material

Penetanguishene: Discovery Harbour / Havre de la Découverte
93 Jury Dr.
Penetanguishene, ON L9M 1G1
Tel: 705-549-8064; *Fax:* 705-549-4858
www.discoveryharbour.on.ca
Other contact information: TTY: 705-528-7697
Ontario's leading Marine Heritage Site; orginally built as a military base with its roots tracing back to the War of 1812. Tours, interactive daily activies in the summer. Open weekdays late-May to July 1; open daily July 1 to Labour Day weekend

Penetanguishene: Penetanguishene Centennial Museum & Archives
13 Burke St.
Penetanguishene, ON L9M 1C1
Tel: 705-549-2150; *Fax:* 705-549-7542
info@pencenmuseum.com
www.pencenmuseum.com
www.facebook.com/1787791345 28
Penetanguishene's museum is housed in the former C. Beck Lumber Office & General Store which was built in 1875. The location also features a Genealogy & History Research Center & Archives, which houses the the Georgian Bay Heritage League Collection with more than 500 genealogical files & local history books. Penetanguishene Centennial Museum & Archives is open year-round.
Nicole Jackson, Curator, njackson@pencenmuseum.com
Janice Gadsdon, Curatorial Assistant, jgadsdon@pencenmuseum.com

Perth: The Perth Museum
11 Gore St. East
Perth, ON K7H 1H9
Tel: 613-267-1947
www.perth.ca/content/perth-museummatheson-house
Year Founded: 1967 1840 stone home of Senator Matheson; open year round; National Historic Site; 2 galleries; historic gardens
Karen Rennie, Contact

Petawawa: Canadian Airborne Forces Museum / Musée des Forces aéroportées canadiennes
Canadian Forces Base Petawawa, PO Box 9999 Main, 63 Colborne Rd.
Petawawa, ON K8H 2X3
Tel: 613-588-6238
basemuseumcalendar@forces.gc.ca
petawawamuseums.org/website/airborne/introduction.htm
The Canadian Airborne Forces Museum preserves & honours the memory of airborne forces that served Canada since World War II. Their history is presented through historical artifacts, dioramas, videos, & a large screen mini-theatre. The museum is a member of the following organizations: the Organization of Military Museums of Canada, the Canadian Museums Association, the Ontario Museums Association, the Ottawa Valley Tourist Association, & the Renfrew County Museums Network. The Canadian Airborne Forces Museum is open year-round.

Petawawa: Canadian Forces Base Petawawa Military Museum
Canadian Forces Base Petawawa, PO Box 9999 Main, 63 Colborne Rd.
Petawawa, ON K8H 2X3
Tel: 613-588-6238
info@petawawamuseums.com
www.petawawamuseums.com
The Canadian Forces Base Petawawa Military Museum collects, preserves, & interprets items related to the history of individuals & units of CFB Petawawa since 1905. Museum staff also assist with research requests. Hours: Open Daily, 11:00-4:00.

Petawawa: Petawawa Heritage Village
Parent: Petawawa Heritage Society
176 Civic Centre Rd.
Petawawa, ON K8H 3B5
Tel: 613-687-5054
www.petawawaheritagevillage.com
twitter.com/kitchisibi
www.facebook.com/PHV1999
Year Founded: 2005 Local history
Ann McIntyre, President, Petawawa Historical Society, annmcintyre21@gmail.com

Peterborough: The Canadian Canoe Museum
910 Monaghan Rd.
Peterborough, ON K9J 5K4
Tel: 705-748-9153; *Fax:* 705-748-0616
Toll-Free: 866-342-2663
info@canoemuseum.ca
www.canoemuseum.ca
Social Media: canoemuseum.wordpress.com
twitter.com/CndnCanoeMuseum
www.facebook.com/CndnCanoeMuseum
Year Founded: 1997 Collection of over 600 canoes & kayaks, plus related artifacts; open year round
Richard Tucker, Executive Director

Peterborough: Hope Water-Powered Saw Mill
c/o Otonabee Region Conservation Authority, 250 Milroy Dr.
3414 Hope Mill Rd., Keene, ON, K0L 2G0
Peterborough, ON K9H 7M9
Tel: 705-745-5791
hopemill.ca
twitter.com/thehopemill
www.facebook.com /hopemill.ca
Year Founded: 1966 Built in 1835 by Scottish immigrant Squire William Lang, the Otonabee Conservation Authority purchased the mill from his great grandson in 1966. The saw-powered Hope Mill has been restored to its original charm and is fully functional. Demonstrations and tours are offered. A collection of 19th-century carpentry tools, as well as larger pieces of equipment (lathe, planer, drill-press), are on exhibit. The mill is

located at 3414 Hope Mill Rd. on the banks of the Indian River in Lang, ON.
Robert Rehder, Restoration Team Leader,
rrehder@sympatico.ca
Kathryn Campbell, Contact, kcampbell@trentu.ca

***Peterborough:* Hutchison House Museum**
***Parent:* Peterborough Historical Society**
270 Brock St.
Peterborough, ON K9H 2P9
Tel: 705-743-9710
info@hutchisonhouse.ca
www.hutchisonhouse.ca
www.facebook.com/120961071272046
Year Founded: 1978 Living history museum owned & operated by the Peterborough Historical Society open to all interested in the history of Upper Canada in the 1800s

***Peterborough:* Lang Grist Mill**
470 Water St.
Peterborough, ON K9H 3M3
Tel: 705-745-5791; *Fax:* 705-295-6644
Fully operational water-powered grist mill located on the west bank of the Indian River at Lang Pioneer Village (Otonabee-South Monaghan Township-County of Peterborough).

***Peterborough:* Lang Pioneer Village**
c/o County of Peterborough, Attn: Lang Pioneer Village Museum, 470 Water St.
Location: 104 Lang Rd., Keene, ON K0L 2G0
Peterborough, ON K9H 3M3
Tel: 705-295-6694; *Fax:* 705-295-6644
Toll-Free: 866-289-5264
info@langpioneervillage.ca
langpioneervillage.ca
Social Media: ca.linkedin.com/pub/lang-pioneer-village-museum/56/aa/547
twitter.com/La ngPioneer
www.facebook.com/langpioneervillage
Year Founded: 1967 Living history museum from 1800-1900; over 20 restored buildings with costumed interpreters; open Mon.-Fri. May 15-June 30, Sat.-Fri. July 1 to Labour Day; call or see website for hours of operation, admission prices & list of special events

***Peterborough:* Peterborough Museum & Archives**
Ashburnham Memorial Park, PO Box 143, 300 Hunter St. East
Peterborough, ON K9J 6Y5
Tel: 705-743-5180; *Fax:* 705-743-2614
www.peterboroughmuseumandarchives.ca
Social Media: www.youtube.com/channel/UCSARKb_GQSRs5DEI5pSCvgg
twitter.com/OntheHill3
www.facebook.com/112608310308
The heritage & culture of Peterborough & the surrounding area is preserved & presented at Peterborough Museum & Archives. The Museum houses a variety of artifacts, such as archaeological collections, technological artifacts, & military collections. The Archives holds over 2,000 fonds, including personal letters, maps, photographs, association records, early Peterborough Examiner newspapers, & the early records of Peterborough County Court. The Museum & Archives is open year-round. Appointments are required to visit the Archives.
Kim Reid, Curator

***Peterborough:* Trent-Severn Waterway National Historic Site of Canada, Lock 21 - Peterborough Lift Lock**
PO Box 567
Peterborough, ON K9J 6Z6
Tel: 705-750-4900; *Fax:* 705-742-9644
Toll-Free: 888-773-8888
Ont.Trentsevern@pc.gc.ca
www.pc.gc.ca/eng/lhn-nhs/on/t rentsevern/visit/visit6/lock21.aspx
twitter.com/TrentSevernNHS
www.fac ebook.com/TrentSevernNHS
Other contact information: Teletypewriter (TTY): 705-750-4949
Opened in 1904, the Peterborough Lift Lock is the highest hydraulic lift lock in the world. Located next to Lock 21 is the Peterborough Lift Lock Visitor Centre, which contains exhibits & films. The Peterborough Lift Lock Visitor Centre is open during the navigation season.

***Petrolia:* Petrolia Discovery**
PO Box 1480, 4381 Discovery Line
Petrolia, ON N0N 1R0
Tel: 519-381-5979
petdisc@xcelco.on.ca
petroliadiscovery.com
www.facebook.com/189976557685990
Petrolia Discovery depicts the history of the pioneer oil men of Lambton County, Ontario. The museum is located at an oilfield which was established in the 1870s. This 19th century oilfield has been restored & is still operational. Petrolia Discovery is open from Victoria Day until Labour Day. School & educational tours may be arranged after the summer season.

***Pickering:* Pickering Museum Village**
c/o City of Pickering, 1 The Esplanade
Located at 2365 Concession Rd. 6, Greenwood, ON, L0H 1H0
Pickering, ON L1V 6K7
Tel: 905-683-8401; *Fax:* 905-686-4079
Toll-Free: 866-683-2760
www.pickering.ca/en/museum.asp
Social Media: www.youtube.com/user/PickeringMuse
twitter.com/pickeringmuse
www.faceb ook.com/pickeringmuse
Other contact information: TTY: 905-420-1739
Year Founded: 1961 The Pickering Museum Village features fifteen restored heritage buildings, including a schoolhouse, churches, a blacksmith shop, houses, & barns.

***Picton:* Macaulay Heritage Park**
35 Church St.
Picton, ON K0K 2T0
Tel: 613-476-3833; *Fax:* 613-476-8356
pecounty.on.ca/government/community_development/museums/macaulay.php
www .facebook.com/museumspec
Year Founded: 1973 The site encompasses the 1830 Macaulay House, home of the Rev. William Macaulay, carriage house, heritage gardens & former St. Mary Magdalene Church and cemetary; open Tues.-Sun. 1-4:30 from long weekend in May to Thanksgiving; 10-4:30 (July & Aug.)
Jennifer Lyons, Head Curator, Museums of Prince Edward County, 613-476-2148

***Picton:* Rose House Museum**
3333 County Rd. 8
Picton, ON K0K 2T0
Tel: 613-476-5439
museums@pecounty.on.ca
pecounty.on.ca/government/community_development/museums/rose_house.php
w ww.facebook.com/museumspec
1804 original homestead; home to five generations of the Rose family; living history depicting life in 1800s; guided tours
Jennifer Lyons, Head Curator, Museums of Prince Edward County, 613-476-3833, Fax: 613-476-8356
Diane Denyes-Wenn, Site Curator

***Port Burwell:* Port Burwell Marine Museum & Historic Lighthouse**
20 Pitt St.
Lighthouse located at 17 Robinson St., Port Burwell, ON
Port Burwell, ON N0J 1T0
Tel: 519-874-4807
Local history

***Port Carling:* Muskoka Lakes Museum**
PO Box 432
Located at 100 Joseph St., Port Carling, ON
Port Carling, ON P0B 1J0
Tel: 705-765-5367
info@mlmuseum.com
www.mlmuseum.com
twitter.com/mlmus eum
www.facebook.com/MuskokaLakesMuseum
Year Founded: 1964 Log home from 1875; artifacts of early settlers & lumber industry; displays related to boat building & water transportation; archives of Muskoka region; open Victoria Day - Thanksgiving

***Port Colborne:* Port Colborne Historical & Marine Museum & Heritage Village**
PO Box 572, 280 King St.
Port Colborne, ON L3K 5X8
Tel: 905-834-7604; *Fax:* 905-834-6198
museum@portcolborne.ca
portcolborne.ca/page/museum
The Port Colborne Historical & Marine Museum depicts the history of Port Colborne & the Welland Canala. The museum features heritage buildings, such as an 1869 home & carriage house, a log schoolhouse, & an 1850 marine blacksmith shop. A reproduction of the parapet of Port Colborne's Lighthouse contains ship models & marine artifacts. The museum, heritage village, & gift shop are open from May to December.
Stephanie Powell Baswick, Director & Curator
Michelle Mason, Assistant Curator, michellemason@portcolborne.ca
Michelle Vosburgh, Technician, Heritage Research, archives@portcolborne.ca

***Port Dover:* Port Dover Harbour Museum**
PO Box 1298, 44 Harbour St.
Port Dover, ON N0A 1N0
Tel: 519-583-2660
portdover.museum@norfolkcounty.ca
www.portdovermuseum.ca
www.facebook.com/340416399319352
The Port Dover Harbour Museum tells the story of Port Dover's fishing industry, ship building, Lake Erie shipwrecks, rum running, & other parts of lakeside life. The museum is open year round.
Angela Wallace, Curator/Director

***Port Hope:* Canadian Fire Fighters Museum**
PO Box 325
Located at 95 Mill St. South, Port Hope, ON
Port Hope, ON L1A 3W3
Tel: 905-885-8985; *Fax:* 905-885-8985
info@firemuseumcanada.com
www.firemuseumcanada.com
www.facebook.com/Fi reMuseumCanada
Year Founded: 1985 The museum's collection represents the history of firefighting in Canada, including vehicles, gear, fire alarms, & photos. Open daily, except Wednesdays, May-Oct., 10:00-4:00.
Ken Burgin, Chair, burgin@firemuseumcanada.com

***Port Hope:* Dorothy's House Museum**
***Parent:* Port Hope & District Historical Society**
PO Box 116, 3632 Ganaraska Rd.
Port Hope, ON L1A 3V9
Tel: 905-885-2981
info@porthopehistorical.ca
www.porthopehistorical.ca
Other contact information: Alt. Phone: 905-885-2634
Artifacts from the Port Hope & Hope Township area; house built around 1869; barn; driveshed; open May - Aug.
Joan Parrott, President

***Port Perry:* Scugog Shores Heritage Centre & Archives**
1655 Reach St.
Port Perry, ON L9L 1P2
Tel: 905-985-8698; *Fax:* 905-985-2697
www.scugogshoresmuseum.com
twitter.com/ScugogMuseum
www.facebook.com/3 00750283308118
Formerly housed in the Scugog Shores Museum Village, the Scugog Heritage Centre & Archives is now located in the Scugog Arena & is accessible to the public. Galleries showcase local history & First Nations history, as well as rotating art shows & travelling exhibits.
Craig Belfry, Manager, Recreation & Culture, Township of Scugog

***Port Perry:* Scugog Shores Museum Village**
16210 Island Rd.
Port Perry, ON L9L 1B4
Tel: 905-985-8698; *Fax:* 905-985-2697
www.scugogshoresmuseum.com
twitter.com/ScugogMuseum
www.facebook.com/3 00750283308118
Historic village, comprising a log cabin, Lee House, blacksmith & woodright shops, print shop, school, church, barns, heritage flower, herb & dye plant gardens, & Ojibway Heritage Interpretive Lands; special events & programming, themed artifact kits for rent, tours, building rentals
Shannon Kelly, Curator, Township of Scucog

***Prescott:* Fort Wellington National Historic Site of Canada**
PO Box 479, 370 Vankoughnet St.
Prescott, ON K0E 1T0
Tel: 613-925-2896; *Fax:* 613-925-1536
ont-wellington@pc.gc.ca
www.pc.gc.ca/lhn-nhs/on/wellington/index.aspx
Other contact information: TTY: 613-925-2896
Built during the War of 1812, Fort Wellington defended the St. Lawrence River shipping route between Kingston & Montréal. It was rebuilt in 1838 to once again defend against possible attack by the United States. Today, the Visitor Centre at the site displays exhibits related to the War of 1812 & the Upper Canada Rebellion. The site is open from Victoria Day weekend to the end of September. During the off-season, groups of ten or more may make an appointment.

Prescott: The Forwarders' Museum
201 Water St.
Prescott, ON K0E 1T0
Tel: 613-925-1861
www.prescott.ca
Forwarding trade; St Lawrence River & local history; open June-Labour Day

Prescott: Stockade Barracks & Hospital Museum
PO Box 446
Located at 356 East St., Prescott, ON
Prescott, ON K0E 1T0
Tel: 613-925-4894
The oldest military building in Ontario.

Queenston: Brock's Monument National Historic Site
Parent: Friends of Fort George
14184 Niagara Pkwy.
Queenston, ON L0S 1P0
Tel: 905-262-4759
www.friendsoffortgeorge.ca
twitter.com/fofg
www.facebook.com/102031676507960
A 185-foot-high monument to Major-General Sir Isaac Brock, situated on the Queenston Heights battlefield.

Queenston: Mackenzie Printery & Newspaper Museum
Parent: Niagara Parks Commission
1 Queenston St.
Queenston, ON L0S 1L0
printer@mackenzieprintery.org
www.mackenzieprintery.org
Year Founded: 1991 Printing history & its influence on society.

Red Lake: Red Lake Regional Heritage Centre
PO Box 64, 51A Hwy. 105
Red Lake, ON P0V 2M0
Tel: 807-727-3006
heritage@redlake.ca
www.redlakemuseum.com
www.facebook.com/154411087917525
At the Red Lake Regional Heritage Centre, visitors will discover Aboriginal, fur trade, gold mining, & immigration history. The centre also provides information about Woodland Caribou Park. The Red Lake Regional Heritage Centre is open year-round.
Michele Alderton, Director/Curator

Renfrew: McDougall Mill Museum
Parent: The Renfrew & District Historical & Museum Society
PO Box 554
Located at 65 Arthur Ave., Renfrew, ON, K7V 3S1
Renfrew, ON K7V 4B1
www.renfrewmuseum.ca
Year Founded: 1969 Housed in a stone, 1855 grist mill built on the Bonnechere River by Hudson's Bay Company agent, John Lorne McDougall, the museum displays 3 floors of artifacts, including early appliances from Renfrew's industrial days. There are also exhibits of military articles, Victorian clothing & a wedding dress gallery.

Renfrew: The NHA/NHL Birthplace Museum
249 Raglan St. South
Renfrew, ON K7V 1R3
Tel: 343-361-0550
nhabirthplacemuseum@cogeco.net
www.nhlbirthplace.ca/Museum.html
www.facebook.com/375277432568370
Year Founded: 2002 The museum details the history of the National Hockey Association & the National Hockey League, starting with the influence of hockey enthusiast & founder of the Town of Renfrew, M.J. O'Brien.
Raymond Dunbar, Contact

Richards Landing: Fort St. Joseph National Historic Site of Canada
PO Box 220
Richards Landing, ON P0R 1J0
Tel: 705-246-2664; *Fax:* 705-246-1796
fortstjoseph-info@pc.gc.ca
www.pc.gc.ca/lhn-nhs/on/stjoseph/index_e.asp
Ruins of a fort erected after 1796 to serve as a fur trade centre; artifacts from excavation of site

Richards Landing: St. Joseph Island Museum Complex
RR#2
Richards Landing, ON P0R 1J0
Tel: 705-246-2672
info@stjoemuseum.com
stjoemuseum.com
Year Founded: 1963 Six artifact buildings represent the pioneer era (1820-1880) & the settlement era after the Homestead Act of 1868; over 6,000 artifacts; farming, lumbering, maple syruping & early navigation displays; 2 schools, a church, a store, a barn, an 1880 log cabin & a general store
Carrie Kennedy-Uusitalo, Curator

Richmond Hill: Canadian Museum of Hindu Civilization (CMOHC)
8640 Yonge St.
Richmond Hill, ON L4C 6Z4
Tel: 905-764-5516
curator@cmohc.com
www.cmohc.com
www.facebook.com/134385929921864
The museum is the first of its kind in North America, celebrating Hinduism's contributions to philosophy, the arts, & science.
Shylee Someshwar, Chair
Dr. Budhendra Doobay, President
Avinash Persaud, Director

Richmond Hill: Richmond Hill Heritage Centre
19 Church St. North
Richmond Hill, ON L4C 3E6
Tel: 905-780-3802
maggie.mackenzie@richmondhill.ca
www.richmondhill.ca
Social Media: www.youtube.com/user/TownRichmondHill
twitter.com/myrichmondhill
www.f acebook.com/myrichmondhill
The Centre offers historic galleries & exhibits, as well as an archive of material related to the history of Richmond Hill. Visitors can also take the Museum of the Streets self-guided tour of the Richmond Hill area.

Ridgetown: Ridge House Museum
PO Box 550, 53 Erie St. South
Ridgetown, ON N0P 2C0
Tel: 519-674-2223*Toll-Free:* 800-714-7497
ckridgehouse@chatham-kent.ca
www.chatham-kent.ca/RidgeHouseMuseum
Year Founded: 1975 The Ridge Hose Museum depicts the life of a middle class family in Ridgetown around 1875. Interactive tours & interpretive programs are provided.Open daily from Mar - Dec.
Lydia Burggraaf, Curator, 519-647-2223, lydiab@chatham-kent.ca

Ridgeway: Fort Erie Historical Museum
Parent: Fort Erie Museum Services
402 Ridge Rd.
Ridgeway, ON L0S 1N0
Tel: 905-894-5322
www.town.forterie.ca/pages/FortErieHistoricalMuseum
Exhibits on archaelogy, genealogy, Fenian Raids, local history & archives; open year-round Sun.-Fri.; daily in July & Aug.
Jane Davies, Curator

Ridgeway: Ridgeway Battlefield National Historic Site
Parent: Fort Erie Museum Services
3388 Garrison Rd.
Ridgeway, ON L0S 1N0
Tel: 905-871-1600
www.museum.forterie.ca/battlefield.html
The Ridgeway Battlefield national historic site marks the location where in 1866 Irish-American soldiers, known as Fenians, fought Canadian forces in an attempt to gain Ireland's independence of England. Fort Erie Museum Services maintains the original cabin at the battle site, where visitors can see a visual account of the Battle of Ridgeway.
Jane Davies, Museum Administrator BA, Fort Erie Museum Services

Rockton: Westfield Heritage Village (WHV)
1049 Kirkwall Rd.
Rockton, ON L0R 1X0
Tel: 519-621-8851
westfield@speedway.ca
westfieldheritage.ca
The Heritage Village presents more than thirty-five historical & reproduction buildings. The site also features Ontario's oldest log cabin & a T.H. & B. steam locomotive.
Rondalyn Brown, Manager, Rondalyn.Brown@conservationhamilton.ca

Russell: Keith M. Boyd Museum
PO Box 307
Located at 1150 Concession St., Russell, ON
Russell, ON K4R 1E1
Tel: 613-445-3849
info@russellmuseum.ca
www.russellmuseum.ca
Year Founded: 1989 Local history.
Dorothy Kinkaid, Curator

St Catharines: Lincoln & Welland Regiment Museum (LWRM)
c/o 81 Lake St.
St Catharines, ON L2R 5X3
Tel: 905-468-0888
lwrm@lwmuseum.ca
www.lwmuseum.ca
Social Media:
www.youtube.com/channel/UCgc0DqUQAP71KeyAw1uf-Pw
twitter.com/lwmuseum
www.facebook.com/217453061745660
Year Founded: 2001 Exhibits the origins & heritage of the Lincoln & Welland Regiment.

St Catharines: Morningstar Mill
2714 Decew Rd.
St Catharines, ON L2R 6P7
Tel: 905-688-6050
info@morningstarmill.ca
www.morningstarmill.ca
www.facebook.com/morningstar.mill
Year Founded: 1962 Museum site is made up of a number of buildings: the water-powered gristmill (built in 1872 & known as Morningstar Mill), the turbine shed, the millers house, the icehouse, sawmill & the barn which houses the blacksmith shop & carpentry shop. School tours are welcome. Admission by donation.

St Catharines: St. Catharines Museum
PO Box 3012, 1932 Welland Canals Pkwy.
St. Catharines, ON L2R 7C2
Tel: 905-984-8880; *Fax:* 905-984-6910
Toll-Free: 800-305-5134
museum@stcatharines.ca
www.stcatharines.ca/en/St-Catha rines-Museum.asp
twitter.com/StCMuseum
www.facebook.com/StCatharinesMu seum
Other contact information: TTY: 905-688-4889
Year Founded: 1965 Major collection of artifact, archival & art material related to the history of St. Catharines & the Welland Canal; collections include Girl Guides, Fred Pattison Aviation Collection (BCATP), St. Lawrence Seaway, family papers, marine photographs, Ferranti-Packard & the DeCew Falls Waterworks Collection; guided tours; summer camps, edu-fun camps; guest speakers; tours & special events
Kathleen Powell, Curator & Supervisor, Historical Services, 905-984-8880, kpowell@stcatharines.ca

St George: Adelaide Hunter Hoodless Homestead
359 Blue Lake Rd.
St George, ON N0E 1N0
Tel: 519-448-1130
curator@adelaidehoodless.ca
www.adelaidehoodless.ca
twitter.com/AddieHoodless
www.facebook.com/130 185503729776
Year Founded: 1959 Birthplace of Adelaide Hunter Hoodless, an educational reformer, one of Canada's early feminists and a co-founder of a number of organizations promoting the cause of women's well-being, including: the Women's Institute, the Victorian Order of Nurses, the YWCA, & the National Council of Women. Hunter Hoodless was instrumental in establishing domestic science on the curriculum of Ontario schools, & wrote the first textbook to be used. Before her untimely death at the age of 53, she was engaged in the cause of promoting technical trades education for women. Her childhood home, built in 1830, is an example of mid-nineteenth century Ontario Neo Gothic style. The homestead property includes picnic facilities & grounds that can be rented for gatherings & other special occasions. Guided tours, & school programs available. Open year round.

***St George:* St George Museum & Archives**
***Parent:* South Dumfries Historical Society**
c/o South Dumfries Historical Society, PO Box 472
Located at 36 Main St. South, St George, ON
St. George, ON N0E 1N0
Tel: 519-448-3265
info@southdumfrieshistory.ca
southdumfrieshistory.ca
Local history

***St Jacobs:* The Maple Syrup Museum**
Country Mill, 1441 King St. North, 3rd Fl.
St Jacobs, ON N0B 2N0
Tel: 519-664-1232
www.stjacobs.com
History of maple syrup production; artifacts; photographs

***St Marys:* Canadian Baseball Hall of Fame & Museum**
PO Box 1838, 140 Queen St.
Location: 386 Church St. East, St Marys, ON
St Marys, ON N4X 1C2
Tel: 519-284-1838; *Fax:* 519-284-1234
Toll-Free: 877-250-2255
baseball@baseballhalloffame.ca
baseballhalloffame.ca
Social Media: www.youtube.com/user/CanadianHallofFame
twitter.com/CDNBaseballHOF
www.facebook.com/135326447763
Year Founded: 1983 Open May - Thanksgiving; displays include exclusive collection of Ferguson Jenkins memorabilia & artifacts of the Montréal Expos & Toronto Blue Jays
Scott Crawford, Director, Operations, scott@baseballhalloffame.ca

***St Marys:* St Marys Museum**
PO Box 998, 177 Church St. South
St Marys, ON N4X 1B6
Tel: 519-284-3556
museum@town.stmarys.on.ca
www.stmarysmuseum.ca
www.facebook.com/stmarysmuseum
Changing exhibits; seasonal activities; research facilities for genealogy & area history in 1850s limestone house
Amy Cubberley, Curator & Archives Assistant
Trisha McKibbin, Manager, Museum & Archives

***St Thomas:* Elgin County Museum**
450 Sunset Dr.
St Thomas, ON N5R 5V1
Tel: 519-631-1460; *Fax:* 519-631-9209
www.elgincounty.ca/museum
twitter.com/ecpmcounty
www.facebook.com/page s/Elgin-County-Museum/750866584990608
Year Founded: 1957 History of Elgin County; changing exhibits in gallery, workshops & special events
Mike Baker, Curator, 519-631-1460
Georgia Sifton, Assistant, 519-631-1460

***St Thomas:* Elgin County Railway Museum**
225 Wellington St.
St Thomas, ON N5R 2S6
Tel: 519-637-6284
thedispatcher@ecrm5700.org
ecrm5700.org
Year Founded: 1988 The museum seeks to preserve the heritage of the St. Thomas & Elgin County railroad, & to educate the public on the railroad's contributions to the community. Open May-Sept., Tu-Su 10:00-4:00.
Jeremy Locke, President
Dawn Miskelly, Manager

***St Thomas:* The Elgin Military Museum**
30 Talbot St.
St Thomas, ON N5P 1A3
Tel: 519-633-7641
curator@elginmilitarymuseum.ca
elginmilitarymuseum.ca
www.facebook.com/ElginMMuseum
Year Founded: 1982 Information on veterans from Elgin County; archive collection with military documents & publications

***Sarnia:* Discovery House Museum**
PO Box 134
Located at 475 Christina St., Sarnia, ON
Sarnia, ON N7T 7H8
Tel: 519-332-1556; *Fax:* 519-383-8042
centre@ebtech.net
www.sarnia.com/groups/discovery/welcome.htm
Other contact information: Alt Phone: 519-383-8472
Local railroad & marine heritage.

***Sarnia:* Stones 'N Bones Museum**
233 North Christina St.
Sarnia, ON N7T 5V1
Tel: 519-336-2100
stonesnbones@cogeco.net
www.stonesnbones.ca
www.facebook.com/StonesnBonesMuseum
The collection includes fossils, mounted wildlife, minerals, stones & RCMP memorabilia.

***Sault Ste Marie:* Canadian Bushplane Heritage Centre (CBHC)**
50 Pim St.
Sault Ste Marie, ON P6A 3G4
Tel: 705-945-6242; *Fax:* 705-942-8947
Toll-Free: 877-287-4752
retail@bushplane.com
www.bushplane.com
Social Media:
pinterest.com/strokeguy/canadian-bushplane-heritage-centre
twitter.com/BushplaneCentre
www.facebook.com/canadian.centre
Year Founded: 1987 The centre celebrates the heritage of bushplanes & forest fire protection in Canada through hands-on displays, including flight simulators. Open May-Oct., daily 9:00-6:00; daily 10:00-4:00 during the rest of the year.
Ron Common, President
Mike Delfre, Executive Director, mdelfre@bushplane.com
Todd Fleet, Curator, display@bushplane.com

***Sault Ste Marie:* Ermatinger-Clergue National Historic Site**
c/o Historic Sites Board, PO Box 580, 99 Foster Dr.
Location: 831 Queen St. East, Sault Ste Marie, ON
Sault Ste Marie, ON P6A 5N1
Tel: 705-759-5443; *Fax:* 705-541-7023
old.stone.house@cityssm.on.ca
www.ermatingerclerguenationalhistoricsite. ca
1814 stone house: features historic crop gardens, recreated rooms, costumed interpreters, hands-on activities; Blockhouse: exhibits & period furnishings; open Mid-Apr. - Nov.
Kathryn Fisher, Curator

***Sault Ste Marie:* St. Mary's River Marine Heritage Centre**
PO Box 23099 Mall
Sault Ste Marie, ON P6A 6W6
Tel: 705-256-7447
www.norgoma.org
Year Founded: 1981 An 188-foot passenger/cargo vessel built in 1950; open June - Oct.

***Sault Ste Marie:* Sault Ste Marie Canal National Historic Site**
1 Canal Dr.
Sault Ste Marie, ON P6A 6W4
Tel: 705-941-6262; *Fax:* 705-941-6206
info-saultcanal@pc.gc.ca
www.parkscanada.gc.ca/sault
Operates a recreational lock between May & Oct. & offers school programming, guided tours & a large open space for the enjoyment of visitors (boat watching, nature trail, birdwatching, cycling, fishing)

***Sault Ste Marie:* Sault Ste Marie Museum**
690 Queen St. East
Sault Ste Marie, ON P6A 2A4
Tel: 705-759-7278; *Fax:* 705-759-3058
saultmuseum@gmail.com
www.saultmuseum.com
Social Media: www.youtube.com/user/saultmuseum
www.facebook.com/143320129039949
Maintained by the Sault St. Marie & 49th Field Regiment R.C.A. Historical Society; the museum collects & preserves artifacts & archival material illustrating the history of Sault Ste Marie & area

***Selkirk:* Cottonwood Mansion Museum**
***Parent:* Cottonwood Mansion Preservation Foundation**
PO Box 56
Located at 740 Regional Road #53, Lot 1, Concession 4, Rainham Township, Haldimand County
Selkirk, ON N0A 1P0
Tel: 905-776-2538
cottonwoodmansion@gmail.com
www.cottonwoodmansion.ca
www.facebook.com/cottonwood.mansion
A restored Italianate-style mansion, circa 1870. Open May-Sept., Th & Sa 11:00-3:00.

***Selkirk:* Wilson MacDonald Memorial School Museum**
3513 Rainham Rd.
Selkirk, ON N0A 1P0
Tel: 905-776-3319; *Fax:* 905-776-0683
wmacdonald.museum@haldimandcounty.on.ca
www.haldimandcounty.on.ca
Wilson MacDonald Memorial School Museum presents the story of poet Wilson Pugsley MacDonald, rural education, & Selkirk, Ontario & its surrounding area. Archival research is available for a fee. The museum is open from mid March to mid December.
Dana B. Stavinga, Curator

***Shakespeare:* Fryfogel Tavern**
***Parent:* Perth County Historical Foundation**
Perth County Historical Foundation, 1931 Perth Line 34
Shakespeare, ON N0B 2P0
Tel: 519-271-1178
perthhistorical@yahoo.ca
www.stratfordperthheritage.ca/tavern.html
www.facebook.com/1486958485552 54
Year Founded: 1990 Stagecoach stop & resting place 1844-45; history of Perth County's settlers; open by appt.
Eric Adams, Chair, 519-273-1955
David Hastie, Vice-Chair, 519-275-2866

***Sharon:* Sharon Temple National Historic Site & Museum**
18974 Leslie St.
Sharon, ON L0G 1V0
Tel: 905-478-2389
info@sharontemple.ca
www.sharontemple.ca
The Sharon Temple National Historic Site features nine historic buildings. The centerpiece of the site is the Temple of the Children of Peace, which was completed in 1832. Sharon Temple is open from mid May to mid October. Group & scholars may make appointments at other times of the year.

***Simcoe:* Eva Brook Donly Museum & Archives**
***Parent:* Norfolk Historical Society**
109 Norfolk St. South
Simcoe, ON N3Y 2W3
Tel: 519-426-1583; *Fax:* 519-426-1584
office@norfolklore.com
www.norfolklore.com
twitter.com/museumnorfolk
www.facebook.com/evabrookdonly
Other contact information: Archive/Genealogy E-mail: genealogy@norfolklore.com
Year Founded: 1942 The Museum & Archives feature information about the people, heritage, & history of Norfolk County. Museum artifacts are housed in a two storey brick home which was erected in the 1840s. Archives include family histories, documents, records, & phototgraphs.
Keitha Davis, President, Norfolk Historical Society
Helen Bartens, Curator & Manager, curator@norfolklore.com

***Sioux Lookout:* Sioux Lookout Community Museum**
PO Box 158
Located at 25 - 5 Ave., Sioux Lookout, ON
Sioux Lookout, ON P8T 1A4
Tel: 807-737-2700
museum@siouxlookout.ca
www.siouxlookoutmuseum.ca
Year Founded: 1981 First Nations artifacts; pioneer artifacts related to logging, mining, aviation & the Canadian National Railway
Stu Finn, Coordinator, 807-737-2700

***Smiths Falls:* Heritage House Museum / Musée de la maison du patrimoine**
PO Box 695, 11 Old Slys Rd.
Smiths Falls, ON K7A 4T6
Tel: 613-283-6311
heritagehouse@smithsfalls.ca
www.smithsfalls.ca/heritagehouse
Year Founded: 1981 Built in 1860-1861 by Joshua Bates, the house is located near the Rideau River & displays 7 rooms, including kitchen, parlor & bedroom, all restored to Victorian style. Workshops & programs for children are offered. There is a gift shop. Tours available; open year round.
Carol Miller, Curator, cmiller@smithsfalls.ca

***Smiths Falls:* Industrial Heritage Complex Merrickville Lockstation**
34A Beckwith St. South
Smiths Falls, ON K7A 2A8
Tel: 613-283-5170

19th century construction on Rideau Canal, with emphasis on Merrickville; collection includes power generation machinery; located on County Rd. #2 in Merrickville, ON.

***Smiths Falls:* Rideau Canal National Historic Site of Canada**
34 Beckwith St. South
Smiths Falls, ON K7A 2B3
Tel: 613-283-5170; *Fax:* 613-283-0677
Toll-Free: 888-773-8888
RideauCanal-info@pc.gc.ca
www.pc.gc.ca/lhn-nhs/on/ride au/index.aspx
twitter.com/RideauCanalNHS
www.facebook.com/RideauCanalN HS
Other contact information: TTY: 1-866-787-6221
The historic Rideau Canal is operated by Parks Canada in an effort to preserve the canal's historic features as well as to provide a navigable waterway for boaters.

***Smiths Falls:* Smiths Falls Railway Museum of Eastern Ontario**
PO Box 962
Located at 90 William St. West, Smith Falls, ON
Smiths Falls, ON K7A 5A5
Tel: 613-283-5696
info@rmeo.org
rmeo.org
www.facebook.com/rmeo.smithsfalls
Railway Museum at the historic CNR station

***Sombra:* Sombra Museum Cultural Centre**
3470 St. Clair Parkway
Sombra, ON N0P 2H0
Tel: 519-892-3982
sombramuseum@hotmail.com
sombramuseum.webs.com
twitter.com/SombraMuseum
www.facebook.com/Sombra Museum
Year Founded: 1959 Local historical artifacts housed in 1881 Victorian frame home; stories of the St. Clair River illustrated through photos & artifacts in 3 rooms; log cabin circa 1830; reference collection & family archives; marine room featuring nautical equipment & photos relating to the St. Clair River & the Great Lakes; special events & programming.
Shelley Lucier, Curator, shelley.lucier@county-lambton.on.ca

***South Baymouth:* Little Schoolhouse & Museum South Baymouth**
113 Church St.
South Baymouth, ON P0P 1Z0
Tel: 705-859-3663; *Fax:* 705-859-3663
sbmuseum@volnetmmp.net
www.manitoulin-island.com/museums/little_schoolho use.htm
Displays the history of this fishing village through artifacts & pictures.

***Southampton:* Bruce County Museum & Cultural Centre**
33 Victoria St. North
Southampton, ON N0H 2L0
Tel: 519-797-2080*Toll-Free:* 866-318-8889
museum@brucecounty.on.ca
www.brucemuseum.ca
twitter.com/brucemuseum
www.facebook.com/124282581140
Year Founded: 1955 Permanent galleries at the Bruce County Museum & Cultural Centre include the following: Creation Stories; Our Tropical Past; Geology & The Ice Ages; First People's Gallery; A Time To Remember, featuring military exhibits; Telephone Beginnings, depicting the history of telephone service in Bruce County; Living On The Land, showcasing the area's agricultural history; The Land; Living On The Water, with information about lighthouses, shipbuilding, fishing, & shipwrecks; & Living in Balance, with information about resources & industries.

***Stirling:* Hastings County Museum of Agricultural Heritage**
PO Box 174, 437 West Front St.
Stirling, ON K0K 3E0
Tel: 613-395-0015
info@agmuseum.ca
farmtownpark.ca
www.facebook.com/pages/Farmtown-Park/227554350595013
Year Founded: 1986 Agricultureal history & lifestyle in rural Ontario.
Margaret Grotek, Contact

***Stittsville:* Goulbourn Museum**
2064 Huntley Rd.
Stittsville, ON K2S 1A7
Tel: 613-831-2393
goulbmus@rogers.com
goulbournmuseum.ca
twitter.com/GoulbournMuseum
www.facebook.com/Goulbo urnMuseum
Year Founded: 1990 Collection housed in 1873 Township Hall & 1961 Clerk's Building; displays about a family farms & rural schools; exhibit of military service from 1812 to present; genealogical data & library. Hours: W-Su 1:00-4:00
Kathryn Jamieson, Curator/Manager, kathryn@goulbournmuseum.ca

***Stoney Creek:* Battlefield House Museum & Park**
77 King St. West
Stoney Creek, ON L8G 5E5
Tel: 905-662-8458; *Fax:* 905-546-4141
battlefield@hamilton.ca
www.battlefieldhouse.ca
The Gage Homestead was built in 1796. During the War of 1812 & the Battle of Stoney Creek, the Gage family fled to the cellar of the home. The Battlefield Monument commemorates the soldiers who died during the battle. Each June, the Battlefield House Museum & Park is the site of a military re-enactment of the Battle of Stoney Creek. The site is open from July 1st to Labour Day.

***Stoney Creek:* Erland Lee (Museum) Home**
***Parent:* Federated Women's Institutes of Ontario (FWIO)**
552 Ridge Rd.
Stoney Creek, ON L8J 2Y6
Tel: 905-662-2691
erlandleehome@fwio.on.ca
www.fwio.on.ca/erland
Year Founded: 1972 Birthplace of the Women's Institutes. Features artifacts from a Victorian lifestyle.

***Stratford:* Brocksden Country School Museum**
2830 Perth Line 37, R.R.#1
Stratford, ON N5A 6S2
Tel: 519-271-0499; *Fax:* 519-271-1978
Year Founded: 1969 The school which opened in 1853 presents a living history program for classes. Open May 15 - September 15 by appointment.
Wilma McCaig, Secretary, 519-271-0499

***Stratford:* Stratford Perth Museum**
***Parent:* Stratford Perth Museum Association**
4275 Huron Rd.
Stratford, ON N5A 6S6
Tel: 519-393-5311; *Fax:* 519-393-5318
www.stratfordperthmuseum.ca
twitter.com/StratPerthMuse
www.facebook.co m/pages/The-Stratford-Perth-Museum/252829452896
Year Founded: 1997 Local history
John Kastner, General Manager, johnkastner@stratfordperthmuseum.ca

***Strathroy:* Museum Strathroy-Caradoc**
34 Frank St.
Strathroy, ON N7G 2R4
Tel: 519-245-0492; *Fax:* 519-245-1073
www.strathroymuseum.ca
Social Media: www.youtube.com/user/strathroymuseum
twitter.com/strathroymuseum
www.f acebook.com/museumstrathroycaradoc
Open year-round; medical theme room; military display; 1930s electric kitchen; printing shop; archival material
Andrew Meyer, Curator & Manager, Community Development, agmeyer@strathroy-caradoc.ca
Crystal Loyst, Coordinator, Collections & Research, cloyst@strathroy-caradoc.ca

***Stratton:* Kay-Nah-Chi-Wah-Nung Historical Centre**
***Parent:* Rainy River First Nations**
PO Box 100
Stratton, ON P0W 1N0
Tel: 807-483-1163; *Fax:* 807-483-1263
mounds.rrfn@bellnet.ca
www.manitoumounds.com
The Manitou Mounds are the centre's focal point. The Mounds are sacred First Nations ground, & were integral to the continent-wide aboriginal trading network. Visitors can explore the site on nature trails, & also learn about the area's history in the visitors centre.

***Sturgeon Falls:* Musée Sturgeon River House Museum**
250, ch Fort Rd.
Sturgeon Falls, ON P2B 2N7
Tél: 705-753-4716
admin@sturgeonriverhouse.com
www.sturgeonriverhouse.com
Le musée se trouve sur un site de la Compagnie de la Baie d'Hudson; l'exposition traite de fourrure et les animaux de la région.

***Sudbury:* Anderson Farm Museum**
***Parent:* Anderson Farm Museum Heritage Society**
PO Box 6400
Location: 564 Main St., Lively, ON P3Y 1J3
Sudbury, ON P3A 3B7
Tel: 705-692-4448; *Fax:* 705-692-4448
Open year round

***Sudbury:* Centre franco-ontarien de folklore (CFOF)**
Université de Sudbury, 935, ch du Lac Ramsay
Sudbury, ON P3E 2C6
Tél: 705-675-8986; *Téléc:* 705-675-5809
cfof@cfof.on.ca
www.cfof.on.ca
twitter.com/LeCFOF
www.facebook.com/1 26335660730527
Fondée en: 1972 A pour mission de mettre en valeur le folklore et le patrimoine franco-ontarien; musée; activités éducatives; bibliothèque; archives; publications; magasin virtuel
Janik Aubin-Robert, Présidente

***Sudbury:* Flour Mill Museum**
245 St. Charles St.
Sudbury, ON P3Y 0A6
Tel: 705-671-2489
www.sudburymuseums.ca
Year Founded: 1974 The museum is made out of two buildings: a heritage house built in 1902 & a log cabin built in 1983 to celebrate Sudbury's centennial. Open July & Aug., W-Su 10:00-4:00.
Samantha Morel, Curator, samantha.morel@greatersudbury.ca

***Sudbury:* Greater Sudbury Heritage Museums**
c/o Greater Sudbury Public Library, 74 MacKenzie St.
Sudbury, ON P3C 4X8
Tel: 705-671-2489
www.sudburymuseums.ca
www.facebook.com/SudburyMuseums
Greater Sudbury Heritage Museums is the collective name for the following four heritage sites located in & around Sudbury: Anderson Farm Museum, Copper Cliff Museum, Flour Mill Museum, & Rayside-Balfour Museum. The Greater Sudbury Virtual Museum is the online collection of photos, videos, archives, & more hosted on www.sudburymuseums.ca.
Samantha Morel, Curator

***Sudbury:* Irish Regiment of Canada Regimental Museum**
Sudbury Armoury, 333 Riverside Dr.
Sudbury, ON P3E 1H5
Tel: 705-669-2300

***Sudbury:* Sudbury Region Police Museum**
190 Brady St.
Sudbury, ON P3E 1C7
Tel: 705-675-9171; *Fax:* 705-674-7090
museum@police.sudbury.on.ca
www.gsps.ca/en/yourpolice/Museum.asp
www.f acebook.com/130223547044054
Police history

***Sutton West:* Eildon Hall Sibbald Memorial Museum**
Sibbald Point Provincial Park, 26071 York Rd. 18
Sutton West, ON L0E 1R0
Tel: 905-722-8061
Year Founded: 1835 Situated by the shore of Lake Simcoe, Eildon Hall was the Sibbald family home. Open from Jul. 1 - Sept. 1., 1:00 - 4:00.

***Tavistock:* Tavistock & District Historical Society**
PO Box 280
Located at 37 Maria St., Tavistock, ON
Tavistock, ON N0B 2R0
Tel: 519-655-3342
info@tavistockhistory.ca
www.tavistockhistory.ca
Other contact information: Alt. Phone: 519-655-9915
Local history

***Teeterville:* Teeterville Pioneer Museum**
194 Teeter St.
Teeterville, ON N0E 1S0
Tel: 519-426-5870; *Fax:* 519-428-3069
teeterville.museum@norfolkcounty.ca
teetervillemuseum.ca
www.facebook. com/teetervillemuseum
Other contact information: Victoria Day - Labour Day: 519-443-4400
Year Founded: 1967 Features historical buildings & picnic grounds.
Jodie Keene, Coordinator, jodie.keene@norfolkcounty.ca

***Thorold:* Thorold Museum**
***Parent:* Thorold & Beaverdams Historical Society**
Chestnut Hall, 14 Ormond St. North
Thorold, ON L2V 1Y8
Tel: 905-227-1632
www.tbhs.ca
Local history
Randy Barnes, President, 905-984-4435

***Thunder Bay:* Centennial Park 1910 Logging Camp & Museum**
c/o City of Thunder Bay Parks Division, 111 Syndicate Ave. South
Thunder Bay, ON P7E 6S4
Tel: 807-625-2941; *Fax:* 807-625-3588
Toll-Free: 888-711-5094
www.thunderbay.ca/parks
Full scale replica of a 1910 logging camp re-creates the early history of Northern Ontario's forest industry; park open year round; logging camp and museum open mid-June to Labour Day, 8:00 am.m to 8:00 p.m.; Muskeg Express logging train; Winter sleigh rides; craft shop; picnic area; trails

***Thunder Bay:* Definitely Superior Artist-Run Centre & Gallery**
PO Box 21015 Grandview Mall
Located at #101, 250 Park Ave., Thunder Bay, ON
Thunder Bay, ON P7A 8A9
Tel: 807-344-3814; *Fax:* 807-344-3814
defsup@tbaytel.net
www.definitelysuperior.com
Social Media: definitelysuperior.tumblr.com
twitter.com/DefSup
www.facebook.com/defs up
Year Founded: 1988 An artist-run centre for contemporary arts, hosting exhibitions as well as workshops, lectures, film & video screenings, performance, music & literary events. Open Tu-Sa 12:00-6:00.
Rusty Brown, President
David Karasiewicz, Director

***Thunder Bay:* Duke Hunt Museum**
3218 Rosslyn Rd.
Thunder Bay, ON P7C 5N5
Tel: 807-939-1262
www.oliverpaipoonge.ca
Year Founded: 1952 Reflecting the history of the Municipality of Oliver/Paipoonge & area during the late 1800s & early 1900s. Collection of pioneer material and farm machinery, old school room, kitchen and bedroom displays. Hours: May 1 - Aug 31Tu - Su 1:00 - 5:00, or by appointment.
Lois Garrity, Curator & Director

***Thunder Bay:* Fort William Historical Park (FWHP)**
1350 King Rd.
Thunder Bay, ON P7K 1L7
Tel: 807-577-8461; *Fax:* 807-473-2327
info@fwhp.ca
www.fwhp.ca
Social Media: www.youtube.com/user/FortWilliamHistPark
twitter.com/FWHPtweets
www.fa cebook.com/fortwilliamhistoricalpark
Year Founded: 1973 A living history site that depicts the fur trade activities of the North West Company in the early 1800s; 42 reconstructed buildings on a 225-acre site. Touts that it is the largest Fur Trade Post. Hours: 10:00-5:00
Sergio Buonocore, General Manager

***Thunder Bay:* Northwestern Ontario Sports Hall of Fame**
219 May St. South
Thunder Bay, ON P7E 1B5
Tel: 807-622-2852; *Fax:* 807-622-2736
nwosport@tbaytel.net
www.nwosportshalloffame.com
twitter.com/nwosports
www.facebook.com/105561449476479
Year Founded: 1978 The Hall's mission is to preserve and honour Northwestern Ontario's sports heritage, with displays, photos, archival material, artifacts and other documentation on over 200 athletes; reference library; educational programming. Open all year, Tu - Sa 12:00 - 5:00.
Diane Imrie, Executive Director

***Thunder Bay:* Thunder Bay Military Museum**
The Armoury, 317 Park Ave.
Thunder Bay, ON P7B 1C7
Tel: 807-343-5175
army.ca/inf/lssrmus.php
Georg Hoegel Art Collection - paintings & drawings done by Mr. Hoegel when he was a prisoner of war in Canada from 1941-1946; other military art; tri-service collection, representing all three services, rotated regularly; open 4 afternoons, 2 evenings & by request
L.Col./Dr. T.M.S. Kaipio, President C.D., Ph.D.
Myles G. Penny, Curator C.D., B.A., B.Ed., pennym@air.on.ca

***Thunder Bay:* Thunder Bay Museum**
***Parent:* Thunder Bay Historical Museum Society**
425 East Donald St.
Thunder Bay, ON P7E 5V1
Tel: 807-623-0801
info@thunderbaymuseum.com
www.thunderbaymuseum.com
Social Media: www.pinterest.com/tbaymuseum
twitter.com/tbaymuseum
www.facebook.com/T hunderbaymuseum
A museum, historical society & archives for Thunder Bay & Northwestern Ontario
Dr. Tory Tronrud, Curator, director@thunderbaymuseum.com
Nick Sottile, Chief Administrative Officer, cao@thunderbaymuseum.com

***Tillsonburg:* Annandale National Historic Museum**
30 Tillson Ave.
Tillsonburg, ON N4G 2Z8
Tel: 519-842-2294; *Fax:* 519-842-5355
www.tillsonburg.ca/Visitors/AnnandaleHouse.aspx
Nationally designated for its interior, representing the Victorian "Aesthetic Art Movement," Annandale House is restored to the 1880's period; location of tourist information for Tillsonburg; open year round
Patricia Phelps, Curator, pphelps@tillsonburg.ca

***Tillsonburg:* Backus Heritage Conservation Area & Village (BHCA)**
c/o Long Point Region Conservation Authority, 4 Elm St.
Tillsonburg, ON N4G 0C4
Tel: 519-586-2201
conservation@lprca.on.ca
www.lprca.on.ca/NHW.htm
Other contact information: Phone, Administration Office: 519-842-4242; Fax: 519-842-7123
Owned & operated by the Long Point Region Conservation Authority, the Backus Heritage Conservation Area features a conservation education centre & a heritage village. The village consists of restored & reconstructed buildings, including the John C. Backhouse Mill, the Teeterville Baptist Church, the Vittoria Carriage Shop, & the Forbes Barn. The history of the Long Point Region Watershed is depicted through exhibits & artifacts.

***Timmins:* Timmins Museum: National Exhibition Centre / Musée de Timmins: Centre national d'exposition**
220 Algonquin Blvd. East
Located at 325 - 2 Ave., Timmins, ON
Timmins, ON P4N 1B3
Tel: 705-360-2617; *Fax:* 705-360-2693
museum@timmins.ca
www.timminsmuseum.ca
twitter.com/TimminsMNEC
www.f acebook.com/129963747035410
Year Founded: 1975 Preserves, presents & studies the history of the Porcupine Gold Camp, Timmins Ontario. The South Porcupine location closed in 2006 due to structural damage; the new site at 325 Second Ave. will be opening soon.
Karen Bachmann, Director/Curator, karen.bachmann@timmins.ca

***Tobermory:* The Peninsula & St. Edmunds Township Museum**
PO Box 250, 7072 Highway #6
Tobermory, ON N0H 2R0
Tel: 519-373-7032
Year Founded: 1967 Housed in the former St. Edmunds Settlement School (ca. 1898), the museum's holdings include land deeds and registers, photographs, and exhibits on lumbering, fishing, and hunting activities; the upper floor of the museum is dedicated to area marine history and includes maps, tools, and relics from shipwrecks. An 1875 furnished log house is located on the grounds and is open by appointment only. Located south of Tobermory Harbour, on the east side of Hwy 6. Open weekends from Victoria Day to Thanksgiving, and weekdays from July 1 to Labour Day.

***Toronto:* 48th Highlanders Museum**
73 Simcoe St.
Toronto, ON M5J 1W9
Tel: 416-596-1382
www.48highlanders.com/04_03.html
Year Founded: 1959 The museum seeks to collect, preserve, & present the legacy of the 48th Highlanders of Canada. Open year-round, W & Th 10:00-3:00.

***Toronto:* Aga Khan Museum (BCHCC)**
77 Wynford Dr.
Toronto, ON M3C 1K1
information@agakhanmuseum.org
www.agakhanmuseum.org
twitter.com/agakhanmuseum
www.facebook.com/agakhanmuseumtoronto
Year Founded: 2014 The Aga Khan Museum in Toronto, Canada offers visitors a window into worlds unknown or unfamiliar: the artistic, intellectual, and scientific heritage of Islamic civilizations across the centuries from the Iberian Peninsula to China.
His Highness the Aga Khan , Chair
Henry Kim, Director & CEO

***Toronto:* Applewood: The James Shaver Woodsworth Homestead**
450 The West Mall
Toronto, ON M9C 1E9
Tel: 416-622-4124
www.applewoodshaverhouse.org
www.facebook.com/ApplewoodShaverHouse
The homestead is an historic building that now offers space for meetings, weddings, & other parties. Open M-F 10:00-5:00, Sa & Su by appointment.

***Toronto:* The Bata Shoe Museum (BSM)**
327 Bloor St. West
Toronto, ON M5S 1W7
Tel: 416-979-7799
www.batashoemuseum.ca
Social Media: pinterest.com/batashoemuseum; batashoemuseum.tumblr.com
twitter.com/batashoemuseum
www.facebook.com/batashoemuseum
Other contact information: Blog: astepintothebatashoemuseum.blogspot.ca
Explores footwear in the social & cultural life of humankind from ancient times to present. Exhibits vary but there is a permanant exhibit which includes a pair of Elton John platform shoes and shoes which date back hundreds of years.
Elizabeth Semmelhack, Senior Curator, elizabeth@batashoemuseum.ca

***Toronto:* Beth Tzedec Reuben & Helene Dennis Museum**
c/o Beth Tzedec Synagogue, 1700 Bathurst St.
Toronto, ON M5P 3K3
Tel: 416-781-3514; *Fax:* 416-781-0150
www.beth-tzedec.org/page/museum
Year Founded: 1965 The museum features a major Judaica collection, including Jewish art & history from ancient times to the present. Appointments may be made for tours. Hours are M, W, Th 11:00 - 1:00, 2:00 - 5:00 and Su 11:00 - 2:00. Closed on Jewish holidays and weekends in July and August.
Dorion Liebgott, Curator, 416-781-3514, dliebgott@beth-tzedec.org

***Toronto:* Black Creek Pioneer Village**
1000 Murray Ross Pkwy.
Toronto, ON M3J 2P3
Tel: 416-736-1733
bcpvinfo@trca.on.ca
www.blackcreek.ca
Social Media: www.flickr.com/groups/blackcreekpioneervillage
twitter.com/blackcreeknew s
www.facebook.com/BlackCreekPioneerVillage
Operated by the Toronto & Region Conservation Authority (TRCA), Black Creek Pioneer Village is a living history experience, which spans over 30 acres. It exemplifies a small south central Ontario community between the 1790s & the 1860s. Demonstrations & special activities depict rural life. Black Creek Village also features the historic Black Creek Historic Brewery. The village is open from the beginning of May to the end of December.
Wendy Rowney, Supervisor, Historic Programs, wrowney@trca.on.ca

***Toronto:* Cabbagetown Regent Park Community Museum**
Residence House, Riverdale Farm, 201 Winchester St.
Toronto, ON M4X 1B8
Tel: 416-392-6794
farm@toronto.ca
www.crpmuseum.com
Year Founded: 2004 The museum collects, preserves, & displays the history of the Cabbagetown & Regent Park neighbourhoods in Toronto. Open year-round, Sa & Su 11:00-4:00.
Carol Moore-Ede, President, cmooreede@rogers.com

***Toronto:* Campbell House**
160 Queen St. West
Toronto, ON M5H 3H3
Tel: 416-597-0227; *Fax:* 416-597-0750
info@campbellhousemuseum.ca
www.campbellhousemuseum.ca
twitter.com/Cam pbellHouseTO
www.facebook.com/365449410187802
Built in 1822, the Campbell House is the oldest remaining building from the original town of York. The Sir William Campbell Foundation operates the museum. Special programs are available for groups. The Home is open from the beginning of May until Thanksgiving.

***Toronto:* Canadian Advertising Museum (CAM)**
c/o Bev Atkinson, Humber ITAL - Lakeshore Campus, Bldg. F, #F102, 3199 lakeshore Boul. West
Toronto, ON M8V 1K8
Tel: 416-675-6622; *Fax:* 416-251-3797
info@canadianadvertisingmuseum.com
www.canadianadvertisingmuseum.com
Social Media: www.linkedin.com/groups/Canadian-Advertising-Museum-CAM-4260094
twitter. com/cam_tweets
www.facebook.com/canadianadvertisingmuseum
The museum seeks to preserve Canadian business & culture through advertising, both online & in their physical collection.
Kate Taylor, Chair
Bev Atkinson, Director

***Toronto:* Canadian Air & Space Museum (TAM)**
Parc Downsview Park, PO Box 1, 65 Carl Hall Rd.
Toronto, ON M3K 2E1
Tel: 416-638-6078 *Toll-Free:* 866-585-2227
casm@casmuseum.org
www.casmuseum.org
Social Media: www.youtube.com/user/CASMuseum
twitter.com/CASMuseum
www.facebook.com/ casmuseum
The museum focuses on the aviation industry & history in the Toronto region, with a collection that includes artifacts & full-size aircraft (including a full-scale metal replica of the AVRO Arrow). Currently the museum is between locations, having been evicted from Downsview Park in 2011. As of 2012, the museum is in talks with the Greater Toronto Airports Authority to relocate the collection to Pearson International Airport. The former Downsview Park address is still used for mailing purposes.
Ian McDougall, Chair

***Toronto:* Canadian Broadcasting Corporation Museum & Graham Spry Theatre**
PO Box 500 A, 250 Front St. West
Toronto, ON M5W 1E6
Tel: 416-205-5574
www.cbc.ca/museum
Year Founded: 1936 The CBC Museum presents the story of CBC's broadcasting history.

***Toronto:* The Canadian Business Hall of Fame / Le Temple de la renommée de l'entreprise canadienne**
***Parent:* Junior Achievement of Canada Foundation**
#218, 1 Eva Rd.
Toronto, ON M9C 4Z5
Tel: 416-622-4602; *Fax:* 416-622-6861
Toll-Free: 800-265-0699
cbhof.org
Year Founded: 1979
Samantha Strong, Contact

***Toronto:* Canadian Language Museum / Musée Canadien des Langues**
150 Walmer Rd.
Toronto, ON M5R 2X9
www.languagemuseum.ca
Year Founded: 2011 Designs travelling exhibits about Canadian English, French & Inuit languages in order to promote the languages spoken in Canada.
Elaine Gold, Chair

***Toronto:* Canadian Sculpture Centre**
***Parent:* Sculptors Society of Canada**
500 Church St.
Toronto, ON M4Y 2C8
Tel: 647-435-5858
gallery@cansculpt.org
cansculpt.org
The Sculptors Society of Canada hosts a sculpture gallery on Church St. in Toronto that displays temporary exhibits. Please see the website for details.

***Toronto:* Canadian Transit Heritage Foundation (CTHF)**
PO Box 30, 260 Adelaide St. East
Toronto, ON M5A 1N1
webmaster@transitheritage.ca
www.transitheritage.ca
The Foundation collects & preserves items relating to transit in Canada, including a small collection of old transit busses. No formal museum exists yet, but a public access program is in the works.
Chris Prentice, President

***Toronto:* Casa Loma**
1 Austin Terrace
Toronto, ON M5R 1X8
Tel: 416-923-1171; *Fax:* 416-923-5734
info@casaloma.org
www.casaloma.org
Social Media: www.instagram.com/Casalomatoronto
twitter.com/casalomatoronto
Year Founded: 1937 Owned by the City of Toronto & operated by The Kiwanis Club of Casa Loma, Casa Loma is the former home of Sir Henry Pellatt, a Canadian financier, industrialist, & military man. The decorated castle contains an 800 foot tunnel, secret passages, towers, & stables. A self-guided audio tour is available in eight languages.
Nick Di Donato, Chief Executive Officer

***Toronto:* Chinese Cultural Centre of Greater Toronto (CCCGT)**
5183 Sheppard Ave. East
Toronto, ON M1B 5Z5
Tel: 416-292-9293; *Fax:* 416-292-9215
www.cccgt.org
www.facebook.com/171784883266
Year Founded: 1998 The cultural centre contains a collection of Chinese artifacts, as well as a library, art gallery, theatre, exhibition hall, classrooms & offices.
Dr. Ming-Tat Cheung, Chair & President

***Toronto:* Colborne Lodge**
c/o Museum Services, Metro Hall, 55 John St., 8th Fl.
Toronto, ON M5V 3C6
Tel: 416-392-6916
clodge@toronto.ca
www.toronto.ca/museums/colbornelodge
twitter.com/ColborneLodgeTO
www.f acebook.com/colbornelodge
Site of the 19th century home of High Park founders, John & Jemmina Howard; contains many of their original furnishings, watercolours of early Toronto, & other artifacts; coach house, tomb & restored gardens on the property; special events & programming; party room rentals; located at the south end of High Park, Colborne Lodge Dr., just north of the Queensway. Open year round.
Bob Webber, Contact, bwebber@toronto.ca

***Toronto:* Dance Collection Danse (DCD)**
145 George St.
Toronto, ON M5A 2M6
Tel: 416-365-3233; *Fax:* 416-365-3169
Toll-Free: 800-665-5320
talk@dcd.ca
www.dcd.ca
twitter.com/DanceCollection
www.facebook.com/14927618346
Dance Collection Danse is an archive of Canadian dance history. The organization also runs an online store & produces exhibitions relating to dance history in Canada.
Miriam Adams, Co-Founder & Director
Amy Bowring, Director, Collections & Research

***Toronto:* Design Exchange (DX)**
PO Box 18 TD Centre, 234 Bay St.
Toronto, ON M5K 1B2
Tel: 416-363-6121; *Fax:* 416-368-0684
info@dx.org
www.dx.org
Social Media: youtube.com/designexchange;
flickr.com/photos/thedesignexchange
twitter.com/designexchange
www.fac ebook.com/DesignExchange
Year Founded: 1994 The DX is the only museum in Canada dedicated to preserving design heritage. The museum is housed in the old Toronto Stock Exchange building in downtown Toronto. Hours of Operation: M-Sa 10:00-5:00, Su 12:00-5:00.
Shauna Levy, President, shauna@dx.org
Sara Nickleson, Curator, sara@dx.org

***Toronto:* The Enoch Turner Schoolhouse (1848)**
106 Trinity St.
Toronto, ON M5A 3C6
Tel: 416-863-0010
www.enochturnerschoolhouse.ca
One of Toronto's oldest institutions & the city's first free school
P. Lynne Kurylo, Chair
Anne Mcarty, Administrator, amcarty@enochturnerschoolhouse.ca

***Toronto:* Fort York National Historic Site**
250 Fort York Blvd.
Toronto, ON M5V 3K9
Tel: 416-392-6907; *Fax:* 416-392-6917
fortyork@toronto.ca
www.toronto.ca/museums/fortyork
twitter.com/fortyo rk
www.facebook.com/fortyork
Other contact information: Alternate URL: www.fortyork.ca
Year Founded: 1934 Built by Lieutenant-Governor John Graves Simcoe as a garrison in 1793, Fort York was purchased by the City of Toronto in 1909 & restored as a museum in 1934. Its fortified walls contain the largest collection of original War of 1812 buildings in Canada. Some of the restored interiors reflect the life of the garrison community, while others serve as exhibit space for artifacts on a military theme. The site offers seasonal guided tours as well as musket, drill & music demonstrations.
David O'Hara, Manager

***Toronto:* Gardiner Museum of Ceramic Art**
111 Queen's Park
Toronto, ON M5S 2C7
Tel: 416-586-8080; *Fax:* 416-586-8085
mail@gardinermuseum.on.ca
www.gardinermuseum.on.ca
Social Media: www.youtube.com/user/gardinermuseum
twitter.com/gardinermuseum
www.fac ebook.com/16720993289
Containing 3,000+ historical & contemporary pieces, the Gardiner Museum is North America's premier specialized ceramic museum; gift shop; Gail Brooker Ceramic Research Library; Gardiner Bistro; permanent & special exhibits; studio spaces & ceramic courses; talks, book launches, films & other programs.
Kelvin Browne, Executive Director & CEO

***Toronto:* Gibson House Museum**
5176 Yonge St.
Toronto, ON M2N 5P6
Tel: 416-395-7432
gibsonhouse@toronto.ca
www.toronto.ca
www.facebook.com/gibsonzion
Gibson House, built in 1851, was the home of Scottish immigrant David Gibson and his family. Gibson, a land surveyor, played a role in the mapping of early Toronto and spent some years in exile in the U.S. for his participation in the Rebellion of 1837 in Upper Canada.
Dorie Billich, Curator

***Toronto:* Historic Zion Schoolhouse**
1091 Finch Ave. East
Toronto, ON M2J 2X3
Tel: 416-395-7435
zionschool@toronto.ca
www.toronto.ca
A City of Toronto Museum, the Zion Schoolhouse offers modern students a roleplaying experience into the lives of children circa 1910.

Toronto: L Space Gallery
Lakeshore Campus, Humber College, #L1002, 21 Colonel Samuel Smith Park Dr.
Toronto, ON M8V 4B6
Tel: 416-675-6622
www.humber.ca/lakeshorecampus/lspacegallery
Social Media: lspacegallery.wordpress.com
twitter.com/HumberGallery
www.facebook.com /HumberGallery
Year Founded: 2012 Work by students & local artists.
Ashley Watson, Curator, ashley.watson@humber.ca

Toronto: Lambton House
4066 Old Dundas St.
Toronto, ON M6S 4S1
Tel: 416-767-5472
postmaster@lambtonhouse.org
www.lambtonhouse.org
twitter.com/LambtonHouse
www.facebook.com/Lambton House
Year Founded: 2012 The last remaining building from the Village of Lambton Mills.

Toronto: Mackenzie House
82 Bond St.
Toronto, ON M5B 1X2
Tel: 416-392-6915
machouse@toronto.ca
www.toronto.ca/museums/mackenziehouse
twitter.com/MackenzieHouse
www.f acebook.com/mackenziehouse
Year Founded: 1950 The final home of Toronto's first mayor, William Lyon Mackenzie who gained notoriety during the 1837 Upper Canada Rebellion, this 1858 Georgian rowhouse has been refurnished in period style and also showcases a print shop.

Toronto: Montgomery's Inn
4709 Dundas St. West
Toronto, ON M9A 1A8
Tel: 416-394-8113; *Fax:* 416-394-6027
montinn@toronto.ca
www.montgomerysinn.com
twitter.com/MontINNTO
www. facebook.com/montgomerysinn
Year Founded: 1975 Built in 1830, the restored inn reflects life in 1847. Its library holds photographs, artifacts, and archival materials documenting the history of Etobicoke; tearoom; gift shop; seasonal programs; community theatre and music; workshops

Toronto: The Morris & Sally Justein Heritage Museum
Baycrest Hospital, 3560 Bathurst St., Main Fl.
Toronto, ON M6A 2E1
Tel: 416-785-2500; *Fax:* 416-785-2378
www.baycrest.org/culture-arts-innovation-15.php
Social Media: www.youtube.com/thebaycrestchannel
twitter.com/baycrest
www.facebook.c om/baycrestcentre
The Morris & Sally Justein Heritage Museum displays Judaica exhibits. The historical & cultural Judaica exhibits & permanent collections are designed for Baycrest Hospital & Home's elderly clients.
Cassandra Zita, Museum Assistant MMSt, BA, czita@baycrest.org

Toronto: MZTV Museum of Television
64 Jefferson Ave.
Toronto, ON M6K 1Y4
Tel: 416-599-7339
mztv@mztv.com
www.mztv.com
www.facebook.com/239799029379279
The museum seeks to protect & preserve television sets & related technologies, as well as books, magazines, original papers, discs, toys & ephemera of television; interactive 3D gallery; museum; e-gallery online at website; guided tours Tues - Fri.

Toronto: National Presbyterian Museum
PO Box 35007 Ellerback, 180 Danforth Ave.
Toronto, ON M4K 1N1
Tel: 416-469-1345
presbyterianmuseum@presbyterian.ca
www.presbyterianmuseum.ca
Year Founded: 2002 The museum is dedicated to preserving the history of the Presbyterian Church in Canada.

Toronto: Osborne Collection of Early Children's Books
Lillian H. Smith Branch, Toronto Public Library, 239 College St., 4th Fl.
Toronto, ON M5T 1R5
Tel: 416-393-7753
www.torontopubliclibrary.ca/osborne
The collection of historic children's books includes the following: The Osborne Collection; The Lillian H. Smith Collection; The Canadiana Collection; & The Jean Thomson Collection of Original Art.

Toronto: Parliament Interpretive Centre
265 Front St, East
Toronto, ON M5A 1G1
Tel: 416-212-8897
programs@heritagetrust.on.ca
www.heritagetrust.on.ca/Conservation/Museums/Parliament.asp x
Year Founded: 2012 Exhibits the history of the site as well as rotating displays.

Toronto: The Queen's Own Rifles of Canada Regimental Museum
Casa Loma, 1 Austin Terrace
Toronto, ON M5R 1X8
Tel: 416-605-9159
museum@qormusuem.org
qormuseum.org
twitter.com/qormu seum
www.facebook.com/qormuseum
Year Founded: 1956 Display artifacts pertinent to the history of the regiment from 1860-present; open year round
Dorit Leo, Curator, dleo@casaloma.org

Toronto: Queen's York Rangers Regimental Museum
Fort York Armoury, 660 Fleet St. West
Toronto, ON M5V 1A9
qyrang.ca/about/history
Traces the history of the Queen's York Rangers, an active reconnaissance unit of the Army Reserve; displays begin wth the Seven Year's War, through the American Revolution & settlement of Upper Canada & through the campaigns of 19th century & two world wars
L.Col. Diane Kruger, Curator, qyrangcentralregistry@intern.mil.ca

Toronto: Redpath Sugar Museum
95 Queen's Quay East
Toronto, ON M5E 1A3
Tel: 416-366-3561 *Toll-Free:* 800-267-1517
Consumer-Canada@redpathsugar.com
www.redpathsugars.com
Social Media: www.youtube.com/redpathsugar
twitter.com/actsofsweetness
www.facebook.com/redpathsugar
Year Founded: 1979 The Redpath Sugar Museum displays the history of sugar production & refining, models of transportation that bring sugar to the refinery, as well as the story of the Redpath family. The museum offers a program for schools.
Richard Feltoe, Curator & Corporate Archivist, Richard.Feltoe@asr-group.com

Toronto: Royal Canadian Military Institute Museum (RCMI)
426 University Ave.
Toronto, ON M5G 1S9
Tel: 416-597-0286; *Fax:* 416-597-6919
Toll-Free: 800-585-1072
info@rcmi.org
www.rcmi.org
twitter.com/rcmiHQ
Artifacts related to Canadians' participation in the military; library open to researchers & members; open year round
Gregory Loughton, Curator, gregory.loughton@rcmi.org

Toronto: The Royal Regiment of Canada Museum
Fort York Armoury, 660 Fleet St.
Toronto, ON M5V 1A9
Tel: 416-755-1727
Year Founded: 1996 Military artifacts, dating from 1862, of the The Royal Regiment of Canada, & predecessors: the 10th Royal Grenadiers (Toronto Regiment), & the 3rd, 123rd, 124th, 204th & 58th Battalions; archives; school tours by appointment. Located next to the Royals' WO's & Sergeants' Mess on the 2nd floor, at the east end of Fort York Armoury.

Toronto: St. Mark's Coptic Museum
41 Glendinning Ave.
Toronto, ON M1W 3E2
Tel: 416-494-4449
stmarkmuseum@yahoo.com
www.copticmuseum-canada.org
Year Founded: 1996 The only Coptic museum outside of Egypt; collection contains artwork & artifacts
Father Marcos Marcos, President
Helene Moussa, Volunteer Curator

Toronto: The Salvation Army Museum
2 Overlea Blvd.
Toronto, ON M4H 1P4
Tel: 416-285-4344
heritage_centre@can.salvationarmy.org
salvationist.ca/ about-us/history/museum-archives
Open to public & gives a pictorial outline of Salvation Army history, particularly as it pertains to Canada & Bermuda, through the use of artifacts, photographs & special techniques; no fee; wheelchair accessible; open Mon.-Fri., closed all statutory holidays

Toronto: Sarah & Chaim Neuberger Holocaust Education Centre
UJA Federation of Greater Toronto, Lipa Green Centre, Sherman Campus, 4600 Bathurst St., 4th Fl.
Toronto, ON M2R 3V2
Tel: 416-631-5689
neuberger@ujafed.org
www.holocaustcentre.com
Social Media: neubergerhec.tumblr.com
twitter.com/holocaust_ed
www.facebook.com/HoloCentre
Year Founded: 1985 The centre is dedicated to educating the public about the Holocaust & creating dialogue about civil society through programs, exhibitions, an on-site museum, & library. Open M-Th 9:00-4:30, F 9:00-1:00, or by appointment.
Marilyn Sinclair, Chair
Mira Goldfarb, Executive Director
Rachel Libman, Head, Programs & Exhibitions
Carol Fox, Administrative Assistant

Toronto: Scadding Cabin
Parent: York Pioneer & Historical Society
c/o York Pioneer & Historical Society, PO Box 45026, 2482 Yonge St.
Toronto, ON M4P 3E3
Tel: 416-219-2454
yorkpioneers@gmail.com
www.yorkpioneers.org/cabin.html
Built for John Scadding, clerk to Lieutenant-Governor John Graves Simcoe, the cabin is Toronto's oldest dwelling. Located at Exhibition Place, southeast of 25 British Columbia Rd.; wooden house, built in late 1700s, contains furniture which belonged to John Graves Simcoe; open late Aug.-Labour Day (during CNE)

Toronto: Scarborough Historical Museum
1007 Brimley Rd.
Toronto, ON M1P 3E8
Tel: 416-338-8807
shm@toronto.ca
www.toronto.ca/scarboroughmuseum
twitter.com/ScarbMuseum
www.facebook. com/scarboroughmuseum
Includes Cornell House, McCowan Log Cabin & Hough Carriage Works; picnic area; parking

Toronto: Sesquicentennial Museum & Archives
263 McCaul St.
Toronto, ON M5T 1W7
Tel: 416-397-3680; *Fax:* 416-397-3685
toes.tdsb.on.ca/day/tusc/location/sesqui.asp
Preserves the history of the TDSB & its schools; collects, documents, researches, exhibits, & historical artifacts, fine art, & archival, & published material for its educational community - students, parents, staff & trustees & its citizens

Toronto: Spadina Museum: Historic House & Gardens
285 Spadina Rd.
Toronto, ON M5R 2V5
Tel: 416-392-6910
spadina@toronto.ca
www.toronto.ca/museums/spadina
twitter.com/SpadinaMuseum
www.facebook. com/spadinamuseum
Year Founded: 1984 1866 mansion contains four generations of décor, reflecting art movements such as Art Nouveau
Karen Edwards, Administrator

***Toronto:* Taras H. Shevchenko Museum**
1614 Bloor St. West
Toronto, ON M6P 1A7
Tel: 416-534-8662; *Fax:* 416-535-1063
shevchenkomuseum@bellnet.ca
www.infoukes.com/shevchenkomuseum
www.face book.com/ShevchenkoMuseum
The museum is dedicated to the art, life and literary legacy of Ukraine's renowned poet, Taras Schevchenko; the Toronto site is the only Shevchenko museum in the Americas; library; art exhibits; Ukrainian folk art and handicrafts. Open year round.

***Toronto:* Tenda do Louro Jewellery Museum (TdLJM)**
#200, 158 Davenport Rd.
Toronto, ON M5R 1J2
Tel: 647-343-7350
www.tendadolourojewellerymuseum.com
Year Founded: 2013 The first jewellery museum in Canada

***Toronto:* Textile Museum of Canada**
55 Centre Ave.
Toronto, ON M5G 2H5
Tel: 416-599-5321
info@textilemuseum.ca
www.textilemuseum.ca
twitter.com/tmctoronto
www.facebook.com/textilemu seumofcanada
Year Founded: 1975 Unique exhibitions & programming; focus on the traditions & aesthetics of historic & contemporary textiles
Shauna McCabe, Executive Director, 416-599-5321, smccabe@textilemuseum.ca

***Toronto:* Theatre Museum Canada (TMC)**
#309, 15 Case Goods Lane
Toronto, ON M5A 3C4
Tel: 416-413-7847; *Fax:* 416-923-0226
www.theatremuseumcanada.ca
Social Media: www.youtube.com/theatremuseumcanada
www.facebook.com/TheatreMuseumCanada
Year Founded: 1991 While no physical location yet exists, the Theatre Museum Canada's collection consists of memorabilia & artifacts that document the history of Canadian theatre.
Michael Wallace, Executive Director, mwallace@theatremuseumcanada.ca

***Toronto:* Todmorden Mills Heritage Museum & Art Centre**
67 Pottery Rd.
Toronto, ON M4K 2B8
Tel: 416-396-2819
todmorden@toronto.ca
www.toronto.ca/culture/museums/todmorden.htm
twitter.com/TodmordenMills
www.facebook.com/TodmordenMills
Depicts early industry in Toronto; new papermill galleries & theatre feature frequent exhibitions & is available for rental

***Toronto:* Toronto Police Museum & Discovery Centre**
40 College St.
Toronto, ON M5G 2J3
Tel: 416-808-7020
museum@torontopolice.on.ca
www.torontopolice.on.ca/museum
Interactive displays; collection includes uniforms, badges, communication & transportation equipment; high profile crimes; open year round

***Toronto:* Toronto Railway Museum**
***Parent:* Toronto Railway Historical Association**
#15, 255 Bremner Blvd.
Toronto, ON M5V 3M9
Tel: 416-214-9229
www.torontorailwaymuseum.com
Social Media: pinterest.com/TOrailwayMuseum
twitter.com/TORailwayMuseum
www.facebook .com/pages/Toronto-Railway-Museum/338897312846580
Year Founded: 2010 Toronto & Ontario railway history.

***Toronto:* Toronto Scottish Regiment Museum**
70 Birmingham St.
Toronto, ON M8V 3W6
tsrpd.com
Year Founded: 1984 Military artifacts.
Tim Stewart, Curator

***Toronto:* Toronto's First Post Office (TFPO)**
***Parent:* Town of York Historical Society**
260 Adelaide St. East
Toronto, ON M5A 1N1
Tel: 416-865-1833; *Fax:* 416-865-9414
tfpo@total.net
www.townofyork.com
twitter.com/tos1stpo
www.facebook. com/TOs1stPO
Year Founded: 1983 Canada's only surviving pre-1851 Post Office; restored as a museum & full postal service operation; gift shop
Janet Walters, Curator

***Toronto:* Ukrainian Museum of Canada (UMC) Ontario Branch**
***Parent:* Ukrainian Women's Association of Canada**
620 Spadina Ave.
Toronto, ON M5S 2H4
Tel: 416-923-3318; *Fax:* 416-923-8266
museum@stvladimir.ca
www.umcontario.com
www.facebook.com/265231800201546
Year Founded: 1944 Open Mon.-Fri., Sat.-Sun. by appointment only.

***Tweed:* Tweed & Area Heritage Centre**
PO Box 665, 40 Victoria St. North
Tweed, ON K0K 3J0
Tel: 613-478-3989; *Fax:* 613-478-6457
tweedheritageinfo@on.aibn.com
Year Founded: 1988 An information centre, art gallery, museum, archives & genealogical research centre; local arts & crafts promotional centre; Hours: M-Sa 9:00am-12:00pm, 1:00-5:00
Evan Morton, Curator, 613-478-3989, Fax: 613-478-6457, tweedheritageinfo@on.aibn.com

***Uxbridge:* Thomas Foster Memorial Temple**
9449 Concession Rd. 7
Uxbridge, ON L0C 1C0
Tel: 905-640-3966
www.fostermemorial.com
www.facebook.com/foster.memorial
Built by former mayor of Toronto, Thomas Foster, in 1935/36 as a memorial to his wife, unique in the design of Byzantine architecture; holds tours on the 1st & 2nd Sun., June-Sept.; special concerts throughout the year, with special program in Oct.

***Uxbridge:* Uxbridge Historical Centre**
PO Box 1301
Located at 7230 Concession Rd. 6, Uxbridge, ON
Uxbridge, ON L9P 1R2
Tel: 905-852-5854
museum@town.uxbridge.on.ca
www.uxbridgehistoricalcentre.com
twitter.com/UxbridgeMuseum
www.facebo ok.com/uxbridgehistoricalcentre
Year Founded: 1972 Displays of artifacts & photos to help tell the story of the Uxbridge area; special display on The Oak Ridges Moraine; 10 heritage buildings on site; picnic grounds; Hours for Tours: May-Oct.: W-Su 10:00-4:00
Nancy Marr, Curator

***Vankleek Hill:* Musée Vankleek Hill Museum**
PO Box 537
Located at 95 Main St. East, Vankleek Hill, ON
Vankleek Hill, ON K0B 1R0
Tel: 613-678-2323
info@vankleek.ca
www.vankleek.ca
www.facebook.com/vankleekhillmuseum
Year Founded: 1997 Local history

***Vaughan:* The Soccer Hall of Fame & Museum**
7601 Martin Grove Rd.
Vaughan, ON L4L 9E4
Tel: 905-264-9390; *Fax:* 905-264-9445
museum@thesoccerhalloffame.ca
thesoccerhalloffame.ca
Social Media: www.youtube.com/user/soccerhalloffame
twitter.com/Hall_Of_Fame
www.fac ebook.com/SoccerHallofFame
Year Founded: 2000 Artifacts & archives relating to Canadian soccer history
Kim Watson, Curator & Project Manager, kwatson@soccer.on.ca

***Vernon:* Osgoode Township Historical Society & Museum**
PO Box 74, 7814 Lawrence St.
Vernon, ON K0A 3J0
Tel: 613-821-4062; *Fax:* 613-821-3140
manager@osgoodemuseum.ca
www.osgoodemuseum.ca
twitter.com/OsgoodeMuseu m
www.facebook.com/125725207465630
The Osgoode Township Historical Society & Museum preserves the development of the Township of Osgoode, situated south of Ottawa, Ontario. Artifacts include indigenous Native & pioneer articles & documents, such as historic furniture & clothing, & agricultural tools & equipment. The Museum is open Tuesdays to Saturdays.
Robin Cushnie, Museum Manager, manager@osgoodemuseum.ca

***Vienna:* Edison Museum of Vienna**
14 Snow St.
Vienna, ON N0J 1Z0
Tel: 519-874-4999; *Fax:* 519-874-4999
Other contact information: Off season phone: 519-866-5521
Artifacts that belonged to relatives of Thomas Edison who lived in Vienna. Open mid-May to Labour Day.

***Wallaceburg:* Wallaceburg & District Museum**
505 King St.
Wallaceburg, ON N8A 1J1
Tel: 519-627-8962
curator@kent.net
www.kent.net/wallaceburg-museum
www.facebook.com/137635349604851
Year Founded: 1984 Local history

***Wallacetown:* Backus-Page House Museum**
PO Box 26, 29424 Lakeview Line
Wallacetown, ON N0L 2M0
Tel: 519-762-3072
info@backuspagehouse.ca
www.backuspagehouse.ca
Social Media: tyrconnellheritagesociety.blogspot.ca
twitter.com/BackusPageHouse
www. facebook.com/backuspagehouse
Year Founded: 1993 A living history museum featuring costumed interpreters & period artifacts. May-Oct., Tu-F 10:00-4:30, Sa & Su 12:00-4:30; open year-round by appointment.
David Ford, Cultural Manager

***Wasaga Beach:* Nancy Island Historic Site**
c/o Wasaga Beach Provincial Park, 11 - 22nd St. North
Location: 119 Mosley St., Wasaga Beach, ON
Wasaga Beach, ON L9Z 2V9
Tel: 705-429-2516; *Fax:* 705-429-7983
www.wasagabeachpark.com
Social Media: nancyislandblog.wordpress.com
twitter.com/FriendsofNancy
Remains of the British schooner "Nancy"; replica of Upper Lakes lighthouse; artifacts related to marine aspects of War of 1812
John Fisher, Superintendent, Wasaga Beach Provincial Park

***Waterford:* Waterford Heritage & Agricultural Museum**
159 Nichol St.
Waterford, ON N0E 1Y0
Tel: 519-443-4211
www.waterfordmuseum.ca
www.facebook.com/147540755302855
History of the Waterford & Townsend area; includes unique collection of agricultural equipment representative of southern Ontario
Melissa Collver, Curator & Director, melissa.collver@norfolkcounty.ca
James Christison, Museum Assistant, james.christison@norfolkcounty.ca

***Waterloo:* Brubacher House Museum**
c/o University of Waterloo, North Campus
Waterloo, ON N2L 3G6
Tel: 519-886-3855
bhouse@uwaterloo.ca
uwaterloo.ca
Built in 1850, the Brubacher House was later purchased by the University of Waterloo. The home's interior was rebuilt to reflect a Pennsylvania German Mennonite home from the 1850 to 1890 era. Many of the furnishings in the Brubacher House, collected from local Mennonite families, also reflect the time period. Operated by Conrad Grebel University College & the Mennonite Historical Society of Ontario, the House is open from the beginning of May to the end of October.

Waterloo: City of Waterloo Museum
Conestoga Mall, 550 King St. North
Waterloo, ON N2L 5W6

Tel: 519-885-8828
www.waterloo.ca/en/government/cityofwaterloomuseum.asp
Permanent collection is comprised of artifacts that relate to the Seagram family & the Seagram Distillery.

Waterloo: Earth Sciences Museum
Centre for Environmental & Information Technology, University of Waterloo, 200 University Ave. West
Waterloo, ON N2L 3G1

Tel: 519-888-4567
earthmuseum@uwaterloo.ca
uwaterloo.ca/earth-sciences-museum
Year Founded: 1967 Dinosaurs, gems, minerals & a 60-tonne rock garden
Corina McDonald, Curator, corina.mcdonald@uwaterloo.ca

Waterloo: Elliott Avedon Virtual Museum & Archive of Games
University of Waterloo, 200 University Avenue West
Waterloo, ON N2L 3G1

Tel: 519-888-4567
www.gamesmuseum.uwaterloo.ca
Year Founded: 1971 Specializes in the collection, presentation & display of games, both Canadian & international collections; researchers act as a resource for archiving related materials related to games & also provide research facilities & expertise to persons interested in pursuing the study of Games. The physical collection was relocated to the Canadian Museum of Civilization in 2009; the University of Waterloo currently maintains information about the collection on its website as a virtual museum.

Waterloo: Museum of Visual Science & Optometry
School of Optometry & Vision Science, University of Waterloo
Waterloo, ON N2L 3G1

Tel: 519-888-4567
optometry.uwaterloo.ca/museum-of-vision-science
Antique spectacles; eye examining equipment; historical documents & books; open; year round
Paul Lofthouse, Curator, plofthou@uwaterloo.ca

Wawa: Lake Superior Provincial Park Visitor Centre
PO Box 267
Wawa, ON P0S 1K0

Tel: 705-856-2284; *Fax:* 705-856-1333
info@lakesuperiorpark.ca
www.lakesuperiorpark.ca
Open from May - Oct., this interpretive centre includes information on the Lake Superior Provincial Park's natural & cultural features & the area's recreational opportunities

Welland: Welland Historical Museum
140 King St.
Welland, ON L3B 3J3

Tel: 905-732-2215; *Fax:* 905-732-9169
wellandhistoricalmuseum@cogeco.net
www.wellandmuseum.ca
twitter.com/We llandMuseum
www.facebook.com/212024838829918
History of Welland including the Welland Canal & its industries; open Tue.-Sat.; kids summer camps in July & Aug.; children's museum
Nora Reid, Executive Director, nr.wm@cogeco.net
Penny Morningstar, Curator, pm.wm@cogeco.net

Wellington: Wellington Heritage Museum
290 Main St.
Wellington, ON K0K 3L0

Tel: 613-399-5015
wellmuseum@pecounty.on.ca
pecounty.on.ca/government/community_development/museums/wellington.php
The local history collection of the Wellington Heritage Museum is housed within a Quaker Meeting House, which was built in 1885. The museum features a tribute to the Society of Friends, who helped develop the county. A special collection is the Douglas A. Crawford Canning Industry Collection. Wellington Heritage Museum is open from May to mid October.
Jennifer Lyons, Head Curator, Museums of Prince Edward County, 613-476-3833, museums@pecounty.on.ca

Westport: Rideau District Museum
29 Bedford St.
Westport, ON K0G 1X0

rdmuseum@kingston.net
www.rideaudistrictmuseum.webs.com
Year Founded: 1961 Housed in 1850s blacksmith & carriage shop with forges & bellows intact & showing many artifacts from the local district, including a 9-foot tall 19th-century statue of Sally Grant, the Blind Lady of Justice

White Lake: Waba Cottage Museum & Gardens
24 Museum Rd.
White Lake, ON K0A 3L0

Tel: 613-623-8853 *Toll-Free:* 800-957-4621
garden_visit@sympatico.ca
www3.sympatico.ca/jsktyrrell/museum.html
www .facebook.com/WabaCottageMuseumGardens
Year Founded: 1967 Situated in an 8-acre park amongst heritage buildings, boat launch & flower gardens.

White River: White River Heritage Museum
PO Box 583
Located 200 Elgin St., White River, ON
White River, ON P0M 3G0

Tel: 807-822-2657
Local history & Winnie the Pooh exhibit

Whitney: Algonquin Visitor Centre, Algonquin Logging Museum & Algonquin Art Centre
PO Box 219
Whitney, ON K0J 2M0

Tel: 613-637-2828; *Fax:* 613-637-2138
www.algonquinpark.on.ca
Social Media: www.youtube.com/user/FOAPAlgonquinPark
twitter.com/AlgonquinPark
www.f acebook.com/TheFriendsofAlgonquinPark
Other contact information: Park Information: 705-633-5572
Visitor Centre contains exhibits on the Park's natural & human history, restaurant, & bookstore; wheelchair accessible; Logging Museum presents the history of logging from 1830's to current times; exhibits include a recreated Camboose camp & a steam powered amphibious tug; Art Centre has indoor & outdoor galleries & offers art activities. Visitor Centre open year round. Logging Museum open daily 9:00-5:00 from late June until Thanksgiving.
Rick Stronks, Chief Park Naturalist

Wiarton: The Gallery of Early Canadian Flight
c/o Brian Reis, RR#3
Located at Wiarton-Keppel Airport, Wiarton, ON
Wiarton, ON N0H 2T0

Tel: 519-534-4090; *Fax:* 519-534-3184
earlycanflight@sympatico.ca
www.canflightmuseum.org
Located in the Wiarton-Keppel Airport, the museum's collection includes photos, posters, & artists' prints of significant moments in Canadian aviation history, as well as models of pioneering aircraft, & historically important videos. Open year-round, daily 8:30-6:30, or by appointment.

Williamstown: Bethune-Thompson House
19730 John St.
Williamstown, ON K0C 2J0

Tel: 613-347-7192
Year Founded: 1977 The house was first built in 1784 by an early settler to the Williamstown area, & is now a National Historic Site.

Williamstown: The Nor'Westers & Loyalist Museum
PO Box 69
Located at 19651 County Rd. 17, Williamstown, ON
Williamstown, ON K0C 2J0

Tel: 613-347-3547
info@norwestersandloyalistmuseum.ca
norwestersandloyal istmuseum.ca
twitter.com/NorWestLoyalist
www.facebook.com/NorWestersAn dLoyalistMuseum
Year Founded: 1967 Housed in a Georgian-style building; stories of loyalist pioneers & partners of the Northwest Fur Trade Company
Graham Wells, Co-Chair
Robin Flockton, Co-Chair

Windsor: Ojibway Nature Centre
5200 Matchette Rd.
Windsor, ON N9C 4E8

Tel: 519-966-5852
www.ojibway.ca
twitter.com/OjibwayPark
The Ojibway Nature Centre presents displays about the natural history & ecology of the Ojibway Prairie Complex. Visitors will also discover a live exhibit area, featuring the Eastern Fox Snake & the Eastern Massasauga Rattlesnake. The Centre is staffed by naturalists, who provide lessons & conducted tours. Events & programs are available for all ages.

Windsor: Serbian Heritage Museum of Windsor (SHM)
6770 Tecumseh Rd. East
Windsor, ON N8T 1E6

Tel: 519-944-4884
info@serbianheritagemuseum.com
www.serbianheritagemuseum.com
Social Media: www.youtube.com/user/shmuseum
www.facebook.com/shmuseum
Year Founded: 1987 Artifacts & archival material of Serbian people in Windsor dating back to 1920s; tours, educational programming & lectures; gift shop; open year round

Windsor: Willistead Manor
1899 Niagara St.
Windsor, ON N8Y 1K3

Tel: 519-253-2365; *Fax:* 519-253-5101
willistead@city.windsor.on.ca
36-room mansion, built 1904-1906; viewing by appt. Available for special events.

Windsor: Windsor's Community Museum
254 Pitt St. West
Windsor, ON N9A 5L5

Tel: 519-253-1812; *Fax:* 519-253-0919
wmuseum@city.windsor.on.ca
www.citywindsor.ca/residents/Culture/Windsors-Community-Museum
Year Founded: 1958 The Museum includes the François Baby House on Pitt St. W., & the Duff-Baby Interpretation Centre, located at 221 Mill St.; changing exhibits on the history of the Windsor region; houses over 15,000 artifacts, paintings, drawings, prints & photos, maps, newspapers & books, & a large archival collection. Open year round.

Wingham: North Huron District Museum
PO Box 1522
Located at 273 Josephine St., Wingham, ON
Wingham, ON N0G 2W0

Tel: 519-357-1096; *Fax:* 519-357-1110
nhmuseum@northhuron.ca
Special events & bi-monthly exhibits featuring the history of North Huron's writers, painters, businesses, farmers & people; Special exhibit & garden dedicated to Alice Munro

Woodstock: Woodstock Museum National Historic Site
Museum Square, 466 Dundas St.
Woodstock, ON N4S 1C4

Tel: 519-537-8411; *Fax:* 519-537-7235
museum@city.woodstock.on.ca
www.woodstockmuseum.ca
The Woodstock Museum National Historic Site exhibits the local history of Woodstock from 10,000 B.C. to 2001. At the former Town Hall & Market House, which was built in 1853, visitors can see the 1879 Council Chambers & the 1889 Grand Hall. The museum contains a research room, with books & vertical files. It is open to the public by appointment only. School education programs are available, by phoning 519-539-2382, extension 2903. The museum is open year-round.
Karen Houston, Curator, khouston@city.woodstock.on.ca

Prince Edward Island

Provincial Museum

Prince Edward Island Museum & Heritage Foundation / Le Musée et la Fondation du patrimoine de l'Ile-du-Prince-Édouard
2 Kent St.
Charlottetown, PE C1A 1M6

Tel: 902-368-6600; *Fax:* 902-368-6608
mhpei@gov.pe.ca
www.peimuseum.com
Social Media: www.flickr.com/photos/pei_museum
twitter.com/PEIMUSEUM
www.facebook.co m/124989037532122
The organization is the operator of seven provincial museums & heritage sites across Prince Edward Island. Sites include the Elmira Railway Museum, Basin Head Fisheries Museum, Orwell Corner Historic Village & Agricultural Museum, Beaconsfield Historic House, Eptek Art & Culture Centre, The Acadian Museum of Prince Edward Island, & Green Park Shipbuilding Museum & Yeo House. Open year-round are the Beaconsfield Historic House, the Eptek Art & Culture Centre, & the The Acadian Museum of Prince Edward Island. The others are open during the summer months. The Prince Edward Island Museum & Heritage Foundation also has the responsibility for the provincial collection of over 90,000 artifacts.

Local Museums

Alberton: Alberton Museum
PO Box 515
Located at 457 Church St., Alberton, PE
Alberton, PE C0B 1B0
Tel: 902-853-4048; *Fax:* 902-853-4066
ahf@isn.net
www.townofalberton.ca/history/museum.htm
Year Founded: 1964 Genealogy resources on area families; old photo collection; history of the fox industry; Micmac Indian displays; displays of antique furniture, glassware, textiles & toys. Open June - Sept.

Belfast: Point Prim Lighthouse
1178 Point Prim Rd., RR#1
Belfast, PE C0A 1A0
Tel: 902-659-2559
info@heroncovepei.com
The oldest lighthouse in PEI, built in 1845; now serves as a museum featuring historical displays & artifacts; open mid-June through mid-Sept., with guided tours offered in July & Aug.

Bideford: Bideford Parsonage Museum
#166, 784 Bideford Rd.
Bideford, PE C0B 1J0
Tel: 902-831-3133
bpm.bideford@pei.sympatico.ca
www.bidefordparsonagemuseum.com
Owned & operated by the West Country Historical Society Inc.; Lucy Maud Montgomery boarded at the home from 1894-95.

Cavendish: Ripley's Believe It or Not! Museum
8863 Cavendish Rd.
Cavendish, PE C0A 1M0
Tel: 902-963-2242
cavendishentertainment.com
Ripley's presents displays of unual events & things; open June - Sept.
Thom McMillan, Contact, thom.mac@pei.aibn.com

Charlottetown: Ardgowan National Historic Site of Canada
2 Palmers Lane
Charlottetown, PE C1A 5V8
Tel: 902-566-7050; *Fax:* 902-566-7226
www.pc.gc.ca/eng/lhn-nhs/pe/ardgowan/index.aspx
Restored house originally belonging to William Henry Pope, one of the Fathers of Confederation.

Charlottetown: Car Life Museum Inc.
45 Oak Dr.
Charlottetown, PE C1A 6T6
Tel: 902-675-3555
carlifemuseum.com
Other contact information: Cell Phone: 902-629-9777
Located on Highway 1 in Bonshaw, Prince Edward Island, the Car Life Museum features restored cars which date back to 1898. The museum also houses farm machinery from the early 1800s & the early 1900s. The Car Life Museum is open from June to September.
Doris MacKay, Contact

Charlottetown: Founder's Hall - Canada's Birthplace Pavillion / Salle des fondateurs
6 Prince St.
Charlottetown, PE C1A 4P5
Tel: 902-368-1864 *Toll-Free:* 800-955-1864
www.foundershall.ca
Founder's Hall stands on the site where deleates to the Charlottetown Conference arrived, & presents the story of Canada's growth as a nation; also the site of the Charlottetown Visitor Information Centre.

Charlottetown: Green Gables Heritage Place
2 Palmers Lane
Charlottetown, PE C1A 5V8
Tel: 902-963-7874; *Fax:* 902-963-7869
greengables.info@pc.gc.ca
www.pc.gc.ca/eng/lhn-nhs/pe/greengables/visit.aspx
Dedicated to Anne of Green Gables, a fictional but nonetheless, famous character created by Lucy Maud Montgomery for her book series "Anne of Green Gables". Open May 1 - Oct. 31

Charlottetown: Port-la-Joye-Fort Amherst National Historic Site of Canada
c/o Parks Canada, 2 Palmer's Lane
Located at 191 Hache Gallant Lane, Rocky Point, PEI
Charlottetown, PE C1A 5V8
Tel: 902-566-7626; *Fax:* 902-566-8295
pljfa.info@pc.gc.ca
www.pc.gc.ca/lhn-nhs/pe/amherst/activ.aspx
Other contact information: Summer Phone: 902-675-2220
Visitors to the Port-la-Joye-Fort Amherst National Historic Site of Canada learn the history of the Mi'kmaq of Prince Edward Island. Interpretive services are available in July & August. Guided tours are offered in both English & French. The grounds are open from June to October.

Charlottetown: Prince Edward Island Regiment (RCAC) Museum
Queen Charlotte Armouries, PO Box 1480
Located at 2 Halivand St., Charlottetown, PE
Charlottetown, PE C1A 7N1
Tel: 902-368-0108; *Fax:* 902-368-3034
www.facebook.com/107780305912036

Charlottetown: Province House National Historic Site of Canada
c/o Parks Canada, 2 Palmer's Lane
Location: 165 Richmind St., Charlottetown, PEI C1A 1J1
Charlottetown, PE C1A 5V6
Tel: 902-566-8287; *Fax:* 902-566-8295
www.pc.gc.ca/eng/lhn-nhs/pe/provincehouse/index.aspx
Includes Confederation Chamber, site of historic discussions regarding union of the BNA colonies; remains of the Legislative Bldg. for PEI; open year round

Charlottetown: Spoke Wheel Car Museum
RR#3
Charlottetown, PE C1A 7J7
Antique automobiles

Hunter River: Farmers' Bank of Rustico Museum & Doucet House
RR#3
Hunter River, PE C0A 1N0
Tel: 902-963-3168; *Fax:* 902-963-2906
info@farmersbank.ca
www.farmersbank.ca
twitter.com/farmersbankpei
ww w.facebook.com/219236821451017
Other contact information: Off-season: 902-963-2194
Banking artifacts; precursor to the Credit Union movement in North America; also an early Acadian Doucet House, one of the oldest houses in the province
J.D. MacDonald, President

Kensington: Anne of Green Gables Museum at Silver Bush
5 Gerald McCarville Dr.
Location: 4542 Rte. 20, Park Corner, PE
Kensington, PE C0B 1M0
Tel: 902-886-2884 *Toll-Free:* 800-665-2663
info@annemuseum.com
www.annemuseum.com
Open May - Thanksgiving

Kensington: The Keir Memorial Museum
2214 Rte. 20
Kensington, PE C0B 1M0
Tel: 902-836-3054
kmmuseum@bellaliant.com
www.malpequebay.ca/keirmuseum.htm
Open July - Sept.

Kensington: Veterans' Memorial Military Museum
PO Box 182, 88 Victoria St.
Kensington, PE C0B 1M0
Tel: 902-836-3600
www.kata.pe.ca/attract/veteran/veteran.htm
Military memorabilia mostly from WWI & WWII; Boer War items
Fred Thibeau, Manager

Miminegash: Irish Moss Interpretive Centre & Museum
Rte. 14
Miminegash, PE C0B 1S0
Tel: 902-882-4313
Details the history of Irish moss harvesting through photographs & artifacts; next door visitors can sample dishes made from Irish moss, such as seeweed pie.

Montague: Garden of the Gulf Museum
PO Box 1237, 564 Main St.
Montague, PE C0A 1R0
Tel: 902-838-2467
www.montaguemuseumpei.com
Other contact information: Off-season Phone: 902-838-2820
Year Founded: 1958 Early island history; open June - Sept. PEI's oldest Museum.
Donna Collings, Curator

Montague: Roma at Three Rivers / Roma à Trois Rivières
Three Rivers Roma Inc., PO Box 758
Montague, PE C0A 1R0
Tel: 902-838-3413
roma1732@gmail.com
www.roma3rivers.com
twitter.com/Roma_3_Rivers
www.facebook.com/RomaAtT hreeRivers
A national historic site depicting the settlement established in 1732 by Jean Pierre Roma.
Marlo Dodge, Site Manager

O'Leary: Canadian Potato Museum
PO Box 602
O'Leary, PE C0B 1V0
Tel: 902-859-2039 *Toll-Free:* 800-565-3457
info@peipotatomuseum.com
www.peipotatomuseum.com
www.facebook.com/grou ps/138711350502
The history of the potato industry is depicted at the Prince Edward Island Potato Museum. Visitors will see a collection of machinery & farm implements related to growing & harvesting potatoes. The museum also includes the Potato Hall of Fame, & a 14-foot-high potato sculpture. It is open from mid May to mid October.
Donna Rowley, Manager, 902-853-2312

Richmond: The Bottle Houses / Les Maisons de Bouteilles
PO Box 72
Richmond, PE C0B 2E0
Tel: 902-854-2987
www.teleco.org/SitesWebs/bouteilles/index.html
Other contact information: Off season: 902-854-2254
Three buildings made of over 25,000 vari-coloured bottles; the in sides are lit in a variety of colours; located in Cape Egmont; flower gardens; giftshop; bilingual service
Réjeanne Arsenault, Owner & Operator

Sherwood: Prince Edward Island Sports Hall of Fame & Museum Inc.
PO Box 20044
Sherwood, PE C1A 9E3
Tel: 902-436-0423; *Fax:* 902-368-4548
publicrelations@sportpei.pe.ca
www.peisportshalloffame.ca
Year Founded: 1968 Open July-Aug., Mon-Fri.; other times by appointment

Summerside: Bishop's Machine Shop Museum
PO Box 1510, 101 Water St.
Summerside, PE C1N 4K4
Tel: 902-432-1296; *Fax:* 902-432-1328
culturesummerside.com/bishops-machine-shop-museum
Social Media: www.youtube.com/user/culturesummerside
twitter.com/culturesside
www.fa cebook.com/CultureSummerside
Historical machine shop complete with lathes & machining tools.
Lori Ellis, Manager, Heritage & Cultural Properties, lori.ellis@city.summerside.pe.ca

Summerside: International Fox Museum & Hall of Fame Inc.
286 Fitzroy St.
Summerside, PE C1N 1J2
Tel: 902-436-0177
toxpei@isn.net
Located at historic Holman Homestead & Gardens; museum tells the story of the PEI silver fox industry heyday between 1894 & WWII
Julie Simmons, Contact

***Summerside:* Lefurgey Cultural Centre**
PO Box 1510, 205 Prince St.
Summerside, PE C1N 4K4
Tel: 902-432-1327; *Fax:* 902-432-1328
info@wyattheritage.com
www.wyattheritage.com/mainsite/lefurgey
Social Media: www.youtube.com/user/culturesummerside
twitter.com/culturesside
www.facebook.com/CultureSummerside
Other contact information: Alt. URL:
culturesummerside.com/lefurgey-cultural-center
An 1867 shipbuilder's home, now dedicated to arts education; operated by Wyatt Heritage Properties
Lori Ellis, Manager, Heritage & Cultural Properties, lori.ellis@city.summerside.pe.ca

***Summerside:* MacNaught History Centre & Archives**
PO Box 1510, 75 Spring St.
Summerside, PE C1N 4K4
Tel: 902-432-1296; *Fax:* 902-432-1328
www.wyattheritage.com/mainsite3/macnaughthouse.asp
Social Media: www.youtube.com/user/culturesummerside
twitter.com/culturesside
www.fa cebook.com/CultureSummerside
Other contact information: Alt. URL:
culturesummerside.com/macnaught-history-centre
Administrative headquarters for Wyatt Heritage Properties, featuring exhibits on local Summerside history.
Lori Ellis, Manager, Heritage & Cultural Properties, lori.ellis@city.summerside.pe.ca

***Summerside:* The Wyatt House Museum**
PO Box 1510, 85 Spring St.
Summerside, PE C1N 4K4
Tel: 902-432-1296; *Fax:* 902-432-1328
www.wyattheritage.com/mainsite3/macnaughthouse.asp
Social Media: www.youtube.com/user/culturesummerside
twitter.com/culturesside
www.fa cebook.com/CultureSummerside
Other contact information: Alt. URL:
culturesummerside.com/wyatt-historic-house-museum
Restored 1867 house of Wanda Lefurgey Wyatt, operated by Wyatt Heritage Properties.
Lori Ellis, Manager, Heritage & Cultural Properties, lori.ellis@city.summerside.pe.ca

***Tignish:* Tignish Cultural Centre**
103 School St.
Tignish, PE C0B 2B0
Tel: 902-882-7363
www.tignish.com
Local history

***Vernon Bridge:* The Macphail Homestead**
Sir Andrew Macphail Foundation
Vernon Bridge, PE COA 2E0
Tel: 902-651-2789
info@macphailhomestead.ca
www.macphailhomestead.ca
An educational facility & interpretive centre dedicated to honouring Sir Andrew Macphail.
Mary Elliott, Site Manager

***West Point:* West Point Lighthouse**
Lot 8, 364 Cedar Dunes Park Rd.
West Point, PE C0B 1V0
Tel: 902-859-3605*Toll-Free:* 800-764-6854
westpointlighthouse1@gmail.com
www.westpointlighthouse.com
Year Founded: 1983 The West Point Development Corporation restored the historic West Point Lighthouse, which was built in 1875 & had a keeper until 1963. The lighthouse is one of the tallest on Prince Edward Island. Today, the lighthouse continues to operate as a navigational aid.

***Woods Islands:* Woods Islands Lighthouse**
173 Lighthouse Rd.
Woods Islands, PE C0A 1B0
Tel: 902-962-3110
lightkeepers@woodislandslighthouse.com
www.woodislands lighthouse.com
The restored 1876 lighthouse acts as an interpretive museum with 10 themed rooms & historical displays.
Kris Rollins, Contact, 902-962-3498
Bev Stewart, Contact, 902-962-3110

Québec

Provincial Museums

Canadian Centre for Architecture (CCA) / Centre Canadien d'Architecture
1920, rue Baile
Montréal, QC H3H 2S6
Tel: 514-939-7026
info@cca.qc.ca
www.cca.qc.ca
twitter.com/ccawire
www.facebook.com/cca.conversation
Other contact information: Phone, Administration: 514-939-7000
Year Founded: 1979 The Canadian Centre for Architecture is a museum & an international research centre. The Centre raises awareness of the role of architecture, stimulates design innovation, & promotes scholarly research.
Mirko Zardini, Director & Chief Curator

McCord Museum of Canadian History / Musée McCord d'histoire canadienne
690, rue Sherbrooke ouest
Montréal, QC H3A 1E9
Tel: 514-398-7100
info.mccord@mccord-stewart.ca
www.mccord-museum.qc.ca
Social Media: www.youtube.com/user/MuseeMcCordMuseum
twitter.com/MuseeMcCord
www.fac ebook.com/museemccord
Year Founded: 1921 The museum started with the collections of David Ross McCord & a building from McGill University. It conserves a variety of objects reflecting the social history & material culture of Montréal, Québec & Canada. Exhibits include over 1,440,000 pieces & range from paintings, costumes & decorative arts, to archives of texts & photographs. Open year round with summer/winter hours.
Suzanne Sauvage, President & CEO
Sylvie Durand, Director, Programs
Philip Leduc, Director, Operations

Musée de l'Amerique francophone (MAF)
2, côte de la Fabrique
Québec, QC G1R 3V6
Tél: 418-692-2843; *Téléc:* 418-646-9705
renseignements@mcq.org
www.mcq.org/en/maf/index.html
Le plus ancien musée au Canada; la collection regroupe des instruments d'enseignement des sciences, monnaies anciennes, médailles, collections de minéralogie, de géologie, de numismatique, de zoologie, de botanique, de fossiles, livres anciens, et de peinture; expositions et activités; centre de référence; boutique; café.
Stéphan La Roche, Directeur-général

Musée de la civilisation (MCQ)
CP 155 B, 85, rue Dalhousie
Québec, QC G1K 8R2
Tél: 418-643-2158; *Téléc:* 418-646-9705
Ligne sans frais: 866-710-8031
renseignements@mcq.org
www.mcq.org
Médias sociaux: www.youtube.com/mcqpromo
twitter.com/mcqorg
www.facebook.com/museedelacivilisation
Fondée en: 1988 Le musée est doté de la plus importante collection ethnographique et historique du Québec et se distingue par sa muséologie innovatrice; programmation thématique; activités éducatives et culturelles; ateliers, visites commentées; boutique; café.
Stéphan La Roche, Directeur général

Pointe-à-Callière, Montréal Museum of Archaeology & History
Angle de la Commune, 350, place Royale
Montréal, QC H2Y 3Y5
Tel: 514-872-9150
info@pacmusee.qc.ca
www.pacmusee.qc.ca
twitter.com/PointeaCalliere
www.facebook.com/637800 79931
Year Founded: 1992 The Montréal Museum of Archaeology & History is situated on the site where, in 1642, a mass celebrated the founding of Montréal. Pointe-à-Callière was also the location of a home built in 1688 by the third governor of Montréal, Chevalier Louis Hector de Callière. The site features architectural remains, & the museum houses hundreds of artifacts.
Andrew Molson, President
Francine Lelièvre, Executive Director
John LeBoutillier, Secretary-Treasurer

Local Museums

***Alma:* L'Odyssée des Bâtisseurs**
1671, av du Pont Nord
Alma, QC G8B 5G2
Tél: 418-668-2606; *Téléc:* 418-668-5851
Ligne sans frais: 866-668-2606
info@odysseedesbatisseurs.com
www.odysseedesbatisseurs.com
www.facebook.com/OdysseeDesBatisseurs
Axé sur l'importance de l'eau au coeur du développement, le parc thématique L'Odyssée des Bâtisseurs vous invite à visiter des expositions vivantes, admirer un panorama naturel et industriel extraordinaire et vivre une expérience multimédia 360 saisissante à l'intérieur d'un ancien château d'eau.
Alexandre Garon, Directeur générale, 418-668-2606, agaron@shlsj.org

***Alouette:* Musée de la Défense aérienne de Bagotville / Bagotville Air Defense Museum**
CP 567 Main
6513, ch. St-Anicet, La Baie, QC, G7B 3N8
Alouette, QC G0V 1A0
Tél: 418-677-7159; *Téléc:* 418-677-4104
museebagotville@forces.qc.ca
www.museebagotville.ca
www.facebook.com/m useedefenseaerienne
Fondée en: 1997 Le musée présente une collection d'uniformes et les avions qui ont été employés par l'armée de l'air canadienne. Il est ouvert chaque jour du juin au sept, du 9h à 17h.

***Angliers:* Site historique T.E Draper/Chantier de Gédéon**
***Parent:* Les Promoteurs d'Angliers inc.**
CP 82, 14, rue de la Baie Miller
Angliers, QC J0Z 1A0
Tél: 819-949-4431; *Téléc:* 819-949-4431
tedraper@tlb.sympatico.ca
www.tedraper.ca
Montez à bord du remorqueur de bois T.E. Draper; visitez le chantier de Gédéon, la reconstitution d'un camp de bûcherons des années 1930-1940.
Cathy Fraser, Contact, tedraper@hotmail.com

***Authier:* École du Rang II d'Authier**
269, rang II
Authier, QC J0Z 1C0
Tél: 819-782-3289; *Téléc:* 819-782-2421
Ligne sans frais: 866-336-3289
info@ecoledurang2.com
www.ecoledurang2.com
www.faceb ook.com/172772349545122
Fondée en: 1983 Représente les écoles de rang qui ont meublé le paysage rural du Québec dans les années quarantes

***Batiscan:* Vieux presbytère de Batiscan**
340, rue Principale
Batiscan, QC G0X 1A0
Tél: 418-362-2051; *Téléc:* 418-362-1373
direction@presbytere-batiscan.com
www.presbytere-batiscan.com
Datant de 1816, propose une reconstitution fidèle de l'intérieur de la maison au milieu du 19e siècle; aperçu du quotidien du curé Fréchette et de sa ménagère Adéline, les deux habitants du presbytère à cette époque; exposition temporaire à chaque année; sentier ornithologique; aire de repos et de pique-nique; boutique souvenir.

***Beauharnois:* Pointe-du-Buisson/Musée québécois d'archéologie**
***Parent:* Société d'archéologie préhistorique du Québec**
333, rue Émond
Beauharnois, QC J6N 0E3
Tel: 450-429-7857; *Fax:* 450-429-5921
administration@pointedubuisson.com
www.pointedubuisson.com
twitter.com /PointeDuBuisson
www.facebook.com/pointedubuisson.museeQuébecoisdarcheol ogie
Year Founded: 1986 Site archéologique; objets préhistoriques qui forment une collection qui est reconnu dans le monde scientifique comme l'un des plus importants dans le nord-est du continent; recherche, l'éducation de sensibilisation; plus de deux millions d'objets et fragments d'objets et écofacts qui marquent SW Québec.
Caroline Nantel, Directrice générale, direction@pointedubuisson.com

Beaumont: Moulin de Beaumont
2, rte du Fleuve
Beaumont, QC G0R 1C0
Tél: 418-833-1867
Moulin à farine de 1821

Beloeil: Muséobus - Le Musée des enfants
10, rue St-Matthieu
Beloeil, QC J3G 2W1
Tél: 450-464-0201; Téléc: 450-446-4644
info@museobus.qc.ca
www.museobus.qc.ca
www.facebook.com/12637187070714 6
Musée mobile aménagé dans des autobus scolaires; propose des expositions scientifiques interactives et des sentiers d'interprétation; piste d'hébertisme et aire de pique-nique; programmation; Camp Éco Nature.

Bergeronnes: Centre Archéo Topo
498, rue de la Mer
Bergeronnes, QC G0T 1G0
Tél: 418-232-6286; Téléc: 418-232-6695
Ligne sans frais: 866-832-6286
archeo95@bellnet.ca
www.archeotopo.com
L'histoire de la région de La Haute-Côte-Nord; exposition interactive retrace la vie des tribus amérindiennes dans la région; jeux didactiques; ateliers pour les enfants et les jeunes; excursions; spectacle multimédia; boutique.
Joëlle Pierre, Directrice générale, archeo95@bellnet.ca

Bergeronnes: Centre d'interprétation et d'observation de Cap-de-Bon-Désir
13, ch du Cap-de-Bon-Désir
Bergeronnes, QC G0T 1G0
Tel: 418-232-6751; Fax: 418-235-4192
Toll-Free: 888-773-8888
information@pc.gc.ca
www.Québecmaritime.ca
Other contact information: hors saison: 418-235-4703
Promontoire naturel pour l'observation des mammifères marins; guides-interprètes; salle d'exposition, phare. Ouvert mi-juin-mi-octobre.

Berthierville: Chapelle des Cuthbert de Berthier
461, rue de Bienville
Berthierville, QC J0K 1A0
Tél: 450-836-7336
www.lachapelledescuthbert.com
www.facebook.com/125624117520547
Autre numéros: hors saison: 450-836-8158
Fondée en: 1958 La plus ancien temple protestant au Québec; expositions, visites commentées; pique-nique sur place; ouverte tous les jours, du juin au fête du Travil, 10h-18h

Berthierville: Musée Gilles-Villeneuve
960, av Gilles-Villeneuve
Berthierville, QC J0K 1A0
Tél: 450-836-2714; Téléc: 450-836-3067
Ligne sans frais: 800-639-0103
museegillesvilleneuve@bellnet.ca
www.museegillesvilleneuve.com
www.facebook.com/MuseeGillesVilleneuveMuse um
Fondée en: 1995 Le musée a pour mandat perpétuer le souvenir de Gilles Villeneuve, le grand coureur automobile du F1; voitures, photographies, Galerie M. Trudel.
Alain Bellehumeur, Président et directeur général

Bonaventure: Musée acadien du Québec à Bonaventure
95, av Port Royal
Bonaventure, QC G0C 1E0
Tél: 418-534-4000; Téléc: 418-534-4105
reception@museeacadien.com
www.museeacadien.com
www.facebook.com/20592 9912758086
Louise Cyr, Directeur, 418-538-4000, direction@museeacadien.com

Boucherville: Maison Louis-Hippolyte Lafontaine
314, boul Marie-Victorin
Boucherville, QC J4B 1X1
Tél: 514-449-8347
maison.lh.lafontaine@boucherville.ca
Expose des objets de la vie de Louis-Hippolyte La Fontaine et l'histoire de Boucherville.

Cascapédia-Saint-Jules: Musée de la rivière Cascapédia / The Cascapedia River Museum
275, rte 299
Cascapédia-Saint-Jules, QC G0C 1T0
Tél: 418-392-5079
cascapedia_museum@globetrotter.net
www.cascapediariver.com/museum.shtml
Le musée raconte l'histoire de la région autour de la rivière Cascapédia, la pêche au saumon, et le patrimoine gaspésien; boutique.
Mary Robertson, Contact

Causapscal: Maison Dr. Joseph-Frenette
3, rue Frenette
Causapscal, QC G0J 1J0
Tél: 418-756-5999; Téléc: 418-756-3344
www.maisondrjosephfrenette.ca
Joseph Frenette exerçait la profession, aujourd'hui disparue, de médecin de campagne. Il consacra sa vie à soigner des malades et des blessés, à faire naître des enfants, à sauver des vies. Tel un livre ouvert, cette exposition fait découvrir son univers familial et professionnel et à comprendre le rôle primordial du médecin de campagne dans l'histoire du Québec.

Causapscal: Site historique Matamajaw
53, rue Saint-Jacques sud
Causapscal, QC G0J 1J0
Tél: 418-756-5999; Téléc: 418-756-3344
faucuscar@globetrotter.net
www.sitehistoriquematamajaw.com
www.faceboo k.com/SitehistoriqueMatamajaw
Ancien lieu de villégiature de Sir John A. McDonald et de Lord Mount Stephen, le Matamajaw Salmon Club a attiré les membres de la haute société anglaise, américaine et canadienne durant la fin du 19e et au début du 20e siècle. Le Site Matamajaw est le seul ancien établissement privé accessible au public en Amérique du Nord.

Chambly: Lieu historique du Fort-Chambly
2, rue Richelieu
Chambly, QC J3L 2B9
Tél: 514-658-1585; Téléc: 514-658-7216
Ligne sans frais: 888-773-8888
parcscanada-que@pc.gc.ca
www.pc.gc.ca/fra/lhn-nhs/qc/fortchambly/index.aspx
Autre numéros: TTY: 1-866-787-6221
Présente l'histoire et les coutumes de la Nouvelle-France de 1665-1760; expositions; activités.

Chambord: Village Historique de Val-Jalbert / Historical Village of Val-Jalbert
95, rue St-Georges
Chambord, QC G0W 1G0
Tél: 418-275-3132; Téléc: 418-275-5875
Ligne sans frais: 888-675-3132
valjalbert@valjalbert.com
www.valjalbert.com
Médias sociaux: www.youtube.com/user/valjalbert1901
www.facebook.com/426543094744
Partiellement restauré ville morte; créée par l'ouverture d'une usine de pâtes et papiers 1901; au fil des années par la ville a prospéré et plusieurs services et les bâtiments ont été ajoutés, notamment une gare, couvent, hôtel et un magasin général; le 13 août 1927, la plante arrêté obligeant les travailleurs à quitter Val-Jalbert; aujourd'hui, il est un patrimoine historique, industriel et religieux.
Dany Bouchard, Directeur général, dbouchard@valjalbert.com

Château-Richer: Centre d'interpretation de la Côte-de-Beaupré
CP 40, 7976, av Royale
Château-Richer, QC G0A 1N0
Tél: 418-824-3677; Téléc: 418-824-5907
Ligne sans frais: 877-824-3677
info@histoire-cotedebeaupre.org
www.histoire-cotedebeaupre.org
www.facebook.com/centredinterpretationdel acotedebeaupre
Fondée en: 1984 Présente les aspects culturels, géographiques, historiques et patrimoniaux qui témoignent de la beauté de la région; activités pédagogiques complémentaires au programme d'enseignement; ouvert tous les jours, 9h30-16h30
Luc Trépanier, Directeur général

Château-Richer: Musée de l'Abeille
8862, boul Sainte-Anne
Château-Richer, QC G0A 1N0
Tél: 418-824-4411; Téléc: 418-824-4422
info@musee-abeille.com
www.musee-abeille.com
www.facebook.com/25518447 6641
Centre d'interprétation; l'exposition Des Abeilles et Des Hommes; visites guidées; informations sur le miel; boutique.
Redmond Hayes, President

Chelsea: Mackenzie King Estate / Domaine Mackenzie-King
c/o Gatineau Park Visitor Centre, 33 Scott Rd.
Chelsea, QC J9B 1R5
Tel: 819-827-2020 Toll-Free: 800-465-1867
info@ncc-ccn.ca
www.canadascapital.gc.ca/places-to-visit/mackenzie-king- estate
Other contact information: TTY: 1-866-661-3530
Located in Gatineau Park; open daily from mid-May to the end of Oct.

Chicoutimi: Centre historique des Soeurs de Notre-Dame du Bon-Conseil de Chicoutimi (NDBC)
700, rue Racine est
Chicoutimi, QC G7H 1V2
Tél: 418-543-4861; Téléc: 418-543-7194
centrehistorique@sndbc.qc.ca
www.centrehistoriquesndbc.com
www.faceboo k.com/284659404922937

Chicoutimi: La Pulperie de Chicoutimi / Musée régional
300, rue Dubuc
Chicoutimi, QC G7J 4M1
Tél: 418-698-3100; Téléc: 418-698-3158
Ligne sans frais: 877-998-3100
info@pulperie.com
www.pulperie.com
Médias sociaux: www.youtube.com/user/PulperieChicoutimi
www.facebook.com/PulperiedeChicoutimi
Collection de plus de 26 000 ojets et oeuvres; maison Arthur-Villeneuve; expositions d'art et d'ethnologie; vestiges restaurés des anciennes installations de la Compagnie de pulpe de Chicoutimi; parc.
Jacques Fortin, Directeur général, 418-698-3100, jfortin@pulperie.com

Claybank: Claybank Brick Plant Historical Museum & National Historic Site
Parent: Claybank Brick Plant Historical Society
PO Box 2-5
Claybank, S0H 0W0
Tel: 306-868-4774; Fax: 306-868-4854
claybank@sasktel.net
claybank.sasktelwebsite.net
The museum is a well-preserved brick plant dating from 1914, & has been designated a National Historic Site. Visitors can also explore the surrounding Massold Clay Canyons area, & hike on a variety of nature trails. Open May-Aug., daily 10:00-12:00 & 1:00-5:00, or by appointment.

Coaticook: Beaulne Museum / Musée Beaulne
96, rue Union
Coaticook, QC J1A 1Y9
Tel: 819-849-6560; Fax: 819-849-9519
info@museebeaulne.qc.ca
www.museebeaulne.qc.ca
www.facebook.com/163224 930454865
Other contact information: Alternative E-mail: bonjour@museebeaulne.qc.ca
Year Founded: 1964 Beaulne Museum depicts the history & achievements of the local Norton family, who were known for manufacturing railway jacks & their philanthropy. The museum is located in Château Arthur Osmore Norton, a Victorian-style mansion which was built in 1912. Beaulne Museum is open year-round from Tuesday to Sunday.

Cookshire-Eaton: Compton County Historical Museum Society / Société d'histoire du musée du comté Compton
374 Rte 253
Cookshire-Eaton, QC J0B 1M0
Tel: 819-875-5256; Fax: 819-875-3182
mus.eatoncorner@gmail.com
www.mus.eatoncorner.com
Year Founded: 1959 Housed in a former Congregationalist Church built in 1842. Address is 374 Route 253, Eaton Corner, Québec.

Pat Boychuck, President, 819-875-5256,
mus.eatoncorner@gmail.com

Coteau-du-Lac: Lieu historique national du Canada de Coteau-du-Lac / Coteau-du-Lac National Historic Site of Canada
308A, ch du Fleuve
Coteau-du-Lac, QC J0P 1B0
Tél: 450-763-5631; *Téléc:* 450-763-1654
Ligne sans frais: 888-773-8888
information@pc.gc.ca
www.pc.gc.ca/fra/lhn-nhs/qc/coteaudulac/index.aspx
Autre numéros: **ATS: 1-866-787-6221**
Exposition et activités: le site stratégique de Coteau-du-Lac, le Blockhaus, coin de famille, circuit nature, jardin archéologique, reconstitution militaire, marché champêtre.

Cowansville: Musée Bruck
225, rue Principale
Cowansville, QC J2K 1J4
Tél: 450-263-6101; *Téléc:* 450-266-7547
www.ville.cowansville.qc.ca

Desbiens: Centre d'histoire et d'archéologie de la Métabetchouane
243, rue Hébert
Desbiens, QC G0W 1N0
Tél: 418-346-5341
cham@digicom.ca
www.chamans.com
www.facebook.com/centre.metabetchouane
Fondée en: 1995 Site historique et archéologique; histoire d'il y a 5,000 ans; poste de traite; salle de découverte; animation; exposition thématique; 20 juin - sept. ou par réservation
Caroline Lemieux, Présidente

La Doré: Le Moulin des Pionniers de La Doré
4205, ch des Peupliers
La Doré, QC G8J 1E4
Tél: 418-256-8242; *Téléc:* 418-256-3539
Ligne sans frais: 866-272-2842
moulindespionniers@live.ca
moulindespionniers.com
Moulin à scie à pouvoir hydraulique, toujours à l'oeuvre depuis 1889; Maison de Marie, une des plus anciennes maisons de La Doré, avec un potager et une grange-étable; petite ferme avec des animaux; camp qui abrite un restaurant et un bar; auberge "La Nuit Boréale"; sentiers pédestres; tour d'observation; expositions; programmation.
Rodrigue Tremblay, Président
Guylaine Lapointe, Directrice générale,
guylainemoulin@hotmail.com

Dorval: Musée d'histoire et du patrimoine de Dorval
1850, ch Bord-du-Lac
Dorval, QC H9S 2E6
Tél: 514-633-4314
musee@ville.dorval.qc.ca
www.ville.dorval.qc.ca

Drummondville: Musée populaire de la photographie
217, rue Brock
Drummondville, QC J2C 1M2
Tél: 819-474-5782; *Téléc:* 819-474-5782
museedelaphoto@cgocable.ca
www.museedelaphoto.ca
www.facebook.com/1725 92636109220

Drummondville: Le Village Québecois d'Antan inc.
1425, rue Montplaisir
Drummondville, QC J2C 0M2
Tél: 819-478-1441; *Téléc:* 819-478-8155
Ligne sans frais: 877-710-0267
renseignements@villageQuébecois.com
www.villageQuébecois.com
www.facebook.com/villageQuébecois
Fondée en: 1977 Reconstitution d'un village canadien-français du siècle dernier (1810-1910); le village est ouvrir du juin à sept
Eric Verreault, Directeur général, 819-478-1441,
eric.verreault@villageQuébecois.com
France Lemoine, Directrice Administrative, 819-478-1441,
france@villageQuébecois.com

Duhamel-Ouest: Lieu historique national du Canada du Fort-Témiscamingue / Fort Témiscamingue National Historic Site of Canada
834, ch du Vieux-Fort
Duhamel-Ouest, QC J9V 1N7
Tél: 819-629-3222; *Téléc:* 819-629-2977
Ligne sans frais: 888-773-8888
info.metropolitain@pc.gc.ca
www.pc.gc.ca/eng/lhn-nhs/qc/temiscamingue/index.aspx
Autre numéros: **TTY: 1-866-787-6221; Off season phone: 514-283-2282**
Rappelle la présence millénaire des algonquins et l'histoire de ce poste de traite situé au détroit du Lac Témiscamingue.

Forestville: Petite Anglicane
CP 147
Situé à #2, 2e rue, Forestville, QC
Forestville, QC G0T 1E0
Tél: 418-587-2109; *Téléc:* 418-587-6212
Archéologie locale, les gardes-feu, les remèdes d'autrefois, la vie domestique, nos pionniers, l'histoire de Forestville en photos; expositions temporaires; visites guidées

Gaspé: Magasin générale Hyman & Sons et l'entrepôt
Parc national du Canada Forillon, 122, boul Gaspé
Gaspé, QC G4X 1A9
Tél: 418-368-5505; *Téléc:* 418-368-6837
Ligne sans frais: 888-773-8888
information@pc.gc.ca
www.pc.gc.ca/pn-np/qc/forillon.aspx
twitter.com/ForillonNP
www.faceboo k.com/ForillonNP
Autre numéros: **ATS: 1-866-787-6221**
Magasin au centre du village, de l'époque 1920, autrefois la propriété de la compagnie de pêche "William Hyman & Sons," au Parc national du Canada Forillon; animation en costumes; programmation; visites guidées.

Gaspé: Manoir Le Boutillier, lieu historique national du Canada
CP 37
Situé à 578, boul Griffon, Gaspé, QC
Gaspé, QC G4X 6A4
Tél: 418-892-5150
manoir.leboutillier@lanseaugriffon.ca
manoirleboutilli er.ca
Médias sociaux: www.pinterest.com/1850manoir/
www.facebook.com/573248999384144
Construit dans les années 1850 par John Le Boutillier; ouverte de juin à octobre.

Gaspé: Musée de la Gaspésie
80, boul de Gaspé
Gaspé, QC G4X 1A9
Tél: 418-368-1534; *Téléc:* 418-368-1535
info@museedelagaspesie.ca
www.museedelagaspesie.ca
Médias sociaux: www.youtube.com/user/musee1534
twitter.com/MG1534
www.facebook.com/pages/Musée-de-la-Gaspésie/11072457562 4365
Fondée en: 1962 Le musée favoriser la connaissance et l'appréciation de l'histoire et du patrimoine gaspésiens; activités de conservation et de recherche; collections y compris les disciplines de l'ethnologie, l'histoire, les beaux-arts, les sciences naturelles, l'archéologie; archives; boutique; programmation.
Nathalie Spooner, Directrice générale,
direction@museedelagaspesie.ca

Gaspé: Parc national du Canada Forillon / Forillon National Park of Canada
122, boul Gaspé
Gaspé, QC G4X 1A9
Tél: 418-368-5505; *Téléc:* 418-368-6837
Ligne sans frais: 888-787-6221
information@pc.gc.ca
www.pc.gc.ca/pn-np/qc/forillon.aspx
twitter.com/ForillonNP
www.faceboo k.com/ForillonNP
Autre numéros: **ATS: 1-866-787-6221**

Gatineau: Fort George National Historic Site of Canada
c/o Parks Canada National Office, 25-7-N Eddy St.
Location: 51 Queen's Parade, Niagara-on-the-Lake, ON L0S 1J0
Gatineau, QC K1A 0M5
Tel: 905-468-6614; *Fax:* 905-468-4638
Toll-Free: 888-773-8888
ont-niagara@pc.gc.ca
www.pc.gc.ca/eng/lhn-nhs/on/fortg eorge/index.aspx
twitter.com/fofg
www.facebook.com/102031676507960
Other contact information: Friends of Fort George URL: www.friendsoffortgeorge.ca
Recontructed fort built in 1799

Gatineau: Musée de l'Auberge Symmes / Symmes Inn Museum
PO Box 311
Situé à 1, rue Front, Gatineau, QC
Gatineau, QC J9H 5E6
Tel: 819-682-0291; *Fax:* 819-682-6594
symmes@ca.inter.net
www.symmes.ca
twitter.com/CharlesSymmes
www.face book.com/130585520302457
Year Founded: 1988 Histoire régionale de Gatineau

Gatineau: Le Musée de l'outil traditionnel en Outaouais est un musée privé
207, rue des Bernaches
Gatineau, QC J8M 1K8
Tél: 819-281-1628; *Téléc:* 819-281-1628
jacques.decarie@musee-outil.info
www.musee-outil.info
Patrimoine ouvrier; patrimoine domestique; collections numériques/centre de documentation; collection de tableaux

Godbout: Musée amérindien et inuit de Godbout
134, ch Pascal-Comeau
Godbout, QC G0H 1G0
Tél: 418-568-7306

Granby: Centre d'interpretation de la Nature du Lac Boivin (CINLB)
700, rue Drummond
Granby, QC J2G 0K6
Tél: 450-375-3861; *Téléc:* 450-375-3736
info@cinlb.org
www.cinlb.org
www.facebook.com/cinlb.org
Fondée en: 1980 A pour mission de conserver le territoire, les habitats, la faune et la flore de la région
Mario Fortin, Directeur général

Guérin: Musée de Guérin
932, rue Principale Nord
Guérin, QC J0Z 2E0
Tél: 819-784-7014
musee-guerin@tlb.sympatico.ca
www.museedeguerin.com
Le Musée de Guérin offre deux expositions permanentes: "Autour du clocher" et "Le Réveil rural" qui retracent la vie religieuse et agricole des années 1940-50. Situé sur la "Terre de la Fabrique", concédée au début de la paroisse, le site du musée comprend encore un lieu du culte et la ferme de Monsieur le Curé

Harrington Harbour: Centre d'interprétation de la maison Rowsell / Rowsell House Interpretation Center
Parent: Association touristique de Harrington Harbour
CP 147, 1, place Harding
Harrington Harbour, QC G0G 1N0
Tél: 418-795-3131
hhtourism@globetrotter.net
www.tourismlowernorthshore.com

Havre-Aubert: Aquarium des Iles-de-la-Madeleine / Island Aquarium
982 route 199, La Grave
Havre-Aubert, QC G4T 9C7
Tél: 418-937-2277
info@aquariumdesiles.ca
www.facebook.com/aquariumdesiles

Hâvre-Aubert: Musée de la Mer Inc.
1023, Rte. 199, La Grave
Hâvre-Aubert, QC G4T 9C8
Tél: 418-937-5711; Fax: 418-937-2449
info@museedelamer-im.com
www.museedelamer-im.com
www.facebook.com/2694 77289781053
L'histoire des Iles-de-la-Madeleine, l'évolution de la navigation, l'histoire de la pêche; collections de roches, de minéraux, de coquillages; photos et objets marins. Ouvert à l'année.
Michelle Joannette, Directrice générale, directiongenerale@museedelamer-im.com

Inukjuak: Musée commémoratif et Centre de transmission de la culture Daniel Weetaluktuk / Daniel Weetaluktuk Commemorative Museum & Cultural Transmission Centre
c/o Institut culturel Avataq, General Delivery
Inukjuak, QC J0M 1M0
Tél: 819-254-8919; Téléc: 819-254-8148
Ligne sans frais: 866-897-2287
avataq-inukjuak@avataq.qc.ca
www.avataq.qc.ca
Autre numéros: **Tél: 819 254-8939**
Le centre contribue à la protection et à la diffusion de la culture des Inuits d'Inukjuak et du Nunavik; collection de plus de 400 objets anciens et contemporains présentés dans leur contexte culturel d'origine; oeuvres d'art, vêtements traditionnels, artefacts; exposition permanente; expositions temporaires.
Louis Gagnon, Conservateur, louisgagnon@avataq.qc.ca

Inverness: Musée du Bronze d'Inverness
1760, ch Dublin
Inverness, QC G0S 1K0
Tél: 418-453-2101; Téléc: 418-453-7711
info@museedubronze.com
www.museedubronze.com
Médias sociaux: www.youtube.com/user/museedubronze
www.facebook.com/museedubronze
Voué à la recherche, la mise en valeur, la diffusion, la fabrication, l'interprétation et l'éducation relative à l'art du bronze; fonderie; ateliers; visites guidées; jardin; programmation.
Roxanne Huard, Chargée de projet à l'exposition, aazroxanne@gmail.com

L'Islet-sur-Mer: Musée maritime du Québec
55, ch des Pionniers est
L'Islet-sur-Mer, QC G0R 2B0
Tél: 418-247-5001
info@mmq.qc.ca
www.mmq.qc.ca
Médias sociaux: www.youtube.com/user/museemaritimeQuébec
www.facebook.com/MuseeMaritimeQ cCapitaineJEBernier
Fondée en: 1968 Le musée a pour mission la sauvegarde, l'étude, et la mise en valeur du patrimoine maritime se rattachant au fleuve Saint-Laurent, et de la porte des Grands Lacs; la conservation des navires historiques; expositions permanentes: "Gens du pays, gens du fleuve", "Capt. Joseph-Elzéar Bernier", "Ilititaa...Bernier, ses hommes et les Inuits", et "Pirates ou corsaires?"; boutique; visites guidées; accessible aux personnes à mobilité réduite.
Marie-Ôve Brisson, Directrice

Jonquiére: Centre d'histoire Sir-William-Price / Sir William Price Heritage Centre
CP 2314, 1994, rue Price
Jonquiére, QC G7X 7X8
Tél: 418-695-7278; Téléc: 418-695-7172
sirwilliamprice@bellnet.ca
sirwilliamprice.com
www.facebook.com/112289 542151626

Kahnawake: Musée Kateri Tekakwitha
Mission Saint-François-Xavier, PO Box 70
Kahnawake, QC J0L 1B0
Tél: 450-632-6030; Fax: 450-632-6031
saintkaterishrine@yahoo.ca
kateritekakwitha.net
Religious & ethnic artifacts dating back to the 17th century; historical mission buildings (rectory 1717, church 1845) contain Blessed Kateri's tomb (1656-1680) & precious works of art including the Deerfield Bell (17th - 19th cent.); open all year 10-5; Kahnawake is a native Mohawk reservation

Kamouraska: Musée régional de Kamouraska
Place de l'église, 69, av Morel
Kamouraska, QC G0L 1M0
Tél: 418-492-9783; Téléc: 418-492-9783
museekam@videotron.ca
www.museekamouraska.com
www.facebook.com/2371912 11412
Fondée en: 1977 Le musée assume fidèlement sa mission de protection, conservation et diffusion du riche patrimoine historique et culturel de tout Kamouraska. Il est ouvert du mai au déc; du jan au avr sur réservation.
Yvette Raymond, Directrice générale

Knowlton: Brome County Historical Museum (BCHS)
PO Box 690, 130 Lakesid Rd.
Knowlton, QC J0E 1V0
Tel: 450-243-6782
bchs@endirect.qc.ca
bromemuseum.com
www.facebook.com /214500035256431
Year Founded: 1898 Managed by the Brome County Historical Society, the Brome County Museum presents the history of Brome County & the surrounding region. The museum's grounds feature an old fire hall from 1904, an academy building from 1854, & the Brome County Court House from 1858-1859. The court house contains the archives of the Brome County Historical Society. The museum is open from mid May to mid September. The archives are open year round.

Lac-Drolet: Maison du Granit
301, rte du Morne
Lac-Drolet, QC G0Y 1C0
Tél: 819-549-2566; Téléc: 819-549-2566
info@maisondugranit.ca
www.maisondugranit.ca
www.facebook.com/15339869 8016458
Fondée en: 1989 A pour mission de collecter et de diffuser l'histoire de l'industrie du granit et de ses artisans les tailleurs de pierre; exposition permanente; expositions thématiques; visites guidées; jardin panoramique.

Lachine: Centre historique des Soeurs de Sainte-Anne
1280, boul Saint-Joseph
Lachine, QC H8S 2M8
Tél: 514-637-4616
musee@ssacong.org
www.ssacong.org/musee
Fondée en: 1918 Musée communautaire de la Congrégation des Soeurs de Sainte-Anne. Le musée a pour mission de faire découvrir la vie des Soeurs de Sainte-Anne marquée par les lieux et les époques où elles ont évolué; ouvert toute l'année.
Murielle Gagnon, Directrice, murielle.gagnon@bellnet.ca

Lachine: Musée de Lachine
1, ch du Musée
Lachine, QC H8S 4L9
Tél: 514-634-3478; Téléc: 514-637-6784
museedelachine@lachine.ca
lachine.ville.Montréal.qc.ca/musee
Comprend Maison LeBer-LeMoyne et la Dépendance, les anciens bâtiments complets sur l'île de Montréal ainsi que le Benoît-Verdickt Pavillion, un centre d'exposition d'art contemporain; le Pavillon de l'Entrepôt présente des expositions pluridisciplinaires et multiculturelles; programme d'éducation disponibles pour les visiteurs d'âge scolaire ainsi que d'autres; ouvert au public d'avril à novembre
Marc Pitre, Directeur

Lac-Mégantic: Musée Namesokanjic
#200, 5527, rue Frontenac
Lac-Mégantic, QC G6B 1H6
Tél: 819-583-2441; Téléc: 819-583-5920
greffier@ville.lac-megantic.qc.ca
www.lac-megantic.qc.ca
Outils forestiers, objets domestiques, photographies, costumes; programmation et activités.

Lasalle: Moulin Fleming, centre d'interprétation historique
9675, boul LaSalle
Lasalle, QC H8R 4A8
Tél: 514-367-6439; Téléc: 514-367-6606
ville.Montréal.qc.ca/lasalle
Fondée en: 1991 Ouvert mai - sept.

Laval: Centre d'interprétation de l'eau (C.I.EAU)
12, rue Hotte
Laval, QC H7L 2R3
Tél: 450-963-6463
info@cieau.qc.ca
www.cieau.qc.ca
www.facebook.com/C.I.EAU
André Perrault, Président

Laval: Musée Armand-Frappier, Centre d'interprétation des biosciences / Armand-Frappier Museum
531, boul des Prairies
Laval, QC H7V 1B7
Tél: 450-686-5641; Téléc: 450-686-5391
musee-afrappier@iaf.inrs.ca
www.musee-afrappier.qc.ca
Médias sociaux: www.youtube.com/user/bcarmandfrappier
www.facebook.com/BiocentreArmandFrappie
Fondée en: 1992 Le musée offre des activités pour favoriser la compréhension d'enjeux scientifiques reliés à la santé humaine, animale & environnementale; il fait connaître l'oeuvre du Dr Armand Frappier, microbiologiste.
Guylaine Archambault, Directrice Générale, 450-686-5641, Fax: 450-686-5665, guylaine.archambault@iaf.inrs.ca
Caroline Labelle, Agente de réservation, 450-686-5641, caroline.labelle@iaf.inrs.ca
Martine Isabelle, Directrice des opérations et des communications, 450-686-5641, Fax: 450-686-5665, martine.isabelle@iaf.inrs.ca

Laval: Musée écologique - (C.J.N.) Vanier
3995, boul Lévesque
Laval, QC H7E 2R3

Lavaltrie: Maison Rosalie-Cadron
Parent: Corporation de la Maison Rosalie-Cadron
1997, rue Notre-Dame
Lavaltrie, QC J5T 1S6
Tél: 450-586-0361
info@maisonrosaliecadron.org
maisonrosaliecadron.org
Médias sociaux: www.youtube.com/user/MaisonRosalieCadron
www.facebook.com/Maison.Rosalie
Fondée en: 2003
Michelle Picard, Directrice, 450-586-1575

Lévis: Maison Alphonse-Desjardins (SHAD)
6, rue du Mont-Marie
Lévis, QC G6V 1V9
Tel: 418-835-2090; Fax: 418-835-9173
Toll-Free: 866-835-8444
info@maisonalphonsedesjardins.com
www.desjardins.com
www.facebook.com/MaisonAlphonseDesjardins
Year Founded: 1982 La maison de style néo-gothique fut construite en 1883 pour Alphonse Desjardins, fondateur des caisses populaires. C'est là que Desjardins a conçu son grand projet coopératif et qu'ont débuté, en 1901, les activités de la Caisse populaire de Lévis
Esther Normand, Conservation & Administration Agent

Lévis: Musée du College de Lévis
9, rue Mgr Gosselin
Lévis, QC G6V 5K1
Tél: 418-837-8600
Fermé au public, ouvert sur demande

Lévis: Musée Le Régiment de la Chaudière
Manège militaire de Lévis, 10, rue de l'Arsenal
Lévis, QC G6V 4P7
Tél: 418-835-0340
Ligne sans frais: 877-748-3783

Longueuil: Musée Marie-Rose Durocher
80, rue St-Charles est
Longueuil, QC J4H 1A9
Tél: 450-651-8104
centremarierose@yahoo.ca
www.snjm.org
Le Centre Marie-Rose est ouvert au public; le musée présente des expositions à caractère religieux et historique de la vie de Marie-Rose Durocher, fondatrice de la Congrégation des Soeurs des Saints Noms de Jésus et de Marie; collection de tableaux et d'artefacts.

Lourdes-de-Blanc-Sablon: Musée Monseigneur Scheffer
Église Notre-Dame-de-Lourdes
Lourdes-de-Blanc-Sablon, QC G0G 1W0
Tél: 418-461-2000
www.tourismebassecotenord.com

Malartic: Musée minéralogique de l'Abitibi-Témiscamingue
650, rue de la Paix
Malartic, QC J0Y 1Z0
Tél: 819-757-4677; Téléc: 819-757-4140
info@museemalartic.qc.ca
www.museemalartic.qc.ca
Expositions de roches rares

La Malbaie: **Musée de Charlevoix**
10, ch du Hâvre
La Malbaie, QC G5A 2Y8
Tél: 418-665-4411; *Téléc:* 418-665-4560
info@museedecharlevoix.qc.ca
museedecharlevoix.qc.ca
twitter.com/Musee Charlevoix
www.facebook.com/MuseeDeCharlevoix
Fondée en: 1975 Principaux domaines d'intérêt: l'ethnohistoire et folklorique art; art textuel; arts décoratifs; beaux-arts; histoire
Raymond Lavoie, Président
Annie Breton, Directrice générale, directiongenerale@bellnet.ca

Maniwaki: **Le centre d'interprétation de l'historique de la protection de la forêt contre le feu**
8, rue Comeau
Maniwaki, QC J9E 2R8
Tél: 819-449-7999; *Téléc:* 819-449-5102
info@ci-chateaulogue.qc.ca
www.ci-chateaulogue.qc.ca
Le Château Logue; centre d'interprétation; expositions y compris l'histoire des grands feux de forêts au Québec, la forêt exploitée, et la forêt protégée; visites et randonnées gratuites; tour d'observation.
François Ledoux, Directeur

La Martre: **Corporation du Centre d'interprétation archéologique de la Gaspésie**
6, rue des Fermières
La Martre, QC G0E 2H0
Tél: 418-288-1318; *Téléc:* 418-288-1318
ci_archéologie_gaspésie@hotmail.com
Interprète sur la préhistoire gaspésienne dont l'accent est mis sur la période paléoindienne récente; exposition et sentier d'interprétation

Mashteuiatsh: **Musée amérindien de Mashteuiatsh / The Native Museum of Mashteuiatsh**
1787, rue Amishk
Mashteuiatsh, QC G0W 2H0
Tél: 418-275-4842; *Téléc:* 418-275-7494
Ligne sans frais: 888-875-4042
museeilnu@cgocable.ca
www.museeilnu.ca
www.facebook.com/212038752166309
Sauvegarde l'héritage ilnu et permet aux autochtones, la population et les touristes d'en prendre connaissance; expositions permanentes et temporaires; programmes éducatifs.
Jean-Denis Gill, Directeur, direction.museeilnu@cgocable.ca
Louise Siméon, Responsable, secteur muséal, archive.museeilnu@cgocable.ca

Matane: **Musée du Vieux-Phare**
#300, 235, av Saint-Jerome
Situé à 968, ave du Phare ouest, Matane, QC G4W 1V7
Matane, QC G4W 3A7
Tél: 418-562-1065; *Téléc:* 418-562-1917
cldtourisme@globetrotter.net

Melbourne: **Richmond County Historical Society Museum (RCHS)**
1296 Rte. 243
Melbourne, QC J0B 2B0
Tel: 819-826-1332
www.richmondcountyhistoricalsociety.com
To research & preserve historical facts in the Richmond County area; museum refurbished as a typical home of the late 1800s; archives centre
Esther Healy, Archivist, e-dhealy@sympatico.ca

Métabetchouan-Lac-à-la-Croix: **Centre d'interprétation de l'agriculture et de la ruralité**
281, rue St-Louis
Métabetchouan-Lac-à-la-Croix, QC G8G 2C8
Tél: 418-349-3633; *Téléc:* 418-349-5013
Ligne sans frais: 877-611-3633
ciar@cgocable.ca
ciar-lacalacroix.com
Fondée en: 1976 Situé au coeur d'une plaine agricole, le CIAR est un site désigné pour découvrir la richesse du patrimoine agricole du Saguenay-Lac-Saint-Jean. A travers l'exposition Gens de la terre, découvrez 150 ans d'histoire, us et coutumes des ancêtres, qui ont bâti le paysage actuel. Labyrinthe dans un Champ de Maïs; ferme pédagogique; camp d'étabissement (1868); programmes éducatifs.
France Lemoine, Directrice générale

Middle Bay: **Centre d'interprétation de Middle Bay**
Parent: **Fondation pour le développement du tourisme de Bonne-Espérance**
Middle Bay, QC G0G 1Z0
Tél: 418-461-2445
www.tourismebassecotenord.com
Melva Flynn, Contact

Mont Saint-Hilaire: **Centre de la nature Mont Saint-Hilaire**
422, ch des Moulins
Mont Saint-Hilaire, QC J3G 4S6
Tél: 450-467-1755; *Téléc:* 450-467-8015
Ligne sans frais: 866-382-2962
info@centrenature.qc.ca
www.centrenature.qc.ca
A pour mission d'assurer l'intégrité du patrimoine naturel de la montagne, offrir un contact avec la nature et une gamme d'activités éducatives et culturelles, et promouvoir la conservation des milieux naturels de la région; ouvert 365 jours par année; offre un réseau de 24 km de sentiers, et un trottoir de bois accessible aux personnes à mobilité restreinte
Kees Vanderheyden, Directeur

Montebello: **Lieu historique national du Canada du Manoir-Papineau / Manoir-Papineau National Historic Site of Canada**
500, rue Notre-Dame
Montebello, QC J0V 1L0
Tél: 819-423-6965; *Téléc:* 819-423-6455
Ligne sans frais: 888-773-8888
info.soulange-outaouais@pc.gc.ca
www.pc.gc.ca/eng/lhn-nhs/qc/manoirpapineau/index.aspx
Autre numéros: **TTY: 1-866-787-6221**
La maison de la famille Papineau, 1848-1850; plus de 800 objets, meubles, vêtements, oeuvres d'art, livres et documents; fresques de Napoléon Bourassa; Concerts d'Amédée; jardin.

Montmagny: **Musée de l'accordéon**
301, boul Taché est
Montmagny, QC G5V 1C5
Tél: 418-248-7927; *Téléc:* 418-248-1596
accordeon@montmagny.com
accordeonmontmagny.com
Fondée en: 1992 Centre de recherche et de collecte des accordéons.

Montréal: **Basilique Notre-Dame de Montréal**
110, rue Notre-Dame ouest
Montréal, QC H2Y 1T2
Tél: 514-842-2925; *Téléc:* 514-842-3370
info@basiliquenddm.org
www.basiliquenddm.org
Fondée en: 1829 Construite entre 1824 & 1829, la basilique acceuille des centaines de milliers de visiteurs chaque année; réputée pour la richesse de sa décoration intérieure: les vitraux, les éléments d'architecture, et les oeuvres d'art; visites guidées (individuels/groupes); visites scolaires; services religieux; événements; concerts; location de salles; boutique.
Yoland Tremblay, Directeur général

Montréal: **Biodôme de Montréal**
4777, av Pierre-De Coubertin
Montréal, QC H1V 1B3
Tél: 514-868-3000
espacepourlavie.ca/biodome
Médias sociaux: www.youtube.com/Espacepourlavie
twitter.com/espacepourlavie
www.facebo ok.com/Espacepourlavi
Le Biodôme recrée des Écosystèmes des Amériques: forêt tropicale, forêt laurentienne, Saint-Laurent marin, monde polaire. Notez que le Biodôme est fermé pour une durée indéterminée en raison d'un conflit de travail à la Ville de Montréal.

Montréal: **The Black Watch of Canada (RHR) Regimental Memorial Museum**
2067, rue Bleury
Montréal, QC H3A 2K2
Tel: 514-496-1686; *Fax:* 514-496-2758
museum@blackwatchcanada.com
www.blackwatchcanada.com
twitter.com/bwrhc
www.facebook.com/blackwatchcanada
Uniforms, photographs & artifacts from early 1860s to present; open Tue. evenings, 7-9 pm & by appt.

Montréal: **Canadian Grenadier Guards Regimental Museum**
4171, av Esplanade
Montréal, QC H2W 1S9
Tel: 514-496-1984

Montréal: **Centre d'exposition de l'Université de Montréal**
2940, ch. Côte-Ste.-Catherine
Pavillon de la Faculté de l'aménagement, C.P. 6128, succursale Centre-ville, Montréal, QC, H3C 3J7
Montréal, QC H3T 1B9
Tél: 514-343-6111; *Téléc:* 514-343-2183
informations@expo.uMontréal.ca
www.expo.uMontréal.ca
twitter.com/ExpoU deM
www.facebook.com/CentreExpoUdeM
Comment s'y rendre: Pavillon de la faculté de l'Aménagement, 2940, ch d la Côte-Sainte-Catherine, local 0056, Montréal. Centre d'exposition multidisciplinaire. Comprend: collection herbier Marie-Victorin; collection du département d'anthropologie; collection du Laboratoire de recherche sur les musiques du monde; oeuvres d'art; design industriel
Louise Grenier, Directrice, 514-343-6111, l.grenier@uMontréal.ca
Sophie Banville, Adjointe administrative, 514-343-6111
Patrick Mailloux, Coordonnateur des expositions et de la collection, 514-343-6111

Montréal: **Centre d'histoire de Montréal (CHM) / Montréal History Centre**
335, Place d'Youville
Montréal, QC H2Y 3T1
Tél: 514-872-3207; *Téléc:* 514-872-9645
chm@ville.Montréal.qc.ca
ville.Montréal.qc.ca
www.facebook.com/chmmtl
Fondée en: 1983 This city museum is located in an old firehall. Here Montréal's story is told through exhibits, models, sets, videos & 8,000 photographs from 1642 until today.
Jean-François Leclerc, Director
Catherine Charlebois, Muséologue

Montréal: **Chapelle Notre-Dame-de-Bon-Secours/Musée Marguerite Bourgeoys**
400, rue Saint-Paul est
Montréal, QC H2Y 1H4
Tél: 514-282-8670; *Téléc:* 514-282-8672
info@marguerite-bourgeoys.com
www.marguerite-bourgeoys.com
twitter.com /margbourg
www.facebook.com/margueritebourgeoys
Fondée en: 1998 Chapelle, musée d'histoire, et site archéologique; programmation diversifiée, visites guidées, boutique, location des salles.

Montréal: **Cité Historia**
10897, rue du Pont
Montréal, QC H2B 2H3
Tél: 514-850-4222; *Téléc:* 514-850-0607
info@citehistoria.qc.ca
www.citehistoria.qc.ca
Médias sociaux: pinterest.com/citehistoria
twitter.com/cite_historia
www.facebook.com/ Citehistoria
Fondée en: 2001 Maison du Pressoir; site des moulins
Michel Le Coester, Directeur général, direction@citehistoria.qc.ca

Montréal: **Écomusée du fier monde**
2050, rue Amherst
Montréal, QC H2L 3L8
Tél: 514-528-8444; *Téléc:* 514-528-8686
info@ecomusee.qc.ca
www.ecomusee.qc.ca
twitter.com/EcomuseeEFM
www.f acebook.com/Ecomuseedufiermonde
Fondée en: 1980 Highlights the history of the Centre-Sud heritage, which is a mircososm of the industrial revoltuion which took place in Canada during the latter half of the 19th century.

Montréal: **The Edward Bronfman Museum**
450, av Kensington
Montréal, QC H3Y 3A2
Tel: 514-937-9471; *Fax:* 514-937-2067
admin@theshaar.org
www.shaarhashomayim.org
Antique artwork & texts; congregation documents & memorabilia; ceremonial objects; open daily; special tours by appointment

Penni Kolb, Executive Director, pkolb@theshaar.org
Elaine Hershenfield, Co-chair & Curator
Deanna Mendelson, Co-chair & Curator

Montréal: Insectarium de Montréal / Montréal Insectarium
4581, rue Sherbrooke est
Montréal, QC H1X 2B2
Tél: 514-872-1400
espacepourlavie.ca/insectarium
Médias sociaux: www.youtube.com/Espacepourlavie
twitter.com/espacepourlavie
www.facebo ok.com/Espacepourlavie
Autre numéros: **Administration, tél: 514-872-0663**
Largest insectarium in North America; 140,000 scientific specimens collection; 20,000 exhibition collection (including 4,000 on public display); about 100 species of arthropods live collection

Montréal: Lieu historique national de Sir George-Etienne Cartier / Sir George-Étienne Cartier National Historic Site
458, rue Notre-Dame est
Montréal, QC H2Y 1C8
Tel: 514-283-2282; *Fax:* 514-283-5560
Toll-Free: 888-773-8888
information@pc.gc.ca
www.pc.gc.ca/lhn-nhs/qc/etienneca rtier.aspx
Other contact information: ATS: 1-866-558-2950
Year Founded: 1985 Commemorates the life and accomplishments of Sir George-Étienne Cartier; Cartier family homes; performances and re-enactments that vary depending on season; Open June - December

Montréal: Lieu historique national du Canada du Commerce-de-la-fourrure-à-Lachine / The Fur Trade at Lachine National Historic Site
1255, boul Saint-Joseph, Lachine Borough
Montréal, QC H8S 2M2
Tel: 514-637-7433; *Fax:* 514-637-5325
Toll-Free: 888-733-8888
info.metropolitain@pc.gc.ca
www.pc.gc.ca/lhn-nhs/qc/la chine.aspx
Other contact information: TTY: 1-866-787-6221; off season phone: 514-283-2282
A bord d'un canot, découvrez le point de départ des grands explorateurs du continent nord-américain; programmes et activités; exposition sur l'apogée du commerce des fourrures; visites thématiques.

Montréal: Maison de Mère d'Youville
138, rue Saint-Pierre
Montréal, QC H2Y 2L7
Tél: 514-842-9411; *Téléc:* 514-842-0142
asscong@sgm.ca
www.sgm.qc.ca
Fondée en: 1981 Ancien couvent des Soeurs Grises; l'hospice et le couvent restauré en 1981; la chapelle mise en valeur en 1991; les anciens magasins-entrepôts rénovés; par rendez-vous.

Montréal: Maison Saint-Gabriel
2146, Place Dublin, Pointe-Sainte-Charles
Montréal, QC H3K 2A2
Tél: 514-935-8136; *Téléc:* 514-935-5692
msgrcip@globetrotter.qc.ca
www.maisonsaint-gabriel.qc.ca
Médias sociaux: www.youtube.com/user/MaisonSaintGabriel
www.facebook.com/255220478149
Fondée en: 1966 La Maison est la maison d'accueil des Filles du Roy et pendant 300 ans, la maison de ferme de la Congrégation de Notre-Dame; un exemple de l'architecture du Régime français; expositions qui expliquent le rôle de Marguerite Bourgeoys et la vie à la colonie de l'Ile de Montréal pendant le 17e siècle; jardin; visites guidées.
Madeleine Juneau, Directrice générale

Montréal: The Montréal Holocaust Memorial Centre / Le Centre commémoratif de l'Holocauste à Montréal
Maison Cummings, 5151, ch. de la Côte-Sainte-Catherine
Montréal, QC H3W 1M6
Tel: 514-345-2605; *Fax:* 514-344-2651
info@mhmc.ca
www.mhmc.ca
www.facebook.com/78382729139
Year Founded: 1976 To collect, research & preserve historical, cultural & ethnographic material related to Jewish communities in Europe & North Africa which fell under Nazi rule
Alice Herscovitch, Executive Director

Montréal: Musée de BMO Banque de Montréal / BMO Bank of Montréal Museum
129, rue St-Jacques, #D
Montréal, QC H2Y 1L6
Tél: 514-877-6810; *Téléc:* 514-877-7341
Le bureau de la Caisse de la plus ancienne institution bancaire du Canada est recréé; ouvert toute l'année (fermé les jours non bancaires); , visite gratuite de l'auto-guidée.
Yolaine Toussaint, Archivist, yolaine.toussaint@bmo.com

Montréal: Musée de L'Oratoire Saint-Joseph du Mont-Royal / Museum of Saint Joseph Oratory of Mount-Royal
3800, ch Queen Mary
Montréal, QC H3V 1H6
Tél: 514-733-8211; *Téléc:* 514-733-9735
Ligne sans frais: 877-672-8647
pastorale@saint-joseph.org
www.saint-joseph.org
Médias sociaux:
www.youtube.com/channel/UClx9rJUB8Mb-Dsd4P0_TgWA
twitter.com/osjmr
www .facebook.com/osaintjoseph
Fondée en: 1955 Le musée se consacre à l'art chrétien et à l'histoire et le patrimoine québécoise; expositions thématiques. L'Oratoire mise en valeur la vie et l'oeuvre de frère André; visites commentées; boutique; bibliothèque/archives/centre de recherche.

Montréal: Musée des Hospitalières de l'Hôtel-Dieu de Montréal
201, av des Pins ouest
Montréal, QC H2W 1R5
Tél: 514-849-2919; *Téléc:* 514-849-4199
museehospitalieres@bellnet.ca
www.museedeshospitalieres.qc.ca
www.face book.com/85965398327
Fondée en: 1992 Le musée introduit l'histoire des Hospitalières de Saint-Joseph et des Hospitalières de l'Hôtel-Dieu; exposition permanent; programmation et activités; boutique; salles de conférence à louer; 20 000 objets; archives.
Louise Verdant, Directrice générale

Montréal: Musée des ondes Émile Berliner
1050, rue Lacasse, local C-220
Montréal, QC H4C 2Z3
Tél: 514-932-9663
info@berliner.Montréal.museum
www.berliner.Montréal.museum
www.facebook.com/368583116562909
Fondée en: 1996 Émile Berliner a inventé le gramophone, le disque horizontal, et la matrice pour imprimer les disques. Le musée possède plus de 30 000 objets et se consacre à l'histoire de l'industrie des ondes; archives; activités.

Montréal: Musée des Soeurs de Miséricorde
12435, av de la Miséricorde
Montréal, QC H4J 2G3
Tél: 514-332-0550; *Téléc:* 514-336-0621
musee_misericorde@yahoo.ca
www.smisericorde.org/Fmusee.htm
www.faceboo k.com/musee.misericorde
Soins de santé et services sociaux; sage-femmerie; Hôpital de la Miséricorde de Montréal; crèche de la Miséricorde; femmes; mentalités

Montréal: Musée du Château Ramezay / Château Ramezay Museum
280, rue Notre-Dame est
Montréal, QC H2Y 1C5
Tél: 514-861-3708; *Téléc:* 514-861-8317
info@chateauramezay.qc.ca
www.chateauramezay.qc.ca
www.facebook.com/Ch ateau.Ramezay
Fondée en: 1895 Le musée est consacré à la conservation, et la mise en valeur d'une collection axée sur l'histoire de Montréal et du Québec; plus de 25 000 objets, oeuvres d'art, artefacts ethnologiques et archéologiques, objets numismatiques; photographies; meubles; costumes; bibliothèque; jardin; boutique; café.
André J. Delisle, Directeur général/Conservateur

Montréal: Musée du Château-Dufresne
2929, av Jeanne-d'Arc
Montréal, QC H1W 3W2
Tél: 514-259-9201; *Téléc:* 514-259-6466
info@chateaudufresne.com
www.chateaudufresne.com
twitter.com/chateaudu fresne
www.facebook.com/234003475426
Le Château, construit entre 1915 et 1918 pour servir de résidence aux frères Oscar et Marius Dufresne, met en pratique les principes du style Beaux-Arts. Programmation culturelle; visites guidées; expositions; salles à louer pour réceptions.
Paul Labonne, Directeur général, plabonne@chateaudufresne.com

Montréal: Musée du Cinéma/Cinémathèque québécoise
335, boul de Maisonneuve est
Montréal, QC H2X 1K1
Tél: 514-842-9763; *Téléc:* 514-842-1816
info@cinematheque.qc.ca
www.cinematheque.qc.ca
Médias sociaux: instagram.com/cinemathequeqc
twitter.com/cinematheqeqc
www.facebook.c om/cinematheque.Québecoise
Fondée en: 1963 La Cinémathèque a le mandat de conserver, documenter et mettre en valeur le patrimoine cinématographique et télévisuel national et international.
Iolande Cadrin-Rossignol, Directrice générale

Montréal: Musée du costume et du textile du Québec
385, rue de la commune Est
Montréal, QC H2Y 1J3
Tél: 514-419-2300; *Téléc:* 514-419-2330
info@mctq.org
mctq.org
twitter.com/MCTQ_MTL
www.facebook.com/1119280 18835551
Fondée en: 1979 Le musée se consacre à la recherche, la conservation, l'éducation, et la diffusion; expositions de costume, textiles, et de la fibre; boutique.
Jean-Claude Poitras, Président
Joanne Watkins, Directrice générale, joanne.watkins@mctq.org

Montréal: Musee du Sault-au-Récollet
Parent: Cité Historia
10865, rue du Pressoir
Montréal, QC H2B 2L1
Tél: 514-280-6783
info@citehistoria.qc.ca
www.citehistoria.qc.ca
Médias sociaux: pinterest.com/citehistoria
twitter.com/cite_historia
www.facebook.com/ Citehistoria
Michel Le Coester, Directeur général, direction@citehistoria.qc.ca

Montréal: Musée Édouard-Dubeau
Cliniques dentaires, Université de Montréal, CP 6123 Centre-ville
Montréal, QC H3C 3J7
Tél: 514-343-6750; *Téléc:* 514-343-2233
musee@medent.uMontréal.ca
www.expo.uMontréal.ca/collections/dentaire.htm
Affiche des formes primitives d'outils de dentisterie moderne.

Montréal: Musée régimentaire les Fusiliers Mont-Royal
3721, av Henri-Julien
Montréal, QC H2X 3H4
Tél: 514-283-7444; *Téléc:* 514-496-5086
museo@lesfusiliersmont-royal.com
lesfusiliersmont-royal.com
twitter.co m/museefmr
w.facebook.com/museeregimentaire.fusiliersmontroyal
Fondée en: 1977

Montréal: Le Musée Stewart au Fort de l'Ile Sainte-Hélène / The Stewart Museum at the Fort Ile Sainte-Hélène
British Military Depot, St. Helen's Island, Parc Jean-Drapeau, 20 ch. du Tour-de-l'Isle
Montréal, QC H3C 0K7
Tél: 514-861-6701; *Téléc:* 514-284-2211
info@stewart-museum.org
www.stewart-museum.org
www.facebook.com/121301 634610186
Fondée en: 1955 Fermeture temporaire; l'exposition permanente renouvelée du musée sera accessible au public dès l'automne 2010; activités scolaires et culturelles.
Guy Vadeboncoeur, Executive Directeur & Chief Curator Ph. D., FCMA, 514-861-6703

***Montréal:* Museum of Jewish Montréal / Musée du Montréal juif**
#215, 1590 Dr. Penfield Ave.
Montréal, QC H3G 1C5
Toll-Free: 888-405-8645
info@mimj.ca
imjm.ca
Social Media: thirdsolitude.tumblr.com
twitter.com/musee_mtl_juif
www.facebook.com/m useeduMontréaljuif
Zev Moses, Director

***Montréal:* Phonothèque québécoise, Musée du son**
335, boul de Maisonneuve est
Montréal, QC H2X 1K1
Tél: 514-282-0703; *Téléc:* 514-282-0019
phono@bellnet.ca
www.phonotheque.org
Histoire des archives sonores, de l'industrie du disque, etc.
History of sound archives, sound recording & radio industry.

***Montréal:* Redpath Museum**
McGill University, 859 Sherbrooke St. West
Montréal, QC H3A 2K6
Tel: 514-398-4086; *Fax:* 514-398-3185
redpath.museum@mcgill.ca
www.mcgill.ca/redpath
Social Media: pinterest.com/redpathmuseum
twitter.com/RedpathMuseum
www.facebook.com /308943939115940
Year Founded: 1882 Extensive collections in paleontonlogy, mineralogy, zoology & ethnology; family workshop series "Discovery Workshop"
Dr. David M. Green, Director/Curator B.Sc., M.Sc., Ph.D., Vertebrates, david.m.green@mcgill.ca
Dr. Virginie Millien, Asst. Prof./Chief Curator Ph.D., D.E.A., Paleontology & Zoology, virginie.millien@mcgill.ca

***Montréal:* Royal Canadian Ordnance Corps Museum**
Longue-Pointe Garrison, CP 4000 K, 6560, rue Hochlega
Montréal, QC H1N 3R9
Tél: 514-252-2777
www.rcocassn.com
www.facebook.com/115520415149693
Fondée en: 1962 An accredited military museum of the Department of National Defence, the Royal Canadian Ordnance Corps Museum depicts the historical mission of the Royal Canadian Ordnance Corps, & other pre-unification support elements of the Canadian Army, the RCAF, & the RCN. These service elements united in 1968 to create the Logistics Branch of the Canadian Forces. The collection of the RCOC Museum is housed in a 1943 building, which originally served as Longue-Pointe Garrison's St-Barbara Catholic & Protestant chapels.
Andrew Gregory, Curator Ph.D, agregory17@cogeco.ca

***Mont-Saint-Grégoire:* Centre d'interprétation du milieu écologique du Haut-Richelieu**
16, ch du Sous-Bois
Mont-Saint-Grégoire, QC J0J 1K0
Tél: 450-346-0406
services@cimehautrichelieu.qc.ca
www.cimehautrichelieu.qc.ca
A pour mission la conservation du Mont-Saint-Grégoire, et d'autres sites naturels dans la région du Haut-Richelieu
Renée Gagnon, Directice générale, r.gagnon@cimehautrichelieu.qc.ca

***Mont-Saint-Hilaire:* Maison amérindienne**
510, Montée des Trente
Mont-Saint-Hilaire, QC J3H 2R8
Tél: 450-464-2500; *Téléc:* 450-464-0071
info@maisonamerindienne.com
www.maisonamerindienne.com
www.facebook.co m/lamaison.amerindienne
Fondée en: 2000 Un lieu d'échanges, de partage et de rapprochement des peuples à travers des activités culturelles (expositions, contes et légendes, conférences), environnementales et gastronomiques; seul site multinations, situé dans une érablière.
André Michel, Fondateur

***New Richmond:* Gaspesian British Heritage Village**
351, boul Perron ouest
New Richmond, QC G0C 2B0
Tel: 418-392-4487; *Fax:* 418-392-5907
info@gaspesianvillage.org
www.gaspesianvillage.org
www.facebook.com/ga spesianvillagegaspesien
British heritage in Gaspé from 1760 to 1900s; June 24th - Aug. 22nd
Mike Geraghty, President, 418-301-6097

Kim Harrison, Director, kharrison_village@globetrotter.net

***Nicolet:* Musée des religions du monde**
900, boul Louis-Fréchette
Nicolet, QC J3T 1V5
Tél: 819-293-6148; *Téléc:* 819-293-4161
musee@museedesreligions.qc.ca
www.museedesreligions.qc.ca
twitter.com/ museereligions
www.facebook.com/museedesreligionsdumonde
Le musée se consacre à l'histoire des rites religieux du bouddhisme, de l'hindouisme, de l'islam, du judaïsme, et du christianisme; location de salle; boutique; programmation et activités; les installations du musée sont adaptées pour les personnes à mobilité réduite.
Jean-François Royal, Directeur

***Nicolet:* Musée historique des Soeurs de l'Assomption de la Sainte Vierge**
***Parent:* Musée des religions du monde**
900, boul Louis-Fréchette
Nicolet, QC J3T 1V5
Tél: 819-293-6148
musee@museedesreligions.qc.ca
www.museedesreligions.qc.ca/musee-soeurs-assomption
twitter.com/museerel igions
www.facebook.com/museedesreligionsdumonde
Fondée en: 1979 Collection permanente du patrimoine des fondatrices et des fondateurs de la Congrégation; costume religieux; tableaux; meubles; instruments de musique; sculptures; objets liturgiques.
Jean-François Royal, Directeur, Musée des religions du monde

***Notre-Dame-de-l'Ile-Perrot:* Parc historique Pointe-du-Moulin**
2500, boul Don-Quichotte
Notre-Dame-de-l'Ile-Perrot, QC J7V 7P2
Tél: 514-453-5936; *Téléc:* 514-453-8744
info@pointedumoulin.com
www.pointedumoulin.com
Fondée en: 1979
Ani Kataroyan, Directrice générale

***Notre-Dame-du-Nord:* Centre thématique fossilifère du lac Témiscamingue / Lake Timiskaming Fossil Centre**
5, rue Principale
Notre-Dame-du-Nord, QC J0Z 3B0
Tél: 819-723-2500; *Téléc:* 819-723-2369
musee@fossiles.qc.ca
www.fossiles.qc.ca
www.facebook.com/Fossilarium
Fondée en: 1997 A pour mission de mettre en valeur la période Orodovicien-Silurien dans la région; recherche; expositions; boutique.

***Nouvelle:* Musée d'histoire naturelle du parc de Miguasha**
231, rte Miguasha ouest
Nouvelle, QC G0C 2E0
Tél: 418-794-2475; *Téléc:* 418-794-2033
parc.miguasha@sepaq.com
maritime.musees.qc.ca/en/museums/miguasha/index. php
www.facebook.com/parcnationaldemiguasha
Protège et affiche le site de fossiles à la Gaspésie

***Odanak:* Musée des Abénakis**
Société historique d'Odanak, 108, Waban-Aki
Odanak, QC J0G 1H0
Tél: 450-568-2600; *Téléc:* 450-568-5959
info@museedesabenakis.ca
www.museedesabenakis.ca
twitter.com/MuseeAben akis
www.facebook.com/musee.desabenakis
Ouvert en 1962 et complètement rénové en 2005, le premier musée amérindien au Québec vous souhaite la bienvenue. Au coeur d'un site historique, un ensemble d'activité est offert pour plaire à toute la famille. Spectacle multimédia, expositions, belvédère, église catholique, chapelle et aire de pique-nique rendront la visite inoubliable.
Michelle Bélanger, Directrice générale

***Oujé-Bougoumou:* Aanischaaukamikw Cree Cultural Institute**
PO Box 1168
Located at 205 Opemiska Meskino, Oujé-Bougoumou, QC
Oujé-Bougoumou, QC G0W 3C0
Tel: 418-745-2444; *Fax:* 418-745-2324
info@creeculture.ca
www.creeculturalinstitute.ca
twitter.com/CreeCultu re
www.facebook.com/210316972365081
Year Founded: 2010 The centre serves as museum, archive, library & teaching centre. The museum collection includes traditional Cree artifacts.
Stephen Inglis, Executive Director, stephen.inglis@creeculture.ca

***Pabos Mills:* Centre d'interprétation du Parc du Bourg de Pabos**
75, rue de la Plage
Pabos Mills, QC G0C 2J0
Tél: 418-689-6043; *Téléc:* 418-689-4240
bourg@globetrotter.net
www.lebourgdepabos.com
Promouvoir l'histoire de la seule seigneurie de la Nouvelle-France à exploiter commercialement la pêche; ouvert tous le jours, juin-septembre.

***Paspébiac:* Site historique du Banc-de-Pêche-de-Paspébiac**
CP 430, 3e rue, rte du Banc
Paspébiac, QC G0C 2K0
Tél: 418-752-6229; *Téléc:* 418-752-6408
shbp@globetrotter.net
www.shbp.ca
twitter.com/shbppaspebiac
www.face book.com/206470989394772
Sea heritage & traditional trades; tours; gift shop; restaurant; open June - Oct.

***Percé:* Centre d'interprétation du Parc national de l'Ile-Bonaventure et du Rocher-Percé**
4, rue du Quai
Percé, QC G0C 2L0
Tél: 418-782-2240; *Téléc:* 418-782-2241
parc.ibrperce@sepaq.com
www.sepaq.com/pq/bon
A pour mission de protéger un refuge d'oiseaux migrateurs, et le patrimoine historique de la région
Rémi Plourde, Directeur

***Percé:* Musée Le Chafaud**
145, rte 132
Percé, QC G0C 2L0
Tél: 418-782-5100; *Téléc:* 418-782-5565
www.musee-chafaud.com
Expose l'art qui a été inspiré par Percé, la pointe de la péninsule gaspésienne.

***Péribonka:* Musée Louis-Hémon**
700, rte Maria-Chapdelaine
Péribonka, QC G0W 2G0
Tél: 418-374-2177; *Téléc:* 418-374-2516
museelh@destination.ca
www.museelh.ca
Expositions qui illustrent l'histoire de la MRC de Maria-Chapdelaine.

***Plaisance:* Centre d'interprétation du patrimoine de Plaisance**
276, rue Desjardins
Plaisance, QC J0V 2S0
Tél: 819-427-6400; *Téléc:* 819-427-5062
info@cipplaisance.qc.ca
www.ville.plaisance.qc.ca

***La Pocatière:* Musée François-Pilote**
100, 4e av
La Pocatière, QC G0R 1Z0
Tél: 418-856-3145; *Téléc:* 418-856-5611
museefpilote@leadercsa.com
www.museefrancoispilote.ca
www.facebook.com /musee.francoispilote
Fondée en: 1973 Voir la paroisse rurale d'autrefois sous tous ses aspects, des salles reconstituées d'habitations, de bureaux de professionnels et d'artisans, une collection de sciences naturelles, agriculture et sciences pures, enseignement agricole; expositions; programmes scolaires; rampe d'acces et ascenseur disponible.

***Pointe-à-la-Croix:* Battle of the Restigouche National Historic Site of Canada**
PO Box 359, rte 132
Pointe-à-la-Croix, QC G0C 1L0
Tel: 418-788-5676; *Fax:* 418-788-5895
information@pc.gc.ca
www.pc.gc.ca/eng/lhn-nhs/qc/ristigouche/index.aspx
Other contact information: TTY: 1-866-787-6221
Located at the mouth of the Restigouche River, the Battle of the Restigouche National Historic Site is the scene of the last naval battle between France & England for possession of North America in 1760. Visitors to the site can see the vestiges of the vessel, The Machault, as well as several artifacts from the

wreck. The national historic site is open daily from June to mid-October.

***Pointe-Claire:* Canadian Ski Museum & Canadian Ski Hall of Fame (CSMus) / Musée canadien du ski et Temple de la renommée du ski canadien**
317, ch du Bord-du-Lac
Pointe-Claire, QC H9S 4L6
Tel: 514-429-8444
info@skimuseum.ca
www.skimuseum.ca
Social Media: www.linkedin.com/groups/Canadian-Ski-Hall-Fame-Museum-4174287
www.facebook.com/pages/Ottawa-ON/Canadian-Ski-Museum/59397511258
The Canadian Ski Museum & Canadian Ski Hall of Fame preserves Canadian skiing history & celebrates Canadian skiing & snowboarding traditions & achievements. The Hall of Fame honours Canada's accomplished skiers, snowboarders, coaches, officials, & builders of the sport.
Stephen Finestone, Chair

***La Prairie:* Société d'histoire de la Prairie de la Magdeleine (SHLM)**
249, rue Sainte-Marie
La Prairie, QC J5R 1G1
Tél: 450-659-1393
info@shlm.info
shlm.info
Fondée en: 1972 La société historique actif dans les domaines de la généalogie, de la recherche historique et visites guidées.
Stéphane Tremblay, Président
Johanne Doyle, Coordinatrice

***Québec:* La Citadelle de Québec & Le Musée du Royal 22e Régiment**
La Citadelle, 1 Côte de la Citadelle
Québec, QC G1R 3R2
Tél: 418-694-2815; *Téléc:* 418-694-2853
information@lacitadelle.qc.ca
www.lacitadelle.qc.ca
Médias sociaux: www.youtube.com/user/museeroyal
www.facebook.com/CitadelleQuébec
Fondée en: 1980 Située sur le Cap Diamant, La Citadelle est un site du patrimoine mondial de l'UNESCO, et la résidence officielle du Royal 22e Régiment. Le musée offre des visites guidées, activités, et collections d'artefacts militaires (médailles, insignes, uniformes et textiles, armes).
Dany Hamel, Directeur, d.hamel@lacitadelle.qc.ca

***Québec:* Commission des Champs-de-Bataille nationaux / National Battlefields Commission**
390, av de Bernières
Québec, QC G1R 2L7
Tél: 418-648-3506; *Téléc:* 418-648-3638
information@ccbn-nbc.gc.ca
www.ccbn-nbc.gc.ca
Les Plaines d'Abraham; Parc des Braves; Maison de la découverte des plaines d'Abraham; Exposition multimédia Odyssée Canada; Tours Martello; Souper mystère de 1814 à la tour Martello 2; Bus d'Abraham: tour guidé des plaines d'Abraham, Maison patrimoniale Louis S.-St-Laurent, Kiosque Edwin-Bélanger, Jardin Jeanne d'Arc

***Québec:* Lieu historique national du Canada Cartier-Brébeuf / Cartier-Brébeuf National Historic Site of Canada**
CP 10 B, 175, rue de l'Espinay
2 D'Auteuil St., Québec, QC, G1R 5C2
Québec, QC G1L 3W6
Tél: 418-648-7016; *Téléc:* 418-648-7931
Ligne sans frais: 888-773-8888
information@pc.gc.ca
www.pc.gc.ca/eng/lhn-nhs/qc/cartierbrebeuf/index.aspx
Autre numéros: TTY: 418-648-7931
Commémore l'hivernage de Jacques Cartier et de ses compagnons en 1535-1536, à proximité du village iroquoïen de Stadaconé.

***Québec:* Lieu historique national du Canada de la Grosse-Ile-et-le-Mémorial-des-Irlandais / Grosse-Ile & the Irish Memorial National Historic Site of Canada**
2, rue d'Auteuil
Québec, QC G1K 7R3
Tél: 418-248-8841; *Téléc:* 866-790-8991
Ligne sans frais: 888-773-8888
information@pc.gc.ca
www.pc.gc.ca/fra/lhn-nhs/qc/grosseile/index.aspx
Médias sociaux: www.youtube.com/parcscanada
twitter.com/parcscanada
www.facebook.com/P arcsCanada
Autre numéros: **ATS: 1-866-787-6221**
Commémore l'importance de l'immigration au Canada, plus particulièrement via la porte d'entrée de Québec, et les événements tragiques vécus par les immigrants irlandais en ce lieu, notamment l'épidémie de typhus de 1847.

***Québec:* Lieu historique national du Canada des Fortifications-de-Québec / Fortifications of Québec National Historic Site of Canada**
2, rue d'Auteuil
Québec, QC G1R 5C2
Tél: 418-648-7016; *Téléc:* 418-648-7931
Ligne sans frais: 888-773-8888
information@pc.gc.ca
www.pc.gc.ca/fra/lhn-nhs/qc/fortifications/index.aspx
Autre numéros: **TTY: 1-866-787-6221**
Trésor de l'UNESCO; la Citadelle et ses environs, terrasse Dufferin, Château Frontnac; visites guidées.

***Québec:* Lieu historique national du Canada des Forts-de-Lévis**
41, ch du Gouvernement
Québec, QC G1K 7R3
Tél: 418-835-5182; *Téléc:* 418-948-9119
Ligne sans frais: 888-773-8888
information@pc.gc.ca
www.pc.gc.ca/fra/lhn-nhs/qc/levis/index.aspx
Autre numéros: **ATS: 1-866-787-6221**

***Québec:* Maison Henry-Stuart**
82, Grande Allée ouest
Québec, QC G1R 2G6
Tél: 418-647-4347; *Téléc:* 418-647-6483
Ligne sans frais: 800-494-4347
info@actionpatrimoine.ca
actionpatrimoine.ca/mhs
Construite en 1849, la maison représente un exemple d'un type d'habitation courant aux 19e siècle à Québec; collection d'objets, meubles; visites thématiques; jardin.
Pierre B. Landry, Directeur général, direction@actionpatrimoine.ca

***Québec:* Moulin des Jésuites**
7960, boul Henri-Bourassa
Québec, QC G1H 3G3
Tél: 418-624-7720; *Téléc:* 418-624-7519
moulindesjesuites@bellnet.ca
www.trait-carre.org
Joanne Timmons, Directrice générale

***Québec:* Musée Bon-Pasteur**
14, rue Couillard
Québec, QC G1R 3S9
Tél: 418-694-0243; *Téléc:* 418-694-6233
info@museebonpasteur.com
www.museebonpasteur.com
Fondée en: 1992 L'histoire de la Congrégation des Servantes du Coeur Immaculé de Marie (Soeurs du Bon-Pasteur de Québec); condition féminine au XIXe siècle; meubles et peintures d'époque; visites personnalisées en français et en anglais (portugais sur demande)
Claudette Ledet, Directrice

***Québec:* Musée de géologie**
Pavillon Adrien-Pouliot, Université Laval, 1065, av de la Médecine
Québec, QC G1V 0A6
Tél: 418-656-2131; *Téléc:* 418-656-7339
www.musee-geologie.ulaval.ca
Possède la plus ancienne collection géologique du Québec.
Olivier Rabeau, Conservateur, olivier.rabeau@ggl.ulaval.ca

***Québec:* Musée de la place Royale**
***Parent:* Musée de la civilisation**
27, rue Notre-Dame
Québec, QC G1K 4E9
Tél: 418-646-3167
Ligne sans frais: 866-710-8031
mcqweb@mcq.org
www.mcq.org/fr/cipr
Fondée en: 1999 Site historique; le Centre est situé au premier établissement français permanent en Amérique; expositions, visites commentées, animations historiques, espace découverte, activités éducatives, ateliers.

***Québec:* Musée des Augustines de l'Hôtel-Dieu de Québec**
32, rue Charlevoix
Québec, QC G1R 5C4
Tél: 418-692-2492; *Téléc:* 418-692-2668
www.augustines.org
Fondée en: 1958 Tableaux canadiens et européens, meubles, vaisselle, broderies, instruments médicaux. Le musée est en réaménagement et est fermée jusqu'en 2011.

***Québec:* Musée des Ursulines de Québec**
12, rue Donnacona
Québec, QC G1R 3Y7
Tél: 418-694-0694; *Téléc:* 418-694-0136
murq-info@vmuq.com
www.museedesursulines.com
www.facebook.com/13636963 6435729
Le musée met en valeur la collection pédagogique des Ursulines de Québec; documents; instruments de musique; objets scientifiques; spécimens d'histoire naturelle; photographies; broderies; tableaux.

***Québec:* Musée les Voltigeurs de Québec**
835, boul Pierre-Bertrand
Québec, QC G1M 2E7
Tel: 418-648-4422; *Fax:* 418-648-3040
info@voltigeursdeQuébec.net
voltigeursdeQuébec.net/musee.html
Social Media: www.youtube.com/voltigeursdeQuébec
twitter.com/voltigeurs
Year Founded: 1964 Expose des objets militaires et des véhicules.
Raymond Falardeau, Conservateur du musée
L'adjudant-chef (r) Éric Godbout, Directeur des projets

***Québec:* Musée Lucienne-Maheux de l'Institut universitaire en santé mentale de Québec**
2601, ch de la Canardière
Québec, QC G1J 2G3
Tél: 418-663-5000
www.institutsmq.qc.ca/a-propos-de/musee-lucienne-maheux
www.facebook.com /210820778947856
Documents d'archives; photographies anciennes; meubles et objets d'époque; équipements médicaux; oeuvres d'art
France St-Hilaire, Responsable du musée, 418-663-5000, musee@institutsmq.qc.ca

***Québec:* Musée Naval de Québec / Naval Museum of Québec**
170, rue Dalhousie
Québec, QC G1K 8M7
Tél: 418-694-5387; *Téléc:* 418-694-5550
info@museenavaldeQuébec.com
museenavaldeQuébec.com
Médias sociaux: www.youtube.com/user/MuseeNavalDeQuébec
twitter.com/museenaval
www.facebook.com/museenavaldeQuébec
Le musée a pour mission de conserver et communiquer l'histoire navale du Saint-Laurent, et de la Réserve navale du Canada.

***Québec:* Site patrimonial du Parc-de-L'Artillerie**
2, rue d'Auteuil
Québec, QC G1K 7A1
Tél: 418-648-7016; *Téléc:* 418-648-7931
Ligne sans frais: 888-773-8888
information@pc.gc.ca
www.pc.gc.ca/fra/lhn-nhs/qc/artiller/index.aspx
Autre numéros: **TTY: 1-866-787-6221**

***Québec:* Villa Bagatelle**
1563, ch St-Louis
Québec, QC G1S 1G1
Tél: 418-654-0259; *Téléc:* 418-654-0991
www.Québecregion.com
Centre d'exposition et de jardin.

***Richmond:* Centre d'interprétation de l'ardoise**
5, rue Belmont
Richmond, QC J0B 2H0
Tél: 819-826-3313
info@centreardoise.ca
www.centreardoise.ca
Fondée en: 1992 A pour mission de promouvoir le patrimoine de l'ardoise dans la vallée du Saint-Françcois; le centre est logé dans une église presbytérienne construite en 1889, ayant une toiture en ardoise; métiers, techniques et divers usages de cette pierre; histoires de l'industrie sont racontées

***Rimousk:* Site historique de la Maison Lamontagne**
707, boul du Rivage
Rimousk, QC G5L 1E9
Tél: 418-722-4038
maisonlamontagne@globetrotter.net
www.maisonlamontagne.com
Open - 24 juin - 5 sept.

***Rimouski:* Musée régional de Rimouski**
35, rue Saint-Germain ouest
Rimouski, QC G5L 4B4
Tél: 418-724-2272; *Téléc:* 418-725-4433
info@museerimouski.qc.ca
museerimouski.qc.ca
www.facebook.com/museerim ouski
Autre numéros: **Alt. E-mail: mrdr@globetrotter.net**
Le musée, qui loge dans la plus ancienne église de pierre de la région, présente des collections thématiques sur l'art contemporain, histoire et sciences; oeuvres et artefacts; guides interprétifs; activités.
Franck Michel, Directeur général, direction@museerimouski.qc.ca

***Rimouski:* Site historique maritime de la Pointe-au-Père**
1000 rue du Phare
Rimouski, QC G5M 1L8
Tél: 418-724-6214; *Téléc:* 418-721-0815
info@shmp.qc.ca
www.shmp.qc.ca
Médias sociaux: www.instagram.com/shmp.qc.ca
twitter.com/SHMP_officiel
www.facebook.co m/SitehistoriquePointeauPere
Fondée en: 1980 Le musée regroupe les artefacts du navire l'Empress of Ireland, et met en valeur le Phare-de-Pointe-au-Père et le sous-marin ONONDAGA, désarmé par la Défense nationale en 2000.

***Rivière-du-Loup:* Musée des bateaux miniatures et de légendes du Bas-Saint-Laurent**
80, boul Cartier
Rivière-du-Loup, QC G5R 2M7
Tél: 418-868-0800; *Téléc:* 418-868-0800
Ligne sans frais: 866-868-0800
info@museedebateauxminiatures.com
www.museebateauxminiatures.com
www.facebook.com/tourismebassaintlaurent
Autre numéros: **Hors saison: 418-498-4250**
Exposition de 160 bateaux miniatures faits par 20 artistes de la région; boutique souvenir; petite galerie d'art; visites guidées.

***Rivière-du-Loup:* Musée du Bas-St-Laurent**
300, rue St-Pierre
Rivière-du-Loup, QC G5R 3V3
Tél: 418-862-7547; *Téléc:* 418-862-3019
musee@mbsl.qc.ca
www.mbsl.qc.ca
www.facebook.com/71648123407
Fondée en: 1975 Consacré à la photographie ethnologique, art moderne, et à l'éducation; conservation, recherche, et diffusion; plus de 2 000 objets ethnologiques, et plus de 300 objets d'art; plus de 125 000 photographies anciennes; expositions itinérantes; publication; boutique; location de salles.
Pierre Landry, Directeur général, p.landry@mbsl.qc.ca

***Rivière-Éternite:* Centre de découverte et de services Le Béluga (secteur Baie Sainte-Marguerite)**
Parc National du Saguenay, 91, rue Notre-Dame
Rivière-Éternite, QC G0V 1P0
Tél: 418-272-1556; *Téléc:* 418-272-3438
Ligne sans frais: 800-665-6527
parc.saguenay@sepaq.com
www.sepaq.com/pq/sag/fr/interpretation.html
Exposition permanente "Baie comme bélugas"; l'histoire et l'importance de protéger le béluga dans son milieu naturel; activités de découverte.

***Rivière-Éternite:* Centre de découverte et de services le Fjord du Saguenay (secteur de la Baie-Éternité)**
Parc National du Saguenay, 91, rue Notre-Dame
Rivière-Éternite, QC G0P 1P0
Tél: 418-272-1556; *Téléc:* 418-272-3438
parc.saguenay@sepaq.com
www.sepaq.com/pq/sag/fr/interpretation.html
Découvrez les secrets du fjord; exposition permanente

***Rivière-St-Paul:* Musée Whiteley Museum**
Rivière-St-Paul, QC G0G 2P0
Tél: 418-379-2996
info@whiteleymuseum.com
www.whiteleymuseum.com
Priscilla Griffin, Présidente

***Rouyn-Noranda:* La Maison Dumulon**
CP 242, 191, av du Lac
Rouyn-Noranda, QC J9X 5C3
Tél: 819-797-7125; *Téléc:* 819-797-7109
maison.dumulon@rouyn-noranda.ca
www.maison-dumulon.ca
www.facebook.com /162847260393368
Fondée en: 1980 La maison de la famille Dumulon est une reconstitution fidèle du bâtiment d'origine; visites guidées; animation; activités spéciales; location de salles; boutique. L'église orthodoxe russe Saint-Georges est administrée par la Corporation de La maison Dumulon.
Alain Flageol, Directeur générale

***Saguenay:* Musée du Fjord**
3346, boul de la Grande-Baie sud
Saguenay, QC G7G 1G2
Tél: 418-697-5077; *Téléc:* 418-697-5079
Ligne sans frais: 866-697-5077
info@museedufjord.com
www.museedufjord.com
Médias sociaux: www.youtube.com/user/museedufjord
twitter.com/Musee_du_Fjord
www.faceb ook.com/118098813663
Fondée en: 1960 Consacré à la préservation et la mise en valeur du patrimoine historique, naturel et artistique du territoire du fjord du Saguenay; exposition permanente; expositions temporaires thématiques; programmation; artefacts historiques; photographies; documents.

***Saint-André-Avellin:* Musée des Pionniers de Saint-André-Avellin**
20, rue Bourgeois
Saint-André-Avellin, QC J0V 1W0
Tél: 819-983-2624
www.museedespionniers.qc.ca
Relate la vie rurale des 19e et 20e siècles; meubles, objets, outils et machines en expositions; livres du XIXe siècle; photographies.
Raymond Whissell, Président
Ginette Labrosse-Lafleur, Secrétaire-archiviste

***Saint-André-d'Argenteuil:* Musée régional d'Argenteuil / Caserne-de-Carillon - Lieu historique national du Canada (MRA)**
44, rte du Long-Sault
Saint-André-d'Argenteuil, QC J0V 1X0
Tél: 450-537-3861; *Téléc:* 450-537-1983
info@museearg.com
www.museeregionaldargenteuil.ca
twitter.com/mrargent euil
www.facebook.com/184512031562388
Fondée en: 1938 Expositions historiques: 8 salles d'exposition; Le musée est installé dans l'ancienne Caserne-de-Carillon.
Luc Grondin, Président
Lyne St-Jacques, Directrice

***Saint-Constant:* Exporail: Musée ferroviaire canadien / Exporail: Canadian Railway Museum**
***Parent:* Association canadienne d'histoire ferroviaire**
110, rue St-Pierre
Saint-Constant, QC J5A 1G7
Tél: 450-632-2410; *Téléc:* 450-638-1563
info@exporail.org
www.exporail.org
Médias sociaux: www.youtube.com/user/Exporail110
twitter.com/Exporail
www.facebook.com /Exporail
Fondée en: 1961 La plus grande collection au Canada de matériel ferroviaire (150 véhicules, un plateau tournant, 2 gares, un nouveau pavillon d'exposition).
Nadine Cloutier, Directrice, Opérations et gestion des bénévoles, nadine.cloutier@exporail.org

***Saint-Denis-de-la-Bouteillerie:* Maison Chapais**
2, rte 132 est
Saint-Denis-de-la-Bouteillerie, QC G0L 2R0
Tél: 418-498-2353; *Téléc:* 418-498-4070
infos@maisonchapais.com
www.maisonchapais.com
twitter.com/MaisonChapai s
www.facebook.com/213524838684198
Fondée en: 1990 Monument historique daté de 1834; trois étages et diverses dépendances; réservations préférables pour les groupes; visites guidées de la maison et ses jardins oubliés; galerie-boutique offre cadeaux et souvenirs, livres.

***Sainte-Anne-de-Beaupré:* Musée de Sainte-Anne-de-Beaupré**
10018, av Royale
Sainte-Anne-de-Beaupré, QC G0A 3C0
Tél: 418-827-3782; *Téléc:* 418-827-8771
musee@ssadb.qc.ca
www.shrinesaintanne.org
Le musée retrace l'histoire d'un pèlerinage et rend hommage à la Vierge Marie; expositions permanentes et temporaires; visites guidées; jardins; magasin du Sanctuaire.

***Sainte-Famille:* Maison de nos Aïeux**
***Parent:* Fondation François-Lamy**
3907, chemin Royal
Sainte-Famille, QC G0A 3P0
Tél: 418-829-0330
www.fondationfrancoislamy.org

***Sainte-Famille:* Maison Drouin**
***Parent:* Fondation François-Lamy**
4700, chemin Royal
Sainte-Famille, QC G0A 3P0
Tél: 418-829-0330
www.fondationfrancoislamy.org

***Sainte-Foy:* Maison Hamel-Bruneau**
CP 700, 2608, ch Saint-Louis
Sainte-Foy, QC G1R 4S9
Tél: 418-641-6280
patrimoinestefoysillery@ville.Québec.qc.ca
www.maisonsdupatrimoine.com
Construit vers 1857; maison historique abrite un centre de diffusion culturelle; programmation thématique variée; concerts; activités; jardins, aire de pique-nique.

***Sainte-Marie:* Maison J.A. Vachon**
383, rue de la Coopérative
Sainte-Marie, QC G6E 3X5
Tél: 418-387-4052; *Téléc:* 418-387-2652
Ligne sans frais: 866-387-4052
maisonjavachon@globetrotter.net
www.vachon.com/en/history/maison

***Saint-Eustache:* Maison de la Culture et du Patrimoine**
235, rue Saint-Eustache
Saint-Eustache, QC J7R 2L8
Tél: 450-974-5170; *Téléc:* 450-974-2632
Fondée en: 2005 Expose des objets qui mettent en valeur l'histoire de la ville

***Saint-Eustache:* Moulin Légaré / Légaré Mill**
232, rue St-Eustache
Saint-Eustache, QC J7R 2L7
Tél: 450-974-5400; *Téléc:* 450-974-2632
www.corporationdumoulinlegare.com
Fondée en: 1975 Ce moulin à farine construit en 1762 n'a jamais cessé de travailler une fois depuis son achèvement. Le meunier y produit du blé et de farine de sarrasin avec les meules d'origine et la farine est vendue sur place. Les activités sont disponibles pour les étudiants.
Mélanie Séguin, Directrice, 450-974-5001, mseguin@corporationdumoulinlegare.com

***Saint-Hyacinthe:* Musée du Centre Élisabeth-Bergeron**
805, av Raymond
Saint-Hyacinthe, QC J2S 5T9
Tél: 450-773-6067; *Téléc:* 450-773-8044
www.sjsh.org/centre-elisabeth-bergeron.html
Médias sociaux: www.youtube.com/soeurssaintjoseph
twitter.com/sjsh_org
www.facebook.co m/SJSH.org
Présente la vie et l'oeuvre de la fondatrice des Soeurs de Saint-Joseph-de Saint-Hyacinthe; l'histoire d'une communauté

de religieuses enseignantes, fondée en terre Maskoutaine; quatre salles d'exposition, visite commentée comprenant une présentation audiovisuelle, un arrêt au tombeau de la vénérable Élisabeth Bergeron ainsi qu'à la chapelle; ouvert tous les jours.

Saint-Hyacinthe: Musée du séminaire de Saint-Hyacinthe
650, rue Girouard est
Saint-Hyacinthe, QC J2S 7B7
Tél: 450-774-8977; *Téléc:* 450-774-7101
Musée des sciences naturelles, de l'archéologie, de l'ethnologie, patrimoine religieux et des ouvres d'art

Saint-Hyacinthe: Société du patrimoine religieux du diocèse de Saint-Hyacinthe
650, rue Girouard est
Saint-Hyacinthe, QC J2S 2Y2
Tél: 450-261-0593; *Téléc:* 450-252-3018
www.prah.org
Fondée en: 1995 La collection virtuelle
Anick Chandonnet, Directrice, anick@prah.org

Saint-Jean-Port-Joli: Musée de la mémoire vivante
710, av De Gaspé Ouest
Saint-Jean-Port-Joli, QC G0R 3G0
Tél: 418-358-0518; *Téléc:* 418-358-0519
information@memoirevivante.org
www.memoirevivante.org
Médias sociaux: www.youtube.com/user/MUSEEMEMOIREVIVANTE
twitter.com/Memoire_vivante
www.facebook.com/369537525226

Saint-Jean-Port-Joli: Musée de sculpture sur bois des Anciens Canadiens
332, av de Gaspé ouest
Saint-Jean-Port-Joli, QC G0R 3G0
Tél: 418-598-3392; *Téléc:* 418-598-3329
info@museedesancienscanadiens.com
www.museedesancienscanadiens.com
Collection de plus de 250 sculptures originales, et un vidéo sur la sculpture sur bois et sur neige. Le musée est ouvert du mai jusqu'au novembre.

Saint-Jean-sur-Richelieu: Musée Du Fort St-Jean
15, rue Jacques-Cartier nord
Saint-Jean-sur-Richelieu, QC J3B 8R8
Tél: 450-358-6500; *Téléc:* 450-358-6909
info@museedufortsaintjean.ca
www.museedufortsaintjean.ca
Fondée en: 1965 Expose des objets militaires et des véhicules
Col. (ret.) Pierre Cadotte, Président O.M.M., M.S.M., C.D.
Eric Ruel, Conservateur

Saint-Jean-sur-Richelieu: Musée du Haut-Richelieu
182, Jacques-Cartier nord
Saint-Jean-sur-Richelieu, QC J3B 7W3
Tél: 450-347-0649; *Téléc:* 450-347-9994
info@museeduhaut-richelieu.com
www.museeduhaut-richelieu.com
Médias sociaux: www.youtube.com/user/MuseeHR
twitter.com/musee_hr
www.facebook.com/79573645828
Fondée en: 1971 L'histoire du Haut-Richelieu; presente l'objets qui font à la ceramique, les objets de nature ethnographique et des photographies qui étaient photographié par Joseph-Laurent Pinsonneault.

Saint-Jérôme: Musée d'art contemporain des Laurentides (MACL)
101, place du Curé-Labelle
Saint-Jérôme, QC J7Z 1X6
Tél: 450-432-7171; *Téléc:* 450-432-8171
musee@museelaurentides.ca
www.museelaurentides.ca
twitter.com/MACLaure ntides
www.facebook.com/MACLaurentides
Serge Tessier, Président

Saint-Jérôme: Société d'histoire de la Rivière-du-Nord (SHRN)
CP 206, 101, place du Curé-Labelle
Saint-Jérôme, QC J7Z 1X6
Tél: 450-436-1512; *Téléc:* 450-436-1211
courriel@shrn.org
www.shrn.org
Suzanne Marcotte, Présidente

Saint-Joseph-de-Beauce: Musée Marius-Barbeau
139, rue Sainte-Christine
Saint-Joseph-de-Beauce, QC G0S 2V0
Tél: 418-397-4039; *Téléc:* 418-397-6151
info@museemariusbarbeau.com
www.museemariusbarbeau.com
www.facebook.co m/267176070016503
Le musée a pour mission la conservation, la recherche et la mise en valeur le patrimoine de la Beauce, tant du point de vue historique, ethnologique et artistique.
Lucie Duval, Personne ressource

Saint-Joseph-de-la-Rive: Musée maritime de Charlevoix
305, rue de l'Église
Saint-Joseph-de-la-Rive, QC G0A 3Y0
Tél: 418-635-1131; *Téléc:* 418-635-2600
expom@charlevoix.net
www.museemaritime.com
www.facebook.com/1002668367 89490
Conserve et communique le patrimoine maritime à travers l'histoire des goélettes qui ont naviguées sur le Saint-Laurent; bâtiment central thématique, scierie, atelier et magasin de l'époque; exposition sur l'astroblème; archives; boutique.
Serge Labbé, Direction générale, sl@museemaritime.com

Saint-Joseph-de-la-Rive: Papeterie Saint-Gilles
CP 40
Situé à 304, rue Félix Antoine-Savard,
Saint-Joseph-de-la-Rive, QC
Saint-Joseph-de-la-Rive, QC G0A 3Y0
Tél: 418-635-2430; *Téléc:* 418-635-2613
Ligne sans frais: 866-635-2430
papier@papeteriesaintgilles.com
www.papeteriesaintgilles.com
Papier fait à la main, 100% coton, sans acide et chiné de pétales de fleurs de la région, selon des techniques traditionnelles datant du XVIIe siècle

Saint-Prime: Musée du fromage cheddar
148, av Albert-Perron
Saint-Prime, QC G8J 1L4
Tél: 418-251-4922; *Téléc:* 418-251-1172
Ligne sans frais: 888-251-4922
cheddar@bellnet.ca
www.museecheddar.org
www.facebook .com/MuseeDuFromageCheddar
La vieille Fromagerie Perron est la seule survivante de sa catégorie au Québec. Aujourd'hui transformée en lieu d'interprétation elle vous raconte la fabrication traditionnelle du cheddar; visites guidées; boutique souvenir, vente de fromage; casiers verrouillés pour vélos; ouverte au public juin - sept. et sur réservation pour le reste de l'année.
Diane Hudon, Directrice générale

Salaberry-de-Valleyfield: Écomusée des Deux-Rives
75, rue St-Jean-Baptiste
Situé à 758, av Grande-île, Salaberry-de-Valleyfield, QC J6S 3N8
Salaberry-de-Valleyfield, QC J6T 1Z6
Tél: 450-370-4855; *Téléc:* 450-370-4861
info@museedesdeuxrives.com

Sept-îles: Musée régional de la Côte-Nord (MRCN)
500, boul Laure
Sept-îles, QC G4R 1X7
Tél: 418-968-2070; *Téléc:* 418-968-8323
mrcn@mrcn.qc.ca
www.mrcn.qc.ca
Fondée en: 1976 Beaux-Arts; archéologie; photographie; sciences naturelles; ethnologie

Sept-Îles: Musée Shaputuan / Shaputuan Museum
290, boul des Montagnais
Sept-Îles, QC G4R 5R2
Tél: 418-962-4000
A pour mission de perpétuer la culture des Innus; le musée s'engage a acquérir, étudier et interpréter la culture; expositions; activités.

Shawinigan: Cité de l'Énergie
CP 156
Situé à 1000, av Melville, Shawinigan, QC
Shawinigan, QC G9N 6T9
Tél: 819-536-8516; *Téléc:* 819-536-2982
Ligne sans frais: 866-900-2483
infocite@citedelenergie.com
www.citedelenergie.com
Médias sociaux: www.youtube.com/user/CiteEnergie
twitter.com/citedelenergie
www.facebo ok.com/CiteEnergie
Fondée en: 1997 Centre de sciences, expositions, spectacle multimédia, tour d'observation Hydro-Québec

Shawinigan-Sud: Église Notre-Dame-de-la-Présentation
825, 2e Avenue
Shawinigan-Sud, QC G9P 1E1
Tél: 819-536-3652; *Téléc:* 819-536-4170
eglisendp@cgocable.ca
www.oziasleducenmauricie.com
www.facebook.com/Oz iasLeducenMauricie
Fondée en: 1977 Lieu historique national du Canada; protection et mise en valeur des oeuvres de Leduc dans l'église

Sherbrooke: Centre culturel et du patrimoine Uplands / Uplands Cultural & Heritage Centre
Parent: Société d'histoire et de musée Lennoxville-Ascot
9, rue Speid
Sherbrooke, QC J1M 1R9
Tél: 819-564-0409; *Téléc:* 819-564-8951
uplands@uplands.ca
uplands.ca
twitter.com/Uplands1
www.facebook.com/ 138071916264187
Oeuvres d'artistes locaux et régionaux; des ateliers; thé à l'anglaise; des activités et des concerts; importante collection d'antiquités
Nancy Robert, Directrice

Sherbrooke: Musée de la nature et des sciences de Sherbrooke / Sherbrooke Museum of Nature & Science
225, rue Frontenac
Sherbrooke, QC J1H 1K1
Tél: 819-564-3200; *Téléc:* 819-564-0287
Ligne sans frais: 877-434-3200
info@naturesciences.qc.ca
www.naturesciences.qc.ca
twitter.com/naturescience
www.facebook.com/na turesciencessherbrooke
Fondée en: 1879 Situé dans une ancienne usine de textile, le Musée renferme une collection de près de 100 000 objets dont 65 000 en sciences naturelles; expositions; théâtre d'objets intéractifs sur la fonction du cerveau; services d'animation et d'éducation et une salle multifonctionnelle disponible en location.
Mme Marie-Claude Bibeau, Directrice générale, marie-claude.bibeau@naturesciences.qc.ca

Sherbrooke: Musée Régimentaire des Fusiliers de Sherbrooke
64, rue Belvédère sud
Sherbrooke, QC J1H 4B4
Tél: 819-564-5940; *Téléc:* 819-564-5641
musee.fusdesher@videotron.ca
www.fusiliersdesherbrooke.ca
Attirail militaire

Sherbrooke: La Société d'histoire de Sherbrooke
275, rue Dufferin
Sherbrooke, QC J1H 4M5
Tél: 819-821-5406; *Téléc:* 819-821-5417
info@histoiresherbrooke.com
www.histoiresherbrooke.com
Médias sociaux: plus.google.com/111475291093887610216/
www.facebook.com/22243800789
Fondée en: 1927 A pour mission de préserver le patrimoine local, et promouvoir l'histoire de Sherbrooke et les Cantons-de-l'Est
Michael Harnois, Directeur général, michel.harnois@histoiresherbrooke.com
Karine Savary, Archiviste, karine.savary@histoiresherbrooke.com

***Sorel-Tracy:* Biophare**
6, rue St-Pierre
Sorel-Tracy, QC J3P 3S2
Tél: 450-780-5740; *Téléc:* 450-780-5734
Ligne sans frais: 877-780-5740
info@biophare.com
www.biophare.com
www.facebook.com/Biophare.observatoire
Fondée en: 1994 Dédiée à la réserve de la biosphère du lac Saint-Pierre; présente une exposition permanente "l'observatoire du lac Saint-Pierre"; musée, groupes scolaires, boutique, location de salles.
Marc Mineau, Directeur général

***Stanbridge East:* Missisquoi Museum / Musée Missisquoi**
2 River St.
Stanbridge East, QC J0J 2H0
Tel: 450-248-3153; *Fax:* 450-248-0420
info@missisquoimuseum.ca
www.museemissisquoi.ca
www.facebook.com/10551 8399495582
Year Founded: 1964 Museum is house in the 1830 three-story, red brick, Cornell Mill. Exhibitions include Missisquoi County Archives, and explore the historic development of the county. Other buildings on site are the Walbridge Barn and Hodge's General Store.
Pamela Realffe, Executive Secretary, prealffe@missisquoimuseum.ca
Heather Darch, Curator, hdarch@missisquoimuseum.ca
Judy Antle, Archivist, jantle@missisquoimuseum.ca

***Stanstead:* Stanstead Historical Society (SHS) / Société Historique de Stanstead**
535, rue Dufferin
Stanstead, QC J0B 3E0
Tel: 819-876-7322; *Fax:* 819-876-7936
info@colbycurtis.ca
www.colbycurtis.ca
Other contact information: Archives E-mail: archives@colbycurtis.ca
Year Founded: 1929 Operates the Colby Curtis Museum & Carrollcroft Property

***St-Lin-Laurentides:* Lieu historique national du Canada de Sir-Wilfrid-Laurier / Sir Wilfrid Laurier National Historic Site of Canada**
945, 12e av
St-Lin-Laurentides, QC J5M 2W4
Tél: 450-439-3702; *Téléc:* 450-439-5721
Ligne sans frais: 888-787-8888
information@pc.gc.ca
www.pc.gc.ca/fra/lhn-nhs/qc/wilfridlaurier/index.aspx
Autre numéros: **ATS: 1-866-787-6221**
Centre d'interprétation; exposition présente la vie et l'oeuvre de Sir Wilfrid Laurier.

***St-Paul-de-l'Ile-aux-Noix:* Lieu historique national du Canada du Fort-Lennox / Fort Lennox National Historic Site of Canada**
1, 61e Avenue
St-Paul-de-l'Ile-aux-Noix, QC J0J 1G0
Tél: 450-291-5700; *Téléc:* 450-291-4389
Ligne sans frais: 888-773-8888
information@pc.gc.ca
www.pc.gc.ca/fra/lhn-nhs/qc/lennox/index.aspx
Autre numéros: **ATS: 1-866-787-6221**
Visites guidées; activités; caserne, poudrière, corps de garde, et prison; expositions: "Ces messieurs les officiers", et "Le fort Lennox, Oeuvre des ingénieurs royaux".

***Sutton:* Eberdt Museum of Communications**
30A, rue Principale sud
Sutton, QC J0E 2K0
Tél: 450-538-2883
mchs@aide-internet.org
Special collection for TV & radio

***Sutton:* Musée des communications et d'histoire de Sutton**
32, rue Principale sud
Sutton, QC J0E 2K0
Tél: 450-538-2883
www.museedesutton.com
www.facebook.com/224180200996688
Expose des objets ayant à voir avec l'histoire de la ville de Sutton et de l'histoire du comté de Brome-Missisquoi.

***Tadoussac:* Centre d'interprétation des mammifères marins**
108, rue de la Cale-Sèche
Tadoussac, QC G0T 2A0
Tél: 418-235-4701; *Téléc:* 418-235-4325
info@gremm.org
www.gremm.org
Fondée en: 2005 A pour mission la conservation du milieu marin & la recherche scientifique sur les mammifères marins du Saint-Laurent

***Tadoussac:* La maison des Dunes**
750, ch du Moulin Baude
Tadoussac, QC G0T 2A0
Tél: 418-235-4238
Ligne sans frais: 800-665-6527
Maison faisant partie du patrimoine local, transformée en centre d'interprétation; exposition permanente; présentations, par des naturalistes, sur le phénomène des dunes de sable

***Tadoussac:* La Petite chapelle de Tadoussac**
CP 69, rue Bord de l'Eau
Tadoussac, QC G0T 2A0
Tél: 418-235-4657
Autre numéros: **Alt. Phone: 418-235-1415**

***Tadoussac:* Poste de Traite Chauvin Trading Post**
157, rue du Bord-de-l'Eau
Tadoussac, QC G0T 2A0
Tél: 418-235-4657
culture@tadoussac.com
Réplique du premier poste de traite des fourrures du 17e siècle; présente des objets se rapportant à la vie des autochtones et les produits d'échange; dégustation de phoque tous les dimanches

***Témiscouata-sur-le-Lac:* Fort Ingall Site Historique**
***Parent:* Société d'Histoire et d'Archéologie du Témiscouata**
81, rue Caldwell
Témiscouata-sur-le-Lac, QC G0L 1E0
Tél: 418-854-2375; *Téléc:* 418-854-6477
Ligne sans frais: 866-242-2437
info@fortingall.ca
www.fortingall.ca
www.facebook.com/fortingall
Expositions, animations et visites guidées
Raymonde Gratton, Présidente

***Terrebonne:* Site historique de l'île-des-Moulins**
866, rue St-Pierre
Terrebonne, QC J6W 1E5
Tél: 450-471-0619; *Téléc:* 450-471-8311
info@iledesmoulins.qc.ca
www.iledesmoulins.qc.ca
www.facebook.com/iled esmoulins.vieuxterrebonne
Bureau seigneurial; le Moulin neuf; le Moulin à scie et le Moulin à farine; la Boulangerie

***Tête-à-la-Baleine:* Centre d'interprétation de l'île Providence et Musée Jos Hébert**
***Parent:* Association touristique de Tête-à-la-Baleine**
Tête-à-la-Baleine, QC G0G 2W0
Tél: 418-242-2015
www.tourismebassecotenord.com

***Thetford Mines:* Musée minéralogique et minier de Thetford Mines**
711, boul Frontenac ouest
Thetford Mines, QC G6E 7Y8
Tél: 418-335-2123; *Téléc:* 418-335-5605
Ligne sans frais: 855-335-2123
service.client@museemineralogique.com
www.museemineralogique.com
www.facebook.com/333048121773
Fondée en: 1976 Présente l'histoire géologique, minière & social de la région de L'Amiante; expositions; activités educatives; excursions
François Cinq-Mars, Directeur, f.cinq-mars@museemineralogique.com

***Trois-Pistoles:* Parc de l'aventure basque en Amérique (PABA)**
66, rue du Parc
Trois-Pistoles, QC G0L 4K0
Tél: 418-851-1556
info@aventurebasque.ca
www.aventurebasque.ca
www.facebook.com/Aventurebasque
Fondée en: 1996

***Trois-Rivières:* Boréalis - Centre d'histoire de l'industrie papetière**
CP 368, 200, av des Draveurs
Trois-Rivières, QC G9A 5H3
Tél: 819-372-4633; *Téléc:* 819-374-1900
borealis@v3r.net
www.borealis3r.ca
Médias sociaux: www.youtube.com/user/borealis3r
www.facebook.com/borealis3r
Boréalis s'engage à vous faire découvrir l'histoire de la région papetière du Québec; activités; groupes scolaires et adultes; ouvert tous les jours 10h-18h, du 26 mai au 30 septembre et sur réservation pour les groupes
Valérie Bourgeois, Directrice

***Trois-Rivières:* Lieu historique national du Canada des Forges-du-Saint-Maurice / Forges du Saint-Maurice National Historic Site of Canada**
10 000, boul des Forges
702 - 5e rue, Shawinigan, QC, G5N 1E9
Trois-Rivières, QC G9C 1B1
Tél: 819-378-5116; *Téléc:* 819-378-0887
Ligne sans frais: 888-773-8888
info.metropolitain@pc.gc.ca
www.pc.gc.ca/fra/lhn-nhs/qc/saintmaurice/index.aspx
Autre numéros: **Off season phone: 514-283-2282; Off season fax: 514-238-5560**
A 20 minutes de Trois-Rivières, commémore l'établissement de la première communauté industrielle au Canada; ouvert de mi-mai à mi-oct.; groupes sur réservation.

***Trois-Rivières:* Musée des Filles de Jésus**
1193, boul Saint-Louis
Trois-Rivières, QC G8Z 2M8
Tél: 819-376-3741; *Téléc:* 819-376-8107
fjtrmuse@infoteck.qc.ca
www.musee-fdj.com

***Trois-Rivières:* Musée des Ursulines de Trois-Rivières**
734, rue des Ursulines
Trois-Rivières, QC G9A 5B5
Tél: 819-375-7922; *Téléc:* 819-375-0238
info@musee-ursulines.qc.ca
www.musee-ursulines.qc.ca
twitter.com/musee ursulines
www.facebook.com/musee.desursulines
Autre numéros: **Alt. URL: www.ursulines-uc.com**
Conserve et met en valeur l'histoire des Ursulines dès 1697; expositions thématiques, visites guidées, galerie d'art.

***Trois-Rivières:* Musée militaire de Trois-Rivières**
574, rue St-François-Xavier
Trois-Rivières, QC G9A 1R6
Tél: 819-371-5290
www.12rbc.ca
www.facebook.com/129458170486545
Musée et manège militaire; exposition retraçant l'histoire du régiment; salles d'armes; collections d'uniformes, pièces d'équipements, armes blanches et armes à feu en usage dans les Forces canadiennes.

***Trois-Rivières:* Musée Pierre Boucher**
858, rue Laviolette
Trois-Rivières, QC G9A 5S3
Tél: 819-376-4459; *Téléc:* 819-378-0607
museepierre-boucher@ssj.qc.ca
www.museepierreboucher.com
Musée fondé en 1920 par Mgr Albert Tessier pour protéger et sauvegarder le patrimoine local et régional; art contemporain (québecois et canadien); un programme d'animation adapté pour les groupes scolaires et les groupes d'adultes est centré sur les expositions temporaires, consacrées aux artistes contemporains et aux collections du musée; le musée est ouvert gratuitement du mardi au dimanche

***Trois-Rivières:* Musée québécois de culture populaire / Museum of Québec Folk Culture**
200, rue Laviolette
Trois-Rivières, QC G9A 6L5
Tél: 819-372-0406; *Téléc:* 819-372-9907
info@culturepop.qc.ca
www.culturepop.qc.ca
Médias sociaux: www.youtube.com/user/Museeculturepop
twitter.com/Museeculturepop
www.f acebook.com/culturepop
Fondée en: 2001 Le Musée propose six expositions audacieuses, non conventionnelles et empreintes de plaisir à la manière des Québécois; reliée au Musée, la Vieille prison de Trois-Rivières, offre une visite-expérience, guidée par des

ex-détenus. Heures: 24 juin à la fête du Travail: L-D 10h-18h; Automne, hiver, printemps: Ma-D 10h-17h
Yvon Noël, Directrice, ynoel@culturepop.qc.ca

Ulverton: Moulin à laine d'Ulverton / Ulverton Woolen Mills
210, ch Porter
Ulverton, QC J0B 2B0
Tél: 819-826-3157; _Téléc:_ 819-826-6266
moulin@moulin.ca
www.moulin.ca
twitter.com/Moulinalaine
www.facebook .com/UlvertonWoolenMills
Fondée en: 1982 Initie aux méthodes artisanales et industrielles de production et de traitement de la laine

Upton: Musée Saint-Éphrem
351, rue Monseigneur Desmarais
Upton, QC J0H 2E0
Tél: 450-549-4533; _Téléc:_ 450-549-4563
info@museestephrem.com
museestephrem.com
www.facebook.com/139545639458 480
Autre numéros: **Courriel: fondation@museestephrem.com**

Valcourt: Musée J. Armand Bombardier
1001, av J.A. Bombardier
Valcourt, QC J0E 2L0
Tél: 450-532-5300; _Téléc:_ 450-532-2260
info@museebombardier.com
www.museebombardier.com
Médias sociaux: www.youtube.com/MuseeJAB
www.facebook.com/MuseeBombardier
Fondée en: 1971 Le musée présente la vie et l'oeuvre de Joseph-Armand Bombardier, mécanicien, inventeur et entrepreneur; retrace l'évolution de l'industrie de la motoneige; expositions; activités.

Val-d'Or: La Cité de l'Or
Parent: La Corporation du Village minier de Bourlamaque
CP 212, 90, av Perreault
Val-d'Or, QC J9P 4P3
Tél: 819-825-1274; _Téléc:_ 819-825-9853
Ligne sans frais: 855-825-1274
courrier@citedelor.qc.ca
www.citedelor.com
Fondée en: 1995 Site historique du patrimoine minier en Abitibi-Témiscamingue; visites guidées à la seule mine d'or du Québec accessible à 91 mètre sous terre; expositions; boutique; par réservation.

Vaudreuil-Dorion: Centre d'histoire La Presqu'île
431, av St-Charles
Vaudreuil-Dorion, QC J7V 2N3
Tél: 450-424-5627; _Téléc:_ 450-424-5675
www.chlapresquile.qc.ca
Jean-Luc Brazeau, Archiviste

Vaudreuil-Dorion: Musée régional de Vaudreuil-Soulanges (MRVS)
431, av St-Charles
Vaudreuil-Dorion, QC J7V 2N3
Tél: 450-455-2092; _Téléc:_ 450-455-6782
Ligne sans frais: 877-455-2092
info@mrvs.qc.ca
www.mrvs.qc.ca
www.facebook.com/Cyprienne.la.souris
Exposition permanente et expositions temporaires; collections spécialisées; ethnologie et histoire; collection beaux-arts; circuits patrimoniaux; centre de documentation en généalogie et histoire régionale; visities guidées, activités, ateliers, programmation; location de salles; boutique; café.
Daniel Bissonnette, Directeur générale

Victoriaville: Musée Laurier
16, rue Laurier ouest
Victoriaville, QC G6P 6P3
Tél: 819-357-8655; _Téléc:_ 819-357-8655
info@museelaurier.com
museelaurier.com
Médias sociaux:
www.youtube.com/channel/UCsyfFCBlzwKYRkL1eFEiolQ
www.facebook.com/musee. laurier
Fondée en: 1929 Résidence de Sir Wilfrid Laurier, ancien premier ministre du Canada, et sa femme Lady Laurier, maintenant la propriété de la Société du Musée Laurier; collection d'objets d'art et de meubles, sculpture, et oeuvres en art contemporain.
Richard Pedneault, Directeur/Conservateur

Westmount: Aron Museum
Temple Emanu-El-Beth Sholom, 4100, rue Sherbrooke ouest
Westmount, QC H3Z 1A5
Tel: 514-937-3575; _Fax:_ 514-937-7058
www.templeMontréal.ca/about-us/museum-and-gallery
twitter.com/templemont real
Jewish ceremonial art objects

Westmount: Royal Montréal Regiment Museum
4625, rue Ste-Catherine ouest
Westmount, QC H3Z 1S4
Tel: 514-496-2003; _Fax:_ 514-496-5085
royalMontréalregiment.com
twitter.com/rmtlr
www.facebook.com/royalmont realregiment

Windsor: Parc histoique de la Poudrière de Windsor / Windsor Powder Mill Historical Park
342, rue St-Georges
Windsor, QC J1S 2Z5
Tél: 819-845-5284
poudriere@villedewindsor.qc.ca
www.poudriere-windsor.com
www.facebook.com/195123797205009
Fondée en 1864, dans la foulée de la guerre de session, la Poudrière de Windsor s'est investie dans la fabrication de poudre noire, un composé essentiel des explosifs. Jusqu'en 1922, la ville de Windsor a vécu au rythme de cette industrie dangereuse. On peut maintenant découvrir les secrets, le comment et le pourquoi de cette industrie via une toute nouvelle exposition permanente et la visite guidé

Saskatchewan

Provincial Museums

Royal Saskatchewan Museum (RSM)
2445 Albert St.
Regina, SK S4P 4W7
Tel: 306-787-2815; _Fax:_ 306-787-2820
info@royalsaskmuseum.ca
www.royalsaskmuseum.ca
Social Media: www.youtube.com/user/royalsaskmuseum
twitter.com/royalsaskmuseum
www.f acebook.com/Royal.Saskatchewan.Museum
Saskatchewan's natural & human history; archaeology; entomology; botany; natural history; paleontology; geology. Life Sciences Gallery; Earth Sciences Gallery; First Nations Gallery; Paleo Pit interactive gallery for children ; Megamunch, a half-size robotic Tyrannosaurus rex. Publication of informational booklets & nature notes, giftshop, research library.
Harold Bryant, Museum Director

Western Development Museum (WDM) Curatorial Centre
2935 Lorne Ave.
Saskatoon, SK S7J 0S5
Tel: 306-934-1400; _Fax:_ 306-934-4467
Toll-Free: 800-363-6345
info@wdm.ca
www.wdm.ca
Social Media: www.instagram.com/wdm.ca
twitter.com/wdmtweets
www.facebook.com/skwdm
The Western Development Museum preserves Saskatchewan's collective heritage, in order to raise awareness of & interest in the cultural & economic development of western Canada. The Curatorial Centre in Saskatoon coordinates services for the museum's branches in Moose Jaw, North Battleford, Saskatoon, & Yorkton. Tours of the Curatorial Centre may be arranged through the education & extension staff.
Joan Kanigan, Chief Executive Officer, jkanigan@wdm.ca

Local Museums

Abernethy: Abernethy Nature-Heritage Museum
PO Box 125, Main St.
Abernethy, SK S0A 0A0
Tel: 306-333-2202
anhm@sasktel.net
www.facebook.com/AbernethyNatureHeritageMuseum
Other contact information: Alt. Phones: 306-333-2102; 306-333-2125
Heritage & antique artifacts with a core exhibit of more than 300 wildlife specimens mounted by the late Ralph Stueck (1897-1979); video presentation of Stueck's "talking goose" & other folklore; activities/hands-on displays for children; small art gallery; 1930's classroom. Open daily May - Sept. Wheelchair accessible.

Abernethy: Motherwell Homestead Natural Historic Site
PO Box 70
Abernethy, SK S0A 0A0
Tel: 306-333-2116; _Fax:_ 306-333-2210
motherwell.homestead@pc.gc.ca
www.pc.gc.ca/lhn-nhs/sk/motherwell.aspx
Year Founded: 1983 The site includes Lanark Place, the farmstead estate of pioneer farmer & politician, W.R. Motherwell, who had a significant influence on the development of scientific agriculture in Western Canada. The homestead depicts the lifestyles, costumes & architecture of the early 20th century, with costumed guides. Open Victoria Day - Labour Day.

Alameda: Alameda & District Heritage Museum
PO Box 195
Alameda, SK S0C 0A0
Tel: 306-483-5099
Open Wed. July-Aug., or by appointment.

Alida: Gervais Wheels Museum
PO Box 40
Alida, SK S0C 0B0
Tel: 306-443-2303
Pioneer artifacts, music boxes, gramophones, North American automobiles

Allan: Allan Community Heritage Society & Museum
326 Main St.
Allan, SK S0K 0C0
Tel: 306-257-3511; _Fax:_ 306-257-4249
allanskmuseum@sasktel.net
www.facebook.com/AllanSKMuseum
Other contact information: Alternate Phone: 306-257-3634
Year Founded: 2005

Arborfield: Dickson Hardie Interpretive Centre at Pasquia Regional Park
PO Box 339
Arborfield, SK S0E 0A0
Tel: 306-768-3239; _Fax:_ 306-769-8307
pasquia1@xplornet.ca
www.pasquia.com
The museum features fossil castings of archaeological finds from around the Carrot River, & pieces from throughout the region collected by locals. Open May-Sept.

Arcola: Arcola Museum
PO Box 354
Arcola, SK S0C 0G0
Tel: 306-455-2462
Open May-Sept.

Assiniboia: Assiniboia & District Museum
PO Box 1211, 506 - 3rd Ave. West
Assiniboia, SK S0H 0B0
Tel: 306-642-5353; _Fax:_ 306-642-5622
assini.museum@sasktel.net
southcentralmuseums.ca/assiniboia.html
www.f acebook.com/173848239361722
The Assiniboia & District Museum features vintage cars from 1916 to 1964, a grain elevator, a Pole Shed with agricultural machinery, a school room & a military display. The museum is open seven days a week during July & August, & Monday to Friday from September to June.

Avonlea: Avonlea Heritage Museum
PO Box 401
Located at 219 Railway Ave., Avonlea, SK
Avonlea, SK S0H 0C0
Tel: 306-868-2101
www.avonleamuseum.ca
Year Founded: 1980 The Avonlea Heritage Museum displays artifacts which depict the geological age, plus the history of native people, pioneers, & ranchers in the area. The Truax Anglican Church is situated on the grounds. The museum is open from June to September. At other times of the year, appointments can be arranged. Hours: June, July, Aug. 10:00-5:00 or by Appointment
Richard Geisler, President
Joyce Holland, Secretary
Debra Penner, Treasurer

Battleford: Fort Battleford National Historic Site of Canada
PO Box 70
Battleford, SK S0M 0E0
Tel: 306-937-2621; _Fax:_ 306-937-3370
battleford.info@pc.gc.ca
www.parkscanada.gc.ca/battleford
Other contact information: TTY: 306-937-3199

Year Founded: 1876 The site features camping grounds, year round special events and learning opportunities for children, as well as access to other museums in the area; open three days a week May - Jun, seven days a week from Jul - Sept, 10:00 - 4:00.

***Battleford:* Fred Light Museum**
PO Box 40
Battleford, SK S0M 0E0
Tel: 306-937-7111
flm@sasktel.net
fredlightmuseum.webs.com
Year Founded: 1980 Pioneer artifacts, gun collection, military artifacts; open May - Aug.
Bernadette Leslie, Director

***Battleford:* Saskatchewan Baseball Hall of Fame & Museum**
PO Box 1388, 292 - 22nd St. West
Battleford, SK S0M 0E0
Tel: 306-446-1983; *Fax:* 306-446-0509
saskbaseballmuseum@sasktel.net
www.saskbaseball.ca/index.php?id=30
Year Founded: 1983 Has over 3,000 artifacts dealing with baseball plus 6,000 items of archival nature such as pictures, books & magazines. Open year round, M - F 9:00 - 4:00.
Mike Ramage, Executive Director, 306-780-9237, Fax: 306-352-3669, mramage@sasktel.net

***Beauval:* Frazer's Museum**
PO Box 64
Beauval, SK S0M 0G0
Year Founded: 1969 Aboriginal & pioneer artifacts, including articles from Hudson's Bay Company, missionaries & Métis people; aboriginal owned & operated

***Bengough:* Bengough & District Museum**
190 - 1st Ave. West
Bengough, SK S0C 0K0
Tel: 306-268-2909
www.southcentralmuseums.ca/bengough.html
Other contact information: Alternate Phone: 306-268-2927
Local history; open daily from July-Aug., & by appointment Sept.-May.

***Big River:* Big River Memorial Museum**
PO Box 220, 205 Third Ave. North
Big River, SK S0J 0E0
Tel: 306-469-2112
The Big River Memorial Museum contains items from fishing & logging in the area.

***Biggar:* Biggar Museum & Gallery**
PO Box 400, 105 - 3rd Ave. West
Biggar, SK S0K 0M0
Tel: 306-948-3451; *Fax:* 306-948-3478
biggarmuseum@sasktel.net
biggarmuseum.webs.com
www.facebook.com/Biggar Museum
Year Founded: 1972 The museum collects historical artifacts from the settlement of the town of Biggar & the surrounding district. Among it collections are a general store display & a reconstruction of the Biggar train station. Biggar Museum & Gallery is open year round, M - F in the winter, and M - Sa in the summer, 9:00 - 5:00.
Anne Livingston, Executive Director

***Birch Hills:* Birch Hills & District Historical Society**
PO Box 693
Birch Hills, SK S0J 0G0
Tel: 306-749-2262
bhmuseum@yahoo.ca
birchhills.ca/recreation/museum.html
The museum's collection contains restored agricultural machines, a memorial wall, & a lending library of over 200 Saskatchewan history books. Buildings on-site include a log barn, a milk house, & a CPR station. Open year round, W 2:00-4:00, also by appointment.

***Blaine Lake:* General Store Memories, Museum & Antiques**
PO Box 457
Blaine Lake, SK S0J 0J0
Tel: 306-226-4646
12-40andbeyond.com
The General Store contains antiques on the first floor & a museum preserving local history on the second floor.
Billy Nemish, Contact
Vivian Nemish, Contact

***Bonnyville:* Bonnyville & District Museum**
***Parent:* Bonnyville & District Historical Society**
4401 - 54 Ave.
Bonnyville, SK T9N 2H4
Tel: 780-826-4925
bvmuseum@mcsnet.ca
bonnyvillemuseum.ca
Year Founded: 1991 The museum features 250,000 artifacts pertaining to local history.
Germaine Prybysh, Manager/Curator

***Borden:* Borden & District Historical Museum**
PO Box 5
Located at 200 Main St., Borden, SK
Borden, SK S0K 0N0
Tel: 306-997-4517
Year Founded: 1990 Artifacts housed in a one-room schoolhouse & former Masonic Lodge; site also includes a replica of the Diefenbaker homestead, as well as a butcher shop & barber shop. Open June-Sept., or by appointment.

***Briercrest:* Briercrest & District Museum**
PO Box 216
Located at 400 Main St., Briercrest, SK
Briercrest, SK S0H 0K0
Tel: 306-799-4951
briercrestmuseum.ca
Year Founded: 1987 The Briercrest & District Museum houses collections from the Briercrest area's earliest settlers & their descendants. Examples of the museum's artifacts include household items & small farm equipment. Open by appointment.
Marge Cleave, Curator
Georgina Gadd, Curator
Chuck Alton, Chair

***Broadview:* Broadview Historical Museum**
PO Box 556, 10th Ave. North
Broadview, SK S0G 0K0
Tel: 306-696-3244
town.of.broadview@sk.sympatico.ca
www.broadview.ca/museum
Year Founded: 1972 Articles related to Broadview's history are collected & displayed. Visitors can see the Highland School, a blacksmith shop, a post office, a sod house, a log home, & a Canadian Pacific Railway station & caboose. Broadview Historical Museum is open from the beginning of June to the end of August 12:00 - 5:00 from F - Su.

***Cabri:* Cabri & District Museum**
PO Box 467
Cabri, SK S0N 0J0
Tel: 306-587-2339
Displays include artifacts from World War I & World War II, First Nations, & household & farm items. The museum is open from May to Sept.

***Cadillac:* Cadillac Museum**
PO Box 8, Centre St.
Cadillac, SK S0N 0K0
Tel: 306-785-2042; *Fax:* 306-785-2042
Household articles & early 20th century tools; clothing; fire-fighting equipment; quilt exhibit; demonstrations. Open upon request
Luanne Hancock, Contact

***Canora:* CN Station House Museum**
PO Box 717
Located at 418 Main St., Canora, SK
Canora, SK S0A 0L0
Tel: 306-563-4591
cdo.canora@sasktel.net
The museum contains CN & pioneer artifacts, & is housed in the oldest Class 2 station left in Saskatchewan. Part of the museum is being integrated into the town's new Visitor Centre. Open July-Sept., daily 10:00-4:00.

***Canwood:* Canwood Museum**
PO Box 269, 635 - 3rd Ave. East
Canwood, SK S0J 0K0
Tel: 306-468-2258
Year Founded: 1971 Canwood Museum is a community museum located in an old schoolhouse. Displays include farm artifacts, clothing, & pictures. There is a miniature golf course on site.

***Carlyle:* Rusty Relics Museum Inc.**
PO Box 840
Located at 115 Railway Ave. West, Carlyle, SK
Carlyle, SK S0C 0R0
Tel: 306-453-2266
rustyrelicsmuseum@gmail.com
Other contact information: Alternate Phone: 306-453-2363
A museum of pioneer life in Saskatchewan; artifacts relating to Carlyle area displayed in room settings in a 1910 CN railway station; includes a 1943 CPR caboose, a CN Motor car, CN tool shed with railway tools, furnished 1905 one-room country school, agricultural machinery & old church

***Choiceland:* Choiceland Historical Society**
PO Box 234
Choiceland, SK S0J 0M0
Tel: 306-428-2850
choiceland.ca/museum.html
Local & military history. Open May-Sept., F 1:00-4:00

***Climax:* Climax Community Museum Inc.**
PO Box 59
Climax, SK S0N 0N0
Tel: 306-293-2051; *Fax:* 306-293-2051
Pioneer collection - domestic, tools, farm machinery, military, hospital & sports, community archives. Open May to Aug daily 10:00 - 12:00, 1:00 - 5:00 or by appointment.

***Consul:* Consul Museum**
PO Box 144
Consul, SK S0N 0P0
Tel: 306-299-4493
consulmuseum@gmail.com
www.consulmuseum.ca
Year Founded: 2005 The Consul Museum is the first Saskatchewan museum to exist solely as a website. The site contains pictures, videos, & stories of local history.

***Coronach:* Coronach District Museum**
PO Box 449, 240 - 1st. St. West
Coronach, SK S0H 0Z0
Tel: 306-267-4403
www.southcentralmuseums.ca/coronach.html
Features historical displays, records, photos & artifacts representing the lives of pioneers of the area. Open Jul - Aug, Su - M from 1:00 - 4:00, or by appointment.
Helen Foley, Contact, 306-267-4403

***Craik:* Craik Oral History Museum**
PO Box 144
Craik, SK S0G 0V0
Tel: 306-734-2751
Local history; collection contains photographs, slides, videos, documents & record books, & 600 hours of audio cassette recordings. Open Jan.-Dec., or by appointment.

***Craik:* Prairie Pioneer Museum**
PO Box 157, 541 Parks Rd.
Craik, SK S0G 0V0
Tel: 306-734-2480
www.craik.ca
Other contact information: Alt. Phones: 306-734-5125; 306-734-2676
Year Founded: 1966 The pioneer way of life in Craik & rural Saskatchewan is portrayed at the Prairie Pioneer Museum. Buildings include two rural schools & a heritage house, which was built in 1906. Artifacts, such as household furnishings & medical & veterinary instruments, are on display. The museum is open during the summer, & is accessible year-round by request.

***Creighton:* Royal Northwest Mounted Police Post Museum**
216 Creighton Ave.
Creighton, SK S0P 0A0
Tel: 306-688-3538
creightontourism@sasktel.net
www.townofcreighton.ca/museum.html
A reconstruction of the original Royal Northwest Mounted Police Post in Beaver City, circa 1915. Located at the Creighton Recreation Culture & Tourism Centre. Open May-Sept.

***Cudworth:* Cudworth Museum**
PO Box 69
Cudworth, SK S0K 1B0
Tel: 306-256-3492; *Fax:* 306-256-3515
town.cudworth@sasktel.net
Year Founded: 2004 Local history; former CN station.

***Cupar:* Cupar & District Heritage Museum**
PO Box 164
Cupar, SK S0G 0Y0
Tel: 306-723-4324
www.townofcupar.com/pages/museum.php
Social Media: cuparmuseum.blogspot.ca
twitter.com/cuparmuseum
www.facebook.com/283870338379373
Year Founded: 1995 Housed in two buildings: an old Masonic Hall & a curling rink; open May - Sept. or by appt.
Wes Bailey, Chair

Cut Knife: **Clayton McLain Memorial Museum (CMMM)**
PO Box 8, 111A Hill Ave.
Cut Knife, SK S0M 0N0
Tel: 306-398-2920; *Fax:* 306-398-2951
cmmmcutknife@gmail.com
www.cmmmcutknife.ca
Social Media: cmmmcutknife.blogspot.com
Located in Tomahawk Park, site of the world's largest tomahawk; local history, including First Nations artifacts from early life & Battle of Cutknife Hill, & McLain family collection; archives include personal papers, photgraphs, and a complete collection of the local newspaper; educational programming; research services; open June-Sept.

Denare Beach: **Northern Gateway Museum**
PO Box 70
Located on Moody Dr., Denare Beach, SK
Denare Beach, SK S0P 0B0
Tel: 306-362-2141
www.northerngatewaymuseum.com
Year Founded: 1957 The Northern Gateway Museum houses artifacts from fur trade excavations, First Nations life, gold rush activities, & mining operations. Archives include architectural records, photographs, & films.

Dinsmore: **Yester-Years Community Museum**
PO Box 216
Located on Main St., Dinsmore, SK
Dinsmore, SK S0L 0T0
Features the main museum, blacksmith shop, butter & post office buildings; open July & Aug. upon request

Dodsland: **Dodsland & District Museum**
PO Box 171
Dodsland, SK S0L 0V0
Tel: 306-356-2228
Old grocery store on lower floor represents a village of the past; top floor represents living quarters of the past; located at Main St. & 1st Ave; open May-Nov., Tu & Th 1:30-4:30, or by appointment.

Duck Lake: **Duck Lake Regional Interpretive Centre**
PO Box 328
Duck Lake, SK S0K 1J0
Tel: 306-467-2057; *Fax:* 306-467-2257
Toll-Free: 866-467-2057
duckmuf@sasktel.net
www.dlric.org
Year Founded: 1959 Frontier of First Nation, Métis & Pioneer Society, 1870-1905; artifact & art galleries, theatre, gift shop, 24m viewing tower, conference facilities; open daily May - Sept 10:00 - 5:30 or by appointment.

Duff: **Duff Community Heritage Museum**
PO Box 57
Duff, SK S0A 0S0
Tel: 306-728-3592
Open by appointment only, this tourist attraction has been built out of an old church & features a recreational pioneer-era kitchen & old rural schoolhouse, along with various other historical items & photos from the village's history.

Dysart: **Dysart & District Museum**
PO Box 327
Dysart, SK S0G 1H0
Tel: 306-432-2255
Other contact information: Alternate Phone: 306-432-2100
Local history; replicas of area country schools; Wall of Honour war memorial; open June-Sept., Th & Sa 1:30-4:00.

Eastend: **Eastend Museum & Cultural Centre**
306 Red Coat Drive
Eastend, SK S0N 0T0
Tel: 306-295-3375
eastendhistoricalmuseum.com
www.facebook.com/EastendHistoricalMuseum
Tie Rail Ranch House, blacksmith shop, operating 1903 Cae Steam Engine, 1927 Federal Truck, & a stage coach; LaRose Building contains 1500 items; Open daily May - Labour Day; by appointment in the winter.
Shelly Parker, President
Glen Duke, Treasurer
Doreen Stewart, Secretary

Eastend: **T.rex Discovery Centre**
PO Box 460, 1 T-rex Dr.
Eastend, SK
Tel: 306-295-4009
www.trexcentre.ca
Social Media: www.youtube.com/user/trexcentre
www.facebook.com/trexcentre
The T.rex Discovery Centre is home to Scotty, the largest & most complete fossilized skeleton of a Tyrannosaurus rex in Canada. The Royal Saskatchewan Museum Fossil Research Station is also located on-site.
Tim Tokaryk, Contact P.Geo., Royal Saskatchewan Museum Fossil Research Station, 306-295-4701

Eatonia: **Eatonia Heritage Park**
PO Box 189
Located at 100 Railway Ave., Eatonia, SK
Eatonia, SK S0L 0Y0
Tel: 306-967-2251
eatonia@yourlink.ca
Municipal Heritage Property featuring a train caboose & wood-frame railway station & house from the early 1900s.

Edam: **Harry S. Washbrook Museum**
PO Box 182
Located on 2nd Ave., Edam, SK
Edam, SK S0M 0V0
Tel: 306-397-2260
Local pioneer & First Nations artifacts

Elbow: **Elbow Museum & Historical Society**
PO Box 207
Elbow, SK S0H 1J0
Tel: 306-854-2290; *Fax:* 306-854-2229
elbow@sasktel.net
www.elbowsask.com
Housed in an old schoolhouse; sodhouse built in 1965 & July 1999; artifacts represent era of late 1800s & early 1900s; open daily May - Sept. 1:00 - 5:00 or by appointment

Elrose: **Elrose Museum**
Parent: **Elrose Heritage Society**
PO Box 556
Located at 102 - 4th Ave., Elrose, SK
Elrose, SK S0L 0Z0
Tel: 306-378-7969
elrosemuseum@hotmail.com
www.facebook.com/pages/Elrose-Museum/382380058543349
Directors collect, restore & catalogue artifacts & antiques; open May-Sept.
Amber Jennett, Secretary
Carolyn Andreas, President

Esterhazy: **Esterhazy Community Museum**
PO Box 1744
Esterhazy, SK S0A 0X0
Tel: 306-745-5406
museum.esterhazy@sasktel.net
Pioneer artifacts, taxidermy & music rooms, old store, model of potash mine; fashion show; antique doll and toy show; open May - Sept. or by appointment.

Esterhazy: **Kaposvar Historic Site**
PO Box 13
Esterhazy, SK S0A 0X0
Tel: 306-745-2715
1907 church & rectory; Annual Pilgrimage on the fourth Sun. in Aug.

Estevan: **Estevan Art Gallery & Museum**
118 - 4th St.
Estevan, SK S4A 0T4
Tel: 306-634-7644; *Fax:* 306-634-2490
eagm@sasktel.net
estevanartgallery.com
NWMP Museum, local artifacts; open summer season; plus art with 2 contemporary exhibiting galleries, with travelling exhibitions, giftshop; open open year round; winter M - F 10:00 - 6:00; summer M - Sa 10:00 - 6:00.
Kaitlyn Pilloud, Museum and Gallery Assistant, office.eagm@sasktel.net
Amber Anderson, Director/Curator, curator.eagm@sasktel.net

Eston: **Prairie West Historical Centre & Society**
PO Box 910
Located at 946 - 2 St. East, Eston, SK
Eston, SK S0L 1A0
Tel: 306-962-3772
Other contact information: Alternate Phones: 206-962-2559; 306-962-4578
Local history museum & art gallery; wildflower garden

Foam Lake: **Foam Lake Museum**
PO Box 1041, 113 Bray Ave. West
Foam Lake, SK S0A 1A0
Tel: 306-272-4292
Local pioneer museum documenting the settlement of the area. Open June 1st - Aug. 31st, W, F 9:00 - 5:00 and by appointment.
Ruth Gushulak, President, 306-272-3360

Fort Qu'appelle: **Fort Qu'Appelle Museum**
PO Box 1093, 198 Bay Ave. North
Fort Qu'appelle, SK S0G 1S0
Tel: 306-332-6033
museum@fortquapelle.com
www.fortquappelle.com/history.html
1864 Hudson Bay Co. post; open June-Sept. 1:00 - 5:00; otherwise by appointment.
Lynn Anderson, President

Frenchman Butte: **Frenchman Butte Museum**
PO Box 114
Frenchman Butte, SK S0M 0W0
Tel: 306-344-4478; *Fax:* 306-344-4566
info@frenchmanbuttemuseum.ca
www.frenchmanbuttemuseum.ca
www.facebook. com/frenchmanbuttemuseum
Other contact information: Off season: 306-825-2246
Year Founded: 1979 Pioneer & CNR artifacts; arrowhead & gun collections, mounted birds; open Jul - Sept 9:00 - 6:00; winter by appointment.
Rudy Buchta, Contact, 306-825-2029

Frobisher: **Frobisher Threshermen's Museum**
PO Box 194
Frobisher, SK S0C 0Y0
Tel: 306-486-4513
Steam engines, wooden threshing separators, gas & diesel tractors, ploughshares, household items & photographs

Glaslyn: **Glaslyn & District Museum**
PO Box 363
Glaslyn, SK S0M 0Y0
Tel: 306-342-7993
Museum contains artifacts from the 1800's, housed in a restored CNR station house circa 1926; CNR water tank & caboose also on-site; taxidermy articles, including a rare two-headed calf.

Glen Ewen: **Glen Ewen Community Antique Centre**
Sports Grounds
Glen Ewen, SK S0C 1C0
Tel: 306-925-2221
Features a collection of antique cars that includes a 1910 Ford & a 1937 Packard; also showcases guns, dishes & household articles from the early 1900s; open seasonally or by request

Glenavon: **Glenavon Museum**
PO Box 246
Location: 309 Railway Ave., Glenavon, SK S0G 1Y0
Glenavon, SK S0G 1Y0
Tel: 306-429-2011; *Fax:* 306-429-2260
www.glenavonsk.ca
Open July & Aug., Tue & Th 1:00-4;00.

Glentworth: **Glentworth Museum**
PO Box 174
Glentworth, SK S0H 1V0
Tel: 306-266-4320
Local history artifacts

Goodsoil: **Goodsoil Historical Museum**
PO Box 370, 401 Main St.
Goodsoil, SK S0M 1A0
Tel: 306-238-7776; *Fax:* 306-238-4991
Year Founded: 1977 Natural stone school building built in 1945; first teacherage built in 1934 of logs; miniature church with original steeple from church destroyed by tornado; over 2,500 artifacts, many dating from 1800s; old machinery; doll house with hundreds of dolls from around the world. Open June 30 - Aug. 31
Alex Schamber, President, 306-238-4565, schamber@sasktel.net
Rudy Leiter, Secretary

Gravelbourg: **Gravelbourg & District Museum**
300 Main St.
Gravelbourg, SK S0H 1X0
Tel: 306-648-2332
www.southcentralmuseums.ca/gravelbourg.html
Open July & Aug.
Louis Stringer, Manager

Grenfell: **Grenfell Museum**
PO Box 1156, 711 Wolseley Ave.
Grenfell, SK S0G 2B0
Tel: 306-697-2839; *Fax:* 306-697-2500
Year Founded: 1973 Restored 1904 Queen Anne turreted house; added attraction is the annex with furniture & tools of bygone days as well as an outstanding military display; open Jun - Aug, F - Su and by appointment.

Gull Lake: **Gull Lake Museum**
3570 Rutland Ave.
Gull Lake, SK S0N 1A0
Tel: 306-672-4377
gulllakesk.ca/museum.htm
The museum site features artifacts housed in three buildings: a vintage house, an old country schoolhouse, & a pole structure with farm-related items.

Hague: **Saskatchewan River Valley Museum**
PO Box 630
Hague, SK S0K 1X0
Tel: 306-225-2112; *Fax:* 306-225-4642
rivervalleymuseum@sasktel.net
Other contact information: Alternate phone: 306-225-4361
Approx. 6,000 artifacts, including First Nations & Mennonite; original European house/barn; country school; Mennonite church; horse-drawn farming machinery, blacksmith tools, pre-1950 furniture & appliances; open May long weekend - Thanksgiving

Harris: **Harris Museum**
PO Box 131, 204 Railway Ave.
Harris, SK S0L 1K0
Tel: 306-656-2002
Year Founded: 1989 The volunteer operated Harris Museum features local history & archives, plus a C.N. Water Tower & a gas engine water pump. The museum is open from May to Sept., or by appointment.
Betty McFarlane, Contact, 306-656-4725
Dolores Neil, Contact, 306-656-2172

Hazenmore: **Heritage Hazenmore Museum**
PO Box 103
Hazenmore, SK S0N 1C0
Tel: 306-264-5149
Local history; open on request

Hepburn: **Hepburn Museum of Wheat**
PO Box 69
Hepburn, SK S0K 1Z0
Tel: 306-947-4351
Other contact information: Alternate Phone: 306-947-2042
Museum collection housed in an original grain elevator. Open Sat. in the summer.

Herbert: **Herbert CPR Train Station Museum**
Parent: **Herbert Heritage Association**
625 Railway Ave.
Herbert, SK S0H 2A0
Tel: 306-784-3411
www.townofherbert.com/herbert_train_station.html
Year Founded: 1986 The museum's collection is housed in a restored CPR station circa 1910, with a caboose on-site. Open June-Sept.
Frances Schwartz, President
Doreen Schroeder, Manager

Herschel: **Ancient Echoes Interpretive Centre**
PO Box 40
Herschel, SK S0L 1L0
Tel: 306-377-2045
ancientechoes@sasktel.net
www.ancientechoes.ca
www.facebook.com/herschelancientechoes
Year Founded: 1994 The Centre contains local artifacts, including petroglyph rock carvings & the remains of a Pleisosaur.

Hodgeville: **Country Craft Shoppe & Homestead Museum**
PO Box 264
Located at 102 - 1st St. West, Hodgeville, SK
Hodgeville, SK S0H 2B0
Tel: 306-677-2693; *Fax:* 306-677-2707
Eight rooms depicting an early homestead; crafts, gifts & tearoom

Hudson Bay: **Al Mazur Memorial Heritage Park**
PO Box 37
Hudson Bay, SK S0E 0Y0
Tel: 306-865-2180
1910heritage@sasktel.net
www.townofhudsonbay.com/default.aspx?page=80
Year Founded: 1984 Local history; artifacts housed in original buildings; 16-acre museum park; located at the junction of Hwy. 3 & 9; open May-Sept., daily 9:00-5:00

Hudson Bay: **Hudson Bay Museum**
Parent: **Hudson Bay & District Cultural Society**
c/o Hudson Bay & District Cultural Society, PO Box 931, 512 Churchill St.
Hudson Bay, SK S0E 0Y0
Tel: 306-865-2170
hbmuseum@hotmail.com
www.townofhudsonbay.com
Preserving artifacts of the area; open June - Sept.

Humboldt: **Humboldt & District Museum & Gallery**
PO Box 2349
Located at 602 Main St., Humboldt, SK
Humboldt, SK S0K 2A0
Tel: 306-682-5226; *Fax:* 306-682-1430
humboldt.museum@sasktel.net
www.humboldtmuseum.ca
Social Media:
www.youtube.com/channel/UCvmWCuqMil5iut7hA8YJEtQ
twitter.com/Hum_Muse_in gs
www.facebook.com/120057151339718
Year Founded: 1982 Focus on the Humboldt Telegraph Station of 1878, as well as the settlement of Humboldt & district, & the spiritual influence of St. Peter's Abbey; housed in a 1912 post office building
Jennifer Hoesgen, Curator

Imperial: **Nels Berggren Museum**
PO Box 125
Imperial, SK S0G 2J0
Tel: 306-963-2033
Lamps, clocks, sewing machines, musical instruments, & art.

Indian Head: **Bell Barn Society of Indian Head**
PO Box 1882
Indian Head, SK S0G 2K0
Tel: 306-695-2355
bellbarn.ca
Year Founded: 2006 The society helps preserve the Bell Barn, a 125-year-old structure that once belonged to the Qu'Appelle Valley Farming Company. Open May-Sept., daily 10:00-4:00, or by appointment.
Kay Dixon, Chair
Jerry Willerth, Barn Boss, 306-695-2086, gdwillerth@sasktel.net
Connie Billett, Secretary, 306-695-3456, cbillett@sasktel.net

Indian Head: **Indian Head Museum**
PO Box 566
Indian Head, SK S0G 2K0
Tel: 306-695-2584
www.townofindianhead.com/our-history/history-resources.html
1907 two-storey fire hall displaying artifacts of local pioneer days; also 1926 one-room school, 1883 Bell Farm Cottage; replica of 1930s one-bay village garage; farm implements
Tim Keslering, Contact

Ituna: **Ituna & District Museum**
Ituna Branch, Parkland Regional Library, 518 - 5th Ave. NE
Ituna, SK S0A 1N0
Tel: 306-785-2835
www.ituna.ca/libraryandmuseum.html
Other contact information: Alternate Phones: 306-795-3458; 306-795-2484
Year Founded: 1971 Local history including Ukrainian & aboriginal artifacts.

Kamsack: **Kamsack & District Museum**
PO Box 991, Queen Elizabeth Boul.
Kamsack, SK S0A 1S0
Tel: 306-542-4415
kphm@gmail.com
Other contact information: Alt. Phone: 306-542-3055
Exhibits focus on both First Nations & European history; housed in a former power plant; features one of the original diesel engines which generated the town's electricity until 1958; rooms furnished in the style of a typical 1920s pioneer dwelling. Open May - Sept.; car show & shine mid-June

Kelliher: **Kelliher & District Heritage Museum Inc.**
PO Box 111
Kelliher, SK S0A 1V0
Tel: 306-675-2183
www.kelliher.ca
Year Founded: 1992 One of the oldest buildings in Kelliher; now contains a collection of local artifacts; open Sundays; hosts school tours
Carole Thompson, President, 306-675-6125
Lenore Fincati, Vice-President, 306-675-2210
Chris Fincati, Secretary-Treasurer, 306-675-2210

Kenosee Lake: **Cannington Manor Provincial Park**
PO Box 220
Kenosee Lake, SK S0C 2S0
Tel: 306-739-5251; *Fax:* 306-577-2622
manor.cannington@gov.sk.ca
www.saskparks.net/CanningtonManor
Other contact information: Phone, Off Season: 306-577-2600
In the late 1800s, partners in the Moose Mountain Trading Company established the village of Cannington Manor. Buildings from this village have been reconstructed or restored for visitors. Buildings at the site include a Land Titles Office, a bachelor's cabin, a Moose Mountain Trading Company store, a carpenter's shop, a blacksmith shop, a flour mill, & the Mitre Hotel. Cannington Manor is open from Victoria Day to Labour Day.

Kerrobert: **Kerrobert & District Museum**
PO Box 452
Located at the Historic Courthouse, 433 Manitoba Ave., Kerrobert, SK S0L 1R0
Tel: 306-834-5277
Other contact information: Alternate Phone: 306-834-2991
Replica of the first tent store & pioneer furniture.
Darren Obritsch, President, 306-834-2934
Bobbi Hebron, Secretary, 306-834-2409

Kincaid: **Kincaid Museum**
PO Box 177
Kincaid, SK S0H 2J0
Tel: 306-264-3910
Local historical material

Kindersley: **Kindersley & District Plains Museum**
PO Box 599
Located at 903 - 11th Ave. East, Kindersley, SK
Kindersley, SK S0L 1S0
Tel: 306-463-6620
kindersleymuseum@sasktel.net
www.facebook.com/KDPMuseum
Year Founded: 1978 Wide collection of early farm machinery & tools, household items, education items & items from school & churches; fire hall & fire truck; military display, a general store, post office & print shop; an archaeological display; open May to Sept.

Kinistino: **Kinistino & District Pioneer Museum Inc.**
510 Main St.
Kinistino, SK S0J 1H0
Tel: 306-864-2838
Displays of artifacts from fur trade & pioneer times; oldest purely agricultural settlement in Saskatchewan.

Kipling: **Kipling & District Historical Society**
PO Box 414
Kipling, SK S0G 2S0
Tel: 306-736-8254

Kisbey: **Kisbey Museum**
PO Box 117
Kisbey, SK S0C 1L0
Tel: 306-462-2162
Detailed history & pictures of Kisbey's namesake, R. Claude Kisbey; 1,000+ objects; open Thu. through July & Aug. & by request

Kronau: **Kronau Heritage Society**
Parent: **Kronau Bethlehem Heritage Society Inc.**
PO Box 1
Kronau, SK S0G 2T0
Tel: 306-781-3082; *Fax:* 306-781-2267
4efarms@sasktel.net
www.facebook.com/pages/Kronau-Heritage-Society/248288010817
The museum collection is housed in the restored Kronau Lutheran Church building, circa 1912. Open May-Sept., Wed.-Su 10:00-4:00.

Kyle: **Kyle & District Museum**
PO Box 543
Kyle, SK S0L 1T0
Tel: 304-375-2525; *Fax:* 206-375-2534
Local history; collection housed in former Tuberose Red Cross outpost hospital; artifacts include World War I & II items, machinery & vehicles, fossils, & items relating to Wooly Mammoth remains found in 1964.
Bill Stepple, Contact, 306-375-2336

Lancer: **Lancer Centennial Museum**
PO Box 3
Lancer, SK S0N 1G0
Tel: 306-689-2925
Open June-Sept.

Langenburg: **Langenburg Homestead Museum**
PO Box 864
Located at 305 Carl Ave. East, Lagenburg, SK
Langenburg, SK S0A 2A0
Tel: 306-743-2432; *Fax:* 306-743-2625
Local history; open June-Aug.
Kay Klopstock, Contact, 306-743-2625

Langham: **Langham & District Heritage Village & Museum**
PO Box 516, 302 Railway St.
Langham, SK S0K 2L0
Tel: 306-283-4342; *Fax:* 306-283-4772
www.langham.ca
www.facebook.com/LanghamAndDistrictHeritageVillageMuseum
Year Founded: 1993 Preserves & exhibits artifacts illustrating the history & culture of Langham & area; special events & programming. Open May long weekend to Sept. 30, Wed. 9-12 & Sat. 9-3, or by appointment.
Doreen Nickel, President, 306-283-4342

Lanigan: **Lanigan & District Heritage Centre**
Parent: **Lanigan & District Heritage Association**
PO Box 424
Lanigan, SK S0K 2M0
Tel: 306-365-2569; *Fax:* 306-365-2960
lanigan.dist.heritage@sasktel.net
lanigandistheritage.wix.com/homepage
www.facebook.com/184809704901859
Year Founded: 1994 The Lanigan & District Heritage Association's mission is to preserve the Lanigan CPR Station, where the Centre is currently housed; includes a museum, tourism information, agricultural interpretive display, potash exposition, caboose, recreation & coffee area & storage. Located at 75 Railway Ave., Lanigan. Open June 1 to Labour Day.
Ruth Wildeman, Secretary, 306-365-4230

Lashburn: **Lashburn Centennial Museum**
PO Box 275
Lashburn, SK S0M 1H0
Tel: 306-285-4145
lashburncentennialmuseum@gmail.com
Other contact information: Town Office: 306-285-3533
Vetern's Gallery with artifacts from the Boer War to Korean War; 1908 Gully School; artifacts of the Barr Colony settlers; log cabin & blacksmith shop; open July & Aug.

Leross: **Kellross Heritage Museum**
PO Box 10, 2nd Ave.
Leross, SK S0A 1V0
Tel: 306-274-4946
Year Founded: 2000 Open from June to Sept. or by appointment.

Leroy: **Leroy & District Heritage Museum**
PO Box 47
Leroy, SK S0K 2P0
Tel: 306-286-3464
Open July & Aug.

Lloydminster: **Lloydminster Cultural & Science Centre (LCSC)**
4515 - 444th St.
Lloydminster, SK S9V 0C6
Tel: 780-874-3720; *Fax:* 780-874-3721
www.lloydminster.ca/index.aspx?nid=400
Social Media: instagram.com/yourlcsc
www.facebook.com/LCSC5655
Other contact information: Phone, City of Lloydminster: 780-875-6184; Fax: 780-871-8345
Located at Highway 16 & 45th Avenue, the Barr Colony Heritage Cultural Centre consists of an antique museum, the Imhoff art collection, the OTS Heavy Oil Science Centre, & the Fuchs wildlife exhibit. The Richard Larsen Museum presents antiques of the Barr Colonists. Artifacts include funiture & agricultural equipment. Visitors can also see Lloydminster's first church, a log cabin, a filling station, & a 1906 schoolhouse. The centre is open year-round.
Kyra Stefanuk, Manager, kstefanuk@lloydminster.ca

Loon Lake: **Steele Narrows Provincial Historic Park**
PO Box 39
Loon Lake, SK S0M 1L0
Tel: 306-837-7410; *Fax:* 306-837-2415
makwalake@gov.sk.ca
www.saskparks.net/SteeleNarrows
The park rests on the site of the last battle of the 1885 North West Rebellion. The battle is depicted on interpretive panels located at the top of a hill overlooking the park. The burial ground containing the remains of the Cree killed in the battle is located across the road.

Lucky Lake: **Lucky Lake Museum**
PO Box 268
Lucky Lake, SK S0L 1Z0
Tel: 306-858-2641

Lumsden: **Lumsden Heritage Museum**
PO Box 91
Located at 50 Qu'Appelle Dr. West, Lumsden, SK
Lumsden, SK S0G 3C0
Tel: 306-731-2905
The museum consists of five pioneer buildings, a machine shed, a livery stable, & a blacksmith shop. Four of the pioneer buildings contain artifacts depicting the district's early history.

Luseland: **Luseland & Districts Museum**
PO Box 8
Located at 600 Grand Ave., Luseland, SK
Luseland, SK S0L 2A0
Tel: 306-372-4258
Other contact information: Alternate Phone: 306-372-4331
Year Founded: 1990 Hours: May - Oct Sa 1:00-4:00 or open upon request

Macklin: **Macklin & District Museum**
PO Box 444
Macklin, SK S0L 2C0
Tel: 306-753-2078
town.macklin@sasktel.net
www.macklin.ca/museum.htm
Other contact information: Alt. Phone: 306-753-2469
Year Founded: 1990 Built in 1919 by Frank Shaw, the town's first bank manager, the house later became a hospital during the 1920s. Open Tu, Th & F in the summer.
Bob Dawson, Contact

Macrorie: **Macrorie Museum**
PO Box 177
Macrorie, SK S0L 2E0
Tel: 306-243-4327
www.macrorie.com/04-history.html
Other contact information: Alternate Phones: 306-243-4507; 306-243-4207
Consists of 3 sites: an old post office, insurance office, & living quarters which depict the local farming area; an old brick school, heritage site; a caboose & jigger; open Mon. in July & Aug. 2-4, or by appt.

Maidstone: **Maidstone & District Historical & Cultural Society Inc.**
PO Box 250
Maidstone, SK S0M 1M0
Tel: 306-893-2890
May - Sept.

Main Centre: **Main Centre Heritage Museum**
c/o Dora Wall, PO Box 42
Main Centre, SK S0H 2V0
Tel: 306-784-2903
Local history & early pioneering artifacts; school & church history; Herbert Ferry Crossing display; open by appt. Jan.-Dec.

Maple Creek: **Fort Walsh National Historic Site**
PO Box 278
Maple Creek, SK S0N 1N0
Tel: 306-662-2645; *Fax:* 306-662-2711
fort.walsh@pc.gc.ca
www.pc.gc.ca/eng/lhn-nhs/sk/walsh/index.aspx
Other contact information: TTY: 306-662-3124
NWMP fort & Cypress Hills Massacre site; open mid May - Sept. 1.

Maple Creek: **Jasper Cultural & Historical Centre**
PO Box 1504
Maple Creek, SK S0N 1N0
Tel: 306-662-2434; *Fax:* 306-662-4359
jasper.centre@sasktel.net
www.jaspercentre.ca
www.facebook.com/5062203 06082521
Year Founded: 1988 Open Mon.-Fri. in winter; daily in summer
Heather Wickstrom, Manager/Curator, 306-332-2434, jasper.centre@sasktel.net

Maple Creek: **St. Victor Petroglyph Provincial Historic Park**
c/o Cypress Hills Interprovincial Park, PO Box 850
c/o Friends of the St. Victor Petroglyphs Cooperative Ltd., PO Box 1716, Assiniboia, SK S0H 0B0
Maple Creek, SK S0N 1N0
Tel: 306-662-5411
CypressHills@gov.sk.ca
stvictor.sasktelwebsite.net
Other contact information: Alt. URL: www.saskparks.net/St.Victor
The St. Victor Petroglyphs are an enduring mystery; their origin & purpose is unknown, yet they provide a clue as to who populated the plains in the era pre-dating written records. The petroglyphs are best viewed in the early morning on a clear day; an interpretive panel & reproduction of a few of the petroglyphs are provided for visitors at the site, which is located south of St. Victor. Admission is free.

Maple Creek: **Southwest Saskatchewan Oldtimers Museum**
PO Box 1540
Located at 218 Jasper St., Maple Creek, SK
Maple Creek, SK S0N 1N0
Tel: 306-662-2474; *Fax:* 206-662-2711
oldtimers@sasktel.net
Ranching, First Nations, NWMP, firearms; open May 20 to Sept. 30

Maple Creek: **Wood Mountain Post Provincial Park**
c/o Cypress Hills Interprovincial Park, PO Box 850
Maple Creek, SK S0N 1N0
Tel: 306-662-5411; *Fax:* 306-662-5482
cypresshills@gov.sk.ca
www.saskparks.net
The post was an important site for the North-West Mounted Police around the turn of the century, where the local detachment patrolled the Canada-USA border. Visitors to the park will find two reconstructed buildings with displays inside, & staff hosting guided tours. Open June-Aug., daily 10:00-5:00.

Maryfield: **Maryfield Museum**
PO Box 262
Maryfield, SK S0G 3K0
Tel: 306-646-2201
Clocks, tools, record players, telephones

McCord: **McCord & District Museum**
PO Box 82
McCord, SK S0H 2T0
Tel: 306-478-2522
ba.wilson@xplornet.com
www.southcentralmuseums.ca/mccord.html
Other contact information: Alt. Phone: 306-478-2559
Year Founded: 1973 Museum is housed in a 1928 CPR railway station & exibits include historical items from households & businesses in the area. Of note is an actual caboose on tracks beside the museum. A companion museum is the 1913 church at the opposite end of the street which displays religious articles from various churches in the region.

Meadow Lake: **Meadow Lake Museum**
PO Box 1028
Meadow Lake, SK S9X 1Y5
Tel: 306-234-2455
www.meadowlake.ca
Exhibits are related to pioneers, farming, lumbering, & birds. The museum is open from Victoria Day to Labour Day.
Cecil Midgett, Contact, 306-234-2455

Melfort: **Melfort & District Museum**
PO Box 3222, 401 Melfort St. West
Melfort, SK S0E 1A0
Tel: 306-752-5870; *Fax:* 306-752-5556
melfort.museum@sasktel.net
www.melfortmuseum.org
twitter.com/MelfortMu seum
www.facebook.com/329483827062438
Year Founded: 1973 Community museum, archives, pioneer village; agricultural machinery displays; located adjacent to the Melfort fairgrounds; open M - F 9:00 - 4:30 year round.
Gailmarie Anderson, Curator

Melville: **Melville Heritage Museum Inc.**
PO Box 2528
Located at 100 Heritage Dr., Melville, SK
Melville, SK S0A 2P0
Tel: 306-728-2070; *Fax:* 306-728-2038
melmus@sasktel.net
Regional museum, located in the former Luther Academy (1913-1926); artifacts & histories of local, provincial & national interest; includes chapel, library, Grand Trunk Pacific/CNR & Military; over 100 original B & W framed photographs depict Melville's first quarter century; gift shop; murals; limited wheelchair access

Melville: **Melville Railway Museum**
PO Box 2863
Melville, SK S0A 2P0
Tel: 306-728-3722
Year Founded: 1986 Former CNR steam locomotive #5114; a J-4-5 class 4-6-2 built in 1919; also former Grand Trunk Pacific station from Duff, Saskatchewan containing artifacts including

exhibits of communications equipment, from telegraphs, and telephones. There are also records from the Grand Trunk Railway and CNR, including employee records
Jennifer Mann, Tourism Manager, 306-728-3722, Fax: 306-728-2443, jmann@melville.ca

***Midale:* Souris Valley Antique Association**
PO Box 352
Midale, SK S0C 1S0
Tel: 306-458-2374
Other contact information: Alternate Phones: 306-458-2409; 306-458-2476
Year Founded: 1966 The association runs a 33-acre Heritage Village consisting of two pioneer houses, a barn, blacksmith shop, church, service station, & rural school. Open June-Sept.

***Middle Lake:* Middle Lake Museum**
PO Box 157
Middle Lake, SK S0K 2X0
Pioneer artifacts

***Milden:* Milden Community Museum**
PO Box 218
Milden, SK S0L 2L0
Tel: 306-935-4511
A community museum holding local artifacts including those of an old-time school, hospital & bedroom; open July-Aug.

***Moose Jaw:* 15 Wing Military Aviation Museum**
PO Box 5000, 15 Wing Moose Jaw
Moose Jaw, SK S6H 7Z8
Tel: 306-694-2222; *Fax:* 306-694-2813
15wingpao@forces.gc.ca
www.cg.cfpsa.ca/cg-pc/moosejaw

***Moose Jaw:* Moose Jaw Museum & Art Gallery**
Crescent Park
Moose Jaw, SK S6H 0X6
Tel: 306-692-4471; *Fax:* 306-694-8016
mjamchin@sasktel.net
www.mjmag.ca
Year Founded: 1966 The building houses art, history & science exhibits, with a wide range of human history artifacts with strong representation of First Nations beadwork, women's clothing, and clothing-related artifacts from 1880 onward. There is a gift shop. The Learning Centre offers programs for school children and art classes for all ages. Open year round; admission by donation.
Heather Smith, Curator, mjamchin@sasktel.net

***Moose Jaw:* Sukanen Ship Pioneer Village & Museum**
PO Box 2071
Moose Jaw, SK S6H 7T2
Tel: 306-693-7315
Museum.mail@sukanenmuseum.ca
www.sukanenmuseum.ca
38 acres of land; pioneer village of 20 buildings; antique farm with machinery; 100 collector tractors; 40 cars & trucks; open mid-May to mid-Sept.

***Moose Jaw:* Western Development Museum (WDM) Moose Jaw Branch**
50 Diefenbaker Dr.
Moose Jaw, SK S6J 1L9
Tel: 306-693-5989; *Fax:* 306-691-0511
moosejaw@wdm.ca
www.wdm.ca/mj.html
www.facebook.com/skwdm
Moose Jaw is one of four exhibit branches of Saskatchewan's Western Development Museum. The other branches are located in North Battleford, Saskatoon, & Yorkton. The Moose Jaw Western Development Museum displays the history of transportation, from the canoe to the railway. The museum also features the Snowbirds Gallery, which presents Canadian military aerobatic flight history.
Katherine Fitton, Manager, kfitton@wdm.ca
David Samson, Museum Technician, dsamson@wdm.ca
James Herrem, Supervisor, Maintenance, jherrem@wdm.ca
Shirley Stenko, Officer, Museum Operations, sstenko@wdm.ca

***Moosomin:* Jamieson Museum**
PO Box 236
Located at 306 Gertie St., Moosomin, SK
Moosomin, SK S0G 3N0
Tel: 306-435-3156
Pre-1900 house, church, military collection; open May - Oct.

***Moosomin:* Moosomin Regional Museum**
PO Box 1654
Moosomin, SK S0G 3N0
Tel: 306-435-7604
Open July & Aug.

***Morse:* Morse Museum & Cultural Centre**
PO Box 308
Morse, SK S0H 3C0
Tel: 306-629-3230
morsemuseum@sasktel.net
sites.google.com/site/morsemuseum1
www.facebook.com/8511642284
Year Founded: 1980 Former school, built in 1912; open year round.

***Mortlach:* Mortlach Museum & Drop In Centre**
PO Box 163
Mortlach, SK S0H 3E0
Tel: 306-355-2268
Other contact information: Chair, Phone: 306-355-2214
Located in the town's old fire hall; pioneer & aboriginal artifacts; replica courthouse & jail cell; open year-round, M-F, or by appointment.

***Mossbank:* Mossbank & District Museum Inc.**
PO Box 172, 517 Main St.
Mossbank, SK S0H 3G0
Tel: 306-354-2889
django@sasktel.net
www.southcentralmuseums.ca/mossbank.html
A community history museum dedicated to the history of No. 2 Bombing & Gunnery School which was located three miles east of Mossbank during WWII; blacksmith shop & blacksmith's house are now classified as provincial heritage property
Roy Tollefson, President
Don Smith, Contact, 306-354-2491

***Naicam:* Naicam Museum**
PO Box 93
Naicam, SK S0K 2Z0
Tel: 306-874-2280
www.townofnaicam.ca/museum.htm
History & archives of Naicam & District in Heritage building (pioneer school)

***Neilburg:* Manitou Pioneers Museum**
PO Box 336
Located at 301 - 4th Ave. East, Neilburg, SK
Neilburg, SK S0M 2C0
Tel: 306-823-4264
The museum features the largest collection of arrowheads & stone hammers in Saskatchewan, as well as salt & pepper shakers, & lamps. Open July & Aug., or by appointment.

***Nipawin:* Nipawin & District Living Forestry Museum**
PO Box 1917
Located at Old Hwy. 35 West, Nipawin, SK
Nipawin, SK S0E 1E0
Tel: 306-862-9299
www.nipawin.com/forestrymuseum.php
Situated on 14 acres; open May - Aug.

***Nokomis:* Nokomis District Museum & Heritage Co-op**
PO Box 417
Nokomis, SK S0G 3R0
Tel: 306-528-2979
Displays & artifacts of early days & local history; open June 1 - Labour Day daily 10-5

***North Battleford:* Western Development Museum (WDM) North Battleford Branch**
PO Box 183, Hwys 16 & 40
North Battleford, SK S9A 2Y1
Tel: 306-445-8033; *Fax:* 306-445-7211
nbattleford@wdm.ca
www.wdm.ca/nb.html
www.facebook.com/skwdm
North Battleford is one of four exhibit branches of Saskatchewan's Western Development Museum. The other branches are located in Moose Jaw, Saskatoon, & Yorkton. The North Battleford Western Development Museum provides visitors with the opportunity to explore a Heritage Farm & Village. Sights include a Wheat Pool grain elevator, a 1910 Case 110 tractor, A Co-op store, homes, & churches. The museum is located at the intersection of Highways 16 & 40.
Joyce Smith, Manager, jsmith@wdm.ca
Cheryl Stewart-Rahm, Coordinator, Programs & Volunteer, cstewart@wdm.ca
David Gilbert, Museum Technician, dgilbert@wdm.ca

***Ogema:* Deep South Pioneer Museum (DSPM)**
510 Government Rd.
Ogema, SK S0C 1Y0
Tel: 306-459-7909
deepsouthpioneermuseum@gmail.com
www.deepsouthpioneermuseum.ca
Year Founded: 1977 28 buildings dipicting early pioneer life in Saskatchewan. Open May-Oct., Sa-Su 1:00-5:00, or by appointment.

***Outlook:* Outlook & District Heritage Museum & Gallery**
PO Box 1095
Located at 100 Railway Ave. East, Outlook, SK
Outlook, SK S0L 2N0
Tel: 306-867-8285
Located in a former railway station, the Outlook & District Heritage Museum & Gallery is open from June to August. Exhibits include a caboose & an old jail cell. The Museum also keeps copies of the local newspaper, entitled "The Outlook", dating back to 1910.

***Oxbow:* Ralph Allen Memorial Museum**
PO Box 911
Located at 802 Railway Ave., Oxbow, SK
Oxbow, SK S0C 2B0
Tel: 306-483-5177
ralphallenmemorialmuseum@outlook.com
www.facebook.com/ RalphAllenMuseumOxbow

***Paynton:* Bresaylor Heritage Museum**
PO Box 33, Main St.
Paynton, SK S0M 2J0
Tel: 306-895-4813
The Bresaylor Heritage Museum collects artifacts from the Bresaylor & Paynton area. Items date back to 1882, when the earliest residents settled in Bresaylor. The museum also holds the Joe Sayers Collection. The museum is open in July & August, & at other times of the year by appointment.

***Pelly:* Fort Pelly-Livingston Museum**
PO Box 217, 1st Ave. South
Pelly, SK S0A 2Z0
Tel: 306-595-4743
pellymuseum@gmail.com
www.pelly.ca/museum.html
School room; pioneer artifacts; scale models of the two forts

***Perdue:* Perdue Museum**
PO Box 243
Perdue, SK S0K 3C0
Tel: 306-237-9161

***Plenty:* Plenty & District Museum**
General Delivery
Plenty, SK S0L 2R0
Tel: 306-377-4717
Other contact information: Alt. Phone: 306-932-4406
Situated in a 1911 building, which once served as Plenty's post office & hardware store, the Plenty & District Museum depicts pioneer life in the community & surrounding area. Farming equipment is featured in a separate building.

***Ponteix:* Notukeu Heritage Museum**
PO Box 603
Located at 110 Railway Ave. East, Ponteix, SK
Ponteix, SK S0N 1Z0
Tel: 306-625-3340; *Fax:* 306-625-3965
auvergnois@sasktel.net
The museum's collection includes fossils, Paleo-Indian artifacts, & the collection of amateur archaeologist Henri Liboiron.

***Porcupine Plain:* Porcupine Plain & District Museum**
PO Box 171
Located at 137 Windsor Ave., Porcupine Plain, SK
Porcupine Plain, SK S0E 1H0
Tel: 306-278-2317
www.porcupineplain.com
Other contact information: Alternate Phone: 306-278-2073
Year Founded: 1968 The Porcupine Plain & District Museum features local pioneer artifacts, such as antique machinery & clothing. The museum also houses a bird displat, with birds from the Porcupine Plain & Somme area. The soldier settlement consists of a log home, a schoolhouse, & a church. The Porcupine Plain & District Museum is open from the beginning of July to the Labour Day weekend in September. At other times, tours may be arranged.

***Prairie River:* Prairie River Museum**
PO Box 86
Prairie River, SK S0E 1J0
Tel: 306-889-4248
prairierivermuseum@yourlink.ca
Railway, agriculture, lumbering, trapping, First Nations artifacts. Located in an old CN railway station. Open Jan.-Dec., or by appointment.

***Preeceville:* Preeceville & District Heritage Museum**
PO Box 511
Located at 239 Highway Ave. East, Preeceville, SK
Preeceville, SK S0A 3B0
Tel: 306-547-2774
www.townofpreeceville.ca/default.aspx?page=52
www.facebook.com/142550417 4354539
Year Founded: 1985 Local history

***Prelate:* Blumenfeld & District Heritage Site**
PO Box 220
Prelate, SK S0N 2B0
Tel: 306-673-2200; *Fax:* 306-673-2635
The museum's collection includes the history of St. Peter & St. Paul Blumenfeld Church, as well as other churches in the area, & artifacts of early pioneers.

***Prelate:* St. Angela's Museum & Archives**
PO Box 220
Located at 201 - 3rd Ave., Prelate, SK
Prelate, SK S0N 2B0
Tel: 306-673-2200; *Fax:* 306-673-2635
stangela.acad01@sk.sympatico.ca
To preserve valuable history of pioneer Saskatchewan & of the pioneer Ursulines of St. Angela's Convent Academy at Prelate Saskatchewan; collection tells story of Ursuline life & apostolate that were used in chapel, classroom & other departments

***Prince Albert:* Cumberland House Provincial Historic Park**
Prince Albert Park Area, PO Box 3003
Prince Albert, SK S6V 6G1
Tel: 306-953-3571
cumberlandhousehistpark@gov.sk.ca
Site of the first Hudson's Bay Company post.

***Prince Albert:* Diefenbaker House**
246 - 19th St. West
Prince Albert, SK S6V 8A9
Tel: 306-764-2992
historypa@citypa.com
historypa.com/museums/diefenbaker_house.html
twitter.com/historypa
www .facebook.com/PrinceAlbertHistoricalSociety
Residence of John G. Diefenbaker immediately prior to his becoming Prime Minister of Canada; museum furnished as it was in Mr. Diefenbaker's day & also includes phtographic displays of his life & associations in Prince Albert; administered by the Prince Albert Historical Society
James Benson, Manager

***Prince Albert:* Evolution of Education Museum**
10 River St. East
Prince Albert, SK S6V 8A9
Tel: 306-764-2992
historypa@citypa.com
historypa.com/museums/evolution_education.html
twitter.com/historypa
w ww.facebook.com/PrinceAlbertHistoricalSociety
Year Founded: 1963 Housed in the original Claytonville one-room rural school & features a class-room setting, plus displays of many early educational materials & artifacts. Administered by the Prince Albert Historical Society.
James Benson, Manager

***Prince Albert:* Prince Albert Historical Museum**
10 River St. East
Prince Albert, SK S6V 8A9
Tel: 306-764-2992
historypa@citypa.com
historypa.com/museums/historical.html
twitter.com/historypa
www.facebo ok.com/PrinceAlbertHistoricalSociety
History, life-styles & people of Prince Albert & area; souvenir shop & tea room; administered by the Prince Albert Historical Society
James Benson, Manager

***Prince Albert:* Rotary Museum of Police & Corrections**
10 River St. East
Prince Albert, SK S6V 8A9
Tel: 306-764-2992
historypa@citypa.com
historypa.com
twitter.com/histo rypa
www.facebook.com/PrinceAlbertHistoricalSociety
Housed in the guardhouse of the Prince Albert division of the NorthWest Mounted Police & Royal Northwest Mounted police; features artifacts, equipment & uniforms from the RCMP, Prince Albert City Police, the Provincial Correctional Service & the Correctional Service of Canada, as well as from the Saskatchewan Provincial Police; administered by the Prince Albert Historical Society
James Benson, Manager

***Prud'homme:* Prud'homme Museum**
PO Box 38
Prud'homme, SK S0K 3K0
Tel: 306-654-2001; *Fax:* 306-654-2007
voprud@sasktel.net
www.prudhommevillage.com
Open year-round.

***Punnichy:* Punnichy & District Museum**
PO Box 396
Located at 223 Main St., Punnichy, SK
Punnichy, SK S0A 3C0
Tel: 306-835-2887
Local history; open July & Aug., Tu & Th 2:00-4:00, or by appointment.

***Radville:* Radville CN Station/Firefighters Museum**
c/o Tourism Radville, PO Box 253
Radville, SK S0C 2G0
Tel: 306-869-3237
Open by appointment only.

***Raymore:* Raymore Pioneer Museum Inc.**
PO Box 453
Raymore, SK S0A 3J0
Tel: 306-476-2180
Collection of local pioneer artifacts

***Regina:* Alex Youck School Museum**
1600 - 4th Ave.
Regina, SK S4R 8C8
Tel: 306-791-8200
Open by appt. only

***Regina:* Government House Museum & Heritage Property (GH)**
4607 Dewdney Ave.
Regina, SK S4T 1B7
Tel: 306-787-5773; *Fax:* 306-787-5714
governmenthouse@gov.sk.ca
www.governmenthouse.gov.sk.ca
twitter.com/Go vt_House
www.facebook.com/governmenthouse
Year Founded: 1980 Former residence of the Lieutenant Governor of the Northwest Territories & the Province of Saskatchewan

***Regina:* RCMP Heritage Centre**
5907 Dewdney Ave.
Regina, SK S4T 0P4
Tel: 306-522-7333; *Fax:* 306-522-7340
Toll-Free: 866-567-7267
info@rcmphc.com
www.rcmpheritagecentre.com
twitter.c om/RCMP_HC
www.facebook.com/RCMPHC
Year Founded: 2007 The complete history of the RCMP is told through exhibits, multimedia, & programs.
Tracy Fahlman, Chair
Al Nicholson, CEO

***Regina:* Regina Plains Museum**
1835 Scarth St., 2nd Fl.
Regina, SK S4P 2G9
Tel: 306-780-9435; *Fax:* 306-565-2979
rp.museum@sasktel.net
www.reginaplainsmuseum.com
twitter.com/RegPlains Museum
www.facebook.com/regina.plains
Year Founded: 1960 Regina Plains Museum is the civic history museum of the city. It is open year-round.
Shari Sokochoff, Executive Director
Rose Schmidlechner, Administrative Assistant, Communications

***Regina:* Saskatchewan African Canadian Heritage Museum Inc.**
PO Box 1171
Regina, SK S4P 3B4
Tel: 306-545-8824; *Fax:* 306-543-6181
info@sachm.org
www.sachm.org
SACHM is a virtual museum dedicated to preserving the history of people of African ancestry who lived & currently live in Saskatchewan.
Muna DeCiman, Chair

***Regina:* Saskatchewan Military Museum**
The Armouries, 1600 Elphinstone St.
Regina, SK S4T 3N1
Tel: 306-347-9349
saskatchewanmilitarymuseum@hotmail.ca
www.saskatchewan militarymuseum.com
Social Media: pinterest.com/saskmilmuseum/
twitter.com/SaskMilMuseum
www.facebook.com/SaskMilitaryMuseum
Collects & preserves Saskatchewan's military history from 1885 to the present; artifacts, uniforms, badges & medals, vehicles, ammunition; photos, archival material & paintings; open M, Th 7:00 - 9:00 or by appointment.
Maj. (Ret'd) C. Keith Inches, Curator, 306-586-8198, keithinches@sasktel.net
Kristian Peachey, Assistant Curator, 306-552-9092

***Regina:* Saskatchewan Pharmacy Museum**
***Parent:* Saskatchewan Pharmacy Museum Society**
#700, 4010 Pasqua St.
Regina, SK S4S 6S4
Tel: 306-584-2292; *Fax:* 306-584-9695
saskpharm@sk.sympatico.ca
www.skpharmacists.ca
Collection & preservation of pharmacy artifacts, documentation of pharmacy history; no physical location
Bill Paterson, President
Brenda Prystupa, Treasurer, brenda.prystupa@skpharmacists.ca

***Regina:* Saskatchewan Sports Hall of Fame & Museum**
2205 Victoria Ave.
Regina, SK S4P 0S4
Tel: 306-780-9232
sasksportshalloffame.com
twitter.com/SaskSportsHF
www.facebook.com/SaskSportsHF
Year Founded: 1966 3,000 sq. ft. of exhibit space celebrating the sport heritage of Saskatchewan; open year round with extended summer hours
Sheila Kelly, Executive Director, skelly@sshfm.com

***Regina Beach:* Lakeside Heritage Museum**
PO Box 102
Regina Beach, SK S0G 4C0
Tel: 306-729-2671
Located beside the Cultural Centre, near South Shore School; open May-Sept., Su.

***Regina Beach:* Last Mountain House Provincial Historic Park**
PO Box 215
Regina Beach, SK S0G 4C0
Tel: 306-725-5203; *Fax:* 306-725-5207
www.saskparks.net/LastMountainHouse
Other contact information: July & Aug., Phone: 306-731-4409
The Last Mountain House dates from 1869, & was used by the Hudson's Bay Company as a winter outpost for its Fort Qu'Appelle fur trade operation. The museum is a reconstruction, featuring three buildings, a privy, & an ice house. Open July-Sept., Th-Su.
John Currie, Contact, john.currie@gov.sk.ca

***Riverhurst:* F.T. Hill Museum**
PO Box 201
Located at 324 Teck St., Riverhurst, SK
Riverhurst, SK S0H 3P0
Tel: 306-353-2220
villageofriverhurst@sasktel.net
Year Founded: 1963 Gun collection, aboriginal artifacts, pioneer items; open June 15 - Aug. 31 & by appt.

***Rocanville:* Rocanville & District Museum**
PO Box 490, 220 Qu'Appelle Ave.
Rocanville, SK S0A 3L0
Tel: 306-645-2113; *Fax:* 306-645-2087
roc.cap@sasktel.net
Other contact information: Phone, Appointments: 306-645-2164

Year Founded: 1989 Located at the corner of Qu'appelle Avenue & St. Albert Street, the Rocanville & District Museum showcases a CPR station, a church, a schoolhouse, a blacksmith shop, & a Masonic Lodge. The museum is open during July & August, & by appointment at other times of the year.

La Ronge: Mistasinihk Place Interpretive Centre
c/o Saskatchewan Family Foundation, PO Box 5000, La Ronge Ave.
La Ronge, SK S0J 1L0
Tel: 306-425-4350
Aboriginal artifacts, artwork by northern artists, displays about northern industries & activites

Rose Valley: Rose Valley & District Heritage Museum
PO Box 123
Located at 115 Centre St., Rose Valley, SK
Rose Valley, SK S0E 1M0
Tel: 306-322-4642
Museum with artifacts from area 1900 to present; open July & Aug., Mon.-Fri.; off season viewing available by request

Rosetown: Rosetown & District Museum
PO Box 37
Located at 605 Colwell Rd. East, Rosetown, SK
Rosetown, SK S0L 2V0
Tel: 306-882-2199
rdmuseum@sasktel.net
Natural history specimens, photographs, handicrafts

Rosthern: Mennonite Heritage Museum
PO Box 116
Rosthern, SK S0K 3R0
Tel: 306-232-4415
Museum housed in school, artifacts from 1800 to present, collection of World Wheat champion; open May to Sept.

Rouleau: Rouleau & District Museum
PO Box 132, 1001 Knox Ave.
Rouleau, SK S0G 4H0
Tel: 306-776-2363
A rural town street setting with houses, barn, blacksmith shop, school & other buildings; archives; special events, such as the annual threshing bee in Aug., & other programming. Open by appt., May - Sept.

St Brieux: Musée St. Brieux Museum
CP 224
Situé à 300, ch Barbier, St. Brieux, SK
St Brieux, SK S0K 3V0
Tél: 306-275-2123
Documentation au sujet de la vie des pionniers, de leurs origines, des missions environnantes et de l'église catholique pré-Vatican II; des tournées en français ou en anglais sont offertes

St Victor: Le Beau Village Museum
PO Box 58
St Victor, SK S0H 3T0
Tel: 306-642-3215; *Fax:* 306-642-3215
Religious & pioneer artifacts; open by appointment only.

St Victor: McGillis House
St Victor, SK S0H 3T0
Tel: 306-642-3171
www.willowbunch.ca
Located in St. Victor's regional park, McGillis House was built in 1890. Artifacts in the home include Métis items, kerosene lanterns, early saddles & bridles, & a feathered buffalo skull.

St Walburg: St. Walburg & District Historical Museum
PO Box 368
St Walburg, SK S0M 2T0
Tel: 306-248-3232
Local exhibits from pioneer days to 1945

Saltcoats: Saltcoats Museum
PO Box 309
Saltcoats, SK S0A 3R0
Tel: 306-744-2977
Local history; open July & Aug., or by appointment.

Saskatoon: Children's Discovery Museum on the Saskatchewan
Market Mall, #116, 2325 Preston Ave.
Saskatoon, SK S7J 2G2
Tel: 306-683-2555
discovery@museumforkids.sk.ca
www.museumforkids.sk.ca
www.facebook.com/museumforkids.sk.ca
Year Founded: 2009 The museum provides hands-on exhibits & programs to children ten & under, in an effort to promote creativity, curiosity, & a love of learning.
Erica Bird, President

Saskatoon: Diefenbaker Canada Centre
University of Saskatchewan, 101 Diefenbaker Pl.
Saskatoon, SK S7N 5B8
Tel: 306-966-8384; *Fax:* 306-966-1967
dief.centre@usask.ca
www.usask.ca/diefenbaker
twitter.com/DiefCentre
www.facebook.com/diefenbakercent
Year Founded: 1980 The Diefenbaker Canada Centre includes a museum, archives, & research centre. The centre houses artifacts, such as a personal library, papers, & memorabilia, that were bequeathed to the University of Saskatchewan by former prime minister of Canada, John G. Diefenbaker. The archives features collections of press clippings, photographs, & documents related to Diefenbaker's life & Canadian history.
Teresa Carlson, Curator & Collections Manager, 306-966-8383, teresa.carlson@usask.ca
Terresa Ann DeMong, Manager, 306-966-8382, terresa.demong@usask.ca

Saskatoon: Fort Carlton Provincial Park
#102, 112 Research Dr.
Saskatoon, SK S7K 2H6
Tel: 306-467-5205; *Fax:* 306-467-5215
fortcarlton@gov.sk.ca
www.saskparks.net
Located 26 km. west of Duck Lake on Hwy. 212; a reconstructed Hudson's Bay Company fur trade post; guided tours; picnic grounds; hiking; camping; open May - Sept.

Saskatoon: Gabriel Dumont Institute of Native Studies & Applied Research (GDI) The Virtual Museum of Métis History & Culture
c/o Saskatoon Publishing Office, #2, 604 - 22nd St. West
Saskatoon, SK S7M 5W1
Tel: 306-934-4941; *Fax:* 306-244-0252
general@gdi.gdins.org
www.metismuseum.com
twitter.com/gdins_org
www.facebook.com/gabrieldumontinstitute
Other contact information: Alt. URL: www.gdins.org
Year Founded: 1980 A joint project between GDI & Saskatchewan Department of Learning, the Department of Canadian Heritage's Canadian Culture Online Program, the Canada Council for the Arts, SaskCulture, the Government of Canada, & the University of Saskatchewan Division of Media & Technology; the virtual museum provides users with a comprehensive study of Métis history & culture, including many primary documents such as oral history interviews, photos, & other archival materials.
Darren R. Préfontaine, Project Leader

Saskatoon: Marr Residence
326 - 11th St. East
Saskatoon, SK S7N 0E7
Tel: 306-652-1201
themarr.ca
Year Founded: 1982 The oldest building in Saskatchewan (built in 1884) that's still on its original site, now designated a heritage site by the City of Saskatoon.

Saskatoon: Meewasin Valley Authority (MVA)
402 - 3rd Ave. South
Saskatoon, SK S7K 3G5
Tel: 306-665-6887; *Fax:* 306-665-6117
meewasin@meewasin.com
www.meewasin.com
Year Founded: 1979 Conservation agency for the South Saskatchewan River
Lloyd Isaak, CEO, 306-665-6887

Saskatoon: Musée Ukraina Museum Inc. (MUM)
PO Box 26072
Saskatoon, SK S7K 8C1
Tel: 306-244-4212
ukrainamuseum@sasktel.net
www.mumsaskatoon.com
Year Founded: 1955 The museum's goal is to collect & preserve Ukranian cultural heritage, & make it available to the public.

Saskatoon: Museum of Antiquities
#116, College Bldg., University of Saskatchewan, 107 Administration Pl.
Saskatoon, SK S7N 5A2
Tel: 306-966-7818; *Fax:* 306-966-1954
museum_antiquities@usask.ca
www.usask.ca/antiquities/
twitter.com/MofA ntiquities
Year Founded: 1974 A collection of Near Eastern, Egyptian, Greek, Roman & Medieval sculpture in full scale replica as well as original works & coinage
Tracene Harvey, Director & Curator
Brittney Sproule, Contact, 306-966-7818, museum_antiquities@usask.ca

Saskatoon: Museum of Natural Sciences
Dept. of Biology & Geological Sciences, University of Saskatchewan, 112 Science Pl.
Saskatoon, SK S7N 5E2
Tel: 306-966-4399; *Fax:* 306-966-4461
biology.dept@usask.ca
artsandscience.usask.ca/museumofnaturalsciences
www.youtube.com/user/artsandscienceUofS
www.facebook.com/Arts.Science.Uo fS
Designed to show evolution through time beginning with marine invertebrates & ending with evolution of animals; displays of living plants & animals correspond to fossils & create an integrated learning experience; free self-guided tours year-round; brochures downloaded from website
Dr. P. Bonham-Smith, Head, Biology, peta.bonhams@usask.ca
Dr. B. Pratt, Geology, brian.pratt@usask.ca

Saskatoon: Royal Canadian Legion Artifacts Room
The Royal Canadian Legion, Nutana Branch, 3021 Louise St.
Saskatoon, SK S7J 3L1
Tel: 306-374-6303; *Fax:* 306-374-3233
nutana.legion@sasktel.net
www.museum.nutanalegion.ca
Social Media: www.pinterest.com/nutanamuseum
twitter.com/MuseumWar
www.facebook.com/613019275419606
The collection is located in the basement of the Legion building, & features a variety of military memorabilia. Open Th 9:00 AM - 10:30 AM or by appointment
Shirley Timpson, Manager, stimpson@sasktel.net

Saskatoon: Saskatchewan Railway Museum *Parent:* Saskatchewan Railroad Historical Association
PO Box 21117
Saskatoon, SK S7H 5N9
Tel: 306-382-9855
srha@saskrailmuseum.org
www.saskrailmuseum.org
www.facebook.com/SaskatchewanRailwayMuseum
Year Founded: 1990 The museum site features locomotives, cabooses, a sleeping car, & streetcars that visitors can board. Visitors can also ride the museum's "speeder."

Saskatoon: Ukrainian Museum of Canada (UMC) *Parent:* Ukrainian Women's Association of Canada
910 Spadina Cres. East
Saskatoon, SK S7K 3H5
Tel: 306-244-3800; *Fax:* 306-652-7620
ukrmuse@sasktel.net
www.umc.sk.ca
Year Founded: 1936 The Ukrainian Museum preserves & encourages Ukrainian folk arts in Canada. The permanent gallery tells the story of Ukrainian immigration to Canada with displays of folk arts, including costumes, embroideries, weaving, ceramics, & Easter eggs. The museum's collection of textiles is one of the largest of its kind in North America.
Sonia Korpus, President
Janet C.P. Danyliuk, Director & CEO

Saskatoon: Wanuskewin Heritage Park
Penner Rd., RR#4
Saskatoon, SK S7K 3J7
Tel: 306-931-6767; *Fax:* 306-931-4522
www.wanuskewin.com
www.facebook.com/Wanuskewin
Year Founded: 1992 The Wanuskewin Heritage Park represents the life of the Northern Plains First Nations people. Visitors will find tipi rings, bison kill sites, a medicine wheel, & pottery fragments. The 116 hectare park operates under the leadership & guidance of First Nations people. It is open year-round.
Dana Soonias, Chief Executive Officer, dana.soonias@wanuskewin.com

Saskatoon: Western Development Museum (WDM) Saskatoon Branch
2610 Lorne Ave.
Saskatoon, SK S7J 0S6
Tel: 306-931-1910; *Fax:* 306-934-0525
saskatoon@wdm.ca
www.wdm.ca/stoon.html
www.facebook.com/skwdm
Saskatoon is one of four exhibit branches of Saskatchewan's Western Development Museum. The other branches are located in Moose Jaw, North Battleford, & Yorkton. The Saskatoon Western Development Museum presents a 1910 Boomtown. Visitors can explore more than thirty buildings, including a blacksmith shop & a general store. The museum is also home to the Saskatchewan Agricultural Hall of Fame.
Jason Wall, Manager, jwall@wdm.ca
Scott Whiting, Coordinator, Education & Public Programs, swhiting@wdm.ca
Dean Fey, Museum Technician, dfey@wdm.ca

Sceptre: Great Sandhills Museum & Interpretive Centre
***Parent:* Great Sandhills Historical Society**
PO Box 29, Hwy. 32
Sceptre, SK S0N 2H0
Tel: 306-623-4345; *Fax:* 306-623-4612
gshs@sasktel.net
www.greatsandhillsmuseum.com
Dedicated to collect, portray & preserve the heritage of the "Great Sandhills" District in SW Saskatchewan through natural history specimens

Scout Lake: St. Mary's Historical Society of Maxstone, Inc.
PO Box 33
Scout Lake, SK S0H 3V0
Tel: 306-642-4079
lornesfarm@sasktel.net
www.southcentralmuseums.ca/maxstone.html
Other contact information: Alternate Phone: 306-642-3150
Heritage site includes old church (1917) & graveyard, oldschool; open year round, by appt. only
Lorne Kwasnicki, Director

Semans: Semans & District Museum
PO Box 205
Semans, SK S0A 3S0
Tel: 306-524-2020
Year Founded: 1983 The museum is housed in an old school-turned-Oddfellows Hall. The collection contains artifacts & archives on local history. The museum is located on the corner of Main Street & 4th Ave.; open June-Sept.

Shaunavon: Grand Coteau Heritage & Cultural Centre
PO Box 966, 440 Centre St.
Shaunavon, SK S0N 2M0
Tel: 306-297-3882; *Fax:* 306-297-3668
gchcc@sasktel.net
www.shaunavonmuseum.ca
Natural history museum, heritage museum, art gallery, public library; open year-round
Wendy Thienes, Director
Kelly Attrell, Collections Manager

Shell Lake: Shell Lake Museum
PO Box 280
Shell Lake, SK S0J 2G0
Tel: 306-427-2272
The Shell Lake Museum is located in the historic station house. The site also features a log house. It is open on weekends during the summer.

Shellbrook: Shellbrook & Districts Museum
PO Box 40
Shellbrook, SK S0J 2E0
Tel: 306-747-4949; *Fax:* 306-747-3111
Open year-round.

Spalding: Reynold Rapp Museum
PO Box 308
Spalding, SK S0K 4C0
Tel: 306-872-2276
www.facebook.com/spaldingmuseum
Year Founded: 1972 Housed in Reynold Rapp M.P.'s family home

Spiritwood: Spiritwood & District Museum
PO Box 34
Spiritwood, SK S0J 2M0
Tel: 306-883-2828
townofspiritwood.ca/museum
www.facebook.com/SpiritwoodAndDistrictMuseum
Local history, with an emphasis on agriculture & vintage machinery & vehicles. Open year-round by appointment.
Auralia Wasden, Contact, awasden@sasktel.net
Geraldine Lavoie, Contact, 306-883-8891, geraldinemarie65@hotmail.com

Spy Hill: Spy Hill Museum
PO Box 268
Spy Hill, SK S0A 3W0
Tel: 306-534-4462; *Fax:* 306-534-2227
Year Founded: 1954 The museum has three buildings depicting the history of Spy Hill, from prehistoric days to the present. Open July & Aug., M, Tu, Th-Su 2:00-4:00.

Spy Hill: Wolverine Hobby & Historical Society Inc.
PO Box 191
Spy Hill, SK S0A 3W0
Tel: 306-534-2200
Three buildings, former country school, former retail outlet & Lutheran church; touring/visiting on request

Star City: Star City Heritage Museum
PO Box 38, 217 - 5th St.
Star City, SK S0E 1P0
Tel: 306-863-2282
Year Founded: 1970 Star City's Heritage Museum presents World War I & World War II memorabilia, personal & household items, & farm equipment. The museum is open from June to August & by appointment during the off season.

Stoughton: Stoughton & District Museum
PO Box 492
Located at 327 Main St., Stroughton, SK
Stoughton, SK S0G 4T0
Tel: 306-457-2413
stoughtontown@sasktel.net
Pioneer items; open July to Sept.

Strasbourg: Strasbourg & District Museum
PO Box 369
Strasbourg, SK S0G 4V0
Tel: 306-725-3443
www.facebook.com/StrasbourgAndDistrictMuseum
Year Founded: 1971 Pioneer & First Nations artifacts, mounted animals & birds
Ingrid Youck, Curator

Sturgis: Sturgis Station House Museum
PO Box 255
Located at 306 Railway Ave. SE., Strugis, SK
Sturgis, SK S0A 4A0
Tel: 306-548-5565
sturgismuseumfile@yahoo.ca
sturgismuseumsk.ca
Year Founded: 1986 Aboriginal & early settlers artifacts; open May-Aug.
Lorraine Sept-Drayer, Curator

Swift Current: Doc's Town Heritage Village
***Parent:* Swift Current Agricultural & Exhibition Association**
Kinetic Exhibition Park, PO Box 146, 17th Ave. SE & South Railway St.
Swift Current, SK S9H 3V5
Tel: 306-773-2944; *Fax:* 306-773-7015
kineticpark@swiftcurrent.ca
www.swiftcurrentex.com
twitter.com/SCAGEX
www.facebook.com/DocsTownHeritageVillage
A reconstructed town depicting Saskatchewan life in the early 1900s.
Tracey Stevenson, Contact, 306-773-2944, kineticpark@swiftcurrent.ca

Swift Current: Swift Current Museum
44 Robert St. West
Swift Current, SK S9H 4M9
Tel: 306-778-2775; *Fax:* 306-778-4818
www.swiftcurrent.ca
www.facebook.com/SwiftCurrentMuseum
Year Founded: 1949 The museum hosts a featured exhibit on how human activities impact the environment, as well as temporary exhibits throughout the year. The museum also houses the Swift Current & district archives. Open year-round, M-F, 8:00-5:00.
Lloyd Begley, Contact, l.begley@swiftcurrent.ca

Tisdale: Tisdale & District Museum
PO Box 1528
Tisdale, SK S0E 1T0
Tel: 306-873-4999
tmuseum@hotmail.com
www.facebook.com/TisdaleAndDistrictMuseum
Year Founded: 1986 The museum features vintage cars, the history of Tisdale bee farming, & artifacts from a historic shoot-out between the Provincial Police & four Russian Bolsheviks. Open May-Sept., 9:00-6:00.

Turtleford: Turtleford & District Museum
PO Box 43
Turtleford, SK S0M 2Y0
Tel: 306-845-2433
dmbleakney@littleloon.ca
townofturtleford.ca
Local history, science & technology; located in Lions Park, south of Turtleford; open May-Sept daily.

Unity: Unity & District Heritage Museum
Unity Regional Park, General Delivery
Unity, SK S0K 4L0
Tel: 306-228-4464; *Fax:* 306-228-2149
www.townofunity.com/recreation/museum.php
The Unity & District Heritage Museum includes the following attractions: a 1909 CP Rail Station, the 1908 St. Thomas Anglican Church, the 1926 St.zwarthmore United Church, restored schools, an original home of Unity, a blacksmith shop, & a harness shop. The museum is open from mid-May to October.

Vanguard: Vanguard Centennial Museum
PO Box 208
Vanguard, SK S0N 2V0
Tel: 306-582-2244
vanguard@chinook.lib.sk.ca
Pioneer articles

Veregin: National Doukhobor Heritage Village (NDHV)
PO Box 99
Veregin, SK S0A 4H0
Tel: 306-542-4441
ndhv@yourlink.ca
www.ndhv.ca
Year Founded: 1980 The Village is a National & Provincial Historical Site, depicting the life of the Russian Doukhobor people who immigrated to Canada in the late 1800s. The Village features 12 buildings, a gift shop, & an on-site picnic area. Open May-Sept., daily 10:00-6:00.

Verigin: National Doukhobour Heritage Village
PO Box 99
Verigin, SK S0A 4H0
Tel: 306-542-4441
ndhv@yourlink.ca
www.ndhv.ca
Year Founded: 1980 Doukhobour artifacts, photos, handicrafts, clothing, hand tools; barns, a blacksmith shop & agricultural equipment; model of early Doukhobour village

Verwood: Verwood Community Museum
PO Box 213
Verwood, SK S0H 4G0
Tel: 306-642-5767
Pioneer articles housed in former church built in 1916

Wadena: Wadena & District Museum & Gallery
PO Box 1208
Wadena, SK S0A 4J0
Tel: 306-338-3454; *Fax:* 306-338-3804
wadena.museum@sasktel.net
townofwadena.com
www.facebook.com/pages/Wade na-Museum
Year Founded: 1986 Early settlers; 1904 CNR station house; 1907 Sunderland School No.1; blacksmith shop; furnishings; artifacts; open June - Aug., Tue.-Sun.
Doug Fitch, Chairman, 306-338-3685, wadena.museum@sasktel.net
Donna Zarowny, Secretary/Treasurer, 306-338-2091, wadena.museum@sasktel.net

Wakaw: Batoche National Historic Site of Canada (BNHS)
PO Box 1040, RR#1
Wakaw, SK S0K 4P0
Tel: 306-423-6227; *Fax:* 306-423-5400
batoche.info@pc.gc.ca
www.pc.gc.ca/eng/lhn-nhs/sk/batoche/index.aspx
Other contact information: TTD: 306-423-5540
The Batoche National Historic Site of Canada, on the banks of the South Saskatchewan River, is the scene of the last battlefield

in the Northwest Rebellion of 1885. The site displays the remains & several restored buildings of the village of Batoche. The life of the Métis at Batoche between 1860 & 1900 is depicted. The site is open from May to September.

***Wakaw:* Diefenbaker Law Office**
PO Box 760
Wakaw, SK S0K 4P0
Tel: 306-233-5157
Year Founded: 1971 Replica of the former prime minister's law office, located in Wakaw from 1918-1925

***Wakaw:* Wakaw Heritage Society Museum**
PO Box 520
Located at 315 - 1 St. South, Wakaw, SK
Wakaw, SK S0K 4P0
Tel: 306-233-4296
Year Founded: 1983 Collections associated with pioneer life
Isabelle McCulloch, Chair, 306-233-4843

***Waskesiu Lake:* Prince Albert National Park of Canada**
Northern Prairies Field Unit, PO Box 100
Waskesiu Lake, SK S0J 2Y0
Tel: 306-663-4522
panp.info@pc.gc.ca
www.pc.gc.ca/eng/pn-np/sk/princealbert/index.aspx
Protecting part of the boreal forest, Prince Albert National Park features the cabin of conservationist Grey Owl, a white pelican nesting colony, & a free-ranging herd of plains bison. Visitors to the park can participate in interpretive programs & special events. The park is open year-round, & the Interpretive Centre is open from the end of June to September.

***Waskesiu Lake:* Waskesiu Heritage Museum**
928 Waskesiu Dr.
Waskesiu Lake, SK S0J 2Y0
waskesiuheritagemuseum@hotmail.com
waskesiuheritagemuseum.org
Year Founded: 2005 Located in Prince Albert National Park, in the Friends of the Park Bookstore; open May & June, Sa-Su 10:00-6:00, July & Aug., daily, 10:00-6:00.

***Watson:* Watson & District Heritage Museum**
PO Box 736
Watson, SK S0K 4V0
Tel: 306-287-3783
The museum is housed in a National Heritage Site building, originally belonging to the Canadian Bank of Commerce, circa 1907. 2,000 artifacts are on display, including farm machinery, tools, ladies' fashion, & sports memorabilia. Open June-Aug., Tu-Sa 10:00-5:00.

***Wawota:* Wawota & District Museum**
PO Box 179, 101 Main St.
Wawota, SK S0G 5A0
Tel: 306-739-2110
www.wawota.com/museum.shtml
Year Founded: 1980 The Wawota & District Museum consists of the following buildings: the main building which was built in the early 1900s & used as a municipal office, a 1909 fire hall, the Bethany Schoolhouse, & a farm equipment shed. The museum is open during July & August, & by appointment at other times.

***Weekes:* Dunwell & Community Museum**
PO Box 120
Weekes, SK S0E 1V0
Tel: 306-278-2906
Restored CNR station, pioneer artifacts & Ukrainian clothes

***Weyburn:* Soo Line Historical Museum**
PO Box 1016, 411 Industrial Lane
Weyburn, SK S4H 2L2
Tel: 306-842-2922; *Fax:* 306-842-2922
slhm@sasktel.net
www.ascasonline.org/articoloOTTO66.html
www.facebook. com/118758801502753
Other contact information: Alt. URL: www.southcentralmuseums.ca/sooline.html
Year Founded: 1960 Largest private collection of silver in the world; collection of artifacts that were used by Weyburn & District pioneers
Jacquie Mallory, Curator

***Weyburn:* Turner Curling Museum**
PO Box 370
Located at 327 Mergens St. NW, Weyburn, SK
Weyburn, SK S4H 2K6
Tel: 306-848-3218
www.weyburn.ca
The museum was established by the late Don Turner & his wife Elva Turner; collection includes curling stones, brooms, clothing, pins, crests & books from around the world; tours available; open by appointment.

***Weyburn:* Weyburn & Area Heritage Village**
PO Box 370
Located at 424 - 10 Ave. South, Weyburn, SK
Weyburn, SK S4H 2K6
Tel: 306-842-6377
www.weyburn.net/attractions.html
Reproduction of a village community from the early 1900s; open May-Aug., daily 1:00-8:00.

***White Fox:* White Fox Museum**
PO Box 399
White Fox, SK S0J 3B0
Trapper's cabin, tool & harness shop, pioneer items; open June-Sept.

***Whitewood:* Whitewood Historical Museum**
PO Box 752
Located at 603 North Railway, Whitewood, SK
Whitewood, SK S0G 5C0
Tel: 306-735-2380
Other contact information: Alternate Phone: 306-735-2210
The museum consists of 5 buildings, including a pioneer school room & home, military display, Hungarian, French, Finnish & Swedish collections; open July - Aug.

***Wilcox:* Athol Murray College of Notre Dame Archives & Museum**
Archives / Museum Bldg., Athol Murray College of Notre Dame Campus, PO Box 100
Wilcox, SK S0G 5E0
Tel: 306-732-2080; *Fax:* 306-732-4409
nd.archives@notredame.sk.ca
www.notredame.sk.ca
The Athol Murray College of Notre Dame Archives & Museum collects & preserves items that tell the story of Père Athol Murray & the history of the Athol Murray College of Notre Dame. The archives & museum features Père Athol Murray's collection of Rare Books, the Rex Beach Repository, the Parthenon Frieze, the Nicholas de Grandmaison Art Portrait collection, sculptures, & stained glass windows. The archives & museum is open seven days a week in July & August, & Monday to Friday from September to June.
Terry McGarry, Curator

***Wilkie:* Wilkie & District Museum**
PO Box 868
Located at 209 - 1 St. East, Wilkie, SK
Wilkie, SK S0K 4W0
Tel: 306-843-2717
wilkiemuseum@gmail.com
Open summer; by appt. the rest of the year

***Willow Bunch:* Willow Bunch Museum**
***Parent:* Willow Bunch Museum & Heritage Society**
PO Box 157, 16 Édouard Beaupré St.
Willow Bunch, SK S0H 4K0
Tel: 306-473-2806
www.willowbunch.ca/museum
Other contact information: Phone, Mid Sept. - Mid May: 306-473-2762, 306-473-2279 & 306-473-2711
Year Founded: 1972 The Willow Bunch Museum is located in a Convent school which was built in 1914 by the Sisters of the Cross. One attraction is the display about Edouard Beaupré, an eight foot, three inch tall circus performer who was born in Willow Bunch in 1881. The museum is open from mid-May to mid-September. Tours may be arranged during the off-season.
Doris O'Reilly, Director

***Wolseley:* Wolseley & District Museum**
PO Box 218
Wolseley, SK S0G 5H0
Tel: 306-698-2360
Local history of the Wolseley including decorative arts, furnishings, household objects, & maps.

***Wood Mountain:* Wood Mountain Rodeo Ranch Museum**
PO Box 53
Wood Mountain, SK S0H 4L0
Tel: 306-266-4953
woodmtnhistoricalsoc@sasktel.net
www.woodmountain.ca/RodRanc.html
Other contact information: Phone, Tour Bookings: 306-266-2000
Located in the Wood Mountain Regional Park, Wood Mountain Rodeo Ranch Museum offers a glimpse into the life of ranchers & cowboys who arrived in the area in the 1880s. Exhibits include the history of the Wood Mountain Stampede, which is the oldest continuous rodeo in Canada. An extensive archival collection is also housed at the museum. The museum is open from May to September.
Lois Todd, Museum Contact

***Wynyard:* Frank Cameron Museum**
PO Box 734
Located at 520 - 1st St., West, Wynyard, SK
Wynyard, SK S0A 4T0
Tel: 306-554-3661
recreation.wynyard@sasktel.net
Local history; houses in a country schoolhouse; open May-Aug.

***Wynyard:* Wynyard & District Museum**
***Parent:* Wynyard & District Museum Society**
c/o Town of Wynyard, PO Box 220
Wynyard, SK S0A 4T0
Tel: 306-554-2123; *Fax:* 306-554-3224
www.facebook.com/875423055807635
CPR hand car, household accesories, farm implements, WWI materials

***Yorkton:* Western Development Museum (WDM) Yorkton Branch**
PO Box 98, Hwy. 16 A West
Yorkton, SK S3N 2V6
Tel: 306-783-8361; *Fax:* 306-782-1027
yorkton@wdm.ca
www.wdm.ca/yk.html
www.facebook.com/skwdm
Yorkton is one of four exhibit branches of Saskatchewan's Western Development Museum. The other branches are located in Moose Jaw, North Battleford, & Saskatoon. The Yorkton Western Development Museum presents the times when immigrants settled in western Canada, including the English, Ukrainians, Doukhobors, Germans, Swedes, & Icelanders.
Susan Mandziuk, Manager, smandziuk@wdm.ca
Carla Madsen, Coordinator, Education & Public Programs, cmadsen@wdm.ca

Yukon Territory

Territorial Museum

MacBride Museum of Yukon History
1124 Front St.
Whitehorse, YT Y1A 1A4
Tel: 867-667-2709
info@macbridemuseum.com
www.macbridemuseum.com
twitter.com/MacBrideMuseum
www.facebook.com/Mac BrideMuseum
Year Founded: 1952 The Yukon Historical Society acquired the unoccupied Government Telegraph Office built in 1900, & in the 1960s opened it to the public as a museum to house the growing collection of cultural & natural history: Yukon heritage from pre-history to present. Exhibits include archeological & paleontological specimens; ethnographic artifacts, historic artifacts, photographs & archival materials; large industrial & transportation artifacts. Also there are outdoor displays, two heritage buildings.
Keith Halliday, Chair, MacBride Museum Society
Patricia Cunning, Executive Director

Local Museums

***Burwash Landing:* Kluane Museum of Natural History**
PO Box 45
Located at Historic Mile 1093 on the Alaska Highway, Burwash Landing, YT
Burwash Landing, YT Y0B 1V0
Tel: 867-841-5561
klvanemus@yknet.yk.ca
www.yukonmuseums.ca/museum/kluane/kluane.html
Workclass wildlife display, native handicrafts; open Victoria Day - Labour Day

***Carmacks:* Tagé Cho Hudän Interpretive Centre**
PO Box 135
Carmacks, YT Y0B 1C0
Tel: 867-863-5831; *Fax:* 867-863-5710
tagechohudan@northwestel.net
Other contact information: Alternate Fax: 867-863-5831
The centre's collection includes traditional boats, stone & bone tools, & traditional clothing. Visitors can also explore the outside area, which features a walking trail & a mammoth snare diorama. Open May-Sept., daily 9:00-6:00; off-season by appointment.

***Dawson City:* Dänojà Zho Cultural Centre**
PO Box 599
Located at 1131 Front St., Dawson City, YT
Dawson City, YT Y0B 1G0
Tel: 867-993-6768; *Fax:* 867-993-6553
cultural.centre@trondek.ca
www.facebook.com/DanojaZhoCulturalCentre
Year Founded: 1998 The centre presents Tr'ondëk Hwëch'in heritage through galleries, exhibits, & walking tours. Operated by the Tr'ondëk Hwëch'in First Nation Heritage Department.

***Dawson City:* Dawson City Museum**
PO Box 303
Located at 959 - 5th Ave., Dawson City, YT
Dawson City, YT Y0B 1G0
Tel: 867-993-5291; *Fax:* 867-993-5839
info@dawsonmuseum.ca
www.dawsonmuseum.ca
twitter.com/dcmuseum
www.facebook.com/pages/Dawson-City-Museum/118073228250444
Year Founded: 1959 Three main galleries include objects and photographs which tells of the story of the Klondike era through the Gold Rush; native history; open mid-May to Sept.; other times by appt.
Laura Mann, Executive Director, lmann@dawsonmuseum.ca
Molly MacDonald, Archivist, mmacdonald@dawsonmuseum.ca

***Dawson City:* Klondike Institute of Art & Culture (KIAC)**
Odd Fellows Hall, PO Box 8000, 902 Second Ave.
Dawson City, YT Y0B 1G0
Tel: 867-993-5005; *Fax:* 867-993-5838
kiac@kiac.ca
kiac.ca
twitter.com/kiactweets
www.facebook.com/7329752 7596
Operated by the Dawson City Arts Society, the KIAC hosts arts & culture-related courses, presentations, festivals & exhibitions.
Karen DuBois, Executive Director, kdubois@kiac.ca
Tara Rudnickas, Director, Gallery/Residence, gallery@kiac.ca
Dan Sokolowski, Producer, Dawson City International Short Film Festival, filmfest@kiac.ca

***Dawson City:* Klondike National Historic Sites**
PO Box 390
Dawson City, YT Y0B 1G0
Tel: 867-993-7200; *Fax:* 867-993-7203
dawson.info@pc.gc.ca
www.pc.gc.ca/lhn-nhs/yt/klondike/index.aspx
twitter.com/ParksCanYukon
www.facebook.com/ParksCanadaYukon
Historic buildings; artifacts; documents; related to Klondike history, Yukon Consolidated Gold Corp. & the Dawson Daily News

***Dawson City:* Tr'ondëk Hwëch'in First Nation Heritage Department**
1242 Front St.
Dawson City, YT Y0B 1G0
Toll-Free: 877-993-3400
trondek.ca/heritage.php
The Heritage Department oversees Tr'ondëk Hwëch'in First Nation hertiage resources, including research, traditional knowledge & oral histories, archeology projects, storage of heritage material, development of heritage sites & operation of the Dänojà Zho Cultural Centre.
Jackie Olson, Director, 867-993-7114
Glenda Bolt, Manager, Dänojà Zho Cultural Centre, 867-993-6768
Sue Parsons, Manager, Collections, 867-993-7144
Jody Beaumont, Specialist, Traditional Knowledge, 867-993-7137

***Faro:* Campbell Region Interpretive Centre**
PO Box 580
Faro, YT Y0B 1K0
Tel: 867-994-2288
cric@faroyukon.ca
www.faroyukon.ca
Other contact information: Year-Round Phone: 867-994-2728
The centre is housed in a log building, & offers visitors information on the area's tourist destinations, hiking trails, & heritage sites. The centre also features displays on the area's history, geology, & wildlife. Hours of Operation: May, daily 9:00-5:00; June-Aug., daily 8:00-6:00; Sept., daily 9:00-5:00.

***Haines Junction:* Kluane National Park**
PO Box 5495
Located at 119 Logan Pl., Haines Junction, YT
Haines Junction, YT Y0B 1L0
Tel: 867-634-7207; *Fax:* 867-634-7208
kluane.info@pc.gc.ca
www.pc.gc.ca/kluane
twitter.com/parkscanyukon
www.facebook.com/ParksCanadaYukon
Other contact information: Administration Phone: 867-634-7250; Conservation Phone: 867-634-7279
Natural & cultural history of Kluane National Park & Reserve of Canada; information on park services, hiking & other activities

***Keno City:* Keno City Mining Museum**
PO Box 17, Site 1
Location: End of the Silver Trail, Main St., Keno City, YK Y0B 1M1
Keno City, YT Y0B 1M0
Tel: 867-995-3103; *Fax:* 867-995-3103
www.yukonmuseums.ca/museum/keno/keno.html
History of mining of gold & silver in the early 1900s (tools, equipment artifacts); open May-Sept.

***Mayo:* Binet House**
PO Box 160
Located at 304 - 2 Ave., Mayo, YT
Mayo, YT Y0B 1M0
Tel: 867-996-2926; *Fax:* 867-996-2907
mayo@northwestel.net
www.yukonmuseums.ca/interp/binet/binet.html
Other contact information: Off-Season Phone: 867-996-2317
A restored heritage building with displays on area history, early medical equipment, wildlife, & geology; open May-Sept.

***Old Crow:* John Tizya Centre**
PO Box 94
Old Crow, YT Y0B 1N0
Tel: 867-966-3261; *Fax:* 867-966-3800
info@vgfn.net
www.vgfn.ca
Situated in the only Yukon community north of the Arctic Circle, the centre presents Vuntut Gwitchin's culture, oral history, & surrounding landscape. Open year-round, weekdays 9:00-12:00, 1:00-4:30.

***Teslin:* George Johnston Tlingit Indian Museum**
PO Box 146
Located at Km 1294 Mile 804, Alaska Hwy., Teslin, YT
Teslin, YT Y0A 1B0
Tel: 867-390-2550; *Fax:* 867-390-8810
manager.teslinhms@gmail.com
www.gjmuseum.yk.net
Inland Tlingit ethnographic & 20th centrury artifacts; open June 1-Aug. 30

***Teslin:* Teslin Tlingit Heritage Centre**
PO Box 133
Teslin, YT Y0A 1B0
Tel: 867-390-2532
admin@ttc-teslin.com
www.ttc-teslin.com/heritage-centre.html
Year Founded: 2001 Visitors to the centre can explore the Tlingit people's day-to-day life; the centre's collection includes traditional masks & artifacts. Open June-Sept., daily 9:00-5:00; off-season by appointment.

***Whitehorse:* Copperbelt Railway & Mining Museum**
***Parent:* Miles Canyon Historic Railway Society**
c/o Miles Canyon Historic Railway Society, 1127 First Ave.
Location: 91928 Alaska Hwy., North of Whitehorse, YK
Whitehorse, YT Y1A 0G5
Tel: 867-667-6355
copperbelt@yukonrails.com
www.yukonrails.com/museum
twitter.com/MCHRSYukon
www.facebook.com/MCHR SYukon
The museum site features a working railway, station museum, & picnic area; open May-Sept.

***Whitehorse:* Fort Selkirk**
c/o Tourism & Culture, Cultural Services Branch, PO Box 2703
Whitehorse, YT Y1A 2C6
Tel: 867-667-3463; *Fax:* 867-667-8023
museevirtuel-virtualmuseum.ca/sgc-cms/expositions-exhibitions/fort_selkirk
Accessible only by boat or plane; co-owned & managed by the Yukon Government and the Selkirk First Nation; open mid-May - mid-Sept. URL is a portal to the virtual museum.

***Whitehorse:* Kwanlin Dün Cultural Centre**
1171 Front St.
Whitehorse, YT Y1A 0G9
Tel: 867-456-5322
info@kdcc.ca
www.kwanlindunculturalcentre.com
twitter.com/KDCulture
www.facebook.co m/KwanlinDunCulturalCentre
The centre seeks to benefit the Kwanlin Dün people by reviving & preserving their culture, heritage, & way of life. Visitors can experience Kwanlin Dün culture through programs, exhibits, & events. Open June-Sept., M-F 9:00-5:00, Sa-Su 10:00-4:00.
Amanda Buffalo, Executive Director, amanda@kdcc.ca

***Whitehorse:* Old Log Church Museum**
PO Box 31461
Located on the corner of 3rd Ave. & Elliot St., Whitehorse, YT
Whitehorse, YT Y1A 6K8
Tel: 867-668-2555; *Fax:* 867-667-6258
logchurch@klondiker.com
www.oldlogchurchmuseum.ca
www.facebook.com/old logchurchmuseum
Year Founded: 1962 Open May - Labour Day

***Whitehorse:* Yukon Beringia Interpretive Centre**
PO Box 2703
Whitehorse, YT Y1A 2C6
Tel: 867-667-8855; *Fax:* 867-667-8854
beringia@gov.yk.ca
www.beringia.com
www.facebook.com/126598970843
Beringia was an ancient place, situated between two continents on the edge of the Arctic. The land connection between Siberia & Alaska was part of the larger area known as Beringia. The land of ice was home to huge mammals, such as woolly mammoths & scimitar cats, & the first people of North America. The Yukon Beringia Interpretive Centre is open from May to September. During the winter, it is open on Sundays, or by appointment.

***Whitehorse:* Yukon Historical & Museums Association**
Donnenworth House, 3126 - 3rd Ave.
Whitehorse, YT Y1A 1E7
Tel: 867-667-4704; *Fax:* 867-667-4506
info@heritageyukon.ca
www.heritageyukon.ca
twitter.com/Yukonheritage
www.facebook.com/26079672887
Year Founded: 1977 The Association offers visitors a 45-minute walking tour of Whitehorse's heritage sites. Donnenworth House features a photographic display depicting various heritage sites around the Yukon. The website offers downloadable audio walking tours.
Sally Robinson, President
Nancy Oakley, Executive Director

***Whitehorse:* Yukon Transportation Museum**
30 Electra Cres.
Whitehorse, YT Y1A 6E6
Tel: 867-668-4792; *Fax:* 867-633-5547
info@goytm.ca
goytm.ca
www.facebook.com/120797977963812
Year Founded: 1995 Transportation displays depicting the first commercial aircraft in the Yukon; construction of the Alaska Highway, the White Pass & Yukon Route Railway. Open daily 10-6, mid-May - end of August.
Casey Mclaughlin, Executive Director
Janna Swales, Director, Collections & Research

National Parks & Outdoor Education Centres

Alberta

***Banff:* Banff National Park**
PO Box 900
Banff Information Centre: 224 Banff Ave., Banff, AB
Banff, AB T1L 1K2
Tel: 403-762-1550; *Fax:* 403-762-1551
Toll-Free: 888-927-3367
banff.vrc@pc.gc.ca
www.pc.gc.ca/eng/pn-np/ab/banff/ind ex.aspx
Social Media:
www.youtube.com/view_play_list?p=7ABD4B2249F753EB
twitter.com/banffnp
www.facebook.com/BanffNP
Other contact information: Backcountry Trail Reservations, Phone: 403-762-1556

Banff National Park was Canada's first national park. It spans 6,641 square kilometres (2,564 square miles) of valleys, mountains, glaciers, forests, meadows, & rivers. Hours of Operation, Banff Visitor Centre: June - Sept, 9:00-7:00, Oct - May, 9:00 - 5:00

Fort Saskatchewan: Elk Island National Park
Site 4, RR#1
Fort Saskatchewan, AB T8L 2N7
Tel: 780-922-5790; *Fax:* 780-992-2951
elk.island@pc.gc.ca
www.pc.gc.ca/pn-np/ab/elkisland/index_E.asp
Elk Island National Park of Canada protects the aspen parkland, which is one of the most endangered habitats in Canada. The park is home to herds of plains bison, wood bison, moose, deer, & elk. The park is also home to over 250 species of birds. Hours: Campground Reservations, Administration Building open year round, 8:00-4:00; Sandy Beach Campground open May-Sept. weather permitting.

Jasper: Jasper National Park of Canada
PO Box 10
Jasper Townsite Information Centre: 500 Connaught Dr., Jasper, AB
Jasper, AB T0E 1E0
Tel: 780-852-6176; *Fax:* 780-852-6152
pnj.jnp@pc.gc.ca
www.pc.gc.ca/pn-np/ab/jasper/index_E.asp
Social Media: www.youtube.com/ParksCanadaAgency
twitter.com/JasperNP
www.facebook.com/JasperNP
Other contact information: Backcountry Trail Reservations, Phone: 780-852-6177
Jasper is the largest & most northerly Canadian rocky mountain national park, part of a World Heritage Site. The park is comprised of carefully protected ecosystems, & includes destinations such as Sunwapta Falls, Mount Edith Cavell, Athabasca Glacier, Miette Hotsprings, & 1,000-plus kilometres of trails.

Waterton Park: Waterton Lakes National Park of Canada
PO Box 200
Waterton Park, AB T0K 2M0
Tel: 403-859-5133; *Fax:* 403-859-5152
waterton.info@pc.gc.ca
www.pc.gc.ca/eng/pn-np/ab/waterton/index.aspx
t witter.com/watertonlakesnp
www.facebook.com/WatertonLakesNP
Waterton Lakes National Park helps protect the unique physical, biological & cultural resources found in one of the narrowest places in the Rocky Mountains. Upper Waterton Lake is the deepest lake in the Canadian Rockies. In 1932, the park was joined with Montana's Glacier National Park to form the Waterton-Glacier International Peace Park. Hours of Operation: Park Receptionist year round, M-F 8:00-4:00; Campsites & Parkways May-Sept.

British Columbia

Field: Yoho National Park of Canada
PO Box 99
Field, BC V0A 1G0
Tel: 250-343-6783
yoho.info@pc.gc.ca
www.pc.gc.ca/eng/pn-np/bc/yoho/index.aspx
twitter.com/YohoNP
www.faceb ook.com/YohoNP
Year Founded: 1886 Yoho National Park is situated on the western slopes of the Canadian Rocky Mountains. 'Yoho' is a Cree experession of awe & wonder, given to the park because of its immense rock walls, waterfalls, & mountain peaks. Hours of Operation: Parklands are open year round; Visitor Centre open only Spring-Fall.
Melanie Kwong, Superintendant, llyk.superintendent@pc.gc.ca

Queen Charlotte: Gwaii Haanas National Park Reserve & Haida Heritage Site
PO Box 37
Haida Heritage Centre: 60 Second Beach Rd., Skidegate, BC
Queen Charlotte, BC V0T 1S0
Tel: 250-559-8818; *Fax:* 250-559-8366
Toll-Free: 877-559-8818
gwaii.haanas@pc.gc.ca
pc.gc.ca/gwaiihaanas
www.faceb ook.com/GwaiiHaanas
Gwaii Haanas National Park is jointly managed by the Government of Canada & the Council of the Haida Nation, through an agreement signed in 1993, although the question of ownership is unresolved.

Radium Hot Springs: Kootenay National Park of Canada
PO Box 220
Information Centre: 7556 Main Street East, Radium, B.C.
Radium Hot Springs, BC V0A 1M0
Tel: 250-347-9505*Toll-Free:* 888-927-3367
kootenay.info@pc.gc.ca
www.pc.gc.ca/eng/pn-np/bc/kootenay/index.aspx
t witter.com/KootenayNP
www.facebook.com/KootenayNP
Year Founded: 1920 Kootenay National Park represents the south-western region of the Canadian Rocky Mountains. The park contains such diverse landscapes as glaciers-topped mountains & semi-arid grasslands that harbour plants such as cactus. Hours of Operation: Parklands are open year round. Hours of operation: the park is open year-round; the Kootenay National Park Visitor Centre is open May-Oct 9:00-5:00.
Melanie Kwong, Superintendant, llyk.superintendent@pc.gc.ca

Revelstoke: Glacier National Park of Canada
PO Box 350
Revelstoke, BC V0E 2S0
Tel: 250-837-7500; *Fax:* 250-837-7536
revglacier.reception@pc.gc.ca
parkscanada.gc.ca/revelstoke
www.faceboo k.com/MRGnationalparks
Other contact information: TTY: 1-866-787-6221
Glacier National Park of Canada protects part of the Columbia Mountains Natural Region in British Columbia's interior, which includes stands of old-growth cedar & hemlock, & habitat for endangered species such as mountain caribou, mountain goat, & grizzly bear. Also located in the park is The Rogers Pass National Historic Site, which commemorates the construction of the country's first major national transportation route.

Revelstoke: Mount Revelstoke National Park of Canada
PO Box 350
Revelstoke Office: 301B - 3rd St. West, Revelstoke, BC
Revelstoke, BC V0E 2S0
Tel: 250-837-7500; *Fax:* 250-837-7536
www.pc.gc.ca/eng/pn-np/bc/revelstoke/index.aspx
Other contact information: TTY: 1-866-787-6221
Mount Revelstoke National Park contains old-growth rainforest of giant cedar & pine, subalpine forest, & alpine meadows & tundra. The Monashee & Selkirk Mountains are also in the park. Hiking trails take visitors through various landscapes, including Western Red Cedars & jungle-like wetland. Hours of Operation: The Revelstoke Office is open year-round, M-F 8:00-4:30.

Sidney: Gulf Islands National Park Reserve of Canada
2220 Harbour Rd.
Sidney, BC V8L 2P6
Tel: 250-654-4000; *Fax:* 250-654-4014
Toll-Free: 866-944-1744
gulf.islands@pc.gc.ca
www.pc.gc.ca/pn-np/bc/gulf/index _E.asp
twitter.com/GulfIslandsNPR
www.facebook.com/GulfIslandsNPR
Year Founded: 2003 Gulf Islands National Park Reserve protects part of British Columbia's southern Gulf Islands archipelago. These islands represent the Strait of Georgia Lowlands, which is one of the most ecologically sensitive regions in southern Canada. The park includes fifteen islands, many islets & reefs, & around twenty-six square kilometres of marine areas. Hours of Operation: Some parks are closed during the off-season & camping is prohibited; please see the website for detailed information.

Ucluelet: Pacific Rim National Park Reserve of Canada (PRNPR)
PO Box 280, 2040 Pacific Rim Hwy.
Ucluelet, BC V0R 3A0
Tel: 250-726-3500; *Fax:* 250-726-3520
pacrim.info@pc.gc.ca
www.pc.gc.ca/eng/pn-np/bc/pacificrim/index.aspx
t witter.com/pacificrimNPR
www.facebook.com/PacificRimNPR
Pacific Rim National Park Reserve of Canada is backed by the Insular Mountains Range of Vancouver Island, & faces the Pacific Ocean. Pacific Rim presents the rich natural and cultural heritage of Canada's west coast. Its cool, wet maritime climate produces an abundance of life in the water & on land. Coastal temperate rainforest gives way to diverse intertidal & subtidal areas. Also presented is the history of the Nuu-chah-nulth First Nations, as well as that of European explorers & settlers. Hours of Operation: year round.

Manitoba

Churchill: Wapusk National Park of Canada
PO Box 127
Churchill, MB R0B 0E0
Tel: 204-675-8863; *Fax:* 204-675-2026
Toll-Free: 888-773-8888
wapusk.np@pc.gc.ca
www.pc.gc.ca/eng/pn-np/mb/wapusk/in dex.aspx
Other contact information: TTY: 866-787-6221
Wapusk National Park of Canada, & is home to one of the world's largest polar bear maternity denning areas ("Wapusk" is a Cree word meaning "White Bear"). The park encompasses the Hudson James Lowlands region, bordering on Hudson Bay, & lies on the transition area between boreal forest & Arctic tundra. Note: Access to the park is via authorized commercial tour operators in Churchill. The park currently has limited visitor capacity. Parks Canada does not recommend unescorted visits to the park. For the most current list of operators, please contact the park office or visit the website.

Wasagaming: Riding Mountain National Park of Canada
133 Wasagaming Dr.
Wasagaming, MB R0J 2H0
Tel: 204-848-7275; *Fax:* 204-848-2596
rmnp.info@pc.gc.ca
www.pc.gc.ca/eng/pn-np/mb/riding/index.aspx
twitter .com/RidingNP
www.facebook.com/RidingNP
Other contact information: TTY: 866-787-6221
Riding Mountain forms part of the Manitoba Escarpmet, & protects a variety of wildlife & vegetation. The park features many hiking trails & Agassiz Tower, which offers visitors a panoramic view of the prairies to the north. Visitor services can be found in Wasagaming, the park's town site, including accommodation, restaurants, & shopping. Hours of Operation: Administration Office M-F 8:00-12:00, 12:30-4:00; Visitor Centre, Spring & Fall Th-M 9:30-5:00, Summer 9:30-8:00.

New Brunswick

Alma: Fundy National Park of Canada
PO Box 1001
Alma, NB E4H 1B4
Tel: 506-887-6000; *Fax:* 506-887-6008
fundy.info@pc.gc.ca
www.pc.gc.ca/eng/pn-np/nb/fundy/index.aspx
Other contact information: TTY: 506-887-6015
Fundy National Park of Canada protects some of the only remaining wilderness in southern New Brunswick, including the Caledonia Highlands & Bay of Fundy. Inland, visitors can explore forests & stream valleys. Hours of Operation: Vistor Reception Centre, Spring & Fall 9:00-4:45; Summer 8:00 am-9:45 pm.

Kouchibouguac National Park: Kouchibouguac National Park of Canada
186 Rte. 117
Kouchibouguac National Park, NB E4X 2P1
Tel: 506-876-2443; *Fax:* 506-876-4802
kouch.info@pc.gc.ca
www.pc.gc.ca/eng/pn-np/nb/kouchibouguac/index.aspx
twitter.com/KouchibouguacNP
www.facebook.com/KouchibouguacNP
Other contact information: TTY: 506-876-4205
Year Founded: 1969 Kouchibouguac National Park of Canada is a Canadian Heritage protected area, & is one of only two wilderness national parks in New Brunswick. The landscape of the 238 km2 park is characteristic of the Maritime Plain Natural Region in which it is located, including such features as bogs, salt marshes, tidal rivers, freshwater systems, lagoons, abandoned fields, & forests. The name Kouchibouguac is of Mi'kmaq origin & means "river of the long tides." Visitors can explore 60 km of paths for hikers & cyclists, as well as partaking in canoeing, kayaking, swimming, camping, bird watching, & cross country skiing, snowshoeing, & tobogganing in winter.

Newfoundland & Labrador

Glovertown: Terra Nova National Park of Canada
General Delivery
Glovertown, NL A0G 2L0
Tel: 709-533-2801; *Fax:* 709-533-2706
info.tnnp@pc.gc.ca
www.pc.gc.ca/eng/pn-np/nl/terranova/index.aspx
Terra Nova National Park of Canada encompasses the North Atlantic Ocean & the boreal forest of Eastern Newfoundland. The park's landscape varies from cliffs & inlets to forested hills, bogs, & ponds. Visitors can also explore the remnants of sawmills & past human cultures found within the park. Hours of Operation: Administration Building, M-F 8:30-4:30; Visitor

Centre, May-June 10:00-4:00, June-Sept. 10:00-6:00, Sept.-Oct. 10:00-4:00.

Nain: Torngat Mountains National Park of Canada
PO Box 471
Nain, NL A0P 1L0
Tel: 709-922-1290; Fax: 709-922-1294
Toll-Free: 888-922-1290
torngats.info@pc.gc.ca
www.pc.gc.ca/eng/pn-np/nl/torng ats/index.aspx
Other contact information: French Phone: 709-458-2417
Year Founded: 2005 The Torngat Mountains National Park of Canada, in northern Labrador, encompasses nearly 10,000 km2. It extends from Saglek Fjord in the south, to the northern tip of Labrador; & from the province's boundary with Québec in the west, to the Labrador Sea in the east. The national park protects an area of Arctic wilderness, featuring mountains (the highest peaks in eastern North America), small glaciers, fjords, river valleys, & rugged coastal landscapes. This land has been home to the Inuit & their ancestors for thousands of years. Hours of operation: Park office hours are M-F 8:00-4:30, except holidays. The park itself is a remote wilderness, with no on-site facilities or road access. As a result, visitors are encouraged to come only in late winter/early spring & summer.

Rocky Harbour: Gros Morne National Park of Canada
PO Box 130
Rocky Harbour, NL A0K 4N0
Tel: 709-458-2417; Fax: 709-458-2059
grosmorne.info@pc.gc.ca
www.pc.gc.ca/pn-np/nl/grosmorne/index_E.asp
Other contact information: TTY: 709-772-4564
Gros Morne National Park of Canada was designated a UNESCO World Heritage Site in 1987. Visitors can hike through mountains or camp by the sea. Boat tours are offered, & waterfalls, marine inlets, sea stacks, beaches, & nearby fishing villages can all be explored. Hours of Operation: Park Headquaters, M-F 8:00-12:00, 1:00-4:30; Visitor Centre, May-June 9:00-5:00, June-Sept. 8:00-8:00, Sept-Oct. 9:00-5:00.

Northwest Territories

Fort Simpson: Nahanni National Park Reserve of Canada
PO Box 348
Located at 10002 - 100 St., Fort Simpsonm NT
Fort Simpson, NT X0E 0N0
Tel: 867-695-7750; Fax: 867-695-2446
nahanni.info@pc.gc.ca
www.pc.gc.ca/pn-np/nt/nahanni/index_E.asp
Nahanni National Park Reserve of Canada protects a portion of the Mackenzie Mountains Natural Region. A key feature of the park is the Naha Dehé (South Nahanni River), and the park's diverse landscape offers a home to many species of birds, fish & mammals. The Ford Simpson visitor centre features displays on the history, culture & geography of the area. The park was inscribed on UNESCO's World Heritage List in 1978. Hours of Operation: Winter, M-F 8:30-12:00, 1:00-5:00; Summer, daily 8:00-12:00, 1:00-5:00.

Fort Smith: Wood Buffalo National Park of Canada
PO Box 750
Fort Chipewyan Satellite Office: PO Box 38, Fort Chipewyan, AB T0P 1B0
Fort Smith, NT X0E 0P0
Tel: 867-872-7960; Fax: 867-872-3910
wbnp.info@pc.gc.ca
www.pc.gc.ca/pn-np/nt/woodbuffalo.aspx
Other contact information: TTY: 867-872-7961; 24-Hour Hotline: 867-872-7962
Year Founded: 1922 Wood Buffalo National Park is Canada's largest national park & one of the largest in the world. It was established to protect the last herds of bison in northern Canada, & today it protects an example of Canada's Northern Boreal Plains. Hours of Operation: Park is open year round; Fort Smith Visitor Reception Centre open seven days a week in the summer, and Mon.-Fri. in the winter; Fort Chipewyan Visitor Reception Centre open Mon.-Fri. year-round, with most weekends open in summer as well.

Inuvik: Ivvavik National Park of Canada
c/o Western Arctic Field Unit, PO Box 1840
Inuvik, NT X0E 0T0
Tel: 867-777-8800; Fax: 867-777-8820
inuvik.info@pc.gc.ca
www.pc.gc.ca/eng/pn-np/yt/ivvavik/index.aspx
Ivvavik National Park of Canada is the first national park in Canada to be created as a result of an aboriginal land claim agreement. The park protects a portion of the calving grounds of the Porcupine caribou herd and represents the Northern Yukon and Mackenzie Delta natural regions. Hours of Operation: Park is open year round, with no available services.

Paulatuk: Tuktut Nogait National Park of Canada
PO Box 91
Parks Canada office in Inuvik: PO Box 1840, Inuvik, NT X0E 0T0
Paulatuk, NT X0E 1N0
Tel: 867-580-3233; Fax: 867-580-3234
inuvik.info@pc.gc.ca
www.pc.gc.ca/eng/pn-np/nt/tuktutnogait/index.aspx
The park is located 170 kilometres north of the arctic circle & is home to the Bluenose West caribou herd, as well as wolves, grizzly bears, muskoxen, arctic char, & a large number of raptors. Hours of Operation: open year round.

Sachs Harbour: Aulavik National Park of Canada
PO Box 29
Sachs Harbour, NT X0E 0Z0
Tel: 867-690-3904; Fax: 867-690-4808
inuvik.info@pc.gc.ca
www.pc.gc.ca/eng/pn-np/nt/aulavik/index.aspx
Aulavik National Park protects more than 12,000 square kilometres of arctic lowlands on the north end of Banks Island. At the heart of the park lies the Thomsen River, one of Canada's most northerly navigable waterways, which visitors can paddle. The park is home to the endangered Peary caribou and the highest density of muskoxen in the world. Hours of operation: open year round.

Tulita: Náátsʼihchʼoh National Park Reserve of Canada
c/o Parks Canada Agency, PO Box 157
Tulita, NT X0E 0K0
naats'ihch'oh.info@pc.gc.ca
www.pc.gc.ca/eng/pn-np/nt/naatsihchoh
Year Founded: 2012 Canada's newest national park.
Laani Uunila, Superintendent

Nova Scotia

Halifax: Sable Island National Park Reserve of Canada
c/o Halifax Citadel National Historic Site, PO Box 9080 A
Halifax, NS B3K 5M7
Tel: 902-426-1993; Fax: 902-426-4228
sable@pc.gc.ca
www.pc.gc.ca/eng/pn-np/ns/sable/index.aspx
Year Founded: 2013 Sable Island is Canada's newest National Park. The island is located in the Atlantic Ocean, 175 km southest of mainland Nova Scotia, making it one of Canada's most remote parks. Visitor access is by charter plane & boat only, & visitors are responsible for their own travel arrangements to & from the island. Parks Canada & Environment Canada operate a research post called Main Station, which serves as the hub of all island activities & programs. The island itself features a landscape devoid of trees & an abundance of protected wildlife, including the free-roaming Sable Island horses, as well as Harbour & Grey seals. Culturally, the island was once known as the "Graveyard of the Atlantic" due to the over 350 recorded shipwrecks that have occurred there. Visitors can access the island from June to the end of October, with August to October being the most favourable time, & must register in advance.

Ingonish Beach: Cape Breton Highlands National Park of Canada
Ingonish Beach, NS B0C 1L0
Tel: 902-224-2306; Fax: 902-285-2866
cbhnp.info@pc.gc.ca
www.pc.gc.ca/pn-np/ns/cbreton/index_E.asp
twitter. com/ParksCanada_NS
www.facebook.com/CBHNP
Year Founded: 1936 Cape Breton Highlands National Park of Canada is home to the Cabot Trail, & offers visitors scenery, wildlife, & human history stretching back to the last Ice Age. Hours of Operation: park is open year round; Visitor Centre Spring 9:00-5:00, Summer 8:30-7:00, Fall 9:00-5:00.

Maitland Bridge, Annapolis County: Kejimkujik National Park & National Historic Site of Canada
PO Box 236
Maitland Bridge, Annapolis County, NS B0T 1B0
Tel: 902-682-2772; Fax: 902-682-3367
kejimkujik.info@pc.gc.ca
www.pc.gc.ca/eng/pn-np/ns/kejimkujik/index.aspx
twitter.com/ParksCanada_NS
www.facebook.com/Kejimkujik
Kejimkujik is the sole inland national park in the Maritimes, featuring lakes & rivers, woodlands, & a variety of wildlife. Visitors can explore historic canoe routes, portages, & hiking trails in the park.

Nunavut

Iqaluit: Quttinirpaaq National Park of Canada
PO Box 278
Iqaluit, NU X0A 0H0
Tel: 867-975-4673; Fax: 867-975-4674
nunavut.info@pc.gc.ca
www.pc.gc.ca/eng/pn-np/nu/quttinirpaaq/index.aspx
Year Founded: 1988 Hours of Operation: Warden station only staffed furing the summer field season. Parks Canada Office in Iqaluit is open M-F 8:30-12:00, 1:00-5:00 year round.
Joadamee Amagoalik, Chair, Quttinirpaaq Joint Inuit/Gov't Park Committee
Nancy Anilniliak, Field Unit Superintendent, Nunavut, Parks Canada

Pangnirtung: Auyuittuq National Park of Canada
PO Box 353
Pangnirtung, NU X0A 0R0
Tel: 867-473-2500; Fax: 867-473-8612
nunavut.info@pc.gc.ca
www.pc.gc.ca/eng/pn-np/nu/auyuittuq/index.aspx
Year Founded: 1976 Auyuittuq National Park of Canada protects 19,089 km2 of terrain. Auyuittuq is an Inuktitut word meaning "land that never melts." The park is located in the eastern Arctic, on southern Baffin Island, & includes the highest peaks of the Canadian Shield, the Penny Ice Cap, coastal fiords, & Akshayuk Pass, which was a traditional corridor used by the Inuit for thousands of years. Hours of Operation: Visitor Centre open year-round, M-F 8:30-5:00; summer hours are posted in June.

Pond Inlet: Sirmilik National Park of Canada
PO Box 300
Pond Inlet, NU X0A 0S0
Tel: 867-899-8092; Fax: 867-899-8104
sirmilik.info@pc.gc.ca
www.pc.gc.ca/eng/pn-np/nu/sirmilik/contact.aspx
Year Founded: 2001 Sirmilik National Park represents the Northern Eastern Arctic Lowlands Natural Region & portions of the Lancaster Sound Marine Region. The park features wilderness hiking & camping, & a prominent seabird colony near of Baillarge Bay. Hours of Operation: Administration & Visitor Centre, M-F 8:30-12:00, 1:00-5:00.

Repulse Bay: Ukkusiksalik National Park of Canada
PO Box 220
Repulse Bay, NU X0C 0H0
Tel: 867-462-4500; Fax: 867-462-4095
ukkusiksalik.info@pc.gc.ca
www.pc.gc.ca/eng/pn-np/nu/ukkusiksalik
twit ter.com/ParksCanNunavut
www.facebook.com/ParksCanadaNunavut
Year Founded: 2003 The park grounds are used for hiking, camping, boating & traditional Inuit use. The office is open all year, M-F 8:30-5:00. The park does not have any facilities or services.

Ontario

Heron Bay: Pukaskwa National Park of Canada
PO Box 212
Heron Bay, ON P0T 1R0
Tel: 807-229-0801; Fax: 807-229-2097
ont-pukaskwa@pc.gc.ca
www.pc.gc.ca/pn-np/on/pukaskwa/index_E.asp
twitt er.com/PukaskwaNP
www.facebook.com/PukaskwaNP
Year Founded: 1978 Pukaskwa National Park is the only wilderness national park in Ontario, & protects 1878 square km of boreal forest & Lake Superior shoreline. Hours of Operation: Administration Office M-F 8:30-4:30 year-round.

Leamington: Point Pelee National Park of Canada
407 Monarch Lane, RR#1
Location: 1118 Point Pelee Dr., Leamington, ON N8H 3V4
Leamington, ON N8H 3V4
Tel: 519-322-2365; Fax: 519-322-1277
Toll-Free: 888-773-8888
pelee.info@pc.gc.ca
www.pc.gc.ca/eng/pn-np/on/pelee/in dex.aspx
twitter.com/PointPeleeNP
www.facebook.com/PointPeleeNP
Other contact information: TTY: 1-866-787-6221
Point Pelee National Park is located at the southern tip of Canada, 50 km (30 miles) south-east of Windsor, Ontario. It is one of Canada's smallest national parks, but features picnic areas & a Visitor Centre, as well as the famous Tip, & Marsh Boardwalk. Hours of Operation: April-May 6:00-10:00, May 5:00-10:00, May-Oct. 6:00-10:00, Oct-March 7:00-7:00.

***Mallorytown:* Thousand Islands National Park**
2 County Road 5, RR#3
Mallorytown, ON K0E 1R0
Tel: 613-923-5261; *Fax:* 613-923-1021
ont-sli@pc.gc.ca
www.pc.gc.ca/eng/pn-np/on/lawren/index.aspx
twitter.c om/slinationalpark
www.facebook.com/160237280773786
St. Lawrence Islands National Park was conceived in the 1870s, & is located in the heart of the Thousand Islands tourist area. Hours of Operation: Administration Office, M-F 8:00-4:30 year round; Islands, May-Oct; Mallorytown Landing Visitor Centre open weekends & holidays May-June 10:00-4:00, & Th-M June-Sept.

***Midland:* Georgian Bay Islands National Park of Canada**
PO Box 9, 901 Wye Valley Rd.
Midland, ON L4R 4K6
Tel: 705-527-7200; *Fax:* 705-526-5939
Toll-Free: 877-737-3783
info.gbi@pc.gc.ca
www.pc.gc.ca/eng/pn-np/on/georg/inde x.aspx
twitter.com/GBINP
Other contact information: Summer Weekend & Holiday Phone: 705-427-2532
Georgian Bay Islands National Park of Canada protects the Canadian Shield, including the Honey Harbour area to Twelve Mile Bay in southern Georgian Bay. The islands are accessible by boat only. Beausoleil, the largest island, offers tent camping, overnight & day docking, heritage education programs, & hiking trails. Wheelchair accessible & reserved campsites are also available at the Cedar Spring campground on Beausoleil. Hours of Operation: Midland administration office open year-round, 8:00-4:00; Cedar Spring Welcome Centre open Su-Th 9:00-5:00, F 9:00-7:00, Sa 9:00-6:00.

***Tobermory:* Bruce Peninsula National Park of Canada**
PO Box 189
Tobermory, ON N0H 2R0
Tel: 519-596-2233; *Fax:* 519-596-2298
bruce-fathomfive@pc.gc.ca
www.pc.gc.ca/eng/pn-np/on/bruce/index.aspx
t witter.com/BrucePNP
www.facebook.com/BrucePeninsulaNP
Other contact information: Camping Office, Phone: 519-596-2263
Bruce Peninsula National Park of Canada is located inside a World Biosphere Reserve. The cliffs of the park are inhabited by thousand-year-old cedar trees, & the park is comprised of habitats ranging from alvars to forests & lakes. All together the ecosystem is the largest remaining chunk of natural habitat in southern Ontario. Hours of Operation: Administration Office, M-F 8:00-4:30; Cyprus Lake Campground Office, Fall Sa-Th 9:00-5:00, F 9:00-9:00, Summer 8:00-11:00.

Prince Edward Island

***Charlottetown:* Prince Edward Island National Park of Canada**
2 Palmers Lane
Charlottetown, PE C1A 5V8
Tel: 902-672-6350; *Fax:* 902-672-6370
pnipe.peinp@pc.gc.ca
www.pc.gc.ca/pn-np/pe/pei-ipe/index_E.asp
twitter .com/ParksCanadaPEI
www.facebook.com/PEInationalpark
Year Founded: 1937 The landscape of Prince Edward Island National Park of Canada includes sand dunes, barrier islands & sand pits, beaches, sandstone cliffs, wetlands, & forests. Various plants & animals call these habitats home, including the endangered Piping Plover. The Park also features Green Gables & Dalvay-by-the-Sea National Historic Site. In 1998, six kilometres of the Greenwich Peninsula were added to the Park in order to protect unique dune formations, rare plants & animals, & archaeological discoveries dating back 10,000 years.

Québec

***Gaspé:* Forillon National Park of Canada**
122 Gaspé Blvd.
Gaspé, QC G4X 1A9
Tel: 418-368-5505; *Fax:* 418-368-6837
Toll-Free: 888-773-8888
information@pc.gc.ca
www.pc.gc.ca/pn-np/qc/forillon/in dex_E.asp
twitter.com/ForillonNP
www.facebook.com/ForillonNP
Other contact information: TTY: 1-866-787-6221
Year Founded: 1970 Forillon National Park of Canada is located at the farthest point of the Gaspé Peninsula, & covers a 244 km2 area. It protects a portion of the Notre-Dame & Mégantic mountain regions, & elements of the Gulf of St. Lawrence marine region. Present in the park are ten different rock formations, colonies of seabirds, & arctic-alpine plants. The Grande-Grave National Heritage Site is located within the park & reveals the way of life of fishing families in the region.

***Havre-Saint-Pierre:* Mingan Archipelago National Park Reserve of Canada**
1340 de la Digue St.
Havre-Saint-Pierre, QC G0G 1P0
Tel: 418-538-3331; *Fax:* 418-538-3595
Toll-Free: 888-773-8888
information@pc.gc.ca
www.pc.gc.ca/eng/pn-np/qc/mingan/ index.aspx
twitter.com/MinganNPR
www.facebook.com/MinganNPR
Other contact information: TTY: 1-866-787-6221
Year Founded: 1984 The Mingan Archipelago National Park Reserve of Canada is situated along the North Shore of the Gulf of St. Lawrence, & is comprised of about forty limestone islands, & and over 1,000 islets & reefs. This territory is home to an abundance of vegetation & wildlife, including seabird colonies, seals, dolphins, & whales. Hours of Operation: Havre-Saint-Pierre Reception & Interpretation Center & Longue-Pointe-de-Mingan Reception & Interpretation Centre open June-Sept.

***Shawinigan:* La Mauricie National Park of Canada**
702 - 5 St.
Shawinigan, QC G9N 6T9
Tel: 819-538-3232; *Fax:* 819-536-3661
Toll-Free: 888-773-8888
parkscanada-que@pc.gc.ca
www.pc.gc.ca/pn-np/qc/maurici e/index_E.asp
www.facebook.com/MauricieNP
Year Founded: 1970 La Mauricie National Park of Canada covers an area of 536 km2, protecting a sample of the southernmost part of the Canadian Shield. Hours of Operation: Reception Centre, May & Sept-Oct. Sa-Th 9:00-4:30, F 9:00-9:30, May-Sept. every day 7:00-9:30.

Saskatchewan

***Val Marie:* Grasslands National Park of Canada**
PO Box 150
Val Marie, SK S0N 2T0
Tel: 306-298-2257; *Fax:* 306-298-2042
grasslands.info@pc.gc.ca
www.pc.gc.ca/eng/pn-np/sk/grasslands/index.aspx
twitter.com/parkscanada_sk
www.facebook.com/grasslandsNP
Other contact information: TTY: 1-866-787-6221
Grasslands is the first national park of Canada to preserve a section of the mixed prairie grasslands. Visitor activities include guided hikes, interpretive trails, bird watching, & nature photography. Hours of Operation: Parklands are open year round.

***Waskesiu Lake:* Prince Albert National Park of Canada**
c/o Northern Prairies Field Unit, PO Box 100
Waskesiu Lake, SK S0J 2Y0
Tel: 306-663-4522
panp.info@pc.gc.ca
www.pc.gc.ca/eng/pn-np/sk/princealbert/index.aspx
Prince Albert National Park protects a portion of the boreal forest, & serves as a transition zone between the parkland & the northern forest. The park features the only protected white pelican nesting colony in Canada, the lakeside cabin of conservationist Grey Owl, & a free-ranging herd of plains bison. Special events & interpretive programs are also offered. Visitor services are provided in the townsite of Waskesiu, located in the park. Hours of Operation: Parklands are open year-round; Information Centre open daily 8:00-8:00 from mid-May - early Sept.

Yukon Territory

***Haines Junction:* Kluane National Park & Reserve of Canada**
PO Box 5495
Haines Junction, YT Y0B 1L0
Tel: 867-634-7207; *Fax:* 867-634-7208
kluane.info@pc.gc.ca
www.pc.gc.ca/pn-np/yt/kluane/index_E.asp
twitter. com/ParksCanYukon
Kluane National Park & Reserve of Canada covers an area of 21,980 km2, & features mountains (including Mount Logan, Canada's highest peak at 5,959 m/19,545 ft.), icefields, & valleys that are home to a variety of plant & wildlife species.

***Old Crow:* Vuntut National Park of Canada**
PO Box 19
Old Crow, YT Y0B 1N0
Tel: 867-667-3910; *Fax:* 867-393-6701
vuntut.info@pc.gc.ca
www.pc.gc.ca/eng/pn-np/yt/vuntut/index.aspx
twitt er.com/ParksCanYukon
www.facebook.com/ParksCanadaYukon
Year Founded: 1995 Vuntut National Park was established after negotiations through the Vuntut Gwitchin First Nation's Final Land Claims Agreement, between the Vuntut Gwitchin of Old Crow & the Government of Canada & the Yukon. The park encompasses 4,345. sq. km of land in the northwestern corner of the Yukon Territory. Hours of Operation: Park is open year round, with no services available.

Observatories

Alberta

***Calgary:* Rothney Astrophysical Observatory (RAO)**
Physics & Astronomy Dept., University of Calgary, #605, 2500 University Dr. NW
Calgary, AB T2N 1N4
Tel: 403-931-2366
rao@phas.ucalgary.ca
www.ucalgary.ca/rao
Other contact information: Open House Info: 403-220-7977; 403-220-5385
Year Founded: 1972 The RAO is the University of Calgary's astronomical facility which is home to the following telescopes: the 0.4-m Clarke-Milone Telescope (which is controlable via the internet), the 0.5-m Baker Nunn Telescope (used to search for asteroids), & the 1.8-m A.R. Cross Telescope (one of the 3 largest in Canada).
Dr. Phil Langill, Director, pplangil@ucalgary.ca

***Edmonton:* University of Alberta Observatory**
Dept. of Physics, University of Alberta, 4-181 Centennial Center for Interdisciplinary Science
Edmonton, AB T6G 2J1
Tel: 780-492-5286; *Fax:* 780-492-0714
stars@ualberta.ca
www.ualberta.ca/~stars
twitter.com/UofAObservatory
www.facebook.com/UofAObservatory
Consists of a 0.5m-diameter telescope equipped with a prime focus CCD camera; research programs are directed toward stellar photometry & the detection of faint, extended sources such as HII regions & supernova remnants; Campus Observatory has permanently mounted 12 & 14 inch telescopes & an exhibit area; facility used for undergraduate instruction & public observing during academic year; admission is free.

British Columbia

***Kamloops:* Thompson Rivers University Observatory**
900 McGill Rd.
Kamloops, BC V2C 0C8
Tel: 250-371-5989; *Fax:* 250-828-5450
physics@tru.ca
www.tru.ca/science/programs/physics/observatory.html
tw itter.com/TRUObservatory
Year Founded: 2005
Colin Taylor, Chair, Physics & Astronomy Department, ctaylor@tru.ca

***Kamuela:* Canada-France-Hawaii Telescope**
c/o CFHT Corporation, #65, 1238 Mamalahoa Hwy.
Kamuela, HI 96743 USA
Tel: 808-885-7944; *Fax:* 808-885-7288
info@cfht.hawaii.edu
www.cfht.hawaii.edu
Other contact information: FTP: ftp.cfht.hawaii.edu
The CFH observatory hosts a world-class, 3.6 meter optical/infrared telescope. The observatory is located atop the summit of Mauna Kea, a 4,200 meter, dormant volcano located on the island of Hawaii. By appointment only.
Dr. Pierre-Olivier Lagage, Chair, pierre-olivier.lagage@cea.fr
Doug Simons, Executive Director, simons@cfht.hawaii.edu

Penticton: Dominion Radio Astrophysical Observatory (DRAO)
PO Box 248
Located at 717 White Lake Rd., Penticton, BC
Penticton, BC V2A 6J9
Tel: 250-497-2300
nrc.drao-ofr.cnrc@nrc-cnrc.gc.ca
www.nrc-cnrc.gc.ca/eng/solutions/facilities/drao.html
Year Founded: 1960 Used for research in the areas of astronomical sciences & technology development.
Sean Dougherty, Contact, Sean.Dougherty@nrc-cnrc.gc.ca

Prince George: Prince George Astronomical Observatory (PGAO)
***Parent:* Royal Astronomical Society of Canada Prince George Centre**
c/o Royal Astronomical Society of Canada Prince George Centre, 7365 Tedford Rd.
Prince George, BC V2N 6S2
Tel: 250-964-3600
pgrasc.org
Public viewings held on Friday nights during the fall and spring.
Bill Stunder, President, blair.s@shaw.ca

Vancouver: Gordon MacMillan Southam Observatory (GSO)
***Parent:* H.R. MacMillan Space Centre**
1100 Chestnut St.
Vancouver, BC V6J 3J9
Tel: 604-738-2855; *Fax:* 604-736-5665
info@spacecentre.ca
www.spacecentre.ca/gms
Social Media: www.youtube.com/user/MacMillanSpaceCentre
twitter.com/AskAnAstronomer
www.facebook.com/MacMillanSpaceCentre
Part of the H.R. MacMillan Space Centre.
Raylene Marchand, Executive Director

Victoria: Centre of the Universe Astronomy Interpretive Centre / Centre de l'Univers - Centre d'interprétation en astronomie
5071 West Saanich Rd.
Victoria, BC V9E 2E7
Tel: 250-363-8262; *Fax:* 250-363-8290
cu@nrc-cnrc.gc.ca
www.nrc-cnrc.gc.ca/eng/outreach/cu/index.html
The Centre offers telescope tours, planetarium presentations, & a multimedia theatre. Public observations are held in the summer. Open year-round.

Victoria: Climenhaga Observatory
Dept. of Physics & Astronomy, University of Victoria, PO Box 1700 CSC
Victoria, BC V8W 3P6
Tel: 250-721-7700; *Fax:* 250-721-7715
physgen@uvic.ca.ca
www.uvic.ca/science/physics/index.php
Russell Robb, Contact, robb@uvic.ca

Manitoba

Winnipeg: Glenlea Astronomical Observatory (GAO)
Allen Bldg., Faculty of Physics & Astronomu, University of Manitoba
Winnipeg, MB R3T 2N2
Tel: 204-474-9817; *Fax:* 204-474-7622
www.physics.umanitoba.ca

Winnipeg: The Lockhart Planetarium
Dept. of Physics & Astronomy, University of Manitoba, 380 University College, 500 Dysart Rd.
Winnipeg, MB R3T 2M8
Tel: 204-474-9785
www.physics.umanitoba.ca/planetarium
Year Founded: 1964 Planetarium theatre; display area; astronomy reference library

Winnipeg: Manitoba Planetarium
***Parent:* The Manitoba Museum**
190 Rupert Ave.
Winnipeg, MB R3B 0N2
Tel: 204-956-2830; *Fax:* 204-942-3679
info@manitobamuseum.ca
manitobamuseum.ca/main/visit/planetarium
Year Founded: 1968 A 287 seat space theatre equipped with Zeiss MkV star projector, which is capable of reproducing the night sky as seen from any location on Earth; complimented with advanced video project & multmedia projectors; shows & programs change throughout the year
Mike Jensen, Supervisor, Science Gallery & Planetarium Programs, 204-988-0613

New Brunswick

Sackville: Mount Allison Gemini Observatory
c/o Physics Department, Mount Allison University, 67 York St.
Sackville, NB E4L 4R6
Tel: 506-364-2530
gemini@mta.ca
www.mta.ca/gemini
Year Founded: 2008

Newfoundland & Labrador

Corner Brook: Grenfell Campus Observatory
Arts & Science Extension, Grenfell Campus, Memorial University, 20 University Dr., 4th Fl.
Corner Brook, NL A2H 5G4
observatory@grenfell.mun.ca
www.grenfell.mun.ca/observatory
Year Founded: 2012

Nova Scotia

Halifax: Burke-Gaffney Observatory (BGO)
Department of Astronomy & Physics, Saint Mary's University, 923 Robie St.
Halifax, NS B3H 3C3
Tel: 902-420-5633; *Fax:* 902-420-5141
www.smu.ca/academic/science/ap/bgo.html
Other contact information: Info Line: 902-496-8257
40 cm reflecting telescope; public tours held on the 2nd & 4th Fro. of each month at 7 pm (Nov.-Mar.) or 9 pm or 10 pm (Apr.-Oct.), weather permitting; Mon. evening group tours by arrangement
David J. Lane, Director, dlane@ap.smu.ca

Halifax: Halifax Planetarium
Sir James Dunn Bldg., Dalhousie University, #120, 6310 Coburg Rd.
Halifax, NS B3H 4R2
planetarium@dal.ca
Year Founded: 1954

Ontario

Buckhorn: Buckhorn Observatory
2254 County Rd. 507
Buckhorn, ON K0L 1J0
Tel: 705-657-2544
www.buckhornobservatory.com
www.facebook.com/pages/Buckhorn-Observatory/175211951986
Year Founded: 2003
John Crossen, Contact, johnstargazer@xplornet.com

Hamilton: W.J. McCallion Planetarium
Dept. of Physics & Astronomy, McMaster University, 1280 Main St. West
Hamilton, ON L8S 4M1
Tel: 905-525-9140; *Fax:* 905-546-1252
planetarium@physics.mcmaster.ca
www.physics.mcmaster.ca/planetarium/
w ww.facebook.com/136771806379731
The McCallion Planetarium was the first one in Ontario to offer public showings, with the original projector having been purchased in 1949.

Kingston: Queen's Observatory
Ellis Hall, Queen's University, 58 University Ave.
Kingston, ON K7L 3N6
Tel: 613-533-2711
observatory@astro.queensu.ca
observatory.phy.queensu.ca
Social Media: queensobservatory.tumblr.com
Open houses are held the 2nd Saturday of each month.
Nathalie Ouellette, Coordinator

Kingsville: Hallam Observatory
c/o Royal Astronomical Society of Canada - Windsor Center, 1508 Greenwood Rd.
Located at 3989 South Middle Rd., Woodslee, ON
Kingsville, ON N9Y 2V7
www.rascwindsor.com
Open houses are held once a month.
John Marn, Director, marnys@gosfieldtel.com

Lively: Sudbury Neutrino Observatory (SNO)
PO Box 159
Lively, ON P3Y 1M3
Tel: 705-692-7000; *Fax:* 705-692-7001
snoinfo@surf.sno.laurentian.ca
www.sno.phy.queensu.ca
Used to study neutrinos & the core of the sun
A.B. McDonald, Project Director, 613-533-2702, Fax: 613-533-6813

London: Hume Cronyn Memorial Observatory
c/o Physics & Astronomy Bldg., University of Western Ontario, #138, 1151 Richmond St.
London, ON N6A 3K7
Tel: 519-661-2111
p-a.info@uwo.ca
physics.uwo.ca/community/cronyn/index.html
twitter.com/westernuCRONYN
www.facebook.com/westernuCronyn
Year Founded: 1940 Built in 1939, observatory houses a 25 cm refactor currently used for teaching & visitor programs
Aaron Sigut, Coordinator, asigut@uwo.ca

London: University of Western Ontario Astronomical Observatory
Dept. of Physics & Astronomy, University of Western Ontario, 1151 Richmond St.
London, ON N6A 3K7
Tel: 519-661-2111
p-a.info@uwo.ca
www.astro.uwo.ca
Year Founded: 1969 The telescope is no longer in regular use, however the observatory site serves as a home to research projects.
Dr. Peter Brown, Director, pbrown@uwo.ca

Neebing: Thunder Bay Observatory
243 Klages Rd.
Neebing, ON P7L 0C5
Tel: 807-577-3617
thunderbayobservatory.com
Randy McAllister, Owner/Operator, astrorandy@tbaytel.net

Ottawa: Helen Sawyer Hogg Observatory
Canada Science & Technology Museum, PO Box 9724 T
Ottawa, ON K1G 5A3
Tel: 613-991-3044 *Toll-Free:* 866-442-4416
www.sciencetech.technomuses.ca
Year Founded: 1974
Melanie Hall, Contact, mhall@technomuses.ca

Ottawa: Kessler Observatory
Carlton University, 1125 Colonel By Dr.
Ottawa, ON K1S 5B6
observatory@physics.carleton.ca
physics.carleton.ca/observatory
Uses a 14 inch Schmidt Cassegrain telescope and a small refractor telescope.
Etienne Rollin, Contact

Pembroke: Algonquin Radio Observatory (ARO)
***Parent:* Thoth Technology Inc.**
RR#6
Pembroke, ON K8A 6W7
Tel: 905-713-2884
aro@thoth.ca
www.arocanada.com
Year Founded: 1959

Richmond Hill: David Dunlap Observatory (DDO)
***Parent:* Metrus Development Inc.**
Observatory Hill, 123 Hillsview Dr.
Richmond Hill, ON L4C 1T3
Tel: 905-883-0174
www.theddo.ca
Other contact information: Alternate URL: www.observatoryhill.ca
Year Founded: 1935 The observatory was sold to Metrus Development in 2008, & is now part of the Observatory Hill site. Public programs are scheduled throughout the summer, & Viewing Nights are held most Saturday nights for the public to drop in & use the facilities.
Paul Mortfield, Chair, paul@theddo.ca

St Catharines: Niagara Community Observatory
c/o Brock University, 500 Glenridge Ave.
St Catharines, ON L2S 3A1
Tel: 905-688-5550
www.brocku.ca/niagara-community-observatory
Barry Wright, Director, 905-688-5550, bwright@brocku.ca

Sudbury: Doran Planetarium
Fraser Bldg., Laurentian University, 935 Ramsey Lake Rd.
Sudbury, ON P3E 2C6
Tel: 705-675-1151 *Toll-Free:* 800-461-4030
laurentian.ca/planetarium
Astronomical presentation, show & lecture in both French & English

***Thunder Bay:* David Thompson Astronomical Observatory (DTAO)**
c/o Fort William Historical Park, 1350 King Rd.
Thunder Bay, ON P7K 1L7
Tel: 807-473-2344
reservations@fwhp.ca
www.fwhp.ca
The largest telescope in central Canada

***Toronto:* University of Toronto Planetarium**
Astronomy Bldg., 50 St. George St.
Toronto, ON M5S 3H4
universe.utoronto.ca/planetarium

***Toronto:* York University Observatory**
Petrie Science Bldg., York University, #405, 4700 Keele St.
Toronto, ON M3J 1P3
Tel: 416-736-2100
observe@yorku.ca
www.yorkobservatory.com
twitter.com/yorkobservatory
www.facebook.com/3 54102802826
Public viewings are held every Wednesday, in addition to online viewings every Monday. The observatory is also used in order to research various stars.
Paul Delaney, Director, pdelaney@yorku.ca

***Waterloo:* Gustav Bakos Observatory**
Physics Bldg., University of Waterloo, 200 University Ave. West
Waterloo, ON N2L 3G1
Tel: 519-885-1211; *Fax:* 519-746-8115
observe@astro.uwaterloo.ca
astro.uwaterloo.ca/observatory/index.html
Year Founded: 1967 Open for public tours on the 1st Wednesday of every month.

Québec

***Champlain:* Observatoire du Cégep de Trois-Rivières**
300, route Sainte-Marie
Champlain, QC G0X 1C0
Tél: 819-295-3043
observatoire@cegeptr.qc.ca
www.cegeptr.qc.ca/observatoire
www.facebook.com/observatoire
Fondée en: 1980 Ouvert 25 juin au 30 août du mardi au samedi.

***Laval:* Observatoire astronomique de Laval**
***Parent:* Club des Astronomes Amateurs de Laval**
825, av du Parc
Laval, QC H7E 2T7
observatoire@astronomielaval.org
www.astronomielaval.org/lobservatoire
twitter.com/ObsDeLaval
www.faceb ook.com/ObservatoireLaval
Ouvert du 1er mai au 31 octobre.
Jean-Marc Richard, Administrateur

***Montréal:* Observatoire du Mont-Mégantic (OMM)**
***Parent:* Centre de recherche en astrophysique du Québec**
Département de physique, Université de Montréal, CP 6128 Centre-Ville
Situé à 189, route du Parc, Notre-Dame-des-Bois, QC
Montréal, QC H3C 3J7
Tél: 514-343-6667; *Téléc:* 514-343-2071
info@craq-astro.ca
omm.craq-astro.ca
twitter.com/OMM_Officiel
www.fa cebook.com/OMMastro
L'observatoire est situé au sommet du mont Mégantic dans les Cantons de l'est, à une altitude de 1111m.
René Doyon, Directeur, 514-343-6111, Fax: 514-343-2071, doyon@astro.uMontréal.ca
Robert Lamontagne, Directeur exécutif, 514-343-6111, Fax: 514-343-2071, lamont@astro.uMontréal.ca

***Notre-Dame-des-Bois:* Astrolab du Parc National du Mont Mégantic**
189, rte du Parc
Notre-Dame-des-Bois, QC J0B 2E0
Tél: 819-888-2941; *Téléc:* 819-888-2943
Ligne sans frais: 800-665-6527
parc.mont-megantic@sepaq.com
astrolab-parc-national-mont-megantic.org
www.facebook.com/MontMegantic

***Saint-Elzéar-de-Beauce:* Observatoire du Mont Cosmos**
750, rang du Haut Sainte-Anne
Saint-Elzéar-de-Beauce, QC G0S 2J0
Tél: 418-554-0326
info@montcosmos.com
montcosmos.com
www.facebook.com/pages/Observatoire-du-Mont-Cosmos/45816422667
Fondée en: 1971

***Sherbrooke:* Bishop's University Astronomical Observatory**
#401, 2600 College St.
Sherbrooke, QC J1M 1Z7
Tel: 819-822-9600
observ@ubishops.ca
physics.ubishops.ca/observatory

Saskatchewan

***Saskatoon:* University of Saskatchewan Observatory**
Dept. of Physics & Engineering Physics, University of Saskatchewan, 116 Science Pl.
Location: 108 Wiggins Rd., Saskatoon, SK S7N 5E6
Saskatoon, SK S7N 5E2
Tel: 306-966-6429; *Fax:* 306-966-6400
artsandscience.usask.ca/physics/observatory
Open every Saturday evening after dark for public viewing through the telescope; admission is free

Yukon Territory

***Watson Lake:* Northern Lights Centre (NLC)**
PO Box 590
Watson Lake, YT Y0A 1C0
Tel: 867-536-7827; *Fax:* 867-536-2823
nlc@northwestel.net
www.northernlightscentre.ca
Year Founded: 1996 The NLC presents the aurora borealis phenomenon & explains the science behind it through displays & a video broadcast in the centre's domed theatre during the summer. In the winter visitors can experience the real northern lights.

Performing Arts - Dance

Alberta Ballet
Nat Christie Centre, 141 - 18 Ave. SW, Calgary AB T2S 0B8
Tel: 403-245-4222; *Fax:* 403-245-6573
info@albertaballet.com
www.albertaballet.com
To enrich & bring beauty to people's lives through creating, performing & teaching ballet
Chris George, Executive Director
Jean Grand-Maître, Artistic Director
Peter Dala, Music Director

Alberta Dance Alliance (ADA)
Percy Page Centre, 11759 Groat Rd., 2nd Fl., Edmonton AB T5M 3K6
Tel: 780-422-8107; *Fax:* 780-422-2663
Toll-Free: 888-422-8107
info@abdancealliance.ab.ca
www.abdancealliance.ab.ca
To foster & promote the appreciation & practice of dance in Alberta, through administrative, technical, & informative services, programs, advocacy, & special events; to support professional development through consultation in grant research, preparation, and production
Bobbi Westman, Executive Director

Alberta Square & Round Dance Federation
6501 - 46 Ave., Camrose AB T4V 0E6
Tel: 403-672-5669
www.squaredance.ab.ca
Wayne Lowther, Co-President
Helen Lowther, Co-President

Amethyst Scottish Dancers of Nova Scotia
c/o 61 Richardson Dr., Fall River NS B2T 1E7
www.amethystscottishdancersns.ca
Marla MacInnis, Artistic Director

Ballet British Columbia
601 Smithe St., Vancouver BC V6G 5G1
Tel: 604-732-5003; *Fax:* 604-732-4417
info@balletbc.com
www.balletbc.com
To commission & perform a balanced repertoire rooted in classical technique, which encompasses the best new ballets & late 20th century classics
Branislav Henselmann, Executive Director

Ballet Creole
61 Primrose Ave., Toronto ON M6H 3V2
Tel: 416-960-0350; *Fax:* 416-960-2067
info@balletcreole.org
www.balletcreole.org
Preserves and perpetuates traditional and contemporary African culture and increases awareness of the rich African culture that exists in Canada. Establishes a dynamic new Canadian artistic tradition based on a fusion of diverse dance and music traditions. Promotes multicultural understanding through education and quality entertainment to national and international audiences.
Patrick Parson, Artistic Director

Ballet Jörgen
c/o George Brown College, Casa Loma Campus, Building C, #126, 160 Kendal Ave., Toronto ON M5R 1M3
Tel: 416-961-4725; *Fax:* 416-415-2865
info@balletjorgen.ca
www.balletjorgen.ca
To operate exclusively as a charitable organization to administer & employ its property, assets & rights for the purpose of raising the public's awareness of ballet as an art form by establishing, maintaining & operating a ballet company; to advance knowledge & increase public recognition of ballet by developing a repertoire of original dance productions for performance, film & video for the benefit of the community at large; to advance artistic appreciation & education of the general public of choreography as a distinctive art form by commissioning & making available to the public presentations by a variety of choreographers
Bengt Jörgen, Artistic Director & CEO

Ballet West / Ballet Ouest
#218, 269, boul St. Jean, Pointe-Claire QC H9R 3J1
Tel: 514-783-1245
reception@balletouest.com
www.balletouest.com
To provide a milieu that encourages young dancers to express themselves through dance & to move from amateur to professional status; educate & develop audiences; present an alternative view to counteract the mass culture that is being fed to our youth
Claude Caron, Artistic Director

Les Ballets Jazz de Montréal (BJM)
1210, rue Sherbrooke est, Montréal QC H2L 1L9
Tél: 514-982-6771; *Téléc:* 514-982-9145
info@bjmdanse.ca
www.bjmdanse.ca
Crée, produit et diffuse à l'échelle nationale et internationale des spectacles de danse contemporaine; offre à ses danseurs un entraînement professionnel; permet aux chorégraphes invités et aux danseurs de développer leur propre recherche; génère un répertoire exclusif et conserve l'esprit novateur qui anime la compagnie de puis sa création
Louis Robitaille, Directeur artistique
Céline Cassone, Coordinatrice, Artistique et répétitrice

Border Boosters Square & Round Dance Association (BBSRDA)
Toll-Free: 866-206-6696
www.borderboosters.qc.ca
To promote square & round dancing in the Québec, eastern Ontario & northern New York area
Ruth Cunningham, President

Brian Webb Dance Co.
PO Box 53092, Edmonton AB T5N 48A
Tel: 780-452-3282
webbcdf@shaw.ca
www.bwdc.ca
To produce & present contemporary dance; to build work through collaboration
Brian Webb, Artistic Director

British Columbia Square & Round Dance Federation
c/o President, 1459 Claudia Pl., Port Coquitlam BC V3C 2V5
Tel: 604-941-6392; *Toll-Free:* 800-335-9433
www.squaredance.bc.ca
To provide healthy recreation at the community level for an affordable cost
Ken Crisp, President

Canada Dance Festival Society
PO Box 1376, Stn. B, Ottawa ON K1P 5R4
Tel: 613-947-7000
cdffdc@nac-cna.ca
www.canadadance.ca
To hold a festival of dance every two years
Jeanne Holmes, Artistic Director
Sébastien Audette, President

Canadian Alliance of Dance Artists (CADA ON) / Alliance canadiennes des artistes de danse
476 Parliament St., 2nd Fl., Toronto ON M4X 1P2
Tel: 416-657-2276
office@cada-on.ca
cadaontario.camp8.org
To advance the socioeconomic status & working conditions of professional dance artists in Ontario; To support the professional & artistic development of Ontario's dance artists
Michael Caldwell, Co-Chair
Brodie Stevenson, Co-Chair
Amelia Ehrhardt, Administrative Director
Lesley Bramhill, Coordinator, Membership Services

Canadian Children's Dance Theatre (CCDT)
509 Parliament St., Toronto ON M4X 1P3
Tel: 416-924-5657; *Fax:* 416-924-4141
info@ccdt.org
www.ccdt.org
To promote dance theatre to young people
Deborah Lundmark, Artistic Director & Resident Choreographer
Michael de Coninck Smith, Co-Artistic Director & Production Manager

Canadian Dance Teachers' Association (CDTA) / Association canadienne des professeurs de danse
#38, 6033 Shawson Dr., Mississauga ON L5T 1H8
Tel: 905-564-2139; *Fax:* 905-564-2211
canadiandanceteachers@bellnet.ca
www.cdtanational.ca
To advance education in the field of dance & maintain throughout Canada an organization of qualified dance teachers; to promote friendship & the exchange of ideas & information among the dance teachers of Canada, to provide an organization to represent Canadian dance teachers internationally
Sue Romeril, President

Canadian Square & Round Dance Society (CSRDS)
c/o Lorraine Kozera, 24 Aspen Villa Dr., Oak Bank MB R0E 1J2
Toll-Free: 866-206-6696
info@squaredance.ca
www.csrds.ca
To link information about Canadian square & round dancing associations together in order to promote awareness, inspire activity, & to offer information
Lorraine Kozera, Secretary
John Kozera, Director, Manitoba
Eric McCormack, President

Le Carré des Lombes
#401, 2022, rue Sherbrooke Est, Montréal QC H2K 1B9
Tél: 514-287-9339
info@lecarredeslombes.com
www.lecarredeslombes.com
Diffuser des spectacles de danse; promouvoir la danse comme discipline artistique
Danièle Desnoyers, Directrice artistique et chorégraphe

Catalyst Theatre Society of Alberta
8529 Gateway Blvd., Edmonton AB T6E 6P3
Tel: 780-431-1750; *Fax:* 780-433-3060
info@catalysttheatre.ca
www.catalysttheatre.ca
To create & present original Canadian work that explores new possibilities for theatre
Jonathan Christenson, Artistic Director

Cercle d'expression artistique Nyata Nyata
4374, boul St-Laurent, 2e étage, Montréal QC H2W 1Z5
Tél: 514-849-9781;
Ligne sans frais: 877-692-8208
info@nyata-nyata.org
www.nyata-nyata.org
Pour créer musical et l'art chorégraphique dans le but de développer l'art de la danse et les compétences des artistes.
Zab Maboungou, Directrice artistique

Compagnie de danse Migrations
880, av Père-Marquette, Québec QC G1S 2A4
Tél: 418-684-3132
migrationsdanse@gmail.com
www.migrationsdanse.com
Création, formation, production et diffusion de la danse et musique traditionnelle québécoise et des cultures du monde

Compagnie Marie Chouinard
4499, av de l'esplanade, Montréal QC H2W 1T2
Tél: 514-843-9036; *Téléc:* 514-843-7616
info@mariechouinard.com
www.mariechouinard.com
Pour être dédié à des interprétations modernes et uniques de la danse, nouvelle chorégraphie artistique, et l'expression à travers les mouvements du corps humain.
Marie Chouinard, Directrice générale et artistique
Bernard Dubreuil, Directeur général délégué

The Dance Centre (TDC)
Scotiabank Dance Centre, 677 Davie St., 6th Fl., Vancouver BC V6B 2G6
Tel: 604-606-6400; *Fax:* 604-606-6401
info@thedancecentre.ca
www.thedancecentre.ca
To increase the exposure of performing arts through the presentation of interdisciplinary performances & workshops; to present contemporary dance work & interdisciplinary dance/theatre/music performances of the highest quality; to act as a catalyst & animator for dance & associated arts in the community & to offer infrastructure & presentation support of that activity
Mima Zagar, Executive Director

Dance Manitoba Inc.
Pantages Playhouse Theatre, #204, 180 Market Ave. East, Winnipeg MB R3B 0P7
Tel: 204-989-5260; *Fax:* 204-989-5268
info@dancemanitoba.org
www.dancemanitoba.org
To promote the development of dance through festivals, workshops, & showcases
Nicole Owens, Executive Director

Dance Nova Scotia
1113 Marginal Rd., Halifax NS B3H 4P7
Tel: 902-422-1749; *Fax:* 902-422-0881
office@dancens.ca
www.dancens.ca
To promote, stimulate & encourage the development of dance as a cultural, educational & social activity
Cliff Le Jeune, Executive Director

Dance Ontario Association / Association Ontario Danse
The Distillery District, #304, 15 Case Goods Lane, Toronto ON M5A 3C4
Tel: 416-204-1083; *Fax:* 416-204-1085
contact@danceontario.ca
www.danceontario.ca
To support the advancement of all forms of dance; To offer a unified voice on dance issues
Samara Thompson, Chair
Jennifer Watkins, Vice-Chair
Rosslyn Jacob Edwards, Executive Director
Jade Jager Clark, Secretary
Debbie Kapp, Treasurer

Dance Oremus Danse (DOD)
PO Box 322, 8023 Palmer Rd., Combermere ON K0J 1L0
Tel: 613-756-3284
www.danceoremusdanse.org
To increase the public's appreciation of the aesthetic arts by promoting & encouraging the philosophy, movement practices & dance forms of Isadora Duncan (1877-1927) & European neo-classical dance, via seminars, workshops, courses on dance, performance, publishing & other media
Paul James Dwyer, Founder/Artistic Director

Dance Saskatchewan Inc.
205A Pacific Ave., Saskatoon SK S7K 1N9
Tel: 306-931-8480; *Fax:* 306-244-1520
Toll-Free: 800-667-8480
dancesask@sasktel.net
www.dancesask.com
To support & enhance the development of all dance forms; to preserve & promote dance in Saskatchewan; to represent & educate about dance; to encourage a passion for dance; to create a viable, unified organization which represents & advocates dance interests; to foster a respect & acceptance of dance which encourages free expression of cultural identity; to establish an active, vibrant environment which focuses on job creation, performance & cultural diversity within a central dance facility
Linda Coe-Kirkham, Executive Director

Dance Umbrella of Ontario (DUO)
476 Parliament St., Toronto ON M4X 1P2
Tel: 416-504-6429; *Fax:* 416-504-8702
duo@danceumbrella.net
www.danceumbrella.net
To assist & support professional dance creators in Ontario dance centres
Jennifer Bennett, Managing Director

Dancemakers
#301, 15 Case Goods Ln., Toronto ON M5A 3C4
Tel: 416-367-1800
info@dancemakers.org
dancemakers.org
To bring dance of challenging physicality & emotional impact to audiences by drawing on the diverse talents & individual strengths of its artists; To develop & support works which both provoke & entertain
Amelia Ehrhardt, Artistic Director

Dancer Transition Resource Centre (DTRC) / Centre de ressources et transition pour danseurs (CRTD)
The Lynda Hamilton Centre, #500, 250 The Esplanade, Toronto ON M5A 1J2
Tel: 416-595-5655; *Fax:* 416-595-0009
Toll-Free: 800-667-0851
nationaloffice@dtrc.ca
www.dtrc.ca
TO hels dancers make necessary transitions into, within & from professional performing, as well as operating a resource centre for the dance community & the public, offering seminars, education materials & information.
Amanda Hancox, Executive Director
Garry Neil, Chair

Danse-Cite inc
#426, 3680, rue Jeanne-Mance, Montréal QC H2X 2K5
Tél: 514-525-3595
info@danse-cite.org
www.danse-cite.org
Création et production de spectacles de danse contemporain
Daniel Soulières, Directeur artistique

Decidedly Jazz Danceworks
1514 - 4th St. SW, Calgary AB T2R 0Y4
Tel: 403-245-3533; *Fax:* 403-245-3584
djd@decidedlyjazz.com
www.decidedlyjazz.com
To create concert jazz dance that sustains the spirit and traditions of jazz; to mix groove, African roots, rhythm, improvisation, interplay with musicians, and deeply human soul, has distinguished DJD on the international jazz dance stage; to offer a season of performances, touring, and jazz classes.
Kimberley Cooper, Artistic Director
Kathi Sundstrom, Executive Director

EDAM Performing Arts Society (EDAM)
303 East 8th Ave., Vancouver BC V5T 1S1
Tel: 604-876-9559
info@edamdance.org
www.edamdance.org
To explore new directions in dance & the performing arts
Peter Bingham, Artistic Director
Mona Hamill, General Manager

Fédération des loisirs-danse du Québec (FLDQ)
4545, av Pierre-de Coubertin, Montréal QC H1V 3N7
Tél: 514-252-3029
France Dagenais, Présidente

Federation of Dance Clubs of New Brunswick (FDCNB)
c/o President, 35 Berwick St., Fredericton NB E3A 4Y2
Tel: 506-472-1444
www.squaredancenb.ca
Strives to be New Brunswick's family of dancers, expounding the virtues of dance-related recreational activity in each and every region of the province, actively involved with training, teaching, instructing, informing & assisting others to learn more about new & not so new dance-related ideas.
Terry Hebert, President

Fortier Danse-Création
#301, 2022, rue Sherbrooke Est, Montréal QC H2K 1B9
Tél: 514-529-8158; *Téléc:* 514-529-1222
admin@fortier-danse.com
www.fortier-danse.com

Création et diffusion des oeuvres du chorégraphe Paul-André Fortier
Paul-André Fortier, Directeur artistique
Gilles Savary, Directeur général

Fujiwara Dance Inventions
PO Box 8039, Toronto ON M2R 1Z1
Tel: 416-593-8455
info@fujiwaradance.com
www.fujiwaradance.com
To dance into insight, through the creation, performance, & teaching of dance; To encounter & express the mysteries of human nature as they are manifest in the body, before words
Denise Fujiwara, Artistic Director

Gina Lori Riley Dance Enterprises
Jackman Dramatic Art Centre, #210, 401 Sunset Ave., Windsor ON N9B 3P4
Tel: 519-253-3000
www.ginaloririleydanceenterprises.com
To advance the art of dance through the development of new work, performance & through community education in an exemplary manner as a contemporary modern professional Canadian dance company
Gina Lori Riley, Artistic Director

Goh Ballet Society
2345 Main St., Vancouver BC V5T 3C9
Tel: 604-872-4014; *Fax:* 604-872-4011
admin@gohballet.com
www.gohballet.com
To prepare aspiring dancers for professional careers by providing rigorous training in the vocabulary & artistry of classical ballet.
Chan Hon Goh, Director

Les Grands Ballets Canadiens de Montréal (GBCM)
4816, rue Rivard, Montréal QC H2J 2N6
Tél: 514-849-8681
info@grandsballets.com
www.grandsballets.com
Maintenir la tradition du ballet classique et élargir le champ d'expression de cette forme artistique par la création; faire connaître et apprécier la danse à tous les publics grâce à la qualité de nos presentations et de nos productions
Alain Dancyger, Directeur général
Gradimir Pankov, Directeur artistique

Kinesis Dance Society
Scotia Bank Dance Centre, 677 Davie St., Level 7, Vancouver BC V6B 2G6
Tel: 604-684-7844; *Fax:* 604-684-7834
admin@kinesisdance.org
www.kinesisdance.org
To contribute new & provocative works of contemporary dance to the local, national & international dance scene; to educate through workshops & cultural exchanges & to collaborate with other media, such as film, video & theatre
Paras Terezakis, Artistic Director

La La La Human Steps
#206, 5655, av du Parc, Montréal QC H2V 4H2
Tél: 514-277-9090; *Téléc:* 514-277-0862
info@lalalahumansteps.com
www.lalalahumansteps.com
Présenter les spectacles crées par Édouard Lock sur les plus grandes scènes du monde; compagnie de danse contemporaine
Édouard Lock, Directeur artistique

Louise Bédard Danse
#300, 2022, rue Sherbrooke Est, Montréal QC H2K 1B9
Tél: 514-982-4580
infos@lbdanse.org
www.lbdanse.org
De poursuivre les activités modernes création de danse, de sensibilisation et d'éducation, et en offrant des créations chorégraphiques originales pour le grand public.
Louise Bédard, Directrice artistique

Lucie Grégoire Danse
6811, rue de Laundière, Montréal QC H2G 3B2
Tél: 514-278-1620
luciegregoire3@sympatico.ca
www.luciegregoire.ca
Lucie Grégoire, Directrice artistique

Manitoba Square & Round Dance Federation
c/o President, #2, 297 Enfield Cres., Winnipeg MB R2H 1C1
Tel: 204-224-3742
www.squaredancemb.com
To promote and govern square, round, clog, and line dancing in Manitoba

Sam Dunn, Co-President
Anne Wiebe, Co-President

Margie Gillis Dance Foundation / Fondation de danse Margie Gillis
#304, 1908, rue Panet, Montréal QC H2L 3A2
Tel: 514-845-3115; *Fax:* 514-845-4526
info@margiegillis.org
www.margiegillis.org
To reach as large a public as possible with a dance program of physical & emotional integrity; to make the audience aware of the potential of their own lives.
Margie Gillis, Artistic Director
Valerie Buddle, General Manager

Mascall Dance
1130 Jervis St., Vancouver BC V6E 2C7
Tel: 604-669-9337
admin@mascalldance.ca
www.mascalldance.ca
To provide a forum for research, creation, performance, education, documentation & dissemination of contemporary dance & related disciplines
Jennifer Mascall, Artistic Director

Montréal Danse
#109, 372, rue Sainte-Catherine ouest, Montréal QC H3B 1A2
Tél: 514-871-4005
questions@Montréaldanse.com
www.Montréaldanse.com
Se voue à la création de vibrantes oeuvres chorégraphiques avec le concours de plusieurs chorégraphes nationaux et internationaux
Kathy Casey, Directrice artistique

National Ballet of Canada
Walter Carsen Centre, 470 Queens Quay West, Toronto ON M5V 3K4
Tel: 416-345-9686; *Fax:* 416-345-8323
info@national.ballet.ca
national.ballet.ca
Karen Kain, Artistic Director
Barry Hughson, Executive Director
David Briskin, Music Director/Principal Conductor

O Vertigo Danse
175, rue Sainte-Catherine ouest, Montréal QC H2X 1Z8
Tél: 514-251-9177; *Téléc:* 514-251-7358
info@overtigo.com
www.overtigo.com
Se consacre à la création en nouvelle danse et la diffusion des oeuvres de la fondatrice et directrice artistique de la compagnie
Ginette Laurin, Directrice générale
Vecerina Jacques, Directeur administratif

Ontario Ballet Theatre
1133 St. Clair Ave. West, Toronto ON M6E 1B1
Tel: 416-656-9568; *Fax:* 416-651-4803
www.ontarioballettheatre.com
To nurture & develop an appreciation of contemporary & classical ballet by reaching new audiences through artistic excellence

Ontario Folk Dance Association (OFDA)
Toronto ON
ontariofolkdancers@gmail.com
www.ofda.ca
To promote the practice of international folk arts & dance; to prepare, collect & disseminate information & material relating to folk arts & dance

Ontario Square & Round Dance Federation (OSRDF)
c/o President, 8 Seven Oaks Circle, St Catharines ON L2P 3N6
Tel: 905-641-1872; *Toll-Free:* 866-206-6696
info@squaredance.on.ca
www.squaredance.on.ca
Wayne Hall, President

Opéra Atelier (OA)
St. Lawrence Hall, 157 King St. East, 4th Fl., Toronto ON M5C 1G9
Tel: 416-703-3767; *Fax:* 416-703-4895
opera.atelier@operaatelier.com
www.operaatelier.com
To produce opera, ballet, & drama from the 17th & 18th centuries; to educate and instruct young performers
Alexandra Skoczylas, Executive Director
Jeannette Lajeunesse Zingg, Co-Artistic Director/Choreographer
Marshall Pynkoski, Co-Artistic Director/Director
David Fallis, Resident Music Director
Trini Mitra, Director, Finance & Administration

Les Productions DansEncorps Inc.
Centre Culturel Aberdeen, #14A, 140, rue Botsford, Moncton NB E1C 4X5
Tél: 506-855-0998; *Téléc:* 506-852-3401
dansencorps@bellaliant.com
www.dansencorps.ca
De contribuer au développement des arts au Nouveau-Brunswick

Regroupement québécois de la danse (RQD)
#440, 3680 rue Jeanne-Mance, Montréal QC H2X 2K5
Tél: 514-849-4003; *Téléc:* 514-849-3288
info@Québecdanse.org
www.Québecdanse.org
Promouvoir, encourager et soutenir le développement artistique, social et économique des danseurs, chorégraphes et de tout intervenant professionnel de la communauté de la danse au Québec
Anik Bissonette, Présidente

Royal Academy of Dance Canada
#601, 1210 Sheppard Ave. East, Toronto ON M2K 1E3
Tel: 416-489-2813; *Fax:* 416-489-3222
Toll-Free: 888-709-0895
info@radcanada.org
www.radcanada.org
To provide dance education & training
Clarke MacIntosh, National Director, Canada

The Royal Scottish Country Dance Society (RSCDS)
12 Coates Cres., Edinburgh EH15 1EY UK
info@rscds.org
www.rscds.org
To preserve & further the practice of traditional Scottish Country Dancing; to provide or assist in providing special education or instruction in the practice of Scottish Country Dances
Gillian Wilson, Executive Officer

Royal Winnipeg Ballet (RWB)
380 Graham Ave., Winnipeg MB R3C 4K2
Tel: 204-956-0183; *Fax:* 204-943-1994
Toll-Free: 800-667-4792
customerservice@rwb.org
www.rwb.org
To enrich the human experience by teaching, creating & performing outstanding dance
David Reid, Chair
André Lewis, Artistic Director

Saskatchewan Square & Round Dance Federation
SK
Tel: 306-463-3620
www.sksquaredance.ca
To guide & promote Square & Round Dancing & Clogging throughout the province as a recreation for people of all ages & in all walks of life to enjoy
Pat Campbell, Co-President
Earl Campbell, Co-President

Springboard Dance
205 - 8th Ave. SE, 2nd Fl., Calgary AB T2G 0K9
Tel: 403-265-3230
springboardperformance.com
To produce, create & perform intellectually & sensually stimulating modern dance
Nicole Mion, Artistic Director & Curator
Selina Clary, Managing Director

Square & Round Dance Federation of Nova Scotia
c/o Ralph MacDonald, PO Box 16, Goshen NS B0H 1M0
Tel: 902-783-2731
www.chebucto.ns.ca
To provide liaison between clubs & the provincial government; to suggest guidelines & provide an organizational framework for operating & coordinating activities of member clubs; to encourage cooperation in advertising, promoting & operating Square & Round Dance classes throughout the province of Nova Scotia; to support & supplement the work of the Association of Nova Scotia Square & Round Dance Teachers
Paul Langille, Co-President
Cathy Langille, Co-President

Sun Ergos, A Company of Theatre & Dance
130 Sunset Way, Priddis AB T0L 1W0
Tel: 403-931-1527; *Fax:* 403-931-1534
Toll-Free: 800-743-3351
waltermoke@sunergos.com
www.sunergos.com
To witness, maintain & develop the ethnocultural roots of theatre & dance, without prejudice of race, creed, sex, or cultural background, to celebrate the differences & recognize the similarities among all peoples; to provide the best possible

theatre & dance within the urban & rural communities, nationally & internationally
Robert Greenwood, Artistic & Managing Director
Dana Luebke, Artistic & Production Director

Toronto & District Square & Round Dance Association
c/o Bob & Betty Beck, 62 Tupper Dr., Thorold ON L2V 4C8
Tel: 905-227-7264
www.td-dance.ca
To promote, encourage & foster wider knowledge of square & round dancing; to provide for mutual exchange of philosophy & material pertaining to square & round dancing between callers, teachers, & leaders; to improve quality of square & round dancing; to encourage use of standards of uniformity relating to square & round dancing
Sharron Hall, Co-President
Wayne Hall, Co-President

Toronto Dance Theatre (TDT)
80 Winchester St., Toronto ON M4X 1B2
Tel: 416-967-1365; *Fax:* 416-963-4379
info@tdt.org
www.tdt.org
To develop Canadian dance works of art; to perform nationally & internationally; to explore new ideas in choreographic expression while embracing the fresh & vital aspects of inherited traditions
Andrea Vagianos, Managing Director
Christopher House, Artistic Director

Two Planks & a Passion Theatre Association (TP&aP)
PO Box 190, 555 Ross Creek Rd., Canning NS B0P 1H0
Tel: 902-582-3842; *Fax:* 902-582-7943
mail@twoplanks.ca
www.twoplanks.ca
To develop & present high quality, professional theatre both regionally & nationally which reflects Canadian life, with strong roles for women; to develop & build an artistic centre in Canning, NS, accessible to both the local community & to artists of all disciplines & residencies
Ken Schwartz, Artistic Director

Vancouver Moving Theatre (VMT)
PO Box 88270, Stn. Chinatown, Vancouver BC V6A 4A4
Tel: 604-628-5672
vancouvermovingtheatre@shaw.ca
www.vancouvermovingtheatre.com
To develop a new form of interdisciplinary art influenced by the Pacific Rim culture of Vancouver; to present services & products to affirm the importance of art in questions of healing, humanity & the soul
Savannah Walling, Artistic Director
Terry Hunter, Executive Director

Vinok Worldance
PO Box 4867, Edmonton AB T6E 5G7
Tel: 780-454-3739; *Fax:* 780-454-3436
vinok@vinok.ca
www.vinok.ca
To present music & dances of the world to audiences all across Canada; to reflect world dance as a way of celebrating life, involving dance, music, song, improvisation & the expression of a people

Winnipeg's Contemporary Dancers
#204, 211 Bannatyne Ave., Winnipeg MB R3B 3P2
Tel: 204-452-0229
wcd@mts.net
www.winnipegscontemporarydancers.ca
To create a place on the local, national and international arts landscape that enables vital intersections, linkages and exchange among dance creators, dance interpreters, spectators and communities
Kathy Fenton, General Manager

Performing Arts - Music

Académie de musique du Québec (AMQ)
CP 818, Succ. C, Montréal QC H2X 4L6
Tél: 514-528-1961
prixdeurope@videotron.ca
www.prixdeurope.ca/lacademie.html
Promouvoir le goût et l'avancement de la musique au Québec, aux professeurs oeuvrant dans le secteur privé et soucieux à la fois d'autonomie et d'encadrement, aux élèves qui désirent une reconnaissance officielle de leur travail
Frédéric Bednarz, Conseiller artistique

African Nova Scotian Music Association (ANSMA)
PO Box 931, Halifax NS B3J 2V9
Tel: 902-404-3036; *Fax:* 902-434-0462
ansma@eastlink.ca
www.ansma.com
The African Nova Scotian Music Association (ANSMA) is a not for profit organization dedicated to the development, promotion and enhancement of African Nova Scotia Music locally, nationally and internationally.
Louis (Lou) Gannon Jr., President

Alberta Band Association (ABA)
#104, 4818 - 50 Ave., Red Deer AB T4N 4A3
Tel: 403-347-2237; *Fax:* 403-347-2241
Toll-Free: 877-687-4239
www.albertabandassociation.com
To promote & develop the musical, educational & cultural values of bands & band music in Alberta
Darwin Krips, President

Alberta Music Industry Association (AMIA)
#301, 10526 Jasper Ave., Edmonton AB T5J 1Z7
Tel: 780-428-3372; *Fax:* 780-426-0188
Toll-Free: 800-465-3117
info@albertamusic.org
www.albertamusic.org
To help music professionals succeed by providing professional development, education, mentoring & training opportunities; to lobby government agencies in support of the music industry; to conduct fundraising & sponsorship activities
Aimee Hill, Chair
Chris Wynters, Executive Director
Carly Klassen, Program Manager

Alliance Chorale Manitoba
340, boul Provencher, Winnipeg MB R2H 0G7
Tél: 204-233-7423; *Téléc:* 204-233-8972
De promouvoir le chant choral en français et de favoriser ainsi l'épanouissement de la culture francophone du Manitoba.

Alliance des chorales du Québec (ACQ)
CP 1000, Succ. M, 4545, av Pierre de Coubertin, Montréal QC H1V 0B2
Tél: 514-252-3020; *Téléc:* 514-252-3222
Ligne sans frais: 888-924-6387
information@chorale.qc.ca
www.chorale.qc.ca
Regrouper des chorales de tous styles et de tous niveaux; donner des moyens de mieux chanter; promouvoir et développer le chant choral au Québec
Decroix Charles, Directeur général

Alliance for Canadian New Music Projects (ACNMP) / Alliance pour des projets de musique canadienne nouvelle
20 St. Joseph St., Toronto ON M4Y 1J9
Tel: 416-963-5937; *Fax:* 416-961-7198
acnmp@rogers.com
www.acnmp.ca
To provide young musicians with an opportunity to celebrate & enjoy the music of their own time & country through the organization's syllabus & its festival, Contemporary Showcase
Paige Reid, General Manager

Association des orchestres de jeunes de la Montérégie (AOJM)
CP 36573, 58, rue Victoria, Saint-Lambert QC J4P 3S8
Tél: 450-923-3733
courrier@aojm.org
www.aojm.org
De promouvoir le développement et la formation de jeunes musiciens
Sophie Roberge, Présidente

Association of Canadian Choral Communities (ACCC) / Association des communautés chorales canadiennes
A-1422 Bayview Ave., Toronto ON M4G 3A7
Tel: 647-606-2467
info@choralcanada.org
www.choralcanada.org
To promote choral music, particularly Canadian works, in schools, post-secondary institutions, churches & communities throughout Canada; to support and encourage participation in all levels of choral music through training and resources
Marta McCarthy, President
John Wiebe, President Elect
Denise Gress, Treasurer

Association québécoise de l'industrie du disque, du spectacle et de la vidéo (ADISQ)
6420, rue Saint-Denis, Montréal QC H2S 2R7
Tél: 514-842-5147; *Téléc:* 514-842-7762
info@adisq.com
www.adisq.com
Promouvoir les intérêts des producteurs de disques, spectacles et vidéos
Julie Gariépy, Directrice générale

Bach Elgar Choir
86 Homewood St., Hamilton ON L8P 2M4
Tel: 905-527-5995; *Fax:* 905-527-0555
bachelgar@gmail.com
www.bachelgar.com
To provide choral music of excellent quality & broad-based appeal to the community; To act as a cultural & educational resource
Alexander Cann, Artistic Director

Barbershop Harmony Society
110 - 7th Ave. North, Nashville TN 37203-3704 USA
Tel: 615-823-9339; *Fax:* 615-313-7620
Toll-Free: 800-876-7464
info@barbershop.org
www.barbershop.org
To perpetuate the old American institution, the barbershop quartet; to promote & encourage vocal harmony & good fellowship among its members by the formation of local chapters & districts; to encourage & promote the education of its members & the public in music appreciation
Marty Monson, CEO & Executive Director

Bluegrass Music Association of Canada (BMAC)
c/o Secretary, 339 Wellington St. N, Woodstock ON N4S 6S6
Tel: 519-539-8967
bluegrasscanada.ca
The Bluegrass Music Association is dedicated to the preservation and promotion of Bluegrass and Old-time music throughout Canada. The BMAC works to support individuals, groups and organizations involved in bluegrass and old-time music and provide leadership and promote education among fans, clubs, bands and artists.
Denis Chadbourn, President

Brandon University School of Music
Queen Elizabeth II Music Building, 270 - 18th St., Brandon MB R7A 6A9
Tel: 204-727-7388; *Fax:* 204-728-6839
music@brandonu.ca
www.brandonu.ca/music
Greg Gatien, Dean

Calgary Opera Association
Arrata Opera Centre, 1315 - 7 St. SW, Calgary AB T2R 1A5
Tel: 403-262-7286; *Fax:* 403-263-5428
info@calgaryopera.com
www.calgaryopera.com
To enrich the cultural life of the community by celebrating musical art through the performance of professional opera
W.R. (Bob) McPhee, General Director & CEO

Calgary Philharmonic Society (CPO)
#205, 8 Ave. SE, Calgary AB T2G 0K9
Tel: 403-571-0270; *Fax:* 403-294-7424
info@calgaryphil.com
www.calgaryphil.com
To provide audience with a rich, diverse & unequalled symphonic musical experience which earns broad community support
Paul Dornian, President & CEO

Calgary Youth Orchestra
c/o Mount Royal University Conservatory, 4825 Mount Royal Gate SW, Calgary AB T3E 6K6
Tel: 403-440-5978; *Fax:* 403-440-6594
cyo@mtroyal.ca
www.cyo.ab.ca
To provide the best possible musical experience for the talented young musicians of the Calgary region, in an art form that is considered one of the highest forms of expression
George Fenwick, Orchestra Manager

Canadian Academy of Recording Arts & Sciences (CARAS) / Académie canadienne des arts et des sciences de l'enregistrement (ACASE)
345 Adelaide St. West, 2nd fl., Toronto ON M5V 1R5
Tel: 416-485-3135; *Fax:* 416-485-4978
Toll-Free: 888-440-5866
info@carasonline.ca
carasonline.ca

To promote Canadian artists and music; To identify & reward the achievements of Canadian artists
Mark Cohon, Chair
Allan Reid, President & CEO, CARAS, The JUNO Awards & MusiCounts
Meghan McCabe, Senior Manager, Communications

Canadian Amateur Musicians (CAMMAC) / Musiciens amateurs du Canada
85 Cammac Rd., Harrington QC J8G 2T2
Tel: 819-687-3938; *Fax:* 819-687-3323
Toll-Free: 888-622-8755
national@cammac.ca
www.cammac.ca
To create opportunities for musicians of all levels & ages to play music in a non-competitive environment
Raymond Vies, President
Caroline Rider, Secretary
Urseula Kobel, Treasurer
Margaret Little, Executive Director
Patricia Abbott, Artistic Director
Jacques Turner, Controller

Canadian Association for Music Therapy (CAMT) / Association de musicothérapie du Canada (AMC)
#5, 1124 Gainsborough Rd., London ON N6H 5N1
Fax: 519-641-0431
Toll-Free: 800-996-2268
info@musictherapy.ca
www.musictherapy.ca
To promote excellence in music therapy practice & education in Canadian clinical, educational, & community settings

Canadian Association for the Advancement of Music & the Arts (CAAMA)
920 Woodbine Ave., Toronto ON M4C 4B7
info@caama.org
www.caama.org
To further the independent music industry, in Canada & abroad; to ensure that laws regarding the music industry are favourable to members
Patti Jannetta, President

Canadian Band Association (CBA) / Association canadienne des harmonies
#305, 1820 Henderson Hwy., Winnipeg MB R2G 1P2
Tel: 204-663-1226; *Fax:* 204-663-1226
cbaband@shaw.ca
www.canadianband.ca
To promote & develop the musical educational & cultural values of band & band music in Canada
Ken Epp, Executive Director

Canadian Bureau for the Advancement of Music (CBAM)
#208, 40 Wynford Dr., Toronto ON M3C 1J5
Tel: 647-352-4015
www.cbam.ca
To promote music (piano) education program for elementary school students
Nancy Manning, CAO

Canadian Children's Opera Chorus (CCOC)
227 Front St. East, Toronto ON M5A 1E8
Tel: 416-366-0467; *Fax:* 416-366-9204
info@canadianchildrensopera.com
www.canadianchildrensopera.com
To be the foremost children's operatic chorus in Canada & to achieve international recognition
Ken Hall, General Manager
Ann Cooper Gay, Executive Artistic Director

Canadian Country Music Association (CCMA) / Association de la musique country canadienne
#200, 120 Adelaide St. East, Toronto ON M5C 1K9
Tel: 416-947-1331; *Fax:* 416-947-5924
country@ccma.org
www.ccma.org
The federally chartered non-profit professional organization protects the heritage, & advocates the development of Canadian country music both in Canada & worldwide.
Don Green, President
Ted Ellis, Chair
Louis O'Reilly, Secretary-Treasurer

Canadian Federation of Music Teachers' Associations (CFMTA) / Fédération canadienne des associations des professeurs de musique
#302, 550 Berkshire Dr., London ON N6J 3S2
Tel: 519-471-6051
admin@cfmta.org
www.cfmta.org
To promote high musical & academic qualifications among members
Charline Farrell, President

Canadian Independent Music Association (CIMA)
30 St. Patrick St., 2nd Fl., Toronto ON M5T 3A3
Tel: 416-485-3152
www.cimamusic.ca
To lobby governments for support & copyright reform; To raise the profile of Canadian music abroad by promoting the industry at international events
Stuart Johnston, President
Donna Murphy, Vice-President, Operations
Lisa Fiorilli, Coordinator, Research & Communications

Canadian Independent Recording Artists' Association (CIRAA)
118 Berkeley St., Toronto ON M5A 2W9
Toll-Free: 866-482-4722
memberservices@ciraa.ca
www.ciraa.ca
To stimulate increased government funding for unsigned artists in Canada; to promote greater airplay for emerging artists
Gregg Terrence, President
Kathryn Rose, Secretary
James Porter, Treasurer

Canadian League of Composers / La Ligue canadienne de compositeurs
Chalmers House, 20 St. Joseph St., Toronto ON M4Y 1J9
Tel: 416-964-1364; *Fax:* 416-961-7189
Toll-Free: 877-964-1364
clcomposers@gmail.com
composition.org
To represent the interests of composers & to monitor & influence the conditions that affect their livlihood and public image.
Jennifer Butler, President
Elisha Denbrug, General Manager

Canadian Music Centre (CMC) / Centre de musique canadienne
20 St. Joseph St., Toronto ON M4Y 1J9
Tel: 416-961-6601
info@musiccentre.ca
www.musiccentre.ca
To stimulate the awareness, appreciation & performance of Canadian music
Glenn Hodgins, Executive Director
Ana-Maria Lipoczi, Manager, Music Services

Canadian Music Competitions Inc. (CMC) / Concours de musique du Canada inc.
69, rue Sherbrooke ouest, Montréal QC H2X 1X2
Tel: 514-284-5398; *Fax:* 514-284-6828
Toll-Free: 877-879-1959
info@cmcnational.com
www.cmcnational.com
Faire participer a une véritable expérience nationale de musique, en étroite collaboration avec les institutions et les professeurs de musique du pays, les plus doués de nos jeunes musiciennes et musiciens canadiens.
Marie-Claude Matton, Directrice

Canadian Music Educators' Association (CMEA) / Association canadienne des éducateurs de musique
#A-430A, Wilfrid Laurier University, Waterloo ON N2L 3C5
Tel: 778-896-7343
www.cmea.ca
To nurture a vital music learning community throughout Canada
Mark Reid, President
Kirsten MacLaine, Vice-President

Canadian Music Festival Adjudicators' Association (CMFAA)
c/o School of Music, Queen's University, Kingston ON K7L 3N6
Tel: 613-533-6000; *Fax:* 613-533-6808
www.cmfaa.ca
John Hansen, President

Canadian New Music Network (CNMN) / Réseau canadien pour les musiques nouvelles (RCMN)
#200, 1085, Côte du Beaver Hall, Montréal QC H2Z 1S5
admin@reseaumusiquesnouvelles.ca
www.newmusicnetwork.ca
To improve communication, understanding & knowledge within the new music community; To represent the community in Canadian society, by working with the media, Canadian government & arts organizations
Emily Hall, Administrator
Kyle Brenders, President

Canadian Opera Company (COC) / Compagnie d'opéra canadienne
227 Front St. East, Toronto ON M5A 1E8
Tel: 416-363-6671; *Fax:* 416-363-5584
info@coc.ca
www.coc.ca
To produce opera of the highest international standard while attracting growing public support & participation in opera through increased accessibility & education; To attract, develop & promote young Canadian singers, musicians, stage directors, conductors, designers, technical personnel & administrators; To encourage Canadian librettists & composers to compose new works
Alexander Neef, General Director
Johannes Debus, Music Director

Canadian Sinfonietta Youth Orchestra (CSYO)
c/o Canadian Sinfonietta, 107 Glengrove Ave. West, Toronto ON M4R 1P1
Tel: 416-716-6997
cs.youthorchestra@gmail.com
www.csyo.wordpress.com
To provide young musicians with quality orchestral experience to further their musical development
Tak-Ng Lai, Music Director

Canadian Society for Traditional Music (CSTM) / Société canadienne pour les traditions musicales (SCTM)
University of Alberta, 3-47 Arts Building, Edmonton AB T6G 2E6
cstmsctm@ualberta.ca
www.yorku.ca/cstm
Study & promotion of musical traditions of all cultures & communities in all their aspects
Judith Klassen, President
Chris McDonald, Treasurer
Jessica Roda, Secretary

Canadian University Music Society (CUMS) / Société de musique des universités canadiennes (SMUC)
c/o Secretariat, #202, 10 Morrow Ave., Toronto ON M6R 2J1
Tel: 416-538-1650; *Fax:* 416-489-1713
journals@interlog.com
www.cums-smuc.ca
To stimulate research, musical performance & composition; to improve instructional methods in university teaching; to provide a forum to exchange views on common problems, scholarly research in music & other matters of professional concern; to advise on new university programs & monitor existing programs
Mary Ingraham, President

Carl Orff Canada Music for Children (COC)
c/o Joan Linklater, 88 Tunis Bay, Winnipeg MB R3T 2X1
Tel: 204-261-1893
www.orffcanada.ca
To encourage the development of a wholistic music education evolved from the pedagogical philosophy & approach of Carl Orff
Beryl Peters, President

Cathedral Bluffs Symphony Orchestra (CBSO)
PO Box 51074, 18 Eglinton Sq., Toronto ON M1L 2K2
Tel: 416-879-5566
info@cathedralbluffs.com
www.cathedralbluffs.com
To provide residents of Greater Toronto with an opportunity to hear classical symphonic music performed by a live orchestra; to provide both skilled and amateur musicians with an opportunity to perform
Peggy Wong, Orchestra Manager
Tim Hendrickson, President

Chants Libres, compagnie lyrique de création
#303, 1908, rue Panet, Montréal QC H2L 3A2
Tél: 514-841-2642
creation@chantslibres.org
www.chantslibres.org
Réunir des créateurs de toutes les disciplines (musique, théâtre, arts plastiques, arts électroniques, vidéo etc.) autour d'un point commun: la voix
Pauline Vaillancourt, Directrice générale

Choir Alberta (ACF)
#103, 10612 - 124 St., Edmonton AB T5N 1S4
Tel: 780-488-7464; *Fax:* 780-488-6403
info@albertachoralfederation.ca
www.albertachoralfederation.ca
To promote choral music within the communities of Alberta; to gain support for choral music through public policy
Lord Brendan, Executive Director

Choirs Ontario
1442 Bayview Ave., #A, Toronto ON M4G 3A7
Tel: 416-923-1144; *Fax:* 416-929-0415
Toll-Free: 866-935-1144
www.choirsontario.org
To promote choral singing in communities, schools & universities, places of worship, etc. throughout Ontario.
Rachel Rensink-Hoff, President
Elizabeth Shannon, Executive Director

Conservatory Canada
#61, 45 King St., London ON N6A 1B8
Tel: 519-433-3147; *Fax:* 519-433-7404
Toll-Free: 800-461-5367
officeadmin@conservatorycanada.ca
www.conservatorycanada.ca
To promote achievement in music through a comprehensive program of study, evaluation & recognition for teachers & students; to foster the development of musical talent & potential
Warwick Victoria, National Executive Director

Counterpoint Community Orchestra
PO Box 41, 552 Church St., Toronto ON M4Y 2E3
Tel: 416-654-9806
info@ccorchestra.org
www.ccorchestra.org
To foster pride as a LGBT positive orchestra; to perform for the community & promote equality within Toronto
Terry Kowalczuk, Music Director

Crowsnest Pass Symphony
PO Box 416, Blairmore AB T0K 0E0
Tel: 403-562-2405; *Fax:* 403-562-7501
To provide a vehicle for young people to learn & perform music; to give amateur adult musicians the opportunity to play classical music recreationally
Jerry Lonsbury, Conductor

Deep River Symphony Orchestra (DRSO)
PO Box 398, Deep River ON K0J 1P0
Tel: 613-584-4264
drsoemail@gmail.com
www.drso.ca
To promote the development & enjoyment of music in the Upper Ottawa Valley
Peter Morris, Music Director
Jane Craig, President

Deep Roots Music Cooperative
PO Box 2360, Wolfville NS B4P 2G9
Tel: 902-542-7668
info@deeprootsmusic.ca
www.deeprootsmusic.ca/cooperative
To develop year-round musical programs culminating in an annual festival, and to encourage meaningful connections between cultures, community groups, artists and audiences.
Peter Mowat, Chair

Early Music Vancouver (EMV)
1254 - 7 Ave. West, Vancouver BC V6H 1B6
Tel: 604-732-1610; *Fax:* 604-732-1602
www.earlymusic.bc.ca
To foster increased understanding & appreciation of early music by providing educational programs, high quality concerts at reasonable prices featuring both local & internationally acclaimed musicians & by providing informative publications
Tim Rendell, Managing Director
Matthew White, Artistic Director

East Coast Music Association (ECMA) / Association de la musique de la côte est
PO Box 31237, Halifax NS B3K 5Y1
Tel: 902-423-6770; *Fax:* 888-519-0346
Toll-Free: 800-513-4953
www.ecma.com
To develop, foster, promote & celebrate East Coast music locally & globally
Andy McLean, Executive Director

Edmonton Jazz Society (EJS)
11 Tommy Banks Way, Edmonton AB T6E 2M2
Tel: 780-432-0428; *Fax:* 780-433-3773
programming@yardbirdsuite.com
www.yardbirdsuite.com
To present, promote & develop the performance of live Jazz music in the City of Edmonton
Adrian Albert, President

Edmonton Opera Association
15230 - 128 Ave., Edmonton AB T5V 1A8
Tel: 780-424-4040; *Fax:* 780-429-0600
edmopera@edmontonopera.com
www.edmontonopera.com
To develop & promote opera as a dynamic & progressive art form; to attract & challenge audiences & artists through a creative program of opera production & education
Tim Yakimec, General Manager

Edmonton Symphony Orchestra (ESO)
9720 - 102 Ave. NW, Edmonton AB T5J 4B2
Tel: 780-428-1108
info@winspearcentre.com
www.edmontonsymphony.com
To foster appreciation & enjoyment of live, professional orchestral music through presenting concert performances, educational & community programs
Annemarie Petrov, Executive Director
Rob McAlear, Artistic Administrator

Edmonton Youth Orchestra Association (EYO)
PO Box 66041, Stn. Heritage, Edmonton AB T6J 6T4
Tel: 780-436-7932; *Fax:* 780-436-7932
eyo@shaw.ca
www.eyso.com
To provide young musicians with the opportunity to develop their orchestral skills & increase their knowledge & appreciation of music, while enriching the cultural life of the community through concerts & benefit performances
Michael Massey, Music Director

Ensemble contemporain de Montréal (ECM+)
3890, rue Clark, Montréal QC H2W 1W6
Tél: 514-524-0173; *Téléc:* 514-524-0179
info@ecm.qc.ca
www.ecm.qc.ca
Promouvoir la création de la musique canadienne par la performance, la formation et le recherche multidisciplinaire
Natalie Watanabe, Directrice générale
Véronique Lacroix, Directrice artistique

Ensemble vocal Ganymède
CP 476, Succ. C, Montréal QC H2L 4K4
Tél: 514-528-6302
contacter@evganymede.com
www.evganymede.com
Choeur d'hommes
Yvan Sabourin, Directeur

Etobicoke Philharmonic Orchestra (EPO)
PO Box 60002, 1500 Islington Ave, Toronto ON M9A 5G2
Tel: 416-239-5665
info@eporchestra.ca
www.eporchestra.ca
To provide an opportunity for trained amateur musicians to perform together & become acquainted with an orchestral repertoire; to provide the community with symphonic music, competently performed in a local setting; to assist serious music students in their studies through performance experience & a scholarship program
Judy Allan, President
Judy Gargaro, General Manager

Fédération des harmonies et des orchestres symphoniques du Québec (FHOSQ)
4545, av Pierre-de Coubertin, Montréal QC H1V 0B2
Tél: 514-252-3026; *Téléc:* 514-252-3115
info@fhosq.org
www.fhosq.org
Contribuer au développement et à l'amélioration des harmonies en tant que loisir éducatif et culturel
Chantal Isabelle, Directrice générale

Festival Chorus of Calgary
EPCOR Centre for Performing Arts, 205 - 8 Ave. SE, Calgary AB T2G 0K9
Tel: 403-294-7400
info@festivalchorus.ca
www.festivalchorus.ca
To present two concerts per year for the Marblehead community
Mel Kirby, Artistic Director

Foundation Assisting Canadian Talent on Recordings (FACTOR)
247 Spadina Ave., 3rd Fl., Toronto ON M5T 3A8
Tel: 416-696-2215; *Fax:* 416-351-7311
Toll-Free: 877-696-2215
general.info@factor.ca
www.factor.ca
To provide financial assistance for production of sound recordings, videos, syndicated radio programs & international tour support; English-language counterpart of Musicaction
Duncan McKie, President
Allison Outhit, Vice President, Operations

Fraser Valley Symphony Society (FVS)
PO Box 122, Abbotsford BC V2S 4N8
Tel: 604-744-9110
info@fraservalleysymphony.org
www.fraservalleysymphony.org
Lindsay Mellor, Music Director

Friends of Chamber Music
PO Box 38046, Stn. King Edward Mall, Vancouver BC V5Z 4L9
Tel: 604-722-1264
www.friendsofchambermusic.ca
To present the best in chamber music
Eric Wilson, Contact

Georgian Bay Symphony (GBS)
PO Box 133, 994 3rd Ave. East, Owen Sound ON N4K 5P1
Tel: 519-372-0212; *Fax:* 519-372-9023
gbs@bmts.com
www.georgianbaysymphony.ca
To enhance appreciation of music which includes growth & development of regional orchestra
François Koh, Music Director

Greater Victoria Youth Orchestra (GVYO)
1611 Quadra St., Victoria BC V8W 2L5
Tel: 250-360-1121; *Fax:* 250-381-3573
gvyo@telus.net
www.gvyo.org
To affirm & nourish the love of music in young people; to foster musical development of orchestra members; to serve as musical resource to the community at large
Sheila Redhead, Manager
Yariv Aloni, Music Director

Halton Mississauga Youth Orchestra (HMYO)
159 Cavendish Ct., Oakville ON L6J 5S3
Tel: 905-842-5569
info@hmyo.ca
www.hmyo.ca
To inspire, encourage & challenge young musicians to build their musical skills through the experience of various forms of orchestral music; to create an enjoyable environment that promotes teamwork, leadership & community involvement
Gregory Burton, Music Director

Hamilton Philharmonic Orchestra
10 MacNab St. South, Hamilton ON L8P 4Y3
Tel: 905-526-1677
communications@hpo.org
www.hpo.org
To provide artistically excellent music to patrons; to educate music students of all ages
Carol Kehoe, Executive Director
Neil Spaulding, Operations and Personnel Manager
Gemma New, Music Director

Hamilton Philharmonic Youth Orchestra (HPYO)
#129, 2 - 140 King St. East, Hamilton ON L8N 1B2
Tel: 905-869-4796
info@hpyo.com
www.hpyo.com
To provide young people with the joy & discipline of orchestral music and perform regular concerts to enrich the cultural landscape of Hamilton & area.
Debra French, Executive Director
Colin Clarke, Music Director

Hart House Orchestra
University of Toronto, 7 Hart House Circle, Toronto ON M5S 3H3
www.harthouseorchestra.ca
Zoe Dille, Programme Advisor
Henry Janzen, Director, Music

Huronia Symphony Orchestra (HSO)
PO Box 904, Stn. Main, Barrie ON L4M 4Y6
Tel: 705-721-4752
office@huroniasymphony.ca
www.huroniasymphony.ca
To operate & support a symphony orchestra in Simcoe County; to provide symphonic music for people of the area as well as an opportunity for children & youth to receive instruction in orchestral music
John Hemsted, President
Don MacLeod, General Manager

Oliver Balaburski, Artistic Director & Conductor

International Symphony Orchestra of Sarnia, Ontario & Port Huron, Michigan
251 North Vidal St., Sarnia ON N7T 5Y5
Tel: 519-337-7775
iso@rivernet.net
www.theiso.org
To provide cultural enrichment within the community by providing high calibre choral & symphonic performances; To reinforce strong commitment to youth music education and initiatives
Thomas K. Andison, President
Anne Brown, Executive Director
Douglas Bianchi, Music Director & Conductor

International Symphony Orchestra Youth String Ensemble
225 Davis St., Sarnia ON N7T 1B2
Tel: 519-337-7775; *Fax:* 519-337-1822
iso@rivernet.net
Anne Brown, Executive Director

Jazz Yukon
PO Box 31307, Whitehorse YT Y1A 5P7
Tel: 867-633-3300
info@jazzyukon.ca
www.jazzyukon.ca
To promote & present jazz in the Yukon through an annual integrated program of live jazz presentations & jazz education outreach

La Jeunesse Youth Orchestra (LJYO)
PO Box 134, Port Hope ON L1A 3W3
Toll-Free: 866-460-5596
info@ljyo.ca
www.ljyo.ca
To provide young musicians from the Port Hope area with the enriching experience of performing a wide range of symphonic music.
Michael Lyons, Music Director
Laurie Mitchell, Music Director

Jeunesses Musicales du Canada (JMC) / Jeunesses Musicales of Canada (JMC)
305, av du Mont-Royal est, Montréal QC H2T 1P8
Tél: 514-845-4108; *Téléc:* 514-845-8241
Ligne sans frais: 877-377-7951
www.jmcanada.ca
To promote Canadian musical artists & develop audiences
Danièle LeBlanc, Directeur général et artistique
Claudia Morissette, Directrice, Artistic Operations
Nathalie Allen, Directrice, Services financiers
Marie Lamoureux, Directrice, Communications

Kamloops Symphony (KSO)
PO Box 57, Kamloops BC V2C 5K3
Tel: 250-372-5000; *Fax:* 250-372-5089
info@kamloopssymphony.com
www.kamloopssymphony.com
To operate & promote a symphony orchestra for the Kamloops region
Kathy Humphreys, General Manager
Bruce Dunn, Music Director

Kingston Symphony Association (KSA)
PO Box 1616, #206, 11 Princess St., Kingston ON K7L 5C8
Tel: 613-546-9729; *Fax:* 613-546-8580
info@kingstonsymphony.on.ca
www.kingstonsymphony.on.ca
To maintain & produce professional orchestral & symphonic music in the Kingston area
Andrea Haughton, General Manager
Evan Mitchell, Music Director

Kingston Youth Orchestra
c/o Kingston Symphony Association, PO Box 1616, Kingston ON K7L 5C8
Tel: 613-546-9729; *Fax:* 613-546-8580
info@kingstonsymphony.on.ca
www.kingstonsymphony.on.ca/youth.cfm
Linda Craig, Manager

Kitchener-Waterloo Chamber Orchestra (KWCO)
F-168 Lexington Ct., Waterloo ON N2J 4R9
info@kwchamberorchestra.ca
www.kwchamberorchestra.ca
To present lesser-known orchestral music from the 18th and 19th century to the residents of the Kitchener-Waterloo area
Matthew Jones, Music Director

Kitchener-Waterloo Symphony Orchestra Association Inc. (KWSOA)
36 King St. West, Kitchener ON N2G 1A3
Tel: 519-745-4711; *Fax:* 519-745-4474
Toll-Free: 888-745-4717
info@kwsymphony.on.ca
kwsymphony.on.ca
To cultivate the tradition of live performance through the presentation of classical orchestral & popular music for the edification, enrichment, education & excitement of our community & beyond
Andrew Bennett, Executive Director
Edwin Outwater, Music Director, Artistic

Kitchener-Waterloo Symphony Youth Orchestra (KWSYO)
36 King St. West, Kitchener ON N2G 1A3
Tel: 519-745-4711; *Fax:* 519-745-4474
Toll-Free: 888-745-4717
info@kwsymphony.on.ca
www.kwsymphony.on.ca
Barbara Kaplanek, Education & Community Programs Manager, Youth Orchestra & Schools
Evan Mitchell, Youth Orchestra Conductor

Kiwanis Music Festival Association of Greater Toronto
1422 Bayview Ave., #A, Toronto ON M4G 3A7
Tel: 416-487-5885; *Fax:* 416-487-5784
kiwanismusic@bellnet.ca
kiwanismusictoronto.org
To bring together various choirs in music competitions
Pam Allen, General Manager

Korean-Canadian Symphony Orchestra (KGSO)
#203, 28 Finch Ave. West, Toronto ON M2N 2G7
Tel: 647-532-2578
info@kcso.ca
www.kcso.ca
To provide concerts to people in the GTA & to promote Korean-Canadian musicians
June Choi, President
Richard Lee, Music Director

Ladies' Morning Musical Club (LMMC) / Les Matinées de musique de chambre
#12, 1410 Guy St., Montréal QC H3H 2L7
Tel: 514-932-6796; *Fax:* 514-932-0510
lmmc@qc.aibn.com
www.lmmc.ca
Constance V. Pathy, President
Rosemary Neville, Secretary-Treasurer

Lethbridge Symphony Orchestra (LSO)
PO Box 1101, Lethbridge AB T1J 4A2
Tel: 403-328-6808; *Fax:* 403-380-4418
info@lethbridgesymphony.org
www.lethbridgesymphony.org
To promote the orchestra & provide memorable musical experiences for their audiences.
Nick Sullivan, Executive Director
Melanie Gattiker, Manager, Operations
Glenn Klassen, Music Director

London Community Orchestra (LCO)
838 Wellington St., London ON N6A 3S7
info@lco-on.ca
lco-on.ca
To give concerts & to sponsor local young artists as soloists
Sally Vernon, President
Leonard Ingrao, Music Director

London Youth Symphony (LYS)
PO Box 553, Stn. B, London ON N6A 4W8
Tel: 519-868-6983
lysymphony@hotmail.com
www.windmillwebworks.ddns.net/londonyouthsymphony/
To provide the region's most talented young musicians with the opportunity to build self-discipline, confidence & team spirit within an outstanding symphonic environment that offers professional directorship & coaching
Len Ingrao, Artistic Director

Manitoba Band Association
131 Rouge Road, Winnipeg MB R3K 1J5
Tel: 204-663-1226
mbband@shaw.ca
www.mbband.org
To promote growth & development of bands in Manitoba
John Balsillie, Executive Director

Manitoba Chamber Orchestra (MCO)
Portage Place, #y300, 393 Portage Ave., Winnipeg MB R3B 3H6
Tel: 204-783-7377; *Fax:* 204-783-7383
info@themco.ca
www.manitobachamberorchestra.org
To perform chamber orchestra repertoire with emphasis on premiering new Canadian works & Canadian soloists
Anne Manson, Music Director
Vicki Young, General Manager

Manitoba Music
#1, 376 Donald St., Winnipeg MB R3B 2J2
Tel: 204-942-8650; *Fax:* 204-942-6083
info@manitobamusic.com
www.manitobamusic.com
To develop and sustain the Manitoba music community and industry to their fullest potential
Sean McManus, Executive Director

Manitoba Opera Association Inc.
#1060, 555 Main St., Winnipeg MB R3B 1C3
Tel: 204-942-7479; *Fax:* 204-949-0377
mbopera@manitobaopera.mb.ca
www.manitobaopera.mb.ca
To present & develop appreciation for art of opera in Manitoba; to assist in development of Canadian talent, with emphasis on Manitobans
Larry Desrochers, General Director & CEO

Mariposa Folk Foundation
PO Box 383, Orillia ON L3V 6J8
Tel: 705-326-3655; *Fax:* 705-326-5963
officemanager@mariposafolk.com
www.mariposafolk.com
To promote & preserve folk arts in Canada through song, story, dance, & craft.
Pam Carter, President

McGill Chamber Orchestra / Orchestre de chambre McGill
5459 Earnscliffe Ave., Montréal QC H3X 2P8
Tel: 514-487-5190; *Fax:* 514-487-7390
info@ocm-mco.org
www.ocm-mco.org
Boris Brott, Artistic Director
Taras Kulish, Executive Director

Music BC Industry Association (PMIA)
#100, 938 Howe St., Vancouver BC V6Z 1N9
Tel: 604-873-1914; *Fax:* 604-873-9686
Toll-Free: 888-866-8570
info@musicbc.org
www.musicbc.org
To address key issues; to implement positive change by presenting a strong voice to government, business & community; To enhance the profile of the BC music industry in the international marketplace; To promote communication; To stimulate activity & employment
Savannah Wellman, Program Manager

Music Canada
85 Mowat Ave., Toronto ON M6K 3E3
Tel: 416-967-7272; *Fax:* 416-967-9415
info@musiccanada.com
www.musiccanada.com
To develop & promote high ethical standards in the creation, manufacture and marketing of sound recordings.
Graham Henderson, President

Music for Young Children (MYC) / Musique pour jeunes enfants
39 Leacock Way, Kanata ON K2K 1T1
Tel: 613-592-7565; *Fax:* 613-592-9353
Toll-Free: 800-561-1692
myc@myc.com
www.myc.com
To develop, deliver & support comprehensive entry level music education programs of the finest quality
Janice Reade, Manager, Public Relations

Music Industries Association of Canada (MIAC) / Association canadienne des industries de la musique
#310, 3-1750 The Queensway, Toronto ON M9C 5H5
Tel: 416-490-1871; *Fax:* 866-524-0037
Toll-Free: 877-480-6422
info@miac.net
www.miac.net
To represent Canadian manufacturers, distributors, retailers & wholesalers of musical instruments & accessories, sound

reinforcement/lighting products, published music & computer music software

Music Managers Forum Canada
1731 Lawrence Ave. East, Toronto ON M1R 2X7
Tel: 416-462-9160
info@musicmanagersforum.ca
musicmanagersforum.ca
To be a source of information for Canadian musicians, artists & managers
Ryhna Thompson, President
Jamie New Johnson, Manager, Operations

Music Nova Scotia
2157 Gottingen St., 2nd Fl., Halifax NS B3K 3B5
Tel: 902-423-6271; *Fax:* 902-423-8841
Toll-Free: 888-343-6426
info@musicnovascotia.ca
www.musicnovascotia.ca
To encourage the creation, development, growth and promotion of Nova Scotia's music industry.
Scott Long, Executive Director

Music NWT
PO Box 127, Yellowknife NT X1A 2N1
info@musicnwt.ca
www.musicnwt.ca
To bring together musicians, offers workshops & other resources, & provides networking opportunities
Mike Filipowitsch, Executive Director

Music PEI
PO Box 2371, Charlottetown PE C1A 8C1
Tel: 902-894-6734; *Fax:* 902-894-4404
music@musicpei.com
www.musicpei.com
To promote, foster and develop artists and the music industry on PEI.
Rob Oakie, Executive Director

Music Yukon
#416, 108 Elliott St., Whitehorse YT Y1A 6C4
Tel: 867-456-8742
office@musicyukon.com
www.musicyukon.com
To promote the Yukon music industry
Kelly Proudfoot, President
Kim Winnicky, Executive Director

Music/Musique NB
#9, 140 Botsford St., Moncton NB E1C 4X4
Tel: 506-383-4662; *Fax:* 506-383-6171
contact@musicnb.org
musicnb.org
To support musicians, managers & businesses involved in the music industry in New Brunswick.
Richard Hornsby, President
Jean Surette, Executive Director

Musicaction
#2, 4385, rue Saint-Hubert, Montréal QC H2J 2X1
Tél: 514-861-8444; *Téléc:* 514-861-4423
Ligne sans frais: 800-861-5561
info@musicaction.ca
www.musicaction.ca
Développement de la musique vocale francophone au Canada
Louise Chenail, Directrice générale

MusicNL
186 Duckworth St., St. John's NL A1C 1G5
Tel: 709-754-2574; *Fax:* 709-754-5758
info@musicnl.ca
www.musicnl.ca
To promote, encourage & develop the music from Newfoundland & Labrador, in all its forms, whether written, recorded or in live performances
David Chafe, President
Denis Parker, Executive Director

National Arts Centre Orchestra of Canada (NACO) / Orchestre du Centre national des Arts (OCNA)
PO Box 1534, Stn. B, Ottawa ON K1P 5W1
Tel: 613-947-7000; *Toll-Free:* 866-850-2787
info@nac-cna.ca
nac-cna.ca
Peter Herrndorf, President & Chief Executive Officer
Alexander Shelley, Music Director

National Shevchenko Musical Ensemble Guild of Canada
626 Bathurst St., Toronto ON M5S 2R1
Tel: 416-533-2725; *Fax:* 416-533-6348
info-sme@bellnet.ca
www.shevchenkomusic.com
To provide instruction in vocal, instrumental & dance for youth & adults by maintaining the Shevchenko Musical Ensemble & Shevchenko School of Dance & Music; to perpetuate Ukrainian cultural traditions
Ginger Kautto, Administrator

National Youth Orchestra Canada (NYOC) / Orchestre national des jeunes Canada (ONJC)
#500, 59 Adelaide St. East, Toronto ON M5C 1K6
Tel: 416-532-4470; *Fax:* 416-532-6879
Toll-Free: 888-532-4470
info@nyoc.org
www.nyoc.org
To provide comprehensive training for Canada's best young classical musicians
Barbara Smith, Executive Director

Newfoundland Symphony Orchestra Association (NSO)
Arts & Culture Centre, PO Box 23125, Stn. Churchill Square, St. John's NL A1B 4J9
Tel: 709-722-4441; *Fax:* 709-753-0561
nso@nsomusic.ca
www.nso-music.com
To foster & promote in all age groups of the general public of the province an interest in & an appreciation of music; to provide the province with a symphony orchestra of the highest possible standard; to provide professional musicians, highly skilled amateur players & talented students with the opportunity of performing
Neil Edwards, CEO
Marc David, Music Director

Newfoundland Symphony Youth Orchestra (NSYO)
18 Hazelwood Cres., St. John's NL A1E 6B3
Tel: 709-690-2259
info@nsyo.ca
www.nsyo.ca
To encourage and develop the musical abilities of young musicians; To play high quality orchestral music
Laura Ivany, Executive Director
Grant Etchegary, Artistic Director

Niagara Youth Orchestra Association
#148, 12 - 111 Fourth Ave., St Catharines ON L2S 3P5
Tel: 905-323-5892
music@niagarayouthorchestra.ca
www.niagarayouthorchestra.ca
To foster an interest & understanding of orchestral music in the youth of the Niagara Region
Laura Thomas, Music Director

Northumberland Orchestra Society (NOC)
PO Box 1012, Cobourg ON K9A 4W4
Tel: 905-376-3021
www.northumberlandmusic.ca
To perform orchestral and choral music to the Northumberland area; To encourage young local musicians through inclusion and education
John Kraus, Music Director & Conductor

Nova Scotia Band Association
108 Grindstone Dr., Halifax NS B3R 0A6
www.novascotiabandassociation.com
To support and promote the development of bands throughout the province of Nova Scotia through communication, coordination, program development, advocacy and lobbying at the provincial level.
Mark Hopkins, President

Nova Scotia Youth Orchestra
6199 Chebucto Rd., Halifax NS B3L 1K7
Tel: 902-423-5984
nsyo@ns.sympatico.ca
www.novascotiayouthorchestra.com
To provide young musicians with the finest orchestral training; to provide live orchestral music to audiences in Nova Scotia
Dinuk Wijeratne, Music Director

Oakville Chamber Orchestra
PO Box 76036, 1500 Upper Middle Rd. West, Oakville ON L6M 3H5
Tel: 905-483-6787
mail@oakvillechamber.org
www.oakvillechamber.org
To enrich the cultural landscape of Oakville by performing chamber music concerts, developing local amateur musicians, and promoting Canadian soloists
Kevin Fernandez, President
Charles Demuynck, Music Director

Oakville Symphony Orchestra (OSO)
#310, 200 North Service Rd. West, Oakville ON L6M 2Y1
Tel: 905-338-1462; *Fax:* 905-338-7954
oakville.symphony@cogeco.ca
www.oakvillesymphony.com
To bring audiences a variety of music for all ages & to contribute to the cultural growth of the community
Peggy Steele, General Manager

Okanagan Symphony Society
865 Bernard Ave., Kelowna BC V1Y 6P6
Tel: 250-763-7544
admin@okanagansymphony.com
okanagansymphony.com
To provide the communities of the Okanagan Valley with an orchestra that is committed to excellence in the performance of classical music
Robert Barr, Executive Director
Rosemary Thomson, Music Director

Ontario Band Association
c/o Membership Co-ordinator, 198 Fincham Ave., Markham ON L3P 4B5
membership@onband.ca
www.onband.ca
To promote & develop musical, educational & cultural values of bands in Ontario by sponsoring annual band & solo instrument competition, composition competition, original works
Andria Kilbride, President

Ontario Philharmonic (OP)
PO Box 444, Oshawa ON L1H 7L5
Tel: 905-579-6711
contact@ontariophil.ca
www.ontariophil.ca
To bring fine orchestral music to residents of Durham Region, Toronto, and the GTA
Laura Vaillancourt, Executive Director
Marco Parisotto, Music Director

L'Opéra de Montréal (ODM) / Montréal Opera
260, boul de Maisonneuve ouest, Montréal QC H2X 1Y9
Tél: 514-985-2222; *Téléc:* 514-985-2219
Ligne sans frais: 877-385-2222
info@operadeMontréal.com
www.operadeMontréal.com
Afin de présenter des productions d'opéra de comparable qualité et originalité à ceux observés dans les plus grands opéras du monde; cherche la contribution du personnel de création de niveaux local et national; ainsi que d'inviter les meilleurs artistes de l'étranger; soutient l'émergence de nouveaux talents opéra canadienne
Pierre Dufour, Directeur général
Louis Bouchard, Directrice, Services financiers et administratifs
Michel Beulac, Directeur Artistique
Monique Denis, Responsable, Dons et commandites
Pierre Vachon, Directeur, Communications, communauté et éducation
Bernard Stotland, Président
Chantal Lambert, Directrice, Atelier Lyrique

Opéra de Québec
1220, av Taché, Québec QC G1R 3B4
Tél: 418-529-4142; *Téléc:* 418-529-3735
operaqc@mediom.qc.ca
www.operadeQuébec.qc.ca
Produire des spectacles d'opéra professionnels à Québec
Gaston Déry, Président
Grégoire Legendre, Directeur général et artistique

Opera Lyra
#110, 2 Daly Ave., Ottawa ON K1N 6E2
Tel: 613-233-9200; *Fax:* 613-233-5431
Toll-Free: 877-233-5972
frontdesk@operalyra.ca
www.operalyra.ca
Opera Lyra's mandate is to produce and present opera productions in the National Capital Region of the highest quality; to promote opera as an art form and make it as accessible to as large a segment of the population as possible through community outreach and education; and, wherever possible, to encourage, nurture and support Canadian artists.
Elizabeth Howarth, General Director

Opera.ca
#6286, 2100 Bloor St. West, Toronto ON M6S 5A5
Tel: 416-591-7222
www.opera.ca
Opera.ca works with members across the country to advance the interests of Canada's opera community and create greater opportunity for opera audiences and professionals alike.
Christina Loewen, Executive Director
D. Liu, Coordinator, Membership & Communications

Orchestra Toronto (OT)
5040 Yonge St., Toronto ON M2N 6R8
Tel: 416-467-7142
info@orchestratoronto.ca
orchestratoronto.ca
To provide affordable family entertainment, music education, & full repertoire in all its programs
Samantha Little, Executive Director
Kevin Mallon, Music Director

Orchestras Canada (OC) / Orchestres Canada
PO Box 2386, Peterborough ON K9J 2Y8
Tel: 416-366-8834
info@oc.ca
www.orchestrascanada.org
To strengthen Canada's orchestral community through leadership in advocacy, education, & professional development
Katherine Carleton, Executive Director

Orchestras Mississauga
Living Arts Centre, 4141 Living Arts Dr., 2nd Fl., Mississauga ON L5B 4B8
Tel: 905-615-4405; *Fax:* 905-615-4402
www.mississaugasymphony.ca
To perform & promote orchestral music; to ensure its accessibility to all segments of the community
Denis Mastromonaco, Music Director
Eileen Keown, General Manager

Orchestre de chambre de Montréal (OCM) / Montréal Chamber Orchestra (MCO)
#2001, 1, Place Ville Marie, Montréal QC H3B 2C4
Tél: 514-871-1224
info@mco-ocm.qc.ca
www.mco-ocm.qc.ca
Se consacrer au répertoire pour ensemble de chambre & oeuvres canadiennes
Natalia Boureaud, Executive Director
Wanda Kaluzny, Music Director

Orchestre symphonique de Montréal
1600, rue Saint-Urbain, Montréal QC H2X 0S1
Tél: 514-840-7400; *Téléc:* 514-842-0728
Ligne sans frais: 888-842-9951
www.osm.ca
De diffuser, au plus large public possible, le répertoire mondial de la musique symphonique, & les artistes de niveau international; assumer son rôle social & institutionnel
Madeleine Careau, Président Directeur Général
Kent Nagano, Directeur musical

Orchestre symphonique de Québec
#250, 437, Grande Allée Est, Québec QC G1R 2J5
Tél: 418-643-8486
www.osq.org
Interpréter le répertoire symphonique; être le principal moteur de l'activité musicale de la région. L'OSM est reconnu comme un organisme de grande qualité, dynamique, accessible, et financièrement sain
Elizabeth Tessier, Présidente-directrice générale par intérim
Tristan Lemieux, Directeur musical

Orchestre symphonique de Sherbrooke (OSS) / Sherbrooke Symphony Orchestra
135, rue Don Bosco Nord, Sherbrooke QC J1L 1E5
Tél: 819-821-0227;
Ligne sans frais: 866-821-0227
info@ossherbrooke.com
www.ossherbrooke.com
Faire connaître la musique symphonique dans la région et permettre aux musiciens de la région de jouer dans un orchestre professionnel
Nicolas Bélanger, Président Directeur Général
Stéphane Laforest, Directeur artistique

Orchestre symphonique de Trois-Rivières (OSTR)
CP 1281, Trois-Rivières QC G9A 5K8
Tél: 819-373-5340; *Téléc:* 819-373-6693
administration@ostr.ca
www.ostr.ca
Poursuivre l'atteinte des objectifs inhérents à ses axes de développement: éducation, implication dans son milieu, diffusion de musique symphonique, création musicale et diffusion de nouveaux produits
Natalie Rousseau, Directrice générale
Jacques Lacombe, Directeur artistique

Orchestre symphonique des jeunes de Montréal (OSJM)
CP 83566, Succ. Garnier, Montréal QC H2J 4E9
Tél: 514-645-0311; *Téléc:* 514-524-9894
osjMontréal@gmail.com
www.osjm.org
Présenter le jeune musicien de talent à un auditoire et lui fournir une expérience formative sous la supervision d'artistes reconnus; encourager et soutenir le choix d'une carrière musicale qui peut mener à un grand orchestre; promouvoir un intérêt dans les concerts et développer un soutien plus diversifié dans les activités de l'orchestre; fournir à l'entreprise privée l'occasion de participer plus activement dans une activité culturelle d'envergure et l'aider à faire apprécier son rôle dans la communauté
Anne-Marie Desbiens, Directrice générale

Orchestre symphonique des jeunes du West Island (OSJWI) / West Island Youth Symphony Orchestra (WIYSO)
CP 1028, Succ. Pointe-Claire, Pointe-Claire QC H9S 4H9
Tél: 514-912-5451
info@osjwi.qc.ca
www.osjwi.qc.ca
Permettre aux jeunes de 8-25 ans de jouer dans un orchestre regroupant tous les instruments sous la direction d'un chef professionel
Jackie Landry-Bigelow, Coordinatrice
Stewart Grant, Directeur artistique

Orchestre symphonique des jeunes Philippe-Filion
1200, boul des Hêtres, Shawinigan QC G9N 6V3
Tél: 819-539-6000
info@aosjpf.ca
www.aosjpf.ca
Offrir une formation orchestrale spécialisé pour jeunes musiciens.
Michel Kozlovsky, Chef d'orchestre

Orchestre symphonique du Saguenay-Lac-St-Jean (OSSLSJ)
202, rue Jacques-Cartier Est, Chicoutimi QC G7H 6R8
Tél: 418-545-3409; *Téléc:* 418-545-8287
info@lorchestre.org
www.lorchestre.org
Produire et diffuser des concerts professionnels à travers tout le Saguenay-Lac-Saint-Jean en regard des enjeux financiers et des structures d'accueil existantes. Ses qualités artistiques et administratives en constante évolution lui permettent d'exercer un leadership au sein des organismes musicaux régionaux, basé sur un partenariat serré avec le milieu, au service du développement de sa discipline et de sa communauté
Jacques Clément, Directeur artisique

Orchestre symphonique régional Abitibi-Témiscamingue
CP 2305, Rouyn-Noranda QC J9X 5A9
Tél: 819-762-0043
info@osrat.ca
www.osrat.ca
Diffusion de la musique classique et integration de la relève
Jacques Marchand, Directeur artistique

Orillia Youth Symphony Orchestra (OYSO)
c/o Mayumi Kumagai, 168 Parkview Ave., Orillia ON L3V 4M3
Tel: 702-241-9502
orilliayouthsymphonyorchestra@gmail.com
www.oyso.ca
To offer youth 6-24 years of age to play in a symphonic orchestra; to participate in community events
Mayumi Kumagai, Music Director

Ottawa Symphony Orchestra Inc. (OSO) / Orchestre symphonique d'Ottawa
#250, 2 Daly Ave., Ottawa ON K1N 6E2
Tel: 613-231-7802; *Fax:* 613-231-3610
gm@ottawasymphony.com
www.ottawasymphony.com
To develop the highest possible artistic level of performance of symphonic repertoire among local musicians, local & Canadian soloists, Canadian music, partnership opportunities for performance with other local performing arts organizations, educational outreach opportunities for young audiences & young performers
Vanessa Sutton, General Manager

Ottawa Youth Orchestra Academy (OYO) / L'Orchestre des jeunes d'Ottawa
#38, 2450 Lancaster Rd., Ottawa ON K1B 5N3
Tel: 613-233-9318; *Fax:* 613-233-5038
info@oyoa-aojo.ca
www.oyoa-aojo.ca
To provide high-quality orchestral training to youth in the Ottawa region
John Gomez, Conductor

Pacific Opera Victoria (POV)
#500, 1815 Blanshard St., Victoria BC V8T 5A4
Tel: 250-382-1641; *Fax:* 250-382-4944
www.pov.bc.ca
To create a dynamic operatic experience, & to inspire audiences, artists & community
Timothy Vernon, Artistic Director
Patrick Corrigan, Director, Markting & Development

Pembroke Symphony Orchestra
PO Box 374, Pembroke ON K8A 6X6
Tel: 613-587-4826
pembrokesymphony.org
To provide members with the opportunity to perform classical and modern music in an orchestral setting; To share orchestral music with the listening public
Angus Armstrong, Music Director
Gail Marion, President

Peterborough Symphony Orchestra (PSO)
PO Box 1135, Peterborough ON K9J 7H4
Tel: 705-742-1992
info@thepso.org
www.thepso.org
To perform & develop excellence in symphonic music that will enrich, stimulate & attract the widest possible audience by presenting quality orchestral music to the people of Peterborough & beyond
Deanna Guttman, Executive Director
Michael Newnham, Music Director

Prairie Saengerbund Choir Association
4823 Claret St. NW, Calgary AB T2L 1B9
Tel: 403-284-3731; *Fax:* 403-284-1470
To share, enhance, encourage & celebrate our wonderful German musical heritage
Ellen Rossi, Contact

Prince Edward Island Symphony Society (PEISO)
PO Box 185, Charlottetown PE C1A 7K4
Tel: 902-892-4333
admin@peisymphony.com
www.peisymphony.com
To establish & promote symphonic music; to further & foster appreciation of musical education; to promote the welfare of musicians; to give & arrange performances, entertainments & concerts; to employ teachers & instructors to inform the public & awaken interest
Mark Shapiro, Music Director

Prince George Symphony Orchestra Society (PGSO)
2880 - 15 Ave., Prince George BC V2M 1T1
Tel: 250-562-0800; *Fax:* 250-562-0844
www.pgso.com
To provide symphonic music for Prince George & region consistent with Prince George Symphony Orchestra artistic policy that facilitates artistic development of its players; to foster & facilitate positive community image & financial responsiblity so that a wide spectrum of musical experiences is offered to players & audiences alike
Jeremy Stewart, General Manager

The Queen of Puddings Music Theatre Company
The Case Good Warehouse, Bldg. 74, Studio 206, 55 Mill St., Toronto ON M5A 3C4
Tel: 416-203-4149; *Fax:* 416-203-8027
queenofpuddings@bellnet.ca
www.queenofpuddingsmusictheatre.com
Queen of Puddings has consistently produced provocative, dramatic presentations that have challenged the parameters of the opera genre. The company works solely with Canadian artists.
Dairine Ni Mheadhra, Artistic Director
John Hess, Artistic Director

Quinte Symphony
c/o Quinte Arts Council, PO Box 22113, Belleville ON K8N 2Z5
Tel: 613-962-7430
info@quintesymphony.com
www.quintesymphony.com

Committed to enriching the Quinte community by actively promoting an appreciation of Classical & Canadian orchestral music
Dan Tremblay, Music Director

Radio Starmaker Fund
#203, 372 Bay St., Toronto ON M5H 2W9
Tel: 416-597-6622; *Fax:* 416-597-2760
Toll-Free: 888-256-2211
info@starmaker.ca
www.starmaker.ca
To provide funding for Canadian musicians, bands & labels that have achieved a proven "track record" with previous work
Chip Sutherland, Executive Director

Red Deer Symphony Orchestra
Culture Services Centre, 3827 - 39th St., Red Deer AB T4N 0Y6
Tel: 403-340-2948
reddeersymphony@telus.net
www.rdso.ca
To provide nationally-recognized, quality symphonic music to central Alberta; To encourage an appreciation for the performance and development of symphonic music in central Alberta
Chandra Kastern, Executive Director
Claude Lapalme, Music Director

Regina Symphony Orchestra (RSO)
2424 College Ave., Regina SK S4P 1C8
Tel: 306-791-6395; *Fax:* 306-586-2133
info@reginasymphony.com
reginasymphony.com
To promote & enhance the performance & enjoyment of live orchestral music in Regina & southern Saskatchewan & contribute to the cultural life of the city, province & nation
Tanya Derksen, Executive Director
Victor Sawa, Music Director

Richmond Delta Youth Orchestra
PO Box 26064, Stn. Central, Richmond BC V6Y 3V3
Tel: 604-365-3584
admin@rdyo.ca
www.rdyo.ca
To encourage young musicians to excel through education and performance; To provide a comprehensive and balanced musical education as a member of an ensemble; To promote an understanding and appreciation of orchestral music in the community at large
Stephen Robb, Music Director

Richmond Orchestra & Chorus Association
#130, 10691 Shellbridge Way, Richmond BC V6X 2W8
Tel: 604-276-2747; *Fax:* 604-270-3644
www.roca.ca
To build community connections and enrich the Richmond cultural scene by performing orchestral & choral music; To nurture musical talent and provide community service
Paul Dufour, Administrator

Royal Canadian College of Organists (RCCO) / Collège royal canadien des organistes (CRCO)
#202, 204 St. George St., Toronto ON M5R 2N5
Tel: 416-929-6400; *Fax:* 416-929-2265
info@rcco.ca
www.rcco.ca
To promote a high standard of organ playing, choral directing, church music & composition; to hold examinations in organ playing, choir directing, theory & general knowledge of music; to encourage recitals; to increase the understanding among church musicisans, authorities & the public of matters relating to church music
Peter Bishop, President
Elizabeth Shannon, Executive Director

Royal Conservatory Orchestra
273 Bloor St. West, Toronto ON M5S 1W2
Tel: 416-408-2824; *Fax:* 416-408-5025
www.rcmusic.ca

Saskatchewan Band Association (SBA)
34 Sunset Dr. North, Yorkton SK S3N 3K9
Tel: 306-783-2263; *Fax:* 866-221-1879
Toll-Free: 877-475-2263
sask.band@sasktel.net
www.saskband.org
To promote & support instrumental music in Saskatchewan; To act as a voice on issues that affect bands in Saskatchewan
Chad Huel, President

Saskatchewan Orchestral Association, Inc. (SOA)
2042 Princess St., Regina SK S4T 3Z4
Tel: 306-546-3050
info@saskorchestras.com
www.saskorchestras.com
To serve as resource base & coordinating body for orchestral & string programs in Saskatchewan; To procure funds to make achievement of goals & objectives of SOA possible
Tara Solheim, Executive Director

Saskatchewan Recording Industry Association (SRIA)
1831 College Ave., 3rd Fl., Regina SK S4P 4V5
Tel: 306-347-7735; *Fax:* 306-347-7735
Toll-Free: 800-347-0676
info@saskmusic.org
www.saskmusic.org
To develop & promote the music & sound recording industry of Saskatchewan
Mike Dawson, Executive Director

Saskatoon Symphony Society (SSO)
408 - 20 St. West, Saskatoon SK S7M 0X4
Tel: 306-665-6414; *Toll-Free:* 888-639-7770
marketing@saskatoonsymphony.org
saskatoonsymphony.org
To promote, encourage & support symphonic & classical music in Saskatoon & elsewhere in Saskatchewan
Mark Turner, Executive Director
Eric Paetkau, Music Director

Saskatoon Youth Orchestra
PO Box 21108, Saskatoon SK S7H 5N9
Tel: 306-955-6336
info@syo.ca
syo.ca
To provide young musicians in the Saskatoon area with an opportunity to improve their playing skills in a full orchestral ensemble; To enruch the cultural landscape of the city of Saskatoon and the province of Saskatchewan at large
Paul Sinkewicz, Executive Director
Richard Carnegie, Music Director
Bernadette Wilson, Music Director

Sault Symphony Association / Orchestre symphonique de Sault Ste-Marie
864 Queen St. East, Sault Ste Marie ON P6A 2B4
Tel: 705-945-5337; *Fax:* 705-945-8865
saultsymphonyorchestra@gmail.com
www.saultsymphony.ca
To promote symphonic music in Sault Ste Marie, Ontario & the surrounding region
Angela Rasaiah, President
John Wilkinson, Artistic Director

Scarborough Philharmonic Orchestra
#209, 3007 Kingston Rd., Toronto ON M1M 1P1
Tel: 416-429-0007
spo@spo.ca
www.spo.ca
To enrich the cultural life of Scarborough, through the promotion & presentation of high calibre musical performances; To develop a strong & financially viable organization
Sue Payne, Executive Director
Ronald Royer, Music Director

Scotia Chamber Players
6181 Lady Hammond Rd., Halifax NS B3K 2R9
Tel: 902-429-9467; *Fax:* 902-425-6785
admin@scotiafestival.ns.ca
www.scotiafestival.ns.ca
To enhance the quality of music by producing an annual festival of world-class chamber music in study & performance for the benefit of musicians, students & audiences
Christopher Wilcox, Managing Director

Screen Composers Guild of Canada (SCGC)
41 Valleybrook Dr., Toronto ON M3B 2S6
Tel: 416-410-5076; *Fax:* 416-410-4516
Toll-Free: 866-657-1117
info@screencomposers.ca
www.screencomposers.ca
To improve the status & quality of music as it applies to film/tv/new media through education & the professional development of its members & the producing community; to represent & communicate the interests of its members to the music & film/tv/new media industries as well as other institutions; to collaborate with trade & industry associations with common interests; to represent all Canadian composers within the certified territories & producer entities detailed in our certification under the Canadian Status of the Artist Act, as the exclusive organization for collective negotiations

Maria Topalovich, Executive Director
Tonya Dedrick, Manager, Operations

Société chorale de Saint-Lambert / St. Lambert Choral Society
CP 36546, Saint-Lambert QC J4P 2S8
Tél: 450-878-0200
info.choeur.scsl@gmail.com
www.chorale-stlambert.qc.ca
De promouvoir et de recueillir une appréciation pour la musique chorale
David Christiani, Directeur Artistique

Société Pro Musica Inc. / Pro Musica Society Inc.
#201, 3505, rue Ste-Famille, Montréal QC H2X 2L3
Tél: 514-845-0532; *Téléc:* 514-845-1500
Ligne sans frais: 877-445-0532
concerts@promusica.qc.ca
www.promusica.qc.ca
Promouvoir et présenter à Montréal la plus belle musique de chambre par les meilleurs interprètes d'ici et d'ailleurs; dans la série TOPAZE, promouvoir et offrir aux jeunes familles de meilleures conditions pour assister aux concerts avec un atelier d'animation musicale pour les enfants
Louise-Andrée Baril, Directrice artistique
Monique Dubé, Directrice générale

Songwriters Association of Canada (SAC) / Association des auteurs-compositeurs canadiens
41 Valleybrook Dr., Toronto ON M3B 2S6
Tel: 416-961-1588; *Fax:* 416-961-2040
Toll-Free: 866-456-7664
sac@songwriters.ca
www.songwriters.ca
To protect & develop the creative & business environments for songwriters in Canada & around the world
Isabel Crack, Managing Director
Greg Johnston, President

Soundstreams Canada
#302, 579 Richmond St. West, Toronto ON M5V 1Y6
Tel: 416-504-1282; *Fax:* 416-504-1285
info@soundstreams.ca
www.soundstreams.ca
To foster & promote the development of 20th century music & music by Canadian composers, through the sponsorship of concerts, musical theatre works for young audiences, festivals & special events, recording projects, the commissioning of new works by Canadian composers & touring of Canadian artists
Ben Dietschi, Executive Director

South Saskatchewan Youth Orchestra (SSYO)
PO Box 868, Lumsden SK S0G 3C0
Tel: 306-761-2576
www.ssyo.ca
To provide orchestral training to young musicians in Southern Saskatchewan
Alan Denike, Music Director

Sudbury Symphony Orchestra Association Inc. (SSO) / Orchestre symphonique de Sudbury inc
303 York St., Sudbury ON P3E 2A5
Tel: 705-673-1280; *Fax:* 705-673-1434
info@sudburysymphony.com
www.sudburysymphony.com
To provide the opportunity for a broad spectrum of the public in the Sudbury Region & surrounding area to attend a stimulating program of concerts; to maintain an environment & organization which encourages artistic responsibility & commitment; to attract & maintain private & public funding in order to achieve accessibility & continuity through financial stability; to increase the awareness & appreciation of music in the community; to provide a vehicle for the participation in & ongoing development of the performance of orchestral music; to increase the awareness, appreciation & performance of Canadian music in the community
Jennifer McGillivray, Executive Director

Sudbury Youth Orchestra Inc.
PO Box 2241, Stn. A, Sudbury ON P3A 4S1
Tel: 705-566-8101
sudburyyouthorch@gmail.com
www.sudburyyouthorchestra.ca
To foster an appreciation of orchestral music; to create opportunities for orchestral performance; to provide access to education & training in an orchestral setting for the youth of Sudbury & area
Jamie Arrowsmith, Music Director

Surrey Symphony Society (SSS)
PO Box 39083, Stn. Panorama, #100, 15157 - 56th Ave., Surrey BC V3S 9A0
www.surreysymphony.com
To expand an appreciation of orchestral music among young musicians & to share this with the community through public performance
Heather Christiansen, General Manager

Symphony New Brunswick / Symphonie Nouveau-Brunswick
Brunswick Square, 39 King St., Level III, Saint John NB E2L 4W3
Tel: 506-634-8379; *Fax:* 506-634-0843
symphony@nbnet.nb.ca
www.symphonynb.com
To present high-quality, live orchestral & chamber music from all periods & to promote the appreciation of music through educational activities in New Brunswick
Jennifer Grant, General Manager
Michael Newnham, Music Director

Symphony Nova Scotia (SNS)
Park Lane Mall, PO Box 218, #301, 5657 Spring Garden Rd., Halifax NS B3J 3R4
Tel: 902-421-1300; *Fax:* 902-422-1209
info@symphonyns.ca
www.symphonynovascotia.ca
To enhance the quality of life of the citizens of Nova Scotia through high quality, professionally performed orchestral music
Christopher Wilkinson, Chief Executive Officer
Bernhard Gueller, Music Director

Symphony on the Bay
#300, 1100 Burloak Dr., Burlington ON L7L 6B2
Tel: 905-526-6690
info@symphonyonthebay.ca
symphonyonthebay.com
To enrich the cultural life of the Hamilton & surrounding area by maintaining a full-size community symphony orchestra; to perform a wide repertoire of symphonic music, including works by Canadian composers; to make great symphonic music accessible to a larger public by offering attractive concert programs at affordable prices
Fonda Loft, President
Aaron Hutchinson, Orchestra Operations Manager
Andrea Armstrong, Personnel Manager

Tafelmusik Baroque Orchestra & Chamber Choir
Trinity-St. Paul's Centre, PO Box 14, 427 Bloor St. West, Toronto ON M5S 1X7
Tel: 416-964-9562; *Fax:* 416-964-2782
info@tafelmusik.org
www.tafelmusik.org
Bringing baroque music to Toronto & the world, through concerts, recordings, & a music education programme
William Norris, Managing Director

Thunder Bay Symphony Orchestra Association (TBSO)
PO Box 29192, Thunder Bay ON P7B 6P9
Tel: 807-474-2284; *Fax:* 807-622-1927
info@tbso.ca
www.tbso.ca
To maintain & nurture a professional, regional orchestra of artistic integrity & excellence; to offer a variety of programs to enrich & encourage the widest possible audience; to support the development of local young musicians
Shannon Whidden, Executive Director
Arthur Post, Music Director

Timmins Symphony Orchestra
35 Pine St. South, 2nd Fl., Timmins ON P4N 7N2
Tel: 705-267-1006; *Fax:* 705-267-1006
info@timminssymphony.com
www.timminssymphony.com
Roy Takayesu, President
Matthew Jones, Music Director

Toronto Downtown Jazz Society
82 Bleecker St., Toronto ON M4X 1L8
Tel: 416-928-2033; *Fax:* 416-928-0533
tdjs@tojazz.com
www.torontojazz.com
To produce the Toronto Downtown Jazz Festival, as well as many other events & programs to further develop jazz talent & audience appreciation; To operate as a registered charity (No. 12969 0269 RR0001); To promote community involvement, artistic excellence, & outstanding production standards
Patrick Taylor, CEO/Executive Producer
Josh Grossman, Artistic Director

The Toronto Mendelssohn Choir
#404, 720 Bathurst St., Toronto ON M5S 2R4
Tel: 416-598-0422
admin@tmchoir.org
www.tmchoir.org
Cynthia Hawkins, Executive Director

Toronto Sinfonietta
400 St. Clair Ave. East, Toronto ON M4T 1P5
Tel: 416-488-8057
info@torontosinfonietta.com
www.torontosinfonietta.com
Matthew Jaskiewicz, Music Director

Toronto Symphony Orchestra (TSO)
212 King St. West, 6th Fl., Toronto ON M5H 1K5
Tel: 416-598-3375
www.tso.ca
To present concerts of both established & new music at the highest artistic standard possible, while recognizing audiences' needs; to play a role in the development of future musicians & audiences
Sonia Baxendale, Interim President & Chief Executive Officer
Peter Oundjian, Music Director

Toronto Symphony Youth Orchestra (TSYO)
212 King St. West, 6th Fl., Toronto ON M5H 1K5
Tel: 416-593-7769; *Fax:* 416-977-2912
www.tso.ca
To provide a high-level orchestral experience for young musicians aged 22 and under; To encourage significant achievement for participants through education and performance
Rachel Robbins, Manager
Shalom Bard, Conductor

University of Toronto Symphony Orchestra
Faculty of Music, University of Toronto, 80 Queen's Park Cres., Toronto ON M5S 2C5
Tel: 416-978-3750; *Fax:* 416-946-3353
performance.music@utoronto.ca
www.music.utoronto.ca
Uri Mayer, Conductor

University of Western Ontario Symphony Orchestra (UWOSO)
Faculty of Music, University of Western Ontario, Lambton Dr., London ON N6A 3K7
Tel: 519-661-2111
music@uwo.ca
www.music.uwo.ca

Vancouver Island Symphony
PO Box 661, Nanaimo BC V9R 5L9
Tel: 250-754-0177; *Fax:* 250-754-0165
info@vancouverislandsymphony.com
www.vancouverislandsymphony.com
To promote & present orchestra music in the Central Vancouver Island Region
Margot Holmes, Executive Director
Pierre Simard, Artistic Director

Vancouver New Music (VNM)
837 Davie St., Vancouver BC V6Z 1B7
Tel: 604-633-0861
info@newmusic.org
www.newmusic.org
To foster connections in the community to bring new music to a wider audience; To commission & premiere new work by Canadian composers; To produce music-theatre & electroacoustic music; To explore the interaction of contemporary music with other disciplines
Giorgio Magnanensi, Artistic Director

Vancouver Opera (VOA) / Association de l'opéra de vancouver
1945 McLean Dr., Vancouver BC V5N 3J7
Tel: 604-682-2871; *Fax:* 604-682-3981
online@vancouveropera.ca
www.vancouveropera.ca
To share the power of opera with all who are open to receiving it, through superior performances & meaningful education programs for all ages
James W. Wright, General Director
Jonathan Darlington, Music Director

Vancouver Philharmonic Orchestra (VPO)
PO Box 27503, Stn. Oakridge, Vancouver BC V5Z 4M4
Tel: 604-878-9989
vancouver.philharmonic@gmail.com
www.vanphil.ca
To provide non-professional musicians with an opportunity to perform orchestral music with a full symphony orchestra; To train aspiring professional conductors and musicians; To inspire and entertain the Vancouver community through performance
Jin Zhang, Music Director

Vancouver Symphony Society (VSO)
#500, 833 Seymour St., Vancouver BC V6B 0G4
Tel: 604-876-3434; *Fax:* 604-684-9264
customerservice@vancouversymphony.ca
www.vancouversymphony.ca
Provides stewardship for the Vancouver Symphony Orchestra to achieve recognition as one of Canada's highest quality symphony orchestras; to perform at all times with artistic distinction & thereby enrich BC's quality of life; to expand the enjoyment & appreciation of the finest orchestral music of the past & present
Kelly Tweeddale, President

Vancouver Youth Symphony Orchestra Society (VYSO)
3214 - 10 Ave. West, Vancouver BC V6K 2L2
Tel: 604-737-0714
vyso2@telus.net
www.vyso.com
To provide orchestral training & experience to music students in Greater Vancouver & the Lower Mainland from beginner to advanced level career student; To contribute to the cultural landscape of the local and provincial community by offering education and support to school & community groups
Roger Cole, Artistic Director
Holly Littleford, Orchestra Manager

Victoria Symphony Society
#610, 620 View St., Victoria BC V8W 1J6
Tel: 250-385-6515
boxoffice@victoriasymphony.ca
www.victoriasymphony.ca
To advance musical culture; to advance musical education among younger members of community; to encourage, foster, & promote performance of Canadian & other contemporary musicians
Mitchell Krieger, Executive Director
Tania Miller, Music Director

Western Canadian Music Alliance (WCMA)
#1, 118 Sherbrook St., Winnipeg MB R3C 2B4
Tel: 204-943-8485; *Fax:* 204-453-1594
info@breakoutwest.ca
breakoutwest.ca
The music industry associations of Manitoba, Alberta, and Saskatchewan work in tandem towards the shared vision of developing the infrastructure of the independent music industry in Western Canada.
Robyn Stewart, Executive Director

Wilfrid Laurier University Symphony Orchestra
Faculty of Music, 75 University Ave. West, Waterloo ON N2L 3C5
Tel: 519-884-0710; *Fax:* 519-884-5285
www.wlu.ca/academics/faculties/faculty-of-music/
To train music students to be musicians with solid knowledge of music theory & history,& competent performers
Paul Pulford, Conductor

Windsor Symphony Orchestra (WSO)
121 University Ave. West, Windsor ON N9A 5P4
Tel: 519-973-1238; *Fax:* 519-973-0764
Toll-Free: 888-327-8327
www.windsorsymphony.com
To enrich community life & serve as an educational resource through high quality live performance of orchestral music
Sheila Wisdom, Executive Director
Robert Franz, Music Director

Winnipeg Symphony Orchestra Inc. (WSO)
1650 - 1 Lombard Pl., Winnipeg MB R3B 0X3
Tel: 204-949-3950
lmarks@wso.mb.ca
www.wso.ca
To perform a wide variety of orchestral music including classical, contemporary, pop & children's music in Manitoba & Northwestern Ontario; To enrich the cultural landscape by engaging with the community
Trudy Schroeder, Executive Director
Alexander Mickelthwate, Music Director

York Symphony Orchestra Inc.
PO Box 355, Richmond Hill ON L4B 4R6
Tel: 416-410-0860; *Fax:* 416-410-0860
yorksymphonyorchestra@hotmail.com
www.yorksymphony.ca

To provide musical enjoyment for audiences & musicians, with the goal of being recognized & supported throughout York Region
Denis Mastromonaco, Music Director

Youth Singers of Calgary (YSC)
1371 Hastings Cres. SE, Calgary AB T2G 4C8
Tel: 403-234-9549; *Fax:* 403-234-9590
yscadmin@youthsingers.org
www.youthsingers.org
To develop & deliver a comprehensive choral program for young performers; to train them in the performance of classical music, jazz, folk & contemporary music, musical theatre & dance
Keith Heilman, Financial Administrator/Office Mgr.
Shirley Penner, CEO & Artistic Director

Performing Arts - Theatre

The Actors' Fund of Canada / La Caisse des acteurs du Canada inc.
#301, 1000 Yonge St., Toronto ON M4W 2K2
Tel: 416-975-0304; *Fax:* 416-975-0306
Toll-Free: 877-399-8392
contact@actorsfund.ca
www.actorsfund.ca
The Actors' Fund of Canada promotes artistic excellence for performers, creators, technicians & other members of creative & production teams in all entertainment industry sectors. The Fund carries out this mission by providing encouragement & short-term financial aid to help entertainment industry workers maintain their health, housing & ability to work after an illness, injury or sudden unemployment.
Fiona Reid, President
David Hope, CGA, Executive Director

Alberta Playwrights' Network (APN)
2633 Hochwald Ave. SW, Calgary AB T3E 7K2
Tel: 403-269-8564; *Fax:* 403-265-6773
Toll-Free: 800-268-8564
dramaturg@albertaplaywrights.com
www.albertaplaywrights.com
To foster playwriting in Alberta.
Trevor Rueger, Executive Director

Associated Designers of Canada (ADC)
#201, 192 Spadina Ave., Toronto ON M5T 2C2
Tel: 416-410-4209; *Fax:* 416-703-6601
associateddesigners@gmail.com
www.designers.ca
To promote, pursue & protect the interests & needs of theatrical designers working in Canada
April Viczko, President
William Mackwood, Vice-President
Michael Walsh, Secretary-Treasurer

Association of Summer Theatres 'Round Ontario (ASTRO)
c/o Theatre Ontario, #350, 401 Richmond St. West, Toronto ON M5V 3A8
Tel: 416-408-4556; *Fax:* 416-408-3402
info@summertheatre.org
www.summertheatre.org
To act as an information & resource network for its members; to support the professional development of its members; to act as a liaison for its membership with arts & business organizations, the media & the community; to advocate for its membership with government, government agencies & other organizations; to undertake projects to increase awareness of the activities of its membership among the general public
Derek Ritschel, President

Association québécoise des marionnettistes (AQM)
Centre UNIMA-CANADA (section Québec), #300, 7755, boul Saint-Laurent, Montréal QC H2R 1X1
Tél: 514-522-1919
info@aqm.ca
www.aqm.ca
Représenter ses membres et créer un terrain propice aux échanges, aux actions communes et à la réflexion sur la pratique de l'art de la marionnette
Hélène Ducharme, Présidente

Bard on the Beach Theatre Society
#203, 456 West Broadway, Vancouver BC V5Y 1R3
Tel: 604-737-0625; *Fax:* 604-737-0425
info@bardonthebeach.org
www.bardonthebeach.org
To provide Vancouver residents & visitors with affordable, accessible Shakespearean productions of the finest quality
Christopher Gaze, Artistic Director
Claire Sakaki, Managing Director

Black Theatre Workshop (BTW)
#432, 3680, Jeanne-Mance, Montréal QC H2X 2K5
Tel: 514-932-1104
info@blacktheatreworkshop.ca
www.blacktheatreworkshop.ca
To encourage & promote the development of a Black & Canadian theatre, rooted in a literature that reflects the creative will of Black Canadian writers & artists, & the creative collaborations between Black & other artists; To strive to create a greater cross-cultural understanding by its presence & the intrinsic value of its work
Quincy Armorer, Artistic Director
Adele Benoit, General Manager

British Columbia Drama Association
Old Courthouse Cultural Centre, 7 Seymour St. West, Kamloops BC V2C 1E4
Tel: 778-471-5620; *Fax:* 778-471-5639
Toll-Free: 888-202-2913
info@theatrebc.org
www.theatrebc.org
To promote the development of theatre in BC & Canada through a wide range of programs, services, activities, competitions, festivals & events
Peter Wienold, President

Buddies in Bad Times Theatre
12 Alexander St., Toronto ON M4Y 1B4
Tel: 416-975-9130
buddiesinbadtimes.com
To promote gay, lesbian, & queer theatrical expression
Brendan Healy, Artistic Director

Canadian Association for Theatre Research (CATR) / Association canadienne de la recherche théâtrale (ACRT)
c/o Peter Kuling, #2507, 140 Erskine Ave., Toronto ON M4P 1Z2
Tel: 416-303-0441; *Fax:* 647-344-6198
catr.membership@gmail.com
www.catr-acrt.ca
To focus on theatre, drama, & performance in a Canadian context, including acting, directing, practical matters of theatre, historiography, & the teaching, reception, theory, & literary criticism of drama
Jenn Stephenson, Secretary
Stephen Johnson, President
James Dugan, Treasurer

Canadian Institute for Theatre Technology (CITT) / L'Institut Canadien des Technologies Scénographiques (ICTS)
PO Box 85041, 345 Laurier Blvd., Mont-Saint-Hilaire QC J3H 5W1
Tel: 613-482-1165; *Fax:* 613-482-1212
Toll-Free: 888-271-3383
info@citt.org
www.citt.org
To work for the betterment of the Canadian live performance community; To promote safe & ethical work practices
Adam Mitchell, President
Gerry van Hezewyk, Vice-President
Mike Dickinson, Secretary
Eric Mongerson, Treasurer
Monique Corbeil, National Coordinator

The Canadian Stage Company
26 Berkeley St., Toronto ON M5A 2W3
Tel: 416-367-8243; *Fax:* 416-367-1768
www.canstage.com
To develop, produce & export the best in Canadian & international contemporary theatre
Matthew Jocelyn, Artistic & General Director

Canadian Theatre Critics Association (CTCA) / Association des critiques de théâtre du Canada
c/o Anton Wagner, #2306 - 201 Sherbourne St., Toronto, ON M5A 3X2
www.canadiantheatrecritics.ca
To promote excellence in theatre criticism; to encourage the dissemination of information on theatre on a national level; to encourage the awareness & development of Canadian theatre nationally & internationally through theatre criticism in all the media; to promote & encourage excellence in Canadian theatre through national awards; to improve the status & working conditions of theatre critics
Martin Morrow, President

Centre des auteurs dramatiques (CEAD)
#200, 261, rue du Saint-Sacrement, Montréal QC H2Y 3V2
Tél: 514-288-3384; *Téléc:* 514-288-7043
cead@cead.qc.ca
www.cead.qc.ca
Promotion et diffusion ici et à l'étranger des textes d'auteurs québécois et d'auteurs franco-canadiens; développement dramaturgique
Nicole Doucet, Directrice générale
Lise Vaillancourt, Présidente

Le Cercle Molière
340, boul Provencher, Winnipeg MB R2H 0G7
Tél: 204-233-8053; *Téléc:* 204-233-2373
info@cerclemoliere.com
www.cerclemoliere.com
Présenter des spectacles de théâtre en français au Manitoba
Geneviève Pelletier, Directrice artistique et générale

Compagnie vox théâtre
#202, 112, rue Nelson, Ottawa ON K1N 5R7
Tél: 613-241-1090; *Téléc:* 613-241-0250
info@voxtheatre.ca
www.voxtheatre.ca
Avec son travail de création, ses productions de théâtre chanté, ses accueils de spectacle pluridisciplinaires et ses tournées, la compagnie Vox Théâtre présente une programation complète pour les enfants et leur propose aussi des activités de formation
Pier Rodier, Direction artistique et générale

Conseil québécois du théâtre (CQT)
#808, 460, rue Ste-Catherine Ouest, Montréal QC H3B 1A7
Tél: 514-954-0270; *Téléc:* 514-954-0165
Ligne sans frais: 866-954-0270
cqt@cqt.qc.ca
www.cqt.ca
Promouvoir et défendre les intérêts du milieu théâtral et le représenter auprès des diverses instances; concerter, animer et informer la communauté théâtrale sur toutes les questions qui touchent la pratique théâtrale; promouvoir et développer le théâtre
Hélène Nadeau, Directrice générale
Pier DuFour, Adjointe à la direction

Evergreen Theatre Society
2633 Hochwald Ave. SW, Calgary AB T3E 7K2
Tel: 403-228-1384; *Fax:* 403-229-1385
Toll-Free: 877-840-9746
info@evergreentheatre.com
www.evergreentheatre.com
To create innovative, entertaining, accessible education-tangible choices for a healthy & sustainable future
Valmai Goggin, Artistic Producer
Sean Fraser, Executive Director

Fédération québécoise du théâtre amateur (FQTA)
CP 211, Succ. Saint-Élie-d'Orford, Sherbrooke QC J1R 1A1
Tél: 819-571-9358;
Ligne sans frais: 877-752-2501
info@fqta.ca
www.fqta.ca
Promouvoir le théâtre amateur en réunissant tous les individus et les groupes de théâtre pour contribuer à l'éducation artistique, esthétique et sociale de la population; établir un contact permanent entre les individus; fournir des occasions d'échange, de travaux, de recherches, de méthodes, de matériel et d'information ayant trait au théâtre
Yoland Roy, Directeur général

First Pacific Theatre Society
1440 West 12 Ave., Vancouver BC V6H 1M8
Tel: 604-731-5483
info@pacifictheatre.org
www.pacifictheatre.org
To produce high quality theatre; to operate with artistic, spiritual, relational & financial integrity
Ron Reed, Artistic & Executive Director
Alison Chisholm, Senior Operations Manager
Frank Nickel, Senior Business Manager
Andrea Loewen, Communications Manager

First Vancouver Theatre Space Society (FVTS)
PO Box 203, 1398 Cartwright St., Vancouver BC V6H 3R8
Tel: 604-257-0350
communications@vancouverfringe.com
www.vancouverfringe.com
To promoting interest in the arts in Vancouver; to nurture & support artists
Eduardo Ottoni, Production Manager
David Jordan, Executive Director

Globe Theatre Society
Globe Theatre, Prince Edward Bldg., 1801 Scarth St., Regina SK S4P 2G9
Tel: 306-525-9553; *Fax:* 306-352-4194
Toll-Free: 866-954-5623
onstage@globetheatrelive.com
www.globetheatrelive.com
To create & produce professional theatre & make it accessible with a view to entertain, educate & challenge
Ruth Smillie, Artistic Director

Greater Vancouver Professional Theatre Alliance (GVPTA)
1405 Anderson St., 3rd Fl., Vancouver BC V6H 3R5
Tel: 604-608-6799; *Fax:* 604-608-6923
info@gvpta.ca
www.gvpta.ca
To promote live theatre & foster a thriving environment for the continued growth & development of theatre in Greater Vancouver
Dawn Brennan, Director

Harbourfront Centre
235 Queens Quay West, Toronto ON M5J 2G8
Tel: 416-973-4600; *Fax:* 416-973-6055
info@harbourfrontcentre.com
www.harbourfrontcentre.com
To nurture the growth of new cultural expression; to stimulte Canadian & international interchange; to provide a dynamic, accessible environment for the public to experience the marvels of the creative imagination
Marah Braye, CEO

Intrepid Theatre Co. Society
#2, 1609 Blanshard St., Victoria BC V8W 2J5
Tel: 250-383-2663
www.intrepidtheatre.com
To educate & enhance the public's awareness & aesthetic appreciation of contemporary & progressive styles of modern theatre by encouraging, developing & producing new or experimental works for public performance; by coordinating & producing the annual Fringe Theatre Festival in Victoria
Janet Munsil, Artistic Director/Producer
Heather Lindsay, Executive Director

Manitoba Association of Playwrights (MAP)
#503, 100 Arthur St., Winnipeg MB R3B 1H3
Tel: 204-942-8941
mbplay@mts.net
www.mbplays.ca
To provide support for playwrights in Manitoba through the operation of programs for emerging & established playwrights
James Durham, President

Manitoba Theatre Centre (MTC)
174 Market Ave., Winnipeg MB R3B 0P8
Tel: 204-942-6537; *Fax:* 204-947-3741
Toll-Free: 877-446-4500
patronservices@mtc.mb.ca
www.mtc.mb.ca
Canada's first English-language regional theatre, with a mandate to study, practise & promote all aspects of the dramatic arts, with particular emphasis on professional production
Steven Schipper, Artistic Director
Camilla Holland, General Manager

Native Earth Performing Arts Inc. (NEPA)
#250, 585 Dundas St. East, Toronto ON M5A 2B7
Tel: 416-531-1402; *Fax:* 416-531-6377
Toll-Free: 877-854-9708
office@nativeearth.ca
www.nativeearth.ca
To enable Native actors, writers, designers, directors & technicians to work together to produce quality theatre that is vital to their development as artists & their identity as Native people; to encourage the use of theatre as form of communication within the Native community, including the use of the Native languages
Ryan Cunningham, Artistic Director
Isaac Thomas, General Manager

Neptune Theatre Foundation
1593 Argyle St., Halifax NS B3J 2B2
Tel: 902-429-7300; *Fax:* 902-429-1211
Toll-Free: 800-565-7345
info@neptunetheatre.com
www.neptunetheatre.com
To pursue theatrical excellence with artistic vision; to develop local & Canadian artistic talent; to encourage the youth of our community to develop a life-long interest in live theatre
Amy Melmock, General Manager
George Pothitos, Artistic Director

New West Theatre Society
#111, 210A - 12A St. North, Lethbridge AB T1H 2J1
Tel: 403-381-9378
info@newwesttheatre.com
www.newwesttheatre.com
To provide Lethbridge & surrounding region with a broad-based & diverse program of professional quality theatrical, musical & dramatic performances
Jeremy Mason, Artistic Director
Natascha Hainsworth, General Manager

Ontario Puppetry Association
c/o Mike Harding, 160 Baronwood Ct., Brampton ON L6V 3H8
Tel: 416-895-3492
www.onpuppet.ca
To promote recognition of puppetry as art; to distribute information on all aspects; to assist in eventual formation of national puppet theatre
Mike Harding, President
Jamie Ashby, Vice-President

Playwrights Guild of Canada (PGC)
#350, 401 Richmond St. West, Toronto ON M5V 3A8
Tel: 416-703-0201; *Fax:* 416-703-0059
Toll-Free: 800-561-3318
info@playwrightsguild.ca
www.playwrightsguild.ca
To encourage Canadian playwriting; to publish, promote & distribute Canadian plays; to provide current information of Canadian plays & their authors; to offer copyright protection; to promote the study & appreciation of Canadian plays; to safeguard freedom of expression on the stage
Robin Sokoloski, Executive Director

Playwrights Theatre Centre
#202, 739 Gore Ave., Vancouver BC V6A 2Z9
Tel: 604-685-6228
plays@playwrightstheatre.com
www.playwrightstheatre.com
To develop new Canadian plays; to provide support to experienced, emerging, & aspiring playwrights from across the country through dramaturgy, workshops, writers' groups and other programs
Heidi Taylor, Artistic & Executive Director

Prairie Theatre Exchange (PTE)
Portage Place, #Y300, 393 Portage Ave., 3rd Fl., Winnipeg MB R3B 3H6
Tel: 204-942-7291; *Fax:* 204-942-1774
pte@pte.mb.ca
www.pte.mb.ca
To operate a professional theatre of high calibre for the entertainment & edification of a broad spectrum of people; to operate a school to encourage appreciation of theatre & to provide accessible, high quality, innovative drama education; to support the development of new plays; to foster theatre arts-related endeavours of others through use of our facilities & expertise; to manage one or more community theatre arts centres
Greg Doyle, President
Cherry Karpyshin, General Manager

Professional Association of Canadian Theatres (PACT)
#555, 215 Spadina Ave., Toronto ON M5T 2C7
Tel: 416-595-6455; *Fax:* 416-595-6450
info@pact.ca
www.pact.ca
To gain recognition & support for professional theatre in Canada; To support the development of Canadian theatre companies by sharing resources & knowledge; to develop working standards & relationships with theatre professionals through their associations; To inform & connect theatres across Canada through a communications network; To act as a major force in influencing cultural policy at all levels of government
Sara Meurling, Executive Director
Jeremy Stacey, Manager, Professional Development
Janice Dowson, Manager, Business

Saskatchewan Playwrights Centre (SPC)
#700, 601 Spadina Cres. East, Saskatoon SK S7K 3G8
Tel: 306-665-7707; *Fax:* 306-244-0255
sk.playwrights@sasktel.net
www.saskplaywrights.ca
To develop playwrights.
Charlie Peters, President

Shaw Festival
PO Box 774, Niagara-on-the-Lake ON L0S 1J0
Tel: 905-468-2153; *Fax:* 905-468-5438
Toll-Free: 800-657-1106
dlg@shawfest.com
www.shawfest.com
To create intellectually challenging & entertaining theatre at an affordable price
Jackie Maxwell, Artistic Director
Elaine Calder, Executive Director

Tarragon Theatre
30 Bridgman Ave, Toronto ON M5R 1X3
Tel: 416-531-1827
info@tarragontheatre.com
www.tarragontheatre.com
To develop & produce new Canadian plays
Richard Rose, Artistic Director
Laura Dinner, President
Giles Meikle, Treasurer

Theatre Alberta Society
11759 Groat Rd., 3rd Fl., Edmonton AB T5M 3K6
Tel: 780-422-8162; *Fax:* 780-422-2663
Toll-Free: 888-422-8160
theatreab@theatrealberta.com
www.theatrealberta.com
To encourage the growth of theatre in Alberta through high quality support & training opportunities to theatre professionals, educators & community theatre practitioners
Keri Mitchell, Executive Director

Theatre Calgary
220 - 9 Ave. SE, Calgary AB T2G 5C4
Tel: 403-294-7440; *Fax:* 403-294-7493
info@theatrecalgary.com
www.theatrecalgary.com
To produce classical and modern theatre.
Mark Thompson, Chair
Dennis Garnhum, Artistic Director

Théâtre de la Vieille 17
204, av King Edward, Ottawa ON K1N 7L7
Tél: 613-241-8562; *Téléc:* 613-241-9507
info@vieille17.ca
www.vieille17.ca
Créer et diffuser des spectacles pour la jeunesse et pour les adultes à l'échelle régionale, nationale et internationale
Esther Beauchemin, Directrice artistique et générale

Théâtre des épinettes
55, rue Laframboise, Chibougamau QC G8P 2S5
Tél: 418-748-4682
Guy Lalancette, Responsable

Théâtre du Nouvel-Ontario (TNO)
21, boul Lasalle, Sudbury ON P3A 6B1
Tél: 705-525-5606
tno@letno.ca
www.letno.ca
Dédié à la création, à la dramaturgie franco-ontarienne et à l'accueil d'oeuvres principalement canadiennes
Geneviève Pineault, Directrice artistique

Théâtre du Trillium
#5, 109, rue Murray, Ottawa ON K1N 5M5
Tél: 613-789-7643; *Téléc:* 613-789-7641
comm@theatre-trillium.com
www.theatre-trillium.com
Pour effectuer des productions théâtrales contemporaines
Anne-Marie White, Directrice artistique et générale

Théâtre français de Toronto
#610, 21, rue College, Toronto ON M5G 2B3
Tél: 416-534-7303
www.theatrefrancais.com
Le Théâtre français de Toronto est un théâtre professionnel de langue française, de répertoire et de création. Il s'adresse à tous les amateurs de théâtre en français, tant les francophones que les francophiles : ce faisant, il contribue au développement culturel et pédagogique de la communauté de Toronto. Théâtre français de Toronto is a professional French-language theatre presenting répertoire as well as new work. While appealing to all lovers of French-language theatre, it contributes to the cultural and educational development of Toronto's francophone community.
Guy Mignault, Directeur artistique
Ghislain Caron, Directeur administratif

Théâtre l'Escaouette
170, rue Botsford, Moncton NB E1C 4X6
Tél: 506-855-0001; *Téléc:* 506-855-0010
escaouette@nb.aibn.com
www.escaouette.com
Pour effectuer productions acadiennes theatricial originaux
Marcia Babineau, Direction artistique & codirection générale

Théâtre la Catapulte
#4, 124, av King-Edward, Ottawa ON K1N 7L1
Tél: 613-562-0851; *Téléc:* 613-562-0631
communications@catapulte.ca
catapulte.ca
Le Théâtre la Catapulte est une compagnie professionnelle de création, de production et de diffusion enracinée en Ontario français, proposant aux adolescents et au grand public des expériences théâtrales audacieuses et éclectiques nourries par la fougue de la relève et par des artistes établis. Il assure à ses productions une diffusion importante dans la région d'Ottawa-Gatineau et dans l'ensemble du Canada tout en cultivant sa relation avec ses publics.
Jean Stéphane Roy, Directeur artistique
Maurice Demers, Président

Théâtre la Seizième
#266, 1555, 7e av Ouest, Vancouver BC V6J 1S1
Tel: 604-736-2616; *Fax:* 604-736-9151
info@seizieme.ca
www.seizieme.ca
Promouvoir le théâtre professionnel francophone en Colombie-Britannique
Craig Holzschuh, Directeur général et artistique

Theatre Network (1975) Society
10708 - 124 St., Edmonton AB T5M 0H1
Tel: 780-453-2440; *Fax:* 780-453-2596
info@theatrenetwork.ca
theatrenetwork.ca
To promote original regional drama
Bradley Moss, Artistic Director

Theatre New Brunswick (TNB)
55 Whitting Rd., Fredericton NB E3B 5Y5
Tel: 506-460-1381; *Fax:* 506-453-9315
general@tnb.nb.ca
www.tnb.nb.ca
To provide live professional theatre to the people of New Brunswick by touring & performing in nine centres throughout the province; to entertain by providing quality theatre & acting as a theatrical resource for playwrights, actors & young people interested in the field
Susan Ready, General Manager

Theatre Newfoundland Labrador
PO Box 655, Corner Brook NL A2H 6G1
Tel: 709-639-7238; *Fax:* 709-639-1006
www.theatrenewfoundland.com
To create & produce professional theatre which reflects the lives and dirversity of the audiences on the province's west coast, extending to labrador and across the island of Newfoundland.
Jeff Pitcher, Artistic Director

Theatre Nova Scotia (TNS)
1113 Marginal Rd., Halifax NS B3H 4P7
Tel: 902-425-3876; *Fax:* 902-422-0881
theatrens@theatrens.ca
www.theatrens.ca
To provide services, training & resources to professional & amateur theatre community throughout Nova Scotia
Elizabeth Murphy, Chair
Nancy Morgan, Executive Director

Theatre Ontario
#350, 401 Richmond St. West, Toronto ON M5V 3A8
Tel: 416-408-4556; *Fax:* 416-408-3402
info@theatreontario.org
www.theatreontario.org
To promote the continued development of theatre arts & artists in Ontario; to support the continued development of vital & broadly accessible theatre training of the highest quality to all sectors of Ontario's theatre community; to encourage the continued development of high quality theatre & drama programs within the educational system of Ontario; to ensure that Ontario's community theatres & educators obtain access to the resources of professional theatre; to facilitate interaction & communication between community, educational & professional theatre
Bruce Pitkin, Executive Director

Théâtre populaire d'Acadie (TPA)
#302, 220, boul. St-Pierre Ouest, Caraquet NB E1W 1A5
Tél: 506-727-0920; *Téléc:* 506-727-0923
Ligne sans frais: 800-872-0920
tpa@tpacadie.ca
www.tpacadie.ca
Créer, produire, diffuser et faire rayonner le théâtre d'ici et d'ailleurs
Maurice Arsenault, Directeur artistique et général

Theatre Saskatchewan
402 Broad St., Regina SK S4R 1X3
Tel: 306-352-0797; *Fax:* 306-569-7888
www.theatresaskatchewan.com
To strive to build a strong foundation for theatre which allows all people in Saskatchewan accessibility to live drama
Melissa Brio, Executive Director

Theatre Terrific Society
#430, 111 West Hastings St., Vancouver BC V6B 1H4
Tel: 604-222-4020; *Fax:* 604-669-2662
info@theatreterrific.ca
www.theatreterrific.ca
To provide theatrical opportunities to people with disabilities
Susanna Uchatius, Artistic Director

Théâtres associés inc. (TAI)
#405, 1908, rue Panet, Montréal QC H2L 3A2
Tél: 514-842-6361; *Téléc:* 514-842-9730
info@theatresassocies.ca
www.theatresassocies.ca
Se faire la voix d'institutions théâtrales francophones québécoises
Pierre Rousseau, Président
Suzanne Thomas, Secrétaire-Trésorière

Théâtres unis enfance jeunesse (TUEJ)
#217, 911, rue Jean-Talon Est, Montréal QC H2R 1V5
Tél: 514-380-2337
info@tuej.org
tuej.org
Défendre les intérêts des producteurs dans le domaine du théâtre pour la jeunesse
Marie-Eve Huot, Présidente
Danielle Bergevin, Directrice générale

Toronto Alliance for the Performing Arts (TAPA)
#350, 401 Richmond St. West, Toronto ON M5V 3A8
Tel: 416-536-6468; *Fax:* 416-536-3463
www.tapa.ca
To foster greater respect & support for the arts by advocating on behalf of Canadian theatre & dance, representing all cultural backgrounds, to government, supporters, & the general public; To provide services which enhance the artistic, technical, & administrative development of members
Jacoba Knaapen, Executive Director
Alexis Da Silva-Powell, Manager, Corporate Partnerships & Membership

La Troupe du Jour (LTDJ)
914, 20e rue Ouest, Saskatoon SK S7M 0Y4
Tél: 306-244-1040
communication@latroupedujour.ca
www.latroupedujour.ca
La Troupe du Jour Inc. develops professional and community French-language theatre through the creation of new works, training, performance, and outreach. La Troupe du Jour is dedicated to the development of French-language theatre in Saskatchewan.
Denis Rouleau, Directeur artistique et général

Vancouver TheatreSports League (VTSL)
1502 Duranleau St., Vancouver BC V6H 3S4
Tel: 604-738-7013; *Fax:* 604-738-8013
info@vtsl.com
www.vtsl.com
To challenge & inspire the community by growing & exploring exceptional improv-based work
Jay Ono, Executive Director

Western Canada Theatre Company Society (WCT)
PO Box 329, 1025 Lorne St., Kamloops BC V2C 5K9
Tel: 250-372-3216; *Fax:* 250-374-7099
www.wctlive.ca
To provide the regional community with challenging professional theatre; to entertain, educate, enrich & interact with the cultural mosaic of its community; to promote & assist the performing arts through the provision of educational, theatrical & artistic opportunities & services & through the management & operation of facilities
Lori Marchand, General Manager

Young People's Theatre (YPT)
165 Front St. East, Toronto ON M5A 3Z4
Tel: 416-862-2222
online@youngpeoplestheatre.ca
www.youngpeoplestheatre.ca
To make a positive impact on the intellectual, social, & emotional development of young people; To produce plays for young audiences; To operate a year-round drama school for youth
Nancy J. Webster, Executive Director
Alexis Buset, Technical Director
Allen MacInnis, Artistic Director
Rick Banville, Director, Production
Jill Ward, Manager, Education & Participation
Marilyn Hamilton, Director, Marketing

Science Centres

Alberta

Local Science Centres

***Calgary:* TELUS Spark**
220 St. George's Dr. NE
Calgary, AB T2E 5T2
Tel: 403-817-6800
info@sparkscience.ca
www.sparkscience.ca
Social Media: www.youtube.com/telusworldofscience
twitter.com/telus_spark
www.facebo ok.com/telusspark
Year Founded: 1967 The new TELUS Spark science centre features the following exhibits & installations: Prototype Lab; Being Human; Earth & Sky; Energy & Innovation; Open Studio; Creative Kids Museum; Presentation Theatre; Temperature Adventure; & HD Digital Dome Theatre. Open year round.
Brent Poohkay, Chair
Jennifer Martin, President & CEO, ceo@sparkscience.ca

***Edmonton:* TELUS World of Science - Edmonton**
11211 - 142 St. NW
Edmonton, AB T5M 4A1
Tel: 780-452-9100
info@twose.ca
telusworldofscienceedmonton.ca
twitter.com/twosedm
www.facebook.com/Ed montonScience
IMAX theatre; planetarium; exhibit galleries; observatory; giftshop; café; Ham Radio Station; science & computer lab
Jackson von der Ohe, Chair
Alan Nursall, President & CEO
Mike Steger, Vice-President, Marketing & Communications

British Columbia

Local Science Centres

***Kamloops:* BIG Little Science Centre (BLSC)**
PO Box 882 Main
Located at 655 Holt St., Kamloops, BC
Kamloops, BC V2C 5M8
Tel: 250-554-2572
blscs.org
Social Media: www.youtube.com/user/BIGLittleScience
twitter.com/BIGLittleScienc
www. facebook.com/190315953017
Year Founded: 2000 A child-friendly science centre located in the Happyvale School.
Gord Stewart, Operator, gord@blscs.org

***Vancouver:* H.R. MacMillan Space Centre (HRMSC)**
1100 Chestnut St.
Vancouver, BC V6J 3J9
Tel: 604-738-7827; *Fax:* 604-736-5665
info@spacecentre.ca
www.spacecentre.ca
Social Media: www.youtube.com/user/MacMillanSpaceCentre
twitter.com/AskAnAstronomer
www.facebook.com/178662617057
Year Founded: 1968 Western Canada's premier earth, space science & astronomy attraction & educational resource
Eric K. Pringle, President
Raylene Marchand, Acting Executive Director

Vancouver: **Science World at TELUS World of Science**
1455 Québec St.
Vancouver, BC V6A 3Z7
Tel: 604-443-7440
info@scienceworld.ca
www.scienceworld.ca
Social Media: www.youtube.com/scienceworldtv
twitter.com/scienceworldca
www.facebook .com/scienceworldca
Year Founded: 1977 Hands-on exhibits; demonstrations; Omnimax theatre
Walter Segsworth, Chair
Bryan Tisdall, President/CEO

Vernon: **Okanagan Science Centre**
Polson Park, 2704 Hwy. 6
Vernon, BC V1T 5G5
Tel: 250-545-3644
info@okscience.ca
www.okscience.ca
twitter.com/Okana ganScience
www.facebook.com/141544795902551
Year Founded: 1990 All of the centre's exhibits are based on scientific principals, in an effort to inspire visitors to appreciate the universal nature of science. Hours of Operation: M-F 10:00-5:00, Sa 11:00-5:00.

New Brunswick

Local Science Centres

Fredericton: **Science East**
Parent: **Science East Association**
668 Brunswick St.
Fredericton, NB E3B 1H6
Tel: 506-457-2340; *Fax:* 506-462-7687
science@scienceeast.nb.ca
www.scienceeast.nb.ca
twitter.com/science_ea st
www.facebook.com/ScienceEast
Year Founded: 1999 Science East offers hands-on science & education exhibits & programs. The centre is located in the historic York County Gaol (c.1842), with exhibits housed in the jail's old cells. Open year-round.
David Desjardins, Chief Executive Officer Ph.D, david.desjardins@scienceeast.nb.ca
Michael Edwards, Director MSc, Programming, michael.edwards@scienceeast.nb.ca
Karen Matheson, Director BSc, BEd, MSc, Education, karen.matheson@scienceeast.nb.ca

Newfoundland & Labrador

Local Science Centre

St. John's: **Johnson Geo Centre**
175 Signal Hill Rd.
St. John's, NL A1A 1B2
Tel: 709-737-7880; *Fax:* 709-737-7885
Toll-Free: 866-868-7625
info@geocentre.ca
www.geocentre.ca
Year Founded: 2002 Mainly focuses on Newfoundland geology.
Melissa Churchill, Manager, Office Administration, melissa.churchill@geocentre.ca

Nova Scotia

Local Science Centre

Halifax: **Discovery Centre**
1593 Barrington St.
Halifax, NS B3J 1Z7
Tel: 902-492-4422; *Fax:* 902-492-3170
handsonfun@discoverycentre.ns.ca
www.discoverycentre.ns.ca
Social Media: www.youtube.com/user/discoverycentre1593
twitter.com/DiscoveryCntr
www.facebook.com/DiscoveryCentre
Year Founded: 1990 Discovery Centre is an interactive science centre with hands-on exhibits, films, science shows & special events. Exhibits include the Lindsay Building Centre, Water & Our World, Tension on Suspension, the Bubble Room & Build Your Own Coaster. Educational programs are also offered.
Dov Bercovici, President & CEO, 902-492-4422, dbercovici@discoverycentre.ns.ca
Linda Laurence, Manager, Operations, 902-492-4422, llaurence@discoverycentre.ns.ca
Jeff McCarron, Manager, Exhibits, 902-492-4422, jmccarron@discoverycentre.ns.ca
Steve Thurbride, Manager, Science Education, 902-492-4422, sthurbide@discoverycentre.ns.ca

Ontario

Provincial Science Centre

Ontario Science Centre / Centre des sciences de l'Ontario
770 Don Mills Rd.
Toronto, ON M3C 1T3
Tel: 416-696-1000; *Fax:* 416-696-3166
Toll-Free: 888-696-1110
contact.centre@OntarioScienceCentre.ca
www.ontarioscie ncecentre.ca
Social Media: www.youtube.com/user/OntarioScienceCentre
twitter.com/ontsciencectr
ww w.facebook.com/ontariosciencecentre
Other contact information: TTY: 416-696-3202
Year Founded: 1969 Over 800 interactive exhibits on the environment, technology, food, chemistry, communications, sport & space; exhibits, programs, demonstrations, workshops & films for the public; special programs for school groups, children, adults & senior citizens; gift shops & restaurant; Ontario's only IMAX Dome theatre, featuring a 24-metre dome screen with wrap-around sound; open year round
Brian Chu, Chair
Maurice Bitran, CEO & Chief Science Officer

Local Science Centres

Sudbury: **Science North**
100 Ramsey Lake Rd.
Sudbury, ON P3E 5S9
Tel: 705-522-3701; *Fax:* 705-522-4954
Toll-Free: 800-461-4898
contactus@sciencenorth.ca
www.sciencenorth.ca
Social Media: www.youtube.com/user/sciencenorth
twitter.com/ScienceNorth
www.facebook.com/ScienceNorth
Year Founded: 1984 Science centre, IMAX Theatre, planetarium, living butterfly gallery & special exhibits hall; exhibit design & consulting services.
Brandi Braithwaite, Manager, Development, 705-522-3701, braithwaite@sciencenorth.ca

Windsor: **Canada South Science City**
930 Marion Ave.
Windsor, ON N9A 2J2
Tel: 519-973-3667; *Fax:* 519-973-3676
info@cssciencecity.com
www.cssciencecity.com
www.facebook.com/CanadaSo uthScienceCity
Year Founded: 2004 A child-friendly science centre that serves the Science & Technology component of the elementary school curriculum, but is also open to the general public. Hours of Operation: Sept.-June, Th, F & Sa 12:00-5:00, Su 1:00-5:00; July & Aug., M-Sa 10:00-5:00; after-hours tours available on request.
William E. Baylis, President, baylis@uwindsor.ca
Tony Sabo, Operations Manager, anthony_sabo@yahoo.ca

Québec

Provincial Science Centre

The Montréal Science Centre (MSC) / Centre des sciences de Montréal
King-Edward Quay, 333 de la Commune St. West
Montréal, QC H2Y 2E2
Tel: 514-496-4724*Toll-Free:* 877-496-4724
information@oldportofMontréal.com
www.Montréalsciencecentre.com
www.fa cebook.com/centredessciences
Year Founded: 2000 Visitors acquire an understanding of science & technology & how it affects daily living; three interactive science exhibition halls; IMAX TELUS Cinema

Local Science Centres

Laval: **Cosmodôme - Centre des sciences de l'espace et Camp spatial Canada / Cosmodôme - Space Science Centre & Space Camp**
2150, rte des Laurentides
Laval, QC H7T 2T8
Tél: 450-978-3600; *Téléc:* 450-978-3624
Ligne sans frais: 800-565-2267
info@cosmodome.org
www.cosmodome.org
Médias sociaux: www.youtube.com/user/LeCosmodome
twitter.com/LeCosmodome
www.facebook.com/cosmodome
Hôte au Centre des sciences de l'espace et à la Space Camp, le Cosmodôme de Laval lance ses visiteurs dans un voyage à travers la conquête de l'espace.
Marc DeBlois, Directeur général MA

Montréal: **Biosphère**
160, ch Tour-de-L'Isle
Montréal, QC H3C 4G8
Tel: 514-283-5000; *Fax:* 514-283-5021
Toll-Free: 855-773-8200
info.biosphere@ec.gc.ca
www.ec.gc.ca/biosphere
twitt er.com/biospheremtl
www.facebook.com/biospheremtl
Museum of environment; the domed structure housing the museum was built for Expo 67.

Montréal: **Planétarium Rio Tinto Alcan**
4801, av Pierre-de Coubertin
Montréal, QC H1V 3V4
Tél: 514-868-3000
espacepourlavie.ca/planetarium
Médias sociaux: www.youtube.com/Espacepourlavie
twitter.com/espacepourlavie
www.facebo ok.com/Espacepourlavie
Productions multimédias sur l'astronomie sur un dôme géant hémisphérique de 20 mètres de diamètre. Le Planétarium de Montréal a fermé en 2011 en raison du manque de fonds, mais a été rouverte en 2013 comme le Planétarium Rio Tinto Alcan.

Saint-Louis-du-Ha-Ha: **Aster, La Station scientifique du BSL**
59, ch Bellevue
Saint-Louis-du-Ha-Ha, QC G0L 3S0
Tél: 418-854-2172; *Téléc:* 418-854-1898
directionaster@bellnet.ca
www.asterbsl.ca
Médias sociaux: www.youtube.com/user/observatoireaster
www.facebook.com/263103340448096
Fondée en: 1976 La culture scientifique et technique; des ateliers éducatifs pour les écoles
Maurice Fallu-Landry, Directeur

Saskatchewan

Local Science Centres

Regina: **Saskatchewan Science Centre**
2903 Powerhouse Dr.
Regina, SK S4N 0A1
Tel: 306-522-4629*Toll-Free:* 800-667-6300
www.sasksciencecentre.com
Social Media: www.youtube.com/user/sasksciencecentre
twitter.com/SkScienceCentre
www .facebook.com/SaskScienceCentre
Other contact information: Administration Phone: 306-791-7900
Year Founded: 1989 Interactive science museum featuring hands-on exhibits, Kramer Imax theatre; open year-round
Sandy Baumgartner, Executive Director

Zoos

Alberta

Calgary: **Bow Habitat Station**
1440 - 17A St. SE
Calgary, AB T2G 4T9
Tel: 403-297-6561; *Fax:* 403-592-8552
bow.habitat@gov.ab.ca
www.bowhabitat.gov.ab.ca
Social Media: www.flickr.com/photos/srdalberta/sets
www.facebook.com/BowHabitatStation
Year Founded: 2009 Includes: a Visitor Centre, which is an interpretive centre about fresh water, fish, and aquatic habitats; the Sam Livingston Fish Hatchery, a large trout hatchery; and

the Pearce Estate Park Interpretive Wetland, a unique collection of constructed wetlands, self-guided trails and interpretive signs.

Calgary: Calgary Zoo, Botanical Garden & Prehistoric Park
1300 Zoo Rd. NE
Calgary, AB T2E 7V6
Tel: 403-232-9300; *Fax:* 403-237-7582
Toll-Free: 800-588-9993
guestrelations@calgaryzoo.ab.ca
www.calgaryzoo.org
Social Media: www.youtube.com/calgaryzoo1
twitter.com/calgaryzoo
www.facebook.com/thecalgaryzoo
Year Founded: 1929 136 acres + 320 acre off-site breeding & conservation facility; educational programs; gift shop; open year round
Hugh Gillard, Chair
Dr. Clément Lanthier, President/CEO

Calgary: Inglewood Bird Sanctuary
2425 - 9 Ave. SE
Calgary, AB T2G 4T4
Tel: 403-268-2489
www.calgary.ca
Offers more than two km. of level trails; more than 270 species of birds & 300 species of plants plus several kinds of mammals have been observed in area; visitor centre; two classrooms where nature-related programs are presented by the Sanctuary's professional naturalists. The trails are currently closed due to flood damage.

Edmonton: Edmonton Valley Zoo
PO Box 2359
Located at 13315 Buena Vista Rd., Edmonton, AB
Edmonton, AB T5J 2R7
Tel: 780-442-5311
attractions@edmonton.ca
www.edmonton.ca/valleyzoo
Year Founded: 1959 Features more than 350 endangered & exotic animals; main zoo & children's zoo; minature train, merry-go-round & camel rides available; open daily except Christmas Day

Lacombe: Ellis Bird Farm
PO Box 5090
Lacombe, AB T4L 1W7
Tel: 403-346-2211
info@ellisbirdfarm.ca
www.ellisbirdfarm.ca
Social Media: www.youtube.com/user/ellisbirdfarm
twitter.com/EllisBirdFarm
Other contact information: Summer phone 403-885-4477
Nestboxes; wildlife gardens; tea house; open May - Aug.
Ken Wigmore, Chair
Myrna Pearman, Biologist/Manager, Site Services
Cynthia Pohl, Head Gardener

British Columbia

Aldergrove: Greater Vancouver Zoo
5048 - 264th St.
Aldergrove, BC V4W 1N7
Tel: 604-856-6825; *Fax:* 604-857-9008
info@gvzoo.com
www.gvzoo.com
twitter.com/GVZooChat
www.facebook.com/ 350349281684818
Year Founded: 1970 Over 960 animals representing 176 species; world's only albino black bear; one of North America's largest grizzly bear habitats.
Jody Henderson, General Manager

Coombs: Butterfly World & Gardens
PO Box 36, 1080 Winchester Rd.
Coombs, BC V0R 1M0
Tel: 250-248-7026; *Fax:* 250-752-1091
www.nature-world.com
The Butterfly World & Gardens is a nature park with tropical gardens, orchids, ponds, birds, & butterflies.

Creston: Creston Valley Wildlife Management Area (CVWMA)
PO Box 640
Creston, BC V0B 1G0
Tel: 250-402-6900; *Fax:* 250-402-6910
askus@crestonwildlife.ca
www.crestonwildlife.ca
twitter.com/crestonwil dlife
www.facebook.com/149782131736839
17,000-acre wetland habitat. This diverse wildlife resource provides many recreational and educational opportunities. Hiking, cycling, canoeing, picnicking, wildlife viewing, hunting, fishing, and many other outdoor activities can be experienced here.
Marc-André Beaucher, Head, Operations

Kamloops: British Columbia Wildlife Park
9077 Dallas Dr.
Kamloops, BC V2C 6V1
Tel: 250-573-3242; *Fax:* 250-573-2406
info@bczoo.org
www.bczoo.org
twitter.com/bcwildlifepark
www.facebook .com/BCzoo
Year Founded: 1965 A non-profit organization dedicated to the conservation of BC wildlife through display, interpretation, education, wildlife rehabilitation, endangered species & direct action.
Glenn Grant, General Manager, 250-573-3242, glenn@bczoo.org

Kelowna: Speedwell Bird Sanctuary
PO Box 144
Kelowna, BC V1Y 7N3
Tel: 250-766-2081
Social Media:
www.youtube.com/playlist?list=PL24A1A0A91EC2638B
Year Founded: 1985 Breeding facility for amazon parrots, pheasants; botanical garden featuring trees, shrubs & roses; by appt.
Dan Bruce, Contact

Port Hardy: Quatse Salmon Stewardship Centre
***Parent:* Northern Vancouver Island Salmonid Enhancement Association**
PO Box 1409
Located at 8400 Byng Rd., Port Hardy, BC
Port Hardy, BC V0N 2P0
Tel: 250-902-0336
salmon@nvisea.org
www.thesalmoncentre.org
www.facebook.com/quatsesalmon.stewardshipcentre
Year Founded: 1983 The centre features an interperative centre & a working salmon hatchery that visitors can observe. All proceeds go towards salmon conservation. Open daily 10:00-5:00.

Richmond: Richmond Nature Park
11851 Westminster Hwy.
Richmond, BC V6X 1B4
Tel: 604-718-6188; *Fax:* 604-718-6189
nature@richmond.ca
www.richmond.ca/parks/parks/naturepark/about.htm
Features 5 km. of well-groomed trails through bog & forest; more than 100 species of birds, mammals, reptiles & amphibians may be sighted; seasonal programs & events
Brenda Bartley-Smith, President, Nature Park Society
Kristine Bauder, Nature Park Coordinator
Richard Kenny, Community Facilities Programmer

Vancouver: Stanley Park Ecology Society
PO Box 5167
Vancouver, BC V6B 4B2
Tel: 604-257-6908; *Fax:* 604-257-8378
info@stanleyparkecology.ca
stanleyparkecology.ca
twitter.com/StanleyPk EcoSoc
www.facebook.com/StanleyPkEcoSoc
Year Founded: 1988 Encourages stewardship of the natural world through education & action & by fostering awareness; provides public programs for adults & families, school programs, wildlife information & resources promoting coexistence between people & its wild neighbours
Patricia Thomson, Executive Director, 604-718-6523, exec@stanleyparkecology.ca

Victoria: Swan Lake Christmas Hill Nature Sanctuary
***Parent:* Swan Lake Christmas Hill Nature Sanctuary Society**
3873 Swan Lake Rd.
Victoria, BC V8X 3W1
Tel: 250-479-0211; *Fax:* 250-479-0132
info@swanlake.bc.ca
www.swanlake.bc.ca
twitter.com/swanlakenature
ww w.facebook.com/SwanLakeChristmasHillNatureSanctuary
Nature education centre; 125 acres including marshy lowlands surrounding Swan Lake & rocky, oak-forested highlands of Christmas Hill.
Blaine Benson, Chair
Renée Cenerini, Program Manager

Victoria: Victoria Butterfly Gardens
PO Box 190, 1461 Benvenuto Ave.
Victoria, BC V8M 1R3
Tel: 250-652-3822; *Fax:* 250-652-4683
Toll-Free: 877-722-0272
info@butterflygardens.com
www.butterflygardens.com
Social Media: www.youtube.com/user/VicButterflyGardens
twitter.com/bflygrdns
www.facebook.com/butterfly.gardens
Indoor tropical gardens, fish, birds, & butterflies. Open year round.
David Roberts, General Manager, david@butterflygardens.com

Manitoba

Rennie: Alfred Hole Goose Sanctuary & Visitor Centre (AHGS)
c/o Manitoba Conservation, PO Box 130
Rennie, MB R0E 1R0
Tel: 204-369-5470
parkinterpretation@gov.mb.ca
www.gov.mb.ca/conservation/parks/act_interp/centres/alf_hole.ht ml
Other contact information: Whiteshell Park Interpreter: 204-369-3157
Year Founded: 1939 Located in Whiteshell Provincial Park; wheelchair accessible Visitor Centre interprets the history of the site as well as the biology of geese; spring, summer & fall program features hands-on activities, guided hikes, school programming & special events

Thompson: Thompson Zoo
***Parent:* Thompson Zoological Society**
Thompson, MB
Tel: 204-677-7982; *Fax:* 204-778-4186
thompzoo@mts.net
Year Founded: 1978 Over 100 animals and birds. The Thompson Zoo is the only northern Wildlife Rehab Cetnre in Manitoba. Open year round.
Erin Wilcox, Director

Winnipeg: Assiniboine Park Zoo
2595 Roblin Blvd.
Winnipeg, MB R3P 2N7
Tel: 204-927-6000
info@assiniboinepark.ca
www.assiniboineparkzoo.ca
Social Media: www.youtube.com/user/AssiniboinePark
twitter.com/assiniboinezoo
www.fa cebook.com/assiniboineparkzoo
Year Founded: 1904 Open daily & currently has over 2,000 animals of 200 different species
Margaret Redmond, President & CEO, Assiniboine Park Conservancy

New Brunswick

Moncton: Magnetic Hill Zoo
100 Worthington Ave.
Location: 125 Magic Mountain Rd., Moncton, NB, E1C 9Z3
Moncton, NB E1C 9Z3
Tel: 506-877-7718; *Fax:* 506-853-3569
info.zoo@moncton.ca
www.moncton.org/zoo
The Magnetic Hill Zoo is committed to safeguarding animal species & raising public awareness of endangered species. The zoo is designed with the well-being of the animals, as well as the safety of the public, in mind.
Bruce Dougan, Manager

Saint John: Cherry Brook Zoo Inc.
901 Foster Thurston Dr.
Saint John, NB E2K 5H9
Tel: 506-634-1440; *Fax:* 506-634-0717
noahsark@bellaliant.net
www.cherrybrookzoo.com
Year Founded: 1978 A non-for profit zoo situated in a 35-acre woodland that is located in the northern section of the city's 2200-acre Rockwood Park. Utilizing the unusual natural terrain of Rockwood Park, the animals are surrounded by a natural setting.
Leonard Collrin, Chief Administrative Director
Lynda Collrin, Director, Zoo Development
Hugh P. O'Hara, Senior Zoo Keeper

Newfoundland & Labrador

***Holyrood:* Salmonier Nature Park**
PO Box 190
Holyrood, NL A0A 2R0
Tel: 709-229-7888; *Fax:* 709-229-7078
www.env.gov.nl.ca/env/snp
www.facebook.com/pages/Salmonier-Nature-Park/1446191848972765
Open June to Thanksgiving
Brenda Pike, Manager, brendapike@gov.nl.ca

Nova Scotia

***Aylesford:* Oaklawn Farm Zoo**
1007 Ward Rd. RR#1
Aylesford, NS B0P 1C0
Tél: 902-847-9790
www.oaklawnfarmzoo.ca
www.facebook.com/OaklawnFarmZoo
Fondée en: 1984 The largest zoo in Nova Scotia, Oaklawn is also home to the largest collection of big cats & primates in Eastern Canada.

***Dartmouth:* Maritime Reptile Zoo Limited**
Burnside Industrial Park, #10, 75 Akerley Blvd.
Dartmouth, NS B3B 1R7
Tel: 902-465-6049*Toll-Free:* 877-204-3838
info@maritimereptilezoo.com
www.maritimereptilezoo.com
twitter.com/Mar itimeReptile
www.facebook.com/MaritimeReptileZooNS
Largestly locally owned & operated reptile zoo in the province. Animals housed in the zoo includes alligators, crocodiles, snakes, lizards & tortoises.

***Shubenacadie:* Shubenacadie Provincial Wildlife Park**
PO Box 299
Shubenacadie, NS B0N 2H0
Tel: 902-758-2040
wildlifepark@gov.ns.ca
wildlifepark.novascotia.ca
45 exhibits featuring native & exotic species in natural enclosures along a 2.3 km walking trail; picnic area & playground; open daily May 15-Oct. 15 & weekends only during winter season.

Ontario

***Bowmanville:* Bowmanville Zoo**
340 King St. East
Bowmanville, ON L1C 3K5
Tel: 905-623-5655; *Fax:* 905-623-0957
info@bowmanvillezoo.com
bowmanvillezoo.com
Social Media: www.youtube.com/user/BowmanvilleZoo1919
twitter.com/Bowmanville_Zoo
ww w.facebook.com/BowmanvilleZoo
Year Founded: 1919 Canada's oldest private zoo, featuring Animal Kingdom shows, elephant rides, restaurant & gift shop; CAZA accredited; open May - Oct.

***Brantford:* Brantford Twin Valley Zoo**
84 Langford Church Rd.
Brantford, ON N3T 5L4
Tel: 519-752-0607
www.twinvalleyzoo.com
www.facebook.com/twinvalleyzoo
Year Founded: 1991 In addition to animal exhibits, the zoo features a nature trail, pony rides & picnic areas. Hours: May - Labour Day 9:00-6:00 daily; Sept - Thanksgiving M-F 10:00-4:00, Sa-Su 10:00-5:00.

***Caledonia:* Killman Zoo**
***Parent:* Killman's Wildlife Sanctuary**
237 Unity Rd. East
Caledonia, ON N3W 2H7
Tel: 905-765-5966
info@thekillmanzoo.com
www.thekillmanzoo.com
Year Founded: 1988 Home to one of the largest big cat collections in Ontario.

***Cambridge:* African Lion Safari & Game Farm**
RR#1
Location: 1386 Cooper Rd., Hamilton, ON
Cambridge, ON N1R 5S2
Tel: 519-623-2620; *Fax:* 519-623-9542
Toll-Free: 800-461-9453
admin@lionsafari.com
www.lionsafari.com
Social Media: www.pinterest.com/lionsafari
www.facebook.com/AfricanLionSafariCanada
Year Founded: 1969 African Lion Safari is a Canadian-owned family business that seeks to both entertain its guests & act as a conservation park for its animals. Open May-Oct.

***Cambridge:* Cambridge Butterfly Conservatory**
2500 Kossuth Rd.
Cambridge, ON N3H 4R7
Tel: 519-653-1234; *Fax:* 519-650-2582
info@cambridgebutterfly.com
www.cambridgebutterfly.com
twitter.com/con servatory_
www.facebook.com/CambridgeButterflyConservatory
Year Founded: 2001 Live butterfly conservatory & tropical garden, also featuring birds & bugs; open daily 10:00-5:00.

***Elmvale:* Elmvale Jungle Zoo**
PO Box 3003
Located at 14191 County Rd. 27, Elmvale, ON
Elmvale, ON L0L 1P0
Tel: 705-322-1112; *Fax:* 705-322-2245
elmvalezoo@sympatico.ca
www.elmvalejunglezoo.com
Year Founded: 1967 The zoo occupies 25 acres of land with over 300 animals on-site, including lions, tigers, jaguars, monkeys, lemurs, giraffes, zebras, & more. Open late May - Thanksgiving.

***Indian River:* Indian River Reptile Zoo**
2206 County Rd. 38
Indian River, ON K0L 2B0
Tel: 705-639-1443
reptilezoo.dinopark@gmail.com
reptilezoo.org
Social Media: www.youtube.com/user/Indianriverreptilezo
twitter.com/Reptilezoo1
www.facebook.com/pages/Indian-River-Reptile-Zoo/426618677381462
Home to over 200 reptiles. Open daily May - Sept., 10:00-5:00.

***Kingsville:* Jack Miner Bird Sanctuary**
360 Rd. 3 West
Kingsville, ON N9Y 2E5
Tel: 519-733-4034; *Fax:* 519-733-0932
www.jackminer.com
twitter.com/JM_Sanctuary
www.facebook.com/JackMinerM igratoryBirdSanctuary
Year Founded: 1931 Centre for the conservation of migrating Canada geese & wild ducks, originating from the waterfowl refuge management system. Open year-round, free admission.
Mary E. Baruth, Executive Director, mbaruth@jackminer.com

***Midland:* Wye Marsh Wildlife Centre**
PO Box 100, 16160 Hwy. 12 East
Midland, ON L4R 4K6
Tel: 705-526-7809; *Fax:* 705-526-3294
info@wyemarsh.com
www.wyemarsh.com
Social Media: www.youtube.com/user/WyeMarshTV
twitter.com/WyeMarsh
www.facebook.com/ wyemarshwildlifecentre
Year Founded: 1984 Indoor & outdoor natural history exhibits; environmental education & recreation programs; fully accessible nature centre & trails; assistive equipment available
Sara Street, Executive Director, sstreet@wyemarsh.com

***Morrisburg:* Upper Canada Migratory Bird Sanctuary (UCMBS) / Sanctuaire des oiseaux migrateurs Upper Canada**
c/o Parks of the St. Lawrence, 13740 County Rd. 2
Located at 5591 County Road 2, Ingleside, ON
Morrisburg, ON K0C 1X0
Tel: 613-543-4328*Toll-Free:* 800-437-2233
ucmbs@parks.on.ca
www.uppercanadabirdsanctuary.com
www.facebook.com/14 6312528725287
Year Founded: 1961 A natural area with over 8 km. of nature trails, visitor centre & gift shop, campground & group camping area; offers a duck banding program, fall goose feeding program, outdoor education topics & special events such as the Annual Waterfowl Day
Darren Dalgleish, General Manager & CEO, St. Lawrence Parks Commission

***Orono:* Jungle Cat World Inc. (JCW)**
3667 Concession Rd. 6
Orono, ON L0B 1M0
Tel: 905-983-5016; *Fax:* 905-983-9858
info@junglecatworld.com
www.junglecatworld.com
Social Media: www.youtube.com/user/SafariZooCamp1
twitter.com/JungleCatWorld
www.fac ebook.com/123056467776168
Year Founded: 1983 Jungle Cat World is a wildlife park located on 15 acres of land. Though Jungle Cat World is home to a variety of threatened & endangered species such as lemurs, gibbons, cotton-top tamarins & spider monkeys, the park specializes in wild felines. They include the world's largest, the Siberian tiger, to the rarest, the Amur leopard, to some of the smallest like the sand cats from the African deserts.
Wolfram Klose, Founder & Owner
Christa Klose, Founder & Owner

***Oshawa:* Oshawa Zoo & Fun Farm**
3441 Grandview St. North
Oshawa, ON L1H 8L7
Tel: 905-655-5236
info@oshawazoo.ca
www.oshawazoo.ca
www.facebook.com/ pages/Oshawa-Zoo/155046104563187
Year Founded: 1993 The zoo is home to 40 species of birds & animals.

***Ottawa:* Little Ray's Reptile Zoo**
5305 Bank St.
Ottawa, ON K1X 1H2
Tel: 613-822-8924; *Fax:* 613-822-8926
Toll-Free: 877-522-8440
raysreptiles.com
Social Media: www.youtube.com/user/LittleRaysReptileZoo
twitter.com/raysreptiles
www.facebook.com/pages/Little-Rays-Reptile-Zoo/70322645099
Year Founded: 1995 The zoo also serves as an animal rescue & has a large animal education outreach program.
Paul Goulet, Co-Founder
Sheri Goulet, Co-Founder
Matthew Korhonen, Curator

***Peterborough:* Riverview Park & Zoo**
***Parent:* Peterborough Utilities Group**
1300 Water St.
Peterborough, ON K9H 6Z4
Tel: 705-745-6866
www.peterboroughutilities.ca/Park_and_Zoo
twitter.com/RiverviewZoo
www.facebook.com/pages/Riverview-Park-Zoo/156583231031582
Year Founded: 1933 The zoo's activities include 27 exhibits & 48 species such as Camels, Wallabies, Monkies & other exotic creatures. It is also home to gardens, trails & a frisbee golf course.
John Stephenson, President & CEO, Peterborough Utilities Group

***St Catharines:* Happy Rolph Bird Sanctuary & Children's Petting Farm**
c/o St Catharines Recreation & Community Services, 320 Geneva St.
Location: 2 Northrup Cres., St Catharines, ON L2M 7M3
St Catharines, ON L2R 7C2
Tel: 905-937-7210; *Fax:* 905-646-9262
A 15-acre municipal park on the shores of Lake Ontario boasts gardens & pathways, petting farm (open Victoria Day to Thanksgiving weekend), picnic area & playground facilities.

***Stevensville:* Safari Niagara**
2821 Stevensville Rd.
Stevensville, ON L0S 1S0
Tél: 905-382-6996; *Téléc:* 905-382-1619
Ligne sans frais: 866-367-9669
info@safariniagara.com
www.safariniagara.com
Médias sociaux: www.youtube.com/SafariNiagara
twitter.com/SafariNiagara
www.facebook.c om/SafariNiagara
Fondée en: 2002 Safari Niagara is home to over 750 mammals, reptiles & birds.

***Thunder Bay:* Chippewa Wildlife Park**
***Parent:* Chippewa Park**
c/o Thunder Bay Parks Division, Victoriaville Civic Centre, 111 Syndicate Ave. South
Thunder Bay, ON P7E 6S4
Tel: 807-623-5111; *Fax:* 807-625-3588
Toll-Free: 888-711-5094
info@chippewapark.ca
www.chippewapark.ca
The municipally operated zoological park contains bird & mammal species, which are indigenous to northwestern Ontario. The Chippewa Wildlife Park features an elevated walkway (pedestrian boardwalk) for viewing the animals.

***Toronto:* High Park Zoo**
c/o Parks, Forestry & Recreation, City Hall, 100 Queen St. West
Park is located at 1873 Bloor St. West, Toronto, ON
Toronto, ON M5H 2N2
Tel: 416-392-6599; *Fax:* 416-397-4899
parks@toronto.ca
www.toronto.ca/parks
Located on Deer Pen Road, the animal paddocks have always been one of the most popular attractions, dating back to 1890 when deer were kept in High Park. Today, visitors will find domestic & exotic species including bison, llamas, peacocks, deer, highland cattle & sheep.
Helen Sousa, Supervisor, Parks - Etobicoke York

***Toronto:* Riverdale Farm**
201 Winchester St.
Toronto, ON M4X 1B8
Tel: 416-392-6794
www.toronto.ca/parks/featured-parks/riverdale-farm
Riverdale Farm is a Toronto Parks, Forestry & Recreation Division facility featuring animals & gardens in the surrounding park. Located in the heart of downtown Toronto, in the area known as Cabbagetown. Admission is free. Parking on neighbouring city streets only.

***Toronto:* Toronto Zoo**
361A Old Finch Ave.
Toronto, ON M1B 5K7
Tel: 416-392-5929; *Fax:* 416-392-5934
tzwebmaster@torontozoo.ca
www.torontozoo.com
Social Media: instagram.com/thetorontozoo
www.facebook.com/TheTorontoZoo
Year Founded: 1974 The Toronto Zoo is one of Canada's premier Zoos, offering interactive education & partaking in conservation activities. The Zoo has over 5,000 animals representing over 500 species. Open year round.
John Tracogna, CEO

***Vaughan:* Reptilia Inc.**
2501 Rutherford Rd.
Vaughan, ON L4K 2N6
Tel: 905-761-6223; *Fax:* 905-303-9478
zoo@reptilia.org
www.reptilia.org
Social Media: www.youtube.com/user/ReptiliaZoo
twitter.com/ReptiliaCanada
www.facebo ok.com/ReptiliaZoo
One of the largest reptile zoos in the country. Open M-F 10:00-8:00, Sa-Su 10:00-6:00.
Cheryl Sheridan, Zoo Manager, cheryl.sheridan@reptilia.org

***Woodbridge:* Kortright Centre for Conservation**
9550 Pine Valley Dr.
Woodbridge, ON L4L 1A6
Tel: 905-832-2289
info@trca.on.ca
www.kortright.org
www.facebook.com/K ortrightCentre
Year Founded: 1982 An environmental education & demonstration centre, situated on 325 hectares of woodland.

Québec

***Bonaventure:* Bioparc de la Gaspésie**
123, des Vieux Ponts
Bonaventure, QC G0C 1E0
Tél: 418-534-1997; *Téléc:* 418-534-1998
Ligne sans frais: 866-534-1997
info@bioparc.ca
www.bioparc.ca
Médias sociaux: www.youtube.com/user/BioparcGaspesie
twitter.com/BioparcGaspesie
www.facebook.com/BioparcGaspesie
Autre numéros: **Blog: bioparcgaspesie.blogspot.ca**
Fondée en: 1998 Centre d'observation de la faune de la Gaspésie; par un chemin que l'on mile de marche, les visiteurs découvrent une collection de faune et de flore sauvages indigènes de la région présentés dans leurs cinq écosystèmes respectifs: la baie, la lagune, la rivière, la forêt et la toundra.
Aurélien Bisson, Président
Marie-Josée Bernard, Directrice générale, mjbernard@bioparc.ca

***Frampton:* Miller ZOO**
20, route Hurley
Frampton, QC G0R 1M0
Tél: 418-420-5550; *Téléc:* 418-420-5550
millerzoo.ca
www.facebook.com/www.millerzooframpton.ca
Fondée en: 2013
Émilie Ferland, Fondateur
Clifford Miller, Fondateur

***Granby:* Zoo de Granby / Granby Zoo**
525, rue St-Hubert
Situé à 1050, boul David-Bouchard, Granby, QC
Granby, QC J2G 5P3
Tél: 450-372-9113; *Téléc:* 450-372-5531
Ligne sans frais: 877-472-6299
info@zoodegranby.com
www.zoodegranby.com
Médias sociaux: www.youtube.com/user/ZOOdeGRANBYOfficiel
twitter.com/zoodegranby
www.facebook.com/zoogranby
Le Zoo de Granby offre aux visiteurs une expérience de l'enseignement, attirer des visiteurs à proximité de animaux en danger et exotiques, tout en favorisant la conservation et le développement scientifique.
Serge Bernier, Président
Paul Gosselin, Directeur général et secrétaire exécutif

***Hemmingford:* Parc Safari Africain (Québec) Inc.**
Bureau administratif, 850, route 202
Safari est situé à 280, rang Roxham, Saint-Bernard-de-Lacolle, QC
Hemmingford, QC J0L 1H0
Tél: 450-247-2727; *Téléc:* 450-247-3563
www.parcsafari.com
www.facebook.com/ParcSafari
Fondée en: 1972 Le parc s'efforce de protéger et préserver les espèces menacées, tout en offrant aux visiteurs une aventure safari. Le parc abrite 500 animaux de 75 espèces différentes, y compris des éléphants, des rhinocéros, des girafes, des zèbres, des lions, des macaques, des chimpanzés, des tigres blancs, et plus. Il comprend aussi un parc aquatique.

***Sainte-Anne-de-Bellevue:* Ecomuseum**
21125, ch Sainte-Marie
Sainte-Anne-de-Bellevue, QC H9X 3Y7
Tél: 514-457-9449; *Téléc:* 514-457-0769
info@ecomuseum.ca
www.ecomuseum.ca
Médias sociaux: instagram.com/zooecomuseum
twitter.com/ZooEcomuseum
www.facebook.com/z ooecomuseum
Fondée en: 1988 Ouvert toute l'année; centre d'interprétation de la faune; animaux de la vallée du Saint-Laurent.
David Rodrigue, Directeur général

***Saint-Eustache:* Ferme de Reptiles Exotarium inc.**
846, ch Fresniere
Saint-Eustache, QC J7R 4K3
Tel: 450-472-1827; *Fax:* 450-472-8122
exotarium@videotron.ca
www.exotarium.net
Year Founded: 1990 Reptiles rares et menacées d'extinction, les amphibiens et les invertébrés.
Hervé Maranda, Fondateur/propriètaire

***Saint-Félicien:* Zoo Sauvage de Saint-Félicien**
CP 90
Situé à 2230, boul du Jardin, Saint-Félicien, QC
Saint-Félicien, QC G8K 2P8
Tél: 418-679-0543; *Téléc:* 418-679-3647
Ligne sans frais: 800-667-5687
infozoo@zoosauvage.org
www.zoosauvage.org
twitter.co m/zoostfelicien
www.facebook.com/zoosauvage
Fondée en: 1960 Affiche faune nord-américaine dans un contexte d'innovation; aucun des cages ou des barres; ouvert tous les jours de mai 15 à octobre 14, 9h-17h.
Lauraine Gagnon, Directrice générale

***Saint-Joachim:* Rèserve Nationale de Faune du Cap Tourmente (RNFCT)**
570, ch du Cap-Tourmente
Saint-Joachim, QC G0A 3X0
Tél: 418-827-3776; *Téléc:* 418-827-6225
cap.tourmente@ec.gc.ca
www.ec.gc.ca/ap-pa
Fondée en: 1978

***St-Édouard-de-Maskinongé:* Zoo de St-Édouard**
3381, rang des Chutes
St-Édouard-de-Maskinongé, QC J0K 2H0
Tél: 819-268-5150
www.betes.com
Fondée en: 1989 Le zoo abrite plus de 90 espèces animales ainsi que d'une mini-ferme.

Saskatchewan

***Moose Jaw:* Saskatchewan Burrowing Owl Interpretive Centre (SBOIC)**
250 Thatcher Dr. East
Moose Jaw, SK S6J 1L7
Tel: 306-692-8710; *Fax:* 306-692-2762
sboic@sasktel.net
www.skburrowingowl.ca
www.facebook.com/1179452016309 85
Year Founded: 1997 The centre has displays, a gift store, a travelling education program, & a small population of captive burrowing owls.
Lori Johnson, Owl Coordinator

***Regina:* Wascana Waterfowl Park**
Wascana Centre, PO Box 7111, 2900 Wascana Dr.
Regina, SK S4P 3S7
Tel: 306-522-3661; *Fax:* 306-565-2742
wca@wascana.sk.ca
www.wascana.sk.ca
twitter.com/wascanacentre
www.fa cebook.com/WascanaCentreRegina
The Wascana Waterfowl Park is a 223 hectare thriving marshland within Regina's city limits.
Bernadette McIntyre, CEO, bernadette.mcintyre@wascana.ca

***Saskatoon:* Saskatoon Forestry Farm Park & Zoo**
1903 Forestry Farm Park Dr.
Saskatoon, SK S7S 1G9
Tel: 306-975-3382
zoo@saskatoon.ca
www.saskatoon.ca
The zoo is home to gardens, restored heritage buildings & a playground. It is Saskatchewan's only member of Canada's Accredited Zoos & Aquariums.

Yukon Territory

***Whitehorse:* Yukon Wildlife Preserve**
CP 20191
Whitehorse, YT Y1A 7A2
Tél: 867-456-7300; *Téléc:* 867-633-2425
info@yukonwildlife.ca
www.yukonwildlife.ca
www.facebook.com/yukonwildl ife
Fondée en: 2004 Exhibits northern Canadian animals.
Greg Meredith, Executive Director, greg@yukonwildlife.ca

SECTION 3
ASSOCIATIONS

Associations in this section are listed alphabetically by subject. Directly following this page is an Entry Index arranged alphabetically by entry name, regardless of subject. Many subjects are also represented in other sections throughout the book. For example, Section 2: Arts & Culture includes Art Galleries, while this section includes Art Gallery Associations.

Association Name Index

B

C

D

G

H

N

S

T

Y

Z

Accounting

Canadian Academic Accounting Association (CAAA) / Association canadienne des professeurs de comptabilité (ACPC)
245 Fairview Mall Dr., Toronto ON M2J 4T1
Tel: 416-486-5361; *Fax:* 416-486-6158
admin@caaa.ca
www.caaa.ca
Social Media:
twitter.com/caaa_acpc
To promote excellence in accounting education & research in Canada with particular reference to Canadian post-secondary accounting programs & Canadian issues
Alan J. Richardson, President
Jamison Aldcorn, Vice-President, Colleges
Sarah Gumpinger, Vice-President
Chi Ho Ng, Treasurer
Gina Létourneau, Secretary

Canadian Bookkeepers Association
#482, 283 Danforth Ave., Toronto ON M4K 1N2
Fax: 866-804-4617
Toll-Free: 866-451-2204
www.c-b-a.ca
To promote, support, provide for & encourage Canadian bookkeepers; to promote & increase the awareness of Bookkeeping in Canada as a professional discipline; to support national, regional & local networking among Canadian Bookkeepers; to provide information on leading-edge procedures, education & technologies that enhance the industry, as well as, the Canadian bookkeeping professional; to support & encourage responsible & accurate bookkeeping practices throughout Canada
Guy Desmarais, President

Canadian Insurance Accountants Association (CIAA) / Association canadienne des comptables en assurance
#301, 250 Consumers Rd., Toronto ON M2J 4V6
Tel: 416-494-1440
ciaa@ciaa.org
www.ciaa.org
To promote study, research, & development of management & insurance accounting
Lisa Isaacs, Account Executive

Certified General Accountants Association of the Northwest Territories & Nunavut
PO Box 128, 5016 - 50th Ave., Yellowknife NT X1A 2N1
Tel: 867-873-5620; *Fax:* 867-873-4469
admin@cga-nwt-nu.org
www.cga-nwt-nu.org
To provide training & professional support services to accountants in the Northwest Territories & Nunavut; To grant the exclusive rights to the CGA designation; To advance the interests of members; To protect the public; To advocate for the public interest
Biswanath Chakrabarty, CGA, President

Chartered Professional Accountants Canada (CPA) / Comptables professionnels agréés du Canada
277 Wellington St. West, Toronto ON M5V 3H2
Tel: 416-977-3222; *Fax:* 416-977-8585
Toll-Free: 800-268-3793
member.services@cpacanada.ca
www.cpacanada.ca
Social Media: www.youtube.com/cpacanada
linkedin.com/company/cpa-canada
twitter.com/CPAcanada
To foster public confidence in the chartered accountant profession; To assist members to excel; To oversee a single, unified professional accounting designation known as CPA, including all 40 of the accounting bodies in Canada (note that some provinces/regions will be represented by a merged CPA body, while others will be represented by the legacy bodies until integration is complete)
Joy Thomas, President & CEO
Stephen Anisman, CPA, CMA, Chief Financial Officer
Tashia Batstone, MBA, FCPA, FCA, Vice-President, Education Services
Gord Beal, CPA, CA, M.Ed., Vice-President, Research, Guidance & Support
Nicholas Cheung, CPA, CA, Vice-President, Member Services
Gale Evans, CPA, CMA, C.Dir, Vice-President, Administration
Nancy Foran, CMA, FCMA, C.Di, Vice-President, International - The Americas
Stephenie Fox, CPA, CA, Vice-President, Financial Reporting & Assurance Standards
Lyle Handfield, CPA, FCGA, Vice-President, International - Asia
Gabe Hayos, FCPA, FCA, Vice-President, Taxation
Heather Whyte, MBA, APR, Vice-President, Strategic Communications, Branding & Public Affairs
Cairine Wilson, MBA, CAE, Vice-President, Corporate Citizenship
Michele Wood-Tweel, FCPA, FCA, Vice-President, Regulatory Affairs

Chartered Professional Accountants of Alberta
#300, 1210 - 8th St. SW, Calgary AB T2R 1L3
Tel: 403-269-5341; *Fax:* 403-262-5477
Toll-Free: 855-306-9390
reception@cma-alberta.com
www.cpaalberta.ca
Social Media:
www.facebook.com/CPAalberta
twitter.com/cpa_ab
To bring together the former Canadian accounting programs (Certified Management Accountants, Certified General Accountants & Chartered Accountants) in Alberta; to be the primary, internationally recognized Canadian accounting designation
Rachel Miller, FCA, FCPA, Chief Executive Officer
Gordon Turtle, Senior Vice-President, Communications

Chartered Professional Accountants of Bermuda
Sofia House, 48 Church St., 1st Fl., Hamilton HM 12 Bermuda
Tel: 441-292-7479; *Fax:* 441-295-3121
info@cpabermuda.bm
www.icab.bm
To build a reputation of reliability on behalf of members among the public
Annarita G. Marion, JP, CA, President & CEO

Chartered Professional Accountants of British Columbia (CPABC)
#800, 555 West Hastings St., Vancouver BC V6B 4N6
Tel: 604-872-7222
www.bccpa.ca
Social Media: www.youtube.com/user/cpabritishcolumbia
www.facebook.com/cpabc
twitter.com/cpa_bc
To administer the CPA designation in BC; To train & certify CPA students
Richard Rees, FCPA, FCA, Chief Executive Officer
Amy Lam, FCPA, FCA, Executive Vice-President, Operations
James (Jamie) Midgley, FCPA, FCA, Executive Vice-President, Regulation & Registrar
Jan Sampson, FCPA, FCA, Executive Vice-President, Member Engagement & IT
Vinetta Peek, FCPA, FCMA, Executive Vice-President, Marketing & Business Development

Chartered Professional Accountants of Manitoba (CPAMB)
#1675, 1 Lombard Place, Winnipeg MB R3B 0X3
Tel: 204-943-1538; *Fax:* 204-943-7119
Toll-Free: 800-841-7148
cpamb@cpamb.ca
www.cpamb.ca
Social Media:
linkedin.com/groups/CPA-Manitoba-6573960
www.facebook.com/CPAmanitoba
twitter.com/CPAManitoba
To oversee the integration of the Institute of Chartered Accountants of Manitoba (CA Manitoba), the Certified General Accountants Association of Manitoba (CGA Manitoba), & the Certified Management Accountants of Manitoba (CGA Manitoba) under the Chartered Professional Accountants (CPA) banner; To administer the CPA designation in MB
Gary Hannaford, FCPA, FCA, Chief Executive Officer
Grant Christensen, FCPA, FCA, Chief Operating Officer
Kathy Zapiltny, CPA, CA, Senior Director, Regulatory Affairs & Member Services

Chartered Professional Accountants of New Brunswick (CPANB) / Comptables professionnels agréés Nouveau-Brunswick
#602, 860 Main St., Moncton NB E1C 1G2
Tel: 506-830-3300; *Fax:* 506-830-3310
info@cpanewbrunswick.ca
www.cpanewbrunswick.ca
Social Media:
twitter.com/CPAnewbrunswick
To train & certify CPA candidates/students; To regulate professional development of members; To protect the public through ethical standards & discipline
Nancy Whipp, CPA, CA, Chief Executive Officer
Kristen Steeves, Senior Manager, Operations
Mylène Lapierre, CPA, CA, CFE, Manager, Professional Standards & Professional Conduct
Danielle Pieroni, Manager, Communications
Murielle Cormier, Coordinator, Member Services

Chartered Professional Accountants of Newfoundland & Labrador (CPA NL)
#500, 95 Bonaventure Ave., St. John's NL A1B 2X5
Tel: 709-753-3090; *Fax:* 709-753-3609
www.cpanl.ca
Social Media:
linkedin.com/company/5268250
twitter.com/CPANL
To enhance the influence, relevance & value of the Canadian CPA profession through the protection of the public & support to its members & students
Jason Hillyard, CPA, CGA, Chief Executive Officer
Kim Mayo, CPA, CA, Director, Professional Services & Operations

Chartered Professional Accountants of Nova Scotia
#300, 1871 Hollis St., Halifax NS B3J 0C3
Tel: 902-425-7273
info@cpans.ca
www.cpans.ca
To protect & serve the public & members by providing exceptional services & resources within a well-regulated CPA profession
Patricia (Patti) Towler, BA, JD, LLM, CI, CEO

Chartered Professional Accountants of Ontario
69 Bloor St. East, Toronto ON M4W 1B3
Tel: 416-962-1841; *Fax:* 416-962-8900
Toll-Free: 800-387-0735
customerservice@cpaontario.ca
www.cpaontario.ca
Social Media:
linkedin.com/company/cpa-ontario
twitter.com/CPA_Ontario
To foster public confidence in the Chartered Professional Accountant profession, by acting in the public interest & helping members excel. CPA Ontario sets & enforces high standards of practice, qualification & education; promotes professional excellence & ethical conduct; encourages continuous improvement of capabilities among members; promotes the profession while serving as it's primary voice in Ontario
Carol Wilding, FCPA, FCA, President & CEO

Chartered Professional Accountants of Prince Edward Island (CPA PEI)
PO Box 301, #600, 97 Queen St., Charlottetown PE C1A 7K7
Tel: 902-894-4290; *Fax:* 902-894-4791
info@cpapei.ca
www.cpapei.ca
To foster the growth & evolution of the accounting profession in Prince Edward Island
Tanya O'Brien, CPA, CA, Chief Executive Officer

Chartered Professional Accountants of Saskatchewan (CPA SK)
#101, 4581 Parliament Ave., Regina SK S4W 0G3
Tel: 306-359-0272; *Fax:* 306-347-8580
Toll-Free: 800-667-3535
info@cpask.ca
www.cpask.ca
To administer the CPA designation in Saskatchewan
Shelley Thiel, FCPA, FCA, Chief Executive Officer

Chartered Professional Accountants of the Yukon (CPAYT)
c/o Chartered Professional Accountants of British Columbia, #800, 555 West Hastings St., Vancouver BC V6B 4N6
Tel: 604-872-7222
info@bccpa.ca
www.bccpa.ca
Social Media: www.youtube.com/user/cpabritishcolumbia
linkedin.com/company/cpabritishcolumbia
www.facebook.com/cpabc
twitter.com/cpa_bc
To administer the CPA designation in the Yukon

CMA Canada - Northwest Territories & Nunavut (CMA NWT&NU)
PO Box 512, Yellowknife NT X1A 2N4
Tel: 867-876-1290; *Fax:* 867-920-2503
www.cma-nwt.com
George Blandford, CMA, Contact

Guild of Industrial, Commercial & Institutional Accountants / Guilde des comptables industriels, commerciaux et institutionnels
36 Tandian Ct., Woodbridge ON L4L 8Z9
Tel: 905-264-2713; *Fax:* 905-264-1043
iciaguild@aol.com
www.guildoficia.ca

To support & promote interest in vocational accountancy; To encourage acceptance of modern accounting methods & procedures

Institute of Chartered Accountants of the Northwest Territories & Nunavut (ICANTNU)
PO Box 2433, 5016 - 50th Ave., Yellowknife NT X1A 2P8
Tel: 867-873-3680; *Fax:* 867-873-4469
info@icanwt.nt.ca
www.icanwt.nt.ca
To use financial management in order to improve the function of businesses
Tara Clowes, CA, CFP, President

L'Ordre des comptables professionels agréés du Québec
#800, 5, Place Ville Marie, Montréal QC H3B 2G2
Tél: 514-288-3256; *Ligne sans frais:* 800-363-4688
info@cpaquebec.ca
cpaquebec.ca
Média social: www.youtube.com/cpaquebec;
www.instagram.com/cpaquebec
linkedin.com/groups/3996221/profile
www.facebook.com/CPAquebec
twitter.com/CPAquebec
Tous les comptables professionnels du Québec sont regroupés au sein de l'Ordre des comptables professionnels agréés depuis le 2012
Geneviève Mottard, CPA, CA, Président et chef de la direction
Jean-François Lasnier, FCPA, FCMA, Premier vice-président

Petroleum Accountants Society of Canada (PASC)
PO Box 4520, Stn. C, #400, 1040 - 7 Ave. SW, Calgary AB T2T 5N3
Tel: 403-262-4744; *Fax:* 403-244-2340
info@petroleumaccountants.com
www.petroleumaccountants.com
Social Media:
linkedin.com/groups/Petroleum-Accountants-Society-Canada-38 14298
To contribute to the long term success of the Canadian petroleum industry by staying abreast of the constantly changing needs of the industry & striving to satisfy those needs
Josh Molcak, President
Tracy Kozak, Treasurer

The Society of Professional Accountants of Canada (SPAC) / La Société des comptables professionnels du Canada
#1007, 250 Consumers Rd., Toronto ON M2J 4V6
Tel: 416-350-8145; *Fax:* 416-350-8146
Toll-Free: 877-515-4447
registrar@professionalaccountant.org
www.professionalaccountant.org
To provide ongoing education & to set qualifying standards, to ensure the professional competence of its members in the practice of accountancy
William O. Nichols, President

Addiction

Addictions Foundation of Manitoba (AFM) / Fondation manitobaine de lutte contre les dépendances
1031 Portage Ave., Winnipeg MB R3G 0R8
Tel: 204-944-6236; *Fax:* 204-944-7082
Toll-Free: 866-638-2561
execoff@afm.mb.ca
afm.mb.ca
To be a sensitive, caring, learning organization dedicated to continuously improving our services related to addiction & to collaborate with community members in providing a holistic approach, resulting in an improved quality of life for Manitobans; provides prevention, education & treatment programs related to addictions to individuals & communities; conducts research into the negative effects of addictions
Don McCaskill, Chair
Yvonne Block, CEO

Adult Children of Alcoholics (ACA)
PO Box 75061, 20 Bloor St. East, Toronto ON M5W 3T3
Tel: 416-631-3614
acatoronto@hotmail.com
acatoronto.org
To find freedom & improve members' lives through the 12 step program

Airspace Action on Smoking & Health
PO Box 18004, 1215C - 56th St., Delta BC V4L 2M4
Tel: 778-899-4832
airspace.bc.ca
Social Media:
www.facebook.com/234024210003649
twitter.com/airspace_bc
To educate non-smokers on the effects that smoking has on them & of their legal right to smoke-free air; to help establish laws to protect the comfort, safety & health of non-smokers; to help reduce the number of future smokers

Al-Anon Family Groups (Canada), Inc. / Groupe familiaux Al-Anon
PO Box 57012, 163 Bell St. North, Ottawa ON K1R 1A1
Tel: 613-860-3431
wso@al-anon.org
al-anon.alateen.on.ca
Social Media:
www.facebook.com/172402452825446
twitter.com/AlAnon_WSO

Alcoholics Anonymous (GTA Intergroup) (AA)
#202, 234 Eglinton Ave. East, Toronto ON M4P 1K5
Tel: 416-487-5591; *Fax:* 416-487-5855
Toll-Free: 877-404-5591
TTY: 866-831-4657
office@aatoronto.org
aatoronto.org
Fellowship of men & women who share their experience, strength & hope with each other so that they may solve their common problem & help others recover from alcoholism; the primary purpose is to stay sober & help other alcoholics to achieve sobriety

Alcooliques Anonymes du Québec
Bureau des services de la Région 87, 3920, rue Rachel est, Montréal QC H1X 1Z3
Tél: 514-374-3688; *Téléc:* 514-374-2250
region@aa87.org
aa-quebec.org
Demeurer abstinent et aider d'autres alcooliques à le devenir
Diane H., Présidente

Alcooliques Anonymes Groupe La Vallée du Cuivre
CP 21, Chibougamau QC G8P 2K5
Ligne sans frais: 866-376-6279

Canadian Assembly of Narcotics Anonymous (CANA)
PO Box 25073 RPO West Kildonan, Winnipeg MB R2V 4C7
www.canaacna.org
To help the addict who suffers from the disease of addiction

Canadian Centre on Substance Abuse (CCSA) / Centre canadien de lutte contre l'alcoolisme et les toxicomanies (CCLAT)
#300, 75 Albert St., Ottawa ON K1P 5E7
Tel: 613-235-4048; *Fax:* 613-235-8101
info@ccsa.ca
www.ccsa.ca
Social Media: www.youtube.com/user/CCSACCLAT
linkedin.com/company/canadian-centre-on-substance-abuse-ccs a-
twitter.com/CCSAcanada
To minimize the harm associated with addictions, including substance abuse & problem gambling
Rita Notarandrea, CEO
Jody Brian, Director, Public Affairs & Communications
Amy Porath-Waller, Interim Director, Research & Policy

Centre for Addiction & Mental Health (CAMH) / Centre de toxicomanie et de santé mentale
250 College St., Toronto ON M5T 1R8
Tel: 416-535-8501; *Toll-Free:* 800-463-6273
info@camh.net
www.camh.net
Social Media: www.youtube.com/camhtv
linkedin.com/company/camh
www.facebook.com/CentreforAddictionandMentalHealth
twitter.com/CAMHnews
To provide treatment for & research into substance abuse & mental health issues. Clinical & research sites in Toronto & across Ontario
Catherine Zahn, President/CEO

Council on Drug Abuse (CODA)
#120, 215 Spadina Ave., Toronto ON M5T 2C7
Tel: 416-763-1491; *Fax:* 416-979-3936
info@drugabuse.ca
drugabuse.ca
Social Media:
www.facebook.com/186232391465114
To prevent & reduce substance abuse, primarily among youth, by sponsoring education programs in schools
Lorraine Patterson, Chair

Drug Prevention Network of Canada (DPNC)
#102, 1595 West 14th Ave., Vancouver BC V6J 2J1
Tel: 604-731-2425; *Fax:* 905-770-1117
www.dpnoc.ca
Social Media: www.drugpreventionnetworkofcanada.blogspot.ca
To advance abstinence-based drug & alcohol treatment recovery programs; To promote healthy lifestyles free of drugs; To oppose the legalization of drugs in Canada
David Berner, Executive Director

MADD Canada / Les mères contre l'alcool auvolant
#500, 2010 Winston Park Dr., Oakville ON L6H 5R7
Tel: 905-829-8805; *Fax:* 905-829-8860
Toll-Free: 800-665-6233
info@madd.ca
www.madd.ca
Social Media:
www.facebook.com/maddcanada.ca
twitter.com/maddcanada
To stop death & injury caused by impaired driving; To support victims of this crime
Andrew Murie, CEO
Wayne Kauffeldt, Chairperson
Denise Dubyk, President

Narcotiques Anonymes
Chibougamau QC
Ligne sans frais: 800-463-0162
www.naquebec.org

Parent Action on Drugs (PAD)
#121, 7 Hawksdale Rd., Toronto ON M3K 1W3
Tel: 416-395-4970; *Fax:* 866-591-7685
Toll-Free: 877-265-9279
pad@parentactionondrugs.org
www.parentactionondrugs.org
Social Media:
www.facebook.com/pages/Parent-Action-on-Drugs-PAD/390301 531674
twitter.com/PAD_Ontario
To address issues of substance use among youth through outreach, prevention, education & parent support; enhances the capacity of parents, youth & communities to promote an environment that encourages youth to make informed choices
Diane Buhler, Executive Director

Physicians for a Smoke-Free Canada / Médecins pour un Canada sans fumée
134 Caroline Ave., Ottawa ON K1Y 0S9
Tel: 613-600-5794; *Fax:* 613-728-9049
psc@NOSPAMsmoke-free.ca
www.smoke-free.ca
Atul Kapur, President
James Walker, Sec.-Treas.

Responsible Gambling Council (Ontario) (RGC(O)) / Le Conseil ontarien pour le jeu responsable
#205, 411 Richmond St. East, Toronto ON M5A 3S5
Tel: 416-499-9800; *Fax:* 416-499-8260
www.responsiblegambling.org
To increase awareness of compulsive gambling among families, community & service club leaders & supports research into the causes & treatment.
Robin Boychuk, Chair
Jon E. Kelly, Executive Director

Advertising & Marketing

The Advertising & Design Club of Canada (ADCC)
#235, 401 Richmond St. West, Toronto ON M5V 3A8
Tel: 416-423-4113; *Fax:* 416-423-3362
info@theadcc.ca
www.theadcc.ca
Social Media:
www.facebook.com/TheADCC
twitter.com/TheADCC
To recognize, support & promote creative excellence in the Canadian advertising, publishing & design community
Fidel Peña, President
Dawn Wickstrom, Executive Director

Advertising Standards Canada (ASC) / Les normes canadiennes de la publicité
South Tower, #1801, 175 Bloor St. East, Toronto ON M4W 3R8
Tel: 416-961-6311; *Fax:* 416-961-7904
www.adstandards.com

To ensure the integrity & viability of advertising through industry self-regulation.
Linda J. Nagel, President/CEO

Alliance for Audited Media
Canadian Member Service Office, #850, 151 Bloor St. West, Toronto ON M5S 1S4
Tel: 416-962-5840; *Fax:* 416-962-5844
www.accessabc.com
Social Media: www.youtube.com/auditedmedia
linkedin.com/groups?about=&gid=2975919
www.facebook.com/auditedmedia
twitter.com/auditedmedia
To be the pre-eminent self-regulatory auditing organization, responsible to advertisers, advertising agencies, & the media they use, for the verification & dissemination of members' circulation data & other information for the benefit of the advertising marketplace in the United States & Canada
Michael J. Lavery, President & Managing Director

Association canadienne des annonceurs inc.
#925, 2015, rue Peel, Montréal QC H3A 1t8
Tél: 514-842-6422; *Téléc:* 514-964-0771
Ligne sans frais: 800-565-0109
www.acaweb.ca
Média social: linkedin.com/company/2553878
twitter.com/aca_tweets
Pour représenter les intérêts des entreprises de publicité et de marketing au Canada
Ron Lund, Président/Chef de la direction

Association des agences de publicité du Québec (AAPQ) / Association of Québec Advertising Agencies
#925, 2015, rue Peel, Montréal QC H3A 1T8
Tél: 514-848-1732; *Téléc:* 514-848-1950
Ligne sans frais: 877-878-1732
aapq@aapq.ca
www.aapq.ca
Promouvoir et défendre les intérêts des agences membres
Dominique Villeneuve, Directrice générale

Association of Canadian Advertisers Inc. (ACA) / Association canadienne des annonceurs
#1103, 95 St. Clair Ave. West, Toronto ON M4V 1N6
Tel: 416-964-3805; *Fax:* 416-964-0771
Toll-Free: 800-565-0109
www.acaweb.ca
Social Media:
linkedin.com/company/2553878
twitter.com/aca_tweets
To promote the common interests of advertisers & to provide expertise, education & information
Ronald S. Lund, President & CEO
Susan Charles, Vice President, Member Services

Canadian Automatic Merchandising Association (CAMA) / L'Association canadienne d'auto-distribution
Member Services, #100, 2233 Argentia Rd., Mississauga ON L5N 2X7
Fax: 905-826-4873
Toll-Free: 888-849-2262
info@vending-cama.com
www.vending-cama.com
Social Media:
www.facebook.com/10047975738697
twitter.com/CAMA_Vending
To represt the intersts of Vending Operators, Machine Manufacturers, and Product and Service Suppliers in Canada.
Ed Kozma, President
Amanda Curtis, Executive Director

Canadian Media Directors' Council (CMDC)
#1097, 1930 Yonge St., Toronto ON M4S 1Z4
Tel: 416-967-7282
www.cmdc.ca
To advance media advertising in Canada; To create more efficient processes to execute and administer media transactions by adopting industry-wide standards
Penny Stevens, President
Janet Callaghan, Executive Director

Canadian Out-of-Home Measurement Bureau (COMB)
#500, 111 Peter St., Toronto ON M5V 2B8
Tel: 416-968-3823; *Fax:* 416-968-9396
Toll-Free: 800-866-1189
www.comb.org
Karen Best, President

Conseil des directeurs médias du Québec (CDMQ)
#925, 2015, rue Peel, Montréal QC H3A 1T8
Tél: 514-990-1899
www.cdmq.ca
Média social: www.facebook.com/170319683021723
Etre un point de convergence d'opinions et d'information, un instrument de défense des intérêts des clients/agences et un outil de promotion et de stimulation de la fonction média
Michèle Savard, Présidente

Institute of Communication Agencies (ICA) / Institut des communications et de la publicité (ICP)
#3002, 2300 Yonge St., Toronto ON M4P 1E4
Tel: 416-482-1396; *Fax:* 416-482-1856
Toll-Free: 800-567-7422
ica@icacanada.ca
www.icacanada.ca
To anticipate, serve & promote the collective interests of ICA members, with regard to defining, developing & helping to maintain the highest possible standards of professional practice
Jani Yates, President
Gillian Graham, CEO

National Advertising Benevolent Society (NABS) / Société nationale de bienfaisance en publicité
#403, 55 St. Clair Ave. West, Toronto ON M4V 2Y7
Tel: 416-962-0446; *Fax:* 416-962-9149
Toll-Free: 800-661-6227
www.nabs.org
Social Media: www.youtube.com/user/NABSCan
linkedin.com/company/nabs-canada
www.facebook.com/pages/NABS-Canada/113033972042210
twitter.com/NABS_Canada
To relieve the suffering of individuals & their families who have derived the majority of their income from advertising
Manuela Yarhi, Executive Director

National Association of Major Mail Users, Inc. (NAMMU) / Association nationale des grands usagers postaux inc. (ANGUP)
#302, 517 Wellington St. West, Toronto ON M5V 1G1
Tel: 416-977-3703; *Fax:* 416-977-4513
Toll-Free: 800-453-1308
admin@nammu.ca
nammu.ca
Social Media:
linkedin.com/company/national-association-of-major-mail-users
To work in cooperation with Canada Post to improve cost & service

Promotional Product Professionals of Canada Inc. / Professionnels en produits promotionnels du Canada
#202, 455 Fénelon Blvd., Montréal QC H9S 5T8
Tel: 514-489-5359; *Fax:* 514-489-7760
Toll-Free: 866-450-7722
info@pppc.ca
www.pppc.ca
Social Media: www.youtube.com/user/pppcinc;
www.flickr.com/photos/pppc/sets/
www.facebook.com/PPPC.ca
twitter.com/PPPCInc
To advance the promotional products industry; To act as the voice of the predominant advertising medium in Canada
Edward Ahad, President & Chief Executive Officer
Chantal Fontaine, Director, Professional Development & Certification
Marc C. Phillips, Director, Information Technology
Catherine Dubois, Coordinator, Membership Services
Mara Welch, Coordinator, Events
Alec Raffa, Coordinator, Communications

Retail Advertising & Marketing Club of Canada (RAC)
#800, 1255 Bay St., Toronto ON M5R 2A9
Tel: 416-495-6826; *Fax:* 416-922-8011
info@raccanada.ca
www.raccanada.ca
To provide a forum for retail advertising & marketing professionals to meet, discuss vital issues, explore trends, exchange ideas & experience dynamic presentations featuring renowned retailing experts
Lisa Tompkins, Chair

Sign Association of Canada (SAC) / Association canadienne de l'enseigne (ACE)
#301, 216 Chrislea Rd., Woodbridge ON L4L 8S5
Tel: 905-856-0000; *Fax:* 905-856-0064
Toll-Free: 877-470-9787
info@sac-ace.ca
www.sac-ace.ca
To represent & support association members

Bob Bronk, Executive Director
Perry Brooks, President

Trans-Canada Advertising Agency Network (T-CAAN)
#300, 25 Sheppard Ave. West, Toronto ON M2N 6S6
Tel: 416-221-6984; *Fax:* 416-221-8260
bill@waginc.ca
www.tcaan.ca
To serve & support its members in every type of marketing & communications endeavour; Focuses on advertising, communications, & marketing
Bill Whitehead, Managing Director

Vividata
Tel: 416-961-3205
info@vividata.ca
www.vividata.ca
To conduct research on the topics of print readership, non-print media exposure, product usage & lifestyles.
Donald Williams, Director, Research
Tosha Kirk, Manager, Client Services

Agriculture & Farming

Agricultural Alliance of New Brunswick (AANB) / Alliance agricole du Nouveau-Brunswick
#303, 259 Brunswick St., Fredericton NB E3B 1G8
Tel: 506-452-8101; *Fax:* 506-452-1085
alliance@fermenbfarm.ca
www.fermenbfarm.ca
To promote & advance the social & economic conditions of those engaged in agricultural pursuits; to formulate & promote agricultural policies to meet changing economic conditions
Nicole Arseneau, Office Manager
Mélanie Godin, Coordinator, Environmental Farm Plan

Agricultural Institute of Canada (AIC) / Institut agricole du Canada
#320, 176 Gloucester St., Ottawa ON K2P 0A6
Tel: 613-232-9459; *Fax:* 613-594-5190
office@aic.ca
www.aic.ca
Social Media:
twitter.com/aginstitute
To provide the voice for national knowledge & expertise; To promote the creation, production, & delivery of safe foods & sustainable use of related national resources in Canada & beyond
Serge Buy, Chief Executive Officer
Jim Downey, Manager, Finance

Agricultural Institute of Canada Foundation (AICF)
#233, 300 Earl Grey Dr., Ottawa ON K2T 1C1
www.aicfoundation.ca
To enhance agriculture & the role it plays in providing Canadians with a safe, affordable, nutritious food supply
Frances Rodenburg, General Manager

Agricultural Producers Association of Saskatchewan (APAS)
140 - 4th Ave. East, Regina SK S4P 4Z4
Tel: 306-789-7774; *Fax:* 306-789-7779
info@apas.ca
www.apas.ca
To provide farmers & ranchers with a democratically elected, grassroots, non-partisan producer organization based on rural municipal boundaries
Duane Haave, General Manager
Norm Hall, President

Agricultural Research & Extension Council of Alberta (ARECA)
#211, 2 Athabascan Ave., Sherwood Park ON T8A 4E3
Tel: 780-416-6046; *Fax:* 780-416-8915
www.areca.ab.ca
To provide agricultural producers with access to field research and new technology, in order to enhance & improve their operations
Gerald Keufler, Chair
Ty Faechner, Executive Director

Alberta Association of Agricultural Societies (AAAS)
J.G. O'Donoghue Building, #200, 7000 - 113 St., Edmonton AB T6H 5T6
Tel: 780-427-2174; *Fax:* 780-422-7755
aaas@gov.ab.ca
www.albertaagsocieties.ca
To preserve & enhance the viability of agricultural societies in Alberta
Tim Carson, Chief Executive Officer
Lisa Hardy, Executive Director

Monica Bradley, Treasurer

Alberta Barley Commission
#200, 6815 - 8 St. NE, Calgary AB T2E 7H7
Tel: 403-291-9111; *Fax:* 403-291-0190
Toll-Free: 800-265-9111
barleyinfo@albertabarley.com
www.albertabarley.com
Social Media: www.youtube.com/user/GoBarleyTV
www.facebook.com/209980095717832
twitter.com/AlbertaBarley
To supprt barley farmers & help advance the industry
Rob Davies, General Manager

Alberta Canola Producers Commission (ACPC)
Vantage Business Park, 14560 - 116 Ave. NW, Edmonton AB T5M 3E9
Tel: 780-454-0844; *Fax:* 780-451-6933
web@albertacanola.com
www.albertacanola.com
Social Media: www.youtube.com/albertacanola
www.facebook.com/albertacanola
twitter.com/albertacanola
To provide leadership in a vibrant canola industry for the benefit of Alberta canola producers; to strive to improve the long-term profitability of Alberta canola producers
Ward Toma, General Manager

Alberta Institute of Agrologists
#1430, 5555 Calgary Trail NW, Edmonton AB T6H 5P9
Tel: 780-435-0606; *Fax:* 780-464-2155
Toll-Free: 855-435-0606
www.albertaagrologists.ca
Social Media:
linkedin.com/company/alberta-institute-of-agrologists
twitter.com/ABagrologists
To serve as a regulatory body within the province for matters related to agrology
David Lloyd, CEO & Registrar

Alberta Milk
1303 - 91 St. SW, Edmonton AB T6X 1H1
Tel: 780-453-5942; *Fax:* 780-455-2196
Toll-Free: 877-361-1231
cblatz@albertamilk.com
www.albertamilk.com
Social Media: www.youtube.com/user/albertamilk
linkedin.com/company/alberta-milk
www.facebook.com/MoreAboutMilk
twitter.com/MoreAboutMilk
To promote the sustainability of the dairy industry in Alberta
Tom Kootstra, Chair
Mike Southwood, General Manager
Denise Brattinga, Manager, Finance
Mike Slomp, Manager, Industry & Member Services
Katherine Loughlin, Manager, Marketing, Nutrition & Education
Gerd Andres, Manager, Policy and Transportation

Animal Nutrition Association of Canada (ANAC) / Association de nutrition animale du Canada
#1301, 150 Metcalfe St., Ottawa ON K2P 1P1
Tel: 613-241-6421; *Fax:* 613-241-7970
info@anacan.org
www.anacan.org
ANAC advocates on behalf of the livestock & poultry feed industry with government regulators & policy-makers, & works to maintain high standards of feed & food safety.
Des Gelz, Chair
Graham Cooper, Executive Director

Association des jeunes ruraux du Québec (AJRQ)
65, rang 3 est, Princeville QC G6L 4B9
Tél: 819-364-5606; *Téléc:* 819-364-5006
info@ajrq.qc.ca
www.ajrq.qc.ca
Promouvoir la formation auprès de nos membres; soutenir leur sentiment d'appartenance au milieu rural
Cindy Jaton, Présidente
Annie Chabot, Directrice générale

Association québécoise des industries de nutrition animale et céréalière (AQINAC)
#200, 4790, rue Martineau, Saint-Hyacinthe QC J2R 1V1
Tél: 450-799-2440; *Téléc:* 450-799-2445
info@aqinac.com
www.aqinac.com
Média social: twitter.com/AQINAC
Yvan Lacroix, Président-directeur général
Cynthia Vallée, Agente, Communication/Événements

Atlantic Dairy Council (ADC)
PO Box 9410, Stn. A, #700, 6009 Quinpool Rd., Halifax NS B3K 5S3
Tel: 902-425-2445; *Fax:* 902-425-2441
info@adcrecycles.com
www.adcrecycles.com
To maintain good relations among those engaged in dairy processing & distribution industries; to provide opportunities for industry training courses; & to enable united action on any matter concerning the welfare of the dairy trade
John K. Sutherland, Executive Secretary

British Columbia Agriculture Council
#230, 32160 South Fraser Way, Abbotsford BC V2T 1W5
Tel: 604-854-4454; *Fax:* 604-854-4485
Toll-Free: 866-522-3477
info@bcac.bc.ca
www.bcac.bc.ca
Social Media:
twitter.com/bcagcouncil
To provide leadership in representing, promoting, & advocating the collective interests of all agriculture producers in the province of British Colombia; To foster cooperation & a collective response to matters affecting the future of agriculture in the province; To facilitate programs & service delivery for a number of programs that benefit the industry
Reg Ens, Executive Director

British Columbia Dairy Association
3236 Beta Ave., Burnaby BC V5G 4K4
Tel: 604-294-3775; *Fax:* 604-294-8199
Toll-Free: 800-242-6455
contactus@bcdairy.ca
www.bcdairyfoundation.ca
Social Media: www.youtube.com/MustDrinkMoreMilkTV
linkedin.com/company/bcdairy
www.facebook.com/bcdairy
twitter.com/bcmilk
To coordinate, plan, produce & administer dairy products promotion, education & public relations programs best suited to meet the needs of the dairy industry in British Columbia.
Dave Eto, Executive Director

British Columbia Fruit Growers' Association
1473 Water St., Kelowna BC V1Y 1J6
Tel: 250-762-5226; *Fax:* 250-861-9089
info@bcfga.com
www.bcfga.com
Social Media:
www.facebook.com/pages/BC-Fruit-Growers-Association/20833
1935875260
To represent fruit growers' interests in British Columbia
Joe Sardinha, President

British Columbia Grapegrowers' Association (BCGA)
451 Atwood Rd., Grand Forks BC V0H 1H9
Tel: 877-762-4652; *Fax:* 250-442-4076
Toll-Free: 877-762-4652
www.grapegrowers.bc.ca
The Association represents all commercial Columbia on agricultural issues and concerns. It works with other industry organizations, with procincial and federal agricultural organizations and all levels of government to represent, promote and advance the interests of all grapegrowers in British Columbia.
Manfred Freese, President

British Columbia Institute of Agrologists (BCIA)
2777 Claude Rd., Victoria BC V9B 3T7
Tel: 250-380-9292; *Fax:* 250-380-9233
Toll-Free: 877-855-9291
admin@bcia.com
www.bcia.com
Robert Moody, Executive Director

Canada Beef Inc.
Plaza 4, #101, 2000 Argentia Rd., Mississauga ON L5N 1W1
Tel: 905-821-4900; *Fax:* 905-821-4915
Toll-Free: 888-248-2333
info@canadabeef.ca
www.canadabeef.ca
Social Media: www.youtube.com/user/LoveCDNBeef
www.facebook.com/ILoveCanadianBeef
twitter.com/canadianbeef
To build consumer demand for beef

Canada Grains Council (CGC)
#1215, 220 Portage Ave., Winnipeg MB R3C 0A5
Tel: 204-925-2130; *Fax:* 204-925-2132
office@canadagrainscouncil.ca
www.canadagrainscouncil.ca
To be the primary networking group for those involved in the grain industry
Chantelle Donahue, Chair
Patti Miller, Vice-Chair

Canadian 4-H Council / Conseil des 4-H du Canada
Central Experimental Farm, 960 Carling Avenue, Building 106, Ottawa ON K1A 0C6
Tel: 613-759-1013; *Fax:* 613-759-1016
info@4-h-canada.ca
www.4-H-canada.ca
Social Media: www.youtube.com/4hcanada
www.facebook.com/4HCanada
twitter.com/4HCanada
To inspire youth across Canada to become contributing leaders in their communities; To support the development of Canada's rural youth
Shannon Benner, Chief Executive Officer
Sue Wood, Manager, Admissions

Canadian Canola Growers Association (CCGA)
#400, 1661 Portage Ave., Winnipeg MB R3J 3T7
Tel: 204-788-0090; *Fax:* 204-788-0039
Toll-Free: 866-745-2256
ccga@ccga.ca
www.ccga.ca
To supprt canola producers by voicing their concerns about national & international issues
Rick White, General Manager
Kelly Green, Director, Communications

Canadian Consulting Agrologists Association (CCAA) / Association canadienne des agronomes-conseils
#510, 5920 1A St. SW, calgary AB T2H 0G3
Tel: 403-686-8407; *Fax:* 403-255-4592
info@ccaa.bz
To provide excellence in agricultural consulting; To promote standards of competency; To maintain Standards of Ethical Conduct
Adele Buettner, Executive Director
Terry Betker, President

Canadian Federation of Agriculture (CFA) / Fédération canadienne de l'agriculture (FCA)
21 Florence St., Ottawa ON K2P 0W6
Tel: 613-236-3633; *Fax:* 613-236-5749
info@canadian-farmers.ca
www.cfa-fca.ca
Social Media:
www.facebook.com/189161978085033
twitter.com/CFAFCA
To coordinate the efforts of agricultural producer organizations throughout Canada for the purpose of promoting their common interests through collective action; to promote & advance the social & economic conditions of those engaged in agricultural pursuits; to assist in formulating & promoting national agricultural policies to meet changing national & international conditions
Ron Bonnett, President
Errol Halkai, Acting Executive Director
Jessica Goodfellow, Director, Communications

Canadian Honey Council / Conseil canadien du miel
36 High Vale Cres., Calgary AB T3A 5K8
Tel: 403-475-3882; *Toll-Free:* 877-356-8935
chc-ccm@honeycouncil.ca
www.honeycouncil.ca
To promote, develop & maintain cooperation among all persons, organizations & government personnel involved with Canadian beekeeping industry
Rod Scarlett, Executive Director

Canadian Pest Management Association (CPMA) / Association canadienne de la gestion parasitaire (ACGP)
PO Box 1748, Moncton NB E1C 9X5
Fax: 866-957-7378
Toll-Free: 866-630-2762
cpma@pestworld.org
www.pestworldcanada.org
To provide pest management information; To act as the voice of the pest management industry throughout Canada; Upholding the association's Code of Ethics
Bill Melville, President
Karen Furgiuele-Percy, Director, Business Development
Randy Hobbs, Director, Government Affairs
Sean Rollo, Treasurer

Canadian Plowing Organization
38 Parkin St., Salisbury NB E4J 2N4
Tel: 506-372-9427
info@canadianplowing.ca
www.canadianplowing.ca

To preserve the art of match plowing in Canada; to promote the efficient operation & use of farm machinery; to promote improved farm productivity & yield efficiency through proper seed bed preparation & soil management
Gary Keith, Secretary

Canadian Seed Growers' Association (CSGA) / Association canadienne des producteurs de semences
PO Box 8455, #202, 240 Catherine St., Ottawa ON K1G 3T1
Tel: 613-236-0497; *Fax:* 613-563-7855
seeds@seedgrowers.ca
www.seedgrowers.ca
To advance the Canadian seed industry; To advocate for the use of the seed certification as an integral part of quality & identity assurance programs; To develop & provide seed crop certification standards & regulations
Glyn Chancey, Executive Director

Canadian Seed Trade Association (CSTA) / Association canadienne du commerce des semences (ACCS)
#505, 2039 Robertson Rd., Ottawa ON K2H 8R2
Tel: 613-829-9527; *Fax:* 613-829-3530
www.cdnseed.org
Social Media:
www.facebook.com/cdnseed
twitter.com/SeedInnovation
To foster an environment conducive to researching, developing, distributing & trading seed and associated technologies
Patty Townsend, Chief Executive Officer
Peter Entz, President

Canadian Society for Bioengineering (CSBE) / Société canadienne de génie agroalimentaire et de bioingénierie (SCGAB)
2028 Calico Crescent, Orléans ON K4A 4L7
Tel: 613-590-0975
bioeng@csbe-scgab.ca
csbe-scgab.ca
Social Media:
linkedin.com/groups/Canadian-Society-Bioengineering-8152433
www.facebook.com/home.php#%21/group.php?gid=1568753910 12250
To provide expertise in the areas of farm power & machinery, structures & environment, soil & water & electrical power & processing
Greg Clark, President
John Feddes, Society Manager

Canadian Society of Agronomy
S.C. Sheppard, PO Box 637, Pinawa MB R0E 1L0
Tel: 204-753-2747; *Fax:* 204-753-8478
www.agronomycanada.com
The mission of The Canadian Society of Agronomy is dedicated to enhancing cooperation and coorindation among agronomists, to recognizing significant achievements in agronomy and to providing the opportunity to report and evaluate information pertinent to agronomy in Canada. The goals and objects include networking; external relations and awareness; and internal communications and coordination.
Steve Sheppard, PhD, Executive Director

Canadian Sphagnum Peat Moss Association (CSPMA) / Association canadienne Tourbe de Sphaigne
#2208, 13 Mission Ave., St Albert AB T8N 1H6
Tel: 780-460-8280; *Fax:* 780-459-0939
cspma@peatmoss.com
www.peatmoss.com
Social Media: pinterest.com/peatmosscanada/
www.facebook.com/peatmoss.canada
To promote the benefits of peat moss to horticulturists and home gardeners throughout North America.
Paul Short, President

Canola Council of Canada
#400, 167 Lombard Ave., Winnipeg MB R3B 0T6
Tel: 204-982-2100; *Fax:* 204-942-1841
Toll-Free: 866-834-4378
admin@canolacouncil.org
www.canolacouncil.org
To enhance the Canadian canola industry's ability to profitably produce & supply seed, oil, & meal products that offer superior value to customers throughout the world.
Terry Youzwa, Chair
Patti Miller, President

Certified Organic Associations of British Columbia (COABC)
#202, 3002 - 32nd Ave., Vernon BC V1T 2L7
Tel: 250-260-4429; *Fax:* 250-260-4436
office@certifiedorganic.bc.ca
www.certifiedorganic.bc.ca
To maintain a credible set of organic production & processing standards
Jen Gamble, Administrator

Christian Farmers Federation of Ontario (CFFO)
642 Woolwich St., Guelph ON N1H 3Y2
Tel: 519-837-1620; *Fax:* 519-824-1835
Toll-Free: 855-800-0306
cffomail@christianfarmers.org
www.christianfarmers.org
Social Media: www.youtube.com/user/ChristianFarmers
www.facebook.com/CFFOnt
twitter.com/CFFOnt
A professional organization for Christian family farm entrepreneurs; a general farm organization with an interest in a broad range of agricultural, rural & social issues that impact upon the quality of the family life & family businesses of members; as a professional organization, committed to enabling members as producers, as marketers & as citizens, developing both the entrepreneurial & community leadership of members; through involvement in public policy, promotes a family farm & stewardship perspective; as a confessional organization, committed to being upfront about the Christian value system that motivates members, in order to make the wisdom of the Christian faith available to farm practice & farm policy
Clarence Nywening, President
Suzanne Armstrong, Director, Research & Board Manager

Les Clubs 4-H du Québec
6500, boulevard Arthur-Sauvé, bur. 202, Laval QC H7R 3X7
Tél: 450-314-1942; *Téléc:* 450-314-1952
info@clubs4h.qc.ca
www.clubs4h.qc.ca
Média social: www.facebook.com/groups/31231553700/
To develop life skills, such as leadership, cooperation, responsibility, & independence, for the English speaking rural youth of Québec, through achievement & skill-development
Andrée Gignac, Directrice

Coalition of Rail Shippers (CRS)
c/o Canadian Industrial Transportation Association, #405, 580 Terry Fox Dr., Ottawa ON K2L 4C2
Tel: 613-599-3283; *Fax:* 613-599-1295
To provide input to government on matters affecting Canadian, rail freight transportation.
Robert H. Ballantyne, Chair

Commercial Seed Analysts Association of Canada Inc. (CSAAC)
#208, 301 Rothesay St., Douglas MB R0K 0K0
Tel: 204-763-4610
csaacexecutivedirector@gmail.com
www.seedanalysts.ca
To help determine the future of the seed industry; to enhance professionalism through ongoing education; to provide customers with seed analysis services & information
Christine DeRooy, President
Betty Girard, Executive Director

Conseil des industriels laitiers du Québec inc. (CILQ) / Québec Dairy Council Inc.
2035, av Victoria, Saint-Lambert QC J4S 1H1
Tél: 514-381-5331; *Téléc:* 514-381-6677
info@cilq.ca
cilq.ca
Regrouper les entreprises laitières industrielles du Québec qui s'occupent des différentes phases de la transformation, distribution et commercialisation du lait et des produits laitiers; promotion, protection et développement de leurs intérêts économiques, sociaux et professionnels
Charles Langlois, Président-directeur général
Youenn Soumahoro, Économiste
Yolaine Villeneuve, Directrice, Affaires publiques & corporatives

La Coop Fédérée
#200, 9001, boul de l'Acadie, Montréal QC H4N 3H7
Tél: 514-384-6450; *Téléc:* 514-384-7176
information@lacoop.coop
www.lacoop.coop
Média social: www.youtube.com/user/LaCoopfederee
linkedin.com/company/55527
twitter.com/LaCoop_federee
Fournit aux agriculteurs, directement ou par l'entremise de ses coopératives sociétaires, une vaste gamme de biens et de services nécessaires à l'exploitation de leur entreprise, y compris des produits pétroliers; de plus, elle transforme et commercialise sur les marchés locaux et internationaux divers produits agricoles: viande porcine, volaille, etc.
Denis Richard, Président

CropLife Canada
#612, 350 Sparks St., Ottawa ON K1R 7S8
Tel: 613-230-9881
www.croplife.ca
Social Media: www.youtube.com/croplifecanada
twitter.com/croplifecanada
To represent Canada's plant science industry; To foster the developmment of the industry; To build Canadians' trust & appreciation for plant science innovations
Lorne Hepworth, President
Maria Trainer, Managing Director, Regulatory Affairs
Nadine Sisk, Vice President, Communications & Member Services
Russel Hurst, Executive Director, Stewardship & Sustainability
Annie Hsu, Vice-President, Finance & Administration
Pierre Petelle, Vice-President, Chemistry
Dennis Prouse, Vice-President, Government Affairs
Janice Tranberg, Vice-President, Western Canada

Dairy Farmers of Canada (DFC) / Les Producteurs laitiers du Canada (PLC)
21 Florence St., Ottawa ON K2P 0W6
Tel: 613-236-9997; *Fax:* 613-236-0905
info.policy@dfc-plc.ca
www.dairyfarmers.ca
Social Media:
twitter.com/dfc_plc
To coordinate action of dairy producer organizations on all issues of national scope; To collaborate with relevant agencies in elaboration of national policies of interest to Canadian dairy industry
Wally Smith, President

Dairy Farmers of Nova Scotia (DFNS)
#100, 4060 Hwy. 236, Lower Truro NS B6L 1J9
Tel: 902-893-6455; *Fax:* 902-897-9768
www.dfns.ca
To provide a regulatory & administrative service to Nova Scotia's dairy producers
Brian Cameron, General Manager

Egg Farmers of Canada (EFC) / Producteurs d'oufs du Canada
21 Florence St., Ottawa ON K2P 0W6
www.eggfarmers.ca
Social Media:
twitter.com/eggsoeufs
To forcast demand for eggs; To promote eggs nationally; To develop national standards for egg farming
Peter Clarke, Chair
Tim Lambert, CEO

Éleveurs de porcs du Québec
#120, 555, boul Roland-Therrien, Longueuil QC J4H 4E9
Tél: 450-679-0540; *Téléc:* 450-679-0102
leseleveursdeporcs@upa.qc.ca
www.leseleveursdeporcsduquebec.com
Média social: www.youtube.com/user/leporcduquebec
www.facebook.com/Porcduquebec
twitter.com/PorcQc
A l'ordre du jour du Plan agroenvironnemental de la production porcine on trouve; l'application de plans de fertilisation sur toutes les fermes; la diminution des rejets de phosphore et d'azote pour éviter la surfertilisation; la réduction des odeurs; l'utilisation du lisier comme matière fertilisante; mise en place d'actions collectives.
David Boissonneault, Président

Farmers of North America (FNA)
320 - 22nd St. East, Saskatoon SK S7K 0H1
Tel: 306-665-2294; *Fax:* 306-651-0444
Toll-Free: 877-362-3276
www.fna.ca
Social Media:
linkedin.com/company/farmers-of-north-america
www.facebook.com/farmersofnorthamerica
To improve farm profitability across Canada
James Mann, President & CEO

Farmers of North America Strategic Agriculture Institute (FNA-SAG)
320 - 22nd St. East, Saskatoon SK S7K 0H1
Tel: 306-665-2294; *Fax:* 306-651-0444
www.fnastag.ca
To identify new methods for farm profitability; To identify policy & regulatory issues affecting profitability, & to help advocate for change; To identify areas of needed research
Bob Friesen, CEO

Fédération d'agriculture biologique du Québec (FABQ)
#100, 555, boul Roland-Therrien, Longueuil QC J4H 3Y9
Tél: 450-679-0530; *Téléc:* 450-670-4867
fabq@upa.qc.ca
www.fabqbio.ca
Promouvoir l'étude, la défense et le développement des intérêts économiques, sociaux et moraux de ses membres; administrer tout le programme de la mise en marché; étudier des problèmes relatifs à la production; coopérer à la vulgarisation des techniques de production biologique; renseigner le producteur sur la production et la vente de produits biologiques certifiés
Gérard Bouchard, Président

Fédération des agricultrices du Québec (FAQ)
555, boul Roland-Therrien, Longueuil QC J4H 4E7
Tél: 450-679-0540; *Téléc:* 450-463-5228
fed.agricultrices@upa.qc.ca
www.agricultrices.com
Valoriser la profession; créer un réseau entre les femmes; avoir une force politique capable de défendre les intérêts des agricultrices; prodiguer de la formation

Fédération des producteurs de bovins du Québec (FPBQ) / Federation of Québec Beef Producers
#305, 555, boul Roland-Therrien, Longueuil QC J4H 4G2
Tél: 450-679-0530; *Téléc:* 450-442-9348
www.bovin.qc.ca
Regrouper et défendre les intérêts professionnels et économiques des producteurs de bovins du Québec; administrer et appliquer le plan conjoint des producteurs de bovins du Québec
Claude Viel, Président
Guy Gallant, Vice-président

Flax Council of Canada
#465, 167 Lombard Ave., Winnipeg MB R3B 0T6
Tel: 204-982-2115; *Fax:* 204-982-2128
flax@flaxcouncil.ca
www.flaxcouncil.ca
To provide a central focus for industry, producers, government, research institutions & marketing organizations; to promote flax worldwide through crop, market & product development.
William Hill, President

Foreign Agricultural Resource Management Services (FARMS)
#706, 5995 Avebury Rd., Mississauga ON L5R 3P9
Fax: 905-568-4175
Toll-Free: 866-271-0826
www.farmsontario.ca
To facilitate & coordinate requests for foreign seasonal agricultural workers
Ken Forth, President
Sue Williams, General Manager

Grain Growers of Canada (GGC)
#912, 350 Sparks St., Ottawa ON K1R 7S8
Tel: 613-233-9954; *Fax:* 613-236-3590
office@ggc-pgc.ca
www.ggc-pgc.ca
To supprt policies that allow for a competitive global farming industry
Stephen Vandervalk, President
Janet Krayden, Manager, Public Affairs

Horticulture Nova Scotia (HORT NS)
Kentville Agricultural Centre, 32 Main St., Kentville NS B4N 1J5
Tel: 902-678-9335; *Fax:* 902-678-1280
info@horticulturens.ca
www.horticulturens.ca
To enhance collaborative efforts among members which will strengthen & provide leadership to the horticultural industry
Marlene Huntley, Executive Director
Mark Sawler, President

Inland Terminal Association of Canada (ITAC)
PO Box 283, Elbow SK S0H 1J0
Tel: 306-854-4554
www.inlandterminal.ca
To supprt & promote the interests of people working with inland terminals
Kevin Hursh, Executive Director

Keystone Agricultural Producers (KAP)
#203, 1700 Ellice Ave., Winnipeg MB R3H 0B1
Tel: 204-697-1140; *Fax:* 204-697-1109
kap@kap.mb.ca
www.kap.mb.ca
Social Media:
twitter.com/KAP_Manitoba
To be a democratic & effective policy organization, promoting the social, economic & physical well-being of all Manitoban agricultural producers
James Battershill, General Manager
Dan Mazier, President

Manitoba Institute of Agrologists (MIA)
#201, 38 Dafoe Ave., Winnipeg MB R3T 2N2
Tel: 204-275-3721; *Fax:* 888-315-6661
agrologist@mia.mb.ca
www.mia.mb.ca
Social Media:
linkedin.com/company/manitoba-institute-of-agrologists
To act in accordance with the Agrologists Act of Manitoba; To regulate the practice of agrology in Manitoba; To ensure the knowledge, competence, & integrity of institute members, in order to protect the public interest; To act as the voice of the agrology profession
Jim Weir, Executive Director & Registrar

Mushrooms Canada (CMGA)
7660 Mill Rd., RR#4, Guelph ON N1H 6J1
Tel: 519-829-4125; *Fax:* 519-837-0729
info@canadianmushroom.com
www.mushrooms.ca
Social Media: www.youtube.com/cdnmushroom
www.facebook.com/mushroomscanada
twitter.com/mushroomscanada
To encourage cooperation & communication within the Canadian industry, with various levels of government, & with related organizations internationally; To promote mushroom consumption

National Farmers Foundation
2717 Wentz Ave., Saskatoon SK S7K 4B6
Tel: 306-652-9465; *Fax:* 306-664-6226
nationalfarmersfoundation@gmail.com
www.nfu.ca/about/national-farmers-foundation
To stimulate rural/urban cooperation; to fund education & research that will further the progressive farm movement in Canada
Jim Phelps, President

National Farmers Union (NFU) / Syndicat national des cultivateurs
2717 Wentz Ave., Saskatoon SK S7K 4B6
Tel: 306-652-9465; *Fax:* 306-664-6226
nfu@nfu.ca
www.nfu.ca
Social Media:
www.facebook.com/nfuCanada
twitter.com/NFUcanada
To improve economic & social well-being of rural people & rural communities
Terry Boehm, President
Joan Brady, Women's President
Cammie Harbottle, Youth President

New Brunswick Institute of Agrologists (NBIA) / L'Institut des agronomes du Nouveau-Brunswick (IANB)
PO Box 3479, Stn. B, Fredericton NB E3B 5H2
Tel: 506-459-5536; *Fax:* 506-454-7837
www.ianbia.com
To maintain high competency & professional standards for those practicing agrology in New Brunswick; To uphold the NBIA Code of Ethics; to offer advice to the public about agriculture & related areas; To formulate policies & improve the agriculture & food industry
Pat Toner, President
Duncan Fraser, Secretary
Rita Rattray, Office Administrator

Newfoundland & Labrador Federation of Agriculture
PO Box 1045, 308 Brookfield Rd., Bldg. 4, Mount Pearl NL A1N 3C9
Tel: 709-747-4874; *Fax:* 709-747-8827
info@nlfa.ca
www.nlfa.ca
Social Media:
www.facebook.com/nlfarms
twitter.com/NLFarms
To act as the united voice of farmers in Newfoundland & Labrador; To improve the agricultural industry in Newfoundland & Labrador; To advance the economic & social conditions of those in the agricultural industry
Melvin Rideout, President
Paul Connors, Executive Director
Nicole Parrell, Financial Officer

Newfoundland & Labrador Institute of Agrologists (NLIA)
PO Box 978, Mount Pearl NL A1N 3C9
Tel: 709-772-4170
www.aic.ca/agrology/nlia.cfm
Dedicated to the professional aspects of Canadian agriculture.
Gary Bishop, President/Treasurer
Samir Debnath, Registrar

Nova Scotia Federation of Agriculture (NSFA)
Perennia Innovation Park, 60 Research Dr., Bible Hill NS B6L 2R2
Tel: 902-893-2293; *Fax:* 902-893-7063
info@nsfa-fane.ca
www.nsfa-fane.ca
To act as the voice for the agricultural community in Nova Scotia; To ensure a competitive & sustainable future for agriculture in Nova Scotia; To build financially viable, ecologically sound, & socially responsible farm businesses in the province
Chris van den Heuvel, President
Henry Vissers, Executive Director

Nova Scotia Fruit Growers' Association (NSFGA)
Kentville Agricultural Centre, 32 Main St., Kentville NS B4N 1J5
Tel: 902-678-1093; *Fax:* 902-678-1567
contact@nsapples.com
www.nsfga.com
Social Media:
www.facebook.com/nsfga
twitter.com/nsfga1863
To serve the interests of tree fruit growers in Nova Scotia
C. Andrew Parker, President

Nova Scotia Institute of Agrologists (NSIA)
Annapolis Building, 60 Research Dr., Bible Hill NS B6L 2R2
Tel: 902-897-6742
info@nsagrologists.ca
www.nsagrologists.ca
Carolyn Van Den Heuvel, President

Ontario Agri Business Association (OABA)
#104, 160 Research Lane, Guelph ON N1G 5B2
Tel: 519-822-3004; *Fax:* 519-822-8862
info@oaba.on.ca
www.oaba.on.ca
To serve & represent firms engaged in the crop inputs, country grain elevator, & feed & farm supply industry, plus related agricultural businesses operating within Ontario
Dave Buttenham, Chief Executive Officer
Darcy Oliphant, President
Dave Bender, Vice-President
Cassandra Loomans, Treasurer

Ontario Agri-Food Technologies (OAFT)
#200, 120 Research Lane, Guelph ON N1G 0B4
Tel: 519-826-4195; *Fax:* 519-821-7361
info@oaft.org
www.oaft.org
To generate wealth & sustainability for the Ontario agriculture & food industries by utilizing current technologies
Gord Surgeoner, President
Kathy Derksen, Office Manager

Ontario Beekeepers' Association (OBA)
#476, 8560 Tremaine Rd., Milton ON L9T 4Z1
Tel: 905-636-0661; *Fax:* 905-636-0662
info@ontariobee.com
www.ontariobee.com
To coordinate & advance the beekeeping industry in Ontario
Maureen Vandermarel, Business Administrator
Dan Davidson, President

Ontario Creamerymen's Association
26 Dominion St., Alliston ON L9R 1L5
Tel: 705-435-6751; *Fax:* 705-435-6797
Lloyd Kennedy, President

Ontario Dairy Council (ODC)
6533D Mississauga Rd., Mississauga ON L5N 1A6
Tel: 905-542-3620; *Fax:* 905-542-3624
Toll-Free: 866-542-3620
info@ontariodairies.ca
www.ontariodairies.ca
To represent interests of dairy product processors, marketers & distributors in Ontario
Christina Lewis, President

Ontario Federation of Agriculture (OFA)
Ontario AgriCentre, #206, 100 Stone Rd. West, Guelph ON N1G 5L3
Tel: 519-821-8883; *Fax:* 519-821-8810
Toll-Free: 800-668-3276
www.ofa.on.ca
Social Media: www.youtube.com/user/ontariofarms
www.facebook.com/ontariofarms
twitter.com/ontariofarms
To represent farm families throughout Ontario; To champion the interests of Ontario farmers; To work towards a sustainable future for farmers
Don McCabe, President

Ontario Fruit & Vegetable Growers' Association (OFVGA) / L'Association des fruiticulteurs et des maraîchers de l'Ontario
#105, 355 Elmira Rd. North, Guelph ON N1K 1S5
Tel: 519-763-6160; *Fax:* 519-763-6604
info@ofvga.org
www.ofvga.org
Social Media:
www.facebook.com/ofvga
twitter.com/OntFruitVeg
Dedicated to the advancement of horticulture, working proactively through effective lobbying for the betterment of the industry & producers as a whole through advocacy, research, education, communication & marketing
Jason Verkaik, Chair
John Kelly, Executive Vice President

Ontario Institute of Agrologists (OIA)
Ontario AgriCentre, #108, 100 Stone Rd. West, Guelph ON N1G 5L3
Tel: 519-826-4226; *Fax:* 519-826-4228
Toll-Free: 866-339-7619
www.oia.on.ca
Social Media:
www.youtube.com/playlist?list=PLEF3F4C0E83C69744
ca.linkedin.com/company/ontario-institute-of-agrologists
www.facebook.com/ontarioinstituteofagrologists
To regulate Ontario's Professional Agrologists & ensure that competencies meet a Standard of Practice within a specific scope of agrology
Drew Orosz, President
Terry Kingsmill, Registrar

Ontario Maple Syrup Producers' Association (OMSPA)
275 Country Rd. 44, RR#4, Kemptville ON K0G 1J0
Tel: 613-258-2294; *Fax:* 613-258-0207
Toll-Free: 866-566-2753
admin@ontariomaple.com
www.ontariomaple.com
To promote Ontario maple products through research & education
Rhonda Roantree, Office Administrator

Ontario Plowmen's Association (OPA)
188 Nicklin Rd., Guelph ON N1H 7L5
Tel: 519-767-2928; *Fax:* 519-767-2101
Toll-Free: 800-661-7569
eventadmin@plowingmatch.org
www.plowingmatch.org
Provides ledership to local plowing associations; oversees the International Plowing Match; mission is to advance interest & involvement in agriculture by promoting new technologies, environmental & safety issues; preserving the history of soil cultivation
Cathy Lasby, Executive Director
Charles Leduc, President

Ordre des agronomes du Québec (OAQ)
#810, 1001, rue Sherbrooke Est, Montréal QC H2L 1L3
Tél: 514-596-3833; *Téléc:* 514-596-2974
agronome@oaq.qc.ca
www.oaq.qc.ca
Assurer les utilisateurs de services agronomiques et les consommateurs de la compétence, du professionnalisme et de l'engagement des agronomes et ainsi favoriser le mieux-être de la société
René Mongeau, Président
Guillaume LaBarre, Directeur général

Prince Edward Island Federation of Agriculture (PEIFA)
#110, 420 University Ave., Charlottetown PE C1A 7Z5
Tel: 902-368-7289; *Fax:* 902-368-7204
www.peifa.ca
Social Media:
www.facebook.com/peifederationofagriculture
To provide a united voice for Island farmers
Mary Robinson, President
Robert Godfrey, Executive Director

Prince Edward Island Institute of Agrologists (PEIIA)
PO Box 2712, Charlottetown PE C1A 8C3
info@peiia.ca
www.peiia.ca
Social Media:
www.facebook.com/PEIInstituteofAgrologists
twitter.com/PEIAgrologists
To safeguard the public by ensuring its members are qualified & competent to provide knowledge & advice on agriculture & related areas
Paul MacDonald, Registrar

Prince Edward Island Vegetable Growers Co-op Association
PO Box 1494, 280 Sherwood Rd., Charlottetown PE C1A 7J7
Tel: 902-892-5361; *Fax:* 902-566-2383
Don Read, Manager

Les producteurs de lait du Québec (PLQ)
#415, 555, boul Roland-Therrien, Longueuil QC J4H 4G3
Tél: 450-679-0530; *Téléc:* 450-679-5899
plq@upa.qc.ca
www.lait.org
Mèdia social: www.youtube.com/user/FPLQ
twitter.com/ProdLaitQc
Défense et promotion des intérêts professionnels et sociaux des producteurs de lait et mise en marché du lait de la ferme.
Alain Bourbeau, Directeur général

Québec Farmers' Association (QFA)
#255, 555, boul Roland-Therrien, Longueuil QC J4H 4E7
Tel: 450-679-0540; *Fax:* 450-463-5291
qfa@upa.qc.ca
www.quebecfarmers.org
Social Media:
www.facebook.com/groups/306871089363565
twitter.com/quebecfarmers
To defend the rights of the English-speaking agricultural community within the province of Québec.
Dougal Rattray, Executive Director
Andrew McClelland, Director, Communications

Saskatchewan Agricultural Graduates' Association Inc. (SAGA)
College of Agriculture, University of Saskatchewan, Rm 2D27, 51 Campus Dr., Saskatoon SK S7N 5A8
saga.uofs@usask.ca
www.saskaggrads.com
To promote the social well-being of graduates of the School & College of Agriculture; to ensure close relationships among graduates & between the College & School, including faculty & students; to keep graduates informed of some of the most recent developments in various fields of agriculture; to cooperate with University of Saskatchewan Alumni Association in promoting interests of the University as a whole
Jill Turner, President

Saskatchewan Agricultural Hall of Fame (SAHF)
2610 Lorne Ave. South, Saskatoon SK S7J 0S6
Tel: 306-931-4057
www.sahf.ca
To honour Saskatchewan people who have contributed to the field of agriculture
Jack Hay, Chair
Valerie Pearson, Secretary

Saskatchewan Association of Agricultural Societies & Exhibitions (SAASE)
PO Box 31025, Regina SK S4R 8R6
Tel: 306-565-2121; *Fax:* 306-565-2079
www.saase.ca
To provide the forum for exchange of ideas among Association members; to provide educational opportunities for members; to address relevant issues affecting members; to provide for district, board & provincial meetings of members; to promote fair & agricultural industry; to help promote & form new societies; to provide a liaison with the extension program of University of Saskatchewan; to assist governments & universities to reach their agricultural & educational objectives
Glen Duck, Executive Director

Saskatchewan Beekeepers Association (SBA)
PO Box 55, RR#3, Yorkton SK S3N 2X5
Tel: 306-743-5469; *Fax:* 306-743-5528
whowland@accesscomm.ca
www.saskatchewanbeekeepers.ca
To support Saskatchewan's beekeeping industry; To represent the province's beekeeping industry at both the provincial & national levels
Calvin Parsons, President
Corey Bacon, Vice-President
Wink Howland, Secetary-Treasurer
Dennis Glennie, Coordinator, SBA Bear Fence Program

Saskatchewan Canola Development Commission
#212, 111 Research Dr., Saskatoon SK S7N 3R2
Tel: 306-975-0262; *Fax:* 306-975-0136
Toll-Free: 877-241-7044
info@saskcanola.com
www.saskcanola.com
SaskCanola enhances canola producers' competitiveness and profitability through research, market development, extension, and policy development.
Catherine Folkersen, Executive Director
Franck Groeneweg, Chair
Ellen Grueter, Manager

SeCan Association / Association SeCan
#400, 300 Terry Fox Dr., Kanata ON K2K 0E3
Tel: 613-592-8600; *Fax:* 613-592-9497
Toll-Free: 800-764-5487
seed@secan.com
www.secan.com
As Canada's Seed Partner, SeCan actively seeks partnerships which promote profitability in Canadian agriculture. SeCan is the largest supplier of certified seed to Canadian farmers with more than 1,000 members from coast to coast engaged in seed production, processing and marketing. They are a private, not-for-profit, member corporation with the primary goal of accessing and promoting leading genetics.
Jeff Reid, General Manager

SHARE Agriculture Foundation
14110 Kennedy Rd., Caledon ON L7C 2G3
Tel: 905-838-0897; *Fax:* 905-838-0794
Toll-Free: 888- 33-7427
info@shareagfoundation.org
www.shareagfoundation.org
Social Media:
www.facebook.com/119869878092172
To help improve the quality of life for agriculturally impoverished communities worldwide; SHARE stands for "Sending Help & Resources Everywhere."
Murray Brownridge, Chair
Les Frayne, Project Manager, Central America
Bob Thomas, Project Manager, South America

Society of Ontario Nut Growers (SONG)
RR#3, Niagara-on-the-Lake ON L0S 1J0
Tel: 905-935-9773; *Fax:* 905-935-6887
nuttrees@grimonut.com
www.songonline.ca
To promote the interests of nut growers; to encourage scientific research in the breeding & culture of nut-bearing plants suited to Ontario conditions; to disseminate information on propagation techniques & cultural practices
Ernie Grimo, Treasurer

Union des producteurs agricoles (UPA)
#100, 555, boul. Roland-Therrien, Longueuil QC J4H 3Y9
Tél: 450-679-0530
www.upa.qc.ca
Mèdia social: www.youtube.com/user/upa1972
www.facebook.com/pageUPA
twitter.com/upaqc
Promouvoir, défendre et développer les intérêts professionnels, économiques, sociaux et moraux des producteurs agricoles et forestiers, sans distinction de race, de nationalité, de sexe, de langue et de croyance
Marcel Groleau, Président général

Vegetable Growers' Association of Manitoba (VGAM)
PO Box 894, Portage la Prairie MB R1N 3C4
Tel: 204-857-4581; *Fax:* 204-239-0260
vgamveggies@hotmail.com
www.vgam.ca
To support Manitoba's vegetable growers
Todd Giffin, President

Western Barley Growers Association (WBGA)
Agriculture Centre, 97 East Lake Ramp NE, Airdrie AB T4A 0C3
Tel: 403-912-3998; *Fax:* 403-948-2069
wbga@wbga.org
www.wbga.org
To provide farmers with an informed & effective voice in the agriculture industry of Western Canada
Doug Robertson, President
Douglas McBain, Treasurer
Tom Hewson, Saskatchewan Vice-President

Western Canadian Shippers' Coalition (WCSC)
31 Centennial Pkwy., Delta BC V4L 2C3
Tel: 604-943-8984; *Fax:* 604-943-8936
contact@westshippers.com
www.westshippers.com
Social Media: www.youtube.com/user/Rhobot?feature=mhee
twitter.com/Westshippers
Ian May, Chair

Western Canadian Wheat Growers
3602 Taylor St. East, Bay 6A, Saskatoon SK S7H 5H9
Tel: 306-586-5866; *Fax:* 306-244-4497
info@wheatgrowers.ca
www.wheatgrowers.ca
To promote changes that improve the wheat industry for its members
Blair Rutter, Executive Director

Western Grains Research Foundation (WGRF)
#306, 111 Research Dr., Saskatoon SK S7N 3R2
Tel: 306-975-0060; *Fax:* 306-975-0316
info@westerngrains.com
www.westerngrains.com
To fund & invest in agricultural research that benefits western Canadian crop producers; To give producers a voice in funding decisions; To encourage the long-term sustainability of crop research in western Canada
Garth Patterson, Executive Director

Wild Rose Agricultural Producers
5033 - 52 St., Lacombe AB T4L 2A6
Tel: 403-789-9151; *Fax:* 780-789-9152
Toll-Free: 855-789-9151
info@wrap.ab.ca
www.wrap.ab.ca
Social Media:
www.facebook.com/122046961202493
twitter.com/WildRoseGFO
To represent its members at the regional, provincial & national level for the benefit of agriculture; to create an atmosphere of cooperation & communication to ensure that areas of common concern among all producers are dealt with to the benefit of agriculture as a whole
Sheryl Rae, Executive Director

Yukon Agricultural Association
#203, 302 Steele St., Whitehorse YT Y1A 2E5
Tel: 867-668-6864; *Fax:* 867-393-3566
admin@yukonag.ca
www.yukonag.ca
To provide resources and opportunities to agricultural producers in the Yukon.
Mike Blumenschein, President
Bev Buckway, Executive Director

AIDS

African & Caribbean Council on HIV/AIDS in Ontario (ACCHO)
20 Victoria St., 4th Fl., Toronto ON M5C 2N8
Tel: 416-977-9955; *Fax:* 416-977-7664
www.accho.ca
Social Media: www.youtube.com/ACCHOntario
www.facebook.com/ACCHOntario
twitter.com/ACCHOntario
To provide support & resources to members of the African, Caribbean & Black communities in Ontario affected by HIV/AIDS.
Valérie Pierre-Pierre, Director

The AIDS Foundation of Canada
#505, 744 West Hastings St., Vancouver BC V6C 1A5
Tel: 604-688-7294
www.aidsfoundationofcanada.ca
To address the growing problem of HIV disease in Canada; to fund new & innovative ways of assisting infected/affected people with HIV; to support new ways to heighten awareness of HIV disease among the general population

Black Coalition for AIDS Prevention
20 Victoria St., 4th Fl., Toronto ON M5C 2N8
Tel: 416-977-9955; *Fax:* 416-977-7664
info@black-cap.com
www.black-cap.com
Social Media:
www.facebook.com/264852343610058
To reduce the spread of HIV infection in the Black communities & to enhance the quality of life for Black people living with or affected by HIV/AIDS
Shannon Thomas Ryan, Executive Director

Blood Ties Four Directions Centre
307 Strickland St., Whitehorse YT Y1A 2J9
Tel: 867-633-2437; *Fax:* 867-633-2447
Toll-Free: 877-333-2437
bloodties@klondiker.com
www.bloodties.ca
To acts as an information & support centre; to promote public awareness of AIDS/AIDS & hepatitis C and aid in their prevention; to assist people living with HIV/AIDS & hep C.
Patricia Bacon, Executive Director

Canadian AIDS Society (CAS) / Société canadienne du sida (SCS)
#100, 190 O'Connor St., Ottawa ON K2P 2R3
Tel: 613-230-3580; *Fax:* 613-563-4998
Toll-Free: 800-499-1986
casinfo@cdnaids.ca
www.cdnaids.ca
Social Media:
www.facebook.com/aidsida
twitter.com/CDNAIDS
To strengthen the response to HIV/AIDS across Canada; To enrich the lives of people living with HIV/AIDS
Albert McNutt, Chair
Jim Kane, Vice-Chair
Monique Doolittle-Romas, Chief Executive Officer
Simonne LeBlanc, Secretary
Gary Lacasse, Treasurer
Ahmed Bechir, Director, Youth

Canadian AIDS Treatment Information Exchange (CATIE) / Réseau canadien d'info-traitements sida
PO Box 1104, #505, 555 Richmond St. West, Toronto ON M5V 3B1
Tel: 416-203-7122; *Fax:* 416-203-8284
Toll-Free: 800-263-1638
info@catie.ca
www.catie.ca
Social Media: www.youtube.com/catieinfo
www.facebook.com/CATIEInfo
twitter.com/CATIEInfo
To improve the health & quality of life of all people living with HIV/AIDS (PHAs) in Canada; to provide HIV/AIDS treatment information to PHAs, caregivers & AIDS service organizations who are encouraged to be active partners in achieving informed decision-making & optimal health care
Laurie Edmiston, Executive Director

Canadian Foundation for AIDS Research (CANFAR) / Fondation canadienne de recherche sur le SIDA
#602, 200 Wellington St. West, Toronto ON M5V 3C7
Tel: 416-361-6281; *Fax:* 416-361-5736
Toll-Free: 800-563-2873
www.canfar.com
Social Media: www.youtube.com/user/CANFAR;
www.flickr.com/photos/canfar
www.facebook.com/canfar
twitter.com/canfar
National, privately funded, charitable foundation created to raise awareness in order to fund research into all aspects of HIV infection & AIDS
Christopher Bunting, President & CEO

Canadian HIV/AIDS Legal Network / Réseau juridique canadien VIH/sida
#600, 1240 Bay St., Toronto ON M5R 2A7
Tel: 416-595-1666; *Fax:* 416-595-0094
info@aidslaw.ca
www.aidslaw.ca
Social Media: www.youtube.com/aidslaw
www.facebook.com/CanadianHIVAIDSLegalNetwork
twitter.com/aidslaw
To promote the human rights of people living with & vulnerable to HIV/AIDS, in Canada & internationally; through research, legal & policy analysis, education, advocacy & community mobilization
Richard Elliot, Executive Director
Janet Butler-McPhee, Director of Communications

Coalition des organismes communautaires québécois de lutte contre le sida (COCQ-SIDA)
1, rue Sherbrooke Est, Montréal QC H2X 3V8
Tél: 514-844-2477; *Téléc:* 514-844-2498
Ligne sans frais: 866-535-0481
info@cocqsida.com
www.cocqsida.com
Média social: www.facebook.com/COCQSIDA
twitter.com/COCQSIDA
Représenter les membres afin de favoriser l'émergence et le soutien d'une action concertée dans les dossiers d'intérêt commun; faire reconnaître l'expertise et l'apport des organismes communautaires et non-gouvernementaux dans la lutte contre le sida.
Hélène Légaré, Présidente
Ken Monteith, Directeur général

Healing Our Spirit BC Aboriginal HIV/AIDS Society
137 East 4 Ave., Vancouver BC V5T 1G4
Tel: 604-879-8884; *Fax:* 604-879-9926
Toll-Free: 866-745-8884
info@healingourspirit.org
www.healingourspirit.org
To prevent & reduce the spread of HIV infection in First Nation communities & to support those affected by HIV/AIDS.
Winston Thompson, Executive Director
Leonard George, President

Maison Plein Coeur
1611, rue Dorion, Montréal QC H2K 4A5
Tél: 514-597-0554; *Téléc:* 514-597-2788
infompc@maisonpleincoeur.org
www.maisonpleincoeur.org
Contribuer à prévenir le VIH-SIDA, et à promouvoir la santé chez les personnes vivant avec la maladie; offrir des services sans aucune discrimination
Gary Lacasse, Directeur général
Elaine Mayrand, Présidente

Positive Living BC
1107 Seymour St., 2nd Fl., Vancouver BC V6B 5S8
Tel: 604-893-2200; *Fax:* 604-893-2251
Toll-Free: 800-994-2437
info@positivelivingbc.org
www.positivelivingbc.org
Social Media:
www.facebook.com/positivelivingbc
twitter.com/pozlivingbc
To empower persons in British Columbia who live with AIDS & HIV disease
John Bishop, Chair
Wayne Campbell, Vice-Chair

RÉZO
CP 246, Succ. C, Montréal QC H2L 4K1
Tél: 514-521-7778; *Téléc:* 514-521-7665
www.rezosante.org
Média social: www.youtube.com/REZOsante
www.facebook.com/REZOsante
twitter.com/rezosante
Développer et coordonner des activités d'éducation et de prévention du VIH-sida et des autres ITSS dans un contexte de promotion de la santé sexuelle auprès des hommes gais, bisexuels et hommes ayant des relations sexuelles avec d'autres hommes de Montréal.
Robert Rousseau, Directeur général

Animal Breeding

Appaloosa Horse Club of Canada (ApHCC)
PO Box 940, Claresholm AB T0L 0T0
Tel: 403-625-3326; *Fax:* 403-625-2274
registry@appaloosa.ca
www.appaloosa.ca
Social Media:
www.facebook.com/255499284509
To collect records & historical data relating to origin of the Appaloosa; to file records & issue certificates of registration; to preserve, improve & standardize the breed
Sharon Duncan, Executive Secretary

Ayrshire Breeders Association of Canada (ABAC) / Associaton des éleveurs Ayrshire du Canada
4865, boul Laurier ouest, Saint-Hyacinthe QC J2S 3V4
Tel: 450-778-3535; *Fax:* 450-778-3531
info@ayrshire-canada.com
www.ayrshire-canada.com
Social Media:
www.facebook.com/ayrshire.canada
twitter.com/AyrshireCanada
To bring Ayrshire breeders together for the purpose of cooperating in their efforts to further the interests of the breed; To promote breeding of purebred Ayrshire cattle in Canada; To establish breeding standards; To cooperate with industry partners to enhance programs
Michel Bourdeault, Executive Director

Canadian Angus Association (CAA) / L'Association canadienne Angus
#142, 6715 - 8 St. NE, Calgary AB T2E 7H7
Tel: 403-571-3580; *Fax:* 403-571-3599
Toll-Free: 888-571-3580
www.cdnangus.ca
Social Media:
www.youtube.com/user/CanadianAngusAssoc/videos
www.facebook.com/CanadianAngusAssociation

To offer services to enhance the growth & position of the Angus breed; To maintain breed purity
Doug Fee, Chief Executive Officer
Bob Switzer, President
Sharmayne Byrgesen, Registrar

Canadian Arabian Horse Registry
#113, 37 Athabascan Ave., Sherwood Park AB T8A 4H3
Tel: 780-416-4990; *Fax:* 780-416-4860
cahr@cahr.ca
www.cahr.ca
To register purebred Arabian horses in Canada; to establish standards of breeding practices; To serve the needs of Arabian horse owners
Christine Tribe, Registrar
Marcia Friesen, President
Robert Sproule, Secretary-Treasurer

Canadian Belgian Horse Association
17150 Concession 10, Schomberg ON L0G 1T0
Tel: 905-939-1186; *Fax:* 905-939-7547
cbha@csolve.net
www.canadianbelgianhorse.com
To promote the Belgian breed of horse
Terry Morrow, President

Canadian Bison Association (CBA) / Association canadienne du bison
PO Box 3116, #200, 1660 Pasqua St., Regina SK S4P 3G7
Tel: 306-522-4766; *Fax:* 306-522-4768
cba1@sasktel.net
www.canadianbison.ca
To develop the bison industry; to maintain the production of bison in a natural state (no growth hormones, chemicals, feed lots, free-range management); to be the voice for commercial breeders; to assist in the formation of regulations & guidelines in commercial production & management of Canadian Plains Bison & to promote the product & awareness of the bison industry
Gavin Conacher, Executive Director

Canadian Blonde d'Aquitaine Association
c/o Canadian Livestock Records Corp., 2417 Holly Ln., Ottawa ON K1V 0M7
Tel: 613-731-7110; *Fax:* 613-731-0704
cbda@clrc.ca
www.canadianblondeassociation.ca
To improve the practice of breeding Blonde d'Aquitaine cows
Myrna Flesch, President

Canadian Brown Swiss & Braunvieh Association / L'association canadienne de la Suisse Brune et de la Braunvieh
RR#5 5653 Hwy. 6 North, Guelph ON N1H 6J2
Tel: 519-821-2811; *Fax:* 519-763-6582
brownswiss@gencor.ca
www.browncow.ca
Social Media:
www.facebook.com/117089315003708
To encourage, develop & regulate breeding of Brown Swiss & Braunvieh dairy cattle.
Renald Dumas, President
Jessie Weir, Secretary Manager

Canadian Cattle Breeders' Association (CCBA) / Société des éleveurs de bovins canadiens (SEBC)
4865, boul Laurier ouest, Saint-Hyacinthe QC J2S 3V4
Tel: 450-774-2775; *Fax:* 450-774-9775
info@cqrl.org
www.clrc.ca/canadiancattle.shtml
Angèle Hébert, Sec.-trés.

Canadian Cattlemen's Association (CCA)
#180, 6815 - 8 St. NE, Calgary AB T2E 7H7
Tel: 403-275-8558; *Fax:* 403-274-5686
feedback@cattle.ca
www.cattle.ca
Social Media: www.instagram.com/Canadiancattlemens
www.facebook.com/Canadian-Cattlemens-Association-333965336775693/
twitter.com/CdnCattlemen
To act as the national voice of beef producers across Canada; To produce high-quality beef products; To maintain a profitable Canadian beef industry; To use management practices that protect the health of the animal & protect the environment
Dan Darling, President
Dennis Laycraft, Executive Vice President
Rob McNabb, General Manager, Operations
Fawn Jackson, Manager, Environment and Sustainability

Canadian Charolais Association (CCA)
2320 - 41 Ave. NE, Calgary AB T2E 6W8
Tel: 403-250-9242; *Fax:* 403-291-9324
cca@charolais.com
www.charolais.com
Social Media:
www.facebook.com/cdncharolais
twitter.com/canCharolais
To be leaders in predictable beef genetics; to register, record, transfer & promote Canadian Charolais; to provide services for membership
Wade Beck, President

Canadian Co-operative Wool Growers Ltd. (CCWG)
PO Box 130, 142 Franktown Rd., Carleton Place ON K7C 3P3
Tel: 613-257-2714; *Fax:* 613-257-8896
ccwghq@wool.ca
www.wool.ca
To operate as a producer-owned wool marketing cooperative; To collect, grade, & market, the majority of the Canadian wool clip to the global market; To retail farm supplies & animal health & identification products
Eric Bjergso, General Manager

Canadian Cutting Horse Association (CCHA)
RR#3, Innisfail AB T4G 1T8
Tel: 403-227-4444; *Fax:* 403-227-3030
www.ccha.ca
To promote the cutting horse, a specially trained horse to isolate or cut an individual animal from large cattle herds
Les Timmons, President
Jamie Couilliard, Vice-President
Connie Delorme, National Administrator
Geoff Thomas, Secretary-Treasurer

Canadian Dexter Cattle Association (CDCA) / Société canadienne des bovins Dexter
2417 Holly Lane, Ottawa ON K1V 0M7
Tel: 613-731-7110; *Fax:* 613-731-0704
ron.black@clrc.ca
www.dextercattle.ca
To preserve & promote the breeding of good quality Dexter cattle in Canada
Adrian Hykaway, President

Canadian Donkey & Mule Association (CDMA)
PO Box 12716, Lloydminster AB T7V 0Y4
Tel: 780-875-6362
donkeyandmule@live.ca
www.donkeyandmule.com
To operate registry for donkeys & recordation for mules; to promote use, well-being & protection of donkeys & mules; to assist in training & placing donkeys for disabled riding.
Chris Schlosser, Secretary
Kim Baerg, President

Canadian Fjord Horse Association
c/o Canadian Livestock Records Corporation, 2417 Holly Ln., Ottawa ON K1V 0M7
Tel: 613-731-7110; *Fax:* 613-731-0704
directors@cfha.org
www.cfha.org
Social Media: www.youtube.com/canadianfjord
www.facebook.com/canadianfjord
twitter.com/canadianfjord
To operate under the Animal Pedigree Act; To assure the success of the purebred registered Norwegian Fjord Horse in Canada
Carol Boehm, President
Lauralee Mills, CLRC Contact

Canadian Galloway Association (CGA) / Société canadienne Galloway
c/o CLRC, 2417 Holly Lane, Ottawa ON K1V 0M7
Tel: 613-731-7110; *Fax:* 613-731-0704
galloway@clrc.ca
www.galloway.ca
To promote & regulate the breeding of Galloways, Belted Galloways & White Galloways in Canada
John Toon, President
Ron Black, Sec.-Treas.

Canadian Gelbvieh Association (CGA)
5160 Skyline Way NE, Calgary AB T2E 6V1
Tel: 403-250-8640; *Fax:* 403-291-5624
gelbvieh@gelbvieh.ca
www.gelbvieh.ca
To promote Gelbvieh cattle in Canada & their registration.
Darrell Hickman, President
Wendy Belcher, Secretary Manager

Canadian Goat Society (CGS) / La Société canadienne des éleveurs de chèvres
2417 Holly Ln., Ottawa ON K1V 0M7
Tel: 613-731-9894; *Fax:* 613-731-0704
cangoatsoc@rogers.com
goat.softcorp.ca
To maintain the integrity of herdbooks, providing accurate evaluation programs for performance and type and promoting the responsible and humane treatment of goats.
Arnold Steeves, President

Canadian Guernsey Association
5653 Hwy. 6 North, RR#5, Guelph ON N1H 6J2
Tel: 519-836-2141; *Fax:* 519-763-6582
info@guernseycanada.ca
www.guernseycanada.ca
To provide services to breeders of Guernsey dairy cattle including records, awards, promotion, sales & shows.
Jesse Weir, Administrator

Canadian Hereford Association (CHA) / Association canadienne Hereford
5160 Skyline Way NE, Calgary AB T2E 6V1
Tel: 403-275-2662; *Fax:* 403-295-1333
Toll-Free: 888-836-7242
herefords@hereford.ca
www.hereford.ca
Social Media:
twitter.com/CAN_Hereford
To promote the consistent & economical production of beef; To strive to meet & exceed consumer expectations for tender, juicy, & flavourful beef products, through performance measurement, genetic selection, appropriate handling, feeding, & processing
Gordon Stephenson, General Manager

Canadian Highland Cattle Society (CHCS) / Société canadienne des éleveurs de bovins Highland
121 Rang 5 East, Saint-Donat-de-Rimouski QC G0K 1L0
Tel: 418-739-4477; *Fax:* 418-739-4477
highland@chcs.ca
www.chcs.ca
To regulate & promote breeding of Highland cattle in Canada.
Marise Labrie, Secretary-Manager

Canadian Icelandic Horse Federation (CIHF)
c/o Maria Badyk, PO Box 1, Stn. Site 1, RR#2, High River AB T1V 1N2
Tel: 403-603-7949
www.cihf.ca
To promote & maintain the purity of the Icelandic horse; to keep record of breeding and registration of Icelandic horse under the Canadian National Livestock Record System; to promote the awareness and secure the integrity of purebred Icelandic horses.
Maria Badyk, President
Victoria Stoncius, Vice-President

Canadian Limousin Association (CLA)
#13, 4101 - 19th St. NE, Calgary AB T2E 7C4
Tel: 403-253-7309; *Fax:* 403-253-1704
Toll-Free: 866-886-1605
limousin@limousin.com
www.limousin.com
Social Media:
www.facebook.com/CanadianLimousin
twitter.com/cdnlimousin
To provide collective service for Limousin breeders in Canada; To record registration & produce Records of Performance on all registered anirnals; To promote & inform producers about Limousin cattle; To develop & implement educational agricultural programs
Tessa Verbeek, General Manager

Canadian Livestock Records Corporation (CLRC) / Société canadienne d'enregistrement des animaux
2417 Holly Lane, Ottawa ON K1V 0M7
Tel: 613-731-7110; *Fax:* 613-731-0704
Toll-Free: 877-833-7110
clrc@clrc.ca
www.clrc.ca
To serve the Canadian seed stock industry; to be responsible to the member breed associations & Agriculture Canada for the maintenance of records, issuance of certificates, endorsement of changes of ownership, enrolment of members, registration of individuals, identification letters, collection of fees & the deposit of same into the appropriate breed association account
Ron Black, General Manager

Canadian Maine-Anjou Association (CMAA)
5160 Skyline Way NE, Calgary AB T2E 6V1
Tel: 403-291-7077; *Fax:* 403-291-0274
cmaa@maine-anjou.ca
www.maine-anjou.ca

To encourage, develop, & regulate the breeding of Main-Anjou cattle in Canada
Stuart Byman, President
Murray Preece, Secretary
Brian Brown, Treasurer

Canadian Milking Shorthorn Society (CMSS)
203 Ferry Rd., Cornwall PE C0A 1H4
Tel: 902-439-9386; *Fax:* 902-436-0551
milking.shorthorn@gmail.com
www.cmss.on.ca
Social Media: www.facebook.com/milkingshorthorn
To promote & encourage the development of milking shorthorn cattle.
Ryan Barrett, Secretary-Manager
Dave Prinzen, President

Canadian Morgan Horse Association (CMHA) / Association des chevaux Morgan canadien inc.
PO Box 286, Port Perry ON L9L 1A3
Tel: 905-982-0060; *Fax:* 905-982-0097
info@morganhorse.ca
www.morganhorse.ca
Bob Watson, President
Melissa MacKenzie, Eastern Vice-President
Laurie Ann Lyons, Western Vice-President
Mark Grootelaar, Treasurer

Canadian Murray Grey Association (CMGA)
PO Box 157, Bragg Creek AB T0L OKO
Tel: 403-949-2199
cmgareg@telus.net
www.cdnmurraygrey.ca
To promote the genetics of Murray Grey Beef Cattle

Canadian Palomino Horse Association (CPHA)
c/o Lorraine Holdaway, 631 Hendershott Rd., RR#1, Hannon ON L0R 1P0
Tel: 905-692-4328
canadianpalomino@gmail.com
www.clrc.ca/palomino.shtml
To develop & promote the breeding of Palomino horses in Canada; To establish standards of breeding
Lorraine Holdaway, Secretary
Laura Lee Mills, Registrar

Canadian Percheron Association / Association canadienne du cheval Percheron
Rolla BC
Tel: 250-759-4981; *Fax:* 888-423-0049
canadapercheron@uniserve.com
www.canadianpercherons.com
To develop & encourage the breeding of purebred Percheron horses in Canada; To establish standards of breeding; To regulate the breeding of purebred Percheron horses
David Logies, President
Kathy Ackles, Contact

Canadian Pork Council (CPC) / Conseil canadien du porc (CCP)
#900, 200 Laurier Ave. West, Ottawa ON K1P 5Z9
Tel: 613-236-9239; *Fax:* 613-236-6658
info@cpc-ccp.com
www.cpc-ccp.com
To provide a leadership role in a concerted effort involving all levels of industry & government toward a common understanding & action plan for achieving a dynamic & prosperous pork industry in Canada.
Jean-Guy Vincent, Chair

Canadian Quarter Horse Association (CQHA)
c/o Sherry Clemens, Secretary, PO Box 2132, Moose Jaw SK S6H 7T2
Tel: 306-692-8393
admin@huntseathorses.com
www.cqha.ca
Social Media: www.facebook.com/192652444096322
To address issues of concern to Canadian owners of American Quarter Horses; to be a communications vehicle for and with Canadian owners of American Quarter Horses; and to promote and market - both globally and within Canada - Canadian-bred and/or Canadian-owned American Quarter Horses.
Haidee Landry, President

Canadian Red Poll Cattle Association / Société Canadienne des Bovins Red Poll
2417 Holly Lane, Ottawa ON K1V 0M7
Tel: 613-731-7110; *Fax:* 613-731-0704
Toll-Free: 877-731-7110
redpoll@clrc.ca
www.clrc.ca/redpoll.shtml
To encourage development & regulation of breeding of purebred Red Poll cattle in Canada for improvement of Canadian beef cattle industry
Ron Black, Sec.-Treas.

Canadian Sheep Breeders' Association (CSBA) / La société canadienne des éleveurs de moutons
PO Box 46, RR#2, Site 7, Bluffton AB T0C 0M0
Fax: 877-207-2541
Toll-Free: 866-956-1116
www.sheepbreeders.ca
To represent & promote sheep breeders
Trenholm Nelson, President
Kim MacDougall, Vice President
Stacey White, General Manager

Canadian Sheep Federation / Fédération canadienne du mouton
130 Malcolm Rd., Guelph ON N1K 1B1
Tel: 613-652-1824; *Fax:* 866-909-5360
Toll-Free: 888-684-7739
info@cansheep.ca
www.cansheep.ca
To set national policy for the sheep industry; to endeavour to further the viability, expansion & prosperity of the Canadian sheep & wool industry.
Philip Kolodychuk, Chair
Carlena Patterson, Executive Director

Canadian Shorthorn Association
Canada Centre Bldg., Exhibition Park, PO Box 3771, Regina SK S4P 3N8
Tel: 306-757-2212; *Fax:* 306-525-5852
info@canadianshorthorn.com
www.canadianshorthorn.com
Belinda Wagner, Sec.-Treas.

Canadian Simmental Association
#13, 4101 - 19 St. NE, Calgary AB T2E 7C4
Tel: 403-250-7979; *Fax:* 403-250-5121
Toll-Free: 866-860-6051
cansim@simmental.com
www.simmental.com
To encourage, develop, & regulate the breeding of Simmental cattle in Canada
Fraser Redpath, President
Kelly Ashworth, First Vice-President
Randy Mader, Second Vice-President
Bruce Holmquist, General Manager

Canadian Swine Breeders' Association (CSBA) / L'Association canadienne des éleveurs de porcs
#2, 408 Dundas St., Woodstock ON N4S 1B9
Tel: 519-421-2354; *Fax:* 519-421-0887
info@canswine.ca
www.canswine.ca
To improve & promote Canadian purebred swine; to lobby on behalf of purebred swine breeders in Canada; to direct & regulate purebred swine industry; to be involved in registration & transfer of following breeds: Berkshire, British Saddleback, Chester White, Duroc, Hampshire, Large Black, Pietrain, Poland China, Spotted, Tamworth, Welsh, Yorkshire, Landrace, Lacombe, Red Wattle (registration forms can be obtained from Canadian Livestock Records Corporation).
Rosemary Smart, General Manager

Canadian Tarentaise Association (CTA)
c/p Rosalyn Harris, PO Box 1156, Shellbrook SK S0J 2E0
Toll-Free: 800-450-4181
canadiantarentaise@sasktel.net
www.canadiantarentaise.com
To develop, register & promote Tarentaise cattle in Canada.
Wayne Collette, President
Rosalyn Harris, Secretary

Canadian Thoroughbred Horse Society (CTHS) / Société canadienne du cheval Thoroughbred
PO Box 172, Toronto ON M9W 5L1
Tel: 416-675-1370; *Fax:* 416-675-9525
info@cthsnational.com
www.cthsnational.com
Social Media: www.facebook.com/CanadianThoroughbredHorseSocietyNationalDivision
To assist & afford a means for promotion of interests of those engaged in breeding of thoroughbreds; to protect members against unbusinesslike methods; to diffuse information among members & others; to secure uniformity in usage & business conditions; to determine requirements of horses as thoroughbreds by the Society; to promote, encourage & assist in livestock & agricultural exhibitions, fairs & racing; to sponsor, assist & conduct sales of thoroughbred stock; to compile statistics of the industry; to maintain efficient supervision of breeders of thoroughbred horses; to prevent, detect & punish fraud (ie. in registration of throughbreds).
Grant Watson, President
Fran Okihiro, Manager

Canadian Trakehner Horse Society (CTHS)
PO Box 6009, New Hamburg ON N3A 2K6
Tel: 519-662-3209
cantrakhsivh@golden.net
www.cantrak.on.ca
Social Media: www.facebook.com/pages/Canadian-Trakehner/203491652994222
To maintain a public registry of Trakehner horses, under the Canadian Livestock Records Corporation; to promote & preserve Trakehner horses in Canada
Judy Kirkby, President
Ingrid von Hausen, Registrar & Secretary
Laurel Glanfield, Treasurer

Canadian Welsh Black Cattle Society (CWBCS) / Société Canadienne des bovins Welsh Black
c/o Canadian Livestock Records Corporation, 2417 Holly Lane, Ottawa ON K1V 0M7
Tel: 613-731-7110; *Fax:* 613-731-0704
www.clrc.ca/welshblack.shtml
Randy Scott, President
Randy Kaiser, Vice-President
Arlin Strohschein, Secretary-Treasurer

EastGen
7660 Mill Rd., Guelph ON N1H 6J1
Tel: 519-821-2150; *Fax:* 519-763-6582
Toll-Free: 888-821-2150
info@eastgen.ca
www.eastgen.ca
Social Media: www.facebook.com/EastGen
twitter.com/EastGenGenetics
To act as a farmer-directed AI cooperative & offer services to members in Ontario, New Brunswick, PEI, & Newfoundland & Labrador
Alan Brown, President

Farm & Food Care Ontario
#106, 100 Stone Rd. West, Guelph ON N1G 5L3
Tel: 519-837-1326; *Fax:* 519-837-3209
www.farmfoodcare.org
Social Media: www.youtube.com/user/FarmandFoodCare
www.facebook.com/FarmFoodCare
twitter.com/farmfoodcare
To support & promote the responsible production & marketing of livestock & poultry by Ontario farmers & through a variety of initiatives, to better inform the public of the excellence of animal agriculture

Holstein Canada
PO Box 610, 20 Corporate Pl., Brantford ON N3T 5R4
Tel: 519-756-8300; *Fax:* 519-756-3502
Toll-Free: 855-756-8300
www.holstein.ca
Social Media: www.instagram.com/holstein_canada
www.facebook.com/HolsteinCanada
twitter.com/HolsteinCanada
To improve the Holstein breed by ascertaining the most desirable characteristics of the breed for current & prospective conditions in Canada; To prepare, maintain & make available a genealogical record of the breed; To promote the best interests of breeders & owners of Holstein cattle
Ann Louise Carson, Chief Executive Officer

Jersey Canada (JC)
#9, 350 Speedvale Ave. West, Guelph ON N1H 7M7
Tel: 519-821-1020; *Fax:* 519-821-2723
info@jerseycanada.com
www.jerseycanada.com
To represent & promote the Jersey breed & encourage market development domestically & internationally; To provide & maintain a registration system, catalogues, & pedigree information; To update classification & milk production records
Mathieu Larose, President
Brian Raymer, First Vice-President
Mark Anderson, Second Vice-President
Kathryn Kyle, General Manager
Jill Dann, Registrar

National Chinchilla Breeders of Canada (NCBC)
9575 Winston Churchill Blvd., Brampton ON L6X 0A4
Tel: 905-451-8736; *Fax:* 905-457-5326
ncbc@idirect.com
Marie Riedstra, Secretary-Manager

Nova Scotia Mink Breeders' Association
c/o Dan Mullen, 2124 Black Rock Rd., Waterville NS B0P 1V0
Tel: 902-680-5360; *Fax:* 902-538-7799
To foster better mink breeding among the members; to help secure market advantage.
Dan Mullen, President

Salers Association of Canada (SAC) / Association salers du Canada
5160 Skyline Way NE, Calgary AB T2E 6V1
Tel: 403-264-5850; *Fax:* 403-264-5895
info@salerscanada.com
www.salerscanada.com
To develop & register Salers cattle
Gar Williams, President
Ray Depalme, Treasurer
Lois Chivilo, Registrar

Sask Pork
#2, 502 - 45th St. West, Saskatoon SK S7L 6H2
Tel: 306-244-7752; *Fax:* 306-244-1712
info@saskpork.com
www.saskpork.com
To position the Saskatchewan pork industry as a preferred supplier of high quality, competitively priced pork products for the global market.
Neil Ketilson, General Manager

Saskatchewan Stock Growers Association (SSGA)
Main Floor, Canada Centre Building, Evraz Place, PO Box 4752, Regina SK S4P 3Y4
Tel: 306-757-8523; *Fax:* 306-569-8799
skstockgrowers.com
To serve, protect, & advance the interests of the beef industry in Saskatchewan; To represent the cattle industry in Saskatchewan on the legislative front
Chad MacPherson, General Manager
Harold Martens, President

Standardbred Canada (SC)
2150 Meadowvale Blvd., Mississauga ON L5N 6R6
Tel: 905-858-3060; *Fax:* 905-858-3111
www.standardbredcanada.ca
Social Media: www.youtube.com/user/jporchak
www.facebook.com/standardbred.canada
twitter.com/TrotInsider
To encourage & develop the breeding of Standardbred Horses
John Gallinger, President & CEO
Val Boom, Manager, Member Services, Identification & Field Services

The Western Stock Growers' Association (WSGA)
PO Box 179, 900 Village Lane, Okotoks AB T1S 1Z6
Tel: 403-250-9121
office@wsga.ca
www.wsga.ca
To support & protect livestock growers by lobbying the government on legislation & proposed new legislation; to promote environmentally sound range management practices
Phil Rowland, President

Animals & Animal Science

Alberta Society for the Prevention of Cruelty to Animals
10806 - 124 St., Edmonton AB T5M 0H3
Tel: 780-447-3600; *Fax:* 780-447-4748
info@albertaspca.org
www.albertaspca.org
Social Media:
www.facebook.com/AlbertaSPCA
To promote education of public about welfare of domestic animals & livestock; To deal with wildlife issues; To work on improving legislation; To concentrate on enforcement & education; To have every animal in Alberta humanely treated
Terra Johnston, Executive Director

Alberta Veterinary Medical Association (AVMA)
Weber Centre, #950, 5555 Calgary Trail NW, Edmonton AB T6H 5P9
Tel: 780-489-5007; *Toll-Free:* 800-404-2862
www.avma.ca
Social Media: www.youtube.com/abvma
linkedin.com/company/alberta-veterinary-medical-association
www.facebook.com/ABVMA
twitter.com/abvma
To represent Alberta veterinarians in small animal, large animal & mixed practice as well as those employed in government, industry or other institutions
Duane Landals, Senior Advisor

Animal Alliance Environment Voters Party of Canada (AAEVPC)
#101, 221 Broadview Ave., Toronto ON M4M 2G3
Tel: 416-462-9541; *Fax:* 416-462-9647
www.environmentvoters.org
Social Media:
www.facebook.com/150318548422896
twitter.com/AAEVPC
To promote a principle of just and equitable human progress that respects, protects, and enhances the environment and the lives of the animals.
Liz White, Leader
Stephen Best, Chief Agent

Animal Alliance of Canada (AAC) / Alliance animale du Canada
#101, 221 Broadview Ave., Toronto ON M4M 2G3
Tel: 416-462-9541; *Fax:* 416-462-9647
contact@animalalliance.ca
www.animalalliance.ca
Social Media: www.youtube.com/user/AACoffice
www.facebook.com/132125293547127
twitter.com/Animal_Alliance
To preserve & protect all animals; to promote harmonious relationship between people, animals & the environment; to address issues including pound seizure, cosmetic & product testing, puppy mills, pet overpopulation, exotic pet trade, the fur trade, sport hunting, factory farming, animals as "entertainment"
Liz White, Coordinator, Fundraising
Lia Laskaris, Coordinator, Donor Relations

Animal Welfare Foundation of Canada (AWF) / Fondation du bien-être animal du Canada
#343, 300 Earl Grey Dr., Ottawa ON K2T 1C1
info@awfc.ca
www.awfc.ca
The Animal Welfare Foundation of Canada is a registered charity, supported by donors and administered by a volunteer Board of Directors. The Foundation seeks to improve the quality of life for animals in this country. Since the 1960s the Foundation, an independent watchdog organization, has been at the forefront of issues of humane care of animals in Canada.
Alice Crook, President & Chair
Frances Rodenberg, Secretary

Assiniboine Park Conservancy
55 Pavilion Cres., Winnipeg MB R3P 2N7
Tel: 204-927-6001
info@assiniboinepark.ca
www.zoosociety.com
Social Media: www.youtube.com/user/AssiniboinePark
www.facebook.com/assiniboineparkzoo
twitter.com/assiniboinepark
To redevelop & manage the Park's operations & ongoing financial viability.
Hartley Richardson, Chair
Margaret Redmond, President & CEO

Atlantic Canadian Anti-Sealing Coalition
contact@antisealingcoalition.ca
www.antisealingcoalition.ca
Social Media:
www.facebook.com/260618610812
twitter.com/GreySealHugger
The Atlantic Canadian Anti-Sealing Coalition is a collection of individuals and groups from across the Atlantic Region working to end the commercial seal hunt by peaceful and legal means.

Brandon Humane Society
2200 - 17 St. East, Brandon MB R7A 7M6
www.brandonhumanesociety.ca
Social Media:
www.facebook.com/307039086058890
To provide care for & homes for abused companion animals; To educate the public about the value of humane treatment of animals
Tracy Munn, Shelter Manager

British Columbia Society for the Prevention of Cruelty to Animals
1245 East 7th Ave., Vancouver BC V5T 1R1
Tel: 604-681-7271; *Toll-Free:* 800-665-1868
info@spca.bc.ca
www.spca.bc.ca
Social Media: www.youtube.com/user/bcspcabc
www.facebook.com/bcspca
twitter.com/BC_SPCA
To protect & enhance the quality of life for domestic, farm, & wild animals in British Columbia
Marylee Davies, President

Calgary Humane Society
4455 - 110 Ave. SE, Calgary AB T2C 2T7
Tel: 403-205-4455; *Fax:* 403-723-6050
www.calgaryhumane.ca
Social Media: www.youtube.com/user/CalgaryHumaneSociety
www.facebook.com/CalgaryHumaneSociety
twitter.com/CalgaryHumane
To foster humane treatment of animals & to promote values which demonstrate respect for animals
Carrie Fritz, Executive Director

Canada's Accredited Zoos and Aquariums (CAZA) / Aquariums et zoos accrédités du Canada (AZAC)
#400, 280 Metcalfe St., Ottawa ON K2P 1R7
Tel: 613-567-0099; *Fax:* 613-233-5438
Toll-Free: 888-822-2907
info@caza.ca
www.caza.ca
Social Media:
linkedin.com/company/canada's-accredited-zoos-and-aquariums—aqua
www.facebook.com/CAZA.AZAC
To promote the welfare of animals; To provide input into legislative matters & government policy affecting the zoo & aquarium industry
Massimo Bergamini, Executive Director

Canadian Animal Health Institute (CAHI) / Institut canadien de la santé animale (ICSA)
#102, 160 Research Lane, Guelph ON N1G 5B2
Tel: 519-763-7777; *Fax:* 519-763-7407
cahi@cahi-icsa.ca
www.cahi-icsa.ca
To work closely with allied industry groups for the betterment of Canadian agriculture; To foster & maintain a regulatory & legislative climate which will encourage member companies to develop & market useful animal health products & services; To promote the proper use of animal health & nutrition products by livestock & poultry farmers through user education information programs; To develop a public information program which enhances appreciation of the contributions the animal health & nutrition industry makes to the economy & society
Jean Szkotnicki, President
Tracey Firth, Director, Programs

Canadian Association for Laboratory Animal Science (CALAS) / Association canadienne pour la science des animaux de laboratoire (ACSAL)
#640, 144 Front St., Toronto ON M5J 2L7
Tel: 416-593-0268; *Fax:* 416-979-1819
office@calas-acsal.org
calas-acsal.org
To elevate standards of laboratory animal science; To promote excellence in research; To eliminate inhumane & unnecessary use of animals in research; To enhance animal welfare
Jacqui Sullivan, Board Liaison
Khadijah Hewitt, Contact, Membership & Registry Relations
Wendy Ansell, Registrar, Symposium
Alysone Will, Contact, Finance
Khadijah Hewitt, Coordinator, Membership & Registry

Canadian Association of Animal Health Technologists & Technicians (CAAHTT) / Association canadienne des techniciens et technologistes en santé animale (ACTTSA)
339 Booth St., Ottawa ON K1R 7K1
Tel: 800-567-2862
info@caahtt-acttsa.ca
www.caahtt-acttsa.ca
To provide coordination & resources to support members in the delivery of animal health care services
Phyllis Mierau, Executive Director
Michele Moroz, President
Chantal Cormier, Vice-President

Canadian Association of Professional Pet Dog Trainers (CAPPDT)
PO Box 85, 156097 Highway 10, Shelburne ON L0N 1S0
Toll-Free: 877-748-7829
info@cappdt.ca
www.cappdt.ca
To further the concept of dog-friendly & humane training techniques; to provide forum whereby professional pet dog trainers can be educated, exchange & generate ideas & network with other professionals
Pat Renshaw, Chair

Canadian Council on Animal Care (CCAC) / Conseil canadien de protection des animaux (CCPA)
#800, 190 O'Connor St., Ottawa ON K2P 2R3
Tel: 613-238-4031; *Fax:* 613-238-2837
ccac@ccac.ca
www.ccac.ca
To act on behalf of the people of Canada to ensure, through programs of education, assessment & persuasion, that the use of animals in Canada, where necessary for research, teaching & testing, employs physical & psychological care according to acceptable scientific standards; To promote an increased level of knowledge, awareness, & sensitivity to the relevant ethical principles
Louise Desjardins, Executive Director
Michael Baar, Director, Assessment & Certification Program
Gilly Griffin, Director, Standards
Pascale Belleau, Director, Public Affairs & Communications
Felicetta Celenza, Coordinator, Events & Publications

Canadian Federation of Humane Societies (CFHS) / Fédération des sociétés canadiennes d'assistance aux animaux
#102, 30 Concourse Gate, Ottawa ON K2E 7V7
Tel: 613-224-8072; *Fax:* 613-723-0252
Toll-Free: 888-678-2347
info@cfhs.ca
www.cfhs.ca
Social Media: www.youtube.com/user/CanadianHumane
linkedin.com/company/canadian-federation-of-humane-societies
www.facebook.com/HumaneCanada
twitter.com/cfhs/
As the national voice of societies and SPCAs, the CFHS supports its member animal welfare organizations across Canada in promoting respect & humane treatment toward all animals
Barbara Cartwright, CEO
Luna Allison, Communications & Marketing Manager

Canadian Kennel Club (CKC) / Club canin canadien
#400, 200 Ronson Dr., Toronto ON M9W 5Z9
Tel: 416-675-5511; *Fax:* 416-675-6506
Toll-Free: 855-364-7252
information@ckc.ca
www.ckc.ca
Social Media: instagram.com/ckc4thedogs
www.facebook.com/pages/The-Canadian-Kennel-Club/300439867556
twitter.com/CKC4thedogs
To provide registry services for all officially recognized breeds of purebred dogs; To provide governance for all CKC approved events; To encourage, guide, & advance the interests of purebred dogs & their responsible owners & breeders in Canada
Lance Novak, Executive Director
Sherry Weiss, Manager, Events
Andrew Patton, Manager, Marketing & Communications
Diane Draper, Manager, Regulatory

Canadian Society of Animal Science (CSAS) / Société canadienne de science animale
c/o University of Alberta, Agriculture & Forestry Centre, #4-10, Edmonton AB T6G 2C8
Tel: 780-248-1700; *Fax:* 780-248-1900
www.csas.net
To provide opportunities to discuss the problems of the Canadian animal & poultry industries, with the objective of furthering advancements in these industries; To assist in the coordination of research, teaching & technology transfer related to the animal & poultry industries; To encourage publication of scientific information; To provide an annual forum for professionals in the agricultural industry to meet & discuss the most recent technological advancements in the field of animal & poultry science
John Baah, President
Carolyn Fitzsimmons, Secretary-Treasurer

Canadian Society of Zoologists (CSZ) / Société canadienne de zoologie (SCZ)
c/o Biology Department, University of Western Ontario, London ON N6A 5B7
Tel: 519-661-3869
www.csz-scz.ca
To promote advancement & public awareness of zoology; To facilitate sharing of knowledge & ideas among all persons interested in science & practice of zoology; To organize discussions & debates of general interest
Helga Guderley, Secretary
Louise Milligan, President

Canadian Veterinary Medical Association (CVMA) / Association canadienne des médecins vétérinaires (ACMV)
339 Booth St., Ottawa ON K1R 7K1
Tel: 613-236-1162; *Fax:* 613-236-9681
admin@cvma-acmv.org
www.canadianveterinarians.net
Social Media:
twitter.com/CanVetMedAssoc
To represent the interests of the veterinary profession in Canada; commits to excellence within the profession & to the well-being of animals; promotes public awareness of the contribution of animals & veterinarians to society
Jost Am Rhyn, Executive Director
Suzanne Lavictoire, Director, Membership Services & Communications

Canadians for Ethical Treatment of Food Animals (CETFA)
PO Box 18024, 2225 - 41 Ave. West, Vancouver BC V6M 4L3
care@cetfa.com
www.cetfa.com
Social Media:
www.facebook.com/cetfa.news
CETFA is an investigation-based, farm animal advocacy organization that promotes the humane treatment of animals raised for food. It works to educate the public about Canada's food industry by providing information on factory farming practices.
Patricia Oswald, President
Twyla Francois, Head, Investigation

College of Veterinarians of British Columbia (CVBC)
#107, 828 Harbourside Dr., North Vancouver BC V7P 3R9
Tel: 604-929-7090; *Fax:* 604-929-7095
Toll-Free: 800-463-5399
reception@cvbc.ca
www.cvbc.ca
To serve members by promoting their professional image, providing a forum for addressing issues of importance to the profession, offering continuing education & protecting their interests & rights; to protect & serve animals & animal custodians through evaluation of veterinary competence & facility quality & by enforcing the Veterinarians Act & Bylaws
Larry W. Odegard, Registrar & CEO
John Brocklebank, Deputy Registrar

College of Veterinarians of Ontario (CVO)
2106 Gordon St., Guelph ON N1L 1G6
Tel: 519-824-5600; *Fax:* 519-824-6497
Toll-Free: 800-424-2856
inquiries@cvo.org
www.cvo.org
To protect the public by regulating & enhancing the veterinary profession in Ontario
Ken Bridge, President
Christine Simpson, Acting Registrar

East Coast Aquarium Society (ECAS)
c/o 91 Deerbrooke Dr., Dartmouth NS B2V 1X2
ECAS.ca
Social Media:
www.facebook.com/eastcoastaquariumsociety
To further the aquarium hobby and promote the practice of keeping tropical fish.
Kathryn Purdy, President
Kelly Lively Jones, Director, Membership

Fort McMurray Society for the Prevention of Cruelty to Animals
155 MacAlpine Cres., Fort McMurray AB T9H 4A5
Tel: 780-743-8997
info@fortmcmurrayspca.ca
www.fortmcmurrayspca.ca
Social Media:
www.facebook.com/307296965992025
To ensure the humane treatment of all animals

Humane Society Yukon
126 Tlingit Rd., Whitehorse YT Y1A 6J2
Tel: 867-633-6019; *Fax:* 867-633-2210
info@humanesocietyyukon.ca
www.humanesocietyyukon.ca
Social Media:
www.facebook.com/153522391419947
To foster a caring, compassionate atmosphere; To promote a humane ethic & responsible pet ownership; To prevent cruelty to animals
Brent Slobodin, President

Manitoba Veterinary Medical Association (MVMA)
1590 Inkster Blvd., Winnipeg MB R2X 2W4
Tel: 204-832-1276; *Fax:* 204-832-1382
Toll-Free: 866-338-6862
www.mvma.ca
To enhance professional excellence for the health & welfare of animals & Manitobans.
Andrea Lear, Executive Director

Montréal SPCA
5215, rue Jean-Talon Ouest, Montréal QC H4P 1X4
Tél: 514-735-2711; *Téléc:* 514-735-7448
admin@spcamontreal.com
www.spcamontreal.com
Média social: www.facebook.com/SPCAMontreal
twitter.com/SPCAMontreal
Recueiller, héberger et soigner les animaux errants ou abandonnés; Rendre les animaux perdus à leurs propriétaires; mettre en adoption les animaux en santé; Inspecter et enquêter sur les plaintes de cruauté
Nicholas Gilman, Directeur général

National Retriever Club of Canada
c/o Mark Laberge, 1970 Paris St., Sudbury ON P3E 3C8
Tel: 613-797-4330
secretary@nrcc-canada.com
www.nrcc-canada.com
Social Media:
www.facebook.com/679064212138775
Jim Ling, President
Mark Laberge, Treasurer

New Brunswick Society for the Prevention of Cruelty to Animals / Société protectrice des animaux du Nouveau-Brunswick
PO Box 1412, Stn. A, Fredericton NB E3B 5E3
Tel: 506-458-8208; *Fax:* 506-458-8209
www.spca-nb.ca
To prevent cruelty to & encourage consideration for all animals; To pursue program of humane education
Hilary Howes, Executive Director

New Brunswick Veterinary Medical Association (NBVMA) / Association des médecins vétérinaires du Nouveau-Brunswick (AMVNB)
c/o Dr. George Whittle, 1700 Manawagonish Rd., Saint John NB E2M 3Y5
Tel: 506-635-8100
registrar@nbvma-amvnb.ca
www.nbvma-amvnb.ca
To act as the regulatory body for the practice of veterinary medicine in New Brunswick; To establish standards of practice in the profession; To promote animal health & welfare; To prevent public health problems related to animal disease
George Whittle, Registrar

Newfoundland & Labrador Society for the Prevention of Cruelty to Animals
PO Box 29053, St. John's NL A1A 5B5
Tel: 709-726-0301; *Fax:* 709-579-8089
shelter@spcastjohns.com
www.spcastjohns.org
Social Media: www.instagram.com/spcastjohns;
www.youtube.com/user/SPCAVideos
www.facebook.com/SPCAStJohns
twitter.com/spcastjohns
To act as the voice for animal welfare in Newfoundland & Labrador; To promote humane treatment toward all animals
Carolyn Hickey, Secretary

Newfoundland & Labrador Veterinary Medical Association (NALVMA)
PO Box 818, Mount Pearl NL A1N 3C8
nalvmacouncil@gmail.com
www.nalvma.ca
To promote better animal health care; to educate the general public & strive towards continued excellence in veterinary medicine.
Heather Hillier, President

Northwest Territories Society for the Prevention of Cruelty to Animals (NWTSPCA)
PO Box 2278, Yellowknife NT X1A 2P7
Tel: 867-920-7722; *Fax:* 867-920-7723
nwtspcayk@gmail.com
www.nwtspca.com
Social Media:
www.facebook.com/nwtspca
To provide animal rescue services in the north; to educate the public about the proper ways to protect & take care of animals
Nicole Spencer, President

Nova Scotia Society for the Prevention of Cruelty to Animals (NS SPCA)
PO Box 38073, 11 Akerley Blvd., Dartmouth NS B3B 1X2
Tel: 902-835-4798; *Fax:* 902-835-7885
Toll-Free: 844-835-4798
animals@spcans.ca
www.spcans.ca
Social Media:
www.facebook.com/nsspca
To prevent abuse & neglect of all animals in Nova Scotia; To provide leadership in humane education through outreach activities & adoption services; To enforce laws on animal cruelty by issuing orders, warrants & laying charges
Elizabeth Murphy, Chief Executive Officer

Nova Scotia Veterinary Medical Association
15 Cobequid Rd., Lower Sackville NS B4C 2M9
Tel: 902-865-1876; *Fax:* 902-865-2001
info@nsvma.ca
www.nsvma.ca
To license Nova Scotia veterinarians in small animal, large animal & mixed practice as well as those employed in government, industry or other institutions
Frank Richardson, Registrar
Rob Doucette, President

Ontario Society for the Prevention of Cruelty to Animals (OSPCA)
16586 Woodbine Ave., RR#3, Newmarket ON L3Y 4W1
Tel: 905-898-7122; *Fax:* 905-853-8643
Toll-Free: 888-668-7722
info@ospca.on.ca
www.ontariospca.ca
Social Media: www.youtube.com/user/OntarioSPCA
www.facebook.com/OntarioSPCA
twitter.com/ontariospca
To provide care & shelter for animals, especially pets; To enforce animal cruelty laws in the province; To investigate cruelty complaints; To carry out rescues & bring perpetrators to court; To advocates for humane laws; To promote humane education & public awareness of the humane treatment of animals; To operate a Wildlife Rehabilitation Centre in Midland, ON
Kate MacDonald, Chief Executive Officer
Tom Stephenson, Chief Financial Officer
Connie Mallory, Chief Inspector
Alison Cross, Director, Marketing & Communications

Ontario Veterinary Medical Association (OVMA)
#205, 420 Bronte St. South, Milton ON L9T 0H9
Tel: 905-875-0756; *Fax:* 905-875-0958
Toll-Free: 800-670-1702
info@ovma.org
www.ovma.org
Social Media: www.youtube.com/user/TheOVMA
www.facebook.com/onvetmedassoc
twitter.com/OnVetMedAssoc
To represent Ontario veterinarians in small animal, large animal & mixed practice as well as those employed in government, industry or other institutions; programs include government & public relations, humane veterinary practice, continuing education in veterinary science & practice management & direct services to members.
Doug Raven, CEO
Melissa Carlaw, Manager, Communications & Public Relations

Ordre des médecins vétérinaires du Québec (OMVQ)
#200, 800, av Ste-Anne, Saint-Hyacinthe QC J2S 5G7
Tél: 450-774-1427; *Téléc:* 450-774-7635
Ligne sans frais: 800-267-1427
omvq@omvq.qc.ca
www.omvq.qc.ca
Protection du public; contribuer à l'amélioration de la santé et du bien-être des animaux; formation des membres; maintien de la qualité des services vétérinaires
Joël Bergeron, Président
Suzie Prince, Directrice générale/Secrétaire

Pet Industry Joint Advisory Council (PIJAC)
#14, 1010 Polytek St., Ottawa ON J1J 9H9
Tel: 613-730-8111; *Fax:* 613-730-8111
Toll-Free: 800-667-7452
information@pijaccanada.com
www.pijaccanada.com
Social Media:
www.youtube.com/channel/UCliDAXG-Cbme73ac3hGVy4A
linkedin.com/company/pijac-canada
www.facebook.com/PIJAC-Canada
www.twitter@pijaccanada
To promote the highest level of pet care for all sectors of the Canadian pet industry; To support research into the best attainable pet care; To engage in legislation & regulation affecting the Canadian pet industry at all levels of government; To promote the humane treatment of animals
Louis McCann, President & Chief Executive Officer
Renald Sabourin, Assistant Executive Director

PIJAC Canada / Conseil consultatif mixte de l'industrie des animaux de compagnie
#14, 1010 Polytek, Ottawa ON K1J 9H9
Tel: 613-730-8111; *Fax:* 613-730-9111
Toll-Free: 800-667-7452
information@pijaccanada.com
www.pijaccanada.com
Social Media:
linkedin.com/company/pijac-canada
To ensure the highest level of pet care attainable & a guarantee of a fair & equitable representation for all facets of the Canadian pet industry.
Louis McCann, President & CEO
Rénald Sabourin, Assistant Executive Director

Prince Edward Island Humane Society (PEIHS)
PO Box 20022, 309 Sherwood Rd., Charlottetown PE C1A 9E3
Tel: 902-892-1190; *Fax:* 902-892-3617
info@peihumanesociety.com
www.peihumanesociety.com
Social Media:
www.facebook.com/peihumanesociety
twitter.com/peihs
To promote & provide the humane treatment of animals recognizing that each is deserving of moral concern
Marla Somersall, Executive Director
Beckie MacLean, Manager, Shelter

Prince Edward Island Veterinary Medical Association (PEIVMA)
PO Box 21097, Stn. 465 University Ave., Charlottetown PE C1A 9h6
Tel: 902-367-3757; *Fax:* 902-367-3176
admin.peivma@gmail.com
www.peivma.com
To represent PEI veterinarians in small animal, large animal & mixed practice as well as those employed in government, industry or other institutions; to licence & regulate veterinarians in PEI
Wade Sweet, President
Jenn Reid, Vice-President

Red Deer & District SPCA
4505 - 77 St., Red Deer AB T4P 2J1
Tel: 403-342-7722; *Fax:* 403-341-3147
office@reddeerspca.com
www.reddeerspca.com
Social Media: www.instagram.com/reddeerspca;
www.pinterest.com/reddeerspca
www.facebook.com/233609360018185
twitter.com/RedDeerSPCA
To care for & protect companion animals & promote humane treatment of animals & responsible pet ownership
Tara Hellewell, Executive Director

Regina Humane Society Inc.
PO Box 3143, Regina SK S4P 3G7
Tel: 306-543-6363; *Fax:* 306-545-7661
Crisis Hot-Line: 306-543-6363
info@reginahumane.ca
www.reginahumanesociety.ca
Social Media: www.instagram.com/reginahumanesociety
www.facebook.com/reginahumane
twitter.com/reginahumane
To provide care & shelter for animals; To encourage the humane treatment of animals
Louise Yates, President

Responsible Dog Owners of Canada (RDOC)
9 Liette Crt., RR1, Kemptville ON K0G 1J0
Tel: 613-206-6885
inquiries@responsibledogowners.ca
www.responsibledogowners.ca
To promote responsible dog ownership and public safety through education and support, cultivate respect for the public rights and privileges of all members of society, both dog-owning and non-dog owning, encourage and foster recognition of the contribution that canines make in society through companionship, service/assistance and therapy and assemble a strong network of responsible dog owners to ensure the restoration and preservation of a dog-friendly society.
Candice O'Connell, Chair

Saskatchewan Society for the Prevention of Cruelty to Animals
519 - 45th St. West, Saskatoon SK S7L 5Z9
Tel: 306-382-7722; *Fax:* 306-384-3425
Toll-Free: 877-382-7722
info@sspca.ca
www.sspca.ca
Social Media:
www.facebook.com/SaskSPCA
twitter.com/SaskSPCA
To promote humane treatment of animals
Frances Wach, Executive Director

Société québécoise pour la défense des animaux (SQDA) / Québec Society for the Defense of Animals (QSDA)
#102, 847, rue Cherrier, Montréal QC H2L 1H6
Tél: 514-524-1976
sqda1976@gmail.org
www.sqda.org
Faire connaître et respecter le monde animal par tous les moyens possibles; obtenir une législation modifiée pour la protection de toute espèce; Combattre la destruction de notre faune; exposer l'aberration de l'élevage intensif; Contrôler l'expérimentation animale

World Animal Protection (WSPA) / Société mondiale pour la protection des animaux
#960, 90 Eglinton Ave. East, Toronto ON M4P 2Y3
Tel: 416-369-0044; *Fax:* 416-369-0147
Toll-Free: 800-363-9772
info@worldanimalprotection.ca
www.worldanimalprotection.ca
Social Media: www.instagram.com/worldanimalprotectioncanada
www.facebook.com/WorldAnimalProtectionCanada
twitter.com/movetheworldca
To promote effective means for the prevention of cruelty to, & relief of suffering of animals in any part of the world
Dominique Bellemare, President

Yukon Schutzhund Association
Whitehorse YT
yukon.schutzhund@gmail.com
Social Media:
www.facebook.com/yukonysa
To promote dog training for the sport of Schutzhund in the Yukon Territory.

ZOOCHECK Canada Inc.
788 1/2 O'Connor Dr., Toronto ON M4B 2S6
Tel: 416-285-1744
zoocheck@zoocheck.com
www.zoocheck.com
Social Media:
www.facebook.com/pages/Zoocheck/118864269587
Zoocheck works to improve wildlife protection in Canada and to end the abuse, neglect and exploitation of individual wild animals through: investigation & research; public education & awareness campaigns; capacity building initiatives; legal programs; legislative actions.

Antiques

Antiquarian Booksellers' Association of Canada (ABAC) / Association de la librairie ancienne du Canada (ALAC)
c/o #301, 368 Dalhousie St., Ottawa ON K1N 7G3
info@abac.org
www.abac.org
Social Media:
www.facebook.com/210124119032896
twitter.com/A_B_A_C
To maintain high standards in the antiquarian book trade; To promote interest in rare books & manuscripts
Roger Auger, President
Alexandre Arjomand, Secretary

Historic Vehicle Society of Ontario (HVSO)
c/o Canadian Transportation Museum & Heritage Village, 6155 Arner Town Line, RR#2, Kingsville ON N9Y 2E5
Tel: 519-776-6909; *Fax:* 519-776-8321
Toll-Free: 886-776-6909
info@ctmhv.com
www.ctmhv.com
To collect, restore & display vehicles, buildings & artifacts that serve to demonstrate the founding settlement of Essex County; to preserve the past to enhance the future.
Kim Brimner, Contact

Manitoba Antique Association
PO Box 2881, Winnipeg MB R3C 4B4
manitobaantique@gmail.com
www.manitobaantiqueassociation.com
To preserve & restore antiques; To promote the admiration of all antiques
Frank Coelho, President

Archaeology

Archaeological Society of Alberta (ASA)
97 Eton Rd. West, Lethbridge AB T1K 4T9
Tel: 403-381-2655
www.arkyalberta.com
To promote the regulations of the Alberta Historical Act & to disseminate archaeological information by means of publications & seminars
Janice Andreas, President
Jim McMurchy, Executive Sec.-Treas.
Christie Grekul, Provincial Coordinator

Archaeological Society of British Columbia (ASBC)
PO Box 520, Stn. Bentall, Vancouver BC V6C 2N3
info@asbc.bc.ca
www.asbc.bc.ca
To protect the archaeological heritage of British Columbia; to promote public understanding of the scientific approach to archaeology; to encourage government to preserve archaeological & pre-historic sites

Association des archéologues du Québec (AAQ)
CP 322, Succ. Haute-Ville, Québec QC G1R 4P8
info@archeologie.qc.ca
www.archeologie.qc.ca
Définir les standards de la profession; veiller à la saine gestion et la mise en valeur du patrimoine archéologique à cause d'une éthique exemplaire et de la qualité de ses membres; agir comme interlocuteur privilégié pour tout ce qui regarde la question archéologique auprès des gouvernements et des organismes, privés ou publics, qui ont à coeur la préservation de notre patrimoine collectif

Association of Professional Archaeologists (APAA)
#600, 3250 Bloor St. West, Toronto ON M8X 2X9
Tel: 647-775-1674
info@apaontario.ca
Social Media:
www.facebook.com/APAOntario
To integrate the concerns of archaeologists in Ontario for all avenues of employment; To maintain commonly recognized standards for dealing with issues affecting archaeological resources
Margie Kenedy, President

Canadian Anthropology Society (CASCA) / Société canadienne d'Anthropologie
c/o Department of Sociology & Anthropology, Carleton University, 1125 Colonel By Dr., Ottawa ON K1S 5B6
www.cas-sca.ca
To promote anthropology in Canada
Regna Darnell, President
Robert Adlam, Treasurer

Canadian Archaeological Association (CAA) / Association d'archéologie canadienne
c/o William Ross, 189 Peter St., Thunder Bay ON P7A 5H8
Tel: 807-345-2733
www.canadianarchaeology.com
To publish & disseminate archaeological knowledge in Canada; To encourage archaeological research & conservation efforts; To promote cooperation among archaeological societies & agencies
William Ross, President
Jennifer Birch, Vice-President
Jeff Hunston, Secretary-Treasurer

Nova Scotia Archaeology Society (NSAS)
PO Box 36090, Halifax NS B3J 3S9
Tel: 902-880-3021
www.novascotiaarchaeologysociety.com
Social Media:
www.facebook.com/pages/Nova-Scotia-Archaeology-Society/126145457490785
twitter.com/NSArchSociety
To promote the preservation of Nova Scotia's archaeological sites & resources
Brittany Houghton, President
Natalie Lavoie, Vice-President
Terry Deveau, Secretary
Rob Ferguson, Treasurer

The Ontario Archaeological Society
PO Box 62066, Stn. Victoria Terrace, #102, 1444 Queen St. E, Toronto ON M4A 2W1
Tel: 416-406-5959; *Fax:* 416-406-5959
info@ontarioarchaeology.org
www.ontarioarchaeology.org
Social Media: www.youtube.com/user/OntarioArchaeology
twitter.com/ontarchsoc
To preserve, promote, investigate, record & publish an archaeological record of the province of Ontario
Lorie Harris, Executive Director
Chris Dalton, Director, Chapter Services
Dana Millson, Director, Membership

Save Ontario Shipwrecks (SOS)
PO Box 2389, Blenheim ON N0P 1A0
Tel: 519-676-4110; *Fax:* 519-676-7058
www.saveontarioshipwrecks.on.ca
To promote & preserve Ontario's marine heritage
Chris Phinney, President
Nicole AuCoin, Secretary

Underwater Archaeological Society of British Columbia (UASBC)
c/o Vancouver Maritime Museum, 1905 Ogden Ave., Vancouver BC V6J 1A3
www.uasbc.com
Social Media: vimeo.com/uasbc
To promote the science of underwater archaeology; to conserve, preserve & protect the maritime heritage lying beneath our coastal & inland waters

Architecture

Alberta Association of Architects (AAA)
Duggan House, 10515 Saskatchewan Dr., Edmonton AB T6E 4S1
Tel: 780-432-0224; *Fax:* 780-439-1431
info@aaa.ab.ca
www.aaa.ab.ca
To regulate the practice of architecture & interior design in Alberta for the protection of the public & the administration of the profession; to bring architects together in order to channel the energies of unique, creative individuals spiritually committed to a superior architecture
Dianne Johnstone, Executive Director

Amis et propriétaires de maisons anciennes du Québec (APMAQ)
2050, rue Amherst, Montréal QC H2L 3L8
Tél: 514-528-8444; *Téléc:* 514-528-8686
apmaq@globetrotter.net
www.maisons-anciennes.qc.ca

Architects Association of Prince Edward Island (AAPEI)
PO Box 1766, Charlottetown PE C1A 7N4
Tel: 902-566-3699; *Fax:* 902-566-1235
info@aapei.com
www.aapei.com
To increase awareness and understanding of architecture and its professional services.
Heather Mader, President

Architects' Association of New Brunswick (AANB) / Association des architectes du Nouveau-Brunswick
PO Box 5093, 36 Maple Ave., Sussex NB E4E 2N5
Tel: 506-433-5811; *Fax:* 506-432-1122
aanb@nb.aibn.com
www.aanb.org
To govern & regulate persons in New Brunswick who offer architectural services; To advance & maintain the standards of architecture in New Brunswick
Christian Hébert, President
Fernand Daigie, Treasurer
John Leroux, Registrar

The Architectural Conservancy of Ontario (ACO)
#403, 10 Adelaide St. East, Toronto ON M5C 1J3
Tel: 416-367-8075; *Fax:* 416-367-8630
Toll-Free: 877-264-8937
manager@arconserv.ca
www.arconserv.ca
Social Media:
www.facebook.com/119712261437141
twitter.com/arconserve
To preserve buildings & structures of architectural merit & places of natural beauty or interest
Susan Ratcliffe, President
Rollo Myers, Manager

Architectural Institute of British Columbia (AIBC)
#100, 440 Cambie St., Vancouver BC V6B 2N5
Tel: 604-683-8588; *Fax:* 604-683-8568
Toll-Free: 800-667-0753
info@aibc.ca
www.aibc.ca
Social Media:
twitter.com/AIBConnected
To regulate the profession of architecture in accordance with the Architects Act; to promote & increase the knowledge, skill & proficiency of its members in all things relating to the practice of architecture; to advance & maintain high standards of qualification & professional ethics; to promote public appreciation of architecture, allied arts, sciences & the professions
Mark Vernon, Chief Executive Officer
Grace Battiston, Director, Communications
Paul Becker, Director, Professional Services

Association des Architectes en pratique privée du Québec (AAPPQ) / Association of Architects in Private Practice of Québec
#302, 420, rue McGill, Montréal QC H2Y 2G1
Tél: 514-937-4140; *Téléc:* 514-937-2329
aappq@aappq.qc.ca
www.aappq.qc.ca

Association of Architectural Technologists of Ontario (AATO)
#38, 2355 Derry Rd. East, Mississauga ON L5S 1V6
Tel: 905-405-0840; *Fax:* 905-405-9882
Toll-Free: 866-805-2286
aato@bellnet.ca
aato.on.ca
To maintain the standard of professional conduct of its members, as well as advocates to all levels of government on behalf of them & the industry.
Sharon Creasor, President

Canadian Architectural Certification Board (CACB) / Conseil canadien de certification en architecture (CCCA)
#710, 1 Nicholas St., Ottawa ON K1N 7B7
Tel: 613-241-8399; *Fax:* 613-241-7991
info@cacb.ca
www.cacb.ca
The Canadian Architectural Certification Board fulfills two seperate but related mandates: 1- Administer a program of accreditation of the Canadian schools of architecture in accordance with "Conditions and Procedures for Accreditation" approved by the CCAC and the CCUSA and 2- Administer a program of certification of the educational qualifications of indivdual applicants in accordance withe criteria contained within the "Education Standard" approved by the CCAC.
Branko Kolarevic, President
Myriam Blais, Vice-President

Canadian Centre for Architecture (CCA) / Centre Canadien d'Architecture
1920, rue Baile, Montréal QC H3H 2S6
Tel: 514-939-7026
info@cca.qc.ca
www.cca.qc.ca
Social Media: www.youtube.com/CCAChannel
www.facebook.com/cca.conversation
twitter.com/ccawire
To advance knowledge, promote public understanding, widen thought & debate on the art of architecture, its history, theory, practice & role in society

Conseil de l'enveloppe du bâtiment du Québec (CEBQ) / Québec Building Envelope Council (QBEC)
12465 - 94E av, Montréal QC H1C 1H6
Tél: 514-943-0251; *Téléc:* 514-943-0300
www.cebq.org
Organiser des forums afin de faciliter la discussion et le transfert de technologies auprès de l'industrie de la construction
Mario D. Gonçalves, Président
Nathalie Martin, CPA, CGA, Directrice

Design Exchange (DX)
Toronto Dominion Centre, PO Box 18, 234 Bay St., Toronto ON M5K 1B2
Tel: 416-363-6121; *Fax:* 416-368-0684
info@dx.org
www.dx.org
To provide a design museum & centre for design research & education; To raise awareness & understanding of design
Tim Gilbert, Interim President

Manitoba Association of Architects (MAA)
137 Bannatyne Ave., 2nd Fl., Winnipeg MB R3B 0R3
Tel: 204-925-4620; *Fax:* 204-925-4624
info@mbarchitects.org
www.mbarchitects.org
To protect the public interest and advance the profession of architecture.
Judy Pestrak, Executive Director

Newfoundland Association of Architects
PO Box 5204, 7 Downing St., St. John's NL A1C 5V5
Tel: 709-726-8550; *Fax:* 709-726-1549
nlaa@newfoundlandarchitects.com
www.newfoundlandarchitects.com
To support architecture & architects in Newfoundland and Labrador.

Northwest Territories Association of Architects (NWTAA)
Administrative Office, Northern Frontier Visitors Centre, PO Box 1394, Yellowknife NT X1A 2P1
Tel: 867-766-4216; *Fax:* 867-973-3654
nwtaa@yk.com
www.nwtaa.ca
To maintain the Register of Architects, in accordance with the NWT Architects Act
Ben Russo, Executive Director
Rod Kirkwood, President

Nova Scotia Association of Architects (NSAA)
1359 Barrington St., Halifax NS B3J 1Y9
Tel: 902-423-7607; *Fax:* 902-425-7024
info@nsaa.ns.ca
www.nsaa.ns.ca
To administer the practice of architecture in Nova Scotia
Mark Atwood, Registrar
Therese LeBlanc, President

Ontario Association of Architects (OAA)
111 Moatfield Dr., Toronto ON M3B 3L6
Tel: 416-449-6898; *Fax:* 416-449-5756
Toll-Free: 800-565-2724
oaamail@oaa.on.ca
www.oaa.on.ca
To operate in accordance with the Government of Ontario's Architects Act; To serve & protect the public interest by promoting & increasing the knowledge, skill, & proficiency of members
I. Hillel Roebuck, Registrar
Gordon Masters, Director, Operations
Kristi Doyle, Director, Policy
Andrew Fuller, Administrator, Accounting & Information Technology
Gail Hanselman, Administrator, Certificate of Practice
Tamara La Pierre King, Administrator, Web site & Communications
Jessica O'Rafferty, Administrator, Admission
Ellen Savitsky, Administrator, Continuing Education
Kim Sumi, Administrator, Licence

Ordre des architectes du Québec (OAQ)
#200, 420 rue McGill, Montréal QC H2Y 2G1
Tél: 514-937-6168; *Téléc:* 514-933-0242
Ligne sans frais: 800-599-6168
info@oaq.com
www.oaq.com
Média social: vimeo.com/user2657182
www.facebook.com/133353596740232
twitter.com/OAQenbref
D'assurer la protection du public en régissant l'exercice de la profession d'architecte au Québec.
Jean-Pierre Dumont, Directeur général

Royal Architectural Institute of Canada (RAIC) / Institut royal d'architecture du Canada
#330, 55 Murray St., Ottawa ON K1N 5M3
Tel: 613-241-3600; *Fax:* 613-241-5750
info@raic.org
www.raic.org
To represent Canadian architects nationally & internationally; to foster public awareness & appreciation of architecture; to engage in architectural research & education; to lobby government on architectural issues
Jim McKee, Executive Director
Paule Boutin, President

Saskatchewan Association of Architects (SAA)
#200, 642 Broadway Ave., Saskatoon SK S7N 1A9
Tel: 306-242-0733; *Fax:* 306-664-2598
www.saskarchitects.com
To regulate the profession of architecture in Saskatchewan, in order to ensure the protection of the public interest; To advance the profession of architecture in the province; To ensure that high standards for practice & conduct are followed
Robert Croft, President
Paul Blaser, 1st Vice-President
Bob Burnyeat, 2nd Vice-President
Jeff Howlett, Secretary-Treasurer
Janelle Unrau, Executive Director

Society for the Study of Architecture in Canada (SSAC) / Société pour l'étude de l'architecture au Canada (SEAC)
PO Box 2302, Stn. D, Ottawa ON K1P 5W5
ssac.seac@gmail.com
canada-architecture.org
Social Media: www.flickr.com/photos/ssac_photos
To promote the study of Canadian architecture including an examination of both historical & cultural issues relating to buildings, districts, cities & the cultural landscapes; to encourage the collection & preservation of Canada's architectural records; to encourage preservation of the built environment
Peter Coffman, President

Arts

Alberta Foundation for the Arts (AFA)
10708 - 105 Ave., Edmonton AB T5H 0A1
Tel: 780-427-9968; *Fax:* 780-422-1162
Toll-Free: -310-0000
www.affta.ab.ca
Social Media: www.youtube.com/user/GOACCS
www.facebook.com/AlbertaFoundationfortheArts
twitter.com/AFA1991
To create the best possible climate for the arts in Alberta
Joan Udell, Chair
Jeffrey Anderson, Secretary
Erin McDonald, Acting Executive Director

Alliance for Arts & Culture
#100, 938 Howe St., Vancouver BC V6Z 1N9
Tel: 604-681-3535; *Fax:* 604-681-7848
info@allianceforarts.com
www.allianceforarts.com
Social Media: www.youtube.com/user/AllianceArtsCulture
www.facebook.com/AllianceforArtsandCulture
twitter.com/AllianceArts
To project a strong voice for the local arts community; To promote the activities of the arts through a variety of programs, services, & marketing strategies; To increase public awareness of & accessibility to the arts & culture
Rob Gloor, Executive Director
Kevin Dale McKeown, Director, Communications & Special Events
Kevin Teichroeb, Director, Interactive Media
Melissa Flagg, Administrator, Members Services

Assembly of BC Arts Councils
PO Box 28533, Stn. Willingdon, Burnaby BC V5C 2H9
Tel: 604-291-0046; *Fax:* 604-648-9454
Toll-Free: 888-315-2288
info@artsbc.org
www.artsbc.org
Social Media:
twitter.com/artsbcdotorg
To promote & advance the role of arts & culture in building community; to work with community based organizations in furthering the impact & contribution of the arts locally, regionally & province-wide
Stephen Parsons, President

Business for the Arts / Affairs pour les arts
174 Avenue Rd., Toronto ON M5R 2J1
Tel: 416-869-3016; *Fax:* 416-869-0435
www.businessforthearts.org
Social Media: www.flickr.com/photos/businessforthearts
linkedin.com/company/businessforthearts
www.facebook.com/businessforthearts
twitter.com/businessftarts
To make the partnership between business & the arts more effective in supporting the nation's creative minds.
James D. Fleck, Chair
Nichole Anderson, President & CEO

Canadian Artists' Representation (CARFAC) / Le Front des artistes canadiens
#250, 2 Daly Ave., Ottawa ON K1N 6E2
Tel: 613-233-6161; *Fax:* 613-233-6162
Toll-Free: 866-344-6161
www.carfac.ca
Social Media:
www.facebook.com/155665580277
twitter.com/carfacnational
To act as a national voice for Canada's professional visual artists; To promote a socio-economic climate that is conducive to the production of visual arts
Grant McConnell, National President & Spokesperson
Deirdre Logue, Vice-President
Barbara Gamble, Secretary
Julie McIntyre, Treasurer
April Britski, Executive Director
Taylor Norris, Coordinator, Membership
Melissa Gruber, Director, Advocacy & Communications

Canadian Arts Presenting Association (CAPACOA) / Association canadienne des organismes artistiques
#200, 17 York St., Ottawa ON K1N 9J6
Tel: 613-562-3515; *Fax:* 613-562-4005
mail@capacoa.ca
www.capacoa.ca
Social Media:
www.facebook.com/CAPACOA
twitter.com/capacoa
To promote the development of the presentation of the arts in Canada; to promote & encourage greater knowledge & appreciation of the presentation of the performing arts; To encourage touring of artists & attractions throughout all regions of Canada; To provide information on artists & attractions touring regionally & nationally; To assist presenters of the arts in Canada with coordination of bookings; To provide opportunities for professional development of presenters in Canada; To promote communication & understanding between presenters of the arts in Canada; To provide forum for exchange of views concerning presentation of the performing arts generally; To provide information on regional & federal policies which relate to presentation of the arts; To provide the opportunity to make contacts nationwide
Paul Gravett, President
Sue Urquhart, Executive Director
Mélanie Bureau, Operations Manager

Canadian Celtic Arts Association
c/o Jean Talman, 81 St. Mary St., Toronto ON M5S 1J4
info@canadiancelticarts.ca
www.canadiancelticarts.ca
To promote Celtic culture; To serve as a link between the diverse Celtic communities in Canada
Janice Chan, President
Donald Gillies, Treasurer
Jean Talman, Membership Secretary & Coordinator, Programmes

Canadian Conference of the Arts (CCA) / Conférence canadienne des arts
#406, 130 Slater St., Ottawa ON K1P 6E2
Tel: 613-238-3561; *Fax:* 613-238-4849
info@ccarts.ca
www.ccarts.ca
Social Media:
linkedin.com/company/canadian-conference-of-the-arts-la-conf-rence
www.facebook.com/CanArts
twitter.com/CanadianArts
To ensure the lively existence & continued growth of the arts & the cultural industries in Canada; To increase the Canadian materials (works created, produced, & performed by Canadians) available to Canadians; To improve the quality of life for all artists & arts groups; To unite members to work for interests of all artists & whole cultural community; To work closely with other arts service organizations to formulate policies & advocate their adoption by governments
Alain Pineau, National Director
Anne-Marie Des Roches, Associate Director, Senior Policy Advisor

The Canadian Society for Mesopotamian Studies (CSMS) / La Société canadienne des études mésopotamiennes
c/o RIM Project, University of Toronto, 4 Bancroft Ave., 4th Fl., Toronto ON M5S 1C1
Tel: 416-978-4531; *Fax:* 416-978-3305
csms@chass.utoronto.ca
www.chass.utoronto.ca/csms
To stimulate interest among the general public in the culture, history & archaeology of Mesopotamia, in particular the civilizations of Sumer, Babylon & Assyria, as well as neighbouring ancient civilizations
Pail-Alain Beaulieu, President
Roy Thomas, Secretary-Treasurer
N.J. Johnson, Administrator

Chorale Les Voix de la Vallée du Cuivre de Chibougamau inc.
CP 129, Chibougamau QC G8P 2K6
Tél: 418-748-6892

Bruno Marceau, Président

Conseil des arts et des lettres du Québec
79, boul René Lévesque est, 3e étage, Québec QC G1R 5N5
Tél: 418-643-1707; *Téléc:* 418-643-4558
Ligne sans frais: 800-897-1707
info@calq.gouv.qc.ca
www.calq.gouv.qc.ca
Média social: www.youtube.com/user/LeCALQ
www.facebook.com/12468994038
twitter.com/LeCALQ
Soutenir dans toutes les régions du Québec la création, l'expérimentation, la production et la diffusion dans les domaines des arts de la scène (théâtre, danse, musique, chanson, arts du cirque), des arts médiatiques (arts numériques, cinéma et vidéo), des arts multidisciplinaires, des arts visuels, de la littérature et du conte, des métiers d'art et de la recherche architecturale et d'en favoriser la reconnaissance et le rayonnement au Québec, au Canada et à l'étranger.
Marie DuPont, Président du conseil d'administration
Stéphan La Roche, Président & Directeur général

Conseil québécois des arts médiatiques (CQAM)
3995, rue Berri, Montréal QC H2L 4H2
Tél: 514-527-5116; *Ligne sans frais:* 888-527-5116
www.cqam.org
Robin Dupuis, Président
Isabelle L'Italien, Directrice générale

Federation of Canadian Artists (FCA)
1241 Cartwright St., Vancouver BC V6H 4B7
Tel: 604-681-2744; *Fax:* 604-681-2740
fcaoffice@artists.ca
artists.ca
Social Media:
www.facebook.com/111266735581892
To share & promote the visual arts
Andrew McDermott, President
Alfonso Tejada, 1st Vice-President
Kathy Hildebrandt, 2nd Vice-President
Patrick Meyer, Office Administrator
Mila Kostic, Director, Gallery
Peter Kiidumae, Secretary
Susie Cipolla, Treasurer

Governor General's Performing Arts Awards Foundation (GGPAAF) / Les Prix du Gouverneur Général pour les arts de la scène
#804, 130 Albert St., Ottawa ON K1P 5G4
Tel: 613-241-5297; *Fax:* 613-238-4849
www.bell.ca/ggawards
To celebrate outstanding lifetime achievement in various performing arts disciplines in Canada; To raise awareness of the contributions of Canadian performing artists; To foster awareness of Francophone artists in English Canada & Anglophone artists in French Canada; To inspire future performing artists
Whitney Taylor, Director
Peter Herrndorf, President/CEO
Harold Redekopp, Co-Chair
Albert Millaire, Co-Chair

International Association of Art Critics - Canada (IAAC) / Association internationale des Critiques d'art - Canada (AICA)
c/o Ninon Gauthier, President, #301, 150, rue Berlioz, Montréal QC H3E 1K3
Tel: 514-658-2538
aica-canada.org
To contribute to the promotion of contemporary art & freedom of expression in the visual arts; to develop national & international cooperation in art criticism
Ninon Gauthier, President
Earl Miller, Treasurer & Secretary

Manitoba Arts Council (MAC) / Conseil des arts du Manitoba (CAM)
#525, 93 Lombard Ave., Winnipeg MB R3B 3B1
Tel: 204-945-2237; *Fax:* 204-945-5925
Toll-Free: 866-994-2787
info@artscouncil.mb.ca
artscouncil.mb.ca
Social Media:
www.facebook.com/190664875839
An arms-length agency of the provincial government dedicated to artistic excellence; offers a broad based grant program for professional artists & arts organizations; promotes, preserves, supports & advocates for the arts as essential to the quality of life of all people of Manitoba.
Keith Bellamy, Chair
Douglas Riske, Executive Director
David R. Scott, Associate Director, Granting Programs

National Arts Centre Foundation
PO Box 1534, Stn. B, Ottawa ON K1P 5W1
Tel: 613-947-7000
donorscircle@nac-cna.ca
nacfoundation.ca
To raise money on behalf on behalf of the National Arts Centre which funds performing arts projects across Canada
Jayne Watson, CEO

New Brunswick Arts Board
649 Queen Street, 2nd Fl., Fredericton NB E3B 1C3
Tel: 506-444-4444; *Fax:* 506-444-5543
Toll-Free: 866-460-2787
artsnb.ca
Social Media:
www.youtube.com/channel/UCjUQTjWrTYsMQ0aRu6VIRvw?feature=mhee
www.facebook.com/pages/artsnb/259770517370657?ref=ts
twitter.com/#!/artsnb
To achieve the vision of New Brunswick as a place where all residents attend a diversity of quality, live performances in their own community; all students attend performances in their own school by performing artists; artists residing in New Brunswick find a supportive arts community & the resources necessary to establish a career in the performing arts in New Brunswick & beyond; maintain a resource centre; assume an advocacy for the performing arts in the community
Akoulina Connell, Executive Director
Pierre McGraw, Chair

Newfoundland & Labrador Arts Council (NLAC)
PO Box 98, 1 Springdale St., St. John's NL A1C 5H5
Tel: 709-726-2212; *Fax:* 709-726-0619
Toll-Free: 866-726-2212
nlacmail@nlac.ca
www.nlac.ca
To foster & promote the arts of the province; to carry on financial assistance programs for individual artists & arts groups; to work with the government & the community for development in the arts
Reg Winsor, Executive Director
Tom Gordon, Chair

Northwest Territories Arts Council / Conseil des arts des TNO
c/o GNWT Education, Culture & Employment, PO Box 1320, Yellowknife NT X1A 2L9
Tel: 867-920-6370; *Fax:* 867-873-0205
Toll-Free: 877-445-2787
www.nwtartscouncil.ca
To promote and encourage the arts in the Northwest Territories.
Boris Atamanenko, Manager, Community Programs

Ontario Arts Council (OAC) / Conseil des arts de l'Ontario
121 Bloor St. East, 7th Fl., Toronto ON M4W 3M5
Tel: 416-961-1660; *Fax:* 416-961-7796
Toll-Free: 800-387-0058
info@arts.on.ca
www.arts.on.ca
Social Media:
www.facebook.com/118143304897633
twitter.com/ONArtsCouncil
Ontario's primary funding body for professional arts activity; promotes & assists the development of the arts & artists; offers 50+ funding programs
Peter Caldwell, Director & CEO
Kirsten Gunter, Director, Communications
Carolyn Vesely, Director, Granting

Organization of Saskatchewan Arts Councils (OSAC)
1102 - 8th Ave., Regina SK S4R 1C9
Tel: 306-586-1250; *Fax:* 306-586-1550
info@osac.ca
www.osac.ca
Social Media: instagram.com/osacsask
www.facebook.com/OSACsask
twitter.com/OSACsask
To assist the membership in their endeavors to develop, promote & present the visual arts &/or performing arts
Kevin Korchinski, Executive Director

Prince Edward Island Council of the Arts (PEICA)
115 Richmond St., Charlottetown PE C1A 1A7
Tel: 902-368-4410; *Toll-Free:* 888-734-2784
www.peiartscouncil.com
Social Media:
www.facebook.com/peiartscouncil
twitter.com/peiartscouncil
To make the Arts integral to the lives of all Prince Edward Islanders; Through advocacy, education, distribution of funds, management of the Arts Guild & program of prizes & awards.

Darrin White, Exeutive Director

SaskCulture Inc.
#404, 2125 - 11th Ave., Regina SK S4P 3X3
Tel: 306-780-9284
saskculture.info@saskculture.sk.ca
www.saskculture.sk.ca
Social Media: www.youtube.com/user/SaskCult
www.facebook.com/SaskCulture
twitter.com/SaskCulture
To bring together organizations which work to further the course of culture
Rose Gilks, General Manager
Diane Ell, Communications Manager

Société de Promotion et de Diffusion des Arts et de la Culture (SPDAC)
Festival International Montréal en Arts, CP 653, Succ. C, Montréal QC H2L 4L5
Tél: 514-370-2269; *Ligne sans frais:* 877-522-4646
info@festivaldesarts.org
www.festivaldesarts.org
Organisme à but non lucratif qui favorise un rapprochement entre les communautés locales et les artistes; le Festival International Montréal en Arts accueille plus de 250 artistes en arts visuels et métiers d'arts.
Stéphane Mabilais, Directeur général

Automotive

Alberta Motor Association (AMA)
PO Box 8180, Stn. South, Edmonton AB T6H 5X9
Tel: 780-430-5555
www.ama.ab.ca
Tania Willumsen, Chair
Don Smitten, President

Association des concessionnaires Ford du Québec
16, rue Marguerite-Bourgeoys, Boucherville QC J4B 2H3
Tél: 450-655-2090

Association des spécialistes du pneus et Mécanique du Québec (ASPQ)
CP 1033, Drummondville QC J2A 0B1
Tél: 514-461-1035; *Téléc:* 514-461-1035
Ligne sans frais: 866-454-0477
info@aspmq.ca
www.aspq.ca/aspq
Daniel Dubuc, Président
Danny Houle, Vice-président
Wendy Allain, Directrice éxécutive

Atlantic Recreation Vehicle Dealers' Association (ARVDA)
PO Box 9410, Stn. A, Halifax NS B3K 5S3
Tel: 902-425-2445; *Fax:* 902-425-2441
www.arvda.ca
George Goodrick, President
John K. Sutherland, Executive Director

Automobile Journalists Association of Canada (AJAC) / Association des journalistes automobile du Canada
PO Box 398, Stn. Main, Cobourg ON K9A 4L1
Tel: 519-563-8417
www.ajac.ca
To report on new vehicles & new industry trends in various print and broadcast media.
Siobhan Duffield, Event Coordinator

Automobile Protection Association (APA) / Association pour la protection automobile
292, boul St. Joseph ouest, Montréal QC H2V 2N7
Tel: 514-272-5555; *Fax:* 514-273-0797
apamontreal@apa.ca
www.apa.ca
To inform & represent the public on major automobile-related issues

Automotive Industries Association of Canada (AIAC) / Association des industries de l'automobile du Canada
#1400, 180 Elgin St., Ottawa ON K2P 2K3
Tel: 613-728-5821; *Fax:* 613-728-6021
Toll-Free: 800-808-2920
info@aia@aiacanada.com
www.aiacanada.com
Social Media: www.youtube.com/c/aiacanada
linkedin.com/company/aia-canada
www.facebook.com/AIAofCanada
twitter.com/AIAOFCANADA

To represent the automotive aftermarket industry in Canada; To promote, educate, & represent members
Tony Canade, Chair
Jean-François Champagne, President
Therese Santostefano, Senior Director, Operations & Finance
Andrew Shepherd, Senior Director, Industry Programs
Luciana Nechita, Manager, Communications

Automotive Parts Manufacturers' Association (APMA)
#801, 10 Four Seasons Pl., Toronto ON M9B 6H7
Tel: 416-620-4220; *Fax:* 416-620-9730
www.apma.ca
Social Media: linkedin.com/groups/2654454
twitter.com/APMACanada
To promote the manufacture in Canada of automotive parts, systems, components, materials, tools, equipment & supplies, & also the provision of services used in the automotive industry & in particular for the original equipment market; To engage in activities in support of the welfare of the members of the Association
Barry Jones, Chair
Flavio Volpe, President

Automotive Recyclers of Canada (ARC)
134 Langarth St. East, London ON N6C 1Z5
Tel: 519-858-8761
info@autorecyclers.ca
autorecyclers.ca
Social Media: www.youtube.com/watch?v=wlmtDORQeOw&feature=youtu.be
twitter.com/autorecyclersCA
To act as the national voice for provincial member automotive recycling associations
Steve Fletcher, Managing Director

Automotive Retailers Association of British Columbia
#1, 8980 Fraserwood Ct., Burnaby BC V5J 5H7
Tel: 604-432-7987; *Fax:* 604-432-1756
reception@ara.bc.ca
www.ara.bc.ca
Social Media: www.facebook.com/autoretailers
twitter.com/autoretailers
To enhance the image & competitive status of association members throughout BC & ensure high quality service to protect the road safety of the motoring public
Ken McCormack, President

BCADA - The New Car Dealers of BC
#70, 10551 Shellbridge Way, Richmond BC V6X 2W9
Tel: 604-214-9964; *Fax:* 604-214-9965
info@newcardealers.ca
www.newcardealers.ca
To promote benefits & heighten awareness of issues of interest to members
Blair Qualey, President & CEO

British Columbia Automobile Association (BCAA)
4567 Canada Way, Burnaby BC V5G 4T1
Tel: 604-268-5000; *Fax:* 604-268-5585
Toll-Free: 800-268-2222
info@bcaa.com
www.bcaa.com
To provide motoring, travel, & insurance services to members in British Columbia & the Yukon
Vacant, President & CEO
Brenda Lowden, Senior Vice-President & Chief People Officer
Clayton Buckingham, Senior Vice-President & CFO
Ken Ontko, Senior Vice-President & CIO
Linda Bowyer, Sr. VP & Chief Member Experience Officer
Brent Cuthbertson, Sr. Vice-President & Chief Marketing Officer

CAA Manitoba
870 Empress St., Winnipeg MB R3C 2Z3
Tel: 204-262-6100
contact@caamanitoba.com
www.caamanitoba.com
Social Media: www.facebook.com/caamanitoba
twitter.com/caamanitoba
Bohdan (Bud) V. Halkewycz, Chair
Michael R. Mager, President & Chief Executive Officer

CAA-Québec
444, rue Bouvier, Québec QC G2J 1E3
Tél: 418-624-2424; *Ligne sans frais:* 800-686-9243
info@caa-quebec.qc.ca
www.caaquebec.com
Mèdia social: www.pinterest.com/caaquebec
linkedin.com/company/caa-quebec
www.facebook.com/caaQc
twitter.com/CAA_Quebec
Veut assurer la sécurité et paix d'esprit à chacun de ses membres ainsi qu'à ses clients en leur offrant des services et des produits de très haute qualité dans les domaines de l'automobile, du voyage, de l'habitation et des services financiers

Canadian Automobile Association Maritimes
Corporate Office & Saint John Member Service Centre, 378 Westmorland Rd., Saint John NB E2J 2G4
Tel: 506-634-1400; *Fax:* 506-653-9500
Toll-Free: 800-471-1611
www.caa.ca/atlantic
To serve New Brunswick, Newfoundland & Labrador, Nova Scotia, & Prince Edward Island

Canadian Automobile Association Niagara
3271 Schmon Pkwy., Thorold ON L2V 4Y6
Tel: 905-984-8585; *Fax:* 905-688-0289
www.caa.niagara.net

Canadian Automobile Association North & East Ontario
Administration Centre, PO Box 8350, Stn. T CSC, Ottawa ON K1G 3T2
Tel: 613-820-1890; *Fax:* 613-820-4646
Toll-Free: 800-267-8713
contactcaa@caaneo.on.ca
caaneo.ca
Social Media: www.youtube.com/user/TheCAANEOChannel
www.facebook.com/CAANEO
twitter.com/CAANEO
To deliver automotive, travel, insurance & related services to members & advocate on their behalf
Jack Campbell, Chair

Canadian Automobile Association Saskatchewan
200 Albert St. North, Regina SK S4R 5E2
Tel: 306-791-4314; *Fax:* 306-949-4461
caa.admin@caasask.sk.ca
www.caasask.sk.ca
Social Media: www.youtube.com/caasask
linkedin.com/company/521051
twitter.com/caasaskatchewan
To guarantee excellent emergency road assistance, travel, & insurance services; To provide services, products, programs, & representations to government in order to meet the needs of members, clients, & employees
Fred Titanich, President

Canadian Automobile Association South Central Ontario
60 Commerce Valley Dr. East, Thornhill ON L3T 7P9
Tel: 905-771-3000; *Fax:* 905-771-3101
Toll-Free: 866-988-8878
membership@caasco.ca
www.caasco.com
Social Media: www.youtube.com/caasouthcentralON
www.facebook.com/106112779480473
twitter.com/caasco
To enrich the driving experience of members by providing travel, insurance & automotive services & information
Bill Carter, Chair
Jay Woo, President & CEO
Jeff LeMoine, Consultant, Communications

Canadian Automobile Association Windsor
1215 Ouellette Ave., Windsor ON N8X 1J3
Tel: 519-255-1212; *Fax:* 519-255-7379
windsor@caasco.ca
www.caa.ca/csg-gce/cgs-offices-locations-e.cfm

Canadian Automobile Dealers' Association (CADA) / Corporation des associations de détaillants d'automobiles (CADA)
85 Renfrew Dr., Markham ON L3R 0N9
Tel: 905-940-4959; *Fax:* 905-940-6870
Toll-Free: 800-463-5289
www.cada.ca
To deal with issues of a national nature which affect the well-being of franchised automobile & truck dealers in Canada
Harry Mertin, Chair
Peter MacDonald, D.Litt, Secretary-Treasurer
Richard C. Gauthier, President & CEO

Canadian Automobile Sport Clubs - Ontario Region Inc. (CASC-OR)
1100 Barmac Dr., Toronto ON M9L 2X3
Tel: 416-667-9500; *Fax:* 416-667-9555
Toll-Free: 877-667-9505
office@casc.on.ca
www.casc.on.ca
To provide leadership, management, advocacy & the administrative services, facilities & equipment necessary to enable members to maximize their enjoyment & participation in motorsport; to maintain controls & standards necessary for safe competition
Peter Jackson, Secretary
Perry Iannuzzi, President

Canadian Automotive Repair & Service Council
c/o Cars Training Network, 81 Osborne Rd., Courtice ON L1E 2R3
Fax: 855-813-2111
Toll-Free: 855-813-2101
info@carstraining.net
www.carsondemand.com
To serve as a virtual gathering place to access training & education programs, to research industry issues, & to learn of new skills, technologies & trends.

Canadian Vehicle Manufacturers' Association (CVMA) / Association canadienne des constructeurs de véhicules
#400, 170 Attwell Dr., Toronto ON M9W 5Z5
Tel: 416-364-9333; *Fax:* 416-367-3221
Toll-Free: 800-758-7122
info@cvma.ca
www.cvma.ca
To create a framework within which member companies work together to achieve shared industry objectives on a range of important issues such as consumer protection, the environment, and vehicle safety
Mark A. Nantais, President

Corporation des concessionnaires d'automobiles du Québec inc. (CCAQ)
#750, 140, Grande-Allée est, Québec QC G1R 5M8
Tél: 418-523-2991; *Téléc:* 418-523-3725
Ligne sans frais: 800-463-5189
info@ccaq.com
www.ccaq.com
Mèdia social: plus.google.com/114145954123226218123
www.facebook.com/LaCCAQ
twitter.com/CCAQ
Offre une multitude de services aux membres; représenter ses membres
Jacques Béchard, Président-directeur général

Japan Automobile Manufacturers Association of Canada
#460, 151 Bloor St. West, Toronto ON M5S 1S4
Tel: 416-968-0150; *Fax:* 416-968-7095
jama@jama.ca
www.jama.ca
To promote increased understanding of economic & trade matters pertaining to the motor vehicle industry; To encourage closer cooperation between Canada & Japan; To represent the interests of members
Takashi Sekiguchi, Chairman

Manitoba Motor Dealers Association (MMDA)
#230, 530 Century St., Winnipeg MB R3H 0Y4
Tel: 204-985-4200; *Fax:* 204-775-9125
Toll-Free: 800-949-6632
info@mmda.mb.ca
www.mmda.mb.ca
To represent franchised automobile & truck dealers in Manitoba by dealing with provincial issues that affect this membership; To advance the automotive industry in Manitoba; To uphold the code of ethics
Neil Metcalfe, President
Geoff Sine, Executive Director

Motor Dealers' Association of Alberta (MDA)
9249 - 48 St., Edmonton AB T6B 2R9
Tel: 780-468-9552; *Fax:* 780-465-6201
info@mdaalberta.com
www.mdaalberta.com
Social Media: www.facebook.com/MDAofAlberta
To serve the collective interest of all its members and promote positive relationships with government, industry, suppliers, consumers and media, by offering needed and effective programs and services.
Denis Ducharme, President

Nova Scotia Automobile Dealers' Association (NSADA)
#700, 6009 Quinpool Rd., Halifax NS B3K 5S3
Tel: 902-425-2445; *Fax:* 902-425-2441
info@nsada.ca
www.nsada.ca
To assist & protect association members; To act as the voice of new vehicle franchised dealers in Nova Scotia
John K. Sutherland, Executive Vice-President

Ontario Tire Dealers Association
PO Box 516, 22 John St., Drayton ON N0G 1P0
Tel: 888-207-9059; *Fax:* 866-375-6832
www.otda.com
Social Media:
www.facebook.com/168955833458608
To represent members; To educate members in all areas that impact the continued growth of the tire industry
Robert Bignell, Executive Director

Prince Edward Island Automobile Dealers Association
PO Box 22004, Charlottetown PE C1A 9J2
Tel: 902-566-3639; *Fax:* 902-368-7116
peiada@eastlink.ca
Lisa Doyle-MacBain, Manager

Recreation Vehicle Dealers Association of Alberta
10561 - 172 St. NW, Edmonton AB T5S 1P1
Tel: 780-455-8562; *Fax:* 780-453-3927
Toll-Free: 888-858-8787
rvda@rvda-alberta.org
www.rvda-alberta.org
To develop professionalism & customer confidence in the RV industry

Recreation Vehicle Dealers Association of British Columbia (RVDABC)
#201, 17700 - 56th Ave., Surrey BC V3S 1C7
Tel: 604-575-3868; *Fax:* 604-575-3869
info@rvda.bc.ca
www.rvda.bc.ca
To promote, protect, educate, & enhances benefits for its members
Joan Jackson, Executive Director

Recreation Vehicle Dealers Association of Canada (RVDA) / Association des commerçants de véhicules recréatifs du Canada
#204, 6411 Buswell St., Richmond BC V6Y 2G5
Tel: 604-718-6325; *Fax:* 604-204-0154
info@rvda.ca
www.rvda.ca
Social Media:
www.facebook.com/RVDAofCanada
To promote professionalism in the RV industry through educational programs & events; to present the views of the industry to government & the general public
Eleonore Hamm, President

Recreation Vehicle Dealers Association of Manitoba
#503, 386 Broadway, Winnipeg MB R3C 3R6
Tel: 204-975-8219; *Fax:* 204-947-9767
rvshow@mbrvda.ca
www.manitobarvda.com
To build & improve the RV industry
Richard Willard, President
Geoff Powell, Executive Director

Recreation Vehicle Dealers Association of Saskatchewan
342 Armstrong Way, Saskatoon SK S7N 3N1
Tel: 306-955-7832; *Fax:* 306-955-7952
skrvda@sasktel.net
www.saskatchewanrvda.ca
Garret Porten, President

Saskatchewan Automobile Dealers Association (SADA)
610 Broad St., Regina SK S4R8H81
Tel: 306-721-2208; *Fax:* 306-721-1009
Susan Buckle, Executive Director

Trillium Automobile Dealers' Association (TADA)
85 Renfrew Dr., Markham ON L3R 0N9
Tel: 905-940-6232; *Fax:* 905-940-6235
Toll-Free: 800-668-6510
info@tada.ca
www.tada.ca
Social Media:
www.facebook.com/149581915142339
twitter.com/tada_gr
Brenda Sachdev, Contact

Used Car Dealers Association of Ontario (UCDA)
230 Norseman St., Toronto ON M8X 6A2
Tel: 416-231-2600; *Fax:* 416-232-0775
Toll-Free: 800-268-2598
web@ucda.org
www.ucda.org
To enhance the image of the industry through member education, consumer awareness of the benefits members provide, & mediation of consumer/dealer disputes
Robert G. Beattie, Executive Director
Steve Peck, President

Aviation & Aerospace

Canada's Aviation Hall of Fame (CAHF)
PO Box 6090, Wetaskiwin AB T9A 2G1
Tel: 780-361-1351; *Fax:* 780-361-1239
Toll-Free: 800-661-4726
cahf2@telus.net
www.cahf.ca
Social Media: www.youtube.com/user/cahf1973
www.facebook.com/pages/Canadas-Aviation-Hall-of-Fame/7078424647
To preserve & publicize the names & deeds of those who have made a significant contribution to Canadian aviation; to house an extensive collection of personal items & memorabilia, as well as a library of about 2,500 books & over 12,000 periodicals.
Tom Appleton, Chair

Helicopter Association of Canada (HAC)
#500, 130 Albert St., Ottawa ON K1P 5G4
Tel: 613-231-1110; *Fax:* 613-369-5097
www.h-a-c.ca
To ensure the financial viability of the Canadian civil helicopter industry; To promote flight safety; To expand utilization of helicopter transport
Teri Northcott, Chair
Fred L. Jones, BA LLB, President & Chief Executive Officer
Sylvain Seguin, Vice-President & Director, Marketing
Gary McDermid, Secretary
Maureen Crockett, Treasurer

International Civil Aviation Organization: Legal Affairs & External Relations Bureau
999, boul Robert-Bourassa, Montréal QC H3C 5H7
Tel: 514-954-8219; *Fax:* 514-954-6077
icaohq@icao.int
www.icao.int
Social Media: www.youtube.com/icaovideo
twitter.com/icao
To promote the safe & orderly development of civil aviation in the world; To set international standards & regulations necessary for the safety, security, efficiency & regularity of air transport & To serve as the medium for cooperation in all fields of civil aviation
John V. Augustin, Director

Ontario Aerospace Council (OAC)
1701 Aberfoyle Ct., Pickering ON L1V 4W4
Tel: 905-492-2296
www.theoac.ca
Social Media:
linkedin.com/company/ontario-aerospace-council
To enhance Ontario's aerospace industry in the global market; to ensure growth & prosperity
Moira Harvey, Executive Director

Better Business Bureaux

Better Business Bureau of Central & Northern Alberta
16102 - 100 Ave. NW, Edmonton AB T5P 0P3
Tel: 780-482-2341; *Fax:* 780-482-1150
Toll-Free: 800-232-7298
info@edmonton.bbb.org
edmonton.bbb.org
Social Media:
www.facebook.com/BBBCentralandNorthernAlberta
twitter.com/EdmontonBBB
To handle inquiries & complaints; To provide an ad review program; To educate the public
Chris Lawrence, President & CEO

Better Business Bureau of Eastern & Northern Ontario & the Outaouais / Bureau d'éthique commerciale de l'Est et Nord de l'Ontario et l'Outaouais
#505, 700 Industrial Ave., Ottawa ON K1G 0Y9
Tel: 613-237-4856; *Fax:* 613-237-4878
info@ottawa.bbb.org
ottawa.bbb.org
To promote & foster the highest ethical relationship between business & the public through voluntary self regulation, consumer & business education, & service excellence
Spencer Nimmons, Vice-President, Business Relations

Better Business Bureau of Mainland BC
#404, 788 Beatty St., Vancouver BC V6B 2M1
Tel: 604-682-2711; *Fax:* 604-681-1544
Toll-Free: 888-803-1222
contactus@mbc.bbb.org
mbc.bbb.org
Social Media:
linkedin.com/groups?gid=1323147
www.facebook.com/BBBmainlandBC
twitter.com/BBB_BC
To promote, develop & encourage an ethical marketplace

Better Business Bureau of Manitoba & Northwest Ontario
1030B Empress St., Winnipeg MB R3G 3H4
Tel: 204-989-9010; *Fax:* 204-989-9016
Toll-Free: 800-385-3074
ceo@bbbmb.ca
manitoba.bbb.org
Social Media:
www.facebook.com/197313847036123
To encourage ethical business practices through self-regulation in Manitoba.

Better Business Bureau of Mid-Western & Central Ontario
354 Charles St., Kitchener ON N2G 4L5
Tel: 519-579-3080; *Fax:* 519-570-0072
Toll-Free: 800-459-8875
mwco.bbb.org
Social Media:
www.facebook.com/234049259942145
To encourage ethical business practices through self-regulation in Mid-Western Ontario.
Ric Borski, President

Better Business Bureau of Saskatchewan
980 Albert St., Regina SK S4R 2P7
Tel: 306-352-7601; *Fax:* 306-565-6236
Toll-Free: 888-352-7601
info@bbbsask.com
sask.bbb.org
Social Media:
twitter.com/BBBSask
To promote & foster high ethical relationships between business & the public through voluntary self-regulation, consumer & business education, & service excellence
Patrick Heffernan, Chief Executive Officer

Better Business Bureau of Vancouver Island
#220, 1175 Cook St., Victoria BC V8V 4A1
Tel: 250-386-6348; *Fax:* 250-386-2367
Toll-Free: 877-826-4222
info@vi.bbb.org
vi.bbb.org
Social Media: www.youtube.com/user/BBBVancouverIsland
linkedin.com/company/better-business-bureau-of-vancouver-island
www.facebook.com/BBBVancouverIsland
twitter.com/VIBBB
Committed to the principle that fair dealing is good business for both buyer & seller & the majority of buyers & sellers are honest & responsible
Vern Fischer, President
Rosalind Scott, Executive Director

Better Business Bureau of Western Ontario
PO Box 2153, #308, 200 Queens Ave., London ON N6A 4E3
Tel: 519-673-3222; *Toll-Free:* 877-283-9222
info@westernontario.bbb.org
westernontario.bbb.org
Social Media:
www.facebook.com/BBBWesternOnt
twitter.com/BBB_Western_Ont
To promote the vitality of the free enterprise system & ethical business practices; To serve the concerns of business & the consuming public
Jan Delaney, President
Chris Lavoie, Manager, Operations
Marlene Aquilina-Bock, Coordinator, Business Development

Better Business Bureau Serving Southern Alberta & East Kootenay
#350, 7330 Fisher St. SE, Calgary AB T2H 2H8
Tel: 403-531-8784; *Fax:* 403-640-2514
info@calgary.bbb.org
calgary.bbb.org
Social Media: www.youtube.com/user/BBBServingSouthernAB
www.facebook.com/CalgaryBBB
twitter.com/calgarybbb
To promote & encourage ethical practices in retail market for goods & services through provision of a wide range of consultative, informative & conciliatory arbitration services for businesses & consumers.

Better Business Bureau Serving the Atlantic Provinces
#303, 1888 Brunswick St., Halifax NS B3J 3J8
Tel: 902-422-6581; *Fax:* 902-429-6457
Toll-Free: 877-663-2363
info@ap.bbb.org
atlanticprovinces.bbb.org
To promote and foster the highest ethical relationships between business and the public through voluntary self-regulation, consumer and business education and service excellence
J. Colin Dodds, Chair

Better Business Bureau Serving the Atlantic Provinces
#303, 1888 Brunswick St., Halifax NS B3J 3J8
Tel: 902-422-6581; *Fax:* 902-429-6457
Toll-Free: 877-663-2363
info@ap.bbb.org
atlanticprovinces.bbb.org
Social Media:
www.facebook.com/300802543311820
twitter.com/BBBAtlantic
To provide mutually beneficial relationships between buyer & seller based on responsible business practices
Don MacKinnon, President

Council of Better Business Bureaus / Conseil des bureaux d'éthique commerciale
#600, 3033 Wilson Blvd., Arlington VA 22201 USA
Tel: 703-276-0100
www.bbb.org
Social Media: pinterest.com/BBBConsumerNews/
linkedin.com/groups?about=&gid=1917928&trk=anet_ug_grppro
www.facebook.com/BetterBusinessBureau
twitter.com/bbb_us
To protect consumers & the vitality of the free enterprise system; To foster the highest standards of responsibility & probity in business practice by advocating truth in advertising, by assuring integrity in performance of business services, & by voluntary regulation & monitoring activities designed to enhance public trust & confidence in business
Jim Deane, Vice-Chair
David Steele, Treasurer
Spencer Nimmons, Vice-President, Business Relations

Breeders

Westgen
PO Box 40, 6681 Glover Rd., Milner BC V0X 1T0
Tel: 604-530-1141; *Fax:* 604-534-3036
Toll-Free: 800-563-5603
www.westgen.com
To provide Semex Alliance Genetics & other value-added products & services which enhance herd improvement to livestock producers in western Canada
Brent Belluk, General Manager
Darcie Kaye, Marketing Manager

Broadcasting

Audio Engineering Society (AES)
AES Toronto Section, PO Box 292, #32E, 223 Pioneer Dr., Kitchener ON N2P 1L9
Tel: 519-894-5308
torontoaes@torontoaes.org
www.torontoaes.org
Social Media:
linkedin.com/groups?mostPopular=&gid=2023730
Dedicated to audio technology.
Blair Francey, Chair
Karl Machat, Secretary
Frank Lockwood, Vice Chair

British Columbia Association of Broadcasters (BCAB)
BC
www.bcab.ca
Social Media:
www.facebook.com/126523200745913
twitter.com/bcabinfo
To unify the broadcasting community in British Columbia
James Stewart, President

Broadcast Educators Association of Canada (BEAC) / Association Canadienne de educateurs en radiodiffusion
beac.ca
Social Media: www.flickr.com/photos/beacanada;
vimeo.com/user6518105
www.facebook.com/BEACanada
twitter.com/BEACanada
To be dedicated to the professional development of staff, faculty & administrators of provincially accredited colleges & universities throughout Canada that specialize in radio, television, broadcast journalism & new media programs.
Dan Pihlainen, President
Anna Rodrigues, Vice-President
Michelle Grimes, Secretary
Stephen Melanson, Treasurer

Broadcast Executives Society (BES)
PO Box 75150, 20 Bloor St. East, Toronto ON M4W 3T3
Tel: 416-899-0370
www.bes.ca
To serve as forum for the broadcast industry.
John Tucker, Administrator

Broadcast Research Council of Canada (BRC)
#1005, 160 Bloor St. East, Toronto ON M4W 1B9
Tel: 416-413-3864; *Fax:* 416-413-3879
brc@tvb.ca
www.brc.ca
Social Media:
ca.linkedin.com/pub/brc-broadcast-research-council-of-canada/2 4/462/11
www.facebook.com/117260268358077
twitter.com/BroadcastBRC
To provide a forum for presentations relating to the broadcast advertising business; to provide awards to the most promising students at colleges that train people to enter the advertising business.
Robert DaSilva, President

Canadian Association of Broadcasters (CAB) / Association canadienne des radiodiffuseurs (ACR)
#770, 45 O'Connor St., Ottawa ON K1P 1A4
Tel: 613-233-4035; *Fax:* 613-233-6961
www.cab-acr.ca
To act as the national voice of Canada's private broadcasters
Sylvie Bissonnette, CFO & Vice-President, Finance

Canadian Association of Ethnic (Radio) Broadcasters (CAEB) / Association canadienne des radiodiffuseurs ethniques
c/o CHIN Radio, #400, 622 College St., Toronto ON M6G 1B6
Tel: 416-531-9991; *Fax:* 416-531-5274
info@chinradio.com
www.chinradio.com
Social Media:
www.facebook.com/pages/CHIN-Radio-Canada/1095528757502 38
twitter.com/chinradiocanada
To foster & promote the development of multilingual / multicultural radio broadcasting in Canada
Lenny Lombardi, President

Canadian Communications Foundation (CCF)
Toronto ON
www.broadcasting-history.ca
To document the history of Canadian broadcasting on the foundation's online electronic database.
Pip Wedge, President
Fil Fraser, Vice-President

Central Canada Broadcast Engineers (CCBE)
3 Jasmine Dr., Paris ON N3L 3P7
Fax: 519-442-1912
Toll-Free: 800-481-4649
information@ccbe.ca
www.ccbe.ca
To provide up-to-date technical information regarding the broadcast industry, including the following areas: television, radio, post production, towers & safety issues.
Peter Warth, President

Friends of Canadian Broadcasting (FCB)
#200-238, 131 Bloor St. West, Toronto ON M5S 1R8
Tel: 416-968-7496; *Fax:* 416-968-7406
friends@friends.ca
www.friends.ca
Social Media: www.youtube.com/user/FriendsCB
www.facebook.com/sharer.php?u=/&t="Welcome
twitter.com/friendscb
To defend & enhance the quality & quantity of Canadian programming in the Canadian audio-visual system
Ian Morrison, Spokesperson

Friends of Music Therapy / Association de Musicothérapie du Canada
#202, 4056 Dorchester Rd., Niagara Falls ON L2E 6M9
Tel: 905-374-8878; *Fax:* 888-665-1307
www.friendsofmusictherapy.com
Social Media: www.youtube.com/user/norriswhitney
www.facebook.com/pages/Friends-Of-Music-Therapy/17943535 8395
The Friends of Music Therapy Endowment Fund was established at SickKids Foundation to provide permanent financial support to the Music Therapy Program at The Hospital for Sick Children.
Kevin Goranson, Co-Founder
Jim Norris, Co-Founder

Interactive Ontario (IO)
#600, 431 King St. West, Toronto ON M5V 1K4
Tel: 416-516-0077
info@interactiveontario.com
www.interactiveontario.com
Social Media: www.flickr.com/photos/32406922@N04/
linkedin.com/groups?about=&gid=2096721&trk=anet_ug_grppro
www.facebook.com/28971906704
twitter.com/ionews
To advance the digital media industry in Ontario, including e-Learning, video & online games, mobile, television & social media.
Peter Miller, Chair
Lucie Lalumière, Vice-Chair
Spence McDonnell, Treasurer
David Dembroski, Secretary
Christa Dickenson, Executive Director

National Campus & Community Radio Association (NCRA) / Association nationale des radio étudiantes et communautaires (ANREC)
#608, 180 Metcalfe St., Ottawa ON K2P 1P5
Tel: 613-321-1440; *Fax:* 613-321-1442
Toll-Free: 866-859-8086
office@ncra.ca
www.ncra.ca
To encourage development of community & student radio in Canada by providing core services to community-oriented radios & representing them to government, industry & the public
Brian Cleveland, President
Shelley Robinson, Executive Director

North American Broadcasters Association (NABA)
PO Box 500, Stn. A, #6C300, 25 John St., Toronto ON M5W 1E6
Tel: 416-598-9877; *Fax:* 416-598-9774
contact@nabanet.com
www.nabanet.com
To provide a framework for the identification, study & active solution of international questions affecting broadcasting
Robert J. Ross, President
Michael McEwen, Director General
Anh Ngo, Director, Administration

Numeris
1500 Don Mills Rd., 3rd Fl., Toronto ON M3B 3L7
Tel: 416-445-9800; *Fax:* 416-445-8644
en.numeris.ca
To provide broadcast measurement & consumer behaviour data to broadcasters, advertisers, & agencies
Jim MacLeod, President & CEO
Glen Shipp, Executive Vice-President & CFO
Lisa Eaton, Senior Vice-President, Member Engagement
Anna Giagkou, Vice-President, Finance
Ricardo Gomez-Insausti, Vice-President, Research
Jane Hill, Vice-President, Operations
Randy Missen, Vice-President, Technical Implementation
Dorena Quinn, Vice-President, Human Resources & Corporate Services

Ontario Association of Broadcasters (OAB)
PO Box 54040, 5762 Hwy. 7 East, Markham ON L3P 7Y4
Tel: 905-554-2730; *Fax:* 905-554-2731
www.oab.ca
Doug Kirk, President
Dave Hughes, Vice-President

Ross Davies, Treasurer

Radio Advisory Board of Canada (RABC) / Conseil consultatif canadien de la radio
#811, 116 Albert St., Ottawa ON K1P 5G3
Tel: 613-230-3261; *Toll-Free:* 888-902-5768
rabc.gm@on.aibn.com
www.rabc-cccr.ca
To consult & advise Industry Canada on behalf of industry on the development, management, & regulation of radio services in Canada
Roger Poirier, General Manager

Radio Amateurs of Canada Inc. (RAC) / Radio Amateurs du Canada inc.
#217, 720 Belfast Rd., Ottawa ON K1G 0Z5
Tel: 613-244-4367; *Toll-Free:* 877-273-8304
www.rac.ca
To act as coordinating body of amateur radio organizations in Canada, liaison agency between members & other amateur organizations in Canada & other countries, coordinating & advisory agency between members & industry Canada; to promote interests of amateur radio operators through program of technical & general education in amateur matters
Geoff Bawden, President
Sukwan Widajat, Corporate Secretary

Radio Television Digital News Association (Canada) (RTDNA Canada) / Association canadienne des directeurs de l'information en radio-télévision
439 University Ave., 5th Fl., Toronto ON M5G 1Y8
Tel: 437-836-3088
admin@rtdnacanada.com
www.rtdnacanada.com
Social Media:
linkedin.com/groups/RTDNA-Canada-1800955
www.facebook.com/RTDNA.CAN
twitter.com/RTDNA_Canada
To represent electronic & digital journalists & news managers in Canada; To act as a progressive voice in the Canadian broadcast news industry; To foster education, professional development & recognition while encouraging active dialogue within its membership
Ian Koenigsfest, President
Yuliana Paspalovski, Coordinator, Membership

Television Bureau of Canada, Inc. (TVB) / Bureau de la télévision du Canada
#1005, 160 Bloor St. East, Toronto ON M4W 1B9
Tel: 416-923-8813; *Fax:* 416-413-3879
Toll-Free: 800-231-0051
tvb@tvb.ca
www.tvb.ca
Social Media:
twitter.com/TVB_CA
To promote sales, marketing & research of commercial television industry in Canada
Rita Fabian, Chair
Theresa Treutler, President & CEO
Rhonda-Lynn Bagnall, Director, Telecaster Services
Duncan Robertson, Director, Media Insights & Research

Western Association of Broadcast Engineers (WABE)
#300, 8120 Beddington Blvd. NW, Calgary AB T3K 2A8
Tel: 403-630-4907; *Fax:* 403-295-3135
info@wabe.ca
www.wabe.ca
Social Media:
linkedin.com/company/western-association-of-broadcast-engineers
Brian Mayer, President

Western Association of Broadcasters (WAB)
#507, 918 - 16th Ave. NW, Calgary AB T2M 0K3
Toll-Free: 877-814-2719
info@wab.ca
www.wab.ca
To represent private television & radio stations in Alberta, Saskatchewan & Manitoba.
Tom Newton, President

Women in Film & Television - Toronto
#601, 110 Eglinton Ave. East, Toronto ON M4P 2Y1
Tel: 416-322-3430; *Fax:* 416-322-3703
wift@wift.com
www.wift.com
Social Media: vimeo.com/wift
linkedin.com/groups/Women-in-Film-Television-Toronto-2908431
www.facebook.com/WIFT.Toronto
twitter.com/WIFT
To provide year-round training programs, industry events, & professional awards for women & men in Canadian screen based media
Prentiss Fraser, Chair
Heather Webb, Executive Director

Women in Film & Television Alberta (WIFT-A)
c/o Luanne Morrow, Borden Ladner Gervais, #1000 Canterra Tower, 400 3rd Ave. SW, Calgary AB T2P 4H2
admin@wifta.ca
www.wifta.ca
Social Media:
linkedin.com/groups/WIFTA-Women-in-Film-Television-4165901
www.facebook.com/WIFTAlberta
twitter.com/WIFTAlberta
WIFT-A is a non-profit organization that promotes and assists the professional development, equitable treatment, recognition of achievements and the creation of new opportunities for professionals, especially women in the film, video, multimedia and television industries
Kathy Fedori, President
Coralie Braum, Vice-President
Astrid Kuhn, Treasurer

Women in Film & Television Vancouver (WIFTV)
Dominion Building, #306, 207 West Hastings St., Vancouver BC V6B 1H7
Tel: 604-685-1152; *Fax:* 604-685-1124
info@womeninfilm.ca
www.womeninfilm.ca
Social Media: www.youtube.com/user/wiftv
www.facebook.com/Womeninfilm
twitter.com/WIFTV
To support, advance, promote & celebrate the professional development & achievements of women working in British Columbia's film, television, video & multimedia industries
Rachelle Chartrand, President
Michelle Billy Povill, Vice-President
Christine Larsen, Secretary

Youth Media Alliance (AMJ) / Alliance Médias Jeunesse (AET)
#107, 1400, boul René-Lévesque est, Montréal QC H2L 2M2
Tel: 514-597-5417; *Fax:* 514-597-5205
alliance@ymamj.org
www.ymamj.org
Social Media: www.youtube.com/alliancemediasjeunes
www.facebook.com/150380741707933
twitter.com/YMAMJ
To promote the production & carriage of quality Canadian television programming for children; to ensure the development of critical viewing skills so that families are able to use media more effectively in the home; to promote awareness of the need to help young people make the most of their experience of television & other screen-based media
Chantal Brown, Executive Director

Building & Construction

Alberta Construction Association (ACA)
18012 - 107 Ave., Edmonton AB T5S 2J5
Tel: 780-455-1122; *Fax:* 780-451-2152
info@albertaconstruction.net
www.albertaconstruction.net
To represent & promote Alberta's construction industry
Ken Gibson, Executive Director
Shelley Andrea, Director, Administration

Alberta Ready Mixed Concrete Association (ARMCA)
9653 - 45 Ave., Edmonton AB T6E 5Z8
Tel: 780-436-5645; *Fax:* 780-436-6503
info@armca.ca
www.armca.ca
To provide industry representation for the advancement of quality concrete in Alberta; To market & promote the use of concrete; To provide a consolidated industry approach to regulatory bodies; To provide networking opportunities; to provide education & training
Laura Reschke, Executive Director
Edward Kalis, Director, Technical Services & Training

Alberta Roadbuilders & Heavy Construction Association (ARHCA)
#201, 9333 - 45 Ave., Edmonton AB T6E 5Z7
Tel: 780-436-9860; *Fax:* 780-436-4910
Toll-Free: 866-436-9860
administration@arhca.ab.ca
www.arhca.ab.ca
Gene Syvenky, Chief Executive Officer
Kimberley Barrett, Director, Finance & Administration
Heidi Harris-Jensen, Director, External Affairs
Dawn Fenske, Coordinator, Communications

Alberta Roofing Contractors Association (ARCA)
2380 Pegasus Rd. NE, Calgary AB T2E 8G8
Tel: 403-250-7055; *Fax:* 403-250-1702
Toll-Free: 800-382-8515
info@arcaonline.ca
www.arcaonline.ca
To provide continuing education for roofing contractors, their personnel & interested others; to represent the roofing contracting industry in its relationships with legislative & regulating bodies; to work closely with affiliate organizations & liaison groups in advancing professionalism of roofing contracting; to provide a forum for interaction of members; to encourage high standards of professional conduct among roofing contractors; to develop a comprehensive body of knowledge about roofing management & technology, & disseminate ideas & knowledge to members & others; to monitor new products & systems; to work for cooperation & greater understanding between contracting, inspection, manufacturing & supply segments of the roofing industry

Architectural Woodwork Manufacturers Association of British Columbia (AWMA-BC)
#101, 4238 Lozells Ave., Burnaby BC V5A 0C4
Tel: 604-298-3555; *Fax:* 604-298-3558
bc.awmac.org
To advance the highest standards of education, quality workmanship, warranties & business practices in architectural woodwork manufacturing in British Columbia
Mike Harskamp, President

Architectural Woodwork Manufacturers Association of Canada (AWMAC)
516 - 4 St. West, High River AB T1V 1B6
Tel: 403-652-7685; *Fax:* 403-652-7384
info@awmac.com
www.awmac.com
To foster & advance the interests of those who are engaged in or who are directly or indirectly connected with or affected by the production & installation of architectural woodwork; to endeavour to achieve a closer relationship & a better understanding among the various branches of the industry
Rick Koehn, Vice-President
Frank VanDonzel, Secretary/Manager
Myron Jonzon, President

Architectural Woodwork Manufacturers Association of Canada - Atlantic
135 Driscoll Cres., Moncton NB E1E 4C8
info@awmac-atlantic.ca
awmac-atlantic.ca
AWMAC-Atlantic is an association of millwork manufacturers, suppliers, installers, designers and educators in the provinces of Atlantic Canada.
Drew Parks, President

Architectural Woodwork Manufacturers Association of Canada - Manitoba
1447 Waverly St., Winnipeg MB R3T 0P7
manitoba@awmac.com
www.awmac.com
To foster and advance the intersts of those who are engaged in or who are directly or indirectly connected with or affected by the production and installation of architectural woodwork; to endeavor to achieve a closer relationship and a better understanding among the various branches of the industry.
Curtis Popel, President
Richard Wroblewski, Vice-President
Nancy Carpenter, Secretary
Greg Pallone, Treasurer

Architectural Woodwork Manufacturers Association of Canada - Northern Alberta
c/o Margo Love, 12816 - 89 St. NW, Edmonton AB T5E 3J9
Tel: 780-937-8572
nab.awmac.com
Dan Zacharko, President

Architectural Woodwork Manufacturers Association of Canada - Ontario Chapter (AWMAC-ON)
70 Leek Cres., Richmond Hill ON L4B 1H1
Tel: 416-499-4000; *Fax:* 416-499-8752
gis@awmacontario.com
www.awmacontario.com
To foster & advance the interests of those engaged in the production & installation of architectural woodwork in Ontario
Jeff Clemount, President
Micah Gingrich, Secretary-Treasurer

Architectural Woodwork Manufacturers Association of Canada - Québec
3875 Isabelle, Brossard QC J4Y 2R2
Tel: 514-346-2511
quebec@awmac.com
awmac-quebec.blogspot.com
Marc Pepin, President

Architectural Woodwork Manufacturers Association of Canada - Saskatchewan
PO Box 26032, Stn. Lawson Heights, Saskatoon SK S7K 8C1
Tel: 306-652-2704; *Fax:* 306-664-2552
awmac.sask@sasktel.net
www.awmac.com
To foster and advance the interests of those who are engaged in or who are directly or indirectly connected with or affected by the production and installation of architectural woodwork; to endeavor to achieve a closer relationship and a better understanding among the various branches of the lbirary.
Kerry DePape, President

Architectural Woodwork Manufacturers Association of Canada - Southern Alberta
#2A, 4803 Centre St. NW, Calgary AB T2E 2Z6
Tel: 403-264-5979; *Fax:* 403-286-9400
southernalberta@awmac.com
sab.awmac.com
To advance the interests of those related to the production & installation of architectural woodwork; to foster a closer relationship among the various branches of the industry.
Rob Hodgins, President
Blaine Wickerson, Secretary
Larry White, AWNAC Director

Association de la construction du Québec (ACQ) / Construction Association of Québec
9200, boul Métropolitain est, Anjou QC H1K 4L2
Tél: 514-354-0609; *Téléc:* 514-354-8292
Ligne sans frais: 888-868-3424
info@prov.acq.org
www.acq.org
Média social: www.youtube.com/user/ACQprovinciale
linkedin.com/company/association-de-la-construction-du-qu-bec
www.facebook.com/ACQprovinciale
twitter.com/ACQprovinciale
Promotion et défense des intérêts des entreprises de construction, de gestionnaire de plans de garantie des bâtiments résidentiels neufs (Qualité Habitation) et d'agent patronal négociateur pour tous les employeurs des secteurs institutionnel/commercial et industriel (IC/I)
Manon Bertrand, Présidente
Francis Roy, Vice-présidente, IC/I
Jean-François Arbour, Vice-président, Finances
René Hamel, Vice-président, Habitation
Laberge Yvan, Vice-président, Régions

Association des constructeurs de routes et grands travaux du Québec (ACRGTQ) / Québec Road Builders & Heavy Construction Association
435, av Grande-Allée est, Québec QC G1R 2J5
Tél: 418-529-2949; *Téléc:* 418-529-5139
Ligne sans frais: 800-463-4672
acrgtq@acrgtq.qc.ca
www.acrgtq.qc.ca
Défendre les intérêts des entrepreneurs en génie civil et voirie du Québec
Alexis Loisel, Président
Louise Morin, Trésorière
Gisèle Bourque, Directrice générale

Association des entrepreneurs en construction du Québec (AECQ) / Association of Building Contractors of Québec (ABCQ)
#101, 7905, boul Louis-H. Lafontaine, Anjou QC H1K 4E4
Tél: 514-353-5151; *Téléc:* 514-353-6689
Ligne sans frais: 800-361-4304
info@aecq.org
www.aecq.org
Étudier, promouvoir, protéger et défendre les intérêts des employeurs en matière de relations de travail; négocier les clauses du tronc commun à chacune des quatre conventions collectives sectorielles
Pierre Dion, Directeur général

Association des maîtres couvreurs du Québec (AMCQ) / Québec Master Roofers Association
3001, boul Tessier, Laval QC H7S 2M1
Tél: 450-973-2322; *Téléc:* 450-973-2321
Ligne sans frais: 888-973-2322
amcq@amcq.qc.ca
www.amcq.qc.ca
Promouvoir les intérêts généraux des entreprises de couvertures et ceux de diverses entreprises des secteurs connexes dans la province de Québec; promouvoir la hausse de la qualité des travaux de couvertures

Association of Commercial & Industrial Contractors of PEI
PO Box 1685, Charlottetown PE C1A 7N4
Tel: 902-566-3456; *Fax:* 902-368-2754
wmm@wmm93.pe.ca
Mary MacDonald, Contact

Association québécoise de la quincaillerie et des matériaux de construction (AQMAT) / The Building Materials Retailers Association of Québec
#200, 476, rue Jean-Neveu, Longueuil QC J4G 1N8
Tél: 450-646-5842; *Téléc:* 450-646-6171
www.aqmat.org
Promouvoir l'intérêt général de ses membres-clients engagés dans la vente au détail de matériaux de construction et de quincaillerie, en leur offrant une panoplie de produits et services visant à faciliter la gestion de leurs commerces, des Québécois et la rénovation
Richard Darveau, Président-directeur général

Atlantic Building Supply Dealers Association (ABSDA)
70 Englehart St., Dieppe NB E1A 8H3
Tel: 506-858-0700; *Fax:* 506-859-0064
www.absda.ca
Social Media:
twitter.com/absdadealers
To keep membership informed of new trends & developments in the industry; to provide a forum to discuss mutual problems & ideas; to provide continuing education programs for members
Don Sherwood, President
Brian Warr, Chair

Atlantic Provinces Ready-Mixed Concrete Association (APRMCA) / Association des fabricants de béton préparé des provinces atlantiques
c/o Mary Macaulay, #301, 3845 Joseph Howe Dr., Halifax NS B3L 4H9
Tel: 902-443-4456; *Fax:* 902-404-8074
info@atlanticconcrete.ca
www.aprmca.com
To promote the use of ready-mixed concrete while providing leadership to the industry through the exchange of ideas & information.
Mary Macaulay, Executive Director

British Columbia Construction Association (BCCA)
#401, 655 Tyee Rd., Victoria BC V9A 6X5
Tel: 250-475-1077; *Fax:* 250-475-1078
www.bccassn.com
Social Media: www.youtube.com/user/BCCASSN
linkedin.com/company/british-columbia-construction-association-bcc
www.facebook.com/WeBuildBC
twitter.com/WeBuildBC
To provide excellence in the representation of & service to British Columbia's construction industry
Manley McLachlan, President
Abigail Fulton, Vice-President
Warren Perks, Vice-President & Director, Industry Practices
Stephen Richter, Administrator, Marketing & Communications

British Columbia Construction Association - North (BCCA-N)
3851 - 18 Ave., Prince George BC V2N 1B1
Tel: 250-563-1744; *Fax:* 250-563-1107
www.bccanorth.ca
To act as a united voice on behalf of all sectors of the construction industry on concerns of the industry; To promote education, training, safety, standard practices, high standards, & investment in the construction industry of northern British Columbia
Rosalind Thorn, President
Ken Morland, Chair
Lee Bedell, Secretary
Bonnie Griffith, Treasurer

British Columbia Ready Mixed Concrete Association
26162 - 30A Ave., Aldergrove BC V4W 2W5
Tel: 604-626-4141; *Fax:* 604-626-4143
info@bcrmca.ca
www.bcrmca.ca
To work cooperatively with all levels of government to ensure the ready-mix concrete industry operates with a focus on the communities & the environment
Charles Kelly, President

British Columbia Road Builders & Heavy Construction Association (BCRB&HCA)
#307, 8678 Greenall Ave., Burnaby BC V5J 3M6
Tel: 604-436-0220; *Fax:* 604-436-2627
info@roadbuilders.bc.ca
www.roadbuilders.bc.ca
To represent the interests of member companies to government, media, other organizations, & the public
Jack W. Davidson, President
Jackson Yu, Administrator
Kate Cockerill, Manager, Communications & Membership

Building Supply Industry Association of British Columbia (BSIA of BC)
#2, 19299 - 94th Ave., Surrey BC V4N 4E6
Tel: 604-513-2205; *Fax:* 604-513-2206
Toll-Free: 888-711-5656
www.bsiabc.ca
To act as the official voice of the building supply industry in British Columbia; To provide services to members
Thomas Foreman, President
Marijoel Chamberlain, Coordinator, Member Services, & Manager, Trade Show
Jackie Trafton, Administrator

Canadian Concrete Masonry Producers Association (CCMPA)
PO Box 1345, 1500 Avenue Rd., Toronto ON M5M 3X0
Tel: 416-495-7497; *Fax:* 416-495-8939
Toll-Free: 888-495-7497
information@ccmpa.ca
www.ccmpa.ca
Works on behalf of concrete masonry producers to build an industry as strong and as enduring as the products it manufactures
Marina de Souza, Managing Director

Canadian Concrete Pipe Association (CCPA) / Association canadienne des fabricants de tuyaux de béton (ACTB)
205 Miller Dr., Halton Hills ON L7G 6G4
Tel: 905-877-5369; *Fax:* 905-877-5369
info@ccpa.com
www.ccpa.com
Social Media: www.youtube.com/user/CanadianConcretePipe
linkedin.com/groups?trk=groups_management_submission_que ue-h-dsc&g
To coordinate research & development, promotion, education & federal government relations programs pertaining to the marketing of high quality precast concrete waste water & storm drainage products in Canada.
John Greer, Chair

Canadian Construction Association (CCA) / Association canadienne de la construction (ACC)
#1900, 275 Slater St., Ottawa ON K1P 5H9
Tel: 613-236-9455; *Fax:* 613-236-9526
cca@cca-acc.com
www.cca-acc.com
Social Media: www.youtube.com/user/ConstructionCAN
linkedin.com/company/canadian-construction-association—associati
twitter.com/ConstructionCAN
To act as the national voice of the construction industry; To serve, promote, & enhance the construction industry by acting on behalf of its members in matters of national concern
Anibal Valente, Chair
Michael Atkinson, President
Eric Lee, Senior Director, Industry Practices
Mark Belton, Director, Finance
Bill Ferreira, Vice-President, Government Relations & Public Affairs
Chantal Montpetit, Director, Meetings & Conferences
Kirsi O'Connor, Director, Marketing & Communications
Aneel Rangi, General Counsel & Corporate Secretary

Canadian Masonry Contractors' Association (CMCA)
Canada Masonry Centre, 360 Superior Blvd., Mississauga ON L5T 2N7
Tel: 905-564-6622; *Fax:* 905-564-5744
www.canadamasonrycentre.com/cmca
To advance masonry technology, skills development & the use of masonry products in construction across Canada.

Canadian Mechanical Contracting Education Foundation (CMCEF)
#601, 280 Albert St., Ottawa ON K1P 5G8
Tel: 613-232-5169; *Fax:* 613-235-2793
cmef@cmcef.org
www.cmcef.org
To ensure a stronger Mechanical Contracting Industry by initiating and conducting essential educational and research

programs which enhance this industry's ability to operate efficiently and economically for the benefit of those served by the industry.
Tania Johnston, Executive Director

Canadian Paint & Coatings Association (CPCA) / Association canadienne de l'industrie de la peinture et du revêtement
#608, 170 Laurier Ave. West, Ottawa ON K1P 5V5
Tel: 613-231-3604; *Fax:* 613-231-4908
cpca@cdnpaint.org
www.cdnpaint.org
To represent the paint industry among the provincial, federal & municipal governments
Dale Constantinoff, Chair

Canadian Precast / Prestressed Concrete Institute (CPCI) / Institut canadien du béton préfabriqué et précontraint
#100, 196 Bronson Ave., Ottawa ON K1R 6H4
Tel: 613-232-2619; *Fax:* 613-232-5139
Toll-Free: 877-937-2724
info@cpci.ca
www.cpci.ca
Social Media:
www.facebook.com/121188924614844
To stimulate & advance the common interests & general welfare of the structural precast/prestressed concrete industry, the architectural precast concrete industry & the post-tensioned concrete industry in Canada
Rob Burak, President

Canadian Roofing Contractors' Association (CRCA) / Association canadienne des entrepreneurs en couverture (ACEC)
#100, 2430 Don Reid Dr., Ottawa ON K1H 1E1
Tel: 613-232-6724; *Fax:* 613-232-2893
crca@on.aibn.com
www.roofingcanada.com

Canadian Welding Bureau (CWB)
8260 Parkhill Dr., Milton ON L9T 5V7
Fax: 905-542-1318
Toll-Free: 800-844-6790
info@cwbgroup.org
www.cwbgroup.org
Social Media: www.youtube.com/user/cwbgroup
www.facebook.com/134949822909
twitter.com/cwbgroupandcwa
To administrator certification programs for CSA Standards W47.1, W47.2, W186, W178.1 & W48 series; to provide support for welding-based programs in schools, education institutions, welding professionals & companies employing welding technology.
Douglas Luciano, President

Cement Association of Canada (CAC) / Association canadienne du ciment
#502, 350 Sparks St., Ottawa ON K1R 7S8
Tel: 613-236-9471; *Fax:* 613-563-4498
www.cement.ca
Represents all of Canada's cement producers; aims to improve & extend the uses of cement & concrete through market development, engineering, research, education, & public affairs work
Michael McSweeney, President & CEO

Construction Association of New Brunswick Inc. (CANB)
59 Avonlea Ct., Fredericton NB E3C 1N8
Tel: 506-459-5770; *Fax:* 506-457-1913
canb4@nbnet.nb.ca
www.constructnb.ca
To co-ordinate a consensus to effectively present the Industry's collective views to various client groups, partic-ularly to relevant departments and agencies of the provincial government.
John Landry, Executive Director

Construction Association of Nova Scotia
#3, 260 Brownlow Ave., Dartmouth NS B3B 1V9
Tel: 902-468-2267; *Fax:* 902-468-2470
cans@cans.ns.ca
www.cans.ns.ca
To represent the interests of its members
Duncan Williams, President

Construction Association of Prince Edward Island (CAPEI)
PO Box 728, Charlottetown PE C1A 7L3
Tel: 902-368-3303; *Fax:* 902-894-9757
admin@capei.ca
www.capei.ca
To foster, promote & advance the interests & efficiency of Prince Edward Island's construction industry
Ross D. Barnes, General Manager
Grant MacPherson, President

Construction Specifications Canada (CSC) / Devis de construction Canada
#312, 120 Carlton St., Toronto ON M5A 4K2
Tel: 416-777-2198; *Fax:* 416-777-2197
www.csc-dcc.ca
Social Media:
linkedin.com/company/construction-specifications-canada
www.facebook.com/120516191352386?ref=ts
To improve communication, contract documentation, & technical information in the construction industry
Peter S. Emmett, President
Nick Franjic, Executive Director

Council of Ontario Construction Associations (COCA)
#2001, 180 Dundas St. West, Toronto ON M5G 1Z8
Tel: 416-968-7200; *Fax:* 416-968-0362
info@coca.on.ca
www.coca.on.ca
Social Media:
linkedin.com/company/2397076
www.facebook.com/172643879452017
twitter.com/ICIconstruction
To contribute to the long-term growth & profitability of the construction industry in Ontario; To speak with a unified voice to government, the industry & the public
Ian Cunningham, President
Martin Benson, Manager, Operations & Member Services

Glass & Architectural Metals Association (GAMA)
c/o Calgary Construction Association, 2725 - 12 St. NE, Calgary AB T2E 7J2
www.pgaa.ca/gama
To advance the glass & architectural metals industry
Al Ryland, President
Becky McLaughlin, Treasurer & Contact, Membership

Heavy Civil Association of Newfoundland & Labrador, Inc. (HCANL)
PO Box 23038, St. John's NL A1B 4J9
Tel: 709-364-8811; *Fax:* 709-364-8812
heavycivilnl.ca
To act as the voice of the heavy construction industries in Newfoundland & Labrador; To develop standard tendering & contractual practices & procedures
Jim Organ, Executive Director
Lorraine Richards, Manager, Operations

Lumber & Building Materials Association of Ontario (LBMAO)
#27, 5155 Spectrum Way, Mississauga ON L4W 5A1
Tel: 905-625-1084; *Fax:* 905-625-3006
Toll-Free: 888-365-2626
www.lbmao.on.ca
To promote the welfare of members so that they are able to build a competitive advantage & remain at the leading edge of the lumber & building materials industry
David W. Campbell, President
Bob Lockwood, Chair
Dwayne Sprague, Vice-Chair

Manitoba Heavy Construction Association (MHCA)
#3, 1680 Ellice Ave., Winnipeg MB R3G 0Z2
Tel: 204-947-1379; *Fax:* 204-943-2279
info@mhca.mb.ca
www.mhca.mb.ca
Social Media:
twitter.com/ManitobaHeavy
To promote a safe workplace for employees in Manitoba's heavy construction industry; To represent the heavy construction industry in Manitoba
Christopher Lorenc, President
Wendy Greund Summerfield, Manager, Finance
Greg Huff, Manager, MHC Training Academy
Christine Miller, Manager, Events & Membership
Jason Rosin, Manager, Communications

Manitoba Ready Mixed Concrete Association Inc. (MRMCA)
3 Park Ridge Dr., East St Paul MB R2E 1H7
Tel: 204-667-8539; *Fax:* 204-668-9740
info@mrmca.com
www.mrmca.com
To represent the concrete industry in Manitoba; To advance the quality of concrete in Manitoba
Jayson Chale, President

Master Insulators' Association of Ontario Inc.
Building 1, #101, 2600 Skymark Ave., Mississauga ON L4W 5B2
Tel: 905-279-6426; *Fax:* 905-279-6422
miapublic1@miaontario.org
www.miaontario.org
To promote & advance the insulation industry
Caroline O'Keeffe, Office Manager

Master Painters & Decorators Association (MPDA)
2800 Ingleton Ave., Burnaby BC V5C 6G7
Tel: 604-298-7578; *Fax:* 604-298-5183
Toll-Free: 888-674-8708
info@paintinfo.com
www.paintinfo.com/assoc/mpda/
To set & raise standards of industrial organizations
Greg Boshard, President
Alan Kelly, Vice President

Mechanical Contractors Association of Alberta
#204, 2725 - 12 St. NE, Calgary AB T2E 7J2
Tel: 403-250-7237; *Fax:* 403-291-0551
Toll-Free: 800-251-0620
www.mca-ab.com
To promote plumbing & mechanical contractors; To provide educational programs to foster improved management & productivity in mechanical contracting; To represent mechanical contractors with their various publics - governments, design authorities, labour; To foster professional advancement & profitability of the plumbing, heating & mechanical contracting industry through its member services
Russ Evans, Executive Director

Mechanical Contractors Association of British Columbia (MCABC)
#223, 3989 Henning Dr., Burnaby BC V5C 6N5
Tel: 604-205-5058; *Fax:* 604-205-5075
Toll-Free: 800-663-8473
www.mcabc.org
Social Media: www.flickr.com/photos/mcabc
linkedin.com/company/mechanical-contractors-association-of-bc
twitter.com/mcabc
To encourage, support & promote the advancement of the mechanical contracting industry; to provide leadership, assistance & training to members.
Dana Taylor, Executive Vice President

Mechanical Contractors Association of Canada (MCAC) / Association des entrepreneurs en mécanique du Canada
#601, 280 Albert St., Ottawa ON K1P 5G8
Tel: 613-232-0492; *Fax:* 613-235-2793
mcac@mcac.ca
www.mcac.ca
To promote plumbing & mechanical contractors; to provide educational programs to foster improved management & productivity in mechanical contracting; to represent mechanical contractors to their various publics - governments, design authorities, labour.
Richard McKeagan, President

Mechanical Contractors Association of Manitoba (MCAM)
#1, 860 Bradford St., Winnipeg MB R3H 0N5
Tel: 204-774-2404; *Fax:* 204-772-0233
mcam@mts.net
www.mca-mb.com
To continually improve mechanical industry standards while providing a high level of value performance & customer service for our members
Betty McInerney, Executive Director

Mechanical Contractors Association of New Brunswick / Association des entrepreneurs en mécanique du N.-B.
c/o Moncton Northeast Construction Association, 297 Collishaw St., Moncton NB E1C 9R2
Tel: 506-857-4128; *Fax:* 506-857-8861
bdixon@mneca.ca
www.mneca.ca
To provide leadership & service to members; to act on behalf of members in labour relations matters, including collective bargaining; to advance & develop the industry, primarily in New Brunswick; to endeavour to improve legislation affecting the industry; to promote sound labour relations
Bill Dixon, Executive Director

Mechanical Contractors Association of Newfoundland & Labrador
PO Box 745, Stn. Mount Pearl, Mount Pearl NL A1N 2Y2
Tel: 709-747-5577; *Fax:* 709-368-5342
ddawe@nfld.net
David Dawe, Executive Director

Mechanical Contractors Association of Nova Scotia
c/o Construction Association of Nova Scotia, #3, 260 Brownlow Ave., Dartmouth NS B3B 1V9
Tel: 902-468-2267; *Fax:* 902-468-2470
cans@cans.ns.ca
www.cans.ns.ca
Donna Cruickshank, Manager

Mechanical Contractors Association of Ontario (MCAO)
#103, 10 Director Ct., Woodbridge ON L4L 7E8
Tel: 905-856-0342; *Fax:* 905-856-0385
mcao@mcao.org
www.mcao.org
Steve Coleman, Executive Vice-President

Mechanical Contractors Association of Saskatchewan Inc. (MCAS)
Heritage Business Park, #105, 2750 Faithfull Ave., Saskatoon SK S7K 6M6
Tel: 306-664-2154; *Fax:* 306-653-7233
admin@mca-sask.com
www.mca-sask.com
To represent plumbing & heating contractors in relation to the construction industry, legislative departments of municipal & provincial government & other industry-related bodies.
Ryan Tynning, President
Carolyn Bagnell, Executive Director

Mechanical Service Contractors of Canada (MSCC)
#601, 280 Albert St., Ottawa ON K1P 5G8
Tel: 613-232-0492; *Fax:* 613-235-2793
Toll-Free: 877-622-2668
daryl@mcac.ca
www.servicecontractor.ca
The Mechanical Service Contractors of Canada (MSCC), a division of the Mechanical Contractors Association of Canada, is dedicated to mechanical service, repair and retrofit contractors.
Daryl Sharkey, Chief Operating Officer

National Building Envelope Council (NBEC) / Conseil National de l'Enveloppe du Bâtiment (CNEB)
c/o 5041 Regent St., Burnaby BC V5C 4H4
Tel: 604-473-9587
nbec@cebq.org
www.nbec.net
To pursue excellence in the design, construction & performance of the building envelope
Dominique Derome, President Elect

National Elevator & Escalator Association (NEEA)
#708, 6299 Airport Rd., Mississauga ON L4V 1N3
Tel: 905-678-9940
Andrew Reistetter, Executive Director

New Brunswick Road Builders & Heavy Construction Associatoin (NBRBHCA)
#5, 59 Avonlea Ct., Fredericton NB E3C 1N8
Tel: 506-454-5079; *Fax:* 506-452-7646
rbanb@nb.aibn.com
www.rbanb.com
To foster & enhance relations between the members, & between the members of other associations in construction; to acquire & disseminate information of value to the industry & to its membership; to improve & extend standards, conditions, methods & practices within the industry
Marc Losier, President
Tom McGinn, Executive Director

New Brunswick Roofing Contractors Association, Inc. (NBRCA) / Association des entrepreneurs en couverture du Nouveau-Brunswick
PO Box 7242, 24 Coborg St., Saint John NB E2L 4S6
Tel: 506-652-7003; *Fax:* 506-696-0380
info@nbrca.ca
www.nbrca.ca
To protect the public's interest in relation to roofing; To act as the voice of New Brunswick's roofing industry; To facilitate a competent & profitable roofing & sealed membrane system industry in the province; To foster excellence in roofing related activities; to ensure that members uphold the code of ethics
Ron Hutton, Executive Director
Gilles Boudreau, President
Andrew Lunn, Vice-President
Guy LeBlanc, Secretary
Jean Claude Vienneau, Treasurer

Newfoundland & Labrador Construction Association (NLCA)
#201, 333 Pippy Pl., St. John's NL A1B 3X2
Tel: 709-753-8920; *Fax:* 709-754-3968
info@nfld.com
www.nlca.ca
To act as the voice of the construction industry in Newfoundland & Labrador; To enhance the professionalism & productivity of members through the development of policies
Keith McCarthy, Chair
Rhonda Neary, President & Chief Operating Officer
Frank Collins, Secretary-Treasurer
Susan Casey, Coordinator, Events
Adelle Connors, Coordinator, Member Services

Northwest Territories Construction Association (NWTCA)
PO Box 2277, 4921 - 49th St., 3rd Fl., Yellowknife NT X1A 2P7
Tel: 867-873-3949; *Fax:* 867-873-8366
director@nwtca.ca
www.nwtca.ca
To act as a voice for construction-related business in the Northwest Territories & Nunavut
Bob Doherty, President
Dave Brothers, Vice-President, Northwest Territories
Gary Collins, Vice-President, Nunavut
Trina Rentmeister, Secretary-Treasurer

Nova Scotia Construction Labour Relations Association Limited (NSCLRA)
#1, 260 Brownlow Ave., Dartmouth NS B3B 1V9
Tel: 902-468-2283; *Fax:* 902-468-3705
admin@nsclra.ca
www.nsclra.ca
Social Media: www.youtube.com/user/ReseauFADOQ
www.facebook.com/reseaufadoq
To represent construction industry employers in collective bargaining with trade unions in the industrial & commercial sectors
Allan Stapleton, President
Nancy Canales, Administrator

Nova Scotia Road Builders Association
#217, 11 Thornhill Dr., Dartmouth NS B3B 1R9
www.nsrba.ca
To speak for the heavy construction industry in Nova Scotia; to liaise with provincial Department of Transportation
Grant Feltmate, Executive Director
Carol Ingraham, Office Manager

Ontario Concrete Pipe Association (OCPA)
447 Frederick St., 2nd Fl, Kitchener ON N2H 2P4
Tel: 519-489-4488; *Fax:* 519-578-6060
admin@ocpa.com
www.ocpa.com
To represent the concrete pipe & maintenance hole industry throughout Ontario; to promote engineered concrete products of permanence
Brian Wood, President
Mike Leathers, Vice President
John Munro, Sec.-tres.

Ontario Formwork Association (OFA)
#7, 951 Wilson Ave., Toronto ON M3K 1Z7
Tel: 416-630-7912; *Fax:* 416-630-7181
info@ontarioformworkassociation.com
www.ontarioformworkassociation.com
To discuss issues related to the formwork sector of the construction industry in Ontario.

Ontario General Contractors Association (OGCA)
#703, 6299 Airport Rd., Mississauga ON L4V 1N3
Tel: 905-671-3969; *Fax:* 905-671-8212
www.ogca.ca
To offer experience & expertise dealing with contracts, architects, engineers and owners
Clive Thurston, President

Ontario Industrial Roofing Contractors' Association (OIRCA)
#301, 940 The East Mall, Toronto ON M9B 6J7
Tel: 416-695-4114; *Fax:* 416-695-9920
Toll-Free: 888-336-4722
oirca@ontarioroofing.com
www.ontarioroofing.com
To act as the voice of the industrial-commercial roofing industry in Ontario; To promote excellence in roofing construction
Rob Kucher, President, Board of Directors
Peter Serino, Treasurer

Ontario Painting Contractors Association (OPCA)
#10, 7611 Pine Valley Dr., Woodbridge ON L4L 0A2
Tel: 416-498-1897; *Fax:* 416-498-6757
Toll-Free: 800-461-3630
info@opca.org
www.ontpca.org
To foster, develop & maintain unity & stability among members by acting as a bargaining agent; providing services & educational opportunities; acting as a liaison between industry groups; upholding & improving the standards of the industry; promoting the use of modern specifications; advancing an attitude of ethical responsibility & pride
Thomas Corbett, President
Andrew Sefton, Executive Director

Ontario Pipe Trades Council
#206, 400 Dundas St. East, Whitby ON L1N 3X2
Tel: 905-665-3500; *Fax:* 905-665-3400
info@optc.org
www.optc.org
Social Media:
www.facebook.com/pipetradescouncil
twitter.com/Pipe_Trades
To promote the many technical, commercial & environmental benefits of the Pipe Trades & maximize their use in the construction industry; to promote the interest of the plumbing, pipe fitting, sprinkler fitting & HVAC industry in the province of Ontario
Neil McCormack, Business Manager

Ontario Stone, Sand & Gravel Association (OSSGA)
#103, 5720 Timberlea Blvd., Mississauga ON L4W 4W2
Tel: 905-507-0711; *Fax:* 905-507-0717
www.ossga.com
Social Media:
twitter.com/_OSSGA
Moreen Miller, CEO

Prince Edward Island Roadbuilders & Heavy Construction Association
PO Box 1901, Charlottetown PE C1A 7N5
Tel: 902-894-9514; *Fax:* 902-894-9512
pei.roadbuilders@pei.sympatico.ca
www3.pei.sympatico.ca/pei.roadbuilders/
To be a strong, effective voice in the Heavy Construction industry.
Joe Murphy, Manager

Ready Mixed Concrete Association of Ontario (RMCAO)
#3, 365 Brunel Rd., Mississauga ON L4Z 1Z5
Tel: 905-507-1122; *Fax:* 905-890-8122
www.rmcao.org
Social Media: www.youtube.com/concreteontario
linkedin.com/company/ready-mixed-concrete-association-of-ontario
www.facebook.com/ConcreteOntario
twitter.com/ConcreteOntario
To promote & further the business, technology & use of quality concrete through partnership between producers & the construction & specifying industries
Chris Conway, President & CEO
Bart Kanters, P.Eng., MBA, Director, Technical Services
Ross Monsour, Director, Marketing
Nancy Chapman, Director, Operations & Finance

Roofing Contractors Association of British Columbia (RCABC)
9734 - 201st St., Langley BC V1M 3E8
Tel: 604-882-9734; *Fax:* 604-882-1744
bporth@rcabc.org
www.rcabc.org
To provide continuing education for roofing contractors, their workers & interested others; to represent the roofing contracting industry in its relationships with legislative & regulating bodies; to work closely with affiliate organizations & liaison groups in advancing the professionalism of roofing contracting; to provide a forum for the interaction of members; to encourage high standards of professional conduct among roofing contractors; to develop a comprehensive body of knowledge about roofing management & technology; to disseminate ideas & knowledge to members & others; to monitor new products & systems; to work for cooperation & greater understanding between contracting, inspection, manufacturing & supply segments of the roofing industry
Ivan van Spronsen, Executive Vice-President

Roofing Contractors Association of Manitoba Inc. (RCAM)
1447 Waverley St., Winnipeg MB R3T 0P7
Tel: 204-783-6365; *Fax:* 204-783-6446
www.rcam.ca
Marian Boles, Contact

Roofing Contractors Association of Nova Scotia (RCANS)
7 Frederick Ave., Mount Uniacke NS B0N 1Z0
Tel: 902-866-0505; *Fax:* 902-866-0506
Toll-Free: 888-278-0133
contact@rcans.ca
www.rcans.ca

To promote quality workmanship in the commerical, industrial & institutional roofing industry; to encourage training for roofers
Mike Croft, President
Marg Woodworth, Office Manager

Saskatchewan Construction Safety Association Inc. (SCSA)
498 Henderson Dr., Regina SK S4N 6E3
Tel: 306-525-0175; *Fax:* 306-525-1542
Toll-Free: 800-817-2079
scsainfo@scsaonline.ca
www.scsaonline.ca
Social Media:
linkedin.com/company/saskatchewan-construction-safety-association-
www.facebook.com/SCSAonline
twitter.com/scsaonline
To provide safety programs & servies to construction employers & employees in order to reduce human & financial loss associated with injuries in the construction industry
Blake Schneider, Director, Operations
Heidi Tiller, Coordinator, Human Resources
Lara Abu-Ghazaleh, Coordinator, Publications & Communications

Saskatchewan Heavy Construction Association
1939 Elphinstone St., Regina SK S4T 3N3
Tel: 306-586-1805; *Fax:* 306-585-3750
slipp@saskheavy.ca
www.saskheavy.com
Social Media: www.youtube.com/saskheavy
www.facebook.com/SaskHeavy
twitter.com/saskheavy
The Saskatchewan Heavy Construction Association is committed to the heavy construction industry by actively promoting quality, cost-effective, socially responsible services for the public & its members.
Dave Paslawski, Chair
Shantel Lipp, President
Ellie Weare, Financial Officer

Saskatchewan Ready Mixed Concrete Association Inc. (SRMCA)
#203, 1801 McKay St., Regina SK S4N 6E7
Tel: 306-757-2788; *Fax:* 306-569-9144
srmca@sasktel.net
www.concreteworksharder.com
To maintain the highest quality of concrete produced by its members; To improve the industry in all aspects & represents its members in relation to governments, environmental agencies & other industry-related associations
Rod Smith, President
Garth Sanders, Executive Director, Finance

Sealant & Waterproofing Association (SWA)
70 Leek Cres., Richmond Hill ON L4B 1H1
Tel: 416-499-4000; *Fax:* 416-499-8752
info@swao.com
www.swao.com
To promote the exchange of ideas for the development of the highest standards & operating efficiency within the sealant & waterproofing industry
Robert J. Montpetit, President
Andrew Porciello, Vice President

Southern Interior Construction Association (SICA)
#104, 151 Commercial Dr., Kelowna BC V1X 7W2
Tel: 250-491-7330; *Fax:* 250-491-3929
www.sica.bc.ca
Social Media: www.youtube.com/user/SICA1969
linkedin.com/company/southern-interior-construction-association
www.facebook.com/SICABC
twitter.com/sicabc
To offer members' plans & specifications for viewing; to promote standard tendering practices
William E. Everitt, Chief Operating Officer

Terrazzo Tile & Marble Association of Canada (TTMAC) / Association canadienne de terrazzo, tuile et marbre
#8, 163 Buttermill Ave., Concord ON L4K 3X8
Tel: 905-660-9640; *Fax:* 905-660-0513
Toll-Free: 800-201-8599
association@ttmac.com
www.ttmac.com
To standardize terrazzo, tile, marble, & stone installation techniques, so that the industry will grow & proper; To support the hardsurface industry & its members
Elaine Cook, Eastern Editor, The Analyst

Toronto Construction Association
70 Leek Cres., Richmond Hill ON L4B 1H1
Tel: 416-499-4000; *Fax:* 416-499-8752
www.tcaconnect.com
To develop & promote excellence within the construction industry of the Greater Toronto Area
Chris Fillingham, Chair
John G. Mollenhauer, President & CEO
Kim F. McKinney, Executive Vice-President

Western Canada Roadbuilders Association
c/o Manitoba Heavy Construction Association, #3, 1680 Ellice Ave., Winnipeg MB R3H 0Z2
Tel: 204-947-1379; *Fax:* 204-943-2279
www.wcrhca.org
To represent four western provincial roadbuilders & heavy construction associations at the provincial & federal level
Chris Lorenc, President

Western Retail Lumber Association (WRLA)
Western Retail Lumber Association Inc., #1004, 213 Notre Dame Ave., Winnipeg MB R3B 1N3
Tel: 204-957-1077; *Fax:* 204-947-5195
Toll-Free: 800-661-0253
wrla@wrla.org
www.wrla.org
To serve & promote needs & common interests of lumber, building materials & hard goods industry on the Prairies
Gary Hamilton, Executive Director
Dwight Dixon, President

Winnipeg Construction Association
1447 Waverly St., Winnipeg MB R3T 0P7
Tel: 204-775-8664; *Fax:* 204-783-6446
wca@winnipegconstruction.ca
www.winnipegconstruction.ca
To encourage a high level of standards among the construction industry in Manitoba & to promote the industry as a whole
Ryan Einarson, President
Ronald Hambley, Executive Vice-President

Business

Alliston & District Chamber of Commerce
PO Box 32, 60B Victoria St. West, Alliston ON L9R 1T9
Tel: 705-435-7921; *Fax:* 705-435-0289
www.adcc.ca
Social Media: www.youtube.com/user/AllistonChamber
www.facebook.com/allistonchamber
twitter.com/allistonchamber
Crystal Kellard, Executive Director

Assiniboia Chamber of Commerce (MB) (ACC)
PO Box 42122, Stn. Ferry Road, 1867 Portage Ave., Winnipeg MB R3J 3X7
Tel: 204-774-4154; *Fax:* 204-774-4201
info@assiniboiacc.mb.ca
www.assiniboiacc.mb.ca
Social Media:
twitter.com/assiniboiacc
To promote entrepreneurship & competitive enterprise in West Winnipeg
Ernie Nairn, Executive Director

Association for Corporate Growth, Toronto Chapter (ACG)
#202, 720 Spadina Ave, Toronto ON M5S 2T9
Tel: 416-868-1881; *Fax:* 416-292-5256
acgtoronto@managingmatters.com
www.acg.org/toronto
To foster sound corporate growth by providing its members with an opportunity to gain new ideas from speakers, seminars & discussions with people working in the field of corporate growth; to develop additional skills & techniques which will contribute to the growth of their respective organizations; to meet other corporate growth professionals who can provide counsel & valuable contacts
Stephen B. Smith, President

The Brampton Board of Trade (BBOT)
#101, 36 Queen St. East, Brampton ON L6V 1A2
Tel: 905-451-1122
admin@bramptonbot.com
www.bramptonbot.com
Social Media: www.youtube.com/user/BramptonBoT
linkedin.com/company/2087561
www.facebook.com/BramptonBOT
twitter.com/BramptonBOT
To represent & actively promote the interests of Brampton business, members & the private enterprise system
Steve Sheils, Chief Executive Officer
Carrie Andrews, Operations Manager

Glenn Williams, Chair

Brandon Chamber of Commerce
1043 Rosser Ave., Brandon MB R7A 0L5
Tel: 204-571-5340; *Fax:* 204-571-5347
info@brandonchamber.ca
brandonchamber.ca
Social Media:
www.facebook.com/156031967812208
twitter.com/BdnChamber
To encourage growth in the Brandon community by fostering a progressive business environment, favourable to enhancing existing & attracting new business
Carolynn Cancade, General Manager

British Columbia Chamber of Commerce
#1201, 750 West Pender St., Vancouver BC V6C 2T8
Tel: 604-683-0700; *Fax:* 604-683-0416
bccc@bcchamber.org
www.bcchamber.org
Social Media: www.youtube.com/user/bcchamberofcom
linkedin.com/company/1134700
www.facebook.com/bcchamber
twitter.com/bcchamberofcom
To make British Columbia a great place to do business; to be the leadership voice of B.C. business; to build a strong Chamber of Commerce network
Rod Cox, Chair
John Winter, President & CEO

Burlington Chamber of Commerce
#201, 414 Locust St., Burlington ON L7S 1T7
Tel: 905-639-0174; *Fax:* 905-333-3956
info@burlingtonchamber.com
www.burlingtonchamber.com
Social Media: www.youtube.com/user/BurlingtonChamber
www.facebook.com/burlington.chamber
twitter.com/burlingtoncofc
To be the focus for business in Burlington; to encourage & promote a strong Burlington business community through sound practices that support social & economic development
Bruce Nicholson, Chair
Keith Hoey, President

Business Professional Association of Canada (BPA Canada)
www.bpacanada.com
Social Media:
twitter.com/bpacanada
To give members quality referrals while helping them build their client relationships
Mike Hurley, Director

Calgary Chamber of Commerce
#600, 237 - 8th Ave. SE, Calgary AB T2G 5C3
Tel: 403-750-0400
info@calgarychamber.com
www.calgarychamber.com
Social Media:
linkedin.com/company/calgary-chamber-of-commerce
www.facebook.com/CalgaryChamber
twitter.com/calgarychamber
To lead & serve the Calgary business community valuing its diversity
Rob Hawley, Chair
Adam Legge, President & CEO
Rebecca Wood, Director, Member Services

Cambridge Chamber of Commerce
750 Hespler Rd., Cambridge ON N3H 5L8
Tel: 519-622-2221; *Fax:* 519-622-0177
Toll-Free: 800-749-7560
cchamber@cambridgechamber.com
www.cambridgechamber.com
Social Media: www.youtube.com/thecambridgechamber
ca.linkedin.com/in/cambridgechamber
twitter.com/My_Chamber
Greg Durocher, President & CEO

Campbell River & District Chamber of Commerce
900 Alder St., Campbell River BC V9W 2P6
Tel: 250-287-4636; *Fax:* 250-286-6490
admin@campbellriverchamber.ca
www.campbellriverchamber.ca
Social Media: www.youtube.com/user/CampbellRiverChamber
www.facebook.com/CampbellRiverChamber
twitter.com/ChamberCR
Colleen Evans, President & CEO

Canada Czech Republic Chamber of Commerce (CNACC)
Stn. A, 115 George St, Oakville ON L6J 0A2
Tel: 905-845-9606
admin@ccrcc.net
www.ccrcc.net
To provide a forum for members to discuss ideas; To promote business; To liaise with Canadian & Czech government agencies, such as CzechTrade, to further the interests of members; To cooperate with Czech cultural organizations on programs; To inform & support members
Miroslav Princ, Chamber President

Canada-Finland Chamber of Commerce
c/o Finnish Credit Union, 191 Eglinton Ave. East, Toronto ON M4P 1K1
Tel: 416-486-1533; *Fax:* 416-486-1592
info@canadafinlandcc.com
www.canadafinlandcc.com
Social Media:
linkedin.com/e/eabb6b-gbb4qf6x-6u/vgh/3194405/
www.facebook.com/?sk=2361831622
Lauri Asikainen, President

Canadian Association of Family Enterprise (CAFE) / Association canadienne des enterprises familiales
#112, 465 Morden Rd., Oakville ON L6K 3W6
Tel: 905-337-8375; *Fax:* 905-337-0572
Toll-Free: 866-849-0099
info@cafecanada.ca
www.cafecanada.ca
Social Media: www.youtube.com/user/CAFECanada1
linkedin.com/groups?home=&gid=1883375
www.facebook.com/fambizsupport
twitter.com/CAFECanada
To improve succession statistics for family businesses across Canada where Canadian family businesses connect with peers & resources for success.
Paul MacDonald, Executive Director
Lorraine Bauer, Managing Director

The Canadian Chamber of Commerce / La Chambre de commerce du Canada
#420, 360 Albert St., Ottawa ON K1R 7X7
Tel: 613-238-4000; *Fax:* 613-238-7643
info@chamber.ca
www.chamber.ca
Social Media: www.youtube.com/user/CdnChamberofCommerce
linkedin.com/company/the-canadian-chamber-of-commerce-canada-
www.facebook.com/CanadianChamberofCommerce
twitter.com/CdnChamberofCom
To create a climate for competitiveness, profitability & job creation for enterprises of all sizes in all sectors across Canada. Offices in Ottawa, Toronto, Montreal & Calgary
David Paterson, Chair
Perrin Beatty, President & CEO
Guillaum (Will) Dubreuil, Director, Public Affairs & Media Relations

The Canadian Council for Public-Private Partnerships (CCPPP) / Le Conseil canadien pour les partenariats public-privé
1 First Canadian Place, #1600, 100 King St. West, Toronto ON M5X 1G5
Tel: 416-861-0500; *Fax:* 416-862-7661
partners@pppcouncil.ca
www.pppcouncil.ca
To act as a proponent for improvements in the quality & cost of public services provided to Canadians through innovative partnerships between the public & private sectors
Mark Romoff, President

Canadian Council for Small Business & Entrepreneurship (CCSBE) / Conseil canadien des PME et de l'entrepreneuriat (CCPME)
c/o Pat Sargeant, Women's Enterprise Centre of Manitoba, #100, 207 Donald St., Winnipeg MB R3C 1M5
Tel: 204-988-1873; *Fax:* 902-988-1871
ccsbesecretariat@wecm.ca
www.ccsbe.org
Social Media:
linkedin.com/groups/CCSBE-CCPME-2431087
www.facebook.com/pages/CCSBE-2011-Annual-Conference/244886798884450
twitter.com/CCSBE2013
The Canadian Council for Small Business and Entrepreneurship (CCSBE-CCPME) is a national membership-based organization promoting and advancing the developmet of small business and entreprenurship through research, education and training, networking, and dissemination of scholarly and policy-oriented information.
Sandra Altner, President
Francine Schlosser, Secretary

Canadian Council of Chief Executives (CCCE) / Conseil canadien des chefs d'entreprise
#1001, 99 Bank St., Ottawa ON K1P 6B9
Tel: 613-238-3727; *Fax:* 613-238-3247
info@ceocouncil.ca
www.ceocouncil.ca
Social Media:
twitter.com/CdnCEOCouncil
To engage in policy work in Canada, North America, & the world
John Manley, P.C., O.C., President & CEO
Susan Scotti, Senior Vice-President
John R. Dillon, Corporate Counsel & Vice-President, Policy
Ross H. Laver, Vice-President, Policy & Communications
Nancy Wallace, Vice-President, Corporate Services
Isabelle Duchaine, Communications Officer

Canadian Deals & Coupons Association (CDCA)
Toronto ON
Toll-Free: 888-958-2948
info@canadiandealsassociation.com
www.canadiandealsassociation.com
Social Media:
linkedin.com/company/canadian-deals-association
www.facebook.com/CanadianDealsandCouponAssociation
twitter.com/DealsCouponsCAN
To provide services to companies in the retail industry, in order to promote specials & coupons.

Canadian Federation of Independent Business (CFIB) / Fédération canadienne de l'entreprise indépendante
#401, 4141 Yonge St., Toronto ON M2P 2A6
Tel: 416-222-8022; *Fax:* 416-222-6103
Toll-Free: 888-234-2232
cfib@cfib.ca
www.cfib-fcei.ca
Social Media: www.youtube.com/user/cfibdotca
www.facebook.com/pages/CFIB/142739089079987
twitter.com/cfib
To act as the voice for small businesses in Canada
Dan Kelly, President & CEO
Laura Jones, Executive Vice-President
Corinne Pohlmann, Senior Vice-President, National Affairs
Ted Mallett, Vice-President & Chief Economist
Doug Bruce, Vice-President, Research

Canadian Franchise Association (CFA) / Association canadienne de la franchise
#116, 5399 Eglinton Ave. West, Toronto ON M9C 5K6
Tel: 416-695-2896; *Fax:* 416-695-1950
Toll-Free: 800-665-4232
info@cfa.ca
www.cfa.ca
To promote & represent franchise excellence through a national association of businesses united by a common interest in ethical franchising
Lorraine McLachlan, President & CEO
Gary Martini-Wong, Manager, Finance & Accounting

Canadian German Chamber of Industry & Commerce Inc. (CGCIC) / Deutsch-Kanadische Industrie- und Handelskammer
#1500, 480 University Ave., Toronto ON M5G 1V2
Tel: 416-598-3355; *Fax:* 416-598-1840
info@germanchamber.ca
kanada.ahk.de
Social Media:
www.facebook.com/AHKCanada
twitter.com/ahkcanada
To promote trade & investment between Germany & Canada; offices in Toronto, Montreal & Vancouver
Gerd U. Wengler, Chair
Thomas Beck, President & CEO

Canadian Institute of Chartered Business Valuators (CICBV) / L'Institut canadien des experts en évaluation d'entreprises
#710, 277 Wellington St. West, Toronto ON M5V 3H2
Tel: 416-977-1117; *Fax:* 416-977-7066
Toll-Free: 866-770-7315
admin@cicbv.ca
cicbv.ca
To develop high professional standards for Canadian Chartered Business Valuators; To manage the Chartered Business Valuator (CBV) designation; To govern members of the Institute with a strict Code of Ethics & Practice Standards
Mary Jane Andrews, President & CEO
Bob Boulton, Director, Education & Standards
Isabel Natale, Coordinator, Program
Megan Rousseau, Manager, Communications
Deborah Pelle Hanlon, Manager, Events
Judith Roth, Manager, Information Technology & Member Services

Canadian International Institute of Applied Negotiation (CIIAN) / L'Institut international canadien de la négociation pratique
68B Raddarz Rd., RR#2, Eganville ON K0J 1T0
Tel: 613-237-9050
ciian@ciian.org
www.ciian.org
Social Media:
www.facebook.com/145938635447384
twitter.com/CIIAN
To build sustainable peace at local, national, & international levels
Benjamin Hoffman, President
Evan Hoffman, Executive Director

Canadian Organization of Small Business Inc. (COSBI)
5405, 129 Ave. NW, Edmonton AB T5A 0A3
Tel: 780-423-2672
To support & promote the interests of small business & independent professionals throughout Canada; to protect the free enterprise system & the interests of independent business; to function as a lobby & service organization dealing with all levels of government or large bureaucracy; to provide members with access to information vital to business success & to present the owner/manager's point of view to decision makers in both political & private sectors
Donald Richard Eastcott, Managing Director
Roy E. Shannon, Chair

Canadian Professional Sales Association (CPSA) / Association canadienne des professionnels de la vente
#400, 655 Bay St., Toronto ON M5G 2K4
Tel: 416-408-2685; *Fax:* 416-408-2684
Toll-Free: 888-267-2772
customerservice@cpsa.com
www.cpsa.com
Social Media:
linkedin.com/groups?gid=1589497
www.facebook.com/CanadianProfessionalSalesAssociation
twitter.com/cpsa
To develop & serve sales professionals
Bob Medland, Chair
Harvey Copeman, CSP, President & CEO
Sylvain Tousignant, Vice-Chair
Ian Macdonald, Treasurer

Canadian Society of Customs Brokers (CSCB) / Société canadienne des courtiers en douane
#320, 55 Murray St., Ottawa ON K1N 5M3
Tel: 613-562-3543; *Fax:* 613-562-3548
cscb@cscb.ca
www.cscb.ca
To act as voice of the industry to all levels of government; To provide information to members on all matters affecting customs brokerage
Bedard Melanie, Chair

Canadian Society of Technical Analysts (CSTA)
#436, 157 Adelaide St. West, Toronto ON M5H 4E7
Tel: 519-807-9178
Toronto@csta.org
www.csta.org
To provide a forum for those interested in & working in technical analysis; to promote technical analysis within the financial community
Reagan Yuke, Business Manager
William Chin, President

Canadian-Croatian Chamber of Commerce
630 The East Mall, Toronto ON M9B 4B1
Tel: 416-641-2829; *Fax:* 416-641-2700
contactus@croat.ca
www.croat.ca
Social Media:
linkedin.com/groups/CanadianCroatianChamberofCommerce
www.facebook.com/CanadianCroatianChamberofCommerce
twitter.com/CroatChamber
The Canadian-Croatian Chamber of Commerce is a not-for-profit network of Croatian-Canadian businesses, professionals and organizations that has emerged as the voice of Croatian-Canadian business in Canada.
Wanita Kelava, Manager

Caribbean & African Chamber of Commerce of Ontario (CACCO)
PO Box 55328, Stn. Scarborough Town Centre, Toronto ON M1P 4Z7
Tel: 416-265-8603; *Fax:* 416-269-2081
www.cacco.ca
To promote, encourage & support the achievement of economic viability within the community it serves & enable advancement of the greater Canadian business community
Worrick Russel, Executive Chair

Castlegar & District Chamber of Commerce (CDCoC)
1995 - 6th Ave., Castlegar BC V1N 4B7
Tel: 250-365-6313; *Fax:* 250-365-5778
info@castlegar.com
www.castlegar.com
To encourage a business climate which enables our membership & community to prosper
Jane Charest, President

Centre for Entrepreneurship Education & Development Inc. (CEED)
Halifax Shopping Centre, Tower 1, PO Box 196, #103, 7001 Mumford Rd., Halifax NS B3L 2H8
Tel: 902-421-2333; *Fax:* 902-482-0291
Toll-Free: 800-590-8481
info@ceed.ca
www.ceed.ca
Social Media: www.youtube.com/ceedhalifax
linkedin.com/company/ceed-centre-for-entrepreneurship-education-an
www.facebook.com/ceed.ca
twitter.com/ceed_halifax
To build entrepreneurial awareness & capacity throughout Atlantic Canada
Paul Joudrey, Chair
Heather Spidell, President & CEO

Cereal & District Board of Trade
PO Box 85, Cereal AB T0J 0N0
Tel: 403-326-3818; *Fax:* 403-326-3800

Chambre de commerce au Coeur de la Montérégie (CCCM)
#101, 2055, rue Du Pont, Marieville QC J3M 1J8
Tél: 450-460-4019; *Téléc:* 450-460-2362
info@coeurmonteregie.com
www.coeurmonteregie.com
Regroupement volontaire de personnes du milieu dans un but de développement économique, civique et social des membres
Yanick Marchand, Président

Chambre de commerce Canado-Suisse (Québec) Inc. (SCCCQ) / Swiss Canadian Chamber of Commerce (Québec) Inc.
#152, 3450, rue Drummond, Montréal QC H3G 1Y4
Tél: 514-937-5822
www.cccsqc.ca
D'assumer un rôle de premier plan dans la promotion des relations commerciales, industrielles et financières entre la Suisse et le Canada, tout en se concentrant sur l'est du Canada
Christian G. Dubois, Président

Chambre de commerce Canado-Tunisienne (CCCT) / Tunisian Canadian Chamber of Commerce
#710, 276, rue Saint-Jacques, Montréal QC H2Y 1N3
Tél: 514-847-1281
info@cccantun.com
www.cccantun.ca
Le fer de lance du partenariat canado-tunisien; fournir des informations privilégiées sur les spécificités du marché tunisien; soutenir dans votre recherche de partenaires d'affaires tunisiens; appuyer dans la démarche de mise en marché de vos produits et services en Tunisie

Chambre de commerce de Charlevoix
#209, 11, rue Saint-Jean-Baptiste, Baie-Saint-Paul QC G3Z 1M1
Tél: 418-760-8648
info@creezdesliens.com
www.creezdesliens.com
Mèdia social: www.facebook.com/chambrecommercecharlevoix
De promouvoir les intérêts de ses membres afin de les aider à prospérer
Johanne Côté, Coordonnatrice

Chambre de commerce de Clair
CP 1025, Clair NB E7B 2J5
Tél: 506-992-6030; *Téléc:* 506-992-6041
info@chambrecommerceclair.com
www.chambrecommerceclair.com
Pour promouvoir les entreprises locales et les aider à grandir
Marie-Josée Michaud, Responsable

Chambre de commerce de Danville-Shipton
CP 599, Danville QC J0A 1A0
Tél: 819-839-2742; *Téléc:* 819-839-2347
info@ccdanville.com
www.ccdanville.com
Isabelle Lodge, Présidente
Martine Satre, Vice-Présidente
Pierre Picard, Trésorier
Sylvie Beauchemin, Secrétaire

Chambre de commerce de Forestville
40, route 138 Ouest, Forestville QC G0T 1E0
Tél: 418-587-1585
www.repertoire-chambres.fccq.ca

Chambre de commerce de l'Ouest-de-l'Ile de Montréal / West Island Chamber of Commerce
#602, 1000, boul Saint-Jean, Pointe-Claire QC H9R 5P1
Tél: 514-697-4228; *Téléc:* 514-697-2562
info@wimcc.ca
www.ccoim.ca
Mèdia social: www.facebook.com/CCOIM.WIMCC
D'assurer le bien-être économique de ses membres et de sa communauté d'affaires.
Joseph Huza, Directeur exécutif

Chambre de commerce de la Haute-Matawinie
521, rue Brassard, Saint-Michel-des-Saints QC J0K 3B0
Tél: 450-833-1334; *Téléc:* 450-833-1334
infocchm@satelcom.qc.ca
www.haute-matawinie.com
Regrouper les leaders de tout son territoire intéressés à travailler au bien-être économique, civique et social du milieu et au développement de ses ressources
France Chapdelaine, Directrice générale

Chambre de commerce de la région d'Acton
Édifice de la Gare, 980, rue Boulay, Acton Vale QC J0H 1A0
Tél: 450-546-0123; *Téléc:* 450-546-2709
ccracton@cooptel.qc.ca
www.chambredecommerce.info
Promouvoir l'action commerciale, sociale, communautaire.
Joanne Joannette, Directrice générale

Chambre de commerce de la région d'Asbestos
CP 34, Asbestos QC J1T 3M9
Tél: 819-300-1484
ccidessources@lives.ca
www.lccra.com
A pour objectif de regrouper en association les gens d'affaires et les personnes qui s'occupent de promotion, d'entraide et de planification économique, commerciale et industrielle sur le territoire immédiat de la MRC de la région d'Asbestos
Denis Beaubien, Président

Chambre de commerce de la region de Cap-Pelé
CP 1219, Cap-Pelé NB E4N 3B1
Tél: 506-332-0118
chambredecommerce@yahoo.ca
www.cap-pele.com/chamber.cfm
Albert E. LeBlanc, Président
Gilles Haché, Secrétaire

Chambre de commerce de la région de Weedon
280, 9e av, Weedon QC J0B 3J0
Tél: 819-560-8555
admin@ccweedon.com
www.ccweedon.com
Favoriser le développement économique par le réseautage et la concertation

Chambre de commerce de Lac-Brome
CP 3654, #316, 1, rue Knowlton, Lac-Brome QC J0E 1V0
Tél: 450-242-2870
info@cclacbrome.com
www.cclacbrome.com
Pour promouvoir le commerce dans la ville et d'offrir à ses membres des services pour aider à développer leur entreprise
Suzanne Gregory, Directrice générale

Chambre de commerce de Saint-Côme
1661A, rue Principale, Saint-Côme QC J0K 2B0
Tél: 450-883-2730
info@stcomelanaudiere.ca
www.stcomelanaudiere.com
Mèdia social:
www.facebook.com/chambredecommercesaintcome
Carole Lachance, Présidente

Chambre de commerce de Sainte-Adèle
Promenades Sainte-Adèle, #134, 555, boul de St-Adèle, Sainte-Adèle QC J8B 1A7
Tél: 450-229-2644; *Téléc:* 450-229-1436
chambredecommerce@sainte-adele.net
www.sainte-adele.net
Pour promouvoir le commerce et à aider leurs membres à prospérer
Guy Goyer, Directeur général

Chambre de commerce de Ste-Justine
167, rte 204, Sainte-Justine QC G0R 1Y0
Tél: 418-383-3207; *Téléc:* 418-383-3223
chambredecommercestejustine@sogetel.net
stejustine.net/chambre
Pour maintenir une économie saine à Saint-Justine
Bruno Turcotte, Président

Chambre de commerce de Saint-Quentin Inc.
144D, rue Canada, Saint-Quentin NB E8A 1G7
Tél: 506-235-3666; *Téléc:* 506-235-1804
Mèdia social:
www.facebook.com/ChambreDeCommerceDeStQuentin
Réunir ceux et celles qui veulent promouvoir et protéger les intérêts de la ville de Saint-Quentin et de sa région immédiate; encourager tous les citoyens à participer à la prospérité et croissance de la communauté; favoriser et améliorer l'industrie, le commerce et le bien-être économique, civique et social de la communauté
Marc Beaulieu, Président
Pascale Bellavance, Secrétaire

Chambre de commerce de Sherbrooke
#202, 9, rue Wellington Sud, Sherbrooke QC J1H 5C8
Tél: 819-822-6151; *Téléc:* 819-822-6156
info@ccsherbrooke.ca
www.ccsherbrooke.ca
Mèdia social: www.facebook.com/ccsherbrooke
De favoriser et promouvoir le développement socio-économique de l'entreprise privée, défendre les intérêts de ses membres grâce à l'exercice de son leadership et assurer le maintien de conditions propices à la croissance des affaires de sa communauté
Louise Bourgault, Directrice générale

Chambre de commerce de St-Léonard
8370, boul. Lacordaire, Saint-Léonard QC H1R 3Y6
Tél: 514-325-4232; *Téléc:* 514-955-8544
info@saintleonardenaffaires.com
saintleonardenaffaires.com
Mèdia social: fr-ca.facebook.com/207992709237477
twitter.com/chambrestleo
Défendre des intérêts de ses membres et de la communauté d'affaires de son territoire
Nick Fiasche, Président

Chambre de commerce de Valcourt et Région
980, rue St-Joseph, Valcourt QC J0E 2L0
Tél: 450-532-3263; *Téléc:* 450-532-5855
info@valcourtregion.com
www.valcourtregion.com
Mèdia social: ca.linkedin.com/pub/valcourt-région/80/52/1ab
twitter.com/valcourtregion
D'améliorer les activités économiques, sociales et civiques de la région de vacourt
Sonia Gauthier, Présidente

Chambre de commerce du grand de Châteauguay
#100, 15, boul Maple, Châteauguay QC J6J 3P7
Tél: 450-698-0027; *Téléc:* 450-698-0088
info@ccgchateauguay.ca
www.ccgchateauguay.ca
Mèdia social:
www.facebook.com/ChambreDeCommerceChateauguay
La Chambre de commerce et d'industrie de Châteauguay a un conseil d'administration dynamique et responsable, engagé et motivant par leurs expériences et leurs connaissances. Des plus présentes dans le milieu la CCIC par des actions et des présences dans des comités et autres.
Isabelle Poirier, Directrice générale par intérim

Chambre de commerce du Grand Tracadie-Sheila
#399, 124, rue de Couvent, Tracadie NB E1X 1E1
Tel: 506-394-4028; *Fax:* 506-394-4899
ccgtracadie-sheila@nb.aibn.com
Social Media:
ca.linkedin.com/pub/chambre-de-commerce-du-grand-tracadie-sheila-inc/4
www.facebook.com/111012852315372
De promouvoir et de développer le commerce dans la région
Rebecca Preston, Directrice générale

Chambre de commerce du Haut-Richelieu
Centre Ernest-Thuot, 75, 5e av, Saint-Jean-sur-Richelieu QC J2X 1T1
Tél: 450-346-2544; *Téléc:* 450-346-3812
info@cchautrichelieu.qc.ca
www.cchautrichelieu.qc.ca
Média social: linkedin.com/company/chambre-de-commerce-du-haut-richelieu
www.facebook.com/94909227051
Pour aider à développer l'économie de la région et aider à développer le commerce
Claude Demers, Directeur général

Chambre de commerce et d'industrie Beauharnois-Valleyfield
#400, 100, rue Sainte-Cécile, Salaberry-de-Valleyfield QC J6T 1M1
Tél: 450-373-8789; *Téléc:* 450-373-8642
ccibv@rocler.com
www.ccibv.ca
Média social: www.facebook.com/ccibv
De miser sur pied d'activités et de services propres à aider les gens d'affaires; de promouvoir des intérêts économiques régionaux face aux décideurs politiques et cela sous forme d'études, de consultations, d'expertises, de propositions et de représentations et enfin promotion du commerce local et régional
Sylvie Villemure, Directrice générale

Chambre de commerce et d'industrie de la région de Richmond
CP 3119, Richmond QC J0B 2H0
Tél: 819-826-5854
info@ccrichmond.com
www.ccrichmond.com
De travailler au bien être économique, civique, et social de la région de Richmond, et au développement de ses ressources en stimulant le commerce, l'industrie et le tourisme
Hélène Tousignant, Présidente
Christian Bazinet, Vice-président
Rémi-Mario Mayette, Secrétaire
Ginette Coutu-Poirier, Trésorière

Chambre de commerce et d'industrie de la Rive-Sud
#101, 85, rue Saint-Charles ouest, Longueuil QC J4H 1C5
Tél: 450-463-2121; *Téléc:* 450-463-1858
info@ccirs.qc.ca
www.ccirs.qc.ca
Média social: linkedin.com/groups?mostPopular=&gid=1621977
www.facebook.com/184970904850383
twitter.com/CCIRS2010
De représenter les entreprises agissant sur son territoire; De prendre position sur les grands enjeux; D'offrir des services en lien avec leurs objectifs de réussite; en développant des partenariats et des occasions de maillage.
Hélène Bergeron, Directrice générale

Chambre de commerce et d'industrie de la Vallée-du-Richelieu
#102, 230, rue Brébeuf, Beloeil QC J3G 5P3
Tél: 450-464-3733; *Téléc:* 450-446-4163
www.ccivr.com
Média social: linkedin.com/groups/CCIVR-Chambre-commerce-dindustrie-Vall éeduRich
www.facebook.com/CCIVR
twitter.com/CCIVR
De développer continuellement de nouveaux services pour ses membres, des services et des activités qui peuvent contribuer à faire connaître leur entreprise.
Anne Durocher, Directrice générale

Chambre de commerce et d'industrie de Québec
17, rue St-Louis, Québec QC G1R 3Y8
Tél: 418-692-3853; *Téléc:* 418-694-2286
info@ccquebec.ca
www.ccquebec.ca
Média social: linkedin.com/groups?mostPopular=&gid=1833061
www.facebook.com/154731684555439
fr.twitter.com/ccquebecca
Pour représenter les entreprises au Québec
Eric Lavoie, Président, Conseil d'administration
Alain Kirouac, Président et chef de la direction

Chambre de commerce et d'industrie de St-Laurent
#204, 935, Décarie, Saint-Laurent QC H4L 3M3
Tél: 514-333-5222; *Téléc:* 514-333-0937
info@ccstl.qc.ca
www.ccstl.qc.ca
De rassembler, informer et défendre les intérêts de ses membres.
Sylvie Séguin, Directrice générale

Chambre de commerce et d'industrie de Varennes (CCIV)
2368, boul Marie-Victorin, Varennes QC J3X 1R7
Tél: 450-652-4209; *Téléc:* 450-652-4244
info@cciv.ca
www.cciv.ca
De défendre les intérêts de ses membres afin de faire prospérer leur entreprise
Marie-Claude Lévesque, Coordonnatrice

Chambre de commerce et d'industrie MRC de Deux-Montagne (CCI2M)
67A, boul Industriel, Saint-Eustache QC J7R 5B9
Tél: 450-491-1991; *Téléc:* 450-491-1648
info@chambrecommerce.com
www.chambrecommerce.com
Média social: www.facebook.com/CCI2M
twitter.com/CCISE
Michel Goyer, Directeur

Chambre de commerce et d'industrie régionale de Saint-Léonard-d'Aston
#1, 370, rue Principale, Saint-Léonard-d'Aston QC J0C 1M0
Tél: 819-399-2020

Chambre de commerce et d'industrie Sorel-Tracy métropolitain
#112, 67, rue George, Sorel-Tracy QC J3P 1C2
Tél: 450-742-0018; *Téléc:* 450-742-7442
info@ccstm.qc.ca
www.ccstm.qc.ca
La loi fédérale des chambres de commerce au Canada donne leur mandat aux chambres de commerce dans les termes suivant : "... Aux fins de favoriser et d'améliorer le commerce et le bien-être économique, civique et social de son district."
Marcel Robert, Directeur général

Chambre de commerce et d'industrie Thérèse-De Blainville (CCITB)
#202, 141, rue St-Charles, Ste-Thérèse QC J7E 2A9
Tél: 450-435-8228; *Téléc:* 450-435-0820
info@ccitb.ca
www.ccitb.ca
Média social: www.youtube.com/user/CCITB85
linkedin.com/company/chambre-de-commerce-et-d'industrie-th-r-se-de
www.facebook.com/CCITB
twitter.com/laccitb
Samuel Bergeron, Président

Chambre de commerce et d'industries de Trois-Rivières
CP 1045, #200, 225, rue des Forges, Trois-Rivières QC G9A 5K4
Tél: 819-375-9628; *Téléc:* 819-375-9083
info@ccitr.net
www.ccitr.net
Défendre les entreprises privées et d'améliorer la communauté
Caroline Beaudry, Directrice générale

Chambre de commerce française au canada (CCFC) / French Chamber of Commerce
#202, 1819, boul René-Lévesque Ouest, Montréal QC H3H 2P5
Tél: 514-281-1246; *Téléc:* 514-289-9594
info@ccfcmtl.ca
www.ccfcmtl.ca
Média social: ca.linkedin.com/pub/chambre-de-commerce-française-au-canad a/26/148/374
www.facebook.com/147358495336342
twitter.com/CCFCcanada
Favoriser les échanges entre la France et le Canada; aider à trouver des partenaires
Véronique Loiseau, Directrice générale

Chambre de commerce gaie du Québec (CCGQ) / The Québec Gay Chamber of Commerce
#100, 1307 rue Ste-Catherine Est, Montréal QC H2L 2H4
Tél: 514-522-1885; *Ligne sans frais:* 888-647-2247
info@ccgq.ca
www.ccgq.ca
Média social: linkedin.com/groups?home=&gid=946577
www.facebook.com/ccgq.ca
Défendre et promouvoir les intérêts de la communauté lesbienne et gaie d'affaires du Québec et favoriser le rayonnement de ses membres
Marc-Antoine Saumier, Président

Chambre de commerce régionale de St-Raymond (CCRSR)
#100, 1, av St-Jacques, Saint-Raymond QC G3L 3Y1
Tél: 418-337-4049; *Téléc:* 418-337-8017
ccrsr@cite.net
www.ccrsr.qc.ca
De soutenir et appuyer ses membres commerçants, entrepreneurs, gens d'affaires et individus évoluant dans le milieu des affaires de Saint-Raymond, Saint-Léonard et de Rivière-à-Pierre
Hughes Genois, Président

Chambre de commerce régionale de Windsor
CP 115, Windsor QC J1S 2L7
Tél: 819-434-5936
www.ccrwindsor.com
Pour aider à développer le commerce dans la région de Windsor afin que leurs membres sont en mesure de prospérer
Guillaumme Lussier, Président

Chambre de commerce Ste-Émélie-de-l'Énergie
400, rue St-Michel, Sainte-Émélie-de-l'Énergie QC J0K 2K0
Tél: 450-886-1658

Chambre de commerce St-Félix de Valois
15, ch Joliette, Saint-Félix-de-Valois QC J0K 2M0
Tél: 450-889-8161; *Téléc:* 450-889-1590
ccst-flx@stfelixdevalois.qc.ca
www.stfelixdevalois.qc.ca
La mission de la Chambre de Commerce de Saint-Félix-de-Valois est de travailler au bien-être économique, civique et social de Saint-Félix-de-Valois et au développement de ses ressources en regroupant les leaders de tout son territoire intéressés à oeuvrer en ce sens
Johanne Dufresne, Directrice générale

Chambre de commerce St-Jean-de-Matha
204L, rue Principale, Saint-Jean-de-Matha QC J0K 2S0
Tél: 450-886-0599; *Téléc:* 450-886-3123
info@chambrematha.com
www.chambrematha.com
Travailler à la promotion de ses membres, ainsi qu'au développement commercial, culturel et social de son village
Sylvain Binette, Président
Sophie Moreau, Coordinatrice

Chambre de commerce St-Martin de Beauce
CP 2022, 131, 1e av Est, Saint-Martin QC G0M 1B0
Tél: 418-382-5549
chambre@st-martin.qc.ca
www.st-martin.qc.ca
Travailler au développement économique civique et social de la localité de St-Martin-De-Beauce
Pascal Bergeron, Président

Chambre de commerce Vallée de la Missisquoi
858, rte Missisquoi, Bolton Centre QC J0E 1G0
Tél: 450-292-4217; *Téléc:* 450-292-4224
Promouvoir la région et ses commerces; encourager la venue de nouveaux commerces; encourager et accueillir les jeunes entrepreneurs

Chambre de commerce Vallée de la Petite-Nation
185, rue Henri-Bourassa, Papineauville QC J0V 1R0
Tél: 819-427-8450
ccvpn@videotron.ca
www.ccvpn.org
Média social: www.facebook.com/ccvpn
Pour stimuler l'économie et la croissance des entreprises locales à travers des projets d'intérêt commun
Jean Careau, Directeur général

Chatham-Kent Chamber of Commerce
54 - 4th St., Chatham ON N7M 2G2
Tel: 519-352-7540
www.chatham-kentchamber.ca
Social Media: linkedin.com/company/chatham-kent-chamber-of-commerce
www.facebook.com/ChathamKentChamberofCommerce
twitter.com/CKChamber
G.A. (Gail) Antaya, President & CEO

Comox Valley Chamber of Commerce (CVCC)
2040 Cliffe Ave., Courtenay BC V9N 2L3
Tel: 250-334-3234; *Fax:* 250-334-4908
Toll-Free: 888-357-4471
admin@comoxvalleychamber.com
www.comoxvalleychamber.com
Social Media: www.facebook.com/ComoxValleyChamber
twitter.com/cxValleyChamber
To support, promote & represent the best interests of our members in municipal, provincial & national issues.
Tracey McGinnis, Chair

Dianne Hawkins, President & CEO

Conseil du patronat du Québec (CPQ) / Québec Employers Council
#510, 1010, rue Sherbrooke ouest, Montréal QC H3A 2R7
Tél: 514-288-5161; *Téléc:* 514-288-5165
Ligne sans frais: 877-288-5161
www.cpq.qc.ca
Mèdia social: www.youtube.com/user/CPQ2010
linkedin.com/groups/Conseil-patronat-Québec-2908454
www.facebook.com/conseilpatronat
twitter.com/conseilpatronat
Le Conseil du patronat du Québec a pour mission de s'assurer que les entreprises puissent disposer au Québec des meilleures conditions possibles- notamment en metiére de capital humain-afin de prosperer de fason durable dans un contexte de concurrence mondiale.
Yves-Thomas Dorval, Président
Patrick Lemieux, Conseiller, Communications

Cranbrook & District Chamber of Commerce
Cranbrook & District Chamber of Commerce, PO Box 84, Cranbrook BC V1C 4H6
Tel: 250-426-5914; *Fax:* 250-426-3873
Toll-Free: 800-222-6174
info@cranbrookchamber.com
www.cranbrookchamber.com
Social Media:
www.facebook.com/cranbrookchamber
twitter.com/cranbrookchambr
To promote the community & its businesses; To protect the interests of businesses; To attract new businesses to the area
David Struthers, President
David Hull, Executive Director

Duncan-Cowichan Chamber of Commerce (DCCC)
381 Trans-Canada Hwy., Duncan BC V9L 3R5
Tel: 250-748-1111; *Fax:* 250-746-8222
chamber@duncancc.bc.ca
www.duncancc.bc.ca
Social Media:
www.facebook.com/DuncanCowichanChamber
twitter.com/DuncanCowichan
To advocacy, service, education, support, & opportunity to engage the business community
Sonja Nagel, Executive Director

Edmonton Chamber of Commerce
World Trade Centre, Sun Life Place, #700, 9990 Jasper Ave., Edmonton AB T5J 1P7
Tel: 780-426-4620; *Fax:* 780-424-7946
info@edmontonchamber.com
www.edmontonchamber.com
Social Media: www.youtube.com/edmontonchamber
ca.linkedin.com/in/edmontonchamber
www.facebook.com/EdmontonChamber
twitter.com/edmontonchamber
To facilitate economic growth by providing information, business opportunities, educational programs & services in the area of international trade; to positively influence Edmonton's business environment
James Cumming, President/CEO
Robin Bobocel, Vice President, Public Affairs

European Union Chamber of Commerce in Toronto (EUCOCIT)
#1500, 480 University Ave., Toronto ON M5G 1V2
Tel: 416-598-7087; *Fax:* 416-598-1840
info@eucocit.com
www.eucocit.com
Social Media:
linkedin.com/groups/European-Union-Chamber-Commerce-in-2924006
www.facebook.com/111523778875074
To strengthen economic ties between Canada & Europe; to act as the business voice of and the one point of contact for European business interests in Canada
Thomas Beck, President

Flin Flon & District Chamber of Commerce
#235, 35 Main St., Flin Flon MB R8A 1J7
Tel: 204-687-4518
flinflonchamber@mymts.net
www.flinflondistrictchamber.com
Social Media:
www.facebook.com/flinflondistrictchamber
twitter.com/FlinFlonChamber
To promote & improve trade & commerce & the economic, civic & social welfare of the district; the Chamber represents the communities of Flin Flon, Creighton, Denare Beach, & Cranberry Portage.
Dianne Russell, President
Karen MacKinnon, President Elect

Fredericton Chamber of Commerce / La Chambre de Commerce de Fredericton
PO Box 275, #200, 364 York St., Fredericton NB E3B 4Y9
Tel: 506-458-8006; *Fax:* 506-451-1119
fchamber@frederictonchamber.ca
www.frederictonchamber.ca
Social Media:
www.facebook.com/frederictonchamber
twitter.com/Fton_Chamber
To contribute to the economic development of the community by being the advocate of business in the Greater Fredericton area
Stephen Hill, President
Krista Ross, Chief Executive Officer

Futurpreneur Canada
#700, 133 Richmond St. West, Toronto ON M5H 2L3
Fax: 877-408-3234
Toll-Free: 866-646-2922
www.futurpreneur.ca
Social Media: www.youtube.com/user/CYBF
linkedin.com/company/futurpreneur-canada
www.facebook.com/futurpreneur
twitter.com/@Futurpreneur
A national, non-profit organization that provides financing, mentoring and support tools to aspiring business owners aged 18-39.
Julia Deans, CEO
Rebecca Dew, CFO

Glendon & District Chamber
PO Box 300, Glendon AB T0A 1P0
Tel: 780-635-2557

Greater Bathurst Chamber of Commerce / Chambre de commerce du Grand Bathurst
Keystone Bldg., #101, 270 Douglas Ave., Bathurst NB E2A 1M9
Tel: 506-546-8100; *Fax:* 506-548-2200
info@bathurstchamber.ca
www.bathurstchamber.ca
Social Media:
www.facebook.com/335718759975
twitter.com/bathurstchamber
To facilitate economic growth in the Chaleur area; To advocate for the business community of Greater Bathurst
Mitch Poirier, General Manager
Bernard Cormier, President
Linda Rogers, Treasurer

Greater Charlottetown & Area Chamber of Commerce
National Bank Tower, 134 Kent St., Charlottetown PE C1A 7K2
Tel: 902-628-2000; *Fax:* 902-368-3570
chamber@charlottetownchamber.com
www.charlottetownchamber.com
Social Media:
www.facebook.com/117356628329546
To be the voice of business on economic issues; to provide services & opportunities for members to enhance their ability to do business
Quentin Bevan, President
Kathy Hambly, Executive Director
Wendy Watts, Manager, Membership & Marketing Sales

Greater Kingston Chamber of Commerce (GKCC)
945 Princess St., Kingston ON K7L 3N6
Tel: 613-548-4453; *Fax:* 613-548-4743
info@kingstonchamber.on.ca
www.kingstonchamber.on.ca
Social Media:
www.youtube.com/channel/UC1Pmf1i3uKXFF7PM_3_5cAA
linkedin.com/company/greater-kingston-chamber-of-commerce
www.facebook.com/greaterkingstonchamber
twitter.com/kingstonchamber
To advance economic progress, free enterprise, & the quality of life
Martin Sherris, CEO

Greater Kitchener & Waterloo Chamber of Commerce
PO Box 2367, 80 Queen St. North, Kitchener ON N2H 6L4
Tel: 519-576-5000; *Fax:* 519-742-4760
admin@greaterkwchamber.com
www.greaterkwchamber.com
Social Media: www.youtube.com/user/GreaterKWChamber
linkedin.com/groups/Greater-KW-Chamber-Commerce-2056325
www.facebook.com/GKWCC
twitter.com/gkwcc
To serve business in the Greater Kitchener Waterloo area & be its voice in the betterment of the community
Ian McLean, President & CEO

Greater Moncton Chamber of Commerce (GMCC) / Chambre de commerce du Grand Moncton
#200, 1273 Main St., Moncton NB E1C 0P4
Tel: 506-857-2883
info@gmcc.nb.ca
www.gmcc.nb.ca
Social Media: www.youtube.com/user/GreaterMonctonCham
linkedin.com/company/greater-moncton-chamber-of-commerce
www.facebook.com/GreaterMonctonChamberOfCommerce
twitter.com/MonctonChamber
To strengthen business & community in the Greater Moncton area through leadership, member services, & advocacy on business issues at the municipal, provincial, & national levels
Carol O'Reilly, CEO
Scott Lewis, Chair

Greater Nanaimo Chamber of Commerce
2133 Bowen Rd., Nanaimo BC V9S 1H8
Tel: 250-756-1191; *Fax:* 250-756-1584
info@nanaimochamber.bc.ca
www.nanaimochamber.bc.ca
To act as the voice of business in Greater Nanaimo; To ensure a healthy economic base & socio-economic structure to benefit the central Vancouver Island area
Kim Smythe, CEO
David Littlejohn, Chair
Justin Schley, Treasurer

Greater Niagara Chamber of Commerce (GNCC)
PO Box 940, #103, 1 St. Paul St., St Catharines ON L2R 6Z4
Tel: 905-684-2361; *Fax:* 905-684-2100
info@gncc.ca
www.greaterniagarachamber.com
Social Media:
linkedin.com/groups/Greater-Niagara-Chamber-Commerce-4151488
www.facebook.com/NiagaraChamber
twitter.com/NiagaraCoC
The Greater Niagara Chamber of Commerce is a non-partisan, non-sectarian association of businesses, groups and individuals who support business growth and effective government fostering a sustainable and vibrant Niagara.
Kithio Mwanzia, Interim CEO
Walter Sendzik, CEO

Greater Peterborough Chamber of Commerce (GPCC)
175 George St. North, Peterborough ON K9J 3G6
Tel: 705-748-9771; *Fax:* 705-743-2331
Toll-Free: 887-640-4037
info@peterboroughchamber.ca
www.peterboroughchamber.ca
Social Media: www.youtube.com/user/PeterboroughChamber
linkedin.com/groups/Peterborough-Chamber-2934106
www.facebook.com/peterboroughchamber
twitter.com/ptbochamber
To create a prosperous community by promoting the free enterprise system, a healthy business environment, & acting as the voice of business
Stuart Harrison, President & CEO

Greater Summerside Chamber of Commerce (GSCC)
#10, 263 Heather Moyse Dr., Summerside PE C1N 5P1
Tel: 902-436-9651; *Fax:* 902-436-8320
info@summersidechamber.com
www.summersidechamber.com
Social Media: www.instagram.com/summersidechamber
linkedin.com/groups/8208866/profile
www.facebook.com/120850442004
twitter.com/GSSideCC
To provide a voice on behalf of business in the City of Summerside & area; To work towards the prosperity & betterment of Greater Summerside
Jan Sharpe, Executive Director

Greater Victoria Chamber of Commerce (GVCC)
#100, 852 Fort St., Victoria BC V8W 1H8
Tel: 250-383-7191; *Fax:* 250-385-3552
chamber@victoriachamber.ca
www.victoriachamber.ca
Social Media: www.youtube.com/user/victoriachamber
linkedin.com/groups?mostPopular=&gid=1795424
www.facebook.com/VictoriaChamber
twitter.com/ChamberVictoria
To act as the voice of business for the Greater Victoria region; To ensure that the area maintains & enhances its prosperous & vibrant business climate
Bruce Carter, CEO
Frank Bourree, Chair
Sang-Kiet Ly, Treasurer

Greenwood Board of Trade
c/o City of Greenwood, PO Box 129, 202 South Government Ave., Greenwood BC V0H 1J0
Tel: 250-445-6644; *Fax:* 250-445-6441
greenwoodbot@gmail.com
www.greenwoodbot.com
Social Media:
www.facebook.com/100003967639871
To promote Greenwood & enhance it with the aid of grants.
Dave Evans, President

Grimsby & District Chamber of Commerce
15 Main St. East, Grimsby ON L3M 1M7
Tel: 905-945-8319; *Fax:* 905-945-1615
info@grimsbychamber.com
www.grimsbychamber.com
Social Media:
www.facebook.com/grimsbychamberofcommerce
To promote commerce in the community
Naomi Beirnes, President

Guelph Chamber of Commerce (GCC)
PO Box 1268, 111 Farquhar St., Guelph ON N1H 3N4
Tel: 519-822-8081; *Fax:* 519-822-8451
chamber@guelphchamber.com
www.guelphchamber.com
Social Media: www.youtube.com/user/GuelphChamberComerc1
linkedin.com/groups/Guelph-Chamber-Commerce-2053342?trk=myg_ugrp_
www.facebook.com/192083367496898?sk=info
To serve as the voice of the business community in Guelph; to help strengthen the economy of Guelph & adjacent townships; provide a forum for the development of discussion & programs that will contribute to the social, economic & physical quality of life in Guelph; to promote Guelph as a good place to live, work & visit
Kithio Mwanzia, President & CEO

Halifax Chamber of Commerce
#100, 32 Akerley Blvd., Dartmouth NS B3B 1N1
Tel: 902-468-7111; *Fax:* 902-468-7333
info@halifaxchamber.com
www.halifaxchamber.com
Social Media:
linkedin.com/groups/Lnkdln-Group-Halifax-Chamber-Commerce-1865797
www.facebook.com/halifaxchamberofcommerce
twitter.com/halifaxchamber
To build & strengthen the business culture in Metro Halifax through advocacy, networking & leadership
Valerie Payn, President & CEO

Hamilton Chamber of Commerce (HCC)
Plaza Level, #507, 120 King St. West, Hamilton ON L8P 4V2
Tel: 905-522-1151; *Fax:* 905-522-1154
hcc@hamiltonchamber.ca
www.hamiltonchamber.ca
Social Media:
linkedin.com/company/hamilton-chamber-of-commerce
www.facebook.com/140038556040986
twitter.com/hamiltonchamber
To make greater Hamilton a great place to live, work, play, visit & invest; & to recognize the importance of the individual as the most significant contributor to achieving community objectives
Diane Stephenson, Manager, Advertising & Promotions

Hong Kong-Canada Business Association (HKCBA) / L'Association commerciale Hong Kong-Canada
#600, 1285 West Broadway, Vancouver BC V6H 3X8
Tel: 604-684-2410; *Fax:* 604-684-6208
nationaled@hkcba.com
national.hkcba.com
To encourage & promote trade & commercial activities across a broad range of industries between Canada & Hong Kong, & through Hong Kong to China & the Asia Pacific Region.
Wayne Berg, National Chair
Joyce Chung, Executive Director

IntegrityLink
#302, 880 Ouellette Ave., Windsor ON N9A 1C7
Tel: 519-258-7222; *Fax:* 519-258-1198
info@integritylink.ca
www.integritylink.ca
Their mission is to promote & foster the highest ethical relationship between businesses & the public through voluntary self-regulation, consumer & business education & service education.
Joe Amort, President & CEO

International Coaching Federation (ICF)
#A325, 2365 Harrodsburg Rd., Lexington KY 40504 USA
Tel: 859-219-3580; *Fax:* 859-226-4411
Toll-Free: 888-423-3131
www.coachfederation.org
Social Media: www.youtube.com/icfheadquarters
linkedin.com/groups/International-Coach-Federation-87212?home=&gid
www.facebook.com/icfhq
twitter.com/icfhq
ICF is the support network for these professional coaches. Whether it's Life Coaching, Executive Coaching, Leadership Coaching or any other skilled coaching
Dave Wondra, Chair

Italian Chamber of Commerce of Ontario (ICCO)
201, 622 College St., Toronto ON M6G 1B6
Tel: 416-789-7169; *Fax:* 416-789-7160
info@italchambers.ca
www.italchambers.ca
Social Media:
linkedin.com/company/icco-italian-chamber-of-commerce-of-ontario
www.facebook.com/IccoItalianChamberOfCommerceOfOntario
twitter.com/Italchambers
To enhance & promote business, trade & cultural relations between Canada & Italy.
George Visintin, President
Corrado Paina, Executive Director

Kapuskasing & District Chamber of Commerce
25 Millview St., Kapuskasing ON P5N 2X6
Tel: 705-335-2332
info@kapchamber.ca
www.kapchamber.ca
To help businesses & the community thrive & grow
Martin Proulx, President
Jammy Pouliot, Contact, Administration

Kelowna Chamber of Commerce
544 Harvey Ave., Kelowna BC V1Y 6C9
Tel: 250-861-3627; *Fax:* 250-861-3624
info@kelownachamber.org
www.kelownachamber.org
Social Media:
linkedin.com/groups/Kelowna-Chamber-Commerce-3972388
www.facebook.com/KelownaChamberofCommerce
twitter.com/KelownaChamber
To improve trade & commerce & the economic, civic & social welfare of the city of Kelowna
Dave Bond, President
Caroline Grover, Chief Executive Officer

Lethbridge Chamber of Commerce
#200, 529 - 6 St. South, Lethbridge AB T1J 2E1
Tel: 403-327-1586; *Fax:* 403-327-1001
office@lethbridgechamber.com
www.lethbridgechamber.com
Social Media: www.youtube.com/lethchamber
www.facebook.com/LethbridgeChamber
twitter.com/lethchamber
To serve and represent the interests of its members by promoting and enhancing free enterprise, for the benefit of the social and economic environment of the City of Lethbridge
Karla Pyrch, Executive Director

Lindsay & District Chamber of Commerce
20 Lindsay St. South, Lindsay ON K9V 2L6
Tel: 705-324-2393; *Fax:* 705-324-2473
info@lindsaychamber.com
www.lindsaychamber.com
Social Media:
www.facebook.com/lindsay.chamber
twitter.com/LDChamber
Ann Gibbons, President
Gayle Jones, General Manager

Lloydminster Chamber of Commerce
4419 - 52 Ave., Lloydminster AB T9V 0Y8
Tel: 780-875-9013; *Fax:* 780-875-0755
contact_lcc@lloydminsterchamber.com
www.lloydminsterchamber.com
Social Media: www.youtube.com/user/LloydminsterChamber
www.facebook.com/LloydChamber
twitter.com/LloydChamber
To enhance private enterprise in Lloydminster & surrounding area
Pat Tenney, Executive Director
Michael Holden, President

Manitoba Quality Network
#660, 175 Hargrave St., Winnipeg MB R3C 3R8
Tel: 204-949-4999; *Fax:* 204-949-4990
www.qnet.ca
To help organizations pursue continuous excellence & improvement
Trish Wainikka, Executive Director

Maple Ridge Pitt Meadows Chamber of Commerce
12492 Harris Rd., Pitt Meadows BC V3Y 2J4
Tel: 604-457-4599; *Fax:* 604-457-4598
info@ridgemeadowschamber.com
www.ridgemeadowschamber.com
Social Media: instagram.com/pmmrchamber
www.facebook.com/RidgeMeadowsChamber
twitter.com/PMMRChamber
Andrea Madden, Executive Director

Markham Board of Trade (MBT)
Markham Convergence Centre, 7271 Warden Ave., Markham ON L3R 5X5
Tel: 905-474-0730; *Fax:* 905-474-0685
info@markhamboard.com
www.markhamboard.com
To enhance the success of members & the Markham business community
Richard Cunningham, President/CEO
Mary Ann Quagliara, Director, Member Services

Medicine Hat & District Chamber of Commerce
413 - 6th Ave. SE, Medicine Hat AB T1A 2S7
Tel: 403-527-5214; *Fax:* 403-527-5182
info@medicinehatchamber.com
www.medicinehatchamber.com
Social Media:
linkedin.com/company/medicine-hat-and-district-chamber-of-commerce
www.facebook.com/MHChamber
twitter.com/mhdchamber
To promote a healthy business environment
Khrista Vogt, President
Lisa Kowalchuk, Executive Director

Mission Regional Chamber of Commerce
34033 Lougheed Hwy., Mission BC V2V 5X8
Tel: 604-826-6914; *Fax:* 604-826-5916
info@missionchamber.bc.ca
www.missionchamber.bc.ca
Social Media: www.youtube.com/TheMissionChamber
www.facebook.com/Mission.Business.Network
twitter.com/MissionCommerce
To foster a network for entrepreneurial leaders to partner in education, communication & representation.
Sean Melia, President

Mouvement québécois de la qualité (MQQ)
#1710, 360, rue Saint-Jacques ouest, Montréal QC H2Y 1P5
Tél: 514-874-9933; *Téléc:* 514-866-4600
Ligne sans frais: 888-874-9933
mqq@qualite.qc.ca
www.qualite.qc.ca
Média social: www.facebook.com/MouvementQuebecoisQualite
Promouvoir et rendre accessibles aux organisations les meilleures pratiques d'affaire pour accroître leur performance et leur compétitivité
Roch Dubé, Président

The National Citizens Coalition / Coalition nationale des citoyens inc.
#501, 27 Queen St. East, Toronto ON M5C 2M6
Tel: 416-869-3838; *Fax:* 416-869-1891
Toll-Free: 888-703-5553
ncc@nationalcitizens.ca
www.nationalcitizens.ca
Social Media:
www.facebook.com/nationalcitizens
To promote free markets, individual freedom & responsibility under limited government & a strong defence
Colin T. Brown, Chair
Peter Coleman, President & CEO

National Quality Institute (NQI) / Institut national de la qualité (INQ)
#307, 2275 Lakeshore West Blvd., Toronto ON M8V 3Y3
Tel: 416-251-7600; *Fax:* 416-251-9131
Toll-Free: 800-263-9648
info@excellence.ca
www.nqi.ca
Social Media:
www.facebook.com/82765064279
twitter.com/excellencecan
To inspire & foster excellence in Canadian organizations; to enhance Canada's national well-being & global leadership

through the incorporation of quality principles in business, government, education & health care; to promote, encourage & support the understanding & adoption of total quality principles & practices in all sectors of the economy across Canada; & to recognize outstanding achievement through the Canada Awards for Excellence
Allan Ebedes, President & CEO

New Brunswick Chamber of Commerce (NBCC)
1, ch Canada, Edmundston NB E3V 1T6
Tel: 506-737-1868; *Fax:* 506-737-1862
info@nbchamber.ca
www.nbchamber.ca
Judith Murray, Chair

North Grenville Chamber of Commerce
PO Box 1047, 509 Kernahan St., Kemptville ON K0G 1J0
Tel: 613-258-4838
www.northgrenvillechamber.com
To promote business community & quality of life
Mark Thornton, Chair

North Queens Board of Trade
PO Box 189, Caledonia NS B0T 1B0
Tel: 902-682-3116
discovercaledonia.com/board-of-trade.php
To support & promote commerce and trade in the North Queens area.
Peter van Dyk, President
Mary Keirstead, Secretary

North Vancouver Chamber of Commerce (NVCC)
1250 Lonsdale Ave., Vancouver BC V7M 2H6
Tel: 604-987-4488; *Fax:* 604-987-8272
www.nvchamber.ca
Social Media: www.instagram.com/nvchamber
linkedin.com/company/north-vancouver-chamber-of-commerce
www.facebook.com/nvchamber
To ensure a healthy socio-economic base for the benefit of the North Shore region by supporting business prosperity, economic growth, & diversification
Louise Ranger, Chief Executive Officer
Misha Wilson, Manager, Membership

Northwest Territories Chamber of Commerce
NWT Commerce Place, #13, 4802 - 50th Ave., Yellowknife NT X1A 1C4
Tel: 867-920-9505; *Fax:* 867-873-4174
admin@nwtchamber.com
www.nwtchamber.com
To act as the voice for northern business; To create a business climate of profitability & competitiveness in the Northwest Territories; To foster business development; To promote business in the Northwest Territories; To involve & assist First Nations organizations; To conduct operations in an environmentally responsible manner
Chuck Parker, President
Kathy Gray, First Vice-President
Hughie Graham, Second Vice-President
John-Eric Petersson, Secretary-Treasurer

L'Office de Certification Commerciale du Québec Inc. (OCCQ) / Québec Commercial Certification Office Inc. (QCCO)
#206, 1565, boul de l'Avenir, Laval QC H7S 2N5
Tél: 514-905-3893; *Téléc:* 450-663-6316
info@occq-qcco.com
www.occq-qcco.com

Ontario Chamber of Commerce (OCC)
#505, 180 Dundas St. West, Toronto ON M5G 1Z8
Tel: 416-482-5222; *Fax:* 416-482-5879
info@occ.on.ca
www.occ.ca
Social Media: www.youtube.com/user/OntarioChamber
linkedin.com/company/876425
twitter.com/OntarioCofC
As "Ontario's Business Advocate", the Ontario Chamber of Commerce is a ISO certified organization providing leadership to the province's business community. The focus is on the development of soundly research policy positions, representing the business community to government, & providing consultation, information & programs to the membership
Allan O'Dette, President & CEO
Ali Mirza, Vice-President, Finance

Ontario Gay & Lesbian Chamber of Commerce
39 River St., Toronto ON M5A 3P1
Tel: 416-646-1600; *Fax:* 416-646-9460
info@oglcc.com
www.oglcc.com
To create an environment in which the Ontario gay & lesbian business & professional communities can thrive through the sharing of knowledge, resources, & communications
Ryan Tollofson, President

Ontario Public Buyers Association, Inc. (OPBA)
Ridley Square, #361, 111 Fourth Ave., St Catharines ON L2S 3P5
Tel: 905-682-2644
info@opba.ca
www.opba.ca
To promote the ethical & effective expenditure of public funds through the principles of professional procurement
Lisa Buitenhuis, President
James Macintyre, Vice President
Bart Menage, Secretary
Barbara Cosby, Treasurer

Ottawa Chamber of Commerce (OCC)
328 Somerset St. West, Ottawa ON K2P 0J9
Tel: 613-236-3631; *Fax:* 613-236-7498
info@ottawachamber.ca
www.ottawachamber.ca
Social Media:
www.facebook.com/ottawachamberofcommerce
twitter.com/ottawachamber
To provide leadership in the community to enhance economic prosperity & quality of life
Alexa Ryan, Interim Executive Director
Laura Haber, Director, Events & Partnerships
Scott Williams, Director, Member Services
Kenny Leon, Manager, Communications

Penticton & Wine Country Chamber of Commerce
553 Vees Dr., Penticton BC V2A 8S3
Tel: 250-492-4103
admin@penticton.org
www.penticton.org
Social Media:
www.facebook.com/200338503334345
twitter.com/PentChamber
Brandy Maslowski, Executive Director
Jason Cox, President

Pictou County Chamber of Commerce
#3C, 115 MacLean St., New Glasgow NS B2H 4M5
Tel: 902-755-3463
info@pictouchamber.com
www.pictouchamber.com
Social Media:
linkedin.com/company/pictou-county-chamber-of-commerce
www.facebook.com/173337132712998
twitter.com/PCChamberCommer
To distinguish itself as the pre-eminent voice of business in our region
Jack Kyte, Executive Director

Portage la Prairie & District Chamber of Commerce
56 Royal Rd. North, Portage la Prairie MB R1N 1V1
Tel: 204-857-7778; *Fax:* 204-856-5001
info@portagechamber.com
www.portagechamber.com
Social Media:
www.facebook.com/PortageLaPrairieDistrictChamberOfCommerce
To foster an environment which will enhance the commercial development of the district
Dave Omichinski, President
Cindy McDonald, Executive Director

Powell River Chamber of Commerce
6807 Wharf St., Powell River BC V8A 2T9
Tel: 604-485-4051
office@powellriverchamber.com
www.powellriverchamber.com
Social Media:
www.facebook.com/188501364559861
Jack Barr, President
Kim Miller, General Manager

Prince George Chamber of Commerce (PGCOC)
890 Vancouver St., Prince George BC V2L 2P5
Tel: 250-562-2454; *Fax:* 250-562-6510
chamber@pgchamber.bc.ca
www.pgchamber.bc.ca
Social Media:
linkedin.com/company/prince-george-chamber-of-commerce
www.facebook.com/124651797620486
twitter.com/PGChamber1
The PG Chamber of Commerce strives to connect, engage and enhance the quality of life in our community by providing opportunities for businesses to succeed.
Jennifer Brandle-McCall, CEO

Red Deer Chamber of Commerce
3017 Gaetz Ave., Red Deer AB T4N 5Y6
Tel: 403-347-4491; *Fax:* 403-343-6188
rdchamber@reddeerchamber.com
www.reddeerchamber.com
Social Media:
linkedin.com/groups?gid=2518693
www.facebook.com/109831038638
twitter.com/RedDeerChamber
To promote a thriving environment by advocating for Red Deer & area members on issues affecting business in the community
Bradley Williams, President
Tim Creedon, Executive Director

Richmond Chamber of Commerce
North Tower, #202, 5811 Cooney Rd., Richmond BC V6X 3M1
Tel: 604-278-2822; *Fax:* 604-278-2972
rcc@richmondchamber.ca
www.richmondchamber.ca
Social Media: www.youtube.com/user/RichmondchamberBC
linkedin.com/company/1026185
www.facebook.com/pages/Richmond-Chamber-of-Commerce/122125354491676
twitter.com/richmondchamber
To support & represent the interests of business in the city on behalf of its membership; to promote, enhance & improve trade & commerce, & the economic, civic & social well-being of Richmond; to support & communicate to all levels of government the informed opinion & positions of policy of its members on key local, provincial & national issues
Matt Pitcairn, President & CEO

Richmond Hill Chamber of Commerce (RHCOC)
376 Church St. South, Richmond Hill ON L4C 9V8
Tel: 905-884-1961; *Fax:* 905-884-1962
info@rhcoc.com
www.rhcoc.com
Social Media: www.youtube.com/user/richmondhillchamber
linkedin.com/groups?mostPopular=&gid=1443337
www.facebook.com/RHCOC
twitter.com/RHChamber
To foster a business enviornment that enhances the success of our members & improves the quality of life in Richmond Hill
Bryon Wilfert, Chair
Elio Fulan, Executive Director

St Thomas & District Chamber of Commerce
#115, 300 South Edgeware Rd., St Thomas ON N5P 4L1
Tel: 519-631-1981; *Fax:* 519-631-0466
mail@stthomaschamber.on.ca
www.stthomaschamber.on.ca
To serve as the voice of the business community & to work to ensure economic success in central Elgin county
Bob Hammersley, President & CEO

Saskatchewan Chamber of Commerce
The Saskatchewan Chamber of Commerce, #1630, 1920 Broad St., Regina SK S4P 3V2
Tel: 306-352-2671; *Fax:* 306-781-7084
info@saskchamber.com
www.saskchamber.com
Social Media: www.youtube.com/user/SaskChamber
linkedin.com/company/saskatchewan-chamber-of-commerce
www.facebook.com/saskchamber
twitter.com/SaskChamber
To act as the voice of business in Saskatchewan; To make Saskatchewan a better place for living, working, & investing; To promote commercial & industrial progress in Saskatchewan; To improve the competitiveness of Saskatchewan's economy
Steve McLellan, CEO

Sechelt & District Chamber of Commerce
PO Box 360, #102, 5700 Cowrie St., Sechelt BC V0N 3A0
Tel: 604-885-0662; *Fax:* 604-885-0691
sdcoc9@telus.net
www.secheltchamber.bc.ca
Social Media:
www.facebook.com/SecheltChamberofCommerce
twitter.com/SecheltChamber
To provide resources & services to members, including business information, community profiles, discounts & benefits plans, payroll services & networking opportunities
Kim Darwin, President
Colleen Clark, Executive Director

Stratford & District Chamber of Commerce
55 Lorne Ave. East, Stratford ON N5A 6S4
Tel: 519-273-5250; *Fax:* 519-273-2229
info@stratfordchamber.com
www.stratfordchamber.com
Social Media:
www.facebook.com/100003043038197
twitter.com/stratfordchambr
To maintain & improve trade & commerce, conservation & good management of community resources; to promote the economic, commercial, industrial, tourist & convention, civic, agricultural & environmental welfare of the City of Stratford & the surrounding district
Garry Lobsinger, General Manager

Swiss Canadian Chamber of Commerce (Ontario) Inc. (SCCC)
756 Royal York Rd., Toronto ON M8Y 2T6
Tel: 416-236-0039; *Fax:* 416-551-1011
sccc@swissbiz.ca
www.swissbiz.ca
Social Media:
linkedin.com/company/2231465
www.facebook.com/swiss.chamber
To assume a prominent role in promoting commercial, industrial & financial relations between Switzerland & Canada, with primary focus on membership in Ontario
Ernst Notz, President

Thunder Bay Chamber of Commerce (TBCC)
#102, 200 Syndicate Ave. South, Thunder Bay ON P7E 1C9
Tel: 807-624-2626; *Fax:* 807-622-7752
chamber@tbchamber.ca
www.tbchamber.ca
Social Media:
linkedin.com/company/thunder-bay-chamber-of-commerce
www.facebook.com/tbchamber
twitter.com/tbchamber
To serve the membership by providing leadership & influencing effective change for a healthy business environment
Charla Robinson, President

Truro & Colchester Chamber of Commerce
605 Prince St., Truro NS B2N 1G2
Tel: 902-895-6328; *Fax:* 902-897-6641
oa@tcchamber.ca
www.trurocolchesterchamber.com
Social Media:
linkedin.com/profile/view?id=88974880
www.facebook.com/tdcoc
twitter.com/TruColCoC
To be the principal advocate for business in Truro & the Colchester Region in matters of economic, social & political importance
Sherry Martell, Executive Director
Trish Petrie, Office Administrator

Vaughan Chamber of Commerce (VCC)
#2, 25 Edilcan Dr., Vaughan ON L4K 3S4
Tel: 905-761-1366; *Fax:* 905-761-1918
info@vaughanchamber.ca
www.vaughanchamber.ca
To be the voice of business working together to promote & improve business in the City of Vaughan
Paula Curtis, President & CEO
Joanne Taibi, Accounting

Wellesley & District Board of Trade
c/o Wendy Sauder, Wellesley Service Centre, 1220 Queens Bush Rd., Wellesley ON N0B 2T0
Tel: 519-656-3494
wellesleyboardoftrade@gmail.com
wellesleyboardoftrade.com
Chris Franklin, President

West Vancouver Chamber of Commerce
2235 Marine Dr., West Vancouver BC V7V 1K5
Tel: 604-926-6614; *Fax:* 604-926-6647
info@westvanchamber.com
www.westvanchamber.com
Social Media:
linkedin.com/company/west-vancouver-chamber-of-commerce
www.facebook.com/WestVanChamber
twitter.com/westvanchamber
To promote, enhance, & facilitate business in the community
Leagh Gabriel, Executive Director

Whitby Chamber of Commerce (WCC)
128 Brock St. South, Whitby ON L1N 4J8
Tel: 905-668-4506; *Fax:* 905-668-1894
info@whitbychamber.org
www.whitbychamber.org
Social Media:
linkedin.com/company/whitby-chamber-of-commerce
www.facebook.com/93725729133
twitter.com/whitbychamber
To act as the recognized voice of business for Whitby; To provide leadership & innovation of services & programs in support of members & the community, through advocacy, networking, education, communication, government liaison, value-added programs, & leadership opportunities
Tracy Hanson, Chief Executive Officer

Whitecourt & District Chamber of Commerce
Synergy Business Centre, PO Box 1011, 4907 - 52 Ave., Whitecourt AB T7S 1N9
Tel: 780-778-5363; *Fax:* 780-778-2351
manager@whitecourtchamber.com
www.whitecourtchamber.com
Social Media:
www.facebook.com/whitecourtchamber
To promote trade & commerce & the economic, civic & social welfare of the district
Pat VanderBurg, General Manager
Neil Shewchuk, President

Whitehorse Chamber of Commerce (WCC)
#101, 302 Steele St., Whitehorse YT Y1A 2C5
Tel: 867-667-7545; *Fax:* 867-667-4507
business@whitehorsechamber.ca
www.whitehorsechamber.ca
To promote & improve trade & commerce; to contribute to the economic, civic & social well-being of Whitehorse
Rick Karp, President

Windsor-Essex Regional Chamber of Commerce
2575 Ouellette Place, Windsor ON N8X 1L9
Tel: 519-966-3696
info@windsorchamber.org
www.windsorchamber.org
Social Media:
linkedin.com/groups?home=&gid=2762020
www.facebook.com/125412597496221
twitter.com/WERCofC
To serve the business community of Windsor & district by providing networking opportunities, & by communicating positions & opinions on government policy & other issues on behalf of its membership.
Carolyn Brown, Chair
Matt Marchand, President & CEO

Winnipeg Chamber of Commerce (WCC) / Chambre de commerce de Winnipeg
#100, 259 Portage Ave., Winnipeg MB R3B 2A9
Tel: 204-944-8484; *Fax:* 204-944-8492
info@winnipeg-chamber.com
www.winnipeg-chamber.com
Social Media: www.youtube.com/wpgchamber;
www.instagram.com/wpgchamber
linkedin.com/company/the-winnipeg-chamber-of-commerce
www.facebook.com/WpgChamber
twitter.com/TheWpgChamber
To act as the voice of business in Winnipeg; To foster an environment in which Winnipeg businesses can proper
Dave Angus, President & Chief Executive Officer
Maxine Kashton, Vice-President, Finance & Operations
Karen Weiss, Vice-President, Membership & Marketing

Worldwide Association of Business Coaches (WABC)
c/o WABC Coaches Inc., PO Box 215, Saanichton BC V8M 2C3
www.wabccoaches.com
Social Media:
linkedin.com/groups?about=&gid=3262807
twitter.com/wabccoaches
To develop, advance & promote the emerging profession of business coaching, worldwide
Wendy Johnson, President/CEO

Yarmouth & Area Chamber of Commerce (YCC)
PO Box 532, #1, 342 Main St., Yarmouth NS B5A 4B4
Tel: 902-742-3074; *Fax:* 902-749-1383
info@yarmouthchamberofcommerce.com
www.yarmouthchamberofcommerce.com
Social Media:
linkedin.com/groups?about=&gid=2910385
www.facebook.com/YarmouthNSChamber
To promote a positive economic & business climate in Yarmouth county

Dave Hall, President
Karen Churchill, 1st Vice-President
Mike Mercier, 2nd Vice-President

Yellowknife Chamber of Commerce
#21, 4802 - 50th Ave., Yellowknife NT X1A 1C4
Tel: 867-920-4944; *Fax:* 867-920-4640
admin@ykchamber.com
www.ykchamber.com
Social Media:
www.facebook.com/pages/Yellowknife-Chamber-of-Commerce/194561107260153
twitter.com/YKChamber
Daneen Everett, Executive Director

Yukon Chamber of Commerce (YCC)
#205, 2237 - 2 Ave., Whitehorse YT Y1A 0K7
Tel: 867-667-2000; *Fax:* 867-667-2001
office@yukonchamber.com
www.yukonchamber.com
Social Media:
www.facebook.com/YukonChamberOfCommerceYukonCanada
To create a climate conducive to a strong private sector economy by providing leadership & representation
Peter Turner, President

Centraide

Centraide Abitibi Témiscamingue et Nord-du-Québec
1009, 6e rue, Val-d'Or QC J9P 3W4
Tél: 819-825-7139; *Téléc:* 819-825-7155
courrier@centraide-atnq.qc.ca
www.centraide-atnq.qc.ca
Média social: www.facebook.com/Centraide.ATNQ
Huguette Boucher, Directrice générale

Chemical Industry

Alberta Sulphur Research Ltd. (ASRL)
Center for Applied Catalysts & Industrial Sulfur Chemistry, #6, 3535 Research Rd. NW, Calgary AB T2L 2K8
Tel: 403-220-5346; *Fax:* 403-284-2054
asrinfo@ucalgary.ca
www.chem.ucalgary.ca/asr
Provides technological support for producers & users of sulfur; research & technology training through seminars & courses; provides contact between industry & academia for applied catalysis & industrial sulfur chemistry; examination of the chemistry & technology of sulfur & its compunds; emphasis on research relevant to sour gas, sulfur & refining industries
Richard Surprenant, President & Chair
Jon Gorrie, 1st Vice-President & Treasurer

Canadian Association of Agri-Retailers (CAAR)
#628, 70 Arthur St., Winnipeg MB R3B 1G7
Tel: 204-989-9300; *Fax:* 204-989-9306
Toll-Free: 800-463-9323
info@caar.org
www.caar.org
Social Media:
linkedin.com/company/caar---canadian-association-of-agri-retailers
twitter.com/CdnAgRetail
To represent & protect the interests of Canadian agricultural retailers
Delaney Ross Burtnack, President & Chief Executive Officer
Lynda Nicol, Manager, Communications & Membership
Lisa Beardsley, Manager, Event & Creative
Carla Jesson, Coordinator, Programs

Canadian Association of Chemical Distributors (CACD) / Association canadienne des distributeurs de produits chimiques (ACDPC)
#1, 1160 Blair Rd., Burlington ON L7M 1K9
Tel: 905-332-8777; *Fax:* 905-332-0777
www.cacd.ca
Social Media: www.youtube.com/user/CatherineCACD
linkedin.com/company/canadian-association-of-chemical-distributors
www.facebook.com/youbethechemistcanada
twitter.com/cacd_cathy
Cathy Campbell, President

Canadian Consumer Specialty Products Association (CCSPA) / Association canadienne de produits de consommation spécialisés (ACPCS)
#800, 130 Albert St., Ottawa ON K1P 5G4
Tel: 613-232-6616; *Fax:* 613-233-6350
assoc@ccspa.org
www.ccspa.org
Social Media:
twitter.com/CCSPA_ACPCS
Represents the specialty chemical & formulated products industry; promotes the interests of member companies by providing a national voice, encouraging ethical practices, negotiating with government, & fostering industry cooperation
Shannon Coombs, President
Nancy Hitchins, Director, Administration & Member Services

Canadian Fertilizer Institute (CFI) / Institut canadien des engrais
#907, 350 Sparks St., Ottawa ON K1R 7S8
Tel: 613-230-2600; *Fax:* 613-230-5142
info@cfi.ca
www.cfi.ca
Social Media: www.youtube.com/user/CanadianFertilizer/feed
twitter.com/CdnFertInst
The Canadian Fertilizer Institute (CFI) is an industry association that represents manufacturers, wholesale and retail distributors of nitrogen, phosphate and potash fertilizers.
Clyde Graham, Acting President
Cassandra Cotton, Director, Sustainability
Catherine King, Director, Public Outreach
Emily Pearce, Director, Government Relations
Amanda Foster, Environment & Safety Advisor
Elizabeth Smith, Manager, Communications
Monique MacDonald, Manager, Finance & Corporate Services

Chemical Institute of Canada (CIC) / Institut de chimie du Canada
#400, 222 Queen St., Ottawa ON K1P 5V9
Tel: 613-232-6252; *Fax:* 613-232-5862
Toll-Free: 888-542-2242
info@cheminst.ca
www.cheminst.ca
Social Media: www.flickr.com/photos/61234653@N08
linkedin.com/company/chemical-institute-of-canada
www.facebook.com/ChemicalInstituteOfCanada
fr.twitter.com/CIC_ChemInst
To maintain all branches of the professions of chemical sciences & chemical engineering in their proper status among other learned & scientific professions; To encourage original research & develop & maintain high standards in profession; To enhance usefulness of profession to the public
Roland Andersson, Executive Director
Joan Kingston, Director, Finance & Administration
Gale Thirlwall, Manager, Awards & Local Sections
Bernadette Dacey, Director, Communications & Marketing
Lyndsay Burman, Leader, Membership Communications

Ordre des chimistes du Québec (OCQ)
Place du Parc, #2199, 300 rue Léo-Pariseau, Montréal QC H2X 4B3
Tél: 514-844-3644; *Téléc:* 514-844-9601
information@ocq.qc.ca
www.ocq.qc.ca
L'Ordre est une corporation professionnelle dont la raison d'être est la protection du public
Guy Collin, Président du Conseil d'administration

Child & Family Services

Affected Families of Police Homicide (AFPH)
Tel: 289-880-9950
grief2action@gmail.com
Social Media:
www.facebook.com/groups/BFRJC
To promote change in the methods that police officers utilize to deal with mental illness & use of force in Ontario
Karyn Greenwood-Graham, Contact

Centre Sportif de la Petite Bourgogne / Little Burgundy Sports Centre
1825, rue Notre-Dame ouest, Montréal QC H3J 1M5
Tel: 514-932-0800
centresportifdelapetitebourgogne.com
Dickens Mathurin, Director General

Elizabeth House / Maison Elizabeth
2131 Marlowe, Montréal QC H4A 3L4
Tel: 514-482-2488; *Fax:* 514-482-9467
questions@maisonelizabethhouse.com
www.maisonelizabethhouse.com
To provide a continuum of specialized services to pregnant adolescents & women, mothers & babies, fathers, & families experiencing significant difficulty in adjusting to pregnancy & to their new roles as parents & caregivers; To support clients as they make choices & are directed to appropriate resources either in-house or in the community; To serve the anglophone community throughout the province of Quebec
Linda Schachtler, Executive Director

Federation of BC Youth in Care Networks (FBCYICN)
#500, 625 Agnes St., New Westminster BC V3M 5Y4
Tel: 604-527-7762; *Toll-Free:* 800-565-8055
info@fbcyicn.ca
www.fbcyicn.ca
Social Media:
linkedin.com/company/federation-of-bc-youth-in-care-networks
www.facebook.com/YouthInCareBC
twitter.com/fbcyicn
To improve the lives of young people in & from government care in BC
Jules Wilson, Executive Director
Chris Buchner, Director, Programs

Missing Children Society of Canada (MCSC)
#219, 3501 - 23 St. NE, Calgary AB T2E 6V8
Tel: 403-291-0705; *Fax:* 403-291-9728
Toll-Free: 800-661-6160
info@mcsc.ca
www.mcsc.ca
Social Media: www.youtube.com//MissingChildCanada
www.facebook.com/MissingChildrenSocietyofCanada
twitter.com/MCSCanada
To reunite abducted & runaway children with their searching families
Amanda Pick, Executive Director
Darcy Tuer, Chair
Jeff Davison, Vice-Chair
David Grout, Secretary

New Brunswick Youth in Care Network
535 Beaverbrook Ct., #B-10, Fredericton NB E3B 1X6
Tel: 506-462-0323; *Fax:* 506-462-0328
www.partnersforyouth.ca/nbyicn
Social Media:
www.facebook.com/NBYICN
twitter.com/VoicesMYICN
To advocate for & support youth in or from government care in New Brunswick
Robyn Lippett, Coordinator

Saskatchewan Youth in Care and Custody Network (SYICCN)
Cornwall Professional Building, #510, 2125 - 11th Ave., Regina SK S4P 3X3
Tel: 306-522-1533; *Fax:* 306-522-1507
info@syiccn.ca
www.syiccn.ca
Social Media:
www.facebook.com/SYICCN
twitter.com/syiccninc
To advocate for & support youth in or from government care or young offender systems in Saskatchewan; To ensure that youth in care or custody have a voice in their lives & communities
Stephanie Bustamante, Executive Director
Candace Fairley, Coordinator, Provincial Outreach

Voices: Manitoba's Youth in Care Network
61 Juno St., 3rd Fl., Winnipeg MB R3A 1T1
Tel: 204-982-4956; *Fax:* 204-982-4950
info@voices.mb.ca
www.voices.mb.ca
Social Media:
www.facebook.com/VoicesMB
twitter.com/VoicesMYICN
To advocate for & support youth in or from government care in Manitoba
Marie Christian, Director

Youth in Care Canada
#263, 223 Main St., Ottawa ON K1S 1C4
Tel: 613-327-4317; *Toll-Free:* 800-790-7074
info@youthincare.ca
www.youthincare.ca
Social Media:
www.facebook.com/565533686914575
twitter.com/nyicn
To increase the awareness of the needs of youth in & from government care by researching the issues & presenting the results to youth, professionals & the general public through publications & speaking engagements; To provide emotional support to youth in or from government care & to guide the development of youth in care groups
Lisa Barleben, President

Yukon Child Care Association (YCCA)
PO Box 31103, Whitehorse YT Y1A 5P7
Tel: 867-668-5130
ycca1974@gmail.com
www.yukonchildcareassociation.org
Social Media:
www.facebook.com/YukonCCA
twitter.com/YukonChildCare
To develop a high quality, universally accessible, & affordable child care system in the Yukon; To represent caregivers & families
Cyndi Desharnais, President

Childbirth

Alberta Association of Midwives (AAM)
#166, 63 - 4307-130 Ave. SE, Calgary AB T2Z 3V8
Tel: 403-214-1882; *Fax:* 888-859-5228
info@alberta-midwives.com
www.alberta-midwives.com
To promote awareness of the profession of midwifery, supports midwifery-centered research, participates in a provincial education program.
Joan Margaret Laine, President
Alex Andrews, Executive Director

Association of Ontario Midwives (AOM) / Association des sages-femmes de l'Ontario
#301, 365 Bloor St. E., Toronto ON M3W 3L4
Tel: 416-425-9974; *Fax:* 416-425-6905
Toll-Free: 866-418-3773
admin@aom.on.ca
www.aom.on.ca
To represent midwives & the practice of midwifery in Ontario
Kelly Stadelbauer, Executive Director

College of Midwives of British Columbia (CMBC)
#207, 1682 West 7th Ave., Vancouver BC V6J 4S6
Tel: 604-742-2230; *Fax:* 604-730-8908
information@cmbc.bc.ca
www.cmbc.bc.ca
To serve & protect the public interest by registering competent midwives who will practise safely & ethically in British Columbia
Jane Kilthei, Registrar & Executive Director

Infant Feeding Action Coalition
533 Colborne St., London ON N6B 2T5
Tel: 416-595-9819
info@infactcanada.ca
www.infactcanada.ca
To protect, promote & support breastfeeding in Canada & globally; to promote better infant & maternal health; to foster appropriate mother & infant nutrition
Elisabeth Sterken, National Director

La Leche League Canada (LLLC) / Ligue La Leche Canada
PO Box 700, Winchester ON K0C 2K0
Tel: 613-774-4900; *Fax:* 613-774-2798
ofm@LLLC.ca
www.lllc.ca
To act as a support network for breastfeeding mothers; To promote the importance of breastfeeding in Canada; To disseminate information on how to help mothers succeed in breastfeeding
Fiona Audy, Chair
Lisa Loeppky, Secretary
Wendy Dale, Treasurer

Multiple Births Canada (MBC) / Naissances multiples Canada
PO Box 432, Wasaga Beach ON L0L 2P0
Tel: 613-834-8946; *Toll-Free:* 866-228-8824
office@multiplebirthscanada.org
www.multiplebirthscanada.org
Social Media:
www.facebook.com/MultipleBirthsCanada
twitter.com/Multiple_Births
To improve the quality of life for multiple birth individuals & their families through research, education, service & advocacy

Ordre des sages-femmes du Québec
#300, 4126, rue Saint-Denis, Montréal QC H2W 2M5
Tél: 514-286-1313; *Ligne sans frais:* 877-711-1313
info@osfq.org
www.osfq.org
Pour surveiller les pratiques des sages-femmes au Québec
Lorena Garrido, Directrice générale

Serena Canada
151 Holland Ave., Ottawa ON K1Y 0Y2
Tel: 613-728-6536; *Toll-Free:* 888-373-7362
sc@serena.ca
www.serena.ca
To promote natural family planning methods based on information from a woman's body

Children & Youth

Adoption Council of Ontario (ACO)
#202, 36 Eglinton Ave West, Toronto ON M4R 1A1
Fax: 877-543-0009
Toll-Free: 877-236-7820
info@adoptontario.ca
www.adoption.on.ca
Social Media:
www.facebook.com/adoptioncouncilontario
twitter.com/ontarioadopts
To education, support & advocate on behalf of those touched by adoption in Ontario
Wendy Hayes, Contact

Alberta Associations for Bright Children (AABC)
c/o Action for Bright Children Calgary Society, PO Box 36093, Stn. Lakeview, Calgary AB T3E 7C6
Tel: 403-463-9612
www.edmontonabc.org/aabc
To inform & support professionals & parents who are facing the challenge of dealing with bright, gifted, talented children; to advocate at the school board & government levels to ensure that resources & expertise are allocated in a manner that serves the children best

Alberta Child Care Association (ACCA)
#54, 9912 - 106 St., Edmonton AB T5K 1C5
Tel: 780-421-7544; *Fax:* 780-428-0080
Toll-Free: 877-421-9937
www.albertachildcare.org
ACCA is non-profit, member-based society with a mission to strengthen and advance the early learning & child care profession in Alberta.
Rosetta Sanders, Chair
Sheri Magnuson, Administrator

Alberta Family Child Care Association (AFCCA)
Gail Blixt, Calgary & Region Family Dayhomes, 3224 - 28 St. SW, Calgary AB T3E 2J6
Tel: 403-217-5394; *Fax:* 403-240-2668
www.afcca.ca
To promote a high standard of well being for children & the child care industry
Gail Blixt, Contact

Association for Bright Children (Ontario) (ABC Ontario) / Société pour enfants doués et surdoués (Ontario)
c/o 135 Brant St., Oakville ON L6K 2Z8
Tel: 416-925-6136
abcinfo@abcontario.ca
www.abcontario.ca
To provide information & support to parents of bright & gifted children; To increase the understanding & acceptance of bright & gifted children/youth at home, at school & in the community
Kathleen Keane, President

Association francophone à l'éducation des services à l'enfance de l'Ontario (AFÉSEO)
#222. 135, rue Alice, Ottawa ON K1L 7X5
Tél: 613-741-5107; *Téléc:* 613-746-6140
communications@afeseo.ca
afeseo.ca
Média social: www.facebook.com/245499925585517
Pour aider les personnes en Ontario qui ont un intérêt dans l'éducation de la petite enfance
Martine St-Engo, Directrice générale
Bianca Nugent, Agente en communications

Association of Day Care Operators of Ontario (ADCO)
6 Davidson St., St Catharines ON L2R 2V4
Fax: 705-733-2154
www.adco-o.on.ca
To promote the growth of private & independent (non-profit) licensed child care programs & safeguard the interests of the providers of this service in Ontario through public education, advocacy, professional (management) development & advisory activities locally & provincially

Association of Early Childhood Educators of Quebec (AECEQ)
1001 Lenoir St., #A2-10, Montréal QC H4C 2Z6
membership@aeceq.ca
www.aeceq.ca
To improve the quality of early childhood education in Quebec
Julie Butler, Contact

Association québécoise des centres de la petite enfance (AQCPE)
#200, 6611, rue Jarry est, Montréal QC H1P 1W5
Tél: 514-326-8008; *Téléc:* 514-326-3322
Ligne sans frais: 888-326-8008
info@aqcpe.com
www.aqcpe.com
A pour mandat la concertation des acteurs du réseau, la représentation politique de ses membres et la promotion des centres de la petite enfance, et services de soutien; représente les employeurs du secteur des CPE à l'occasion de négociations, en matière de relations du travail et de main-d'oeuvre; l'AQCPE est reconnue par le Min. de la Famille et des Aînés pour les négociations provinciales.
Louis Senécal, Directeur général
Viriya Thach, Responsable des communications

B'nai Brith Youth Organization (BBYO)
Lake Ontario Region, #1-22, 4700 Bathurst St., Toronto ON M2R 1W8
Tel: 416-398-2004; *Fax:* 416-398-5780
info@bbyo.ca
www.bbyo.ca
Social Media:
www.facebook.com/lorbbyo
twitter.com/lorbbyo
To educate young people about the richness of Jewish culture & heritage
Kevin Goodman, Executive Director

Boys & Girls Clubs of Canada (BGCC) / Clubs garçons & filles du Canada
National Office, #400, 2005 Sheppard Ave. East, Toronto ON M2J 5B4
Tel: 905-477-7272; *Fax:* 416-640-5331
info@bgccan.com
www.bgccan.com
Social Media: www.youtube.com/user/bgccan
www.facebook.com/BGCCAN
twitter.com/BGCCAN
To provide safe, supportive place where children & youth can experience new opportunities, overcome barriers, build positive relationships, & develop confidence & skills for life
Robert Livingston, Chair
Pam Jolliffe, President & CEO
Marlene Deboisbriand, Vice-President, Member Services
Susan Bower, CMA, Vice-President, Business Operations
Sue Sheridan, Director, Resource Development
Denise Silverstone, Director, National Programs
Mary O'Connell, Manager, Communications Services
Karen McCullagh, Western Region Director
Sandra Morris, Central Region Director
Jennifer Bessell, Newfoundland & Labrador Region Director
Debbie Cooper, Maritime Region Director
Line St-Amour, Québec Region Director
Carrie Wagner-Miller, Pacific Regional Director

Boys & Girls Clubs of Canada Foundation / Fondation des Clubs Garçons et Filles du Canada
Boys and Girls Clubs of Canada, #400, 2005 Sheppard Ave. East, Toronto ON M2J 5B4
Tel: 905-477-7272; *Fax:* 416-640-5331
www.bgccan.com/en/AboutUs/BGCCFoundation
To support the Boys & Girls Clubs of Canada
Peter Wallace, Chair

British Columbia Family Child Care Association (BCFCCA)
#100, 6878 King George Blvd., Surrey BC V3W 4Z9
Tel: 604-590-1497; *Fax:* 604-590-1427
Toll-Free: 800-686-6685
office@bcfcca.ca
www.bcfcca.ca
Social Media:
www.facebook.com/1433767050225700
twitter.com/BCFCCA
To act as a voice for family child care providers in British Columbia; To promote awareness of professionalism in family child care
Janeen Fowler, Administrator

Canadian Association for Young Children (CAYC) / Association canadienne pour les jeunes enfants (ACJE)
c/o Vicki Brown, 356B Prospect Bay Rd., Prospect Bay NS B3T 1Z7
www.cayc.ca
To influence policies & programs affecting critical issues related to the education & welfare of Canadian young children from birth through age nine
Margaret Fair, President
Iris Berger, Chair, Publications
Vicki Brown, Contact, Membership Dervice

Canadian Centre for Child Protection
615 Academy Rd., Winnipeg MB R3N 0E7
Tel: 204-945-5735; *Fax:* 204-948-2461
Toll-Free: 800-532-9135
www.protectchildren.ca
Social Media:
www.facebook.com/184856436064
twitter.com/CdnChildProtect
To assist in the location & prevention of missing children; to increase the provincial awareness of issues relating to missing children & to advocate for the protection & rights of children
Lianna McDonald, Executive Director

Canadian Child Care Federation (CCCF) / Fédération canadienne des services de garde à l'enfance (FCSGE)
#600, 700 Industrial Ave., Ottawa ON K1G 0Y9
Tel: 613-729-5289; *Fax:* 613-729-3159
Toll-Free: 800-858-1412
info@cccf-fcsge.ca
www.cccf-fcsge.ca
Social Media: www.youtube.com/user/Qualitychildcare
www.facebook.com/208512635846134
twitter.com/CCCFed
To promote excellence in child care & early learning
Don Giesbrecht, President & CEO
Linda Skinner, Treasurer
Claire McLaughlin, Manager, Publications & Marketing

Canadian Young Judaea
788 Marlee Ave., Toronto ON M6B 3K1
Tel: 416-781-5156; *Fax:* 416-787-3100
www.youngjudaea.ca
Social Media:
www.facebook.com/youngjudaea
twitter.com/CdnYoungJudaea
To empower its members through their Jewish indentity
Risa Epstein, National Executive Director

Child Find British Columbia
#208, 2722 Fifth St., Victoria BC V8T 4B2
Tel: 250-382-7311; *Fax:* 250-382-0227
Toll-Free: 888-689-3463
childvicbc@shaw.ca
childfindbc.com
To assist in the search & location of missing children, providing support to law enforcement & families; To educate & prevent the abduction & exploitation of children & provide awareness
Steve Orcherton, Executive Director

Child Find Canada Inc. (CFC)
PO Box 237, Oakville MB R0H 0Y0
Tel: 204-870-1298
childcan@aol.com
Supports provincial Child Find organizations in the location of & education in the prevention of missing children; increases national awareness of issues relating to missing children; advocates for the protection & rights of children.

Child Find Newfoundland/Labrador
#217, 31 Peet St., St. John's NL A1B 3W8
Tel: 709-738-4400; *Toll-Free:* 800-387-7962
childnfld@aol.com
www.childfind.ca
To prevent missing children; To support the search for missing children

Child Find Ontario
#303B, 75 Front St. East, Toronto ON M5E 1V9
Tel: 416-987-9684; *Toll-Free:* 866-543-8477
mail@childfindontario.ca
www.childfindontario.ca
To assist in the search & recovery process of missing children

Child Find PEI Inc.
8 Belvedere Ave., Charlottetown PE C1A 6A1
Tel: 902-566-5935; *Fax:* 902-368-1389
Toll-Free: 800-387-7962
childfind@pei.aibn.com
www.childfindpei.com
Social Media: www.facebook.com/459667334088816
To assist in the location of missing children; to increase awareness of the problem of missing children; to teache ways to prevent abduction; to provide assistance & support to families of a missing child.
Megan DeCoste, President

Child Find Saskatchewan Inc.
#202, 3502 Taylor St. East, Saskatoon SK S7H 5H9
Tel: 306-955-0070; *Fax:* 306-373-1311
Toll-Free: 800-513-3463
childfind@childfind.sk.ca
www.childfind.sk.ca
Social Media: www.facebook.com/pages/Child-Find-Saskatchewan/121799723998
To locate missing & abducted children & reunite them with their lawful parent or guardian; To increase public awareness of the need to protect children; To educate both parents & child on street proofing technology & to support families of missing children
Phyllis Hallatt, President

Children's Miracle Network
#C10, 4220 Steeles Ave. West, Woodbridge ON L4L 3S8
Tel: 905-265-9750; *Fax:* 905-265-9749
childrensmiraclenetwork.ca
Social Media: www.youtube.com/cmnhospitals
www.facebook.com/cmnhospitals
twitter.com/cmncanada
To raise funds for children's hospitals
John Lauck, President & CEO
Jenni Debartolo, Chief People Officer
John Hartman, Chief Operating Officer
Craig Sorensen, Chief Concept Officer
Clark Sweat, Chief Corporate Partnership Officer

Children's Wish Foundation of Canada / Fondation canadienne rêves d'enfants
#350, 1101 Kingston Rd., Pickering ON L1V 1B5
Tel: 905-839-8882; *Fax:* 905-839-3745
Toll-Free: 800-700-4437
nat@childrenswish.ca
www.childrenswish.ca
Social Media: linkedin.com/company/children's-wish-foundation-of-canada
www.facebook.com/ChildrensWish
twitter.com/Childrens_wish
The Foundation grants wishes to children suffering from a high risk, life-threatening illnesses
Chris Kotsopoulos, CEO
Linda Marco, Vice-President, Development
Paul St-Germain, Director, Communications

Concerned Children's Advertisers
#200, 10 Alcorn Ave., Toronto ON M4V 3A9
Tel: 416-484-0871; *Fax:* 416-484-6564
info@cca-arpe.ca
cca-arpe.ca
To produce campaigns such as public service announcements, curricula & advice for families, in order to responsibly handle issues such as drug abuse, child abuse, child safety, self-esteem, bullying, media literacy & healthy lifestyles.
Craig Hutchison, Chair
Sherry MacLauchlan, Vice-Chair
Russ Ward, Treasurer

Enfant-Retour Québec / Missing Children Quebec
#420, 6830, av du Parc, Montréal QC H3N 1W7
Tél: 514-843-4333; *Téléc:* 514-843-8211
Ligne sans frais: 888-692-4673
info@enfant-retourquebec.ca
www.enfant-retourquebec.ca
Média social: www.facebook.com/182144014082
twitter.com/enfantretourqc
Assister les parents à la recherche de leurs enfants portés disparus; aider également les professionnels, avocats, policiers, travailleurs sociaux impliqués dans une situation de disparition d'enfant ou de prévention contre une disparition; réseau international de communication et d'aide qui oeuvre également à sensibiliser la population au problème des enfants disparus et exploités par des affiches, émissions, documents
Yves J. Beauchesne, Président
Pina Arcamone, Directrice générale
Nancy Duncan, Directrice, Programmes d'assistance aux familles

Fondation Rêves d'Enfants, div. Nord-du-Québec
CP 553, 14, chemin Lac Cumming, Chibougamau QC G8P 2Y8
beaudoinmarca@hotmail.com
Marc-André Beaudoin, Responsable

Girl Guides of Canada (GGC) / Guides du Canada
50 Merton St., Toronto ON M4S 1A3
Tel: 416-487-5281; *Fax:* 416-487-5570
www.girlguides.ca
Social Media: www.youtube.com/user/ggcanada
linkedin.com/groups/Girl-Guides-Canada-Guides-du-3598633
www.facebook.com/GirlGuidesofCanada.GuidesduCanada
twitter.com/girlguidesofcan
To prepare girls to meet the challenges of life, in a safe environment, by teaching them such skills as bandaging wounds & coping with bullies; to encourage girls to foster friendships & develop a sense of leadership; to make girls. It is part of a global organization of 145 countries, the largest for girls in the world
Pamela Rice, Chief Commissioner
Sharron Callahan, International Commissioner
Deborah Del Duca, CEO

Junior Achievement Canada (JACAN) / Jeunes Entreprises du Canada
#218, 1 Eva Rd., Toronto ON M9C 4Z5
Tel: 416-622-4602; *Fax:* 416-622-6861
Toll-Free: 800-265-0699
www.jacan.org
Social Media: www.youtube.com/user/juniorachievementcan
linkedin.com/groups?mostPopular=&gid=3027142
www.facebook.com/JAchievement
twitter.com/ja_canada
To provide practical business & economic education programs & experience for young people, through partnerships with business & education communities
Keith Publicover, President & CEO
Kevin Dane, Chair
Stephen Lippa, Vice President, Education & Digital Strategy
Aliya Ansari, National Director, CBHF & Signature Events
Sarah Hull, National Fundraising Manager

Junior Chamber International Canada / Jeune chambre internationale du Canada
14 Bruce Farm Dr., Toronto ON M2H 1G3
Tel: 416-226-9756; *Fax:* 416-221-9389
Toll-Free: 800-265-0484
administration@jcicanada.com
www.jcicanada.com
To contribute to the advancement of the global community by providing the opportunity for young people to develop the leadership skills, social responsibility & fellowship necessary to create positive change. Chapters across Canada.
Francois Begin, Chairman of the Board
Jason Ranchoux, National President

Justice for Children & Youth (JFCY)
#1203, 415 Yonge St., Toronto ON M5B 2E7
Tel: 416-920-1633; *Fax:* 416-920-5855
Toll-Free: 866-999-5329
info@jfcy.org
www.jfcy.org
To assist & empower children & youth in obtaining fair & equal access to legal, educational, medical & social resources; to provide direct legal assistance in all areas of children's law to eligible children & youth of Metro Toronto & vicinity; to provide summary legal advice, information & assistance to young people, parents, professionals & community groups on a province-wide basis; to advocate for law & policy reform; to monitor & respond to developments & changes to the laws which affect children
Mary Birdsell, Executive Director
Emily Chan, Community Development Lawyer

Make-A-Wish Canada / Fais-Un-Voeu Canada
#520, 211 Yonge St., Toronto ON M2P 2A9
Tel: 416-224-9474; *Fax:* 416-224-8795
Toll-Free: 888-822-9474
nationaloffice@makeawish.ca
makeawish.ca
Social Media: www.youtube.com/user/makeawishcanada
linkedin.com/company/422218
www.facebook.com/makeawish.ca
twitter.com/MakeAWishCA
The Foundation grants wishes to children suffering from a high risk, life-threatening illnesses
Jennifer Klotz-Ritter, Chief Executive Officer

Manitoba Child Care Association (MCCA)
2350 McPhillips St., 2nd Fl., Winnipeg MB R2V 4J6
Tel: 204-586-8587; *Fax:* 204-589-5613
Toll-Free: 888-323-4676
info@mccahouse.org
www.mccahouse.org
Social Media: twitter.com/MCCAHOUSE
To act as the voice of child care in Manitoba; To advocate for a quality system of child care; To advance early childhood education as a profession
Pat Wege, Executive Director

National Alliance for Children & Youth (NACY) / Alliance nationale pour l'enfance et la jeunesse (ANEJ)
#707, 331 Cooper St., Ottawa ON K2P 0G5
Tel: 613-292-0569
info@nacy.ca
www.nacy.ca
Social Media: www.facebook.com/189588222849
twitter.com/NACY_ANEJ
To promote the health & well being of children in Canada.
Gordon Floyd, Chair

Nova Scotia Child Care Association / Association des services de garde à l'enfance de la Nouvelle-Écosse
#161, 1083 Queen St., Halifax NS B3H 0B2
Tel: 902-423-8199; *Fax:* 902-492-8106
Toll-Free: 800-565-8199
info@nschildcareassociation.org
nschildcareassociation.org
To promote high standards in service in the child care industry; to be a voice for its members
Kathleen Couture, Chair

Parachute
#300, 150 Eglinton Ave. East, Toronto ON M4P 1E8
Tel: 647-776-5100; *Toll-Free:* 888-537-7777
info@parachutecanada.org
www.parachutecanada.org
Social Media: linkedin.com/company/parachute—leaders-in-injury-prevention
www.facebook.com/parachutecanada
twitter.com/parachutecanada
To promote effective strategies to prevent unintentional injuries; to build partnerships & uses a comprehensive approach to advance safety & reduce the burden of injuries to Canada's children & youth
Louise Logan, President & CEO

Ranch Ehrlo Society
Pilot Butte Campus, PO Box 570, Pilot Butte SK S0G 3Z0
Tel: 306-781-1800; *Fax:* 306-757-0599
inquiries@ranchehrlo.ca
www.ehrlo.com
Social Media: www.youtube.com/user/ranchehrlo1
www.facebook.com/RanchEhrlo
twitter.com/RanchEhrlo
To provide a range of quality assessment, treatment, education & support services that improves the social & emotional functioning of children & youth referred to our program
Marion MacIver, President & CEO

Scouts Canada / Scouts du Canada
National Office, 1345 Baseline Rd., Ottawa ON K2C 0A7
Toll-Free: 888-855-3336
helpcentre@scouts.ca
www.scouts.ca
Social Media: www.youtube.com/scoutscanada
linkedin.com/company/scouts-canada
www.facebook.com/scoutscanada
twitter.com/scoutscanada
To contribute to the education of young people through a value system based on the Scout Promise & Law; To emphasize learning by doing, particularly in small groups, with outdoor activities as a learning resource
Doug Reid, National Commissioner
Kaylee Galipeau, National Youth Commissioner
Andrew Price, Executive Commissioner & CEO
Valarie Dillon, Executive Director, Human Resources & Volunteer Services
Ian Mitchell, Executive Director, Field Services
John Petitti, Executive Director, Marketing and Communications
Peter Valters, Executive Director, Business Services

Citizenship & Immigration

Canadian Association of Professional Immigration Consultants (CAPIC) / Association Canadienne des Conseillers Professionnels en Immigration (ACCPI)
#602, 245 Fairview Mall Dr., Toronto ON M2J 4T1
Tel: 416-483-7044; *Fax:* 416-309-1985
info@capic.ca
www.capic.ca
Social Media:
www.facebook.com/684073984953919
twitter.com/capicaccpi
To represent Certified Canadian Immigration Consultants (CCIC), or full members of the Canadian Society of Immigration Consultants (CSIC)
Katarina Onuschak, Executive Director
Monica Poon, National Coordinator
Christopher Daw, Director, Lobbying
Lynn Gaudet, Director, Communications
Deepak Kohli, Director, Membership
Tanveer Sharief, Director, Education & Training

Canadian Ukrainian Immigrant Aid Society (CUIAS)
2383 Bloor St. West, 2nd Fl., Toronto ON M6S 1P9
Tel: 416-767-4595; *Fax:* 416-767-2658
www.cuias.org
To sponsor & aid in settlement of Ukrainian refugees.
Ludmila Kolesnichenko, Executive Director

Centre for Immigrant & Community Services (CICS)
c/o Immigrant Resource Centre, 2330 Midland Ave., Toronto ON M1S 5G5
Tel: 416-292-7510; *Fax:* 416-292-7579
Crisis Hot-Line: 416-292-2832
info@cicscanada.com
www.cicscanada.com
Social Media:
www.facebook.com/cicscanada
twitter.com/cicscanada
To provide a wide range of cost-effective, culturally-sensitive & professional services; to empower newcomers to settle & integrate into Canadian society; to promote active citizenship in the community; committed to excellence & to be a leading agency in settlement, education & social services
Moy Wong-Tam, Executive Director
Suba Satgunaraj, Director, Finance & Operations

Immigrant Centre Manitoba Inc.
100 Adelaide St., Winnipeg MB R3A 0W2
Tel: 204-943-9158; *Fax:* 204-949-0734
info@icmanitoba.com
icmanitoba.com
To encourage pride in Canada & appreciation of Canadian citizenship; to encourage intercultural understanding in multicultural Canada; to support immigration & provide caring services to newcomers.
Cec Hanec, President

Jewish Immigrant Aid Services of Canada (JIAS) / Services canadiens d'assistance aux immigrants juifs
#300, 2255 Carling Ave., Ottawa ON K2B 7Z5
Tel: 613-722-2225; *Fax:* 613-722-5750
national@jias.org
www.jias.org
To serve the needs of Jewish immigrants & refugees; To facilitate the legal entry of Jewish immigrants to Canada; to provide services for immigration, naturalization, resettlement & integration
Mark Zarecki, Executive Director

National Organization of Immigrant & Visible Minority Women of Canada (NOIVMWC) / Organisation nationale des femmes immigrantes et des femmes appartenant à une minorité visible du Canada (ONFIFAMVC)
#225, 219 Argyle St., Ottawa ON K2P 2H4
www.noivmwc.org
To ensure equality for immigrant & visible minority women within bilingual Canada by putting into place strategies that will combat sexism, racism, poverty, isolation & violence & by acting as an advocate on issues dealing with immigrant & visible minority women.

Ontario Council of Agencies Serving Immigrants (OCASI)
#200, 110 Eglinton Ave. West, Toronto ON M4R 1A3
Tel: 416-322-4950; *Fax:* 416-322-8084
TTY: 416-322-1498
generalmail@ocasi.org
www.ocasi.org
Social Media:
twitter.com/OCASI_Policy
To act as a collective voice for immigrant services; to provide access for immigrants & refugees to settlement services; to provide social organizational development with community groups, policy analysis & government relations, professional development of member agency staff & research into issues facing immigrant service agencies
Carl Nicholson, President
Debbie Douglas, Executive Director

Ottawa Community Immigrant Services Organization (OCISO) / Organisme communautaire des services aux immigrants d'Ottawa
959 Wellington St. West, Ottawa ON K1Y 2X5
Tel: 613-725-0202; *Fax:* 613-725-9054
info@ociso.org
www.ociso.org
Social Media: www.youtube.com/user/OCISOTV
linkedin.com/profile/view?trk=hb_tab_pro_top&id=229386541
twitter.com/intent/user?screen_name=OttawaOCISO
To enable newcomers & their families to fully participate in an open & welcoming Ottawa, through innovative services, community building & public engagement
Leslie Emory, Executive Director

Colleges

Alberta College of Combined Laboratory & X-Ray Technologists (ACCLXT)
#830, 4445 Calgary Trail, Edmonton AB T6H 5R7
Tel: 780-438-3323; *Fax:* 855-299-0829
www.acclxt.ca
To be responsible for the registration, discipline & competency of all registered Combined Laboratory & X-Ray Technicians / Technologists currently practicing in the province of Alberta; To strive to provide excellence in the combined fields of laboratory, radiography, & electrocardiography medicine
Sheila Joyce, President
Anna Steblyk, Vice President
Lyndsay Arndt, Executive Director/Registrar
Sandra Toepfer, Competency Co-ordinator

Community Planning

Provincial Association of Resort Communities of Saskatchewan (PARCS)
PO Box 52, Elbow SK S0H 1J0
Tel: 306-545-6253; *Fax:* 306-854-4412
parcs@sasktel.com
www.parcs-sk.com
To promote the interests of resort communities in Saskatchewan; To promote fair & equitable policies & procedures for all resort communities
Shirley Gange, President
Lynne Saas, Contact, Member Servivces

Conservation

Lloydminster & District Fish & Game Association (LDFGA)
PO Box 116, Lloydminster AB T9V 0X9
Tel: 780-875-5100
admin@lloydfishandgame.org
www.lloydfishandgame.org
To advocate for & assist in the conservation & management of fish, wildlife & habitat for the continuing benefit of association members & the general public
Bill Armstrong, President

Nova Scotia Federation of Anglers & Hunters (NSFAH)
PO Box 654, Halifax NS B3J 2T3
Tel: 902-477-8898; *Fax:* 902-444-3883
tonyrodgers@eastlink.ca
www.nsfah.ca
The Nova Scotia Federation of Anglers and Hunters is dedicated to the conservation and propagation of the wildlife in the province for those who hunt, fish, trap or otherwise wish to enjoy the wildlife resources of Nova Scotia. This will be accomplished by education, cooperation and exchange of information will all people and by uniting provincial organizations having similar objectives.
Tony Rodgers, Executive Director

Construction

Association des professionnels à l'outillage municipal (APOM)
11, av du Ruisseau, Montréal QC H4K 2C8
Téléc: 866-334-1264
Ligne sans frais: 866-337-5136
info@apom-quebec.ca
www.apom-quebec.ca
Média social: www.facebook.com/apomquebec
Répondre aux besoins créés par l'achat, l'entretien et la réparation de l'outillage utilisé dans l'exécution des travaux publics municipaux; Encourager la coopération entre ses organisations membres
Eric Landry, President

Ontario Road Builders' Association (ORBA)
#1, 365 Brunel Rd., Mississauga ON L4Z 1Z5
Tel: 905-507-1107; *Fax:* 905-890-8122
www.orba.org
Social Media:
www.facebook.com/OntarioRoadBuildersAssociation
twitter.com/onroadbuilders
To act as the voice of the Ontario road building industry; To maintain high standards in the road building industry; To promote worker health & safety
Geoff Wilkinson, Executive Director
Karen Renkema, Director, Government Relations
Kathryn Thomas, Director, Member Services
Kim Le Fort, Office Manager & Coordinator, Events
Patrick McManus, Policy Analyst

Consumers

Consumers Council of Canada (CCC)
Commercial Bldg., #201, 1920 Yonge St., Toronto ON M4S 3E2
Tel: 416-483-2696
www.consumerscouncil.com
Aubrey LeBlanc, President
Ken Whitehurst, Executive Director

Consumers' Association of Canada (CAC) / Association des consommateurs du Canada
Ottawa ON
Tel: 604-418-8359
consumer@rogers.com
www.consumer.ca
Social Media:
www.facebook.com/consumercanada
twitter.com/ConsumerCanada
To represent & articulate the best interests of Canadian consumers to all levels of government & to all sectors of society by continually earning recognition as the trusted voice of the consumer on a national basis; to inform & educate consumers on marketplace issues; To work with government & industry to solve marketplace problems; To focus its work in the areas of food, health, trade, standards, financial services, communications industries & other marketplace issues as they emerge
Bruce Cran, President & Director
Trevor Todd, Director

Copyright

Canadian Artists Representation Copyright Collective Inc. (CARCC) / Société des droits d'auteur du Front des artistes canadiens inc
214 Barclay Rd., Ottawa ON K1K 3C2
Tel: 613-232-3818; *Fax:* 613-232-8384
carcc@carcc.ca
www.carcc.ca
Operating as a coyright collecting society
Janice Seline, Executive Director

Culture

Assemblée communautaire fransaskoise (ACF)
#215, 1440, 9 av Nord, Regina SK S4R 8B1
Tél: 306-569-1912; *Téléc:* 306-781-7916
Ligne sans frais: 800-991-1912
acf@sasktel.net
www.fransaskois.sk.ca
Média social:
www.facebook.com/assembeecommunautairefransaskoise.acf
Travaille au développement, à l'épanouissement et au rayonnement de tous ses membres; est l'entité gouvernante de la communauté fransaskoise
Françoise Sigur-Cloutier, Présidente
Marc Masson, Agente aux communications
Francis Potié, Directeur général

Assemblée de la francophonie de l'Ontario (AFO)
1492B, ch Star Top, Ottawa ON K1B 3W6
Tél: 613-744-6649; *Téléc:* 416-744-8861
Ligne sans frais: 866-596-4692
ad@monassemblee.ca
www.monassemblee.ca
Média social: www.youtube.com/monassemblee
www.facebook.com/monassemblee.ca
twitter.com/MonAssemblee
Pour représenter la voix politique des francophones en Ontario
Peter Hominuk, Directeur général

Assemblée parlementaire de la Francophonie (APF)
Région Amérique, Assemblée nationale, 1020, rue des Parlementaires, 6e étage, Québec QC G1A 1A3
Tél: 418-643-7391; *Téléc:* 418-643-1865
mvermette@assnat.qc.ca
www.regionamerique-apf.org
Promouvoir la langue et la culture francaise; promouvoir les droits de l'homme et la démocratie
André Lavoie, Secrétaire administrative régionale

Association canadienne-française de l'Alberta (ACFA)
#303, Pav. II, 8627, rue Marie-Anne-Gaboury, Edmonton AB T6C 3N1
Tél: 780-466-1680; *Téléc:* 780-465-6773
acfa@acfa.ab.ca
www.acfa.ab.ca
Média social: www.youtube.com/user/acfaab
www.facebook.com/acfaab
Représenter la population francophone de l'Alberta; promouvoir le bien-être intellectuel, culturel et social des francophones de l'Alberta; encourager, faciliter et développer l'enseignement en français; entretenir des relations amicales avec les groupes de différentes origines ethniques et anglophones dans la province
Isabelle Laurin, Directeur général (par intérim)

Association canadienne-française de l'Ontario, Mille-îles (ACFOMI)
Kingston ON
Tél: 613-546-7863; *Téléc:* 613-507-7794
www.acfomi.org/acfo
Appuyer le développement communautaire; rassembler les forces vives de la communauté franco-ontarienne; faire des représentations politiques
Lucie Mercier, Directrice générale

Association des francophone du Nunavut (AFN)
CP 880, Iqaluit NU X0A 0H0
Tél: 867-979-4606; *Téléc:* 867-979-0800
cuerrier@nunafranc.ca
Pour représenter la communauté française et l'aider à développer
Éric Corneau, Président

Association des francophones de Fort Smith (AFFS)
212, ch McDougal, Fort Smith NT X0E 0P0
Tél: 867-872-2338; *Téléc:* 867-872-5710
affs@northwestel.net
www.associationfrancophonesfortsmith.ca
Afin de préserver et de développer la communauté francophone de Fort Smith
Marie-Christine Aubrey, Présidente

Association des francophones du delta du Mackenzie Association des francophones du delta du Mackenzie (AFDM)
CP 2845, Inuvik NT X0E OTO
Tél: 867-678-2661; *Téléc:* 867-777-2799
afdm@hotmail.ca
www.afdm.ca
Pour représenter les intérêts et les droits de la communauté francophone de delta du Mackenzie
André Church, Président

Association des parents ayants droit de Yellowknife (APADY)
CP 2103, Yellowknife NT X1A 2P5
Tél: 867-446-8285
apady@franco-nord.com
www.apady.ca
Pour promouvoir l'éducation de la langue française à Yellowknife
Jacques Lamarche, Président

Association franco-culturelle de Hay River
CP 4482, 77A, rue Woodland, Hay River NT X0E 1G2
Tél: 867-674-3171
afchr.ca
Média social:
www.facebook.com/AssociationFrancoCulturelleDeHayRiver
Pour représenter la communauté francophone de Hay River et de défendre leurs droits
Christian Girard, Président

Association Franco-culturelle de Yellowknife (AFCY)
CP 1586, Succ. Principale, 5016, 48 rue, Yellowknife NT X1A 2P2
Tél: 867-873-3292; *Téléc:* 867-873-2158
dgafcy@franco-nord.com
afcy.info
Média social: www.facebook.com/afcy.yellowknife
twitter.com/AFCYTNO
Pascaline Gréau, Direction générale

Association franco-yukonnaise (AFY)
302, rue Strickland, Whitehorse YT Y1A 2K1
Tél: 867-668-2663; *Téléc:* 867-663-3511
afy@afy.yk.ca
www.afy.yk.ca
Média social: www.facebook.com/AFY.Yukon
D'offrir plusieurs activités sociales, culturelles et artistiques.
Isabelle Salesse, Codirectrice générale

Association of Canadian Clubs / Association des cercles canadiens
#211, 2415 Holly Lane, Ottawa ON K1V 2P2
Tel: 613-236-8288; *Fax:* 613-236-8299
support@istcl.com
www.canadianclub.ca
To promote Canadian identity; to encourage Canadian unity; to foster throughout Canada an interest in public affairs; to cultivate attachment to Canadian institutions
Lyn Goldman, National President
Christine Merrikin, Executive Secretary
Jim Waters, Regional Director, British Columbia
Marjorie Nickerson, Regional Director, Alberta
Maura Gillis-Cipywnyk, Regional Director, Saskatchewan
Jacqui Blanchard, Regional Director, Manitoba
Allan Mutart, Regional Director, Southern Ontario
Clara Edwardson, Regional Director, Eastern & Northern Ontario
Cynthia Dinsmore, Regional Director, Québec

Calgary Exhibition & Stampede
PO Box 1060, Stn. M, 1410 Olympic Way SE, Calgary AB T2P 2K8
Tel: 403-261-0101; *Fax:* 403-265-7197
Toll-Free: 888-883-3828
info@calgarystampede.com
www.calgarystampede.com
Social Media: www.youtube.com/calgarystampede
www.facebook.com/calgarystampede
twitter.com/calgarystampede
To preserve & promote Western heritage & values
Bill Gray, President & Chair
Warren Connell, CEO

Calgary Stampede Foundation (CSF)
Calgary Stampede Headquarters, PO Box 1060, Stn. M, 1410 Olympic Way SE, Calgary AB T2P 2K8
Tel: 403-261-9155; *Fax:* 403-261-9390
CSF_Administration@calgarystampede.com
www.stampedefoundation.com
To generate income to support the development of youth in Southern Alberta
Ann McCaig, Chair
Sarah Hayes, Executive Director
Bianca von Nagy, Foundation Manager

Canada-Israel Cultural Foundation (CICF) / Fondation culturelle Canada-Israël
4700 Bathurst St., 2nd Fl., Toronto ON M2R 1W8
Tel: 416-932-2260
cicf@bellnet.ca
www.cicfweb.ca
To act as a cultural bridge between Canada and Israel, promoting and supporting intercultural exchange with a special focus on young artists, and developing artistic life by awarding scholarships and grants
Cheryl Wetstein, Executive Director

Canadian Italian Heritage Foundation (CIHF)
11 Director Ct., Woodbridge ON L4L 4S5
Tel: 905-850-4500; *Fax:* 905-850-4516
To work with the Italian Canadian community to undertake projects in collaboration with other existing organizations that support & promote Italian heritage & culture through activities within Canada
Michael Tibollo, President

Canadian-Scandinavian Foundation (CSF) / Fondation Canada-Scandinavie
1438, rue Fullum, Montréal QC H2K 3M1
www.thecsfoundation.com
To raise funds to distribute to Canadian students who wish to travel to Denmark, Finland, Iceland, Norway or Sweden, to undertake studies at a Scandinavian institution; to promote study/research projects by offering travel busaries.
Noami Kramer, President

Centre culturel franco-manitobain (CCFM)
340, boul Provencher, Winnipeg MB R2H 0G7
Tél: 204-233-8972; *Téléc:* 204-233-3324
communication@ccfm.mb.ca
www.ccfm.mb.ca
Média social:
www.facebook.com/people/Centre-Culturel-Franco-Manitobain/1549747456
De maintenir, d'encourager, de favoriser et de patronner, par tous les moyens possibles, toutes les formes d'activités culturelles de langue française, et de rendre la culture canadienne-française accesible à tous les résidents de la province.
Sylviane Lanthier, Directrice générale

Centre francophone de Toronto (CFT)
#303, 555, rue Richmond ouest, Toronto ON M5V 3B1
Tél: 416-922-2672; *Téléc:* 416-203-1165
infos@centrefranco.org
www.centrefranco.org
Média social:
www.youtube.com/channel/UCK-ySdR14l29fBcm-xBVFYw
www.facebook.com/Centre.francophone.de.Toronto
twitter.com/CentrefrancoT
Permettre à la population francophone du grand Toronto d'avoir accès à des services d'information, d'orientation et d'encadrement susceptibles de promouvoir la dimension humaine, culturelle et communautaire des multiples visages de la francophonie
Lise Marie Baudry, Directrice générale

Chateauguay Valley English-Speaking Peoples' Association (CVESPA)
1493, rte 138, CP 1357, Huntingdon QC J0S 1H0
Tel: 450-264-5386; *Fax:* 450-264-5387
To assure preservation, maintenance & on-going development of English-speaking population in Southwest Québec; to encourage continuous development of their institutions & cultural heritage; to assure full participation & representation of English-speaking community in all aspects of Québec society; to promote positive attitudes in English-speaking community to participate fully & harmoniously with French-speaking population; to foster activities which would bring the two communities together to improve their mutual understanding

Chinese Canadian Association of Prince Edward Island (CCAPEI)
36 Massey Dr., Charlottetown PE C1E 1R6

Commission nationale des parents francophones (CNPF)
2445, boul St-Laurent, #B182, Ottawa ON K1G 6C3
Tél: 613-288-0958; *Téléc:* 613-688-1367
Ligne sans frais: 800-665-5148
cnpf@cnpf.ca
cnpf.ca
Média social: www.vimeo.com/cnpf
www.facebook.com/219249894852875
twitter.com/parentsfranco
Pour soutenir les branches provinciales de l'organisation et les aider à fournir de l'aide aux parents
Adèle David, Directrice générale
Véronique Legault, Présidente

The Council of Canadians (COC) / Le Conseil des Canadiens
#300, 251 Bank St., Ottawa ON K2P 1X3
Tel: 613-233-2773; *Fax:* 613-233-6776
Toll-Free: 800-387-7177
inquiries@canadians.org
www.canadians.org
Social Media: www.youtube.com/councilofcanadians
www.facebook.com/CouncilofCDNS?rf=105965852767091
twitter.com/councilofcdns
With chapters across the country, The Council of Canadians is Canada's largest citizens' organization, working to protect Canadian independence in areas such as energy & environment, health care & fair trade. The Council provides a critical voice on key national issues: safeguarding our social programs, promoting economic justice, renewing Canada's democracy, asserting Canadian sovereignty, promoting alternatives to corporate-style free trade & preserving the environment
Maude Barlow, National Chairperson

Fédération acadienne de la Nouvelle-Écosse (FANE)
La Maison acadienne, 54, rue Queen, Dartmouth NS B2Y 1G3
Tél: 902-433-0065; *Téléc:* 902-433-0066
fane@federationacadienne.ca
www.federationacadienne.ca
Un regroupement d'organismes régionaux, provinciaux et institutionnels d'expression française qui s'engage à promouvoir l'épanouissement et le développement global de la communauté acadienne et francophone de la Nouvelle-Écosse.
Marie-Claude Rioux, Directrice générale

Fédération culturelle canadienne-française (FCCF)
Place de la Francophonie, #405, 450 Rideau St., Ottawa ON K1N 5Z4
Tél: 613-241-8770; *Téléc:* 613-241-6064
Ligne sans frais: 800-267-2005
info@fccf.ca
www.fccf.ca
Mèdia social: www.facebook.com/infofccf
twitter.com/infofccf
Défendre et promouvoir les arts et la culture de la francophonie canadienne hors-Québec.
Éric Dubeau, Directeur général

Fédération de la jeunesse canadienne-française inc. (FJCF)
#403, 450 Rideau St., Ottawa ON K1N 5Z4
Tél: 613-562-4624; *Téléc:* 613-562-3995
Ligne sans frais: 800-267-5173
fjcf@fjcf.ca
www.fjcf.ca
Mèdia social: www.flickr.com/photos/fjcf_canada
www.facebook.com/fjcf.ca
twitter.com/FJCF_Canada
Etre le porte-parole national de la jeunesse canadienne-française et acadienne; assurer l'épanouissement de la jeunesse dans les secteurs de l'éducation, des arts et communications, des loisirs et de l'économie; augmenter la visibilité de la FJCF et de ses membres auprès de leurs différentes clientèles; augmenter les occasions pour les jeunes d'utiliser la langue française; renforcer le sentiment d'appartenance des jeunes, pour qu'ils soient des agents de changement dans leur communauté.
Sylvian Groulx, Directeur Général

Fédération des communautés francophones et acadienne du Canada (FCFAC)
#300,450, rue Rideau, Ottawa ON K1N 5Z4
Tél: 613-241-7600; *Téléc:* 613-241-6046
info@fcfa.ca
www.fcfa.ca
Mèdia social: www.facebook.com/FCFACanada
twitter.com/fcfacanada
Défendre et promouvoir les droits et les intérêts des communautés francophones et acadiennes qu'elle représente
Suzanne Bossé, Directrice générale
Sylviane Lanthier, Présidente

Fédération franco-ténoise (FFT)
CP 1325, Yellowknife NT X1A 2N9
Tél: 867-920-2919; *Téléc:* 867-873-2458
info@franco-nord.com
www.federation-franco-tenoise.com
Afin de promouvoir et de préserver la communauté francophone des Territoires du Nord-Ouest
Richard Létourneau, Président

Fondation franco-ontarienne (FFO)
CP 7340, Ottawa ON K1L 8E4
Tél: 613-565-4720; *Téléc:* 613-565-8539
info@fondationfranco-ontarienne.ca
www.fondationfranco-ontarienne.ca
Mèdia social: www.facebook.com/Fondationfranco
twitter.com/fondationfranco
La Fondation franco-ontarienne appuie financièrement la réalisation d'initiatives qui assurent la vitalité de la communauté franco-ontarienne
Marie-Michèle Laferrière, Directrice générale

L'Institut canadien de Québec (ICQ)
350, rue Saint-Joseph est, 4e étage, Québec QC G1K 3B2
Tél: 418-641-6788; *Téléc:* 418-641-6787
courrier@institutcanadien.qc.ca
www.institutcanadien.qc.ca
Mèdia social:
linkedin.com/company/l'institut-canadien-de-qu-bec
www.facebook.com/176468254731
twitter.com/ICQ_Quebec
Démocratiser l'accès au savoir et aux oeuvres d'imagination par un service de bibliothèque universellement accessible; Sensibiliser le public aux arts et à la culture; Gestion de bibliothèques publiques de la Ville de Québec
Marie-Claire Lévesque, Présidente

The Japan Foundation, Toronto / Kokosai Koryu Kikin Toronto Nihon Bunka Centre
#213, 131 Bloor St. West, Toronto ON M5S 1R1
Tel: 416-966-1600; *Fax:* 416-966-9773
info@jftor.org
www.japanfoundationcanada.org
Social Media:
www.facebook.com/pages/The-Japan-Foundation-Toronto/2802 13815446606
twitter.com/JFToronto
To promote Japanese culture abroad; to offer a broad range of programs designed to further cultural exchange with Japan, with an emphasis on Japanese studies at the post-secondary level & Japanese language study
Ishida Takashi, Executive Director
Chieko Kono, Director

The Royal Commonwealth Society of Canada (RCS) / La Société royale du Commonwealth du Canada
c/o RCS Ottawa, PO Box 8023, Stn. T, Ottawa ON K1G 3H6
www.rcs.ca
Social Media:
www.facebook.com/RCSCanada
twitter.com
A charitable, non-partisan organization which promotes knowledge of the Commonwealth & its member countries; fosters unity in diversity in matters of common concern; promotes international understanding, cooperation & peace; upholds the best traditions of the Commonwealth
Norman Macfie, Chair

Société de développement des entreprises culturelles (SODEC)
#800, 215, rue Saint-Jacques, Montréal QC H2Y 1M6
Tél: 514-841-2200; *Téléc:* 514-841-8606
Ligne sans frais: 800-363-0401
info@sodec.gouv.qc.ca
www.sodec.gouv.qc.ca
Mèdia social: www.facebook.com/SODEC.gouv.qc.ca
twitter.com/la_sodec
Soutient la production et la diffusion de la culture québécoise dans le champ des industries culturelles
Pierre Laporte, Président du conseil
Monique Simard, Présidente et chef de la direction

Société des Acadiens et Acadiennes du Nouveau-Brunswick (SANB)
#204, 702, rue Principale, Petit-Rocher NB E8J 1V1
Tél: 506-783-4205; *Téléc:* 506-783-0629
Ligne sans frais: 888-722-2343
sanb@nb.aibn.com
www.saanb.org
Mèdia social: www.facebook.com/sanb.ca
twitter.com/SANB2012
La Société vise à unir tous les Acadiens et Acadiennes du Nouveau-Brunswick et les sensibiliser aux problèmes sociaux, économiques, culturels et politiques qu'ils doivent affronter; s'occuper de tout sujet ayant trait à la protection et à la promotion des droits et à l'avancement des intérêts des Acadiens et Acadiennes du Nouveau-Brunswick; entretenir des liens aussi étroits que possible avec les groupements analogues des autres provinces canadiennes et de l'étranger.
Jeanne d'Arc Gaudet, Présidente
Bruno Godin, Directeur général

Société franco-manitobaine (SFM)
#106, 147, boul. Provencher, Saint-boniface MB R2H 0G2
Tél: 204-233-4915; *Téléc:* 204-977-8551
Ligne sans frais: 800-665-4443
sfm@sfm-mb.ca
www.sfm-mb.ca
Veiller à l'épanouissement de cette communauté
Daniel Boucher, Président/Directeur général

Société nationale de l'Acadie (SNA)
307, rue Amirault Dieppe, Dieppe NB E1A 1G1
Tél: 506-853-0404; *Téléc:* 506-853-0400
www.snacadie.org
Mène différentes activités sur les scènes interprovinciales et internationales afin de promouvoir et de défendre les droits et intérêts du peuple acadien
Martin Arseneau, Directeur, Comunications

Société Saint-Jean-Baptiste de Montréal (SSJBM)
82, rue Sherbrooke ouest, Montréal QC H2X 1X3
Tél: 514-843-8851; *Téléc:* 514-844-6369
www.ssjb.com
Mèdia social: fr-ca.facebook.com/SSJBM
twitter.com/ssjbm
Une société nationale qui participe de façon non partisane à l'évolution politique, sociale, économique et culturelle du Québec par ses actions, ses études, ses interventions et ses campagnes d'opinion
Mario Beaulieu, Président général

Townshippers' Association (TA) / Association des Townshippers
#100, 257, rue Queen, Sherbrooke QC J1M 1K7
Tel: 819-566-5717; *Fax:* 819-566-0271
Toll-Free: 866-566-5717
ta@townshippers.qc.ca
www.townshippers.qc.ca
Social Media:
twitter.com/townshippersTA
To promote the interests of the English-speaking community in the historical Eastern Townships; to strengthen the cultural identity of this community; to encourage the full participation of the English-speaking population in the community at large
Ingrid Marini, Executive Director
Gerald Cutting, President

L'Union culturelle des Franco-Ontariennes (UCFO)
#302, 450, rue Rideau, Ottawa ON K1N 5Z4
Tél: 613-741-1334; *Téléc:* 613-741-8577
Ligne sans frais: 877-520-8226
ucfo@on.aibn.com
www.unionculturelle.ca
Améliorer les conditions et les réalités sociales des femmes francophones de l'Ontario; faciliter l'épanouissement de la femme tout en favorisant son autonomie
Madeleine Chabot, Présidente provinciale

Dental

Alberta Dental Association & College (ADAC)
#101, 8230 - 105 St., Edmonton AB T6E 5H9
Tel: 780-432-1012; *Fax:* 780-433-4864
Toll-Free: 800-843-3848
reception@adaandc.com
www.dentalhealthalberta.ca
To provide guidance & leadership to dentists in Alberta; to maintain patient care standards set by the association

Association des assistant(e)s-dentaires du Québec (CDAA/AADQ)
#410, 7400, boul. Les Galeries d'Anjou, Montréal QC H1M 3M2
Tél: 514-722-9900; *Téléc:* 514-355-4159
aadq@spg.qc.ca
www.aadq.ca
Aider ses membres à parfaire leurs connaissances par des cours pratiques et théoriques; moderniser le domaine dentaire; règlementer les assistants-dentaires
Denise Longpré, Présidente

Association des denturologistes du Québec (ADQ)
#230, 8150, boul Métropolitain Est, Anjou QC H1K 1A1
Tél: 514-252-0270; *Téléc:* 514-252-0392
Ligne sans frais: 800-563-6273
denturo@adq-qc.com
www.adq-qc.com
Mèdia social: www.facebook.com/denturo
Protéger et développer les intérêts professionnels, moraux, sociaux et économiques de ses membres
Marie-France Brisson, Directrice générale

British Columbia Dental Association
#400, 1765 - 8th Ave. West, Vancouver BC V6J 5C6
Tel: 604-736-7202; *Fax:* 604-736-7588
Toll-Free: 888-396-9888
post@bcdental.org
www.bcdental.org
To act as the voice of dentistry in British Columbia; To prevent oral disease

Canadian Academy of Endodontics / L'Académie canadienne d'endodontie
c/o Wayne Maillet, #301, 400 St. Mary Ave., Winnipeg MB R3C 4K5
info@caendo.ca
www.caendo.ca
To advance the art & science of endodontics by providing learning experiences through lectures, providing teachers of endodontics a forum for interaction, providing information & acting as a resource to dental governing bodies, & ultimately to improving the health of the public.
Douglas Conn, President
Wayne Maillet, Executive Secretary

Canadian Association for Dental Research (CADR) / Association canadienne de recherches dentaires (ACRD)
c/o Dr. C. Birek, Faculty of Dentistry, University of Manitoba, 780 Bannatyne Ave., Winnipeg MB R3E 0W2
Tel: 204-789-3256; *Fax:* 204-789-3913
birek@ms.umanitoba.ca
www.cadr-acrd.ca
To advance research & increase knowledge in order to improve oral health in Canada; To support & represent Canadian oral health researchers
Edward Putnins, President
Michael Greene, President, CADR Student Research Group
Debora Matthews, Vice-President
Catalena Birek, Secretary-Treasurer

Canadian Association of Orthodontists (CAO) / Association canadienne des orthodontists (aco)
#310, 2175 Sheppard Ave. East, Toronto ON M2J 1W8
Tel: 416-491-3186; *Fax:* 416-491-1670
Toll-Free: 877-226-8800
cao@taylorenterprises.com
www.cao-aco.org
To advance the science & art of orthodontics; To promote the highest quality of orthodontic care in Canada; To act as the official voice of Canadian orthodontic specialists
Howard Steiman, President
Paul Major, First Vice-President
Garry A. Solomon, Second Vice-President
Michael W. Patrician, Secretary-Treasurer
Dan Pollit, Chair, Communications

Canadian Dental Assistants Association (CDAA) / Association canadienne des assistants(es) dentaires (ACAD)
#202, 110 Clarence St., Ottawa ON K1N 5P6
Tel: 613-521-5495; *Fax:* 613-521-5572
Toll-Free: 800-345-5137
info@cdaa.ca
www.cdaa.ca
Social Media:
twitter.com/CDAA_ACAD
Strives to foster opportunities for growth, to be the voice for Canadian dental assistants, & to represent the interests of provincial & military dental associations
Calla Effa, President
Michelle Fowler, Vice-President

Canadian Dental Association (CDA) / L'Association dentaire canadienne (ADC)
1815 Alta Vista Dr., Ottawa ON K1G 3Y6
Tel: 613-523-1770; *Fax:* 613-523-7736
reception@cda-adc.ca
www.cda-adc.ca
Social Media:
www.facebook.com/pages/Canadian-Dental-Health/2034526896 66842
twitter.com/mydentalhealth
The authoritative national voice of dentistry, dedicated to the representation & advancement of the profession, nationally & internationally, & to the achievement of optimum oral health
Peter Doig, President

Canadian Dental Hygienists Association (CDHA) / Association canadienne des hygiènistes dentaires
96 Centrepointe Dr., Ottawa ON K2G 6B1
Tel: 613-224-5515; *Fax:* 613-224-7283
Toll-Free: 800-267-5235
info@cdha.ca
www.cdha.ca
Social Media:
www.facebook.com/theCDHA
twitter.com/theCDHA
To act as the collective voice of dental hygiene in Canada; to advance the profession in support of our members; to contribute to the health & well-being of the public.
Ondina Love, Executive Director

Certified Dental Assistants of BC (CDABC)
#504, 602 West Hastings St., Vancouver BC V6B 1P2
Tel: 604-714-1766; *Fax:* 604-714-1767
Toll-Free: 800-579-4440
info@cdabc.org
www.cdabc.org
Marlene Robinson, Executive Director
Arlene Cearns, President

College of Dental Hygienists of Nova Scotia (CDHNS)
Armdale Professional Centre, #11, 2625 Joseph Howe Dr., Halifax NS B3L 4G4
Tel: 902-444-7241; *Fax:* 902-444-7242
info@cdhns.ca
cdhns.ca
To advance the profession & contribute to the health of the public
Wendy Stewart, Chair
Joyce Lind, Vice-President

College of Dental Surgeons of British Columbia (CDSBC)
#500, 1765 West 8th Ave., Vancouver BC V6J 5C6
Tel: 604-736-3621; *Fax:* 604-734-9448
Toll-Free: 800-663-9169
info@cdsbc.org
www.cdsbc.org
Registers, licenses & regulates dentists & certified dental assistants. Assures British Columbians of professional standards of health care, ethics, & competence by regulating dentistry in a fair & reasonable manner; administers the Dentists Act
Jerome Marburg, Registrar & CEO

College of Dental Surgeons of Saskatchewan
Tower at Midtown, #1202, 201 - 1 Ave. South, Saskatoon SK S7K 1J5
Tel: 306-244-5072; *Fax:* 306-244-2476
cdss@saskdentists.com
www.saskdentists.com
To operate as a provincial licensing body
Bernie White, Registrar
Frank Hohn, President
Brent Dergousoff, Vice-President

College of Dental Technologists of Ontario
#300, 2100 Ellesmere Rd., Toronto ON M1H 3B7
Tel: 416-438-5003; *Fax:* 416-438-5004
Toll-Free: 877-391-2386
info@cdto.ca
www.cdto.ca
To serve & protect the public interest by regulating & guiding the dental technology profession
Judy Rigby, Registrar

Dental Association of Prince Edward Island (DAPEI)
184 Belvedere Ave., Charlottetown PE C1A 2Z1
Tel: 902-892-4470
dapei@pei.sympatico.ca
www.dapei.ca
DAPEI sees itself as a partner, a policy advisor, and decision maker with the public, government and its members, regarding the availability, accessibility, and affordibility of appropriate and high quality dental services for islanders.
Travis McLean, President
Brian Barrett, Executive Director

Dental Council of Prince Edward Island
184 Belvedere Ave., Charlottetown PE C1A 2Z1
Tel: 902-892-4470; *Fax:* 902-892-4470

Denturist Association of British Columbia
PO Box 1802, Gibsons BC V0N 1V0
Tel: 604-886-1705
info@denturist.bc.ca
www.denturist.bc.ca
Kore Connolly, President

Denturist Association of Canada (DAC) / Association des denturologistes du Canada (ADC)
66 Dundas St. East, Belleville ON K8N 1C1
Tel: 613-968-9467; *Toll-Free:* 877-538-3123
dacdenturist@bellnet.ca
www.denturist.org
To promote oral health in Canada through the profession of denturism.

Denturist Association of Manitoba
PO Box 69012, RPO Tuxedo Park, Winnipeg MB R3P 2G9
Tel: 204-897-1087; *Fax:* 204-488-2872
administrator@denturistmb.org
www.denturistmb.org
To represent Manitoba denturists & ensure high quality, low cost delivery of dentures direct to the public

Denturist Association of Newfoundland & Labrador
9 Bay Bulls Rd., Kilbride NL A1G 1A2
Tel: 709-364-4813
info@denturistassociationnl.ca
www.denturistassociationnl.ca
To promote denturist as a profession & provide services for its members
Steve Browne, President

Denturist Association of Northwest Territories
PO Box 1506, Yellowknife NT X1A 2P2
Tel: 867-766-3666; *Fax:* 867-669-0103

Denturist Association of Ontario (DAO)
#106, 5780 Timberlea Blvd., Mississauga ON L4W 4W8
Tel: 905-238-6090; *Fax:* 905-238-7090
Toll-Free: 800-284-7311
info@denturistassociation.ca
denturistassociation.ca
To develop services that address current needs & future concerns & are the primary providers of dental prosthetics & related services.
Nancy Tomkins, President
Susan Tobin, Chief Administrative Officer

Denturist Society of Nova Scotia
c/o Della Sangster, 134 Arthur St., Truro NS B2N 1Y1
Tel: 902-893-8010; *Fax:* 902-893-1094
info@nsdenturistsociety.ca
www.nsdenturistsociety.ca
Della Sangster, Vice President

Denturist Society of Prince Edward Island
Down East Mall, PO Box 1589, 500 Main St., Montague PE C0A 1R0
Tel: 902-569-5511; *Fax:* 902-692-2607
David Murphy, Registrar

Manitoba Dental Assistants Association
#17, 595 Clifton St., Winnipeg MB R3G 2X5
Tel: 204-586-7378; *Fax:* 204-783-9631
mdaa@mdaa.ca
www.mdaa.ca

Manitoba Dental Association (MDA)
#103, 698 Corydon Ave., Winnipeg MB R3M 0X9
Tel: 204-988-5300; *Fax:* 204-988-5310
office@manitobadentist.ca
www.manitobadentist.ca
To act as the governing body for dentists & dental assistants in Manitoba; To ensure that that the oral health of Manitobans is met
Joel Antel, President
Allan Cogan, Vice-President
Rafi Mohammed, Sec.-Treas.

National Dental Examining Board of Canada / Le bureau national d'examen dentaire du Canada
80 Elgin St., 2nd Fl., Ottawa ON K1P 6R2
Tel: 613-236-5912; *Fax:* 613-236-8386
director@ndeb.ca
www.ndeb.ca
To establish qualifying conditions for a national standard of dental competence for general practitioners; to establish & maintain an examination facility to test for this national standard of dental competence; to issue certificates to dentists who successfully meet this national standard.
W. Judson, President

New Brunswick Dental Assistants Association (NBDAA) / Association des Assistantes Dentaires du Nouveau-Brunswick (AADNB)
PO Box 8997, Shediac NB E4P 8W5
Tel: 506-532-9189; *Fax:* 506-532-3635
Toll-Free: 866-530-9189
nbdaa.ca
Social Media:
www.facebook.com/pages/NBDAA/309506835839025
To provide opportunities Dental Assistants in New Brunswick.
Amber Caissie, President
Bernice Léger, Office Coordinator

New Brunswick Dental Society / Société dentaire du Nouveau-Brunswick
HSBC Place, PO Box 488, Stn. A, #820, 520 King St., Fredericton NB E3B 4Z9
Tel: 506-452-8575; *Fax:* 506-452-1872
nbds@nb.aibn.com
www.nbdental.com
Social Media:
www.facebook.com/NBDentalSociety
twitter.com/NBDentalNB
To regulate & promote the dentistry profession in New Brunswick. To promote professional growth, high ethical standards and quality care giving through communication, education, and regulation of denistry in New Brunswick.
Lia A. Daborn, Executive Director

New Brunswick Denturists Society / Société des denturologistes du Nouveau-Brunswick
PO Box 5566, 288 West St. Pierre Blvd., Caraquet NB E1W 1B7
Tel: 506-727-7411; *Fax:* 506-727-6728
www.nbdenturistsociety.ca
Daniel J. Robichaud, President
Claudette Boudreau, Administrative Assistnat

Newfoundland & Labrador Dental Association
#102, 1 Centennial St., Mount Pearl NL A1N 0C9
Tel: 709-579-2362; *Fax:* 709-579-1250
nfdental@nfld.net
www.nlda.net
To promote & advance dentistry or dental surgery & related arts & sciences in all their branches; to increase the knowledge, skill, standard & proficiency of its members in the practice of dentistry or dental surgery; to maintain the honour & integrity of the dental profession; to aid in the furtherance of measures designed to improve dental health & prevent disease & disability; to cooperate with & to assist public & private dental associations, agencies & commissions in the task of providing or financing dental care; to promote measures designed to improve standards of dental care & the practice of dentistry or dental surgery; to improve the welfare & social standards of its members & encourage the cooperation of its members in the protection of their rights.
Anthony Patey, Executive Director

Newfoundland & Labrador Dental Board
#204, 49-55 Elizabeth Ave., St. John's NL A1A 1W9
Tel: 709-579-2391; *Fax:* 709-579-2392
nldb@nf.aibn.com
nldb.ca
To establish qualifying conditions for a national standard of dental competence for general practitioners; to establish & maintain an examination facility to test for this national standard of dental competence & to issue certificates to dentists who successfully meet this national standard.
Paul O'Brien, Secretary-Registrar

Newfoundland Dental Assistants Association (NLDAA)
#274, 38 Pearson St., St. John's NL A1A 3R1
Tel: 709-579-2391
nldaa@yahoo.ca
www.nldaa.ca
To advance the career of dental assisting in Newfoundland
Vera Walsh, President

Northwest Territories & Nunavut Dental Association
PO Box 283, Yellowknife NT X1A 2N2
Tel: 867-873-6416; *Fax:* 877-389-6876
nwtnudentalassoc@theedge.ca
nwtnudentalassociation.ca
Roger Armstrong, President

Nova Scotia Dental Assistants' Association (NSDAA)
PO Box 9142, Stn. A, Halifax NS B3K 5M8
Tel: 902-405-1122; *Fax:* 902-405-1133
nsdaa@eastlink.ca
www.nsdaa.ca
To affiliate at local, provincial & national levels for the betterment of the dental assistant profession & patient care
Michelle Fowler, President
Lynda Foran, Executive Director

Nova Scotia Dental Association (NSDA)
#101, 1559 Brunswick St., Halifax NS B3J 2G1
Tel: 902-420-0088; *Fax:* 902-423-6537
nsda@eastlink.ca
www.nsdental.org
To help dentists in Nova Scotia better serve their patients

Ontario Dental Assistants Association (ODAA)
869 Dundas St., London ON N5W 2Z8
Tel: 519-679-2566; *Fax:* 519-679-8494
info@odaa.org
www.odaa.org
Social Media:
www.facebook.com/yourODAA
To act as the certifying body for dental assistants in Ontario
Jennifer Gill, President
Nancy Niely, Vice-President
Judy Melville, Executive Director

Ontario Dental Association (ODA)
4 New St., Toronto ON M5R 1P6
Tel: 416-922-3900; *Fax:* 416-922-9005
Toll-Free: 800-387-1393
info@oda.ca
www.oda.ca
Social Media: www.youtube.com/user/OntarioDentalAssoc
www.facebook.com/203452689666842
To represent the dentists of Ontario; to provide exemplary oral health care & promote the attainment of optimal health for the people of Ontario
Rick Caldwell, President
Gerald Smith, President-Elect
Victor Kutcher, Vice-President
Tom Magyarody, Executive Director

Ordre des dentistes du Québec (ODQ)
#1640, 800, boul René-Lévesque ouest, Montréal QC H3B 1X9
Tél: 514-875-8511; *Téléc:* 514-393-9248
Ligne sans frais: 800-361-4887
www.odq.qc.ca
Mèdia social: www.youtube.com/webmestreodq
www.facebook.com/102225303175310
twitter.com/ordredentistes
Assurer la qualité des services en médecine dentaire par le respect de normes élevées de pratique et d'éthique et de promouvoir la santé bucco-dentaire auprès de la population du Québec
Caroline Daoust, Directrice générale et secrétaire

Ordre des denturologistes du Québec (ODQ)
395, rue du Parc-Industriel, Longueuil QC J4H 3V7
Tél: 450-646-7922; *Téléc:* 450-646-2509
Ligne sans frais: 800-567-2251
info@odq.com
www.odq.com
Monique Bouchard, Directrice générale et secrétaire
Robert Cabana, Président

Provincial Dental Board of Nova Scotia
#102, 1559 Brunswick St., Halifax NS B3J 2G1
Tel: 902-420-0083; *Fax:* 902-492-0301
admin@pdbns.ca
www.pdbns.ca
To protect the public in the delivery of dental care by licensure & regulation
Martin Gillis, Registrar

Royal College of Dental Surgeons of Ontario
6 Crescent Rd., Toronto ON M4W 1T1
Tel: 416-961-6555; *Fax:* 416-961-5814
Toll-Free: 800-565-4591
info@rcdso.org
www.rcdso.org
To operate as the governing body for dentists in Ontario; To protect the public's right to quality dental services by providing leadership to the dental profession in self-regulation
Irwin W. Fefergrad, Registrar
Ronald Yarascavitch, President

Royal College of Dentists of Canada (RCDC) / Collège Royal des Chirurgiens Dentistes du Canada
#2404, 180 Dundas St. West, Toronto ON M3G 1Z8
Tel: 416-512-6571; *Fax:* 416-512-6468
office@rcdc.ca
www.rcdc.ca
To provide examinations for dental sciences & for nationally recognized dental specialties in Canada
Hugh Lamont, President
Christopher Robinson, Vice-President
Peter McCutcheon, Secretary
Garnet Packota, Acting Registrar
Paul Jackson, Examiner-in-Chief

Saskatchewan Dental Assistants' Association (SDAA)
PO Box 294, 603 - 3rd St., Kenaston SK S0G 2N0
Tel: 306-252-2769; *Fax:* 306-252-2089
sdaa@sasktel.net
www.sdaa.sk.ca
To promote excellence in dental health care; To advance public protection through enforcement of regulations, education, ethical practice, & standardization
Susan Anholt, Executive Director
Calla Effa, President
Robin McKay Ganshorn, Coordinator, Professional Development

Yukon Denturist Association
#1, 106 Main St., Whitehorse YT Y1A 2A7
Tel: 867-668-6818; *Fax:* 867-668-6811

Developing Countries

Canadian Christian Relief & Development Association (CCRDA)
374 North Scugog Crt., Bowmanville ON L1C 3K2
Tel: 289-385-7307; *Fax:* 519-885-5225
ccrdacoordinator@gmail.com
www.ccrda.ca
Building partnerships to effectively provide emergency relief, facilitate sustainable development, promote justice, and speak with one voice on behalf of the world's poor and disadvantaged peoples.

Dignitas International
#35, 550 Queen St. East, Toronto ON M5A 1V2
Tel: 416-260-3100; *Toll-Free:* 866-576-3100
info@dignitasinternational.org
dignitasinternational.org
Social Media: www.instagram.com/dignitasintl;
www.youtube.com/dignitasonline
linkedin.com/company/dignitas-international
www.facebook.com/DignitasInternational
twitter.com/dignitasintl
To improve access to quality health care for people facing a high burden of disease & unequal access to services; To educate health care workers in remote areas on ways to treat HIV, TB, & malaria; To work towards the eradication of the AIDS epidemic in Malawi
Heather Johnston, President & Chief Executive Officer
Emmay Mah, Director, Programs & Policy
Joep Van Oosterhout, Director, Medical & Research

Teamwork Children's Services International
5983 Ladyburn Cres., Mississauga ON L5M 4V9
Tel: 905-542-1047
jchacha@teamworkchildrenservices.com
www.teamworkchildrenservices.com
To provide orphaned & disadvantaged children in rural areas of Africa a safe & secure faith-based home environment; To provide the children with good health, education, & vocational training, enabling them to become self-supporting & productive citizens
Joel Chacha, Program Director

Disabled Persons

AboutFace
PO Box 72, 1057 Steeles Ave. West, Toronto ON M2R 3X1
Tel: 416-597-2229; *Fax:* 416-597-8494
Toll-Free: 800-665-3223
info@aboutface.ca
aboutface.ca
Social Media:
www.youtube.com/user/AboutFaceEvents?feature=mhum
linkedin.com/pub/anna-pileggi/a/7a2/91a
www.facebook.com/191138150916182
twitter.com/AboutFace0
To provide emotional support & information to, & on behalf of, individuals who have a facial difference & their families
Anna Pileggi, Executive Director

Alberta Association of Rehabilitation Centres (AARC)
#19, 3220 - 5 Ave. NE, Calgary AB T2A 5N1
Tel: 403-250-9495; *Fax:* 403-291-9864
acds@acds.ca
www.acds.ca

To support organizations that provide services & supports to people with disabilities; To act as a voice for the field of community rehabilitation to the political & administrative arms of government; To focus on human resource initiatives for the services sector; To provide in-service training opportunities for people employed in the field; To accredit & certify service in Alberta
Ann Nicol, CEO
Helen Ficocelli, President
Bob Diewold, Vice-President

Alberta Committee of Citizens with Disabilities (ACCD)
#106, 10423 - 178 St. NW, Edmonton AB T5S 1R5
Tel: 780-488-9088; *Fax:* 780-488-3757
Toll-Free: 800-387-2514
accd@accd.net
www.accd.net
Social Media:
www.facebook.com/accdisabilities
twitter.com/accdisabilities
To promote full participation in society for Albertans with disabilities
Beverley D. Matthiessen, Executive Director

Alberta Easter Seals Society
#103, 811 Manning Rd. NE, Calgary AB T2E 7L4
Tel: 403-235-5662; *Fax:* 403-248-1716
Toll-Free: 877-732-7837
calgary@easterseals.ab.ca
www.easterseals.ab.ca
Social Media: pinterest.com/clienttell
www.facebook.com/EasterSealsAlberta
twitter.com/eastersealsAB
To represent interests of all people with disabilities in Alberta; to promote change at all policy-making levels through public awareness campaigns, projects, seminars; to provide mobility equipment; to conduct public awareness programs; to provide recreational activities through summer camp - Camp Horizon; to provide a residential home program - Easter Seals McQueen Residence
Susan Boivin, Chief Executive Officer

ARCH Disability Law Centre
#110, 425 Bloor St. East, Toronto ON M4W 3R5
Tel: 416-482-8255; *Fax:* 416-482-2981
Toll-Free: 866-482-2724
TTY: 416-482-1254
archlib@lao.on.ca
www.archdisabilitylaw.ca
Social Media:
www.youtube.com/channel/UCZI_6YpK8XB7LJ_dQxdonlg
www.facebook.com/ARCHDisabilityLawCentre
twitter.com/ARCHDisability
To defend & advance the equality rights of persons with disabilities; assisting individuals with disabilities to understand their rights & how to enforce them; working with groups representing people with disabilities throughout Ontario; representing in precedent setting cases where client cannot be represented appropriately by other legal services; summary advice & referral - lawyers who specialize in areas of law as they relate to disability provide free, confidential, basic legal advice & referral to other sources of assistance
Ivana Petricone, Executive Director

Association du Québec pour enfants avec problèmes auditifs (AQEPA)
3700, rue Berri, #A-446, Montréal QC H2L 4G9
Tél: 514-842-8706; *Téléc:* 514-842-4006
Ligne sans frais: 877-842-4006
info@aqepa.org
www.aqepa.org
Média social: www.facebook.com/AQEPA
Regrouper les parents d'enfants sourds et malentendants; informer et sensibiliser les parents et le public

Association du Québec pour l'intégration sociale / Institut québécois de la déficience intellectuelle (AQIS-IQDI) / Québec Association for Community Living / Québec Institute for Intellectual Disability
3958, rue Dandurand, Montréal QC H1X 1P7
Tél: 514-725-7245; *Téléc:* 514-725-2796
info@aqis-iqdi.qc.ca
www.aqis-iqdi.qc.ca
Média social: www.facebook.com/151177351568742
Défendre les droits et promouvoir les intérêts des personnes ayant une déficience intellectuelle
Jacqueline Babin, Présidente
Diane Milliard, Directrice générale

Association for Vaccine Damaged Children
c/o Mary James, 67 Shier Dr., Winnipeg MB R3R 2H2
To inform parents of the risks of immunization; To support parents in any challenging situation with public health authorities
Mary James, Contact

Association québécoise pour le loisir des personnes handicapées (AQLPH)
CP 1000, Succ. M, 4545, av Pierre-de Coubertin, Montréal QC H1V 3R2
Tél: 514-252-3144
info@aqlph.qc.ca
www.aqlph.qc.ca
Promouvoir le droit à un loisir de qualité (éducatif, sécuritaire, valorisant et de détente); promouvoir la participation et la libre expression de la personne face à son loisir; promouvoir l'accès à tous les champs d'application du loisir (tourisme, plein air, sport et activité physique, loisir scientifique, socio-éducatif et socioculturel) pour toutes les personnes handicapées du Québec sans restriction d'âge, de sexe, ni de type d'handicap
Guylaine Laforest, Directrice générale

BALANCE for Blind Adults
#302, 4920 Dundas St. West, Toronto ON M9A 1B7
Tel: 416-236-1796; *Fax:* 416-236-4280
info@balancefba.org
www.balancefba.org
Social Media:
www.facebook.com/balanceforblindadults
twitter.com/balancefba
To provide instruction & support to individuals with visual impairment to enable them to live independently & confidently in their community; To promote independence, decision making, & self-fulfillment
Susan Archibald, Executive Director

BC People First Society
BC
www.selfadvocatenet.com
Social Media:
www.facebook.com/bcpeoplefirst/timeline?ref=page_internal
To change attitudes towards individuals with disabilities; To encourage self-advocacy among individuals with disabilities; To provide information & mentoring services; To raise public awareness about disabilities in the community
Bryce Schaufelberger, Contact

The Bob Rumball Centre for the Deaf (BRCD)
2395 Bayview Ave., Toronto ON M2L 1A2
Tel: 416-449-9651; *Fax:* 416-449-8881
TTY: 416-449-2728
info@bobrumball.org
www.bobrumball.org
Social Media:
www.facebook.com/86097284911
To provide opportunities for a higher quality of life for deaf people while preserving & promoting their language & culture; to foster & develop good relations with the community at large & actively promote the Centre; to work closely with the various ministries of the provincial government & related agencies.
Alistair M. Fraser, Chairman

British Columbia Coalition of People with Disabilities (BCCPD)
#204, 456 West Broadway, Vancouver BC V5Y 1R3
Tel: 604-875-0188; *Fax:* 604-875-9227
Toll-Free: 800-663-1278
TTY: 604-875-8835
feedback@bccpd.bc.ca
www.bccpd.bc.ca
To raise public & political awareness of issues concerning people with disabilities; to facilitate full participation of disabled people in society by promoting independence & the self-help model; to lobby government on policies & attitudes which affect people with disabilities
Pat Danforth, President

Canadian Abilities Foundation
#803, 255 Duncan Mill Rd., Toronto ON M3B 3H9
Tel: 416-421-7944; *Fax:* 416-421-8418
abilities@bcsgroup.com
www.abilities.ca
Social Media:
twitter.com/abilitiescanada
To provide information, inspiration & opportunity to Canadians with disabilities
Cameron Graham, Chair

Canadian Association for Community Living (CACL) / Association canadienne pour l'intégration communautaire
Kinsmen Building, York University, 4700 Keele St., Toronto ON M3J 1P3
Tel: 416-661-9611; *Fax:* 416-661-5701
inform@cacl.ca
www.cacl.ca
Social Media: www.youtube.com/canadianacl
www.facebook.com/canadianacl
twitter.com/cacl_acic
To ensure the following for people with intellectual disabilities: the same rights, & access to choice, services, & supports as others; the same opportunities to live in freedom & dignity with the necessary supports to do so; & the ability to articulate & realize their rights & aspirations
Laurie Larson, President
Michael Bach, Executive Vice-President
John Cairns, Director, Finance & Administration
Cam Crawford, Director, Research & Knowledge Management
Doris Rajan, Director, Social Development & Public Education
Neil Wiernik, Manager, Online Community & Communications

Canadian Association of the Deaf (CAD) / Association des sourds du Canada (ASC)
#303, 251 Bank St., Ottawa ON K2P 1X3
Tel: 613-565-2882; *Fax:* 613-565-1207
TTY: 613-565-8882
info@cad.ca
www.cad.ca
To protect & promote the rights, needs, & concerns of deaf Canadians
Frank Folino, President
Marie-Josée Blier, Secretary

The Canadian Council of the Blind (CCB) / Le Conseil canadien des aveugles
#100, 20 James St., Ottawa ON K2P 0T6
Tel: 613-567-0311; *Fax:* 613-567-2728
Toll-Free: 877-304-0968
www.ccbnational.net
Social Media:
www.facebook.com/ccbnational?v=wall
twitter.com/ccbnational
To promote the well-being of individuals who are blind or vision-impaired through higher education, profitable employment, & social association; To create a closer relationship between blind & sighted friends; To organize a nation-wide organization of people who are blind & vision-impaired & groups of blind persons throughout Canada; To promote measures for the conservation of sight & the prevention of blindness
Louise Gillis, National President
Lori Fry, First Vice-President
Jim Tokos, Second Vice-President

Canadian Council on Rehabilitation & Work (CCRW) / Le Conseil canadien de la réadaptation et du travail (CCRT)
#1202, 1 Yonge St., Toronto ON M5E 1E5
Tel: 416-260-3060; *Fax:* 416-260-3093
Toll-Free: 800-664-0925
TTY: 416-260-9223
info@ccrw.org
www.ccrw.org
To improve employment opportunities for persons with disabilities in Canada; To promote the equitable & meaningful employment of persons with disabilities
Carole J. Barron, President & Chief Executive Officer
Venatius Babu, Chief Financial Officer
Georgia Whalen, Director, Information Technology & Standards
Elizabeth Smith, Manager, Employer Consultations & Partnerships
Monica Winkler, Senior Administrator

Canadian Cultural Society of The Deaf, Inc. (CCSD)
The Distillery Historic District, 34 Distillery Lane, Toronto ON M5A 3C4
info@deafculturecentre.ca
www.deafculturecentre.ca
Social Media:
www.facebook.com/pages/Deaf-Culture-Centre/93708438725
twitter.com/DeafCulture
To ensure that the cultural needs of deaf & hard-of-hearing people are being met; To concentrate efforts in the areas of the performing arts, sign language, deaf literature, the visual arts, & heritage resources
Joanne Cripps, Executive Director

Canadian Deafblind Association (National) (CDBA) / Association canadienne de la surdicécité (Bureau National)
2000 Appleby Line, Burlington ON L7L 7H7
Fax: 905-319-2027
Toll-Free: 866-229-5832
info@cdbanational.com
www.cdbanational.com
Social Media:
www.facebook.com/cdbanational
twitter.com/CDBANational
To promote awareness, education & support for people who are deafblind, in order to enhance their well-being
Carolyn Monaco, President
Tom McFadden, National Executive Director

Canadian Foundation for Physically Disabled Persons (CFPDP)
#265, 6 Garamond Ct., Toronto ON M3C 1Z5
Tel: 416-760-7351; *Fax:* 416-760-9405
whynot@sympatico.ca
www.cfpdp.com
To provide financial assistance to organizations sharing concern for physically disabled adults; to help create awareness in the public & business communities, & in government of the needs of physically disabled adults in the areas of housing, employment, education, accessibility, sports & recreation, & research.
Vim Kochhar, Chair
Dorothy Price, Executive Director

Canadian Guide Dogs for the Blind (CGDB)
National Office & Training Centre, PO Box 280, 4120 Rideau Valley Dr. North, Manotick ON K4M 1A3
Tel: 613-692-7777; *Fax:* 613-692-0650
info@guidedogs.ca
www.guidedogs.ca
To assist visually-impaired Canadians with their mobility by providing & training them in the use of professionally trained guide dogs
Jane Thornton, Co-Founder & Chief Operating Officer

Canadian Hard of Hearing Association (CHHA) / Association des malentendants canadiens (AMEC)
#205, 2415 Holly Lane, Ottawa ON K1V 7P2
Tel: 613-526-1584; *Fax:* 613-526-4718
Toll-Free: 800-263-8068
TTY: 613-526-2692
chhanational@chha.ca
www.chha.ca
Social Media:
www.facebook.com/144214962320170
twitter.com/CHHA_AMEC
To act as the voice of all hard of hearing Canadians; To promote the integration of hard of hearing people into society
Robert Corbeil, Executive Director
Myrtle Barrett, President

Canadian Hearing Society (CHS) / Société canadienne de l'ouïe
271 Spadina Rd., Toronto ON M5R 2V3
Tel: 416-928-2535; *Fax:* 416-928-2506
Toll-Free: 877-347-3427
TTY: 877-216-7310
info@chs.ca
www.chs.ca
Social Media: www.youtube.com/user/CHSCanadaTV
www.facebook.com/pages/The-Canadian-Hearing-Society/1646 04840229034
twitter.com/wwwCHSca
To provide services that enhance the independence of deaf, deafened, & hard of hearing people, & that encourage prevention of hearing loss
Julia Dumanian, President/CEO
Stephanus Greeff, Vice-President, Finance & Corporate Services
Gary Malkowski, Vice-President, Stakeholder & Employer Relations

Canadian National Institute for the Blind (CNIB) / INCA (INCA)
1929 Bayview Ave., Toronto ON M4G 3E8
Toll-Free: 800-563-2642
info@cnib.ca
www.cnib.ca
Social Media: www.youtube.com/cnibnatcomm
www.facebook.com/myCNIB
twitter.com/CNIB
To ameliorate the condition of persons with vision loss in Canada; To prevent blindness; To promote sight enhancement services; To direct services to more than 100,000 Canadians with vision loss, provided through a network of more than 57 service centres, within 13 provincial & territorial operating divisions; To provide library services, research, advocacy, public education, & accessible design consulting; To produce materials in alternative formats, including Braille & DAISY talking books; To supply assistive technologies for persons with vision loss
John M. Rafferty, President
Craig Lillico, CFO, Treasurer, & Vice-President
Margaret McGrory, Executive Director & Vice-President, CNIB Library
Tim Alcock, Vice-President, Marketing & Fund Development
Keith Gordon, Vice-President, Research

Centre de réadaptation Constance-Lethbridge (CRCL) / Constance Lethbridge Rehabilitation Centre
7005, boul de Maisonneuve Ouest, Montréal QC H4B 1T3
Tél: 514-487-1770; *Ligne sans frais:* 866-487-1891
www.constance-lethbridge.qc.ca
Média social:
linkedin.com/company/centre-de-readaptation-constance-lethbridge-r
www.facebook.com/ConstanceLethbridge
Offrer des services spécialisés et ultraspécialisés à des adultes ayant une déficience motrice, en externe ou à domicile, de réadaptation, d'adaptation, de préparation et de support à l'intégration sociale ou professionnelle aux clientèles ayant des problèmes orthopédiques, neurologiques et rhumatologiques; offrer aussi une expertise d'évaluation de la conduite automobile, d'évaluation et d'orientation des capacités de travail de la personne handicapée

Community Living Manitoba
#6, 120 Maryland St., Winnipeg MB R3G 1L1
Tel: 204-786-1607; *Fax:* 204-789-9850
aclmb@aclmb.ca
www.aclmb.ca
Social Media:
www.facebook.com/370890112967949
twitter.com/aclmanitoba
To promote the welfare of people with handicaps & their families; To speak on behalf of people with developmental disabilities in Manitoba; To ensure that every person in Manitoba has access to supports necessary to live with dignity & to participate fully in the community of his/her choice
Terry Masse, Co-President
Val Surbey, Co-President
Anne Kresta, Project Manager
Cheryl Duffy, Office Manager

Community Living Ontario (CLO) / Intégration communautaire Ontario
#201, 1 Valleybrook Dr., Toronto ON M3B 2S7
Tel: 416-447-4348; *Fax:* 416-447-8974
Toll-Free: 800-278-8025
info@communitylivingontario.ca
www.communitylivingontario.ca
Social Media: www.youtube.com/user/comlivon
www.facebook.com/communitylivingontario
twitter.com/CLOntario
To lobby on behalf of people with intellectual disablilities in Ontario; To ensure that every person in Ontario has access to supports to live with dignity & to participate in the community of his/her choice
Chris Beesley, CEO
Ron Laroche, Director, Communications, Marketing & Fund Development
Keith Dee, Director, Membership Services
Gordon Kyle, Director, Social Policy & Government Relations
Kimberly Gavan, Director, Community Development

Council of Canadians with Disabilities (CCD) / Conseil des Canadiens avec déficiences
#926, 294 Portage Ave., Winnipeg MB R3C 0B9
Tel: 204-947-0303
TTY: 204-947-4757
ccd@ccdonline.ca
www.ccdonline.ca
Social Media: www.youtube.com/ccdonline
www.facebook.com/ccdonline
twitter.com/ccdonline
To improve the status of disabled citizens in Canadian society; to promote self-help for persons with disabilities; to provide a democratic structure for disabled citizens to voice concerns; to monitor federal legislation; to share information & cooperate with disabled persons' organizations in Canada & in other countries; to establish a positive image of disabled Canadians
Laurie Beachell, National Coordinator
Tony Dolan, Chair

DIRECTIONS Council for Vocational Services Society
#920, 99 Wyse Rd., Dartmouth NS B3A 4S5
Tel: 902-466-2220; *Fax:* 902-461-2220
www.directionscouncil.org
To promote the abilities & inclusion of persons with disabilities by supporting member agencies
Bob Bennett, President

DisAbled Women's Network of Canada / Réseau d'Action des Femmes Handicapées du Canada
#505, 110, rue Ste. Thérèse, Montréal QC H2Y 1E6
Tel: 514-396-0009; *Fax:* 514-396-6585
Toll-Free: 866-396-0074
admin@dawncanada.net
www.dawncanada.net
Social Media:
www.facebook.com/dawnrafhcanada
DAWN Canada's mission is to end the poverty, isolation, discrimination & violence experienced by women with disabilities; to ensure that they get the services & support needed, as well as the access to opportunities granted non-disabled people; to engage all levels of government & the wider disability & women's sectors & other stakeholders in addressing key issues.
Carmela Sebastiana Hutchison, President
Bonnie L. Brayton, National Executive Director

The Easter Seal Society (Ontario) (TESS) / Société du timbre de Pâques de l'Ontario
#700, 1 Concorde Gate, Toronto ON M3C 3C6
Tel: 416-421-8377; *Fax:* 416-696-1035
Toll-Free: 800-668-6252
info@easterseals.org
www.easterseals.org
Social Media: www.youtube.com/user/Eastersealsont
linkedin.com/company/107859
www.facebook.com/MoneyMart24HourRelay
twitter.com/eastersealsont
To help children with physical disabilities achieve their full individual potential & future independence
Duncan Hawthorne, Chair
Carol Lloyd, President & CEO

Easter Seals Canada / Timbres de Pâques Canada
#401, 40 Holly St., Toronto ON M4S 3C3
Tel: 416-932-8382; *Fax:* 416-932-9844
Toll-Free: 877-376-6362
info@easterseals.ca
www.easterseals.ca
Social Media:
www.facebook.com/eastersealscanada
twitter.com/easterseals
To enhance the quality of life, self-esteem, & self-determination of Canadians with physical disabilities; To support the social & economic integration of people with disabilities
Dave Starrett, Chief Executive Officer
Alex Krievins, National Director, Programs & Development
Frank Williamson, Director, Finance

Easter Seals New Brunswick (ESNB) / Les Timbres de Pâques N.-B.
65 Brunswick St., Fredericton NB E3B 1G5
Tel: 506-458-8739; *Fax:* 506-457-2863
info@easterseals.nb.ca
www.easterseals.nb.ca
Social Media:
www.facebook.com/246795441998452
twitter.com/EasterSealsNB
To provide rehabilitation services & programs to persons with disabilities in New Brunswick; To improve public attitudes towards disabled persons; To provide disabled persons with new opportunities; to provide orthopedic appliances, rehabilitative equipment, technical aids & computers; To advocate on behalf of disabled persons; To serve as information resource centre for disabled persons, students, the public & health professionals; To hold the franchise for the Easter Seals campaign; To provide interprovincial transportation assistance to treatment & diagnostic centres
Julia Latham, Executive Director

Easter Seals Newfoundland & Labrador
Husky Energy Easter Seals House, 206 Mount Scio Rd., St. John's NL A1B 4L5
Tel: 709-754-1399; *Fax:* 709-754-1398
info@easterseals.nf.ca
www.easterseals.nf.ca
Social Media:
linkedin.com/company/easter-seals-newfoundland-and-labrador
www.facebook.com/EasterSealsNL
twitter.com/eastersealsnl

To maximize the abilities & enhancing the lives of children & youth with physical disabilities through recreational, social & other therapeutic programs, direct assistance, education & advocacy
Mark Bradbury, Chief Executive Officer

Easter Seals Nova Scotia (AFNS)
3670 Kempt Rd., Halifax NS B3K 4X8
Tel: 902-453-6000
mailing@easterseals.ns.ca
www.easterseals.ns.ca
Social Media: www.youtube.com/user/eastersealsns
www.facebook.com/ESnovascotia
twitter.com/Eastersealsns
To enable Nova Scotians with physical disabilities to enhance their quality of life by realizing their individual potential
Henk van Leeuwen, President & CEO

Entrepreneurs with Disabilities Network (EDN)
PO Box 44, #504, 5475 Spring Garden Rd., Halifax NS B3J 3T2
ednns.ca
Social Media:
www.facebook.com/EntrepreneurswithDisabilitiesNetwork
twitter.com/EDNns
To encourage entrepreneurship to people with disabilities; to understand the needs of entrepreneurs with disabilities & to represent them; to work on behalf of entrepreneurs with disabilities to advise government, business service providers & others on how best to serve them
Brian Aird, Executive Director

La fédération des mouvements personne d'abord du Québec
3958, rue Dandurand, #S-4, Montréal QC
Tél: 514-723-7507; *Téléc:* 514-723-2517
Ligne sans frais: 877-475-1617
fmpdaq@bellnet.ca
www.fmpdaq.org
Défendre les droits et intérêts des personnes ayant une déficience intellectuelle; Promouvoir l'auto-défense
Françoise Charbonneau, Coordinatrice

Handicap International Canada
#400, 50, rue Sainte-Catherine ouest, Montréal QC H2X 3V4
Tel: 514-908-2813; *Fax:* 514-937-6685
Toll-Free: 877-908-2813
info@handicap-international.ca
www.handicap-international.ca
Social Media: www.youtube.com/user/HandicapInterCan
www.facebook.com/Handicap.International.Canada
twitter.com/HI_Canada
To provide assistance through work in various fields for people in developing countries with disabilities; To prevent disabilities through the clearing of anti-personnel mines & cluster munitions; To provide support for disabled persons in the aftermath of natural disasters and other humanitarian crises
Jérôme Bobin, Executive Director

Inclusion Alberta (AACL)
11724 Kingsway Ave., Edmonton AB T5G 0X5
Tel: 780-451-3055; *Fax:* 780-453-5779
Toll-Free: 800-252-7556
mail@inclusionalberta.org
inclusionalberta.org
Social Media:
linkedin.com/company/3831926
www.facebook.com/InclusionAlberta
twitter.com/inclusionAB
To advocate for fully inclusive community lives for children & adults with developmental disabilities
Bruce Uditsky, Chief Executive Officer
Shawn Ergang, Chief Operating Officer
Trish Bowman, Executive Director, Community Devlopment

Inclusion BC
227 - 6th St., New Westminster BC V3L 3A5
Tel: 604-777-9100; *Fax:* 604-777-9394
Toll-Free: 800-618-1119
info@inclusionbc.org
www.inclusionbc.org
Social Media: www.youtube.com/user/BCACL
www.facebook.com/pages/Inclusion-BC/112557852110381
twitter.com/InclusionBC
To enhance the lives of persons with developmental disabilities & their families; To promote the participation of people with developmental disabilities in all aspects of community life; To support activities dedicated to building inclusive communities that value the diverse abilities of all people
Annette Delaplace, President
Faith Bodnar, Executive Director
Karen De Long, Director, Community Development
Rick O'Brien, Director, Resource Development

Frank Peng, Director, Finance & Administration
Charlotte Kates, Coordinator, Communications

Independent Living Canada (ILC) / Vie autonome Canada (VAC)
#402, 214 Montréal Rd., Ottawa ON K1L 8L8
Tel: 613-563-2581; *Fax:* 613-563-3861
TTY: 613-563-4215
info@ilc-vac.ca
www.ilcanada.ca
To represent & coordinate the network of independent living centres; To guide & support independent living centres in the delivery of programs & services
Cecilia Carroll, National Chair
Steve Lind, Financial Officer

Kinsmen Foundation of British Columbia & Yukon (KRF)
c/o David Owen, #3, 33361 Wren Cres., Abbotsford BC V2S 5V9
Tel: 604-852-4501; *Fax:* 604-852-4501
kinsmenfoundationofbc@shaw.ca
www.kinsmenfoundationofbc.ca
Committed to providing funding for services & technologies empowering British Columbians with physical disabilities to live more independently
David Owen, Volunteer Chief Administrative Officer

LakeCity Employment Services Association
386 Windmill Rd., Dartmouth NS B3A 1J5
Tel: 902-465-5000; *Fax:* 902-465-5009
lesa@lakecityemployment.com
www.lakecityemployment.com
To assist mental health consumers in improving their quality of life by helping them to assume responsibility & independence through work
Andre McConnell, Chair
Chris Fyles, Executive Director

Nanaimo Association for Community Living (NACL)
#201, 96 Cavan St., Nanaimo BC V9L 2V1
Tel: 250-741-0224; *Fax:* 250-741-0227
info@nanaimoacl.com
www.nanaimoacl.com
Social Media:
www.facebook.com/nanaimoacl
To support all people with disabilities to achieve the highest quality of life through participation, independence, inclusion & education
Graham Morry, Executive Director

National Institute of Disability Management & Research (NIDMAR) / Institut national de recherche et de gestion de l'incapacité au travail
c/o Pacific Coast University for Workplace Health Sciences, 4755 Cherry Creek Rd., Port Alberni BC V9Y 0A7
Tel: 778-421-0821; *Fax:* 778-421-0823
nidmar@nidmar.ca
www.nidmar.ca
Committed to reducing the human, social, & economic cost of disability to workers, employers, & society by providing education, research, policy development, & implementation resources to promote workplace-based integration programs
Wolfgang Zimmermann, Executive Director

New Brunswick Association for Community Living (NBACL) / Association du Nouveau-Brunswick pour l'intégration communautaire
800 Hanwell Rd., Fredericton NB E3B 2R7
Tel: 506-453-4400; *Fax:* 506-453-4422
Toll-Free: 866-622-2548
nbacl@nbnet.nb.ca
www.nbacl.nb.ca
Social Media: www.youtube.com/communitylivingnb
www.facebook.com/nbacl
twitter.com/nbacl
To promote the welfare of people with handicaps & their families; To lobby for developmentally disabled people in New Brunswick; To ensure that every person in New Brunswick has access to supports to live with dignity & participate in the community of his/her choice
Krista Carr, Executive Director
Tammy Gallant, Director, Finance & Office Administration

Newfoundland & Labrador Association for Community Living (NLACL)
PO Box 8414, 74 O'Leary Ave., St. John's NL A1B 3N7
Tel: 709-722-0790; *Fax:* 709-722-1325
Toll-Free: 800-701-8511
nlacl@nlacl.ca
www.nlacl.ca
Social Media:
www.facebook.com/nlacl
twitter.com/nlacl1
To develop communities in Newfoundland & Labrador that welcome individuals with developmental disabilities
Dennis Gill, President
Gail St. Croix, Vice-President
Una Tucker, Secretary
Helen O'Rourke, Treasurer
Sherry Gambin-Walsh, Executive Director

Nova Scotia Association for Community Living (NSACL)
#100, 22-24 Dundas St., Dartmouth NS B2Y 4L2
Tel: 902-469-1174; *Fax:* 902-461-0196
nsacl@accesswave.ca
nsacl.wordpress.com
Social Media:
facebook.com/nsacl
twitter.com/NSACL
To work for the benefit of persons of all ages who have an intellectual disability in Nova Scotia; To ensure those with an intellectual disability have the same rights & access as all other persons
Jean Coleman, Executive Director

Nova Scotia Hearing & Speech Foundation
PO Box 120, #401, 5657 Spring Garden Rd., Halifax NS B3S 3R4
Tel: 902-492-8201
contact@hearingandspeech.ca
www.hearingandspeech.ca
Social Media:
twitter.com/NSHSF
To provide hearing services to all Nova Scotians & speech-language services to preschool children & adults; To work with community volunteer leaders, the families & friends of those who are hearing or speech impaired, our partners in government, & the medical & academic communities; To raise funds to support critical Centres' needs
Gordon Moore, Chair

Nunavummi Disabilities Makinnasuaqtiit Society (NDMS) / Société Nunavummi Disabilities Makinnasuaqtiit
PO Box 4212, #105, 8 Storey Bldg., Iqaluit NU X0A 1H0
Tel: 867-979-2228; *Fax:* 867-979-2293
Toll-Free: 877-354-0916
ndms@qiniq.com
www.nuability.ca
To improve the quality of life for people with disabilities in Nunavut through encouragement, advocacy & promotion of opportunities.

Ontario Federation for Cerebral Palsy (OFCP)
#104, 1630 Lawrence Ave. West, Toronto ON M6L 1C5
Tel: 416-244-9686; *Fax:* 416-244-6543
Toll-Free: 877-244-9686
TTY: 866-740-9501
info@ofcp.ca
www.ofcp.ca
Social Media:
www.facebook.com/OntarioFederationforCerebralPalsy
twitter.com/OntarioFCP
To improve the quality of life of persons with cerebral palsy through a broad range of programs, education, support of research & the delivery of needed services to people with cerebral palsy & other physical disabilities & their families.
Cathy Samuelson, Executive Director

Ontario March of Dimes (OMOD) / Marche des dix sous de l'Ontario
10 Overlea Blvd., Toronto ON M4H 1A4
Tel: 416-425-3463; *Fax:* 416-425-1920
Toll-Free: 800-263-3463
www.marchofdimes.ca
Social Media: www.youtube.com/user/marchofdimescda
www.facebook.com/marchofdimescanada
twitter.com/modcanada
To maximize the independence, personal empowerment & community participation of people with physical disabilities
Andria Spindel, President & CEO
Jerry Lucas, Vice-President & COO

Pamiqsaiji Association for Community Living
PO Box 708, Rankin Inlet NU X0C 0G0
Tel: 867-645-2542; *Fax:* 867-645-2543
pamiqad@qiniq.com
Yvonne Cooper, Manager

PEI People First
81 Prince St., Charlottetown PE C1A 4R3
Tel: 902-892-8989
Social Media:
www.facebook.com/312960685412957
To encourage self-advocacy among individuals labelled with an intellectual disability

People First Nova Scotia
568A Prince St., Truro NS B2N 1G3
Tel: 902-893-3033; *Toll-Free:* 877-454-3860
pfns2014@gmail.com
www.peoplefirstns.ca
To promote equality for individuals who have been labelled with an intellectual disability; To promote & encourage self-advocacy among labelled individuals; To educate the community on issues affecting labelled individuals
Cindy Carruthers, Coordinator

People First of Canada (PFC) / Personnes d'abord du Canada
#5, 120 Maryland St., Winnipeg MB R3G 1L1
Tel: 204-784-7362; *Fax:* 204-784-7364
info@peoplefirstofcanada.ca
www.peoplefirstofcanada.ca
Social Media: www.youtube.com/user/PeopleFirstofCanada
www.facebook.com/PeopleFirstofCanada
twitter.com/PeopleFirstCA
To educate the public on issues faced by persons with intellectual disabilities; To promote equality; To work toward the deinstitutionalization of persons with intellectual disabilities
Shelley Fletcher, Executive Director

People First of Manitoba
AB
To promote & educate the community about the values of inclusion; To assist individuals labelled with a disability in living a full & inclusive life

People First of Newfoundland & Labrador
#5A, Limerick Pl., St. John's NL A1B 2H2
peoplefirst@nl.rogers.com
www.peoplefirstnl.ca
To educate the public about issues that affect individuals labelled with a disability; To encourage self-advocacy among labelled individuals

People First of Ontario
#4, 2495 Parkedale Ave., Brockville ON
Tel: 613-213-3214; *Fax:* 613-345-4092
info@peoplefirstontario.ca
www.peoplefirstontario.com
Social Media: www.youtube.com/user/PeopleFirstofCanada
www.facebook.com/peoplefirstontario
twitter.com/people1ontario
To promote equality for all persons; To foster & encourage self-advocacy; To teach members about the rights, abilities, & strengths of individuals labelled with a disability
Richard Ruston, President
Reina Soltis, Coordinator

People First Society of Yukon
PO Box 31478, Whitehorse YT Y1A 6K8
Tel: 867-667-4606; *Fax:* 867-668-8169
peoplefirstyukon@hotmail.com
Social Media:
www.facebook.com/PeopleFirstSocietyOfYukon
To encourage self-advocacy among individuals labelled with an intellectual disability

Prince Edward Island Association for Community Living (PEIACL)
13A Myrtle St., Stratford PE C1B 1P4
Tel: 902-393-3507
familysupport@peiacl.org
www.peiacl.org
Social Media:
www.youtube.com/channel/UCR951HZ9Ah9xD6VjYTsb8mQ
www.facebook.com/PEIACL
twitter.com/PEIACL
To work on behalf of individuals with an intellectual disability & their families; To empower families to increase options available to Islanders with an intellectual disability
Bridget Cairns, Executive Director

Prince Edward Island Council of People with Disabilities (PEICOD)
Landmark Plaza, #2, 5 Lower Malpeque Rd., Charlottetown PE C1E 1R4
Tel: 902-892-9149; *Fax:* 902-566-1919
Toll-Free: 888-473-4263
peicod@peicod.pe.ca
www.peicod.pe.ca
Social Media:
www.facebook.com/PEICOD
To improve the quality of life of people with disabilities on PEI
Marcia Carroll, Executive Director

Saskatchewan Abilities Council
2310 Louise Ave., Saskatoon SK S7J 2C7
Tel: 306-374-4448; *Fax:* 306-373-2665
provincialservices@abilitiescouncil.sk.ca
www.abilitiescouncil.sk.ca
Social Media:
linkedin.com/company/saskatchewan-abilities-council
www.facebook.com/saskatchewanabilitiescouncil
twitter.com/skabilitiesyqr
To enhance the independence & community participation of people of varying abilities in Saskatchewan
Ian Wilkinson, Executive Director

Saskatchewan Association for Community Living (SACL)
3031 Louise St., Saskatoon SK S7J 3L1
Tel: 306-955-3344; *Fax:* 306-373-3070
sacl@sacl.org
www.sacl.org
Social Media: www.youtube.com/SACL3031
www.facebook.com/SaskACL
twitter.com/thesacl
To enhance the lives of individuals with intellectual disabilities throughout Saskatchewan; To develop programs & services to meet the needs of people with intellectual disabilities
Kevin McTavish, Executive Director
Andrea Young, Coordinator, Youth Programs
Bonnie Cherewyk, Advocate, Communications & Research

Silent Voice Canada Inc.
#300, 50 St. Clair Ave. East, Toronto ON M4T 1M9
Tel: 416-463-1104; *Fax:* 416-778-1876
TTY: 416-463-3928
silent.voice@silentvoice.ca
www.silentvoice.ca
Social Media:
www.facebook.com/silentvoice.canada
twitter.com/silentvoiceca
To serve deaf children, deaf youth & adults & their families in the GTA; to improve communication & relationships between the deaf & hearing in families & in our community; to provide services in a sign language environment
Kelly MacKenzie, Executive Director
Mike Cyr, Director, Child & Family Services

Société pour les enfants handicapés du Québec (SEHQ) / Quebec Society for Disabled Children
2300, boul René-Lévesque ouest, Montréal QC H3H 2R5
Tél: 514-937-6171; *Téléc:* 514-937-0082
Ligne sans frais: 877-937-6171
sehq@enfantshandicapes.com
www.enfantshandicapes.com
Média social: www.facebook.com/enfantshandicapes
twitter.com/SEHQ
Voué au bien-être des enfants handicapés et de leur famille; grâce aux contributions publiques qui lui sont versées et aux efforts conjugués de bénévoles et des permanents, la société offre des services directs et professionnels qui favorisent le développement personnel des enfants et leur intégration dans la communauté
Ronald Davidson, Directeur général
Carolle Desjardins, Directrice, Financement
Nicole Amzallag, Séjours de groupes et classes nature

Society for Manitobans with Disabilities Inc. (SMD)
825 Sherbrook St., Winnipeg MB R3A 1M5
Tel: 204-975-3010; *Fax:* 204-975-3073
Toll-Free: 866-282-8041
TTY: 204-784-3012
info@smd.mb.ca
smd.mb.ca
To promote the full participation & equality of people with disabilities: To provide a full range of rehabilitation services; To facilitate the development of a receptive & supportive environment

Special Needs Planning Group
70 Ivy Cres., Stouffville ON L4A 5A9
Tel: 905-640-8285
www.specialneedsplanning.ca
The "Special Needs" Planning Group is an organization that is made up entirely of parents of people with disabilities. They use a team approach to planning using Planners, Lawyers and Accountants, all of whom are specialists in planning for people with disabilities.
Graeme S. Treeby, Contact

The Speech & Stuttering Institute
#2, 150 Duncan Mill Rd., Toronto ON M3B 3M4
Tel: 416-491-7771; *Fax:* 416-491-7215
info@speechandstuttering.com
www.speechandstuttering.com
Social Media:
www.facebook.com/pages/The-Speech-Stuttering-Institute/1218
32407856560
twitter.com/SpchStutterInst
To provide treatment of & foster the development of innovative speech/language therapy programs; to support education & research in communication disorders
Paul L'Heureux, Chair
Robert Kroll, Executive Director

Vecova Centre for Disability Services & Research
3304 - 33 St. NW, Calgary AB T2L 2A6
Tel: 403-284-1121; *Fax:* 403-284-1146
info@vecova.ca
www.vecova.ca
Social Media: www.youtube.com/user/Vecovadisability
linkedin.com/company/vecova
www.facebook.com/Vecova
twitter.com/Vecova
To be leaders in innovative services & research that support persons with disabilities to live as contributing & valued members of the community
John Lee, CEO
Neil MacKenzie, Chair

Vision Institute of Canada (VIC)
York Mills Centre, #110, 16 York Mills Rd., Toronto ON M2P 2E5
Tel: 416-224-2273; *Fax:* 416-224-9234
visioninstitute.optometry.net
To improve the quality of vision care in the community; to provide eye & vision care to persons with special needs
Paul Chris, Executive Director
Catherine Chiarelli, Chief of Clinical Services

Yellowknife Association for Community Living (YKACL)
Abe Miller Bldg., PO Box 981, 4912 - 53 St., Yellowknife NT X1A 2N7
Tel: 867-920-2644; *Fax:* 867-920-2348
info@ykacl.ca
www.ykacl.ca
Social Media:
www.facebook.com/124566867584059
To promote the welfare of people with handicaps & their families; to lobby on behalf of people with developmental disabilities in the Northwest Territories; to ensure that every person in Northwest Territories has access to supports to live with dignity & to participate in the community of his/her choice
Lynn Elkin, Executive Director
Janice McKenna, President
Anita Griffore, Vice-President

Yukon Association for Community Living (YACL)
#7, 4230 - 4 Ave., Whitehorse YT Y1A 1K1
Tel: 867-667-4606; *Fax:* 867-667-4606
yaclwhse@northwestel.net
www.ycommunityliving.com
Social Media:
www.facebook.com/YCommunityLiving
To promote the welfare of people with intellectural disabilities & their families; To ensure that every person in the Yukon has access to supports necessary to live with dignity & to participate fully in the community of his/her choice

Disarmament

Coalition to Oppose the Arms Trade (COAT)
541 McLeod St., Ottawa ON K1R 5R2
Tel: 613-231-3076
overcoat@rogers.com
coat.ncf.ca
To actively oppose the arms trade and support the anti-war movement.
Richard Sanders, Coordinator

Drilling

Alberta Water Well Drilling Association (AWWDA)
PO Box 130, Lougheed AB T0B 2V0
Tel: 780-386-2335; *Fax:* 780-386-2344
awwda@xplornet.com
www.awwda.com
To assist, promote, encourage, & support the interest and welfare of the water well industry in all of its phases; To foster aid and promote scientific education, standard research, and technique in order to improve methods of well construction: To advance the science of groundwater in Alberta
Michael Schmidt, Secretary Manager

Association des enterprises spécialiseés en eau du Québec
5930, boul Louis-H. Lafontaine, Montréal QC H1M 1S7
Tél: 514-353-9960; *Téléc:* 514-352-5259
Ligne sans frais: 800-468-8160
contact@aeseq.com
www.aeseq.com
Regrouper les entrepreneurs de construction oeuvrant dans tous les secteurs du cycle de l'eau décentralisé au Québec
Daniel Schanck, Directeur général

British Columbia Ground Water Association (BCGWA)
1708 - 197A St., Langley BC V2Z 1K2
Tel: 604-530-8934; *Fax:* 604-530-8934
secretary@bcgwa.org
www.bcgwa.org
Joan Perry, Secretary

Canadian Association of Oilwell Drilling Contractors (CAODC)
#2050, 717 - 7th Ave. SW, Calgary AB T2P 0Z3
Tel: 403-264-4311; *Fax:* 403-263-3796
info@caodc.ca
www.caodc.ca
Social Media: www.youtube.com/user/TheCAODC
twitter.com/markascholz
To represent drilling rig contractors; to provide ongoing means of communication between drilling & well servicing contractors, governments, other industry sector participants, & the general public; To improve standards for safety & training, equipment & technical procedures; To coordinate programs between government bodies & contractors; To oversee the Rig Technician Trade & Apprenticeship Program in Alberta, British Columbia, & Saskatchewan
Duane Carol, Chair
Mark A. Scholz, President

Canadian Diamond Drilling Association (CDDA)
City Centre Building, #337, 101 Worthington St. East, North Bay ON P1B 1G5
Tel: 705-476-6992; *Fax:* 705-476-9494
office@cdda.ca
www.canadiandrilling.com
To foster the commercial interests of members; to promote the simplifications, standardization & interchangeability of diamond drilling equipment; to recognize the safety & health of employees; to foster the protection of the natural environment; to secure the elimination of unfair or uneconomic practices within the industry & freedom from unjust or unlawful exactions; to establish & maintain uniformity & equity in the customs & commercial usages of the diamond drilling business; to acquire & disseminate valuable business information; to promote communication among those engaged in the industry
Louise Lowe, Manager

Manitoba Water Well Association (MWWA)
PO Box 1648, Winnipeg MB R3C 2Z6
Tel: 204-479-3777
info@mwwa.ca
www.mwwa.ca
To promote & support the water well industry in Manitoba
Jeff Bell, President
Ray Ford, Vice-President
Lynn Giersch, Business Manager
Marilyn Schneider, Secretary-Treasurer

New Brunswick Ground Water Association
1278 Route 260, St-Martin de Restigouche NB E8A 2M8
Tel: 506-235-5002
nbgwa@nb.sympatico.ca
www.nbgwa.ca
To preserve & protect New Brunswick's water; To promote education of members & the public; To encourage the development of ground water guidelines & strategies
Danny Constantine, President
Terry Burpee, Sec.-Treas.

Newfoundland/Labrador Ground Water Association
PO Box 160, Doyles NL A0N 1J0
Tel: 709-955-2561; *Fax:* 709-955-3402
gwater@nf.sympatico.ca
To promote the protection & management of ground water in Newfoundland & Labrador
Francis Gale, Contact

Nova Scotia Ground Water Association (NSGWA)
#417, 3 - 644 Portland St., Dartmouth NS B2W 2M3
Fax: 902-435-0089
Toll-Free: 888-242-4440
nsgwa@ns.aliantzinc.ca
www.nsgwa.ca
To act as the voice of the industry to all levels of government; To encourage the management & protection of ground water
Arthur Jefferson, President
Noreene McGuire, Secretary-Treasurer

Ontario Ground Water Association (OGWA)
48 Front St. East, Strathroy ON N7G 1Y6
Tel: 519-245-7194; *Fax:* 519-245-7196
www.ogwa.ca
To protect & promote Ontario's ground water; To provide guidance to members, government representatives, & the public
Greg Bullock, President
Rob MacKinnon, Secretary-Treasurer
Anne Gammage, Office Manager

Prince Edward Island Ground Water Association
PO Box 857, RR#2, Cornwall PE C0A 1H0
Tel: 902-675-2360; *Fax:* 902-675-2360
To promote the protection of ground water in Prince Edward Island
Watson MacDonald, Contact

Saskatchewan Ground Water Association (SGWA)
PO Box 9434, Saskatoon SK S7K 7E9
Tel: 306-244-7551; *Fax:* 306-343-0001
teksmarts.com/skgwa
To act as the voice of the ground water industy throughout Saskatchewan; To promote the management of ground water throughout the province
Kathleen Watson, Contact

Economics

Association des économistes québécois (ASDÉQ)
#7118, 385, rue Sherbrooke Est, Montréal QC H2X 1E3
Tél: 514-342-7537; *Téléc:* 514-342-3967
Ligne sans frais: 866-342-7537
info@economistesquebecois.com
www.economistesquebecois.com
Média social: linkedin.com/groups/3809359
www.facebook.com/127117010671812
twitter.com/EconomistesQc
Assurer la promotion professionnelle des économistes
Bernard Barrucco, Directeur général

Association des professionnels en développement économique du Québec (APDEQ) / Economic Development Professionals Association of Québec
CP 297, Magog QC J1X 3W8
Tél: 819-868-9778; *Téléc:* 819-868-9907
Ligne sans frais: 800-361-8470
info@apdeq.qc.ca
www.apdeq.qc.ca
Média social: linkedin.com/companies/111964
twitter.com/apdeq
Pour aider les artisans du Développement économique à acquérir des compétences et de la formation afin de les aider à réussir
Patrice Gagnon, Directeur général

Association of Professional Economists of British Columbia (APEBC)
#102, 211 Columbia St., Vancouver BC V6A 2R5
Tel: 604-689-1455; *Fax:* 604-681-4545
info@apebc.ca
www.apebc.ca
To encourage a high standard of professional competence; To foster continuing education
Jacob Helliwell, President

Atlantic Association of Applied Economists (AAAE)
1701 Hollis St., 13th Fl., Halifax NS B3J 3M8
Tel: 902-420-4601
www.cabe.ca/jmv3/index.php/cabe-chapters/aaae
To provide forums for current economic & public policy issues
Michael Milloy, President
Tara Ainsworth, Treasurer

Atlantic Provinces Economic Council (APEC) / Conseil économique des provinces de l'Atlantique
#500, 5121 Sackville St., Halifax NS B3J 1K1
Tel: 902-422-6516; *Fax:* 902-429-6803
info@apec-econ.ca
www.apec-econ.ca
Social Media:
twitter.com/APECatlantic
To be the leading advocate for the economic development of the Atlantic region and accomplishes this by: monitoring and analysing current and emerging economic trends and policies; communicating the results of this analysis to its mbmers on a regular basis; consulting with a wide audience; dissminating its research and policy analysis to business, gov't, and the community at large; advocating the appropriate public and private sector policy responses.
Elizabeth Beale, President & CEO

Canada West Foundation (CWF)
#900, 105 - 12th Ave. SE, Calgary AB T2G 5A5
Tel: 403-264-9535; *Toll-Free:* 888-825-5293
cwf@cwf.ca
www.cwf.ca
Social Media:
linkedin.com/groups?home=&gid=2343545
www.facebook.com/canadawestfoundation?ref=ts
twitter.com/CanadaWestFdn
A leading source of strategic insight, conducting and communicating non-partisan economic and public policy research of importance to the four western provinces and all Canadians.
Dylan Jones, President & Chief Executive Officer
Shawna Stirrett, Interim Vice-President, Operations
Robert Roach, Vice-President, Research
Barry Spencer, Director, Finance
Doug Firby, Director, Communications

Canada's Public Policy Forum / Forum des politiques publiques du Canada
#1405, 130 Albert St., Ottawa ON K1P 5G4
Tel: 613-238-7160; *Fax:* 613-238-7990
mail@ppforum.ca
www.ppforum.com
Social Media: www.youtube.com/user/PublicPolicyForum;
flickr.com/photos/ppforumdotca
www.facebook.com/publicpolicyforum
twitter.com/ppforumca
To promote better public policy & better public management through dialogue among leaders from the public, private, labour & voluntary sectors
Larry Murray, Chair
David J. Mitchell, President & CEO
Julie Cafley, Vice-President
Natasha Gauthier, Director, Communications

Canadian Agricultural Economics Society (CAES) / Société canadienne d'agroéconomie (SCAE)
University Of Victoria, PO Box 1700, Stn. CSC, Rm. 360, Business & Economics Bldg., Victoria BC V8W 2Y2
Fax: 866-543-7613
caes.usask.ca
Social Media:
www.facebook.com/CanadianAgriculturalEconomicsSociety
twitter.com/CAES_AgEcon
To address problems related to the economics of food production & marketing & the quality of rural life through extension, research, teaching, & policy making in government & private industry
Valerie Johnson, Executive Director

Canadian Association for Business Economics (CABE) / Association canadienne de science économique des affaires
PO Box 898, Stn. B, Ottawa ON K1P 5P9
Toll-Free: 855-222-3321
info@cabe.ca
www.cabe.ca
Social Media:
www.facebook.com/CABEconomics
twitter.com/CABE_Economics
To represent the interests of business economists in Canada; To enhance the professionalism of business economists
Paul Jacobson, President

Canadian CED Network / Réseau canadien de DÉC
PO Box 199E, 59, rue Monfette, Victoriaville QC G6P 1J8
Tel: 819-795-3056; *Fax:* 819-795-3056
Toll-Free: 877-202-2268
info@ccednet-rcdec.ca
ccednet-rcdec.ca
Social Media: www.youtube.com/user/ccednet
linkedin.com/company/canadian-community-economic-development-network
www.facebook.com/CCEDNet
twitter.com/CCEDNet_RCDEC
To strengthen communities in Canada by creating economic opportunities that improve local social & environmental conditions.
Mike Toye, Executive Director

Canadian Economics Association (CEA) / Association canadienne d'économique
Department of Economics, Brock Univ., 500 Glenridge Ave., St Catharines ON L2S 3A1
Tel: 905-688-5550
www.economics.ca
To represent academic economists; To advance economic knowledge
Vivian Tran, Executive Director
Charles Beach, President
Frances Woolley, Vice-President
Robert Diamond, Secretary-Treasurer

Canadian Law & Economics Association
Faculty of Law, University of Toronto, 84 Queen's Park Cres., Toronto ON M5S 2C5
Tel: 416-978-0210; *Fax:* 416-978-7899
www.canlecon.org
Nadia Gulezko, Contact

C.D. Howe Institute / Institut C.D. Howe
#300, 67 Yonge St., Toronto ON M5E 1J8
Tel: 416-865-1904; *Fax:* 416-865-1866
cdhowe@cdhowe.org
www.cdhowe.org
Social Media:
linkedin.com/company/c.d.-howe-institute
www.facebook.com/pages/CD-Howe-Institute/254245404682417
twitter.com/cdhoweinstitute
To identify current & emerging economic & social policy issues facing Canadians; to recommend particular policy options; to communicate conclusions of research to domestic & international audiences.
William B.P. Robson, President & CEO
Daniel Schwanen, Vice-President, Research

Centre interuniversitaire de recherche en économie quantitative (CIREQ)
Pavillon Lionel-Groulx, Université de Montréal, CP 6128, Succ. Centre-Ville, 3150, rue Jean-Brillant, local C-6088, Montréal QC H3C 3J7
Tél: 514-343-6557; *Téléc:* 514-343-5831
www.cireqmontreal.com
Recherches dans les domaines de l'économétrie théorique et appliquée, de l'économie financière et de la théorie économique
Emanuela Cardia, Dirctrice

The Conference Board of Canada / Le Conference Board du Canada
255 Smyth Rd., Ottawa ON K1H 8M7
Tel: 613-526-3280; *Fax:* 613-526-4857
Toll-Free: 866-711-2262
www.conferenceboard.ca
To be dedicated to applied research, notably in public policy, economic trends, & organizational performance
Anne Golden, President & CEO
Glen Hodgson, Sr. VP & Chief Economist
Perry Eisenschmid, Vice-President, Marketing, Sales & IT

Economic Developers Association of Canada (EDAC) / Association canadienne de développement économique (ACDE)
#200, 7 Innovation Dr., Hamilton ON L9H 7H9
Tel: 905-689-8771
info@edac.ca
www.edac.ca
Social Media:
twitter.com/E_D_A_C
To contribute to Canada's economic, social, & environmental well-being by advancing economic development; To enhance professional competence & ethical service
Penny A. Gardiner, Chief Executive Officer
Greg Borduas, President
David Emerson, 1st Vice-President
Kevin Rose, 2nd Vice-President
Gerry Gabinet, Treasurer

Economic Developers Council of Ontario Inc. (EDCO)
6506 Marlene Ave., Cornwall ON K6H 7H9
Tel: 613-931-9827; *Fax:* 613-931-9828
edco@edco.on.ca
www.edco.on.ca
Social Media:
linkedin.com/company/economic-developers-council-of-ontario
twitter.com/edco1edco
To provide a forum for economic development related educational activities; to increase the profile of EDCO & the profession; to encourage & create an awareness of economic development issues with relevant government agencies; to promote & develop Ontario as a premier location for economic activity by increasing employment & prosperity, & enhancing the quality of life within the Ontario municipalities.
Jennifer Patterson, President
Heather Lalonde, Executive Director

The Fraser Institute
1770 Burrard St., 4th Fl., Vancouver BC V6J 3G7
Tel: 604-688-0221; *Fax:* 604-688-8539
info@fraserinstitute.ca
www.fraserinstitute.ca
Social Media: www.youtube.com/FraserInstitute
linkedin.com/company/the-fraser-institute
www.facebook.com/fraserinstitute
twitter.com/FraserInstitute
To redirect public attention to the role competitive markets play in the economic well-being of all Canadians
Peter Brown, Chair
Niels Veldhuis, President
Kenneth P. Green, Senior Director, Centre for Natural Resources

Manitoba Association for Business Economics (MABE)
MB
www.cabe.ca/jmv3/index.php/cabe-chapters/mabe
To provide a forum for people in Manitoba who are interested in economics; to foster education in the field of economics
John Harper, President

The North-South Institute (NSI) / L'Institut Nord-Sud
#500, 55 Murray St., Ottawa ON K1N 5M3
Tel: 613-241-3535; *Fax:* 613-241-7435
nsi@nsi-ins.ca
www.nsi-ins.ca
Social Media:
www.facebook.com/NSIINS
twitter.com/NSI_INS
To analyze, for Canadians & others, the economic, social, & political implications of global change & to propose policy alternatives to promote global development & justice
Joseph K. Ingram, President & CEO
Rodney Schmidt, Vice-President & COO

Ottawa Economics Association (OEA)
PO Box 264, Stn. B, Ottawa ON K1P 6C4
Tel: 613-837-9415
www.cabe.ca/jmv3/index.php/cabe-chapters/oea
To organize programs of interest to members
Joe Macaluso, Membership Chair/Contact
Stephen Tapp, Treasurer

Rotman Institute for International Business (RIIB)
University of Toronto, 105 St. George St., Toronto ON M5S 3E6
Tel: 416-978-5781
riib@utoronto.ca
www.rotman.utoronto.ca
RIIB merges the former Institute for Policy Analysis & the Institute for International Business, & focusses on research on the global business environment, enterprise decision making in the global economy, & the urban service economy.
Wendy Dobson, Co-Director
Ig Horstman, Co-Director, Prof. of Economics

Saskatchewan Economic Development Association (SEDA)
PO Box 113, #202, 120 Sonnenschein Way, Saskatoon SK S7K 3K1
Tel: 306-384-5817; *Fax:* 306-384-5818
Toll-Free: 877-551-7332
seda@seda.sk.ca
www.seda.sk.ca
Social Media:
linkedin.com/in/saskecdevassoc
www.facebook.com/148408781882152
twitter.com/saskecdevassoc
To secure the economic future of Saskatchewan by helping communities to grow
Russ McPherson, President

Verona Thibault, Executive Director

Saskatchewan Economics Association (SEA)
c/o Rahatjan Judge, Treasurer, 826 Ave. K south, Saskatoon SK S7M 2E8
sea@cabe.ca
www.cabe.ca/jmv3/index.php/cabe-chapters/oskaer
To provide a forum for individuals & agencies interested in economics, including the following: economic policy analysts; certified financial, management and accounting officials; economic development consultants; statisticians; banking officials; university officials; & students of economics.
Aaron Murray, President
Rahatjan Judge, Treasurer

Toronto Association for Business Economics Inc. (TABE)
PO Box 955, 31 Adelaide St. East, Toronto ON M5C 2K3
Tel: 647-693-7418
tabe@cabe.ca
www.cabe.ca/chapters/TABE
Social Media:
twitter.com/TABE_Economics
To promote a better understanding of economic issues; to contribute to the professional development of members; to encourage the availability of economic information & to broaden awareness of business economics; to recognize achievement of business economists
Ingrid Porter, Executive Director
Jane Voll, President

Education

Agence universitaire de la Francophonie (AUF)
CP 49714, Succ. Musée, 3034, boul Edouard-Montpetit, Montréal QC H3T 1J7
Tél: 514-343-6630; *Téléc:* 514-343-5783
recorat@auf.org
www.auf.org
Média social: www.youtube.com/planeteauf
www.facebook.com/profile.php?id=1691871982
twitter.com/planeteauf
Le développement, au sein de l'espace francophone, d'une coopération internationale pour assurer à la fois le dialogue permanent des cultures et la circulation des personnes, des idées, des expériences entre institutions universitaires, dans l'intérêt de l'éducation et du progrès de la science
Bernard Cerquiglini, Recteur

Alberta Assessment Consortium (AAC)
#700, 11010 - 142 St., Edmonton AB T5N 2R1
Tel: 780-761-0530; *Fax:* 780-761-0533
info@aac.ab.ca
www.aac.ab.ca
Social Media:
twitter.com/AACinfo
Develops a broad range of classroom assessment materials, directly aligned to Alberta curriculum, that address both formative and summative processes.
Sherry Bennett, Executive Director

Alberta Association of Family School Liaison Workers (AAFSLW)
c/o Tonia Koversky, St. Albert Family & Community Support Services, #10, 50 Bellerose Dr., St. Albert AB T8N 3L5
Tel: 780-459-1749; *Fax:* 780-458-1260
www.aafslw.ca
Social Media:
linkedin.com/groups/AAFSLW-6609871
www.facebook.com/AAFSLW
AAFSLW provides an opportunity for networking among professionals through conferences, regional meetings, newsletters, resource sharing, and case conferencing.
Christine Payne, President

Alberta Educational Facilities Administrators Association (AEFAA)
7 White Pelican Way, Lake Newell Resort AB T1R 0X5
Tel: 403-376-0461
www.aefaa.ca
Social Media:
twitter.com/AlanKloepper
Alan Kloepper, Executive Director

Alberta Home Education Association (AHEA)
AB
www.aheaonline.com
AHEA serves home schooling parents as needs arise, to support local groups of parents and individuals, and to interact with various levels of government to protect the responsibilities of parents.
Paul van den Bosch, President

Alberta School Boards Association (ASBA)
#1200, 9925 - 109 St., Edmonton AB T5K 2J8
Tel: 780-482-7311
reception@asba.ab.ca
www.asba.ab.ca
Social Media:
twitter.com/ABSchoolBoards
To promote the availability of high quality schooling for all; To assist member boards in fulfilling their mission of achieving excellence in education
Scott McCormack, Executive Director
Heather Massel, Director, Communications
Heather Rogers, Director, Finance & Corporate Services

Alberta School Councils' Association (ASCA)
#1200, 9925 - 109 St., Edmonton AB T5K 2J8
Tel: 780-454-9867; *Fax:* 780-455-0167
Toll-Free: 800-661-3470
parents@albertaschoolcouncils.ca
www.albertaschoolcouncils.ca
Social Media:
www.youtube.com/channel/UCY9v9ogRIoU4GK26D5dmiGw
linkedin.com/in/alberta-school-councils-association-5aa73a84
www.facebook.com/180244032050548
twitter.com/ABschoolcouncil
To be the voice of parents/families committed to the best possible education for Alberta children, so that they may reach their potential to participate in society in a meaningful & responsible way
Jacquie Hansen, Executive Director
Brad Vonkeman, President
Tasha Schindel, Vice-President

Alberta Teachers' Association (ATA)
Barnett House, 11010 - 142 St. NW, Edmonton AB T5N 2R1
Tel: 780-447-9400; *Fax:* 780-455-6481
Toll-Free: 800-232-7208
postmaster@ata.ab.ca
www.teachers.ab.ca
Social Media:
linkedin.com/company/the-alberta-teachers'-association
www.facebook.com/ABteachers
twitter.com/albertateachers
To advance the cause of education in Alberta; To improve the teaching profession; To increase public interest in & support for education; To cooperate with other bodies having similar objectives
Brian Andrais, Coordinator, Member Services
Mark Yurick, Coordinator, Professional Development
Caroline Inacio, Chief Financial Officer, Member Services

Alliance canadienne des responsables et enseignants en français (langue maternelle) (ACREF) / Canadian Association for the Teachers of French as a First Language
Place de la Francophonie, Succ. A, #401, 450, rue Reideau, Ottawa ON K1N 5Z4
Tél: 613-744-3192; *Téléc:* 613-744-0154
acref@franco.ca
Développer un réseau d'identification nationale des professeurs de français langue maternelle; favoriser le développement et l'épanouissement des associations provinciales vouées à l'enseignement du français langue maternelle; promouvoir la diffusion de l'information en matière de théories pédagogiques, de formation à l'approche communicative, et de pratiques scolaires et d'idéologie visant l'identité des francophones, l'égalité en tant que groupe national et le contrôle des structures éducatives; appuyer les organismes provinciaux lors de leur rencontre annuelle; développer des instruments de diffusion de l'information à l'intention de ses membres; favoriser le développement d'une politique nationale en ce qui a trait à la gestion des institutions d'enseignement et voir à ce qu'elle respecte l'autonomie des francophones

Association canadienne d'éducation de langue française (ACELF)
#303, 265, rue de la Couronne, Québec QC G1K 6E1
Tél: 418-681-4661; *Téléc:* 418-681-3389
info@acelf.ca
www.acelf.ca
Média social: www.youtube.com/acelfcanada
www.facebook.com/acelf.ca
twitter.com/_ACELF
L'ACELF inspire et soutient le développement et l'action des institutions éducatives francophones du Canada
Yves St-Maurice, Président
Richard Lacombe, Direction générale

Association canadienne des professeurs d'immersion (ACPI) / Canadian Association of Immersion Teachers (CAIT)
#310, 176, rue Gloucester, Ottawa ON K2P 0A6
Tél: 613-230-9111; *Téléc:* 613-230-5940
bureau@acpi.ca
www.acpi.ca
Chantal Bourbonnais, Directrice générale

Association des cadres des centres de la petite enfance (ACCPE) / Association of Managers of Childcare Centers (AMCC)
CP 4042, Succ. D, Montréal QC
Tél: 514-933-3954
info@associationdescadres.ca
www.associationdescadres.ca
Réunir les cadres de centres de la petite enfance; Travailler en collaboration avec le Ministère de la Famille
Isabelle Palardy, Directrice générale

Association des cadres scolaires du Québec
#170, 1195, av Lavigerie, Québec QC G1V 4N3
Tél: 418-654-0014; *Téléc:* 418-654-1719
acsq@acsq.qc.ca
www.acsq.qc.ca
Valoriser le statut professionnel de ses membres et promouvoir leurs intérêts professionnels et éconimiques; Collaborer avec les autorités gouvernementales et les organismes intéressés, au développement ordonné du système scolaire, par une participation constante et adéquate à l'élaboration et à la mise en oeuvre des politiques relatives à l'éducation
Lucie Godbout, Directrice général
Lucie Demers, Présidente
Mario Vachon, Vice-Président
Jean-François Lussier, Secrétaire-trésorier

Association des collèges privés du Québec (ACPQ)
1940, boul Henri-Bourassa est, Montréal QC H2B 1S2
Tél: 514-381-8891; *Téléc:* 514-381-4086
Ligne sans frais: 888-381-8891
acpq@cadre.qc.ca
www.acpq.net
Défendre les intérêts de ses collèges membres et contribuer au développement de l'enseignement collégial privé au Québec
Guy Forgues, Directeur général
Lucie Leduc, Adjointe administrative

Association des directeurs généraux des commissions scolaires du Québec (ADIGECS)
a/s Directeur exécutif, #212, 195 ch de Chambly, Longueuil QC J4H 3L3
Tél: 450-674-6700; *Téléc:* 450-674-7337
adigecs.qc.ca
Contribuer à l'avancement de l'éducation au Québec; protéger les intérêts de ses membres notamment au chapitre des conditions de travail
Raynald Thibeault, Président
Serge Lefebvre, Directeur exécutif

Association des enseignantes et des enseignants franco-ontariens (AEFO) / Franco-Ontarian Teachers' Association
#801, 1420, place Blair, Ottawa ON K1J 9L8
Tél: 613-244-2336; *Téléc:* 613-563-7718
Ligne sans frais: 800-267-4217
aefo@aefo.on.ca
www.aefo.on.ca
Média social: www.facebook.com/155281931200167
twitter.com/AEFO_ON_CA
De regrouper les travailleuses et les travailleurs au service des établissements publics et privés francophones en Ontario
Pierre Léonard, Directeur général
Nicole Beauchamp, Responsable des communications

Association des enseignantes et des enseignants francophones du Nouveau-Brunswick (AEFNB)
CP 712, 650, rue Montgomery, Fredericton NB E3B 5B4
Tél: 506-452-8921; *Téléc:* 506-452-1838
www.aefnb.ca
Média social:
www.youtube.com/channel/UCjZukUoeNt4styGTFsrxF0A
www.facebook.com/aefnb/
twitter.com/aefnb
Représenter les intérêts des enseignantes et des enseignants francophones de la province; favoriser et maintenir au Nouveau-Brunswick des services éducatifs de langue française de première qualité
Marc Arseneau, Président

Association for Canadian Studies (ACS) / Association d'études canadiennes (AEC)
1822A, rue Sherbooke ouest, Montréal QC H3H 1E4
Tel: 514-925-3099; *Fax:* 514-925-3095
general@acs-aec.ca
www.acs-aec.ca
Social Media:
plus.google.com/113769569781539301984?prsrc=3
www.facebook.com/acs.aec.canadianstudies
twitter.com/Canadianstudies
To initiate & supports activities in the areas of research, teaching, communications, & the training of students in the field of Canadian studies, especially in interdisciplinary & multidisciplinary perspectives; To strive to raise public awareness of Canadian issues; To provide the Canadian Studies community, principally within Canada, with a wide range of activities & programs
Jack Jedwab, Executive Director
James Ondrick, Director, Programs & Administration

Association francophone pour le savoir (ACFAS)
425, rue de la Gauchetière, Montréal QC H2L 2M7
Tél: 514-849-0045; *Téléc:* 514-849-5558
www.acfas.ca
Média social:
linkedin.com/company/acfas—association-francophone-pour-le-savoir
www.facebook.com/Acfas/
twitter.com/_Acfas
Promouvoir et soutenir la science et la technologie pour encourager le développement culturel et économique de la société
Esther Gaudreault, Directrice générale
Isabelle Gandilhon, Conseillère principale

Association of Atlantic Universities (AAU) / Association des universités de l'Atlantique
#403, 5657 Spring Garden Rd., Halifax NS B3J 3R4
Tel: 902-425-4230; *Fax:* 902-425-4233
info@atlanticuniversities.ca
www.atlanticuniversities.ca
To assist in assuring the quality & coordination of higher education in Atlantic Provinces; to provide a forum for university administrators to discuss & coordinate their views, interests & concerns in support of higher education in the Atlantic provinces
Peter Halpin, Executive Director

Association of British Columbia Teachers of English as an Additional Language (BC TEAL)
#206, 640 West Broadway, Vancouver BC V5Z 1G4
Tel: 604-736-6330; *Fax:* 604-736-6306
admin@bcteal.org
www.bcteal.org
To foster & promote effective instruction in English as a second language in BC; to raise the professional status of BC ESL teachers; to promote communication among BC ESL professionals
Shawna Williams, President

Association of Canadian Faculties of Dentistry (ACFD) / Association des facultés dentaires du Canada (AFDC)
#350, 2194 Health Sciences Mall, Vancouver BC V6T 1Z3
Tel: 604-827-1083; *Fax:* 604-822-4532
admin@acfd.ca
www.acfd.ca
To assure the quality of dental education & research in Canada. It also strives to keep its members informed of issues regarding University-based dental education and promote communication between its members.
Daniel Haas, President
Tom Boran, Vice-President & Treasurer

Association of Canadian Universities for Northern Studies (ACUNS) / Association universitaire canadienne d'études nordiques
PO Box 321, Stn. A, Ottawa ON K1N 8V3
Tel: 613-669-8162
office@acuns.ca
www.acuns.ca
Social Media:
www.facebook.com/110949402264676
twitter.com/acunsaucen
To encourage the government & private sector to support polar scholarship, which fosters programs to increase public awareness of polar sciences & research; to represent its member universities & colleges, encouraging the establishment of funds & resources to ensure a network of trained researchers, regional managers & educators.
Peter Geller, President
Monique Bernier, Vice-President
Gary Wilson, Secretary-Treasurer

Heather Cayouette, Program Manager

Association of Deans of Pharmacy of Canada (ADPC) / Association des doyens de pharmacie du Canada (ADPC)
c/o Association of Faculties of Pharmacy of Canada, PO Box 21053, Stn. Terwilligar, Edmonton AB T6R 2V4
afpc.info/council-of-deans
To represent the interests of the academic pharmaceutical community.
Harold Lopatka, Executive Director
Pierre Moreau, President

Association of Early Childhood Educators Ontario (AECEO)
#211, 40 Orchard View Blvd., Toronto ON M4R 1B9
Tel: 416-487-3157; *Fax:* 416-487-3758
Toll-Free: 866-932-3236
info@aeceo.ca
www.aeceo.ca
Social Media:
www.facebook.com/189978994376068
twitter.com/AECEO
To support early childhood educators throughout Ontario
Rachel Langford, President
Eduarda Sousa, Executive Director
Lena DaCosta, Coordinator, Professional Development, Marketing & Advertising
Sue Parker, Coordinator, Membership Services & Office Manager
Goranka Vukelich, Secretary
Gaby Chauvet, Treasurer

Association of Educational Researchers of Ontario (AERO) / Association ontarienne des chercheurs et chercheuse en éducation
c/o Research & Information Services, Toronto District School Board, 1 Civic Centre Court, Lower Level, Toronto ON M9C 2B3
Tel: 416-394-4929; *Fax:* 416-394-4946
info@aero-aoce.org
www.aero-aoce.org
To promote & improve research, education, planning & development pertaining to education in the Ontario school system
Terry Spencer, President

Association of Faculties of Medicine of Canada (AFMC) / L'Association des facultés de médecine du Canada (AFMC)
#800, 265 Carling Ave., Ottawa ON K1S 2E1
Tel: 613-730-0687; *Fax:* 613-730-1196
username@afmc.ca
www.afmc.ca
Social Media:
twitter.com/afmc_e
To represent the interests of members in medical research policy formulation; to promote & advance academic medicine through the review & development of standards for medical education, through the development of national policies appropriate to the aims & purposes of Canadian faculties of medicine, through the fostering of research, & through representation of Canadian faculties of medicine to professional associations & governments
Genevieve Moineau, President & CEO

Association of Independent Schools & Colleges in Alberta (AISCA)
#201, 11830 - 111 Ave., Edmonton AB T5X 5Y3
Tel: 780-469-9868; *Fax:* 780-469-9880
office@aisca.ab.ca
www.aisca.ab.ca
To defend & promote the right of parents to determine the context for their children's education; to create a positive social, fiscal & political environment in which independent schools are free to maintain their identity as they serve the public interest; to support & encourage independent schools in providing significant educational choices for parents & their children; to foster public understanding & appreciation of independent schools & their services
Duane Plantinga, Executive Director

Association of Registrars of the Universities & Colleges of Canada (ARUCC) / Association des registraires des universités et collèges du Canada
c/o Angelique Saweczko, Thompson Rivers University, 900 McGill Rd., Kamloops BC V2C 0C8
Tel: 250-828-5019
www.arucc.ca
ARUCC was developed in response to the professional needs of student administrative services personnel in universities.
Hans Rouleau, President

Association of University Forestry Schools of Canada (AUFSC) / Association des écoles forestières universitaires du Canada
c/o Faculty of Agric., Life & Environ. Sciences, University of Alberta, 751 General Services Building, Edmonton AB T6G 1H1
Tel: 780-492-6722
www.aefuc-aufsc.ca
Vic Lieffers, Chair

Association provinciale des enseignantes et enseignants du Québec (APEQ) / Québec Provincial Association of Teachers (QPAT)
#1, 17035, boul Brunswick, Kirkland QC H9H 5G6
Tél: 514-694-9777; *Téléc:* 514-694-0189
Ligne sans frais: 800-361-9870
www.qpat-apeq.qc.ca
Média social:
www.facebook.com/pages/Kirkland-QC/QPATAPEQ/243536577025
Alan Lombard, Executive Director

Association québécoise des professeurs de français (AQPF)
773, rue Sainte-Hélène, Longueuil QC J4K 3R5
Tél: 450-332-5885; *Téléc:* 450-332-5888
Ligne sans frais: 800-267-0947
info@aqpf.qc.ca
www.aqpf.qc.ca
Les principaux champs d'intervention sont - la didactique et l'enseignement du français langue maternelle du préscolaire à l'université; l'enseignement du français aux adultes; l'alphabétisation; l'enseignement du français langue seconde; promotion de la langue française, de la culture québécoise et de la francophonie
Érick Falardeau, Président, Section de Québec-et-Est-du-Québec
Danielle Lefebvre, Présidente, Section Centre du Québec
Geneviève Messier, Présidente, Section de Montréal-et-Ouest-du-Québec
Suzanne Richard, Présidente
Isabelle Péladeau, Directrice générale

Association québécoise des troubles d'apprentissage (AQETA) / Learning Disabilities Association of Québec (LDAQ)
#502, 740, rue Saint-Maurice, Montréal QC H3C 1L5
Tél: 514-847-1324; *Téléc:* 514-281-5187
Ligne sans frais: 877-847-1324
adj.adm@aqeta.qc.ca
www.aqeta.qc.ca
Média social: www.facebook.com/aqeta.provinciale
twitter.com/AQDRnationale
Faire connaître les troubles d'apprentissage; faire la promotion des besoins et des droits collectifs des enfants et des adultes qui vivent avec des troubles d'apprentissage
Lise Bibaud, Directrice générale

Association québécoise du personnel de direction des écoles (AQPDE)
#235, 3291, ch Ste-Foy, Québec QC G1X 3V2
Tél: 418-781-0700; *Téléc:* 418-781-0276
info@aqpde.ca
www.aqpde.ca
Défendre et promouvoir les intérêts professionnels, sociaux et économiques des membres, favoriser leur participation et établir une concertation avec les autres organismes du réseau de l'éducation pour assurer les meilleures conditions de ses membres
Danielle Boucher, Présidente

Black Educators Association of Nova Scotia (BEA)
2136 Gottingen St., Halifax NS B3K 3B3
Tel: 902-424-7036; *Fax:* 902-424-0636
Toll-Free: 800-565-3398
info@theblackeducators.ca
www.theblackeducators.ca
To monitor & ensure the development of an equitable education system, so that African Nova Scotians are able to achieve their maximum potential
Ken Fells, President
Robert Upshaw, Executive Director

British Columbia Career College Association (BCCCA)
PO Box 40528, #11, 200 Burrard, Vancouver BC V6C 3L0
Tel: 604-874-4419; *Fax:* 604-874-4420
thebccca@gmail.com
www.bccca.com
Social Media:
linkedin.com/pub/bc-career-colleges-association/89/95/31b
www.facebook.com/pages/BC-Career-Colleges-Association/370318143114942
twitter.com/@thebccca
This association's aim is to promote and support post secondary schools, stakeholders, students and all interested parties involved in private post-secondary education and training in BC.
Amanda Steele, Executive Director
Jeremy Sabell, President

British Columbia Confederation of Parent Advisory Councils (BCCPAC)
#200, 4170 Still Creek Dr., Burnaby BC V5C 6C6
Tel: 604-687-4433; *Fax:* 604-687-4488
Toll-Free: 866-529-4397
info@bccpac.bc.ca
www.bccpac.bc.ca
Social Media:
www.facebook.com/153750724696021
twitter.com/bccpac
To advance the public school education & well-being of children in British Columbia
Terry Berting, President
Carla Giles, COO

British Columbia School Trustees Association (BCSTA) / Association des commissaires d'écoles de Colombie-Britannique
1580 West Broadway, 4th Fl., Vancouver BC V6J 5K9
Tel: 604-734-2721; *Fax:* 604-732-4559
bcsta@bcsta.org
www.bcsta.org
Social Media:
linkedin.com/company/bc-school-trustees-association
www.facebook.com/pages/BC-School-Trustees-Association
twitter.com/bc_sta
To promote effective boards of public school trustees working together for BC students; To improve student achievement through community engagement
Mike Roberts, Chief Executive Officer
Jodi Olstead, Director, Finance & Human Resources
Mike P. Gagel, Director, Information & Education Technology

British Columbia Science Teachers' Association (BCScTA)
c/o Ashcroft Secondary School, PO Box 669, Ashcroft BC V0K 1A0
Tel: 250-453-9144; *Fax:* 250-453-2368
bcscta@gmail.com
www.bcscta.ca
Grahame Rainey, President
Tim McCracken, 1st Vice-President

British Columbia Teachers of English Language Arts
c/o B.C. Teachers' Federation, #100, 550 West 6th Ave., Vancouver BC V5Z 4P2
Tel: 604-871-1848; *Toll-Free:* 800-663-9163
www.bctela.ca

British Columbia Teachers' Federation (BCTF) / Fédération des enseignants de la Colombie-Britannique
#100, 550 West 6th Ave., Vancouver BC V5Z 4P2
Tel: 604-871-2283; *Toll-Free:* 800-663-9163
webinfo@bctf.ca
www.bctf.ca
Social Media: www.youtube.com/bctfvids
www.facebook.com/BCTeachersFederation
twitter.com/bctf
To represent 41,000 public school teachers in the province of British Columbia; To support 32 provincial specialist associations, such as the British Columbia Teacher-Librarians' Association & the British Columbia Music Educators' Association; To advocate for the professional, economic, & social goals of teachers
Glen Hansman, President
Teri Mooring, Second Vice-President

Canadian Accredited Independent Schools (CAIS)
PO Box 3013, 2 Ridley Rd., St Catharines ON L2R 7C3
Tel: 905-683-5658; *Fax:* 905-684-5057
director@cais.ca
www.cais.ca
Anne-Marie Kee, Executive Director

Canadian Alliance of Student Associations (CASA) / Alliance canadienne des associations étudiantes (ACAE)
130 Slater St., Ottawa ON K1P 6E2
Tel: 613-236-3457; *Fax:* 613-236-2386
www.casa-acae.com
Social Media: www.youtube.com/user/CASAACAE; www.flickr.com/photos/casa-acae
www.facebook.com/casa.acae
twitter.com/casadaily
Chris Saulnier, Chair
Zach Dayler, National Director
Michael McDonald, Manager, Stakeholder Relations
Matthew McMillan, Secretary
Ghislain LeBlanc, Treasurer

Canadian Asian Studies Association (CASA) / Association canadienne des études asiatiques (ACEA)
c/o Dept. of Geography, Université du Québec à Montréal, PO Box 8888, Stn. Centre Ville, Pavillon Hubert Aquin Local A-4310, Montréal QC H3C 3P8
Tel: 514-848-2280; *Fax:* 514-848-4514
casa_acea@yahoo.ca
www.casa-acea.ca
To expand & disseminate knowledge about Asia in Canada
André Laliberté, Secretary
Prashant Keshavmurthy, Treasurer

Canadian Association for American Studies (CAAS) / Association d'études américaines au Canada (AEAC)
c/o Jennifer Harris, Assoc. Prof., Mount Allison University, 63D York St., Sackville NB E4L 1G9
webmaster@american-studies.ca
www.american-studies.ca
Social Media: twitter.com/CAASCanada
To encourage study & research concerning the United States; To examine the implications of American studies for Canada & the world
Jennifer Harris, President
Jason Haslam, Vice-President
Jennifer Harris, Secretary
Percy Walton, Treasurer

Canadian Association for Co-operative Education (CAFCE) / Association canadienne de l'enseignement coopératif
#202, 720 Spadina Ave., Toronto ON M5S 2T9
Tel: 416-929-5256
cafce@cafce.ca
www.cafce.ca
To act as the voice for post-secondary co-operative education in Canada; To advance post-secondary co-operative education throughout the country; To establish national standards
Rachel King, Director, Operations

Canadian Association for Graduate Studies (CAGS) / Association canadienne pour les études supérieures (ACES)
#301, 260 St. Patrick St., Ottawa ON K1N 5K5
Tel: 613-562-0949; *Fax:* 613-562-9009
info@cags.ca
www.cags.ca
To promote excellence in graduate education; To foster research, scholarship, & creative activity; To provide a nationwide link for the exchange of information between graduate schools & granting councils, research, business, & industrial sectors, & all levels of government; To hold meetings & conferences; To publish materials to advance graduate education; To develop & maintain national standards for graduate degree programs; To support the regular external evaluation of these standards; To deal with other matters of concern to Deans & Associate Deans of graduate studies
Sally Rutherford, Executive Director
John Doering, President
Gary Slater, Vice-President
Sue Horton, Sec.-Treas.

Canadian Association for Scottish Studies (CASS)
Dept. of History, Centre for Scottish Studies, University of Guelph, 1008 MacKinnon Ext., Guelph ON N1G 2W1
Tel: 519-824-4120; *Fax:* 519-766-9516
scottish@uoguelph.ca
www.uoguelph.ca/scottish
Social Media: www.facebook.com/scottishstudies
twitter.com/ScottishStudies
To promote interest in Scottish history, literature, & culture
Graeme Morton, General Editor, IRSS

Canadian Association for Social Work Education (CASWE) / Association canadienne pour la formation en travail social (ACFTS)
#410, 383 Parkdale Ave., Ottawa ON K1Y 4R4
Tel: 613-792-1953; *Toll-Free:* 888-342-6522
admin@caswe-acfts.ca
caswe-acfts.ca
To advance university education for the profession of social work; To accredit professional social work educational programs, based on high educational standards; To increase understanding of the nature & role of social work practice & social welfare
Carolyn Campbell, President, -
Sylvie Renaud, Coordinator, Accreditation
Sheri McConnell, Vice-President
John Flynn, Treasurer
Sharon Leslie, Office Administrator
Alexandra Wright, PhD, Executive Director

Canadian Association for Teacher Education (CATE) / Association canadienne pour la formation des enseignants (ACFE)
c/o The Canadian Society for the Study of Education, #204, 260 Dalhousie St., Ottawa ON K1N 7E4
Tel: 613-241-0018; *Fax:* 613-241-0019
www.csse-scee.ca/cate
To encourage scholarly study & research in education, with special emphasis on teacher education; to provide for the membership a national forum for the presentation & discussion of significant studies in education, with special emphasis on teacher education
Lynn Thomas, President

Canadian Association for the Advancement of Netherlandic Studies (CAANS) / Association canadienne pour l'avancement des études néerlandaises (ACAEN)
c/o Secretary, 613 Huycks Point Rd., Wellington ON K0K 3L0
www.caans-acaen.ca
Social Media: www.facebook.com/29784957106215
To stimulate awareness & interest in & to promote the study of Netherlandic languages (Dutch, Flemish, Afrikaans), as well as Netherlandic literature, history & culture; to provide a forum for discussion in these areas, hold an annual conference, publish research & sponsor relevant cultural & scholarly activities such as meetings, presentations, lectures & discussions
Michiel Horn, President
Paul de Laat, Secretary-Treasurer

Canadian Association for the Study of Discourse & Writing (CASDW) / Association canadienne de rédactologie (ACR)
c/o W. Brock MacDonald, Woodsworth College, University of Toronto, 119 St. George St., Toronto ON M5S 1A9
casdwacr.wordpress.com
To advance the study & teaching of discourse, writing, & communication in both academic & nonacademic settings
W. Brock MacDonald, Treasurer, Membership

Canadian Association for University Continuing Education (CAUCE) / Association pour l'éducation permanente dans les universités du Canada (AEPUC)
c/o Centre for Continuing & Distance Education, U. of Saskatchewan, #464, 221 Cumberland Ave. North, Saskatoon SK S7N 1M3
Tel: 306-966-5604; *Fax:* 306-966-5590
cauce.secretariat@usask.ca
www.cauce-aepuc.ca
To enlarge the quality & scope of educational opportunities for adults at the university level
Cathy Kelly, President

Canadian Association of College & University Student Services (CACUSS) / Association des services aux étudiants des universités et collèges du Canada (ASEUCC)
#202, 720 Spadina Ave., Toronto ON M5S 2T9
Tel: 647-345-1116
contact@cacuss.ca
www.cacuss.ca
Social Media: www.facebook.com/cacuss
twitter.com/cacusstweets
To represent & serve persons who work in Canadian post-secondary institutions in student affairs & services; To offer advocacy & assistance on issues that affect the quality of student life on Canadian university & college campuses
Janet Mee, President
David Newman, President-Elect
Jennifer Hamilton, Executive Director

Canadian Association of Foundations of Education (CAFE) / Association canadienne des fondements de l'éducation (ACFE)
c/o The Canadian Society for the Study of Education, #204, 260 Dalhousie St., Ottawa ON K1N 7E4
Tel: 613-241-0018; *Fax:* 613-241-0019
csse-scee@csse.ca
www.csse-scee.ca/cafe
To provide a forum for discussing the contribution of the social sciences & humanities (eg. history of education, philosophy of education, sociology of education) to educational theory, research & practice
Michael O'Sullivan, President

Canadian Association of Geographers (CAG) / Association canadienne des géographes
Department of Geography, McGill University, #425, 805, rue Sherbrooke ouest, Montréal QC H3A 2K6
Tel: 514-398-4946; *Fax:* 514-398-7437
valerie.shoffey@cag-acg.ca
www.cag-acg.ca
To promote the discipline of geography in Canada & internationally
Anne Godlewska, President
Mary-Louise Byrne, Secretary-Treasurer
Ian MacLachlan, Editor, The Canadian Geographer
Valerie Shoffey, Editor, The CAG Newsletter

Canadian Association of Montessori Teachers (CAMT)
312 Oakwood Crt., Newmarket ON L3Y 3C8
Tel: 416-755-7184; *Fax:* 866-328-7974
info@camt100.ca
www.camt100.ca
To advance the standards of Montessori teaching to improve the quality of Montessori education throughout Canada; To promote the interests of Montessori teachers
Barton Graff, President
Shaza Tehseen, Vice-President

Canadian Association of Principals (CAP) / Association canadienne des directeurs d'école
#220, 300 Earl Grey Dr., Kanata ON K2T 1C1
Tel: 613-839-0768; *Fax:* 613-622-0258
info@cdnprincipals.org
www.cdnprincipals.org
Social Media: www.facebook.com/599842980034960
twitter.com/CdnPrincipals
To represent the professional perspectives of principals & vice-principals at the national level & to provide the leadership necessary to ensure quality educational opportunities for Canadian students.
Jill Sooley-Perley, Executive Assistant
Jameel Aziz, President

Canadian Association of Research Administrators (CARA) / Association canadienne des administratrices et des administrateurs de recherche (ACAAR)
#1710, 350 Albert St., Ottawa ON K1R 1B1
Tel: 289-244-3744
webinars@cara-acaar.ca
cara-acaar.ca
Social Media: linkedin.com/groups/4978586/profile
twitter.com/@cara_acaar
To advance the research administrator profession; To improve the efficiency & effectiveness of research administration at post-secondary institutions; To advocate for its membership through representation & unity; To foster & encourage collaboration with organizations in related disciplines
Sarah Lampson, Executive Director

Canadian Association of School Social Workers & Attendance Counsellors (CASSWAC)
c/o Rolling River School Div., PO Box 1170, Minnedosa MB R0J 0P0
Tel: 204-867-2754
www.casswac.ca
Rebecca Gray, President

Canadian Association of Schools of Nursing (CASN) / Association canadienne des écoles de sciences infirmières (ACESI)
#450, 1145 Hunt Club Rd., Ottawa ON K1V 0Y3
Tel: 613-235-3150; *Fax:* 613-235-4476
inquire@casn.ca
www.casn.ca
Social Media: twitter.com/CASN43

CASN/ACESI represents Canadian nursing programs. The association is the national voice for nursing education & nursing research.
Cynthia Baker, Executive Director

Canadian Association of Second Language Teachers (CASLT) / Association canadienne des professeurs de langues secondes (ACPLS)
2490 Don Reid Dr., Ottawa ON K1H 1E1
Tel: 613-727-0994; *Fax:* 613-727-3831
Toll-Free: 877-727-0994
admin@caslt.org
www.caslt.org
Social Media: www.youtube.com/user/casltcaslt
twitter.com/CASLT_ACPLS
To promote & advance nationally learning of second languages; to encourage activities & research in field of second language
Guy Leclair, Executive Director
Caroline Turnbull, President

Canadian Association of Slavists (CAS) / Association canadienne des slavistes
Alumni Hall, Dept. of History & Classics, University of Alberta, #2, 28 Tory Bldg., Edmonton AB T6G 2H4
Tel: 780-492-2566; *Fax:* 780-492-9125
csp@ulberta.ca
www.ualberta.ca/~csp/cas/contact.html
To operate a learned society comprising scholars & professionals with interests in the social, economic, & political life of Slavic people, in addition to their languages, cultures, & histories; To promote understanding of Slavic societies & dialogue; To disseminate information about the past & present of the Slavic world
Megan Swift, President
R. Carter Elwood, Honorary President
Bohdan Nebesio, Sec.-Treas.
Elena Baraban, Vice-President
Reid Allan, Vice-President
Bohdan Nebesio, Sec.-Treas.

Canadian Association of University Business Officers (CAUBO) / Association canadienne du personnel administratif universitaire (ACPAU)
#320, 350 Albert St., Ottawa ON K1R 1B1
Tel: 613-230-6760; *Fax:* 613-563-7739
info@caubo.ca
www.caubo.ca
To promote the professional & effective management of the administrative, financial & business affairs of higher education; to have the professional standards of its members & to strengthen the contribution of higher education to the well being of Canada
Nathalie Laporte, Executive Director

Canadian Association of University Teachers (CAUT) / Association canadienne des professeures et professeurs d'université (ACPPU)
2705 Queensview Dr., Ottawa ON K2B 8K2
Tel: 613-820-2270; *Fax:* 613-820-7244
acppu@caut.ca
www.caut.ca
Social Media:
linkedin.com/company/canadian-association-of-university-teachers
www.facebook.com/CAUT.ACPPU
twitter.com/CAUT_ACPPU
To act as the national voice for academic staff; To promote academic freedom; To improve the quality & accessibility of post-secondary education in Canada
David Robinson, Executive Director
Sylvain Schetagne, Director, Research & Political Action
Valérie Dufour, Director, Communications

Canadian Bureau for International Education (CBIE) / Bureau canadien de l'éducation internationale (BCEI)
#1550, 220 Laurier Ave. West, Ottawa ON K1P 5Z9
Tel: 613-237-4820; *Fax:* 613-237-1073
info@cbie.ca
www.cbie-bcei.ca
Social Media: www.youtube.com/user/cbiebcei
www.facebook.com/pages/CBIE-BCEI/347318151976441
twitter.com/cbie_bcei
Karen McBride, President
Basel Alashi, Vice-President
Margaux Béland, Vice-President
Bashir Hassanali, Vice-President
Jennifer Humphries, Vice-President

Canadian Council for the Advancement of Education (CCAE) / Le Conseil canadien pour l'avancement de l'éducation
#310, 4 Cataraqui St., Kingston ON K7K 1Z7
Tel: 613-531-9213; *Fax:* 613-531-0626
admin@ccaecanada.org
www.ccaecanada.org
Social Media:
twitter.com/CCAECanada
To promote excellence in educational advancement through networking opportunities, professional development, & mutual support
Mark Hazlett, Executive Director
Melana Soroka, President
Kathy Arney, Vice-President
Kathy Butler, Vice-President
Ivan Muzychka, Vice-President

Canadian Council of Teachers of English Language Arts (CCTELA)
#10, 730 River Rd., Winnipeg MB R2M 5A4
Tel: 204-255-1676; *Fax:* 204-253-2562
cctela.52@gmail.com
www.cctela.ca
To provide a national voice in education relating to English Language Arts; to serve as a forum for communication among provincial councils concerning English Language Arts; to provide a system of communication & cooperation for teachers of English Language Arts at all levels in Canada; to encourage research, experimentation & investigation in English Language Arts teaching; to sponsor, promote & lobby for programs of benefit to Canadian students.
Linda Ferguson, Executive Director

Canadian Education & Training Accreditation Commission (CETAC)
#310, 590 Queen St., Fredericton NB E3B 7H9
Tel: 613-800-0340
www.cetac.ca
To assure students & the general public of the quality of Canada's post-secondary institutions & the programs they offer; To assist the institutions in continuously improving themselves & the education provided to students

Canadian Education Association (CEA) / Association canadienne d'éducation (ACE)
#705, 119 Spadina Ave., Toronto ON M5V 2L1
Tel: 416-591-6300; *Fax:* 416-591-5345
Toll-Free: 866-803-9549
info@cea-ace.ca
www.cea-ace.ca
Social Media: www.youtube.com/user/CdnEducAssn
www.facebook.com/cea.ace
twitter.com/cea_ace
Ron Canuel, President & Chief Executive Officer
Gilles Latour, Chief Operating Officer
Max Cooke, Director, Communications
Cailey Crawford, Director, Strategic Partnerships

Canadian Faculties of Agriculture & Veterinary Medicine (CFAVM) / Facultés d'agriculture et de médecine vétérinaire du Canada
77 Townsend Dr., Nepean ON K2J 2V3
Tel: 613-825-6873
info@cfavm.ca
www.cfavm.ca

Canadian Federation for Humanities & Social Sciences (CFHSS) / Fédération canadienne des sciences humaines (FCSH)
#300, 275 Bank St., Ottawa ON K2P 2I6
Tel: 613-238-6112; *Fax:* 613-238-6114
info@ideas-idees.ca
www.ideas-idees.ca
Social Media:
www.youtube.com/channel/UCirwy—DhRDqgLIujCUY4VA
linkedin.com/company/canadian-federation-for-the-humanities-and-social-sciences
www.facebook.com/ideas.idees
twitter.com/ideas_idees
The Federation represents the Canadian research community by working to support & advance research in the humanities & social sciences in Canada.
Stephen Toope, President
Jean-Marc Mangin, Executive Director

Canadian Federation of Business School Deans (CFBSD) / Fédération canadienne des doyens des écoles d'administration (FCDEA)
3000, ch de la Côte-Sainte-Catherine, Montréal QC H3T 2A7
Tel: 514-340-7116; *Fax:* 514-340-7275
info@cfbsd.ca
www.cfbsd.ca
To encourage the professional development of business school administrators; To promote excellence in management education; To represent management education to the government, the business community, & the media
Timothy Daus, Executive Director
Bahram Dadgostar, Chair
Jerry Tomberlin, Vice-Chair
Robert Mantha, Secretary-Treasurer

Canadian Federation of Students (CFS) / Fédération canadienne des étudiantes et étudiants (FCEE)
338C Somerset St. West, Ottawa ON K2P 0J9
Tel: 613-232-7394; *Fax:* 613-232-0276
web@cfs-fcee.ca
www.cfs-fcee.ca
Social Media: instagram.com/cfsfcee
twitter.com/CFSFCEE
To represent the collective interests of college & university students across Canada; To act as a unified voice for Canadian university & college students
Jessica McCormick, National Chair
Bilan Arte, National Deputy Chair
Gabe Hoogers, National Treasurer
Kevin Godbout, Representative, Graduate Students
Anne-Marie Roy, Representative, Francophone Students
Yolen Bollo-Kamara, Representative, Women
Simka Marshall, Representative, Aboriginal Students
Rajean Hoilett, Representative, Racialised Students

Canadian Federation of University Women (CFUW) / Fédération canadienne des femmes diplômées des universités (FCFDU)
Head Office, #502, 331 Cooper St., Ottawa ON K2P 0G5
Tel: 613-234-8252; *Fax:* 613-234-8221
cfuwgen@rogers.com
www.cfuw.org
Social Media:
www.facebook.com/CFUW.Ottawa
To pursue knowledge; to promote education; to improve the status of women & human rights; To participate actively in public affairs in a spirit of cooperation & friendship
Susan Murphy, President
Robin Jackson, Executive Director
Janice Pillon, Coordinator, Member Services
Betty Dunlop, Manager, Fellowship Program
Tara Fischer, Coordinator, Advocacy
Ryszard Kowalski, Developer, Bookkeeper & Software

Canadian Foundation for Economic Education (CFEE) / Fondation d'éducation économique
#201, 110 Eglinton Ave. West, Toronto ON M4R 1A3
Tel: 416-968-2236; *Fax:* 416-968-0488
Toll-Free: 888-570-7610
mail@cfee.org
www.cfee.org
Social Media: vimeo.com/cfee/videos
twitter.com/cfee1
To enhance the economic capabilities of Canadians
Gary Rabbior, President

Canadian History of Education Association (CHEA) / L'Association canadienne d'histoire de l'éducation (ACHE)
University of Saskatchewan, College of Education, 28 Campus Dr., Saskatoon SK S7N 0X1
www.ache-chea.ca
Social Media:
www.facebook.com/achechea
twitter.com/CHEA_ACHE
Kristina Llewellyn, President

Canadian Home & School Federation (CHSF) / Fédération canadienne des associations foyer-école (FCAFE)
#110, 99-1500 Bank St., Ottawa ON K1H 1B8
www.canadianhomeandschoolfederation.org
To improve the quality of Canadian public education available to children & youth; To act as the national voice of parents with children in public schools
Cynthia Richards, President
Deb Giesbrecht, First Vice-President
Charla Dorrington, Second Vice-President
Michelle Ercolini, Secretary-Treasurer

Canadian Network for Innovation in Education (CNIE) / Réseau canadien pour l'innovation en éducation (RCIÉ)
#204, 260 Dalhousie St., Ottawa ON K1N 7E4
Tel: 613-241-0018; *Fax:* 613-241-0019
cnie-rcie@cnie-rcie.ca
www.cnie-rcie.ca
Social Media:
www.facebook.com/pages/CNIE-RCIÉ/178940428810638
twitter.com/CNIE_RCIE
To develop & promote the use of technologies, practices, & policies that foster access to learning for students
Lorraine Carter, Interim Co-President
Diane Janes, Interim Co-President
Sandy Hughes, Secretary-Treasurer

Canadian School Boards Association (CSBA) / Association canadienne des commissions/conseils scolaires
#515, 1410 rue Stanley, Montréal QC H3A 1P8
Tel: 514-289-2988; *Fax:* 514-849-8228
info@cdnsba.org
www.cdnsba.org
Social Media:
www.facebook.com/124194330966818
twitter.com/cdnsba
To provide leadership for school boards throughout Canada by supporting the efforts of the provincial/territorial school board/trustee associations; To promote educational excellence at the elementary/secondary levels as a national imperative; To foster & promote the maintenance of the principles of local autonomy in education in Canada through elected representation; To provide for & maintain liaison with the Cabinet & all branches of the federal government & members of Parliament & to make representation on behalf of school boards in Canada; To maintain a national profile for school boards & to make representation on their behalf to other national organizations; To provide for interprovincial communication on issues & developments in public education that take place on a provincial/territorial, national or international level
Sandi Urban Hall, President

Canadian Society for Education through Art (CSEA) / Société canadienne d'éducation par l'art (SCEA)
PO Box 1700, Stn. CSC, University of Victoria, Victoria BC V8W 3N4
Tel: 250-721-7896; *Fax:* 250-721-7598
office.csea@gmail.com
www.csea-scea.ca
Social Media:
twitter.com/CSEA_SCEA
The Canadian Society for Education through Art, is a voluntary association and is the only Canadian national organization that brings together art educators, gallery educators, and others wtih similar intersts and concerns.
Miriam Cooley, President

Canadian Society for the Study of Education (CSSE) / Société canadienne pour l'étude de l'éducation (SCÉÉ)
#204, 260 Dalhousie St., Ottawa ON K1N 7E4
Tel: 613-241-0018; *Fax:* 613-241-0019
csse-scee@csse.ca
www.csse-scee.ca
Social Media:
www.facebook.com/csse.scee
twitter.com/CSSESCEE
To advance knowledge & inform practice in educational settings; to promote the advancement of Canadian research & scholarship in education; to provide for the discussion of studies, issues & trends in education, & for the dissemination of research findings; to promote exchange among members & other educational researchers in Canada & internationally; to foster partnerships &, through educational research, influence public policy & help determine the nature, structure & funding of the research agenda
Victor Glickman, President

Canadian Society for the Study of Higher Education (CSSHE) / La Société canadienne pour l'étude de l'enseignement supérieur (SCEES)
#204, 260 Dalhousie St., Ottawa ON K1N 7E4
Tel: 613-241-0018; *Fax:* 613-241-0019
csshe-scees@csse.ca
www.csshe-scees.ca
Social Media:
twitter.com/csshescees
To advance the knowledge of post-secondary education through the promotion of research & its dissemination through publications & learned meetings
Kathleen Matheos, Treasurer
Walter Archer, President

Canadian Teachers' Federation (CTF) / Fédération canadienne des enseignantes et des enseignants (FCE)
2490 Don Reid Dr., Ottawa ON K1H 1E1
Tel: 613-232-1505; *Fax:* 613-232-1886
Toll-Free: 866-283-1505
info@ctf-fce.ca
www.ctf-fce.ca
Social Media: www.youtube.com/user/canadianteachers
www.facebook.com/pages/Canadian-Golf-Teachers-Federation/321967620898
twitter.com/CanTeachersFed
To promotes a strong publicly funded education system for Canada, one that enhances the country's competitiveness in a knowledge based global economy & gives children the opportunity to become active, engaged citizens
Heather Smith, President
Cassandra Hallett DaSilva, Secretary General

Canadian Test Centre Inc. (CTC) / Services d'évaluation pédagogique
#10, 80 Citizen Ct., Markham ON L6G 1A7
Tel: 905-513-6636; *Fax:* 905-513-6639
Toll-Free: 800-668-1006
info@canadiantestcentre.com
www.canadiantestcentre.com
Social Media: www.youtube.com/user/CanadianTestCentre
To publish & distribute test products; to support teachers to make their testing programs work; to invest in research & development projects which aim to improve the measurement & evaluation of student ability & achievement.
Ernest W. Cheng, Managing Director

Canadian University & College Conference Organizers Association (CUCCOA) / Association des coordonnateurs de congrès des universités et des collèges du Canada (ACCUCC)
312 Oakwood Ct., Newmarket ON L3Y 3C8
Tel: 905-954-0102; *Fax:* 905-895-1630
inquiries@cuccoa.org
www.cuccoa.org
Exists for the purpose of information sharing, professional development & group marketing
Carol Ford, Manager

Career Colleges Ontario (CCO)
#2, 155 Lynden Rd., Brantford ON N3R 8A7
Tel: 519-752-2124; *Fax:* 519-752-3649
www.careercollegesontario.ca
Social Media:
linkedin.com/company/ontario-association-of-career-colleges
www.facebook.com/careercollegesontario
twitter.com/c_c_ontario
To act as the voice for the private career college sector in Ontario
Paul Kitchin, Executive Director
Lorna Mills, Manager, Office & Financial Aid

Centre d'animation de développement et de recherche en éducation (CADRÉ)
1940, boul Henri-Bourassa est, Montréal QC H2B 1S2
Tél: 514-381-8891; *Téléc:* 514-381-4086
www.cadre.qc.ca
Paul Boisvenu, Directeur général

Centre franco-ontarien de ressources pédagogiques (CFORP)
435, rue Donald, Ottawa ON K1K 4X5
Tél: 613-747-8000; *Téléc:* 613-747-2808
Ligne sans frais: 877-742-3677
cforp@cforp.ca
www.cforp.ca
Média social: twitter.com/CFORP
Produit et diffuse des ressources pédagogiques et offrir des services destinés à soutenir l'éducation en langue française
Gilles Leroux, Directeur général
Penny Bell, Directrice exécutive, Finances et Ressources humaines
Simone Saint-Pierre, Directrice, Communications et marketing

Colleges and Institutes Canada (CICan) / Collèges et instituts Canada
#701, 1 Rideau St., Ottawa ON K1N 8S7
Tel: 613-746-2222; *Fax:* 613-746-6721
info@collegesinstitutes.ca
www.collegesinstitutes.ca
Social Media: instagram.com/College_can
www.facebook.com/collegesinstitutes
twitter.com/CollegeCan
Colleges and Institutes Canada (CICan) is the national, voluntary membership organization representing publicly supported colleges, institutes, cégeps and polytechnics in Canada and internationally.
Denise Amyot, President & CEO

Colleges Ontario
PO Box 88, #1600, 20 Bay St., Toronto ON M5J 2N8
Tel: 647-258-7670; *Fax:* 647-258-7699
www.collegesontario.org
Social Media:
www.youtube.com/user/CollegesOntario1?feature=mhee
linkedin.com/company/network-for-innovation-and-entrepreneurship
www.facebook.com/CollegesOntario
twitter.com/CollegesOntario
To represent Ontario colleges; To advocate on provincial & national issues on behalf of its membership
Linda Franklin, President & CEO
Rob Savage, Director, Communications
Caroline Donkin, Director, Member Services & Special Projects
Bill Summers, Vice-President, Research & Policy

The Commonwealth of Learning (COL)
#2500, 4710 Kingsway, Burnaby BC V5H 4M2
Tel: 604-775-8200; *Fax:* 604-775-8210
info@col.org
www.col.org
Social Media: www.youtube.com/user/comlearn
linkedin.com/company/commonwealth-of-learning
www.facebook.com/COL4D
twitter.com/COL4D
To create & widen access to education & to improve its quality, utilising distance education techniques & associated communications technologies to meet the particular requirements of member countries
Asha S. Kanwar, President & CEO

The Comparative & International Education Society of Canada (CIESC) / La Société canadienne d'éducation comparée et internationale (SCECI)
University of Western Ontario, #2, 1151 Richmond St., London ON N6A 5B8
www.edu.uwo.ca/ciesc/
To promote international knowledge & understanding in education; To examine educational systems in international & comparative framework
Lynette Shultz, President

Confederation of Alberta Faculty Associations (CAFA)
Univ. of Alberta, 11043 - 90 Ave., Edmonton AB T6G 2E1
Tel: 780-492-5630; *Fax:* 780-436-0516
www.ualberta.ca/~cafa/
Social Media:
twitter.com/cafaab
CAFA is a professional organization of faculty and faculty association in Alberta Universities. The objects of the Conferdation are to promote the quality of education in the province and to promote the well-being of Alberta Universities and their academic staff. Comprised of four associations: The Association of Academic Staff University of Alberta, Athabasca University Faculty Association, The Faculty Association of the University of Calgary and The University of Lethbridge Faculty Association.
John Nicholls, Executive Director
Lori Morinville, Administrative Officer

Confederation of University Faculty Associations of British Columbia (CUFA BC)
#315, 207 West Hastings St., Vancouver BC V6B 1H7
Tel: 604-646-4677; *Fax:* 604-646-4676
www.cufa.bc.ca
Robert Clift, Executive Director
David Mirhady, President

Conférence des recteurs et des principaux des universités du Québec (CREPUQ) / Conference of Rectors & Principals of Quebec Universities
c/o Conférence des recteurs et des principaux, #200, 500, rue Sherbrooke ouest, Montréal QC H3A 3C6
Tél: 514-288-8524; *Téléc:* 514-288-0554
info@crepuq.qc.ca
www.crepuq.qc.ca
Est un organisme privé qui regroupe, sur une base volontaire, tous les établissements universitaires québécois; sert de forum permanent d'échanges et de concertation qui permet aux gestionnaires de partager leurs expériences en vue d'améliorer l'efficacité générale du système universitaire québécois.
Daniel Zizian, Directeur général

Conference of Independent Schools (Ontario) (CIS)
PO Box 27, Whitby ON L1N 5R7
Tel: 905-665-8622; *Fax:* 905-665-8635
admin@cisontario.ca
www.cisontario.ca
Social Media:
twitter.com/CISOntario
To provide a collegial forum to promote excellence in education among its member schools
Ian Campbell, Executive Director

Council of Atlantic Ministers of Education & Training (CAMET) / Conseil atlantique des ministres de l'Éducation et de la Formation (CAMEF)
PO Box 2044, Halifax NS B3J 2Z1
Tel: 902-424-5352; *Fax:* 902-424-8976
camet-camef@cap-cpma.ca
www.camet-camef.ca
To allow the ministers responsible for education & training in New Brunswick, Nova Scotia, Newfoundland & Labrador, & Prince Edward Island to collaborate & respond to needs identified in public & post-secondary education; To enhance cooperation in public & post-secondary education to improve learning for Atlantic Canadians
Rhéal Poirier, Secretary
Sylvie Martin, Regional Coordinator

Council of Canadian Law Deans (CCLD) / Conseil des doyens et des doyennes des facultés de droit du Canada (CDFDC)
c/o Bridgitte Pilon, Executive Director, 57 Louis Pasteur, Ottawa ON K1N 6N5
Tel: 613-824-9233; *Fax:* 613-824-9233
brigitteccld@rogers.com
www.ccld-cdfdc.ca
Brigitte Pilon, Executive Director

Council of Ontario Universities (COU) / Conseil des universités de l'Ontario
#1100, 180 Dundas St. West, Toronto ON M5G 1Z8
Tel: 416-979-2165; *Fax:* 416-979-8635
cou@cou.on.ca
www.cou.on.ca
Social Media:
www.facebook.com/CouncilofOntarioUniversities
twitter.com/OntUniv
To work with & on behalf of members to meet public policy expectations related to accountability, diversity of educational opportunity, financial self-reliance, & responsiveness to educational & marketplace needs
Alastair Summerlee, Chair
Bonnie M. Patterson, President & CEO
Nancy Sullivan, Interim Executive Director, Corporate Services
Barbara Hauser, Secretary to Council & Sr. Advisor

Dufferin Peel Educational Resource Workers' Association (DPERWA)
#106, 5805 Whittle Rd., Mississauga ON L4Z 2J1
Tel: 905-501-1622; *Fax:* 905-501-1623
www.dperwa.com
DPERWA is the official, certified bargaining body for all Educational Assistants, Designated Early Childhood Educators & Supply ERWs employed with the Dufferin Peel Catholic District School Board.
Diane Kossel, President

EduNova
#200, 1533 Barrington St., Halifax NS B3J 1Z4
Tel: 902-424-8274; *Fax:* 902-424-8134
info@edunova.ca
www.edunova.ca
Social Media: www.youtube.com/edun0va
www.facebook.com/pages/EduNova/212866282085259
twitter.com/edunova_news
To work with members in order to raise the profile of education & training expertise in Nova Scotia. EduNova is the only provincial education & training cooperative in Canada
Wendy Luther, President & CEO

Elementary Teachers' Federation of Ontario (ETFO) / Fédération des enseignantes et des enseignants de l'élémentaire de l'Ontario (FEEO)
136 Isabella St., Toronto ON M4Y 1P6
Tel: 416-962-3836; *Fax:* 416-642-2424
Toll-Free: 888-838-3836
www.etfo.ca
Social Media: www.youtube.com/user/ETFOprovincial
www.facebook.com/ETFOprovincialoffice
twitter.com/etfonews
To regulate relations between employees & employer, including but not limited to securing & maintaining, through collective bargaining, the best possible terms & conditions of employment; To advance the cause of education & the status of teachers & educational workers; To promote a high standard of professional ethics & a high standard of professional competence; To foster a climate of social justice in Ontario & continue a leadership role in such areas as anti-poverty, non-violence & equity; To promote & protect the interests of all members of the Federation & the students in their care; To cooperate with other organizations in Ontario, Canada & elsewhere, having the same or like objects
Sam Hammond, President
Susan Swackhammer, First Vice-President

Fédération des cégeps
500, boul Crémazie est, Montréal QC H2P 1E7
Tél: 514-381-8631; *Téléc:* 514-381-2263
comm@fedecegeps.qc.ca
www.fedecegeps.qc.ca
Média social: www.facebook.com/monretouraucegep
De promouvoir le développement de l'enseignement collégial; au nom de ses membres, la Fédération établit des contacts et étudie des dossiers communs avec différents partenaires gouvernementaux et privés, notamment en ce qui concerne les affaires pédagogiques, étudiantes, matérielles et financières, et les ressources humaines du réseau
François Dornier, Président
Jean Beauchesne, Président-directeur général

Fédération des comités de parents du Québec inc. (FCPQ)
2263, boul Louis-XIV, Québec QC G1C 1A4
Tél: 418-667-2432; *Téléc:* 418-667-6713
Ligne sans frais: 800-463-7268
courrier@fcpq.qc.ca
www.fcpq.qc.ca
Média social: www.facebook.com/fcpq.parents
twitter.com/fcpq
De défendre et de promouvoir les droits et les intérêts des parents des élèves des écoles publiques primaires et secondaires de façon à assurer la qualité de l'éducation offerte aux enfants
Gaston Rioux, Président
Marc Charland, Directeur général
Jonatan Bérubé, Conseiller aux communications

La Fédération des commissions scolaires du Québec (FCSQ)
CP 10490, Succ. Sainte-Foy, 1001, av Bégon, Québec QC G1V 4C7
Tél: 418-651-3220; *Téléc:* 418-651-2574
info@fcsq.qc.ca
www.fcsq.qc.ca
Média social: www.youtube.com/user/fcsq2011/videos
twitter.com/fcsq
Tout en conservant ses tâches premières de coordination et d'unification, la mission de la Fédération s'est élargie, au fil des ans, pour rencontrer deux objectifs principaux : contribuer à promouvoir l'éducation ainsi que représenter et défendre avec détermination les intérêts des commissions scolaires.
Josée Bouchard, Présidente
Pâquerette Gagnon, Directrice générale

Fédération des établissements d'enseignement privés (FEEP)
1940, boul Henri-Bourassa est, Montréal QC H2B 1S2
Tél: 514-381-8891; *Téléc:* 514-381-4086
Ligne sans frais: 888-381-8891
info@feep.qc.ca
www.feep.qc.ca
Média social: twitter.com/lafeep
Soutien des établissements membres sur les plans administratifs, pédagogiques et de la vie scolaire; représentation auprès du gouvernement
Nancy Brosseau, Directrice générale

Fédération des parents du Manitoba (FPCP)
MB
www.lapfm.com
Appuyer les membres dans le développement des milieux, familial, éducatif (préscolaire et scolaire) et communautaire, propices à l'épanouissement des familles francophones

Fédération étudiante universitaire du Québec (FEUQ) / Québec University Students' Federation
15, Marie-Anne Ouest, 2e étage, Montréal QC H2W 1B6
Tél: 514-396-3380; *Téléc:* 514-396-7140
Ligne sans frais: 877-396-3380
feuq@feuq.qc.ca
www.feuq.qc.ca
Média social: www.flickr.com/photos/feuq
www.facebook.com/page.FEUQ
twitter.com/feuq
Défendre et promouvoir les droits des étudiantes et étudiants universitaires du Québec
Jonathan Bouchard, Président
Alex Goyer, Vice-président exécutive

Fédération nationale des enseignants et des enseignantes du Québec (FNEEQ) / National Federation of Québec Teachers
1601, av de Lorimier, Montréal QC H2K 4M5
Tél: 514-598-2241; *Téléc:* 514-598-2190
fneeq.reception@csn.qc.ca
www.fneeq.qc.ca
Média social: www.facebook.com/FneeqCSN
twitter.com/FneeqCSN
La Fédération nationale des enseignantes et des enseignants du Québec (FNEEQ) est une fédération de la CSN qui regroupe les syndicats de l'enseignement. La mission première de la FNEEQ est l'amélioration des conditions de travail par l'entremise de la négociation et de l'application d'une convention collective entre un employeur et le personnel enseignant et salarié
Jean Trudelle, Président

Federation of Independent School Associations of BC (FISA)
150 Robson St., Vancouver BC V6B 2A7
Tel: 604-684-6023; *Fax:* 604-684-3163
info@fisabc.ca
www.fisabc.ca
To assist independent schools in maintaining their independence while seeking fair treatment for them in legislative & financial terms.
Peter Froese, Executive Director
Doug Lauson, President

Federation of New Brunswick Faculty Associations (FNBFA) / Fédération des associations de professeures et professeurs d'université du Nouveau-Brunswick (FAPPUNB)
#204, 361 Victoria St., Fredericton NB E3B 1W5
Tel: 506-458-8977; *Fax:* 506-458-5620
www.fnbfa.ca
To promote interests of teachers, librarians & researchers in universities & colleges of New Brunswick; To advance standards of professions & to seek to improve quality of higher education in the Province
Jean Sauvageau, President
Elisabeth Hans, Executive Director

Fédération québécoise des directeurs et directrices d'établissements d'enseignement (FQDE)
#100, 7855, boul Louis-H-Lafontaine, Anjou QC H1K 4E4
Tél: 514-353-7511; *Téléc:* 514-353-2064
Ligne sans frais: 800-361-4258
info@fqde.qc.ca
www.fqde.qc.ca
Média social: twitter.com/fqde/
Défendre les droits des directeurs, directrices, directeurs adjoints, directrices adjointes d'établissements d'enseignement, sans oublier de promouvoir l'excellence dans la direction des établissements d'enseignement au Québec: en supportant des associations de directions d'établissement d'enseignement; en faisant en sorte que les directions d'établissement d'enseignement aient un environnement de travail favorisant la réalisation du projet éducatif; en s'assurant que les directions d'établissement d'enseignement maintiennent une compétence de gestionnaire de haute qualité.
Marc Brunelle, Secrétaire
Chantal Longpré, Présidente

Fédération québécoise des professeures et professeurs d'université (FQPPU) / Québec Federation of University Professors
#300, 666, rue Sherbrooke, Montréal QC H3A 1E7
Tél: 514-843-5953; *Téléc:* 514-843-6928
Ligne sans frais: 888-843-5953
federation@fqppu.org
www.fqppu.org
Média social: twitter.com/fqppu
Ouvrer au maintien, à la défense, à la promotion et au développement de l'université comme service public; défendre une université accessible et de qualité
Jean-Marie Lafortune, Président

First Nations SchoolNet (FNS)
Indian & Northern Affairs Canada, Education Program Directorate, 10 Wellington St., North Tower, Gatineau QC K1A 0H4
Toll-Free: 800-567-9604
TTY: 866-553-0554
pnr-fns@ainc-inac.gc.ca
www.ainc-inac.gc.ca/edu/ep/index1-eng.asp
Established by the federal government, FNS provides internet access, computer equipment & technical support to First Nations schools on reserves across the country. Students can connect with each other, develop new skills, & participate in national &

international events. Six non-profit, regional management organizations deliver the program in their respective region, working with Indian & Northern Affairs Canada.

Foundation for Educational Exchange Between Canada & the United States of America
#2015, 350 Albert St., Ottawa ON K1R 1A4
Tel: 613-688-5540; *Fax:* 613-237-2029
info@fulbright.ca
www.fulbright.ca
Social Media: www.youtube.com/user/FulbrightCanada
www.facebook.com/pages/Fulbright-Canada/193768967190
twitter.com/FulbrightPrgrm
To support outstanding graduate students, faculty, professionals, & independent researchers in order to enhance understanding between the people of Canada & the United States
Michael K. Hawes, Executive Director
Ava Kovats, Sr. Finance Officer

IAESTE Canada (International Association for the Exchange of Students for Technical Experience) (IAESTE)
c/o Gordon Hall, Queens University, 74 Union St., Kingston ON K7L 3N6
Tel: 613-533-2992; *Fax:* 613-533-2535
canada@iaeste.org
www.queensu.ca/iaeste
To provide technical students with international work experience related to their studies
Michele Lee, National Secretary

Institut de coopération pour l'éducation des adultes (ICEA)
#303, 55, ave Mont-Royal ouest, Montréal QC H2T 2S6
Tél: 514-948-2044; *Téléc:* 514-948-2046
Ligne sans frais: 877-948-2044
icea@icea.qc.ca
www.icea.qc.ca
Promouvoir l'exercice du droit des adultes à l'éducation tout au long de la vie
Diane Dupuis, Directrice générale

Learning Assistance Teachers' Association (LATA)
c/o BC Teachers' Federation, #100, 550 West 6th Ave., Vancouver BC V5Z 4P2
Fax: 250-377-0860
www.latabc.com
Social Media:
www.facebook.com/LATABC
twitter.com/latabc
To provide equal access to the educational system, a position that supports the opportunity for students to pursue their goals in all aspects of education; To work together with parents and the community, and give all students the best opportunities for success
Janice Neden, President
Gail Bailey, Vice-President

Learning Disabilities Association of Alberta (LDAA) / Troubles d'apprentissage - Association de l'Alberta
PO Box 29011, Stn. Pleasantview, Edmonton AB T6H 5Z6
Tel: 780-448-0360
www.ldalberta.ca
To foster & promote public understanding & cultivate support networks to discover potential in individuals with learning disabilities; To provide direct support to children, families, & adults affected by learning disabilities & ADHD
Ellie Shuster, Executive Director

Learning Disabilities Association of British Columbia (LDAV) / Troubles d'apprentissage - Association de la Colombie-Britannique
3292 East Broadway, Vancouver BC V5M 1Z8
Tel: 604-873-8139; *Fax:* 604-873-8140
info@ldav.ca
www.ldav.ca
Social Media:
www.facebook.com/LDAVancouver
twitter.com/LDAVancouver
To advance the education, employment, social development, legal rights & general well-being of people with learning disabilities; to operate as a coordinating body, information centre & provincial representative for chapters within BC. The provincial administration is provided out of the Vancouver chapter office; the Vancouver chapter serves the Vancouver, Richmond & Burnaby areas.
Susan Keyes, Executive Director
Sofia Fortin, Officer, Resource Development & Communications

Learning Disabilities Association of Canada (LDAC) / L'association Canadienne des troubles d'apprentissage (ACTA)
#20, 2420 Bank St., Ottawa ON K1V 8S1
Tel: 613-238-5721; *Toll-Free:* 877-238-5332
info@ldac-acta.ca
www.ldac-acta.ca
Social Media: www.youtube.com/ldacacta
www.facebook.com/ldacacta
twitter.com/ldacacta
To advance the education, employment, social development, legal rights & general well-being of people with learning disabilities; to create a greater public awareness & understanding of learning disabilities; to promote & develop early recognition, diagnosis, treatment & appropriate educational, social, recreational & career-oriented programs for people with learning disabilities; to promote legislation, research & training of personnel in the field of learning disabilities
Claudette Larocque, Executive Director
Thealzel Lee, Chair

Learning Disabilities Association of Manitoba (LDAM) / Troubles d'apprentissage - Association de Manitoba
617 Erin St., Winnipeg MB R3G 2W1
Tel: 204-774-1821; *Fax:* 204-788-4090
ldamb@mts.net
www.ldamanitoba.org
To provide support to all those who are concerned with learning disabilities; To represent individuals & families with learning disabilities
Marilyn MacKinnon, Executive Director

Learning Disabilities Association of New Brunswick (LDANB) / Troubles d'apprentissage - Association du Nouveau-Brunswick (TA-ANB)
#203, 403 Regent St., Fredericton NB E3B 3X6
Tel: 506-459-7852; *Fax:* 506-455-9300
Toll-Free: 877-544-7852
admin@ldanb-taanb.ca
www.ldanb-taanb.ca
Social Media: vimeo.com/user19549796
www.facebook.com/LDANBTAANB
twitter.com/LDANB
Promotes the understanding & acceptance of the ability of persons with learning disabilities to lead meaningful & successful lives. Satellite office in Saint John.
Deschênes André, Executive Director

Learning Disabilities Association of Newfoundland & Labrador Inc. (LDANL)
The Board of Trade Bldg., #301, 66 Kenmount Rd., St. John's NL A1B 3V7
Tel: 709-753-1445; *Fax:* 709-753-4747
info@ldanl.ca
www.ldanl.ca
Social Media:
www.facebook.com/103104129749204
twitter.com/ldanl
To work towards to the advancement of legal rights, social development, education, employment, & the general well-being of people with learning disabilities
David Banfield, Executive Director

Learning Disabilities Association of Ontario (LDAO) / Troubles d'apprentissage - Association de l'Ontario
#202, 365 Evans Ave., Toronto ON M8Z 1K2
Tel: 416-929-4311; *Fax:* 416-929-3905
resource@ldao.ca
www.ldao.ca
Social Media:
www.facebook.com/LDAOntario
twitter.com/ldaofontario
To provide leadership in learning disabilities advocacy, research, education & services; to advance the full participation of children, youth & adults with learning disabilites in today's society
Lawrence Barns, President & CEO
Karen Quinn, Director, Operations

Learning Disabilities Association of Prince Edward Island (LADPEI)
#149, 40 Enman Cres., Charlottetown PE C1E 1E6
Tel: 902-894-5032
ldapei@eastlink.ca
www.ldapei.ca
Social Media:
www.facebook.com/ldapei
twitter.com/LDAPEI
To advance the interests of people with learning disabilities; To act as a voice for learning disabled people of Prince Edward Island
Martin Dutton, Executive Director

Learning Disabilities Association of Saskatchewan (LDAS) / Troubles d'apprentissage - Association de la Saskatchewan
221 Hanselman Ct., Saskatoon SK S7L 6A8
Tel: 306-652-4114; *Fax:* 306-652-3220
reception@ldas.org
www.ldas.org
To advance the education, employment, social development, legal rights & general well-being of people with learning disabilities. Branches in Regina & Prince Albert.
Dale Rempel, Provincial Executive Director

Learning Disabilities Association of The Northwest Territories (LDA-NWT)
PO Box 242, Yellowknife NT X1A 2N2
Tel: 867-873-6378; *Fax:* 867-873-6378
lda-nwt@arcticdata.ca
To help people with learning disabilities achieve their potential in school, the workplace, & in society

Learning Disabilities Association of Yukon Territory (LDAY)
128A Copper Rd., Whitehorse YT Y1A 2Z6
Tel: 867-668-5167; *Fax:* 867-668-6504
office@ldayukon.com
www.ldayukon.com
To provide services & programs for Yukoners with learning disabilities so that they reach their potential & become productive members of society
Stephanie Hammond, Executive Director
Barb Macrae, President

Learning Enrichment Foundation (LEF)
116 Industry St., Toronto ON M6M 4L8
Tel: 416-769-0830; *Fax:* 416-769-9912
info@lefca.org
www.lefca.org
To provide programs & services to help individuals become contributors to their community's social & economic development
Ed Lamoureux, President
James McLeod, Vice-President
Kathleen Macdonald, Secretary

Manitoba Association of Parent Councils (MAPC)
#1005, 401 York Ave., Winnipeg MB R3C 0P8
Tel: 204-956-1770; *Fax:* 204-948-2855
Toll-Free: 877-290-4702
info@mapc.mb.ca
www.mapc.mb.ca
Social Media: www.youtube.com/MBParentCouncils
www.facebook.com/mapcmb
twitter.com/mapcmb
An organization of school-based parent groups throughout Manitoba.
Naomi Kruse, Executive Director

Manitoba Association of School Business Officials (MASBO)
PO Box 547, Morris MB R0G 1K0
Tel: 204-254-7570; *Fax:* 204-254-3606
www.masbo.ca
To provide leadership in the areas of finance, maintenance & transportation
Roy Seidler, Executive Director

Manitoba Association of School Superintendents (MASS)
375 Jefferson Ave., Winnipeg MB R2V 0N3
Tel: 204-487-7972; *Fax:* 204-487-7974
www.mass.mb.ca
To provide leadership for public education by advocating in the best interest of learners, & supports its members through professional services.
Ken Klassen, Executive Director

Manitoba Federation of Independent Schools Inc. (MFIS)
630 Westminster Ave., Winnipeg MB R3C 3S1
Tel: 204-783-4481
www.mfis.ca
To support & encourage high educational standards & values unique to our various school communities; to represent interests & concerns of member independent schools in Manitoba
Susan Eberhard, Executive Director
Robert Praznik, President

Manitoba School Boards Association
191 Provencher Blvd., Winnipeg MB R2H 0G4
Tel: 204-233-1595; *Fax:* 204-231-1356
Toll-Free: 800-262-8836
webmaster@mbschoolboards.ca
www.mbschoolboards.ca
Social Media:
twitter.com/mbschoolboards
To provide services to school boards in Manitoba; To advocate for public education
Josh Watt, Executive Director
Heather Demetrioff, Director, Education & Communication Services
George Coupland, Director, Labour Relations & Human Resource Services

Manitoba Teachers' Society (MTS)
McMaster House, 191 Harcourt St., Winnipeg MB R3J 3H2
Tel: 204-888-7961; *Fax:* 204-831-0877
Toll-Free: 800-262-8803
www.mbteach.org
Social Media:
www.facebook.com/manitobateachers
twitter.com/mbteachers
Envisions a public education system that provides equal accessibility & equal opportunity for all children, that optimizes the potential of all students as individuals & citizens, that fosters lifelong learning & that ensures a safe learning environment respectful of diversity & human dignity
Bobbi Taillefer, General Secretary
Dave Tate, Chief Financial Officer

McMaster University Retirees Association (MURA)
c/o McMaster University, Gilmour Hall, #B108, 1280 Main St. W, Hamilton ON L8S 4L8
Tel: 905-525-9140
mura@mcmaster.ca
mura.mcmaster.ca
The McMaster University Retirees Association seeks to contribute in as many ways as possible to the welfare, prestige, and excellence of the University and to encourage and promote a spirit of fraternity and unity among the members of the Association, and to provide means for continuing the associations which retirees enjoyed as employees of the University.

Mensa Canada Society / La Société Mensa Canada
PO Box 1570, Kingston ON K7L 5C8
Tel: 613-547-0824; *Fax:* 613-531-0626
mensa@eventsmgt.com
www.canada.mensa.org
To identify & foster human intelligence for the benefit of humanity; To encourage research; To provide an intellectual & social environment for members
Millie Norry, President

National Educational Association of Disabled Students (NEADS) / Association nationale des étudiant(e)s handicapé(e)s au niveau postsecondaire
Carleton University, Unicentre, #426, 1125 Colonel By Dr., Ottawa ON K1S 5B6
Tel: 613-380-8065; *Fax:* 613-369-4391
Toll-Free: 877-670-1256
info@neads.ca
www.neads.ca
To encourage the self-empowerment of post-secondary students with disabilities; to advocate for increased accessibility at all levels so that disabled students may gain equal access to a college or university education; to provide an information resource base on services for disabled students nationwide according to a file of material from post-secondary institutions
Frank Smith, National Coordinator

National Reading Campaign, Inc.
#300, 2 Toronto St., Toronto ON M5C 2B6
Tel: 416-847-0309
info@nationalreadingcampaign.ca
www.nationalreadingcampaign.ca
Social Media: www.youtube.com/user/NationalReadCampaign
www.facebook.com/NationalReadingCampaign
twitter.com/readingcampaign
To help make Canada a nation of readers
Sandy Crawley, Executive Director

New Brunswick Federation of Home & School Associations, Inc. (NBFHSA)
921 College Hill Rd., Fredericton NB E3B 6Z9
Tel: 506-451-6247
www.nbfhsa.org
To ensure a quality education, enhanced by parental involvement, & a safe environment for all children.
Cynthia Richards, Interim President
Lynne Roy, 1st Vice President

New Brunswick Teachers' Association (NBTA) / Fédération des enseignants du Nouveau-Brunswick (FENB)
PO Box 752, 650 Montgomery St., Fredericton NB E3B 5G2
Tel: 506-452-8921; *Fax:* 506-453-9795
www.nbta.ca
Social Media:
www.facebook.com/219814221400600
Guy Arseneault, President
Larry Jamieson, Executive Director

Newfoundland & Labrador School Boards Association (NLSBA)
40 Strawberry Marsh Rd., St. John's NL A1B 2V5
Tel: 709-722-7171; *Fax:* 709-722-8214
www.schoolboardsnl.ca
To promote the interests of education in Newfoundland & Labrador
Brian Shortall, Executive Director

Newfoundland & Labrador Teachers' Association (NLTA) / Association des enseignants de Terre-Neuve
3 Kenmount Rd., St. John's NL A1B 1W1
Tel: 709-726-3223; *Fax:* 709-726-4302
Toll-Free: 800-563-3599
mail@nlta.nl.ca
www.nlta.nl.ca
Social Media:
www.facebook.com/nlta.nl.ca
twitter.com/NLTeachersAssoc
To strive towards the professional excellence & personal well-being of teachers
Don Ash, Executive Director

Northwest Territories Teachers' Association (NWTTA)
PO Box 2340, 5018 - 48 St., Yellowknife NT X1A 2P7
Tel: 867-873-8501; *Fax:* 867-873-2366
nwtta@nwtta.nt.ca
www.nwtta.nt.ca
The Northwest Territories Teachers' Association is the professional voice of educators as they provide quality education to Northwest Territories students. With commitment to growth, respect & security for its membership, the Association represents all regions equally, advocates for public education & promotes the teaching profession
Fraser Oliver, President
David Roebuck, Executive Director

Nova Scotia Federation of Home & School Associations (NSFHSA)
#102, 7165 Hwy. 1, Coldbrook NS B4R 1A2
Tel: 902-676-6676; *Toll-Free:* 800-214-8373
nsfhsa@staff.ednet.ns.ca
www.nsfhsa.org
To provide a forum for discussion between the home & school beyond the parent-teacher interview; to promote & secure legislation for the care & protection of & equality of educational opportunities for children; to give parents an understanding of the school & its work, assisting in interpreting the school to the public; to confer & cooperate with organizations other than the schools which concern themselves with the training & development of children & youth
Charla Dorrington, President

Nova Scotia School Boards Association (NSSBA) / Association des conseils scolaires de la Nouvelle-Écosse
#395, 3 Spectacle Lake Dr., Dartmouth NS B3B 1W8
Tel: 902-491-2888
info@nssba.ca
www.nssba.ca
Social Media:
www.youtube.com/user/NSSBA2012?feature=mhee
linkedin.com/company/nova-scotia-school-boards-association
www.facebook.com/NovaScotiaSchoolBoardsAssociation
twitter.com/NSSchoolBoards
To act as the voice for school boards in Nova Scotia; To strive towards excellence in public education for students in the province
Nancy Pynch-Worthylake, Executive Director

Nova Scotia Teachers Union (NSTU) / Syndicat des enseignants de la Nouvelle-Écosse
Dr. Tom Parker Bldg., 3106 Joseph Howe Dr., Halifax NS B3L 4L7
Tel: 902-477-5621; *Fax:* 902-477-3517
Toll-Free: 800-565-6788
centraloffice@nstu.ca
www.nstu.ca
Social Media: www.youtube.com/user/nstuwebcast
www.facebook.com/nsteachersunion
twitter.com/NSTeachersUnion
To unify the teaching profession in Nova Scotia; To improve the quality of education
Joan Ling, Executive Director

Nunavut Teachers' Association (NTA)
PO Box 2458, Iqaluit NU X0A 0H0
Tel: 867-979-0750; *Fax:* 867-979-0780
www.ntanu.ca
To represent & negotiate for teachers, vice-principals, & principals, as well as RSO & TLC coordinators in Nunavut; To ensure that members' rights & benefits are advocated & protected
Terry Young, President
Emile Hatch, Executive Director
Jeff Avery, Coordinator, Professional Improvement

Ontario Association of Deans of Education (OADE)
c/o Council of Ontario Universities, #1100, 180 Dundas St. West, Toronto ON M5G 1Z8
Tel: 416-979-2165; *Fax:* 416-979-8635
cou.on.ca
Peter Gooch, Contact

Ontario Association of School Business Officials (OASBO)
#207, 144 Main St., Markham ON L3P 5T3
Tel: 905-209-9704; *Fax:* 905-209-9705
office@oasbo.org
www.oasbo.org
Dedicated to the pursuit & support of quality education for all students. OASBO is the professional organization for school business officials in Ontario. The purpose is to improve the quality of school business management and the status, competency, leadership qualities and ethical standards of school business officials at all levels; focus is on information sharing, the promotion of learning at all opportunities, the optimization of operational processes, & the development of partnerships to promote & recognize business practices excellence.
Bill Blackie, Executive Director

Ontario Catholic School Trustees' Association (OCSTA)
PO Box 2064, #1804, 20 Eglinton Ave. West, Toronto ON M4R 1K8
Tel: 416-932-9460; *Fax:* 416-932-9459
ocsta@ocsta.on.ca
www.ocsta.on.ca
Social Media: www.youtube.com/user/OCSTAVideo1
www.facebook.com/CatholicEducationInOntario
twitter.com/catholicedu
Kevin Kobus, Executive Director

Ontario Confederation of University Faculty Associations (OCUFA) / Union des associations des professeurs des universités de l'Ontario
17 Isabella St., Toronto ON M4Y 1M7
Tel: 416-979-2117; *Fax:* 416-593-5607
ocufa@ocufa.on.ca
www.ocufa.on.ca
Social Media:
www.facebook.com/OCUFA
twitter.com/ocufa
To act as the voice of Ontario's approximately 15,000 university faculty & academic librarians; To advance the professional & economic interests of university faculty & academic librarians; To enhance the quality of Ontario's higher education system
Kate Lawson, President
Judy Bates, Vice-President
Mark Rosenfeld, Executive Director
Mark Rosenfeld, Associate Executive Director, Research & Communications
Glen Copplestone, Treasurer

Ontario Council for University Lifelong Learning
c/o Lakehead University, Thunder Bay ON P7B 5E1
Tel: 807-343-8210; *Fax:* 807-343-8008
www.ocull.ca
To advocate for adult learners at Ontario universities, a collegial network, and a vehicle for professional development for its members.
Lisa Fanjoy, President

Ontario Council on Graduate Studies (OCGS) / Conseil ontarien des études supérieures
#1100, 180 Dundas St. West, Toronto ON M5G 1Z8
Tel: 416-979-2165; *Fax:* 416-979-8635
cou.on.ca/ocgs-1
To ensure quality graduate education & research across Ontario
Peter Gooch, Secretariat, COU
Clarke Anthony, Chair

Ontario Federation of Home & School Associations Inc. (OFHSA)
51 Stuart St., Hamilton ON L8L 1B5
Tel: 905-308-9563
info@ofhsa.on.ca
www.ofhsa.on.ca
Social Media:
www.facebook.com/159974104078740
To provide facilities for the bringing together of members of Home & School Associations for discussion of matters of general interest & to stimulate cooperative effort; to assist in forming public opinion favorable to reform & advancement of the education of the child; to develop between educators & the general public such united effort as shall secure for every child the highest advantage in physical, mental, moral & spiritual education; to raise the standard of home & national life; to maintain a non-partisan, non-commercial, non-racial & non-sectarian organization
Teresa Blum, President
Sandra Binns, 1st Executive Vice-President
Michelle Ercolini, 2nd Executive Vice-President

Ontario Federation of Independent Schools (OFIS)
PO Box 27011, 101 Holiday Inn Dr., Cambridge ON N3C 0E6
Tel: 519-249-1665
info@ofis.ca
www.ofis.ca
Social Media: www.youtube.com/user/subtlevox
www.facebook.com/OFISOntario
twitter.com/OFIS_Ontario
To secure guarantees from Ontario government for independent schools' right to exist, curricular freedom, self-governance & acceptance by government of its responsibility to let education grants follow a child to any bona fide school that meets acceptable social & educational criteria
Barbara Bierman, Executive Director
Barbara Brown, President

Ontario Modern Language Teachers Association (OMLTA) / Association ontarienne des professeurs de langues vivantes (AOPLV)
PO Box 268, 71 George St., Lanark ON K0G 1K0
omlta@omlta.org
www.omlta.org
Social Media:
www.facebook.com/omlta
twitter.com/omlta
To represent French & international languages teachers in the province of Ontario; To advocate on behalf of language educators; To promote the benefits of learning languages
Jennifer Rochon, President

Ontario Principals' Council (OPC)
180 Dundas St. West, 25th Fl., Toronto ON M5G 1Z8
Tel: 416-322-6600; *Fax:* 416-322-6618
Toll-Free: 800-701-2362
admin@principals.ca
www.principals.ca
Social Media:
www.facebook.com/pages/Ontario-Principals-Council
twitter.com/OPCouncil
To support the work of Ontario's principals & vice-principals to provide excellent leadership in the public education system
Ian McFarlane, Executive Director
Bob Pratt, President
Peggy Sweeney, Senior Communications Consultant

Ontario Public School Boards Association (OPSBA)
#1850, 439 University Ave., Toronto ON M5G 1Y8
Tel: 416-340-2540; *Fax:* 416-340-7571
webmaster@opsba.org
www.opsba.org
Social Media: www.flickr.com/photos/opsba
linkedin.com/company/ontario-public-school-boards'-association
twitter.com/OPSBA
To represent Ontario's public school authorities & public district school boards; To advocate on behalf of the public school system in Ontario; To promote & enhance public education
Michael Barrett, President
Gail Anderson, Executive Director
Florenda Tingle, Executive Coordinator

Ontario Secondary School Teachers' Federation (OSSTF) / Fédération des enseignants des écoles secondaires de l'Ontario (FEESO)
60 Mobile Dr., Toronto ON M4A 2P3
Tel: 416-751-8300; *Toll-Free:* 800-267-7867
www.osstf.on.ca
Social Media: www.youtube.com/user/OSSTF
www.facebook.com/osstfnews
twitter.com/osstf
To protect & enhance Ontario's public education system; To establish working conditions for members
Paul Elliott, President & CEO
Harvey Bischof, Vice-President
Cindy Dubué, Vice-President
Pierre Côté, General Secretary
Earl Burt, Treasurer

Ontario Teachers' Federation (OTF) / Fédération des enseignantes et des enseignants de l'Ontario (FEO)
#200, 1300 Yonge St., Toronto ON M4T 1X3
Tel: 416-966-3424; *Fax:* 416-966-5450
Toll-Free: 800-268-7061
www.otffeo.on.ca
Social Media:
www.youtube.com/channel/UCkcSWDBDWNmFvv-QsvokCPw
www.facebook.com/otffeo
twitter.com/otffeo
To represent the interests of all registered teachers in Ontario's publicly funded schools
Francine LeBlanc-Lebel, President
Rhonda Kimberley-Young, Secretary-Treasurer
Lindy Amato, Director, Professional Affairs

Ontario University Registrars' Association (OUSA)
900 McGill Rd., Kamloops BC V2C 0C8
Tel: 250-828-5019
www.oura.ca
Lucy Bellissimo, President

ORT Canada
c/o ORT Toronto, #604, 3101 Bathurst St., Toronto ON M6A 2A6
Tel: 416-787-0339; *Fax:* 416-787-9420
Toll-Free: 866-991-3045
info@ort-toronto.org
www.ortcanada.com
Social Media:
www.facebook.com/pages/ORT-Toronto/299243785455
To fundraise in support of the worldwide vocational-training-school network of ORT.
Janis Finkelstein, President
Lindy Meshwork, Executive Director

Parent Cooperative Preschools International (PCPI)
8725 Westport Dr., Niagara Falls ON L2H 0A2
Tel: 905-374-6605
www.preschools.coop
Social Media: plus.google.com/118022490917296587831
www.facebook.com/parentcooperatives
To promote the family & community; to strengthen & expand the parent cooperative movement & community appreciation of parent education for adults & preschool education for children; to promote desirable standards for program, practices & conditions in parent cooperative preschools & encourage continuing education for parents, teachers & directors; to promote interchange of information among parent cooperative nursery schools, kindergartens & other parent-sponsored preschool programs; to cooperate with family living, adult education & early childhood educational organizations in the interest of more effective service relationships with parents of young children; to study & promote legislation designed to further the health & well-being of children & families
Lesley Romanoff, President
Maria Campbell, Canadian Secretary

Parents as First Educators (PAFE)
PO Box 84556, Toronto ON M6S 4Z7
Tel: 416-763-7233
pafe4you@gmail.com
www.p-first.com
Social Media:
www.facebook.com/pafe4
twitter.com/PAFE4
To ensure Ontario Catholic school board trustees are promoting Catholic teachings & to make parents aware of the work trustees are doing

Parents partenaires en éducation (PPE)
#B-150, 2445, boul St-Laurent, Ottawa ON K1G 6C3
Tél: 613-741-8846; *Téléc:* 613-741-7322
Ligne sans frais: 800-342-0663
www.ppeontario.ca
Média social: www.youtube.com/reseauppe
www.facebook.com/ppeontario
twitter.com/ppeontario
Travailler en étroite collaboration avec ses partenaires en éducation, outiller les parents dans leur rôle de partenaires en éducation et agir comme porte-parole provincial des parents; promouvoir l'excellence de l'éducation de langue française et l'épanouissement global des enfants francophones
Janine Brydges, Présidente
Sylvie Ross, Directrice générale

Pathways to Education Canada
439 University Ave., 16th Fl., Toronto ON M5G 1Y8
Tel: 416-646-0123; *Fax:* 416-646-0122
Toll-Free: 877-516-0123
info@pathwayscanada.ca
www.pathwaystoeducation.ca
Social Media:
www.facebook.com/pathwaystoeducationcanada
twitter.com/PathwaysCanada
To assist youth in low-income communities graduate high school & transition into post-secondary education opportunities
Sue Gillespie, President & CEO
Colleen Ryan, Director, Marketing & Communications

People for Education (P4E)
641 Bloor St. West, Toronto ON M6G 1L1
Tel: 416-534-0100; *Fax:* 416-536-0100
info@peopleforeducation.ca
www.peopleforeducation.ca
Social Media:
www.facebook.com/peopleforeducation
www.twitter.com/Anniekidder
People for Education is an independent organization working to support public education in Ontario's English, Catholic and French schools.
Annie Kidder, Executive Director

Prince Edward Island Home & School Federation Inc. (PEIHSF)
PO Box 1012, 40 Enman Cres., Charlottetown PE C1A 7M4
Tel: 902-620-3186; *Fax:* 902-620-3187
Toll-Free: 800-916-0664
peihsf@edu.pe.ca
peihsf.ca
Social Media:
www.facebook.com/peihsf
twitter.com/peihsf
Wendy MacDonald, President
Shirley Jay, Executive Director

Prince Edward Island Teachers' Federation (PEITF) / Fédération des enseignants de l'Île-du-Prince-Édouard
PO Box 6000, Charlottetown PE C1A 8B4
Tel: 902-569-4157; *Fax:* 902-569-3682
Toll-Free: 800-903-4157
www.peitf.com
Social Media:
www.facebook.com/PEITF
twitter.com/PEITF
To promote & support education as well as the professional & economic well-being of PEI teachers
McLeod Bethany, President
Shaun MacCormac, General Secretary

Québec Association of Independent Schools (QAIS) / Association des écoles privées du Québec
PO Box 398, Stn. Snowdon, Montréal QC H3X 3T6
Tel: 514-483-6111; *Fax:* 514-483-0865
Toll-Free: 866-909-6111
qais@qc.aibn.com
www.qais.qc.ca
To promote collaboration, provide services that further educational leadership & advocate for independent English language education in Quebec on behalf of its member schools.
Sidney Benudiz, Executive Director

Québec Board of Black Educators (QBBE)
#310, Cavendish Blvd., Montréal QC H4B 2M5
Tel: 514-481-9400; *Fax:* 514-481-0611
qbbe@videotron.ca
www.qbbe.org
The Quebec Board of Black Educators mission is to promote the development of educational services for Black Youth and other youth between the ages of 5 to 25 who reside in the Greater Montreal area.
Phylicia Burke, Contact

Clarence Bayne, President

Québec English School Boards Association (QESBA) / Association des commissions scolaires anglophones du Québec (ACSAQ)
#515, 1410, rue Stanley, Montréal QC H3A 1P8
Tel: 514-849-5900; *Fax:* 514-849-9228
Toll-Free: 877-512-7522
qesba@qesba.qc.ca
www.qesba.qc.ca
Social Media:
twitter.com/qesba
To represent English school boards in Québec
Marcus Tabachnick, Executive Director

Québec Federation of Home & School Associations Inc. (QFHSA) / Fédération des associations foyer-école du Québec Inc.
#560, 3285, boul Cavendish, Montréal QC H4B 2L9
Tel: 514-481-5619; *Fax:* 514-481-5610
Toll-Free: 888-808-5619
info@qfhsa.org
www.qfhsa.org
Social Media:
www.facebook.com/QFHSA
To provide facilities for the bringing together of members of Home & School Associations for discussion of matters of general interest & to stimulate cooperative effort; To assist in forming public opinion favorable to reform & advancement of the education of the child; to develop between educators & the general public such a united effort as shall secure for every child the highest advantage in physical, mental, moral & spiritual education; To raise the standard of home & national life; To maintain non-partisan, non-commercial, non-racial & non-sectarian organization
Brian Rock, President

Le Réseau d'enseignement francophone à distance du Canada (REFAD)
CP 47542, Succ. Plateau Mont-Royal, Montréal QC H2H 2S8
Tél: 514-284-9109; *Téléc:* 514-284-9363
refad@sympatico.ca
www.refad.ca
Mèdia social: twitter.com/_refad
Favoriser la collaboration entre les personnes et les organisations intéressées par l'enseignement à distance en français; rassembler en réseau les établissements qui ont recours à la formation à distance en français; appuyer et compléter d'autres réseaux d'enseignement à distance existant déjà à travers le Canada; promouvoir et accroître la qualité et la quantité des programmes et des cours offerts dans la francophonie canadienne.
Caroll-Ann Keating, Présidente
Alain Langlois, Directeur général

The Retired Teachers of Ontario (RTO) / Les Enseignants et enseignantes retraités de l'Ontario (ERO)
#300, 18 Spadina Rd., Toronto ON M5R 2S7
Tel: 416-962-9463; *Fax:* 416-962-1061
Toll-Free: 800-361-9888
info@rto-ero.org
www.rto-ero.org
Social Media: www.youtube.com/erorto
www.facebook.com/rto.ero
twitter.com/rto_ero
To promote the interests of persons in receipt of a pension under the Ontario Teachers' Pension Act
Howard Braithwaite, Executive Director

Saskatchewan Association for Multicultural Education (SAME)
2454 Atkinson St., Regina SK S4N 3X5
Tel: 306-780-9428
same@sk.sympatico.ca
To promote multicultural & anti-racist education throughout Saskatchewan; To raise awareness & acceptance of cultural diversity in the province; To respond to changes in multicultural policies & demographics; To address social justice issues

Saskatchewan Association of Historical High Schools (SAHHS)
c/o Luther College High School, 1500 Royal St., Regina SK S4T 6G3
Tel: 306-791-9150; *Fax:* 306-359-6962
lutherhs@luthercollege.edu
www.luthercollege.edu
Mark Anderson, Principal

Saskatchewan Association of School Councils (SASC)
#301, 221 Cumberland Ave. North, Saskatoon SK S7N 1M3
Tel: 306-955-5723; *Fax:* 306-445-7707
sasc@sasktel.net
To enhance the education & general well-being of children & youth; To promote the involvement of parents, students, educators & the community at large in the advancement of learning & to act as a voice for parents; To promote effective communication between the home & the school; To encourage parents to participate in educational activities & decision making

Saskatchewan School Boards Association (SSBA)
#400, 2222 - 13th Ave., Regina SK S4P 3M7
Tel: 306-569-0750; *Fax:* 306-352-9633
admin@saskschoolboards.ca
www.saskschoolboards.ca
Social Media:
www.youtube.com/channel/UCHNAF7Vjq91-XbpSRUbdNJQ
www.facebook.com/saskschoolboards
twitter.com/saskschoolboard
To represent boards of education, including division boards, conseils scolaires, & local or district boards; To ensure advocacy, leadership & support for member boards by speaking as the voice for quality public education for all children; To offer opportunities for trustee development
Darren McKee, Executive Director
Catherine Vu, Director, Corporate Services
Jill Welke, Director, Communications Services

Saskatchewan Teachers' Federation (STF) / Fédération des enseignants et des enseignantes de la Saskatchewan
2317 Arlington Ave., Saskatoon SK S7J 2H8
Tel: 306-373-1660; *Fax:* 306-374-1122
Toll-Free: 800-667-7762
stf@stf.sk.ca
www.stf.sk.ca
Social Media:
www.youtube.com/channel/UClw3RFPZPxTzbldiTocbknA
twitter.com/SaskTeachersFed
To help provide the best possible education to children
Patrick Maze, President
Gwen Dueck, Executive Director

Skills/Compétences Canada
#201, 294 Albert St., Ottawa ON K1P 6E6
Tel: 343-883-7545; *Fax:* 613-691-1404
Toll-Free: 877-754-5226
www.skillscanada.com
Social Media: www.youtube.com/user/SkillsCanadaOfficial
www.facebook.com/pages/Skills-Canada-Competences-Canada/11736117829828
twitter.com/Skills_Canada
To create dynamic synergies between industry, government, youth, educators & labour; to raise awareness of the value of a technical or skilled trade career; to champion & stimulate the development of technological & employability skills in Canadian youth to strengthen our competitive edge in the global marketplace
John Oates, President
Shaun Thorson, Chief Executive Officer
Jennifer Cavanagh, Director, Communications

Society for Educational Visits & Exchanges in Canada (SEVEC) / Société éducative de visites et d'échanges au Canada
#201, 1150 Morrison Dr., Ottawa ON K2H 8S9
Tel: 613-727-3832; *Fax:* 613-727-3831
Toll-Free: 800-387-3832
info@sevec.ca
www.sevec.ca
Social Media: www.youtube.com/user/SEVECanada
www.facebook.com/SEVECanada
twitter.com/sevec
To create, facilitate & promote enriching educational opportunities within Canada for the development of mutual respect & understanding through programs of exploration in language & culture
Mary Reeves, Chair
Françoise Gagnon, Executive Director
Heather Daly, Director, Finance & Administration

Society for Quality Education (SQE)
57 Twyford Rd., Toronto ON M9A 1W5
Tel: 416-231-7247; *Fax:* 416-237-0108
Toll-Free: 888-856-5535
info@societyforqualityeducation.org
www.societyforqualityeducation.org
Social Media:
www.facebook.com/SQEducation
twitter.com/SQESocQualEd
To advance public & private education in Canada by disseminating authoritative information on educational governance & methodology.
Doretta Wilson, Executive Director
Malkin Dare, President

Society for the Promotion of the Teaching of English as a Second Language in Quebec (SPEAQ) / Société pour la promotion de l'enseignement de l'anglais, langue seconde, au Québec
#2, 6818, Rue Saint-Denis, Montréal QC H2S 2S2
Tel: 514-271-3700; *Fax:* 514-271-4587
speaq@speaq.qc.ca
www.speaq.qc.ca
To bring together persons engaged or interested in the teaching of English as a second language in Quebec; To promote & develop the professional & economic interests of its members; To create a favourable climate for the development of teaching English as a second language in Quebec//Promouvoir l'enseignement de l'anglais, langue seconde au Québec
Micheline Schinck, President
Monique Mainella, Vice President

South Western Alberta Teachers' Convention Association (SWATCA)
c/o Roxane Holmes, 1215 - 19 Ave., Coaldale AB T1M 1A4
Tel: 403-308-8761
www.swatca.ca
Social Media:
twitter.com/swatca
Kim Yearous, President

TESL Canada Federation (TESL Canada)
3751 - 21 St. NE, Calgary AB T2E 6T5
Tel: 403-538-7300; *Fax:* 403-538-7392
Toll-Free: 800-393-9199
info@tesl.ca
www.tesl.ca
To support the sharing of knowledge & experiences across Canada; To represents diverse interests in TESL nationally & internationally
Sumana Barua, Executive Director
Ron Thomson, President

TESL Ontario
#405, 27 Carlton St., Toronto ON M5B 1L2
Tel: 416-593-4243; *Fax:* 416-593-0164
Toll-Free: 800-327-4827
administration@teslontario.org
www.teslontario.org
Social Media:
linkedin.com/groups/TESL-Ontario-1813872
www.facebook.com/101601733235647
twitter.com/TESLOntario
Sheila Nicholas, Chair
Marilyn Johnston, Vice-Chair

United World Colleges
Lester B. Pearson College of the Pacific, 650 Pearson College Dr., Victoria BC V9C 4H7
Tel: 250-391-2411
alumni@pearsoncollege.ca
www.pearsoncollege.ca
Social Media: www.youtube.com/user/PearsonUWC
linkedin.com/groups?gid=49277&home=
www.facebook.com/PearsonUWC
twitter.com/PCUWC
To encourage young people to become responsible citizens, politically & environmentally aware, committed to the ideals of peace, justice, understanding & cooperation, & to the implementation of these ideals through action & personal example
David B. Hawley, Director

Universities Canada (AUCC) / Universités Canada
#1710, 350 Albert St., Ottawa ON K1R 1B1
Tel: 613-563-1236; *Fax:* 613-563-9745
info@univcan.ca
www.univcan.ca
Social Media: www.pinterest.com/univcan;
www.youtube.com/user/auccweb
twitter.com/univcan
To act as the voice of Canadian universities; To present a unified voice for higher education, research, & innovation
Paul Davidson, President/CEO
Helen Murphy, Assistant Director, Communications
Heather Cayouette, Manager, Higher Education Scholarships

Yukon Teachers' Association (YTA) / Association des enseignantes et des enseignants du Yukon
2064 - 2 Ave., Whitehorse YT Y1A 1A9
Tel: 867-668-6777; *Fax:* 867-667-4324
Toll-Free: 866-668-2097
admin@yta.yk.ca
www.yta.yk.ca
To promote & support public education; To represent the professional & economic needs of Yukon educators
Jill Mason, President
Douglas Rody, General Secretary

Electronics & Electricity

Canadian Electrical Contractors Association (CECA) / Association canadienne des entrepreneurs électriciens (ACEE)
#460, 170 Attwell Dr., Toronto ON M9W 5Z5
Tel: 416-675-3226; *Fax:* 416-675-7736
Toll-Free: 800-387-3226
ceca@ceca.org
www.ceca.org
To represent electrical contractors at the national level
Colin Campbell, President
David Mason, Vice-President
Eryl Roberts, Executive Secretary

Canadian Electrical Manufacturers Representatives Association (CEMRA)
#300, 180 Attwell Dr., Toronto ON M9W 6A9
Tel: 647-258-7476; *Fax:* 416-679-9234
Toll-Free: 866-602-8877
info@electrofed.com
www.electrofed.com
To represent over 300 member companies that manufacture, distribute & service electrical, electronics & telecommunications products
Jim Taggart, President & CEO
Jeff Miller, Executive Director

Consumer Electronics Marketers of Canada: A Division of Electro-Federation Canada (CEMC)
#300, 180 Attwell Dr., Mississauga ON M9W 6A9
Tel: 905-602-8877; *Fax:* 416-679-9234
info@electrofed.com
www.cemc-efc.ca
To represent the consumer electronic marketing industry; To provide information for CEMC members to help them make good business decisions; To report on the status of the consumer electronics market
Robert Gumiela, Chair
Susan Winter, Vice-President

Corporation des maîtres électriciens du Québec (CMEQ) / Corporation of Master Electricians of Québec
5925, boul Décarie, Montréal QC H3W 3C9
Tél: 514-738-2184; *Téléc:* 514-738-2192
Ligne sans frais: 800-361-9061
www.cmeq.org
Augmenter la compétence des membres; règlementer la conduite des membres et de la profession; faciliter et encourager les membres à se familiariser avec des nouvelles techniques; chercher des solutions pratiques aux problèmes communs de l'industrie électrique

Electrical Contractors Association of Alberta (ECAA)
17725 - 103 Ave., Edmonton AB T5S 1N8
Tel: 780-451-2412; *Fax:* 780-455-9815
Toll-Free: 800-252-9375
ecaa@ecaa.ab.ca
www.ecaa.ab.ca
Social Media:
www.facebook.com/179555132080555
To work towards increased contractors knowledge & efficiency; improved communication between industry sections; government liaison for training qualifications & regulations; overall improvement of the electrical industry
Sheri McLean, Executive Director

Electrical Contractors Association of BC (ECA-BC)
#201, 3989 Henning Dr., Burnaby BC V5C 6N5
Tel: 604-294-4123; *Fax:* 604-294-4120
www.eca.bc.ca
Social Media: www.youtube.com/ecabctv
To promote use of electricity; to strengthen, encourage & promote electrical contracting industry; to promote functions assisting businessmen to become more efficient & profitable.
Deborah Cahill, President

Electrical Contractors Association of New Brunswick Inc. (ECANB)
PO Box 322, Fredericton NB E3B 4Y9
Tel: 506-452-7627; *Fax:* 506-452-1786
dwe@eca.nb.ca
www.eca.nb.ca
David Ellis, Executive Director

Electrical Contractors Association of Ontario (ECAO)
#460, 170 Attwell Dr., Toronto ON M9W 5Z5
Tel: 416-675-3226; *Fax:* 416-675-7736
Toll-Free: 800-387-3226
ecao@ecao.org
www.ecao.org
Social Media:
linkedin.com/company/electrical-contractors-association-of-ontario
www.facebook.com/141086522621754
To serve & represent the interests of the electrical contracting industry
Jeff Koller, Executive Director

Electrical Contractors Association of Saskatchewan
c/o Michael Fougere, 320 Gardiner Park Ct., Regina SK S4V 1R9
Tel: 306-525-0171
To voice the concerns of electrical contractors in Saskatchewan; To improvethe electrical industry
Michael Fougere, Executive Director

Institute of Electrical & Electronics Engineers Inc. - Canada
PO Box 63005, Stn. University, 102 Plaza Dr., Dundas ON L9H 4H0
Tel: 905-628-9554
www.ieee.ca
To advance the theory & practice of electrical, electronics, & computer engineering & computer science
Cathie Lowell, IEEE Canada Administrator
Keith Brown, President
Amir Aghdam, President Elect
Ashfaq Husain, Treasurer

Manitoba Electrical League Inc. (MEL)
#104, 1780 Wellington Ave., Winnipeg MB R3H 1B3
Tel: 204-783-4125; *Fax:* 204-783-4216
www.meleague.net
To advise & inform all people of Manitoba on effective use of electricity toward maintenance & betterment of standards of living; to encourage cooperation of various branches of electrical industry in developing programs in support of common marketing objectives.
Gord Macpherson, Executive Director

National Electricity Roundtable (NER)
c/o Bryan Simonson, 148 Park Estates Pl. SE, Calgary AB T2J 3W5
Tel: 403-619-8967
nationaler@shaw.ca
www.nationalelectricityroundtable.com
To act as a forum for companies operating in the Canadian electric power industry; to work with government to develop a sustainable industry
Richard Wunderlich, Chair
Bryan Simonson, President

Ontario Electrical League (OEL)
#300, 180 Attwell Dr., Toronto ON M9W 6A9
Tel: 905-238-1382; *Fax:* 905-238-1420
communications@oel.org
www.oel.org
Social Media:
linkedin.com/oeleague
www.facebook.com/132812900129239?fref=ts
twitter.com/OEL3
To represent & strengthen the electrical industry in Ontario
Stephen Sell, President
Sheila Sage, Manager, Operations
Cynthia Kenth, Editor, Dialogue

Emergency Response

Canadian Avalanche Association (CAA)
PO Box 2759, 110 MacKenzie Ave., Revelstoke BC V0E 2S0
Tel: 250-837-2435; *Fax:* 250-837-4624
Toll-Free: 800-667-1105
info@avalanche.ca
www.avalanche.ca
To foster & support a professional environment for avalanche safety operations in Canada; To represent the avalanche community to stakeholders
Ian Tomm, Executive Director
Mary Clayton, Director, Communications
Kristin Anthony-Malone, Manager, Operations
Emily Grady, Manager, Industry Training Program

Canadian Fallen Firefighters Foundation / Fondation canadienne des pompiers morts en service
#200, 440 Laurier Ave. West, Ottawa ON K1R 7X6
Tel: 613-786-3024; *Fax:* 613-782-2228
info@cfff.ca
www.cfff.ca
Social Media:
www.facebook.com/CFFF.FCPMS
To serve all firefighters & their families in time of need. This registered, non-profit, charitable organization is made up of members of the Canadian Fire Service and other interested citizens dedicated to honouring Canada's fallen firefighters.
Robert Kirkpatrick, President
Douglas Wylie, 1st Vice-President
Mike McKenna, 2nd Vice-President
John Clare, Treasurer

Canadian Red Cross (CRC) / La Société la Croix-Rouge canadienne
170 Metcalfe St., Ottawa ON K2P 2P2
Tel: 613-740-1900; *Fax:* 613-740-1911
Toll-Free: 800-418-1111
WeCare@redcross.ca
www.redcross.ca
Social Media: www.youtube.com/user/canadianredcross
www.facebook.com/canadianredcross
twitter.com/redcrossCanada
To help people deal with situations that threaten: their survival & safety, their security & well-being, their human dignity, in Canada & around the world; To improve the lives of vulnerable people by mobilizing the power of humanity
Conrad Sauvé, Secretary General & Chief Executive Officer
Jimmy Mui, Chief Financial Officer
Samuel Schwisberg, General Counsel & Corporate Secretary

Civil Air Search & Rescue Association (CASARA)
Tel: 204-953-2290
www.casara.ca
To promote aviation safety; To support Canada's Search & Rescue (SAR) program
Frank Schuurmans, President

Corporation des services d'ambulance du Québec
#205, 455, rue Marais, Vanier QC G1M 3A2
Tél: 418-681-4448; *Téléc:* 418-681-4667
Ligne sans frais: 800-463-6773
info@csaq.org
www.csaq.org
Pour offrir une gamme de services et d'avantages à ses membres et à défendre les intérêts de ces derniers auprès des différentes instances gouvernementales, auprès de ses membres au Québec.
Denis Perrault, Directeur général

Humanity First Canada
#40, 600 Bowes Rd., Concord ON L6A 4A3
Tel: 416-440-0346; *Fax:* 416-440-0346
info@humanityfirst.ca
www.humanityfirst.ca
to provide hunmanitarian aid and to arrange response to disasters and help restore communities and help them build a future in addition to relieve poverty by establishing, operating and maintaining training centres in developing countries.
Aslam Daud, President
Ejaz Khan, Secretary

Lifesaving Society / Société de sauvetage
400 Consumers Rd., Toronto ON M2J 1P8
Tel: 416-490-8844; *Fax:* 416-490-8766
www.lifesavingsociety.com
Social Media:
www.facebook.com/lifesavingsocietyON
twitter.com/LifesavingON
To prevent drowning & water-related incidents by providing lifesaving, lifeguarding & leadership education
Yvan Chalifour, Executive Director

Occupational First Aid Attendants Association of British Columbia (OFAAA)
#108, 2323 Boundary Rd., Vancouver BC V5M 4V8
Tel: 604-294-0244; *Fax:* 604-294-0289
Toll-Free: 800-667-4566
ofaaa@ofaaa.bc.ca
www.ofaaa.bc.ca
Social Media:
www.facebook.com/119440864766772
twitter.com/OFAAABC

To enhance the professional status of first aid attendants & to promote accessibility to high standards of first aid for the workers of the province of British Columbia
Allan Zdunic, President

REACT Canada Inc.
32 The Queensway North, Keswick ON L4P 1E3
Tel: 905-476-5231
react@react-canada.org
www.react-canada.org
To provide skilled volunteer two-way radio communications for safety; To provide volunteer emergency radio communications for travellers; To provide safety communications for walkathons & parades.; To offer speakers to community groups on correct use of radio in emergencies
Ronald W. McCracken, Director

St. John Ambulance / Ambulance Saint-Jean
#400, 1900 City Park Dr., Ottawa ON K1J 1A3
Tel: 613-236-7461; *Toll-Free:* 888-840-5646
www.sja.ca
Social Media:
www.youtube.com/channel/UCKqDpzz1BjDqUglmjquTC7w
www.facebook.com/St.John.Ambulance.TO
twitter.com/sja_canada
To enable Canadians to improve their health, safety & quality of life by providing training & community service. Courses in CPR, emergency first aid, & safety training are offered, as well as community service programs (medical first response, therapy dog services, emergency preparedness, youth programs), & first aid kits
Robert White, Chancellor
Jerry Rankin, Interim Chief Operating Officer

Search & Rescue Volunteer Association of Canada (SARVAC)
24 McNamara Dr., Paradise NL A1L 0A6
Tel: 709-368-5533; *Fax:* 709-368-1298
Toll-Free: 866-972-7822
info@sarvac.ca
www.sarvac.ca
A national voice for ground search and rescue volunteers in Canada to address issues of common concern, to develop consistency and promote standardization or portability of programs and volunteers and deliver initiatives that benefit and support all ground search and rescue volunteers in Canada as well as the general public.

Employment & Human Resources

Association of Canadian Search, Employment & Staffing Services (ACSESS) / Association nationale des entreprises en recrutement et placement de personnel
#100, 2233 Argentia Rd., Mississauga ON L5N 2X7
Tel: 905-826-6869; *Fax:* 905-826-4873
Toll-Free: 888-232-4962
acsess@acsess.org
www.acsess.org
Social Media: www.youtube.com/user/acsess123
linkedin.com/company/281336
twitter.com/ACSESS_
To promote the advancement & growth of the employment & staffing services industry in Canada
Neil Smith, National President
Amanda Curtis, Executive Director

Association of Career Professionals Internatinal (ACPI)
PO Box 38179, Toronto ON M5N 3A8
Tel: 416-233-4440; *Fax:* 866-605-0657
info@acpinternational.org
www.acpinternational.org
Social Media:
twitter.com/ACPIntl
A global organization dedicated to advancing public awareness of the career management profession, as well as in promoting the international profile and credibility of its varied membership.

Association of Professional Recruiters of Canada
#2210, 1081 Ambleside Dr., Ottawa ON K2B 8C8
Tel: 613-721-5957; *Fax:* 613-721-5850
Toll-Free: 888-421-0000
www.workplace.ca/resources/aprc_assoc.html
Social Media:
www.facebook.com/InstituteofProfessionalManagement
To establish standards & practices for the recruitment & selection of human resources in Canada & to provide members with the tools to practice at the highest professional levels

Canadian Association of Career Educators & Employers (CACEE) / Association canadienne des spécialistes en emploi et des employeurs (ACSEE)
#202, 720 Spadina Ave., Toronto ON M5S 2T9
Tel: 416-929-5156; *Toll-Free:* 866-922-3303
www.cacee.com
Social Media:
linkedin.com/groups?home=&gid=882447
twitter.com/followCACEE
To facilitate the process of matching graduates with employment; a partnership of employer recruiters & career educators providing information, advice & services to students, employers & career centre personnel in the areas of career planning & student recruitment.
Paul Smith, Executive Director
Jennifer McCleary, President

Canadian Career Information Association (CCIA) / Association canadienne de documentation professionnelle (ACADOP)
cciainquiries@gmail.com
www.ccia-acadop.ca
To promote the development & effective delivery of Canadian career information
Christine Colosimo, Co-Chair
Angella Nunes, Co-Chair

Canadian Council of Human Resources Associations (CCHRA) / Conseil canadien des associations en ressources humaines (CCARH)
#603, 150 Metcalfe St., Ottawa ON K2P 1P1
Tel: 613-567-2477; *Fax:* 613-567-2478
Toll-Free: 866-560-1288
info@cchra-ccarh.ca
www.cchra-ccarh.ca
To establish national core standards for the human resources profession; to foster communications among participating associations; to be the recognized resource on equivalency for human resources qualifications across Canada; & to provide a national & international collective voice on human resources issues
Patrick Hartling, Chair

HRMS Professionals Association (HRMSP) / Association des professionnels en SGRH (PSGRH)
#301, 250 Consumers Rd., Toronto ON M2J 4V6
Tel: 416-221-4559; *Fax:* 416-495-8723
Toll-Free: 866-878-3899
info@hrmsp.org
www.hrmscanada.com
To serve human resource management systems professionals by sharing knowledge, best practices, & industry trends
Richard Rousseau, President
Martine Castellani, Vice-President & Treasurer
John Allen Doran, Secretary

Human Resource Management Association of Manitoba (HRMAM)
#1810, 275 Portage Ave., Winnipeg MB R3B 2B3
Tel: 204-943-2836; *Fax:* 204-943-1109
hrmam@hrmam.org
www.hrmam.org
To enhance & promote the value of the human resource profession & practices across Manitoba
Ron Gauthier, Executive Director

Human Resources Professionals Association (HRPA)
#200, 150 Bloor St. West, Toronto ON M5S 2X9
Tel: 416-923-2324; *Fax:* 416-923-7264
Toll-Free: 800-387-1311
TTY: 866-620-3848
info@hrpa.org
www.hrpa.ca
Social Media: www.youtube.com/user/HRPATV
linkedin.com/company/HRPA
www.facebook.com/pages/HRPA/192819190690
twitter.com/HRPA
To empower human resources professionals by providing management & leadership support, through information resources, events, professional development, & networking opportunities.
Philip C. Wilson, Chair
William (Bill) Greenhalgh, CEO
Louise Tagliacozzo, Manager, Board Relations & Administration

Ordre des conseillers en ressources humaines agréés (CRHA)
#1400, 1200, av McGill Collège, Montréal QC H3B 4G7
Tél: 514-879-1636; *Ligne sans frais:* 800-214-1609
info@portailrh.org
www.portailrh.org
Média social: linkedin.com/groups?mostPopular=&gid=3233907
www.facebook.com/OrdreCRHACRIA
twitter.com/crha_quebec
De promouvoir l'importance stratégique de la gestion des ressources humaines dans la gestion des organisations ainsi que la promotion des nouveaux concepts et champs de développement qui caractérisent son évolution
Florent Francoeur, Président-directeur général

Energy

Canadian Coalition for Nuclear Responsibility (CCNR) / Regroupement pour la surveillance du nucléaire (RSN)
53 Dufferin Rd., Hampstead QC H3X 3T4
Tel: 514-489-5118
ccnr@web.ca
www.ccnr.org
To research all issues related to nuclear energy, whether civilian or military — including non-nuclear alternatives — especially those pertaining to Canada.
Gordon Edwards, President

Canadian National Energy Alliance (CNEA)
www.cnea.co
Social Media:
twitter.com/CNEA_for_AECL
To unite Canada's leading engineering & technology companies to manage Canada's radioactive waste & decommissioning responsibilities; To ensure that Canada's nuclear science capabilities continue to support the federal government's needs & responsibilities; To create & maintain an innovative agenda that not only supports Canada's existing science & technology needs but allows the association to pursue global nuclear initiatives
Lou Riccoboni, Contact

Canadian Nuclear Association (CNA) / Association nucléaire canadienne
#1610, 130 Albert St., Ottawa ON K1P 5G4
Tel: 613-237-4262; *Fax:* 613-237-0989
info@cna.ca
www.cna.ca
Social Media: www.youtube.com/talknuclear
linkedin.com/company/canadian-nuclear-association
www.facebook.com/TalkNuclear
twitter.com/talknuclear
To promote the orderly & sound development of nuclear energy for peaceful purposes in Canada & abroad; To promote & foster an environment favourable to the healthy growth of the uses of nuclear energy & radioisotopes; To encourage cooperation between various industries, utilities, educational institutions, government departments & agencies, which may have a common interest in the development of economic nuclear power & the uses of radioisotopes; To provide a forum for the discussion & resolution of problems which are of concern to the members, the industry, or the Canadian public; To stimulate cooperation with other associations with similar objectives & purposes
John Barrett, President & Chief Executive Officer
George Christidis, Director, Government Affairs
Malcolm Bernard, Director, Communications
John Stewart, Director, Policy & Research
Marie-danielle Davis, Corporate Secretary/Director, Member Services

Canadian Nuclear Society (CNS) / Société nucléaire canadienne (SNC)
655 Bay St., 17th Fl., Toronto ON M5G 2K4
Tel: 416-977-7620; *Fax:* 416-977-8131
cns-snc@on.aibn.com
www.cns-snc.ca
To promote the exchange of information about nuclear science & technology & its applications; To foster the beneficial utilization of nuclear science
Adriaan Buijs, President
K.L. (Ken) Smith, Financial Administrator
Denise Rouben, Office Manager

Canadian Renewable Fuels Association (CRFA) / Association canadienne des carburants renouvelables

#450, 55 Murray St., Ottawa ON K1N 5M3
Tel: 613-594-5528; *Fax:* 613-594-3076
www.greenfuels.org
Social Media:
linkedin.com/company/canadian-renewable-fuels-association
www.facebook.com/CanadianRenewableFuels
twitter.com/CanGreenfuels
To promote renewable fuel development & usage
Andrea Kent, President
Tyler Bjornson, Executive Director

Earth Energy Society of Canada (EESC) / Société canadienne de l'énergie du sol (SCES)

7885 Jock Trail, Richmond ON K0A 2Z0
Tel: 613-822-4987; *Fax:* 613-822-4987
info@earthenergy.ca
www.earthenergy.ca
To represent the ground-source/geothermal heat pump industry by promoting quality installations & earth energy technology
Bill Eggertson, Consultant

Wood Energy Technology Transfer Inc. (WETT)

#1, 189 Queen St. East, Toronto ON M5A 1S2
Tel: 416-968-7718; *Fax:* 416-968-6818
Toll-Free: 888-358-9388
WETT@funnel.ca
www.wettinc.ca
To promote the safe & effective use of wood burning systems, WETT maintains a training program designed to confirm & recognize the knowledge & skills of practising wood energy professionals; to provide training to new people entering the industry; to provide training to non-industry professionals such as inspectors; to provide training to specialty audiences such as volunteer firefighters & carpenters in remote communities
Anthony Laycock, Executive Director

Engineering & Technology

Applied Science Technologists & Technicians of British Columbia (ASTTBC)

10767 - 148 St., Surrey BC V3R 0S4
Tel: 604-585-2788; *Fax:* 604-585-2790
techinfo@asttbc.org
www.asttbc.org
Social Media: www.youtube.com/user/ASTTBC
linkedin.com/company/asttbc
www.facebook.com/ASTTBC
twitter.com/asttbc
To advance the profession of applied science technology & the professional recognition of applied science technologists, certified technician, & other members in a manner that serves & protects the public interest
Keith Trulson, AScT, President
John E. Leech, AScT, CAE, Chief Executive Officer
Cindy Aitken, Manager, Governance & Events
Anne Sharp, Manager, Marketing & Communications
Jason Jung, Manager, Professional Practice & Development
Nicky Malli, Manager, Finance
Geoff Sale, AScT, Manager, Internationally Trained Professionals
Jacqueline de Raadt, Manager, Executive Initiatives
Karen Taylor, DipBM, Manager, Operations

Association des firmes de génie-conseil - Québec (AFG) / Association of Consulting Engineering Companies - Quebec

#930, 1440, rue Ste-Catherine ouest, Montréal QC H3G 1R8
Tél: 514-871-2229; *Téléc:* 514-871-9903
info@aicq.qc.ca
www.aicq.qc.ca
Média social: www.youtube.com/aicqtv
linkedin.com/company/association-des-ing-nieurs-conseils-du-qu-bec
www.facebook.com/forumAICQ
Promouvoir et développer l'industrie du génie-conseil en regroupant des membres qui offrent des services de qualité
Robert Landry, Président du Conseil
André Rainville, Président-directeur général
Pierre Nadeau, Directeur, Communications

Association des ingénieurs municipaux du Québec (AIMQ) / Association of Québec Municipal Engineers

CP 792, Succ. B, Montréal QC H3B 3K5
Tél: 514-845-5303
admin@aimq.net
www.aimq.net
Améliorer les connaissances et le statut de l'ingénieur municipal par l'échange d'information, la coopération entre ingénieurs municipaux et avec d'autres associations professionnelles et la promotion des intérêts communs des membres de l'Association
Mathieu Richard, Directeur général
Richard Lamarche, Adjoint administratif

Association of Consulting Engineering Companies - British Columbia (ACEC-BC)

#1258, 409 Granville St., Vancouver BC V6C 1T2
Tel: 604-687-2811; *Fax:* 604-688-7110
info@acec-bc.ca
www.acec-bc.ca
To improve the commercial environment for consulting engineering firms
Catherine Fritter, Chair
Keith Sashaw, President & CEO
Alla Samusevich, Coordinator, Accounting & Events

Association of Consulting Engineering Companies - Canada (ACEC) / L'Association des firmes d'ingénieurs-conseils - Canada (AFIC)

#420, 130 Albert St., Ottawa ON K1P 5G4
Tel: 613-236-0569; *Fax:* 613-236-6193
Toll-Free: 800-565-0569
info@acec.ca
www.acec.ca
Social Media: www.youtube.com/ACECAFIC
linkedin.com/groups/ACECCanada-7450101?trk=my_groups-b-grp-v
www.facebook.com/ACECAFIC
twitter.com/ACECCanada
To assist in promoting satisfactory business relations between its Member Firms & their clients; To promote cordial relations among the various consulting engineering firms in Canada & to foster the interchange of professional, management & business experience & information among them; To safeguard the interest of the consulting engineer; To further the maintenance of high professional standards in the consulting engineering profession
Anne Poschmann, Chair
John D. Gamble, CET, P.Eng., President
Jean-Marc Carrière, Vice-President, Finance & Administration
Susie Grynol, CAE, Vice-President, Policy & Public Affairs

Association of Consulting Engineering Companies - Manitoba (ACEC-MB)

PO Box 1547, Stn. Main, Winnipeg MB R3C 2Z4
Tel: 204-774-5258; *Fax:* 204-779-0788
acec-mb.ca
Social Media:
twitter.com/acec_manitoba
To promote & enhance the business interests of the consulting engineers of Manitoba; to lead in the application of technology for the benefit of society
Cameron Dyck, P.Eng., P.E., President
Shirley E. Tillett, Executive Director

Association of Consulting Engineering Companies - New Brunswick (ACEC-NB) / Association des firmes d'ingénieurs-conseils - Nouveau-Brunswick

PO Box 415, Moncton NB E1C 8L4
Tel: 506-380-5776
info@acec-nb.ca
www.acec-nb.ca
To develop & support member firms; To improve the business environment for member firms & their clients; To further the professional standards of the consulting engineering profession
Nadine Boudreau, Executive Director

Association of Consulting Engineering Companies - Prince Edward Island (ACEC-PEI)

c/o James C Johnson Associates Inc., #2, Pickard Bldg., Harbourside II, Charlottetown PE C1A 8R4
Tel: 902-629-5895; *Fax:* 902-368-2196
Hal Brothers, Acting Executive Director

Association of Consulting Engineering Companies - Saskatchewan (ACEC-SK)

#12, 2010 - 7 Ave., Regina SK S4R 1C2
Tel: 306-359-3338; *Fax:* 306-522-5325
info@acec-sk.ca
www.acec-sk.ca
To further the maintenance of high professional standards in consulting engineering profession; To promote cordial relations among various consulting firms in Saskatchewan; To foster interchange of professional management & business experience & information among consulting engineers; To develop regional representation & participation in affairs of the association
Jason Gasmo, P.Eng, Chair
Beverly MacLeod, Executive Director

Association of Engineering Technicians & Technologists of Newfoundland & Labrador (AETTNL)

Donovan's Industrial Park, PO Box 790, 22 Sagona Ave., Mount Pearl NL A1N 2Y2
Tel: 709-747-2868; *Fax:* 709-747-2869
Toll-Free: 888-238-8600
aettnl@aettnl.com
www.aettnl.com
To advance the profession of Applied Science/Engineering Technology & the professional recognition of Certified Technicians & Technologists.
Newton Pritchett, President
Donna Parsons, Registrar

Association of Professional Engineers & Geoscientists of Alberta (APEGA)

Scotia One, #1500, 10060 Jasper Ave. NW, Edmonton AB T5J 4A2
Tel: 780-426-3990; *Fax:* 780-426-1877
Toll-Free: 800-661-7020
email@apega.ca
www.apega.ca
To register & set practice standards & codes of professional conduct & ethics for professional engineers, geologists, & geophysicists in Alberta, according to The Engineering, Geological & Geophysical Professions Act
Mark Flint, Chief Executive Officer
Krista Nelson-Marciano, Director, Operations
Pat Lobregt, Director, Executive & Government Relations
Philip Mulder, Director, Communications
D.S. (Pal) Mann, Director, Corporate Services

Association of Professional Engineers & Geoscientists of British Columbia (APEGBC)

#200, 4010 Regent St., Burnaby BC V5C 6N2
Tel: 604-430-8035; *Fax:* 604-430-8085
Toll-Free: 888-430-8035
apeginfo@apeg.bc.ca
www.apeg.bc.ca
Social Media:
linkedin.com/company/apegbc
twitter.com/APEGBC
To protect the public interest in matters related to geoscience & engineering; To regulate & govern the professions of professional engineers & geoscientists in British Columbia, according to the Engineers & Geoscientists Act; To strive for professional excellence, by establishing academic, experience, & professional practice standards
Ann English, P.Eng., CEO & Registrar
Tony Chong, P.Eng., Chief Regulatory Officer & Deputy Registrar
Janet Sinclair, COO
Jennifer Cho, CGA, Director, Finance & Administration
Peter Mitchell, P.Eng., Director, Professional Practice, Standards, & Development

Association of Professional Engineers & Geoscientists of British Columbia Foundation

#200, 4010 Regent St., Burnaby BC V5C 6N2
Tel: 604-430-8035; *Fax:* 604-430-8085
Toll-Free: 888-430-8035
www.apeg.bc.ca/services/foundation.html
To operate at arms-length from the APEGBC & to promote education in engineering & geoscience through the granting of bursaries & scholarships

Association of Professional Engineers & Geoscientists of Manitoba (APEGM)

870 Pembina Hwy., Winnipeg MB R3M 2M7
Tel: 204-474-2736; *Fax:* 204-474-5960
Toll-Free: 866-227-9600
apegm@apegm.mb.ca
www.apegm.mb.ca
To serve & protect the public interest by governing & advancing the practice of engineering in accordance with the Engineering Profession Act of Manitoba
Grant Koropatnick, P.Eng., FEC, CEO & Registrar
Michael Gregoire, P.Eng., FEC, Director, Professional Standards
Sharon E. Sankar, P.Eng., FEC, Director, Admissions
Lorraine Dupas, Coordinator, Professional Standards
Angela Moore, Coordinator, Operations
Diana Vander Aa, Coordinator, Volunteer & Government Relations

Association of Professional Engineers & Geoscientists of New Brunswick (APEGNB) / Association des ingénieurs et géoscientifiques du Nouveau-Brunswick (AINB)
183 Hanwell Rd., Fredericton NB E3B 2R2
Tel: 506-458-8083; *Fax:* 506-451-9629
Toll-Free: 888-458-8083
info@apegnb.com
www.apegnb.com
Social Media: twitter.com/APEGNB
To establish, maintain & develop standards of knowledge & skill, qualification & practice, & professional ethics; To promote public awareness of the role of the association
Annie Dietrich, P.Eng./P.Geo, President
Matt Hayes, P.Eng., Vice-President
Andrew McLeod, FEC/FGC (Hon.), CEO

Association of Professional Engineers & Geoscientists of Saskatchewan (APEGS)
#300 - 4581 Parliament Ave., Regina SK S4W 0G3
Tel: 306-525-9547; *Fax:* 306-525-0851
Toll-Free: 800-500-9547
apegs@apegs.sk.ca
www.apegs.sk.ca
To achieve a safe & prosperous future through engineering & geoscience
Andrew Loken, P.Eng., FEC, President
Dennis Paddock, P.Eng., FEC, FC, Executive Director & Registrar
Bob McDonald, P.Eng., LL.B., Deputy Registrar
Kate MacLachlan, Ph.D., P.Geo., Director, Academic Review
Tina Maki, P.Eng., FEC, FG, Director, Registration
Chris Wimmer, P.Eng., FEC, Director, Professional Standards

Association of Professional Engineers of Prince Edward Island (APEPEI)
135 Water St., Charlottetown PE C1A 1A8
Tel: 902-566-1268; *Fax:* 902-566-5551
www.engineerspei.com
Social Media: twitter.com/EngineersPEI
To regulate the practice of professional engineering in the province, with authority over members, licensees, engineers-in-training, & holders of certificates of authorization.
Richard MacEwan, President
Jim Landrigan, Executive Director/Registrar

Association of Professional Engineers of Yukon (APEY)
312B Hanson St., Whitehorse YT Y1A 1Y6
Tel: 867-667-6727; *Fax:* 867-668-2142
staff@apey.yk.ca
www.apey.yk.ca
To establish, maintain & develop standards of knowledge & skill, standards of qualification & practice & standards of professional ethics; to promote public awareness of the role of the association

Association of Science & Engineering Technology Professionals of Alberta (ASET)
#1600, 9888 Jasper Ave., Edmonton AB T5J 5C6
Tel: 780-425-0626; *Fax:* 780-424-5053
Toll-Free: 800-272-5619
asetadmin@aset.ab.ca
www.aset.ab.ca
Social Media: www.youtube.com/channel/UCLp53oRwqj7En352luQiLhQ
linkedin.com/company/asetmembers
www.facebook.com/ASETmembers
twitter.com/asetmembers
To benefit the public & the profession by regulating & promoting safe, high quality, professional technology practice; To focus on the engineering technology, applied science, & information technology fields; To issue credentials to qualified individuals; To accredit training programs. There are 9 chapters across the province
Norman Kyle, R.E.T., P.L.(En, President
Barry Cavanaugh, CEO & General Counsel
Mat Steppan, Director, Stakeholder Relations
Kimberly McDonald, MA, Director, Communications & Member Services
Norman Viegas, Director, Finance & Administration & Privacy Officer
Norman Viegas, CMA, CAE, Director, Finance & Administration

Canadian Acoustical Association (CAA) / Association canadienne d'acoustique (ACA)
c/o C. Laroche, Faculty of Health Sciences, University of Ottawa, #3062, 451 Smyth Rd., Ottawa ON K1H 8M5
Tel: 613-562-5800; *Fax:* 613-562-5248
www.caa-aca.ca
To foster communication among people working in all areas of acoustics in Canada; To promote the growth & practical application of knowledge in acoustics; To encourage education, research, & employment in acoustics
Christian Giguère, President
Dalila Giusti, Treasurer
Chantal Laroche, Executive Secretary

Canadian Advanced Technology Alliance (CATA Alliance) / Association canadienne de technologie de pointe
National Headquarters, #416, 207 Bank St., Ottawa ON K2P 2N2
Tel: 613-236-6550
info@cata.ca
www.cata.ca
Social Media: twitter.com/CATAAlliance
To provide members with a network to establish partnerships, to match up with global business opportunities; To offer communication & advocacy services, notably in dealing with the government; To work to ensure that policies are favourable to Canadian technology companies; To maintain a research repository where members can access information to advance their agendas
John Reid, President & CEO
Barry Gander, Executive Vice-President
Charles Duffet, Senior Vice-Presient & CIO Advisor
Russ Roberts, Senior Vice-President, Tax & Finance
Kevin Wennekes, Chief Business Officer

Canadian Air Cushion Technology Society (CACTS)
c/o Canadian Aeronautics & Space Institute, #104, 350 Terry Fox Dr., Kanata ON K2K 2W5
Tel: 613-591-8787; *Fax:* 613-591-7291
www.casi.ca/canadian-air-cushion-tech-soc
To serve the air cushion technology (hovercraft) community throughout Canada; To advance the science, technologies, & applications of air cushion technology
Jacques Laframboise, Society Chair

Canadian Association for Composite Structures & Materials (CACSMA) / Association canadienne pour les structures et matériaux composites (ACSMAC)
c/o J. Denault, Industrial Materials Institute, Ntl. Research Council, 75 Mortange Blvd., Boucherville QC J4B 6Y4
Tel: 450-641-5149; *Fax:* 450-641-5105
www.cacsma.ca
To support composites companies in Canada; To promote Canadian composites capabilities; To encourage the application of composites in all sectors
Suong V. Hoa, President
Mehdi Hojjati, Secretary
Johanne Denault, Treasurer

Canadian Council of Technicians & Technologists (CCTT) / Conseil canadien des techniciens et technologues
#405, 2197 Riverside Dr., Ottawa ON K1H 7X3
Tel: 613-238-8123; *Fax:* 613-238-8822
cctadm@cctt.ca
www.cctt.ca
Social Media: linkedin.com/company/canadian-council-of-technicians-&-technologis
twitter.com/CCTTCanada
To advocate on behalf of Canada's certified technicians & technologists; To establish & maintain national competency standards
Rick Tachuk, President & CEO
Darlene Pilon, Manager, Finance
Valery Vidershpan, Manager, Projects
Lorry Fortin, Coordinator, Programs

Canadian Hydrogen & Fuel Cell Association (CHFCA)
#900, 1188 West Georgia St., Vancouver BC V6E 4A2
Tel: 604-283-1040; *Fax:* 604-283-1043
info@chfca.ca
www.chfca.ca
Social Media: www.youtube.com/chfca
linkedin.com/groups?mostPopular=&gid=3145006?mostPopular=&gid=3145
www.facebook.com/poweringnow
twitter.com/poweringnow
To act as the collective voice of the hydrogen & fuel cell technologies & products sector; To support Canadian corporations, educational institutions, & governments which develop & deploy hydrogen & fuel cell products & services in Canada
Eric Denhoff, President & Chief Executive Officer

Canadian Remote Sensing Society (CRSS) / Société canadienne de télédétection
c/o Canadian Aeronautics & Space Institute, #104, 350 Terry Fox Dr., Kanata ON K2K 2W5
Tel: 613-591-8787; *Fax:* 613-591-7291
casi@casi.ca
www.crss-sct.ca
To advance the art, science, engineering, & application of remote sensing in Canada; To uphold the Society's Code of Ethics
Monique Bernier, Chair
Anne Smith, Vice-Chair
Richard Fournier, Secretary-Treasurer

Canadian Society for Civil Engineering (CSCE) / Société canadienne de génie civil
4877, rue Sherbrooke ouest, Montréal QC H3Z 1G9
Tel: 514-933-2634; *Fax:* 514-933-3504
info@csce.ca
www.csce.ca
To develop & maintain high standard of civil engineering practice in Canada; To enhance the public image of the civil engineering profession
Doug Salloum, Executive Director
Mahmoud Lardjane, Manager, Programs
Louise Newman, Manager, Communications
Andrea Grimaud, Officer, Membership Liaison

Canadian Society for Engineering Management (CSEM) / Société canadienne de gestion en ingénierie
1295 Hwy. 2 East, Kingston ON K7L 4V1
Tel: 613-547-5989
louisem@cogeco.ca
www.csem-scgi.org
Social Media: linkedin.com/groups/Canadian-Engineering-Management-4865922
To represent the interests & enhance the capabilities of engineers in management in order to promote & advance efficient management of commerce, industry & public affairs.
Aidan Gordon, President
Dominique Janssens, Sec.-Treas.

Canadian Society for Mechanical Engineering (CSME) / Société canadienne de génie mécanique (SCGM)
1295 Hwy. 2 East, Kingston ON K7L 4V1
Tel: 613-547-5989; *Fax:* 613-547-0195
csme@cogeco.ca
www.csme-scgm.ca
To benefit Canada & the world by fostering excellence in the practice of mechanical engineering; To support members
Rama B. Bhat, President

Canadian Technical Asphalt Association (CTAA) / Association technique canadienne du bitume
#300, 895 Fort St., Victoria BC V8W 1H7
Tel: 250-361-9187; *Fax:* 250-361-9187
admin@ctaa.ca
www.ctaa.ca
Social Media: linkedin.com/groups/3266673/profile
www.facebook.com/254383501294589
To organize efforts of membership on a non-profit, public service basis; To assemble, correlate & disseminate technical information on characteristics & uses of bituminous materials; To encourage research on uses of asphaltic materials; To encourage colleges to teach students to study asphalt technology
Chuck McMillan, Secretary-Treasurer

Certified Technicians & Technologists Association of Manitoba (CTTAM)
#602, 1661 Portage Ave., Winnipeg MB R3J 3T7
Tel: 204-784-1088; *Fax:* 204-784-1084
admin@cttam.com
www.cttam.com
To advance the professional recognition & development of certified applied science technicians & technologists in a manner that serves the public interest
Neil Klassen, CET, President
Terry Gifford, CAE, Executive Director
Robert D. Okabe, CET; IntET, Registrar

Consulting Engineers of Alberta (CEA)
Phipps-McKinnon Building, #870, 10020 - 101A Ave., Edmonton AB T5J 3G2
Tel: 780-421-1852; *Fax:* 780-424-5225
info@cea.ca
www.cea.ca
Social Media:
linkedin.com/company/consulting-engineers-of-alberta
www.facebook.com/749479441765790
twitter.com/ConsultingEngAB
To provide leadership to foster a positive business environment for the consulting engineering firms in Alberta; To promote the engineering industry; To enhance interests & opportunities of CEA members; To provide society with high standards of engineering design & safety
Matt Brassard, President
Ken Pilip, CEO & Registrar
Lisa Krewda, Director, Operations
Chantal Sargent, Manager, Events

Consulting Engineers of Newfoundland & Labrador (CENL)
PO Box 1236, St. John's NL A1C 5M9
Tel: 709-726-3468
www.consultingengineersofnl.ca
To unite the local industry; to promote & advocate common business interests; to support the development & successs of member firms.
Mike Brady, P.Eng., PMP, President

Consulting Engineers of Nova Scotia (CENS)
PO Box 613, Stn. M, Halifax NS B3J 2R7
Tel: 902-461-1325; *Fax:* 902-461-1321
cens@eastlink.ca
www.cens.org
To enable the consulting engineering industry in Nova Scotia to capitalize on opportunities to grow; To promote employment of member firms
Scott Kyle, President
Skit Ferguson, Executive Director

Consulting Engineers of Ontario (CEO)
#405, 10 Four Seasons Pl., Toronto ON M9B 6H7
Tel: 416-620-1400; *Fax:* 416-620-5803
www.ceo.on.ca
Social Media: www.youtube.com/user/CEOYT
linkedin.com/company/consulting-engineers-of-ontario
www.facebook.com/ConsultingEngON
twitter.com/ConsultingEngON
To further the maintenance of high professional standards in consulting engineering profession; to promote cordial relations among various consulting firms in Ontario; to foster interchange of professional management & business experience & information among consulting engineers; to develop regional representation & participation in affairs of the association
Bruce Potter, Chair
Barry Steinburg, Chief Executive Officer
Jennifer Parent, Manager, Events & Member Services
Diane Lee, Coordinator, Communications

Consulting Engineers of the Northwest Territories (CENT)
c/o NAPEG, Bowling Green Bldg., #201, 4817 - 49th St., Yellowknife NT X1A 3S7
info@cent-nt.ca
www.cent-nt.ca
To promote positive business relationships between member firms & clients; to promote members' business interests.
Carlos Philipovsky, President

Consulting Engineers of Yukon (CEY)
c/o EBA Engineering Consultants Ltd., #6, 151 Industrial Rd., Whitehorse YT Y1A 2V3
Tel: 867-668-3068; *Fax:* 867-668-4349
cey@eba.ca
www.cey.ca
To maintain high professional standards in the consulting engineering profession; To promote cordial relations among various consulting firms in the Yukon; to foster interchange of professional management & business experience & information among consulting engineers; To develop regional representation & participation in affairs of the association

Continental Automated Buildings Association (CABA) / Association continentale pour l'automatisation des bâtiments
#210, 1173 Cyrville Rd., Ottawa ON K1J 7S6
Tel: 613-686-1814; *Fax:* 613-744-7833
Toll-Free: 888-798-2222
caba@caba.org
www.caba.org
Social Media: www.youtube.com/cabaconf
linkedin.com/company/continental-automated-buildings-associati on-c
www.facebook.com/108759039149175?fref=ts
twitter.com/caba_news
To promote advanced technologies for the automation of homes & buildings in North America; To create opportunities for members
Ronald J. Zimmer, President & Chief Executive Officer
Noranda Haasper, Financial Administrator
Greg Walker, Director, Research
Rawlson O'Neil King, Director, Communications

The Engineering Institute of Canada (EIC) / L'Institut canadien des ingénieurs (ICI)
PO Box 40140, Ottawa ON K1V 0W8
www.eic-ici.ca
Social Media:
linkedin.com/company/the-engineering-institute-of-canada
To further the development of engineering in Canada; to stimulate the advancement of the quality & scope of Canadian engineering; to meet regularly with other engineering organizations & industries to promote understanding & improvement of the profession, the diffusion of engineering information & to provide Canadian representation in specialized engineering fields; to interact with government agencies & departments for the purpose of influencing decision making on matters relating to engineering & technology; to cooperate with the provincial engineering licensing bodies, The Canadian Council of Professional Engineering, The Association of Consulting Engineers of Canada, The Canadian Academy of Engineering & other engineering organizations in matters of common interest; to promote interaction with specific interest groups; to collaborate with universities & educational institutions
Guy Gosselin, Executive Director
Mohammud Emamally, Administrative Officer, admin.officer@eic-ici.ca

Engineers Canada / Ingénieurs Canada
#1100, 180 Elgin St., Ottawa ON K2P 2K3
Tel: 613-232-2474; *Fax:* 613-230-5759
Toll-Free: 877-408-9273
info@engineerscanada.ca
www.engineerscanada.ca
Social Media: www.youtube.com/user/EngineersCanada
linkedin.com/company/engineers-canada
www.facebook.com/EngineersCanada
twitter.com/engineerscanada
To establish & maintain a common bond between constituent associations; To assist constituent associations to meet their common needs & those of their members by coordinating standards, procedures, & programs across Canada; To represent the engineering profession with respect to national & international affairs; To increase the profile & prestige of the engineering profession
Paul Amyotte, FEC, P.Eng., President
Kim Allen, FEC, P.Eng., CEO
Guy Legault, MBA, FCPA, FCGA, Vice-President, Business Development & Services
Kathryn Sutherland, P.Eng., FEC, LL, Vice-President, Regulatory Affairs

Engineers Nova Scotia
1355 Barrington St., Halifax NS B3J 1Y9
Tel: 902-429-2250; *Fax:* 902-423-9769
Toll-Free: 888-802-7367
info@engineersnovascotia.ca
www.engineersnovascotia.ca
To establish, maintain & develop standards of knowledge & skill, standards of qualification & practice, & standards of professional ethics; To promote public awareness of the role of the association
Len White, P.Eng., Chief Executive Officer & Registrar
Perry Mitchelmore, P.Eng., President

Ingénieurs Sans Frontières Québec (ISFQ) / Engineers Without Borders Quebec
2330, rue Notre-Dame ouest, Montréal QC H3J 2Y2
Tél: 514-940-7704
www.isfq.ca
Média social:
linkedin.com/company/ing-nieurs-sans-fronti-res-qu-bec-isfq-
www.facebook.com/ingenieurssansfrontieresquebec
Améliorer la qualité de vie dans les pays en développement à travers le développement durable; Fournir des services d'ingénierie dans les pays en développement; Informer le public sur l'importance de la coopération internationale
Jean-Yves Bourdages, Directeur général
Charles Ghayad, Coordonateur, Projets

Innovate Calgary
Alastair Ross Technology Centre, 3553 - 31 St. NW, Calgary AB T2L 2K7
Tel: 403-284-6400; *Fax:* 403-267-5699
info@innovatecalgary.com
www.innovatecalgary.com
Social Media:
linkedin.com/company/innovate-calgary
www.facebook.com/innovatecalgary
twitter.com/innovatecalgary
To aid in acceleration & innovation in the technology sector
Peter Garrett, Interim President

Institut national d'optique (INO) / National Optics Institute
2740, rue Einstein, Québec QC G1P 4S4
Tél: 418-657-7006; *Téléc:* 418-657-7009
Ligne sans frais: 866-657-7406
info@ino.ca
www.ino.ca
To be an international leader in optics & photonics R&D, promoting economic expansion in the country by providing assistance to companies seeking to be more competitive
Jean-Yves Roy, President & CEO

ISIS Canada Research Network (ISIS)
Agricultural & Civil Engineering Building, University of Manitoba, #A250, 96 Dafoe Rd., Winnipeg MB R3T 2N2
muftia@cc.umanitoba.ca
www.isiscanada.com
To advance civil engineering in Canada to a world leadership position through the development & application of fibre-reinforced polymers & integrated intelligent fibre optic sensing technologies, for the benefit of all Canadians
Donald Whitmore, Chair
Aftab Mufti, President & Scientific Director
Edward Pentland, Chair, Technology Transfer & Commercialization Committee

Island Technology Professionals (ITP)
PO Box 1436, 92 Queen St., Charlottetown PE C1A 7N1
Tel: 902-892-8324
registrar@techpei.ca
www.techpei.ca
Social Media:
www.facebook.com/IslandTechnologyProfessionals
twitter.com/Tech_PEI
To benefit society by advancing the professions of applied science & engineering technology in Prince Edward Island
Bryan Burt, CET, President
Marea O'Halloran, CET, Vice-President
Laurie Eveleigh, CET, Treasurer
Troy Livingstone, CET, Registrar

New Brunswick Society of Certified Engineering Technicians & Technologists (NBSCETT) / Société des techniciens et des technologues agréés du génie du Nouveau-Brunswick (STTAGN-B)
#12B 102 Main St., Fredericton NB E3A 9N6
Tel: 506-454-6124; *Fax:* 506-452-7076
Toll-Free: 800-665-8324
nbscett@nbscett.nb.ca
www.nbscett.nb.ca
To grant certification to applied science & engineering technology technicians & technologists; to protect titles & powers of discipline for its members
Jean-Luc Michaud, PTech, President
Edward F. Leslie, Executive Director & CEO

Northwest Territories & Nunavut Association of Professional Engineers & Geoscientists (NAPEG)
#201, 4817 - 49 St., Yellowknife NT X1A 3S7
Tel: 867-920-4055; *Fax:* 867-873-4058
www.napeg.nt.ca
Social Media:
linkedin.com/groups?gid=4169273
www.facebook.com/208781715979685
twitter.com/napeg_north
To license professional engineers & professional geoscientists in the Northwest Territories & Nunavut; To regulate the practices of professional engineering & professional geoscience; To establish & maintain standards of knowledge, skill, care, & professional ethics among registrants
Linda Golding, FEC (Hon), FGC, Executive Director & Registrar

Ontario Association of Certified Engineering Technicians & Technologists (OACETT)
#404, 10 Four Seasons Pl., Toronto ON M9B 6H7
Tel: 416-621-9621; *Fax:* 416-621-8694
info@oacett.org
www.oacett.org
Social Media:
linkedin.com/groups/official-oacett-group-149199
www.facebook.com/OACETT
twitter.com/OACETT
To advance the profession of applied science & engineering technology through standards for society's benefit.
David J. Thomson, CEO
Stephen Morley, President

Ordre des ingénieurs du Québec (OIQ)
Gare Windsor, #350, 1100, av des Canadiens-de-Montréal, Montréal QC H3B 2S2
Tél: 514-845-6141; *Téléc:* 514-845-1833
Ligne sans frais: 800-461-6141
info@oiq.qc.ca
www.oiq.qc.ca
Média social: www.youtube.com/user/ordredesingenieurs
linkedin.com/company/604039
www.facebook.com/oiq.qc.ca
twitter.com/OIQ
Faire de la promotion et s'assurer de la qualité des services rendus à la société par les ingénieurs, individuellement et collectivement, en tant que membres d'un corps professionnel; Favoriser leur épanouissement professionnel et personnel; Contribuer au développement socio-économique de la société
Kathy Baig, Président
Chantal Michaud, ing., Directrice générale
Claude Soucy, Directeur général adoint, Ressources humaines
Lorraine Godin, CPA-CA, Directrice, Administration-finances
Louis Tremblay, ing., Directeur, Affaires professionnelles
Luc Vagneux, CRIA, Directeur, Profession et communications

Ordre des technologues professionnels du Québec (OTPQ)
#505, 606, rue Cathcart, Montréal QC H3B 1K9
Tél: 514-845-3247; *Téléc:* 514-845-3643
Ligne sans frais: 800-561-3459
info@otpq.qc.ca
www.otpq.qc.ca
Média social: www.youtube.com/user/TechnologuePro1
linkedin.com/groups/4134994/profile
www.facebook.com/TechnologuesProfessionnels
twitter.com/otpq
Promouvoir et assurer la compétence des technologues professionnels dans l'intérêt public
Denis Beauchamp, Directeur général et secrétaire

Plant Engineering & Maintenance Association of Canada (PEMAC)
#402, 6 - 2400 Dundas St. West, Mississauga ON L5K 2R8
Fax: 905-823-8001
Toll-Free: 877-532-7255
admin@pemac.org
www.pemac.org
To be recognized as a nationwide centre of excellence in plant engineering & maintenance; To form positive & constructive links with industry & service sectors, in support of local & nationwide developments & productivity; To deliver strongly identifiable services & commitments across the range of disciplines embraced by the association; to educate & introduce new concepts; To provide representation at all government levels; To provide career enhancement & networking opportunities; To promote research in the field of plant engineering & maintenance
Rob Lash, President

Professional Engineers & Geoscientists Newfoundland & Labrador (PEG-NL)
PO Box 21207, #203, 10 Fort William Pl., St. John's NL A1A 5B2
Tel: 709-753-7714; *Fax:* 709-753-6131
main@pegnl.ca
www.pegnl.ca
To provide competent & ethical practice of engineering & geoscience in Newfoundland & Labrador; To ensure public confidence, sustainability, & stewardship of the professions; To provide leadership to enhance quality of life through the application & management of engineering & geoscience
Geoff Emberley, P. Eng., FEC, CEO & Registrar
Mark Fewer, B. Comm., COO & Deputy Registrar
Leo White, P. Eng., Director, Professional Standards

Professional Engineers Ontario (PEO)
#101, 40 Sheppard Ave. West, Toronto ON M2N 6K9
Tel: 416-224-1100; *Fax:* 416-224-9527
Toll-Free: 800-339-3716
www.peo.on.ca
To meet the needs of Ontario society by licensing & regulating the entire practice of professional engineering in an open, transparent, inclusive manner. There are 36 chapters across the province
Thomas Chong, M.Sc., P.Eng., President
Gerard McDonald, P.Eng., MBA, Registrar
Scott Clark, LL.B., CAO
Linda Latham, P.Eng., Deputy Registrar, Regulatory Compliance
Michael Price, P.Eng., MBA, Deputy Registrar, Licensing & Registration
Johnny Zuccon, P.Eng., Deputy Registrar, Tribunals & Regulatory Affairs
Connie Mucklestone, Director, Communications

Saskatchewan Applied Science Technologists & Technicians (SASTT)
363 Park St., Regina SK S4N 5B2
Tel: 306-721-6633; *Fax:* 306-721-0112
info@sastt.ca
www.sastt.ca
To regulate the professional conduct of applied science technologists & certified technicians in Saskatchewan, in order to protect the public

Shad Valley International
8 Young St. East, Waterloo ON N2J 2L3
Tel: 519-884-8844; *Fax:* 519-884-8191
info@shad.ca
www.shad.ca
Social Media: www.youtube.com/ShadValleyOfficial
linkedin.com/groups?mostPopular=&gid=2101
www.facebook.com/ShadValley
twitter.com/shadvalley
To advance the scientific & technological capabilities of youth, integrated with the development of their entrepreneurial spirit; To collaborate with education, business & other communities, both domestic & international, to provide exceptional development opportunities
Barry Bisson, President
Wendy Zufelt-Baxter, Vice President, Advancement
Mary Hamoodi, Vice President, Finance & Operations

TechNova
#308, 202 Brownlow Ave., Dartmouth NS B3B 1T5
Tel: 902-463-3236; *Fax:* 902-465-7567
Toll-Free: 866-723-8867
info@technova.ca
www.technova.ca
Social Media:
twitter.com/NSTechNova
To certify engineering & applied science technicians & technologists for the betterment of the public & the welfare of the environment
Eric Jury, President
Joe Simms, Executive Officer

Environmental

Alberta Ecotrust Foundation
#1020, 105 - 12 Ave. SE, Calgary AB TSG 1A1
Tel: 403-209-2245; *Toll-Free:* 800-465-2147
info@albertaecotrust.com
albertaecotrust.com
Social Media:
twitter.com/AlbertaEcotrust
To provide grants to environmental groups that work towards improving Alberta's eco health
Pat Letizia, Executive Director

Alberta Environmental Network (AEN)
PO Box 4541, Edmonton AB T6E 5G4
Tel: 780-757-4872
admin@aenweb.ca
www.aenweb.ca
Social Media:
twitter.com/ABEnvNet
To facilitate communication & cooperation among environmental groups in Alberta in order to contribute to the enhancement & protection of the environment
Melissa Gorrie, Co-Chair
Nikki Way, Co-Chair

Alberta Fish & Game Association (AFGA)
6924 - 104 St., Edmonton AB T6H 2L7
Tel: 780-437-2342; *Fax:* 780-438-6872
office@afga.org
www.afga.org
Social Media:
www.facebook.com/120693761350755
twitter.com/AlbertaFishGame
To ensure fish & wildlife habitat & resources in Alberta
Martin Sharren, Executive Vice-President

Alberta Water Council
Petroleum Plaza, South Tower, #1400, 9915 - 108 St., Edmonton AB T5K 2G8
Tel: 780-644-7380
info@awchome.ca
www.albertawatercouncil.ca
The Alberta Water Council is a stakeholder partnership that provides leadership, expertise and advocacy, to engage and empower individuals, organizations, business and governments to achieve the outcomes of the Water for Life strategy.
Gord Edwards, Executive Director

Alberta Wilderness Association (AWA)
455 - 12 St. NW, Calgary AB T2N 1Y9
Tel: 403-283-2025; *Fax:* 403-270-2743
Toll-Free: 866-313-0713
awa@abwild.ca
albertawilderness.ca
Social Media: www.youtube.com/AlbertaWilderness
www.facebook.com/AlbertaWilderness
twitter.com/ABWilderness
To promote the protection of Alberta's rivers & wildlands areas; To restore the natural ecosystems of Alberta; To educate Albertans on wilderness conservation & sustainable use of natural lands & waters
Owen McGoldrick, President
Christyann Olson, Executive Director

Arctic Institute of North America (AINA)
University of Calgary, 2500 University Dr. NW, Calgary AB T2N 1N4
Tel: 403-220-7515; *Fax:* 403-282-4609
arctic@ucalgary.ca
www.arctic.ucalgary.ca
Social Media:
www.facebook.com/ArcticInstituteofNorthAmerica
twitter.com/ASTISdatabase
To encourage & support scientific research pertaining to the polar regions
Marybeth Murray, Executive Director
Mary Li, Institute Manager

Association for Literature, Environment, & Culture in Canada (ALECC) / Association pour la littérature, l'environnement et la culture au Canada
c/o Department of English, University of Calgary, 2500 University Dr. NW, 11th Fl., Calgary AB T2N 1N4
contactus@alecc.ca
www.alecc.ca
To promote and support artistic, critical and cultural studies work on a wide range of environmental issues.
Robert Boschman, President

Big Rideau Lake Association (BRLA)
PO Box 93, Portland ON K0G 1V0
Tel: 613-272-3629
brla@brla.on.ca
www.brla.on.ca
To protect & conserve Big Rideau Lake and share its resources.
Doug Good, President

BIOQuébec / Québec Bio-Industries Business Network
#205, 1460, boul de l'innovation, Bromont QC J2L 0J8
Tél: 514-360-4565; *Téléc:* 450-919-0827
direction@bioquebec.com
www.bioquebec.com
Ôtre le porte-parole des entreprises biotechnologiques du Québec; favoriser le développement et la mise en valeur des biotechnologies et des bioindustries québécoises, et ce au bénéfice de ses membres; To promote the development & the upgrading of biotechnologies; to supply strategic information of technical & economical content as well as carry out projects, events & activities; to stimulate collaboration between private industry, governments & universities; to stimulate the growth of structuring economical activities in this field; to act as a spokesman for the bio-industry in Québec
Anie Perrault, Directrice générale

British Columbia Environment Industry Association (BCEIA)
#400, 602 West Hastings St., Vancouver BC V6B 1P2
Tel: 604-683-2751; *Fax:* 604-677-5960
info@bceia.com
www.bceia.com
Social Media:
twitter.com/BCEIA_
To develop the environmental industry in British Columbia; To promote technological development
Frank Came, President
Charles Bois, Secretary-Treasurer

British Columbia Environmental Network (BCEN)
PO Box 1209, Mile House BC V0K 2G0
Tel: 604-515-1969
www.ecobc.org
To facilitate communication among environmental groups & individuals so that ecological sustainability & economic stability prevail, & biological diversity & human health remain viable
Dave Stevens, Chair
Rod Marining, Coordinator, Communications

BurlingtonGreen Environmental Association
3281 Myers Lane, Burlington ON L7N 1K6
Tel: 905-466-2171
www.burlingtongreen.org
Social Media:
www.facebook.com/burlington.green.environment
twitter.com/burlingtongreen
To advocate for local environmental issues
Amy Schnurr, Executive Director

Campaign for Nuclear Phaseout (CNP)
#412, 1 Nicholas St., Ottawa ON K1N 7B7
www.cnp.ca
The Campaign for Nuclear Phaseout (CNP) represents a coalition of Canadian public interest organizations concerned with the environmental consequences of nuclear power generation.

Canadian Arctic Resources Committee
488 Gladstone Ave., Ottawa ON K1N 8V4
Tel: 613-759-4284; *Fax:* 613-237-3845
Toll-Free: 866-949-9006
davidg@carc.org
www.carc.org
Social Media:
www.facebook.com/168782596508551
The Canadian Arctic Resources Committee (CARC) is a citizens' organization dedicated to the long-term environmental and social well being of northern Canada and its peoples.
Ben McDonald, Acting Chair

Canadian Association for Laboratory Accreditation Inc. (CALA)
#310, 1565 Carling Ave., Ottawa ON K1Z 8R1
Tel: 613-233-5300; *Fax:* 613-233-5501
www.cala.ca
Social Media:
linkedin.com/company/canadian-association-for-laboratory-accreditation
www.facebook.com/161209647296775
To provide internationally-recognized accreditation services; To assist laboratories in the achievement of high levels of scientific & management excellence; To improve environmental quality & public health & safety
Charlie Brimley, President & CEO
Brenda Dashney, Chief Financial Officer
Tim Delaney, Chair
Ken Middlebrook, Manager, Proficiency Testing
Andrew Morris, Manager, Data & Information

Canadian Association of Environmental Law Societies (CAELS)
info@caels.org
caels.org
Social Media:
facebook.com/CAELSorg
twitter.com/CAELSorg
The Canadian Association of Environmental Law Societies (CAELS) is a networking project connecting environmental law students across the country. CAELS will allow law students to interact with their peers and professors, practitioners and environmental professionals.

Canadian Association of Recycling Industries (CARI) / Association canadienne des industries du recyclage (ACIR)
#1906, 130 Albert St., Ottawa ON K1P 5G4
Tel: 613-728-6946; *Fax:* 705-835-6196
info@cari-acir.org
www.cari-acir.org
Social Media:
linkedin.com/company/canadian-association-of-recycling-industries-
twitter.com/CARI_Recycling
To address issues facing the recycling industry in Canada & internationally; To promote commercial recycling activities
Tracy Shaw, President & CEO
Donna Turner, Director, Events
Marie Binette, Manager, Communications

Canadian Environment Industry Association (CEIA)
#410, 215 Spadina Ave., Toronto ON M5T 2C7
Tel: 416-531-7884
info@oneia.ca
www.oneia.ca
Social Media: www.youtube.com/user/ONEIAmedia
linkedin.com/groups/3999411/profile
twitter.com/ONEIAnetwork
To promote the interests and development of Canadian companies supplying environmental technologies, products & services
Derek Webb, President & Chief Executive Officer
Alex Gill, Executive Director
Marjan Lahuis, Manager, Operations

Canadian Environmental Certification Approvals Board (CECAB) / Bureau canadien de reconnaissance professionnelle des spécialistes de l'environnement
#200, 308 - 11th Ave. SE, Calgary AB T2G 0Y2
Tel: 403-233-7484; *Fax:* 403-264-6240
certification@eco.ca
www.cecab.org
CECAB is a professional autonomous body providing national certification for Canadian environmental practitioners.
Victor Nowicki, Chair

Canadian Environmental Law Association (CELA) / Association canadienne du droit de l'environnement
#301, 130 Spadina Ave., Toronto ON M5V 2L4
Tel: 416-960-2284; *Fax:* 416-960-9392
articling@cela.ca
www.cela.ca
Social Media:
www.facebook.com/CanadianEnvironmentalLawAssociation
twitter.com/CanEnvLawAssn
To advocate for environmental law reform; To act in court or during hearings on behalf of citizens' groups & individuals who would otherwise be unable to afford legal assistance
Tracy Tucker, Office Manager/Executive Assistant

Canadian Environmental Network (RCEN) / Réseau canadien de l'environnement
14 Manchester Ave., Ottawa ON K1Y 1Y9
Tel: 613-728-9810; *Fax:* 613-728-2963
secretary@rcen.ca
rcen.ca
Social Media: www.youtube.com/user/RCEN1
www.facebook.com/CanadianEnvironmentalNetwork
twitter.com/RCEN
To promote ecologically sound ways of life; To enhance members' work to restore, protect, & promote a clean & sustainable environment
Josh Brandon, Chair

Canadian Environmental Technology Advancement Corporation - West (CETAC)
3608 - 33rd St. NW, Calgary AB T2L 2A6
Tel: 403-777-9595; *Fax:* 403-777-9599
cetac@cetacwest.com
cetacwest.com
Social Media:
www.facebook.com/431936763529236
Established by Environment Canada, CETAC-West is a private sector, not-for-profit corporation committed to helping small & medium-sized enterprises that are engaged in the development & commercialization of new environmental technologies. To this end, it has created a network of technology producers, industry experts, & investment sources.

Canadian Institute of Resources Law (CIRL) / Institut canadien du droit des ressources
Murray Fraser Hall, University of Calgary, #3353, 2500 University Dr. NW, Calgary AB T2N 1N4
Tel: 403-220-3200; *Fax:* 403-282-6182
cirl@ucalgary.ca
www.cirl.ca
Social Media:
twitter.com/ResourcesLaw
To undertake and promote research, education and publication on the law relating to Canada's renewable and non-renewable natural resources.
Allan Ingelson, LLM; JD; BSc; B, Executive Director
Ian Holloway, PhD, Chair

Canadian Land Reclamation Association (CLRA) / Association canadienne de réhabilitation des sites dégradés (ACRSD)
c/o ManageWise, Inc., PO Box 21085, Edmonton AB T6R 2V4
Tel: 780-437-0044
www.clra.ca
Social Media:
linkedin.com/company/canadian-land-reclamation-association
To encourage involvement in reclamation projects of disturbed land
Andrea McEachern, President
Shauna Prokopchuk, Coordinator
Marisa Hemmes, Coordinator, Membership & Communications

Canadian Network for Environmental Education & Communication (EECOM) / Réseau canadien d'éducation et de communication relatives à l'environnement
c/o 336 Rosedale Ave., Winnipeg MB R3L 1L8
nswayze@eecom.org
www.eecom.org
Social Media:
www.facebook.com/112287385502920?ref=sgm
To advance environmental learning in Canada; To promote environmental literacy & environmental stewardship; To contribute to a sustainable future
Natalie Swayzer, Executive Director
Grant Gardner, Chair
Rick Wishart, Treasurer

Canadian Parks Partnership (CPP) / Partenaires des parcs canadiens
#360, 1414 - 8th St. SW, Calgary AB T2R 1J6
Tel: 613-567-0099
To support the overall enhancement of Canada's parks, historic sites & canals system & to foster public awareness, appreciation, understanding of & involvement in the system

Canadian Peregrine Foundation (CPF)
#20, 25 Crouse Rd., Toronto ON M1R 5P8
Tel: 416-481-1233; *Toll-Free:* 888-709-3944
info@peregrine-foundation.ca
www.peregrine-foundation.ca
The Canadian Peregrine Foundation is a registered charity dedicated to assisting the recovery of the peregrine falcon and other raptors at risk.

Canadian Society of Environmental Biologists (CSEB) / Société canadienne des biologistes de l'environnement
PO Box 962, Stn. F, Toronto ON M4Y 2N9
www.cseb-scbe.org
To further the conservation of natural resources of Canada & to promote the prudent management of these resources so as to minimize adverse environmental effects; to ensure high professional standards in education, research & management related to resources & environment; to advance the education of the public & to protect public interest on matters pertaining to the use of natural resources & the protection & management of the environment; to undertake environmental research & education programs; to assess & evaluate administrative & legislative policies having ecological significance in terms of conservation of resources & quality of the environment; to develop & promote policies that seek to achieve balance among resource management & utilization, protection of the environment & quality of life; to foster liaison among environmental biologists working within governmental, industrial & educational frameworks across Canada
Robert Stedwill, President

Canadian Wildlife Federation (CWF) / Fédération canadienne de la faune
350 Michael Cowpland Dr., Ottawa ON K2M 2W1
Tel: 613-599-9594; *Fax:* 613-599-4428
Toll-Free: 800-563-9453
info@cwf-fcf.org
www.cwf-fcf.org
Social Media: www.youtube.com/user/CanadianWildlifeFed
ca.linkedin.com/company/canadian-wildlife-federation
www.facebook.com/CanadianWildlifeFederation
twitter.com/CWF_FCF
To promote the conservation of fish & wildlife, wildlife habitat & quality aquatic environments; To foster an understanding of natural processes; To ensure adequate stocks of wildlife for the use & enjoyment of all Canadians; To sponsor research; To cooperate with legislators, government & non-government agencies in achieving conservation objectives
Bates Rick, Acting Executive Vice-President & CEO

Canadians for Clean Prosperity
#503, 460 Richmond St. West, Toronto ON M5V 1Y1
Tel: 416-777-2327; *Fax:* 416-777-2524
info@cleanprosperity.ca
www.cleanprosperity.ca
Social Media:
www.facebook.com/cleanprosperity
twitter.com/CleanProsperity
To build a strong economy using pollution fees to cut taxes
Mark Cameron, Executive Director
Tom Chervinsky, Acting Executive Director & Vice-President, Campaigns
Mollie Anderson, Coordinator, Engagement

Carolinian Canada Coalition
Grosvenor Lodge, 1017 Western Rd., London ON N6G 1G5
Tel: 519-433-7077; *Fax:* 519-645-0981
info@carolinian.org
www.carolinian.org
Social Media: www.youtube.com/user/CarolinianCanada
www.facebook.com/caroliniancanada
twitter.com/caroliniancan
To promote the protection and conservation of the Carolinian Life Zone of Southwestern Ontario.
Michelle Kanter, Executive Director

Citizens for a Safe Environment (CSE)
Tel: 416-461-1092
info@csetoronto.org
www.csetoronto.org
To promomote waste management practices that protect the health of Toronto citizens, their communities and the environment.

Citizens Opposed to Paving the Escarpment (COPE)
PO Box 20014, 2211 Brant St., Burlington ON L7P 0A4
mail@cope-nomph.org
www.cope-nomph.org
Social Media:
www.facebook.com/pages/Highway-No-Way/146644585393483?v=wall
twitter.com/StopHwy
To preserve the Niagara Escarpment, by ensuring that no new highway corridors are paved across the Niagara Escarpment & that all viable alternatives to the proposed Mid-Peninsula Highway are fully considered

Citizens' Environment Watch (CEW)
#380, 401 Richmond St. West, Toronto ON M5V 3A8
Tel: 647-258-3280; *Fax:* 416-979-3155
info@citizensenvironmentwatch.org
www.citizensenvironmentwatch.org
To provide communities the tools for education, monitoring and influencing positive change and to encourage people to take an active role in restoring and sustaining nature.
Meredith Cochrane, Executive Director

Clean Nova Scotia (CNS)
126 Portland St., Dartmouth NS B2Y 1H8
Tel: 902-420-3474; *Fax:* 902-982-6768
Toll-Free: 855-736-3473
info@clean.ns.ca
www.clean.ns.ca
Social Media: www.youtube.com/CleanFoundation
www.facebook.com/CleanFoundation
twitter.com/CleanFoundation
To inspire positive environmental change in Nova Scotia
Chris Morrissey, Executive Director
Vanessa Peckford, Director, Human Resources & Office Services
Geoff McCain, Manager, Business
Carl Little, Coordinator, Energy Programs
Charlynne Robertson, Coordinator, Waste Programs
Camilla Melrose, Coordinator, Water Programs

Compost Council of Canada / Conseil canadien du compost
16 Northumberland St., Toronto ON M6H 1P7
Tel: 416-535-0240; *Fax:* 416-536-9892
Toll-Free: 877-571-4769
info@compost.org
www.compost.org
Social Media:
www.facebook.com/people/Compost-Council/100001137258465
To advance organics residuals recycling & compost use; To contribute to environmental sustainability
Susan Antler, Executive Director

Conservation Council of New Brunswick (CCNB) / Conseil de la conservation du Nouveau-Brunswick
180 St. John St., Fredericton NB E3B 4A9
Tel: 506-458-8747; *Fax:* 506-458-1047
info@conservationcouncil.ca
www.conservationcouncil.ca
Social Media: www.youtube.com/user/ccnbactiontv
www.facebook.com/ccnbaction
twitter.com/cc_nb
To generate awareness of the ecological foundations of our quality of life; To promote public policies with respect to the integrity of natural systems & to contribute to a sustainable society; To advocate appropriate remedies to pressing environmental problems such as ground water contamination & hazardous wastes
Céline Delacroix, Executive Director
Stephanie Coburn, President

Conservation Council of Ontario (CCO) / Conseil de conservation de l'Ontario
#132, 215 Spadina Ave., Toronto ON M5T 2C7
Tel: 416-533-1635; *Fax:* 416-979-3936
cco@web.ca
www.weconserve.ca
To build a strong conservation movement across Ontario
Ben Marans, President
Chris Winter, Executive Director
Karen Sun, Secretary

Conservation Ontario
PO Box 11, 120 Bayview Pkwy., Newmarket ON L3R 4W3
Tel: 905-895-0716; *Fax:* 905-895-0751
info@conservationontario.ca
www.conservation-ontario.on.ca
Social Media: instagram.com/con_ont
www.facebook.com/126861190733330
twitter.com/conont
To represent & support a network of community-based environmental organizations; To ensure conservation, restoration, & responsible management of Ontario's wetlands, woodlands, & natural habitat
Dick Hibma, Chair
Kim Gavine, General Manager
Bonnie Fox, Manager, Policy & Planning
Jane Lewington, Specialist, Marketing & Communications

Construction Resource Initiatives Council (CRI) / Conseil d'initiatives des ressources de construction
#609 Donald B. Munro Dr., Carp ON K0A 1L0
Tel: 613-795-4632; *Fax:* 613-839-0704
info@cricouncil.com
www.cricouncil.com
Social Media:
linkedin.com/groups/Construction-Resource-Initiatives-Council-3819
www.facebook.com/330962370266752
twitter.com/CRICouncil
To develop strategies that help the building industry achieve the goal of zero waste production.
Renée L. Gratton, President & CEO

Cumulative Environmental Management Association (CEMA)
Morrison Center, #214, 9914 Morrison St., Fort McMurray AB T9H 4A4
Tel: 780-799-3947; *Fax:* 780-714-3081
info@cemaonline.ca
www.cemaonline.ca
Social Media:
www.facebook.com/111309945551863
twitter.com/cemacomms
To study the cumulative environmental effects of industrial development in the region and produce guidelines and management frameworks.
Glen Semenchuk, Executive Director

Ducks Unlimited Canada (DUC) / Canards Illimités Canada
PO Box 1160, Mallard Bay at Hwy. 220, Stonewall MB R0C 2Z0
Fax: 204-467-9028
Toll-Free: 800-665-3825
webfoot@ducks.ca
www.ducks.ca
Social Media: www.youtube.com/user/DucksUnlimitedCanada
www.facebook.com/ducksunlimitedcanada
twitter.com/ducanada
To conserve, restore & manage wetlands & associated habitats for waterfowl, as well as for the benefit of other wildlife & people
Malcolm M. Dunfield, Chair
Gregory E. Siekaniec, Chief Executive Officer
James A. Fortune, Chief Fundraising Officer
Marcy Sullivan, Chief Financial Officer
Karla Guyn, National Director, Conservation
Linda Monforton, National Director, Human Resources
Gary Goodwin, Executive Corporate Secretary & Counsel

Earth Day Canada (EDC) / Jour de la terre Canada
#503, 111 Peter St., Toronto ON M5V 2H1
Tel: 416-599-1991; *Fax:* 416-599-3100
Toll-Free: 888-283-2784
info@earthday.ca
www.earthday.ca
Social Media: www.youtube.com/user/EarthDayCanada
www.facebook.com/EarthDayCanada
twitter.com/earthdaycanada
To improve the state of the environment by motivating & helping Canadians to achieve local solutions
Jed Goldberg, President
Keith Treffry, Director, Communications
Paul Bubelis, Chair

Ecojustice Canada Society
#214, 131 Water St., Vancouver BC V6B 4M3
Tel: 604-685-5618; *Fax:* 604-685-7813
Toll-Free: 800-926-7744
www.ecojustice.ca
Social Media:
www.facebook.com/ecojustice
twitter.com/ecojustice_ca
To provide legal representation to environmental groups that cannot afford to go to court against large institutions when important wilderness values are at stake; to bring selected cases with the ultimate goal of establishing an aggregate of strong legal precedents that recognize environmental values; to provide professional advice on the development of environmental legislation
Cathy Wilkinson, President & Chair
Deborah Curran, Vice-Chair
Mike Cormack, Treasurer
Ronald H. Pearson, Secretary
Devon Page, Executive Director

Ecology Action Centre (EAC)
2705 Fern Lane, Halifax NS B3K 4L3
Tel: 902-429-2202; *Fax:* 902-405-3716
info@ecologyaction.ca
www.ecologyaction.ca
Social Media:
www.facebook.com/EcologyActionCentre
twitter.com/ecologyaction
To act as a voice for Nova Scotia's environment; To build a healthier, more sustainable Nova Scotia
Maggy Burns, Managing Director
Rochelle Owen, Co-Chair

Ecotrust Canada
#90, 425 Carrall St., Vancouver BC V6B 6E3
Tel: 604-682-4141; *Fax:* 604-862-1944
info@ecotrust.ca
ecotrust.ca
Social Media: www.youtube.com/user/EcotrustCanada
www.facebook.com/ecotrust.ca
twitter.com/ecotrustcanada
To improve environmental sustainability in British Columbia
Brenda Reid-Kuecks, President

Elsa Wild Animal Appeal of Canada
PO Box 45051, 2482 Yonge St., Toronto ON M4P 3E3
Tel: 416-489-8862
info@elsacanada.com
www.elsacanada.com
To help save endangered wildlife species in Canada
Betty Henderson, President

Enviro-Accès Inc.
#150, 85, rue Belvédère nord, Sherbrooke QC J1H 4A7
Tél: 819-823-2230; *Téléc:* 819-823-6632
enviro@enviroaccess.ca
www.enviroaccess.ca
Supporter les petites et moyennes entreprises qui oeuvrent dans le domaine de l'environnement en leur offrant les services professionnels nécessaires au développement de leurs projets et de leurs affaires.
Manon Laporte, Présidente-directrice générale

Environmental Careers Organization of Canada / L'Organisation pour les carrières en environnement du Canada
#200, 308 - 11th Ave. SE, Calgary AB T2G 0Y2
Tel: 403-233-0748; *Fax:* 403-269-9544
info@eco.ca
www.eco.ca
Social Media:
www.facebook.com/ecocanada
twitter.com/ecocanada
To provide services to all participants in the environmental sector, including educators, students, practitioners, & employers
Hubert Bourque, Chair
Jon Ogryzlo, Sec.-Treas.
Grant S. Trump, President/CEO
Michael Kerford, Vice-President
Janelle Thomlinson, Director, Marketing & Communications

Environmental Education Association of the Yukon (EEAY)
Whitehorse YT
eeyukon@gmail.com
taiga.net/YukonEE
To promote environmental education in the Yukon and foster communication between individuals and groups with and interest in environmental education.

Environmental Health Association of British Columbia (EHABC)
PO Box 30033, RPO Reyolds, Victoria BC V8X 5E1
Tel: 250-658-2027
info@ehabc.org
www.ehabc.org
Social Media:
www.facebook.com/353025931439290
To raise awareness within the medical community, educational institutions, and the general public to prevent further cases of environmental sensitivity from occurring.

The Environmental Law Centre (Alberta) Society (ELC)
#800, 10025 - 106 St., Edmonton AB T5J 1G4
Tel: 780-424-5099; *Fax:* 780-424-5133
Toll-Free: 800-661-4238
elc@elc.ab.ca
www.elc.ab.ca
Social Media: www.youtube.com/ELCAlberta
www.facebook.com/environmentallawcentre
twitter.com/ELC_Alberta
To conduct research in environmental & natural resources law, policy & procedure; To educate the public on environmental law; To operate an environmental law information & referral service for the benefit of the public; To monitor relevant municipal, provincial & federal environmental laws, policies & procedures, & make recommendations for reform
Josephine Victoria Yam, Executive Director

Environmental Managers Association of British Columbia (EMABC)
PO Box 3741, Vancouver BC V6B 3Z8
Tel: 604-998-2226; *Fax:* 604-998-2226
info@emaofbc.com
www.emaofbc.com
Social Media:
linkedin.com/groups/Environmental-Managers-Association-BC-1856767
twitter.com/emaofbc
To encourage education, share knowledge among members and create a forum for environmental management issues in the industrial, commercial and institutional sectors, serve as a key resource of environmental information for members and explore existing and emerging environmental issues.
Patrick Johnstone, President
Don Bryant, Executive Director

Environmental Services Association of Alberta (ESAA)
#102, 2528 Ellwood Dr. SW, Edmonton AB T6X 0A9
Tel: 780-429-6363; *Fax:* 780-429-4249
Toll-Free: 800-661-9278
info@esaa.org
www.esaa.org
To act as the voice of Alberta's environment industry
Craig Robertson, President
Randy Neumann, Secretary
Skip Kerr, Treasurer
Joe Barraclough, Director, Industry & Government Relations
Joe Chowaniec, Director, Program & Event Development

Environmental Services Association of Nova Scotia (ESANS)
Woodside Industrial Park, #211-2, 1 Research Dr., Dartmouth NS B2Y 4M9
Tel: 902-463-3538; *Fax:* 902-466-6889
contact@esans.ca
www.esans.ca
ESANS is a province-wide business organization dedicated to the promotion of environmental products, services & organizations within the environmental industry.
Norval Collins, President
Sandra Lynch, Operations Manager

Environnement jeunesse
Maison du développement durable, #400, 50, rue Sainte-Catherine Ouest, Montréal QC H2X 3V4
Tél: 514-252-3016; *Téléc:* 514-254-5873
Ligne sans frais: 866-377-3016
infoenjeu@enjeu.qc.ca
enjeu.qc.ca
Média social: vimeo.com/channels/enjeu
www.facebook.com/environnement.jeunesse
twitter.com/ENJEUquebec
Promouvoir la conservation et l'amélioration de la qualité de l'environnement; développer chez les jeunes les qualités favorisant leur implication sociale.
Jérôme Normand, Directeur général

Evergreen
#300, 550 Bayview Ave, Toronto ON M4W 3X8
Tel: 416-596-1495; *Fax:* 416-596-1443
Toll-Free: 888-426-3138
info@evergreen.ca
www.evergreen.ca
To bring communities & nature together for the benefit of both; To create sustaining, healthy, dynamic outdoor spaces by engaging people & encouraging local stewardship
Geoff Cape, Executive Director
Seana Irvine, Chief Operating officer

FaunENord
CP 422, 512, rte 167 sud, Chibougamau QC G8P 2X8
Tél: 418-748-4441; *Téléc:* 418-748-1110
faunenord@lino.com
www.faunenord.org
Média social:
www.facebook.com/pages/FaunENord/220907094605740
Une entreprise vouée à la promotion & à l'aménagement durable des ressources fauniques & des écosystèmes
Isabelle Milord, Présidente

Fédération québécoise des chasseurs et pêcheurs
162, rue du Brome, Québec QC G3A 2P5
Tél: 418-878-8901; *Téléc:* 418-878-8980
Ligne sans frais: 888-523-2863
info@fedecp.qc.ca
www.fedecp.qc.ca
Média social: www.facebook.com/116805682100
twitter.com/FederationCP
Contribuer, dans le respect de la faune et de ses habitats, à la gestion du développement et à la perpétuation de la chasse et de la pêche comme activités traditionnelles et sportives
Pierre Latraverse, Président

Fédération québécoise pour le saumon atlantique (FQSA)
42B, rue Racine, Québec QC G2B 1C6
Tél: 418-847-9191; *Téléc:* 418-847-9279
Ligne sans frais: 888-847-9191
secretariat@saumon-fqsa.qc.ca
www.FQSA.ca
Média social: instagram.com/fqsa_saumon
www.facebook.com/85717316801?fref=ts
twitter.com/SaumonFQSA
Organisme à but non lucratif dont la raison d'être est d'unir et de représenter les intérêts de l'ensemble des saumoniers du Québec
Michel Jean, Directeur général

First Nations Environmental Network
PO Box 394, Tofino BC V0R 2Z0
Tel: 250-726-5265; *Fax:* 250-725-2357
councilfire@hotmail.com
www.fnen.org
The First Nations Environmental Network is a circle of First Nations people committed to protecting, defending, and restoring the balance of all life by honouring traditional Indigenous values and the path of our ancestors.

Fondation de la faune du Québec (FFQ)
#420, 1175, av Lavigerie, Sainte-Foy QC G1V 4P1
Tél: 418-644-7926; *Téléc:* 418-643-7655
Ligne sans frais: 877-639-0742
ffq@fondationdelafaune.qc.ca
www.fondationdelafaune.qc.ca
Média social: www.facebook.com/fondationdelafauneduquebec
Promouvoir la conservation et la mise en valeur de la faune et de son habitat
André Martin, Président-directeur général

FortWhyte Alive
1961 McCreary Rd., Winnipeg MB R3P 2K9
Tel: 204-989-8355; *Fax:* 204-895-4700
info@fortwhyte.org
www.fortwhyte.org
Social Media:
www.facebook.com/pages/FortWhyte-Alive/471614835647
twitter.com/fortwhytealive
FortWhyte Alive is dedicated to providing programming, natural settings and facilities for environmental education and outdoor recreation. In so doing, FortWhyte promotes awareness and understanding of the natural world and actions leading to sustainable living.
Bill Elliott, President/CEO

Fraser Basin Council (FBC)
Basin-Wide Office, 470 Granville St., 1st Fl., Vancouver BC V6C 1V5
Tel: 604-488-5350; *Fax:* 604-488-5351
info@fraserbasin.bc.ca
www.fraserbasin.bc.ca
To advance sustainability in the Fraser River Basin & across British Columbia
David Marshall, Executive Director
Charlotte Argue, Assistant Manager, Climate Change & Air Quality Program

Fresh Outlook Foundation (FOF)
12510 Ponderosa Rd., Lake Country BC V4V 2G9
Tel: 250-766-1777; *Fax:* 250-766-1767
www.freshoutlookfoundation.org
Social Media:
www.facebook.com/FreshOutlookFoundation?ref=website
twitter.com/FreshOutlook
The Fresh Outlook Foundation (FOF) builds sustainable communities through a focus on the social, cultural, environmental, and economic aspects of community sustainability.
Joanne de Vries, CEO

Friends of Red Hill Valley
PO Box 61536, Hamilton ON L8T 5A1
Tel: 905-664-8796
redhill@hwcn.org
To protect & enhance the Red Hill Valley in Hamilton, Ontario
Don McLean, Chair

Friends of the Earth Canada (FoE) / Les Ami(e)s de la Terre Canada
#200, 251 Bank St., Ottawa ON K2P 1X3
Tel: 613-241-0085; *Fax:* 613-566-3449
Toll-Free: 888-385-4444
foe@foecanada.org
www.foecanada.org
Social Media: www.youtube.com/user/FOECanada
www.facebook.com/foe.canada
twitter.com/FoE_Canada
To serve as a national voice for the environment, working with others to inspire the renewal of our communities & the earth, through research, education, advocacy & cooperation
Beatrice Olivastri, Chief Executive Officer
Stephen Barg, President

Friends of the Greenbelt Foundation
#500, 661 Yonge St., Toronto ON M4Y 1Z9
Tel: 416-960-0001; *Fax:* 416-960-0030
info@greenbelt.ca
www.greenbelt.ca
Social Media:
linkedin.com/company/friends-of-the-greenbelt-foundation
www.facebook.com/ontariogreenbelt
twitter.com/greenbeltca
To help foster the Greenbelt's living countryside by nurturing & supporting activities that preserve its environmental & agricultural integrity
Burkhard Mausberg, CEO

Fuse Collective
Scrubfield Hall, #199B, 2500 University Dr., Calgary AB T2N 1N4
info@iseeesa.ca
fusecollective.org
Social Media:
www.facebook.com/ISEEESA
twitter.com/iseeesa
To promote and create initiatives that reflect the growing movement to obtain a cleaner energy supply, healthy environment, and efficient economy.
Arathi Haridas, President

Green Action Centre (RCM)
303 Portage Ave., 3rd Fl., Winnipeg MB R3B 2B4
Tel: 204-925-3777; *Fax:* 204-942-4207
Toll-Free: 866-394-8880
info@greenactioncentre.ca
greenactioncentre.ca
Social Media: www.pinterest.com/gacentre/
www.facebook.com/GreenActionCentre
twitter.com/greenactionctr
To promote ecological sustainability by developing alternatives to currently unsustainable practices; their principal activity is environmental education; our partners & clients include businesses, schools, non-profit groups, governments, recyclers, home gardeners & general public
Tracy Hucul, Executive Director

Greenpeace Canada
33 Cecil St., Toronto ON M5T 1N1
Tel: 416-597-8408; *Fax:* 416-597-8422
Toll-Free: 800-320-7183
supporter.ca@greenpeace.org
www.greenpeace.org/canada
Social Media: www.youtube.com/user/GreenpeaceCanada
www.facebook.com/greenpeace.canada
twitter.com/greenpeaceCA
Greenpeace is an independent, non-profit organization best known for non-violent direct actions to raise awareness on issues such as biodiversity, pollution of the Earth, nuclear threats & disarmament; it brings public opinion to bear on decisions makers. Public protest is only one of many Greenpeace strategies; it conducts scientific, economic & political research, publicizes environmental problems, recommends environmentally sound solutions & lobbies for change.
Joanna Kerr, Executive Director
Sue Birge, Chair

Greenspace Alliance of Canada's Capital
PO Box 55085, 240 Sparks St., Ottawa ON K1P 1A1
greenspace@greenspace-alliance.ca
www.greenspace-alliance.ca
To preserve green spaces in the National Capital area.
Amy Kempster, Chair

Hamilton Industrial Environmental Association (HIEA)
PO Box 35545, Hamilton ON L8H 7S6
Tel: 905-561-4432
info@hiea.org
www.hiea.org
To improve the local environment - air, land and water - through joint and individual activities, and by partnering with the community to enhance future understanding of environmental issues and help establish priorities for action.
Jim Stirling, Chair

Harmony Foundation of Canada / Fondation Harmonie du Canada
PO Box 50022, #15, 1594 Fairfield Rd., Victoria BC V8S 1G1
Tel: 250-380-3001; *Fax:* 250-380-0887
harmony@islandnet.com
www.harmonyfdn.ca
Social Media: www.youtube.com/user/harmonyfdn
www.facebook.com/117724434937243
To encourage development which is socially & environmentally sustainable; To strive towards ecological stability, long-term prosperity, & social harmony
Michael Bloomfield, Founder & Executive Director
Robert Bateman, Honorary Chair
Jean-Pierre Soublière, President
Nick Mosky, Secretary
Robert Van Tongerloo, Treasurer

Hope for Wildlife Society
5909 Hwy. 207, Seaforth NS B0J 1N0
Tel: 902-452-3339
Crisis Hot-Line: 902-407-9453
info@hopeforwildlife.net
www.hopeforwildlife.net
Social Media:
www.facebook.com/hopeforwildlife
twitter.com/hopeforwildlife
Specializing in the care, treatment and rehabilitation of injured or orphaned native fur bearing mammals, sea birds and songbirds both indigenous to the Nova Scotia area as well as non-indigenous species and pets.
Hope Swinimer, Founder & Director

Institut de recherche en biologie végétale (IRBV) / Plant Biology Research Institute (PBRI)
4101, rue Sherbrooke est, Montréal QC H1X 2B2
Tél: 514-343-2121; *Téléc:* 514-343-2288
irbv@irbv.umontreal.ca
www.irbv.umontreal.ca
To develop a centre of excellence in plant biology; both in fundamental research and its applicaitons; train students in plant biology at the master, doctoral, and post-doctoral levels; further training and knowledge of its researchers and technical personnel; promote the technological transfer of its scientific research results to users; provide complementary services to the community in fields relevant to plant biology, where expertise in the field is lacking.
Anne Bruneau, Directrice

International Council for the Exploration of the Sea (ICES)
H.C. Andersens Blvd. 44-46, Copenhagen VDK-1553 Denmark
info@ices.dk
www.ices.dk
To coordinate research & monitor activities to understand the marine environment & resources & man's impact upon them, including the identification of priority marine contaminants, their distribution, transport & effects; to provide advice regarding marine resources & pollution to member governments & international regulatory commissions; to publish & disseminate the results of research
Gerd Hubold, General Secretary
David Gillis, ICES Delegate, Canada
Ariane Plourde, ICES Delegate, Canada

International Institute for Sustainable Development (IISD) / Institut international du développement durable (IIDD)
161 Portage Ave. East, 6th Fl., Winnipeg MB R3B 0Y4
Tel: 204-958-7700; *Fax:* 204-958-7710
info@iisd.ca
www.iisd.org
Social Media:
www.facebook.com/IISDnews
twitter.com/IISD_news
To promote sustainable development in decision-making in Canada & abroad by undertaking sustainable development research, advising government, business & organizations, analyzing & reporting on issues & events, & publishing & disseminating sustainable development information. Offices in Winnipeg, Ottawa, New York, & Geneva.
Scott Vaughan, President/CEO
Grace Mota, Treasurer and Chief Financial Officer
Janice Gair, VP, Human Resources & Corporate Services
Joel Trenaman, Director, Communications & Publishing

Jasper Environmental Association (JEA)
PO Box 2198, Jasper AB T0E 1E0
Tel: 780-852-4152
jea2@telus.net
www.jasperenvironmental.org
To support Parks Canada in administering Jasper National Park in accordance with Canadian legislation, Parks Canada principles and policies and the wishes of the Canadian public.

Manitoba Conservation Districts Association (MCDA)
#4, 940 Princess Ave., Brandon MB R7A 0P6
Tel: 204-570-0164
info@mcda.ca
www.mcda.ca
Social Media:
www.youtube.com/channel/UCNM4SLi9ZNTxurTbQcYWWpQ
www.facebook.com/176771465790644
twitter.com/MBConsDistAssoc
Manitoba Conservation Districts Association (MCDA) is a non-profit organization which represents the 18 Conservation Districts (CD's) within Manitoba.
Shane Robins, Executive Director

Manitoba Eco-Network Inc. (MEN) / Réseau écologique du Manitoba inc.
#3, 303 Portage Ave., Winnipeg MB R3B 2B4
Tel: 204-947-6511; *Fax:* 866-237-3130
info@mbeconetwork.org
www.mbeconetwork.org
Social Media: www.youtube.com/user/ManitobaEcoNetwork
www.facebook.com/Manitoba.Eco.Network
twitter.com/MB_EcoNetwork
To educate the public on environmental issues; to conduct research on environmental issues; to facilitate communications between environmental groups & the general public
Peters Karen, Executive Director

Manitoba Environment Officers Association Inc. (MEOA)
147 Norcross Cres., Winnipeg MB R3X 1J2
meoa@mts.net
www.meoa.ca
To enhance the public health and safety of Manitobans and to protect, maintain and rehabilitate Manitoba's environment ecosystems through the diligent duties of educated Environment Officers and to obtain for Environment Officers continued education and recognition of their efforts.
Bill Barr, President

Manitoba Environmental Industries Association Inc. (MEIA)
#100, 62 Albert St., Winnipeg MB R3B 1E9
Tel: 204-783-7090; *Fax:* 204-783-6501
admin@meia.mb.ca
www.meia.mb.ca
To assist members in the business of the environment; To connect business, government, & stakeholders with environmental issues
John Fjeldsted, Executive Director
Vaughn Bullough, President
Rosemary Deans, Coordinator, Education & Training
Deb Tardiff, Coordinator, Education & Training
Sheldon McLeod, Secretary
John Pikel, Treasurer

Manitoba Wildlife Federation (MWF)
70 Stevenson Rd., Winnipeg MB R3H 0W7
Tel: 204-633-5967; *Toll-Free:* 877-633-4868
info@mwf.mb.ca
www.mwf.mb.ca
To devote members to the causes of conservation & the participation in the wise use of natural resources; To encourage the propagation of game & fish; To promote the enforcement of game laws; To cooperate with government departments
Rob Olson, Managing Director

Municipal Waste Association (MWA)
PO Box 1894, Guelph ON N1H 7A1
Tel: 519-823-1990; *Fax:* 519-823-0084
www.municipalwaste.ca
To expedite the flow of information regarding 3R programs to municipalities & other community & government groups; To act as an information forum for municipal recycling coordinators; To allow member municipalities to act as a unified voice in promoting progressive waste reduction & recycling alternatives
Ben Bennett, Executive Director
Melissa Campbell, Coordinator, Membership

The Nature Conservancy of Canada (NCC) / Société canadienne pour la conservation de la nature
#400, 36 Eglinton Ave. West, Toronto ON M4R 1A1
Tel: 416-932-3202; *Toll-Free:* 800-465-0029
nature@natureconservancy.ca
www.natureconservancy.ca
Social Media: www.instagram.ca/ncc_cnc
linkedin.com/company/the-nature-conservancy-of-canada
www.facebook.com/natureconservancy.ca
twitter.com/NCC_CNC
To protect Canada's biodiversity through long-term stewardship & property securement
John Lounds, President & Chief Executive Officer
Michael Bradstreet, Vice-President, Conservation

New Brunswick Environmental Network (NBEN) / Réseau environnemental du Nouveau-Brunswick (RENB)
167 Creek Rd., Waterford NB E4E 4L7
Tel: 506-433-6101; *Fax:* 506-433-6111
nben@nben.ca
www.nben.ca
Social Media:
www.facebook.com/pages/NBEN-RENB/134259049952351
To strengthen the environmental movement throughout New Brunswick; To promote ecologically sound ways of life
Mary Ann Coleman, Executive Director
Joanna Brown, Coordinator, Youth Outreach & Events

Raissa Marks, Coordinator, Education & Outreach Programs

New Brunswick Wildlife Federation (NBWF) / Fédération de la faune du Nouveau-Brunswick
PO Box 549, Moncton NB E1C 8L9
nbwildlifefederation.org
To foster sound management & wise use of the renewable & non-renewable natural resources of New Brunswick; To assist & encourage the enforcement of those game laws which are in keeping with the objectives of the Federation & to strive for better management & game laws where & when necessary; To educate membership & the public, with particular emphasis upon conservation & safety; To represent the interests & concerns of New Brunswick sportsmen; to cooperate with government departments & all related groups, where interests are mutual
Charlie Leblanc, President

Newfoundland & Labrador Environmental Industry Association (NEIA)
#207, 90 O'Leary Ave., St. John's NL A1B 2C7
Tel: 709-237-8090
info@neia.org
neia.org
Social Media:
linkedin.com/company/3194901
www.facebook.com/NEIAssoc
twitter.com/NEIAssoc
To promote the growth & development of the environmental industry of Newfoundland & Labrador; to promote ethical behavior & high standards for environmental products & services; to provide a strong, unified voice toward all private sector, government & non-profit entities involved in the Newfoundland environmental industry.
Ted Lomond, Executive Director
Frank Ricketts, Chair

Newfoundland & Labrador Wildlife Federation (NWLF)
15 Conran St., St. John's NL A1E 5L8
Tel: 709-364-8415
www.nlwf.ca
To foster awareness & enjoyment of the natural world; To promote the sustainable use of natural resources; To protect wildlife & its habitat through conservation & effective wildlife management
Rick Bouzan, President

North American Recycled Rubber Association (NARRA)
#24, 1621 McEwen Dr., Whitby ON L1N 9A5
Tel: 905-433-7769; *Fax:* 905-433-0905
narra@oix.com
www.recycle.net/recycle/assn/narra
The Association provides a unified voice, as well as a communication network & research facility, for issues of concern to those involved in rubber recycling across North America.
Diane Sarracini, Office Manager

Nova Scotia Nature Trust (NSNT)
PO Box 2202, 2085 Maitland St., Halifax NS B3J 3C4
Tel: 902-425-5263; *Fax:* 902-429-5263
Toll-Free: 877-434-5263
nature@nsnt.ca
www.nsnt.ca
Social Media: www.youtube.com/user/naturetrust/videos
www.facebook.com/novascotianaturetrust
twitter.com/nsnaturetrust
To protect Nova Scotia's outstanding natural legacy through land conservation.
Corey Miller, President
Bonnie Sutherland, Executive Director

Oak Ridges Moraine Foundation (ORMF)
120 Bayview Pkwy., Newmarket ON L3Y 4X1
Tel: 289-279-5733
support@ormf.com
www.ormf.com
Social Media:
twitter.com/ormoraine
To provide support and encouragement for activities that preserve, protect, and restore the environmental integrity of the Oak Ridges Moraine and support a trail along it.
Michele Donnelly, Senior Administrative Assistant

Ontario Environment Industry Association (ONEIA)
#410, 215 Spadina Ave., Toronto ON M5T 2C7
Tel: 416-531-7884; *Fax:* 416-644-0116
info@oneia.ca
www.oneia.ca
Social Media: www.youtube.com/user/ONEIAmedia
twitter.com/ONEIAnetwork
To promote the growth of environment business in Ontario
Alex Gill, Executive Director

Marjan Lahuis, Operations Manager

Ontario Environmental Network (OEN)
PO Box 192, Georgetown ON L7G 4T1
oen@oen.ca
www.oen.ca
Social Media: www.youtube.com/ontarioenvironment
www.facebook.com/OntarioEnvironmentNetwork
To encourage discussions of ways to protect the environment; To increase environmental awareness throughout Ontario; To serve the environmental non-profit, non-governmental community in Ontario
Phillip Penna, Coordinator

Ontario Federation of Anglers & Hunters (OFAH)
PO Box 2800, 4601 Guthrie Dr., Peterborough ON K9J 8L5
Tel: 705-748-6324; *Fax:* 705-748-9577
ofah@ofah.org
www.ofah.org
Social Media: www.youtube.com/ofahcommunications
www.facebook.com/theOFAH
twitter.com/ofah
To save & defend from waste the natural resources of Ontario, its soils, minerals, air, water, forests & wildlife
Angelo Lombardo, Executive Director

Ontario Pollution Control Equipment Association (OPCEA)
PO Box 137, Midhurst ON L0L 1X0
Tel: 705-725-0917; *Fax:* 705-725-1068
opcea@opcea.com
www.opcea.com
To assist members in the promotion of their services & equipment in Ontario
Kelly Manden, Executive Administrator
Brian Allen, President
Wayne Harrison, Vice-President
Heinz Held, Treasurer

Ontario Steelheaders
PO Box 604, Brantford ON N3T 5T3
president@ontariosteelheaders.ca
www.ontariosteelheaders.ca
Social Media:
www.facebook.com/pages/Ontario-Steelheaders/117486061781254
twitter.com/ONSteelheaders
To improve access and habitat for migratory rainbow trout, provide young rainbow trout with suitable nursery habitat, provide relevent and appropriate input to government, agencies and other organizations, and to educate members and the public on relevent issues, conservation practices and proper angling techniques.
Karl Redin, President

Ontario Streams
50 Bloomington Rd. West, Aurora ON L4G 3G8
Tel: 905-713-7399; *Fax:* 905-713-7361
www.ontariostreams.on.ca
To promote the conservation & rehabilitation of streams & wetlands, through education & community involvement
Doug Forder, General Manager

Ontario Waste Management Association (OWMA) / Société ontarienne de gestion des déchets
#3, 2005 Clark Blvd., Brampton ON L6T 5P8
Tel: 905-791-9500; *Fax:* 905-791-9514
info@owma.org
www.owma.org
Social Media:
linkedin.com/company/ontario-waste-management-association
twitter.com/OWMA1
To act as the voice of the private sector waste industry in Ontario; To protect the enviroment by properly managing waste & recyclable materials

Ottawa Riverkeeper / Sentinelle Outaouais
#301, 1960 Scott St., Ottawa ON K1Z 8L8
Tel: 613-321-1120; *Fax:* 613-822-5258
Toll-Free: 888-953-3737
info@ottawariverkeeper.ca
www.ottawariverkeeper.ca
To protect and promote the ecological health and diversity of the Ottawa River and its tributaries; To ensure swimmable, fishable, drinkable waterways
Meredith Brown, Executive Director

The Pembina Institute
219 - 19 St. NW, Calgary AB T2N 2H9
Tel: 403-269-3344; *Fax:* 403-269-3377
www.pembina.org
To develop & promote public policy & educational programs which protect the environment & encourage environmentally sound resource management strategies; to implement a conserver society
Ed Whittingham, Executive Director

Pitch-In Canada (PIC) / Passons à l'action Canada
PO Box 45011, RPO Ocean Park, White Rock BC V4A 9L1
Tel: 604-536-4726; *Fax:* 604-535-4653
Toll-Free: 877-474-8244
pitch-in@pitch-in.ca
www.pitch-in.ca
Social Media:
www.facebook.com/pitchin.canada
twitter.com/@pitch_in_canada
To improve communities & the envionment by providing programs to reduce, re-use, recycle, & properly manage & dispose waste
Misha Cook, Executive Director
Erika Tibbe, Marketing & Program Coordinator

The Pollution Probe Foundation (PPF)
#200, 150 Ferrand Dr., Toronto ON M3C 3E5
Tel: 416-926-1907; *Fax:* 416-926-1601
pprobe@pollutionprobe.org
www.pollutionprobe.org
Social Media:
linkedin.com/company/989805
www.facebook.com/PollutionProbe
twitter.com/PollutionProbe
A registered Canadian charity which seeks to define environmental problems through research; to promote understanding through education & to press for practical solutions through advocacy. The organization is non-partison & works collaboratively with government agencies, other non-profit organizations, & private business to engage key issues & find solutions. Offices in Toronto & Ottawa
Bob Oliver, CEO
Husam Mansour, COO

Prince Edward Island Eco-Net (PEIEN)
#216, 40 Enman Cres., Charlottetown PE C1E 1E6
Tel: 902-566-4170; *Fax:* 902-566-4037
network@eastlink.ca
Social Media:
www.facebook.com/peieconet?ref=ts
To promote communication & cooperation among ENGO's (Environmental NGO's) & between ENGO's & governments; to provide referral services; to coordinate workshops & conferences; to provide consultations; to publish & distribute information
Matthew McCarville, Executive Director

Prince Edward Island Wildlife Federation
#103B, 420 University Ave., Charlottetown PE C1A 7Z5
Tel: 902-626-9699
Social Media:
www.facebook.com/145488672186392
To foster sound management & wise use of the renewable resources of PEI; to assist & encourage the enforcement of those game laws which are in keeping with the objectives of the Federation & to strive for better management & game laws where & when necessary; to cooperate with government departments & related groups where interests are mutual; to educate membership & the public, with particular emphasis upon conservation & safety; to represent the interests & concerns of PEI sportsmen
Duncan Crawford, Contact

Recycling Council of Alberta (RCA)
PO Box 23, Bluffton AB T0C 0M0
Tel: 403-843-6563; *Fax:* 403-843-4156
info@recycle.ab.ca
www.recycle.ab.ca
Social Media:
www.facebook.com/RecyclingCouncilOfAlberta
twitter.com/3RsAB
To promote & facilitate waste reduction, recycling, & resource conservation in Alberta
Jason London, President
Sharon Howland, Vice-President
Maegan Lukian, Secretary
Anne Auriat, Treasurer

Recycling Council of British Columbia (RCBC)
#10, 119 West Pender St., Vancouver BC V6B 1S5
Tel: 604-683-6009; *Fax:* 604-683-7255
Toll-Free: 800-667-4321
rcbc@rcbc.ca
www.rcbc.ca
Social Media:
www.facebook.com/RecyclingBC
twitter.com/RecyclingBC
To promote the principles of zero waste; To decrease British Columbia's environmental footprint

Brock Macdonald, Chief Executive Officer
Anna Rochelle, Director, Finance
Harvinder Aujala, Manager, Information Services
Ben Ramos, Manager, Member Services

Recycling Council of Ontario (RCO) / Conseil du recyclage de l'Ontario
#225, 215 Spadina Ave., Toronto ON M5T 2C7
Tel: 416-657-2797; *Toll-Free:* 888-501-9637
rco@rco.on.ca
www.rco.on.ca
Social Media:
www.facebook.com/372107118725
twitter.com/RCOntario
To inform & educate society about the generation & avoidance of waste; To encourage recycling & the efficient use of resources
Jo-Anne St. Godard, Executive Director
Diane Blackburn, Manager, Events
Meirav Even-Har, Program Manager, Waste Diversion Certification Program

Réseau environnement
#220, 911, rue Jean Talon est, Montréal QC H2R 1V5
Tél: 514-270-7110; *Téléc:* 514-270-7154
info@reseau-environnement.com
www.reseau-environnement.com
Regrouper des entreprises spécialisées dans la gestion des déchets commerciaux, industriels et des services municipaux reliés à l'environnement; Assurer l'avancement des technologies et de la science, la promotion des expertises et le soutien des activités en environnement
Stéphanie Myre, Présidente-directrice générale
Mario Laplante, Directeur général adjointé
Josianne Lafantaisie, Coordonnatrice principale, Communications et relations publiques
Romy Regis, Coordonnatrice, Événements
Lyne Dubois, Merlicom
Mihaela Sandor, Comptable

Réseau québécois des groupes écologistes (RQGE)
454, av Laurier Est, Montréal QC H2J 1E7
Tél: 514-587-8194
info@rqge.qc.ca
www.rqge.qc.ca
Média social: www.youtube.com/user/RQgroupesecologistes
www.facebook.com/Reseau.quebecois.des.groupes.ecologistes
twitter.com/InfoRQGE
Pour recueillir de services et d'information pour les groupes écologiques du Québec; aider les groupes à communiquer entre eux
Stéphane Gingras, Président
Bruno Massé, Coordonnateur général

Resource Efficient Agricultural Production (REAP Canada)
PO Box 125, Stn. Centennial Centre CCB13, #21, 111 Lakeshore Rd., Sainte-Anne-de-Bellevue QC H9X 3V9
Tel: 514-398-7743; *Fax:* 514-398-7972
info@reap-canada.com
www.reap-canada.com
To improve farm profits & productivity while minimizing adverse health & environmental effects
Roger Samson, Executive Director

Rideau Environmental Action League (REAL)
PO Box 1061, Smiths Falls ON K7A 5A5
Tel: 613-283-9500
info@realaction.ca
www.realaction.ca
Social Media:
twitter.com/RideauEnvActL
To conduct community-wide environmental projects and promote environmental improvements within the Town of Smiths Falls and Lanark, Leeds and Grenville Counties.
Larry Manson, President

Rideau Valley Conservation Authority (RVCA)
PO Box 599, 3889 Rideau Valley Dr., Manotick ON K4M 1A5
Tel: 613-692-3571; *Fax:* 613-692-0831
Toll-Free: 800-267-3504
info@rvcf.ca
www.rvca.ca
Social Media: www.flickr.com/photos/64684563@N08
www.facebook.com/108941882522595
twitter.com/RideauValleyCA
To advocate for clean water, natural shorelines & sustainable land use throughout the Rideau Valley watershed
Sommer Casgrain-Robertson, General Manager
Diane Downey, Director, Communications

Sackville Rivers Association (SRA)
PO Box 45071, Sackville NS B4E 2Z6
Tel: 902-865-9238; *Fax:* 902-864-3564
sackvillerivers@ns.sympatico.ca
www.sackvillerivers.ns.ca
To promote the preservation, restoration and enhancement of the Sackville River Watershed.
Damon Conrad, Contact

Saskatchewan Eco-Network (SEN)
535 - 8 St. East, Saskatoon SK S7K 0P9
Tel: 306-652-1275
info@econet.ca
www.econet.sk.ca
To provide educational activities to develop an awareness of conservation & enhancement of the environment
Rick Morrell, Executive Director

Saskatchewan Environmental Industry & Managers' Association (SEIMA)
2341 McIntyre St., Regina SK S4P 2S3
Tel: 306-543-1567; *Fax:* 306-543-1568
info@seima.sk.ca
www.seima.sk.ca
Social Media:
www.facebook.com/146987992039835
To act as the voice of practitioners in Saskatchewan's environmental industry on environmental matters; To promote responsible environmental management in the province; To develop the environmental industry in Saskatchewan
Kathleen Livingston, Executive Director & COO
Al Shpyth, President
Lenore Swystun, Vice-President
Lois Miller, Treasurer
Cheryl Hender, Secretary

Saskatchewan Environmental Society (SES)
PO Box 1372, Saskatoon SK S7K 3N9
Tel: 306-665-1915
info@environmentalsociety.ca
www.environmentalsociety.ca
Social Media: www.youtube.com/user/EnvironmentalSociety
linkedin.com/company/saskatchewan-environmental-society
www.facebook.com/environmentalsociety
twitter.com/skenvsociety
To maintain the integrity of Saskatchewan's forests, farmlands & natural prairie landscapes; To promote energy conservation & the development of renewable energy resources; To build sustainable communities, enhanced waste management, & enhanced water quality in the province's lakes & rivers
Allyson Brady, Executive Director
Peter Prebble, Director, Environmental Policy
Angie Bugg, Coordinator, Energy Conservation
Lynette Suchar, Coordinator, Communications

Saskatchewan Soil Conservation Association (SSCA)
PO Box 1360, Indian Head SK S0G 2K0
Tel: 306-695-4233; *Fax:* 306-695-4236
Toll-Free: 800-213-4287
info@ssca.ca
www.ssca.ca
To improve the land & environment; To increase public awareness of soil conservation; To promote conservation production systems to Saskatchewan producers
Tim Nerbas, President
Marilyn Martens, Office Manager

Saskatchewan Waste Reduction Council (SWRC)
The Two-Twenty, #208, 220 - 20th St. West, Saskatoon SK S7M 0W9
Tel: 306-931-3242; *Fax:* 306-955-5852
info@saskwastereduction.ca
www.saskwastereduction.ca
To lead in addressing the underlying causes of waste by identifying opportunities, creating connections & promoting solutions.
Joanne Fedyk, Executive Director
Martha Hollinger, Contact, Member Services & Administration

Saskatchewan Wildlife Federation (SWF)
9 Lancaster Rd., Moose Jaw SK S6J 1M8
Tel: 306-692-8812; *Fax:* 306-692-4370
Toll-Free: 877-793-9453
sask.wildlife@sasktel.net
www.swf.sk.ca
Social Media:
www.facebook.com/pages/Saskatchewan-Wildlife-Federation/178255362147
twitter.com/saskwildlife
To promote the wise use & management of natural resources in Saskatchewan
Darrell Crabbe, Executive Director

Darren Newberry, Coordinator, Habitat Land Trust
Laurel Waldner, Coordinator, Education Program
Adam Matichuk, Coordinator, Fisheries Project
Darby Briggs, Coordinator, Communications

Sea Shepherd Conservation Society (SSCS)
PO Box 48446, Vancouver BC V7X 1A2
Tel: 604-688-7325
canada@seashepherd.org
www.seashepherd.org
Social Media:
www.facebook.com/SeaShepherdVancouver
To investigate & document violations of international laws, regulations & treaties protecting marine wildlife species
Farley Mowat, International Chair

SEEDS Foundation
#400, 144 - 4th Ave. SW., Calgary AB T2P 3N4
Tel: 403-221-0884; *Fax:* 403-221-0876
Toll-Free: 800-661-8751
seeds@telusplanet.net
www.seedsfoundation.ca
Social Media:
ca.linkedin.com/pub/seeds-foundation/3a/909/44
www.facebook.com/117021191648133
To provide educational support materials & professional assistance to teachers in the area of energy, environment & sustainable development; To work toward the development of a society which understands & is committed to actions leading to wise stewardship of resources, resource use & the environment
Corinne Craig, Executive Director

Sierra Club of Canada (SCC) / Sierre club du Canada
#412, 1 Nicholas St., Ottawa ON K1N 7B7
Tel: 613-241-4611; *Fax:* 613-241-2292
Toll-Free: 888-810-4204
info@sierraclub.ca
www.sierraclub.ca
Social Media: www.youtube.com/sierraclubcanada
www.facebook.com/sierraclubcanada
twitter.com/SierraClubCan
To develop a diverse, well-trained grassroots network, working to protect the integrity of our global ecosystems; To focus on five overriding threats: loss of animal & plant species, deterioration of the planet's oceans & atmosphere, the ever-growing presence of toxic chemicals in all living things, destruction of our remaining wilderness, spiralling population growth & overconsumption
John Bennett, Executive Director
Anowara Baqi, CFO
Tania Beriau, Development Director
Daniel Spence, Director, Communications

Small Water Users Association of BC
4167 Highway 3A, Nelson BC V1L 6N1
Tel: 250-825-4308
smallwaterusers@shaw.ca
www.smallwaterusers.com
The Small Water Users Association of BC is a new non-profit society dedicated to serving the interests of small water systems (1 to 300 connections) throughout British Columbia.
Denny Ross-Smith, Executive Director

Society Promoting Environmental Conservation (SPEC)
2060 Pine St., Vancouver BC V6J 4P8
Tel: 604-736-7732; *Fax:* 604-736-7115
admin@spec.bc.ca
www.spec.bc.ca
Social Media: www.youtube.com/user/SPECbc
www.facebook.com/137945192900176
To address environmental issues in British Columbia, with a focus on urban communities in the Lower Mainland & the Georgia Basin; To encourage policies that lead to urban sustainability
Rob Baxter, President
Oliver Lane, Coordinator

Southeast Environmental Association (SEA)
41 Woods Islands Hill, Montague PE C0A 1R0
Tel: 902-838-3351; *Fax:* 902-838-0610
seapei.org
To protect, maintain, and enhance the ecology of south eastern Prince Edward Island for the environmental, social, and economic well being of area residents.
Jackie Bourgeois, Executive Director
Lawrence Millar, Chair

Sustainable Urban Development Association (SUDA)
2637 Council Ring Rd., Mississauga ON L5L 1S6
Tel: 416-400-0553
mail@suda.ca
www.suda.ca

To foster a healthy natural environment by providing information about ways in which cities can become more efficient in the land, material, water and energy resources, and highly supportive of sustainable transportation.
John Banka, President

TD Friends of the Environment Foundation / Fondation des amis de l'environnement TD
TD Bank Tower, PO Box 1, 66 Wellington St., Toronto ON M5K 1A2
Toll-Free: 800-361-5333
tdfef@td.com
www.fef.td.com
To protect & preserve the Canadian environment
Natasha Alleyne-Martin, Manager, National Programs
Sarah Lawless-Ajibade, Regional Manager, Ontario North & East, Quebec and Atlantic Provinces
Mandip Kharod, Regional Manager, BC, Alberta, Yukon & Northwest Territories, Saskatchewan & Manito
Carolyn Scotchmer, Regional Manager, Greater Toronto Region & Western Ontario

Water Environment Association of Ontario (WEAO)
PO Box 176, Milton ON L9T 4N9
Tel: 416-410-6933; *Fax:* 416-410-1626
weao@weao.org
www.weao.org
Social Media:
twitter.com/WEAOYP
To advance the water environment industry; To promote sound public policy
Julie Vincent, Executive Administrator

Western Canada Water (WCW)
PO Box 1708, 240 River Ave., Cochrane AB T4C 1B6
Tel: 403-709-0064; *Fax:* 403-709-0068
Toll-Free: 877-283-2003
member@wcwwa.ca
www.wcwwa.ca
To advance support for water professionals throughout western Canada
Audrey Arisman, Executive Director

Wild Bird Care Centre (WBCC)
PO Box 11159, Nepean ON K2H 7T9
Tel: 613-828-2849; *Fax:* 613-828-2194
mojo@wildbirdcarecentre.org
www.wildbirdcarecentre.org
To assess, treat, and rehabilitate sick, orphaned, or injured wild birds before releasing them back to the wild.
Kathy Nihei, Founder

Wilderness Committee (WCWC)
46 East 6th Ave., Vancouver BC V5T 1J4
Tel: 604-683-8220; *Fax:* 604-683-8229
Toll-Free: 800-661-9453
info@wildernesscommittee.org
www.wildernesscommittee.org
Social Media: www.instagram.com/wildernews
www.facebook.com/wildernesscommittee
twitter.com/wildernews
To work for the protection of Canadian & the Earth's wilderness through research & education; To promote the principles which achieve ecologically sustainable communities
Beth Clarke, Director, Development & Program
Gwen Barlee, Director, Policy
Joe Foy, Director, National Campaign

Wildlife Habitat Canada (WHC) / Habitat faunique Canada (HFC)
#247, 2039 Robertson Rd., Ottawa ON K2H 8R2
Tel: 613-722-2090; *Fax:* 613-722-3318
Toll-Free: 800-669-7919
wildlifehabitatcanada@gmail.com
www.whc.org
Social Media:
www.facebook.com/124492716000
twitter.com/WildlifeHCanada
To promote the conservation, restoration & enhancement of wildlife habitat to retain diversity, distribution & abundance of wildlife; To provide a funding mechanism for the conservation, restoration & enhancement of wildlife habitat in Canada; To foster coordination & leadership in the conservation, restoration & enhancement of wildlife habitat in Canada
Cameron Mack, Executive Director

Wildlife Preservation Canada (WPC) / Conservation de la faune au Canada
RR#5, 5420 Hwy. 6 North, Guelph ON N1H 6J2
Tel: 519-836-9314; *Toll-Free:* 800-956-6608
admin@wildlifepreservation.ca
www.wildlifepreservation.ca
Social Media:
www.facebook.com/WildlifePreservationCanada
twitter.com/WPCWild911
To save endangered animal species from extinction in Canada & internationally
Elaine Williams, Executive Director
Ian Glen, President
Jessica Steiner, Recovery Biologist

World Wildlife Fund - Canada (WWF-Canada) / Fonds mondial pour la nature
#410, 245 Eglinton Ave. East, Toronto ON M4P 3J1
Tel: 416-489-8800; *Fax:* 416-489-3611
Toll-Free: 800-267-2632
www.wwf.ca
Social Media: www.youtube.com/wwfcanada
www.facebook.com/WWFCanada
twitter.com/wwfcanada
To conserve wild animals, plants & habitats for their own sake & the long-term benefit of people; to protect the diversity of life on earth; to stop, & eventually reverse, the accelerating degradation of our planet's natural environment, & to help build a future in which humans live in harmony with nature
Alex Himelfarb, Chair
David Miller, President & CEO
Mary MacDonald, Chief Conservation Officer & Senior VP
Sara Oates, CFO & Vice-President, Finance & Administration
Jay Hooper, Vice-President, Development

Yukon Conservation Society (YCS)
302 Hawkins St., Whitehorse YT Y1A 1X6
Tel: 867-668-5678; *Fax:* 867-668-6637
ycs@ycs.yk.ca
www.yukonconservation.org
To pursue ecosystem well-being throughout the Yukon & beyond
Karen Baltgailis, Executive Director
Georgia Greetham, Coordinator, Office
Sue Kemmett, Coordinator, Forestry
Anne Middler, Coordinator, Energy
Lewis Rifkind, Coordinator, Mining

Yukon Fish & Game Association (YFGA)
509 Strickland St., Whitehorse YT Y1A 2K5
Tel: 867-667-4263; *Fax:* 867-667-4273
yfga@klondiker.com
www.yukonfga.ca
Social Media: www.flickr.com/photos/74103579@N03/
www.facebook.com/yukonfga
To ensure the long-term management of fish, wildlife, & outdoor recreational resources in the Yukon; To improve wildlife habitat
Gord Zealand, Executive Director

Yukon Territory Environmental Network
302 Hawkins St., Whitehorse YT Y1A 1X6
Tel: 867-668-5678; *Fax:* 867-668-6637
yukonenvironet@gmail.com
Susan Davis, Coordinator

Equipment & Machinery

Agricultural Manufacturers of Canada (AMC)
Evraz Place, Stockman's Arena, PO Box 636, Stn. Main, Regina SK S4P 3A3
Tel: 306-522-2710; *Fax:* 306-781-7293
amc@a-m-c.ca
www.a-m-c.ca
To foster & promote the growth & development of the agricultural equipment manufacturing industry; to identify industry problems & take remedial action; to encourage governments to enact legislation & offer programs that enhance the growth potential of industry; to provide a forum for members to exchange ideas & discuss their industry as it relates to the national & international economy
James Umlah, Chair
Jerry Engel, President

Association des marchands de machines aratoires de la province de Québec (AMMAQ)
7, rue Bernier, Bedford QC J0J 1A0
Tél: 450-248-7946; *Téléc:* 450-248-3264
info@ammaq.ca
www.ammaq.ca
Aider et regrouper tous les concessionnaires de machineries agricoles de toute la province; compiler des statistiques et des renseignements sur la vente de machines aratoires dans la province du Québec; obtenir une plus grande coopération entre les marchands de machines aratoires des diverses régions de la province; promouvoir la vente et l'utilisation des machines aratoires
Peter Maurice, Directeur général

Association des propriétaires de machinerie lourde du Québec inc. (APMLQ)
Plaza Laval, #259, 2750, ch Ste-Foy, Sainte-Foy QC G1V 1V6
Tél: 418-650-1877; *Téléc:* 418-650-3361
Ligne sans frais: 800-268-7318
info@apmlq.com
www.apmlq.com
Informer et instruire ses membres au moyen de publications; maintenir un secrétariat permanent dans un but de liaison entre les membres et de contact avec différentes autorités; négocier avec les autorités publiques toutes ententes susceptibles de promouvoir les buts de l'Association et ceux de ses membres
Jacques Guimond, Président
Yvan Grenier, Directeur général

Association of Equipment Manufacturers - Canada (AEM-Canada)
World Exchange Plaza, PO Box 81067, #880, 111 Albert St., Ottawa ON K1P 1B1
Tel: 613-566-4568; *Fax:* 613-566-2026
www.aem.org
To act as a voice for its members to the public & on a governmental level. It is also a regulatory body setting standars for safety, offering a variety of educational programs & seminars.
Dennis Slater, President
Howard Mains, Canada Consultant, Public Policy

Canada East Equipment Dealers' Association (CEEDA)
580 Bryne Dr, #C1, Barrie ON L4N 9P6
Tel: 705-726-2100; *Fax:* 705-726-2187
www.ceeda.ca
Social Media:
linkedin.com/groups/Canada-East-Equipment-Dealers-Association-3210
www.facebook.com/189673951062605
twitter.com/@ceedaCanadaEast
To promote the welfare of equipment trade retailers in the Maritimes & Ontario; To represent dealer interests in government legislation & regulation; To foster cooperation among manufacturers & distributors; To promote high standards for the retail equipment industry
Craig Smith, Chair
Keith Stoltz, 1st Vice-Chair
Beverly J. Leavitt, President & CEO
Carol Schoen, Secretary-Treasurer

Canadian Association of Defence & Security Industries (CADSI) / Association des industries canadiennes de défense et de sécurité (AICDS)
#300, 251 Laurier Ave. West, Ottawa ON K1P 5J6
Tel: 613-235-5337; *Fax:* 613-235-0784
cadsi@defenceandsecurity.ca
www.defenceandsecurity.ca
Social Media:
twitter.com/cadsicanada
To represent Canadian defence & security industries domestically & internationally
Janet Thorsteinson, Vice-President, Policy & Government Relations
Jennifer Giguere, Director, Domestic & International Events
Steven Hillier, Director, Development, Marketing, & Membership
Nicolas Todd, Director, Policy & Government Relations

Canadian Process Control Association (CPCA)
#25, 1250 Marlborough Ct., Oakville ON L6H 2W7
Tel: 905-844-6822; *Fax:* 905-901-9913
cpca@cpca-assoc.com
www.cpca-assoc.com
To promote the industry & its members to customers, academia, & public bodies; To provide a forum to exchange technical, industry, & regulatory information; To develop industry statistics; To encourage professional & ethical behaviour & quality standards among members
Peter Dello, President

Ethnic Groups

African Canadian Social Development Council (ACSDC)
#107B, 2238 Dundas St. West, Toronto ON M6R 3A9
Tel: 647-352-5775
www.acsdc.net
Social Media:
www.facebook.com/AfricanCanadianSDC
twitter.com/acsdc_1
To promote social, economic & cultural development within the continental African community in Canada
Kayode (Kay) Alabi, Executive Director/CEO

Canadian Ethnic Media Association (CEMA)
24 Tarlton Rd., Toronto ON M5P 2M4
Tel: 416-764-3081; *Fax:* 416-764-3245
webmaster@canadianethnicmedia.com
canadianethnicmedia.com
To promote & preserve the value of the ethnic media in Canada; To advance understanding of Canada's cultural diversity
Kiumars Rezvanifar, President
Madaine Ziniak, Chair
Gina Valle, Secretary
Irene Chu, Treasurer

Canadian Ethnic Studies Association (CESA) / Société canadienne d'études ethniques (SCEE)
c/o Dept. of Sociology, University of Calgary, 2500 University Dr. NW, Calgary AB T2N 1N4
Tel: 403-220-6502; *Fax:* 403-282-9298
cesa@uwinnipeg.ca
cesa.uwinnipeg.ca
To encourage scholarly debate about theoretical & practical issues in Canadian ethnic studies
Lloyd Wong, President
Lori Wilkinson, Vice-President
Amal Madibbo, Secretary-Treasurer

Jamaica Association of Montréal Inc.
4065, Jean-Talon ouest, Montréal QC H4P 1W6
Tel: 514-737-8229
www.jam-montreal.com
Social Media:
www.facebook.com/JamaicaAssociationOfMontrealInc
Educational, cultural & social activities for the Jamaican community; after-school & evening classes & programs for youth & adults; Saturday morning program for children; restaurant on site

New Brunswick African Association Inc.
NB
nbaa.ca
To support the African community in New Brunswick
Andrew Gbongbor, President

Events

Alberta Music Festival Association
Alberta College, Edmonton AB
Tel: 780-633-3725
info@albertamusicfestival.org
www.albertamusicfestival.org
Social Media:
www.facebook.com/AlbertaMusicFestivalOrganization
To coordinate, regulate & assist activities of local Alberta festivals of music & speech arts; To encourage formation of additional local festivals
Heather Bedford-Clooney, President
Wendy Durieux, Provincial Administrator

Associated Manitoba Arts Festivals, Inc. (AMAF)
#2, 88 St. Anne's Rd., Winnipeg MB R2M 2Y7
Tel: 204-231-4507; *Fax:* 204-231-4510
www.amaf.mb.ca
To promote & encourage participation in growth & development of & appreciation for creative & performing arts in partnership with local festivals
William Gordon, President
Judith Oatway, Secretary
Tannie Lam, Treasurer

Association des professionnels en exposition du Québec (APEQ)
868, rue Brisette, Sainte-Julie QC J3E 2B1
Tél: 514-990-0224; *Téléc:* 450-922-7238
info@apeq.org
www.apeq.org
Faire reconnaître le rôle vital de l'industrie des expositions dans la vie économique, industrielle, culturelle et sociale au Québec; promouvoir, auprès du monde des affaires, l'efficacité des expositions comme moyen de promotion, de commercialisation et de communication; favoriser l'éducation de ses membres
Jacques Perreault, Directeur général

Canadian Association of Exposition Management (CAEM) / Association canadienne des directeurs d'expositions
PO Box 218, #2219, 160 Tycos Dr., Toronto ON M6B 1W8
Tel: 416-787-9377; *Fax:* 416-596-1808
Toll-Free: 866-441-9377
info@caem.ca
www.caem.ca
To represent & improve the exposition & trade show industry in Canada
Serge Micheli, Executive Director
Lisa McDonald, President
Sherry Kirkpatrick, 1st Vice-President
Catherine MacNutt, 2nd Vice-President
Jennifer Allaby, Secretary
Mike Russell, Treasurer
Michael Dargavel, Office Manager

Canadian Association of Fairs & Exhibitions (CAFE) / Association canadienne des foires et expositions
PO Box 21053, Stn. WEPO, Brandon MB R7B 3W8
Tel: 204-571-6377; *Toll-Free:* 800-663-1714
info@canadian-fairs.ca
www.canadian-fairs.ca
Social Media:
www.facebook.com/463750700351384
twitter.com/CdnAssocofFairs
To provide leadership in the development of the Canadian Fair Industry; To represent the Canadian fairs & exhibitions sector at the national level
Jim Laurendeau, President
Karen Oliver, Executive Director

Carnaval de Québec / Québec Winter Carnival
205, boul des Cèdres, Québec QC G1L 1N8
Tél: 418-626-3716; *Ligne sans frais:* 866-422-7628
bonhomme@carnaval.qc.ca
www.carnaval.qc.ca
Média social: www.pinterest.com/carnavalquebec
www.facebook.com/CarnavaldeQuebec
twitter.com/CarnavalQc
Organiser annuellement une fête populaire hivernale dans le but de faire bénéficier à Québec une activité économique, touristique et sociale de première qualité dont les gens de la région seront fiers
Alain April, Président

Exhibitions Association of Nova Scotia (EANS)
40 Gateway Rd., Halifax NS B3M 1M9
Tel: 902-443-2039
www.eans.ca
To promote such events as fairs & exhibitions across the province.
Glen E. Jefferson, Executive Director

Federation of Canadian Music Festivals (FCMF) / La Fédération canadienne des festivals de musique
c/o Heather Beford Clooney, Executive Director, 14004 - 75th Ave. NW, Edmonton AB T5R 2Y5
Fax: 780-758-1227
Toll-Free: 877-323-3263
info@fcmf.org
www.fcmf.org
Social Media:
www.facebook.com/nationalmusicfestival
To act as an umbrella organization for 230+ local & provincial festivals; To develop & encourage Canadian talent in the performance & knowledge of classical music; To encourage the study & practice of the art of music alone or in conjunction with related arts; To organize the National Music Festival in which winners from each province participate
Jerry Lonsbury, President
Joy McFarlane-Burton, Vice-President
Heather Bedford Clooney, Executive Director

Federation of Music Festivals of Nova Scotia
PO Box 31, Lunenburg NS B0J 2C0
Tel: 902-640-2448
www.musicfestivalsnovascotia.ca
Pamela Rogers, Secretary

Festivals & Events Ontario (FEO)
#301, 5 Graham St., Woodstock ON N4S 6J5
Tel: 519-537-2226; *Fax:* 519-537-2226
info@festivalsandeventsontario.ca
www.festivalsandeventsontario.ca
Social Media:
www.facebook.com/FestivalsandEventsOntario
twitter.com/FEOntario
Festivals & Events Ontario (FEO) is an association devoted to the growth and stability of the festival and event industry in Ontario. FEO provides festival and event organizers across the province with a networking forum offering professional development opportunities and resources aimed to encourage professionalism and excellence in the delivery of festivals and special events.
Debbie Mann, Interim Executive Director
Martha Cookson, Administrative Coordinator

Festivals et Événements Québec (FEQ)
CP 1000, Succ. M, 4545, av Pierre-de Coubertin, Montréal QC H1V 3R2
Tél: 514-252-3037; *Téléc:* 514-254-1617
Ligne sans frais: 800-361-7688
info@satqfeq.com
www.evenementsquebec.qc.ca
Regrouper les fêtes, festivals et événements, de les promouvoir et de leur offrir des services qui favorisent leur développement
Pierre-Paul Leduc, Directeur general
Luc Martineau, Directeur marketing
Sylvain Martineau, Dir. Ventes
Lyne Voyer, Dir. Communications
Sylvie Theberge, Dir. Services Membres
Robert Aucoin, Dir. recherche
Claude Latour, Dir. web

International Special Events Society - Toronto Chapter (ISES)
312 Oakwood Ct., Newmarket ON L3Y 3C8
Tel: 905-898-7434; *Fax:* 905-895-1630
Toll-Free: 866-729-4737
info@isestoronto.com
www.isestoronto.com
Social Media:
linkedin.com/company/international-special-events-society-toronto
www.facebook.com/ISESToronto
twitter.com/isestoronto
To educate, advance & promote the special events industry & its network of professionals along with related industries; to uphold the integrity of the special events profession to the public through "Principles of Professional Conduct & Ethics"; to acquire & disseminate useful business information; to foster a spirit of cooperation among members & other special events professionals
Aaron Kaufman, President

New Brunswick Federation of Music Festivals Inc. (NBFMF) / La Fédération des festivals de musique du Nouveau-Brunswick inc. (FFMNB)
NB
info@nbfmf.org
nbfmf.org
Barbara Long, Executive Director/President

Newfoundland Federation of Music Festivals
1 Marigold Place, St. John's NL A1A 3T1
Tel: 709-722-9376
To coordinate activities of local music festivals & conduct a provincial music festival annually; to participate in the CIBC National Music Festival.
Joan Woodrow, Provincial Administrator

Ontario Music Festivals Association (OMFA)
c/o Pam Allen, Festival Administrator, 1422 Bayview Ave., #A, Toronto ON M4G 3A7
Toll-Free: 888-307-6632
mail@omfa.info
www.omfa.info
Social Media:
www.facebook.com/ONTMUSFEST
To promote the performance of classical music by Ontario's youth; To encourage knowledge of classical music
Martha Gregory, President
Quinte Bell, Secretary
Pam Allen, Festival Administrator

Performing Arts BC
PO Box 1484, Stn. A, Comox BC V9M 8A2
Tel: 250-493-7279
festival@bcprovincials.com
www.bcprovincials.com

Prince Edward Island Kiwanis Music Festival Association
c/o Diane Campbell, Administrator, 227 Keppoch Rd., Stratford PE C1B 2J5
Tel: 902-569-2885
www.peikiwanismusicfestival.ca
To make possible performances of young & older musicians in a semi-professional atmosphere; To adjudicate using professionals; & to encourage performance & study in music

Diane Campbell, Provincial Administrator

Provincial Exhibition of Manitoba
115 - 10th St., Brandon MB R7A 4E7
Tel: 204-726-3590; *Fax:* 204-725-0202
Toll-Free: 877-729-0001
info@provincialexhibition.com
www.provincialexhibition.con
Social Media:
www.facebook.com/provincial.exhibition
twitter.com/ProvincialEx
To showcase agriculture; To link urban & rural regions through education & awareness while providing entertainment, community pride & economic enhancement to the region
Ron Kristjansson, General Manager

Québec Competitive Festival of Music / Festival de concours du Québec
136 Duke-of-Kent Ave., Pointe-Claire QC H9R 1X9
Tel: 514-398-4535; *Fax:* 514-398-8061
Tom Davidson, Provincial Administrator

Royal Agricultural Winter Fair Association (RAWF) / Foire agricole royale d'hiver
The Ricoh Coliseum, 100 Prince's Blvd., Toronto ON M6K 3C3
Tel: 416-263-3400
info@royalfair.org
www.royalfair.org
Social Media: theroyalagriculturalwinterfair.tumblr.com
www.facebook.com/royalfair
twitter.com/THERAWF
To promote excellence in agricultural & equestrian activities through world class competition, exhibitions & education
Sandra G. Banks, Chief Executive Officer

Saskatchewan Music Festival Association Inc.
PO Box 37005, Regina SK S4S 7K3
Tel: 306-757-1722; *Fax:* 306-347-7789
Toll-Free: 888-892-9929
sask.music.festival@sasktel.net
www.smfa.ca
Social Media:
twitter.com/SKMusicFestival
To provide a classical competitive music festival system of the highest standard at the local, provincial & national levels
Carol Donhauser, Executive Director

Vancouver International Children's Festival
402 - 873 Beatty St., Vancouver BC V6B 2M6
Tel: 604-708-5655; *Fax:* 604-708-5661
info@childrensfestival.ca
www.childrensfestival.ca
Social Media: www.youtube.com/user/VanKidsFest
www.facebook.com/KidsFest
twitter.com/VICF
To provide performing arts programs to young people in a festival environment; To encourage critical thinking & a lifelong interest in learning, the arts & cultural development
Tom Stulberg, Chair
Katharine Carol, Artistic & Executive Director

Farming

Association des producteurs maraîchers du Québec (APMQ) / Québec Produce Growers Association (QPGA)
905, rue du Marché-Central, Montréal QC H4N 1K2
Tél: 514-387-8319
apmq@apmquebec.com
www.apmquebec.com
Favorise le développement du secteur horticole québécois et veille à la promotion des fruits et légumes cultivés au Québec, sur le marché local et sur les marchés extérieurs.

Canadian Agricultural Safety Association (CASA) / Association canadienne de sécurité agricole (ACSA)
3325-C Pembina Hwy., Winnipeg MB R3V 0A2
Tel: 204-452-2272; *Fax:* 204-261-5004
Toll-Free: 877-452-2272
info@casa-acsa.ca
www.casa-acsa.ca
Social Media: www.youtube.com/planfarmsafety
linkedin.com/company/canadian-agricultural-safety-association
www.facebook.com/planfarmsafety
twitter.com/planfarmsafety
To address problems of illness, injuries & accidental death in farmers, their families & agricultural workers; To improve health & safety conditions of those that live or work on Canadian farms
Marcel L. Hacault, Executive Director
Denis Bilodeau, Chair
Dean Anderson, Vice-Chair

Lauranne Sanderson, Treasurer

Ontario Ginseng Growers Association
PO Box 587, 1283 Blueline Rd., Simcoe ON N3Y 4N5
Tel: 519-426-7046; *Fax:* 519-426-9087
info@ginsengontario.com
www.ginsengontario.com
To conduct research on how to improve ginseng growing, as well as new varieties of ginseng; to help market North American ginseng
Rebecca Coates, Executive Director

Ontario Greenhouse Vegetable Growers (OGVG)
32 Seneca Rd., Leamington ON N8H 5H7
Tel: 519-326-2604; *Fax:* 519-326-7824
Toll-Free: 800-265-6926
admin@ogvg.com
www.ontariogreenhouse.com
Social Media:
www.youtube.com/channel/UCk9o96iBk6TUUgHnkfHjGQA
www.facebook.com/ONgreenhouseVeg
twitter.com/ONgreenhouseVeg
To represent growers' interests & ensure that they have the necessary resources to continue to prosper
Rick Seguin, General Manager

Potatoes New Brunswick / Pommes de terre Nouveau-Brunswick
PO Box 7878, Grand Falls NB E3Z 3E8
Tel: 506-473-3036; *Fax:* 506-473-4647
gfpotato@potatoesnb.com
www.potatoesnb.com
Social Media:
www.facebook.com/pages/Potatoes-New-Brunswick/223361891051973
To work in close collaboration with industry partners in advocating, coordinating, promoting, negotiating, & leading growth & development of New Brunswick potato producers
Joe Brennan, Chair
Matt Hemphill, Executive Director
Robert Corriveau, Director, Finance
Gisele Beardsley, Bookkeeper & Translator

Prince Edward Island Certified Organic Producers Co-op
PO Box 1776, #110, 420 University Ave., Charlottetown PE C1A 7Z5
Tel: 902-894-9999; *Toll-Free:* 866-850-9799
www.organicpei.com
Social Media:
www.facebook.com/organicpei
To increase organic production, research and market development; invite growers into the organic industry and promote and educate Islanders about organic food.
Fred Dollar, President

Union des cultivateurs franco-ontariens (UCFO)
2474 rue Champlain, Clarence Creek ON K0A 1N0
Tél: 613-488-2929; *Téléc:* 613-488-2541
Ligne sans frais: 877-425-8366
info@ucfo.ca
www.ucfo.ca
Média social: www.facebook.com/UCFO.ca
Regrouper les franco-ontariens et les franco-ontariennes qui oeuvrent dans le secteur agricole; concerter pour la protection de nos droits; promouvoir nos intérêts; informer notre communauté; appuyer les institutions et groupements qui favorisent notre développement; développer notre sentiment et fierté; stimuler le développement social et économique des régions agricoles et rurales
Marc Laflèche, Président
Simon Durand, Directeur exécutif
Marc-André Tessier, Agent, Communication et développement du leadership

Fashion & Textiles

Alberta Men's Wear Agents Association
PO Box 66037, Stn. Heritage, Edmonton AB T6J 6T4
Tel: 780-455-1881
amwa@shaw.ca
www.trendsapparel.com
Ken Melnychuk, President

Allied Beauty Association (ABA)
#26-27, 145 Traders Blvd. East, Mississauga ON L4Z 3L3
Tel: 905-568-0158; *Fax:* 905-568-1581
abashows@abacanada.com
www.abacanada.com
Social Media: www.youtube.com/user/TheABACanada
www.facebook.com/ABACanada
twitter.com/abacanada
To encourage & create a greater understanding & knowledge of the professional beauty industry to the salons, the public, the federal & provincial governments, & to members
Marc Speir, Executive Director

Apparel Manufacturers Association of Ontario
#504, 124 O'Connor St., Ottawa ON K1P 5M9
Tel: 613-231-3220; *Fax:* 613-231-2305
Bob Kirke, Executive Director

BeautyCouncil (BC)
899 West 8th Ave., Vancouver BC V5Z 1E3
Tel: 604-871-0222; *Fax:* 604-871-0299
Toll-Free: 800-663-9283
info@beautycouncil.ca
beautycouncil.ca
Social Media: www.pinterest.com/beautycouncil
www.facebook.com/beautycouncilwesterncanada
twitter.com/beautycouncil
To strive for the highest standards of excellence in professional cosmetology services through its member enhancement programs & to service the public through education & knowledge.
Bill Moreland, Chair
Debbie Nickel, Executive Director

Canadian Apparel Federation (CAF) / Fédération canadienne du vêtement
#708, 151 Slater St., Ottawa ON K1P 5H3
Tel: 613-231-3220; *Fax:* 613-231-2305
info@apparel.ca
www.apparel.ca
Social Media:
linkedin.com/company/canadian-apparel-federation
www.facebook.com/102242196491712
twitter.com/caf_apparel
To provide a forum for provincial apparel associations representing the vast majority of the country's manufacturers; To exercise leadership in relations with government, suppliers & the general public
Bob Kirke, Executive Director

Canadian Association of Wholesale Sales Representatives (CAWS) / Association canadienne des représentants de ventes en gros
PO Box 70003, 1725 Avenue Rd., Toronto ON M5M 0A3
Tel: 416-782-8961; *Fax:* 416-782-5876
info@caws.ca
www.caws.ca
To represent comission sales agents on a national level; To serve as an umbrella organization for affiliate markets across Canada
Kim Crawford, President

Canadian Textile Association (CTA) / La Fédération canadienne du textile
13 Interlacken Dr., Brampton ON L6X 0Y1
Tel: 647-821-4649
www.cdntexassoc.com
To advance & disseminate knowledge of textiles; to promote sound procedures of textile processing; to encourage & sponsor textile research & investigation; to assist in the establishment of standards in the textile industry; to promote & encourage schools, classes & libraries for the study of textile technology; to collaborate with international groups in advancing the foregoing objectives
John Secondi, President

Cosmetology Association of Nova Scotia (CANS)
126 Chain Link Dr., Halifax NS B3S 1A2
Tel: 902-468-6477; *Fax:* 902-468-7147
Toll-Free: 800-765-8757
www.nscosmetology.ca
To apply standards ensuring the safety of the public & practitioners
Lloyd Petrie, Chair

Groupe CTT Group
3000, rue Boullé, Saint-Hyacinthe QC J2S 1H9
Tél: 450-778-1870; *Téléc:* 450-778-3901
Ligne sans frais: 877-288-8378
info@gcttg.com
www.groupecttgroup.com
Favoriser le développement des matériaux textiles et de stimuler l'avancement technologique de l'industrie textile et géosynthétique par des activités telles que la recherche et le développement, l'assistance technique, la formation sur mesure, l'information spécialisé et l'animation du milieu
Jacek Mlynarek, Président & PDG
Martin Filteau, Vice-Président

Luggage, Leathergoods, Handbags & Accessories Association of Canada (LLHA)
PO Box 144, Stn. A, Toronto ON M9C 4V2
Fax: 519-624-6408
Toll-Free: 866-872-2420
info@llha.ca
www.llha.ca
To promote the growth of the industry in Canada; To foster the interchange of ideas
Catherine Genge, Executive Administrator

METROSHOW Vancouver
#103, 1951 Glen Dr., Vancouver BC V6A 4J6
Tel: 604-929-8995; *Fax:* 604-357-1995
info@metroshow.ca
www.metroshow.ca
Social Media:
www.facebook.com/MetroShowVan
twitter.com/MetroShowVan
To produce the METROSHOW, an event held four times a year in Vancouver which houses vendors selling apparel, footwear & giftware
Karen James, President

Ontario Fashion Exhibitors (OFE)
PO Box 218, #2219, 160 Tycos Dr., Toronto ON M6B 1W8
Tel: 416-596-2401; *Fax:* 416-596-1808
Toll-Free: 800-765-7508
info@profileshow.ca
www.profileshow.ca
To produce fashion marketplace events
Serge Micheli, Executive Director
Michael Dargavel, Show Manager

Prairie Apparel Market
PO Box 55065, Stn. Dakota Crossing, Winnipeg MB R2N 0A8
Tel: 204-973-3256; *Fax:* 204-947-0561
To sell women's & children's apparel
Dan Kelsch, President

Shoe Manufacturers' Association of Canada (SMAC) / Association des manufacturiers de chaussures du Canada
#203, 90, rue Morgan, Baie d'Urfe QC H9X 3A8
Tel: 514-457-3436; *Fax:* 514-457-8004
To represent & serve Canadian footwear manufacturers; To protect the Canadian domestic shoe industry
George P. Hanna, President

Western Canada Children's Wear Markets (WCCWM)
#245, 1868 Glen Dr., Vancouver BC V6A 4K4
Tel: 604-634-0909; *Fax:* 888-595-9360
www.wccwm.com
To provide showcases for children's & maternity goods
Doug Fulton, President

Film & Video

Academy of Canadian Cinema & Television (ACCT) / Académie canadienne du cinéma et de la télévision
#501, 49 Ontario St., Toronto ON M5A 2V1
Tel: 416-366-2227; *Fax:* 416-366-8454
Toll-Free: 800-644-5194
info@academy.ca
www.academy.ca
Social Media:
www.facebook.com/acctv
To promote & celebrate exceptional creative achievement in the Canadian film & television industries; To heighten public awareness & increase audience appreciation of Canadian film & television productions through its national Award program
Martin Katz, Chair
Helga Stephenson, Chief Executive Officer

Alberta Motion Picture Industries Association (AMPIA)
#318, 8944 - 182 St. NW, Edmonton AB T5T 2E3
Tel: 780-944-0707; *Fax:* 780-426-3057
Toll-Free: 800-814-7779
info@ampia.org
www.ampia.org
Social Media:
twitter.com/yourampia
To develop & sustain the motion picture industry indigenous to Alberta
Josh Miller, President
Camille Beaudoin, Director

Association des producteurs de films et de télévision du Québec (APFTQ)
Edifice City Centre, #1030, 1450, rue City Councillors, Montréal QC H3A 2E6
Tél: 514-397-8600; *Téléc:* 514-392-0232
info@apftq.qc.ca
www.apftq.qc.ca
Représente ses membres auprès des gouvernements et organismes et encourage la coopération étroite entre tous les intervenants de l'industrie cinématographique et télévisuelle
Claire Samson, President and CEO

Association des réalisateurs et réalisatrices du Québec (ARRQ)
5154, rue St-Hubert, Montréal QC H2J 2Y3
Tél: 514-842-7373; *Téléc:* 514-842-6789
realiser@arrq.qc.ca
www.arrq.qc.ca
Défendre les intérêts et les droits professionnels, économiques, culturels, sociaux et moraux des réalisateurs pigistes membres, travaillant principalement dans les domaines du cinéma et de la télévision
Caroline Fortier, Directrice générale

Atlantic Filmmakers Cooperative (AFCOOP)
PO Box 2043, Stn. M, Halifax NS B3J 2Z1
Tel: 902-405-4474; *Fax:* 902-405-4485
membership@afcoop.ca
afcoop.ca
Social Media: www.youtube.com/afcoophalifax
www.facebook.com/117025119810
twitter.com/afcoop
To provide a space where media artists can meet & produce films; to give members access to production equipment & facilities
Martha Cooley, Executive Director

Canadian Association of Film Distributors & Exporters (CAFDE) / Association canadienne des distributeurs et exportateurs de films (ACDEF)
#1605, 85 Albert St., Ottawa ON K1P 6A4
Tel: 613-238-3557
info@CAFDE.ca
cafde.ca
To foster & promote the health of the Canadian motion picture industry by strengthening the Canadian owned & controlled distribution/export sector
Hussain Amarshi, President

Canadian Film Centre (CFC) / Centre canadien du film
2489 Bayview Ave., Toronto ON M2L 1A8
Tel: 416-445-1446; *Fax:* 416-445-9481
info@cdnfilmcentre.com
www.cfccreates.com
Social Media: www.youtube.com/user/CanadianFilmCentre
www.facebook.com/cfccreates
twitter.com/cfccreates
To operate as Canada's foremost film, televion, & new media institution; To advance Canadian creative talent, content, & values worldwide, through training, production, promotion & investment
Slawko Klymkiw, Chief Executive Officer

Canadian Film Institute (CFI) / Institut canadien du film (ICF)
#120, 2 Daly Ave., Ottawa ON K1N 6E2
Tel: 613-232-6727; *Fax:* 613-232-6315
info@cfi-icf.ca
www.cfi-icf.ca
To promote Canadian cinema; To assist in locating sources for rental or purchase of individual films & videos; To give subject & content information on theatrical & non-theatrical films & videos from both private & public sources; To give general information on Canadian & international film, video, & television production, distribution, exhibition, & related subjects
Jack Horwitz, Chair
Tom McSorley, Executive Director & Secretary
Jerrett Zaret, Coordinator, Sponsorship
Michael Leong, Treasurer

Canadian Filmmakers Distribution Centre (CFMDC)
#245, 401 Richmond St. West, Toronto ON M5V 3A8
Tel: 416-588-0725
cfmdc@cfmdc.org
www.cfmdc.org
Social Media:
www.facebook.com/cfmdcmembers
To promote & distribute the work of independent Canadian filmmakers.
Lauren Howes, Executive Director

Canadian Media Production Association (CMPA)
601 Bank St., 2nd Fl., Ottawa ON K1S 3T4
Tel: 613-233-1444; *Fax:* 613-233-0073
Toll-Free: 800-656-7440
ottawa@cmpa.ca
www.cmpa.ca
Social Media: www.youtube.com/CMPAOnline
linkedin.com/company/canadian-media-production-association-cmpa-
www.facebook.com/theCMPA
twitter.com/CMPA_Updates
To represent the interests of media companies engaged in the production & distribution of English language television programs, feature films, & new media content throughout Canada
Michael Hennessy, President & Chief Executive Officer
Jane Cheesman, Chief Financial Officer
Marc Séguin, Senior Vice-President, Policy
Jay Thomson, Vice-President, Broadcasting Policy & Regulatory Affairs
Susanne Vaas, Vice-President, Corporate & International Affairs
Anne Trueman, Director, Communications & Media
Sarolta Csete, Manager, National Mentorship Program & e-Services
Lisa Moreau, Manager, Member Services & Special Events

Canadian Picture Pioneers (CPP)
#1762, 250 The East Mall, Toronto ON M9B 6L3
Tel: 416-368-1139; *Fax:* 416-368-1139
cdnpicturepioneers@rogers.com
www.canadianpicturepioneers.ca
Social Media:
www.facebook.com/groups/116714111684364/?fref=ts
twitter.com/PicturePioneers
To provide assistance for the welfare of those in the motion picture industry in Canada
John Freeborn, Executive Director
Phil May, President
Paul Wroe, Secretary-Treasurer

Canadian Society of Cinematographers (CSC)
#131, 3007 Kingston Rd., Toronto ON M1M 1P1
Tel: 416-266-0591; *Fax:* 416-266-3996
admin@csc.ca
www.csc.ca
To promote the art & craft of cinematography
Joan Hutton, President
Susan Saranchuk, Executive Director

La Cinémathèque québécoise
335, boul de Maisonneuve est, Montréal QC H2X 1K1
Tél: 514-842-9763; *Téléc:* 514-842-1816
info@cinematheque.qc.ca
www.cinematheque.qc.ca
Conservation et mise en valeur du patrimoine cinématographique et télévisuel; promouvoir la culture cinématographique; créer des archives de cinéma; acquérir et conserver des films ainsi que toute la documentation qui s'y rattache; projeter ces films et exposer ces documents de facon non commerciale à des fins historique, pédagogique et artistique.
Iolande Cadrin-Rossignol, Directrice générale
Fabrice Montal, Directeur, Programmation
Jean Gagnon, Directeur, Collections
Claude Bouffard, Directrice, Administration et finances
Jeanine Basile, Directrice, Communications et marketing

Directors Guild of Canada (DGC) / La Guilde canadienne des réalisateurs
#600, 111 Peter St., Toronto ON M5V 2H1
Tel: 416-925-8200; *Fax:* 416-925-8400
Toll-Free: 888-972-0098
mail@dgc.ca
www.dgc.ca
Social Media: vimeo.com/dgcnational;
www.flickr.com/photos/dgcnational
twitter.com/DGCnational
To represent key creative & logistical personnel in the film & television industry; to promote & advance the quality & vitality of Canadian feature film
Tim Southam, President
Brian Baker, National Executive Director

FilmOntario
625 Church St., 2nd Fl., Toronto ON M4Y 2G1
Tel: 416-642-6704
www.filmontario.ca
To market Ontario as a creator of film content & a location for film & television production
Sarah Ker-Hornell, Executive Director & CEO

The Harold Greenberg Fund
Astral Media, Brookfield Place, PO Box 787, #100, 181 Bay St., Toronto ON M5J 2T3
Tel: 416-956-5432; *Fax:* 416-956-2087
hgfund@astral.com
www.astral.com/en/about-astral/astrals-harold-greenberg-fund
To foster the development & production of feature-length movies written by Canadians & the production of family television series
John Galway, President

Independent Media Arts Alliance (IMAA) / Alliance des arts médiatiques indépendants (AAMI)
#200-A, 4067 boul Saint-Laurent, Montréal QC H2W 1Y7
Tel: 514-522-8240; *Fax:* 514-987-1862
info@imaa.ca
www.imaa.ca
Social Media: www.youtube.com/channel/UC4dulDEsR21dbEg_0hTqNiw?feature=mhee
www.facebook.com/imaa.aami
twitter.com/IMAA_AAMI
To promote discussion among media art centres; To coordinate independent film & video centres
Emmanuel Madan, National Director
Mercedes Pacho, Director, Communications & Development

Motion Picture Association - Canada / Association Cinématographique - Canada
#210, 55 St. Clair Ave. West, Toronto ON M4V 2Y7
Tel: 416-961-1888; *Fax:* 416-968-1016
info@mpa-canada.org
mpa-canada.org
Social Media: twitter.com/mpacanada
To act as the voice of U.S.A. studios who market feature films, prime time entertainment programming for television & pay TV, & pre-recorded videos & DVDs in Canada; To coordinate recommendations on matters affecting national distributors of feature films, pre-recorded videocassettes, & television programs; To protect the rights of copyright owners
Katherine Ward, Director, Public Affairs

NABET 700 CEP
#203, 100 Lombard St., Toronto ON M5C 1M3
Tel: 416-536-4827; *Fax:* 416-536-0859
info@nabet700.com
www.nabet700.com
To be a union serving television & film technicians in Toronto; in 1994 NABET 700 merged with the Communications, Energy & Paperworkers Union of Canada (CEP).
Jonathan Ahee, President
Craig Steele, Senior Vice-President
Frank Iacobucci, Secretary-Treasurer

National Screen Institute - Canada (NSI)
#400, 141 Bannatyne Ave., Winnipeg MB R3B 0R3
Tel: 204-956-7800; *Fax:* 204-956-5811
Toll-Free: 800-952-9307
info@nsi-canada.ca
www.nsi-canada.ca
To supply innovative, focused, applied professional training, leading participants to successful careers as writers, directors & producers in Canada's film & television industry
John Gill, Chief Executive Officer

North of Superior Film Association (NOSFA)
#352, 1100 Memorial Ave., Thunder Bay ON P7B 4A3
Tel: 807-625-5450
info@nosfa.ca
www.nosfa.ca
To promote film and appreciation of film in the Thunder Bay area.
Marty Mascarin, President
Catherine Powell, Festival Coordinator

Northern Film & Video Industry Association (NFVIA)
PO Box 31340, Whitehorse YT Y1A 5P7
Tel: 867-456-2978
info@nfvia.com
www.nfvia.com
To support the film & video sector in the Yukon by focussing on areas such as human resource development in the industry, development of infrastructure & production support, marketing, strategic alliances & partnerships, & membership services

On Screen Manitoba
#003, 100 Albert St., Winnipeg MB R3B 1H3
Tel: 204-927-5898; *Fax:* 204-272-8792
info@onscreenmanitoba.com
www.onscreenmanitoba.com
Social Media: www.youtube.com/user/OnScreenManitoba
www.facebook.com/onscreenmanitoba
twitter.com/OnScreenMB
To build & represent the motion picture industry in Manitoba; To foster excellence & innovation in the industry
Nicole Matiation, Executive Director
Trevor Suffield, Coordinator, Communications

Saskatchewan Motion Picture Industry Association (SMPIA)
PO Box 31088, Regina SK S4R 6R8
Tel: 306-529-1832
office@smpia.sk.ca
www.smpia.sk.ca
Social Media: www.facebook.com/SaskatchewanMediaProductionIndustryAssociation
twitter.com/smpiaoffice
Committed to the intrinsic cultural & economic value of motion pictures;to work toward the creation & advancement of opportunities for the production, promotion & appreciation of motion pictures in Saskatchewan
Holly Baird, President
Vanessa Bonk, Executive Director

Yukon Film Society (YFS)
212 Lambert St., Whitehorse YT Y1A 1Z4
Tel: 867-393-3456; *Fax:* 867-393-3456
yfs@yukonfilmsociety.com
www.yukonfilmsociety.com
To present independent and alternative media art works to Yukon audiences and to support the production and distribution of works by Yukon media artists.
Noel Sinclair, President
Zoë Toupin, General Manager

Film Festivals

The Atlantic Film Festival Association (AFFA)
PO Box 36139, Halifax NS B3J 3S9
Tel: 902-422-3456; *Fax:* 902-422-4006
festival@atlanticfilm.com
www.atlanticfilm.com
To promote & to build a strong film industry in Atlantic Canada
Wayne Carter, Executive Director

Canadian Labour International Film Festival (CLiFF)
Toronto ON
Tel: 416-579-0481
info@labourfilms.ca
labourfilms.ca
To produce a labour-oriented film festival in Canada, featuring films about workers & their conditions from Canada & around the world; To provide a venue where working people can tell their own stories in their own words & images; To encourage the production of films about working people
Frank Saptel, Festival Founder & Director

Edmonton International Film Festival Society (EIFFS)
#201, 10816A - 82nd Ave., Edmonton AB T6E 2B3
Tel: 780-423-0844
info@edmontonfilmfest.com
www.edmontonfilmfest.com
Social Media: www.youtube.com/user/Edmontonfilmfest
www.facebook.com/edmontonfilmfest
twitter.com/edmfilmfest
To produce a film festival for 9 days each autumn showing international, independent films in categories that include contemporary, world cinema, Canadian, documentary, alternative, shorts.
Kerrie Long, Festival Producer

Greater Vancouver International Film Festival Society (VIFF)
1181 Seymour St., Vancouver BC V6B 3M7
Tel: 604-685-0260; *Fax:* 604-688-8221
viff@viff.org
viff.org
Social Media: www.facebook.com/pages/Vancouver-Film-and-TV-Forum/99910045387
twitter.com/VIFForum
To operate the Annual Vancouver International Film Festival, bringing to British Columbia the best in current art cinema from around the world as well as buried treasures from past international cinema
Alan Franey, Festival Director

ReelWorld Film Festival
#300, 438 Parliament St., Toronto ON M5A 3A2
Tel: 416-598-7933
www.reelworld.ca
Social Media: www.youtube.com/ReelWorldFestival;
www.flickr.com/photos/reelworldfilm
www.facebook.com/ReelWorld.Film.Festival.Toronto
twitter.com/ReelWorldFilm
To present a culturally & racially diverse film festival showcasing films & music videos, & to connect filmmakers with producers, acquisitions personnel & distributors through The RealWorld Foundation.
Moe Jiwan, Chair & Treasurer
Tonya Lee Williams, Founder, Executive Director & Head, Programming

St. John's International Women's Film Festival (SJIWFF)
PO Box 984, Stn. C, St. John's NL A1C 5M3
Tel: 709-754-3141; *Fax:* 709-754-0049
info@womensfilmfestival.com
www.womensfilmfestival.com
Social Media: www.youtube.com/user/womensfilmfest
linkedin.com/company/st-john%27s-international-women%27s-film-fest
www.facebook.com/womensfilmfestival
twitter.com/sjiwff
To promote international women filmmakers through the annual film festival
Noreen Golfman, Chair
Kelly Davis, Executive Director

Toronto International Film Festival Inc. (TIFF)
TIFF Bell Lightbox, 250 King St. West, Toronto ON M5V 3K5
Tel: 416-599-8433; *Toll-Free:* 888-599-8433
customerrelations@tiff.net
www.tiff.net
Social Media: www.youtube.com/user/tiff
www.facebook.com/TIFF
To lead in creative & cultural discovery through the moving image
Lisa de Wilde, Chair

Finance

Association de planification fiscale et financière (APFF) / Fiscal & Financial Planning Association
#660, 1100, boul. René-Lévesque ouest, Montréal QC H3B 4N4
Tél: 514-866-2733; *Téléc:* 514-866-0113
Ligne sans frais: 877-866-0113
apff@apff.org
www.apff.org
Média social: linkedin.com/groups/Association-planification-fiscale-financière-A
Regrouper les personnes intéressées à la planification fiscale successorale et financière; publier et diffuser l'information dans ces domaines; favoriser la recherche
Maurice Mongrain, Président et directeur général

Association des cadres municipaux de Montréal (ACMM)
#305, 7245, rue Clark, Montréal QC H2R 2Y4
Tél: 514-499-1130; *Téléc:* 514-499-1737
acmm@acmm.qc.ca
www.acmm.qc.ca
A pour objet l'établissement de relations ordonnées entre l'employeur et les membres ainsi que l'étude, la défense et le développement des intérêts économiques sociaux, moraux et professionnels de ces derniers
Pascale Tremblay, Présidente

Association of Canadian Pension Management (ACPM) / Association canadienne des administrateurs de régimes de retraite
#304, 1255 Bay St., Toronto ON M5R 2A9
Tel: 416-964-1260; *Fax:* 416-964-0567
info@acpm.com
www.acpm.com
Social Media: linkedin.com/company/the-association-of-canadian-pension-management
To act as the voice of Canada's pension industry; To foster the growth of the the national retirement income system
Hugh Wright, Chair
Bryan Hocking, Chief Executive Officer
Ric Marrero, Director, Marketing, Communications & Membership

ATM Industry Association Canada Region (ATMIA)
c/o Curt Binns, Executive Director, #218, 10520 Yonge St., Unit 35B, Richmond Hill ON L4C 3C7
Tel: 416-970-7954; *Fax:* 905-770-6230
www.atmia.com/regions/canada
Social Media:
linkedin.com/company/atm-industry-association
To promote ATM convenience, growth, & usage worldwide; to protect the ATM industry's assets, interests, & reputation; to provide education, networking opportunities, & best practices
Curt Binns, Executive Director, Canada

Caisse Groupe Financier / Caisse Financial Group
#400, 205 Provencher Blvd., Winnipeg MB R2H 0G4
Tél: 204-237-8988; *Téléc:* 204-233-6405
Ligne sans frais: 866-926-0706
info@caisse.biz
www.caisse.biz
Contribuer à l'essor économique et socio-culturel des manitobains en poursuivant le développement des services et du réseau financiers dont les avoirs sont gérés, administrés et contrôlés par des francophones
Réal Déquier, President
Joël Rondeau, Chief Executive Officer

Canada's Venture Capital & Private Equity Association (CVCA) / Association canadienne du capital de risque et d'investissement (ACCR)
#1201, 372 Bay St., Toronto ON M5H 2W9
Tel: 416-487-0519
cvca@cvca.ca
www.cvca.ca
Social Media:
linkedin.com/company/cvca
twitter.com/cvcacanada
To provide advocacy, networking, information & professional development for venture capital & private equity professionals.
Dave Mullen, Chair
Mike Woollatt, Chief Executive Officer

Canadian Association of Insolvency & Restructuring Professionals (CAIRP) / Association canadienne des professionnels de l'insolvabilité et de la réorganisation (ACPIR)
277 Wellington St. West, Toronto ON M5V 3H2
Tel: 416-204-3242; *Fax:* 416-204-3410
info@cairp.ca
www.cairp.ca
Social Media:
linkedin.com/company/3239103
www.facebook.com/CAIRP.ca
twitter.com/CAIRP_ACPIR
To develop, educate, support & give value to members; To foster the provision of insolvency, business recovery service with integrity, objectivity & competence, in a manner that instils the highest degree of public trust; To advocate for a fair, transparent, & effective system of insolvency/business recovery administration throughout Canada
Mark Yakabuski, President & COO
Bea Casey, Director, CAIRP Education Programs
Ali R. Hemani, Director, Finance & Administration

Canadian Association of Pension Supervisory Authorities (CAPSA) / Association canadienne des organismes de contrôle des régimes de retraite (ACOR)
c/o CAPSA Secretariat, PO Box 85, 5160 Yonge St., 18th Fl., Toronto ON M2N 6L9
Tel: 416-590-7081; *Fax:* 416-226-7878
Toll-Free: 800-668-0128
capsa-acor@fsco.gov.on.ca
www.capsa-acor.org
To facilitate an efficient & effective pension regulatory system in Canada
Neil Mohindra, Manager, Policy

Canadian Association of Student Financial Aid Administrators (CASFAA)
c/o Treasurer, University of Manitoba, 422 University Centre, Winnipeg MB R3T 2N2
Tel: 204-474-9532
info@casfaa.ca
www.casfaa.ca
Represents financial aid administrators & awards officers in universities & colleges across Canada
John Boylan, President
Jane Lastra, Treasurer

Canadian Bankers Association (CBA) / Association des banquiers canadiens
PO Box 348, Stn. Commerce Court West, 199 Bay St., 30th Fl., Toronto ON M5L 1G2
Tel: 416-362-6093; *Fax:* 416-362-7705
inform@cba.ca
www.cba.ca
Social Media: www.youtube.com/user/cdnbankers
linkedin.com/company/1820482
twitter.com/CdnBankers
To advocate for policies that contribute to a beneficial banking system
Anatol von Hahn, Chair, Executive Council
Terry Campbell, President
Kate Payne, Manager, Media Relations

Canadian Community Reinvestment Coalition (CCRC)
PO Box 821, Stn. B, Ottawa ON K1P 241
Tel: 613-789-5753; *Fax:* 613-241-4758
info@cancrc.org
www.cancrc.org
To increase the accountability of Canada's financial institutions, increase their reinvestment in the Canadian ecomony, strengthen Canada's economy, strengthen community economic development efforts across Canada, & develop leadership in the Canadian financial sevices consumer movement.

Canadian Co-operative Association (CCA) / Association des coopératives du Canada (ACC)
#400, 275 Bank St., Ottawa ON K2P 2L6
Tel: 613-238-6711; *Fax:* 613-567-0658
info@coopscanada.coop
www.coopscanada.coop
Social Media: www.youtube.com/user/CCAottawa
www.facebook.com/361648435712
twitter.com/CoopsCanada
To develop co-operatives in other countries; To promote the co-operative model; To unite co-operatives from various industry sectors & regions of Canada
Bill Dobson, President
Jo-Anne Ferguson, Executive Director
Julie Breuer, Director, Engagement
Vijaya Venkatesh-Mannar, Director, Finance
Michael Wodzicki, Director, Market Development

Canadian Credit Union Association (CCUA) / Association canadienne des coopératives financières (ACCF)
Corporate Office, #1000, 151 Yonge St., Toronto ON M5C 2W7
Tel: 416-232-1262; *Toll-Free:* 800-649-0222
inquiries@ccua.com
www.ccua.com
Social Media:
www.youtube.com/channel/UCFUZjJj6jCnYLYfBgDU7EA
linkedin.com/company/canadian-credit-union-association
www.facebook.com/CCUA.ACCF
twitter.com/CCUA_ACCF
To act as the national voice for the Canadian credit union system; To facilitate the national cooperative movement; To provide services to ensure best practices are met at all credit unions; To develop opportunities for cooperative growth
Martha Durdin, President & CEO
Korinne Collins, Vice-President, Professional Development & Education
Stephen Fitzpatrick, Vice-President & CFO, Corporate Services
Jennifer McGill, Vice-President, Communications & Marketing
Brenda O'Connor, Vice-President, General Counsel & Corporate Secretary
Chris White, Vice-President, Government Relations

Canadian ETF Association (CETFA)
c/o Horizons Exchange Traded Funds, #700, 26 Wellington St. East, Toronto ON M5E 1S2
www.cetfa.ca
Social Media: www.youtube.com/cetfassn
twitter.com/cetfassn
To promote awareness of the Canadian exchange trade fund (ETF) industry
Howard Atkinson, Founding Managing Director & Chair

Canadian Finance & Leasing Association (CFLA) / Association canadienne de financement et de location (ACFL)
#301, 15 Toronto St., Toronto ON M5C 2E3
Tel: 416-860-1133; *Fax:* 416-860-1140
Toll-Free: 877-213-7373
info@cfla-acfl.ca
www.cfla-acfl.ca
Social Media:
linkedin.com/company/1360377
To ensure an environment in Canada where asset-based financing, equipment & vehicle-leasing industry can be profitable
David Powell, President & CEO
Matthew Poirier, Director, Policy
Lalita Sirnaik, Manager, Finance & Administration

Canadian Institute of Financial Planners (CIFPs)
#600, 3660 Hurontario St., Mississauga ON L5B 3C4
Tel: 647-723-6450; *Fax:* 647-723-6457
Toll-Free: 866-933-0233
cifps@cifps.ca
www.cifps.ca
To train & qualify advisors to become Certified Financial Planners; To represent members on matters of common interest
Keith Costello, President & Chief Executive Officer
Anthony Williams, Vice-President, Academic Affairs
Andrew Cunningham, Director, Information Services
Robert Jeffrey, Director, Member Relations
Odele Burton, Corporate Secretary

Canadian Investor Relations Institute (CIRI) / Institut canadien de relations avec les investisseurs
#601, 67 Yonge St., Toronto ON M5E 1J8
Tel: 416-364-8200; *Fax:* 416-364-2805
enquiries@ciri.org
www.ciri.org
To advance the practice of investor relations; To raise the stature of the profession in Canada; To act as the voice of investor relations professionals throughout Canada
Yvette Lokker, President & Chief Executive Officer
Salisha Hosein, Director, Professional Development & Communications
Kaitlin Beca, Coordinator, Programming
Karen Clutsam, Coordinator, Membership
Jane Maciel, Executive Assistant & Specialist, Publications

Canadian Payments Association (CPA) / Association canadienne des paiements (ACP)
180 Elgin St., 12th Fl., Ottawa ON K2P 2K3
Tel: 613-238-4173; *Fax:* 613-233-3385
info@cdnpay.ca
www.cdnpay.ca
To establish & operate safe & efficient national clearing & settlements systems; To facilitate the interaction of its systems with others involved in the exchange, clearing & settlement of payments; To facilitate the development of new payment methods & technologies
Janet Cosier, Chair
Eric Wolfe, Deputy Chair

Canadian Payroll Association (CPA) / L'Association canadienne de la paie (ACP)
#1600, 250 Bloor St. East, Toronto ON M4W 1E6
Tel: 416-487-3380; *Fax:* 416-487-3384
Toll-Free: 800-387-4693
infoline@payroll.ca
www.payroll.ca
Social Media:
linkedin.com/company/the-canadian-payroll-association
twitter.com/cdnpayroll
To provide payroll leadership, through advocacy & education
Patrick Culhane, President & CEO

Canadian Pension & Benefits Institute (CPBI) / Institut canadien de la retraite et des avantages sociaux (ICRA)
CPBI National Office, 1175 Union Ave., Montréal QC H3B 3C3
Tel: 514-288-1222; *Fax:* 514-288-1225
info@cpbi-icra.ca
www.cpbi-icra.ca
Social Media:
linkedin.com/company/canadian-pension-&-benefits-institute
twitter.com/cpbi_icra
Peter G. Casquinha, Chief Executive Officer

Canadian Securities Administrators (CSA) / Autorités canadiennes en valeurs mobilières (ACVM)
CSA Secretariat, Tour de la Bourse, #2510, 800, Victoria Sq., Montréal QC H4Z 1J2
Tel: 514-864-9510; *Fax:* 514-864-9512
csa-acvm-secretariat@acvm-csa.ca
www.securities-administrators.ca
Social Media:
twitter.com/CSA_News
To coordinate & harmonize regulation of the Canadian capital markets; To foster fair & efficient capital markets; To reduce the risk of failure of market intermediaries
Tom Cotter, Interim Chair
Kim Lachapelle, Secretary General

Canadian Securities Institute (CSI) / L'Institut canadien des valeurs mobilières
200 Wellington St. West, 15th Fl., Toronto ON M5V 3C7
Tel: 416-364-9130; *Fax:* 416-359-0486
Toll-Free: 866-866-2601
customer_support@csi.ca
www.csi.ca
Social Media: csiblog.csi.ca
linkedin.com/groups?gid=3720042
www.facebook.com/csiglobal
twitter.com/CSIGlobalEd
To enhance the knowledge of securities & financial industry professionals & promote knowledge & understanding of investing among the public
Simon Parmar, Managing Director

Canadian Security Traders Association, Inc. (CSTA)
PO Box 3, 31 Adelaide St. East, Toronto ON M5C 2J6
janice.cooper@canadiansta.org
www.canadiansta.org
Peggy Bowie, President

Chambre de commerce Canada-Pologne
5570 Waverly Rue, Montréal QC H2T 2Y1

Co-operatives & Mutuals Canada (CMC) / Coopératives et mutuelles Canada
#400, 275 Bank St., Ottawa ON K2P 2L6
Tel: 613-238-6712; *Fax:* 613-567-0658
info@coopscanada.coop
canada.coop
Social Media:
www.facebook.com/792260167456516
twitter.com/CoopsCanada
To unite co-operatives & mutuals from various industry sectors & regions of Canada
Leo Leblanc, President
Denyse Guy, Executive Director
Madeleine Brillant, Director, Corporate Affairs

Council of Ukrainian Credit Unions of Canada
145 Evans Ave., Toronto ON M8Z 5X8
Tel: 416-323-3495; *Fax:* 416-923-7904
info@cucuc.ca
www.cucuc.ca
To unite & promote Ukrainian member credit unions in Canada; To assist with the development of credit unions in Ukraine
Olya Sheweli, President

Credit Counselling Canada (CCC) / Conseil en crédit du Canada
#1600, 401 Bay St., Toronto ON M5H 2Y4
Toll-Free: 866-398-5999
contact@creditcounsellingcanada.ca
www.creditcounsellingcanada.ca
Social Media:
www.youtube.com/channel/UCj1dgARyEE1aya5RtJxvuUw
twitter.com/Creditcc
To ensure all Canadians have access to not-for-profit credit counselling; to ensure a quality of service is provided to Canadians by member agencies; to advocate on issues relevant to money management & the wise use of credit along with public policy & legislative issues around these; to promote awareness of the existence & availability of non-profit credit counselling; to cultivate positive working relationships with stakeholders

Credit Institute of Canada (CIC) / L'Institut canadien du crédit
#216C, 219 Dufferin St., Toronto ON M6K 3J1
Tel: 416-572-2615; *Fax:* 416-572-2619
Toll-Free: 888-447-3324
geninfo@creditedu.org
www.creditedu.org
Social Media: www.youtube.com/user/creditinstitute
linkedin.com/groups/Credit-Collections-Management-Professionals-23
www.facebook.com/creditedu
twitter.com/creditinstitute
To provide credit education for credit & financial professionals in Canada
Dana Swekla, President & Dean
Nawshad Khadaroo, General Manager

Fédération des caisses populaires acadiennes
Édifice Martin-J.-Légère, CP 5554, 295, boul St-Pierre ouest, Caraquet NB E1W 1B7
Tél: 506-726-4000; *Téléc:* 506-726-4001
www.acadie.com
Média social: www.facebook.com/caissespopulairesacadiennes
twitter.com/CPAcadiennes
Améliorer la qualité de vie de ceux et celles qui y adhèrent tout en contribuant à l'autosuffisance socio-économique de la collectivité acadienne du Nouveau-Brunswick, dans le respect de son identité linguistique et ses valeurs coopératives
Camille H. Thériault, Président/Directeur général

Financial Executives International Canada (FEIC)
#1201, 170 University Ave., Toronto ON M5H 3B3
Tel: 416-366-3007; *Fax:* 416-366-3008
Toll-Free: 866-677-3007
www.feicanada.org
Social Media:
linkedin.com/company/fei-canada
twitter.com/financial_execs
To promote ethical conduct in the practice of financial management; To contribute to the legal & policy making process in Canada
William G. Ross, Chair
Tim Zahavich, Vice-Chair
Michael Conway, President & CEO
Line Trudeau, Chief Financial Officer & Secretary
Don Comish, Director, Sponsorship
Liz Bowell, Coordinator, Membership

Financial Planning Standards Council (FPSC)
#902, 375 University Ave., Toronto ON M5G 2J5
Tel: 416-593-8587; *Fax:* 416-593-6903
Toll-Free: 800-305-9886
inform@fpsc.ca
www.fpsc.ca
Social Media: www.youtube.com/user/FPVision2020
linkedin.com/company/100790
www.facebook.com/FPSC.Canada
twitter.com/FPSC_Canada
To develop, enforce, & promote competency & ethical standards in financial planning by those who have earned the designation of Certified Financial Planner (CFP)
Lisa Pflieger, Chair
Dawn Hawley, Vice-Chair
Cary List, President & Chief Executive Officer
Kimberley Ney, Vice-President, Communications & Program Development
Stephen Rotstein, Vice-President, Policy & Regulatory Affairs
Heather Terrence, Vice-President, Operations
Joan Yudelson, Vice-President, Professional Practice
Isabelle Gonthier, Director, Certification Process & Examinations

The Institute of Internal Auditors (IIA) / L'Institut des vérificateurs internes
247 Maitland Ave., Altamonte Springs FL 32701-4201 USA
Tel: 407-937-1111; *Fax:* 407-937-1101
customerrelations@theiia.org
www.theiia.org
Social Media:
linkedin.com/groups?home=&gid=107948
www.facebook.com/TheInstituteofInternalAuditors
twitter.com/theiia
To provide leadership for the global profession of internal auditing; To advocate for the profession's value
Richard F. Chambers, President & CEO

Interac Association / L'Association Interac
Royal Bank Plaza, North Tower, #2400, 200 Bay St., Toronto ON M5J 2J1
Tel: 416-362-8550; *Toll-Free:* 855-789-2979
info@interac.org
www.interac.org
Social Media: youtube.ca/InteracBrand
linkedin.com/companies/1328202/Interac+Association
www.facebook.com/interac
twitter.com/interac
The Association is a recognized leader in debit card services in Canada
Mark O'Connell, President & CEO

Investment Funds Institute of Canada (IFIC) / L'Institut des fonds d'investissement du Canada
11 King St. West, 4th Fl., Toronto ON M5H 4C7
Tel: 416-363-2150; *Toll-Free:* 866-347-1961
member-services@ific.ca
www.ific.ca
Social Media:
linkedin.com/company/266541
twitter.com/ific
To act as the voice of the investment funds industry in Canada; To enhance the integrity & growth of the Canadian mutual fund industry
John Adams, Chair
Ross Kappele, 1st Vice-Chair
Paul C. Bourque, Q.C., President & CEO
Parker John, CFO & Vice-President, Finance

Investment Industry Regulatory Organization of Canada (IIROC) / Organisme canadien de réglementation du commerce des valeurs mobilières (OCRCVM)
#2000, 121 King St. West, Toronto ON M5H 3T9
Tel: 416-364-6133; *Fax:* 416-364-0753
Toll-Free: 877-442-4322
publicaffairs@iiroc.ca
www.iiroc.ca
To oversee investment dealers & trading activity on debt & equity marketplaces in Canada; To focus on regulatory & investment industry standards, protecting investors & strengthening market integrity
Andrew J. Kriegler, President & CEO

Municipal Finance Officers' Association of Ontario (MFOA)
2169 Queen St. East, 2nd Fl., Toronto ON M4L 1J1
Tel: 416-362-9001; *Fax:* 416-362-9226
office@mfoa.on.ca
www.mfoa.on.ca
To represent the interests of municipal finance officers throughout Ontario; To promote the interests of members
Dan Cowin, Executive Director
Shelley Stedall, President
Nancy Taylor, Vice-President

Mutual Fund Dealers Association of Canada (MFDA) / Association canadienne des courtiers de fonds mutuels
#1000, 121 King St. West, Toronto ON M5H 3T9
Tel: 416-361-6332; *Toll-Free:* 888-466-6332
mfda@mfda.ca
www.mfda.ca
To be the national self-regulatory organization (SRO) for the distribution side of the Canadian mutual fund industry
Roderick M. McLeod, Q.C., Chair
Mark T. Gordon, LLB, President & CEO
Shaun Devlin, Senior Vice-President, Member Regulation - Enforcement
Karen L. McGuinness, Senior Vice-President, Member Regulation - Compliance
Paige L. Ward, General Counsel, Corporate Secretary & VP, Policy

Ontario Association of Credit Counselling Services (OACCS)
ON
info@oaccs.ca
www.indebt.org
To represent member agencies & provide them with a forum for the pursuit of common interests in order to support, strengthen & enhance not-for-profit credit counselling services; to enhance the quality & availability of not-for-profit credit counselling
Henrietta Ross, Executive Director

Parksville & District Chamber of Commerce
PO Box 99, Parksville BC V9P 2G3
Tel: 250-248-3613; *Fax:* 250-248-5210
info@parksvillechamber.com
www.parksvillechamber.com
Social Media: www.youtube.com/user/ParksvilleChamber1
www.facebook.com/parksvillechamber
twitter.com/parksvillechmbr
Kim Burden, Executive Director
Linda Tschorz, Manager, Member Services
Lynda Schneider, Bookkeeper
Patti Lee, Manager, Visitor Centre

Pension Investment Association of Canada (PIAC) / Association canadienne des gestionnaires de fonds de retraite
#123, 20 Carlton St., Toronto ON M5B 2H5
Tel: 416-640-0264
www.piacweb.org
To promote the financial security of pension fund beneficiaries through sound investment policy & practices
Peter Waite, Executive Director

Portfolio Management Association of Canada (PMAC)
#1210, 155 University Ave., Toronto ON M5H 3B7
Tel: 416-504-1118; *Fax:* 416-504-1117
info@portfoliomanagement.org
www.portfoliomanagement.org
Social Media:
linkedin.com/company/portfolio-management-association-of-canada
twitter.com/PMACnews
To represent the Investment Counsel & portfolio managers in Canada; To advocate high standards of unbiased portfolio management in the interest of investors

Katie Walmsley, President
Alex Stephen, Manager, Sponsorship, Events & General Inquiries

Registered Deposit Brokers Association (RDBA)
#614, 55 Cedar Pointe Dr., Barrie ON L4N 5R7
Tel: 705-730-7599; *Fax:* 705-730-0477
Toll-Free: 866-261-6263
headoffice@rdba.ca
www.rdba.ca
To represent interests of deposit clients & independent deposit brokers

Responsible Investment Association (RIA)
#300, 215 Spadina Ave., Toronto ON M5T 2C7
Tel: 416-461-6042
staff@riacanada.ca
riacanada.ca
Social Media:
linkedin.com/company/responsible-investment-association
www.facebook.com/ResponsibleInvestmentAssociation
twitter.com/riacanada
To take a leadership role in coordinating the responsible investing (RI) agenda in Canada; to raise public awareness of RI in Canada; to reach out to other groups interested in RI; to provide information on RI to members & the public
Deb Abbey, Chief Executive Officer
Wendy Mitchell, Financial Coordinator
Dustyn Lanz, Director, Research & Communications

Smiths Falls & District Chamber of Commerce
Town Hall, 77 Beckwith St. North, Smiths Falls ON K7A 2B8
Tel: 613-283-1334; *Fax:* 613-283-4764
info@smithsfallschamber.ca
www.smithsfallschamber.ca
Social Media:
linkedin.com/company/2345454
www.facebook.com/SmithsFallsChambers
twitter.com/sfchambers
Rebecca White, Marketing Coordinator
Ashley Lennox, Office Co-ordinator

Society of Actuaries (SOA)
#600, 475 North Martingale Rd., Schaumburg IL 60173 USA
Tel: 847-706-3500; *Fax:* 847-706-3599
customerservice@soa.org
www.soa.org
Social Media:
twitter.com/soasupport
To advance actuarial knowledge & improve decision making to benefit society
Errol Cramer, President
Greg Heidrich, Executive Director

Startup Canada
Ottawa ON
Tel: 613-316-6203
hello@startupcan.ca
www.startupcan.ca
Social Media: youtube.com/user/StartupCanada;
flickr.com/photos/62463248@N06
linkedin.com/groups/Startup-Canada-Campaign-3895252
twitter.com/Startup_Canada
To be a national, grassroots, non-profit organization dedicated to strengthening & enhancing Canada's entrepreneurial culture.
Adam Chowaniec, Founding Chair
Victoria Lennox, Co-Founder & CEO
Cyprian Szalankiewicz, Co-Founder & Vice-President, Multimedia & Technology

Women in Capital Markets (WCM) / Les femmes sur les marchés financiers
#402, 357 Bay St., Toronto ON M5H 2T7
Tel: 416-502-3614
info@wcm.ca
www.wcm.ca
Social Media:
www.youtube.com/channel/UC0B0i-RA-uKeUL-msjrhxmA
linkedin.com/groups/1681457
www.facebook.com/WomenInCapitalMarkets
twitter.com/WCMCanada
To enable capital markets professionals to reach their greatest potential for success; to advance woment within Canadian financial services
Michele Goddard, Chair
Jennifer Reynolds, President

World Council of Credit Unions, Inc. (WOCCU)
PO Box 2982, 5710 Mineral Point Rd., Madison WI 53705-4493 USA
Tel: 608-395-2000; *Fax:* 608-395-2001
mail@woccu.org
www.woccu.org
Social Media: www.youtube.com/user/WOCCU/featured
linkedin.com/company/world-council-of-credit-unions
www.facebook.com/woccu
twitter.com/woccu
To promote the sustainable growth & expansion of credit unions & financial cooperatives worldwide; to provide technical assistance & trade association services to members
Grzegorz Bierecki, Chair
Manfred Alfonso Dasenbrock, Secretary
Brian Branch, President & CEO

Fisheries & Fishing Industry

Association québécoise de l'industrie de la pêche (AQIP) / Québec Fish Processors Association
#860, 2600, boul Laurier, Sainte-Foy QC G1V 4W2
Tél: 418-654-1831; *Téléc:* 418-654-1376
aqip@globetrotter.net
www.quebecweb.com/aqip
Défendre les intérêts professionnels des industries québécoises de la transformation des produits marins; travailler au développement des services; aider à l'amélioration de la productivité en usines

Atlantic Canada Fish Farmers Association (ACFFA)
226 Limekiln Rd., Letang NB E5C 2A8
Tel: 506-755-3526; *Fax:* 506-755-6237
info@atlanticfishfarmers.com
atlanticfishfarmers.com
Social Media: www.youtube.com/user/acffavideos
www.facebook.com/150506105026651
twitter.com/AtlFishFarmers
To act as the voice of Atlantic Canada's salmon farming industry; To implement fish health initiatives to produce high-quality finfish
Pamela Parker, Executive Director
Tobi Taylor, Manager, Operations
Betty House, Coordinator, Research & Development
Jim Hanley, Manager, Wharf

Atlantic Fishing Industry Alliance
#10, 3045 Robie St., Halifax NS B3K 4P6
Tel: 902-446-4477
To represent organizations in the harvesting, processing and marketing sectors of the commercial fishing industry in the Maritime Provinces.

Atlantic Salmon Federation (ASF) / Fédération du saumon atlantique
PO Box 5200, St Andrews NB E5B 3S8
Tel: 506-529-4581; *Fax:* 506-529-1070
Toll-Free: 800-565-5666
savesalmon@asf.ca
www.asf.ca
Social Media: www.youtube.com/user/ASFatlanticsalmon
www.facebook.com/pages/Atlantic-Salmon-Federation/1435962 65564
twitter.com/SalmonNews
To protect, conserve & restore wild Atlantic salmon & their ecosystems
Bill Taylor, President & Chief Executive Officer
Geoff Griffin, Executive Director, Regional Programs
Jonathan Carr, Director, Research & Environment
Bill Mallory, Executive Vice-President & CFO
Kirsten Rouse, Executive Director, Development
Sue Ann Scott, Vice-President, Communications
Holly Johnson, Manager, Public Information
Martin Silverstone, Editor, Atlantic Salmon Journal

British Columbia Salmon Farmers Association (BCSFA)
#201, 909 Island Hwy., Campbell River BC V9W 2C2
Tel: 250-286-1636; *Toll-Free:* 800-661-7256
info@bcsalmonfarmers.ca
www.bcsalmonfarmers.ca
Social Media:
www.youtube.com/channel/UCmOkdMmXlRq1PW_WyKV0iag
www.facebook.com/BCSalmonFarmers
twitter.com/BCSalmonFarmers
To act as the voice of British Columbia's farmed salmon industry; To advance the competitiveness & sustainable growth of the salmon farming industry
Jeremy Dunn, Executive Director
Sabrina Santoro, Manager, Communications
David Minato, Coordinator, Community & Regulatory Affairs
Neha Prihar, Coordinator, Communications

British Columbia Seafood Alliance (BCSA)
#1100, 1200 West 73rd Ave., Vancouver BC V6P 6G5
Tel: 604-377-9213; *Fax:* 604-683-4510
www.bcseafoodalliance.com
To represent the interests & values of a majority of BC's seafood industries to the federal & provincial governments & to the general public; to promote the conservation & environmentally sustainable use & production of seafood resources in BC; to foster an economically viable & internationally competitive seafood industry
Christina Burridge, Executive Director
Gina McKay, Coordinator, Safety & Assistance

British Columbia Shellfish Growers Association (BCSGA)
2002 Comox Ave., Unit F, Comox BC V9M 3M6
Tel: 250-890-7561; *Fax:* 250-890-7563
www.bcsga.ca
Advancing the sustainable growth & prosperity of the BC shellfish industry in a global economy by providing leadership & advocacy to members & stakeholders while maintaining the integrity of the marine environment
Roberta Stevenson, Executive Director

Canadian Aquaculture Industry Alliance (CAIA) / Alliance de l'industrie canadienne de l'aquiculture
PO Box 81100, Stn. World Exchange Plaza, #705, 116 Albert St., Ottawa ON K1P 1B1
Tel: 613-239-0612; *Fax:* 613-239-0619
info@aquaculture.ca
www.aquaculture.ca
Social Media:
www.youtube.com/channel/UCgg1cyvyiLcDP8lF81oHAWg
www.facebook.com/155794491097836
twitter.com/CDNaquaculture
To represent the interests of aquaculture operators, feed companies, suppliers, & provincial finfish & shellfish aquaculture associations on both the national & international scenes; To ensure the international competitiveness of the Canadian aquaculture industry
Ruth Salmon, Executive Director
Clare Backman, President

Canadian Association of Prawn Producers (CAPP)
1362 Revell Dr., Manotick ON K4M 1K8
Tel: 613-692-8249; *Fax:* 613-692-8250
office@shrimp-canada.com
www.shrimp-canada.org
To represent the interests of Canadian at-sea producers of coldwater shrimp; To advocate for sustainable & responsible resource management; To provide a platform through which Canadian prawn producers can communicate their issues to government & the general public
Bruce Chapman, Executive Director

Canadian Centre for Fisheries Innovation (CCFI) / Centre canadien d'innovations des pêches
PO Box 4920, St. John's NL A1C 5R3
Tel: 709-778-0517; *Fax:* 709-778-0516
ccfi@mi.mun.ca
www.ccfi.ca
To work with the fishing industry to improve productivity & profitability of fishery through science & technology
Robert Verge, Managing Director

Canadian Council of Professional Fish Harvesters (CCPFH) / Conseil canadien des pêcheurs professionnels (CCPP)
#712, 1 Nicholas St., Ottawa ON K1N 7B7
Tel: 613-235-3474; *Fax:* 613-231-4313
www.ccpfh-ccpp.org
To represent the interests of professional fish harvesters across Canada in their dealings with the federal, provincial & territorial governments on national issues of common concern; To provide organizational structure & leadership for the development of a program of professionalization for fish harvesters in collaboration with the organizations representing professional fishers across Canada; To act as a national industry sector council to plan & implement training & adjustment programs for the fish harvesting industry in Canada
John Sutcliffe, Executive Director
Earle McCurdy, President
Dan Edwards, Vice-President
Ronnie Heighton, Vice-President
Daniel Landry, Secretary
O'Neil Cloutier, Treasurer

Environment Resources Managament Association
PO Box 857, Grand Falls-Windsor NL A2A 2P7
Tel: 709-489-7350
info@exploitsriver.ca
www.exploitsriver.ca/association.php
To promote the development of the Exploits River as a major Atlantic Salmon producing river.

Fisheries Council of Canada (FCC) / Conseil Canadien des Pêches
#610, 170 Laurier Ave. West, Ottawa ON K1P 5V5
Tel: 613-727-7450; *Fax:* 613-727-7453
info@fisheriescouncil.org
www.fisheriescouncil.ca
To represent Canada's fish & seafood industry
Gilbert Linstead, Chair

Fishermen & Scientists Research Society (FSRS)
PO Box 25125, Halifax NS B3M 4H4
Tel: 902-876-1160; *Fax:* 902-876-1320
www.fsrs.ns.ca
To establish and maintain a network of fishermen and scientific personnel that are concerned with the long-term sustainability of the marine fishing industry in the Atlantic Region.
Patricia King, General Manager

North Atlantic Salmon Conservation Organization (NASCO)
11 Rutland Sq., Edinburgh EH1 2AS United Kingdom
hq@nasco.int
www.nasco.int
To promote the conservation, restoration, enhancement & rational management of salmon stocks in North Atlantic
Mary Collingan, President
Peter Hutchinson, Secretary

North Pacific Anadromous Fish Commission (NPAFC)
#502, 889 West Pender St., Vancouver BC V6C 3B2
Tel: 604-775-5550; *Fax:* 604-775-5577
secretariat@npafc.org
www.npafc.org
To promote the conservation of anadromous stocks in the North Pacific Ocean
Vladimir Fedorenko, Executive Director

Northwest Atlantic Fisheries Organization (NAFO)
PO Box 638, #100, 2 Morris Dr., Dartmouth NS B2Y 3Y9
Tel: 902-468-5590; *Fax:* 902-468-5538
info@nafo.int
www.nafo.int
To contribute through consultation & cooperation to the optimum utilization, rational management & conservation of the fishery resources of the Convention Area
Vladimir Shibanov, Executive Secretary
Lisa LeFort, Office Manager

Nova Scotia Salmon Association (NSSA)
PO Box 396, Chester NS B0J 1J0
info@nssalmon.ca
www.nssalmon.ca
To further the conservation & wise management of wild Atlantic salmon & trout
Rene Aucoin, President

Prince Edward Island Finfish Association
c/o Dover Fish Hatchery, RR#2, Murray River PE C0A 1W0
Tel: 902-962-3446
To represent the interests of the finfish aquaculture sector in Prince Edward Island
Leon Moyaert, President
Dawn Runighan, Vice-President
Mike Murray, Secretary-Treasurer

Prince Edward Island Fishermen's Association Ltd. (PEIFA)
#102, 420 University Ave., Charlottetown PE C1A 7Z5
Tel: 902-566-4050; *Fax:* 902-368-3748
adminpeifa@pei.eastlink.ca
www.peifa.org
To represent fishermen across Prince Edward Island; To act as a single, united voice on behalf of Island fishers on industry issues
Craig Avery, President
Ian MacPherson, Manager

Seafood Producers Association of Nova Scotia
#900, 45 Alderney Dr., Dartmouth NS B2Y 3Z6
Tel: 902-463-7790; *Fax:* 902-469-8294
spans@ns.sympatico.ca
Roger C. Stirling, President

Food & Beverage Industry

Association des brasseurs du Québec (ABQ) / Québec Brewers Association
#888, 2000, rue Peel, Montréal QC H3A 2W5
Tél: 514-284-9199; *Téléc:* 514-284-0817
Ligne sans frais: 800-854-9199
asbq@brasseurs.qc.ca
brasseurs.qc.ca
De représenter les intérêts de ses membres à des organismes et des intervenants government
Philippe Batani, Directeur général

Association of Canadian Distillers (ACD) / Association des distillateurs canadiens
#704, 255 Albert St., Ottawa ON K1P 6A9
Tel: 613-238-8444; *Fax:* 613-238-3411
www.acd.ca
To protect & advance the interests of its members; To promote & protect, both nationally & internationally, the well-being & viability of the Canadian distilling industry; To foster responsible attitudes toward the consumption of distilled spirits (gin, vodka, rum, Canadian Whisky) in Canada; To aggressively pursue & enhance the recognition of the name & positive reputation of Canadian Whisky as Canada's unique appellation distilled spirits product; To preserve & protect the integrity & standards of all distilled products

Atlantic Food & Beverage Processors Association
500 St. George St., Moncton NB E1C 1Y3
Tel: 506-389-7892; *Fax:* 506-854-5850
info@atlanticfood.ca
www.atlanticfood.ca
To actively support the food processors in the region in their efforts to operate efficiently and profitably.
Don Newman, Executive Director

Breakfast Cereals Canada (BCC)
#600, 100 Sheppard Ave. East, Toronto ON M2N 6N5
Tel: 416-510-8024; *Fax:* 416-510-8043
breakfastcereals.ca
To provide a forum for members to review issues of significance to the breakfast industry; to represent industry with government
Kathryn Fitzwilliam, Contact

Brewers Association of Canada / L'Association des brasseurs du Canada
#650, 45 O'Connor St., Ottawa ON K1P 1A4
Tel: 613-232-9601; *Fax:* 613-232-2283
info@beercanada.com
www.beercanada.com
Social Media:
linkedin.com/company/beer-canada
twitter.com/beercanada
To represent brewing companies operating in Canada; to collect information & statistics about the brewing industry; to provide information about the industry to the public
John Sleeman, Chair
André Forin, Director, Public & Government Affairs
Edwin P. Gregory, Director, Policy & Research
Linda Andrusek, Executive Assistant & Manager, Administrative Services
Peter A.B. MacPhail, Accountant

Brewing & Malting Barley Research Institute (BMBRI) / Institut de recherche - brassage et orge de maltage
PO Box 1497, Stn. Main, Winnipeg MB R3C 2Z4
Tel: 204-927-1407
info@bmbri.ca
www.bmbri.ca
To support the development & evaluation of new malting barley varieties in Canada
Michael Brophy, President & CEO

CanadaGAP
#312, 245 Stafford Rd. West, Ottawa ON K2H 9E8
Tel: 613-829-4711; *Fax:* 613-829-9379
info@canadagap.ca.
www.canadagap.ca
To operate a food safety program for companies that produce & handle fruits & vegetables; To develop & disseminate manuals for Greenhouse & fruit & vegetable operations; To encourage Good Agricultural Practices (GAPs); To encourage best practices for food supply management
Heather Gale, Executive Director

Canadian Association of Foodservice Professionals (CAFP) / Association canadienne des professionnels des services alimentaires
CAFP National Office, #130, 10691 Shellbridge Way, Richmond BC V6X 2W8
Tel: 604-248-0215; *Fax:* 604-270-3644
Toll-Free: 877-599-2237
national@cafp.com
www.cafp.com
Social Media:
twitter.com/wearecafp
To enhance the prestige of the food service profession through improving standards of service; To promote education in the industry & to provide increased opportunity for youth to train for the food service profession; to promote research in food service & nutrition; To work for food service regulation & legislation in the public interest; To promote through good fellowship & personal association new opportunities for increased management efficiency & exchange of professional information
Andrea Gillespie, National President
Leslie Smith, Vice-President, Membership
Dwayne Botchar, Secretary-Treasurer

Canadian Beverage Association / Association canadienne des boissons
WaterPark Place, 20 Bay St., 11th Fl., Toronto ON M5J 2N8
Tel: 416-362-2424; *Fax:* 416-362-3229
info@canadianbeverage.ca
www.canadianbeverage.ca
To represent soft drink bottlers, distributors, franchise houses & industry suppliers on a variety of issues
Jim Goetz, President
Stephanie Baxter, Senior Director, Communications
Anthony Van Heyningen, Senior Director, Research & Policy

Canadian Bottled Water Association (CBWA) / Association canadienne des embouteilleurs d'eau
#617, 7357 Woodbine Ave., Markham ON L3R 6R3
Tel: 416-618-1763; *Fax:* 877-354-2788
www.cbwa.ca
To represent the Canadian bottled water industry; To ensure a high standard of quality for bottled water
Elizabeth Griswold, Executive Director

Canadian College & University Food Service Association (CCUFSA)
c/o Drew Hall, University of Guelph, Gordon St., Guelph ON N1G 2W1
Tel: 519-824-4120; *Fax:* 519-837-9302
mcollins@hrs.uoguelph.ca
www.ccufsa.on.ca
To enhance the quality of campus life through the growth & development of food service operations in colleges & universities
Lee Elkas, President
David Boeckner, Executive Director
Gerard Hayes, Secretary-Treasurer

Canadian Federation of Independent Grocers (CFIG) / Fédération canadienne des épiciers indépendants
#401, 105 Gordon Baker Rd., Toronto ON M2H 3P8
Tel: 416-492-2311; *Fax:* 416-492-2347
Toll-Free: 800-661-2344
info@cfig.ca
www.cfig.ca
Social Media:
www.facebook.com/CFIGFCEI
twitter.com/cfigfcei
To equip & enable independent, franchised, & specialty grocers for sustainable success; To act as a united voice for independent grocers across Canada
Thomas A. Barlow, President & Chief Executive Officer
Ward Hanlon, Vice-President, Industry Relations & Business Services
Nancy Kwon, Director, Communications & Marketing

Canadian Health Food Association (CHFA) / Association canadienne des aliments de santé
#302, 235 Yorkland Blvd., Toronto ON M2J 4Y8
Tel: 416-497-6939; *Fax:* 905-479-3214
Toll-Free: 800-661-4510
info@chfa.ca
www.chfa.ca
Social Media: instagram.com/canadianhealthfoodassociation
www.facebook.com/CanadianHealthFoodAssociation
twitter.com/cdnhealthfood
To act as the voice of the natural products industry; To promote natural & organic products as an integral part of health & well-being; To ensure the growth of the natural & organic industry
Matthew James, Chair

Canadian Meat Council (CMC) / Conseil des viandes du Canada
#407, 1545 Carling Ave., Ottawa ON K1Z 8P9
Tel: 613-729-3911; *Fax:* 613-729-4997
info@cmc-cvc.com
www.cmc-cvc.com
To express the views of the membership with government, all elements of the food industry, consumer organizations, the research & academic community, & the media; To foster high standards of industry integrity, & a vast range of wholesome, nutritional meat products
James M. Laws, Executive Director
Ray Price, First Vice President-Treasurer

Canadian Meat Science Association (CMSA) / Association scientifique canadienne de la viande (ASCB)
Dept. of Agricultural, Food & Nutritional Science, Univ. of Alberta, #4-10, Agriculture / Forestry Centre, Edmonton AB T6G 2P5
Tel: 780-492-3651; *Fax:* 780-492-5771
ruth.ball@ales.ualberta.ca
www.cmsa-ascv.ca
To promote the application of science & technology to the production, processing, packaging, distribution, preparation, evaluation, & utilization of all meat & meat products; To develop & promote useful, coordinated research, educational techniques, & service activities
Peter Purslow, President
Sandra Gruber, President-Elect
Manuel Juárez, Sec.-Treas.
Sylvain Fournaise, Director at Large

Canadian National Millers Association (CNMA)
#200, 265 Carling Ave., Ottawa ON K1S 2E1
Tel: 613-238-2293; *Fax:* 613-235-5866
www.canadianmillers.ca
To serve as a vehicle for consultation between the milling industry, government departments & agencies; to promote regulatory & public policy environment that enhances international competitiveness; to provide international trade development to the industry; to disseminate information about the industry & Canadian wheat flour quality; to work directly & in cooperation with the trade offices abroad
Gordon Harrison, President
Donna Wiggins, Director, Administration

Canadian Snack Food Association (CSFA) / Association canadienne des fabricants des grignotines
c/o Ileana Lima, PO Box 42252, 128 Queen St. South, Mississauga ON L5M 4Z0
Tel: 289-997-1379
ileanal@4reflections.com
canadiansnack.com
To provide the leadership required for sustained growth & competitiveness of the industry; to influence policy formulation, legislation & regulations at all levels of government in the best interests of the industry
Calum MacLeod, President
Ileana Lima, Contact

Canadian Sugar Institute (CSI) / Institut canadien du sucre
Water Park Pl., #620, 10 Bay St., Toronto ON M5J 2R8
Tel: 416-368-8091; *Fax:* 416-368-6426
info@sugar.ca
www.sugar.ca
Sandra Marsden, President
Tristin Brisbois, Manager, Nutrition & Scientific Affairs

Canadian Vintners Association (CVA) / L'Association des vignerons du Canada
#200, 440 Laurier Ave. West, Ottawa ON K1R 7X6
Tel: 613-782-2283; *Fax:* 613-782-2239
info@canadianvintners.com
www.canadianvintners.com
Social Media:
www.facebook.com/CVAwine
twitter.com/cvawine
To formulate & promote policies that will advance the interests & goals of the Canadian wine sector.
Dan Paszkowski, President & CEO

Coffee Association of Canada (CAC) / Association du café du Canada
#1100, 120 Eglinton Ave. East, Toronto ON M4P 1E2
Tel: 416-510-8032; *Fax:* 416-320-5075
info@coffeeassoc.com
www.coffeeassoc.com
Social Media:
ca.linkedin.com/groups?gid=5060649
To address industry-wide issues on behalf of members, keeping them fully informed, & allowing them to focus on the proprietary concerns of building their businesses
Sandy McAlpine, President

Confectionery Manufacturers Association of Canada (CMAC) / Association canadienne des fabricants de confiseries
#301, 885 Don Mills Rd., Toronto ON M3C 1V9
Tel: 416-510-8034; *Fax:* 416-510-8043
info@cmaconline.ca
www.confectioncanada.com
To increase confectionery consumption & production; to achieve global competitiveness; to grow confectionery consumption in a responsible manner as an enjoyable food that is part of a healthy, active lifestyle.
Leslie Ewing, Executive Director

Conseil de la transformation agroalimentaire et des produits de consommation (CTAC) / Council of Food Processing & Consumer Products
216, rue Denison est, Granby QC J2H 2R6
Tél: 450-349-1521; *Téléc:* 450-349-6923
info@conseiltac.com
www.conseiltac.com
Média social: linkedin.com/company/1237456
Le porte-parole officiel des manufacturiers de produits alimentaires du Québec qui s'y regroupent à titre de membres fabricants; canalise les représentations des manufacturiers, en particulier auprès des gouvernements; coordonne l'action des membres en vue de promouvoir leurs intérêts économiques, sociaux et professionnels; suscite l'éducation des consommateurs sur les valeurs d'une bonne alimentation; favorise la promotion des produits fabriqués par les membres; établit des liaisons entre les manufacturiers, les producteurs, les fournisseurs, les distributeurs, les consommateurs et les autres maillons de la chaîne alimentaire; encourage la recherche dans les domaines de l'agriculture, de l'alimentation et du marketing
Sylvie Cloutier, Présidente-directrice générale

Flavour Manufacturers Association of Canada (FMAC) / Association canadienne de fabricants des arômes
#600, 100 Sheppard Ave. East, Toronto ON M2N 5N6
Tel: 416-510-8036; *Fax:* 416-510-8043
info@flavourcanada.ca
www.flavorcanada.com
To serve the needs of the Canadian flavour industry by providing a forum for the examination of industry problems, assisting in the implementation of solutions, & fostering a global perspective for creativity, innovation & competition.

Food & Consumer Products of Canada (FCPC) / Produits alimentaires et de consommation du Canada (PACC)
#600, 100 Sheppard Ave. East, Toronto ON M2N 6N5
Tel: 416-510-8024; *Fax:* 416-510-8043
info@fcpc.ca
www.fcpc.ca
Social Media:
linkedin.com/company/food-&-consumer-products-of-canada
twitter.com/FCPC1
To represent the food & consumer products industry, from small independently-owned companies to large multinationals
Nancy Croitoru, President & Chief Executive Officer
Paula Pergantis, Vice-President, Finance & Corporate Services
Rachel Kagan, Vice-President, Environment & Sustainability Policy
Tom Arnold, Director, Communications

Food Processors of Canada (FPC) / Fabricants de produits alimentaires du Canada
#900, 350 Sparks St., Ottawa ON K1R 7S8
Tel: 613-722-1000; *Fax:* 613-722-1404
fpc@foodprocessors.ca
www.foodprocessors.ca
To provide professional services & advice to members on matters such as manufacturing, trade, & commerce
Christopher J. Kyte, President
Mel Fruitman, Vice-President

New Brunswick Maple Syrup Association (NBMSA)
#223, 1350 Regent St., Fredericton NB E3C 2G6
Tel: 506-458-8889; *Fax:* 506-454-0652
yrp@nb.aibn.com
www.maple.infor.ca
The New Brunswick Maple Syrup Association (NBMSA) is a non-profit organization, dedicated to representing the interests of its members, and facilitating the industry through advertisement and the constant improvement of quality and standards by collaborating with various organizations towards the enrichment of the ever-growing maple industry.
Yvon Poitras, General Manager

Ontario Food Protection Association (OFPA)
PO Box 51575, 2140A Queen St. East, Toronto ON M4E 1C0
Tel: 519-265-4119; *Fax:* 416-981-3368
info@ofpa.on.ca
www.ofpa.on.ca
Provides a common forum for those associated with food safety in the food industry and enables those interested in food safety to exchange ideas, experiences and information.
Jeff Hall, President

Ontario Independent Meat Processors (OIMP)
7660 Mill Rd., RR#4, Guelph ON N1H 6J1
Tel: 519-763-4558; *Fax:* 519-763-4164
info@oimp.ca
www.oimp.ca

Pet Food Association of Canada (PFAC) / Association des fabricants d'aliments pour animaux familiers du Canada
PO Box 35570, 2528 Bayview Ave., Toronto ON M2L 2Y4
Tel: 416-447-9970; *Fax:* 416-443-9137
www.pfac.com
To provide association members with a unified voice on issues that affect the pet food industry in Canada

Tea Association of Canada (TAC) / Association du thé du Canada
#602, 133 Richmond St. West, Toronto ON M5H 2L3
Tel: 416-510-8647
info@tea.ca
www.tea.ca
Social Media:
www.facebook.com/teaassociationofcanada
twitter.com/Canadatea
To represent & advance the interests of Canada's tea industry to all levels of government in an effort to improve the conditions under which the industry operates & to promote better business relations between the industry's players
Louise Roberge, President

Wine Council of Ontario
PO Box 4000, 4890 Victoria Ave. North, Vineland ON L0R 2E0
Tel: 905-684-8070; *Fax:* 905-562-1993
info@winesofontario.org
winecountryontario.ca
Social Media:
www.facebook.com/WineCountryOntario
twitter.com/winecountryont
A non-profit trade association which plays a leadership role in the marketing, promotion, and future directions of the Ontario wine industry
Magdalena Kaiser-Smit, Director, Public Relations, Marketing & Tourism

Forestry & Forest Products

Alberta Forest Products Association (AFPA)
#900, 10707 - 100 Ave., Edmonton AB T5J 3M1
Tel: 780-452-2841; *Fax:* 780-455-0505
www.albertaforestproducts.ca
To represent companies that manufacture forest products throughout Alberta
Neil Shelly, Executive Director
Brady Whittaker, President & Chief Executive Officer
Norm Dupuis, Director, Grade Bureau
Brock Mulligan, Director, Communications
Keith Murray, Director, Policy & Regulation
Carola von Sass, Director, Health & Safety

Association of British Columbia Forest Professionals (ABCFP)
#330 - 321 Water St., Vancouver BC V6B 1B8
Tel: 604-687-8027; *Fax:* 604-687-3264
info@abcfp.ca
www.abcfp.ca
Social Media: www.youtube.com/user/TheABCFP
www.facebook.com/79659811198
twitter.com/abcfp
To protect the public interest in the practice of professional forestry by ensuring the competence, independence & integrity of its members; to ensure that every person practising professional forestry is accountable to the association & to the public
Sharon Glover, Chief Executive Officer
Mike Larock, Director, Professional Practice & Forest Stewardship
Amanda Brittain, Director, Communications

Association of Registered Professional Foresters of New Brunswick (ARPFNB) / Association des forestiers agréés du Nouveau-Brunswick (AFANB)
#221, 1350 Regent St., Fredericton NB E3C 2G6
Tel: 506-452-6933; *Fax:* 506-450-3128
info@arpfnb.ca
www.arpfnb.ca
Social Media:
www.facebook.com/arpfnb
To manage the forest resources of New Brunswick for the sustained development of these resources; To assure the proficiency & competency of Registered Professional Foresters in New Brunswick
Edward Czerwinski, Executive Director
Jody Jenkins, President
Jasen Golding, Secretary-Treasurer

Canadian Forestry Association (CFA) / Association forestière canadienne
c/o the Canadian Institute of Forestry:, PO Box 99, 6905 Hwy. 17 West, Mattawa ON P0H 1V0
Tel: 705-744-1715; *Fax:* 705-744-1716
Toll-Free: 866-441-4006
www.canadianforestry.com
To advocate for the wise use & protection of Canada's forest, water, & wildlife resources; To nurture economic & environmental health, through the management & conservation of forest resources; To provide a national voice for provincial forestry agencies
Dave Lemkay, General Manager
Kathy Abusow, President & Chief Executive Officer

Canadian Forestry Association of New Brunswick (CFANB) / Association forestière canadienne du Nouveau-Brunswick (AFCNB)
#248, 1350 Regent St., Fredericton NB E3C 2G6
Tel: 506-452-1339; *Fax:* 506-452-7950
Toll-Free: 866-405-7000
info@cfanb.ca
www.cfanb.ca
Social Media: www.youtube.com/cfanb
www.facebook.com/#!/pages/Envirothon-NB/166340680083948
To champions trees & forests of New Brunswick; To promote environmental, commercial, recreational, & inspirational benefits; To encourages conservation & wise use of natural resources
Bernard Daigle, President
Doug Hiltz, Treasurer/Secretary

Canadian Hardwood Plywood & Veneer Association (CHPVA) / Association canadienne du Contreplaqué et de Placages de bois dur (ACCPBD)
89 Godfrey Ave., St. Sauveur QC J0R 1R5
Tel: 450-227-4048; *Fax:* 450-227-7827
www.chpva.com
To protect the interests & conserve the rights of those involved in the manufacture & distribution of hardwood veneer & plywood & their suppliers in Canada.
Gaëtan Lauzon, Executive Vice President
Carole Aussant, Coordinator

Canadian Institute of Forestry (CIF) / Institut forestier du Canada (IFC)
PO Box 99, 6905 Hwy. 17 West, Mattawa ON P0H 1V0
Tel: 705-744-1715; *Fax:* 705-744-1716
admin@cif-ifc.org
www.cif-ifc.org
Social Media: youtube.com/user/CIFtube
facebook.com/groups/5380633929
twitter.com/cif_ifc
To act as the national voice of forest practitioners
Johnathan Lok, President
Megan Smith, Vice President
Alex Drummond, 2nd Vice President
Al Stinson, Past President

Canadian Lumber Standards Accreditation Board (CLSAB)
#102, 28 Deakin St., Ottawa ON K2E 8B7
Tel: 613-482-2480; *Fax:* 613-482-6044
info@clsab.ca
www.clsab.ca
Alphonse Caouette, Chair
Chuck Dentelbeck, Secretary-Treasurer

Canadian Pallet Council (CPC) / Conseil des palettes du Canada
239 Division St., Cobourg ON K9A 3P9
Tel: 905-372-1871; *Fax:* 905-373-0230
info@cpcpallet.com
www.cpcpallet.com
Belinda Junkin, President/CEO

Canadian Plywood Association
#100, 375 Lynn Ave., North Vancouver BC V7J 2C4
Tel: 604-981-4190; *Fax:* 604-985-0342
info@canply.org
www.canply.org
Canadian plywood organization.
Judy White, Office Manager
Nick Nagy, President

Canadian Well Logging Society (CWLS)
Scotia Centre, #2200, 700 - 2nd St. SW, Calgary AB T2P 2W1
Tel: 403-269-9366; *Fax:* 403-269-2787
www.cwls.org
Mike Seifert, Membership Chair
Harold S. Hovdebo, President

Canadian Wood Council (CWC) / Conseil canadien du bois (CCB)
#400, 99 Bank St., Ottawa ON K1P 6B9
Tel: 613-747-5544; *Fax:* 613-747-6264
www.cwc.ca
Social Media:
twitter.com/CdnWoodFacts
To represent Canadian manufacturers of wood products; To ensure market access for wood products; To communicate technical information; To organize educational programs for students & construction professionals
Michael Giroux, President
Wanda Thompson, Chief Financial Officer
Natalie Tarini, Manager, Communications

Canadian Wood Pallet & Container Association (CWPCA) / Association canadienne des manufacturiers de palettes et contenants (ACMPC)
#11, 1884 Merivale Rd., Ottawa ON K2G 1E6
Tel: 613-521-6468; *Fax:* 613-521-1835
Toll-Free: 877-224-3555
info@canadianpallets.com
www.canadianpallets.com
Social Media:
twitter.com/canadianpallets
To promote the general welfare of the wooden pallet & container manufacturing industry; to improve services directly or otherwise; to cooperate with officers of government & business in any program considered essential to the national welfare or economy; to engage in any other lawful activities & enjoy powers, rights & privileges granted or conferred upon associations of a similar nature.
Bill Eggertson, Executive Director
Lori Devlin, Director, Member Services
Stephanie Poirier, CWPCP
Blair McEwen, President

Canadian Wood Preservers Bureau (WPC) / Préservation du bois Canada
#202, 2141 Thurston Dr., Ottawa ON K1G 6C9
Tel: 613-737-4337; *Fax:* 613-247-0540
www.woodpreservation.ca
To provide a quality assurance program for the treated wood industry
Henry Walthert, Executive Director

Christmas Tree Farmers of Ontario (CFTO)
9251 County Rd. 1, Palgrave ON L0N 1P0
Fax: 905-729-0548
Toll-Free: 800-661-3530
www.christmastrees.on.ca
Shirley Brennan, Executive Director

College of Alberta Professional Foresters
#200, 10544 - 106 St., Edmonton AB T5H 2X6
Tel: 780-432-1177; *Fax:* 780-432-7046
office@capf.ca
www.capf.ca
To maintain an accurate register of registered professional foresters in Alberta; To set standards of professional conduct & competence for members; To administer the title, Registered Professional Forester (RPF)
Noel St. Jean, President
Doug Krystofiak, Executive Director & Registrar

Conseil de l'industrie forestière du Québec (CIFQ) / Québec Forestry Industry Council (QFIC)
#200, 1175, av Lavigerie, Sainte-Foy QC G1V 4P1
Tél: 418-657-7916; *Téléc:* 418-657-7971
info@cifq.qc.ca
www.cifq.qc.ca
Média social:
linkedin.com/company/conseil-de-l'industrie-foresti-re-du-qu-bec
twitter.com/CIFQ
Représente la très grande majorité des entreprises de sciage résineux, de pâtes, papiers, cartons et panneaux oeuvrant au Québec; Consacre à la défense des intérêts de ces entreprsies, à la promotion de leur contribution au développement socio-économique, à la gestion intégrée et à l'aménagement durable des forêts, de même qu'à l'utilisation optimale des ressources naturelles; Oeuvre auprès des instances gouvernementales, des organismes publics et parapublics, des organisations et de la population; Encourage un comportement responsable de ses membres en regard des dimensions environnementales, économiques et sociales de leurs activités
André Tremblay, Président-CEO
Mario St-Laurent, Directeur, Communications
Pierre Vézina, Directeur, Energy & Environment

Consulting Foresters of British Columbia
PO Box 98, Pender Island BC V0N 2M0
Tel: 250-656-8818
info@cfbc.bc.ca
www.cfbc.bc.ca
To maintain high professional standards in forestry consulting; To advance contact between its members, client groups, & the public at large
Bruce Blackwell, President
Mike Trepanier, Secretary

Council of Forest Industries (COFI)
Pender Place I Business Building, #1501, 700 Pender St. West, Vancouver BC V6C 1G8
Tel: 604-684-0211; *Fax:* 604-687-4930
info@cofi.org
www.cofi.org
To be the voice of the British Columbia interior forest industry; To offer member companies services in areas such as international market & trade development, community relations, public affairs, quality control, & forest policy
Ken Higginbotham, Chair
John Allan, President & Chief Executive Officer
Paul J. Newman, Executive Director, Market Access & Trade
Doug Routledge, Vice-President, Forestry & Northern Operations
Anne Mauch, Director, Regulatory Issues

La Fédération des producteurs de bois du Québec (FPBQ)
#565, 555, boul Roland-Therrien, Longueuil QC J4H 4E7
Tél: 450-679-0530; *Téléc:* 450-679-4300
bois@upa.qc.ca
www.fpbq.qc.ca
Défendre les intérêts de l'ensemble des propriétaires de boisés du Québec ainsi que l'élaboration et la promotion des politiques souhaitables et nécessaires pour atteindre cet objectif; représenter les propriétaires de boisés privés auprès des pouvoirs publics et des autres groupes de la société au niveau provincial et national; coordonner l'ensemble des activités des Syndicats et Offices de producteurs de bois ainsi que l'établissement, le maintien et le développement entre eux d'une étroite collaboration
Marc-André Côté, Directeur

Forest Nova Scotia
PO Box 696, Truro NS B2N 5E5
Tel: 902-895-1179; *Fax:* 902-893-1197
forestns.ca
To act as the voice of the forest industry in Nova Scotia; To cooperate with industry, federal, provincial, & municipal governments, & other stakeholders to ensure adherence to forest management & stewardship policies; To promote sustainable management & viability of the forest industry

Forest Products Association of Canada (FPAC) / Association des produits forestiers du Canada
#410, 99 Bank St., Ottawa ON K1P 6B9
Tel: 613-563-1441; *Fax:* 613-563-4720
ottawa@fpac.ca
www.fpac.ca
Social Media: www.youtube.com/ForestProdsAssocCan
www.facebook.com/FPAC.APFC
twitter.com/FPAC_APFC
To be the voice of Canada's wood, pulp & paper producers nationally & internationally in the areas of government, trade, & environmental affairs; To advance the Canadian forest products industry's global competitiveness & sustainable stewardship; To operate in a mannner which is economically viable, environmentally responsible, & socially desirable
David Lindsay, President & Chief Executive Officer
Susan Murray, Executive Director, Public Relations

Forests Ontario
#700, 144 Front St. West, Toronto ON MSJ 2L7
Tel: 416-646-1193; *Fax:* 416-493-4608
Toll-Free: 877-646-1193
info@treesontario.ca
www.forestsontario.ca
Social Media: www.youtube.com/user/ontforest
linkedin.com/company/1243400?trkInfo=tas%3Aontario+fores%2Cidx%3A1
www.facebook.com/Forests.Ontario?ref=ts
twitter.com/Forests_Ontario
To promote sound land use & full development protection & utilization of Ontario's forest resources for maximum public advantage; to increase public awareness, school education & natural appreciation of forests; to bring about better understanding of forests to people of all ages & backgrounds
Rob Keen, CEO
Al Corlett, Director of Programs
Shelley McKay, Director of Communications & Development

Manitoba Forestry Association Inc.
900 Corydon Ave., Winnipeg MB R3M 0Y4
Tel: 204-453-3182; *Fax:* 204-477-5765
www.thinktrees.org
To promote the wise use & management of all natural renewable resources, with emphasis on forests; to promote the planting of trees; to promote private land forestry (woodlots); to act as liaison among government, industry & the general public.
Patricia Pohrebnuk, Executive Director
Christina McDonald, President

Maritime Lumber Bureau (MLB) / Bureau de bois de sciage des Maritimes
PO Box 459, Amherst NS B4H 4A1
Tel: 902-667-3889; *Fax:* 902-667-0401
Toll-Free: 800-667-9192
info@mlb.ca
www.mlb.ca
An accredited quality control agency for the lumber industry in the region.
Diana L. Blenkhorn, President & CEO

National Aboriginal Forestry Association (NAFA)
#302, 359 Kent St., Ottawa ON K2P 0R6
Tel: 613-233-5563; *Fax:* 613-233-4329
www.nafaforestry.org
To promote & support increased Aboriginal involvement in forest management & related commercial opportunities; to assist Aboriginal communities in their quest to achieve a standard of land care which is balanced, sustainable & reflective of the traditional knowledge & forest values of Aboriginal peoples; to facilitate capacity-building in forest management through the development of human resource strategies & models for increased participation in natural resource decision making; to address the need for Aboriginal forest land rehabilitation & increased Aboriginal control over forest resources through the development of appropriate policy & programming
Bradley Young, Executive Director
Janet Pronovost, Office Manager

New Brunswick Forest Products Association Inc. (NBFPA) / L'Association des produits forestiers du Nouveau-Brunswick (APFNB)
Hugh John Flemming Forestry Centre, 1350 Regent St., Fredericton NB E3C 2G6
Tel: 506-452-6930; *Fax:* 506-450-3128
info@nbforestry.com
www.nbforestry.com
To represent forest industry members by serving as a common voice in relations with the government and the public, promoting a healthy New Brunswick forest, raise public awareness of sustainable forest management practices & provide a forum for the exchange of information, ideas & concerns.
Jacques Cormier, Chair

Nova Scotia Forestry Association (NSFA)
PO Box 696, Truro NS B2N 5E5
Tel: 902-895-1179; *Fax:* 902-893-1197
kari@nsfa.ca
www.nsfa.ca
Social Media:
www.facebook.com/NSENVIROTHON
twitter.com/envirothonns
To conserve Nova Scotia's forests; To promote the wise use & management of forest resources
Debbie Waycott, Executive Director

Ontario Forest Industries Association (OFIA) / l'Industrie forestière de l'Ontario
#1704, 8 King St. East, Toronto ON M5C 1B5
Tel: 416-368-6188; *Fax:* 416-368-5445
info@ofia.com
www.ofia.com
To act as a unified voice on behalf of member companies to ensure industry positions are considered; To respond to industry issues, such as economic, environmental, & technological developments

Ontario Lumber Manufacturers' Association (OLMA) / Association des manufacturiers de bois de sciage de l'Ontario
244 Viau Rd., Noelville ON P0M 2N0
Tel: 705-618-3403; *Fax:* 705-898-3403
info@olma.ca
olma.ca
To ensure a sound & renewable forest economy; To oversee lumber grading licenses & quality control at member sawmills in Ontario; To ensure market access within Northern America, Europe, & Japan
André G. Boucher, President/Chief Lumber Grading Inspector

Ontario Professional Foresters Association (OPFA)
#201, 5 Wesleyan St., Georgetown ON L7G 2E2
Tel: 905-877-3679; *Fax:* 905-877-6766
opfa@opfa.ca
www.opfa.ca
To operate as a regulatory body for the practice of professional forestry in Ontario; To govern members in accordance with the Ontaro Professional Foresters Act 2000
Tony Jennings, R.P.F, Executive Director; Registrar

Ontario Urban Forest Council (OUFC)
Mount Pleasant Group of Cemeteries, #23/25, 1523 Warden Ave., Toronto ON M1R 4Z8
Tel: 416-936-6735; *Fax:* 416-291-5709
info@oufc.org
www.oufc.org
To promote & assist in the protection & preservation of shade trees; to cooperate with all associations, government agencies, industry & individuals with a mutual interest in preserving & developing Ontario's shade tree heritage & landscape; to promote management of urban forest in Ontario
Jack Radecki, Executive Director

Ordre des ingénieurs forestiers du Québec (OIFQ)
#110, 2750, rue Einstein, Québec QC G1P 4R1
Tél: 418-650-2411; *Téléc:* 418-650-2168
oifq@oifq.com
www.oifq.com
Assurer la protection du public; assurer la qualité des services rendus au public québécois; favoriser l'amélioration continue de l'expertise et de la compétence des ingénieurs forestiers; mettre en place des actions favorisant la durabilité de l'aménagement forestier pour le bénéfice de l'ensemble de la société
Denis Villeneuve, Président

Prince Edward Island Forest Improvement Association (PEIFIA)
RR#1, York PE C9A 1P0
Tel: 902-672-2114; *Fax:* 902-672-2620
Wanson Hemphill, Contact

Pulp & Paper Centre
University of British Columbia, 2385 East Mall, Vancouver BC V6T 1Z4
Tel: 604-822-8560
ppc-info@ubc.ca
www.ppc.ubc.ca
To act as a university-industry partnership for innovation & education; to house inter-disciplinary, cross-faculty post-graduate research programs
James Olson, Ph.D., P.Eng., Director & Professor, Mechanical Engineering
George Soong, Safety & Operations Officer, Building/Technical Inquiries
Richard Kerekes, Director

Registered Professional Foresters Association of Nova Scotia (RPFANS)
PO Box 1031, Truro NS B2N 5G9
Tel: 902-893-0099
contact@rpfans.ca
www.rpfans.ca
To improve the holistic management of forest resources in Nova Scotia
Roger Aggas, Registrar
John Ross, President
Mike Brown, Treasurer

Regroupement des associations forestières régionales du Québec
#100, 138, rue Wellington nord, Sherbrooke QC J1H 5C5
Tél: 819-562-3388
info@afce.qc.ca
www.afce.qc.ca
Daniel Archambault

Saskatchewan Forestry Association (SFA)
#139, 1061 Central Ave., Prince Albert SK S6V 4V4
Tel: 306-763-2189; *Fax:* 306-763-6456
info@whitebirch.ca
www.whitebirch.ca
To promote the wise use, protection, & management of forests, water, & wildlife in Saskatchewan
Sindy Nicholson, President

Wood Preservation Canada (WPC) / Préservation du bois Canada
#202, 2141 Thurston Dr., Ottawa ON K1G 6C9
Tel: 613-737-4337; *Fax:* 613-247-0540
www.woodpreservation.ca
To represent, support & promote the treated wood industry in Canada

Francophones in Canada

Association des parents fransaskois (APF) / Fransaskois Parents Association
910, 5, rue est, Saskatoon SK S7N 2C6
Tél: 306-653-7444; *Téléc:* 306-653-7001
Ligne sans frais: 855-653-7444
apf.direction@sasktel.net
www.parentsfransaskois.ca
Média social: www.facebook.com/148583571881687
Assurer la mise sur pied et le développement d'un système scolaire complet de qualité, conforme au Projet éducatif de la communauté des familles fransaskoises
Danielle Raymond, Directrice générale
Brigitte Chassé, Agente à la petite enfance

Le Collège du Savoir
20, rue Nelson ouest, Brampton ON L6X 2M5
Tél: 905-457-7884
www.lecollegedusavoir.com
Média social: linkedin.com/in/le-collège-du-savoir-040077b0
Assurer l'éducation et la formation de l'emploi aux francophones de la région de Peel; Préparer les adultes pour obtenir une équivalence d'études secondaires
Anna Veltri, Directrice

La Passerelle - Intégration et Développement Économique
2, rue Carlton, Mezzanine ouest, Toronto ON M5B 1J3
Tél: 416-934-0558; *Téléc:* 416-934-0590
info@passerelle-ide.com
www.paserelle-ide.com
Média social: www.youtube.com/user/passerelleide/videos
www.facebook.com/lapasserelleide
twitter.com/Passerelle_IDE
Pour répondre aux besoins d'intégration et économiques des francophones dans la Région du Grand Toronto (RGT)
Léonie Tchatat, Directrice générale

Reflet Salvéo
#202B, 1415 Bathurst St., Toronto ON M5R 3H8
Tél: 647-345-5502; *Téléc:* 647-345-5520
TTY: 800-855-0511
info@refletsalveo.ca
www.refletsalveo.ca
Média social: www.facebook.com/pagerefletsalveo
twitter.com/refletsalveo
Assurer que les francophones ont un accès égal à des soins de santé de qualité, en français, indépendamment de l'origine, la race, l'orientation, ou le statut
Gilles Marchildon, Directeur général

Fraternal

Benevolent & Protective Order of Elks of Canada
#100, 2629 - 29 Ave., Regina SK S4S 2N9
Tel: 306-359-9010; *Fax:* 306-565-2860
Toll-Free: 888-843-3557
grandlodge@elks-canada.org
www.elks-canada.org
To promote & support community needs, through volunteer efforts of local lodges
Bill Blake, National Executive Director
Sebastian Merk, Manager, Finance & Administration

The Canadian Club of Toronto
Royal York Hotel, 100 Front St. West, Fl. MM, Toronto ON M5J 1E3
Tel: 416-364-5590; *Fax:* 416-364-5676
info@canadianclub.org
www.canadianclub.org
Social Media:
www.facebook.com/193517383995
twitter.com/cdnclubto
To host speakers & leaders from politics, business, science, art & the media; programming is accessible to everyone through cable broadcasts & online webcasts.
Alison Loat, President
Lynn Chou, Executive Director

Les Chevaliers de Colomb du Québec / Knights of Columbus of Québec
670, av Chambly, Saint-Hyacinthe QC J2S 6V4
Tél: 450-768-0616; *Téléc:* 450-768-1660
Ligne sans frais: 866-893-3681
conact@chevaliersdecolomb.com
www.chevaliersdecolomb.com
Un groupe d'entraide et une société fraternelle, qui unit des hommes de foi; l'ordre n'est pas rattaché à la structure juridique de l'Église catholique mais c'est un ordre de laïcs catholiques et exclusivement masculin

Les Chevaliers de Colomb du Québec, District No 37, Conseil 5198
124, rue des Forces Armées, Chibougamau QC G8P 2K5
Tél: 418-748-2411
dd37cc@hotmail.com
www.chevaliersdecolomb.com
Danny Bouchard, Député de district
Gaston Deroy, Grand Chevalier

Empire Club of Canada
Fairmont Royal York Hotel, 100 Front St. West, Level H, Toronto ON M5J 1E3
Tel: 416-364-2878; *Fax:* 416-364-7271
info@empireclub.org
www.empireclub.org
Social Media: www.flickr.com/photos/empire_club
linkedin.com/groups/Empire-Club-Canada-2488065
www.facebook.com/169851787973
twitter.com/Empire_Club
To present prominent speakers from professions such as businesses, labour, education, government & cultural organizations.
Noble Chummar, President

Foresters
ON
Tel: 416-429-3000; *Fax:* 416-467-2518
Toll-Free: 800-828-1540
service@foresters.com
www.foresters.com
Social Media: www.youtube.com/c/foresters;
www.pinterest.com/foresters
www.facebook.com/Foresters
twitter.com/weareforesters
A fraternal benefit society which provides life insurance & other financial products to its members
Anthony M. (Tony) Garcia, President & Chief Executive Officer

IODE Canada (IODE)
#219, 40 Orchard View Blvd., Toronto ON M4R 1B9
Tel: 416-487-4416; *Fax:* 416-487-4417
iodecanada@bellnet.ca
www.iode.ca
To operate as a women's charitable organization
A. Mason, Contact

Knights Hospitallers, Sovereign Order of St. John of Jerusalem, Knights of Malta, Grand Priory of Canada (OSJ)
#301, 2800 Hwy. 7 West, Concord ON L4K 1W8
To propagate the principles of chivalry; care for the sick, aged, invalid, poor & children in need; protect & defend Christianity throughout the world; combat errors; champion the truth; promote & encourage the spirit of Brotherhood & charity within the order; members are expected to be united in brotherhood & charity
Mario Cortellucci, Contact

Knights of Pythias - Domain of British Columbia
BC
knightsofpythiasbritishcolumbia.ca
Roger Murray, Chancellor

Ladies' Orange Benevolent Association of Canada (LOBA)
c/o Grand Orange Lodge of Canada, 94 Sheppard Ave. West, Toronto ON M2N 1M5
Tel: 416-223-1690; *Fax:* 416-223-1324
Toll-Free: 800-565-6248
To promote women with an opportunity to practice Orange beliefs & participate in benevolent activities
John Chalmers, Grand Secretary, Grand Lodge of Canada

Order of Sons of Italy in Canada
1375 Main St., Cambridge ON N1R 5S7
Tel: 905-388-9328; *Fax:* 905-383-9926
www.ordersonsofitalycanada.com
To assist the needy, the ill, and disabled through financial support, the provision of housing, and other support programs; To encourage the active participation of our members in the political, social and economic life of our community; to participate in programs combating discrimination, racism, and social injustice; To promote and preserve the Italian language, culture, and traditions in our country.
Josie Cumbo, National President
Patsy Giammarco, National Administative Secretary

The Order of United Commercial Travelers of America (UCT)
Canadian Office, #300, 901 Centre St. North, Calgary AB T2E 2P6
Tel: 403-277-0745; *Fax:* 403-277-6662
Toll-Free: 800-267-2371
customerservice@uct.org
www.uct.org
Social Media: www.youtube.com/UCTinaction;
www.flickr.com/photos/uctinaction
linkedin.com/company/united-commercial-travelers
www.facebook.com/UCTinAction
To provide members with affordable insurance & support through fraternal benefit & discount programs
Tom Hoffman, President
Joseph Hoffman, CEO

Réseau Hommes Québec (RHQ)
Centre Jean-Marie Gauvreau, #134, 911, rue Jean-Talon est, Montréal QC H2R 1V5
Tél: 514-276-4545; *Ligne sans frais:* 877-908-4545
rhquebec.ca
Média social: www.facebook.com/114381705296554
Organisme sans but lucratif; a pour mission d'entretenir un réseau de groupes autogérés d'écoute, de parole & d'entraide aux hommes
Éric Maisonneuve, Président
Léo-Paul Provencher, Directeur général intérimaire

Royal Arch Masons of Canada
361 King St. West. 2nd Fl., Hamilton ON L8P 1B4
Tel: 905-522-5775; *Fax:* 905-522-5099
office@royalarchmasons.on.ca
www.royalarchmasons.on.ca
Melvyn J. Duke, Grand Scribe E.

Society of Kabalarians of Canada
1160 West 10th Ave., Vancouver BC V6H 1J1
Tel: 604-263-9551; *Fax:* 604-263-5514
Toll-Free: 866-489-1188
info1@kabalarians.com
www.kabalarians.com
To promote Kabalarian philosophy, which teaches a constructive way of life through the understanding of the Mathematical Principle, encouraging people to live a more progressive, constructive life.
Lorenda Bardell, President

Funeral Services

Alberta Funeral Service Association (AFSA)
3030 - 55 St., Red Deer AB T4P 3S6
Tel: 403-342-2460; *Fax:* 403-342-2495
Toll-Free: 800-803-8809
inquiry@afsa.ca
www.afsa.ca
To promote & improve funeral service in Alberta
Deanna Schroeder, Executive Administrator

British Columbia Funeral Association (BCFA)
#211, 2187 Oak Bay Ave., Victoria BC V8R 1G1
Tel: 250-592-3213; *Fax:* 250-592-4362
Toll-Free: 800-665-3899
info@bcfunerals.com
www.bcfunerals.com
Social Media:
www.facebook.com/bcfunerals
twitter.com/bcfunerals
To promote, through education, communication, & leadership, the highest standards of ethics & service in the funeral profession
Sharla MacKay, President
Lori Cascaden, Executive Director

Corporation des thanatologues du Québec (CTQ)
#115, 4600, boul Henri-Bourassa, Québec QC G1H 3A5
Tél: 418-622-1717; *Téléc:* 418-622-5557
Ligne sans frais: 800-463-4935
info@corpothanato.com
www.domainefuneraire.com
Média social:
www.facebook.com/corporation.thanatologues.quebec?fref=ts
twitter.com/corpothanato
Représenter le domaine funéraire, supporter son évolution promouvoir l'excellence et contribuer au développement d'affaire de ses membres pour le mieux être de la population
René Goyer, Président

Funeral & Cremation Services Council of Saskatchewan (FCSCS)
3847C Albert St., Regina SK S4S 3R4
Tel: 306-584-1575; *Fax:* 306-584-1576
Toll-Free: 800-892-0116
administration@fcscs.ca
www.fcscs.ca
To outline standard practices for the funeral industry for the benefit of the public
Phil Fredette, Chair
Sandy Mahon, Registrar

Funeral Advisory & Memorial Society (FAMS)
55 St. Phillips Rd., Toronto ON M9P 2N8
Tel: 416-241-6274
info@fams.ca
www.fams.ca
To provide unbiased consumer advice on funeral planning
Margaret Adamson, Chair
Paul Siemens, Vice-Chair & Secretary
Johanna Ntiforo, Office Administrator

Funeral Service Association of Canada (FSAC) / L'Association des services funéraires du Canada
#304, 555 Legget Dr., Ottawa ON K2K 2K3
Tel: 613-271-2107; *Fax:* 613-271-3737
Toll-Free: 866-841-7779
info@fsac.ca
www.fsac.ca
Social Media:
www.facebook.com/FuneralAssociation
To provide a collective voice for the Canadian funeral professional; To provide high quality professional services with dignity & competence; To ensure compliance with all provisions of the law; To provide information about services
Faye Doucette, President
Phil Fredette, Vice-President

Manitoba Funeral Service Association (MFSA)
#610, 55 Garry St., Winnipeg MB R3C 4H4
Tel: 204-947-0927
info@mfsa.mb.ca
www.mfsa.mb.ca
To serve funeral directors & funeral homes throughout Manitoba; To advance funeral service; To uphold a code of ethics
Owen McKenzie, President
Thorunn Petursdottir, Executive Director
Matt Nichol, Secretary-Treasurer

Newfoundland & Labrador Funeral Services Association (NLFSA)
PO Box 138, Winterton NL A0G 3M0
Tel: 709-586-2721; *Fax:* 709-586-2888
To offer funeral service support for the province.

Ontario Association of Cemetery & Funeral Professionals (OACFP)
PO Box 10173, 27 Legend Ct., Ancaster ON L9K 1P3
Tel: 905-383-6528; *Fax:* 905-383-2771
Toll-Free: 888-558-3335
info@oacfp.com
www.oacfp.com
To promote high standards of service & the professional operation of cemeteries, funeral homes, crematoria, & related bereavement services
Anita Mazzara, President
Terry Eccles, First Vice-President
Tim Vreman, Sec.-Treas.
Jo-Anne Rogerson, Executive Director

Ontario Funeral Service Association (OFSA)
#103, 3228 South Service Rd., Burlington ON L7N 3N1
Tel: 905-637-3371; *Fax:* 905-637-3583
Toll-Free: 800-268-2727
info@ofsa.org
www.ofsa.org
Social Media:
www.facebook.com/ofsa.socialmedia
twitter.com/OFSAsocialmedia
To maintain high standards of services & ethical business practices among Ontario's funeral homes for the welfare of the public; To represent & support Ontario's independently owned funeral establishments
Scott Davidson, President
Kerri Douglas, Executive Director

Prince Edward Island Funeral Directors & Embalmers Association
PO Box 540, Kensington PE C0B 1M0
Tel: 902-836-3313; *Fax:* 902-836-4461
To ensure professional services of the highest standards

Fur Trade

Canadian Association for Humane Trapping (CAHT)
PO Box 36534, Stn. Eastgate, 75 Centennial Pkwy North, Hamilton ON L8E 2P0
info@caht.ca
www.caht.ca
To reduce & eliminate suffering of animals trapped for whatever reason; To work with governments, trappers, the commercial fur industry, animal welfare organizations & the public-at-large to bring about actual trapping improvements
Carl Bandow, Executive Director
Donald Mitton, Project Director
Donna Bandow, Coordinator, Grants & Fundraising

The Fur Council of Canada (FCC) / Conseil canadien de la fourrure
#1270, 1435 St. Alexandre Rd., Montréal QC H3A 2G4
Tel: 514-844-1945; *Fax:* 514-844-8593
info@furcouncil.com
www.furcouncil.com
Social Media: www.youtube.com/user/EcoFurs
To promote all aspects of the fur trade

Fur Institute of Canada (FIC) / Institut de la fourrure du Canada (IFC)
#701, 331 Cooper St., Ottawa ON K2P 0G5
Tel: 613-231-7099; *Fax:* 613-231-7940
info@fur.ca
www.fur.ca
To promote the sustainable & wise use of Canadian fur resources
Robert B. Cahill, Executive Director
Bruce Williams, Chair
Mary Baskin, Manager, Corporate & Communications

Fur-Bearer Defenders (FBD)
179 West Broadway, Vancouver BC V5Y 1P4
Tel: 604-435-1850
fbd@furbearerdefenders.com
furbearerdefenders.com
Social Media: www.youtube.com/furbearerdefenders
ca.linkedin.com/pub/fur-bearer-s-assoc/20/52/587
www.facebook.com/FurFree
twitter.com/FurBearers
To stop trapping cruelty & protect fur-bearing animals
Lesley Fox, Executive Director

Furriers Guild of Canada
#211, 4174 Dundas St. West, Toronto ON M8X 1X3
Tel: 416-234-9494; *Fax:* 416-234-2244
furriersguildca@ica.net
To promote Canadian fur retailers

Galleries & Museums

Alberta Museums Association
#404, 10408, 124 St., Edmonton AB T5N 1R5
Tel: 780-424-2626; *Fax:* 780-425-1679
info@museums.ab.ca
www.museums.ab.ca
To promote understanding, access & excellence within Alberta's museums for the benefit of society
Bill Peters, President

Association Museums New Brunswick (AMNB) / Association des musées du Nouveau-Brunswick
668 Brunswick St., Fredericton NB E3B 1H6
Tel: 506-454-3561; *Fax:* 506-462-7687
info@amnb.ca
www.amnb.ca
Social Media:
www.facebook.com/AMNB2012
To preserve New Brunswick's heritage by uniting, promoting & advancing our heritage workers, supporters & organizations
David Desjardins, President
Chantal Brideau, Administrative Officer

Association of Manitoba Museums (AMM)
#1040, 555 Main St., Winnipeg MB R3B 1C3
Tel: 204-947-1782; *Fax:* 204-942-3749
www.museumsmanitoba.com
To strengthen the museum community by promoting excellence in preserving & presenting Manitoba's heritage; To improve the AMM's ability to communicate with its members; To continue a training program
Monique Brandt, Executive Director
Beryth Strong, Coordinator, Training
Jame Dalley, Conservator, Cultural Stewardship Program

Association of Nova Scotia Museums (ANSM)
1113 Marginal Rd., Halifax NS B3H 4P7
Tel: 902-423-4677; *Fax:* 902-422-0881
Toll-Free: 800-355-6873
admin@ansm.ns.ca
ansm.ns.ca
Social Media:
www.facebook.com/113166268748419
The Association of Nova Scotia Museums, using a consultative regional representative model, proactively champions museums through education, outreach, networking and advocacy to achieve excellence.
Anita Price, Managing Director

Atlantic Provinces Art Gallery Association (APAGA)
c/o MSVU Art Gallery, 166 Bedford Hwy., Halifax NS B3M 2J6
Tel: 902-457-6160; *Fax:* 902-457-2447
info@apaga.com
To pursue & promote high standards of excellence in care & presentation of works of art in public art galleries in the Atlantic region; To encourage the closest possible cooperation between art galleries, museums & artists; To serve as an advisory body in matters of professional interest
Ingrid Jenkner, Director

British Columbia Museums Association (BCMA)
675 Belleville St., Victoria BC V8W 9W2
Tel: 250-356-5700
bcma@museumsassn.bc.ca
www.museumsassn.bc.ca
Social Media:
www.facebook.com/BCMuseumsAssn
twitter.com/bcmuseumsassn
To promote the protection & preservation of the objects, specimens, records & sites significant to the natural, creative & human history of British Columbia; to aid in the improvement of museums & galleries as educational institutions; to assist in the development of the museum profession.
Theresa Mackay, Executive Director
Heather Jeliazkov, Manager, Marketing and Membership Services

Canadian Federation of Friends of Museums (CFFM) / Fédération canadienne des amis de musées (FCAM)
#400, 280 Metcalfe St., Ottawa ON K2P 1R7
Tel: 613-567-0099; *Fax:* 613-233-5438
www@cffm-fcam.ca
www.cffm-fcam.ca
Social Media:
www.facebook.com/146503988697066
To serve as source of information & expertise for friends of museums; To serve as communications network & national voice for those who are dedicated to the support & promotion of museums for the benefit of all Canadians
Tony Bowland, Co-President
Marie Senécal-Tremblay, Co-President
Yves Dagenais, Treasurer

Canadian Museums Association (CMA) / Association des musées canadiens
#400, 280 Metcalfe St., Ottawa ON K2P 1R7
Tel: 613-567-0099; *Fax:* 613-233-5438
Toll-Free: 888-822-2907
info@museums.ca
www.museums.ca
Social Media: www.youtube.com/museumsdotca
www.facebook.com/pages/Canadian-Museums-Association/107410072621904
twitter.com/musecdnCached
To advance a strong, vital, & valued Canadian museum sector
Bill Greenlaw, President
Nancy Noble, Vice-President
John G. McAvity, Executive Director & CEO

Community Museums Association of Prince Edward Island
PO Box 22002, Charlottetown PE C1A 9J2
Tel: 902-892-8837; *Fax:* 902-892-1459
info@museumspei.ca
www.museumspei.ca
Social Media:
wwww.facebook.com/116764358400112
To foster & support museums, historical societies & other non-profit organizations concerned with heritage of PEI.
David Panton, President
Barry King, Executive Director

ICOM Museums Canada / ICOM Musées Canada
#400, 280 Metcalfe St., Ottawa ON K2P 1R7
Tel: 613-567-0099
Social Media:
linkedin.com/groups/ICOM-Canada-4263110
www.facebook.com/150364635019516
twitter.com/ICOMCanada
To advance the cause of museums throughout the world & in Canada; to provide liaison with International Council of Museums in Paris; to hold annual meeting in conjunction with Canadian Museums Association.
Audrey Vermette, Director, Programs & Public Affairs

Museum London
421 Ridout St. North, London ON N6A 5H4
Tel: 519-661-0333
www.museumlondon.ca
To enrich public knowledge & enjoyment of the art & history of the London region & Canada
Brian Meehan, Executive Director

Museums Association of Saskatchewan (MAS)
424 McDonald St., Regina SK S4N 6E1
Tel: 306-780-9279; *Fax:* 306-780-9463
Toll-Free: 866-568-7386
mas@saskmuseums.org
www.saskmuseums.org
Social Media:
www.facebook.com/saskmuseums
twitter.com/saskmuseums
To work for the advancement of strong & vibrant museums in Saskatchewan; To encourage the preservation & understanding of the province's cultural & natural heritage; To serve Saskatchewan museums
Wendy Fitch, Executive Director
Robert Hubick, President

Ontario Association of Art Galleries (OAAG)
#125, 111 Peter St., Toronto ON M5V 2H1
Tel: 416-598-0714; *Fax:* 416-598-4128
oaag@oaag.org
oaag.org
To encourage the highest standards for the exhibition, interpretation, & conservation of the visual arts; to develop tools to assist gallery professionals in achieving institutional goals; to advance positive, responsive relations with government, its agencies & the citizens of Ontario
Demetra Christakos, Executive Director
Veronica Quach, Assistant Director

Ontario Museum Association (OMA) / Association des musées de l'Ontario
George Brown House, 50 Baldwin St., Toronto ON M5T 1L4
Tel: 416-348-8672; *Fax:* 416-348-0438
Toll-Free: 866-662-8672
www.museumsontario.com
To enhance the mission of museums as significant cultural resources in the service of Ontario society & its development
Marie Lalonde, Executive Director

Organization of Military Museums of Canada, Inc. (OMMC) / L'Organisation des musées militaires du Canada inc.
PO Box 60042, Stn. Unicity, Winnipeg MB R3K 2E7
ommcinc@gmail.com
www.ommcinc.ca
To preserve the military heritage of Canada by encouraging the establishment & operation of military museums; to educate museum staffs through lectures, discussions, workshops, visits, publications & exhibits; to cooperate with others having the same or similar purposes.
Marilyn Gurney, President
Stuart Beaton, Vice President

Prince Edward Island Museum & Heritage Foundation (PEIMHF) / Le Musée et la fondation du patrimoine de l'Île-du-Prince-Édouard
2 Kent St., Charlottetown PE C1A 1M6
Tel: 902-368-6600; *Fax:* 902-368-6608
mhpei@gov.pe.ca
www.peimuseum.com
Social Media: www.facebook.com/124989037532122
twitter.com/PEIMUSEUM
To study, preserve, interpret & protect the human & natural heritage of PEI
David L. Keenlyside, Executive Director
Nora J. Young, Executive Assistant

Société des musées québécois (SMQ)
CP 8888, Succ. Centre-Ville, Montréal QC H3C 3P8
Tél: 514-987-3264; *Téléc:* 514-987-3379
info@smq.qc.ca
www.musees.qc.ca
Média social: www.facebook.com/museesadecouvrir
twitter.com/museesdecouvrir
Au service du développement de la muséologie au Québec
Michel Perron, Directeur général

Yukon Historical & Museums Association (YHMA)
3126 - 3 Ave., Whitehorse YT Y1A 1E7
Tel: 867-667-4704; *Fax:* 867-667-4506
info@heritageyukon.ca
heritageyukon.ca
Social Media: twitter.com/Yukonheritage
To preserve & foster an appreciation of the Yukon's history & culture; to act as forum for other museum & heritage organizations in the region
Nancy Oakley, Executive Director

Gas & Oil

Association pétrolière et gazière du Québec (APGQ) / Quebec Oil and Gas Association (QOGA)
#200, 140, Grande Allée est, Québec QC G1R 5P7
Tél: 418-261-2941
info@apgq-qoga.com
www.apgq-qoga.com
L'APGQ a été créée afin d'encourager le dialogue sur le potentiel d'une nouvelle industrie au Québec.

Canadian Heavy Oil Association (CHOA)
#400, 500 - 5th Ave. SW, Calgary AB T2P 3L5
Tel: 403-269-1755; *Fax:* 403-453-0179
www.choa.ab.ca
Social Media: linkedin.com/groups?gid=2795817
twitter.com/CDN_CHOA
To provide a technical, educational, & social forum for people employed in, or associated with, the oil sands & heavy oil industries
Kym Fawcett, President
Kerri Markle, Executive Director

Gems & Jewellery

Alberta Federation of Rock Clubs (AFRC)
2073 Blackmud Creek Dr. SW, Edmonton AB T6W 1G8
Tel: 780-430-6694
paulinez8@shaw.ca
www.afrc.ca
To assist member clubs by providing information & expertise; to promote the study of the Earth Sciences
Alice Watts, President
Pauline Zeschuk, Secretary

Canadian Gemmological Association (CGA)
#1301, 55 Queen St. East, Toronto ON M5C 1R6
Tel: 647-466-2436; *Fax:* 416-366-6519
info@canadiangemmological.com
www.canadiangemmological.com
To set a standard for excellence in the practice of gemmology
Duncan Parker, President
Brad Wilson, Vice-President
Glen King, Treasurer

Canadian Institute of Gemmology (CIG) / Institut canadien de gemmologie
c/o School of Jewellery Arts, PO Box 57010, Vancouver BC V5K 5G6
Tel: 604-530-8569
info@cigem.ca
www.cigem.ca
Social Media: www.facebook.com/pages/Canadian-Institute-of-Gemmology/135719129830957
twitter.com/CIGemNews
To serve the jewellery industry & the general public
Wolf Kuehn, Executive Director

Canadian Jewellers Association (CJA)
#600, 27 Queen St. East, Toronto ON M5C 2M6
Tel: 416-368-7616; *Fax:* 416-368-1986
Toll-Free: 800-580-0942
www.canadianjewellers.com
To provide its members with information, services & techonology that allow them to flourish in their profession
David Ritter, President & CEO

Corporation des bijoutiers du Québec (CBQ) / Québec Jewellers' Corporation
868, rue Brissette, Sainte-Julie QC J3E 2B1
Tél: 514-485-3333; *Téléc:* 450-649-8984
info@cbq.qc.ca
www.cbq.qc.ca
La promotion des membres, la défence de leurs intérêts économiques et sociaux et le développement du professionnalisme chez les membres; garantir au public un meilleur service et l'intégrité des bijoutiers membres; accroître la compétence des gens du métier; favoriser l'exercise du métier selon l'art et la science
André Marchand, Président
Lise Petitpas, Directrice générale

Gem & Mineral Federation of Canada (GMFC) / Fédération canadienne des gemmes et des minéraux
PO Box 42015, RPO North, Winfield BC V4V 1Z8
Tel: 250-766-4353
president@gmfc.ca
www.gmfc.ca
To promote earth sciences; to protect collecting sites; to educate collectors; to foster good will, friendship & rapport among all
Peter Hagar, President

Jewellers Vigilance Canada Inc. (JVC)
#600, 27 Queen St. East, Toronto ON M5C 2M6
Tel: 416-368-4840; *Fax:* 416-368-5552
Toll-Free: 800-636-9536
info@jewellersvigilance.ca
www.jewellersvigilance.ca
To advance ethical practices, establish a level playing field for the Canadian jewellery industry & provide crime prevention education for the trade.

Government & Public Administration

Alberta Association of Municipal Districts & Counties (AAMDC)
2510 Sparrow Dr., Nisku AB T9E 8N5
Tel: 780-955-3639; *Fax:* 780-955-3615
Toll-Free: 855-548-7233
aamdc@aamdc.com
www.aamdc.com
Social Media: www.flickr.com/photos/45829734@N03
twitter.com/aamdc
Bob Barss, President
Gerald Rhodes, Executive Director

Alberta Municipal Clerks Association (AMCA)
c/o City of Spruce Grove, 315 Jespersen Dr., Spruce Grove AB T7X 3E8
Tel: 780-962-7634
communications@albertamunicipalclerks.com
www.albertamunicipalclerks.com
To provide a forum for exchange of ideas among the municipal clerks of the municipalities of Alberta; to provide a means for presentation of suggested amendments in legislation to senior government; to work in conjunction with any other organization, having as its objective the betterment of administration of local government
Doug Tymchyshyn, President

Alberta Rural Municipal Administrators Association
6027 - 4th St. NE, Calgary AB T2K 4Z5
Tel: 403-275-0622; *Fax:* 403-275-8179
www.armaa.ca
To represent administrators in Alberta municipal governments
Valerie Schmaltz, Executive Director
Sheila Kitz, President

Alberta Urban Municipalities Association (AUMA)
#300, 8616 51 Ave., Edmonton AB T6E 6E6
Tel: 780-433-4431; *Fax:* 780-433-4454
Toll-Free: 877-421-6644
main@auma.ca
www.auma.ca
Social Media: www.youtube.com/channel/UC_HJ3RFfvOwFpdVDcLifGLw/feed
linkedin.com/company/alberta-urban-municipalities-association?trk=
www.facebook.com/theauma?fref=ts
twitter.com/theauma
To provide leadership in advocating local government interests to the provincial government & other organizations, & to provide services that address the needs of its membership
Sue Bohaichuk, FCPA (CMA); ICD, Chief Executive Officer

Association des directeurs généraux des municipalités du Québec
#470, 43, rue de Buade, Québec QC G1R 4A2
Tél: 418-660-7591; *Téléc:* 418-660-0848
adgmq@adgmq.qc.ca
adgmq.qc.ca
Permettre l'amélioration des connaissances et du statut de ses membres et la promotion de la formule de gestion conseil/directeur général
Jack Benzaquen, Président
Martine Lévesque, Directrice génerale

Association des directeurs municipaux du Québec (ADMQ)
Hall Est, #535, 400, boul. Jean-Lesage, Québec QC G1K 8W1
Tél: 418-647-4518; *Téléc:* 418-647-4115
admq@admq.qc.ca
admq.qc.ca
De voir à la promotion et à la défense des membres en plus d'offrir un soutien professionnel constant au niveau des outils de formation et de communication
Charles Ricard, Président
Marc Laflamme, Directeur général

Association francophone des municipalités du Nouveau-Brunswick Inc. (AFMNB)
#322, 702, rue Principale, Petit-Rocher NB E8J 1V1
Tél: 506-542-2622; *Téléc:* 506-542-2618
Ligne sans frais: 888-236-2622
afmnb@afmnb.org
www.afmnb.org
Promouvoir le développement des municipalités francophones du Nouveau-Brunswick
Frédérick Dion, Directeur général
Roger Doiron, Président

Association internationale des maires francophones - Bureau à Québec (AIMF)
CP 700, Succ. Haute-Ville, #312, 2, rue des Jardins, Québec QC G1R 4S9
Tél: 418-641-6188; *Téléc:* 418-641-6437
Favoriser les échanges et la coopérations entre les villes membres

Association of Manitoba Municipalities (AMM)
1910 Saskatchewan Ave. West, Portage la Prairie MB R1N 0P1
Tel: 204-857-8666; *Fax:* 204-856-2370
amm@amm.mb.ca
www.amm.mb.ca
Social Media: www.facebook.com/124665930946719
twitter.com/AMMManitoba
To provide communications link between municipalities; to lobby for municipal governments with senior levels of government
Joe Masi, Executive Director
Doug Dobrowolski, President

Association of Municipal Administrators of New Brunswick (AMANB) / Association des administrateurs municipaux du Nouveau-Brunswick (AAMNB)
20 Courtney St., Douglas NB E3G 8A1
Tel: 506-453-4229; *Fax:* 506-444-5452
amanb@nb.aibn.com
www.amanb-aamnb.ca
To promote & advance status of persons employed in field of municipal administration; to advance quality of administration of municipal services; to encourage closer official & personal relationship among members to facilitate interchange of ideas & experience; to establish & maintain standards of performance for members; to assist in provision of formal training & educational facilities
Melanie MacDonald, President
Danielle Charron, Executive Director

Association of Municipal Administrators, Nova Scotia (AMANS)
CIBC Building, #1106, 1809 Barrington St., Halifax NS B3J 3K8
Tel: 902-423-2215; *Fax:* 902-425-5592
info@amans.ca
www.amans.ca
To improve the quality of local government in Nova Scotia through the development of educational programs; To provide a forum for the exchange of ideas; to provide a resource to municipal officials; To provide service to members to improve their professional capabilities
Janice Wentzell, Executive Director
Kristy Hardie, Event Coordinator/ Financial Officer

Association of Municipal Managers, Clerks & Treasurers of Ontario (AMCTO) / Association des directeurs généraux, secrétaires et trésoriers municipaux de l'Ontario (ASTMO)
#610, 2680 Skymark Ave., Mississauga ON L4W 5L6
Tel: 905-602-4294; *Fax:* 905-602-4295
amcto@amcto.com
www.amcto.com
To foster administrative excellence in local government; to identify & meet training & education needs in local government; to be an influential voice for local government; to provide an effective communication forum for local government; to promote public awareness of & confidence in local government; to facilitate change within AMCTO
Andy Koopmans, Executive Director
Roger Ramkissoon, Manager, Finance & Administration

Association of Municipalities of Ontario (AMO)
#801, 200 University Ave., Toronto ON M5H 3C6
Tel: 416-971-9856; *Fax:* 416-971-6191
Toll-Free: 877-426-6527
amo@amo.on.ca
www.amo.on.ca
To support & enhance strong & effective municipal government in Ontario; To represent almost all of Ontario's 444 municipal governments
Pat Vanini, Executive Director
Nancy Plumridge, Director, Administration & Business Development
Monika Turner, Director, Policy

Association of Yukon Communities (AYC)
#140, 2237 2nd Ave., Whitehorse YT Y1A 0K7
Tel: 867-668-4388; *Fax:* 867-668-7574
www.ayc-yk.ca
To further the establishment of responsible government at the community level; To provide a united approach to issues affecting local governments; To advance ambitions & goals of member communities by developing a shared common vision of the future; To represent members in matters affecting them & the welfare of their communities; To provide programs & services of common interest & benefit to members
Bev Buckway, Executive Director

Association québécoise du loisir municipal (AQLM)
4545, av Pierre-de Coubertin, Montréal QC H1V 0B2
Tél: 514-252-5244; *Téléc:* 514-252-5220
infoaqlm@loisirmunicipal.qc.ca
www.loisirmunicipal.qc.ca
Intégrer le domaine de vie communautaire au mandat de loisir; Affirmer la maîtrise d'oeuvre de la municipalité en loisir; faire valoir le service municipal de loisir comme partenaire du réseau des organisations locales (institutionnelles et associatives); Promouvoir l'expertise des professionnels du loisir; démontrer l'utilité et les bénéfices du loisir; Développer des pratiques professionnelles en loisir
Luc Toupin, Directeur général
Pierre Waters, Directeur, Services aux membres associés
Joëlle Derulle, Conseillère, Formations et développement

Canadian Association of Municipal Administrators (CAMA)
PO Box 128, Stn. A, Fredericton NB E3B 4Y2
Tel: 866-771-2262
admin@camacam.ca
www.camacam.ca
To advance excellence in municipal management throughout Canada
Jacques Des Ormeaux, President
Ron Shaw, Treasurer

Canadian Council on Social Development (CCSD) / Conseil canadien de développement social (CCDS)
PO Box 13713, Kanata ON K2K 1X6
Tel: 613-236-8977
info@ccsd.ca
www.ccsd.ca
Social Media:
www.facebook.com/CanadianCouncilonSocialDevelopment
twitter.com/the_ccsd
To develop & promote progressive social policies, on issues such as child well-being, poverty, housing, employment, cultural diversity, & social inclusion
Peggy Taillon, President & CEO
Katherine Scott, Vice-President, Research & Policy
Michel Frojmovic, Manager, Community Data Program
Nancy Shipman, Vice-President, Strategic Communications & Social Media

Cities of New Brunswick Association
PO Box 1421, Stn. A, Fredericton NB E3B 5E3
Tel: 506-452-9292; *Fax:* 506-452-9898
cnba_acnb@bellaliant.com
Denis Roussel, Executive Director

Corporation des officiers municipaux agréés du Québec (COMAQ) / Corporation of Chartered Municipal Officers of Québec
Édifice Lomer-Gouin, #R02, 575, rue Saint-Amable, Québec QC G1R 2G4
Tél: 418-527-1231; *Téléc:* 418-527-4462
Ligne sans frais: 800-305-1031
info@comaq.qc.ca
www.comaq.qc.ca
Regrouper les cadres municipaux des cités et villes du Québec; promouvoir la formation professionnelle par l'organisation de cours; protéger les intérêts sociaux-économiques des membres.
Julie Faucher, Diretrice générale

Council of Atlantic Premiers (CAP)
Council Secretariat, PO Box 2044, #1006, 5161 George St., Halifax NS B3J 2Z1
Tel: 902-424-7590; *Fax:* 902-424-8976
info@cap-cpma.ca
www.cap-cpma.ca
The mandate of the Council is to promote Atlantic Canadian interests on national issues. To accomplish this, the Council seeks to establish common views & positions to ensure that Atlantic Canadians & their interests are well represented in national debates. The work of the Council of Atlantic Premiers builds on the ongoing work of the Council of Maritime Premiers & the Conference of Atlantic Premiers. The premiers are committed to work together on behalf of Atlantic Canadians to strengthen the economic competitiveness of the region, improve the quality of public services to Atlantic Canadians and/or improve the cost-effectiveness of delivering public services to Atlantic Canadians.
Tim Porter, Secretary to Council

Democracy Watch
PO Box 821, Stn. B, #412, 1 Nicholas St., Ottawa ON K1P 5P9
Tel: 613-241-5179; *Fax:* 613-241-4758
info@democracywatch.ca
democracywatch.ca
Social Media: www.youtube.com/dwatchcda
www.facebook.com/DemocracyWatch
twitter.com/democracywatchr
To advocate for democratic reform, government accountability, and corporate responsibility.
Duff Conacher, Coordinator

Federation of Canadian Municipalities (FCM) / Fédération canadienne des municipalités
24 Clarence St., Ottawa ON K1N 5P3
Tel: 613-241-5221; *Fax:* 613-241-7440
info@fcm.ca
www.fcm.ca
Social Media: www.youtube.com/user/FCMChannel
linkedin.com/company/federation-of-canadian-municipalities
www.facebook.com/pages/FCM/201746766534992
twitter.com/FCM_online
FCM is the national voice of municipal government that represents the interests of municipalities on policy & program matters that fall within federal jurisdiction. Its goal in serving elected municipal officials is the improvement of the quality of life in all communities.
Clark Somerville, President
Jenny Gerbasi, First Vice-President

Federation of Northern Ontario Municipalities (FONOM)
88 Riverside Dr., Kapuskasing ON P5N 1B3
Tel: 705-337-4454; *Fax:* 705-337-1741
fonom.info@gmail.com
www.fonom.org
To act as the voice for the people of northeastern Ontario communities; To work for the betterment of municipal government by striving for improved legislation respecting local government in northern Ontario
Alan Spacek, President

Federation of Prince Edward Island Municipalities Inc. (FPEIM)
1 Kirkdale Rd., Charlottetown PE C1E 1R3
Tel: 902-566-1493; *Fax:* 902-566-2880
info@fpeim.ca
www.fpeim.ca
To represent the interests of the cities, towns & communities within PEI; To secure united action for the protection of individual municipalities & municipal interests as a whole; To act as a clearing house for the collection, exchange & dissemination of information of concern & interest to member municipalities; To provide training, education & development opportunities for elected & appointed municipal officials
John Dewey, Executive Director
Bruce MacDougall, President

Fédération Québécoise des Municipalités (FQM)
#560, 2954, boul Laurier, Sainte-Foy QC G1V 4T2
Tél: 418-651-3343; *Téléc:* 418-651-1127
Ligne sans frais: 866-951-3343
info@fqm.ca
www.fqm.ca
Média social: www.facebook.com/FQMenligne
twitter.com/fqmenligne
Etre la porte-parole des régions; défendre les intérêts de ses membres
Bernard Généreux, Président
Ann Bourget, Directrice générale

Foreign Service Community Association (FSCA) / Association de la communauté du service extérieur (ACSE)
L.B. Pearson Building, 125 Sussex Dr., Ottawa ON K1A 0G2
Tel: 613-944-5729; *Fax:* 613-995-9335
fsca.acse@international.gc.ca
www.fsca-acse.org
To support the employees, spouses, & dependants of Canadian foreign service departments; To act as a liaison between families of the Canadian Foreign Service & Foreign Affairs Canada (FAC), the Canadian International Development Agency (CIDA), International Trade Canada (ITCan), Citizenship & Immigration Canada (CIC), & the Department National Defence (DND)
Helen Boutilier-Inglis, President

Institute of Public Administration of Canada (IPAC) / Institut d'administration publique du Canada (IAPC)
#401, 1075 Bay St., Toronto ON M5S 2B1
Tel: 416-924-8787; *Fax:* 416-924-4992
www.ipac.ca
Social Media:
https://linkedin.com/grps?gid=1937184
twitter.com/IPAC_IAPC
To advance public service excellence, by sharing effective practices & policy in public administration; To lead public administration research in Canada; To further professional, non-artisan public service
Robert P. Taylor, Chief Executive Officer
Gabriella Ciampini, Director, Special Events
Andrea Migone, Director, Research & Outreach
Marta Guzik, Lead, Membership
Suzanne Patterson, Director, Finance & Special Projects
Christy Paddick, Managing Editor & Manager, Public Sector Management Magazine

Institute On Governance (IOG) / Institut sur la gouvernance
60 George St., Ottawa ON K1N 1J4
Tel: 613-562-0090; *Fax:* 613-562-0087
info@iog.ca
www.iog.ca
Social Media:
linkedin.com/groups/Institute-On-Governance-4179557
www.facebook.com/IOGca
twitter.com/IOGca
To explore, share & promote responsible & responsive governance in Canada & abroad
Maryantonett Flumian, President
Philip Bolger, Vice-President, Operations
Todd Cain, Vice-President, Crown & Organization Governance
Laura Edgar, Vice-President, Partnerships & International Programming
Toby Fyfe, Vice-President, Learning Lab
Marion Lefebvre, Vice-President, Aboriginal Governance

Local Government Management Association of British Columbia (LGMA)
Central Building, 620 View St., 7th Fl., Victoria BC V8W 1J6
Tel: 250-383-7032; *Fax:* 250-384-4879
office@lgma.ca
www.lgma.ca
To promote professional management & leadership excellence in local government; To create awareness of local government officers' roles in the community
Nancy Taylor, Executive Director
Ana Fuller, Manager, Programs
Randee Platz, Officer, Finance

Manitoba Municipal Administrators' Association Inc.
533 Buckingham Rd., Winnipeg MB R3R 1B9
Tel: 204-255-4883
Crisis Hot-Line: 800-668-9920
mmaa@mts.net
www.mmaa.mb.ca
To promote the needs of membership & their professional development.
Mel Nott, Executive Director

Municipalities Newfoundland & Labrador
460 Torbay Rd., St. John's NL A1A 5J3
Tel: 709-753-6820; *Fax:* 709-738-0071
Toll-Free: 800-440-6536
info@municipalnl.ca
www.municipalitiesnl.com
To assist communities in their endeavour to achieve & sustain strong & effective local government thereby improving the quality of life for all the people of this province.
Terry Taylor, General Manager
Churence Rogers, President

National Association of Federal Retirees (FSNA) / L'Association nationale des retraités fédéraux (ANRF)
1052 St. Laurent Blvd., Ottawa ON K1K 3B4
Tel: 613-745-2559; *Fax:* 613-745-5457
Toll-Free: 855-304-4700
info@fsna.com
www.fsna.com
Social Media:
www.facebook.com/HonourYourPromise
To protect & enhance the rights & benefits of retired federal employees, & seniors in general, & to cooperate with other seniors'/pensioners' organizations on objectives of mutual interest
Gary Oberg, National President
Sylvia Ceacero, Executive Director

Northwest Territories Association of Communities (NWTAC)
Finn Hansen Bldg., #200, 5105 - 50th St., Yellowknife NT X1A 1S1
Tel: 867-873-8359; *Fax:* 867-873-3042
Toll-Free: 866-973-8359
communications@nwtac.com
www.nwtac.com
Social Media: www.flickr.com/photos/nwtac
twitter.com/nwtac
To promote the exchange of information amongst the community governments of the Northwest Territories and to provide a united front for the realization of goals.
Sara Brown, CEO

Northwestern Ontario Municipal Association (NOMA)
PO Box 10308, Thunder Bay ON P7B 6T8
Tel: 807-683-6662
admin@noma.on.ca
www.noma.on.ca
To consider matters of interest to municipalities in northwestern Ontario; To procure enactment of legislation which may be advantageous to northwestern Ontario's municipalities
Charla Robinson, Executive Director
Dennis Brown, President
Iain Angus, Vice-President

Ontario Municipal Human Resources Association (OMHRA)
#307, 1235 Fairview St., Burlington ON L7S 2K9
Tel: 905-631-7171; *Fax:* 905-631-2376
customerservice@omhra.on.ca
www.omhra.ca
To provide direction on issues of human resources management; To represent the interests of the association, related to legislation & policies
Elizabeth Bourns, President
Louise Ann Riddell, Vice-President
Christine A. Ball, Executive Officer

Ontario Municipal Management Institute (OMMI)
618 Balmoral Dr., Oshawa ON L1J 3A7
Tel: 905-434-8885; *Fax:* 905-434-7381
www.ommi.on.ca
To enhance management skills, in order to strengthen local government administration
Bill McKim, Executive Director
Shea-Lea Latchford, Administrative Assistant

Ontario Small Urban Municipalities (OSUM)
c/o Association of Municipalities of Ontario, #801, 200 University Ave., Toronto ON M5H 3C6
Tel: 416-971-9856; *Fax:* 416-971-6191
Toll-Free: 877-426-6527
amo@amo.on.ca
www.osum.ca
To take matters which affect Ontario's small urban communities to the attention of the provincial & federal governments
Paul Grenier, Chair
Jim Collard, Vice-Chair & Conference Chair
Larry McCabe, Administrative Member, OSUM Executive Committee

The Public Affairs Association of Canada (PAAC) / Association des affaires publiques du Canada
c/o John Capobianco, Fleishman-Hillard Canada Inc., #1500, 33 Bloor St. East, Toronto ON M4W 3H1
Tel: 416-645-8182; *Fax:* 416-361-2447
info@publicaffairs.ca
www.publicaffairs.ca
Social Media:
linkedin.com/groups/Public-Affairs-Association-Canada-PAAC-4790500
twitter.com/PAAC84
To improve the professionalism of members to enhance the relations of members' organizations with their publics
John Capobianco, President
Jennifer Dent, Events Chair
Stephen Andrews, Secretary-Treasurer
Rick Hall, Vice-President

Rural Municipal Administrators' Association of Saskatchewan (RMAA)
PO Box 130, Wilcox SK S0G 5E0
Tel: 306-732-2030; *Fax:* 306-732-4495
rmaa@sasktel.net
www.rmaa.ca
To address the needs of rural administrators in Saskatchewan
Kevin Ritchie, Executive Director
Tim Leurer, President

Rural Ontario Municipal Association (ROMA)
#801, 200 University Ave., Toronto ON M5H 3C6
Tel: 416-971-9856; *Fax:* 416-971-6191
Toll-Free: 877-426-6527
www.roma.on.ca
Social Media:
twitter.com/share
The Rural Ontario Municipal Association (ROMA) is the rural arm of the Association of Municipalities of Ontario (AMO).
Ron Eddy, Chair

Saskatchewan Association of Rural Municipalities (SARM)
2075 Hamilton St., Regina SK S4P 2E1
Tel: 306-757-3577; *Fax:* 306-565-2141
Toll-Free: 800-667-3604
sarm@sarm.ca
www.sarm.ca
To represent & advocate for rural municipal government in Saskatchewan
Dale Harvey, Executive Director
David Marit, President

Saskatchewan Urban Municipalities Association (SUMA)
#200, 2222 - 13th Ave., Regina SK S4P 3M7
Tel: 306-525-3727; *Fax:* 306-525-4373
suma@suma.org
www.suma.org
To work to enhance urban life in Saskatchewan, by providing administrative & consultative services to members, a forum for the discussion & resolution of current issues, & a negotiating vehicle for improvements in legislation, financing & programs. SUMA provides information & training for aldermen & mayors, and group benefits for its members
Laurent Mougeot, CEO
Sean McEachern, Director, Policy & Communication

Society of Local Government Managers of Alberta
PO Box 308, 4629 - 54 Ave., Bruderheim AB T0B 0S0
Tel: 780-796-3836; *Fax:* 780-796-2081
www.clgm.net
To govern & promote the profession of municipal government managers
Linda M. Davies, Executive Director/Registrar

Union des municipalités du Québec (UMQ)
#680, 680, rue Sherbrooke ouest, Montréal QC H3A 2M7
Tél: 514-282-7700; *Téléc:* 514-282-8893
info@umq.qc.ca
www.umq.qc.ca
Média social: twitter.com/UMQuebec
Au bénéfice des citoyens, représenter les municipalités auprès du gouvernement et contribuer à l'efficience de gestion des municipalités
Jasmin Savard, Directeur général
Martine Painchaud, Directrice, Relations Internationales
Diane Simard, Directrice/Secrétaire, Affaires juridiques

Union of British Columbia Municipalities (UBCM)
#60, 10551 Shellbridge Way, Richmond BC V6X 2W9
Tel: 604-270-8226; *Fax:* 604-270-9116
www.ubcm.ca
Social Media:
twitter.com/UBCM
To provide a common voice for local government
Mary Sjostrom, President
Gary MacIsaac, Executive Director
Marie Crawford, Associate Executive Director
Anna-Maria Wijesinghe, Manager, Member & Association Services

Union of Municipalities of New Brunswick (UMNB) / Union des municipalités du Nouveau-Brunswick
#4, 79 Main St., Rexton NB E4W 1Z9
Tel: 506-523-7991; *Fax:* 506-523-7992
umnb@nb.aibn.com
www.umnb.ca
To unite the municipalities of New Brunswick through their respective councils into a body whose common efforts shall be devoted solely to the achievement of that which is the common good of all
Tom Gillett, Director

Union of Nova Scotia Municipalities (UNSM)
#1106, 1809 Barrington St., Halifax NS B3J 3K8
Tel: 902-423-8331; *Fax:* 902-425-5592
info@unsm.ca
www.unsm.ca
To research, promote & represent provincial interests of local government
Betty MacDonald, Executive Director
Judy Webber, Event Planner/Financal Officer

Urban Municipal Administrators' Association of Saskatchewan (UMAAS)
PO Box 730, Hudson Bay SK S0E 0Y0
Tel: 306-865-2261; *Fax:* 306-865-2800
umaas@sasktel.net
www.umaas.ca
Richard Dolezsar, Executive Director

Health & Medical

Acoustic Neuroma Association of Canada (ANAC) / Association pour les neurinomes acoustiques du Canada
PO Box 193, Buckhorn ON K0L 1J0
Tel: 416-546-6426; *Fax:* 705-657-2365
Toll-Free: 800-561-2622
info@anac.ca
www.anac.ca
To provide support & information for those who have experienced acoustic neuromas or other tumors affecting the cranial nerves; To furnish information on patient rehabilitation to

physicians & health care personnel; To promote & support research; To educate the public regarding symptoms suggestive of acoustic neuromas, thus promoting early diagnosis & consequent successful treatment
Theresa Forson, National Coordinator

Active Healthy Kids Canada / Jeunes en forme Canada
#1205, 77 Bloor St. West, Toronto ON M5S 1M2
Tel: 416-913-0238; *Fax:* 416-913-1541
info@activehealthykids.ca
www.activehealthykids.ca
Social Media: www.youtube.com/user/ActiveHealthyKids
www.facebook.com/ActiveHealthyKidsCanada
twitter.com/ActiveHealthyKi
To advocate the importance of quality, accessible & enjoyable physical activity participation experiences for children & youth; To provide expertise & direction to decision makers at all levels, from policy-makers to parents, in order to increase the attention given to, investment in, & effective implementation of physical activity opportunities for all Canadian children & youth
Jennifer Cowie Bonne, Chief Executive Officer

Acupuncture Foundation of Canada Institute (AFCI) / Institut de la fondation d'acupuncture du Canada
#204, 2131 Lawrence Ave. East, Toronto ON M1R 5G4
Tel: 416-752-3988; *Fax:* 416-752-4398
afciweb@afcinstitute.com
www.afcinstitute.com
To define & maintain the highest professional standards for the use of acupuncture; to gain recognition of acupuncture's legitimate place in western medicine as a safe, efficient complement to conventional medical treatment; to design educational training programs for physicians, physiotherapists, RNs, dentists, chiropractors & naturopaths in the methodology & practice of acupuncture
Mac Mierzejewski, President/Chair
Cathy Donald, Treasurer
Ronda Kellington, Managing Director

African Medical & Research Foundation Canada (AMREF Canada)
#403, 489 College St., Toronto ON M6G 1A5
Tel: 416-961-6981; *Fax:* 416-961-6984
Toll-Free: 888-318-4442
info@amrefcanada.org
www.amrefcanada.org
Social Media: www.youtube.com/amrefcanada
www.facebook.com/amrefcanada
twitter.com/amrefcanada
Development agency working to enhance community health in East & Southern Africa; headquartered in Nairobi, Kenya; eleven national offices in both Europe & America; acts as support office in raising private & public funds for overseas health programs & also plays active role in maintaining working relations with Canadian International Development Agency (CIDA)
Anne-Marie Kamanye, Executive Director

Alberta & Northwest Territories Lung Association
PO Box 4500, Stn. South, #208, 17420 Stony Plain Rd., Edmonton AB T5E 6K2
Tel: 780-488-6819; *Fax:* 780-488-7195
Toll-Free: 888-566-5864
info@ab.lung.ca
www.ab.lung.ca
Social Media:
www.facebook.com/lungassociationabnwt?ref=ts
twitter.com/lungabnwt
To educate the public & medical professionals about lung health
Anne Marie Downey, Chair
Kate Hurlburt, Vice-Chair
Tom Watts, Secretary
Paul Borrett, Treasurer

Alberta Association of Optometrists (AAD)
#100, 8407 Argyll Rd., Edmonton AB T6C 4B2
Tel: 780-451-6824; *Fax:* 780-452-9918
Toll-Free: 800-272-8843
www.optometrists.ab.ca
Social Media: www.youtube.com/DoctorsofOptometry
www.facebook.com/AskaDoctorofOptometry
twitter.com/AAOOptometrists
To promote excellence in the practice of Optometry, to enhance public recognition of Optometry as the primary vision care provider in Alberta, and to advance the interests of the profession.
Brian Wik, Executive Director

Alberta Children's Hospital Foundation
2888 Shaganappi Trail NW, Calgary AB T3B 6A8
Tel: 403-955-8818; *Fax:* 403-955-8840
Toll-Free: 877-715-5437
www.childrenshospital.ab.ca
To raise money on behalf of the Alberta Children's Hospital in order to improve the services provided to patients & to fund research
Saifa Koonar, President & CEO

Alberta College & Association of Chiropractors (ACAC)
Manulife Place, 11203 - 70 St. NW, Edmonton AB T5B 1T1
Tel: 780-420-0932; *Fax:* 780-425-6583
office@albertachiro.com
www.albertachiro.com
Social Media: www.youtube.com/user/albertachiro
www.facebook.com/AlbertaChiropractors
twitter.com/AlbertaChiro
To ensure quality chiropractic care that enhances the well-being & protects the rights of the people of Alberta; To promote the art, science, & philosophy of chiropractic & its value in the health care community
Deb Manz, Chief Executive Officer

Alberta Hospice Palliative Care Association (AHPCA)
#1245, 70 Ave. SE, Calgary AB T2H 2X8
Tel: 403-206-9938; *Fax:* 403-206-9958
director@ahpca.ca
ahpca.ca
Social Media: www.youtube.com/watch?v=6Z3044hPlrl
www.facebook.com/AlbertaHospicePalliativeCare
twitter.com/AHPCA
To engage in actions & strategies that result in comprehensive, equitable & quality end of life care for Albertans
Terri Woytkiw, Chair
Leslie Penny, Treasurer
Jennifer Elliott, Executive Director
Theresa Bellows, Road Show Coordinator
Jon Angevine, Web Consultant

Alberta Innovates - Health Solutions
#1500, 10104 - 103 Ave., Edmonton AB T5J 4A7
Tel: 780-423-5727; *Fax:* 780-429-3509
Toll-Free: 877-423-5727
health@albertainnovates.ca
www.aihealthsolutions.ca
Social Media: www.youtube.com/user/AIHSChannel
www.facebook.com/179968058752241?sk=wall
twitter.com/ABInnovates
To support basic biomedical, clinical & health research in Alberta; contributes funds to scientific community to carry out research
Cyril (Cy) B. Frank, CEO
Kathleen Thurber, Director, Communications & Education

Alberta Medical Association (AMA)
12230 - 106 Ave. NW, Edmonton AB T5N 3Z1
Tel: 780-482-2626; *Fax:* 780-482-5445
Toll-Free: 800-272-9680
amamail@albertadoctors.org
www.albertadoctors.org
Social Media: www.youtube.com/user/ABMedAssoc
linkedin.com/company/alberta-medical-association
www.facebook.com/AlbertaMedicalAssociation
twitter.com/Albertadoctors
To advocate on behalf of its physician members; to provide leadership & support for their role in the provision of quality health care
Richard Johnston, President
Michael A. Gormley, Executive Director
Cameron N. Plitt, Chief Financial Officer

Alberta Occupational Health Nurses Association (AOHNA)
c/o College & Association of Registered Nurses of Alberta (CARNA), 11620 - 168 St., Edmonton AB T5M 4A6
Fax: 866-877-0228
Toll-Free: 888-566-3343
info@aohna.org
aohna.org
Social Media:
linkedin.com/company/alberta-occupational-health-nurses%27-association
twitter.com/AOHNA1
To promote healthy work environments for Occupational Health Nurses in Alberta; To provide growth & develop opportunities for its membership
Shannon Jacobi, President

Alberta Public Health Association (APHA)
c/o University of Alberta, 4075 RTF, 8308 - 114th St., Edmonton AB T6G 2E1
Tel: 780-492-6014; *Fax:* 780-492-7154
info@apha.ab.ca
www.apha.ab.ca
To promote & protect the health of the public through advocacy, partnerships, & education
PK (Tish) Doyle-Baker, President

Allergy Asthma Information Association (AAIA) / Allergie Asthme association d'information
#118, 295 The West Mall, Toronto ON M9C 4Z4
Tel: 416-621-4571; *Fax:* 416-621-5034
Toll-Free: 800-611-7011
admin@aaia.ca
www.aaia.ca
Social Media:
www.facebook.com/AllergyAsthmaInformationAssociation
To create a safer environment for Canadians with allergies, asthma, & anaphylaxis; To assist persons coping with allergies; To act as a national voice for individuals affected by allergy, asthma, & anaphylaxis
Sharon Van Gyzen, Chair
Mary Allen, CEO
Louis Isabella, Treasurer

ALS Society of Canada (ALS) / La Société canadienne de la SLA (SLA)
#200, 3000 Steeles Ave. East, Markham ON L3R 4T9
Tel: 905-248-2052; *Fax:* 905-248-2019
Toll-Free: 800-267-4257
www.als.ca
Social Media:
linkedin.com/company/als-society-of-canada
www.facebook.com/ALSCanada1
twitter.com/alscanada
To support research towards a cure for ALS; To support ALS partners in their provision of quality care for persons affected by ALS
Tammy Moore, Chief Executive Officer

Alzheimer Manitoba
#10, 120 Donald St., Winnipeg MB R3C 4G2
Tel: 204-943-6622; *Fax:* 204-942-5408
Toll-Free: 800-378-6699
alzmb@alzheimer.mb.ca
www.alzheimer.mb.ca
Social Media: www.youtube.com/AlzheimerMB
www.facebook.com/AlzheimerSocietyManitoba
twitter.com/AlzheimerMB
To alleviate the individual, family & social consequences of Alzheimer type dementia while supporting the search for a cure
Wendy Schettler, CEO

Alzheimer Society Canada (ASC) / Société Alzheimer Canada
#1600, 20 Eglinton Ave. West, Toronto ON M4R 1K8
Tel: 416-488-8772; *Fax:* 416-322-6656
Toll-Free: 800-616-8816
info@alzheimer.ca
www.alzheimer.ca
Social Media: www.youtube.com/thealzheimersociety
www.facebook.com/AlzheimerSociety
twitter.com/AlzSociety
Identifies, develops & facilitates national priorities that enable members to alleviate personal & social consequences of Alzheimer's disease & related disorders; promotes research & leads the search for a cure
John O'Keefe, President

Alzheimer Society of Alberta & Northwest Territories
10531 Kingsway Ave., Edmonton AB T5H 4K1
Tel: 780-488-2266; *Fax:* 780-488-3055
Toll-Free: 866-950-5465
info@alzheimer.ab.ca
www.alzheimer.ab.ca
The Society strives to alleviate the personal & social consequences of Alzheimer disease through the development, support & coordination of local societies & chapters. It also promotes the search for a cure through education & research. It is a registered charity, BN: 129690343RR0001.
Bill Gaudette, CEO
Christene Gordon, Director, Clinet Services & Programs

Alzheimer Society of British Columbia
#300, 828 West 8th Ave., Vancouver BC V5Z 1E1
Tel: 604-681-6530; *Fax:* 604-669-6907
Toll-Free: 800-667-3742
info@alzheimerbc.org
www.alzheimerbc.org
Social Media: www.youtube.com/AlzheimerBC
linkedin.com/company/alzheimer-society-of-b.c.
www.facebook.com/AlzheimerBC
twitter.com/AlzheimerBC
To alleviate the personal & social consequences of Alzheimer disease & related dementias; to promote public awareness & to search for the causes & the cures
Maria Howard, CEO

Alzheimer Society of New Brunswick / Société alzheimer du nouveau brunswick
PO Box 1553, Stn. A, Fredericton NB E3B 5G2
Tel: 506-459-4280; *Fax:* 506-452-0313
Toll-Free: 800-664-8411
info@alzheimernb.ca
www.alzheimernb.ca
Social Media:
www.facebook.com/127071537361985
twitter.com/AlzheimerNB
To alleviate the personal & social consequences of Alzheimer disease; to promote the search for a cause & cure

Alzheimer Society of Newfoundland & Labrador
#107, 835 Topsail Rd., Mount Pearl NL A1N 3J6
Tel: 709-576-0608; *Fax:* 709-576-0798
Toll-Free: 877-776-0608
alzheimersociety@nf.aibn.com
www.alzheimernl.org
Social Media:
www.facebook.com/ASNL2
twitter.com/asnl2
To support the search for the cause & cure of Alzheimer Disease; To raise public awareness of the personal & social impact of the disease; To promote the provision of support to families & caregivers in Newfoundland
Shirley Lucas, Executive Director

Alzheimer Society of Nova Scotia
#112, 2719 Gladstone St., Halifax NS B3K 4W6
Tel: 902-422-7961; *Fax:* 902-422-7971
Toll-Free: 800-611-6345
alzheimer@asns.ca
www.alzheimer.ca/ns
Social Media: www.youtube.com/user/alzheimerns
www.facebook.com/alzheimersocietyns
twitter.com/alzheimerns
To enhance the quality of life of people with Alzheimer disease through providing & promoting public education & family support; to engage in advocacy on behalf of people with Alzheimer disease & their families; to promote research at the provincial & national levels
Lloyd O. Brown, Executive Director
Chris Wilson, President

Alzheimer Society of PEI
166 Fitzroy St., Charlottetown PE C1A 1S1
Tel: 902-628-2257; *Fax:* 902-368-2715
Toll-Free: 866-628-2257
society@alzpei.ca
www.alzheimer.ca/pei
Social Media: www.youtube.com/user/Alzpei
www.facebook.com/AlzheimerPEI
twitter.com/AlzheimerPEI
To support & assist Islanders affected by Alzheimer Disease; To raise the level of awareness & educate the public at large about the disease
Corrine Hendricken-Eldershaw, CEO

Alzheimer Society Of Saskatchewan Inc. (ASOS)
#301, 2550 - 12 Ave., Regina SK S4P 3X1
Tel: 306-949-4141; *Toll-Free:* 800-263-3367
info@alzheimer.sk.ca
www.alzheimer.sk.ca
Social Media: www.youtube.com/thealzheimersociety
www.facebook.com/217901721605861
twitter.com/AlzheimerSK
To alleviate the personal & social consequences of Alzheimer's disease & related disorders & to promote the search for a cause & a cure
Joanne Bracken, CEO

Alzheimer Society Ontario / Société Alzheimer Ontario
20 Eglinton Ave. West, 16th Fl., Toronto ON M4R 1K8
Tel: 416-967-5900; *Fax:* 416-967-3826
Toll-Free: 800-879-4226
staff@alzheimeront.org
www.alzheimer.ca/en/on
Social Media: www.youtube.com/alzheimersocietyont
www.facebook.com/AlzheimerSocietyofOntario
twitter.com/alzheimeront
To improve the quality of life for persons with Alzheimer disease & their families; to inform & educate the public & health care professionals about Alzheimer disease; to coordinate a chapter network & liaison in order to present a united voice to the Government of Ontario & other provincial groups on matters relating to legal concerns, health care, research, & community needs; to raise funds for research
Gale Carey, CEO
Rosemary Corbett, Chair

Alzheimer's Foundation for Caregiving in Canada, Inc. (AFCC) / Fondation d'Alzheimer pour les proches aidants au Canada inc. (FAPAC)
#600, 95 rue Mural, Toronto ON L4B 3G2
Tel: 905-882-3141; *Fax:* 905-882-3132
Toll-Free: 877-321-2594
info@alzfdn.ca
www.alzfdn.ca
To provide optimal care & services to individuals confronting dementia & to their caregivers & families - through member organizations dedicated to improving quality of life

Aplastic Anemia & Myelodysplasia Association of Canada (AAMAC)
#321, 11181 Yonge St., Richmond Hill ON L4S 1L2
Tel: 905-780-0698; *Fax:* 905-780-1648
Toll-Free: 888-840-0039
info@aamac.ca
www.aamac.ca
To disseminate information concerning the disease; To form a nation-wide support network for patients, families & medical professionals; To support Canadian Blood Services & their programs; To raise funds for research
Pam Wishart, President
Michelle Joseph, Secretary
Janice Cook, Coordinator, British Columbia
Bob Ross, Coordinator, Ontario

Arthritis Society / Société de l'arthrite
#1700, 393 University Ave., Toronto ON M5G 1E6
Tel: 416-979-7228; *Fax:* 416-979-8366
Toll-Free: 800-321-1433
info@arthritis.ca
www.arthritis.ca
Social Media:
www.facebook.com/arthritissociety
twitter.com/arthritissoc
To fund & promote arthritis research, programs & patient care. There are division offices in each province & nearly 1,000 community branches throughout Canada
Drew McArthur, Chair
Janet Yale, President & CEO
Derek Rodrigues, CFO

Association d'orthopédie du Québec
Tour de L'Est, CP 216, Succ. Desjardins, 2, Complexe Desjardins, 30e étage, Montréal QC H5B 1G8
Tél: 514-844-0803; *Téléc:* 514-844-6786
aoq@fmsq.org
www.orthoquebec.ca
Valoriser le statut professionnel de ses membres; promouvoir leurs intérêts économiques; contribuer au développement de la chirurgie orthopédique et de la traumatologie par le biais d'activités de formation médicale continue
Louis Bellemare, Président
Louise Leclaire, Secrétariat

Association d'oto-rhino-laryngologie et de chirurgie cervico-faciale du Québec
#3000, 2, Complexe Desjardins, Montréal QC H5B 1G8
Tél: 514-350-5125; *Téléc:* 514-350-5165
assorl@fmsq.org
www.orlquebec.org
Valoriser le statut professionnel de ses membres, promouvoir leurs intérêts scientifiques, économiques et professionnels, et contribuer au développement de l'oto-rhino-laryngologie
Frédéric Hélie, Secrétaire
Yanick Larivée, Président

Association de neurochirurgie du Québec (ANCQ)
CP 216, Succ. Desjardins, #3000, 2, Complexe Desjardins, Montréal QC H5B 1G8
Tél: 514-350-5120; *Téléc:* 514-350-5100
ancq@fmsq.org
www.ancq.net
Pour représenter les médecins spécialistes et de promouvoir leurs intérêts
Alain Bouthillier, Président
David Mathieu, Secrétaire

L'Association de spina-bifida et d'hydrocéphalie du Québec (ASBHQ)
#303, 55, av Mont-Royal Ouest, Montréal QC H2T 2S6
Tél: 514-340-9019; *Ligne sans frais:* 800-567-1788
info@spina.qc.ca
www.spina.qc.ca
Média social: www.facebook.com/asbhq
twitter.com/ASBHQ
Promouvoir et défendre les droits, les intérêts et le bien-être des personnes ayant le spina-bifida et l'hydrocéphalie; sensibiliser le public à la nature du spina-bifida et de l'hydrocéphalie ainsi qu'aux besoins des personnes ayant ces malformations; favoriser et soutenir la recherche sur les causes, les nouveaux traitements et les techniques de prévention du spina-bifida et de l'hydrocéphalie
Marc Picard, Président

Association des Allergologues et Immunologues du Québec
CP 216, Succ. Desjardins, #3000, 2, Complexe Desjardins, Montréal QC H5B 1G8
Tél: 514-350-5101
aaiq@fmsq.org
www.allerg.qc.ca

Association des bénévoles du don de sang (ABDS) / Association of Blood Donation Volunteers (ABDV)
4045, boul Côte-Vertu, Montréal QC H4R 2W7
Tél: 514-832-5000; *Téléc:* 514-832-0872
Ligne sans frais: 888-666-4362
abdsdondesang@gmail.com
www.abdsdondesang.com
Média social: linkedin.com/in/abdsdondesang
www.facebook.com/ABDS-333369506845428
Soutenir le recrutement de nouveaux donneurs en partenariat avec Héma-Québec; Promouvoir le don de sang
Florentina Costache, Directrice des opérations

Association des cardiologues du Québec (ACQ)
CP 216, Succ. Desjardins, #3000, 2, Complexe Desjardins, Montréal QC H5B 1G8
Tél: 514-350-5106; *Téléc:* 514-350-5156
acq@fmsq.org
Gilles O'Hara, Président
Louise Girard, Directrice

Association des chiropraticiens du Québec
7960, boul Métropolitain Est, Montréal QC H1K 1A1
Tél: 514-355-0557; *Téléc:* 514-355-0070
Ligne sans frais: 866-292-4476
acq@chiropratique.com
www.chiropratique.com
Média social: www.youtube.com/user/AssoDesChirosQc
www.facebook.com/AssoDesChirosQc
twitter.com/AssoChiroQc
Défendre les intérêts professionnels, sociaux et économiques de ses membres

Association des conseils des médecins, dentistes et pharmaciens du Québec (ACMDP) / Association of Councils of Physicians, Dentists & Pharmacists of Québec
#212, 560, boul Henri-Bourassa ouest, Montréal QC H3L 1P4
Tél: 514-858-5885; *Téléc:* 514-858-6767
acmdp@acmdp.qc.ca
www.acmdp.qc.ca
Offrir l'information, la motivation, et la formation médico-administrative nécessaire aux Conseils des médecins, dentistes, et pharmaciens membres afin qu'ils accomplissent adéquatement leurs tâches
Annick Lavoie, Directrice générale

Association des dermatologistes du Québec (ADQ) / Association of Dermatologists of Québec
CP 216, Succ. Desjardins, #3000, 2, Complexe Desjardins, Montréal QC H5B 1G8
Tél: 514-350-5111; *Téléc:* 514-350-5161
www.adq.org
Syndicat professionnel: assure la défense des intérêts économiques, professionnels et scientifiques de ses membres
Dominique Hanna, Présidente

Association des gastro-entérologues du Québec (AGEQ)
CP 216, Succ. Desjardins, 2, Complexe Desjardins, Montréal QC H5B 1G8
Tél: 514-350-5112; *Téléc:* 514-350-5146
www.ageq.qc.ca
D'informer et de formations aux médecins de première ligne, aux patients souffrant de pathologies gastro-intestinales et aux autres médecins intéressés par la gastro-entérologie; de créer des liens avec la communauté médicale internationale.
Josée Parent, Président

Association des médecins biochimistes du Québec (AMBQ)
CP 216, Succ. Desjardins, #3000, 2, Complexe Desjardins, Montréal QC H5B 1G8
Tél: 514-350-5105
ambq@fmsq.org
www.ambq.med.usherbrooke.ca
Promouvoir l'utilisation optimale des tests de laboratoire au Québec en offrant, au professionnel de la santé et au patient, les meilleurs services de diagnostic et de dépistage de maladies grâce à des techniques biochimiques et immunologiques
Jean Dubé, Président

Association des médecins endocrinologues du Québec
CP 216, Succ. Desjardins, #3000, 2, Complexe Desjardins, Montréal QC H5B 1G8
Tél: 514-350-5135; *Téléc:* 514-350-5049
Ligne sans frais: 800-561-0703
ameq@fmsq.org
www.ameq.qc.ca
L'Association est un porte-parole des endocrinologues; elle favorise les intérêts scientifiques de ses membres et organise plusieurs réunions afin de permettre une formation médicale continue des endocrinologues

Association des médecins généticiens du Québec
#300, 2, Complexe Desjardins, Montréal QC H5B 1G8
Tél: 514-350-5141; *Téléc:* 514-350-5116
Bruno Maranda, M.D., Présidente
Sandrine Guillot, Directrice

Association des médecins gériatres du Québec
CP 216, Succ. Desjardins, #3000, 2, Complexe Desjardins, Montréal QC H5B 1G8
Tél: 514-350-5145
info@amgq.ca
www.amgq.ca
Maurice St-Laurent, Président

Association des médecins hématologistes-oncologistes du Québec (AMHOQ)
CP 216, Succ. Desjardins, 2, Complexe Desjardins, Montréal QC H5B 1G8
Tél: 514-350-5121; *Téléc:* 514-350-5126
info@amhoq.org
amhoq.org
Média social: www.facebook.com/311775155609901
Daniel Bélanger, Président
Nathalie Latendresse, Directrice administrative

Association des médecins microbiologistes-infectiologues du Québec (AMMIQ)
#3000, 2, Complexe Desjardins, Montréal QC H5B 1G8
Tél: 514-350-5104; *Téléc:* 514-350-5144
info@ammiq.org
www.ammiq.org
L'Association regroupe des médecins (de laboratoire et dans le diagnostic clinique) spécialisés dans l'épidémiologie, le traitement et la prévention des maladies infectieuses
Karl Weiss, Président

Association des médecins ophtalmologistes du Québec (AMOQ)
CP 216, Succ. Desjardins, 2, Complexe Desjardins, Montréal QC H5B 1G8
Tél: 514-350-5124; *Téléc:* 514-350-5174
amoq@fmsq.org
www.amoq.org
Promouvoir les intérêts professionnels et économiques de ses membres; se préoccuper du maintien de la compétence; susciter et appuier des activités scientifiques susceptibles de favoriser l'avancement de l'ophtalmologie; se préoccuper de l'accessibilité aux soins ophtalmologiques
Côme Fortin, Président

Association des médecins rhumatologues du Québec (AMRQ)
CP 216, Succ. Desjardins, Montréal QC H5B 1G8
Tél: 514-350-5136; *Téléc:* 514-350-5029
Ligne sans frais: 800-561-0703
info@rhumatologie.org
www.rhumatologie.org
La rhumatologie se consacre au diagnostic et au traitement des pathologies qui touchent les articulations, les os, les muscles et tendons et parfois tout organe dans le cadre de maladies systémiques. Ceci regroupe au-delà de 100 conditions pouvant aller de l'arthrite rhumatoïde au lupus érythémateux disséminé en passant par l'arthrose, les vasculites et l'ostéoporose.
Frédéric Morin, Président

Association des médecins spécialistes en médecine nucléaire du Québec (AMSMNQ)
CP 216, Succ. Desjardins, #3000, 2, Complexe Desjardins, Montréal QC H5B 1G8
Tél: 514-350-5133; *Téléc:* 514-350-5151
Ligne sans frais: 800-561-0703
amsmnq@fmsq.org
www.medecinenucleaire.com
Pour former ses membres et maintenir un haut niveau de professionnalisme
François Lamoureux, Président
Jean Guimond, Vice-président

Association des médecins spécialistes en santé communautaire du Québec (AMSSCQ)
#3000, 2, Complexe Desjardins, Montréal QC H5B 1G8
Tél: 514-350-5138; *Téléc:* 514-350-5151
amsscq@fmsq.org
www.amsscq.org
De promouvoir les intérêts professionnels et économiques de ses membres
Yv Bonnier Viger, Président
Michelle Laviolette, Directrice

Association des néphrologues du Québec
CP 216, Succ. Desjardins, #3000, 2, Complexe Desjardins, Montréal QC H5B 1G8
Tél: 514-350-5134; *Téléc:* 514-350-5151
nephrologie@fmsq.org
Robert Charbonneau, Président
Lillian Plasse, Directrice

Association des neurologues du Québec (ANQ)
CP 216, Succ. Desjardins, #3000, 2, Complexe Desjardins, Montréal QC H5B 1G8
Tél: 514-350-5122; *Téléc:* 514-350-5172
anq@fmsq.org
www.anq.qc.ca
Représenter des médecins spécialistes qui diagnostique et traite les maladies affectant le système nerveux central ainsi que le système nerveux périphérique
Ginette Guilbeault, Directrice
J. Marc Girard, Président
Anne Lortie, Secrétaire

Association des obstétriciens et gynécologues du Québec (AOGQ)
#3000, 2, Complexe Desjardins, Montréal QC H5B 1G8
Tél: 514-849-4969; *Téléc:* 514-849-5011
info@gynecoquebec.com
www.gynecoquebec.com
Promouvoir l'intérêt professionnel scientifique et économique de ses membres
Isabelle Girard, Présidente

Association des optométristes du Québec (AOQ) / Québec Optometric Association
#740, 1265, rue Berri, Montréal QC H2L 4X4
Tél: 514-288-6272; *Téléc:* 514-288-7071
info@aoqnet.qc.ca
www.aoqnet.qc.ca
Média social: www.facebook.com/109631962406806
De développer meilleures conditions de pratique économiques et professionnelles pour les optométristes du Québec
Maryse Nolin, Directeur général
Steven Carrier, Président

Association des pathologistes du Québec (APQ)
CP 216, Succ. Desjardins, #3000, 2, Complexe Desjardins, Montréal QC H5B 1G8
Tél: 514-350-5102; *Téléc:* 514-350-5152
Ligne sans frais: 800-561-0703
patho@fmsq.org
www.apq.qc.ca
Danielle Joncas, Directrice

Association des pédiatres du Québec
CP 216, Succ. Desjardins, #3000, 2, Complexe Desjardins, Montréal QC H5B 1G8
Tél: 514-350-5000; *Téléc:* 514-350-5100
Ligne sans frais: 800-561-0703
www.fmsq.org
Média social: www.youtube.com/user/LaFMSQ
www.facebook.com/laFMSQ
twitter.com/FMSQ
Gaétan Barrette, Président

Association des pharmaciens des établissements de santé du Québec (APES)
#320, 4050, rue Molson, Montréal QC H1Y 3N1
Tél: 514-286-0776; *Téléc:* 514-286-1081
info@apesquebec.org
www.apesquebec.org
Linda Vaillant, Directrice générale
France Boucher, Directrice générale adjointe

Association des physiatres du Québec (APQ)
CP 216, Succ. Desjardins, #3000, 2, Complexe Desjardins, Montréal QC H5B 1G8
Tél: 514-350-5119; *Téléc:* 514-350-5147
apq@fmsq.org
www.fmsq.org
Pour ouvrer à la prévention, au diagnostic et au traitement médical des douleurs et des troubles de l'appareil locomoteur (la colonne vertébrale, les os, les muscles, les tendons, les articulations, les vaisseaux et le cerveau)

Claude Bouthillier, Président

Association des pneumologues de la province de Québec (APPQ)
#3000, 2, Complexe Desjardins, Montréal QC H5B 1G8
Tél: 514-350-5117; *Téléc:* 514-350-5153
appq@fmsq.org
www.fmsq.org
Promouvoir les intérêts professionnels et économiques de ses membres; se préoccuper du maintien de leur compétence; se prononcer sur les problématiques de la pneumologie dans les meilleurs intérêts de la population
Dionne Raymonde, Directrice
Alain Beaupré, Président

Association des radiologistes du Québec
CP 216, Succ. Desjardins, Montréal QC H5B 1G8
Tél: 514-350-5129; *Téléc:* 514-350-5179
bureau@arq.qc.ca
www.arq.qc.ca
Média social: www.facebook.com/496349387128403
twitter.com/SCFRQuebec
Regrouper les médecins spécialisés en radiologie; défendre leurs intérêts et promouvoir leur spécialité
André Constantin, Président

Association des radio-oncologues du Québec (AROQ)
CP 216, Succ. Desjardins, #3000, 2, Complexe Desjardins, Montréal QC H5B 1G8
Tél: 514-350-5130; *Téléc:* 514-350-5126
aroq@fmsq.org
www.aroq.ca
De fournir un forum où ses membres peuvent échanger des idées afin d'aider à améliorer leurs méthodes de traitement
Khalil Sultanem, Président

Association des sexologues du Québec (ASQ)
#709, 1100, boul Crémazie Est, Montréal QC H2P 2X2
Tél: 514-270-9289; *Téléc:* 514-270-6351
info@associationdessexologues.com
www.associationdessexologues.com
Susciter auprès du public une meilleure connaissance de la sexologie et du rôle du sexologue, en favorisant et en maintenant les normes scientifiques et professionnelles les plus élevées dans l'exercice de la sexologie et dans la formation des sexologues

Association des spécialistes en chirurgie plastique et esthétique du Québec (ASCPEQ)
CP 216, Succ. Desjardins, 2, Complexe Desjardins, Montréal QC H5B 1G8
Tél: 514-350-5109; *Téléc:* 514-350-5246
ascpeq@fmsq.org
www.ascpeq.org
L'Association entend se consacrer essentiellement au développement continu de l'art et de la science de la chirurgie plastique et esthétique, entre autres par la diffusion de renseignements pertinents auprès du public, par la promotion d'une relation médecin-patient fondée sur la communication, la compréhension et le respect mutuel, ainsi que par une contribution active aux programmes d'éducation et de formation continue et par une participation critique aux débats relatifs au rôle et à la place des professionnels de la santé au sein de la société québécoise
Éric Bensimon, Président

Association des spécialistes en médecine d'urgence du Québec
Tour de l'Est, #3000, 2, Complexe Desjardins, Montréal QC H5B 1G8
Tél: 514-350-5115; *Téléc:* 514-350-5116
www.asmuq.org
François Dufresne, Président

Association des spécialistes en médecine interne du Québec
Tour Est, 2, Complexe Desjardins, 30e étage, Montréal QC H5B 1G8
Tél: 514-350-5118; *Téléc:* 514-350-5168
asmiq.org
Mario Dallaire, Président

Association des urologues du Québec (AUQ) / Quebec Urological Association (QUA)
Tour de l'est, 2, Complexe Desjardins, 32e étage, Montréal QC H5B 1G8
Tél: 514-350-5131; *Téléc:* 514-350-5181
info@auq.org
www.auq.org
Serge Carrier, Président
Steven Lapointe, Secrétaire

Association médicale du Québec (AMQ) / Québec Medical Association (QMA)
#3200, 380, rue Saint-Antoine Ouest, Montréal QC H2Y 3X7
Tél: 514-866-0660; *Téléc:* 514-866-0670
Ligne sans frais: 800-363-3932
admin@amq.ca
www.amq.ca
Média social:
www.facebook.com/Association.medicale.du.Quebec
twitter.com/amquebec
Rassembler et soutenir les médecins du Québec afin de garantir à la population québécoise des conditions et des soins de santé de qualité
Normand Laberge, Directeur général

Association of Local Public Health Agencies (ALPHA)
#1306, 2 Carlton St., Toronto ON M5G 1T6
Tel: 416-595-0006; *Fax:* 416-595-0030
info@alphaweb.org
www.alphaweb.org
To provide leadership in public health management to health units in Ontario; To assist local public health units in the provision of efficient & effective services
Linda Stewart, Executive Director
Gordon Fleming, Manager, Public Health Issues
Tannisha Lambert, Manager, Administrative & Association Services

Association of Medical Microbiology & Infectious Disease Canada (AMMI Canada) / Association pour la microbiologie médicale et l'infectiologie Canada
192 Bank St., Ottawa ON K2P 1W8
Tel: 613-260-3233; *Fax:* 613-260-3235
communications@ammi.ca
www.ammi.ca
To represent the broad interests of researchers & physicians who specialize in the fields of infectious diseases & medical microbiology in Canada; To contribute to the health of people at risk of, or affected by, infectious diseases; To promote & facilitate research; To develop policies for the prevention, diagnosis, & management of infectious diseases
Riccarda Galioto, Chief Operating Officer
Paul Glover, Coordinator, Meetings & Membership
Tamara Nahal, Coordinator, Communications

Association pour la santé publique du Québec (ASPQ) / Québec Public Health Association
#102, 4529, rue Clark, Montréal QC H2T 2T3
Tél: 514-528-5811; *Téléc:* 514-528-5590
info@aspq.org
www.aspq.org
Média social:
fr-ca.facebook.com/AssociationPourLaSantePubliqueDuQuebecaspq
twitter.com/ASPQuebec
Favoriser un regard critique sur les enjeux de santé publique au Québec en constituant un regroupement volontaire, autonome, multidisciplinaire et multisectoriel de personnes et d'organisations provenant des milieux tant institutionnels et professionnels que communautaires. L'Association constitue un forum qui offre un espace à ses membres pour développer des prises de position communes ou concertées, appuyer des politiques favorables à la santé et au bien-être et développer des coalitions et des projets en collaboration avec d'autres partenaires de santé publique ou du milieu.
Lucie Granger, Directrice Générale
Lilianne Bertrand, Présidente

Association Québécoise de chirurgie
CP 216, Succ. Desjardins, #3000, 2, Complexe Desjardins, Montréal QC H5B 1G8
Tél: 514-350-5107; *Téléc:* 514-350-5157
info@chirurgiequebec.ca
www.chirurgiequebec.ca
Média social: www.facebook.com/DPCAQC
twitter.com/AQCChirurgieQub
Objectifs sont la protection et défense des intérêts professionnels collectifs des chirurgiens et l'enseignement chirurgical continu
Mario Viens, Président
Chantale Jubinville, Directrice

Association québécoise de l'épilepsie
#204, 1650, boul de Maisonneuve Ouest, Montréal QC H3H 2P3
Tél: 514-875-5595; *Téléc:* 514-875-6734
aqe@cooptel.qc.ca
www.associationquebecoiseepilepsie.com
Veiller au mieux-être des personnes épileptiques et à leurs familles; promouvoir les droits des personnes épileptiques; sensibiliser le public à l'épilepsie; promouvoir l'intégration scolaire et au travail

Association québécoise des infirmières et infirmiers en urologie (AQIIU)
342, rue Morin, Laval QC H7L 4V2
Tél: 450-625-0214
infoaqiiu@gmail.com
www.aqiiu.com
Annie Taillefer, Présidente

Asthma Society of Canada (ASC) / Société canadienne de l'asthme
#401, 124 Merton St., Toronto ON M4S 2Z2
Tel: 416-787-4050; *Fax:* 416-787-5807
Toll-Free: 866-787-4050
info@asthma.ca
www.asthma.ca
Social Media:
www.facebook.com/AsthmaSocietyofCanada
twitter.com/AsthmaSociety
To optimize the health of people with asthma through education and asthma awareness.
Robert Oliphant, President & CEO
Noah Farber, Director, Communications & Government Relations

Autism Northwest Territories
4904 Matonabee St., Yellowknife NT X1A 1X8
Tel: 867-920-4206
autism.nwt@hotmail.com
Lynn Elkin, Contact

Autism Nova Scotia (ANS)
5945 Spring Garden Rd., Halifax NS B3H 1Y4
Tel: 902-446-4995; *Fax:* 902-446-4997
Toll-Free: 877-544-4495
info@autismns.ca
www.autismnovascotia.ca
Social Media:
www.facebook.com/AutismNovaScotia
twitter.com/autismns
To advocate for, educate the public about, & provide support to, persons with autism/pervasive developmental disorders & their families

Autism Ontario
#004, 1179 King St. West, Toronto ON M6K 3C5
Tel: 416-246-9592; *Fax:* 416-246-9417
Toll-Free: 800-472-7789
mail@autismontario.com
www.autismontario.com
Social Media:
www.facebook.com/autismontarioprovincial
twitter.com/AutismONT
To ensure that each individual with autism spectrum disorders is provided the means to achieve quality of life as a respected member of society
Marg Spuelstra, Executive Director

Autism Society Alberta (ASA)
#101, 11720 Kingsway Ave., Edmonton AB T5G 0X5
Tel: 780-453-3971; *Fax:* 780-447-4948
autism@autismedmonton.org
www.autismedmonton.org
Social Media:
www.facebook.com/autismedmonton
twitter.com/AutismEdmonton
To improve the understanding of autism throughout Alberta by the dissemination of information to parents, health care workers, educators, government, private agencies & the public
Shane Lynch, President
Jenni Schwetz, Secretary

Autism Society Canada (ASC) / Société canadienne d'autisme
PO Box 22017, 1670 Heron Rd., Ottawa ON K1V 0W2
Tel: 613-789-8943; *Toll-Free:* 866-476-8440
info@autismsocietycanada.ca
www.autismsocietycanada.ca
To provide support on a national basis to people affected by autism & related conditions through the collective efforts of Canadian provincial & territorial autism societies; to provide information & general referrals to the public regarding autism & related conditions; to promote public awareness of autism & related conditions; to encourage research in fields related or relevant to autism & related conditions; to communicate with government, agencies, & other organizations on behalf of persons affected by autism & related conditions; to promote actions to ensure people with autism & related conditions live in an environment that supports their well-being & enables them to reach their full potential; to promote & encourage the convening of conferences focused on autism & related conditions
Michael Lewis, President
Richard Burelle, Executive Director

Autism Society Manitoba
825 Sherbrook St., 2nd Fl., Winnipeg MB R3A 1M5
Tel: 204-783-9563; *Fax:* 204-975-3027
Toll-Free: 888-444-9563
info@autismmanitoba.com
www.autismmanitoba.com
Social Media:
www.facebook.com/AutismSocietyOfManitoba
twitter.com/manitobaautism
To promote the quality of life for people with Pervasive Developmental Disorder/Autism & their families; to promote full inclusion, dignity & development of personal skills & abilities for our members

Autism Society Newfoundland & Labrador (ASNL)
PO Box 14078, St. John's NL A1B 4G8
Tel: 709-722-2803; *Fax:* 709-722-4926
info@autism.nf.net
www.autism.nf.net
Social Media:
twitter.com/AutismSocietyNL
To promote the diagnosis, treatment, education & integration into the community of all autistic persons; to provide information about autism; to promote research; to promote integrated care for autistic persons; to encourage the formation of parent support groups around the province
Scott Crocker, Executive Director

Autism Society of British Columbia
#303, 3701 East Hastings St., Burnaby BC V5C 2H6
Tel: 604-434-0880; *Fax:* 604-434-0801
Toll-Free: 888-437-0880
info@autismbc.ca
www.autismbc.ca
Social Media:
www.facebook.com/autismbc
twitter.com/AutismSocietyBC
To promote awareness of autism & the needs of families with a child or adult with autism; to provide advocacy, resources, & referrals to families of people with autism in BC
Michael Lewis, President

Autism Society of PEI
PO Box 3243, Charlottetown PE C1A 8W5
Tel: 902-566-4844; *Toll-Free:* 888-360-8681
www.autismsociety.pe.ca
Social Media:
www.facebook.com/autismsocietypei
twitter.com/AutismSocietyPE
To provide austim resources to families in PEI
Nathalie Walsh, Executive Director

Autism Treatment Services of Canada (ATSC) / Association canadienne pour l'obtention des services aux personnes autistiques
404 - 94 Ave. SE, Calgary AB T2J 0E8
Tel: 403-253-2291; *Fax:* 403-253-6974
Toll-Free: 888-301-2872
autismtreatment@sta-ab.com
www.autism.ca
To ensure that a comprehensive range of services exists across Canada to meet the needs of individuals with autism & their families, & that autistic people are given the opportunity to achieve maximum independence & productivity within the community.
Peter Johnson, Chair
Dave Mikkelsen, Executive Director

Autism Yukon
503B Steele St., Whitehorse YT Y1A 2E1
Tel: 867-667-6406; *Fax:* 867-667-6408
executive@autismyukon.org
www.autismyukon.org
Social Media:
www.facebook.com/162869033819118

Barth Syndrome Foundation of Canada
#115, 162 Guelph St., Georgetown ON L7G 5X7
Tel: 905-873-2391; *Fax:* 905-877-5952
Toll-Free: 888-732-9458
www.barthsyndrome.ca
To find research grants into the cause, treatments & cure for Barth Syndrome; to assist Canadian families & physicians dealing with the disease.
Lynn Elwood, President

Bladder Cancer Canada (BCC) / Cancer de la vessie Canada
#1000, 4936 Yonge St., Toronto ON M2N 6S3
Toll-Free: 866-674-8889
info@bladdercancercanada.org
www.bladdercancercanada.org
Social Media: www.youtube.com/user/BladderCancerCA
linkedin.com/company/2599127?trk=NUS_CMPY_TWIT
www.facebook.com/BladderCancerCanada
twitter.com/BladderCancerCA
Bladder Cancer Canada aims to improve patient support by having a patient to patient support system in place; be a source of information about available treatment options and create greater awareness of bladder cancer.
David Guttman, CHair
Tammy Udall, Executive Director

Brain Tumour Foundation of Canada (BTFC) / La Fondation canadienne sur les tumeurs cérébrales
#301, 620 Colborne St., London ON N6B 3R9
Tel: 519-642-7755; *Fax:* 519-642-7192
Toll-Free: 800-265-5106
www.braintumour.ca
Social Media: www.youtube.com/user/BrainTumourFdn
www.facebook.com/BrainTumourFoundationofCanada
twitter.com/BrainTumourFdn
To find a cure for brain tumors & to improve the quality of life for those affected; To fund brain tumor research; to provide patient & family support services; To educate the public
Carl Cadogan, CEO

Breast Cancer Action (BCA) / Sensibilisation au cancer du sein
#301, 1390 Prince of Wales Dr., Ottawa ON K2C 3N6
Tel: 613-736-5921; *Fax:* 613-736-8422
info@bcaott.ca
www.bcaott.ca
Social Media:
www.facebook.com/106397202723177
twitter.com/bcaott
To advocate establishment of a national resource office, directed by women affected by breast cancer, to serve as clearinghouse for information about treatment, legislative action, access to treatments & support services; to advocate for a designated centre for excellence to accelerate research; to advocate greater emphasis on developing earlier detection; to promote increased survivor participation in cancer care planning & policy making; to promote better education of family physicians & women in early detection & follow-up
Karen Graszat, Executive Director

Breast Cancer Society of Canada (BCSC) / Société du cancer du sein du Canada
420 East St. North, Sarnia ON N7T 6Y5
Tel: 519-336-0746; *Fax:* 519-336-5725
Toll-Free: 800-567-8767
bcsc@bcsc.ca
www.bcsc.ca
Social Media: www.youtube.com/user/BreastCancerSociety
linkedin.com/company/2260739
www.facebook.com/breastcancersocietyofcanada
twitter.com/bcsctweet
To support research into the prevention, detection, & treatment of breast cancer
Kimberly Carlson, Chief Executive Officer

The British Columbia Association of Optometrists (BCAO)
#610, 2525 Willow St., Vancouver BC V5Z 3N8
Tel: 604-737-9907; *Fax:* 604-737-9967
Toll-Free: 888-393-2226
info@optometrists.bc.ca
www.optometrists.bc.ca
Social Media: www.youtube.com/BCDoctorsofOptometry
www.facebook.com/AskaDoctorofOptometry
To maintain standards; to represent membership to government & other health care professions; to raise public levels of awareness about optometry, good vision & eye care.
Cheryl Williams, CEO
Sherman Tung, President

British Columbia Cancer Foundation (BCCF)
#150, 686 West Broadway, Vancouver BC V5Z 1G1
Tel: 604-877-6040; *Fax:* 604-877-6161
Toll-Free: 888-906-2873
bccfinfo@bccancer.bc.ca
www.bccancerfoundation.com
Social Media:
www.facebook.com/BCCancerFoundation
twitter.com/bccancer
To reduce the incidence of cancer, reduce the mortality rate from cancer, & improve the quality of life for those living with cancer, through the acquisition, development, & stewardship of resources
Douglas Nelson, President & Chief Executive Officer
Luigi (Lou) Del Gobbo, Chief Financial Officer & Vice-President
Patsy Worrall, Vice-President, Marketing & Communications
Cindy Dopson, MBA, CHRP, Director, Human Resources

British Columbia Centre for Ability Association (BCCFA)
2805 Kingsway, Vancouver BC V5R 5H9
Tel: 604-451-5511; *Fax:* 604-451-5651
info@bc-cfa.org
bc-cfa.org
Social Media:
www.facebook.com/sharer.php
twitter.com/bccfa
To provide community-based services that enhance the quality of life for children, youth & adults with disabilities & their families in ways that facilitate & build competencies & foster inclusion in all aspects of life
Jennifer Baumbusch, President

British Columbia Chiropractic Association (BCCA)
#125, 3751 Shell Rd., Richmond BC V6X 2W2
Tel: 604-270-1332; *Fax:* 604-278-0093
Toll-Free: 866-256-1474
info@bcchiro.com
www.bcchiro.com
Social Media: www.youtube.com/bcchiropractic
twitter.com/bcchiro
To represent BC chiropractors in matters relating to health policy, public relations & health authorities
Jay Robinson, President

British Columbia Lung Association (BCLA)
2675 Oak St., Vancouver BC V6H 2K2
Tel: 604-731-5864; *Fax:* 604-731-5810
Toll-Free: 800-665-5864
info@bc.lung.ca
www.bc.lung.ca
Social Media:
www.facebook.com/home.php?#!/BCLungAssociation
To support lung health research, education, prevention, & advocacy; To help people manage respiratory diseases, including asthma, COPD (chronic bronchitis and emphysema), lung cancer, sleep apnea, & tuberculosis
Scott McDonald, Executive Director
Kelly Ablog-Morrant, Director, Health Education & Program Services
Chris Lam, Manager, Development
Katrina van Bylandt, Manager, Communications
Debora Wong, Manager, Finance & Administration
Marissa McFadyen, Coordinator, Specia Events

British Columbia Lupus Society (BCLS)
#210, 888 West 8th Ave., Vancouver BC V5Z 3Y1
Tel: 604-714-5564; *Toll-Free:* 866-585-8787
info@bclupus.org
www.bclupus.org
To provide education & support to Lupus patients & their friends & families; to increase public awareness of lupus
Josie Bradley, President

British Columbia Naturopathic Association (BCNA)
2238 Pine St., Vancouver BC V6J 5G4
Tel: 604-736-6646; *Fax:* 604-736-6048
Toll-Free: 800-277-1128
bcna@bcna.ca
www.bcna.ca
Social Media: www.youtube.com/user/BCNaturopathicAssoc
www.facebook.com/BCNaturopathicAssociation
twitter.com/BCnaturopath
To act on behalf of the naturopathic profession in British Columbia; To advance the welfare of members of the profession

British Columbia Transplant Society (BCTS)
West Tower, 555 West 12th Ave., 3rd Fl., Vancouver BC V5Z 3X7
Tel: 604-877-2240; *Fax:* 604-877-2111
Toll-Free: 800-663-6189
BCTS_Webmaster@bcts.hnet.bc.ca
www.transplant.bc.ca
Social Media:
www.facebook.com/BCTransplant
twitter.com/bc_transplant
To lead & coordinate all activities related to organ transplantation & donation, ensuring high standards of quality & efficient management.

Calgary Health Trust
#800, 11012 Macleod Trail SE, Calgary AB T2J 6A5
Tel: 403-943-0615; *Fax:* 403-943-0628
fundraising@calgaryhealthtrust.ca
www.calgaryhealthtrust.ca
Social Media: www.youtube.com/user/YYCHealthTrust
linkedin.com/company/calgary-health-trust
www.facebook.com/YYCHealthTrust
twitter.com/YYCHealthTrust
To receive & distribute philanthropic health care gifts & funds across Calgary; To work closely with Alberta Health Services to identify key priorities for allocation of philanthropic support; To enhance the development of health care, patient care, technology, & services at medical centres across Calgary
Jill Olynyk, Chief Executive Officer
Susan Cuerrier, Chief Financial Officer

Canada Health Infoway / Inforoute Santé du Canada
#1200, 1000, rue Sherbrooke ouest, Montréal QC H3A 3G4
Tel: 514-868-0550; *Fax:* 514-868-1120
Toll-Free: 866-868-0550
info@infoway-inforoute.ca
www.infoway-inforoute.ca
Social Media: www.youtube.com/user/InfowayInforoute
linkedin.com/company/canada-health-infoway
www.facebook.com/CanadaHealthInfoway
twitter.com/infoway
To accelerate the development of compatible electronic health information systems, which provide healthcare professionals with rapid access to complete & accurate patient information, enabling better decisions about diagnosis & treatment.
Richard C. Alvarez, President & CEO

Canadian Agency for Drugs & Technologies in Health (CADTH) / Agence canadienne des médicaments et des technologies de la santé (ACMTS)
#600, 865 Carling Ave., Ottawa ON K1S 5S8
Tel: 613-226-2553; *Fax:* 613-226-5392
Toll-Free: 866-988-1444
requests@cadth.ca
www.cadth.ca
Social Media: www.youtube.com/user/CADTHACMTS
linkedin.com/company/canadian-agency-for-drugs-and-technologies-in
twitter.com/CADTH_ACMTS
To offer evidence-based information & impartial advice to health care decision makers about the effectiveness of drugs & other health technologies
Brian O'Rourke, President & CEO

Canadian Alliance of Physiotherapy Regulators / Alliance canadienne des organismes de réglementation de la physiothérapie
#501, 1243 Islington Ave., Toronto ON M8X 1Y9
Tel: 416-234-8800; *Fax:* 416-234-8820
email@alliancept.org
www.alliancept.org
To facilitate the sharing of information & build consensus on national regulatory issues in order to assist member regulators in fulfilling their mandate of protecting the public interest
Katya Duvalko, Chief Executive Officer

Canadian Anesthesiologists' Society (CAS) / Société canadienne des anesthésiologistes (SCA)
#208, 1 Eglinton Ave. East, Toronto ON M4P 3A1
Tel: 416-480-0320; *Fax:* 416-480-0602
anesthesia@cas.ca
www.cas.ca
Social Media:
twitter.com/CASUpdate
To advance the medical practice of anesthesia throughout Canada
Susan O'Leary, President
Douglas DuVal, Vice-President
Stanley Mandarich, Executive Director
Salvatore Spadafora, Secretary
François Gobeil, Treasurer

Canadian Association for Clinical Microbiology & Infectious Diseases (CACMID) / Association canadienne de microbiologie clinique et des maladies contagieuses
c/o National Microbiology Laboratory, 1015 Arlington St., Winnipeg MB R3E 3R2
Fax: 204-789-2097
www.cacmid.ca
Social Media:
www.facebook.com/CACMID
twitter.com/cacmid
To enhance the cooperation of professionals specializing in clinical microbiology & infectious disease; To act as the voice for

clinical microbiology & infectious disease professionals; To develop standards in the field of clinical microbiology
Jeff Fuller, President
Matthew W. Gilmour, Secretary-Treasurer

Canadian Association for Health Services & Policy Research (CAHSPR) / Association canadienne pour la recherche sur les services et les politiques de la santé (ACRSPS)
292 Somerset St. West, Ottawa ON K2P 0J6
Tel: 613-288-9239; *Fax:* 613-599-7805
info@cahspr.ca
www.cahspr.ca
Social Media: www.youtube.com/CAHSPR
www.facebook.com/CAHSPR
twitter.com/CAHSPR
To provide a multidisciplinary association fostering and supporting linkages between researchers and decision makers; knowledge translation and exchange; education and training; and advocacy for research and its more effective use in planning, practice and policy-making.
Steve Morgan, President
Adalsteinn (Steini) Brown, President-Elect

The Canadian Association for HIV Research (CAHR) / L'Association Canadienne de recherche sur le HIV (ACRV)
#744, 1 Rideau St., Ottawa ON K1N 8S7
Tel: 613-241-5785; *Fax:* 613-670-5701
info@cahr-acrv.ca
www.cahr-acrv.ca
Social Media:
www.facebook.com/CanadianAssociationforHIVResearch
twitter.com/CAHR_ACRV
Focuses on HIV/AIDS research & education
Robert Hogg, President
Carol Strike, Secretary
Curtis Cooper, Treasurer
Andrew Matejcic, Executive Director
Shelley Mineault, Project Coordinator
Erin Love, Project Coordinator

Canadian Association for Neuroscience (CAN)
can-acn.org
To promote communication amongst Canadian neuroscientists & encourage research related to the nervous system; To educate about current neuroscience research

Canadian Association of Cardio-Pulmonary Technologists (CACPT)
PO Box 848, Stn. A, Toronto ON M5W 1G3
contactus@cacpt.ca
www.cacpt.ca
To establish maintain high standards for Registered Cardio-Pulmonary Technologists
Glenda Ryan, President

Canadian Association of Centres for the Management of Hereditary Metabolic Diseases
c/o London Health Sciences Centre, 800 Commissioners Rd. East, London ON N6C 2V5
Tel: 519-685-8140
www.garrod.ca
To coordinate of the management of inherited metabolic disorders; to provide a forum for the exchange of information & develops guidelines for the investigation & treatment of the diseases.
Chitra Prasad, Chair
Pierre Allard, Secretary-Treasurer

Canadian Association of Child Neurology (CACN) / L'Association canadienne de neurologie pédiatrique (ACNP)
#709, 7015 Macleod Trail SW, Calgary AB T2H 2K6
Tel: 403-229-9544; *Fax:* 403-229-1661
www.cnsfederation.org
To advance knowledge about the development of the nervous system from conception, as well as the diseases of the nervous system in children; To improve treatment of young people with neurological handicaps

Canadian Association of Emergency Physicians (CAEP) / Association canadienne des médecins d'urgence (ACMU)
#808, 180 Elgin St., Ottawa ON K2P 2K3
Tel: 613-523-3343; *Fax:* 613-523-0190
Toll-Free: 800-463-1158
admin@caep.ca
www.caep.ca
Social Media:
ca.linkedin.com/pub/canadian-assoc-of-emergency-physicians/2 2/b06/4a5
www.facebook.com/275451855826447
twitter.com/CAEP_Docs
To act as the national voice of emergency medicine; To empower physicians to provide excellent emergency care, through leadership, continuing education, & advocacy
Vera Klein, Executive Director
Christina Bova, Manager, Member Services & CTAS
Lee Arbon, Manager, Communications & Marketing
Janice MacIsaac, Manager, Continuing Professional Development
Heather King, Manager, Finance
Jennifer Artz, PhD, Manager, Academic Section & Research

Canadian Association of Gastroenterology / Association canadienne de gastroentérologie
#224, 1540 Cornwall Rd., Oakville ON L6J 7W5
Tel: 905-829-2504; *Fax:* 905-829-0242
Toll-Free: 888-780-0007
general@cag-acg.org
www.cag-acg.org
To support & engage in the study of gastroenterology; to promote patient care, research, teaching and professional development in the field; to promote and maintain the highest ethical standards of practice.
Paul Sinclair, Executive Director

Canadian Association of General Surgeons (CAGS) / Association canadienne des chirurgiens généraux (ACCG)
PO Box 1428, Stn. B, Ottawa ON K1P 5R4
Tel: 613-882-6510
cags@cags-accg.ca
www.cags-accg.ca
Social Media:
www.facebook.com/220880261312881
twitter.com/CAGS_ACCG
To assist all general surgeons with continuing education; facilitate & promote surgical research; develop policies & new ideas in the areas of clinical care, education & research
Debrah Wirtzfeld, President
Jasmin Lidington, Executive Director

Canadian Association of Medical Biochemists (CAMB) / Association des médecins biochimistes du Canada (AMBC)
2083 Black Friars Rd., Ottawa ON K2A 3K6
Tel: 613-680-8526; *Fax:* 613-249-3557
camb.ambc@gmail.com
www.camb-ambc.ca
Andrew don Wauchope, President

Canadian Association of Medical Device Reprocessing (CAMDR)
147 Parkside Dr., Oak Bluff MB R4G 0A6
info@camdr.ca
www.camdr.ca
CAMDR seeks to address numerous issues including patient safety, infection prevention & control, technology assessments, vendor relations, organizational management, and education.
Abdool Karim, President

Canadian Association of Medical Oncologists (CAMO) / Association canadienne des oncologues médicaux (ACOM)
PO Box 35164, Stn. Westgate, Ottawa ON K1Z 1A2
Tel: 613-415-6033; *Fax:* 866-839-7501
camo@royalcollege.ca
www.cos.ca/camo
Christopher Lee, President
Alexi Campbell, Executive Director
Bruce Colwell, Secretary-Treasurer

Canadian Association of Medical Radiation Technologists (CAMRT) / Association canadienne des technologues en radiation médicale (ACTRM)
#1000, 85 Albert St., Ottawa ON K1P 6A4
Tel: 613-234-0012; *Fax:* 613-234-1097
Toll-Free: 800-463-9729
editorialoffice@camrt.ca
www.camrt.ca
To act as the certifying body for medical radiation technologists & therapists throughout Canada
Charles Shields, Chief Executive Officer
Michelle Charest, Director, Finance & Administration
Elaine Dever, Director, Education
Mark Given, Director, Professional Practice
Leacy O'Callaghan O'Brien, Director, Advocacy, Communications, & Events

The Canadian Association of Naturopathic Doctors (CAND) / Association canadienne des docteurs en naturopathie
#200, 20 Holly St., Toronto ON M2S 3B1
Tel: 416-496-8633; *Fax:* 416-496-8634
Toll-Free: 800-551-4381
www.cand.ca
Social Media:
www.facebook.com/NaturopathicDrs
twitter.com/naturopathicdrs
CAND is a not-for-profit professional organization that promotes naturopathic medicine to the public, insurance companies & corporations. CAND encourages professional, educational & networking activities among its members, & standardization of educational requirements for practitioners
Shawn O'Reilly, Executive Director
Alex McKenna, Marketing Director

Canadian Association of Neuropathologists (CANP) / Association canadienne de neuropathologistes
c/o Department of Pathology, Vancouver General Hospital, 855 West 12th Ave., Vancouver BC V5Z 1M9
Tel: 604-875-4111; *Fax:* 604-875-4988
canp.medical.org
To organize the annual scientific meeting; to promote the professional & educational objectives of neuropathologists.
Ian MacKenzie, President
Peter Gould, Secretary-Treasurer

Canadian Association of Nuclear Medicine (CANM) / Association canadienne de médecine nucléaire (ACMN)
PO Box 4383, Stn. E, Ottawa ON K1S 5B4
Tel: 613-882-5097
canm@canm-acmn.ca
www.canm-acmn.ca
To strive for excellence in the practice of diagnostic & therapeutic nuclear medicine; to promote the continued professional competence of nuclear medicine specialists; to establish guidelines of clinical practice; to encourage biomedical research
Andrew Ross, President
Francois Lamoureux, Vice-President
Glenn Ollenberger, Secretary-Treasurer

Canadian Association of Occupational Therapists (CAOT) / Association canadienne des ergothérapeutes (ACE)
#100, 34 Colonnade Rd., Ottawa ON K2E 7J6
Tel: 613-523-2268; *Fax:* 613-523-2552
Toll-Free: 800-434-2268
insurance@caot.ca
www.caot.ca
Social Media:
www.facebook.com/CAOT.ca
twitter.com/CAOT_ACE
To develop & promote the profession of occupational therapy in Canada & abroad; To assist occupational therapists achieve excellence in their professional practice by offering services, products, events, & networking opportunities
Janet M. Craik, Executive Director
Mike Brennan, Chief Operating Officer
Havelin Anand, Director, Government Affairs & Policy
Vicky Wang, Director, Finance

Canadian Association of Occupational Therapists - British Columbia (CAOT-BC)
PO Box 30042, RPO Parkgate Village, N., Vancouver BC V7H 2Y8
Fax: 613-523-2552
Toll-Free: 800-434-2268
www.caot.ca
To promote the profession of occupational therapy throughout the province & represent its members to regional health boards & government, health professional groups & the public; to foster the growth & development of the profession in BC; to provide a variety of services to its members including continuing education, reentry & participation in professional issues
Giovanna Boniface, Managing Director

Canadian Association of Optometrists (CAO) / Association canadienne des optométristes (ACO)
234 Argyle Ave., Ottawa ON K2P 1B9
Tel: 613-235-7924; *Fax:* 613-235-2098
Toll-Free: 888-263-4676
info@opto.ca
www.opto.ca
Social Media:
linkedin.com/company/canadian-association-of-optometrists
www.facebook.com/CanadianOpto
twitter.com/CanadianOpto
To represent & assist the profession of optometry in Canada; To improve the quality, availability, & accessibility of vision & eye care
Laurie Clement, Executive Director
Doug Dean, Director
Debra Yearwood, Director, Marketing & Communications
Danielle Paquette, Manager, Canadian Certified Optometric Assistant (CCOA) Program

Canadian Association of Oral & Maxillofacial Surgeons (CAOMS) / Association canadienne de spécialistes en chirurgie buccale et maxillo-faciale (ACSCBMF)
#100, 32 Colonnade Rd., Ottawa ON K2E 7J6
Tel: 613-721-1816; *Fax:* 613-721-3581
Toll-Free: 888-369-5641
caoms@caoms.com
www.caoms.com
Kevin McCann, Chair, Membership

Canadian Association of Paediatric Surgeons (CAPS) / Association de la chirurgie infantile canadienne
c/o Children's Hospital Of Winnipeg, 840 Sherbrook St., #AE401, Winnipeg MB R3A 1S1
Tel: 204-787-1246; *Fax:* 204-787-4618
www.caps.ca
To improve the surgical care of infants and children in Canada.
B.J. Hancock, Secretary Treasurer

Canadian Association of Pathologists (CAP) / Association canadienne des pathologistes (ACP)
#310, 4 Cataraqui St., Kingston ON K7K 1Z7
Tel: 613-507-8528; *Toll-Free:* 866-531-0626
info@cap-acp.org
cap-acp.org
Social Media:
linkedin.com/in/capacp
www.facebook.com/canadian.association.pathologists
twitter.com/CAPACP
To maintain high standards for patient practices and care for pathologists and laboratory medicine.
Martin Trotter, President
Heather Dow, Manager

Canadian Association of Radiologists (CAR) / L'Association canadienne des radiologistes
#600, 294 Albert St., Ottawa ON K1P 6E6
Tel: 613-860-3111; *Fax:* 613-860-3112
info@car.ca
www.car.ca
Voluntary organization representing the goals & the interests of imaging specialists; to promote the clinical, educational, research & political goals of Canadian radiology to members, organized radiology, medical associations, government & the public
Adele Fifield, CEO

Canadian Association of Thoracic Surgeons (CATS) / Association canadienne des chirurgiens thoraciques
#300, 421 Gilmour St., Ottawa ON K2P 0R5
cats@canadianthoracicsurgeons.ca
www.canadianthoracicsurgeons.ca
To represent thoracic surgeons across Canada
Richard I. Inculet, President
Sean C. Grondin, Secretary-Treasurer & Chair, Programs

Canadian Association of Transplantation
114 Cheyenne Way, Ottawa ON K2J 0E9
Toll-Free: 877-968-9449
admin@cst-transplant.ca
www.cst-transplant.ca
Health professionals committed to facilitating & enhancing the transplant process
Steven Paraskevas, President

Canadian Blood & Marrow Transplant Group (CBMTG) / Société Canadienne de greffe de cellules souches hematopoietiques
#400, 570 West 7th Ave., Vancouver BC V5Z 1B3
Tel: 604-874-4944; *Fax:* 604-874-4378
cbmtg@malachite-mgmt.com
www.cbmtg.org
To provide leadership in the field of blood & marrow transplantation (BMT); to recognize & promote advances in clinical care; to promote basic, translational & clinical research & education; to represent BMT issues to government agencies, health care organizations & the public; to collaborate with fellow organizations
Ana Torres, Executive Director

Canadian Blood Services (CBS) / Société canadienne du sang
1800 Alta Vista Dr., Ottawa ON K1G 4J5
Tel: 613-739-2300; *Fax:* 613-731-1411
Toll-Free: 888-236-6283
feedback@blood.ca
www.bloodservices.ca
Social Media: www.youtube.com/18882DONATE
www.facebook.com/canadianbloodservices
twitter.com/itsinyoutogive
To manage the blood supply for Canadians; to ensure blood safety in every branch of its structure & in every decision
Leah Hollins, Chair
Graham D. Sher, Chief Executive Officer

Canadian Brain Tumour Tissue Bank
London Health Sciences Centre, University of Western Ontario, 339 Windermere Rd., #C7108, London ON N6A 5A4
Tel: 519-663-3427; *Fax:* 519-663-2930
www.braintumor.ca
To supply optimally collected brain tumour tissue to researchers all over the country, internationally & locally in the hopes that some day the cause of & the cure for brain tumours will be found.
Marcela White, Coordinator

Canadian Cancer Society (CCS) / Société canadienne du cancer
National Office, #300, 55 St. Clair Ave. West, Toronto ON M4V 2Y7
Tel: 416-961-7223; *Fax:* 416-961-4189
Toll-Free: 888-939-3333
ccs@cancer.ca
www.cancer.ca
Social Media: www.youtube.com/user/CDNCancerSociety
www.facebook.com/canadiancancersociety
twitter.com/cancersociety
To collect donations to fund cancer research in Canada; to disseminate information on cancer prevention & treatments, advocating for healthy environment & lifestyle to reduce the incidence of cancer; to offer individual & group support programs for caregivers, family & friends of cancer patients
Stephen Baron, Chair
Pamela Fralick, President & CEO
Monique Porlier, Vice President & Chief Financial Officer
Arlene Teti, Vice President, Human Resources

Canadian Cancer Society Research Institute
#300, 55 St. Clair Ave. West, Toronto ON M4V 2Y7
Tel: 416-961-7223; *Fax:* 416-961-4189
ccsri@cancer.ca
www.cancer.ca/research
To act as a strong voice in the cancer research community; To support a broad range of projects that involve Canadian investigators across the spectrum of cancer research
Sian Bevan, Director, Research
Christine Williams, Vice President, Research

Canadian Cardiovascular Society (CCS) / Société canadienne de cardiologie
#1403, 222 Queen St., Ottawa ON K1P 5V9
Tel: 613-569-3407; *Fax:* 613-569-6574
Toll-Free: 877-569-3407
info@ccs.ca
www.ccs.ca
Social Media:
www.facebook.com/141084722576966
twitter.com/SCC_CCS
To promote cardiovascular health & care through knowledge translation, dissemination of research & encouragement of best practices, professional development & leadership in health policy
Heather Ross, President
Anne Ferguson, Chief Executive Officer

Canadian Celiac Association (CCA) / L'Association canadienne de la maladie coeliaque
Bldg. 1, #400, 5025 Orbitor Dr., Mississauga ON L4W 4Y5
Tel: 905-507-6208; *Fax:* 905-507-4673
Toll-Free: 800-363-7296
info@celiac.ca
www.celiac.ca
Social Media:
twitter.com/gfbri
To increase awareness of celiac & dermatitis herpetiformis among government institutions, health care professionals & the public; to provide information about the disease & a gluten-free diet, & encourges research through the establishment of the J.A. Campbell Research Fund
Anne Wraggett, President
Leo Turner, Treasurer

Canadian Chiropractic Association (CCA) / Association chiropratique canadienne (ACC)
#6, 186 Spadina Ave., Toronto ON M5T 3B2
Tel: 416-585-7902; *Fax:* 416-585-2970
Toll-Free: 877-222-9303
info@chiropractic.ca
www.chiropracticcanada.ca
Social Media: www.youtube.com/CanChiroAssoc
linkedin.com/company/canadian-chiropractic-association
www.facebook.com/canadianchiropracticassociation
twitter.com/CanChiroAssoc
To see every Canadian have full & equitable access to chiropractic care; To promote the integration of chiropractic into the Canadian health care system
Alison Dantas, CEO

Canadian Coalition for Genetic Fairness (CCGF) / Coalition Canadienne pour L'Equité Génétique (CCEG)
#400, 151 Frederick St., Kitchener ON N2H 2M2
Tel: 519-749-7063; *Fax:* 519-749-8965
Toll-Free: 800-998-7398
info@ccgf-cceg.ca
www.ccgf-cceg.ca
Social Media:
www.facebook.com/pages/Fighting-Genetic-Discrimination/218530198176435
twitter.com/GeneticFairness
The CCGF/CCEG is a coalition of organizations dedicated to preventing genetic discrimination for all Canadians.

Canadian College of Health Leaders (CCHL) / Collège canadien des leaders en santé
292 Somerset St. West, Ottawa ON K2P 0J6
Tel: 613-235-7218; *Fax:* 613-235-5451
Toll-Free: 800-363-9056
info@cchl-ccls.ca
www.cchl-ccls.ca
Social Media: www.youtube.com/HealthLeadersCanada
linkedin.com/company/canadian-college-of-health-leaders
www.facebook.com/CCHL.National
twitter.com/CCHL_CCLS
To advance excellence in health leadership; To act as a collective voice for the profession
Ray J. Racette, President & Chief Executive Office
Jaime M. Cleroux, Vice-President, Membership & Corporate Services
Sylvie M. Deliencourt, Director, LEADS Support & Certification
Carolyn Farrington, CFO
Kathy Ivey, Manager, Marketing & Communications

Canadian College of Medical Geneticists (CCMG) / Collège canadien de généticiens médicaux
#310, 4 Cataraqui St., Kingston ON K7K 1Z7
Tel: 613-507-8345; *Fax:* 866-303-0626
info@ccmg-ccgm.org
www.ccmg-ccgm.org
To establish & maintain professional & ethical standards for medical genetics services in Canada; To certify individuals who provide medical genetics services; to encourage research activities
Gail Graham, President
Sean Young, Treasurer

Canadian Critical Care Society (CCCS) / Société canadienne de soins intensifs
c/o Toronto General Hospital, 10 Eaton North, Room 220, 200 Elizabeth St., Toronto ON M5G 2C4
Tel: 416-340-4800; *Fax:* 416-340-4211
info@canadiancriticalcare.org
www.canadiancriticalcare.org
Social Media:
www.facebook.com/269898849687697
To promote & develop critical care medicine in Canada
Claudio Martin, President

Canadian Dermatology Association (CDA) / Association canadienne de dermatologie (ACD)
#425, 1385 Bank St., Ottawa ON K1H 8N4
Tel: 613-738-1748; *Fax:* 613-738-4695
Toll-Free: 800-267-3376
info@dermatology.ca
www.dermatology.ca
Social Media:
www.facebook.com/CdnDermatology
twitter.com/cdndermatology
To advance the science of medicine & surgery related to the health of the skin; To support & advance patient care; To represent dermatologists in Canada
Vince Bertucci, President
Chantal Courchesne, Chief Executive Officer
Robyn Hopkins, Director, Finance
Nimmi Sidhu, Coordinator, Communications

Canadian Diabetes Association (CDA) / Association canadienne du diabète
#1400, 522 University Ave., Toronto ON M5G 2R5
Tel: 416-363-3373; *Fax:* 416-363-7465
Toll-Free: 800-226-8464
info@diabetes.ca
www.diabetes.ca
Social Media: www.youtube.com/user/CDA1927
www.facebook.com/CanadianDiabetesAssociation
twitter.com/DiabetesAssoc
To advance the welfare of Canadians with diabetes; to support research into the causes, complications, treatment, & cure of diabetes; To promote & strengthen services for people affected by diabetes & their families; To work with health professionals to improve standards in care the & treatment of diabetes; To develop guidelines for diabetes education in Canada; To promote the rights of Canadians affected by diabetes in an effort to bring about positive change in the areas of public awareness, government policy, health policy issues, & employment
Suzanne Deuel, Chair
Rick Blickstead, President & CEO
Walter Kurz, CFO & Vice-President, Organizational Excellence & Shared Services
Aileen Leo, Executive Directpr, Government Relations & Public Affairs
Janelle Robertson, Vice-President, Business Operations
Jovita Sundaramoorthy, Vice-President, Research & Education

Canadian Down Syndrome Society (CDSS) / Société canadienne du syndrome de Down
#103, 2003 - 14 St. NW, Calgary AB T2M 3N4
Tel: 403-270-8500; *Fax:* 403-270-8291
info@cdss.ca
www.cdss.ca
Social Media:
www.facebook.com/cdndownsyndrome
twitter.com/CdnDownSyndrome
To ensure equitable opportunities for all Canadians with Down syndrome.
Kevin Whyte, Board Chair
Kirk Crowther, Executive Director
Jonathan A. Bateman, Coordinator, Event & Fund Development
Kaitlyn Pecson, Coordinator, Design & Communication
Ashlee Stone, Coordinator, Advocacy Research

Canadian Dyslexia Association (CDA) / Association canadienne de la dyslexie
57, rue du Couvent, Gatineau QC J9H 3C8
Tel: 613-853-6539; *Fax:* 819-684-0672
info@dyslexiaassociation.ca
www.dyslexiaassociation.ca

Canadian Epilepsy Alliance (CAE) / L'Alliance canadienne de l'épilepsie (ACE)
c/o President, 351 Kenmount Rd., St. John's NL A1B 3P9
Tel: 709-722-0502; *Fax:* 709-722-0999
www.epilepsymatters.com
To promote independence & quality of life for people with epilepsy & their families, through support services, information, advocacy, & public awareness
Gail Dempsey, President

Canadian Fabry Association / L'association canadienne de fabry
PO Box 40036, 4250 1re ave, Québec QC G1H 7J6
www.fabrycanada.com
Social Media:
www.facebook.com/27694413535
To educate the public & offer information on treatments; to encourage & support research; to increase facilities for those suffering from the disease.

Canadian Federation of Aromatherapists / La fédération canadienne d'aromathérapistes
124 Sweet Water Cres., Richmond Hill ON L4S 2B4
Tel: 519-746-1594; *Fax:* 519-746-9493
cfamanager@cfacanada.com
www.cfacanada.com
Social Media:
www.facebook.com/CanadianAromatherapy
twitter.com/cfaaromatherapy
To maintain a register of aromatherapy practitioners, schools, & instructors who meet established minimum standards; To act as a unified voice of the profession; To maintain the highest ethical standards of the profession
Danielle Sade, President

Canadian Foundation for Dietetic Research (CFDF)
#604, 480 University Ave., Toronto ON M5G 1V2
Tel: 519-267-0755; *Fax:* 416-596-0603
www.cfdr.ca
Provides grants for research in dietetics and nutrition.
Isla Horvath, Executive Director

Canadian Foundation for the Study of Infant Deaths (CFSID) / Fondation canadienne pour l'étude de la mortalité infantile
PO Box 21053, St Catharines ON L2R 7X2
Tel: 905-688-8884; *Fax:* 905-688-3300
Toll-Free: 800-363-7437
sidsinfo@sidscanada.org
www.sidscanada.org
Social Media:
www.facebook.com/sidscanada
twitter.com/SIDSCanada
To provide information & emotional support to families of infants who have died due to Sudden Infant Death Syndrome (SIDS); to carry out programs of public education & awareness; to promote & support research activities into the cause(s) of SIDS & its effects on families

Canadian Health Coalition (CHC) / Coalition canadienne de la santé
#212, 251 Bank St., Ottawa ON K2P 1X3
Tel: 613-688-4973
contact@healthcoalition.ca
www.healthcoalition.ca
Social Media: www.youtube.com/user/HealthCoalition
twitter.com/healthcoalition
To create good health; To preserve & strengthen the Canada Health Act, the foundation of Medicare; To make the health care system democratic, accountable & representative; To provide a continuum of care from large institutions to the home; To protect our investment in the skills & abilities of our health care workers; To ensure fair wages for all health care providers; To eliminate profit-making from illness; To reduce over-prescribing & make drugs affordable; to stop fee-for-service payments; To expand methods of health care & the role of non-physician health providers
Adrienne Silnicki, National Coordinator

Canadian Hematology Society (CHS) / Société canadienne d'hématologie
#199, 435 St. Laurent Blvd., Ottawa ON K1K 2Z8
Tel: 613-748-9613; *Fax:* 613-748-6392
chs@uniserve.ca
www.canadianhematologysociety.org
To represent members of the Society & provide information about hematology
Aaron Schimmer, President

Canadian Hemochromatosis Society (CHS) / Société canadienne de l'hémochromatose
#285, 7000 Minoru Blvd., Richmond BC V6Y 3Z5
Tel: 604-279-7135; *Fax:* 604-279-7138
Toll-Free: 877-223-4766
office@toomuchiron.ca
www.toomuchiron.ca
Social Media: www.youtube.com/user/toomuchiron
linkedin.com/groups/Canadian-Hemochromatosis-Society-1096237
www.facebook.com/TooMuchIron
twitter.com/IronOutCanada
To increase awareness among the public & medical community with regards to the importance of family screening, early diagnosis & treatment of Hemochromatosis
Patrick Haney, President & Chair
Bob Rogers, Executive Director & CEO

Canadian Hemophilia Society (CHS) / Société canadienne de l'hémophilie (SCHQ)
#301, 666 Sherbrooke St. West, Montréal QC H3A 1E7
Tel: 514-848-0503; *Fax:* 514-848-9661
Toll-Free: 800-668-2686
chs@hemophilia.ca
www.hemophilia.ca
Social Media: www.youtube.com/user/CanadianHemophilia
www.facebook.com/CanadianHemophiliaSociety
To find a cure & to provide services to people with hemophilia or other inherited bleeding disorders; to serve persons infected with HIV or hepatitis through blood & blood products
David Page, National Executive Director
Hélène Bourgaize, National Director, Chapter Relations & Human Resources
Deborah Franz Currie, National Director, Resource Development

Canadian Hospice Palliative Care Association (CHPCA) / Association canadienne de soins palliatifs (ACSP)
Annex D, Saint-Vincent Hospital, 60 Cambridge St. North, Ottawa ON K1R 7A5
Tel: 613-241-3663; *Fax:* 613-241-3986
Toll-Free: 800-668-2785
www.chpca.net
Social Media:
www.facebook.com/CanadianHospicePalliativeCare
twitter.com/CanadianHPCAssn
CHPCA provides leadership in the pursuit of excellence in the care of people approaching death in Canada, in order to lessen suffering, loneliness, & grief. The national association works to develop national standards of practice for hospice palliative care.
Laurie Anne O'Brien, President
Jeff Christiansen, Secretary-Treasurer
Sharon Baxter, Executive Director

Canadian Hypnotherapy Association (CHA)
121 Wallis St., Parksville BC V9P 1K7
Tel: 250-248-9297
To determine standards for hypnotherapy in Canada & to promote the therapeutic value of hypnotherapy
Joe Friede, President

Canadian Institute of Child Health (CICH) / Institut canadien de la santé infantile
#300, 384 Bank St., Ottawa ON K2P 1Y4
Tel: 613-230-8838; *Fax:* 613-230-6654
cich@cich.ca
www.cich.ca
To promote the health & well-being of Canadian children through consultation, collaboration, research & advocacy by building alliances & coalitions & by creating resources on health promotion, disease & injury prevention relevant to child & family health in Canada; To identify issues of concern by monitoring the health & well-being of children in Canada; To promote & improve the health & well-being of mothers & infants in all settings; To promote the healthy physical development of children in a safe environment & reduce childhood injuries; To promote the healthy psycho-social development of children in supportive & nurturing environments; To facilitate empowerment of individuals & communities to achieve the above goals for Canadian children & their families; To facilitate collaborative work between consumers, professional, non-professional & government agencies that results in appropriate actions for identified needs
Robin Moore-Orr, D.Sc., R.D., Chair
Lynne Westlake, Secretary
Eleonore Benesch, Treasurer

Canadian Institute of Public Health Inspectors (CIPHI) / Institut Canadien des inspecteurs en santé publique (ICISP)
#720, 999 West Broadway Ave., Vancouver BC V5Z 1K5
Tel: 604-739-8180; *Fax:* 604-738-4080
Toll-Free: 888-245-8180
questions@ciphi.ca
www.ciphi.ca
To protect the health of all Canadians; To advance the environmental & health sciences; To enhance the field of public health inspection through certification, information, & advocacy
Adam Grant, National President

Canadian League Against Epilepsy (CLAE)
c/o Secretariat Centreal, #6, 20 Crown Steel Dr., Markham ON L3R 9X9
Tel: 905-415-3917
clae@secretariatcentral.com
claegroup.org
To help Canadians affected by epilepsy; To develop therapeutic & preventative strategies to avoid the consequences of epilepsy
S. Nizam Ahmed, President
Elizabeth Donner, Secretary-Treasurer

Canadian Liver Foundation (CLF) / Fondation canadienne du foie (FCF)
#801, 3100 Steeles Ave. East, Toronto ON L3R 8T3
Tel: 416-491-3353; *Fax:* 905-752-1540
Toll-Free: 800-563-5483
clf@liver.ca
www.liver.ca
Social Media: www.youtube.com/user/clfwebmaster
www.facebook.com/6584473365
twitter.com/CdnLiverFdtn
To reduce the incidence & impact of all liver disease by funding liver research & education; promote liver health through programs & publications
Morris Sherman, Chairman
Elliot M. Jacobson, Sec.-Treas.

Canadian Lung Association (CLA) / Association pulmonaire du Canada
National Office, #300, 1750 Courtwood Cres., Ottawa ON K2C 2B5
Tel: 613-569-6411; *Toll-Free:* 888-566-5864
info@lung.ca
www.lung.ca
Social Media: www.youtube.com/user/TheLungAssociation
www.facebook.com/canadianlungassociation
twitter.com/canlung
To improve & promote lung health across Canada
Debra Lynkowski, President & Chief Executive Officer
Terry Dean, Senior Vice President, Federation Development & Partnerships
Debbie Smith, Vice President, Finance & Operations
Janet Sutherland, Director, Canadian Thoracic Society/Canadian Respiratory Health Professiona
Marketa Stastna, Manager, Marketing & Communications
Amy Henderson, Manager, Public Policy & Health Communications
Kristen Curren, Manager, Education & Knowledge Translation

Canadian Lyme Disease Foundation / Fondation canadienne de la maladie de lyme
2495 Reece Rd., Westbank BC V4T 1N1
Tel: 250-768-0978; *Fax:* 250-768-0946
www.canlyme.org
Social Media:
www.facebook.com/143033619666
twitter.com/canlyme
To advance research about Lyme Disease in Canada
Jim Wilson, President & Founder

Canadian Marfan Association (CMA) / Association du syndrome de Marfan
PO Box 42257, Stn. Centre Plaza, 128 Queen St. South, Mississauga ON L5M 4Z0
Tel: 905-826-3223; *Fax:* 905-826-2125
Toll-Free: 866-722-1722
info@marfan.ca
www.marfan.ca
Social Media:
www.facebook.com/CanadianMarfanAssociation
twitter.com/CanadianMarfan
Barry Edington, Executive Director

Canadian Massage Therapist Alliance (CMTA) / Alliance Canadienne de Massothérapeutes
#16, 1724 Quebec Ave., Saskatoon SK S7K 1V9
Tel: 306-384-7077
info@crmta.ca
www.crmta.ca
Social Media:
www.facebook.com/CRMTA
To foster & advance the art, science & philosophy of massage therapy through nationwide cooperation in a professional, ethical & practical manner for the betterment of health care in Canada

Canadian Medical Association (CMA) / Association médicale canadienne (AMC)
1209 Michael St., Ottawa ON K1J 7T2
Tel: 613-731-8610; *Fax:* 613-236-8864
Toll-Free: 888-855-2555
cmamsc@cma.ca
www.cma.ca
Social Media: www.youtube.com/user/CanadianMedicalAssoc
linkedin.com/company/canadian-medical-association
www.facebook.com/CanadianMedicalAssociation
twitter.com/CMA_Docs
To act as the national voice of physicians in Canada; To serve the Canadian medical community; To promote the highest standards of health & health care
Cindy Forbes, President
Brian Brodie, Chair
Granger Avery, President-Elect

Canadian Medical Foundation (CMF) / La Fondation médicale canadienne
1870 Alta Vista Dr., Ottawa ON K1G 6R7
Fax: 613-526-7555
Toll-Free: 866-530-4979
info@cmf.ca
www.medicalfoundation.ca
Social Media: www.youtube.com/CdnMedicalFoundation
twitter.com/CdnMedicalFound
Physicians striving for excellence in health care through charitable action together & in partnership with others; organized, guided & funded by physicians CMF makes decisive, targeted funding decisions in areas physicians feel will provide the best impact
Ruth Collins-Nakai, Chair
Lee Gould, President & CEO

The Canadian Medical Protective Association / Association canadienne de protection médicale
PO Box 8225, Stn. T, Ottawa ON K1G 3H7
Tel: 613-725-2000; *Fax:* 613-725-1300
Toll-Free: 800-267-6522
inquiries@cmpa.org
www.cmpa-acpm.ca
Social Media: www.youtube.com/user/cmpamembers
linkedin.com/company/canadian-medical-protective-association
twitter.com/CMPAmembers
Founded by a group of Canadian doctors for their mutual protection against legal actions based on allegations of malpractice or negligence
Edward Crosby, Chair
Hartley Stern, Executive Director & CEO

Canadian MedicAlert Foundation / Fondation canadienne MedicAlert
#800, 2005 Sheppard Ave. East, Toronto ON M2J 5B4
Tel: 416-696-0267; *Fax:* 800-392-8422
Toll-Free: 800-668-1507
www.medicalert.ca
Social Media: www.youtube.com/medicalertCA
www.facebook.com/medicalertcanada
twitter.com/medicalertCA
To provide lifelong access to personal & medical information in order to protect & save the lives of its members; MedicAlert is a non-profit organization that provides all Canadians with medical protection in an emergency situation
Robert Ridge, President
Dorothy Scanlon, Director, Finance & Corporate Affairs

Canadian Memorial Chiropractic College (CMCC)
6100 Leslie St., Toronto ON M2H 3J1
Tel: 416-482-2340; *Fax:* 416-482- 362
communications@cmcc.ca
www.cmcc.ca
To advance the art, science & philosophy of chiropractic; To educate chiropractors; To further the development of the chiropractic profession; To improve the health of society
Mark Symchych, Chair
Jean A. Moss, DC, MBA, President
David Gryfe, Secretary-Treasurer

Canadian Natural Health Association (CNHA)
#105, 5 Wakunda Pl., Toronto ON M4A 1A2
Tel: 416-686-7056
To establish leadership in healthy, natural lifestyle education & support services; to assist by providing resources to help make people healthier

Canadian Network of Toxicology Centres (CNTC) / Réseau canadien des centres de toxicologie
University of Guelph, 50 Stone Rd E, Guelph ON N1G 2W1
Tel: 519-824-4120
To be recognized & respected for excellence in research, training, analysis & communication of information focused on critical toxicology issues for ecosystem & human health; to achieve this through innovative, multi-disciplinary teamwork & partnerships between the public & private sector
Leonard Ritter, Executive Director

Canadian Neurological Sciences Federation (CCNS) / Fédération des sciences neurologiques du Canada
#709, 7015 Macleod Trail SW, Calgary AB T2H 2K6
Tel: 403-229-9544; *Fax:* 403-229-1661
info@cnsfederation.org
www.cnsfederation.org
To enhance the care of patients with diseases of the nervous system; To act as the umbrella organization for the following societies: Canadian Neurological Society, Canadian Neurosurgical Society, Canadian Society of Clinical Neurophysiologists, & Canadian Association of Child Neurologists
Dan Morin, Chief Executive Officer
Marika Fitzgerald, Manager, Finance & Administration
Donna Irvin, Administrator, Membership Services
Lisa Bicek, Coordinator, Professional Development
Cindy Leschyshyn, Editorial Coordinator, Journal

Canadian Neurological Society (CNS) / Société canadienne de neurologie
#709, 7015 Macleod Trail SW, Calgary AB T2H 2K1
Tel: 403-229-9544; *Fax:* 403-229-1661
www.cnsfederation.org
To promote & encourage all aspects of neurology, including research, education, assessment & accreditation; provide for annual scientific sessions to promote the knowledge & practice of neurology
Dan Morin, CNSF CEO
Marika Fitzgerald, CNSF Controller

Canadian Occupational Therapy Foundation (COTF) / La Fondation canadienne d'ergothérapie (FCE)
CTTC Bldg., #3401, 1125 Colonel By Dr., Ottawa ON K1S 5R1
Tel: 613-523-2268; *Fax:* 613-523-2552
Toll-Free: 800-434-2268
www.cotfcanada.org
Social Media:
www.facebook.com/239464269434993
To fund & promote research & scholarship in occupational therapy in Canada
Sangita Kamblé, Executive Director
Anne McDonald, Executive Assistant

Canadian Oncology Societies
c/o Ottawa Hospital, 501 Smyth Rd., Ottawa ON K1H 8K6
Fax: 613-247-3511
Toll-Free: 877-990-9044
info@cos.ca
cos.ca
To increase & exchange knowledge in the field of oncology; to promote the application of such knowledge in the prevention and diagnosis of cancer and the care of cancer patients and their families; to promote interdisciplinary approaches to patient care and research in cancer; to provide a forum for the presentation and discussion of scientific knowledge and advances in oncology; to further continuing education for groups and indivduals involved in the care of patients who require special attention; support public cancer education programs; to support and assist the Canadian Cancer Society and the National Cancer Insitute; to advise government and other agencies on the provision of health services relevent to oncology.
Charles Pitts, Administrator

Canadian Ophthalmological Society (COS) / Société canadienne d'opthalmologie (SCO)
#610, 1525 Carling Ave., Ottawa ON K1Z 8R9
Tel: 613-729-6779; *Fax:* 613-729-7209
cos@eyesite.ca
www.eyesite.ca
To assure the provision of optimal eye care to all Canadians by promoting excellence in ophthalmology & providing services to support its members in practice
Jennifer Brunet-Colvey, Chief Executive Officer

Canadian Organization for Rare Disorders (CORD)
#600, 151 Bloor St. West, Toronto ON M5S 1S4
Tel: 416-969-7464; *Fax:* 416-969-7420
Toll-Free: 877-302-7273
info@raredisorders.ca
raredisorders.ca
Social Media:
www.facebook.com/RareDisorders
twitter.com/Durhane
To advocate for health policy that works for people with rare disorders; to promote research & services for all rare disorders in Canada; To increase access to genetic screening & genetic counselling for rare disorders
Durhane Wong-Rieger, President & CEO
John Adams, Chair

Canadian Orthopaedic Association (COA) / Association canadienne d'orthopédie
#360, 4150, rue Ste-Catherine ouest, Montréal QC H3Z 2Y5
Tel: 514-874-9003; *Fax:* 514-874-0464
cynthia@canorth.org
www.coa-aco.org
Social Media:
twitter.com/CdnOrthoAssoc
To provide continuing medical education for orthopaedic surgeons
Douglas C. Thomson, CEO

Canadian Orthopaedic Foundation (COF) / Fondation orthopédique du Canada (FOC)
PO Box 1036, Toronto ON M5K 1P2
Tel: 416-410-2341; *Fax:* 416-352-5078
Toll-Free: 800-461-3639
mailbox@canorth.org
www.canorth.org
Social Media:
www.facebook.com/pages/Canadian-Orthopaedic-Foundation/175163319218018
twitter.com/CanOrthoFound
To foster excellence in the provision of health care to patients with musculoskeletal disease or injury, in a cost effective manner, based on significant outcome studies, by supporting research, educating its members & securing funding from government & other health care funding agencies
Geoffrey Johnston, Chair & President
James Hall, Vice Chair

Canadian Orthoptic Council / Conseil canadien d'orthoptique
CHUL, 2705, boul Laurier, Ste. Foy QC G1V 4G2
Fax: 418-654-2188
info@orthopticscanada.org
www.orthopticscanada.org
To establish standards in the training of orthoptic students; to establish standards for orthoptic training centres; to provide examinations of orthoptic students in order to determine their proficiency in orthopotics & to award a certificate of competency to qualified students who pass the examinations; to require evidence of continuing education of certified orthoptists; to establish standards for the professional ethical conduct of certified orthoptists.
Louis-Etienne Marcoux, Secretary-Treasurer
Cathie Day, Administrative Coordinator

Canadian Paediatric Society (CPS) / Société canadienne de pédiatrie
2305 St. Laurent Blvd., Ottawa ON K1G 4J8
Tel: 613-526-9397; *Fax:* 613-526-3332
info@cps.ca
www.cps.ca
Social Media: www.youtube.com/canpaedsociety
linkedin.com/company/canadian-paediatric-society
www.facebook.com/CanadianPaediatricSociety
twitter.com/canpaedsociety
To advocate for the health needs of children & youth; to provide continuing education to paediatricians; to establish national guidelines for paediatric care & practice
Andrew Lynk, President
Marie Adèle Davis, Executive Director
Elizabeth Moreau, Director, Communications & Public Education

Canadian Pain Society / Société canadienne pour le traitement de la douleur
#202, 1143 Wentworth St. West, Oshawa ON L1J 8P7
Tel: 905-404-9545; *Fax:* 905-404-3727
office@canadianpainsociety.ca
www.canadianpainsociety.ca
Social Media:
www.facebook.com/CanadianPain
twitter.com/canadianpain
To foster research on pain; To improve the management of patients with acute & chronic pain
M. Catherine Bushnell, President
Diane LaChapelle, Secretary
Michael McGillion, Treasurer
Ellen Maracle-Benton, Office Manager
Judy Watt-Watson, President Elect

Canadian Pediatric Foundation (CPF) / La fondation canadienne de pédiatrie
2305 St. Laurent Blvd., Ottawa ON K1G 4J8
Tel: 613-526-9397; *Fax:* 613-526-3332
cpf@cps.ca
www.cps.ca
Social Media: www.youtube.com/canpaedsociety
linkedin.com/company/canadian-paediatric-society/
www.facebook.com/CanadianPaediatricSociety
twitter.com/canpaedsociety
To promote improved health care & social well-being for the children of Canada, particularly for disadvantaged groups; to promote better standards of health care for children throughout the world, particularly where Canadian aid is active.
Marie Adèle Davis, Executive Director

Canadian Physiotherapy Association (CPA) / L'Association canadienne de physiothérapie
955 Green Valley Cres., Ottawa ON K2C 3V4
Tel: 613-564-5454; *Fax:* 613-564-1577
Toll-Free: 800-387-8679
information@physiotherapy.ca
www.physiotherapy.ca
Social Media:
linkedin.com/company/canadian-physiotherapy-association
www.facebook.com/CPA.ACP
twitter.com/physiocan
To provide leadership & direction to the profession; To foster excellence in practice, education & research; To promote high standards of health in Canada
Robert Werstine, President

Canadian PKU and Allied Disorders Inc.
#180, 260 Adelaide St. East, Toronto ON M5A 1N1
Tel: 416-207-0064; *Toll-Free:* 877-226-7581
info@canpku.org
www.canpku.org
Social Media:
twitter.com/canpku
To provide news, information & support to families and professionals dealing with phenylketonuria and similar, rare, inherited metabolic disorders
John Adams, President & CEO

Canadian Podiatric Medical Association (CPMA) / Association médicale podiatrique canadienne
#2063, 61 Broadway Blvd., Sherwood Park AB T8H 2C1
Toll-Free: 888-220-3338
askus@podiatrycanada.org
www.podiatrycanada.org
To effectively serve & provide guidance to its members & the podiatry profession in Canada; to serve the public; to provide the authoritative national voice for podiatrists in Canada; to recognize a particular responsibility to contribute to the development of national positions & standards related to the podiatric medical profession through education, research, materials & personnel
Jayne Jeneroux, Executive Director

Canadian Porphyria Foundation Inc. (CPF) / La Fondation canadienne de la porphyrie
PO Box 1206, Neepawa MB R0J 1H0
Tel: 204-476-2800; *Fax:* 204-476-2800
Toll-Free: 866-476-2801
porphyria@cpf-inc.ca
www.cpf-inc.ca
Dedicated to improving the quality of life for Canadians affected by the porphyrias through programs of awareness, education, service, advocacy & research; committed to promoting public & medical professional awareness; assembling, printing & distributing up-to-date educational information to physicians, health care personnel, individuals & others affected by porphyria; offering support programs to affected individuals & their families; promoting the family social welfare of affected individuals; educating & informing physicians & others in health care about the porphyrias so that early diagnosis & proper treatment will be realized; promoting & providing financial assistance for research; committed to encouraging, supporting & serving physicians & researchers in their efforts to find more effective treatments & to increasing physician, patient & community awareness & thereby cultivating support for research
Lois J. Aitken, President/Executive Director

Canadian Post-MD Education Registry (CAPER) / Système informatisé sur les stagiaires post-MD en formation clinique
#800, 265 Carling Ave., Ottawa ON K1S 2E1
Tel: 613-730-1204; *Fax:* 613-730-1196
caper@afmc.ca
www.caper.ca
Social Media:
twitter.com/CAPERCanada
To provide accurate & timely data pertaining to Post-MD training & physician resources in Canada to assist medical schools, governments & other work longitudinal research pertaining to physicians training & supply
Lynda Buske, Interim Director

Canadian Public Health Association (CPHA) / Association canadienne de santé publique (ACSP)
#404, 1525 Carling Ave., Ottawa ON K1Z 8R9
Tel: 613-725-3769; *Fax:* 613-725-9826
info@cpha.ca
www.cpha.ca
Social Media:
www.youtube.com/channel/UC_SDgqaCLW1YKWKYqlO4evg
linkedin.com/company/113746
www.facebook.com/cpha.acsp
twitter.com/CPHA_ACSP
To represent public health in Canada; To support universal & equitable access to the necessary conditions to achieve health for all Canadians; To provide links to the international public health community
Ardene Robinson Vollman, PhD, RN, CCHN(C, Chair
Susan Jackson, PhD, MSc, BSc, Chair-Elect
Annie Duchesne, MScPH, Director
Jacqueline Gahagan, PhD, Director
James Mintz, BA, Director
Manasi Parikh, Director

Canadian Public Health Association - NB/PEI Branch NB
nbpei.pha@gmail.com
To maintain & improve the level of personal & community health
Kathleen Brennan, President
Anne Lebans, Secretary-Treasurer

Canadian Public Health Association - NWT/Nunavut Branch (NTNUPHA)
PO Box 1709, Yellowknife NT X1A 2P3
Faye Stark, President

Canadian Rheumatology Association (CRA) / Société canadienne de rhumatologie
#244, 12 - 16715 Yonge St., Newmarket ON L3X 1X4
Tel: 905-952-0698; *Fax:* 905-952-0708
info@rheum.ca
rheum.ca
To represent Canadian rheumatologists & promote their pursuit of excellence in arthritis care & research in Canada through leadership, education & communication
Cory Baillie, President
Jacob Karsh, Sec.-Treas.

Canadian Society for Clinical Investigation (CSCI) / Société canadienne de recherches cliniques (SCRC)
114 Cheyenne Way, Ottawa ON K2J 0E9
Fax: 613-491-0073
Toll-Free: 877-968-9449
info@csci-scrc.ca
www.csci-scrc.ca
To promote research in the field of human health throughout Canada; to lobby for research funding; to support Canadian researchers in their endeavours & at all stages of their careers by supporting knowledge translation & fostering communities of health science researchers
Norman Rosenblum, President

Canadian Society for International Health (CSIH) / Société canadienne de la santé internationale
#726, 1 Nicholas St., Ottawa ON K1N 7B7
Tel: 613-241-5785
csih@csih.org
www.csih.org
Social Media:
linkedin.com/groups/CSIH-Global-Health-Forum-3671985
www.facebook.com/CSIH.org
twitter.com/globalsante
To promote international health & development through mobilization of Canadian resources; To advocate & facilitate research, education, & service activities in international health; To further Canadian strengths of progressive health policy & programming in all fields where global & domestic health concerns meet; To contribute to the evolving global understanding of health & development
Kate Dickson, Co-Chair
L. Duncan Saunders, Co-Chair
Eva Slawecki, Acting Director

Canadian Society for Medical Laboratory Science (CSMLS) / Société canadienne de science de laboratoire médical (SCSLM)
33 Wellington Ave. North, Hamilton ON L8R 1M7
Tel: 905-528-8642; *Fax:* 905-528-4968
Toll-Free: 800-263-8277
www.csmls.org
Social Media: www.youtube.com/user/csmls
www.facebook.com/csmls
twitter.com/csmls

To promote & maintain a nationally accepted standard of medical laboratory technology; To promote, maintain, & protect professional identity & interests of medical laboratory technologists
Tricia Vandenakker, President
Christine Nielsen, Executive Director

Canadian Society for Pharmaceutical Sciences (CSPS) / Société canadienne des sciences pharmaceutiques (SCSP)
Katz Group Centre, University of Alberta, #2-020L, 11361 - 87 Ave., Edmonton AB T6G 2E1
Tel: 780-492-0950; *Fax:* 780-492-0951
www.cspscanada.org
To advance pharmaceutical R&D & education; to provide a forum for researchers, industry & government to advance pharmaceutical sciences & increase drug discovery & development in Canada
Barbara Scollick, Executive Director
Bev Berekoff, Administrator

Canadian Society for Surgical Oncology (CSSO) / Société canadienne d'oncologie chirurgicale
c/o Jane Hanes, Princess Margaret Hospital, #3-130, 610 University Ave., Toronto ON M5G 2M9
Tel: 416-946-6583; *Fax:* 416-946-6590
www.cos.ca/csso
To encourage optimum cancer patient care through a multi-disciplinary treatment approach; To promote surgical oncology training programs in Canadian universities
Andy McFadden, President
Jane Hanes, Executive Coordinator

Canadian Society for the History of Medicine (CSHM) / Société canadienne d'histoire de la médecine (SCHM)
c/o Brock University, Community Health Sciences, 500 Glendridge Ave., St Catharines ON L2S 3A1
Tel: 905-688-5550; *Fax:* 905-688-8954
www.cshm-schm.ca
To promote the study & communication of the history of health & medicine
James Moran, President
Sasha Mullaly, Vice-President
Dan Malleck, Secretary-Treasurer & Membership Coordinator

Canadian Society for Transfusion Medicine (CSTM) / Société canadienne de médecine transfusionnelle
#6, 20 Crown Steel Dr., Markham ON L3R 9X9
Tel: 905-415-3917; *Fax:* 905-415-0071
Toll-Free: 855-415-3917
office@transfusion.ca
www.transfusion.ca
Social Media:
www.facebook.com/290163767690083
twitter.com/CanSocTransMed
To promulgate throughout Canada a high level of ethics & professional standards; to create national & regional opportunities for the presentation & discussion of research & developments in this & allied fields; to initiate & maintain a program of continuing education; to promote good laboratory & good manufacturing practices; to establish mutually beneficial working relationships with relevant national & international societies & organizations & to be the primary voice for transfusion medicine in Canada
Gwen Clarke, President

Canadian Society for Vascular Surgery (CSVS) / Société canadienne de chirurgie vasculaire
PO Box 58062, Ottawa ON K1C 7H4
Tel: 613-286-7583
info@canadianvascular.ca
canadianvascular.ca
Social Media:
twitter.com/canadianvascul1
To promote vascular health for Canadians
Greg Browne, President

Canadian Society of Allergy & Clinical Immunology (CSACI) / Société canadienne d'allergie et d'immunologie clinique
PO Box 51045, Orléans ON K1E 3W4
Tel: 613-986-5869; *Fax:* 866-839-7501
info@csaci.ca
www.csaci.ca
Social Media:
www.facebook.com/471713226291440
twitter.com/csacimeeting
To ensure optimal patient care by advancing the knowledge & practice of allergy, clinical immunology, & asthma
Sandy Kapur, President
David Fischer, Vice-President

Harold Kim, Secretary-Treasurer

Canadian Society of Cardiac Surgeons / Société des chirurgiens cardiaques
#1403, 222 Queen St., Ottawa ON K1P 5V9
Toll-Free: 877-569-3407
cscs@ccs.ca
www.ccs.ca/cscs
To promote cardiac surgery as a profession
David Ross, President
Roderick MacArthur, Secretary-Treasurer

Canadian Society of Clinical Neurophysiologists (CSCN) / Société canadienne de neurophysiologistes cliniques
#709, 7015 Macleod Trail SW, Calgary AB T2H 2K6
Tel: 403-229-9544; *Fax:* 403-229-1661
www.cnsfederation.org
To promote & encourage all aspects of neurophysiology, including research & education, in addition to assessment & accreditation in the field
Dan Morin, CNSF CEO

Canadian Society of Cytology (CSC) / Société canadienne de cytologie
c/o Canadian Association of Pathologists, #310, 4 Cataraqui St., Kingston ON K7K 1Z7
Tel: 613-507-8528; *Fax:* 866-531-0626
www.cap-acp.org/cytology.php
To promote & support education in cytology; To maintain a high standard of practice within the discipline of cytopathology; To foster the development of cytopathology in Canada
Janine Benoit, Chair

Canadian Society of Endocrinology & Metabolism (CSEM) / Société canadienne d'endocrinologie et métabolisme (SCEM)
#1403, 222 Queen St., Ottawa ON K1P 5V9
Tel: 613-594-0005; *Fax:* 613-569-6574
info@endo-metab.ca
www.endo-metab.ca
To advance the discipline of endocrinology & metabolism in Canada
Stephanie Kaiser, President
Jean-Patrice Baillargeon, Secretary-Treasurer

Canadian Society of Gastroenterology Nurses & Associates (CSGNA)
#224, 1540 Cornwall Rd., Oakville ON L6J 7W5
Tel: 905-829-8794; *Fax:* 905-829-0242
Toll-Free: 866-544-8794
csgnaexecutiveassistant@csgna.com
www.csgna.com
To enhance the educational & professional growth of the membership within the resources available.
Lisa Westin, President
Jacqui Ho, Treasurer

Canadian Society of Hand Therapists (CSHT) / Societe canadienne des therapeutes de la main (SCTM)
csht.org
Social Media:
www.facebook.com/324550384259629
twitter.com/handtherapists
Trevor Fraser, President

Canadian Society of Internal Medicine (CSIM) / Société canadienne de médecine interne (SCMI)
#300, 421 Gilmour St., Ottawa ON K2P 0R5
Tel: 613-422-5977; *Fax:* 613-249-3326
Toll-Free: 855-893-2746
info@csim.ca
csim.ca
Social Media:
www.facebook.com/canadiansocietyofinternalmedicine
twitter.com/CSIMSCMI
To promote healthy living among Canadians; to provide leadership for physicians; to conduct research & education.
Benjamin Chen, President

Canadian Society of Nephrology (CSN) / Société canadienne de néphrologie (SCN)
PO Box 25255, Stn. RDP, Montréal QC H1E 7P9
Tel: 514-643-4985
info@csnscn.ca
www.csnscn.ca
Social Media:
www.facebook.com/1498868453774190
twitter.com/CSNSCN
To advance the practice of Nephrology; To promote the highest quality of care for patients with renal diseases, by setting high standards for medical training & education; To encourage research in biomedical sciences related to the kidney, kidney disorders & renal replacement therapies
Braden Manns, President
Filomena Picciano, Director, Operations

Canadian Society of Nutrition Management / Société canadienne de gestion de la nutrition
#300, 1370 Don Mills Rd., Toronto ON M3B 3N7
Fax: 416-441-0591
Toll-Free: 866-355-2766
csnm@csnm.ca
www.csnm.ca
Social Media:
ca.linkedin.com/in/thecsnm
twitter.com/TheCSNM
To foster an environment in which members can achieve success in their chosen field.
Barbara Cockwell, President Elect
Jean Van Nus, President

Canadian Society of Otolaryngology - Head & Neck Surgery (CSO-HNS) / Société canadienne d'otolaryngologie et de chirurgie cervico-faciale
Administrative Office, 221 Millford Cres., Elora ON N0B 1S0
Tel: 519-846-0630; *Fax:* 519-846-9529
Toll-Free: 800-655-9533
cso.hns@sympatico.ca
www.entcanada.org
To improve patient care in otolaryngology - head & neck surgery; To maintain high professional & ethical standards
Dale Brown, President
Sam Spafford, Secretary
Martin Corsten, Treasurer
Donna Humphrey, General Manager

Canadian Society of Palliative Care Physicians (CSPCP) / Société canadienne des médecins de soins palliatifs (SCMSP)
c/o Fraser Health Authority, #400, 13450 - 102 Ave., Surrey BC V3T 0H1
Tel: 604-341-3174; *Fax:* 604-587-4644
office@cspcp.ca
www.cspcp.ca
The CSPCP is a membership organization for patients and their families, though the advancement and improvement of palliative medicine and training.
Susan MacDonald, President
Kim Taylor, Executive Director

Canadian Society of Plastic Surgeons (CSPS) / Société canadienne des chirurgiens plasticiens
#4, 1469, boul St-Joseph est, Montréal QC H2J 1M6
Tel: 514-843-5415; *Fax:* 514-843-7005
csps_sccp@bellnet.ca
www.plasticsurgery.ca
To represent, promote & provide leadership for the descipline fo plastic surgery across Canada
Karyn Wagner, Executive Director
Patricia Bortoluzzi, President
Douglas Ross, Vice-President
Bryan Callaghan, Sec.-Treas.

Canadian Society of Respiratory Therapists (CSRT) / La Société canadienne des thérapeutes respiratoires (SCTR)
#400, 301 Cooper St., Ottawa ON K1G 3Y6
Tel: 613-731-3164; *Fax:* 613-521-4314
Toll-Free: 800-267-3422
info@csrt.com
www.csrt.com
Social Media:
www.facebook.com/csrt.sctr
twitter.com/@CSRT_tweets
To provide leadership toward the advancement of cardiorespiratory care; To achieve excellence through the definition of roles, standards, & scope of clinical practice
Christiane Ménard, Executive Director
James McCormick, President
Angela Coxe, President-Elect
Jeff Dmytrowich, Treasurer

Canadian Society of Transplantation (CST) / Société canadienne de transplantation
774 Echo Dr., Ottawa ON K1S 5N8
Tel: 613-730-6274; *Fax:* 613-730-1116
cst@rcpsc.edu
www.cst-transplant.ca
To provide leadership for the advancement of educational, scientific, & clinical aspects of transplantation in Canada
Marcelo Cantarovich, President
Shaf Keshavjee, Secretary-Treasurer

Canadian Spinal Research Organization (CSRO)
#2, 120 Newkirk Rd., Richmond Hill ON L4C 9S7
Tel: 905-508-4000; *Fax:* 905-508-4002
Toll-Free: 800-361-4004
www.csro.com
Social Media: www.youtube.com/user/CSROVideos
www.facebook.com/196341387063476
To improve the physical quality of life for people with spinal injuries; to reduce the incidence of spinal cord injuries through awareness programs for the public & prevention programs with targeted groups
Kent Bassett-Spiers, Executive Director
Barry Munro, President

Canadian Thoracic Society (CTS) / Société canadienne de thoracologie (SCT)
c/o National Office, The Lung Association, #300, 1750 Courtwood Cres., Ottawa ON K2C 2B5
Tel: 613-569-6411; *Fax:* 613-569-8860
Toll-Free: 888-566-5864
ctsinfo@lung.ca
www.lung.ca/cts
To enhance the prevention & treatment of respiratory diseases
George Fox, President
Janet Sutherland, Director
Jean Bourbeau, Secretary
Mark FitzGerald, Treasurer
Suzanne Desmarais, Manager, Communications & Membership
Suzanne McCoy, Manager, Continuing Professional Development

Canadian Tinnitus Foundation
#404, 1688 - 152 St., Surrey BC V4A 4N2
Tel: 604-317-2952
info@findthecurenow.org
www.findthecurenow.org
Social Media:
www.facebook.com/CanadianTinnitusFoundation
A not-for-profit organization working to expand awareness & generate funding for tinnitus research
Nathan Nowak, President
John Jabat, Vice-President
Brian Cassidy, Treasurer

Canadian Transplant Association (CTA) / Association canadienne des greffes
26 Morris St., Ottawa ON K1S 4A7
Toll-Free: 877-779-5991
cta@txworks.ca
www.organ-donation-works.org
Social Media:
www.facebook.com/CanadianTransplantAssociationandGames
twitter.com/CTACanada
To promote a healthy lifestyle for transplant recipients
Aubrey Goldstein, President
Neil Folkins, Director, Membership
Kathy Tachynski, Secretary
Michael J. Sullivan, Treasurer

Canadian Urological Association (CUA) / Association des urologues du Canada
#1303, 1155, University St., Montréal QC H3B 3A7
Tel: 514-395-0376; *Fax:* 514-395-1664
cua@cua.org
www.cua.org
Tiffany Pizioli, Executive Director
Josephine Sciortino, Editorial Director CUAJ

Canadians for Health Research (CHR) / Les Canadiens pour la recherche médicale
PO Box 126, Westmount QC H3Z 2T1
Tel: 514-398-7478; *Fax:* 514-398-8361
info@chrcrm.org
www.chrcrm.org
Social Media:
www.facebook.com/300688209959308
To further understanding & communication among the public, the scientific community & government; To promote stability & quality in Canadian health research; to meet goals through the direct provision of information on request, & development & circulation of literature & special programming; To sponsor periodic conferences, workshops, a journalism award, & a student essay competition
Tim Lougheed, Chair

CancerCare Manitoba (CCMB)
MacCharles Unit, 675 McDermot Ave., Winnipeg MB R3E 0V9
Tel: 204-787-2197; *Toll-Free:* 866-561-1026
donate@cancercare.mb.ca
www.cancercare.mb.ca
Social Media: www.youtube.com/user/CancerCareMB
twitter.com/cancercaremb
To provide exceptional care for patients & their families
Sri Navaratnam, President & CEO
Valerie Wiebe, Vice-President & Chief Officer, Patient Services
Bill Funk, Interim Chief Operating Officer

Cape Breton Regional Hospital Foundation
#209, 45 Weatherbee Rd., Sydney NS B1M 0A1
Tel: 902-567-7752
foundation@cbdha.nshealth.ca
www.becauseyoucare.ca
Social Media:
www.youtube.com/channel/UC_GsK8t5w3UR8HTqjoxTJGQ
www.facebook.com/CapeBretonCares
twitter.com/BecauseUCare
To raise money on behalf of the Cape Breton Regional Hospital in order to improve the services provided to patients & to fund research
Brad Jacobs, CEO

Carcinoid NeuroEndocrine Tumour Society Canada
#4103, 3219 Yonge St., Toronto ON M4N 3S1
Tel: 416-628-3189; *Toll-Free:* 844-628-6788
info@cnetscanada.ca
www.cnetscanada.org
Social Media:
www.facebook.com/cnetscanada
twitter.com/CNETSCanada
To raise awareness about neuroendocrine tumours; to provide help & support to those suffering from this type of cancer; to fund research that treats neuroendocrine tumours
Jackie Herman, President

Cerebral Palsy Association of British Columbia (CPABC)
#330, 409 Granville St., Vancouver BC V6C 1T2
Tel: 604-408-9484; *Fax:* 604-408-9489
Toll-Free: 800-663-0004
www.bccerebralpalsy.com
Social Media:
www.facebook.com/cerebral.palsy.39
To raise awareness of cerebral palsy in the community; To assist those living with cerebral palsy to reach to maximum; To work to see those living with cerebral palsy realize their place as equals within a diverse society; To provide support & services that facilitate these needs; To make a Life Without Limits for people with disabilities
Andy Yu, President
Feri Dehdar, Executive Director

Childhood Cancer Canada Foundation
#801, 21 St. Clair Ave. East, Toronto ON M4T 1L9
Tel: 416-489-6440; *Fax:* 416-489-9812
Toll-Free: 800-363-1062
info@childhoodcancer.ca
www.childhoodcancer.ca
Social Media:
www.facebook.com/ChildhoodCancerCanada
twitter.com/chldhdcancercan
To help improve the lives of children suffering from cancer through family support programs; to fund cancer research
Megan Davidson, President & CEO

Children's Hospital Foundation of Manitoba
#CE501, 840 Sherbrook St., Winnipeg MB R3A 1S1
Tel: 204-787-4000; *Fax:* 204-787-4114
Toll-Free: 866-953-5437
goodbear.mb.ca
Social Media: www.youtube.com/user/DRGoodbear1
www.facebook.com/childrenshospitalfoundation
twitter.com/chfmanitoba
To help raise funds for the Winnipeg Children's Hospital & the Manitoba Institute of Child Health in order to provide patients with improved health care services & to fund research
Lawrence Prout, President & CEO

Children's Hospital Foundation of Saskatchewan
#1, 345 - 3 Ave. South, Saskatoon SK S7K 1M6
Tel: 306-931-4887; *Toll-Free:* 888-808-5437
info@chfsask.ca
www.childrenshospitalsask.ca
Social Media: www.youtube.com/user/ChildHospitalSK
www.facebook.com/CHFSask
twitter.com/childhospitalsk
To help raise funds for the Children's Hospital of Saskatchewan in order to provide patients with improved health care services & to fund research
Robert Hawkins, Chair

Chiropractic Awareness Council (CAC)
#126, 17A - 218 Silvercreek Pkwy. North, Guelph ON N1H 9E9
Tel: 519-822-1879; *Fax:* 519-822-1239
Toll-Free: 877-997-9927
totalhealth@chiropracticawarenesscouncil.org
www.chiropracticawarenesscouncil.org
To promote public awareness of chiropractic life principles by promoting an awareness of the devastating effects of vertebral subluxation complex on the expression of human health potential; To educate the public with the conviction that chiropractic care is a integral aspect of health for people of all ages & to society in general
Steven Silk, Chair

Chronic Pain Association of Canada (CPAC)
PO Box 66017, Stn. Heritage, Edmonton AB T6J 6T4
Tel: 780-482-6727; *Fax:* 780-433-3128
cpac@chronicpaincanada.com
www.chronicpaincanada.com
To advance the treatment & management of chronic intractable pain; to develop research projects to promote the discovery of a cure for this disease; to educate both the health care community & the public
Terry Bremner, President
Barry Ulmer, Executive Director

Collège des médecins du Québec (CMQ)
2170, boul René-Lévesque Ouest, Montréal QC H3H 2T8
Tél: 514-933-4441; *Téléc:* 514-933-3112
Ligne sans frais: 888-633-3246
info@cmq.org
www.cmq.org
Média social: www.facebook.com/257741694238490
twitter.com/CMQ_org
Promouvoir une médecine de qualité pour protéger le public et contribuer à l'amélioration de la santé des Québécois
Charles Bernard, Président-directeur général
Yves Robert, Secrétaire

College of Dietitians of Alberta
#740, 10707 - 100 Ave., Edmonton AB T5J 3M1
Tel: 780-448-0059; *Fax:* 780-489-7759
Toll-Free: 866-493-4348
office@collegeofdietitians.ab.ca
www.collegeofdietitians.ab.ca
The College is the regulatory body of registered dieticians/nutritionists in Alberta, setting entry requirements, standards of practice. It is accountable to both the government & the public.
Doug Cook, Executive Director & Registrar

College of Dietitians of British Columbia (CDBC)
#409, 1367 West Broadway, Vancouver BC V6H 4A7
Tel: 604-736-2016; *Fax:* 604-736-2018
Toll-Free: 877-736-2016
info@collegeofdietitiansbc.org
www.collegeofdietitiansbc.org
To serve & protect the nutritional health of the public through quality dietetic practice
Fred Hubbard, Registrar

College of Dietitians of Manitoba
#36, 1313 Border St., Winnipeg MB R3H 0X4
Tel: 204-694-0532; *Fax:* 204-889-1755
Toll-Free: 866-283-2823
office.cdm@mts.net
www.manitobadietitians.ca
To act as the regulating body within the province for dietitians & the profession of dietetics, setting education standards, ensuring competency of members.
Michelle Hagglund, Registrar

College of Dietitians of Ontario (CDO) / L'Ordre des diététistes de l'Ontario
PO Box 30, #1810, 5775 Yonge St., Toronto ON M2M 4J1
Tel: 416-598-1725; *Fax:* 416-598-0274
Toll-Free: 800-668-4990
information@collegeofdietitians.org
www.collegeofdietitians.org
Social Media:
www.facebook.com/CollegeDietitiansOntario
twitter.com/CDOntario
To promote awareness of & access to competent, high quality nutritional care for Ontarians
Melisse L. Willems, Registrar & Executive Director

College of Family Physicians of Canada (CFPC) / Collège des médecins de famille du Canada
2630 Skymark Ave., Mississauga ON L4W 5A4
Tel: 905-629-0900; *Fax:* 905-629-0893
Toll-Free: 800-387-6197
info@cfpc.ca
www.cfpc.ca
Social Media: www.youtube.com/user/CFPCMedia
twitter.com/FamPhysCan
To improve the health of Canadians by promoting high standards of medical education & care in family practice, by contributing to public understanding of healthful living, by supporting ready access to family physician services, & by encouraging research & disseminating knowledge about family medicine
Marie-Dominique Beaulieu, MD, CCFP, FCFP, President
Kathy Lawrence, MD, CCFP, FCFP, President-Elect & Chair
Calvin Gutkin, MD, CCFP (EM), Executive Director/CEO

College of Naturopathic Doctors of Alberta (CNDA)
813 - 14th St. NW, Calgary AB T2N 2A4
Tel: 403-266-2446; *Fax:* 403-226-2433
secretary@cnda.net
www.cnda.net
Social Media:
twitter.com/CollegeNDAB
To maintain a high standard of practice among naturopathic doctors.
Alissa Gaul, President

College of Occupational Therapists of British Columbia (COTBC)
Yarrow Bldg., #219, 645 Fort St., Victoria BC V8W 1G2
Tel: 250-386-6822; *Fax:* 250-383-4144
Toll-Free: 866-386-6822
info@cotbc.org
www.cotbc.org
To establish standards of practice & conduct; To enhance quality assurance; To monitor quality of practice & continuing competence; To improve competence of occupational therapists; To investigate complaints; To enforce standards
Kathy Corbett, Registrar-CEO
Cindy McLean, Deputy Registrar

College of Physicians & Surgeons of Alberta (CPSA)
#2700, 10020 - 100 St. NW, Edmonton AB T5J 0N3
Tel: 780-423-4764; *Fax:* 780-420-0651
Toll-Free: 800-561-3899
info@cpsa.ab.ca
www.cpsa.ab.ca
To serve the public & guide the medical profession; to identify factors affecting competent medical practice; to promote quality improvement in medical practice; to ensure practitioners meet our registration standards; to resolve complaints involving practitioners fairly & effectively.
Trevor Theman, Registrar

College of Physicians & Surgeons of British Columbia (CPSBC)
#300, 699 Howe St., Vancouver BC V6C 0B4
Tel: 604-733-7758; *Fax:* 604-733-3503
Toll-Free: 800-461-3008
www.cpsbc.ca
Social Media:
linkedin.com/company/2905395
twitter.com/cpsbc_ca
L.C. Jewett, President
Heidi Oetter, Registrar

College of Physicians & Surgeons of Manitoba (CPSM)
#1000, 1661 Portage Ave., Winnipeg MB R3J 3T7
Tel: 204-774-4344; *Fax:* 204-774-0750
Toll-Free: 877-774-4344
cpsm@cpsm.mb.ca
cpsm.mb.ca
Brent Kvern, President
Anna Ziomek, Registrar

College of Physicians & Surgeons of New Brunswick / Collège des médecins et chirurgiens du Nouveau-Brunswick
#300, 1 Hampton Rd., Rothesay NB E2E 5K8
Tel: 506-849-5050; *Fax:* 506-849-5069
Toll-Free: 800-667-4641
info@cpsnb.org
www.cpsnb.org
Lisa Jean Sutherland, President

College of Physicians & Surgeons of Newfoundland & Labrador
#W100, 120 Torbay Rd., St. John's NL A1A 2G8
Tel: 709-726-8546; *Fax:* 709-726-4725
cpsnl@cpsnl.ca
www.cpsnl.ca
To protect the public; to regulate the practice of medicine & medical practitioners
Linda Inkpen, Registrar
Arthur Rideout, Chair

College of Physicians & Surgeons of Nova Scotia (CPSNS)
#5005, 7071 Bayers Rd., Halifax NS B3L 2C2
Tel: 902-422-5823; *Fax:* 902-422-7476
Toll-Free: 877-282-7767
info@cpsns.ns.ca
www.cpsns.ns.ca
Social Media:
linkedin.com/company/2497006
www.facebook.com/291670920671
To govern the practice of medicine in the public interest
James MacLachlan, President

College of Physicians & Surgeons of Ontario (CPSO)
80 College St., Toronto ON M5G 2E2
Tel: 416-967-2603; *Fax:* 416-961-3330
Toll-Free: 800-268-7096
feedback@cpso.on.ca
www.cpso.on.ca
Social Media: www.youtube.com/user/theCpso
linkedin.com/groups/College-Physicians-Surgeons-Ontario-4760466
www.facebook.com/144601285573797
twitter.com/cpso_ca
To ensure the best quality care for the people of Ontario by the doctors of Ontario
Carol Leet, President
Rocco Gerace, Registrar

College of Physicians & Surgeons of Prince Edward Island
14 Paramount Dr., Charlottetown PE C1E 0C7
Tel: 902-566-3861; *Fax:* 902-566-3986
cpspei.ca
To act as the regulatory body for physicians in the province, responsible for licensing all medical doctors, maintaining medical standards, handling complaints from the public, & delivering disciplinary action.
Cyril Moyse, Registrar

College of Physicians & Surgeons of Saskatchewan (CPSS)
#500, 321A - 21st St. East, Saskatoon SK S7K 0C1
Tel: 306-244-7355; *Fax:* 306-244-0090
Toll-Free: 800-667-1668
cpss@quadrant.net
www.quadrant.net/cpss/
To be responsible for licencing properly qualified medical practitioners, developing and ensuring the standards of practice in all fields of medicine, investigating and disciplining of all doctors whose standards of medical care, ethical or professional conduct are questioned.
Bryan Salte, Associate Registrar
David Pulin, Deputy Registrar
Karen Shaw, Registrar

Community & Hospital Infection Control Association Canada / Association pour la prévention des infections à l'hôpital et dans la communauté - Canada
PO Box 46125, RPO Westdale, Winnipeg MB R3R 3S3
Tel: 204-897-5990; *Fax:* 204-895-9595
Toll-Free: 866-999-7111
admin@ipac-canada.org
www.chica.org
Social Media: plus.google.com/110560934212739734281
linkedin.com/company/3590721
www.facebook.com/179334712101680
twitter.com/CHICACanada
To promote excellence in the practice of infection prevention & control; to employ evidence based practice & application of epidemiological principles to improve the health of Canadians
Gerry Hansen, Execurive Director

Conseil communauté en santé du Manitoba (CCS)
#400, 400, av Taché, Saint-Boniface MB R2H 3C3
Tél: 204-235-2393; *Téléc:* 204-237-0984
ccs@ccsmanitoba.ca
ccsmanitoba.ca
Annie Bédard, Directrice générale

Conseil québécois sur le tabac et la santé / Québec Council on Tobacco & Health
#302, 4126, rue St-Denis, Montréal QC H2W 2M5
Tél: 514-948-5317; *Téléc:* 514-948-4582
info@cqts.qc.ca
www.cqts.qc.ca
Média social: www.facebook.com/317301810228
twitter.com/cqts
Promouvoir la santé du fumeur et du non-fumeur; faire le lien entre les associations, groupes bénévoles et autres intéressés à la santé publique; trouver des approches et des moyens pour améliorer l'éducation face à l'usage du tabac
Mario Bujold, Directeur général
Marie-Soleil Boivin, Agente, Communication et relations médias

Consumer Health Organization of Canada (CHOC)
#1901, 355 St. Clair Ave. West, Toronto ON M5P 1N5
Tel: 416-924-9800; *Fax:* 416-924-6404
info@consumerhealth.org
www.consumerhealth.org
To encourage the prevention of all kinds of illness through knowledge; to help the individual, the family & the community to enjoy the benefits of a more wholesome lifestyle; to promote harmony & cooperation between like-minded groups.
Libby Gardon, President

Crohn's & Colitis Canada / Crohn's et Colitis Canada
#600, 60 St. Clair Ave. East, Toronto ON M4T 1N5
Tel: 416-920-5035; *Fax:* 416-929-0364
Toll-Free: 800-387-1479
support@crohnsandcolitis.ca
www.crohnsandcolitis.ca
Social Media: www.youtube.com/user/getgutsy
www.facebook.com/crohnsandcolitis.ca
twitter.com/getgutsyCanada
To find a cure for Crohn's disease & ulcerative colitis; To raise funds for medical research; To educate individuals with inflammatory bowel disease, their families, health professionals, & the public
Lindee David, CEO
Har Grover, Chair
Mark Ram, Secretary
Byron Sonberg, Treasurer

Cystic Fibrosis Canada / Fibrose Kystique Canada
National Office, #800, 2323 Yonge St., Toronto ON M4P 2C9
Tel: 416-485-9149; *Fax:* 416-485-0960
Toll-Free: 800-378-2233
info@cysticfibrosis.ca
www.cysticfibrosis.ca
Social Media: www.youtube.com/CysticFibrosisCanada
www.facebook.com/CysticFibrosisCanada
twitter.com/CFCanada
To help people with Cystic Fibrosis through funding research towards a cure or control; To support high quality care; To promote public awareness; To raise & allocate funds
Norma Beauchamp, President & CEO

Diabète Québec (ADQ) / Diabetes Quebec
#300, 8550, boul Pie-IX, Montréal QC H1Z 4G2
Tél: 514-259-3422; *Téléc:* 514-259-9286
Ligne sans frais: 800-361-3504
info@diabete.qc.ca
www.diabete.qc.ca
Média social: www.facebook.com/179747505687
twitter.com/DiabeteQuebec
Regrouper les diabétiques et favoriser l'entraide; les renseigner sur les façons de faire face à la maladie; informer le grand public et le sensibiliser à la condition de personnes souffrant du diabète; ouvrir de nouvelles voies dans le domaine de la recherche pour en venir à triompher du diabète
Serge Langlois, Président-directeur général
Sylvie Lauzon, Chef des opération, Directrice, Développement

Dietitians of Canada (DC) / Les diététistes du Canada
#604, 480 University Ave., Toronto ON M5G 1V2
Tel: 416-596-0857; *Fax:* 416-596-0603
centralinfo@dietitians.ca
www.dietitians.ca
To advance health, through food & nutrition; To act as the voice of the profession in Canada
Marsha Sharp, Chief Executive Officer
Corinne Eisenbraun, Director, Professional Practice Development
Janice Macdonald, Director, Communications
Marlene Wyatt, Director, Professional Affairs
Patricia Sierra, Manager, Finance & Administration

Doctors Manitoba
20 Desjardins Dr., Winnipeg MB R3X 0E8
Tel: 204-985-5888; *Fax:* 204-985-5844
Toll-Free: 888-322-4242
general@docsmb.org
www.docsmb.org
To unite & advocate for Manitoba physicians; To encourage the highest standards of health care for the people of Manitoba
Robert Cram, Chief Executive Officer
Rick Sawyer, Chief Administrative Officer

Doctors Nova Scotia
25 Spectacle Lake Dr., Dartmouth NS B3B 1X7
Tel: 902-468-1866; *Fax:* 902-468-6578
Toll-Free: 800-563-3427
info@doctorsns.com
www.doctorsns.com
Social Media:
twitter.com/Doctors_NS
To maintain the integrity of the medical profession; To represent members; To promote high quality health care & disease prevention in Nova Scotia
Nancy MacCready-Williams, CEO
John Sullivan, President

Doctors of BC
#115, 1665 West Broadway, Vancouver BC V6J 5A4
Tel: 604-736-5551; *Fax:* 604-638-2917
Toll-Free: 800-665-2262
communications@doctorsofbc.ca
www.doctorsofbc.ca
Social Media:
twitter.com/doctorsofbc
To promote a social, economic & political climate in which members can provide the citizens of British Columbia with the highest standard of health care while achieving maximum professional satisfaction & fair economic reward.
William Cunningham, President

Dystonia Medical Research Foundation Canada / Fondation de recherches médicales sur la dystonie
#305, 121 Richmond St. West, Toronto ON M5H 2K1
Tel: 416-488-6974; *Fax:* 416-488-5878
Toll-Free: 800-361-8061
www.dystoniacanada.org
Social Media:
www.facebook.com/DMRFC
To advance & support research relating to dystonia; to build awareness about the illness in order to educate both medical & lay communities; to sponsor patient & family support groups & programs.
Diane S. Gillespie, Executive Director

Eating Disorder Association of Canada (EDAC) / Association des Troubles Alimentaires du Canada (ATAC)
ON
edacatac@gmail.com
www.edac-atac.ca
Social Media:
twitter.com/EDACATAC
EDAC-ATAC aims to serve the needs of those whose lives are impacted by eating disorders.
Jadine Cairns, President

Edmonton (Alberta) Nerve Pain Association (EANPA)
14016 - 91 A Ave., Edmonton AB T5R 5A7
Tel: 780-217-9306
Neuropathy_nervepain@hotmail.com
www.edmontonnervepain.ca
To support people suffering from neuropathic pain.
Claude M. Roberto, President

effect:hope
#200, 90 Allstate Pkwy., Markham ON L3R 6H3
Tel: 905-886-2885; *Fax:* 905-886-2885
Toll-Free: 888-537-7679
info@effecthope.org
effecthope.org
Social Media: www.youtube.com/user/effecthope
linkedin.com/company/3068053
www.facebook.com/effecthope
twitter.com/effecthope
To provide care & support to leprosy patients in many parts of the world including India, Bangladesh, and Nigeria.
Peter Derrick, Executive Director

Epilepsy & Seizure Association of Manitoba
#4, 1805 Main St., Winnipeg MB R2V 2A2
Tel: 204-783-0466; *Fax:* 204-784-9689
Toll-Free: 866-374-5377
epilepsy.seizures.mb@mts.net
www.manitobaepilepsy.org
To improve the quality of life of persons with epilepsy through a broad range of programs, education, support of research & services.
Jim Cook, President
Chris Vander Aa, Vice-President
Diane Wall, Secretary
Ruby Fife, Treasurer

Epilepsy Canada (EC) / Épilepsie Canada
#2B, 2900 John St., Markham ON L3R 5G3
Fax: 905-764-1231
Toll-Free: 877-734-0873
epilepsy@epilepsy.ca
www.epilepsy.ca
To enhance the quality of life for persons affected by epilepsy; To promote & support research into all aspects of epilepsy; To facilitate educational initiatives; To increase public & professional awareness of epilepsy; To fund research; To encourage governments to address the needs of people with epilepsy
Jacques Brunelle, National President
Gary N. Collins, Executive Director

Epilepsy Ontario / Épilepsie Ontario
#803, 3100 Steeles Ave. East, Markham ON L3R 8T3
Tel: 905-474-9696; *Fax:* 905-474-3663
Toll-Free: 800-463-1119
info@epilepsyontario.org
epilepsyontario.org
Social Media:
www.facebook.com/epilepsyontario1
twitter.com/EpilepsyOntario
To promote optimal quality of life for people living with seizure disorders; to advocate for awareness, support services & research into these disorders and maintains a network of local agencies, contacts & associates to provide services, counselling & referrals.
Rozalyn Werner-Arcé, Executive Director

Ethiopiaid
#900, 275 Slater St., Ottawa ON K1P 5H9
Tel: 613-697-4843
info@ethiopiaid.ca
www.ethiopiaid.ca
Social Media:
twitter.com/EthiopiaidCAN
Ethiopiaid aims to create lasting and positive change in Ethiopia by tackling the problems of poverty, ill health and poor education.
As a fundraising organisation, it donates directly to local community projects in Ethiopia.

Evangelical Medical Aid Society Canada (EMAS)
#1, 20 Freel Lane, Stouffville ON L4A 5B9
Tel: 905-642-4661; *Fax:* 905-642-1616
Toll-Free: 866-648-0664
www.emascanada.org
To heal, teach & serve in a Christlike manner
Peter Agwa, Executive Director
Ellen Watson, Director, Administration

Eye Bank of BC (EBBC)
Jim Pattison Pavilion North - B205, 855 West 12th Ave, Vancouver BC V5Z 1M9
Tel: 604-875-4567; *Fax:* 604-875-5316
Toll-Free: 800-667-2060
eyebankofbc@vch.ca
www.eyebankofbc.ca
Social Media:
www.facebook.com/EyeBankBC
To acquire human donor eye tissue for the purposes of corneal transplant, scelra grafts & medical research.
Linda Wong, Manager
J. Martin McCarthy, Medical Director

Eye Bank of Canada - Ontario Division
Dept. of Ophthalmology, University of Toronto, 1929 Bayview Ave., Toronto ON M4G 0A1
Tel: 416-978-7355; *Fax:* 416-978-1522
eye.bank@utoronto.ca
www.eyebank.utoronto.ca
To provide donated eye tissue for surgical use in those whose vision can be restored or improved through corneal transplantation or other eye surgery
Fides Coloma, Manager

Fédération des médecins omnipraticiens du Québec (FMOQ) / Québec Federation of General Practitioners
2, Place Alexis Nihon, #2000, 3500, boul. de Maisonneuve ouest, Montréal QC H3G 1R8
Tél: 514-878-1911; *Téléc:* 514-878-4455
Ligne sans frais: 800-361-8499
info@fmoq.org
www.fmoq.org
Étude et défense des intérêts économiques, sociaux, moraux et scientifiques des associations et de leurs membres; promouvoir et développer le rôle de l'omnipraticien dans les sphères de la vie économique, sociale, scientifique et culturelle en définissant d'une façon objective le statut propre à l'omnipraticien
Louis Godin, Président-directeur général

Fédération des médecins spécialistes du Québec (FMSQ)
CP 216, Succ. Desjardins, #3000, 2, Complexe Desjardins, Montréal QC H5B 1G8
Tél: 514-350-5000; *Téléc:* 514-350-5100
Ligne sans frais: 800-561-0703
communications@fmsq.org
www.fmsq.org
Média social: www.facebook.com/laFMSQ
twitter.com/FMSQ
Défendre et promouvoir les intérêts économiques, professionnels et scientifiques des médecins spécialistes
Gaétan Barrette, Président

Federation of Medical Regulatory Authorities of Canada (FMRAC) / Fédération des ordres des médecins du Canada
#103, 2283 St. Laurent Blvd., Ottawa ON K1G 5A2
Tel: 613-738-0372; *Fax:* 613-738-9169
info@fmrac.ca
www.fmrac.ca
To provide a national structure for the provincial & territorial medical regulatory authorities; To present & pursue issues of common concern & interest; To share, consider, & develop positions on such matters
Fleur-Ange Lefebvre, Executive Director & CEO

Fédération québécoise de l'autisme et des autres troubles envahissants du développement (FQATED) / Québec Federation for Autism & Other Pervasive Developmental Disorders
#200, 7675, boul Saint-Laurent, Montréal QC H2R 1W9
Tél: 514-270-7386; *Téléc:* 514-270-9261
Ligne sans frais: 888-830-2833
info@autisme.qc.ca
www.autisme.qc.ca
Média social: www.facebook.com/198123333548170
Promouvoir et défendre les droits et les intérêts de la personne autiste ou ayant un trouble envahissant du développement afin qu'elle accède à une vie digne et à une meilleure autonomie sociale possible.
Jo-Ann Lauzon, Directrice générale

Fédération québécoise des massothérapeutes (FQM)
#400, 4428, boul St-Laurent, Montréal QC H2W 1Z5
Tél: 514-597-0505; *Téléc:* 514-597-0141
Ligne sans frais: 800-363-9609
administration@fqm.qc.ca
www.fqm.qc.ca
Média social: www.youtube.com/user/FQMmassotherapie
www.facebook.com/massotherapie.FQM
twitter.com/FederationFQM
Regrouper les massothérapeutes afin de promouvoir la massothérapie sous l'intérêt public et de valoriser la profession de la massothérapie
Sylvie Bédard, Présidente directrice générale

Fédération québécoise des sociétés Alzheimer (FQSA) / Federation of Québec Alzheimer Societies
#211, 5165, rue Sherbrooke ouest, Montréal QC H4A 1T6
Tél: 514-369-7891; *Téléc:* 514-369-7900
Ligne sans frais: 888-636-6473
info@alzheimerquebec.ca
www.alzheimerquebec.ca
Média social: www.youtube.com/user/FQSA1
www.facebook.com/LaFederationQuebecoiseDesSocietesAlzheimer
twitter.com/FqsaAlzh
Alléger les conséquences personnelles et sociales de la maladie d'Alzheimer; diffuser l'information auprès du public sur la maladie d'Alzheimer et sur les services offerts par notre réseau; soutenir les sociétés qui offrent aide et formation; promouvoir et encourager la recherche sur la maladie d'Alzheimer entre autres par la gestion d'un fonds provincial de la recherche; établir des

relations et faire des représentations auprès des autorités concernées
Réal Leahey, Président
Diane Roch, Directrice générale

Fibrose kystique Québec (FKQ) / Cystic Fibrosis Québec (CFQ)
625 av du Président-Kennedy, Montréal QC H3A 1K2
Tél: 514-877-6161; *Téléc:* 514-877-6116
Ligne sans frais: 800-363-7711
www.fibrosekystiquequebec.com
Mèdia social: plus.google.com/106908476349956061911
www.facebook.com/162576157129896
twitter.com/FKQuebec
Sensibiliser la population sur la fibrose kystique; amasser des fonds pour la recherche médicale; améliorer la qualité de vie des personnes atteintes de FK; découvrir un remède ou un moyen de contrôler la fibrose kystique.
Benoit Vigneau, Président-directeur général

A fleur de sein
313 3e Rue, Chibougamau QC G8P 1N4
Tél: 418-748-7914; *Téléc:* 418-748-4422
Offrir solidarité, présence, écoute & entraide à ceux & celles qui sont atteints d'un cancer, quel qu'il soit
Suzanne Hamel Migneaul, Présidente, A fleur de sein

La Fondation canadienne du rein, section Chibougamau
CP 462, Chibougamau QC G8P 2Y8
Hélène Ross-Arseneault

Fondation de la banque d'yeux du Québec inc. / Québec Eye Bank Foundation
5415, boul de l'Assomption, Montréal QC H1T 2M4
Tél: 514-252-3886; *Téléc:* 514-252-3821
Financement de la recherche sur les maladies de l'oeil et plus particulièment de la cornée (greffe)
Daniel Michaluk, Coordonnatrice administrative

Fondation des étoiles / Foundation of Stars
#205, 370, rue Guy, Montréal QC H3J 1S6
Tél: 514-595-5730; *Téléc:* 514-595-5745
Ligne sans frais: 800-665-2358
info@fondationdesetoiles.ca
www.fondationdesetoiles.ca
Mèdia social: instagram.com/fondation_des_etoiles
linkedin.com/in/fondation-des-%C3%A9toiles-77a55063
www.facebook.com/FondationDesEtoiles
twitter.com/EnfantsEtoiles
Amasser des fonds pour la recherche sur les maladies infantiles au Québec; ces fonds sont distribués aux quatre centres de recherche suivants: Centre de recherche de l'Hôpital Ste-Justine, Institut de recherche de l'Hôpital de Montréal pour enfants, Centre Hospitalier Universitaire de Québec et Centre Hospitalier Universitaire de Sherbrooke
Josée Saint-Pierre, Présidente-directrice générale
Étienne Lalonde, Directeur, Développement

Fondation des maladies du coeur du Québec (FMCQ) / Heart & Stroke Foundation of Québec
#500, 1434, rue Sainte-Catherine ouest, Montréal QC H3G 1R4
Tél: 514-871-1551; *Téléc:* 514-871-9385
Ligne sans frais: 800-567-8563
www.fmcoeur.qc.ca
Mèdia social: www.youtube.com/heartandstrokefdn
www.facebook.com/fmcoeur
twitter.com/FMCoeur
Forte de l'engagement de ses donateurs, de ses bénévoles et de ses employés, a pour mission de contribuer à l'avancement de la recherche et de promouvoir la santé du coeur, afin de réduire les invalidités et les décès dus aux maladies cardiovasculaires et aux accidents vasculaires cérébraux
Edmée Métivier, Chef de la direction
Éric Champagne, Président du conseil

Fondation québécoise du cancer
2075, rue de Champlain, Montréal QC H2L 2T1
Tél: 514-527-2194; *Téléc:* 514-527-1943
Ligne sans frais: 877-336-4443
cancerquebec.mtl@fqc.qc.ca
www.fqc.qc.ca
Mèdia social: www.facebook.com/fqcancer
Vouée à l'amélioration de la condition de la personne atteinte de cancer et de ses proches; offrir des services d'hôtellerie, d'écoute et d'information pour gens atteints du cancer; améliorer la qualité de vie des patients et celle de leurs proches.
Pierre-Yves Gagnon, Directeur général

The Foundation Fighting Blindness (FFB)
890 Yonge St., 12th Fl., Toronto ON M4W 3P4
Tel: 416-360-4200; *Fax:* 416-360-0060
Toll-Free: 800-461-3331
info@ffb.ca
www.ffb.ca
Social Media: www.youtube.com/user/FFBCanada
www.facebook.com/187447074652378
twitter.com/FFBCanada
To support & promote research directed to finding the causes, treatments & ultimately the cures for retinitis pigmentosa, macular degeneration & related retinal diseases
Sharon M. Colle, President & CEO
Rahn Dodick, Treasurer
Malcolm Hunter, Corporate Secretary

Genesis Research Foundation
92 College St., 3rd Fl., Toronto ON M5G 1L4
Tel: 416-978-2667
www.genesisresearch.org
Social Media:
linkedin.com/company/genesis-research-foundation
twitter.com/GenesisOrg
To fund & promote research & understanding in women's health in the areas of obstetrics & gynaecology
Alan Bocking, MD, FRCSC, Chair

Geneva Centre for Autism (GCA)
112 Merton St., Toronto ON M4S 2Z8
Tel: 416-322-7877; *Fax:* 416-322-5894
Toll-Free: 866-436-3829
info@autism.net
www.autism.net
Social Media:
linkedin.com/company/geneva-centre-for-autism
www.facebook.com/genevacentre
twitter.com/geneva_centre
To empower individuals with autism & other related disorders & their families, to fully participate in their communities
Debbie Irish, Chief Executive Officer
Jim Gilmour, Chief Financial Officer
Debbie Drewett, Director, Development

GI (Gastrointestinal) Society
#231, 3665 Kingsway, Vancouver BC V5R 5W2
Tel: 604-873-4876; *Fax:* 604-875-4429
Toll-Free: 866-600-4875
www.badgut.org
Social Media: www.youtube.com/user/badgutcanada
www.facebook.com/CISociety
twitter.com/GISociety
To improve the lives of people with GI and liver conditions, support research, advocate for appropriate patient access to healthcare & promote gastrointestinal & liver health
Lynda Cranston, Chairperson
Gail Attara, Co-Founder & President/CEO

Glaucoma Research Society of Canada / Société canadienne de recherche sur le glaucome
#215E, 1929 Bayview Ave., Toronto ON M4G 3E8
Tel: 416-483-0200; *Toll-Free:* 877-483-0204
info@glaucomaresearch.ca
www.glaucomaresearch.ca
The Glaucoma Research Society of Canada is a national registered charity committed to funding research into the causes, diagnosis, prevention and treatment of glaucoma.
Martin Chasson, President

Headache Network Canada (HNC)
210 Georgian Drive, Oakville ON L6H 6T8
Tel: 905-330-9657
headachenetwork.ca
To raise awareness about headache disorders in Canada; To encourage government assistance to the field; To educate the public about headache disorders

Health Action Network Society (HANS)
#214, 5589 Rumble Rd., Burnaby BC V5J 3J1
Tel: 604-435-0512; *Fax:* 604-435-1561
Toll-Free: 855-787-1891
hans@hans.org
www.hans.org
Social Media:
www.facebook.com/HANSHealthAction
twitter.com/JoinHANS
To support complementary & alternative health care; To provide resources about preventive medicine & natural therapeutics; To facilitate delivery of integrated health care; To act as a voice for natural health consumers in Canada
Lorna Hancock, Director

Health Association of African Canadians (HAAC)
c/o Black Cultural Centre for Nova Scotia, 10 Cherry Brook Rd., Cherry Brook NS B2Z 1A8
Tel: 902-405-4222
info@africancanadianhealth.ca
africancanadianhealth.ca
To promote and improve the health of African Canadians in Nova Scotia through community engagement, education, policy recommendations, partnerships, and research participation.
Donna Smith Darrell, President/Treasurer

Health Care Public Relations Association (HCPRA) / Association des relations publiques des organismes de la santé (ARPOS)
PO Box 36029, 1106 Wellington St., Ottawa ON K1Y 4V3
Tel: 613-729-2102; *Fax:* 613-729-7708
info@hcpra.org
www.hcpra.org
Social Media:
linkedin.com/HCPRA
www.facebook.com/165490196835523
twitter.com/HCPRA
To address the concerns of the public relations professionals in Canadian health care settings
Jane Adams, National Coordinator
Judy Brown, HCPRA President

Health Sciences Centre Foundation (HSCF)
Thorlakson Building, 820 Sherbrook St., #MS107, Winnipeg MB R3A 1R9
Tel: 204-787-2022; *Fax:* 204-787-2804
Toll-Free: 800-679-8493
hsc_foundation@hsc.mb.ca
www.hscfoundation.mb.ca
Social Media:
www.facebook.com/hscfdn
twitter.com/hscfoundation
HSC Foundation supports the men and women who provide health care at Health Sciences Centre Winnipeg by funding research, education, advanced technology and infrastructure enhancements.
Jonathon Lyon, President & CEO
Sue Graham, Vice-President

Heart & Stroke Foundation of Alberta, NWT & Nunavut (HSFA)
#100, 119 - 14 St. NW, Calgary AB T2N 1Z6
Tel: 403-351-7030; *Fax:* 403-237-0803
Toll-Free: 888-473-4636
www.hsf.ab.ca
To disseminate information about heart disease & stroke; to promote research into new drugs, therapies, treatments in disorders leading to heart disease & stroke; to conduct several events to campaign for funds.
Michael Hill, Chair
Donna Hastings, CEO

Heart & Stroke Foundation of British Columbia & Yukon (HSFBCY)
#200, 1212 West Broadway, Vancouver BC V6H 3V2
Tel: 778-372-8000
www.heartandstroke.bc.ca
Social Media:
www.facebook.com/heartandstrokebcyukon
To further the study, prevention & relief of cardiovascular disease
Adrienne Bakker, CEO

Heart & Stroke Foundation of Canada (HSFC) / Fondation des maladies du coeur du Canada
#1402, 222 Queen St., Ottawa ON K1P 5V9
Tel: 613-569-4361; *Fax:* 613-569-3278
www.heartandstroke.ca
Social Media: www.youtube.com/heartandstrokefdn
www.facebook.com/heartandstroke
twitter.com/TheHSF
To further the study, prevention & reduction of disability & death from heart disease & stroke through research, education & the promotion of healthy lifestyles
David Sculthorpe, CEO
Douglas B. Clement, Chair

Heart & Stroke Foundation of Manitoba (HSFM)
The Heart & Stroke Bldg., #200, 6 Donald St., Winnipeg MB R3L 0K6
Tel: 204-949-2000; *Fax:* 204-957-1365
www.heartandstroke.mb.ca
To eliminate heart disease & stroke through education, advocacy, & research
Debbie Brown, CEO

Heart & Stroke Foundation of New Brunswick / Fondation des maladies du coeur du Nouveau-Brunswick
133 Prince William St., 5th Fl, Saint John NB E2L 2B5
Tel: 506-634-1620; *Fax:* 506-648-0098
Toll-Free: 800-663-3600
www.heartandstroke.nb.ca
To improve the health of residents of New Brunswick by preventing & reducing disability & death from heart disease & stroke, through research, health promotion & advocacy
Kurtis Sisk, CEO

Heart & Stroke Foundation of Newfoundland & Labrador
1037 Topsail Rd., Mount Pearl NL A1N 5E9
Tel: 709-753-8521; *Fax:* 709-753-3117
www.heartandstroke.nf.ca
To work in Newfoundland & Labrador to advance research, advocate, & promote healthy lifestyles so that heart disease & stroke will be eliminated & their impact reduced
Mary Ann Butt, CEO

Heart & Stroke Foundation of Nova Scotia (HSFNS)
Park Lane - Mall Level 3, PO Box 245, 5657 Spring Garden Rd., Halifax NS B3J 3R4
Tel: 902-423-7530; *Fax:* 902-492-1464
Toll-Free: 800-423-4432
www.heartandstroke.ns.ca
To eliminate heart disease & stroke; To advance research; To promote healthy living; To engage in advocacy activities
Menna MacIsaac, CEO

Heart & Stroke Foundation of Ontario (HSFO)
PO Box 2414, #1300, 2300 Yonge St., Toronto ON M4P 1E4
Tel: 416-489-7111; *Fax:* 416-489-6885
www.heartandstroke.on.ca
To eliminate heart disease & stroke by advancing research & promoting healthy living; To advocate in areas such as a smoke-free world, equal access to quality stroke care, obesity targeting, elimination of trans-fat, & resuscitation/CPR
Barry Cracower, Chair

Heart & Stroke Foundation of Prince Edward Island Inc.
PO Box 279, 180 Kent St., Charlottetown PE C1A 7K4
Tel: 902-892-7441; *Fax:* 902-368-7068
www.heartandstroke.pe.ca
To improve the health of Islanders through the funding of heart disease & stroke research & the provision of heart & stroke education & programs
Charlotte Comrie, CEO
Sharon Hollingsworth, Manager, Communications
Sarah Crozier, Manager, Health Promotion

Heart & Stroke Foundation of Saskatchewan (HSFS) / Fondation des maladies du coeur de la Saskatchewan
279 - 3 Ave. North, Saskatoon SK S7K 2H8
Tel: 306-244-2124; *Fax:* 306-664-4016
Toll-Free: 888-473-4636
heart.stroke@hsf.sk.ca
www.heartandstroke.sk.ca
Social Media: www.youtube.com/saskheart
linkedin.com/company/heart-and-stroke-foundation-saskatchewan
www.facebook.com/heartandstrokesask
To eliminate & reduce the impact of heart disease & stroke; to advance research, promote healthy living, & advocates a healthy public policy.

Hepatitis Outreach Society of Nova Scotia (HepNS)
PO Box 29120, RPO Halifax Shopping Centre, #201, 5571 Cunard St., Halifax NS B3J 4T8
Tel: 902-420-1767; *Fax:* 902-463-6725
Toll-Free: 800-521-0572
info@hepns.ca
www.hepns.ca
Social Media: www.youtube.com/user/HepNSca
www.facebook.com/114379611934070
twitter.com/HepNSca
To educate Nova Scotians about Hepatitis and its prevention, reduce social stigmatization and isolation; and prevent the spread of Hepatitis.
Angus Campbell, Executive Director

Hospital for Sick Children Foundation (HSCF)
525 University Ave., 14th Fl., Toronto ON M5G 2L3
Tel: 416-813-6166; *Fax:* 416-813-5024
Toll-Free: 800-661-1083
www.sickkidsfoundation.com
Social Media: www.youtube.com/sickkidsfoundation
www.facebook.com/sickkidsfoundation
twitter.com/sickkids
To invest contributions in paediatric care, research & education to help children at The Hospital for Sick Children, throughout Canada, & around the world
Ted Garrard, President/CEO
Kathleen Taylor, Chair
L. Robin Cardozo, Chief Operating Officer
Josee Bertrand, Director, Finance
Noelle de la Mothe, Director, Direct Marketing
Nora Paradis, Director, Human Resources

Huntington Society of Canada (HSC) / Société Huntington du Canada
#400, 151 Frederick St., Kitchener ON N2H 2M2
Tel: 519-749-7063; *Fax:* 519-749-8965
Toll-Free: 800-998-7398
info@huntingtonsociety.ca
www.huntingtonsociety.ca
Social Media: www.youtube.com/user/HuntSocCanada
linkedin.com/company/huntington-society-of-canada
www.facebook.com/HuntingtonSC
twitter.com/HuntingtonSC
To aspire for a world free of Huntington disease; To maximize the quality of life of people living with HD
Bev Heim-Myers, CEO

Hypertension Canada
c/o Judi Farrell, #211, 3780 - 14th Ave., Markham ON L3R 9Y5
Tel: 905-943-9400; *Fax:* 905-943-9401
www.hypertension.ca
Social Media: www.youtube.com/user/hypertensioncanada
twitter.com/HTNCANADA
To advance health by preventing & controlling high blood pressure
Ernesto Schiffrin, President
Angelique Berg, Chief Executive Officer
Laura Syron, Vice-President
Robert Brooks, Treasurer

Immunize Canada / Immunisation Canada
c/o Canadian Public Health Association, #404, 1525 Carling Ave., Ottawa ON K1Z 8R9
Tel: 613-725-3769; *Fax:* 613-725-9826
immunize.ca
Social Media: www.youtube.com/user/ImmunizeCanada
www.facebook.com/ImmunizeCanada
twitter.com/immunizedotca
To contribute to the control/elimination/eradication of vaccine preventable diseases in Canada by increasing awareness of the benefits & risks of immunization for all ages.
Susan Bowles, BSc, Phm, Pharm, Chair
Shelly McNeil, MD, FRCPC, Vice-Chair

International Association for Medical Assistance to Travellers (IAMAT)
#036, 67 Mowat Ave., Toronto ON M6K 3E3
Tel: 416-652-0137; *Fax:* 416-652-1983
www.iamat.org
Social Media: www.flickr.com/photos/iamat_photo_contest/
www.facebook.com/IAMATHealth
twitter.com/IAMAT_Travel
To make competent care available to the traveller around the world; to make direct grants to medical institutions
Assunta Uffer-Marcolongo, President
Tullia Marcolongo, Director, Programs & Development
Nadia Sallete, Director, Membership Services

International Dyslexia Association (IDA)
40 York Rd., 4th Fl/, Baltimore MD 21204 USA
Tel: 410-296-0232; *Fax:* 410-321-5069
info@interdys.org
eida.org
Social Media: www.youtube.com/user/idachannel
linkedin.com/company/international-dyslexia-association
www.facebook.com/interdys
twitter.com/IntlDyslexia
The IDA actively promotes effective teaching approaches and related clinical educational intervention strategies for dyslexics.

Juvenile Diabetes Research Foundation Canada (JDRF)
#800, 2550 Victoria Park Ave., Toronto ON M2J 5A9
Tel: 647-789-2000; *Fax:* 416-491-2111
Toll-Free: 877-287-3533
general@jdrf.ca
www.jdrf.ca
Social Media: www.youtube.com/JDRFCanada
www.facebook.com/JDRFCanada
twitter.com/JDRF_Canada
To support research to find a cure for diabetes & its complications; To increase awareness of diabetes, particularly Juvenile (Type 1) diabetes
Matt Varey, Chair

Dave Prowten, President/CEO
David Kozloff, Secretary
Alex Davidson, Treasurer

Kidney Cancer Canada (KCC)
PO Box 25034, 411 The Queensway Ave. South, Keswick ON L4P 4C2
Tel: 905-476-1935; *Fax:* 866-806-1720
Toll-Free: 866-598-7166
www.kidneycancercanada.ca
Social Media: www.youtube.com/KidneyCancerCanada
www.facebook.com/KidneyCancerCanada
twitter.com/KidneyCancer_Ca
To support & improve the lives of patients & families living with kidney cancer
Deb Maskens, Chair
Catherine Madden, Executive Director

Kidney Foundation of Canada (KFOC) / Fondation canadienne du rein
#310, 5160, boul Decarie, Montréal QC H3X 2H9
Tel: 514-369-4806; *Fax:* 514-369-2472
Toll-Free: 800-361-7494
info@kidney.ca
www.kidney.ca
Social Media: www.youtube.com/kidneycanada
www.facebook.com/kidneyfoundation
twitter.com/kidneycanada
To improve the health & quality of life of people living with kidney disease; To fund research & related clinical education; To provide services for the special needs of individuals living with kidney disease; To advocate for access to high quality health care; To actively promote awareness of & commitment to organ donation
Paul Kidston, National President
Silvana Anania, Interim National Executive Director
Elisabeth Fowler, National Director, Research
Teresa Havill, National Director, Human Resources
Carole Larouche, National Director, Finance

Leucan - Association pour les enfants atteints de cancer / Leucan - Association for Children with Cancer
#505, 5800, rue St-Denis, Montréal QC H2S 3L5
Tél: 514-731-3696; *Téléc:* 514-731-2667
Ligne sans frais: 800-361-9643
info@leucan.qc.ca
www.leucan.qc.ca
Média social: www.youtube.com/user/associationleucan
linkedin.com/company/1115189
www.facebook.com/leucanpageprovinciale
twitter.com/Leucan_Org
Accroître la confiance en l'avenir des enfants atteints de cancer et de leurs familles
Sandro Di Cori, Directeur général

The Leukemia & Lymphoma Society of Canada (LLSC) / Société de leucémie et lymphome du Canada
#804, 2 Lansing Square, Toronto ON M2J 4P8
Tel: 416-661-9541; *Fax:* 416-661-7799
Toll-Free: 877-668-8326
AdminCanada@lls.org
www.llscanada.org
Social Media: www.youtube.com/llscanada
www.facebook.com/LLSCanada
twitter.com/llscanada
To cure leukemia, lymphoma, Hodgkin's disease & myeloma, & to improve the quality of life of patients & their families
Shelagh Tippet-Fagyas, President
Gilles B. Legault, Chair

Lieutenant Governor's Circle on Mental Health & Addiction
#208, 14925 - 111th Ave., Edmonton AB T5M 2P6
Tel: 780-453-2201
execdir@lgcirclealberta.ca
www.lgcircle.ca
Social Media:
www.facebook.com/LGCircle
Sol Rolingher, Chair

The Lung Association of Nova Scotia (LANS)
6331 Lady Hammond Rd., Halifax NS B3K 2S2
Tel: 902-443-8141; *Fax:* 902-445-2573
Toll-Free: 888-566-5864
info@ns.lung.ca
www.ns.lung.ca
Social Media: www.youtube.com/LungNovaScotia
linkedin.com/company/the-lung-association-of-nova-scotia
www.facebook.com/LungNS
twitter.com/NSLung

To control & prevent lung disease in Nova Scotia; To help people who live with lung disease
Louis Brill, President & Chief Executive Officer
Robert MacDonald, Manager, Health Initiatives
Hilton Botma, Manager, Finance & Administration
Lex Dunn, Manager, Communications
Lynette Hollett, Coordinator, Donor Relations
Mohammad Al-hamdani, Manager, Health Initiatives

Lupus Canada
#14, 3555 14th Ave., Markham ON L3R 0H5
Tel: 905-513-0004; *Fax:* 905-513-9516
Toll-Free: 800-661-1468
info@lupuscanada.org
www.lupuscanada.org
To improve the lives of people living with lupus; To encourage cooperation among the lupus organizations in Canada
Catherine Madden, Executive Director
Kendra MacDonald, President
Karen Chow, Vice-President
Leanne Mielczarek, Manager, National Operations

Lupus Foundation of Ontario (LFO)
PO Box 687, 294 Ridge Rd. North, Ridgeway ON L0S 1N0
Tel: 905-894-4611; *Fax:* 905-894-4616
Toll-Free: 800-368-8377
lupusont@vaxxine.com
www.lupusfoundationofontario.com
To serve the lupus patient community as a charitable organization
Laurie Kroeker, President

Lupus New Brunswick
#17, 55 Grant St., Moncton NB E1A 3R3
Toll-Free: 877-303-8080
lupins@rogers.com
www.lupusnb.ca
To promote eduction & public awarness of lupus; to bring together lupus patients, friends, family, & other interested persons for a network of support.

Lupus Newfoundland & Labrador
PO Box 8121, Stn. A, St. John's NL A1B 3M9
Tel: 709-368-8130
lupus.nl.ca@gmail.com
www.envision.ca/webs/lupusnfldlab
To support individuals with lupus; to promote education & awareness of lupus; to support research & treatment of the disease

Lupus Nova Scotia
PO Box 38038, Dartmouth NS B3B 1X2
Tel: 902-425-0358; *Fax:* 902-798-0772
Toll-Free: 800-394-0125
info@lupusns.org
www.lupuscanada.org/novascotia
Social Media: www.flickr.com/photos/65268085@N06
www.facebook.com/208993942462906
To inform, educate & support all those afflicted with lupus; to promote public & professional awareness of the disease as a prevalent & controllable one, as well as funding research for its cure.

Lupus Ontario
#301, 2900 John St., Markham ON L3R 5G3
Tel: 905-415-1099; *Fax:* 905-415-9874
Toll-Free: 877-240-1099
info@lupusontario.org
www.lupusontario.org
Social Media:
twitter.com/LupusON
To serve the needs of Lupus sufferers in Ontario
Michael Stewart, President
Karen Furlotte, Coordinator

Lupus PEI
PO Box 23002, Charlottetown PE C1E 1Z6
Tel: 902-892-3875; *Fax:* 902-626-3585
Toll-Free: 800-661-1468
info@lupuscanada.org
www.lupuscanada.org/pei
To promote public awareness of lupus on PEI, while offering support & educational materials to lupus patients, their families & friends.

Lupus SK Society
c/o Royal University Hospital, PO Box 88, 103 Hospital Dr., Saskatoon SK S7N 0W0
Toll-Free: 877-566-6123
lupus@lupussk.com
www.lupussk.com
Social Media: www.youtube.com/user/sasklupus?
www.facebook.com/pages/Lupus-SK/254959414545218
twitter.com/Lupus_SK
To provide support for those affected by lupus through understanding, education, public awareness & research
Lloyd Driedger, President

Lupus Society of Alberta (LESA)
#202, 1055 - 20 Ave. NW, Calgary AB T2M 1E7
Tel: 403-228-7956; *Fax:* 403-228-7853
Toll-Free: 888-242-9182
lupuslsa@shaw.ca
www.lupus.ab.ca
Social Media: www.youtube.com/user/LupusSocietyofAB
To provide education & support on lupus issues & enable research to find a cure.
Rosemary E. Church, Executive Director
Mike Sewell, President

Lupus Society of Manitoba
#105, 386 Broadway Ave., Winnipeg MB R3X 1G2
Tel: 204-942-6825; *Fax:* 204-942-4894
lupus@mymts.net
www.lupusmanitoba.com
Social Media:
www.facebook.com/lupus.manitoba
To provide support, encouragement & education to lupus patients & their families
Debbie Dohan, President

Manitoba Association of Optometrists (MAO)
#217, 530 Century St., Winnipeg MB R3H OY4
Tel: 204-943-9811; *Fax:* 204-943-1208
mao@optometrists.mb.ca
www.optometrists.mb.ca
To regulate the practice of optometry in Manitoba, in accordance with The Optometry Act & Regulation; To represent optometrists in Manitoba; To protect & promote the vision care needs & eye health of Manitobans
Neil Campbell, President
Laureen Goodridge, Executive Director
Lorne Ryall, Registrar

Manitoba Chiropractors' Association (MCA)
#610, 1445 Portage Ave., Winnipeg MB R3G 3P4
Tel: 204-942-3000; *Fax:* 204-942-3010
www.mbchiro.org
To act as both a regulatory body & a professional association to serve the public & the chiropractors of Manitoba; To foster high standards of chiropractic health care for Manitobans; To ensure that safe, ethical, & competent servicew are provided by Manitoba chiropractors
Taras Luchak, Executive Director
Ernie Miron, Registrar

Manitoba Lung Association
629 McDermot Ave., Winnipeg MB R3A 1P6
Tel: 204-774-5501; *Fax:* 204-772-5083
Toll-Free: 888-566-5864
info@mb.lung.ca
www.mb.lung.ca
Social Media: www.youtube.com/user/ManitobaLung
www.facebook.com/manitobalungassociation
twitter.com/ManitobaLung
To improve lung health
Margaret Bernhardt-Lowdon, Executive Director
Tracy Fehr, Director, Tobacco Reduction Initiatives
Kris Kamenz, Director, Finance

Manitoba Medical Service Foundation Inc. (MMSF)
PO Box 1046, Stn. Main, Winnipeg MB R3G 3P3
Tel: 204-788-6801; *Fax:* 204-774-1761
info@mmsf.ca
www.mmsf.ca
To consider the provision of funds for the advancement of scientific, educational, & other activities to maintain & improve the health & welfare of the citizens of Manitoba
Greg Hammond, Executive Director
Lindsay Du Val, Chair

Manitoba Naturopathic Association (MNA)
PO Box 434, 971 Corydon Ave., Winnipeg MB R3M 0Y0
Tel: 204-947-0381
info@mbnd.ca
www.mbnd.ca
To act as a regulatory body for the profession of naturopathy, in accordance with The Naturopathic Act of Manitoba

Lesley Phimister, Executive Director/Registrar

Manitoba Paraplegia Foundation Inc.
825 Sherbrook St., Winnipeg MB R3A 1M5
Tel: 204-786-4753; *Fax:* 204-786-1140
winnipeg@canparaplegic.org
www.cpamanitoba.ca/mpf
To provide support for research & prevention activities; to provide direct aid to paraplegics & quadriplegics for home modifications, vocational aid & other items to assist spinal cord injured Manitobans to lead independent lives within the community; to provide support for special projects undertaken on behalf of spinal cord injured persons in Manitoba
Doug Finkbeiner, President

Manitoba Public Health Association (MPHA)
c/o Klinic Community Health Centre, 870 Portage Ave., Winnipeg MB R3G 0P1
manitobapha@mts.net
www.manitobapha.ca
To influence health, social, environmental, & economic policy decisions, in order to improve the well-being of people in Manitoba; To ensure that health promotion, health protection, & disease protection are part of services
Barb Wasilewski, President

Médecins francophones du Canada
8355, boul Saint-Laurent, Montréal QC H2P 2Z6
Tél: 514-388-2228; *Téléc:* 514-388-5335
Ligne sans frais: 800-387-2228
www.medecinsfrancophones.ca
Marie-Françoise Mégie, Présidente
Céline Monette, Directrice générale

Medical Council of Canada (MCC) / Le Conseil médical du Canada (CMC)
#100, 2283 St. Laurent Blvd., Ottawa ON K1G 5A2
Tel: 613-521-6012; *Fax:* 613-521-9509
service@mcc.ca
www.mcc.ca
Social Media: www.youtube.com/user/medicalcouncilcanada
linkedin.com/company/medical-council-of-canada
www.facebook.com/MedicalCouncilOfCanada
twitter.com/MedCouncilCan
To establish & promote a qualification in medicine, known as the Licentiate of the Medical Council of Canada, such that the holders thereof are acceptable to medical licensing authorities for the issuance of a licence to practise medicine
Ian Bowmer, Executive Director

Medical Devices Canada
#900, 405 The West Mall, Toronto ON M9C 5J1
Tel: 416-620-1915; *Toll-Free:* 866-586-3332
www.medec.org
To achieve a business & regulatory environment favourable to the growth of the industry & ensuring the availability of new cost-effective medical technologies that benefit Canadians
Paul Bradley, Chair
Brian Lewis, President & CEO

Medical Society of Prince Edward Island (MSPEI)
2 Myrtle St., Stratford PE C1B 2W2
Tel: 902-368-7303; *Fax:* 902-566-3934
Toll-Free: 888-368-7303
www.mspei.org
Social Media:
twitter.com/MSPEI_Docs
To promote health & improvement of medical services; to prevent disease; to represent members at national bodies & government; to consider all matters concerning the professional welfare of members.
Kathy Maher, Director, Operations & Communications

The Michener Institute for Applied Health Sciences
222 St. Patrick St., Toronto ON M5T 1V4
Tel: 416-596-3101; *Toll-Free:* 800-387-9066
info@michener.ca
www.michener.ca
Social Media: www.youtube.com/user/TheMichenerInstitute
www.facebook.com/TheMichenerInstitute
twitter.com/michenerinst
To design, develop & deliver the best educational programs, products & services in applied health sciences
Cliff Nordal, Chair
President Adamson, President & CEO

Multiple Sclerosis Society of Canada (MS) / Société canadienne de la sclérose en plaques
North Tower, #500, 250 Dundas St. West, Toronto ON M5T 2Z5
Tel: 416-922-6065; *Fax:* 416-922-7538
Toll-Free: 800-268-7582
info@mssociety.ca
www.mssociety.ca
Social Media: www.youtube.com/MSSocietyCanada
www.facebook.com/MSSocietyCanada
twitter.com/mssocietycanada
To be a leader in finding a cure for multiple sclerosis & enabling people affected by MS to enhance their quality of life
Charles Ford, Chair
Yves Savoie, President & CEO

Muscular Dystrophy Canada (MDC) / Dystrophie musculaire Canada (DMC)
#900, 2345 Yonge St., Toronto ON M4P 2E5
Tel: 416-488-0030; *Fax:* 416-488-7523
Toll-Free: 866-687-2538
info@muscle.ca
www.muscle.ca
Social Media: www.youtube.com/user/musculardystrophycan
linkedin.com/company/466761
www.facebook.com/muscle.ca
twitter.com/md_canada
To improve the quality of life of persons who have muscular dystrophy through a broad range of programs, education, support of research & the delivery of needed services to people with muscular dystrophy & their families
Nancy Cumming, Chair
Catherine Sherrard, CEO
Melanie Towell, CFO

Myasthenia Gravis Association of British Columbia (MGABC)
2805 Kingsway, Vancouver BC V5R 5H9
Tel: 604-451-5511; *Fax:* 604-451-5651
mgabc@centreforability.bc.ca
www.myastheniagravis.ca
To provide information & support to British Columbians who suffer from Myasthenia Gravis (Grave Muscular Disease) & to their caregivers; to increase public awareness of the disease; to gather & disseminate specific information on Myasthenia Gravis to healthcare providers in British Columbia; to foster & support research into the causes & treatment of Myasthenia Gravis
Brenda Kelsey, President

National Eating Disorder Information Centre (NEDIC)
ES 7-421, 200 Elizabeth St., Toronto ON M5G 2C4
Tel: 416-340-4156; *Fax:* 416-340-4736
Toll-Free: 866-633-4220
nedic@uhn.ca
www.nedic.ca
Social Media:
www.facebook.com/267097966860
twitter.com/NEDIC85
The National Eating Disorder Information Centre (NEDIC) is a non-profit organization founded in 1985 to provide information and resources on eating disorders and food and weight preoccupation. One of their main goals is to inform the public about eating disorders and related issues.
Merryl Bear, Director

National ME/FM Action Network / Réseau national d'action EM/FM encéphalomyélite myalgique/fibromyalgie
#512, 33 Banner Rd., Nepean ON K2H 8V7
Tel: 613-829-6667
mefminfo@mefmaction.com
www.mefmaction.net
Social Media:
www.facebook.com/MEFMActionNetwork
twitter.com/mefmaction
To offer support, advocacy, education & research into the many, varied, anomalies connected with Myalgic Encephalomyelitis/Chronic Fatigue Syndrome & Fibromyalgia (ME/FM)
Margaret Parlor, President
Lydia E. Neilson, M.S.M., Founder & CEO

Neurological Health Charities Canada (NHCC)
#316, 4211 Yonge St., Toronto ON M2P 2A9
Tel: 416-227-9700; *Fax:* 416-227-9600
Toll-Free: 800-565-3000
info@mybrainmatters.ca
www.mybrainmatters.ca
Social Media: www.youtube.com/MyBrainMatters
www.facebook.com/MyBrainMatters
twitter.com/MyBrainMatters
To improve quality of life for persons with chronic brain conditions & their caregivers; To increase awareness in the government about neurological issues; To support research

New Brunswick Association of Dietitians (NBAD) / Association des diététistes du Nouveau-Brunswick (ADNB)
530 Main St., Woodstock NB E7M 2C3
Tel: 506-324-9396; *Fax:* 506-328-2686
registrar@adnb-nbad.com
www.adnb-nbad.com
To regulate the practice of dietitians within New Brunswick
Jensen Thomas, President

New Brunswick Association of Naturopathic Doctors (NBAND)
c/o Crystal Charest, 2278 King George Hwy., Miramichi NB E1V 6N6
Tel: 506-773-3700; *Fax:* 506-773-3704
www.nband.ca
Social Media:
twitter.com/NewBrunswickNDs
To educate the public on the philosophies and values of Naturopathic Medicine and to promote the profession within the province.
Martin Gleixner, President

New Brunswick Association of Optometrists (NBAO) / Association des optométristes du Nouveau-Brunswick
#1, 490 Gibson St., Fredericton NB E3A 4E9
Tel: 506-458-8759; *Fax:* 506-450-1271
nbao@nbnet.nb.ca
www.nbao.ca
To represent Doctors of Optometry in New Brunswick
Krista McDevitt, President

New Brunswick Chiropractors' Association (NBCA) / Association des chiropraticiens du Nouveau-Brunswick
#206, 944 Prospect St., Fredericton NB E3B 9M6
Tel: 506-445-6800; *Fax:* 506-455-4430
comments@nbchiropractic.ca
www.nbchiropractic.ca
To regulate the practice of chiropractic & govern its members in accordance with the Act & the by-laws, in order to serve & protect the public interests; to establish, maintain, develop & enforce standards of qualification for the practice of chiropractic, including the required knowledge, skill & efficiency; to establish, maintain, develop & enforce standards of professional ethics; to promote public awareness of the role of the Association & the work of chiropractic, & to communicate & cooperate with other professional organizations for the advancement of the best interests of the Association, including the publication of books, papers & journals; & to encourage studies in chiropractic & provide assistance & facilities for special studies & research
Mohamed El-Bayoumi, Executive Director

New Brunswick Lung Association / Association pulmonaire du Nouveau-Brunswick
65 Brunswick St., Fredericton NB E3B 1G5
Tel: 506-455-8961; *Fax:* 506-462-0939
Toll-Free: 800-565-5864
Info@nb.lung.ca
www.nb.lung.ca
To promote wellness throughout New Brunswick & prevent lung disease
Barbara MacKinnon, President & Chief Executive Officer
Ted Allingham, Director, Finance & Administration
Arthur Thomson, Vice President
Barbara Walls, Director, Health Initiatives

New Brunswick Medical Society (NBMS) / Société médicale du Nouveau-Brunswick
21 Alison Blvd., Fredericton NB E3C 2N5
Tel: 506-458-8860; *Fax:* 506-458-9853
nbms@nb.aibn.com
www.nbms.nb.ca
Social Media:
www.facebook.com/CareFirstLasanteenpremier
twitter.com/nb_docs
To advance medical science in all its branches; to promote improvement of medical services; to prevent disease in cooperation with health officers & all others engaged in such work; to maintain high scientific & professional status for its members; to promote medical science & related arts & sciences
Camille Haddad, President

Newfoundland & Labrador Association of Optometrists (NLAO)
PO Box 8042, St. John's NL A1B 3M7
Tel: 709-739-8284; *Fax:* 709-739-8378
nlao@nl.rogers.com
www.nao.opto.ca
To provide an online resource for Doctors of Optometry & other healthcare providers in Newfoundland & Labrador
Ed Breen, Executive Director

Newfoundland & Labrador Chiropractic Association
#285W, 120 Torbay Rd., St. John's NL A1A 2G8
Tel: 709-739-7762; *Fax:* 709-739-7703
www.nlchiropractic.ca

Newfoundland & Labrador College of Dietitians (NLCD)
PO Box 1756, Stn. C, St. John's NL A1C 5P5
Tel: 709-753-4040; *Fax:* 709-781-1044
Toll-Free: 877-753-4040
registrar@nlcd.ca
www.nlcd.ca
To regulate Registered Dietitians & to ensure competency in the dietetic profession, in the interest of the people in Newfoundland

Newfoundland & Labrador Lung Association (NLLA)
PO Box 13457, Stn. A, St. John's NL A1B 4B8
Tel: 709-726-4664; *Fax:* 709-726-2550
Toll-Free: 888-566-5864
info@nf.lung.ca
www.nf.lung.ca
To achieve healthy breathing for the people of Newfoundland & Labrador
Greg Noel, Executive Director

Newfoundland & Labrador Medical Association (NLMA)
164 MacDonald Dr., St. John's NL A1A 4B3
Tel: 709-726-7424; *Fax:* 709-726-7525
Toll-Free: 800-563-2003
nlma@nlma.nl.ca
www.nlma.nl.ca
Social Media: www.youtube.com/user/nlmavideo
www.facebook.com/nlma.nl.ca
twitter.com/_nlma
To represent & support physicians in Newfoundland & Labrador; provide leadership in the promotion of good health & the provision of quality health care to the people of the province
Wendy Graham, President
Robert Thompson, Executive Director

Newfoundland & Labrador Public Health Association (NLPHA)
PO Box 8172, St. John's NL A1B 3M9
Tel: 709-364-1589
info@nlpha.ca
www.nlpha.ca
To advocate for the physical, emotional, social, & environmental well-being of Newfoundland & Labrador's people & communities
Lynn Vivian-Book, President
Elizabeth Wright, Secretary
Pat Murray, Treasurer

Northwest Territories Medical Association (NWTMA)
PO Box 1732, Yellowknife NT X1A 2P3
Tel: 867-920-4575; *Fax:* 867-920-4575
nwtmedassoc@ssimicro.com
www.nwtma.ca
To advocate on behalf of its members and the citizens of the North for access to high quality health care, and provides leadership and guidance to its members.
David Pontin, President

Nova Scotia Association of Naturopathic Doctors (NSAND)
PO Box 245, Lower Sackville NS B4C 2S9
Tel: 902-431-8001
info@nsand.ca
www.nsand.ca
Social Media:
www.facebook.com/44570499509
twitter.com/NSAND_
To be a resource for its members & to inform the public about naturopathic medicine.
Colin Huska, President

Nova Scotia Association of Optometrists (NSAO)
PO Box 9410, Stn. A, #700, 6009 Quinpool Rd., Halifax NS B3K 5S3
Tel: 902-435-2845; *Fax:* 902-425-2441
info@ns.doctorsofoptometry.ca
ns.doctorsofoptometry.ca

To foster excellence in the delivery of vision & eye health services in Nova Scotia; To act as the voice of optometry in Nova Scotia

Nova Scotia College of Chiropractors (NSCC)
PO Box 9410, Stn. A, Halifax NS B3K 5S3
Tel: 902-407-4255; *Fax:* 902-425-2441
inquiries@chiropractors.ns.ca
www.chiropractors.ns.ca
To promote & improve the proficiency of chiropractors in all matters relating to the practice of chiropractic; to protect the public from untrained & unqualified persons acting as chiropractors; to advance the chiropractic profession
John K. Sutherland, Executive Director

Nova Scotia Dietetic Association (NSDA)
#212, 1496 Bedford Hwy., Bedford NS B4A 1E5
Tel: 902-835-0253; *Fax:* 902-835-0523
info@nsdassoc.ca
www.nsdassoc.ca
To regulate dietitions & nutritionists in the province, & register & discipline (when necessary) practitioners to ensure safe, ethical & competent dietetic practice
Patti Simpson, President
Jennifer Garus, Executive Manager (ex-officio)

Occupational & Environmental Medical Association of Canada (OEMAC) / Association canadienne de la médecine du travail et de l'environnement (ACMTE)
#503, 386 Broadway, Winnipeg MB R3C 3R6
Toll-Free: 888-223-3808
info@oemac.org
oemac.org
To act as the voice of the Canadian occupational & environmental medicine sector
Maureen Cividino, President

Ontario Association of Naturopathic Doctors (OAND)
#603, 789 Don Mills Rd., Toronto ON M3C 1T5
Tel: 416-233-2001; *Fax:* 416-233-2924
Toll-Free: 877-628-7284
info@oand.org
www.oand.org
Social Media:
www.facebook.com/ndontario
twitter.com/OANDorg
To act as a voice for naturopathic doctors in Ontario
Chrystine Langille, CEO
Alfred Hauk, Chair
Angeli Chitale, Secretary

Ontario Association of Optometrists (OAO)
PO Box 16, #801, 20 Adelaide St. East, Toronto ON M5C 2T6
Tel: 905-826-3522; *Fax:* 905-826-0625
Toll-Free: 800-540-3837
info@optom.on.ca
www.optom.on.ca
Social Media: www.youtube.com/user/OntarioOptometrists
www.facebook.com/pages/Ontario-Association-of-Optometrists/28166312427
twitter.com/ONOptometrists
To advance the profession of optometry at the government, regulatory, & public levels
Beth Witney, Chief Executive Officer
Bethany Carey, Director, Member Services
Melissa Secord, Director, Professional Affairs
Sandra Ng, Manager, Policy & Government Relations

Ontario Chiropractic Association (OCA) / Association chiropratique de l'Ontario
#200, 20 Victoria St., Toronto ON M5C 2N8
Tel: 416-860-0070; *Fax:* 416-860-0857
Toll-Free: 877-327-2273
oca@chiropractic.on.ca
www.chiropractic.on.ca
Social Media:
www.facebook.com/ontariochiropracticassociation
twitter.com/ON_Chiropractic
To serve its members by promoting the philosophy, art, & science of chiropractic & thereby enhance the health & well-being of the citizens of Ontario
Kristina Peterson, President

Ontario Gerontology Association (OGA) / Association ontarienne de gérontologie
#601, 90 Eglinton Ave. East, Toronto ON M4P 2Y3
Tel: 416-535-6034; *Fax:* 416-535-6907
www.gerontario.org
Social Media:
linkedin.com/company/9320422
www.facebook.com/ONgerontology
twitter.com/gerontario

Terri Stonehewer, Administrator

Ontario Lung Association (OLA)
#401, 18 Wynford Dr., Toronto ON M3C 0K8
Tel: 416-864-9911; *Fax:* 416-864-9916
Toll-Free: 888-344-5864
olalung@on.lung.ca
www.on.lung.ca
Social Media: www.youtube.com/user/ONLungAssociation
www.facebook.com/OntarioLungAssociation?ref=ts
twitter.com/OntarioLung
To provide lung health information & support to people affected by lung disease; To prevent & control chronic lung disease
John Granton, Chair
George Habib, President & Chief Executive Officer
John Martin, Treasurer

Ontario Medical Association (OMA)
#900, 150 Bloor St. West, Toronto ON M5S 3C1
Tel: 416-599-2580; *Fax:* 416-340-2944
Toll-Free: 800-268-7215
info@oma.org
www.oma.org
Social Media: www.youtube.com/user/OntMedAssociation
linkedin.com/company/ontario-medical-association
www.facebook.com/Ontariosdoctors
twitter.com/OntariosDoctors
To represent the clinical, political, & economic interests of Ontario physicians; To promote an accessible, quality health-care system
Tom Magyarody, Chief Executive Officer
Danielle Milley, Senior Advisor, Media Relations

Ontario Occupational Health Nurses Association (OOHNA)
#605, 302 The East Mall, Toronto ON M9B 6C7
Tel: 416-239-6462; *Fax:* 416-239-5462
Toll-Free: 866-664-6276
administration@oohna.on.ca
www.oohna.on.ca
Social Media:
linkedin.com/groups/OOHNA-Ontario-Occupational-Health-Nurses-51484
twitter.com/OOHNA1
To foster a climate of excellence, innovation & partnership enabling Ontario Occupational Health Nurses to achieve positive workplace health & safety objectives
Ken Storen, President
Brian Verrall, Executive Director

Ontario Public Health Association (OPHA) / Association pour la santé publique de l'Ontario
#1850, 439 University Ave., Toronto ON M5G 1Y8
Tel: 416-367-3313; *Fax:* 416-367-2844
Toll-Free: 800-267-6817
info@opha.on.ca
www.opha.on.ca
Social Media: twitter.com/nutritionrc
linkedin.com/company/ontario-public-health-association
www.facebook.com/195756817126713
twitter.com/OPHA_Ontario
To provide leadership on issues affecting public health in Ontario, such as preserving the environment, promoting disease prevention, narrowing health disparities & reducing poverty; To strengthen the influence of persons involved in public & community health across Ontario
Sue Makin, President
Barb Prud'homme, Knowledge Management Coordinator

Ontario Rheumatology Association (ORA)
#244, 12 - 16715 Yonge St., Newmarket ON L3X 1X4
Tel: 905-952-0698; *Fax:* 905-952-0708
admin@ontariorheum.ca
ontariorheum.ca
To represent Ontario Rheumatologists and promote their pursuit of excellence in Arthritis care in Ontario.
Arthur Karasik, President

Ontario Society of Occupational Therapists (OSOT)
#210, 55 Eglinton Ave. East, Toronto ON M4P 1G8
Tel: 416-322-3011; *Fax:* 416-322-6705
Toll-Free: 877-676-6768
osot@osot.on.ca
www.osot.on.ca
Social Media:
linkedin.com/company/ontario-society-of-occupational-therapists
www.facebook.com/161471573904550
twitter.com/osotvoice
To promote & represent the profession of occupational therapy in the areas of government affairs, education, professional issues & public relations in Ontario
Christie Benchley, Executive Director
Rob Linkiewicz, Manager, Operations

Seema Sindwani, Manager, Professional Development & Practice Support

Opticians Association of Canada (OAC)
#2706, 83 Garry St., Winnipeg MB R3C 4J9
Tel: 204-982-6060; *Fax:* 204-947-2519
Toll-Free: 800-842-3155
canada@opticians.ca
www.opticians.ca
Social Media: www.youtube.com/user/opticianstv
linkedin.com/company/opticians-association-of-canada
www.facebook.com/215512795151373
twitter.com/OACexecutiveDr
Robert Dalton, Executive Director

Ordre des ergothérapeutes du Québec (OEQ)
#920, 2021, av Union, Montréal QC H3A 2S9
Tél: 514-844-5778; *Téléc:* 514-844-0478
Ligne sans frais: 800-265-5778
ergo@oeq.org
www.oeq.org
Protéger le public; assurer la qualité d'ergothérapie; promouvoir l'accessibilité aux services d'ergothérapie; soutenir la pratique professionnelle et son évolution; favoriser le rayonnement de la profession
Alain Bibeau, Président-directeur général
Louise Tremblay, Secrétaire générale

Ordre des orthophonistes et audiologistes du Québec (OOAQ)
#601, 235, boul René-Levesque Est, Montréal QC H2X 1N8
Tél: 514-282-9123; *Téléc:* 514-282-9541
Ligne sans frais: 888-232-9123
info@ooaq.qc.ca
www.ooaq.qc.ca
D'assurer la protection du public en regard du domaine d'exercice de ses membres, soit les troubles de la communication humaine; surveiller l'exercice professionnel des orthophonistes et des audiologistes et voir à favoriser l'accessibilité du public à des services de qualité; contribuer à l'intégration sociale des individus et à l'amélioration de la qualité de vie de la population québécoise
Marie-Pierre Caouette, Présidente et directrice générale

Ordre des techniciens et techniciennes dentaires du Québec (OTTDQ)
#900, 500, rue Sherbrooke Ouest, Montréal QC H3A 3C6
Tél: 514-282-3837; *Téléc:* 514-844-7556
www.ottdq.com
Média social: www.facebook.com/OTTDQ
De réglementer la profession des techniciens dentaires afin de protéger le public et d'assurer la meilleure qualité de service possible est fournie
Linda Carbone, Secrétaire

Ordre professionnel de la physiothérapie du Québec (OPPQ)
#1000, 7151, Jean Talon est, Anjou QC H1M 3N8
Tél: 514-351-2770; *Téléc:* 514-351-2658
Ligne sans frais: 800-361-2001
physio@oppq.qc.ca
www.oppq.qc.ca
Assurer la protection du public en surveillant l'exercice de la physiothérapie par ses membres et en contribuant à leur développement professionnel
Lucie Forget, Présidente
Claude Laurent, Directeur général et Secrétaire

Ordre professionnel des diététistes du Québec (OPDQ)
#1220, 2155, rue Guy, Montréal QC H3H 2R9
Tél: 514-393-3733; *Téléc:* 514-393-3582
Ligne sans frais: 888-393-8528
opdq@opdq.org
www.opdq.org
Assurer la protection du public en contrôlant notamment l'exercice de la profession par ses membres.
Annie Chapados, Directrice générale et secrétaire

Ordre professionnel des sexologues du Québec (OPSQ)
#300, 4126, rue St-Denis, Montréal QC H2W 2M5
Tél: 438-386-6777; *Ligne sans frais:* 855-386-6777
info@opsq.org
opsq.org
De réglementer la profession des sexologues afin de protéger le public et d'assurer la meilleure qualité de service possible est fournie
Isabelle Beaulieu, Directrice générale et secrétaire de l'Ordre

Orthotics Prosthetics Canada (OPC)
National Office, #202, 300 March Rd., Ottawa ON K2K 2E2
Tel: 613-595-1919; *Fax:* 613-595-1155
info@opcanada.ca
www.opcanada.ca
To promote high standards of patient care & professionalism in the prosthetic & orthotic profession throughout Canada; To represent members with government, related organizations, & the general public
Dan Mead, President
Dana Cooper, Executive Director

Osteoporosis Canada / Ostéoporose Canada
#301, 1090 Don Mills Rd., Toronto ON M3C 3R6
Tel: 416-696-2663; *Fax:* 416-696-2673
Toll-Free: 800-463-6842
www.osteoporosis.ca
Social Media: www.youtube.com/osteoporosisca
linkedin.com/company/2610844
www.facebook.com/osteoporosiscanada
twitter.com/OsteoporosisCA
To encourage research into the prevention, diagnosis, & treatment of osteoporosis; To improve access to osteoporosis care & support
Famida Jiwa, President & CEO
Emily Bartens, Chair

Ostomy Canada Society
#501, 344 Bloor St. West, Toronto ON M5S 3A7
Tel: 416-595-5452; *Fax:* 416-595-9924
Toll-Free: 888-969-9698
info1@ostomycanada.ca
www.ostomycanada.ca
Social Media:
www.youtube.com/channel/UCjHdm7WOJokLkXgKS9Gnjng
linkedin.com/company/united-ostomy-association-of-canada-inc-?trk=
www.facebook.com/OstomyCanada
twitter.com/UOACweb
To assist all persons with gastrointestinal or urinary diversions, & their families & caregivers, by providing emotional & practical support & help, information & instruction
Peter Folk, President
Ann Ivol, Vice-President

Ovarian Cancer Canada (OCC) / Cancer de l'ovaire Canada (COC)
#205, 145 Front St. East, Toronto ON M5A 1E3
Tel: 416-962-2700; *Fax:* 416-962-2701
Toll-Free: 877-413-7970
info@ovariancanada.org
www.ovariancanada.org
Social Media: www.youtube.com/ovariancancercanada
linkedin.com/company/728166
www.facebook.com/pages/Ovarian-Cancer-Canada/102394063730
twitter.com/OvarianCanada
To support women & their families living with the disease; to raise awareness in the general public & with health care professionals; to fund research to develop reliable early detection techniques, improved treatments & ultimately, a cure.
Tammy Brown, Chair
Elisabeth Baugh, CEO
Karen Cinq Mars, Vice-President, Marketing & Business Innovation
Hoda Brooke, Finance Director

Pain Society of Alberta (PSA)
132 Warwick Rd., Edmonton AB T5X 4P8
Tel: 780-457-5225; *Fax:* 780-475-7968
info@painsocietyofalberta.org
painsocietyofalberta.org
Gaylord Wardell, President

Parkinson Alberta Society (PAS)
Westech Building, #102, 5636 Burbank Cres. SE, Calgary AB T2H 1Z6
Tel: 403-243-9901; *Fax:* 403-243-8283
Toll-Free: 800-561-1911
info@parkinsonalberta.ca
www.parkinsonalberta.ca
Social Media: www.youtube.com/user/ParkinsonAlberta
www.facebook.com/281448621909497
twitter.com/ParkinsonAB
PAS is dedicated to helping people and families of Southern Alberta who live with Parkinson's and related disorders
John Petryshen, CEO

Parkinson Society British Columbia (PSBC)
#600, 890 West Pender St., Vancouver BC V6C 1J9
Tel: 604-662-3240; *Fax:* 604-687-1327
Toll-Free: 800-668-3330
info@parkinson.bc.ca
www.parkinson.bc.ca
Social Media: www.youtube.com/user/ParkinsonSocietyBC
www.facebook.com/191326604220827
twitter.com/ParkinsonsBC
Jean Blake, CEO

Parkinson Society Canada (PSC) / Société Parkinson Canada
#316, 4211 Yonge St., Toronto ON M2P 2A9
Tel: 416-227-9700; *Fax:* 416-227-9600
Toll-Free: 800-565-3000
general.info@parkinson.ca
www.parkinson.ca
To raise funds for research into the causes & treatment of Parkinsons; to provide services which support Parkinsonians & their families; to disseminate information about the condition to individuals & organizations across Canada
Joyce Gordon, President & CEO
Marina Joseph, Director, Marketing & Communication

Parkinson Society Central & Northern Ontario
#321, 4211 Yonge St., Toronto ON M2P 2A9
Tel: 416-227-1200; *Fax:* 416-227-1520
Toll-Free: 800-565-3000
info.cno@parkinson.ca
www.cno.parkinson.ca
Social Media:
www.facebook.com/101248525517
twitter.com/ParkinsonCNO
Debbie Davis, CEO

Parkinson Society Manitoba
#7, 414 Westmount Dr., Winnipeg MB R2J 1P2
Tel: 204-786-2637; *Toll-Free:* 866-999-5558
parkinson@mymts.net
www.parkinsonmanitoba.ca
Social Media:
www.facebook.com/ParkinsonSocietyManitobaSuperwalk2013
Howard Koks, CEO

Parkinson Society Maritime Region (PSMR) / Société Parkinson - Region Maritime (SPRM)
#150, 7071 Bayers Rd., Halifax NS B3L 2C2
Tel: 902-422-3656; *Fax:* 902-422-3797
Toll-Free: 800-663-2468
psmr@parkinsonmaritimes.ca
www.parkinsonmaritimes.ca
Social Media:
www.youtube.com/channel/UCo1IYTO_WaeyIOiUhkrnjXg
www.facebook.com/parkinsonmaritimes
twitter.com/psmr
To give information to people with Parkinson & their family, children & caregivers
Jim Horwich, Chair
Robert Shaw, Regional CEO

Parkinson Society Newfoundland & Labrador
The Viking Bldg., #305, 136 Crosbie Rd., St. John's NL A1B 3K3
Tel: 709-574-4428; *Fax:* 709-754-5868
Toll-Free: 800-567-7020
parkinson@nf.aibn.com
www.parkinsonnl.ca
Social Media:
www.facebook.com/ParkinsonSocietyNewfoundlandAndLabrador
twitter.com/Parkinsons_NL
Derek Staubitzer, Executive Director

Parkinson Society of Eastern Ontario / Société Parkinson de l'est de l'Ontario
#1, 200 Colonnade Rd., Ottawa ON K2E 7M1
Tel: 613-722-9238; *Fax:* 613-722-3241
psoc@toh.on.ca
www.parkinsons.ca
Social Media:
twitter.com/ParkinsonEastOn
Dennise Taylor-Gilhen, CEO
Hilary Evans, Director, Resource Development

Parkinson Society Saskatchewan (PSS)
610 Duchess St., Saskatoon SK S7K 0R1
Tel: 306-933-4481; *Fax:* 888-775-1402
Toll-Free: 888-685-0059
saskatchewan@parkinson.ca
www.parkinsonsaskatchewan.ca
To provide education & support services in Saskatchewan to ease the burdens of people living with Parkinson's disease & their families; To support research to find a cure for Parkinson's disease
Travis Low, Executive Director

Partenariat communauté en santé (PCS)
#328, 302, rue Strickland, Whitehorse YT Y1A 2K1
Tél: 867-268-2663
pcsyukon@francosante.ca
www.francosante.org
Sandra St-Laurent, Directrice

Patients Canada
3560 Bathurst St., Toronto ON M6A 2E1
Tel: 416-785-2500
communications@patientsassociation.ca
patientsassociation.ca
Social Media:
www.facebook.com/113395605361806
twitter.com/PatientsAssocCa
To highlight instances where the health care system worked & where it needs improvement, from the perspective of patients.
Sholom Glouberman, President

Post-Polio Awareness & Support Society of BC (PPASS/BC)
102 - 9775 - 4th St., Sidney BC V8L 2Z8
Tel: 250-655-8849; *Fax:* 250-655-8859
ppass@ppassbc.com
www.ppassbc.com
To develop awareness, communication & education between society & community; to disseminate information concerning research & treatment about Post-Polio Syndrome; to support polio survivors other than through direct financial aid
Joan Toone, President

Post-Polio Network Manitoba Inc. (PPN-MB)
c/o SMD Self-Help Clearinghouse, 825 Sherbrook St., Winnipeg MB R3A 1M5
Tel: 204-975-3037; *Fax:* 204-975-3027
postpolionetwork@gmail.com
www.postpolionetwork.ca
To serve as a support group & information centre for polio survivors throughout Manitoba, especially those suffering from post-polio syndrome; To acquaint the medical community & those responsible for government services as to the nature & extent of the problems associated with the late effects of polio
Cheryl Currie, President
Donna Remillard, Treasurer
Estelle Boissonneault, Secretary

Prince County Hospital Foundation (PCHF)
PO Box 3000, 65 Roy Boates Ave., Summerside PE C1N 2A9
Tel: 902-432-2547; *Fax:* 902-432-2551
info@pchcare.com
www.pchcare.com
Social Media:
www.facebook.com/PCHFoundation
To raise money for Prince County Hospital in order to keep up with medical equipment needs
Heather Matheson, Managing Director
Gord Coffin, President

Prince Edward Island Association of Optometrists (PEIAO)
PO Box 1812, Charlottetown PE C1A 7N5
visionpei@gmail.com
www.peioptometrists.ca
To promote the professional interests of optometrists in Prince Edward Island Association; To improve optometrists' proficiency
Jayne Toombs, President
David McKenna, Vice-President
Carolyn Acorn, Secretary
J.E. Hickey, Treasurer

Prince Edward Island Chiropractic Association (PEICA)
228 Grafton St., Charlottetown PE C1A 1L5
Tel: 902-894-4400; *Fax:* 902-894-3762
dtownchiro@pei.aibn.com
To represent the chiropractic profession in Prince Edward Island; To advance the chiropractic profession in the province; To encourage high standards of service; To protect the residents of Prince Edward Island from unqualified individuals acting as chiropractors
Christopher MacCarthy, Chair

Prince Edward Island Dietetic Association (PEIDA)
c/o Prince Edward Island Dietitians Registration Board, PO Box 152, Summerside PE C1N 4Y8
Tel: 902-436-2438
peidietitians@gmail.com
www.peidietitians.ca
Social Media: www.facebook.com/peidieteticassociation
To promote, encourage & improve the status of dietitians & nutritionists in the province of PEI; to promote & increase the knowledge & proficiency of its members in all matters relating to nutrition & dietetics; to promote public awareness
Mary Laura Coady, President

Prince Edward Island Lung Association
#2, 1 Rochford St., Charlottetown PE C1A 9L2
Tel: 902-892-5957; *Fax:* 902-566-9901
Toll-Free: 888-566-5864
info@pei.lung.ca
www.pei.lung.ca
To improve the respiratory health of Islanders through education, advocacy & research; To raise funds to support medical research
Margaret Munro, President
Judy Hansen, Vice-President
Joanne Ings, Executive Director
Bev McCormick, Treasurer

Prince Edward Island Society for Medical Laboratory Science (PEIMLS)
PO Box 20061, Stn. Sherwood, 161 St. Peters Rd., Charlottetown PE C1A 9E3
peismls.com
Social Media: www.facebook.com/320495861437823
twitter.com/peismls
To promote, maintain & protect professional identity & interests of medical laboratory technologist & of the profession; to promote development of continuing education; to provide information on current developments in medical laboratory technology
Carolyn McCarville, President
Andrea Dowling, Vice-President
Gerard Fernando, Treasurer

Psoriasis Society of Canada / Société psoriasis du Canada
National Office, PO Box 25015, Halifax NS B3M 4H4
Fax: 902-443-2073
Toll-Free: 800-656-4494
www.psoriasissociety.org
To provide programs & services to people who suffer from psoriasis in Canada; to encourage formation of support groups where individual sufferers may share experiences & exchange information; to provide facts about psoriasis to medical community, general public & teaching profession; to promote & encourage research directed towards treatment & cure for psoriasis
Judy Misner, President

Public Health Association of British Columbia (PHABC)
#210, 1027 Pandora Ave., Victoria BC V8V 3P6
Tel: 250-595-8422; *Fax:* 250-595-8622
staff@phabc.org
www.phabc.org
To constitute a special resource in BC for the betterment & maintenance of the population's health at the community & personal level

Public Health Association of Nova Scotia (PHANS)
PO Box 33074, Halifax NS B3L 4T6
www.phans.ca
To build public health capacity & to make progress on the determinants of health in Nova Scotia

Québec Black Medical Association
#180, 2021 av Atwater, Montréal QC H3H 2P2
Tel: 514-937-8822
www.qbma.ca
The Québec Black Medical Association aims to enable young people from the Black community to pursue careers as health professionals and to advance medical practice and research in Quebec.
Edouard Tucker, President

Québec Lung Association (QLA) / Association pulmonaire du Québec (APQ)
#104, 6070, rue Sherbrooke Est, Montréal QC H1N 1C1
Tel: 514-287-7400; *Fax:* 514-287-1978
Toll-Free: 888-768-6669
info@pq.poumon.ca
www.pq.poumon.ca
Social Media: www.youtube.com/user/PoumonAPQ
www.facebook.com/poumon.qc
twitter.com/AssoPulmonaireQ
To provide resources in Québec about lung cancer, chronic obstructive pulmonary disease, sarcoidosis, tuberculosis, asthma, chronic bronchitis, sleep apnea, pneumonia, & emphysema
Dominique Massie, Executive Director
Raymond Jabbour, Chief Financial Officer & Director, Direct Marketing & Information Technology
Mathieu Leroux, Admisor, Development & Communications

Regroupement québécois des maladies orphelines (RQMO) / Québec Coalition for Orphan Diseases
l'Institut de recherches cliniques de Montréal (IRCM), 110, av des Pins ouest, Montréal QC H2W 1R7
Tél: 514-987-5659
administration@rqmo.org
www.rqmo.org
Média social: www.youtube.com/user/RQMOMalOrph
www.facebook.com/139256366104757
twitter.com/maladorphelines
Améliorer la recherche, le financement, et la sensibilisation concernant les maladies rares au Québec
Gail Ouellette, Directrice générale

Research & Education Foundation of the College of Family Physicians of Canada (REF)
2630 Skymark Ave., Mississauga ON L4W 5A4
Tel: 905-629-0900; *Fax:* 888-843-2372
Toll-Free: 800-387-6197
ref@cfpc.ca
www.cfpc.ca/REF
To raise funds in order to support family doctors
Saeah Delaney, Director, Awards & Development

Réseau de Santé en Français au Nunavut (SAFRAN)
CP 1516, Iqaluit NU X0A 0H0
Tél: 867-222-2107
resefan.nu@gmail.com
www.resefan.ca
Daniel Hubert, Directeur général

Réseau des services de santé en français de l'Est de l'Ontario
#300, 1173, ch Cyrville, Ottawa ON K1J 7S6
Tél: 613-747-7431; *Téléc:* 613-747-2907
Ligne sans frais: 877-528-7565
reseau@rssfe.on.ca
www.rssfe.on.ca
Jacinthe Desaulniers, Directrice générale

Réseau du mieux-être francophone du Nord de l'Ontario
435, av Notre-Dame, Sudbury ON P3C 5K6
Tél: 705-674-9381; *Téléc:* 705-675-5106
Ligne sans frais: 866-489-7484
reseaudumieuxetre.ca
Diane Quintas, Directrice générale par intérim

Réseau franco-santé du Sud de l'Ontario (RFSSO)
CP 90057, 1000, rue Golf Links, Ancaster ON L9K 0B4
Tél: 416-413-1717; *Ligne sans frais:* 888-549-5775
info@francosantesud.ca
francosantesud.ca
Julie Lantaigne, Directrice générale

Réseau québécois de l'asthme et de la MPOC (RQAM)
Institut universitaire de cardiologie et de pneumologie de Québec, #U-3771, 2723, ch Sainte-Foy, Québec QC G1V 4G5
Tél: 418-650-9500; *Téléc:* 418-650-9391
Ligne sans frais: 877-441-5072
info@rqam.ca
qww.rqam.ca
De fournir un soutien aux professionnels travaillant dans l'asthme dans le secteur de la santé et de leurs patients
Jean Bourbeau, Président

Réseau Santé - Nouvelle-Écosse
#227, 1589, rue Walnut, Halifax NS B3H 3S1
Tél: 902-222-5871
reseau@reseausantene.ca
www.reseausantene.ca
Jeanne-Françoise Caillaud, Directrice générale

Réseau santé albertain
8627, rue Marie-Anne-Gaboury, Edmonton AB T6C 4S8
Tél: 780-466-9816
info@reseausantealbertain.ca
www.reseausantealbertain.ca
Média social: www.youtube.com/user/reseausantealbertain
www.facebook.com/162905357095396
twitter.com/inforsab
Luc Therrien, Directeur général

Réseau Santé en français de la Saskatchewan (RSFS)
#103, 308, 4 av Nord, Saskatoon SK S7K 2L7
Tél: 306-653-7445; *Téléc:* 306-664-6447
rsfs@shaw.ca
www.rsfs.ca
Roger Gauthier, Directeur

Réseau Santé en français I.-P.-É
CP 58, 48, ch Mill, Wellington PE C0B 2E0
Tél: 902-854-7440; *Téléc:* 902-854-7255
info@santeipe.ca
www.santeipe.ca
Média social: www.facebook.com/RSFIPE
Élise Arsenault, Directrice

Réseau santé en français Terre-Neuve-et-Labrador
Centre scolaire et communautaire des Grads-Vants, #233, 65 ch Ridge, St. John's NL A1B 4P5
Tél: 709-575-2862; *Téléc:* 709-722-9904
reseauSante@fftnl.ca
www.francotnl.ca
Jean-Marc Bélanger, Coordonnateur

Réseau TNO Santé en français
CP 1325, 5016, 48 rue, Yellowknife NT X1A 2N9
Tél: 867-920-2919; *Téléc:* 867-873-2158
santetno@franco-nord.com
reseautnosante.ca
Jean de Dieu Tuyishime, Coordonnateur

Réso Santé Colombie Britannique (RSCB)
#201, 2929, rue Commercial, Vancouver BC V5N 4C8
Tél: 604-629-1000
www.resosante.ca
Louis Giguère, Directeur générale

Ronald McDonald House Toronto
240 McCaul St., Toronto ON M5T 1W5
Tel: 416-977-0458; *Fax:* 416-977-8807
info@rmhtoronto.org
www.rmhtoronto.org
To provide a home away from home for out-of-town families whose children are receiving treatment in Toronto hospitals for serious illness.
Jane Marco, Executive Director
G. Keith Graham, President

The Royal College of Physicians & Surgeons of Canada (RCPSC) / Le Collège royal des médecins et chirurgiens du Canada (CRMCC)
774 Echo Dr., Ottawa ON K1S 5N8
Tel: 613-730-8177; *Fax:* 613-730-8830
Toll-Free: 800-668-3740
feedback@royalcollege.ca
www.royalcollege.ca
Social Media: www.facebook.com/TheRoyalCollege
twitter.com/Royal_College
To oversee the medical education of specialists in Canada; To set the highest standards in postgraduate medical education, through national certification examinations & lifelong learning programs; To promote sound health policy
Andrew Padmos, CEO

Saint Elizabeth Health Care (SEHC) / Les soins de santé Sainte-Elizabeth
#300, 90 Allstate Pkwy., Markham ON L3R 6H3
Tel: 905-940-9655; *Fax:* 905-940-9934
Toll-Free: 800-463-1763
communications@saintelizabeth.com
www.saintelizabeth.com
Social Media: www.youtube.com/user/SaintElizabethSEHC
linkedin.com/company/saint-elizabeth-health-care
www.facebook.com/SaintElizabethSEHC
twitter.com/stelizabethSEHC
To serve the physical, emotional, & spiritual needs of people in their homes & communities
Shirlee M. Sharkey, President & CEO
Noreen Taylor, Chair
Heather McClure, Treasurer
Janet Holder, Secretary

Saskatchewan Association of Naturopathic Practitioners (SANP)
2146 Robinson St., #2A, Regina SK S4T 2P7
Tel: 306-757-4325; *Fax:* 306-522-0745
info@sanp.ca
www.sanp.ca
Social Media:
www.facebook.com/169544933105033
To act as the governing body for naturopathic doctors in Saskatchewan; To license & regulate naturopathic physicians in the province; To ensure members are educated & trained according to strict standards
Julie Zepp Rutledge, President
Tim Mrazek, Vice-President
Amy Velichka, Secretary
Jacqui Fleury, Treasurer
Allison Ziegler, Registrar

Saskatchewan Association of Optometrists (SAO)
#108, 2366 Ave. C North, Saskatoon SK S7L 5X5
Tel: 306-652-2069; *Fax:* 306-652-2642
Toll-Free: 877-660-3937
saskop@sasktel.net
optometrists.sk.ca
To license the delivery of optometric care in Saskatchewan; To regulate doctors of optometry throughout the province; To ensure excellence in the delivery of vision & eye health services across Saskatchewan; To enforce high standards of optometric eye care, in order to protect the public; To act as the voice of optometry in Saskatchewan
Leland Kolbenson, Registrar

Saskatchewan Dietitians Association (SDA)
#17, 2010 - 7th Ave., Regina SK S4R 1C2
Tel: 306-359-3040; *Fax:* 306-359-3046
registrar@saskdietitians.org
www.saskdietitians.org
To protect the public by registering competent dietitians; To set standards of practice; To uphold codes of conduct; To provide a framework for continuing competence, consisting of a self-assessment tool, a learning plan, & a quality assurance audit
Charlotte Pilat Burns, President
Lana Moore, Registrar

Saskatchewan Families for Effective Autism Treatment (SASKFEAT)
PO Box 2150, Tisdale SK S0E 1T0
Tel: 306-862-4768
saskfeat@hotmail.com
www.saskfeat.com
To act as a voice for the concerns & needs of parents & families of autistic children & individuals in Saskatchewan; To find the most effective treatment for autistic children & individuals
Tim Verklan, President
Carolyn Forsey, Vice-President
Ron Luciw, Secretary
Brad Hayes, Treasurer

Saskatchewan Lung Association
Saskatoon Office, 1231 - 8 St. East, Saskatoon SK S7H 0S5
Tel: 306-343-9511; *Fax:* 306-343-7007
Toll-Free: 888-566-5864
info@sk.lung.ca
www.sk.lung.ca
Social Media: www.youtube.com/user/LungAssociationSK
www.facebook.com/LungSask
twitter.com/lungsk
To improve respiratory health & overall quality of life; To advocate for support of education & research
Helen Cotton, Chair
Pat Smith, Vice-Chair
Brian Graham, President & CEO
Jennifer Miller, Vice-President, Health Promotion
Sharon Kremeniuk, Vice-President, Development
Leah Sullivan, Vice-President, Finance & Operations
Karen Davis, Treasurer

Saskatchewan Medical Association (SMA)
#402, 321A - 21st St. East, Saskatoon SK S7K 0C1
Tel: 306-244-2196; *Fax:* 306-653-1631
Toll-Free: 800-667-3781
sma@sma.sk.ca
www.sma.sk.ca
Social Media:
www.facebook.com/SMAdocs
twitter.com/SMA_docs
To represent physicians in Saskatchewan; To advance the professional, educational, & economic welfare of physicians in the province
Vino Padayachee, CEO
Maria Derzko, Coordinator, Communications
Ed Hobday, Administrative Director

Clare Kozroski, President

Saskatchewan Public Health Association Inc.
PO Box 845, Regina SK S4P 3B1
saskpha@gmail.com
To constitute a resource in Saskatchewan for the improvement & maintenance of health
Greg Riehl, President

Société canadienne de la sclérose en plaques (Division du Québec) (SCSP) / Multiple Sclerosis Society of Canada (Québec Division)
Tour Est, #1010, 550, rue Sherbrooke Ouest, Montréal QC H3A 1B9
Tél: 514-849-7591; *Téléc:* 514-849-8914
Ligne sans frais: 800-268-7582
info.qc@mssociety.ca
www.mssociety.ca/qc
Média social: www.youtube.com/SocieteSPCanada
linkedin.com/company/soci-t-canadienne-de-la-scl-rose-en-plaques-d
www.facebook.com/SocieteSPCanada
twitter.com/SocCanDeLaSP
Soutenir la recherche sur la SP; offrir des services aux personnes atteintes de la maladie et à leurs familles; sensibiliser le public à la sclérose en plaques et maintenir les relations avec les gouvernements.
Louis Adam, Directeur général

Société Huntington du Québec (SHQ) / Huntington Society of Québec (HSQ)
2300, boul René-Lévesque Ouest, Montréal QC H3H 2R5
Tél: 514-282-4272; *Téléc:* 514-937-0082
Ligne sans frais: 877-220-0226
shq@huntingtonqc.org
huntingtonqc.org
Pour aider les personnes atteintes de la maladie de Huntington à faire face
Francine Lacroix, Directrice générale

Société Parkinson du Québec / Parkinson Society Québec
#1080, 550 rue Sherbrooke Ouest, Montréal QC H3A 1B9
Tél: 514-861-4422; *Ligne sans frais:* 800-720-1307
info@parkinsonquebec.ca
www.parkinsonquebec.ca
Média social:
www.youtube.com/channel/UCMo6s0d7FXkc46ThRFScExQ
www.facebook.com/pages/Societe-Parkinson-du-Quebec/442004702608772
twitter.com/parkinsonquebec
Nicole Charpentier, Directrice générale

Société Santé en français (SSF)
#201, 291, rue Dalhousie, Ottawa ON K1N 7E5
Tél: 613-244-1889; *Téléc:* 613-244-0283
info@santefrancais.ca
www.santefrancais.ca
Pour améliorer l'accès et la qualité des services de soins de santé en français au Canada
Michel Tremblay, Directeur général
Aurel Schofield, Président

Société Santé et Mieux-être en français du Nouveau-Brunswick (SSMEFFNB)
CP 1764, Moncton NB E1C 9X6
Tél: 506-389-3351; *Téléc:* 506-389-3366
ssmefnb@nb.aibn.com
www.ssmefnb.ca
Média social: www.facebook.com/SSMEFNB
twitter.com/SSMEFNB
Gilles Vienneau, Directeur général

Society of Obstetricians & Gynaecologists of Canada (SOGC) / Société des obstétriciens et gynécologues du Canada
780 Echo Dr., Ottawa ON K1S 5R7
Tel: 613-730-4192; *Fax:* 613-730-4314
Toll-Free: 800-561-2416
helpdesk@sogc.com
www.sogc.org
To promote excellence in the practice of obstetrics & gynaecology; To produce national clinical guidelines for medical education on women's health issues; To promote optimal, comprehensive women's health care
Ward Murdock, President
Jennifer Blake, Chief Executive Officer

Society of Rural Physicians of Canada (SRPC) / Société de la médecine rurale du Canada
PO Box 893, 269 Main St., Shawville QC J0X 2Y0
Fax: 819-647-2485
Toll-Free: 877-276-1949
info@srpc.ca
www.srpc.ca
To provide equitable medical care for rural communities; to provide sustainable working conditions for rural physicians
John Soles, President
Lee Teperman, Administrative Officer

Speech-Language & Audiology Canada (SAC) / Orthophonie et Audiologie Canada (OAC)
#1000, 1 Nicholas St., Ottawa ON K1N 7B7
Tel: 613-567-9968; *Fax:* 613-567-2859
Toll-Free: 800-259-8519
info@sac-oac.ca
www.sac-oac.ca
Social Media:
www.youtube.com/channel/UCmg6LP26_eRR72hBEFfnRug
linkedin.com/groups/SAC-Members-4226965/about
www.facebook.com/sac.oac
twitter.com/sac_oac
To support & represent the professional needs & development of speech-language pathologists & audiologists; to champion the needs of people with communication disorders
Judy Meintzer, President
Roula Baali, Treasurer
Joanne Charlebois, Chief Executive Officer
Jessica Bedford, Director, Communications and Marketing

Spina Bifida & Hydrocephalus Association of Canada (SBHAC) / Association de spina-bifida et d'hydrocephalie du Canada
#647, 167 Lombard Ave., Winnipeg MB R3B 0V3
Tel: 204-925-3650; *Fax:* 204-925-3654
Toll-Free: 800-565-9488
info@sbhac.ca
www.sbhac.ca
Social Media:
www.facebook.com/167743789940812
To improve the quality of life of all individuals with spina bifida &/or hydrocephalus & their families through awareness, education, advocacy & research; to reduce the incidence of neural tube defects
Colleen Talbot, President

Spinal Cord Injury Canada / Lésions Médullaires Canada
Varette Bldg., #512, 130 Albert St., Ottawa ON K1P 5G4
Tel: 613-723-1913; *Fax:* 613-723-1060
info@sciontario.org
www.sciontario.org
Social Media:
www.facebook.com/223239864405595
To assist persons with spinal cord injuries & other physical disabilitieto to cope with the changes caused by their injury, to become independent & self-reliant, & to lead productive lives. The Canadian Paraplegic Association officially changed its name to Spinal Cord Injury Canada in 2012. Member associations are in the process of also changing their names & are aiming to share the Spinal Cord Injury title in 2013.
Eddie Joyce, President
Myrtle Jenkins-Smith, Vice-President/Secretary
Ron Swan, Treasurer

The Terry Fox Foundation / La Fondation Terry Fox
#303, 46165 Yale Rd., Chilliwack BC V2P 2P2
Tel: 604-701-0246; *Fax:* 604-701-0247
national@terryfoxrun.org
www.terryfoxrun.org
Social Media: www.youtube.com/terryfoxcanada
www.facebook.com/TheTerryFoxFoundation
twitter.com/TerryFoxCanada
To maintain the vision & principles of Terry Fox while raising money for cancer research through the annual Terry Fox Run, memoriam donations & planned gifts. All money raised by the Foundation is distributed through the National Cancer Institute of Canada
Bill Pristanski, Chair
Judith Fox-Alder, International Director

Thalidomide Victims Association of Canada (TVAC) / Association canadienne des victimes de la thalidomide (ACVT)
Centre commercial Joseph Renaud, #211, 6830, boul Joseph Renaud, Montréal QC H1K 3V4
Tel: 514-355-0811; *Fax:* 514-355-0860
Toll-Free: 877-355-0811
tvac.acvt@sympatico.ca
www.thalidomide.ca

To monitor the drug thalidomide & to meet the needs of thalidomide survivors; to empower & enhance the quality of life of Canadian thalidomidors
Mercedes Benegbi, Executive Director

The 3C Foundation of Canada / Fondation Canadienne des 3c
#200, 1 Hines Rd., Kanata ON K2K 3C7
Tel: 613-237-6690
info@3cfoundation.org
www.3cfoundation.org
Social Media: www.facebook.com/GutTogether
Michele Hepburn, President

Thyroid Foundation of Canada / La Fondation canadienne de la Thyroïde
PO Box 298, Bath ON K0H 1G0
Toll-Free: 800-267-8822
www.thyroid.ca
To provide leadership to the fight against thyroid disease
Donna Miniely, President
Rinda Hartner, Treasurer

Tourette Syndrome Foundation of Canada (TSFC) / La Fondation canadienne du syndrome de Tourette
#175, 5945 Airport Rd., Mississauga ON L4V 1R9
Tel: 905-673-2255; *Fax:* 905-673-2638
Toll-Free: 800-341-3120
tsfc@tourette.ca
www.tourette.ca
Social Media: www.youtube.com/TSFCanada
www.facebook.com/TSFCanada
twitter.com/TSFCanada
Through education, advocacy, self-help, & the promotion of research, the TSFC assists individuals affected by Tourette Syndrome & its associated disorders.
Lynn McLarnon, Executive Director

Tourette Syndrome Foundation of Canada (TSFC)
#175, 5945 Airport Rd., Mississauga ON L4V 1R9
Tel: 905-673-2255; *Fax:* 905-673-2638
Toll-Free: 800-361-3120
tsfc@tourette.ca
www.tourette.ca
Social Media: www.youtube.com/TSFCanada
www.facebook.com/TSFCanada
twitter.com/TSFCanada
To educate & increase public awareness about Tourette Syndrome

Trillium Gift of Life Network
#900, 522 University Ave., Toronto ON M5G 1W7
Tel: 416-363-4001; *Fax:* 416-363-4002
Toll-Free: 800-263-2833
www.giftoflife.on.ca
Social Media: linkedin.com/company/1426658
www.facebook.com/TrilliumGiftofLife
twitter.com/TrilliumGift
To enable every Ontario resident to make an informed decision to donate organs & tissue; to support healthcare professionals in implementing their wishes; maximize organ & tissue donation in Ontario in a respectful & equitable manner through education, research, services & support
Ronnie Gavsie, President & CEO

Turner's Syndrome Society (TSS) / Société du syndrome de Turner
#9, 30 Clearly Ave., Ottawa ON K2A 4A1
Tel: 613-321-2267; *Fax:* 613-321-2268
Toll-Free: 800-465-6744
info@turnersyndrome.ca
www.turnersyndrome.ca
Social Media: www.facebook.com/TurnerSyndromeSocietyOfCanada
To improve the quality of life for individuals & families affected by Turner's Syndrome; to strive to accomplish this through providing public & professional awareness about the needs & concerns of individuals with Turner's Syndrome & their families through the development of communication networks to provide mutual support
Krista Kamstra-Cooper, President

Vocational Rehabilitation Association of Canada (VRA Canada)
#310, 4 Cataraqui St., Kingston ON K7K 1Z7
Tel: 613-507-5530; *Fax:* 888-441-8002
Toll-Free: 888-876-9992
info@vracanada.com
www.vracanada.com
Social Media: linkedin.com/groups?home=&gid=374132
www.facebook.com/VRACanada
twitter.com/VRACanada
To support members in promoting & providing the professional delivery of rehabilitation services
Lesley McIntyre, President

VOICE for Hearing Impaired Children
#302, 177 Danforth Ave., Toronto ON M4K 1N2
Tel: 416-487-7719; *Fax:* 416-487-7423
Toll-Free: 866-779-5144
TTY: 416-487-7719
info@voicefordeafkids.com
www.voicefordeafkids.com
Social Media: www.youtube.com/channel/UCtqS6zWzpmW9Tq6DRRbZubw
www.facebook.com/VOICEforHearingImpairedChildren
twitter.com/VOICE4DEAFKIDS
To ensure that all hearing impaired children have the right to develop their ability to listen & speak & have access to services which will enable them to listen & speak

Yukon Medical Association
5 Hospital Rd., Whitehorse YT Y1A 3H7
Tel: 867-393-8749
office@yukondoctors.ca
www.yukondoctors.ca
A voluntary association of Yukon doctors; advocates on behalf of members; promotes professionalism in medical practice & accessibility to quality health care for Yukoners
Ken Quong, President

Heating, Air Conditioning, Plumbing

Canadian Institute of Plumbing & Heating (CIPH) / Institut canadien de plomberie et de chauffage
#504, 295 The West Mall, Toronto ON M9C 4Z4
Tel: 416-695-0447; *Toll-Free:* 800-639-2474
info@ciph.com
www.ciph.com
Social Media: www.youtube.com/channel/UCx8_LwmTSuOmOr0lyp7sLGQ
linkedin.com/company/ciph
www.facebook.com/pages/CIPH/355926634482039
www.twitter.com/ciphnews
To act as a unified voice for plumbing, heating, hydronic, PVF, & waterworks across Canada
Ralph Suppa, CAE, President & General Manager
Elizabeth McCullough, CDE, General Manager, Trade Shows
Kevin Wong, Technical Advisor
Stephen Apps, Manager, Program
Matt Wiesenfeld, Manager, Program

Heating, Refrigeration & Air Conditioning Institute of Canada (HRAI) / Institut canadien du chauffage, de la climatisation et de la réfrigération (ICCCR)
Bldg. 1, #201, 2800 Skymark Ave., Mississauga ON L4W 5A6
Tel: 905-602-4700; *Fax:* 905-602-1197
Toll-Free: 800-267-2231
hraimail@hrai.ca
www.hrai.ca
Social Media: www.youtube.com/hraichannel
linkedin.com/company/heating-refrigeration-and-air-conditioning-institute-of-canada
www.facebook.com/322711681086830
twitter.com/HRAI_Canada
To serve the HRAI membership & HVACR industry in Canada by facilitating industry solutions, coordinating a strong national membership, representing the industry to their publics, conducting accountable association activities, providing quality member/customer services, & educating & training industry members
Warren J. Heeley, President
Martin Luymes, Director, Programs & Relations
Frank Diecidue, Director, Operations & Services

Ontario Geothermal Association (OGA)
#201, 2800 Skymark Ave., Mississauga ON L4W 5A6
Tel: 905-602-4700; *Fax:* 905-602-1197
Toll-Free: 800-267-2231
www.ontariogeothermal.ca
John Bosman, President

Ontario Plumbing Inspectors Association (OPIA)
129 Dumble Ave., Peterborough ON K9H 5A9
Tel: 705-748-0120
opia@opia.info
www.opia.info/members
To promote uniform enforcement of plumbing regulations; close liaison & interchange of ideas & knowledge between members of the OPIA & members of other associations; provide education & training to members & the industry
Doug Flucker, President
Rainier Blundel, Vice President

Ontario Refrigeration & Air Conditioning Contractors Association (ORAC)
#43, 6770 Davand Dr., Mississauga ON L5T 2G3
Tel: 905-670-0010; *Fax:* 905-670-0474
contact@oraca.ca
www.oraca.ca
To represent Ontario's contractor practitioners in the refrigeration & air conditioning trade; To enhance quality & efficiency in the industry to benefit customers
Dino Russo, President
David Sinclair, Vice-President
Mike Verge, Interim Managing Director
Gregg Little, Treasurer

Plumbing Officials' Association of British Columbia (POABC)
2328 Hollyhill Pl., Victoria BC V8N 1T9
Tel: 250-361-0342; *Fax:* 250-385-1128
bhusband@victoria.ca
www.bcplumbingofficials.com
Brian Husband, President

Refrigeration Service Engineers Society (Canada) (RSES Canada)
PO Box 3, Stn. B, Toronto ON M9W 5K9
Tel: 905-842-9199; *Toll-Free:* 877-955-6255
www.rsescanada.com
To lead all segments of the HVAC industry by providing superior educational & training programs; to create an environment that encourages maximum member participation in the development & decision process of the Society
Denis Hebert, President
Nick Reggi, Secretary

Thermal Environmental Comfort Association (TECA)
PO Box 73105, Stn. Evergreen RO, Surrey BC V3R 0J2
Tel: 604-594-5956; *Fax:* 604-594-5091
Toll-Free: 888-577-3818
training@teca.ca
www.teca.ca
To offer the residential heating, cooling & ventilation industry up-to-date training courses & a collective voice in local & provincial issues
Katharine Czycz, President

History, Heritage, Genealogy

Action Patrimoine
82, Grande-Allée ouest, Québec QC G1R 2G6
Tél: 418-647-4347; *Téléc:* 418-647-6483
Ligne sans frais: 800-494-4347
info@actionpatrimoine.ca
actionpatrimoine.ca
Média social: www.facebook.com/Actionpatrimoine
Afin de préserver et de promouvoir repères culturels au Québec
Émilie Vézina-Doré, Directrice générale

Alberta Family History Society (AFHS)
712 - 16 Ave. NW, Calgary AB T2M 0J8
Tel: 403-214-1447
www.afhs.ab.ca
To encourage accuracy & thoroughness in family histories & genealogical research; to establish relations with related societies to promote common interests
Irene Oickle, Membership Chair
Lorna Loughton, President

Alberta Historical Resources Foundation (AHRF)
Old St. Stephen's College, 8820 - 112 St., Edmonton AB T6G 2P8
Tel: 780-431-2300; *Fax:* 780-427-5598
culture.alberta.ca/ahrf
To assist in the preservation of Alberta's historic sites, buildings & objects; to encourage & promote public awareness of the province's past; grants are awarded in the spring & fall at each year to a wide variety of community-based heritage initiatives
David Link, Director

Antique Motorcycle Club of Manitoba Inc. (AMCM)
1377 Niakwa Rd. East, Winnipeg MB R2J 3T3
Tel: 204-831-8165
www.amcm.ca
Ross Metcalfe, President
Mike Baraschuk, Librarian

Architectural Heritage Society of Saskatchewan (AHSS)
202 - 1275 Broad St., Regina SK S4R 1Y2
Tel: 306-359-0933; *Fax:* 306-359-3899
sahs@sasktel.net
www.ahsk.ca
To promote, support & facilitate the preservation, conservation, restoration & reuse of distinct architectural & historical heritage properties (designated or potential) throughout the province, ensuring that our built heritage is maintained for present & future citizens to appreciate the contributions & craftsmanship of past generations; to enhance the current social, economic & environmental quality of life

Association québécoise d'interprétation du patrimoine (AQIP)
CP 11003, Succ. Le Plateau, Gatineau QC J9A 0B6
Tél: 819-595-2190
aqip@aqip.ca
www.aqip.ca
Stimuler la communication entre les individus et les organismes intéressés à l'interprétation du patrimoine naturel, culturel, historique et industriel; promouvoir l'interprétation du patrimoine québécois auprès des gouvernements, des organismes, des médias et du public en général; stimuler l'acquisition de connaissances et la recherche liée à l'interprétation du patrimoine
Denis Lavoie, Président

British Columbia Genealogical Society (BCGS)
PO Box 88054, Stn. Lansdowne Mall, Richmond BC V6X 3T6
Tel: 604-502-9119; *Fax:* 604-502-9119
bcgs@bcgs.ca
www.bcgs.ca
To perpetuate the heritage of BC; to collect, preserve & publish material relevant to promotion of ethical principles, scientific methods & effective techniques in genealogical & historical research
Lorraine Irving, President

British Columbia Historical Federation (BCHF)
PO Box 5254, Stn. B, Victoria BC V8R 6N4
info@bchistory.ca
www.bchistory.ca
Social Media:
www.facebook.com/bchistoricalfederation
To encourage interest in the history of British Columbia through financial support, research, & presentation
Gary Mitchell, President
Sandra Martins, Secretary

Bus History Association, Inc. (BHA)
c/o Bernie Drouillard, 965 McEwan Ave., Windsor ON N9B 2G1
www.bus-history.org
To preserve & record data, information & other related materials of the bus industry, both within North America & worldwide
Paul A. Leger, Chair
Bernard Drouillard, Secretary-Treasurer

Canada's History / Histoire Canada
PO Box 118, Stn. Main, Markham ON L3P 3J5
Tel: 905-946-8790; *Fax:* 905-946-1679
Toll-Free: 888-816-0997
memberservices@canadashistory.ca
www.canadashistory.ca
Social Media: www.youtube.com/canadashistory;
www.flickr.com/photos/canadas_history
www.facebook.com/CanadasHistory
twitter.com/canadashistory
To promote greater popular interest in Canadian history
Janet Walker, President & CEO
Danielle Chartier, Manager, Marketing & Circulation
Joel Ralph, Director, Programs

Canadian Association for Conservation of Cultural Property (CAC) / Association canadienne pour la conservation et la restauration des biens culturels (ACCR)
c/o Danielle Allard, #419, 207 Bank St., Ottawa ON K2P 2N2
Tel: 613-231-3977; *Fax:* 613-231-4406
coordinator@cac-accr.com
www.cac-accr.ca
Social Media:
www.facebook.com/289264431135291
To promote conservation of Canadian cultural property
Cindy Colford, President
Jessica Lafrance, Vice-President
Susannah Kendall, Secretary
Michael Harrington, Treasurer

Canadian Association of Heritage Professionals (CAPHC) / Association canadienne d'experts-conseils en patrimoine (ACECP)
190 Bronson Ave., Ottawa ON K1R 6H4
Tel: 613-569-7455
admin@cahp-acecp.ca
www.caphc.ca
Social Media:
www.facebook.com/pages/CAHP-Acecp/121466461265655
To represent & further the professional interests of heritage consultants active in both the private & public sectors; To establish & maintain principles & standards of practice for heritage consultants; To enhance awareness & appreciation of heritage resources, & the contribution of heritage consultants; To foster communication among private practitioners, public agencies, & the public at large in matters related to heritage conservation
Jill Taylor, President
Julie Harris, Secretary

Canadian Heritage Information Network (CHIN) / Réseau canadien d'information sur le patrimoine (RCIP)
15 Eddy St., 7th Fl., Gatineau QC K1A 0M5
Tel: 819-994-1200; *Fax:* 819-994-9555
Toll-Free: 800-520-2446
TTY: 888-997-3123
service@chin.gc.ca
www.rcip-chin.gc.ca
To engage national & international audiences in Canadian heritage, through leadership & innovation in digital content, partnerships, & lifelong learning opportunities
Claudette Lévesque, Acting Director General
Paul Lima, Senior Policy Advisor
Julie Marion, Director, Program Development

Canadian Historical Association (CHA) / Société historique du Canada (SHC)
#1201, 130 Albert St., Ottawa ON K1P 5G4
Tel: 613-233-7885; *Fax:* 613-565-5445
www.cha-shc.ca
Social Media:
www.facebook.com/215430858536628
twitter.com/CndHistAssoc
To encourage historical research; To stimulate public interest in history; To promote the preservation of Canadian heritage
Michel Duquet, Executive Director

Canadian Oral History Association (COHA) / Société canadienne d'histoire orale (SCHO)
c/o University of Winnipeg, 515 Portage Ave., Winnipeg MB R3B 2E9
www.canoha.ca
To encourage & support the creation & preservation of sound recordings which document the history & culture of Canada; to develop standards of excellence & increase competence in the field of oral history through study, education & research.
Nolan Reilly, President
Janis Thiessen, Secretary-Treasurer

Canadian Society for the Study of Names (CSSN) / Société canadienne d'onomastique (SCO)
PO Box 2164, Stn. Hull, Gatineau QC J8X 3Z4
www.csj.ualberta.ca/sco
CSSN promotes the study of all aspects of names & naming in Canada & elsewhere.
Carol J. Léonard, Chair
Léo La Brie, Secretary-Treasurer

Canadian Society of Mayflower Descendants
c/o Lynne Webb, 2927 Highfield Cres., Ottawa ON K2B 6G4
administrator@csmd.org
csmd.org
Social Media:
www.facebook.com/canadiansocietyofmayflowerdescendants
twitter.com/CanMayflower
To promote the memory of the Mayflower pilgrims & to inform the public of this era of Canadian history
Joyce Cutler, Governor

Canadian Society of Presbyterian History
c/o Burns Presbyterian Church, 765 Myrtle Rd. West, Ashburn ON L0B 1A0
Tel: 905-655-8509
www.csph.ca
To study Presbyterian & Reformed history
A. Donald MacLeod, President

Canadian Vintage Motorcycle Group (CVMG)
33 Station Rd., Toronto ON M8V 2R1
secretary@cvmg.ca
www.amcm.ca
Bill Hoar, President
Betty Anne Clark, Correspondence Secretary
Anthony Petti, Membership Secretary

Canadian Warplane Heritage (CWH)
9280 Airport Rd., Mount Hope ON L0R 1W0
Tel: 905-679-4183; *Fax:* 905-679-4186
Toll-Free: 877-347-3359
museum@warplane.com
www.warplane.com
To acquire documents; perserve & maintain a complete collection of aircraft that were flown by Canadians & the Canadian military services from the beginning of World War II to the present, including other related aviation artifacts & memorabilia of significant historic importance to this period; to instruct, educate & entertain the general public through the maintenance & rotation of displays, flight demonstrations, special events & activities, & to encourage Canadians of all ages to become actively involved in the preservation of these aircraft & artifacts; to provide facilities for the restoration & protection, interpretation & exhibits of the collection; to maintain supportive exhibits in tribute to the thousands of men & women who built, serviced & flew these aircraft & in memory of those who did not return
Pamela Rickards, Vice President of Operations
Al Mickeloff, Manager, Marketing

Canadiana
#200, 440 Laurier Ave. West, Ottawa ON K1R 7X6
Tel: 613-235-2628; *Fax:* 613-235-9752
info@canadiana.org
www.canadiana.ca
Social Media: www.flickr.com/photos/canadiana_org
www.facebook.com/CanadianaCA
twitter.com/CanadianaCA
To specialize in the digitization of, preservation of, & access to documentary heritage
Ron Walker, Executive Director
Ulrich Werneburg, Manager, Partnerships
Daniel Velarde, Officer, Communications

Family History Society of Newfoundland & Labrador
PO Box 8008, #101A, 66 Kenmount Rd., St. John's NL A1B 3V7
Tel: 709-754-9525; *Fax:* 709-754-6430
fhs@fhsnl.ca
www.fhsnl.ca
Social Media:
www.facebook.com/144749998869923
twitter.com/fhsnl
To encourage & promote the study of family history in Newfoundland & Labrador; To collect & preserve local genealogical & historical records & materials; to foster education in genealogical research
Smith Frederick, President
Dunne Paul, Secretary

Fédération des sociétés d'histoire du Québec
4545, av Pierre-de Coubertin, Montréal QC H1V 0B2
Tél: 514-252-3031; *Téléc:* 514-251-8038
Ligne sans frais: 866-691-7207
fshq@histoirequebec.qc.ca
www.histoirequebec.qc.ca
Média social: twitter.com/FederationHQ
Regrouper les organisations historiques de Québec.
Richard M. Bégin, Président

Fédération québécoise des sociétés de généalogie (FQSG)
CP 9454, Succ. Sainte-Foy, 1055, av du Séminaire, Québec QC G1V 4B8
Tél: 418-653-3940; *Téléc:* 418-653-3940
federationgenealogie@bellnet.ca
www.federationgenealogie.qc.ca
Représenter les sociétés de généalogie locales et régionales; la promotion et l'épanouissement de la généalogie au Québec et son rayonnement à l'étranger sont les buts visés
Albert J. Cyr, Président

Genealogical Association of Nova Scotia (GANS) / Association généalogique de la Nouvelle-Écosse
PO Box 333, 3045 Robie St., Halifax NS B3K 4P6
Tel: 902-454-0322
info@novascotiaancestors.ca
www.novascotiaancestors.ca
Social Media:
www.facebook.com/NovaScotiaAncestors
twitter.com/NSAncestors

To encourage interest in & to raise standards of research in genealogy through workshops & publications; to acquaint members with research materials & methods to serve as medium of exchange for genealogical information; to support the collection & preservation of documents & other genealogical materials; to foster recognition of the value of genealogy to a proper study of the social sciences.
Allan Marble, President

Genealogical Institute of The Maritimes (GIM) / Institut généalogique des Provinces Maritimes
PO Box 36022, 5675 Spring Garden Rd., Halifax NS B3J 1G0
nsgna.ednet.ns.ca/gim
To pursue geneaology; to upgrade the quality of professional family history research in the Maritimes
Allen Marble, Contact

L'Héritage canadien du Québec (HCQ) / The Canadian Heritage of Québec (CHQ)
#1201, 1350 rue Sherbrooke ouest, Montréal QC H3G 1J1
Tél: 514-393-1417; *Téléc:* 514-393-9444
mail@hcq-chq.org
www.hcq-chq.org
Média social: www.facebook.com/1723406467941985
Organisme qui se consacre à la préservation des terrains & des constructions revêtant une valeur historique/architecturale dans la province du Québec
Jacques Archambault, General Manager

Heritage Foundation of Newfoundland & Labrador (HFNL)
The Newman Building, PO Box 5171, 1 Springdale St., St. John's NL A1C 5V5
Tel: 709-739-1892; *Fax:* 709-739-5413
Toll-Free: 888-739-1892
info@heritagefoundation.ca
www.heritagefoundation.ca
To stimulate an understanding of & appreciation for the architectural heritage of Newfoundland & Labrador; To support & contribute to the preservation, maintenance & restoration of buildings of architectural or historical significance; To designate buildings & structures as Registered Heritage Structures; may make grants for purpose of preservation, maintenance, or restoration (Deadline for submitting grant application is Mar. 1 & Sept. 1 of each year)
George Chalker, Executive Director
Frank Crews, Chairperson

Heritage Society of British Columbia
914 Garthland Pl. West, Victoria BC V9A 4J5
Tel: 250-384-4840
hsbc@islandnet.com
www.heritagebc.ca
Social Media:
www.facebook.com/pages/Heritage-BC/191841050874008
To represent groups involved with heritage projects & issues
Rick Goodacre, Executive Director
Eric Pattison, President
Jan Thomas, Office Manager, Surrey

Historic Sites Association of Newfoundland & Labrador (HSANL)
PO Box 5542, 10 Barter's Hill, 5th Fl., St. John's NL A1C 5W4
Tel: 709-753-2566; *Fax:* 709-753-0879
Toll-Free: 877-753-9262
info@historicsites.ca
www.historicsites.ca
Social Media:
www.facebook.com//131036186980761
twitter.com/historicsitesnl
To preserve, promote, & interpret the history & heritage of Newfoundland & Labrador, in partnership with Parks Canada
Catherine Dempsey, Executive Director

Historic Theatres' Trust (HTT) / Société des salles historiques
PO Box 387, Stn. Victoria Station, Montréal QC H3Z 2V8
Tel: 514-933-8077; *Fax:* 514-933-8012
theatres@total.net
To develop an increased appreciation within the Canadian public concerning the preservation of historic Canadian theatres; To provide technical documentation & expertise to encourage improved methods of preserving, restoring, maintaining, operating & researching historic theatres
Janet MacKinnon, President

Historical Society of Alberta (HSA)
PO Box 4035, Stn. C, Calgary AB T2T 5M9
Tel: 403-261-3662; *Fax:* 403-269-6029
info@albertahistory.org
www.albertahistory.org
To preserve & promote the history of Alberta; to encourage the study & preservation of Canadian & Albertan history; to rescue from oblivion the memories, experiences & knowledge of early inhabitants.
Belinda Crowson, President

ICOMOS Canada
PO Box 737, Stn. B, Ottawa ON K1P 5P8
Tel: 613-749-0971; *Fax:* 613-749-0971
canada@icomos.org
canada.icomos.org
To further the conservation, protection, rehabilitation, & enhancement of monuments, groups of buildings & sites; To encourage primary research in many important fields
Dinu Bumbaru, President
Alain Dejeans, Vice-président, Comité francophone
John Ward, Vice President, English Speaking Committee

J. Douglas Ferguson Historical Research Foundation
PO Box 5079, Shediac NB E4P 8T8
Tel: 506-532-6025
www.nunet.ca/jdfhrf/main.php
To give financial support to a broad range of activities aimed at preserving the heritage of early historical currency, banks & other issuers of money, coins, tokens & paper money issued throughout Canada since the 18th century.
Geoffrey G. Bell, Deputy Chair
Chris Faulkner, Chairman
Len Buth, Treasurer

Jewish Genealogical Society of Canada (JGSC)
PO Box 91006, 2901 Bayview Ave., Toronto ON M2K 2Y6
Tel: 647-247-6414
info@jgstoronto.ca
www.jgstoronto.ca
To foster interest in Jewish genealogical research; To facilitate the pursuit of Jewish genealogical research domestically & internationally; To provide a forum for the exchange of knowledge & information among people interested in Jewish genealogy
Les Kelman, President
Neil Richler, Coordinator, Membership

Literary & Historical Society of Québec (LHSQ) / Société littéraire et historique de Québec
44 Chaussée des Écossais, Québec QC G1R 4H3
Tel: 418-694-9147; *Fax:* 418-694-0754
info@morrin.org
www.morrin.org
To preserve, develop & share the diverse cultural life of the Québec City region's English-speaking community through innovative, responsive & effective services
Barry McCullough, Executive Director

Manitoba Genealogical Society Inc. (MGS)
1045 St. James St., #E, Winnipeg MB R3H 1B1
Tel: 204-783-9139; *Fax:* 204-783-0190
contact@mbgenealogy.com
www.mbgenealogy.com
Social Media:
www.facebook.com/pages/Manitoba-Genealogical-Society-Inc/7054423205
twitter.com/MbGenealogy
To collect & preserve local genealogical & historical records & materials; To foster education in genealogical research through society workshops & seminars; To encourage production of genealogical publications relating especially to Manitoba
Kathy Stokes, President
Mary Bole, Library Chair

Manitoba Historical Society (MHS)
61 Carlton St., Winnipeg MB R3C 1N7
Tel: 204-947-0559; *Fax:* 204-943-2565
info@mhs.mb.ca
www.mhs.mb.ca
To promote public interest in, and preservation of Manitoba's historical resources; To encourage research relating to the history of Manitoba
Annabelle Mays, President
James Kostuchuk, First Vice-President
Victor Sawelo, Manager, Ross House

Monarchist League of Canada (MLC) / Ligue Monarchiste du Canada
PO Box 1057, Stn. Lakeshore West, Oakville ON L6K 0B2
Tel: 905-912-0916
domsec@monarchist.ca
www.monarchist.ca
Social Media:
www.youtube.com/LigueMonarchLeague?hl=en-GB
www.facebook.com/canadamonarchist
twitter.com/monarchist
To promote loyalty to the Sovereign & a broader understanding of constitutional monarchy as part of Canada's parliament, history, social fabric, culture & traditions
Robert Finch, Dominion Chairman

National Trust for Canada (HCF) / Fondation Héritage Canada
190 Bronson Ave., Ottawa ON K1R 6H4
Tel: 613-237-1066; *Fax:* 613-237-5987
Toll-Free: 866-964-1066
nationaltrust@nationaltrustcanada.ca
www.nationaltrustcanada.ca
Social Media:
www.instagram.com/instagram.com/nationaltrustca
www.facebook.com/NationalTrustCanada
twitter.com/nationaltrustca
To foster & ensure the understanding, protection & sustainable evolution of Canada's heritage buildings & historic places
Natalie Bull, Executive Director
Carolyn Quinn, Director, Communications

New Brunswick Genealogical Society Inc. (NBGS, Inc.) / Société Généalogique du Nouveau-Brunswick Inc.
PO Box 3235, Stn. B, Fredericton NB E3A 5G9
webmanager@nbgs.ca
www.nbgs.ca
To promote & facilitate family historical research in New Brunswick
Stephanie Heenan-Orr, President
Ron Green, Treasurer
Shirley Graves, Secretary

New Brunswick Historical Society
Loyalist House, 120 Union St., Saint John NB E2L 1A3
Tel: 506-652-3590
info@LoyalistHouse.com
www.loyalisthouse.com
To promote the study, research & discussion of New Brunswick history; to collect & preserve New Brunswick history; to publish & educate. The Society owns & operates Loyalist House.

Newfoundland Historical Society (NHS)
PO Box 23154, Stn. Churchill Square, St. John's NL A1B 4J9
Tel: 709-722-3191; *Fax:* 709-722-9035
nhs@nf.aibn.com
www.nlhistory.ca
To promote study, research & public discussion of Newfoundland & Labrador's history; to record the history of the province; to promote preservation of historic sites
Fred Smith, President

Ontario Black History Society (OBHS) / Société historique des Noirs de l'Ontario
#402, 10 Adelaide St. East, Toronto ON M5C 1J3
Tel: 416-867-9420; *Fax:* 416-867-8691
admin@blackhistorysociety.ca
www.blackhistorysociety.ca
Social Media: www.youtube.com/user/OntarioBlackHistory
www.facebook.com/109773629168
twitter.com/tweetOBHS
To study Black history in Canada; to recognize, preserve & promote the contribution of Black peoples & their collective histories through education, research & cooperation; to promote the inclusion of material on Black history in school curricula; to sponsor & support educational conferences & exhibits in this field.

Ontario Electric Railway Historical Association
PO Box 578, Milton ON L9T 5A2
Tel: 519-856-9802; *Fax:* 519-856-1399
streetcar@hcry.org
www.hcry.org
Social Media:
twitter.com/streetcarmuseum
To collect & return to operating capacity, electric railway equipment representing North American city & interurban systems

Ontario Genealogical Society (OGS)
#102, 40 Orchard View Blvd., Toronto ON M4R 1B9
Tel: 416-489-0734; *Fax:* 416-489-9803
provoffice@ogs.on.ca
www.ogs.on.ca
Social Media: www.ogs.on.ca/ogsblog
www.facebook.com/OntarioGenealogicalSociety
To encourage, bring together & assist all those interested in the pursuit of family history; to promote genealogical research; to set standards for genealogical excellence; to make available the knowledge, availability, diversity & comprehensiveness of the genealogical resources of Ontario; to share expertise in other geographic areas
Sarah Newitt, Executive Director

Ruthann LaBlance, Manager, Digitization Division

Ontario Historical Society (OHS) / La Société historique de l'Ontario
34 Parkview Ave., Willowdale ON M2N 3Y2
Tel: 416-226-9011; *Fax:* 416-226-2740
ohs@ontariohistoricalsociety.ca
www.ontariohistoricalsociety.ca
To bring people together who are interested in preserving some aspect of Ontario's history; to encourage & assist museums, historical societies & other heritage groups to research, preserve & interpret artifacts, architecture, archaeological sites & archival resources of local communities; to provide a forum to exchange ideas, research & experiences related to the history of Ontario; to sponsor programs & projects with a wide general appeal that help discover Ontario history
Robert Leverty, Executive Director

Pier 21 Society
1055 Marginal Rd., Halifax NS B3H 4P6
Tel: 902-425-7770; *Fax:* 902-423-4045
Toll-Free: 855-526-4721
info@pier21.ca
www.pier21.ca
Social Media: www.youtube.com/Pier21Museum
www.facebook.com/210412625764977
twitter.com/pier21
To preserve & share information about the Canadian immigration experience through history
Tung Chan, Chair
Marie Chapman, Chief Executive Officer
Monica MacDonald, Manager, Research
Cailin MacDonald, Manager, Communication

Postal History Society of Canada (PHSC)
PO Box 562, Stn. B, Ottawa ON K1P 5P7
secretary@postalhistorycanada.net
www.postalhistorycanada.net
To promote the study of postal history of Canada
Chris Green, Contact

Prince Edward Island Genealogical Society Inc. (PEIGS)
PO Box 2744, Charlottetown PE C1A 8C4
peigs_queries@yahoo.ca
www.peigs.ca
To encourage & promote the study of family history in PEI; to collect & preserve local genealogical & historical records & materials; to foster education in genealogical research

Québec Family History Society (QFHS) / Société de l'histoire des familles du Québec
PO Box 1026, Pointe-Claire QC H9S 4H9
Tel: 514-695-1502; *Fax:* 514-695-3508
qfhs@bellnet.ca
www.qfhs.ca
To promote genealogy & genealogical research in Québec (particularly English & Protestant records) to collect & preserve books, manuscripts & other related material; To conduct workshops & seminars & discuss topics of interest to members
Gary Schroder, President
Joan Benoit, Executive Secretary

Réseau du patrimoine franco-ontarien (RPFO)
#B151, 2445 boul St-Laurent, Ottawa ON K1G 6C3
Tél: 613-729-5769; *Téléc:* 613-729-2209
Ligne sans frais: 866-307-9995
www.rpfo.ca
Permettre à ses membres de découvrir le patrimoine franco-ontarien par l'entremise de l'histoire et de la généalogie
Alexandre Ranger, Coordonnateur administratif
Richard St-Georges, Président
Andréanne Joly, Vice-présidente

Réseau du patrimone franco-ontarien (RPFO)
2445, boul. Saint-Laurent, Ottawa ON K1G 6C3
Tél: 613-729-5769; *Ligne sans frais:* 866-307-9995
www.rpfo.ca
Promouvoir la conservation du patrimoine franco-ontarien
Alexandre Ranger, Coordonnateur administratif

Richard III Society of Canada
c/o 156 Drayton Ave., Toronto ON M4C 3M2
richardiii@cogeco.ca
home.cogeco.ca/~richardiii/
Social Media:
twitter.com/RichardIIICA
To promote research into the life & times of Richard III to secure a re-assessment of the material relating to this period & this monarch's role in English history.

Royal Heraldry Society of Canada / Société royale héraldique du Canada
PO Box 8128, Stn. T, Ottawa ON K1G 3H9
secretary@heraldry.ca
www.heraldry.ca
To maintain, foster & develop the heraldic traditions of Canadians by: increasing public awareness of heraldry & the society; advocating with governments for the protection & proper use of heraldry in Canada; advising the Canadian Heraldic Authority on matters of mutual concern
David E. Rumball, President
Edward McNabb, 1st Vice-President
Vicken Koundakjian, 2nd Vice-President

Saskatchewan Cultural Exchange Society (SCES)
2431 - 8 Ave., Regina SK S4R 5J7
Tel: 306-780-9494; *Fax:* 306-780-9487
sces@sasktel.net
www.sces.ca
Social Media: www.youtube.com/user/theexchangeclub;
www.myspace.com/the_exchange
twitter.com/TheExchangeClub
To support & facilitate cultural exchange & communication by providing a base for sharing community cultural experiences; to attract & involve practising artists in a cultural exchange in Saskatchewan; to enhance the opportunities for residents of smaller communities in Saskatchewan to experience & learn about contemporary cultural production; to provide an alternative for artists to interact with the public
Margaret Fry, CEO
Carol Morin, Chair

Saskatchewan Genealogical Society (SGS)
#110, 1514 - 11th Ave., Regina SK S4P 0H2
Tel: 306-780-9207
saskgenealogy@sasktel.net
www.saskgenealogy.com
Social Media:
www.facebook.com/216892188363312
To provide assistance in researching family history throughout the world; to preserve heritage documents; to collect materials for study
Linda Dunsmore-Porter, Executive Director

Société d'histoire régionale de Chibougamau (SHRC)
646, 3e Rue, Chibougamau QC G8P 1P1
Tél: 418-748-3124; *Téléc:* 418-748-3324
info@shrcnq.com
www.shrcnq.com
Média social: www.facebook.com/720678961296885
Pierre Pelletier, Président

Société généalogique canadienne-française (SGCF)
3440, rue Davidson, Montréal QC H1W 2Z5
Tél: 514-527-1010; *Téléc:* 514-527-0265
info@sgcf.com
www.sgcf.com
Regrouper toutes les personnes désireuses de partager des connaissances généalogiques et leur histoire de famille par les conférences et la publication de travaux de recherche
Gisèle Monarque, Présidente

La Société historique de Québec
#158, 6, rue de la Vieille-Université, Québec QC G1R 5X8
Tél: 418-694-1020
shq1@bellnet.ca
www.societehistoriquedequebec.qc.ca
Média social: www.facebook.com/157594394301478
Étudier et diffuser l'histoire de la ville de Québec et de sa région; relever et mettre en valeur le patrimoine de la même région
Jean Dorval, Président
Jean-François Caron, Trésorier
Doris Drolet, Secrétaire

United Empire Loyalists' Association of Canada (UELAC)
Dominion Office, The George Brown House, #202, 50 Baldwin St., Toronto ON M5T 1L4
Tel: 416-591-1783
uelac@uelac.org
www.uelac.org
Social Media:
www.facebook.com/UELAC
twitter.com/uelac
To unite together descendants of those families who, as a result of the American revolutionary war, sacrificed their homes in retaining their loyalty to the British Crown; to keep alive the knowledge of the early contributions of hundreds of thousands of Loyalists of many cultures, creeds & colours
Bonnie Schepers, President
Barbara J. Andrew, Sr. Vice-President

The Vimy Foundation / La Fondation Vimy
#726, 1470 Peel St., Montréal QC H3A 1T1
Tel: 514-904-1007
info@vimyfoundation.ca
www.vimyfoundation.ca
Social Media:
twitter.com/vimyfoundation
To preserve & promote Canada's First World War legacy as symbolized with the 1917 victory at Vimy Ridge
Rick Hillier, Honorary Chair
Christopher Sweeney, Chair

Horticulture & Gardening

Les Amis du Jardin botanique de Montréal / Friends of the Montréal Botanical Garden
#206A, 4101, rue Sherbrooke est, Montréal QC H1X 2B2
Tél: 514-872-1493; *Téléc:* 514-872-3765
amisjardin@ville.montreal.qc.ca
www.amisjardin.qc.ca
Média social:
www.facebook.com/LesAmisduJardinbotaniquedeMontreal
Maud Fillion, Contact
Paule Lamontagne, Présidente

British Columbia Landscape & Nursery Association (BCLNA)
#102, 5783 - 176A St., Surrey BC V3S 6S6
Tel: 604-575-3500; *Fax:* 604-574-7773
Toll-Free: 800-421-7963
www.bclna.com
Social Media:
linkedin.com/groups?home=&gid=2387526&trk=anet_ug_hm
www.facebook.com/bclna
twitter.com/bclna
To work together to improve quality & standards of the industry
Lesley Tannen, Executive Director

Canadian Horticultural Council (CHC) / Conseil canadien de l'horticulture
#102, 2200 Prince of Wales Dr., Ottawa ON K2E 6Z9
Tel: 613-226-4880; *Fax:* 613-226-4497
webmaster@hortcouncil.ca
www.hortcouncil.ca
To improve horticultural & allied industries including production, grading, packing, transportation, storage & marketing
Keith Kuhl, President
Anne Fowlie, Executive Vice-President

Canadian Iris Society (CIS)
c/o Ed Jowett, 1960 Sideroad 15, RR#2, Tottenham ON L0G 1W0
Tel: 905-936-9941
cdniris@gmail.com
www.cdn-iris.ca
To encourage, improve & extend the cultivation of the Iris & to collaborate with other societies for this purpose, as well as to regulate the nomenclature & colour classification of this flower.
Ed Jowett, President
Nancy Kennedy, Secretary

Canadian Nursery Landscape Association (CNLA)
Stn. Main, 7856 Fifth Line South, R.R.#4, Milton ON L9T 2X8
Tel: 905-875-1399; *Fax:* 905-875-1840
Toll-Free: 888-446-3499
info@canadanursery.com
www.canadanursery.com
Social Media:
twitter.com/cnlavictor
To coordinate provincial member groups in the Canadian horticultural industry; to set national standards; to work with government; to develop national priorities
Victor Santacruz, Executive Director

Canadian Ornamental Plant Foundation (COPF) / Fondation canadienne des plantes ornementales
PO Box 26029, Guelph ON N1E 6W1
Tel: 519-341-6761; *Fax:* 519-341-6748
Toll-Free: 800-265-1629
info@copf.org
www.copf.org
To encourage new plant development by strengthening relations between growers & breeders for the benefit of the horticulture industry
Victoria Turner Shoemaker, Executive Director

Canadian Rose Society (CRS)
116 Belsize Dr., Toronto ON M4S 1L7
Tel: 416-266-6303
Canrosesociety@aol.com
canadianrosesociety.org
Social Media:
www.facebook.com/canadianrosesociety
To provide information about rose growing, speakers, judges, nurseries & suppliers, & rose shows; To correspond with people with similar interests throughout Canada & around the world
Barb Munton, Membership Sec.-Treas.

Canadian Society for Horticultural Science (CSHS) / Société canadienne de science horticole (SCSH)
c/o Dept. of Plant & Animal Sciences, Nova Scotia Agricultural College, PO Box 550, Truro NS B2N 5E3
Tel: 902-893-6032; *Fax:* 902-897-9762
www.cshs.ca
To advance research, teaching, information, & technology related to all horticultural crops
Samir C. Debnath, President
Kris Pruski, Ph.D., Secretary-Treasurer

City Farmer - Canada's Office of Urban Agriculture
PO Box 74567, Stn. Kitsilano, Vancouver BC V6K 4P4
Tel: 604-685-5832
cityfarmer@gmail.com
www.cityfarmer.org
To encourage gardening in an urban environment
Michael Levenston, Executive Director

Fédération des sociétés d'horticulture et d'écologie du Québec (FSHÉQ)
CP 1000, Succ. M, 4545, av Pierre-de Coubertin, Montréal QC H1V 3R2
Tél: 514-252-3010; *Téléc:* 514-251-8038
fsheq@fsheq.com
www.fsheq.com
Mèdia social: www.facebook.com/305119346270307?fref=ts
Regrouper tous les organismes voués à l'horticulture; faire la promotion de l'horticulture.
Thérèse Tourigny, Directrice générale

Fédération interdisciplinaire de l'horticulture ornementale du Québec (FIHOQ)
#300E, 3230, rue Sicotte ouest, Saint-Hyacinthe QC J2S 7B3
Tél: 450-774-2228; *Téléc:* 450-774-3556
fihoq@fihoq.qc.ca
www.fihoq.qc.ca
Mèdia social: www.facebook.com/fihoq
Grouper en fédération les associations professionnelles qui s'occupent d'horticulture ornementale au Québec; étudier, promouvoir, protéger et développer de toutes manières les intérêts économiques, sociaux et professionnels de ses membres; imprimer, éditer des revues, journaux, périodiques et plus généralement, toutes publications du domaine de l'horticulture ornementale aux fins d'information, de culture professionnelle et de propagande; organiser et tenir des cours, conférences, congrès, assemblées, expositions et autres réunions pour la promotion, le développement et la vulgarisation de l'horticulture ornementale; promouvoir la protection du consommateur dans le domaine de l'horticulture ornementale; assurer une représentation tant sur le plan local et national, que sur le plan international des personnes oeuvrant dans le domaine de l'horticulture ornementale au Québec.
Luce Daigneault, Directrice générale
Lise Gauthier, Président

Flowers Canada (FC) / Fleurs Canada
Retail & Distribution Sector, #305, 99 Fifth Ave., Ottawa ON K1S 5P5
Fax: 866-671-8091
Toll-Free: 800-447-5147
flowers@flowerscanada.org
www.flowerscanada.org
To act as the voice of the Canadian floriculture industry; To improve the Canadian floriculture industry
James Fuller, Chairman

Flowers Canada Growers (FCA)
#7, 45 Speedvale Ave. East, Guelph ON N1H 1J2
Tel: 519-836-5495; *Fax:* 519-836-7529
Toll-Free: 800-698-0113
flowers@fco.on.ca
www.flowerscanadagrowers.com
To help members increase their exposure & sales by addressing issues pertaining to the industry
Dean Shoemaker, Executive Director

Landscape Alberta Nursery Trades Association
#200, 10331 - 178 St. NW, Edmonton AB T5S 1R5
Tel: 780-489-1991; *Fax:* 780-444-2152
Toll-Free: 800-378-3198
admin@landscape-alberta.com
www.landscape-alberta.com
Social Media:
linkedin.com/company/landscape-alberta-nursery-trade-associati on
twitter.com/LandscapeAB
To advance the Alberta ornamental horticulture industry through unity, education & professionalism
Joel Beatson, Executive Director

Landscape New Brunswick Horticultural Trades Association (LNBHTA)
PO Box 742, Saint John NB E2L 4B3
Fax: 866-595-5467
Toll-Free: 866-752-6862
lnb@nbnet.nb.ca
www.landscapenbmember.com
Social Media:
www.facebook.com/Landscapenewbrunswick
To further the development of the ornamental horticulture industry by focusing on the environment, education, promotion & professionalism; to represent members & to help them achieve their goals
Joe Wynberg, President

Landscape Newfoundland & Labrador (LNL)
PO Box 8062, St. John's NL A1B 3M9
Fax: 866-833-8603
Toll-Free: 855-872-8722
lnl@landscapenl.com
members.landscapenl.com
Social Media: pinterest.com/landscapenl/
facebook.com/landscapenlevents
twitter.com/@landscapeNL
To promote professionalism at all levels of the Industry, and achieve the highest standards of excellence in delivery of services and products across all sectors of our industry.
David Kiell, Executive Director

Landscape Nova Scotia
Executive Plus Business Centre, Burnside Industrial Park, #44, 201 Brownlow Ave., Dartmouth NS B3B 1W2
Tel: 902-463-0519; *Fax:* 902-446-8104
Toll-Free: 877-567-4769
info@landscapenovascotia.ca
www.landscapenovascotia.ca
Social Media:
www.facebook.com/199135136822813
To promote high standards in product quality, professional service and conduct in the landscape and horticulture industry
Pam Woodman, Executive Director

Landscape Ontario Horticultural Trades Association (LOHTA)
7856 - 5th Line South, RR#4, Milton ON L9T 2X8
Tel: 416-848-7575; *Fax:* 905-875-3942
Toll-Free: 800-265-5656
www.horttrades.com
To be a leader in representing, promoting & fostering a favourable environment for the advancement of the horticultural industry in Ontario
Tony DiGiovanni, Executive Director

North American Native Plant Society (NANPS)
PO Box 84, Stn. D, Toronto ON M9A 4X1
Tel: 416-631-4438
nanps@nanps.org
www.nanps.org
Social Media:
www.facebook.com/nativeplant
Dedicated to the study, conservation & cultivation of North America's wild flora.
Ruth Zaugg, Secretary

Ontario Horticultural Association (OHA)
448 Paterson Ave., London ON N5W 5C7
secretary@gardenontario.org
www.gardenontario.org
Social Media:
twitter.com/gardenontario
To promote civic beautification, preservation of the environment, youth work & education of many aspects of horticulture
Carol Dunk, President

Royal Botanical Gardens (RBG) / Les jardins botaniques royaux
680 Plains Rd. West, Hamilton ON L7T 4H4
Tel: 905-527-1158; *Fax:* 905-577-0375
Toll-Free: 800-694-4769
www.rbg.ca
Social Media: www.youtube.com/user/royalbotanicalgarden
www.facebook.com/140038459379746
twitter.com/RBGCanada
To be recognized in Canada & throughout the world for its unique contribution to the collection, research, exhibition, & interpretation of the plant world & for the development of public understanding & appreciation of the relationship between the plant world, humanity, & the rest of nature
Mark C. Runciman, CEO

Saskatchewan Nursery Landscape Association (SNLA)
c/o Landscape Alberta Nursery Trades Association, #200, 10331 - 178 St., Edmonton AB T5S 1R5
Toll-Free: 888-446-3499
www.snla.ca
To encourage people in the landscaping industry to network in order to spread their wealth of knowledge among each other
Leslie Cornell, President

Seeds of Diversity Canada (SoDC) / Semences du patrimoine Canada
PO Box 36, Stn. Q, Toronto ON M4T 2L7
Toll-Free: 866-509-7333
mail@seeds.ca
www.seeds.ca
To search out & preserve rare & endangered varieties of vegetables, fruits, flowers, herbs & grains
Bob Wildfong, Executive Director

Hospitals

Accreditation Canada / Agrément Canada
1150 Cyrville Rd., Ottawa ON K1J 7S9
Tel: 613-738-3800; *Fax:* 613-738-7755
Toll-Free: 800-814-7769
communications@accreditation.ca
www.accreditation.ca
To improve quality in health services through accreditation; To provide health care organizations with a voluntary, external peer review to assess the quality of their services
Sébastien Audette, Chief Executive Officer & Secretary
Jil Beardmore, Contact

Association des établissements privés conventionnés - santé services sociaux (AEPC)
#200, 1076, rue de Bleury, Montréal QC H2Z 1N2
Tél: 514-499-3630; *Téléc:* 514-873-7063
info@aepc.qc.ca
www.aepc.qc.ca
Mèdia social: www.facebook.com/416653585019212
twitter.com/AEPC_SSS
Promouvoir l'amélioration continue de la qualité des soins et des services donnés au sein des entreprises membres; protéger et promouvoir l'entreprise privée dans le domaine de la santé et du bien-être
Danny Macdonald, Directeur général par intérim

Association of Ontario Health Centres (AOHC) / Association des centres de santé de l'Ontario (ACSO)
#500, 970 Lawrence Ave. West, Toronto ON M6A 3B6
Tel: 416-236-2539; *Fax:* 416-236-0431
mail@aohc.org
www.aohc.org
Social Media:
www.facebook.com/AOHC.ACSO
twitter.com/aohc_acso
To promote community based primary care, health promotion, & illness prevention services, focusing on the broader determinants of health such as education, employment, poverty, isolation, & housing
Adrianna Tetley, Chief Executive Officer
Hugh Hasan, Director, Corporate Services
Sandra Wong, Manager, Human Resources & Administration

Auxiliaires bénévoles de l'Hôpital de Chibougamau
51, 3e Rue, Chibougamau QC G8P 1N1
Tél: 418-748-2676
Priscilla Ratthé, Présidente

Canadian Association of Healthcare Auxiliaries (CAHA) / L'association des auxiliaires bénévoles des soins de santé du Canada
c/o Canadian Healthcare Assn., #100, 17 York St., Ottawa ON K1N 9J6
Tel: 613-236-9364; *Fax:* 613-236-9350
caha.office@rogers.com
www.caha.freeservers.com
To assist provincial members in providing support to local auxiliaries through leadership, education, advocacy, communication & representation

Canadian Association of Paediatric Health Centres (CAPHC) / Association canadienne des centres de santé pédiatriques
c/o Canadian Association of Paediatric Health Centres, #104, 2141 Thurston Dr., Ottawa ON K1G 6C9
Tel: 613-738-4164; *Fax:* 613-738-3247
info@caphc.org
www.caphc.org
Social Media:
www.facebook.com/ACCSP.CAPHC
twitter.com/CAPHCTweets
To improve the health of children within Canada through research activities & through advocacy with governments & health care organizations; To provide information exchange amongst members
Elaine Orrbine, President & Chief Executive Officer
Doug Maynard, Associate Director

Canadian Home Care Association (CHCA) / Association canadienne de soins et services à domicile
7111 Syntex Dr., 3rd Fl., Mississauga ON L5N 8C3
Tel: 289-290-4389; *Fax:* 289-290-4301
chca@cdnhomecare.ca
www.cdnhomecare.ca
Social Media: www.youtube.com/user/cdnhomecare
twitter.com/CdnHomeCare
To promote the development, integration, delivery, public awareness & evaluation of quality home care services in Canada; to provide national leadership to strengthen & unify the home care sector; to collect & disseminate information about home care; to encourage or commission research; to influence policy & legislation; to establish a code of ethics
John Schram, President
Nadine Henningsen, Executive Director

Continuing Care Association of Nova Scotia (CCANS)
c/o Sunshine Personal Home Care, 38A Withrod Dr., Halifax NS B3N 1B1
Tel: 902-446-3140
ccans@eastlink.ca
www.nsnet.org/ccans
To represent continuing care facilities throughout Nova Scotia
Marty Wexler, President

Health Association Nova Scotia
2 Dartmouth Rd., Halifax NS B4A 2K7
Tel: 902-832-8500; *Fax:* 902-832-8505
www.healthassociation.ns.ca
Social Media:
twitter.com/HealthAssnNS
To promote an effective, efficient & integrated quality health system for all Nova Scotians through leadership in influencing the development of public policy, representing & advocating members' interests & providing services to assist its members meet the health care needs of their communities
Gerald Pottier, Chair
Mary Lee, President/CEO
Alex Cross, Communications Assistant

Health Association of PEI (HAPEI)
10 Pownal St., Charlottetown PE C1A 3V6
Tel: 902-368-3901
To influence the change & development of the health delivery system; to provide services which assist members in managing their human, financial & physical resources.

Health Employers Association of British Columbia (HEABC)
#200, 1333 West Broadway, Vancouver BC V6H 4C6
Tel: 604-736-5909; *Fax:* 604-736-2715
contact@heabc.bc.ca
www.heabc.bc.ca
Social Media: www.youtube.com/user/BCHealthCareAwards
linkedin.com/company/heabc
twitter.com/heabcnews
To serve a diverse group of over 250 publicly funded healthcare employers; To deliver high quality labour relations services; To advance the efficiency & productivity of human resources system-wide
David Logan, President & CEO
Lyn Kocher, Executive Director

HealthCareCAN
#100, 17 York St., Ottawa ON K1N 9J6
Tel: 613-241-8005; *Fax:* 613-241-5055
info@healthcarecan.ca
www.healthcarecan.ca
Social Media:
linkedin.com/company/1363724?trk=cws-btn-overview-0-0
www.facebook.com/healthcarecan.soinssantecan
twitter.com/healthcarecan
To improve the delivery of health services in Canada through policy development, advocacy & leadership
Bill Tholl, President/CEO

Hospital Auxiliaries Association of Ontario (HAAO)
#2800, 200 Front St. West, Toronto ON M5V 3L1
Tel: 416-205-1407; *Fax:* 416-205-1596
www.haao.com
Social Media:
www.facebook.com/193203857388754
To advocate for community partnerships to support health care in Ontario; To promote volunteer services

Ontario Association of Medical Laboratories (OAML)
#1802, 5000 Yonge St., Toronto ON M2N 7E9
Tel: 416-250-8555; *Fax:* 416-250-8464
oaml@oaml.com
www.oaml.com
To act as the voice of Ontario's community laboratory sector; To promote professionalism, technical excellence, & accountability in the delivery of laboratory services throughout Ontario

Ontario Hospital Association (OHA)
#2800, 200 Front St. West, Toronto ON M5V 3L1
Tel: 416-205-1300; *Fax:* 416-205-1301
Toll-Free: 800-598-8002
info@oha.com
www.oha.com
Social Media: www.youtube.com/onthospitalassn
linkedin.com/company/ontario-hospital-association
www.facebook.com/onthospitalassn
twitter.com/OntHospitalAssn
To build a strong, innovative, & sustainable health care system that meets patient care needs throughout Ontario; To promote an efficent & effective health care system
Marcia Visser, Chair
Anthony Dale, Interim President & CEO
Warren DiClemente, Chief Operating Officer & VP, Educational Services
Julie Giraldi, Chief Human Resources Officer
Doug Miller, Chief Financial Officer
Colin Goodfellow, Treasurer

Ontario Long Term Care Association (OLTCA)
#500, 425 University Ave., Toronto ON M5G 1T6
Tel: 647-856-3490; *Fax:* 416-642-0635
info@oltca.com
www.oltca.com
Social Media: www.youtube.com/user/OLTCA345
twitter.com/oltcanews
Provides professional leadership to the long-term care sector; to empower long-term care facilities to provide high quality & cost-effective health care & accommodation services
Candace Chartier, CEO
Judy Irwin, Senior Manager, Communications

The Regional Health Authorities of Manitoba (RHAM)
#2, 203 Duffield St., Winnipeg MB R3J 0H6
Tel: 204-833-1721; *Fax:* 204-940-2042
www.rham.mb.ca
To establish programs that help to improve Manitoba health authorities
Monique Vielfaure Mackenzie, Executive Director

Saskatchewan Association of Health Organizations (SAHO)
#500, 2002 Victoria Ave., Regina SK S4P 0R7
Tel: 306-347-1740; *Fax:* 306-347-1043
www.saho.ca
To serve members through services, support, & programs

Housing

Alberta Public Housing Administrators' Association (APHAA)
14220 - 109 Ave. NW, Edmonton AB T5N 4B3
Tel: 780-498-1971; *Fax:* 780-464-7039
www.aphaa.org
Social Media:
twitter.com/AphaaInfo
Works with the Province of Alberta in the publicly-funded housing industry to promote excellence in publicly funded housing administration through education, information and networking
Raymond Swonek, President

Association of Condominium Managers of Ontario (ACMO)
#100, 2233 Argentia Rd., Mississauga ON L5N 2X7
Tel: 905-826-6890; *Fax:* 905-826-4873
Toll-Free: 800-265-3263
www.acmo.org
Social Media:
linkedin.com/groups/ACMOnews-3782859
www.facebook.com/pages/ACMOnews/163609167022080
twitter.com/ACMOnews
To enhance the quality performance of condominium property managers & management companies in Ontario
Steven Christodoulou, R.C.M., President

Association provinciale des constructeurs d'habitations du Québec inc. (APCHQ) / Provincial Association of Home Builders of Québec
5930, boul Louis-H.-Lafontaine, Anjou QC H1M 1S7
Tél: 514-353-9960; *Téléc:* 514-353-4825
Ligne sans frais: 800-468-8160
www.apchq.com
Média social: www.youtube.com/APCHQinc/
linkedin.com/company/apchq/
www.facebook.com/apchq
twitter.com/APCHQ
Depuis 1997, l'APCHQ est la plus importante gestionnaire de mutuelles de prévention du domaine de la construction. Étant le seul agent négociateur patronal des relations de travail dans le secteur résidentiel, elle défend les intérêts de quelque 12 000 employeurs et 25 000 travailleurs
Marc Savard, Directeur général
Frédéric Birtz, Directeur des opérations

Canadian Association of Home & Property Inspectors (CAHPI) / Association canadienne des inspecteurs de biens immobiliers
PO Box 13715, Ottawa ON K2K 1X6
Fax: 866-876-9877
Toll-Free: 888-748-2244
info@cahpi.ca
www.cahpi.ca
To promote & enhance the professionalism & competency of professional home & property inspectors
Blaine Swan, President
Brian Hutchinson, Treasurer
Sharry Featherston, Executive Director

Canadian Condominium Institute (CCI)
#210, 2800 - 14th Ave., Markham ON L3R 0E4
Tel: 416-491-6216; *Fax:* 416-491-1670
Toll-Free: 866-491-6216
cci.national@associationconcepts.ca
www.cci.ca
To serve as a central clearinghouse & research centre on condominium issues & activities across the country; To provide objective research for practitioners & government agencies regarding all aspects of condominium operations; To offer professional assistance; To improve legislation & represent condominiums; to develop standards
Geoff Penney, Chair
Bill Thompson, National President
F. Diane Gaunt, Executive Director
Alison Nash, Administrator

Canadian Federation of Apartment Associations (CFAA) / Fédération canadienne des Associations de propriétaires immobiliers
#640, 1600 Carling Ave., Ottawa ON K1Z 1G3
Tel: 613-235-0101; *Fax:* 613-238-0101
admin@cfaa-fcapi.org
www.cfaa-fcapi.org
Social Media:
twitter.com/CFAAConference
To represent members on political & economic issues at the national level & to facilitate the exchange of information & materials amongst members while maintaining the highest professional & ethical standards in all activities

John Dickie, President
David Benes, Administrator

Canadian Home Builders' Association (CHBA) / Association canadienne des constructeurs d'habitations
#500, 150 Laurier Ave. West, Ottawa ON K1P 5J4
Tel: 613-230-3060; *Fax:* 613-232-8214
chba@chba.ca
www.chba.ca
Social Media:
twitter.com/chbanational
To assist its members in serving the needs & meeting the aspirations of Canadians for housing; To be the voice of the residential construction industry in Canada; To achieve an environment in which members can operate profitably; To promote affordability & choice in housing for all Canadians; To support the professionalism of members
Kevin Lee, Chief Executive Officer
John Bos, Director, Finance
David Foster, Director, Communications
Jack Mantyla, Director, Professional Development
Christopher McLellan, Director, Technical Services

Canadian Housing & Renewal Association (CHRA) / Association canadienne d'habitation et de rénovation urbaine (ACHRU)
#902, 75 Albert St., Ottawa ON K1P 5E7
Tel: 613-594-3007; *Fax:* 613-594-9596
info@chra-achru.ca
www.chra-achru.ca
Social Media: www.youtube.com/user/CanadianHousing/
www.facebook.com/CHRA.ACHRU.ca
twitter.com/CHRAstaff
To provide access to adequate & affordable housing.
Jody Ciufo, Executive Director

Canadian Manufactured Housing Institute (CMHI)
#500, 150 Laurier Ave. West, Ottawa ON K1P 5J4
Tel: 613-563-3520; *Fax:* 613-232-8600
cmhi@cmhi.ca
www.cmhi.ca
Social Media: plus.google.com/105246295798437075142
linkedin.com/company/canadian-manufactured-housing-institute
twitter.com/CMHI_ICHU
To be the voice of the manufactured housing industry in Canada; to seek, identify & solidify the development of new, profitable market opportunities for manufactured housing, both domestically & internationally; to promote housing affordability for all Canadians.
Dale Ball, President

Cooperative Housing Association of Newfoundland & Labrador (CHANAL)
PO Box 453, #204, 75 Barbour Dr., Mount Pearl NL A1N 2C4
Tel: 709-747-5615; *Fax:* 709-747-5606
chanal@nl.rogers.com
www.chfcanada.coop/eng/pages2007/feds_1_1.asp

Cooperative Housing Federation of British Columbia (CHF BC)
#200, 5550 Fraser St., Vancouver BC V5W 2Z4
Tel: 604-879-5111; *Fax:* 604-879-4611
Toll-Free: 866-879-5111
info@chf.bc.ca
www.chf.bc.ca
Social Media: www.youtube.com/user/coopsbc;
www.flickr.com/photos/bchousingcoops
www.facebook.com/pages/CHF-BC/123651397671685
twitter.com/chfbc
To expand non-profit co-operative housing; to promote better housing conditions in BC; to share skills & information with the co-operative housing community; represent housing co-ops to governments & the general public
Thom Armstrong, Executive Director

Cooperative Housing Federation of Canada (CHF Canada) / Fédération de l'habitation coopérative du Canada (FHCC)
#311, 225 Metcalfe St., Ottawa ON K2P 1P9
Tel: 613-230-2201; *Fax:* 613-230-2231
Toll-Free: 800-465-2752
info@chfcanada.coop
www.chfc.ca
Social Media: www.youtube.com/user/coophousing
www.facebook.com/105594649486310
twitter.com/CHFCanada
To unite, represent, & serve the co-op housing community across Canada
Nicholas Gazzard, Executive Director

Federation of Metro Toronto Tenants' Associations (FMTA)
#500, 27 Carlton St., Toronto ON M5B 1L2
Tel: 416-646-1772
Crisis Hot-Line: 416-921-9494
hotline@torontotenants.org
www.torontotenants.org
To inform & educate tenants; To encourage the organization of tenants; To lobby for tenant protection laws; To promote affordable housing

Ontario Association of Property Standards Officers Inc.
PO Box 43209, 3980 Grand Park Dr., Mississauga ON L5B 4A7
www.oapso.org
To provide training for professionals involved in the governing of property & the environment
Warwick Perrin, President

Ontario Non-Profit Housing Association (ONPHA)
#400, 489 College St., Toronto ON M6G 1A5
Tel: 416-927-9144; *Fax:* 416-927-8401
Toll-Free: 800-297-6660
mail@onpha.org
www.onpha.on.ca
Social Media:
linkedin.com/company/ontario-non-profit-housing-association
www.facebook.com/ONPHA
To build a strong non-profit housing sector in Ontario; To strive for excellence in non-profit housing management; To represent non-profit housing
Sharad Kerur, Executive Director
Michelle Coombs, Manager, Member Services
Wyndham Bettencourt-McCarthy, Coordinator, Policy & Research
Christina Friend, Coordinator, Communications & Marketing

Réseau québécois des OSBL d'habitation (RQOH)
#102, rue Fullum, Montréal QC H2K 0B5
Tél: 514-846-0163; *Téléc:* 514-846-3402
Ligne sans frais: 866-846-0163
info@rqoh.com
www.rqoh.com
Média social:
www.facebook.com/ReseauQuebecoisOsblHabitation
twitter.com/RQOH_
Pour représenter les organismes de logement à but non lucratif; Pour répondre aux besoins de logement des personnes vulnérables et exclus de la province
Isabelle Leduc, Présidente
Stéphan Corriveau, Directeur général

ShareOwner Education Inc.
#806, 4 King St. West, Toronto ON M5H 1B6
Tel: 416-595-9600; *Fax:* 416-595-0400
Toll-Free: 800-268-6881
customercare@shareowner.com
www.shareowner.com
To offer practical education & portfolio training to individual investors & investment clubs, so that they may invest successfully in quality growth stocks; To increase stock market literacy
John Bart, Founder & Chief Mentor

Human Rights & Civil Liberties

Alberta Civil Liberties Research Centre (ACLRC)
c/o Murray Fraser Hall, Faculty of Law, University of Calgary, #2350, 2500 University Dr. NW, Calgary AB T2N 1N4
Tel: 403-220-2505; *Fax:* 403-284-0945
aclrc@ucalgary.ca
www.aclrc.com
To promote awareness among Albertans about civil liberties & human rights through research & education
Linda McKay-Panos, Executive Director

Amnesty International - Canadian Section (English Speaking)
312 Laurier Ave. East, Ottawa ON K1N 1H9
Tel: 613-744-7667; *Fax:* 613-746-2411
Toll-Free: 800-266-3789
info@amnesty.ca
www.amnesty.ca
Social Media:
www.facebook.com/amnestycanada
twitter.com/AmnestyNow
AI Canada is part of a worldwide movement which is independent of any government, political grouping, ideology, economic interest or religious creed. It's primary aim is to bring public attention to abuses of human rights standards, particularly cases where people are imprisoned for their beliefs, or "prisoners of conscience." It holds that mass public pressure, expressed through effective forms of action, is critical to preventing & ending human rights violations. It also works to abolish the death penalty, torture, & other cruel treatment of prisoners, to end political killings & "disappearances."
David Smith, Chair
Sharmila Setaram, President
Robert Goodfellow, Executive Director

Amnistie internationale, Section canadienne (Francophone) / Amnesty International, Canadian Section (Francophone)
50 rue Ste-Catherine Ouest bureau 500, Montréal QC H2X 3V4
Tél: 514-766-9766; *Téléc:* 514-766-2088
Ligne sans frais: 800-565-9766
info@amnistie.ca
www.amnistie.ca
Mouvement d'intervention directe formé de bénévoles qui visent à la libération des prisonniers d'opinion, la tenue de procès équitables pour les prisonniers politiques, l'abolition de la torture et la cessation des "disparitions" et assassinats politiques
Beatrice Vaugrante, Direction

Black Coalition of Québec / La Ligue des Noirs du Québec
5201, boul Decarie, Montréal QC H3W 3C2
Tel: 514-489-3830
info@liguedesnoirs.org
www.liguedesnoirs.org
The Coalition speaks for the Black community in the defence of individual human rights and against all forms of discrimination
Peterson Frederick, President

British Columbia Civil Liberties Association (BCCLA)
900 Helmcken St., 2nd Fl., Vancouver BC V6Z 1B3
Tel: 604-687-2919; *Fax:* 604-687-3045
Toll-Free: 866-731-7507
www.bccla.org
Social Media: www.youtube.com/user/BCCivilLiberties
linkedin.com/company/b.c.-civil-liberties-association
www.facebook.com/pages/BC-Civil-Liberties-Association/884126
3601
twitter.com/bccla
To protect & enhance civil liberties & human rights in British Columbia
Josh Paterson, Executive Director
Micheal Vonn, Policy Director

Canada Tibet Committee (CTC)
1425, boul René-Lévesque ouest, 3e étage, Montréal QC H3G 1T7
Tel: 514-487-0665
ctcoffice@tibet.ca
www.tibet.ca
Social Media: www.youtube.com/tibetchannel
www.facebook.com/CanadaTibet
twitter.com/canadatibet
To defend & promote human rights & democratic freedoms of Tibetan people; To encourage support for Tibet from the government of Canada
Carole Samdup, Executive Director

Canadian Association of Statutory Human Rights Agencies (CASHRA) / Association canadienne des commissions et conseil des droits de la personne (ACCCDP)
#170, 99 - 5th Ave., Ottawa ON K1P 5P5
www.cashra.ca
An umbrella organization for the federal, provincial and territorial human rights commissions.

The Canadian Centre/International P.E.N. (PEN)
#301, 24 Ryerson Ave., Toronto ON M5T 2P3
Tel: 416-703-8448; *Fax:* 416-703-3870
queries@pencanada.ca
www.pencanada.ca
Social Media: www.youtube.com/canadapen
www.facebook.com/pages/PEN-Canada/141054639272034
twitter.com/PENCanada
To foster understanding among writers of all nations; to fight for freedom of expression wherever it is endangered; to work for preservation of world's literature
Philip Slayton, President
Tasleem Thawar, Executive Director

Canadian Civil Liberties Association (CCLA) / Association canadienne des libertés civiles
#900, 90 Eglinton Ave. E, Toronto ON M4P 1A6
Tel: 416-363-0321; *Fax:* 416-861-1291
mail@ccla.org
www.ccla.org
Social Media: www.youtube.com/cancivlib
www.facebook.com/cancivlib
twitter.com/cancivlib
To protect the civil liberties, human rights, & democratic freedoms of all Canadians
Sukanya Pillay, Executive Director

Canadian Tribute to Human Rights (CTHR) / Monument canadien pour les droits de la personne (MCDP)
#170, 99 - 5th Ave., Ottawa ON K1P 5P5
info@cthr-mcdp.com
www.cthr-mcdp.com
To ensure public awareness of the presence in Ottawa of the Tribute monument as a symbol of Canadians' committment to preserving & fostering human rights; To promote use of the site as a focal point for all groups working for human rights in Canada & internationally; To spread the concept of public places dedicated to human rights in other capital cities of countries that have affirmed the UN Universal Declaration of Human Rights.

CPJ Corp. (CPJ)
#501, 309 Cooper St., Ottawa ON K2P 0G5
Tel: 613-232-0275; *Fax:* 613-232-1275
Toll-Free: 800-667-8046
cpj@cpj.ca
www.cpj.ca
Social Media: www.youtube.com/user/c4pj
www.facebook.com/citizensforpublicjustice
twitter.com/publicjustice
To promote public justice in Canada byshaping key public policy debates through research & analysis, publishing & public dialogue; CPJ encourages citizens, leaders in society & governments to support policies & practices which reflect God's call for love, justice & stewardship
Joe Gunn, Executive Director

Equitas - International Centre for Human Rights Education / Equitas - Centre international d'éducation aux droits humains
#1100, 666 Sherbrooke St. West, Montréal QC H3A 1E7
Tel: 514-954-0382; *Fax:* 514-954-0659
info@equitas.org
www.equitas.org
Social Media: www.youtube.com/user/EquitasHRE
linkedin.com/groups/Equitas-International-Centre-Human-Rights-1828
twitter.com/equitasintl
To provide human rights education in Canada & abroad, based on the principles elaborated in the Universal Declaration of Human Rights
Rob Yalden, President
Ian Hamilton, Executive Director

League for Human Rights of B'nai Brith Canada / Ligue des droits de la personne de B'nai Brith Canada
15 Hove St., Toronto ON M3H 4Y8
Tel: 416-633-6224; *Fax:* 416-630-2159
Toll-Free: 800-892-2624
Crisis Hot-Line: 800-892-2624
league@bnaibrith.ca
www.bnaibrith.ca/league
To strive for human rights for all Canadians; to improve inter-community relations; to combat racism & racial discrimination; to prevent bigotry & anti-Semitism.
Frank Dimant, CEO

Macedonian Human Rights Movement International (MHRMI) / Mouvement canadien de défense des droits de la personne dans la communauté macédonienne
#434, 157 Adelaide St., Toronto ON M5H 4E7
Tel: 416-850-7125; *Fax:* 416-850-7127
info@mhrmi.org
www.mhrmi.org
Social Media:
www.facebook.com/MHRMI
twitter.com/mhrmi
To secure & maintain the human rights of all Macedonians wherever they live through advocacy & education
Bill Nicholov, President
Luby Vidinovski, Vice-President
Mark Opashinov, Secretary
Andy Plukov, Treasurer

Philanthropic Foundations Canada (PFC) / Fondations philanthropiques Canada (FPC)
#1220, 615 René-Lévesque Blvd. West, Montréal QC H3B 1P5
Tel: 514-866-5446; *Fax:* 514-866-5846
info@pfc.ca
pfc.ca
To encourage public policies that promote philanthropy; to increase awareness of philanthropy & provide opportunities for foundations to learn from one another
Hilary Pearson, President & CEO
Liza Goulet, Director, Research & Member Services

Pivot Legal Society
121 Heatley Ave., Vancouver BC V6A 3E9
Tel: 604-255-9700; *Fax:* 604-255-1552
www.pivotlegal.org
Social Media:
www.facebook.com/PivotLegalSociety
twitter.com/pivotlegal
To use the law to address the root causes of social exclusion & poverty; To pressure authorities in order to shift society's values toward equality & inclusivity
Katrina Pacey, Executive Director

Immigration

Association for New Canadians (ANC) / L'association des nouveaux Canadiens (ANC)
Head Office & Settlement Services, PO Box 2031, Stn. C, 144 Military Rd., St. John's NL A1C 5R6
Tel: 709-722-9680; *Fax:* 709-754-4407
settlement@nfld.net
www.ancnl.ca
To provide full service immigrant settlement programs & services to the newcomer community in Newfoundland & Labrador; To support integration, & cross cultural understanding

Collectif des femmes immigrantes du Québec (CFIQ)
7124, rue Boyer, Montréal QC H2S 2J8
Tél: 514-279-4246; *Téléc:* 514-279-8536
info@cfiq.ca
www.cfiq.ca
Préparation à l'emploi des immigrants, formation, placement à Montréal et en région
Aoura Bizzarri, Directrice générale
Marie-Josée Duplessis, Adjointe à la direction

Information Technology

Association for Image & Information Management International - 1st Canadian Chapter (AIIM Canada)
Toronto ON
www.aiim.org/Community/Chapters/First-Canadian
To connect users & suppliers of e-business technologies & services
Winnie Tsang, President

Association of Professional Computer Consultants - Canada (APCC)
#700, 2200 Yonge St., Toronto ON M4S 2C6
Tel: 416-545-5275; *Toll-Free:* 800-487-2722
information@apcconline.com
www.apcconline.com
Social Media:
linkedin.com/groups?home=&gid=3768080
www.facebook.com/APCCOnline
twitter.com/APCC_Canada
To promote the interests of independent computer consultants; to provide cost-saving services to members; to provide members with a forum for interaction & exchange
Frank McCrea, President

Association québécoise des informaticiennes et informaticiens indépendants (AQIII) / Québec Association for ICT Freelancers
#974, rue Michelin, Laval QC H7L 5B6
Tél: 514-388-6147; *Téléc:* 514-388-7249
Ligne sans frais: 888-858-7777
aqiii@aqiii.org
www.aqiii.org
Média social: www.linked.in/company/691970
www.facebook.com/pages/AQIII/45009582564
twitter.com/aqiii
Réunir le maximum de consultants autonomes et d'expérience en TI afin de bénéficier des avantages d'un réseau solide tout en préservant la liberté du travail indépendant. L'association favorise l'obtention de mandats en TI, le réseautage, le partage d'information entre informaticiens ainsi que les économies d'échelle chez des fournisseurs ciblés
Sylvie Racine, Directrice générale par intérim

Canada's Advanced Internet Development Organization (CANARIE)
#500, 45 O'Connor St., Ottawa ON K1P 1A4
Tel: 613-943-5454; *Fax:* 613-943-5443
info@canarie.ca
www.canarie.ca
Social Media:
linkedin.com/groups?mostPopular=&gid=3712846
www.facebook.com/CanarieInc
twitter.com/CANARIE_Inc
Canada's advanced internet development organization; to facilitate & promote the development of Canada's communications infrastructure; to stimulate next-generation products, applications & services; to communicate the benefits of an information-based society. CANARIE also intends to act as a catalyst and partner with governments, industry and the research community to increase overall IT awareness, ensure continuing promotion of Canadian technological excellence and ultimately, foster long-term productivity and improvement of living standards.
Jim Ghadbane, President & CEO
Nancy E. Carter, Chief Financial Officer

Canadian Association of Internet Providers (CAIP) / Association canadienne des fournisseurs internet (ACFI)
#416, 207 Bank St., Ottawa ON K2P 2N2
Tel: 613-236-6550; *Fax:* 613-236-8189
info@cata.ca
www.caip.ca
To foster the growth of a healthy & competitive Internet service industry in Canada through collective & cooperative action on issues of mutual interest.
Tom Copeland, Chair
Cathi Malette, Manager, Member Services

Canadian Association of SAS Users (CASU) / Association canadienne des utilisateurs SAS (ACUS)
280 King St. East, 5th Fl., Toronto ON M5A 1K7
Tel: 416-363-4424; *Fax:* 416-363-5399
Social Media:
twitter.com/SASCanada
To provide support to all Canadian SAS user groups; to assist them in the most efficient & effective use of the SAS system for information delivery; to provide updates on research & development of institute software & services.
Carl Farrell, Executive Vice President, SAS Americas

Canadian Image Processing & Pattern Recognition Society (CIPPRS) / Association canadienne de traitement d'images et de reconnaissance des formes (ACTIRF)
Dept. of Computer Sciences, Univ. of Western Ontario, Middlesex College 383, London ON N6A 5B7
Tel: 519-661-2111; *Fax:* 519-661-3515
www.cipprs.org
To promote research & development activities in image & signal processing for solving pattern recognition problems.
John Barron, Treasurer
Greg Dudek, President

Canadian Information Processing Society (CIPS) / L'Association canadienne de l'informatique (ACI)
National Office, #801, 5090 Explorer Dr., Mississauga ON L4W 4T9
Tel: 905-602-1370; *Fax:* 905-602-7884
Toll-Free: 877-275-2477
info@cips.ca
www.cips.ca
Social Media:
linkedin.com/groups/71785/profile
www.facebook.com/187610094599781
twitter.com/cips
To define & foster the IT profession; To encourage & support the IT practitioner; To advance the theory & practice of IT, while safeguarding the public interest
Jon Nightingale, Chair, Governance Committee

Centre international pour le développement de l'inforoute en français (CIDIF)
167, boul Hébert, Edmundston NB E3V 4H2
Tél: 506-737-5280; *Téléc:* 506-737-5281
info@cidif.org
www.cidif.org
Média social: linkedin.com/company/cidif
twitter.com/cidif
Fournir des outils et des services spécialisés afin de contribuer à rendre l'utilisation de logiciels et l'internet transparente aux usagers de différentes cultures et de différentes langues

Réal Gervais, Propriétaire et président
Éric Bélanger, Directeur

COACH - Canada's Health Informatics Association (COACH)
#301, 250 Consumers Rd., Toronto ON M2J 4V6
Tel: 416-494-9324; *Fax:* 416-495-8723
Toll-Free: 888-253-8554
info@coachorg.com
www.coachorg.com
Social Media:
www.youtube.com/channel/UCiaVmX9quqgl14MTxJ3Wh6Q
linkedin.com/company/coach-canada's-health-informatics-association
www.facebook.com/COACHORG
twitter.com/COACH_HI
To improve the health of Canadians & enhance the management of Canada's health system by advancing the practice of health information management & effective utilization of associated technologies
Don Newsham, Chief Executive Officer
Shannon Bott, Executive Director, Operations
Linda Miller, Executive Director, CHIEF: Canada's Health Informatics Executive Forum
Mike Barron, President
Jim Mickelson, Sec.-Tres.

Digital Nova Scotia (ITANS)
Technology Innovation Centre, 1 Research Dr., Dartmouth NS B2Y 4M9
Tel: 902-423-5332; *Fax:* 877-282-9506
info@digitalnovascotia.com
www.digitalnovascotia.com
Social Media: www.youtube.com/user/digitalnovascotia
linkedin.com/groups/Digital-Nova-Scotia-1801099/about
www.facebook.com/pages/Digital-Nova-Scotia/686711044710199
twitter.com/digitalns
To be dedicated to the development & growth of the digital technologies industry in Nova Scotia
Ulrike Bahr-Gedalia, President & CEO
Bruce MacDougall, Chair
Emily Boucher, Director, Marketing & Research

Electronic Frontier Canada Inc. (EFC) / Frontière électronique du Canada
20 Richmond Ave., Kitchener ON N2G 1Y9
Tel: 905-525-9140; *Fax:* 905-546-9995
www.efc.ca
To ensure that the principals embodied in the Canadian Charter of Rights & Freedoms are protected as new computing, communications & information technologies emerge.
David Jones, President
Jeffrey Shallit, Vice-President/Treasurer
Richard Rosenberg, Vice-President

GS1 Canada
#800, 1500 Don Mills Rd., Toronto ON M3B 3L1
Tel: 416-510-8039; *Fax:* 416-510-1916
Toll-Free: 800-567-7084
info@gs1ca.org
www.gs1ca.org
To act as a facilitator for the use of electronic information transactions in support of Canadian users.
N. Arthur Smith, President/CEO

Information & Communications Technology Council of Canada (ICTC) / Conseil des technologies de l'information et des communications du Canada (CTIC)
#300, 116 Lisgar St., Ottawa ON K2P 0C2
Tel: 613-237-8551; *Fax:* 613-230-3490
info@ictc-ctic.ca
www.ictc-ctic.ca
Social Media: www.youtube.com/user/DigitalEconomyPulse
linkedin.com/company/information-and-communications-technology-council
www.facebook.com/196829353752455
twitter.com/@ictc_ctic
To serve the software development profession by developing joint ventures in courseware design & delivery, by integrating training & education processes, by helping to ensure sufficient supply & quality of new entrants to the profession & by promoting an attractive image & definition of software workers
Faye West, Chair
Namir Anani, President & CEO
Sandra Saric, Vice-President, Talent Innovation

Information Resource Management Association of Canada (IRMAC)
PO Box 5639, Stn. A, Toronto ON M5W 1N8
Tel: 416-712-9932
www.irmac.ca
To provide a forum for members to exchange information about data administration & information resource management
Ron Klein, President
Ruxandra Petolescu, Vice-President
Jonathan Pinchefsky, Secretary
Rezelline Tan, Treasurer

Information Technology Association of Canada (ITAC) / Association canadienne de la technologie de l'information
#801, 5090 Explorer Dr., Mississauga ON L4W 4T9
Tel: 905-602-8345; *Fax:* 905-602-8346
info@itac.ca
www.itac.ca
Represents 1,300 companies in the computing & telecommunications hardware, software, services & electronic content sectors; identifies & leads on issues that affect the industry; advocates initiatives to enable continued growth & development.
Karna Gupta, President
Bill Munson, Vice President
Carlo Viola, Director, Finance
Alberta Fraccaro, Accounting Coordinator

National Capital FreeNet (NCF) / Libertel de la Capitale Nationale
Trailhead Building, #302, 1960 Scott St., Ottawa ON K1Z 8L8
Tel: 613-520-9001; *Fax:* 613-520-3524
ncf@ncf.ca
www.ncf.ca
Free, computer-based information sharing network; links the people & organization of the National Capital region; provides useful information & enables an open exchange of ideas with the world; prepares people for full participation in a rapidly changing communications environment

Newfoundland & Labrador Association of Technology Companies (NLATC)
#5, 391 Empire Ave., St. John's NL A1E 1W6
Tel: 709-772-8324; *Fax:* 709-757-6284
info@nati.net
www.nati.net
Social Media:
twitter.com/NATI_NL
To act collectively for technical organizations in Newfoundland industry in cooperation with educational & public sectors to promote the growth of innovative technical industries in Newfoundland & Labrador & the rest of Canada
Ron Taylor, Chief Executive Officer

reBOOT Canada
#1, 2450 Lawrence Ave. East, Toronto ON M1P 2R7
Tel: 416-534-6017; *Fax:* 416-534-6083
rose@rebootcanada.ca
www.rebootcanada.ca
Refurbishes old computers received from individual & corporate donors & distributes them, free of charge, to other charitable organizations
Nicholas Brinckman, Executive Director

Insurance Industry

Advocis
#209, 390 Queens Quay West, Toronto ON M5V 3A2
Tel: 416-444-5251; *Fax:* 416-444-8031
Toll-Free: 800-563-5822
info@advocis.ca
www.advocis.ca
Social Media: www.youtube.com/user/AdvocisTFAAC
linkedin.com/company/advocis
www.facebook.com/advocis
twitter.com/Advocis
To represent Advice & Advocacy; to carry on the tradition of effectively representing members' interests with all levels of government, regulators, & industry, always with the intention of putting the interests of consumers first
David Juvet, Chair
Greg Pollock, President & CEO

Canadian Association of Blue Cross Plans (CABCP) / Association Canadienne des Croix Bleue (ACCB)
PO Box 2005, #610, 185 The West Mall, Toronto ON M9C 5P1
Toll-Free: 866-732-2583
www.bluecross.ca
To maintain & monitor standards of performance by association members; to ensure members manage effectively supplementary health, dental, life insurance, & disability income products on an individual and group basis

Canadian Association of Independent Life Brokerage Agencies (CAILBA)
105 King St. East, Toronto ON M5C 1G6
Tel: 416-548-4223; *Fax:* 416-340-9977
info@cailba.com
www.cailba.com
To lobby provincial & federal governments on legislative issues affecting the life & health insurance brokerage industry; to provide a forum for networking & relationship building among members, insurance companies & industry vendors
Michael Williams, President
Bob Ferguson, Executive Director

Canadian Association of Mutual Insurance Companies (CAMIC) / Association canadienne des compagnies d'assurance mutuelles (ACCAM)
#205, 311 McArthur Ave., Ottawa ON K1L 6P1
Tel: 613-789-6851; *Fax:* 613-789-7665
www.camic.ca
To provide information, research, advocacy to its members in areas of general concerns & to negotiate supply agreements for goods & services of common needs. Objectives: to promote a strong, health and competitive insurance market; to support regulatory efficiency and legislative change; to inform member companies on matters affecting the industry and to build consensus on action plans; to promote self-regulation for the property and casualty insurance industry
Normand Lafrenière, President

Canadian Board of Marine Underwriters (CBMU)
#100, 2233 Argentia Rd., Mississauga ON L5N 2X7
Tel: 905-826-4768; *Fax:* 905-826-4873
cbmu@cbmu.com
www.cbmu.com
Social Media:
linkedin.com/groups/4581774/profile
twitter.com/TheCBMU
To procure & disseminate information of interest to marine underwriters & others; To facilitate the exchange of views & ideas which work to improve the marine underwriting industry & marine insurance; To promote & protect the interest of the underwriting community
Roger Fernandes, President
Jennifer Yung, Administrator
Halyna Troian, Secretary-Treasurer

Canadian Independent Adjusters' Association (CIAA) / Association canadienne des experts indépendants (ACEI)
Centennial Centre, #100, 5401 Eglinton Ave. West, Toronto ON M9C 5K6
Tel: 416-621-6222; *Fax:* 416-621-7776
Toll-Free: 877-255-5589
info@ciaa-adjusters.ca
www.ciaa-adjusters.ca
To provide leadership for independent adjusters in Canada; To develop & maintain high standards of professionalism; To represent the interests of independent adjusters at the regional, provincial, & national levels
Patricia M. Battle, Executive Director
Fred R. Plant, President
Heather Matthews, 1st Vice-President
Gary Ellis, 2nd Vice-President
Monica Kuzyk, Secretary
John Seyler, Treasurer

Canadian Institute of Actuaries (CIA) / Institut canadien des actuaires (ICA)
Secretariat, #1740, 360 Albert St., Ottawa ON K1R 7X7
Tel: 613-236-8196; *Fax:* 613-233-4552
head.office@cia-ica.ca
www.cia-ica.ca
Social Media:
twitter.com/CIA_Actuaries
To set & ensure educational & professional standards for members; To operate a review & disciplinary system; To maintain liaison with government authorities & other professions & organizations; To promote research
Michel C. Simard, Executive Director
Lynn Blackburn, Director, Professional Practice & Volunteer Services
Les Dandridge, Director, Communications & Public Affairs
Jacques Leduc, Director, Operations, Finance, & Administration
Alicia Rollo, Director, Membership, Education & Professional Development

Canadian Life & Health Insurance Association Inc. (CLHIA) / Association canadienne des compagnies d'assurances de personnes inc. (ACCAP)
#1700, 1 Queen St. East, Toronto ON M5C 2X9
Tel: 416-777-2221; *Fax:* 416-777-1895
info@clhia.ca
www.clhia.ca
Social Media:
twitter.com/clhia
To represent the interests of member life & health insurance companies
Donald Guloien, Chair
Frank Swedlove, President
Wendy Hope, Vice-President, External Relations

Centre for Study of Insurance Operations (CSIO) / Centre d'étude de la pratique d'assurance
#500, 110 Yonge St., Toronto ON M5C 1T4
Tel: 416-360-1773; *Fax:* 416-364-1482
Toll-Free: 800-463-2746
helpdesk@csio.com
www.csio.com
Social Media:
linkedin.com/company/csio
twitter.com/csio
To act as the national standards association for property & casualty insurance by representing property & casualty industry initiatives; to provide a competitive advantage for the independent broker distribution channel
Steve Whitelaw, Chair
Catherine Smola, President & CEO

Chambre de l'assurance de dommages (CHAD)
#1200, 999, boul de Maisonneuve ouest, Montréal QC H3A 3L4
Tél: 514-842-2591; *Téléc:* 514-842-3138
Ligne sans frais: 800-361-7288
info@chad.qc.ca
www.chad.ca
Média social: linkedin.com/company/2579212
Assurer la protection du public en matière d'assurance de dommages et d'expertise en règlement de sinistres; encadrer de façon préventive et disciplinaire la pratique professionnelle des individus et des organisations oeuvrant dans ces domaines
Diane Beaudry, Chair
Maya Raic, Présidente-directrice générale

Chambre de la sécurité financière (CSF)
300, rue Léo-Pariseau, 26e étage, Montréal QC H2X 4B8
Tél: 514-282-5777; *Téléc:* 514-282-2225
Ligne sans frais: 800-361-9989
renseignements@chambresf.com
www.chambresf.com
Média social: www.youtube.com/chambresf
linkedin.com/company/1004475
www.facebook.com/ChambreSF
twitter.com/ChambreSF
Assurer la protection du public en maintenant la discipline et en veillant à la formation et à la déontologie de ses membres
Luc Labelle, Président et chef de la direction

Facility Association
PO Box 121, #2400, 777 Bay St., Toronto ON M5G 2C8
Tel: 416-863-1750; *Fax:* 416-868-0894
Toll-Free: 800-268-9572
mail@facilityassociation.com
www.facilityassociation.com
To ensure the availability of automobile insurance for owners & licensed drivers of motor vehicles who may otherwise have difficulty obtaining such insurance.
David J. Simpson, President & CEO

Financial Services Commission of Ontario (FSCO) / Commission des services financiers de l'Ontario (CSFO)
PO Box 85, 5160 Yonge St., 17th Fl., Toronto ON M2N 6L9
Tel: 416-250-7250; *Fax:* 416-590-7070
Toll-Free: 800-668-0128
TTY: 800-387-0584
contactcentre@fsco.gov.on.ca
www.fsco.gov.on.ca
To regulate the following sectors in Ontario: insurance; pension plans; loan & trust companies; credit unions & caisses populaires; mortgage brokering; co-operative corporations in Ontario; & service providers who invoice auto insurers for statutory accident benefits claims.
Brian Mills, Interim Chief Executive Officer

GAMA International Canada / GAMA International du Canada
#209, 390 Queens Quay West, Toronto ON M4V 3A2
Tel: 416-444-5251; *Fax:* 416-444-8031
Toll-Free: 800-563-5822
info@gamacanada.com
www.gamacanada.com
Social Media: www.youtube.com/user/AdvocisTFAAC
linkedin.com/groups/GAMA-International-Canada-1952201
twitter.com/Advocis
To focus on professional development for leaders involved in the distribution of financial services
Rob Popazzi, President
Celia Ciotola, Director

Groupement des assureurs automobiles (GAA)
Tour de la Bourse, CP 336, #2410, 800 Place-Victoria, Montréal QC H3A 3C6
Tél: 514-288-4321; *Ligne sans frais:* 877-288-4321
cinfo@gaa.qc.ca
www.gaa.qc.ca
Administrer, de façon efficace et selon les décisions du conseil d'administration, tous les mandats certifiés au Groupement des assureurs automobiles par la Loi sur l'assurance automobile du Québec
Patricia St-Jean, Présidente
Johanne Lamanque, Directrice générale

L'Institut d'assurance de dommages du Québec (IADQ)
#1650, 1200, av McGill College, Montréal QC H3B 4G7
Tél: 514-393-8156; *Téléc:* 514-393-9222
iadq@institutdassurance.ca
www.insuranceinstitute.ca/fr/institutes-and-chapters/Quebec.aspx
Organiser des cours, des séminaires et des conférences; promouvoir le rayonnement des titres professionnels PAA et FPAA d'assurance du Canada (AIAC & FIAC). Organisme sans but lucratif, qui a été mis sur pied par l'industrie de l'assurance de dommages pour donner la formation professionnelle à tous ceux qui oeuvrent dans ce secteur au Québec
François Houle, Directeur général

Insurance Brokers Association of Alberta (IBAA)
3010 Calgary Trail NW, Edmonton AB T6J 6V4
Tel: 780-424-3320; *Fax:* 780-424-7418
Toll-Free: 800-318-0197
ibaa@ibaa.ca
www.ibaa.ca
Social Media:
linkedin.com/company/insurance-brokers-association-of-alberta
www.facebook.com/insurancebrokersassociationofalberta
twitter.com/ibaa1
To preserve & strengthen insurance brokers
George Hodgson, Chief Executive Officer
Rikki McBridge, Chief Operating Officer
Janis Losie, Director, Member Relations, Marketing, & Communications

Insurance Brokers Association of British Columbia (IBABC)
#1600, 543 Granville St., Vancouver BC V6C 1X6
Tel: 604-606-8000; *Fax:* 604-683-7831
www.ibabc.org
Social Media: twitter.com/@ibabcEdu
twitter.com/ibabc
To promote the member insurance broker as the premiere distributor of general insurance products & services in British Columbia
Charles (Chuck) Byrne, Executive Director
Trudy Lancelyn, Deputy Executive Director

Insurance Brokers Association of Manitoba (IBAM)
#600, 1445 Portage Ave., Winnipeg MB R3G 3P4
Tel: 204-488-1857; *Fax:* 204-489-0316
Toll-Free: 800-204-5649
info@ibam.mb.ca
www.ibam.mb.ca
Social Media:
linkedin.com/company/insurance-brokers-association-of-manitoba-iba
www.facebook.com/IBAManitoba
twitter.com/IBAManitoba
To promote insurance brokers as the primary providers of insurance products & services in Manitoba
David Schioler, Chief Executive Officer

Insurance Brokers Association of New Brunswick (IBANB) / Association des courtiers d'assurances du Nouveau-Brunswick
PO Box 1523, #202, 334 Queen St., Fredericton NB E3B 5G2
Tel: 506-450-2898; *Fax:* 506-450-1494
ibanb@nbinsurancebrokers.ca
www.nbinsurancebrokers.ca
Social Media: www.youtube.com/nbbrokerstv
www.facebook.com/nbbrokers
twitter.com/nbbrokers
To champion the professional, independent insurance broker system in New Brunswick
Kirby Curtis, Chair
Andrew McNair, Chief Executive Officer

Insurance Brokers Association of Newfoundland (IBAN)
Chimo Bldg., 151 Crosbie Rd., 3rd Floor, St. John's NL A1B 4B4
Tel: 709-726-4450; *Fax:* 709-726-5850
iban@nfld.net
www.iban.ca
Social Media:
www.facebook.com/InsuranceBrokersNewfoundland
twitter.com/IbanSocial
Association of insurance brokers in Newfoundland. Insurance brokers work on behalf of clients to secure the best coverage in the market from federally regulated insurance companies
CJ Nolan, President

Insurance Brokers Association of Nova Scotia (IBANS)
380 Bedford Hwy, Halifax NS B3M 2L4
Tel: 902-876-0526; *Fax:* 902-876-0527
info@ibans.com
www.ibans.com
Social Media:
linkedin.com/company/3485745
www.facebook.com/brokersns
twitter.com/InsuranceNS
To promote the independent insurance broker as the premier distributor of property & casualty insurance products & other related insurance services in Nova Scotia
Karen Slaunwhite, Executive Director

Insurance Brokers Association of Ontario (IBAO)
#700, 1 Eglinton Ave. East, Toronto ON M4P 3A1
Tel: 416-488-7422; *Fax:* 416-488-7526
Toll-Free: 800-268-8845
www.ibao.org
Social Media:
linkedin.com/groups/Insurance-Brokers-Association-Ontario-3976676
www.facebook.com/IBAO1
twitter.com/IBAOntario
To act as the authoritative voice of independent brokers in Ontario; To serve the interests of member brokers; To preserve & enhance the value & integrity of the independent broker insurance distribution system
Doug Heaman, President
Chris Floyd, Chair
Jim Murphy, CEO

Insurance Brokers Association of Prince Edward Island (IBAPEI)
c/o Cooke Insurance Group, PO Box 666, 125 Pownal St., Charlottetown PE C1A 3W4
Tel: 902-566-5666; *Fax:* 855-566-4662
Mark Hickey, President
Stephanie Cooke-Landry, Secretary

Insurance Brokers' Association of Saskatchewan (IBAS)
#305, 2631 - 28 Ave., Regina SK S4S 6X3
Tel: 306-525-5900; *Fax:* 306-569-3018
www.ibas.ca
Social Media: twitter.com/IBASedu
www.facebook.com/270988899613418
twitter.com/SKbrokers
To promote & preserve the independent insurance brokerage system as a secure, knowledgeable, cost-effective, customer-oriented, professional method of insurance delivery
Sheldon Wasylenko, President
Ernie Gaschler, Executive Director

Insurance Bureau of Canada (IBC) / Bureau d'assurance du Canada
Head Office / Ontario Office, PO Box 121, #2400, 777 Bay St., Toronto ON M5G 2C8
Tel: 416-362-2031; *Fax:* 416-361-5952
Toll-Free: 844-227-5422
www.ibc.ca
Social Media: www.youtube.com/insurancebureau
linkedin.com/company/15105
www.facebook.com/insurancebureau
twitter.com/InsuranceBureau
To foster a healthy property & casualty insurance marketplace & strenghten the ability of our members to serve the needs of Canada's insurance consumers; to advocate public policies that foster a healthy insurance marketplace; to facilitate communication, seek consensus & when in a unique position to do so, undertake industry solutions to common insurance industry concerns
Don Forgeron, President & CEO
Tamara Stoll, Communications Officer

Insurance Institute of British Columbia (IIBC)
#1110, 800 West Pender St., Vancouver BC V6C 2V6
Tel: 604-681-5491; *Fax:* 604-681-5479
Toll-Free: 888-681-5491
IIBCmail@insuranceinstitute.ca
www.insuranceinstitute.ca
Danielle Bolduc, Manager

Insurance Institute of Canada (IIC) / Institut d'assurance du Canada (IAC)
18 King St. East, 6th Fl., Toronto ON M5C 1C4
Tel: 416-362-8586; *Fax:* 416-362-1126
Toll-Free: 866-362-8585
IICmail@insuranceinstitute.ca
www.insuranceinstitute.ca
Social Media:
linkedin.com/company/insurance-institute
To design, develop, & delivers insurance educational programs & texts; To prepare examinations & awards diplomas; To provide a graduate society; To develop career information on behalf of the property/casualty insurance industry
Peter G. Hohman, MBA, FCIP, ICD., President & CEO

Insurance Institute of Manitoba (IIM)
#303, 175 Hargrave St., Winnipeg MB R3C 3R8
Tel: 204-956-1702; *Fax:* 204-956-0758
IIMmail@insuranceinstitute.ca
www.insuranceinstitute.ca
To provide educational services in the general insurance industry in both English and French, such as the Chartered Insurance Professional (CIP), & Fellow Chartered Insurance Professional (FCIP) programs
Holly Anderson, Manager

Insurance Institute of New Brunswick (IINB)
#101, 1010 St-George Blvd., Moncton NB E1E 4R5
Tel: 506-386-5896; *Fax:* 506-386-1130
IINBmail@insuranceinstitute.ca
www.insuranceinstitute.ca
Monique LeBlanc, Manager

Insurance Institute of Newfoundland & Labrador Inc. (IINL)
Chimo Bldg., 151 Crosbie Rd., St. John's NL A1B 4B4
Tel: 709-754-4398; *Fax:* 709-754-4399
IINLmail@insuranceinstitute.ca
www.insuranceinstitute.ca
Leona Rowsell, Manager

Insurance Institute of Northern Alberta (IINA)
#204, 10109 - 106 St., Edmonton AB T5J 3L7
Tel: 780-424-1268; *Fax:* 780-420-1940
IINAmail@insuranceinstitute.ca
www.insuranceinstitute.ca
The Insurance Institute of Northern Alberta provides products and services to the general insurance industry, and ensures the maintenance of a uniform standard of education for the general Insurance Business throughout Canada
Dawn Horne, Manager

Insurance Institute of Nova Scotia (IINS)
#220, 250 Baker Dr., Dartmouth NS B2W 6L4
Tel: 902-433-0070; *Fax:* 902-433-0072
IINSmail@insuranceinstitute.ca
www.insuranceinstitute.ca
Social Media:
twitter.com/insuranceinsns
To provide educational products & services to the general insurance industry, such as the Chartered Insurance Professional (CIP) & the Fellow Chartered Insurance Professional (FCIP) designation programs
Jenny Renyo, Manager

Insurance Institute of Ontario (IIO)
18 King St. East, 16th Fl., Toronto ON M5C 1C4
Tel: 416-362-8586; *Fax:* 416-362-8081
iiomail@insuranceinstitute.ca
insuranceinstitute.ca/en/institutes-and-chapters/Ontario.aspx
To deliver general insurance educational services in English & French, which are consistent with the standardized curriculum offered throughout Canada, such as the Fellow Chartered Insurance Professional (FCIP) & the Fellow Chartered Insurance Professional (FCIP) designation programs
Dawna Matton, BA, FCIP, Senior Director

Insurance Institute of Prince Edward Island (IIPEI)
c/o The Insurance Institute of Canada, 18 King St. East, 6th Fl., Toronto ON M5C 1C4
Tel: 902-892-1692; *Fax:* 902-368-7305
IIPEImail@insuranceinstitute.ca
www.insuranceinstitute.ca
Social Media:
twitter.com/insuranceinspei
Kent Hudson, Marketing Coordinator

Insurance Institute of Saskatchewan (IIS)
#310, 2631 - 28 Ave., Regina SK S4S 6X3
Tel: 306-525-9799; *Fax:* 306-525-8169
IISmail@insuranceinstitute.ca
www.insuranceinstitute.ca
To offer educational products & services to the general insurance industry in both English & French, such as the Fellow Chartered Insurance Professional (FCIP) & the Chartered Insurance Professional (CIP) designation programs
Shannon Karok, Manager

Insurance Institute of Southern Alberta (IISA)
#1110, 833 - 4 Ave. SW, Calgary AB T2P 3T5
Tel: 403-266-3427; *Fax:* 403-269-3199
IISAmail@insuranceinstitute.ca
www.insuranceinstitute.ca
To advance the efficiency, expertise & ability of people employed in the insurance & financial services industry
Seti Mazaheri, Manager

LOMA Canada
East Tower, 675 Cochrane Dr., 6th Floor, Markham ON L3R 0B8
Tel: 905-530-2309; *Fax:* 905-530-2001
lomacanada@loma.org
www.loma.org/canada
To serve its member companies by encouraging & assisting individuals to acquire knowledge & understanding of business of life & health insurance & related financial services.

Marine Insurance Association of British Columbia (MIABC)
c/o Tina Antonio, Aon Risk Solutions, PO Box 3228, #1200, 401 West Georgia St., Vancouver BC V6B 3X8
Tel: 604-844-7654; *Fax:* 604-682-4026
marineinsuranceassociationbc.ca
To represent the goals & interests of the marine insurance industry in British Columbia
Tina Antonio, President

Nuclear Insurance Association of Canada (NIAC) / Association canadienne d'assurance nucléaire
#1600, 401 Bay St., Toronto ON M5H 2Y4
Tel: 416-646-6232
www.niac.biz
Social Media:
www.youtube.com/channel/UCpwR0r-ONaYt6TDZXwf64hA
linkedin.com/company/5279485
www.facebook.com/648772525244971
twitter.com/NIACanada
NIAC is a voluntary, non-profit association of insurers. Members may provide insurance protection by participation in property and liability pools; the association underwrites and accepts nuclear risks located within Canadian territorial limits for Nuclear Liability and Physical Damage (liability &/or property insurance)
Colleen P. DeMerchant, Manager

Ontario Insurance Adjusters Association (OIAA)
29 De Jong Dr., Mississauga ON L5M 1B9
Tel: 905-542-0576; *Fax:* 905-542-1301
Toll-Free: 888-259-1555
manager@oiaa.com
www.oiaa.com
Social Media:
www.facebook.com/OntarioInsuranceAdjustersAssociation
twitter.com/PresidentOIAA
To promote & maintain a high standard of ethics in the business of insurance claims adjusting
Tammie Norn, President

Ontario Mutual Insurance Association (OMIA)
350 Pinebush Rd., Cambridge ON N1T 1Z6
Tel: 519-622-9220; *Fax:* 519-622-9227
info@omia.com
www.omia.com
To assist mutual insurance companies to achieve excellence in service provision

Regroupement des cabinets de courtage d'assurance du Québec (RCCAQ) / Insurance Brokers Association of Québec - Assembly
Complexe Saint-Charles, #550, 1111 rue Saint-Charles Ouest, Tour Est, Longueuil QC J4K 5G4
Tél: 450-674-6258; *Ligne sans frais:* 800-516-6258
info@rccaq.com
www.rccaq.com
Média social:
www.youtube.com/channel/UC6nqrfE3VCXRXkzMvpiiRlw
linkedin.com/company/rccaq
www.facebook.com/RCCAQ
twitter.com/rccaq
Promouvoir les intérêts socio-économiques des membres
Patrick Bouchard, Président
Guy Parent, Directeur général

Reinsurance Research Council (RRC) / Conseil de recherche en réassurance (CRR)
#1, 189 Queen St. East, Toronto ON M5A 1S2
Tel: 416-968-0183; *Fax:* 416-968-6818
mail@rrccanada.org
www.rrccanada.org
Represents the majority of professional reinsurers registered in Canada; conducts research into all lines of property/casualty reinsurance, presents the views of its members where appropriate, and provides liaison with governments, the primary insurance market, & other interested parties; promotes high standards of service and ethical business practices; develops and maintains cordial relations among members and with kindred associations and the public
Anthony Laycock, General Manager

Risk & Insurance Management Society Inc. (RIMS)
c/o Darius Delon, RIMS Canada Council, Mount Royal University, 4825 Mount Royal Gate SW, Calgary AB T3E 6K6
rcc@rimscanada.ca
www.rimscanada.ca
Social Media:
www.facebook.com/RIMSorg
twitter.com/RIMSCdaCouncil
To advance the practice of risk management in Canada
Darius Delon, Chair

Saskatchewan Municipal Hail Insurance Association (SMHI)
2100 Cornwall St., Regina SK S4P 2K7
Tel: 306-569-1852; *Fax:* 306-522-3717
Toll-Free: 877-414-7644
smhi@smhi.ca
www.smhi.ca
Social Media:
twitter.com/MunicipalHail
To provide spot-loss hail insurance coverage to Saskatchewan grain farmers at cost
Rodney Schoettler, Chief Executive Officer
Mark Holfeld, Chief Operating Officer

Society of Public Insurance Administrators of Ontario (SPIAO)
c/o The Municipality Of Clarington, 40 Temperance St., Bowmanville ON L1C 3A6
info@spiao.ca
www.spiao.ca
To exchange knowledge & pursue matters dealing with risk & insurance management; to promote cooperation among all local government bodies which have interests in the field of risk & insurance management; to encourage development of educational training programs; to collect & disperse information
Marie Endicott, President
Catherine Carr, Treasurer

Underwriters' Laboratories of Canada (ULC) / Laboratoires des assureurs du Canada
7 Underwriters Rd., Toronto ON M1R 3A9
Tel: 416-757-3611; *Fax:* 416-757-8727
Toll-Free: 866-937-3852
customerservice@ulc.ca
www.ul.com
To support domestic governmental product safety regulations, & works with international safety systems to help further trade with adherence to local safety requirements.
Keith E. Williams, President & CEO

Interior Design

Association des designers industriels du Québec (ADIQ)
Succ. #406, 420, rue McGill, Montréal QC H2Y 2G1
Tél: 514-287-6531; *Téléc:* 514-278-3049
info@adiq.ca
www.adiq.ca
Média social: www.facebook.com/adiquebec
De soutenir, de représenter et de promourvoir les membres professionels et de mettre en valeur la profession.
Mario Gagnon, Président

Association of Canadian Industrial Designers (ACID) / Association des designers industriels du Canada
#251, 157 Adelaide St. West, Toronto ON M5H 4E7
info@designcanada.org
www.designcanada.org
To represent Canadian industrial designers throughout world. The ACID represents the collective interests of designers and is dedicated to increasing the knowledge, skill and proficiency of its members through networking, discussion forums, seminars and trade events

Association of Interior Designers of Nova Scotia (IDNS)
PO Box 2042, Halifax NS B3J 3B4
Tel: 902-425-4367
idns.ca
To promote the profession; to serve both the interests of public and the interior design industry.
Fran Underwood, President

Association of Registered Interior Designers of New Brunswick (ARIDNB) / Association des designers d'intérieur immatriculés du Nouveau-Brunswick (ADIINB)
PO Box 1541, Fredericton NB E3B 5G2
Tel: 506-459-3014
info@aridnb.ca
www.aridnb.ca
To establish & maintain standards of knowledge, skill, & professional ethics among association members; To serve the public interest by governing the practice of interior design in New Brunswick
Rachel Mitton, President
Lyn Van Tassel, Vice-President
Chrystalla Wilde, Treasurer & Registrar
Ginette Fougère, Secretary

Association of Registered Interior Designers of Ontario (ARIDO)
43 Hanna Ave., #C536, Toronto ON M6K 1X1
Tel: 416-921-2127; *Fax:* 416-921-3660
Toll-Free: 800-334-1180
adminoffice@arido.ca
www.arido.ca
To govern the conduct & professional standards of members; To increase awareness of the profession & ensure rights of interior designers & the public they serve
Sharon Portelli, Registrar

Association professionnelle des designers d'intérieur du Québec (APDIQ)
Maison de l'Architecture, du Design et de l'Urbanisme (MADU), #406, 420, rue McGill, Montréal QC H2Y 2G1
Tél: 514-284-6263
info@apdiq.com
www.apdiq.com
Promouvoir la reconnaissance des designers d'intérieur comme ordre professionnel; assurer la qualité de leurs services; les regrouper pour faire évoluer leur profession; veiller aux intérêts du public; édicter et assurer le respect des règles d'éthique professionnelle
Marie-Claude Parenteau-Lebeuf, Directrice générale

British Columbia Industrial Designer Association (BCID)
PO Box 33943, Vancouver BC V6J 4L7
Tel: 604-608-3204; *Fax:* 604-608-3204
email@bcid.com
www.bcid.com
To act as the public voice for its members; to represent their interests nationally; to maintain a set of standards to preserve the integrity of the profession; to keep a register of professional industrial designers in the province.

Canadian Decorators' Association (CDECA)
#202, 10 Morrow Ave., Toronto ON M6R 2J1
Tel: 416-231-6202; *Fax:* 416-489-1713
Toll-Free: 866-878-2155
info@cdeca.com
www.cdeca.com
Social Media:
linkedin.com/groups?mostRecent=&gid=3909610
www.facebook.com/CanDecorators
twitter.com/CDECAnational
The Canadian Decorators' Association (CDECA) is a professional not-for-profit Association representing interior decorators and interior designers, and Affiliate businesses across Canada.
Seamus Gearin, Executive Director

Interior Designers Association of Saskatchewan (IDAS)
PO Box 32005, Stn. Erindale, Saskatoon SK S7S 1N8
Tel: 306-343-3311
idasadmin@idas.ca
www.idas.ca
To promote an understanding of the profession to the public & to support members in their profession through continuing education & networking
Kenda Owens, President

Interior Designers Institute of British Columbia (IDIBC)
#400, 601 West Broadway, Vancouver BC V5Z 4C2
Tel: 604-298-5211; *Fax:* 604-421-5211
info@idibc.org
www.idibc.org
Social Media:
linkedin.com/company/idibc---the-interior-designers-institute-of-bc
www.facebook.com/IDIBC
twitter.com/idibc
To act as the single representative voice of the Interior Design profession in British Columbia; to advance the profession through public recognition & provide leadership & services to members through programs, communication & education; to benefit public health, safety & welfare, contribute to the enhancement of the environment & increase the perception, appreciation & value of design in the community.
Erica Wickes, President

Interior Designers of Alberta (IDA)
c/o ManageWise Inc., PO Box 21171, #202, 5405 - 99 St., Edmonton AB T6R 2V4
Tel: 780-413-0013; *Fax:* 780-413-0076
info@idalberta.ca
www.idalberta.ca
To develop & maintain standards of practice of interior design; to encourage excellence in interior design; to develop standards of & encourage continuing education of practicing designers; & to provide a liaison between the profession & the general public.
Kelly Vander Hooft, President
Adele Bonetti, Registrar

Interior Designers of Canada (IDC) / Designers d'intérieur du Canada
#C536, 43 Hanna Ave., Toronto ON M6K 1X1
Tel: 416-649-4425; *Fax:* 416-921-3660
Toll-Free: 877-443-4425
www.idcanada.org
Social Media:
www.facebook.com/147037918674277?v=info
twitter.com/IDCanadaTweets
To advance the interior design industry in Canada through high standards of education for the profession, professional responsibility, professional development, & communication
Susan Wiggins, Chief Executive Officer

Interior Designers of Newfoundland and Labrador (IDNL)
NL
idnl.ca

Professional Interior Designers Institute of Manitoba
137 Bannatyne Ave. East, 2nd Fl., Winnipeg MB R3B 0R3
Tel: 204-925-4625
pidim@shaw.ca
www.pidim.ca
To practice interior design in order to improve the lives of the public

International Cooperation/International Relations

AFS Interculture Canada (AFSIC)
#1100, 1425, boul René-Lévesque ouest, Montréal QC H3G 1T7
Tel: 514-288-3282; *Fax:* 514-843-9119
Toll-Free: 800-361-7248
info-canada@afs.org
www.afscanada.org
Social Media: www.pinterest.com/afscanada
www.facebook.com/afsinterculturecanada
twitter.com/afscanada
To promote global education & international development through intercultural exchange programs for both young people & adults; To offer international internships; To work as part of the largest network of international exchange programs in the world
Anisara Creary, National Director

Aga Khan Foundation Canada (AKFC)
The Delegation of the Ismaili Imamat, 199 Sussex Dr., Ottawa ON K1N 1K6
Tel: 613-237-2532; *Fax:* 613-567-2532
Toll-Free: 800-267-2532
info@akfc.ca
www.akfc.ca
To support cost-effective development projects in Asia & Africa in the fields of primary health care, education & rural development, with special attention paid to the needs of women. Major initiatives include: The Pakistan-Canada Social Institutions Development Program; the Tajikistan Institutional Support Program and the Non-Formal Education Program of the Bangladesh Rural Advancement Committee.
Khalil Z. Shariff, CEO

Atlantic Council of Canada (ACC) / Conseil atlantique du Canada (CAC)
#102, 165 University Ave., Toronto ON M5H 3B8
Tel: 416-979-1875; *Fax:* 416-979-0825
info@atlantic-council.ca
www.atlantic-council.ca
Social Media: www.youtube.com/user/TheAtlanticCouncil
linkedin.com/company/atlantic-council-of-canada
www.facebook.com/TheAtlanticCouncilOfCanada
twitter.com/NATOCanada
To inform Canadians of the purpose & benefits of Canada's membership in the Atlantic Alliance & NATO.
Julie Lindhout, President
Hugh Segal, Chair

Canada World Youth (CWY) / Jeunesse Canada Monde (JCM)
#300, 2330, rue Notre-Dame ouest, Montréal QC H3J 1N4
Tel: 514-931-3526; *Fax:* 514-939-2621
Toll-Free: 800-605-3526
info@cwy-jcm.org
www.canadaworldyouth.org
Social Media:
fr-fr.facebook.com/CanadaWorldYouth.JeunesseCanadaMonde
twitter.com/cwyjcm
To increase people's ability to participate actively in the development of just, harmonious & sustainable societies; To create exceptional learning opportunities for communities, groups & individuals wishing to acquire skills & explore new ideas.
Louis Moubarak, President & CEO

Canadian Association for Latin American & Caribbean Studies (CALACS) / Association canadienne des études latino-américaines et caraïbes (ACELAC)
c/o Juan Pablo Crespo Vasquez, York Research Tower, York University, #8-17, 4700 Keele St., Toronto ON M3J 1P3
Tel: 416-736-2100; *Fax:* 519-971-3610
calacs@yorku.ca
www.can-latam.org
To facilitate networking & the exchange of information among those engaged in teaching & research on Latin America & the Caribbean in Canada & abroad; To foster throughout Canada, especially within the universities, colleges, & other centres of higher education, the expansion of information on & interest in Latin America & the Caribbean; To represent the academic & professional interest of Canadian Latin Americanists
Pablo Crespo Vasquez Juan, Contact, Administration
Steven Palmer, Secretary-Treasurer

Canadian Association for the Study of International Development (CASID) / L'Association canadienne d'études du développement international (ACEDI)
c/o The Canadian Federation for the Humanities & Social Sciences, #300, 275 Bank St., Ottawa ON K2P 2L6
Tel: 613-238-6112; *Fax:* 613-238-6114
info@ideas-idees.ca
ideas-idees.ca
National, bilingual, interdisciplinary & pluralistic association devoted to the study of international development in all parts of the world
Ann Miller, Contact

Canadian Commission for UNESCO / Commission canadienne pour l'UNESCO
PO Box 1047, 350 Albert St., Ottawa ON K1P 5V8
Tel: 613-566-4414; *Fax:* 613-566-4405
Toll-Free: 800-263-5588
info@unesco.ca
www.unesco.ca
An arm's length agency of the Government of Canada; to promote Canadian participation in the programmes & activities of UNESCO; to advise the government of Canada on its policies toward UNESCO; to act as a forum for Canadian civil society & government to discuss matters relating to UNESCO
David A. Walden, Secretary-General

Canadian Council for International Co-operation (CCIC) / Conseil canadien pour la coopération internationale
39 McArthur Ave., Ottawa ON K1L 8L7
Tel: 613-241-7007; *Fax:* 613-241-5302
info@ccic.ca
www.ccic.ca
Social Media: www.youtube.com/user/CCICable
www.facebook.com/ccciccic
twitter.com/CCCICCIC
To work globally to achieve sustainable human development; To seek to end global poverty; To promote social justice & human dignity for all
Jim Cornelius, Chair
Julia Sánchez, President & CEO
Anna Campos, Officer, Finance & Administration
Chantal Havard, Officer, Government Relations & Communications
Fraser Reilly-King, Policy Analyst, Aid & International Co-operation

Canadian Foundation for the Americas (FOCAL) / Fondation canadienne pour les Amériques
#720, 1 Nicholas St., Ottawa ON K1N 7B7
Tel: 613-562-0005; *Fax:* 613-562-2525
www.focal.ca
To foster informed & timely debate & dialogue on issues of importance to decision-makers throughout Canada & the Americas; to develop a greater understanding of important hemispheric issues & to help build a stronger community of the Americas
Kathryn Hewlett-Jobes, Chair
Carlo Dade, Executive Director
Madeleine Bélanger, Director, Communications

Canadian Friends of Burma (CFOB) / Les Amis canadiens de la Birmanie
#206, 145 Spruce St., Ottawa ON K1R 6P1
Tel: 613-237-8056; *Fax:* 613-563-0017
cfob@cfob.org
www.cfob.org
To promote democracy & human rights in Burma by working within the global movement, & educating & activating Canadian involvement in the struggle for peace in Burma
Tin Maung Htoo, Executive Director
Toe Kyi, Director, Information Technology
Ashley Stewart, Director, Media & Community Relations
Kevin McLoed, Researcher

Canadian Friends of Ukraine (CFU)
South Building, 620 Spadina Ave., 2nd Fl., Toronto ON M5S 2H4
Tel: 416-964-6644; *Fax:* 416-964-6085
canfun@interlog.com
www.canadianfriendsofukraine.com
Social Media:
www.facebook.com/Canadian-Friends-of-Ukraine-26427389693 9710/
To strengthen Canadian-Ukrainian relations; To promote democracy & reform in Ukraine
Lisa Shymko, Executive Director

Canadian Institute for Conflict Resolution (CICR) / Institut canadien pour la résolution des conflits
c/o St. Paul University, 223 Main St., Ottawa ON K1S 1C4
Tel: 613-235-5800; *Fax:* 613-235-5801
Toll-Free: 866-684-2427
info@cicr-icrc.ca
www.cicr-icrc.ca
To foster, develop & communicate resolution processes for individuals, organizations & communities in Canada & internationally; to embody, within the conflict resolution process, the positive attributes of common sense, sensitivity, compassion & spirituality.
Brian Strom, Executive Director

Canadian Institute of Cultural Affairs / Institut canadien des affaires culturelles
#405, 401 Richmond St. West, Toronto ON M5V 3A8
Tel: 416-691-2316
ica@icacan.org
www.icacan.org
Social Media:
www.facebook.com/ICAInternational
To empower people to develop leadership capacity; To contribute to positive social change
Nan Hudson, Executive Director

Canadian International Council (CIC) / Conseil international du Canada
6 Hoskin Ave., Toronto ON M5S 1H8
Tel: 416-946-7209
info@thecic.org
www.thecic.org
Social Media: www.youtube.com/user/onlinecicvideos
www.facebook.com/CanadianInternationalCouncil
twitter.com/TheCIC
To strengthen Canada's role in international affairs; To advance research & dialogue on international affairs
Keith Martin, Acting President

Canadian Peace Alliance (CPA) / Alliance canadienne pour la paix
PO Box 13, 427 Bloor St. West, Toronto ON M5S 1X7
Tel: 416-588-5555; *Fax:* 416-588-5556
cpa@web.ca
www.acp-cpa.ca
Social Media:
www.facebook.com/268544019838244
twitter.com/CanadianPeace
To involve Canadians in the worldwide movement to stop the arms race, ensure the non-violent settlement of disputes & guarantee the security & well-being of all peoples.
Sid Lacombe, Coordinator

Canadian Physicians for Aid & Relief (CPAR)
1425 Bloor St. West, Toronto ON M6P 3L6
Tel: 416-369-0865; *Fax:* 416-369-0294
Toll-Free: 800-263-2727
info@cpar.ca
www.cpar.ca
Social Media:
www.youtube.com/channel/UC_7_sOan_HyDiTpvn07BH3A
linkedin.com/company/canadian-physicians-for-aid-and-relief
www.facebook.com/cparcan
twitter.com/cpar
To help impoverished communities in developing nations become prosperous, while maintaining harmony with the environment; To tackle all aspects of poverty; To emphasize healthy community empowerment & integrated community based development
Kathy Johnston, Executive Assistant

CARE Canada
#100, 9 Gurdwara Rd., Ottawa ON K2E 7X6
Tel: 613-228-5600; *Fax:* 613-226-5777
Toll-Free: 800-267-5232
info@care.ca
www.care.ca
Social Media: www.youtube.com/carecanada
www.facebook.com/carecanada
twitter.com/CARE_CAN
To serve individuals & families in developing communities; To provide economic opportunity & emergency relief to those in need
Gillian Barth, President/CEO

Carrefour de solidarité internationale inc.
165, rue Moore, Sherbrooke QC J1H 1B8
Tél: 819-566-8595; *Téléc:* 819-566-8076
www.csisher.com
Média social: www.youtube.com/user/CSIsherbrooke
www.facebook.com/carrefour.solidarite.internationale
twitter.com/csisherbrooke
Susciter la solidarité de la population de l'Estrie pour la justice sociale au plan international
Jérémie Roberge, Président
Serge-Étienne Parent, Secrétaire
Marco Labrie, Directeur général

Centre canadien d'étude et de coopération internationale (CECI) / Canadian Centre for International Studies & Cooperation
3000, rue Omer-Lavallée, Montréal QC H1Y 3R8
Tél: 514-875-9911; *Téléc:* 514-875-6469
Ligne sans frais: 877-875-2324
info@ceci.ca
www.ceci.ca
Média social: www.youtube.com/commceci
www.facebook.com/cecicooperation
twitter.com/CECI_Canada
Le CECI combat la pauvreté et l'exclusion; renforce les capacités de développment des communautés défavorisées; appuie des initiatives de paix, de droits humains et d'équité; mobilise des ressources et favorise l'échange de savoir-faire.
Robert Perreault, Président
Claudia Black, Directrice générale

Child Haven International / Accueil international pour l'enfance
19014 - 7th Conc., RR#1, Maxville ON K0C 1T0
Tel: 613-527-2829; *Fax:* 613-527-1118
fred@childhaven.ca
www.childhaven.ca
To assist any child of any nationality who needs in-country care or a private family home; To provide institutions & cottage or village industries for giving training in handcrafts, music, agricultural methods; To promote the integrity of the family by providing help for adolescents or adults who have special needs & by community development & medical aid projects

Children's International Summer Villages (Canada) Inc. (CISV) / Villages internationaux d'enfants
233 Chaplin Cres., Toronto ON M5P 1B1
canada@cisv.org
www.ca.cisv.org
To promote cross-cultural friendship, through educational programs for youth & adults in 60 countries; To prepare indivduals to become active & contributing members of a peaceful society; To stimulate the life-long development of amicable relationships & effective & appropriate leadership towards a fair & just world

CNEC - Partners International
#56, 8500 Torbram Rd., Brampton ON L6T 5C6
Tel: 905-458-1202; *Fax:* 905-458-4339
Toll-Free: 800-883-7697
info@partnersinternational.ca
www.partnersinternational.ca
Social Media: www.youtube.com/user/partnerscanada
twitter.com/Partnersintlcan
Partners Canadians with indigenous Christian ministries to spread the Word of God.
Harry Doxsee, Chair

Coady International Institute (CII)
St. Francis Xavier University, PO Box 5000, Antigonish NS B2G 2W5
Tel: 902-867-3960; *Fax:* 902-867-3907
Toll-Free: 866-820-7835
coady@stfx.ca
www.coady.stfx.ca
Social Media: www.youtube.com/user/CoadyInstitute
www.facebook.com/coady.international.institute
twitter.com/coadystfx
Promotes learning in individuals & organizations engaged in community-driven action to achieve wellbeing, global justice, peace & participating democracy
John Gaventa, Director

CODE
321 Chapel St., Ottawa ON K1N 7Z2
Tel: 613-232-3569; *Fax:* 613-232-7435
Toll-Free: 800-661-2633
codehq@codecan.org
www.codecan.org
Social Media: www.youtube.com/user/TheCodecan
www.facebook.com/code.org
twitter.com/codecan_org
To enable people to learn by developing partnerships that provide resources for learning, to promote awareness & understanding & to encourage self-reliance; To support training for teachers & librarians; To coordinate book donations from North American publishers to schools & libraries in the developing world
Scott Walter, Executive Director
Marc Molnar, Director, Finance & Administration

Allen LeBlanc, Director, Fund Development & Marketing
Marika Escaravage, Manager, Integrated Marketing Communications

CoDevelopment Canada (CODEV)
#260, 2747 East Hastings St., Vancouver BC V5K 1Z8
Tel: 604-708-1495; *Fax:* 604-708-1497
codev@codev.org
www.codev.org
Social Media:
www.facebook.com/CoDevCanada
twitter.com/CoDevCanada
To initiate social change in Latin American, facilitating relationships between Northern & Southern organizations that share a commitment to workers' rights, community development & women's rights.
Joey Hartman, President
Barbara Wood, Executive Director

Compassion Canada
PO Box 5591, London ON N6A 5G8
Tel: 519-668-0224; *Fax:* 866-685-1107
Toll-Free: 800-563-5437
info@compassion.ca
www.compassion.ca
To provide sponsors for children in Third World countries; to aid community development projects in cooperation with Canadian International Development Agency; to be an advocate for children, to release them from their spiritual, economic, social & physical poverty & to enable them to become responsible & fulfilled Christian adults
Barry Slauenwhite, President & CEO

Conseil canadien de la coopération et de la mutualité (CCCM)
#400, 275, rue Bank, Ottawa ON K2P 2L6
Tél: 613-238-6712; *Téléc:* 613-567-0658
info@coopscanada.coop
canada.coop
Média social: www.facebook.com/792260167456516
twitter.com/CoopFrancoCan
Le Conseil vise à promouvoir la coopération en vue du développement socio-économique des communautés francophones du Canada.
Denyse Guy, Directrice générale

Conseil de coopération de l'Ontario (CCO)
#201, 435, boul St-Laurent, Ottawa ON K1K 2Z8
Tél: 613-745-8619; *Téléc:* 613-745-4649
Ligne sans frais: 866-290-1168
info@cco.coop
www.cco.coop
Média social: www.youtube.com/user/conseilcoopontario
linkedin.com/company/conseil-de-la-coop-ration-de-l'ontario
www.facebook.com/LeConseildelacooperationdelOntario
twitter.com/ccocoop
Favoriser la prise en charge socio-économique de la communauté francophone de l'Ontario par le biais de la coopération
Luc Morin, Directeur général

Conseil québécois de la coopération et de la mutualité (CCQ)
#204, 5955, rue Saint-Laurent, Lévis QC G6V 3P5
Tél: 418-835-3710; *Téléc:* 418-835-6322
info@coopquebec.coop
www.coopquebec.qc.ca
Média social: www.facebook.com/quebec.coop
twitter.com/CQCMCOOP
Pour unir des organisations coopératives du Québec pour favoriser l'action concertée de ses membres, promouvoir l'authenticité coopérative, défendre les intérêts de ses membres
Gaston Bédard, Directeur général intérimaire

CUSO International
#200, 44 Eccles St., Ottawa ON K1R 6S4
Tel: 613-829-7445; *Fax:* 613-829-7996
Toll-Free: 888-434-2876
questions@cusointernational.org
www.cusointernational.org
Social Media: www.youtube.com/cusointernational
www.facebook.com/cusovso
twitter.com/CusoIntl
To work through skilled volunteers to aid global social justice; to address poverty, human rights violations, HIV/AIDS, inequity & environmental degradation; to give Canadians information, the experiences & the tools they need to become active global citizens.
Derek Evans, Executive Director

Forum for International Trade Training (FITT) / Forum pour la formation en commerce international
#300, 116 Lisgar St., Ottawa ON K2P 0C2
Tel: 613-230-3553; *Fax:* 613-230-6808
Toll-Free: 800-561-3488
info@fitt.ca
www.fitt.ca
Social Media:
linkedin.com/company/fitt-forum-for-international-trade-training-
www.facebook.com/FITTNews
twitter.com/FITTNews
To provide quality programs' training & certification in international trade designed to prepare businesses & individuals to compete successfully in world markets.
Caroline Tompkins, President

Group of 78 / Groupe des 78
#244, 211 Bronson Ave., Ottawa ON K1R 6H5
Tel: 613-230-0860; *Fax:* 613-563-0017
group78@group78.org
group78.org
Social Media:
www.facebook.com/groupof78
To advocate for peace, disarmament, sustainable development & strengthening of the United Nations.
Richard Harmston, Chair

HOPE International Development Agency
214 Sixth St., New Westminster BC V3L 3A2
Tel: 604-525-5481; *Fax:* 604-525-3471
Toll-Free: 866-525-4673
hope@hope-international.com
www.hope-international.com
Social Media:
twitter.com/HOPEInt
To help the poverty-stricken section of Third World people to attain the basic necessities of life; To inform Canadians regarding issues related to the developing world & HOPE's activities; To provide alternative technological & educational support to people in developing countries where environmental, economic, &/or social circumstances have interfered with the ability of local communities to sustain themselves by using traditional methods. Other offices in Afghanistan, Australia, Cambodia, Ethiopia, Japan, Myanmar, New Zealand, the U.K., & the U.S.
Brian Cannon, Interim Executive Director

Horizons of Friendship (HOF)
PO Box 402, 50 Covert St., Cobourg ON K9A 4L1
Tel: 905-372-5483; *Fax:* 905-372-7095
Toll-Free: 888-729-9928
info@horizons.ca
www.horizons.ca
Social Media: www.youtube.com/user/HorizonsofFriendship
www.facebook.com/horizonsoffriendship
twitter.com/HorizonsFriends
To address the root causes of poverty & injustice through the cooperation of people from the south & north; To support Central American & Mexican partner organizations which undertake local initiatives; To raise awareness in Canada of global issues; To work with Canadian organizations at the local & national levels
Patricia Rebolledo, Executive Director

Inter Pares / Among Equals
221 Laurier Ave. East, Ottawa ON K1N 6P1
Tel: 613-563-4801; *Fax:* 613-594-4704
Toll-Free: 866-563-4801
info@interpares.ca
www.interpares.ca
To build equality of people, North & South, by collaborating with & supporting justice for people around the world; Inter Pares applies 4 principles: Leadership by Women, Participation, Sustainability & Respect for Cultural Values
Rita Morbia, Executive Director

International Relief Agency Inc. (IRA)
#84, 95 Wood St., Toronto ON M4Y 2Z3
Tel: 416-928-0901
ira@ica.net
To promote free enterprise, national freedoms & democracy

Mahatma Gandhi Canadian Foundation for World Peace
PO Box 60002, RPO University of Alberta, Edmonton AB T6G 2S4
Tel: 780-492-5504; *Fax:* 780-492-0113
gandhifoundationcanada@gmail.com
www.gandhi.ca
To conduct programs & activities that promote the teachings & philosophy of Mahatma Gandhi in order to advance peace & understanding amongst peoples of the world
Jaime Beck, Educational Coordinator

Manitoba Council for International Cooperation (MCIC) / Conseil du Manitoba pour la coopération internationale
#302, 280 Smith St., Winnipeg MB R3C 1K2
Tel: 204-987-6420; *Fax:* 204-956-0031
info@mcic.ca
www.mcic.ca
Social Media:
www.facebook.com/mcic.ca
twitter.com/MCIC_CA
To promote international development that protects the environment; To coordinate the development work of member agencies
Janice Hamilton, Executive Director

The Marquis Project, Inc.
PO Box 50045, Brandon MB R7A 7E4
Tel: 204-727-5675; *Fax:* 204-727-5683
marquis@marquisproject.com
www.marquisproject.com
Social Media:
www.facebook.com/pages/The-Marquis-Project/461638847282359
To inform rural Manitobans of global issues; to link concerns to those of Third World peoples; to encourage concrete positive action in response to global concerns
Al Friesen, President

Ontario Council for International Cooperation (OCIC) / Conseil de l'Ontario pour la coopération internationale
#209, 344 Bloor St. West, Toronto ON M5S 3A7
Tel: 416-972-6303; *Fax:* 416-972-6996
info@ocic.on.ca
www.ocic.on.ca
Social Media:
linkedin.com/groups?gid=4146814&trk=hb_side_g
twitter.com/ocictweets
Community of Ontario-based international development and global education organizations and individual associate members working globally for social justice
Kimberly Gibbons, Executive Director

Operation Eyesight Universal
#200, 4 Parkdale Cres. NW, Calgary AB T2N 3T8
Tel: 403-283-6323; *Fax:* 403-270-1899
Toll-Free: 800-585-8265
info@operationeyesight.ca
www.operationeyesight.ca
Social Media: www.youtube.com/user/OpEyesightUniversal
linkedin.com/company/operation-eyesight
www.facebook.com/OperationEyesightUniversal
twitter.com/OpEyesight
To eliminate avoidable blindness through the development & support of permanent, self-sustaining, quality blindness prevention & sight restoration programs for those people in greatest need
Brian Foster, Executive Director

Oxfam Canada
39 McArthur Ave., Ottawa ON K1L 8L7
Tel: 613-237-5236; *Fax:* 613-237-0524
Toll-Free: 800-466-9326
info@oxfam.ca
www.oxfam.ca
Social Media: www.youtube.com/user/OxfamCanada
www.facebook.com/OxfamCanada
twitter.com/oxfamcanada
To build solutions for the creation of a fair world, without poverty & injustice
Margaret Hancock, Chair
Don MacMillan, Treasurer

Peace Brigades International (Canada) (PBI)
323 Chapel St., Ottawa ON K1N 7Z2
Tel: 613-237-6968
info@pbicanada.org
www.pbicanada.org
Social Media:
www.facebook.com/pbicanada
twitter.com/pbicanada
To explore & implement non-violent approaches to peacekeeping & support for basic human rights; to provide protective accompaniment & peace education training in Colombia, Indonesia, & Mexico
Meaghen Simms, Executive Director

Physicians for Global Survival (Canada) (PGS) / Médecins pour la survie mondiale (Canada)
30 Cleary Ave., Ottawa ON K2A 4A1
Tel: 613-233-1982
pgsadmin@web.ca
www.pgs.ca
Social Media: www.youtube.com/user/pgsottawa
www.facebook.com/pages/Physicians-For-Global-Survival/134022454568
Committed to the abolition of nuclear weapons, the prevention of war, the promotion of non-violent means of conflict resolution & social justice in a sustainable world
Juan Carlos Chirgwin, President

Project Ploughshares
140 Westmount Rd. North, Waterloo ON N2L 3G6
Tel: 519-888-6541; *Fax:* 519-888-0018
plough@ploughshares.ca
www.ploughshares.ca
Social Media:
www.facebook.com/pages/Project-Ploughshares/206928856016444
twitter.com/ploughshares_ca
Ecumenical peace agency of the Canadian Council of Churches that identifies, develops & advances approaches that build peace & prevent war
Debbie Hughes, Assistant

Saskatchewan Council for International Co-operation (SCIC) / Conseil de la Saskatchewan pour la co-opération internationale
2138 McIntyre St., Regina SK S4P 2R7
Tel: 306-757-4669; *Fax:* 306-757-3226
scic@earthbeat.sk.ca
www.earthbeat.sk.ca
Social Media: www.youtube.com/user/SCICYouth
www.facebook.com/SaskCIC
www.twitter.com/saskCIC
To act as the umbrella organization for international development agencies in Saskatchewan; To distribute international development funds provided by the Government of Saskatchewan; To facilitate communications among member agencies in Saskatchewan and across Canada; To support cooperative government relations, public education, & fundraising
Jacqui Wasacase, Executive Director

Save a Family Plan (SAFP)
PO Box 3622, London ON N6A 4L4
Tel: 519-672-1115; *Fax:* 519-672-6379
safpinfo@safp.org
www.safp.org
Social Media:
www.facebook.com/pages/Save-A-Family-Plan/117934038235594
twitter.com/SaveaFamilyPlan
Implements sustainable family & community development programs in 5 states in India, with 41 social service societies, 26 homes of health, approximately 10,550 grass roots community organiziations & 15,000 poor families; programs are developed through needs assessments; within all aspects of programming, environmental & gender impact assessments are undertaken. Offices in Canada, the U.S. & India
Lesley Tordoff, Executive Director
Lois Côté, President

Save the Children Canada (SCC) / Aide à l'enfance - Canada
#300, 4141 Yonge St., Toronto ON M2P 2A8
Tel: 416-221-5501; *Fax:* 416-221-8214
Toll-Free: 800-668-5036
info@savethechildren.ca
www.savethechildren.ca
Social Media: www.youtube.com/savethechildrenCA
www.facebook.com/savethechildren.ca
twitter.com/SaveChildrenCan
To fight for children's rights; To deliver immediate & lasting improvements to children's lives worldwide in Canada & 10 countries overseas
Patricia Erb, President/CEO

Science for Peace (SfP) / Science et paix
c/o University College, #045, 15 King's College Circle, Toronto ON M5S 3H7
Tel: 416-978-3606; *Fax:* 416-978-3606
sfp@physics.utoronto.ca
www.scienceforpeace.ca
To understand & act against forces of militarism, social injustice, & environmental destruction
Metta Spencer, President
Margrit Eichler, Secretary
Pieter Basedow, Treasurer

United Nations Association in Canada (UNAC) / Association canadienne pour les Nations Unies (ACNU)
#300, 309 Cooper St., Ottawa ON K2P 0G5
Tel: 613-232-5751; *Fax:* 613-563-2455
info@unac.org
www.unac.org
Social Media: www.flickr.com/photos/106512533@N07
linkedin.com/company/1177974?trk=prof-exp-company-name
www.facebook.com/196640250481693?sk=info&tab=page_info
twitter.com/UNACanada
To study international problems & Canada's relationship to them as a member of the UN & its related agencies; To foster mutual understanding, goodwill & cooperation between the people of Canada & those of other countries, with the object of promoting peace & justice; To study possible courses of action in the field of international affairs; To work for support by the government & the people of Canada for desirable policies; To provide information on & stimulate public interest in the UN & its various agencies which have been established for direct or indirect promotion of international order, justice & security; To foster national commitment to principles of multilateralism & international cooperation
Kathryn White, Executive Director

Vides Canada
178 Steeles Ave. East, Markham ON L3T 1A5
Tel: 416-803-3558
videscanada.ca
Social Media: www.flickr.com/photos/57388169@N05
www.facebook.com/videscanada
To improve the lives of underpriviledged children; to train volunteers & send them to developing countries in order to help the children who live there
Jeannine Landra, Director

World Federalist Movement - Canada (WFMC)
#207, 145 Spruce St., Ottawa ON K1R 6P1
Tel: 613-232-0647; *Fax:* 613-563-0017
wfcnat@web.ca
www.worldfederalistscanada.org
Social Media:
www.facebook.com/pages/World-Federalist-Movement-Canada/14694450199518
twitter.com/WFMCanada
Education, research, political support for strengthening the United Nations & rule of law in world affairs
Warren Allmand, President
Fergus Watt, Executive Director
Simon Rosenblum, Chair

World University Service of Canada (WUSC) / Entraide universitaire mondiale du Canada (EUMC)
1404 Scott St., Ottawa ON K1Y 4M8
Tel: 613-798-7477; *Fax:* 613-798-0990
Toll-Free: 800-267-8699
wusc@wusc.ca
www.wusc.ca
Social Media: www.youtube.com/wusceumc
linkedin.com/groups/WUSC-EUMC-Alumni-2441658
www.facebook.com/wusc.ca
twitter.com/worlduniservice
To foster human development & global understanding through education & training.
Chris Eaton, Executive Director
Ravi Gupta, Associate Executive Director

World Vision Canada (WVC) / Vision Mondiale
1 World Dr., Mississauga ON L5T 2Y4
Tel: 905-565-6100; *Fax:* 866-219-8620
Toll-Free: 866-595-5550
www.worldvision.ca
Social Media: www.youtube.com/WorldVisionCanada;
www.instagram.com/worldvisioncan
www.facebook.com/WorldVisionCan
twitter.com/worldvisioncan
To act as an international partnership of Christians that provides relief to children, families, & communities; To work towards overcoming poverty & injustice; To aid people regardless of religion, race, ethnicity, or gender
Michael Messenger, President & CEO

Labour Relations

ADR Institute of Canada (ADRIC) / Institut d'arbitrage et de médiation du Canada
#405, 234 Eglinton Ave. East, Toronto ON M4P 1K5
Tel: 416-487-4733; *Fax:* 416-487-4429
Toll-Free: 877-475-4353
admin@adrcanada.ca
www.adrcanada.ca
Social Media:
www.youtube.com/channel/UCwA2kIDn6cqf2oUFxzYiN8A
linkedin.com/groups?gid=3303518
www.facebook.com/ADRInstituteOfCanadaADRIC.IAMC
twitter.com/adrcanada
To promote the use of arbitration & mediation (ADR - alternative dispute resolution) to settle disputes; to provide information & education on ADR to practitioners, parties, the public, & the business, professional & government communities; to assist those wishing to use ADR through the provision of Arbitration & Mediation Rules, administrative services, & information about the process & member arbitrators & mediators
Janet McKay, Executive Director

Association canadienne des relations industrielles (ACRI) / Canadian Industrial Relations Association (CIRA)
Département des relations industrielles, Université Laval, #3129, 1025, av. des Sciences-Humaines, Québec QC G1V 0A6
acri-cira@rlt.ulaval.ca
www.cira-acri.ca
Promouvoir la discussion, la recherche, et la formation dans le domaine des relations industrielles
Kelly Williams Whitt, Président
Étienne Cantin, Secrétaire

Association of Workers' Compensation Boards of Canada (AWCBC) / Association des commissions des accidents du travail du Canada
6551B Mississauga Rd., Mississauga ON L5N 1A6
Tel: 905-542-3633; *Fax:* 905-542-0039
Toll-Free: 855-282-9222
contact@awcbc.org
www.awcbc.org
To facilitate cooperation among Canadian Boards & Commissions; To foster greater public understanding or dialogue about workplace health & safety & workers' compensation
Cheryl Tucker, Executive Director

Canadian Association of Administrators of Labour Legislation (CAALL) / Association canadienne des administrateurs de la législation ouvrière (ACALO)
CAALL Secretariat, Phase II, Place du Portage, 165, rue Hôtel-de-Ville, 8e étage, Gatineau QC K1A 0J2
Tel: 819-934-7814; *Fax:* 819-953-9779
CAALL-secretariat@hrsdc-rhdsc.gc.ca
www.caall-acalo.org/en
To provide a forum for federal, provincial, & territorial senior officials; to develop agenda, background papers, & logistics for meetings of Ministers responsible for Labour; To follow-up on issues as directed by Ministers
Margaret MacDonald, President
Debra Young, Secretary
Sandy Jones, Acting Manager, Intergovernmental Relations & Social Dialogue
Nina Chretien, Officer, Research & Project, Intergovernmental Relations & Social Dialogue

Canadian Association of Labour Media (CALM) / Association canadienne de la presse syndicale (ACPS)
PO Box 10624, Stn. Bloorcourt, Toronto ON M6H 4H9
Tel: 581-983-4397; *Fax:* 581-983-4397
editor@calm.ca
www.calm.ca
Social Media:
www.facebook.com/canadian.association.of.labour.media
twitter.com/CanLabourMedia
To provide training, labour-friendly news, & graphics for labour communicators
Chris Lawson, President
Martin Lukacs, Executive Editor
Nora Loreto, Executive Editor

Canadian Committee on Labour History (CCLH) / Comité canadien sur l'histoire du travail
c/o Canadian Committee on Labour History, Athabasca University, #1200, 10011 - 109 St., Edmonton AB T5J 3S8
cclh@athabascau.ca
www.cclh.ca

To promote & publish scholarly research in the area of Canadian labour history & related topics
Alvin Finkel, President
G.S. Kealey, Treasurer

Canadian Injured Workers Alliance (CIWA) / L'Alliance canadienne des victimes d'accidents et de maladies du travail (ACVAMT)
PO Box 10098, 1201 Jasper Dr., Thunder Bay ON P7B 6T6
Tel: 807-345-3429; *Fax:* 807-344-8683
Toll-Free: 877-787-7010
www.ciwa.ca
To support & strengthen the work of local & provincial groups by providing a forum for exchanging information & experiences; To provide training & educational resources in partnership with these groups to ensure that injured workers maintain control over their destinies & that the groups themselves be democratically controlled by the workers
Bill Cheodore, National Coordinator

Cape Breton Injured Workers' Association (CBIWA)
714 Alexandra St., Sydney NS B1S 2H4
Tel: 902-539-4650; *Fax:* 902-539-4171
cbiwa@ns.aliantzinc.ca
The Cape Breton Injured Workers Association is a volunteer group, located in Sydney, Nova Scotia working on behalf of injured workers by providing information, assisting with claims and appeals, and continuing a dialogue with the Workers' Compensation Board of Nova Scotia.

Centre canadien d'arbitrage commercial (CCAC) / Canadian Commercial Arbitration Centre (CCAC)
Place du Canada, #905, 1010, rue de la Gauchetière ouest, Montréal QC H3B 2N2
Tél: 514-448-5980; *Téléc:* 514-448-5948
www.ccac-adr.org
Média social:
linkedin.com/company/centre-canadien-d'arbitrage-commercial
Fournir des services de conciliation, de médiation et d'arbitrage pour les activités commerciales et de consommation; offrir des activités de formation aux arbitres et médiateurs; analyse de dossiers litigieux et études pour des organismes privés et publics
Julie Houle, Coordonnatrice

Construction Labour Relations - An Alberta Association (CLRA)
Calgary Office, #207, 2725 - 12 St. NE, Calgary AB T2E 7J2
Tel: 403-250-7390; *Fax:* 403-250-5516
Toll-Free: 800-450-7204
www.clra.org
To represent construction employers in collective bargaining, collective agreement administration, administrative labour law, lobbying.

Construction Labour Relations Association of British Columbia
PO Box 820, 97 - 6 St., New Westminster BC V3L 4Z8
Tel: 604-524-4911; *Fax:* 604-524-3925
wendym@clra-bc.com
www.clra-bc.com
Clyde Scollan, President
Wendy Mazur, Office Manager

Construction Labour Relations Association of Newfoundland & Labrador Inc. (CLRA)
Ultramar Bldg., Main Floor, PO Box 8144, Stn. A, 39 Pippy Pl., St. John's NL A1B 3M9
Tel: 709-753-5770; *Fax:* 709-753-5771
clranl@clranl.com
www.clranl.com
Neil Chaplin, President

Institut de médiation et d'arbitrage du Québec (IMAQ)
#1501, 1445, rue Stanley, Montréal QC H3A 3T1
Tél: 514-282-3327; *Téléc:* 514-282-2214
Ligne sans frais: 855-482-3327
info@imaq.org
www.imaq.org
Média social: www.youtube.com/user/IMAQuebec
linkedin.com/company/institut-de-m-diation-et-d%27arbitrage-du-quebec
Promouvoir les méthodes alternatives de résolution de conflits (médiation, arbitrage); donner accès par internet à la population et aux entreprises à une banque de médiateurs et d'arbitres accrédités selon leur: spécialité (médiateur ou arbitre), région, langue de communication, catégorie de membre, profession, domaine d'expertise
Pierre Grenier, Président
Ginette Gamache, Directrice, Opérations

Provincial Building & Construction Trades Council of Ontario
35 International Blvd., Toronto ON M9W 6H3
Tel: 416-679-8887; *Fax:* 416-679-8882
info@ontariobuildingtrades.com
www.ontariobuildingtrades.com
Patrick J. Dillon, Business Manager

Pulp & Paper Employee Relations Forum
c/o Westcott Consulting, 6627 Westcott Rd., Duncan BC V9L 6A4
Tel: 250-748-9445; *Fax:* 888-273-7148
westcot@telus.net
paperforum.com
To act primarily as a research & information service for the industry; to service the pulp & paper industry in job evaluation, benefit & pension plan administration & trusteeship, contract interpretation & any other matters relating to labour relations
Fred Oud, Executive Director

Union of Injured Workers of Ontario, Inc.
2888 Dufferin St., Toronto ON M6B 3S6
Tel: 416-785-8787; *Fax:* 416-785-6390
Serving injured workers & their families; advocacy, counselling, information & referral
Philip Biggin, Executive Director

Western Employers Labour Relations Association
#203, 27126 Fraser Hwy., Langley BC V4W 3P6
Tel: 604-857-5540; *Fax:* 604-857-5547
To provide employee relations services for both union & non-union employers

World at Work
PO Box 4520, Stn. A, Toronto ON M5W 4M4
Tel: 480-951-9191; *Fax:* 480-483-8352
Toll-Free: 877-951-9191
customerrelations@worldatwork.com
www.worldatwork.org
Social Media: www.youtube.com/worldatworktv
linkedin.com/groups?about=&gid=84761
www.facebook.com/WorldatWorkAssociation
twitter.com/worldatwork
To promote the education of compensation & benefits professionals
Anne Ruddy, President
Marcia Rhodes, Contact, Media Relations

Labour Unions

Agriculture Union
#1000, 233 Gilmour St., Ottawa ON K2P 0P2
Tel: 613-560-4306; *Fax:* 613-235-0517
www.agrunion.com
To advance the workplace interests of its membership; To fight for a society that recognizes the value of the important public services provided by Agriculture Union members
Bob Kingston, National President

Alberta Federation of Labour (AFL) / Fédération du travail de l'Alberta
#300, 10408 - 124 St., Edmonton AB T5N 1R5
Tel: 780-483-3021; *Fax:* 780-484-5928
Toll-Free: 800-661-3995
afl@afl.org
www.afl.org
Social Media:
twitter.com/abfedlabour
To act as a central labour body, representing Alberta's organized workers & their families; To improve conditions for Alberta's workers, their families & communities
Gil McGowan, President
Gwen Feeny, Director, Policy Analysis & Advocacy
Olav Rokne, Director, Communications

Alberta Union of Provincial Employees / Syndicat de la fonction publique de l'Alberta
10451 - 170 St., Edmonton AB T5P 4S7
Tel: 780-930-3300; *Fax:* 780-930-3392
Toll-Free: 800-232-7284
www.aupe.org
Social Media:
www.facebook.com/yourAUPE
Ron Hodgins, Executive Director
Jamie Oyarzun, Director, Labour Relations

Alliance des professeures et professeurs de Montréal (APPM)
8225, boul Saint-Laurent, Montréal QC H2P 2M1
Tél: 514-384-5756; *Téléc:* 514-383-4880
presidence@alliancedesprofs.qc.ca
www.alliancedesprofs.qc.ca
Alain Marois, Président

Alliance du personnel professionnel et technique de la santé et des services sociaux (APTS)
#1050, 1111 rue Saint-Charles Ouest, Longueuil QC J4K 5G4
Tél: 450-670-2411; *Téléc:* 450-679-0107
Ligne sans frais: 866-521-2411
info@aptsq.com
www.aptsq.com
Média social:
www.youtube.com/channel/UC1srtPhluOjUv_ohjlMhM0g
www.facebook.com/SyndicatAPTS
twitter.com/APTSQ
Regrouper les organisations syndicales représentant toutes les catégories des personnes salariées professionnelles ou paramédicales travaillant dans le domaine de la santé; défendre, promouvoir et sauvegarder les intérêts collectifs des membres
Carolle Dubé, Présidente
Dominique Aubertin, Directrice générale

Alliance of Canadian Cinema, Television & Radio Artists (ACTRA) / Alliance des artistes canadiens du cinéma, de la télévision et de la radio
#300, 625 Church St., Toronto ON M4Y 2G1
Tel: 416-489-1311; *Fax:* 416-489-8076
Toll-Free: 800-387-3516
national@actra.ca
www.actra.ca
Social Media: www.youtube.com/user/ACTRANational
www.facebook.com/pages/Actra-National/125652344169446
twitter.com/ACTRAnat
To represent performers in recorded media; To negotiate & administer collective agreements which set minimum rates & basic conditions governing work; To advocate public policies designed to create strong Canadian broadcasting & film industries in order to provide work opportunities for members in their own country
Daintry Dalton, Regional Executive Director
Stephen Waddell, National Executive Director
Ferne Downey, National President
Theresa Tova, National Treasurer

Association canadienne des métiers de la truelle, section locale 100 (CTC) / Trowel Trades Canadian Association, Local 100 (CLC)
#2000, 565, rue Crémazie est, Montréal QC H2M 2V6
Tél: 514-326-3691; *Téléc:* 514-326-5562
Ligne sans frais: 888-326-3691
acmt@qc.aira.com
truellelocal100.org
Média social:
www.facebook.com/pages/ACMT-Local-100/364336873624899/
La FTQ-Construction a, bien entendu, de manière très précise le mandat de négocier les conventions collectives applicables dans les sous secteurs d'activités (industriel, commercial et institutionnel, génie civil et voirie, résidentiel) et de voir à leur application. Mais bien au-delà de ce mandat traditionnel, la FTQ-Construction veut s'assurer d'être présent dans l'ensemble des débats représentant un intérêt pour les travailleurs et les travailleuses qu'il représente.
Roger Poirier, Directeur-général

Association nationale des peintres et métiers connexes, section locale 99 (CTC) (ANPMC) / National Association of Painters & Allied Trades, Local 99 (CLC)
#200, 5275, rue Jean-Talon est, Saint-Léonard QC H1S 1L2
Tél: 514-593-5413; *Téléc:* 514-727-8331
Aider nos membres dans leur métier; faire respecter les conventions collectives sur les chantiers

Association of Allied Health Professionals: Newfoundland & Labrador (Ind.) (AAHP) / Association des professionnels unis de la santé: Terre-Neuve et Labrador (ind.)
6 Mount Carson Ave., Mount Pearl NL A1N 3K4
Tel: 709-722-3353; *Fax:* 709-722-0987
Toll-Free: 800-728-2247
info@aahp.nf.ca
www.aahp.nf.ca

Association of Canadian Film Craftspeople
Local 2020 Communications, Energy & Paperworkers Union of Canada, #108, 3993 Henning Dr., Burnaby BC V5C 6P7
Tel: 604-299-2232; *Fax:* 604-299-2243
info@acfcwest.com
www.acfcwest.com
Benoit Lamarche, President
Richard Chilton, Ssecretary/Treasurer
Greg Chambers, Business Manager

Association of Canadian Financial Officers (ACFO) / Association canadienne des agents financiers (ACAF)
#400, 2725 Queensview Dr., Ottawa ON K2B 0A1
Tel: 613-728-0695; *Fax:* 613-761-9568
Toll-Free: 877-728-0695
information@acfo-acaf.com
www.acfo-acaf.com
Social Media:
www.youtube.com/channel/UCW-ozDw9aTM6rT389Rf0C6w
linkedin.com/company/401947
twitter.com/acfoacaf
To unite in a democratic organization all public service financial administrators for which the association becomes or applies to become a bargaining agent; to serve the welfare of its members through effective collective bargaining with their employers; to obtain for members the best levels of compensation for services rendered to their employers & the best terms & conditions of employment; to protect the rights & interests of all members in all matters upon their employment or upon their relationship with their employers; to seek to maintain high professional standards & promote their professional development; to affiliate as appropriate with other associations, unions or labour organizations for the purpose of enhancing the interests of members in the attainment of their professional & bargaining goals
Milt Isaacs, President

Association of New Brunswick Professional Educators (ANBPE) / Association des éducateurs professionnels du Nouveau-Brunswick
c/o Wayne Milner, Counselling Services, NBCC Moncton, #1101A, 1234 Mountain Rd., Moncton NB E1C 8H9
To operate as a bargaining unit of the New Brunswick Union of Public & Private Employees (NBUPPE / NUPGE)
Wayne Milner, President & Director

Association professionnelle des ingénieurs du gouvernement du Québec (ind.) (APIGQ) / Association of Professional Engineers of the Government of Québec (Ind.)
Complexe Iberville Trois, #218, 2960, boul. Laurier, Québec QC G1V 4S1
Tél: 418-683-3633; *Téléc:* 418-683-6878
info@apigq.qc.ca
www.apigq.qc.ca
Pour représenter les intérêts de leurs membres
Michel Gagnon, Président

Atlantic Federation of Musicians, Local 571 (AFM, Local 571)
32B St. Margaret's Bay Rd., Halifax NS B3N 1J7
Tel: 902-479-3200; *Fax:* 902-479-1312
Toll-Free: 866-240-4809
571@bellaliant.com
www.cfm571.ca
Varun Vyas, Secretary-Treasurer

Bakery, Confectionery, Tobacco Workers & Grain Millers International Union (AFL-CIO/CLC) - Local 154-G (BCTGM)
1051 Dundas St., London ON N5W 3A4
Tel: 519-432-2024; *Fax:* 519-432-2153
bctgm154@execulink.com
www.bctgm154.ca
Social Media:
www.facebook.com/bctgm.london
twitter.com/BCTGM154G
To bring economic justice in the workplace to all workers in our jurisdiction & social justice to all workers throughout the United States & Canada.

Bakery, Confectionery, Tobacco Workers & Grain Millers International Union (AFL-CIO/CLC) - Canadian Office
Section locale 480, 293, boul. Vachon Sud, Ste-Marie QC G6E 3C1
Tel: 418-387-5313

Bricklayers, Masons Independent Union of Canada (CLC) / Syndicat indépendant des briqueteurs et des maçons du Canada (CTC)
PO Box 105, #307, 1263 Wilson Ave., Toronto ON M3M 3G3
Tel: 416-247-9841; *Fax:* 416-241-9636
localone.ca
Fernando Da Cunha, Vice President
John Meiorin, Secretary-Treasurer

British Columbia Federation of Labour (BCFL) / Fédération du travail de la Colombie-Britannique
#200, 5118 Joyce St., Vancouver BC V5R 4H1
Tel: 604-430-1421; *Fax:* 604-430-5917
bcfed@bcfed.ca
www.bcfed.com
Social Media:
www.facebook.com/bcfed
twitter.com/bcfed
To promote the interests of affiliated unions & their members; To advance the economic & social welfare of the workers of British Columbia; To act as the single voice for workers' rights in British Columbia
Jim Chorostecki, Executive Director
Jaime Matten, Director, Communications

British Columbia Government & Service Employees' Union (BCGEU) / Syndicat des fonctionnaires provinciaux et de service de la Colombie-Britannique
4911 Canada Way, Burnaby BC V5G 3W3
Tel: 604-291-9611; *Fax:* 604-291-6030
Toll-Free: 800-663-1674
www.bcgeu.ca
Judi Filion, Treasurer
Darryl Walker, President

British Columbia Principals & Vice-Principals Association (BCPVPA)
#200, 525 - 10 Ave. West, Vancouver BC V5Z 1K9
Tel: 604-689-3399; *Fax:* 604-877-5380
Toll-Free: 800-663-0432
www.bcpvpa.bc.ca
Social Media: www.youtube.com/user/BCPVPAVideos
twitter.com/bcpvpa
To provide legal and contractual services advice, organize student leadership activities, and provide professional development programs
Shelley Green, President
Kit Krieger, Executive Director

British Columbia Teacher Regulation Branch (BCCT)
#400, 2025 West Broadway, Vancouver BC V6J 1Z6
Tel: 604-660-6060; *Fax:* 604-775-4859
Toll-Free: 800-555-3684
www.bcteacherregulation.ca
To establish standards for the education, professional responsibility & competence of its members; To certify educators
Alison Hougham, Media Relations Contact

Canada Employment & Immigration Union (CEIU) / Syndicat de l'emploi et de l'immigration du Canada (SEIC)
#1204, 275 Slater St., Ottawa ON K1P 5H9
Tel: 613-236-9634; *Fax:* 613-236-7871
Toll-Free: 855-271-3848
courchs@ceiu-seic.ca
ceiu-seic.ca
To unite all the union members in the Canada Employment & Immigration Commission, the Department of Employment & Immigration & the Immigration Appeal Board, & anyone who wishes to join in a single union acting on their behalf by processing appeals & grievances; To unite all members by fostering an understanding of the fundamental differences between the interests of the members & those of the employer; To assure a union presence at the workplace through collective strength of membership
Marco Angeli, National President
Michelle Henderson, National Executive Vice-President

Canadian Actors' Equity Association (CLC) (CAEA)
44 Victoria St., 12th Fl., Toronto ON M5C 3C4
Tel: 416-867-9165; *Fax:* 416-867-9246
info@caea.com
www.caea.com
To negotiate & administer collective agreements, provides benefit plans, information & support; to act as an advocate for its membership.
Allan Teichman, President
Arden R. Ryshpan, Executive Director
Lynn McQueen, Director, Communications

Canadian Association of Professional Employees (CAPE) / Association canadienne des employés professionnels (ACEP)
World Exchange Plaza, 100 Queen St., 4th Fl., Ottawa ON K1P 1J9
Tel: 613-236-9181; *Fax:* 613-236-6017
Toll-Free: 800-265-9181
general@acep-cape.ca
www.acep-cape.ca
To negotiate & monitor collective agreement for all federal government economists, sociologists & statisticians.
Claude Poirier, President

Canadian Federal Pilots Association (CFPA) / Association des pilotes fédéraux du Canada (APFC)
#107, 18 Deakin St., Ottawa ON K2E 8B7
Tel: 613-230-5476; *Fax:* 613-230-2668
cfpa@cfpa-apfc.ca
www.cfpa-apfc.ca
Greg McConnell, Chair
Denis Brunelle, Vice-Chair
Ron Graham, Secretary-Treasurer
Greg Holbrook, Director, Operations

Canadian Federation of Nurses Unions (CFNU) / La Fédération canadienne des syndicats d'infirmières/infirmiers
2841 Riverside Dr., Ottawa ON K1V 8X7
Tel: 613-526-4661; *Fax:* 613-526-1023
Toll-Free: 800-321-9821
www.nursesunions.ca
Social Media:
www.facebook.com/NursesUnions
twitter.com/CFNU
To advance the social, economic & general welfare of its members; To act on national matters of significant concern to the Federation; To promote unity among nurses' unions & other allied health care workers who share the objectives of the CFNU; To provide a national forum to promote desirable legislation on matters of national significance; To preserve free democratic unionism & collective bargaining in Canada; To support other organizations sharing the Union's objectives
Linda Silas, President
Pauline Worsfold, Secretary-Treasurer

Canadian Labour Congress (CLC) / Congrès du travail du Canada (CTC)
National Headquarters, 2841 Riverside Dr., Ottawa ON K1V 8X7
Tel: 613-521-3400; *Fax:* 613-521-4655
www.canadianlabour.ca
Social Media: www.youtube.com/canadianlabour
www.facebook.com/clc.ctc
twitter.com/canadianlabour
To represent the interests of affiliated workers across Canada; To act as an umbrella organization for affiliated regional labour councils, provincial federations, Canadian unions, & international unions
Hassan Yussuff, President
Kerry Pither, Director, Communications

Canadian Marine Officers' Union (AFL-CIO/CLC) / Syndicat canadien des officiers de la marine marchande (FAT-COI/CTC)
9670, Notre-Dame East, Montréal QC H1L 3P8
Tel: 514-354-8321; *Fax:* 514-354-8368
info@cmou.ca
www.cmou.ca
Richard Vezina, President

Canadian Media Guild (CMG) / La Guilde canadienne des médias
#810, 310 Front St. West, Toronto ON M5V 3B5
Tel: 416-591-5333; *Fax:* 416-591-7278
Toll-Free: 800-465-4149
info@cmg.ca
www.cmg.ca
Social Media:
www.facebook.com/pages/Canadian-Media-Guild/108304249197614
To advance the interests of Guild members through collective bargaining
Carmel Smyth, National President
Karen Wirsig, Coordinator, Communications

Canadian Merchant Service Guild (CMSG) / Guilde de la marine marchande du Canada (GMMC)
#234, 9 Antares Dr., Ottawa ON K2E 7V5
Tel: 613-727-6079; *Fax:* 613-727-6079
cmsgott@on.aibn.com
www.cmsg-gmmc.ca
To promote the social, economic, cultural, educational & material interests of ships' masters, chief engineers, officers, pilots & of other persons whose employment is directly related to maritime operations
Mark Boucher, National President

Canadian National Federation of Independent Unions (CNFIU) / Fédération canadienne nationale des syndicats indépendants (FCNSI)
PO Box 416, 36 Main St. North, Campbellville ON L0P 1B0
Tel: 905-854-6868; *Fax:* 905-854-6869
Toll-Free: 800-638-9438
info@cnfiu.com
www.cnfiu.com
To encourage & promote the formation of independent unions
Ann Waller, National President
Paul Dickson, Secretary-Treasurer

Canadian Office & Professional Employees Union (COPEU) / Le Syndicat canadien des employées et employés professionnels et de bureau (SEPB)
c/o Francine Doyon, #11100, boul 565 East Cremazie, Montréal QC H2M 2W2
copesepb.ca
A national labour union organization made up of 2 regional Councils and 39 Local unions comprising tens of thousands of members in several provinces across Canada.
Serge Cadieux, National President

Canadian Postmasters & Assistants Association (CPAA) / Association canadienne des maîtres de poste et adjoints (ACMPA)
281 Queen Mary St., Ottawa ON K1K 1X1
Tel: 613-745-2095; *Fax:* 613-745-5559
mail@cpaa-acmpa.ca
cpaa-acmpa.ca
Leslie A. Schous, National President
Pierre Charbonneau, National Vice-President
Shirley L. Dressler, National Vice President
Daniel L. Maheux, National Secretary-Treasurer

Canadian Union of Postal Workers (CUPW) / Syndicat des travailleurs et travailleuses des postes (STTP)
377 Bank St., Ottawa ON K2P 1Y3
Tel: 613-236-7238; *Fax:* 613-563-7861
TTY: 613-236-9753
feedback@cupw-sttp.org
www.cupw-sttp.org
Social Media: www.youtube.com/user/cupwsttp
linkedin.com/company/canadian-union-of-postal-workers
www.facebook.com/cupwsttp
twitter.com/cupw
To be involved with various campaigns and activities which help support their members
Mike Palecek, National President
Bev Collins, National Sec.-Treas.

Canadian Union of Public Employees (CUPE) / Syndicat canadien de la fonction publique (SCFP)
1375 St. Laurent Blvd., Ottawa ON K1G 0Z7
Tel: 613-237-1590; *Fax:* 613-237-5508
Toll-Free: 844-237-1590
www.cupe.ca
Social Media:
linkedin.com/company/canadian-union-of-public-employees
www.facebook.com/cupescfp
twitter.com/cupenat
To advance the social, economic, & general welfare of both active & retired employees; To promote required legislation
Mark Hancock, National President
Charles Fleury, National Secretary-Treasurer

Centrale des syndicats démocratiques (CSD)
#600, 900, av de Bourgogne, Québec QC G1X 3E3
Tél: 514-899-1070; *Ligne sans frais:* 866-651-0050
www.csd.qc.ca
Média social: www.facebook.com/CSDCentrale
twitter.com/CSDCentrale
François Vaudreuil, Président

Centrale des syndicats du Québec (CSQ)
9405, rue Sherbrooke est, Montréal QC H1L 6P3
Tél: 514-356-8888; *Téléc:* 514-356-9999
Ligne sans frais: 800-465-0897
communications@csq.qc.net
www.csq.qc.net
Média social: www.youtube.com/user/csqvideos
www.facebook.com/lacsq
twitter.com/csq_centrale
De regrouper dans un même mouvement des personnels salariés ayant des aspirations et des intérêts communs et de promouvoir leurs intérêts professionnels, sociaux, et économiques; dans cette perspective, elle travaille à établir un environnement syndical et professionnel exempt de harcèlement sexuel et favorise la vie syndicale par le partage des ressources; elle intervient au soutien direct de ses affiliés et assure différents services liés aux relations de travail et à la vie professionnelle (recherche dans le domaine de l'éducation, etc.)
Louise Chabot, Présidente

Compensation Employees' Union (Ind.) (CEU) / Syndicat des employés d'indemnisation (ind.)
#120, 13775 Commerce Pkwy., Richmond BC V6V 2V4
Tel: 604-278-4050; *Fax:* 604-278-5002
www.ceu.bc.ca
Social Media:
www.facebook.com/313873122023339
twitter.com/CEUOurUnion
The Compensation Employees' Union was certified in 1974. The CEU is an all inclusive bargaining unit representing all workers at the Workers' Compensation Board that are not excluded by law. The membership ranges from cleaners, support positions, technicial positions, officer level positions, physiologists, and lawyers.
Sandra Wright, President
Candace Philpitt, Secretary

Confédération des syndicats nationaux (CSN) / Confederation of National Trade Unions
1601, av De Lorimier, Montréal QC H2K 4M5
Tél: 514-598-2271; *Téléc:* 514-598-2052
sesyndiquer@csn.qc.ca
www.csn.qc.ca
Média social: www.facebook.com/LaCSN
twitter.com/laCSN
La Confédération limite ses activités principalement au Québec, quoique certains locaux soient établis hors de la province; comprend 9 fédérations, 13 conseils centraux et 2 800 syndicats
Pierre Patry, Trésorier
Jacques Létourneau, Présidente
Jean Lortie, Secrétaire générale

Congress of Union Retirees Canada (CURC) / Association des syndicalistes retraités du Canada (ASRC)
2841 Riverside Dr., Ottawa ON K1V 8X7
Tel: 613-526-7422; *Fax:* 613-521-4655
curc.clc-ctc.ca
Social Media:
www.facebook.com/315702295180775
twitter.com/UnionRetirees
To ensure that the concerns of senior citizens & union retirees are heard across Canada
Pat Kerwin, President
Len Hope, First Vice-President
Doug MacPherson, Second Vice-President
Bob McGarry, Secretary
Betty Ann Bushell, Treasurer

Construction Maintenance & Allied Workers (CMAW)
1450 Kootenay St., Vancouver BC V5K 4R1
Tel: 604-437-0471; *Fax:* 604-437-1110
reception@cmaw.ca
www.cmaw.ca
Social Media:
twitter.com/CMAWunion
The objects of the Council are to organize workers; encourage an apprenticeship system & higher standard of skill; to develop, improve & enforce the program & standards of occupational safety & health; to cultivate friendship; to develop good public relations with the community; to assist each other to secure employment & to reduce the hours of daily labour
Jan Noster, President
Paul Nedelec, Secretary-Treasurer
Kim Ballantyne, Office Administrator

Customs & Immigration Union (CIU) / Syndicat des douanes et de l'immigration (SDI)
1741 Woodward Dr., Ottawa ON K2C 0P9
Tel: 613-723-8008; *Fax:* 613-723-7895
web@ciu-sdi.ca
www.ciu-sdi.ca
Social Media:
www.facebook.com/ciu-sdi
twitter.com/ciusdi_en
To address CIU-SDI members' concerns on a timely basis
Jean-Pierre Fortin, National President
Jason McMichael, First National Vice-President
Michelle Tranche-Montagne, Contact, Communications

Employees' Union of St. Mary's of the Lake Hospital - CNFIU Local 3001 / Association des employés, l'Hôpital Saint Mary's of the Lake (FCNSI)
340 Union St., Kingston ON K7L 5A2
Tel: 613-544-5220; *Fax:* 613-544-8527

Fédération autonome du collégial (ind.) (FAC) / Autonomous Federation of Collegial Staff (Ind.)
#400, 1259, rue Berri, Montréal QC H2L 4C7
Tél: 514-848-9977; *Téléc:* 514-848-0166
Ligne sans frais: 800-701-1369
Défendre et développer les intérêts économiques, sociaux, pédagogiques et professionnels du personnel enseignant des cégeps; défendre le droit d'association, la libre négociation et la liberté d'action syndicale; négocier et s'assurer de l'application des conventions collectives; de représenter ses syndicats affiliés partout où leurs intérêts sont débattus.
Alain Dion, Président

Fédération CSN - Construction (CSN) / CNTU Federation - Construction (CNTU)
2100, boul de Maisonneuve Est, 4e étage, Montréal QC H2K 4S1
Tél: 514-598-2044; *Téléc:* 514-598-2040
www.csnconstruction.qc.ca
Média social: www.facebook.com/csnconstruction
Pour défendre les droits de leurs membres et de leur assurer de bonnes conditions de travail
Pierre Brassard, Président
Karyne Prégent, Secrétaire général

Fédération de l'industrie manufacturière (FIM-CSN)
#204, 2100, boul de Maisonneuve est, Montréal QC H2K 4S1
Tél: 514-529-4937; *Téléc:* 514-529-4935
Ligne sans frais: 877-529-4977
fim@csn.qc.ca
www.fim.csn.qc.ca
Média social: www.facebook.com/FIMCSN
Alain Lampron, Président
Kathy Beaulieu, Secrétaire-Trésorier

Fédération de la santé et des services sociaux (FSSS)
1601, av de Lorimier, Montréal QC H2K 4M5
Tél: 514-598-2210; *Téléc:* 514-598-2223
www.fsss.qc.ca
Média social: www.youtube.com/user/f3scsn
www.facebook.com/FSSSCSN
twitter.com/FSSSCSN
De promouvoir et sauvegarder la santé, la sécurité et les intérêts des personnes employées des établissements affiliés ou en voie d'affiliation; de représenter ses membres auprès de la Confédération des syndicats nationaux en lui soumettant toutes questions d'intérêt général; de représenter ses membres, de concert avec le CSN, partout où les intérêts généraux des travailleuses et travailleurs le justifient; d'aider à conclure, en faveur des syndicats affiliés, des conventions collectives de travail et en favoriser l'application; de collaborer à l'éducation des travailleuses et travailleurs et à la formation de responsables et militantes et militants syndicaux; d'assurer les services à ses syndicats affiliés; de favoriser et d'établir des liens inter-syndicaux avec les autres travailleuses et travailleurs dans le secteur public et para-public et dans le secteur privé du Québec et du Canada
Jeff Begley, Président
Denyse Paradis, Secrétaire-trésorière

Fédération des employées et employés de services publics inc. (CSN) (FEESP) / Federation of Public Service Employees Inc. (CNTU)
1601, av de Lorimier, Montréal QC H2K 4M5
Tél: 514-598-2231; *Téléc:* 514-598-2398
feesp.courrier@csn.qc.ca
www.feesp.csn.qc.ca
Média social: www.facebook.com/feespcsn
Il est composé de quatre personnes élues, du coordonnateur ou coordonnatrice des services et de la personne déléguée syndicale.
Nathalie Arguin, Secéraire-générale

Fédération des enseignants de cégeps
9405, rue Sherbrooke Est, Montréal QC H1L 6P3
Tél: 514-356-8888; *Téléc:* 514-354-8535
Ligne sans frais: 800-465-0897
fec@csq.qc.net
www.fec.csq.qc.net
Média social: www.facebook.com/feccsq
twitter.com/feccsq
De protéger les intérêts de ses membres
Mario Beauchemin, President

Fédération des intervenantes en petite enfance du Québec (FIPEQ)
9405, rue Sherbrooke Est, Montréal QC H1L 6P3
Tél: 514-356-8888; *Téléc:* 514-356-9999
Ligne sans frais: 800-465-0897
fipeq@csq.qc.net
La Fédération des intervenantes en petite enfance du Québec (FIPEQ) est vouée à la promotion de la profession, à la défense

des droits et des intérêts ainsi qu'à l'amélioration des conditions de vie de toutes les intervenantes, tant travailleuses autonomes que salariées, oeuvrant au service des centres de la petite enfance.
Kathleen Courville, Présidente

Fédération des médecins résidents du Québec inc. (ind.) (FMRQ) / Québec Federation of Residents (Ind.)
#510, 630, rue Sherbrooke ouest, Montréal QC H3A 1E4
Tél: 514-282-0256; *Téléc:* 514-282-0471
Ligne sans frais: 800-465-0215
fmrq@fmrq.qc.ca
www.fmrq.qc.ca
Média social: www.facebook.com/fmrqc
D'étudier, de défendre et de développer des intérêts économiques, sociaux, moraux et scientifiques des syndicats et des leurs membres.
Jean Gouin, Executive Director
Patrick Labelle, Administrative Director

Fédération des policiers et policières municipaux du Québec (ind.) (FPMQ) / Québec Federation of Policemen (Ind.)
7955, boul Louis-Hippolyte-La Fontaine, Anjou QC H1K 4E4
Tél: 514-356-3321; *Téléc:* 514-356-1158
Ligne sans frais: 800-361-0321
info@fpmq.org
www.fpmq.org
Média social: www.facebook.com/policiersMun
twitter.com/policiersmun
L'étude et la défense des intérêts économiques, professionnels, sociaux et moraux de ses associations-membres et de tous les policiers que celles-ci regroupent.
Denis Côté, Président
Luc Lalonde, Directeur exécutif

Fédération des professionnèles (FPCSN) / Quebec Federation of Managers & Professional Salaried Workers (CNTU)
1601, av de Lorimier, Montréal QC H2K 4M5
Tél: 514-598-2143; *Téléc:* 514-598-2491
Ligne sans frais: 888-633-2143
www.fpcsn.qc.ca
Regroupe plus de 7000 professionnèles oeuvrant dans différents secteurs d'activités: santé et services sociaux, organismes gouvernementaux, éducation, secteur municipal, médecines alternatives, secteur juridique, intégration à l'emploi, professionnèles autonomes, organismes communautaires, etc
Michel Tremblay, Président
Lucie Dufour, Secrétaire générale

Fédération des professionnelles et professionnels de l'éducation du Québec (FPPE) / Québec Federation of Professional Employees in Education
9405, rue Sherbrooke est, Montréal QC H1L 6P3
Tél: 514-356-0505; *Téléc:* 514-356-1324
infos@fppe.qc.ca
www.fppe.qc.ca
Média social: www.youtube.com/user/FPPECSQ
twitter.com/FPPECSQ
De promouvoir et de développer les intérêts professionnels, sociaux et économiques des professionnelles et professionnels de l'éducation du Québec ainsi que de défendre les droits fondamentaux compris à l'intérieur des chartes, le droit d'association, le droit à la libre négociation et le droit à la liberté d'action syndicale; de représenter ses syndicats affiliés à un niveau national; d'orienter et de coordonner la représentation de ses syndicats affiliés auprès des instances de la Centrale; de diriger et de coordonner la négociation des conventions collectives; de concilier les conflits qui peuvent naître entre les syndicats affiliés; de mettre à la disposition des syndicats affiliés et de leurs membres des services de qualité en matière de négociation et d'application des conditions de travail et des droits sociaux, d'information et de formation syndicale
Johanne Pomerleau, Président
Jean-Marie Comeau, Vice-présidente

Fédération des Syndicats de l'Enseignement (FSE)
CP 100, 320, rue Saint-Joseph est, Québec QC G1K 9E7
Tél: 418-649-8888; *Téléc:* 418-649-1914
Ligne sans frais: 877-850-0897
fse@csq.qc.net
www.fse.qc.net
Média social: www.youtube.com/user/z00lantp
www.facebook.com/FSECSQ
twitter.com/FSECSQ
Promouvoir les intérêts professionnels, sociaux et économiques du personnel enseignant des commissions scolaires; orienter et coordonner la représentation des syndicats affiliés auprès des instances de la Centrale et de représenter les syndicats affiliés là où leurs intérêts et leurs droits sont débattus; assumer prioritairement la responsabilité des négociations, les aspects sectoriels des relations du travail et de l'action juridique ainsi que les questions professionnelles à caractère sectoriel; favoriser la concertation entre les syndicats affiliés et concilier les divergences qui pourraient naître entre eux.
Laurier Caron, Directeur général

Fédération des syndicats de la santé et des services sociaux (F4S-CSQ)
9405, rue Sherbrooke est, Montréal QC H1L 6P3
Tél: 514-356-8888; *Téléc:* 514-356-2845
info@f4s.gs
www.f4s.gs
S'assurer que ses membres travaillent dans des conditions de sécurité; de représenter les intérêts de ses membres au cours des conventions collectives
Claude Demontigny, Président

Fédération des travailleurs et travailleises du Québec (FTQ) / Québec Federation of Labour
#12100, 565, boul Crémazie Est, Montréal QC H2M 2W3
Tél: 514-383-8000; *Téléc:* 514-383-8004
Ligne sans frais: 877-897-0057
www.ftq.qc.ca
Média social: www.facebook.com/laFTQ
twitter.com/FTQnouvelles
Michel Arsenault, Président

Fédération des travailleurs et travailleuses du Québec - Construction
#2900, 565, boul Crémazie est, Montréal QC H2M 2V6
Tél: 514-381-7300; *Téléc:* 514-381-5173
Ligne sans frais: 877-666-4060
www.ftqconstruction.org
Média social: www.youtube.com/user/FTQconstruction
www.facebook.com/Construction
twitter.com/FTQConstruction
On peut facilement affirmer que la mission d'une association syndicale est quasi sans limite. La FTQ-Construction a, bien entendu, de manière très précise le mandat de négocier les conventions collectives applicables dans les sous secteurs d'activités (industriel, commercial et institutionnel, génie civil et voirie, résidentiel) et de voir à leur application. Mais bien au-delà de ce mandat traditionnel, la FTQ-Construction veut s'assurer d'être présent dans l'ensemble des débats représentant un intérêt pour les travailleurs et les travailleuses qu'il représente.
Yves Ouellette, Directeur général

Fédération du commerce (CSN)
1601, av De Lorimier, Montréal QC H2K 4M5
Tél: 514-598-2421; *Téléc:* 514-598-2304
infofc@csn.qc.ca
www.fc-csn.ca
Serge Fournier, Président

Fédération du personnel de l'enseignement privé (FPEP)
9405, rue Sherbrooke est, Montréal QC H1L 6P3
Tél: 514-356-8888; *Téléc:* 514-356-1866
fpep@csq.qc.net
www.fpep.csq.qc.net
Francine Lamoureux, Présidente
Martine Dion, Première Vice-Présidente
Denis Benoit, Deuxième Vice-Président
Stéphane Lévis, Secrétaire
Marie-Josée Noël, Trésorerie

Fédération du personnel de soutien scolaire (CSQ) (FPSS) / Federation of Support Staff
9405, rue Sherbrooke est, 4e étage, Montréal QC H1L 6P3
Tél: 514-356-8888; *Téléc:* 514-493-3697
webfpss@csq.qc.net
www.fpss.csq.qc.net
Média social: www.facebook.com/fpss.csq
twitter.com/FPSSCSQ
Le seul regroupement au Québec représentant exclusivement du personnel de soutien scolaire des écoles et des centres. Elle est affiliée à la Centrale des syndicats du Québec (CSQ)
Diane Cinq-Mars, Présidente

Fédération du personnel du loisir, de la culture et du communautaire (CEQ) (FPLCC)
9405, rue Sherbrooke est, Montréal QC H1L 6P3
Tél: 514-356-8888; *Téléc:* 418-649-8888
Ligne sans frais: 877-850-0897
fplcc@csq.qc.net
www.csq.qc.net
Regroupe les syndicats qui représentent le personnel oeuvrant dans les secteurs du loisir, du sport, de la culture du tourisme et du communautaire
Réjean Parent, Président

Fédération du personnel professionnel des collèges (FPPC)
9405, rue Sherbrooke est, Montréal QC H1L 6P3
Tél: 514-356-8888; *Téléc:* 514-356-3377
fppc@csq.qc.net
www.fppc.csq.qc.net
Média social: www.facebook.com/166365983458347
twitter.com/fppc_csq
Défendre et promouvoir la fonction professionnelle dans les collèges
Bernard Bérubé, Président

Fédération du personnel professionnel des universités et de la recherche (FPPU)
873, rue du Haut-Boc, Trois-Rivières QC G9A 4W7
Tél: 819-840-4544; *Téléc:* 819-840-4294
info@fppu.ca
www.fppu.ca
Média social: www.facebook.com/518734318146156
La FPPU est la seule organisation syndicale regroupant exclusivement le personnel professionnel des universités et de la recherche

Fédération indépendante des syndicats autonomes (FISA) / Independent Federation of Autonomous Unions
#201, 1778, boul Wilfrid-Hamel, Québec QC G1N 3Y8
Tél: 418-529-4571; *Téléc:* 418-529-4695
Ligne sans frais: 800-407-3472
info@fisa.ca
www.fisa.ca
Fournir des services d'organisation, de conseils, de représentation et d'aide financière aux associations membres.
Jean Gagnon, Président

Fédération nationale des communications (CSN) (FNC) / National Federation of Communication Workers (CNTU)
1601, av de Lorimier, Montréal QC H2K 4M5
Tél: 514-598-2132; *Téléc:* 514-598-2431
fnc@fncom.org
www.fncom.org
La défense des intérêts économiques, sociaux, politiques et professionnels des membres.
Pierre Roger, Président

Fraternité interprovinciale des ouvriers en électricité (CTC) (FIPOE) / Interprovincial Brotherhood of Electrical Workers (CLC)
10200, boul Golf, Montréal QC H1J 2Y7
Tél: 514-385-3476; *Téléc:* 514-385-9298
Ligne sans frais: 855-453-4763
info@fipoe.org
www.fipoe.org
Média social: www.youtube.com/fipoeorg
www.facebook.com/FIPOE
twitter.com/fipoeorg
Regrouper des électriciens de construction, des installateurs de systèmes d'alarmes et des monteurs de ligne
Styve Grenier, Président
Arnold Guérin, Directeur général

Fraternité nationale des forestiers et travailleurs d'usine (CTC) / National Brotherhood of Foresters & Industrial Workers (CLC)
Locale 9, #8, rue Père Divet, Sept-Iles QC G4R 3N2
Tél: 418-968-3008
L'étude, la sauvegarde et le développement des intérêts économiques, et l'application de conventions collectives
Yves Guérette, Président

Government Services Union (GSU) / Syndicat des services gouvernementaux
#705, 233 Gilmour St., Ottawa ON K2P 0P2
Tel: 613-560-4395; *Fax:* 613-230-6774
www.gsu-ssg.ca
Their members provide compensation, audit, procurement, disposal telecommunications and informatics, translation, real property and reciever general services to some 100 federal government departments and agencies. They also provide information about government programmes and research the opinions of Canadians.
Donna Lackie, President

Grain Services Union (CLC) (GSU) / Syndicat des services du grain (CTC)
2334 McIntyre St., Regina SK S4P 2S2
Tel: 306-522-6686; *Fax:* 306-565-3430
Toll-Free: 866-522-6686
gsu.regina@sasktel.net
www.gsu.ca

They represent Saskatchewan Wheat Pool Workers and represent members working for a variety of companies within Canada.
Carolyn Illerbrun, President
Hugh J. Wagner, Secretary/Manager

Health Sciences Association of Alberta (HSAA) / Association des sciences de la santé de l'Alberta (ind.)
10212 - 112 St., Edmonton AB T5K 1M4
Tel: 780-488-0168; *Fax:* 780-488-0534
Toll-Free: 800-252-7904
www.hsaa.ca
Social Media: www.facebook.com/349561555109272
twitter.com/HSAAlberta
To conduct activities as a labour union to enhance the quality of life for HSAA members & society
Elisabeth Ballermann, President
Lynette McAvoy, Executive Director

Health Sciences Association of Saskatchewan (HSAS) / Association des sciences de la santé de la Saskatchewan (ind.)
#42, 1736 Quebec Ave., Saskatoon SK S7K 1V9
Tel: 306-955-3399; *Fax:* 306-955-3396
Toll-Free: 888-565-3399
hsasstoon@hsas.ca
www.hsas.ca
Social Media: www.youtube.com/user/HealthScienceSask
www.facebook.com/124779960928913
To conduct activities as an independent union representing its members who are health sciences professionals in Saskatchewan
Karen Wasylenko, President
Bill Feldbruegge, Vice-President
Maureen Kraemer, Secretary

Hospital Employees' Union (HEU) / Syndicat des employés d'hôpitaux
5000 North Fraser Way, Burnaby BC V5J 5M3
Tel: 604-438-5000; *Fax:* 604-739-1510
Toll-Free: 800-663-5813
info@heu.org
www.heu.org
Social Media: twitter.com/HospEmpUnion
To unite & associate together all employees employed in hospital, medical or related work for the purpose of securing concerted action in whatever may be regarded as conducive to their best interests; to embrace the concept of equality of treatment for all in hospital, medical or related employment, with respect to wages & job opportunities, recognizing their obligation to provide high-quality care; to defend & preserve the right of all persons to high standards of medical & hospital treatment
Victor Elkins, President
Bonnie Pearson, Secretary & Business Manager

International Longshore & Warehouse Union (CLC) / Syndicat international des débardeurs et magasiniers (CTC)
1188 Franklin St., 4th Fl., San Francisco CA 94109 USA
Tel: 415-775-0533; *Fax:* 415-775-1302
www.ilwu.org
To represent the rights of their members, who work in the warehouse industry
Robert McEllrath, President

International Union of Bricklayers & Allied Craftworkers (AFL-CIO/CFL) (BAC) / Union internationale des briqueteurs et métiers connexes (FAT-COI/FCT)
620 F St. NW, Washington DC 20004 USA
Tel: 202-783-3788; *Toll-Free:* 888-880-8222
askbac@bacweb.org
www.bacweb.org
Social Media: www.youtube.com/user/BACInternational
www.facebook.com/IUBAC
twitter.com/IUBAC
To improve the quality of life of their members
James Boland, President

International Union, United Automobile, Aerospace & Agricultural Implement Workers of America (UAW) / Syndicat international des travailleurs unis de l'automobile, de l'aérospatiale et de l'outillage agricole d'Amérique
8000 East Jefferson Ave., Detroit MI 48214 USA
Tel: 313-926-5000; *Toll-Free:* 800-243-8829
www.uaw.org
Social Media: www.youtube.com/uaw
www.facebook.com/uaw.union
twitter.com/uaw
To act as the collective bargaining body for its members, negotiating for wages & benefits.
Dennis Williams, President
Gary Casteel, Sec.-Treas.

Manitoba Association of Health Care Professionals (MAHCP) / Association des professionnels de la santé du Manitoba
#101, 1500 Notre Dame Ave., Winnipeg MB R3E 0P9
Tel: 204-772-0425; *Fax:* 204-775-6829
info@mahcp.ca
mahcp.com
To protect, advocate for & advance the rights of its members through labour relations activities.
Bob Moroz, President

Manitoba Federation of Labour / Fédération du travail du Manitoba
#303, 275 Broadway, Winnipeg MB R3C 4M6
Tel: 204-947-1400; *Fax:* 204-943-4276
admin@mfl.mb.ca
www.mfl.mb.ca
Social Media: www.youtube.com/user/MFLabour/featured
www.facebook.com/ManitobaLabour
twitter.com/MFLabour
To advance economic & social welfare of working people in Manitoba; To encourage workers to vote & exercise full rights & responsibilities
Kevin Rebeck, President
Sylvia Farley, Executive Director

Manitoba Government & General Employees' Union (MGEU)
#601, 275 Broadway, Winnipeg MB R3C 4M6
Tel: 204-982-6438; *Fax:* 204-942-2146
Toll-Free: 866-982-6438
TTY: 204-982-6599
resourcecentre@mgeu.ca
www.mgeu.ca
Social Media: www.youtube.com/user/mgeulogin
www.facebook.com/174238299256105
twitter.com/MGEUnion
Michelle Gawronsky, President
Debbie O'Hare, Executive Assistant

Maritime Fishermen's Union (CLC) (MFU) / Union des pêcheurs des Maritimes (CTC) (UPM)
408 Main St., Shediac NB E4P 2G1
Tel: 506-532-2485; *Fax:* 506-532-2487
shediac@mfu-upm.com
www.mfu-upm.com
To maintain a sustainable inshore fishery & defend the principal of the fishermen/owner-operator.
Christian Brun, Executive Secretary

Mount Royal Staff Association (MRSA)
#W301, 4825 Mount Royal Gate SW, Calgary AB T3E 6K6
Tel: 403-440-5993; *Fax:* 403-440-6763
mrsa@mtroyal.ca
www.mrssa.ca
To ensure Mount Royal University staff work in a fair environment
Baset Zarrugr, President

National Health Union (NHU) / Syndicat national de la santé (SNS)
#1202, 233 Gilmour St., Ottawa ON K2P 0P2
Tel: 613-237-2732; *Fax:* 613-237-6954
Toll-Free: 888-454-6305
www.nhu-sns.ca
To protect their members by ensuring safe working conditions & fair wage rights & benefits
Tony Tilley, President

National Union of Public & General Employees (NUPGE)
15 Auriga Dr., Nepean ON K2E 1B7
Tel: 613-228-9800; *Fax:* 613-228-9801
nupge.ca
A family of 11 component unions that works to deliver public services of every kind to the citizens of their home provinces.
James Clancy, National President

Native Brotherhood of British Columbia (NBBC) / Fraternité des Indiens de la Colombie-Britannique
#110, 100 Park Royal South, West Vancouver BC V7T 1A2
Tel: 604-913-3372
nativebrotherhood.ca
To advance the social, spiritual, economic & physical conditions of its members, including higher standards of education, health & living conditions; to cooperate with other organizations which concern themselves with the advancement of Indian welfare; focus is on capacity building, including fisheries, marine resources, tourism & eco-tourism, forestry & other resources with economic potential & opportunities

Natural Resources Union (NRU)
#600, 233 Gilmour St., Ottawa ON K2P 0P2
Tel: 613-560-4378; *Fax:* 613-233-7012
www.nru-srn.com
Mike Sargent, National President

New Brunswick Federation of Labour (NBFL) / Fédération des travailleurs et travailleuses du Nouveau-Brunswick
#314, 96 Norwood Ave., Moncton NB E1C 6L9
Tel: 506-857-2125; *Fax:* 506-383-1597
info@fednb.ca
www.nbfl-fttnb.ca
Social Media: www.facebook.com/NewBrunswickFederationOfLabour
twitter.com/NBFL_FTTNB
To act as the central voice of labour in New Brunswick; To build solidarity & support between unions; To advance the economic & social welfare of New Brunswick's workers
Patrick Colford, President
John Gagnon, First Vice-President

Newfoundland & Labrador Association of Public & Private Employees (NAPE)
PO Box 8100, 330 Portugal Cove Pl., St. John's NL A1B 3M9
Tel: 709-754-0700; *Fax:* 709-754-0726
Toll-Free: 800-563-4442
www.nape.nf.ca
The largest union in Newfoundland & Labrador
Bert Blundon, Secretary-Treasurer
Carol Furlong, President
Arlene Sedlickas, General Vice-President

Newfoundland & Labrador Federation of Labour (NLFL) / Fédération du travail de Terre-Neuve et du Labrador
NAPE Bldg., PO Box 8597, Stn. A, 330 Portugal Cove Pl., 2nd Fl., St. John's NL A1B 3P2
Tel: 709-754-1660; *Fax:* 709-754-1220
fed@nlfl.nf.ca
www.nlfl.nf.ca
Social Media: www.youtube.com/user/NLLABOUR
www.facebook.com/189773034381902
twitter.com/NLFL_labour
To represent the interests of its members
Mary Shortall, President
Linda Rideout, Executive Secretary

Northern Territories Federation of Labour / Fédération du travail des Territoires du Nord
PO Box 2787, Yellowknife NT X1A 2R1
Tel: 867-873-3695; *Fax:* 867-873-6979
Toll-Free: 888-873-1956
ntfl@yk.com
www.ntfl.ca
Social Media: www.facebook.com/NTFed
To promote the interests of its members
Gayla Thunstrom, Acting President

Nova Scotia Federation of Labour / Fédération du travail de la Nouvelle-Écosse
#225, 3700 Kempt Rd., Halifax NS B3K 4X8
Tel: 902-454-6735; *Fax:* 902-454-7671
nsfl@ns.aliantzinc.ca
www.nsfl.ns.ca
To speak on behalf of & represent the interests of organized & unorganized workers; to promote decent wages & working conditions, improved health & safety laws & lobbies for fair taxes & strong social programs; to work for social equality & to end racism & discrimination.
Rick Clarke, President
Kyle Buott, Secretary-Treasurer

Nova Scotia Government & General Employees Union (NSGEU) / Syndicat de la fonction publique de la Nouvelle-Écosse
255 John Savage Ave., Dartmouth NS B3B 0J3
Tel: 902-424-4063; *Fax:* 902-424-2111
Toll-Free: 877-556-7438
www.nsgeu.ns.ca
Joan Jessome, President
Keiren Tompkins, Executive Director

Nova Scotia Union of Public & Private Employees (CCU) (NSUPE) / Syndicat des employés du secteur public de la Nouvelle-Écosse (CCU)
#402A, 7020 Mumford Rd., Halifax NS B3L 4S9
Tel: 902-422-9495; *Fax:* 902-429-7655
www.nsupe.ca
To better & protect the livelihood and the social and economic well-being of its members, their families and fellow citizens.
Joe Kaiser, President
Claudia MacFarlane, Vice-President

Nunavut Employees Union (NEU)
PO Box 869, Iqaluit NU X0A 0H0
Tel: 867-979-4209; *Fax:* 867-979-4522
Toll-Free: 877-243-4424
reception@neu.ca
www.neu.ca
The Nunavut Employees Union represents the interests of the employees of the Government of Nunavut, the Northwest Territories Power Corporation who live in Nunavut, Workers Compensation Board in Nunavut, Nunavut Housing Corporation, and the unionized employees of Nunavut municipalities and Housing Associations. Most of our members work for the Government of Nunavut and live all across the territory. Others belong to Canada Labour Code bargaining units representing Housing Associations and Authorities, Hamlet and town employees, and support staff in schools. NEU members are social workers and nurses, health care professionals, power plant workers, security guards, hamlet bylaw officers, renewable resource officers, engineers, and many more.
Bill Fennell, President
Brian Boutilier, Executive Director

Office & Professional Employees International Union (AFL-CIO/CLC) / Union internationale des employés professionnels et de bureau (FAT-COI/CTC)
80 - 8 Ave., 20th Fl., New York NY 10011 USA
Tel: 800-346-7348
www.opeiu.org
Michael Goodwin, President

Ontario Federation of Labour (OFL) / Fédération du travail de l'Ontario
#202, 15 Gervais Dr., Toronto ON M3C 1Y8
Tel: 416-441-2731; *Fax:* 416-441-0722
Toll-Free: 800-668-9138
TTY: 416-443-6305
info@ofl.ca
www.ofl.ca
Social Media:
linkedin.com/company/ontario-federation-of-labour
www.facebook.com/OFLabour
twitter.com/OFLabour
To represent the interests of organized workers in Ontario; To provide support services to its affiliated local unions & labour councils
Chris Buckley, President
Patty Coates, Sec.-Treas.

Ontario Professional Fire Fighters Association (OPFFA) / Association des pompiers professionnels de l'Ontario (ind.)
292 Plains Rd. East, Burlington ON L7T 2C6
Tel: 905-681-7111; *Fax:* 905-681-1489
www.opffa.org
Fred LeBlanc, President
Mark McKinnon, Executive Vice-President
Barry Quinn, Secretary-Treasurer
Jeff Braun-Jackson, Office Manager & Researcher

Ontario Public Service Employees Union (OPSEU) / Syndicat des employées et employés de la fonction publique de l'Ontario
100 Lesmill Rd., Toronto ON M3B 3P8
Tel: 416-443-8888; *Fax:* 416-443-9670
Toll-Free: 800-268-7376
opseu@opseu.org
www.opseu.org
Social Media: www.youtube.com/user/OPSEUSEFPO
www.facebook.com/OPSEU?v=app_4949752878
twitter.com/OPSEU
To negotiate collective agreements; to conduct membership education; to lobby governments to maintain & improve public services; to defend the principle of social unionism by speaking out on public policy issues such as taxes, free trade, privatization, health care, social services, occupational health & safety, & employment equity.
Warren (Smokey) Thomas, President

Operative Plasterers' & Cement Masons' International Association of the US & Canada (AFL-CIO/CFL) - Canadian Office
Varette Bldg., #1902, 130 Albert St., Ottawa ON K1P 5G4
Tel: 613-236-0653; *Fax:* 613-230-5138
www.buildingtrades.ca
Social Media: www.youtube.com/user/Buildingtrades12
twitter.com/CDNTrades
To represent the interests of those employed in the building, construction, fabrication & maintenance industry in Canada ensuring safe working conditions
Robert Blakely, Canadian Operating Officer

Prince Edward Island Federation of Labour / Fédération du travail de l'Île-du-Prince-Édouard
326 Patterson Dr., Charlottetown PE C1A 8K4
Tel: 902-368-3068
peifed@pei.aibn.com
www.peifl.ca
Carl Pursey, President

Prince Edward Island Union of Public Sector Employees / Syndicat de la fonction publique de l'Île-du-Prince-Édouard
4 Enman Cres., Charlottetown PE C1E 1E6
Tel: 902-892-5335; *Fax:* 902-569-8186
Toll-Free: 800-897-8773
peiupse@peiupse.ca
www.peiupse.ca
To represent & advocate on behalf of its members in order to ensure safe & fair working conditions
Debbie Bovyer, President

Professional Association of Foreign Service Officers (Ind.) (PAFSO) / L'Association professionnelle des agents du service extérieur (ind.) (APASE)
#412, 47 Clarence St., Ottawa ON K1N 9K1
Tel: 613-241-1391; *Fax:* 613-241-5911
info@pafso.com
www.pafso.com
Ron Cochrane, Executive Director

Professional Association of Internes & Residents of Newfoundland (PAIRN) / Association professionnelle des internes et résidents de Terre-Neuve
c/o Student Affairs, Health Sciences Complex, Memorial University, #2713, 300 Prince Philip Dr., St. John's NL A1B 3V6
Tel: 709-777-7118; *Fax:* 709-777-6968
pairn@mun.ca
www.pairn.ca
To collaborate with local & national health care organizations to advocate on behalf of internes, resident physicians, & fellows of Newfoundland & Labrador; To advocate for the acknowledgement of the resident's role in medical education
Sarah Kean, President
Robert Mercer, Vice-President
Heather O'Reilly, Secretary
Erika Hansford, Treasurer

Professional Association of Interns & Residents of Saskatchewan (PAIRS) / Association professionnelle des internes et résidents de la Saskatchewan (ind.)
C Wing, Royal University Hospital, PO Box 23, #5687, 103 Hospital Dr., 5th Fl., Saskatoon SK S7N 0W8
Tel: 306-655-2134; *Fax:* 306-655-2134
pairs.sk@usask.ca
www.saskresidents.ca
To represent resident physicians of Saskatchewan at the university & hospital levels, as well as provincially & nationally; To improve education, salaries, & other benefits for resident physicians
Paul Dhillon, President
Dilip Gill, Vice-President
Laura Weins, Secretary-Treasurer
Kristin Johnson, Executive Director

Professional Association of Residents & Interns of Manitoba (PARIM) / Association professionnelle des résidents et internes du Manitoba
#AD107, 720 McDermot Ave., Winnipeg MB R3E 0T3
Tel: 204-787-3673; *Fax:* 204-787-2692
parim.office@gmail.com
www.parim.org
To represent the concerns of all residents & interns in Manitoba; To advocate for the well-being of residents & interns; To promote quality medical education & excellent patient care
Elizabeth Berg, Co-President
Markus Ziesmann, Co-President
Debarsi Das, Vice-President, Communications

Professional Association of Residents in the Maritime Provinces (PARI-MP) / Association professionnelle des résidents des provinces maritimes
Halifax Professional Centre, #460, 5991 Spring Garden Rd., Halifax NS B3H 1Y6
Tel: 902-404-3597; *Toll-Free:* 877-972-7467
www.parimp.ca
To represent the interests of resident physicians who train at Dalhousie University; To improve the well-being & working conditions of residents in the Maritimes; To advocate on the behalf of residents
Philip Davis, President
Sandi Carew Flemming, Executive Director

Professional Association of Residents of Alberta (PARA) / Association professionnelle des résidents de l'Alberta
Garneau Professional Center, #340, 11044 - 82 Ave., Edmonton AB T6G 0J2
Tel: 780-432-1749; *Fax:* 780-432-1778
Toll-Free: 877-375-7272
para@para-ab.ca
www.para-ab.ca
To represent physicians completing further training in residency programs; To promote excellence in education & patient care; To advocate for health care issues & for improvement in working conditions, salary, & benefits for resident physicians of Alberta
David Weatherby, President
Tana Findlay, Interim Chief Executive Officer
Aimee Kozun, Coordinator, Communications

Professional Association of Residents of British Columbia (PAR-BC) / Association professionnelle des résidents de la Colombie-Britannique
#2010, 401 West Georgia St., Vancouver BC V6B 5A1
Tel: 604-876-7636; *Toll-Free:* 888-877-2722
par@par-bc.org
www.par-bc.org
Social Media:
www.facebook.com/PARBC
twitter.com/PAR_BC
To bargain collectively on behalf of residents in British Columbia; To foster the personal well-being of members
Arun Jagdeo, President
Paul Hentz, Vice-President
Mary Masotti, Director, Communications
Michael Suen, Director, Finance

Professional Employees Association (Ind.) (PEA) / Association des employés professionnels (ind.)
#505, 1207 Douglas St., Victoria BC V8W 2E7
Tel: 250-385-8791; *Fax:* 250-385-6629
Toll-Free: 800-779-7736
www.pea.org
Social Media: www.youtube.com/user/PEAblogger
www.facebook.com/peaonline
twitter.com/pea_online
To provide collective bargaining representation to professionals employed in the provincial public service & elsewhere in the BC public sector
Scott McCannell, Executive Director
Ben Harper, Communications Officer

Professional Engineers Government of Ontario
4711 Yonge St., 10th Fl., Toronto ON M2N 6K8
Tel: 416-784-1284; *Fax:* 416-784-1366
pego@pego.on.ca
www.pego.on.ca
The Professional Engineers Government of Ontario (PEGO) is a certified bargaining association representing Professional Engineers and Ontario Land Surveyors working directly for the Government of the Province of Ontario.

The Professional Institute of the Public Service of Canada (PIPSC) / Institut professionnel de la fonction publique du Canada
250 Tremblay Rd., Ottawa ON K1G 3J8
Tel: 613-228-6310; *Fax:* 613-228-9048
Toll-Free: 800-267-0446
www.pipsc.ca
Social Media: www.youtube.com/user/PIPSCOMM/videos
www.facebook.com/PIPSC.IPFPC/
twitter.com/PIPSC_IPFPC
To serve members by serving as their collective bargaining agent & by providing representational services
Debi Daviau, President
Edward Gillis, COO/Executive Secretary

Public Service Alliance of Canada (PSAC) / Alliance de la Fonction publique du Canada (AFPC)
233 Gilmour St., Ottawa ON K2P 0P1
Tel: 613-560-4200; *Fax:* 613-567-0385
Toll-Free: 888-604-7722
www.psacunion.ca
Social Media: www.youtube.com/psacafpc
www.facebook.com/psac.national
twitter.com/psacnat
To unite all workers in a single democratic organization; To obtain for all public service employees the best standards of compensation & other conditions of employment & to protect the rights & interests of all public service employees; To maintain & defend the right to strike
Robyn Benson, National President
Jeannie Baldwin, Regional Executive Vice-President, Atlantic
Bob Jackson, Regional Executive Vice-President, B.C.
Marianne Hladun, Regional Executive Vice-President, Prairies
Chris Aylwarde, National Executive Vice-President
Sharon DeSousa, Regional Executive Vice-President, Ontario
Magali Picard, Vice-président exécutif régional, Québec
Julie Docherty, Regional Executive Vice-President, North
Larry Rousseau, Regional Executive Vice-President, National Capital Region

Pulp, Paper & Woodworkers of Canada (PPWC)
#201, 1184 - West 6 Ave., Vancouver BC V6H 1A4
Tel: 604-731-1909; *Fax:* 604-731-6448
Toll-Free: 888-992-7792
www.ppwc.ca
Social Media: www.youtube.com/user/PPWCUnion
www.facebook.com/PulpPaperandWoodworkersofCanada
To ensure fair working conditions for its members
Arnold Bercov, President

Research Council Employees' Association (Ind.) (RCEA) / Association des employés du conseil de recherches (ind.) (AECR)
PO Box 8256, Stn. Alta Vista Terminal, Ottawa ON K1G 3H7
Tel: 613-746-9341; *Fax:* 613-745-7868
office@rcea.ca
www.rcea.ca
To act as the certified bargaining agent for six groups and categories and represents the majority of NRC employees, which are: AD (Administrative Support) Group, AS (Administrative Services) Group, CS (Computer Systems Administration) Group, OP (Operational) Category, PG (Purchasing and Supply) Group, and TO(Technical) Category.
Cathie Fraser, President

Royal Newfoundland Constabulary Association (RNCA) / Association de la gendarmerie royale de Terre-Neuve
125 East White Hills Rd., St. John's NL A1A 5R7
Tel: 709-739-5946; *Fax:* 709-739-6276
office@rnca.ca
www.rnca.ca
To improve benefits & working conditions for police officers; to improve public safety & strive to create a positive relationship between the police & the community they protect
Tim Buckle, President
Warren Sullivan, 1st Vice-President
Albert Gibbons, 2nd Vice-President

Saskatchewan Government & General Employees' Union (SGEU) / Syndicat de la fonction publique de la Saskatchewan
1440 Broadway Ave., Regina SK S4P 1E2
Tel: 306-522-8571; *Fax:* 306-352-1969
Toll-Free: 800-667-5221
general@sgeu.org
www.sgeu.org
Social Media: www.youtube.com/user/SGEUtube
www.facebook.com/SGEU.SK
twitter.com/sgeu
To represent & protect the interests of its members who work in the public sector in Saskatchewan
Bob Bymoen, President

Saskatchewan Joint Board, Retail, Wholesale & Department Store Union (CLC) / Conseil mixte du syndicat des employés de gros, de détail et de magasins à rayons de la Saskatchewan (CTC)
1233 Winnipeg St., Regina SK S4R 1K1
Tel: 306-569-9311; *Fax:* 306-569-9521
Toll-Free: 877-747-9378
rwdsu.regina@sasktel.net
www.rwdsu.sk.ca
Chris Banting, Secretary-Treasurer

Schneider Employees' Association (Ind.) / Association des employés de Schneider (ind.)
321 Courtland Ave. East, Kitchener ON N2G 3X8
Tel: 519-741-5000; *Fax:* 519-744-5099
schneider@cwa-scacanada.ca
Sandy Russell, National President

Seafarers' International Union of Canada (AFL-CIO/CLC) / Syndicat international des marins canadiens (FAT-COI/CTC)
#200, 1333, rue Saint-Jacques, Montréal QC H3C 4K2
Tel: 514-931-7859; *Fax:* 514-931-3667
siuofcanada@seafarers.ca
www.seafarers.ca
Social Media:
www.facebook.com/pages/SIU-of-Canada/221924054504351
twitter.com/SIUCanada
To ensure its members safe & fair working conditions
James Given, President

Société des Auteurs de Radio, Télévision et Cinéma (SARTEC) / Society of Writers in Radio, Television & Cinema
1229, rue Panet, Montréal QC H2L 2Y6
Tél: 514-526-9196; *Téléc:* 514-526-4124
information@sartec.qc.ca
www.sartec.qc.ca
Média social: vimeo.com/user8816585
twitter.com/SARTEC_auteur
Regroupe les auteurs de langue française oeuvrant au Canada dans les domaines de la radio, de la télévision, du cinéma ou de l'audiovisuel; a pour objet l'étude, la défense et le développement des intérêts économiques, sociaux et moraux de ses membres
Yves Légaré, Directeur général
Sylvie Lussier, Présidente

Société des technologues en nutrition (STN)
CP 68568, Succ. Seugneuriale, 3333, rue du Carrefour, Québec QC G1C 0G7
Tél: 418-990-0309
info@stnq.ca
www.stnq.ca
Média social:
ca.linkedin.com/groups/Société-technologues-nutrition-STN-4543978
Signer des contrats collectifs de travail; surveiller la mise en application des conditions de travail des membres; promouvoir la défense et les intérêts économiques et professionnels des membres
Sylvie Gignac, Présidente

Society of Professional Engineers & Associates (SPEA) / Société des ingénieurs professionnels et associés
#2, 2275 Speakman Dr., Mississauga ON L5K 1B1
Tel: 905-823-3606; *Fax:* 905-823-9602
www.spea.ca
To represent scientists, engineers, technologists, & tradespeople who work for Atomic Energy of Canada Limited (AECL) in Mississauga, Ontario & abroad
Michael Ivanco, President
Brian Girard, Chair, Membership
Vincent Tume, Secretary
Val Aleyaseen, Treasurer

Syndicat de la fonction publique du Québec inc. (ind.) (SFPQ) / Québec Government Employees' Union (Ind.)
5100, boul des Gradins, Québec QC G2J 1N4
Tél: 418-623-2424; *Téléc:* 418-623-6109
Ligne sans frais: 855-623-2424
communication@sfpq.qc.ca
www.sfpq.qc.ca
Média social: www.youtube.com/user/SFPQ
linkedin.com/company/syndicat-de-la-fonction-publique-du-qu-bec
www.facebook.com/SFPQ.Syndicat
twitter.com/SFPQ_Syndicat
Assurer la défense des intérêts économiques, politiques et sociaux des membres et le développement de leurs conditions de vie; faire la promotion des services publics comme moyen démocratique de répondre aux besoins de la population
Lucie Martineau, Présidente général

Syndicat de professionnelles et professionnels du gouvernement du Québec (SPGQ) / Union of Professional Employees of the Québec Government
7, rue Vallière, Québec QC G1K 6S9
Tél: 418-692-0022; *Téléc:* 418-692-1338
Ligne sans frais: 800-463-5079
courrier@spgq.qc.ca
www.spgq.qc.ca
Média social: www.youtube.com/spgqinformation
www.facebook.com/lespgq
twitter.com/spgq
Richard Perron, Président
Francine Belleau, Secrétaire
Maurice Fortier, Directeur général

Syndicat des Agents Correctionnels du Canada (CSN) (SACC-CSN) / Union of Canadian Correctional Officers (UCCO-CSN)
1601, av De Lorimier, Montréal QC H2K 4M5
Tel: 514-598-2263; *Fax:* 514-598-2943
Toll-Free: 866-229-5566
ucco-sacc@csn.qc.ca
www.ucco-sacc.csn.qc.ca
Social Media:
www.facebook.com/216852691687729
Kevin Grabosky, Président

Syndicat des agents de la paix en services correctionnels du Québec (ind.) (SAPSCQ) / Union of Prison Guards of Québec (Ind.)
4906, boul Gouin est, Montréal QC H1G 1A4
Tél: 514-328-7774; *Téléc:* 514-328-0889
Ligne sans frais: 800-361-3559
www.sapscq.com
Service syndical pour les agents de la paix en services correctionnels du Québec
Stéphane Lemaire, Président national
Tony Vallières, Vice-président
Sylvain Maltais, Secrétaire général

Syndicat des agents de maîtrise de TELUS (ind.) (SAMT) / TELUS Professional Employees Union (Ind.) (TPEU)
#605, 2, St-Germain est, Rimouski QC G5L 8T7
Tél: 418-722-6144; *Téléc:* 418-724-0765
info@samt.qc.ca
www.samt.qc.ca/apropos.php
La sauvegarde et la promotion des intérêts professionnels, scientifiques, économiques, sociaux, culturels et politiques de ses membres; faire bénéficier les membres et les travailleurs en général des avantages de l'entraide et des négociations collectives; obtenir pour ses membres un meilleur niveau de vie et de meilleures conditions de travail; représenter les membres auprès de l'employeur
Harold Morrissey, Président
Lynda Fortin, Secrétaire

Syndicat des employé(e)s de magasins et de bureau de la Société des alcools du Québec (ind.) (SEMB SAQ) / Québec Liquor Board Store & Office Employees Union (Ind.)
1065, rue St-Denis, Montréal QC H2X 3J3
Tél: 514-849-7754; *Téléc:* 514-849-7914
Ligne sans frais: 800-361-8427
info@semb-saq.com
www.semb-saq.com
Média social: www.facebook.com/semb.saq
Katia Lelièvre, Présidente

Syndicat des employés en radio-télédiffusion de Télé-Québec (CSQ) / Télé-Québec Television Broadcast Employees' Union
c/o Télé-Québec, 1000, rue Fullum, Montréal QC H2K 3L7
Tél: 514-529-2805
sert@colba.net
Sylvain Leboeuf, Président

Syndicat des pompiers et pompières du Québec (CTC) (SPQ) / Québec Union of Firefighters (CLC)
#3900, 565, boul Crémazie Est, Montréal QC H2M 2V6
Tél: 514-383-4698; *Téléc:* 514-383-6782
Ligne sans frais: 800-461-4698
www.spq-ftq.com
Daniel Pépin, Président

Syndicat des professeures et professeurs de l'Université du Québec à Chicoutimi (SPPUQAC)
#P2-1000, 555, boul de l'Université, Chicoutimi QC G7H 2B1
Tél: 418-545-5378; *Téléc:* 418-545-6659
sppuqac@uqac.ca
www.uqac.ca/sppuqac
Lison Bergeron, Secrétaire

Syndicat des professeurs de l'État du Québec (ind.) (SPEQ) / Union of Professors for the Government of Québec (Ind.)
#1003, 2120, rue Sherbrooke Est, Montréal QC H2K 1C3
Tél: 514-525-7979; *Téléc:* 514-525-4655
Ligne sans frais: 877-525-7979
info@speq.org
www.speq.org
Pour représenter les fonctionnaires enseignants salariés.
Claude Tanguay, Président

Syndicat des professionnels et des techniciens de la santé du Québec (SPTSQ) / Québec Union of Health Professionals & Technicians
7595, boul St-Michel, Montréal QC H2A 3A4
Tél: 514-723-0422; *Téléc:* 514-723-5248
Ligne sans frais: 800-567-2022
secretariat@stepsq.org
stepsq.org
Média social: www.facebook.com/STEPSQ.org
twitter.com/STEPSQ
Défense des intérêts socio-économiques de ses membres
Nancy Corriveau, Présidente

Syndicat des technicien(ne)s et artisan(e)s du réseau français de Radio-Canada (ind.) (STARF) / CBC French Network Technicians' Union (Ind.)
1250, rue de la Visitation, Montréal QC H2L 3B4
Tél: 514-524-1100; *Téléc:* 514-524-6023
Ligne sans frais: 888-838-1100
secretariat@starf.qc.ca
www.starf.qc.ca
Benoît Celestino, Président
Marie-Lou Faille, Secrétaire-trésorier

Syndicat des technologues en radiologie du Québec (ind.) (STRQ) / Union of Radiology Technicians of Québec
#850, 1001, rue Sherbrooke est, Montréal QC H2L 1L3
Tél: 514-521-4469; *Téléc:* 514-521-0086
Étude, développement et la défense des intérêts professionnels, économiques, sociaux et éducatifs de ses membres et particulièrement la négociation et l'application de conventions collectives.

Syndicat des travailleurs de la construction du Québec (CSD)
#300, 801, 4e rue, Québec QC G1J 2T7
Tél: 418-522-3918; *Téléc:* 418-529-6323
info@csdconstruction.qc.ca
www.csdconstruction.qc.ca
Média social: www.youtube.com/user/LaCSDConstruction
www.facebook.com/csdconstruction
twitter.com/csdconstruction
Défendre et promouvoir les intérêts sociaux et économiques de ses membres
Daniel Laterreur, Président
Guy Terrault, Vice-président
Gilles C. Coulombe, Secrétaire

Syndicat du personnel technique et professionnel de la Société des alcools du Québec (ind.) (SPTP-SAQ) / Québec Liquor Board's Union of Technical & Professional Employees (Ind.)
905, rue de Lorimier, Montréal QC H2K 3V9
Tél: 514-873-5878; *Téléc:* 514-873-5896
intra.sptp-saq.ca
Steve d'Agostino, Président
Patrick Bray, Vice-Président
Hélène Daneault, Directrice
Johanne Morrisseau, Directrice
Lisanne Racine, Directrice

Syndicat interprovincial des ferblantiers et couvreurs, la section locale 2016 à la FTQ-Construction
#200, 8300, boul Métropolitain Est, Anjou QC H1K 1A2
Tél: 514-374-1515; *Téléc:* 514-448-2265
Ligne sans frais: 866-374-1515
info@ftq2016.org
www.ftq2016.org
Voir à la promotion et à la défense des intérêts économiques et sociaux des membres; assurer l'intégrité du métier de ferblantier et couvreur en défendant sa jurisdiction professionnelle et en assurant sa sécurité d'emploi; représenter les travailleurs, que leur travail soit effectué à l'intérieur du chantier de construction ou non; cultiver des sentiments de solidarité parmis les travailleurs; obtenir des améliorations dans les conditions de travail de ses membres
Dorima Aubut, Directeur provincial

Syndicat professionnel des diététistes et nutritionnistes du Québec (SPDNQ) / Québec Professional Union of Dieticians (Ind.)
2665, rue Beaubien est, Montréal QC H1Y 1G8
Tél: 514-725-5535; *Téléc:* 514-725-4433
Claudette Péloquin-Antoun, Présidente

Syndicat professionnel des médecins du gouvernement du Québec (ind.) (SPMGQ) / Professional Union of Government of Québec Physicians (Ind.)
1390, rue du Père-Jamet, Sainte-Foy QC G1W 3G5
Tél: 418-266-4670
Représenter les médecins à l'emploi du gouvernement du Québec
Christine Gagné, Présidente

Syndicat québécois de la construction (SQC) / North Shore Construction Inc. (Ind.)
2121, av Sainte-Anne, Saint-Hyacinthe QC J2S 5H5
Tél: 450-773-8833; *Téléc:* 450-773-2232
Ligne sans frais: 888-773-8834
info@sqc.ca
www.sqc.ca
Média social:
www.facebook.com/SyndicatQuebecoisConstruction
Sylvain Gendron, Président

Teaching Support Staff Union (TSSU)
Academic Quadrangle, Simon Fraser University, #5129/5130, 8888 University Dr., Burnaby BC V5A 1S6
Tel: 778-782-4735
tssu@tssu.ca
www.tssu.ca
Social Media:
www.facebook.com/TSSU.ca
twitter.com/TSSU
To represent teaching support staff during collective bargaining agreements & in employee-employer conflicts.
Melissa Roth, Organizer

Teamsters Canada (CLC) (TC)
#804, 2540, boul Daniel Johnson, Laval QC H7T 2S3
Tél: 450-682-5521; *Téléc:* 450-681-2244
Ligne sans frais: 866-888-6466
lantonin@teamsters.ca
www.teamsters-canada.org
Média social: twitter.com/TCYC1
www.facebook.com/TeamstersCanada
twitter.com/TeamstersCanada
Robert Bouvier, Président
Don McGill, Vice-président, International
Tom Fraser, Vice-président, International

Toronto Musicians' Association (TMA)
#500, 15 Gervais Dr., Toronto ON M3C 1Y8
Tel: 416-421-1020; *Fax:* 416-421-7011
Toll-Free: 800-762-3444
info@tma149.ca
www.torontomusicians.org
Social Media:
www.facebook.com/146633580744
twitter.com/TMA149
To represent professional musicians in all facets of music in the greater Toronto area; To offer legal protection, assistance, & advice; To help musicians have a successful professional career
Jim Biros, Executive Director

UNIFOR
205 Placer Ct., Toronto ON M2H 3H9
Tel: 416-497-4110; *Toll-Free:* 800-268-5763
communications@unifor.org
www.unifor.org
Social Media: www.youtube.com/user/UniforCanada
www.facebook.com/UniforCanada
twitter.com/UniforTheUnion
To improve the working conditions & general economic & social conditions of Canadian workers in the industries of: aerospace, mining, fishing, auto & specialty vehicle assembly, auto parts, hotels, airlines, rail, education, hospitality, retail, road transportation, health care, manufacturing, shipbuilding, & others
Jerry Dias, National President
Peter Kennedy, National Secretary-Treasurer

UniforACL
c/o Unifor Local 2289, #100, 6300 Lady Hammond Rd., Halifax NS B3K 2R6
Tel: 902-425-2440; *Fax:* 902-422-4647
Toll-Free: 800-565-2289
unifor-acl.ca
Penny Fawcett, Chair

Union canadienne des travailleurs en communication (ind.) / Canadian Union of Communication Workers (Ind.)
502, 90e av, LaSalle QC H8R 2Z7
Tél: 514-595-9095; *Téléc:* 514-595-8911

Union des artistes (UDA) / Artists' Union
#400, 1441, boul. René-Lévesque ouest, Montréal QC H3G 1T7
Tél: 514-288-6682; *Téléc:* 514-285-6789
info@uda.ca
www.uda.ca
Média social:
www.facebook.com/75AnsDeLUnionDesArtistes?notif_t=page_new_likes
twitter.com/udaquebec
Identification, étude, défense et développement des intérêts économiques, sociaux et moraux de ses membres
Sophie Prègent, Président
Sylvie Brousseau, Directrice générale

Union of Environment Workers (UEW) / Syndicat des travailleurs de l'environnement (STE)
2181 Thurston Dr., Ottawa ON K1G 6C9
Tel: 613-736-5533; *Fax:* 613-736-5537
www.uew-ste.ca
Social Media:
www.facebook.com/pages/Union-of-Environment-Workers/111345079011371
twitter.com/UEWCanada
To protect their members by ensuring safe working conditions & fair wage rights & benefits
Luc Paquette, Service Officer

Union of National Defence Employees (UNDE) / Union des employés de la Défense nationale (UEDN)
#700, 116 Albert St., Ottawa ON K1P 5G3
Tel: 613-594-4505; *Fax:* 613-594-8233
Toll-Free: 866-594-4505
www.unde-uedn.com
Social Media:
www.youtube.com/channel/UCHq7kXfLm2OP2EpPj4L58DA
twitter.com/UNDEUEDN
To represent the interests of their members & ensure safe working conditions for them
John MacLennan, National President

Union of National Employees (UNE) / Syndicat des employées et employés nationaux (SEN)
#900, 150 Isabella St., Ottawa ON K1S 1V7
Tel: 613-560-4364; *Fax:* 613-560-4208
Toll-Free: 800-663-6685
une-sen.org
Social Media: www.youtube.com/user/UnionNESyndicatEN
www.facebook.com/Union.NE.Syndicat.EN
twitter.com/my_UNE
To protect their members by ensuring safe working conditions & fair wage rights & benefits
Georges St-Jean, Acting Coordinator & Finance Officer

Union of Northern Workers / Syndicat des travailleurs du Nord
#200, 5112 - 52 St., Yellowknife NT X1A 3Z5
Tel: 867-873-5668; *Fax:* 867-920-4448
Toll-Free: 877-906-4447
hq@unw.ca
www.unw.ca
Social Media:
twitter.com/UNW_NWT
To represent the interests of its members in contract negotiations & grievances
Todd Parsons, President

Union of Postal Communications Employees (UPCE) / Syndicat des employés des postes et des communications (SEPC)
#701, 233 Gilmour St., Ottawa ON K2P 0P2
Tel: 613-560-4342; *Fax:* 613-594-3849
sepc-upce@psac.com
www.upce.ca
Represents Canada Post members employed in administrative, clerical, technical & professional capacities
François Paradis, National President

Union of Solicitor General Employees (USGE) / Syndicat des employés du Solliciteur général (SESG)
#603, 233 Gilmour St., Ottawa ON K2P 0P2
Tel: 613-232-4821; *Fax:* 613-232-3311
www.usge-sesg.com
Stan Stapleton, National President

Union of Taxation Employees (UTE) / Syndicat des employé(e)s de l'impôt (SEI)
#800, 233 Gilmour St., Ottawa ON K2P 0P2
Tel: 613-235-6704; *Fax:* 613-234-7290
www.ute-sei.org
Social Media:
www.facebook.com/pages/Union-of-Taxation-Employees/12540 2707475856
Robert Campbell, National President

Union of Veterans' Affairs Employees (UVAE) / Syndicat des employé(e)s des affaires des anciens combattants (SEAC)
#703, 233 Gilmour St., Ottawa ON K2P 0P2
Tel: 613-560-5460; *Fax:* 613-237-8282
uvae-seac.ca
To represent the interests of employees of Veterans' Affairs Canada
Carl Gannon, National President

UNITE HERE Canada
OFL Bldg., 15 Gervais Dr., 3rd Fl., Toronto ON M3C 1Y8
Tel: 416-384-0983; *Fax:* 416-384-0991
info@uniteherecanada.org
www.uniteherecanada.org
Nick Worhaug, Canadian Director
Karen Grella, International Vice-President
Amarjeet Kaur Chhabra, Media Contact

United Brotherhood of Carpenters & Joiners of America (AFL-CIO/CLC) / Fraternité unie des charpentiers et menuisiers d'Amérique (FAT-COI/CTC)
101 Constitution Ave. NW, Washington DC 20001 USA
Tel: 202-546-6206; *Fax:* 202-543-5724
www.carpenters.org
Social Media:
www.facebook.com/905962876138436
twitter.com/UBCJA_Official
Douglas J. McCarron, General President

United Food & Commercial Workers Canada (UFCW CANADA)
#300, 61 International Blvd., Toronto ON M9W 6K4
Tel: 416-675-1104; *Fax:* 416-675-6919
ufcw@ufcw.ca
www.ufcw.ca
Social Media: www.youtube.com/user/UFCWCanada
www.facebook.com/ufcwcanada
twitter.com/ufcwcanada
One of Canada's largest private sector unions
Paul Meinema, National President

United Mine Workers of America (CLC) / Mineurs unis d'Amérique (CTC)
#200, 18354 Quantico Gateway Dr., Triangle VA 22172-1179 USA
Tel: 703-291-2400
www.umwa.org
Cecil Roberts, President

Yukon Employees Union (YEU) / Syndicat des employés du Yukon
#201, 2285 - 2nd Ave., Whitehorse YT Y1A 1C9
Tel: 867-667-2331; *Fax:* 867-667-6521
Toll-Free: 888-938-2331
contact@yeu.ca
www.yeu.ca
Social Media: www.youtube.com/user/YukonEmployeesUnion
www.facebook.com/YukonEmployeesUnion
twitter.com/YEUPSAC
To unite all members of the Alliance over which this Union has jurisdiction into a single union capable of acting on their behalf; to obtain through democratic means for all members the best possible standards of wages, salaries & other conditions of employment, & to protect the interests, rights & privileges of all such employees
Steve Geick, President
Laura Hureau, Executive Director

Yukon Federation of Labour (YFL) / Fédération du travail du Yukon
#102, 106 Strickland St., Whitehorse YT Y1A 2J5
Tel: 867-456-8250; *Fax:* 867-668-3426
yfl@yukonfed.com
www.yukonfed.com
Social Media:
www.facebook.com/pages/Yukon-Federation-of-Labour/1378215 25367
twitter.com/yukonworkers
To advocate on behalf of its memebers
Vikki Quocksister, President

Landscape Architecture

Alberta Association of Landscape Architects (AALA)
PO Box 21052, Edmonton AB T6R 2V4
Tel: 780-435-9902; *Fax:* 780-413-0076
aala@aala.ab.ca
www.aala.ab.ca
To advance the quality of the professional practice of landscape architecture in Alberta
Jill Lane, Manager
Mark Nolan, Registrar
Brian Charanduk, Treasurer
Michelle Lefebre, Secretary

Association des architectes paysagistes du Québec (AAPQ)
#406, 420, rue McGill, Montréal QC H2Y 2G1
Tél: 514-526-6385; *Téléc:* 514-526-6385
info@aapq.org
www.aapq.org
Média social: www.facebook.com/pageaapq
twitter.com/AAPQ_paysages
Promouvoir la création et la valorisation du paysage en milieu naturel et construit dans le but de constituer un cadre de vie sain, fonctionnel, esthétique, axé sur les besoins de la population et répondant aux exigences écologiques
Édith Normandeau, Directrice générale par intérim

Atlantic Provinces Association of Landscape Architects (APALA)
PO Box 653, Stn. Halifax CRO, Halifax NS B3J 2Z1
info@apala.ca
www.apala.ca
To promote, improve & advance the profession; to maintain standards of professional practice & conduct consistent with the need to serve & to protect the public interest; to support improvement &/or conservation of the natural, cultural, social & built environment
Angela Morin, Secretary-Treasurer
Daniel Glenn, President

British Columbia Society of Landscape Architects (BCSLA)
#110, 355 Burrard St., Vancouver BC V6C 2G8
Tel: 604-682-5610; *Fax:* 604-681-3394
admin@bcsla.org
www.bcsla.org
Social Media:
linkedin.com/groups/BC-Society-Landscape-Architects-5074296
www.facebook.com/BCSocietyofLandscapeArchitects
twitter.com/BCSLA
To promote, improve & advance the profession; to maintain standards of professional practice & conduct consistent with the need to serve & to protect the public interest; to support the improvement &/or conservation of the natural, cultural, social & built environment.
Robert Evans, President

Canadian Society of Landscape Architects (CSLA) / Association des architectes paysagistes du Canada (AAPC)
12 Forillon Cres., Ottawa ON K2M 2S5
Tel: 866-781-9799; *Fax:* 866-871-1419
info@csla.ca
www.csla.ca
Social Media:
linkedin.com/groups/Canadian-Society-Landscape-Architects-48 49978?
www.facebook.com/177312791600
twitter.com/CSLA_AAPC
To support the improvement &/or conservation of the natural, cultural, social & built environment; to promote visibility, recognition, acceptance & understanding of the profession by communicating its value in relation to that of the public good
Elizabeth A. Sharpe, Executive Director

Manitoba Association of Landscape Architects (MALA)
131 Callum Cres., Winnipeg MB R2G 2C7
Tel: 204-663-4863; *Fax:* 204-668-5662
www.mala.net
To promote, improve & advance the profession; to maintain standards of professional practice & conduct consistent with the need to serve & protect public interest; to support improvement &/or conservation of the natural, cultural, social & built environment
Monica Giesbrecht, President

Newfoundland & Labrador Association of Landscape Architects (NLALA)
77 Gower St., St. John's NL A1C 1N6
Tel: 709-579-7744
www.nlala.com
Jim Floyd, President

Northwest Territories Association of Landscape Architects (NWTALA)
PO Box 1394, Yellowknife NT X1A 2P1
Tel: 867-920-2986; *Fax:* 867-920-2986
atborow@internorth.com
To represent landscape architects in the Northwest Territories

Ontario Association of Landscape Architects (OALA)
#407, 3 Church St., Toronto ON M5E 1M2
Tel: 416-231-4181; *Fax:* 416-231-2679
oala@oala.ca
www.oala.ca
Social Media:
twitter.com/OALA_ON
To promote, improve & advance the profession; to maintain standards of professional practice & conduct consistent with the need to serve & to protect the public interest; to support improvement &/or conservation of the natural, cultural, social & built environment
Linda MacLeod, Registrar
Sarah Culp, President

Saskatchewan Association of Landscape Architects (SALA)
PO Box 20015, Regina SK S4P 4J7
www.sala.sk.ca
To promote, improve, & advance the profession of landscape architecture; To maintain standards of professional practice & conduct
Laureen Snook, President

Language, Linguistics, Literature

ABC Life Literacy Canada
#604, 110 Eglinton Ave. East, Toronto ON M4P 2Y1
Tel: 416-218-0010; *Fax:* 416-218-0457
Toll-Free: 800-303-1004
info@abclifeliteracy.ca
abclifeliteracy.ca
Social Media:
www.youtube.com/channel/UCQP3kFeNaDadqk739mgj7Gg
www.facebook.com/abclifeliteracy
twitter.com/abclifeliteracy
To inspire Canadians to increase their literacy skills
Gillian Mason, President
Stephanie Wells, Manager, Communications

L'arc-en-ciel littéraire
CP 180, Succ. C, Montréal QC H2L 4K1
arcencliellitteraire@yahoo.ca
arcenciellitteraire.site.voila.fr
Le seul regroupement d'écrivains GLBT au Québec; promouvoit la littérature gaie et des auteurs gais
Réjean Roy, Président fondateur

Association canadienne de traductologie (ACT) / Canadian Association for Translation Studies (CATS)
a/s École de traduction et d'interprétation, Université d'Ottawa, 70, av Laurier est, Ottawa ON K1N 6N5
www.act-cats.ca
Société savante qui regroupe des chercheurs, des professeurs et des praticiens qui se consacrent ou s'intéressent à l'étude ou à l'enseignement de la traduction et des disciplines apparentées
Marco Fiola, Président
Denise Nevo, Vice-présidente

Association of Canadian Corporations in Translation & Interpretation (ACCTI) / Association canadienne de compagnies de traductions et d'interpretation
#306, 421 Bloor St. East, Toronto ON M4W 3T1
Tel: 416-975-5000; *Fax:* 416-975-0505
english_info@accti.org
www.accti.org
To unite the Canadian translation industry, providing a quality standard to protect the public & service providers alike; to arrange for arbitration in the event of a dispute; to operate in the best interest of members
Paul Penzo, President
Maryse M. Benhoff, Vice-President

Association of Translators & Interpreters of Alberta (ATIA) / Association des traducteurs et interprètes de l'Alberta
PO Box 546, Stn. Main, Edmonton AB T5J 2K8
Tel: 780-434-8384
www.atia.ab.ca
To protect the interests of their members
Hellen Martinez, President

Association of Translators & Interpreters of Nova Scotia (ATINS) / Association des traducteurs et interprètes de la nouvelle-écosse
PO Box 372, Halifax NS B3J 2P8
info@atins.org
www.atins.org
To ensure that clients have access to a body of qualified professionals; to promote the profession & the development of its members
Bassima Jurdak O'Brien, President

Association of Translators & Interpreters of Ontario (ATIO) / Association des traducteurs et interprètes de l'Ontario
#1202, 1 Nicholas St., Ottawa ON K1N 7B7
Tel: 613-241-2846; *Fax:* 613-241-4098
Toll-Free: 800-234-5030
info@atio.on.ca
www.atio.on.ca
To promote a high degree of professionalism & to protect the interest of those who use the language services provided by its members; to organize professional development activities & to encourage exchanges among its members
Catherine Bertholet-Schweizer, Executive Director
Barbara Collishaw, President

Association of Translators & Interpreters of Saskatchewan (ATIS) / Association des traducteurs et interprètes de la Saskatchewan
50 Harvard Cres., Regina SK S7H 3R1
www.atis-sk.ca
Social Media:
www.facebook.com/ATIS.SK.CA
To provide a collective voice for members; to ensure that members exercise the profession in accordance with their code of ethics; to administer admission procedures of national certification examination; to provide a list of current certified members
Robert Jerrett, President
Estelle Bonetto, Vice-President

Association of Translators, Terminologists & Interpreters of Manitoba (ATIM) / Association des traducteurs, terminologues et des interprètes du Manitoba
PO Box 83, 200 Cathédrale Ave., Winnipeg MB R2H 0H7
Tel: 204-797-3247
info@atim.mb.ca
www.atim.mb.ca
To provide a collective voice for its members, ensure that members exercise their profession in accordance with its Code of Ethics, & protect the public interest by ensuring the quality of the services rendered by its members.

Association of Visual Language Interpreters of Canada (AVLIC) / Association des interprètes en langage visuel du Canada
#110, 39012 Discovery Way, Squamish BC V8B 0E5
Tel: 604-617-8502; *Fax:* 604-567-8502
avlic@avlic.ca
www.avlic.ca
Social Media: www.youtube.com/user/TheAVLIC
www.facebook.com/AVLIC
To represent interpreters whose working languages are English & American Sign Language (ASL); To promote high standards & uniformity within the profession of interpreting
Christie Reaume, President
Caroline Tetreault, Secretary
Cindy Haner, Treasurer
Jane Pannell, Administrative Manager

Association québécoise des enseignants de français langue seconde (AQEFLS) / Québec Association of Teachers of French as a Second Language
#228, 7400, boul Saint-Laurent, Montréal QC H2R 2Y1
Tél: 514-276-6470; *Téléc:* 514-276-3350
info@aqefls.org
www.aqefls.org
Média social: twitter.com/AQEFLS
Promouvoir l'enseignement du français langue seconde et les aspects qui s'y rattachent; coordonner et encourager les recherches d'ordre pratique dans le domaine de la pédagogie et dans tout autre domaine touchant l'enseignement du français langue seconde; permettre la diffusion des derniers développements de la recherche et les techniques dans le domaine de l'enseignement du français langue seconde
Carlos Carmona, Président

The Bronte Society
7 West Rivers St., Oakville ON L6L 6N9
Tel: 905-825-5552
brontehistoricalsociety@bellnet.ca
www.brontehistoricalsociety.ca
To bring closer together all who honour the Brontë sisters; to act as the guardian of such letters, writings & personal belongings as could be acquired for the Museum; to dispel legend & false sentiments regarding the Brontë story
Judith Watkins, Canadian Representative

Canadian Association for Commonwealth Literature & Language Studies (CACLALS) / Association canadienne pour l'étude des langues et de la littérature du Commonwealth
c/o Kristina Fagan, Department of English, University of Saskatchewan, 9 Campus Dr., Saskatoon SK S7N 5A5
www.caclals.ca
To promote the study of Commonwealth literature in Canada; To encourage the reading of Canadian literature abroad
Susan Gingell, President
Kristina Fagan, Secretary-Treasurer
Neil ten Kortenaar, Editor, Chimo

Canadian Comparative Literature Association (CCLA) / Association canadienne de littérature comparée (ACLC)
c/o Markus Reisenleitner, Department of Humanities, York University, 217 Vanier College, Toronto ON M3H 1P3
complit.ca
Karin Beeler, President
Susan Ingram, Vice-President
Pascal Gin, Secretary
Markus Reisenleitner, Treasurer

Canadian Linguistic Association (CLA) / Association canadienne de linguistique (ACL)
c/o University of Toronto Press, Journals Division, 5201 Dufferin Ave., Toronto ON M3H 5T8
www.chass.utoronto.ca/~cla-acl
To advance scientific study of linguistics & language in Canada
France Martineau, President
Ileana Paul, Secretary
Carrie Dyck, Treasurer

Canadian Literacy & Learning Network (CLLN) / Rassemblement canadien pour l'alphabétisation (RCA)
342A Elgin St., Ottawa ON K2P 1M6
Tel: 613-563-2464; *Fax:* 613-563-2504
clln@literacy.ca
www.literacy.ca
Social Media:
www.facebook.com/195237923820101
twitter.com/Cdn_Literacy
To act as a national voice for literacy for Canadians
Lindsay Kennedy, President & CEO

Canadian Literary & Artistic Association / Association littéraire et artistique canadienne inc.
PO Box 20035, Stn. De Vinci, Repentigny QC J5Y 0K6
Tel: 514-993-1556
alaican@aei.ca
www.alai.ca
To promote & protect copyright as well as to study questions regarding the protection and the applicability of these rights.
Madeleine Lamothe-Samson, President

Canadian Parents for French (CPF)
#1104, 170 Laurier Ave. West, Ottawa ON K1P 5V5
Tel: 613-235-1481; *Fax:* 613-230-5940
cpf@cpf.ca
www.cpf.ca
Social Media:
www.facebook.com/CanadianParentsForFrench
twitter.com/CDNP4F
To provide educational opportunities for young Canadians to learn & use the French language; To recognize & support English & French as Canada's two official languages; To create & promote opportunities for young Canadians to learn & use French as a second language
Philip Fenez, President
Cathy Stone, Director, Operations

Canadian Translators, Terminologists & Interpreters Council (CTTIC) / Conseil des traducteurs, terminologues et interprètes du Canada (CTTIC)
#1202, One Nicholas St., Ottawa ON K1N 7B7
Tel: 613-562-0379; *Fax:* 613-241-4098
info@cttic.org
www.cttic.org
To ensure uniform standards for the practice of the profession; to make available to the public a body of reliable professionals in translation, terminology & interpretation
Kristel Blais, Administrative Director
Faith Cormier, President

The Canadian Writers' Foundation Inc. (CWF) / La Fondation des écrivains canadiens inc.
PO Box 13281, Stn. Kanata, Ottawa ON K2K 1X4
Tel: 613-256-6937; *Fax:* 613-256-5457
info@canadianwritersfoundation.org
www.canadianwritersfoundation.org
Strives to continue building the capital fund through donations
Marianne Scott, President
Suzanne Williams, Executive Secretary

Centre interdisciplinaire de recherches sur les activités langagières (CIRAL)
Pavillon Charles-de-Koninck, Université Laval, #2260-A, Faculté des lettres, Québec QC G1V 0A6
Tél: 418-656-2131
www.ciral.ulaval.ca
Le Centre interdisciplinaire de recherches sur la activités langagières (CIRAL) regroupe cinq équipes régulières, une vingtaine de chercheurs et quelque soixante-dix étudiants de deuxième et troisième cycles. Tous partagent la même conception des questions linguistiques : la langue est indissociable de l'histoire et de la culture des groupes qui la parlent, et elle évolue en fonction des contacts interethniques et des pressions socioculturelles qui s'exercent sur elle.
Aline Francoeur, Directrice

Copian
Sterling House, 767 Brunswick St., Fredericton NB E3B 1H8
Tel: 506-457-6900; *Fax:* 506-457-6910
Toll-Free: 800-720-6253
contact@copian.ca
www.copian.ca
Social Media:
twitter.com/Copian_E
To provide an information network, in both official languages; to support the Canadian literacy community: adult learners, practitioners, organizations & governments
Bill Stirling, CEO

Corporation des traducteurs, traductrices, terminologues et interprètes du Nouveau-Brunswick (CTINB) / Corporation of Translators, Terminologists & Interpreters of New Brunswick
CP 427, Fredericton NB E3B 4Z9
Tél: 506-458-1519
ctinb@nbnet.nb.ca
www.ctinb.nb.ca
Donner à ses membres une voix collective; promouvoir le perfectionnement professionnel de ses membres; veiller à ce que ses membres respectent son Code de déontologie; faire connaître le rôle professionnel de ses membres dans la société; protéger l'intérêt public en faisant subir des examens d'admission à la CTINB et d'agrément des membres ainsi qu'en examinant les plaintes reçues à l'égard des membres; entretenir des liens avec les organismes semblables et avec les établissements de formation universitaire dans les domaines de la traduction, de la terminologie et de l'interprétation

Esperanto Association of Canada (KEA) / Association canadienne d'esperanto
277, rue Regina, Montréal QC H4G 2G6
www.esperanto.ca/en/kea

To promote & teach the neutral international language of Esperanto
Paul Hopkins, President
Tamara Anna Kozeij, Director

Jane Austen Society of North America (JASNA)
#105, 195 Wynford Dr., Toronto ON M3C 3P3
Toll-Free: 800-836-3911
info@jasna.org
www.jasna.org
Social Media:
www.facebook.com/285332054855712
To promote an appreciation of Jane Austen & her writings
Nancy Stokes, Canadian Membership Secretary

L. M. Montgomery Institute (LMMI)
University of Prince Edward Island, 550 University Ave., Charlottetown PE C1A 4P3
Tel: 902-628-4346; *Fax:* 902-628-4345
lmmi@upei.ca
www.lmmontgomery.ca
With a focus on scholarship & teaching, the Institute provides resources & educational opportunities to students & scholars researching the life, works & influence of L.M. Montgomery
Mark Leggott, Chair

Languages Canada / Langues Canada
5886 - 169A St., Surrey BC V3S 6Z8
Tel: 604-574-1532; *Fax:* 888-277-0522
info@languagescanada.ca
www.languagescanada.ca
Social Media:
www.facebook.com/languagescanada
twitter.com/LangCanada
To promote quality, accredited English & French language training in Canada, & to represent Canada as a destination for excellent English & French language training
Michael Armour, Contact

Literary Translators' Association of Canada (LTAC) / Association des traducteurs et traductrices littéraires du Canada (ATTLC)
Concordia University LB 601, 1455 Maisonneuve Blvd. West, Montréal QC H3G 1M8
Tel: 514-848-2424
info@attlc-ltac.org
www.attlc-ltac.org
Social Media:
www.facebook.com/111956408910924
To promote literary translation & interests of literary translators.
Nicola Danby, President

Ordre des traducteurs, terminologues et interprètes agréés du Québec (OTTIAQ)
#1108, 2021, rue Union, Montréal QC H3A 2S9
Tél: 514-845-4411; *Téléc:* 514-845-9903
Ligne sans frais: 800-265-4815
info@ottiaq.org
www.ottiaq.org
L'OTTIAQ assure la protection du public en octroyant les titres de traducteur agréé, de terminologue agréé et d'interprète agréé, en veillant au respect de son code de déontologie et des normes professionnelles et en mettant en ouvre les mécanismes prévus au Code des professions.
Johanne Boucher, Directrice générale

Quebec English Literacy Alliance (QELA)
PO Box 3542, #236, 410 St. Nicholas St., Montréal QC H2Y 2P5
Tel: 450-242-2360; *Fax:* 450-242-2543
Toll-Free: 866-942-7352
info@qela.qc.ca
qela.qc.ca
To be the unified voice of Quebec English literacy providers nationally & provincially
Louise Quinn, Executive Director

Regroupement de Bouches à Oreilles (RBO)
#1, 317, rue Lanctôt, Chibougamau QC G8P 2P5
Tél: 418-748-2239; *Téléc:* 418-748-2761
bouchesaoreilles@yahoo.ca
www.abc02.org
Formation de base: compter, lire, écrire
Isabelle Lamontagne, Coordonnatrice

Réseau pour le développement de l'alphabétisme et des compétences (RESDAC)
#205, 235 ch Montréal, Ottawa ON K1L 6C7
Tél: 613-749-5333; *Téléc:* 613-749-2252
Ligne sans frais: 888-906-5666
info@resdac.net
www.resdac.net
Média social: www.facebook.com/128384640568102
Promouvoir l'alphabétisation en français au Canada; assurer une concertation des intervenantes en alphabétisation en français au Canada.
Normand Lévesque, Directeur général
Isabelle Salesse, Présidente
Donald Desroches, Vice-président

Saskatchewan Elocution & Debate Association (SEDA) / Association d'élocution et des débats de la Saskatchewan
1860 Lorne St., Regina SK S4P 2L7
Tel: 306-780-9243; *Fax:* 306-781-6021
info@saskdebate.com
www.saskdebate.com
Social Media:
www.facebook.com/sask.debate
twitter.com/SaskDebate
To foster debate & public speaking
Lorelie DeRoose, Executive Director

Saskatchewan Organization for Heritage Languages Inc. (SOHL)
2144 Cornwall St., Regina SK S4P 2K7
Tel: 306-780-9275; *Fax:* 306-780-9407
sohl@sasktel.net
www.heritagelanguages.sk.ca
Social Media:
linkedin.com/in/sohl-sk-aa554151
www.facebook.com/sohl.sask
twitter.com/sohl_sk
To promote & develop teaching of heritage languages in Saskatchewan; to act in advocacy capacity to make representation to government, institutions & boards regarding matters pertaining to heritage languages; to promote cooperation with & mutual support of provincial organizations with similar aims & objectives; to encourage inter-provincial & national liaison
Tamara Ruzic, Executive Director

Société québécoise d'espéranto (SQE) / Québec Esperanto Society (QES)
6358A, rue de Bordeaux, Montréal QC H2G 2R8
www.esperanto.qc.ca
Faire connaître et aider à l'apprentissage de l'espéranto; organiser des rencontres et favoriser l'utilisation de la langue; présenter les avantages de la langue et le mouvement mondial
Normand Fleury, Président
Sylvano Auclair, Secrétaire-trésorier

Society of Translators & Interpreters of British Columbia (STIBC)
PO Box 33, #511, 850 West Hastings St., Vancouver BC V6C 1E1
Tel: 604-684-2940; *Fax:* 604-684-2947
www.stibc.org
To promote the interests of translators & interpreters in BC; to serve the public by applying a Code of Ethics members must comply with; by setting & maintaining high professional standards through education & certification
Golnaz Aliyarzadeh, President

Stephen Leacock Associates
PO Box 854, Orillia ON L3V 6K8
Tel: 705-835-3218; *Fax:* 705-835-5171
www.leacock.ca
Social Media:
www.facebook.com/148060321915484
twitter.com/leacockmedal
To honour & promote Stephen Leacock & his body of writing
Michael Hill, President

World Literacy of Canada (WLC) / Alphabétisation mondiale Canada
#281, 401 Richmond St. West, Toronto ON M5V 3A8
Tel: 416-977-0008; *Fax:* 416-977-1112
info@worldlit.ca
www.worldlit.ca
Social Media: www.youtube.com/user/worldliteracycanada
www.facebook.com/worldlit
twitter.com/WorldLit
To promote international development & social justice through support of community-based programs that emphasize adult literacy & non-formal education
Ken Setterington, President
Jasmine Gill, Vice-President
Virginia Bosomworth, Secretary
Mamta Mishra, Executive Director

Law

The Advocates' Society
#2700, 250 Yonge St., Toronto ON M5B 2L7
Tel: 416-597-0243; *Fax:* 416-597-1588
mail@advocates.ca
www.advocates.ca
Social Media:
linkedin.com/company/the-advocates%27-society
www.facebook.com/TheAdvocatesSociety
twitter.com/Advocates_Soc
To teach the skills & ethics of advocacy through information sharing, educational programs, seminars, conferences, & workshops; To speak out on behalf of advocates; To protect the right to representation by an independent bar; To initiate appropriate reforms to the legal system
Alan H. Mark, President
Alexandra Chyczij, Executive Director

Alberta Association of Police Governance (AAPG)
PO Box 36098, Stn. Lakeview Post Office, Calgary AB T3E 7C6
Tel: 587-892-7874
admin@aapg.ca
www.aapg.ca
The AAPG is an association of police commissions and RCMP policing committees created pursuant to Alberta's Police Act.
Terry Noble, Chair

Alberta Civil Trial Lawyers' Association (ACTLA)
#550, 10055 - 106 St., Edmonton AB T5J 2Y2
Tel: 780-429-1133; *Fax:* 780-429-1199
Toll-Free: 800-665-7248
admin@actla.com
www.actla.com
To advocate for a strong civil justice system that protects the rights of all Albertans
Lyn Bromilow, Executive Director
James D. Cuming, President

Alberta Federation of Police Associations (AFPA)
Energy Square, #100, 7024 - 101 Ave., Edmonton AB T6A 0H7
Fax: 403-795-7173
information@albertapolice.ca
www.albertapolice.ca
To address local, provincial, & national police association issues
Bob Walsh, President

Alberta Law Foundation (ALF)
#300, 407 - 8 Ave. SW, Calgary AB T2P 1E5
Tel: 403-264-4701; *Fax:* 403-294-9238
infoo@albertalawfoundation.org
www.albertalawfoundation.org
To conduct research into & recommend reform of law & administration of justice; to establish, maintain & operate law libraries; to contribute to legal education & knowledge of people of Alberta; to provide assistance to Native people's legal & student programs
David Aucoin, Executive Director
Diana M. Porter, Administrative Assistant

Association canadienne des juristes-traducteurs (ACJT) / Canadian Association of Legal Translators (CALT)
a/s OOTTIAQ, #1108, 2021 Union Ave., Montréal QC H3A 2S9
info@acjt.ca
www.acjt.ca
Pour promouvoir le double qualification comme avocat (ou juriste) et comme traducteur pour la traduction de documents juridiques.
Louis Fortier, President

Association des juristes d'expression française de l'Ontario (AJEFO)
#201, 214 ch Montréal, Ottawa ON K1L 8L8
Tél: 613-842-7462; *Téléc:* 613-842-8389
bureau@ajefo.ca
www.ajefo.ca
Média social: www.facebook.com/ajefo?fref=nf
Représenter les intérêts des avocates, des avocats, des juges, des fonctionnaires de la justice, des professeures, des professeurs, des étudiantes et des étudiants en droit, et des autres participants et participantes du monde juridique, qui travaillent à la promotion des services juridiques en français sur le territoire de l'Ontario; viser à assurer un accès égal à la justice, sans pénalité, délai, obstacle ou hésitation à l'utilisation du français par l'appareil judiciaire, les membres du Barreau ou la population francophone de notre province
Paul Le Vay, Président
Danielle Manton, Directrice générale

Association des juristes d'expression française de la Saskatchewan (AJEFS) / French Jurists Association of Saskatchewan
#219, 1440, 9e av Nord, Regina SK S4R 8B1
Tél: 306-924-8543; *Téléc:* 306-781-7916
Ligne sans frais: 800-991-1912
ajefs@sasktel.net
www.ajefs.ca
Média social: www.facebook.com/ajefs.saskatchewan
twitter.com/AJEFS1
Développer et promouvoir les droits et services en français auprès des instances juridiques et gouvernementales; informer et sensibiliser la population fransaskoise sur la vulgarisation des lois et l'utilisation des services juridiques en français
Francis Poulin, Président

Association des policières et policiers provinciaux du Québec (ind.) (APPQ) / Québec Provincial Police Association (Ind.)
1981, rue Léonard-De Vinci, Sainte-Julie QC J3E 1Y9
Tél: 450-922-5414; *Téléc:* 450-922-5417
www.appq-sq.qc.ca
Média social: www.youtube.com/watch?v=2AWQQrHbx20
Promouvoir le bien-être de ses membres et voir à leurs intérêts sociaux, moraux et culturels
Pierre Veilleux, Président
Jocelyn Boucher, Vice-président, Ressources humaines
Luc Fournier, Vice-président, Finances
Jacques Painchaud, Vice-président, Discipline et déontologie
Pierre Lemay, Vice-président, Griefs et formation
Daniel Rolland, Vice-président, Ress. matérielles et santé et sécurité du travail

Barreau de Montréal / Bar of Montréal
Palais de Justice, #980, 1, rue Notre Dame est, Montréal QC H2Y 1B6
Tél: 514-866-9392; *Téléc:* 514-866-1488
info@barreaudemontreal.qc.ca
www.barreaudemontreal.qc.ca
Administrer une corporation professionnelle
Doris Larrivée, Directrice générale
Gislaine Dufault, Directrice des communications

Black Law Students' Association of Canada (BLSA) / L'Association des etudiants noirs en droit du Canada
Admin@blsacanada.com
www.blsacanada.com
Social Media:
www.facebook.com/blsacanada
twitter.com/BLSAC
A national organization committed to supporting and enhancing academic and professional opportunities for black law students in both official languages.
Moses Gashirabake, President

British Columbia Law Institute (BCLI)
University of British Columbia, 1822 East Mall, Vancouver BC V6T 1Z1
Tel: 604-822-0142; *Fax:* 604-822-0144
Toll-Free: 800-565-5297
bcli@bcli.org
www.bcli.org
A not-for-profit law reform agency that performs research & studies to change & modernize British Columbian law.
D. Peter Ramsay, Q.C., Chair
R.C. (Tino) DiBella, Vice-Chair
W. James Emmerton, Executive Director
Krista James, National Director

British Columbia Police Association
#202, 190 Alexander St., Vancouver BC V6A 1B5
Tel: 604-685-6486; *Fax:* 604-685-5228
contact@bc-pa.ca
www.bc-pa.ca
To represent the interests of its members
Tom Stamatakis, President

British Columbia Public Interest Advocacy Centre (BCPIAC)
#208, 1090 West Pender St., Vancouver BC V6E 2N7
Tel: 604-687-3063; *Fax:* 604-682-7896
support@bcpiac.com
www.bcpiac.com
Social Media:
www.facebook.com/443550842340768
twitter.com/BCPIAC
To advance the interests of groups that are generally unrepresented or underrepresented in issues of major public concern, such as welfare, disability, human, farmworkers & consumers rights
Tannis Braithwaite, Executive Director

Grace Matsutani, Administrator

Canadian Association of Black Lawyers (CABL) / L'Association des Avocats Noirs du Canada
#300, 20 Toronto St., Toronto ON M5C 2B8
www.cabl.ca
Andrew Alleyne, President

Canadian Association of Chiefs of Police (CACP) / Association canadienne des chefs de police (ACCP)
#100, 300 Terry Fox Dr., Kanata ON K2K 0E3
Tel: 613-595-1101; *Fax:* 613-383-0372
cacp@cacp.ca
www.cacp.ca
To encourage & develop cooperation among all Canadian police organizations & members in pursuit & attainment of common objects to create & develop the highest standards of efficiency in law enforcement through the fostering & encouragement of police training, education & research; To promote & maintain a high standard of ethics, integrity, honour & conduct in profession of law enforcement; To encourage & advance the study of modern & progressive practices in prevention & detection of crime; To foster uniformity of police practices & cooperation for the protection & security of the people of Canada
Dale McFee, O.O.M., President

Canadian Association of Crown Counsel (CACC) / Association canadienne des juristes de l'État (ACJE)
PO Box 30, #1015, 180 Dundas St. West, Toronto ON M5G 1Z8
Tel: 416-260-4888; *Fax:* 416-977-1460
info@cacc-acje.ca
www.cacc-acje.ca
To represent the collective interests of its members on a national level
Rick Woodburn, President

Canadian Association of Police Governance (CAPG) / Association canadienne des commissions de police
#302, 157 Gilmour St., Ottawa ON K2P 0N8
Tel: 613-235-2272; *Fax:* 613-235-2275
capg.ca
To express views & positions of municipal governing authorities; To provide means for collection & sharing of information & discussion of matters relating to policing services; To consider matters of national interest; To comment on social, economic, cultural, & legislative questions which may affect the quality, efficiency, & costs of policing services; To promote the quality & uniformity of policing services; To educate the public on matters relating to the governance of policing services; To act as a lobbying group to liaise between federal, provincial & municipal governmental authorities, & the federal & provincial solicitors general; To provide a forum for participation by civilian governors of municipal policing services & other agencies; To promote & encourage greater cooperation to serve the interest of the public; To advance criminal justice
Jennifer Malloy, Executive Director

Canadian Association of Provincial Court Judges (CAPCJ) / L'Association canadienne des juges de cours provinciales
c/o Judge Alan T. Tufts, Nova Scotia Provincial Court, 87 Cornwallis St., Kentville NS B4N 2E5
Tel: 902-679-6070; *Fax:* 902-679-6190
capcp@judges-juges.ca
www.judges-juges.ca
To ensure the soundness of provincial & territorial courts across Canada
Robert Prince, President
Russell J. Otter, Executive Director
Robin Finlayson, Co-Chair, National Education Committee
Ronald LeBlanc, Co-Chair, National Education Committee
David Orr, Chair, Committee on the Law
Odette Perron, Co-Chair, Provincial Judges' Journal / Journal des juges provinciaux
Robert Prince, Chair, Communications Committee
Karen Ruddy, Chair, CAPCJ Newsletter Editorial Committee
David C. Walker, Co-Chair, Provincial Judges' Journal / Journal des juges provinciaux

Canadian Bar Association (CBA) / Association du barreau canadien (ABC)
#500, 865 Carling Ave., Ottawa ON K1S 5S8
Tel: 613-237-2925; *Fax:* 613-237-0185
Toll-Free: 800-267-8860
info@cba.org
www.cba.org
Social Media: www.youtube.com/user/cbaspin
linkedin.com/company/canadian-bar-association
www.facebook.com/CanadianBarAssociation
twitter.com/CBA_News
To promote improvements in the law; to promote improvements in the administration of justice; to promote individual lawyer training; to advocate in the public interest; to represent the profession on a national & international level; to promote the interests of the CBA; to promote equality in the profession
John Hoyles, CAE, Chief Executive Officer
Janet M. Fuhrer, President

Canadian Corporate Counsel Association (CCCA) / Association canadienne des conseillers juridiques d'entreprises
#1210, 20 Toronto St., Toronto ON M5C 2B8
Tel: 416-869-0522; *Fax:* 416-869-0946
ccca@ccca-cba.org
www.ccca-accje.org
Social Media:
twitter.com/CCCA_News
To provide quality education, information & other services & resources of specific interest to corporate counsel in Canada, & to facilitate communication & networking among such counsel
Christine Staley, Executive Director

Canadian Council on International Law (CCIL) / Conseil canadien de droit international (CCDI)
275 Bay St., Ottawa ON K1R 5Z5
Tel: 613-235-0442; *Fax:* 613-232-8228
manager@ccil-ccdi.ca
www.ccil-ccdi.ca
Social Media:
linkedin.com/groups/Canadian-Council-on-International-Law-4787358?
www.facebook.com/240331419338849
www.twitter.com/ccil_ccdi
To bring together scholars of international law & organizations engaged in teaching & research at Canadian universities; To encourage & conduct studies in international law with a view to its progressive development & codification; To foster the study of legal aspects of Canada's international problems & to advocate their solution in accordance with existing or developing principles of international law.
Adrienne Jarabek, President
Elizabeth Macaulay, Manager

Canadian Criminal Justice Association (CCJA) / Association canadienne de justice pénale (ACJP)
#101, 320 Parkdale Ave., Ottawa ON K1Y 4X9
Tel: 613-725-3715; *Fax:* 613-725-3720
ccja-acjp@rogers.com
www.ccja-acjp.ca
Social Media:
www.facebook.com/186547581359601
To promote a humane, equitable & effective criminal justice system in Canada
Roland LaHaye, President
Irving Kulik, Executive Director

Canadian Institute for the Administration of Justice (CIAJ) / Institut canadien d'administration de la justice (ICAJ)
Faculté de droit, Univ. de Montréal, PO Box 6128, Stn. Centre-Ville, #A3421, 3101, chemin de la Tour, Montréal QC H3C 3J7
Tel: 514-343-6157; *Fax:* 514-343-6296
ciaj@ciaj-icaj.ca
www.ciaj-icaj.ca
Social Media:
linkedin.com/groups?about=&gid=4113891
www.facebook.com/ciaj.icaj
twitter.com/ciaj_icaj
To improve the quality of justice for all Canadians
Michèle Moreau, Executive Director
Donna Ventress, Coordinator, Publications & Communications

Canadian Law & Society Association (CLSA) / Association canadienne droit et société (ACDS)
info@acds-clsa.org
www.acds-clsa.org
To encourage socio-legal inquiry both domestically & internationally
Lyndsay Campbell, President
Nicole O'Byrne, Vice President

Thomas McMorrow, Vice President

Canadian Maritime Law Association / Association canadienne de droit maritime
#900, 1000, rue de la Gauchetiére ouest, Montréal QC H3B 5H4
Tel: 514-849-4161; *Fax:* 514-849-4167
cmla@cmla.org
www.cmla.org
To represent all Canadian commercial maritime interests for the uniform development of Canadian & international maritime law affecting marine transportation & related aspects
John G. O'Connor, President
David G. Colford, National Vice-President

Canadian Police Association (CPA) / Association canadienne des policiers (ACP)
#100, 141 Catherine St., Ottawa ON K2P 1C3
Tel: 613-231-4168; *Fax:* 613-231-3254
cpa-acp@cpa-acp.ca
www.cpa-acp.ca
Tom Stamatakis, President
Denis Côté, Vice-President

Chambre des notaires du Québec
#600, 1801, av McGill College, Montréal QC H3A 0A7
Tél: 514-879-1793; *Téléc:* 514-879-1923
Ligne sans frais: 800-263-1793
www.cnq.org
Média social: www.youtube.com/user/ChambreDesNotaires
D'assurer principalement la protection du public utilisateur des services professionnels de notaire.
Christian Tremblay, Directeur général

Community Legal Education Association (Manitoba) Inc. (CLEA) / Association d'éducation juridique communautaire (Manitoba) inc.
#205, 414 Graham Ave., Winnipeg MB R3C 0L8
Tel: 204-943-2382; *Fax:* 204-943-3600
mctroszko@communitylegal.mb.ca
www.communitylegal.mb.ca
Social Media:
www.facebook.com/339159352882635
To provide legal education & information programs to Manitobans
Mary Troszko, Executive Director
Geof Langen, President

Community Legal Education Ontario (CLEO)
#600, 119 Spadina Ave., Toronto ON M5V 2L1
Tel: 416-408-4420; *Fax:* 416-408-4424
cleo@cleo.on.ca
www.cleo.on.ca
To provide public legal education services & programs that benefit the low income community, disadvantaged persons, such as immigrants & refugees, seniors, women, & injured workers in Ontario

Community Legal Information Association of Prince Edward Island (CLIA PEI)
Royalty Centre, #11, 40 Enman Cres., Charlottetown PE C1A 7K4
Tel: 902-892-0853; *Toll-Free:* 800-240-9798
clia@cliapei.ca
www.cliapei.ca
Social Media: www.youtube.com/CLIAPEI
www.facebook.com/CLIAPEI
twitter.com/cliapei
To provide Islanders with understandable, useful information about the Canadian laws & the justice system
Warren Banks, President
David Daughton, Executive Director

Community Planning Association of Alberta (CPAA)
#205, 10940 - 166A St., Edmonton AB T5P 3V5
Tel: 780-432-6387; *Fax:* 780-452-7718
cpaa@cpaa.biz
www.cpaa.biz
The Community Planning Association of Alberta is an organization dedicated to the promotion of community planning in the Province of Alberta.
Gloria Wilkinson, Chair

Congress of Black Lawyers & Jurists of Québec
#500, 445, boul St-Laurent, Montréal QC H3S 2B8
Tel: 514-954-3471; *Fax:* 514-954-3451
Please call prior to visit

Continuing Legal Education Society of BC
#500, 1155 West Pender St., Vancouver BC V6E 2P4
Tel: 604-669-3544; *Fax:* 604-669-9260
Toll-Free: 800-663-0437
custserv@cle.bc.ca
www.cle.bc.ca
Social Media: www.youtube.com/user/TheCLEBC
linkedin.com/company/continuing-legal-education-society-of-bc
www.facebook.com/clebc
www.twitter.com/clebc
To meet the present & future educational needs of the legal profession in British Columbia
Gwendoline C. Allison, Chair
Ronald G. Friesen, Chief Executive Officer

Criminal Lawyers' Association (CLA)
#1, 189 Queen St. East, Toronto ON M5A 1S2
Tel: 416-214-9875; *Fax:* 416-968-6818
www.criminallawyers.ca
To be the voice for criminal justice & civil liberties in Canada
Anthony Laycock, Executive Director
Norm Boxall, President

Fédération des associations de juristes d'expression française de common law (FAJEF)
117B, rue Egénie, Winnipeg MB R2H 0X9
Tél: 204-415-7551; *Téléc:* 204-415-4482
reception@fajef.com
www.accesjustice.ca
Pour fournir un soutien et de représenter ses membres
Rénald Rémillard, Directeur général
Allan Damer, Président

Federation of Law Reform Agencies of Canada (FOLRAC)
c/o Manitoba Law Reform Commission, 405 Broadway, 12th Fl., Winnipeg MB R3C 3L6
Tel: 604-822-0142; *Fax:* 604-822-0144
folracanada@gmail.com
www.folrac.com
Collection of 8 law reform agencies, from various provinces, who meet yearly to exchange information.
Greg Steele, President

Federation of Law Societies of Canada (FLSC) / Fédération des ordres professionnels de juristes du Canada
World Exchange Plaza, #1810, 45 O'Connor St., Ottawa ON K1P 1A4
Tel: 613-236-7272; *Fax:* 613-236-7233
info@flsc.ca
www.flsc.ca
To coordinate the law societies of Canada; To act as a voice for Canadian law societies
Jeff Hirsch, President
Jonathan G. Herman, Chief Executive Officer
Bob Linney, Director, Communications

Fondation du barreau du Québec
Maison du Barreau, 445, boul Saint-Laurent, Montréal QC H2Y 3T8
Tél: 514-954-3400; *Ligne sans frais:* 800-361-8495
information@barreau.qc.ca
www.barreau.qc.ca
Média social: plus.google.com/101349996276959545722
linkedin.com/groups?gid=2206718
www.facebook.com/barreauduquebec
twitter.com/BarreauduQuebec
Subventionner, primer et supporter des travaux axés vers l'intérêt public et utiles à la pratique du droit.
Bernard Synnott, Président

Foundation for Legal Research (FLR) / La foundation pour la recherche juridique
Cour d'appel du Québec, 100 rue Notre-Dame E., Montréal QC H2Y 4B6
Toll-Free: 800-267-8860
foundationforlegalresearch.org
To support & maintain scholarships, bursaries & prizes in the field of legal research
Nicholas Kasirer, Chair
Francois Letourneaux, Secretary
Stephen Bresolin, Treasurer

Hamilton Police Association (HPA) / Association de la police de Hamilton
555 Upper Wellington St., Hamilton ON L9A 3P8
Tel: 905-574-6044; *Fax:* 905-574-3223
hpa@hpa.on.ca
www.hpa.on.ca
To promote high quality professional policing through labour relations & political activity
Brad Boyce, Administrator

Mike Cruse, Executive Officer

Institute of Law Clerks of Ontario (ILCO)
#502, 20 Adelaide St. East, Toronto ON M5C 2T6
Tel: 416-214-6252; *Fax:* 416-214-6255
reception@ilco.on.ca
www.ilco.on.ca
To provide an organized network for promoting unity, cooperation & mutual assistance among law clerks in Ontario; to advance & protect their status & interests; to promote their education for the purpose of increasing their knowledge, efficiency & professional ability.
Rose Kottis, President
Elsie Karulas, Vice-President

International Centre for Criminal Law Reform & Criminal Justice Policy (ICCLR)
1822 East Mall, Vancouver BC V6T 1Z1
Tel: 604-822-9875; *Fax:* 604-822-9317
icclr@law.ubc.ca
www.icclr.law.ubc.ca
To improve the quality of justice through reform of criminal law, policy & practice; to provide advice, information, research & proposals for policy development & legislation
Kathleen Macdonald, Executive Director

International Commission of Jurists (Canadian Section) (ICJ) / La Commission internationale de juristes (section canadienne) (CIJ)
#500, 865 Carling Ave., Ottawa ON K1S 5S8
Tel: 613-237-2925; *Fax:* 613-237-0185
patw@cba.org
www.icjcanada.org
To works internationally with the parent organization to monitor & promote the rule of law & the impartiality & independence of the judiciary in countries where these are threatened or non-existent; to act nationally & locally to promote awareness of these issues & human rights generally
Paul D.K. Fraser, President
Pat Whiting, Executive Director

Law Foundation of British Columbia
#1340, 605 Robson St., Vancouver BC V6B 5J3
Tel: 604-688-2337; *Fax:* 604-688-4586
info@lawfoundationbc.org
www.lawfoundationbc.org
To allocate funds to programs that will benefit the general public of British Columbia; To act in accordance with The Legal Profession Act & distribute income in areas that promote & advance a just society & the rule of law, such as legal aid, law libraries, legal education, legal research, & law reform; To conduct operations with recognition of the diverse population of British Columbia
Wayne Robertson, Executive Director
Margaret Sasges, Chair
Jo-Anne Kaulius, Director, Finance

Law Foundation of Newfoundland & Labrador
Murray Premises, 2nd Fl., PO Box 5907, #49, 55 Elizabeth Ave., St. John's NL A1C 5X4
Tel: 709-754-4424; *Fax:* 709-754-4320
www.atyp.com/lawfoundationnl
To provide grants for the following services in Newfoundland & Labrador that advance public understanding of the law & access to legal services: the Legal Aid Commission as established under the Legal Aid Act; law libraries; legal research; legal education; scholarships for studies relevant to law; law reform; & legal referral services

Law Foundation of Nova Scotia
Cogswell Tower, #1305, 2000 Barrington St., Halifax NS B3J 3K1
Tel: 902-422-8335; *Fax:* 902-492-0424
nslawfd@nslawfd.ca
www.nslawfd.ca
To establish & maintain a fund to be used for the examination, research, revision & reform of & public access to the law, legal education, the administration of justice in the province & any other purposes incidental or conducive to or consequential upon the attainment of any such objects
Kerry L. Oliver, Executive Director

Law Foundation of Ontario (LFO) / La fondation du droit de l'Ontario
PO Box 19, #3002, 20 Queen St. West, Toronto ON M5H 3R3
Tel: 416-598-1550; *Fax:* 416-598-1526
general@lawfoundation.on.ca
www.lawfoundation.on.ca
Social Media:
www.facebook.com/pages/The-Law-Foundation-of-Ontario/222748937889770
twitter.com/LawFoundationOn

An organization that provides funding to a wide range of organizations to foster excellence in the work of lawyers, paralegals and other legal professionals.
Mark J. Sandler, Chair
Elizabeth Goldberg, Chief Executive Officer

Law Foundation of Prince Edward Island
49 Water St., Charlottetown PE C1A 7K2
Tel: 902-620-1763
info@lawfoundationpei.ca
www.lawfoundationpei.ca
To establish & maintain a fund & use the proceeds for the purposes of: legal education & research on law reform; the editing & printing of decisions of the Supreme Court & the Provincial Court of PEI; the promotion of legal aid; aid in the establishment, operation & maintenance of law libraries in PEI
Sheila Lund MacDonald, Executive Director

Law Foundation of Saskatchewan
#200, 2208 Scarth St., Regina SK S4P 2J6
Tel: 306-352-1121; *Fax:* 306-522-6222
lfsk@virtusgroup.ca
www.lawfoundation.sk.ca
To maintain a fund to support legal aid, law reform, law libraries, legal education, & legal research
Robert Arscott, Secretary
Patricia Quaroni, Chair
Bob Watt, Treasurer

Law Society of Alberta (LSA)
#500, 919 - 11th Ave. SW, Calgary AB T2R 1P3
Tel: 403-229-4700; *Fax:* 403-228-1728
Toll-Free: 800-661-9003
www.lawsocietyalberta.com
Social Media:
linkedin.com/company/the-law-society-of-alberta
twitter.com/LawSocietyofAB
To serve the public by promoting a high standard of legal services & professional conduct through the governance & regulation of an independent legal profession; To govern all lawyers who practise law in Alberta; To admit lawyers to the Bar; To supervise professional conduct & disciplinary actions as required
Don Thompson, Executive Director
James Eamon, President
Drew Thomson, Director, Corporate Services
Ally Taylor, Manager, Communications

Law Society of British Columbia
845 Cambie St., 8th Fl., Vancouver BC V6B 4Z9
Tel: 604-669-2533; *Fax:* 604-669-5232
Toll-Free: 800-902-5300
TTY: 604-443-5700
communications@lsbc.org
www.lawsociety.bc.ca
Social Media: www.youtube.com/user/lawsocietyofbc
linkedin.com/company/law-society-of-british-columbia
twitter.com/LawSocietyofBC
To ensure that the public is well served by a competent, honourable & independent legal profession
E. David Crossin, President
Timothy E. McGee, CEO & Executive Director

Law Society of Manitoba (LSM) / La Société du Barreau du Manitoba
219 Kennedy St., Winnipeg MB R3C 1S8
Tel: 204-942-5571; *Fax:* 204-956-0624
admin@lawsociety.mb.ca
www.lawsociety.mb.ca
To ensure the public in Manitoba is well served by the legal profession
Allan Fineblit, CEO
Marilyn Billinkoff, Deputy CEO

Law Society of New Brunswick / Barreau du Nouveau-Brunswick
68 Avonlea Court, Fredericton NB E3C 1N8
Tel: 506-458-8540; *Fax:* 506-451-1421
general@lawsociety-barreau.nb.ca
www.lawsociety-barreau.nb.ca
The Law Society was officially created in 1846. The Provincial Legislative Assembly adopted Chapter 48 of the Provincial Statutes which in effect incorporated what was then called the "Barristers' Society" for the "purpose of securing in the Province a learned and honourable legal profession, for establishing order and good conduct among its members and for promoting knowledgeable development and reform of the law".
Hélène L. Beaulieu, President
Marc L. Richard, Executive Director

Law Society of Newfoundland & Labrador
PO Box 1028, 196-198 Water St., St. John's NL A1C 5M3
Tel: 709-722-4740; *Fax:* 709-722-8902
thelawsociety@lawsociety.nf.ca
www.lawsociety.nf.ca
To ensure that law students are appropriately educated and trained through articling and Bar Admission programs and exams, and provides continuing legal education to practititoners.
Brenda B. Grimes, Executive Director

Law Society of Nunavut (LSNU)
PO Box 149, Iqaluit NU X0A 0H0
Tel: 867-979-2330; *Fax:* 867-979-2333
administrator@lawsociety.nu.ca
lawsociety.nu.ca
To govern its membership & protect the public
Nalini Vaddapalli, CEO

Law Society of Prince Edward Island
PO Box 128, 49 Water St., Charlottetown PE C1A 7K2
Tel: 902-566-1666; *Fax:* 902-368-7557
lawsociety@lspei.pe.ca
www.lspei.pe.ca
To uphold & protect the public interest in the administration of justice; to establish standards for the education, professional responsibility & competence of members & applicants for membership; to ensure the independence, integrity & honour of the society & its members; to regulate the practice of law; to uphold & protect the interests of members.
Susan M. Robinson, Executive Director & Sec.-Treas.

Law Society of Saskatchewan
#1100, 2002 Victoria Ave., Regina SK S4P 0R7
Tel: 306-569-8242; *Fax:* 306-352-2989
reception@lawsociety.sk.ca
www.lawsociety.sk.ca
To govern the legal profession by upholding high standards of competence & integrity; ensuring the independence of the profession; advancing the administration of justice, the profession & the rule of law, all in the public interest
Tom Schonhoffer, Executive Director
Tim Huber, Counsel

Law Society of the Northwest Territories / Le Barreau des Territoires du Nord-Ouest
PO Box 1298, Stn. Main, Yellowknife NT X1A 2N9
Tel: 867-873-3828; *Fax:* 867-873-6344
info@lawsociety.nt.ca
www.lawsociety.nt.ca
Social Media:
twitter.com/LawSocietyNWT
To serve the public by an independent, responsible & responsive legal profession.
Pamela Naylor, Executive Director

Law Society of Upper Canada / Barreau du Haut-Canada
Osgoode Hall, 130 Queen St. West, Toronto ON M5H 2N6
Tel: 416-947-3300; *Fax:* 416-947-3924
Toll-Free: 800-668-7380
TTY: 416-644-4886
lawsociety@lsuc.on.ca
www.lsuc.on.ca
Social Media: www.youtube.com/lawsocietylsuc
linkedin.com/company/the-law-society-of-upper-canada
www.facebook.com/pages/Law-Society-of-Upper-Canada/110214529001232
twitter.com/LawsocietyLSUC
To govern the legal profession in the public interest by ensuring that the people of Ontario are served by lawyers who meet high standards of learning, competence & professional conduct.
Robert G. W. Lapper, CEO
Diana Miles, Director, Professional Development & Competence

Law Society of Yukon (LSY)
#202, 302 Steele St., Whitehorse YT Y1A 2C5
Tel: 867-668-4231; *Fax:* 867-667-7556
info@lawsocietyyukon.com
www.lawsocietyyukon.com
To govern legal profession in the Yukon.
Lynn Daffe, Executive Director

Legal Education Society of Alberta (LESA)
#2610, 10104 - 103 Ave., Edmonton AB T5J 0H8
Tel: 780-420-1987; *Fax:* 780-425-0885
Toll-Free: 800-282-3900
lesa@lesa.org
www.lesaonline.org
Social Media:
linkedin.com/company/legal-education-society-of-alberta
www.facebook.com/lesaonline
twitter.com/lesaonline
To educate providers of legal services in Alberta; To increase awareness of issues affecting the legal profession; To maintain & increase professional responsibility & competence; To develop & provide education in law, skills, & ethics
Tamara Buckwold, Chair
Aaron D. Martens, Secretary-Treasurer
Jennifer Flynn, Executive Director & Director, Canadian Centre for Professional Legal Education (CPLED) Alberta

Legal Information Society of Nova Scotia (LISNS)
5523B Young St., Halifax NS B3K 1Z7
Tel: 902-454-2198; *Fax:* 902-455-3105
Toll-Free: 800-665-9779
lisns@legalinfo.org
www.legalinfo.org
Social Media:
www.facebook.com/LegalSeagull
twitter.com/LegalInfoNS
To provide Nova Scotians easy access to information & resources about the law
Kevin A. MacDonald, President

The Manitoba Law Foundation / La Fondation manitobaine du droit
#300, 207 Donald St., Winnipeg MB R3C 1M5
Tel: 204-947-3142; *Fax:* 204-942-3221
mblawfoundation@gatewest.net
manitobalawfoundation.org
To provide funds for legal education, legal research, legal aid, law reform & the establishment, operation & maintenance of law libraries
Barbara Palace Churchill, Executive Director

Municipal Law Enforcement Officers' Association (Ontario) Inc.
c/o j. Popple, PO Box 100, #7-8. 100 Dissett St., Bradford ON L3Z 2A7
Tel: 905-775-5366; *Fax:* 905-775-0153
mleo@mleoa.ca
www.mleoa.ca
To bring members into helpful association with each other to maintain professional standards; to encourage & assist in the education & training programs for Municipal Law Enforcement Officers
Randy Berg, President

New Brunswick Law Foundation / La Fondation pour l'avancement du droit au Nouveau-Brunswick
66, rue Avonlea Court, Fredericton NB E3C 1N8
Tel: 506-453-7776; *Fax:* 506-451-1421
amartin@lawsociety-barreau.nb.ca
www.lawsociety.nb.ca
To receive the interest earned on lawyers' mixed trust accounts & to use these funds to support law-related projects to benefit residents of New Brunswick
Alban Martin, Executive Director

Northwest Territories Association of Provincial Court Judges
c/o Judge Garth Malakoe, Territorial Court of Northwest Territories, PO Box 550, 4093 - 49th St., Yellowknife NT X1A 2N4
Tel: 867-873-7604; *Fax:* 867-873-0203
Garth Malakoe, Northwest Territories Director, Canadian Association of Provincial Court Judges

Northwest Territories Law Foundation
PO Box 2594, 5212 - 55th St., Yellowknife NT X1A 2P9
Tel: 867-873-8275; *Fax:* 867-873-6383
www.lawsociety.nt.ca/LawFoundation
To provide funding in the Northwest Territories in the following areas: the establishment & operation of law libraries; the provision of legal education; research in law & the administration of justice; recommendations for law reform; legal aid programs & similar programs; & the Assurance Fund
Wendy Carter, Executive Manager
Emerald Murphy, Chair

Nova Scotia Barristers' Society (NSBS)
800 - 2000 Barrington St., Halifax NS B3J 3K1
Tel: 902-422-1491; *Fax:* 902-429-4869
www.nsbs.org
Social Media:
https://linkedin.com/company/ns-barristers'-society
www.facebook.com/NSBarristers
twitter.com/nsbs
To set & enforce standards of professional responsibility & ethics for lawyers; To license & discipline members of the profession, in accordance with the Legal Profession Act
Darrel Pink, Executive Director

Ontario Association of Police Services Boards (OAPSB)
Suite A, 10 Peel Centre Dr., Brampton ON L6T 4B9
Tel: 905-458-1488; *Fax:* 905-458-2260
Toll-Free: 800-831-7727
admin@oapsb.ca
www.oapsb.ca
To act as the voice of police services boards to government; To provide services to assist police services boards in Ontario
Fred Kaustinen, Executive Director

Ontario Criminal Justice Association (CJAO)
PO Box 949, Stn. K, Toronto ON M4P 2V3
cjao.info
To encourage co-operation among individuals, groups & governmental organizations interested & active in the field of criminal justice; to further the study of criminal justice issues.

Ontario Crown Attorneys Association (OCAA) / Association des procureurs de la couronne de l'Ontario (APCO)
PO Box 30, #1905, 180 Dundas St. West, Toronto ON M5G 1Z8
Tel: 416-977-4517; *Fax:* 416-977-1460
reception@ocaa.ca
www.ocaa.ca
To promote & protect the professional interests of crown counsels, assistant crown attorneys, & articling students
Scott Childs, President

People's Law School
#150, 900 Howe St., Vancouver BC V6Z 2M4
Tel: 604-331-5400; *Fax:* 604-331-5401
info@publiclegaled.bc.ca
www.publiclegaled.bc.ca
Social Media: www.youtube.com/user/plsbc
linkedin.com/company/2024453?trk=tyah
www.facebook.com/pages/Peoples-Law-School-BC/181366371905105
twitter.com/PLSBC
To make law & the legal system understandable & accessible to residents of British Columbia
Terresa Augustine, Executive Director

Police Association of Nova Scotia (PANS) / Association des policiers de la Nouvelle-Écosse
#2, 1000 Windmill Rd., Dartmouth NS B3B 1L7
Tel: 902-468-7555; *Fax:* 902-468-2202
Toll-Free: 888-468-2798
www.pansguide.com
David W. Fisher, CEO

Police Association of Ontario (PAO) / Association des policiers de l'Ontario
#302, 1650 Yonge St., Toronto ON M4T 2A2
pao@pao.ca
www.pao.ca
Social Media:
www.facebook.com/PoliceAssociationofOntario
To act as the official voice & representative body for Ontario's front line police personnel; To represent & support Ontario police associations
Stephen Reid, Executive Director

Police Sector Council (PSC) / Conseil sectoriel de la police (CSP)
#303, 1545 Carling Ave., Ottawa ON K1Z 8P9
Tel: 613-729-2789
info@policecouncil.ca
www.policecouncil.ca
Social Media:
twitter.com/PoliceCouncil
Improving the ways in which human resource planning & management support police operations & enhance police service in communities across Canada
Geoff Gruson, Executive Director

Probation Officers Association of Ontario (POAO)
#6245, 2100 Bloor St. West, Toronto ON M6S 5A5
www.poao.org
Social Media:
www.facebook.com/POAOntario
twitter.com/POAOntario
To represent the professional interests of the probation & parole Officers across the province; to provide representation on legislative issues to policy makers; to act as a forum for exchange of experience & information.
Elana Lamese, President

The Public Interest Advocacy Centre (PIAC) / Centre pour la défense de l'intérêt public
#1204, 1 Nicholas St., Ottawa ON K1N 7B7
Tel: 613-562-4002
piac@piac.ca
www.piac.ca
To provide legal services on a non-profit basis to groups & individuals addressing public interest issues of broad concern who would not otherwise have access to such services; the centre's special interests are telecommunications, energy, transportation, broadcasting, privacy, technical services & consumer protection
John Lawford, Executive Director & General Counsel

Public Legal Education Association of Saskatchewan, Inc. (PLEA Sask.)
#500, 333 - 25th St. East, Saskatoon SK S7K 0L4
Tel: 306-653-1868; *Fax:* 306-653-1869
plea@plea.org
www.plea.org
To provide the public with information regarding the law
Heather Jensen, President
Joel Janow, Executive Director

Public Legal Information Association of Newfoundland (PLIAN)
Tara Place, #227, 31 Peet St., St. John's NL A1B 3W8
Tel: 709-722-2643; *Fax:* 709-722-0054
Toll-Free: 888-660-7788
info@publiclegalinfo.com
www.publiclegalinfo.com
Social Media:
twitter.com/PLIAN_NL
To provide plain language legal information to the general public of Newfoundland, in both official languages, through a telephone enquiry line, public speaking engagements, publications, & a lawyer referral service
Kevin O'Shea, Executive Director

Saskatchewan Federation of Police Officers (SFPO)
SK
Tel: 306-539-0960
www.saskpolice.com
To advance police work as a profession; To support members in their police careers
Bernie Eiswirth, Executive Officer
Evan Bray, President
Jason Stonechild, Executive Vice-President

Société de criminologie du Québec (SCQ)
#201, 2000, boul Saint-Joseph est, Montréal QC H2H 1E4
Tél: 514-529-4391; *Téléc:* 514-529-6936
crimino@societecrimino.qc.ca
www.societecrimino.qc.ca
Média social: www.facebook.com/SocieteCrimino
twitter.com/societecrimino
Mission: de contribuer à l'évolution du système de justice pénale, de favoriser les échanges & les débats entre tous les intéressés à l'avancement de la justice pénale, & de favoriser & encourager la recherche
Caroline Savard, Directrice générale

The Society of Notaries Public of British Columbia
PO Box 44, #1220, 625 Howe St., Vancouver BC V6C 2T6
Tel: 604-681-4516; *Fax:* 604-681-7258
Toll-Free: 800-663-0343
www.notaries.bc.ca
To ensure that its members provide high quality services to their clients
G.W. Wayne Braid, Chief Executive Officer/Secretary
Akash Sablok, President

Toronto Police Association (TPA) / Association de la police de Toronto
180 Yorkland Blvd., Toronto ON M2J 1R5
Tel: 416-491-4301; *Fax:* 416-494-4948
information@tpa.ca
www.tpa.ca
Mike McCormack, President
Douglas Corrigan, Vice-President

Yukon Law Foundation
PO Box 31789, Whitehorse YT Y1A 6L3
Tel: 867-667-7500; *Fax:* 867-393-3904
info@yukonlawfoundation.com
www.yukonlawfoundation.com
The objects of the Foundation are to maintain & manage a fund accumulated primarily from the interest on lawyers' trust accounts
Mike Reynolds, Chair
Deana Lemke, Executive Director

Yukon Public Legal Education Association (YPLEA)
PO Box 2799, Yukon College, Whitehorse YT Y1A 5K4
Tel: 867-668-5297; *Toll-Free:* 866-667-4305
www.yplea.com
To provide free legal information to Yukoners & promote greater accessibility to the legal system

LGBTQ

Alliance des gais et lesbiennes Laval-Laurentides (AGLLL Inc.)
CP 98030, 95, boul Labelle, Sainte-Thérèse QC J7E 5R4
aglll@hotmail.com
www.algi.qc.ca/asso/aglll/
Groupe de discussion; activités

AlterHéros
CP 56073, Succ. Alexis-Nihon, Montréal QC H3Z 1X5
Tél: 514-360-1320
info@alterheros.com
www.alterheros.com
Média social: www.facebook.com/alterheros
twitter.com/alterheros
Organisme communautaire bénévole à but non lucratif qui favorise l'insertion sociale des personnes d'orientation homosexuelle, bisexuelle et d'identité transsexuelle
Véronique Daneau, Directrice générale

Amazones des grands espaces
Montréal QC
Tél: 514-525-3663
info@plein-air-amazones.org
www.plein-air-amazones.org
Club de plein air pour lesbiennes

ARC: Aînés et retraités de la communauté
Montréal QC
Tél: 514-730-8870
arcssc2@gmail.com
www.algi.qc.ca/asso/retraitesgais
Média social: www.facebook.com/arc.montreal
Groupement de personnes gaies aînées ou retraitées; activités sociales, culturelles ou sportives. Contactez Raymond B. au 514-529-7471 ou Nicholas au 514-343-1117

Association des Gais et Lesbiennes Sourds (AGLS)
Montréal QC
agls@live.ca
www.agls.ca
Média social: www.facebook.com/214130285283518
L'Association des Gais et Lesbiennes Sourds est un organisme provincial à but non lucratif qui offre des activités sociales et des ateliers sur l'homophobie auprès de la communauté sourde et malentendante du Québec et du Grand Montréal.

Association des lesbiennes et des gais sur Internet (ALGI)
CP 476, Succ. C, Montréal QC H2L 4K4
Tél: 514-528-8424
info@algi.qc.ca
www.algi.qc.ca
Média social: www.facebook.com/algi.qc.ca
Favoriser l'expression des lesbiennes et des gais au moyen de l'Internet; favoriser l'échange entre les individus et les organismes de la communauté gaie et lesbienne dans un esprit d'entraide

Association des pères gais de Montréal inc. (APGM) / Gay Fathers of Montréal Inc.
4245, rue Laval, Montréal QC H2W 2J6
Tél: 514-528-8424; *Téléc:* 514-528-9708
peresgais@gmail.com
www.algi.qc.ca/asso/apgm/
Regrouper les hommes qui sont à la fois pères et gais; offrir support et aide aux hommes gais soucieux d'éduquer leurs enfants; permettre au père gai de se situer face à la condition de vie au moyen d'échanges, de discussion et d'information; promouvoir la condition des pères gais et la défense de leurs intérêts communs

BC Rainbow Alliance of the Deaf
BC
info@bcrad.com
www.bcrad.com
Social Media:
www.facebook.com/BCRAD.YVR?fref=ts
The British Columbia Rainbow Alliance of the Deaf (BCRAD) is an educational and social recreation organization for all people on the Deaf and queer spectrums.
Zoée Montpetit, President

Bi Unité Montréal (BUM)
CP 476, Succ. C, Montréal QC H2L 4K4
info@biunitemontreal.org
www.algi.qc.ca/asso/bum/
Association à but non lucratif; a pour mission de fair connaître la bisexualité et de rassembler les bisexuel(le)s dans un lieu commun pour qu'ils/qu'elles puissent s'informer, se divertir, et se supporter.

Les Bolides
3350, rue Ontario Est, Montréal QC H1W 1P7
Tél: 514-522-7773
info@lesbolides.org
www.lesbolides.org
Ligue de quilles

Canadian Lesbian & Gay Archives (CLGA)
PO Box 699, Stn. F, 34 Isabella St., Toronto ON M4Y 1N1
Tel: 416-777-2755
queeries@clga.ca
www.clga.ca
Social Media:
www.facebook.com/116735553447
twitter.com/clgarchives
To acquire, preserve & make available to the public information in any medium about lesbians & gays, with an emphasis on Canada.
Robert Windrum, President

Canadian Professional Association for Transgender Health (CPATH)
#201, 1770 Fort St., Ottawa ON V8R 1J5
Tel: 250-592-6183; *Fax:* 250-592-6123
info@cpath.ca
www.cpath.ca
CPATH is an interdisciplinary professional organization which works to support the health, wellbeing, and dignity of trans and gender diverse people.
Devon MacFarlane, President

Centre communautaire des gais et lesbiennes de Montréal (CCGLM)
CP 476, Succ. C, Montréal QC H2L 4K4
Tél: 514-528-8424; *Téléc:* 514-528-9708
info@ccglm.org
www.ccglm.org
Média social: www.facebook.com/ccglm
Organisme sans but lucratif qui agit pour améliorer la condition des membres de nos communautés - lesbiennes, gais, bisexuel(les), transexuel(les), transgenres, et allosexuel(les); bibliothèque
Christian Tanguay, Director-General

Centre d'orientation sexuelle de l'université McGill (COSUM) / McGill University Sexual Identity Centre (MUSIC)
Dép. de psychiatrie, Hôpital général de Montréal, #A2-160, 1650, av Cedar, Montréal QC H3G 1A4
Tél: 514-934-1934; *Téléc:* 514-934-8471
music-cosum@mcgill.ca
www.mcgill.ca/cosum
Offre des psychothérapies individuelles à court terme, psychothérapies de groupe & de couple ou familiales
Karine J. Igartua, Psychiatre

Centre de solidarité lesbienne
#301, 4126, rue St-Denis, Montréal QC H2W 2M5
Tél: 514-526-2452; *Téléc:* 514-526-3570
info@solidaritelesbienne.qc.ca
www.solidaritelesbienne.qc.ca
Le Centre est accessible aux personnes à mobilité réduite; organisme sans but lucratif qui a pour mission d'améliorer les conditions de vie des lesbiennes en leur offrant des services et des interventions adaptés à leur réalité et ce, dans les domaines de la violence conjugales, du bien-être et de la santé.

Coalition des familles LGBT / LGBT Family Coalition
Montréal QC
Tél: 514-846-7600
info@familleslgbt.org
www.familleslgbt.org
Milite pour la reconnaissance légale et sociale des familles homoparentales; groupe bilingue de parents lesbiens, gais, bisexuels et transgenres. Québec: 418-523-5572
Mona Greenbaum, Directrice générale

Coalition for Lesbian & Gay Rights in Ontario (CLGRO) / Coalition pour les droits des lesbiennes et personnes gaies en Ontario
PO Box 822, Stn. A, Toronto ON M5W 1G3
Tel: 416-392-6878
www.clgro.org
To work towards feminism, lesbian, gay & bisexual liberation by engaging in public struggle for full human rights, by promoting access & diversity within our communities, & by strengthening cooperative networks for lesbian, gay & bisexual activism

Community One Foundation
PO Box 760, Stn. F, Toronto ON M4Y 2N6
Tel: 416-920-5422
info@communityone.ca
www.communityone.ca
To raise & disburse funds for the advancement of lesbian, gay, bisexual & transgender projects, artists & organizations; to fund projects in the areas of health & social services, arts & culture, research & education, political & legal
Craig Daniel, Board Co-Chair
Andrea Love, Board Co-Chair
Calvin Chiu, Treasurer

Conseil central du Montréal métropolitain (CCMM-CSN)
1601, av De Lorimier, Montréal QC H2K 4M5
Tél: 514-598-2021; *Téléc:* 514-598-2020
receptionccmm@csn.qc.ca
www.ccmm-csn.qc.ca
Média social:
www.facebook.com/Conseil.Central.Montreal.Metropolitain.CSN
Mireille Bénard, Coordonnatrice

Conseil québécois des gais et lesbiennes du Québec (CQGL)
CP 182, Succ. C, Montréal QC H2L 4K1
Tél: 514-759-6844
info@conseil-lgbt.ca
www.cqgl.ca
Média social: www.facebook.com/CQLGBT
twitter.com/cqlgbt
A pour mission concrétiser notre leitmotive 'S'engager pour l'égalité sociale'. Adresse civique: #100, 1307, rue Sainte-Catherine Est, Montréal, QC.
Steve Foster, Directeur général

Egale Canada
185 Carlton St., Toronto ON M5A 2K7
Tel: 416-964-7887; *Fax:* 416-963-5665
Toll-Free: 888-204-7777
egale.canada@egale.ca
www.egale.ca
Social Media:
www.facebook.com/EgaleCanada
twitter.com/egalecanada
To advance equality & justice for lesbian, gay, bisexual & transgendered persons, & their families in Canada
Helen Kennedy, Executive Director

Fondation Mario-Racine / Mario Racine Foundation
#110, 2075, rue Plessis, Montréal QC H2L 2Y4
Tél: 514-528-5940
fondationmarioracine99@gmail.com
www.algi.qc.ca/asso/fmr
A pour mission de favoriser le développement communautaire et culturel des gais et lesbiennes à Montréal; est engagée dans la réalisation du Centre communautaire des gais et lesbiennes de Montréal.
Michel Durocher, Président

GRIS-Mauricie/Centre-du-Québec
#232, 255 rue Brock, Drummondville QC J2C 1M5
Tél: 819-445-0007; *Ligne sans frais:* 877-745-0007
info@grismcdq.org
www.grismcdq.org
De promouvoir la diversité de l'acceptation
Nathalie Niquette, Directrice générale

Groupe de recherche et d'intervention sociale (GRIS-Montréal)
CP 476, Succ. C, Montréal QC H2L 4K4
Tél: 514-590-0016; *Téléc:* 514-590-0764
info@gris.ca
www.gris.ca
Média social: www.facebook.com/grismontreal
twitter.com/GRISmontreal
Favoriser un meilleure connaissance des réalités homosexuelles et de faciliter l'intégration des gais, lesbiennes et bisexuel(les) dans la société
David Platts, Président

Groupe gai de l'Outaouais
#003, 109, rue Wright, Gatineau QC J8X 2G7
Tél: 819-776-2727; *Téléc:* 819-776-2001
Ligne sans frais: 877-376-2727
info@lebras.qc.ca
www.algi.qc.ca/asso/gdhgfo/
Discussions, rencontres, activités sociales; les rencontres ont lieu les mercredis soir à 19h30, au Bureau régional d'action sida, 109, rue Wright, local 003 (Gatineau, secteur Hull).

Groupe gai de l'Université Laval (GGUL)
Pavillon Mauice-Pollack, #2223, 2305, rue de l'Université, Québec QC G1V 0A6
Tél: 418-656-2131
ggul@public.ulaval.ca
www.ggul.org
Média social: www.youtube.com/user/GGULULAVAL
ca.linkedin.com/pub/ggul-ulaval/28/37a/23
twitter.com/ggul_ulaval

Groupe régional d'intervention social - Québec (GRIS-Québec)
#202, 363, rue de la Couronne, Québec QC G1K 6E9
Tél: 418-523-5572
info@grisquebec.org
www.grisquebec.org
Média social: www.facebook.com/GrisQuebec
André Tardiff, Directeur général

Hors sentiers
10229, rue Chambord, Montréal QC H2C 2R3
Tél: 450-433-7508
sentiers@hotmail.ca
www.algi.qc.ca/asso/horssentiers/
Groupe de plein air

Jeunesse Lambda
CP 321125, Succ. Saint-André, Montréal QC H2L 4Y5
Tél: 514-528-7535
info@jeunesselambda.org
www.algi.qc.ca/asso/jlambda/
Média social:
www.facebook.com/pages/Jeunesse-Lambda/139443476158956
Groupe d'accueil francophone de discussion et d'activités par et pour les jeunes gais, lesbiennes, bisexuel(les).

Ontario Rainbow Alliance of the Deaf (ORAD)
c/o The 519 Community Centre, 519 Church St., Toronto ON M4Y 2C9
info@orad.ca
new2.orad.ca
Social Media: www.youtube.com/ontariorad
www.facebook.com/176398609081793
www.twitter.com/OntarioRAD
Ontario Rainbow Alliance for the Deaf (ORAD) is a not for profit organization serving Deaf, deaf, deafened, hard of hearing and hearing people who are LGBTTIQQ2S* communities in the Province of Ontario.
Nicka Noble, Acting President/Vice-President

Projet 10 / Project 10
1575, rue Amherst, Montréal QC H2L 3L4
Tél: 514-989-0001
questions@p10.qc.ca
www.p10.qc.ca
Média social: www.facebook.com/P10montreal
Ligne d'entraide anonyme et confidentielle; services pour les jeunes lesbiennes, gais, bisexuel(le)s, intersexuel(le)s, allosexuel(le)s, trans, et bispirituel(le)s
Remy Attig, Co-coordinatrice
Sarah Butler, Co-coordinatrice

Réseau des lesbiennes du Québec (RLQ) / Québec Lesbian Network
#110, 2075, rue Plessis, Montréal QC H2L 2Y4
Tél: 438-929-6928; *Téléc:* 514-528-9708
rlqln.info@gmail.com
rlq-qln.algi.qc.ca
Média social: www.facebook.com/RLQQLN

La Trame
CP 845, Succ. Desjardins, Montréal QC H5B 1B9
Tél: 514-374-0227
la.trame@hotmail.com
la-trame.ca
Regroupement pour lesbiennes dans le domaine des arts, de la culture et du loisir
Mireille Robillard, Contact

Welcome Friend Association
PO Box 242, 76 Dawson St., Thessalon ON P0R 1L0
Toll-Free: 888-909-2234
registration@welcomefriend.ca
www.welcomefriend.ca
Social Media:
www.facebook.com/welcomefriendassociation
Welcome Friend Association educates and promotes awareness in society regarding gender, sexual identities and expressions.
Harry Stewart, President

Libraries & Archives

Alberta Association of Academic Libraries (AAAL)
c/o Leigh Cunningham, Medicine Hat College Library Services, 299 College Dr. SE, Medicine Hat AB TIA 3Y6
aaal.ca
Social Media: www.facebook.com/AlbertaAssociationofAcademicLIbraries
twitter.com/AlbertaAAL
To facilitate planning, cooperation, & communication among Alberta's academic libraries; To promote continuing education
Sonya Betz, Co-Chair
Robyn Hall, Co-Chair
Leigh Cunningham, Secretary-Treasurer

Alberta Association of Library Technicians (AALT)
PO Box 700, Edmonton AB T5J 2L4
Toll-Free: 866-350-2258
secretary@aalt.org
www.aalt.org
Social Media: linkedin.com/in/librarytechnicians
www.facebook.com/AALTLibraryTech
twitter.com/AALTLibraryTech
To foster & enhance the professional image of library technicians in Alberta; To support library technicians throughout the province
Sarah Stephens, President
Kristy Nicholls, Director, Membership
Lynda Shurko, Secretary

Alberta Library Trustees Association (ALTA)
#6-24, 7 Sir Winston Churchill Sq., Edmonton AB T5J 2V5
Tel: 780-761-2582; *Fax:* 866-419-1451
admin@librarytrustees.ab.ca
www.librarytrustees.ab.ca
Social Media: linkedin.com/company/alberta-library-trustees-association
www.facebook.com/librarytrustees
twitter.com/librarytrustees
To act as the collective voice for library trustees in Alberta; To develop effective trustees
Heather Coulson, Executive Director

Alberta School Learning Commons Council (ASLC)
c/o Alberta Teachers' Association, Barnett House, 11010 - 142 St. NW, Edmonton AB T5N 2R1
admin@aslc.ca
www.aslc.ca
To advance teaching & learning excellence through effective school library practices; To cultivate & enhance effective school library operation through leadership, information, & professional development
Lissa Davies, President
Keith Fiels, Executive Director
Mark Leon, Chief Financial Officer
Cheryl Malden, Officer, Programs
Dan Hoppe, Director, Human Resources

Archives Association of British Columbia (AABC)
#249, 34A-2755 Lougheed Hwy., Port Coquitlam BC V3B 5Y9
info@aabc.ca
www.aabc.ca
Social Media: www.facebook.com/576282679111715
To act as the voice of archivists & archival institutions in British Columbia; To undertake projects that strengthen the archival network in the province; To preserve & promote access to British Columbia's documentary heritage
Cindy McLellan, President
Sarah Jensen, Secretary
Sarah Romkey, Treasurer

Archives Association of Ontario (AAO) / L'Association des archives de l'Ontario
#202, 720 Spadina Ave., Toronto ON M5S 2T9
Tel: 647-343-3334
aao@aao-archivists.ca
aao-archivists.ca
Social Media: linkedin.com/company/archives-association-of-ontario
www.facebook.com/ArchivesAssociationOfOntario
twitter.com/AAO_tweet
To encourage, through the establishment of networks, the public knowledge & appreciation of archives & their function; to promote the advancement of general education in the preservation of the cultural heritage & identity of the various regions of the province; to represent the interests of the archival community before the government of Ontario, local government & other provincial institutions of a public or private nature; to provide professional guidance & leadership through communication & cooperation with all persons, groups & associations interested in the preservation & use of records of the human experience in Ontario
Ned Struthers, President
Laura Hallman, Secretary

Archives Council of Prince Edward Island
PO Box 1000, Charlottetown PE C1A 7M4
acpei@gov.pe.ca
www.archives.pe.ca
To facilitate the development of the archival system in PEI; To make recommendations about the system's operation & financing; To develop & facilitate the implementation & management of programs to assist the archival community; To communicate archival needs & concerns to decision-makers, researchers & the general public
Simon Lloyd, President

Archives Society of Alberta (ASA)
#407, 10408 - 124 St. NW, Edmonton AB T5N 1R5
Tel: 780-424-2697; *Fax:* 780-425-1679
info@archivesalberta.org
www.archivesalberta.org
To provide professional leadership among persons engaged in practice of archival science; to promote development of archives & archivists in Alberta; to encourage cooperation of archivists & archives with all those interested in preservation & use of documents of human experience
Shamin Malmas, President
Meribeth Plenert, Acting Director/Archives Advisor

Association des archivistes du Québec (AAQ)
CP 9768, Succ. Sainte-Foy, Québec QC G1V 4C3
Tél: 418-652-2357; *Téléc:* 418-646-0868
infoaaq@archivistes.qc.ca
www.archivistes.qc.ca
Média social: linkedin.com/groups/2311475/profile
www.facebook.com/ArchivistesQc
twitter.com/archivistesQc
Regrouper les personnes qui offrent aux organisations et à leurs clientèles des services liés à la gestion de leur information organique et consignée; offrir à ses membres des services en français et propres à assurer le développement, l'enrichissement et la promotion de leur profession et de leur discipline; assurer aux membres les services susceptibles de favoriser et d'accroître les échanges et la communication internes et externes des idées et des connaissances; promouvoir le développement professionnel des membres en s'impliquant activement au plan de la formation et du perfectionnement, en favorisant la recherche et le développement et en assurant une représentation adéquate de la profession au sein de la société et auprès des corps politiques
Carole Saulnier, Présidente
Charles Cormier, Directeur général

Association des bibliothécaires francophones de l'Ontario (ABFO)
a/s Association des bibliothèques de l'Ontario, 2, rue Toronto, 3e étage, Toronto ON M5C 2B6
Tél: 416-363-3388; *Téléc:* 416-941-9581
Ligne sans frais: 866-873-9867
Média social: twitter.com/ABO_FRANCO
L'ABFO est l'Association des Bibliothécaires Francophones de l'Ontario qui oeuvrent dans le domaine public, collégial, universitaire ou scolaire et qui ont à coeur la culture francophone.
Joanne Plante, Présidente

Association des bibliothécaires professionnel(le)s du Nouveau-Brunswick (ABPNB) / Association of Professional Librarians of New Brunswick (APLNB)
NB
Promouvoir les bibliothécaires et les services de bibliothèques au Nouveau-Brunswick

Association des bibliothèques de droit de Montréal (ABDM) / Montréal Association of Law Libraries (MALL)
CP 482, 800, carre Victoria, Montréal QC H4Z 1J7
www.abdm-mall.org
Vise à permettre aux gens qui travaillent dans les bibliothèques de droit et qui exercent des fonctions connexes de communiquer et d'échanger des idées; d'encourager l'avancement de la profession; de maintenir et d'accroître l'utilité des bibliothèques de droit; promouvoir la coopération
Sophie Lecoq, Présidente

Association des bibliothèques publiques de l'Estrie (ABIPE)
1002, av J.-A.-Bombardier, Valcourt QC J0E 2L0
Tél: 450-532-1532; *Téléc:* 450-532-5807
www.bpq-estrie.qc.ca
Regrouper les bibliothèques publiques d'Estrie pour en favoriser le développement; informer les membres et échanger sur toute question pertinente au dossier des bibliothèques; représenter les intérêts des bibliothèques membres de la région 05 en étant leur porte-parole officiel auprès des instances gouvernementales et autres; organiser et réaliser des activités d'animation culturelle; sensibiliser le milieu au rôle et à l'importance de la bibliothèque publique dans la communauté
Karine Corbeil, Présidente

Association des bibliothèques publiques du Québec (ABPQ)
#215, 1453, rue Beaubien est, Montréal QC H2G 3C6
Tél: 514-886-7779; *Téléc:* 514-845-1618
info@abpq.ca
www.abpq.ca
Média social: www.facebook.com/ABPQc
Agit à titre de représentant officiel des bibliothèques publiques du Québec
Eve Lagacé, Directrice générale

Association for Manitoba Archives (AMA)
600 Shaftesbury Blvd., Winnipeg MB R3P 0M4
Tel: 204-942-3491
ama1@mts.net
mbarchives.ca
To promote understanding & awareness of the role & use of archives; to promote standards, procedures & practices in the management of archives; to provide assistance & education to persons seeking to improve their skills in the development, management or operation of archives
Emma Prescott, Chair

Association of Canadian Archivists (ACA) / Association canadienne des archivistes
PO Box 2596, Stn. D, #911, 75 Albert St., Ottawa ON K1P 5W6
Tel: 613-234-6977; *Fax:* 613-234-8500
www.archivists.ca
Social Media: www.youtube.com/user/archivistsdotca
linkedin.com/company/2154820
www.facebook.com/AssociationofCanadianArchivists
twitter.com/archivistsdotca
To ensure the preservation & accessibility of Canada's documentary heritage; To provide professional leadership among persons engaged in the discipline & practice of archival science; To promote the development of archives & archivists in Canada; To encourage cooperation of archivists with all those interested in the preservation & use of documents of human experience

Association of Canadian Map Libraries & Archives (ACMLA) / Association des cartothèques et archives cartographiques du Canada (ACACC)
c/o Deena Yanofsky, Humanities & Social Sciences Library, McGill U, 3459 McTavish St., Montréal QC H3A 0C9
Tel: 514-398-1087
www.acmla-acacc.ca
To represent Canadian map librarians & cartographic archivists, as well as others who are interested in geographic information; To develop professional standards & international cataloguing rules for the management & access to geographic information; To promote the contributions of map libraries & cartographic archives
Deena Yanofsky, President
Irene M.H. Herold, President
Mary Ellen K. Davis, Executive Director

Association of Newfoundland & Labrador Archives (ANLA)
PO Box 23155, St. John's NL A1B 4J9
Tel: 709-726-2867; *Fax:* 709-722-9035
anla@nf.aibn.com
www.anla.nf.ca
To provide professional leadership among persons engaged in practice of archival science; to promote development of archives & archivists in Newfoundland & Labrador; to encourage cooperation of archivists with all those interested in preservation & use of documents of human experience
Emily Gushue, President

Association of Parliamentary Libraries in Canada (APLIC) / Association des bibliothèques parlementaires au Canada (ABPAC)
c/o Valerie Footz, Alberta Legislature Library, 216 Legislature Bldg., 10800 - 97th Ave., Edmonton AB T5K 2B6
Tel: 780-427-0202; *Fax:* 780-427-6016
www.aplic-abpac.ca
To improve parliamentary library service in Canada; To encourage cooperation with related officials & organizations
Valerie Footz, President

Association of Professional Librarians of New Brunswick (APLNB) / Association des bibliothécaires professionnel(le)s de Nouveau-Brunswick (ABPNB)
c/o Tyler Griffin, Fredericton Public Library, 12 Carleton St., Fredericton NB E3B 5P4
www.aplnb-abpnb.ca
Social Media: twitter.com/APLNB
To promote librarians & libraries in New Brunswick
Tyler Griffin, President

Association pour l'avancement des sciences et des techniques de la documentation (ASTED)
#387, 2065, rue Parthenais, Montréal QC H2K 3T1
Tel: 514-281-5012; *Fax:* 514-281-8219
info@asted.org
asted.org
Social Media: www.facebook.com/asted.org
Pour promouvoir les intérêts de ses membres
Cossette, Président par intérim
Gagnon, Secrétaire-trésorière

Association pour la promotion des services documentaires scolaires (APSDS)
#5, 7870, rue Madeleine-Huguenin, Montréal QC H1L 6M7
Tél: 514-588-9400
apsds@apsds.org
apsds.org
Média social: facebook.com/APSDS.QC
twitter.com/apsds_
APSDS est une association professionnelle qui contribue au développement des services documentaires dans les commissions scolaires du Québec, dans les écoles primaires et secondaires, publiques et privées, et qui en assure la promotion.
Marie-Josée Proulx St-Pierre, Présidente

Atlantic Provinces Library Association (APLA)
c/o School of Information Management, Kenneth C. Rowe Management Bldg., Stn. 15000, #4010, 6100 University Ave., Halifax NS B3H 4R2
www.apla.ca
Social Media: linkedin.com/groups/4224326/profile
twitter.com/APLAcontact
To promote library & information service & workers throughout the Atlantic region; To represent & support the interests of persons who work in libraries in the Atlantic provinces; To cooperate with other library associations & similar organizations; To develop & offer effective continuing education programs
Suzanne van den Hoogen, President

Les bibliothèques publiques des régions de la Capitale-Nationale et Chaudière-Appalaches
a/s Réseau BIBLIO de la Capitale-Nationale, 3189, rue Albert-Demers, Charny QC G6X 3A1
Tél: 418-832-6166; *Téléc:* 418-832-6168
www.abpq.ca/fr/capitale-nationale-et-chaudieres-appalaches
Regrouper les responsables des bibliothèques publiques de ces régions; promouvoir et défendre les intérêts de ces bibliothèques; représenter le secteur des bibliothèques publiques des ces régions au sein des organismes à caractères culturel et social.
Marjorie Gagnon, Administratrice

British Columbia Courthouse Library Society
800 Smithe St., Vancouver BC V6Z 2E1
Tel: 604-660-2841; *Fax:* 604-660-2821
Toll-Free: 800-665-2570
librarian@courthouselibrary.ca
www.courthouselibrary.ca
Social Media: twitter.com/theclbc
Alan Ross, Chair

British Columbia Library Association (BCLA)
#150, 900 Howe St., Vancouver BC V6Z 2M4
Tel: 604-683-5354; *Fax:* 604-609-0707
Toll-Free: 888-683-5354
office@bcla.bc.ca
www.bcla.bc.ca
To encourage library development throughout British Columbia; To coordinate library services to various parts of the province; To promote cooperation between libraries; To advance the mutual interests of libraries & library personnel
Annette DeFaveri, Executive Director
Allie Douglas, Office Manager

British Columbia Library Trustees' Association (BCLTA)
#108, 9865 - 140th St., Surrey BC V3T 4M4
Tel: 604-913-1424; *Toll-Free:* 888-206-1245
office@bclta.ca
www.bclta.ca
Social Media: www.facebook.com/392761817401045
twitter.com/BCLTA
To develop & support library trustees who govern local public libraries in British Columbia; To advance public library service in the province
Barbara Kelly, Executive Director

British Columbia Teacher-Librarians' Association (BCTLA)
c/o Grahame Rainey, Treasurer, #1607 - 511 Rochester Ave., Coquitlam BC V3K 0A2
www.bctf.ca/bctla
Social Media: linkedin.com/groups/BCTLA-4726189
www.facebook.com/bctlaofficial
twitter.com/bctla
To promote the essential role of teacher-librarians within British Columbia's education community; To improve the learning & working condition in school library resource centres
Heather Daly, President
Grahame Rainey, Treasurer
Patricia Baisi, Secretary

Canadian Association for Information Science (CAIS) / Association canadienne des sciences de l'information (ACSI)
www.cais-acsi.ca
To advance information science in Canada by encouraging & facilitating the exchange of information on the use, access, retrieval, organization, management, & dissemination of information
Heidi Julien, President
Deborah Hicks, Vice-President
Philippe Mongeon, Secretary & Treasurer

Canadian Association of Family Resource Programs / Association canadienne des programmes de ressources pour la famille
#149, 150 Isabella St., Ottawa ON K1S 1V7
Tel: 613-237-7667; *Fax:* 613-237-8515
Toll-Free: 866-637-7226
info@frp.ca
www.frp.ca
Social Media: www.youtube.com/user/FRPCanada
www.facebook.com/frpcanada
twitter.com/frpcanada
To promote the well-being of families, through provision of leadership, consultation, & resources to organizations which care for children & support families; To act as the national voice for family resource programs; To advance social policy, research, resource development, & training for those who support the capacity of families to raise their children
Kelly Stone, Executive Director

Canadian Association of Law Libraries (CALL) / Association canadienne des bibliothèques de droit (ACBD)
#202, 720 Spadina Ave., Toronto ON M5S 2T9
Tel: 647-346-8723
office@callacbd.ca
www.callacbd.ca
Social Media: linkedin.com/groups/2006070/profile
www.facebook.com/callacbd
twitter.com/callacbd
To promote law librarianship; To develop Canadian law libraries; To promote access to legal information
Connie Crosby, President

Canadian Association of Music Libraries, Archives & Documentation Centres (CAML) / Association canadienne des bibliothèques, archives et centres de documentation musicaux inc. (ACBM)
Edward Johnson Bldg., University of Toronto, 80 Queen's Park Cres., Toronto ON M5S 2X5
library.music.utoronto.ca/caml-acbm
To represent librarians, researchers, & archivists in the field of music
Brian McMillan, President
Kyla Jemison, Membership Secretary

Canadian Association of Professional Academic Librarians (CAPAL)
capalibrarians@gmail.com
capalibrarians.org
Social Media: twitter.com/CAPALacbap
CAPAL is a national membership association representing the interests of professional academic librarians in relation to the areas of education, standards, professional practice, ethics, and core principles.
Eva Revitt, Chair

Canadian Association of Research Libraries (CARL) / Association des bibliothèques de recherche du Canada (ABRC)
#203, 309 Cooper St., Ottawa ON K2P 0G5
Tel: 613-482-9344
info@carl-abrc.ca
www.carl-abrc.ca
Social Media: www.youtube.com/channel/UCK59-sdDLfQgUUoAuiOVQeQ
twitter.com/carlabrc
To provide leadership to the Canadian research library community; To address issues affecting research libraries, such as federal research policy, copyright, open access publication, & preservation; To encourage broad access to scholarly information; To seek public policy encouraging of research
Susan Haigh, Executive Director
Katherine McColgan, Manager, Programs & Administration

Canadian Committee on Cataloguing / Comité canadien de catalogage
Library & Archives Canada, 550, boul de la Cité, Gatineau QC K1A 0N4
Tel: 613-996-5115; *Toll-Free:* 866-578-7777
standards@bac-lac.gc.ca
www.bac-lac.gc.ca
To formulate policy on questions concerning cataloguing & bibliographic control including subject analysis, referred to it by any of the organizationsrepresented on the Committee; to provide representative Canadian opinion for presentation at international meetings, committees & working groups; actively involved with the revision of the Anglo-American Cataloguing Rules.
Christine Oliver, Chair

Canadian Committee on MARC / Comité canadien du MARC
Description Division, Service Branch, Library & Archives Canada, 395 Wellington St., Ottawa ON K1A 0N4
Fax: 819-934-4388
BAC.MARC21.LAC@bac-lac.gc.ca
www.marc21.ca/040010-203-e.html
Acts as a Canadian MARC Advisory Committee to the National Library by examining the MARC 21 communication formats & making recommendations on the formats; examines MARC 21 communication formats as a medium for the exchange of machine-readable bibliographic information in Canada; establishes procedures for receiving, evaluating & making recommendationss on proposed national & international standards for the representation in machine-readable form of bibliographic information & other related standards; maintains liaison with its constituent organizations & relevant outside agencies
Leonard Bill, Contact

Canadian Council of Archives (CCA) / Conseil canadien des archives
#1201, 130 Albert St., Ottawa ON K1P 5G4
Tel: 613-565-1222; *Fax:* 613-565-5445
Toll-Free: 866-254-1403
cca@archivescanada.ca
archivescanada.ca/AboutCCA
To facilitate development of Canadian archival system & its coordination; to make recommendations to system's operation & financing; to develop & facilitate implementation & management of programs to assist archival community; to communicate archival needs & concerns to decision-makers, researchers & the general public.
Lara Wilson, Chair
Christina Nicholas, Executive Director

Canadian Federation of Library Associations (CFLA) / Fédération canadienne des associations de bibliothèques (FCAB)
#400, 1150 Morrison Dr., Ottawa ON K2H 8S9
info@cla.ca
www.cla.ca
Social Media: twitter.com/CLA_web
linkedin.com/company/canadian-library-association
www.facebook.com/CanadianLibraryAssociation
twitter.com/CFLAFCAB

To serve as the national public voice for Canada's library communities; To champion library values & the value of libraries; To influence public policy impacting libraries; To inspire & support learning; To collaborate to strengthen the library community.
On January 27, 2016, the membership of the Canadian Library Association voted to dissolve the CLA, based on a proposal for the creation of a new national association called the Canadian Federation of Library Associations. The innagural Annual General Meeting is planned for January or February 2017.
Paul Takala, Chair

Canadian Health Information Management Association (CHIMA)
99 Enterprise Dr. South, London ON N6N 1B9
Tel: 519-438-6700; *Fax:* 519-438-7001
Toll-Free: 877-332-4462
www.echima.ca
Social Media:
linkedin.com/groups/4445368/profile
www.facebook.com/OfficialCHIMA
twitter.com/E_CHIMA
To contribute to the promotion of wellness & the provision of quality healthcare through excellence in health information management; to assure competency of practice through credentialling, standards & continuing education; to promote value of health information management professionals
Gail Crook, CEO & Registrar
Tasha Clipperton, Coordinator, Member Services

Canadian Health Libraries Association (CHLA) / Association des bibliothèques de la santé du Canada (ABSC)
#LL02, 468 Queen St. East, Toronto ON M5A 1T7
Tel: 416-646-1600; *Fax:* 416-646-9460
info@chla-absc.ca
www.chla-absc.ca
Social Media: instagram.com/chla_absc
linkedin.com/grps/Canadian-Health-Libraries-Association-Association-8457293
www.facebook.com/CHLA.ABSC
twitter.com/chlaabsc
To lead health librarians towards excellence
Lindsay Alcock, President
Sophie Regalado, Secretary
Lindsey Sikora, Director, Public Relations

Canadian Urban Libraries Council (CULC)
349 Main St., Bloomfield ON K0K 1G0
Tel: 416-699-1938; *Fax:* 866-211-2999
www.culc.ca
To identify the issues & choices available in developing urban public library services; to explore the philosophy & principles that govern public library service in urban areas; to comment on the state of public library service in Canada; to facilitate the exchange of ideas & information between member libraries; to influence legislation & financing of urban public libraries; to promote & work in conjunction with other library organizations in Canada to achieve an urban public library service which is comprehensive, economic & efficient; to provide the means for communication & information sharing between members of the public library community; to promote formal & informal cooperation with organizations & institutions in Canada & outside Canada whose goals & objectives are relevant to large urban public library service
Jefferson Gilbert, Executive Director
Paul Takala, Chair

Church Library Association of British Columbia (CLABC)
c/o Membership Secretary, 1732 - 10 St. East, Courtenay BC V9N 7H7
clabc.ca@gmail.com
www.clabc.ca
Social Media:
www.facebook.com/ca.clabc
To help church libraries in British Columbia make the most of their resources

Church Library Association of Ontario (CLAO)
c/o Alice Meems, Treasurer, 112 Bristol St., Guelph ON N1H 3L6
treasurer@clao.ca
www.clao.ca
Social Media:
www.facebook.com/churchlibraryassociationofontario
To help church libraries in Ontario make the most of their resources
Medda Burnett, President
Laurie Lee Sproule, Coordinator, Outreach
Michelle Rickard, Coordinator, Communications
Alice Meems, Treasurer

Corporation des bibliothécaires professionnels du Québec (CBPQ) / Corporation of Professional Librarians of Québec
#215, 1453 rue Beaubien est, Montréal QC H2G 3C6
Tél: 514-845-3327; *Téléc:* 514-845-1618
info@cbpq.qc.ca
www.cbpq.qc.ca
Média social: www.facebook.com/bibliothecairesprofessionels
twitter.com/CBPQ_QC
Développer les services de bibliothèques; établir des normes de compétence; encourager et stimuler la recherche en bibliothéconomie; promouvoir et développer les intérêts professionnels de ses membres
Isabelle Pilon, Présidente

Council of Archives New Brunswick (CANB) / Conseil des archives du Nouveau-Brunswick
PO Box 1204, Stn. A, Fredericton NB E3B 5C8
Tel: 506-453-4327; *Fax:* 506-453-3288
archives.advisor@gnb.ca
www.canbarchives.ca/canb
Social Media:
twitter.com/CANBarchives
To address the needs of the archival institutions in New Brunswick; To provide training & information on developments in the profession; To encourage information sharing & cooperation in educational opportunities with Maritime sister provinces & national associations
Anne LeClair, President

Council of Nova Scotia Archives (CNSA)
6016 University Ave., Halifax NS B3H 1W4
Tel: 902-424-7093
advisor@councilofnsarchives.ca
www.councilofnsarchives.ca
Social Media:
www.facebook.com/536190566445902
To foster education of archival standards & practices to preserve Nova Scotia's documentary heritage; To promote archival standards, procedures, & practices
Jamie Serran, Advisor, Archives

Council of Prairie & Pacific University Libraries (COPPUL)
University of Calgary, 2500 University Dr. NW, 6th Fl., Calgary AB T2N 1N4
Tel: 403-220-8133; *Fax:* 403-282-1218
www.coppul.ca
Social Media:
twitter.com/coppul
To work together to leverage members' collective expertise, resources & influence; to increase capacity & infrastructure; to enhance learning, teaching, student experiences & research at member institutions
Andrew Waller, Executive Director

Federal Libraries Coordination Secretariat
Place de la Cité, 550,boul de la Cité, Gatineau QC K1A 0N4
Tel: 613-410-9752; *Fax:* 819-934-7539
BAC.SCBGF-FLCS.LAC@canada.ca
To coordinate federal libraries service reports to the Recordkeeping & Library Coordination Office of the Government Records Branch
Anne Chartrand, Resources Officer, Federal Libraries Consortium

Federation of Ontario Public Libraries (FOPL)
c/o North York Central Library, 5120 Yonge St., Toronto ON M2N 5N9
Tel: 416-395-5638; *Fax:* 416-395-0743
admin@fopl.ca
www.fopl.ca
Social Media:
www.facebook.com/160173540675944
twitter.com/foplnews
To represent Ontario's public library systems; To advocate for support, programs, & resources that will contribute to the success of Ontario public libraries
Stephen Abram, Executive Director

Halifax Library Association
Nova Scotia Community College, Waterfront Campus Library Tech Services, 80 Mawiomi Pl., Halifax NS B2Y 0A5
halifaxlibraryassociation@gmail.com
halifaxla.wordpress.com
To promote libraries and their services, and to encourage more extensive cooperation and interdependence among libraries in the geographic area of Halifax Regional Municipality
Bill Slauenwhite, President

Health Libraries Association of British Columbia (HLABC)
c/o Antje Helmuth, Ministry of Health, Health & Human Services Library, PO Box 9637, Stn. Prov Govt, 1515 Blanshard St., 7th Fl., Victoria BC V8W 9P1
Tel: 250-952-1478; *Fax:* 250-952-2180
hlabc.exec@gmail.com
hlabc.chla-absc.ca
To support the work of health librarians throughout British Columbia
Kristina McDavid, President
Chantelle Jack, Secretary
Antje Helmuth, Treasurer & Contact, Membership

Indexing Society of Canada (ISC) / Société canadienne d'indexation (SCA)
133 Major St., Toronto ON M5S 2K9
administrator@indexers.ca
www.indexers.ca
Social Media: www.pinterest.com/iscsci
linkedin.com/groups/8248555/profile
twitter.com/indexerscanada
To encourage the production & use of indexes & abstracts; To promote the recognition of indexers & abstractors; To improve indexing & abstracting techniques; To improve communication among individual indexers & abstractors
Margaret de Boer, President
Frances Robinson, Membership Secretary
Sergey Lobachev, Treasurer

Library Association of Alberta (LAA)
80 Baker Cres. NW, Calgary AB T2L 1R4
Tel: 403-284-5818; *Toll-Free:* 877-522-5550
info@laa.ca
www.laa.ca
Social Media: plus.google.com/114726559596090866928
linkedin.com/groups/Library-Association-Alberta-4735949
www.facebook.com/LibraryAssociationOfAlberta
twitter.com/Lib_Assn_AB
To facilitate the improvement of library services in Alberta; To promote library service throughout Alberta; To encourage cooperation among libraries & information centres across the province; To promote intellectual freedom in Alberta
Christine Sheppard, Executive Director

Library Association of the National Capital Region (LANCR) / Association des bibliothèques de la région de la capitale nationale
Ottawa ON
lancrinfo@gmail.com
lancr.wordpress.com
Social Media:
twitter.com/LANCR_ABRCN
To create a forum for library personnel & friends of libraries from the Ottawa-Hull region, where members can discuss library issues of general interest, share information related to library matters, promote an esprit de corps among librarians, library technicians, & all others interested in libraries & library work
Sarah Simpkin, President

Library Boards Association of Nova Scotia (LBANS)
135 North Park St., Bridgewater NS B4V 9B3
Tel: 902-543-2548
www.standupforlibraries.ca
To preserve & support quality public library service throughout Nova Scotia
Christina Pottie, Executive Secretary

Manitoba Association of Health Information Providers (MAHIP)
c/o Neil John Maclean Health Sciences Library, University of Manitoba, 727 McDermott Ave., Winnipeg MB R3E 3P5
Fax: 204-789-3922
contact.mahip@gmail.com
mahip.chla-absc.ca
To promote the provision of quality library service to the health community in Manitoba by communication & mutual assistance.
Laura Hochheim, President
Andrea Szwajcer, Secretary

Manitoba Association of Library Technicians (MALT)
PO Box 1872, Winnipeg MB R3C 3R1
malt.mb.ca@gmail.com
www.malt.mb.ca
Social Media:
www.facebook.com/malt.mb.ca
To promote & advance the role of library technicians throughout Manitoba; To respond to issues that relate to the library & information services community
Christine Janzen, President
Cassie Page, Secretary
Ebony Novakowski, Coordinator, Communications
Leslie McDonald, Coordinator, Membership

Darren Wesselius, Editor, Newsletter

Manitoba Library Association (MLA)
#606, 100 Arthur St., Winnipeg MB R3B 1H3
Tel: 204-943-4567; *Fax:* 866-202-4567
www.mla.mb.ca
Social Media:
linkedin.com/in/manitoba-library-association-2a24325b
www.facebook.com/MBLibAssn
twitter.com/MB_Lib_Assn
To develop, support, & promote library & information services in Manitoba for the benefit of the library community & Manitoba residents
Alix-Rae Stefanko, President
Sarah Clark, Director, Membership
Kyle Feenstra, Director, Communications
Vickie Albrecht, Secretary

Manitoba Library Trustees Association (MLTA)
MB
Tel: 204-726-0025
www.mlta.ca
Social Media: manitobalibrarytrusteesassn@gmail.com
To foster & promote the effectiveness of public library boards through leadership & advocacy; To promote a better understanding of the role of the library trustee; To maintain channels of communication between other trustee associations to exchange information & ideas
Donna Kormilo, Chair

Manitoba School Library Association (MSLA)
307 Shaftesbury Blvd., Winnipeg MB R3P 0L9
www.manitobaschoollibraries.com
Social Media:
twitter.com/_MSLA_
To advocate for school library programs in Manitoba; To provide professional development opportunities for members
Jo-Anne Gibson, President
Dorothy McGinnis, Secretary

Maritimes Health Libraries Association (MHLA) / Association des bibliothèques de la santé des Maritimes (ABSM)
c/o Robin Parker, W.K. Kellogg Health Sciences Library, Dalhousie Uni., PO Box 1500, 5850 College St., Halifax NS B3H 4R2
mhla.absm@gmail.com
libguides.cdha.nshealth.ca/MHLA
To support members in the provision of quality information services for the health care community in the maritime provinces
Jackie Phinney, President

New Brunswick Library Trustees' Association (NBLTA) / Association des commissaires de bibliothèque du Nouveau-Brunswick, inc.
PO Box 34, St. Antoine NB E0A 2X0
To train effective library trustees in New Brunswick

Newfoundland & Labrador Health Libraries Association (NLHLA)
c/o Health Sciences Library, Memorial University of Newfoundland, St. John's NL A1B 3V6
nlhla@chla-absc.ca
nlhla.chla-absc.ca
To promote the provision of a high quality library service to the health community in Newfoundland & Labrador through mutual assistance & communication; to provide professional support to the membership by offering continuing education opportunities
Shannon McAlorum, President
Alison Farrell, Secretary/Treasurer

Northern Alberta Health Libraries Association
c/o J.W. Scott Health Sciences Library, University of Alberta, 2K3.28 Walter MacKenzie Ctr., Edmonton AB T6G 2R7
contact.nahla@gmail.com
nahla.chla-absc.ca
This chapter of NAHLA exists to provide a forum for networking among libararians, library technicians and other interested in health libraries and health information.
Robin Featherstone, President
Morgan Truax, Secretary

Northwest Territories Archives Council (NWTAC)
c/o NWT Archives Council, PO Box 1320, Yellowknife NT X1A 2L9
www.pwnhc.ca/nwtac
To facilitate development of the archival system in the Northwest Territories; To make recommendations about the system's operation & financing; to develop & facilitate implementation & management of programs to assist the archival community; To communicate archival needs & concerns to decision-makers, researchers & the general public.

Erin Suliak, President

Northwest Territories Library Association (NWTLA)
PO Box 2276, Yellowknife NT XIA 2P7
nwtlibraryassociation@gmail.com
nwtlibraryassociation.wordpress.com
Social Media:
www.facebook.com/NWTLA
To facilitate the exchange of ideas among persons involved inlibrary services in the Northwest Territories; To recommend policies for the provision of library services; To promote intellectual freedom
John Mutford, President

Nova Scotia Government Libraries Council (NSGLC)
NS
Tel: 902-424-7214
www.nsglc.ednet.ns.ca
To provide a forum for government libraries to discuss common problems & share information
Ruth Hart, Chair
Natalie MacPherson, Secretary
Anne Van Iderstine, Treasurer

Nova Scotia Library Association (NSLA)
c/o Nova Scotia Provincial Library, PO Box 456, Stn. Central, 1741 Brunswick St., 2nd Fl., Halifax NS B3J 3X8
www.nsla.ns.ca
To promote the value of libraries; To facilitate the exchange of ideas & information among library workers in Nova Scotia
Cindy Lelliott, President
Meghan Fillmore, Secretary

Nunavut Library Association (NLA)
c/o Nunavut Court of Justice Law Library, PO Box 297, Iqaluit NU X0A 0H0
nunavutlibraryassociation@gmail.com
www.nunavutlibraryassociation.ca
To support persons who work in Nunavut libraries; To advocatefor excellent library services for Nunavut; To promote library services & literacy; To provide professional development for members.

Ontario Association of Library Technicians (OALT) / Association des bibliotechniciens de l'Ontario (ABO)
Abbey Market, PO Box 76010, 1500 Upper Middle Rd. West, Oakville ON L6M 3H5
info@oaltabo.on.ca
oaltabo.on.ca
Social Media:
linkedin.com/company/oalt-abo
www.facebook.com/OALTABO
twitter.com/OALTABO
To promote the interests of library & information technician graduates & students throughout Ontario; To advance library & information technician graduates & students
Carolin Toppan, President
Lori O'Connor, Treasurer
Jillann Rothwell, Coordinator, Membership

Ontario College & University Library Association (OCULA)
c/o Ontario Library Association, 2 Toronto St., 3rd Fl., Toronto ON M5C 2B6
Tel: 416-363-3388; *Fax:* 416-941-9581
Toll-Free: 866-873-9867
info@accessola.com
www.accessola.org
To support librarians & to improve Library Science in Ontario's college & university libraries
Denise Smith, President

Ontario Council of University Libraries (OCUL)
Robarts Library, 130 St. George St., 7th Fl., Toronto ON M5S 1A5
ocul@ocul.on.ca
www.ocul.on.ca
To collaborate in the delivery & development of effective information resources for Ontario's universities
John Barnett, Executive Director

Ontario Health Libraries Association (OHLA)
c/o Ontario Library Association, 2 Toronto St., 3rd Fl., Toronto ON M5C 2B6
Tel: 416-363-3388; *Fax:* 416-941-9581
Toll-Free: 866-873-9867
askohla@accessola.com
www.ohla.on.ca
Social Media:
linkedin.com/groups/2670522/profile
www.facebook.com/303797462978073
twitter.com/ohlacommunity

To represent views of members; To advocate for the value of health libraries & specialists; To provide a forum for leadership, education, & communications; To build & strengthen relationships with members & other organizations.
Rachel Couban, President

Ontario Library & Information Technology Association (OLITA)
c/o Ontario Library Association, 2 Toronto St., 3rd Fl., Toronto ON M5C 2BS
Tel: 416-363-3388; *Fax:* 416-941-9581
Toll-Free: 866-873-9867
www.accessola.com/olita/
Planning, development, design, application & integration of technology in the library & information environment with the impact of emerging technologies on library service, & with the effect of automated technologies on people
Sarah Simpkin, President

Ontario Library Association (OLA)
2 Toronto St., 3rd Fl., Toronto ON M5C 2B6
Tel: 416-363-3388; *Fax:* 416-941-9581
Toll-Free: 866-873-9867
info@accessola.com
www.accessola.org
Social Media: www.youtube.com/user/ONLibraryAssoc
linkedin.com/groups/Ontario-Library-Association
www.facebook.com/accessola
twitter.com/ollibraryassoc
To provide opportunities for people in the library & information field to share experience & expertise, & to create innovative solutions
Shelagh Paterson, Executive Director
Stephanie Pimentel, Manager, Operations
Beckie MacDonald, Manager, Member Services
Michelle Arbuckle, Manager, Education Programs
Meredith Tutching, Director, Forest of Reading

Ontario Library Boards' Association (OLBA)
c/o Ontario Library Association, 2 Toronto St., 3rd Fl., Toronto ON M5C 2B6
Tel: 416-363-3388; *Fax:* 416-941-9581
Toll-Free: 866-873-9867
info@accessola.com
www.accessola.org/olba
To represent Ontario public library board members on issues that affect library board leadership; To advance public library board development & improve the management & services of libraries throughout Ontario; To enhance the visibility of library boards
Pierre Mercier, President

Ontario Public Library Association (OPLA)
c/o Ontario Library Association, 2 Toronto St., 3rd Fl., Toronto ON M5C 2B6
Tel: 416-363-3388; *Fax:* 416-941-9581
Toll-Free: 866-873-9867
info@accessola.com
www.accessola.org
To foster the expansion & improvement of public library service in Ontario; To support public librarians throughout Ontario; To encourage standards & certification for public library workers
Alexandra Yarrow, President

Ontario School Library Association (OSLA)
c/o Ontario Library Association, 2 Toronto St., 3rd Fl., Toronto ON M5C 2B6
Tel: 416-363-3388; *Fax:* 416-941-9581
Toll-Free: 866-873-9867
info@accessola.com
www.accessola.org/osla
To act as the voice of elementary & secondary school teacher-librarians in Ontario; To promote teacher-librarians as curriculum leaders; To support student success
Kate Johnson-McGregor, President

Ottawa Valley Health Libraries Association (OVHLA) / Association des bibliothèques de santé de la Vallée d'Outaouais
c/o Canadian Agency for Drugs and Technologies in Health (CADTH), #600, 875 Carling Ave., Ottawa ON K1S 591
Tel: 613-725-9965
ovhla.chla-absc.ca
The Ottawa Valley Health Libraries Association / l'Association des Bibliothèques de la Santé de la Vallée de l'Outaouais is an association of over twenty health-related libraries whose purpose is to promote the provision of quality library services in the health sciences throughout the Ottawa Valley and the Outaouais. It was formed in 1994 through the amalgamation of the Ottawa-Hull Health Libraries Association and the OHA Region 9 chapter of the Ontario Health Libraries Association and is a chapter of the Ontario Health Libraries Association (OHLA) and the Canadian Health Libraries Association (CHLA).

Alexandra Hickey, President

PEI Teacher-Librarians' Association (PEITLA)
c/o Carrie St. Jean, PO Box 6500, Glen Stewart Primary School, Charlottetown PE C1l 8B5
To represent Teacher-Librarians in PEI
Carrie St. Jean, President

Prince Edward Island Professional Librarians Association (PEIPLA)
c/o Louise Mould, 4 Sydney St., Charlottetown PE C1A 1E9
www.peipla.wordpress.com
To advocate for librarians & library services in the province
Louise Mould, President
Roseanne Gauthier, Secretary/Treasurer

Provincial & Territorial Public Library Council (PTPLC) / Conseil provincial et territorial des bibliotheques (CPTBP)
www.bclibraries.ca/ptldc
To act as a forum in which provincial & territorial public libraries can share experience, informatiom, & resources; To serve as a point of contact between national library organizations & the federal government

Québec Library Association (QLA) / Association des bibliothécaires du Québec (ABQLA)
PO Box 26717, Stn. Beaconsfield, Montréal QC H9W 6G7
Tel: 514-697-0146; *Fax:* 514-697-0146
www.abqla.qc.ca
Social Media:
linkedin.com/groups/5071380/profile
www.facebook.com/124766477552846
twitter.com/ABQLA
To promote the role of library & information specialists in the greater Québec community; To foster & encourage the exchange of information on library-related issues; To strengthen relationships with national, provincial, & local library associations
Sonia Smith, President

Reseau Biblio de l'Abitibi-Témiscamingue Nord-du-Québec
20, av Québec, Rouyn-Noranda QC J9X 2E6
Tél: 819-762-4305; *Téléc:* 819-762-5309
info@reseaubiblioatnq.qc.ca
mabiblio.quebec
Média social: www.youtube.com/user/Mouvi1
www.facebook.com/335729189842131
Promotion du livre et de la lecture en Abitibi-Témiscamingue; promotion des bibliothèques
Louis Dallaire, Directeur général

Réseau BIBLIO de la Côte-Nord
QC
www.reseaubiblioduquebec.qc.ca
Promouvoir les bibliothèques publiques; concertation dans des dossiers concernant les bibliothèques publiques; faire connaître nos services
Jean-Roch Gagnon, Directeur général

Réseau BIBLIO du Québec
c.o Jacques Côté, 3189, rue Albert-Demers, Charny QC G5R 4T6
Tél: 418-867-1682; *Téléc:* 418-867-3434
www.reseaubiblioduquebec.qc.ca
Le Réseau BIBLIO du Québec est un regroupement national qui vise à unir les ressources des Réseaux BIBLIO régionaux pour maintenir et développer leur réseau de bibliothèques et de les représenter auprès des diverses instances sur des dossiers d'intérêts communs.
Jacques Côté, Secrétaire général

Réseau BIBLIO du Saguenay-Lac-Saint-Jean (RBSLSJ)
100, rue Price ouest, Alma QC G8B 4S1
Tél: 418-662-6425; *Téléc:* 418-662-7593
Ligne sans frais: 800-563-6425
info@reseaubibliosIsj.qc.ca
www.mabibliotheque.ca/saguenay-lac-saint-jean/fr/index.aspx
Média social: www.facebook.com/reseaubiblioSLSJ
twitter.com/reseaubiblio
Promouvoir les bibliothèques publiques; concertation dans des dossiers concernant les bibliothèques publiques; faire connaître nos services
Sophie Bolduc, Directrice générale

Réseau des services d'archives du Québec (RAQ)
a/s Archives nationales du Québec à Montréal, #5.27.1, 535, av Viger Est, Montréal QC H2L 2P3
Tél: 514-864-9213
archiviste.conseil.raq@gmail.com
archivisteraq.com
Média social: www.facebook.com/293550674109606
twitter.com/reseauraq
Promouvoir le développement et la mise en valeur des archives historiques; favoriser l'échange et la mise en commun d'information, d'expérience et de ressources; devenir un instrument de consultation et un groupe de pression reconnu des divers intervenants des milieux archivistiques
Theresa Rowat, Présidente

Saskatchewan Association of Library Technicians, Inc. (SALT)
PO Box 24019, Saskatoon SK S7K 8B4
Fax: 306-543-4487
sasksalt@gmail.com
www.libraries.gov.sk.ca/salt
To promote the value of library technicians in Saskatchewan
Carole-Anne Wilson-Hough, President
Elisabeth Eilinger, Secretary

Saskatchewan Council for Archives & Archivists (SCAA)
#202, 1275 Broad St., Regina SK S4R 1Y2
Tel: 306-780-9414; *Fax:* 306-585-1765
scaa@sasktel.net
www.scaa.sk.ca
Social Media:
www.facebook.com/SCAArchivists/
To facilitate the development of the archival system in Saskatchewan; To develop standard archival policies & practices; To promote public awareness of the use of archives
Sandy Doran, Executive Director
Donald Johnson, President
Cameron Hart, Archives Advisor

Saskatchewan Health Libraries Association (SHLA)
SK
shlasask@gmail.com
shla.chla-absc.ca
To promote access to health care literature for physicians & allied health care staff
Lukas Miller, President
Ashley Booth, Secretary/Treasurer

Saskatchewan Library Association (SLA)
#15, 2010 - 7th Ave., Regina SK S4R 1C2
Fax: 306-780-9447
www.saskla.ca
Social Media:
www.facebook.com/sasklibraryassociation
twitter.com/sklibrary
To further the development of library services in Saskatchewan
Judy Nicholson, Executive Director
Anne Pennylegion, Program Coordinator

Saskatchewan Library Trustees' Association (SLTA)
c/o Nancy Kennedy, 79 Mayfair Cres., Regina SK S4S 5T9
Tel: 306-584-2495; *Fax:* 306-585-1473
www.slta.ca
Social Media:
www.facebook.com/sasklibrarytrusteesassoc
twitter.com/yourslta
To foster the development of libraries & library services throughout Saskatchewan
Nancy Kennedy, Executive Director
Dennis Taylor, President
Donna Hartley, Treasurer

Southern Alberta Health Libraries Association (SAHLA)
c/o Chelsea Ambler, Health Sciences Library, University of Calgary, 3330 University Dr. NW, Calgary AB T2N 4N1
www.chla-absc.ca/sahla
To promote good health information service in southern Alberta; To encourage cooperation & communication among members; To promote educational development
Carrie Sherlock, President
Chelsea Ambler, Secretary

Southwestern Ontario Health Libraries & Information Network (SOHLIN)
c/o London Health Sciences Centre, PO Box 5165, London ON N9A 4L6
sohlin.chla-absc.ca
To build communication lines among members; to provide opportunities for continued education & professional development
Jill McTavish, President

Toronto Health Libraries Association (THLA)
c/o Raluca Serban, UHN - Toronto Rehabilitation Institute, 550 University Ave., Toronto ON M5G 2A2
secretary@thla.ca
www.thla.ca
To promote the provision of quality library service to the health community; to encourage communication & cooperation among members & to foster their professional development; to consult & collaborate with other professional, technical & scientific organizations in matters of mutual interest
Ashley Farrell, President

Wellington Waterloo Dufferin Health Library Network (WWDHLN)
ON
wwdhln-l@mailman.uwaterloo.ca
wwdhln.chla-absc.ca
To support & enhance the ability of its members to provide high quality knowledge information services to member organizations; To promote communication among members; To co-operate with other health library networks to promote the efficient delivery of service; To support health library development
Tracy Morgan, President

Yukon Council of Archives (YCA)
PO Box 31089, Whitehorse YT Y1A 5P7
Fax: 867-393-6253
yukoncnclarch@gmail.com
www.yukoncouncilofarchives.ca
To facilitate the development of the archival system in the Yukon; To make recommendations about the system's operation & financing; To develop & facilitate implementation & management of programs to assist the archival community; To communicate archival needs & concerns to decision-makers, researchers & the general public
Linda Johnson, President

Management & Administration

Administrative Sciences Association of Canada (ASAC) / Association des sciences administratives du Canada
c/o Sobey School of Business, Saint Mary's University, Halifax NS B3H 3C3
Tel: 902-496-8139
jean.mills@smu.ca
www.asac.ca
To develop teaching & research in management studies at Canadian universities
Tanya Mark, Secretary
Travor Brown, President

ARMA Canada (ARMA)
c/o Yvonne Perry-White, 195 Summerlea Rd., Brampton ON L6T 4P6
www.armacanada.org
Social Media:
linkedin.com/groups/6629965/profile
twitter.com/armacanada
To work to advance records & information management as a discipline & a profession; To organize programs of research, education, training & networking
Jolynne Jackson, Region Director
Yvonne Perry-White, Treasurer

Association des MBA du Québec (AMBAQ)
1970, rue Notre-Dame Ouest, Montréal QC H3C 1K8
Tél: 514-323-8480; *Téléc:* 514-282-4292
info@ambaq.com
www.ambaq.com
Média social:
linkedin.com/groups/Association-MBA-Québec-78306
www.facebook.com/ambaq
twitter.com/AMBAQ
Ötre le porte-parole des MBA du Québec; constituer un réseau actif de diplômés et étudiants MBA; favoriser le développement personnel et professionnel des membres; valoriser et promouvoir le diplôme MBA
Ivan Roy, Directeur général

Association of Administrative Assistants (AAA) / Association des adjoints administratifs
c/o 11110 - 108 St., Edmonton AB T5G 2T2
Tel: 780-423-2929; *Fax:* 780-407-3340
registrar@aaa.ca
www.aaa.ca
Social Media:
linkedin.com/pub/association-of-administrative-assistants/3a/356/4
To establish a national standard of qualifications for an administrative assistant; to help assistants to reach this standard

by providing opportunities for advanced education; to make management aware of the value of the fully-qualified administrative assistant
Doris Kurtz, Director

Association of Fundraising Professionals (AFP)
#300, 4300 Wilson Blvd., Arlington VA 22203 USA
Tel: 703-684-0410; *Fax:* 703-684-0540
Toll-Free: 800-666-3863
afp@afpnet.org
www.afpnet.org
Social Media:
linkedin.com/company/878282
www.facebook.com/AFPFan
twitter.com/afpihq
To promote stewardship, donor trust & effective & ethical fundraising
Bob Carter, Chair
Derek Fraser, Chair, AFP Canadian Council
Andrew Watt, President & CEO

Association of MBAs in Canada (AMBA)
admin@ambac.ca
ambac.ca
Social Media:
linkedin.com/company/the-association-of-mbas-in-canada
The prominent body in Canada representing and supporting those who have invested in an MBA.
Muradali Amir, President

Association of Professional Executives of the Public Service of Canada (APEX) / L'Association professionnelle des cadres de la fonction publique du Canada
#508, 75 Albert St., Ottawa ON K1P 5E7
Tel: 613-995-6252; *Fax:* 613-943-8919
info@apex.gc.ca
www.apex.gc.ca
The association focuses on issues such as compensation, the work environment and public service management reform.
Nadir Patel, Chair
Lisanne Lacroix, Chief Executive Officer

Canadian Association of Management Consultants (CMC-Canada) / Association canadienne des conseillers en management
#2004, 401 Bay St., Toronto ON M5H 2Y4
Tel: 416-860-1515; *Fax:* 416-860-1535
Toll-Free: 800-268-1148
consulting@cmc-canada.ca
www.cmc-canada.ca
Social Media: cmc-yonemitsu.blogspot.ca;
ww.youtube.com/user/CMCCanada1
linkedin.com/groups?mostPopular=&gid=80782
www.facebook.com/153670124764294
twitter.com/CMCCanada1
To foster excellence & integrity in the management consulting profession; To administer the Certified Management Consultant (CMC) designation in Canada; To advance the practice & profile of the profession of management consulting in Canada; To promote ethical standards
Glenn Yonemitsu, Chief Executive Officer
Lynn Bennett, Vice Chair
Glenn Yonemitsu, Chief Executive Officer
Mary Blair, Managing Director

Canadian Association of School System Administrators (CASSA) / Association canadienne des administrateurs et des administratrices scolaires (ACGCS)
1123 Glenashton Dr., Oakville ON L6H 5M1
Tel: 905-845-2345; *Fax:* 905-845-2044
www.cassa-acgcs.ca
Social Media:
twitter.com/CASSAACGCS
To promote & enhance effective administration & leadership in provision of quality education in Canada; to provide a national voice on educational matters; to promote & provide opportunity for professional development to the membership; to promote communication & liaison with national & international organizations having an interest in education; to provide a variety of services to the membership; to recognize outstanding contributions to education in Canada
Ken Bain, Executive Director

Canadian Council of Professional Certification (CCPC)
1 Edenmills Dr., Toronto ON M1E 4L1
Tel: 416-724-5339; *Fax:* 905-727-1061
www.ccpcglobal.com
Social Media:
linkedin.com/company/ccpc-global
www.facebook.com/267324543281480
twitter.com/CCPCGlobal
To grant certification & professional designation to qualified applicants

Canadian Executive Service Organization (CESO) / Service d'assistance canadienne aux organismes (SACO)
PO Box 800, #800, 700 Bay St., Toronto ON M5G 1Z6
Fax: 416-961-1096
Toll-Free: 800-268-9052
toronto@ceso-saco.com
www.ceso-saco.com
Social Media: www.youtube.com/CESOSACO
linkedin.com/company/ceso-canadian-executive-service-organization
www.facebook.com/cesosaco
twitter.com/cesosaco
To enhance the socio-economic well-being of the peoples & the communities of Canada, developing nations & emerging market economies
Wendy Harris, President & Chief Executive Officer
Janet Lambert, Chief Operating Officer, Public Affairs & National Services
Gale Lee, Director, International Services (Asia, Americas & the Caribbean)
Apollinaire Ihaza, Director, International Services (Africa & Haiti)

Canadian Institute of Management (CIM) / Institut canadien de gestion
National Office, 15 Collier St., Lower Level, Barrie ON L4M 1G5
Tel: 705-725-8926; *Fax:* 705-725-8196
Toll-Free: 800-387-5774
office@cim.ca
www.cim.ca
To promote the senior management profession by offering a series of educational programs from single courses to professional certification
Matthew Jelavic, President
Betty Smith, Secretary
Deb Daigle, Treasurer

Canadian Management Centre
150 York St., 5th Fl., Toronto ON M5H 3S5
Fax: 416-214-6047
Toll-Free: 877-262-2519
cmcinfo@cmcoutperform.com
www.cmctraining.org
Social Media: www.youtube.com/user/CdnMgmtCtr
linkedin.com/company/35861
twitter.com/canadianmgmt
To play a key role in strengthening the ability of Canada's business leaders, managers & organizations to compete & succeed in today's challenging & changing business environment; To provide a full range of professional development & management education services to companies, government agencies, & individuals
John Wright, President & Managing Director
Jo Bouchard, Vice-President, Business Development
Bernadette Smith, Vice-President, Learning Solutions

Canadian Public Relations Society Inc. (CPRS) / La Société canadienne des relations publiques
#346, 4195 Dundas St. West, Toronto ON M8X 1Y4
Tel: 416-239-7034; *Fax:* 416-239-1076
admin@cprs.ca
www.cprs.ca
Social Media:
twitter.com/CPRSNational
To oversee the practice of public relations practitioners in Canada, to ensure the protection of the public interest; To advance the professional stature of public relations practitioners; To promote the ethical practice of public relations & communications management
Karen Dalton, Executive Director
Jorge de Mendonca, Director, Finance & Information Systems
Monica Simmie, Director, Professional Development & Sponsorship
Elizabeth Tang, Manager, Membership, Communications, & Awards

Canadian Society of Association Executives (CSAE) / Société canadienne d'association (SCDA)
#1100, 10 King St. East, Toronto ON M5C 1C3
Tel: 416-363-3555; *Fax:* 416-363-3630
Toll-Free: 800-461-3608
www.csae.com
Social Media:
linkedin.com/company/csae-canadian-society-of-association-executives
www.facebook.com/AssociationExecutives
twitter.com/csaeconnect
To provide members with the environment, knowledge, & resources to develop excellence in not-for-profit leadership through networking, education, advocacy, information, & research
Michael Anderson, President & CEO
Danielle Lamothe, Director, Education
Stewart Laszlo, Director, Marketing
Gail McHardy, Director, Conferences & Events

Canadian Society of Corporate Secretaries (CSCS)
#255, 55 St. Clair Ave. West, Toronto ON M4V 2Y7
Tel: 416-921-5449; *Fax:* 416-967-6320
Toll-Free: 800-774-2850
info@cscs.org
www.cscs.org
To provide members with the tools necessary to become expert in corporate secretarial practice & to strengthen the corporate secretary's profile in the company.
Pamela Smith, Administrative Director
Lynn Beauregard, President

Canadian Society of Physician Executives (CSPE) / Société canadienne des médecins gestionnaires
PO Box 59005, 1559 Alta Vista Dr., Ottawa ON K1G 5T7
Tel: 613-731-9331; *Fax:* 613-731-1779
www.cspexecs.com
Social Media:
twitter.com/CSPExecs
To develop physician leaders to be successful in health care leadership & management roles
Carol Rochefort, Executive Director

Canadian Student Leadership Association (CSLA)
2460 Tanner Rd., Victoria BC V8Z 5R1
studentleadership.ca
Social Media:
www.facebook.com/CanadianStudentLeadershipAssociation
twitter.com/CSLA_Leaders
Don Homan, Chair
Bill Conconi, Executive Director

CIO Association of Canada (CIOCAN)
National Office, #204, 7270 Woodbine Ave., Markham ON L3R 4B9
Tel: 905-752-1899; *Fax:* 905-513-1254
Toll-Free: 877-865-9009
www.ciocan.ca
Social Media:
linkedin.com/company/cio-association-of-canada
twitter.com/CIO_CAN
To facilitate networking, sharing of best practices & executive development, & to drive advocacy on issues facing IT Executives/CIOs. Chapters: Calgary, Edmonton, Manitoba, Ottawa, Toronto & Vancouver
Gary Davenport, President, National Board of Directors

Corporation des approvisionneurs du Québec (CAQ)
Complexe Tassé, #302, 895, boul Séminaire nord, Saint-Jean-sur-Richelieu QC J3A 1J2
Tél: 450-357-0033; *Téléc:* 450-357-0044
Ligne sans frais: 800-977-1877
info@caq.qc.ca
www.caq.qc.ca
Média social: www.facebook.com/CorpoAppQc
La Corporation des approvisionneurs du Québec assure le développement professionnel de ses membres et veille à promouvoir et favoriser l'implantation des meilleures pratiques en matière de gestion de la chaîne d'approvisionnement au sein des entreprises québécoises afin que la valeur stratégique de l'approvisionnement puisse contribuer pleinement à l'essor des entreprises et à la société québécoise.
Pierre St-Jean, Président

Couchiching Institute on Public Affairs (CIPA)
#301, 250 Consumers Rd., Toronto ON M2J 4V6
Tel: 416-642-6374; *Fax:* 416-495-8723
Toll-Free: 866-647-6374
couch@couchichinginstitute.ca
www.couchichinginstitute.ca
Social Media: couchichinginstitute.tumblr.com
www.facebook.com/couchichinginstitute
twitter.com/couchiching

To bring together interested Canadians to discuss important public policy issues with experts & other members of the general public
Amanuel Melles, President
Shannon Bott, Executive Director

Fédération des secrétaires professionnelles du Québec (FSPQ)
#390-1, 1173, boul Charest ouest, Québec QC G1N 2C9
Tél: 418-527-5041; *Téléc:* 418-527-2160
Ligne sans frais: 866-527-5041
info@fspq.qc.ca
www.fspq.qc.ca
Média social: linkedin.com/groups?gid=2340718
twitter.com/FSPQ
Travail à la valorisation de la profession.
Anick Blouin, Présidente

Global Network of Director Institutes (GNDI)
c/o Institute of Corporate Directors, #2701, 250 Yonge St., Toronto ON M5B 2L7
Tel: 416-593-7741; *Fax:* 416-593-0636
Toll-Free: 877-593-7741
www.gndi.org
To help members stay abreast of leading practices as well as current & emerging governance issues; to foster closer cooperation between members
Stan Magidson, Chair
Simon Walker, Deputy Chair
Maliha Aqeel, Director, Communications, Institute of Corporate Directors

Institute of Certified Management Consultants of Alberta (CMC-Alberta)
c/o CMC-Canada National Office, PO Box 20, #2004, 410 Bay St., Toronto ON M5H 2Y4
Tel: 416-860-1515; *Fax:* 416-860-1535
Toll-Free: 800-268-1148
consulting@cmc-canada.ca
www.cmc-canada.ca/provincial_institutes.cfm?Portal_ID=1
To act under the regulations of the Professional & Occupational Associations Registration Act; To work as the regulatory authority for provisional registrants, certified management consultants, & fellow certified management consultants in Alberta; To ensure that members abide by professional & ethical standards
Greg McIntyre, Vice-President
Jeff Griffiths, Registrar

Institute of Certified Management Consultants of Atlantic Canada
c/o CMC-Canada National Office, PO Box 20, #2004, 401 Bay St., Toronto ON M5H 2Y4
Tel: 416-860-1515; *Fax:* 416-860-1535
Toll-Free: 800-268-1148
consulting@cmc-canada.ca
www.cmc-canada.ca/provincial_institutes.cfm?Portal_ID=2
To foster excellence & integrity in the management consulting profession.
Jerrold White, President
Blaine Atkinson, Registrar

Institute of Certified Management Consultants of British Columbia (CMC-BC)
c/o CMC-Canada National Office, PO Box 20, #2004, 401 Bay St., Toronto ON M5H 2Y4
Tel: 416-860-1515; *Fax:* 416-860-1535
Toll-Free: 800-268-1148
consulting@camc.com
www.cmc-canada.ca/provincial_institutes.cfm?Portal_ID=3
To protect the general public & clients by ensuring that the Institute's Code of Professional Conduct is followed by the certified management consultant profession; To ensure that certified members comply with all applicable legislation & laws
Stephen Spooner, President
Lyn Blanchard, Vice-President
Shayda Kassam, Treasurer

Institute of Certified Management Consultants of Manitoba (CMC-Manitoba) / Institut manitobain des conseillers en administration agréés
c/o CMC-Canada National Office, PO Box 20, #2004, 401 Bay St., Toronto ON M5H 2Y4
Tel: 416-860-1515; *Fax:* 416-860-1535
Toll-Free: 800-268-1148
consulting@cmc-canada.ca
www.cmc-canada.ca/provincial_institutes.cfm?Portal_ID=4
To foster & promote the development & acceptance of the profession of management consulting; to promote excellence in the practice of the profession for the benefit of members, clients & the community at large.
Timothy Wildman, President
Warren Thompson, Registrar

Institute of Certified Management Consultants of Saskatchewan
c/o CMC-Canada National Office, PO Box 20, #2004, 401 Bay St., Toronto ON M5H 2Y4
Tel: 416-860-1515; *Fax:* 416-860-1535
Toll-Free: 800-662-2972
consulting@cmc-canada.ca
www.cmc-canada.ca/provincial_institutes.cfm?Portal_ID=7
Social Media:
www.facebook.com/CMC.Saskatchewan
Richmond Graham, President
Jeremy Hall, Registrar

Institute of Chartered Secretaries & Administrators - Canadian Division (ICSA Canada) / Institut des secrétaires et administrateurs agréés au Canada
#202, 300 March Rd., Ottawa ON K2K 2E2
Tel: 613-595-1151; *Fax:* 613-595-1155
Toll-Free: 800-501-3440
info@icsacanada.org
www.icsacanada.org
The organization represents and serves Chartered Secretaries & Administrators, professionals who are hired by organizations to administer key areas such as corporate governance, director/officer/shareholder matters, compliance & regulatory matters, & financial matters.
Nancy Barrett, Executive Director

Institute of Corporate Directors (ICD) / Institut des administrateurs de sociétés
#2701, 250 Yonge St., Toronto ON M5B 2L7
Tel: 416-593-7741; *Fax:* 416-593-0636
Toll-Free: 877-593-7741
info@icd.ca
www.icd.ca
Social Media:
linkedin.com/groups?gid=4163769
twitter.com/ICDCanada
To enhance the quality of corporate governance in Canada
Stan Magidson, President & CEO
Maliha Aqeel, Director, Communications
Al-Azhar Khalfan, Director, Marketing & Sales

Institute of Professional Management (IPM)
#2210, 1081 Ambleside Dr., Ottawa ON K2B 8C8
Tel: 613-721-5957; *Fax:* 613-721-5850
info@workplace.ca
www.workplace.ca
Social Media:
www.facebook.com/InstituteofProfessionalManagement

International Personnel Management Association - Canada (IPMA-Canada)
National Office, 20 Edwards Pl., Mount Pearl NL A1N 3V5
Fax: 613-226-2298
Toll-Free: 888-226-5002
national@ipma-aigp.ca
ipma-aigp.com
Social Media:
www.facebook.com/IPMACanada
twitter.com/IPMACanada
To promote excellence in the practice of human resource management; to promote & enhance the HR profession in Canada & globally; to provide professional development & training for the HR community; to maintain a code of ethics & standards of practice; to recognize excellence through national & local awards programs
Glenn Saunders, Executive Director
Rick Brick, President
Heather Bowser, Director, Communications

Ontario Association of Emergency Managers (OAEM)
c/o McCauley Nichols, 14 Caledonia Terrace, Goderich ON N7A 2M8
Tel: 519-524-5992; *Fax:* 519-612-1992
secretary@oaem.ca
www.oaem.ca
To unite emergency management professionals in Ontario; To promote, support, & improve the profession of emergency management in Ontario
Amber Rushton, Coordinator, Membership

Ordre des administrateurs agréés du Québec (OAAQ)
#360, 1050, côte du Beaver Hall, Montréal QC H2Z 0A5
Tél: 514-499-0880; *Téléc:* 514-499-0892
Ligne sans frais: 800-465-0880
info@adma.qc.ca
www.adma.qc.ca
Média social:
linkedin.com/groups/Ordre-administrateurs-agréés-Québec-OAAQ-43624
www.facebook.com/OrdreAdmA
twitter.com/OrdreAdmA
Favorise auprès des professionnels de l'administration, l'innovation et l'atteinte d'un niveau de compétence supérieur pour qu'ils contribuent de façon proactive et dynamique au développement des entreprises et des organisations; Assure la protection du public en garantissant le respect des normes et standards professionnels en administration, en conformité avec le code de déontologie et par le biais des mécanismes prévus au code des professions; Contribue à l'avancement de l'administration, discipline essentielle au développement social et économique du Québec
France Vézina, Directrice générale et Secrétaire

Strategic Leadership Forum (SLF)
165 Thamesview Cres., St Marys ON N4X 1E1
Tel: 416-628-8262
membership@slftoronto.com
strategicleadershipforum.camp9.org
Social Media:
linkedin.com/company/strategic-leadership-forum
www.facebook.com/SLFToronto
twitter.com/Letstalkstrat
To provide our community of members with an independent & intellectually challenging forum that delivers practical insights & interactions on strategic management & leadership
Augustin Manchon, President

Supply Chain Management Association (SCMA) / Association de la gestion de la chaîne d'approvisionnement (AGCA)
PO Box 112, #2701, 777 Bay St., Toronto ON M5G 2C8
Tel: 416-977-7111; *Fax:* 416-977-8886
Toll-Free: 888-799-0877
info@scmanational.ca
www.scmanational.ca
Social Media:
linkedin.com/groups/Supply-Chain-Management-Association-SCMA-28889
www.facebook.com/scmanational
twitter.com/scmanational
To advance strategic supply chain management by providing training, education, & professional development for supply chain management professionals in Canada
Cheryl Paradowski, President & CEO
Cori Ferguson, Director, Public Affairs & Communications
Mike Whelan, Chair

Supply Chain Management Association - Alberta (SCMAAB)
Sterling Business Centre, #115, 17420 Stony Plain Rd., Edmonton AB T5S 1K6
Tel: 780-944-0355; *Fax:* 780-944-0356
Toll-Free: 866-610-4089
info@scmaab.ca
www.scmaab.ca
Social Media:
linkedin.com/groups?gid=4259963&trk=hb_side_g
www.facebook.com/332429763455410
twitter.com/SCMA_alberta
To develop the profession by ensuring that professional status is accessible to all purchasing practitioners in the province; high standards of eligibility & professional conduct will be developed, maintained & enforced to enhance the profession & protect public interest in the province of Alberta
Allan To, President

Supply Chain Management Association - British Columbia (SCMABC)
#300, 435 Columbia St., New Westminster BC V3L 5N8
Tel: 604-540-4494; *Fax:* 604-540-4023
Toll-Free: 800-411-7622
info@scmabc.ca
www.scmabc.ca
Social Media:
linkedin.com/groups/Supply-Chain-Management-Association-SCMA-28889
www.facebook.com/scmanational
twitter.com/scmabc
BC Institute PMAC is an incorporated, not-for-profit association that maintains a code of ethics for the profession to regulate quality & integrity.

Barrie Lynch, Executive Director
Ron Wiebe, President

Supply Chain Management Association - Manitoba (SCMAMB)
#200, 5 Donald St., Winnipeg MB R3L 2T4
Tel: 204-231-0965; *Fax:* 204-233-1250
Toll-Free: 877-231-0965
info@scmamb.ca
www.scmamb.ca
Social Media:
linkedin.com/groups/SCMA-Manitoba-4546716
www.facebook.com/140785209269900
twitter.com/scmanational
SCMAMB is committed to offering a professional development program coupled with networking opportunities to advance supply chain management.
Jay Anderson, President
Rick Reid, Executive Director

Supply Chain Management Association - New Brunswick (SCMANB)
#402, 527 Dundonald St., Fredericton NB E3B 1X5
Tel: 506-458-9414
info@scmanb.ca
www.scmanb.ca
Social Media:
linkedin.com/groups?about=&gid=2888933
www.facebook.com/NBPMI
twitter.com/scmanational
NBPMI is dedicated to being the leading source of education, training, & development in the field of purchasing & supply chain management. It provides members with networking opportunities & offers them training for a Supply Chain Management Professional (SCMP) designation.
Ryan McPherson, President
Wendy Piercy, Administrator

Supply Chain Management Association - Newfoundland & Labrador (SCMANL)
PO Box 29011, Stn. Torbay Road, St. John's NL A1A 5B5
Tel: 709-778-4033; *Fax:* 709-724-5625
info@scmanl.ca
www.scmanl.ca
Social Media:
linkedin.com/groups?about=&gid=2888933
www.facebook.com/scmanational
twitter.com/scmanational
To deliver education, training, & professional development programs in the province, so members may earn a Supply Chain Management Professional (SCMP) designation
Shauna Clark, President

Supply Chain Management Association - Northwest Territories (SCMANWT)
PO Box 2736, Yellowknife NT X1A 2R1
Tel: 867-873-9324
info@scmanwt.ca
www.scmanwt.ca
A non profit organization registered with the Societies Act in the Northwest Territories. They provide information and Education leading to a professional designation as a C.P.P. (Certified Professional Purchaser) the only accredited and legally recognized designation in the fields of Purchasing and Supply Management in Canada.
John Vandenberg, President

Supply Chain Management Association - Nova Scotia (SCMANS)
PO Box 21, Stn. CRO, Halifax NS B3J 2L4
Tel: 902-425-4029; *Fax:* 902-431-7220
info@scmans.ca
www.scmans.ca
Social Media:
linkedin.com/groups?about=&gid=2888933
www.facebook.com/140785209269900
twitter.com/scmanational
NSIPMAC delivers education, training & professional development programs in the province, so members may earn a Supply Chain Management Professional (SCMP) designation.
Joe McKenna, President

Supply Chain Management Association - Ontario (SCMAO)
PO Box 64, #2704, 1 Dundas St. West, Toronto ON M5G 1Z3
Tel: 416-977-7566; *Fax:* 416-977-4135
Toll-Free: 877-726-6968
info@scmao.ca
www.scmao.ca
Social Media: www.youtube.com/user/OIPMAC
linkedin.com/groups?gid=5139410&trk=my_groups-b-grp-v
twitter.com/SCMAOnt
The preeminent supply chain managemen organisation in Ontario, supporting a growing global SCM community of over 20,00 active members and program participants in meeting their professional and lifelong learning goals. Their programs taught by leading North American academics and professional trainers, are designed to build/enhance the professional competence and strategic perspective of practitioners at all levels of career progression, from entry-, to mid-, to senior/executive levels of functional responsibility.
Kelly Duffin, Executive Director

Supply Chain Management Association - Saskatchewan (SCMASK)
#221A, 3521 - 8th St. East, Saskatoon SK S7H 0W5
Tel: 306-653-8899; *Fax:* 306-653-8870
Toll-Free: 866-665-6167
info@scmask.ca
www.scmask.ca
Social Media:
linkedin.com/company/3549789
www.facebook.com/SCMASK
twitter.com/SCMASK
To promote & improve supply management practices in the profession through education & raising the awareness of the supply management profession within Saskatchewan
Nicole Burgess, Executive Director

Manufacturing & Industry

Association de la recherche industrielle du Québec (ADRIQ)
#1120, 555, boul. René-Lévesque Ouest, Montréal QC H2Z 1B1
Tél: 514-337-3001; *Téléc:* 514-337-2229
adriq@adriq.com
www.adriq.com
Média social: linkedin.com/groups?gid=2999463
twitter.com/ADRIQ_RCTi
De promouvoir les nouvelles technologies afin d'accroître le commerce concurrentiel au Québec et à l'étranger
Jean-Louis Legault, Président-directeur général

Association for Operations Management (APICS)
#300, 1370 Don Mills Rd., Toronto ON M3B 3N7
Tel: 416-366-5388; *Fax:* 416-381-4054
info@apics.ca
www.apics.ca
To offer programs & materials on business management techniques; To promotes education in resource management
Shari Bricks, Executive Director
Lina DeMatteo, Manager, Events
Anthony Nijmeh, Manager, Technical Support
Greg Mulroney, Coordinator, Membership Support

Association of Home Appliance Manufacturers Canada Council (AHAM)
PO Box 45560, Stn. Chapman Mills, 3151 Strandherd Dr., Ottawa ON K2J 5N1
Tel: 613-823-3223
info@ahamcanada.ca
www.ahamcanada.ca
To represent member interests in the establishment of product standards & in environmental legislation; To advocate the safe removal of mercury & other ozone depleting substances from older appliances; To support the development of energy efficient products
Steve Caldow, Chair

Association of Independent Corrugated Converters
PO Box 73063, Stn. White Shields, 2300 Lawrence Ave. East, Toronto ON M1P 4Z5
Tel: 905-727-9405; *Fax:* 905-727-1061
info@aicc11.com
aiccbox.ca
Social Media:
linkedin.com/company/aicc-canada
To provide a forum for the independent corrugated converter on legitimate matters of mutual interest; To enhance the level of professionalism of the independent converter in the operation of his/her business; To implement democratically determined goals on matters civil & governmental which have a positive effect on all independent corrugated converters
Jana Marmei, Executive Director

British Columbia Paint Manufacturers' Association (BCPMA)
c/o Cloverdale Paint Inc., 6950 King George Blvd., Surrey BC V3W 4Z1
Tel: 604-596-6261; *Fax:* 604-597-2677
helpdesk@cloverdalepaint.com
To act as the voice of paint manufacturers in British Columbia; To promote the welfare of association members
Ed Linton, President
Ron Vanderdrift, Vice-President
Deryk Pawsey, Secretary
Yvon Poitras, Treasurer

Canadian Association of Moldmakers (CAMM)
c/o St. Clair College (FCEM), PO Box 16, 2000 Talbot Rd. West, Windsor ON N9A 6S4
Tel: 519-255-7863; *Fax:* 519-255-9446
info@camm.ca
www.camm.ca
To address the concerns of Canadian mould making companies & to present a united voice on legislative issues to provincial & federal governments
Dan Moynahan, President
Diane Deslippe, Executive Director, Office

Canadian Carpet Institute / Institut canadien du tapis
#200, 435 St. Laurent Blvd., Ottawa ON K1K 2z8
Tel: 613-749-3265; *Fax:* 613-745-8753
info@canadiancarpet.org
www.canadiancarpet.org
To serve as a forum in developing industry consensus for action on common problems & opportunities; To enhance the well-being of the Canadian carpet industry by any & all means consistent with the members, & the public interest
Walter Eckhardt, President
Karel Vercruyssen, Vice-President
Raymonde Lemire, Manager, Administration

Canadian Cosmetic, Toiletry & Fragrance Association (CCTFA) / Association canadienne des cosmétiques, produit de toilette et parfums
#102, 420 Britannia Rd. East, Mississauga ON L4Z 3L5
Tel: 905-890-5161; *Fax:* 905-890-2607
cctfa@cctfa.ca
www.cctfa.ca
To encourage trust & confidence in the Canadian cosmetic, toiletry & fragrance industry & in the safety, efficacy & quality of its products; To be the princiapal voice of the personal care industry, including cosmetic-like drug products & cosmetic-like natural health products (NHP), interfacing on a timely basis with governemtn & elected representatives, to ensure development & effective representationof industry positions on a ll regulatory issues; to have the personal care industyr perceived by consumers at large as being socially concerned, responsible & involved with Canadian society; this will be primarily achieved through the CCTFA Foundation & the Look Good Feel Better program.
Myles Robinson, Chair

Canadian Explosives Industry Association (CEAEC)
#903, 3590 Rivergate Wy., Ottawa ON K1V 1V6
Tel: 613-249-8488; *Fax:* 613-723-0013
www.ceaec.ca
To promote & represent the general interests of distributors, manufacturers, & users of explosives; To promote & maintain high standards concerning the use, handling, & transport of explosives; To co-operate with government authorities in the promotion of safety standards; To encourage the adoption & adherence to uniform legislation concerning the Canadian explosives industry
Rene A. (Moose) Morin, Manager

Canadian Hardware & Housewares Manufacturers' Association (CHHMA) / Association canadienne des fabricants de produits de quincaillerie et d'articles ménagers
#101, 1335 Morningside Ave., Toronto ON M1B 5M4
Tel: 416-282-0022; *Fax:* 416-282-0027
Toll-Free: 800-488-4792
www.chhma.ca
Social Media:
twitter.com/theCHHMA
To assist members to sell more & do it more profitably
Vaughn Crofford, President
Maureen Hizaka, Director, Operations
Michael Jorgenson, Manager, Marketing & Communications
Pam Winter, Coordinator, Events

Canadian Innovation Centre (CIC)
c/o Waterloo Research & Technology Park, #15, 295 Hagey Blvd., Waterloo ON N2L 6R5
Tel: 519-885-5870; *Fax:* 519-513-2421
Toll-Free: 800-265-4559
info@innovationcentre.ca
www.innovationcentre.ca
Social Media:
linkedin.com/company/canadian-innovation-centre
twitter.com/innovationctre

To advance innovation by helping our clients make better business decisions through information, education & commercialization.
Ted Cross, Chair
Josie Graham, CEO & Director, Projects and Studies

Canadian Kitchen Cabinet Association (CKCA) / Association canadienne de fabricants d'armoires de cuisine (ACAC)
1485 Laperriere Ave., Ottawa ON K1Z 7S8
Tel: 613-567-9171; *Fax:* 613-729-6206
info@ckca.ca
www.ckca.ca
To promote the interests & conserve the rights of those engaged in the manufacture of kitchen cabinets, bathroom vanities & related millwork as well as their suppliers & dealers.
Jake Wolter, President

Canadian Laboratory Suppliers Association (CLSA) / Association canadienne de fournisseurs de laboratoire
#131, 525 Highland Rd. West, Kitchener ON N3M 5P4
Tel: 519-650-8028; *Fax:* 519-653-8749
www.clsassoc.com
The Canadian Labratory Suppliers Association is a group of scientific companies committed to promoting and serving the Canadian laboratory marketplace. It provides a non-competitive environment for executives of Canada's leading scientific suppliers to share ideas and concepts. The CLSA's objective is to provide market analysis on the scientific industry, and to understand and discuss issues that influence the Canadian laboratory scientific market.
Alan Koop, President & Chair

Canadian Manufacturers & Exporters (CME) / Manufacturiers et Exportateurs Canada
#1500, 1 Nicholas St., Ottawa ON K1N 7B7
Tel: 613-238-8888; *Fax:* 613-563-9218
www.cme-mec.ca
Social Media: www.youtube.com/manufacturingTV
twitter.com/cme_mec
To continuously improve the competitiveness of Canadian industry & to expand export business by: aggressive, effective advocacy to government at all levels; delivering timely, relevant information, programs & support of superior quality & value; providing opportunities for education, learning & professional growth; & promoting the development & implementation of advanced technology
Jayson Myers, President & Chief Executive Officer
Mathew Wilson, Senior Vice-President
Jeff Brownlee, Vice-President, Public Affairs & Partnerships
Joanne Heighway, Vice-President, Organizational Excellence
John Knox, Vice-President, Sales & Marketing
Philip Turi, General Counsel & Director, Global Business Services

Canadian Office Products Association (COPA)
#101, 1335 Morningside Ave., Toronto ON M1B 5M4
Tel: 905-624-9462; *Fax:* 905-624-0830
info@copa.ca
www.copa.ca
Social Media:
linkedin.com/company/2675440
www.facebook.com/CanadianOfficeProductsAssociation
twitter.com/COPA_network
To help their memebers by providing them with business solutions that allow them to grow
Sam Moncada, President

Canadian Plastics Industry Association (CPIA) / Association canadienne de l'industrie des plastiques
#125, 5955 Airport Rd., Mississauga ON L4V 1R9
Tel: 905-678-7748; *Fax:* 905-678-0774
www.plastics.ca
Social Media:
linkedin.com/company/canadian-plastics-industry-association
www.facebook.com/CanadianPlasticsIndustryAssociation
twitter.com/CPIA_ACIP
To advance the prosperity & international competitiveness of the Canadian plastics industry in an environmentally & socially responsible manner
Carol Hochu, President & CEO
Krista Friesen, Vice-President, Sustainability
Shannon Laszlo, Coordinator, Projects & Administration

Canadian Sanitation Supply Association (CSSA) / Association canadienne des fournisseurs de produits sanitaires
PO Box 10009, 910 Dundas St. West, Whitby ON L1P 1P7
Tel: 905-665-8001; *Fax:* 905-430-6418
Toll-Free: 866-684-8273
www.cssa.com
Social Media:
linkedin.com/company/canadian-sanitation-supply-association
www.facebook.com/CSSA1957
twitter.com/CSSA1957
To provide a high degree of professionalism, technical knowledge & business ethics within the membership; To promote greater public awareness, appreciation & understanding of the sanitation industry
Mike Nosko, Executive Director

Canadian Tooling & Machining Association (CTMA)
#3, 140 McGovern Dr., Cambridge ON N3H 4R7
Tel: 519-653-7265; *Fax:* 519-653-6764
Toll-Free: 888-437-3661
info@ctma.com
www.ctma.com
To be an effective, broad-based, respected organization, representing the Canadian tooling & machining industry, nationally & internationally
Les Payne, Executive Director

Canadian Toy Association / Canadian Toy & Hobby Fair (CTA) / L'Association canadienne du Jouet
#212, 7777 Keele St., Concord ON L4K 1Y7
Tel: 905-660-5690; *Fax:* 905-660-6103
info@cdntoyassn.com
www.cdntoyassn.com
Carol McDonald, Contact, Media Relations

Door & Hardware Institute in Canada
#310, 2175 Sheppard Ave. East, Toronto ON M2J 1W8
Tel: 416-492-6502; *Fax:* 416-491-1670
www.dhicanada.ca
Social Media:
twitter.com/dhicanada
To serve Canadian members as the professional development, information, advocate & certification resource for the total distribution process in the architectural openings industry.
Lawrence Beatty, President
Carolyne Vigon, Executive Director

Fenestration Association of BC (FEN-BC)
#101, 20351 Duncan Way, Langley BC V3A 7N3
Tel: 778-571-0245; *Fax:* 866-253-9979
info@fen-bc.org
www.fen-bc.org
Social Media: www.youtube.com/user/FenBC?feature=mhee
www.facebook.com/pages/Fen-Bc/561853500522221?ref=ts&fref=ts
twitter.com/fenbc
A nonprofit trade association representing the interests of businesses engaged in the fenestration industry in BC.
Zana Gordon, Executive Director

Fenestration Canada
#1208, 130 Albert St., Ottawa ON K1P 5G4
Tel: 613-235-5511; *Fax:* 613-235-4664
info@fenestrationcanada.ca
www.fenestrationcanada.ca
To represents its members in all aspects of the window & door manufacturing industry, including formulating & promoting high standards of quality in manufacturing, design, marketing, distribution, sales, & application of all types of window & door products
Yvan Banman, President
Eva Ryterband, Treasurer

The Metal Working Association of New Brunswick (MWANB) / Association des entreprises métallurgiques du Nouveau-Brunswick
PO Box 7129, #12, 567 Coverdale Rd., Riverview NB E1B 4T8
Tel: 506-861-9071; *Fax:* 506-857-3059
nb@cme-mec.ca
www.mwanb.com
To be a voice for the metal working sector in New Brunswick; to be a forum for members to network discuss opportunities
Marco Gagnon, President
David Plante, Manager

National Floor Covering Association (NFCA) / Association nationale des revêtements de sol
987 Clarkson Rd. South, Mississauga ON L5J 2V8
Tel: 905-822-2280; *Fax:* 905-822-2494
www.nfcaonline.ca
To unite the Canadian regional & provincial associations in a spirit of cooperation; to improve & enhance the floorcovering industry; to share information & ideas; to undertake & support programs which will improve communications at all levels of the industry

Organization of CANDU Industries (OCI) / Association des industries CANDU
#2, 1730 McPherson Ct., Pickering ON L1W 3E6
Tel: 905-839-0073; *Fax:* 905-839-7085
www.oci-aic.org
To represent companies in the Canadian private sector engaged in the supply of goods & services for CANDU power plants in export markets; to provide a focal point for industrial collaboration between the private sector of Canada's nuclear industry & foreign purchasers of a CANDU plant; functions separately from AECL, but participates with it in the design, manufacture, construction & commissioning of CANDU facilities in foreign countries
Ron Oberth, President
Marina Oeyangen, Manager, Member Services

Saskatchewan Trade & Export Partnership Inc. (STEP)
PO Box 1787, #320, 1801 Hamilton St., Regina SK S4P 3C6
Tel: 306-933-6551; *Fax:* 306-933-6556
Toll-Free: 888-976-7875
inquire@sasktrade.com
www.sasktrade.com
To work in partnership with Saskatchewan exporters & emerging exporters to maximize commercial success in global ventures; To deliver custom export solutions & market intelligence to member companies; To coordinate international development projects
Lionel LaBelle, President & Chief Executive Officer
Angela Krauss, Executive Director, Export Services
Brad Michnik, Executive Director, Trade Development
Pam Bartoshewski, Controller

Sous-Traitance Industrielle Québec (STIQ)
#900, 1080, côte du Beaver Hall, Montréal QC H2Z 1S8
Tél: 514-875-8789; *Ligne sans frais:* 888-875-8789
info@stiq.com
www.stiq.com
Normand Voyer, Vice-président executive

Tire and Rubber Association of Canada (TRAC) / L'Association canadienne du pneu et du caoutchouc
Plaza 4, #100, 2000 Argentia Rd., Mississauga ON L5N 1W1
Tel: 905-814-1714; *Fax:* 905-814-1085
info@rubberassociation.ca
www.tracanada.ca
Social Media:
linkedin.com/company/the-rubber-association-of-canada
twitter.com/GTRadials
To upgrade & maintain good industry/government working relations; to explore ways of improving industry competitiveness & efficiency; To promote safety in members' products, in their use & in the workplace; To promote expansion & profitability of Canadian rubber manufacturing units; To enhance standing of Canadian rubber industry worldwide; To provide members with industry marketing statistics
Glenn Maidment, President
Ralph Warner, Director, Operations
Antonia Issa, Communications Manager

Toronto Japanese Association of Commerce & Industry
PO Box 104, #122, 20 York Mills Rd., Toronto ON M2P 2C2
Tel: 416-360-0235; *Fax:* 416-360-0236
office@torontoshokokai.org
www.torontoshokokai.org
To promote business relations between Canada & Japan through the activities of the members of the Japanese School of Toronto Shokokai Inc. (commonly known as the Hoshuko).
Tetsuo Komuro, President
Yukio Arita, Executive Director & Secretary

Marine Trades

Boating BC Association
#130, 10691 Shellbridge Way, Richmond BC V6X 2W8
Tel: 604-248-8906; *Fax:* 604-270-3644
info@boatingbc.ca
www.boatingbc.ca
Social Media:
www.youtube.com/channel/UCyvMWT5_eNm_0LBJFbXiZSw
linkedin.com/company/boating-bc-association
www.facebook.com/BoatingBC
twitter.com/boatingbc

To act as the voice of the BC recreational marine industry
Don Prittie, President
Lisa Geddes, Executive Director
Mike Short, First Vice-President & Treasurer

British Columbia Maritime Employers Association (BCMEA)
349 Railway St., Vancouver BC V6A 1A4
Tel: 604-688-1155; *Fax:* 604-684-2397
www.bcmea.com
Andy Smith, President & Chief Executive Officer
John Beckett, Vice-President, Training, Safety, & Recruitment
Terry Duggan, Vice-President, Finance & Secretary
Mike Leonard, Vice-President, Labour Relations
Eleanor Marynuik, Vice-President, Human Resources
Greg Vurdela, Vice-President, Marketing & Information Services

The Canadian Marine Industries and Shipbuilding Association (CMISA) / Association de la construction navale du Canada
#1502, 222 Queen St., Ottawa ON K1P 5V9
Tel: 613-232-7127; *Fax:* 613-238-5519
canadianshipbuilding.com
Represents the interests of the Canadian shipbuilding, ship repair & associated marine equipment & services industries
Peter Cairns, President

Canadian Navigation Society (CNS)
c/o Canadian Aeronautics & Space Institute, #104, 350 Terry Fox Dr., Kanata ON K2K 2W5
Tel: 613-591-8787; *Fax:* 613-591-7291
www.casi.ca/canadian-navigation-society
To advance the science, technologies, & applications of navigation
Susan Skone, Society Chair

The Great Lakes Marine Heritage Foundation
55 Ontario St., Kingston ON K7L 2Y2
Tel: 613-542-2261; *Fax:* 613-542-0043
marmus@marmuseum.ca
www.marmuseum.ca
Doug Cowie, Manager

National Marine Manufacturers Association Canada (NMMA)
#8, 14 McEwan Dr., Bolton ON L7E 1H1
Tel: 905-951-0009; *Fax:* 905-951-0018
sanghel@nmma.org
www.cmma.ca
The CMMA is committed to being a leader; in promoting boating, advocacy with government and providing value added services to foster the financial success of the marine industry.
Sara Anghel, Executive Director

Marketing

Association of Internet Marketing & Sales (AIMS)
#650, 99 Spadina Ave., Toronto ON M5V 3P8
admin@aimscanada.com
www.aimscanada.com
To assist business professionals to leverage the internet in their daily business
Bruce Powell, Member, Executive Board

Atlantic Publishers Marketing Association (APMA)
1484 Carlton St., Halifax NS B3H 3B7
Tel: 902-420-0711; *Fax:* 902-423-4302
apma.admin@atlanticpublishers.ca
www.atlanticpublishers.ca
Social Media:
www.facebook.com/AtlanticBooksToday
twitter.com/abtmagazine
To promote the growth & development of Canadian-owned publishing houses based in Atlantic Canada
Carolyn Guy, Executive Director
Lauren D'Entremont, Managing Editor

British Columbia Cranberry Marketing Commission (BCCMC)
PO Box 162, Stn. A, Abbotsford BC V2T 6Z5
Tel: 604-897-9252
cranberries@telus.net
www.bccranberries.com
Social Media: instagram.com/bccranberries
www.facebook.com/bccranberries
twitter.com/BCcranberries
To regulate cranberry farming in BC

British Columbia Egg Marketing Board
#250, 32160 South Fraser Way, Abbotsford BC V2T 1W5
Tel: 604-556-3348; *Fax:* 604-556-3410
bcemb@bcegg.com
www.bcegg.com
Social Media: www.youtube.com/user/BCEggProducers
www.facebook.com/bcegg
twitter.com/bceggs
To regulate British Columbia's egg farming industry
Richard King, Chair

British Columbia Hog Marketing Commission
PO Box 8000-280, Abbotsford BC V2S 6H1
Tel: 604-287-4647; *Fax:* 604-820-6647
info@bcpork.ca
bcpork.ca
Geraldine Auston, Contact

British Columbia Milk Marketing Board
#200, 32160 South Fraser Way, Abbotsford BC V2T 1W5
Tel: 604-556-3444; *Fax:* 604-556-7717
info@milk-bc.com
www.milk-bc.com
To promote, control and regulate the production, transportation, packing, storing and marketing of milk, fluid milk and manufactured milk products within British Columbia
Bob Ingratta, Chief Executive Officer
Jim Byrne, Chair

British Columbia Turkey Marketing Board
#106, 19329 Enterprise Way, Surrey BC V3S 6J8
Tel: 604-534-5644; *Fax:* 604-534-3651
info@bcturkey.com
www.bcturkey.com
Michel Benoit, General Manager
Ron Charles, Chair

British Columbia Vegetable Marketing Commission (BCVMC)
#207, 15252- 32nd Ave., Surrey BC V3S 0R7
Tel: 604-542-9734; *Fax:* 604-542-9735
tom@bcveg.com
www.bcveg.com
Tom Demma, General Manager
David Taylor, Chair

Canadian Agencies Practicing Marketing Activation (CAPMA)
#107, 1 Eva Rd., Toronto ON M9C 4Z5
info@capma.org
www.capma.org
To raise the profile of the industry
Christine Ross, Executive Director
Mike Armstrong, President
Matthew Diamond, Vice-President
Chad Grenier, Secretary
Rick Takamatsu, Treasurer

Canadian Agri-Marketing Association (CAMA)
22 Guyers Dr., RR#3, Port Elgin ON N0H 2C7
Tel: 519-389-6552
info@cama.org
www.cama.org
To promote the exchange & application of agricultural marketing ideas; To encourage high professional standards of agricultural marketing in Ontario
Mary Thornley, Executive Director

Canadian Agri-Marketing Association (Alberta) (CAMA)
c/o CAMA, 22 Guyers Dr., RR#3, Port Elgin ON N0H 2C7
Alberta@cama.org
www.cama.org/alberta/AlbertaHome.aspx
To increase knowledge of ideas related to agri-marketing; To promote high professional standards of agricultural marketing
Jenn Norrie, CAMA AB Treasurer

Canadian Agri-Marketing Association (Manitoba)
210 - 1600 Kenaston Blvd., Winnipeg MB R3P 0Y4
Tel: 204-799-2019; *Fax:* 204-257-5651
camamb@mts.net
www.cama.org/manitoba/ManitobaHome.aspx
To promote excellence in agrimarketing
Barbara Chabih, President

Canadian Agri-Marketing Association (Saskatchewan)
PO Box 4005, Regina SK S4P 3R9
Tel: 306-262-0733
camask@sasktel.net
www.cama.org/saskatchewan/saskatchewanHome.aspx
To operate as a networking organization for all sectors of Saskatchewan's agricultural industry
Lesley Kelly, President

Canadian Broiler Hatching Egg Marketing Agency (CBHEMA) / Office canadien de commercialisation des oeufs d'incubation de poulet à chair (OCCOIPC)
21 Florence St., Ottawa ON K2O 0W6
Tel: 613-232-3023; *Fax:* 613-232-5241
info@chep-poic.ca
www.chep-poic.ca
To ensure that our members produce enough hatching eggs to meet the needs of the broiler industry
Jack Greydanus, Chair
Giuseppe Caminiti, General Manager

Canadian Hotel Marketing & Sales Executives (CHMSE)
26 Avonhurst Rd., Toronto ON M9A 2G8
Tel: 416-252-9800; *Fax:* 416-252-7071
info@chmse.com
www.chmse.com
Social Media:
linkedin.com/groups?home=&gid=3020813
twitter.com/CHMSE
To be the leading association in providing professional development opportunities to sales & marketing executives within the Canadian hospitality industry
Shelley Macdonald, Executive Director
Christopher White, President

Canadian Institute of Marketing / Institut canadien du marketing
205 Miller Dr., Georgetown ON L7G 6G4
Tel: 905-877-5369
www.professionalmarketer.ca
Social Media: www.youtube.com/user/canadianmarketer
linkedin.com/groups?mostPopular=&gid=105823
twitter.com/regprofmarketer
To improve the practice of marketing in Canada by encouraging the adoption of professional standards & qualifications by practitioners & employers, & by sponsoring activities related to marketing education & training; To be a means by which those engaged in all aspects of marketing as a professional activity can represent their views & interests to governments & agencies
A. Grant Lee, Executive Director
Faythe Pal, Chair
John Jackson, Secretary-Treasurer
Shiv Seechurn, Registrar

Canadian Marketing Association (CMA) / Association canadienne du marketing (ACM)
#607, 1 Concorde Gate, Toronto ON M3C 3N6
Tel: 416-391-2362; *Fax:* 416-441-4062
Toll-Free: 800-267-8805
info@the-cma.org
www.the-cma.org
Social Media: www.youtube.com/user/canadianmarketing
linkedin.com/groups?mostPopular=&gid=47336
www.facebook.com/cdnmarketing
twitter.com/Cdnmarketing
To be the pre-eminent marketing association in Canada representing the integration & convergence of all marketing disciplines, channels & technologies
John Gustavson, President & CEO
Stephen Brown, Chair

Canadian Produce Marketing Association (CPMA) / Association canadienne de la distribution de fruits et légumes
162 Cleopatra Dr., Ottawa ON K2G 5X2
Tel: 613-226-4187; *Fax:* 613-226-2984
question@cpma.ca
www.cpma.ca
To increase the market for fresh fruits & vegetables in Canada, by encouraging cooperation & information exchange in all segments, at the domestic & international level
Jim DiMenna, Chair
Ron Lemaire, President

Marketing Research & Intelligence Association (MRIA) / L'Association de la recherche et de l'intelligence marketing (ARIM)
Bldg. 4, #104, 2600 Skymark Ave., Mississauga ON L4W 5B2
Tel: 905-602-6854; *Fax:* 905-602-6855
Toll-Free: 888-602-6742
info@mria-arim.ca
mria-arim.ca
Social Media:
linkedin.com/groups/MRIA-113690
www.facebook.com/MRIAARIM
twitter.com/MRIAARIM
To benefit the public & its members by developing & delivering ethical, professional practice standards, promoting the industry,

& advocating for public policy that balances the need for research with privacy & consumer rights.
Anastasia Arabia, President
John Ball, Interim Executive Director
Tricia Benn, Secretary-Treasurer

Multicultural Marketing Society of Canada
c/o Gautam Nath, Monsoon Communications, 37 Bulwer St., Toronto ON M5T 1A1
Tel: 647-477-3167
Social Media: linkedin.com/groups/Multicultural-Marketing-Society-Canada-3853327
Gautam Nath, Founder

Natural Products Marketing Council
PO Box 890, Truro NS B2N 5G6
Tel: 902-893-6511; *Fax:* 902-893-6573
www.novascotia.ca
To assure the orderly marketing of natural products
Elizabeth Crouse, General Manager
Ken Peacock, Chair

New Brunswick Egg Marketing Board (NBEMB) / L'Office de commercialisation des oeufs de Nouveau Brunswick
#101, 275 Main St., Fredericton NB E3A 1E1
www.nbegg.ca

Newfoundland & Labrador Farm Direct Marketing Association
PO Box 317, 1 Goose Pond Rd., Shearstown NL A0A 3V0
Tel: 709-786-2943
bamhaadmin@hotmail.com
Committed to development, promotion, leadership and representation.
Perry A. Mercer, President

North Shore Forest Products Marketing Board
PO Box 386, Bathurst NB E2A 3Z3
Tel: 506-548-8958
nsfpmb@nb.aibn.com
www.forestrysyndicate.com
To negotiate with industry & government on behalf of the private wood producers of the regulated area for fair prices for the products of the woodlots & to promote improved forest management
Alain Landry, General Manager
Patrick Doucet, Sylviculture Manager

Nova Scotia Wool Marketing Board
c/o Natural Products Marketing Council, NS Dept. of Agriculture, PO Box 190, Halifax NS B3J 2M4
To foster the production of high-quality wool in Nova Scotia, & the effective marketing of this product

Ontario Farm Fresh Marketing Association (OFFMA)
2002 Vandorf Sideroad, Aurora ON L4G 7B9
Tel: 905-841-9278; *Fax:* 905-726-3369
info@ontariofarmfresh.com
ontariofarmfresh.com
Social Media: www.youtube.com/user/OntarioFarmFresh
www.facebook.com/OntarioFarmFresh
twitter.com/OFFMA
To assist members in marketing skills; To liaise with other farm-oriented organizations such as Ontario Fruit & Vegetable Growers Association
Cathy Bartolic, Executive Director

Ontario Flue-Cured Tobacco Growers' Marketing Board (OFCTGMB)
4B Elm St., Tillsonburg ON N4G 0C4
Tel: 519-842-3661; *Fax:* 519-842-7813
otb@ontarioflue-cured.com
www.ontarioflue-cured.com
To administer & enforce the provisions of Regulation 207/09 (Tobacco - Plan) & Regulation 208/09 (Tobacco - Powers of Local Board), made under the Farm Products Marketing Act; To control & regulate the production & marketing of tobacco, within the limits imposed by the Farm Products Marketing Act

Ontario Pork Producers' Marketing Board
655 Southgate Dr., Guelph ON N1G 5G6
Tel: 519-767-4600; *Fax:* 519-829-1769
Toll-Free: 877-668-7675
www.ontariopork.on.ca
Tess Raay, Director, Strategic Management

Ontario Sheep Marketing Agency (OSMA)
130 Malcolm Rd., Guelph ON N1K 1B1
Tel: 519-836-0043; *Fax:* 519-836-2531
www.ontariosheep.org
To represent all aspects of the sheep, lamb, & wool industry in Ontario; To improve the marketing of sheep & enhance producers' returns; To provide the public with safe, quality lamb & related products
Jennifer MacTavish, General Manager

Out-of-Home Marketing Association of Canada (OMAC) / Association marketing canadienne de l'affichage (AMCA)
#500, 111 Peter St., Toronto ON M5V 2H1
Tel: 416-968-3435; *Fax:* 416-968-6538
rcaron@omaccanada.ca
www.omaccanada.ca
To increase out-of-home's share of ad dollars by promoting the benefits & effectiveness of out-of-home media to agencies & advertisers; to develop & implement new initiatives that serve as a resource to the industry & increase understanding of out-of-home media; to foster development of standards & guidelines that make out-of-home easier to plan & buy; to serve as the united voice of the industry through involvement in issues that represent the interests of its members
Rosanne Caron, President

Photo Marketing Association International - Canada (PMAI)
PO Box 81191, Ancaster ON L9G 4X2
Tel: 905-304-8800; *Fax:* 905-304-7700
Toll-Free: 800-461-4350
www.pmai.org/content.aspx?id=21982
To disseminate timely information while providing market research & business improvement products & services that contribute to increased profitability & business growth for its membership
Bob Moggach, Director of Canadian Activities

Prince Edward Island Hog Commodity Marketing Board
#209, 420 University Ave., Charlottetown PE C1A 7Z5
Tel: 902-892-4201; *Fax:* 902-892-4203
peipork@hotmail.com
www.peipork.pe.ca
Social Media: www.youtube.com/user/SwineTV
twitter.com/porkisyummy
To provide information to the pork production industry of Prince Edward Island; To voice the concerns of hog farmers
Tim Seeber, Executive Director
Paul Larsen, Chair

Prince Edward Island Marketing Council
PO Box 1600, Charlottetown PE C1A 7N3
Tel: 902-569-7575; *Fax:* 902-569-7745
To administer the Natural Products Marketing Act under which commodity boards & groups
Ian MacIssac, Secretary & General Manager

Prince Edward Island Poultry Meat Commodity Marketing Board
RR#6, Cardigan PE C0A 1G0
Tel: 902-838-4108; *Fax:* 902-838-4108
mmyles@dfpei.pe.ca
Janet Murphy Hilliard, Secretary-Manager

Saskatchewan Turkey Producers' Marketing Board (STPMB)
1438 Fletcher Rd., Saskatoon SK S7M 5T2
Tel: 306-931-1050; *Fax:* 306-931-2825
saskaturkey@sasktel.net
To manage the supply managed system in Saskatchewan, which includes negotiating the province's quota levels with the CTMA, negotiating price levels with local processors and developing a long-term strategic focus for Saskatchewan's turkey industry
Rose Olson, Executive Director

Mental Health

Alberta Psychiatric Association (APA)
#400, 1040 - 7 Ave. SW, Calgary AB T2P 3G9
Tel: 403-244-4487; *Fax:* 403-244-2340
info@albertapsych.org
www.albertapsych.org
Thomas Raedler, President

Association des médecins-psychiatres du Québec (AMPQ) / Québec Psychiatrists' Association
CP 216, Succ. Desjardins, Montréal QC H5B 1G8
Tél: 514-350-5128; *Téléc:* 514-350-5198
www.ampq.org
Promouvoir les intérêts professionnels et économiques de ses membres
Karine J. Igartua, Présidente
Guillaume Dumont, Secrétaire

Canadian Alliance on Mental Illness & Mental Health (CAMIMH)
#702, 141 Laurier Ave. West, Ottawa ON K1P 5J3
Tel: 613-237-2144; *Fax:* 613-237-1674
Social Media: www.flickr.com/photos/45033589@N02
www.facebook.com/FaceMentalIllness
twitter.com/miawcanada
An alliance of mental health organizations comprised of health care providers and organizations representing persons with mental illness and their families and caregivers.

Canadian Art Therapy Association (CATA) / L'association canadienne d'art thérapie
26 Earl Grey Rd., Toronto ON M4J 3L2
www.catainfo.ca
To promote the development & maintenance of professional standards of art therapy training, registration, research, & practice in Canada; To heighten awareness of art therapy as an important mental health discipline
Nick Zwaagstra, President
Lori Boyko, Registrar
Marie Alexander, Chair, Ethics
Olena Darewych, Chair, Membership

Canadian Association for Suicide Prevention (CASP) / L'Association canadienne pour la prévention du suicide (ACPS)
870 Portage Ave., Winnipeg MB R3G 0P1
Tel: 204-784-4073
casp@casp-acps.ca
www.suicideprevention.ca
To reduce the suicide rate; To minimize the harmful consequences of suicide
Dammy Damstrom Albach, President
Renée Ouimet, Vice-President
Yvonne Bergmans, Secretary
Ian Ross, Treasurer
Tim Wall, Executive Director

Canadian Centre for Stress & Well-Being
#1801, 1 Yonge St., Toronto ON M5E 1W7
Tel: 416-363-6204; *Fax:* 416-658-9536
smcen@yahoo.com
To provide education about stress management; To increase health & wellness

Canadian Group Psychotherapy Association (CGPA)
c/o First Stage Enterprises, #109, 1 Corcorde Gate, Toronto ON M3C 3N6
Tel: 416-426-7229; *Fax:* 416-726-7280
Toll-Free: 866-433-9695
admin@cgpa.ca
www.cgpa.ca
Social Media: linkedin.com/company/5054194
twitter.com/National_CGPA
To promote excellence in standards of training, practice, & research; To encourage & provide for the education of mental health professionals in group psychotherapy
Joan-Dianne Smith, President
Colleen Wilkie, Secretary
Jessica Kerr, Contact

Canadian Institute of Stress (CIS)
Toronto ON
Tel: 416-236-4218
info@stresscanada.org
www.stresscanada.org
Social Media: www.facebook.com/TheCanadianInstituteOfStress
To provide programs & tools for individuals & workplaces to handle stress

Canadian Mental Health Association (CMHA) / Association canadienne pour la santé mentale (ACSM)
#1110, 151 Slater St., Ottawa ON K1P 5H3
Tel: 613-745-7750; *Fax:* 613-745-5522
www.cmha.ca
Social Media: www.youtube.com/user/cmhanational
www.facebook.com/CANMentalHealth
twitter.com/CMHA_NTL
To promote mental health as well as support the resilience & recovery of people experiencing mental illness, through advocacy, education, research & service
Peter Coleridge, National Chief Executive Officer
Irene Merien, Chair
Sarah Smith, National Director, Fund Development
Mark Ferdinand, National Director, Public Policy

Canadian Psychiatric Association (CPA) / Association des psychiatres du Canada
#701, 141 Laurier Ave. West, Ottawa ON K1P 5J3
Tel: 613-234-2815; *Fax:* 613-234-9857
Toll-Free: 800-267-1555
cpa@cpa-apc.org
www.cpa-apc.org
To forge a strong, collective voice for Canadian psychiatrists & to promote an environment that fosters excellence in the provision of clinical care, education & research
Ted Callanan, Sec.-Treas.
Alex Saunders, CEO

Canadian Psychiatric Research Foundation (CPRF) / Fondation canadienne de recherche en psychiatrie (FCRP)
#500, 2 Toronto St., Toronto ON M5C 2B6
Tel: 416-351-7757; *Fax:* 416-351-7765
Toll-Free: 800-915-2773
admin@healthymindscanada.ca
healthymindscanada.ca
Social Media:
www.facebook.com/healthymindscanada
twitter.com/Healthy_Minds
To discover better treatments & cures for mental illness & addiction, by funding mental health & addiction research to improve the health of Canadians
Katie W. Robinette, Executive Director
Andrea Swinton, Director, Fund Development & Marketing

Canadian Psychoanalytic Society (CPS) / Société canadienne de psychanalyse (SCP)
7000 Côte-des-Neiges Chemin, Montréal QC H3S 2C1
Tel: 514-738-6105
www.psychoanalysis.ca
Andrew Brook, President

Canadian Psychological Association (CPA) / Société canadienne de psychologie (SCP)
#702, 141 Laurier Ave. West, Ottawa ON K1P 5J3
Tel: 613-237-2144; *Fax:* 613-237-1674
Toll-Free: 888-472-0657
cpa@cpa.ca
www.cpa.ca
Social Media: www.youtube.com/user/CPAVideoChannel
linkedin.com/groups/3766289/profile
www.facebook.com/146082642130174
twitter.com/CPA_SCP
To improve the health & welfare of Canadians by promoting psychological research, education, & practice
Karen R. Cohen, Chief Executive Officer
David Dozois, President
Phil Bolger, Chief Financial Officer
John Service, Director, Practice Directorate
Melissa Tiessen, Registrar & Director, Education Directorate

Centre de ressources et d'intervention pour hommes abusés sexuellement dans leur enfance (CRIPHASE) / Resource and Intervention Center for Men Sexually Abused during their Childhood
#100, 8105, rue de Gaspé, Montréal QC H2P 2J9
Tél: 514-529-5567; *Téléc:* 514-529-0571
info@criphase.org
www.criphase.org
Mèdia social: www.facebook.com/168619389848314
Services et ressources pour hommes abusés sexuellement dans leur enfance; groupes, activités/ateliers
Alice Charasse, Coordinatrice

Child & Parent Resource Institute (CPRI)
600 Sanatorium Rd., London ON N6H 3W7
Tel: 519-858-2774; *Fax:* 519-858-3913
Toll-Free: 877-494-2774
TTY: 519-858-0257
www.cpri.ca
To enhance the quality of life of children & youth with complex mental health or developmental challenges; to assist their families so these children & youth can reach their full potential

Children's Mental Health Ontario (CMHO) / Santé Mentale pour Enfants Ontario (SMEO)
#309, 40 St. Clair Ave. East, Toronto ON M4T 1M9
Tel: 416-921-2109; *Fax:* 416-921-7600
Toll-Free: 888-234-7054
info@cmho.org
www.kidsmentalhealth.ca
Social Media: www.youtube.com/2013changetheview
www.facebook.com/kidsmentalhealth
twitter.com/kidsmentalhlth
To promote, support & strengthen a sustainable system of mental health services for children, youth & their families
Gordon Floyd, President & CEO

Fédération des familles et amis de la personne atteinte de maladie mentale (FFAPAMM) / Federation of Families & Friends of Persons with a Mental Illness
#203, 1990, rue Jean-Talon nord, Sainte-Foy QC G1N 4K8
Tél: 418-687-0474; *Téléc:* 418-687-0123
Ligne sans frais: 800-323-0474
info@ffapamm.com
www.ffapamm.qc.ca
La FFAPAMM se veut le porte-parole provincial des associations de familles et amis de la personne atteinte de maladie mentale. Tout en ayant à coeur de défendre et promouvoir les intérêts de ses membres, elle a également le mandat de les soutenir dans leur développement, de sensibiliser l'opinion publique aux problèmes reliés à la maladie mentale et de créer des programmes de communication et d'éducation.
Hélène Fradet, Directrice générale

Fondation des maladies mentales / Mental Illness Foundation
#804, 55, av du Mont-Royal West, Montréal QC H2T 2S6
Tél: 514-529-5354; *Téléc:* 514-529-9877
Ligne sans frais: 888-529-5354
info@fondationdesmaladiesmentales.org
www.fondationdesmaladiesmentales.org
Pour mettre des services cliniques en place et les maintenir
Brigitte Germain, Directrice générale

Healthy Minds Canada
#500, 2 Toronto St., Toronto ON M5C 2B6
Tel: 416-351-7757; *Fax:* 416-351-7765
Toll-Free: 800-915-2773
admin@healthymindscanada.ca
www.healthymindscanada.ca
Social Media:
www.facebook.com/healthymindscanada
twitter.com/Healthy_Minds
Katie W. Robinette, Executive Director

International Schizophrenia Foundation (ISF)
16 Florence Ave., Toronto ON M2N 1E9
Tel: 416-733-2117; *Fax:* 416-733-2352
centre@orthomed.org
www.isfmentalhealth.org
Social Media:
www.facebook.com/178337749007188
twitter.com/ISFMentalHealth
To raise the levels of diagnosis, treatment & prevention of the schizophrenias & related disorders; to reduce the fear & stigma; to provide the best possible treatment & rehabilitation services.
Trevor Roberts, Executive Director

Mood Disorders Association of Ontario (MDAO)
#602, 36 Eglinton Ave., Toronto ON M4R 1A1
Tel: 416-486-8046; *Fax:* 416-486-8127
Toll-Free: 888-486-8236
www.mooddisorders.on.ca
To provide information, education & support to those affected by depression & manic depression, their families & friends; to develop & maintain a network of supportive self-help groups; to improve the quality of life of people who experience mood disorders, their families & friends; to advocate for a flexible & responsive system of care
Anne Davis, President & Chair
Ann Marie MacDonald, Executive Director

Mood Disorders Society of Canada (MDSC) / La Société pour les troubles de l'humeur du Canada
#736, 3-304 Stone Rd. West, Guelph ON N1G 4W4
Tel: 519-824-5565; *Fax:* 519-824-9569
info@mooddisorderscanada.ca
www.mooddisorderscanada.ca
Social Media: www.youtube.com/user/MDSofC?
linkedin.com/company/3204824
www.facebook.com/MoodDisordersSocietyCanada
twitter.com/MoodDisordersCa
The MDSC works nationally to ensure that issues related to mood disorders are understood and considered in the setting of research priorities, the development of treatment strategies, and the creation of government programs and policies. The Mood Disorders Society of Canada is one of the leading national, voluntary health organizations in the fields of depression, bipolar illness, and associated mood disorders
Phil Upshall, National Executive Director
John Starzynski, President

Ontario Psychological Association (OPA)
#403, 21 St. Clair Ave. East, Toronto ON M4T 1L8
Tel: 416-961-5552
opa@psych.on.ca
www.psych.on.ca
Social Media:
www.facebook.com/114986531859137
To advance the practice & science of psychology in Ontario communities; To promote the highest ethical standards in the profession
Connie Kushnir, President
Janet Kasperski, Chief Executive Officer

L'Ordre des psychologues du Québec (OPQ)
#510, 1100, av Beaumont, Montréal QC H3P 3H5
Tél: 514-738-1881; *Téléc:* 514-738-8838
Ligne sans frais: 800-363-2644
info@ordrepsy.qc.ca
www.ordrepsy.qc.ca
Assurer la protection du public; contrôler l'exercice de la profession par ses membres; veiller à la qualité des services dispensés par ses membres; favoriser le développement de la compétence professionnelle, le respect des normes déontologiques et l'accessibilité aux services psychologiques
Rose-Marie Charest, Présidente

Saskatchewan Psychiatric Association
Saskatoon SK
www.cpa-apc.org/browse/documents/276
To increase psychiatric knowledge in Saskatchewan
Declan Quinn, President
Keriem, Secretary

Schizophrenia Society of Canada (SSC) / Société canadienne de schizophrénie
#100, 4 Fort St., Winnipeg MB R3C 1C4
Tel: 204-786-1616; *Fax:* 204-783-4898
Toll-Free: 800-263-5545
info@schizophrenia.ca
www.schizophrenia.ca
Social Media:
www.facebook.com/pages/Schizophrenia-Society-of-Canada/19
7088263635191
twitter.com/SchizophreniaCa
To improve the quality of life for those affected by schizophrenia & psychosis; To advocate on behalf of individuals & families affected by schizophrenia for improved treatment & services
Chris Summerville, D. Min, CPRP, Chief Executive Officer

Your Life Counts (YLC)
Seaway Mall, #GG5B, 800 Niagara St. North, Welland ON L3C 5Z4
Tel: 289-820-5777
info@yourlifecounts.org
www.yourlifecounts.org
Social Media: www.youtube.com/user/YOURLIFECOUNTSTV
www.facebook.com/YourLifeCounts
twitter.com/yourlifecounts
Works with youth, families, veterans and emergency services in the battle against trauma, addictions and overwhelming life situations that may lead to thoughts of suicide.
Kevin Bolibruck, Chair

Military & Veterans

Air Cadet League of Canada / Ligue des cadets de l'air du Canada
66 Lisgar St., Ottawa ON K2P 0C1
Tel: 613-991-4349; *Fax:* 613-991-4347
Toll-Free: 877-422-6359
webadmin@aircadetleague.com
www.aircadetleague.com
Social Media: www.youtube.com/user/AirCadetLeague
www.facebook.com/Air.Cadet.League.of.Canada
twitter.com/AirCadetLeague
To promote & encourage a practical interest in aeronautics among young people; To assist those intending to pursue a career in aviation
Donald W. Doern, CD, National President
Sarah Matresky, Executive Director

Air Force Association of Canada (AFAC) / L'Association des forces aériennes du Canada
PO Box 2460, Stn. D, Ottawa ON K1P 5W6
Tel: 613-232-2303; *Fax:* 613-232-2156
Toll-Free: 866-351-2322
rcafassociation.ca
Social Media:
www.facebook.com/RCAFAssociationARC
twitter.com/RCAFAssociation
To promote a viable well-equipped air force & a strong Canadian aerospace industry
Terry Chester, National President
Dean Black, National Executive Director

Army Cadet League of Canada (ACLC) / Ligue des cadets de l'armée du Canada
66 Lisgar St., Ottawa ON K2P 0C1
Tel: 613-991-4348; *Fax:* 613-990-8701
Toll-Free: 877-276-9223
national@armycadetleague.ca
www.armycadetleague.ca
Social Media:
www.facebook.com/132804156762142
twitter.com/ArmyCadetLeague
To provide accommodation, transportation, & financial support for the army cadets; To promote the corps & assists in recruitment
Wayne Foster, President

Canadian Aboriginal Veterans & Serving Members Association (CAV)
34 Kingham Pl., Victoria BC V9B 1L8
Tel: 250-900-5768
national-president@nationalalliance.ca
canadianaboriginalveterans.ca

Canadian Association of Veterans in United Nations Peacekeeping (CAVUNP) / Association Canadienne des Vétérans des Forces de la Paix pour les Nations Unies
PO Box PO Box 46026, RPO Beacon Hill, 2339 Ogilvie Rd., Gloucester ON K1J 9M7
Tel: 613-746-3302
cavunp@rogers.com
www.cavunp.org
To perpetuate the memories of fallen comrades; to provide assistance to serving & retired Canadian peacekeepers & their families; to provide education about peacekeeping & peacekeepers
Ronald R. Griffis, National President
J. Robert O'Brien, Chair
Paul Greensides, National Secretary-Treasurer

Canadian Battlefields Foundation
c/o Canadian War Museum, 1 Vimy Pl., Ottawa ON K1R 1C2
Tel: 613-731-7767
cbf.fccb@gmail.com
www.canadianbattlefieldsfoundation.ca
Social Media:
www.facebook.com/220483754647284?ref=ts&fref=ts
twitter.com/CBFFCCB
To act with Le Mémorial to educate the international public with respect to Canada's role in the Second World War & to educate Canadians through providing scholarships, bursaries & prizes to carry on research into military history; to raise & disburse funds to support these activities.
H.G. Needham, Treasurer
Charles Belzile, President
Antonio Lamer, Honorary Patron

Canadian Corps Association
201 Niagara St., Toronto ON M5V 1C9
Tel: 416-504-6694

The Canadian Corps of Commissionaires / Le Corps Canadien des Commissionnaires
National Office, #201, 100 Gloucester St., Ottawa ON K2P 0A4
Tel: 613-688-0710; *Fax:* 613-688-0719
Toll-Free: 888-688-0715
info@commissionaires.ca
www.commissionaires.ca
Social Media:
linkedin.com/company/commissionaires-canada
www.facebook.com/pages/Commissionaires-Canada/210055862403710
To create meaningful employment opportunities for former members of the Canadian Forces, the Royal Canadian Mounted Police & others who wish to contribute to the security & well-being of Canadians
W.G.S. (Bill) Sutherland, CD, Chair
J. Douglas Briscoe, OMM, CD, Executive Director
Greg Richardson, Business Manager
Lynne Bermel, Contact

Canadian Merchant Navy Veterans Association Inc. (CMNVA) / L'Association des Anciens Combattants de la marine marchande canadienne Inc.
2108 Melrick Pl., Sooke BC V9Z 0M9
Tel: 250-642-2638; *Fax:* 250-642-3332
To renew old friendships & bring together ex-Canadian merchant seamen; to promote increased recognition of the role of the merchant navy during wartime; to liaise with government to obtain full benefits & pension as recognized veterans
Bruce Ferguson, President

Canadian Peacekeeping Veterans Association (CPVA)
PO Box 905, Kingston ON K7L 4X8
Tel: 506-627-6437
info@cpva.ca
www.cpva.ca
To assist Canadians who have served on peacekeeping missions
Ray Kokkonen, President

Commission canadienne d'histoire militaire (CCHM) / Canadian Commission of Military History (CCMH)
Quartier général de la Défense nationale, 101 Colonel By Dr., Ottawa ON K1A 0K2
Téléc: 613-990-8579
La CCHM est une organisation bénévole, ne comptant qu'un Conseil de direction, sans membres, collaborant à la Commission internationale d'histoire militaire (CIHM) du Comité international des Sciences historiques (CISH) de Genève, Suisse; La Commission canadienne cherche à servir de lien entre les historiens militaires canadiens et la communauté internationale des chercheurs et écrivains en histoire militaire; La Commission canadienne travaille aussi à mieux faire connaître l'histoire militaire canadienne au Canada et à l'étranger
Serge Bernier, Directeur

Commonwealth War Graves Commission - Canadian Agency (CWGC) / Commission des sépultures de guerre du Commonwealth - Agence canadienne (CSGC)
#1707, 66 Slater St., Ottawa ON K1A 0P4
Tel: 613-992-3224; *Fax:* 613-995-0431
cwgc-canada@vac-acc.gc.ca
www.cwgc-canadianagency.ca
To ensure Commonwealth War Burials in the Americas (including the Caribbean) are marked & maintained; To ensure maintenance of memorials to the missing; To keep records & registers; To discharge Commission duties for Commonwealth war graves in the Americas (comprising some 3,350 cemeteries & over 20,000 commemorations)
David Kettle, Canandian Agency Director

Conference of Defence Associations (CDA) / Conférence des associations de la défense
#412A, 151 Slater St., Ottawa ON K1P 5H3
Tel: 613-236-1252; *Fax:* 613-236-8191
cda@cda-cdai.ca
www.cdacanada.ca
Social Media:
twitter.com/CDAInstitute
To place before people of Canada problems of defence & the well-being of Canada's Armed Forces
Alain Pellerin, Executive Director
Peter Forsberg, Officer, Public Affairs

Korea Veterans Association of Canada Inc., Heritage Unit (KVA) / Association canadienne des vétérans de la Corée (ACVC)
246 Huntington Cres., Courtice ON L1E 3J5
Tel: 905-579-0751; *Fax:* 905-579-0527
www.kvacanada.com
To promote awareness of Canada's role in the Korean War; To represent veterans & their families
Douglas Finney, President
Peter Siereson, National Vice-President
Alphonse Marel, National Treasurer
Gordon Strathy, National Secretary

Military Collectors Club of Canada (MCC of Canada)
c/o John Zabarylo, Secretary-treasurer, PO Box 64009, 525 London St., Winnipeg MB R2K 3Y4
Tel: 204-669-0871
militarycollectorsclubofcanada@yahoo.ca
www.mccofc.org
John Zabarylo, Sec.-Treas.
Jim Simmons, President

National Council of Veteran Associations (NCVA) / Conseil national des associations d'anciens combattants au Canada (CNAAC)
2827 Riverside Dr., Ottawa ON K1V 0C4
Tel: 613-731-3821; *Fax:* 613-731-3234
Toll-Free: 800-465-2677
ncva@waramps.ca
www.ncva-cnaac.ca
Social Media:
twitter.com/NCVACanada
The National Council of Veteran Associations is an umbrella organization of some 60 distinct Veterans' Associations formed to ensure a strong and independent voice on issues which are of significant interest to the Veterans' community at large.
Brian N. Forbes, Chair

The Naval Officers' Association of Canada (NOAC) / L'Association des officiers de la marine du Canada
c/o Ottawa Branch, PO Box 505, Stn. B, Ottawa ON K1P 5P6
Tel: 613-841-4358
noacexdir@msn.com
www.navalassoc.ca
To maintain active interest in the Maritime affairs of Canada; To oversee 15 member branches in major cities from coast to coast & a member branch in Brussels, Belgium
Jim Carruthers, President
Ken Lait, Executive Director

Navy League of Canada / Ligue navale du Canada
66 Lisgar St., Ottawa ON K2P 0C1
Fax: 613-990-8701
Toll-Free: 800-375-6289
info@navyleague.ca
www.navyleague.ca
Social Media:
twitter.com/NavyLeagueCA
To promote an interest in maritime affairs generally throughout Canada; To prepare, publish & disseminate information & encourage debate relating to the role & importance of maritime matters in the interests of Canada; To promote, organize, sponsor, support & encourage the education & training of the youth of the country through Cadet movements & other youth groups with a maritime orientation; To hold conferences, symposia & meetings for the discussion & exchange of views in matters relating to the objects of The League; To raise funds as may be deemed necessary, for the welfare & benefit of seamen, for their dependents & for Seamen's Homes, Hostels & other institutions in Canada, including the establishment, operation & maintenance thereof; To co-operate with any kindred society having either in whole or in part comparable objects to The League
Douglas J. Thomas, National Executive Director

New Brunswick Signallers Association (NB Sigs)
c/o 3 ASG Signal Squadron, CFB Gagetown, PO Box 17000, Stn. Forces, Oromocto NB E2V 4J5
Tel: 506-357-7314
admin@nbsigs.net
www.nbsigs.net
Al Lustig, President

Princess Patricia's Canadian Light Infantry Association
PO Box 210, Denwood AB T0B 1B0
Tel: 780-842-1363; *Fax:* 780-842-4106
www.army.gc.ca/ppclic
Bud Hawkins, President, Manitoba/Northwest Ontario Branch

The Royal Canadian Legion (RCL) / La Légion royale canadienne
Dominion Command, 86 Aird Place, Ottawa ON K2L 0A1
Tel: 613-591-3335; *Fax:* 613-591-9335
Toll-Free: 888-556-6222
info@legion.ca
www.legion.ca
Social Media: www.youtube.com/user/RCLDominionCommand
www.facebook.com/CanadianLegion
twitter.com/RoyalCdnLegion
To serve veterans, ex-military & military members, their families, communities & Canada
Larry Murray, Grand President
Tom Eagles, Dominion President
Mark Barham, Dominion Treasurer
Bradley Kenneth White, Dominion Secretary

Royal Canadian Military Institute (RCMI)
426 University Ave., Toronto ON M5G 1S9
Tel: 416-597-0286; *Fax:* 416-597-6919
Toll-Free: 800-585-1072
info@rcmi.org
www.rcmi.org
To promote the navy, army & air force art, science, literature & interests; promotion of good fellowship & esprit de corps amongst the officers of the various branches of the services; to maintain of a clubhouse for the accommodation, recreation, enlightenment, convenience & entertainment of its members.
Chris Corrigan, Executive Director

Royal Canadian Mounted Police Veterans' Association / Association des anciens de la Gendarmerie royale du Canada
1200 Vanier Pkwy., Ottawa ON K1A 0R2
Tel: 613-993-8633; *Fax:* 613-993-4353
Toll-Free: 877-251-1771
rcmp.vets@rcmp-grc.gc.ca
www.rcmpvetsnational.ca

Royal Canadian Naval Benevolent Fund (RCNBF)
PO Box 505, Stn. B, Ottawa ON K1P 5P6
Tel: 613-996-5087; *Fax:* 613-236-8830
Toll-Free: 888-557-8777
rcnbf@rcnbf.com
www.rcnbf.ca
To relieve distress & promote the well-being of members & former members of the naval forces of Canada & Canadian merchant navy war veterans & of their dependants
L.F. Harrison, Secretary-Treasurer

Ukrainian War Veterans Association of Canada (UWVA)
145 Evans Ave., Toronto ON M8Z 5X8
Tel: 416-925-2770
www.unfcanada.ca/uwva
To promote national unity & maintain Ukrainian identity; To support the Ukrainian National Federation of Canada

Mines & Mineral Resources

Association de l'exploration minière de Québec (AEMQ) / Quebec Mineral Exploration Assocation (QMEA)
#203, 132, av du Lac, Rouyn-Noranda QC J9X 4N5
Tél: 819-762-1599; *Téléc:* 819-762-1522
info@aemq.org
www.aemq.org
Média social:
www.linkedin.com/company/association-de-l%27exploration-mini-re-du-qu-bec-aemq-
www.facebook.com/AEMQ1975
twitter.com/AEMQ_
Développer, défendre et promouvoir l'exploration minière au Québec
Philippe Cloutier, Président
Valerie Fillion, Directrice générale

Association for Mineral Exploration British Columbia (AMEBC)
#800, 889 West Pender St., Vancouver BC V6C 3B2
Tel: 604-689-5271; *Fax:* 604-681-2363
info@amebc.ca
www.amebc.ca
Social Media:
linkedin.com/company/association-for-mineral-exploration-bc
www.facebook.com/Association.for.Mineral.Exploration.BC
twitter.com/ame_bc
To promote & assist development & growth of mining of mineral exploration in BC
Gavin C. Dirom, President & CEO
Jonathan Buchanan, Director, Communications & Public Affairs
Simone Hill, Director, Member Relations & Events

Association minière du Québec (AMQ) / Québec Mining Association (QMA)
Place de la Cité - Tour Belle Cour, #720, 2590, boul Laurier, Québec QC G1V 4M6
Tél: 418-657-2016; *Téléc:* 418-657-2154
amq@amq-inc.com
www.amq-inc.com
Promouvoir le développement de l'industrie des mines, de la métallurgie et des industries connexes; défendre les intérêts généraux de ses membres; soutenir les efforts de ses membres quant au bien-être, à la sécurité et à la prévention des accidents au travail
Claude Bélanger, Directeur générale

Association of Applied Geochemists (AEG)
PO Box 26099, 72 Robertson Rd., Nepean ON K2H 9R0
Tel: 613-828-0199; *Fax:* 613-828-9288
office@appliedgeochemists.org
www.appliedgeochemists.org
To promote interest in the applications of geochemistry to mineral & petroleum exploration, resource evaluation & related fields
David R. Cohen, President
Betty Arseneault, Business Manager

Canada's Oil Sands Innovation Alliance (COSIA)
#1700, 520 5th Ave. SW, Calgary AB T2P 3R7
Tel: 403-444-5282
info@cosia.ca
www.cosia.ca
Social Media:
twitter.com/COSIA_ca
Canada's Oil Sands Innovation Alliance (COSIA) is an alliance of oil sands producers focused on accelerating the pace of improvement in environmental performance in Canada's oil sands through collaborative action and innovation.
Dan Wicklum, Chief Executive

John Brogly, Director, Water EPA
Donna Dunlop, Director, Land EPA
Wayne Hillier, Director, Greenhouse Gases EPA

Canadian Copper & Brass Development Association (CCBDA)
#415, 49 The Donway West, Toronto ON M3C 3M9
Tel: 416-391-5599; *Fax:* 416-391-3823
Toll-Free: 877-640-0946
coppercanada@onramp.ca
www.coppercanada.ca
To promote, foster & stimulate use of products of Canadian copper & brass industry. To represent and support the primary producers fabricators, manufacturers, and consumers of copper and copper alloys in Canada, by increasing industry and public awareness of copper's capabilites and advantages compared to other metals and materials, and by providing technical services related to copper's use.
Stephen A.W. Knapp, Executive Director

Canadian Mineral Analysts (CMA) / Analystes des minéraux canadiens
c/o John Gregorchuk, 444 Harold Ave. West, Winnipeg MB R2C 2E2
Tel: 204-224-1443
www.canadianmineralanalysts.com
To promote communication among analysts in the mining industry & persons engaged in analytical procedures & the development of methods
John Gregorchuk, Managing Secretary
Sean Murry, Treasurer

Chamber of Mines of Eastern British Columbia
215 Hall St., Nelson BC V1L 5X4
Tel: 250-352-5242
chamberofmines@netidea.com
cmebc.com
Social Media:
www.facebook.com/ChamberOfMinesEasternBC
To act as advocate for the mining industry in British Columbia; to provide a collective voice on behalf of prospectors & miners; to provide information on exploration & mining; to educate the public through accessibility to mineral museum & library.

Chrysotile Institute / Instit du Chrysotile
#1640, 1200, av McGill College, Montréal QC H3B 4G7
Tel: 514-877-9797; *Fax:* 514-877-9717
info@chrysotile.com
www.chrysotile.com
To promote the implementation & enforcement of effective regulations, standards, work practices & techniques for the safe use of asbestos.
Denis Hamel, Director General

Coal Association of Canada (CAC)
#150, 205 - 9th Ave. SE, Calgary AB T2G 0R3
Tel: 403-262-1544; *Fax:* 403-265-7604
Toll-Free: 800-910-2625
info@coal.ca
www.coal.ca
Social Media:
twitter.com/coalcanada
To promote coal as a vital energy source that is abundant, safe, reliable, environmentally and economically acceptable.
Ann Marie Hann, President
Michelle Mondeville, Director, Communications and Stakeholder Relations

East Kootenay Chamber of Mines
#201, 12 - 11th Ave. South, Cranbrook BC V1C 2P1
Tel: 250-489-2255; *Fax:* 250-426-8755
www.ekcm.org/chamber2
Ross Stanfield, President

Mineralogical Association of Canada (MAC) / Association minéralogique du Canada
490, rue de la Couronne, Québec QC G1K 9A9
Tel: 418-653-0333; *Fax:* 418-653-0777
office@mineralogicalassociation.ca
www.mineralogicalassociation.ca
To promote & advance knowledge of mineralogy & the allied disciplines of petrology, crystallography, mineral deposits, & geochemistry
Lee A. Groat, President
Johanne Coran, Manager, Business

Mining Association of British Columbia (MABC)
#900, 808 West Hastings St., Vancouver BC V6C 2X4
Tel: 604-681-4321; *Fax:* 604-681-5305
mabcinfo@mining.bc.ca
www.mining.bc.ca
Social Media:
www.facebook.com/MABCMining
twitter.com/ma_bc
To speak on behalf of mineral producers; To represent the interests of British Columbia's mining industry; To communicate with senior government decision-makers, communities, NGOs, First Nations, & the media; To act as the industry's voice regarding issues such as environmental regulations, taxation, infrastructure demands, labour issues, health & safety, & international trade
Karina Briñño, President & CEO
Bryan Cox, Vice-President, Corporate Affairs

Mining Association of Canada (MAC) / Association minière du Canada
#1100, 275 Slater St., Ottawa ON K1P 5H9
Tel: 613-233-9392; *Fax:* 613-233-8897
communications@mining.ca
www.mining.ca
Social Media:
twitter.com/theminingstory
To represent the interests of member companies engaged in mineral exploration, extraction & refining; To work with governments on public policy pertaining to minerals
Pierre Gratton, President & CEO
Justyna Laurie-Lean, Vice-President, Environment & Regulatory Affairs
Jessica Draker, Director, Communications

Mining Association of Manitoba Inc. (MAMI)
#700, 305 Broadway Ave., Winnipeg MB R3C 3J7
Tel: 204-989-1890
www.mines.ca
Social Media:
linkedin.com/company/the-mining-association-of-manitoba-inc-
To represent mining & exploration companies in Manitoba
Lovro Paulic, Chair

Mining Association of Nova Scotia (MANS)
7744 St. Margaret's Bay Rd., Ingramport NS B3Z 3Z8
Tel: 902-820-2115
info@tmans.ca
tmans.ca
Social Media:
www.facebook.com/MiningNS
twitter.com/MiningNS
To ensure Nova Scotia is recognized internationally as having mineral resources worthy of investment; to develop mineral deposits; to work for government policies that provide a framework for a competitive mining industry within the global marketplace; to promote mining as a corporate industry creating wealth & long-term stable employment, with responsible environmental & social attitudes
Sean Kirby, Executive Director

Mining Industry NL
Prince Charles Bldg., PO Box 21463, #W280, 120 Torbay Rd., St. John's NL A1A 2G8
Tel: 709-722-9542; *Fax:* 709-722-8588
info@miningnl.com
www.miningnl.com
To represent all sectors of the mineral industry in the province; to be a central contact for government, media & the public
Ed Moriarity, Executive Director
Jennifer Kelly, Communications Advisor

Mining Society of Nova Scotia
88 Leeside Dr., Sydney NS B1R 1S6
Tel: 902-567-2147; *Fax:* 902-567-2147
www.miningsocietyns.ca
To provide services in order to help & improve the mining industry
Bob MacDonald, President

Northwest Territories & Nunavut Chamber of Mines
PO Box 2818, #103, 5102-50 Ave., Yellowknife NT X1A 2R1
Tel: 867-873-5281; *Fax:* 867-920-2145
info@miningnorth.com
www.miningnorth.com
To promote & assist the development & growth of mining & mineral exploration in NWT & Nunavut
Tom Hoefer, Executive Director

Ontario Mining Association (OMA)
#1201, 5775 Yonge St., Toronto ON M2M 4J1
Tel: 416-364-9301; *Fax:* 416-364-5986
info@oma.on.ca
www.oma.on.ca
Social Media: www.youtube.com/user/miningontario; www.pinterest.com/ontminingassoc
twitter.com/OntMiningAssoc
To help improve the competitiveness of the Ontario mineral industry
Chris Hodgson, President

Prospectors & Developers Association of Canada (PDAC) / Association canadienne des prospecteurs & entrepreneurs
135 King St. East, Toronto ON M5C 1G6
Tel: 416-362-1969; *Fax:* 416-362-0101
info@pdac.ca
www.pdac.ca
Social Media:
linkedin.com/company/prospectors-and-developers-association-of-canada
www.facebook.com/thePDAC
twitter.com/the_pdac
To protect & promote the interests of the Canadian mineral exploration & development sector
Andrew Cheatle, Executive Director
Lisa McDonald, Chief Operations Officer
Cameron Ainsworth-Vincze, Senior Manager, Communications
Lesley Williams, Manager, Aboriginal Affairs & Resource Development

Saskatchewan Mining Association (SMA)
#1500, 2002 Victoria Ave., Regina SK S4P 0R7
Tel: 306-757-9505; *Fax:* 306-569-1085
info@saskmining.ca
www.saskmining.ca
Social Media:
twitter.com/SaskMiningAssoc
To ensure the safe & profitable development of mineral resources in Saskatchewan; To act as the voice of the mining industry throughout the province; To promote understanding of the development of mineral resources in Saskatchewan
Neil McMillan, President
Pamela Schwann, Executive Director

Yukon Chamber of Mines (YCM)
3151B - 3rd Ave., Whitehorse YT Y1A 1G1
Tel: 867-667-2090; *Fax:* 867-668-7127
info@yukonminers.ca
www.yukonminers.ca
To provides services to members, with a focus on the mining industry; To promote responsible exploration & sustainable mining practices
Mark Ayranto, President
Hugh Kitchen, Vice President

Yukon Mine Training Association (YMTA)
2099 - 2nd Ave., Whitehorse YT Y1A 1B5
Tel: 867-633-6463; *Toll-Free:* 877-986-4637
info@ymta.org
ymta.org
To maximize employment opportunities emerging from the growth of the mining and related resource sectors in the North for First Nations and other Yukoners.
P. Jerry Asp, Chair
Sascha Weber, Executive Director

Multiculturalism

Affiliation of Multicultural Societies & Service Agencies of BC (AMSSA)
#205, 2929 Commercial Dr., Vancouver BC V5N 4C8
Tel: 604-718-2777; *Fax:* 604-298-0747
Toll-Free: 888-355-5560
amssa@amssa.org
www.amssa.org
Social Media:
www.facebook.com/amssabc
twitter.com/safeharbourcdn
To provide leadership in advocacy & education in British Columbia for anti-racism, human rights & social justice; to support members in serving immigrants, refugees & culturally diverse communities
Tim Welsh, Program Director
Lynn Moran, Executive Director

Association of Latvian Craftsmen in Canada / Latviesu Dailamatnieku Savieniba
Latvian Canadian Cultural Centre, 4 Credit Union Dr., Toronto ON M4A 2N8
Tel: 416-759-4900; *Fax:* 416-759-9311

The Atlantic Jewish Council
#508, 5670 Spring Garden Rd., Halifax NS B3J 1H6
Tel: 902-422-7491; *Fax:* 902-425-3722
atlanticjewishcouncil@theajc.ns.ca
theajc.ns.ca
Social Media: www.flickr.com/photos/atlanticjewishcouncil
www.facebook.com/AtlanticJewishCouncil
Jon M. Goldberg, Executive Director

Australia-New Zealand Association (ANZA)
3 West 8 Ave., Vancouver BC V5Y 1M8
Tel: 604-876-7128
info@anzaclub.org
www.anzaclub.org
Social Media:
www.facebook.com/anzaclubvancouver
twitter.com/anzaclub
To foster friendly relations between British Columbia, Canada, Australia & New Zealand

B'nai Brith Canada (BBC)
15 Hove St., Toronto ON M3H 4Y8
Tel: 416-633-6224; *Fax:* 416-630-2159
toronto@bnaibrith.ca
www.bnaibrith.ca
Social Media:
www.facebook.com/bnaibrithcanada
twitter.com/bnaibrithcanada
To bring men & women of the Jewish faith together in fellowship to serve the Jewish community through combating anti-Semitism, bigotry & racism in Canada & abroad; To carry out activities which ensure the security & survival of the State of Israel & Jewish communities worldwide
Michael Mostyn, Chief Executive Officer

B'nai Brith Canada Institute for International Affairs
15 Hove St., Toronto ON M3H 4Y8
Tel: 416-633-6224; *Fax:* 416-630-2159
bnb@bnaibrith.ca
www.bnaibrith.ca/institute.html
To identify & fight human rights abuses throughout the world, with special emphasis on Jewish communities worldwide
Eric Bissell, President
Frank Dimant, Executive Vice-President

Baltic Federation in Canada
c/o Andris Kesteris, 1754 Turnberry Rd., Orléans ON K1E 3T7
Tel: 416-755-2352
www.balticfederation.ca
To provide political representation for its member organizations of Estonian, Latvian & Lithuanian Canadians
Andris Kesteris, President

Black Cultural Society for Nova Scotia
10 Cherry Brook Rd., Cherry Brook NS B2Z 1A8
Tel: 902-434-6223; *Fax:* 902-434-2306
Toll-Free: 800-465-0767
contact@bccns.com
www.bccns.com
Social Media:
www.facebook.com/188265867860941
To create among members of the Black community an awareness of their past, their heritage & identity; to provide programs & activities to explore, learn about, understand & appreciate Black history, achievements & experiences in Canadian life.
Leslie Oliver, President

Canadian Arab Federation (CAF) / La Fédération Canado-Arabe
1057 McNicoll Ave., Toronto ON M1W 3W6
Tel: 416-493-8635; *Fax:* 416-493-9239
Toll-Free: 866-886-4675
info@caf.ca
www.caf.ca
To represent Canadian Arabs on issues related to public policy; To protect civil liberties & the equality of human rights
Farid Ayad, President
Abdallah Alkrunz, Vice-President, East
Mohamed El Rashidy, Vice-President, West

The Canadian Doukhobor Society (CDS)
215 - 33 Ave. South, Creston BC V0G 1G1
Tel: 250-204-2931
spirit-wrestlers.com/CDS
To promote brotherhood, universal peace & the spiritual growth of our members
Beth Terriff, Secretary-Treasurer
Alex Wishlow, President

Canadian Ethnocultural Council (CEC) / Conseil ethnoculturel du Canada
#205, 176 Gloucester St., Ottawa ON K2P 0A6
Tel: 613-230-3867; *Fax:* 613-230-8051
cec@web.net
www.ethnocultural.ca
Social Media: www.youtube.com/user/EthnoCanada
To represent a cross-section of ethnocultural groups across Canada.
Lou Seulovski, President
Anna Chiappa, Executive Director

Canadian Institute for Jewish Research (CIJR) / Institut canadien de recherche sur le Judaïsme (ICRJ)
PO Box 175, Stn. H, Montréal QC H3G 2K7
Tel: 514-486-5544; *Fax:* 514-486-8284
cijr@isranet.org
www.isranet.org
Social Media:
www.facebook.com/162536567136089
twitter.com/cijr
To increase public understanding of Jewish Israel & general Jewish world issues
Jack Kincler, National Chair
Baruch Cohen, Research Chair
Frederick Krantz, Director
Ira Robinson, Associate Director

Canadian Polish Congress (CPC) / Congrès canadien polonais
3055 Lake Shore Blvd. West, Toronto ON M8V 1K6
Tel: 416-532-2876; *Fax:* 416-532-5730
kongres@kpk.org
www.kpk.org
To represent Polish-Canadians & to defend their interests; To coordinate & support the work of Polish-Canadian organizations in Canada; To foster Polish culture & assist Polish immigrants; To inform Canadians about Poland's contribution to culture & to maintain liaisons with Poland
Teresa Berezowski, President
Jan Cytowski, First Vice-President, Polish Affairs
Ludwik Klimkowski, Vice-President, Canadian Affairs
Teresa Szramek, Secretary-General
Elizabeth Morgan, Treasurer

Canadian Race Relations Foundation (CRRF)
#225, 6 Garamond Crt., Toronto ON M3C 1Z5
Tel: 416-703-4164; *Fax:* 416-441-2752
Toll-Free: 888-240-4936
info@crrf-fcrr.ca
www.crr.ca
Social Media:
linkedin.com/company/the-canadian-race-relations-foundation
www.facebook.com/699059076842903
twitter.com/CRRF
To eliminate racism and all forms of racial discrimination, and promote Canadian identity, belonging and the mutuality of citizenship rights and responsibilities for a more harmonious Canada.
Anita Bromberg, Executive Director

Canadian Slovak League
#6, 259 Traders Blvd. East, Mississauga ON L4Z 2E5
Tel: 905-507-8004
administrator@kanadskyslovak.ca
www.ksliga.com

Canadian Tibetan Association of Ontario (CTAO)
40 Titan Rd., Toronto ON M8Z 2J8
Tel: 416-410-5606; *Fax:* 416-410-5606
www.ctao.org
To represent Tibetans in Ontario; To serve the needs of the Tibetan community in the province; To promote cross-cultural understanding
Tsering Tsomo, President
Ngawang Diki, Coordinator, Cultural

Canadian Zionist Federation (CZF) / La fédération sioniste canadienne
4600 Bathurst St., 4th Fl., Toronto ON M2R 3V2
Tel: 416-633-3988; *Fax:* 416-633-2758
czf@jazo.org.il
To promote the Zionist ideal among the Jewish population in Canada; To assist in strengthening the Jewish State of Israel; To enrich Canadian Jewish life through the provision of Jewish education & information on Israel & Zionism, through the promotion of Aliyah & activities among Jewish youth in Canada

Florence Simon, National Executive Director

Canadian-Croatian Congress (CCC) / Kanadsko-Hrvatski Kongres
3550 Commercial St., Vancouver BC V5A 4E9
Tel: 604-871-7190; *Fax:* 604-879-2256
crocc@shaw.ca
www.crocc.org
To represent the Croatian Canadian community before the people & Government of Canada
Mijo Maric, President

The Centre for Israel & Jewish Affairs (CIJA)
PO Box 19514, Stn. Manulife Centre, 55 Bloor St. West, Toronto ON M4W 3T9
Tel: 416-925-7499
info@cija.ca
www.cija.ca
Social Media: www.instagram.com/cijainfo
www.facebook.com/cijainfo
twitter.com/cijainfo
To act as decision-making body of the Jewish community in Canada; To act on behalf of Canadian Jewish community on issues & concerns affecting Jews in Canada & around the world; To foster interaction between interests & needs of Jewish community in Canada & Canadian society at large on a broad range of political, charitable & social justice issues
David J. Cape, Chair

Chinese Canadian National Council (CCNC) / Conseil national des canadiens chinois
#507, 302 Spadina Ave., Toronto ON M5T 2E7
Tel: 416-977-9871; *Fax:* 416-977-1630
national@ccnc.ca
www.ccnc.ca
To promote the rights of all individuals, in particular, those of Chinese Canadians & to encourage their full & equal participation in Canadian society; to create an environment in Canada in which the rights of all individuals are fully recognized & protected; to promote understanding & cooperation between Chinese Canadians & all other ethnic, cultural, & racial groups in Canada; to encourage & develop in persons of Chinese descent, a desire to know & respect their historical & cultural heritage, & to educate them in adopting a creative & positive attitude towards the Chinese Canadian contribution to society & the Chinese Canadian heritage
Victor Wong, Executive Director

Clans & Scottish Societies of Canada (CASSOC)
c/o Secretary, #78, 24 Fundy Bay Blvd., Toronto ON M1W 3A4
Tel: 416-492-1623
editor@cassoc.ca
www.cassoc.ca
To foster the organization of & cooperation between Scottish associations, federations, clans, societies & groups through initiation & coordination of projects & undertakings; to advance Scottish cultural heritage in Canada
Ian A. Munro, Chair
Jo Ann M. Tuskin, Secretary

Cypriot Federation of Canada / Fédération chypriote du Canada
6 Thorncliff Park Dr., Toronto ON M4H 1H1
Tel: 416-696-7400; *Fax:* 416-696-9465
cypriotfederation@rogers.com
cypriotfederation.ca

Czech & Slovak Association of Canada
PO Box 564, 3044 Bloor St. West, Toronto ON M8X 2Y8
Tel: 416-925-2241; *Fax:* 416-925-1940
ustredi@cssk.ca
www.cssk.ca
To develop the highest standards of citizenship in Canadians of Czech or Slovak origin by encouraging, carrying on & participating in activities of national, patriotic, cultural & humanitarian nature; to act in matters affecting status rights & welfare of Canadians of Czech or Slovak origin; to cultivate in members appreciation of their mother tongue, cultural heritage & historical traditions; to promote growth of spirit in toleration, understanding & goodwill between all ethnic elements in Canada; to conduct research & encourage studies.
Marie Fuchsová, President

Federation for Scottish Culture in Nova Scotia (FSCNS)
PO Box 811, Lower Sackville NS B4C 3V3
info@scotsns.ca
www.scotsns.ca
To act as the voice for Nova Scotia's clans, Scottish-cultural communities, & cultural associations; To create appreciation for the Scottish culture, traditions, & heritage
Thomas (Tom) E.S. Wallace, President

Daniel G. Campbell, 1st Vice-President
Audrey Manzer, Secretary
Al Matheson, Treasurer

Federation of Canada-China Friendship Associations
159 Oakmount Rd. SW, Calgary AB T2V 4X3
Tel: 819-777-8434
www.fccfa.ca
To work with students from the Peoples' Republic of China studying in Canada; To take groups to China; To welcome delegations coming from China; To promote cultural exchanges
Sheila Foster, President

Federation of Canadian Turkish Associations (FCTA)
#15, 1170 Sheppard Ave. West, Toronto ON M3K 2A3
Tel: 647-955-1923; *Fax:* 647-776-3111
info@turkishfederation.ca
www.turkishfederation.ca/en/home_en.html
To support & encourage activities of member associations aimed at making Turkish culture & Turks better known; To promote closer relations with Canadians & other ethnic communities

Federation of Chinese Canadian Professionals (Ontario) (FCCP)
Coral Place, 55 Glenn Hawthorne Blvd., Mississauga ON L5R 3S6
Tel: 905-890-3235; *Fax:* 905-568-5293
www.fccpontario.com
Fosters the promotion, cooperation, & growth among Chinese Canadian Professionals from various disciplines, including: accounting, architecture, biomedical, chiropractic, dental, education, engineering, information technology, legal, medical, pharmacy, & physiotherapy
Josephine Kiang, President

Federation of Chinese Canadian Professionals (Québec) (FCCP Québec) / Fédération des professionnels chinois canadiens (Québec)
PO Box 1004, Stn. B, Montréal QC H3B 3K5
Tel: 514-747-2488
htan222@yahoo.ca
www.fccp.ca
To promote the well-being of Chinese Canadian professionals in Québec; To liaise & cooperate with Chinese Canadian professionals in other parts of Canada & throughout the world; To provide a strong voice for the group
Howard Tan, President
John Chen, Vice-President
Renee Chin, Treasurer

Federation of Danish Associations in Canada / Fédération des associations danoises du Canada
679 Eastvale Ct., Gloucester ON K1J 6Z7
home.ca.inter.net/~robuch/dan-fed.htm
To promote cooperation among Danish Canadian organizations; To promote preservation & understanding of Danish tradition & heritage
Rolf Buschardt Christensen, National President
Ole D. Larsen, National Vice-President
Ella Wolder, National Secretary
Sue Anne Nielsen, National Treasurer

Finnish Canadian Cultural Federation / Fédération culturelle finno-canadienne
128 Quartz Ave., Timmins ON P4N 4L6
finnsincanada.org
To act as non-political coordinator between associations, congregations, clubs & other groups of Finnish ethnic background; To promote Finland & Canadians of Finnish origin; To promote Canada & its Finnish ethnic community in Finland; To support Annual Finnish Canadian Grand Festival
Margaret Kangas, Treasurer

German-Canadian Congress (GCC) / Congrès germano-canadien
#58, 81 Garry St., Winnipeg MB R3C 4J9
Tel: 204-989-8300
gccmb@hotmail.com
www.gccmb.com
To serve as official voice for 2.7 million Canadians of German-speaking background

Goethe-Institut (Toronto)
North Tower, PO Box 136, #201, 100 University Ave., Toronto ON M5J 1V6
Tel: 416-593-5257; *Fax:* 416-593-5145
info@toronto.goethe.org
www.goethe.de/toronto
Social Media:
www.facebook.com/GoetheToronto
twitter.com/GoetheToronto
To provide cultural programs, international cultural cooperation, German language teaching, & library & information services
Uwe Rau, Director

Greater Vancouver Japanese Canadian Citizens' Association (JCCA)
Nikkei Heritage Centre, #200, 6688 Southoaks Cres., Burnaby BC V5E 4M7
Tel: 604-777-5222; *Fax:* 604-777-5223
jccabulletin-geppo.ca/about-2/jcca-bulletin
Ron Nishimura, President

Hellenic Canadian Congress of BC (HCC(BC))
PO Box 129, 4500 Arbutus St., Vancouver BC V6J 4A2
Tel: 604-780-2460
info@helleniccongressbc.ca
www.helleniccongressbc.ca
Social Media:
www.facebook.com/124766634268645
Fosters education, communication, and cooperation between Hellenic Canadians and other ethnic groups, and promotes the development of just and equitable policies and legislation concerning all citizens.
Jimmy Sidiropoulos, President

Holocaust Education Centre
Lipa Green Centre, Sherman Campus, 4600 Bathurst St., 4th Fl., Toronto ON M2R 3V2
Tel: 416-635-2883; *Fax:* 416-635-0925
neuberger@ujafed.org
www.holocaustcentre.com
Social Media:
twitter.com/Holocaust_Ed
Mira Goldfarb, Executive Director
Carson Phillips, Head, Education
Mary Siklos, Manager, Operations
Anna Skorupsky, Librarian

Hungarian Canadian Cultural Centre
1170 Sheppard Ave. West, Toronto ON M3K 2A3
Tel: 416-654-4926
office@hccc.org
www.hccc-e.org
To preserve & showcase Hungarian heritage in the Canadian mosaic.

Icelandic National League of North America (INL/NA)
#103, 94 - 1st Ave., Gimli MB R0C 1B1
Tel: 204-642-5897
inl@mymts.net
www.inlofna.org
Social Media:
www.facebook.com/115047545201629
To foster & promote good citizenship among people of Icelandic descent; to foster & strengthen a mutual understanding of kinship, language, literature & cultural bonds among people of Icelandic origin & descent in North America & the people of Iceland; to cooperate with organizations which have similar purposes & objectives; to actively support various cultural & ethnic developments including education, history, publishing & the arts
Gail Einarson-McCleery, President
Gwen Grattan, Executive Secretary

International Organization of Ukrainian Communities "Fourth Wave"
#2, 15 Canmotor Ave., Toronto ON M8Z 4E4
Tel: 416-251-2244
canadafourthwave@hotmail.com
www.4thwave.org
To contribute to the strengthening & development of the Ukrainian community in Canada; To develop & promote Ukrainian national heritage as an element of the Canadian multicultural environment; To liaise with Ukrainian in Ukraine to promote mutual achievements of Ukrainian Canadians in science, technology, culture, & business; To provide social support to Ukrainian Canadians who are in need
Anna Kisil, President

Irish Canadian Cultural Association of New Brunswick (ICCA NB)
c/o Patricia O'Leary-Coughlan, 189 Carlisle Rd., Douglas NB E3A 7M8
info@newirelandnb.ca
www.newirelandnb.ca
To recognize & honour the contributions made by our ancestors to Canada by holding an annual Irish Festival, promoting an Irish Studies program at universities & sponsoring Irish cultural & social programs & events
Patricia O'Leary-Coughlan, Contact

Italian Cultural Institute (Istituto Italiano di Cultura)
496 Huron St., Toronto ON M5R 2R3
Tel: 416-921-3802; *Fax:* 416-962-2503
iicToronto@esteri.it
www.iictoronto.esteri.it
Social Media: www.youtube.com/user/IICCulturalToronto
www.facebook.com/iictoronto
twitter.com/IICToronto
To promote Italian culture & language in its many expressions in a spirit of vital interaction with the host country; To provide information on Italy's cultural heritage & contemporary cultural production
Adriana Frisenna, Director
Carlo Settembrini, Technical Manager
Tiziana Miano brini, Assistant to the Manager

Jamaican Canadian Association (JCA)
995 Arrow Rd., Toronto ON M9M 2Z5
Tel: 416-746-5772; *Fax:* 416-746-7035
info@jcaontario.org
jcaontario.org
To provide social interaction among members & to facilitate desirable relations with Canadian society; to represent the Caribbean community on public matters; to respond to the diverse social service needs of members; to facilitate economic, social & cultural integration of Caribbean people within Canadian society
Audrey Campbell, President

Japanese Canadian Association of Yukon (JCAY)
531 Grove St., Whitehorse YT Y1A 5J9
Tel: 867-393-2588
jcayukon@gmail.com
Fumi Torigai, President

Jewish Federations of Canada - UIA (JFC-UIA)
#315, 4600 Bathurst St., Toronto ON M2R 3V3
Tel: 416-636-7655; *Fax:* 416-636-9897
info@jfcuia.org
www.jewishcanada.org
Social Media: www.youtube.com/user/JewishFedofCanada
www.facebook.com/JewishFederationsofCanadaUIA
twitter.com/jfcuia
To raise money for Canadian Jewish organizations & to promote their efforts
Linda Kislowicz, President & CEO

Kashmiri Canadian Council (KCC)
#44516, 2376 Eglinton Ave. East, Toronto ON M1K 5K3
Tel: 416-282-6933; *Fax:* 416-282-7488
kcc@kashmiri-cc.ca
www.kashmiri-cc.ca

Latvian Canadian Cultural Centre (LCCC)
4 Credit Union Dr., Toronto ON M4A 2N8
Tel: 416-759-4900; *Fax:* 416-759-9311
office@latviancentre.org
www.latviancentre.org
Social Media:
www.facebook.com/143970339032047
To acquire, maintain & operate a Centre; to foster & sustain the Latvian heritage & cultural tradition; to provide social & cultural exchange with the various cultural communities in Canada; to provide facilities for meetings, concerts, dances, seminars, theatre & film shows & similar social/recreational activities for the general public & members
Sylvia Shedden, President & CEO

Latvian National Federation in Canada / Fédération nationale lettone au Canada
4 Credit Union Dr., Toronto ON M4A 2N8
Tel: 416-755-2353
lnak@lnak.net
www.lnak.net/eng
Social Media:
www.facebook.com/latviannationalfederationincanada
To represent the interests of Latvian Canadians at the city, provincial & federal levels; To maintain contact with other Canadian non-governmental organizations & expedite projects both in Canada & in Latvia
Andris Kesteris, Chair
Ilze Maksina, Administrator

The Latvian Relief Society of Canada
4 Credit Union Dr., Toronto ON M4A 2N8
Tel: 647-727-4310
dvkvbirojs@gmail.com
www.daugavasvanagi.ca
To provide financial assistance to Latvian-Canadians who demonstrate financial need; To encourage Latvian-Canadian youth to pursue post-secondary education
Gunta Reynolds, President
Astride Sile, Secretary

League of Ukrainian Canadian Women (LUCW)
#204, 2282 Bloor St. West, Toronto ON M6S 1N9
Tel: 416-763-8907
info@lucw.ca
www.lucw.ca
To support the development & sustainment of a strong Ukrainian community in Canada; To promote Ukraine's right to protect is national independence & security in the European family of nations
Lisa Shymko, President

League of Ukrainian Canadians
9 Plastics Ave., Toronto ON M8Z 4B6
Tel: 416-516-8223; *Fax:* 416-516-4033
luc@lucorg.com
www.lucorg.com
Social Media:
www.facebook.com/LeagueofUkrainianCanadians
To aid Ukrainian people living in Canada & in Ukraine; To contribute to the growth & development of a prosperous Ukrainian community in Canada
Orest Steciw, President

The Lithuanian Canadian Community / La Communauté lithuanienne du Canada
1 Resurrection Rd., Toronto ON M9A 5G1
Tel: 416-533-3292; *Fax:* 416-533-2282
info@klb.org
www.klb.org
To promote, maintain, & encourage the survival of the Lithuanian culture & language in Canada & abroad
Joana Kuraite-Lasiene, President

Maltese-Canadian Society of Toronto, Inc. (MCST)
3132 Dundas St. West, Toronto ON M6P 2A1
Tel: 416-767-3645
The organization strives for the betterment of the Maltese community in Toronto. It also preserves & promotes the Maltese language & culture in Canada.

Mizrachi Organization of Canada
296 Wilson Ave., Toronto ON M3H 1S8
Tel: 416-630-9266; *Fax:* 416-630-2305
mizrachi@rogers.com
www.mizrachi.ca
Social Media:
www.facebook.com/186778775014
twitter.com/MizrachiCanada
To coordinate Zionist-oriented programming for the Orthodox Jewish communities in Canada; to raise funds for educational & social welfare institutions in Israel
Meir Rosenberh, Executive Director

Multicultural Association of Northwestern Ontario (MANWO)
511 East Victoria Ave., Thunder Bay ON P7C 1A8
Tel: 807-622-4666; *Fax:* 807-622-7271
Toll-Free: 800-692-7692
manwoyc@tbaytel.net
To promote the concept of multiculturalism; to provide information, training & resources on citizenship, multiculturalism & race relations.

Multicultural Association of Nova Scotia (MANS) / Association multiculturelle de la Nouvelle-Écosse
1113 Marginal Rd., Halifax NS B3H 4P7
Tel: 902-423-6534; *Fax:* 902-422-0881
admin@mans.ns.ca
www.mans.ns.ca
To develop & influence multicultural policy & to promote equality; To create a sense of belonging & respect for all cultures
Sylvia Parris, Vice-President

Multicultural History Society of Ontario (MHSO)
c/o Oral History Museum, #307, 901 Lawrence Ave. West, Toronto ON M5S 1C3
Tel: 416-979-2973; *Fax:* 416-979-7947
mhso.mail@utoronto.ca
www.mhso.ca
Social Media: www.youtube.com/user/MulticulturalHistory
www.facebook.com/multiculturalhistorysociety
Working with communities, schools, cultural agencies and institutions to preserve, record and make accessible archival and other material which demonstrate the role of immigration and ethnicity in shaping the culture and economic growth of Ontario and Canada. Library is located at St. Michael's College, University of Toronto.
Cathy Leekam, Program Manager

National Association of Canadians of Origin in India (NACOI) / Association nationale des Canadiens d'origine indienne
PO Box 2308, Stn. D, Ottawa ON K1P 5W5
dbdavis@web.net
www.nacoi.ca
To encourage Canadians of origins in India to fully participate in Canadian society; to provide a national voice to Canadian of origins in India; to provide a forum for exchanges of ideas, issues, & common concerns; to facilitate communication within & with other organizations; to assure & protect rights of Canadians of origins in India
Dharam Pal Verma, President

National Association of Japanese Canadians (NAJC)
207 Donald St., 3rd Fl., Winnipeg MB R3C 1M5
Tel: 204-943-2910; *Fax:* 888-515-3192
national@najc.ca
www.najc.ca
To promote & develop a strong Japanese Canadian identity, thereby strengthening local communities & the national organization; to strive for equal rights & liberties for all persons & racial & ethnic minorities in particular.
Ken Noma, President

National Congress of Italian Canadians (NCIC) / Congrès national des italo-canadiens
#202, 340 Falstaff Ave., Toronto ON M6L 3E8
Tel: 416-531-9964; *Fax:* 416-531-9966
www.canadese.org
Michael Tibollo, President
Catherine Tinaburri, Coordinator

National Council of Trinidad & Tobago Organizations in Canada (NCTTOC)
66 Oakmeadow Blvd., Toronto ON M1E 4G5
Tel: 416-283-9672; *Fax:* 416-283-9672
To provide a national focus for representing the concerns of Trinidad & Tobago Nationals; to advocate on behalf of Trinidad & Tobago Nationals & their families in Canada; to develop & maintain a system of communication, information sharing & networking among Trinidad & Tobago organizations; to provide information, referrals, advocacy & support to new arrivals from Trinidad & Tobago
Emmanuel Dick, Contact

National Federation of Pakistani Canadians Inc. (NFPC)
#1100, 251 Laurier Ave. W, Ottawa ON K1P 5J6
Tel: 613-232-5346; *Fax:* 613-232-6607
www.cool.mb.ca/nfpc
To preserve & promote the heritage, culture & language of Pakistani Canadians; to generate goodwill & understanding among ethnic & mainstream communities; to provide support to new immigrants; to create awareness of Canadian issues in the Pakistani community

New Brunswick Multicultural Council (NBMC) / Conseil multiculturel du Nouveau-Brunswick (CMNB)
#200, 361 Victoria St., Fredericton NB E3B 1W5
Tel: 506-453-1091; *Fax:* 866-644-1956
nbmc@nb-mc.ca
www.nb-mc.ca
To represent multicultural & multi-racial interests of all member associations; to encourage development & formation of new associations; to encourage member associations in their multicultural, inter-cultural & inter-racial programs & activities
Dexter Noel, President

Pacific Peoples Partnership (PPP)
#407, 620 View St., Victoria BC V8W 1J6
Tel: 250-381-4131; *Fax:* 250-388-5258
info@pacificpeoplespartnership.org
www.pacificpeoplespartnership.org
To promote increased understanding of social justice, environment, development, health & other issues of importance to the people of the Pacific Islands; To support equitable, environmentally sustainable development & social justice in the region
April Ingham, Executive Director

Polish Alliance of Canada (PAC)
c/o Mississauga Branch, 3060 Eden Oak Cres., Mississauga ON L5L 5V2
Tel: 905-569-7139
www.polishalliance.ca
To promote Polish history, culture & interests
Robert Zawierucha, President

Polish-Jewish Heritage Foundation of Canada
#61, 396 Woodsworth Rd., Toronto ON M2L 2T9
www.pjhftoronto.ca

To preserve the unique heritage of Polish Jews & to actively foster better understanding & cooperation between Polish & Jewish communities in Canada
Peter Jassem, Chair

Serbian National Shield Society of Canada
#303, 1900 Sheppard Ave. East, Toronto ON M2J 4T4
Tel: 416-496-7881; *Fax:* 416-493-0335
To promote & inform about interests & heritage of Canadian Serbs
Diane Dragasevich, Contact

Turkish Community Heritage Centre of Canada (TCHHC)
#35B, 234-10520 Yonge St., Richmond Hill ON L4C 3C7
Tel: 416-644-9909
info@TurkishCommunityCentre.org
www.turkishcommunitycentre.org
Social Media: www.facebook.com/178208095522790?sk=info
twitter.com/tchcc
Provides and maintains a community centre for the Canadian Turkish community.
Musabay Figen, President

UJA Federation of Greater Toronto
4600 Bathurst St., Toronto ON M2R 3V2
Tel: 416-635-2883
info@jewishtoronto.com
www.jewishtoronto.com
Social Media: www.youtube.com/user/UJAFederation;
www.instagram.com/UJAFederation
www.facebook.com/UJAFederationToronto
twitter.com/UJAFederation
To preserve & strengthen Jewish life in Toronto, Canada & Israel, through philanthropic, volunteer & professional leadership. The UJA is committed to social justice on behalf of the Jewish poor & vulnerable locally & internationally, to strengthening ties with Israel & its people, to supporting Israel's struggle to meet its social welfare needs, to combatting antisemitism in all its forms around the world, to nurturing shared values with Canadians of all faiths, to promoting Jewish education, to building a vibrant Jewish communal life. The following Pillars identify main areas of focus for UJA: Jewish Education & Identity; Strategic Planning & Community Engagement; Integrated Development; Operations & Corporate Relations; Business & Finance
Ted Sokolsky, President & CEO

Ukrainian Canadian Congress (UCC) / Congrès des ukrainiens canadiens
#203, 952 Main St., Winnipeg MB R2W 3P4
Tel: 204-942-4627; *Fax:* 204-947-3882
Toll-Free: 866-942-4627
ucc@ucc.ca
www.ucc.ca
Social Media: www.youtube.com/user/UkrainianCanCongress
linkedin.com/company/ukrainian-canadian-congress
www.facebook.com/pages/Ukrainian-Canadian-Congress/195065046451
twitter.com/ukrcancongress
To protect, promote & enhance cultural identity of Ukrainians throughout Canada & beyond; to maintain, develop & enhance Ukrainian culture & language as integral elements of Canada's multicultural mosaic; to encourage participation of Ukrainian Canadians in cultural, social, economic, & political life in Canada; to actively advance better communication, understanding & mutual respect between Ukrainian Canadians & other ethnocultural communities; to foster sense of unity, cohesiveness & cooperation among member organizations
Paul Grod, President

Ukrainian Canadian Research & Documentation Centre (UCRDC) / Centre canadien-ukrainien de recherches et de documentation
620 Spadina Ave., Toronto ON M5S 2H4
Tel: 416-966-1819; *Fax:* 416-966-1820
info@ucrdc.org
www.ucrdc.org
Social Media: www.facebook.com/261703763950638
To collect, store & promote information pertaining to Ukrainian historical events & Ukrainian Canadian experiences
Jurij Darewych, Chair & President

Ukrainian Democratic Youth Association (ODUM)
3029 Bloor St. West, Toronto ON M8X 1C5
www.odum.org
To unite Ukrainian Canadians & other Ukrainians across North America

Ukrainian National Federation of Canada (UNF) / Fédération nationale Ukrainienne du Canada
#210, 145 Evans Ave., Toronto ON M8Z 5X8
Tel: 416-925-2770
info@unfcanada.ca
www.unfcanada.ca
Social Media: www.facebook.com/unfcanada
To unite Ukrainian Canadians while promoting good Canadian citizenship; To represent the interests & needs of the Ukrainian Canadian community; To inform Canadians about Ukrainian history & culture while strengthening the place of the Ukrainian community in Canadian society at large
Olya Grod, Executive Director

Ukrainian Self-Reliance League of Canada (CYC)
455 Habkirk St., Regina SK S4S 6B2
Tel: 306-586-6805; *Fax:* 306-585-7945
www.usrl-cyc.org
To preserve Canadian heritage while advancing Ukrainian Canadian culture; To enhance the future growth of the Ukrainian Orthodox Church of Canada
Tony Harras, President

Ukrainian Women's Association of Canada (UWAC)
10611 - 110 Ave. NW, Edmonton AB T5H 1H7
Tel: 780-456-4141; *Fax:* 780-425-3991
info@uwac-national.ca
www.uwac-national.ca
To support the continual growth of the Ukrainian Orthodox Church of Canada; To preserve, develop, & nurture Ukrainian heritage; To foster & encourage cooperation within Canadian society; To support education of Ukrainian Canadian youth in church schools, Ukrainian schools, & bilingual schools; To maintain the growth of the Ukrainian Museum of Canada of the UWAC
Geraldine Nakonechny, President

Ukrainian Youth Association of Canada
83 Christie St., Toronto ON M6G 3B1
Tel: 416-537-2007; *Fax:* 416-516-4033
KY-Canada@CYM.org
archive.cym.org/ca/index.asp
Social Media: www.facebook.com/CYM.Canada
To encourage Ukrainian children & youth to discover their Ukrainian heritage; To promote Ukrainian traditions & language; To emphasize the development of Christian ethics & leadership skills
Tamara Tataryn, President

Urban Alliance on Race Relations (UARR)
#507, 302 Spadina Ave., Toronto ON M5T 2E7
Tel: 416-703-6607; *Fax:* 416-703-4415
info@urbanalliance.ca
www.urbanalliance.ca
To promote a stable & healthy multiracial environment in the community, by creating awareness of current issues, assisting institutions to develop solid policies & practices, & promoting full participation by the community to dismantle barriers to equal opportunity
Sharon Simpson, President
Yumei Lin, Administrative Assistant

Vietnamese Canadian Federation (VCF) / Fédération vietnamienne du Canada
2476 Regatta Ave., Ottawa ON K2J 5V6
Tel: 780-708-0876; *Fax:* 780-425-0799
lhnvc1980vcf@gmail.com
www.vietfederation.ca
Social Media: www.flickr.com/photos/vietnamesecanadianfederationcentre
www.facebook.com/vietnamesecanadian.centre
twitter.com/VietCdnCentre
To provide focal point for activities of the Vietnamese community in the National Capital Region & across Canada; to serve as resource centre on Vietnamese culture & issues related to resettlement & integration of Vietnamese refugees & immigrants in Canada; to maintain solidarity among the Vietnamese associations across Canada; to harmonize their activities for a better achievement of their common objectives; to work for the preservation & development of Vietnamese culture & for the enrichment of Canadian culture; to foster the spirit of mutual help & community responsibility

Music Festivals

Canadian Music Week Inc. (CMW)
5355 Vail Ct., Mississauga ON L5M 6G9
Tel: 905-858-4747; *Fax:* 905-858-4848
cmw.net
Social Media: www.facebook.com/canadianmusicweek
twitter.com/CMW_Week
To organize the annual Canadian Music Week festival, convention & trade show
Neill Dixon, President
Verle Mobbs, General Manager
Cameron Wright, Director, Festival

Native Peoples

Aboriginal Agricultural Education Society of British Columbia (AAESBC)
PO Box 1186, Stn. Main, 7410 Dallas Dr., Kamloops BC V2C 6H3
Tel: 778-469-5040; *Fax:* 778-469-5030
info@aaesbc.ca
www.aaesbc.ca
To provide culturally appropriate & respectful training for First Nations agricultural businesses, so that they may excel in the agricultural industry

Aboriginal Friendship Centres of Saskatchewan
115 Wall St., Saskatoon SK S7K 6C2
Tel: 306-955-0762; *Fax:* 306-955-0972
www.afcs.ca
Social Media: www.youtube.com/user/theAFCS
www.facebook.com/192129454182112
twitter.com/afcsk
The objectives of the Aboriginal Friendship Centres (AFC) of Sask. are: the promotion of the goals and objectives of its member Friendship Centres; the facilitation of communication and cooperation amongst all Centres w/in SK,; the providing of information regarding the operation and dvlp. of AFCs to the public; negotiation with all tiers of gov't on matters of concern to the member Centres; assistance in Program Dvlp.; and assistance to all members in terms of funding information, debt recovery plans, financial negotiation, and networking.
Gwen Bear, Executive Director

Aboriginal Head Start Association of British Columbia (AHSABC)
PO Box 271, Cobble Hill BC V0R 1L0
Tel: 250-858-4543; *Fax:* 250-743-2478
www.ahsabc.com
To promote excellence in Aboriginal early childhood learning programs across British Columbia
Leona Antoine, President
Peggy Abou, Secretary
Joan Gignac, Executive Director

Aboriginal Nurses Association of Canada (ANAC) / Association des infirmières et infirmiers autochtones du Canada
#600, 16 Concourse Gate, Ottawa ON K2E 7S8
Tel: 613-724-4677; *Fax:* 613-724-4718
Toll-Free: 866-724-3049
info@anac.on.ca
www.anac.on.ca
Social Media: twitter.com/aboriginalnurse
To work with & on behalf of Aboriginal nurses to promote the development & practice of Aboriginal nursing in order to improve the health of Aboriginal people
Rhonda Goodtrack, President
Sherri Di Lallo, Vice-President
Lisa Bourque-Bearskin, Secretary-Treasurer

Aboriginal Women's Association of Prince Edward Island
172 Eagle Feather Trail, Lennox Island PE C0B 1P0
Tel: 902-831-3059; *Fax:* 902-831-3181
info@awapei.org
Social Media: www.facebook.com/193334154037222
The purpose of the project is to address issues of concern to off-reserve Aboriginal women and to improve the educational, social and economic environments in which they live. The resource centre offers culturally sensitive programs and services to off-reserve Aboriginal families and children from birth to age 6.

Alberta Aboriginal Women's Society
PO Box 5168, Stn. Main, Peace River AB T8S 1R8
Tel: 780-624-3416; *Fax:* 780-624-3409
aaws@telusplanet.net

Ruth Kidder, President

Alberta Native Friendship Centres Association (ANFCA)
10336 - 121 St., Edmonton AB T5N 1K8
Tel: 780-423-3138; *Fax:* 780-425-6277
www.anfca.com
To assist friendship centres in communication, funding & training
Nelson Mayer, Executive Director

Alliance autochtone du Québec inc. / Native Alliance of Québec Inc.
21, rue Brodeur, Gatineau QC J8Y 2P6
Tél: 819-770-7763; *Téléc:* 819-770-6070
info@aaqnaq.com
www.aaqnaq.com
Robert Bertrand, Président Grand Chef

Assembly of First Nations (AFN) / Assemblée des Premières Nations (APN)
#1600, 55 Metcalfe St., Ottawa ON K1P 6L5
Tel: 613-241-6789; *Fax:* 613-241-5808
Toll-Free: 866-869-6789
www.afn.ca
Social Media: www.youtube.com/user/afnposter
www.facebook.com/AFN.APN
twitter.com/AFN_Updates
The AFN Secretariat acts as an advocate for First Nations on many issues, including Aboriginal & Treaty Rights, economic development, education, languages & literacy, health, housing, social development, justice, land claims & the environment
Perry Bellgarde, National Chief

Assembly of Manitoba Chiefs
#200, 275 Portage Ave., Winnipeg MB R3B 2B3
Tel: 204-956-0610; *Fax:* 204-956-2109
Toll-Free: 888-324-5483
info@manitobachiefs.com
www.manitobachiefs.com
To promote & preserve Aboriginal and treaty rights while striving to improve the quality of life of the First Nation citizens in Manitoba.
Derek Nepinak, Grand Chief

Association for Native Development in the Performing & Visual Arts (ANDPVA)
#10, 610 Baldwin St., Toronto ON M5T 3K7
Tel: 416-535-4567; *Fax:* 416-535-9331
info@andpva.com
www.andpva.com
To coordinate & develop programs that will encourage Indigenous peoples & communities to become more actively involved in the arts; to act as liaison for Native groups & individuals who are seeking funds for specific arts projects
Millie Knapp, Executive Director

Association of Iroquois & Allied Indians
387 Princess Ave., London ON N6B 2A7
Tel: 519-434-2761; *Fax:* 519-675-1053
Toll-Free: 888-269-9593
www.aiai.on.ca
To advocate for the political interests of eight member nations in Ontario
Geoff Stonefish, Office Manager

British Columbia Association of Aboriginal Friendship Centres (BCAAFC)
551 Chatham St., Victoria BC V8T 1E1
Tel: 250-388-5522; *Fax:* 250-388-5502
Toll-Free: 800-990-2432
frontdesk@bcaafc.com
www.bcaafc.com
Social Media:
www.facebook.com/pages/BC-Friendship-Centres/16002765735 3593
To promote the betterment of Aboriginal Friendship Centres in British Columbia by acting as a unifying body for the Centres; To establish & maintain communications between Aboriginal Friendship Centres, other associations, & government
Paul Lacerte, Executive Director

British Columbia Native Women's Association
144 Briar Ave., Kamloops BC V2B 1C1
Tel: 250-554-4556; *Fax:* 250-554-4573
Social Media:
www.facebook.com/bc.nativewomensassociation

Canadian Aboriginal & Minority Supplier Council (CAMSC)
95 Berkeley St., Toronto ON M5A 2W8
Tel: 416-941-0004; *Fax:* 416-941-9282
info@camsc.ca
www.camsc.ca
Dedicated to the economic empowerment of Aboriginal & visible minority communities through business development & employment; to identify & certify Aboriginal & minority-owned businesses, & to integrate them into the supply chain of major corporations in Canada.
Cassandra Dorrington, President

Canadian Association for the Study of Indigenous Education (CASIE) / Association canadienne pour l'etude de l'education des autochtones (ACÉÉA)
c/o Canadian Society for the Study of Education, #204, 260 Dalhousie St., Ottawa ON K1N 7E4
Dwayne Donald, President

Canadian Council for Aboriginal Business (CCAB) / Conseil canadien pour le commerce autochtone
#204, 250 The Esplanade, Toronto ON M5A 1J2
Tel: 416-961-8663; *Fax:* 416-961-3995
info@caab.com
www.ccab.com
To promote full participation of Aboriginal communities in the Canadian economy
J.P. Gladu, President & CEO

Canadian Native Friendship Centre (CNFC)
15001 - 112 Ave., 2nd Fl., Edmonton AB T5G 2A4
Tel: 780-760-1900
www.cnfcedmonton.com
Social Media: www.youtube.com/user/cnfcedmonton
twitter.com/EdmontonCNFC
To improve the quality of life of Aboriginal Peoples in an urban environment by supporting self-determined activities encouraging equal access to & participation in Canadian society while respecting Aboriginal cultural distinctiveness
Adam North Peigan, Executive Director

Centre indien cri de Chibougamau
95, rue Jaculet, Chibougamau QC G8P 2G1
Tél: 418-748-7667
cicc@lino.com
Centre social pour les Autochtones de la région; centre d'exposition pour les artisans cri
Jo-Ann Toulouse, Directice générale

Chiefs of Ontario
#804, 111 Peter St., Toronto ON M5V 2H1
Tel: 416-597-1266; *Fax:* 416-597-8365
Toll-Free: 877-517-6527
www.chiefs-of-ontario.org
Social Media: vimeo.com/chiefsofontario;
www.flickr.com/photos/chiefsofontario
twitter.com/chiefsofontario
To enable the political leadership to discuss regional, provincial & national priorities affecting First Nation people in Ontario & to provide a unified voice on these issues.
Pam Montour, Executive Director

Confederacy of Mainland Mi'kmaq (CMM)
PO Box 1590, 57 Martin Cresc., Truro NS B2N 6N7
Tel: 902-895-6385; *Fax:* 902-893-1520
Toll-Free: 877-892-2424
www.cmmns.com
To proactively promote and assist Mi'kmaw communities' initiatives toward self determination and enhancement of community.
Donald M. Julien, Executive Director

Congress of Aboriginal Peoples (CAP) / Congrès des Peuples Autochtones
867 St. Laurent Blvd., Ottawa ON K1K 3B1
Tel: 613-747-6022; *Fax:* 613-747-8834
Toll-Free: 888-997-9927
reception@abo-peoples.org
www.abo-peoples.org
Social Media: www.youtube.com/user/TheCAPOttawa
www.facebook.com/178584242154616
twitter.com/CAPChief
To represent approximately 3/4 million Aboriginal people living off-reserve in Canada
Dwight Dorey, National Chief
Jim Devoe, Chief Executive Officer

Council of Yukon First Nations (CYFN)
2166 - 2nd Ave., Whitehorse YT Y1A 4P1
Tel: 867-393-9200; *Fax:* 867-668-6577
reception@cyfn.net
www.cyfn.ca
The Council of Yukon First Nations is the central political organization for the First Nation people of the Yukon. It's mission is to serve the needs of First Nations within the Yukon and the MacKenzie delta.
Ruth Massie, Grand Chief
Michelle Kolla, Executive Director

Federation of Saskatchewan Indian Nations
Asimakaniseekan Askiy Reserve, #100, 103A Packham Ave., Saskatoon SK S7N 4K4
Tel: 306-665-1215; *Fax:* 306-244-4413
www.fsin.com
To honour the spirit & intent of the First Nations Treaties & their rights; to foster the economic, educational & social endeavours of the First Nation people & adherence to democratic procedure & civil law.
Kim Jonathan, Interim Chief

Femmes autochtones du Québec inc. (FAQ) / Québec Native Women Inc.
CP 1989, Kahnawake QC J0L 1B0
Tél: 450-632-0088; *Téléc:* 450-632-9280
info@faq-qnw.org
www.faq-qnw.org
Média social: vimeo.com/user14258370
www.facebook.com/FAQQNW
twitter.com/FAQQNW
Appuyer les efforts des femmes autochtones pour l'amélioration de leurs conditions de vie par la promotion de la non-violence, de la justice et de l'égalité des droits et de les soutenir dans leur engagement au sein de leur communauté.
Aurelie Arnaud, Contact, Médias

First Nations Agricultural Association (FNAA)
PO Box 1186, Stn. Main, 7410 Dallas Dr., Kamloops BC V2C 6H3
Tel: 778-469-5040; *Fax:* 778-469-5030
info@fnala.com
www.fnala.com
To further the social & economic well-being of Aboriginal agricultural businesses
Harold Aljam, President

First Nations Agricultural Lending Association (FNALA)
PO Box 1186, Stn. Main, 7410 Dallas Dr., Kamloops BC V2C 6H3
Tel: 778-469-5040; *Fax:* 778-469-5030
info@fnala.com
www.fnala.com/fnala.php
To provide loans of up to up to $350,000 to Aboriginal agricultural & agri-food businesses (on & off-reserve projects); to provide First Citizen's Fund loans & mortgages

First Nations Breast Cancer Society
#309, 1333 East 7th Ave., Vancouver BC V5N 1R6
Tel: 604-872-4390; *Fax:* 604-875-0779
echoes@fnbreastcancer.bc.ca
www.fnbreastcancer.bc.ca
Offers breast cancer education and support to First Nations women.
Jacqueline Davis, President

First Nations Confederacy of Cultural Education Centres
#302, 666 Kirkwood Ave., Ottawa ON K1Z 5X9
Tel: 613-728-5999; *Fax:* 613-728-2247
www.fnccec.com
Social Media:
www.facebook.com/134419529944964
twitter.com/fnccec
To advocate for the recovery, maintenance, enhancement & preservation of First Nations languages, cultures & traditions
Claudette Commanda, Executive Director
Donna Goodleaf, National President
Tiffany Sark-Carr, Vice-President
Dorothy Myo, Secretary-Treasurer

Grand Council of the Crees / Grand Conseil des Cris
2, rue Lakeshore, Nemaska QC J0Y 3B0
Tel: 819-673-2600; *Fax:* 819-673-2606
cree@cra.qc.ca
www.gcc.ca
Social Media:
linkedin.com/companies/grand-council-of-the-crees
www.facebook.com/gcccra
twitter.com/gcccra
To representg the Cree people; to foster, promote, protect & assist in preserving the way of life, values & traditions of the Cree people of Quebec.
Mathew Coon Come, Grand Chief
Bill Namagoose, Executive Director

Indigenous Bar Association
c/o Anne Chalmers, 70 Pineglen Cres., Ottawa ON K2G 0G8
www.indigenousbar.ca
To recognize & respect the spiritual basis of our Indigenous laws, customs & traditions; To promote the advancement of legal & social justice for Indigenous peoples in Canada; To promote reform of policies & laws affecting Indigenous peoples in

Canada; To foster public awareness within the legal community, the Indigenous community & the general public in respect of legal & social issues of concern to Indigenous peoples in Canada; To provide a forum & network amongst Indigenous lawyers
Koren Lightning-Earle, President
Anne Chalmers, Administrative Support

Indspire
Six Nations of the Grand River, PO Box 5, 50 Generations Dr., Oshweken ON N0A 1M0
Tel: 519-445-3021; *Fax:* 866-433-3159
Toll-Free: 855-463-7747
communications@indspire.ca
indspire.ca
Social Media:
www.facebook.com/Indspire
twitter.com/Indspire
To provide scholarships to Indigenous people that help them pay for a post-secondary educations
Roberta Jamieson, President & CEO

Inuit Art Foundation (IAF) / Fondation d'art Inuit
c/o Centre of Social Innovation, #400, 215 Spadina Ave., Toronto ON M5T 2C7
Tel: 647-498-7717; *Toll-Free:* 855-274-0109
info@inuitartfoundation.org
www.inuitartfoundation.org
To facilitate the creative expression of Inuit artists; To foster an increased understanding of this expression in a local & global context; To assist in the marketing of Inuit art; To promote Inuit art through exhibits, publications & public events
Jimmy Manning, President
William Huffman, Director, Development & Stakeholder Relations

Inuit Tapiriit Kanatami (ITK)
#1101, 75 Albert St., Ottawa ON K1P 5E7
Tel: 613-238-8181; *Fax:* 613-234-1991
Toll-Free: 866-262-8181
info@itk.ca
www.itk.ca
Social Media: www.youtube.com/inuitofcanada
www.facebook.com/pages/Inuit-Tapiriit-Kanatami/149359161748927
twitter.com/ITK_CanadaInuit
To ensure the survival of Inuit culture in Canada
Natan Obed, President
Elizabeth Ford, Acting Executive Director

Labrador Native Women's Association
PO Box 542, Stn. B, Happy Valley-Goose Bay NL A0P 1S0
Tel: 709-896-5071; *Fax:* 709-896-5071

Makivik Corporation / Société Makivik
PO Box 179, Kuujjuaq QC J0M 1C0
Tel: 819-964-2925; *Toll-Free:* 877-625-4825
www.makivik.org
A non-profit organization owned by the Inuit of Nunavik, the Corporation promotes the social & economic interests of the Inuit people; receives, administers & invests Inuit compensation funds received under the James Bay & Northern Québec Agreement, & promotes the political, social & economic development of the Nunavik region. Offices in Kuujjuaq, Montreal, Ottawa, Quebec City
Jobie Tukkiapik, President
Andy Pirti, Treasurer
Andy Moorhouse, Corporate Secretary

Manitoba Association of Friendship Centres (MAC)
#11, 150 Henry Ave., Winnipeg MB R3B 0J7
Tel: 204-942-6299; *Fax:* 204-942-6308
www.mac.mb.ca
Social Media:
www.facebook.com/FriendshipCentres
To assist friendship centres in communication, funding & training.
Joan Church, President
Adam Blanchard, Executive Director

Manitoba Indian Cultural Education Centre (MICEC)
119 Sutherland Ave., Winnipeg MB R2W 3C9
Tel: 204-942-0228; *Fax:* 204-947-6564
info@micec.com
www.micec.com
Social Media:
www.facebook.com/micec.mb
To stimulate, reidentify, maintain, expand & promote the cultural interests, lives & identity of Manitoba First Nations in every manner & respect whatsoever, & to promote an awareness of the traditional history of the First Nation Peoples of Manitoba; to advance the interests of First Nation Peoples who are registered members of the reserves within Manitoba, whether residing on or outside them; to cooperate with other organizations concerned with the interests of First Nation Peoples; to establish & promote research services; to assist in the development of accurate curriculum for use in schools within Manitoba; to produce audio, visual, & written materials relevant to cultural education development

Manitoba Métis Federation / Fédération des Métis du Manitoba
Head Office, #300, 150 Henry Ave., Winnipeg MB R3B 0J7
Tel: 204-586-8474; *Fax:* 204-947-1816
mmf@mmf.mb.ca
www.mmf.mb.ca
Social Media: www.youtube.com/ManitobaMetisMMF
www.facebook.com/ManitobaMetisFederationOfficial
twitter.com/MBMetis_MMF
To promote & instill pride in the history & culture of the Métis people; to educate members with respect to their legal, political, social & other rights; to promote the participation & represention of the Métis people in key political & economic bodies & organizations; to promote the political, legal, social and economic interests & rights of its members.
David Chartrand, President

Maritime Aboriginal Peoples Council (MAPC)
172 Truro Heights Rd., Truro NS B6L 1X1
Tel: 902-895-2982; *Fax:* 902-895-3844
mapcorg.ca
Represents the Traditional Ancestral Homeland Mi'Kmaq, Maliseet, and Passamaquoddy Aboriginal Peoples of Canada.

Métis Nation - Saskatchewan
231 Robin Cres., Saskatoon SK S7L 6M8
Tel: 306-343-8285; *Fax:* 306-343-0171
Toll-Free: 888-343-6667
reception@mn-s.ca
www.mn-s.ca
Social Media: www.youtube.com/user/MetisSK2012
www.facebook.com/metisnationsaskatchewan
twitter.com/metisnationsask
To represent Saskatechwan Métis & act as its legislative assembley

Métis Nation of Alberta
Delia Gray Bldg., #100, 41738 Kingsway Ave., Edmonton AB T5G 0X5
Tel: 780-455-2200; *Fax:* 780-452-8948
Toll-Free: 800-252-7553
www.albertametis.com
Social Media:
www.facebook.com/pages/Metis-Nation-of-Alberta/339682308115
twitter.com/AlbertaMetis
To represent the interests of the Métis people of Alberta & ensure the advancement of their culture & well-being
Audrey Poitras, President

Métis Nation of Ontario
#3, 500 Old St. Patrick St., Ottawa ON K1N 9G4
Tel: 613-798-1488; *Fax:* 613-722-4225
Toll-Free: 800-263-4889
www.metisnation.org
Social Media:
www.facebook.com/147602041992683
To bring Métis people together to celebrate and share their rich culture and heritage and to forward the aspirations of the Métis people in Ontario as a collective.
Gary Lipinski, President

Métis National Council (MNC) / Ralliement national des Métis
#4, 340 MacLaren St., Ottawa ON K2P 0M6
Tel: 613-232-3216; *Fax:* 613-232-4262
Toll-Free: 800-928-6330
info@metisnation.ca
www.metisnation.ca
Social Media: www.youtube.com/user/MetisNationalCouncil
www.facebook.com/186735084697421
twitter.com/MNC_tweets
To represent the Métis both nationally & internationally; To secure a healthy space for the Métis Nation's existence within Canada
Clément Chartier, President

Métis National Council of Women (MNCW) / Conseil national des femmes métisses, inc. (CNFM)
PO Box 293, Woodlawn ON K0A 3M0
Tel: 613-567-4287; *Fax:* 613-567-9644
Toll-Free: 888-867-2635
info@metiswomen.ca
www.metiswomen.ca
To unite & organize Métis women in Canada and to maintain & promote respect for the individual rights, freedoms & gender equality of Métis women.
Sheila D. Genaille, President

Métis Provincial Council of British Columbia
30691 Simpson Rd., Abbotsford BC V2T 2C7
Tel: 604-557-5851; *Fax:* 604-557-2024
Toll-Free: 800-940-1150
reception@mnbc.ca
www.mnbc.ca
Social Media:
www.facebook.com/metisnationbc
To support the Métis population in British Columbia.
Bruce Dumont, President
Dale Drown, Chief Executive Officer

Métis Settlements General Council
#101, 10335 - 172 St., Edmonton AB T5S 1K9
Tel: 780-822-4096; *Fax:* 780-489-9558
Toll-Free: 888-213-4400
reception@msgc.ca
www.msgc.ca
Social Media: www.youtube.com/user/MSGCHistoryOnline
www.facebook.com/alberta.settlements
To represent settlements & address socio-economic issues on their behalf; to promote good governance & community involvement
Randy Hardy, President

Mi'Kmaq Association for Cultural Studies (MACS)
PO Box 243, Sydney NS B1P 6H1
Tel: 902-567-1752; *Fax:* 902-567-0776
macs@mikmaq-assoc.ca
www.mikmaqculture.com
To promote, maintain & protect the customs, language, history, tradition & culture of the Mi'Kmaq people; to facilitate & promote understanding & awareness of our culture among the public; to teach the culture, language & history of the Mi'Kmaq people to others
Deborah Ginnish, Executive Director

Mi'kmaq Native Friendship Centre
2158 Gottingen St., Halifax NS B3K 3B4
Tel: 902-420-1576; *Fax:* 902-423-6130
www.mymnfc.com
Social Media:
www.facebook.com/121366117945828
To promote the educational & cultural advancement of native people in & about the Halifax/Dartmouth area; to assist people of native descent who have newly arrived in the area to settle in; to strive to create & improve mutual understanding between people of native descent & others.
Pam Glode-Desrochers, Executive Director

Mother of Red Nations Women's Council of Manitoba (MORN)
#300, 141 Bannatyne Ave., Winnipeg MB R3B 0R3
Tel: 204-942-6676
morn.cimnet.ca/cim/92C270_397T18346.dhtm
To represent Aboriginal women in Manitoba & serve as their primary political & advocacy organization; To promote, protect & support the spiritual, emotional, physical & mental well-being of all Aboriginal women & children in the province

National Aboriginal Circle Against Family Violence
Kahnawake Business Complex, PO Box 2169, Kahnawake QC J0L 1B0
Tel: 450-638-2968; *Fax:* 450-638-9415
www.nacafv.ca
To reduce & eliminate family violence in our Aboriginal communities; programs are culturally appropriate, & support shelters & family violence prevention centres
Brenda Combs, Chair

National Association of Friendship Centres (NAFC) / Association nationale des centres d'amitié
275 MacLaren St., Ottawa ON K2P 0L9
Tel: 613-563-4844; *Fax:* 613-594-3428
Toll-Free: 877-563-4844
nafcgen@nafc.ca
nafc.ca
Social Media:
www.facebook.com/131454736880978
twitter.com/AYC_NAFC
To assist friendship centres in communication, funding & training
Jeffrey Cyr, Executive Director

Native Addictions Council of Manitoba (NACM)
160 Salter St., Winnipeg MB R2W 4K1
Tel: 204-586-8395; *Fax:* 204-589-3921
info@nacm.ca
www.mts.net/~nacm/

To provide traditional holistic healing services to First Peoples through treatment of addictions; each member of First Peoples has the right to wellness.

Native Council of Nova Scotia (NCNS)
129 Truro Heights Rd., Truro NS B6L 1X2
Tel: 902-895-1523; *Fax:* 902-895-0024
Toll-Free: 800-565-4372
www.ncns.ca
To aid & assist people of Aboriginal ancestry in Nova Scotia; to work with all levels of government, public & private agencies, & industry to improve social, educational & employment opportunities for Aboriginal people; to foster & strengthen cultural identity & pride; to inform the public of the special needs of Native People; to cooperate with other Native organizations
Grace Conrad, Chief & President
Theresa Hare, Finance

Native Council of Prince Edward Island
6 F.J. McAuley Ct., Charlottetown PE C1A 9M7
Tel: 902-892-5314; *Fax:* 902-368-7464
Toll-Free: 877-591-3003
admin@ncpei.com
www.ncpei.com
The Native Council of Prince Edward Island is a Community of Aboriginal People residing off reserve in traditional Mi'kmaq territory. NCPEI is the self governing authority for all off reserve Aboriginal people living on Epekwitk (PEI).
Jamie Thomas, President & Chief
Rikki Schock, Vice-President
Lisa Cooper, Director, Operations

Native Counselling Services of Alberta (NCSA)
10975 - 124 St., Edmonton AB T5M 0H9
Tel: 780-451-4002; *Fax:* 780-428-0187
www.ncsa.ca
To promote wellness for Aboriginal individuals, families and communities.
Allen Benson, CEO

Native Friendship Centre of Montréal Inc. (NFCM) / Centre d'amitié autochtone de Montréal Inc.
2001 St. Laurent Blvd., Montréal QC H2X 2T3
Tel: 514-499-1854; *Fax:* 514-499-9436
Toll-Free: 855-499-1854
info@nfcm.org
www.nfcm.org
Social Media:
www.facebook.com/nfcm.montreal
To promote, develop & enhance the quality of life of the urban Aboriginal community of Montréal
Brett W. Pineau, Executive Director

Native Investment & Trade Association (NITA)
6520 Salish Dr., Vancouver BC V6N 2C7
Tel: 604-275-6670; *Fax:* 604-275-0307
Toll-Free: 800-337-7743
mail@aboriginal-business.com
To promote, establish & maintain trade/investment opportunities in Native communities; encourages free enterprise solutions to economic & social problems confronting Native communities, but remains sensitive to their special cultural heritage, needs, requirements; views non-governmental business involvement with First Nations as a vital step towards greater self-reliance; fosters business ventures with high employment potential; promotes projects with potential for sustainable economic growth; conducts research into innovative approaches to economic development of Native communities

Native Women's Association of Canada (NWAC) / L'Association des femmes autochtones du Canada (AFAC)
1 Nicholas St., 9th Fl., Ottawa ON K1N 7B7
Fax: 613-722-7687
Toll-Free: 800-461-4043
www.nwac.ca
Social Media:
www.facebook.com/283649502474
To enhance, promote & foster the social, economic, cultural & political well-being of First Nations & Métis women with First Nations & Canadian societies; to help empower women by being involved in developing & changing legislation which affects them, & by involving them in the development & delivery of programs promoting equal opportunity for Aboriginal women. Satellite office located at 1292 Wellington St. West, Ottawa, 613-722-3033.
Michèle Audette, President

New Brunswick Aboriginal Peoples Council (NBAPC)
320 St. Mary's St., Fredericton NB E3A 2S4
Tel: 506-458-8422; *Fax:* 506-451-6130
Toll-Free: 800-442-9789
www.nbapc.org
To represent Status & Non-status First Nations who reside in New Brunswick
Wendy Wetteland, Chief & President
Carol LaBillios-Slocum, Executive Director

New Brunswick Aboriginal Women's Council
29 Big Cove Rd., Elsipogtog NB E4W 2S5
Tel: 506-523-9518; *Fax:* 506-523-8350
nbawca@nb.aibn.com
Sarah Rose, President

Newfoundland Native Women's Association
PO Box 22, Benoits Cove NL A0L 1A0
Tel: 709-789-3430; *Fax:* 709-789-2207
nf.nativewomen@nf.aibn.com
To enhance, promote & foster the social, economic, cultural and political well-being of First Nations and Métis women within First Nation, Métis and Canadian societies.

Northeastern Alberta Aboriginal Business Association (NAABA)
PO Box 5993, Stn. Main, #100, 425 Gregoire Dr., Fort McMurray AB T9H 4V9
Tel: 780-791-0478; *Fax:* 780-714-6485
admin@naaba.ca
www.naaba.ca
Social Media:
www.facebook.com/203534376346311
twitter.com/NAABA_RMWB
To create partnerships between Aboriginal businesses & industry; to support economic development of Aboriginal people in the Wood Buffalo region
Boyd Madsen, President
Debbie Hahn, General Manager

Northwest Territories/Nunavut Council of Friendship Centres
PO Box 2285, #209, 4817 - 49th St., Yellowknife NT X1A 2P6
Tel: 867-669-7063; *Fax:* 867-669-7064
ntnucfc.wildapricot.org
To assist friendship centres in the Northwest Territories & Nunavut

Nova Scotia Native Women's Society (NSNWA)
PO Box 805, Truro NS B2N 5E8
Tel: 902-893-7402; *Fax:* 902-897-7162
Social Media:
www.facebook.com/nsnwa

Ontario Coalition of Aboriginal Peoples (OCAP)
PO Box 189, Wabigoon ON P0V 2W0
Tel: 807-938-1321
www.o-cap.ca
To represent the rights & interests of Métis, Status & Non-Status Aboriginal peoples living off-reserve in urban, rural or remote areas
Brad Maggrah, President

Ontario Federation of Indian Friendship Centres (OFIFC)
219 Front St. East, Toronto ON M5A 1E8
Tel: 416-956-7575; *Fax:* 416-956-7577
Toll-Free: 800-772-9291
ofifc@ofifc.org
www.ofifc.org
Social Media:
www.facebook.com/TheOFIFC
twitter.com/theofifc
To represent the collective interests of Ontario's friendship centres; To administer programs delivered by friendship centres, such as justice, health, employment, & family support; To improve the quality of life for Aboriginal people for equal access & participation in Canadian society
Sheila McMahon, President

Ontario Native Women's Association (ONWA)
380 Ray Blvd., Thunder Bay ON P7B 4E6
Tel: 807-623-3442; *Fax:* 807-623-1104
Toll-Free: 800-667-0816
www.onwa-tbay.ca
Social Media:
www.facebook.com/onwa7
twitter.com/_onwa_
To foster & promote the economic, social, cultural, & political well-being of First Nations & Métis women in Ontario; To represent Native women on issues that affect their lives
Dawn Harvard, President

Qalipu Mi'kmaq First Nations Band
3 Church St., Corner Brook NL A2H 6J3
Tel: 709-634-0996; *Fax:* 709-639-3997
Toll-Free: 800-561-2266
qalipu.ca
Annie Randell, Chief Executive Officer

Quaker Aboriginal Affairs Committee (QAAC)
c/o Canadian Friends Service Committee, 60 Lowther Ave., Toronto ON M5R 1C7
Tel: 416-920-5213; *Fax:* 416-920-5214
quakerservice.ca
Support for Aboriginal fights & justice, public education & campaigns
Jennifer Preston, Program Coordinator

Red Road HIV/AIDS Network (RRHAN)
#61-1959 Marine Dr., North Vancouver BC V7P 3G1
Tel: 778-340-3388; *Fax:* 778-340-3328
info@red-road.org
www.red-road.org
Social Media:
twitter.com/RRHAN
The Red Road HIV/AIDS Network works to reduce or prevent the spread of HIV/AIDS; improve the health and wellness of Aboriginal people living with HIV/AIDS; and increase awareness about HIV/AIDS and establish a network which supports the development and delivery of culturally appropriate, innovative, coordinated, accessible, inclusive and accountable HIV/AIDS programs and services
Kim Louie, Executive Director
Heidi Standeven, Provincial Coordinator

Regroupement des centres d'amitié autochtone du Québec (RCAAQ)
#100, 85, boul Maurice-Bastien, Wendake QC G0A 4V0
Tél: 418-842-6354; *Téléc:* 418-842-9795
Ligne sans frais: 877-842-6354
infos@rcaaq.info
www.rcaaq.info
Média social: www.youtube.com/rcaaq
www.facebook.com/RCAAQ
twitter.com/rcaaq
Etre la voix provinciale des centres existants ou en voie de développement et de leurs communautés; appuyer ses membres dans l'atteinte de leurs objectifs; favoriser leur concertation et les représenter collectivement pour qu'ils remplissent au mieux leur mandat
Tanya Sirois, Directrice générale

Saskatchewan Aboriginal Women's Circle Corporation
PO Box 1174, Yorkton SK S3N 2X3
Tel: 306-783-1228; *Fax:* 306-783-1771
communications@sawcc.sk.ca
www.sawcc.sk.ca
To walk in balance with guidance by the creator; to unite people together as healthy nations to ensure a better life for future generations
Judy Hughes, President

2-Spirited People of the First Nations (TPFN)
#105, 145 Front St. East, Toronto ON M5A 1E3
Tel: 416-944-9300; *Fax:* 416-944-8381
www.2spirits.com
Social Media: www.instagram.com/2spirits_com
www.facebook.com/2spiritsTO
To create a place where Aboriginal 2-Spirited people can grow & learn together as a community, fostering a positive, self-sufficient image, honouring our past & building a future; to work together toward bridging the gap between the 2-Spirited, Lesbian, Gay, Bisexual & Transgendered community & our Aboriginal identity
Art Zoccole, Executive Director

Union of British Columbia Indian Chiefs
#500, 342 Water St., Vancouver BC V6B 1B6
Tel: 604-684-0231; *Fax:* 604-684-5726
ubcic@ubcic.bc.ca
www.ubcic.bc.ca
Social Media: www.youtube.com/UBCIC
www.facebook.com/UBCIC
twitter.com/UBCIC
To settle land claims & aboriginal rights in BC; to improve the social, economic, health, education of Aboriginal people in BC; to provide a political voice for Aboriginal people in BC
Stewart Phillip, President

Union of Nova Scotia Indians (UNSI)
47 Maillard St., Membertou NS B1S 2P5
Tel: 902-539-4107; *Fax:* 902-564-2137
rec@unsi.ns.ca
www.unsi.ns.ca

To promote welfare & progress of Native people in Nova Scotia; to liaise with all Native people on relevant issues; to defend & advise on Native rights; to cooperate with Native & non-Native agencies & organizations to the benefit of Nova Scotia Native people
Joe B. Marshall, Executive Director

Union of Ontario Indians (UOI)
Nipissing First Nation, 1 Miigizi Mikan, North Bay ON P1B 8J8
Tel: 705-497-9127; *Fax:* 705-497-9135
Toll-Free: 877-702-5200
info@anishinabek.ca
www.anishinabek.ca
Social Media: www.youtube.com/user/AnishinabekNation
www.facebook.com/AnishinabekNation
twitter.com/anishnation
To represent 42 First Nations throughout the province of Ontario from Golden Lake in the east, Sarnia in the south, Thunder Bay & Lake Nipigon in the north
Patrick Madahbee, Grand Council Chief
Gordon Waindubence, Grand Council Elder

United Native Nations Society
#6, 534 Cedar St., Campbell River BC V9W 2V6
Tel: 250-287-9249
administration@unitednativenation510.com
www.unitednativenation510.com
Bill Williams, Contact

Yukon Aboriginal Women's Council
#202, 307 Jarvis St., Whitehorse YT Y1A 2H3
Tel: 867-667-6162; *Fax:* 867-668-7539
admin@yawc.ca
yawc.ca
To create equal opportunities for Aboriginal women by implementing programs aimed to improving their quality of life
Marian Horne, President

Naturalists

Avicultural Advancement Council of Canada (AACC)
c/o #109, 1633 Hillside Ave., Victoria BC VBT 2C4
www.aacc.ca
To establish & maintain a national association of interested societies & individuals to promote the advancement of aviculture in Canada; To represent the Canadian avicultural community internationally; To disseminate information; to support recognized expert aviculturalists; To assist all levels of government in preparing informed legislation & policy relating to aviculture; To establish standards for the exhibition of birds in Canada; To provide a national identification leg band registry; To establish an avian species preservation program in Canada
Dunstan H. Browne, President
Denise Antler, Ring Registrar

British Columbia Nature (Federation of British Columbia Naturalists) (FBCN)
c/o Parks Heritage Centre, 1620 Mount Seymour Rd., North Vancouver BC V7G 2R9
Tel: 604-985-3057
manager@bcnature.ca
www.bcnature.ca
To protect biodiversity, species at risk, & natural areas throughout British Columbia; To present a unified voice on conservation & environmental issues
Betty Davison, Office Manager
Bev Ramey, President
Rosemary Fox, Chair, Conservation
Elisa Kreller, Treasurer
Maria Hamann, Office Manager
Joan Snyder, Chair, Education
Pat Westheuser, Chair, Awards

British Columbia Waterfowl Society
5191 Robertson Rd., RR#1, Delta BC V4K 3N2
Tel: 604-946-6980
www.reifelbirdsanctuary.com/bcws2.html
To encourage conservation of wetlands; to spur public awareness on importance of conservation of estuaries; to operate George C. Reifel Migratory Bird Sanctuary.
Kathleen Fry, Manager
Jack Bates, President

Canadian Biomaterials Society (CSB) / Société canadienne des biomatériaux (SCB)
www.biomaterials.ca
Social Media:
linkedin.com/groups/Canadian-Biomaterials-Society-Societe-Canadien
To develop biomaterials science, technology, & education in Canadian industries, universities, & governments
Diego Mantovani, Representative, International Union of Societies - Biomaterials Science/Engineeri
Ze Zhang, Representative, International Union of Societies - Biomaterials Science/Engineeri
Rosalind Labow, Treasurer
Lauren Flynn, Secretary

Jack Miner Migratory Bird Foundation, Inc.
PO Box 39, 360 RR#3 WeEst, Kingsville ON N9Y 2E5
Tel: 519-733-4034; *Toll-Free:* 877-289-8328
info@jackminer.com
www.jackminer.com
Social Media:
www.facebook.com/JackMinerMigratoryBirdSanctuary
The sanctuary provides food, shelter & protection to migratory water fowl, tags birds & tracks migration patterns
Kirk W. Miner, Executive Director

Natural History Society of Newfoundland & Labrador
PO Box 1013, St. John's NL A1C 5M3
naturenl@naturenl.ca
naturenl.ca
Social Media:
www.facebook.com/128262310581874
To promote the enjoyment & protection of all wildlife and natural history resources in the Province of Newfoundland & Labrador & surrounding waters.
Dave Innes, Secretary

Nature Alberta
Percy Page Centre, 11759 Groat Rd., 3rd Fl., Edmonton AB T5M 3K6
Tel: 780-427-8124; *Fax:* 780-422-2663
info@naturealberta.ca
naturealberta.ca
Social Media: www.youtube.com/user/naturealberta
www.facebook.com/NatureAB
twitter.com/naturealberta
To encourage Albertans to increase knowledge & understanding of natural history & ecological processes; to provide a unified voice for naturalists on conservation issues; to organize field meetings, conferences, nature camps, research symposia, & other activities.
Petra Rowell, Executive Director

Nature Canada / Canada Nature
#300, 75 Albert St., Ottawa ON K1P 5E7
Tel: 613-562-3447; *Toll-Free:* 800-267-4088
info@naturecanada.ca
www.naturecanada.ca
Social Media: www.youtube.com/user/NatureCanada1;
www.pinterest.com/NatureCanada
linkedin.com/company/nature-canada
www.facebook.com/NatureCanada
twitter.com/NatureCanada
To protect & conserve wildlife & habitats throughout Canada
Eleanor Fast, Executive Director
Stephen Hazell, Director, Conservation & General Counsel
Jodi Joy, Director, Development

Nature Manitoba
Hammond Building, #401, 63 Albert St., Winnipeg MB R3B 1G4
Tel: 204-943-9029; *Fax:* 204-943-9029
info@naturemanitoba.ca
www.naturemanitoba.ca
Social Media:
www.facebook.com/pages/Nature-Manitoba/67945358869
To foster the popular & scientific study of nature; To preserve the natural environment; To act as a voice for people interested in the outdoors & natural history
Roger Turenne, President
Donald Himbeault, Executive Vice-President
Alain Louer, Secretary
Sean Worden, Treasurer
Susan McLarty, Office Administrator

Nature NB
#110, 924 Prospect St., Fredericton NB E3B 2T9
Tel: 506-459-4209; *Fax:* 506-459-4209
nbfn@nb.aibn.com
www.naturenb.ca
Social Media:
www.facebook.com/naturenb
twitter.com/NatureNB
To preserve wildlife & protect its natural habitat; to promote a public interest in & a knowledge of natural history; to promote, encourage & cooperate with organizations & individuals who have similar interests & objectives; to consider matters of environmental concern.
Danielle Smith, Executive Director

Nature Nova Scotia (Federation of Nova Scotia Naturalists)
c/o Nova Scotia Museum of Natural History, 1747 Summer St., Halifax NS B3H 3A6
Tel: 902-582-7176
doug@fundymud.com
www.naturens.ca
To support the interests of naturalists clubs; To represent naturalists clubs throughout Nova Scotia
Bob Bancroft, President
Sue Abbot, Vice-President
Doug Linzey, Secretary
Jean Gibson, Treasurer

Nature Québec
#207, 870, av de Salaberry, Québec QC G1R 2T9
Tél: 418-648-2104; *Téléc:* 418-648-0991
conservons@naturequebec.org
www.naturequebec.org
Média social:
linkedin.com/company/nature-qu-bec?trx=hb_tab_compy_id_2794658
www.facebook.com/naturequebec
twitter.com/NatureQuebec
Regrouper les individus et les sociétés oeuvrant en sciences naturelles et en environnement; maintenir des processus écologiques essentiels; préserver la diversité génétique; utiliser soutenablement des espèces et des écosystèmes
Christian Simard, Directeur général

Nature Saskatchewan
#206, 1860 Lorne St., Regina SK S4P 2L7
Tel: 306-780-9273; *Fax:* 306-780-9263
Toll-Free: 800-667-4668
info@naturesask.ca
www.naturesask.ca
Social Media:
linkedin.com/pub/nature-sask-gary-seib/38/7b6/39a
www.facebook.com/NatureSask
twitter.com/naturesask
To foster appreciation & understanding for the natural environment; To document & protect the biological diversity of Saskatchewan; To preserve the natural eco-systems of the province
Gary Seib, General Manager
Deanna Trowsdale-Mutafov, Manager, Conservation & Education
Melissa Ranalli, Manager, Species at Risk
Ellen Bouvier, Office Coordinator

Ontario Nature
#612, 214 King St. West, Toronto ON M5H 3S6
Tel: 416-444-8419; *Fax:* 416-444-9866
Toll-Free: 800-440-2366
info@ontarionature.org
www.ontarionature.org
Social Media: www.youtube.com/user/ONNature
www.facebook.com/OntarioNature?ref=ts
twitter.com/ontarionature
To promote knowledge, understanding & respect for Ontario's natural heritage & commitment to its conservation & protection on the part of the FON membership, landowners, decision makers & the general public; To seek legislation, policies, practices & institutions which permanently protect Ontario's natural ecosystem & indigenous biodiversity, including the establishment of a comprehensive natural heritage system for Ontario with an enlarged system of parks & other protected areas linked by a network of existing & rehabilitated natural corridors
Angela Martin, President
Caroline Schultz, Executive Director

Society of Canadian Ornithologists (SCO) / Société des ornithologistes du Canada (SOC)
C/O Lance Laviolette, Membership Secretary, 22350 County Rd. 10, RR #1, Glen Robertson ON KOB 1H0
www.sco-soc.ca
To support research to understand & conserve Canadian birds; To represent Canadian ornithologists
Greg Robertson, President
Lance Laviolette, Membership Secretary

Newspapers

National NewsMedia Council (NNC)
#200, 890 Yonge St., Toronto ON M4W 3P4
Tel: 416-340-1981; *Toll-Free:* 844-877-1163
info@mediacouncil.ca
www.mediacouncil.ca
To promote ethical practice in the news media industry; To serve as a forum for complains against its member news

organizations; To represent the rights of the public in regards to free speech & freedom of the media
John Fraser, President & Chief Executive Officer
Don McCurdy, Coordinator, Complaints

Nursing

Academy of Canadian Executive Nurses (ACEN)
#400, 331 Cooper St., Ottawa ON K2P 0G5
Tel: 613-235-3033
www.acen.ca
To advance nursing practice, education, research, & leadership; To work in partnership with other national organizations to influence health policy & set direction of healthcare in Canada to assure quality of care to Canadians
Lori Lamont, President

Alberta Gerontological Nurses Association (AGNA)
PO Box 67040, Stn. Meadowlark, Edmonton AB T5R 5Y3
info@agna.ca
www.agna.ca
Social Media:
twitter.com/AGNAtweets
To promote a high standard of nursing care & related health services for older adults; To enhance professionalism in the practice of gerontological nursing
Lynne Moulton, President

British Columbia Nurses' Union (BCNU) / Syndicat des infirmières de la Colombie-Britannique
4060 Regent St., Burnaby BC V5C 6P5
Tel: 604-433-2268; *Fax:* 604-433-7945
Toll-Free: 800-663-9991
www.bcnu.org
Social Media: www.youtube.com/user/TheBCNursesUnion
linkedin.com/company/british-columbia-nurses'-union
www.facebook.com/OurNursesMatter
twitter.com/BCNursesUnion
To defend nurses' individual rights & the rights of the nursing profession as a whole; To protect & advance the well-being of members & the community at large
Gayle Duteil, President

Canadian Association for Nursing Research (CANR) / Association canadienne pour la recherche infirmière
c/o Caroline Park, Athabasca University, Faculty of Health Disciplines, 1 University Dr., Athabasca AB T9S 3A3
www.canr.ca
To foster practice-based nursing research & research-based nursing practice across Canada
Caroline Park, President
Pam Hawranik, Secretary
Riek van den Berg, Treasurer

Canadian Association for the History of Nursing (CAHN) / Association canadienne pour l'histoire du nursing
c/o Jayne Elliot, School of Nursing, University of Ottawa, 451 Smyth Rd., Ottawa ON K1H 8M5
www.cahn-achn.ca
To promote interest in the history of nursing; To develop scholarship in the field
Margaret Scaia, President
Lydia Wytenbroek, Vice-President

Canadian Association of Burn Nurses (CABN) / Association canadienne des infirmières et infirmiers en soins aux brûlés
c/o Judy Sleith, 6483 - 68 St. NE, Calgary AB T3J 2N7
www.cabn.ca
Social Media:
www.facebook.com/canadianburnnurses
To provide education related to burn care; To research & develop national burn standards; To promote & support nurses & other care providers
Nora-Gene Goodwin, President
Catherine McAndie, Vice-President
Judy Knighton, Treasurer

Canadian Association of Foot Care Nurses (CAFCN)
c/o Pat MacDonald, President, 110 Linden Park Bay, Winnipeg MB R2R 1Y3
www.cafcn.ca
To advance the practice of foot care through a collaborative and networking process for all individuals providing foot care.
Pat MacDonald, President

Canadian Association of Nephrology Nurses & Technologists (CANNT) / Association canadienne des infirmières et infirmiers et technologues de néphrologie (ACITN)
PO Box 10, 59 Millmanor Place, Delaware ON N0L 1E0
Tel: 519-652-6767; *Fax:* 519-652-5015
Toll-Free: 877-720-2819
cannt@cannt.ca
www.cannt.ca
Social Media:
www.facebook.com/160999717295820
twitter.com/CANNT1
To improve the care of renal patients through support of educational opportunities for association members; To evaluate the performance & competence of nephrology nurses & technologists against the CANNT Standards of Practice
Anne Moulton, RN, CNeph(C), President
Melanie Wiggins, Treasurer & Coordinator, Website

Canadian Association of Neuroscience Nurses (CANN) / Association canadienne des infirmiers et infirmières en sciences neurologiques (ACIISN)
c/o Aline Mayer, Membership Chairperson, CANN, 30 Chantilly Gate, Stittsville ON K2S 2B1
canninfo@cann.ca
www.cann.ca
To prevent illness & to improve health outcomes for people with, or at risk for, neurological disorders; To establish standards of practice for neuroscience nurses
Sandra Bérubé, President
Deb Holtom, Vice-President & Secretary
Mark Bonin, Treasurer
Aline Mayer, Chair, Membership

Canadian Association of Nurses in HIV/AIDS Care (CANAC) / Association canadienne des infirmières et infirmiers en sidologie
St. Paul's Hospital, #B552, 1081 Burrard St., Vancouver BC V6Z 1Y6
admin@canac.org
www.canac.org
The Canadian Association of Nurses in AIDS Care (CANAC) is a national professional nursing organization committed to fostering excellence in HIV/AIDS nursing, promoting the health, rights and dignity of persons affected by HIV/AIDS and to preventing the spread of HIV infection.
Janna Campbell, Executive Assistant

Canadian Association of Nurses in Oncology (CANO) / Association canadienne des infirmières en oncologie (ACIO)
#201, 375 West 5th Ave., Vancouver BC V5Y 1J6
Tel: 604-874-4322; *Fax:* 604-874-4378
cano@malachite-mgmt.com
www.cano-acio.ca
Social Media: www.youtube.com/user/CANOACIO
www.facebook.com/336467099484
twitter.com/CANO_ACIO
To advocate for improved cancer care for all Canadians.
Barbara Fitzgerald, President
Ana Torres, Executive Director

Canadian Council of Cardiovascular Nurses (CCCN) / Conseil canadien des infirmières et infirmiers en nursing cardiovasculaire (CCINC)
#202, 300 March Rd., Ottawa ON K2K 2E2
Tel: 613-599-9210; *Fax:* 613-595-1155
info@cccn.ca
www.cccn.ca
Social Media:
www.facebook.com/124535634406687
To promote & maintain high standards of cardiovascular nursing through education, research, health promotion, strategic alliances, & advocacy
David Miriguay, Executive Director

Canadian Council of Practical Nurse Regulators (CCPNR)
c/o College of Licensed Practical Nurses of Newfoundland and Labrador, 9 Paton St., St. John's NL A1B 4S8
Tel: 709-579-3843; *Fax:* 709-579-3095
www.ccpnr.ca
Responsible for the safety of the public through the regulation of Licensed/Registered Practical Nurses.
Paul D. Fisher, Chair

Canadian Federation of Mental Health Nurses (CFMHN) / Fédération canadienne des infirmières et infirmiers en santé mentale
#109, 1 Concorde Gate, Toronto ON M3C 3N6
Tel: 416-426-7029; *Fax:* 416-426-7280
info@cfmhn.ca
www.cfmhn.ca
Social Media:
twitter.com/CFMHN
The CFMHN is a national voice for psychiatric and mental health (PMH) nursing. They wish to assure leadership in the development and application of nursing standards that inform and affect psychiatric and mental health nursing practice; examine and influence government policy, and address national issues related to mental health and mental illness; communicate and collaborate with national and international groups that share our professional interests; faciliate excellence in psychiatric and mental health nursing by providing members with educational and networking resources.
Chris Davis, President

Canadian Gerontological Nursing Association (CGNA) / Association canadienne des infirmières et infirmiers en gérontologie
#1202, 71 Charles St. East, Toronto ON M4Y 2T3
Tel: 416-927-8654; *Fax:* 604-874-4378
cgna@malachite-mgmt.com
www.cgna.net
To promote high standards of gerontological nursing practice; to promote educational programs in gerontological nursing; to participate in affairs which promote the health of elderly persons; to promote networking opportunities for nurses; to promote & disseminate gerontological nursing research; to present the views of the Association to government, education, professional & other appropriate bodies.
Lynn McCleary, RN, PhD, President

Canadian Holistic Nurses Association (CHNA) / Association canadienne des infirmières en soins holistiques
www.chna.ca
Social Media:
www.facebook.com/CHNA.ca
To further the development of holistic nursing practice; To promote CHNA standards of practice
Linda Turner, President
Jane Aitken-Herring, Secretary
Susan Morris, Acting Contact, Membership

Canadian Nurse Continence Advisors Association (CNCA)
c/o Jennifer Skelly, St. Joseph's Healthcare, King Campus, 2757 King St. East, Hamilton ON L8G 5E4
Tel: 905-573-4823
www.cnca.ca
To protect the quality standard associated with being an NCA
Jennifer Skelly, President

Canadian Nurses Association (CNA) / Association des infirmières et infirmiers du Canada
50 Driveway, Ottawa ON K2P 1E2
Tel: 613-680-0879; *Fax:* 613-237-3520
Toll-Free: 844-204-0124
info@cna-aiic.ca
www.cna-aiic.ca/en
Social Media: www.youtube.com/user/CNAVideos
www.facebook.com/cnf.fiic
twitter.com/theCNF
To advance the discipline of nursing; to advocate for public policy that incorporates the principles of primary health care & respects the principles, conditions & spirit of the Canada Health Act; To advance the regulation of Registered Nurses in the interest of the public; To advance international health policy & development in Canada
Karima A. Velji, President
Anne Sutherland Boal, CEO
Joanne Lauzon, Director, Finance and Administration

Canadian Nurses Foundation (CNF) / Fondation des infirmières et infirmiers du Canada
50 Driveway, Ottawa ON K2P 1E2
Tel: 613-237-2133; *Fax:* 613-237-3520
Toll-Free: 800-361-8404
info@cnf-fiic.ca
www.cnf-fiic.ca
Social Media:
www.facebook.com/CNA.AIIC
twitter.com/canadanurses
To promote the health of Canadians by enhancing nursing education & research.
Christine Rieck Buckley, Executive Director

Canadian Nurses Protective Society (CNPS) / Société de protection des infirmières et infirmiers du Canada (SPIIC)
#510, 1545 Carling Ave., Ottawa ON K1Z 8P9
Tel: 613-237-2092; *Fax:* 613-237-6300
Toll-Free: 800-267-3390
info@cnps.ca
www.cnps.ca
To offer legal liability protection related to nursing practice to eligible Registered Nurses
Chantal Léonard, CEO

Canadian Occupational Health Nurses Association (COHNA) / Association canadienne des infirmières et infirmiers en santé du travail (ACIIST)
karen.mazerolle@imperialgroup.ca
www.cohna-aciist.ca
To promote national standards for occupational health nursing practice; to advance the profession by providing a national forum for the exchange of ideas & concerns; to enhance the profile of occupational health nurses; to improve the health & safety of workers; to contribute to the health of the community by providing quality health services to workers; to encourage continuing education
Karen Mazerolle, President
Marg Creen, Secretary/Treasurer
Ellen Coe, Vice President

Canadian Orthopaedic Nurses Association (CONA) / Association canadienne des infirmières et infirmiers en orthopédie
2035 Rosealle In, West Kelowna BC V1Z 3Z5
Tel: 250-769-3640
www.cona-nurse.org
To foster professional growth of the membership in the assessment, treatment & rehabilitation of individuals with neuromuscular & skeletal alterations; to promote nursing research related to orthopaedics
Angela Dunklee-Clark, President

Canadian Vascular Access Association (CVAA) / Association canadienne d'Accès Vasculaire
PO Box 68030, 753 Main St. East, Hamilton ON L8M 3M7
Tel: 289-396-8824; *Fax:* 289-396-1624
cvaa@cvaa.info
www.cvaa.info
Social Media:
www.facebook.com/165776480198722
To establish & promote standards of intravenous therapy to enhance patient care & safety
Jocelyn Hill, President
Melissa McQueen, Executive Director

The College & Association of Registered Nurses of Alberta (CARNA)
11620 - 168 St., Edmonton AB T5M 4A6
Tel: 780-451-0043; *Fax:* 780-452-3276
Toll-Free: 800-252-9392
carna@nurses.ab.ca
www.nurses.ab.ca
Social Media: www.youtube.com/carnavideo
www.facebook.com/albertarns
twitter.com/albertarns
To set nursing practice standards & to ensure Albertans receive safe, competent, & ethical nursing services
Shannon Spenceley, President

College of Licensed Practical Nurses of Alberta (CLPNA)
13163 - 146 St., Edmonton AB T5L 4S8
Tel: 780-484-8886; *Fax:* 780-484-9069
Toll-Free: 800-661-5877
info@clpna.com
www.clpna.com
Social Media: www.youtube.com/clpna
linkedin.com/company/college-of-licensed-practical-nurses-of-alberta
www.facebook.com/CLPNA
twitter.com/clpna
To regulate & lead the profession in a manner that protects & serves the public through excellence in Practical Nursing.
Linda L. Stanger, Executive Director/Registrar

College of Licensed Practical Nurses of BC (CLPNBC)
#260, 3480 Gilmore Way, Burnaby BC V5G 4Y1
Tel: 778-373-3101; *Fax:* 778-373-3102
Toll-Free: 877-373-2201
info@clpnbc.org
www.clpnbc.org
To regulate practical nursing in the public interest

College of Licensed Practical Nurses of Manitoba (CLPNM)
463 St. Anne's Rd., Winnipeg MB R2M 3C9
Tel: 204-663-1212; *Fax:* 204-663-1207
Toll-Free: 877-663-1212
www.clpnm.ca
The governing body for the Licensed Practical Nurses in Manitoba. The College's duty is to carry out its activities and govern its members in a manner that serves and protects the public interest. The College establishes requirements to enter the profession and assures the quality of the practice of LPNs through the development and enforcement of standards and practice and continuing competence programs.
Jennifer Breton, LPN, RN, BN, Executive Director
Barb Palz, Business Manager

College of Licensed Practical Nurses of Newfoundland & Labrador (CLPNNL)
9 Paton St., St. John's NL A1B 4S8
Tel: 709-579-3843; *Fax:* 709-579-8268
Toll-Free: 888-579-2576
info@clpnnl.ca
www.clpnnl.ca
To regulate the practice of Licensed Practical Nurses in Nnewfound & Labrador; to promote safety and protection of the general public through the provision of safe, competent and ethical nursing care.
Paul D. Fisher, Executive Director/Registrar

College of Licensed Practical Nurses of Nova Scotia (CLPNNS)
Starlite Gallery, #302, 7071 Bayers Rd., Halifax NS B3L 2C2
Tel: 902-423-8517; *Fax:* 902-425-6811
Toll-Free: 800-718-8517
www.clpnns.ca
To represent licensed practical nurses within the health care system; to protect the public by providing safe, competent nursing care.
Ann Mann, Executive Director/Registrar

College of Nurses of Ontario (CNO) / Ordre des infirmières et infirmiers de l'Ontario
101 Davenport Rd., Toronto ON M5R 3P1
Tel: 416-928-0900; *Fax:* 416-928-6507
Toll-Free: 800-387-5526
www.cno.org
Social Media: www.youtube.com/user/cnometrics
linkedin.com/company/college-of-nurses-of-ontario
www.facebook.com/collegeofnurses
To protect the public's right to quality nursing services by providing leadership to the nursing profession in self-regulation
Anne Coghlan, Executive Director

College of Registered Nurses of British Columbia (CRNBC)
2855 Arbutus St., Vancouver BC V6J 3Y8
Tel: 604-736-7331; *Fax:* 604-738-2272
Toll-Free: 800-565-6505
info@crnbc.ca
www.crnbc.ca
Social Media:
www.facebook.com/CRNBC
twitter.com/CRNBC
To provide safe & appropriate nursing practice regulated by nurses in the public interest; To promote good practice, prevent poor practice & intervene when practice is unacceptable
Cynthia Johansen, CEO/Registrar
Mary Kjorven, Chair

College of Registered Nurses of Manitoba (CRNM)
890 Pembina Hwy., Winnipeg MB R3M 2M8
Tel: 204-774-3477; *Fax:* 204-775-6052
Toll-Free: 800-665-2027
info@crnm.mb.ca
www.crnm.mb.ca
Social Media:
www.facebook.com/collegeofrnsmb
To regulate the practice of registered nurses & to advance the quality of nursing to protect the public interest
Katherine Stansfield, Executive Director
Tammy Murdoch, Director, Registration Services
Kristin Hancock, Manager, Communications

College of Registered Nurses of Nova Scotia (CRNNS)
#4005, 7071 Bayers Rd., Halifax NS B3L 2C2
Tel: 902-491-9744; *Fax:* 902-491-9510
Toll-Free: 800-565-9744
info@crnns.ca
www.crnns.ca
Registered nurses regulating their profession to promote excellence in nursing practice.
Sue Smith, CEO & Registrar

College of Registered Psychiatric Nurses of Alberta
#201, 9711 - 45 Ave., Edmonton AB T6E 5V8
Tel: 780-434-7666; *Fax:* 780-436-4165
Toll-Free: 877-234-7666
crpna@crpna.ab.ca
www.crpna.ab.ca
To protect & servce the public interest by ensuring members provide safe, competent and ethical practice; to address the needs of members and the public through education, regulation, advocacy.
Chris Watkins, President
Barbara Lowe, Executive Director

College of Registered Psychiatric Nurses of British Columbia
#307, 2502 St. Johns St., Port Moody BC V3H 2B4
Tel: 604-931-5200; *Fax:* 604-931-5277
Toll-Free: 800-565-2505
www.crpnbc.ca
To serve & protect the public; to assure a safe, accountable & ethical level of psychiatric nursing practice
Dorothy Jennings, Chair
Kyong-ae Kim, Executive Director & Registrar

College of Registered Psychiatric Nurses of Manitoba (CRPNM)
1854 Portage Ave., Winnipeg MB R3J 0G9
Tel: 204-888-4841; *Fax:* 204-888-8638
www.crpnm.mb.ca
To ensure that members of the profession provide safe & effective psychiatric nursing services to the public of Manitoba, in accordance with the Registered Psychiatric Nurses Act
Laura Panteluk, Executive Director

Community Health Nurses of Canada (CHNC) / Infirmières et infirmiers en santé communautaire au Canada
75 New Cove Rd., Toronto ON A1A 2C2
Tel: 709-738-3541
info@chnc.ca
www.chnc.ca
Social Media:
www.facebook.com/250569078355380
To act as the voice of community health nurses across Canada; To respond to issues which affect community health nurses
Ann Manning, Executive Director
Cheryl Reid-Haughian, Secretary
Karen Curry, Officer, Communications

Corporation des infirmières et infirmiers de salle d'opération du Québec (CIISOQ)
CP 63, 10, Place du Commerce, Brossard QC J4W 3L7
info@ciisoq.ca
www.ciisoq.ca
Média social: facebook.com/ciisoq
Philippe Willame, Président

Fédération de la santé du Québec - CSQ (FSQ-CSQ)
9405, rue Sherbrooke Est, Montréal QC H1L 6P3
Tél: 514-356-8888; *Téléc:* 514-667-5590
fsq@csq.qc.net
www.fsq.lacsq.org
La FSQ assure la représentation de ses membres, donne aux syndicats une structure politique et fournit, en collaboration avec la CSQ, des services aux membres en matière de relations de travail, de professionnel, de négociation et de formation
Claire Montour, Présidente

Fédération interprofessionnelle de la santé du Québec (FIQ)
1234, av Papineau, Montréal QC H2K 0A4
Tél: 514-987-1141; *Téléc:* 514-987-7273
Ligne sans frais: 800-363-6541
info@fiqsante.qc.ca
www.fiqsante.qc.ca
Média social: www.youtube.com/FIQSante
www.facebook.com/FIQSante
WWW.twitter.com/FIQSante
Améliorer les conditions de travail des infirmières, infirmiers & cardiorespiratoires; s'associer aux luttes des femmes et être présente dans les débats concernant les orientations du système de santé
Régine Laurent, Présidente

Gerontological Nursing Association of British Columbia (GNABC)
c/o 328 Nootka St., New Westminster BC V3L 4X4
Tel: 604-484-5698; *Fax:* 604-874-4378
gnabc@shaw.ca
gnabc.com
To promote a high standard of nursing care & related health services for older adults; To enhance professionalism in the practice of gerontological nursing

Kim Martin, President

Gerontological Nursing Association of Ontario (GNAO)
PO Box 368, Stn. K, Toronto ON M4P 2E0
info@gnaontario.org
www.gnaontario.org
To promote a high standard of nursing care & related health services for older adults; To enhance professionalism in the practice of gerontological nursing
Julie Rubel, President
Gwen Harris, Treasurer

Licensed Practical Nurses Association & Regulatory Board of PEI
#204, 155 Belvedere Ave., Charlottetown PE C1A 2Y9
Tel: 902-566-1512; *Fax:* 902-892-6315
info@lpna.ca
www.lpna.ca
To represent practical nurses within the health care system
Alana Essery, Executive Director/Registrar

Manitoba Gerontological Nurses' Association (MGNA)
c/o Leslie Dryburgh, 300 Booth Dr., Winnipeg MB R3J 3M7
Tel: 204-831-2547
info@mbgna.com
mbgna.ca
To promote a high standard of nursing care & related health services for older adults; To enhance professionalism in the practice of gerontological nursing
Poh Lin Lim, President

Manitoba Nurses' Union (MNU) / Syndicat des infirmières du Manitoba
#301, 275 Broadway, Winnipeg MB R3C 4M6
Tel: 204-942-1320; *Fax:* 204-942-0958
Toll-Free: 800-665-0043
manitobanurses.ca
Social Media: www.youtube.com/user/mbnursesunion
www.facebook.com/ManitobaNurses
twitter.com/ManitobaNurses
To represent & support all categories of licensed nurses in Manitoba; To safeguard the role of nurses in the health care system of Manitoba
Sandi Mowat, President
Kirsten Andersson, Director, Labour Relations
Bill Crawford, Director, Communications & Government Relations
Janice Grift, Director, Operations

Manitoba Operating Room Nurses Association (MORNA)
MB
Karen Sagness, President

National Emergency Nurses Affiliation (NENA) / Affiliation des infirmières et infirmiers d'urgence
112 Old River Rd., RR#2, Mallorytown ON K0E 1R0
www.nena.ca
Social Media:
www.facebook.com/103455173059386
To represent the Canadian emergency nursing specialty.
Landon James, President

New Brunswick Nurses Union (NBNU) / Syndicat des infirmières et infirmiers du Nouveau-Brunswick (SIINB)
103 Woodside Lane, Fredericton NB E3C 2R9
Tel: 506-453-0820; *Fax:* 506-453-0828
Toll-Free: 800-442-4914
nbnu1@nbnu.ca
www.nbnu.ca
Social Media:
www.facebook.com/212365802133370
twitter.com/NBNU_SIINB
To enhance the social, economic, and general worklife of nurses and their vision is NBNU as a professional, credible, and respected voice advocating for nurses and quality health care.
David Brown, Executive Director
Marilyn Quinn, President

New Brunswick Operating Room Nurses (NBORN)
NB
Charlotte Roach, President

Newfoundland & Labrador Nurses' Union (NLNU) / Syndicat des infirmières de Terre-Neuve et du Labrador
PO Box 416, 229 Major's Path, St. John's NL A1C 5J9
Tel: 709-753-9961; *Fax:* 709-753-1210
Toll-Free: 800-563-5100
info@nlnu.ca
www.nlnu.ca
Social Media: www.youtube.com/user/RNUNL
www.facebook.com/rnunl
John Vivian, Executive Director
Karyn Whelan, Communications Specialist

Newfoundland and Labrador Operating Room Nurses Association (N&LORNA)
NL
Margot Walsh, President

Nova Scotia Gerontological Nurses Association (NSGNA)
PO Box 33101, Stn. Quinpool, Halifax NS B3L 4T6
ssavage@ssdha.nshealth.ca
www.nsgna.com
To promote a high standard of nursing care & related health services for older adults; To enhance professionalism in the practice of gerontological nursing
Sohani Welcher, President

Nova Scotia Nurses' Union (NSNU)
30 Frazee Ave., Dartmouth NS B3B 1X4
Tel: 902-469-1474; *Fax:* 902-466-6935
Toll-Free: 800-469-1474
www.nsnu.ns.ca
Social Media: www.youtube.com/user/NSNursesUnion
twitter.com/TheNSNU
To represent Registered Nurses & Licensed Practical Nurses working in acute and long term care, with the VON and Canadian Blood Services
Jean Candy, Executive Director
Janet Hazelton, President

Nurses Association of New Brunswick (NANB) / Association des infirmières et infirmiers du Nouveau-Brunswick (AIINB)
165 Regent St., Fredericton NB E3B 7B4
Tel: 506-458-8731; *Fax:* 506-459-2838
Toll-Free: 800-442-4417
www.nanb.nb.ca
To act as the professional voice & regulatory body of nursing in New Brunswick; To protect the public by maintaining standards for nursing education & practice
France Marquis, President
Roxanne Tarjan, Executive Director

Ontario Nurses' Association (ONA) / Association des infirmières et infirmiers de l'Ontario
#400, 85 Grenville St., Toronto ON M5S 3A2
Tel: 416-964-8833; *Fax:* 416-964-8864
Toll-Free: 800-387-5580
onamail@ona.org
www.ona.org
Social Media: www.youtube.com/OntarioNurses
www.facebook.com/OntarioNurses
twitter.com/ontarionurses
To improve the socio-economic welfare of members
Linda Haslam-Stroud, President
Marie Kelly, Interim CEO/Chief Administrative Office

Operating Room Nurses Association of Canada (ORNAC) / Association des infirmières et infirmiers de salles d'opération du Canada
info@ornac.ca
www.ornac.ca
Social Media:
www.facebook.com/491656354213298
To promote operating nursing for the betterment of surgical patient care
Rupinder Khotar, President
Liz Beck, RN, CPN(C), Treasurer
Catherine Harley, Executive Director

Operating Room Nurses Association of Nova Scotia (ORNANS)
NS
www.ornans.ca
Ida Berry, President

Operating Room Nurses Association of Ontario (ORNAO)
ON
info@ornao.org
www.ornao.org
Debra Bastone, President

Operating Room Nurses of Alberta Association (ORNAA)
AB
info@ornaa.org
www.ornaa.org
Lucia Pfeuti, President
Charlotte Parker, Secretary

Ordre des infirmières et infirmiers auxiliaires du Québec (OIIAQ)
531, rue Sherbrooke Est, Montréal QC H2L 1K2
Tél: 514-282-9511; *Téléc:* 514-282-0631
Ligne sans frais: 800-283-9511
oiiaq@oiiaq.org
www.oiiaq.org
Favoriser le développement professionnel des infirmières et infirmiers auxiliaires du Québec pour viser l'excellence dans l'exercice professionnel et tendre à une plus grande humanisation des soins
Régis Paradis, Président et directeur général

Ordre des infirmières et infirmiers du Québec (OIIQ)
4200, rue Molson, Montréal QC H1Y 4V4
Tél: 514-935-2501; *Téléc:* 514-935-1799
Ligne sans frais: 800-363-6048
www.oiiq.org
Mèdia social: www.flickr.com/photos/ordreinf/sets/
www.facebook.com/Ordre.infirmieres.infirmiers.Quebec
twitter.com/OIIQ
Assurer la protection du public; contrôler l'exercice de la profession par ses membres
Lucie Tremblay, Présidente
Ginette Bernier, Vice-présidente
Denise Brosseau, Directrice générale

Perioperative Registered Nurses Association of British Columbia (PRNABC)
BC
www.prnabc.ca
Marlene Skucas, President
Coleen Newland, Treasurer

Prince Edward Island Gerontological Nurses Association (PEIGNA)
PE
www.cgna.net/PEIGNA.html
To promote a high standard of nursing care & related health services for older adults; To enhance professionalism in the practice of gerontological nursing
Elaine E. Campbell, President

Prince Edward Island Nurses' Union (PEINU) / Syndicat des infirmières de l'Île-du-Prince-Édouard
10 Paramount Dr., Charlottetown PE C1E 0C7
Tel: 902-892-7152; *Fax:* 902-892-9324
Toll-Free: 866-892-7152
office@peinu.com
www.peinu.com
Social Media: vimeo.com/user2758462
twitter.com/PEINursesUnion
To regulate employment relations between nurses & employers through collective bargaining & negotiation of written contracts with employers implementing progressively better conditions of employment
Mona O'Shea, President
Kendra Gunn, Executive Director

Provincial Nurse Educator Interest Group (PNEIG)
c/o First Stage Enterprises, #109, 1 Concorde Gate, Toronto ON M3C 3N6
Tel: 416-426-7234
secretary@pneig.ca
www.pneig.ca
To promote the professional development of Ontario nurse educators through continuing education resources; To foster & encourage an interest in the role of nurse educator as a career choice; To share & support the vision & mission of the Registered Nurses Association of Ontario (RNAO)
Priya Herne, President
Mary Guise, Coordinator, Membership & Services

The Registered Nurses Association of the Northwest Territories & Nunavut (RNANT/NU)
PO Box 2757, Yellowknife NT X1A 2R1
Tel: 867-873-2745; *Fax:* 867-873-2336
info@rnantnu.ca
www.rnantnu.ca
Social Media:
www.facebook.com/www.rnantnu.ca
To promote & ensure competent nursing practice for the people of the NWT
Donna Stanley-Young, Executive Director

Registered Nurses' Association of Ontario (RNAO) / L'Association des infirmières et infirmiers autorisés de l'Ontario
158 Pearl St., Toronto ON M5H 1L3
Tel: 416-599-1925; *Fax:* 416-599-1926
Toll-Free: 800-268-7199
www.rnao.org
Social Media: www.youtube.com/RNAOVideo
www.facebook.com/RNAOHomeOffice
twitter.com/rnao
To promote excellence in nursing practice; Ro advocate the role of nursing in empowering the people of Ontario to achieve & maintain their optimal health; To provide membership-centred services
Rhonda Seidman-Carlson, RN, MN, President
Doris Grinspun, RN, MSN, PhD, L, Chief Executive Officer

Registered Practical Nurses Association of Ontario (RPNAO)
Bldg. 4, #200, 5025 Orbitor Dr., Mississauga ON L4W 4Y5
Tel: 905-602-4664; *Fax:* 905-602-4666
Toll-Free: 877-602-4664
info@rpnao.org
www.rpnao.org
Social Media:
www.facebook.com/RPNAO
twitter.com/rpnao
Dedicated to decisions that enhance professional practical nursing
Dianne Martin, RPN, RN, BScN, Executive Director
Beth McCracken, RPN, CAE, Nursing Practice & Outreach Specialist
Pia Ramos-Javellana, BSc., CGA, Director, Finance

Registered Psychiatric Nurses Association of Saskatchewan (RPNAS)
2055 Lorne St., Regina SK S4P 2M4
Tel: 306-586-4617; *Fax:* 306-586-6000
www.rpnas.com
To regulate psychiatric nursing as a distinct profession
Marion Palidwor, President
Robert Allen, Executive Director

Saskatchewan Association of Licensed Practical Nurses (SALPN)
#700A, 4400 - 4th Ave., Regina SK S4T 0H8
Tel: 306-525-1436; *Fax:* 306-347-7784
Toll-Free: 888-257-2576
www.salpn.com
To regulate Licensed Practical Nurses (LPNs) in Saskatchewan, in order to ensure public safety; To ensure that Saskatchewan's Licensed Practical Nurses provide professional nursing care; To maintain an efficient investigation & disciplinary process
Lynsay Donald, Executive Director
Kari Pruden, President
Cara Brewster, Registrar

Saskatchewan PeriOperative Registered Nurses' Group (SORNG)
SK
Candace Franke, President

Saskatchewan Registered Nurses' Association (SRNA)
2066 Retallack St., Regina SK S4T 7X5
Tel: 306-359-4200; *Fax:* 306-359-0257
Toll-Free: 800-667-9945
info@srna.org
www.srna.org
Social Media:
twitter.com/SRNAdialogue
To ensure competent, knowledge-based, & ethical nursing in Saskatchewan, for the protection of the public; To establish registration & licensure requirements
Signy Klebeck, President
Karen Eisler, Executive Director

Saskatchewan Union of Nurses (SUN) / Syndicat des infirmières de la Saskatchewan
2330 - 2nd Ave., Regina SK S4R 1A6
Tel: 306-525-1666; *Fax:* 306-522-4612
Toll-Free: 800-667-7060
regina@sun-nurses.sk.ca
www.sun-nurses.sk.ca
Social Media:
www.facebook.com/SUNnurses
twitter.com/sunnurses
To advocate to protect the rights of members; to enhance the socio-economic & general welfare of members through collective bargaining, research, & education
Tracy Zambory, President
Donna Trainor, Executive Director

United Nurses of Alberta (UNA) / Infirmières unies de l'Alberta
#700, 11150 Jasper Ave., Edmonton AB T5K 0L1
Tel: 780-425-1025; *Fax:* 780-426-2093
Toll-Free: 800-252-9394
ProvincialOffice@una.ab.ca
www.una.ab.ca
Social Media: www.youtube.com/user/UnitedNursesAlberta
www.facebook.com/UnitedNurses
twitter.com/unitednurses
To advance the social, economic & general welfare of nurses & other allied personnel
Heather Smith, President

Victorian Order of Nurses for Canada (VON Canada) / Infirmières de l'Ordre de Victoria du Canada
110 Argyle Ave., Ottawa ON K2P 1B4
Tel: 613-233-5694; *Fax:* 613-230-4376
Toll-Free: 888-866-2273
national@von.ca
www.von.ca
Social Media: www.youtube.com/VONCanadaFD
linkedin.com/company/von-canada
twitter.com/VON_Canada
To be a leader in the delivery of innovative comprehensive health & social services & to influencing the development of health & social policy in Canada; to meet rapidly changing social & external challenges
Judith Shamian, President & CEO
John Gallinger, Chief Operationg Officer

Yukon Registered Nurses Association (YRNA)
#204, 4133 - 4th Ave., Whitehorse YT Y1A 1H8
Tel: 867-667-4062; *Fax:* 867-668-5123
admin@yrna.ca
www.yrna.ca
Social Media:
www.facebook.com/190306321094679
twitter.com/YrnaExec
To establish & promote standards of practice for registered nurses; to regulate nursing practice & to advance professional excellence; to speak out on health care issues; to advocate for the development of healthy public policy in the interest of the public.
Joy Peacock, Executive Director
Sean Secord, President

Packaging

Canadian Corrugated Containerboard Association / Association canadienne du cartonnage ondulé et du carton-caisse
#3, 1995 Clark Blvd., Brampton ON L6T 4W1
Tel: 905-458-1247; *Fax:* 905-458-2052
info@cccabox.org
www.cccabox.org
To represent containerboard mill sites, corrugator plants, sheet plants & related industries; to work together with other players in the paper industry to develop an agenda of common concerns & issues
Peter Moore, Chair
David Andrews, Executive Director

Packaging Association of Canada (PAC) / Association canadienne de l'emballage
#607, 1 Concorde Gate, Toronto ON M3C 3N6
Tel: 416-490-7860
pacinfo@pac.ca
www.pac.ca
Social Media:
linkedin.com/company/the-packaging-association
www.facebook.com/ThePackagingAssociation
To represent both users & suppliers on the strength of environmental & economic policy
James D. Downham, President & CEO

Patents & Copyright

Access Copyright
#800, One Yonge St., Toronto ON M5E 1E5
Tel: 416-868-1620; *Fax:* 416-868-1621
Toll-Free: 800-893-5777
info@accesscopyright.ca
www.accesscopyright.ca
To licence copyright users who wish to reproduce copyright-protected works; to collect a fee for this service & to distribute royalties to the copyright owners whose works have been copied; to provide protection for copyright owners as well as legal access to published works for copyright users
Maureen Cavan, Executive Director

Brian O'Donnell, Director, Business Development
Roanie Levy, Director, Legal & External Affairs

Canadian Copyright Institute (CCI)
#107, 192 Spadina Ave., Toronto ON M5T 2C2
Tel: 416-975-1756; *Fax:* 416-975-1839
info@thecci.ca
www.thecci.ca
To encourage a better understanding of the law of copyright on the part of members, public & users of copyright material; To engage in & foster research in copyright law
Anne McClelland, Administrator

Canadian Musical Reproduction Rights Agency (CMRRA) / Agence canadienne des droits de production musicaux limitée
#320, 56 Wellesley St. West, Toronto ON M5S 2S3
Tel: 416-926-1966; *Fax:* 416-926-7521
inquiries@cmrra.ca
www.cmrra.ca
Represents the majority of music publishers & copyright owners doing business in Canada; on their behalf, issues licences & collects royalties for the reproduction of copyrighted musical works on CDs, cassettes & other sound carriers, & in films, TV programs & advertising; owned by the Canadian Music Publishers Association
David A. Basskin, President
Fred Merritt, Vice-President, Finance & Administration

Intellectual Property Institute of Canada (IPIC) / Institut de la Propriété Intellectuelle du Canada (IPIC)
#606, 60 Queen St., Ottawa ON K1P 5Y7
Tel: 613-234-0516; *Fax:* 613-234-0671
info@ipic.ca
www.ipic.ca
To promote the protection of intellectual property in Canada & abroad in order to enhance Canada's economic prospects as a sovereign nation & to foster cooperation between Canada & its trading partners around the world.

Re:Sound
#900, 1235 Bay St., Toronto ON M5R 3K4
Tel: 416-968-8870; *Fax:* 416-962-7797
info@resound.ca
www.resound.ca
To obtain fair compensation for artists and record companies for their performance rights
Matthew Fortier

Society of Composers, Authors & Music Publishers of Canada (SOCAN) / Société canadienne des auteurs, compositeurs et éditeurs de musique
41 Valleybrook Dr., Toronto ON M3B 2S6
Tel: 416-445-8700; *Fax:* 416-445-7108
Toll-Free: 800-557-6226
socan@socan.ca
www.socan.ca
Social Media: www.youtube.com/SOCANmusic
www.facebook.com/SOCANmusic
twitter.com/SOCANmusic
SOCAN is the Canadian copyright collective that administers the performing rights of members & of affiliated international organizations by licensing the use of music in Canada
Stan Meissner, President
Eric Baptiste, CEO
David Wood, CFO
Randy Wark, CAO & Vice-President, Human Resources
Jennifer Brown, Vice-President, Licensing
Michael McCarty, Chief Membership Officer
Janice Scott, Vice-President, Information Technology
Gilles M. Daigle, General Counsel, Legal Services

Peace

Canadian Friends of Peace Now (Shalom Achshav) (CFPN)
#517, 119-660 Eglinton Ave. East, Toronto ON M4G 2K2
Tel: 416-322-5559; *Fax:* 416-322-5587
Toll-Free: 866-405-5387
info@peacenowcanada.org
www.peacenowcanada.org
Social Media:
www.facebook.com/CanadianFriendsofPeaceNow
CFPN supports Peace Now, a peace movement in Israel that sponsors dialogue between Israelis & Palestinians, & advocates a 2-state solution for co-existence. CFPN organizes lectures in Canada & sponsors visits by Israeli & Palestinian peace activists. It is a registered charity, BN: 119147320RR0001.
David Brooks, Co-Chair, Ottawa
Gabriella Goliger, Co-Chair, Ottawa

Sheldon Gordon, Chair, Toronto
Stephen Scheinberg, Chair, Montréal

Development & Peace / Développement et paix
1425, boul René-Lévesque ouest, 3e étage, Montréal QC H3G 1T7
Tel: 514-257-8711; *Fax:* 514-257-8497
info@devp.org
www.devp.org
Social Media: www.youtube.com/devpeacetv; www.flickr.com/photos/devpedu/sets
www.facebook.com/devpeace
twitter.com/DevPeace
G. Gagnon, Contact

Performing Arts

For Performing Arts organizations, please see the Arts & Culture section on page 123.

Pharmaceutical

Alberta College of Pharmacists (ACP)
#1100, 8215 - 112 St. NW, Edmonton AB T6G 2C8
Tel: 780-990-0321; *Fax:* 780-990-0328
Toll-Free: 877-227-3838
acpinfo@pharmacists.ab.ca
www.pharmacists.ab.ca
Social Media:
linkedin.com/company/alberta-college-of-pharmacists
www.facebook.com/ACPharmacists
twitter.com/ACPharmacists
Greg Eberhart, Registrar

Association of Faculties of Pharmacy of Canada (AFPC) / Association des facultés de pharmacie du Canada
PO Box 21053, Stn. Terwilligar, Edmonton AB T6R 2V4
admin@afpc.info
www.afpc.info
To develop & implement policies & programs which will provide a forum for exchange of ideas, ensure a liaison with other organizations; to foster & promote excellence in pharmaceutical education & research in Canada
Harold Lopatka, Executive Director

Association professionnelle des pharmaciens salariés du Québec (APPSQ)
3560, rue la Verendrye, Sherbrooke QC J1L 1Z6
Tél: 819-563-6464; *Téléc:* 819-563-6464
Ligne sans frais: 877-565-6464
appsq@hotmail.com
De defendre des intérêts des pharmaciens salariés du Québec

Association québécoise des pharmaciens propriétaires (AQPP) / Québec Association of Pharmacy Owners
4378, av Pierre-de Coubertin, Montréal QC H1V 1A6
Tél: 514-254-0676; *Téléc:* 514-254-1288
Ligne sans frais: 800-361-7765
info@aqpp.qc.ca
www.aqpp.qc.ca
Mèdia social: www.youtube.com/user/VotrePharmacien
twitter.com/VotrePharmacien
Assurer l'étude, la défense et le développement des intérêts économiques, sociaux et professionnels de ses membres.
Normand Cadieux, Vice-président exécutif et directeur général

British Columbia Pharmacy Association (BCPhA)
#1530, 1200 West 73rd Ave., Vancouver BC V6P 6G5
Tel: 604-261-2092; *Fax:* 604-261-2097
Toll-Free: 800-663-2840
info@bcpharmacy.ca
www.bcpharmacy.ca
To support & advance the economic & professional well-being of members, with the goal that they will provide improved health care in British Columbia
Marnie Mitchell, Chief Executive Officer
Parkash Ragsdale, Deputy Chief Executive Officer & Director, Professional Services
Kate Hunter, Director, Communications
Cyril Lopez, Director, Member & Corporate Services

Canada's Research-Based Pharmaceutical Companies (Rx&D) / Les companies de recherche pharmaceutique du Canada
#1220, 55 Metcalfe St., Ottawa ON K1P 6L5
Tel: 613-236-0455; *Toll-Free:* 800-363-0203
info@canadapharma.org
www.canadapharma.org
Social Media:
twitter.com/rxandd
To discover new medicines that improve the quality of health care available for every Canadian
John Helou, Chair
Russell Williams, President

Canadian Association for Pharmacy Distribution Management (CAPDM) / Association canadienne de la gestion de l'approvisionnement pharmaceutique (ACGAP)
#301A, 3800 Steeles Ave. West, Woodbridge ON L4L 4G9
Tel: 905-265-1706; *Fax:* 905-265-9372
www.capdm.ca
Social Media:
ca.linkedin.com/company/canadian-association-for-pharmacy-distribution
www.facebook.com/pages/CAPDM/182173808506667?sk=info&tab=overview
To act as a resource & an advocacy voice for its members to advance the pharmacy distribution system as an effective, efficient, & safe delivery system for patient health care in Canada
Brent Teulon, Chair
David W. Johnston, President & CEO
Allan Reynolds, Vice-President, Industry & Member Relations
Allison Chan, Manager, Member Services & Events

Canadian Association of Pharmacy Students & Interns (CAPSI) / Association canadienne des étudiants et internes en pharmacie (ACEIP)
PO Box 68552, 360A Bloor St. West, Toronto ON M5S 1X0
www.capsi.ca
To prepare members for moral, social, ethical obligations to be upheld in the profession of pharmacy; to promote high standards of pharmacy education throughout Canada; to promote means by which members may enhance their professional knowledge & skills; to promote mutual interests & liaison with international pharmacy students, interns & society at large
Amber-lee Carriere, President

Canadian Association of Pharmacy Technicians (CAPT)
#164, 9-6975 Meadowvale Town Centre Circle, Mississauga ON L5N 2V7
Tel: 416-410-1142
info@capt.ca
www.capt.ca
Social Media:
www.facebook.com/capt.ca
To act as the voice of pharmacy assistants
Mary Bozoian, President
Colleen Norris, Vice-President
Mona Sousa, Director, Membership
Robert Solek, Director, Promotions & Public Relations
Lois Battcock, Director, Administration

The Canadian Council for Accreditation of Pharmacy Programs (CCAPP) / Le Conseil canadien de l'agrément des programmes de pharmacie
Leslie Dan Faculty of Pharmacy, University of Toronto, #1207, 144 College St., Toronto ON M5S 3M2
Tel: 416-946-5055; *Fax:* 416-978-8511
ccappinfo@phm.utoronto.ca
www.ccapp-accredit.ca
To accredit pharmacy academic programs offered at Canadian universities
Wayne Hindmarsh, Executive Director
Catherine Schuster, Coordinator, Pharmacy Technician Programs Accreditation

The Canadian Council on Continuing Education in Pharmacy (CCCEP) / Le conseil canadien de l'éducation permanente en pharmacie
#210, 2002 Quebec Ave., Saskatoon SK S7K 1W4
Tel: 306-652-7790; *Fax:* 306-652-7795
cccep@cccep.ca
www.cccep.ca
To act as the national coordinating & accrediting body for continuing education in pharmacy in Canada; To enhance the quality of continuing pharmacy education; To advance pharmacy practice
Barbara Thomas, President

Canadian Foundation for Pharmacy (CFP) / Fondation canadienne pour la pharmacie
5809 Fieldon Rd., Mississauga ON L5M 5K1
Tel: 905-997-3238; *Fax:* 905-997-4264
www.cfpnet.ca
Social Media:
linkedin.com/groups/Canadian-Foundation-Pharmacy-7473036
To provide programs for the advancement of the pharmacy profession in Canada
Marshall Moleschi, President
Dayle Acorn, Executive Director

Canadian Generic Pharmaceutical Association (CGPA) / L'Association canadienne du médicament générique (ACMG)
#409, 4120 Yonge St., Toronto ON M2P 2B8
Tel: 416-223-2333; *Fax:* 416-223-2425
info@canadiangenerics.ca
www.canadiangenerics.ca
Social Media:
www.facebook.com/CanadianGenerics
twitter.com/CdnGenerics
To promote an environment which supports & enhances the provision of affordable generic & innovative medications to Canadians & patients around the world through research, development & manufacturing of pharmaceuticals & fine chemicals in Canada
Jeff Connell, President

Canadian Pharmacists Association (CPhA) / Association des pharmaciens du Canada
1785 Alta Vista Dr., Ottawa ON K1G 3Y6
Tel: 613-523-7877; *Fax:* 613-523-0445
Toll-Free: 800-917-9489
info@pharmacists.ca
www.pharmacists.ca
Social Media:
www.facebook.com/cpha
twitter.com/CPhAAPhC
To advance the profession of pharmacy to contribute to the health of Canadians; To represent & support pharmacists across Canada
Jeff Poston, Executive Director
Paula MacNeil, President

Canadian Society of Hospital Pharmacists (CSHP) / Société canadienne des pharmaciens d'hôpitaux
#3, 30 Concourse Gate, Ottawa ON K2E 7V7
Tel: 613-736-9733; *Fax:* 613-736-5660
info@cshp.ca
www.cshp.ca
To advance safe, effective medication use & patient care in hospitals & related health care settings throughout Canada; To act as an influential voice for hospital pharmacy; To encourge professional growth & practice excellence
Myrella Roy, Executive Director
Desarae Davidson, Administrator, Conferences
Colleen Drake, Administrator, Publications
Anna Dudek, Administrator, Finance
Robyn Rockwell, Administrator, Membership

College of Pharmacists of British Columbia
#200, 1765 West 8 Ave., Vancouver BC V6J 5C6
Tel: 604-733-2440; *Fax:* 604-733-2493
Toll-Free: 800-663-1940
info@bcpharmacists.org
www.bcpharmacists.org
Social Media:
twitter.com/BCPharmacists
Safe & effective pharmacy practice outcomes for the people of British Columbia.
Anar Dossa, Chair
Bob Nakagawa, Registrar
Ashifa Keshavji, Director, Practice Reviews & Competency

College of Pharmacists of Manitoba
200 Tache Ave., Winnipeg MB R2H 1A7
Tel: 204-233-1411; *Fax:* 204-237-3468
info@cphm.ca
mpha.in1touch.org
To administer the Manitoba Pharmaceutical Act; to give license to & monitors pharmacists in the province, setingt standards of practice & investigating complaints.
Glenda Marsh, President
Ronald Guse, Registrar

Consumer Health Products Canada
#406, 1111 Prince of Wales Dr., Ottawa ON K2C 3T2
Tel: 613-723-0777; *Fax:* 613-723-0779
info@chpcanada.ca
www.chpcanada.ca
Social Media: www.youtube.com/CHPCanada0
linkedin.com/company/consumer-health-products-canada
www.facebook.com/chpcanada
twitter.com/chp_can
To contribute to quality of life & cost-effective health care for Canadians by creating & maintaining an environment for the growth of responsible self-medication.
Adam Kingsley, Acting President
Gerry Harrington, Director, Public Affairs

Council for Continuing Pharmaceutical Education (CCPE) / Conseil de formation pharmaceutique continue (CFPC)
#350, 3333 boul de la Côte-Vertu, Saint-Laurent QC H4R 2N1
Tel: 514-333-8362; *Fax:* 514-333-1119
Toll-Free: 888-333-8362
www.ccpe-cfpc.com
To provide educational programs to establish improved professional standards within the Canadian pharmaceutical industry; To better meet the needs & expectations of our internal & external stakeholders in the healthcare industry
Jim Shea, General Manager

Manitoba Society of Pharmacists Inc. (MSP)
#202, 90 Garry St., Winnipeg MB R3C 4H1
Tel: 204-956-6680; *Fax:* 204-956-6686
Toll-Free: 800-677-7170
www.msp.mb.ca
To act as the voice of pharmacists in Manitoba on economic & professional issuess
Brenna Shearer, Executive Director

National Association of Pharmacy Regulatory Authorities (NAPRA) / Association nationale des organismes de réglementation de la pharmacie
#750, 220 Laurier Ave. West, Ottawa ON K1P 5Z9
Tel: 613-569-9658; *Fax:* 613-569-9659
info@napra.ca
www.napra.ca
To facilitate the activities of provincial pharmacy regulatory authorities in their service of public interest
Carole Bouchard, Executive Director

New Brunswick Pharmaceutical Society (NBPhS) / Ordre des pharmaciens du N.-B.
#8, 1224 Mountain Rd., Moncton NB E1C 2T6
Tel: 506-857-8957; *Fax:* 506-857-8838
Toll-Free: 800-463-4434
info@nbpharmacists.ca
www.nbpharmacists.ca
To protect the public by regulating the profession of pharmacy in New Brunswick.
Sam Lanctin, Registrar
Karen DeGrace, Communications Manager

New Brunswick Pharmacists' Association (NBPA) / Association des pharmaciens du Nouveau-Brunswick (APNB)
#410, 212 Queen St., Fredericton NB E3B 1A8
Tel: 506-459-6008; *Fax:* 506-453-0736
Toll-Free: 888-358-2345
nbpa@nbnet.nb.ca
www.nbpharma.ca
Social Media:
twitter.com/PharmacistsNB
To advance the profession of pharmacy in New Brunswick; To represent the interests of members & the profession of pharmacy
Paul Blanchard, Executive Director

Nova Scotia College of Pharmacists (NSCP)
#200, 1559 Brunswick St., Halifax NS B3J 2G1
Tel: 902-422-8528; *Fax:* 902-422-0885
info@nspharmacists.ca
www.nspharmacists.ca
To govern the practice of pharmacy in Nova Scotia to benefit the health & well being of the public
Shelagh Campbell-Palmer, Manager, Professional Practice
Susan Wedlake, Registrar

Ontario College of Pharmacists (OCP)
483 Huron St., Toronto ON M5R 2R4
Tel: 416-962-4861; *Fax:* 416-847-8200
Toll-Free: 800-220-1921
ocpclientservices@ocpinfo.com
www.ocpinfo.com
Social Media:
twitter.com/ocpinfo
To administer the Regulated Health Professions Act; To regulate the practice of pharmacy, in accordance with standards of practice; To ensure that members provide quality pharmaceutical service & care to the public

Ontario Pharmacists' Association (OPA)
#800, 375 University Ave., Toronto ON M5G 2J5
Tel: 416-441-0788; *Fax:* 416-441-0791
mail@opatoday.com
www.opatoday.com
To promote excellence in the practice of pharmacy & the wellness of patients; To act as the voice of pharmacists throughout Ontario
Dennis Darby, Chief Executive Officer
Amedeo Zottola, CFO & COO
Allan H. Malek, Vice-President, Professional Affairs
Lisa Mayeski, Director, Corporate Development & Partnerships
Deborah McNorgan, Director, Communications
Eija Kanniainen, Manager, Insurance Services
Eric Li, Manager, Pharmacy Policy
Wendy Furtenbacher, Coordinator, Membership

Ordre des pharmaciens du Québec (OPQ)
#301, 266, rue Notre Dame Ouest, Montréal QC H2Y 1T6
Tél: 514-284-9588; *Téléc:* 514-284-3420
Ligne sans frais: 800-363-0324
ordrepharm@opq.org
www.opq.org
Média social: www.youtube.com/user/ordrepharmaciensqc
www.facebook.com/OrdredespharmaciensduQuebec
twitter.com/ordrepharmaQc
Protection du public en matières de services pharmaceutiques.
Bertrand Bolduc, Président
Manon Lambert, Directrice générale et secrétaire

Pharmacy Association of Nova Scotia (PANS)
#225, 170 Cromarty Dr., Dartmouth NS B3B 0G1
Tel: 902-422-9583; *Fax:* 902-422-2619
pans@pans.ns.ca
pans.ns.ca
Social Media: www.youtube.com/pharmacyassocns
www.facebook.com/152014618179908
twitter.com/pharmacyns
To advance the professional, academic, & commercial aspects of pharmacy & pharmacists throughout Nova Scotia; To represent the interests of Nova Scotia's pharmacists; To improve public health in Nova Scotia
Allison Bodnar, CEO

The Pharmacy Examining Board of Canada (PEBC) / Le Bureau des examinateurs en pharmacie du Canada (BEPC)
717 Chursh St., Toronto ON M4W 2M4
Tel: 416-979-2431; *Fax:* 416-599-9244
pebcinfo@pebc.ca
www.pebc.ca
To establish qualifications for pharmacists; To provide for examinations of those qualifications
Shawn Bugden, President
Catherine Schuster, Vice-President

Prince Edward Island Pharmacy Board (PEIPB)
PO Box 89, 20454 Trans Canada Hwy., Crapaud PE C0A 1J0
Tel: 902-658-2780; *Fax:* 902-658-2528
info@pepharmacists.ca
www.pepharmacists.ca
To prescribe qualifications, grant authorization & monitor adherence to established standards, so as to promote high standards & safeguard the public with regard to pharmaceutical service
Alicia McCallum, Chair
Michelle Wyand, Registrar
Rachel Lowther-Doiron, Administrative Assistant

Saskatchewan College of Pharmacists (SCP)
#700, 4010 Pasqua St., Regina SK S4S 7B9
Tel: 306-584-2292; *Fax:* 306-584-9695
info@saskpharm.ca
www.napra.ca/pages/Saskatchewan
To regulate pharmacists, pharmacies, & drugs in Saskatchewan; To register pharmacists who meet the education & training qualifications specified in "The Pharmacy Act, 1996"; To issue permits to operate pharmacies
Spiro Kolitsas, President
Justin Kosar, Vice-President
Ray Joubert, Registrar

Photography

Alberta Professional Photographers Association
c/o Professional Photographers of Canada, 209 Light St., Woodstock ON N4S 6H6
Tel: 519-537-2555; *Fax:* 888-831-4036
Toll-Free: 888-643-7762
www.ppoc-alberta.ca
To maintain a strong national identity for all those involved in the photographic industry and includes provincial factions which abide by a specific code of ethics.
Cameron Colclough, Director

Canadian Association for Photographic Art (CAPA) / L'Association canadienne d'art photographique
PO Box 357, Logan Lake BC V0K 1W0
Tel: 604-523-2378; *Fax:* 604-523-2333
capa@capacanada.ca
capacanada.ca
Social Media:
www.facebook.com/TheCanadianAssociationForPhotographicArt
To promote the advancement of photography as an art form in Canada
Jacques S. Mailloux, President

Canadian Association of Professional Image Creators (CAPIC) / Association canadienne de photographes et illustrateurs de publicité
#202, 720 Spadina Ave., Toronto ON M5S 2T9
Tel: 416-462-3677; *Fax:* 416-929-5256
Toll-Free: 888-252-2742
info@capic.org
www.capic.org
Social Media:
ca.linkedin.com/pub/capic-national-office-bureau-national/a/a76/713
www.facebook.com/pages/CAPIC/33315648062
twitter.com/followCAPIC
To safeguard & promote the rights of photographers, illustrators, & digital artists who work in the Canadian communications industry
Hai Au Bui, President

Canadian Imaging Trade Association (CITA) / Association canadienne de l'industrie de l'imagerie
#300, 180 Attwell Dr., Toronto ON M9W 6A9
Tel: 905-602-8877
cita@electrofed.com
www.electrofed.com/cita/
To promote traditional & emerging imaging technologies (manufacturers/importers & distributors of photographic & electronic imaging equipment & sensitized materials)
Dori Gospodaric, General Manager

Paved Arts New Media Inc.
424 - 20th St. West, Saskatoon SK S7M 0X4
Tel: 306-652-5502
www.pavedarts.ca
To develop photography & photo-based art
Biliana Velkova, Executive Director
David LaRiviere, Artistic Director

Photographes professionnels du Québec (PPDQ) / Professional Photographers of Québec
23, rue Frère André Daoust, Rigaud QC J0P 1P0
Tél: 438-397-8182
web@ppdq.ca
www.ppdq.ca
Média social: www.youtube.com/user/cmpqadmin
www.facebook.com/PhotographesProfessionnelsduQuebec
twitter.com/PhotographesQc
Pour faire avancer la photographie professionnelle tout en assurant aux consommateurs la protection et un haut niveau de qualité.
Nathalie Mathieu, Présidente

Photographic Historical Society of Canada (PHSC)
PO Box 239, 6021 Yonge St., Toronto ON M2M 3W2
Tel: 416-691-1555; *Fax:* 416-693-0018
info@phsc.ca
www.phsc.ca
To facilitate the sharing of photographic knowledge; To help research & preserve Canada's photographic heritage
Clint Hyrorijiw, President

Professional Photographers Association of Canada - Atlantic / Atlantique (PPAC Atlantic)
c/o Cindi-Lee Campbell, 9195 Rte. 102, Morrisdale NB E5K 4N3
Tel: 506-757-1198
www.mppaphoto.com
To uphold the association's code of ethics

Berni Wood, President
Cindi-Lee Campbell, Secretary-Treasurer

Professional Photographers of Canada - British Columbia (PPOC-BC)
PO Box 1329, 4543 - 201 St., Langley BC V3A 6M5
Tel: 604-857-1569; *Fax:* 604-857-1570
Toll-Free: 877-857-1569
contact@ppoc-bc.ca
www.ppoc-bc.ca
Social Media: twitter.com/PPOC_BC
To promote & foster the personal ethics & professional development of the working photographer &/or specialist through education, fellowship & public awareness
Jillian Chateauneuf, PPOC Director, British Columbia
Melissa Walsh, President

Professional Photographers of Canada - Ontario Branch
209 Light St., Woodstock ON N4S 6H6
Tel: 519-537-2555; *Fax:* 888-831-4036
Toll-Free: 888-643-7762
bureauduppoc@ppoc.ca
www.ppocontario.com
Social Media: www.youtube.com/ppocontario
www.facebook.com/PPOC.ONTARIO
twitter.com/PPOC_Ontario
To provide an educational, business & creative environment for professional photographers & with the purpose of promoting the highest standard of personal & creative excellence within the craft
Robert Nowell, President
Tanya Thompson, Executive Director

Professional Photographers of Canada 1970 Incorporated (PPOC) / Photographes Professionnels du Canada
209 Light St., Woodstock ON N4S 6H6
Tel: 519-537-2555; *Fax:* 519-537-5573
Toll-Free: 888-643-7762
www.ppoc.ca
To promote excellence in professional imaging; To elevate professional standards & ethics; To act as a voice for the photographic profession on legal matters & legislative issues
Tanya Thompson, Executive Director
Chris Stambaugh, President
Brian Boyle, Vice-President
John Beesley, Corporate Secretary
Cam Colclough, Corporate Treasurer

Saskatchewan Professional Photographers Association Inc.
c/o Professional Photographers Association of Canada, 209 Light St., Woodstock ON N4S 6H6
Tel: 519-537-2555; *Fax:* 888-831-4036
Toll-Free: 888-643-7762
admin@sppa.org
ppoc-sk.com
To advance professional photography through educational seminars, fellowship & competitions
Wayne Inverarity, President
Tanya Thompson, Administrative Coordinator

Planning & Development

Alberta Professional Planners Institute (APPI)
PO Box 596, Edmonton AB T5J 2K8
Tel: 780-435-8716; *Fax:* 780-452-7718
Toll-Free: 888-286-8716
admin@albertaplanners.com
www.albertaplanners.com
To expand the depth & enhance the credibility of the association; To promote professional growth of practicing planners throughout Alberta, the Northwest Territories, & Nunavut; To maximize membership potential; To provide an effective level of service to the membership
Eleanor Mohammed, RPP, MCIP, President
MaryJane Alanko, Executive Director

Atlantic Planners Institute (API) / Institut des Urbanistes de l'atlantique (IVA)
35 Ascot Ct., Fredericton NB E3B 6C4
Tel: 506-455-7203; *Fax:* 506-455-1113
apiexecutivedirector@gmail.com
www.atlanticplanners.org
To represent professional planners in New Brunswick, Prince Edward Island, Nova Scotia, Newfoundland & Labrador.
Jennifer Griffiths, Executive Director

Canadian Association of Certified Planning Technicians (CACPT)
PO Box 69006, 1900 King St. East, Hamilton ON L8K 6R4
Tel: 905-578-4681; *Fax:* 905-578-9581
director@cacpt.org
www.cacpt.org
To maintain high standards for Planning Technicians & other related planning professionals
Danielle Stevens, President
Norman Pearson, Registrar
Diane LeBreton, CPT, MCIP, RPP, Executive Director

Canadian Institute of Planners (CIP) / Institut canadien des urbanistes (ICU)
#1112, 141 Laurier Ave. West, Ottawa ON K1P 5J3
Tel: 613-237-7526; *Fax:* 613-237-7045
Toll-Free: 800-207-2138
general@cip-icu.ca
www.cip-icu.ca
To advance professional planning excellence, through the delivery of membership & public services in Canada & abroad
Steven Brasier, CAE, Executive Director

Manitoba Professional Planners Institute (MPPI)
137 Bannatyne Ave., 2nd Fl., Winnipeg MB R3B 0R3
Tel: 204-943-3637; *Fax:* 204-925-4624
mppiadmin@shaw.ca
www.mppi.mb.ca
To handle membership applications & services & to enforce the Code of Professional Conduct.
Valdene Buckley, President
Kari MacKinnon, Administrator

Muniscope (ICURR)
#210, 40 Wynford Dr., Toronto ON M3C 1J5
Fax: 647-345-7004
www.muniscope.ca
Social Media: twitter.com/muniscope
To support local and regional governments, as well as private & non-profit companies through subsidized information & networking services; to act as a national resource on municipal issues, with subscription-based research & library services available on economic development, finance and taxation, housing and infrastructure, transportation, planning, & sustainability
Mathieu Rivard, Director
Mark Rose, Manager, Information Services

Ontario Professional Planners Institute (OPPI) / Institut des planificateurs professionnels de l'Ontario
#201, 234 Eglinton Ave. East, Toronto ON M4P 1K5
Tel: 416-483-1873; *Fax:* 416-483-7830
Toll-Free: 800-668-1448
info@ontarioplanners.ca
www.ontarioplanners.ca
Social Media: www.youtube.com/user/OntarioPlanners
linkedin.com/company/3068747
www.facebook.com/OntarioProfessionalPlannersInstitute
twitter.com/OntarioPlanners
To act as the voice of Ontario's planning profession; To provide leadership on policies related to planning & development
Andrea Bourrie, President
Mary Ann Rangam, Executive Director
Robert Fraser, Director, Finance & Administration
Loretta Ryan, Director, Public Affairs
Brian Brophey, Registrar & Director, Member Relations

Ordre des urbanistes du Québec (OUQ)
#410, 85, rue St-Paul ouest, Montréal QC H2Y 3V4
Tél: 514-849-1177; *Téléc:* 514-849-7176
info@ouq.qc.ca
www.ouq.qc.ca
Média social: www.facebook.com/666855766761080
Assurer la protection du public dans l'exercice de la profession par ses membres et la promotion de la pratique de l'urbanisme au Québec
Karina Verdon, Directrice générale

Planning Institute of British Columbia (PIBC)
#1750, 355 Burrard St., Vancouver BC V6C 2G8
Tel: 604-696-5031; *Fax:* 604-696-5032
Toll-Free: 866-696-5031
info@pibc.bc.ca
www.pibc.bc.ca
To promote orderly use of land, buildings & natural resources; to maintain high standard of professional competence; to protect rights & interests of those engaged in planning profession
Andrew Young, President
Dave Crossley, Executive Director

Saskatchewan Professional Planners Institute (SPPI)
2424 College Ave., Regina SK S4P 1C8
Tel: 306-584-3879; *Fax:* 306-352-6913
msteranka@sasktel.net
sppi.ca
Social Media: www.facebook.com/SaskPlanning
twitter.com/SaskPlanning
To promote & maintain professionalism in planning field
Marilyn Steranka, Executive Director
Bill Delainey, Secretary
Ryan Walker, Treasurer

Urban Development Institute of Canada (UDI) / Institut de développement urbain du Canada
200-602 West Hastings St., Vancouver BC V6B 1P2
Tel: 604-669-9585; *Fax:* 604-689-8691
www.udi.bc.ca
Social Media: www.youtube.com/UDIPacific; www.instagram.com/udibc
linkedin.com/company/urban-development-institute---pacific-region
www.facebook.com/UDIBC
twitter.com/udibc
To promote wise, efficient & productive urban growth; To be an effective voice of the land development & property management industry at all levels of government; To serve as a forum for the exchange of knowledge, experience & research on land use planning & development
Anne McMullin, President & CEO
Jeff Fisher, Vice President
Elsie Edillor, Manager, Finance
Patrick Santoro, Manager, Policy & Projects

Police

Canadian Association of Police Educators (CAPE) / Association canadienne des intervenants en formation policière (ACIFP)
c/o Wayne Jacobsen, 1430 Victoria Ave. East, Brandon MB R7A 2A9
Tel: 204-725-8700
cape.educators@gmail.com
cape-educators.ca
Social Media: www.facebook.com/593948850654424
To promote law enforcement training & education through the guidance of research, program development, knowledge transfer, network facilitation & collaborative training initiatives; to providve advice & input on national & regional law enforcement training & educations trends/needs; to promote a commitment to training
Catherine Wareham, Secretary
Wayne Jacobsen, President

Canadian Search Dog Association (CSDA)
PO Box 37103, Stn. Lynnwood Postal Outlet, Edmonton AB T5R 5Y2
calgary.csda@outlook.com
canadiansearchdog.com
Social Media: www.facebook.com/156258481071770
To generate a group of trained search workers & search dogs to aid the RCMP & other tasking agencies in the search for lost or missing persons

International Police Association - Canada (IPA Canada)
179 Greak Oak Trail, Binbrook ON L0R 1C0
www.ipa.ca
To encourage contact in social & cultural activities among members throughout the world

Ontario Association of Chiefs of Police (OACP)
#605, 40 College St., Toronto ON M5G 2J3
Tel: 416-926-0424; *Fax:* 416-926-0436
Toll-Free: 800-816-1767
oacpadmin@oacp.ca
www.oacp.on.ca
Social Media: www.youtube.com/OACPOfficial
www.facebook.com/OACPOfficial
twitter.com/OACPOfficial
The Association coordinates police training & education. It advocates on behalf of its membership, expressing concerns & priorities to the government, public & to any other bodies.
Ron Bain, Executive Director
Joe Couto, Director, Government Relations & Communications
Sharon Seepersad, Manager, Administration/Member Services
Jennifer Evans, President

Ontario Provincial Police Association (OPPA)
119 Ferris Lane, Barrie ON L4M 2Y1
Fax: 705-721-4867
www.oppa.ca
To represent members in negotiations with the Ontario government; to promote safe & healthy work environments
Jim Christie, President
Martin Bain, Vice-President

Prince Edward Island Police Association (PEIPA)
PE
Toll-Free: 800--
www.peipolice.com
To help members of the community become more familiar with the Prince Edward Island Police force; To promote the public's role in crime prevention; To support Youth Development; To speak for Prince Edward Island's municipal police officers
Ron MacLean, Corporal, President
Jason Blacquiere, Vice-President West
John Flood, Vice-President East

Politics

Alberta Liberal Party
10247 - 124 St. NW, Edmonton AB T5N 1P8
Tel: 780-414-1124
www.albertaliberal.com
Social Media: www.youtube.com/albertaliberalcaucus
www.facebook.com/ablib
twitter.com/abliberal
To elect Liberals to the Legislative Assembly of Alberta; to enunciate & promote liberal principles & policies; to initiate & maintain effective electoral constituencies
David Swann, Party Leader
Karen Sevcik, President

Beaver Party of Canada (BPOC) / Parti Castor du Canada (PCDC)
PO Box 3100, Stn. Pacific Institute U2, Abbotsford BC V2S 4P4
Tel: 250-755-1183
info@beaverparty.ca
www.beaverparty.ca
To become a majority government in the Canadian parliament; to focus on the following issues: restorative justice, pro-life, immigration, free education, national housing, animal rights, increased military, equal & fair taxes, universal health care, upgraded infrastructure, new transportation technologies, legalization & taxation of marijuana, nationwide unemployment insurance & welfare reform, & enhanced government oversight.
Kelvin Purdy, Leader
Ian Rowe, Chief Executive Officer
Riley Quin, Media Officer
Leona Whiting, Records Officer

Bloc québécois (BQ)
#502, 3750, boul Crémazie est, Montréal QC H2A 1B4
Tél: 514-526-3000; *Téléc:* 514-526-2868
www.blocquebecois.org
Mèdia social:
www.youtube.com/user/blocquebecois?feature=results_main
www.facebook.com/blocquebecois
twitter.com/blocquebecois
Rhéal Fortin, Chef
Mario Beaulieu, Président

Canadian Action Party (CAP)
333 Sockeye Creek St., Terrace BC V8G 0G5
Tel: 250-638-0011
www.canadianactionparty.ca
Christopher Porter, Leader

Canadian Political Science Association (CPSA) / Association canadienne de science politique (ACSP)
#204, 260 Dalhousie St., Ottawa ON K1N 7E4
Tel: 613-562-1202; *Fax:* 613-241-0019
cpsa-acsp@cpsa-acsp.ca
www.cpsa-acsp.ca
To encourage & develop political science & its relationship with other disciplines
Silvina Danesi, Executive Director

Canadian Political Science Students' Association (CPSSA) / Association des Étudiants de Science Politique du Canada (AESPC)
University of Calgary, Dept. of Political Science, 2500 Universtiy Dr. NW, Calgary AB T2N 1N4
Tel: 613-562-1202; *Fax:* 613-241-0019
contact@cpssa.ca
www.cpssa.ca
Social Media: instagram.com/cpssa_aespc
www.facebook.com/CPSSAAESPC
twitter.com/cpssa_aespc
A national student organization representing students and student groups studying Political Science across the country.

Christian Heritage Party of Canada (CHP) / Parti de l'héritage du Canada
PO Box 4958, Stn. E, Ottawa ON K1S 5J1
Fax: 819-281-7174
Toll-Free: 888-868-3247
nationaloffice@chp.ca
www.chp.ca
Social Media: www.youtube.com/user/christianheritage
www.facebook.com/CHP.ca.Canada
twitter.com/CHPCanada
To provide true Christian leadership & uphold biblical principles in federal legislation; To attain the leadership of the federal government of Canada through the existing democratic process
Rod Taylor, National Leader
Dave Bylsma, President

Communist Party of Canada (CPC) / Parti Communiste du Canada
Central Committee, 290A Danforth Ave., Toronto ON M4K 1N6
Tel: 416-469-2446
info@cpc-pcc.ca
www.communist-party.ca
Social Media: flickr.com/photos/communist-party-of-canada
www.facebook.com/CommunistPartyOfCanada
twitter.com/compartycanada
To establish a socialist society in Canada, in which the principal means of producing & distributing wealth will be the common property of society as a whole.
Miguel Figueroa, Party Leader

Communist Party of Canada (Marxist-Leninist) (CPC(ML)) / Parti communiste du Canada (marxiste-léniniste)
National Headquarters, 1876, rue Amherst, Montréal QC H2L 3L7
Tel: 514-522-1373; *Fax:* 514-522-1373
Toll-Free: 800-263-4203
office@cpcml.ca
www.cpcml.ca
The Party holds that the attainment of communism will bring the complete emancipation of the working class. It holds that all people have claims on the society by virtue of being human and that this is the overriding principle of society, along with gender equality and freedom of conscience & lifestyle.
Anna Di Carlo, Party Leader
Hélène Héroux, Chief Agent

Conservative Party of Canada / Parti conservateur du Canada
#1204, 130 Albert St., Ottawa ON K1P 5G4
Toll-Free: 866-808-8407
www.conservative.ca
Social Media: www.youtube.com/cpcpcc
www.facebook.com/cpcpcc
twitter.com/CPC_HQ
The Conservative Party provided Canadians with an alternative to the Liberal government. It developed innovative and practical new policy ideas such as the Federal Accountability Act, the Public Transit Tax Credit and the Apprenticeship Incentive Grant- ideas Conservatives would later implement in government.
Hon. Rona Ambrose, Interim Leader

Federal Liberal Association of Nunavut
c/o Liberal Party of Canada, #600, 81 Metcalf St., Ottawa ON K1P 6M8
Toll-Free: 888-542-3725
assistance@liberal.ca
Representing the Liberal Party in Nunavut
Michel Potvin, President

Forces et Démocratie
CP 4, Succ. Matane, Québec QC G4W 2B0
Ligne sans frais: 855-667-7344
www.forcesetdemocratie.org
Mèdia social:
www.youtube.com/channel/UCq5iKfnw0vA5gk3Z2XFL09w
www.facebook.com/forcesdemocratie
twitter.com/Forcedemocratie
Jean-François Fortin, Chef du parti

The Green Party of Alberta
PO Box 45066, Stn. Brentwood, #319, 3630 Brentwood Rd. NW, Calgary AB T2L 1Y4
Tel: 403-293-4593
greenpartyofalberta.ca
Social Media:
www.facebook.com/GreenPartyOfAlberta
twitter.com/greenpartyab
To encourage the development of an attitude that everyone is part of the land; to encourage strict control of all forms of pollution; to promote programs teaching consensus & facilitation; to facilitate the process of all interested community members becoming involved in education, both learning & teaching, guided by the long-term sustainability of the Earth community; to create the opportunity for Albertans to become involved in the strategic planning process
Janet Keeping, Party Leader
Carl Svoboda, President
Matt Burnett, Chief Financial Officer

Green Party of Canada (GPC) / Parti vert du Canada
PO Box 997, Stn. B, #204, 396 Cooper St., Ottawa ON K1P 5R1
Tel: 613-562-4916; *Fax:* 613-482-4632
Toll-Free: 888-868-3447
info@greenparty.ca
www.greenparty.ca
Social Media: www.youtube.com/user/canadiangreenparty
www.facebook.com/GreenPartyofCanada
twitter.com/canadiangreens
To promote a platform that includes debt reduction, eco-jobs, saving Canada's forests, supporting small business, use of soft energies, sovereignty for First Nations, & a guarantee of full rights for women
Elizabeth May, Party Leader
Daniel Green, Deputy Leader
Bruce Hyer, Deputy Leader
Bob MacKie, Interim President

The Green Party of Manitoba
PO Box 26023, Stn. Maryland, 120 Sherbrook St., Winnipeg MB R3C 3R3
Tel: 204-488-2831; *Toll-Free:* 866-742-4292
www.greenparty.mb.ca
Social Media: www.youtube.com/user/GreenPartyofManitoba
www.facebook.com/GreenPartyofManitoba
twitter.com/Green_Party_MB
James R. Beddome, Party Leader
Drew Fenwick, President

Green Party of New Brunswick / Parti Vert du Nouveau Brunswick
#102, 403 Regent St., Fredericton NB E3B 3X6
Tel: 506-447-8499; *Fax:* 506-447-8489
Toll-Free: 888-662-8683
www.greenpartynb.ca
Social Media: www.youtube.com/user/GPVNB
www.facebook.com/GPNB.PVNB
twitter.com/greenpartynb
David Coon, Party Leader
Derek Simon, Party Leader

Green Party of Nova Scotia
PO Box 36044, 5665 Spring Garden Rd., Halifax NS B3J 3S9
Tel: 902-252-3995; *Toll-Free:* 877-707-5775
gpns@greenparty.ns.ca
greenparty.ns.ca
Social Media:
facebook.com/134420653259017
twitter.com/JohnPercyGPNS
John Percy, Party Leader

The Green Party of Ontario (GPO) / Parti Vert d'Ontario
PO Box 1132, Stn. F, #035, 67 Mowat Ave., Toronto ON M4Y 2T8
Tel: 416-977-7476; *Fax:* 416-977-5476
Toll-Free: 888-647-3366
admin@gpo.ca
www.gpo.ca
Mike Schreiner, Party Leader
Becky Smit, Executive Director

Green Party of Prince Edward Island
PO Box 104, 101 Kent St., Charlottetown PE C1A 7K2
Tel: 902-658-2041
info@greenparty.pe.ca
greenparty.pe.ca
Social Media:
www.facebook.com/109519535816769
twitter.com/PEIgreens
Peter Bevan-Baker, Party Leader

Green Party Political Association of British Columbia (GPBC)
PO Box 8088, Stn. Central, Victoria BC V8W 3R7
Fax: 250-590-4537
Toll-Free: 888-473-3686
info@greenparty.bc.ca
www.greenparty.bc.ca
Social Media: www.instagram.com/GreenPartyBC
www.facebook.com/BCGreens
twitter.com/BCGreens
To form healthy communities with diverse economies by involving the citizens of British Columbia in the political process; To offer voters in British Columbia fiscal responsibility, socially progressive policies, & environmental sustainability
Andrew Weaver, Party Leader

International Political Science Association (IPSA) / Association internationale de science politique (AISP)
#331, 1590, av Docteur-Penfield, Montréal QC H3G 1C5
Tel: 514-848-8717; *Fax:* 514-848-4095
info@ipsa.org
www.ipsa.org
Social Media:
www.facebook.com/IPSA.AISP
twitter.com/IPSN_AISP
To promote the advancement of political science through the collaboration of scholars in different parts of the world; IPSA has consultative status with the Economic & Social Council of the United Nations & with UNESCO
Guy Lachapelle, Secretary General
Helen Milner, President
Mathieu St-Laurent, Manager, Membership Services & External Relations

The Island Party of Prince Edward Island
PE
theislandparty@yahoo.com
theislandpartypei.ca
Billy Cann, Party Leader
Sandra Sharpe, President

The Liberal Party of Canada (LPC) / Le Parti Libéral du Canada (PLC)
#920,350 Albert St., Ottawa ON K1P 6M8
Fax: 613-235-7208
Toll-Free: 888-542-3725
assistance@liberal.ca
www.liberal.ca
Social Media: www.youtube.com/user/liberalvideo
linkedin.com/company/liberal-party-of-canada
www.facebook.com/LiberalCA
twitter.com/Liberal_party
To seek a common ground of understanding among the people of the provinces & territories of Canada; To advocate liberal philosophies, principles & policies; To promote the election of candidates of the Liberal Party to the Parliament of Canada
Rt. Hon. Justin Trudeau, Prime Minister & Party Leader
Anna Gainey, National President
Christina Topp, Acting National Director
Chris MacInnes, National Vice-President, English
Marie Tremblay, National Vice-President, French

The Liberal Party of Canada (British Columbia) (LPCBC) / Parti libéral du Canada (Colombie-Britannique)
#460, 580 Hornby St., Vancouver BC V6C 3B6
Fax: 613-235-7208
Toll-Free: 888-411-6511
assistance@liberal.ca
bc.liberal.ca
Social Media: www.youtube.com/user/liberalvideo
www.facebook.com/LPCBC
twitter.com/lpcbc
Shaun Govender, Executive Director

The Liberal Party of Canada (Manitoba)
Molgat Place, 635 Broadway, Winnipeg MB R3C 0X1
Tel: 204-988-9540; *Fax:* 204-988-9549
Toll-Free: 888-542-3725
manitoba.liberal.ca
Social Media:
www.facebook.com/LPCMB.PLCMB
twitter.com/liberalpartymb
David Johnson, Executive Director

Liberal Party of Canada (Ontario) (LPC(O)) / Parti libéral du Canada (Ontario)
#420, 10 St. Mary St., Toronto ON M4Y 1P9
Tel: 416-921-2844; *Fax:* 416-921-3880
Toll-Free: 800-361-3881
ontario@liberal.ca
ontario.liberal.ca
Social Media:
www.facebook.com/LPCO.PLCO
twitter.com/lpc_o
Tyler Banham, President
Kunal Parmar, Director, Operations

Liberal Party of Canada in Alberta (LPC(A))
#308, 10240 - 124 St., Edmonton AB T5N 3W6
Tel: 705-328-3889; *Fax:* 613-235-7208
alberta@liberal.ca
alberta.liberal.ca
Social Media:
www.facebook.com/lpcalberta
twitter.com/lpca
Robbie Schuett, President

Liberal Party of Newfoundland & Labrador / Parti libéral de Terre-Neuve et du Labrador
Beothuk Bldg., #205, 20 Crosbie Place, St. John's NL A1B 3Y8
Tel: 709-754-1813; *Fax:* 709-754-0820
Toll-Free: 866-726-7116
info@nlliberals.ca
nlliberals.ca
Social Media: www.youtube.com/nlliberals
www.facebook.com/nlliberals
twitter.com/nlliberals
Hon. Dwight Ball, Leader

Liberal Party of Nova Scotia
PO Box 723, #1400, 5151 George St., Halifax NS B3J 2T3
Tel: 902-429-1993; *Fax:* 902-423-1624
office@liberal.ns.ca
www.liberal.ns.ca
Social Media: www.youtube.com/nsliberalparty
www.facebook.com/StephenMcNeilLiberal
twitter.com/NSLiberal
Hon. Stephen McNeil, Leader
Michael Mercer, Executive Director
Marney Bentley, Director, Operations & Compliance

Liberal Party of Prince Edward Island / Parti libéral de l'Ile du Prince Édouard
PO Box 2559, #205, 129 Kent St., Charlottetown PE C1A 8C2
Tel: 902-368-3449; *Fax:* 902-368-3687
Toll-Free: 877-740-3449
officialagent@liberalpei.ca
www.liberal.pe.ca
Social Media: www.youtube.com/user/peiliberals?feature=mhee
www.facebook.com/pages/PEI-Liberals/183212951743526
twitter.com/peiliberalparty
Hon. Wade MacLauchlan, Leader
Jamie MacPhail, Executive Director

The Libertarian Party of Canada
#205, 372 Rideau St., Ottawa ON K1N 1G7
Toll-Free: 888-785-7930
www.libertarian.ca
Social Media:
linkedin.com/company/libertarian-party-of-canada
www.facebook.com/libertarianCDN
twitter.com/libertarianCDN
Tim Moen, Party Leader

Manitoba Liberal Party (MLP)
635 Broadway, Winnipeg MB R3C 0X1
Tel: 204-988-9380; *Fax:* 204-284-1492
Toll-Free: 800-567-5746
rana@manitobaliberals.ca
www.manitobaliberals.ca
Social Media: www.youtube.com/user/manitobaliberals
www.facebook.com/manitobaliberals
Rana Bokhari, Party Leader

New Brunswick Liberal Association
715 Brunswick St., Fredericton NB E3B 1H8
Tel: 506-453-3950; *Fax:* 506-453-2476
Toll-Free: 800-442-4902
www.nbliberal.ca
Social Media: www.youtube.com/user/NBLiberalTV
www.facebook.com/nbla.alnb
twitter.com/NBLA_ALNB
Hon. Brian Gallant, Leader
Joel Reed, President

New Democratic Party (NDP) / Nouveau Parti Démocratique
Federal Office, #300, 279 Laurier West, Ottawa ON K1P 5J9
Tel: 613-236-3613; *Fax:* 613-230-9950
Toll-Free: 866-525-2555
TTY: 866-776-7742
www.ndp.ca
Social Media: www.youtube.com/user/NDPCanada
www.facebook.com/NewDemocraticParty
twitter.com/ThomasMulcair
To offer Canadians an alternative political vision based on the principles of democratic socialism; To protect & expand programs such as Medicare & the Old Age Pension through prudent & effective government, & through a truly fair tax system
Hon. Tom Mulcair, Party Leader
Rebecca Blaikie, President

Nova Scotia Progressive Conservative Association
#1003, 1660 Hollis St., Halifax NS B3J 1V7
Tel: 902-429-9470; *Fax:* 902-423-2465
Toll-Free: 800-595-8779
www.pcparty.ns.ca
Social Media: www.youtube.com/user/pcnovascotia
www.facebook.com/people/Jamie-Baillie/634725469
twitter.com/JamieBaillie
The Progressive Conservative Association of Nova Scotia is one of the oldest political parties in the province, with a mission to form a fiscally responsible, socially progressive government.
Jamie Baillie, Party Leader
Jim David, Provincial Director

Online Party of Canada
#411, 637 Lake Shore Blvd. West, Toronto ON M5V 3J6
Tel: 416-567-6913
Contact@OnlineParty.ca
www.onlineparty.ca
Social Media:
www.facebook.com/onlinepartyca
Michael Nicula, Leader

Ontario Liberal Party (OLP)
#210, 10 St. Mary St., Toronto ON M4Y 1P9
Fax: 416-323-9425
Toll-Free: 800-268-7250
info@ontarioliberal.ca
www.ontarioliberal.ca
Social Media: www.youtube.com/user/OntarioLiberalTV
linkedin.com/groups/Ontario-Liberal-Party-3410725
www.facebook.com/OntarioLiberalParty
twitter.com/OntLiberal
Hon. Kathleen Wynne, Leader
Vince Borg, President

Ontario Progressive Conservative Party
59 Adelaide St. East, 4th Fl., Toronto ON M5C 1K6
Tel: 416-861-0020; *Fax:* 416-861-9593
Toll-Free: 800-903-6453
www.ontariopc.com
Social Media: www.youtube.com/user/ontariopcparty
www.facebook.com/OntarioPC
twitter.com/OntarioPCParty
Patrick Brown, Party Leader
Richard Ciano, President

Parti communiste du Québec (PCQ)
CP 482, Succ. Place d'Armes, Montréal QC H2Y 3H3
Tél: 514-528-6142
info@pcq.qc.ca
www.pcq.qc.ca
Unifier avec la classe ouvrière et les couches populaires pour que s'installe le pouvoir populaire dans le but de construire le socialisme
André Parizeau, Party Leader

Parti libéral du Québec (PLQ) / Québec Liberal Party (QLP)
254, rue Queen, Montréal QC H3C 2N8
Tél: 514-288-4364; *Téléc:* 514-288-9455
Ligne sans frais: 800-361-1047
info@plq.org
www.plq.org
Média social: www.youtube.com/PartiLiberalduQuebec
www.facebook.com/liberalquebec
twitter.com/LiberalQuebec
Hon. Philippe Couillard, Chef du Parti

Parti québécois (PQ)
#150, 1200 ave. Papineau, Montréal QC H2K 4R5
Tél: 514-526-0020; *Téléc:* 514-526-0272
Ligne sans frais: 800-363-9531
info@pq.org
www.pq.org
Média social: www.instagram.com/partiquebecois
www.facebook.com/lepartiquebecois
twitter.com/PartiQuebecois
Réaliser démocratiquement la souveraineté du Québec pour s'épanouir comme peuple francophone, pour ne plus être minoritaire, pour mettre fin au gaspillage, pour se doter d'une politique économique qui répond aux intérêts du Québec; donner au Québec une place dans le monde
Sylvain Gaudreault, Chef
Raymond Archambault, Président
Danielle Gagné, Secrétaire nationale

Parti Vert du Québec (PVQ) / Green Party of Québec
#208, 6575, av Somerled, Montréal QC H4V 1T1
Tél: 514-612-3365
info@pvq.qc.ca
www.pvq.qc.ca
Média social: www.facebook.com/partivert
twitter.com/partivertqc
Alex Tyrrell, Chef

Pirate Party of Canada
#155, 3-212 Henderson Hwy., Winnipeg MB R2L 1L8
Tel: 778-800-2744; *Toll-Free:* 877-978-2023
info@pirateparty.ca
www.pirateparty.ca
Social Media:
facebook.com/piratepartyca
twitter.com/piratepartyca
James Wilson, Leader

Progressive Conservative Association of Alberta
PC Alberta Office, #300, 1000 - 9 Ave. SW, Calgary AB T2P 2Y6
Tel: 780-423-1624; *Fax:* 780-423-1634
Toll-Free: 800-461-4443
www.albertapc.ab.ca
Social Media: www.youtube.com/user/PCAlberta
www.facebook.com/pc.alberta
twitter.com/pc_alberta
To assist in nominating & supporting Progressive Conservative canadidates in Alberta provincial elections; To promote the Progressive Conservative Association of Alberta
Ric McIver, Party Leader
Terri Beaupre, President
Courtney Day, Secretary
Ron Renaud, Treasurer

Progressive Conservative Association of Prince Edward Island
PO Box 578, 30 Pond St., #B, Charlottetown PE C1A 7L1
Tel: 902-628-8679; *Fax:* 902-628-6428
Toll-Free: 800-859-4221
info@peipcparty.ca
peipcparty.ca
Social Media:
www.facebook.com/peipcparty
twitter.com/PEIPCParty
To form a government that is socially progessive
Jamie Fox, Interim Party Leader

Progressive Conservative Party of Manitoba
23 Kennedy St., Winnipeg MB R3C 1S5
Tel: 204-594-4080; *Toll-Free:* 800-663-8679
www.pcmanitoba.com
Social Media:
www.facebook.com/PCManitoba
twitter.com/PC_Manitoba
Hon. Brian Pallister, Party Leader

Progressive Conservative Party of New Brunswick / Le Parti Progressiste-Conservateur de Nouveau-Brunswick
336 Regent St., Fredericton NB E3B 3X4
Tel: 506-453-3456; *Fax:* 506-444-4713
info@pcng.org
www.pcnb.ca
Social Media: www.youtube.com/pcnbtv
www.facebook.com/PCNBca
twitter.com/pcnbca
Bruce Fitch, Interim Leader
J.P. Soucy, Executive Director

Progressive Conservative Party of Saskatchewan
72 High St. East, Moose Jaw SK S6H 0B8
Tel: 306-693-7572; *Fax:* 306-693-7580
pcsask@sasktel.net
www.pcsask.ca
Social Media: plus.google.com/109797344778550107038
www.facebook.com/sask.pc.7
twitter.com/PC_Saskatchewan
Rick Swenson, Party Leader

Rhinoceros Party
4540, av de l'Hôtel-de-Ville, Montréal QC H2T 2B1
Tel: 514-903-9450
www.neorhino.ca
François Yo Gourd, Leader

Saskatchewan Liberal Association
845A McDonald St., Regina SK S4N 2X5
Fax: 613-235-7208
assistance@liberal.ca
saskatchewan.liberal.ca
Social Media:
www.facebook.com/LPC.SK
twitter.com/lpcsask
Evatt Merchant, President

Socialist Party of Canada (SPC) / Parti Socialiste du Canada
PO Box 4280, Victoria BC V8X 3X8
spc@iname.com
www.worldsocialism.org/canada/
To promote the establishment of socialism - a system of society based upon the common ownership & democratic control of the means & instruments for producing & distributing wealth by & in the interest of society as a whole
John Ayers, Contact

United Party of Canada
119 Oakcrest Dr., Keswick ON L4P 3J2
Tel: 905-476-0000
www.unitedpartyofcanada.com
Robert (Bob) Kesic, Leader

Western Arctic Liberal Association
PO Box 965, Yellowknife NT XIA 2N7
Tel: 867-445-2377; *Fax:* 867-766-4915

Western Block Party
PO Box 24052, 4420 West Saanich Rd., Victoria BC V8Z 7E7
Tel: 250-479-6270; *Fax:* 250-479-3294
www.westernblockparty.com
Paul St. Laurent, Leader

Yukon Green Party
PO Box 31603, Whitehorse YT Y1A 3r3
Tel: 867-633-6334; *Fax:* 867-633-3392
yukongreenparty@gmail.com
www.yukongreenparty.ca
Kristina Calhoun, Party Leader

Yukon Liberal Party
PO Box 183, #108 Elliot St., Whitehorse YT Y1A 2C6
Tel: 867-667-4748; *Fax:* 867-667-4720
www.ylp.ca
Social Media:
www.facebook.com/yukonliberalparty
twitter.com/YukonLiberal
Sandy Silver, Leader
Ranj Pillai, President

Poultry & Eggs

Alberta Egg Producers' Board (EFA)
#101, 90 Freeport Blvd. NE, Calgary AB T3J 5J9
Tel: 403-250-1197; *Fax:* 403-291-9216
Toll-Free: 877-302-2344
info@eggs.ab.ca
eggs.ab.ca
To be the best producers & marketers of eggs
Ben Waldner, Chair
David Webb, Manager, Marketing & Communications

British Columbia Broiler Hatching Egg Producers' Association (BCBHEC)
PO Box 191, Abbotsford BC V4X 3R2
Tel: 604-864-7556
association@bcbhec.com
www.bcbhec.com
To establish a better understanding & appreciation with the public & other interested parties regarding the industry; to stimulate & encourage improvements related to sales & scientific development in the field; to promote the exchange of ideas in an effort to find solutions to problems in the broiler hatching egg industry; to encourage economical plans to assists producers; & to provide better contact with hatcheries, feed suppliers, processors, & broiler growers.
Bryan Brandsma, President

Chicken Farmers of Canada (CFC) / Les Producteurs de poulet du Canada
#1007, 350 Sparks St., Ottawa ON K1R 7S8
Tel: 613-241-2800; *Fax:* 613-241-5999
cfc@chicken.ca
www.chickenfarmers.ca
Social Media: www.pinterest.com/chickendotca
www.facebook.com/chickenfarmers
twitter.com/chickenfarmers
To build an evidence-based, consumer driven Canadian chicken industry that provides opportunities for profitable growth for all stakeholders
Mike Dungate, Executive Director
Lisa Bishop-Spencer, Manager, Communications

Éleveurs de volailles du Québec
#250, 555, boul Roland-Therrien, Longueuil QC J4H 4G1
Tél: 450-679-0530; *Téléc:* 450-679-5375
evq@upa.qc.ca
volaillesduquebec.qc.ca
A pour mission l'étude, la défense et le développement des intérêts économiques, sociaux et moraux de ses membres; favorise et stimule la mobilisation et la participation de ses membres tout en les consultant et en les informant; développe et renforce la mise en marché collective des poulets et des dindons produits au Québec, en mettant en place des services garantissant le fonctionnement optimal du plan conjoint et des autres outils de mise en marché
Jean-Paul Bouchard, Président

Fédération des producteurs d'oeufs de consommation du Québec (FPOCQ)
#320, 555, boul Roland-Therrien, Longueuil QC J4H 4E7
Tél: 450-679-0530; *Téléc:* 450-679-0855
www.oeuf.ca
Média social: www.facebook.com/lesoeufs?v=wall
Favoriser le développement durable de l'industrie québécoise des oeufs et ce par: le respect de l'environnement et le bien-être des animaux; en procurant un revenu équitable aux intervenants du secteur; en répondant aux attentes des consommateurs avec des oeufs et produits de haute qualité
Serge Lefebvre, Président

Turkey Farmers of Canada (TFC) / Les éleveurs de dindon du Canada (ÉDC)
Bldg. One, #202, 7145 West Credit Ave., Mississauga ON L5N 6J7
Tel: 905-812-3140; *Fax:* 905-812-9326
www.turkeyfarmersofcanada.ca
Social Media:
www.facebook.com/TastyTurkey
twitter.com/tastyturkey
To develop & strengthen the Canadian Turkey market through an effective supply management systems that stimulates growth & profitability for stakeholders
Mark Davies, Chair

Printing Industry & Graphic Arts

British Columbia Printing & Imaging Association (BCPIA)
PO Box 75218, Stn. White Rock, Surrey BC V4A 0B1
Tel: 604-542-0902
www.bcpia.org
To be the voice of the BC printing industry & its employees; to provide services & benefits which encourage fellowship, education, community involvement & high standards in business conduct.
Marilynn Knoch, Executive Director

Canadian Printing Industries Association (CPIA) / Association canadienne de l'imprimerie (ACI)
#407, 2-2026 Lanthier Dr., Orleans ON K4A 0N6
Tel: 613-236-7208; *Fax:* 613-232-1334
Toll-Free: 800-267-7280
info@cpia-aci.ca
www.cpia-aci.ca
Social Media: linkedin.com/company/canadian-printing-industries-association
To advance the quality of management in the printing & allied trades; to offer services through a network of local & related organizations including representations to various sectors; to enhance the image & profile of the industry
Brian Ellis, Executive Director
Sandy Stephens, Chair

Canadian Printing Ink Manufacturers' Association (CPIMA)
ON
Tel: 905-665-9310; *Fax:* 647-439-1572
www.cpima.org
To exchange information that will be of benefit to members, the ink industry, & the printing industry
Steve Marshall, President
Michelle Connolly, Executive Director

Ontario Printing & Imaging Association (OPIA)
#135, 3-1750 The Queensway, Toronto ON M9C 5H5
Tel: 905-602-4441; *Fax:* 905-602-9798
www.opia.on.ca
To provide leadership for a successful printing & imaging industry in Ontario
Kim Stewart, Chair

Printing & Graphics Industries Association of Alberta (PGIA)
PO Box 61229, RPO Kensington, Calgary AB T2N 4S6
Tel: 403-281-1421; *Fax:* 403-225-1421
info@pgia.ca
www.pgia.ca
Committed to the advancement of a healthy, effective & ethical graphic arts industry by providing leadership in the development of imaged communications; by enabling members to work to strengthen the industry
Caron Evans, Association Manager
Dean McElhinney, President

Printing Equipment & Supply Dealers' Association of Canada (PESDA)
11 Alderbrook Place, Bolton ON L7E 1V3
Tel: 416-524-1954; *Fax:* 905-951-6374
www.pesda.com
To promote & advance the interests of the printing equipment, consumables & related services industries in Canada
Richard Armstrong, President
Bob Kirk, General Manager

Saskatchewan Graphic Arts Industries Association (SGAIA)
PO Box 7152, Saskatoon SK S7K 4J1
Tel: 306-373-3202; *Fax:* 306-373-3246
info@sgaia.ca
sgaia.ca
To promote the interests of Saskatchewan's printing & allied industries; To increase the influence of graphic arts industry to the government & the general business community; To promote programs for the graphic arts industry at universities & technical institutions
Don Breher, Executive Director

Society of Graphic Designers of Canada (GDC) / Société des designers graphiques du Canada
Arts Court, 2 Daly Ave., Ottawa ON K1N 6E2
Tel: 613-567-5400; *Fax:* 613-564-4428
Toll-Free: 877-496-4453
info@gdc.net
www.gdc.net
Social Media: linkedin.com/groups?home=&gid=124328
www.facebook.com/GDCNational
twitter.com/gdcntl
To maintain a defined, recognized & competent body of graphic designers; To promote high standards of graphic design for benefit of Canadian industry, commerce, public service & education
Adrian Jean, President
Melanie MacDonald, Executive Director

Prisoners & Ex-Offenders

Canadian Association of Elizabeth Fry Societies (CAEFS) / Association canadienne des sociétés Elizabeth Fry (ACSEF)
#701, 151 Slater St., Ottawa ON K1P 5H3
Tel: 613-238-2422; *Fax:* 613-232-7130
Toll-Free: 800-637-4606
admin@caefs.ca
www.elizabethfry.ca
Social Media: www.youtube.com/user/CAEFSElizabethFry
www.facebook.com/138252919680859
twitter.com/CAEFS
To work with & on behalf of women & girls involved with the justice system, in particular criminalized women; To offer services & programs to women in need, advocating for reforms & offering fora within which the public may be informed about & participate in all aspects of the justice system as it affects women
Kim Pate, Executive Director

Canadian Coalition Against the Death Penalty (CCADP) / Coalition canadien contre la peine de mort
80 Lillington Ave., Toronto ON M1N 3K7
Tel: 416-693-9112; *Fax:* 416-693-9112
info@ccadp.org
www.ccadp.org
Social Media: www.youtube.com/ccadpmedia
www.facebook.com/70610338689
To provide information about abuses of the death penalty internationally; To ensure Canada does not return to the death penalty
Tracy Lamourie, Director & Founder
Dave Parkinson, Director & Founder

The John Howard Society of British Columbia
763 Kingsway, Vancouver BC V5V 3C2
Tel: 604-872-5651; *Fax:* 604-872-8737
info@johnhowardbc.ca
www.johnhowardbc.ca
To prevent crime & reform the justice system through alternative programming
Tim Veresh, Executive Director

The John Howard Society of Canada / Société John Howard du Canada
809 Blackburn Mews, Kingston ON K7P 2N6
Tel: 613-384-6272; *Fax:* 613-384-1847
national@johnhoward.ca
www.johnhoward.ca
Social Media: twitter.com/JohnHoward_Can
To promote effective, just, & humane responses to the causes & consequences of crime; To assist individuals who have come into conflict with the law; To advocate for change in the criminal justice process; To educate the community on matters involving prison conditions, criminal law, & its applications today
Catherine Latimer, Executive Director

Operation Springboard
#800, 2 Carlton St., Toronto ON M5B 1J3
Tel: 416-977-0089; *Fax:* 416-977-2840
info@operationspringboard.on.ca
www.operationspringboard.on.ca
Social Media: www.youtube.com/user/OperationSpringbord
linkedin.com/company/springboard-services
www.facebook.com/OperationSpringboard
twitter.com/OpSpringboard
To design & provide services & programs that effectively reintegrate offenders into the community as responsible individuals; to develop crime prevention strategies; To promote community involvement in design & provision of services along with continuous effort to encourage understanding & support; To bring forward recommendations that will improve effectiveness of the criminal justice system.
Brad Lambert, President & Chair
Margaret Stanowski, Executive Director
Alain Mootoo, Chief Administrative Officer

Quakers Fostering Justice (QFJ)
c/o Canadian Friends Service Committee, 60 Lowether Ave., Toronto ON M5R 1C7
Tel: 416-920-5213; *Fax:* 416-920-5214
qfj@quakerservice.ca
quakerservice.ca/our-work/justice
To build caring community without need for prisons; to explore alternatives to prison based on economic, social justice & fulfillment of human needs; to foster awareness within & outside Quaker community of roots of crime & violence in society; to reach & support prisoners, guards, victims & families
Tasmin Rajotte, Program Coordinator

St. Leonard's Society of Canada (SLSC) / Société St-Léonard du Canada
Bronson Centre, #208, 211 Bronson Ave., Ottawa ON K1R 6H5
Tel: 613-233-5170; *Fax:* 613-233-5122
Toll-Free: 888-560-9760
info@stleonards.ca
www.stleonards.ca
Social Media: www.facebook.com/SLSCanada
twitter.com/StLeonards_Can
Committed to the prevention of crime through programs which promote responsible community living & safer communities
Elizabeth White, Executive Director

Seventh Step Society of Canada
#2017, 246 Stewart Green SW, Calgary AB T3H 3C8
Tel: 403-650-1902
seventh@7thstep.ca
www.7thstep.ca
Self-help organization dedicated to help adult & young offenders to become useful & productive members of society; to provide follow-up to those who wish to use organization as means to maintain freedom
Patrick Graham, Executive Director

Psychology

Bereavement Ontario Network (BON)
174 Oxford St., Woodstock ON N4S 6B1
Tel: 519-266-4747
info@BereavementOntarioNetwork.ca
www.bereavementontarionetwork.ca
Bereavement Ontario Network is a diverse group of organizations and individuals throughout the province that work in the field of grief, bereavement, and mourning as professionals and volunteers.
Janet Devine, Chair

Publishing

Alberta Weekly Newspapers Association (AWNA)
3228 Parsons Rd., Edmonton AB T6H 5R7
Tel: 780-434-8746; *Fax:* 780-438-8356
Toll-Free: 800-282-6903
info@awna.com
www.awna.com
Social Media: releases@awna.com
To assist members to publish high quality community newspapers; To serve advertisers by providing information about the markets of community newspapers in Alberta
Dennis Merrell, Executive Director
Ossie Sheddy, President
Murray Elliott, Vice-President
Chrissie Hamblin, Controller
Maurizia Hinse, Coordinator, Professional Development & Communication
Fred Gorman, Corporate Secretary

The Alcuin Society
PO Box 3216, Vancouver BC V6B 3X8
info@alcuinsociety.com
www.alcuinsociety.com
Social Media: www.flickr.com/photos/alcuinsociety
www.facebook.com/alcuinsociety
twitter.com/alcuin
To sponsor educational programs; Yo publish a journal; To offer awards & citations for excellence in book arts
Howard Greaves, Chair

Association des libraires du Québec (ALQ)
#801, 407, boul St-Laurent, Montréal QC H2Y 2Y5
Tél: 514-526-3349; *Téléc:* 514-526-3340
info@alq.qc.ca
www.alq.qc.ca
Regrouper, pour leur bénéfice mutuel, les libraires engagées dans la vente au détail au Québec et celles engagées dans la vente du livre en langue française au Canada; fournir des services, faire des études, fournir de l'information, tenir des réunions et des rencontres et contribuer à des programmes pour le bénéfice et l'amélioration de ses membres; encourager la vente au détail du livre au Québec; encourager la communication et la collaboration entre les éditeurs, les distributeurs et les autres participants de l'industrie du livre; aider les libraires à encourager la lecture; lutter contre toute forme de censure
Katherine Fafard, Directrice générale

Association nationale des éditeurs de livres (ANEL)
2514, boul Rosemont, Montréal QC H1Y 1K4
Tél: 514-273-8130; *Téléc:* 514-273-9657
Ligne sans frais: 866-900-2635
info@anel.qc.ca
anel.qc.ca
Média social: anel.qc.ca/blogue
www.facebook.com/61084204798
twitter.com/ANEL_QE
Soutenir le développement d'une industrie nationale de l'édition québécoise et canadienne de langue française; établir entre ses membres des rapports de bonne confraternité; étudier et défendre les intérêts tant généraux que politiques et économiques de ses membres; étudier toute question relative à la profession et diffuser l'information auprès de ses membres; constituer une représentation réelle et efficace de la profession à toute les instances pertinentes
Jean-François Bouchard, Président
Richard Prieur, Directeur général

Association of Book Publishers of British Columbia (ABPBC)
#600, 402 West Pender St., Vancouver BC V6B 1T6
Tel: 604-684-0228; *Fax:* 604-684-5788
admin@books.bc.ca
books.bc.ca
To encourage writing, publishing, distribution & promotion of books written by BC & Canadian authors; to cooperate with other associations & organizations to further the reading & studying of books; to work for the development & maintenance of strong competitive book publishing houses owned & controlled in BC & Canada; to further professional training for individuals engaged in book publishing
Ruth Linka, President
Margaret Reynolds, Executive Director

Association of Canadian Publishers (ACP) / Association des éditeurs canadiens
#306, 174 Spadina Ave., Toronto ON M5T 2C2
Tel: 416-487-6116; *Fax:* 416-487-8815
admin@canbook.org
www.publishers.ca
To encourage writing, publishing, distribution & promotion of books written by Canadian authors in particular, & reading & study of books in general; To represent the members at international book fairs; To facilitate the exchange of information & professional expertise among members
Matt Williams, President
Kate Edwards, Executive Director
Emily Kellogg, Manager, Programs

Association of Canadian University Presses (ACUP) / Association des presses universitaires canadiennes (APUC)
#700, 10 St. Mary St., Toronto ON M4Y 2W8
Tel: 416-978-2239; *Fax:* 416-978-4738
www.acup.ca
To support scholarly publishing by university presses in Canada
John Yates, President

Association of English Language Publishers of Québec (AELAQ) / Association des éditeurs de langue anglaise du Québec
#3, 1200 Atwater Ave., Montréal QC H3Z 1X4
Tel: 514-932-5633
admin@aelaq.org
www.aelaq.org
To raise the profile of English-language books published in Québec
Julia Kater, Executive Director

Association of Manitoba Book Publishers (AMBP)
#404, 100 Arthur St., Winnipeg MB R3B 1H3
Tel: 204-947-3335; *Fax:* 204-956-4689
To promote Manitoba publishing industry
Michelle Peters, Executive Director

Association québécoise des salons du livre (AQSL)
#100, 60, rue St-Antoine, Trois-Rivières QC G9A 0C4
Téléc: 819-376-4222
Ligne sans frais: 888-542-2075
info@aqsl.org
www.aqsl.org
De promouvoir du livre, du périodique et de la lecture; De défendre les intérêts des Salons membres et favorise la recherche, la documentation, les contacts professionnels, la création et la diffusion du livre
Julie Brosseau, Présidente

Book & Periodical Council (BPC)
#107, 192 Spadina Ave., Toronto ON M5T 2C2
Tel: 416-975-9366; *Fax:* 416-975-1839
info@thebpc.ca
www.thebpc.ca
To increase the level of awareness & the use of Canadian materials by the general public & in educational systems at all levels; To ensure the public has an adequate & representative range of Canadian books & periodicals in sales outlets, library systems & educational institutions; To strengthen book & periodical distribution systems; To support the development of new & existing Canadian-owned companies & encourage their growth & expansion; To improve market conditions & contractual arrangements as well as promotion & publicity given to Canadian writers & their work; To encourage the development of writing & publishing projects of social & cultural importance; To improve the cultural & economic climate in which the Canadian book & periodical industries exist; To discourage expansion of foreign ownership in all sectors of the book & periodical publishing industries
Anita Purcell, Chair

Book Publishers Association of Alberta (BPAA)
10523 - 100 Ave., Edmonton AB T5J 0A8
Tel: 780-424-5060; *Fax:* 780-424-7943
info@bookpublishers.ab.ca
www.bookpublishers.ab.ca
To work for maintenance & growth of strong book publishing houses owned & controlled in Alberta; to speak for common interests of constituent members; to liaise & cooperate with other associations for the good of the Canadian publishing industry
Kieran Leblanc, Executive Director

British Columbia & Yukon Community Newspapers Association (BCYCNA)
9 West Broadway, Vancouver BC V5Y 1P1
Tel: 604-669-9222; *Fax:* 604-684-4713
Toll-Free: 866-669-9222
info@bccommunitynews.com
www.bccommunitynews.com
Social Media:
linkedin.com/company/220705
To encourage excellence in the publishing of community newspapers
George Affleck, General Manager
Kerry Slater, Manager, Special Projects
Connor Barnsley, Manager, Communications & Member Services
Cora Schupp, Accounting Manager

Canadian Book Professionals Association (CanBPA)
info@canbpa.ca
canbpa.ca
Social Media:
www.facebook.com/136875019696314
twitter.com/canbpa
To foster networking, provide educational opportunities & idea sharing, & job & career information & postings for book professionals of all kinds, including publishers, librarians, booksellers & agents
David Ward, President

Canadian Bookbinders & Book Artists Guild (CBBAG) / Guilde canadienne des relieurs et des artisans du livre
#207, 80 Ward. St., Toronto ON M6H 4A6
Tel: 416-581-1071
cbbag@cbbag.ca
www.cbbag.ca
Social Media:
www.facebook.com/groups/77394956232
To create a spirit of community among hand workers in the book arts & those who love books; to promote greater awareness of the book arts; to increase educational opportunities, & foster excellence through exhibitions, workshops, lectures, & publications.
Mary McIntyre, President

Canadian Booksellers Association (CBA)
#902, 1255 Bay St., Toronto ON M5R 2A9
Tel: 416-467-7883; *Fax:* 416-467-7886
Toll-Free: 866-788-0790
enquiries@cbabook.org
www.cbabook.org
To promote a high standard of business methods & ethics among members; to define & expand the role of booksellers within the Canadian publishing process; to provide professional advice to prospective & practising booksellers
Mark Lefebvre, President
Christopher Smith, Vice-President
Ellen Pickle, Treasurer

Canadian Children's Book Centre (CCBC)
#217, 40 Orchard View Blvd., Toronto ON M4R 1B9
Tel: 416-975-0010; *Fax:* 416-975-8970
info@bookcentre.ca
www.bookcentre.ca
Social Media:
www.facebook.com/kidsbookcentre
twitter.com/kidsbookcentre
To promote the reading, writing, & illustrating of Canadian books for young readers, providing programs, publications & resources for teachers, librarians, authors, illustrators, publishers, booksellers & parents.
Todd Kyle, President
Charlotte Teeple, Executive Director
Dawn Todd, General Manager

Canadian Circulations Audit Board Inc. (CCAB) / Office canadien de vérification de la diffusion
Div. of BPA International, #800, 1 Concorde Gate, Toronto ON M3C 3N6
Tel: 416-487-2418; *Fax:* 416-487-6405
www.bpaww.com
To issue standardized statements of data reported by a member; to verify the figures shown in these statements by auditors' examination of any & all records considered by the corporation to be necessary; to disseminate these data for the benefit of any individual or company requiring such information
Tim Peel, Contact

Canadian Community Newspapers Association (CCNA)
#200, 890 Yonge St., Toronto ON M4W 3P4
Tel: 416-923-3567; *Fax:* 416-923-7206
Toll-Free: 877-305-2262
info@newspaperscanada.ca
www.newspaperscanada.ca
To be the national voice of the community press in Canada
John Hinds, President & CEO

The Canadian Press (CP) / La presse canadienne
36 King St. East, Toronto ON M5C 2L9
Tel: 416-364-0321; *Fax:* 416-364-0207
editorial@thecanadianpress.com
www.thecanadianpress.com
Social Media:
linkedin.com/company/the-canadian-press
www.facebook.com/thecanadianpress
twitter.com/CdnPress
To operate as a national news cooperative, owned & financed by Canada's daily newspapers
Stephen Meurice, Editor-in-Chief
Rose Kingdon, Director, Broadcast News
Graeme Roy, Director, News Photography
Andrea Baillie, Managing Editor, News Desks/Beats

Canadian Publishers' Council (CPC)
#203, 250 Merton St., Toronto ON M4S 1B1
Tel: 416-322-7011; *Fax:* 416-322-6999
www.pubcouncil.ca
To represent the interests of 18 companies who publish books & other media for elementary & secondary schools, colleges & universities, professional & reference, retail & library markets
David Swail, Executive Director, External Relations

Canadian University Press (CUP) / Presse universitaire canadienne
#5, 411 Richmond St. East, Toronto ON M5A 3S5
Tel: 416-962-2287; *Fax:* 416-966-3699
Toll-Free: 866-250-5595
president@cup.ca
www.cup.ca
Social Media: www.youtube.com/user/CUPonline
www.facebook.com/canadianuniversitypress
twitter.com/canunipress
To elevate the standard of post-secondary student journalism; to foster communication among post-secondary student newspapers; to provide a national press service for post-secondary student newspapers; to provide facilities for the dissemination of news of importance to post-secondary students
Erin Hudson, President
Brendan Kergin, National Bureau Chief

Circulation Management Association of Canada (CMC) / Association canadienne des chefs de tirage
c/o Target Audience Management Inc., #6, 50 Main St. East, Beeton ON L0G 1A0
Tel: 905-729-1046; *Fax:* 905-729-4432
admin@thecmc.ca
thecmc.ca
Social Media:
www.facebook.com/180627152014026
twitter.com/CircCanada

To provide professional development, promotes fellowship within the circulation profession & raises the profile of circulation professionals by rewarding outstanding achievement.
Tony Danas, President
Ron Sellwood, Director, Communications
Brian Gillet, Administrator

Connexions Information Sharing Services
#201, 812A Bloor St. West, Toronto ON M6G 1L9
Tel: 416-964-7799
mailroom@connexions.org
www.connexions.org
Social Media:
www.facebook.com/ConnexionsOnline
twitter.com/connexi0ns
To connect people working for social justice with information, ideas, groups & the history of social change movements.
Ulli Diemer, Coordinator

Hebdos Québec
#345, 2250, boul Daniel-Johnson, Laval QC H7T 2L1
Tél: 514-861-2088
communications@hebdos.com
www.hebdos.com
Média social: www.facebook.com/hebdosqc
twitter.com/HebdosQuebec
Favoriser et stimuler le développement du secteur des hebdomadaires en offrant à ses membres divers services en matière de recherche, de marketing et de formation; projeter une image crédible de la presse hebdomadaire, de la défendre, et de la rendre plus visible et plus accessible
Gilber Paquette, Directeur général

International Board on Books for Young People - Canadian Section (IBBY - Canada) / Union internationale pour les livres de jeunesse
c/o Canadian Children's Book Centre, #217, 40 Orchard View Blvd., Toronto ON M4R 1B9
Tel: 416-975-0010; *Fax:* 416-975-8970
info@ibby-canada.org
www.ibby-canada.org
Social Media: flickr.com/photos/50914640@N08
www.facebook.com/ibbycanada
twitter.com/IBBYCanada
To promote the belief that all children everywhere should have the ability to read a wide & rich selection of books at the level of their needs & interests; To build bridges of understanding & tolerance through children's books
Susane Duchesne, President
Stephanie Dror, Secretary, Membership

The Literary Press Group of Canada (LPG)
#501, 192 Spadina Ave., Toronto ON M5T 2C2
Tel: 416-483-1321; *Fax:* 416-483-2510
info@lpg.ca
www.lpg.ca
A not-for-profit association of Canadian literary book publishers, with a mandate to advocate on behalf of its members, & to foster the survival, growth & maintenance of strong Canadian-owned & controlled literary book publishing houses
Jack Illingworth, Executive Director
Petra Morin, Sales & Marketing Manager

Livres Canada Books
#504, 1 Nicholas St., Ottawa ON K1N 7B7
Tel: 613-562-2324; *Fax:* 613-562-2329
info@livrescanadabooks.com
www.livrescanadabooks.com
Social Media:
www.facebook.com/LivresCanadaBooks
The association defends the interests of Canadian book publishers by providing market intelligence products and services, information and resources on digital publishing, as well as financial, promotion and logisitical support; the association administers the Foreign Rights Marketing Assistance Program, a component of the Canada Book Fund, as well as mentoring programs and other funding initiatives
Caroline Fortin, Chair
François Charette, Executive Director

Magazines Canada
#700, 425 Adelaide St. West, Toronto ON M5V 3C1
Tel: 416-504-0274; *Fax:* 416-504-0437
info@magazinescanada.ca
www.magazinescanada.ca
Social Media: www.youtube.com/magazinescanada
linkedin.com/company/magazines-canada
www.facebook.com/MagazinesCanada
twitter.com/magscanada
Mark Jamison, Chief Executive Officer
Barbara Zatyko, General Manager
Barbara Bates, Executive Director, Circulation Marketing
Jim Everson, Executive Director, Public Affairs
Gary Garland, Executive Director, Advertising Services

Manitoba Community Newspapers Association (MCNA)
943 McPhillips St., Winnipeg MB R2X 2J9
Tel: 204-947-1691; *Fax:* 204-947-1919
Toll-Free: 800-782-0051
www.mcna.com
To serve community newspaper publishers in Manitoba; To act as the industry voice for the issues of community newspaper publishers; To encourage high standards in publishing
Tanis Hutchinson, Manager, Display Ad Sales

National Magazine Awards Foundation (NMAF) / Fondation nationale des prix du magazine canadien
#3500, 2 Bloor St. East, Toronto ON M4W 1A8
Tel: 416-422-1358
staff@magazine-awards.com
www.magazine-awards.com
Social Media: youtube.com/magazineawards
linkedin.com/groups/4002310/profile
www.facebook.com/190062084384867?
twitter.com/magawards
To recognize & promote excellence in the content & creation of Canadian print & digital publications through an annual program of awards & national publicity efforts
Barbara Gould, Managing Director

Newspapers Atlantic
#216, 7075 Bayers Rd., Halifax NS B3L 2C2
Tel: 902-832-4480; *Fax:* 902-832-4484
Toll-Free: 877-842-4480
info@newspapersatlantic.ca
newspapersatlantic.ca
To promote excellence, credibility, & the economic well-being of member community newspapers throughout Atlantic Canada
Inez Forbes, President
Mike Kierstead, Executive Director

Newspapers Canada (CNA) / Journaux Canadiens (ACJ)
#200, 37 Front St. East, Toronto ON M5E 1B3
Tel: 416-923-3567; *Fax:* 416-923-7206
Toll-Free: 877-305-2262
info@newspaperscanada.ca
www.newspaperscanada.ca
Social Media:
linkedin.com/company/newspapers-canada
www.facebook.com/newspaperscanada
twitter.com/newspapercanada
To ensure the continuance of a free press to serve readers effectively, by combining the experience, expertise, & dedication of members; To increase the profile & effectiveness of Canada's newspaper industry
John Hinds, President & Chief Executive Officer

Ontario Community Newspapers Association (OCNA)
#200, 890 Yonge St., Toronto ON M4W 3P4
Tel: 905-639-8720; *Fax:* 905-639-6962
www.ocna.org
Social Media:
www.facebook.com/171125688577
To support members with information about the Ontario community newspaper industry & market; to improve the competitive position of the industry
Dave Adsett, President
John Willems, Secretary-Treasurer
Caroline Medwell, Executive Director
Todd Frees, Controller
Karen Shardlow, Coordinator, Member Services
Lucia Shepherd, Coordinator, Accounting/Newsprint

Periodical Marketers of Canada (PMC)
South Tower, #1007, 175 Bloor St. East, Toronto ON M4W 3R8
Tel: 416-968-7547; *Fax:* 416-968-6281
info@periodical.ca
www.periodical.ca
To represent Canadian wholesalers; To promote Canadian magazines
Ray Argyle, Executive Director

Québec Community Newspaper Association (QCNA) / Association des journaux régionaux du Québec (AJRQ)
#5, 400, boul Grand, L'Ile-Perrot QC J7V 4X2
Tel: 514-453-6300; *Fax:* 514-453-6330
info@qcna.qc.ca
www.qcna.org
To promote Québec community English media; To serve as clearinghouse for information; To promote good journalism among members; to enhance the role of the media as social catalysts; To represent its members to pertinent government departments; To interact with other provincial & national newspaper associations in Canada; To help members better their financial condition
Greg Duncan, Executive Director

Saskatchewan Publishers Group (SPG)
2405 - 11th Ave., Regina SK S4P 0K4
Tel: 306-780-9808; *Fax:* 306-780-9810
info@saskbooks.com
www.skbooks.com
Social Media:
twitter.com/SaskBooks
To promote the Saskatchewan book publishing industry; to provide a forum for sharing information & ideas; to speak for the common interests of its members; to undertake specific projects, programs & studies; to work closely with other publishing & cultural organizations across Canada
Brenda Niskala, Co-Executive Director
Jillian Bell, Co-Executive Director

Saskatchewan Weekly Newspapers Association (SWNA)
#14, 401 - 45th St. West, Saskatoon SK S7L 5Z9
Tel: 306-382-9683; *Fax:* 306-382-9421
Toll-Free: 800-661-7962
www.swna.com
Social Media:
www.facebook.com/sask.newspaper
twitter.com/swnainfo
To assist persons to issue press releases, buy advertising, & place classifieds in member newspapers in central Saskatchewan & the Northwest Territories
Steven Nixon, Executive Director
Rob Clark, President
Louise Simpson, Treasurer & Office Manager

Société de développement des périodiques culturels québécois (SODEP)
#716, 460, rue Ste-Catherine ouest, Montréal QC H3B 1A7
Tél: 514-397-8669; *Téléc:* 514-397-6887
info@sodep.qc.ca
www.sodep.qc.ca
Média social: www.facebook.com/sodep.qc.ca?ref=ts
twitter.com/cultureenrevues
Travailler à l'essor et au rayonnement des revues culturelles; établir et entretenir des liens avec le milieu de l'enseignement, les bibliothèques, les médias et les maisons de distribution; représenter et promouvoir les intérêts professionnels, éthiques et économiques des éditeurs; favoriser les échanges internationaux
Éric Perron, Président
Isabelle Lelarge, Vice-président
Francine Bergeron, Directrice générale
Josiane Ouellet, Secrétaire-trésorier

Toronto Press & Media Club
#101, 1755 Rathburn Rd. East, Mississauga ON L4W 2M8
info@torontopressclub.net
www.torontopressclub.net
Social Media:
www.facebook.com/TorontoPressAndMediaClub
Ed Patrick, President

Radio Broadcasting

Alliance des radios communautaires du Canada
#1206, 1, rue Nicholas, Ottawa ON K1N 7B7
Tél: 613-562-0000; *Téléc:* 613-562-2182
radiorfa.com
Média social: www.youtube.com/arcducanada
www.facebook.com/arcducanada
twitter.com/arcducanada
François Coté, Secrétaire général

Real Estate

Alberta Building Officials Association
12010 - 111 Avenue, Edmonton AB T5G 0E6
www.aboa.ab.ca
To improve standards of building inspection; To be a discussion forum for shared issues and concerns; To assist in education of building inspectors in various fields
Ryan Nixon, President
Brian Boddez, Director, Membership

Alberta Real Estate Association (AREA)
#300, 4954 Richard Rd. SW, Calgary AB T3E 6L1
Tel: 403-228-6845; *Fax:* 403-228-4360
Toll-Free: 800-661-0231
info@areahub.ca
www.areahub.ca
Dan Russel, CEO

Annapolis Valley Real Estate Board
PO Box 117, 2110 Hwy. 1, Auburn NS B0P 1A0
Tel: 902-847-9336; *Fax:* 902-847-9869
avreb@eastlink.ca
Cathy Simpson, Executive Officer

Appraisal Institute of Canada (AIC) / Institut canadien des évaluateurs (ICE)
#403, 200 Catherine St., Ottawa ON K2P 2K9
Tel: 613-234-6533; *Fax:* 613-234-7197
Toll-Free: 888-551-5521
info@aicanada.ca
www.aicanada.ca
Social Media:
linkedin.com/groups/2967439
www.facebook.com/AppraisalInstitute.Canada
twitter.com/aic_canada
To grant professional designations in real estate appraisal (Accredited Appraiser Canadian Institute (AACI) & Canadian Residential Appraiser (CRA)); To strive to maintain high standards in real estate appraisal to protect the public interest
Keith Lancastle, Chief Executive Officer
Rosmarie Buxbaum, Director, Finance & Administration
Sheila Roy, Director, Marketing & Communications
Nathalie Roy-Patenaude, Director, Professional Practice

Appraisal Institute of Canada - Alberta (AIC-AB)
#245, 495 - 36 St. NE, Calgary AB T2A 6K3
Tel: 403-207-7892; *Fax:* 403-207-7857
aic.alberta@shawlink.ca
www.aicanada.ca/province-alberta/alberta
To maintain professional ethics & standards in real estate valuation; to qualify real estate appraisers in Alberta, Nunavut & the Northwest Territories
Sanjit Singh, President
Christine Vandelinder, Executive Director

The Appraisal Institute of Canada - British Columbia (AIC-BC)
#210, 10451 Shellbridge Way, Richmond BC V6X 2W8
Tel: 604-284-5515; *Fax:* 604-284-5514
info@appraisal.bc.ca
www.aicanada.ca/province-british-columbia/british-columbia
To represent, promote & support members as leaders in the counselling, analysis & evaluation of real property. Chapters: Fraser Valley, Nanaimo, Okanagan, Vancouver, Kamloops, The North, Victoria, & Kootenay.
Steve Blacklock, President
Janice P. O'Brien, Executive Director

The Appraisal Institute of Canada - Manitoba (AIC-MB)
5 Donwood Dr., Winnipeg MB R2G 0V9
Tel: 204-771-2982; *Fax:* 204-654-9583
mbaic@mts.net
www.aicanada.ca
To maintain professional ethics & standards in real estate valuation; to qualify real estate appraisers in the province
Dan Diachun, President
Pamela Wylie, Executive Director

The Appraisal Institute of Canada - Newfoundland & Labrador (AIC-NL)
PO Box 1571, Stn. C, St. John's NL A1C 5P3
Tel: 709-759-5769
naaic@nf.aibn.com
www.aicanada.ca/province-newfoundland-labrador
To promote the appraisal profession throughout Newfoundland & Labrador.
Greg Bennett, President
Sherry House, Executive Director

Appraisal Institute of Canada - Ontario (AIC-ON)
#108, 16 Four Seasons Place, Toronto ON M9B 6E5
Tel: 416-695-9333; *Fax:* 877-413-4081
info@oaaic.on.ca
www.aicanada.ca/ontario
To serve the public interest by advancing high standards in the analysis & valuation of real property matters by enhancing the professional competence of its members. Chapters: Credit Valley, Hamilton-Niagara, Huronia, Kingston, London, North Bay, Oshawa/Durham, Ottawa, Peterborough/Lindsay, Sudbury & Sault Ste. Marie, Thunder Bay, Toronto, Waterloo/Wellington, Windsor, York.
Robin Jones, President
Bonnie Prior, Executive Director

The Appraisal Institute of Canada - Prince Edward Island (AIC-PEI)
PO Box 1796, Charlottetown PE C1A 7N4
Tel: 902-368-3355; *Fax:* 902-368-3582
peiaic@bellaliant.net
www.aicanada.ca/province-prince-edward-island
To promote the appraisal profession throughout Prince Edward Island; to assist members, those wishing to become members & the public
Boyce Costello, President
Suzanne Pater, Executive Director

The Appraisal Institute of Canada - Saskatchewan (AIC-SK)
#505, 2300 Broad St., Regina SK S4P 1Y8
Tel: 306-352-4195
skaic@sasktel.net
sk.aicanada.ca
To assist members, those hoping to become appraisers & the public
Wanda Styre, President
Marilyn Sterdnica, Executive Director

Association des propriétaires du Québec inc. (APQ) / Quebec Landlords Association (QLA)
10720, boul St-Laurent, Montréal QC H3L 2P7
Tél: 514-382-9670; *Téléc:* 514-382-9676
Ligne sans frais: 888-382-9670
www.apq.org
Média social: www.youtube.com/user/assoproprietaires
www.facebook.com/141154527095
twitter.com/apquebec
Défendre les droits et les intérêts des propriétaires de logements locatifs du Québec

L'Association du Québec de l'Institut canadien des évaluateurs (AQICE) / The Appraisal Institute of Canada - Québec (AIC-QC)
#400, 200 Catherine St., Ottawa ON K2P 2K9
Tél: 613-234-6533; *Ligne sans frais:* 888-551-5521
aqice@aicanada.ca
www.aicanada.ca/province-quebec
La mission de l'Institut canadien des évaluateurs est de protéger l'intérêt du public en s'assurant que ses membres offrent des services d'expert-conseil selon des normes élevées de pratique professionnelle
Daniel Pinard, President
Nicole Laflèche Anderson, Executive Director

Association of Battlefords Realtors
PO Box 611, North Battleford SK S9A 2Y7
Tel: 306-445-6300; *Fax:* 306-445-9020
bfords.realestate@sasktel.net
To advance & promote interest of those engaged in real estate as brokers, agents, valuators, examiners, & experts; To increase public confidence in & respect for those engaged in real estate
Rick Cann, Executive Officer

Association of Regina Realtors Inc.
1854 McIntyre St., Regina SK S4P 2P9
Tel: 306-791-2700; *Fax:* 306-781-7940
www.reginarealtors.com
Social Media:
www.facebook.com/ReginaREALTORS
twitter.com/ReginaREALTORS
Mike Duggleby, President
Stacy Svendsen, President-Elect

Association of Saskatchewan Realtors (ASR)
2811 Estey Dr., Saskatoon SK S7J 2V8
Tel: 306-373-3350; *Fax:* 306-373-5377
Toll-Free: 877-306-7732
info@saskatchewanrealestate.com
www.saskatchewanrealestate.com
Social Media:
www.facebook.com/69418510914
twitter.com/saskREALTORS
Represents real estate boards & their realtor members on government affairs & provincial issues; develops standards of professional practice; administers training; provides information to members, governments & the public; provides support services to members; registers brokers & salespeople; develops special projects for the educational benefit of all registrants in Saskatchewan
Bill Madder, Executive Vice President
Patty Kalytuk, Director, Communication & Administration
Arvid Kuhnle, Director, Professional Development
Linda Minor, Member Services Coordinator

Bancroft District Real Estate Board
PO Box 1522, 69 Hastings St. North, Bancroft ON K0L 1C0
Tel: 613-332-3842; *Fax:* 613-332-3842

Barrie & District Association of REALTORS Inc.
30 Mary St., Barrie ON L4N 1S8
Tel: 705-739-4650
www.barrie.realtors.ca
Social Media:
linkedin.com/company/barrie-&-district-association-of-realtors-inc
www.facebook.com/BDARInc
twitter.com/barrierealtors
To provide continuing education, Multiple Listing Service (MLS), statistical information & many other services to its members; To promote a high standard of business practices

BC Northern Real Estate Association
2609 Queensway, Prince George BC V2L 1N3
Tel: 250-563-1236; *Fax:* 250-563-3637
inquiries@bcnreb.bc.ca
Alexandra Goseltine, Executive Director

Brampton Real Estate Board (BREB)
#401, 60 Gillingham Dr., Brampton ON L6X 0Z9
Tel: 905-791-9913; *Fax:* 905-791-9430
info@breb.org
www.breb.org
Social Media: www.youtube.com/user/TheBREBTV
www.facebook.com/theBREB
To help members achieve their real estate related goals
Gerry Verdone, Executive Officer

Brandon Real Estate Board (BREB)
857 - 18 St., Unit B, Brandon MB R7A 5B8
Tel: 204-727-4672; *Fax:* 204-727-8331
info@breb.mb.ca
www.breb.mb.ca
To provide real estate support for Realtors in Brandon.
Cam Toews, President
Annette Wiebe, Executive Officer

Brantford Regional Real Estate Association Inc. (BRREA)
106 George St., Brantford ON N3T 2Y4
Tel: 519-753-0308; *Fax:* 519-753-8638
brantfordreb@rogers.com
www.brrea.com
Social Media: www.youtube.com/BRREAssociation
linkedin.com/company/brantford-regional-real-estate-association
www.facebook.com/BrantfordRegionalRealEstateAssociation
twitter.com/_BRREA
To provide real estate support for realtors working in Brantford
Viktoria Tumilowicz, Executive Officer

British Columbia Northern Real Estate Board
2609 Queensway, Prince George BC V2L 1N3
Tel: 250-563-1236; *Fax:* 250-563-3637
inquiries@bcnreb.bc.ca
boards.mls.ca/bcnreb
Dorothy Friesen, President

British Columbia Real Estate Association (BCREA)
PO Box 10123, #1420, 701 Georgia St. West, Vancouver BC V7Y 1C6
Tel: 604-683-7702; *Fax:* 604-683-8601
bcrea@bcrea.bc.ca
www.bcrea.bc.ca
Social Media:
twitter.com/bcrea
To promote the interests of & advocate for the real estate profession; To secure public support & trust in the profession; To promote property rights & real estate related issues; To ensure high standards of ethics & professionalism through ongoing education of realtors
Robert Laing, Chief Executive Officer
Melinda Entwistle, Chief Operating Officer
Damian Stathonikos, Director, Communications & Public Affairs

Building Owners & Managers Association - Canada
PO Box 61, #1801, 1 Dundas St. West, Toronto ON M5G 1Z3
Tel: 416-214-1912; *Fax:* 416-214-1284
info@bomacanada.ca
www.bomacanada.ca
Social Media:
linkedin.com/groups/3958628/profile
www.facebook.com/pages/BOMA-Canada/107613392698316
twitter.com/BOMA_CAN
To represent the Canadian commerical real estate industry on matters of national concern; To develop a strong communications network between local associations; To promote professionalism of members through education programs & effective public relations activity
Benjamin L, Shinewald, President/CEO

Building Owners & Managers Association Toronto
#1800, 1 Dundas St. West, Toronto ON M5G 1Z3
Tel: 416-596-8065; *Fax:* 416-596-1085
info@bomatoronto.org
www.bomatoronto.org
Social Media: www.youtube.com/user/BOMAtoronto
linkedin.com/company/boma-toronto
www.facebook.com/bomatoronto
twitter.com/bomatoronto
To represent the interests & concerns of building owners & managers in the commercial & office space industry in the Greater Toronto Area
Maryanne McDougald, Chair
Susan Allen, President & Chief Staff Officer
Tamara Orlova, Director, Finance, Administration & Information Technology
Robyn Sauret, Manager, Events & Education
Kirsten Martin, Manager, Marketing & Communication

Calgary Real Estate Board Cooperative Limited (CREB)
300 Manning Rd. NE, Calgary AB T2E 8K4
Tel: 403-263-0530; *Fax:* 403-218-3688
info@creb.com
www.creb.com
Alan Tennant, CEO

Cambridge Association of Realtors Inc.
2040 Eagle St. North, Cambridge ON N3H 0A1
Tel: 519-623-3660; *Fax:* 519-623-8253
cambridge-admin@rogers.com
cambridgeassociationofrealtors.com
Social Media:
www.facebook.com/CambridgeAssociationOfRealtors
twitter.com/CamRealtors

Canadian National Association of Real Estate Appraisers (CNAREA)
PO Box 157, Qualicum Beach BC V9K 1S7
Fax: 866-836-6369
Toll-Free: 844-792-3679
HQ@cnarea.ca
www.cnarea.ca
To certify & regulate real property appraisers in Canada; To raise the standards of the real property appraising profession; To protect consumers
Steven G. Coull, Chief Executive Officer
Robert B. Fraser, National President & Treasurer
James Carty, National Vice-President
Rob MacDonald, National Secretary

The Canadian Real Estate Association (CREA) / Association canadienne de l'immeuble
200 Catherine St., 6th Fl., Ottawa ON K2P 2K9
Tel: 613-237-7111; *Fax:* 613-234-2567
Toll-Free: 800-842-2732
info@crea.ca
www.crea.ca
Social Media: www.youtube.com/user/CREACHANNEL
linkedin.com/company/1400987
www.facebook.com/CREA.ACI
twitter.com/CREA_ACI
To enhance member professionalism, competency & profitability; To advocate government policies which improve the industry's market environment & enhance individual rights with respect to the ownership of real property
Gary Simonsen, Chief Executive Officer
Pauline Aunger, President

Central Alberta Realtors Association
4922 - 45 St., Red Deer AB T4N 1K6
Tel: 403-343-0881; *Fax:* 403-347-9080
office@CARAssociation.ca
www.rdreb.ca
Social Media:
www.facebook.com/243909398990726
twitter.com/CaraRedDeer
Judy Ferguson, Executive Officer
Ken Devoe, President

Chambre immobilière Centre du Québec Inc.
139C, rue Hériot, Drummondville QC J2C 2B1
Tél: 819-477-1033; *Téléc:* 819-474-7913
Ligne sans frais: 877-546-8320
chambre@cgocable.ca
www.immobiliercentreduquebec.com
Marie-Paule Landry, Adjointe exécutive
Denis A. Jackson, Présidente

Chambre immobilière de l'Abitibi-Témiscamingue Inc. (CIAT)
#203, 33, av Horne, Rouyn-Noranda QC J9X 4S1
Tél: 819-762-1777; *Téléc:* 819-762-4030
ciat@cablevision.qc.ca
www.ciat.qc.ca
Robert Brière, Président
Gilles Langlais, Directeur général

Chambre immobilière de l'Estrie inc.
19, rue King ouest, Sherbrooke QC J1H 1N4
Tél: 819-566-7616; *Téléc:* 819-566-7688
info@mon-toit.net
www.mon-toit.net
Promouvoir et protéger les intérêts de l'industrie immobilière du Québec afin que les Chambres et les membres accomplissent avec succès leurs objectifs d'affaires.
Lucien Choquette, Président

Chambre immobilière de l'Outaouais
106, boul Sacré-Coeur, Gatineau QC J8X 1E1
Tél: 819-771-5221; *Téléc:* 819-771-8715
info@avecunagent.com
www.avecunagent.com
Média social: www.facebook.com/104740336281495
twitter.com/avecuncourtier
De fournir à ses membres les outils nécessaires pour réussir
Chantal Legault, Directrice générale

Chambre immobilière de la Haute Yamaska Inc. (CIHY) / Haute Yamaska Real Estate Board
#3, 45, rue Centre, Granby QC J2G 5B4
Tél: 450-378-6702; *Téléc:* 450-375-5268
administration.cihy@videotron.ca
Offrir des services de formation et d'information pour les agents immobiliers.
Lise Desrochers, Directrice générale

Chambre immobilière de la Mauricie Inc. / Trois-Rivières Real Estate Board
1275, boul des Forges, Trois-Rivières QC G8Z 1T7
Tél: 819-379-9081; *Téléc:* 819-379-9262
info@cimauricie.com
www.cimauricie.com
Lise Girardeau, Directrice générale

Chambre immobilière de Lanaudière Inc.
765, boul Manseau, Joliette QC J6E 3E8
Tél: 450-759-8511; *Téléc:* 450-759-6557
cil@immobilierlanaudiere.com
www.immobilierlanaudiere.com
Louise Renaud, Directrice générale

Chambre immobilière de Québec
600, ch du Golf, Ile-des-Soeurs QC H3E 1A8
Tél: 514-762-0212; *Téléc:* 514-762-0365
Ligne sans frais: 866-882-0212
info@fciq.ca
www.fciq.ca
Média social: twitter.com/fciq_eco
Promouvoir et protéger les intérêts de l'industrie immobilière du Québec afin que les Chambres et les membres accomplissent avec succès leurs objectifs d'affaires.
Gina Gaudreault, Président

Chambre immobilière de Saint-Hyacinthe Inc.
CP 667, Saint-Hyacinthe QC J2S 7P5
Tél: 450-799-2210; *Téléc:* 450-799-2230
chimmob@cgocable.ca
www.chambreimmobiliersthyacinthe.com
Promouvoir et protéger les intérêts de l'industrie immobilière du Québec afin que les Chambres et les membres accomplissent avec succès leurs objectifs d'affaires.
Pierre Tanguay, Président

Chambre immobilière des Laurentides (CIL)
570, boul. des Laurentides, Piedmont QC J0R 1K0
Tél: 450-240-0006; *Ligne sans frais:* 800-263-3511
info@cilaurentides.ca
www.cilaurentides.ca
Média social: www.facebook.com/OptionLaurentides
De promouvoir et à développer des intérêts professionnels, économiques et sociaux de ses membres
Francine Soucy, Présidente
Daniel Vandal, Directrice générale

Chambre immobilière du Grand Montréal / Greater Montréal Real Estate Board
600, ch du Golf, Ile-des-Soeurs QC H3E 1A8
Tél: 514-762-2440; *Téléc:* 514-762-1854
Ligne sans frais: 888-762-2440
cigm@cigm.qc.ca
www.cigm.qc.ca
De protéger les intérêts commerciaux de ses membres afin de développer leur succès
Éric Charbonneau, Directeur général

Chambre immobilière du Saguenay-Lac St-Jean Inc. (CISL)
#140, 2655, boul du Royaume, Jonquière QC G7S 4S9
Tél: 418-548-8808; *Téléc:* 418-548-2588
chambre@immobiliersaguenay.com
www.immobiliersaguenay.com
Média social: www.facebook.com/immobilier.saguenay
Regrouper les membres afin de leur fournir des services, assurer la qualité de leur travail, défendre et promouvoir leurs intérêts; protéger et promouvoir le commerce de l'immobilier et encourager l'accès à la propriété; offrir de la formation et du perfectionnement dans le domaine immobilier afin d'assurer et de garantir le professionnalisme de l'industrie; faciliter au public en général l'accès à l'information dans le domaine immobilier
Ginette Gaudreault, Directrice générale

Chatham-Kent Real Estate Board
252 Wellington St. W., Chatham ON N7M 1K1
Tel: 519-352-4351
ckreb@mnsi.net
boards.mls.ca/chatham
Social Media:
www.facebook.com/153823918039312
Jamie Winkler, President

Chilliwack & District Real Estate Board
#1, 8433 Harvard Pl., Chilliwack BC V2P 7Z5
Tel: 604-792-0912; *Fax:* 604-792-6795
cadreb@telus.net
cadreb.com
Social Media:
twitter.com/ChilliwackREB
To serve the real estate needs of Chilliwack, Agassiz, Hope, Boston Bar and Harrison.
Steve Lerigny, Executive Officer

Cornwall & District Real Estate Board
407B Pitt St., Cornwall ON K6J 3R3
Tel: 613-932-6457; *Fax:* 613-932-1687
www.mls-cornwall.com
Dani Tedesco-Derouchie, Executive Officer

Durham Region Association of REALTORS (DRAR)
#14, 50 Richmond St. East, Oshawa ON L1G 7C7
Tel: 905-723-8184; *Fax:* 905-723-7531
Reception@DurhamRealEstate.org
www.durhamrealestate.org
Social Media:
twitter.com/DurhamRENews
To pursue excellence & professionalism in real estate through commitment & service
Nancy Shaw, Executive Officer

Fédération des Chambres immobilières du Québec (FCIQ)
600, ch du Golf, Ile-des-Soeurs QC H3E 1A8
Tél: 514-762-0212; *Téléc:* 514-762-0365
Ligne sans frais: 866-882-0212
info@fciq.ca
www.fciq.ca
Média social: twitter.com/fciq_eco
Promouvoir et protéger les intérêts de l'industrie immobilière du Québec afin que les Chambres et les membres accomplissent avec succès leurs objectifs d'affaires
Normand Racine, Président du conseil d'administration
Chantal de Repentigny, Directrice adjointe, Communication et relations avec l'industrie

Fort McMurray Realtors Association
9909 Sutherland St., Fort McMurray AB T9H 1V3
Tel: 780-791-1124; *Fax:* 780-743-4724
boards.mls.ca/fortmcmurray
Chris Moskalyk, Executive Officer

Fraser Valley Real Estate Board
15463 - 104 Ave., Surrey BC V3R 1N9
Tel: 604-930-7600; *Fax:* 604-588-0325
Toll-Free: 877-286-5685
mls@fvreb.bc.ca
www.fvreb.bc.ca
Social Media:
linkedin.com/company/fraser-valley-real-estate-board
www.facebook.com/FVREB
twitter.com/FVREB
To provide the most efficient real estate marketing service.
Ron Todson, President
Rob Philipp, Chief Executive Officer

Greater Moncton Real Estate Board Inc.
541 St. George Blvd., Moncton NB E1E 2B6
Tel: 506-857-8200; *Fax:* 506-857-1760
gmreb@nb.aibn.com
www.monctonrealestateboard.com
To provide its members with the strcuture & services to enhance REALTOR professionalism, standards of business practice and ethics in meeting the real estate needs of the community.
Kerry Rakuson, Executive Officer
Roxanne Maillet, President

Guelph & District Real Estate Board
400 Woolwich St., Guelph ON N1H 3X1
Tel: 519-824-7270
info@gdar.ca
www.gdar.ca
Social Media:
linkedin.com/company/guelph-&-district-association-of-realtors-r-
www.facebook.com/AssociationofREALTORS
twitter.com/_gdar_

Hamilton-Burlington & District Real Estate Board (HBDREB)
505 York Blvd., Hamilton ON L8R 3K4
Tel: 905-529-8101; *Fax:* 905-529-4349
info@rahb.ca
www.rahb.ca
To pursue excellence & professionalism in real estate through commitment & service
George O'Neill, Chief Executive Officer

Huron Perth Association of Realtors
#6, 55 Lorne Ave. East, Stratford ON N5A 6S4
Tel: 519-271-6870; *Fax:* 519-271-3040
www.hpar.ca
To maintain a professional standard among its members in order to better serve the public
Gwen Kirkpatrick, Executive Officer

Institute of Municipal Assessors
#206, 10720 Yonge St., Richmond Hill ON L4C 3C9
Tel: 905-884-1959; *Fax:* 905-884-9263
Toll-Free: 877-877-8703
info@assessorsinstitute.ca
www.assessorsinstitute.ca
The IMA is the largest Canadian professional association representing members that practice in the field of Property Assessment and related Property Taxation functions.
Terry Tomkins, President
Colleen Vercouteren, 1st Vice President

Kamloops & District Real Estate Association (KADREA)
#101, 418 St. Paul St., Kamloops BC V2C 2J6
Tel: 250-372-9411
kadrea.realtyserver.com

Kawartha Lakes Real Estate Association
31 Kent St. East, Lindsay ON K9V 2C3
Tel: 705-324-4515
www.kawarthalakes-mls.ca
Social Media:
www.facebook.com/184458454969478
To provide its members with resources that allow them to grow within the profession
Susan Schell, Executive Officer

Kingston & Area Real Estate Association
720 Arlington Park Pl., Kingston ON K7M 8H9
Tel: 613-384-0880; *Fax:* 613-384-0863
info@karea.ca
www.karea.ca
Adam Rayner, President

Kootenay Real Estate Board (KREB)
#208, 402 Baker St., Nelson BC V1L 4H8
Tel: 250-352-5477; *Fax:* 250-352-7184
Toll-Free: 877-295-9375
kreb@telus.net
www.kreb.ca
Social Media:
www.facebook.com/217611504946687
To promote interest in real estate markets in all aspects through service to members & the public.
Cathy Graham, President
Marianne Bond, Executive Officer

Lethbridge & District Association of Realtors
522 - 6 St. South, Lethbridge AB T1J 2E2
Tel: 403-328-8838; *Fax:* 403-328-8906
eo@ldar.ca
www.ldar.ca
Social Media:
twitter.com/LDAR2013
To provide real estate information on the Lethbridge area; to serve as a forum to network & build connections within the real estate community.

London & St. Thomas Association of Realtors
342 Commissioners Rd. West, London ON N6J 1Y3
Tel: 519-641-1400; *Fax:* 519-641-4613
info@lstar.ca
www.lstar.ca
Social Media: www.youtube.com/user/LSTARMembers
www.facebook.com/LSTAR.REALTORS
twitter.com/LSTARtweets
To provide its members with the necessary tools that enable them to deliver excellent service to the community
Betty Doré, Executive Vice President
Joanne Shannon, Director, Administration

Manitoba Building Officials Association
PO Box 2063, Winnipeg MB R3C 3R4
Tel: 204-832-1512; *Fax:* 204-897-8094
info@mboa.mb.ca
www.mboa.mb.ca
To promote building safety through training & awareness in order to help their members
Rick Grimshaw, President

Manitoba Real Estate Association (MREA)
1873 Inkster Blvd., Winnipeg MB R2R 2A6
Tel: 204-772-0405; *Fax:* 204-775-3781
Toll-Free: 800-267-6019
cduheme@mrea.mb.ca
www.realestatemanitoba.com
Social Media:
www.facebook.com/144040815612760
To represent the interest of Manitoba's licensed realtors
Brian M. Collie, Executive Director

Medicine Hat Real Estate Board Co-operative Ltd.
403 - 4 St. SE, Medicine Hat AB T1A 0K5
Tel: 403-526-2879; *Fax:* 403-526-0307
www.mhreb.ca
Murray Schlenker, President
Randeen Bray, Executive Officer

Melfort Real Estate Board
PO Box 3157, Melfort SK S0E 1A0
Tel: 306-752-5751; *Fax:* 306-752-5754
Derwood Dodds, President

Mississauga Real Estate Board
#1, 3450 Ridgeway Dr., Mississauga ON L5L 0A2
Tel: 905-608-6732; *Fax:* 905-608-9988
membership@mreb.ca
www.mreb.ca
Social Media:
twitter.com/MREBca
To represent its members & keep them informed about events involving real estate so that they are able to provide knowledgable service to the public
Donna Metcalfe, Executive Officer

Moose Jaw Real Estate Board
88 Saskatechewan St. East, Moose Jaw SK S6H 0V4
Tel: 306-693-9544; *Fax:* 306-692-4463
eo.mjreb@sasktel.net
www.moosejawrealestateboard.com
To promote the real estate sector in the area & provides a forum for local realtors to exchange information.
Jami Thorn, President
Jim Millar, Executive Officer

New Brunswick Association of Real Estate Appraisers (NBAREA) / Association des évaluateurs immobiliers du Nouveau-Brunswick (AEIN-B)
#204, 403 Regent St., Fredericton NB E3B 3X6
Tel: 506-450-2016; *Fax:* 506-450-3010
nbarea@nb.aibn.com
www.nbarea.org
To enhance the profession & to protect the public
Andrew Leech, President

New Brunswick Building Officials Association (NBBOA) / L'Association des officiels de la construction du Nouveau-Brunswick
PO Box 3193, Stn. B, Fredericton NB E3A 5G9
Tel: 506-470-3375; *Fax:* 506-450-4924
admin@nbboa.ca
www.nbboa.ca
Social Media:
www.facebook.com/NBBOA
twitter.com/THENBBOA
To achieve & maintain the highest levels of professionalism in membership, education & qualifications; legislative interpretation; building inspection service; building & construction safety.
Sherry Sparks, President
Robert Pero, Secretary
Lucas Roze, Executive Director

New Brunswick Real Estate Association (NBREA) / Association des agents des immeubles du Nouveau-Brunswick
#1, 22 Durelle St., Fredericton NB E3C 1N8
Tel: 506-459-8055; *Fax:* 506-459-8057
Toll-Free: 800-762-1677
info@nbrea.ca
nbrea.ca
Social Media:
www.facebook.com/NBREALTORS
twitter.com/NBREALTORS
To strengthen & promote standards of professionalism in the real estate industry
Jamie Ryan, CEO

Newfoundland & Labrador Association of Realtors (NLAR)
28 Logy Bay Rd., St. John's NL A1A 1J4
Tel: 709-726-5110; *Toll-Free:* 855-726-5110
reception@nlar.ca
www.nlar.ca
Social Media:
linkedin.com/company/newfoundland-and-labrador-association-of-realtors-
www.facebook.com/NLAREALTORS
twitter.com/_NLAR
Bill Stirling, Chief Executive Officer

Niagara Association of REALTORS (NAR)
116 Niagara St., St Catharines ON L2R 4L4
Tel: 905-684-9459; *Fax:* 905-684-4778
www.niagararealtor.ca
Social Media: www.pinterest.com/niagararealtors
linkedin.com/company/niagara-association-of-realtors
www.facebook.com/NiagaraRealtors
twitter.com/NiagaraREALTORS
To provide members with the structure & services to facilitate the marketing of real estate; To ensure a high standard of business practices & ethics; To effectively serve the real estate needs of the members
Stephen Oliver, President

North Bay Real Estate Board
926 Cassells St., North Bay ON P1B 4A8
Tel: 705-472-6812; *Fax:* 705-472-0529
admin@nbreb.com
www.nbreb.com
To represent real estate agents and member offices in North Bay
Susan Nosko, President

Northumberland Hills Association of Realtors
#14, 975 Elgin St. West, Cobourg ON K9A 5J3
Tel: 905-372-8630; *Fax:* 905-372-1443
districtrealestate@bellnet.ca
boards.mls.ca/northumberland

Nova Scotia Association of REALTORS (NSAR)
#100, 7 Scarfe Ct., Dartmouth NS B3B 1W4
Tel: 902-468-2515; *Fax:* 902-468-2533
Toll-Free: 800-344-2001
nshomeguide.ca
Social Media:
linkedin.com/company/2406082
www.facebook.com/nsarcommunications
twitter.com/NSAR_RealEstate
Provides Realtors with services & representation to enable them to best serve the public in real estate transactions
Roger Boutilier, Executive Officer
Bonnie Wigg, Director, MLSr & Member Services
Monica MacLean, Acting Director, Communications

Nova Scotia Real Estate Appraisers Association (NSREAA)
#602, 5670 Spring Garden Rd., Halifax NS B3J 1H6
Tel: 902-422-4077; *Fax:* 902-422-3717
nsreaa@nsappraisal.ns.ca
nsreaa.ca
The Association regulates the practice of real estate appraisal in Nova Scotia, establishes & promotes the interests of appraisers, develops & maintains high standards of knowledge & best practices in the field, develops & enforces professional ethics, promotes public awareness of the profession, & encourages studies in real estate appraisal.
Carla Dempsey, President
Davida Mackay, Executive Director & Registrar

The Oakville, Milton & District Real Estate Board
125 Navy St., Oakville ON L6J 2Z5
Tel: 905-844-6491; *Fax:* 905-844-6699
info@omdreb.on.ca
www.omdreb.on.ca
Social Media: www.youtube.com/user/omdreb
linkedin.com/company/the-oakville-milton-and-district-real-estate-board-omdreb-
www.facebook.com/OMDREB
twitter.com/OMDREB_Official
To represent its members & provide them with services to help further their career
Marta Sponder, Executive Officer

Okanagan Mainline Real Estate Board (OMREB)
#112, 140 Commercial Dr., Kelowna BC V1X 7X6
Tel: 250-491-4560; *Fax:* 250-491-4580
admin@omreb.com
www.omreb.com
Social Media:
www.facebook.com/okanaganmainlineREB
twitter.com/OMREB1
To provide a forum for the exchange of property-related information between members so that they may provide the public with outstanding service; to establish & maintain optimum standards of business practices; to provide continuing education for the betterment of the members' knowledge; to monitor proposed & legislated laws which inhibit or restrict the right of Canadians or British Columbians to own or use real property

Ontario Building Officials Association Inc. (OBOA) / Association de l'Ontario des officers en bâtiment inc.
#8, 200 Marycroft Ave., Woodbridge ON L4L 5X4
Tel: 905-264-1662; *Fax:* 905-264-8696
admin@oboa.on.ca
www.oboa.on.ca
To foster & cooperate in the establishment of uniform regulations relating to the fire protection & structural adequacy of buildings & the safety & health of the occupants; to promote the understanding & uniform interpretation & enforcement of these regulations & their companion documents; to provide assistance in the development & improvement of these regulations & their companion documents; to promote a close liaison & interchange of ideas on these regulations with related associations, the building industry, government & the consumer public
Ronald M. Kolbe, CAO
Leo Cusumano, President

Ontario Real Estate Association (OREA)
99 Duncan Mill Rd., Toronto ON M3B 1Z2
Tel: 416-445-9910; *Fax:* 416-445-2644
Toll-Free: 800-265-6732
info@orea.com
www.orea.com
Social Media: www.youtube.com/OREAinfo
www.facebook.com/OREAinfo
twitter.com/oreainfo
To represent the vocational interests of members; To advocate for a better working environment; To communicate with members & the public; To develop educational opportunities for the betterment of the real estate profession; To develop programs to assist members in providing quality services to the public; To develop & administer the educational courses required for registration to trade in real estate on behalf of The Real Estate Council of Ontario
Tim Hudak, Chief Executive Officer

Orangeville & District Real Estate Board (ODREB)
228 Broadway Ave., Orangeville ON L9W 1K5
Tel: 519-941-4547
www.odreb.com
Social Media:
twitter.com/odrebrealtors
David Grime, President

Organisme d'autoréglementation du courtage immobilier du Québec (OACIQ) / Québec Real Estate Association
#2200, 4905, boul Lapinière, Brossard QC J4Z 0G2
Tél: 450-676-4800; *Téléc:* 450-676-7801
Ligne sans frais: 800-440-5110
www.oaciq.com
Protéger le public par l'encadrement des activités professionnelles de tous les courtiers et agents immobiliers exerçant au Québec
Serge Brousseau, Président du conseil

Ottawa Real Estate Board (OREB) / Chambre d'immeuble d'Ottawa
1826 Woodward Dr., Ottawa ON K2C 0P7
Tel: 613-225-2240; *Fax:* 613-225-6420
Admin@oreb.ca
www.ottawarealestate.org
Social Media:
twitter.com/OREB1

Parry Sound & Area Association of REALTORS
47A James St., Parry Sound ON P2A 1T6
Tel: 705-746-4020; *Fax:* 705-746-2955
psreb@vianet.on.ca
www.parrysoundrealestateboard.ca
To set a high standard of practice & ethics for its members so that they may better serve the public

Peterborough & the Kawarthas Association of Realtors Inc. (PKAR)
PO Box 1330, 273 Charlotte St., Peterborough ON K9J 7H5
Tel: 705-745-5724; *Fax:* 705-745-9377
info@peterboroughrealestate.org
www.peterboroughrealestate.org
Social Media:
linkedin.com/company/peterborough-and-the-kawarthas-association-of-realtors-inc
www.facebook.com/PtboRealtors
twitter.com/pkarrealestate
Mike Heffernan, President

Portage La Prairie Real Estate Board
PO Box 1288, Portage la Prairie MB R1N 3L5
Tel: 204-857-4111

Powell River Sunshine Coast Real Estate Board
PO Box 307, Powell River BC V8A 5C2
Tel: 604-485-6944; *Fax:* 604-485-6944
prscreb@shaw.ca
www.thesunshinecoast.com
Geri Powell, Board Administrator

Prince Albert & District Association of Realtors
615 Branion Dr., Prince Albert SK S6V 2R9
Tel: 306-764-8755; *Fax:* 306-763-0555
pareb@sasktel.net
www.princealbertrealtors.ca
To support realtors in the Prince Albert Real Estate community.
Candy Marshall, Executive Officer

Prince Edward Island Real Estate Association
75 St. Peter's Rd., Charlottetown PE C1A 5N7
Tel: 902-368-8451; *Fax:* 902-894-9487
office@peirea.com
www.peirea.com
Jim "Benson" Carragher, President
Jane Brewster, First Vice-President, Education
Greg Lipton, Second Vice-President, Finance

Quinte & District Association of REALTORS Inc.
PO Box 128, 51 Cannifton Rd. North, Cannifton ON K0K 1K0
Tel: 613-969-7873; *Fax:* 613-962-1851
ExecOfficer@Quinte-mls.com
www.quinte-mls.com
Social Media:
twitter.com/quinte_REALTORS
Jamie Troke, President

Real Estate Board of Greater Vancouver
2433 Spruce St., Vancouver BC V6H 4C8
Tel: 604-730-3000; *Fax:* 604-730-3100
Toll-Free: 800-304-0565
www.rebgv.org
Social Media: www.youtube.com/user/rebgv
www.facebook.com/rebgv
twitter.com/rebgv
Robert K. Wallace, CEO

Real Estate Board of the Fredericton Area Inc. (FREB)
544 Brunswick St., Fredericton NB E3B 1H5
Tel: 506-458-8163; *Fax:* 506-459-8922
freb01@rogers.com
www.frederictonrealestateboard.com
To address member education, motivation & appreciation
Edie Whitman, Executive Officer

Real Estate Institute of Canada (REIC) / Institut canadien de l'immeuble (ICI)
#208, 5407 Eglinton Ave. West, Toronto ON M9C 5K6
Tel: 416-695-9000; *Fax:* 416-695-7230
Toll-Free: 800-542-7342
infocentral@reic.com
www.reic.ca
Social Media:
linkedin.com/company/real-estate-institute-of-canada
www.facebook.com/reicnational
twitter.com/reicnational
To advance opportunities for persons involved in real estate; To offer certification & designation for real estate professionals
Maura McLaren, Executive Director
Lesley Lucas, Director, Education & Business Development
Britny Rodé, Coordinator, Marketing & Communications
Shelley Barfoot-O'Neill, Director, Admissions & Membership

Real Property Association of Canada
#1410, One University Ave., Toronto ON M5J 2P1
Tel: 416-642-2700; *Fax:* 416-642-2727
Toll-Free: 855-732-5722
info@realpac.ca
www.realpac.ca
Social Media: www.youtube.com/user/REALpacVideos
linkedin.com/company/realpac
www.facebook.com/111245762249174
twitter.com/realpac_news
To represent the real estate industries point of view to government at all levels on legislative & regulatory matters
Paul Morse, CEO
Deborah Prestwich, Manager, Events & Office Services
Julia St. Michael, Manager, Research & Environmental Programs

Realtors Association of Edmonton
14220 - 112 Ave., Edmonton AB T5M 2T8
Tel: 780-451-6666; *Fax:* 780-452-1135
Toll-Free: 888-674-7479
www.ereb.com
Marc Perras, President
Ron Hutchinson, Executive Vice-President

REALTORS Association of Grey Bruce Owen Sound (RAGBOS)
517 - 10 St., Lower Level, Hanover ON N4N 1R4
Tel: 519-364-3827
www.ragbos.ca
To provide a web-based multiple listing service for its members
Dawn Lee McKenzie, President

Realtors Association of Lloydminster & District
#203, 5009 - 48 St., Lloydminster AB T9V 0H7
Tel: 780-875-6939; *Fax:* 780-875-5560
lloydreb@telus.net
rald.realtyserver.com

Realtors Association of South Central Alberta
PO Box 997, Brooks AB T1R 1B8
Tel: 403-362-4643; *Fax:* 403-362-3276
Carol Breakell, Executive Officer
Creitia Morishita, President

Renfrew County Real Estate Board (RCREB)
197 Pembroke St. East, Pembroke ON K8A 3J6
Tel: 613-735-5840; *Fax:* 613-735-0405
www.renfrewcountyrealestateboard.com
Social Media:
www.facebook.com/RCREB
To promote standard practices among its members in order to unify & strengthen their abilities
Sue Martin, Executive Officer

Rideau-St. Lawrence Real Estate Board
#12, 1275 Kensington Pkwy., Brockville ON K6V 6C3
Tel: 613-342-3103; *Fax:* 613-342-1637
rideau@bellnet.ca
boards.mls.ca/rideau

Saint John Real Estate Board Inc.
#100, 55 Drury Cove Rd., Saint John NB E2K 2Z8
Tel: 506-634-8772; *Fax:* 506-634-8775
www.sjrealestateboard.ca
Social Media:
twitter.com/SJ_REALTORS
To provide services to & set standards for members; to preserve & promote the MLS marketing system to benefit buyers & sellers of real property
Jason Stephen, President

Sarnia-Lambton Real Estate Board (SLREB)
555 Exmouth St., Sarnia ON N7T 5P6
Tel: 519-336-6871; *Fax:* 519-344-1928
www.mls-sarnia.com
Social Media:
www.facebook.com/152351484834475
David Burke, Executive Officer

Saskatchewan Building Officials Association Inc. (SBOA)
PO Box 1671, Prince Albert SK S6V 5T2
Tel: 306-445-1733; *Fax:* 306-445-1739
membership@sboa.sk.ca
www.sboa.sk.ca
Dan Knutson, President
Todd Russell, Secretary-Treasurer

Saskatoon Region Association of REALTORS (SRAR)
1149 - 8 St. East., Saskatoon SK S7H 0S3
Tel: 306-244-4453; *Fax:* 306-343-1420
info@srar.ca
www.srar.ca
To represent the real estate interests of its members & the public; to provide services & programs to enhance the professionalism, competency & effectiveness of its members; to advocate public policy towards improving the real estate market environment
Jason Yochim, Executive Officer
Darrin Sych, Director, Advertising

Sault Ste Marie Real Estate Board (SSMREB)
372 Albert St. East, Sault Ste Marie ON P6A 2J6
Tel: 705-949-4560; *Fax:* 705-949-5935
www.saultstemarierealestate.ca
Social Media:
www.facebook.com/SaultSteMarieRealEstateBoard
Andrea Gagne, Executive Officer

Simcoe & District Real Estate Board
191 Queensway West, Simcoe ON N3Y 2M8
Tel: 519-426-4454; *Fax:* 519-426-9330
www.norfolk-mls.ca
Social Media:
www.facebook.com/sdreb

South Okanagan Real Estate Board (SOREB)
365 Van Horne St., Penticton BC V2A 8S4
Tel: 250-492-0626; *Fax:* 250-493-0832
www.soreb.org
Social Media:
www.facebook.com/151180668308444
twitter.com/soreb1
To pursue excellence & professionalism in real estate, through quality education & high ethical standards; To protect the interest of the membership & the public

Southern Georgian Bay Association of REALTORS
243 Ste. Marie St., Collingwood ON L9Y 2K6
Tel: 705-445-7295
info@sgbREALTORS.com
www.sgbrealtors.com
To deliver MLS & real estate services
Sandy Raymer, Executive Officer

Tillsonburg District Real Estate Board
#202, 1 Library Lane, Tillsonburg ON N4G 4W3
Tel: 519-842-9361; *Fax:* 519-688-6850
tburgreb@bellnet.ca
www.tburgreb.ca
To provide its members with the tools they need to best serve the public
Frank Catry, President

Toronto Real Estate Board (TREB)
1400 Don Mills Rd., Toronto ON M3B 3N1
Tel: 416-443-8100
membership@trebnet.com
www.torontorealestateboard.com
Social Media: www.youtube.com/TREBChannel;
www.pinterest.com/trebhome
linkedin.com/company/treb?trk=prof-following-company-logo
www.facebook.com/TorontoRealEstateBoard
twitter.com/TREBhome
Mark McLean, President

Vancouver Island Real Estate Board (VIREB)
6374 Metral Dr., Nanaimo BC V9T 2L8
Tel: 250-390-4212; *Fax:* 250-390-5014
info@vireb.com
www.vireb.com
Social Media:
linkedin.com/pub/vancouver-island-real-estate-board/4a/926/332
www.facebook.com/117416804932
twitter.com/vireb
To provide cost-effective tools, services & information necessary to foster professionalism & maintain the realtor's position as the primary focus in the real estate industry
Guy Bezeau, President
Bill Benoit, CAE, Executive Officer
Darrell Paysen, Manager, Member Services

Victoria Real Estate Board (VREB)
3035 Nanaimo St., Victoria BC V8T 4W2
Tel: 250-385-7766; *Fax:* 250-385-8773
info@vreb.org
www.vreb.org
To promote & enhance the use of the real estate services that its members provide to the public
David Corey, Executive Officer
Carol Crabb, President

West Central Alberta Real Estate Board
162 Athabasca Ave., Hinton AB T7V 2A5
Tel: 780-865-7511; *Fax:* 780-865-7517
wcareb@shaw.ca
boards.mls.ca/wcab

Windsor-Essex County Real Estate Board
3020 Deziel Dr., Windsor ON N8W 5H8
Tel: 519-966-6432; *Fax:* 519-966-4469
www.windsorrealestate.com
Social Media: www.youtube.com/wecrealtors
www.facebook.com/wecrealtors
twitter.com/wecrealtors
Norm Langlois, President

Winnipeg Real Estate Board (WREB)
1240 Portage Ave., Winnipeg MB R3G 0T6
Tel: 204-786-8854; *Fax:* 204-784-2343
websupport@winnipegrealtors.ca
www.winnipegrealtors.ca
Social Media: www.youtube.com/user/winnipegrealtors
To serve members & to promote the benefits of organized real estate

Woodstock-Ingersoll & District Real Estate Board
#6, 65 Springbank Ave. North, Woodstock ON N4S 8V8
Tel: 519-539-3616; *Fax:* 519-539-1975
admin@widreb.ca
woodstockingersolldistrictrealestateboard.com
Social Media:
www.facebook.com/widreb1
Nicole Bowman, Executive Officer

Yellowknife Real Estate Board
#201, 5204 - 50 Ave., Yellowknife NT X1A 1E2
Tel: 867-920-4624; *Fax:* 867-873-6387
boards.mls.ca/yellowknife

Yorkton Real Estate Association Inc. (YREA)
#040, 41 Broadway West, Yorkton SK S3N 0L6
Tel: 306-783-3067; *Fax:* 306-782-3231
yrea@sasktel.net
To promote a high level of professionalism among members by providing leadership in the real estate industry & in the community
Judy Pfeifer, Executive Officer
Ron Skinner, President

Yukon Real Estate Association
3 Bonanza Pl., Whitehorse YT Y1A 5M4
Tel: 867-633-5565; *Fax:* 867-667-7005
admin@yrea.ca
www.yrea.ca
To promote interest in marketing of real estate in all its aspects & to advance & improve relations of members of society with public

Recreation, Hobbies & Games

Aéroclub des cantons de l'est
Aéroport Roland-Désourdy, 101, rue du Ciel, Bromont QC V6B 3X9
Tél: 514-862-1216
Média social: www.facebook.com/AeroclubDesCantonsDeLEst
Marc Arsenault, Contact

Air Currency Enhancement Society (ACES)
c/o Bud Bernston, 13 Casavechia Ct., Dartmouth NS B2X 3G7
www.soaraces.ca
Social Media: www.youtube.com/user/soaraces
www.facebook.com/AirCurrencyEnhancementSociety
twitter.com/soaraces
To promote & improve standards in aviation
Robert Francis, Chairman
Patrick Dalton, Contact, Communications

Alberta Camping Association (ACA)
Percy Page Centre, 11759 Groat Rd., Edmonton AB T5M 3K6
Tel: 403-477-5443
info@albertacamping.com
www.albertacamping.com
Social Media:
www.facebook.com/AlbertaCampingAssociation
twitter.com/Alberta_Camping
To promote & coordinate organized camping in Alberta by providing camp information & leadership direction as well as promoting high standards of camp programs & activities for all populations; to take a leading role in the recognition & promotion of professional standards for organized camps in Alberta
Gerrit Leewes, President
Gwen Dell'Anno, Executive Director

Alberta Recreation & Parks Association (ARPA)
11759 Groat Rd., Edmonton AB T5M 3K6
Tel: 780-415-1745; *Fax:* 780-451-7915
Toll-Free: 877-544-1747
arpa@arpaonline.ca
arpaonline.ca
Social Media:
www.youtube.com/channel/UCWpGvr7VoeGnxXeivhcuETQ
linkedin.com/company/alberta-recreation-and-parks-association
www.facebook.com/arpaonline
twitter.com/arpaonline
To promote accessibility to recreation & parks & their benefits to Albertans; To work toward economic sustainability, natural resource protection, & conservation within provincial parks & natural environments
Bill Wells, Chief Executive Officer
Steve Allan, Director, Finance & Operations
Anna Holtby, Coordinator, Communications

Alberta Whitewater Association (AWA)
Percy Page Centre, 11759 Groat Rd., Edmonton AB T5M 3K6
Tel: 403-628-2336
admin@albertawhitewater.ca
www.albertawhitewater.ca
Social Media:
www.facebook.com/alberta.whitewater
To encourage whitewater paddlesport activities
Chuck Lee, Executive Director

All Terrain Vehicle Association of Nova Scotia (ATVANS)
PO Box 46020, Stn. Novalea, Halifax NS B3K 5V8
Tel: 902-241-3200; *Toll-Free:* 877-288-4244
admin@atvans.org
www.atvans.org
To represent the interest of ATV'ers to Government, Land owners, other recreation user groups and the general public and educate, inform and organize ATV'ers to preserve and expand ATV recreational opportunities to promote safe family activities.
Vince Sawler, President
Barry Barnet, Executive Director

Association chasse & pêche de Chibougamau
CP 171, Chibougamau QC G8P 2K6
Tél: 418-748-2021
info@acpcchibougamau.com
www.acpcchibougamau.com
Favoriser et développer parmi les membres l'esprit sportif en préservant la conservation des richesses naturelles
Serge Picard, Président

Association des camps du Québec inc. (ACQ) / Québec Camping Association
CP 1000, Succ. M, 4545, av Pierre-de Coubertin, Montréal QC H1V 3R2
Tél: 514-252-3113; *Téléc:* 514-252-1650
Ligne sans frais: 800-361-3586
info@camps.qc.ca
www.camps.qc.ca
Média social: www.instagram.com/campsduquebec
www.facebook.com/130062375961
Assurer le développement, la promotion et la qualité des camps de vacances; s'assurer de la formation du personnel des camps
Eric Beauchemin, Directeur

Boating Ontario
15 Laurier Rd., Penetanguishene ON L9M 1G8
Tel: 705-549-1667; *Fax:* 705-549-1670
Toll-Free: 888-547-6662
info@boatingontario.ca
www.boatingontario.ca
To promote recreational boating throughout Ontario
Dick Peever, President
Graham Lacey, Vice-President
Al Donaldson, Executive Director
Ed Leeman, Secretary
Bob Eaton, Director, Environmental Services

British Columbia Camping Association
BC
info@bccamping.org
bccamping.org
Social Media:
www.facebook.com/BCcampingassociation
To facilitate the development of organized camping in order to provide educational, character-building & constructive recreational experiences for all people; to develop awareness & appreciation of the natural environment
Margo Dunnet, President
Stephanie Mikalishen, Secretary
Conor Lorimer, Treasurer

British Columbia Recreation & Parks Association (BCRPA)
#301, 470 Granville St., Vancouver BC V6C 1V5
Tel: 604-629-0965; *Fax:* 604-629-2651
Toll-Free: 866-929-0965
bcrpa@bcrpa.bc.ca
www.bcrpa.bc.ca
Social Media:
twitter.com/bcrpa
To establish & sustain healthy lifestyles & communities in British Columbia
Darryl Condon, President
Holly-Ann Burrows, Manager, Communication
Sandra Couto, Manager, Finance
Sara Ferguson, Clerk

The Bruce Trail Conservancy
PO Box 857, Hamilton ON L8N 3N9
Tel: 905-529-6821; *Fax:* 905-529-6823
Toll-Free: 800-665-4453
info@brucetrail.org
www.brucetrail.org
Social Media:
www.facebook.com/TheBruceTrailConservancy
To secure, develop & manage the Bruce Trail as a public footpath along the Niagara Escarpment from Queenston to Tobermory, thereby promoting preservation of the escarpment's ecological & cultural integrity & fostering an appreciation of its natural beauty. The Bruce Trail, designated as a UNESCO World Biosphere Reserve, is Canada's oldest and longest footpath.
Beth Gilhespy, Executive Director

Campground Owners Association of Nova Scotia (COANS)
c/o Tourism Industry Association of Nova Scotia, 2089 Maitland St., Halifax NS B3K 2Z8
Tel: 902-496-7474
www.campingnovascotia.com
To provide the best camping experience possible throughout our diverse province; To improve standards at all the province's campgrounds; to provide leadership to this important segment of the provincial economy
Jennifer Falkenham, General Manager

Canada's National Firearms Association (NFA)
PO Box 49090, Edmonton AB T6E 6H4
Tel: 780-439-1394; *Fax:* 780-439-4091
Toll-Free: 877-818-0393
info@nfa.ca
nfa.ca
Social Media:
www.facebook.com/NFACANADA
To support hunting & sport shooting rights in Canada
Sheldon Clare, President

Canadian Aerophilatelic Society (CAS) / La société canadienne d'aérophilatélie (SCA)
203A Woodfield Dr., Nepean ON K2G 4P2
www.aerophilately.ca
To represent Canadian aerophilatelists nationally & internationally
Steve Johnson, President
Brian Wolfenden, Secretary-Treasurer

Canadian Association of Numismatic Dealers (CAND) / Association canadienne des marchands numismatiques
c/o Jo-Anne Simpson, Executive Secretary, PO Box 10272, Stn. Winona, Stoney Creek ON L8E 5R1
Tel: 905-643-4988; *Fax:* 905-643-6329
email@cand.org
www.cand.org
To ensure professionalism by members of the association
Michael Findlay, President
Paul Koolhaas, Vice-President
Wendy Hoare, Secretary-Treasurer

Canadian Association of Wooden Money Collectors (CAWMC)
PO Box 2643, Stn. M, Calgary AB T2P 3C1
www.nunet.ca/cawmc
Norm Belsten, Contact

Canadian Boating Federation / Fédération nautique du Canada
#330, 24 St-Louis, Salaberry-De-Valleyfield QC J6T 1M4
Tel: 450-377-4122; *Fax:* 450-377-5282
cbfnc@cbfnc.ca
www.cbfnc.ca
Derek Anderson, President

Canadian Bridge Federation (CFB) / La Fédération canadienne incorporée de bridge
2719 East Jolly Pl., Regina SK S4V 0X8
Tel: 306-761-1677; *Fax:* 306-789-4919
www.cbf.ca
Social Media:
www.facebook.com/Canadian.Bridge.Federation
To conduct grassroot bridge events in Canada; to select & subsidize teams to World Championships.
Janice Anderson, Executive Director
Nader Hanna, President

Canadian Camping Association (CCA) / Association des camps du Canada (ACC)
c/o Jill Dundas, Girl Guides Ontario, 100-180 Duncan Mill Rd., Toronto ON M3B 1Z6
www.ccamping.org
Social Media:
www.facebook.com/CanadianCampingAssociation
twitter.com/ccampingorg
To develop & promote organized camping for all populations across Canada; To further the interests & welfare of children, youth, & adults through camping; To encourage high standards in camping
Jill Dundas, President

Canadian Casting Federation
c/o Toronto Sportsmen's Association, #66, 2700 Dufferin St., Toronto ON M6B 4J3
Tel: 416-487-4477; *Fax:* 416-487-4478
info@torontosportsmens.ca
www.torontosportsmens.ca/Casting.html
To teach casting skills, covering fly, bait, & spinning

Canadian Correspondence Chess Association (CCCA) / L'Association canadienne des échecs par correspondance (ACEC)
c/o Manny Migicovsky, 1669 Country Rd. 4, RR#1, L'Orignal QC K0B 1K0
Tel: 613-632-3166
ccca@cogeco.ca
correspondencechess.com/ccca
To promote chess playing via mail & e-mail both nationally & internationally
Manny Migicovsky, President

Canadian Flag Association (CFA) / Association canadienne de vexillologie (ACV)
409 - 60 C Line, Orangeville ON L9W 0A9
cfa.acv@gmail.com
cfa-acv.tripod.com
Social Media:
www.facebook.com/317266027131
To gather, organize & disseminate flag information with particular emphasis on flags having some association with Canada; to promote vexillology; to encourage & facilitate exchange of ideas between flag scholars, flag makers, flag collectors, flag designers & flag historians
Kevin Harrington, President

Canadian International DX Club (CIDX)
PO Box 67063, Stn. Lemoyne, St. Lambert QC J4R 2T8
cidxclub@yahoo.com
www.anarc.org/cidx
To serve radio enthusiasts throughout the world

Canadian Paper Money Society (CPMS)
Attn: Dick Dunn, PO Box 562, Pickering ON L1V 2R7
info@cpmsonline.ca
www.nunetcan.net/cpms.htm
To encourage & support historical studies of banks & other paper money issuing authorities in Canada, to preserve their history & statistical records, & through research & publishing the results thereof, ensure that information, documents & other evidence of Canada's financial development will be preserved.
Dick Dunn, Secretary-Treasurer
Jared Stepleton, President

Canadian Parks & Recreation Association (CPRA) / Association canadienne des parcs et loisirs
PO Box 83069, 1180 Walkley Rd., Ottawa ON K1V 2M5
Tel: 613-523-5315
info@cpra.ca
www.cpra.ca
Social Media:
www.facebook.com/168910893249240?ref=hl
twitter.com/CPRA_ACPL
To advocate on the benefits of parks & recreation services
Dean Gibson, President
CJ Noble, Executive Director
Sarah Wayne, Accountant

Canadian Parks & Wilderness Society (CPAWS) / Société pour la nature et les parcs du Canada (SNAP)
#506, 250 City Centre Ave., Ottawa ON K1R 6K7
Tel: 613-569-7226; *Fax:* 613-569-7098
Toll-Free: 800-333-9453
www.cpaws.org
Social Media: www.youtube.com/cpawsnational;
www.instagram.com/cpaws_national
www.facebook.com/cpaws
twitter.com/cpaws
To act as the Canadian voice for public wilderness protection
Éric Hébert-Daly, National Executive Director
Ellen Adelberg, Director, Communications & Marketing

Canadian Racing Pigeon Union Inc.
#C, 261 Tillson Ave., Tillsonburg ON N4G 5X2
Tel: 519-842-9771; *Fax:* 519-842-8809
Toll-Free: 866-652-5704
crpu@crpu.ca
www.crpu.ca
To promote the sport of pigeon racing in Canada
Brad Foster, President
Denise Luscher, Administrator

Canadian Senior Pro Rodeo Association (CSPRA)
PO Box 393, Carseland AB T0J 0M0
Tel: 403-875-3242
info@canadaseniorrodeo.com
www.canadianseniorrodeo.com
To allow individuals over 40 to compete in rodeo events across Canada & North America
Lynn Turcato, President

Canadian Stamp Dealers' Association (CSDA) / Association canadienne des négociants en timbres-poste (ACNTP)
PO Box 81, Stn. Lambeth, London ON N6P 1P9
director@csdaonline.com
www.csdaonline.com
Social Media:
www.facebook.com/214870458990?ref=ts
John Sheffield, Executive Director
Rick Day, President
Ian Kimmerly, Vice-President

Canadian Toy Collectors' Society Inc. (CTCS)
#245, 91 Rylander Blvd., Unit 7, Toronto ON M1B 5M5
ctcsweb@hotmail.com
www.ctcs.org
To promote interest in the collection & display of all types of toys, childhood memorabilia & literature; to acquire, maintain & house a collection of toys & to restore & preserve Canadian toys of historic significance.
Ron Blair, President

Chess Federation of Canada / Fédération canadienne des échecs
#356, 17A-218 Silvercreek Pkwy. North, Guelph ON N1H 8E8
Tel: 519-265-1789
info@chess.ca
www.chess.ca
Social Media: www.youtube.com/ChessCanada
linkedin.com/groups?home=&gid=3949499
www.facebook.com/163031117086480
twitter.com/ChessCanada
To coordinate chess play across Canada
Vlad Drkulec, President
Michael von Keitz, Executive Director

Citizens for Safe Cycling (CfSC)
PO Box 248, Stn. B, Ottawa ON K1P 6C4
Tel: 613-722-4454; *Fax:* 613-722-4454
info@safecycling.ca
www.safecycling.ca
Social Media:
www.facebook.com/safecycling
twitter.com/CfSC_Ott
To promote cycling as fun, healthy, safe, economical, and environmentally-friendly transportation and recreation.
Hans Moor, President

Classical & Medieval Numismatic Society (CMNS)
3329 Queen St. East, Toronto ON M4E 1E8
cmns.info@gmail.com
www.cmns.ca
To promote & encourage study & research in the field of numismatics & history as they relate to ancient & medieval coinage & related subjects; to publish the writings that are the result of such activity.

Climb Yukon Association
YT
info@climbyukon.net
www.climbyukon.net
To develop to the climbing community in the Yukon as a recreational opportunity for adults & youth, to raise awareness of & address access & safety concerns.

Cycle Toronto
#307, 720 Bathurst St., Toronto ON M5S 2R4
Tel: 416-644-7188
www.cycleto.ca
Social Media:
www.facebook.com/cycletoronto
twitter.com/cycletoronto
Cycle Toronto is a member-supported organization that advocates for a healthy, safe, cycling-friendly city for all.
Jared Kolb, Executive Director

Federation of Ontario Cottagers' Associations (FOCA)
#201, 159 King St., Peterborough ON K9J 2R8
Tel: 705-749-3622; *Fax:* 705-749-6522
info@foca.on.ca
www.foca.on.ca
Social Media:
www.facebook.com/foca.on.ca
To ensure a healthy future for waterfront Ontario; To support the interests of Ontario's cottagers
Terry Rees, Executive Director

Fédération québécoise de camping et de caravaning inc. (FQCC)
CP 100, #100, 1560, rue Eiffel, Boucherville QC J4B 5Y1
Tél: 450-650-3722; *Téléc:* 450-650-3721
Ligne sans frais: 877-650-3722
info@fqcc.ca
www.fqcc.ca
Média social: www.youtube.com/user/LaFQCC
www.facebook.com/LaFQCC
Unir les adepts du camping et du caravaning; Entreprendre et coordonner des actions relatives au camping et au caravaning
Yvan Lafontaine, Président
Michel Quintal, Trésorier

Fédération québécoise de la marche
4545, av Pierre-de Coubertin, Montréal QC H1V 0B2
Tél: 514-252-3157; *Téléc:* 514-252-5137
Ligne sans frais: 866-252-2065
infomarche@fqmarche.qc.ca
www.fqmarche.qc.ca
Média social: www.youtube.com/user/fqmarche
www.facebook.com/138582999548977
twitter.com/QuebecMarche
Promotion de la marche et de la randonnée pedestre; support au développement de lieux de marche
Daniel Pouplot, Directeur général

Fédération québécoise des échecs (FQE) / Québec Chess Federation
CP 1000, Succ. M, Montréal QC H1V 3R2
Tél: 514-252-3034; *Téléc:* 514-251-8038
info@fqechecs.qc.ca
www.fqechecs.qc.ca
Média social: www.facebook.com/eqechecs
twitter.com/fqechecs
Promouvoir l'étude, l'enseignement et la pratique du jeu d'échecs au Québec
Richard Bérubé, Directeur Général

Fédération québécoise des jeux récréatifs (FQJR)
4545, av Pierre-de Coubertin, Montréal QC H1V 0B2
Tél: 514-252-3032
info@quebecjeux.org
www.quebecjeux.org
Média social: www.youtube.com/user/FQJRJeux
www.facebook.com/355560369062
De promouvoir les sports de loisirs et jeux
Dominic Robitaille, Président

Guide Outfitters Association of British Columbia (GOABC)
#103, 19140 - 28th Ave., Surrey BC V3S 6M3
Tel: 604-541-6332; *Fax:* 604-541-6339
info@goabc.org
www.goabc.org
Social Media:
twitter.com/GOABC
Dale Drown, General Manager

Halifax North West Trails Association (HNWTA)
c/o 27 Warwick Lane, Halifax NS B3M 4J3
Tel: 902-443-5051
info@halifaxnorthwesttrails.ca
www.halifaxnorthwesttrails.ca
Social Media:
www.facebook.com/124497311008207
twitter.com/HalifaxNWTrails
To promote the creation, protection and maintenance of trails within the Halifax Mainland North area.
Todd Beal, Chair

Hike Ontario
#800, 165 Dundas St. West, Mississauga ON L5B 2N6
Tel: 905-277-4453; *Toll-Free:* 800-894-7249
info@hikeontario.com
www.hikeontario.com
To act as the voice for hikers & walkers in Ontario; To encourage hiking, walking & trail development in Ontario; To promote trail maintenance. best practices, & safe hiking; To enhance environmental awareness, conservation & sustainable trails
Bill Wilson, President
Fran Rawlings, Secretary
Asvin Parsad, Treasurer

H.R. MacMillan Space Centre Society (HRMSC)
1100 Chestnut St., Vancouver BC V6J 3J9
Tel: 604-738-7827; *Fax:* 604-736-5665
info@spacecentre.ca
www.spacecentre.ca
Social Media: www.youtube.com/user/MacMillanSpaceCentre
www.facebook.com/MacMillanSpaceCentre
twitter.com/AskAnAstronomer
To educate, inspire & evoke a sense of wonder about the universe, our planet & space exploration
Raylene Marchand, Interim Executive Director
Lisa McIntosh, Director, Learning

Manitoba Camping Association (MCA)
Manitoba Camping Association Sunshine Fund, 545 Telfer St. South, Winnipeg MB R3G 2Y4
Tel: 204-784-1134
sunshinefund@mbcamping.ca
www.mbcamping.ca
Social Media:
www.facebook.com/sunshinefundmb
twitter.com/SunshineFundMB
To act as a coordinating body for organized camping in Manitoba; To promote organized camping as an educational and recreational experience
Liz Kovach, Executive Director
Kelly Giddings, Coordinator, Outdoor Learning & Member Services
Sydney Kazina, Coordinator, Sunshine Fund

Model Aeronautics Association of Canada Inc. (MAAC) / Modélistes Aéronautiques Associés du Canada
#9, 5100 South Service Rd., Burlington ON L7L 6A5
Tel: 905-632-9808; *Fax:* 905-632-3304
Toll-Free: 855-359-6222
www.maac.ca
To foster, enhance, assist, aid & engage in scientific development; To provide central organization to record & disseminate information relating to model aeronautics; To guide & direct national model aviation activities; To direct technical organization of national & international model aircraft contests
Ronald R. Dodd, President
Linda Patrick, Secretary-Treasurer

Newfoundland & Labrador Camping Association
c/o Malcolm Turner, President, 27 Earle Dr., Pasadena NL A0L 1K0
Tel: 709-686-2363
To facilitate the development of organized camping in order to provide educational, character-building & constructive recreational experiences for all people; to develop awareness & appreciation of the natural environment
Malcolm Turner, President

Northwest Territories Recreation & Parks Association (NWTRPA)
PO Box 841, Yellowknife NT X1A 2N6
Tel: 867-873-5340; *Fax:* 867-669-6791
admin@nwtrpa.org
www.nwtrpa.org
Social Media:
www.facebook.com/260257614047483
To increase public awareness of recreation & parks; to enhance the quality of life of residents of the NWT through fostering the development of recreation & parks services
Geoff Ray, Executive Director

Nova Scotia Trails Federation (NSTF)
5516 Spring Garden Rd., 4th Fl., Halifax NS B3Z 1E8
Tel: 902-425-5450; *Fax:* 902-425-5606
www.novascotiatrails.com
Social Media:
www.facebook.com/nstrails
twitter.com/NSTrails
To promote the development & responsible use of recreational trails for the benefit & enjoyment of all Nova Scotians & visitors to the province
Holly Woodill, President
Vanda Jackson, Executive Director

Ontario Camps Association (OCA)
70 Martin Ross Ave., Toronto ON M3J 2L4
Tel: 416-485-0425; *Fax:* 416-485-0422
info@ontariocamps.ca
www.ontariocamps.ca
Social Media:
www.facebook.com/OntarioCampsAssociation
twitter.com/OCACamps
To promote youth camping throughout Ontario; To maintain high standards for organized camping; To advocate on issues which impact members
Adam Kronick, President
Heather Heagle, Executive Director
Jen Gilbert, Coordinator, Membership & Volunteer

Ontario Numismatic Association (ONA)
c/o Bruce Raszmann, PO Box 40033, Stn. Waterloo Square, 75 King St. South, Waterloo ON N2J 4V1
the-ona.ca
Paul Petch, President
Len Trakalo, Secretary
Bruce Raszmann, Treasurer & Chair, Membership

Ontario Parks Association (OPA)
7856 - 5th Line South, RR#4, Milton ON L9T 2X8
Tel: 905-864-6182; *Fax:* 905-864-6184
Toll-Free: 866-560-7783
opa@ontarioparksassociation.ca
www.ontarioparksassociation.ca
To develop & protect parks & green spaces in Ontario
Paul Ronan, Executive Director
Eric Trogdon, Executive Director
Shelley May, Coordinator, Operations & Administration
Maureen Sinclair, President

Bill Harding, Vice-President

Ontario Recreation Facilities Association Inc. (ORFA)
#102, 1 Concorde Gate, Toronto ON M3C 3N6
Tel: 416-426-7062; *Fax:* 416-426-7385
Toll-Free: 800-661-6732
info@orfa.com
www.orfa.com
To provide leadership for the recreation facility profession in Ontario; To promote the professional operation of recreation facilities throughout the province
Steve Hardie, RRFA, CIT, CPT, President & Chair
John Milton, Chief Administrative Officer
Remo Petrongolo, Director, Business Development
Terry Piche, RRFA, CIT, Director, Technical
Hubie Basilio, Coordinator, Public Relations & Communications
Rebecca Russell, Facilities Librarian

Ontario Research Council on Leisure (ORCOL) / Conseil Ontarien de Recherche en Loisir
c/o Recreation & Leisure Studies, Faculty of Applied Health Sciences, University of Waterloo, Waterloo ON N2L 3G1
ahsweb@healthy.uwaterloo.ca
www.orcol.uwaterloo.ca
To disseminate research about leisure & recreation, including culture, tourism, fitness, & sports
Bryan Smale, President
Don Reid, Treasurer

Ontario Trails Council
PO Box 500, Deseronto ON K0K 1X0
ontrails@gmail.com
www.ontariotrails.on.ca
Social Media: www.youtube.com/user/ontrails
www.facebook.com/OntarioTrails?ref=mf
twitter.com/ontrails
To promote the creation, development, preservation, management & use of an integrated, recreational, multi-seasonal trail network in Ontario; To show interest in all types of trails for non-motorized & motorized (where applicable) use in all seasons; To acquire & convert Ontario's abandoned railway rights-of-way to linear greenways for year-round recreational activities for the people of Ontario
Chris Laforest, President
Forbes Symon, Vice-President
Patrick Connor, CAE, Executive Director
Damian Braley, Secretary

Ontario Vintage Radio Association (OVRA)
ON
www.ovra.ca
To preserve Canada's radio history, literature & equipment; to serve as a forum for members to exchange information & continue the legacy of the original club.

Outdoor Recreation Council of British Columbia (ORC)
47 West Broadway, Vancouver BC V5Y 1P1
Tel: 604-873-5546
outdoorrec@orcbc.ca
www.orcbc.ca
To advise industry & government in the development & implementation of outdoor recreation & conservation plans for BC; to contribute to the coordination of regional outdoor recreation by assisting in the establishment of a provincial network of outdoor recreationists to address recreational use conflicts & to advise government & industry on local & regional needs for noncompetitive outdoor recreation; to encourage active participation by the residents of BC in outdoor recreation activities; to promote the quality & diversity of outdoor recreation opportunities in BC by working cooperatively with government, industry, business & the public.
Dennis Webb, Chair
Jeremy McCall, Executive Director

Outward Bound Canada
Centre for Green Cities, #404, 550 Bayview Ave., Toronto ON M4W 3X8
Fax: 705-382-5959
Toll-Free: 888-688-9273
info@outwardbound.ca
www.outwardbound.ca
Social Media: www.youtube.com/user/OutwardBoundCanada
linkedin.com/company/outward-bound-canada
www.facebook.com/pages/Outward-Bound-Canada/8376438193?ref=ts
twitter.com/OutwardBoundCan
To promote self-reliance, care & respect for others, responsibility to community & concern for the environment
Sarah Wiley, Executive Director

Parks & Recreation Ontario (PRO) / Parcs et loisirs de l'Ontario
#302, 1 Concorde Gate, Toronto ON M3C 3N6
Tel: 416-426-7142; *Fax:* 416-426-7371
pro@prontario.org
www.prontario.org
Social Media: www.facebook.com/PROntario
twitter.com/prontario
To enhance the quality of life, health & well-being of people, their communities & their environments; To advocate provincially for parks & recreation issues; To provide networking as well as multi-discipline professional development opportunities
Larry Ketcheson, CEO

Recreation & Parks Association of the Yukon (RPAY)
4061 - 4th Ave., Whitehorse YT Y1A 1H1
Tel: 867-668-3010; *Fax:* 867-668-2455
rpay@klondiker.com
www.rpay.org
Social Media: facebook.com/goRPAY
twitter.com/RPAY1
To promote, encourage and foster the growth and development of all areas of recreation throughout the Yukon Territory.
Ian Spencer, President
Anne Morgan, Executive Director

Recreation Facilities Association of British Columbia (RFABC)
PO Box 112, Powell River BC V8A 4Z5
Toll-Free: 877-285-3421
info@rfabc.com
www.rfabc.com
To promote safe & successful operating standards for community centres, swimming pools, arenas, stadiums, & parks in British Columbia; To encourage professionalism among recreation facility operators
Lori Blackman, Executive Director
Steve McLain, President
Karin Carlson, Secretary/Treasurer
Chante Patterson-Elden, Chair, Marketing

Recreation New Brunswick
#34, 55 Whiting Rd., Fredericton NB E3B 5Y5
Tel: 506-459-1929; *Fax:* 506-450-6066
www.recreationnb.ca
Social Media: www.facebook.com/RecreationNB
twitter.com/RecreationNB
To develop a professional organization for members; To enhance the image of recreation to government & the general public; To develop liaisons with other recreation groups; To affect legislation in the field of recreation & parks; to expand the NB Skills Program for Management Volunteers; To promote the need for education for leisure
Sarah Wagner, Executive Director

Recreation Newfoundland & Labrador
PO Box 8700, St. John's NL A1B 4J6
Tel: 709-729-3892; *Fax:* 709-729-3814
info@recreationnl.com
www.recreationnl.com
Social Media: www.facebook.com/455370901173112
To promote, foster & develop recreation; to provide a full range of services to enrich the concept of leisure throughout Newfoundland & Labrador; to enable individual citizens to improve their quality of life.
Dawn Sharpe, President
Gary Milley, Executive Director

Recreation Nova Scotia (RNS)
#309, 5516 Spring Garden Rd., Halifax NS B3J 1G6
Tel: 902-425-1128; *Fax:* 902-422-8201
www.recreationns.ns.ca
Social Media: linkedin.com/company/recreation-nova-scotia
www.facebook.com/RecreationNovaScotia
twitter.com/recreationns
To build healthier futures through programs & services that promote the benefits of recreation
Rhonda Lemire, Executive Director
Rae Gunn, President

Roller Sports Canada / Sports à roulettes du Canada
1 Bancroft Cres., Whitby ON L1R 2E6
Tel: 905-666-9343
rollersports@hotmail.com
rollersports.ca
Wayne Burret, President

Royal Canadian Numismatic Association (RCNA)
#432, 5694 Hwy. 7 East, Markham ON L3P 1B4
Tel: 647-401-4014; *Fax:* 905-472-9645
info@rcna.ca
www.rcna.ca
To encourage & promote education in the science of numismatics, through the study of coins, paper money, medals, tokens, & all other numismatic items, with special emphasis on material pertaining to Canada
Kevin McCann, Chair, Membership

The Royal Philatelic Society of Canada (RPSC) / La Société royale de philatélie du Canada (SRPC)
PO Box 929, Stn. Q, Toronto ON M4T 2P1
Tel: 416-921-2077; *Fax:* 416-921-1282
Toll-Free: 888-285-4143
info@rpsc.org
www.rpsc.org
To promote the hobby of stamp collecting; to use stamps & postal history in education for youths & adults
George Pepall, President
Peter Butler, Executive Director

Saskatchewan Association of Recreation Professionals (SARP)
2205 Victoria Ave., Regina SK S4P 0S4
Tel: 306-780-9267; *Fax:* 306-525-4009
Toll-Free: 800-667-7780
sarp.sk@sasktel.net
www.sarp-online.ca
To represent & support present & future recreation professionals; To promote the pursuit of excellence in the profession; To advocate for the profession
Nicole Goldsworthy, Chair

Saskatchewan Camping Association (SCA)
3950 Castle Rd., Regina SK S4S 6A4
Tel: 306-586-4026; *Fax:* 306-790-8634
info@saskcamping.ca
www.saskcamping.ca
To promote the development of quality organized camping in Saskatchewan; To act as the voice for leaders of organized camps throughout Saskatchewan
Donna Wilkinson, Executive Director

Saskatchewan Parks & Recreation Association (SPRA)
#100, 1445 Park St., Regina SK S4N 4C5
Tel: 306-780-9231; *Fax:* 306-780-9257
Toll-Free: 800-563-2555
office@spra.sk.ca
www.spra.sk.ca
To stimulate & advance parks, recreation & leisure activities, facilities, & programs in Saskatchewan

Trail Riders of the Canadian Rockies
PO Box 6742, Stn. D, Calgary AB T2P 2E6
Tel: 403-874-4408
admin@trail-rides.ca
trailridevacations.com
Social Media: www.facebook.com/189174017824540
To encourage travel on horseback through the Canadian Rockies; to foster the maintenance & improvement of old trails & the building of new trails; to promote good fellowship among those who visit & live in the Canadian Rockies; to encourage the appreciation of outdoor life & the study & conservation of mountain ecology; to assist in every way possible to ensure the preservation of the National Parks of Canada for the use & enjoyment of the public; to cooperate with other organizations with similar aims
Robert Vanderzweerde, Secretary-Treasurer

Trans Canada Trail Foundation (TCTF) / Fondation du sentier transcanadien
#300, 321 de la Commune West, Montréal QC H2Y 2E1
Tel: 514-485-3959; *Fax:* 514-485-4541
Toll-Free: 800-465-3636
info@tctrail.ca
www.tctrail.ca
Social Media: www.youtube.com/user/TheTransCanadaTrail
linkedin.com/company/trans-canada-trail
www.facebook.com/transcanadatrail
twitter.com/TCTrail
To promote & coordinate the planning, designing & building of a continuous, shared-use recreation trail that winds its way through every Province & Territory
Jane Murphy, National Director of Trail
Gay Decker, Director of Communications
Amparo Jardine, Director of Development

Tunnelling Association of Canada (TAC) / Association canadienne des tunnels
8828 Pigott Rd., Richmond ON V7A 2C4
Tel: 604-241-1297; *Fax:* 604-241-1399
admin@tunnelcanada.ca
www.tunnelcanada.ca
To promote Canadian tunnelling & underground excavation technologies, & safe design, construction & maintenance; to facilitate information exchange; to represent the tunnelling community in matters of public & technical concern; to publish a Canadian registry of tunnels, underground excavations & similar works
Derek Zoldy, Secretary-Treasurer
Rick Staples, President

Velo Halifax Bicycle Club
PO Box 125, Dartmouth NS B2Y 3Y2
cycling@chebucto.ns.ca
www.velohalifax.com
Terry Walker, President

Vintage Road Racing Association (VRRA)
c/o Karen Duncan, Membership Secretary, 499 Fiddick Rd., Brighton ON K0K 1H0
Tel: 613-475-9052
vrramembership@gmail.com
www.vrra.ca
Social Media:
www.facebook.com/vrra.ca
twitter.com/VRRACANADA
To promote & maintain the sport & traditions of racing classic & vintage machines
Mike Vinten, President
Karen Duncan, Membership Secretary

YMCA Canada
#601, 1867 Younge St., Toronto ON M4S 1Y5
Tel: 416-967-9622; *Fax:* 416-967-9618
www.ymca.ca
Social Media:
www.facebook.com/YMCACanada
twitter.com/YMCA_Canada
Dedicated to the growth of all persons in spirit, mind & body, & in a sense of responsibility to each other & the global community; fosters & stimulates the development of strong member associations & advocates on their behalf regionally, nationally & internationally
Scott Haldane, President/CEO
Bahadur Madhani, Chair

Yukon Outdoors Club (YOC)
4061 - 4th Ave., Whitehorse YT Y1A 1H1
yukonoutdoorsclub@gmail.com
www.yukonoutdoorsclub.ca
To co-ordinate trips that promote the enjoyment of the outdoors.

YWCA Canada / Association des jeunes femmes chrétiennes du Canada
104 Edward St., 1st Fl., Toronto ON M5G 0A7
Tel: 416-962-8881; *Fax:* 416-962-8084
national@ywcacanada.ca
www.ywcacanada.ca
Social Media: www.instagram.com/ywcacanada
www.facebook.com/ywcacanada
twitter.com/YWCA_Canada
To coordinate the YWCA movement in Canada, & advocate for the equity & equality rights of women; To raise awareness on the prevention of violence against women, and the need for universal, accessible and quality child care
Paulette Senior, Chief Executive Officer
Ann Decter, Director, Advocacy & Public Policy
Raine Liliefeldt, Director, Membership Services & Development

Recycling

Association of Alberta Coordinated Action for Recycling Enterprises
5212 - 49 St., Leduc AB T9E 7H5
Tel: 780-980-0035; *Fax:* 780-980-0232
Toll-Free: 866-818-2273
www.albertacare.org
To support waste management & recycling activities at the community level in Alberta
Linda McDonald, Executive Director

Automotive Recyclers Association of Manitoba (ARM)
PO Box 43049, Stn. Kildonan Place, Winnipeg MB R2C 5G5
Tel: 204-654-2726
www.arm.mb.ca
To provide quality recycled auto parts; To serve its customers & communities; To help the environment

Alec Gilman, President

New Brunswick Solid Waste Association (NBSWA) / l'Association des déchets solides du Nouveau-Brunswick (ADSNB)
32 Wedgewood Dr., Rothesay NB E2E 3P7
Tel: 506-849-4218; *Fax:* 506-847-1369
Toll-Free: 877-777-4218
nbswa@nbnet.nb.ca
To promote environmentally friendly solid waste management practices in New Brunswick.

Reproductive Issues

Action Canada for Sexual Health & Rights
251 Bank St., 2nd Fl., Ottawa ON K2P 1X3
Tel: 613-241-4474; *Toll-Free:* 888-642-2725
access@sexualhealthandrights.ca
www.sexualhealthandrights.ca
Social Media:
www.facebook.com/actioncanadaSHR
twitter.com/acpdcanada
To advance sexual & reproductive health & rights in Canada & abroad through Public education & awareness; Support for the delivery of programs & services in Canada.
Sandeep Prasad, Executive Director
Frédérique Chabot, Health Information Officer

Birthright International / Accueil Grossesse
777 Coxwell Ave., Toronto ON M4C 3C6
Tel: 416-469-4789; *Fax:* 416-469-1772
Crisis Hot-Line: 800-550-4900
info@birthright.org
www.birthright.org
To provide non-judgmental support to women facing an unplanned pregnancy, helping them carry their baby to term.
Louise R. Summerhill, Co-President & Founder
Mary Berney, Co-President

Canadian Fertility & Andrology Society (CFAS) / Société canadienne de fertilité et d'andrologie
#1107, 1255, rue University, Montréal QC H3B 3W7
Tel: 514-524-9009; *Fax:* 514-524-2163
info@cfas.ca
www.cfas.ca
To speak on behalf of interested parties in the field of assisted reproductive technologies & research in reproductive sciences
Carl A. Laskin, President
Mathias Gysler, Vice-President
Agneta Holländer, Executive Director
Jeff Roberts, Director, Continuing Professional Development
Janet Fraser, Secretary-Treasurer

Fédération du Québec pour le planning des naissances (FQPN)
#405, 110, rue Ste-Thérèse, Montréal QC H2Y 1E6
Tél: 514-866-3721; *Téléc:* 514-866-1100
info@fqpn.qc.ca
www.fqpn.qc.ca
Promouvoir les droits des femmes dans le domaine de la santé, particulièrement la reproduction et la sexualité; promouvoir l'accès à une information critique et fiable, la liberté de choix et le consentement des femmes face à leur propre corps.
Sophie de Cordes, Coordonnatrice générale

Infertility Awareness Association of Canada (IAAC) / Association canadienne de sensibilisation à l'infertilité (ACSI)
#201, 475 av Dumont, Dorval QC H9S 5W2
Tel: 514-633-4494; *Toll-Free:* 800-263-2929
info@iaac.ca
www.iaac.ca
Social Media: www.pinterest.com/iaac1
www.facebook.com/57435550753
twitter.com/iaac_acsi
To offer assistance, support & education to individuals with infertility concerns; to increase the awareness & understanding of the causes, treatments & the emotional impact of infertility through the development of educational programs.
Janet Fraser, President

Life's Vision
388 Portage Ave., #A, Winnipeg MB R3C 0C8
Tel: 204-233-8047; *Fax:* 204-233-0523
Toll-Free: 877-233-8048
lifesvision@shaw.ca
lifesvision.ca
Social Media:
www.facebook.com/pages/Lifes-Vision/244848322240237
twitter.com/LifesVision1
To engage in non-sectarian educational activities in order to encourage & promote among the general public an understanding & awareness of the dignity & worth of each individual human life, whatever its state & circumstances; to foster respect for all human life. Life's Vision provides information & referral services dealing with pregnancy & end of life issues, such as abortion, euthanasia & assisted suicide, & provides a voice for those opposed to abortion.

Natural Family Planning Association
c/o #205, 3050 Yonge St., Toronto ON M4N 2K4
Tel: 416-481-5465
www.naturalfamilyplanning.ca
To promote the Billings Ovulation Method of natural family planning which is based on an awareness of a woman's physical systems to gauge optimum fertility state.
Christian Elia, Executive Director

Newfoundland & Labrador Right to Life Association
PO Box 5427, 195 Freshwater Rd., St. John's NL A1C 5W2
Tel: 709-579-1500; *Fax:* 709-579-1600
centreforlife@centreforlife.ca
www.centreforlife.ca
The Association upholds the sacredness & inviolability of human life from conception to natural death. It disseminates information on such to authorities & the public, supporting mothers during & after pregnancy. It networks with similar organizations, & promotes medical research to support its beliefs.
Linda Holden, President

Ontario Coalition for Abortion Clinics (OCAC)
PO Box 495, Stn. P, 427 Bloor St. West, Toronto ON M5S 2Z1
Tel: 416-969-8463; *Fax:* 416-789-0762
ocac88@gmail.com
ocac-choice.com
Social Media:
www.facebook.com/OCAC88
twitter.com/OCAC25
To work for reproductive rights & access to abortions

Options for Sexual Health (OPT)
3550 East Hastings St., Vancouver BC V5K 2A7
Tel: 604-731-4252; *Fax:* 604-731-4698
info@optbc.org
www.optionsforsexualhealth.org
Social Media:
www.facebook.com/optbc
twitter.com/optbc
To promote optimal sexual health for all British Columbians by supporting reproductive choice, reducing unplanned pregnancy, & providing quality education, information & clinical services
Jennifer Breakspear, Executive Director

Planned Parenthood - Newfoundland & Labrador Sexual Health Centre (NLSHC)
203 Merrymeeting Rd., St. John's NL A1C 2W6
Tel: 709-579-1009; *Fax:* 709-726-2308
Toll-Free: 877-666-9847
info@nlsexualhealthcentre.org
www.nlsexualhealthcentre.org
Social Media:
www.facebook.com/PlannedParenthoodNL
twitter.com/NLSexualHealth
To promote positive sexual health attitudes & practices throughout Newfoundland & Labrador; To support & respect individual choice
Angie Brake, Executive Director

Planned Parenthood Saskatoon Centre (PPSC)
210 - 2 Ave. North, Saskatoon SK S7K 2B5
Tel: 306-244-7989; *Fax:* 306-652-4034
info@shcsaskatoon.ca
sexualhealthcentresaskatoon.ca
To ensure that information, resources & support services of the highest quality regarding sexuality, contraception & reproduction are available & accessible to all in our community who need them; to encourage responsible decision-making & behaviour which is respectful of the needs & of the choices available to each individual
Linzi Williamson, Interim Executive Director
Patrick LaPointe, Interim Executive Director

The Right to Life Association of Toronto & Area
#302, 120 Eglinton Ave. East, Toronto ON M4P 1E2
Tel: 416-483-7869
www.righttolife.to
Social Media:
www.facebook.com/righttolifeto
To uphold the right to life as the basic human right on which all others depend; to provide information & services to that end

Sexuality Education Resource Centre Manitoba (SERC)
#200, 226 Osborne St. North, Winnipeg MB R3C 1V4
Tel: 204-982-7800; *Fax:* 204-982-7819
www.serc.mb.ca
Social Media: www.youtube.com/user/sercmbca
www.facebook.com/sercmb
To promote universal access to comprehensive, reliable information & services on sexuality & related health issues by fostering awareness, understanding, & support through education
Holly Banner, Acting Executive Director

Signal Hill
PO Box 45076, RPO Langley Crossing, Langley BC V2Y 0C9
Tel: 604-532-0023; *Fax:* 604-532-0094
Toll-Free: 877-774-4625
www.thesignalhill.com
Social Media: www.youtube.com/thesignalhill
www.facebook.com/thesignalhill
twitter.com/TheSignalHill
To offer education about life issues, women's health, & human rights; To promote the value of human life

World Organization Ovulation Method Billings Inc.
1506 Dansey Ave., Coquitlam BC V3K 3J1
Tel: 604-936-4472; *Fax:* 604-936-5690
www.woomb.ca
To teach fertility awareness & natural family planning

Research & Scholarship

Advanced Foods & Materials Network / Réseau des aliments et des matériaux d'avant-garde
#215, 150 Research Lane, Guelph ON N1G 4T2
Tel: 519-822-6253; *Fax:* 519-824-8453
www.afmnet.ca
Rickey Yada, Scientific Director

AllerGen NCE Inc.
Michael DeGroote Centre for Learning & Discovery, McMaster University, #3120, 1200 Main St. West, Hamilton ON L8N 2A5
Tel: 905-525-9140; *Fax:* 905-524-0611
info@allergen-nce.ca
www.allergen-nce.ca
To support research, capacity building activities, & networking regarding allergic disease in Canada; To reduce the morbidity, mortality & socio-economic impacts of allergy, asthma, & related immune diseases
Judah Denburg, CEO & Scientific Director
Diana Royce, Chief Operating Officer & Managing Director
Mark Mitchell, Manager, Research & Partnerships
Marta Rudyk, Manager, Communications & Coordinator, Knowledge Mobilization
Allison Brown, Coordinator, Research
Michelle Harkness, Coordinator, Highly Qualified Personnel & Events

AquaNet - Network in Aquaculture
Ocean Sciences Centre, Memorial University of Newfoundland, St. John's NL A1C 5S7
Tel: 709-737-3245; *Fax:* 709-737-3500
info@aquanet.ca
www.aquanet.ca
To foster a sustainable aquaculture sector in Canada through high quality research & education

ArcticNet Inc.
Pavillon Alexandre-Vachon, Université Laval, #4081, 1045, av de la Médecine, Québec QC G1V 0A6
Tel: 418-656-5830; *Fax:* 418-656-2334
arcticnet@arcticnet.ulaval.ca
www.arcticnet.ulaval.ca
Social Media:
twitter.com/arcticnet
To study the impacts of climate change in the coastal Canadian Arctic; To engage Inuit organizations, northern communities, universities, research institutes, industry, government, & international agencies as partners in the scientific process
Martin Fortier, Executive Director
Louis Fortier, Scientific Director

AUTO21 Network of Centres of Excellence
401 Sunset Ave., Windsor ON N9B 3P4
Tel: 519-253-3000; *Fax:* 519-971-3626
info@auto21.ca
www.auto21.ca
Social Media: www.youtube.com/user/AUTO21NCE
linkedin.com/groups?about=&gid=2804256
www.facebook.com/AUTO21
twitter.com/auto21nce
To partner the public & private secotrs in applied automotive R&D
Peter Frise, CEO & Scientific Director
Michelle Watters, COO & Executive Director
Stephanie Campeau, Director, Public Affairs & Communications

Canada Media Fund (CMF)
#4, 50 Wellington St. East, Toronto ON M5E 1C8
Tel: 416-214-4400; *Fax:* 416-214-4420
Toll-Free: 877-975-0766
info@cmf-fmc.ca
www.cmf-fmc.ca
Social Media:
www.facebook.com/cmf.fmc
twitter.com/cmf_fmc
To provide funding to Canada's television & digital media industries through the following two streams: Experimental & Convergent.
Louis L. Roquet, Chair
Valerie Creighton, President & CEO
Stéphane Cardin, Vice-President, Industry & Public Affairs
Sandra Collins, Vice-President & CFO, Operations

Canadian Arthritis Network (CAN) / Le Réseau canadien de l'arthrite
#8-400-6-1, 700 University Ave., Toronto ON M5G 1Z5
Tel: 416-586-4770; *Fax:* 416-586-8395
can@arthritisnetwork.ca
www.arthritisnetwork.ca
Social Media:
www.facebook.com/102841629761794
twitter.com/commcan
To improve the quality of life for people with arthritis; To support integrated, trans-disciplinary research & development, with a focus upon inflammatory joint diseases, osteoarthritis, & bioengineering for restoration of joint function
Robin Armstrong, Chair
Kate Lee, Managing Director
Claire Bombardier, Co-Scientific Director
Monique Gignac, Co-Scientific Director

Canadian Association of Aesthetic Medicine (CAAM) / L'association canadienne de médecine esthétique
#220, 445 Mountain Hwy., North Vancouver BC V7J 2L1
Tel: 604-988-0450; *Fax:* 604-929-0871
info@caam.ca
www.caam.ca
CAAM is the face of aesthetic medicine in Canada, comprising of a multidisciplinary group of aesthetic physicians from various backgrounds and interests.
Susan Roberts, Executive Director

Canadian Carbonization Research Association (CCRA)
c/o Ted Todoschuk, PO Box 2460, 1330 Burlington St. East, Hamilton ON L8N 3J5
Tel: 905-548-4796; *Fax:* 905-548-4653
www.cancarb.ca
To fund coke & coal research in Canada for benefit of member companies
Ted Todoschuk, Contact

Canadian Committee of Byzantinists
Talbot College, Univ. of Western Ontario, London ON N6A 3K7
Tel: 519-661-3045; *Fax:* 519-850-2388
To network among Canadian Byzantinists; to promote communications & exchange of information; to promote Byzantine Studies in Canada
Geoffrey Greatrex, President

Canadian Federation for Robotics / Fédération canadienne de robotique
#301, 126 York St., Ottawa ON K1N 5T5
To promote interest in the use of & the application of robotics technologies by Canadian firms
Paul Johnston, Director

Canadian Genetic Diseases Network (CGDN) / Réseau canadien sur les maladies génétiques (RCMG)
#201, 2150 Western Pkwy., Vancouver BC V6T 1Z4
Tel: 604-221-7300
A nation-wide consortium of Canada's top investigators & core-technology facilities in human genetics, partnered with colleagues from industry to conduct leading-edge research within an "Institute without Walls"; to achieve international competitiveness in scientific research with social & economic benefits

Canadian Institute for Advanced Research (CIFAR) / Institut canadien de recherches avancées (ICRA)
#1400, 180 Dundas St. West, Toronto ON M5G 1Z8
Tel: 416-971-4251; *Fax:* 416-971-6169
Toll-Free: 888-738-1113
info@cifar.ca
www.ciar.ca
Social Media:
linkedin.com/company/canadian-institute-for-advanced-research
www.facebook.com/CIFAR
twitter.com/cifar_news
To stimulate leading-edge research projects vital to Canada's future prosperity.
Alan Bernstein, President/CEO

Canadian Institute for Mediterranean Studies (CIMS) / Institut canadien d'études méditerranéennes
c/o Carr Hall, Department of Italian Studies, University of Toronto, 100 St. Joseph St., Toronto ON M5S 1J4
www.utoronto.ca/cims
To study all aspects of Mediterranean culture & civilization, past & present
Mario Crespi, Executive Director

Canadian Institute for Photonics Innovations (CIPI)
Université Laval, Pavillon d'optique-photonique, #2111, 2375 rue de la Terrasse, Québec QC G1V 0A6
Tel: 418-656-3013; *Fax:* 418-656-2995
cipi@cipi.ulaval.ca
www.cipi.ulaval.ca
Photonics - science of generating, manipulating, transmitting & detecting light
Robert Corriveau, President

Canadian Institute for Research in Nondestructive Examination (CINDE)
135 Fennell Ave. West, Hamilton ON L8N 3T2
Tel: 905-387-1655; *Fax:* 905-574-6080
Toll-Free: 800-964-9488
www.cinde.ca
Social Media:
linkedin.com/groups/Canadian-Institute-NDE-4510204?trk=myg_ugrp_ov
www.facebook.com/pages/Canadian-Institute-for-NDE-CINDE/297023083473
To foster, coordinate & disseminate results of research, development & application of new or advanced NDE techniques in Canada; to promote technology transfer by encouraging collaboration between universities, research organizations & industrial or governmental users; to raise the profile of NDE research in Canada by publicizing the need for & economic benefits arising from advances in NDE
Larry Cote, President and CEO

Canadian Institute of Ukrainian Studies (CIUS) / Institut canadien d'études ukrainiennes
#4-30, Pembina Hall, University of Alberta, Edmonton AB T6G 2H8
Tel: 780-492-2972; *Fax:* 780-492-4967
cius@ualberta.ca
www.cius.ca
Social Media:
www.facebook.com/canadian.institute.of.ukrainian.studies
To develop Ukrainian scholarship in Canada; To organize research in Ukrainian & Ukrainian-Canadian studies
Volodymyr Kravchenko, Director

Canadian Mathematical Society (CMS) / Société mathématique du Canada
#209, 1785 St Laurent Blvd., Ottawa ON K1G 3Y4
Tel: 613-733-2662; *Fax:* 613-733-8994
office@cms.math.ca
www.cms.math.ca
Social Media:
www.facebook.com/canmathsoc
twitter.com/canadmathsoc
To promote & advance the discovery, learning & application of mathematics.
Johan Rudnick, Executive Director

Canadian Mining Industry Research Organization (CAMIRO)
1545 Maley Dr., Sudbury ON P3A 4R7
Tel: 705-673-6595; *Fax:* 705-673-6588
info@camiro.org
www.camiro.org
To manage collaborative mining research in the divisions of exploration, mining, & metallurgical processing; To contribute to the safety, growth, & competitiveness of the Canadian mineral industry
Peter Golde, Managing Director

Canadian Nautical Research Society (CNRS) / Société canadienne pour la recherche nautique
PO Box 34029, Ottawa ON K2J 4B0
www.cnrs-scrn.org
Social Media: www.facebook.com/150946001632212
To stimulate & promote nautical research in Canada; to enhance Canada's understanding of its maritime heritage; to foster communication in nautical affairs, to organize meetings, & to cooperate with other agencies promoting nautical research
Marice D. Smith, President

Canadian Numismatic Research Society (CNRS)
PO Box 1351, Victoria BC V8W 2W7
www.nunetcan.net/cnrs/cnrs.htm
To promote reseach & study of numismatics
Ronald Greene, Secretary/Treasurer

Canadian Operational Research Society (CORS) / Société canadienne de recherche opérationelle (SCRO)
PO Box 2225, Stn. D, Ottawa ON K1P 5W4
www.cors.ca
To advance the theory & practice of O.R. in Canada; to stimulate & promote contacts between people interested in the subject
Corinne MacDonald, President
Dionne Aleman, Secretary

Canadian Philosophical Association (CPA) / Association canadienne de philosophie (ACP)
c/o Louise Morel, Saint Paul University, 223 Main St., Ottawa ON K1S 1C4
Tel: 613-236-1393; *Fax:* 613-782-3005
administration@acpcpa.ca
www.acpcpa.ca
Social Media: www.facebook.com/164300999481
twitter.com/acp_cpa
To advance the discipline of philosophy in Canada
Louise Morel, Executive Director
Judy Pelham, Secretary
Patrice Philie, Treasurer
Eric Dayton, English Editor, Dialogue: Canadian Philosophical Review
Mathieu Marion, Éditeur Francophone, Dialogue: Revue canadienne de philosophie

Canadian Quaternary Association / Association canadienne pour l'étude du Quaternaire
c/o Kathryn Hargan, Department of Biology, Queen's University, 116 Barrie St., Kingston ON K7L 3N6
Tel: 613-533-6000
www.canqua.com
To study & advance knowledge of the quaternary period
Sarah Finkelstein, President
Patrick Lajeunesse, Vice-President
Kathryn Hargan, Secretary-Treasurer

Canadian Research Institute for the Advancement of Women (CRIAW) / Institut canadien de recherches sur les femmes (ICREF)
c/o Institute of Women's Studies, University of Ottawa, 143 Séraphin-Marion, Ottawa ON K1N 6N5
Tel: 613-562-5800
info@criaw-icref.ca
www.criaw-icref.ca
To advance the position of women in society through feminist & women-centred research; to encourage, coordinate & communicate research about the reality of women's lives & ensure an equal place for women & their experiences in the body of knowledge about Canada; to recognize & affirm the diversity of women's experiences; to demystify the research process & promote connections between research, social action & social change; to facilitate communication among feminist researchers & research organizations world-wide
Maria-Héléna Pacelli, Administrative Officer
Ann Denis, President

Canadian Society for Aesthetics (CSA) / Société canadienne d'esthétique (SCE)
c/o Dawson College, 4729, av de Maisonneuve, Westmount QC H3Z 1M3
www.csa-sce.ca
To keep aesthetic theorists in close touch with the creative & critical practices that are the basis of their discipline; to increase awareness of aesthetic issues among Canadian citizens & develop the intellectual & conceptual resources for dealing with them.
Ira Newman, Anglophone President
Carl Simpson, Secretary, Membership

Canadian Society for Eighteenth-Century Studies (CSECS) / Société canadienne d'étude du dix-huitième siècle (SCEDS)
c/o Department of French, University of Manitoba, 427 Fletcher Argue Bldg., Winnipeg MB R3T 2N2
Tel: 204-474-9206
www.csecs.ca
To sustain, in Canada, interest in eighteenth-century civilization in Europe & the New World; to encourage, from a wide interdisciplinary base, research on the eighteenth-century; to make known to eighteenth-century specialists the work done in this area in Canada.
Armelle St-Martin, President
Isabelle Tremblay, Secretary
Julie Murray, Treasurer

Canadian Sociological Association (CSA)
PO Box 98014, 2126 Burnhamthorpe Rd. West, Mississauga ON L5L 5V4
Tel: 438-880-2182
office@csa-scs.ca
www.csa-scs.ca
Social Media: linkedin.com/groups?mostPopular=&gid=3188569
www.facebook.com/134213209935255
To promote research, publication & teaching in sociology in Canada
J.S. Frideres, President

Canadian Stroke Network (CSN) / Réseau canadien contre les accidents cérébrovasculaires
#301, 600 Peter Morand Cres., Ottawa ON K1G 5Z3
Tel: 613-562-5696; *Fax:* 613-521-9215
info@canadianstrokenetwork.ca
www.canadianstrokenetwork.ca
Social Media: www.youtube.com/user/strokenetwork
linkedin.com/groups?gid=3012927&trk=myg_ugrp_ovr
www.facebook.com/canadianstrokenetwork
twitter.com/strokenetwork
To reduce the physical, social, & economic consequences of stroke on individuals & society through leadership in research; To develop & implement national strategies in stroke research; To maximize health & economic benefits; To build a consensus across Canada on stroke policy
Pierre Boyle, Chair
Antoine Hakim, CEO & Scientific Director
Kevin Willis, Executive Director
Robin Millbank, Manager, Professional Development

Canadian Water Network (CWN) / Réseau canadien de l'eau
University of Waterloo, 200 University Ave. West, Waterloo ON N2L 3G1
Tel: 519-888-4567; *Fax:* 519-883-7574
info@cwn-rce.ca
www.cwn-rce.ca
Social Media: linkedin.com/company/canadian-water-network
www.facebook.com/CanadianWaterNetwork
twitter.com/CdnWaterNetwork
To create a national partnership in innovation that promotes environmentally responsible stewardship & opportunities with respect to Canada's water resources resulting in sustained prosperity & improved quality of life for Canadians.
Bernadette Conant, Executive Director
Mark Servos, Scientific Director

Cancer Research Society / Société de recherche sur le cancer
#402, 625, av Président-Kennedy, Montréal QC H3A 3S5
Tel: 514-861-9227; *Fax:* 514-861-9220
Toll-Free: 888-766-2262
info@src-crs.ca
www.crs-src.ca
Social Media: linkedin.com/company/cancer-research-society-soci-t-de-recherche-s
www.facebook.com/cancerresearchsociety
To support basic cancer research through funding & seed money; To allocate grants & fellowships to universities & hospitals involved in research across Canada
Andy Chabot, Executive Director
Nathalie Giroux, Vice-President & Chief Operating Officer

Centre for Research on Latin America & The Caribbean (CERLAC)
8th Fl., York Research Tower, York University, 4700 Keele St., Toronto ON M3J 1P3
Tel: 416-736-5237; *Fax:* 416-736-5688
cerlac@yorku.ca
www.yorku.ca/cerlac
To offer an interdisciplinary research unit concerned with economic development, political & social organization & cultural contributions of Latin America & the Caribbean; to build academic & cultural links between these regions & Canada; informs researchers, policy advisors & public on matters concerning the regions; to assist in development of research & teaching institutions that directly benefit people of the regions
Eduardo Canel, Director

Classical Association of Canada (CAC) / Société canadienne des études classiques (SCEC)
c/o Guy Chamberland, Thornloe College at Laurentian University, Laurentian University, Sudbury ON P3E 2C6
www.cac-scec.ca
To advance the study of the civilizations of the Roman & Greek worlds; To promote teaching of classical civilizations & languages in Canadian schools; To encourage research in classical studies
Guy Chamberland, Secretary

Commission canadienne pour la théorie des machines et des mécanismes (CCToMM) / Canadian Committee for the Theory of Machines & Mechanisms
Faculté de génie mécanique, Université du Nouveau Brunswick, CP 4400, Fredericton NB E3B 5A3
Tél: 506-458-7454; *Téléc:* 506-453-5025
www.cctomm.mae.carleton.ca
Promouvoir le développement dans le domaine des machines et des mécanismes par la recherche théorique et expérimentale et leurs applications pratiques.
Marc Arsenault, Secrétaire général
Scott Nokleby, Responsable des communications

FPInnovations
570, boul Saint-Jean, Pointe-Claire QC H9R 3J9
Tel: 514-630-4100; *Fax:* 514-630-4134
info@fpinnovations.ca
fpinnovations.ca
Social Media: twitter.com/fpinnovations
To develop & assist with the implementation of innovative & safe forest operational solutions, which encompass areas such as the engineering, environmental, & human aspects of forestry & wildland fire operations; To improve sustainable forest operations in Canada; To provide members with knowledge & technology, based on research, to conduct cost-competitive, quality forest operations
Pierre Lapointe, President & CEO
Hervé Deschênes, Vice-President, Business Development

Geomatics for Informed Decisions Network
Pavillon Louis-Jacques-Casault, Cité Universitaire, #2306, 1055, av du Séminaire, Québec QC G1V 0A6
Tel: 418-656-7758; *Fax:* 418-656-2611
info@geoide.ulaval.ca
www.geoide.ulaval.ca
Chantal Arguin, President
Nicholas Chrisman, Scientific Director

Great Lakes Institute for Environmental Research (GLIER)
401 Sunset Ave., Windsor ON N9B 3P4
Tel: 519-253-3000; *Fax:* 519-971-3616
glier@uwindsor.ca
www.uwindsor.ca/glier
Multidisciplinary facility with members from many disciplines, including biology, geology, chemistry, engineering, marine biology, molecular biology, genetics and ecology.
Brian Fryer, Contact

Humanist Canada (HC) / Humaniste Canada (HC)
#1150, 45 O'Connor St., Ottawa ON K1P 1A4
Fax: 613-739-5969
Toll-Free: 877-486-2671
info@humanistcanada.com
www.humanistcanada.com
To bring together people who share a non-theistic view of the world; to educate the public about humanism & its ethics & values

Innovation Management Association of Canada (IMAC) / Association canadienne de la gestion de l'innovation (ACGI)
c/o CATAAlliance, #416, 207 Bank St., Ottawa ON K2P 2N2
Tel: 613-236-6550; *Fax:* 613-236-8189
info@cata.ca
www.cata.ca/imac/
To enhance the productivity & effectiveness of Canadian research development & technology-based innovations
Cathi Malette, Membership Coordinator

Institute for Research on Public Policy / Institut de recherche en politiques publiques
#200, 1470, rue Peel, Montréal QC H3A 1T1
Tel: 514-985-2461; *Fax:* 514-985-2559
irpp@irpp.org
www.irpp.org
To improve public policy in Canada by generating research, providing insight, & sparking debate that will contribute to the public policy decision-making process & strengthen the quality of public policy decisions made by Canadian governments, citizens, institutions, & organizations
Graham Fox, President

Institute for Stuttering Treatment & Research & the Communication Improvement Program (ISTAR, CIP)
College Plaza, #1500, 8215 - 112 St., Edmonton AB T6G 2C8
Tel: 780-492-2619; *Fax:* 780-492-8457
istar@ualberta.ca
www.istar.ualberta.ca
Social Media: www.youtube.com/user/RehabMedicineUofA
www.facebook.com/UofARehabMedicine
twitter.com/ISTAR_UofA
To provide treatment solutions to adults & children who stutter; to conduct research regarding stuttering.
Deryk Beal, Executive Director

Institute of Urban Studies (IUS)
University of Winnipeg, #103, 520 Portage Ave., Winnipeg MB R3C 0G2
Tel: 204-982-1140; *Fax:* 204-943-4695
ius@uwinnipeg.ca
ius.uwinnipeg.ca
To undertake policy-oriented research in the field of Urban Studies; to serve as a resource centre for the community; to provide educational services to the University community & the community-at-large.
Jino Distasio, Director

International Council for Canadian Studies (ICCS) / Conseil international d'études canadiennes (CIEC)
PO Box 64016, Stn. Holland Cross, #8, 1620 Scott St., Ottawa ON K1R 6K7
Tel: 613-789-7834; *Fax:* 613-789-7830
www.iccs-ciec.ca
Social Media:
www.facebook.com/ICCS.CIEC.page
twitter.com/ICCS_CIEC
To promote scholarly study, research, teaching & publication about Canada in all disciplines & all countries; to enhance communications among its members to facilitate & develop such scholarly activities; to disseminate research results & to publicize researchers' activities in the area of Canadian Studies; to encourage the development of an international community of Canadianists.
Cristina Frias, Executive Director
Nadyne Lacroix, Coordinator, Finance & Programs

International Council for Central & East European Studies (Canada) (ICCEES) / Conseil international d'études de l'Europe centrale et orientale (Canada)
c/o Dept. Government & International Relations, University of Sydney, Sydney NSW 2006 Australia
www.iccees.org
To foster study of East European affairs & to encourage dissemination of this knowledge among specialists; To create an international community of scholars.
Graeme Gill, President
Andrii Krawchuk, Member, Canada

International Geographical Union - Canadian Committee
Dept. of Geography & Environmental Management, University of Waterloo, 200 University Ave. West, Waterloo ON N2L 3G1
Tel: 519-504-7985; *Fax:* 519-746-0658
www.igu-net.org
To promote international programs in geography within Canada; to promote activities within IGU programs relevant to Canada & to coordinate Canadian participation; to formulate Canadian position & advise the National Research Council on Canadian participation in IGU activities
Jean Andrey, Contact

International Society for Research in Palmistry Inc. / Société internationale de recherches en chirologie inc.
576 rte 315, ChénéVille QC J0V 1E0
Tel: 819-428-4298; *Fax:* 819-428-4495
Toll-Free: 866-428-3799
info@birlacenter.com
www.birlacenter.com/palmistry
The Society offers individual & group counselling through palmistry & astrology based on Eastern Vedic System.

Mathematics of Information Technology & Complex Systems (MITACS)
Technology Enterprise Facility, University of British Columbia, #301, 6190 Agronomy Rd., Vancouver BC V6T 1Z3
Tel: 604-822-9189; *Fax:* 604-822-3689
mitacs@mitacs.ca
www.mitacs.math.ca
Social Media:
linkedin.com/company/mitacs
www.facebook.com/MITACS
twitter.com/DiscoverMITACS
MITACS leads Canada's effort in the generation, application and commercialization of new mathematical tools and methodologies within a world-class research program. The network initiates and fosters linkages with industrial, governmental, and not-for-profit organizations that require mathematical technologies to deal with problems of strategic importance to Canada. MITACS is driving the recruiting, training, and placement of a new generation of highly mathematically skilled personnel that is vital to Canada's future social and economic wellbeing. Offices in Vancouver, Toronto, Montréal, St. John's & Fredericton.
Arvind Gupta, CEO & Scientific Director

The M.S.I. Foundation
12230 - 106 Ave. NW, Edmonton AB T5N 3Z1
Tel: 780-421-7532; *Fax:* 780-425-4467
info@msifoundation.ca
www.msifoundation.ca
To foster & support research into any aspect of the provision of medical & allied health services to the people of Alberta
Doug Wilson, Chairperson

Ontario Centres of Excellence (OCE)
#200, 156 Front St. West, Toronto ON M5J 2L6
Tel: 416-861-1092; *Fax:* 416-971-7164
Toll-Free: 866-759-6014
www.oce-ontario.org
Social Media: www.youtube.com/ocediscovery;
www.instagram.com/oceinnovation
linkedin.com/groups/1811772/profile
www.facebook.com/OCEInnovation
twitter.com/oceinnovation
To create new jobs, products, services, technologies & businesses by creating partnerships between industry & academia
Tom Corr, President & CEO
Tanya Dunn, Executive Assistant
Bob Civak, Senior Vice-President, Business Development & Commercialization
Sharon Jobity, Vice-President, Human Resources & Talent Acquisition

Ontario Public Interest Research Group (OPIRG) / Groupe de recherche d'intérêt public de l'Ontario
North Borden Building, #101, 563 Spadina Ave., Toronto ON M5S 2J7
Tel: 416-978-7770; *Fax:* 416-971-2292
opirg.toronto@utoronto.ca
www.opirg.org
To make information available to the general public that enables them to make informed decisions on issues & understand & possibly influence decisions made by others on their behalf; to provide an alternative to the information provided by the academic community, government & business; to offer an analysis of environmental & social issues aimed at motivating change & placing issues in the broader social, economic & political perspective in which they need to be understood
Sarom Rho, Director

Pulp & Paper Technical Association of Canada (PAPTAC) / Association technique des pâtes et papiers du Canada
#1070, 740, rue Notre-Dame ouest, Montréal QC H3C 3X6
Tel: 514-392-0265; *Fax:* 514-392-0369
tech@paptac.ca
www.paptac.ca
To provide means for the interchange of knowledge & expertise among its members; to improve the skill levels & effectiveness of present & future employees through training & education; to provide technical & practical information on pulp & paper manufacture & use
Greg Hay, Executive Director

The Royal Canadian Geographical Society (RCGS) / La Société géographique royale du Canada (SGRC)
#200, 1155 Lola St., Ottawa ON K1K 4C1
Tel: 613-745-4629; *Fax:* 613-744-0947
rcgs@rcgs.org
www.rcgs.org
Social Media:
www.facebook.com/theRCGS
twitter.com/RCGS_SGRC
To impart a broader knowledge of Canada, including its environmental, economic, & social challenges, as well as it natural & cultural heritage
John Geiger, Chief Executive Officer
Gilles Gagnier, Chief Operating Officer and Publisher
André Préfontaine, Chief Development Officer

Royal Canadian Institute (RCI)
#H7D, 700 University Ave., Toronto ON M5G 1X6
Tel: 416-977-2983; *Fax:* 416-962-7314
royalcanadianinstitute@sympatico.ca
www.royalcanadianinstitute.org
Social Media: www.youtube.com/RCIonline
www.facebook.com/481071185037
twitter.com/RCI_Canada
To increase public understanding of science; to create an environment in which science can flourish & be appreciated
Helle Tosine, President
John W. Johnston, Treasurer

The Royal Society of Canada (RSC) / La Société royale du Canada
Walter House, 282 Somerset West, Ottawa ON K2P 0J6
Tel: 613-991-6990; *Fax:* 613-991-6996
www.rsc.ca
Social Media: www.youtube.com/user/RSCSRC1
linkedin.com/pub/the-royal-society-of-canada-rsc/23/592/418
www.facebook.com/RSC.SRC
twitter.com/rsctheacademies
To promote learning & research in the arts, humanities & sciences in Canada; in its role as a National Academy, to draw on the breadth of knowledge & expertise of its members to recognize & honour distinguished accomplishments; to advise on the state of scholarship & culture across Canada; to inform the public on noteworthy social, scientific & ethical questions of the day; it is organized into three academies covering the arts & humanities, the social sciences, & the natural & applied sciences
Darren Gilmour, Executive Director

Shevchenko Scientific Society of Canada
516 The Kingsway, Toronto ON M9A 3W6
ntsh.ca@gmail.com
www.ntsh.ca
Social Media:
www.youtube.com/channel/UCobh6boBPbiYHSxLFYQL07Q
www.facebook.com/1594608770752854
twitter.com/NtshCanada
To promote scholarly research & publication; To advance education in the field of Ukrainian & Ukrainian Canadian studies
Daria Darewych, President

Society for the Study of Egyptian Antiquities (SSEA) / Société pour l'Étude de l'Égypte Ancienne
PO Box 19004, Stn. Walmer, 360A Bloor St. West, Toronto ON M5S 3C9
Tel: 647-520-4339
info@thessea.org
www.thessea.org
Social Media:
www.facebook.com/SocietyfortheStudyofEgyptianAntiquities
To stimulate interest in Egyptology; To assist with research & training in the field; To sponsor & promote archaeological expeditions to Egypt
Lyn Green, National President

Stem Cell Network (SCN) / Réseau de cellules souches
#CCW-6189, 501 Smyth Rd., Ottawa ON K1H 8L6
Tel: 613-739-6675
info@stemcellnetwork.ca
www.stemcellnetwork.ca
Social Media: vimeo.com/stemcellnetwork
www.facebook.com/CanadianStemCellNetwork
twitter.com/StemCellNetwork
To investigate the immense therapeutic potential of stem cells for the treatment of diseases currently incurable by conventional approaches
Philip Welford, Executive Director
Lisa Willemse, Director of Communications

Technion Canada
#206, 970 Lawrence Ave. West, Toronto ON M6A 3B6
Tel: 416-789-4545; *Fax:* 416-789-0255
Toll-Free: 800-935-8864
info@technioncanada.org
www.technioncanada.org
Social Media:
linkedin.com/groups/Canadian-Technion-Society-4351525
www.facebook.com/pages/Canadian-Technion-Society/1200727 21377514
To support Technion Israel Institute of Technology; to promote exchange of scientific information between Israel & Canada, scholarships, research, etc.
Marvin Ostin, National President
Cheryl Koperwas, National Executive Director
Edward Nagel, National Vice-President

Traffic Injury Research Foundation (TIRF) / Fondation de recherches sur les blessures de la route
#200, 171 Nepean St., Ottawa ON K2P 0B4
Tel: 613-238-5235; *Fax:* 613-238-5292
Toll-Free: 877-238-5235
tirf@tirf.ca
www.tirf.ca
To reduce traffic related deaths & injuries, through the design, promotion, & implementation of prevention programs & policies based on sound research
Robyn D. Robertson, President & CEO
Sara Oglestone, Manager, Marketing & Communications

Restaurants & Food Services

Association des fournisseurs d'hôtels et restaurants inc. (AFHR) / Hotel & Restaurant Suppliers Association Inc. (HRSA)
#230, 9300, boul Henri-Bourassa ouest, Saint-Laurent QC H4S 1L5
Tel: 514-334-3404; *Fax:* 514-334-1279
info@afhr.com
www.afhr.com
Informer et parfaire les connaissances des professionnels de l'industrie; offrir une vitrine aux fournisseurs par le biais du site web de l'association; centre d'information pour les hôtels, restaurants et institutions à la recherche de fournisseurs; programme d'escomptes pour les membres sur divers services; l'AFHR organise le Salon Rendez-vous HRI
Victor Francoeur, President & CEO
Isabelle Julien, Operation Manager
Hughes Moisan, Vice-President, Business Development

Association des restaurateurs du Québec (ARQ) / Québec Restaurant Association
6880, boul Louis-H.-La Fontaine, Montréal QC H1M 2T2
Tél: 514-527-9801; *Téléc:* 514-527-3066
Ligne sans frais: 800-463-4237
arqc@arqc.qc.ca
www.restaurateurs.ca
Média social: www.facebook.com/167396323369138
twitter.com/ARQ_resto
Fournir à l'ensemble des restaurateurs du Québec des services complets d'information, de formation, d'escomptes, d'assurances et de représentation gouvernementale
Bernard Fortin, Président directeur général

British Columbia Restaurant & Foodservices Association (BCRFA)
#2, 2246 Spruce St., Vancouver BC V6H 2P3
Tel: 604-669-2239; *Fax:* 604-669-6175
Toll-Free: 877-669-2239
info@bcrfa.com
www.bcrfa.com
Social Media:
linkedin.com/company/bc-restaurant-&-foodservices-association-bcrf
www.facebook.com/BCRFA
twitter.com/BCRFA
To be the voice of the hospitality industry in British Columbia; the advocat of the restaurant industry.
Ian Tostenson, President & CEO

Canadian Culinary Federation (CCFCC) / Fédération Culinaire Canadienne
30 Hamilton Ct., Riverview NB E1B 3C3
Tel: 506-387-4882; *Fax:* 506-387-4884
admin@ccfcc.ca
www.ccfcc.ca
Social Media:
www.facebook.com/CCFCC
twitter.com/CdnChefs
To promote a Canadian food culture both nationally & internationally; To encourage professional excellence among chefs & cooks throughout Canada
Judson Simpson, Chair
Donald A. Gyurkovits, President
Roy Butterworth, Executive Director
Ahron Goldman, Secretary
Simon Smotkowicz, Treasurer

Manitoba Restaurant & Food Services Association (MRFA)
103-D Scurfield Blvd., Winnipeg MB R3Y 1M6
Tel: 204-783-9955; *Fax:* 204-783-9909
Toll-Free: 877-296-2909
info@mrfa.mb.ca
www.mrfa.mb.ca
Social Media:
www.facebook.com/105407752852372
twitter.com/ManRFA
To lobby government and other regulatory bodies on issues affecting you and your business; to present educational seminars and social programs; to provide member services such as insurance programs and credit card savings; to represent the restaurant and foodservice industry effectively through a large membership.
Scott Jocelyn, Executive Director

Restaurants Canada
1155 Queen St. West, Toronto ON M6J 1J4
Tel: 416-923-8416; *Fax:* 416-923-1450
Toll-Free: 800-387-5649
info@restaurantscanada.org
www.restaurantscanada.org
Social Media: www.instagram.com/restaurantscanada
www.facebook.com/RestaurantsCanada
twitter.com/RestaurantsCA
To create a favourable business environment & deliver tangible value to members in all sectors of Canada's foodservice industry
Donna Dooher, President & Chief Executive Officer
Joyce Reynolds, Executive Vice-President, Government Affairs
Jill Holroyd, Senior Vice-President, Communications & Research

Société des chefs, cuisiniers et pâtissiers du Québec (SCCPQ)
CP 47536, Succ. Plateau Mont-Royal, Montréal QC H2H 2S8
Tél: 514-528-1083; *Téléc:* 514-528-1037
bureau-national@sccpq.ca
www.sccpq.ca
Média social: www.youtube.com/user/sccpq
www.facebook.com/sccpq
twitter.com/SCCPQ
Mise en valeur et émulation de la profession; reconnaissance professionnelle au niveau national
René Derrien, Président national
Patrick Gérôme, Secrétaire

Retail Trade

Association des détaillants en alimentation du Québec (ADA) / Québec Food Retailers' Association
#900, 2120, rue Sherbrooke Est, Montréal QC H2K 1C3
Tél: 514-982-0104; *Téléc:* 514-849-3021
Ligne sans frais: 800-363-3923
info@adaq.qc.ca
www.adaq.qc.ca
Média social: vimeo.com/adaquebec
www.facebook.com/ADAQuebec
twitter.com/ADAquebec
Représenter et défendre les intérêts professionnels, socio-politiques et économiques de tous les détaillants du Québec, et ce, quels que soient leur bannière et le type de surface qu'ils opèrent
Daniel Choquette, Président
Florent Gravel, Président-directeur général

Association nationale des distributeurs aux petites surfaces alimentaires (ANDPSA) / National Convenience Stores Distributors Association (NACDA)
#410, 1695, boul Laval, Laval QC H7S 2M2
Toll-Free: 800-686-2823
nacda@nacda.ca
www.nacda.ca
Promouvoir le bien-être et les intérêts de nos membres distributeurs-grossistes ainsi que de l'industrie
Raymond Bouchard, Président du conseil d'administration

Association Québécoise des dépanneurs en alimentation (AQDA)
#501, 1, av Holiday, Montréal QC H9R 5N3
Tél: 514-240-3934; *Téléc:* 514-630-6989
info@acda-aqda.ca
www.acda-aqda.ca
Michel Gadbois, Président

Atlantic Convenience Store Association (ACSA)
#B, 100 Ilsley Ave., Dartmouth NB B3B 1L3
Tel: 902-880-9733
theacsa.ca
To represent convenience store retailers in the Atlantic provinces
Mike Hammoud, President

Canadian Convenience Stores Association (CCSA) / Association Canadienne des dépanneurs en alimentation (ACDA)
#103, 220 Wyecroft Rd., Oakville ON L6K 3V1
Tel: 905-845-9339; *Fax:* 905-845-9340
Toll-Free: 877-934-3968
www.theccsa.ca
To be the industry voice for all convenience store matters; to provide a forum for concerns & issues; to educate members
Alex Scholten, President
Lynda Watson, Secretary

Canadian Gift Association / Association canadienne de cadeaux
42 Voyager Ct. South, Toronto ON M9W 5M7
Tel: 416-679-0170; *Fax:* 416-679-0175
Toll-Free: 800-611-6100
info@cangift.org
www.cangift.org
Social Media: www.youtube.com/user/cgtassoc
linkedin.com/company/3520259
www.facebook.com/CanadianGift
twitter.com/cangift
To create & manage sales opportunities for the gift industry
Peter Moore, President & CEO

Canadian Sporting Goods Association (CSGA) / Association canadienne d'articles de sport (ACAS)
#1272, 10 - 225 The East Mall, Toronto ON M9B 0A9
Toll-Free: 844-350-9902
info@csga.ca
www.csga.ca
Social Media: www.instagram.com/csgahub
linkedin.com/company/canadian-sporting-goods-association
www.facebook.com/211952635634448
twitter.com/CSGAhub
To conduct quality trade shows; To provide forum responsive to the professional needs of its members; To initiate programs designed to stimulate sports activity participation as considered feasible
Kelly Falls, Coordinator, Membership & Advertising: North America

Conseil québécois du commerce de détail (CQCD) / Retail Council of Québec
#910, 630, rue Sherbrooke ouest, Montréal QC H3A 1E4
Tél: 514-842-6681; *Téléc:* 514-842-7627
Ligne sans frais: 800-364-6766
cqcd@cqcd.org
www.cqcd.org
Promouvoir, représenter et valoriser le secteur du commerce de détail au Québec et les détaillants qui en font partie afin d'assurer le sain développement et la prospérité du secteur
Léopold Turgeon, Président
Chantale Bélanger, Directrice, Comptabilité et administration

Direct Sellers Association of Canada (DSA) / Association de ventes directes du Canada
#250, 180 Attwell Dr., Toronto ON M9W 6A9
Tel: 416-679-8555; *Fax:* 416-679-1568
info@dsa.ca
www.dsa.ca
Social Media:
www.facebook.com/322698510777
twitter.com/dsacanada
To represent companies that manufacture & distribute goods & services through independent sales contractors, away from a fixed retail location; To encourage strong consumer protection, through Codes of Ethics & Business Practices; To engage in discussion with government & industry; To act as the voice of the direct selling industry to government in pursuit of better business opportunities for Canadian entrepreneurs.
Angela Abdallah, Chair
Ross Creber, President & Secretary

Neighbourhood Pharmacy Association of Canada
#301, 45 Sheppard Ave. East, Toronto ON M2N 5W9
Tel: 416-226-9100; *Fax:* 416-226-9185
info@neighbourhoodpharmacies.ca
www.cacds.com
Neighbourhood Pharmacy Association of Canada strives to ensure a strong chain drug store sector access to high quality products & health care services to Canadians.
Denise Carpenter, President/CEO
Vivek Sood, Chair

Ontario Convenience Store Association (OCSA)
#217, 466 Speers Rd., Oakville ON L6K 3W9
Tel: 905-845-9152; *Fax:* 905-849-9947
www.conveniencestores.ca
Social Media:
twitter.com/ontariocstores
To represent convenience store retailers in Ontario
Dave Bryans, Chief Executive Officer

Pool & Hot Tub Council of Canada (PHTCC) / Conseil canadien des piscines et spas
5 MacDougall Dr., Brampton ON L6S 3P3
Tel: 905-458-7242; *Fax:* 905-458-7037
Toll-Free: 800-879-7066
info@poolcouncil.ca
www.poolcouncil.ca
Social Media:
www.facebook.com/273144795787
To promote the image & sales of the pool, spa & hot tub industry throughout Canada; to promote & enhance consumer awareness of the industry's products; to encourage & promote increased health & safety standards within the industry; to support efforts to improve pool, hot tub & spa equipment facilities, services & products; &, generally, to promote & advance the common interests of members
Robert Wood, National Executive Director

Retail Council of Canada (RCC) / Conseil canadien du commerce de détail
#800, 1881 Yonge St., Toronto ON M4S 3C4
Tel: 416-922-6678; *Fax:* 416-922-8011
Toll-Free: 888-373-8245
info@retailcouncil.org
www.retailcouncil.org
Social Media: www.youtube.com/user/RetailCouncil
linkedin.com/company/retail-council-of-canada
www.facebook.com/retailcouncil
twitter.com/RetailCouncil
To be the best at delivering the services our retail members value most; To serve, promote & represent the diverse needs of Canada's retailing industry to the highest standards of quality
Anna Martini, Chair
Diane J. Brisebois, CAE, President & CEO
David Wilkes, Senior Vice-President, Grocery Division & Government Relations
Andrew Siegwart, Vice-President, Membership Services

Surrey Board of Trade (SBOT)
#101, 14439 - 104 Ave., Surrey BC V3R 1M1
Tel: 604-581-7130; *Fax:* 604-588-7549
Toll-Free: 866-848-7130
info@businessinsurrey.com
www.businessinsurrey.com
Social Media:
www.facebook.com/pages/Surrey-Board-of-Trade/14153105258 1905
twitter.com/SBofT
To provide advocacy, resources, experience & networking to members & fosters best business practices to ensure growth & prosperity of members
Anita Huberman, Chief Executive Officer
Bijoy Samuel, President
Gerard Breamault, Vice-President

Western Convenience Store Association (WCSA)
AB
Tel: 778-987-4440; *Toll-Free:* 800-734-2487
andrew@conveniencestores.ca
www.thewcsa.com
Social Media:
linkedin.com/groups/Western-Convenience-Stores-Association-4 191541
To represent convenience store retailers in Manitoba, Saskatchewan, Alberta, British Columbia, Yukon, Northwest Territories & Nunavut
Andrew Klukas, President

Safety & Accident Prevention

Alberta Fire Chiefs Association (AFCA)
AB
Tel: 780-719-7939; *Fax:* 780-892-3333
www.afca.ab.ca
William Purdy, Executive Director

Alberta Safety Council
4831 - 93 Ave., Edmonton AB T6B 3A2
Tel: 780-462-7300; *Fax:* 780-462-7318
Toll-Free: 800-301-6407
info@safetycouncil.ab.ca
www.safetycouncil.ab.ca
Social Media:
www.facebook.com/189043441145255
twitter.com/ABSafetycouncil
To create awareness & provide educational & training programs to citizens of Alberta on how to maintain a safe environment at home, in traffic, at work & at play
Laurie Billings, Executive Director

Association de la santé et de la sécurité des pâtes et papiers et des industries de la forêt du Québec (ASSIFQ-ASSPPQ)
Place Iberville II, #210, 1175, av Lavigerie, Québec QC G1V 4P1
Tél: 418-657-2267; *Téléc:* 418-651-4622
Ligne sans frais: 888-632-9326
info@santesecurite.org
www.santesecurite.org
De soutenir et d'accompagner les entreprises dans l'amélioration continue de la santé et de la sécurité du travail
Jacques Laroche, Président-directeur général
Suzanne Lavoie, Adjointe administrative

Association des chefs en sécurité incendie du Québec (ACSIQ) / Québec Association of Fire Chiefs
5, rue Dupré, Beloeil QC J3G 3J7
Tél: 450-464-6413; *Téléc:* 450-467-6297
Ligne sans frais: 888-464-6413
administration@acsiq.qc.ca
www.acsiq.qc.ca
Regrouper les personnes détenant un poste de commande dans le domaine de la prévention et de la lutte contre les incendies
Daniel Brazeau, Président

Association paritaire pour la santé et la sécurité du travail - Administration provinciale
#10, 1220, boul Lebourgneuf, Québec QC G2K 2G4
Tél: 418-624-4801; *Téléc:* 418-624-4858
apssap@apssap.qc.ca
apssap.qc.ca
Supporter la prise en charge paritaire de la prévention en matière de santé, de sécurité et d'intégrité physique des personnes du secteur de l'Administration provinciale
Colette Trudel, Directrice générale
Sylvie Bédard, Technicienne, Administration

Association paritaire pour la santé et la sécurité du travail - Imprimerie et activités connexes
#450, 7450, boul Galeries d'Anjou, Anjou QC H1M 3M3
Tél: 514-355-8282; *Téléc:* 514-355-6818
info@aspimprimerie.qc.ca
www.aspimprimerie.qc.ca
Fournir aux employeurs et aux travailleurs du secteur imprimerie et activités connexes des services d'information, de formation, de conseil et de recherche pour favoriser la prise en charge de la prévention dans les entreprises
Marie Ménard, Directrice générale

Association paritaire pour la santé et la sécurité du travail du secteur affaires sociales
#950, 5100, rue Sherbrooke Est, Montréal QC H1V 3R9
Tél: 514-253-6871; *Téléc:* 514-253-1443
Ligne sans frais: 800-361-4528
www.asstsas.qc.ca
Média social: ca.linkedin.com/in/asstsas
www.facebook.com/305696879444973
twitter.com/InfosASSTSAS
Pour promouvoir la santé et la sécurité et à assurer la formation et l'information du public
Diane Parent, Directrice générale

Association sectorielle services automobiles
#150, 8, rue de la Place-du-Commerce, Brossard QC J4W 3H2
Tél: 450-672-9330; *Téléc:* 450-672-4835
Ligne sans frais: 800-363-2344
info@autoprevention.org
www.autoprevention.org
Média social: www.youtube.com/autoprevention
twitter.com/AutoPrevention
Aider les travailleurs et les employeurs du secteur des services automobiles à prendre en charge la santé et la sécurité au travail, afin d'éliminer les risques d'accidents et de maladies professionnelles
Sylvie Mallette, Directrice Générale

Board of Canadian Registered Safety Professionals (BCRSP) / Conseil canadien des professionnels en securité agréés
#100, 6700 Century Ave., Mississauga ON L5N 6A4
Tel: 905-567-7198; *Fax:* 905-567-7191
Toll-Free: 888-279-2777
info@bcrsp.ca
www.bcrsp.ca
Social Media:
linkedin.com/company/board-of-canadian-registered-safety-profe ssionals
www.twitter.com/bcrsp
To protect & promote occupational health & safety, environmental safety, & public safety, through the registration of qualified health & safety professionals committed to a code of ethics
Daniel T. Lyons, Chair
Nicola Wright, Executive Director

Canada Safety Council (CSC) / Conseil canadien de la sécurité (CCS)
1020 Thomas Spratt Pl., Ottawa ON K1G 5L5
Tel: 613-739-1535; *Fax:* 613-739-1566
csc@safety-council.org
www.canadasafetycouncil.org
Social Media:
www.facebook.com/canada.safety
twitter.com/CanadaSafetyCSC
Jack Smith, President
Raynard Marchand, General Manager, Programs

Canadian Association of Fire Chiefs (CAFC) / Association canadienne des chefs de pompiers (ACCP)
#702, 280 Albert St., Ottawa ON K1P 5G8
Tel: 613-270-9138; *Toll-Free:* 800-775-5189
www.cafc.ca
Social Media:
ca.linkedin.com/pub/canadian-association-of-fire-chiefs/2a/a05/8 2b
twitter.com/cafc2
To lead & represent the Canadian Fire Service on public safety issues with the vision of being nationally recognized as the fire service voice of authority
Robert Simonds, President
Pierre Voisine, Secretary
Lee Grant, Treasurer

Canadian Association of Road Safety Professionals (CARSP) / Association canadienne des professionnels de la sécurité routière (ACPSER)
St Catharines ON
info@casp.ca
www.carsp.ca
Social Media:
ca.linkedin.com/pub/canadian-association-of-road-safety-profess ionals/
twitter.com/CARSPInfo
The association preserves & shares professional experience regarding road safety. It promotes research & professional development & facilitates communication & cooperation among road safety groups & agencies.
Brenda Suggett, Executive Administrator
Brian Jonah, President
Jennifer Kroeker-Hall, Vice-President

Canadian Automatic Sprinkler Association (CASA)
#302, 335 Renfrew Dr., Markham ON L3R 9S9
Tel: 905-477-2270; *Fax:* 905-477-3611
info@casa-firesprinkler.org
www.casa-firesprinkler.org
Social Media:
www.youtube.com/user/CASAFiresprinkler1?blend=1&ob=5
linkedin.com/groups/CASA-Canadian-Automatic-Sprinkler-Assoc iation-
twitter.com/CASAFS

To advance the fire sprinkler art as applied to the conservation of life & property from fire
John Galt, President

Canadian Centre for Occupational Health & Safety (CCOHS) / Centre canadien d'hygiène et de sécurité au travail (CCHST)
135 Hunter St. East, Hamilton ON L8N 1M5
Tel: 905-572-2981; *Fax:* 905-572-4500
Toll-Free: 800-668-4284
clientservices@ccohs.ca
www.ccohs.ca
Social Media:
linkedin.com/company/canadian-centre-for-occupational-health-and-s
www.facebook.com/CCOHS
twitter.com/ccohs
Promotes the total well-being—physical, psychological & mental health—of working Canadians by providing information, training, education, management systems & solutions that support health, safety, & wellness programs
S. Len Hong, President/CEO
Patabendi K. Abeytunga, Vice-President

Canadian Fire Safety Association (CFSA)
#310, 2175 Sheppard Ave. East, Toronto ON M2J 1W8
Tel: 416-492-9417; *Fax:* 416-491-1670
cfsa@taylorenterprises.com
www.canadianfiresafety.com
Social Media:
twitter.com/CFSA4
To promote fire safety through seminars, safety training courses, scholarships & regular meetings.
Matteo Gilfillan, President
Carolyne Vigon, Administrator

Canadian Radiation Protection Association (CRPA) / Association canadienne de radioprotection (ACRP)
PO Box 83, Carleton Place ON K7C 3P3
Tel: 613-253-3779; *Fax:* 888-551-0712
secretariat@crpa-acrp.ca
www.crpa-acrp.ca
Social Media:
linkedin.com/groups?gid=4296889
To develop scientific knowledge for protection from the harmful effects of radiation; To encourage research; To assist in the development of professional standards in the discipline
Jeff Dovyak, President
Ray Ilson, Treasurer

Canadian Security Association (CANASA) / L'Association canadienne de la sécurité
National Office, #201, 50 Acadia Ave., Markham ON L3R 0B3
Tel: 905-513-0622; *Fax:* 905-513-0624
Toll-Free: 800-538-9919
staff@canasa.org
www.canasa.org
Social Media:
linkedin.com/groups?mostPopular=&gid=3663787
www.facebook.com/169077016452968
twitter.com/CANASA_News
To act as the national voice of the security industry; To promote & protect the interests of members; To increase public awareness of the security industry's effectiveness in reducing risk; To develop & promote programs consistent with the needs of members; To develop & promote programs which will lead to the reduction of false dispatches & improved response; To influence regulations affecting the members
Richard McMullen, President
Heather Terrence, Executive Director
Steve Basnett, Director, Trade Shows & Events
Mona Emond, Director, Marketing & Communications
Dave Kushner, Manager, Finance

Canadian Society of Air Safety Investigators (CSASI)
139 West 13th Ave., Vancouver BC V5Y 1V8
avsafe@shaw.ca
www.beyondriskmgmt.com
To ensure air safety through investigation
Barbara M. Dunn, President
Elaine M. Parker, Vice-President

Canadian Society of Safety Engineering, Inc. (CSSE) / Société canadienne de la santé et de la sécurité, inc.
468 Queen St. East, LL-02, Toronto ON M5A 1T7
Tel: 416-646-1600; *Fax:* 416-646-9460
Toll-Free: 877-446-2674
www.csse.org
Social Media:
linkedin.com/groups?gid=1558517
www.facebook.com/39373429711
twitter.com/csse
To be the voice of safety in Canada
Wayne Glover, Executive Director
Jim B. Hopkins, President

Centre patronal de santé et sécurité du travail du Québec (CPSSTQ) / Employers Center for Occupational Health & Safety of Quebec
#1000, 500, rue Sherbrooke ouest, Montréal QC H3A 3C6
Tél: 514-842-8401; *Téléc:* 514-842-9375
www.centrepatronalsst.qc.ca
Fournir de l'information et de la formation en SST aux entreprises regroupées par les associations patronales membres du Centre patronal
Claude Gosselin, Président
Denise Turenne, Direction générale
Diane Rochone, Directrice, Communications

Council of Canadian Fire Marshals & Fire Commissioners (CCFMFC) / Conseil canadien des directeurs provinciaux et des commissaires des incendies
c/o 491 McLeod Hill Rd., Fredericton NB E3A 6H6
Tel: 506-453-1208; *Fax:* 506-457-0793
CCFMFC@rogers.com
www.ccfmfc.ca
To contribute to a reduction in the number of fire deaths
Duane McKay, President
Harold Pothier, Vice-President
Philippa Gourley, Secretary-Treasurer

Council of Private Investigators - Ontario (CPIO)
#204, 43 Keefer Crt., Hamilton ON L8E 4V4
Tel: 416-955-9450
www.cpi-ontario.com
To represent the interests of private investigators in Ontario
Debbra MacDonald, President
Charlie Robb, Administration Manager

Federal Association of Security Officials (FASO) / Association fédérale des représentants de la sécurité
PO Box 2384, Stn. D, Ottawa ON K1P 5W5
Fax: 613-773-5787
Toll-Free: 888-330-3276
info@faso-afrs.ca
faso-afrs.ca
To enhance the performance & career development of federal security officers through enhancing the security function in government & improving the professionalism of security officers.
Claude J.G. Levesque, President

Fédération Québécoise des Intervenants en Sécurité Incendie (FQISI)
CP 40025, Granby QC J2G 9SI
Tél: 514-990-1338; *Téléc:* 514-666-9119
info@fqisi.org
www.fqisi.org
Média social:
linkedin.com/company/fqisi---f-d-ration-qu-b-coise-des-intervenant
www.facebook.com/FQISI.org
Aider à promouvoir la prévention des incendies; aider, soutenir et susciter des efforts en vue de réduire les pertes de vie; favoriser le perfectionnement en vue de combattre plus efficacement les incendies; promouvoir l'éducation populaire en général sur la protection et la prévention des incendies; faire des recommandations auprès des corps politiques et gouvernementaux
Jocelyn Lussier, Président
Alain Richard, Directeur Éxécutif

Fire Prevention Canada (FPC)
PO Box 37009, 3332 McCarthy Rd., Ottawa ON K1V 0W0
Tel: 613-749-3844
info@fiprecan.ca
www.fiprecan.ca
To work with the public & private sectors to achieve fire safety through education.
Peter Adamakos, National Manager

Industrial Accident Victims Group of Ontario (IAVGO)
#203, 489 College St., Toronto ON M6G 1A5
Tel: 416-924-6477; *Toll-Free:* 877-230-6311
www.iavgo.org
Social Media:
www.facebook.com/167369409975545
Provides free services to injured workers in Ontario including legal advice, legal representation, public legal education, advocacy training and community development.
Mary DiNucci, Coordinator

Institut de recherche Robert-Sauvé en santé et en sécurité du travail (IRSST) / Robert Sauvé Occupational Health & Safety Research Institute
505, boul de Maisonneuve ouest, 15e étage, Montréal QC H3A 3C2
Tél: 514-288-1551; *Téléc:* 514-288-7636
communications@irsst.qc.ca
www.irsst.qc.ca
Média social: www.facebook.com//207703664186
twitter.com/IRSST
Contribuer par la recherche et le développement à l'amélioration de la santé et de la sécurité des travailleurs et plus spécifiquement, à l'élimination à la source des dangers pour leur santé, leur sécurité et leur intégrité physique ainsi qu'à la réadaptation des travailleurs victimes d'accidents ou de maladies professionnelles; fournir au Réseau public québécois de la prévention en santé et en sécurité du travail - composé de CSST, des Centres locaux de services communautaires, des Régies de la santé et des services sociaux et des associations sectorielles paritaires - les services et l'expertise nécessaires à leur action; diffuser les connaissances issues de ces recherches et de ces expertises auprès des milieux de travail et en favoriser le transfert; accorder des bourses d'études supérieures en santé et en sécurité du travail; agir comme laboratoire de référence au Québec, dans le domaine de l'hygiene industrielle.
Michel Després, Président/Directeur général

Manitoba Association of Fire Chiefs (MAFC)
PO Box 1208, Portage la Prairie MB R1N 3J9
Tel: 204-857-6249
mb.firechiefs@mymts.net
mafc.ca
Martin Haller, President

MultiPrévention
#301, 2271, boul Fernand-Lafontaine, Longueuil QC J4G 2R7
Tél: 450-442-7763; *Téléc:* 450-442-2332
info@multiprevention.org
multiprevention.org
L'union rejoindre de sécurité pour les secteurs de la santé et sécurité:métallique, électricité, vêtements, & gravures
Nathalie Laurenzi, Directrice générale

MultiPrévention ASP: Association paritaire pour la santé et la sécurité au travail des secteurs: métal, électrique, habillement et imprimerie
#150, 2405 boul Fernand-Lafontaine, Longueuil QC J4N 1N7
Tél: 450-442-7763; *Téléc:* 450-442-2332
multiprevention.org
Média social:
www.facebook.com/MultiPrévention-214272358763722/
Marie-Josée Ross, Conseillère en gestion
Caroline Godin, Conseiller technique

Ontario Association of Fire Chiefs (OAFC)
#22, 520 Westney Rd. South, Ajax ON L1S 6W6
Tel: 905-426-9865; *Fax:* 905-426-3032
Toll-Free: 800-774-6651
info@oafc.on.ca
www.oafc.on.ca
Social Media: www.flickr.com/photos/96578349@N02
linkedin.com/company/ontario-association-of-fire-chiefs
www.facebook.com/570718659627505
twitter.com/ONFireChiefs
To provide a voice for matters relating to the management & delivery of fire & emergency services in Ontario; To represent fire chief officers in Ontario
Richard Boyes, Executive Director

Ontario Industrial Fire Protection Association (OIFPA)
193 James St. South, Hamilton ON L8P 3A8
Tel: 905-527-0700; *Fax:* 905-527-6254
oifpa@interlynx.net
www.oifpa.org
To unite individuals with a concern for fire protection within Ontario's industrial community

Ontario Safety League (OSL) / Ligue de sécurité de l'Ontario
#212, 2595 Skymark Ave., Mississauga ON L4W 4L5
Tel: 905-625-0556; *Fax:* 905-625-0677
info@osl.org
www.ontariosafetyleague.com
Safety through education with an emphasis on traffic & child safety
Brian J. Patterson, President & General Manager

Opération Nez rouge / Operation Red Nose
Maison Couillard, Université Laval, 2539, rue Marie-Fitzbach, Québec QC G1V 0A6
Tél: 418-653-1492; *Téléc:* 418-653-3315
Ligne sans frais: 800-463-7222
info@operationnezrouge.com
www.operationnezrouge.com
Média social: www.youtube.com/user/OperationNezrouge
www.facebook.com/OperationNezrouge
twitter.com/ORNose
Service de chauffeur privé gratuit & bénévole offert pendant la période des Fêtes à tout automobiliste qui a consommé de l'alcool, our qui ne se sent pas en état de conduire son véhicule.
Guylaine Beaupré, Directrice générale

Préventex - Association paritaire du textile
1936, rue Rossignol, Brossard QC J4X 2C6
Tél: 450-671-6925; *Téléc:* 450-671-9267
www.preventex.qc.ca
Amener les employeurs et les travailleurs du secteur à prendre charge activement de la prévention des accidents du travail et des maladies professionnelles
François Lauzon, Co-président
Daniel Vallée, Co-président

Radiation Safety Institute of Canada / Institut de radioprotection du Canada
Head Office & National Education Centre, #300, 165 Avenue Rd., Toronto ON M5R 3S4
Tel: 416-650-9090; *Fax:* 416-650-9920
Toll-Free: 800-263-5803
info@radiationsafety.ca
www.radiationsafety.ca
Social Media:
www.facebook.com/143472245714096
To be an independent source for knowledge about radiation safety in the environment, the community, & the workplace
Fergal Nolan, President & Chief Executive Officer
R. Moridi, Vice-President, Chief Scientist
Bruce Sylvester, Vice-President, Finance & Administration
Mike Haynes, Scientific Director
Natalia Mozayani, Program Manager
Tara Hargreaves, Scientist & Coordinator, Training

Safety Services Manitoba (SSM)
#3, 1680 Notre Dame Ave., Winnipeg MB R3H 1H6
Tel: 204-949-1085; *Fax:* 204-949-2897
Toll-Free: 800-661-3321
registrar@safetyservicesmanitoba.ca
www.safetyservicesmanitoba.ca
Social Media:
ca.linkedin.com/in/gotosafetyservicesmanitoba
www.facebook.com/SafetyServicesManitoba
twitter.com/SafetyServMB
To prevent accidental injury or occupational illness in Manitoba by providing effective safety & health programs.
Judy Murphy, President & CEO

Safety Services New Brunswick (SSNB) / Services de Sécurité Nouveau-Brunswick
#204, 440 Wilsey Rd., Fredericton NB E3B 7G5
Tel: 506-458-8034; *Fax:* 506-444-0177
Toll-Free: 877-762-7233
info@safetyservicesnb.ca
www.safetyservicesnb.ca
Social Media:
www.facebook.com/motorcyclecourse
twitter.com/safetynb
To promote traffic, occupational & public safety issues & practices through safety training courses & programs, educational material, public information, safety campaigns & conferences.
Bill Walker, President & CEO
Jim Arsenault, Director of OSH & Traffic Training

Safety Services Newfoundland & Labrador
1076 Topsail Rd., Mount Pearl NL A1N 5E7
Tel: 709-754-0210; *Fax:* 709-754-0010
info@safetyservicesnl.ca
safetyservicesnl.ca
Social Media:
www.facebook.com/303428916390762
twitter.com/SafetyNL
Safety Services Newfoundland Labrador is dedicated to the prevention of injuries and fatalities; represents all the major sectors of the province's industry, business, government departments, volunteer organizations and many individuals who have a personal interest in safety, both on and off the job.

Safety Services Nova Scotia (SSNS)
#1, 201 Brownlow Ave., Dartmouth NS B3B 1W2
Tel: 902-454-9621; *Fax:* 902-454-6027
Toll-Free: 866-511-2211
www.safetyservicesns.com
Social Media:
www.facebook.com/SafetyNS
twitter.com/SafetyNS
To develop & provide quality safety & health services, education & training programs to improve the quality of life of Nova Scotians.
Jackie Norman, Executive Director

Saskatchewan Safety Council
445 Hoffer Dr., Regina SK S4N 6E2
Tel: 306-757-3197; *Fax:* 306-569-1907
sasksafety.org
Social Media: www.flickr.com/sasksafetycouncil
www.facebook.com/sasksafetycouncil
twitter.com/SkSafetyCouncil
To inform the public in order that they are able to make sound decisions regarding their safety
Harley P. Toupin, Chief Executive Officer
Dianne Wolbaum, Director, Operations

Workplace Safety & Prevention Services (WSPS)
Centre for Health & Safety Innovation, 5110 Creekbank Rd., Mississauga ON L4W 0A1
Tel: 905-614-1400; *Fax:* 905-614-1414
Toll-Free: 877-494-9777
customercare@wsps.ca
www.wsps.ca
Social Media: www.youtube.com/user/WSPSpromo
linkedin.com/company/workplace-safety-&-prevention-services
www.facebook.com/workplacesafetyandpreventionservices
twitter.com/WSPS_NEWS
WSPS is a not-for-profit organization with a mandate to meet the health & safety needs of businesses in the agricultural, manufacturing & service industries. It provides programs, products & services for the prevention of injury & illness.
Elizabeth Mills, CEO

Scientific

Alberta Society of Professional Biologists (ASPB)
#370, 105 - 12 Ave. East, Calgary AB T2G 1A1
Tel: 403-264-1273
pbiol@aspb.ab.ca
www.aspb.ab.ca
Social Media:
linkedin.com/company/alberta-society-of-professional-biologists
twitter.com/albertabiology
To promote excellence in the practice of biology; To provide a voice for professional biologists in Alberta
Jennifer Sipkens, Executive Director

Association des microbiologistes du Québec (AMQ)
5094A, av. Charlemagne, Montréal QC H1X 3P3
Tél: 514-728-1087; *Téléc:* 514-374-3988
amq@microbiologistes.ca
www.microbiologistes.ca
Média social:
www.facebook.com/AssociationDesMicrobiologistesDuQuebec
De regrouper les microbiologistes du Québec oeuvrant principalment en environnement, en alimentaire et en pharmaceutique; d'étudier, de protéger et de développer les intérêts économiques, sociaux et professionnels des microbiologistes et de promouvoir l'essor de la microbiologie en général
Patrick D. Paquette, Président

Association of Canadian Ergonomists (ACE) / L'Association canadienne d'ergonomie
#1003, 105-150 Crowfoot Cres. NW, Calgary AB T3G 3T2
Tel: 403-219-4001; *Fax:* 403-451-1503
Toll-Free: 888-432-2223
info@ace-ergocanada.ca
www.ace-ergocanada.ca
To advance human factors/ergonomics through encouraging a high quality of practice, education & research; To facilitate communication among members; To represent the discipline; To increase awareness of human factors/ergonomics; To identify resources
Margo Fraser, Executive Director
Brenda Mallat, President

Association of Professional Biology (APB)
#300, 1095 McKenzie Ave., Victoria BC V8P 2L5
Tel: 250-483-4283; *Fax:* 250-483-3439
info@professionalbiology.com
professionalbiology.com
Social Media:
linkedin.com/in/probio
twitter.com/BIOLOGYAPBWORLD
To represent biology professionals who are practicing in Western Canada; To promote the professional practice of applied biology
Marie Vander Heiden, Executive Director

Biophysical Society of Canada (BSC) / La société de biophysique du Canada
c/o Department of Physics, Simon Fraser University, 8888 University Dr., Burnaby BC V5A 1S6
www.biophysicalsociety.ca
To promote biophysical research & education; to encourage cross-feeding of ideas between the physical & biological sciences; to foster & support scientific meetings, workshops & discussions in biophysics; to represent Canadian biophysics & biophysicists
John E. Baenziger, President

BIOTECanada
#600, 1 Nicholas St., Ottawa ON K1N 7B7
Tel: 613-230-5585
info@biotech.ca
www.biotech.ca
Social Media:
linkedin.com/company/biotecanada
twitter.com/biotecanada
To provide a unified voice fostering an environment that responds to the needs of the biotechnology industry & research community, both nationally & internationally
David Main, Chair
Andrew Casey, President & CEO

Canadian Association for Anatomy, Neurobiology, & Cell Biology (CAANCB) / Association canadienne d'anatomie, de neurobiologie et de biologie cellulaire (ACANBC)
Dr. W.H. Baldridge, Department of Anatomy, Faculty of Medicine, Dalhousie University, Halifax NS B3H 4H7
Tel: 613-533-2864; *Fax:* 613-533-2566
www.caancb.blogspot.com
To advance knowledge of anatomy; To represent anatomical sciences throughout Canada
William H. Baldridge, Secretary

Canadian Association of Palynologists (CAP) / Association canadienne des palynologues
c/o Dr. Mary A. Vetter, Luther College, University of Regina, Regina SK S4S 0A2
www.scirpus.ca/cap/cap.shtml
To advance all aspects of palynology in Canada
Francine McCarthy, President
Mary A. Vetter, Secretary-Treasurer
Florin Pendea, Editor, CAP Newsletter

Canadian Association of Physicists (CAP) / Association canadienne des physiciens et physiciennes (ACP)
MacDonald Bldg., #112, 150 Louis Pasteur Priv., Ottawa ON K1N 6N5
Tel: 613-562-5614; *Fax:* 613-562-5615
cap@uottawa.ca
www.cap.ca
CAP is a broadly-based national network of physicists working in Canadian educational, industrial, and research settings. They are a strong advocacy group for support of, and excellence in, physics research and education.
Gabor Kunstatter, President
Francine M. Ford, Executive Director

Canadian Association of Science Centres (CASC) / L'Association canadienne des centres de sciences (ACCS)
100 Ramsey Lake Rd., Sudbury ON P3E 5S9
Tel: 705-522-6825
info@casc-accs.com
www.canadiansciencecentres.ca
Creates synergy among Canada's science centres and science-related museums, assists in finding solutions to the challenges faced by these public institutions, and provides a single voice before government.
Catherine Paisley, President
David Desjardins, Treasurer

Canadian Astronomical Society (CASCA) / Société canadienne d'astronomie
c/o R. Hanes, Dept. of Physics, Engineering, Physics & Astronomy, 64 Bader Lane, Stirling Hall, Queen's University, Kingston ON K7L 3N6
Tel: 613-533-6000; *Fax:* 613-533-6463
casca@astro.queensu.ca
www.casca.ca
Gilles Joncas, President
Nadine Manset, Secretary
Leslie Sage, Press Officer

Canadian Botanical Association (CBA) / Association botanique du Canada (ABC)
PO Box 160, Aberdeen SK S0K 0A0
Tel: 306-253-4654; *Fax:* 306-253-4744
Toll-Free: 888-993-9990
www.cba-abc.ca
To represent Canadian Botany & botanists nationally & internationally; to respond quickly & professionally on matters that are of concern to Canadian botanists.
Fédéerique Guinel, President
Anne Bruneau, Vice-President
Santokh Singh, Secretary
Jane Young, Treasurer

Canadian College of Physicists in Medicine (CCPM) / Collège canadien des physiciens en médecine
PO Box 72124, RPO Kanata North, Kanata ON K2K 2P4
Tel: 613-599-3491; *Fax:* 613-435-7257
admin@medphys.ca
www.ccpm.ca
To identify, through certification, individuals who have acquired & maintained a standard of knowledge & skill essential to the practice of medical physics, in order to serve the public
Nancy Barrett, Executive Director
Horacio Patrocinio, CCPM Registrar
Matthew G. Schmid, President

Canadian Federation of Earth Sciences (CFES) / Fédération canadienne des sciences de la Terre
c/o Scott Swinden, 3 Crest Rd., Halifax NS B3M 2W1
Tel: 902-444-3525; *Fax:* 902-444-7802
info@swindengeoscience.ca
earthsciencescanada.com
To promote coordination & cooperation in activities in Canadian geoscientific education; to advise on science policy involving the earth sciences; to provide an informed opinion to the public of Canada on matters of public concern.
Scott Swinden, President

Canadian Hydrographic Association (CHA) / Association canadienne d'hydrographie
#1205, 4900 Yonge St., Toronto ON M2N 6A6
Tel: 416-512-5815
www.hydrography.ca
To advance the development of hydrography & associated activities in Canada; to further the knowledge & professional development of members; to enhance & demonstrate the public need for hydrography; & to help the development of hydrographic sciences in developing countries; & to embrace the desciplines of marine cartography, hydrographic surveying, offshore exploration, marine geodesy, & tidal studies.
Rob Hare, National President
Kirsten Greenfield, National Secretary
Christine Delbridge, National Treasurer

Canadian Institute of Food Science & Technology (CIFST) / Institut canadien de science et technologie alimentaires (ICSTA)
#1311, 3-1750 The Queensway, Toronto ON M9C 5H5
Tel: 905-271-8338; *Fax:* 905-271-8344
cifst@cifst.ca
www.cifst.ca
To advance food science & technology; To act as a voice for scientific issues related to the Canadian food industry
Carol Ann Burrell, Executive Director
Belinda Elysée-Collen, President

Canadian Medical & Biological Engineering Society (CMBES) / Société canadienne de génie biomédical inc. (SCGB)
1485 Laperriere Ave., Ottawa ON K1Z 7S8
Tel: 613-728-1759
secretariat@cmbes.ca
www.cmbes.ca
Social Media:
twitter.com/cmbesociety
To advance the theory & practice of medical device technology; To advance individuals who are engaged in interdisciplinary work involving medicine, engineering, & the life sciences; To represent the interests of biomedical & clinical engineering to government agencies
Martin Poulin, President
Mike Capuano, Vice-President

Canadian Meteorological & Oceanographic Society (CMOS) / Société canadienne de météorologie et d'océanographie (SCMO)
PO Box 3211, Stn. D, Ottawa ON K1P 6H7
Tel: 613-990-0300
cmos@cmos.ca
www.cmos.ca
Social Media:
linkedin.com/groups/Canadian-Meteocean-Group-6515104/about
twitter.com/cmos_scmo
To advance meteorology & oceanography in Canada
Gordon Griffith, Executive Director
Doug G. Steyn, Director, Publications
Bourque Sheila, Director, Education & Outreach
Qing Liao, Office Manager

Canadian Physiological Society (CPS) / Société canadienne de physiologie
c/o Dr. Melanie Woodin, Dept. of Cell & Systems Biology, U. of Toronto, 25 Harbord St., Toronto ON M5S 3G5
www.cpsscp.ca
To disseminate & discuss scientific information of interest to researchers in physiology & biological sciences
Steven Barnes, President
Melanie Woodin, Secretary

Canadian Phytopathological Society (CPS) / Société Canadienne de Phytopathologie (SCP)
c/o Vikram Bisht, PO Box 1149, 65 - 3 Ave. NE, Carman MB R0G 0J0
Tel: 204-745-0260; *Fax:* 204-745-5690
phytopath.ca
Social Media:
www.facebook.com/111761558875337
To encourage & support research, education, & dissemination of knowledge on the nature, cause, & control of plant diseases; To promote communication among plant pathologists; To broaden educational opportunities for members
Janice Elmhirst, President

Canadian Science & Technology Historical Association (CSTHA) / Association pour l'histoire de la science et de la technologie au Canada (AHSTC)
PO Box 8502, Stn. T, Ottawa ON K1G 3H9
cstha-ahstc.ca
To foster the study of Canada's scientific & technological heritage through research, publication, teaching & preservation of artifacts & records
Suzanne Beauvais, Secretary
Bertrum H. MacDonald, President

Canadian Society for Analytical Sciences & Spectroscopy
PO Box 46122, 2339 Ogilvie Rd., Ottawa ON K1J 9M7
Tel: 613-933-3719; *Fax:* 613-954-5984
www.csass.org
To organize programs of scientific & general interest for the educational benefit of members & the public; to organize annual scientific conferences & workshops on various aspects of pure & applied spectroscopy in the chemical, biological, geochemical & metallurgical sciences
Graeme Spiers, President
Ana Delgado, Treasurer

Canadian Society for Molecular Biosciences (CSBM) / Société Canadienne pour Biosciences Moléculaires
c/o Rofail Conference & Management Services, 17 Dossetter Way, Ottawa ON K1G 4S3
Tel: 613-421-7229; *Fax:* 613-421-9811
contact@csmb-scbm.ca
www.csmb-scbm.ca
Christian Baron, President
Kristin Baetz, Vice-President

Canadian Society for the History & Philosophy of Science (CSHPS) / Société Canadienne d'Histoire et Philosophie des Sciences (SCHPS)
c/o Dr. Conor Burns, Department of History, Ryerson University, 350 Victoria St., Toronto ON M5C 2K3
www.yorku.ca/cshps1
To explore all aspects of science, past & present
Lesley Cormack, President
Conor Burns, Secretary-Treasurer

The Canadian Society for the Weizmann Institute of Science (CSWIS)
4700 Bathurst St., 2nd Fl., Toronto ON M2R 1W8
Tel: 416-733-9220; *Fax:* 416-733-9430
Toll-Free: 800-387-3894
info@weizmann.ca
www.weizmann.ca
Social Media: www.youtube.com/user/WeizmannCanada
linkedin.com/company/weizmann-canada
www.facebook.com/129788800406309
To marshal Canadian support for the Weizmann Institute of Science in Rehovot, Israel; to help build & maintain scientific facilities; to acquire costly up-to-date research equipment & instrumentation; to set up endowments for research centres; to establish professional chairs & scholarships
Catherine Beck, Chair
Susan Stern, National Executive Vice-President
Marni Brinder Byk, Manager, Development

Canadian Society of Exploration Geophysicists (CSEG)
#600, 640 - 8th Ave. SW, Calgary AB T2P 1G7
Tel: 403-262-0015
cseg.office@shaw.ca
www.cseg.ca
To promote the science of geophysics
John Townsley, President
Larry Herd, Vice-President
Jim Racette, Managing Director
John Fernando, Director, Educational Services
Kelly Jamison, Director, Finance
Kristy Manchul, Director, Communications
Dave Nordin, Director, Member Service

Canadian Society of Forensic Science (CSFS)
PO Box 37040, 3332 McCarthy Rd., Ottawa ON K1V 0W0
Tel: 613-738-0001; *Fax:* 613-738-1987
csfs@bellnet.ca
www.csfs.ca
Social Media:
facebook.com\csfscanada/
To promote the study of forensic science; To maintain professional standards in the discipline of forensic science
G. Anderson, President
G. Verret, Secretary
D. Camellato, Treasurer

Canadian Society of Microbiologists (CSM) / Société canadienne des microbiologistes
CSM-SCM Secretariat, 17 Dossetter Way, Ottawa ON K1G 4S3
Tel: 613-421-7229; *Fax:* 613-421-9811
info@csm-scm.org
www.csm-scm.org
Social Media:
twitter.com/CSM_SCM
To advance microbiology in all its aspects; to facilitate interchange of ideas between microbiologists
Charles Dozois, President
Mohan Babu, Secretary-Treasurer

Canadian Society of Pharmacology & Therapeutics (CSPT) / Société de pharmacologie du Canada
c/o PATH Research Institute, #200, 25 Main St. West, Hamilton ON L8P 1H1
Tel: 905-523-7284
www.pharmacologycanada.org
To promote research & education in the disciplines of pharmacology & experimental therapeutics
Gaebel Kathryn, Executive Administrator
Richard Kim, President
Fiona Parkinson, Vice-President
Cindy Woodland, Secretary-Treasurer

Canadian Society of Plant Biologists (CSPP) / Société canadienne de biologie végétale (SCPV)
c/o Barry Micallef, Crop Science Building, University of Guelph, 117 Reynolds Walk, Guelph ON N1G 1Y4
secretary@cspb-scbv.ca
www.cspb-scbv.ca
Social Media:
twitter.com/cspbscbv
To promote the teaching & public awareness of plant physiology in Canada
Jean-Benoit Charron, Senior Director
Anja Geitmann, President

Canadian Society of Soil Science (CSSS) / Société canadienne de la science du sol (SCSS)
Business Office, PO Box 637, Pinawa MB R0E 1L0
Tel: 204-282-9486; *Fax:* 204-753-8478
sheppards@ecomatters.com
www.csss.ca

To be actively engaged in land use, soils research, & classification
Maja Krzic, PhD, President
Amanda Dichon, PhD, Secretary
Kent Watson, Treasurer

Canadian Space Society (CSS) / La société canadienne de l'espace
Bldg. E, PO Box 70009, Stn. Rimrock Plaza, 1115 Lodestar Rd., Toronto ON M3J 0H3
www.css.ca
To conduct technical & outreach projects; to promote the involvement of Canadians in space development
Kevin Shortt, President
Marc Fricker, Vice-President
Gary McQueen, Treasurer

Citizen Scientists
1749 Meadowvale Rd., Toronto ON M1B 5W8
info@citizenscientists.ca
www.citizenscientists.ca
To monitor local watersheds, foster local environmental stewardship, and educate volunteers and the public.

Club d'astronomie Quasar de Chibougamau
783, 6e rue, Chibougamau QC G8P 2W4
Tél: 418-748-4642
www.faaq.org/clubs/quasar/
Pierre Bureau, Président

Geological Association of Canada (GAC) / Association géologique du Canada (AGC)
c/o Department of Earth Sciences, Memorial University of Newfoundland, #ER4063, Alexander Murray Bldg., St. John's NL A1B 3X5
Tel: 709-864-7660; *Fax:* 709-864-2532
gac@mun.ca
www.gac.ca
To advance the wise use of geoscience in academic, professional, & public circles
Victoria Yehl, President
Graham Young, Vice-President
James Conliffe, PhD, Secretary-Treasurer
Dène Tarkyth, Chair, Finance
Chris White, Chair, Publications

Innovation & Technology Association of Prince Edward Island (ITAP)
PO Box 241, Charlottetown PE C1A 7K4
Tel: 902-894-4827; *Fax:* 902-894-4867
itap@itap.ca
www.itap.ca
Social Media:
www.facebook.com/pages/ITAP/229205927166908
twitter.com/itapei
To provide advocacy and support to our members, through projects in the key areas of export development, communication and leadership development.
Daniel Lazaratos, President
Mike Gillis, Innovation Director

Institute of Textile Science (ITS) / Institut des sciences textiles
c/o Jerry Bauerle, #105, 4575 Lakeshore Rd., Burlington ON L7L 1E1
Tel: 905-822-4111; *Fax:* 905-823-1446
info@textilescience.ca
www.textilescience.ca
To promote the dissemination & interchange of knowledge concerning textile science; to encourage research & development related to textile science & technology, including the establishment & granting of awards
Aldjia Begriche, President

International Association of Hydrogeologists - Canadian National Chapter (IAH-CNC)
c/o WESA, 3108 Carp Rd., Carp ON K0A 1L0
Tel: 613-839-3053
www.iah.ca
To advance the science of hydrogeology & exchange hydrogeologic information internationally
Nell van Walsum, Secretary

International Association of Science & Technology for Development (IASTED)
Bldg B6, #101, 2509 Dieppe Ave. SW, Calgary AB T3E 7J9
Tel: 403-288-1195; *Fax:* 403-247-6851
calgary@iasted.com
www.iasted.org
Social Media:
www.facebook.com/pages/IASTED/130963346917239
twitter.com/IASTED_Calgary

To further economic development by promoting science & technology

International Oceans Institute of Canada (IOIC)
c/o Dalhousie Univ., PO Box 15000, 6414 Coburg Rd., Halifax NS B3H 4R2
Tel: 902-494-1977; *Fax:* 902-494-1334
ioi@dal.ca
internationaloceaninstitute.dal.ca
To promote responsible management of the world's oceans & sustainable development of marine resources; to protect the integrity of the ocean environment; to promote sustainable resource development; to improve the quality of ocean-dependent human life, including health & safety of maritime communities; to further these objectives, all aspects of the ocean environment are pursued - resource management & development, marine environmental quality, ocean law & policy, high seas management, coastal zone management, marine transportation, ocean science & technology, tourism & recreation, ocean industries & maritime boundary delimitation
Michael J.A. Butler, Director

Life Science Association of Manitoba (LSAM)
1000 Waverley St., Winnipeg MB R3T 0P3
Tel: 204-272-5095; *Fax:* 204-272-2961
info@lsam.ca
www.lsam.ca
Social Media: www.youtube.com/user/LifeScienceMB
linkedin.com/groups/3753791/profile
www.facebook.com/123001494423036
twitter.com/LifeScienceMB
To represent the life science industry in Manitoba; to provide services for companies in the industry; to promote economic development
Tracey Maconachie, President

Microscopical Society of Canada (MSC) / Société de Microscopie du Canada
Brockhouse Inst. of Mat.Res., McMaster Univ., 1280 Main St. West, Hamilton ON L8S 4M1
Tel: 905-525-9140; *Fax:* 905-521-2773
butcher@mcmaster.ca
msc.rsvs.ulaval.ca
Randy Mikula, President
Chris Butcher, Treasurer
Frances Leggett, Executive Secretary

MindFuel
#260, 3512 - 33 St. NW, Calgary AB T2L 2A6
Tel: 403-220-0077; *Fax:* 403-284-4132
info@mindfuel.ca
mindfuel.ca
To increase science literacy by creating innovative programs for all Albertans
Cassy Weber, CEO
Alma Abugov, Director, Development & Community Engagement

North Pacific Marine Science Organization (PICES)
c/o Institute of Ocean Sciences, PO Box 6000, Sidney BC V8L 4B2
Tel: 250-363-6366; *Fax:* 250-363-6827
secretariat@pices.int
www.pices.int
To promote & coordinate marine research in the northern North Pacific & adjacent seas especially northward of 30 degrees North; to advance scientific knowledge about the ocean environment, global weather & climate change, living resources & their ecosystems & the impacts of human activities; to promote the collection & rapid exchange of scientific information on these issues
Alexander Bychkov, Executive Secretary

Nova Scotian Institute of Science (NSIS)
Science Services, Killam Library, Dalhousie Univ., 6225 University Ave., Halifax NS B3H 4H8
Tel: 902-494-3621; *Fax:* 902-494-2062
nsis.chebucto.org
To provide a forum for scientists & those interested in science
Tom Rand, President
Patrick Ryall, Vice-President
Linda Marks, Secretary
Angelica Silva, Treasurer

Ontario Kinesiology Association (OKA)
#100, 6700 Century Ave., Mississauga ON L5N 6A4
Tel: 905-567-7194; *Fax:* 905-567-7191
info@oka.on.ca
www.oka.on.ca
Social Media:
linkedin.com/groups?home=&gid=1264707
www.facebook.com/ontariokinesiologyassociation
twitter.com/ONKinesiology

To promote the application of the science of human movement to other professionals & to the community; to uphold the standards of the profession of kinesiology; to assist kinesiologists in the performance of their duties & responsibilities
Jennifer Chapman, President

Royal Astronomical Society of Canada (RASC) / Société royale d'astronomie du Canada
#203, 4920 Dundas St. West, Toronto ON M9A 1B7
Tel: 416-924-7973; *Fax:* 416-924-2911
Toll-Free: 888-924-7272
www.rasc.ca
Social Media:
www.facebook.com/theRoyalAstronomicalSocietyofCanada
twitter.com/rasc
To promote the advancement of astronomy across Canada
James Edgar, President
Randy Attwood, Executive Director

Science Atlantic / Science Atlantique
Dept. of Psychology & Neuroscience, Dalhousie University, PO Box 15000, Halifax NS B3H 4R2
Tel: 902-494-3421
admin@scienceatlantic.ca
www.scienceatlantic.ca
Social Media:
twitter.com/scienceatlantic
To advance science & technology through education & public awareness & the promotion of scientific literacy education & research throughout the region
David McCorquodale, Chair
Lois Whitehead, Executive Director

Society of Toxicology of Canada (STC) / Société de toxicologie du Canada
PO Box 55094, Montréal QC H3G 2W5
stcsecretariat@mcgill.ca
www.stcweb.ca
To promote acquisition, facilitate dissemination & encourage utilization of knowledge in the science of toxicology
Louise Winn, President
Veronica Atehortua, Information Executive Secretary

Southern Ontario Seismic Network (SOSN)
c/o University of Western Ontario, London ON N6A 5B7
Tel: 519-661-3605; *Fax:* 519-661-3198
www.gp.uwo.ca
To obtain information on the seismicity and seismic hazards of a region of southern Ontario in which a number of nuclear power facilities are located.
R.F. Mereu, Administrator

Statistical Society of Canada (SSC) / Société statistique du Canada
#209, 1725 St. Laurent Blvd., Ottawa ON K1G 3V4
Tel: 613-733-2662; *Fax:* 613-733-1386
info@ssc.ca
www.ssc.ca
To promote the development & use of statistics & probability; To ensure that decisions that affect society are based upon valid & appropriate statistics & interpretation; To encourage high standards for statistical education & practice
John Brewster, President
John J. Koval, Treasurer
Julie Trépanier, Executive Secretary

Youth Science Canada (YSC) / Sciences jeunesse Canada (SJC)
#213, 1550 Kingston Rd., Pickering ON L1V 1C3
Tel: 416-341-0040; *Fax:* 866-613-2542
Toll-Free: 866-341-0040
info@youthscience.ca
youthscience.ca
Social Media:
www.youtube.com/user/YOUTHSCIENCECANADA
www.facebook.com/ysc.sjc
twitter.com/YouthScienceCan
YSF assists Canadian youth to develop skills & knowledge for excellence in science & technology.
Reni Barlow, Executive Director
Malcolm Butler, Chair
Mayur Gahdia, Treasurer
Jennifer Gerritsen, Secretary

Search & Rescue

International Cospas-Sarsat Programme / Mission du Programme Cospas-Sarsat
#4215, 1250, boulevard René-Lévesque West, Montréal QC H3B 4W8
Tel: 514-500-7999; *Fax:* 514-500-7996
mail@cospas-sarsat.int
www.cospas-sarsat.int
Social Media:
linkedin.com/company/international-cospas-sarsat-programme
www.facebook.com/InternationalCospasSarsatProgramme
twitter.com/cospas_sarsat
To provide accurate, reliable distress alert & location data to assist search & rescue authorities using the satellite-based search & rescue (SAR) system
Steven Lett, Director, Secretariat

Senior Citizens

Active Living Coalition for Older Adults (ALCOA) / Coalition d'une vie active pour les ainé(e)s
PO Box 143, Stn. Main, Shelburne ON L9V 3L8
Tel: 519-925-1676; *Toll-Free:* 800-549-9799
alcoa@uniserve.com
www.alcoa.ca
Social Media:
www.facebook.com/726682140748841
To encourage older Canadians to maintain & enhance their well-being & independence through a lifestyle that embraces daily physical activities
Patricia Clark, Executive Director

Advocacy Centre for the Elderly (ACE)
#701, 2 Carlton St., Toronto ON M5B 1J3
Tel: 416-598-2656; *Fax:* 416-598-7924
www.acelaw.ca
To provide legal services to low income senior citizens
Judith Wahl, Executive Director
Timothy Banks, Chair

Alberta Continuing Care Association (ACCA)
8861 - 75 St. NW, Edmonton AB T6C 4G8
Tel: 780-435-0699; *Fax:* 780-436-9785
info@ab-cca.ca
www.ab-cca.ca
To represent owners & operators of long term care & designated assisted living facilities & home care
Tammy Leach, Chief Executive Officer
Heather Aggus, Manager, Communications & Events

Alberta Council on Aging
Circle Square Plaza, PO Box 9, #232, 11808 St. Albert Trail, Edmonton AB T5L 4G4
Tel: 780-423-7781; *Fax:* 780-425-9246
Toll-Free: 888-423-9666
info@acaging.ca
www.acaging.ca
Social Media:
www.facebook.com/albertacouncilonaging
twitter.com/acaging
To define the needs of aging & the aged & to bring the current needs to the attention of government or voluntary agencies & to take action where appropriate; to identify & encourage relevant areas of research & systematic compilation of information affecting aging; to encourage & develop discussion on all problems affecting aging; to inform government at any level on the potential impact of policies & legislation on the aging; to print, publish, distribute & sell publications related to aging; to foster interagency liaison & cooperation

Association des personnes en perte d'autonomie de Chibougamau inc. & Jardin des aînés
101, av du Parc, Chibougamau QC G8P 3A5
Tél: 418-748-4411
jardindesaines@tlb.sympatico.ca
Chantal Lessard, Directrice générale

British Columbia Seniors Living Association (BCSLA)
#300, 3665 Kingsway, Vancouver BC V5R 5W2
Tel: 604-689-5949; *Fax:* 604-689-5946
Toll-Free: 888-402-2722
membership@bcsla.ca
www.bcsla.ca
Marlene Williams, Executive Director
Stuart Bowden, Vice-President, Finance

Canadian Alliance for Long Term Care (CALTC)
info@caltc.ca
www.caltc.ca
To ensure the delivery fo quality care to vulnerable citizens of Canada

Canadian Association on Gerontology (CAG) / Association canadienne de gérontologie (ACG)
#328, 263 McCaul St., Toronto ON M5T 1W7
Toll-Free: 855-224-2240
cagacg@igs.net
www.cagacg.ca
Social Media:
www.facebook.com/CdnAssocGero
twitter.com/cagacg
To develop the theoretical & practical understanding of individual & population aging through multidisciplinary research, practice, education & policy analysis in gerontology; To seek the improvement of the conditions of life of elderly people in Canada
Neena Chappell, President
Anthony Lombardo, PhD, Executive Director
Margaret Denton, Secretary-Treasurer

Canadian Pensioners Concerned Inc. (CPC) / Retraités canadiens en action (RCA)
6 Trinity Sq., Toronto ON M5G 1B1
Tel: 416-368-5222; *Fax:* 416-368-0443
Toll-Free: 888-822-6750
canpension@gmail.com
www.canpension.ca
To provide joint action on seniors issues; To collect authoritative factual material & distribute it in usable form to relevant persons & authorities
Barbara Kilbourn, President
Sylvia Hall, Corporate Secretary
Jane Miller, Treasurer

CARP
30 Jefferson Ave., Toronto ON M6K 1Y4
Tel: 416-363-8748; *Toll-Free:* 888-363-2279
support@carp.ca
www.carp.ca
Social Media: www.zoomers.ca/group/CARP
www.facebook.com/CARP
twitter.com/carpnews
The Association is a national, non-partisan organization that promotes the rights & quality of life of Canadians as they age through advocacy, education, information & CARP-recommended services & programs
Moses Znaimer, President
Susan Eng, Executive Vice-President

LA Centre for Active Living
55 Rankin Cres., Toronto ON M6P 4E4
Tel: 416-452-4875
www.loyolaarrupecentre.com
Social Media:
www.facebook.com/LACentreforActiveLiving
twitter.com/lacseniors
To serve the emotional & physical needs of people 55+; To provide & promote independent community living in an inclusive fashion; To allow seniors to live actively with dignity & confidence
Sandra Cardillo, Executive Director

Club de l'âge d'or Les intrépides de Chibougamau
126, rue des Forces-Armées, Chibougamau QC G8P 3A1
Tél: 418-748-6703
Darquise St-Georges, Présidente

Council for Black Aging / Le Conseil Des Personnes Agées De La Communauté Noire De Montréal
8606, rue Centrale, Montréal QC H4C 1M8
Tel: 514-935-4951
The Council for Black Aging works as an advocate for the needs of Black seniors, undertaking activities designed to advance the interests of Black elders, keeping Black seniors better informed of issues relating to the availability of health and social services, and developing a unique day centre and a nursing home for Black elders.

Fédération des aînées et aînés francophones du Canada (FAAFC)
#300, 450 rue Rideau, Ottawa ON K1N 5Z4
Tél: 613-564-0212; *Téléc:* 613-564-0212
info@faafc.ca
www.faafc.ca/fr
Défendre les droits des personnes à la retraite; défendre les droits des préretraités; programmes intergénérationnels; protection de la langue et la culture française
Roger Doiron, Président
Jean-Luc Racine, Directeur général
Michel Vézina, Premier vice-président, Saskatchewan
André Faubert, Deuxième vice-présidente, Québec
Richard Martin, Trésorier, Terre-Neuve & Labrador
Mélina Gallant, Secrétaire, Ile-du-Prince-Édouard
Marie-Christine Aubrey, Administratrice, Territoire du Nord-Ouest
Louis Bernardin, Administrateur, Manitoba
Roland Gallant, Administrateur, Nouveau-Brunswick
Charles Gaudet, Administrateur, Nouvelle-Écosse
Claire Grisé, Administratrice, Colombie-Britannique
Germaine Lehodey, Administratrice, Alberta
Francine Poirier, Administratrice, Ontario
Roxanne Thibaudeau, Administratrice, Yukon

HelpAge Canada / Aide aux aînés Canada
1300 Carling Ave., Ottawa ON K1Z 7L2
Tel: 613-232-0727; *Fax:* 613-232-7625
Toll-Free: 800-648-1111
info@helptheaged.ca
www.helptheaged.ca
Social Media: www.youtube.com/user/helpage
www.facebook.com/helpagecanada
twitter.com/HelpAgeCanada
To meet the needs of poor or destitute elderly people in Canada & the developing world
Jacques Bertrand, Executive Director
Jack Panozzo, Chair
Ivan Hale, Vice-Chair
Rosalie Gelderman, Secretary
Donald Hefler, Treasurer

National Pensioners Federation (NPF) / Fédération nationale des retraités
c/o Sandy Carricato, Treasurer, 2389 Head Rd., Port Perry ON L9L 1B4
Tel: 905-985-8170
www.nationalpensionersfederation.ca
Social Media: www.youtube.com/user/npfederation
www.facebook.com/NPFederation
twitter.com/npfederation
To act as an advisory body providing central contacts, facilities for research, surveys, uniform objectives & a national expansion of the pensioners movement; To stimulate public interest in the welfare of senior citizens by means of adequate pensions & social security that will provide comfortable housing & decent living; To protect the rights & interests of pensioners & prospective pensioners; To prevent discrimination & undue delay in granting pensions; To project a social friendly fellowship among the pensioners of Canada
Herb John, President
Pat Brady, Secretary
Sandy Carricato, Treasurer

New Brunswick Association of Nursing Homes, Inc. (NBANH) / Association des foyers de soins du Nouveau-Brunswick, inc. (AFSNB)
#206, 1113 Regent St., Fredericton NB E3B 3Z2
Tel: 506-460-6262; *Fax:* 506-460-6253
communication@nbanh.com
www.nbanh.com
Social Media:
www.facebook.com/pages/NBANH-AFSNB/347209608754750
twitter.com/NBANH_AFSNB
To assist members in the provision of quality & efficient care to their residents
Jean-Eudes Savoie, President
Michael Keating, Executive Director
Robert Stewart, Treasurer

New Brunswick Senior Citizens Federation Inc. (NBSCF) / Fédération des citoyens aînés du Nouveau-Brunswick inc. (FCANB)
#214, 23 - 451 Paul St., Dieppe NB E1A 6W8
Tel: 506-857-8242; *Fax:* 506-857-0315
Toll-Free: 800-453-4333
horizons@nbnet.nb.ca
www.nbscf.ca
Social Media:
www.facebook.com/238798849533942
To promote the general welfare & leadership of NB's senior citizens regardless of language, race, colour, sex, or creed; to elevate the social, moral, & intellectual standing of NB's senior citizens; to provide information, coordination, communication, & advocating services to members
Isabelle Arseneault, Director, Operations

New Brunswick Special Care Home Association Inc.
c/o Seely Lodge Inc., 2081 Route 845, Bayswater NB E5S 1J7
Tel: 506-738-8514; *Fax:* 506-738-0892
www.nbscha.com
To assist licensed members of the New Brunswick Special Care Home Association Inc. in providing quality, cost effective long term care for seniors and special needs adults in cooperation with the Department of Social Development.
Jan Seely, President

Older Adult Centres' Association of Ontario (OACAO) / Association des centres pour aînés de l'Ontario
PO Box 65, Caledon East ON L7C 3L8
Tel: 905-584-8125; *Fax:* 905-584-8126
Toll-Free: 866-835-7693
www.oacao.org
To ensure that seniors in Ontario have opportunities & choices that lead to healthy, active lifestyles
Sue Hesjedahl, Executive Director

Ontario Association of Non-Profit Homes & Services for Seniors (OANHSS)
#700, 7050 Weston Rd., Woodbridge ON L4L 8G7
Tel: 905-851-8821; *Fax:* 905-851-0744
www.oanhss.org
To support members in the provision of quality non-profit long term care, seniors' community services, & housing
Kevin Queen, Board Chair
Donna A. Rubin, Chief Executive Officer

Ontario Association of Residents' Councils (OARC)
#207-208, 10155 Yonge St., Toronto ON L4T 1T5
Tel: 905-770-3710; *Fax:* 905-770-2755
Toll-Free: 800-532-0201
info@ontarc.com
www.residentscouncils.ca
To represent the views of residents on issues that affect the quality of their lives in long term care facilities & to promote & support the role & development of Residents' Councils
Sharron Cooke, President
Milly Radford, 1st Vice-President

Ontario Coalition of Senior Citizens' Organizations (OCSCO) / Coalition des organismes d'aînés et d'aînées de l'Ontario (COAAO)
#406, 333 Wilson Ave., Toronto ON M3H 1T2
Tel: 416-785-8570; *Fax:* 416-785-7361
Toll-Free: 800-265-0779
ocsco@ocsco.ca
www.ocsco.ca
To improve the quality of life for Ontario's seniors by encouraging seniors' involvement in all aspects of society, by keeping them informed of current issues, & by focusing on programs to benefit an aging population
Elizabeth Macnab, Executive Director
Jennifer Forde, Specialist, Communications & Program

Prince Edward Island Senior Citizens Federation Inc. (PEISCF)
#214, 40 Enman Cres., Charlottetown PE C1E 1E6
Tel: 902-368-9008; *Fax:* 902-368-9006
Toll-Free: 877-368-9008
peiscf@pei.aibn.com
www.peiscf.com
To advance the education opportunities for seniors on PEI; to improve the quality of life for seniors by advising government & other decision making bodies regarding seniors' concerns; to improve the quality of life for seniors; to increase societal understanding of seniors & the aging process through positive role modelling
Linda Jean Nicholson, Executive Director

Réseau FADOQ / Québec Federation of Senior Citizens
4545, av Pierre-de Coubertin, Montréal QC H1V 0B2
Tél: 514-252-3017; *Ligne sans frais:* 800-828-3344
info@fadoq.ca
www.fadoq.ca
Média social: www.youtube.com/user/ReseauFADOQ
www.facebook.com/reseaufadoq
Promouvoir un concept positif du vieillissement; encourager le maintien et l'amélioration de la qualité de vie et de l'autonomie des aînés; initier et soutenir l'organisation d'activités physiques et de loisirs; redonner aux aînés une nouvelle fierté en les revalorisant à leurs propres yeux comme à ceux de la société; remettre entre les mains des aînés la gestion de leurs affaires
Maurice Duport, Président
Danis Prud'homme, Directeur générale

Road Scholar
11 Ave. de Lafayette, Boston MA 02111 USA
Fax: 613-530-2096
Toll-Free: 866-745-1690
registration@roadscholar.org
www.roadscholar.org
Social Media: www.youtube.com/user/roadscholarorg
www.facebook.com/rsadventures
twitter.com/roadscholarorg
To develop, manage & facilitate educational experiences for older adults through cooperative partnership with educational agents; To balance education & travel in an environment of comradeship & respect; To continue to experiment with pilot projects to reach broader populations of older adults; To be a "learner-centered" organization that responds to the learning needs of older adults; To work towards a better understanding of our relationship with our current populations; To use new methods of reaching out to an ever more diverse multicultural Canada; to promote cost-effective educational opportunities to an ever widening group of older adults
Victoria Pearson, President/CEO

Seniors Association of Greater Edmonton (SAGE)
15 Sir Winston Churchill Sq., Edmonton AB T5J 2E5
Tel: 780-423-5510; *Fax:* 780-426-5175
info@mysage.ca
www.mysage.ca
Social Media:
www.facebook.com/438132792913806
twitter.com/sageYEG
To enhance the quality of life of older persons through service, innovation, advocacy & voluntarism
D. Lynn Skillen, President
Roger E. Laing, Executive Director

United Senior Citizens of Ontario Inc. (USCO)
3033 Lakeshore Blvd. West, Toronto ON M8V 1K5
Tel: 416-252-2021; *Fax:* 416-252-5770
Toll-Free: 888-320-2222
office@uscont.ca
www.uscont.ca
Social Media:
www.facebook.com/uscont
To further the interests & promote the welfare of the senior population in Ontario; To provide for an exchange of ideas for member groups; To assist in the formation of senior citizens clubs
Bernard Jordan, President

Service Clubs

Association des Grands Frères et Grandes Soeurs de Québec (GFGS) / Big Brothers & Big Sisters of Québec
#201, 2380, av du Mont-Thabor, Québec QC G1J 3W7
Tél: 418-624-3304; *Téléc:* 418-624-4013
gfgsquebec@videotron.ca
www.gfgs.qc.ca
Favoriser l'épanouissement de jeunes âgés de 6 à 16 ans privés de la presence d'un de leurs parents en les jumelant avec un adulte mature, qui s'engage à le rencontrer 3-4 heures par semaine pour échanger et faire des activités, selon leurs goûts réciproques

Big Brothers Big Sisters of Canada (BBBSC) / Les Grands Frères Grandes Soeurs du Canada
#113E, 3228 South Service Rd., Burlington ON L7N 3H8
Tel: 905-639-0461; *Fax:* 905-639-0124
Toll-Free: 800-263-9133
www.bigbrothersbigsisters.ca
Social Media: www.youtube.com/bbbscanada
www.facebook.com/bigbrothersbigsistersofcanada
twitter.com/bbbsc
To provide leadership to member agencies as they develop programs to meet the changing needs of young people
Bruce MacDonald, President & CEP

British Columbia Lions Society for Children with Disabilities (BCLS)
3981 Oak St., Vancouver BC V6H 4H5
Tel: 604-873-1865; *Fax:* 604-873-0166
Toll-Free: 800-818-4483
info@lionsbc.ca
www.lionsbc.ca
Social Media:
www.facebook.com/125279254193295
twitter.com/LionsBC
To provide as many services as possible to children with disabilities; to enhance the lives of children with special needs; to continue building, not only specialized services & facilities, but challenging young hearts & minds as well; giving children with disabilities self-esteem, self-confidence & a sense of independence

Canadian Federation of Junior Leagues (CFJL) / Fédération canadienne des jeunes ligues
4 Steeplehill Cres., Carlisle ON L0R 1H3
Tel: 905-659-9339
info@cfjl.org
www.cfjl.org
To promote effective leadership & volunteerism for the betterment of women & the community
Marion Goard, National Coordinator
Fiona Colangelo, Treasurer

Canadian Progress Club / Club progrès du Canada
#143, 75 Lavinia St., New Glasgow NS B2H 1N5
Fax: 888-337-9826
Toll-Free: 877-944-4726
info@progressclub.ca
www.progressclub.ca
Social Media:
twitter.com/ProgressClub
To assist those in need as well as creating & preserving a spirit of friendship that is sincere; to advance the best interests of the community in which that club is located.
Juanita Soutar, National President
Jana Cleary, National Business Administrator

Club Kiwanis Chibougamau
CP 61, Chibougamau QC G8P 2K5
Tél: 418-770-8303
Yves Lachaine, Président

Club Lions de Chibougamau
CP 11, Chibougamau QC G8P 2K5
Tél: 418-770-9366
lionschibougamau@hotmail.com
lionschibougamau.icr.qc.ca
Mario Asselin, Président

Club Optimiste de Rivière-du-Loup inc.
CP 1344, Rivière-du-Loup QC G5R 4L9
Tél: 418-862-8454; *Téléc:* 418-862-3366
service@optimiste.org
www.optimiste.org
Les clubs Optimistes inspirent le meilleur chez les jeunes depuis 1919 en rencontrant les besoins des jeunes de toutes les collectivités du monde. Ils organisent des projets de service communautaire positifs qui visent à tendre la main à la jeunesse.
Jean-Louis Dorval, Trésorier

Kin Canada
PO Box 3460, 1920 Rogers Dr., Cambridge ON N3H 5C6
Fax: 519-650-1091
Toll-Free: 800-742-5546
kinhq@kincanada.ca
www.kincanada.ca
Social Media:
www.facebook.com/kincanada
twitter.com/kincanada
To enrich communities through service, while embracing national pride, positive values, personal development, & lasting friendships; To support Cystic Fibrosis research & care in Canada
Grant Ferron, Executive Director

Kin Canada Foundation
PO Box 3460, 1920 Rogers Dr., Cambridge ON N3H 5C6
Tel: 519-653-1920; *Fax:* 519-650-1091
Toll-Free: 800-742-5546
kinhq@kincanada.ca
www.kincanada.ca/kin-canada-foundation
Social Media:
www.facebook.com/kincanada
twitter.com/kincanada
To support Kin, Kinsmen & Kinette clubs across Canada; To function as the official charitable organization of Kin Canada
Carmen Preston, Contact

Kiwanis International (Eastern Canada & the Caribbean District)
PO Box 26040, Stn. Terrace Hill, Brantford ON N3R 7X4
Tel: 519-304-0745; *Fax:* 519-304-5362
Toll-Free: 888-921-9054
district@kiwanisecc.org
www.kiwanisecc.org
Hope Markes, Governor

Kiwanis International (Western Canada District)
#303, 6010 - 48 Ave., Camrose AB T4V 0K3
Tel: 780-608-1417; *Fax:* 780-672-8369
WeCanDST@gmail.com
www.ikiwanis.ca
Dirk Bannister, Secretary-Treasurer
Richard Le Sueur, Governor
Cheryl Storrs, Governor-Elect

Last Post Fund (LPF) / Fonds du Souvenir
#401, 505, boul René-Lévesque ouest, Montréal QC H2Z 1Y7
Tel: 514-866-2727; *Fax:* 514-866-1471
Toll-Free: 800-465-7113
info@lastpost.ca
www.lastpostfund.ca
To ensure that no war veterans, or certain other persons who meet the wartime service eligibility criteria, are denied a funeral & burial due to lack of funds

Douglas Briscoe, President
Charles Keple, Vice-President, West
Barry Keeler, Vice President (East)
Jean-Pierre Goyer, Executive Director

Soroptimist Foundation of Canada
c/o Treasurer, 2455 Cunningham Blvd., Peterborough ON K9H 0B2
www.soroptimistfoundation.ca
To provide bursaries, scholarships & fellowships to Canadian students & Canadian schools, colleges & universities for the advancement of education & in particular to further the appreciation of social needs, & the study of community, national & international problems
Elizabeth Jane (BJ) Gallagher, Chair
Sheryl Hopkins, Treasurer
Lori Roblesky, Secretary

Variety - The Children's Charity (Ontario)
3701 Danforth Ave., Toronto ON M1N 2G2
Tel: 416-699-7167; *Fax:* 416-367-0028
info@varietyontario.ca
www.varietyontario.ca
To improve the quality of life for children with disabilities & their integration into society
John Wilson, CEO

Variety - The Children's Charity of BC
4300 Still Creek Dr., Burnaby BC V5C 6C6
Tel: 604-320-0505; *Toll-Free:* 800-310-5437
info@variety.bc.ca
www.variety.bc.ca
Social Media: www.youtube.com/user/VarietyBC
www.facebook.com/variety.bc.ca
twitter.com/VarietyBC
To raise funds throughout the province of B.C. for the benefit of B.C.'s children with special needs; to provide funds for capital costs; to create new centres or improve existing facilities & purchase specialized equipment
Bernice Scholten, Executive Director

Variety - The Children's Charity of Manitoba, Tent 58 Inc.
#2, 1313 Border St., Winnipeg MB R3H 0X4
Tel: 204-982-1050; *Fax:* 204-475-3198
admin@varietymanitoba.com
www.varietymanitoba.com
Social Media: www.youtube.com/user/varietymanitoba
www.facebook.com/varietymanitoba
twitter.com/Varietymanitoba
Jerry Maslowsky, Chief Executive Officer

Variety Club of Northern Alberta, Tent 63
#1205 Energy Square, 10109 - 106th St., Edmonton AB T5J 3L7
Tel: 780-448-9544; *Fax:* 780-448-9289
Raises funds for the children of Northern Alberta who have disabilities or are disadvantaged
Sue McEachern, Executive Director

Variety Club of Southern Alberta
Calgary AB
Tel: 403-228-6168
info@varietyalberta.ca
www.varietyalberta.ca
Social Media:
www.facebook.com/VarietyAlberta
To provide disabled & disadvantaged children with the means to enjoy quality life experiences; to support research for the below the knee amputee children; to provide assistance & bursaries to children in special situations

Social Response/Social Services

Agincourt Community Services Association (ACSA)
#100, 4155 Sheppard Ave. East, Toronto ON M1S 1T4
Tel: 416-321-6912; *Fax:* 416-321-6922
info@agincourtcommunityservices.com
www.agincourtcommunityservices.com
Social Media:
linkedin.com/company/agincourt-community-services-association
www.facebook.com/AgincourtCommunityServices
twitter.com/AginComServices
To address a variety of issues including systemic poverty, hunger, housing, homelessness, unemployment, accessibility and social isolation in the Scarborough community.
Lee Soda, Executive Director
Vinitha Gengatharan, Chair

Alberta Association of Marriage & Family Therapy (AAMFT)
907 - 25 Ave NW, Calgary AB T2M 2B5
Tel: 403-519-2198
info@aamft.ab.ca
www.aamft.ab.ca
To provide individual marriage & family therapy; to provide educational seminars for therapists
Lori Limacher, Interim President

Alberta Association of Services for Children & Families (AASCF)
Bonnie Doon Mall, #255, 8330 - 82nd Ave., Edmonton AB T6C 4E3
Tel: 780-428-3660; *Fax:* 780-428-3844
aascf@aascf.com
www.aascf.com
To provide opportunities for deliverers of services to meet with each other to exchange views & develop quality service in Alberta; to establish a structure which can provide information to membership & the public in support of social policy on behalf of Alberta children & families; to create a mechanism for action in social policy & public attitudes relating to the welfare of children & families; to support ongoing development & implementation of standards of service for human service providers & maintain accountability to these standards through an accreditation process; to advocate on behalf of the membership; to promote professional development of member agencies; to support research into child & family welfare issues relevant to member agencies; to advise government on social policy
Rhonda Barraclough, Executive Director

Alberta Block Parent Association (ABPA)
220 Doveview Crescent SE, Calgary AB T2B 1Y6
Tel: 403-262-2864
albertabpa@hotmail.com
www.albertablockparent.com
To assist with the start-up of new programs; to provide ongoing support & resources for established programs; to ensure that faltering programs are properly closed down
Donna Fox, President

Alberta College of Social Workers (ACSW) / Association des travailleurs sociaux de l'Alberta
#550, 10707 - 100 Ave. NW, Edmonton AB T5J 3M1
Tel: 780-421-1167; *Fax:* 780-421-1168
Toll-Free: 800-661-3089
www.acsw.ab.ca
To promote, regulate & govern the profession of social work in the Province of Alberta; To advocate for skilled & ethical social work practices & for policies, programs & services that promote the profession & protect the best interests of the public
Lynn Labrecque King, Executive Director/Registrar

Alberta Family Mediation Society (AFMS)
#1650, 246 Stewart Green SW, Calgary AB T3H 3C8
Tel: 403-233-0143; *Toll-Free:* 877-233-0143
info@afms.ca
www.afms.ca
To advocate for the resolution of family conflict through mediation by qualified professionals
Linda Hancock, Chair

Applegrove Community Complex
60 Woodfield Rd., Toronto ON M4L 2W6
Tel: 416-461-8143; *Fax:* 416-461-5513
applegrove@applegrovecc.ca
www.applegrovecc.ca
Social Media:
www.facebook.com/pages/Applegrove-Community-Complex/99742456574
To provide social service programs for infants, children, teens, adults and seniors living in the Queen-Greenwood area of Toronto.
Susan Fletcher, Executive Director
Ann McKechnie, Chair

Association de médiation familiale du Québec (AMFQ)
4800, ch Queen Mary, Montréal QC H3W 1W9
Tél: 514-990-4011; *Téléc:* 514-733-9081
Ligne sans frais: 800-667-7559
info@mediationquebec.ca
www.mediationquebec.ca
Média social: www.facebook.com/669501183095454
twitter.com/Amfqinfo
L'Association de médiation familiale du Québec a pour mission de développer et promouvoir la médiation familiale et les médiateurs familiaux accrédités, au Québec et à l'étranger.
Jean-François Chabot, Présidente
Gerald Schoel, Trésorier
José Mongeau, Secrétaire

Association des services de réhabilitation sociale du Québec inc. (ASRSQ) / Association of Social Rehabilitation Agencies of Québec Inc.
2000, boul St-Joseph est, Montréal QC H2H 1E4
Tél: 514-521-3733; *Téléc:* 514-521-3753
info@asrsq.ca
www.asrsq.ca
Promouvoir la participation des citoyens dans l'administration de la justice, la prévention du crime et la réhabilitation des délinquants adultes
Josée Rioux, Présidente
Philippe Létourneau, Vice-présidente
Ruth Gagnon, Secrétaire
Serge Arel, Trésorier

The Association of Social Workers of Northern Canada (ASWNC) / L'Association des travailleurs sociaux du Nord canadien (ATSNC)
PO Box 2963, Yellowknife NT X1A 2R2
Tel: 867-699-7964
ed@socialworknorth.com
www.socialworknorth.com
The ASWNC represents social workers practicing in Canada's three Territories in the far north - Nunavut, the Northwest Territories, and the Yukon Territory.
Dana Jennejohn, President

Association québécoise des personnes de petite taille (AQPPT) / Association of Little People of Quebec
#308, 6300, av du Parc, Montréal QC H2V 4H8
Tél: 514-521-9671; *Téléc:* 514-521-3369
info@aqppt.org
www.aqppt.org
Média social: www.facebook.com/AQPPT
Promouvoir des intérêts et défendre les droits des personnes de petite taille et faciliter leur intégration scolaire, sociale et professionnelle.
Normande Gagnon, Co-fondatrice

Association québécoise Plaidoyer-Victimes (AQPV)
#201, 4305, rue d'Iberville, Montréal QC H2H 2L5
Tél: 514-526-9037; *Téléc:* 514-526-9951
aqpv@aqpv.ca
www.aqpv.ca
Défense des droits et des intérêts des victimes d'actes criminels par la discussion, la sensibilisation, la formation, la concertation et la recherche
Marie-Hélène Blanc, Directrice générale

Battlefords United Way Inc.
#203, 891 - 99th St., North Battleford SK S9A 0N8
Tel: 306-445-1717
buw@sasktel.net
www.battlefordsunitedway.ca
To improve lives & build community by engaging individuals & mobilizing collective action
Brendon Boothman, Chair
Jana Blais, Treasurer

BC Society of Transition Houses (BCSTH)
#325, 119 West Pender St., Vancouver BC V6B 1S5
Tel: 604-669-6943; *Fax:* 604-682-6962
Toll-Free: 800-661-1040
info@bcsth.ca
bcsth.ca
Social Media: www.youtube.com/BCYSTH
www.facebook.com/BCSTH
twitter.com/BCSTH
To educate, promote & advocate on issues of violence against women; to support an organization that provides or seeks to provide shelter &/or services to women & their children who experience violence
Shabna Ali, Executive Director

Bereaved Families of Ontario (BFO)
PO Box 10015, Stn. Watline, Mississauga ON L4Z 4G5
info@bereavedfamilies.net
www.bereavedfamilies.net
To create programs, services & resources to support bereaved families; committed to self-help & mutual aid; focus is on families who have experienced the death of a child
Carolyn Baltaz, Chair

Birchmount Bluffs Neighbourhood Centre (BBNC)
93 Birchmount Rd., Toronto ON M1N 3J7
Tel: 416-396-4310; *Fax:* 416-396-4314
contact@bbnc.ca
www.bbnc.ca
Social Media:
www.facebook.com/birchmountbluffs
twitter.com/bbncentre

To provide programs and supports and foster social inclusion within the community, with a focus on individuals that face a barrier to service.
Enrique Robert, Executive Director

Block Parent Program of Canada Inc. (BPPCI) / Programme Parents-Secours du Canada inc.
PO Box 7, 50 Dunlop St. East, Lower Level, Barrie ON L4N 6S7
Tel: 705-792-4245; *Fax:* 705-792-4245
Toll-Free: 800-663-1134
info@blockparent.ca
www.blockparent.ca
To provide immediate assistance through a safety network; to offer supporting community education programs
Linda Patterson, President

Block Parent Program of Winnipeg Inc.
466 Gertrude Ave., Winnipeg MB R3L 0M8
Tel: 204-284-7562
bppw@mts.net
www.winnipegblockparents.mb.ca
To provide a network of police-screened, easily recognizable, safe places for the members of the community, primarily children.
George Jarvis, President

Block Watch Society of British Columbia (BCBPS)
#120, 12414 - 82nd Ave., Surrey BC V3W 3E9
Tel: 604-418-3827; *Fax:* 604-501-2509
Toll-Free: 877-602-3358
blockwatch@blockwatch.com
blockwatch.com
To build safe neighbourhoods across British Columbia; To encourage bonds among local residents & businesses to create a crime free area through community participation; To assist in the reduction of crime; To improve relations between police & communities
Colleen Staresina, President
Gary O'Brien, Vice-President
Jenniffer Sanford, Secretary
Michelle Wulff, Treasurer

Brant United Way (BUW)
125 Morrell St., Brantford ON N3T 4J9
Tel: 519-752-7848; *Fax:* 519-752-7913
info@brantunitedway.org
www.brantunitedway.org
Social Media:
www.facebook.com/pages/Brant-United-Way/33874902961
twitter.com/brantunitedway
To help people in their time of need
Sherry Haines, Executive Director

British Columbia Association of Family Resource Programs
#203, 2590 Granville St., Vancouver BC V6H 3H1
Tel: 604-738-0068; *Fax:* 604-738-0568
info@frpbc.ca
www.frpbc.ca
Mimi Hudson, President
Nicky Logins, Vice-President

British Columbia Association of Social Workers (BCASW) / Association des travailleurs sociaux de la Colombie-Britannique
#402, 1755 West Broadway, Vancouver BC V6J 4S5
Tel: 604-730-9111; *Fax:* 604-730-9112
Toll-Free: 800-665-4747
bcasw@bcasw.org
www.bcasw.org
Represents member concerns regarding the practice of social work in BC, professional education & regulation.
Dianne Heath, Executive Director

British Columbia Council for Families (BCCF)
#208, 1600 West 6th Ave., Vancouver BC V6J 1R3
Tel: 604-678-8884; *Fax:* 604-678-8886
bccf@bccf.ca
www.bccf.ca
Social Media:
linkedin.com/company/bc-council-for-families
www.facebook.com/BCFamilies
twitter.com/BC_Families
To strengthen, encourage & support families through information, education, research & advocacy
Sylvia Tremblay, President
Joel B. Kaplan, Executive Director
Tina Albrecht, Manager, Communications

British Columbia Federation of Foster Parent Associations (BCFFPA)
#207, 22561 Dewdney Trunk Rd., Maple Ridge BC V2X 3K1
Tel: 604-466-7487; *Fax:* 604-466-7490
Toll-Free: 800-663-9999
office@bcfosterparents.ca
www.bcfosterparents.ca
To be the collective voice for all foster parents & to promote fostering; to act as a channel of communication between authorized child welfare agencies & foster parents concerning children & foster children in particular
Heather Bayes, President
Sheila Davis, Secretary

British Columbia Society for Male Survivors of Sexual Abuse (BCSMSSA)
#202, 1252 Burrard St., Vancouver BC V6Z 1Z1
Tel: 604-682-6482; *Fax:* 604-684-8883
bcsmssa@hotmail.com
www.bc-malesurvivors.com
To provide treatment & support services to male survivors of sexual abuse & support for their families & partners; to acquire & develop education material re: male survivors & gather statistics; to establish new programs for male survivors within British Columbia or assist other agencies in setting up programs through training & consultation; to advocate for male survivors with government & the general population
Don Wright, Executive Director

BullyingCanada Inc.
PO Box 27009, Stn. Atl Superstore, 471 Smythe St., Fredericton NB E3B 9M1
Toll-Free: 877-352-4497
info@bullyingcanada.ca
www.bullyingcanada.ca
To offer information, help & support to everyone involved in bullying
Rob Frenette, Co-Executive Director
Katie Neu, Co-Executive Director

Campbell River & District United Way
PO Box 135, Campbell River BC V9W 5A7
Tel: 250-702-2911
bvbayly@uwcnvi.ca
To raise & distribute funds to member agencies that are providing support and services to residents in the Campbell River area

Canada Without Poverty / Canada Sans Pauvreté
251 Bank St., 2nd Fl., Ottawa ON K2P 1X3
Tel: 613-789-0096; *Fax:* 613-566-3449
Toll-Free: 800-810-1076
info@cwp-csp.ca
www.cwp-csp.ca
Social Media:
www.facebook.com/106633876058589
twitter.com/CWP_CSP
To eradicate poverty in Canada by promoting income and social security for all Canadians, and by promoting poverty eradication as a human rights obligation.
Leilani Farha, Executive Director
Megan Yarema, Director, Education & Outreach

Canadian Association for the Prevention of Discrimination & Harassment in Higher Education (CAPDHHE) / Association canadienne pour la prévention de la discrimination et ou harcèlement en milieu d'enseignement supérieur (ACPDHMES)
c/o University of British Columbia, Vancouver BC V6T 1Z2
Tel: 604-822-4859; *Fax:* 604-822-3260
amlong@ubc.ca
www.capdhhe.org
To provide professional development for individuals employed at colleges & universities in the area of discrimination & harassment, including harassment as identified under human rights law
Anne-Marie Long, President

Canadian Association of Sexual Assault Centres (CASAC) / Association canadienne des centres contre les agressions à caractère sexuel (ACCCACS)
77 East 20th Ave., Vancouver BC V5V 1L7
Tel: 604-876-2622; *Fax:* 604-876-8450
casac01@shaw.ca
www.casac.ca
To work for an end to violence against women & toward women's equality; to provide a national voice for anti-rape workers.

Canadian Association of Social Workers (CASW) / Association canadienne des travailleurs sociaux (ACTS)
#402, 383 Parkdale Ave., Ottawa ON K1Y 4R4
Tel: 613-729-6668; *Fax:* 613-729-9608
casw@casw-acts.ca
www.casw-acts.ca
Social Media:
www.facebook.com/Canadian.Association.of.Social.Workers
To represent Canadian professional social workers; To strengthen & advances the social work profession in Canada; To preserve excellence within the profession
Fred Phelps, Executive Director

Canadian Career Development Foundation (CCDF) / Fondation canadienne pour le développement de carrière (FCDC)
#202, 119 Ross Ave., Ottawa ON K1Y 0N6
Tel: 613-729-6164; *Fax:* 613-729-3515
Toll-Free: 877-729-6164
information@ccdf.ca
www.ccdf.ca
Social Media:
twitter.com/CCDFFCDC
To advance the understanding & practice of career development.
Lynne Bezanson, Executive Director
Sareena Hopkins, Co-Executive Director

Canadian Centre for Policy Alternatives (CCPA) / Centre canadien de politique alternative
#500, 251 Bank St., Ottawa ON K2P 1X3
Tel: 613-563-1341; *Fax:* 613-233-1458
ccpa@policyalternatives.ca
www.policyalternatives.ca
Social Media: www.youtube.com/user/policyalternatives
www.facebook.com/policyalternatives
twitter.com/ccpa
To promote research on economic & social issues facing Canada; To monitor current developments in economy & study important trends that affect Canadians; To demonstrate thoughtful alternatives to the limited perspectives of business, research institutes & government agencies; To put forward research that reflects concerns of women & men, labour & business, churches, cooperatives & voluntary agencies, governments, minorities, disadvantaged & fortunate individuals
Bruce Campbell, Executive Director

Canadian Centre for Victims of Torture (CCVT)
194 Jarvis St., 2nd Fl., Toronto ON M5B 2B7
Tel: 416-363-1066; *Fax:* 416-363-2122
www.ccvt.org
Social Media:
www.facebook.com/115015798517911
twitter.com/ccvt_toronto
To offer support & arrange medical, legal & social care for torture victims & their families; to increase public awareness in Canada & abroad of torture & its effects upon survivors & their families
Mulugeta Abai, Executive Director

Canadian Council for Refugees (CCR) / Conseil canadien pour les réfugiés
#302, 6839, rue Drolet, Montréal QC H2S 2T1
Tel: 514-277-7223; *Fax:* 514-277-1447
info@ccrweb.ca
www.ccrweb.ca
Social Media:
www.youtube.com/ccrwebvideos
www.facebook.com/ccrweb
twitter.com/ccrweb
To be committed to the rights & protection of refugees in Canada & around the world & to the settlement of refugees & immigrants in Canada
Janet Dench, Executive Director
Marisa Berry-Méndez, Director, Settlement Policy
Cynthia Beaudry, Coordinator, Youth
Colleen French, Coordinator, Communications & Networking

Canadian Counselling & Psychotherapy Association (CCPA) / L'Association canadienne de counseling et de psychothérapie (ACCP)
#114, 223 Colonnade Rd. South, Ottawa ON K2E 7K3
Tel: 613-237-1099; *Fax:* 613-237-9786
Toll-Free: 877-765-5565
info@ccpa-accp.ca
www.ccpa-accp.ca
Social Media:
www.facebook.com/CCPA.ACCP
twitter.com/ccpa_accp
To enhance the counselling profession in Canada; To promote policies & practices which support the provision of accessible,

competent, & accountable counselling services throughout the human lifespan, & in a manner sensitive to the pluralistic nature of society.
Blythe Shepard, President
Barbara MacCallum, Executive Director

Canadian Crossroads International (CCI) / Carrefour canadien international
#201, 49 Bathurst St., Toronto ON M5V 2P2
Tel: 416-967-1611; *Fax:* 416-967-9078
Toll-Free: 877-967-1611
info@cintl.org
www.cintl.org
Social Media: www.youtube.com/user/CanadianCrossroads
www.facebook.com/CanadianCrossroads
twitter.com/Crossroads_CCI
CCI is a development organization that is reducing poverty & increasing women's rights around the world. It works with local organizations in West Africa, Southern Africa & South America. Organizations in developing countries select Canadian, partner organizations working on similar issues, so that they can help develop programs & meet their development goals. CCI supports the exchange of skilled volunteers. It is a registered charity, BN: 129814570RR0001.
Darlene Bessey, Chair
Karen Takacs, Executive Director
Aranka Somlo, Executive Assistant

Canadian Feed The Children (CFTC)
174 Bartley Dr., Toronto ON M4A 1E1
Tel: 416-757-1220; *Fax:* 416-757-3318
Toll-Free: 800-387-1221
contact@canadianfeedthechildren.ca
www.canadianfeedthechildren.ca
Social Media: www.youtube.com/user/canadianfeed
linkedin.com/company/canadian-feed-the-children
www.facebook.com/CanadianFeedTheChildren
twitter.com/cdnfeedchildren
To alleviate the impact of poverty on children; work with local partners overseas & in Canada to enhance the well-being of children & the self-sufficiency of their families & communities.
Debra Kerby, Executive Director

Canadian Grandparents' Rights Association (CGRA)
#207, 14980 - 104 Ave., Surrey BC V3R 1M9
Tel: 604-585-8242; *Fax:* 604-585-8241
Toll-Free: 866-585-8242
www.CanadianGrandparentsRightsAssociation.com
Promotes, supports, and assists Grandparents and their families in maintaining or re-establishing family ties and family stability where the family has been disrupted; especially those ties between grandparents and grandchildren.

Canadian Social Work Foundation (CSWF) / Fondation canadienne du service social
#402, 383 Parkdale Ave., Ottawa ON K1Y 4R4
Tel: 613-729-6668; *Fax:* 613-729-9608
Toll-Free: 855-729-2279
casw@casw-acts.ca
www.casw-acts.ca
Social Media:
www.facebook.com/Canadian.Association.of.Social.Workers
To edit & publish books, papers, journals & other forms of literature respecting social work in order to disseminate information to the public; to encourage studies; to promote, develop & sponsor activities strengthening social work
Morel Caissie, President
Fred Phelps, Executive Director

Canadian Society for the Prevention of Cruelty to Children (CSPCC)
PO Box 700, 362 Midland Ave., Midland ON L4R 4P4
Tel: 705-526-5647; *Fax:* 705-526-0214
cspcc@bellnet.ca
www.empathicparenting.org
To increase public awareness of the long-term consequences of child abuse & neglect; to encourage primary prevention initiatives for improved nurturing of children in their earliest years of life
E.T. Barker, President

Canadian Urban Institute (CUI)
PO Box 612, #402, 555 Richmond St. West, Toronto ON M5V 3B1
Tel: 416-365-0816; *Fax:* 416-365-0650
cui@canurb.org
www.canurb.org
Social Media:
www.facebook.com/pages/Canadian-Urban-Institute/265253496954
twitter.com/canurb
Fred Eisenberger, President & Chief Executive Officer
Andrew Farncombe, Vice-President, International Partnerships
Glenn R. Miller, FCIP, RPP, Vice-President, Education & Research
Ed Mafa, CMA, Director, Finance
Lisa Cavicchia, Program Manager, International Partnerships
Elena Dinu, Program Manager, International Partnerships
Careesa Gee, Manager, Education & Events
Simon Geraghty, Senior Engineering Researcher, Urban Solutions
Katelyn Margerm, Senior Engineering Researcher

Canadians Concerned About Violence in Entertainment (C-CAVE)
167 Glen Rd., Toronto ON M4W 2W8
info@c-cave.com
www.c-cave.com
To provide public education on research findings related to media violence through popular culture, commodities marketed primarily to children, adolescents & adults.
Rose Anne Dyson, Media Contact

Carrefour communautaire de Chibougamau
330, ch Merrill, Chibougamau QC G8P 2X4
Tél: 418-748-7266
carrefour_com@hotmail.com
Brigitte Rosa, Responsable

Centraide Bas St-Laurent
#303, 1555, boul. Jacques Cartier, Mont-Joli QC G5H 2W1
Tél: 418-775-5555; *Téléc:* 418-775-5525
direction@centraidebsl.org
www.centraidebsl.org
Organisme sans but lucratif de lutte à la pauvreté et de soutien aux personnes démunies.
Michel Daigle, Directeur général

Centraide Centre du Québec
154, rue Dunkin, Drummondville QC J2B 5V1
Tél: 819-477-0505; *Téléc:* 819-477-6719
Ligne sans frais: 888-477-0505
bureau@centraide-cdq.ca
www.centraide-cdq.ca
Média social:
www.facebook.com/pages/Centraide_cdq/152071968150658
twitter.com/centraide_cdq
Rassembler les personnes et les ressources du Centre-du-Québec afin de contribuer au développement social de la communauté et d'améliorer la qualité de vie de ses membres les plus vulnérables et ce, en lien avec les organismes communautaires.
Isabelle Dionne, Directrice générale

Centraide du Grand Montréal / Centraide of Greater Montréal
493, rue Sherbrooke Ouest, Montréal QC H3A 1B6
Tél: 514-288-1261; *Téléc:* 514-350-7282
info@centraide-mtl.org
centraide-mtl.org
Média social: www.youtube.com/user/CentraideMtl
www.facebook.com/centraide.du.grand.montreal
twitter.com/centraidemtl
To maximize financial & volunteer resources in order to promote mutual aid, social commitment, & self-reliance as effective means of improving the quality of life of the community, & especially of its neediest members
Lili-Anna Peresa, Présidente et Directrice générale

Centraide Duplessis
#101, 185, rue Napoléon, Sept-Iles QC G4R 4R7
Tél: 418-962-2011; *Téléc:* 418-968-4694
administration@centraideduplessis.org
www.centraideduplessis.org
Denis Miousse, Directeur général

Centraide Estrie
1150, rue Belvédère sud, Sherbrooke QC J1H 4C7
Tél: 819-569-9281; *Téléc:* 819-569-5195
bureau@estrie.centraide.ca
www.estrie.centraide.ca
Média social: www.youtube.com/user/centraideestrie
www.facebook.com/pages/Centraide-Estrie/177152949010458
Vise à soutenir les organismes bénévoles et communautaires engagés directement auprès des clientèles les plus démunies et vulnérables.
Claude Forgues, Directeur général

Centraide Gaspésie Iles-de-la-Madeleine
#216, 230, rte du Parc, Sainte-Anne-des-Monts QC G4V 2C4
Tél: 418-763-2171; *Téléc:* 418-763-7677
centraidegim@globetrotter.net
www.gim.centraide.ca
Soulager la misère et la souffrance humaine.
Yvon Lemieux, Directeur général

Centraide Gatineau-Labelle-Hautes-Laurentides
671, rue de la Madone, Mont-Laurier QC J9L 1T2
Tél: 819-623-4090; *Téléc:* 819-623-7646
bureau@centraideglhl.ca
www.gatineaulabellehlaurentides.centraide.ca
Média social:
www.facebook.com/Centraide.Gatineau.Labelle.Hautes.Laurentides
Annie Lajoie, Directrice générale

Centraide Haute-Côte-Nord/Manicouagan
#301, 858, rue de Puyjalon, Baie-Comeau QC G5C 1N1
Tél: 418-589-5567; *Téléc:* 418-295-2567
centraidehcnman@globetrotter.net
www.centraidehcnmanicouagan.ca
Christine Brisson, Directrice générale

Centraide KRTB-Côte-du-Sud
100, 4e av, La Pocatière QC G0R 1Z0
Tél: 418-856-5105; *Téléc:* 418-856-4385
centraideportage@bellnet.ca
centraidekrtbcotedusud.org
Notre mission est d'aider les gens, d'affecter les ressources en fonction des besoins, d'améliorer la qualité de vie de chacun et de renforcer le soutien communautaire. Donnez un coup de main au destin et participez aux efforts déployés par le Mouvement Centraide Portage-Taché.
Sylvain Roy, Directeur général

Centraide Lanaudière
674, rue St-Louis, Joliette QC J6E 2Z6
Tél: 450-752-1999
www.centraide-lanaudiere.com
Média social: www.facebook.com/275362692481275
Promouvoir l'entraide, le partage et l'engagement bénévole et communautaire
Nicole Campeau, Directrice générale

Centraide Laurentides
#107, 880, Michèle-Bohec, Blainville QC J7C 5E2
Tél: 450-436-1584; *Téléc:* 450-951-2772
www.centraidelaurentides.org
Média social: www.youtube.com/user/centraidelaurentides
www.facebook.com/CentraideLaurentides
twitter.com/CentraideLauren
Contribuer, par la promotion du partage et de l'engagement bénévole et communautaire, à la construction d'une société d'entraide vouée à l'amélioration de la qualité de vie des personnes en difficulté
Suzanne M. Piché, Directrice générale

Centraide Mauricie
90, Des Casernes, Trois-Rivières QC G9A 1X2
Tél: 819-374-6207; *Téléc:* 819-374-6857
centraide.mauricie@centraidemauricie.ca
www.centraidemauricie.ca
Média social: linkedin.com/company/centraide-mauricie
www.facebook.com/centraide.mauricie
twitter.com/centraidem
Travailler à un changement social pour une société plus juste, plus humaine et plus démocratique à travers la promotion de l'entraide, la solidarité et l'engagement bénévole afin de répondre aux besoins socio-économiques de notre communauté.
Julie Colbert, Directrice générale

Centraide Outaouais
74, boul. Montclair, Gatineau QC J8Y 2E7
Tél: 819-771-7751; *Téléc:* 819-771-0301
Ligne sans frais: 800-325-7751
information@centraideoutaouais.com
www.centraideoutaouais.com
Média social: www.youtube.com/user/centraideoutaouais
www.facebook.com/pages/Centraide-Outaouais/346079120163
Mobiliser le gens et rassembler les ressources pour améliorer la qualité de vie de personnes plus vulnérables et contribuer au développement de collectivités solidaires.
Nathalie Lepage, Directrice générale

Centraide Québec
#101, 3100, av du Bourg-Royal, Québec QC G1C 5S7
Tél: 418-660-2100; *Téléc:* 418-660-2111
centraide@centraide-quebec.com
www.centraide-quebec.com
Média social: www.youtube.com/user/CentraideQuebec
linkedin.com/company/centraide-qu-bec-et-chaudi-re-appalaches
www.facebook.com/centraidequebec
twitter.com/CentraideQc
Levées de fonds et attribution de subventions à 166 organismes communautaires pour aider les personnes les plus démunies
Bruno Marchand, Président/Directeur général

Centraide Richelieu-Yamaska
320, ave. de la Concorde nord, Saint-Hyacinthe QC J2S 4N7
Tél: 450-773-6679; *Téléc:* 450-773-4734
bureau@centraidery.org
www.richelieuyamaska.centraide.ca
Média social:
www.facebook.com/pages/Centraide-Richelieu-Yamaska/19919 6286858982
Centraide Portage-Taché, c'est une organisation charitable, qui repose sur l'engagement bénévole et qui se donne comme mission d'améliorer les conditions de vie des plus démuni(e)s de son territoire.
Daniel Laplante, Directrice générale

Centraide Saguenay-Lac St-Jean
#107, 475, boul. Talbot, Chicoutimi QC G7H 4A3
Tél: 418-543-3131; *Téléc:* 418-543-0665
info@centraideslsj.ca
www.centraidesaglac.ca
Rassembler et développer des ressources financières et bénévoles afin d'aider les diverses communautés du Saguenay-Lac-St-Jean à organiser et à promouvoir l'entreaide, l'engagement social et la prise en charge afin d'améliorer la qualité de vie de sa collectivité et de ses membres les plus démunis et les plus vulnérables.
Martin St-Pierre, Directeur général
Claude Fortin, Agente, Communication

Centraide sud-ouest du Québec
#200, 100, rue Ste-Cécile, Salaberry-de-Valleyfield QC J6T 1M1
Tél: 450-371-2061; *Téléc:* 450-377-2309
centraid@rocler.qc.ca
www.centraidesudouest.org
Média social: www.facebook.com/195796617125646
Grâce à votre don, il y a du changement possible. En effet, la misère qu'elle soit physique, morale, psychologique ou matérielle peut toucher tout le monde, peu importe la classe sociale. Donner à Centraide Sud-Ouest, c'est susciter un changement positif dans notre communauté
Steve Hickey, Directeur général

Centre for Suicide Prevention (CSP)
#320, 105 - 12 Ave. SE, Calgary AB T2G 1A1
Tel: 403-245-3900; *Fax:* 403-245-0299
Crisis Hot-Line: 406-266-4357
csp@suicideinfo.ca
www.suicideinfo.ca
Social Media: suicideinfo.tumblr.com
linkedin.com/company/centre-for-suicide-prevention
twitter.com/cspyyc
CSP educates people with the information, knowledge and skills necessary to respond to the risk of suicide.
Diane Yackel, Executive Director

The Child Abuse Survivor Monument Project (CASMP)
274 Rhodes Ave., Toronto ON M4L 3A3
Tel: 416-469-4764; *Fax:* 416-963-8892
mci@irvingstudios.com
www.irvingstudios.com/child_abuse_survivor_monument
Social Media: www.youtube.com/user/ChildAbuseMonument
www.facebook.com/ChildAbuseMonument
twitter.com/ChildAbuseMnumt
To build a memorial monument for & by survivors of child abuse to assist with the personal & social healing of the ravages of child abuse
Michael C. Irving, Artistic Director

Child Care Advocacy Association of Canada (CCAAC) / Association canadienne pour la promotion des services de garde à l'enfance (ACPSGE)
225 Brunswick Ave., Toronto ON M5S 2M6
Tel: 416-926-8859
www.ccaac.ca
Social Media:
www.facebook.com/childcareadvocacyassociationofcanada
twitter.com/CCAAC_ACPSGE
To work toward expanding the child care system & improving its quality; To advocate for the development of an affordable, comprehensive, high-quality, not-for-profit child care system that is supported by public funds & accessible to every Canadian family who wishes to use it

Child Welfare League of Canada (CWLC) / Ligue pour le bien-être de l'enfance du Canada (LBEC)
226 Argyle Ave., Ottawa ON K2P 1B9
Tel: 613-235-4412; *Fax:* 613-235-7616
info@cwlc.ca
www.cwlc.ca
Social Media:
www.facebook.com/CWLC.LBEC
To provide public education on the needs of all children, youth & their families through research, information & other services directed toward enhancing & improving public awareness; to facilitate the development of standards in services to children, youth & their families; to encourage excellence in the delivery of these services
Mike DeGagné, Chair
Gordon Phaneuf, MSW, RSW, Chief Executive Officer

Christie-Ossington Neighbourhood Centre (CONC)
854 Bloor St. West, Toronto ON M6G 1M2
Tel: 416-534-8941; *Fax:* 416-534-8704
www.conccommunity.org
To improve the quality of life in the Christie Ossington community by working in collaboration with residents, community institutions, agencies, local businesses and stakeholders to create a safe and healthy community.
Lynn Daly, Executive Director

Community Action Resource Centre (CARC)
1652 Keele St., Toronto ON M6M 3W3
Tel: 416-652-2273; *Fax:* 416-652-8992
www.communityarc.ca
Social Media:
www.facebook.com/CommunityActionResourceCentre
twitter.com/communityarc
To build the capacity of communities by mobilizing resources & providing supportive social services, for the empowerment of individuals & groups with a focus on serving the most vulnerable and disadvantaged.

Community Social Services Employers' Association (CSSEA)
Two Bentall Centre, PO Box 232, #800, 555 Burrard St., Vancouver BC V7X 1M8
Tel: 604-687-7220; *Fax:* 604-687-7266
Toll-Free: 800-377-3340
cssea@cssea.bc.ca
www.cssea.bc.ca
To strive for excellence & innovation in human resources & labour relations
Gentil Mateus, Chief Executive Officer
Thomas Marshall, Director, Communications

Confédération des organismes familiaux du Québec (COFAQ)
4657, rue Papineau, Montréal QC H2H 1V4
Tél: 514-521-4777; *Téléc:* 514-521-6272
www.cofaq.qc.ca
Média social: www.facebook.com/CofaqFamille
twitter.com/CofaqFamille
Représenter les familles et revendiquer leurs droits auprès des diverses instances publiques et privées; Promouvoir des projets innovateurs et le développement d'expertises satisfaisant aux besoins des familles et leurs organisations; Réaliser des activités de soutien auprès des membres
Jean-Christophe Filosa, Présidente
Robert Rodrigue, Trésorière

Conflict Resolution Saskatchewan Inc.
PO Box 3765, Regina SK S4P 3N8
Tel: 306-565-3939; *Fax:* 306-586-6711
Toll-Free: 866-565-3938
admin@conflictresolutionsk.ca
www.conflictresolutionsk.ca
Dreena Horner, President

Cooper Institute / L'Institut Cooper
81 Prince St., Charlottetown PE C1A 4R3
Tel: 902-894-4573; *Fax:* 902-368-7180
www.cooperinstitute.ca
Social Media:
www.facebook.com/pages/Cooper-Institute/156027014448502
To promote programs that are focussed on livable income for all, food sovereignty & cultural diversity & inclusion; to conduct research & popular education projects on provincial, national & international level.
Joe Byrne, President

COSTI Immigrant Services
Education Centre, 1710 Dufferin St., Toronto ON M6E 3P2
Tel: 416-658-1600; *Fax:* 416-658-8537
info@costi.org
www.costi.org
To provide educational, social & employment support to help immigrants in the greater Toronto area attain self-sufficiency in Canadian society. Services are provided in over 60 languages.
Bruno M. Suppa, President
Mario J. Calla, Executive Director

Cowichan United Way
1 Kenneth Place, Duncan BC V9L 5G3
Tel: 250-748-1312; *Fax:* 250-748-7652
Toll-Free: 877-748-1312
office@cowichan.unitedway.ca
www.cowichan.unitedway.ca
Social Media:
www.facebook.com/UnitedWayCowichan
twitter.com/uwcowichan
To fundraise for charities; To provide guidance & counsel to charitable organization; To take leadership role in raising awareness of community needs
Mike Murphy, President
Heather Gardiner, Interim Advisor

Davenport-Perth Neighbourhood & Community Health Centre (DPNCHC)
1900 Davenport Rd., Toronto ON M6N 1B7
Tel: 416-656-8025; *Fax:* 416-656-1264
info@dpnchc.ca
dpnchc.com
The Davenport-Perth Neighbourhood Centre (DPNC) is a multi-service agency located in the west end of Toronto dedicated to encouraging people to work together and take action to improve the political, social, economic, spiritual and cultural life of the whole community.
Wade Hilier, President

Dejinta Beesha Multi-Service Centre
8 Taber Rd., Toronto ON M9W 3A4
Tel: 416-743-1286; *Fax:* 416-743-1233
info@dejinta.org
dejinta.org
To provide settlement, integration, recreation, health, employment, education, & social services to the community; Offering services in English, French, Italian, Arabic, Somali, & Kiswahili
Mohamed Gilao, Executive Director

Delta Family Resource Centre
#5, 2972 Islington Ave., Toronto ON M9L 2K6
Tel: 416-747-1172; *Fax:* 416-747-7415
contactus@dfrc.ca
www.dfrc.ca
Social Media:
www.facebook.com/pages/Delta-Family-Resource-Centre/33700 7286321251
twitter.com/DeltaFamilyRC
To support the needs of families & children within the community; Offering services in English, Spanish, Italian, Hindi, Punjabi, Laotian, Gujarati, Somali, Cantonese, Tamil, Mandarin, Thi, Ewe, Twi, Urdu, Dari, & Ga
Rosalyn Miller, Executive Director

Distress Centres Ontario (DCO)
#1016, 30 Duke St. West, Kitchener ON N2H 3W5
Tel: 416-486-2242; *Fax:* 519-342-0970
info@dcontario.org
www.dcontario.org
To transfer best practices between member centres; To promote, support & sustain member agencies
Karen Letofsky, Chair
Elizabeth Fisk, Executive Director

Dixon Hall
58 Sumach St., Toronto ON M5A 3J7
Tel: 416-863-0499; *Fax:* 416-863-9981
info@dixonhall.org
www.dixonhall.org
Social Media:
www.facebook.com/DixonHallToronto
twitter.com/dixon_hall
To create opportunities for people of all ages to dream, to achieve and to live full and rewarding lives.
Kate Stark, Executive Director

Doorsteps Neighbourhood Services
#106, 200 Chalkfarm Dr., Toronto ON M3L 2H7
Tel: 416-243-5480; *Fax:* 416-243-7406
www.doorsteps.ca
To focus on community education, prevention, & the enhancement of resiliency of individuals & communities
Carol Thames, Executive Director

Dying with Dignity (DWD) / Mourir dans la dignité
#802, 55 Eglinton Ave. East, Toronto ON M4P 1G8
Tel: 416-486-3998; *Fax:* 416-486-5562
Toll-Free: 800-495-6156
info@dyingwithdignity.ca
www.dyingwithdignity.ca
Social Media: www.youtube.com/user/DWDCanada
www.facebook.com/DWDCanada
twitter.com/DWDCanada

To improve the quality of dying for all Canadians in accordance with their own wishes, values & beliefs
Wanda Morris, Executive Director

Edmonton Social Planning Council (ESPC)
#37, 9912 - 106 St., Edmonton AB T5K 1C5
Tel: 780-423-2031; *Fax:* 780-425-6244
edmontonspc@gmail.com
www.edmontonsocialplanning.ca
Social Media: www.facebook.com/pages/Edmonton-Social-Planning-Council/37296571206
twitter.com/edmontonspc
To provide leadership within the community by addressing & researching social issues, informing public discussion & influencing social policy
Susan Morrissey, Executive Director
Vasant Chotai, President

Elder Mediation Canada (EMC)
www.eldermediation.ca
To advance the practice of elder mediation in Canada; to improve the qualifications & effectiveness of mediators

Eston United Way
PO Box 23, Eston SK S0L 1A0
Tel: 306-962-3962
cassjacqui@sasktel.net
Raising money in order to create positive and lasting changes in communities.

Family & Community Support Services Association of Alberta (FCSSAA)
Belmead Professional Bldg., #106, 8944 - 182 St., Edmonton AB T5T 2E3
Tel: 780-415-4790; *Fax:* 780-415-4793
fcssaa@telus.net
www.fcssaa.ab.ca
To advocate on behalf of local communities & programs to the general public, municipal governments, regional services, provincial & national agencies, & authorities; To educate individuals, communities, boards, & staff
Sharlyn White, Executive Director
Jeff Carlson, President
Judy Macknee, Executive Assistant

Family Mediation Canada (FMC) / Médiation Familiale Canada
#180, 55 Northfield Dr. East, Waterloo ON N2K 3T6
Tel: 519-585-3118; *Fax:* 416-849-0643
Toll-Free: 877-362-2005
fmc@fmc.ca
www.fmc.ca
To improve the provision for cooperative conflict resolution in areas such as separation & divorce, child welfare, adoption, parent & teen counselling, age-related issues, & wills & estates
Mary Damianakis, President
Linda Bonnell, Secretary
Carrie Cekerevac, Manager, Operations

Family Mediation Manitoba Inc. (FMM)
PO Box 2369, Winnipeg MB R3C 4A6
Tel: 204-989-5330; *Fax:* 204-694-7555
info@familymediationmanitoba.ca
www.familymediationmanitoba.ca
To promote family mediation in Manitoba
Karen Burwash, President

Family Mediation Nova Scotia (FMNS)
c/o Keith Wallis, #306, 35 Commercial St., Truro NS B2N 3H9
mirkwoodmediation@ns.aliantzinc.ca
The purpose of Family Mediation Nova Scotia is to promote accessible, quality mediation services for families. FMNS provides information about family mediation to the public, promotes professional development & establishes standards of practice for family mediators.
Charlene Moore, Past President
Keith Wallis, Vice-President

Family Service Canada (FSC) / Services à la famille - Canada
c/o 312 Parkdale Ave., Ottawa ON K1Y 4X45
Toll-Free: 877-451-1055
www.familyservicecanada.org
To promote families as the primary source of nurturing & development of individuals, their relationship in families & communities, through promoting & ensuring the best policies & services for families in Canada.
Heather Underhill, Manager, Operations

Family Service Toronto (FST)
355 Church St., Toronto ON M5B 1Z8
Tel: 416-595-9230; *Fax:* 416-595-0242
sau@familyservicetoronto.org
www.fsatoronto.com
To help low-income individuals & families in need.
Lan Nguyen, President
Margaret Hancock, Executive Director

Fédération des associations de familles monoparentales et recomposées du Québec (FAFMRQ) / Federation of Single-Parent Family Associations of Québec
584, rue Guizot est, Montréal QC H2P 1N3
Tél: 514-729-6666; *Téléc:* 514-729-6746
fafmrq.info@videotron.ca
www.fafmrq.org
Média social: twitter.com/FAFMRQ
Travailler à améliorer les conditions socio-économiques des familles monoparentales et recomposées du Québec.
Sylvie Lévesque, Directrice générale

Fédération des centres d'action bénévole du Québec (FCABQ)
1557, av Papineau, Montréal QC H2K 4H7
Tél: 514-843-6312; *Téléc:* 514-843-6485
Ligne sans frais: 800-715-7515
info@fcabq.org
www.fcabq.org
Mèdia social: www.facebook.com/fcabq
Promouvoir l'action bénévole au Québec; former un centre d'action bénévole; organiser la semaine de l'action bénévole.
Fimba Tankoano, Directeur général

The 519 Church St. Community Centre
519 Church St., Toronto ON M4Y 2C9
Tel: 416-392-6874; *Fax:* 416-392-0519
info@the519.org
www.the519.org
Social Media: www.youtube.com/The519Toronto
www.facebook.com/The519
twitter.com/The519
To act as a meeting place & focal point for the diverse downtown Toronto community; To respond to the needs of the local neighbourhood and the broader Lesbian, Gay, Bisexual, Transsexual, Transgender, and Queer community
Maura Lawless, Executive Director

Flemingdon Neighbourhood Services
#104, 10 Gateway Blvd., Toronto ON M3C 3A1
Tel: 416-424-2900; *Fax:* 416-424-3455
info@fnservices.org
www.fnservices.org
To enhance the over-all quality of life for residents of Flemingdon Park and the City of Toronto by increasing access to information and community resources for our clients through advocacy, empowerment and education.
John Carey, Executive Director

Food Banks Canada / Banques alimentaires Canada
Bldg. 2, #400, 5025 Orbitor Dr., Mississauga ON L4W 4Y5
Tel: 905-602-5234; *Fax:* 905-602-5614
Toll-Free: 877-535-0958
www.foodbankscanada.ca
Social Media: www.youtube.com/user/FoodBanksCanada1
www.facebook.com/FoodBanksCanada
twitter.com/foodbankscanada
To act as the voice for the hungry in Canada; To find short term & long term solutions for Canadians who are assisted by food banks
Katharine Schmidt, Executive Director
Brian Fraser, Chair
Marc Guay, Vice-Chair
Monica Donahue, Secretary
Allan Cosman, Treasurer

Foster Parent Support Services Society (FPSS)
#145, 735 Goldstream Ave., Victoria BC V9B 2X4
Tel: 778-430-5459; *Fax:* 778-430-5463
Toll-Free: 888-922-8437
admin@fpsss.com
www.fpsss.com
Social Media: www.facebook.com/fpsssociety
twitter.com/FPSSSociety
To provide meaningful and accessible support, education and networking services which will continually enhance the skills and abilities of foster parents to deliver the best care possible to the children in their homes.
Dan Malone, Executive Director

Fred Victor Centre
59 Adelaide St. East, 6th Fl., Toronto ON M5C 1K6
Tel: 416-364-8228; *Fax:* 416-364-4728
www.fredvictor.org
To offer a continuum of community services, housing options and advocacy for adults who are experiencing homelessness, marginalization and poverty. Over 150 beds and spaces are available across 6 sites and programs.
Mark Aston, Executive Director

Frontiers Foundation (FF/OB) / Fondation Frontière
419 Coxwell Ave., Toronto ON M4L 3B9
Tel: 416-690-3930; *Fax:* 416-690-3934
www.frontiersfoundation.ca
Social Media: www.facebook.com/pages/Frontiers-Foundation/66661443145
To implement the enduring relief of human poverty throughout Canada & also abroad in tangible advancement projects.
Marco A. Guzman, Executive Director
Lawrence Gladue, President

Good Jobs for All Coalition
Toronto ON
Tel: 416-937-9378
communications@goodjobsforall.ca
goodjobsforall.ca
Social Media: twitter.com/goodjobsforall
The Good Jobs for All Coalition is an alliance of community, labour, social justice, youth and environmental organizations in the Toronto region. It was formed in 2008 to start a focused dialogue on how to improve living and working conditions in Canada's largest urban centre.
Preethy Sivakumar, Coordinator

Goodwill Industries of Alberta
8761 - 51 Ave., Edmonton AB T6E 5H1
Tel: 780-944-1414; *Toll-Free:* 866-927-1414
media@goodwill.ab.ca
www.goodwill.ab.ca
Social Media: www.youtube.com/GoodwillAB
www.facebook.com/GoodwillAB
twitter.com/goodwillab
To help persons with disabilities & disadvantages; To build a strong future through rehabilitation & training
Larry Brownoff, Chair
Dale Monaghan, President & CEO

Goodwill Industries of Toronto
350 Progress Ave., Toronto ON M1P 2Z4
Tel: 416-362-4711; *Fax:* 416-815-4795
info@goodwill.on.ca
www.goodwill.on.ca
Social Media: www.facebook.com/pages/Goodwill-TECNO/594576443969604
twitter.com/goodwilltecno
To provide effective vocational programs & services to people who face employment barriers to enable them to become as independent as possible
Keiko Nakamura, CEO

GRAND Society
c/o #509, 14 Spadina Rd., Toronto ON M5R 3M4
Tel: 416-513-9404
To provide emotional support to grandparents who have been denied access to their grandchildren; to make the public & professionals aware of this problem; to influence provincial family law to recognize the rights of grandparents
Joan Brooks, President/Chair

Grande Prairie & Region United Way
#213, 11330 - 106 St., Grande Prairie AB T8V 7X9
Tel: 780-532-1105; *Fax:* 780-532-3532
info@unitedwayabnw.org
www.gpunitedway.org
Social Media: www.youtube.com/user/GrowUnitedBreakfast
www.facebook.com/UnitedWayABNW
twitter.com/UnitedWayABNW
To bring people together to strengthen the community; To strengthen the capacity of community & other local agencies to bring about positive change
Brenda Yamkowy, Executive Director

Harbourfront Community Centre (HCC)
627 Queen's Quay West, Toronto ON M5V 3G3
Tel: 416-392-1509; *Fax:* 416-392-1512
hcc@harbourfrontcc.ca
www.harbourfrontcc.ca
To advocate for provision of necessary services to the community, provide a range of responsive programs and services in an atmosphere of belonging and meet the needs of a diverse and changing multicultural community.
Leona Rodall, Executive Director

Human Concern International (HCI)
PO Box 3984, Stn. C, Ottawa ON K1Y 4P2
Tel: 613-742-5948; *Toll-Free:* 800-587-6424
info@humanconcern.org
www.humanconcern.org
Social Media: www.youtube.com/user/HumanConcernInt
www.facebook.com/HCICanada
twitter.com/humanconcernint
To help alleviate human suffering by investing in humanity, through long-term development projects for sustainability, & emergency relief assistance during times of dire need
Kaleem Akhtar, Executive Director
Garnayl Abdi, Program Officer

The Identification Clinic
#101, 260 Wyse Rd., Dartmouth NS B3A 1N3
Tel: 902-292-4587
theidclinic@gmail.com
www.theidclinic.org
Social Media:
www.facebook.com/theidentificationclinic
twitter.com/theidclinic
To assist homeless & disadvantaged individuals in the Halifax area acquire pieces of standard identification
Darren Greer, Founder/Coordinator

Imagine Canada
#700, 65 St. Clair Ave. East, Toronto ON M4T 2Y3
Tel: 416-597-2293; *Fax:* 416-597-2294
Toll-Free: 800-263-1178
info@imaginecanada.ca
www.imaginecanada.ca
Social Media: www.youtube.com/ImagineCanada
linkedin.com/groups/Imagine-Canada-1866345
www.facebook.com/ImagineCanada
twitter.com/ImagineCanada
To support Canada's charities, non-profit organizations, & socially conscious businesses
Owen Charters, Chair
Bruce MacDonald, President & CEO
Cathy Barr, Vice-President, Mission Effectiveness
Stephen Faul, Vice-President, Strategic Communications & Business Development
Bill Harper, Vice-President, Operations
Marnie Grona, Director, Marketing & Communications

InformOntario (IO)
c/o 3010 Forest Glade Dr., Windsor ON N8R 1L5
Tel: 519-735-9344
info@informontario.on.ca
www.informontario.on.ca
To provide leadership to the organizations it represents so that they are able to best serve their members
Sylvia Mueller, President
Barbara McLachlan, Coordinator

International Social Service Canada (ISSC) / Service Social International Canada (SSIC)
#201, 1376 Bank St., Ottawa ON K1H 7Y3
Tel: 613-733-9938; *Fax:* 613-733-4868
www.issc-ssic.ca
To provide linkages to social service organizations worldwide; To help resolve individual & family problems resulting from the movement of people across national borders
Sylvie J. Lapointe, Ditector, Services

Jane Finch Community & Family Centre
#108, 440 Jane St., Toronto ON M3N 2K4
Tel: 416-663-2733; *Fax:* 416-663-3816
admin@janefinchcentre.org
www.janefinchcentre.org
Social Media:
www.facebook.com/people/Jane-Finch-Centre/1518951464
To operate with a strong commitment to social justice, community engagement, & collaboration
Michelle Dagnino, Executive Director

Jewish Family & Child (JFCS)
4600 Bathurst St., 1st Fl., Toronto ON M2R 3V3
Tel: 416-638-7800; *Fax:* 416-638-7943
info@jfandcs.com
www.jfandcs.com
Social Media: www.youtube.com/user/jewishfamilyandchild
linkedin.com/company/jewish-family-&-child
www.facebook.com/JFandCS
To support the healthy development of individuals, families & communities in the Greater Toronto Area through prevention, protection, counselling, education & advocacy services, within the context of Jewish values
Brian Prousky, Executive Director

Kids First Parent Association of Canada
8337 Shaske Cres., Edmonton AB T6R 0B4
Tel: 604-291-0088
info@kidsfirstcanada.org
www.kidsfirstcanada.org
To lobby to protect their right & choice to raise children in a family setting; to provide support to anyone wanting to further this cause in other communities
Helen Ward, President

Kids Help Phone (KHP) / Jeunesse j'écoute
#300, 439 University Ave., Toronto ON M5G 1Y8
Tel: 416-586-5437; *Toll-Free:* 800-668-6868
info@kidshelpphone.ca
kidshelpphone.ca
Social Media: www.youtube.com/user/KidsHelpPhone
linkedin.com/company/kids-help-phone
www.facebook.com/KidsHelpPhone
twitter.com/kidshelpphone
To provide a national, bilingual, 24-hours a day, 365 days of the year, toll-free, professionally staffed, confidential counselling service to young people; To help young people deal with concerns large or small; To contribute to awareness of children's issues & the development of policies & practices to help Canadian children
Sharon Wood, President & CEO

Lakeland United Way
Marina Mall, PO Box 8125, #3, 901 - 10 St., Cold Lake AB T9M 1N1
Tel: 780-826-0045; *Fax:* 780-639-2699
www.lakelandunitedway.com
Ajaz Quraishi, President

Lakeshore Area Multi-Service Project (LAMP)
185 - 5th St., Toronto ON M8V 2Z5
Tel: 416-252-6471; *Fax:* 416-252-4474
www.lampchc.org
Social Media:
www.facebook.com/LAMPCHEALTHC
To offer community health centre services in South Etobicoke, Toronto West
Russ Ford, Executive Director

Lawyers for Social Responsibility (LSR) / Avocats en faveur d'une conscience sociale (AFCS)
Calgary AB
Tel: 403-282-8260
www.peacelawyers.ca
To advise the public, politicians, & government officials on the application of the law to foreign & defence policies; To call for use of law, not use of force, to resolve conflicts
Beverley Delong, President

Lloydminster & District United Way
4419 - 52nd Ave., Lloydminster AB T9V 0Y8
Tel: 780-875-3743; *Fax:* 780-875-3793
luw@telusplanet.net
www.lloydminster.unitedway.ca

Manitoba Association of Women's Shelters (MAWS)
c/o Genesis House, PO Box 389, Winkler MB R6W 4A6
Tel: 204-325-9957
Crisis Hot-Line: 877-977-0007
maws@maws.mb.ca
www.maws.mb.ca
To eliminate violence against women; To provide support to member shelters for abused women & their children; To share information & resources with its member shelters, increase training of staff & increase services for clients.
Karen Peto, Co-Chair
Sharon Morgan, Co-Chair

Manitoba Institute of Registered Social Workers (MIRSW)
#101, 2033 Portage Ave., Winnipeg MB R3J 0K6
Tel: 204-888-9477; *Fax:* 204-831-6359
www.mirsw.mb.ca
To certify members; To act as the regulatory arm of the social work profession; To encourage ethical standards of practice to protect the public
Liz McLeod, President

Mediate BC Society
#177, 800 Hornby St., Vancouver BC V6Z 2C5
Tel: 604-684-1300; *Fax:* 604-684-1306
Toll-Free: 877-656-1300
info@mediatebc.com
www.mediatebc.com
To provide practical, accessible, & affordable dispute resolution choices
Peter C.P. Behie, President
Kari D. Boyle, Executive Director

Mediation PEI Inc.
c/o Elizabeth S. Reagh, 17 West St., Charlottetown PE C1A 3S3
Tel: 902-892-7667; *Fax:* 902-368-8629
mediationpei.com
Frank Bulger, Mediator
Viola Evans-Murley, Mediator
Elizabeth S. Reagh, Q.C., Mediator

Mediation Yukon Society
PO Box 31102, Whitehorse YT Y1A 5P7
mediationyukon@gmail.com
mediationyukon.com
To encourage alternate methods for dispute resolution
Christiane Boisjoly, Mediator

La Mine d'Or, entreprise d'insertion sociale
542, 3e Rue, Chibougamau QC G8P 1N9
Tél: 418-748-4183
dglaminedor@outlook.com
Organisme sans but lucratif, qui a pour mission l'insertion sociale & professionnelle des personnes en situation d'exclusion; offre une passerelle aux participants vers le marché du travail, la formation ou d'autres alternatives
France Bureau, Présidente

Mouvement ATD Quart Monde Canada / ATD Fourth World Movement Canada
6747, rue Drolet, Montréal QC H2S 2T1
Tél: 514-279-0468; *Téléc:* 514-279-7759
www.atdquartmonde.ca
Média social: www.facebook.com/AtdQMCanada
Développer un courant de refus de la misère en donnant la priorité aux plus pauvres, dans le respect des droits et de la dignité de la personne; contribuer à l'action du Mouvement dans le monde

Neepawa & District United Way
PO Box 1545, Neepawa MB R0J 1H0
Tel: 204-476-3410
unitedwayneepawa@mymts.net
www.neepawaunitedway.org
Local United Way Chapter raising funds to help community organization.

New Brunswick Association of Food Banks (NBAFB) / Association des banques alimentaires du Nouveau-Brunswick (ABANB)
4270, Rte. 102, Lower Kingsclear NB E3E 1L3
Tel: 506-363-4217; *Fax:* 506-473-6883
www.foodbanksnb.com
To support member agencies in their efforts to alleviate hunger; to serve as a provincial voice for same
George Piers, President
Stéphane Bourgoin, Vice-President

New Brunswick Association of Social Workers (NBASW) / Association des travailleurs sociaux du Nouveau-Brunswick
PO Box 1533, Stn. A, Fredericton NB E3B 5G2
Tel: 506-459-5595; *Fax:* 506-457-1421
Toll-Free: 877-495-5595
nbasw@nbasw-atsnb.ca
www.nbasw-atsnb.ca
To regulate the profession of social work; to protect the public; To set standards; To promote the profession
Miguel LeBlanc, Executive Director

New Brunswick Block Parent Association (NBBPAI)
#47, 100 Howe Crt., Oromocto NB E2V 2R3
Tel: 506-446-5992; *Fax:* 506-446-5992
nbbpai@nbnet.nb.ca
www.blockparent.ca
To provide immediate assistance to community members, especially children & seniors, through a safety network; To serve 35 communities & 500 homes throughout New Brunswick

Newfoundland & Labrador Association of Social Workers (NLASW) / Association des travailleurs sociaux de Terre-Neuve et Labrador
PO Box 39039, 177 Hamlyn Rd., St. John's NL A1E 5Y7
Tel: 709-753-0200; *Fax:* 709-753-0120
info@nlasw.ca
www.nlasw.ca
To ensure excellence in social work in Newfoundland & Labrador; To speak out & take appropriate action on issues of social concern; To disseminate information & provide opportunities for continuing education; To provide consultation to agencies involved in training for or delivering human services; To promote the development & the enhancement of social service delivery system suited to the needs of Newfoundlanders
Lisa Crockwell, Executive Director

Non-Smokers' Rights Association (NSRA) / Association pour les droits des non-fumeurs
#221, 720 Spadina Ave., Toronto ON M5S 2T9
Tel: 416-928-2900; *Fax:* 416-928-1860
toronto@nsra-adnf.ca
www.nsra-adnf.ca
Social Media:
twitter.com/nsra_adnf
To promote public health by stopping illness & death due to tobacco, including second-hand smoke
Lorraine Fry, Executive Director

North York Community House
Lawrence Square Mall, #226, 700 Lawrence Ave., Toronto ON M6A 3B4
Tel: 416-784-0920
www.nych.ca
Social Media: www.youtube.com/user/nychonline
www.facebook.com/nychonline
twitter.com/nychonline
To assist newcomers settle, integrate and become vibrant members of our community; to help residents improve their economic conditions; and to help build strong neighbourhoods.
Shelley Zuckerman, Executive Director

Northumberland United Way
#700, 600 William St., Cobourg ON K9A 3A5
Tel: 905-372-6955; *Fax:* 905-372-4417
Toll-Free: 800-833-0002
office@nuw.unitedway.ca
www.northumberlandunitedway.ca
Social Media: www.youtube.com/user/NlandUnitedWay
www.facebook.com/pages/Northumberland-United-Way/61851907835
twitter.com/nlanduw
To raise & allocate funds in an efficient manner & to promote the effective delivery of services in response to current & emerging social needs in Northumberland County.
Lynda Kay, CEO

Nova Scotia Association of Social Workers (NSASW) / Association des travailleurs sociaux de la Nouvelle-Écosse
#700, 1888 Brunswick St., Halifax NS B3J 3J8
Tel: 902-429-7799; *Fax:* 902-429-7650
nsasw@nsasw.org
www.nsasw.org
Social Media:
www.facebook.com/NSASW
twitter.com/NSASWNEWS
To promote & regulate the practice of social work so the members can provide a high standard of service that respects diversity, promotes social justice & enhances the worth, self-determination & potential of individuals, families & communities
Robert R. Shepherd, Executive Director

Nova Scotia Block Parent Advisory Board
Tel: 902-849-3525
byrnemg@hotmail.com
www.novascotiablockparent.com

One Parent Families Association of Canada / Association des familles uniparentales du Canada
PO Box 628, Pickering ON L1V 3T3
Tel: 905-831-7098; *Toll-Free:* 877-773-7714
oneparentfamilies@gmx.com
oneparentfamilies.net
To develop & provide a broad comprehensive program for the enlightenment & guidance of single parents & their children on the special problems they encounter & for assistance on the various readjustments involved.
Greg Mercer, President

Ontario Association for Family Mediation (OAFM)
PO Box 102, Almonte ON K0A 1A0
Tel: 416-740-6236; *Fax:* 866-352-1579
Toll-Free: 800-989-3025
www.oafm.on.ca
OAFM is a not for profit association promoting family mediation as a dispute resolution process for separating couples & for families in conflict. OAFM also promotes professionalism within the family mediation community. It is run by a volunteer Board Directors comprised of members from across Ontario, Canada.
Nancy Huntley, President

Ontario Association for Marriage & Family Therapy (OAMFT)
PO Box 693, Tottenham ON L0G 1W0
Tel: 905-936-3338; *Fax:* 905-936-9192
Toll-Free: 800-267-2638
admin@oamft.com
www.oamft.com
To serve members of the association, the profession of marriage & family therapy, & the public; To uphold the Code of Ethics of the American Association for Marriage & Family Therapy
Brenda Spitzer, President
Donna Chamberlain, Administrator

Ontario Association of Children's Aid Societies (OACAS) / Association ontarienne des sociétés de l'aide à l'enfance
#308, 75 Front St. East, Toronto ON M5E 1V9
Tel: 416-987-7725; *Fax:* 416-366-8317
Toll-Free: 800-718-7725
public_editor@oacas.org
www.oacas.org
Social Media:
linkedin.com/company/ontario-association-of-children-s-aid-societi
twitter.com/our_children
To provide leadership for the achievement of excellence in the protection of children & in the promotion of their well-being within their families & communities
Nancy MacGillivray, Executive Director

Ontario Association of Interval & Transition Houses (OAITH)
#1404, 2 Carleton St., Toronto ON M5B 1J3
Tel: 416-977-6619
info@oaith.ca
www.oaith.ca
Social Media: www.youtube.com/user/OAITH
www.facebook.com/OAITH
To work towards social change by ensuring that the voices of abused women are heard; To remove barriers to equality for women & children
Charlene Catchpole, Chair, Board of Directors
Susan H. Young, Director

Ontario Association of Social Workers (OASW) / Association des travailleuses et travailleurs sociaux de l'Ontario (ATTSO)
410 Jarvis St., Toronto ON M4Y 2G6
Tel: 416-923-4848; *Fax:* 416-923-5279
info@oasw.org
www.oasw.org
To act as the voice of social workers in Ontario
Kate Power, President

Ontario Block Parent Program Inc. (OBPPI)
902 Maitland St., London ON N5Y 2X1
Tel: 519-438-2016; *Toll-Free:* 800-563-2771
obppi@live.com
www.blockparent.on.ca
To provide immediate assistance through a safety network & to offer supportive community education programs; to provide a network of police screened, easily recognizable safe homes for members of the community, especially children, to turn to in times of distress; to educate children about the program, safety on the streets & safety within the home; to develop promotions & materials to educate the community about the program, latch key children & streetproofing; to work together with the police, educators & other community groups toward safer communities
Marg Rooke, Acting Chair

Ontario Coalition for Better Child Care (OCBCC)
#206, 489 College St., Toronto ON M6G 1A5
Tel: 416-538-0628; *Fax:* 416-538-6737
Toll-Free: 800-594-7514
info@childcareontario.org
www.childcareontario.org
Social Media:
www.facebook.com/OCBCC
twitter.com/ChildCareON
Advocates on behalf of Ontario's non-profit, licensed child care programs
Tracy Saarikoski, President
Carrol Anne Sceviour, Vice-President

Ontario Coalition of Rape Crisis Centres (OCRCC) / Coalition des centres anti-viol de l'Ontario
PO Box 6597, Stn. A, Toronto ON M5S 1A8
Tel: 416-597-1171
Crisis Hot-Line: 416-597-8808
www.ocrcc.ca
To work for prevention & eradication of sexual assault; to implement legal, social & attitudinal changes regarding sexual assault; to provide mechanism for communication, education & mobilization to alleviate political & geographical isolation of rape crisis centres in Ontario; to encourage, direct & generate research into sexual violence; to work with Canadian Association of Sexual Assault Centres (see listing) on developing national policies; to liaise with other provincial organizations addressing similar issues
Jacqueline Benn-John, President

Ontario Community Justice Association (OCJA)
Tel: 416-304-1974
Social Media:
www.facebook.com/OntarioCommunityJusticeAssociation
twitter.com/OCJA1979
To promote community justice through support to service providers; to endorse service provision that embraces inclusivity and human rights; to advocate for the presence & accessibility of community justice programs
Gemma Napoli, President
Amy Roy, Representative, Public Relations

Ontario Community Support Association (OCSA) / Association ontarienne de soutien communautaire
#104, 970 Lawrence Ave. West, Toronto ON M6A 3B6
Tel: 416-256-3010; *Fax:* 416-256-3021
Toll-Free: 800-267-6272
reception@ocsa.on.ca
www.ocsa.on.ca
Social Media:
twitter.com/OCSAtweets
To support & represent the common goals of community-based, not-for-profit health & social service organizations which assist individuals to live at home in their own community
Deborah Simon, Chief Executive Officer

Ontario Municipal Social Services Association (OMSSA) / Association des services sociaux des municipalités de l'Ontario
#2500, 1 Dundas St West, Toronto ON M5G 1Z3
Tel: 416-646-0513; *Fax:* 416-979-4627
info@omssa.com
www.omssa.com
Social Media:
linkedin.com/company/ontario-municipal-social-services-association
www.facebook.com/theOMSSA
twitter.com/theOMSSA
To promote high standards of competency within the profession to ensure quality delivery of human services in communities; To improve social policies & programs in the areas of affordable housing, homelessness prevention, children's services, & social assistance; To act as the voice for Consolidated Municipal Service Managers in Ontario
Petra Wolfbeiss, Acting Executive Director

The Ontario Trillium Foundation / La Fondation Trillium de l'Ontario
800 Bay St., 5th Fl., Toronto ON M5S 3A9
Tel: 416-963-4927; *Fax:* 416-963-8781
Toll-Free: 800-263-2887
TTY: 416-963-7905
otf@otf.ca
www.otf.ca
Social Media: www.youtube.com/user/trilliumfoundation1
www.facebook.com/213404512034051
twitter.com/ONTrillium
To work with others to make strategic investments to build healthy, sustainable & caring communities in Ontario
Andrea Cohen Barrack, CEO

Ordre professionnel des travailleurs sociaux du Québec (OPTSQ)
#520, 255, boul. Crémazie Est, Montréal QC H2M 1M2
Tél: 514-731-3925; *Téléc:* 514-731-6785
Ligne sans frais: 888-731-9420
info.general@optsq.org
www.optsq.org
Média social: www.facebook.com/OTSTCFQ
twitter.com/OTSTCFQ1
Assurer la protection du public par le contrôle de l'exercice de la profession, par la formation continue, et le développement professionnel.
Ghislaine Brosseau, Directrice générale

Parcelles de tendresse
CP 582, Chibougamau QC G8P 2Y8
Tél: 418-748-3753
Lisa Fradette Caron, Présidente

Parent Finders Ottawa
PO Box 21025, Stn. Ottawa South, Ottawa ON K1S 5N1
Tel: 613-730-8305; *Fax:* 613-730-0345
pfncr@yahoo.com
parentfindersottawa.ca
Social Media:
www.facebook.com/pages/Parent-Finders-Ottawa/120530528033309
twitter.com/ParentFinders
To assist adult adoptees/foster persons & birth relatives to obtain background information from adoption files kept in social services departments; To assist in search & reunion; To promote a feeling of openness about the adoption experience & a better

understanding about the longing for a reunion between adult adoptees & birth relatives
Patricia McCarron, President

Parent Support Services Society of BC (PSSS)
#204, 5623 Imperial St., Burnaby BC V5J 1G1
Tel: 604-669-1616; *Fax:* 604-669-1636
Toll-Free: 877-345-9777
office@parentsupportbc.ca
www.parentsupportbc.ca
Social Media: www.youtube.com/user/ParentSupportBC
www.facebook.com/ParentSupportBC
twitter.com/PSS_BC
To promote parent support circles to help parents & guardians learn positive parenting skills & receive emotional support
Carol Madsen, Executive Director

Parents-secours du Québec inc. (PSQI)
#203, 17, rue Fusey, Trois-Rivières QC G8T 2T3
Ligne sans frais: 800-588-8173
info@parentssecours.ca
www.parentssecours.ca
Média social: www.youtube.com/user/ParentsSecours
www.facebook.com/262687173759603
twitter.com/ParentsSecours
Parents-Secours du Québec inc. (PSQI) est un organisme à but non lucratif qui assure la sécurité et la protection des enfants et des aînés-es en offrant un réseau de foyers-refuges sécuritaires tout en contribuant à promouvoir la prévention par l'information et l'éducation.

People, Words & Change (PWC) / Monde des mots
Heartwood House, 153 Chapel St., Ottawa ON K1N 1H5
Tel: 613-234-2494; *Fax:* 613-234-4223
dee@pwc-ottawa.ca
www.nald.ca/pwc
To teach adults to read & write in English
Dee Sullivan, Coordinator

PFLAG Canada Inc.
265 Montreal Rd., Ottawa ON K1L 6C4
Fax: 888-959-4128
Toll-Free: 888-530-6777
inquiries@pflagcanada.ca
www.pflagcanada.ca
Social Media:
www.facebook.com/PFLAGCA
twitter.com/pflagcanada
To support individuals with questions & concerns about sexual orientation or gender identity; to make Canada a more accepting place for persons of all gender identities & sexual orientations
Stephen Hartley, President & Director
Dino Benganovic, Vice-President
Tim Mt. Pleasant, Treasurer

Plan Canada
#300, 245 Eglinton Ave. East, Toronto ON M4P 0B3
Tel: 416-920-1654; *Fax:* 416-920-9942
Toll-Free: 800-387-1418
info@plancanada.ca
plancanada.ca
Social Media: www.youtube.com/user/plancanadavideos
linkedin.com/company/plan-canada
www.facebook.com/PlanCanada
twitter.com/PlanCanada
To help children, their families, & communities in developing countries; To raise funds through sponsorship program & implement programs in health, education, & community development overseas
Rosemary McCarney, President & CEO

Porcupine United Way
PO Box 984, #312, 60 Wilson Ave., Timmins ON P4N 7H6
Tel: 705-268-9696; *Fax:* 705-268-9700
puw@ntl.sympatico.ca
porcupineunitedway.com
Social Media:
www.facebook.com/pages/Porcupine-United-Way/85026973282
To promote the organized capacity of people to care for one another
Jean Warren, Executive Director

Portage Plains United Way
PO Box 953, 224 Saskatchewan Ave. East, Portage la Prairie MB R1N 3C4
Tel: 204-857-4440; *Fax:* 204-239-1740
info@portageplainsuw.ca
www.portageplainsuw.ca
Social Media:
www.facebook.com/pages/Portage-Plains-United-Way
To unite our community to enhance the quality of life for those in need
Kathee Thurston, President

Powell River & District United Way
PO Box 370, #205, 4750 Joyce Ave., Powell River BC V8A 5C2
Tel: 604-485-2791
admin@unitedwayofpowellriver.ca
www.unitedwayofpowellriver.ca
Social Media:
www.facebook.com/322827261966
twitter.com/PRUnitedway
Ashley Hull, President

Prince Edward Island Association of Social Workers (PEIASW) / Association des travailleurs sociaux de l'Île-du-Prince-Édouard
81 Prince St., Charlottetown PE C1A 4R3
Tel: 902-368-7337; *Fax:* 902-368-7180
contact@peiasw.ca
peiasw.ca
To acknowledge & promote the work of social workers in Prince Edward Island; To advance the social work profession throughout the province, to ensure well-being for residents
Kelly MacWilliams, President

Prince George United Way
1600 - 3rd Ave., Prince George BC V2L 3G6
Tel: 250-561-1040; *Fax:* 250-562-8102
info@unitedwaynbc.ca
www.pguw.bc.ca
Social Media:
www.facebook.com/unitedwaynorthernbc
To promote the organized capacity of persons to care for one another through voluntarism, leadership & education; To ensure the effective raising & allocation of charitable funds for community-based social services; To foster the effective provision of services that are in the best interest of the community
Trevor Williams, Executive Director
Rob Jarvis, Chair

Québec Association of Marriage & Family Therapy (QAMFT) / Association québécoise pour la thérapie conjugale et familiale
#300, 360 Victoria Ave., Westmount QC H3H 2N4
info@qamft.org
www.qamft.org
To promote understanding, research & education in the field of couple & family therapy & to ensure that public needs are met by practitioners of the highest quality
Andrew Sofin, President

Ralph Thornton Centre
765 Queen St. East, Toronto ON M4M 1H3
Tel: 416-392-6810
info@ralphthornton.org
www.ralphthornton.org
Social Media: www.youtube.com/user/ralphthorntoncentre
To create a supportive environment in which the Riverdale community responds to issues and needs.
Paula Fletcher, President
John Campey, Executive Director

Reena
927 Clark Ave. West, Thornhill ON L4J 8G6
Tel: 905-889-6484; *Fax:* 905-889-3827
info@reena.org
www.reena.org
To integrate developmentally disabled people towards independent living within community, with emphasis on Judaic programming
Bryan Keshen, President & CEO
Minnie Ross, Manager, Communications

Regroupement des Auberges du Coeur
#32, 2000, boul Saint-Joseph est, Montréal QC H2H 1E4
Tél: 514-523-8559; *Téléc:* 514-523-5148
www.aubergesducoeur.com
Défendre l'existence & l'autonomie des ressources communautaires d'hébergement pour jeunes adolescents & jeunes adultes en difficulté ou sans abri; agir comme porte-parole des jeunes sans abri; favoriser entre les maisons, les jeunes & les partenaires des communautés d'appartenance de chacune des Auberges des échanges sur les besoins des jeunes
Rémi Fraser, Directeur général

Renfrew County United Way
224 Pembroke St. West, Pembroke ON K8A 5N2
Tel: 613-735-0436; *Fax:* 613-735-2663
Toll-Free: 888-592-2213
info@renfrewcountyunitedway.ca
www.renfrewcountyunitedway.ca
Social Media:
www.facebook.com/182315931870874

To identify & address the needs of our community by organizing the resources of community members to care for one another
Shelley Rolland-Porucks, Chair
Gail Logan, Executive Director

The Right to Die Society of Canada (RTDSC) / Société Canadienne pour le Droit de Mourir (SCDM)
145 Macdonell Ave., Toronto ON M6R 2A4
Tel: 416-535-0690; *Toll-Free:* 866-535-0690
info@righttodie.ca
www.righttodie.ca
To work with legislators, policy makers & the public to expand the range of humane options for people who are suffering intolerably from incurable conditions & who want a self-directed dying; to work with sufferers to expand their awareness of the options that are legal & may be appropriate for them
Ruth von Fuchs, President & Secretary

Ronald McDonald House Charities of Canada (RMHC) / Oeuvres pour enfants Ronald McDonald du Canada
1 McDonald's Place, Toronto ON M3C 3L4
Tel: 416-446-3493; *Fax:* 416-446-3588
Toll-Free: 800-387-8808
rmhc@ca.mcd.com
www.rmhc.ca
Social Media:
www.facebook.com/RMHCCanada
To help children in need by improving the physical & emotional quality of life for children with serious illnesses, disabilities &/or chronic conditions, allowing them to lead happier, healthier & more productive lives
Cathy Loblaw, President & CEO
Richard Ellis, Chair
Roxanna Kassam Kara, Manager, Communications & Marketing

Saskatchewan Association of Social Workers (SASW) / Association des travailleurs sociaux de la Saskatchewan
Edna Osborne House, 2110 Lorne St., Regina SK S4P 2M5
Tel: 306-545-1922; *Fax:* 306-545-1895
Toll-Free: 877-517-7279
sasw@accesscomm.ca
www.sasw.ca
To conduct the work of a professional regulator; To act as the voice of social workers in Saskatchewan; To develop & maintain standards of knowledge, skill, conduct, & competence among members to serve & protect the public interest
Kirk Englot, President

Scadding Court Community Centre (SCCC)
707 Dundas St. West, Toronto ON M5T 2W6
Tel: 416-392-0335; *Fax:* 416-392-0340
www.scaddingcourt.org
Social Media:
www.facebook.com/people/Scadding-Court/100001939237499
twitter.com/scadding_court
To support and foster the well being of individuals, families, and community groups by providing and encouraging both local and international opportunities for recreation, education, athletics, community participation and inclusive social interaction.
Kevin Lee, Executive Director

Secours aux lépreux (Canada) inc. (SLC) / Leprosy Relief (Canada) Inc. (LR)
#305, 1805, rue Sauvé ouest, Montréal QC H4N 3H4
Tél: 514-744-3199; *Téléc:* 514-744-9095
Ligne sans frais: 866-744-3199
info@slc-lr.ca
www.slc-lr.ca
Venir en aide médicalement et socialement aux personnes affectées par la lèpre.
Paul E. Legault, Président
Maryse Legault, Director
Marie Gilbert, Secrétaire
Christiane Beauvois, Trésorière

Sex Information & Education Council of Canada (SIECCAN) / Conseil d'information et éducation sexuelles du Canada
#400, 235 Danforth Ave., Toronto ON M4K 1N2
Tel: 416-466-5304
www.sieccan.org
To ensure that all Canadians have access to sexual health information, education, & health services; To share knowledge & information with health professionals, policymakers, & educators
Alex McKay, Executive Director

Social Planning & Research Council of BC (SPARC BC)
4445 Norfolk St., Burnaby BC V5G 0A7
Tel: 604-718-7733; *Fax:* 604-736-8697
Toll-Free: 888-718-7794
info@sparc.bc.ca
www.sparc.bc.ca
To promote the social, economic & environmental well-being of citizens & communities; to advocate the principles of social justice, equality & the dignity & worth of all people in our multicultural society; to conduct research & planning for public information, education & citizen participation in developing social policies & programs
Lorraine Copas, Executive Director
Irene Willsie, President

Social Planning Council of Ottawa (SPCO) / Conseil de planification sociale d'Ottawa
790 Bronson Ave., Ottawa ON K1S 4G4
Tel: 613-236-9300; *Fax:* 613-236-7060
office@spcottawa.on.ca
www.spcottawa.on.ca
To provide the residents of Ottawa-Carleton with the means to exercise informed leadership on issues affecting their social & economic well-being
Diane Urquhart, Executive Director

Social Planning Council of Winnipeg
#300, 207 Donald St., Winnipeg MB R3C 1M5
Tel: 204-943-2561; *Fax:* 204-942-3221
info@spcw.mb.ca
www.spcw.mb.ca
Social Media:
ca.linkedin.com/company/social-planning-council-of-winnipeg
twitter.com/spcw1919
To identify & define social planning issues, needs & resources in the community; to develop & promote policy & program options to policy-makers; to support community groups & the voluntary human service sector; to raise community awareness of social issues & human service needs, social policy options & service delivery alternatives; to serve as a link between the three levels of government & community neighbourhoods
Dennis Lewycky, Executive Director

Social Planning Toronto (SPT)
#1001, 2 Carlton St., Toronto ON M5B 1J3
Tel: 416-351-0095; *Fax:* 416-351-0107
info@socialplanningtoronto.org
www.socialplanningtoronto.org
Social Media: plus.google.com/112933900589591472077
linkedin.com/company/social-planning-toronto
www.facebook.com/pages/Social-Planning-Toronto/1391415801
35
twitter.com/planningtoronto
To promote community-based, social policy, planning & civic participation at both the local & city-wide levels through analysis & action-oriented research on social issues.
Winston Tinglin, Interim Executive Director
Maria Serrano, Director, Operations

SOS Children's Villages Canada / SOS Villages d'Enfants Canada
#240, 44 By Ward Market Square, Ottawa ON K1N 7A2
Tel: 613-232-3309; *Toll-Free:* 800-767-5111
info@soschildrensvillages.ca
www.soschildrensvillages.ca
Social Media: www.youtube.com/user/soscanada1
www.facebook.com/105288666168351
To assist SOS-Children's Villages in Canada & abroad through financial & operating support; to care for orphaned, abandoned & other children in need of long-term placement; to create opportunities for children to become happy, stable, responsible members of society
Boyd McBride, President & CEO

Springtide Resources
#220, 215 Spadina Ave., Toronto ON M5T 2C7
Tel: 416-968-3422; *Fax:* 416-968-2026
info@womanabuseprevention.com
www.springtideresources.org
Social Media:
www.facebook.com/springtide.resources
twitter.com/Springtide_VAW
To increase public awareness of the many aspects of violence against women & its effect on children; to change the social conditions that subject women to abuse by providing training & resources proactively.
Marsha Sfeir, Executive Director

Swift Current United Way
PO Box 485, #203, 12 Cheadle St. West, Swift Current SK S9H 3W3
Tel: 306-773-4828; *Fax:* 306-773-4870
unitedway@sasktel.net
swiftcurrentunitedway.ca
Social Media: www.youtube.com/user/SwiftUnitedWay
www.facebook.com/swiftunitedway
twitter.com/swiftunitedway
Darla Lindbjerg, Executive Director

Syme-Woolner Neighbourhood & Family Centre (SWNFC)
#3, 2468 Eglinton Ave. West, Toronto ON M6M 5E2
Tel: 416-766-4634; *Fax:* 416-766-8162
swoolner@symewoolner.org
www.symewoolner.org
To create in the community a sense of belonging, to enable individuals, families and groups to support each other and build a better future.
Mark Neysmith, Executive Director

Thompson Crisis Centre
PO Box 1226, Thompson MB R8N 1P1
Tel: 204-677-9668; *Fax:* 204-677-9042
Crisis Hot-Line: 800-442-0613
www.thompsoncrisiscentre.org
To provide immediate assistance through a walk-in facility & a 24-hour emergency telephone service; to provide a safe place for the women & their children who are victims of physical/emotional abuse; to provide services to women & their children needing longer term support
Sue O'Brien, Chair

Thompson, Nicola, Cariboo United Way
177 Victoria St., Kamloops BC V2C 1Z4
Tel: 250-372-9933; *Fax:* 250-372-5926
Toll-Free: 855-372-9933
office@unitedwaytnc.ca
www.unitedwaytnc.ca
Social Media: www.youtube.com/unitedwaytnc
www.facebook.com/unitedwaytnc
twitter.com/unitedwaytnc
To enable all citizens to join in a community wide effort to fund & provide in consort with others, effective delivery of health & social services & programs in response to the needs of the community
Danalee Baker, Acting Executive Director

Toronto Community Foundation (TCF)
#1603, 33 Bloor St. East, Toronto ON M4W 3H1
Tel: 416-921-2035; *Fax:* 416-921-1026
info@tcf.ca
www.tcf.ca
To connect philanthropic individuals and families to charitable organizations in Toronto. TCF invests charitable gifts from donors into income-earning endowment funds, and makes grants from the earnings to support a range of charities
John B. MacIntyre, Chair
Rosalyn Morrison, VP, Community Initiatives
Carol Turner, VP, Finance

United Generations Ontario (UGO) / Générations Unies Ontario
#604B, 1185 Eglinton Ave. East, Toronto ON M3C 3C6
Tel: 416-426-7115; *Fax:* 416-426-7388
info@intergenugo.org
To promote programs that bring young & old together in a spirit of cooperation, mutual support, shared affection & regard; to empower people to take a constructive part in the life of their own communities & to create a vital volunteer exchange in caring & sharing

United Way Central & Northern Vancouver Island
#9, 327 Prideaux St., Nanaimo BC V9R 2N4
Tel: 250-591-8731; *Fax:* 250-591-7340
info@uwcnvi.ca
www.uwcnvi.ca
Social Media: www.youtube.com/user/UnitedWayCNVI
linkedin.com/company/united-way-central-&-northern-vancouver-islan
www.facebook.com/UWCNVI
twitter.com/UWCNVI
To improve lives by engaging individuals & mobilizing collective action
Signy Madden, Executive Director

United Way Elgin-St. Thomas
#103, 10 Mondamin St., St Thomas ON N5P 2V1
Tel: 519-631-3171; *Fax:* 519-631-9253
www.stthomasunitedway.ca
Social Media:
www.facebook.com/UnitedWayElginStThomas
To be a leader in improving the quality of life for all people in Elgin County.
James Todd, President
Melissa Schneider, Campaign/Communications Coordinator

United Way for the City of Kawartha Lakes (UWVC)
50 Mary St. West, Lindsay ON K9V 2N6
Tel: 705-878-5081; *Fax:* 705-878-0475
office@ckl.unitedway.ca
www.ckl.unitedway.ca
Social Media:
www.facebook.com/UWCKL
twitter.com/unitedwayckl
To promote the organized capacity of people & groups in Victoria County to care for each other
Penny Barton Dyke, Executive Director

United Way of Brandon & District Inc.
Scotia Towers, 201-1011 Rosser Ave., Brandon MB R7A 0L5
Tel: 204-571-8929; *Fax:* 204-727-8939
office@brandonuw.ca
www.brandonuw.ca
Social Media:
www.facebook.com/UnitedWayBrandon
Cynamon Mychasiw, Interim CEO

United Way of Burlington & Greater Hamilton
177 Rebecca St., Hamilton ON L8R 1B9
Tel: 905-527-4543; *Fax:* 905-527-5152
uway@uwaybh.ca
www.uwaybh.ca
Social Media:
www.facebook.com/unitedwaybh
twitter.com/UnitedWayBH
To empower a diverse community to achieve positive social development
Len Lifchus, CEO

United Way of Calgary & Area
#600, 105 - 12 Ave SE, Calgary AB T2G 1A1
Tel: 403-231-6265; *Fax:* 403-355-3135
uway@calgaryunitedway.org
www.calgaryunitedway.org
Social Media: www.instagram.com/unitedwaycgy
linkedin.com/companies/united-way-of-calgary-and-area
www.facebook.com/calgaryunitedway
twitter.com/UnitedWayCgy
To invest in 250 programs offered by 130 agencies in Calgary, Airdrie, Cochrane, High River, Okotoks & Strathmore
Lucy Miller, President

United Way of Cambridge & North Dumfries
150 Main St., 2nd Fl., Cambridge ON N1R 6P9
Tel: 519-621-1030; *Fax:* 519-621-6220
www.uwcambridge.on.ca
Social Media:
www.facebook.com/142106829162378?ref=sgm
twitter.com/uwcambridge
To enhance the quality of life in Cambridge & North Dumfries by caring for & contributing to community needs
Ron Dowhaniuk, Executive Director

United Way of Canada - Centraide Canada
#900, 116 Albert St., Ottawa ON K1P 5G3
Tel: 613-236-7041; *Fax:* 613-236-3087
Toll-Free: 800-267-8221
info@unitedway.ca
www.unitedway.ca
Social Media: www.youtube.com/UnitedWayofCanada
ca.linkedin.com/company/united-way-centraide-canada
www.facebook.com/UnitedWayCentraide
twitter.com/UnitedWayCanada
To create opportunities for a better life for all; To inspire Canadians to make a lasting difference in their communities
Jacline A. Nyman, President/CEO

United Way of Cape Breton
245 Charlotte St., Sydney NS B1P 6W4
Tel: 902-562-5226; *Fax:* 902-562-5721
unitedway@ns.aliantzinc.ca
www.sydney.unitedway.ca
Social Media:
www.facebook.com/UnitedWayOfCapeBreton
Brenda Durrah, Executive Director

United Way of Central Alberta
4811 - 48th St., Red Deer AB T4N 1S6
Tel: 403-343-3900; *Fax:* 403-309-3820
info@caunitedway.ca
www.caunitedway.ca
To improve lives & build community by engaging individuals & mobilizing collective action
Robert J. Mitchell, Chief Executive Officer

United Way of Chatham-Kent County
PO Box 606, 425 McNaughton Ave. West, Chatham ON N7M 5K8
Tel: 519-354-0430; *Fax:* 519-354-9511
info@uwock.ca
uwock.ca
Social Media: www.youtube.com/user/UnitedWayChathamKent
www.facebook.com/UnitedWayofChathamKent
twitter.com/UnitedWayCK
To build the organized capacity of people to care for one another
Alison Patrick, President
Karen Kirkwood-Whyte, CEO

United Way of Cumberland County
PO Box 535, 43 Prince Arthur St., Lower Level, Amherst NS B4H 4A1
Tel: 902-667-2203; *Fax:* 902-667-3819
unitedway.cumberland@ns.aliantzinc.ca
amherst.unitedway.ca
Judi Giroux, Chair

United Way of Durham Region
345 Simcoe St. South, Oshawa ON L1H 4J2
Tel: 905-436-7377; *Fax:* 905-436-6414
mail@unitedwaydr.com
www.unitedwaydr.com
Social Media:
www.facebook.com/profile.php?id=100001589175198
Cindy Murray, Executive Director
Robert Howard, Campaign Director

United Way of East Kootenay
PO Box 657, 930 Baker St., Cranbrook BC V1C 4J2
Tel: 250-426-8833; *Fax:* 250-426-5455
office@cranbrook.unitedway.ca
www.cranbrook.unitedway.ca
Social Media:
www.facebook.com/ourunitedway
To ensure the effective raising & allocation of charitable funds for community based social services that are in the best interest of the community
Donna Brady Fields, Executive Director

United Way of Elrose & District Corp.
PO Box 443, Elrose SK S0L 0Z0
Tel: 306-378-2921
delhart@hotmail.com
Jack Elliott, Chair

United Way of Estevan
PO Box 611, Estevan SK S4A 2A5
Tel: 306-634-7375
www.unitedwayofestevan.com
Lori Buchanan, Executive Director

United Way of Fort McMurray
The Redpoll Centre, #200, 10010 Franklin Ave., Fort McMurray AB T9H 2K6
Tel: 780-791-0077
info@fmunitedway.com
fmunitedway.com
Social Media: www.youtube.com/user/fmunitedwaycampaign
www.facebook.com/142299649181047
twitter.com/FMUnitedWay
To provide effective support for social health & welfare services in the community of Fort McMurray
Ben Dutton, President
Diane Shannon, Executive Director
Russell Thomas, Director, Communications & Community Impact

United Way of Greater Moncton & Southeastern New Brunswick (UWGMSENB) / Centraide de la région du Grand Moncton et du Sud-Est du NB Inc. (CGMSENB)
#T210, 22 Church St., Moncton NB E1C 0P7
Tel: 506-858-8600; *Fax:* 506-858-0584
office@moncton.unitedway.ca
www.gmsenbunitedway.ca
Social Media: www.flickr.com/photos/unitedwaygmsenb
www.facebook.com/UnitedWayGMSENBCentraideGMSENB
twitter.com/unitedwaygmsenb
To raise funds to increase the organized capacity of people to care for one another
Debbie McInnis, Executive Director

United Way of Greater Saint John Inc.
#301, 28 Richmond St., Saint John NB E2L 3B2
Tel: 506-658-1212; *Fax:* 506-633-7724
contactus@unitedwaysaintjohn.com
www.unitedwaysaintjohn.com
Social Media: www.youtube.com/UnitedWaySJ
www.facebook.com/21724743048
twitter.com/SJUnitedWay
Wendy MacDermott, Executive Director

United Way of Greater Simcoe County
1110 Hwy. 26, Midhurst ON L0L 1X0
Tel: 705-726-2301; *Fax:* 705-726-4897
info@UnitedWayGSC.ca
www.unitedwaygsc.ca
Social Media: www.youtube.com/user/UnitedWaySimcoeCty
linkedin.com/pub/united-way-of-greater-simcoe-county/20/44/6a3
www.facebook.com/UnitedWayofGreaterSimcoeCounty?ref=ts&sk=wall
twitter.com/greatersimcoeco
United Way of Greater Simcoe County has been making a difference in our community for over 47 years by assessing local needs and distributing resources to help those most in need.
Alison Pickard, CEO

United Way of Guelph, Wellington & Dufferin
85 Westmount Rd., Guelph ON N1H 5J2
Tel: 519-821-0571; *Fax:* 519-821-7847
info@unitedwayguelph.com
www.unitedwayguelph.com
Social Media:
www.facebook.com/unitedwayguelph
twitter.com/uwguelph
Ken Dardano, Executive Director

United Way of Haldimand-Norfolk
45 Kent St. North, Simcoe ON N3Y 3L5
Tel: 519-426-5660; *Fax:* 519-426-0017
Toll-Free: 866-792-7394
uw@unitedwayhn.on.ca
www.unitedwayhn.on.ca
Social Media:
www.facebook.com/UnitedWayOfHaldimandAndNorfolk?ref=ts&fref=ts
twitter.com/UWayHaldimand
To improve people's lives & to strengthen the community
Evelyn Nobbs, Executive Director

United Way of Halifax Region
Royal Bank Bldg., 46 Portland St., 7th Fl.., Dartmouth NS B2Y 1H4
Tel: 902-422-1501; *Fax:* 902-423-6837
info@unitedwayhalifax.ca
www.unitedwayhalifax.ca
Social Media:
www.facebook.com/UnitedWayHalifaxRegion
twitter.com/UWHalifax
To strengthen neighbourhoods & communities by providing programs & services that link people & resources, encourage participation & increase giving
Catherine J. Woodman, President/CEO

United Way of Halton Hills
PO Box 286, Georgetown ON L7G 4Y5
Tel: 905-877-3066; *Fax:* 905-877-3067
office@unitedwayofhaltonhills.ca
www.unitedwayofhaltonhills.ca
To provide leadership in the raising & responsible allocation of funds to meet human needs & to improve social conditions in a caring community
Janet Foster, Executive Director

United Way of Kingston, Frontenac, Lennox & Addington
417 Bagot St., Kingston ON K7K 3C1
Tel: 613-542-2674; *Fax:* 613-542-1379
uway@unitedwaykfla.ca
www.unitedwaykfla.ca
Social Media: www.youtube.com/unitedwaykfla
www.facebook.com/unitedwaykfla
twitter.com/unitedwaykfla
To strengthen & support the organized capacity of our diverse community to care for one another
Bhavana Varma, President & CEO

United Way of Kitchener-Waterloo & Area
Marsland Centre, #801, 20 Erb St. West, Waterloo ON N2L 1T2
Tel: 519-888-6100; *Fax:* 519-888-7737
info@uwaykw.org
www.uwaykw.org
Social Media: www.youtube.com/user/UwayKW
www.facebook.com/uwaykw
twitter.com/UnitedWayKW
Through collaboration, build on our community's resources & strengthen our capacity to improve the quality of life for all
Daniela Seskar-Hencic, Board Chair
Jan Varner, CEO

United Way of Lanark County
15 Bates Dr., Carleton Place ON K7C 4J8
Tel: 613-253-9074; *Fax:* 888-249-9075
www.lanarkunitedway.com
Social Media: www.youtube.com/UnitedWayofCanada
linkedin.com/company/united-way-of-lanark-county
www.facebook.com/pages/United-Way-Lanark-County/124650764256245
twitter.com/UWLanarkCounty
Fraser Scantlebury, Executive Director

United Way of Leeds & Grenville
PO Box 576, 42 George St., Brockville ON K6V 5V7
Tel: 613-342-8889; *Fax:* 613-342-8850
www.uwlg.org
Social Media: www.youtube.com/user/UnitedWayLeedsGrenv
www.facebook.com/pages/United-Way-Leeds-Grenville/132810080337
Judi Baril, Executive Director

United Way of Lethbridge & South Western Alberta
1277 - 3 Ave. South, Lethbridge AB T1J 0K3
Tel: 403-327-1700; *Fax:* 403-317-7940
together@lethbridgeunitedway.ca
www.lethbridgeunitedway.ca
Social Media:
www.facebook.com/unitedwaylethy
twitter.com/unitedwaylethy
To build a better community by organizing the capacity of people to care for one another
Jeff McLarty, Executive Director

United Way of London & Middlesex
409 King St., London ON N6B 1S5
Tel: 519-438-1721; *Fax:* 519-438-9938
uwl@uwlondon.on.ca
www.uwlondon.on.ca
Social Media:
www.facebook.com/unitedwaylm
twitter.com/unitedwaylm
To exercise leadership in coordinating people & organizations to assist those in need in our community
Andrew Lockie, CEO

United Way of Milton
PO Box 212, 1 Chris Hadfield Way, Milton ON L9T 4N9
Tel: 905-875-2550; *Fax:* 905-875-2402
office@miltonunitedway.ca
www.miltonunitedway.ca
Social Media: www.youtube.com/unitedwaymilton
linkedin.com/groups?gid=2558626
www.facebook.com/pages/United-Way-of-Milton/147869698556418
twitter.com/unitedwaymilton
To act as a voluntary fundraising organization to serve the people of the Milton area, reaching out for & with the recognized charitable agencies to ensure human services that enhance the quality of life in our community
Kate Williamson, CEO

United Way of Morden & District Inc.
114 Nelson St., Morden MB R6M 1S2
Tel: 204-822-6992
mordendistrictuw@gmail.com
To serve as an umbrella group representing 17 charitable agencies in Morden & perform only one community-wide canvassing campaign on their behalf
Cindy Kolwalski, Chair

United Way of Niagara Falls & Greater Fort Erie
MacBain Community Ctr., 7150 Montrose Rd., Niagara Falls ON L2H 3N3
Tel: 905-354-9342; *Fax:* 905-354-2717
unitedw@vaxxine.com
www.unitedwayniagara.org
Social Media:
www.facebook.com/UnitedWayNFGFE
Carol Stewart-Kirkby, Executive Director

United Way of North Okanagan Columbia Shuswap
3304 - 30th Ave., Vernon BC V1T 2C8
Tel: 250-549-1346; *Fax:* 250-549-1357
Toll-Free: 866-448-3489
unitedwaynocs@shaw.ca
www.unitedwaynocs.com
Social Media:
www.facebook.com/226411234037024
twitter.com/unitedwaynocs
To promote a healthy, caring inclusive community; To strenghten our community's capacity to address social issues
Linda Yule, Executive Director

United Way of Oakville (UWO)
#200, 466 Speers Rd., Oakville ON L6K 3W9
Tel: 905-845-5571; *Fax:* 905-845-0166
info@uwoakville.org
www.uwoakville.org
Social Media: www.youtube.com/user/UnitedWayofOakville
linkedin.com/company/united-way-oakville
www.facebook.com/UnitedWayOakville
twitter.com/uwoakville
To bring people & resources together to strengthen the Oakville community
Brad Park, CEO
John Armstrong, Chair

United Way of Oxford
#5, 65 Springbank Ave. North, Woodstock ON N4S 8V8
Tel: 519-539-3851; *Fax:* 519-539-3209
Toll-Free: 877-280-1391
info@unitedwayoxford.ca
www.unitedwayoxford.ca
Social Media: www.youtube.com/watch?v=txDpzdNm0Jk
www.facebook.com/pages/United-Way-of-Oxford/36680758990
twitter.com/UnitedWayOxford
To build the organized capacity of the community to care for one another
Kelly Gilson, Executive Director

United Way of Peel Region
PO Box 58, #408, 90 Burnhamthorpe Rd. West, Mississauga ON L5B 3C3
Tel: 905-602-3650; *Fax:* 905-602-3651
TTY: 905-602-3653
www.unitedwaypeel.org
Social Media: www.youtube.com/user/unitedwaypeel
linkedin.com/company/657177
www.facebook.com/unitedwaypeel
twitter.com/Unitedwaypeel
United Way of Peel Region was established in 1967 and serves the communities of Mississauga, Brampton and Caledon, improving social conditions so that everyone can thrive. United Way provides a strong voice for social change that strengthens communities and improves lives.
Shelley White, President/ CEO
Shirley Crocker, Vice President, Finance & Administration
Carol Kotacka, Interim Vice President, Communications & Marketing
Anita Stellinga, Vice President, Community Investment

United Way of Perth-Huron
32 Erie St., Stratford ON N5A 2M4
Tel: 519-271-7730; *Fax:* 519-273-9350
Toll-Free: 877-818-8867
perthhuron@unitedway.ca
www.perthhuron.unitedway.ca
Social Media:
www.youtube.com/user/UnitedWPH?feature=watch
linkedin.com/groups?gid=3966504
www.facebook.com/UWPH1
twitter.com/UnitedWayPH
To strengthen & support the ability of the people of our community to care for one another
Ryan Erb, Executive Director
Ron Cameron, President

United Way of Peterborough & District
277 Stewart St., Peterborough ON K9J 3M8
Tel: 705-742-8839; *Fax:* 705-742-9186
office@uwpeterborough.ca
www.uwpeterborough.ca
Social Media:
www.facebook.com/15103169591
twitter.com/UnitedWayPtbo
To improve lives & build community by engaging individuals & mobilizing collective action; to provide resources, services & programs for community leadership
Jim Russell, CEO

United Way of Pictou County
PO Box 75, 342 Stewart St., New Glasgow NS B2H 5E1
Tel: 902-755-1754; *Fax:* 902-755-0853
info@pictoucountyunitedway.ca
www.pictoucountyunitedway.ca
Social Media:
www.facebook.com/UWPictouCounty
twitter.com/UWPictouCo
To strengthen communities by facilitating programs & services that link people & resources; encourage participation; increase giving
Jessica Smith, Executive Director

United Way of Prince Edward Island / Centraide PEI
180 Kent St., Charlottetown PE C1A 7K4
Tel: 902-894-8202; *Fax:* 902-894-9643
Toll-Free: 877-902-4438
inquiries@peiunitedway.com
www.peiunitedway.com
Social Media:
www.facebook.com/pages/United-Way-of-PEI/398947502165
twitter.com/uwpei
To provide funds needed to meet community needs & build stronger communities
David Hennessey, Executive Director
Kris O'Brien, President

United Way of Quinte
PO Box 815, Belleville ON K8N 5B5
Tel: 613-962-9531; *Fax:* 613-962-4165
www.unitedwayofquinte.ca
Social Media:
www.facebook.com/UnitedWayofQuinte
twitter.com/unitedwayquinte
To provide leadership in a collaborative endeavor with our member agencies & others to increase the capacity of our community to respond to human service needs
Danny Nickle, Chair
Judi Gilbert, Executive Director
Tambra Patrick-MacDonald, Director, Finance & Administration

United Way of Regina
1440 Scarth St., Regina SK S4R 2E9
Tel: 306-757-5671; *Fax:* 306-522-7199
office@unitedwayregina.ca
www.unitedwayregina.ca
Social Media:
www.facebook.com/UnitedWayRegina?ref=stream
twitter.com/unitedwayregina
To improve lives & to build the community by engaging individuals & mobilizing collective action
Joanne Grant, CEO

United Way of St Catharines & District
#3, 80 King St., Ground Fl., St Catharines ON L2R 7G1
Tel: 905-688-5050; *Fax:* 905-688-2997
office@stcatharines.unitedway.ca
www.unitedwaysc.ca
Social Media:
www.facebook.com/148938585140989
twitter.com/UWStCathDis
To increase the organized capacity of people to care for one another
Frances Hallworth, Executive Director

United Way of Sarnia-Lambton
PO Box 548, 420 East St. North, Sarnia ON N7T 6Y5
Tel: 519-336-5452; *Fax:* 519-383-6032
info@theunitedway.on.ca
www.theunitedway.on.ca
To generate resources enabling the community to respond to human care priorities in Sarnia-Lambton
Dave Brown, Executive Director

United Way of Saskatoon & Area
#100, 506 - 25 St. East, Saskatoon SK S7K 4A7
Tel: 306-975-7700; *Fax:* 306-244-0583
office@unitedwaysaskatoon.ca
www.unitedwaysaskatoon.ca
Sheri Benson, Executive Director

United Way of Sault Ste Marie & District
7A Oxford St., Sault Ste Marie ON P6B 1R7
Tel: 705-256-7476; *Fax:* 705-759-5899
uwssm@ssmunitedway.ca
www.ssmunitedway.ca
Social Media:
www.facebook.com/pages/United-Way-of-Sault-Ste-Marie/17258
1389458207
To improve lives & build community by engaging individuals & mobilizing collective action
Gary Vipond, CEO

United Way of Slave Lake Society
PO Box 1985, Slave Lake AB T0G 2A0
Tel: 780-849-7290
gdungsym@telus.net

United Way of South Eastern Alberta
928 Allowance Ave., Medicine Hat AB T1A 7G7
Tel: 403-526-5544; *Fax:* 403-526-5244
www.utdway.ca
Social Media:
www.facebook.com/UnitedWaySEAB
twitter.com/UnitedWaySEAB
Melissa Fandrick, Coordinator, Community Investment

United Way of South Georgian Bay
PO Box 284, #9, 275 First St., Collingwood ON L9Y 3Z5
Tel: 705-444-1141; *Fax:* 705-444-0981
admin@unitedwaysgb.ca
To serve the south Georgian Bay area by promoting, supporting & facilitating the organized capacity of people to help one another
Debbie Kesheshian, Executive Director

United Way of Stormont, Dundas & Glengarry / Centraide de Stormont, Dundas & Glengarry
PO Box 441, Stn. Case Postale, Cornwall ON K6H 5T2
Tel: 613-932-2051; *Fax:* 613-932-7534
info@unitedwaysdg.com
www.unitedwaysdg.com
Social Media:
www.facebook.com/209841445745076
twitter.com/unitedwaysdg
To improve lives & build our community by working together
Kimberley Lauzon-Desjardin, Program Development Director
Heather Paquette, President
Karen Turchetto, Executive Director

United Way of the Alberta Capital Region
15132 Stony Plain Rd., Edmonton AB T5P 3Y3
Tel: 780-990-1000; *Fax:* 780-990-0203
united@myunitedway.ca
myunitedway.ca
Social Media: www.youtube.com/uwacr
www.facebook.com/myUnitedWay
twitter.com/myunitedway
To bring people & resources together to build caring, vibrant communities
Mona Hale, Chair
Anne Smith, Secretary/Treasurer

United Way of the Central Okanagan & South Okanagan/Similkameen
#202, 1456 St. Paul St., Kelowna BC V1Y 2E6
Tel: 250-860-2356; *Fax:* 250-868-3206
info@unitedwaycso.com
unitedwaycso.com
Social Media: www.youtube.com/user/UnitedWayCSO
www.facebook.com/unitedwaycso
twitter.com/UnitedWayCSO
To increase the organized capacity of people in our community to care for one another
Shelley Gilmore, Executive Director

United Way of the Fraser Valley (UWFV)
Sweeney Neighbourhood Centre, #208, 33355 Bevan Ave., Abbotsford BC V2S 0E7
Tel: 604-852-1234; *Fax:* 604-852-2316
Toll-Free: 888-251-7777
info@uwfv.bc.ca
Social Media:
www.facebook.com/unitedwayfraservalley
twitter.com/unitedwayfv
To promote the organized capacity of people to care for one another
Wayne Green, Executive Director

United Way of the Lower Mainland
4543 Canada Way, Burnaby BC V5G 4T4
Tel: 604-294-8929
info@uwlm.ca
www.uwlm.ca
Social Media: www.youtube.com/user/UnitedWayVancouver
linkedin.com/groups?about=&gid=4196396
www.facebook.com/UnitedWayoftheLowerMainland
twitter.com/uwlm
Michael McKnight, President & CEO

United Way of Trail & District
803B Victoria St., Trail BC V1R 3T3
Tel: 250-364-0999; *Fax:* 250-364-1564
www.traildistrictunitedway.com
To raise funds which are allocated to 26 affiliated non-profit organizations

Jodi LeSergent, President

United Way of Windsor-Essex County
#A1, 300 Giles Blvd. East, Windsor ON N9A 4C4
Tel: 519-258-0000; *Fax:* 519-258-2346
united@weareunited.com
www.weareunited.com
Social Media:
www.facebook.com/unitedway.windsoressex
twitter.com/UnitedWayWE
To promote & strengthen the organized capacity of people to care for one another
Sheila Wisdom, Executive Director

United Way of Winnipeg / Winnipeg Centraide
580 Main St., Winnipeg MB R3B 1C7
Tel: 204-477-5360; *Fax:* 204-453-6198
info@unitedwaywinnipeg.mb.ca
www.unitedwaywinnipeg.mb.ca
Social Media: www.youtube.com/user/uwaywinnipeg
www.facebook.com/unitedwaywinnipeg
twitter.com/unitedwaywpg
To support & strengthen the organized capacity of people to care for one another
Susan Lewis, President & CEO

United Way South Niagara (UWSN) / Centraide de Niagara Sud
Seaway Mall, 800 Niagara St., 2nd Fl, Welland ON L3C 5Z4
Tel: 905-735-0490; *Fax:* 905-735-5432
office@southniagara.unitedway.ca
www.unitedwaysouthniagara.ca
Social Media: www.youtube.com/UWSouthNiagara
www.facebook.com/pages/United-Way-of-South-Niagara/227801910292
twitter.com/UnitedWaySN
Tamara Coleman-Lawrie, Executive Director

United Way Toronto & York Region
26 Wellington St. East, 12th Fl., Toronto ON M5E 1S2
Tel: 416-777-2001; *Fax:* 416-777-0962
TTY: 866-620-2993
www.unitedwaytyr.com
Social Media: instagram.com/unitedwaytyr
linkedin.com/company/unitedwaytyr
www.facebook.com/unitedwaytyr
twitter.com/unitedwaytyr
To meet urgent human needs & improve social conditions by mobilizing the community's volunteer & financial resources in a common cause of caring
Vince Timpano, Chair
Daniele Zanotti, President & CEO

United Way/Centraide (Central NB) Inc.
#1A, 385 Wilsey Rd., Fredericton NB E3B 5N6
Tel: 506-459-7773; *Fax:* 506-451-1104
office@unitedwaycentral.com
www.unitedwaycentral.com
Social Media:
www.facebook.com/148382218531358
twitter.com/JessieUnitedWay
To be a leader in helping to create & sustain a caring & healthy community
Blair McLaughlin, President
Jeff Richardson, Executive Director

United Way/Centraide Ottawa (UW/CO)
363 Coventry Rd., Ottawa ON K1K 2C5
Tel: 613-228-6700; *Fax:* 613-228-6730
info@unitedwayottawa.ca
www.unitedwayottawa.ca
Social Media: www.youtube.com/user/unitedwayottawa
linkedin.com/company/united-way-centraide-ottawa
www.facebook.com/unitedwayottawa
twitter.com/UnitedWayOttawa
To bring people & resources together to build a strong, healthy, safe community for all; to build & support a network of high priority, results-oriented community services; to offer leadership in bringing the community together; to excel in fundraising; to invest resources & charitable funds in partnership with the community; to inform & engage community stakeholders
Michael Allen, President/CEO

United Way/Centraide Sudbury & District
#E6, 105 Elm St., Sudbury ON P3C 1T3
Tel: 705-560-3330
www.unitedwaysudbury.com
Social Media:
www.facebook.com/UWSudNip
twitter.com/UWSudNip
To increase the organized capacity of people to care for one another through effective fundraising & allocation of these funds
Michael Cullen, Executive Director

Vanier Institute of The Family (VIF) / Institut Vanier de la famille
94 Centrepointe Dr., Ottawa ON K2G 6B1
Tel: 613-228-8500; *Fax:* 613-228-8007
info@vanierinstitute.ca
www.vanierinstitute.ca
Social Media:
www.facebook.com/vanierinstitute
twitter.com/vanierinstitute
To create awareness of, & to provide leadership on the importance & strengths of families in Canada, & the challenges families face in all their diverse structures; information from the institute's research, consultation & policy development is conveyed through advocacy, education & communications vehicles to elected officials, policymakers, educators, the media, the public & Canadian families themselves
Nora Spinks, Chief Executive Officer
David Northcott, Chair

Victims of Violence Canadian Centre for Missing Children (VOV)
#340, 117 Centrepointe Dr., Ottawa ON K2G 5X3
Tel: 613-233-0052; *Fax:* 613-233-2712
Toll-Free: 888-606-0000
vofv@victimsofviolence.on.ca
www.victimsofviolence.on.ca
Social Media:
www.facebook.com/205047429517768
To help crime victims regain control of their lives by reducing fear & trauma; to prevent future victimization through crime prevention information; to strengthen local efforts to assist crime victims & witnesses
Gary Rosenfeldt, Executive Director

Volunteer Canada / Bénévoles Canada
353 Dalhousie St. 3rd floor, Ottawa ON K1N 7G1
Tel: 613-231-4371; *Fax:* 613-231-6725
Toll-Free: 800-670-0401
info@volunteer.ca
www.volunteer.ca
Social Media: www.youtube.com/VolunteerCanada
www.facebook.com/VolunteerCanada
twitter.com/VolunteerCanada
To support volunteerism & civic participation through special projects & programs

Volunteer Grandparents (VIP)
#203, 2101 Holdom Ave., Burnaby BC V5B 0A4
Tel: 604-736-8271; *Fax:* 604-294-6814
info@volunteergrandparents.ca
www.volunteergrandparents.ca
To support & encourage multigenerational relationships & the concept of extended family by matching screened volunteers (50+) with families with children between the age of 3-14
Stephen Sjoberg, President

The War Amputations of Canada / Les Amputés de guerre du Canada
2827 Riverside Dr., Ottawa ON K1V 0C4
Tel: 613-731-3821; *Fax:* 613-731-3234
Toll-Free: 800-465-2677
customerservice@waramps.ca
www.waramps.ca
Social Media: www.youtube.com/warampsofcanada
www.facebook.com/TheWarAmps
twitter.com/thewaramps
To provide a wide range of assistance to all Canadian war amputees & child amputees; promotes the advancement of prosthetics & prosthetic research through grants to facilities undertaking research in field of prosthetics
David Saunders, Chief Operating Officer
Danita Chisholm, Executive Director, Communications

Warden Woods Community Centre
74 Firvalley Ct., Toronto ON M1L 1N9
Tel: 416-694-1138; *Fax:* 416-694-1161
www.wardenwoods.com
Social Media: www.flickr.com/photos/80046247@N07
www.facebook.com/pages/Warden-Woods-Community-Centre/12257770090
twitter.com/WardenWoodsCC
Warden Woods is a charitable community centre in Scarborough offering programmes to families, seniors, youth.
Ginelle Skerritt, Executive Director

Welfare Committee for the Assyrian Community in Canada
#102, 964 Albion Rd., Toronto ON M9V 1A7
Tel: 416-741-8836; *Fax:* 416-741-8836
assyrianwelfare@aol.com
To sponsor Assyrian refugees for admission into Canada; To provide support for the settlement of Assyrian refugees; To offer referrals & general information

Mizra Shmoli, Chair & Executive Director

Weyburn & District United Way
PO Box 608, Weyburn SK S4H 2K7
Tel: 306-842-7880
weyburn.unitedway@accesscomm.ca
www.weyburnunitedway.com
Social Media:
www.facebook.com/197260380295115
Gary Erickson, President

Winkler & District United Way
PO Box 1528, Winkler MB R6W 4B4
Tel: 204-829-3843
unitedway.wix.com/winkleranddistrict
Social Media:
www.facebook.com/152819198203?ref=nf

Yorkton & District United Way Inc.
180 Broadway St. West, #A, Yorkton SK S3N 0M6
Tel: 306-621-8948
bpohorelic@sasktel.net
To unite & facilitate community fundraising on behalf of our membership of local, charitable organizations
Brian Pohorelic, Chair
Lisa Washington, Secretary

Sports

For Sports organizations, please see the Sports section on page 1993.

Standards & Testing

Canadian Accredited Independent Schools (CAIS)
PO Box 3013, 2 Ridley Rd., St Catharines ON L2R 7C3
Tel: 905-684-5658; *Fax:* 905-684-5057
www.cais.ca
To develop & promote educational standards & to foster compliance with those standards related to independent elementary & secondary school education.
Anne-Marie Kee, Executive Director

Canadian Accredited Independent Schools Advancement Professionals (CAISAP)
communications@caisap.ca
www.caisap.ca
Social Media:
linkedin.com/groups?gid=2071818
www.facebook.com/CAISap.ca
twitter.com/CAISap
The Canadian Accredited Independent Schools Advancement Professionals is an association of development and advancement directors and officers.
Laura Edwards, President

Canadian Evaluation Society (CES) / Société canadienne d'évaluation
#3, 247 Barr St., Renfrew ON K7V 1J6
Fax: 613-432-6840
Toll-Free: 855-251-5721
secretariat@evaluationcanada.ca
www.evaluationcanada.ca
Social Media:
linkedin.com/groups/8172963
facebook.com/ces.sce
twitter.com/CES_SCE
To advance evaluation for its members & the public; To establish & maintain CES as the recognized national organization which represents the evaluation community; To provide a forum for the advancement of theory & practice of evaluation; To develop competencies, ethics, & standards to improve the practice of evaluation; To advocate for high-quality evaluation with practitioners, local chapters, nationally & internationally; To promote the use of evaluation in society
Harry Cummings, President
Rebecca Mellett, Executive Director

Canadian General Standards Board (CGSB) / Office des normes générales du Canada (ONGC)
Place Du Portage III, #6B1, 11 Laurier St., Gatineau QC K1A 1G6
Tel: 819-956-0425; *Fax:* 819-956-1634
Toll-Free: 800-665-2472
ncr.cgsb-ongc@tpsgc-pwgsc.gc.ca
www.tpsgc-pwgsc.gc.ca/ongc-cgsb
To develop standards, through accreditation with the Standards Council of Canada; To offer conformity assessment services, including product certification & registration of quality & environmental management systems, conforming to ISO standards

Begonia Lojk, Acting Director

Canadian Institute for NDE
135 Fennell Ave. West, Hamilton ON L8N 3T2
Tel: 905-387-1655; *Fax:* 905-574-6080
Toll-Free: 800-964-9488
info@cinde.ca
www.cinde.ca
Social Media:
www.facebook.com/297023083473
To advance scientific, engineering, technical knowledge in the field of nondestructive testing; to gather & disseminate information relating to nondestructive testing useful to individuals & beneficial to the general public; to promote nondestructive testing through courses of instruction, lectures, meetings, publications, conferences, etc.
Larry Cote, President & CEO

Steel & Metal Industries

Aluminium Association of Canada (AAC) / Association de l'aluminium du Canada
#1600, 1010, rue Sherbrooke ouest, Montréal QC H3A 2R7
Tél: 514-288-4842; *Téléc:* 514-288-0944
www.thealuminiumdialog.com
Mèdia social: twitter.com/AAC_aluminium
To be a representative for the Canadian aluminium industry & to enhance its presence in industrial sectors, especially road & mass transit infrastructure & the automotive industry.
Jean Simard, President & General Manager

Canadian Die Casters Association (CDCA) / Association canadienne des mouleurs sous pression
#3, 247 Barr St., Renfrew ON K7V 1J6
Fax: 613-432-6840
Toll-Free: 866-809-7032
info@diecasters.ca
www.diecasters.ca
To assist die casters in dealing with governments & other organizations on industry issues; To provide a united voice for members
Bonnie James, Executive Director

Canadian Foundry Association (CFA) / Association des fonderies canadiennes (AFC)
#1500, 1 Nicholas St., Ottawa ON K1N 7B7
Tel: 613-789-4894; *Fax:* 613-789-5957
www.foundryassociation.ca
To assist & represent the membership in dealing with government on industry specific issues; To communicate information to the industry, which will assist its members in strengthening their own competitive position & ensuring a strong Canadian foundry industry
Judith Arbour, Executive Director
William Monaghan, Secretary-Treasurer

Canadian Institute of Steel Construction (CISC) / Institut canadien de la construction en acier (ICCA)
#200, 3760 - 14th Ave., Markham ON L3R 3T7
Tel: 905-946-0864; *Fax:* 905-946-8574
info@cisc-icca.ca
www.cisc-icca.ca
Social Media:
linkedin.com/company/986081
www.facebook.com/cisc.icca.ca
twitter.com/cisc_icca
To promote good design & safety, together with efficient & economical use of steel as a means of expanding the construction markets for structural steel, joists & platework
Jim McLagan, Chair
Ed Whalen, President

Canadian Sheet Steel Building Institute (CSSBI) / Institut canadien de la tôle d'acier pour le bâtiment (ICTAB)
#2A, 652 Bishop St. North, Cambridge ON N3H 4V6
Tel: 519-650-1285; *Fax:* 519-650-8081
info@cssbi.ca
www.cssbi.ca
Social Media:
linkedin.com/groups/Canadian-Sheet-Steel-Building-Institute-388674
www.facebook.com/197469816960835
twitter.com/cssbi
To make steel the material of choice for building construction in Canada.
Meredith Perez, Manager, Marketing

Canadian Steel Construction Council (CSCC) / Conseil canadien de la construction en acier
#300, 201 Consumers Rd., Toronto ON M2J 4G8
Tel: 416-491-9898; *Fax:* 416-491-6461
To represent the manufacturers of steel products, including: open-web steel joists, steel platework, corrugated steel pipe, sheet steel, & steel fasteners; to promote the use of steel in construction through research & engineering

Canadian Steel Producers Association (CSPA) / Association canadienne des producteurs d'acier (ACPA)
#906, 350 Sparks St., Ottawa ON K1R 7S8
Tel: 613-238-6049; *Fax:* 613-238-1832
info@canadiansteel.ca
www.canadiansteel.ca
Social Media:
www.facebook.com/220022834730294
twitter.com/CSPA_ACPA
To represent the steel producers that melt & pour steel in Canada
Ron Watkins, President

Canadian Steel Trade & Employment Congress
#800, 234 Eglinton Ave. East, Toronto ON M4P 1K7
Tel: 416-480-1797; *Fax:* 416-480-2986
general@cstec.ca
www.cstec.ca
Social Media: www.vimeo.com/user8234365
linkedin.com/company/canadian-steel-trade-and-employment-congress
twitter.com/SteelSkills
To provide a forum for communication among steel companies, steelworkers, & governments to work for the betterment of the industry & its workforce
Ken Delaney, Executive Director

Corrugated Steel Pipe Institute (CSPI) / Institut pour tuyaux de tôle ondulée
#2A, 652 Bishop St. North, Cambridge ON N3H 4V6
Tel: 519-650-8080; *Fax:* 519-650-8081
info@cspi.ca
www.cspi.ca
To promote & encourage general & wider use of corrugated steel pipe for drainage & other uses across Canada; to initiate & support research, marketing, promotion, public relations & advertising programs designed to broaden the markets for CSP products; to cooperate with public & private agencies engaged in the formulation of specifications & designs for drainage & other underground structures; to provide the industry & the public with documented experience & up-to-date technical information on CSP products & their proper use & application; to enhance, through responsible public relations practices, the reputation & image of the Canadian CSP industry; to cooperate with allied industry & government authorities; to encourage & participate in educational endeavours in colleges & universities.
David J. Penny, Marketing Manager

Nickel Institute
Brookfield Place, #2700, 161 Bay St., Toronto ON M5J 2S1
Tel: 416-591-7999; *Fax:* 416-572-2201
www.nickelinstitute.org
Social Media:
linkedin.com/company/nickel-institute-brussels
twitter.com/NickelInstitute
To provide information for nickel users, designers, specifiers, educators & others interested in nickel-containing materials & their applications
David Butler, President
Hudson Bates, Executive Director

Ontario Sheet Metal Contractors Association (OSM)
#26, 30 Wertheim Ct., Richmond Hill ON L4B 1B9
Tel: 905-886-9627; *Fax:* 905-886-9959
shtmetal@bellnet.ca
www.osmca.org
To negotiate & administer all provincial collective agreements between OSM, the Ontario Sheet Metal Workers' & Roofers' Conference & the Sheet Metal Workers International Association.
Kim Crossman, President
Wayne Peterson, Executive Director

Reinforcing Steel Institute of Ontario (RSIO)
PO Box 30104, RPO New Westminster, Thornhill ON L4J 0C6
Tel: 416-239-7746; *Fax:* 416-239-7745
rsio@rebar.org
www.rebar.org
To promote reinforced concrete as a building material

Surveying & Mapping

Alberta Land Surveyors' Association (ALSA)
#1000, 10020 - 101A Ave., Edmonton AB T5J 3G2
Tel: 780-429-8805; *Fax:* 888-459-1664
Toll-Free: 800-665-2572
info@alsa.ab.ca
www.alsa.ab.ca
To regulate the practice of land surveying.
Brian Munday, Executive Director
David McWilliam, Registrar
Robert Scott, President
Bruce Clark, Secretary-Treasurer

Association of British Columbia Land Surveyors (ABCLS)
#301, 2400 Bevan Ave., Sidney BC V8L 1W1
Tel: 250-655-7222; *Fax:* 250-655-7223
Toll-Free: 800-332-1193
office@abcls.ca
www.abcls.ca
To protect the public interest & the integrity of the survey system in British Columbia by regulating & governing the practice of land surveying in the province.
R. Chad Rintoul, Chief Administrative Officer
Ian Lloyd, President
Chuck Salmon, Secretary & Treasurer

Association of Canada Lands Surveyors / Association des arpenteurs des terres du Canada
100E, 900 Dynes Rd., Ottawa ON K2C 3L6
Tel: 613-723-9200; *Fax:* 613-723-5558
www.acls-aatc.ca
To establish & maintain standards of qualification for Canada Lands Surveyors; to regulate Canada Lands Surveyors; To establish & maintain standards of conduct, knowledge & skill among members of the Association & permit holders; to govern the activities of members of the Association & permit holders; To cooperate with other organizations for the advancement of surveying; To perform the duties & exercise the powers that are imposed or conferred on the Association by the Act
Jean-Claude Tétreault, Executive Director

Association of Manitoba Land Surveyors
#202, 83 Gary St., Winnipeg MB R3C 4J9
Tel: 204-943-6972; *Fax:* 204-957-7602
www.amls.ca
To license qualified persons becoming commissioned land surveyors; To protect public interests concerning land boundary matters
Lori McKietiuk, Executive Director

Association of New Brunswick Land Surveyors (ANBLS) / Association des arpenteurs-géomètres du Nouveau-Brunswick (AA-GN-B)
#312, 212, Queen St., Fredericton NB E3B 1A8
Tel: 506-458-8266; *Fax:* 506-458-8267
anbls@nb.aibn.com
www.anbls.nb.ca
To regulate & govern the practice of land surveying in New Brunswick; To develop & maintain standards of knowledge, skill, & professional ethics
Doug Morgan, Executive Director

Association of Newfoundland Land Surveyors
#203, 62-64 Pippy Pl., St. John's NL A1B 4H7
Tel: 709-722-2031; *Fax:* 709-722-4104
www.surveyors.nf.ca
To establish & maintain standards of knowledge, skill, & professional conduct in the practice of land surveying, in order to serve & protect the public interest in Newfoundland; to regulate & govern the practice of land surveying in the province
Robert Way, President
Paula Baggs, Executive Director

Association of Nova Scotia Land Surveyors (ANSLS)
325A Prince Albert Rd., Dartmouth NS B2Y 1N5
Tel: 902-469-7962; *Fax:* 902-469-7963
ansls@accesswave.ca
www.ansls.ca
To establish & maintain standards of professional ethics among its members, student members & holders of a certificate of authorization, in order that the public interest may be served & protected; & knowledge & skills among its members, student members & holders of a certificate of authorization; to regulate the practice of professional land surveying & govern the profession in accordance with the Act, the regulations & the by-laws; & to communicate & cooperate with other professional organizations for the advancement of the best interests of the surveying profession
Fred Hutchinson, Executive Director

Association of Ontario Land Economists
#205, 555 St. Clair Ave. West, Toronto ON M4V 2Y7
Tel: 416-283-0440; *Fax:* 866-401-3665
admin@aole.org
www.aole.org
To continue attracting membership-quality professionals engaged in land economics pursuits; To broaden & enrich the professional development of members; To promote & maintain high ethical work standards throughout our membership; To make submissions to government for improvements in law & public administration bearing on land economics
Andrea Calla, President
John Blackburn, Vice-President & Secretary
Naomi Irizawa, Treasurer

Association of Ontario Land Surveyors (AOLS)
1043 McNicoll Ave., Toronto ON M1W 3W6
Tel: 416-491-9020; *Fax:* 416-491-2576
Toll-Free: 800-268-0718
info@aols.org
www.aols.org
Social Media: www.youtube.com/user/AOLSTUBE
linkedin.com/groups/Association-Ontario-Land-Surveyors-AOLS-408320
www.facebook.com/288456831275733
twitter.com/_AOLS
To be responsible for the licensing and governance of professional land surveyors, in accordance with the Surveyors Act.
Blain W. Martin, Executive Director
William D. Buck, Registrar

Association of Prince Edward Island Land Surveyors (APEILS)
PO Box 20100, Charlottetown PE C1A 9E3
Tel: 902-394-3121
info@apeils.ca
www.apeils.ca
To regulate the practice of land surveying in PEI
Serge Bernard, Secretary-Treasurer
John Mantha, President

Canadian Cartographic Association (CCA) / Association canadienne de cartographie
c/o Paul Heersink, 39 Wales Ave., Markham ON L3P 2C4
Fax: 416-446-1639
treasurer@cca-acc.org
www.cca-acc.org
To promote interest in cartographic materials; To encourage research in the field of cartography; To advance education in cartography
Elise Pietroniro, Secretary
Paul Heersink, Treasurer

Canadian Geophysical Union (CGU) / Union géophysique canadienne (UGC)
c/o Dept. of Geology & Geophysics, University of Calgary, ES #278, 2500 University Dr. NW, Calgary AB T2N 1N4
Tel: 403-220-5596; *Fax:* 403-284-0074
cgu@ucalgary.ca
www.cgu-ugc.ca
Social Media:
www.facebook.com/pages/CGU/442350399250129
twitter.com/CGU_UGC
To bring together & promote the geophysical sciences; To provide a focus for geophysicists at Canadian universities, government agencies, & industry in fields of study encompassing the composition & processes of the whole earth, including hydrology, space studies, & geology
Brian Branfireun, President
Richard Petrone, Treasurer
Maria Strack, Secretary

Canadian Institute of Quantity Surveyors (CIQS)
#19, 90 Nolan Ct., Markham ON L3R 4L9
Tel: 905-477-0008; *Fax:* 905-477-6774
admin@ciqs.org
www.ciqs.org
Social Media:
linkedin.com/groups/Canadian-Institute-Quantity-Surveyors-4837923
www.facebook.com/112909992224092
twitter.com/CIQS_Official
To represent the quantity surveying & construction estimating profession in Canada
Lois Metcalfe, Executive Director
Mark Gardin, Chair

Geomatics Industry Association of Canada (GIAC) / Association canadienne des entreprises de géomatique
1460 Merivale Rd., Ottawa ON K2E 1B1
Tel: 613-851-1256
To strengthen business climate; to maintain cooperative relations with government; to promote expanded role for members in provision of geomatics products & services; to encourage adoption by governments of improved policies & practices for procurement of geomatics products & services; to promote member firms as source of high quality, professional services; to promote Canadian geomatics industry abroad.

Ordre des arpenteurs-géomètres du Québec (OAGQ) / Québec Land Surveyors Association
Iberville Quatre, #350, 2954 boul Laurier, Québec QC G1V 4T2
Tél: 418-656-0730; *Téléc:* 418-656-6352
Ligne sans frais: 800-243-6490
oagq@oagq.qc.ca
www.oagq.qc.ca
La protection du public et le contrôle de la profession
Pierre Tessier, Président

Professional Surveyors Canada / Géomètres professionnels du Canada
#101B, 900 Dynes Rd., Ottawa ON K2C 3L6
Tel: 613-695-8333; *Toll-Free:* 800-241-7200
www.psc-gpc.ca
To foster cooperation amongst surveyors in Canada; To advocate for an integrated Canadian surveying profession
Sarah Cornett, BSc, OLS, Executive Director

Saskatchewan Land Surveyors' Association (SLSA)
#230, 408 Broad St., Regina SK S4R 1X3
Tel: 306-352-8999; *Fax:* 306-352-8366
info@slsa.sk.ca
www.slsa.sk.ca
To uphold the stewardship & standards of the legal survey profession in Saskatchewan; To regulate & govern members in the practice of professional land surveying & professional surveying; To ensure the competency of members; To administer the profession to protect the public
Mike Waschuk, President
Carla Stadnick, Executive Director

Taxation

Canadian Property Tax Association, Inc. (CPTA) / Association canadienne de taxe foncière, inc.
#816, 5863 Leslie St., Toronto ON M2H 1J8
Tel: 416-493-3276; *Fax:* 416-493-3276
cpta@on.aibn.com
www.cpta.org
To facilitate the exchange of information about industrial & commercial property tax issues throughout Canada
Monica Keller
Viviane Marcotte, Managing Director, National Office

Canadian Tax Foundation (CTF) / Foundation canadienne de fiscalité (FCF)
#1200, 595 Bay St., Toronto ON M5G 2N5
Tel: 416-599-0283; *Fax:* 416-599-9283
Toll-Free: 877-733-0283
www.ctf.ca
Social Media:
linkedin.com/groups?home=&gid=4000744
twitter.com/cdntaxfdn
To create a greater understanding of the Canadian tax system; To improve the Canadian tax system
Penny Woolford, Chair
Gabrielle Richards, Vice-Chair
Debbie Selley, CGA, Treasurer
Larry Chapman, FCPA, FCA, Executive Director & CEO
Judy Singh, Librarian

Canadian Taxpayers Federation (CTF)
#265, 438 Victoria Ave. East, Regina SK S4N 0N7
Tel: 306-352-7199; *Fax:* 306-205-8339
admin@taxpayer.com
taxpayer.com
Social Media: www.youtube.com/taxpayerdotcom
www.facebook.com/TaxpayerDOTcom
twitter.com/taxpayerdotcom
To advocate for the common interest of taxpayers; To effect public policy change
Michael Binnion, Chair
Troy Lanigan, President & CEO
Shannon Morrison, Vice-President, Operations
Scott Hennig, Vice-President, Communications
Gregory Thomas, Director, Federal
Melanie Harvie, Manager, Finance

Canadian Taxpayers Federation - Alberta (CTF)
PO Box 84171, Stn. Market Mall, 3625 Shaganappi Trail, Calgary AB T3A 5C4
Toll-Free: 800-661-0187
www.taxpayer.com
Social Media:
twitter.com/DFildebrandt
To advocate on behalf of taxpayers across Alberta
Derek Fildebrandt, Director, Alberta

Canadian Taxpayers Federation - Altlantic Canada (CTF)
PO Box 34077, Stn. Scotia Square, 5201 Duke St., Halifax NS B3J 1N0
Tel: 902-407-5757
www.taxpayer.com
To advocate on behalf of taxpayers across Atlantic Canada
Kevin Lacey, Director

Canadian Taxpayers Federation - British Columbia (CTF)
PO Box 20539, Stn. Howe St., Vancouver BC V6Z 2N8
Tel: 604-999-3319
www.taxpayer.com
Social Media:
twitter.com/jordanbateman
To advocate lower taxes, less waste & accountable government
Jordan Bateman, Director, British Columbia

Canadian Taxpayers Federation - Ontario (CTF)
#283, 100 - 2 Toronto St., Toronto ON M5C 2B5
Toll-Free: 800-667-7933
www.taxpayer.com
Social Media:
twitter.com/CandiceMalcolm
To engage in advocacy activities specific to Ontario
Candice Malcolm, Director, Ontario

Canadian Taxpayers Federation - Saskatchewan & Manitoba (CTF)
PO Box 42123, 1881 Portage Ave., Winnipeg MB R3J 3X7
Tel: 204-982-2150; *Fax:* 204-982-2154
Toll-Free: 800-772-9955
www.taxpayer.com
Social Media:
twitter.com/colincraig1
To advocate on behalf of taxpayers in the prairie provinces
Colin Craig, Director, Prairies

Ontario Municipal Tax & Revenue Association (OMTRA)
#119, 14845 - 6 Yonge St., Aurora ON L4G 6H8
webmaster@omtra.ca
www.omtra.ca
Social Media:
www.facebook.com/278364522173943
twitter.com/omtra1
To bring those persons in the municipal field of tax collecting into helpful association with each other; To promote improved standards of ethics & efficiency in tax collection methods & procedures: To consider, resolve, & recommend amendments to Provincial Acts which may improve the tax billing & collection administration; To encourage submissions & disseminate information of interest to its members; To encourage & assist in the development of educational training programs for collection personnel; To cooperate with other municipal associations; To foster good public relations
Connie Mesih, President

Technology

Association professionnelle des techniciennes et techniciens en documentation du Québec (APTDQ)
594, rue des Érables, Neuville QC G0A 2R0
Tél: 418-909-0608; *Téléc:* 418-909-0608
info@aptdq.org
www.aptdq.org
Média social: www.facebook.com/aptdq
twitter.com/aptdq
Regrouper les techniciens en documentation; promouvoir auprès des employeurs le caractère professionnel de ce travail; défendre les intérêts de ses membres auprès des employeurs et de l'État; fournir des services de toute nature en relation avec les buts de l'association; favoriser le développement de la profession; développer les échanges entre professionnels
Christian Fortin, Président

Canadian Printable Electronics Industry Association (CPEIA)
170 Cheyenne Way, Ottawa ON K2J 5S6
Tel: 613-795-8181
cpeia-acei.ca
Social Media: linkedin.com/company/canadian-printable-electronics-industry-assoc
twitter.com/CPEIA_ACEI
The Canadian Printable Electronics Industry Association (CPEIA) connects key Canadian and international players in industry, academia and government to build a strong Canadian PE sector.
Peter Kallai, Executive Director
Leo Valiquette, Director, Marketing and Communications

Telecommunications

Bell Aliant Pioneers
PO Box 1430, Saint John NB E2L 4K2
Toll-Free: 800-565-1436
www.bellaliantpioneers.com
To act as the largest corporate-based volunteer organization in Atlantic Canada
Chantal MacDonald, President

Canadian Call Management Association (CAM-X)
#10, 24 Olive St., Grimsby ON L3M 2B6
Tel: 905-309-0224; *Fax:* 905-309-0225
Toll-Free: 800-896-1054
info@camx.ca
www.camx.ca
Social Media: linkedin.com/groups/CAM-X-Canadian-Association-Message-Exchange-40
www.facebook.com/pages/CAM-X/118064931573806
twitter.com/CAM-XAssociation
To promote the welfare of the message-handling industry & related services through the encouragement & maintenance of high standards of ethics & services; the exchange of information & the rendering of mutual aid & assistance between member organizations.
Linda Osip, Executive Director

Canadian Independent Telephone Association (CITA) / Association canadienne du téléphone indépendant
c/o Creative Events Management, #205, 1402 Queen St. West, Alton ON L7K 0C3
Tel: 519-940-0935; *Fax:* 519-940-1137
www.cita.ca
To promote the increase & improvement of telephone service in Canada; to promote & protect the common business interest of members; to produce & distribute literature; to represent the industry before regulatory bodies, either federal or provincial.
Margi Taylor, General Manager

Canadian Internet Registration Authority (CIRA)
#306, 350 Sparks St., Ottawa ON K1R 7S8
Tel: 613-237-5335; *Fax:* 800-285-0517
www.cira.ca
Social Media: www.youtube.com/ciranews
linkedin.com/groups?gid=2456714
www.facebook.com/cira.ca
twitter.com/ciranews
To operate the dot-ca internet country code.
Byron Holland, President & CEO

Canadian Wireless Telecommunications Association (CWTA) / Association canadienne des télécommunications sans fil (ACTS)
#300, 80 Elgin St., Ottawa ON K1P 6R2
Tel: 613-233-4888; *Fax:* 613-233-2032
info@cwta.ca
www.cwta.ca
Social Media: twitter.com/CWTAwireless
The authority on wireless issues, trends & developments in Canada; represents cellular, PCS, messaging, mobile radio, fixed wireless & mobile satellite service providers as well as companies that develop & produce products & services for the industry.
Bernard Lord, President & Chief Executive Officer
Patrick Jim, Senior Vice-President
Geiger J. Michael, Manager, IT

Frequency Co-ordination System Association (FCSA) / Association pour la coordination des fréquences
#700, 1 Nicholas St., Ottawa ON K1N 7B7
Tel: 613-241-3080; *Fax:* 613-241-9632
www.fcsa.ca
To operate & administer computerized Microwave Information & Coordination System (MICS); to provide cost-effective, timely & high quality centralized administrative & technical services to allow members to be able to effectively plan & coordinate frequencies for microwave communication systems on national basis.
Alejandro Moreno, General Manager/Secretary-Treasurer

Halifax Regional CAP Association (HRC@P)
Halifax NS
Tel: 902-293-8122
admin@halifaxcap.ca
www.halifaxcap.ca
Social Media: www.facebook.com/HRCAP
twitter.com/hrcap
To deliver quality service to communities through their locally operated Community Access Program (CAP) sites.
Paul Hudson, Chair

Information & Communication Technologies Association of Manitoba (ICTAM)
#412, 435 Ellice Ave., Winnipeg MB R3B 1Y6
Tel: 204-943-7133; *Fax:* 204-957-5628
www.ictam.ca
Social Media: linkedin.com/company/information-&-communication-technologies-asso
www.facebook.com/ICTAMMB
twitter.com/ICTAM
To provide programming, advocacy & collaboration to the information & communication technologies industry in Manitoba, in order to accelerate growth, prosperity & sustainability
Charles Loewen, President
Kathy Knight, CEO

Ontario Pioneers
21 Meadowland Dr., Brampton ON L6W 2R5
Tel: 905-451-5607; *Fax:* 905-453-3996
Sheila O'Donoghue, Manager

SaskTel Pioneers
21016 - 1st Ave., Regina SK S4P 3Y2
Tel: 306-777-2515; *Fax:* 306-777-2831
Toll-Free: 866-944-4442
sasktel.pioneers@sasktel.sk.ca
www.sasktelpioneers.com
Social Media: twitter.com/sasktelpioneers
Darrell Liebrecht, Director

Telecommunities Canada Inc.
c/o President, #318, 210-1600 Kenaston Blvd., Winnipeg MB R3P 0Y4
www.tc.ca
To ensure that all Canadians are able to participate in community-based communications & electronic information services by promoting and supporting local community network initiatives; to represent & promote Canadian community networking movement at the national & international level
Clarice Leader, President

TelecomPioneers of Alberta
18 Primrose Place North, Lethbridge AB T1H 4K1
Tel: 403-329-3462
Stan Mills, Manager

TelecomPioneers of Canada
PO Box 880, Halifax NS B3J 2W3
Fax: 902-484-5189
Toll-Free: 888-994-3232
www.telecompioneers.ca
The TelecomPioneers of Canada is a network of current and former telecom industry employees, their partners and their families and are commited to improving the quality of life in Canada's communities.
J. Michael Sears, President

Television

Alliance québécoise des techniciens de l'image et du son (AQTIS)
#300, 533, rue Ontario est, Montréal QC H2L 1N8
Tel: 514-844-2113; *Fax:* 514-844-3540
Toll-Free: 888-647-0681
info@aqtis.qc.ca
www.aqtis.qc.ca
Bernard Arseneau, Président
Jean-Claude Rocheleau, Directeur général

Independent Production Fund (IPF) / Fonds indépendant de production
#1709, 2 Carlton St., Toronto ON M5B 1J3
Tel: 416-977-8966; *Fax:* 416-977-0694
info@ipf.ca
ipf.ca
To support the production of Canadian dramatic television series by independent producers through financial investment.
Charles Ohayon, Chair
Andra Sheffer, Executive Director
Carly McGowan, Program Manager

Shaw Rocket Fund
#210, 2421 - 37th Ave., Calgary AB T2E 6Y7
www.rocketfund.ca
Social Media: www.facebook.com/rocketfund
twitter.com/RocketFund
To provide funding for children's programming
Annabel Slaight, Chair
Agnes Augustin, President & Treasurer

Tenants & Landlords

Action Dignité de Saint-Léonard
9089A, boul Viau, Saint-Léonard QC H1R 2V6
Tél: 514-251-2874
Groupe de défense des droits des locataires

Association des locataires de l'Ile-des-Soeurs (ALIS/NITA) / Nuns' Island Tenants Association
CP 63008, 40, Place du Commerce, Verdun QC H3E 1V6
Tél: 514-767-1003
Défense des droits des locataires

Comité d'action des citoyennes et citoyens de Verdun
3972, rue de Verdun, Verdun QC H4G 1K9
Tél: 514-769-2228; *Téléc:* 514-769-0825
www.cacv-verdun.org
Le CACV soutien les personnes les plus démunies afin qu'elles améliorent leurs conditions de vie dans une optique de prise en charge
Chantal Lamarre, Directrice

Comité d'action Parc Extension (CAPE)
#03, 419, St-Roch, Montréal QC H3N 1K2
Tél: 514-278-6028; *Téléc:* 514-278-0900
A pour mission d'améliorer les conditions de vie de tous les citoyens/citoyennes du quartier Parc Extension
Denis Giraldeau, Coordonnateur

Comité des citoyens et citoyennes du quartier Saint-Sauveur
301, rue Carillon, Québec QC G1K 5B3
Tél: 418-529-6158; *Téléc:* 418-529-9455
cccqss@bellnet.ca
www.cccqss.org
Média social: www.facebook.com/CCCQSS

Comité logement de Lacine-Lasalle
426, rue St-Jacques Ouest, Lachine QC H8R 1E8
Tél: 514-544-4294; *Téléc:* 514-366-0505
logement.lachine-lasalle@videotron.ca
Daniel Chainey, Responsable

Comité logement du Plateau Mont-Royal
#328, 4450, rue St-Hubert, Montréal QC H2J 2W9
Tél: 514-527-3495; *Téléc:* 514-527-6653
clplateau@yahoo.ca
sites.google.com/site/comitelogementplateau

Comité logement Rosemont
#R-145, 5350, rue Lafond, Montréal QC H1X 2X2
Tél: 514-597-2581; *Téléc:* 514-524-9813
info@comitelogement.org
www.comitelogement.org
Média social: www.facebook.com/comitelogement
Défendre et promouvoir les droits des locataires du quartier Rosemont

Martine Poitras, Coordonnatrice

Conseil communautaire Notre-Dame-de-Grâce / Notre-Dame-de-Grâce Community Council
#204, 5964, av Notre-Dame-de-Grâce, Montréal QC H4A 1N1
Tél: 514-484-1471
ndgcc@ndg.ca
www.ndg.ca
Halah Al-Ubaidi, Directrice générale

POPIR-Comité logement (St-Henri, Petite Bourgogne, Ville Émard, Côte St-Paul)
4017, rue Notre-Dame Ouest, Montréal QC H4C 1R3
Tél: 514-935-4649; *Téléc:* 514-935-4067
info@popir.org
popir.org
Média social: twitter.com/lepopir
Antoine Morneau-Sénéchal, Organisateur Communautaire

Tourism & Travel

Alberta Hotel & Lodging Association
2707 Ellwood Dr. SW, Edmonton AB T6X 0P7
Tel: 780-436-6112; *Fax:* 780-436-5404
Toll-Free: 888-436-6112
www.ahla.ca
Social Media:
linkedin.com/company/alberta-hotel-&-lodging-association
www.facebook.com/171333316227097
twitter.com/ABHotelAssoc
To enhance the image, the quality & efficiency of the hotel industry in Alberta
Dave Kaiser, President & CEO

Algoma Kinniwabi Travel Association (AKTA)
334 Bay St., Sault Ste Marie ON P6A 1X1
Tel: 705-254-4293; *Fax:* 705-254-4892
Toll-Free: 800-263-2546
info@algomacountry.com
www.algomacountry.com
Social Media: www.youtube.com/user/OntarioAlgomaCountry
www.facebook.com/pages/Ontarios-Algoma-Country/75801493223
twitter.com/AlgomaCountry
To promote the Algoma Country region to the travelling public
Lori Johnson, President

Almaguin-Nipissing Travel Association
PO Box 351, Stn. Regional Information Centre, North Bay ON P1B 8H5
Tel: 705-474-6634; *Toll-Free:* 800-387-0516
To market Ontario's Near North as a four-seasons family-oriented outdoor vacation destination on behalf of the organized tourist industry

Association Hôtellerie Québec (AHQ)
#100, 450, ch. de Chambly, Longueuil QC J4H 3L7
Tél: 579-721-6215; *Téléc:* 579-721-3663
Ligne sans frais: 877-769-9776
info@hotelleriequebec.org
www.hotelleriequebec.com
Média social: www.facebook.com/HoteliersQuebecAHQ
Regrouper les établissements hôteliers pour les représenter, défendre leurs intérêts et leurs fournir des services et ce, tout en collaborant au développement de la qualité de la profession hôtelière et de l'industrie touristique en général
Benoit Sirard, Président

Association of Canadian Travel Agencies (ACTA) / Association canadienne des agences de voyages
#226, 2560 Matheson Blvd. East, Mississauga ON L4W 4Y9
Tel: 905-282-9294; *Fax:* 905-282-9826
Toll-Free: 866-725-2282
actacan@acta.ca
www.acta.ca
Social Media:
linkedin.com/company/association-of-canadian-travel-agencies-acta
www.facebook.com/ACTACanada
twitter.com/actacanada
To provide leadership for the retail travel professional
Heather Craig-Peddie, Vice-President
Marco Pozzobon, Director, Digital & Communications
Deanne Osborne, Office Coordinator

Association of Canadian Travel Agencies - Atlantic
PO Box 21007, Quispamsis NB E2E 4Z4
Tel: 888-257-2282; *Fax:* 855-349-0658
actaatlantic@acta.ca
www.acta.ca
To represent & defend the interests of the retail travel services industry; To serve as the focal point for the retail travel services industry, where ideas & resources are pooled into initiatives designed to create & maintain a healthly business & legislative environment
Lorie Cohen Hackett, Regional Manager

Association of Canadian Travel Agents - Alberta & NWT
PO Box 21058, Stn. Terwilligar, Edmonton AB T6R 2V4
Tel: 780-437-2555; *Fax:* 855-349-0658
Toll-Free: 888-257-2282
www.acta.ca
To represent the retail travel sector of Canada's tourism industy, with a focus on Albertan travel agents
Doug Boyd, Regional Chair
Barbara Sutherland, Regional Manager

Association of Canadian Travel Agents - British Columbia/Yukon
#213, 5760 Minoru Blvd., Richmond BC V6X 2A9
Tel: 604-231-0544; *Fax:* 604-231-6020
David McCaig, President & CEO

Association of Canadian Travel Agents - Manitoba
#700, 177 Lombard Ave., Winnipeg MB R3B 0W5
Tel: 204-831-0831; *Fax:* 204-925-8000
actambsk@acta.ca
Shelley Morris, Regional Manager

Association of Canadian Travel Agents - Ontario
#226, 2560 Matheson Blvd. East, Mississauga ON L4W 4Y9
Tel: 905-282-9294; *Fax:* 905-282-9826
Toll-Free: 888-257-2282
www.acta.ca
To represent the retail travel sector of Canada's tourism industry, with a focus on Ontario travel agents
Fiona Bowen, Regional Manager
Mike Foster, Regional Chair

Association of Canadian Travel Agents - Québec / Association des agents de voyages du Québec
CP 50043, Succ. Dagenais, Laval QC H7M 0A1
Tél: 450-933-4802; *Téléc:* 450-933-4803
Défense des droits et intérêts de l'industrie du voyage
Jean Luc Beauchemin, Directeur régional

Association touristique des Laurentides (ATL) / Laurentian Tourist Association
14 142, rue de la Chapelle, Mirabel QC J7J 2C8
Tél: 450-436-8532; *Téléc:* 450-436-5309
Ligne sans frais: 800-561-6673
info-tourisme@laurentides.com
www.laurentides.com
Média social: www.youtube.com/notredecor
www.facebook.com/TourismeLaurentides
Unir tous les agents, corporations, corps publics et municipaux, associations et organismes, entreprises, oeuvrant dans le domaine touristique dans la région nord de Montréal; orienter et favoriser le développement et l'activité touristique régionale dans le meilleur intérêt régional; obtenir au nom de toute la région des interventions gouvernementales ou autres propres à favoriser son développement touristique

Association touristique régionale de Charlevoix
495, boul de Comporté, La Malbaie QC G5A 3G3
Tél: 418-665-4454; *Téléc:* 418-665-3811
Ligne sans frais: 800-667-2276
info@tourisme-charlevoix.com
www.tourisme-charlevoix.com
Média social: www.youtube.com/user/TourismeCharlevoix
www.facebook.com/tourismecharlevoix
twitter.com/gocharlevoix
Acceuil, promotion, développement de Charlevoix en tourisme

Association touristique régionale de Duplessis (ATRD)
312, av Brochu, Sept-Iles QC G4R 2W6
Tél: 418-962-0808; *Téléc:* 418-962-6518
Ligne sans frais: 888-463-0808
info@tourismeduplessis.com
www.tourismeduplessis.com
Regrouper efficacement, sur une base géographique et sectorielle, les diverses entreprises touristiques de la région; proposer un plan d'action annuel dans lequel sont déterminés les priorités, les programmes et les services offerts à ses membres
Marie-Soleil Vigneault, Directrice générale
Danys Jomphe, Président

Association touristique régionale du Saguenay-Lac-Saint-Jean
#100, 412, boul. Saguenay Est, Chicoutimi QC G7H 7Y8
Tél: 418-543-3536; *Téléc:* 418-543-1805
Ligne sans frais: 855-253-8387
admin@tourismesaglac.net
www.saguenaylacsaintjean.ca
Média social: www.youtube.com/SaguenayLacStJean
linkedin.com/tourisme-saguenay-lac-saint-jean
www.facebook.com/TourismeSaguenayLacSaintJean
twitter.com/Saguenay_Lac
Au service et à l'écoute de ses membres et de l'industrie touristique régionale dans son ensemble, elle est une organisation de concertation dont les principales activités visent à promouvoir la qualité de l'expérience touristique, à assurer l'accueil et l'information et la mise en marché
Julie Dubord, Directrice générale
Sylvianne Dufour, Adjointe à la direction générale

Association touristique régionale Manicouagan
#304, 337, boul LaSalle, Baie-Comeau QC G4Z 2Z1
Tél: 418-294-2876; *Téléc:* 418-294-2345
Ligne sans frais: 888-463-5319
info@cotenord-manicouagan.com
www.tourismemanicouagan.com/fr/
Média social: www.facebook.com/manicouagancotenord
Promouvoir la région comme destination touristique et mettre en valeur ses attraits
Grétha Fougèrers, Directrice générale

Associations touristiques régionales associées du Québec (ATRAQ) / Québec Regional Tourist Associations Inc.
#330, 1575, boul de l'Avenir, Laval QC H7S 2N5
Tél: 450-686-8358; *Téléc:* 450-686-9630
Ligne sans frais: 877-686-8358
information@atrassociees.com
www.atrassociees.com
Média social: www.youtube.com/user/ATRassociees
www.facebook.com/ATRassociees
twitter.com/atrassociees
Regrouper l'ensemble des associations touristiques régionales oeuvrant au Québec en vue de les représenter et défendre leurs intérêts collectifs; les promouvoir et leur offrir des services; contribuer ainsi au développement de l'industrie touristique québécoise
François-G. Chevrier, Président-Directeur général

British Columbia Lodging & Campgrounds Association (BCLCA)
#209, 3003 St. John's St., Port Moody BC V3H 2C4
Tel: 778-383-1037; *Fax:* 604-945-7606
www.bclca.com
Social Media:
www.facebook.com/TravellinginBritishColumbia
twitter.com/TravellinginBC
To promote the public's utilization of member lodging & campground businesses; to monitor & make representation to governments on legislation affecting the interests of British Columbia's lodging & campground businesses; to speak for the membership on matters of general or specific interest; to encourage members to strive for excellence in accommodation & service
Joss Penny, Executive Director

Cambridge Tourism
750 Hespeler Rd., Cambridge ON N3H 5L8
Tel: 519-622-2336; *Fax:* 519-622-0177
Toll-Free: 800-749-7560
visit@cambridgechamber.com
www.cambridgetourism.com
Social Media: www.pinterest.com/cambridgeon
www.facebook.com/pages/Visit-Cambridge-Ontario/249977815059176
To develop tourism initiatives & build partnerships that pool ideas & resources to promote Cambridge as a viable travel destination, generating greater economic impact for the city & other tourism stakeholders.

Camping in Ontario
#6, 1915 Clements Rd., Pickering ON L1W 3V1
Tel: 289-660-2192; *Fax:* 289-660-2146
Toll-Free: 877-672-2226
info@campinginontario.ca
www.campinginontario.ca
Social Media: plus.google.com/+CampinginontarioCanada
www.facebook.com/pages/Camping-In-Ontario/119145788133338
twitter.com/CampInOntario
To support & improve the operation of private campgrounds in Ontario by establishing standards, disseminating information &

by representation in the tourist industry & at all levels of government
Alexandra Anderson, Executive Director

Camping Québec
#700, 2001, rue de la Métropole, Longueuil QC J4G 1S9
Tél: 450-651-7396; *Téléc:* 450-651-7397
Ligne sans frais: 800-363-0457
www.campingquebec.com
Défendre les intérêts de nos membres; offrir des services de publications et promotion, des activitées, des escomptes sur achats et programmes divers.
Natasha Bouchard, Présidente

Canadian Recreational Vehicle Association (CRVA) / Association canadienne du véhicule récréatif
110 Freelton Rd., Freelton ON L0R 1K0
www.crva.ca
To promote recreational vehicle lifestyle

Canadian Resort Development Association (CRDA)
13061 - 15 Ave., South Surrey BC V4A 1K6
Tel: 604-538-7001; *Fax:* 604-538-7101
info@crda.com
www.crda.com
To raise a better understanding of the value of the vacation ownership product; to ensure fair & ethical treatment by all industry participants, through legislation or industry self-management; to educate & inform within the membership & outwardly to the public.
Jon Zwickel, President & CEO

Canadian Tourism Research Institute
255 Smyth Rd., Ottawa ON K1H 8M7
Tel: 613-526-3280; *Fax:* 613-526-4857
Toll-Free: 866-711-2262
ctri@conferenceboard.ca
www.conferenceboard.ca/ctri/
Gregory Hermus, Associate Director

Cariboo Chilcotin Coast Tourism Association
#204, 350 Barnard St., Williams Lake BC V2G 4T9
Tel: 250-392-2226; *Fax:* 250-392-2838
Toll-Free: 800-663-5885
info@landwithoutlimits.com
www.landwithoutlimits.com
Social Media: www.youtube.com/user/TheCCCTA
www.facebook.com/CaribooChilcotinCoast
twitter.com/CarChiCoa
To promote tourism products of the Cariboo Chilcotin Coast region of BC. Products & services include, access to an extensive image bank, travel guide & DVD, familiarization tour assistance, itinerary planning assistance, property inspection/recommendations, regional knowledge.
Amy Thacker, CEO

Central Nova Tourist Association (CNTA)
65 Treaty Trail, Millbrook NS B6L 1W3
Tel: 902-893-8782; *Fax:* 902-893-2269
Toll-Free: 800-895-1177
info@centralnovascotia.com
www.centralnovascotia.com
Social Media:
www.facebook.com/pages/Central-Nova-Tourist-Association/62069285284
To contribute to the Central Nova area becoming the most important tourist destination in Nova Scotia, resulting in new tourism initiatives & strengthened businesses by working as a team dedicated to effective communication & production of our community
Joyce Mingo, Executive Director

Cornwall & Seaway Valley Tourism
11 Water St. West, Cornwall ON K6J 1A1
Tel: 613-938-4748; *Fax:* 613-938-4751
Toll-Free: 800-937-4748
info@cornwalltourism.com
www.cornwalltourism.com
To promote Cornwall & Seaway Valley as a viable visitor & convention destination
Michael Lalonde, Executive Manager

Council of Tourism Associations of British Columbia (COTA)
PO Box 3636, 349 West Georgia St., Vancouver BC V6B 3Y8
Tel: 604-685-5956
www.cotabc.com
To advocate the interests of members to provincial & federal governments, businesses & media, in order to inform them of the opportunities & concerns of the tourism industry; To promote tourism in British Columbia
Stephen Regan, President & CEO

Kitka Neyedli, Coordinator, Membership & Industry Relations Coordinator
Peter Larose, Director, Policy & Planning

Economic Development Winnipeg Inc. (EDW)
#300, 259 Portage Ave., Winnipeg MB R3B 2A9
Tel: 204-954-1997
www.economicdevelopmentwinnipeg.com
Social Media: www.youtube.com/user/EDWinnipeg
linkedin.com/company/economic-development-winnipeg-inc.
twitter.com/EDWinnipeg
To act as Winnipeg's economic development & tourism services agency, by marketing the city & providing related economic development & tourism services
Marina R. James, President & CEO
Greg Dandewich, Senior Vice-President
Chantal Sturk-Nadeau, Senior Vice-President, Tourism

Fondation Tourisme Jeunesse
3514, av Lacombe, Montréal QC H3T 1M1
Tél: 514-731-1015; *Téléc:* 514-731-1715
www.tourismejeunesse.org
Rendre accessible le tourisme aux jeunes, en développant divers outils et services, notamment par le biais des bureaux d'information voyages et des auberges de jeunesse du Québec
Dragos Cacio, Coordonateur de la Fondation

Fredericton Tourism
11 Carleton St., Fredericton NB E3B 3T1
Tel: 506-460-2041; *Fax:* 506-460-2474
Toll-Free: 888-888-4768
tourism@fredericton.ca
www.tourismfredericton.ca
Social Media: www.youtube.com/user/FrederictonTourism
www.facebook.com/FrederictonTourism
twitter.com/FredTourism
To develop & run a variety of cultural programs largely focused in the Historic Garrison District; to operate 2 municipal Visitor Information Centres, Lighthouse on the Green, & River Valley Crafts retail shop.
Ken Forrest, Director, Growth & Community Planning

The Georgian Triangle Tourist Association & Tourist Information Centre
45 St. Paul St., Collingwood ON L9Y 3P1
Tel: 705-445-7722; *Fax:* 705-444-6158
Toll-Free: 888-227-8667
info@georgiantriangle.com
www.georgiantriangle.com
Social Media:
www.facebook.com/114000537662
twitter.com/SGeorgianBay
To promote tourism & convention industries in the Georgian Triangle

HomeLink International Home Exchange (HLCA)
1707 Platt Cres., North Vancouver BC V7J 1X9
Tel: 604-987-3262
info@homelink.ca
www.homelink.org/canada/
Social Media:
www.facebook.com/HomeLink.CA
To produce directories listing homes for vacation exchange worldwide
Jack Graber, Director

Hospitality Newfoundland & Labrador (HNL)
#102, 71 Goldstone St., St. John's NL A1B 5C3
Tel: 709-722-2000; *Fax:* 709-722-8104
Toll-Free: 800-563-0700
hnl@hnl.ca
hnl.ca
Social Media:
www.facebook.com/HospitalityNL
twitter.com/hospitalitynl
To develop & promote tourism & hospitality industry throughout Newfoundland & Labrador.
Carol-Ann Gilliard, Chief Executive Officer

Hotel Association of Canada Inc. (HAC) / Association des hôtels du Canada
#1206, 130 Albert St., Ottawa ON K1P 5G4
Tel: 613-237-7149; *Fax:* 613-237-8928
info@hotelassociation.ca
www.hotelassociation.ca
Social Media:
linkedin.com/company/hotel-association-of-canada
twitter.com/hotelassoc
To represent members both nationally & internationally; to provide cost-effective services which stimulate & encourage a free market accommodation industry
Philippe Gadbois, Chair
Anthony P. Pollard, President

Linda Hartwell, Director, Marketing Communications & Business Development

Hotel Association of Nova Scotia (HANS)
PO Box 473, Stn. M, Halifax NS B3J 2P8
To make Nova Scotia a year-round travel destination; To act as the official voice of the collective member hotels; To provide support for appropriate advisory boards & committees; To develop & encourage a coordinated joint marketing effort

Hotel Association of Prince Edward Island
c/o Murphy Hospitality Group, 96 Kensington Rd., Charlottetown PE C1A 5J4
Tel: 902-566-3137
Kevin Murphy, President

Institut de tourisme et d'hôtellerie du Québec (ITHQ)
3535, rue Saint-Denis, Montréal QC H2X 3P1
Tél: 514-282-5111; *Téléc:* 514-873-4529
Ligne sans frais: 800-361-5111
info@ithq.qc.ca
www.ithq.qc.ca
Média social: www.facebook.com/ecoleITHQ
twitter.com/ITHQ
l'ITHQ est la plus importante école de gestion hôtelière au Canada spécialisée en tourisme, hôtellerie, restauration et sommellerie.
Lucille Daoust, Directrice générale
Paolo Di Pietrantonio, Président

Klondike Visitors Association (KVA)
PO Box 389, Dawson City YT Y0B 1G0
Tel: 867-993-5575; *Fax:* 867-993-6415
Toll-Free: 877-465-3006
kva@dawson.net
www.dawsoncity.ca
Social Media:
www.facebook.com/dawsoncity
To respond to visitor information requests & liaises with municipal & territorial governments to encourage Tourism-related initiatives; to promote Dawson City, Yukon & the Klondike Region as a year-round tourist destination.
Gary Parker, Executive Director

Kootenay Rockies Tourism
1905 Warren Ave., Kimberley BC V1A 1S2
Tel: 250-427-4838; *Fax:* 250-427-3344
Toll-Free: 800-661-6603
info@kootenayrockies.com
www.krtourism.ca
Social Media: www.youtube.com/user/kootrock
linkedin.com/company/kootenay-rockies-tourism
www.facebook.com/KootRock
twitter.com/kootrock
To coordinate & execute tourism marketing initiatives of private sector partners.
Kathy Cooper, CEO & Travel Trade Manager

Muskoka Tourism
1342 Hwy. 11 North, RR#2, Kilworthy ON P0E 1G0
Tel: 705-689-0660; *Fax:* 705-689-9118
Toll-Free: 800-267-9700
info@muskokatourism.ca
www.discovermuskoka.ca
Social Media: www.youtube.com/user/MuskokaTourism
www.facebook.com/discovermuskoka
twitter.com/DiscoverMuskoka
To market the region's tourism resources to the public, media & group tour travel markets
Michael Lawley, Executive Director

Niagara Falls Tourism (NFT)
5400 Robinson St, Niagara Falls ON L2G 2A6
Tel: 905-356-6061; *Fax:* 905-356-5567
Toll-Free: 800-563-2557
www.niagarafallstourism.com
Social Media: www.youtube.com/user/niagarafallstourism
www.facebook.com/niagarafallstourismcanada
twitter.com/nfallstourism
Niagara Falls Tourism (Visitor and Convention Bureau) is the official tourism marketing organization of the Community, responsible for developing public and private sector programs that produce incremental visitor business and resulting economic development returns for the City, its residents and the business community
Toni Williams, Director, Operations

North of Superior Tourism Association (NOSTA)
#2, 605 Victoria Ave. East, Thunder Bay ON P7C 1B1
Tel: 807-346-1130; *Fax:* 807-346-1135
Toll-Free: 800-265-3951
info@northofsuperior.org
www.northofsuperior.org
Social Media:
www.facebook.com/northofsuperior
twitter.com/northosuperior
To market the tourism opportunities for vacationing in Northwestern Ontario.
Tim Lukinuk, President

North West Commercial Travellers' Association (NWCTA)
39 River St., Toronto ON M5A 3P1
Fax: 877-284-8909
Toll-Free: 800-665-6928
nwcta@nwcta.com
www.nwcta.com
Social Media:
linkedin.com/NorthWestCommercialAssociation
twitter.com/NWCTAI
To protect & introduce benefits for individual business travellers
Peter McClure, President
Wendy Sue Lyttle, Executive Director
Charles Ng, Membership Coordinator

Northeastern Ontario Tourism
#401, 2009 Long Lake Rd., Sudbury ON P3E 6C3
Tel: 705-522-0104; *Toll-Free:* 800-465-6655
www.northeasternontario.com
Social Media:
www.facebook.com/northeasternontario
twitter.com/NeOntario

Northern British Columbia Tourism Association (NBCTA)
1274 - 5th Ave., Prince George BC V2L 3L2
Tel: 250-561-0432
www.travelnbc.com
To promote & develop the tourism industry of northern British Columbia
Anthony Everett, CEO

Northern Frontier Visitors Association (NFVA)
#4, 4807 - 49 St., Yellowknife NT X1A 3T5
Tel: 867-873-4262; *Fax:* 867-873-3654
Toll-Free: 877-881-4262
info@northernfrontier.com
www.northernfrontier.com
Social Media:
www.facebook.com/163871037005160
To promote the Northern Frontier Region as an attractive area for tourism; to foster, encourage & assist in any way the growth of tourism into & within the Northern Frontier Region; to increase awareness within the Northern Frontier Region of the potential tourism holds as a viable, clean, labour intensive industry.

Northern Rockies Alaska Highway Tourism Association (NRAHTA)
PO Box 6850, #300, 9523 - 100 St., Fort St. John BC V1J 4J3
Tel: 250-785-2544; *Fax:* 250-785-4424
Toll-Free: 888-785-2544
info@hellonorth.com
www.hellonorth.com
To coordinate opportunites for sustainable tourism growth & development by fostering memorable year round visitor experiences; promoting social & economic benefits to members & wider community.

Northwest Ontario Sunset Country Travel Association
PO Box 647W, Kenora ON P9N 3X6
Tel: 807-468-5853; *Toll-Free:* 800-665-7567
info@ontariossunsetcountry.ca
www.ontariossunsetcountry.ca
Social Media: sunsetcountry.tumblr.com
www.facebook.com/SunsetCountry
twitter.com/Sunset_Country
To develop, promote & advertise through cooperation, coordination & communication with clients & organizations for the betterment of tourism in Sunset Country & the province.
Gerry Cariou, Executive Director

Northwest Territories Tourism (NWTT)
PO Box 610, Yellowknife NT X1A 2N5
Toll-Free: 800-661-0788
info@spectacularnwt.com
www.spectacularnwt.com
Social Media:
twitter.com/spectacularnwt
To support the development of a strong tourism sector in the Northwest Territories for the benefit of tourists, residents, & communities; To promote pan-territorial tourism; To act as a voice for the tourism industry; To preserve the integrity of the cultural & natural heritage of the Northwest Territories
Brian Desjardins, Executive Director
Ron Ostrom, Director, Marketing
Julie Warnock, Coordinator, Communications
Margo Thorne, Officer, Finance

Nunavut Tourism
PO Box 1450, Iqaluit NU X0A 0H0
Toll-Free: 866-686-2888
info@nunavuttourism.com
www.nunavuttourism.com
Social Media: www.youtube.com/nunavuttourism
www.facebook.com/nunavuttourism
twitter.com/NunavutTourism
To represent the tourism industry for the private sector in Nunavut; to promote & market Nunavut tourism products

Office du tourisme et des congrès de Québec (OTCQ) / Québec City & Area Tourism & Convention Board
399, rue St-Joseph est, Québec QC G1K 8E2
Tél: 418-641-6654; *Téléc:* 418-641-6578
Ligne sans frais: 877-783-1608
www.quebecregion.com
Média social: www.facebook.com/QuebecRegion
Organisme responsable de la mise en marché de la région touristique de Québec
Gabriel Savard, Directeur général
Daniel Gagnon, Directeur, Communication et publicité

Ontario East Tourism Association (OETA)
PO Box 730, #200, 104 St. Lawrence St., Merrickville ON K0G 1N0
Tel: 613-269-4113; *Fax:* 613-659-4306
Toll-Free: 800-567-3278
support@realontario.ca
www.realontario.ca
To encourage visitation to Eastern Ontario by means of cooperative tourism marketing
Rose Bertoia, Executive Director
John Bonser, President

Ontario Restaurant, Hotel & Motel Association (ORHMA)
#8-201, 2600 Skymark Ave., Mississauga ON L4W 5B2
Tel: 905-361-0268; *Fax:* 905-361-0288
Toll-Free: 800-668-8906
info@orhma.com
www.orhma.com
Social Media:
linkedin.com/company/ontario-restaurant-hotel-&-motel-association
www.facebook.com/ORHMA
twitter.com/orhma
To foster a positive business climate for the hospitality industry in Ontario; To represent members before municipal & provincial governments
Steven Robinson, Chair
Tony Elenis, President & CEO
Fatima Finnegan, Director, Corporate Marketing & Business Development

Ottawa Tourism / Tourisme Ottawa
#1800, 130 Albert St., Ottawa ON K1P 5G4
Tel: 613-237-5150; *Fax:* 613-237-7339
Toll-Free: 800-363-4465
info@ottawatourism.ca
www.ottawatourism.ca
Social Media: www.youtube.com/OttawaTourism
www.facebook.com/visitottawa
twitter.com/Ottawa_Tourism
To maximize the number of visits to Ottawa & Canada's Capital Region through effective marketing & communication programs; to help develop & promote awareness of the contribution of tourism in the community; to facilitate the development & promotion of the products, services & needs of members
Noel Buckley, President & CEO

Ottawa Valley Tourist Association (OVTA)
9 International Dr., Pembroke ON K8A 6W5
Tel: 613-732-4364; *Fax:* 613-735-2492
Toll-Free: 800-757-6580
info@ottawavalley.travel
www.ottawavalley.travel
Social Media: www.youtube.com/ottawavalleytravel
www.facebook.com/ottawavalleytravel
twitter.com/theottawavalley
To promote Renfrew County as a prime tourist destination
Alastair Baird, Manager

Chris Hinsperger, President

Peterborough & the Kawarthas Tourism
1400 Crawford Dr., Peterborough ON K9J 6X6
Tel: 705-742-2201; *Fax:* 705-742-2494
Toll-Free: 800-461-6424
info@thekawarthas.net
www.thekawarthas.net
Social Media: www.pinterest.com/pktourism
www.facebook.com/TheKawarthas
twitter.com/pktourism
To help market the Peterborough area to visitors

Pictou County Tourist Association
980 East River Rd., New Glasgow NS B2H 3S8
Tel: 902-752-6383; *Toll-Free:* 877-816-2326
admin@visitdeans.ca
To promote the county to residents & visitors

Regina Regional Opportunities Commission (RROC)
1925 Rose St., Regina SK S4P 3P1
Tel: 306-789-5099; *Fax:* 306-352-1630
Toll-Free: 800-661-5099
info@reginaroc.com
www.reginaroc.com
Social Media: www.youtube.com/user/thereginaroc
linkedin.com/in/reginaroc
www.facebook.com/ReginaRoc
twitter.com/ReginaRoc
To promote tourism in Regina; To support industry growth & diversification through development
John Lee, President & CEO
Kim Exner, Director, Corporate Services

Resorts Ontario
29 Albert St. North, Orillia ON L3V 5J9
Tel: 705-325-9115; *Fax:* 705-325-7999
Toll-Free: 800-363-7227
escapes@resorts-ontario.com
www.resortsofontario.com
Social Media: www.youtube.com/user/ResortsofOntario
www.facebook.com/ResortsofOntario
twitter.com/ResortsOntario
To serve & promote the collective interests of resorts, lodges & inns of Ontario
Grace Sammut, Executive Director

Saskatchewan Hotel & Hospitality Association (SHHA)
#302, 2080 Broad St., Regina SK S4P 1Y3
Tel: 306-522-1664; *Toll-Free:* 800-667-1118
info@skhha.com
www.skhha.com
Glenn Weir, Chair
Jim Bence, Chief Executive Officer

Stratford Tourism Alliance (STA)
47 Downie St., Stratford ON N5A 1W7
Tel: 519-271-5140; *Fax:* 519-273-1818
Toll-Free: 800-561-7926
info@visitstratford.ca
www.welcometostratford.com
A marketing organization promoting Stratford as a destination for leisure travelers & others; provides services to members, assistance, information & guidance to visitors, convention planners, & media contacts about the advantages of Stratford & surrounding area as a destination
Eugene Zakreski, Executive Director
Christina Phillips, Coordinator, On-line & Membership Programme
Cathy Rehberg, Coordinator, Marketing

Thompson Okanagan Tourism Association (TOTA)
2280-D Leckie Rd., Kelowna BC V1X 6G6
Tel: 250-860-5999; *Fax:* 250-860-9993
Toll-Free: 800-567-2275
info@totabc.com
www.totabc.org/corporatesite
Social Media: www.youtube.com/user/thompsonokanagan
www.facebook.com/totabc
twitter.com/totamedia
To increase members' revenue & sustainability through cooperative marketing, ongoing education & government liaison
Glenn Mandziuk, CEO

Tourism Brantford
Brantford Visitor & Tourism Centre, 399 Wayne Gretzky Pkwy., Brantford ON N3R 8B4
Tel: 519-751-9900; *Fax:* 519-751-2617
Toll-Free: 800-265-6299
tourism@brantford.ca
www.discoverbrantford.com

To ensure quality visitor services through awareness, education, marketing & communications; to enhance the development of the tourism industry as an economic generator & to enhance the quality of life in our community
John Frabotta, Director, Economic Development & Tourism Services
Donna Clements, Acting Manager, Tourism & Marketing

Tourism Burlington
414 Locust St., Burlington ON L7S 1T7
Tel: 905-634-5594; *Fax:* 905-634-7220
Toll-Free: 877-499-9989
info@tourismburlington.com
www.tourismburlington.com
Social Media: www.youtube.com/user/TourismBurlington
linkedin.com/groups?gid=4070362
www.facebook.com/TourismBurlington
twitter.com/burlingtontour
To increase tourism, resulting in economic benefits through utilization of recreational, cultural, commercial & personal resources
Pam Belgrade, Executive Director
Victor Szeverenyi, Chair

Tourism Calgary
#200, 238 - 11 Ave. SE, Calgary AB T2G 0X8
Tel: 403-263-8510; *Fax:* 403-262-3809
Toll-Free: 800-661-1678
www.visitcalgary.com
Social Media:
www.facebook.com/visitcalgary
twitter.com/calgary
A non-profit destination marketing organization, providing services to members to promote Calgary as a destination for travel industry professionals, as well as leisure & business travelers
Randy Williams, President & CEO

Tourism Cape Breton
PO Box 1448, Sydney NS B1P 6R7
Tel: 902-563-4636; *Toll-Free:* 888-562-9848
dcb@dcba.ca
www.cbisland.com
Social Media: www.youtube.com/user/CBTourism
www.facebook.com/TourismCB
twitter.com/TourismCB

Tourism Hamilton
The Lister Building, 28 James St. North, Ground Fl., Hamilton ON L8R 2K1
Tel: 905-546-2666; *Fax:* 905-546-2667
Toll-Free: 800-263-8590
tourism@hamilton.ca
www.tourismhamilton.com
Social Media: www.youtube.com/user/HamiltonTourism
www.facebook.com/TourismHamilton
twitter.com/tourismhamilton
To promote & increase the tourism & convention industries in Greater Hamilton
Susan Monarch, Manager

Tourism Industry Association of Canada (TIAC) / Association de l'industrie touristique du Canada (AITC)
#600, 116 Lisgar St., Ottawa ON K2P 0C2
Tel: 613-238-3883
info@tiac.travel
www.tiac.travel
Social Media:
www.facebook.com/106471679403288
twitter.com/tiac_aitc
To enhance Canada's tourism industry by removing regulatory & legislative barriers to growth
Charlotte Bell, President/CEO
Jennifer Taylor, Vice-President, Marketing & Member Relations
Rob Taylor, Vice-President, Public & Industry Affairs

Tourism Industry Association of New Brunswick Inc. (TIANB) / Association de l'industrie touristique du Nouveau-Brunswick inc. (AITNB)
#440, 500 Beaverbrook Ct., Fredericton NB E3B 5X4
Tel: 506-458-5646; *Fax:* 506-459-3634
Toll-Free: 800-668-5313
info@tianb.com
www.tianb.com
Social Media:
www.facebook.com/pages/TIANB-AITNB/127475440600650?sk=wall&filter=12
twitter.com/tianb_aitnb
To act as the provincial tourism & hospitality organization of New Brunswick, existing to fulfill the needs of its membership, in cooperation with both private & public sector partners; committed to be a representative, industry driven organization which provides leadership & direction, making tourism & hospitality the leading & most viably sustainable industry in New Brunswick
Ron Drisdelle, Executive Director
Kathy Weir, President

Tourism Industry Association of Nova Scotia (TIANS)
2089 Maitland St., Halifax NS B3K 2Z8
Tel: 902-423-4480; *Fax:* 902-422-0184
Toll-Free: 800-948-4267
information_central@tians.org
www.tians.org
Social Media:
www.facebook.com/tians.nsthrc
To lead, support, represent & enhance the Nova Scotia tourism industry
Darlene Grant Fiander, President
Glenn Squires, Chair
James Miller, Secretary/Treasurer

Tourism Industry Association of PEI (TIAPEI)
PO Box 2050, 25 Queen St., 3rd Fl., Charlottetown PE C1A 7N7
Tel: 902-566-5008; *Fax:* 902-368-3605
Toll-Free: 866-566-5008
webmaster@tiapei.pe.ca
www.tiapei.pe.ca
Social Media:
www.facebook.com/tiapei
twitter.com/tiapei
To represent tourism related businesses, associations, institutions, & individuals; to encourage tourism to & within PEI
Kevin Mouflier, Chief Executive Officer

Tourism Industry Association of the Yukon
#3, 1109 - 1st Ave., Whitehorse YT Y1A 5G4
Tel: 867-668-3331; *Fax:* 867-667-7379
info@tiayukon.com
www.tiayukon.com
Social Media:
www.facebook.com/232432356772503
To represent all sectors & businesses of the tourism industry; to foster & promote travel in Yukon; to encourage increase & improvement of visitor facilities, services & attractions; to enhance & stimulate business climate in industry; to enhance awareness of importance of tourism; to design & deliver marketing programs
Krista Prochazka, Executive Director

Tourism London
696 Wellington Rd. South, London ON N6C 4R2
Toll-Free: 800-265-2602
www.londontourism.ca
Social Media: www.youtube.com/tourismlondonontario
www.facebook.com/tourismlondon
twitter.com/tourism_london
To promote London through co-operative partnerships as the tourism, sports tourism & meeting destination of choice resulting in positive economic impact on the city of London
Deb Harvey, President

Tourism Saint John / Bureau de tourisme et de congrès de Saint John
PO Box 1971, Saint John NB E2L 4L1
Tel: 506-658-2990; *Fax:* 506-632-6118
Toll-Free: 866-463-8639
visitsj@saintjohn.ca
www.tourismsaintjohn.com
Social Media: www.youtube.com/user/discoversaintjohn
www.facebook.com/DiscoverSaintJohn
twitter.com/visitsaintjohn
To position Saint John as the premier all-season, visitor, meeting & event destination on New Brunswick's Bay of Fundy; to generate revenues & publicity for the city of Saint John & its tourism operators & businesses through increased visitation, service excellence & the provision of advice & partnering opportunities
Ross Jefferson, Executive Director

Tourism Sarnia Lambton (TSL)
556 Christina St. North, Sarnia ON N7T 5W6
Tel: 519-336-3232; *Fax:* 519-336-3278
Toll-Free: 800-265-0316
info@tourismsarnialambton.com
www.tourismsarnialambton.com
Social Media:
www.youtube.com/user/VisitSarniaLambton?feature=watch
www.facebook.com/tourismsarnialambton
To promote tourism to Lambton County, creating economic value for the entire community
Leona Allen, Office Administrator
Marlene Wood, General Manager

Tourism Saskatoon
#101, 202 Fourth Ave. North, Saskatoon SK S7K 0K1
Tel: 306-242-1206; *Fax:* 306-242-1955
Toll-Free: 800-567-2444
info@tourismsaskatoon.com
www.tourismsaskatoon.com
Social Media: www.youtube.com/tourismsaskatoon
www.facebook.com/tourismsaskatoon
twitter.com/visitsaskatoon
To operate as Saskatoon's destination management organization, maximizing the economic benefit for Saskatoon through tourism
Todd Brandt, CEO

Tourism Simcoe County
Simcoe County Museum, 1151 Hwy. 26 West, Minesing ON L0L 1Y2
Toll-Free: 800-487-6642
tourism@simcoe.ca
discover.simcoe.ca
Social Media:
www.facebook.com/TourismSimcoeCounty
twitter.com/simcoecountytsc
The association promotes & develops the tourism industry of Simcoe County & area.
Kathryn Stephenson, Manager, Tourism
Diana Coulson, Coordinator, Marketing & Communications

Tourism Thunder Bay
PO Box 800, 53 Water St. South, Thunder Bay ON P7C 5K4
Tel: 807-625-2564; *Fax:* 807-625-3789
Toll-Free: 800-667-8386
TTY: 807-622-2225
rtarnowski@thunderbay.ca
www.visitthunderbay.com
Social Media:
www.Facebook.com/visitthunderbay
twitter.com/visitthunderbay
To market Thunder Bay as a destination for individuals & groups
Paul Pepe, Tourism Manager
Rose Marie Tarnowski, Convention & Visitor Services Coordinator

Tourism Toronto (TCVA)
Toronto Convention & Visitors Association, PO Box 126, 207 Queen's Quay West, Toronto ON M5J 1A7
Tel: 416-203-2600; *Fax:* 416-203-6753
Toll-Free: 800-499-2514
toronto@torcvb.com
www.seetorontonow.com
Social Media: www.youtube.com/seetorontonow;
www.instagram.com/seetorontonow
www.facebook.com/visittoronto
twitter.com/seetorontonow
To promote Toronto as a convention & visitor destination; To position Toronto as one of the world's great cities & a year-round destination for leisure & business
Johanne R. Bélanger, President/CEO

Tourism Vancouver/Greater Vancouver Convention & Visitors Bureau
The Greater Vancouver Convention & Visitors Bureau, #210, 200 Burrard St., Vancouver BC V6C 3L6
Tel: 604-682-2222; *Fax:* 604-682-1717
VisitVancouver@tourismvancouver.com
www.tourismvancouver.com
Social Media: www.instagram.com/inside_vancouver
www.facebook.com/insidevancouver
twitter.com/myvancouver
To lead the cooperative effort of positioning Greater Vancouver as a preferred travel destination in all targeted markets worldwide, thereby creating opportunities for member & community sharing of the resulting economic, environmental, social & cultural benefits
Ty Speer, President/CEO
Dave Gazley, Vice-President, Meeting & Convention Sales
Ted Lee, CFO

Tourism Victoria/Greater Victoria Visitors & Convention Bureau
Administration Office, #200, 737 Yates St., Victoria BC V8W 1L6
Tel: 250-953-2033; *Fax:* 250-382-6539
Toll-Free: 800-663-3883
info@tourismvictoria.com
www.tourismvictoria.com
Social Media: www.youtube.com/user/TourismVictoriaBC
www.facebook.com/tourismvictoriafan
twitter.com/victoriavisitor
To oversee the development & promotion of the tourism industry in Greater Victoria
Paul Nursey, President & CEO
Alan Paige, Vice-President, Strategy Management & CFO

Tourism Windsor Essex Pelee Island
City Centre, #103, 333 Riverside Dr. West, Windsor ON N9A 5K4
Tel: 519-253-3616; *Fax:* 519-255-6192
Toll-Free: 800-265-3633
info@tourismwindsoressex.com
www.visitwindsoressex.com
Social Media: www.youtube.com/user/visitwindsoressex
www.facebook.com/visitwindsoressex
twitter.com/TWEPI
To promote Windsor, Essex, Pelee Isalnd as a tourist destination.
Gordon Orr, Chief Executive Officer

Tourisme Abitibi-Témiscamingue
#100, 155, av Dallaire, Rouyn-Noranda QC J9X 4T3
Tél: 819-762-8181; *Téléc:* 819-762-5212
Ligne sans frais: 800-808-0706
info@tourisme-abitibi-temiscamingue.org
www.abitibi-temiscamingue-tourism.org
Média social: www.vimeo.com/atrat
www.facebook.com/TourismeAbitibiTemiscamingue
twitter.com/tourismeAT
Promotion du tourisme en Abitibi-Témiscamingue

Tourisme Baie-James (TBJ) / James Bay Tourism
CP 134, 1252, rte 167 sud, Chibougamau QC G8P 2K6
Tél: 418-748-8140; *Téléc:* 418-748-8150
Ligne sans frais: 888-748-8140
info@tourismebaiejames.com
www.tourismebaiejames.com
Assure dans le cadre de ses responsabilités corporatives, des mandats en matière de concertation régionale, d'accueil, d'information, de signalisation, de promotion et de développement touristique
Luc Letendre, Président

Tourisme Bas-Saint-Laurent
148, rue Fraser, 2e étage, Rivière-du-Loup QC G5R 1C8
Tél: 418-867-1272; *Téléc:* 418-867-3245
Ligne sans frais: 800-563-5268
info@bassaintlaurent.ca
bassaintlaurent.ca
Média social: www.facebook.com/tourismebassaintlaurent
Accueil, développement et promotion touristique
Pierre Laplante, Directeur général

Tourisme Cantons-de-l'Est
20, rue Don-Bosco sud, Sherbrooke QC J1L 1W4
Tél: 819-820-2020; *Téléc:* 819-566-4445
Ligne sans frais: 800-355-5755
info@atrce.com
www.cantonsdelest.com
Média social: www.facebook.com/cantonsdelest
twitter.com/cantonsdelest
A pour mission de faire de la région des Cantons-de-l'Est une des meilleures destinations touristique du Québec en toutes saisons
Alain Larouche, Directeur général
Francine Patenaude, Directrice, Marketing & développement

Tourisme Centre-du-Québec
20, boul Carignan Ouest, Princeville QC G6L 4M4
Tél: 819-364-7177; *Téléc:* 819-364-2120
Ligne sans frais: 888-816-4007
info@tourismecentreduquebec.com
www.tourismecentreduquebec.com
Média social: www.youtube.com/TourismCentreduQc
linkedin.com/company/tourisme-centre-du-qu-bec
www.facebook.com/Tourismecentreduquebec
twitter.com/CentreduQuebec
Yves Zahra, Directeur général

Tourisme Chaudière-Appalaches (ATCA)
800, autoroute Jean-Lesage, Saint-Nicolas QC G7A 1E3
Tél: 418-831-4411; *Téléc:* 418-831-8442
Ligne sans frais: 888-831-4411
info@chaudiereappalaches.com
www.chaudiereappalaches.com
Média social: www.facebook.com/ChaudiereAppalaches
twitter.com/ChaudApp
Favoriser le développement et la promotion de l'industrie touristique de son territoire tout en contribuant à la réussite des entreprises qui en sont members
Richard Moreau, Director général

Tourisme Gaspésie
1020, boul Jacques-Cartier, Mont-Joli QC G5H 0B1
Tél: 418-775-2223; *Ligne sans frais:* 877-775-2463
info@tourisme-gaspesie.com
www.tourisme-gaspesie.com
Média social: www.youtube.com/Gaspesiejetaime;
www.pinterest.com/gaspesiejetaime
ca.linkedin.com/company/tourisme-gasp-sie
www.facebook.com/gaspesiejetaime
twitter.com/gaspesiejetaime
Orienter et favoriser la promotion, le développement et l'activité touristique dans le meilleur intérêt de la Gaspésie; promouvoir, organiser et coordonner divers programmes de promotion et de développement touristique ayant comme conséquence d'accroître la clientèle touristique et prolongation des séjours dans la Gaspésie
Joëlle Ross, Directrice générale

Tourisme Iles de la Madeleine
128, ch Principal, Cap-aux-Meules QC G4T 1C5
Tél: 418-986-2245; *Téléc:* 418-986-2327
Ligne sans frais: 877-624-4437
info@tourismeilesdelamadeleine.com
www.tourismeilesdelamadeleine.com
Média social: www.youtube.com/TourismeIDM
www.facebook.com/tourismeilesdelamadeleine
twitter.com/ATRIM
Regrouper les entreprises de l'industrie touristique de l'archipel afin d'accroître les efforts de développement et de promotion
Michel Bonato, Directrice générale

Tourisme Lanaudière
3568, rue Church, Rawdon QC J0K 1S0
Tél: 450-834-2535; *Téléc:* 450-834-8100
Ligne sans frais: 800-363-2788
info@lanaudiere.ca
www.lanaudiere.ca/fr/
Média social: www.facebook.com/tourismelanaudiere
twitter.com/tourlanaud
Faire la promotion, développement, commercialisation de l'offre touristiques de la région auprès des clienteles des différents marchés; améliorer l'accueil & l'information touristique
Évangéline Richard, Présidente

Tourisme Laval
480, Promenade du Centropolis, Laval QC H7T 3C2
Tél: 450-682-5522; *Téléc:* 450-682-7304
info@tourismelaval.com
www.tourismelaval.com
Média social: www.youtube.com/user/tourismelaval
www.facebook.com/tourismelaval
twitter.com/TourismeLaval
De promouvoir Laval comme destination touristique
Geneviève Roy, Directrice générale
Yves Legault, Président

Tourisme Mauricie
CP 100, Shawinigan QC G9N 8S1
Tél: 819-536-3334; *Téléc:* 819-536-3373
Ligne sans frais: 800-567-7603
info@tourismemauricie.com
www.tourismemauricie.com
Média social: www.youtube.com/tourismemauricie
www.facebook.com/tourismemauricie
twitter.com/mauricie
De promovoir la ville de Maurice comme une destination touristique
André Nollet, Directeur général

Tourisme Montérégie
#10, 8940, boul Leduc, Brossard QC J4Y 0G4
Tél: 450-466-4666; *Téléc:* 450-466-7999
Ligne sans frais: 866-469-0069
info@tourisme-monteregie.qc.ca
www.tourisme-monteregie.qc.ca
Média social:
www.facebook.com/pages/Tourisme-Monteregie/283759343997
twitter.com/tourmonteregie
Josée Juliener, Directrice générale
François Trépanier, Directeur, Communications

Tourisme Montréal/Office des congrès et du tourisme du Grand Montréal / Greater Montréal Convention & Tourism Bureau
CP 979, Montréal QC H3C 2W3
Tél: 514-873-2015; *Téléc:* 514-864-3838
Ligne sans frais: 877-266-5687
info@tourisme-montreal.org
www.tourism-montreal.org
Média social: www.youtube.com/user/TourismeMontreal
www.facebook.com/Montreal
twitter.com/montreal
De promouvoir Montréal comme une destination touristique populaire
Yves Lalumière, Président et directeur général

Travel and Tourism Research Association (Canada Chapter) (TTRA)
#600, 116 Lisgar St., Ottawa ON K2P 0C2
Tel: 613-238-6378
info@ttracanada.ca
www.ttracanada.ca
An association of tourism research and marketing professionals with Chapters in the U.S., Canada, Europe, and Asia.
Kelly MacKay, President

Travellers' Aid Society of Toronto (TAS)
Union Station, PO Box 102, 65 Front St. West, Toronto ON M5J 1E6
Tel: 416-366-7788; *Fax:* 416-366-0829
TAID668@gmail.com
www.travellersaid.ca
To provide a base of needed information for travellers as well as shelter & other help in crisis situations

Vancouver, Coast & Mountains Tourism Region
#270, 1651 Commercial Dr., Vancouver BC V5l 3Y3
Tel: 604-739-9011; *Fax:* 604-739-0153
Toll-Free: 800-667-3306
info@vcmbc.com
www.604pulse.com
Social Media:
www.facebook.com/vcmbc
twitter.com/vcmbc
To create tourist experineces for travellers
Kevan Ridgway, President & CEO
Doleen Dean, Visitor Services

Wilderness Tourism Association of the Yukon (WTAY)
#4, 1114 - 1st Ave., Whitehorse YT Y1A 1A3
Tel: 867-668-3369; *Fax:* 867-668-3370
info@wtay.com
wtay.com
To represent the wilderness & adventure tourism industry in the Yukon Territory, Canada; to provide marketing, advocacy, research, consultation, referral & education resources.
Felix Geithner, President

Trade

Asia Pacific Foundation of Canada (APFC) / Fondation Asie Pacifique du Canada
#220, 890 West Pender St., Vancouver BC V6C 1J9
Tel: 604-684-5986; *Fax:* 604-681-1370
info@asiapacific.ca
www.asiapacific.ca
Social Media:
www.facebook.com/asiapacificfoundationofcanada
twitter.com/AsiaPacificFdn
Independent think tank on Canada's relations with Asia; to bring together people & knowledge to provide the most current & comprehensive research, analysis & information on Canada's transpacific relations; to promote dialogue on economic, security, political & social issues, helping to influence public policy & foster informed decision-making in the Canadian public, private & non-governmental sectors
Yuen Pau Woo, President & CEO
Jill Price, Executive Director

Beef Cattle Research Council (BCRC)
#180, 6815 - 8th St. NE, Calgary AB T2E 7H7
Tel: 403-275-8558; *Fax:* 403-274-5686
info@beefresearch.ca
www.beefresearch.ca
Social Media: www.youtube.com/beefresearch
www.facebook.com/BeefResearch
twitter.com/BeefResearch
Canada's national industry-led funding agency for beef research.
Andrea Brocklebank, Research Manager
Reynold Bergen, Science Director

British Canadian Chamber of Trade & Commerce
Dominion Centre, Royal Trust Tower, 2401, 77 King St., Toronto ON M5K 1G8
Tel: 416-816-9154; *Fax:* 647-435-3436
central@bcctc.ca
www.bcctc.ca
Social Media:
twitter.com/bcctc
To foster reciprocal trading between Canada & the U.K.
Thomas O'Carroll, Vice-President, Central
Liam J. Hopkins, Vice President, Western
John Hoblyn, Contact, Eastern

Business Council of British Columbia
#810, 1050 Pender St. West, Vancouver BC V6E 3S7
Tel: 604-684-3384; *Fax:* 888-488-5376
info@bcbc.com
www.bcbc.com
Social Media:
linkedin.com/company/business-council-of-british-columbia
twitter.com/BizCouncilBC
To build a competitive & growing economy that provides opportunities for all who invest, work, & live in British Columbia
Jonathan Whitworth, Chair
Greg D'Avignon, President & CEO
Jock Finlayson, Executive VP & Chief Policy Officer
Cheryl Maitland Muir, Vice-President, Communications
Ken Peacock, Chief Economist & Vice-President

Canada - Albania Business Council (CABC) / Conseil Commercial Canada - Albanie
#701, 165 University Ave., Toronto ON M5H 3B8
Tel: 416-979-1875; *Fax:* 416-979-0825
canadaalbaniabusinesscouncil.ca
To help encourage businesses to invest in & trade with Albania
Robert Baines, Executive Director
Abby Badwi, Chairman, Board of Directors

Canada China Business Council (CCBC) / Conseil commercial Canada Chine
#1501, 330 Bay St., Toronto ON M5H 2S8
Tel: 416-954-3800; *Fax:* 416-954-3806
ccbc@ccbc.com
www.ccbc.com
To build business success in China & Canada by offering service & support, from direct operational support in China, to trade & investment advocacy on its members' behalf
Peter Kruyt, Chair
Sarah Kutulakos, Executive Director

Canada Organic Trade Association (COTA) / Association pour le commerce des produits biologiques (ACPB)
PO Box 13, Stn. A, Ottawa ON kKN 8V1
Tel: 613-482-1717; *Fax:* 613-236-0743
www.ota.com/canada-ota
Social Media:
linkedin.com/company/organic-trade-association
www.facebook.com/OrganicTrade
twitter.com/OrganicTrade
To promote & protect the growth of organic trade in Canada; to benefit organic farmers, consumers, the environment & the economy; to provide information on ingredients, sourcing, certification, marketing, imports & exports, & a range of other concerns
Matthew Holmes, Executive Director

Canada Romania Business Council
c/o DEPAG Deposit Agency of Canada Inc., #1402, 67 Yonge St., Toronto ON M5E 1J8
Tel: 416-364-4112; *Fax:* 416-364-4074
To increase awareness of opportunities in trade, exchange of technology, & investments among members
Charles Janthur, Executive Director

Canada-Arab Business Council (CABC) / Conseil de commerce canado-arabe (CCCA)
#702, 116 Albert St., Toronto ON K1P 5G3
Tel: 613-680-3888; *Fax:* 613-565-3013
info@canada-arabbusiness.org
www.canada-arabbusiness.org
Social Media:
www.facebook.com/216689288352215
twitter.com/CABC1983
To promote trade investment with Arab countries
Hugh O'Donnell, Chairman & CEO

Canada-India Business Council (C-IBC) / Conseil de commerce Canada-Inde
#302, 1 St. Clair Ave. East, Toronto ON M4T 2V7
Tel: 416-214-5947; *Fax:* 416-214-9081
info@canada-indiabusiness.ca
www.canada-indiabusiness.ca
To promote trade & investment between Canada & India by fostering direct contacts between Canadian & Indian business people; To advise the Canadian government with respect to policies & programs affecting Canada's relations with India; To serve as a forum for exchange of information & views between business executives of Canada & India on issues of importance to both countries; To provide information & advice to companies of both countries with respect to trade & investment matters in either country.
Don Stewart, Chair
Peter Sutherland, President & Executive Director

Canada-Sri Lanka Business Council (CSLSC)
PO Box 309, #6A, 170 The Donway West, Toronto ON M3C 2E8
Tel: 416-445-5390; *Fax:* 416-363-4601
info@cslbcbiz.com
www.cslbcbiz.com
To promote trade, investment, technological exchange, tourism, & industrial cooperation between Canada & Sri Lanka
Upali Obeyesekere, President
Mohan Perera, General Secretary

Canadian Armenian Business Council Inc. (CABC) / Conseil commercial canadien-arménien inc.
#102, 2425 de Salaberry, Montréal QC H3M 1L2
Tel: 514-333-7655; *Fax:* 514-333-7280
info@cabc.ca
www.cabc.ca
To promote & serve the Armenian business community; To act as a marketing tool for North American Armenian businesses
Paul Nahabedian, President

Canadian Association of Importers & Exporters / Association canadienne des importateurs & exportateurs
#200, 10 St. Mary St., Toronto ON M4Y 1P9
Tel: 416-595-5333
info@iecanada.com
www.iecanada.com
To act as the voice of Canadian importers & exporters; To support Canadian importers & exporters so that they remain profitable & competitive in a global market
Joy Nott, CCS, P.Log, President
Keith Mussar, VP, Regulatory Affairs & Co-Chair, Food Committee
Carol Osmond, Vice-President, Policy
Amesika Baeta, Director, Member Relations & Development
Andrea MacDonald, Contact, Media Inquiries, I.E. Now, & Special Publications

Canadian Association of Regulated Importers (CARI) / Association canadienne des importateurs règlementés
#206, 1545 Carling Ave., Ottawa ON K1Z 8P9
Tel: 613-738-1729; *Fax:* 613-733-9501
www.cariimport.org
To ensure the right & ability for importers to do business like other businesses & to create one voice for commodities on the import control list or otherwise controlled by regulations.

Canadian Columbian Professional Association (CCPA)
2408 Gladacres Lane, Oakville ON L6M 0G4
info@ccpassociation.com
www.ccpassociation.com
Paula Calderon, President
Adriana Santofimio, Treasurer

Canadian Council for the Americas (CCA) / Conseil Canadien pour les Amériques
PO Box 48612, 595 Burrard St., Vancouver BC V7X 1A3
Tel: 604-868-8678; *Fax:* 604-806-6112
info@cca-bc.com
www.cca-bc.com
Principal private sector link between Canada & the countries of Latin America & the Caribbean.
André Nudelman, Chair
Leon Teicher, Secretary

Canadian Courier & Logistics Association (CCLA)
PO Box 333, #119, 660 Eglinton Ave. East, Toronto ON M4G 2K2
Tel: 416-696-9995; *Fax:* 416-696-9993
Toll-Free: 877-766-6604
info@canadiancourier.org
www.canadiancourier.org
Social Media:
twitter.com/CCLA4
To serve the needs, promote the interests & concerns, & enhance the reputation of the courier industry in Canada regardless of size or type of operation
David Turnbull, President & CEO

Citizens Concerned About Free Trade (CCAFT)
PO Box 8052, Saskatoon SK S7K 4R7
Tel: 306-244-5757; *Fax:* 306-244-3790
ccaftnat@sk.sympatico.ca
www.davidorchard.com/ccaft
To provide information & mobilize those opposed to the Free Trade Agreements & the loss of Canadian sovereignty; to have Canada exercise the termination clauses of both the FTA & NAFTA so that the country can protect its resources & play an independent role in world affairs

Electronics Import Committee (EIC)
PO Box 189, Stn. Don Mills, Toronto ON M3C 2S2
Tel: 416-595-5333
info@iecanada.com
www.iecanada.com
To represent members' interests before government & regulatory bodies.
Joy Nott, President

Global Automakers of Canada (GAC) / Constructeurs mondiaux d'automobiles du Canada (CMAC)
PO Box 5, #1804, 2 Bloor St. West, Toronto ON M4W 3E2
Tel: 416-595-8251; *Fax:* 416-595-2864
auto@globalautomakers.ca
www.globalautomakers.ca
To represent before federal, provincial, & territorial governments the interests of members engaged in the manufacturing, importation, distribution, & servicing of light-duty vehicles
David C. Adams, President
Loulia Kouchaji, Analyst, Policy & Commercial Issues
Greg Overwater, Acting Director, Technical & Regulatory Affairs

Groupe export agroalimentaire Québec - Canada (GEAQC) / Agri-Food Export Group Québec - Canada
1971, rue Léonard-De Vinci, Sainte-Julie QC J3E 1Y9
Tél: 450-649-6266; *Téléc:* 450-461-6255
Ligne sans frais: 800-563-9767
info@groupexport.ca
www.groupexport.ca
Média social: linkedin.com/company/1742471
Développer des services adaptés aux besoins réels de nos membres afin d'augmenter leurs ventes sur les marchés internationaux; faciliter l'accès aux programmes gouvernementaux dont nous avons la gestion.
André A. Coutu, Président-directeur général
Francine Lapointe, Directrice, Programme et affaires gouvernemntale

Hong Kong Trade Development Council
Hong Kong Convention & Exhibition Centre, 1 Expo Dr., Wanchai Hong Kong
hktdc@hktdc.org
www.hktdc.com
To promote external trade in goods & services; to create & facilitate opportunities in international trade for Hong Kong companies; to strengthen Hong Kong as the global trade platform of Asia; to assist manufacturers, traders & service providers through marketing opportunities, trade contacts, market knowledge & competitive skills
Fred Lam, Executive Director

Indonesia Canada Chamber of Commerce (ICCC)
c/o Canadian Education International, Wisma Metropolitan I, 11th Fl., Jl. Jend. Sudirman kav 29-31, Jakarta 12920 Indonesia
secretariat@iccc.or.id
www.iccc.or.id
To promote trade & investment between Canada & Indonesia.
Karina Sherlen, Vice Executive Director

International Cheese Council of Canada (ICCC)
c/o Canadian Association of Importers & Exporters, PO Box 189, Toronto ON M3C 2S2
To act as the representative voice of Canadian importers of cheese, with respect to the activities of the federal & provincial governments & agencies & all other bodies affecting the commercial interests of cheese importers in Canada; To monitor & analyze all developments relating to the importation of cheese into Canada; To contribute to the formulation, revision & amendment of government policy relating to the commercial regulatory framework within which Canadian cheese importers operate their businesses; To promote the commercial interests of members in a public relations capacity; To liaise with other industry & trade associations working in cheese-related sectors
Amesika Baëta, Director, Member Relations & Development

Ontario Association of Trading Houses (OATH)
PO Box 43086, Toronto ON M2N 6N1
Tel: 416-223-2028; *Fax:* 416-223-5707
info@oath.on.ca
www.oath.on.ca
Social Media:
linkedin.com/company/ontario-association-of-trading-houses
To develop & expand international trade; To help Canadian companies to increase their international trade & investment

Parliamentary Centre / Le Centre parlementaire
#1000, 66 Slater St., Ottawa ON K1P 5H1
Tel: 613-237-0143; *Fax:* 613-235-8237
parlcent@parl.gc.ca
www.parlcent.org
Social Media:
linkedin.com/company/parliamentarycentre
www.facebook.com/parliamentarycentre
twitter.com/parlcent
To strengthen legislatures through continuous learning & innovation in parliamentary development, mutual sharing & practical parliamentary experience, & the provision of advisory services
Jean-Paul Ruszkowski, President/CEO

Southeast Asia-Canada Business Council
5294 Imperial St., Burnaby BC V5J 1E4
Tel: 604-439-0779; *Fax:* 604-439-0284
info@aseancanada.com
www.aseancanada.com
To assist Canadian companies, especially small & medium sized enterprises (SMEs), to enter or expand their presence in the ASEAN market
Carmelita Salonga Tapia, President

Trade Facilitation Office Canada / Bureau de promotion du commerce Canada
#300, 56 Sparks St., Ottawa ON K1P 5A9
Tel: 613-233-3925; *Fax:* 613-233-7860
Toll-Free: 800-267-9674
info@tfocanada.ca
www.tfocanada.ca
Social Media:
linkedin.com/company/tfo-canada
twitter.com/TFOcan
To help improve the economic well-being of developing countries through increased integration into the global economy
Brian Mitchell, Executive Director

World Trade Centre Montréal (WTCM)
#6000, 380, rue St-Antoine Ouest, Montréal QC H2Y 3X7
Tél: 514-871-4002; *Téléc:* 514-849-3813
Ligne sans frais: 877-590-4040
wtcmontreal@ccmm.qc.ca
www.btmm.qc.ca/en/international
Appuyer, former et conseiller les entreprises, associations, institutions et organismes de développement économiques dans leurs démarches sur les marchés internationaux
Michel Leblanc, Président et chef de la direction
Lise Aubin, Vice-présidente, Exploitation & Administration

Translation

Association of Legal Court Interpreters & Translators (ALCIT) / Association des traducteurs et interprètes judiciares (ATIJ)
483, rue St-Antoine est, Montréal QC H2Y 1A5
Tel: 514-845-3113; *Fax:* 514-845-3006
admin@atij.ca
www.atij.ca
To provide translation & interpretation services, mainly for the Municipal Court of Montréal and the City of Montréal Police Department

Transportation & Shipping

Association of Ontario Road Supervisors (AORS)
PO Box 129, 160 King St., Thorndale ON N0M 2P0
Tel: 519-461-1271; *Fax:* 519-461-1343
admin@aors.on.ca
www.aors.on.ca
To promote the exchange of ideas & information concerning public works among municipalities
John Maheu, Executive Director

The Association of School Transportation Services of British Columbia (ASTSBC) / Association des transports du Canada
BC
Tel: 250-804-7892; *Fax:* 250-832-2584
info@astsbc.org
www.astsbc.org
Dedicated to the promotion of safe transportation and encourages those associated with it to do likewise.
Robyn Stephenson, President

Canadian Railway Club
PO Box 162, Stn. St-Charles, Kirkland QC H9H 0A3
Tel: 514-428-5903; *Fax:* 514-697-6238
cdnrailwayclub.mtl@hotmail.com
canadianrailwayclub.ca
Heather McGuire, Administrator

iTaxiworkers Association
25 Cecil St., Toronto ON M5T 1N1
Tel: 416-597-6838; *Fax:* 416-597-2195
info@itaxiworkers.ca
www.itaxiworkers.ca
To improve the rights & working conditions of Ontario taxi drivers

Veterinary Medicine

World Small Animal Veterinary Association (WSAVA)
72 Melville St., Dundas ON L9H 2A1
Tel: 905-627-8540
wsavasecretariat@gmail.com
www.wsava.org
Social Media:
linkedin.com/company/world-small-animal-veterinary-association
www.facebook.com/WSAVA
twitter.com/vetswsava
To advance the health & welfare of small companion animals worldwide through a collaborative global community of veterinary peers; To unite veterinary associations that share common goals; To create a unified standard of care for the benefit of animals & humankind
Colin Burrows, President
June Ingwersen, Administrator

Visual Art, Crafts, Folk Arts

Alberta Craft Council (ACC)
10186 - 106 St., Edmonton AB T5J 1H4
Tel: 780-488-6611; *Fax:* 780-488-8855
Toll-Free: 800-362-7238
acc@albertacraft.ab.ca
www.albertacraft.ab.ca
Social Media: www.youtube.com/user/albertacraftcouncil
www.facebook.com/pages/Alberta-Craft-Council/176292132592
twitter.com/abcraftcouncil
To stimulate, develop & support craft in Alberta through communication, education, exhibition, & participation
Tom McFall, Executive Director
Tara Owen, Chair

Art Dealers Association of Canada Inc. (ADAC) / Association des marchands d'art du Canada
#393, 401 Richmond St. West, Toronto ON M5V 3A8
Tel: 416-934-1583; *Fax:* 866-280-9432
Toll-Free: 866-435-2322
info@ad-ac.ca
www.ad-ac.ca
Social Media:
www.facebook.com/ArtDealersAssociationofCanada
twitter.com/ADAC_AMAC
To promote & encourage public awareness of visual arts in Canada & abroad
Elizabeth Edwards, Executive Director
Jeanette Langmann, President

Artists in Stained Glass (AISG)
c/o Elizabeth Steinebach, PO Box 302, Parry Sound ON P2A 2X4
www.aisg.on.ca
To encourage the development of stained glass as a contemporary art form, in Ontario & throughout Canada.
Elizabeth Steinebach, Contact
Robert Brown, President

Association des collections d'entreprises (ACE) / Corporate Art Collectors Association
QC
info@ace-cca.ca
ace-cca.ca
Réunir les conservateurs et les propriétaires de collections corporatives; favoriser l'échange d'information, d'idées, d'expériences, d'expertise, de systèmes ou de services; représenter de façon générale les intérêts de ses membres; favoriser la diffusion de l'art au Québec
Jo-Ann Kane, Présidente et secrétaire
François Rochon, Trésorier
Kimberlee Clarke, Responsable, Logistique

The Canadian Art Foundation
#320, 215 Spadina Ave., Toronto ON M5T 2C7
Tel: 416-368-8854; *Fax:* 416-368-6135
Toll-Free: 800-222-4762
info@canadianart.ca
www.canadianart.ca
Social Media: vimeo.com/channels/canadianart;
canadianart.tumblr.com
www.facebook.com/canadianart
twitter.com/canartca
To foster & support the visual arts in Canada & to celebrate artists & their creativity with a program of events, lectures, competitions, publications & educational initiatives.
Ann Webb, Executive Director
Romina Tina Fontana, Director, Marketing & Communications
Ann Webb, Publisher, Canadian Art
Richard Rhodes, Editor, Canadian Art

Canadian Association of Professional Conservators (CAPC) / Association canadienne des restaurateurs professionnels (ACRP)
c/o Canadian Museums Association, #400, 280 Metcalfe St., Ottawa ON K2P 1R7
Fax: 613-233-5438
www.capc-acrp.ca
To foster high standards within the conservation profession through accreditation; To facilitate public access to professional conservators
Dee Stubbs-Lee, President
Heidi Sobol, Vice-President
Anita Henry, Treasurer

Canadian Craft & Hobby Association (CCHA)
Mono Plaza, PO Box 101, 633419 Hwy. 10 North, Orangeville ON L9W 2Z5
Tel: 519-940-5969; *Fax:* 519-941-0492
Paul.laplante@asi-tapedots.com
www.cdncraft.org
To further the success of every business engaged in Canada's craft & hobby industry by providing an arena for the discussion of goals & plans; to foster industry expansion through development & implementation of dynamic programs & activities; to provide a forum for meeting new people, learning new ideas & profiting from benefits of working together
Paul Laplante, President

Canadian Crafts Federation (CCF) / Fédération canadienne des métiers d'art (FCMA)
PO Box 1231, Fredericton NB E3B 5C8
Tel: 506-462-9560
info@canadiancraftsfederation.ca
www.canadiancraftsfederation.ca
To represent provincial & territorial crafts councils & the Canadian crafts sector; to advance & promote the vitality & excellence of Canadian crafts nationally & internationally to the benefit of Canadian craftspeople & the community at large
Deborah Dumka, President

Canadian Guild of Crafts / Guilde canadienne des métiers d'art
1460B, Sherbrooke St. West, Montréal QC H3G 1K4
Tel: 514-849-6091; *Fax:* 514-849-7351
Toll-Free: 866-477-6091
info@canadianguild.com
www.canadianguildofcrafts.com
Social Media:
www.facebook.com/187315447973358
To preserve, encourage & promote Canadian crafts; to organize & sponsor exhibitions of the work of recognized & promising artists in the fields of arts & crafts; to educate interested groups about Canadian & native crafts through tours & lectures
Diane Labelle, Director

Canadian Quilters' Association (CQA) / Association canadienne de la courtepointe (ACC)
6 Spruce St., Pasadena NL A0L 1K0
administration@canadianquilter.com
www.canadianquilter.com
Social Media:
www.facebook.com/canadianquilterassociation
The promotion of a greater understanding, appreciation & knowledge of the art, techniques & heritage of patchwork, appliqué & quilting; the promotion of the highest standards of workmanship & design in both traditional & innovative work the fostering of a climate of cooperation amongst quiltmakers across the country.
Johanna Alford, President
Vivian Kapusta, Secretary/Publicist

Canadian Society of Painters in Water Colour (CSPWC) / Société canadienne de peintres en aquarelle (SCPA)
80 Birmingham St., #B3, Toronto ON M8V 3W6
Tel: 416-533-5100
info@cspwc.com
www.cspwc.com
To promote the use of experimentation with water-based media; To encourage new artists
William Rogers, President
Anita Cotter, Administrator

Conseil des arts de Montréal (CAM)
Édifice Gaston Miron, 1210, rue Sherbrooke est, Montréal QC H2L 1L9
Tél: 514-280-3580; *Téléc:* 514-280-3784
artsmontreal@ville.montreal.qc.ca
www.artsmontreal.org
Mèdia social: www.facebook.com/ArtsMontreal
twitter.com/ConseilArtsMtl
Soutenir, encourager et harmoniser les initiatives d'ordre artistique et culturel sur le territoire de la ville de Montréal.
Nathalie Maillé, Directrice générale et sec. conseil
France Laroche, Directrice de l'administration

Conseil des métiers d'art du Québec (ind.) (CMA) / Québec Crafts Council (Ind.)
Marché Bonsecours, #400, 390, rue St-Paul Est, Montréal QC H2Y 1H2
Tél: 514-861-2787; *Téléc:* 514-861-9191
Ligne sans frais: 855-515-2787
info@metiersdart.ca
www.metiers-d-art.qc.ca
Pour distribuer les créations métiers d'art auprès des grossistes canadiens et étrangers.
Patrice Bolduc, Adjoint du directeur général

Craft Council of Newfoundland & Labrador
Devon House, 59 Duckworth St., St. John's NL A1C 1E6
Tel: 709-753-2749; *Fax:* 709-753-2766
info@craftcouncil.nl.ca
www.craftcouncil.nl.ca
Social Media: www.flickr.com/photos/craftcouncilnl
www.facebook.com/CraftCouncilNL
twitter.com/CraftCouncilNL
To produce high quality work; To assist & advise members in wide variety of craft-related areas
Anne Manuel, Executive Director

Crafts Association of British Columbia (CABC) / Conseil de l'artisanat de la Colombie-Britannique
Granville Island, 1386 Cartwright St., Vancouver BC V6H 3R8
Tel: 604-687-6511; *Fax:* 604-687-6711
Toll-Free: 888-687-6511
info@cabc.net
www.cabc.net
To develop excellence in crafts
Yvonne Chui, Executive Director

Embroiderers' Association of Canada, Inc. (EAC)
c/o Membership Director, 168 Kroeker Ave., Steinbach MB R5G 0L8
www.eac.ca
To preserve traditional techniques & promote new challenges in embroidery through education & networking; to offer courses in embroidery & certifies teachers.
Beryl Burnett, President
Dianna Thorne, Treasurer

Folklore Canada International (FCI)
2040, rue Alexandre-de-Sève, Montréal QC H2L 2W4
Tel: 514-524-8552; *Fax:* 514-524-0262
patrimoine@qc.aira.com
www.folklore-canada.org
To promote folk arts; to organize cultural exhanges between groups at national & international levels; to organize international folk arts festivals.

Manitoba Crafts Council (MCC)
#553, 70 Arthur St., Winnipeg MB R3B 1G7
Tel: 204-946-0803
media@manitobacraft.ca
manitobacraft.ca
Social Media: pinterest.com/manitobacraft/
www.facebook.com/ManitobaCraftCouncil
twitter.com/mbcraftcouncil
To promote the development & appreciation of fine craft; to facilitate a supportive environment in which fine, contemporary craft may flourish.
Alison Norberg, President

The Metal Arts Guild of Canada (MAGC)
151 Marion St., Toronto ON M6R 1E6
communications@metalartsguild.ca
www.metalartsguild.ca
Social Media:
twitter.com/MAGcanada
To be committed to the exchange of information & ideas encouraging appreciation for the metal arts; To promote & develop the metal arts; To further education in the metal arts; To encourage members to experiment with all the forms that metal takes
Delane Cooper, President

New Brunswick Crafts Council / Conseil d'artisanat du Nouveau-Brunswick
PO Box 1231, Stn. A, Fredericton NB E3B 5C8
Tel: 506-450-8989; *Fax:* 506-457-6010
Toll-Free: 866-622-7238
info@nbcraftscouncil.ca
www.nbcraftscouncil.ca
Social Media:
www.facebook.com/2411474486
To provide opportunities & support to members by developing, promoting & fostering an appreciation of excellence in craft.
Natalie Landry, Executive Director
Kim Bent, President

Nova Scotia Designer Crafts Council (NSDCC)
1113 Marginal Rd., Halifax NS B3H 4P7
Tel: 902-423-3837; *Fax:* 902-422-0881
office@nsdcc.ns.ca
www.nsdcc.ns.ca
Social Media: www.youtube.com/user/nsdcc
www.facebook.com/NSDCC
twitter.com/NSDCC
To encourage & promote the craft movement in Nova Scotia; to increase public awareness & appreciation of craft products & activities
Susan Hanrahan, Executive Director

Ontario Crafts Council (OCC)
990 Queen St. West, Toronto ON M6J 1H1
Tel: 416-925-4222; *Fax:* 416-925-4223
info@craft.on.ca
www.craft.on.ca
Social Media:
www.facebook.com/OntarioCraftsCouncil
twitter.com/OntarioCrafts
To have craft recognized as a valuable part of life and the excellence of Ontario craft and craftspeople acknowledged across Canada and around the world.
Emma Quin, Executive Director

Prince Edward Island Crafts Council (PEICC)
PO Box 20071, Stn. Sherwood, Charlottetown PE C1A PE3
Tel: 902-892-5152; *Fax:* 902-628-8740
info@peicraftscouncil.com
peicraftscouncil.com
Social Media:
www.facebook.com/peicraftscouncil
twitter.com/PECraftsCouncil
To promote the making & acceptance of quality handcrafted items through the provision of programs & services
Suzanne Scott, President
Laura Cole, Executive Director

Royal Canadian Academy of Arts (RCA) / Académie royale des arts du Canada
#375, 401 Richmond St. West, Toronto ON M5V 3A8
Tel: 416-408-2718; *Fax:* 416-408-2286
rcaarts@interlog.com
www.rca-arc.ca
To celebrate the achievement of excellence & innovation by visual artists across Canada; to encourage the new generation of artists; to facilitate the exchange of ideas about visual culture for the benefit of all Canadians
Ann McCall, President
Rachel Wallace, Acting Managing Director

Saskatchewan Craft Council (SCC)
813 Broadway Ave., Saskatoon SK S7N 1B5
Tel: 306-653-3616; *Fax:* 306-244-2711
Toll-Free: 866-653-3616
saskcraftcouncil@sasktel.net
www.saskcraftcouncil.org
Social Media:
www.facebook.com/SaskatchewanCraftCouncil
twitter.com/skcraftcouncil

Sculptors Society of Canada (SSC) / Société des sculpteurs du Canada
c/o Canadian Sculpture Centre, 500 Church St., Toronto ON M4Y 2C8
Tel: 647-435-5858
gallery@cansculpt.org
www.cansculpt.org
To promote Canadian sculpture; to provide encouragement to sculptors through public exhibitions & discussions in Canada & other countries
Judi Michelle Young, President

Society of Canadian Artists (SCA) / Société des artistes canadiens (SAC)
Toronto ON
info@societyofcanadianartists.com
www.societyofcanadianartists.com
To promote recognition of its member-artists through exhibitions, seminars, workshops, travelling shows
Josy Britton, President
Peter Gough, Vice-President

Visual Arts Nova Scotia (VANS)
1113 Marginal Rd., Halifax NS B3H 4P7
Tel: 902-423-4694; *Fax:* 902-422-0881
Toll-Free: 866-225-8267
vans@visualarts.ns.ca
www.visualarts.ns.ca
Social Media:
www.facebook.com/VisualArtsNovaScotia
twitter.com/visualartsns
To promote a better understanding of arts & artists in Nova Scotia; to provide practical assistance to artists; to act in an advisory capacity to public & private interests
Briony Carros, Executive Director

Wildlife

Quetico Foundation
#216, 642 King St. West, Toronto ON M5V 1M7
Tel: 416-941-9388; *Fax:* 416-941-9236
office@queticofoundation.org
www.queticofoundation.org
Social Media:
www.facebook.com/pages/QueticoFoundation
To preserve wilderness areas of Ontario, particularly Quetico Provincial Park, for recreation & scientific use
Glenda McLachlan, Executive Director

Spruce City Wildlife Association (SCWA)
1384 River Rd., Prince George BC V2L 5S8
Tel: 250-563-5437; *Fax:* 250-563-5438
info@scwa.bc.ca
www.scwa.bc.ca
To perform environmental acts that improve the BC wilderness
Jim Glaicar, President

Women

Act To End Violence Against Women
#209, 390 Steeles Ave. West, Thornhill ON L4J 6X2
Tel: 905-695-5372; *Fax:* 905-695-5375
Toll-Free: 866-333-5942
info@acttoendvaw.org
www.acttoendvaw.org
Social Media:
www.facebook.com/acttoendvaw
Works locally, nationally & internationally to strengthen the effectiveness of women in the Jewish community & society; to foster the emotional well-being of children; to perpetuate Jewish values & secure world Jewry. Programs include ending violence towards women, sexual assault awareness, emergency housing for women & children, & advocacy to end child poverty in Canada. Offices in Toronto & Montréal, & chapters in Toronto, Montréal, B.C., Windsor & Winnipeg.
Penny Krowitz, Executive Director

Alberta Women's Institutes (AWI)
AB
awi.athabascau.ca
To help discover, stimulate & develop leadership among women
Evelyn Ellerman, Contact

Alliance des femmes de la francophonie canadienne (AFFC)
Place de la francophonie, #302, 450, rue Rideau, Ottawa ON K1N 5Z4
Tél: 613-241-3500; *Téléc:* 613-241-6679
Ligne sans frais: 866-535-9422
info@affc.ca
www.affc.ca
Média social: www.facebook.com/229810340365531
twitter.com/AFFCfemmes
Favorise l'autonomie des femmes canadiennes-françaises sur tous les plans; assure le respect des droits des femmes francophones vivant en milieu minoritaire; soutien le développement de l'action collective et politique des femmes au Canada français; souligne la spécificité des femmes francophones auprès des instances gouvernementales, des diverses associations et du grand public
Manon Beaulieu, Directrice générale
Lepage Maria, Présidente

Association féminine d'éducation et d'action sociale (AFEAS) / Feminine Association for Education & Social Action
5999, rue de Marseille, Montréal QC H1N 1K6
Tél: 514-251-1636; *Téléc:* 514-251-9023
info@afeas.qc.ca
www.afeas.qc.ca
Média social:
www.youtube.com/results?search_query=afeas&aq=f
www.facebook.com/pages/Afeas/181581728519026
twitter.com/afeas1966
Avec ses Activités femmes d'ici organisées sur tout le territoire québécois, l'Afeas informe ses membres, suscite des échanges et des débats et les incite à participer davantage aux différentes structures de la société

Association Marie-Reine de Chibougamau
CP 295, Chibougamau QC G8P 2K7
Tél: 418-748-4760
Aider les femmes & les enfants victimes de violence
Marie-Paule Lévesque, Présidente

Association of Canadian Women Composers (ACWC) / L'Association des femmes compositeurs canadiennes (AFCC)
c/o Canadian Music Centre, 20 St. Joseph St., Toronto ON M4Y 1J9
acwcafcc@gmail.com
www.acwc.ca
Social Media:
www.facebook.com/215231155239835
To promote the music of Canadian women composers through concerts, commissions, publications, recordings, etc.
Joanna Estelle, Chair

Atlantic Mission Society (AMS)
ams.pccatlantic.ca
To support missions with prayer, study & service
Jennifer Whitfield, President

British Columbia Women's Institutes (BCWI)
PO Box 36, 4395 Mountain Rd., Barriere BC V0E 1E1
Tel: 250-672-0259; *Fax:* 250-672-0259
info@bcwi.org
www.bcwi.ca
Social Media: www.youtube.com/user/BCWomensInstitute
www.facebook.com/185390304847227
twitter.com/bcwi
To help discover, stimulate & develop leadership among women; to assist, encourage & support women to become knowledgeable & responsible citizens; to ensure basic human rights for women & to work towards their equality; to be a strong voice through which matters of utmost concern can reach the decision makers; to network with organizations sharing similar objectives; to promote the improvement of agricultural & other rural communities & to safeguard the environment

Canadian Association of Women Executives & Entrepreneurs (CAWEE) / Association canadienne des femmes cadres et entrepreneurs
#1600, 401 Bay St., Toronto ON M5H 2Y4
Tel: 416-756-0000; *Fax:* 416-756-0000
contact@cawee.net
www.cawee.net
Social Media:
linkedin.com/groups?home=&gid=2294616&trk=anet_ug_hm
To provide an environment for successful businesswomen to grow & develop, both professionally & personally, through business & community involvement
Lois Volk, President
Amya Greenleaf Brassert, Director, Policy & Administration
Heather Freed, Director, Sponsorship
Marie May, Director, Membership

Canadian Board Diversity Council (CBDC) / Conseil canadien pour la diversité administrative (CCDA)
#502, 180 Bloor St. West, Toronto ON M5S 2V6
Tel: 416-361-1475
www.boarddiversity.ca
Social Media:
linkedin.com/company/882730
twitter.com/diverseboards
To conduct research on diversity on Canadian corporate boards; to provide governance education programming; to educate members & the governance community onboard diversity best practices & principles; to build a network of business leaders who are committed to diversity
Pamela Jeffery, Founder
Sherri Stevens, Chief Executive Officer
Paul-Emile McNab, Manager, Research
Lori Brotherton, Manager, Governance Education
Samantha Morton, Senior Coordinator

The Canadian Federation of Business & Professional Women's Clubs (CFBPWC) / Fédération canadienne des clubs des femmes de carrières commerciales et professionnelles (FCCFCCP)
PO Box 62054, Orléans ON K1C 7H8
www.bpwcanada.com
Social Media:
www.ca.linkedin.com/in/bpwcanada
facebook.com/bpw.canada
twitter.com/bpwcan
To develop & encourage women to pursue business, the professions & industry; To work toward the improvement of economic, employment & social conditions for women; To work for high standards of service in business, the professions, industry & public life; To stimulate interest in federal, provincial & municipal affairs; To encourage women to participate in the business of government at all levels; To encourage & assist women & girls to acquire further education & training
Doris Hall, President
Valerie Clarke, First Vice-President
Sue Calhoun, Second Vice President
Sheila Crook, Secretary
Karin Gorgerat, Treasurer

Canadian Hadassah WIZO (CHW)
#208, 90 Eglinton Ave. East, Toronto ON M4P 2Y3
Tel: 416-477-5964; *Fax:* 416-977-5965
info@chw.ca
www.chw.ca
Social Media: www.youtube.com/user/CHWOrganization
linkedin.com/company/chw
www.facebook.com/CanadianHadassahWIZO
twitter.com/CHWdotCA
To extend material & moral support of Jewish women of Canada to needy individuals in Hadassah-WIZO welfare institutions in Israel; To encourage Jewish & Hebrew culture in Canada
Claudia Goldman, National President
Alina Ianson, Executive Director

Canadian Women in Communications (CWC) / Association canadienne des femmes en communication (AFC)
#300, 116 Lisgar St., Ottawa ON K2P 0C2
Tel: 613-706-0607; *Fax:* 613-706-0612
Toll-Free: 800-361-2978
cwcafc@cwc-afc.com
www.cwc-afc.com
To advance the role of women in the communications sector
Joanne Stanley, Executive Director

Canadian Women's Foundation / Fondation canadienne des femmes
#504, 133 Richmond St. West, Toronto ON M5H 2L3
Tel: 416-365-1444; *Fax:* 416-365-1745
Toll-Free: 866-293-4483
TTY: 416-365-1732
info@canadianwomen.org
www.canadianwomen.org
Social Media: www.youtube.com/user/CanadianWomenFdn
linkedin.com/company/the-canadian-women%27s-foundation
www.facebook.com/CanadianWomensFoundation
www.twitter.com/cdnwomenfdn
To raise money to research, fund & share the best approaches to ending violence against women, moving low-income women out of poverty & building strong, resilient girls
Sheherazade Hirji, President & CEO

Centre Afrique au Féminin
#106, 7000, av du Parc, Montréal QC H3N 1X1
Tél: 514-272-3274; *Téléc:* 514-272-8617
info@afriqueaufeminin.org
www.afriqueaufeminin.org
Offre un lieu de recontres pour toutes les femmes, ces familles & ce dans une ambiance conviviale; classes, activités, halte-garderie, dépannage alimentaire
Magdalena Molineros, Coordonatrice Principale

Centre de Femmes Les Elles du Nord
#2, 570, 3e Rue, Chibougamau QC G8P 1N9
Tél: 418-748-7171
ccfc@tlb.sympatico.ca
Linda Boulanger, Responsable

Centre for Women in Business (CWB)
c/o Mount Saint Vincent University, The Meadows, 166 Bedford Hwy., 2nd Fl., Halifax NS B3M 2J6
Tel: 902-457-6449; *Fax:* 902-443-4687
Toll-Free: 888-776-9022
cwb@msvu.ca
www.centreforwomeninbusiness.ca
Social Media: www.youtube.com/user/CentreWomenBusiness
linkedin.com/company/1539340
www.facebook.com/centreforwomeninbusiness
twitter.com/cwb_ns
To help women entrepreneurs start, grow & advance their businesses
Sandi Findlay-Thompson, Chair
Tanya Priske, Executive Director

Cercle des Fermières - Chibougamau
CP 417, Chibougamau QC G8P 2X7
Tél: 418-672-4877
www.cfq.qc.ca
Colombe Bergeron, Responsable

Comité condition féminine Baie-James
#203, 552, 3e Rue, Chibougamau QC G8P 1N9
Tél: 418-748-4408; *Téléc:* 418-748-2486
ccfbj@tlb.sympatico.ca
ccfbj.com
A pour mission l'amélioration des conditions de vie des Jamésiennes
Gérald Lemoine, Présidente

Les EssentiElles
Centre de la francophonie, 302, rue Strickland, Whitehorse YT Y1A 2K1
Tél: 867-668-2636; *Téléc:* 867-668-3511
elles@essentielles.ca
www.lesessentielles.ca
De représenter les intérêts des femmes francophones du Yukon.
Ketsia Houde, Directrice

Federated Women's Institutes of Canada (FWIC) / Fédération des instituts féminins du Canada
PO Box 209, 359 Blue Lake Rd., St George ON N0E 1N0
Tel: 519-448-3873; *Fax:* 519-448-3506
www.fwic.ca
Social Media:
www.facebook.com/WomensInstitutes
twitter.com/fwicanada
To act as a united voice for Women's Institutes of Canada; To promote Canadian women, families, & community living
Kate Belair, Executive Director

Federated Women's Institutes of Ontario (FWIO)
552 Ridge Rd., Stoney Creek ON L8J 2Y6
Tel: 905-662-2691; *Fax:* 905-930-8631
www.fwio.on.ca
Social Media:
twitter.com/fwiontario
To assist & encourage women to become more knowledgeable & responsible citizens; To promote & develop good family life skills; To help discover, stimulate & develop leadership; To help identify & resolve need in the community
Kim Sauder, Executive Administrator
Andrea Morrison, Manager, Program & Communications

Fédération des femmes du Québec (FFQ)
#309, 110, rue St-Thérèse, Montréal QC H2Y 1E6
Tél: 514-876-0166; *Téléc:* 514-876-0162
info@ffq.qc.ca
www.ffq.qc.ca
Média social: www.flickr.com/photos/laffq
www.facebook.com/FFQMMF
twitter.com/LaFFQ
Pour défendre les droits et intérêts des femmes
Alexa Conradi, Présidente
Eve-Marie Lacasse, Coordonnatrice

Federation of Medical Women of Canada (FMWC) / Fédération des femmes médecins du Canada
#170, 774 Prom. Echo Dr., Ottawa ON K1S 5N8
Tel: 613-569-5881; *Fax:* 613-249-3906
Toll-Free: 877-771-3777
fmwcmain@fmwc.ca
www.fmwc.ca
Committed to the professional, social, & personal advancement of women physicians & to the promotion of the well-being of women in the medical profession & in society at large
Mamta Gautam, President

The Group Halifax
Halifax NS
info@thegrouphalifax.com
thegrouphalifax.com
Social Media:
linkedin.com/groups/Group-Professional-Networking-Association-2403
www.facebook.com/TheGroupHalifax
twitter.com/TheGroupHalifax
A Halifax Metro-based business networking association with the aim of bringing together professionals in different sectors and industries to develop new skills, expand business networks, and promote the growth of their businesses.

Immigrant Women Services Ottawa (IWSO) / Services pour femmes immigrantes d'Ottawa
#400, 219 Argyle St., Ottawa ON K2P 2H4
Tel: 613-729-3145; *Fax:* 613-729-9308
infomail@immigrantwomenservices.com
www.immigrantwomenservices.com
Social Media:
www.facebook.com/immigrantwomenservicesottawa
twitter.com/ImmigrantWomen
To empower & enable immigrant women in the Ottawa region to participate in the elimination of all forms of abuse against women; to raise awareness among immigrant women who are abused, in order to break down their isolation & enable them to advocate on their own behalf; to develop a crisis service for immigrant women who are abused to give them full access to mainstream resources; to develop cross-cultural training for shelters & mainstream agencies regarding the special needs of immigrant women in order to ensure that existing services are accessible & appropriate to them & their families; to educate immigrant communities to work toward ending violence against women.

Korean Canadian Women's Association (KCWA)
2, 27 Madison Ave., Toronto ON M5R 2S2
Tel: 416-340-1234; *Fax:* 416-340-8114
kcwa@kcwa.net
www.kcwa.net
To empower Korean Canadian families and other vulnerable members of the community-at-large to live free from violence, poverty and inequity through the provision of culturally sensitive and linguistically appropriate services for the purpose of enhancing the well-being of immigrant families and promoting their successful integration into Canadian society.

Manitoba Women's Institutes (MWI)
1129 Queens Ave., Brandon MB R7A 1L9
Tel: 204-726-7135; *Fax:* 204-726-6260
mbwi.ca
Social Media:
www.facebook.com/557282304320877
Focuses on personal development, the family, agriculture, rural development & community action, locally & globally
Joni Swidnicki, Executive Administrator

MATCH International Women's Fund
1404 Scott St., Ottawa ON K1Y 4M8
Fax: 613-798-0990
Toll-Free: 855-640-1872
info@matchinternational.org
www.matchinternational.org
Social Media: www.youtube.com/user/MATCHIntCentre;
www.instagram.com/thematchfund
www.facebook.com/matchinternational
twitter.com/MATCHIntFund
To encourage sustained development in the global South, through a focus on women's rights & empowerment; To support women in the global South in executing their ideas regarding women's rights & equality; To advance women's rights through international cooperation
Jessica Tomlin, Executive Director

Na'amat Canada Inc.
#6, 7005 Kildare Rd., Montréal QC H4W 1C1
Tel: 514-488-0792; *Fax:* 514-487-6727
Toll-Free: 888-278-0792
naamat@naamatcanada.org
www.naamat.com
Social Media: www.youtube.com/user/NaamatCanada
www.facebook.com/NaamatCanada
twitter.com/NaamatCanada
To support social programs in Canada & Israel; to help protect women, children & families in both nations; to support the state of Israel
Orit Tobe, President

National Action Committee on the Status of Women (NAC) / Comité canadien d'action sur le statut de la femme (CCA)
#417, 215 Spadina Ave., Toronto ON M5T 2C7
Tel: 416-932-1718; *Fax:* 416-979-3936
To shape public opinion, influence decision makers & mobilize membership & the Canadian public to work for equality & justice for all women

National Association of Women & the Law (NAWL) / Association nationale de la femme et du droit (ANFD)
PO Box 46008, 2339 Ogilvie Rd., Gloucester ON K1J 9M7
Tel: 613-241-7570
www.nawl.ca
To promote the equality rights of women through legal education, research & law reform advocacy; to improve the legal status of women in Canada through law reform; to dismantle barriers to all women's equality
Alison Dewar, Chair, National Steering Committee
Jane Bailey, Member, National Steering Committee
Samantha Henrickson, Member, National Steering Committee

The National Council of Women of Canada (NCWC) / Le Conseil national des femmes du Canada
PO Box 67099, Ottawa ON K2A 4E4
Tel: 902-422-8485
ncwc@magma.ca
www.ncwcanada.ca
Social Media:
www.facebook.com/thencwc
To empower all women to work together towards improving the quality of life for women, families & society through a forum of member organizations & individuals
Karen Monnon Dempsey, President

Native Women's Association of the Northwest Territories
Post Office Building, 2nd Fl., PO Box 2321, Yellowknife NT X1A 2P7
Tel: 867-873-5509; *Fax:* 867-873-3152
Toll-Free: 866-459-1114
nativewomensnwt.com
Social Media:
www.facebook.com/NativeWomensAssociationOfTheNwt
Provides training & education programs for native women in the Western Arctic
Marilyn Napier, Executive Director

New Brunswick Women's Institute (NBWI)
681 Union St., Fredericton NB E3A 3N8
Tel: 506-454-0798; *Fax:* 506-451-8949
nbwi@nb.aibn.com
www.nbwi.ca
Social Media:
www.facebook.com/284295801781170
To help discover, stimulate & develop leadership among women; to assist, encourage & support women to become knowledgeable & responsible citizens; to ensure basic human rights for women & work towards their equality; to network with other organizations sharing similar objectives; to promote the improvement of agricultural & other rural communities & to safeguard the environment

Newfoundland & Labrador Women's Institutes
c/o Arts & Culture Centre, PO Box 1854, St. John's NL A1C 5P9
Tel: 709-753-8780; *Fax:* 709-753-8708
nlwi@nfld.com
www.nlwi.ca
To encourage women to work together to expand their skills, broaden their interests, plan meetings, workshops & conferences, & strengthen the quality of life for themselves, their families & their communities
Barbara Taylor, Executive Officer

NSERC Chair for Women in Science & Engineering
350 Albert St., Ottawa ON K1A 1H5
Tel: 613-944-6240; *Fax:* 613-996-2589
cwse-cfsg@nserc-crsng.gc.ca
www.nserc-crsng.gc.ca
To encourage women in Canada to enter careers in science, engineering, mathematics & computer sciences; to encourage women in Canada to attain high levels of professional achievement in these fields; to serve as an information centre for & about women in these fields; to make people aware of Canadian women scientists & engineers & of career opportunities available to them; to provide a forum for discussion of subjects of interest to members
Carolyn J. Emerson, Chair, Atlantic Region

The Older Women's Network (OWN) / Réseau des femmes aînées
115 The Esplanade, Toronto ON M5E 1Y7
Tel: 416-214-1518
info@olderwomensnetwork.org
olderwomensnetwork.org
To initiate & support discussion on issues relevant to the well-being of older women; To develop & support legislation to expand opportunities for housing, economic security, & optimum health; To monitor the media in order to encourage a more realistic & positive portrayal of older women; To support the efforts of young women to achieve equal opportunity, freedom from discrimination, abuse & exploitation, & the right to reproductive choice; To support the needs of children; To liaise with movements for social justice in Canada & abroad

Prince Edward Island Business Women's Association (PEIBWA)
161 St. Peter's Rd., Charlottetown PE C1A 5P7
Tel: 902-892-6040; *Fax:* 902-892-6050
Toll-Free: 866-892-6040
office@peibwa.org
www.peibwa.org
Social Media:
www.facebook.com/PEIBWA
twitter.com/peibwa
To assist women in business to succeed by providing services and programs to meet their objectives.
Michelle Ryder-MacEwen, President

Prince Edward Island Women's Institute (PEIWI)
#105, 40 Enman Cres., Charlottetown PE C1E 1E6
Tel: 902-368-4860; *Fax:* 902-368-4439
wi@gov.pe.ca
www.peiwi.ca
Social Media:
www.facebook.com/PEIWomensInstitute
To help discover, stimulate & develop leadership among women; To assist, encourage & support women to become knowledgeable & responsible citizens; To ensure basic human rights for women & to work towards their equality; To be a strong voice through which matters of utmost concern can reach the decision makers; to network with organizations sharing similar objectives; To promote the improvement of agricultural & other rural communities & to safeguard the environment
Jacquie Laird, President

Québec Women's Institutes (QWI)
177, Rg. Ste-Anne, Saint-Chrysostome QC J0S 160
Toll-Free: 877-781-9293
info@qwi.la
www.qwi.la
Social Media:
www.facebook.com/QuebecWomensInstitute
To help discover, stimulate & develop leadership among women; To assist, encourage & support women to become knowledgeable & responsible citizens; To ensure basic human rights for women & to work toward their equality; To be a strong voice through which matters of utmost concern can reach the decision makers; To promote the improvement of agricultural & other rural communities & to safeguard the environment
Norma Sherrer, President
Pat Clarke, Treasurer

Réseau des femmes d'affaires du Québec inc. (RFAQ)
#201, 476, rue Jean-Neveau, Longueuil QC J4G 1N8
Tél: 514-521-2441; *Téléc:* 514-521-0410
Ligne sans frais: 800-332-2683
info@rfaq.ca
www.rfaq.ca
Média social: www.youtube.com/user/RFAQinc
linkedin.com/groups?gid=2390552
www.facebook.com/RFAQinc
twitter.com/ReseauFAQ
Afin d'encourager et de promouvoir les femmes à devenir des leaders dans les instances sociales, politiques et économiques

Ruth Vachon, Présidente/Directrice générale

Réseau Femmes Québec (RFQ)
#134, 911, rue Jean-Talon est, Montréal QC H2R 1V5
Tél: 514-484-2375
reseau.femmes.quebec@gmail.com
www.reseau-femmes-quebec.qc.ca
Ruth Vachon, Présidente

Saskatchewan Women's Institute (SWI)
SK
saskatchewan@fwic.ca
Social Media:
www.facebook.com/436313276575974
To help discover, stimulate & develop leadership among women; To assist, encourage & support women to become knowledgeable & responsible citizens; To ensure basic human rights for women & to work towards their equality; To be a strong voice through which matters of the utmost concern can reach the decision makers; To promote the improvement of agricultural & other rural communities & to safeguard the environment

Society for Canadian Women in Science & Technology (SCWIST) / Société des canadiennes dans la science et la technologie
#311, 525 Seymour St., Vancouver BC V6B 3H7
Tel: 604-893-8657
esourcecentre@scwist.ca
www.scwist.ca
Social Media:
linkedin.com/groups?gid=1915550
www.facebook.com/167831516563792
twitter.com/SCWIST
To promote equal opportunities for women in scientific, technical & engineering careers; to educate public about careers in science & technology particularly to improve social attitudes on the stereotyping of careers in science; to assist educators by providing current information on careers & career training in sciences & scientific policies
Rosine Hage-Moussa, President

South Asian Women's Centre (SAWC)
8163 Main St., Vancouver BC V5X 3L2
Tel: 604-325-6637; *Fax:* 604-322-6675
sawc@asia.com
www.sawc.8m.com
The South Asian Women's Centre is a space for South Asian women to work actively for social change. The centre strongly believes that women can change their own lives and the lives of others in our communities, in our society, and even globally. The centre supports the development of non-oppressive attitudes and behaviours by critiquing and combating sexism, racism, homophobia, caste/classism, ageism and ableism.

Transition House Association of Nova Scotia (THANS)
#215, 2099 Gottingen St., Halifax NS B3K 3B2
Tel: 902-429-7287; *Fax:* 902-429-0561
coordinator@thans.ca
www.thans.ca
The Transition House Association of Nova Scotia (THANS) member organizations provide transitional services to women (and their children) who are experiencing violence and abuse, including culturally relevant services to Mi'kmaw people. THANS eleven member organizations work with women and their children in thirteen locations across Nova Scotia.
Pamela Harrison, Provincial Coordinator

Women Business Owners of Manitoba (WBOM)
PO Box 2748, Winnipeg MB R3C 4B3
Tel: 204-775-7981; *Fax:* 204-897-8094
info@wbom.ca
www.wbom.ca
Social Media:
linkedin.com/groups?mostPopular=&gid=2573420
www.facebook.com/WomenBusinessOwnersOfManitoba
Supports & inspires excellence, learning & growth in business
Lucy Camara, President
Tracy Ducharme, Vice-President

Women on the Rise Telling her Story (WORTH)
5775 rue Saint-Jacques, Montréal QC H4A 2E8
Tel: 514-485-7418; *Fax:* 514-485-7418
womenontherise@bellnet.ca
To promote the well-being of women and their children, especially in the Black anglophone community, by offering them self-help activities and encouraging them to develop their potential.
Grace Campbell, Director

Women's Art Association of Canada (WAAC)
23 Prince Arthur Ave., Toronto ON M5R 1B2
Tel: 416-922-2060
administration@womensartofcanada.ca
www.womensartofcanada.ca
To provide scholarships for the arts through the following schools & colleges: The Royal Conservatory of Music of Toronto; The Ontario College of Art; The Faculty of Music, University of Toronto; The National Ballet School; Sheridan College

Women's Art Resource Centre (WARC)
#122, 401 Richmond St. West, Toronto ON M5V 3A8
Tel: 416-977-0097
warc@warc.net
www.warc.net

Women's Centre of Montreal / Centre des femmes de Montréal
3585, rue Saint-Urbain, Montréal QC H2X 2N6
Tél: 514-842-1066; *Téléc:* 514-842-1067
cfmwcm@centredesfemmes.com
www.centredesfemmesdemtl.org
The mission of the Women's Centre of Montréal is to provide services to help women help themselves. To accomplish its mission, the Centre offers educational and vocational training, information, counselling and referral services. The Centre communicates women's concerns to the public and acts as a catalyst for change regarding women's issues.
Johanne Bélisle, Directrice générale

Women's Counselling & Referral & Education Centre (WCREC)
#303B, 489 College St., Toronto ON M6G 1A5
Tel: 416-534-8458; *Fax:* 416-534-1704
generalmail@wcrec.org
www.plasmalife.com/WCRECsite
To promote the mental & emotional well-being of women; To provide free community-based, alternative, non-medical mental health services in Toronto & in other areas through contact by phone & e-mail
Barbara Heron, President

Women's Executive Network (WXN) / Réseau des femmes exécutives (RFE)
#502, 180 Bloor St. West, Toronto ON M5S 2V6
Tel: 416-361-1475; *Fax:* 416-361-1652
Toll-Free: 866-465-3996
membership@wxnetwork.com
www.wxnetwork.com
Social Media:
www.facebook.com/WXNevents
www.twitter.com/wxn
Dedicated to the advancement & recognition of executive-minded women in the workplace
Pamela Jeffery, Founder
Sherri Stevens, Chief Executive Officer
Linsay Moran, Vice-President, Programs & Events

Women's Healthy Environments Network (WHEN)
#400, 215 Spadina Ave., Toronto ON M5T 2C7
Tel: 416-928-0880; *Fax:* 416-644-0116
office@womenshealthyenvironments.ca
www.womenshealthyenvironments.ca
Social Media: www.youtube.com/user/WHENwomen
www.facebook.com/WHENonlinex
twitter.com/WHENonline
To provide a forum for communication; to conduct research on issues relating to women in their environments of planning, health, ecology, workplace design, community development & urban & rural sociology & economy
Enida Kule, Chair

Women's Institutes of Nova Scotia (WINS)
#207, 90 Research Dr., Bible Hill NS B6L 2R2
Tel: 902-843-9467; *Fax:* 902-896-7276
novascotiawi@eastlink.ca
www.gov.ns.ca/agri/wins
To provide women with opportunities to enhance their lives through community service & involvement, education & leadership development

Women's International League for Peace & Freedom (WILPF)
c/o Bruna Nota, #901, 70 Mill St., Toronto ON M5A 4R1
Tel: 416-203-1402
www.wilpfinternational.org/canada
To unite women throughout the world into a force working to put an end to war; to work for social, economic & political equality for all people in all nations.
Marlene LeGates, President

Women's Legal Education & Action Fund (LEAF) / Fonds d'action et d'éducation juridiques pour les femmes (FAEJ)
#401, 260 Spadina Ave., Toronto ON M5T 2E4
Tel: 416-595-7170; *Fax:* 416-595-7191
Toll-Free: 888-824-5323
info@leaf.ca
www.leaf.ca
Social Media:
www.facebook.com/23825817618
twitter.com/LEAFNational
The Fund promotes equality for women, primarily by using the gender equality provisions of the Canadian Charter of Rights & Freedoms. It sponsors test cases before the Canadian courts, human rights commissions & government agencies on behalf of women, & provides public education on the issue of gender equality.
Michelle Bullas, Chair
Diane O'Reggio, Executive Director
Kim Stanton, Legal Director

Women's Missionary Society (WMS)
Tel: 416-441-1111; *Toll-Free:* 800-619-7301
www.wmspcc.ca
To encourage people of the Presbyterian Church in Canada to be involved in local & world mission
Sarah Kim, Executive Director

Women's Network PEI
PO Box 233, 40 Enman Cres., Charlottetown PE C1A 7K4
Tel: 902-368-5040; *Fax:* 902-368-5039
Toll-Free: 888-362-7373
www.wnpei.org
Social Media:
www.facebook.com/wnpei
To strengthen & support the efforts of PEI women to improve their status in society
Michelle MacCallum, Executive Director

Writers & Editors

Association de la presse francophone (APF) / Association of Francophone Newspapers
267, rue Dalhousie, Ottawa ON K1N 7E3
Tél: 613-241-1017; *Téléc:* 613-241-6313
admin@apf.ca
www.apf.ca
Média social:
www.facebook.com/Associationdelapressefrancophone
twitter.com/apf_journaux
Promouvoir l'existence d'une presse communautaire écrite en langue française aussi vigoureuse et aussi répandue que possible dans les communautés de langue française à l'extérieur du Québec; Contribuer à l'amélioration de sa qualité et de son rayonnement; défendre énergiquement les principes de la liberté de parole et de la presse écrite
Jean-Patrice Meunier, Directeur général
Sophie Bègue, Chargée, Des communications et projets spéciaux

Canadian Association of Journalists (CAJ) / L'Association canadienne des journalistes
PO Box 117, Stn. F, Toronto ON MRY 2L4
Tel: 647-968-2393
www.caj.ca
Social Media:
linkedin.com/company/canadian-association-of-journalists
www.facebook.com/CdnAssocJournalists
twitter.com/CAJ
To promote excellence in journalism; to encourage & promote investigative journalism
Nick Taylor-Vaisey, President

Canadian Authors Association (CAA)
#203, 6 West St. North, Orillia ON L3V 5B8
Tel: 705-325-3926
admin@canadianauthors.org
canadianauthors.org
To promote & protect Canadian authors & their works; To act as a voice for writers
Anita Purcell, Executive Director
Jessica Wiles, Executive Director

Canadian Farm Writers' Federation (CFWF)
PO Box 250, Ormstown QC J0S 1K0
Fax: 450-829-2226
Toll-Free: 877-782-6456
secretariat@cfwf.ca
cfwf.wildapricot.org
To serve the interests of agricultural journalists
Lisa Guenther, President

Tamara Leigh, Vice-President
Hugh Maynard, Secretary-Treasurer
Christina Franc, Administrator

Canadian Journalism Foundation (CJF) / La Fondation pour le journalisme canadien
#500, 59 Adelaide St. East, Toronto ON M5C 1K6
Tel: 416-955-0394; *Fax:* 416-532-6879
www.cjf-fjc.ca
Social Media:
www.facebook.com/cjfprograms
twitter.com/cjffjc
To honour outstanding achievements in the field of journalism in Canada through grants, awards & scholarships; to promote & support programs & seminars at or in conjunction with qualified educational institutions in journalism.
Natalie Turvey, Executive Director
Wendy Kan, Program Manager

Canadian Science Writers' Association (CSWA) / Association canadienne des rédacteurs scientifiques
PO Box 75, Stn. A, Toronto ON M5W 1A2
Toll-Free: 800-796-8595
office@sciencewriters.ca
www.sciencewriters.ca
To foster excellence in science communication; To increase public awareness of Canadian science & technology
Kristina Bergen, Executive Director
Stephen Strauss, President

Canadian Society of Children's Authors, Illustrators & Performers (CANSCAIP) / La société canadienne des auteurs, illustrateurs et artistes pour enfants
#501, 720 Bathurst St., Toronto ON M5S 2R4
Tel: 416-515-1559
office@canscaip.org
www.canscaip.org
Social Media:
www.facebook.com/CANSCAIP.org
twitter.com/CANSCAIP
To promote the growth of children's literature by establishing the rapport with teachers, librarians & children; to establish communication between publishers & society; to encourage the development of new writers, illustrators & performers
Bill Swan, President

The Crime Writers of Canada (CWC)
#4C, 240 Westwood Rd., Guelph ON N1H 7W9
info@crimewriterscanada.com
www.crimewriterscanada.com
To promote Canadian crime writing
Vicki Delany, Chair

Écrivains Francophones d'Amérique
1995, rue Sherbrooke Ouest, Montréal QC H3A 1H9
Tél: 514-318-2590
lesecrivainsfrancophones@yahoo.ca
ecrivainsfrancophones.com
Média social: www.facebook.com/111361458891464
Grouper en association les écrivains de langue française, de nationalité canadienne, domiciliés ou non au Canada, auteurs d'un ou de plusieurs livres publiés au Canada ou ailleurs par des éditeurs homologués; servir et défendre les intérêts de la littérature canadienne; prendre toutes les mesures nécessaires ou opportunes pour assurer le respect de la propriété littéraire de ses membres.
Gino Levesque, Responsable

Editors' Association of Canada (EAC) / Association canadienne des réviseurs (ACR)
#505, 27 Carlton St., Toronto ON M5B 1L2
Tel: 416-975-1379; *Fax:* 416-975-1637
Toll-Free: 866-226-3348
info@editors.ca
www.editors.ca
Social Media:
twitter.com/eac_acr
To promote & maintain standards of professional editing & publishing; to set guidelines to help editors secure fair pay & good working conditions, fosters networking among editors & cooperates with other publishing associations in areas of common concern.
Anne Louise Mahoney, President
Patrick Banville, Executive Director

Federation of British Columbia Writers (FBCW)
PO Box 3887, Stn. Terminal, Vancouver BC V6B 2Z3
Tel: 604-683-2057
info@bcwriters.ca
www.bcwriters.ca
To develop, support, inform, & promote writers in British Columbia; To foster a community for writing in British Columbia
Ben Nuttall-Smith, President

Fédération québécoise du loisir littéraire (FQLL)
CP 1000, Succ. M, 4545, av Pierre-de Coubertin, Montréal QC H1V 3R2
Tél: 514-252-3033; *Ligne sans frais:* 866-533-3755
www.litteraire.ca
Offre au grand public l'accès à toutes les formes de l'expression littéraire et artistique dans un contexte de loisir, d'éducation et de perfectionnement
Diane Robert, Présidente

The League of Canadian Poets (LCP)
#312, 192 Spadina Ave., Toronto ON M5T 2C2
Tel: 416-504-1657; *Fax:* 416-504-0096
admin@poets.ca
www.poets.ca
To develop the art of poetry; to enhance the status of poets & nurture a professional poetic community; to facilitate the teaching of Canadian poetry at all levels of education; to enlarge the audience for poetry by encouraging publication, performance & recognition of poetry nationally & internationally; to uphold freedom of expression
Joanna Poblocka, Executive Director

Manitoba Writers' Guild Inc. (MWG)
#218, 100 Arthur St., Winnipeg MB R3B 1H3
Tel: 204-944-8013
info@mbwriter.mb.ca
www.mbwriter.mb.ca
To provide services & support writers in Manitoba
Darcia Senft, President
Sharron Arksey, Secretary
Mickey Cuthbert, Treasurer

The Ontario Poetry Society (TOPS)
#710, 65 Spring Garden Ave., Toronto ON M2N 6H9
www.theontariopoetrysociety.ca
To establish a democratic organization for members to unite in friendship for emotional support & encouragement in all aspects of poetry, including writing, editing, performing & publishing
Fran Figge, President
Mel Sarnese, Vice-President
Bunny Iskov, Treasurer
Joan Sutcliffe, Secretary

Professional Writers Association of Canada (PWAC)
#130, 215 Spadina Ave., Toronto ON M5T 2C7
Tel: 416-504-1645
info@pwac.ca
www.pwac.ca
Social Media:
www.youtube.com/channel/UCkMZ2XfVMZeMdfiiwRv6uCA
twitter.com/writersdotca
To protect & promote interests of periodical writers in Canada; to develop & maintain professional standards in editor/writer relationships by instituting use of standard publication agreement in all freelance assignments; to improve quality of periodical writing in Canada; to work actively for survival of periodical writing in a highly competitive communications market; to lobby for higher standard fees for freelance magazine & newspaper writing; to mediate grievances between writers & editors; to provide professional development workshops; to lobby for freedom of press & expression; to offset isolation of freelance writers by circulating news, information on market
Michelle Greysen, President
Sandy Crawley, Executive Director

Québec Writers' Federation (QWF) / Fédération des Écrivaines et Écrivains du Québec
#3, 1200 Atwater Ave., Montréal QC H3Z 1X4
Tel: 514-933-0878
admin@qwf.org
www.qwf.org
To encourage & support English-language writing in Québec to ensure a lasting place for English literature in the province's cultural scene.
David Homel, President
Lori Schubert, Executive Director

Saskatchewan Writers Guild (SWG)
PO Box 3986, Regina SK S4P 3R9
Tel: 306-757-6310; *Fax:* 306-565-8554
info@skwriter.com
www.skwriter.com
Social Media:
www.facebook.com/pages/Saskatchewan-Writers-Guild/917244 4541
twitter.com/SKWritersGuild
To promote excellence in writing by Saskatchewan writers; to advocate for Saskatchewan writers; to promote the teaching of Saskatchewan & Canadian literature & instruction in the art of writing at all levels of education; to improve public access to writers & their work; to develop professionalism in the business of writing; to improve the economic status of Saskatchewan writers
Judith Silverthorne, Executive Director
Tracy Hamon, Program Manager
Rhea McFarlane, Administrative Assistant

Société professionnelle des auteurs et des compositeurs du Québec (SPACQ)
#901, 505, boul René-Lévesque ouest, Montréal QC H2Z 1Y7
Tél: 514-845-3739; *Téléc:* 514-845-1903
Ligne sans frais: 866-445-3739
info@spacq.qc.ca
www.spacq.qc.ca
Média social: www.youtube.com/laspacq
www.facebook.com/213627294934
twitter.com/SPACQ
Défendre les droits et les intérêts moraux, professionnels et économiques des auteurs et des compositeurs, ainsi que les droits qui se rapportent aux oeuvres, auprès des autorités gouvernementales.
Pierre-Daniel Rheault, Directeur général
Sébastien Charest, Responsable, Service aux membres

Union des écrivaines et écrivains québécois (UNEQ)
3492, av Laval, Montréal QC H2X 3C8
Tél: 514-849-8540; *Téléc:* 514-849-6239
Ligne sans frais: 888-849-8540
ecrivez@uneq.qc.ca
www.uneq.qc.ca
Média social: www.facebook.com/152536222994
twitter.com/Ecrivains_QC
Élaborer des politiques et administrer des programmes en vue de favoriser le développement de la littérature québécoise et sa diffusion au Québec comme à l'étranger, en vue également de faire reconnaître la profession d'écrivain de telle sorte que les intérêts moraux, sociaux et économiques des auteurs soient respectés
Danièle Simpson, Présidente
Francis Farley-Chevrier, Directeur général

Writers Guild of Canada (WGC)
#401, 366 Adelaide St. West, Toronto ON M5V 1R9
Tel: 416-979-7907; *Fax:* 416-979-9273
Toll-Free: 800-567-9974
info@wgc.ca
www.wgc.ca
Social Media:
twitter.com/WGCtweet
Voice of professional Canadian screenwriters; to lobby on their behalf; to protect their interests; to raise the profile of screenwriters & screenwriting
Jill Golick, President
Maureen Parker, Executive Director

Writers' Alliance of Newfoundland & Labrador (WANL)
Haymarket Square, #208, 223 Duckworth St., St. John's NL A1C 6N1
Tel: 709-739-5215; *Toll-Free:* 866-739-5215
wanl@nf.aibn.com
wanl.ca
Social Media:
www.facebook.com/writersalliance
twitter.com/WANL
To enhance the quality of writing in Newfoundland & Labrador through such programmes as workshops, meetings, readings; to encourage & develop public awareness & appreciation for the work of writers in Newfoundland & Labrador
Alison Dyer, Executive Director

Writers' Federation of New Brunswick (WFNB)
#151, 527 Dundonald St., Fredericton NB E3B 1X5
Tel: 506-260-3564
info@wfnb.ca
www.wfnb.ca
Social Media:
www.facebook.com/writersfederation
twitter.com/WritersNB
To promote New Brunswick writing; to assist writers of New Brunswick at all stages of their development by providing services; to uphold the right to free artistic expression; to provide additional educational services to schools & libraries; to contribute to the enhancement of literary arts

Writers' Federation of Nova Scotia (WFNS)
1113 Marginal Rd., Halifax NS B3H 4P7
Tel: 902-423-8116; *Fax:* 902-422-0881
talk@writers.ns.ca
www.writers.ns.ca
Social Media:
www.facebook.com/WritersFedNS
twitter.com/WFNS

To foster creative & professional writing; to provide advice & assistance to writers; to encourage greater public recognition of Nova Scotia writers

The Writers' Guild of Alberta (WGA)
Percy Page Centre, 11759 Groat Rd., Edmonton AB T5M 3K6
Tel: 780-422-8174; *Fax:* 780-422-2663
Toll-Free: 800-665-5354
mail@writersguild.ab.ca
www.writersguild.ab.ca
Social Media:
www.facebook.com/139496766118754
twitter.com/WritersGuildAB
To provide a meeting ground & collective voice for the writers of Alberta; to promote excellence in writing in Alberta
Carol Holmes, Executive Director
Patricia MacQuarrie, President
Julie Sedivy, Vice-President

The Writers' Trust of Canada
#600, 460 Richmond St. West, Toronto ON M5V 1Y1
Tel: 416-504-8222; *Fax:* 416-504-9090
Toll-Free: 877-906-6548
info@writerstrust.com
www.writerstrust.com
Social Media:
www.facebook.com/writerstrust
twitter.com/writerstrust
Is a national charitable organization providing support to writers through various programs & awards; celebrates the talents & achievements of our country's writers; is committed to exploring & introducing to future generations the traditions that will enrich our common literary heritage & strengthen Canada's cultural foundations
Peter Kahnert, Chair
Don Oravec, Executive Director
Amanda Hopkins, Program Coordinator

The Writers' Union of Canada (TWUC)
#600, 460 Richmond St. West, Toronto ON M5V 1Y1
Tel: 416-703-8982; *Fax:* 416-504-9090
info@writersunion.ca
www.writersunion.ca
Social Media:
www.facebook.com/thewritersunionofcanada
twitter.com/twuc
To unite writers for the advancement of their common interests; To foster writing in Canada; To maintain relations with publishers; To exchange information among members; To safeguard the freedom to write & to publish; To advance good relations with other writers & their organizations in Canada & all parts of the world
John Degen, Executive Director

Youth

Black Community Resource Centre (BCRC)
#497, 6767, ch de la Côte-des-Neiges, Montréal QC H3S 2T6
Tel: 514-342-2247; *Fax:* 514-342-2283
bcrc@qc.aira.com
www.bcrcmontreal.com/bcrc
BCRC is a resource-based organization committed to helping English-speaking visible minority youth rekindle their dreams and achieve their full potential. The Centre takes a comprehensive approach, with a strategy that is progressive, multi-interventionist and holistic; emphasis is on infrastructure support and training, prevention and empowerment, community-building, collaboration, and an inclusive perspective. BCRC has a mandate to provide support services to individuals, communities, para-public and public organizations, and develops and implements health, education, socio-cultural and economic development programs.

Centre Afrika
1644, rue St-Hubert, Montréal QC H2L 3Z3
Tél: 514-843-4019; *Téléc:* 514-849-4323
centreafrika@centreafrika.com
www.centreafrika.com
Média social:
www.youtube.com/channel/UCh07u7KOPIF43d_Qg-DPjQA
www.facebook.com/centreafrika
Activités sociales & culturelles et activités spirituelles/religieuses

Club Richelieu Boréal de Chibougamau
CP 522, Chibougamau QC G8P 2X9
Tél: 418-748-2398
Julie Poirier, Responsable

ERS Training & Development Corporation (ERS) / Corporation pour la formation et le développement ERS
#810, 5250, rue Ferrier, Montréal QC H4P 1L4
Tel: 514-731-3419; *Fax:* 514-731-4999
ers@erstraining.ca
www.erstraining.ca
To promote development & training; to identify the needs of youth; to develop & promote training skills & employment readiness; to seek out & put in place programs for the improvement of youth circumstances; to implement programs so that all may achieve full potential
Peter L. Clément, Président et directeur général

Force Jeunesse
#322, 1000, rue Saint-Antoine ouest, Montréal QC H3C 3R7
Tél: 514-384-8666; *Téléc:* 514-384-6442
info@forcejeunesse.qc.ca
www.forcejeunesse.qc.ca
Force Jeunesse est un regroupement de jeunes travailleurs issus de différents milieux dont le principe fondateur est l'équité intergénérationnelle; agit concrètement en revendiquant des mesures qui améliorent la situation économique et sociale des jeunes.
Jonathan Plamondon, Président

Head & Hands / A deux mains
5833, rue Sherbrooke ouest, Montréal QC H4A 1X4
Tel: 514-481-0277; *Fax:* 514-481-2336
info@headandhands.ca
www.headandhands.ca
Social Media: www.youtube.com/user/HeadandHands
www.facebook.com/headandhands
twitter.com/headandhands
Medical, social, and legal services with an approach that is harm-reductive, holistic, and non-judgmental.
Jon McPhedran Waitzer, Director
Juniper Belshaw, Contact, Fundraising and Development

Jeunes en partage
CP 441, Chibougamau QC G8P 2X8
Tél: 418-748-2935
Dany Larouche, Responsable

Richelieu International (RI)
#25, 1010 rue Polytek, Ottawa ON K1J 9J1
Tél: 613-742-6911; *Téléc:* 613-742-6916
Ligne sans frais: 800-267-6525
international@richelieu.org
www.richelieu.org
Média social: www.youtube.com/watch?v=7pqgbohjM6A
linkedin.com/company/richelieu-international?trk=company_name
www.facebook.com/277906642896
twitter.com/Le_Richelieu
A pour mission l'épanouissement de la personalité de ses membres & au développement de leurs aptitudes personnelles & collectives; la promotion de la langue française; aider la jeunesse
Laurier Thériault, Directeur général
Denis Daigle, Directeur administratif

SECTION 4
BROADCASTING

The listings in this section are arranged by province, then city within province, except the Major Broadcasting Companies, which are arranged alphabetically by company name.

Major Broadcasting Companies

591987 B.C. Ltd.
Owned by: YTV Canada Inc.*
Corus Conventional Television, 170 Queen St., Kingston, ON K7K 1B2
Tel: 613-544-2340; *Fax:* 613-544-5508
www.corusent.com
591987 B.C. Ltd. is a subsidiary of Corus Entertainment Inc., via YTV Canada Inc., that owns & operates the following TV stations: CHEX & CKWS.

591989 B.C. Ltd.
Owned by: Corus Premium Television Ltd.*
Corus Conventional Television, 170 Queen St., Kingston, ON K7K 1B2
Tel: 613-544-2340; *Fax:* 613-544-5508
www.corusent.com
591989 B.C. Ltd. owns & operates radio stations throughout Ontario.

Access Communications Co-operative Limited
Old Name: Regina Cablevision Co-operative Ltd.
2250 Park St., Regina, SK S4N 7K7
Fax: 306-565-5395
Toll-Free: 866-363-2225
www.myaccess.ca
Social Media: www.youtube.com/myaccessca, www.facebook.com/accesscommunication, twitter.com/MyAccess_ca
Access Communications offers internet access, television & cable, telephone, home security & web hosting services to communities in Saskatchewan.
Jim Deane, Chief Executive Officer
Carmela Haines, Vice-President, Finance & Administration

Arctic Radio
316 Green St., Flin Flon, MB R8A 0H2
Tel: 204-687-3469
Operates 3 AM Radio stations in Northern Manitoba.

Bayshore Broadcasting Corporation
PO Box 280, Owen Sound, ON N4K 5P5
Tel: 519-376-2030; *Fax:* 519-371-4242
Toll-Free: 866-384-0501
info@bayshorebroadcasting.ca
www.bayshorebroadcasting. ca
Social Media: twitter.com/NewsBayshore
Bayshore Broadcasting Corporation is an independent broadcaster. It operates radio stations in Grey, Bruce, Simcoe, & Huron counties in southern Ontario. The following stations are operated by Bayshore Broadcasting: 560 CFOS, Mix 106 (CIXK-FM), Country 93 (CKYC-FM), 98 the Beach (CFPS-FM), 97.7 the Beach (CHGB-FM), 104.9 the Beach (CHWC-FM), & Sunshine 89 (CISO-FM).
Ross Kentner, General Manager
Kevin Brown, Vice-President, Sales & Marketing, sales@bayshorebroadcasting.ca

Bell Media Inc.
Old Name: CTVglobemedia; Bell Globemedia; Baton Broadcasting
Headquarters
299 Queen St. West, Toronto, ON M5V 2Z5
Tel: 416-384-8000
www.bellmedia.ca
Social Media: www.facebook.com/bellmediainc, twitter.com/bellmediapr
Bell Media's subsidiaries are Bell Media TV & Bell Media Radio, which in turn own assets such as CTV, CTV Two, the former CHUM Limited radio properties, & 30 specialty cable television channels. In 2013, Bell Media acquired Astral Media & its assets, dissolving the company.
Mary Ann Turcke, President

Bell Media Radio
Owned by: Bell Media Inc.*
299 Queen St. West, Toronto, ON M5V 2Z5
Tel: 416-384-8000
www.bellmedia.ca
Bell Media Radio owns 30 stations across Canada, including the former CHUM Radio Network.
Randy Lennox, President, Broadcasting & Content

Bell Media TV
Owned by: Bell Media Inc.*
299 Queen St. West, Toronto, ON M5V 2Z5
Tel: 416-384-8000
www.bellmedia.ca
Bell Media TV owns the CTV network of television channels, including 21 stations, as well as CTV Two. The company also owns 30 specialty channels.

Blackburn Radio Inc.
#102, 700 Richmond St., London, ON N6A 5C7
Tel: 519-679-8680; *Fax:* 519-679-5321
www.blackburnradio.com
Social Media: www.linkedin.com/company/blackburn-radio-inc
Blackburn Radio is an AM-FM radio broadcaster which operates stations in Chatham, Leamington, London, Sarnia, Windsor, & Wingham.

Blue Ant Media
#200, 130 Merton St., Toronto, ON M4S 1A4
Tel: 416-646-4434; *Fax:* 416-646-4444
feedback@blueantmedia.ca
blueantmedia.ca
Social Media: www.linkedin.com/company/blue-ant-media, twitter.com/BlueAntMedia
Blue Ant Media is an independent broadcasting & publishing company founded by Michael MacMillan, former Chairman of Alliance Atlantis, & owned by Torstar Corporation (25%), Providence Equity Partners & Fairfax Financial. The company owns former GlassBox Television Inc. channels Aux, BitTV & Travel + Escape, as well as HIFI, bold, eqhd, Oasis HD & radX.
Michael MacMillan, Co-Founder & Chief Executive Officer
Raja Khanna, Chief Executive Officer, Television & Digital
Robb Chase, Chief Operating Officer
Cynthia Schyff, Executive Vice-President & Chief Financial Officer

Canadian Broadcasting Corporation (CBC)
Société Radio-Canada
Also known as: CBC/Radio-Canada
Head Office
PO Box 3220 C, Ottawa, ON K1Y 1E4
Tel: 613-288-6000
www.cbc.radio-canada.ca
Social Media: www.linkedin.com/groups/2280703/profile, www.facebook.com/CBCRadioCanada, twitter.com/CBCRadioCanada
Other information: TTY: 613-288-6455
CBC/Radio-Canada is Canada's national public broadcaster & one of its largest cultural institutions. Services are offered on radio, television, the Internet, satellite radio, digital audio, as well as through its record & music distribution service & wireless WAP & SMS messaging services.
Rémi Racine, Chair
Hubert T. Lacroix, President & CEO, CBC/Radio-Canada

Canadian Broadcasting Corporation - Canadian Broadcasting Centre
Société Radio-Canada
Owned by: Canadian Broadcasting Corporation*
PO Box 500 A, 250 Front St. West, Toronto, ON M5W 1E6
Tel: 416-205-3311
Toll-Free: 866-306-4636
cbcinput@cbc.ca
www.cbc.ca
Other information: TTY: 416-205-6688
The CBC is a Canadian crown corporation & serves as Canada's national public radio & television broadcaster; in French, the CBC is called la Société Radio-Canada (SRC), & the corporation also operates Radio Canada International (RCI); offers programming in English, French & 8 Aboriginal languages on radio, & in 9 languages on RCI; provides regional & local television programming in both official languages; broadcasts locally produced programs in English & native languages for people living in the far north; primarily funded by federal statutory grants.
Rémi Racine, Chair, Board of Directors
Hubert T. Lacroix, President & CEO

Channel Zero Inc.
2844 Dundas St. West, Toronto, ON M6P 1Y7
Tel: 416-492-1595
www.tvchannelzero.com
Social Media: www.linkedin.com/company/channel-zero-inc-
Channel Zero is a media company that owns several television stations including CHCH in Ontario & specialty channels Rewind & Silver Screen Classics.
Romen Podzyhun, Chair & Chief Executive Officer

CityWest
248 - 3rd Ave. West, Prince Rupert, BC V8J 1L1
Tel: 250-624-2111; *Fax:* 250-627-0905
Toll-Free: 800-442-8664
citywest@cwct.ca
www.citywest.ca
Social Media: www.facebook.com/CityWest.BC
Other information: Toll-Free Fax: 1-866-387-7964
CityWest provides television services to the following communitiesin British Columbia: Prince Rupert, Port Edward, Terrace/Thornhill, Kitimat, Hazeltons, Smithers/Telkwa, Houston & Stewart.
Don Holkestad, Chief Executive Officer, 250-627-0972, don.holkestad@cwct.ca
Chris Marett, Chief Financial Officer, 250-627-0925, chris.marett@cwct.ca

CKIK-FM Limited
Corporate Head Office
Owned by: Corus Premium Television Ltd.*
630 - 3rd Ave. SW, 8th Fl., Calgary, AB T2P 4L4
Tel: 403-716-6500; *Fax:* 403-444-4240
www.corusent.com
Other information: Alt. Fax: 403-444-4319
CKIK-FM Limited operates two radio stations in Alberta: CFGQ-FM (Q107) & CHQR-AM. CFGQ used to be called CKIK, but now that call sign belongs to CKIK-FM (KRAZE 101.3), owned by the independent Harvard Broadcasting. Despite this change, CKIK-FM Limited's name remains the same.

CKUA Radio Network
9804 Jasper Ave. NW, Edmonton, AB T5J 0C5
Tel: 780-428-7595; *Fax:* 780-428-7624
Toll-Free: 800-494-2582
www.ckua.com
Social Media: instagram.com/ckuaradio, www.facebook.com/CKUARadio, twitter.com/ckuaradio
CKUA Radio Network originally operated on the University of Alberta campus in Edmonton, but now broadcasts from offices in downtown Edmonton. CKUA is Canada's first educational broadcaster & Canada's first public broadcaster, is carried province-wide on AM & FM, & broadcasts in western Canada on some satellite providers & globally through ckua.com. It also has a large music collection consisting of over 70,000 CDs, 50,000 LPs & other formats. Due to financial constraints, CKUA's AM transmitter is scheduled to be shut down in the spring of 2013.
Ken Regan, Chief Executive Officer, kregan@ckua.com
Katrina Ingram, Chief Operating Officer, kingram@ckua.com
Don Barnes, Manager, Sales, dbarnes@ckua.com

Cogeco Connexion
Détenteur: COGECO Inc.*
#1700, 5 Place Ville-Marie, Montréal, QC H3B 0B3
Tél: 514-764-4700
carriere@cogeco.com
www.cogeco.ca
Médias sociaux: www.linkedin.com/company/cogeco-connexion, www.facebook.com/CogecoQC, twitter.com/CogecoQC
Louis Audet, President & CEO

Cogeco Inc.
#1700, 5, Place Ville-Marie, Montréal, QC H3B 0B3
Tél: 514-764-4700
media@cogeco.com
www.cogeco.ca
Médias sociaux: www.facebook.com/CogecoQC, twitter.com/CogecoQC
COGECO is telecommunications company which provides television & radio broadcasting services in Québec & Ontario. It is the second largest cable system operator in Ontario & Québec, in terms of the number of basic cable service customers served. COGECO owns & operates 13 radio stations in Québec through its subsidiary Cogeco Diffusion.
Jan Peeters, Chair
Louis Audet, President & CEO
Patrice Ouimet, Senior Vice-President & CFO, Finance
René Guimond, Vice-President, Affaires publiques et communications

Cogeco Media Inc.
Old Name: Cogeco Diffusion Inc.
Détenteur: Cogeco Inc.*
#1100, 800, rue de la Gauchetière ouest, Montréal, QC H5A 1M1
Tél: 514-787-7799
web@cogecomedia.com
www.cogecomedia.com
Médias sociaux: www.linkedin.com/company/cogeco-diffusion
Cogeco Diffusion owns & operates 13 radio stations in Québec.
Richard Lachance, President & CEO

Connelly Communications Corp.
c/o CJKL-FM, PO Box 430, 5 Kirkland St., Kirkland Lake, ON P2N 1N9
Tel: 705-567-3366; *Fax:* 705-567-6101
cjkl@cjklfm.com
www.cjklfm.com
Connelly Communications owns CJKL-FM & CJTT-FM.
Robin Connelly, President & General Manager

** For details on this company see listing in Major Broadcasting Companies section; † French language station*

Corus Entertainment Inc.
Corporate Executive Head Office
Corus Quay, 25 Dockside Dr., Toronto, ON M5A 0B5
Tel: 416-479-7000; *Fax:* 416-479-7006
www.corusent.com
Corus Entertainment is an integrated media & entertainment company. Television services include: YTV, Treehouse, W Network, CMT, The Documentary Channel, SCREAM, Discovery Kids, Telelatino & TELETOON (50%); Western Canada's exclusive pay-TV movie service on nine thematic channels under the Movie Central brand; three local over-the-air television stations; Corus Custom Networks advertising services for television & Max Trax, a residential subscription digital music service. They also operate 37 radio stations throughout Canada.
Doug Murphy, President & CEO
Tom Peddie, Executive Vice-President & CFO

Corus Premium Television Ltd.
Owned by: Corus Entertainment Inc.*
Corus Quay, 25 Dockside Dr., Toronto, ON M5A 0B5
www.corusent.com

Corus Radio Company
Owned by: Corus Entertainment Inc.*
Corus Quay, 25 Dockside Dr., Toronto, ON M5A 0B5
Tel: 416-479-6271; *Fax:* 416-479-7002
www.corusent.com

Dauphin Broadcasting Co. Ltd.
1735 Main St. South, Dauphin, MB R7N 2V4
Tel: 204-638-3230; *Fax:* 204-638-8257
ckdm.reception@730ckdm.com
730ckdm.com
Operates 730 CKDM, a community radio station serving Dauphin, Manitoba for over 50 years.

DERYtelecom
PO Box 1154, La Baie, QC G7B 3P3
Tel: 418-544-3358; *Fax:* 418-544-0187
Toll-Free: 866-544-3358
servicesaguenay@derytelecom.ca
www.derytele.com
Rémi Tremblay, Président et directeur général

DHX Media Ltd.
Also known as: Decode Halifax Media
Headquarters
1478 Queen St., Halifax, NS B3J 2H7
Tel: 902-423-0260; *Fax:* 902-422-0752
info@dhxmedia.com
www.dhxmedia.com
Social Media: www.linkedin.com/company/dhx-media, www.facebook.com/dhxmedia, twitter.com/dhxmedia
A production company whose main focus is on children & youth programming. It was created in 2006 through the merger of Decode Entertainment & Halifax Film Company. In 2013, DHX Media aquired Family Channel, Disney XD & Disney Junior after Astral Media merged with Bell Media.
Dana Sean Landry, Chief Executive Officer

Dougall Media
87 Hill St. North, Thunder Bay, ON P7A 5V6
Tel: 807-346-2600; *Fax:* 807-345-9923
www.dougallmedia.com
Dougall Media owns radio stations, television stations & a newspaper, all of which serve the Thunder Bay area.

EastLink
Old Name: Bragg Communications Inc.
PO Box 8660 A, Halifax, NS B3K 5M3
Tel: 902-484-2800
Toll-Free: 888-345-1111
www.eastlink.ca
Social Media: www.facebook.com/EastLink, twitter.com/eastlink
Other information: Business Services, Toll-Free; 1-877-813-1727
EastLink is a privately held telecommunications company providing services including communications, entertainment, television & advertising to residential, business & public sector clients in Atlantic Canada, Ontario, Québec, Alberta, Manitoba, British Columbia (through Coast Cable & Delta Cable) & Bermuda.
Lee Bragg, Chief Executive Officer

EastLink TV
Old Name: Bragg Communications Inc.
Owned by: EastLink*
PO Box 8660 A, Halifax, NS B3K 5M3
Tel: 902-484-2800
Toll-Free: 888-345-1111
eastlinktv.com
Social Media: www.facebook.com/EastLink, twitter.com/eastlink
Other information: Business Services, Toll-Free: 1-877-525-5441
EastLink TV provides services to clients & operates community TV channels in Nova Scotia, Prince Edward Island, Ontario & Alberta.

Evanov Communications Inc.
Old Name: Evanov Radio Group
5312 Dundas St. West, Toronto, ON M9B 1B3
Tel: 416-213-1035; *Fax:* 416-233-8617
info@evanov.radio.com
www.evanovradio.com
Owns 10 radio stations spread across Cetral & Atlantic Canada; promotes independent radio broadcasting
William Evanov, President & Chief Executive Officer

Fabmar Communications Ltd.
Also known as: 1097282 Alberta Ltd.
PO Box 750, Melfort, SK S0E 1A0
Tel: 306-752-2587
fabmarcommunications.com
Fabmar owns three radio stations in Saskatchewan & Alberta: CKJH, CJVR-FM & CIXM-FM.
Ken Singer, Vice-President, Broadcast Operations

Fairchild Media Group
Aberdeen Centre, #3300, 4151 Hazelbridge Way, Richmond, BC V6X 4J7
Tel: 604-295-1313; *Fax:* 604-295-1300
info@fairchildtv.com
www.fairchildgroup.com
Fairchild Media Group owns & operates Fairchild TV, Talentvision & Fairchild Radio.
Thomas Fung, Chair & Founder

Fairchild Radio
Owned by: Fairchild Media Group*
#26-29, 151 Esna Park Dr., Markham, ON L3R 3B1
Tel: 905-415-1430; *Fax:* 905-415-6292
www.fairchildradio.com
Social Media: www.youtube.com/user/fairchildradiotor, www.facebook.com/fairchildradiotoronto
Chinese Canadian multicultural radio network with stations in Toronto, Vancouver, & Calgary. Provides program schedules & internet simulcasting
Thomas Fung, Chair & Founder, Fairchild Media Group

Global National
Also known as: Global News
Owned by: Corus Entertainment Inc.*
7850 Enterprise St., Burnaby, BC V5A 1V7
Tel: 604-420-2288; *Fax:* 604-422-6466
viewers@globalnational.com
www.globalnews.ca
Social Media: twitter.com/globalnational

Global Television Network
Also known as: Global News
Owned by: Corus Entertainment Inc.*
7850 Enterprise St., Burnaby, BC V5A 1V7
Tel: 604-420-2288; *Fax:* 604-422-6466
viewers@globalnational.com
www.globaltv.com
Social Media: twitter.com/globalnational

Golden West Broadcasting Ltd.
Radio Head Office
#201, 125 Centre Ave., Altona, MB R0G 0B0
Tel: 204-324-6464; *Fax:* 888-765-7039
www.goldenwestradio.com
Headquartered in Altona, Manitoba. Golden West has 37 radio stations scattered across Manitoba, Saskatchewan, Alberta & Ontario.
Elmer Hildebrand, CEO
Lyndon Friesen, President

Groupe Radio Antenne 6 Inc.
Owned by: RNC MÉDIA, Inc.*
568, boul St-Joseph, Roberval, QC G8H 2K6
Tel: 418-275-1831; *Fax:* 418-275-2475
www.planeteradio.ca
Operates 5 stations in Lac-Saint-Jean region; also has a presence in Abitibi, Outaouais, & Montreal; operates the Planète brand.
Marc-André Levesque, President, malevesque@rncmedia.ca

Groupe TVA inc.
1600, boul de Maisonneuve est, Montréal, QC H2L 4P6
Tél: 514-526-9251; *Téléc:* 514-599-5502
groupetva.ca
Médias sociaux: www.linkedin.com/company/groupe-tva-inc
Groupe TVA fondée en 1960 sous le nom de Corporation Télé-Métropole inc., est une entreprise de communication intégrée active dans les secteurs de la diffusion, de la production de produits audiovisuels, de la publication de magazines, de l'édition ainsi que de la distribution de films.
Julie Tremblay, Présidente/Chef de la direction

Harvard Broadcasting Inc.
1900 Rose St., Regina, SK S4P 0A9
Tel: 306-546-6200
www.harvardbroadcasting.com
Social Media: www.linkedin.com/company/harvard-broadcasting
Harvard Broadcasting came into being in 1977, when The Hill Companies purchased CKCK-TV, the Regina-based CTV affiliate station. In 1981, Harvard expanded into radio with the purchase of CKRM and CFMQ, also both local stations. Today, Harvard Broadcasting Inc. includes 620 CKRM, MY92FM & 104.9 The Wolf in Regina, X92.9 in Calgary & CFVR-FM in Fort McMurray. In December 2015, Harvard Broadcasting acquired CKIK-FM in Red Deer.
Cam Cowie, Vice-President & COO, ccowie@harvardbroadcasting.com

Hector Broadcasting Co. Ltd.
Also known as: East Coast FM
PO Box 519, 84 Provost St., New Glasgow, NS B2H 5E7
Tel: 902-752-4200; *Fax:* 902-755-2468
info@ecfm.ca
ecfm.ca
Social Media: www.facebook.com/941EastCoastFM, twitter.com/941ECFM
Operates CKEC-FM (94.1 East Coast FM), a community radio station serving Pictou County, NS, & the newly created CKEZ-FM.

ICI Radio-Canada
Old Name: Société Radio-Canada
Détenteur: Canadian Broadcasting Corporation*
CP 6000, 1400, boul René-Lévesque ouest, Montréal, QC H3C 3A8
Tél: 514-597-6000
Ligne san frais: 866-306-4636
www.ici.radio-canada.ca
Médias sociaux: fr-ca.facebook.com/ICIRadioCanada, twitter.com/iciradiocanada
Autre information: ATS: 514-597-6013
ICI Radio-Canada est le radiodiffuseur public national du Canada et l'une des plus grandes institutions culturelles du pays. Avec ses 28 services offerts sur des plateformes comme la radio, la télévision, Internet, la radio par satellite, l'audio numérique, sans compter son service de distribution de disques et de musique et ses services de messagerie sans fil WAP et SMS, CBC/Radio-Canada est maintenant accessible aux Canadiens à leur convenance.
Hubert T. Lacroix, Président-Directeur général, CBC/Radio-Canada

Inuit Broadcasting Corporation (IBC)
Administrative Office
#301, 331 Cooper St., Ottawa, ON K2P 0G5
Tel: 613-235-1892; *Fax:* 613-230-8824
info@inuitbroadcasting.ca
www.nac.nu.ca
The Inuit Broadcasting Corporation provides a window to the Arctic by producing television programming by Inuit, for Inuit. IBC has 5 production centres scattered across Nunavut, with 34 Inuit staff at every level of the production chain, from director of network programming to technical producer to administrative assistant. IBC is a founding member of Television Northern Canada & the Aboriginal Peoples Television Network.
Debbie Brisebois, Executive Director

Island Radio Ltd.
Old Name: Central Island Broadcasting Ltd.
Owned by: The Jim Pattison Broadcast Group*
4550 Wellington Rd., Nanaimo, BC V9T 2H3
Tel: 250-758-1131; *Fax:* 250-758-4644
info@islandradio.bc.ca
www.islandradio.bc.ca
Island Radio consists of six radio stations on Vancouver Island, British Columbia

The Jim Pattison Broadcast Group
460 Pemberton Terrace, Kamloops, BC V2C 1T5
Tel: 250-372-3322; *Fax:* 250-374-0445
info@jpbroadcast.com
jpbroadcast.com
The Jim Pattison Broadcast Group is Canada's largest private western-based broadcasting company
Rod Schween, President
Mark Rogers, Vice-President, Sales
Bill Stovold, Director, IT & Engineering

** For details on this company see listing in Major Broadcasting Companies section; † French language station*

Klondike Broadcasting Ltd.
#203, 4103 - 4th Ave., Whitehorse, YK Y1A 1H6
Tel: 867-668-6100; *Fax:* 867-668-4209
info@ckrw.com
www.ckrw.com
Operates CKRW-FM/AM in Whitehorse, YK.
Eva Birdman, General Manager, eva@ckrw.com

Le5 Communications
#301, 336 Pine St., Sudbury, ON P3C 1X8
Tel: 705-222-8306; *Fax:* 705-222-2805
www.leloupfm.com
Social Media: www.facebook.com/leloupfm
Le5 Communications owns & operates two radio stations in Northern Ontario, with an additional one in the works for 2014, under the brand name Le Loup. The company also owns the newspapers L'Express de Timmins & Le Voyageur, from Timmins & Sudbury, respectively.
Paul Lefebvre, Propriétaire, plefebvre@leloupfm.com

Leclerc Communication Inc.
#505, 815, boul Lebourgneuf, Québec, QC G2J 0C1
Tel: 418-688-0919; *Fax:* 418-682-8430
www.leclerccommunication.ca
Leclerc Communication owns & operates two radio stations in Québec: CJEC-FM (WKND FM) & CFEL-FM (CKOI 102,1 Québec).
Jean-François Leclerc, Co-owner, jf.leclerc@leclerccommunication.ca
Nicolas Leclerc, Co-owner, nicolas.leclerc@leclerccommunication.ca

Mainstream Broadcasting Corporation
#100, 1200 West 73rd Ave., Vancouver, BC V6P 6G5
Tel: 604-263-1320; *Fax:* 604-261-0310
adm@am1320.com
www.am1320.com
Social Media: www.facebook.com/AM1320, twitter.com/AM1320chmb
Other information: www.linkedin.com/company/mainstream-broadcasting-corporation
Mainstream Broadcasting Corporation is a British Columbia media company owned and operated by local Vancouver resident and businessman, James Ho. In 1993, OCV programming was incorporated into the multicultural AM radio station of CHMB AM 1320, serving the needs of Vancouver's multicultural community.
James Ho, President

Maritime Broadcasting System (MBS)
90 Lovett Lake Ct., Halifax, NS B3S 0H6
Tel: 902-425-1225; *Fax:* 902-423-2093
mail@mbsradio.com
www.mbsradio.com
Originally established in 1969 as Eastern Broadcasting Limited, MBS Radio is a 100% maritime-owned, private broadcasting company, with 25 radio stations & 410 employees serving communities in the three Maritime Provinces of Nova Scotia, New Brunswick & Prince Edward Island
Robert L. Pace, Founding President

My Broadcasting Corporation (MBC)
Also known as: myFM
PO Box 961, 321B Raglan St. South, Renfrew, ON K7V 4H4
Tel: 613-432-6936; *Fax:* 613-432-1086
mybroadcastingcorp.weebly.com
The company owns & operates a number of small-market radio stations in Ontario. In 2015, the company purchased Pineridge Broadcasting Inc., which ownws & operates CHUC, CKSG (based in Cobourg) & CJWV (based in Peterborough).
Jon Pole, President & Co-Founder
Andrew Dickson, Vice-President & Co-Founder
Jeff Degraw, Vice-President, Sales

Newcap Radio
Also known as: Newcap Inc.
Old Name: Newcap Broadcasting
8 Bainsview Dr, Dartmouth, NS B3B 1G4
Tel: 902-468-7557; *Fax:* 902-468-7558
ncc@ncc.ca
www.ncc.ca
Robert G. Steele, President & CEO
Ian Lurie, Chief Operating Officer
Scott Weatherby, Chief Financial Officer & Corporate Secretary

Newfoundland Broadcasting Co. Ltd.
PO Box 2020, St. John's, NL A1C 5S2
Tel: 709-722-5015; *Fax:* 709-726-5017
greetings@ntv.ca
www.ntv.ca
Social Media: www.facebook.com/NTVNewsNL, twitter.com/NTVNewsNL
Reaches 8 million households across Canada via digital cable & satellite

NL Broadcasting Ltd.
611 Lansdowne St., Kamloops, BC V2C 1Y6
Tel: 250-372-2292; *Fax:* 250-372-2293
info@radionl.com
www.radionl.com
NL Broadcasting owns the following radio stations: CHNL-AM, CJKC-FM, CKRV-FM & CKMQ-FM (Merritt Broadcasting Ltd.).
Garth Buchko, General Manager, gbuchko@radionl.com

Okalakatiget Society
PO Box 160, Nain, NL A0P 1L0
Tel: 709-922-2187; *Fax:* 709-922-2293
okradio@oksociety.com
www.oksociety.com
Social Media: www.facebook.com/pages/OKâlaKatiget-Society/302939923049908, twitter.com/OKSociety
Other information: Alternate E-mail: okradio@oksociety.com
The OKalaKatiget Society was incorporated in 1982. Stationed in Nain, Labrador the Society provides a regional, native communication service for the people on the North Coast and the Lake Melville region of Labrador. People have come to rely on the Society for information and entertainment via radio and television. Their mandate is to preserve and promote the language and culture of the Inuit within the region
Morris Prokop, Exececutive Director

Quinte Broadcasting Co. Ltd.
PO Box 488, 10 Front St. South, Belleville, ON K8N 5B2
Tel: 613-969-5555; *Fax:* 613-969-8122
www.quinteradio.com

Radio Canada International (RCI)
Owned by: Canadian Broadcasting Corporation*
1400, boul René-Lévesque est, Montréal, QC H2L 2M2
Tel: 514-597-7461
info@rcinet.ca
www.rcinet.ca
Social Media: www.facebook.com/rcinet, twitter.com/RCInet
Radio Canada International has been broadcasting around the World since 1945, with live radio in English, French, Spanish, Portuguese, Arabic, Mandarin, and Russian. RCI's mandate is to increase awareness of Canadian values, as well as its social, economic and cultural activities to specific geographic areas as determined in consultation with the government of Canada. RCI also has the complementary mandate of addressing these same topics to new immigrants to Canada.
Soleïman Mellali, Editor in Chief

Rawlco Radio Ltd.
715 Saskatchewan Cres. West, Saskatoon, SK S7M 5V7
Tel: 306-934-2222; *Fax:* 306-477-0002
www.rawlco.com
Rawlco Radio Ltd. is a Saskatchewan company with radio stations in Saskatoon, Regina, Prince Albert, North Battleford, & Meadow Lake. Operates 13 radio stations
Kristy Werner, Vice-President & General Manager, Rawlco Saskatoon
Tom Newton, Vice-President & General Manager, Rawlco Regina
Kent Newson, Vice-President & General Manager, Rawlco Calgary

Remstar Corporation
85, rue St-Paul ouest, Montréal, QC H2Y 3V4
Tél: 514-847-1136
remstarcorp.com
Remstar is a film & broadcasting company that owns the French-language television network V.

Riding Mountain Broadcasting Ltd.
Owned by: Westman Communications Group*
624 - 14th St. East, Brandon, MB R7A 7E1
Tel: 204-726-8888; *Fax:* 204-726-1270
www.westmancom.com
Riding Mountain Broadcasting owns & operates two radio stations in the Brandon, MB, area: CKLQ-AM & CKLF-FM (Star 94.7)
David Baxter, President & CEO, Westman Communications Group

RNC MÉDIA, Inc.
Old Name: Radio-Nord Communications inc.
#1523, 1, Place Ville Marie, Montréal, QC H3B 2B5
Tél: 514-866-8686; *Téléc:* 514-866-8056
info@rncmedia.ca
www.rncmedia.ca
Radiodiffusion (Planète Radio, Radio X); télédiffusion (TVA Gatineau-Ottawa et Abitibi-Témiscamingue; TQS Gatineau-Ottawa et Abitibi-Témiscamingue; SRC Abitibi-Témiscamingue); programmation de haute qualité et services de publicité.
Mario Cecchini, Président/Directeur général, mcecchini@rncmedia.ca
Pierre R. Brosseau, Président exécutif du conseil, pbrosseau@rncmedia.ca

Rogers Broadcasting Ltd.
Owned by: Rogers Communications Inc.*
333 Bloor St. East, Toronto, ON M4W 1G9
Tel: 416-935-7777
www.rogersmedia.com
Social Media: www.facebook.com/Rogers, twitter.com/rogersbuzz
Rogers Broadcasting has 51 AM & FM radio stations across Canada. Television properties include Toronto multicultural television broadcasters OMNI.1 (CFMT) & OMNI.2, televised & electronic shopping service, The Shopping Channel, Rogers Sportsnet & manages two digital television services.
Rick Brace, President, Media Business Unit

Rogers Communications Inc.
333 Bloor St. East, 10th Fl., Toronto, ON M4W 1G9
Tel: 416-935-7777; *Fax:* 416-935-3597
www.rogers.com
Social Media: www.facebook.com/Rogers, twitter.com/rogersbuzz
Alan D. Horn, Chair
Guy Laurence, President & CEO

Saskatoon Media Group
Old Name: Hildebrand Communications; 629112 Saskatchewan Ltd.
366 - 3 Ave. South, Saskatoon, SK S7K 1M5
Tel: 306-244-1975
www.saskatoonhomepage.ca
Operates the following radio stations in Saskatoon: CJWW-AM, CKBL-FM & CJMK-FM.
Vic Dubois, General Manager
Myles Myrol, General Sales Manager
Tim Kostuik, Retail Sales Manager

SaskTel
Also known as: Saskatchewan Telecommunications Holding Corporation
PO Box 2121, Regina, SK S4P 4C5
Tel: 306-543-1696
Toll-Free: 800-727-5835
www.sasktel.com
Social Media: www.facebook.com/SaskTel, twitter.com/sasktel
Other information: Alternate Phone: 306-373-4791
SaskTel is a crown corporation telecommunications company that offers telephone, internet, digital TV (SaskTel Max), cell phone & wireless data services, among others.
Ron Styles, President & CEO
Charlene Gavel, Chief Financial Officer
Daryl Godfrey, Chief Technology Officer

SaskTel Max
Also known as: maxTV
Owned by: SaskTel*
PO Box 2121, Regina, SK S4P 4C5
Tel: 306-522-1820
Toll-Free: 800-727-5835
www.sasktel.com
Social Media: www.facebook.com/SaskTel, twitter.com/sasktel
SaskTel Max provides digital TV services to clients in Saskatchewan.
Ron Styles, President & CEO, SaskTel

Seneca College
1750 Finch Ave. East, Toronto, ON M2J 2X5
Tel: 416-491-5050
www.senecacollege.ca
Social Media: www.facebook.com/senecacollege, twitter.com/SenecaCollege
David Agnew, President, president@senecacollege.ca
Donna Duncan, Chair

** For details on this company see listing in Major Broadcasting Companies section; † French language station*

Shaw Communications Inc.
Also known as: Shaw Cablesystems G.P.
Old Name: Capital Cable Television
Owned by: Corus Entertainment Inc.*
#900, 630 - 3rd Ave. SW, Calgary, AB T2P 4L4
Tel: 403-750-4500; *Fax:* 403-750-4469
Toll-Free: 888-472-2222
www.shaw.ca
Social Media: www.youtube.com/user/ShawCommunication, www.facebook.com/shaw, twitter.com/shawinfo
Shaw Communications Inc. is a diversified communications company.Its core business is the provision of broadband cable television, high-speed Internet, digital phone, telecommunications services, & satellite direct-to-home services to more than 3 million customers throughout Canada.
Brad Shaw, Chief Executive Officer
Jay Mehr, President

Steele Communications
Owned by: Newcap Radio*
PO Box 8-590, 391 Kenmount Rd., St. Johns, NL A1B 3P5
Tel: 709-726-5590; *Fax:* 709-726-4633
www.vocm.com
Steele Communications is the Newfoundland & Labrador division of Newcap Inc. Owned & operated stations include VOCM & the Big Land network (CFLN-FM).
Harold Steele, Chairman

Stingray Digital Group Inc.
730, rue Wellington, Montréal, QC H3C 1T4
Tel: 514-664-1244; *Fax:* 514-664-1143
info@stingray.com
www.stingray.com
Social Media: www.facebook.com/StingrayBusiness, twitter.com/StingrayBiz
Eric Boyko, Founder, President & CEO

Télé Inter-Rives ltée
Inter-Riverbank Television
15, rue de la Chute, Rivière-du-Loup, QC G5R 5B7
Tél: 418-867-8080; *Téléc:* 418-867-4710
nousjoindre@cimt.ca
cimt.teleinterrives.com
Tele Inter-Rives Ltd. dirige 4 stations de télévision régionales dans l'est du Québec; CKRT-TV (SRC), CIMT-DT, CHAU (TVA), et CFTF (V).

Telelatino Network Inc. (TLN)
Owned by: Corus Entertainment Inc.*
5125 Steeles Ave. West, Toronto, ON M9L 1R5
Tel: 416-744-8200; *Fax:* 416-744-0966
Toll-Free: 800-551-8401
info@tlntv.com
www.tlntv.com
Social Media: www.facebook.com/TLNTelelatino, twitter.com/TLNTV
Telelatino Network is 50.5% owned by Corus Entertainment Inc. The network consists of the following channels: Mediaset Italia, EuroWorld Sport, Sky TG 24 Canada, Telelatino, TeleNiños & TLN en Español.
Aldo DiFelice, President

Télé-Québec
Also known as: Société de télédiffusion du Québec
1000, rue Fullum, Montréal, QC H2K 3L7
Tél: 514-521-2424; *Téléc:* 514-873-7464
Ligne san frais: 800-361-4362
info@telequebec.tv
www.telequebec.tv
Médias sociaux: instagram.com/telequebec, www.facebook.com/TeleQc, twitter.com/telequebec
La Société a pour objet d'exploiter une entreprise de télédiffusion éducative et culturelle afin d'assurer, par tout mode de diffusion, l'accessibilité de ses produits au public. Télé-Québec est une société publique de production et de diffusion, desservant plus de 92 % de la population québécoise à travers son réseau riche de 17 émetteurs, alimenté par un lien satellite portant sa programmation de Montréal.
Marie Collin, Présidente-Directrice générale

Teletoon Canada Inc.
Owned by: Corus Entertainment Inc.*
Brookfield Place, PO Box 787, 181 Bay St., Toronto, ON M5J 2T3
Tel: 416-956-2060; *Fax:* 416-956-2070
www.teletoon.com
Social Media: www.youtube.com/user/Teletoon, www.facebook.com/Teletoon

Touch Canada Broadcasting Limited Partnership
4510 MacLeod Trail South, Calgary, AB T2G 0A4
Tel: 403-276-1111; *Fax:* 403-276-1114
www.shinefm.com
Touch Canada Broadcasting owns & operates the following Christian radio stations in Alberta: CJCA-AM, CJLI-AM (forthcoming), CJRY-FM, CJSI-FM & CKRD-FM.

TVOntario (TVO)
PO Box 200 Q, Toronto, ON M4T 2T1
Tel: 416-484-2600
Toll-Free: 800-613-0513
asktvo@tvo.org
tvo.org
Social Media: www.youtube.com/user/tvochannel, www.facebook.com/tvontario, twitter.com/tvo
In 1970, TVOntario was established by the government of Ontario, for the purpose of using technology to support the province's education priorities. TVO, TVOntario's English-language service, is Canada's oldest educational broadcaster, and is available to over 98% of Ontario homes. TVO provides educational programming and online resources to extend learning at home and in the classroom, and to promote Ontario's cultural identity.
Lisa de Wilde, CEO

V Interactions Inc.
Also known as: V; V Télé
Old Name: TQS inc.
#100, 355, rue Ste-Catherine ouest, Montréal, QC H3B 1A5
Tél: 514-390-6100; *Téléc:* 514-390-6056
vtele.ca
Médias sociaux: www.youtube.com/user/tribuv, www.facebook.com/vtele.ca, twitter.com/vtele
V est un réseau de télévision de langue française privée, avec des stations à travers le Québec.
Maxime Rémillard, Président

Vista Broadcast Group
Also known as: Vista Radio
#110, 5477 - 152 St., Surrey, BC V3S 5A5
Tel: 604-372-1650
info@vistaradio.ca
www.vistaradio.ca
Other information: Phone, Business Office: 250-338-1133
Geoff Poulton, President, gpoulton@vistaradio.net
Andy Boyd, Chief Financial Officer, aboyd@vistaradio.ca
Murray Brookshaw, National Director, Programming, mbrookshaw@vistaradio.ca

Wawatay Native Communications Society
PO Box 1180, 16 - 5th Ave., Sioux Lookout, ON P8T 1B7
Tel: 807-737-2951; *Fax:* 807-737-3224
Toll-Free: 800-243-9059
www.wawataynews.ca
Wawatay Native Communications Society is a self-governing, independent community-driven entrepreneurial native organization dedicated to using appropriate technologies to meet the communication needs of people of Aboriginal ancestry in Northern Ontario
John Gagnon, Chief Executive Officer

Wawatay Radio Network
Owned by: Wawatay Native Communications Society*
PO Box 1180, 16 - 5th Ave., Sioux Lookout, ON P8T 1B7
Tel: 807-737-4040; *Fax:* 807-737-3224
Toll-Free: 800-661-5171
www.wawataynews.ca
Jerry Sawanas, Senior Broadcaster, jerrys@wawatay.on.ca
Bill Morris, Broadcaster & Producer, billm@wawatay.on.ca

Westman Communications Group
Also known as: Westman Cable
Old Name: Westman Cable TV
1906 Park Ave., Brandon, MB R7B 0R9
Tel: 204-725-4300; *Fax:* 204-726-0853
Toll-Free: 800-665-3337
www.westmancom.com
Social Media: www.facebook.com/WestmanCom, twitter.com/WestmanCom
Westman is a telecommunications company offering television, internet & phone services to southwestern Manitoba. The company also owns & operates two radio stations in the Brandon, MB, area through its subsidiary Riding Mountain Broadcasting Ltd.: CKLQ-AM & CKLF-FM (Star 94.7).
David Baxter, President & CEO

YourLink Inc.
204 Cardinal Cres., Saskatoon, SK S7L 6H8
Tel: 306-955-3122; *Fax:* 306-955-3148
Toll-Free: 866-650-5465
moreinfo@yourlink.ca
www.yourlink.ca
Social Media: www.linkedin.com/company/yourlink-inc, www.facebook.com/225941474133051, twitter.com/YourLinkSK
YourLink is primarily a provider of rural high speed internet, but it also operates rural cable subsidiaries such as Columbia Cable, Revelstoke Cable & Omineca Cable.

YTV Canada Inc.
Owned by: Corus Entertainment Inc.*
Corus Quay, 25 Dockside Dr., Toronto, ON M5A 0B5
info@ytv.com
www.ytv.com
Social Media: www.facebook.com/ytv, twitter.com/ytv

ZoomerMedia Ltd.
70 Jefferson Ave., Toronto, ON M6A 1Y4
Tel: 416-368-3194
www.zoomermedia.ca
Moses Znaimer, President

AM Radio Stations

Alberta

***Calgary:* CBR** (Freq: 1010)
Owned by: Canadian Broadcasting Corporation*
PO Box 2640, Calgary, AB T2P 2M7
Tel: 403-521-6000
www.cbc.ca/calgary

***Calgary:* CFAC-AM** (Freq: 960)
Owned by: Rogers Broadcasting Ltd.*
#240, 2723 - 37 Ave. NE, Calgary, AB T1Y 5R8
Tel: 403-246-9696
www.sportsnet.ca/960
Social Media: www.facebook.com/sportsnet960
Kelly Kirch, Program Director, kelly.kirch@rci.rogers.com

***Calgary:* CFFR-AM** (Freq: 660)
Owned by: Rogers Broadcasting Ltd.*
2723 - 37 Ave. NE, Calgary, AB T1Y 5R8
Tel: 403-291-0000
news660@rogers.com
www.660news.com
Social Media: www.facebook.com/660news, twitter.com/660NewsTraffic

***Calgary:* CHQR-AM (News Talk 770)** (Freq: 770)
Owned by: CKIK-FM Limited*
#200, 3320 - 17th Ave. SW, Calgary, AB T3E 0B4
Tel: 403-716-6500
www.newstalk770.com
Social Media: www.youtube.com/user/AM770Calgary, www.facebook.com/NewsTalk770Calgary, twitter.com/NewsTalk770
John Vos, Program Director

***Calgary:* CKMX-AM (Funny 1060 AM)** (Freq: 1060)
Owned by: Bell Media Inc.*
#300, 1110 Centre St. NE, Calgary, AB T2E 2R2
Tel: 403-240-5800
www.funny1060.com
Social Media: www.facebook.com/Funny1060AM, twitter.com/Funny1060AM
Stewart Meyers, General Manager, stewart.meyers@bellmedia.ca

***Drumheller:* CKDQ-AM (910 CFCW)** (Freq: 910; Joined CFCW family in 2016)
Owned by: Newcap Inc.
PO Box 1480, 515 - Hwy. 10 East, Drumheller, AB T0J 0Y0
Tel: 403-823-3384, *Fax:* 403-823-7241
910cfcw.com
Social Media: www.facebook.com/910cfcw/, twitter.com/910CFCW
Jared Waldo, Station Manager, jwaldo@newcap.ca

***Edmonton:* CBX** (Freq: 740)
Owned by: Canadian Broadcasting Corporation*
Edmonton City Centre, #125, 10062 - 102 Ave., Edmonton, AB T5J 2Y8
Tel: 780-468-7500
www.cbc.ca/edmonton

* *For details on this company see listing in Major Broadcasting Companies section; † French language station*

***Edmonton:* CFCW-AM** (Freq: 840)
Owned by: Newcap Radio*
2394 West Edmonton Mall (Entrance 55), 8882 - 170th St., Edmonton, AB T5T 4M2
Tel: 780-468-3939, *Fax:* 780-435-0844
www.cfcw.com
Social Media: www.youtube.com/user/790CFCWAM, www.facebook.com/840CFCW, twitter.com/840CFCW
Neil Cunningham, Station Manager, ncunningham@newcap.ca

***Edmonton:* CFRN-AM (TSN 1260)** (Freq: 1260)
Owned by: Bell Media Inc.*
#100, 18520 Stony Plain Rd., Edmonton, AB T5S 2E2
Tel: 780-486-2800, *Fax:* 780-489-6927
www.tsn1260.ca
Social Media: www.facebook.com/TSN1260, twitter.com/TSN1260
Pat Cardinal, General Manager, patrick.cardinal@bellmedia.ca

***Edmonton:* CHED-AM** (Freq: 630)
Owned by: Corus Premium Television Ltd.*
5204 - 84 St., Edmonton, AB T6E 5N8
Tel: 780-440-6300
www.630ched.com
Social Media: www.youtube.com/630chedEdmonton, www.facebook.com/630CHED, twitter.com/630CHED
Syd Smith, Program Director, SSmith@630ched.com
Peter Wilkes, Sales Manager, Peter.Wilkes@corusent.com

***Edmonton:* CHQT-AM (iNews880)** (Freq: 880)
Owned by: Corus Radio Company*
5204 - 84 St., Edmonton, AB T6E 5N8
Tel: 780-440-6300
www.inews880.com
Social Media: www.youtube.com/user/inews880, www.facebook.com/iNews880, twitter.com/iNews880
Syd Smith, Program Director, ssmith@630ched.com

***Edmonton:* CJCA-AM (The Light)** (Freq: 930)
Owned by: Touch Canada Broadcasting Limited Partnership*
5316 Calgary Trail NW, Edmonton, AB T6H 4J8
Tel: 780-466-4930, *Fax:* 780-469-5335
105.9@shinefm.com
www.am930thelight.com

***High River:* CHRB-AM** (Freq: 1140)
Owned by: Golden West Broadcasting Ltd.*
11 - 5th Ave. SE, High River, AB T1V 1G2
Tel: 403-652-2472, *Toll-Free:* 866-652-2472
www.highriveronline.com
Social Media: www.facebook.com/pages/AM-1140/120693441344363, twitter.com/AM_1140

***Lethbridge:* CRLC The Kodiak** (Freq: Online radio station)
Owned by: Lethbridge College
Student Service Centre, 3000 College Dr. South, Lethbridge, AB T1K 1L6
Tel: 403-320-3394, *Fax:* 403-317-3582
lethcollege.ca/commarts/crlc
Social Media: twitter.com/CRLCTheKodiak

***Peace River:* CKYL-AM** (Freq: 610)
Peace River Office
PO Box 300, Peace River, AB T8S 1T5
Tel: 780-624-2535, *Fax:* 780-624-5424
Toll-Free: 800-610-3610
www.ylcountry.com
Social Media: www.facebook.com/ylcountry, twitter.com/KIX_YL_Newsroom
Chris Black, General Manager, 780-681-4230

***Wetaskiwin:* CKJR-AM** (Freq: 1440)
Owned by: Newcap Radio*
5214A - 50th Ave., Wetaskiwin, AB T9A 0S8
Tel: 780-352-0144, *Fax:* 780-352-5656
www.w1440.com
Larry Donohue, Program Director, 780-490-2487, ldonohue@newcap.com
Kelly Walter, Program Director, 780-437-9209, kwalter@newcap.ca

British Columbia

***100 Mile House:* CKBX-AM (The Wolf)** (Freq: 840)
Owned by: CKCQ-FM (The Wolf)
100 Mile House, BC
pete@reachthecariboo.com
www.wolf100mile.ca
Social Media: www.youtube.com/user/Wolf100MileCA, www.facebook.com/125770480819346, twitter.com/wolf100mileca
Other information: News E-mail: cariboonews@reachthecariboo.com

***Ashcroft:* CINL-AM (Radio NL)** (Freq: 1340)
Owned by: CHNL-AM (Radio NL)*
Ashcroft, BC
www.radionl.com

***Burns Lake:* CFLD-AM** (Freq: 760)
Owned by: CFBV
PO Box 600, Burns Lake, BC V0J 1E0
Tel: 250-692-3414

***Burns Lake:* CFLD-AM (Moose FM)** (Freq: 760)
Owned by: CFBV-AM (The Peak)
Burns Lake, BC
www.mybulkleylakesnow.com

***Clearwater:* CHNL-AM-1 (Radio NL)** (Freq: 1400)
Owned by: CHNL-AM (Radio NL)*
Clearwater, BC
www.radionl.com

***Dawson Creek:* CJDC-AM** (Freq: 890)
Owned by: Bell Media Inc.*
901 - 102 Ave., Dawson Creek, BC V1G 2B6
Tel: 250-782-3341, *Fax:* 250-782-3154
www.cjdccountry.com
Social Media: www.facebook.com/196127377070136
Terry Shepherd, General Manager, terry.shepherd@bellmedia.ca

***Elkford:* CJEV-AM (Mountain Radio)** (Freq: 1340)
Owned by: CJPR-FM
Elkford, BC
Tel: 403-562-2806, *Fax:* 403-562-8114
mountain.requests@newcap.ca
www.mountainradiofm.com

***Fort St. James:* CIFJ-AM (Valley Country)** (Freq: 1480)
Owned by: CIVH-AM (Valley Country)
Fort St. James, BC
www.mynechakovalleynow.com

***Fraser Lake:* CIFL-AM (Valley Country)** (Freq: 1450)
Owned by: CIVH-AM (Valley Country)
Fraser Lake, BC
www.mynechakovalleynow.com

***Granisle:* CFBV-AM-2 (Moose FM)** (Freq: 1480)
Owned by: CFBV-AM (The Peak)
Granisle, BC
www.mybulkleylakesnow.com

***Invermere:* CKIR-AM** (Freq: 870)
Owned by: CKXR-FM (EZ Rock)
Invermere, BC
salmonarm.myezrock.com

***Kamloops:* CHNL-AM (Radio NL)** (Freq: 610)
Owned by: CHNL-AM (Radio NL)*
611 Lansdowne St., Kamloops, BC V2C 1Y6
Tel: 250-372-2292, *Fax:* 250-372-2293
info@radionl.com
www.radionl.com
Social Media: www.facebook.com/radionlkamloops, twitter.com/RadioNLNews
Garth Buchko, General Manager, gbuchko@radionl.com

***Kelowna:* CKFR-AM** (Freq: 1150)
Owned by: Bell Media Inc.*
435 Bernard Ave., Kelowna, BC V1Y 6N8
Tel: 250-860-8600, *Fax:* 250-880-8856
Toll-Free: 866-960-8600
info@am1150.ca
www.am1150.ca
Social Media: www.facebook.com/AM1150, twitter.com/am1150
Ken Kilcullen, General Manager, ken.kilcullen@bellmedia.ca

***Merritt:* CJNL-AM (Radio NL)** (Freq: 1230)
Owned by: CHNL-AM (Radio NL)*
Merritt, BC
www.radionl.com

***Osoyoos:* CJOR-AM (EZ Rock)** (Freq: 1240)
Owned by: Bell Media Inc.*
#203, 8309 Main St., Osoyoos, BC V0H 1V0
Tel: 250-495-7226, *Fax:* 250-495-6841
osoyoos.myezrock.com
Social Media: www.facebook.com/EZRock1240, twitter.com/ezrockosoyoos
Janet Burley, General Manager & Manager, Sales, janet.burley@bellmedia.ca

***Penticton:* CKOR-AM (EZ Rock)** (Freq: 800)
Owned by: Bell Media Inc.*
33 Carmi Ave., Penticton, BC V2A 3G4
Tel: 250-492-2800, *Fax:* 250-493-0370
penticton.myezrock.com
Social Media: www.facebook.com/EZRock800, twitter.com/ezrockpenticton
Mark Burley, Program Director, mark.burley@bellmedia.ca
Janet Burley, General Manager/Sales Manager, janet.burley@bellmedia.ca

***Port Hardy:* CFNI-AM (1240 Coast AM)** (Freq: 1240)
Owned by: Vista Broadcast Group*
7035 A Market St., Port Hardy, BC V0N 2P0
Tel: 250-949-6500, *Fax:* 250-949-6580
www.mytriportnow.com
Social Media: www.facebook.com/theport1240, twitter.com/ThePort1240

***Richmond:* CISL-AM** (Freq: 650)
Owned by: Newcap Radio*
#20, 11151 Horseshoe Way, Richmond, BC V7A 4S5
Tel: 604-241-2100, *Fax:* 604-272-0917
www.cisl650.com
Social Media: www.facebook.com/cisl650, twitter.com/CISL650
Sherri Pierce, Station Manager, spierce@newcap.ca

***Richmond:* CJVB-AM** (Freq: 1470)
Owned by: Fairchild Radio*
Aberdeen Centre, #2090, 4151 Hazelbridge Way, Richmond, BC V6X 4J7
Tel: 604-295-1234, *Fax:* 604-295-1201
sales@am1470.com
www.am1470.com
Social Media: www.youtube.com/fairchildradiovan, www.facebook.com/am1470fm961, twitter.com/am1470fm961
Other information: News E-mail: news@am1470.com

***Smithers:* CFBV-AM (Moose FM)** (Freq: 870)
Owned by: Vista Broadcast Group*
1139 Queen St., Smithers, BC V0J 2N0
Tel: 250-847-2521, *Fax:* 250-847-9411
www.mybulkleylakesnow.com
Alissa Angel, Sales Manager, aangel@vistaradio.ca

***Terrace:* CFTK-AM (EZ Rock)** (Freq: 590)
Owned by: Bell Media Inc.*
4625 Lazelle Ave., Terrace, BC V8G S4
Tel: 250-635-6316, *Fax:* 250-638-6320
terrace.myezrock.com
Social Media: www.facebook.com/NorthEZRock, twitter.com/EZRockNorth
Brian Langston, General Manager, brian.langston@bellmedia.ca

***Vancouver:* CBU** (Freq: 690)
Owned by: Canadian Broadcasting Corporation*
PO Box 4600, Vancouver, BC V6B 4A2
Tel: 604-662-6000
www.cbc.ca/bc

***Vancouver:* CFTE-AM** (Freq: 1410)
Owned by: Bell Media Radio*
#500, 969 Robson St., Vancouver, BC V6Z 1X5
Tel: 604-871-9000, *Fax:* 604-871-2901
www.teamradio.ca
Social Media: www.facebook.com/teamradiovancouver, twitter.com/TEAM1040

***Vancouver:* CHMB-AM** (Freq: 1320)
Owned by: Mainstream Broadcasting Corp.*
#100, 1200 West 73 Ave., Vancouver, BC V6P 6G7
Tel: 604-263-1320, *Fax:* 604-261-0310
adm@am1320.com
www.am1320.com
Social Media: www.youtube.com/am1320chmb, www.facebook.com/am1320, twitter.com/AM1320chmb
Victor Qin, Manager

** For details on this company see listing in Major Broadcasting Companies section; † French language station*

***Vancouver:* CHMJ-AM (AM740)** (Freq: 730)
Owned by: Corus Radio Company*
#2000, 700 West Georgia St., Vancouver, BC V7Y 1K9
Tel: 604-681-7511, *Fax:* 604-331-2722
www.am730.ca
Social Media: www.facebook.com/am730traffic, twitter.com/AM730Traffic
Ian Koenigsfest, Brand Director

***Vancouver:* CKNW-AM** (Freq: 980)
Owned by: Corus Premium Television Ltd.*
#2000, 700 West Georgia St., Vancouver, BC V7Y 1K9
Tel: 604-331-2711, *Fax:* 604-331-2722
Toll-Free: 877-399-9898
www.cknw.com
Social Media: www.facebook.com/cknw980, twitter.com/cknw
Mike Searson, Director, Sales

***Vancouver:* CKST-AM** (Freq: 1040)
Owned by: Bell Media Radio*
#500, 969 Robson St., Vancouver, BC V6Z 1X5
Tel: 604-871-9000, *Fax:* 604-871-2901
www.teamradio.ca
Social Media: www.facebook.com/teamradiovancouver, twitter.com/TEAM1040

***Vancouver:* CKWX-AM** (Freq: 1130)
Owned by: Rogers Broadcasting Ltd.*
2440 Ash St., Vancouver, BC V5Z 4J6
Tel: 604-873-2599, *Fax:* 604-873-0877
news1130@news1130.rogers.com
www.news1130.com
Social Media: www.facebook.com/News1130, twitter.com/news1130radio

***Vanderhoof:* CIVH-AM (Valley Country)** (Freq: 1340)
Owned by: Vista Broadcast Group*
150 West Columbia St., Vanderhoof, BC T0J 3A0
Tel: 250-567-4914
www.mynechakovalleynow.com
Social Media: www.facebook.com/165380483533130, twitter.com/ValleyCountryAM

***Victoria:* CFAX-AM** (Freq: 1070)
Owned by: Bell Media Radio*
1420 Broad St., Victoria, BC V8W 2B1
Tel: 250-386-1070, *Fax:* 250-920-4603
cfaxnews@cfax1070.com
www.cfax1070.com
Social Media: www.facebook.com/cfax1070, twitter.com/cfax1070

***Williams Lake:* CKWL-AM (The Wolf)** (Freq: 570)
Owned by: Vista Broadcast Group*
83 South First Ave., Williams Lake, BC V2G 1H4
Tel: 250-392-6551, *Fax:* 250-392-4142
www.thewolfonline.ca
Social Media: www.facebook.com/164187966948000

***Williams Lake:* CKWL-AM (The Wolf)** (Freq: 570)
Owned by: CKCQ-FM (The Wolf)
83 South First Ave., Williams Lake, BC V2G 1H4
Tel: 250-392-6551, *Fax:* 250-392-4142
pete@reachthecariboo.com
www.thewolfonline.ca
Other information: News E-mail: cariboonews@reachthecariboo.com

Manitoba

***Altona:* CFAM-AM** (Freq: 950)
Owned by: Golden West Broadcasting Ltd.*
PO Box 950, #201, 125 Centre Ave., Altona, MB R0G 0B0
Tel: 204-324-6464, *Toll-Free:* 800-374-3315
cfam@goldenwestradio.com
www.pembinavalleyonline.com
Social Media: www.facebook.com/pages/CFAM-950/243829332352635

***Boissevain:* CJRB-AM** (Freq: 1220)
Owned by: Golden West Broadcasting Ltd.*
PO Box 1220, 420 South Railway, Boissevain, MB ROK 0E0
Tel: 204-534-6000, *Fax:* 888-765-7039
cjrb@goldenwestradio.com
www.discoverwestman.com/cjrb

***Brandon:* CKLQ-AM** (Freq: 880)
Owned by: Riding Mountain Broadcasting Ltd.*
624 - 14 St. East, Brandon, MB R7A 7E1
Tel: 204-726-8888
qcountry@cklq.mb.ca
www.cklq.com
Social Media: www.youtube.com/880CKLQ, www.facebook.com/cklq.qcountry, twitter.com/880cklqsports
Cam Clark, General Manager, clarkc@westmancom.com

***Cross Lake:* CFNC-AM** (Freq: 1490)
PO Box 129, Cross Lake, MB R0B 0J0
Tel: 204-676-2331, *Fax:* 204-676-2911

***Dauphin:* CKDM-AM** (Freq: 730)
Owned by: Dauphin Broadcasting Co. Ltd.*
27 - 3rd Ave., Dauphin, MB R7N 0Y5
Tel: 204-638-3230, *Fax:* 204-638-8257
ckdm.reception@730ckdm.com
730ckdm.ca
Social Media: www.facebook.com/730CKDM, twitter.com/730CKDM
Allan Truman, General Manager, allan.truman@730ckdm.com

***Flin Flon:* CFAR-AM** (Freq: 590)
Owned by: Arctic Radio*
316 Green St., Flin Flon, MB R8A 0H2
Tel: 204-687-3469, *Fax:* 204-687-6786
flinflononline.com
Social Media: www.facebook.com/CFAR590
Other information: Alt. Phone: 204-687-8300

***Portage la Prairie:* CFRY-AM** (Freq: 920)
Owned by: Golden West Broadcasting Ltd.*
PO Box 130, 2390 Sisson Dr., Portage la Prairie, MB R1N 3B2
Tel: 204-239-5111, *Toll-Free:* 866-239-5111
www.portageonline.com
Social Media: twitter.com/cfry_portage

***Steinbach:* CHSM-AM** (Freq: 1250)
Owned by: Golden West Broadcasting Ltd.*
#105, 32 Brandt St., Steinbach, MB R5G 2J7
Tel: 204-326-3737, *Toll-Free:* 866-326-3737
www.steinbachonline.com
Social Media: www.facebook.com/pages/AM1250-Radio/153028841424047, twitter.com/am1250radio

***The Pas:* CJAR-AM** (Freq: 1240)
Owned by: Arctic Radio*
PO Box 2980, 130 - 3rd St. West, The Pas, MB R9A 1R7
Tel: 204-623-5307, *Fax:* 204-623-5337
cjar@arcticradio.ca
www.thepasonline.com
Social Media: www.facebook.com/CJ1240

***Thompson:* CHTM-AM** (Freq: 610)
Owned by: Arctic Radio*
103 Cree Rd., Thompson, MB R8N 0B9
Tel: 204-778-7361, *Fax:* 204-778-5252
chtm@arcticradio.ca
www.thompsononline.ca
Social Media: www.facebook.com/610CHTM, twitter.com/610CHTM

***Winnipeg:* CBW** (Freq: 990)
Owned by: Canadian Broadcasting Corporation*
541 Portage Ave., Winnipeg, MB R3B 2G1
Tel: 204-788-3222
www.cbc.ca/manitoba
Gabriela Kilmes, Manager, Communications, Marketing & Brand, gabriela.klimes@cbc.ca

***Winnipeg:* CFRW-AM** (Freq: 1290)
Owned by: Bell Media Radio*
1445 Pembina Hwy., Winnipeg, MB R3T 5C2
Tel: 204-477-5120
live@tsn1290.ca
www.tsn.ca/Winnipeg
Social Media: www.facebook.com/TSNRADIO1290, twitter.com/TSN1290Radio
Chris Brooke, Program Director

***Winnipeg:* CHFC** (Freq: 1230)
Owned by: Canadian Broadcasting Corporation*
c/o CBC Winnipeg, 541 Portage Ave., Winnipeg, MB R3B 2G1
Tel: 204-788-3205
Other information: TTY/Teletypewriter: 866-220-6045

***Winnipeg:* CJOB-AM** (Freq: 680)
Owned by: Corus Premium Television Ltd.*
#200, 1440 Jack Blick Ave., Winnipeg, MB R3G 0L4
Tel: 204-786-2471, *Fax:* 204-783-4512
www.cjob.com
Social Media: www.youtube.com/cjob680, www.facebook.com/CJOB68, twitter.com/680cjob
Scott Armstrong, General Manager
Steve Dubois, General Sales Manager

***Winnipeg:* CKJS-AM** (Freq: 810)
Owned by: Evanov Communications*
520 Corydon Ave., Winnipeg, MB R3L 0P1
Tel: 204-477-1221, *Fax:* 204-453-8244
www.ckjs.com
Social Media: www.facebook.com/pages/CKJS/107542652608653
Mike Fabian, General Manager, mike@evanovwpg.com

New Brunswick

†*Bathurst:* CKLE-AM (Freq: 810)
Détenteur: CKLE-FM
#301, 270, av Douglas, Bathurst, NB E2A 1M9
Tél: 506-546-4600, *Téléc:* 506-546-6611
superstation@ckle.fm
www.ckle.fm
Médias sociaux: www.facebook.com/cklefm
Armand Roussy, Directeur

***Campbellton:* CKNB-AM** (Freq: 950)
Owned by: Maritime Broadcasting System*
74 Water St., Campbellton, NB E3N 3G7
Tel: 506-753-4415, *Fax:* 506-789-9505
95cknb.ca

***Fredericton:* CKHJ-AM (KHJ)** (Freq: 1260)
Owned by: Bell Media Inc.*
206 Rookwood Ave., Fredericton, NB E3B 2M2
Tel: 506-451-9111, *Fax:* 506-452-2345
feedback@khj.ca
www.khj.ca
Social Media: www.facebook.com/CountryKHJ, twitter.com/CountryKHJ

***Saint John:* CFBC-AM** (Freq: 930)
Owned by: Maritime Broadcasting System*
226 Union St., Saint John, NB E2L 1B1
Tel: 506-658-5100
www.cfbc.am
Social Media: www.facebook.com/pages/93-CFBC/248282851961805

***Sussex:* CJCW-AM** (Freq: 590)
Owned by: Maritime Broadcasting System*
PO Box 5900, Sussex, NB E0E 1P0
Tel: 506-432-2529, *Fax:* 506-433-4900
www.590cjcw.com
Social Media: www.facebook.com/590CJCW

Newfoundland & Labrador

***Baie Verte:* CKIM (VOCM)** (Freq: 1240)
Owned by: CKCM-VOCM*
Baie Verte, NL
Tel: 709-489-2192, *Fax:* 709-489-8626
www.vocm.com
Social Media: twitter.com/vocmnews

***Clarenville:* CKVO-AM (VOCM)** (Freq: 710)
Owned by: Newcap Radio*
Clarenville, NL
Tel: 709-466-1399, *Fax:* 709-596-8626
www.vocm.com
Mike Murphy, General Manager, mmurphy@newcap.ca
Mike Campbell, Program Director, mcampbell@newcap.ca

***Corner Brook:* CBY** (Freq: 990)
Owned by: Canadian Broadcasting Corporation*
162 Premier Dr., Corner Brook, NL A2H 7M6
Tel: 709-634-3141, *Fax:* 709-634-8506
cbrookradio@cbc.ca
www.cbc.ca/nl

** For details on this company see listing in Major Broadcasting Companies section; † French language station*

***Corner Brook:* CFCB-AM** (Freq: 570)
Owned by: Newcap Radio*
345 O'Connell Dr., Corner Brook, NL A2H 7V3
Tel: 709-634-4570, *Fax:* 709-634-4081
onair@cfcbradio.com
www.cfcbradio.com
Social Media: www.facebook.com/570-CFCB/108849352471861, twitter.com/CFCBRadio
Dave Hillier, Station Manager, dhillier@newcap.ca

***Gander:* CBG-AM** (Freq: 1400)
Owned by: Canadian Broadcasting Corporation*
98 Sullivan Ave., Gander, NL A1V 1S2
Tel: 709-256-4311, *Fax:* 709-651-2021
www.cbc.ca/nl

***Gander:* CKGA (VOCM)** (Freq: 650)
Owned by: Newcap Radio*
PO Box 650, Gander, NL A1B 1X2
Tel: 709-651-3650, *Fax:* 709-651-2542
www.vocm.com
David Hillier, Station Manager, dhillier@newcap.ca
Dean Clarke, Program Director, dean.clarke@vocm.com

***Grand Falls-Windsor:* CBT-AM** (Freq: 540)
Owned by: Canadian Broadcasting Corporation*
2 Harris Ave., Grand Falls-Windsor, NL A2A 2Y2
Tel: 709-489-2102, *Fax:* 709-489-1055
centralmorning@cbc.ca
www.cbc.ca/nl
Denise Wilson, Senior Managing Director, Atlantic Canada, denise.wilson@cbc.ca
Peter Gullage, Executive Producer, Newfoundland & Labrador, peter.gullage@cbc.ca
Nadine Antle, Regional Manager, Communications, Marketing & Brand, 902-420-4223, Nadine.Antle@cbc.ca

***Grand Falls-Windsor:* CKCM-VOCM** (Freq: 620)
Owned by: Newcap Radio*
35A Grenfell Heights, Grand Falls-Windsor, NL A2A 2K2
Tel: 709-489-2192, *Fax:* 709-489-8626
www.vocm.com
Social Media: twitter.com/vocmnews
David Hillier, Contact

***Marystown:* CHCM-AM (VOCM)** (Freq: 740)
Owned by: Newcap Radio*
PO Box 560, Marystown, NL A0E 2M0
Tel: 709-279-2560, *Fax:* 709-279-2800
www.vocm.com
Russell Murphy, Station Manager, rmurphy@newcap.ca

***Mount Pearl:* VOAR** (Freq: 1210)
1041 Topsail Rd., Mount Pearl, NL A1N 5E9
Tel: 709-745-8627, *Toll-Free:* 888-740-8627
voar@voar.org
www.voar.org
Social Media: www.flickr.com/photos/69531297@N02, www.facebook.com/VOARRadio, twitter.com/voarRadio
Sherry Griffin, Station Manager

***Port aux Basques:* CFGN-AM** (Freq: 1230)
Owned by: Newcap Radio
Port aux Basques, NL A2N 1C6
Tel: 709-643-2191, *Fax:* 709-643-5025
cfsx@vocm.com
www.cfsxradio.com
Katherine Hogan, Station Manager, khogan@newcap.ca

***St. John's:* CBN-AM** (Freq: 640)
Owned by: Canadian Broadcasting Corporation*
PO Box 12010 A, St. John's, NL A1B 3T8
Tel: 709-576-5000, *Fax:* 709-576-5234
www.cbc.ca/nl
Other information: Phone, CBC Radio One Newsroom: 709-576-5225
Denise Wilson, Senior Managing Director, Atlantic Canada, denise.wilson@cbc.ca
Peter Gullage, Executive Producer, Newfoundland & Labrador, peter.gullage@cbc.ca
Nadine Antle, Regional Manager, Communications, Marketing & Brand, 902-420-4223, Nadine.Antle@cbc.ca

***St. John's:* CJYQ** (Freq: 930)
Owned by: Newcap Radio*
PO Box 8590, 391 Kenmount Rd, St. John's, NL A1B 3P5
Tel: 709-726-5590, *Fax:* 709-726-4633
email@930kixxcountry.ca
www.930kixxcountry.ca
Social Media: www.facebook.com/930kixxcountry, twitter.com/930kixxcountry
Mike Murphy, Station Manager, mmurphy@newcap.ca
Mike Campbell, Program Director, mcampbell@newcap.ca

***St. John's:* VOCM-AM** (Freq: 590)
Owned by: Steele Communications*
PO Box 8-590, 391 Kenmount Rd., St. John's, NL A1B 3P5
Tel: 709-726-5590, *Fax:* 709-726-4633
www.vocm.com
Social Media: www.facebook.com/590VOCM, twitter.com/590vocm
Mike Murphy, Station Manager, mmurphy@newcap.ca
Mike Campbell, Program Director, mcampbell@newcap.ca

***St. John's:* VOWR** (Freq: 800)
PO Box 26006, St. John's, NL A1E 0A5
Tel: 709-579-9233
vowr@vowr.org
www.vowr.org

***Stephenville:* CFSX-AM** (Freq: 870)
VOCM Affiliate
Owned by: Newcap Radio
60 West St., Stephenville, NL A2N 1C6
Tel: 709-643-2191, *Fax:* 709-643-5025
cfsx@vocm.com
www.cfsxradio.com
Social Media: www.facebook.com/pages/CFSX-870/109059929132227, twitter.com/cfsxradio
Katherine Hogan, Sales Manager, 709-214-0258, khogan@newcap.ca
Dave Hillier, Station Manager, dhillier@newcap.ca

Northwest Territories

***Inuvik:* CHAK** (Freq: 860)
Owned by: Canadian Broadcasting Corporation*
100 Mackenzie Rd., Inuvik, NT X0E 0T0
Tel: 867-920-5400
www.cbc.ca/north
Kerry Fraser, Communications Manager

***Yellowknife:* CFYK** (Freq: 1340)
Owned by: Canadian Broadcasting Corporation*
PO Box 160, Yellowknife, NT X1A 2N2
Tel: 867-920-5400
www.cbc.ca/north

Nova Scotia

***Digby:* CKDY-AM** (Freq: 1420)
Owned by: CKEN-FM
PO Box 1420, 53 Sydney St., Digby, NS B0V 1A0
Tel: 902-245-2111, *Fax:* 902-245-9720
www.avrnetwork.com
Social Media: www.facebook.com/avrnetwork

***Middleton:* CKAD-AM** (Freq: 1350)
Owned by: CKEN-FM
PO Box 550, 10 Bridge St., Middleton, NS B0S 1P0
Tel: 902-825-3429, *Fax:* 902-825-6009
www.avrnetwork.com
Social Media: www.facebook.com/avrnetwork

***Sydney:* CBI** (Freq: 1140)
Owned by: Canadian Broadcasting Corporation*
500 George St., Sydney, NS B1P 1K6
Tel: 902-539-5050, *Fax:* 902-539-1562
www.cbc.ca
Denise Wilson, Senior Managing Director, Atlantic Canada, denise.wilson@cbc.ca

***Sydney:* CJCB-AM** (Freq: 1270)
Owned by: Maritime Broadcasting System*
318 Charlotte St., Sydney, NS B1P 1C8
Tel: 902-564-5596, *Fax:* 902-564-1873
www.cjcbradio.com
Social Media: www.facebook.com/1270cjcb
Other information: News & Sports Phone: 902-539-3000

***Windsor:* CFAB-AM** (Freq: 1450)
Owned by: Maritime Broadcasting System*
PO Box 278, 169A Water St., Windsor, NS B0N 2T0
Tel: 902-798-2111, *Fax:* 902-798-8140
www.avrnetwork.com
Social Media: www.facebook.com/avrnetwork

Nunavut

***Iqaluit:* CFFB** (Freq: 1230)
Owned by: Canadian Broadcasting Corporation*
PO Box 490, Iqaluit, NU X0A 0H0
Tel: 867-979-6100
cbc.ca/north
Kerry Fraser, Communications Manager

Ontario

***Belleville:* CJBQ-AM** (Freq: 800)
Owned by: Quinte Broadcasting Co. Ltd.*
PO Box 488, 10 Front St. South, Belleville, ON K8N 5B2
Tel: 613-969-5555, *Fax:* 613-969-8122
www.cjbq.com

***Brantford:* CKPC-AM** (Freq: 1380)
Owned by: Evanov Radio Group*
571 West St., Brantford, ON N3T 5P8
Tel: 519-759-1000, *Fax:* 519-753-1470
www.am1380.ca
Social Media: www.facebook.com/114839388574219
Randy Redden, General Manager, randy@ckpcradio.com

***Guelph:* CJOY-AM** (Freq: 1460)
Owned by: 591989 B.C. Ltd.*
75 Speedvale Ave. East, Guelph, ON N1E 6M3
Tel: 519-824-7000, *Fax:* 519-824-4118
www.cjoy.com
Social Media: www.facebook.com/166142293420594, twitter.com/CJOYMagicNews
Lars Wunsche, General Manager

***Hamilton:* CHAM-AM (Funny 820)** (Freq: 820)
Owned by: Bell Media Inc.*
#401, 883 Upper Wentworth St., Hamilton, ON L9A 4Y6
Tel: 905-574-1150, *Fax:* 905-575-6429
www.funny820.com
Social Media: www.facebook.com/funny820, twitter.com/Funny820
Bob Harris, General Manager, Bell Radio Hamilton, bob.harris@bellmedia.ca
Mike Nabuurs, Brand Director & Host, mike.nabuurs@bellmedia.ca

***Hamilton:* CHML-AM** (Freq: 900)
Owned by: Corus Premium Television Ltd.*
875 Main St. West, Hamilton, ON L8S 4R1
Tel: 905-521-9900
News@900chml.com
www.900chml.com
Social Media: www.youtube.com/AM900CHML, www.facebook.com/AM900CHML, twitter.com/AM900CHML
Jeff Storey, Program Director, jstorey@900chml.com

***Hamilton:* CKOC-AM (Oldies 1150)** (Freq: 1150)
Owned by: Bell Media Inc.*
#401, 883 Upper Wentworth St., Hamilton, ON L9A 4Y6
Tel: 905-574-1150, *Fax:* 905-575-6429
www.1150ckoc.ca
Social Media: www.facebook.com/1150CKOC, twitter.com/oldies1150
Bob Harris, General Manager, Bell Radio Hamilton, bob.harris@bellmedia.ca

***Kitchener:* CKGL-AM** (Freq: 570)
Owned by: Rogers Broadcasting Ltd.*
PO Box 936, Kitchener, ON N2G 4E4
Tel: 519-743-2611
news570@rogers.com
www.570news.com
Social Media: www.facebook.com/570News, twitter.com/570News

***London:* CFPL-AM (AM980)** (Freq: 980)
Owned by: Corus Radio Company*
#222, 380 Wellington St., London, ON N6A 5B5
Tel: 519-931-6000
news@am980.ca
www.am980.ca
Social Media: www.youtube.com/user/Am980News, www.facebook.com/78585693009, twitter.com/AM980News
Nathan Smith, Brand Director

***London:* CJBK-AM (Newstalk 1290)** (Freq: 1290)
Owned by: Bell Media Inc.*
743 Wellington Rd. South, London, ON N6C 4R5
Tel: 519-686-2525
www.cjbk.com
Social Media: www.facebook.com/1290cjbk, twitter.com/CJBK

** For details on this company see listing in Major Broadcasting Companies section; † French language station*

Don Mumford, General Manager, don.mumford@bellmedia.ca

***London:* CKSL-AM (Funny 1410)** (Freq: 1410)
Owned by: Bell Media Inc.*
743 Wellington Rd. South, London, ON N6C 4R5
Tel: 519-686-2525
www.funny1410.ca
Social Media: www.facebook.com/Funny1410, twitter.com/funny1410am
Don Mumford, General Manager, don.mumford@bellmedia.ca

***Markham:* CHKT-AM** (Freq: 1430)
Owned by: Fairchild Radio*
#26-29, 151 Esna Park Dr., Markham, ON L3R 3B1
Tel: 905-415-1430, *Fax:* 905-415-6292
www.am1430.com

***North Bay:* CKAT-AM** (Freq: 600)
Owned by: Rogers Broadcasting Ltd.*
273 Main St. East, North Bay, ON P1B 1B2
Tel: 705-474-2000
www.country600.com
Social Media: www.facebook.com/600ckat, twitter.com/country600ckat
Richard Coffin, News Director, richard.coffin@northbayradio.rogers.com

***Oakville:* CJMR-AM** (Freq: 1320)
284 Church St., Oakville, ON L6J 7N2
Tel: 905-271-1320, *Fax:* 905-845-9171
contact@cjmr1320.ca
www.cjmr1320.ca
Social Media: twitter.com/CJMR1320

***Oakville:* CJYE-AM** (Freq: 1250)
284 Church St., Oakville, ON L6J 7N2
Tel: 905-845-2821, *Fax:* 905-842-1250
contact@joy1250.ca
www.joy1250.ca
Social Media: www.facebook.com/joy1250, twitter.com/JOY1250
Michael H. Caine, Founder

***Oshawa:* CKDO-AM** (Freq: 1580; 107.7)
#207, 1200 Airport Blvd., Oshawa, ON L1J 8P5
Tel: 905-571-0949, *Fax:* 905-571-1150
www.ckdo.ca
Social Media: www.youtube.com/user/ckdoradio, www.facebook.com/ckdoradio, twitter.com/CKDOradio
Steve Kassay, Vice President, Programming, steve@kx96.fm

***Ottawa:* CFGO-AM** (Freq: 1200)
Owned by: Bell Media Radio*
87 George St., Ottawa, ON K1N 9H7
Tel: 613-750-1200, *Fax:* 613-739-4040
Toll-Free: 877-670-1200
webmaster@tsn1200.ca
www.tsn1200.ca
Social Media: www.facebook.com/TSN1200, twitter.com/TSN1200
John Rodenburg, Sports Director, John.Rodenburg@bellmedia.ca

***Ottawa:* CFRA-AM** (Freq: 580)
Owned by: Bell Media Radio*
87 George St., Ottawa, ON K1N 9H7
Tel: 613-789-2486
www.cfra.com
Social Media: www.facebook.com/580CFRA, twitter.com/CFRAOttawa
Steve Winogron, Program Director, Steve.Winogron@bellmedia.ca

***Ottawa:* CIWW-AM** (Freq: 1310)
Owned by: Rogers Broadcasting Ltd.*
2001 Thurston Dr., Ottawa, ON K1G 6C9
Tel: 613-736-2001
tips1310@rogers.com
www.1310news.com
Social Media: www.facebook.com/1310news, twitter.com/1310news
Glennis Lane, Senior Editor

***Owen Sound:* CFOS-AM** (Freq: 560)
Owned by: Bayshore Broadcasting Corporation*
PO Box 280, Owen Sound, ON N4K 5P5
Tel: 519-376-2030, *Fax:* 519-371-4242
www.560cfos.ca
Social Media: www.facebook.com/560cfos
Kevin Brown, Vice-President, Sales & Marketing, sales@bayshorebroadcasting.ca

***Sarnia:* CHOK-AM** (Freq: 1070)
Owned by: Blackburn Radio Inc.*
1415 London Rd., Sarnia, ON N7S 1P6
Tel: 519-542-5500
news@chok.com
www.chok.com
Social Media: www.youtube.com/user/Country1039, www.facebook.com/country1039chok, twitter.com/country1039chok

***St Catharines:* CKTB-AM (Newstalk 610)** (Freq: 610)
Owned by: Bell Media Inc.*
12 Yates St., St Catharines, ON L2R 6Z4
Tel: 905-684-1174, *Fax:* 905-684-4800
newsroom@610cktb.com
www.610cktb.com
Social Media: www.facebook.com/610CKTB, twitter.com/610CKTB
Bob Harris, General Manager, bob.harris@bellmedia.ca

***Stratford:* CJCS-AM** (Freq: 1240)
Owned by: Vista Broadcast Group*
376 Romeo St. South, Stratford, ON N5A 4T9
Tel: 519-271-2450, *Fax:* 519-271-3102
www.mystratfordnow.com
Social Media: twitter.com/1240CJCS

***Timmins:* CHIM-AM** (Freq: 1710)
226 Delnite Rd., Timmins, ON P4N 7C2
Tel: 705-264-2150
info@chimfm.com
www.chimfm.com
Roger de Brabant, General Manager, roger@chimfm.com

***Toronto:* CFMJ-AM (Talk Radio AM640)** (Freq: 640)
Owned by: Corus Premium Television Ltd.*
25 Dockside Dr., Toronto, ON M5A 0B5
Tel: 416-479-7000
www.640toronto.com
Social Media: www.facebook.com/640toronto, twitter.com/am640
Scott Guest, Interim Brand Director

***Toronto:* CFRB-AM (Newstalk 1010)** (Freq: 1010)
Owned by: Bell Media Inc.*
250 Richmond St. West, 3rd Fl., Toronto, ON M5V 1W4
Tel: 416-384-8000
infotoronto@bellmedia.ca
www.newstalk1010.com
Social Media: www.facebook.com/newstalk1010, twitter.com/newstalk1010
Mike Bendixen, Program Director, mike.bendixen@newstalk1010.com

***Toronto:* CFTR-AM** (Freq: 680)
Owned by: Rogers Broadcasting Ltd.*
1 Ted Rogers Way, Toronto, ON M4Y 3B7
Tel: 416-413-3930
680info@680news.com
www.680news.com
Social Media: www.facebook.com/680News, twitter.com/680news

***Toronto:* CFZM-AM** (Freq: 740)
Owned by: ZoomerMedia*
70 Jefferson Ave., Toronto, ON M6K 1Y4
Tel: 416-544-0740
www.zoomerradio.ca
Social Media: www.facebook.com/zoomerradio, twitter.com/am740

***Toronto:* CFZM-AM (Zoomer Radio)** (Freq: 740)
Owned by: ZoomerMedia*
70 Jefferson Ave., Toronto, ON M6K 1Y4
Tel: 416-544-0740
www.zoomerradio.ca
Social Media: www.facebook.com/zoomerradio, twitter.com/am740

***Toronto:* CHIN-AM** (Freq: 1540)
622 College St., Toronto, ON M6G 1B6
Tel: 416-531-9991, *Fax:* 416-531-5274
info@chinradio.com
www.chinradio.com
Social Media: www.facebook.com/chinradiocanada, twitter.com/chinradiocanada

***Toronto:* CHUM-AM (TSN Radio 1050)** (Freq: 1050)
Owned by: Bell Media Radio*
299 Queen St. West, Toronto, ON M5V 2Z5
Tel: 416-870-1050, *Toll-Free:* 855-591-6876
live@tsn1050.ca
www.tsn.ca/toronto
Social Media: twitter.com/TSN1050Radio

***Toronto:* CIAO-AM** (Freq: 530)
Owned by: Evanov Radio Group*
c/o Evanov Radio, 5312 Dundas St. West, Toronto, ON M9B 1B3
Tel: 416-213-1035, *Fax:* 416-233-8617
info@evanovradio.com
www.am530.ca

***Toronto:* CJCL-AM** (Freq: 590)
Owned by: Rogers Broadcasting Ltd.*
1 Ted Rogers Way, Toronto, ON M4Y 3B7
Tel: 416-935-0590
contact@sportsnet590.ca
www.sportsnet.ca/590
Social Media: www.facebook.com/fan590, twitter.com/FAN590
Diane Farrell, Contact, Sales, Diane.Farrell@rci.rogers.com

***Toronto:* S@Y Radio** (Freq: closed circuit)
Owned by: Seneca College
70 The Pond Rd., Toronto, ON M3J 3M6
Tel: 416-491-5050
www.sayradio.ca
Social Media: www.facebook.com/senecaradio, twitter.com/sayradio

***Toronto:* The Scope** (Freq: 1280 (online))
#201, 55 Gould St., Toronto, ON M5B 1E9
Tel: 416-904-6889
admin@thescopeatryerson.ca
www.thescopeatryerson.ca
Social Media: www.facebook.com/pages/The-Scope-at-Ryerson/289318544428603, twitter.com/ScopeatRyerson
Jacky Tuinstra Harrison, Station Manager

***Windsor:* CBE-AM** (Freq: 1550)
Owned by: Canadian Broadcasting Corporation*
825 Riverside Dr. West, Windsor, ON N9A 5K9
Tel: 519-255-3411
www.cbc.ca/windsor

†*Windsor:* CBEF (Freq: 1550)
Détenteur: Canadian Broadcasting Corporation*
825, promenade Riverside Ouest, Windsor, ON N9A 5K9
Tél: 519-255-3411, *Téléc:* 519-255-3573
ici.radio-canada.ca

***Windsor:* CKLW-AM** (Freq: 800)
Owned by: Bell Media Radio*
1640 Ouellette Ave., Windsor, ON N8X 1L1
Tel: 519-258-8888, *Fax:* 519-258-0182
contact@am800cklw.com
www.am800cklw.com
Social Media: www.facebook.com/am800, twitter.com/am800cklw
Eric Proksch, Vice President/General Manager, Eric.Proksch@bellmedia.ca
Keith Chinnery, Program Director, Keith.Chinnery@bellmedia.ca

***Windsor:* CKWW-AM** (Freq: 580)
Owned by: Bell Media Radio*
1640 Ouellette Ave., Windsor, ON N8X 1L1
Tel: 519-258-8888
info@am580radio.com
www.am580radio.com

***Wingham:* CKNX-AM** (Freq: 920)
Owned by: Blackburn Radio Inc.*
215 Carling Terrace, Wingham, ON N0G 2W0
Tel: 519-357-1310, *Fax:* 519-357-1897
info@cknx.ca
cknx.ca
Social Media: www.facebook.com/CKNXAM920

Québec

†*Laval:* CJLV-AM (Radio Laval) (Freq: 1570)
Laval, QC
www.1570.ca

** For details on this company see listing in Major Broadcasting Companies section; † French language station*

†Montréal: CFMB-AM (Freq: 1280)
35, rue York, Montréal, QC H3Z 2Z5
Tél: 514-483-2362, *Téléc:* 514-483-1362
info@cfmb.ca
www.cfmb.ca

Montréal: CJAD-AM (Freq: 800)
Owned by: Bell Media Inc.*
1717 René-Lévesque Blvd. East, Montréal, QC H2L 4T9
Tel: 514-989-2523
yourstory@cjad.com
www.cjad.com
Social Media: www.facebook.com/cjad800, twitter.com/CJAD800
Chris Bury, Contact, Programming, cbury@cjad.com

Montréal: CJLO-AM (Freq: closed circuit)
Owned by: Concordia Student Broadcasting Corporation
7141, rue Sherbrooke ouest, #CC-430, Montréal, QC H4B 1R6
Tel: 514-848-8663, *Fax:* 514-848-7450
feedback@cjlo.com
www.cjlo.com
Social Media: www.facebook.com/cjlo1690am, twitter.com/CJLO1690AM
Michael Sallot, Station Manager, manager@cjlo.com

†Montréal: CJWI-AM (Freq: 1410)
3390, boul Crémazie Est, Montréal, QC H2A 1A4
Tél: 514-790-2726, *Téléc:* 514-287-3299
info@cpam1610.com
www.cpam1610.com

†Montréal: CKAC-AM (Radio Circulation 730) (Freq: 730)
Détenteur: Cogeco Media Inc.*
Place Bonaventure, #1100, 800, rue de la Gauchetière Ouest, Montréal, QC H5A 1M1
Tél: 514-787-0730
www.radiocirculation.net

Montréal: CKGM-AM (Freq: 990)
Owned by: Bell Media Radio*
1717, boul Rene-Levesque Est, Montréal, QC H2L 4T9
Tel: 514-931-4487
www.tsn.ca/Montreal
Social Media: www.facebook.com/TSN690Montreal
Chris Bury, Program Director

†Rimouski: CAJT-AM (Radio étudiante) (Freq: closed circuit)
Cégep de Rimouski, 60, rue de l'Évêché ouest, Rimouski, QC G5L 4H6
Tél: 418-723-1880, *Téléc:* 418-724-4961
Ligne sans frais: 800-463-0617
information.scolaire@cegep-rimouski.qc.ca
www4.cegep-rimouski.qc.ca
Médias sociaux: www.facebook.com/RadioCajt

Saskatchewan

Estevan: CJSL-AM (Freq: 1280)
Owned by: Golden West Broadcasting Ltd.*
#200, 1236 - 5th St., Estevan, SK S4A 0Z6
Tel: 306-634-1280, *Toll-Free:* 800-824-0743
discoverestevan.com
Social Media: www.facebook.com/168180086627809

†Gravelbourg: CBKF-1 (Freq: 690)
Détenteur: CBKF-FM (Première Chaîne)
Gravelbourg, SK

Kindersley: CFYM-AM (Freq: 1210)
Owned by: CJYM-AM
Kindersley, SK
Tel: 306-463-2692, *Toll-Free:* 866-463-2692
www.cjym.com

Melfort: CKJH-AM (Freq: 750)
Owned by: Fabmar Communications Ltd.*
611 Main St. North, Melfort, SK S0E 1A0
Tel: 306-752-2587, *Fax:* 306-752-5932
info@yourtownnews.ca
www.ck750.com
Social Media: www.facebook.com/141244215927372, twitter.com/CK750am

Moose Jaw: CHAB-AM (Freq: 800)
Owned by: Golden West Broadcasting Ltd.*
1704 Main St. North, Moose Jaw, SK S6J 1L4
Tel: 306-694-0800, *Toll-Free:* 800-820-1768
discovermoosejaw.com
Social Media: www.facebook.com/800CHAB, twitter.com/800CHAB

North Battleford: CJNB-AM (Freq: 1050)
Owned by: Jim Pattison Broadcast Group*
1711 - 100 St., North Battleford, SK S9A 0W7
Tel: 306-445-2477
cjnbnews@jpbg.ca
www.cjnb.com
Social Media: www.facebook.com/cjnbcjns, twitter.com/CJNBNews
Karl Johnston, General Manager, karl.johnston@jpbg.ca

Prince Albert: CKBI-AM (Freq: 900)
Owned by: Jim Pattison Broadcast Group*
1316 Central Ave., Prince Albert, SK S6V 7R4
Tel: 306-763-7421
900ckbi@rawlco.com
www.900ckbi.com
Social Media: www.facebook.com/pages/Todays-Country-900-CKBI/151031428275052
Karl Johnston, General Manager, kjohnston@rawlco.com

Regina: CJME-AM (Freq: 980)
Owned by: Rawlco Radio Ltd.*
#210, 2401 Saskatchewan Dr., Regina, SK S4P 4H8
Tel: 306-525-0000
reginanews@rawlco.com
www.cjme.com
Social Media: www.facebook.com/CJMEnews, twitter.com/CJMENews
Tom Newton, General Manager

Regina: CKRM-AM (Freq: 620)
Owned by: Harvard Broadcasting Inc.*
1900 Rose St., Regina, SK S4P 0A9
Tel: 306-546-6200, *Fax:* 306-781-7338
Toll-Free: 866-767-0620
news@620ckrm.com
www.620ckrm.com
Social Media: www.youtube.com/user/620ckrm, www.facebook.com/620ckrm, twitter.com/620ckrm
Jason Huschi, General Manager, jasonh@harvardbroadcasting.com
Grant Biebrick, Program Director, gbiebrick@harvardbroadcasting.com

Rosetown: CJYM-AM (Freq: 1330)
Owned by: Golden West Broadcasting Ltd.*
PO Box 490, 208 Hwy. 4, Rosetown, SK S0L 2V0
Tel: 306-882-2686, *Toll-Free:* 800-667-5313
cjymnews@goldenwestradio.com
www.cjym.com

†Saskatoon: CBKF-2 (Freq: 860)
Détenteur: CBKF-FM (Première Chaîne)
Saskatoon, SK

Saskatoon: CJWW-AM (Freq: 600)
Owned by: Saskatoon Media Group*
366 - 3 Ave. South, Saskatoon, SK S7K 1M5
Tel: 306-938-0600, *Fax:* 306-665-5501
www.cjwwradio.com
Vic Dubois, General Manager

Saskatoon: CKOM-AM (Freq: 650)
Owned by: Rawlco Radio Ltd.*
715 Saskatchewan Cres. West, Saskatoon, SK S7M 5V7
Tel: 306-934-2222
ckomnews@rawlco.com
www.ckom.com
Social Media: www.facebook.com/NewsTalk650CKOM, twitter.com/CKOMNews
Kristy Werner, General Manager
Angela Hill, Program Director

Swift Current: CJSN-AM (Freq: 1490)
Owned by: Golden West Broadcasting Ltd.*
134 Central Ave. North, Swift Current, SK S9H 0L1
Tel: 306-773-4605, *Toll-Free:* 800-821-8073
cmr@goldenwestradio.com
www.swiftcurrentonline.com
Social Media: www.facebook.com/CountryMusicRadio, twitter.com/CKSW_570

Swift Current: CKSW-AM (Freq: 570)
Owned by: Golden West Broadcasting Ltd.*
134 Central Ave. North, Swift Current, SK S9H 0L1
Tel: 306-773-4605, *Toll-Free:* 800-821-8073
cmr@goldenwestradio.com
www.swiftcurrentonline.com
Social Media: www.facebook.com/CountryMusicRadio, twitter.com/CKSW_570

Weyburn: CFSL-AM (Freq: 1190)
Owned by: Golden West Broadcasting Ltd.*
305 Souris Ave., Weyburn, SK S4H 0C6
Tel: 306-848-1190
discoverweyburn.com
Social Media: www.facebook.com/111247462239648, twitter.com/AM1190Weyburn

Yorkton: CJGX-AM (Freq: 940)
Owned by: Harvard Broadcasting Inc.*
120 Smith St. East, Yorkton, SK S3N 3V3
Tel: 306-782-2256, *Fax:* 306-783-4994
ykt-reception@harvardbroadcasting.com
www.gx94radio.com
Social Media: www.youtube.com/user/GX94radio, www.facebook.com/GX94Radio, twitter.com/GX94Radio
Angie Norton, General Manager, anorton@harvardbroadcasting.com

Yukon Territory

Whitehorse: CKRW-FM (The Rush) (Freq: 610)
Owned by: Klondike Broadcasting Ltd.*
#203, 4103 - 4th Ave., Whitehorse, YT Y1A 1H6
Tel: 867-668-6100, *Fax:* 867-668-4209
info@ckrw.com
www.ckrw.com
Eva Bidrman, General Manager

FM Radio Stations

Alberta

Airdrie: CFIT-FM (Air 106.1) (Freq: 106.1)
Owned by: Golden West Broadcasting Ltd.*
#30, 105 Main St. North, Airdrie, AB T4B 0R3
Tel: 403-217-1061, *Toll-Free:* 866-945-1061
air106@goldenwestradio.com
www.discoverairdrie.com
Social Media: www.facebook.com/AIR1061, twitter.com/AIR1061FM

Athabasca: CKBA-FM (The River 94.1) (Freq: 94.1)
Owned by: Newcap Radio*
#1, 4902 - 49 St., Athabasca, AB T9S 1C2
Tel: 780-675-5301, *Fax:* 780-675-4938
www.941theriver.ca
Social Media: www.facebook.com/941theriver, twitter.com/river941
Wray Betts, Station Manager, wbetts@newcap.ca

Athabasca: CKUA-FM-10 (Freq: 98.3)
Owned by: CKUA Radio Network*
Athabasca, AB
Toll-Free: 800-494-2582
www.ckua.com

Banff: CJAY-FM-1 (Freq: 95.1)
Owned by: CJAY-FM (CJAY 92)
Banff, AB
www.cjay92.com

Banff/Canmore: CKUA-FM-14 (Freq: 104.3)
Owned by: CKUA Radio Network*
Banff/Canmore, AB
Toll-Free: 800-494-2582
www.ckua.com

Blairmore: CJPR-FM (Mountain Radio) (Freq: 94.9)
Owned by: Newcap Radio*
PO Box 840, 13213 - 20th Ave, 2nd Fl., Blairmore, AB T0K 0E0
Tel: 403-562-2806, *Fax:* 403-562-8114
mountain.requests@newcap.ca
www.mountainradiofm.com
Barb Kelly, Station Manager, bkelly@newcap.ca
Jenn Dalen, Program Director, jdalen@newcap.ca

** For details on this company see listing in Major Broadcasting Companies section; † French language station*

***Bonnyville:* CFNA-FM (The Wolf)** (Freq: 99.7)
Owned by: Vista Broadcast Group*
#102, 5316 - 54 Ave., Bonnyville, AB T9N 2C9
Tel: 780-573-1745, *Fax:* 780-573-1746
www.997thewolf.com
Social Media: www.facebook.com/99.7TheWolf, twitter.com/997thewolf
Marvin Perry, General Manager, Sales, marvin@borderrock.com

***Bonnyville:* CJEG-FM (101.3 Kool FM)** (Freq: 101.3)
Owned by: Newcap Radio*
PO Box 8251, 4816 - 50th Ave, Bonnyville, AB T9N 2J5
Tel: 780-812-3058, *Fax:* 780-812-3363
www.1013koolfm.com
Social Media: www.facebook.com/kool1013, twitter.com/Kool101dot3
Lisa Fielding, Station Manager, 780-812-7315, lfielding@newcap.ca
Cash Kaye, Program Director, cashk@newcap.ca
Melissa Kelman, Marketing Consultant, mkelman@newcap.ca

***Brooks:* CIBQ-FM (Q 105.7)** (Freq: 105.7)
Owned by: Newcap Radio*
#8, 403 - 2nd Ave. West, Brooks, AB T1R 0S3
Tel: 403-362-3418
q1057@newcap.ca
www.q1057.ca
Social Media: www.facebook.com/Q1057/, twitter.com/Q1057
John Petrie, Station Manager, jpetrie@newcap.ca

***Brooks:* CIXF-FM (101.1 The One)** (Freq: 101.1)
Owned by: Newcap Radio*
#8, 403 - 2nd Ave West, Brooks, AB T1R 0S3
Tel: 403-362-3418, *Fax:* 403-362-8168
www.theonebrooks.com
Social Media: www.facebook.com/theonebrooks, twitter.com/theonebrooks
John Petrie, Station Manager, jpetrie@newcap.ca
Jeff Murray, Program Director, jmurray@newcap.ca

***Calgary:* CBR-FM** (Freq: 102.1)
Owned by: Canadian Broadcasting Corporation*
1724 Westmount Blvd. NW, Calgary, AB T2N 3G7
Tel: 403-521-6000
www.cbc.ca/calgary

***Calgary:* CFGQ-FM (Q107)** (Freq: 107.3)
Owned by: CKIK-FM Limited*
#200, 3320 - 17th Ave. SW, Calgary, AB T3E 0B4
Tel: 403-716-6500, *Fax:* 403-444-4319
www.q107fm.ca
Social Media: www.youtube.com/user/Q107Calgary, www.facebook.com/Q107Calgary, twitter.com/q107calgary
Phil Kallsen, Contact, Programming

***Calgary:* CFXL-FM (XL 103 FM)** (Freq: 103.1)
Owned by: Newcap Radio*
#100, 1110 Centre St. NE, Calgary, AB T2E 2R2
Tel: 403-271-6366, *Fax:* 403-278-6772
feedback@xl103calgary.com
www.xl103calgary.com
Social Media: www.facebook.com/xl103, twitter.com/xl103calgary
Vinka Dubroja, General Manager, vdubroja@newcap.ca
Al Tompson, Program Director, al@xl103calgary.com

***Calgary:* CHFM-FM** (Freq: 95.9)
Owned by: Rogers Broadcasting Ltd.*
#240, 2723 - 37 Ave. NE, Calgary, AB T1Y 5R8
Tel: 403-246-9696
www.lite96.ca
Social Media: www.facebook.com/kiss959calgary, twitter.com/kiss959calgary

***Calgary:* CHKF-FM** (Freq: 94.7)
Owned by: Fairchild Radio*
#109, 2723 - 37th Ave. NE, Calgary, AB T1Y 5R8
Tel: 403-717-1940, *Fax:* 403-717-1945
general@fm947.com
www.fm947.com
Social Media: www.facebook.com/fairchildcal
Other information: News E-mail: news@fm947.com; Sales E-mail: sales@fm947.com

***Calgary:* CIBK-FM (98.5 Virgin Radio)** (Freq: 98.5)
Owned by: Bell Media Inc.*
#300, 1110 Centre St. NE, Calgary, AB T2E 2R2
Tel: 403-240-5800
calgaryweb@virginradio.ca
calgary.virginradio.ca
Social Media: www.facebook.com/virginradiocalgary, twitter.com/VirginRadioYYC
Stewart Meyers, General Manager, stewart.meyers@bellmedia.ca

***Calgary:* CJAY-FM (CJAY 92)** (Freq: 92.1)
Owned by: Bell Media Inc.*
#300, 1110 Centre St. NE, Calgary, AB T2E 2R2
Tel: 403-240-5800
www.cjay92.com
Social Media: www.facebook.com/CJAY92calgary, twitter.com/CJay92
Stewart Meyers, General Manager, stewart.meyers@bellmedia.ca

***Calgary:* CJSI-FM (Shine FM)** (Freq: 88.9)
Owned by: Touch Canada Broadcasting Limited Partnership*
4510 Macleod Trail South, Calgary, AB T2G 0A4
Tel: 403-276-1111, *Fax:* 403-276-1114
www.cjsi.ca
Social Media: www.facebook.com/88.9shinefm, twitter.com/889shinefm
Other information: Shine FM URL: www.shinefm.com

***Calgary:* CJSW-FM** (Freq: 90.9)
#312, MacEwan Hall, University of Calgary, Calgary, AB T2N 1N4
Tel: 403-220-3902, *Fax:* 403-289-8212
office@cjsw.com
www.cjsw.com
Social Media: www.myspace.com/cjsw, www.facebook.com/CJSWFM, twitter.com/cjsw
Myke Atkinson, Station Manager, 403-220-3904, manager@cjsw.com
Joe Burima, Program Director, 403-220-3903, programming@cjsw.com
Whitney Ota, Music Director, 403-220-3085, music@cjsw.com
Marc Affeld, News Director, 403-220-8033, news@cjsw.com

***Calgary:* CKIS-FM** (Freq: 96.9)
Owned by: Rogers Broadcasting Ltd.*
#240, 2723 - 37 Ave. NE, Calgary, AB T1Y 5R8
Tel: 403-250-9797
www.jackfm.ca
Social Media: www.facebook.com/jackfmcalgary, twitter.com/jackfmcalgary

***Calgary:* CKMP-FM (90.3 Amp Radio)** (Freq: 90.3)
Owned by: Newcap Radio*
#100, 1110 Centre St NE, Calgary, AB T2E 2R2
Tel: 403-271-6366, *Fax:* 403-278-6772
feedback@ampcalgary.com
Social Media: www.youtube.com/user/903ampradio, www.facebook.com/ampcalgary, twitter.com/ampcalgary
Vinka Dubroja, Station Manager, vdubroja@newcap.ca
Al Tompson, Program Director, al@xl103calgary.com

***Calgary:* CKRY-FM (Country 105)** (Freq: 105.1)
Owned by: Corus Radio Company*
#200, 3320 - 17th Ave. SW, Calgary, AB T3E 0B4
Tel: 403-716-6500, *Fax:* 403-444-4366
www.country105.com
Social Media: www.facebook.com/Country105, twitter.com/Country105_FM
Phil Kallsen, Program Director

***Calgary:* CKUA-FM-1** (Freq: 93.7)
Owned by: CKUA Radio Network*
Calgary, AB
www.ckua.com

***Calgary:* CMRC The Shift** (Freq: Online radio station)
Mount Royal University, 4825 Richard Rd. SW, Calgary, AB T3E 6K6
Tel: 403-440-6119, *Fax:* 403-440-6563
www.cmrcradio.ca
Social Media: www.facebook.com/pages/The-Shift-Radio/116478261740963, twitter.com/TheShiftRadio
Jillian Hunter, Station Manager

***Camrose:* CFCW-FM (98.1 CAM FM)** (Freq: 98.1)
Owned by: Newcap Radio
5708 - 48th Ave., Camrose, AB T4V 0K1
Tel: 780-672-8255, *Fax:* 780-672-4678
www.981camfm.com
Social Media: www.facebook.com/981CAMFM/#!, twitter.com/981camfm
Neil Cunningham, Station Manager, ncunningham@newcap.ca

***Canmore:* CHMN-FM (Mountain FM)** (Freq: 106.5)
Owned by: Rogers Broadcasting Ltd.*
749 Railway Ave., Canmore, AB T1W 1P2
Tel: 403-678-2222, *Fax:* 403-678-6844
www.mountainfm.ca
Social Media: twitter.com/1065MountainFM, www.facebook.com/106.5mountainfm

***Cold Lake:* CJXK-FM (K-Rock)** (Freq: 95.3)
Owned by: Newcap Radio*
B-5412 - 55 St., Cold Lake, AB T9M 1R5
Tel: 780-594-2459, *Fax:* 780-594-3001
news@k-rock953.com
www.953krock.com
Social Media: www.facebook.com/953KRock, twitter.com/953Krock
Kelli Wispinski, Station Manager, kwispinski@newcap.ca

***Drayton Valley:* CIBW-FM (Big West Country)** (Freq: 92.9)
Owned by: The Jim Pattison Broadcast Group*
PO Box 929, 5164 - 52 Ave., Drayton Valley, AB T7A 1V3
Tel: 780-542-9290, *Toll-Free:* 888-884-2448
www.bigwestcountry.ca
Social Media: www.facebook.com/167537829943069

***Drumheller:* CHOO-FM (99.5 Drum FM)** (Freq: 99.5)
Owned by: Golden West Broadcasting Ltd.*
105 South Railway Ave., Drumheller, AB T0J 0Y0
Tel: 403-823-9936, *Toll-Free:* 877-823-9936
drumfm@goldenwestradio.com
www.drumhelleronline.com
Social Media: www.facebook.com/995drumfm, twitter.com/995drumfm

***Drumheller/Hanna:* CKUA-FM-13** (Freq: 91.3)
Owned by: CKUA Radio Network*
Drumheller/Hanna, AB
Toll-Free: 800-494-2582
www.ckua.com

***Edmonton:* CBX-FM** (Freq: 90.9)
Owned by: Canadian Broadcasting Corporation*
10062 - 102 Ave., Edmonton, AB T5J 2Y8
Tel: 780-462-7500
www.cbc.ca/edmonton

***Edmonton:* CFBR-FM (100.3 The Bear)** (Freq: 100.3)
Owned by: Bell Media Inc.*
#100, 18520 Stony Plain Rd., Edmonton, AB T5S 2E2
Tel: 780-486-2800
www.thebearrocks.com
Social Media: www.facebook.com/TheBearRocks, twitter.com/1003TheBear
Pat Cardinal, General Manager, patrick.cardinal@bellmedia.ca

***Edmonton:* CFMG-FM (104.9 Virgin Radio)** (Freq: 104.9)
Owned by: Bell Media Inc.*
#100, 18520 Stony Plain Rd., Edmonton, AB T5S 2E2
Tel: 780-486-2800
edmonton.virginradio.ca
Social Media: www.facebook.com/1049VirginEdmonton, twitter.com/1049virginyeg
Pat Cardinal, General Manager, patrick.cardinal@bellmedia.ca
Chris Myers, Brand Director, chris.myers@bellmedia.ca

***Edmonton:* CFWE-FM** (Freq: 98.5)
13245 - 146th St., Edmonton, AB T5L 4S8
Tel: 780-455-2700, *Fax:* 780-455-7639
www.cfweradio.ca
Social Media: www.facebook.com/CFWE.FM, twitter.com/cfweradio
Bert Crowfoot, General Manager, bert@cfweradio.ca

***Edmonton:* CHBN-FM** (Freq: 91.7)
Owned by: Rogers Broadcasting Ltd.*
5915 Gateway Blvd., Edmonton, AB T6H 2H3
Tel: 780-423-2005, *Fax:* 780-437-5129
www.thebounce.ca
Social Media: www.youtube.com/917thebounce, www.facebook.com/91.7TheBounce, twitter.com/917thebounce

***Edmonton:* CIRK-FM** (Freq: 97.3)
Owned by: Newcap Radio*
West Edmonton Mall, #2394, 8882 - 170 St., Edmonton, AB T5T 4M2
Tel: 780-437-4996, *Fax:* 780-435-0844
www.k-rock973.com
Social Media: www.facebook.com/K97Edmonton, twitter.com/k97
Neil Cunningham, General Manager, ncunningham@newcap.ca

** For details on this company see listing in Major Broadcasting Companies section; † French language station*

John Roberts, Program Director, jroberts@newcap.ca

Edmonton: CISN-FM (CISN Country 103.9 FM) (Freq: 103.9)
Owned by: Corus Radio Company*
5204 - 84 St., Edmonton, AB T6E 5N8
Tel: 780-440-6300, *Fax:* 780-469-5937
www.cisnfm.com
Social Media: www.youtube.com/cisnfm, www.facebook.com/cisncountry, twitter.com/CISNCountry
Chris Scheetz, Program Director, cscheetz@cisnfm.com

Edmonton: CJRY-FM (Shine FM) (Freq: 105.9)
Owned by: Touch Canada Broadcasting Limited Partnership*
5316 Calgary Trail NW, Edmonton, AB T6H 4J8
Tel: 780-466-4930, *Fax:* 780-469-5335
105.9@shinefm.com
www.cjry.ca
Social Media: www.facebook.com/1059ShineFM, twitter.com/1059shinefm
Other information: Shine FM URL: www.shinefm.com

Edmonton: CJSR-FM (Freq: 88.5)
#0-09 Students Union Bldg., University of Alberta, Edmonton, AB T6G 2J7
Tel: 780-492-2577, *Fax:* 780-492-3121
admin@cjsr.com
www.cjsr.com
Social Media: www.facebook.com/cjsr885, twitter.com/CJSR
Sarah Edwards, Station Manager

Edmonton: CKER-FM (World FM) (Freq: 101.7)
Owned by: Rogers Broadcasting Ltd.*
10212 Jasper Ave., Edmonton, AB T5J 5A3
Tel: 780-424-2222
www.worldfm.ca
Social Media: www.facebook.com/1017WorldFm, twitter.com/1017worldfm

Edmonton: CKNG-FM (925 Fresh FM) (Freq: 92.5)
Owned by: Corus Premium Television Ltd.*
5204 - 84 St., Edmonton, AB T6E 5N8
Tel: 780-440-6300, *Fax:* 780-469-5937
www.925freshfm.com
Social Media: www.youtube.com/925FreshFM, www.facebook.com/925FreshFM, twitter.com/925FreshFM
Greg Johnson, Program Director

Edmonton: CKRA-FM (96.3 Capital FM) (Freq: 96.3)
Owned by: Newcap Radio*
West Edmonton Mall, #2394, 8882 - 170 St., Edmonton, AB T5T 4M2
Tel: 780-437-4996, *Fax:* 780-435-0844
info@963capitafm.com
www.963capitalfm.com
Social Media: www.facebook.com/963capitalfm, twitter.com/capitalfm
Neil Cunningham, General Manager, ncunningham@newcap.ca
John Roberts, Program Director, jroberts@newcap.ca

Edmonton: CKUA-FM (Freq: 94.9)
Owned by: CKUA Radio Network*
9804 Jasper Ave. NW, Edmonton, AB T5J 0C5
Tel: 780-428-7595, *Fax:* 780-428-7624
Toll-Free: 800-494-2582
www.ckua.com
Social Media: www.facebook.com/CKUARadio, twitter.com/ckuaradio
Ken Regan, Chief Executive Officer
Katrina Ingram, Chief Operations Officer

Edson: CFXE-FM (The Eagle) (Freq: 94.3)
Owned by: Newcap Radio*
PO Box 7800, 422 - 50th St., 2nd Fl., Edson, AB T7E 1T1
Tel: 780-723-4461, *Fax:* 780-723-3765
feedback@theeagle.ca
www.theeagle.ca
Social Media: www.facebook.com/theeagleradio/, twitter.com/theeagleradio
Dave Schuck, General Manager, dave@theeagle.ca

Edson: CKUA-FM-8 (Freq: 103.7)
Owned by: CKUA Radio Network*
Edson, AB
Toll-Free: 800-494-2582
www.ckua.com

†Falher: CKRP-FM (Freq: 95.7; 102.9; 90.3)
CP 718, Falher, AB T0H 1M0
Tél: 780-837-2346, *Ligne sans frais:* 866-837-2346
programmation@ckrp.ca
www.ckrp.ca
Médias sociaux: www.facebook.com/CkrpFm

Fort McMurray: CJOK-FM (Country 93.3) (Freq: 93.3)
Owned by: Rogers Broadcasting Ltd.*
9912 Franklin Ave., Fort McMurray, AB T9H 2K5
Tel: 780-743-2246
www.country933.com
Social Media: www.facebook.com/country933, twitter.com/Country933
Rick Walters, General Manager
John Knox, Program Director

Fort McMurray: CKUA-FM-11 (Freq: 96.7)
Owned by: CKUA Radio Network*
Fort McMurray, AB
Toll-Free: 800-494-2582
www.ckua.com

Fort Saskatchewan: CKFT-FM (Mix 107.9 FM) (Freq: 107.9)
Owned by: Golden West Broadcasting Ltd.*
#200, 9940 - 99th Ave., Fort Saskatchewan, AB T8L 4G8
Tel: 780-998-1079, *Toll-Free:* 855-997-1079
fortsaskonline.com
Social Media: www.youtube.com/FortSaskOnline, twitter.com/Mix1079FortSask

Fort Vermilion: CIAM-FM (Freq: 92.7; 104.3; 95.5; 94.1; 102.9)
PO Box 609, Fort Vermilion, AB T0H 1N0
Tel: 780-927-2426, *Fax:* 780-927-2427
Toll-Free: 866-927-2426
info@ciamradio.com
www.ciamradio.com

Fox Creek: CFFC-FM (Freq: 92.1)
Owned by: CKKX-FM
Fox Creek, AB

Fox Creek: CFXW-1 (98.1 The Rig) (Freq: 98.1)
Owned by: CFXW-FM
Fox Creek, AB
Tel: 780-778-5101, *Fax:* 780-778-5137
www.therig.ca

Grande Cache: CFXG-FM (The Eagle) (Freq: 93.3)
Owned by: CFXE-FM 94.3
Grande Cache, AB
Tel: 780-723-4461, *Fax:* 780-723-3765
feedback@theeagle.ca
www.theeagle.ca
Social Media: www.facebook.com/theeagleradio, twitter.com/theeagleradio

Grande Prairie: CFGP-FM (Rock 97.7) (Freq: 97.7)
Owned by: Rogers Broadcasting Ltd.*
#200, 9835 - 101 Ave., Grande Prairie, AB T8V 5V4
Tel: 780-539-9700, *Fax:* 780-532-1600
www.rock977.ca
Social Media: www.facebook.com/ROCK977, twitter.com/ROCK977
Other information: News Phone: 780-532-1044

Grande Prairie: CFRI-FM (104.7 2Day FM) (Freq: 104.7)
Owned by: Vista Broadcast Group*
#1, 11002 - 104 Ave., Grande Prairie, AB T8V 7W5
Tel: 780-357-3733, *Fax:* 780-830-7815
www.mygrandeprairienow.com

Grande Prairie: CJXX-FM (Big Country 93.1) (Freq: 93.1)
Owned by: The Jim Pattison Broadcast Group*
Big Country 93.1 FM, #202, 9817 - 101 Ave., Grande Prairie, AB T8V 0X6
Tel: 780-532-0840, *Fax:* 780-538-1266
info@bigcountryxx.com
www.bigcountryxx.com
Social Media: www.facebook.com/BigCountry931, twitter.com/bigcountry931
Other information: News Phone: 780-538-0841
Ken Norman, General Manager, program@bigcountryxx.com

Grande Prairie: CKUA-FM-4 (Freq: 100.9)
Owned by: CKUA Radio Network*
Grande Prairie, AB
Toll-Free: 800-494-2582
www.ckua.com

High Level: CKHL-FM (Freq: 102.1)
PO Box 3759, High Level, AB T0H 1Z0
Tel: 780-926-4531, *Fax:* 780-926-4564
www.ylcountry.com
Social Media: www.facebook.com/ylcountry, twitter.com/KIX_YL_Newsroom
Chris Black, General Manager, 780-618-4230

High Prairie: CKVH-FM (Prairie FM) (Freq: 93.5)
Owned by: Newcap Radio*
PO Box 2219, 4833 - 52nd Ave., High Prairie, AB T0G 1E0
Tel: 780-523-5120, *Fax:* 780-523-3360
feedback@prairiefm.ca
www.prairiefm.ca
Social Media: www.facebook.com/935PrairieFM/, twitter.com/prairiefm
Wray Betts, Station Manager, wbetts@newcap.ca
Dave Schuck, General Manager, dschuck@newcap.ca

High River: CFXO-FM (SUN Country 99.7) (Freq: 99.7)
Owned by: Golden West Broadcasting Ltd.*
11 - 5th Ave. SE, High River, AB T1V 1G2
Tel: 403-652-2472, *Toll-Free:* 866-652-2472
www.highriveronline.com
Social Media: www.facebook.com/197265794075, twitter.com/suncountry997

Hinton: CFXH-FM (The Eagle) (Freq: 97.5)
Owned by: CFXE-FM 94.3
#102, 506 Carmichael Lane, Hinton, AB T7V 1S4
Fax: 780-865-7792
feedback@theeagle.ca
www.theeagle.ca
Social Media: www.facebook.com/theeagleradio, twitter.com/theeagleradio

Hinton: CKUA-FM-7 (Freq: 102.5)
Owned by: CKUA Radio Network*
Hinton, AB
Toll-Free: 800-494-2582
www.ckua.com

Jasper: CFXP-FM (The Eagle) (Freq: 95.5)
Owned by: CFXE-FM 94.3
Jasper, AB
Tel: 780-723-4461, *Fax:* 780-723-3765
feedback@theeagle.ca
www.theeagle.ca
Social Media: www.facebook.com/theeagleradio, twitter.com/theeagleradio

LLoydminster: CKUA-FM-15 (Freq: 97.5)
Owned by: CKUA Radio Network*
LLoydminster, AB
Toll-Free: 800-494-2582
www.ckua.com

La Crete: CKLA-FM (Freq: 92.1)
Owned by: CKYL
La Crete, AB

Lac La Biche: CILB-FM (Big Dog 103.5) (Freq: 103.5)
Owned by: Newcap Radio*
PO Box 86, #201, 10107 - 102nd Ave, Lac La Biche, AB T0A 2C0
Tel: 780-623-3744, *Fax:* 780-623-3740
www.1035bigdog.com/
Social Media: www.facebook.com/1035BigDog, twitter.com/BigDog1035
Chad Tabish, General Manager, ctabish@newcap.ca
Rick Flumian, Station Manager, rflumian@newcap.ca
Kurt Price, Program Director, kprice@newcap.ca

Lacombe: CJUV-FM (Sunny 94 FM) (Freq: 94.1)
Owned by: L.A. Radio Group Inc.
4720 Hwy. 2A, Lacombe, AB T4L 1H4
Tel: 403-786-0194, *Fax:* 403-786-0199
onair@sunny94.com
sunny94.com
Social Media: www.facebook.com/SUNNY94FM, twitter.com/Sunny94FM
Troy Schaab, President & Co-owner

** For details on this company see listing in Major Broadcasting Companies section; † French language station*

***Lake Louise:* CJAY-FM-2** (Freq: 97.5)
Owned by: CJAY-FM (CJAY 92)
Lake Louise, AB
www.cjay92.com

***Lethbrdge:* CKBD-FM** (Freq: 98.1)
#400, 220 - 3rd Ave. South, Lethbrdge, AB T1J 0G9
Tel: 403-388-2910, *Fax:* 403-388-4648
www.981thebridge.ca
Social Media: www.youtube.com/981theBridge, www.facebook.com/981theBridge, twitter.com/981theBridge

***Lethbridge:* CFRV-FM** (Freq: 107.7)
Owned by: Rogers Broadcasting Ltd.*
1015 - 3rd Ave. South, Lethbridge, AB T1J 0J3
Tel: 403-320-1220, *Fax:* 403-380-1539
www.1077theriver.ca
Social Media: www.facebook.com/1077theriver, twitter.com/1077TheRiver

***Lethbridge:* CHLB-FM (Country 95)** (Freq: 95.5)
Owned by: The Jim Pattison Broadcast Group*
401 Mayor Magrath Dr. South, Lethbridge, AB T1J 3L8
Tel: 403-329-0995, *Fax:* 403-329-0195
events@country95.fm
www.country95.fm
Social Media: pinterest.com/country955, www.facebook.com/pages/Country-955-Lethbridge/117935014929433, twitter.com/country95
Gary Dorosz, General Manager, gdorosz@country95.fm

***Lethbridge:* CJBZ-FM (B-93.3)** (Freq: 93.3)
Owned by: The Jim Pattison Broadcast Group*
401 Mayor Magrath Dr. South, Lethbridge, AB T1J 3L8
Tel: 403-329-0955, *Fax:* 403-329-0165
info@b93.fm
www.b93.fm
Social Media: www.facebook.com/196439890402849, twitter.com/Breakfast_Buzz
Gary Dorosz, General Manager, gdorosz@country95.fm

***Lethbridge:* CJRX-FM** (Freq: 106.7)
Owned by: Rogers Broadcasting Ltd.*
1015 - 3rd Ave. South, Lethbridge, AB TlJ 0J3
Tel: 403-320-1220, *Fax:* 403-380-1539
www.rock106.ca
Social Media: www.facebook.com/rock106lethbridge, twitter.com/Rock106

***Lethbridge:* CKUA-FM-2** (Freq: 99.3)
Owned by: CKUA Radio Network*
Lethbridge, AB
Toll-Free: 800-494-2582
www.ckua.com

***Lloydminster:* CKLM-FM** (Freq: 106.1; 99.7)
Owned by: Vista Broadcast Group*
Atrium Center, 5012 - 49th St., 2nd Fl., Lloydminster, AB T9V 0K2
Tel: 780-875-5400
www.borderrock.com
Social Media: www.facebook.com/1061TheGoat, twitter.com/1061thegoat

***Lloydminster:* CKLM-FM (106.1 The Goat)** (Freq: 106.1)
Owned by: Vista Broadcast Group*
Atrium Centre, 5012 - 49th St., 2nd Fl., Lloydminster, AB T9V 0K2
Tel: 780-875-5400, *Fax:* 780-875-4628
www.mylloydminsternow.com
Social Media: www.youtube.com/thegoat1061, www.facebook.com/1061TheGoat, twitter.com/1061thegoat

***Lloydminster:* CKSA-FM (Lloyd 95.9)** (Freq: 95.9)
Owned by: Newcap Radio*
5026 - 50th St., Lloydminster, AB T9V 1P3
Tel: 780-875-3321, *Fax:* 780-875-4704
Toll-Free: 800-565-2572
Lloyd@newcap.ca
www.959lloydfm.com
Social Media: www.facebook.com/959LLOYDFM, twitter.com/lloydfm
Chad Tabish, General Manager, ctabish@newcap.ca
Dean Martin, Creative Director, dmartin@newcap.ca

***Martin Mountain:* CHSL-FM (92.7 Lake FM)** (Freq: 92.7)
Owned by: Newcap Radio*
#103, 228 - 3rd Ave NW, Martin Mountain, AB T0G 2A1
Tel: 780-849-2569, *Fax:* 780-849-4833
onair@lakefm.ca
www.lakefm.ca
Social Media: www.facebook.com/927LAKEFM, twitter.com/927LakeFM
Wray Betts, Station Manager, wbetts@newcap.ca

***Medicine Hat:* CJLT-FM (Praise FM)** (Freq: 93.7)
Owned by: Vista Broadcast Group*
#206, 1741 Dunmore Rd. SE, Medicine Hat, AB T1A 1Z8
Tel: 403-529-9599
studio@937praisefm.com
www.937praisefm.com
Social Media: www.facebook.com/937Praisefm, twitter.com/937Praisefm
Other information: News E-mail: News@937praisefm.com; Sales: Sales@937praisefm.com

***Medicine Hat:* CKUA-FM-3** (Freq: 97.3)
Owned by: CKUA Radio Network*
Medicine Hat, AB
Toll-Free: 800-494-2582
www.ckua.com

***Okotoks:* CFXL-FM** (Freq: 100.9)
Owned by: Golden West Broadcasting Ltd.*
PO Box 1889, 22 Elizabeth St,. Bay 3, Okotoks, AB T1S 1B7
Tel: 403-995-9611, *Toll-Free:* 866-995-9611
theeagle1009@goldenwestradio.com
www.theeagle1009.com
Social Media: www.facebook.com/pages/The-Eagle-1009/296045543680, twitter.com/TheEagle1009

***Okotoks:* CLUV-FM (100.9 The Eagle)** (Freq: 100.9)
Owned by: Golden West Broadcasting Ltd.*
PO Box 1889, 22 Elizabeth St., Bay 3, Okotoks, AB T1S 1B7
Tel: 403-995-9611, *Toll-Free:* 866-995-9611
theeagle1009@goldenwestradio.com
okotoksonline.com
Social Media: www.facebook.com/296045543680, twitter.com/TheEagle1009

***Peace River:* CKKX-FM** (Freq: 106.1)
PO Box 300, 9807 - 100 Ave., Peace River, AB T8S 1T5
Tel: 780-624-2535, *Fax:* 780-624-5424
www.kix106.net
Social Media: www.facebook.com/pages/KIX-FM/169489399721, twitter.com/KIXFM

***Peace River:* CKUA-FM-5** (Freq: 96.9)
Owned by: CKUA Radio Network*
Peace River, AB
Toll-Free: 800-494-2582
www.ckua.com

***Pincher Creek:* CJPV-FM (Mountain Radio)** (Freq: 92.7)
Owned by: CJPR-FM
Pincher Creek, AB
Tel: 403-562-2806, *Fax:* 403-562-8114
www.mountainradiofm.com

***Red Deer:* CFDV-FM (The Drive)** (Freq: 106.7)
Owned by: The Jim Pattison Broadcast Group*
2840 Bremner Ave., Red Deer, AB T4R 1M9
Tel: 403-343-7105, *Fax:* 403-343-2573
rock@1067thedrive.fm
www.1067thedrive.fm
Social Media: www.facebook.com/14398632969
Paul Mason, General Manager

***Red Deer:* CHUB-FM (Big 105 FM)** (Freq: 105.5)
Owned by: The Jim Pattison Broadcast Group*
2840 Bremner Ave., Red Deer, AB T4R 1M9
Tel: 403-343-7105, *Fax:* 403-343-2573
heydj@big105.fm
www.big105.fm
Social Media: www.youtube.com/user/big105radio, www.facebook.com/147587290330, twitter.com/Big105

***Red Deer:* CIZZ-FM (Zed 98.9)** (Freq: 98.9)
Owned by: Newcap Radio*
PO Box 5339, 4920 - 59th St., Red Deer, AB T4N 6W1
Tel: 403-348-0955, *Fax:* 403-346-1230
zed99@newcap.ca
www.zed99.com
Social Media: www.facebook.com/ZED989, twitter.com/zed99reddeer
Jared Waldo, General Manager, jwaldo@newcap.ca
Jeff Murray, Program Director, jmurray@newcap.ca

***Red Deer:* CKGY-FM (KG Country)** (Freq: 95.5)
Owned by: Newcap Radio*
PO Box 5339, 4920 - 59th St., Red Deer, AB T4N 6W1
Tel: 403-348-0955, *Fax:* 403-346-1230
www.kgcountry.ca
Social Media: www.facebook.com/KGCountry955, twitter.com/kgreddeer
Jared Waldo, General Sales Manager, jwaldo@newcap.com
Jenn Dalen, Program Director, jdalen@newcap.ca

***Red Deer:* CKIK-FM (KRAZE 101.3)** (Freq: 101.3)
Owned by: L.A. Radio Group Inc.
#103, 6751 - 52nd Ave., Red Deer, AB T4N 4K8
Tel: 403-358-3100, *Fax:* 403-309-8311
onair@kraze1013.com
kraze1013.com
Social Media: www.facebook.com/kraze1013, twitter.com/kraze1013

***Red Deer:* CKRD-FM (Shine FM)** (Freq: 90.5)
Owned by: Touch Canada Broadcasting Limited Partnership*
#13, 7619 - 50 Ave., Red Deer, AB T4P 1M6
Tel: 403-356-9052, *Fax:* 403-356-1745
90.5@shinefm.com
www.ckrd.ca
Social Media: www.facebook.com/ShineFMRedDeer, twitter.com/905ShineFM
Other information: Shine FM URL: www.shinefm.com

***Red Deer:* CKUA-FM-6** (Freq: 107.7)
Owned by: CKUA Radio Network*
Red Deer, AB
Toll-Free: 800-494-2582
www.ckua.com

***Redcliff:* CHAT-FM (Chat 94.5)** (Freq: 94.5)
Owned by: The Jim Pattison Broadcast Group*
10 Boundary Rd., Redcliff, AB T0J 2P0
Tel: 403-548-8282, *Fax:* 403-548-8270
chat945@jpbg.com
www.chat945.com
Social Media: www.facebook.com/chat94.5, twitter.com/CHAT945

***Redcliffe:* CFMY-FM (My 96 FM)** (Freq: 96.1)
Owned by: The Jim Pattison Broadcast Group*
10 Boundary Rd., Redcliffe, AB T0J 2P0
Tel: 403-548-8282, *Fax:* 403-548-8270
my96fm@jpbg.com
www.my96fm.com
Social Media: www.facebook.com/my96fm, twitter.com/my96fm

***Rocky Mountain House:* CHBW-FM (B-94)** (Freq: 94.5)
Owned by: The Jim Pattison Broadcast Group*
4814B - 49th St., Rocky Mountain House, AB T4T 1S8
yourb94.ca
Social Media: www.facebook.com/305722079556076

***Siksika:* CHDH-FM** (Freq: 97.7)
Siksika, AB
www.siksikamedia.com

***Spirit River:* CKUA-FM-12** (Freq: 99.5)
Owned by: CKUA Radio Network*
Spirit River, AB
Toll-Free: 800-494-2582
www.ckua.com

***St. Paul:* CHSP-FM (97.7 The Spur)** (Freq: 97.7)
Owned by: Newcap Radio*
#201, 4341 - 50th Ave, St. Paul, AB T0A 3A3
Tel: 780-645-4425, *Fax:* 780-645-2383
www.977thespur.com
Social Media: www.facebook.com/97.7TheSpur, twitter.com/977thespur1
Chad Tabish, General Manager, ctabish@newcap.ca
Kurt Price, Program Director, kprice@newcap.ca
Kevin Bernhardt, Marketing Consultant, kbernhardt@newcap.ca

** For details on this company see listing in Major Broadcasting Companies section; † French language station*

***Stettler:* CKSQ-FM (Q93.3)** (Freq: 93.3)
Owned by: Newcap Radio*
PO Box 2050, 4812A - 50th St., Stettler, AB T0C 2L0
Tel: 403-742-1400, *Fax:* 403-742-0660
Q933@newcap.ca
www.q933.ca
Social Media: www.facebook.com/Q933, twitter.com/Q933Country
Vicki Leuck, General & Sales Manager, vleuck@newcap.ca

***Wabasca:* CHSL-FM-1 (Lake FM)** (Freq: 94.3)
Owned by: CHSL-FM 92.7
Wabasca, AB
Tel: 780-849-2569, *Fax:* 780-849-4833
onair@lakefm.ca
www.lakefm.ca
Social Media: www.facebook.com/927LAKEFM, twitter.com/927LakeFM

***Wainwright:* CKKY-FM** (Freq: 101.9)
Owned by: Newcap Radio*
1037 - 2nd Ave., 2nd Fl., Wainwright, AB T9W 1K7
Tel: 780-842-4311, *Fax:* 780-842-4636
www.krock1019.com
Social Media: www.facebook.com/Krock1019, twitter.com/Krock1019
Chad Tabish, General Manager, ctabish@newcap.ca
Hugh Macdonald, Station/Sales Manager, hmacdonald@newcap.ca
Kurt Price, Alberta Radio Group - East: Program Director, kprice@newcap.ca

***Wainwright:* CKWY-FM (93.7 Wayne FM)** (Freq: 93.7)
Owned by: Newcap Radio*
1037 - 2nd Ave., 2nd Fl., Wainwright, AB T9W 1K7
Tel: 780-842-4311, *Fax:* 780-842-4636
www.waynefm.com
Social Media: www.facebook.com/waynefm, twitter.com/waynefm
Chad Tabish, General Manager, ctabish@newcap.ca
Hugh MacDonald, Station/Sales Manager, hmacdonald@newcap.ca
Kurt Price, Program Director, kprice@newcap.ca

***Westlock:* CKWB-FM (97.9 The Range)** (Freq: 97.9)
Owned by: Newcap Radio*
#17, 10030 - 106 St., Westlock, AB T7P 2K4
Tel: 780-349-4421, *Fax:* 780-349-6259
www.979therange.ca
Social Media: www.facebook.com/979TheRange, twitter.com/979therange
Wray Betts, General Manager, wbetts@newcap.ca
Stuart McIntosh, Program Director, smcintosh@newcap.ca

***Whitecourt:* CFXW-FM (96.7 The Rig)** (Freq: 96.7)
Owned by: Newcap Radio*
PO Box 2288, 5036 - 50th Ave, Whitecourt, AB T7S 1N4
Tel: 780-778-5137, *Fax:* 780-778-5137
www.therig.ca
Social Media: www.facebook.com/967TheRig/, twitter.com/RigRadio
Dave Schuck, General Manager, 780-723-4461, dschuck@newcap.ca
Stuart McIntosh, Program Director, smcintosh@newcap.ca

***Whitecourt:* CIXM-FM** (Freq: 105.3)
Owned by: Fabmar Communications Ltd.*
4912A - 50th Ave., Whitecourt, AB T7S 1P4
Tel: 780-706-1053, *Fax:* 780-706-1017
info@xm105fm.com
www.xm105fm.com
Social Media: www.facebook.com/108298062551705, twitter.com/XM1053FM
Neil Shewchuk, Station Manager & Sales Manager, neil@xm105fm.com

***Whitecourt:* CKUA-FM-9** (Freq: 107.1)
Owned by: CKUA Radio Network*
Whitecourt, AB
Toll-Free: 800-494-2582
www.ckua.com

British Columbia

***100 Mile House:* CFFM-FM-3 (The Goat)** (Freq: 99.7)
Owned by: CFFM-FM (The Rush)
#3, 407 Alder Ave., 100 Mile House, BC V0K 2E0
Tel: 250-395-3848
www.mycariboonow.com

***Abbotsford:* CKQC-FM (Country 107.1)** (Freq: 107.1)
Owned by: Rogers Broadcasting Ltd.*
#318, 31935 South Fraser Way, Abbotsford, BC V2T 5N7
Tel: 604-853-4756, *Fax:* 604-853-1071
Toll-Free: 866-468-1071
country1071.com
Social Media: www.youtube.com/Country1071, www.facebook.com/Country1071, twitter.com/country1071

***Burnaby:* CJSF-FM** (Freq: 90.1)
#TC216, Simon Fraser University, Burnaby, BC V5A 1S6
Tel: 778-782-3727, *Fax:* 778-782-3695
cjsfmgr@sfu.ca
www.cjsf.ca
Social Media: www.facebook.com/cjsfradio, twitter.com/CJSF
Magnus Thyrold, Station Manager
David Swanson, Program Coordinator, cjsfprog@sfu.ca

***Burns Lake:* CJFW-FM-5** (Freq: 92.9)
Owned by: CJFW-FM
Burns Lake, BC

***Campbell River:* CIQC-FM (99.7 2day FM)** (Freq: 99.7)
Owned by: Vista Broadcast Group*
470 - 13th Ave., Campbell River, BC V9W 7J4
Tel: 250-287-7106, *Fax:* 250-287-7170
www.mycampbellrivernow.com/2day-fm
Social Media: www.facebook.com/9972dayfm, twitter.com/9972DayFM_CR
Andrew Davis, Program Director

***Castlegar:* CKQR-FM (The Goat)** (Freq: 99.3)
Owned by: Vista Broadcast Group*
1101 - 4th St., Castlegar, BC V1N 2A8
Tel: 250-365-7600, *Fax:* 250-365-8480
kootenay.thegoatrocks.ca
Social Media: www.facebook.com/114114955319657, twitter.com/GOATFM

***Chetwynd:* CHET-FM** (Freq: 94.5)
PO Box 214, Chetwynd, BC V0C 1J0
Tel: 250-788-9452, *Fax:* 250-788-9402
Toll-Free: 800-788-5330
info@peacefm.ca
www.peacefm.ca
Social Media: www.facebook.com/pages/Peace-FM/178391508895881, twitter.com/Peace_FM
Leo Sabulsky, General Manager, leo@peacefm.ca

***Chilliwack:* CKSR-FM** (Freq: 98.3)
Owned by: Rogers Broadcasting Ltd.*
#309, 46167 Yale Rd., Chilliwack, BC V2P 2N2
Tel: 604-795-5711, *Fax:* 604-795-2983
www.starfm.com
Social Media: pinterest.com/983starfm, www.facebook.com/983starfm, twitter.com/983StarFM

***Christina Lake:* CKGF-1-FM (93.3 The Goat)** (Freq: 93.3)
Owned by: CKQR-FM
Christina Lake, BC

***Courtenay:* CFCP-FM (98.9 the Goat)** (Freq: 98.9)
Owned by: Vista Broadcast Group*
#201A, 910 Fitzgerald Ave., Courtenay, BC V9N 2R5
Tel: 250-334-2421, *Fax:* 250-334-1977
www.mycomoxvalleynow.com/the-goat
Social Media: www.facebook.com/989TheGoat, twitter.com/989theGOAT

***Courtenay:* CKLR-FM (97.3 The Eagle)** (Freq: 97.3)
Owned by: Island Radio Ltd.*
801B - 29th St., Courtenay, BC V9N 7Z5
Tel: 250-703-2200, *Fax:* 250-703-9611
info@973theeagle.com
www.973theeagle.com
Social Media: www.facebook.com/160156290730199, twitter.com/theeagle973
Kent Wilson, Program Director, kwilson@islandradio.bc.ca

***Cranbrook:* CHBZ-FM (Total Country)** (Freq: 104.7)
Owned by: The Jim Pattison Broadcast Group*
19 - 9 Ave. South, Cranbrook, BC V1C 2L9
Tel: 250-426-2224, *Fax:* 250-426-5520
www.b104.ca
Social Media: www.facebook.com/pages/B104-Total-Country/174505095908858
Leo Baggio, Program Director, leo@thedrivefm.ca

***Cranbrook:* CHDR-FM (The Drive)** (Freq: 102.9)
Owned by: The Jim Pattison Broadcast Group*
19 - 9 Ave. South, Cranbrook, BC V1C 2L9
Tel: 250-426-2224
info@thedrivefm.ca
www.thedrivefm.ca
Social Media: www.facebook.com/pages/1029-The-Drive/189645437832891
Leo Baggio, General Manager, leo@thedrivefm.ca

***Crawford Bay:* CBTE-FM** (Freq: 89.9)
Owned by: Canadian Broadcasting Corporation
Crawford Bay, BC

***Crawford Bay:* CHNV-FM-1 (91.9 Juice FM)** (Freq: 91.9)
Owned by: CHNV-FM (103.5 Juice FM)
Crawford Bay, BC
www.mynelsonnow.com/juicefm

***Crawford Bay:* CKKC-1-FM** (Freq: 101.9)
Owned by: CKKC-FM (Kootenays EZ Rock)
Crawford Bay, BC
kootenays.myezrock.com

***Dawson Creek:* CHAD-FM** (Freq: 104.1)
#5, 1017- 103 Ave., Dawson Creek, BC V1G 2G6
Tel: 250-784-2002, *Fax:* 250-784-2002
info@peacefm.ca
peacefm.ca
Leo Sabulsky, General Manager

***Dawson Creek:* CHRX-FM-1 (Sun FM)** (Freq: 95.1)
Owned by: CHRX-FM (Sun FM)
Dawson Creek, BC
www.peacesunfm.com

***Duncan:* CJSU-FM (SUN FM)** (Freq: 89.7)
Owned by: Vista Broadcast Group*
#4, 130 Trans Canada Hwy., Duncan, BC V9L 6W4
Tel: 250-746-4897
onair@897sunfm.com
www.897sunfm.com
Social Media: instagram.com/897sunfm, www.facebook.com/897sunfm, twitter.com/897sunfm
Troy Scott, Program Director, troy@897sunfm.com

***Egmont:* CIEG-FM** (Freq: 107.5)
Owned by: CISQ-FM
Egmont, BC

***Enderby:* CKIZ-FM-1** (Freq: 93.9)
Owned by: CKIZ-FM (107.5 Kiss FM)
Enderby, BC

***Enderby:* CKXR-FM-2** (Freq: 104.3)
Owned by: CKXR-FM (EZ Rock)
Enderby, BC
salmonarm.myezrock.com

***Fernie:* CJDR-FM (The Drive)** (Freq: 99.1)
Owned by: The Jim Pattison Broadcast Group*
Fernie, BC
www.thedrivefm.ca

***Fort Nelson:* CKRX-FM (102.3 The Bear)** (Freq: 102.3)
Owned by: Bell Media Inc.*
5152 Liard St., Fort Nelson, BC V0C 1R0
Tel: 250-774-2525, *Fax:* 250-774-2577
www.1023thebear.com
Social Media: www.facebook.com/The.BEAR.CKRX, twitter.com/1023thebear
Ken Johnson, Station Manager, ken.johnson@bellmedia.ca

***Fort St John:* CHRX-FM (Sun FM)** (Freq: 98.5)
Owned by: Bell Media Inc.*
10532 Alaska Rd., Fort St John, BC V1J 1B3
Tel: 250-785-6634, *Fax:* 250-785-4544
www.peacesunfm.com
Social Media: www.facebook.com/PeaceSunFM, twitter.com/sunfmpeacemusic
Terry Shepherd, General Manager, terry.shepherd@bellmedia.ca

***Fort St John:* CKFU-FM** (Freq: 100.1)
9924 - 101 Ave., Fort St John, BC V1J 2B2
Tel: 250-787-7100
reception@moosefm.ca
energeticcity.ca/moosefm

** For details on this company see listing in Major Broadcasting Companies section; † French language station*

***Fort St John:* CKNL-FM (101.5 The Bear)** (Freq: 101.5)
Owned by: Bell Media Inc.*
10532 Alaska Rd., Fort St John, BC V1J 1B3
Tel: 250-785-6634, *Fax:* 250-785-4544
www.1015thebear.com
Social Media: www.facebook.com/1015thebear, twitter.com/1015thebear
Terry Shepherd, General Manager, terry.shepherd@bellmedia.ca
Dave Lewis, Creative Director, dave.lewis@bellmedia.ca
Andre Da Costa, News Director, andre.dacosta@bellmedia.ca

***Fort St. James:* CIRX-FM-3 (94X)** (Freq: 94.7)
Owned by: CIRX-FM (94X)
Fort St. James, BC

***Gibsons:* CISC-FM** (Freq: 107.5)
Owned by: CISQ-FM (Mountain FM)
Gibsons, BC
www.mountainfm.com
Joe Polito, Manager

***Gold River:* CJGR-FM (100.1 2day FM)** (Freq: 100.1)
Owned by: CIQC-FM (99.7 2Day FM)*
Gold River, BC

***Golden:* CKGR-FM (106.3 EZ Rock)** (Freq: 106.3)
Owned by: Bell Media Inc.*
PO Box 1403, 825 - 10th Ave. South, Golden, BC V0A 1H0
Tel: 250-344-7177, *Fax:* 250-344-7233
golden.myezrock.com
Social Media: www.facebook.com/myezrock, twitter.com/MyEzRock

***Grand Forks:* CKGF-FM (Juice FM)** (Freq: 102.3)
Owned by: CJUI-FM
Grand Forks, BC

***Grand Forks:* CKGF-FM (The Goat)** (Freq: 96.7)
Owned by: CKQR-FM (99.3 The Goat)*
Grand Forks, BC

***Hazelton:* CJFW-FM-8** (Freq: 101.9)
Owned by: CJFW-FM
Hazelton, BC

***Houston:* CFBV-FM-1 (The Peak)** (Freq: 106.5)
Owned by: CFBV-AM (The Peak)
Houston, BC
thepeak@thepeak.ca
www.thepeak.ca

***Houston:* CJFW-FM-7** (Freq: 105.5)
Owned by: CJFW-FM
Houston, BC

***Invermere:* CJAY-FM-3** (Freq: 99.7)
Owned by: CJAY-FM (CJAY 92)
Invermere, BC
www.cjay92.com

***Kamloops:* CFBX-FM** (Freq: 92.5)
Thompsons Rivers University, 900 McGill Rd., House 8, Kamloops, BC V2C 0C8
Tel: 250-377-3988
radio@tru.ca
www.theX.ca
Social Media: www.facebook.com/pages/925-FM-CFBX-the-X/345643872210945, twitter.com/CFBXRadio
Brant Zwicker, Station Manager, bzwicker@tru.ca

***Kamloops:* CIFM-FM** (Freq: 98.3)
Owned by: The Jim Pattison Broadcast Group*
460 Pemberton Terrace, Kamloops, BC V2C 1T5
Tel: 250-372-3322, *Fax:* 250-374-0445
www.98.3cifm.com
Social Media: www.youtube.com/983CIFM, www.facebook.com/162715043755503, twitter.com/983cifm
Rod Schween, President & General Manager, rschween@jpbg.com

***Kamloops:* CJKC-FM (Country 103)** (Freq: 103.1)
Owned by: NL Broadcasting Ltd.*
611 Lansdowne St., Kamloops, BC V2C 1Y6
Tel: 250-571-1031, *Fax:* 250-372-2263
info@radionl.com
www.country103.ca
Social Media: www.facebook.com/Country103, twitter.com/Country103CJKC
Garth Buchko, General Manager, gbuchko@radionl.com

***Kamloops:* CKBZ-FM (B-100)** (Freq: 100.1)
Owned by: The Jim Pattison Broadcast Group*
460 Pemberton Terrace, Kamloops, BC V2C 1T5
Tel: 250-372-3322, *Fax:* 250-374-0445
www.b100.ca
Social Media: www.youtube.com/kamloopsb100, www.facebook.com/215800745108662, twitter.com/kamloopsb100
Rod Schween, President & General Manager, rschween@jpbg.com

***Kamloops:* CKRV-FM (97.5 The River)** (Freq: 97.5)
Owned by: NL Broadcasting Ltd.*
611 Lansdowne St., Kamloops, BC V2C 1Y6
Tel: 250-372-2197, *Fax:* 250-372-2293
info@radionl.com
www.975river.com
Social Media: www.facebook.com/161321237228076, twitter.com/ckrvfm
Garth Buchko, General Manager, gbuchko@radionl.com

***Kaslo:* CKZX-FM-1** (Freq: 95.3)
Owned by: CKKC-FM (Kootenays EZ Rock)
Kaslo, BC
kootenays.myezrock.com

***Kelowna:* CBTK-FM** (Freq: 88.9)
Owned by: Canadian Broadcasting Corporation*
243 Lawrence Ave., Kelowna, BC V1Y 6L2
Tel: 250-861-3781
www.cbc.ca/bc

***Kelowna:* CHSU-FM (99.9 Sun FM)** (Freq: 99.9)
Owned by: Bell Media Inc.*
435 Bernard Ave., Kelowna, BC V1Y 6N8
Tel: 250-860-8600, *Fax:* 250-860-8856
Toll-Free: 866-960-8600
info@thesun.net
www.thesun.net
Social Media: www.facebook.com/99.9SUNFM, twitter.com/999SUNFM
Ken Kilcullen, General Manager, ken.kilcullen@bellmedia.ca

***Kelowna:* CILK-FM (101.5 EZ Rock)** (Freq: 101.5)
Owned by: Bell Media Inc.*
435 Bernard Ave., Kelowna, BC V1Y 6N8
Tel: 250-860-8600, *Fax:* 250-860-8856
kelownainfo@myezrock.com
kelowna.myezrock.com
Social Media: www.facebook.com/101.5EZrockKelowna, twitter.com/1015ezrock
Ken Kilcullen, General Manager, ken.kilcullen@bellmedia.ca

***Kelowna:* CJUI-FM (103.9 Juice FM)** (Freq: 103.9)
Owned by: Vista Broadcast Group*
1729 Gordon Dr., Kelowna, BC V1Y 3H3
Tel: 250-980-9009, *Fax:* 250-980-1038
1039.juicefm.ca
Social Media: www.facebook.com/1039JuiceFM, twitter.com/1039juicefm
Steve Huber, General Manager, shuber@vistaradio.ca

***Kelowna:* CKKO-FM (K963)** (Freq: 96.3)
Owned by: Newcap Radio*
1601 Bertram St, Kelowna, BC VIY 2G5
Tel: 250-861-5693, *Fax:* 250-469-9963
www.k963.ca
Social Media: www.instagram.com/k963classicrock, www.facebook.com/K96.3fm, twitter.com/K963ClassicRock
Peter Angle, General Manager, pangle@newcap.ca
David Larsen, Program Director, dlarsen@newcap.ca

***Kelowna:* CKLZ-FM (Power 104 FM)** (Freq: 104.7)
Owned by: The Jim Pattison Broadcast Group*
3805 Lakeshore Rd., Kelowna, BC V1W 3K6
Tel: 250-763-1047, *Fax:* 250-762-2141
info@power104.fm
www.power104.fm
Social Media: www.facebook.com/Power104, twitter.com/Power104

***Kelowna:* CKQQ-FM (The Q 103.1)** (Freq: 103.1)
Owned by: The Jim Pattison Broadcast Group*
3805 Lakeshore Rd., Kelowna, BC V1W 3K6
Tel: 250-762-3331
theq@q1031.ca
www.q1031.ca
Social Media: www.youtube.com/q1031radio, www.facebook.com/Q1031, twitter.com/q1031

***Keremeos:* CIGV-FM-1** (Freq: 98.9)
Owned by: CIGV-FM
Keremeos, BC

***Kitimat:* CJFW-FM-1** (Freq: 92.9)
Owned by: CJFW-FM
Kitimat, BC

***Lillooet:* CHLS-FM** (Freq: 100.5)
415 Main St., Lillooet, BC V0K 1V0
Tel: 250-256-7561
radiolillooet@gmail.com
radiolillooet.ca

***Mackenzie:* CHMM-FM** (Freq: 103.5)
PO Box 547, Mackenzie, BC V0J 2C0
Tel: 250-997-6277, *Fax:* 250-997-6222
chmm1035@gmail.com
www.chmm.ca

***Masset:* CJFW-FM-4** (Freq: 92.9)
Owned by: CJFW-FM
Masset, BC

***Merritt:* CKMQ-FM (Q101.1 FM)** (Freq: 101.1)
Owned by: Merritt Broadcasting Ltd.*
#201, 2196 Quilchena Ave., Merritt, BC V1K 1A4
Tel: 250-378-4288
www.q101.ca
Social Media: www.facebook.com/pages/Q101-Merritts-Music-Mix/140846484203, twitter.com/Q101Merritt

***Nakusp:* CKBS-FM** (Freq: 103.1)
Owned by: CKKC-FM (Kootenays EZ Rock)
Nakusp, BC
kootenays.myezrock.com

***Nanaimo:* CHLY-FM** (Freq: 101.7)
c/o The Radio Malaspina Society, #2, 34 Victoria Rd., Nanaimo, BC V9R 5B8
Tel: 250-716-3410, *Toll-Free:* 855-740-1017
www.chly.ca
Social Media: www.facebook.com/Radio.Malaspina, twitter.com/chlyradio
Bob Simpson, Executive Director & Interim Station Manager, programdirector@chly.ca

***Nanaimo:* CHWF-FM (106.9 The Wolf)** (Freq: 106.9)
Owned by: Island Radio Ltd.*
4550 Wellington Rd., Nanaimo, BC V9T 2H3
Tel: 250-758-1131, *Fax:* 250-758-4644
info@1069thewolf.com
www.1069thewolf.com
Social Media: www.facebook.com/1069thewolf, twitter.com/1069thewolf
Other information: News Phone: 250-758-2467
Rob Bye, General Manager

***Nanaimo:* CKWV-FM (102.3 The Wave)** (Freq: 102.3)
Owned by: Island Radio Ltd.*
4550 Wellington Rd., Nanaimo, BC V9T 2H3
Tel: 250-758-1131, *Fax:* 250-758-4644
info@1023thewave.com
www.1023thewave.com
Social Media: www.facebook.com/1023thewave, twitter.com/1023thewave
Other information: News Phone: 250-758-2467
Rob Bye, General Manager

***Nelson:* CHNV-FM (103.5 Juice FM)** (Freq: 103.5)
Owned by: CJUI-FM (103.9 Juice FM)
312 Hall St., Nelson, BC V1L 1Y8
Tel: 250-352-1902, *Fax:* 250-352-0301
www.mynelsonnow.com/juicefm
Social Media: www.facebook.com/1035juicefm, twitter.com/1035juicefm
Steve Huber, General Manager, shuber@vistaradio.ca
John Helm, Programming Director, john@thegoatrocks.ca

***Nelson:* CJLY-FM** (Freq: 93.5; 96.5)
308A Hall St., Nelson, BC V1L 1Y8
Tel: 250-352-9600, *Fax:* 250-352-9653
km@kootenaycoopradio.com
www.kootenaycoopradio.com
Social Media: twitter.com/cjly

** For details on this company see listing in Major Broadcasting Companies section; † French language station*

***Nelson:* CKKC-FM (Kootenays EZ Rock)** (Freq: 106.9)
Owned by: Bell Media Inc.*
513C Front St., Nelson, BC V1L 4B4
Tel: 250-368-5510, *Fax:* 250-352-9189
kootenays.myezrock.com
Social Media: www.facebook.com/EZRockKootenayBoundary, twitter.com/ezrockkootenays
Nicole Beetstra, General Manager, 250-368-5510, nicole.beetstra@bellmedia.ca

***New Denver:* CKZX-FM** (Freq: 93.5)
Owned by: CKKC-FM (Kootenays EZ Rock)
New Denver, BC
kootenays.myezrock.com
Lee Sterry, Operations Manager

***Oliver:* CJOR-FM (EZ Rock)** (Freq: 102.9)
Owned by: CJOR-AM (EZ Rock)
Oliver, BC
osoyoos.myezrock.com

***Parksville:* CHPQ-FM (The Lounge 99.9)** (Freq: 99.9)
Owned by: Island Radio Ltd.*
PO Box 1370, 166 East Island Hwy., Parksville, BC V9P 2H3
Tel: 850-248-4211, *Fax:* 250-248-4210
info@thelounge999.com
www.thelounge999.com
Rob Bye, General Manager

***Parksville:* CIBH-FM (88.5 The Beach)** (Freq: 88.5)
Owned by: Island Radio Ltd.*
PO Box 1370, 166 East Island Hwy., Parksville, BC V9P 2H3
Tel: 250-248-4211, *Fax:* 250-248-4210
info@885thebeach.com
885thebeach.com
Other information: News Phone: 250-758-2467
Rob Bye, General Manager, rbye@islandradio.bc.ca
Kent Wilson, Program Director

***Pemberton:* CISP-FM** (Freq: 104.5)
Owned by: CISQ-FM (Mountain FM)
Pemberton, BC
www.mountainfm.com
Gary Miles, President
Joe Polito, Manager

***Pender Harbour:* CIPN-FM** (Freq: 104.7)
Owned by: CISQ-FM (Mountain FM)
Pender Harbour, BC
www.mountainfm.com

***Penticton:* CIGV-FM** (Freq: 100.7)
Owned by: Newcap Radio*
#201, 1301 Main St., Penticton, BC V2A 5E9
Tel: 250-493-6767, *Fax:* 250-493-2851
okanagancountry.com
Social Media: www.youtube.com/channel/UCEPbLLjn9aJVke_tokoFzeQ, www.facebook.com/Country1007, twitter.com/country1007
Peter Angle, General Manager, pangle@newcap.ca
Casey Clarke, Program Director, cclarke@newcap.ca

***Penticton:* CJMG-FM (Sun FM)** (Freq: 97.1)
Owned by: Bell Media Inc.*
33 Carmi Ave., Penticton, BC V2A 3G4
Tel: 250-492-2800, *Fax:* 250-493-0370
www.sunonline.ca
Social Media: www.facebook.com/97.1SUNFM, twitter.com/971sunfm
Mark Burley, Brand Director, mark.burley@bellmedia.ca

***Port Alberni:* CJAV-FM (93.3 The Peak)** (Freq: 93.3)
Owned by: Island Radio Ltd.*
3296 - 3rd Ave., Port Alberni, BC V9Y 4E1
Tel: 250-723-2455, *Fax:* 250-723-0797
info@933thepeak.com
www.933thepeak.com
Social Media: www.facebook.com/933thepeak
David Wiwchar, Operations Manager

***Port Alice:* CFPA-FM (1240 Coast AM)** (Freq: 100.3)
Owned by: CFNI-AM (1240 Coast AM)
Port Alice, BC
www.coastamradio.ca

***Powell River:* CFPW-FM (95.7 Coast FM)** (Freq: 95.7)
Owned by: Vista Broadcast Group*
#103, 7074 Westminster St., Powell River, BC V8A 1C5
Tel: 604-485-4207, *Fax:* 604-485-4210
www.mypowellrivernow.com/coast-fm
Social Media: www.facebook.com/957coastfm, twitter.com/957CoastFM
Allison Mandzuk, General Manager, GSM - The Coast Group, amandzuk@vistaradio.ca
Rob Alexander, Program director, Regional Cluster, ralexander@vistaradio.ca

***Powell River:* CJMP-FM** (Freq: 90.1)
4476 Marine Ave., Powell River, BC V8A 2K2
Tel: 604-483-1712
onair@cjmp.ca
cjmp.ca
Social Media: www.facebook.com/CJMP90.1FM, twitter.com/cjmpfm

***Prince George:* CBYG-FM** (Freq: 91.5)
Owned by: Canadian Broadcasting Corporation*
#1, 890 Victoria St., Prince George, BC V2L 5P1
Tel: 250-562-2888
www.cbc.ca/bc

***Prince George:* CFUR-FM** (Freq: 88.7)
3333 University Way, Prince George, BC V2N 4Z9
Tel: 250-960-7664
www.cfur.ca
Social Media: www.facebook.com/CFURradio
Fraser Hayes, Station Manager, fhayes@cfur.ca

***Prince George:* CIRX-FM (94.3 The Goat)** (Freq: 94.3)
Owned by: Vista Broadcast Group*
#101, 2977 Ferry Ave., Prince George, BC V2N 1L3
Tel: 250-564-2524, *Fax:* 250-562-6611
www.myprincegeorgenow.com
Social Media: twitter.com/943theGOAT

***Prince George:* CJCI-FM (The Wolf)** (Freq: 97.3)
Owned by: Vista Broadcast Group*
1940 - 3rd Ave., Prince George, BC V2M 1G7
Tel: 250-564-2524, *Fax:* 250-562-6611
www.97fm.ca
Social Media: www.facebook.com/10150116163045363, twitter.com/thewolfat97fm

***Prince George:* CKDV-FM (93.3 The Drive)** (Freq: 99.3)
Owned by: The Jim Pattison Broadcast Group*
1810 - 3rd Ave., 2nd Fl., Prince George, BC V2M 1G4
Tel: 250-564-8861, *Fax:* 250-562-8768
www.993thedrive.com
Social Media: www.youtube.com/user/DRIVE993, www.facebook.com/99.3TheDrive, twitter.com/993thedrive
Mike Clotildes, General Manager, mclotildes@ckpg.com
Kelli Moorhead, General Sales Manager, kmoorhead@ckpg.com

***Prince George:* CKKN-FM (The River 101.3)** (Freq: 101.3)
Owned by: The Jim Pattison Broadcast Group*
1810 - 3rd Ave., 2nd Fl., Prince George, BC V2M 1G4
Tel: 250-564-8861, *Fax:* 250-562-8768
1013theriver.com
Social Media: www.youtube.com/user/1013theriver, www.facebook.com/CKKN1013TheRiver, twitter.com/1013theriver
Mike Clotildes, General Manager

***Prince Rupert:* CHTK-FM (EZ Rock)** (Freq: 99.1)
Owned by: Bell Media Inc.*
#230, 215 Cowbay Rd., Prince Rupert, BC V8J 1A8
Tel: 250-624-9111, *Fax:* 250-624-3100
princerupert.myezrock.com
Social Media: www.facebook.com/NorthEZRock, twitter.com/EZRockNorth
Brian Langston, General Manager, brian.langston@bellmedia.ca

***Prince Rupert:* CJFW-FM-2** (Freq: 101.9)
Owned by: CJFW-FM
Prince Rupert, BC

***Princeton:* CIGV-FM-2** (Freq: 98.1)
Owned by: CIGV-FM
Princeton, BC

***Quesnel:* CFFM-FM-2 (The Goat)** (Freq: 94.9)
Owned by: CFFM-FM (The Rush)
#502, 410 Kinchant St., Quesnel, BC V2J 7J5
Tel: 250-992-7046, *Fax:* 250-992-2354
www.mycariboonow.com

***Quesnel:* CKCQ-FM (The Wolf)** (Freq: 100.3)
Owned by: Vista Broadcast Group*
#502, 410 Kinchant St., Quesnel, BC V2J 7J5
Tel: 250-992-7046, *Fax:* 250-992-2354
pete@reachthecariboo.com
www.thewolfonline.ca
Other information: News E-mail: cariboonews@reachthecariboo.com

***Revelstoke:* CKCR-FM (EZ Rock)** (Freq: 106.1)
Owned by: Bell Media Inc.*
PO Box 1420, #207, 555 Victoria Rd., Revelstoke, BC V0E 2F0
Tel: 250-837-2149, *Fax:* 250-837-5577
www.revelstoke.myezrock.com
Social Media: www.facebook.com/myezrock, twitter.com/MyEzRock
Gord Leighton, General Manager, gord.leighton@bellmedia.ca

***Richmond:* CHKG-FM** (Freq: 96.1)
Owned by: Fairchild Radio*
Aberdeen Centre, #2090, 4151 Hazelbridge Way, Richmond, BC V6X 4J7
Tel: 604-295-1234, *Fax:* 604-295-1201
www.fm961.com
Social Media: www.youtube.com/fairchildradiovan, www.facebook.com/am1470fm961, twitter.com/am1470fm961

***Richmond:* CHLG-FM (LG 104.3)** (Freq: 104.3)
Owned by: Newcap Radio*
#20, 11151 Horseshoe Way, Richmond, BC V7A 4S5
Tel: 604-241-2100, *Fax:* 604-272-0917
www.lg1043.com
Social Media: instagram.com/lg1043fm, www.facebook.com/lg1043, twitter.com/lg1043
Sherri Pierce, General Manager, spierce@newcap.ca
Paul Sereda, Program Director, psereda@newcap.ca

***Richmond:* CKZZ-FM (Z95.3)** (Freq: 95.3)
Owned by: Newcap Radio*
#20, 11151 Horseshoe Way, Richmond, BC V7A 4S5
Tel: 604-241-2100, *Fax:* 604-272-0917
www.z953.ca
Social Media: instagram.com/z953fm, www.facebook.com/z953vancouver, twitter.com/Z953VAN
Sherri Pierce, General Manager, spierce@newcap.ca
Jason Manning, Program Director, jmanning@newcap.ca

***Rock Creek:* CKGF-3-FM (103.7 Juice FM)** (Freq: 103.7)
Owned by: CJUI-FM (103.9 Juice FM)
Rock Creek, BC

***Salmon Arm:* CKXR-FM (EZ Rock 91.5)** (Freq: 91.5)
Owned by: Bell Media Inc.*
PO Box 69, 360 Ross St., Salmon Arm, BC V1E 4N2
Tel: 250-832-2161, *Fax:* 250-832-2240
salmonarm.myezrock.com
Social Media: www.facebook.com/myezrock, twitter.com/MyEzRock

***Sandspit:* CJFW-FM-3** (Freq: 92.9)
Owned by: CJFW-FM
Sandspit, BC

***Sechelt:* CKAY-FM (The Coast)** (Freq: 91.7)
Owned by: Vista Broadcast Group*
#1, 1877 Field Rd., Sechelt, BC V0N 3A1
Tel: 604-741-9170, *Toll-Free:* 855-451-9170
917coastfm.com
Social Media: www.facebook.com/917Coastfm, twitter.com/917coastfm
Gord Gauvin, General Manager, Sales, gord@917coastfm.com

***Sechelt:* CKKS-FM** (Freq: 104.7)
Owned by: CISQ-FM (Mountain FM)
Sechelt, BC
www.mountainfm.com

***Smithers:* CJFW-FM-6** (Freq: 92.9)
Owned by: CJFW-FM
Smithers, BC

***Sorrento:* CKXR-FM-1** (Freq: 102.1)
Owned by: CKXR-FM (EZ Rock)
Sorrento, BC
salmonarm.myezrock.com

** For details on this company see listing in Major Broadcasting Companies section; † French language station*

***Squamish:* CISQ-FM (Mountain FM)** (Freq: 107.1)
Owned by: Rogers Broadcasting Ltd.*
#202, 40147 Glenalder Place, Squamish, BC V8B 0G2
Tel: 604-892-1021, *Fax:* 604-892-6383
Toll-Free: 888-429-2724
www.mountainfm.com
Social Media: www.facebook.com/adventurestation, twitter.com/MountainFM

***Summerland:* CHOR-FM (EZ Rock)** (Freq: 98.5)
Owned by: Bell Media Inc.*
#200, 9901 Main St., Summerland, BC V0H 1Z0
Tel: 250-494-0333, *Fax:* 250-404-0263
summerland.myezrock.com
Social Media: www.facebook.com/EZRock98.5
Mark Burley, Brand Director, mark.burley@bellmedia.ca
Janet Burley, General Manager/Sales Manager, janet.burley@bellmedia.ca

***Terrace:* CJFW-FM** (Freq: 103.1)
Owned by: Bell Media Inc.*
4625 Lazelle Ave., Terrace, BC V8G 1S4
Tel: 250-635-6316, *Fax:* 250-638-6320
www.cjfw.ca
Social Media: www.facebook.com/129368130435057, twitter.com/CJFWAstral
Brian Langston, General Manager, brian.langston@bellmedia.ca

***Terrace:* CKTK-FM (EZ Rock)** (Freq: 97.7)
Owned by: Bell Media Inc.*
4625 Lazelle Ave., Terrace, BC V8G 1S4
Tel: 250-635-6316, *Fax:* 250-638-6320
kitimat.myezrock.com
Social Media: www.facebook.com/NorthEZRock, twitter.com/EZRockNorth
Brian Langston, General Manager, blangston@astral.com

***Trail:* CHRT-FM (The Goat)** (Freq: 104.1)
Owned by: CKQR-FM (99.3 The Goat)*
Trail, BC

***Trail:* CJAT-FM (Kootenays EZ Rock)** (Freq: 95.7)
Owned by: Bell Media Inc.*
1560 - 2nd Ave., Trail, BC V1R 1M4
Tel: 250-368-5510, *Fax:* 250-368-8471
kootenays.myezrock.com
Social Media: www.facebook.com/EZRockKootenayBoundary, twitter.com/ezrockkootenays
Nicole Beetstra, General Manager, 250-368-5510, nicole.beetstra@bellmedia.ca

†*Vancouver:* CBUF-FM (Freq: 97.7)
Détenteur: Canadian Broadcasting Corporation*
700, rue Hamilton, Vancouver, BC V6B 4A2
Tél: 604-662-6135
www.radio-canada.ca
Pierre Guerin, Directeur des services francais dans l'ouest, 204-788-3237, pierre.guerin@radio-canada.ca

***Vancouver:* CBU-FM** (Freq: 105.7)
Owned by: Canadian Broadcasting Corporation*
700 Hamilton St., Vancouver, BC V6B 4A2
Tel: 604-662-6000
cbc.ca/bc

***Vancouver:* CBUX-FM** (Freq: 90.9)
Owned by: Canadian Broadcasting Corporation*
700, rue Hamilton, Vancouver, BC V6B 4A2
Tel: 604-662-6135
www.radio-canada.ca/regions/colombie-britannique
Pierre Guérin, Directeur des services français, Régions de l'Ouest, pierre.guerin@radio-canada.ca

***Vancouver:* CFBT-FM** (Freq: 94.5)
Owned by: Bell Media Radio*
#500, 969 Robson St., Vancouver, BC V6Z 1X5
Tel: 604-871-9000, *Fax:* 604-871-2901
feedback@thebeat.com
www.thebeat.com
Social Media: www.facebook.com/BeatVIP, twitter.com/TheBeat945

***Vancouver:* CFMI-FM (Classic Rock 101)** (Freq: 101.1)
Owned by: Corus Premium Television Ltd.*
#2000, 700 West Georgia St., Vancouver, BC V7Y 1K9
Tel: 604-331-2808, *Fax:* 604-331-2722
www.rock101.com
Social Media: www.youtube.com/user/ROCK101Videos, www.facebook.com/ClassicRock101, twitter.com/ClassicRock101
Ronnie Stanton, Program Director

***Vancouver:* CFOX-FM (99.3 The Fox)** (Freq: 99.3)
Owned by: Corus Radio Company*
#2000, 700 West Georgia St., Vancouver, BC V7Y 1K9
Tel: 604-684-7221, *Fax:* 604-331-2722
www.cfox.com
Social Media: www.youtube.com/user/CFOXVideos, www.facebook.com/993thefox, twitter.com/993thefox
Ronnie Stanton, Program Director

***Vancouver:* CFRO-FM** (Freq: 102.7)
#110, 360 Columbia St., Vancouver, BC V6A 4J1
Tel: 604-684-8494
www.coopradio.org

***Vancouver:* CHQM-FM** (Freq: 103.5)
Owned by: Bell Media Radio*
#500, 969 Robson St., Vancouver, BC V6Z 1X5
Tel: 604-871-9000, *Fax:* 604-871-2901
feedback@qmfm.com
www.qmfm.com
Social Media: www.facebook.com/1035qmfm, twitter.com/QMFM

***Vancouver:* CITR-FM** (Freq: 101.9)
#233, 6138 Sub Blvd., Vancouver, BC V6T 1Z1
Tel: 604-822-8648, *Fax:* 604-882-9364
stationmanager@citr.ca
www.citr.ca
Social Media: www.youtube.com/user/CiTR1019fm, www.facebook.com/CiTR101.9, twitter.com/CiTRradio
Brenda Grunau, Station Manager

***Vancouver:* CJJR-FM (JRfm 93.7)** (Freq: 93.7)
Owned by: The Jim Pattison Broadcast Group*
#300, 1401 West 8th Ave., Vancouver, BC V6H 1C9
Tel: 604-731-7772
www.jrfm.com
Social Media: instagram.com/jrfm, www.facebook.com/937jrfm, twitter.com/jrfm

***Vancouver:* CKLG-FM** (Freq: 96.9)
Owned by: Rogers Broadcasting Ltd.*
2440 Ash St., Vancouver, BC V5Z 4J6
Tel: 604-872-2557
www.jackfm.com
Social Media: www.facebook.com/JACKvancouver, twitter.com/969JACK

***Vancouver:* CKPK-FM (102.7 The Peak)** (Freq: 102.7)
#300, 1401 West 8th Ave., Vancouver, BC V6H 1C9
Tel: 604-731-6111
www.thepeak.fm
Social Media: soundcloud.com/thepeak, www.facebook.com/thepeak, twitter.com/thepeak
Other information: Advertising Phone: 604-730-6553

***Vanderhoof:* CIRX-FM-2 (94.7 The Goat)** (Freq: 95.9)
Owned by: CIRX-FM (94X)
Vanderhoof, BC

***Vernon:* CICF-FM (105.7 Sun FM)** (Freq: 105.7)
Owned by: Bell Media Inc.*
2800 - 31 St., Vernon, BC V1T 5H4
Tel: 250-545-9222, *Fax:* 250-542-2083
reception@thesunonline.ca
www.thesunonline.ca
Social Media: www.facebook.com/105.7SUNFM, twitter.com/SunFMVernon
Gord Leighton, General Manager, gord.leighton@bellmedia.ca

***Vernon:* CKIZ-FM (107.5 Kiss FM)** (Freq: 107.5)
Owned by: The Jim Pattison Broadcast Group*
3313 - 32 Ave., Vernon, BC V1T 2E1
Tel: 250-545-2141
1075kiss@1075kiss.com
www.1075kiss.com
Social Media: www.linkedin.com/pub/107-5-kiss-fm/28/916/409, www.facebook.com/1075.KISS, twitter.com/1075KISSFM

***Victoria:* CFUV-FM** (Freq: 101.9)
University of Victoria, PO Box 3035, Victoria, BC V8W 3P3
Tel: 250-721-8607
director@uvic.ca
cfuv.uvic.ca
Social Media: vimeo.com/user7758198, www.facebook.com/CFUV101.9, twitter.com/CFUV
Randy Gelling, Station Manager, 250-721-8607, cfuvman@uvic.ca

***Victoria:* CHBE-FM (107.3 Kool FM)** (Freq: 107.3)
Owned by: Bell Media Radio*
1420 Broad St., Victoria, BC V8W 2B1
Tel: 250-382-1073
www.1073kool.fm
Social Media: www.facebook.com/1073KOOLFM, twitter.com/1073Koolfm
Robin Haggar, Program Director

***Victoria:* CHTT-FM** (Freq: 103.1)
Owned by: Rogers Broadcasting Ltd.*
817 Fort St., Victoria, BC V8W 1H6
Tel: 250-382-0900, *Fax:* 250-382-4358
www.1031jackfm.com
Social Media: www.facebook.com/1031jackfm, twitter.com/jackvictoria

***Victoria:* CIOC-FM** (Freq: 98.5)
Owned by: Rogers Broadcasting Ltd.*
817 Fort St., Victoria, BC V8W 1H6
Tel: 250-382-0900, *Fax:* 250-382-4358
www.ocean985.com
Social Media: www.facebook.com/Ocean985, twitter.com/ocean985

***Victoria:* CJZN-FM (The Zone)** (Freq: 91.3)
Owned by: The Jim Pattison Broadcast Group*
2750 Quadra St., Victoria, BC V8T 4E8
Tel: 250-475-6611, *Fax:* 250-475-6626
www.thezone.fm
Social Media: www.youtube.com/TheZoneDotFM, www.facebook.com/thezone.fm, twitter.com/TheZonedotFM
Rob Bye, General Manager

***Victoria:* CKKQ-FM (The Q!)** (Freq: 100.3)
Owned by: The Jim Pattison Broadcast Group*
2750 Quadra St., Victoria, BC V8T 4E8
Tel: 250-475-0100, *Fax:* 250-475-3299
Toll-Free: 800-717-1003
www.theq.fm
Social Media: www.youtube.com/TheQDotFM, www.facebook.com/theq.fm, twitter.com/TheQdotFM
Rob Bye, General Manager, rbye@TheQ.fm

***Whistler:* CISW-FM** (Freq: 102.1)
Owned by: CISQ-FM (Mountain FM)
#126, 4295 Blackcomb Way, Whistler, BC V0N 1B4
Tel: 604-905-1691, *Fax:* 604-892-6383
www.mountainfm.com
Social Media: instagram.com/mountainfmradio, www.facebook.com/adventurestation, twitter.com/MountainFM

***Williams Lake:* CFFM-FM (The Goat)** (Freq: 97.5)
Owned by: Vista Broadcast Group*
83 South First Ave., Williams Lake, BC V2G 1H4
Tel: 250-392-6551, *Fax:* 250-392-4142
www.mycariboonow.com
Social Media: www.facebook.com/RushFM

Manitoba

***Brandon:* CIWM-FM** (Freq: 91.5)
Owned by: CICY-FM
Brandon, MB

***Brandon:* CJJJ-FM** (Freq: 106.5)
1430 Victoria Ave. East, Brandon, MB R7A 2A9
Tel: 204-725-8700
cj-106.assiniboine.net
Social Media: www.twitter.com/cj106fm
Jill Ferguson, Contact, 204-725-8700

***Brandon:* CKLF-FM (Star 94.7)** (Freq: 94.7)
Owned by: Riding Mountain Broadcasting Ltd.*
624 - 14 St. East, Brandon, MB R7A 7E1
Tel: 204-726-8888, *Toll-Free:* 866-727-7827
starfm@starfmradio.com
www.starfmradio.com
Social Media: www.youtube.com/user/StarFMBrandon, www.facebook.com/starfmbrandonfan, twitter.com/StarfmBrandon
Cam Clark, General Manager, clarkc@westmancom.com

***Brandon:* CKXA-FM (101.1 The Farm)** (Freq: 101.1)
Owned by: Bell Media Inc.*
2940 Victoria Ave., Brandon, MB R7B 3Y3
Tel: 204-728-1150, *Fax:* 204-725-3794
brandonnews@bellmedia.ca
www.1011thefarm.com
Social Media: www.facebook.com/1011thefarm, twitter.com/1011TheFarm

** For details on this company see listing in Major Broadcasting Companies section; † French language station*

Mark Maheu, General Manager, mark.maheu@bellmedia.ca

***Brandon:* CKX-FM (96.1 BOB FM)** (Freq: 96.1)
Owned by: Bell Media Inc.*
2940 Victoria Ave., Brandon, MB R7B 3Y3
Tel: 204-728-1150, *Fax:* 204-725-3794
brandonnews@bellmedia.ca
www.961bobfm.ca
Social Media: www.facebook.com/KX96FM, twitter.com/KX96Westman
Mark Maheu, General Manager, mark.maheu@bellmedia.ca

***Portage La Prairie:* CJPG-FM (Mix 96.5)** (Freq: 96.5)
Owned by: Golden West Broadcasting Ltd.*
PO Box 130, 2390 Sissons Dr., Portage La Prairie, MB R1N 3B2
Tel: 204-239-5111, *Toll-Free:* 866-239-5111
www.portageonline.com
Social Media: www.facebook.com/Mix96.5FM, twitter.com/Mix_96

***Portage la Prairie:* CFRY-FM** (Freq: 93.1)
Owned by: CFRY
Portage la Prairie, MB

***Pukatawagan:* CFPX-FM** (Freq: 98.3)
PO Box 321, Pukatawagan, MB R0B 1G0
Tel: 204-553-2155, *Fax:* 204-553-2158

†*Saint-Boniface:* CKXL-FM (Freq: 91.1)
340, boul Provencher, Saint-Boniface, MB R2H 0G7
Tél: 204-233-4243, *Téléc:* 204-233-3646
Ligne sans frais: 866-894-3691
info@envol91.mb.ca
www.envol91.mb.ca
Médias sociaux: www.youtube.com/user/Envol91FM, www.facebook.com/envol91, twitter.com/Envol91
Annick Boulet, Directrice générale, direction@envol91.mb.ca

***Steinbach:* CILT-FM (Mix 96)** (Freq: 96.7)
Owned by: Golden West Broadcasting Ltd.*
#105, 32 Brandt St., Steinbach, MB R5G 2J7
Tel: 204-326-3737
mix@steinbachonline.com
www.steinbachonline.com
Social Media: www.facebook.com/MIX96.7FM, twitter.com/mix967fm

***The Pas:* CITP-FM** (Freq: 92.7)
Owned by: CICY-FM
The Pas, MB

***Thompson:* CBWK-FM** (Freq: 100.9)
Owned by: Canadian Broadcasting Corporation*
7 Selkirk Ave., Thompson, MB R8N 0M4
www.cbc.ca/manitoba
Social Media: www.facebook.com/cbcmanitoba, twitter.com/CBCManitoba

***Winkler:* CJEL-FM (The Eagle 93.5)** (Freq: 93.5)
Owned by: Golden West Broadcasting Ltd.*
PO Box 399, 277 - 1st, Winkler, MB R6W 4A6
Tel: 204-331-9300, *Fax:* 888-765-7039
Toll-Free: 800-355-7065
www.pembinavalleyonline.com
Social Media: www.facebook.com/Eagle935FM, twitter.com/Eagle935FM

***Winkler:* CKMW-FM** (Freq: 88.9)
Owned by: Golden West Broadcasting Ltd.*
PO Box 339, 277 - 1st, Winkler, MB R6W 4A6
Tel: 204-325-9506, *Fax:* 888-765-7039
Toll-Free: 800-355-7065
www.pembinavalleyonline.com
Social Media: www.facebook.com/country889fm, twitter.com/Country889FM

†*Winnipeg:* CBW-FM (Freq: 98.3)
Détenteur: Canadian Broadcasting Corporation*
607, rue Langevin, Winnipeg, MB R2H 2W2
Tél: 204-788-3235, *Téléc:* 204-788-3245
www.cbc.ca/manitoba
Sylvie Laurencelle-Vermette, Chef des communications

***Winnipeg:* CFEQ-FM (Classical 107 FM)** (Freq: 107.1)
Owned by: Golden West Broadcasting Ltd.*
#2, 20 St. Mary's Rd., Winnipeg, MB R2H 1H1
Tel: 204-256-2525, *Toll-Free:* 855-346-1071
info@classic107.com
classic107.com
Social Media: www.youtube.com/channel/UCqsKhZ6bKTKaQ2J7Q05yX6Q, www.facebook.com/classic107, twitter.com/Classic107FM

Fin Paterson, Station Manager

***Winnipeg:* CFQX-FM (QX104)** (Freq: 104.4)
Owned by: Jim Pattison Broadcast Group*
177 Lombard Ave., 3rd Fl., Winnipeg, MB R3B 0W5
Tel: 204-944-1031, *Fax:* 204-989-5291
www.qx104fm.com
Social Media: www.facebook.com/qx104, twitter.com/QX104winnipeg
Don Shafer, General Manager, dshafer@jpbg.ca

***Winnipeg:* CFWM-FM** (Freq: 99.9)
Owned by: Bell Media Radio
1445 Pembina Hwy., Winnipeg, MB R3T 5C2
Tel: 204-477-5120, *Fax:* 204-453-0815
www.999bobfm.com
Social Media: www.facebook.com/999BOBFM
Mark Maheu, General Manager, mark.maheu@bellmedia.ca
David Drake, Program Director, david.drake@bellmedia.ca

***Winnipeg:* CHIQ-FM** (Freq: 94.3)
Owned by: The Jim Pattison Broadcast Group*
177 Lombard Ave., 3rd Fl., Winnipeg, MB R3B 0W5
Tel: 204-944-1031, *Fax:* 204-989-5291
www.curve943.com
Social Media: www.facebook.com/FAB943FM, twitter.com/FAB943FM
Don Shafer, General Manager, dshafer@jpbg.ca

***Winnipeg:* CHVN-FM** (Freq: 95.1)
Owned by: Golden West Broadcasting Ltd.*
#1, 741 St. Mary's Rd., Winnipeg, MB R2M 3N5
Tel: 204-452-9602, *Toll-Free:* 866-951-2486
info@chvnradio.com
www.chvnradio.com
Social Media: www.facebook.com/chvn951, twitter.com/chvn951

***Winnipeg:* CHWE-FM** (Freq: 106.1)
Owned by: Evanov Radio Group*
520 Corydon Ave., Winnipeg, MB R3L 0P1
Tel: 204-477-1221, *Fax:* 204-453-8244
www.energy106.ca
Social Media: www.youtube.com/user/Energy1061FM, www.facebook.com/energy106fm, twitter.com/energy106fm
Mike Fabian, General Manager, mike@evanovwpg.com

***Winnipeg:* CICY-FM** (Freq: 105.5)
1507 Inkster Blvd., Winnipeg, MB R2X 1R2
Tel: 204-772-8255
www.ncifm.com
Social Media: www.facebook.com/ncifm, twitter.com/NCIWakeUpCrew

***Winnipeg:* CJGV-FM (99.1 Fresh FM)** (Freq: 99.1)
Owned by: Corus Premium Television Ltd.*
#200, 1440 Jack Blick Ave., Winnipeg, MB R3G 0L4
Tel: 204-786-2471, *Fax:* 204-783-4512
www.991freshfm.com
Social Media: www.youtube.com/user/991FreshFM, www.facebook.com/991FreshFM, twitter.com/991FreshFM
Jason Manning, Brand Manager

***Winnipeg:* CJKR-FM (Power 97)** (Freq: 97.5)
Owned by: Corus Premium Television Ltd.*
#200, 1440 Jack Blick Ave., Winnipeg, MB R3G 0L4
Tel: 204-786-2471, *Fax:* 204-783-4512
www.power97.com
Social Media: www.youtube.com/user/power97rocks, www.facebook.com/Power97Rocks, twitter.com/power97
Jason Manning, Brand Manager

***Winnipeg:* CJUM-FM** (Freq: 101.5)
University of Manitoba, #308, University Centre, Winnipeg, MB R3T 2N2
Tel: 204-474-7027, *Fax:* 204-269-1299
cjum@cjum.com
www.umfm.com
Social Media: www.youtube.com/user/CJUMVids, www.facebook.com/umfm1015, twitter.com/UMFM
Jared McKetiak, Station Manager, jared@umfm.com
Michael Elves, Program Director, michael@umfm.com

***Winnipeg:* CKMM-FM (103.1 Virgin Radio)** (Freq: 103.1)
Owned by: Bell Media Inc.*
1445 Pembina Hwy., Winnipeg, MB R3T 5C2
Tel: 204-477-5120, *Fax:* 204-453-0815
winnipeg.virginradio.ca
Social Media: www.facebook.com/1031VirginRadio, twitter.com/1031Virgin
Mark Maheu, General Manager, mark.maheu@bellmedia.ca

***Winnipeg:* CKUW-FM** (Freq: 95.9)
University of Winnipeg, #4CM11, 515 Portage Ave., Winnipeg, MB R3B 2E9
Tel: 204-786-9782, *Fax:* 204-783-7080
ckuw@uwinnipeg.ca
www.ckuw.ca
Social Media: www.facebook.com/pages/CKUW-Radio-959fm/119731854749489, twitter.com/ckuw
Rob Schmidt, Station Manager, manager@ckuw.ca

***Winnipeg:* CKY-FM** (Freq: 102.3)
Owned by: Rogers Broadcasting Ltd.*
#4, 166 Osborne St., Winnipeg, MB R3L 1Y8
Tel: 204-780-3400
www.102clearfm.com
Social Media: instagram.com/1023clearfm, www.facebook.com/1023clearfm, twitter.com/1023clearfm

New Brunswick

†*Balmoral:* CIMS-FM (Freq: 103.9)
CP 2561, Balmoral, NB E8E 2W7
Tél: 506-826-1040, *Téléc:* 506-826-2400
info@cimsfm.ca
cimsfm.ca
Médias sociaux: www.facebook.com/RadioRestigouche
Pierre Bourque, Directeur général

***Bathurst:* CKBC-FM (Max 104.9)** (Freq: 104.9)
Owned by: Bell Media Inc.*
#1, 640 St. Peter Ave., Bathurst, NB E2A 2Y7
Tel: 506-547-1360, *Fax:* 506-547-1367
www.max1049.ca
Social Media: www.facebook.com/MAX104.9, twitter.com/Max1049bathurst
Jamie Robichaud, General Manager, jamie.robichaud@bellmedia.ca

†*Bathurst:* CKLE-FM (Freq: 92.9)
#301, 270, av Douglas, Bathurst, NB E2A 1M9
Tél: 506-546-4600, *Téléc:* 506-546-6611
superstation@ckle.fm
www.ckle.fm
Médias sociaux: www.facebook.com/CKLEFM

†*Edmundston:* CFAI-FM (Freq: 101.1; 105.1)
17, rue Costigan, Edmundston, NB E3V 1W7
Tél: 506-737-5060, *Téléc:* 506-737-5084
radio@cfai.fm
www.cfai.fm
Médias sociaux: www.facebook.com/cfaifm, twitter.com/cfaifm
Michelle Daigle, Directrice, direction@cfai.fm

†*Edmundston:* CJEM-FM (Freq: 92.7)
64, rue Rice, Edmundston, NB E3V 1T2
Tél: 506-735-3351, *Téléc:* 506-739-5803
cjem@cjemfm.com
cjemfm.com
Murillo Soucy, Directeur général, 506-735-3351, direction@cjemfm.com

†*Edmundston:* CKMV-FM (Freq: 92.7)
64, rue Rice, Edmundston, NB E3V 1T2
Tél: 506-735-3351, *Téléc:* 506-739-5803
cjem@cjemfm.com
cjemfm.com
Murillo Soucy, Directeur général, direction@cjemfm.com

***Fredericton:* CBZF-FM** (Freq: 99.5)
Owned by: Canadian Broadcasting Corporation*
1160 Regent St., Fredericton, NB E3B 5G4
Tel: 506-451-4000
www.cbc.ca/nb

***Fredericton:* CFRK-FM (New Country 92.3)** (Freq: 92.3)
Owned by: Newcap Radio*
495-A Prospect St, Fredericton, NB E3B 9M4
Tel: 506-455-3602, *Fax:* 506-455-3602
www.newcountry923.com
Social Media: www.facebook.com/newcountry923, twitter.com/NewCountry923
Kenton Dunphy, Station Manager, kdunphy@newcap.ca
Rod Martens, Program Director, rmartens@newcap.ca

** For details on this company see listing in Major Broadcasting Companies section; † French language station*

***Fredericton:* CFXY-FM (105.3 The Fox)** (Freq: 105.3)
Owned by: Bell Media Inc.*
206 Rookwood Ave., Fredericton, NB E3B 2M2
Tel: 506-454-2444, *Fax:* 506-452-2345
feedback@foxrocks.ca
www.foxrocks.ca
Social Media: www.intagme.com/105thefox, www.facebook.com/105TheFox, twitter.com/105TheFox
Pat Brennan, General Manager, pat.brennan@bellmedia.ca

***Fredericton:* CHSR-FM** (Freq: 97.9)
PO Box 4400, #223, 21 Pacey Dr., Fredericton, NB E3B 5A3
Tel: 506-453-4985
stationmanager@chsrfm.ca
chsrfm.ca
Social Media: www.facebook.com/pages/CHSR-FM-Official/238304316821, twitter.com/CHSR979
Tim Rayne, Station Manager

***Fredericton:* CIBX-FM (106.9 Capital FM)** (Freq: 106.9)
Owned by: Bell Media Inc.*
206 Rookwood Ave., Fredericton, NB E3B 2M2
Tel: 506-451-9111, *Fax:* 506-452-2345
feedback@capitalfm.ca
www.capitalfm.ca
Social Media: www.facebook.com/171723956676, twitter.com/1069Capital
Pat Brennan, General Manager, pat.brennan@bellmedia.ca

***Fredericton:* CIHI-FM (Up! 93.1)** (Freq: 93.1)
Owned by: Newcap Radio*
495-A Prospect St, Fredericton, NB E3B 9M4
Tel: 506-455-0923, *Fax:* 506-455-3602
www.up931.com/
Social Media: www.facebook.com/Up931/, twitter.com/up931
Kenton Dunphy, Station Manager, kdunphy@newcap.ca
Rod Martens, Program Director, rmartens@newcap.ca

***Fredericton:* CIXN-FM** (Freq: 96.5)
#10, 1010 Hanwell Rd., Fredericton, NB E3B 6A4
Tel: 506-454-9600, *Fax:* 506-454-0991
welcome@joyfm.ca
www.joyfm.ca
Social Media: www.facebook.com/JoyFm965

***Fredericton:* CJPN-FM** (Freq: 90.5)
715, rue Priestman, Fredericton, NB E3B 5W7
Tel: 506-454-2576, *Fax:* 506-453-3958
direction@cjpn.ca
www.cjpn.ca
Social Media: www.facebook.com/Cjpn905Fm, twitter.com/cjpnfm

***Grand Falls:* CIKX-FM (K93)** (Freq: 93.5)
Owned by: Bell Media Inc.*
399 Broadway Blvd., Grand Falls, NB E3Z 2K5
Tel: 506-473-9393, *Fax:* 506-473-3893
k93@bellmedia.ca
www.k93.ca
Social Media: www.facebook.com/k93fans, twitter.com/K935
Kirk Davidson, Program Supervisor, 506-473-3124, kirk@k93.ca

***Kedgwick:* CFJU-FM** (Freq: 90.1)
PO Box 1043, Kedgwick, NB E8B 1Z9
Tel: 506-235-9000, *Fax:* 506-235-9001
cfjufm@rogers.com
www.cfjufm.com
Social Media: twitter.com/CFJU_FM
Lucille Thériault, Directrice-Animatrice

***McLeod Hill:* CKTP-FM** (Freq: 95.7)
1036 McLeod Hill Rd., McLeod Hill, NB E3G 6J7
Tel: 506-474-2795, *Fax:* 506-206-3301
info@957thewolf.ca
www.cktpradio.com
Social Media: www.facebook.com/957WOLF, twitter.com/957wolf

***Miramichi:* CFAN-FM (99.3 The River)** (Freq: 99.3)
Owned by: Maritime Broadcasting System*
396 Pleasant St., Miramichi, NB E1V 1X3
Tel: 506-622-3311, *Fax:* 506-627-0335
www.993theriver.com
Social Media: www.facebook.com/187522916587

***Miramichi:* CHHI-FM (95.9 Sun FM)** (Freq: 95.9)
Owned by: Newcap Radio*
202 Pleasant St, Miramichi, NB E1V 1Y5
Tel: 506-622-3969, *Fax:* 506-622-3970
info@959sunfm.com
959sunfm.com
Social Media: www.instagram.com/959sunfm, www.facebook.com/959sunfm, twitter.com/959sunfm
Dan Fagan, Station Manager/Sales Manager, dfagan@newcap.ca
Steve Power, Program Director, steve.power@newcap.ca

***†Moncton:* CBAF-FM** (Freq: Radio-Canada Première Chaîne 88.5 MHz (FM) à Moncton; 102.3 FM à Fredericton/Saint-Jean; 105.7 FM à Allardville; 91.5 FM à Campbellton; 100.3 FM à Edmunston; 90.3 FM à Lamèque/Caraquet; et 91.7 FM à Bon Accord.)
Détenteur: Canadian Broadcasting Corporation*
#15, 165, rue Main, Moncton, NB E1C 1B8
Tél: 506-853-6666, *Ligne sans frais:* 800-561-7010
infoacadie@radio-canada.ca
ici.radio-canada.ca/acadie
Richard Simoens, Directeur, Radio-Canada Acadie

***†Moncton:* CBAL-FM** (Freq: 98.3; 95.3; 101.9; 88.1)
Détenteur: Canadian Broadcasting Corporation*
#15, 165, rue Main, Moncton, NB E1C 1B8
Tél: 506-853-6666, *Ligne sans frais:* 800-561-7010
www.icimusique.ca
Richard Simoens, Directeur

***Moncton:* CBAM** (Freq: 106.1)
Owned by: Canadian Broadcasting Corporation*
#15, 165 Main St., Moncton, NB E1C 1B8
Tel: 506-853-6666
www.cbc.ca/nb
Social Media: twitter.com/cbcnb
Darrow MacIntyre, Executive Producer, News, New Brunswick
Denise Wilson, Senior Managing Director, Atlantic Canada

***Moncton:* CFQM-FM (MAX FM)** (Freq: 103.9)
Owned by: Maritime Broadcasting System*
1000 St. George Blvd., Moncton, NB E1E 4M7
Tel: 506-858-1220
1039maxfm.com
Social Media: www.facebook.com/monctonsgreatesthits

***†Moncton:* CHOY-FM (Choix 99)** (Freq: 99.9)
Détenteur: Maritime Broadcasting System*
Moncton, NB E1E 4M7
Tél: 506-384-2469
choix999.com
Médias sociaux: www.facebook.com/Choix99

***Moncton:* CJMO-FM (C103)** (Freq: 103.1)
Owned by: Newcap Radio*
Moncton Industrial Park, 27 Arsenault Ct., Moncton, NB E1E 4J8
Tel: 506-858-5525, *Fax:* 506-858-5539
c103@c103.com
www.c103.com
Social Media: www.youtube.com/user/C103Moncton, www.facebook.com/c103moncton, twitter.com/c103
Dan Fagan, General Manager, dfagan@newcap.ca
Adam McLaren, Program Director, amclaren@newcap.ca

***Moncton:* CJXL-FM (XL Country)** (Freq: 96.9)
Owned by: Newcap Radio*
Moncton Industrial Park, 27 Arsenault Court, Moncton, NB E1E 4J8
Tel: 506-858-5525, *Fax:* 506-858-5539
reception@xl96.com
www.xl96.com
Social Media: instagram.com/xlcountry969, www.facebook.com/xl969, twitter.com/xlcountry969
Dan Fagan, General Manager, dfagan@newcap.ca
Adam McLaren, Program Director, amclaren@newcap.ca

***Moncton:* CKCW-FM (K94.5)** (Freq: 94.5)
Owned by: Maritime Broadcasting System*
1000 St. George Blvd., Moncton, NB E1E 4M7
Tel: 506-858-1220
k945.ca
Social Media: www.facebook.com/k945moncton, twitter.com/K945Moncton
Krysta Janssen, Manager, Operations

***Moncton:* CKOE-FM** (Freq: 107.3)
3030 Mountain Rd., Moncton, NB E1G 2W8
Tel: 506-384-1009, *Fax:* 506-383-9699
info@ckoefm.com
www.ckoefm.com
Social Media: twitter.com/ckoefm
Jim Houssen, Station Manager

***Pokemouche:* CKRO-FM** (Freq: 97.1)
142 Rte 113, Pokemouche, NB E8P 1K7
Tel: 506-336-9706, *Fax:* 506-336-9058
info@ckro.ca
www.ckro.ca
Social Media: www.facebook.com/radiockro
Donald Noël, Directeur

***Riverview:* CITA-FM** (Freq: 105.9)
#4, 645 Pinewood Rd., Riverview, NB E1B 5J9
Tel: 506-872-2901, *Fax:* 506-872-2234
Toll-Free: 855-330-0335
harvestersoffice@gmail.com
www.citafm.com
Social Media: www.facebook.com/318492205878
Jeff Lutes, Contact, jeff@jefflutes.com

***Sackville:* CHMA-FM** (Freq: 106.9)
62 York St., Sackville, NB E4L 1E2
Tel: 506-364-2221
chma@mta.ca
chmafm.wordpress.com
Social Media: www.facebook.com/pages/CHMA-FM/8928370874, twitter.com/chmaFM
Pierre Malloy, Station Manager

***Saint John:* CBD-FM** (Freq: 91.3)
Owned by: Canadian Broadcasting Corporation*
PO Box 2358, Saint John, NB E2L 3V6
Tel: 506-632-7710
www.cbc.ca/nb
Denise Wilson, Senior Managing Director, Atlantic Canada, denise.wilson@cbc.ca
Darrow MacIntyre, Executive Producer, News, New Brunswick
Steven Webb, Executive Producer, Saint John
Nadine Antle, Regional Manager, Manager, Communications, Marketing & Brand, 902-420-4223
Mary-Pat Schutta, Senior Manager, New Brunswick

***Saint John:* CFMH-FM** (Freq: 107.3)
Thomas J Condon Student Centre, University of New Brunswick Saint John, #235, 100 Tucker Park Rd., Saint John, NB E2L 4L5
Tel: 506-648-5667, *Fax:* 506-648-5541
cfmh@unbsj.ca
localfm.ca
Social Media: www.facebook.com/localfm, twitter.com/local1073fm
Brian Cleveland, Station Manager, brian@cfmh.ca

***Saint John:* CHNI-FM (Rock 88.9)** (Freq: 88.9)
Owned by: Newcap Radio*
#137, 1 Market Square, Saint John, NB E2L 4Z6
Tel: 506-635-6500, *Fax:* 506-635-6505
www.rock889.ca
Social Media: www.facebook.com/rock889, twitter.com/Rock889FM
Jay McNeil, Station Manager, jay.mcneil@newcap.ca
Rod Martens, Program Director, rmartens@newcap.ca

***Saint John:* CHSJ-FM** (Freq: 94.1)
58 King St., Saint John, NB E2L 3T4
Tel: 506-633-3323, *Fax:* 506-644-3485
www.country94.ca
Social Media: www.facebook.com/country94, twitter.com/country94chsj

***Saint John:* CHWV-FM** (Freq: 97.3)
58 King St., Saint John, NB E2L 1G4
Tel: 506-633-3323, *Fax:* 506-644-3485
mail@thewave.ca
www.thewave.ca
Social Media: www.facebook.com/973thewave, twitter.com/973thewave

***Saint John:* CINB-FM** (Freq: 96.1)
PO Box 96, Saint John, NB E2L 3X1
Tel: 506-657-9600
staff@newsongfm.com
newsongfm.com
Social Media: www.facebook.com/NewSongFM, twitter.com/NewSongfm
Don Mabee, Station Manager

** For details on this company see listing in Major Broadcasting Companies section; † French language station*

***Saint John:* CIOK-FM (K-100)** (Freq: 100.5)
Owned by: Maritime Broadcasting System*
226 Union St., Saint John, NB E2L 1B1
Tel: 506-658-5100
www.k100.ca
Social Media: www.facebook.com/k100fm, twitter.com/K100_FM

***Saint John:* CJRP-FM** (Freq: 103.5)
77 King St. East, Saint John, NB E2L 1G9
Tel: 506-657-1035, *Fax:* 888-573-8961
cjrpfm.com
Graham Brown, Contact, graham@saintjohnradio.fm

***Saint John:* CJYC-FM (Kool 98)** (Freq: 98.9)
Owned by: Maritime Broadcasting System*
226 Union St., Saint John, NB E2L 1B1
Tel: 506-658-5100
kool98.fm
Social Media: www.facebook.com/KOOL98SaintJohn, twitter.com/KOOL98FM
Kelly O'Neill, General Manager, Sales

***Shédiac:* CJSE-FM** (Freq: 89.5, 101.7, 107.5)
51, ch Cornwall, Shédiac, NB E4P 8T8
Tel: 506-532-0080, *Fax:* 506-532-0120
cjse@cjse.ca
www.cjse.ca
Social Media: www.facebook.com/CJSEFM89, twitter.com/cjsefm
Patricia Bourque-Chevarie, Directrice générale par intérim

***St Stephen:* CHDT-FM** (Freq: 98.1)
112 Milltown Blvd., St Stephen, NB E3L 1G6
Tel: 506-466-1000, *Fax:* 506-466-4500
mail@thetide.ca
www.thetide.ca
Social Media: www.facebook.com/pages/981-The-Tide/346408628831, twitter.com/TheTide981

***Woodstock:* CJCJ-FM** (Freq: 104.1)
Owned by: Bell Media Inc.*
#2, 131 Queen St., Woodstock, NB E7M 2M8
Tel: 506-325-3030, *Fax:* 506-325-3031
cj104@bellmedia.ca
www.cj104.com
Social Media: www.facebook.com/CJ104, twitter.com/CJ104FM

Newfoundland & Labrador

***Argentia:* CFOZ-FM** (Freq: 100.3)
Owned by: CHOZ-FM
Argentia, NL

***Bonavista:* CJOZ-FM** (Freq: 92.1)
Owned by: CHOZ-FM
Bonavista, NL
Brian O'Connell, Station Manager

***Carbonear:* CHVO-FM (Kixx Country 103.9)** (Freq: 103.9)
Owned by: Newcap Radio*
1 CHVO Dr., Carbonear, NL A1Y 1A2
Tel: 709-596-1560, *Fax:* 709-596-8626
info@kixxcountry.ca
www.kixxcountry.ca
Social Media: www.facebook.com/kixxcountry, twitter.com/kixxcountry

***Churchill Falls:* CFLC-FM** (Freq: 97.9)
Owned by: CFLN-FM (Big Land - Labrador's FM)
Churchill Falls, NL
www.bigland.fm

***Clarenville:* CKLN-FM (Kixx Country 103.9)** (Freq: 97.1)
Owned by: CHVO-FM
Clarenville, NL

***Clarenville:* VOCM-FM1(100.7 K-Rock)** (Freq: 100.7)
Owned by: VOCM-FM 97.5*
Clarenville, NL
Tel: 709-726-5590, *Fax:* 709-726-4633
email@krockrocks.com
www.k-rock975.com
Social Media: www.facebook.com/975krock, twitter.com/975krock

***Corner Brook:* CFLN-FM (Big Land - Labrador's FM)** (Freq: 97.9)
Owned by: Steele Communications*
345 O'Connell Dr, Corner Brook, NL A2H 7V3
Tel: 709-570-1163, *Fax:* 709-726-4633
Toll-Free: 800-356-4570
info@bigland.fm
www.bigland.fm
Social Media: twitter.com/biglandfm
Mike Murphy, Station Manager, mmurphy@newcap.ca
Mike Campbell, Program Director, mcampbell@newcap.ca

***Corner Brook:* CKOZ-FM** (Freq: 92.3)
Owned by: CHOZ-FM
Corner Brook, NL
www.ozfm.com

***Corner Brook:* CKXX-FM (K-Rock 103.9)** (Freq: 103.9)
Owned by: Newcap Radio*
345 O'Connell Dr., Corner Brook, NL A2H 7V3
Tel: 709-634-4570, *Fax:* 709-634-4081
www.k-rock1039.com
Social Media: www.facebook.com/1039krock
Dave Hillier, General Manager, dhillier@newcap.ca
Mike Payne, Program Director, mike.payne@vocm.com

***Deer Lake:* CFDL-FM** (Freq: 97.9)
Owned by: CFCB
Deer Lake, NL
Tel: 709-634-4570, *Fax:* 706-634-4081
onair@cfcbradio.com
www.cfcbradio.com

***Gander:* CKXD-FM (98.7 K-ROCK)** (Freq: 98.7)
Owned by: Newcap Radio*
PO Box 650, Gander, NL A1V 1X2
Tel: 709-651-3650, *Fax:* 709-651-2542
OnAir@987krock.com
www.987krock.com
Social Media: www.youtube.com/user/987Krock, www.facebook.com/pages/987-K-Rock/233634473362049, twitter.com/987krock
David Hillier, Station Manager, dhillier@newcap.ca

***Grand Falls-Windsor:* CKMY-FM** (Freq: 95.9)
Owned by: CHOZ-FM
Grand Falls-Windsor, NL
www.ozfm.com

***Grand Falls-Windsor:* CKXG-FM (102.3 K-Rock)** (Freq: 102.3; 101.3)
Owned by: Newcap Radio*
35A Grenfell Heights, Grand Falls-Windsor, NL A2A 2K2
Tel: 709-489-2192, *Fax:* 709-489-8626
onair@krocknl.com
www.krocknl.com
Social Media: www.facebook.com/krock.grandfallswindsor, twitter.com/krockgfw
David Hillier, General Manager, dhillier@newcap.ca
Richard King, Program Director, rking@vocm.com

***Happy Valley-Goose Bay:* CFGB-FM** (Freq: 89.5)
Owned by: Canadian Broadcasting Corporation*
12 Loring Dr., Happy Valley-Goose Bay, NL A0P 1C0
Tel: 709-896-2911, *Fax:* 709-896-8900
labradormorning@cbc.ca
www.cbc.ca/nl
Denise Wilson, Senior Managing Director, Atlantic Canada, denise.wilson@cbc.ca

***Labrador City:* CBDQ-FM** (Freq: 96.3)
Owned by: Canadian Broadcasting Corporation*
500 Vanier Ave., Labrador City, NL A2V 2W7
Tel: 709-944-3616, *Fax:* 709-944-5472
labradormorning@cbc.ca
www.cbc.ca/nl
Denise Wilson, Senior Managing Director, Atlantic Canada, denise.wilson@cbc.ca
Peter Gullage, Executive Producer, Newfoundland & Labrador, peter.gullage@cbc.ca
Nadine Antle, Regional Manager, Communications, Marketing & Brand, 902-420-4223, Nadine.Antle@cbc.ca

***Marystown:* CIOZ-FM** (Freq: 96.3)
Owned by: CHOZ-FM
Marystown, NL
www.ozfm.com

***Nain:* Okalakatiget Society Radio** (Freq: 99.9)
Owned by: Okalakatiget Society*
PO Box 160, Nain, NL A0P 1L0
Tel: 709-922-2187, *Fax:* 709-922-2293
okradio@oksociety.com
www.oksociety.com

***Northwest River:* CFLN-1-FM** (Freq: 95.9)
Owned by: CFLN-FM
Northwest River, NL
www.bigland.fm

***Springdale:* CKCM-1FM (VOCM)** (Freq: 89.3)
Owned by: CKCM-VOCM*
Springdale, NL
Tel: 709-489-2192, *Fax:* 709-489-8626
www.vocm.com
Social Media: twitter.com/vocmnews

***St Anthony:* CFNN-FM (CFCB 97.9)** (Freq: 97.9)
Owned by: CFCB
St Anthony, NL
www.cfcbradio.com

***St. Andrews:* CFCVFM** (Freq: 97.7)
Owned by: CFSX-AM
St. Andrews, NL
Tel: 709-643-2192, *Fax:* 709-643-5025
www.cfsxradio.com

***St. John's:* CBN-FM** (Freq: 106.9)
Owned by: Canadian Broadcasting Corporation*
95 University Ave., St. John's, NL A1B 1Z4
Tel: 709-576-5000
www.cbc.ca/nl
Denise Wilson, Senior Managing Director, Atlantic Canada, denise.wilson@cbc.ca

***St. John's:* CHMR-FM** (Freq: 93.5)
Memorial University, PO Box A-119, St. John's, NL A1C 5S7
Tel: 709-864-4777, *Fax:* 709-864-7688
chmr@mun.ca
www.mun.ca/chmr
Social Media: www.facebook.com/chmrfmnewsdepartment, twitter.com/chmrmunradio
Kathy Rowe, Station Manager

***St. John's:* CHOZ-FM** (Freq: 94.7)
Owned by: Newfoundland Broadcasting Co. Ltd.*
446 Logy Bay Rd., St. John's, NL A1C 5S2
Tel: 709-273-2255
www.ozfm.com
Social Media: www.youtube.com/user/NewfoundlandsOZFM, www.facebook.com/OZFM.Newfoundland, twitter.com/CHOZFM

***St. John's:* CHOZ-FM** (Freq: 94.7)
Owned by: Newfoundland Broadcasting Co. Ltd.*
446 Logy Bay Rd., St. John's, NL A1C 5S2
Tel: 709-273-2255
www.ozfm.com
Social Media: www.facebook.com/OZFM.Newfoundland, twitter.com/CHOZFM
Brian O'Connell, Station Manager

***St. John's:* CKIX-FM (Hits FM)** (Freq: 99.1)
Owned by: Newcap Radio*
PO Box 8-590, 391 Kenmount Rd., St. John's, NL A1B 3P5
Tel: 709-726-5590, *Fax:* 709-726-4633
hitsmail@991hitsfm.com
www.991hitsfm.com
Social Media: instagram.com/991hitsfm, www.facebook.com/991hitsfm, twitter.com/hitsfm
Mike Murphy, General Manager, mmurphy@newcap.ca
Mike Campbell, Program Director, mcampbell@newcap.ca

***St. John's:* CKSJ-FM** (Freq: 101.1)
#201, 95 Bonaventure Ave., St. John's, NL A1B 2X5
Tel: 709-754-6748, *Fax:* 709-754-6749
onair@coast1011.com
www.coast1011.com
Social Media: www.facebook.com/coast1011, twitter.com/coast1011

***St. John's:* VOCM-FM (97.5 K-Rock)** (Freq: 97.5)
Owned by: Newcap Radio*
PO Box 8590, 391 Kenmount Rd., St. John's, NL A1B 3P5
Tel: 709-726-5590, *Fax:* 709-726-4633
email@krockrocks.com
www.k-rock975.com
Social Media: www.facebook.com/975krock, twitter.com/975krock

** For details on this company see listing in Major Broadcasting Companies section; † French language station*

Stephenville: CIOS-FM (Freq: 98.5)
Owned by: CHOZ-FM
Stephenville, NL
www.ozfm.com

Stephenville: CKXX-FM-1 (Freq: 95.9)
Owned by: CKXX-FM
60 West St., Stephenville, NL

Wabush: CFLW-FM (Big Land FM) (Freq: 94.7)
Owned by: CFLN-FM (Big Land - Labrador's FM)
Wabush, NL
www.bigland.fm

Northwest Territories

Hay River: CJCD-FM-1 (100.1 Moose FM) (Freq: 100.1)
Owned by: CJCD-FM (Mix 100)
Hay River, NT
Toll-Free: 867-873-4663
www.myyellowknifenow.com

†Yellowknife: CIVR-FM (Freq: 103.5)
CP 456, 5106, 48e rue, Yellowknife, NT X1A 2P2
Tél: 867-766-5172
civr@radiotaiga.com
www.radiotaiga.ca
Médias sociaux: www.facebook.com/pages/Radio-Taïga-CIVR-1035-FM/299660494713, twitter.com/radiotaiga

Yellowknife: CJCD-FM (100.1 Moose FM) (Freq: 100.1)
Owned by: Vista Broadcast Group*
PO Box 218, 5114 - 49th St., Yellowknife, NT X1A 2N2
Tel: 867-920-4636, *Fax:* 867-920-4033
www.myyellowknifenow.com

Yellowknife: CJCD-FM (Moose FM) (Freq: 100.1)
5114 - 49 St., Yellowknife, NT X1A 1P8
Tel: 867-920-4636, *Fax:* 867-920-4033
www.cjcd.ca
Social Media: www.facebook.com/Mix100cjcd, twitter.com/1001MooseFMCJCD

Yellowknife: CKLB-FM (Freq: 101.9)
PO Box 2193, Yellowknife, NT X1A 2P6
Tel: 320-295-7700
ask@cklbradio.com
cklbradio.com
Social Media: www.facebook.com/cklbradio.radiocklb, twitter.com/cklbradio
Deneze Nakehk'o, Director of Radio, deneze.nakehko@cklbradio.com

Nova Scotia

Amherst: CKDH-FM (Freq: 101.7)
Owned by: Maritime Broadcasting System*
PO Box 670, Amherst, NS B4H 4B8
Tel: 902-667-3875
www.ckdh.net
Social Media: www.facebook.com/101.7CKDH

Antigonish: CFXU-FM (Freq: 93.3)
St. Francis Xavier University, PO Box 948, Antigonish, NS B2G 2W5
Tel: 902-867-2410
cfxu@stfx.ca
radiocfxu.ca
Social Media: cfxuandu.tumblr.com, www.facebook.com/CFXUTheFox, twitter.com/CFXUradio
Rory Macleod, Station Manager

Antigonish: CJFX-FM (989 XFM) (Freq: 98.9)
c/o Atlantic Broadcasters Limited, PO Box 5800, Antigonish, NS B2G 2R9
Tel: 902-863-4580, *Fax:* 902-863-6300
www.989xfm.ca
Social Media: www.youtube.com/user/989XFMAntigonish, www.facebook.com/pages/989-XFM/228101459666, twitter.com/989xfm
Ken Farrell, General Manager

Bridgewater: CKBW-FM (Freq: 98.1)
#200, 135 North St., Bridgewater, NS B4V 2V7
Tel: 902-543-2401, *Fax:* 902-543-1208
ckbw@ckbw.com
ckbw.ca
Social Media: www.facebook.com/CKBWRadio, twitter.com/ckbwradio

†Cheticamp: CKJM-FM (Freq: 106.1)
CP 699, Cheticamp, NS B0E 1H0
Tél: 902-224-1242, *Téléc:* 902-224-1770
Ligne sans frais: 877-828-1242
info@ckjm.ca
www.ckjm.ca
Médias sociaux: www.facebook.com/radiockjm, twitter.com/RadioCKJM
Angus LeFort, Directeur général, angus@ckjm.ca

Eastern Passage: CFEP-FM (Freq: 105.9)
PO Box 196, Eastern Passage, NS B3G 1M5
Tel: 902-469-9231, *Fax:* 902-463-1935
info@seasidefm.com
www.seasidefm.com
Social Media: www.facebook.com/seasidefmradio, twitter.com/seasidefm
Wayne Harrett, General Manager, wharrett@seasidefm.com

†Halifax: CBAX-FM (Freq: 91.5)
5600 Sackville St., Halifax, NS B3J 1L2
Tél: 902-420-8311
ici.radio-canada.ca

Halifax: CBHA-FM (Freq: 90.5)
Owned by: Canadian Broadcasting Corporation*
#100, 7067 Chebucto Rd., Halifax, NS B3L 4R5
Tel: 902-420-8311, *Fax:* 902-420-4357
Toll-Free: 866-306-4636
www.cbc.ca/ns
Other information: Phone, CBC Radio One Newsroom, Halifax: 902-420-4100
Denise Wilson, Senior Managing Director, Atlantic Canada, denise.wilson@cbc.ca
Chantal Bernard, Senior Officer, Communications, 709-576-5161

Halifax: CBH-FM (Freq: 102.7)
Owned by: Canadian Broadcasting Corporation*
#100, 7067 Chebucto Rd., Halifax, NS B3L 4R5
Tel: 902-420-8311
www.cbc.ca/ns
Denise Wilson, Senior Managing Director, Atlantic Canada, denise.wilson@cbc.ca

Halifax: CFRQ-FM (Q104) (Freq: 104.3)
Owned by: Newcap Radio*
#200, 3770 Kempt Rd., Halifax, NS B3K 4X8
Tel: 902-453-4004, *Fax:* 902-453-3120
halifaxreception@newcap.ca
www.q104.ca
Social Media: www.facebook.com/pages/Q104-FM/141967777087, twitter.com/q104halifax
Ken Geddes, General Manager, kgeddes@newcap.ca
Trevor Wallworth, Program Director, twallworth@newcap.ca

Halifax: CHFX-FM (FX101.9) (Freq: 101.9)
Owned by: Maritime Broadcasting System*
90 Lovett Lake Ct., Halifax, NS B3S 0H6
Tel: 902-422-1651
www.fx1019.ca
Social Media: www.facebook.com/FX101.9

Halifax: CHNS-FM (89.9 The Wave) (Freq: 89.9)
Owned by: Maritime Broadcasting System*
90 Lovett Lake Ct., Halifax, NS B3S 0H6
Tel: 902-422-1651
www.899thewave.fm
Social Media: www.facebook.com/89.9TheWave

Halifax: CIOO-FM (Freq: 100.1)
PO Box 9316 RPO CSC, Halifax, NS B3K 6B2
Tel: 902-453-2524
www.c100fm.com
Social Media: www.facebook.com/C100FM, twitter.com/C100FM
Trent McGrath, General Manager, 902-493-2731, trent.mcgrath@bellmedia.ca
Brad Muir, Program Manager, brad.muir@bellmedia.ca

Halifax: CJCH-FM (101.3 The BOUNCE) (Freq: 101.3)
Owned by: Bell Media Radio*
PO Box 9316 RPO CSC, Halifax, NS B3K 6A7
Tel: 902-453-2524
www.1013thebounce.com
Social Media: www.facebook.com/1013TheBOUNCE, twitter.com/1013TheBOUNCE
Trent McGrath, General Manager, trent.mcgrath@bellmedia.ca

Halifax: CKDU-FM (Freq: 88.1)
Student Union Bldg., 6136 University Ave., Halifax, NS B3H 4J2
Tel: 902-494-6479
info@ckdu.ca
www.ckdu.ca
Social Media: www.youtube.com/user/CKDUFM, www.facebook.com/CKDU88.1FM, twitter.com/CKDU881FM
Gianna Lauren, Station Coordinator, gianna@ckdu.ca

Halifax: CKHY-FM (Freq: 105.1)
Owned by: Evanov Radio Group*
5527 Cogswell St., Halifax, NS B3J 1R2
Tel: 902-429-1035, *Fax:* 902-425-8637
live105@live105.ca
www.live105.ca
Social Media: www.facebook.com/pages/Live-105-Halifax/103161393070787, twitter.com/Live105HRM
Gary Tredwell, Program Director, gtredwell@evanovradio.com

Halifax: CKHZ-FM (Freq: 103.5)
Owned by: Evanov Radio Group*
5527 Cogswell St., Halifax, NS B3J 1R2
Tel: 902-429-1035, *Fax:* 902-425-8637
www.energy1035.ca
Social Media: www.facebook.com/energy1035, twitter.com/energy1035hfx
Gary Tredwell, Program Director, gtredwell@evanovradio.com

Halifax: CKUL-FM (Mix 96.5) (Freq: 96.5)
Owned by: Newcap Radio*
#200, 3770 Kempt Rd., Halifax, NS B3K 4X8
Tel: 902-453-4004, *Fax:* 902-453-3120
www.mix965.ca
Social Media: www.youtube.com/user/radio965hhalifax, www.facebook.com/mix965halifax, twitter.com/mix965hfx
Ken Geddes, General Manager, kgeddes@newcap.ca
Trevor Wallworth, Program Director, twallworth@newcap.ca

Inverness: CJFX-FM (Freq: 102.5)
Owned by: CJFX-FM
Inverness, NS

Kentville: CKEN-FM (AVR) (Freq: 97.7)
Owned by: Maritime Broadcasting System*
PO Box 310, 29 Oakdene Ave., Kentville, NS B4N 1H5
Tel: 902-678-2111, *Fax:* 902-678-9894
www.avrnetwork.com
Social Media: www.facebook.com/avrnetwork

Kentville: CKWM-FM (Magic) (Freq: 94.9)
Owned by: Maritime Broadcasting System*
PO Box 310, 29 Oakdene Ave., Kentville, NS B4N 1H5
Tel: 902-678-2111, *Fax:* 902-678-9894
www.magic949.ca
Social Media: www.facebook.com/250425211647226

New Glasgow: CKEC-FM (94.1 East Coast FM) (Freq: 94.1)
Owned by: Hector Broadcasting Co. Ltd.*
PO Box 519, 84 Provost St., New Glasgow, NS B2H 5E7
Tel: 902-752-4200, *Fax:* 902-755-2468
info@ecfm.com
ecfm.ca
Social Media: www.facebook.com/10388345939, twitter.com/941ECFM
Michael Freeman, Vice-President/General Manager
Doulas Freeman, CEO

New Glasgow: CKEZ-FM (Freq: 97.9)
Owned by: Hector Broadcasting Co. Ltd.*
PO Box 519, 84 Provost St., New Glasgow, NS B2H 5E7
Tel: 902-752-4200, *Fax:* 902-755-2468
classicrock979.ca
Social Media: www.facebook.com/Classicrock979, twitter.com/ROCKEZ979

** For details on this company see listing in Major Broadcasting Companies section; † French language station*

***New Minas:* CIJK-FM (89.3 K-Rock)** (Freq: 89.3)
Owned by: Newcap Radio*
#3, 8794 Commercial St, New Minas, NS B4N 3C5
Tel: 902-365-8930, *Fax:* 902-365-3566
info@893krock.com
www.893krock.com
Social Media: www.instagram.com/893krock, www.facebook.com/893krock, twitter.com/893krock
Ken Geddes, General Manager, kgeddes@newcap.ca
Melanie Sampson, Program Director, msampson@newcap.ca

***Port Hawkesbury:* CIGO-FM (The Hawk)** (Freq: 101.5)
#201, 609 Church St., Port Hawkesbury, NS B9A 2X4
Tel: 902-625-1220, *Fax:* 902-625-2664
news@1015thehawk.com
www.1015thehawk.com
Social Media: www.youtube.com/1015TheHawk, www.facebook.com/pages/1015-The-Hawk, twitter.com/1015_The_Hawk
Bob MacEachern, President & General Manager, bob@1015thehawk.com

***†Saulnierville:* CIFA-FM** (Freq: 104.1)
CP 8, Saulnierville, NS B0W 2Z0
Tél: 902-769-2432, *Téléc:* 902-769-3101
info@cifafm.com
cifafm.com
Médias sociaux: www.facebook.com/radiocifa
Ghislain Boudreau, Directeur général

***Shelburne:* CJLS-FM-2** (Freq: 96.3)
Owned by: CJLS-FM
Shelburne, NS

***Shelburne:* CKBW-FM-2** (Freq: 93.1)
Owned by: CKBW-FM
Shelburne, NS

***Sydney:* CBI-FM** (Freq: CBC Radio 2; 105.1)
Owned by: Canadian Broadcasting Corporation*
500 George St., Sydney, NS B1P 1K6
Tel: 902-539-5050
www.cbc.ca/ns

***Sydney:* CHER-FM (MAX FM)** (Freq: 98.3)
Owned by: Maritime Broadcasting System*
318 Charlotte St., Sydney, NS B1P 1C8
Tel: 902-564-5596, *Fax:* 902-562-1873
983maxfm.com
Social Media: www.facebook.com/max983fm
Dwayne Keller, Manager, Operations

***Sydney:* CHRK-FM (The Giant)** (Freq: 101.9)
Owned by: Newcap Radio*
#300, 500 Kings St, Sydney, NS B1S 1B1
Tel: 902-270-1019, *Fax:* 902-270-3566
info@giant1019.com
www.giant1019.com
Social Media: www.instagram.com/1019thegiant, www.facebook.com/1019TheGiant, twitter.com/1019thegiant
Rob Redshaw, General Manager, rredshaw@newcap.ca
Daryl Stevens, Program Director, dstevens@newcap.ca

***Sydney:* CKCH-FM (103.5 The Eagle)** (Freq: 103.5)
Owned by: Newcap Radio*
#300, 500 Kings Rd, Sydney, NS B1S 1B1
Tel: 902-563-1035, *Fax:* 902-270-3566
info@eagle1035.com
www.eagle1035.com
Social Media: www.instagram.com/1035theeagle/, www.facebook.com/1035TheEagle, twitter.com/1035theeagle
Robert Redshaw, General Manager/ Sales Manager, rredshaw@newcap.ca
Jay Bedford, Program Director, jbedford@newcap.ca
Daryl Stevens, Operations Manager, dstevens@newcap.ca

***Sydney:* CKPE-FM (The Cape)** (Freq: 94.9)
Owned by: Maritime Broadcasting System*
318 Charlotte St., Sydney, NS B1P 1C8
Tel: 902-564-5596, *Fax:* 902-564-1873
949thecape.com
Social Media: www.facebook.com/thecape949
Dwayne Keller, Manager, Operations

***Truro:* CKTO-FM (Big Dog 100.9 FM)** (Freq: 100.9)
Owned by: Bell Media Inc.*
187 Industrial Ave., Truro, NS B2N 6V3
Tel: 902-893-6060, *Fax:* 902-893-7771
Toll-Free: 877-891-6060
truronewsroom@bellmedia.ca
www.bigdog1009.ca
Social Media: www.facebook.com/bigdogfanpage, twitter.com/BigDogTruro
Chris VanTassel, Brand Director, 902-893-6060, cvtassel@bigdog1009.ca

***Truro:* CKTY-FM (Cat Country 99.5 FM)** (Freq: 99.5)
Owned by: Bell Media Inc.*
187 Industrial Ave., Truro, NS B2N 6V3
Tel: 902-893-6060, *Fax:* 902-893-7771
Toll-Free: 877-891-6060
truronewsroom@bellmedia.ca
www.catcountry995.ca
Social Media: www.facebook.com/catcountry995, twitter.com/CatCountryTruro
Chris VanTassel, Brand Director, cvtassel@bigdog1009.ca
Matt Mossman, Sales Manager, matthew.mossman@bellmedia.ca

***Weymouth:* CKDY-FM-1** (Freq: 103.3)
Owned by: CKEN-FM
Weymouth, NS

***Yarmouth:* CJLS-FM** (Freq: 95.5)
#201, 328 Main St., Yarmouth, NS B5A 1E4
Tel: 902-742-7175, *Fax:* 902-742-3143
cjls@cjls.com
www.cjls.com
Social Media: www.facebook.com/pages/CJLS-The-Wave/186605881367192
Jim Grattan, Production Manager

Nunavut

***†Iqaluit:* CFRT-FM** (Freq: 107.3)
CP 880, Iqaluit, NU X0A 0H0
Tél: 867-979-1073
www.cfrt.ca
Médias sociaux: www.facebook.com/130276437094882, twitter.com/CFRT1073FM
Pascal Auger, Directeur du produit

***Iqaluit:* CKIQ-FM** (Freq: 99.9)
PO Box 417, Iqaluit, NU X0A 0H0
Fax: 877-490-2547
Toll-Free: 877-445-2547
icefmiqaluit@gmail.com
www.icefm.ca
Social Media: www.facebook.com/pages/Ice-Fm/208026069253058
Glenn Craig, Station Manager

***Rankin Inlet:* CBQR-FM** (Freq: 105.1)
Owned by: Canadian Broadcasting Corporation*
PO Box 130, Rankin Inlet, NU X0C 0G0
www.cbc.ca/north

Ontario

***Arnprior:* CHMY-FM-1 (myFM)** (Freq: 107.7)
Owned by: CHMY-FM (myFM)
Kenwood Corporate Centre, #50, 160 William St. West, Arnprior, ON K7S 3W4
Tel: 613-623-7772, *Fax:* 613-623-4508
www.arnpriortoday.ca
Social Media: www.facebook.com/1077myfm, twitter.com/1077myFM
Angela Kluke, Contact

***Aylmer:* CHPD-FM** (Freq: 105.9)
16 Talbot St. East, Aylmer, ON N5H 1H4
Tel: 519-773-8555, *Fax:* 519-773-8606
www.mcson.org

***Bancroft:* CHMS-FM (Moose FM)** (Freq: 97.7)
Owned by: Vista Broadcast Group*
PO Box 1240, 30674 Hwy. 28E, Bancroft, ON K0L 1C0
Tel: 613-332-1423, *Fax:* 613-332-0841
www.mybancroftnow.com
Social Media: www.facebook.com/MooseFMBancroft, twitter.com/moosefmchms

***Barrie:* CFJB-FM** (Freq: 95.7)
#10, 431 Huronia Rd., Barrie, ON L4N 9B3
Tel: 705-725-7304, *Fax:* 705-792-7858
www.rock95.com
Social Media: www.facebook.com/Rock95Barrie, twitter.com/rock95barrie

***Barrie:* CHAY-FM (Fresh Radio 93.1)** (Freq: 93.1)
Owned by: Corus Radio Company*
PO Box 937, 1125 Bayfield St. North, Barrie, ON L4M 4Y6
Tel: 705-737-3511
www.931freshradio.ca
Social Media: www.youtube.com/channel/UCycHBBKOK2uKRzFIAePvEVw, www.facebook.com/931freshradio, twitter.com/931freshradio
Deb James, Brand Director

***Barrie:* CIQB-FM (B101)** (Freq: 101.1)
Owned by: 591989 B.C. Ltd.*
PO Box 101, 1125 Bayfield St. North, Barrie, ON L4M 4S9
Tel: 705-726-1011
www.b101fm.com
Social Media: www.facebook.com/b101fmbarrie, twitter.com/B101FMBARRIE
Deb James, Brand Director

***Barrie:* CJLF-FM (Life 100.3)** (Freq: 100.3)
#111, 115 Bell Farm Rd., Barrie, ON L4M 5G1
Tel: 705-735-3370, *Fax:* 705-735-3301
www.lifeonline.fm
Scott Jackson, Station Manager
Janice Baird, CFO & Office Manager

***Barrie:* CKMB-FM** (Freq: 107.5)
#10, 431 Huronia Rd., Barrie, ON L4N 9B3
Tel: 705-725-7304, *Fax:* 705-792-7858
www.1075koolfm.com
Social Media: www.facebook.com/koolfmbarrie, twitter.com/KoolFMBarrie
Tom Manton, General Manager, 705-797-8702, tmanton@cobroadcasting.com.

***Belleville:* CHCQ-FM** (Freq: 100.1)
497 Dundas St. West, Belleville, ON K8P 1B6
Tel: 613-966-0955
www.cool100.fm
Social Media: instagram.com/cool100fm, www.facebook.com/cool100.1, twitter.com/cool100fm
John Sherratt, President & Owner, johns@cool100.ca

***Belleville:* CIGL-FM (Mix 97)** (Freq: 97.1)
Owned by: Quinte Broadcasting Co. Ltd.*
PO Box 488, 10 Front St. South, Belleville, ON K8N 5B2
Tel: 613-969-5555, *Fax:* 613-969-8122
www.mix97.com
Social Media: www.facebook.com/mix97fm, twitter.com/MIX97radio

***Belleville:* CJLX-FM (91X)** (Freq: 91.3)
PO Box 4200, Belleville, ON K8N 5B9
Tel: 613-969-0923, *Fax:* 613-966-0923
contact@91x.fm
www.91x.fm
Social Media: www.youtube.com/user/91xfm, www.facebook.com/91Xfm, twitter.com/91xfm
Other information: Newsroom, Phone: 613-966-6797

***Belleville:* CJOJ-FM** (Freq: 95.5)
497 Dundas St. West, Belleville, ON K8P 1B6
Tel: 613-966-0955
www.955hitsfm.ca
Social Media: instagram.com/955hitsfm, www.facebook.com/955hitsfm, twitter.com/955hitsfm
John Sherratt, President & Owner, johns@cool100.ca

***Belleville:* CJTN-FM (Rock 107)** (Freq: 107.1)
Owned by: Quinte Broadcasting Co. Ltd.*
PO Box 488, 10 Front St. South, Belleville, ON K8N 5B2
Tel: 613-969-5555, *Fax:* 613-969-8122
www.rock107.ca
Social Media: www.facebook.com/276736605697503, twitter.com/Rock_107

***Bracebridge:* CFBG-FM (Moose FM)** (Freq: 99.5)
Owned by: Vista Broadcast Group*
3A Taylor Dr., Bracebridge, ON P1L 1S6
Tel: 705-645-2218, *Fax:* 705-645-5798
www.mymuskokanow.com
Social Media: www.facebook.com/159641740741946

** For details on this company see listing in Major Broadcasting Companies section; † French language station*

Brantford: **CFWC-FM** (Freq: 93.9)
271 Greenwich St., Brantford, ON N3S 2X9
Tel: 519-759-2339, *Fax:* 226-381-0940
info@brant939.faithfm.org
brantford.faithfm.org
Social Media: www.facebook.com/faithfmBrantford
Peter Jackson, Station Manager

Brantford: **CKPC-FM (Jewel 92)** (Freq: 92.1)
Owned by: Evanov Radio Group*
571 West St., Brantford, ON N3R 7C5
Tel: 519-759-1000, *Fax:* 519-753-1470
www.jewel92.com
Social Media: www.facebook.com/fm92thejewel, twitter.com/jewel_92
Mike Rose, Operations Manager, mike@ckpcradio.com

Brighton: **CIYM-FM (myFM)** (Freq: 100.9)
Owned by: My Broadcasting Corporation*
PO Box 1522, Brighton, ON K0K 1H0
Tel: 613-475-6936, *Fax:* 613-475-9026
www.brightontoday.ca
Social Media: www.facebook.com/1009myfm, twitter.com/1009myFM
Pam Oliver, Contact

Brockville: **CFJR-FM** (Freq: 104.9)
Owned by: Bell Media Radio*
601 Stewart Blvd., Brockville, ON K6V 5V9
Tel: 613-345-1666
www.1049jrfm.com
Social Media: www.facebook.com/1049JRfm, twitter.com/1049JRfm
Greg Hinton, Vice President/General Manager, greg.hinton@bellmedia.ca

Brockville: **CJPT-FM** (Freq: 103.7)
Owned by: Bell Media Radio*
601 Stewart Blvd., Brockville, ON K6V 5T4
Tel: 613-345-1666
www.bob.fm
Social Media: www.facebook.com/1037BOBFM, twitter.com/1037BOB_FM
Greg Hinton, Vice President/General Manager, greg.hinton@bellmedia.ca

Caledonia: **CKJN-FM (Moose FM)** (Freq: 92.9)
Owned by: Vista Broadcast Group*
#14, 282 Argyle St. South, Caledonia, ON N3W 1K7
Tel: 289-284-1070, *Fax:* 289-284-1072
www.moosefm.com/ckjn
Social Media: www.facebook.com/145017032213085
Wendy Gray, General Manager, 905-356-6710

Campbellford: **CKOL-FM** (Freq: 93.7)
PO Box 551, Campbellford, ON K0L 1L0
Tel: 705-653-1089
ckol-radio@bell.net
ckol.webs.com
Social Media: www.facebook.com/CKOLRadio, twitter.com/CKOLfm

Chatham: **CKSY-FM** (Freq: 94.3)
Owned by: Blackburn Radio Inc.*
117 Keil Dr. South, Chatham, ON N7M 3H3
Tel: 519-354-2200, *Fax:* 519-354-2880
www.cksyfm.com
Social Media: www.youtube.com/user/cksyfm943, www.facebook.com/943CKSY, twitter.com/943cksy

Chatham: **CKUE-FM** (Freq: 95.1)
Owned by: Blackburn Radio Inc.*
PO Box 100, 117 Keil Dr., Chatham, ON N7M 5K1
Tel: 519-354-2200
info@canadasrock.ca
www.therock951.com
Social Media: www.facebook.com/canadasrock, twitter.com/Canadasrock

Chatham-Kent: **CFCO-FM** (Freq: 630 AM; 92.9 FM)
Owned by: Blackburn Radio Inc.*
117 Keil Dr. South, Chatham-Kent, ON N7M 5K1
Tel: 519-354-2200, *Fax:* 519-354-2880
info@country929.com
country929.com
Social Media: www.youtube.com/Country929fm, www.facebook.com/country929cfco, twitter.com/Country929

Cobourg: **CHUC-FM (107.9 The Breeze)** (Freq: 107.9)
Owned by: Pineridge Broadcasting Inc.
PO Box 520, Cobourg, ON K9A 4L3
Tel: 905-372-5401, *Fax:* 905-372-6280
www.1079thebreeze.com
Social Media: www.facebook.com/1079TheBreeze, twitter.com/1079TheBreeze
Don Conway, President

Cobourg: **CKSG-FM (Star 93.3)** (Freq: 93.3)
Owned by: Pineridge Broadcasting Inc.
PO Box 520, Cobourg, ON K9A 4L3
Tel: 905-372-5401, *Fax:* 905-372-6280
Toll-Free: 866-782-7933
www.star933.com
Social Media: www.facebook.com/STAR933Radio, twitter.com/Star933HitMusic
Don Conway, President
Dave Hughes, General Sales Manager

Cochrane: **CFIF-FM (The Moose)** (Freq: 101.1)
Owned by: Vista Broadcast Group*
171 - 6th Ave., Cochrane, ON P1L 1C0
Tel: 705-272-2520, *Fax:* 705-272-6467

Cochrane: **CHPB-FM (Moose FM)** (Freq: 98.1)
Owned by: Vista Broadcast Group*
PO Box 2604, 22 - 5th St., Cochrane, ON P0L 1C0
Tel: 705-272-6467, *Fax:* 705-272-2520
www.moosefm.com/chpb
Social Media: www.facebook.com/156734384370515
Donna Todd, Contact, Sales

Collingwood: **CHGB-FM (The Beach)** (Freq: 97.7)
Owned by: Bayshore Broadcasting Corporation*
9937 Hwy. 26, Collingwood, ON L9Y 0Y4
Tel: 705-422-0970, *Fax:* 705-422-0468
info@977thebeach.ca
www.977thebeach.ca
Other information: News E-mail: news@977thebeach.ca
Kevin Brown, Vice-President, Sales & Marketing, sales@bayshorebroadcasting.ca

Collingwood: **CKCB-FM (95.1 The Peak FM)** (Freq: 95.1)
Owned by: 591989 B.C. Ltd.*
#200, 186 Hurontario St., Collingwood, ON L9Y 4T4
Tel: 705-446-9510
www.thepeakfm.com
Social Media: www.facebook.com/95.1thepeakfm, twitter.com/thepeakfm
Deb James, Brand Director

Cornwall: **CFLG-FM (Fresh Radio 104.5)** (Freq: 104.5)
Owned by: Corus Radio Company*
709 Cotton Mill St., Cornwall, ON K6H 7K7
Tel: 613-932-5180, *Fax:* 613-938-0355
www.1045freshradio.ca
Social Media: www.youtube.com/variety104, www.facebook.com/variety104, twitter.com/Variety104
Mark Dickie, General Manager

†***Cornwall:*** **CHOD-FM** (Freq: 92.1)
#202, 1111, ch Montréal, Cornwall, ON K6H 1E1
Tel: 613-936-2463
chodfm@chodfm.ca
chodfm.ca
Médias sociaux: www.facebook.com/pages/Chodfm-921/457850440922218, twitter.com/CHODFM
Marc Charbonneau, Responsable, marc@chodfm.ca

Cornwall: **CJSS-FM** (Freq: 101.9)
Owned by: Corus Radio Company*
709 Cotton Mill St., Cornwall, ON K6H 7K7
Tel: 613-932-5180, *Fax:* 613-938-0355
www.cjssfm.com
Social Media: www.facebook.com/1019cjssfm, twitter.com/cjssfm
Mark Dickie, General Manager, mark.dickie@corusent.com

Dryden: **CKDR-FM** (Freq: 92.7)
122 King St., Dryden, ON P8N 1C2
Tel: 807-223-2355, *Fax:* 807-223-5090
Toll-Free: 800-465-7200
www.ckdr.net
Social Media: www.facebook.com/CKDR.Dryden
Michelle Nault, Contact, nault.michelle@radioabl.ca

Elliot Lake: **CKNR-FM (Moose FM)** (Freq: 94.1)
Owned by: Vista Broadcast Group*
144 Ontario Ave., Elliot Lake, ON P5A 1Y3
Tel: 705-848-3608, *Fax:* 705-848-1378
www.myalgomamanitoulinnow.com
Social Media: www.facebook.com/166739240015143, twitter.com/moosefmcknr

Espanola: **CJJM-FM (Moose FM)** (Freq: 99.3)
Owned by: Vista Broadcast Group*
#2, 90 Gray St., Espanola, ON P5E 1G1
Tel: 705-869-0578, *Fax:* 705-869-0578
www.moosefm.com/cjjm
Social Media: www.facebook.com/111251348942369
Mike Trahan, General Manager, 705-475-9991

Exeter: **CKXM-FM** (Freq: 90.5)
Owned by: My Broadcasting Corporation*
#6, 145 Thames Rd. West, Exeter, ON N0M 1S3
Tel: 519-235-3000, *Fax:* 519-235-6262
www.exetertoday.ca
Social Media: www.facebook.com/1057myfm, twitter.com/905myFM
Robin Glenny, Contact

Fort Frances: **CFOB-FM (The Border)** (Freq: 93.1)
210 Scott St., Fort Frances, ON P9A 1G7
Tel: 807-274-5341
info@931theborder.ca
www.b93.ca
Social Media: www.facebook.com/931TheBorder, twitter.com/B93FortFrances

Gananoque: **CJGM-FM (myFM)** (Freq: 99.9)
Owned by: My Broadcasting Corporation*
PO Box 9, Gananoque, ON K7G 2T6
Tel: 613-382-6936, *Fax:* 613-382-8301
www.gananoquenow.ca
Social Media: www.facebook.com/999myfm, twitter.com/999myFM
Terri-Lynn Bayford, Contact

Goderich: **CHWC-FM (The Beach)** (Freq: 104.9)
Owned by: Bayshore Broadcasting Corporation*
300 Suncoast Dr., #E, Goderich, ON N7A 4N7
Tel: 519-612-1149, *Fax:* 519-612-1050
thebeach@1049thebeach.ca
www.1049thebeach.ca
Social Media: www.youtube.com/beachradio, www.facebook.com/1049thebeach, twitter.com/1049thebeach
Kevin Brown, Vice-President, Sales & Marketing, sales@bayshorebroadcasting.ca

Goderich: **CIYN-FM-1 (myFM)** (Freq: 99.7)
Owned by: CIYN-FM (myFM)
Goderich, ON
Tel: 519-565-2675
www.shorelinetoday.ca
Dylan Bartlett, Contact, Advertising

Guelph: **CFRU-FM** (Freq: 93.3)
University Centre, Level 2, University of Guelph, Guelph, ON N1G 2W1
Tel: 519-824-4120
info@cfru.ca
www.cfru.ca
Social Media: www.facebook.com/groups/2221470650, twitter.com/cfru_radio
Vish Khanna, Station Manager

Guelph: **CIMJ-FM (Magic 106.1)** (Freq: 106.1)
Owned by: 591989 B.C. Ltd.*
75 Speedvale Ave. East, Guelph, ON N1E 6M3
Tel: 519-824-7000, *Fax:* 519-824-4118
www.magic106.com
Social Media: www.youtube.com/user/Magic106Guelph, www.facebook.com/112905142082887, twitter.com/magic1061
Lars Wunsche, General Manager

Haliburton: **CFZN-FM (Moose FM)** (Freq: 93.5)
Owned by: Vista Broadcast Group*
PO Box 960, 152 Highland St., Haliburton, ON K0M 1S0
Tel: 705-457-3897, *Fax:* 705-457-3827
Toll-Free: 877-883-7625
www.moosefm.com/cfzn
Social Media: www.facebook.com/131914410197785
Karen Broad, General Manager, kbroad@moosefm.com

** For details on this company see listing in Major Broadcasting Companies section; † French language station*

***Haliburton:* CKHA-FM** (Freq: 100.9)
PO Box 1125, Haliburton, ON K0M 1S0
Tel: 705-457-1009, *Fax:* 705-457-9522
canoefmadmin@bellnet.ca
www.canoefm.com
Social Media: www.facebook.com/canoefm
Roxanne Casey, Station Manager, roxanne@canoefm.com

***Hamilton:* CING-FM (953 Fresh FM)** (Freq: 95.3)
Owned by: Corus Premium Television Ltd.*
875 Main St. West, Hamilton, ON L8S 4R1
Tel: 905-521-9900, *Fax:* 905-521-1691
www.953freshfm.com
Social Media: www.youtube.com/953FreshFM, www.facebook.com/953FreshFm, twitter.com/953FreshFM
Jim McCourtie, Program Director, jim.mccourtie@corusent.com

***Hamilton:* CIOI-FM** (Freq: 101.5)
#F111, 135 Fennell Ave., Hamilton, ON L8N 3T2
Tel: 905-575-2175, *Fax:* 905-575-2420
www.1015thehawk.ca
Social Media: www.facebook.com/thehawkfm, twitter.com/1015TheHawk
Les Palango, Station Manager, les.palango@mohawkcollege.ca

***Hamilton:* CJXY-FM (Y108)** (Freq: 107.9)
Owned by: Corus Radio Company*
875 Main St. West, Hamilton, ON L8S 4R1
Tel: 905-521-9900
www.y108.ca
Social Media: www.facebook.com/Y108Rocks, twitter.com/Y108Rocks
Jim McCourtie, Program Director, jim.mccourtie@corusent.com

***Hamilton:* CKLH-FM (102.9 K-Lite FM)** (Freq: 102.9)
Owned by: Bell Media Inc.*
#401, 883 Upper Wentworth St., Hamilton, ON L9A 4Y6
Tel: 905-574-1150, *Fax:* 905-575-6429
www.k-litefm.com
Social Media: www.facebook.com/1029klite, twitter.com/1029klite
Bob Harris, General Manager, Bell Radio Hamilton, bob.harris@bellmedia.ca
Sarah Cummings, Brand Director, sarah.cummings@bellmedia.ca

***Hamilton:* wave.fm** (Freq: Closed circuit)
589 Upper Wellington, Hamilton, ON L9A 3P8
Tel: 905-388-8911, *Fax:* 905-388-7947
www.wave.fm
Social Media: www.youtube.com/user/wave947, www.facebook.com/waveonlineradio, twitter.com/waveonlineradio
Steve Macaulay, Vice-President, Sales, stevemc@kx96.fm

***Hanover:* CFBW-FM (Bluewater Radio)** (Freq: 91.3)
267 - 10th St., Hanover, ON N4N 1P1
Tel: 519-364-0200, *Fax:* 519-364-5175
Toll-Free: 855-364-0200
info@bluewaterradio.ca
www.bluewaterradio.ca
Social Media: twitter.com/bluewaterradio
Andrew McBride, Station Manager, 519-370-9090

***Hawkesbury:* CKHK-FM (The Jewel)** (Freq: 107.7)
Owned by: Evanov Radio Group*
1320 Main St. East, Hawkesbury, ON K6A 1C5
Tel: 613-872-1077, *Fax:* 613-632-4022
info@1077thejewel.com
www.jewelradio.com/1077
Ted Silver, Administrator

***Hearst:* CHYK-FM-3** (Freq: 92.9)
Owned by: CHYK (Le Loup 104.1)
Hearst, ON

†*Hearst:* CINN-FM (Freq: 91.1)
CP 2648, Hearst, ON P0L 1N0
Tél: 705-372-1011, *Téléc:* 705-362-7411
Ligne sans frais: 866-362-5168
www.cinnfm.com
Médias sociaux: www.facebook.com/cinndirection, twitter.com/CINNFM
Steve McInnis, Directeur général, direction@cinnfm.com

***Huntsville:* CFBK-FM (Moose FM)** (Freq: 105.5)
Owned by: Vista Broadcast Group*
7 John St., Huntsville, ON P1H 1G1
Tel: 705-789-4461, *Fax:* 705-789-1269
www.mymuskokanow.com
Social Media: www.facebook.com/moosefm1055

***Huntsville:* CJLF-FM-3** (Freq: 98.9)
Owned by: CJLF-FM (Life 100.3)
Huntsville, ON
www.lifeonline.fm

***Kapuskasing:* CHYX-FM** (Freq: 93.7)
Owned by: CHYK (Le Loup 104.1)
Kapuskasing, ON

***Kapuskasing:* CKAP-FM (Moose FM)** (Freq: 100.9)
Owned by: Vista Broadcast Group*
#2A, 22 Queen St., Kapuskasing, ON P5N 1G8
Tel: 705-335-2379, *Fax:* 705-337-6391
Toll-Free: 866-505-2379
www.mykapuskasingnow.com
Social Media: www.facebook.com/MooseCKAP, twitter.com/moosefmckap

†*Kapuskasing:* CKGN-FM (Freq: 89.7 Kapuskasing et 94.7 Smooth Rock Falls)
77, ch Brunelle nord, Kapuskasing, ON P5N 2M1
Tél: 705-335-5915, *Téléc:* 705-335-3508
ckgn-fm@nt.net
www.ckgn.ca
Médias sociaux: www.facebook.com/197086727069227
Claude Chabot, Directeur général, claudechabot@ckgn.ca

***Kapuskasing:* CKHT-FM (Moose FM)** (Freq: 94.5)
Owned by: CKAP-FM (Moose FM)
#2A, 22 Queen St., Kapuskasing, ON P5N 1G8
Tel: 705-335-2379, *Fax:* 705-337-6391
Toll-Free: 866-505-2379
moose1009@moosefm.com
www.moosefm.com/ckht

***Kemptville:* CKVV-FM (Star FM)** (Freq: 97.5)
Owned by: Vista Broadcast Group*
#3, 4 Industrial Rd., Kemptville, ON K0G 1J0
Tel: 613-258-1786, *Fax:* 613-258-1786
www.fm975kemptville.com
Social Media: www.facebook.com/star975
Chris Nimigon, National Sales Manager, 416-925-0488

***Kenora:* CJRL-FM (89.5 The Lake)** (Freq: 89.5)
301 - 1st Ave. South, Kenora, ON P9N 1W2
Tel: 807-468-3181, *Fax:* 807-468-4188
www.cjrl.ca
Social Media: www.facebook.com/pages/895-The-Lake/357569390926298, twitter.com/thetide981

***Kenora:* CJRL-FM (89.5 The Lake)** (Freq: 89.5)
301 - 1st Ave South, Kenora, ON P9N 1W2
Tel: 807-468-3181, *Fax:* 807-468-4188
www.895thelake.ca
Social Media: www.facebook.com/357569390926298, twitter.com/CJRLNews

***Kenora:* CKQV-FM (Q104)** (Freq: 103.3)
Owned by: Golden West Broadcasting Ltd.*
619 Lakeview Dr., Kenora, ON P9N 3P6
Tel: 807-468-1045, *Toll-Free:* 855-468-1045
www.kenoraonline.com
Social Media: www.facebook.com/q104fm, twitter.com/q104kenora

***Killaloe:* CHCR-FM** (Freq: 102.9; 104.5)
PO Box 195, Killaloe, ON K0J 2A0
Tel: 613-757-0657, *Fax:* 613-757-0818
radio@chcr.org
www.chcr.org
Social Media: www.facebook.com/FriendsOfChcr

***Kincardine:* CIYN-FM (myFM)** (Freq: 95.5)
Owned by: My Broadcasting Corporation*
756 Queen St., Kincardine, ON N2Z 2Y2
Tel: 519-396-7770, *Fax:* 519-396-7771
www.shorelinetoday.ca
Social Media: www.facebook.com/955myfm, twitter.com/myFMshoreline
Dean Daly, Contact, Advertising

***Kingston:* CFLY-FM** (Freq: 98.3)
Owned by: Bell Media Radio*
#10, 993 Princess St., Kingston, ON K7L 1H3
Tel: 613-544-1380
heydeejay@983flyfm.com
www.983flyfm.comm
Social Media: www.facebook.com/983FLYFM, twitter.com/983FLYFM
Greg Hinton, Vice President/General Manager, greg.hinton@bellmedia.ca

***Kingston:* CFMK-FM (FM 96)** (Freq: 96.3)
Owned by: 591989 B.C. Ltd.*
170 Queen St., Kingston, ON K7K 1B2
Tel: 613-544-2340, *Fax:* 613-544-5508
www.963bigfm.com
Social Media: www.youtube.com/user/KingstonsFM96, www.facebook.com/963bigfm, twitter.com/963bigfm
Peter Mayhew, General Sales Manager
Rudy Chase, Program Director

***Kingston:* CFRC-FM** (Freq: 101.9)
Lower Carruthers Hall, Queen's University, 62 - 5th Field Company Lane, Kingston, ON K7L 3N6
Tel: 613-533-2121
cfrcops@ams.queensu.ca
www.cfrc.ca
Social Media: www.youtube.com/user/CFRC1019, www.facebook.com/cfrcradio, twitter.com/CFRC
Kristiana Clemens, Operations Officer

***Kingston:* CIKR-FM** (Freq: 105.7)
Owned by: Rogers Broadcasting Ltd.*
#301, 863 Princess St., Kingston, ON K7L 5N4
Tel: 613-549-1057, *Fax:* 613-549-5302
www.krock1057.ca
Social Media: plus.google.com/103140346673228495635, www.facebook.com/krock1057, twitter.com/Krock1057
Stephen Peck, General Manager, stephen.peck@rci.rogers.com

***Kingston:* CKLC-FM (98.9 The Drive)** (Freq: 98.9)
Owned by: Bell Media Radio*
PO Box 1380, #10, 993 Princess St., Kingston, ON K7L 1H3
Tel: 613-544-1380
onair@989thedrive.com
www.989thedrive.com
Social Media: www.facebook.com/989THEDRIVE, twitter.com/989THEDRIVE

***Kingston:* CKVI-FM** (Freq: 91.9)
235 Frontenac St., Kingston, ON K7L 3S7
Tel: 613-544-7864
www.thecave.ca
Social Media: www.facebook.com/91.9CaveRadio

***Kingston:* CKWS-FM** (Freq: 104.3)
Owned by: 591989 B.C. Ltd.*
170 Queen St., Kingston, ON K7K 1B2
Tel: 613-544-2340
www.1043freshradio.ca
Social Media: www.youtube.com/channel/UCxjyZrjWcLFXkr7P1NQFuPw, www.facebook.com/1043freshradio, twitter.com/1043freshradio
Peter Mayhew, General Manager, Sales
Rudy Chase, Program Director

***Kirkland Lake:* CJKL-FM** (Freq: 101.5)
Owned by: Connelly Communications Corp.*
PO Box 430, Kirkland Lake, ON P2N 3J4
Tel: 705-567-3366, *Fax:* 705-567-6101
cjkl@cjklfm.com
cjklfm.com
Social Media: www.facebook.com/128034260585970, twitter.com/CJKLFM
Other information: News Phone: 705-567-6200
Robin Connelly, President, General Manager, Programming Director

***Kitchener:* CHYM-FM** (Freq: 96.7)
Owned by: Rogers Broadcasting Ltd.*
305 King St. West, Kitchener, ON N2G 4E4
Tel: 519-743-2611
www.chymfm.com
Social Media: www.youtube.com/user/967CHYMFM, www.facebook.com/CHYMFM, twitter.com/chym967

***Kitchener:* CIKZ-FM** (Freq: 106.7)
Owned by: Rogers Broadcasting Ltd.*
305 King St. West, Kitchener, ON N2G 1B9
Tel: 519-743-2611
www.country1067.com
Social Media: www.facebook.com/country1067, twitter.com/country1067

***Kitchener:* CJDV-FM (107.5 Dave FM)** (Freq: 107.5)
Owned by: 591989 B.C. Ltd.*
#210, 50 Sportsworld Crossing Rd., Kitchener, ON N2P 0A4
Tel: 519-772-1212, *Fax:* 519-772-1213
www.davefm.com
Social Media: www.youtube.com/davefmrock, www.facebook.com/davefmrock, twitter.com/davefmrocks
Scot Turner, Program Director, Scot.Turner@corusent.com

** For details on this company see listing in Major Broadcasting Companies section; † French language station*

***Kitchener:* CJIQ-FM** (Freq: 88.3)
299 Doon Valley Dr., Kitchener, ON N2G 4M4
Tel: 519-748-5220
www.cjiqfm.com
Social Media: www.facebook.com/883cjiq, twitter.com/CJIQFM
Brian Clemens, Station Manager, music@cjiq.fm

***Kitchener:* CJTW-FM** (Freq: 94.3)
#207, 659 King St. East, Kitchener, ON N2G 2M4
Tel: 519-575-9090, *Fax:* 519-575-9119
info@faithfm.org
kitchener.faithfm.org
Social Media: www.facebook.com/943FaithFM
Dave MacDonald, General Manager

***Kitchener:* CKBT-FM (91.5 The Beat)** (Freq: 91.5)
Owned by: Corus Premium Television Ltd.*
#210, 50 Sportsworld Crossing Rd., Kitchener, ON N2P 0A4
Tel: 519-772-1212, *Fax:* 519-772-1213
www.915thebeat.com
Social Media: www.facebook.com/915thebeat, twitter.com/915theBeat
Scot Turner, Program Director

***Kitchener:* CKWR-FM** (Freq: 98.5)
1446 King St. East, Kitchener, ON N2G 2N7
Tel: 519-886-9870, *Fax:* 519-886-0090
general@ckwr.com
www.ckwr.com
Social Media: www.facebook.com/HANSCKWR
Henning Grumme, Contact, hgrumme@ckwr.com

***Leamington:* CHYR-FM** (Freq: 96.7)
Owned by: Blackburn Radio Inc.*
100 Talbot St. East, Leamington, ON N8H 1L3
Tel: 519-326-6171, *Fax:* 519-322-1110
Toll-Free: 800-567-9696
info@blackburnradio.com
mix967.ca
Social Media: www.youtube.com/user/chyrfm, www.facebook.com/mix967, twitter.com/themix967

***Lindsay:* CKLY-FM** (Freq: 91.9)
Owned by: Bell Media Radio*
249 Kent St. West, Lindsay, ON K9V 2Z3
Tel: 705-324-9103, *Fax:* 705-324-4149
bob@919bobfm.com
www.919bobfm.com
Social Media: www.facebook.com/919bobfm, twitter.com/919bobfm
Steve Fawcett, General Manager, Steve.Fawcett@bellmedia.ca

***London:* CBBL-FM** (Freq: 100.5)
Owned by: Canadian Broadcasting Corporation
London, ON
www.cbc.ca

***London:* CBCL-FM** (Freq: 93.5)
Owned by: Canadian Broadcasting Corporation*
208 Piccadilly St., London, ON N6A 1S1
Tel: 519-667-1990
www.cbc.ca/radio

***London:* CFHK-FM (103.1 Fresh FM)** (Freq: 103.1)
Owned by: Corus Radio Company*
#222, 380 Wellington Rd., London, ON N6A 5B5
Tel: 519-931-6000, *Fax:* 519-679-1967
www.1031freshfm.com
Social Media: www.youtube.com/user/Thenew1031freshFM, www.facebook.com/1031freshfm, twitter.com/1031FreshFM
Brad Gibb, Brand Director

***London:* CFPL-FM (FM96)** (Freq: 95.9)
Owned by: Corus Radio Company*
#222, 380 Wellington St., London, ON N6A 5B5
Tel: 519-931-6000, *Fax:* 519-679-1967
www.fm96.com
Social Media: www.youtube.com/user/FM96Tube, www.facebook.com/FM96London, twitter.com/FM96Rocks
Brad Gibb, Brand Director

***London:* CHJX-FM** (Freq: 99.9)
#100, 120 Wellington St., London, ON N6B 2K6
Tel: 519-679-2459, *Fax:* 519-679-8014
info@london.faithfm.org
faithfm.org/london
Social Media: www.facebook.com/faithfm.org, twitter.com/999FaithFM
Dave Wettlaufer, General Manager, davew@faithfm.org

***London:* CHRW-FM** (Freq: 94.9)
Western University, #250, University Community Centre, London, ON N6A 3K7
Tel: 519-661-3601
chrwgm@chrwradio.ca
chrwradio.ca
Social Media: www.youtube.com/user/chrwradio, www.facebook.com/chrwradio, twitter.com/chrwradio
Grant Stein, Station Manager
Allison Brown, Program Director, chrwpd@chrwradio.ca
Ed von Aderkas, News, Sports & Spoken Word Director, chrwnd@chrwradio.ca

***London:* CHST-FM** (Freq: 102.3)
Owned by: Rogers Broadcasting Ltd.*
1 Communications Rd., London, ON N6J 4Z1
Tel: 519-690-0102
www.1023bob.com
Social Media: plus.google.com/105322528118704110567, www.facebook.com/1023BOBFM, twitter.com/1023bobfm
Mike Collins, General Manager, 519-690-0102
Pete Travers, Program Director, 519-690-0102

***London:* CIQM-FM (97.5 Virgin Radio)** (Freq: 97.5)
Owned by: Bell Media Inc.*
743 Wellington Rd. South, London, ON N6C 4R5
Tel: 519-686-2525
london.virginradio.ca
Social Media: instagram.com/975virginlondon, www.facebook.com/975VirginRadioLondon, twitter.com/975VirginLondon
Don Mumford, General Manager, don.mumford@bellmedia.ca

***London:* CIXX-FM** (Freq: 106.9)
PO Box 7005, London, ON N5Y 5R6
Tel: 519-453-2810
www.fanshawemedia.ca
Social Media: www.youtube.com/user/1069TheX, www.facebook.com/1069TheX, twitter.com/1069TheX

***London:* CJBX-FM (BX93)** (Freq: 92.7)
Owned by: Bell Media Inc.*
743 Wellington Rd. South, London, ON N6C 4R5
Tel: 519-685-2525
www.bx93.com
Social Media: www.facebook.com/BX93London, twitter.com/bx93
Don Mumford, General Manager, don.mumford@bellmedia.ca

***Markham:* CHKT-FM** (Freq: 88.9)
Owned by: Fairchild Radio*
#26-29, 151 Esna Park Dr., Markham, ON L3R 3B1
Tel: 905-415-1430, *Fax:* 905-415-6292
www.am1430.com

***Midland:* CICZ-FM** (Freq: 104.1)
355 Cranston Cres., Midland, ON L4R 4L3
Tel: 705-720-1991, *Fax:* 705-526-3060
1041thedock.com
Social Media: www.facebook.com/1041thedock, twitter.com/1041thedock
Mora Austin, General Manager, mora.austin@larchecom.com

***Mississauga:* CFRE-FM** (Freq: 91.9)
University of Toronto, Mississauga, #131, 3359 Mississauga Rd., Mississauga, ON L5L 1C6
Tel: 905-828-2088
info@cfreradio.com
www.cfreradio.com
Social Media: www.youtube.com/user/cfreradio, www.facebook.com/cfreradio, www.twitter.com/cfreradio
Monique Swaby, Station Manager, monique@cfreradio.com

***Napanee:* CKYM-FM (myFM)** (Freq: 88.7)
Owned by: My Broadcasting Corporation*
11 Market Sq., Napanee, ON K7R 1J4
Tel: 613-354-4554, *Fax:* 613-354-3661
www.napaneetoday.ca
Social Media: www.facebook.com/887myfm, twitter.com/887myFM
Pam Oliver, Contact

***New Liskeard:* CJTT-FM** (Freq: 104.5)
Owned by: Connelly Communications Corp.*
PO Box 1058, 55 Whitewood Ave., New Liskeard, ON P0J 1P0
Tel: 705-647-7334, *Fax:* 705-647-8660
cjtt@cjttfm.com
www.cjttfm.com
Social Media: www.facebook.com/171612742872981, twitter.com/1045cjttfm

***Neyaashiinigmiing:* CHFN-FM** (Freq: 100.1)
67 Community Centre Rd., Neyaashiinigmiing, ON N0H 2T0
Tel: 519-534-1003, *Fax:* 519-534-4916
chfn@ymail.com
www.nawash.ca/chfn-100-1
Social Media: www.facebook.com/pages/CHFN-1001/137257499685779
Waylynne Elliott, Contact

***Niagara Falls:* CFLZ-FM (101.1 Juice FM)** (Freq: 101.1)
Owned by: Vista Broadcast Group*
Niagara Falls, ON
Tel: 905-356-6710, *Fax:* 905-356-0644
1011.juicefm.ca
Social Media: www.facebook.com/1011juicefm, twitter.com/1011juicefm

***Niagara Falls:* CJED-FM (105.1 2Day FM)** (Freq: 105.1)
Owned by: Vista Broadcast Group*
4673 Ontario Ave., Niagara Falls, ON L2E 3R1
Tel: 905-356-6710, *Fax:* 905-356-0644
www.1051.2dayfm.ca

***North Bay:* CFXN-FM (Moose FM)** (Freq: 106.3)
Owned by: Vista Broadcast Group*
118 Main St. East, North Bay, ON P1B 1A8
Tel: 705-475-9991, *Fax:* 705-475-9058
www.moosefm.com/cfxn
Social Media: www.facebook.com/MooseFMNorthBay
Mike Trahan, General Manager, Sales, 705-475-9991

***North Bay:* CHUR-FM** (Freq: 100.5)
Owned by: Rogers Broadcasting Ltd.*
273 Main St. East, North Bay, ON P1B 8K8
Tel: 705-479-2000
www.ezrocknorthbay.com
Social Media: www.facebook.com/KISSNorthBay, twitter.com/KISSNorthBay
Holly Cangiano, General Manager, holly.cangiano@northbayradio.rogers.com

***North Bay:* CKFX-FM** (Freq: 101.9)
Owned by: Rogers Broadcasting Ltd.*
743 Main St. East, North Bay, ON P1B 1C2
Tel: 705-474-2000
thefox@foxradio.ca
www.foxradio.ca
Social Media: plus.google.com/114407550964508169733, www.facebook.com/1019thefox, twitter.com/1019thefox
Mitch Belanger, Program Director, mitch.belanger@northbayradio.rogers.com
Holly Cangiano, General Manager, holly.cangiano@northbayradio.rogers.com

***North Bay:* CRFM-FM** (Freq: 89.9)
Canadore College, 100 College Dr., North Bay, ON P1B 8K9
Tel: 705-474-7601
www.ThePanther.ca
Social Media: www.facebook.com/233056936793545, twitter.com/panthertweet

***Orillia:* CICX-FM** (Freq: 105.9)
Owned by: Rogers Broadcasting Ltd.*
7 Progress Dr., RR#1, Orillia, ON L3V 6K2
Tel: 705-722-5429, *Fax:* 705-326-1816
kicx106.com
Social Media: www.facebook.com/kicx106, twitter.com/kicx106
Mora Austrin, General Manager, mora.austin@larchecom.com

***Orillia:* CISO-FM (Sunshine)** (Freq: 89.1)
Owned by: Bayshore Broadcasting Corporation*
#2, 490 West St. North, Orillia, ON L3V 5E8
Tel: 705-325-9786, *Fax:* 705-325-2600
Toll-Free: 888-536-9786
info@sunshine891.ca
www.sunshine891.ca
Social Media: www.facebook.com/sunshine891, twitter.com/sunshineorillia
Other information: News E-mail: news@sunshine891.ca; Sales E-mail: sales@sunshine891.ca
Kevin Brown, Vice-President, Sales & Marketing, sales@bayshorebroadcasting.ca

***Oshawa:* CJKX-FM** (Freq: 95.9; 89.9)
#207, 1200 Airport Blvd., Oshawa, ON L1J 8P5
Tel: 905-571-0949, *Fax:* 905-571-1150
www.kx96.fm
Social Media: www.youtube.com/user/kx96fm, www.facebook.com/KX96Country, twitter.com/kx96
Steve Kassay, Vice-President, Programming, steve@kx96.fm

** For details on this company see listing in Major Broadcasting Companies section; † French language station*

Oshawa: CKGE-FM (Freq: 94.9)
#207, 1200 Airport Blvd., Oshawa, ON L1J 8P5
Tel: 905-571-0949, *Fax:* 905-579-1150
www.therock.fm
Social Media: www.youtube.com/CKGEFM, www.facebook.com/949therock.fm, twitter.com/949therock
Steve Kassay, Vice-President, Programming, steve@kx96.fm

Ottawa: CBOF-FM (Freq: 90.7)
Owned by: Canadian Broadcasting Corporation*
181, rue Queen, Ottawa, ON K1Y 1E4
Tel: 613-288-6000
ici.radio-canada.ca/ottawa-gatineau
Marco Dubé, Directeur, Radio-Canada Ottawa-Gatineau, 613-288-6705, Fax: 613-288-6703, Marco.Dube@radio-canada.ca
Chantal Jolicoeur, Chef de la programmation et des affaires publiques, 613-288-6547, Fax: 613-288-6703, chantal.jolicoeur@radio-canada.ca

Ottawa: CBO-FM (Freq: 91.5)
Owned by: Canadian Broadcasting Corporation*
PO Box 3220 C, Ottawa, ON K1Y 1E4
Tel: 613-288-6000
cbcnewsottawa@cbc.ca
www.cbc.ca/ottawa
Ruth Zowdu, Executive Producer, Radio Current Affairs & local programming

Ottawa: CBOQ-FM (Freq: 103.3)
Owned by: Canadian Broadcasting Corporation*
PO Box 3220 C, Ottawa, ON K1Y 1E4
Tel: 613-288-6000
www.cbc.ca/ottawa

†Ottawa: CBOX-FM (Freq: 102.5)
Détenteur: Canadian Broadcasting Corporation*
181, rue Queen, Ottawa, ON K1Y 1E4
Tél: 613-288-6000
www.icimusique.ca
Marco Dubé, Directeur, Radio-Canada Ottawa-Gatineau, Marco.Dube@radio-canada.ca

Ottawa: CHEZ-FM (Freq: 106.1)
Owned by: Rogers Broadcasting Ltd.*
2001 Thurston Dr., Ottawa, ON K1G 6C9
Tel: 613-736-2001
www.chez106.com
Social Media: www.facebook.com/Chez106, twitter.com/chez106

Ottawa: CHRI-FM (Freq: 99.1)
#3, 1010 Thomas Spratt Pl., Ottawa, ON K1G 5L5
Tel: 613-247-1440, *Fax:* 613-247-7128
Toll-Free: 866-247-1440
chri@chri.ca
www.chri.ca
Social Media: www.youtube.com/user/CHRIradio, www.facebook.com/chriradio, twitter.com/CHRIRadio

Ottawa: CHUO-FM (Freq: 89.1)
#0038, 65 University Pvt., Ottawa, ON K1N 9A5
Tel: 613-562-5965
prog@chuo.fm
chuo.fm
Social Media: instagram.com/chuo891fm, www.facebook.com/chuofm, twitter.com/chuofm
Erin Flynn, Station Manager, erin@chuo.fm

Ottawa: CIHT-FM (Hot 89.9) (Freq: 89.9)
Owned by: Newcap Radio*
#100, 6 Antares Dr., Ottawa, ON K2E 8A9
Tel: 613-723-8990, *Fax:* 613-723-7016
www.hot899.com
Social Media: www.facebook.com/ottawahot899/, twitter.com/newhot899
Scott Broderick, General Manager, sbroderick@newcap.ca
Josie Fenech, Program Director, josie@hot899.com

Ottawa: CILV-FM (Live 88.5) (Freq: 88.5)
Owned by: Newcap Radio*
#100, 6 Antares Dr., Phase 1, Ottawa, ON K2E 8A9
Tel: 613-688-8888, *Fax:* 613-723-7016
www.live885.com
Social Media: www.youtube.com/live885, www.facebook.com/live885, twitter.com/Live885fm
Scott Broderick, Station Manager, sbroderick@newcap.ca
Dan Youngs, Program Director, dyoungs@newcap.ca

Ottawa: CISS-FM (Freq: 105.3)
Owned by: Rogers Broadcasting Ltd.*
2001 Thurston Dr., Ottawa, ON K1G 6C9
Tel: 613-736-2001
www.1053kissfm.com
Social Media: plus.google.com/100055255267223461562, www.facebook.com/1053kissfm, twitter.com/1053kissfm

Ottawa: CJLL-FM (CHIN) (Freq: 97.9)
#100, 30 Murray St., Ottawa, ON K1N 5M4
Tel: 613-244-0979, *Fax:* 613-244-3858
Toll-Free: 866-697-0979
chinottawa@chinradio.com
www.chinradioottawa.com
Social Media: www.youtube.com/chinradioottawa, www.facebook.com/chinradioottawa, twitter.com/CHINRadioottawa
Francesco Di Candia, General Manager

Ottawa: CJMJ-FM (Freq: 100.3)
Owned by: Bell Media Radio*
87 George St., Ottawa, ON K1N 9H7
Tel: 613-789-2486
webmaster@majic100.fm
www.majic100.fm
Social Media: www.facebook.com/Majic100, twitter.com/MAJIC100Ottawa
Ian March, Program Director, ian.march@bellmedia.ca

Ottawa: CJOT-FM (boom 99.7) (Freq: 99.7)
Owned by: Corus Entertainment Inc.*
1504 Merivale Rd., Ottawa, ON K2E 6Z5
Tel: 613-225-1069
www.boom997.com
Social Media: www.youtube.com/user/boom997ottawa, www.facebook.com/boom99.7, twitter.com/boomottawa
Mark Dickie, General Manager, mark.dickie@corusent.com

Ottawa: CJWL-FM (The Jewel 98.5) (Freq: 98.5)
Owned by: Evanov Radio Group*
127 York St., Ottawa, ON K1N 5T4
Tel: 613-241-9850, *Fax:* 613-241-9852
silver@985thejewel.com
www.jewelradio.com/985
Social Media: www.facebook.com/pages/Jewel-985/310233766395, twitter.com/985thejewel

Ottawa: CKBY-FM (Freq: 101.1)
Owned by: Rogers Broadcasting Ltd.*
2001 Thurston Dr., Ottawa, ON K2J 6C9
Tel: 613-736-2001, *Fax:* 613-736-2002
www.y101.fm
Social Media: plus.google.com/111229961884345231553, www.facebook.com/country1011, twitter.com/country1011fm

Ottawa: CKCU-FM (Freq: 93.1)
University Centre, Carleton University, #517, 1125 Colonel By Dr., Ottawa, ON K1S 5B6
Tel: 613-520-2898, *Fax:* 613-520-4060
info@ckcufm.com
www.ckcufm.com
Social Media: www.facebook.com/CKCUFM, twitter.com/ckcufm
Matthew Croiser, Station Manager, 613-520-2600, manager@ckcufm.com

Ottawa: CKDJ-FM (Freq: 107.9)
Algonquin College, 1385 Woodroffe Ave., Ottawa, ON K2G 1V8
Tel: 613-750-2535
ckdj@algonquincollege.com
www.ckdj.net
Social Media: www.youtube.com/user/ckdj1079video, www.facebook.com/CKDJ1079, twitter.com/ckdj1079

Ottawa: CKKL-FM (Freq: 93.9)
Owned by: Bell Media Radio*
87 George St., Ottawa, ON K1N 9H7
Tel: 613-789-2486
www.939bobfm.com
Social Media: www.facebook.com/BOBFMOttawa, twitter.com/bobfmottawa
Ian March, Program Director

Ottawa: CKQB-FM (Jump! 106.9) (Freq: 106.9)
Owned by: Corus Entertainment Inc.*
1504 Merivale Rd, Ottawa, ON K2E 6Z5
Tel: 613-225-1069, *Fax:* 613-226-3381
www.jumpradio.ca
Social Media: www.youtube.com/user/JumpOttawa, www.facebook.com/JumpOttawa, twitter.com/JumpOttawa
Mark Dickie, General Manager, mark.dickie@corusent.com

Owen Sound: CIXK-FM (Mix 106.5) (Freq: 106.5)
Owned by: Bayshore Broadcasting Corporation*
PO Box 280, Owen Sound, ON N4K 5P5
Tel: 519-376-2030, *Fax:* 519-371-4242
www.mix106.ca
Social Media: www.youtube.com/mix1065owensound, www.facebook.com/mix1065owensound, twitter.com/Mix1065OnAir
Kevin Brown, Vice-President, Sales & Marketing, sales@bayshorebroadcasting.ca

Owen Sound: CJLF-FM-1 (Freq: 90.1)
Owned by: CJLF-FM (Life 100.3)
Owen Sound, ON
www.lifeonline.fm

Owen Sound: CKYC-FM (Country 93) (Freq: 93.7)
Owned by: Bayshore Broadcasting Corporation*
PO Box 280, Owen Sound, ON N4K 5P5
Tel: 519-376-2030, *Fax:* 519-371-4242
www.country93.ca
Social Media: www.youtube.com/todaysbestcountry, www.facebook.com/country937, twitter.com/country93
Kevin Brown, Vice-President, Sales & Marketing, sales@bayshorebroadcasting.ca

Parry Sound: CKLP-FM (Moose FM) (Freq: 103.3)
Owned by: Vista Broadcast Group*
#301, 60 James St., Parry Sound, ON P2A 1T5
Tel: 705-746-2163, *Fax:* 705-746-4292
www.myparrysoundnow.com
Social Media: www.facebook.com/mooseckIp, twitter.com/moosefmcklp

Pembroke: CHVR-FM (Star 96) (Freq: 96.7)
Owned by: Bell Media Inc.*
595 Pembroke St. East, Pembroke, ON K8A 3L7
Tel: 613-735-9670, *Fax:* 613-735-7748
star96@bellmedia.ca
www.star96.ca
Social Media: www.facebook.com/star96fm
Richard Gray, General Manager, richard.gray@bellmedia.ca
Tracy McBride, Sales Manager, tracy.mcbride@bellmedia.ca

Pembroke: CIMY-FM (myFM) (Freq: 104.9)
Owned by: My Broadcasting Corporation*
84 Isabella St., Pembroke, ON K8A 5S5
Tel: 613-735-6936, *Fax:* 613-732-4054
www.pembroketoday.ca
Social Media: www.facebook.com/1049myfm, twitter.com/1049myFM
Marc Poirier, Contact

†Penetanguishene: CFRH-FM (Freq: 88.1)
CP 5099, Penetanguishene, ON L9M 2G3
Tél: 705-549-8288, *Téléc:* 705-549-6463
vaguefm@vaguefm.ca
vaguefm.ca
Médias sociaux: www.facebook.com/pages/CFRH-881-VAGUE-FM/104742480799
Mélanie Bouchard, Gérante, mbouchard@lacle.ca

Peterborough: CFFF-FM (Freq: 92.7)
Trent University, 715 George St. North, Peterborough, ON K9H 3T2
Tel: 705-741-4011
Info@TrentRadio.cadio.ca
www.trentu.ca/org/trentradio
Other information: Studio: 705-748-4761
John K. Muir, General Manager

Peterborough: CJWV-FM (Magic 96.7) (Freq: 96.7)
Owned by: Pineridge Broadcasting Inc.
#1, 360 George St. North, Peterborough, ON K9H 7E7
Tel: 705-876-7773, *Fax:* 705-876-1917
Toll-Free: 888-668-0967
magic967.fm
Social Media: www.facebook.com/Magic967fm, twitter.com/magic967fm

Peterborough: CKPT-FM (Freq: 99.7)
Owned by: Bell Media Radio*
PO Box 177, 59 George St. North, Peterborough, ON K9J 6Y8
Tel: 705-742-8844, *Fax:* 705-742-1417
energy997@chumradio.com
www.energy997.ca
Social Media: www.facebook.com/Energy997, twitter.com/energy997
Steve Fawcett, General Manager, steve.fawcett@bellmedia.ca

** For details on this company see listing in Major Broadcasting Companies section; † French language station*

***Peterborough:* CKQM-FM** (Freq: 105.1)
Owned by: Bell Media Radio*
PO Box 177, 59 George St. North, Peterborough, ON K9J 6Y8
Tel: 705-742-8844, *Fax:* 705-742-1417
www.country105.fm
Social Media: www.facebook.com/Country105Peterborough, twitter.com/Country1051
Steve Fawcett, General Manager, 705-742-8844, steve.fawcett@bellmedia.ca
Brian Young, Program Director, brian.young@bellmedia.ca

***Peterborough:* CKRU-FM (100.6 KRUZ FM)** (Freq: 100.5)
Owned by: 591989 B.C. Ltd.*
#200, 151 King St., Peterborough, ON K9J 2R8
Tel: 705-748-6101, *Fax:* 705-742-7708
www.kruzfm.ca
Social Media: www.youtube.com/channel/UCWw9-pkpiVYtFI7MYPLORyg, www.facebook.com/KruzFM, twitter.com/KruzFM
Rob Seguin, Program Director & Brand Manager

***Peterborough:* CKWF-FM (The Wolf 101.5)** (Freq: 101.5)
Owned by: 591989 B.C. Ltd.*
#200, 151 King St., Peterborough, ON K9J 2R8
Tel: 705-748-6101, *Fax:* 705-742-7708
www.thewolf.ca
Social Media: www.facebook.com/thewolf1015, twitter.com/thewolfca
Rob Seguin, Program Director & Brand Manager

***Port Elgin:* CFPS-FM (98 the Beach)** (Freq: 97.9)
Owned by: Bayshore Broadcasting Corporation*
382 Goderich St., Port Elgin, ON N0H 2C1
Tel: 519-832-9800, *Fax:* 519-832-9808
Toll-Free: 877-652-9800
info@98thebeach.ca
www.98thebeach.ca
Social Media: www.youtube.com/beachradio, www.facebook.com/98thebeach, twitter.com/98thebeach
Kevin Brown, Vice-President, Sales & Marketing, sales@bayshorebroadcasting.ca

***Port Elgin:* CIYN-FM-2 (myFM)** (Freq: 90.9)
Owned by: CIYN-FM (myFM)
Port Elgin, ON
Tel: 613-396-7770
www.shorelinetoday.ca
Dylan Bartlett, Contact, Advertising

***Red Lake:* CKDR-5** (Freq: 97.1)
Owned by: CKDR-FM
Red Lake, ON

***Renfrew:* CHMY-FM (myFM)** (Freq: 96.1)
Owned by: My Broadcasting Corporation*
PO Box 961, Renfrew, ON K7V 4H4
Tel: 613-432-6936, *Fax:* 613-432-1086
www.renfrewtoday.ca
Social Media: www.facebook.com/961myfm, twitter.com/961myFM
Angela Kluke, Contact

***Sarnia:* CBEG-FM** (Freq: 90.3)
Owned by: Canadian Broadcasting Corporation
Sarnia, ON
Sandra Porteous, Managing Editor, Radio & Television, 519-255-3563
David Daigneault, Executive Producer, Radio & Television, 519-255-3410

***Sarnia:* CFGX-FM** (Freq: 99.9)
Owned by: Blackburn Radio Inc.*
1415 London Rd., Sarnia, ON N7S 1P6
Tel: 519-542-5500
www.foxfm.com
Social Media: www.youtube.com/foxfmsarnia, www.facebook.com/foxfmsarnia, twitter.com/foxfmsarnia

***Sarnia:* CHKS-FM** (Freq: 106.3)
Owned by: Blackburn Radio Inc.*
1415 London Rd., Sarnia, ON N7S 1P6
Tel: 519-542-5500
rock@k106fm.com
www.k106fm.com
Social Media: www.youtube.com/user/k1063fm, www.facebook.com/K1063, twitter.com/k1063sarnia

***Sault Ste Marie:* CHAS-FM** (Freq: 100.5)
Owned by: Rogers Broadcasting Ltd.*
642 Great Northern Rd., Sault Ste Marie, ON P6B 4Z9
Tel: 705-759-9200, *Fax:* 705-946-3575
www.ezrocksoo.com
Social Media: plus.google.com/112874858720110727380, www.facebook.com/kiss.ssm, twitter.com/kiss_soo
Scott Sexsmith, General Manager, scott.sexsmith@ssmradio.rogers.com

***Sault Ste Marie:* CJQM-FM** (Freq: 104.3)
Owned by: Rogers Broadcasting Ltd.*
642 Great Northern Rd., Sault Ste Marie, ON P6B 4Z9
Tel: 705-759-9200, *Fax:* 705-946-3575
www.qcountry.ca
Social Media: plus.google.com/100580849359302461611, www.facebook.com/country1043, twitter.com/country1043
Gary Creighton, Contact, Programming, gary.creighton@rci.rogers.com

***Simcoe:* CHCD-FM (myFM)** (Freq: 98.9)
Owned by: My Broadcasting Corporation*
PO Box 98, Simcoe, ON N3Y 4K8
Tel: 519-426-7700, *Fax:* 519-426-8574
www.norfolktoday.ca
Social Media: www.facebook.com/171942679620136, twitter.com/myFM989

***Sioux Lookout:* CKWT-FM** (Freq: 89.9)
Owned by: Wawatay Radio Network*
PO Box 1180, 16 - 5th Ave., Sioux Lookout, ON P8T 1B7
Tel: 807-737-2951, *Fax:* 807-737-3224
Toll-Free: 800-243-9059
www.wawataynews.ca/radio
Social Media: www.facebook.com/wawataynews, twitter.com/wawataynews

***Smiths Falls:* CJET-FM** (Freq: 92.3)
Owned by: Rogers Broadcasting Ltd.*
PO Box 430, Smiths Falls, ON K7A 4T4
Tel: 613-283-4630, *Fax:* 613-283-7243
www.923jackfm.com
Social Media: plus.google.com/108995144295544720542, www.facebook.com/923jackfm, twitter.com/923jackfm
Mark Hunter, General Sales Manager, 613-736-2001, markp.hunter@rci.rogers.com
Kalum Figura, Retail Sales Manager, 613-736-2001, kalum.figura@rci.rogers.com

***St Catharines:* CFBU-FM** (Freq: 103.7)
c/o 500 Glenridge Ave., St Catharines, ON L2S 3A1
Tel: 905-688-2644
pd@cfbu.ca
www.cfbu.ca
Social Media: www.facebook.com/brockradio103.7, twitter.com/cfbu1037
Deborah Cartmer, Program Director

***St Catharines:* CHRE-FM (Niagara's EZ Rock)** (Freq: 105.7)
Owned by: Bell Media Inc.*
12 Yates St., St Catharines, ON L2R 5R2
Tel: 905-688-1057
www.1057ezrock.com
Social Media: www.facebook.com/1057ezrock, twitter.com/1057ezrock
Bob Harris, General Manager, bob.harris@bellmedia.ca

***St Catharines:* CHTZ-FM (HTZ-FM)** (Freq: 97.7)
Owned by: Bell Media Inc.*
12 Yates St., St Catharines, ON L2R 5R2
Tel: 905-688-0977, *Fax:* 905-684-4800
www.htzfm.com
Social Media: www.facebook.com/977HTZFM, twitter.com/977HTZFM
Bob Harris, General Manager, bob.harris@bellmedia.ca

***St Thomas:* CKZM-FM (myFM)** (Freq: 94.1)
Owned by: My Broadcasting Corporation*
Grand Central Place, #2, 300 Talbot St., St Thomas, ON N5P 4E2
Tel: 519-633-6936, *Fax:* 519-637-8410
www.stthomastoday.ca
Social Media: www.facebook.com/941myfm, twitter.com/myFM_News941
Rob Mise, Contact

***Stratford:* CHGK-FM** (Freq: 107.7)
Owned by: Vista Broadcast Group*
376 Romeo St. South, Stratford, ON N5A 4T6
Tel: 519-271-2450, *Fax:* 519-271-3102
www.fm1077stratford.com
Social Media: www.facebook.com/229060673782438
Alex Stephens, General Manager, Sales, 519-271-2450

***Strathroy:* CJMI-FM (myFM)** (Freq: 105.7)
Owned by: My Broadcasting Corporation*
85 Zimmerman St. South, Strathroy, ON N7G 0A3
Tel: 519-246-6936, *Fax:* 519-245-6670
www.strathroytoday.ca
Social Media: www.facebook.com/1057myfm, twitter.com/News1057

***Sturgeon Falls:* CFSF-FM (Moose FM)** (Freq: 99.3)
Owned by: Vista Broadcast Group*
#130, 204 King St., Sturgeon Falls, ON P2B 1R7
Tel: 705-475-9991
www.moosefm.com/cfsf
Social Media: www.facebook.com/202065813139933
Mike Trahan, General Manager, 705-475-9991

***†Sudbury:* CBBK-FM** (Freq: 90.9)
Détenteur: Canadian Broadcasting Corporation*
15, rue Mackenzie, Sudbury, ON P3C 4Y1
Tél: 705-688-3200, *Téléc:* 705-688-3220
Ligne sans frais: 800-461-1138
www.icimusique.ca
Robert McMillan, Responsable de l'affectation, robert.mcmillan@radio-canada.ca

***Sudbury:* CBBS-FM** (Freq: 90.1)
Owned by: Canadian Broadcasting Corporation*
15 MacKenzie St., Sudbury, ON P3C 4Y1
Tel: 705-688-3200
www.cbc.ca/sudbury
Fiona Christensen, Managing Editor, 705-688-3232

***†Sudbury:* CBBX-FM** (Freq: 90.9)
Détenteur: Canadian Broadcasting Corporation*
15 MacKenzie St., Sudbury, ON P3C 4Y1
Tél: 705-688-3200
www.icimusique.ca

***Sudbury:* CBCS-FM** (Freq: 99.9)
Owned by: Canadian Broadcasting Corporation*
15 MacKenzie St., Sudbury, ON P3C 4Y1
Tel: 705-688-3200, *Fax:* 705-688-3220
Toll-Free: 866-306-4636
www.cbc.ca/sudbury
Other information: Phone, Sudbury News: 705-688-3240; Toll-Free: 1-800-461-1138
Fiona Christensen, Managing Editor, 705-688-3232

***†Sudbury:* CBON-FM** (Freq: 98.1)
Détenteur: Canadian Broadcasting Corporation*
15 MacKenzie St., Sudbury, ON P3C 4Y1
Tél: 705-688-3200, *Ligne sans frais:* 800-641-1138
www.radio-canada.ca/regions/ontario
Médias sociaux: www.facebook.com/fm1017.ca, twitter.com/Fm1017Info

***Sudbury:* CHNO-FM (Rewind 103.9)** (Freq: 103.9)
Owned by: Newcap Radio*
493B Barrydowne Rd., Sudbury, ON P3A 3T4
Tel: 705-560-8323, *Fax:* 705-560-7765
news@rewind1039.ca
www.rewind1039.ca
Social Media: www.facebook.com/rewind1039sudbury/, twitter.com/Rewind_1039
Mike Cameron, General Manager, mcameron@newcap.ca
Rick Tompkins, Program Director, rtompkins@newcap.ca

***†Sudbury:* CHYC-FM (Le Loup 98.9)** (Freq: 98.9)
Détenteur: Le5 Communications*
#301, 336, rue Pine, Sudbury, ON P3C 1X8
Tél: 705-222-8306, *Téléc:* 705-222-2805
leloupfm.wix.com/leloup
Médias sociaux: www.facebook.com/leloupfm
Paul Lefebvre, Propriétaire, plefebvre@leloupfm.com

***Sudbury:* CIGM-FM (Hot 93.5)** (Freq: 93.5)
Owned by: Newcap Radio*
493-B Barrydowne Rd, Sudbury, ON P3A 3T4
Tel: 705-560-8323, *Fax:* 705-560-7765
info@hot935.ca
www.hot935.ca
Social Media: www.instagram.com/thenewhot935, www.facebook.com/thenewhot93.5, twitter.com/TheNewHot935
Mike Cameron, Station Manager, mcameron@newcap.ca

** For details on this company see listing in Major Broadcasting Companies section; † French language station*

Rick Tompkins, Program Director, rtompkins@newcap.ca

***Sudbury:* CJMX-FM** (Freq: 105.3)
Owned by: Rogers Broadcasting Ltd.*
880 Lasalle Blvd., Sudbury, ON P3A 1X5
Tel: 705-566-4480, *Fax:* 705-560-7232
www.ezrocksudbury.com
Social Media: plus.google.com/117380637041772396884, www.facebook.com/1053EZRock, twitter.com/kisssudbury

***Sudbury:* CJRQ-FM** (Freq: 92.7)
Owned by: Rogers Broadcasting Ltd.*
880 Lasalle Blvd., Sudbury, ON P3A 1X5
Tel: 705-566-4480, *Fax:* 705-560-7232
www.q92rocks.com
Social Media: plus.google.com/106948058024325133344, www.facebook.com/q92sudbury, twitter.com/q92sudbury
Kevin Britton, Contact, Programming/Music, kevin.britton@rci.rogers.com

***Sudbury:* CJTK-FM** (Freq: 95.5)
2150 Lasalle Blvd., Sudbury, ON P3A 2A7
Tel: 705-674-2585, *Fax:* 705-688-1081
Toll-Free: 888-674-2585
mail@kfmradio.ca
www.cjtk.com
Social Media: www.facebook.com/pages/KFM-Sudbury/8680749692
Curtis L. Belcher, Contact

***Sudbury:* CKLU-FM** (Freq: 96.7)
935 Ramsey Rd., Sudbury, ON P3E 2C6
Tel: 705-673-6538
traffic@cklu.ca
www.cklu.ca
Social Media: www.facebook.com/ckluradio, twitter.com/CKLURadio

***Thunder Bay:* CBQ-FM** (Freq: 101.7)
Owned by: Canadian Broadcasting Corporation*
213 Miles St. East, Thunder Bay, ON P7C 1J5
Tel: 807-625-5000
www.cbc.ca/thunderbay

***Thunder Bay:* CBQT-FM** (Freq: 88.3)
Owned by: Canadian Broadcasting Corporation*
213 East Miles St., Thunder Bay, ON P7C 1J5
Tel: 807-625-5000
www.cbc.ca/thunderbay
Sandra Porteus, Deputy Managing Director, Ontario

***Thunder Bay:* CBQX-FM** (Freq: 98.7)
Owned by: Canadian Broadcasting Corporation*
213 East Miles St., Thunder Bay, ON P7C 1J5
Tel: 807-625-5000, *Fax:* 807-625-5035
www.cbc.ca/thunderbay
Social Media: twitter.com/CBCTBay
Susan Porteus, Deputy Managing Director, Ontario, Sandra.Porteus@cbc.ca

***Thunder Bay:* CFNO-FM** (Freq: 93.1; 100.7)
Owned by: Dougall Media*
87 Hill St. North, Thunder Bay, ON P7A 5V6
Toll-Free: 888-621-1989
info@cfno.fm
www.cfno.fm
Bill Malcolm, Programming Director, bmalcolm@dougallmedia.com

***Thunder Bay:* CFQK-FM** (Freq: 103.5; 104.5)
Owned by: Dougall Media*
87 Hill St. North, Thunder Bay, ON P7A 5V6
Tel: 807-346-2600, *Fax:* 807-345-9923
Energy@Energyfm.fm
www.energyfm.fm
Social Media: www.facebook.com/Energy103104, twitter.com/Energy103104
Bill Malcolm, Program Director, bmalcolm@dougallmedia.com

***Thunder Bay:* CJOA-FM** (Freq: 95.1)
#42, 63 Carrie St., Thunder Bay, ON P7A 4J2
Tel: 807-344-9525, *Fax:* 807-344-9525
fm95@cjoa.ca
www.cjoa.org
Social Media: www.facebook.com/Cjoa95.1FmChristianRadioThunderBayOntario

***Thunder Bay:* CJSD-FM** (Freq: 94.3)
Owned by: Dougall Media*
87 Hill St. North, Thunder Bay, ON P7A 5V6
Tel: 807-346-2600, *Fax:* 807-345-9923
rock@rock94.com
www.rock94.com
Social Media: www.facebook.com/943rock
Brad Hilgers, Program Director, bhilgers@rock94.com

***Thunder Bay:* CJUK-FM** (Freq: 99.9)
#200, 180 Park Ave., Thunder Bay, ON P7B 6J4
Tel: 807-344-2000
magic@magic999.ca
www.magic999.ca
Social Media: instagram.com/magic999tbay, www.facebook.com/magicthunderbay, twitter.com/magicthunderbay

***Thunder Bay:* CKPR-FM** (Freq: 91.5)
Owned by: Dougall Media*
87 Hill St. North, Thunder Bay, ON P7A 5V6
Tel: 807-346-2600
radio@ckpr.com
www.ckpr.com
Social Media: www.facebook.com/915ckpr, twitter.com/915ckpr
Brad Hilgers, Program Director, bhilgers@dougallmedia.com

***Tillsonburg:* CKOT-FM** (Freq: 101.3)
PO Box 10, Tillsonburg, ON N4G 4H3
Tel: 519-842-4281, *Fax:* 519-842-4284
info@easy101.com
www.easy101.com
Social Media: www.facebook.com/pages/EASY-101/380722881968423

***Timmins:* CHMT-FM (Moose FM)** (Freq: 93.1)
Owned by: Vista Broadcast Group*
49 Cedar St. South, Timmins, ON P4N 2G5
Tel: 705-267-6070, *Fax:* 705-267-6095
Toll-Free: 866-728-9636
www.moosefm.com/chmt
Social Media: www.facebook.com/117620021634651, twitter.com/moosefmchmt
Barb McCartney, Contact, Sales

†*Timmins:* CHYK-FM (Le Loup) (Freq: 104.1)
Détenteur: Le5 Communications*
136, 3e av, Timmins, ON P4N 1C6
Tél: 705-269-8307, *Téléc:* 705-269-8305
leloupfm.wix.com/leloup
Médias sociaux: www.facebook.com/leloupfm
Paul Lefebvre, Propriétaire

***Timmins:* CJQQ-FM** (Freq: 92.1)
Owned by: Rogers Broadcasting Ltd.*
260 - 2nd Ave., Timmins, ON P4N 8A4
Tel: 705-264-2351, *Fax:* 705-264-2984
reply@q92timmins.com
www.q92timmins.com
Social Media: plus.google.com/104690183905063068352, www.facebook.com/q92timmins, twitter.com/TimminsQ92

***Timmins:* CKGB-FM** (Freq: 99.3)
Owned by: Rogers Broadcasting Ltd.*
260 - 2nd Ave., Timmins, ON P4N 8A4
Tel: 705-264-2351, *Fax:* 705-264-2984
www.kisstimmins.com
Social Media: plus.google.com/118187649916400925109, www.facebook.com/kisstimmins, twitter.com/kisstimmins

***Toronto:* CBLA-FM** (Freq: 99.1)
Owned by: Canadian Broadcasting Corporation*
PO Box 500 A, Toronto, ON M5W 1E6
Tel: 416-205-3311, *Toll-Free:* 866-306-4636
www.cbc.ca/toronto
Social Media: www.facebook.com/radiocbc, twitter.com/cbcradio
Cathy Perry, Managing Director, 416-205-3689

***Toronto:* CBL-FM** (Freq: 94.1)
Owned by: Canadian Broadcasting Corporation*
PO Box 500 A, Toronto, ON M5W 3G7
Tel: 416-205-3311, *Toll-Free:* 866-306-4636
www.cbc.ca/toronto
Cathy Perry, Managing Director, 416-205-3689

***Toronto:* CFIE-FM** (Freq: 106.5)
PO Box 87 E, Toronto, ON M6H 4E1
Tel: 416-703-1287, *Fax:* 416-703-4328
www.aboriginalvoices.com

***Toronto:* CFMZ-FM** (Freq: 96.3)
Owned by: ZoomerMedia*
70 Jefferson Ave., Toronto, ON M6K 1Y4
Tel: 416-367-5353, *Fax:* 416-367-1742
info@classical963fm.com
www.classical963fm.com
Social Media: Www.facebook.com/thenewclassical, twitter.com/classical963fm
John van Driel, Vice-President, Radio Programming & Operations, ZoomerMedia, jvd@mzmedia.com

***Toronto:* CFNY-FM (102.1 The Edge)** (Freq: 102.1)
Owned by: Corus Radio Company*
25 Dockside Dr., Toronto, ON M5A 0B5
Tel: 416-479-7000
www.edge.ca
Social Media: www.youtube.com/1021theedge, www.facebook.com/102edge, twitter.com/the_edge
Ronnie Stanton, Brand Director

***Toronto:* CFXJ-FM (93-5 The Move)** (Freq: 93.5)
Owned by: Newcap Radio*
2 St. Clair Ave. West, 2nd Fl., Toronto, ON M4V 1L6
Tel: 416-482-0973, *Fax:* 416-486-5696
www.935themove.com
Social Media: www.facebook.com/935TheMoveTO, twitter.com/935TheMoveTO
Lorie Russell, General Manager, lrussell@newcap.ca
Paul Parhar, Program Director, pparhar@newcap.ca

***Toronto:* CHBM-FM (Boom 97.3)** (Freq: 97.3)
Owned by: Newcap Radio*
2 St. Clair Ave. West, 20th Fl., Toronto, ON M4V 1L5
Tel: 416-482-0973, *Fax:* 416-486-5696
info@boom973.com
www.boom973.com
Social Media: www.facebook.com/boom973Toronto, twitter.com/boom973
Lorie Russell, General Manager, lrussell@newcap.ca
Troy McCallum, Program Director, tmccallum@boom973.com

***Toronto:* CHFI-FM** (Freq: 98.1)
Owned by: Rogers Broadcasting Ltd.*
1 Ted Rogers Way, Toronto, ON M4Y 3B7
Tel: 416-935-8298, *Fax:* 416-935-8260
www.chfi.com
Social Media: www.youtube.com/user/981chfi, www.facebook.com/981CHFI, twitter.com/981chfi

***Toronto:* CHIN-FM** (Freq: 100.7)
622 College St., Toronto, ON M6G 1B6
Tel: 416-531-9991, *Fax:* 416-531-5274
info@chinradio.com
www.chinradio.com
Social Media: www.facebook.com/chinradiocanada, twitter.com/chinradiocanada

***Toronto:* CHRY-FM** (Freq: 105.5)
York University, Student Centre, #413, 4700 Keele St., Toronto, ON M3J 1P3
Tel: 416-736-5293
chry@yorku.ca
www.chry.fm
Social Media: www.youtube.com/user/CHRYRadio, www.facebook.com/chryradio, twitter.com/chryradio

***Toronto:* CHUM-FM** (Freq: 104.5)
Owned by: Bell Media Radio*
299 Queen St. West, Toronto, ON M5V 2Z5
Tel: 416-925-6666
facebook@chumfm.com
www.chumfm.com
Social Media: www.pinterest.com/1045chumfm, www.facebook.com/1045CHUMFM, twitter.com/1045CHUMFM

***Toronto:* CIDC-FM** (Freq: 103.5)
Owned by: Evanov Communications*
5312 Dundas St. West, Toronto, ON M9B 1B2
Tel: 416-213-1035, *Fax:* 416-233-8617
info@z1035.com
www.z1035.com
Social Media: www.youtube.com/z1035tv, www.facebook.com/Z103.5, twitter.com/Z1035Toronto
Carmela Laurignano, Station Manager, carmela@z1035.com

***Toronto:* CILQ-FM (Q107)** (Freq: 107.1)
Owned by: Corus Premium Television Ltd.*
25 Dockside Dr., Toronto, ON M5A 0B5
Tel: 416-479-7000
www.q107.com
Social Media: www.youtube.com/q107classicrock, www.facebook.com/Q107Toronto, twitter.com/q107toronto

** For details on this company see listing in Major Broadcasting Companies section; † French language station*

Toronto: CIND-FM (Freq: 88.1)
20 Hanna Ave., Toronto, ON M6K 3E7
Tel: 416-588-7595
questions@indie88.com
indie88.com
Social Media: www.youtube.com/user/Indie88toronto, www.facebook.com/indie88toronto, twitter.com/Indie88Toronto
Megan Bingley, General Manager, megan@indie88.com

Toronto: CIRR-FM (Freq: 103.9)
Owned by: Evanov Radio Group*
5312 Dundas St. West, Toronto, ON M9B 1B3
Tel: 416-922-1039, *Fax:* 416-922-3692
www.proudfm.com
Social Media: instagram.com/proudfm, www.facebook.com/1039ProudFM, twitter.com/PROUDFM
Sheila Koenig, Creative Director, sheila@evanovradio.com

Toronto: CIRV-FM (Freq: 88.9)
1087 Dundas St. West, Toronto, ON M6J 1W9
Tel: 416-537-1088, *Fax:* 416-537-2463
info@cirvfm.com
www.cirvfm.com

Toronto: CIUT-FM (Freq: 89.5)
89.5 Tower Rd., 3rd Fl., Toronto, ON M5S 0A2
Tel: 416-978-0909
ciutoutreach@gmail.com
www.ciut.fm
Social Media: www.youtube.com/user/CIUTFM, www.facebook.com/CIUT895FM, twitter.com/CIUT895FM
Ken Stowar, Station Manager & Program Director, ken.stowar@ciut.fm

Toronto: CJAQ-FM (Freq: 92.5)
Owned by: Rogers Broadcasting Ltd.*
1 Ted Rogers Way, Toronto, ON M4Y 3B7
Tel: 416-935-8392
www.kiss925.com
Social Media: www.youtube.com/user/KiSS925Toronto, facebook.com/kiss925, twitter.com/kiss925toronto

†Toronto: CJBC-FM (Freq: 90.3)
Détenteur: Canadian Broadcasting Corporation*
CP 500 A, Toronto, ON M5W 1E6
Tél: 416-205-3311
www.icimusique.ca

Toronto: CJRT-FM (Freq: 91.1)
#100, 4 Pardee Ave., Toronto, ON M6K 3H5
Tel: 416-595-0404, *Fax:* 416-959-9413
info@jazz.fm
www.jazz.fm
Social Media: www.youtube.com/jazzfm91, www.facebook.com/jazzfm91, twitter.com/JAZZFM91
Bernard Webber, Chair
Ross Porter, President & CEO

Toronto: CKDX-FM (Freq: 88.5)
Owned by: Evanov Radio Group*
5312 Dundas St. West, Toronto, ON M9B 1B3
Tel: 416-213-1035, *Fax:* 416-233-8617
info@885thejewel.com
www.jewelradio.com/885
Social Media: www.facebook.com/jewel885, twitter.com/Jewel885
Doug Sexton, General Sales Manager, doug@885thejewel.com

Toronto: CKFM-FM (99.9 Virgin Radio) (Freq: 99.9)
Owned by: Bell Media Inc.*
299 Queen St. West, Toronto, ON M5V 2Z5
Tel: 416-922-9999
toronto.virginradio.ca
Social Media: www.youtube.com/999virginradio, www.facebook.com/999VirginToronto, twitter.com/999VirginTO

Toronto: CKHC-FM (Freq: 96.9)
205 Humber College Blvd., Toronto, ON M9W 5L7
Tel: 416-675-6622
radio.humber.ca
Social Media: instagram.com/radiohumber, www.facebook.com/RadioHumber, twitter.com/RadioHumber
Dean Sinclair, General Manager, Dean.Sinclair@Humber.ca

Toronto: CSCR-FM (Freq: 90.3)
University of Toronto Scarborough, 1265 Military Trail, Toronto, ON M1C 1A4
Tel: 416-287-7051
stationmanager@fusionradio.ca
www.fusionradio.ca
Social Media: instagram.com/fusion_radio, www.facebook.com/FusionRadioCSCR, twitter.com/fusionradio
Rudolf Ray, Station Manager

Waterloo: CFCA-FM (Freq: 105.3)
Owned by: Bell Media Radio*
#207, 255 King St. North, Waterloo, ON N2J 4V2
Tel: 519-884-4470
websupport@koolfm.com
www.koolfm.com
Social Media: instagram.com/kool1053, www.facebook.com/KOOLFM1053, twitter.com/1053koolfm
Paul Fisher, Vice President/General Manager, paul.fisher@bellmedia.ca

Waterloo: CKKW-FM (KFUN 99.5) (Freq: 99.5)
Owned by: Bell Media Radio*
#207, 255 King St. North, Waterloo, ON N2J 4V2
Tel: 519-884-4470
websupport@kfun995.com
www.kfun995.com
Social Media: www.facebook.com/KFUN995, twitter.com/995KFUN
Paul Fisher, Vice-President & General Manager, Bell Media Radio, Kitchener & London, paul.fisher@bellmedia.ca

Waterloo: CKMS-FM (Freq: 100.3)
#2, 108 King St. North, Waterloo, ON N2J 2X6
office@soundfm.ca
soundfm.ca

Wawa: CJWA-FM (Freq: 107.1)
PO Box 1447, 55 Broadway Ave., Wawa, ON P0S 1K0
Tel: 705-856-4555, *Fax:* 705-856-1520
Rick Labbe, President, ceojjam@bellnet.ca

Welland: CRNC-FM (Freq: 90.1)
300 Woodlawn Rd., Welland, ON L3C 7L3
Tel: 905-735-2211
theheat90.1@gmail.com
broadcasting.niagaracollege.ca/content/Radio/CRNCTheHeat.aspx
Social Media: www.facebook.com/901FMTHEHEAT, twitter.com/901FMTHEHEAT
Devin Jorgensen, Program Director

Windsor: CBE-FM (Freq: 89.9)
Owned by: Canadian Broadcasting Corporation*
825 Riverside Dr. West, Windsor, ON N9A 5K9
Tel: 519-255-3411
www.cbc.ca/windsor
Shawna Kelly, Managing Editor, Local News & Programs, 519-255-3563

Windsor: CIDR-FM (Freq: 93.9)
Owned by: Bell Media Radio*
1640 Ouellette Ave., Windsor, ON N8X 1L1
Tel: 519-258-8888
www.939theriverradio.com
Social Media: www.pinterest.com/939theriver, www.facebook.com/939theriverradio, twitter.com/939theriver
Sloane Cummings, Production Director

Windsor: CIMX-FM (Freq: 88.7)
Owned by: Bell Media Radio*
1640 Ouellette Ave., Windsor, ON N8X 1L1
Tel: 519-258-8888, *Fax:* 519-258-0182
programming@89xradio.com
www.89xradio.com
Social Media: www.facebook.com/89XFANS, twitter.com/TheOfficial89X

Windsor: CJAM-FM (Freq: 99.1)
University of Windsor, 401 Sunset Ave., Windsor, ON N9B 3P4
Tel: 519-971-3606, *Fax:* 519-971-3605
www.cjam.ca
Social Media: instagram.com/cjamfm, www.facebook.com/cjamfm, twitter.com/CJAMFM
Vernon Smith, Station Manager, statcjam@gmail.com

Wingham: CKNX-FM (Freq: 101.7)
Owned by: Blackburn Radio Inc.*
215 Carling Terrace, Wingham, ON N0G 2W0
Tel: 519-357-1310, *Fax:* 519-357-1897
Toll-Free: 800-265-3030
www.1017theone.ca
Social Media: www.facebook.com/pages/1017-The-One, twitter.com/1017theOne

Woodstock: CJFH-FM (Freq: 94.3)
1038 Parkinson Rd., Woodstock, ON N4S 7W3
Tel: 519-539-2304, *Fax:* 519-539-2011
www.hopefm.ca
Chris Gordon, Music Director, newmusic@hopefm.ca

Woodstock: CKDK-FM (Country 104) (Freq: 103.9)
Owned by: Corus Radio Company*
290 Dundas St., Woodstock, ON N4S 1B7
Tel: 519-931-6000
www.country104.com
Social Media: www.youtube.com/channel/UC1ftx6De5Ve_rJun47yyhXw, www.facebook.com/Country104, twitter.com/Country104
Brad Gibb, Program Director

Prince Edward Island

Charlottetown: CBCT-FM (Freq: 96.1)
Owned by: Canadian Broadcasting Corporation*
PO Box 2230, Charlottetown, PE C1A 8B9
Tel: 902-629-6400, *Fax:* 902-629-6518
www.cbc.ca/pei
Other information: Phone, News: 902-629-6402
Denise Wilson, Senior Managing Director, Atlantic Canada, denise.wilson@cbc.ca
Donna Allen, Executive Producer, Prince Edward Island News
Nadine Antle, Regional Manager, Partnerships, Communications, Brand, & Promot, 902-420-4223
Chantal Bernard, Senior Officer, Communications, Chantal.Bernard@cbc.ca

Charlottetown: CFCY-FM (Freq: 630)
Owned by: Maritime Broadcasting System*
5 Prince St., Charlottetown, PE C1A 4P4
Tel: 902-892-1066, *Fax:* 902-566-1338
cfcy.fm
Social Media: www.facebook.com/951fmcfcy, twitter.com/cfcy

Charlottetown: CHLQ-FM (Q93) (Freq: 93.1)
Owned by: Maritime Broadcasting System*
5 Prince St., Charlottetown, PE C1A 4P4
Tel: 902-892-1066, *Fax:* 902-566-1338
q93.fm
Social Media: www.facebook.com/Q93ROCKS, twitter.com/Q93ROCKS

Charlottetown: CHTN-FM (Ocean 100) (Freq: 100.3; 99.9; 89.9)
Owned by: Newcap Radio*
176 Great George St., Charlottetown, PE C1A 4K9
Tel: 902-569-1003, *Fax:* 902-569-8693
www.ocean1003.com
Social Media: www.facebook.com/ocean100, twitter.com/ocean100
Jennifer Evans, General Manager, jevans@newcap.ca

Charlottetown: CKQK-FM (Hot 105.5) (Freq: 105.5)
Owned by: Newcap Radio*
176 Great George St, Charlottetown, PE C1A 4K9
Tel: 902-569-1003, *Fax:* 902-569-8693
www.hot1055fm.com
Social Media: www.instagram.com/thenewhot1055, www.facebook.com/Hot1055, twitter.com/thehot1055
Jennifer Evans, General Manager, jevans@newcap.ca
Matt MacLeod, Program Director, mmacleod@newcap.ca

Elmira: CKQK-FM-1 (Hot 105.5) (Freq: 103.7)
Owned by: CKQK-FM*
Elmira, PE
Tel: 902-569-1003, *Fax:* 902-569-8693
www.hot1055fm.com

St. Edwards: CKQK-FM-2 (Hot 105.5) (Freq: 91.1)
Owned by: CKQK-FM*
St. Edwards, PE
Tel: 902-569-1003, *Fax:* 902-569-8693
www.hot1055fm.com

Québec

Akwesasne: CKON-FM (Freq: 97.3)
#2, 22 Hilltop Dr., Akwesasne, QC H0H 1A0
Tel: 613-575-2100, *Fax:* 613-575-2566
frontdesk@ckonfm.com
www.ckonfm.com
Social Media: Www.facebook.com/pages/CKON-Radio/452385308168295, twitter.com/ckonradio
Reen Cook, News Director

* For details on this company see listing in Major Broadcasting Companies section; † French language station

†*Alma:* CFGT-FM (Planète 104.5) (Freq: 104.5)
Détenteur: Groupe Radio Antenne 6 Inc.*
460, rue Sacré-Coeur ouest, Alma, QC G8B 1L9
Tél: 418-662-6888
www.alma.planeteradio.ca
Médias sociaux: www.facebook.com/205430152830652

***Amos:* CHOW-FM** (Freq: 105.3)
42, 1re ave Est, Amos, QC J9T 1H2
Tel: 819-732-6991, *Fax:* 819-732-6988
info@radioboreale.com
www.radioboreale.com
Social Media: www.facebook.com/362476834435, twitter.com/CHOW1053
Guylaine Belley, Coordonnatrice, coordonnatrice@radioboreale.com

†*Amqui:* CFVM-FM (Rouge FM) (Freq: 99.9)
Détenteur: Bell Media Inc.*
111, av Gaétan-Archambault, Amqui, QC G5J 2K1
Tél: 418-629-2025, *Téléc:* 418-629-2599
amqui.rougefm.ca
Médias sociaux: www.youtube.com/Rouge1073Montreal, www.facebook.com/999Rougefm, twitter.com/999Rougefm
André Émond, Directeur Général et Directeur des Ventes

†*Asbestos:* CJAN-FM (Freq: 99.3)
1, rue Hilaire, Asbestos, QC J1T 0A3
Tél: 819-879-5439, *Téléc:* 819-879-7922
info@fm993.ca
fm993.ca
Médias sociaux: www.facebook.com/133076530207940

***Baie-Comeau:* CBMI-FM** (Freq: 93.7)
Owned by: CBVE-FM
Baie-Comeau, QC
www.cbc.ca/montreal

†*Baie-Comeau:* CBSI-FM-24 (Freq: 106.1)
Détenteur: Canadian Broadcasting Corporation
Baie-Comeau, QC
www.radio-canada.ca/regions/quebec

†*Baie-Comeau:* CHLC-FM (Freq: 97.1)
907, rue de Puyjalon, Baie-Comeau, QC G5C 1N3
Tél: 418-589-3771, *Téléc:* 418-589-9086
chlcfm97@globetrotter.net
www.chlc.com
Médias sociaux: www.facebook.com/pages/FM-971-et-1005/217028048325739
Georges Daviault, Directeur Général, direction971-1005@globetrotter.net

***Baie-Saint-Paul:* CHOX-FM-1** (Freq: 94.1)
Owned by: CHOX-FM
Baie-Saint-Paul, QC

†*Cap-aux-Meules:* CFIM-FM (Freq: 92.7)
CP 8192, Cap-aux-Meules, QC G4T 1R3
Tél: 418-986-5233, *Téléc:* 418-986-5319
administration@cfim.ca
www.cfim.ca
Charles Eugene Cyr, Directeur général, direction@cfim.ca

†*Carleton:* CIEU-FM (Freq: 94.9; 106.1)
1645, boul Perron Est, Carleton, QC G0C 1J0
Tél: 418-364-7094, *Téléc:* 418-364-3150
administration@cieufm.com
www.cieufm.com
Médias sociaux: www.facebook.com/cieufm
Claude Roy, Directeur général, direction@cieufm.com

†*Chandler:* CJMC-FM (Freq: 100.3)
#101, 141, rue Commercial Ouest, Chandler, QC G0C 1K0
Tél: 418-689-0963
direction@bleufm.ca
www.bleufm.ca
Médias sociaux: www.facebook.com/bleuFM.ca

***Châteauguay:* CHAI-FM** (Freq: 101.9)
25, boul St-Francis, Châteauguay, QC J6J 1Y2
Tel: 450-698-3131, *Fax:* 450-698-3339
chai@videotron.ca
www.1019fm.net
Social Media: www.facebook.com/pages/1019-Chai-FM/171051749593931, twitter.com/chai1019fm
Sylvain Poirier, Directeur général

†*Chibougamau:* CKXO-FM (Planète 93.5) (Freq: 93.5)
Détenteur: Groupe Radio Antenne 6 Inc.*
#1, 359, 3e rue, Chibougamau, QC G8P 1N4
www.chibougamau.planeteradio.ca

†*Chicoutimi:* CBJ-FM (Freq: 93.7)
Détenteur: Canadian Broadcasting Corporation*
500, rue des Sagueneens, Chicoutimi, QC G7H 6N4
Tél: 418-696-6600
saguenay@radio-canada.ca
ici.radio-canada.ca/saguenay-lac-saint-jean/

†*Chicoutimi:* CFIX-FM (Rouge FM) (Freq: 96.9)
Détenteur: Bell Media Inc.*
CP 8390, Chicoutimi, QC G7H 5C2
Tél: 418-543-9797, *Téléc:* 418-543-7968
webmestre-saguenay@astral.com
saguenay.rougefm.ca
Médias sociaux: www.facebook.com/969Rougefm, twitter.com/969Rougefm

†*Chicoutimi:* CJAB-FM (NRJ Saguenay-Lac-Saint-Jean 94.5) (Freq: 94.5)
Détenteur: Bell Media Inc.*
CP 8390, Chicoutimi, QC G7H 5C2
Tél: 418-545-9450, *Téléc:* 418-543-7968
saguenay.radionrj.ca
Médias sociaux: pinterest.com/radionrj, www.facebook.com/nrj945, twitter.com/NRJ945

†*Chicoutimi:* CKRS-FM (rythme 98,3 Saguenay) (Freq: 98.3)
345, rue Racine, Chicoutimi, QC G7H 1S8
Tél: 418-545-2577
www.rythmefm.com/saguenay
Médias sociaux: www.youtube.com/user/rythmefm, www.facebook.com/983rythmefm, twitter.com/rythmefm983
Sylvain Carbonneau, Directeur général

†*Dégelis:* CFVD-FM (Freq: 95.5)
654, 6e rue est, Dégelis, QC G5T 1Y1
Tél: 418-853-3370, *Téléc:* 418-853-3321
info@fm95.ca
fm95.ca
Médias sociaux: www.facebook.com/90319881621
Autre information: Alt. E-mail: administration@fm95.ca; horizon@fm95.ca
Gilles Caron, Directeur général

†*Dolbeau-Mistassini:* CHVD-FM (Planète 100.3) (Freq: 100.3)
Détenteur: Groupe Radio Antenne 6 Inc.*
1975, boul Wallberg, Dolbeau-Mistassini, QC G8L 1J5
Tél: 418-276-3333
www.dolbeau-mistassini.planeteradio.ca
Médias sociaux: www.facebook.com/115354181826762
Marc-André Levesque, Président

†*Drummondville:* CHRD-FM (Rouge FM) (Freq: 105.3)
Détenteur: Bell Media Inc.*
2070, rue Raphaël-Nolet, Drummondville, QC J2C 5G6
Tél: 819-475-1480, *Téléc:* 819-747-6610
drummondville.rougefm.ca
Médias sociaux: www.youtube.com/user/rougefm, www.facebook.com/1053Rougefm

†*Drummondville:* CJDM-FM (NRJ Drummondville 92.1) (Freq: 92.1)
Détenteur: Bell Media Inc.*
2070, rue Raphaël-Nolet, Drummondville, QC J2C 5G6
Tél: 819-475-1480, *Téléc:* 819-474-6610
drummondville.radionrj.ca
Médias sociaux: www.youtube.com/user/NRJquebec, www.facebook.com/nrj921, twitter.com/NRJ921

***Essipit:* CHME-FM** (Freq: 94.9)
34, rue de la Réserve, Essipit, QC G0T 1K0
Tel: 418-233-2700, *Fax:* 418-233-3326
Toll-Free: 800-661-2701
chme@B2B2C.ca
chme949.jimdo.com
Social Media: www.facebook.com/pages/CHME-Rock-ma-vie/174431196087
Claudine Roussel, Directrice générale

***Fermont:* CBMR-FM** (Freq: 105.1)
Owned by: Canadian Broadcasting Corporation
Fermont, QC
www.cbc.ca/radio

†*Fermont:* CFMF-FM (Freq: 103.1)
20, Place Daviault, Fermont, QC G0G 1J0
Tél: 418-287-5147
infocfmf@diffusionfermont.ca
www.cfmf.ca
Médias sociaux: www.facebook.com/pages/CFMF1031-FM/79719726630, twitter.com/cfmf1031
Karl Gangné Côté, Directeur de station et programmation, dp@diffusionfermont.ca

***Forestville:* CFRP-FM** (Freq: 100.5)
Forestville, QC

†*Fort-Coulonge:* CHIP-FM (Freq: 101.7)
CP 820, Fort-Coulonge, QC J0X 1V0
Tél: 819-683-3155, *Téléc:* 819-683-3211
Ligne sans frais: 888-775-3155
admin@chipfm.com
www.chipfm.com
Médias sociaux: www.facebook.com/chipfm
François Carrier, General Manager, dg@annexef.com

†*Gaspé:* CHGM-FM (Freq: 99.3)
Détenteur: CHNC
155 rue de la Reine, Gaspé, QC G4X 2R1
Tél: 418-368-1150

†*Gaspé:* CJRG-FM (Freq: 94.5)
162, rue Jacques Cartier, Gaspé, QC G4X 1M9
Tél: 418-368-3511, *Téléc:* 418-368-1663
Ligne sans frais: 866-360-3511
www.radiogaspesie.ca
Médias sociaux: www.facebook.com/radiogaspesie
Jacques Chartier, Directeur général, jacques.chartier@radiogaspesie.ca

†*Gatineau:* CFTX-FM (Capitale Rock) (Freq: 96.5)
Détenteur: RNC MÉDIA, Inc.*
171-A, rue Jean-Proulx, Gatineau, QC J8Z 1W5
Tél: 819-503-9659
www.gatineau.capitalerock.ca
Médias sociaux: www.facebook.com/965capitalerock, twitter.com/965capitalerock

†*Gatineau:* CHLX-FM (Planète 97.1) (Freq: 97.1)
Détenteur: RNC MÉDIA, Inc.*
171-A, rue Jean-Proulx, Gatineau, QC J8Z 1W5
Tél: 819-770-1040
www.gatineau.planeteradio.ca
Médias sociaux: www.youtube.com/user/rythmefm, www.facebook.com/planeteradio971, twitter.com/planeteradio971

†*Gatineau:* CIMF-FM (Rouge FM) (Freq: 94.9)
Détenteur: Bell Media Inc.*
15, rue Taschereau, Gatineau, QC J8Y 2V6
Tél: 819-243-5555, *Téléc:* 819-243-6816
gatineau.rougefm.ca
Médias sociaux: www.facebook.com/949Rougefm, twitter.com/949Rougefm

†*Gatineau:* CKOF-FM (104,7) (Freq: 104.7)
Détenteur: Cogeco Media Inc.*
150, rue d'Edmonton, Gatineau, QC J8Y 3S6
Tél: 819-561-8801, *Téléc:* 819-561-3333
www.fm1047.ca
Médias sociaux: www.facebook.com/1047fm.Outaouais, twitter.com/1047_fm

***Gatineau:* CKTF-FM (NRJ Gatineau-Ottawa 104.1)** (Freq: 104.1)
Owned by: Bell Media Inc.*
15, rue Taschereau, Gatineau, QC J8Y 2V6
Tel: 819-243-5555, *Fax:* 819-243-6816
gatineau.radionrj.ca
Social Media: www.youtube.com/user/nrj943montreal, www.facebook.com/NRJ104.1, twitter.com/InfoAstralGat

†*Havre-Saint-Pierre:* CBSI-FM-7 (Freq: 92.5)
Détenteur: Canadian Broadcasting Corporation
Havre-Saint-Pierre, QC
www.radio-canada.ca/regions/quebec

†*Hâvre-Saint-Pierre:* CILE-FM (Freq: 95.1)
992, rue du Bouleau, Hâvre-Saint-Pierre, QC G0G 1P0
Tél: 418-538-2453, *Téléc:* 418-538-3870
info@cilemf.com
www.cilemf.com

** For details on this company see listing in Major Broadcasting Companies section; † French language station*

†*Joliette:* CJLM-FM (Freq: 103.5)
540, rue Thomas, Joliette, QC J6E 3R4
Tél: 450-756-1035, *Téléc:* 450-756-8097
radio@m1035fm.com
www.m1035fm.com
Médias sociaux: www.facebook.com/10196265652614, twitter.com/m1035fm
Normand Masse, Directeur général

†*Jonquière:* CKAJ-FM (Freq: 92.5)
3877, boul. Harvey, 2e étage, Jonquière, QC G7X 0A6
Tél: 418-546-2525, *Téléc:* 418-546-2528
ckaj@ckaj.org
www.ckaj.org
Médias sociaux: www.facebook.com/ckajfm, twitter.com/ckaj925
Johanne Tremblay, Directrice générale

***Kahnawake:* CKRK-FM (K103 Kahnawake)** (Freq: 103.7)
PO Box 1050, Kahnawake, QC J0L 1B0
Tel: 450-638-1313, *Fax:* 450-638-4009
www.k103radio.com
Social Media: www.facebook.com/139720622747580

***Kuujjuaq:* CKUJ-FM** (Freq: 97.3)
PO Box 1082, Kuujjuaq, QC J0M 1C0
Tel: 819-964-2921

***L'Annonciation:* CFLO-FM-1** (Freq: 101.9)
Owned by: CFLO-FM
L'Annonciation, QC

†*La Pocatière:* CHOX-FM (Freq: 97.5)
#50, 601, 1ère rue Poiré, La Pocatière, QC G0R 1Z0
Tél: 418-856-1310, *Téléc:* 418-856-3747
chox@chox97.com
www.chox97.com
Médias sociaux: www.facebook.com/pages/CHOX-FM-975/377928410603, twitter.com/CHOXFM975

†*La Tuque:* CFLM-FM (Freq: 97.1)
CP 850, La Tuque, QC G9X 3P6
Tél: 819-523-4575
routage@cflm.ca
www.cflm.ca

***Lac-Etchemin:* CFIN-FM** (Freq: 100.5)
201, rue Claude-Bilodeau, Lac-Etchemin, QC G0R 1S0
Tel: 418-625-3737, *Fax:* 418-625-3730
www.cfin-fm.com
Sylvie Lamontagne, Coordonnatrice

†*Lac-Mégantic:* CFJO-FM-1 (Freq: 101.9)
Détenteur: CFJO-FM
Lac-Mégantic, QC
www.o973.com
Médias sociaux: www.facebook.com/182494896930, twitter.com/o973

†*Lac-Mégantic:* CJIT-FM (Freq: 106.7)
4766, rue Laval, Lac-Mégantic, QC G6B 1C7
Tél: 819-583-0663
radiocjit@gmail.com
www.cjitfm.com
Médias sociaux: www.facebook.com/103316478096

†*Lachute:* CHPR-FM (Planète Lov' 102.1) (Freq: 102.1)
Détenteur: RNC MÉDIA, Inc.*
11, av Argenteuil, Lachute, QC J8H 1X8
Tél: 450-562-8862, *Téléc:* 450-562-1902
planetelov.ca
Médias sociaux: www.facebook.com/229629290417310, twitter.com/planetelov

***Lachute:* CJLA-FM (Planète Lov' 104.9)** (Freq: 104.9)
Owned by: RNC MÉDIA, Inc.*
11, rue Argenteuil, Lachute, QC J8H 1X8
Tel: 450-562-8862, *Fax:* 450-562-1902
www.planetelov.ca
Social Media: www.facebook.com/229629290417310, twitter.com/planetelov

†*Laval:* CFGL-FM (Rhythme Montréal) (Freq: 105.7)
Détenteur: Cogeco Media Inc.*
#100, 2830, boul St-Martin est, Laval, QC H7E 5A1
Tél: 450-664-4647, *Téléc:* 450-664-4138
Ligne sans frais: 877-984-6336
www.rythmefm.com/montreal
Médias sociaux: www.youtube.com/user/rythmefm, www.facebook.com/104523882938940, twitter.com/rythmefm1057
Jean-Luc Meilleur, Directeur général et vice-président, stations régionales de Cogeco Diffusion

***Listuguj:* CFIC-FM** (Freq: 105.1)
PO Box 304, Listuguj, QC G0C 2R0
Tel: 418-788-5166, *Fax:* 418-788-3524
www.105hotcountry.com
Jake Dedan, General Manager

***Listuguj:* CHRQ-FM** (Freq: 106.9)
PO Box 180, Listuguj, QC G0C 2R0
Tel: 418-788-2121, *Fax:* 418-788-2653
chrq1069@globetrotter.net

***Longueuil:* CHAA-FM** (Freq: 103.3)
91, rue St-Jean, Longueuil, QC J4H 2W8
Tel: 450-646-6800, *Fax:* 450-646-7378
info@fm1033.ca
www.fm1033.ca
Social Media: instagram.com/fm1033, www.facebook.com/fm1033, twitter.com/fm1033
Eric Tetreault, Directeur, admin@fm1033.ca

†*Maniwaki:* CFOR-FM (Freq: 99.3)
139, rue Principal sud, Maniwaki, QC J9E 1Z8
Tél: 819-441-0993, *Téléc:* 819-441-3488
cfor993@b2b2c.ca
www.cforfm.com
Laure Voilquin, Directrice commerciale

†*Maniwaki:* CHGA-FM (Freq: 97.3)
158, rue Laurier, Maniwaki, QC J9E 2K7
Tél: 819-449-9730, *Téléc:* 819-449-7331
Ligne sans frais: 866-767-9730
reception@chga.fm
www.chga.qc.ca
Médias sociaux: www.facebook.com/chga.fm, twitter.com/RadioChga
Gisèle Danis, Directrice générale, gdanis@chga.fm

***Maniwaki:* CKWE-FM** (Freq: 103.9)
PO Box 309, Maniwaki, QC J9E 3C9
Tel: 819-449-5097, *Fax:* 819-449-2327
ckwe.radio@gmail.com
www.ckwe1039.fm
Social Media: www.youtube.com/channel/UCsrPL8A9vOZnFK_-kcXApuw, www.facebook.com/CKWE103.9Radio, twitter.com/CKWERADIO

†*Mashteuiatsh:* CHUK-FM (Freq: 107.3)
1491, rue Ouiatchouan, Mashteuiatsh, QC G0W 2H0
Tél: 418-275-4684, *Téléc:* 418-275-7964
chuk@chukfm.ca
www.chukfm.ca

†*Matagami:* CHEF-FM (Freq: 99.9)
CP 39, Matagami, QC J0Y 2A0
Tél: 819-739-9990, *Téléc:* 819-739-6003
chef99fm@lino.com
www.chef99.ca
Marie-Eve C. Gallant, Directrice générale, meve.chef99fm@lino.com

†*Matane:* CBGA-FM (Freq: 102.1)
Détenteur: Canadian Broadcasting Corporation*
303, av Saint-Jérôme, Matane, QC G4W 3A8
Tél: 418-562-0290
nouvelles.matane@radio-canada.ca
ici.radio-canada.ca

†*Matane:* CHOE-FM (Freq: 95.3)
800, av du Phare ouest, Matane, QC G4W 1V7
Tél: 418-562-8181, *Téléc:* 418-562-0778
www.choefm.com
Médias sociaux: www.facebook.com/117043981639072,

†*Matane:* CHRM-FM (Freq: 105.3)
800, av du Phare ouest, Matane, QC G4W 1V7
Tél: 418-562-4141, *Téléc:* 418-562-0778
www.chrmfm.com
Médias sociaux: www.facebook.com/pages/CHRM-1053-Matane/115997205081095
Michel Desrosiers, Directeur commercial, micheldesrosiers@choefm.com

†*Mont-Laurier:* CFLO-FM (Freq: 104.7)
456, rue du Pont, Mont-Laurier, QC J9L 2R9
Tél: 819-623-6610, *Téléc:* 819-623-7406
Ligne sans frais: 888-623-6610
www.cflo.ca
Médias sociaux: www.facebook.com/178411675560925
Dominic Bell, Directeur général, 819-623-6610, dbell@cflo.ca

†*Montréal:* CBF-FM (Freq: 95.1)
Détenteur: Canadian Broadcasting Corporation*
1400, boul René-Lévesque Est, Montréal, QC H2L 2M2
Tél: 514-597-6000, *Téléc:* 514-597-5545
Ligne sans frais: 866-306-4636
ici.radio-canada.ca

†*Montréal:* CBFX-FM (Freq: 100.7)
Détenteur: Canadian Broadcasting Corporation*
CP 6000 Centre-ville, Montréal, QC H3C 3A8
Tél: 514-597-6000, *Téléc:* 514-597-5545
Ligne sans frais: 866-306-4636
www.icimusique.ca
Médias sociaux: www.youtube.com/user/musiqueRC, www.facebook.com/icimusique, twitter.com/icimusique
Guylaine Picard, Réalisatrice-coordonnatrice

†*Montréal:* CBME-FM (Freq: 88.5)
Détenteur: Canadian Broadcasting Corporation*
CP 6000, Montréal, QC H3C 3A8
Tél: 514-597-6000
www.cbc.ca/montreal
Shelagh Kinch, Directrice général, Anglais service

***Montréal:* CBM-FM** (Freq: 93.5)
Owned by: Canadian Broadcasting Corporation*
1400, boul René-Lévesque Est, Montréal, QC H2L 2M2
Tel: 514-597-6000, *Fax:* 514-597-5545
Toll-Free: 866-306-4636
www.cbc.ca/montreal

†*Montréal:* CHMP-FM (l'actualité 98,5) (Freq: 98.5)
Détenteur: Cogeco Media Inc.*
#1100, 800, rue de la Gauchetière ouest, Montréal, QC H5A 1M1
Tél: 514-789-0985
www.985fm.ca
Médias sociaux: www.facebook.com/985fm, twitter.com/le985fm
Autre information: Sports URL: www.985sports.ca; Twitter: twitter.com/985Sports

***Montréal:* CHOM-FM** (Freq: 97.7)
Owned by: Bell Media Inc.*
1717 René-Lévesque Blvd. East, Montréal, QC H2L 4T9
Tel: 514-931-2466
infodesk@chom.com
www.chom.com
Social Media: www.facebook.com/CHOM977, twitter.com/CHOM977
André Lallier, Program Director, andre.lallier@bellmedia.ca

†*Montréal:* CIBL-FM (Freq: 101.5)
#201, 2, rue Ste-Catherine est, Montréal, QC H2X 1K4
Tél: 514-526-2581, *Téléc:* 514-285-2814
www.cibl1015.com
Médias sociaux: www.facebook.com/CIBLRadioMontreal, twitter.com/CIBLmedia
Gilles Labelle, Directeur général

***Montréal:* CINQ-FM** (Freq: 102.3)
5212, boul St-Laurent, Montréal, QC H2T 1S1
Tel: 514-495-2597, *Fax:* 514-495-2429
cinqfm@radiocentreville.com
www.radiocentreville.com
Social Media: www.facebook.com/pages/Radio-Centre-Ville-Montréal/150733819960, twitter.com/fmcentreville
Marc De Roussan, Directeur général

***Montréal:* CIRA-FM** (Freq: 91.3)
#199, 4020, rue Saint-Ambroise, Montréal, QC H4C 2C7
Tel: 514-382-3913, *Fax:* 514-858-0965
Toll-Free: 855-212-2020
auditoire@radiovm.com
www.radiovm.com
Social Media: www.facebook.com/RadioVilleMarie
Raynald Gagné, Directeur général

†*Montréal:* CISM-FM (Freq: 89.3)
CP 6128 Centre-Ville, Montréal, QC H3C 3J7
Tél: 514-343-7511
info@cism893.ca
www.cism.umontreal.ca
Médias sociaux: www.facebook.com/cism893, twitter.com/cism893
Jarrett Mann, Directeur général, jmann@cism893.ca

** For details on this company see listing in Major Broadcasting Companies section; † French language station*

***Montréal:* CITE-FM (Rouge FM)** (Freq: 107.3)
Owned by: Bell Media Inc.*
1717, boul René-Lévesque Est, Montréal, QC H2L 4T9
Tel: 514-529-3200, *Fax:* 514-529-9308
montreal.rougefm.ca
Social Media: www.facebook.com/1073Rougefm, twitter.com/1073Rougefm

***Montréal:* CJFM-FM (Virgin Radio 96)** (Freq: 95.9)
Owned by: Bell Media Inc.*
1717 René-Lévesque Blvd. East, Montréal, QC H2L 4T9
Tel: 514-989-2536
montreal.virginradio.ca
Social Media: www.facebook.com/virginradio96, twitter.com/VirginRadio96

***Montréal:* CJPX-FM** (Freq: 99.5)
124, ch du Chenal-Le-Moyne, Montréal, QC H3C 1A9
Tel: 514-871-0995, *Fax:* 514-871-0990
cjpx@radioclassique.ca
www.cjpx.ca
Social Media: www.facebook.com/radioclassiquemontreal99.5
Jacques Boiteau, Vice-Président, Ventes et marketing, jacquesboiteau@radioclassique.ca

†*Montréal:* CKBE-FM (The Beat) (Freq: 92.5)
Détenteur: Cogeco Media Inc.*
Place Bonaventure, #1100, 800, rue de la Gauchetière ouest Montréal, QC H5A 1M1
Tél: 514-767-9250, *Téléc:* 514-787-7979
www.thebeat925.ca
Médias sociaux: www.youtube.com/user/925thebeatofmontreal, www.facebook.com/TheBeatofMontreal, twitter.com/thebeat925
Sam Zniber, Program Director

***Montréal:* CKDG-FM** (Freq: 105.1)
4865 Jean-Talon St. West, Montréal, QC H4P 1W7
Tel: 514-273-2481, *Fax:* 514-273-3707
info@mikefm.ca
mikefm.ca
Social Media: www.facebook.com/1051Mike

***Montréal:* CKLX-FM (91.9 Sport)** (Freq: 91.9)
Owned by: RNC MÉDIA, Inc.*
200, av Laurier ouest, Montréal, QC H2T 2N8
Tel: 514-790-0919
919sport.ca
Social Media: instagram.com/919sport, www.facebook.com/919sport, twitter.com/919sport

†*Montréal:* CKMF-FM (NRJ Montréal 94.3) (Freq: 94.3)
Détenteur: Bell Media Inc.*
1717, boul René-Lévesque Est, Montréal, QC H2L 4T9
Tél: 514-529-3200, *Téléc:* 514-529-9308
montreal.radionrj.ca
Médias sociaux: www.youtube.com/nrj943montreal, www.facebook.com/nrj943montreal, twitter.com/nrj943montreal

†*Montréal:* CKOI-FM (Freq: 96.9)
Détenteur: Cogeco Media Inc.*
#1100, 800, rue de la Gauchetière ouest, Montréal, QC H5A 1M1
Tél: 514-789-2564, *Téléc:* 514-787-7982
www.ckoi.com
Médias sociaux: www.youtube.com/c/ckoi969fm, www.facebook.com/969CKOI, twitter.com/ckoi
Jean-Sébastien Lemire, Directeur de la programmation

***Montréal:* CKUT-FM** (Freq: 90.3)
3647 University St., Montréal, QC H3A 2B3
Tel: 514-448-4041
programming@ckut.ca
www.ckut.ca
Social Media: www.facebook.com/RadioCKUT, twitter.com/ckut

†*Natashquan:* CKNA-FM (Freq: 104.1)
29, ch d'en Haut, Natashquan, QC G0G 2E0
Tél: 418-726-3284, *Téléc:* 418-726-3367
ckna@globetrotter.net
pages.globetrotter.net/ckna

†*New Carlisle:* CHNC-FM (Freq: 107.1)
CP 610, New Carlisle, QC G0C 1Z0
Tél: 418-752-2215, *Téléc:* 418-752-6939
Ligne sans frais: 866-470-0462
radiochnc@globetrotter.net
www.radiochnc.com
Médias sociaux: www.youtube.com/user/CHNCFM, www.facebook.com/pages/Radio-CHNC/115816745122190, twitter.com/radiochnc
Brigitte Paquet, Directrice générale, brigitte@radiochnc.com

***Pikogan:* CKAG-FM** (Freq: 100.1)
30, rue David Kistabish, Pikogan, QC J9T 3A3
Tel: 819-727-3237, *Fax:* 819-727-4432
ckagfm@cableamos.com
www.ckagfm.com

†*Pohénégamook:* CFVD-FM-2 (Freq: 92.1)
Détenteur: CFVD-FM
Pohénégamook, QC

†*Port-Cartier:* CIPC-FM (Freq: 99.1)
Port-Cartier, QC
Tél: 418-968-2472, *Téléc:* 418-968-9900
CIPC991@laradioactive.com
www.laradioactive.com
Médias sociaux: www.facebook.com/LaRadioActive, twitter.com/RadioActive991

†*Port-Menier:* CJBE-FM (Freq: 90.1)
CP 15, Port-Menier, QC G0G 2Y0
Tél: 418-535-0292, *Téléc:* 418-535-0497

***Québec:* CBVE-FM** (Freq: 104.7)
Owned by: Canadian Broadcasting Corporation*
888, rue Saint-Jean, Québec, QC G1R 5H6
Tel: 418-654-1341, *Fax:* 418-656-8557
Toll-Free: 866-954-1341
www.cbc.ca/montreal

†*Québec:* CBV-FM (Freq: 106.3)
Détenteur: Canadian Broadcasting Corporation*
CP 18800, Québec, QC G1K 9L4
Tél: 418-654-1341, *Ligne sans frais:* 866-954-1341
nouvelles.quebec@radio-canada.ca
ici.radio-canada.ca

†*Québec:* CBV-FM (Freq: 106.3)
Détenteur: Canadian Broadcasting Corporation*
CP 18800, Québec, QC G1K 9L4
Tél: 418-654-1341, *Ligne sans frais:* 866-954-1341
www.radio-canada.ca

***Québec:* CBVX-FM** (Freq: 95.3)
Owned by: Canadian Broadcasting Corporation*
888, rue Saint-Jean, Québec, QC G1R 5H6
Tel: 418-654-1341, *Fax:* 418-656-8557
nouvelles.quebec@radio-canada.ca
www.icimusique.ca

†*Québec:* CFEL-FM (CKOI 102,1 Québec) (Freq: 102.1)
Détenteur: Leclerc Communication Inc.*
#505, 815, boul Lebourgneuf, Québec, QC G2J 0C1
Tél: 418-529-1021
www.ckoiquebec.com
Médias sociaux: www.facebook.com/1021CKOI, twitter.com/1021ckoi
Pierre-Luc Gilbert, Directeur des ventes
Jean-François Leclerc, Directeur général

†*Québec:* CFOM-FM (M-FM) (Freq: 102.9)
Détenteur: Cogeco Media Inc.*
1305, ch Ste-Foy - 4e étage, Québec, QC G1S 4Y5
Tél: 418-694-1029, *Ligne sans frais:* 877-394-1029
www.m1029.com
Médias sociaux: www.facebook.com/mfm1029, twitter.com/mfm1029
Richard Renaud, Directeur général

†*Québec:* CHIK-FM (NRJ Québec 98.9) (Freq: 98.9)
Détenteur: Bell Media Inc.*
900, rue d'Youville, 1er étage, Québec, QC G1R 3P7
Tél: 418-687-9900, *Téléc:* 418-687-3106
quebec.radionrj.ca
Médias sociaux: www.youtube.com/user/NRJquebec, www.facebook.com/989nrj, twitter.com/NRJ989

†*Québec:* CHOI-FM (CHOI 98.1 Radio X) (Freq: 98.1)
Détenteur: RNC MÉDIA, Inc.*
#300, 1134, Grande-Allée ouest, Québec, QC G1S 1E5
Tél: 418-687-9810
quebec.radiox.com

***Québec:* CHXX-FM (Radio X2 100.9)** (Freq: 100.9)
Owned by: RNC MÉDIA, Inc.*
#300, 1134 Grande-Allée ouest, Québec, QC G1S 1E5
Tel: 418-687-9810
radiox2.com

***Québec:* CHYZ-FM** (Freq: 94.3)
Pavillon Maurice-Pollack, l'Université Laval, #0236, 2305, rue de l'université, Québec, QC G1V 0A6
Tel: 418-656-7007
info@chyz.ca
www.chyz.ca
Social Media: www.youtube.com/chyz943fm, www.facebook.com/chyz943, twitter.com/chyz943
Jean-Philippe Lessard, Directeur général, dg@chyz.ca

***Québec:* CION-FM** (Freq: 90.9; 102.5; 106.7)
3196, ch Sainte-Foy, Québec, QC G1X 1R4
Tel: 418-659-9090, *Fax:* 418-650-3306
Toll-Free: 800-447-2466
cionfm@radiogalilee.qc.ca
www.radiogalilee.com
Denis Veilleux, Directeur

†*Québec:* CITF-FM (Rouge FM) (Freq: 107.5)
Détenteur: Bell Media Inc.*
900, rue d'Youville, 1er étage, Québec, QC G1R 3P7
Tél: 418-687-9900, *Téléc:* 418-687-3106
quebec.rougefm.ca
Médias sociaux: www.youtube.com/Rouge1075Quebec, www.facebook.com/1075Rougefm, twitter.com/1075rougefm

***Québec:* CJEC-FM (WKND FM)** (Freq: 91.9)
Owned by: Leclerc Communication Inc.*
#505, 815, boul Lebourgneuf, Québec, QC G2J 0C1
Tel: 418-688-0919
www.wknd.fm
Social Media: www.facebook.com/wknd.fm, twitter.com/wknd919
Pierre-Luc Gilbert, Directeur des ventes
Jean-François Leclerc, Ditrecteur général

†*Québec:* CJMF-FM (FM93) (Freq: 93.3)
Détenteur: Cogeco Media Inc.*
1305, ch Ste-Foy, Québec, QC G1S 4Y5
Tél: 418-687-9330, *Téléc:* 418-687-9718
www.fm93.com
Médias sociaux: www.facebook.com/fm93quebec, twitter.com/fm93quebec

†*Québec:* CKIA-FM (Freq: 88.3)
#200, 335, rue Saint-Joseph, Québec, QC G1K 3B4
Tél: 418-529-9026
www.ckiafm.org
Médias sociaux: www.facebook.com/pages/CKIA-FM/115737995163836
Lorinne Larouche, Coordonnatrice aux opérations

†*Québec:* CKRL-FM (Freq: 89.1)
405, 3e av, Québec, QC G1L 2W2
Tél: 418-640-2575, *Téléc:* 418-640-1588
programmation@ckrl.qc.ca
www.ckrl.qc.ca
Médias sociaux: www.facebook.com/CKRL891, twitter.com/CKRL891
Dany Fortin, Directeur général, direction@ckrl.qc.ca

†*Radisson:* CIAU-FM (Freq: 103.1)
CP 285, Radisson, QC J0Y 2X0
Tél: 819-638-7033, *Téléc:* 819-638-1031
ciaufm@lino.com
www.ciaufm.ca

†*Rimouski:* CJBR-FM (Freq: 89.1)
Détenteur: Canadian Broadcasting Corporation*
185, boul René-Lepage, Rimouski, QC G5L 1P2
Tél: 418-723-2217
www.radio-canada.ca/radio

†*Rimouski:* CBRX-FM (Freq: 101.5)
Détenteur: Canadian Broadcasting Corporation*
185, boul René-Lepage est, Rimouski, QC G5L 1P2 *Tél:* 418-723-2217, *Téléc:* 418-723-6126
www.icimusique.ca
Josée Bouchard, Rédactrice en chef, Est du Québec, josee.bouchard@radio-canada.ca

†*Rimouski:* CIKI-FM (NRJ Est du Québec 98.7) (Freq: 98.7)
Détenteur: Bell Media Inc.*
#502, 287, rue Pierre-Saindon, Rimouski, QC G5L 9A7
Tél: 418-723-2323, *Téléc:* 418-722-7508
rimouski.radionrj.ca
Médias sociaux: www.facebook.com/nrj987, twitter.com/NRJ987
Mario Fournier, Directeur général et Directeur des ventes

** For details on this company see listing in Major Broadcasting Companies section; † French language station*

†*Rimouski:* CJOI-FM (Rouge FM) (Freq: 102.9)
Détenteur: Bell Media Inc.*
#502, 287, rue Pierre-Saindon, Rimouski, QC G5L 9A7
Tél: 418-723-2323, *Téléc:* 418-722-7508
rimouski.rougefm.ca
Médias sociaux: www.facebook.com/1029Rougefm, twitter.com/1029rougefm
Mario Fournier, Directeur général

†*Rimouski:* CKMN-FM (Freq: 96.5)
323, Montée industrielle et commerciale, Rimouski, QC G5M 1A7
Tél: 418-722-2566, *Téléc:* 418-724-7815
secretariat@ckmn.fm
www.ckmn.fm
Médias sociaux: www.facebook.com/CKMN.FM

***Rivière-au-Renard:* CJRE-FM** (Freq: 97.9)
Owned by: CJRG-FM
Rivière-au-Renard, QC

†*Rivière-du-Loup:* CIBM-FM (Freq: 107.1)
64, rue Hôtel-de-Ville, Rivière-du-Loup, QC G5R 1L5
Tél: 418-867-1071, *Téléc:* 418-867-4940
www.cibm107.com
Médias sociaux: www.facebook.com/pages/CIBM-FM-107/140168673893
Daniel St-Pierre, Directeur de la programmation, dstpierre@cibm107.com

†*Rivière-du-Loup:* CIEL-FM (Freq: 103.7)
64, rue Hôtel-de-Ville, Rivière-du-Loup, QC G5R 1L5
Tél: 418-862-8241, *Téléc:* 418-867-4940
www.ciel103.com
Médias sociaux: www.facebook.com/pages/CIEL-FM-1037/208658131206
Clermont Labrie, Contrôleur, clabrie@ciel103.com
Daniel St-Pierre, Directeur de la programmation, dstpierre@ciel103.com

†*Roberval:* CHRL-FM (Planète 99.5) (Freq: 99.5)
Détenteur: Groupe Radio Antenne 6*
568, boul St-Joseph, Roberval, QC G8H 2K6
Tél: 418-275-1831, *Téléc:* 418-275-2475
www.roberval.planeteradio.ca
Médias sociaux: www.facebook.com/176702051800

***Rouyn-Noranda:* CHGO-FM (Capitale Rock)** (Freq: 104.3)
Owned by: RNC MÉDIA, Inc.*
380, rue Murdoch, Rouyn-Noranda, QC J9X 1G5
Tel: 819-762-0741, *Fax:* 819-762-2466
live@abitibi.capitalerock.ca
www.abitibi.capitalerock.ca
Nancy Deschênes, Directrice générale, ndeschenes@rncmedia.ca

***Rouyn-Noranda:* CHIC-FM** (Freq: 88.7)
PO Box 2185, 120, 9e Rue, Rouyn-Noranda, QC J9X 5A6
Tel: 819-797-4242, *Fax:* 819-797-3803
887@chicfm.org
chicfm.org
Richard Dubé, Responsable, Technique et informatique

†*Rouyn-Noranda:* CHLM-FM (Freq: 90.7)
70, av Principal, Rouyn-Noranda, QC J9X 4P2
Tél: 819-762-8155, *Ligne sans frais:* 877-666-8155
abitibi@radio-canada.ca
www.radio-canada.ca/regions/abitibi
Serge Cossette, Chef des services français, Abitibi-Témiscamingue, serge.cossette@radio-canada.ca

***Rouyn-Noranda:* CHOA-FM (rythme 96,5)** (Freq: 96.5)
Owned by: RNC MÉDIA, Inc.*
380, rue Murdoch, Rouyn-Noranda, QC J9X 1G5
Tel: 819-762-0744, *Toll-Free:* 800-492-2462
www.rythmefm.com/abitibi
Social Media: www.youtube.com/user/rythmefm, www.facebook.com/pages/Rythme-FM-Abitibi/139619569401136 6, twitter.com/rythmefmabitibi
Nancy Deschênes, Directrice générale

†*Rouyn-Noranda:* CJGO-FM (Capitale Rock) (Freq: 102.1)
Détenteur: RNC MÉDIA, Inc.*
380, rue Murdoch, Rouyn-Noranda, QC J9X 1G5
Tél: 819-762-0741, *Téléc:* 819-762-2466
live@abitibi.capitalerock.ca
www.abitibi.capitalerock.ca
Médias sociaux: www.facebook.com/965capitalerock, twitter.com/965capitalerock

***Rouyn-Noranda:* CJMM-FM (NRJ Rouyn-Noranda 99.1)** (Freq: 99.1)
Owned by: Bell Media Inc.*
191, av Murdoch, Rouyn-Noranda, QC J9X 1E3
Tel: 819-797-2566, *Fax:* 819-797-1664
rouyn.radionrj.ca
Social Media: www.facebook.com/nrj991, twitter.com/NRJ991

***Saguenay:* CBJE-FM** (Freq: 102.7FM)
Owned by: CBVE-FM
Saguenay, QC
www.cbc.ca/radio

†*Saguenay:* CBJX-FM (Freq: 100.9FM)
Détenteur: Canadian Broadcasting Corporation*
500, rue des Saguenéens, Saguenay, QC G7H 6N4
Tél: 418-696-6600
www.radio-canada.ca/regions/saguenay-lac

†*Saguenay:* CKYK-FM (KYK Radio X) (Freq: 95.7)
Détenteur: Groupe Radio Antenne 6 Inc.*
345, rue des Saguenéens # 70, Saguenay, QC G7H 6K9
Tél: 418-543-8912
saguenay.radiox.com
Marc-André Levesque, Président

***Saint-Augustin:* CJAS-FM** (Freq: 93.5)
PO Box 100, 558 rue Principal, Saint-Augustin, QC G0G 2R0
Tel: 418-947-2239, *Fax:* 418-947-2664
cjasradio@gmail.com
www.lnscommunityradio.com/CJAS
Lorette Gallibois, General Manager

***Saint-Gabriel-de-Brandon:* CFNJ-FM** (Freq: 99.1)
245, rue Beauvilliers, Saint-Gabriel-de-Brandon, QC J0K 2N0
Tel: 450-835-3437, *Fax:* 450-835-3581
Toll-Free: 888-935-3437
info@cfnj.net
www.cfnj.net

†*Saint-Georges:* CKRB-FM (Freq: 103.5)
CP 100, Saint-Georges, QC G5Y 5C4
Tél: 418-228-1460, *Téléc:* 418-228-0096
Ligne sans frais: 866-535-1035
studio@coolfm.biz
www.coolfm.biz
Médias sociaux: www.facebook.com/1035CoolFm, twitter.com/InfoRadioBeauce
Roger Quirion, Directeur des Opérations, rogerquirion@radiobeauce.com

†*Saint-Hilarion:* CIHO-FM (Freq: 96.3)
315, ch Cartier nord, Saint-Hilarion, QC G0A 3V0
Tél: 418-457-3333, *Téléc:* 418-457-3518
studio@cihofm.com
www.cihofm.com
Médias sociaux: www.facebook.com/pages/Ciho-Fm-963-Charlevoix/1016193666 99027, twitter.com/cihofm
Gervais Desbiens, Directeur général, direction@cihofm.com

†*Saint-Hyacinthe:* CFEI-FM (Boom FM) (Freq: 106.5)
Détenteur: Bell Media Inc.*
2596, boul Casavant ouest, Saint-Hyacinthe, QC J2S 7R8
Tél: 450-774-6486, *Téléc:* 450-774-7785
www.boomfm.com
Médias sociaux: www.facebook.com/radioboom, twitter.com/radioboomfm

†*Saint-Jean-sur-Richelieu:* CFZZ-FM (Boom FM) (Freq: 104.1)
Détenteur: Bell Media Inc.*
104, rue Richelieu, Saint-Jean-sur-Richelieu, QC J3B 6X3
Tél: 450-346-0104, *Téléc:* 450-348-2274
www.boomfm.com
Médias sociaux: www.facebook.com/radioboom, twitter.com/radioboomfm

†*Saint-Jérôme:* CIME-FM (Le Rhythme des Laurentides) (Freq: 101.3; 103.9)
Détenteur: Cogeco Media Inc.*
#102, 300, rue Marie-Victorin, Saint-Jérôme, QC J7Y 2G8
Tél: 450-431-2463, *Téléc:* 450-504-5601
www.cime.fm
Médias sociaux: www.facebook.com/cime.fm, twitter.com/CIMEfm
Joanne Leboeuf, Directrice générale

†*Saint-Rémi:* CHOC-FM (Freq: 104.9)
93, rue Lachapelle est, Saint-Rémi, QC J0L 2L0
Tél: 450-454-5500, *Téléc:* 450-454-9435
www.chocfm.com

***Sainte-Perpétue:* CHOX-FM-2** (Freq: 101.1)
Owned by: CHOX-FM
Sainte-Perpétue, QC

†*Salaberry-de-Valleyfield:* CKOD-FM (Freq: 103.1)
#103, 249, rue Victoria, Salaberry-de-Valleyfield, QC J6T 1A9
Tél: 450-373-0103, *Téléc:* 450-854-8103
fm103@ckod.qc.ca
www.ckod.qc.ca
Médias sociaux: www.facebook.com/CKODFM103, twitter.com/ckodfm
Robert Brunet, Propriétaire

†*Senneterre:* CIBO-FM (Freq: 100.5)
121, 1ère rue Est, Senneterre, QC J0Y 2M0
Tél: 819-737-2222, *Téléc:* 819-737-8599
cibo.fm@cableamos.com
cibofm.wix.com/radio
Médias sociaux: www.youtube.com/user/cibofm, www.facebook.com/cibofm, twitter.com/cibofm

†*Sept-Iles:* CBSI-FM (Freq: 98.1)
Détenteur: Canadian Broadcasting Corporation*
#30, 350, rue Smith, Sept-Iles, QC G4R 3X2
Tél: 418-968-0720, *Ligne sans frais:* 800-463-1731
cbsi@radio-canada.ca
ici.radio-canada.ca/cote-nord

***Sept-Iles:* CKAU-FM** (Freq: 90.1; 104.5)
100, boul des Montagnais, Sept-Iles, QC G4R 4K2
Tel: 418-927-2476
www.ckau.com
Social Media: www.facebook.com/ckaufm
Reginald Volant, Directeur Général, 418-927-2476

†*Sept-Iles:* CKCN-FM (Freq: 94.1)
365, boul Laure, Sept-Iles, QC G4R 1X2
Tél: 418-962-3838, *Téléc:* 418-968-6662
Ckcn941@Purfm.com
www.purfm.com
Médias sociaux: www.facebook.com/pages/PUR-FM-941-Sept-Ies/15678964606, twitter.com/FM941

***Sherbrooke:* CFAK-FM** (Freq: 88.3)
2500, boul de Université, Sherbrooke, QC J1K 2R1
Tel: 819-821-8000, *Fax:* 819-821-7930
info.cfak883@usherbrooke.ca
cfak883.usherbrooke.ca
Social Media: www.facebook.com/CFAK883, twitter.com/CFAK883
Serge Langlois, Directeur général, dg.cfak883@usherbrooke.ca

†*Sherbrooke:* CFGE-FM (Rhythme Sherbrooke) (Freq: 93.7; 98.1)
Détenteur: Cogeco Media Inc.*
4020, boul de Portland, Sherbrooke, QC J1L 2V6
Tél: 819-822-0937, *Téléc:* 819-562-1666
www.rythmefm.com/estrie
Médias sociaux: www.facebook.com/130198797025166, twitter.com/rythmefm937

†*Sherbrooke:* CFLX-FM (Freq: 95.5)
67, rue Wellington Nord, Sherbrooke, QC J1H 5A9
Tél: 819-566-2787, *Téléc:* 819-566-7331
commentaire@cflx.qc.ca
www.cflx.qc.ca
Médias sociaux: twitter.com/cflx955

†*Sherbrooke:* CIMO-FM (NRJ Estrie 106.1) (Freq: 106.1)
Détenteur: Bell Media Inc.*
#200, 2185, rue King ouest, Sherbrooke, QC J1J 2G2
Tél: 819-347-1414, *Téléc:* 819-347-1061
sherbrooke.radionrj.ca
Médias sociaux: www.youtube.com/nrj1061estrie, www.facebook.com/nrj1061, twitter.com/NRJ1061

†*Sherbrooke:* CITE-FM-1 (Rouge FM) (Freq: 102.7)
Détenteur: Bell Media Inc.*
#200, 2185, rue King ouest, Sherbrooke, QC J1L 2E4
Tél: 819-347-1414, *Téléc:* 819-566-1011
estrie.rougefm.ca
Médias sociaux: www.youtube.com/user/1027Rougefm, www.facebook.com/1027Rougefm, twitter.com/1027Rougefm

* *For details on this company see listing in Major Broadcasting Companies section; † French language station*

***Sherbrooke:* CJMQ-FM** (Freq: 88.9)
184 Queen St., Sherbrooke, QC J1M 1J9
Tel: 819-822-1838
cjmqnews@yahoo.ca
www.cjmq.fm
Social Media:
www.facebook.com/pages/CJMQ-889-Radio-Station/87230649091
David Teasdale, Station Manager, 819-570-2094, dteasdale77@yahoo.ca
Maureen Dillon, Program & Music Director, 819-822-1838

†*Sherbrooke:* CKOY-FM (Freq: 107.7)
Détenteur: Cogeco Media Inc.*
4020, boul Portland, Sherbrooke, QC J1L 2V6
Tél: 819-822-0937, *Téléc:* 819-562-1666
www.fm1077.ca
Médias sociaux: www.facebook.com/1077fm, twitter.com/fm1077

†*Sorel-Tracy:* CJSO-FM (Freq: 101.7)
52, rue du Roi, Sorel-Tracy, QC J3P 4M7
Tél: 450-743-2772, *Téléc:* 450-743-0293
Ligne sans frais: 888-489-1017
administration@fm1017.ca
www.fm1017.ca
Médias sociaux: www.facebook.com/fm1017.ca, twitter.com/Fm1017Info
Jean-Marc Belzile, Président et directeur-général

†*Squatec:* CFVD-FM-3 (Freq: 92.1)
Détenteur: CFVD-FM
Squatec, QC

†*St-Georges:* CHJM-FM (Freq: 99.7)
CP 100, St-Georges, QC G5Y 5C4
Tél: 418-227-0997, *Téléc:* 418-228-0096
studio@radiobeauce.com
www.mix997.com
Médias sociaux: www.facebook.com/mix997, twitter.com/MIX997

†*Ste-Marie-de-Beauce:* CHEQ-FM (Freq: 101.5)
373, rte Cameron, Ste-Marie-de-Beauce, QC G6E 3E2
Tél: 418-387-1015, *Téléc:* 418-387-3757
Ligne sans frais: 855-331-1015
studio@fm1015.ca
www.fm1015.ca
Médias sociaux: www.facebook.com/cheqfm
Chantal Baribeau, Directrice générale, cbaribeau@fm1015.ca

†*Témiscaming:* CKVM-FM-1 (Freq: 92.1)
Détenteur: CKVM-FM
Témiscaming, QC

†*Thetford Mines:* CFJO-FM (Freq: 103.1)
327, rue Labbé, Thetford Mines, QC G6G 1Z2
Tél: 418-338-1009
www.o973.com
Médias sociaux: www.facebook.com/182494896930, twitter.com/o973

†*Thetford Mines:* CKLD-FM (Freq: 105.5)
327, rue Labbé, Thetford Mines, QC G6G 1Z2
Tél: 418-335-7533
www.passionrock.com
Médias sociaux: www.facebook.com/113218588716902, twitter.com/prock1055

†*Trois-Rivières:* CHEY-FM (Rouge FM) (Freq: 94.7)
Détenteur: Bell Media Inc.*
#260, 1500, rue Royale, Trois-Rivières, QC G9A 6J4
Tél: 819-378-1023, *Téléc:* 819-378-1360
mauricie.rougefm.ca
Médias sociaux: www.facebook.com/947Rougefm, twitter.com/947rougefm
Marc Thibault, Directeur de la programmation, marc.thibault@bellmedia.ca

†*Trois-Rivières:* CIGB-FM (NRJ Mauricie 102.3) (Freq: 102.3)
Détenteur: Bell Media Inc.*
#260, 1500, rue Royal, Trois-Rivières, QC G9A 6J4
Tél: 819-378-1023, *Téléc:* 819-378-1360
mauricie.radionrj.ca
Médias sociaux: www.youtube.com/user/NRJquebec, www.facebook.com/nrj1023, twitter.com/nrjmauricie

†*Trois-Rivières:* CJEB-FM (Rythme Mauricie) (Freq: 100.1)
Détenteur: Cogeco Media Inc.*
#1200, 1350, rue Royale, Trois-Rivières, QC G9A 4J4
Tél: 819-691-1001, *Téléc:* 819-374-3222
www.rythmefm.com/mauricie
Médias sociaux: www.youtube.com/user/rythmefm, www.facebook.com/104523882938940, twitter.com/rythmefm1001
Daniel Brouillette, Directeur général

†*Trois-Rivières:* CKOB-FM (Freq: 106.9)
Détenteur: Cogeco Media Inc.*
#1200, 1350, rue Royale, Trois-Rivières, QC G9A 4J4
Tél: 819-374-3556, *Téléc:* 819-374-3222
www.fm1069.ca
Médias sociaux: www.facebook.com/fm1069, twitter.com/fm1069

†*Val d'Or:* CJMV-FM (NRJ Val-d'Or 102.7) (Freq: 102.7)
Détenteur: Bell Media Inc.*
1610, 3e Avenue, Val d'Or, QC J9P 1V8
Tél: 819-825-2568, *Téléc:* 819-825-2840
valdor.radionrj.ca
Médias sociaux: www.facebook.com/nrj1027, twitter.com/NRJ1027

†*Victoriaville:* CFDA-FM (Freq: 101.9)
55, rue St-Jean Baptiste, Victoriaville, QC G6P 6T3
Tél: 819-752-5545
www.passionrock.com/centre-du-quebec/accueil.aspx
Médias sociaux: www.facebook.com/114831865223346, twitter.com/prock1019

†*Victoriaville:* CFJO-FM (Freq: 93.7)
55, rue St-Jean-Baptiste, Victoriaville, QC G6P 4E1
Tél: 819-752-2785
www.o973.com

†*Ville-Marie:* CKVM-FM (Freq: 93.1)
62, rue Ste-Anne, Ville-Marie, QC J9V 2B7
Tél: 819-629-2710, *Téléc:* 819-622-0716
www.ckvmfm.com
Médias sociaux: www.facebook.com/ckvmfm

***Windsor:* CIAX-FM** (Freq: 98.3)
49, 6e av, Windsor, QC J1S 1T2
Tel: 819-845-2692
unitewindsor@qc.aira.com
www.ciaxfm.net
Social Media:
www.facebook.com/pages/CIAX-983-fm/185450771483585

Saskatchewan

†*Bellegarde:* CBKF-FM-4 (Freq: 91.9)
Détenteur: CBKF-FM (Première Chaîne)
Bellegarde, SK

***Carlyle Lake:* CIDD-FM** (Freq: 97.7)
Carlyle Lake, SK

***Peterborough:* CJLF-FM-2** (Freq: 89.3)
Owned by: CJLF-FM (Life 100.3)
Peterborough, ON
www.lifeonline.fm

***Carrot River:* CJVR-FM-3** (Freq: 99.7)
Owned by: CJVR-FM (CJVR Country)
Carrot River, SK

***Dafoe:* CJVR-FM-1** (Freq: 100.3)
Owned by: CJVR-FM (CJVR Country)
Dafoe, SK

***Estevan:* CHSN-FM (Sun 102)** (Freq: 102.3)
Owned by: Golden West Broadcasting Ltd.*
#200, 1236 - 5th St., Estevan, SK S4A 0Z6
Tel: 306-634-1280, *Toll-Free:* 800-824-0743
discoverestevan.com
Social Media: www.facebook.com/153908414691570, twitter.com/Sun102FM

***Estevan:* CKSE-FM** (Freq: 106.1)
Owned by: Golden West Broadcasting Ltd.*
#200, 1236 - 5th St., Estevan, SK S4A 0Z6
Tel: 306-636-6106
1061FM@DiscoverEstevan.com
discoverestevan.com
Social Media: www.facebook.com/1061Ckse, twitter.com/1061FMCKSE

***Hudson Bay:* CFMQ-FM** (Freq: 98.1)
PO Box 1272, Hudson Bay, SK S0E 0Y0
Tel: 306-865-3065, *Fax:* 306-865-2227
cfmq@sasktel.net

***Humboldt:* CHBO-FM (107.5 Bolt FM)** (Freq: 107.5)
Owned by: Golden West Broadcasting Ltd.*
PO Box 2888, 640 - 10th St., Humboldt, SK S0K 2A0
Tel: 306-682-2255, *Toll-Free:* 855-476-0155
boltfm@discoverhumboldt.com
www.discoverhumboldt.com
Social Media: www.facebook.com/107.5Humboldt, twitter.com/1075BoltFM

***La Ronge:* CBKA-FM** (Freq: 105.9)
Owned by: Canadian Broadcasting Corporation*
308 La Ronge Ave., La Ronge, SK S0J 1L0
Tel: 306-347-9540
www.cbc.ca/sask

***La Ronge:* CJLR-FM** (Freq: 89.9)
Napoleon T. Gardiner Broadcast Centre, 712 Finlayson St., La Ronge, SK S0J 1L0
Tel: 306-425-4003, *Fax:* 306-425-3123
reception@mbcradio.com
www.mbcradio.com
Social Media: twitter.com/mbcradionews
Deborah A. Charles, CEO, deb@mbcradio.com

***Meadow Lake:* CFDM-FM** (Freq: 105.7)
PO Box 8168, Flying Dust Reserve, Meadow Lake, SK S9X 1T8
Tel: 306-236-1445, *Fax:* 306-236-2861
cfdmradio@hotmail.com
cfdm.sasktelwebhosting.com

***Melfort:* CJVR-FM (CJVR Country)** (Freq: 105.1)
Owned by: Fabmar Communications Ltd.*
611 Main St. North, Melfort, SK S0E 1A0
Tel: 306-752-2587, *Fax:* 306-752-5932
info@cjvr.com
www.cjvr.com
Social Media: www.facebook.com/158719314169212, twitter.com/105CJVR
Ken Singer, Vice-President, k.singer@cjvr.com
Linda Rheaume, Station Manager, linda@cjur.com

***Moose Jaw:* CILG-FM (Country 100)** (Freq: 100.7)
Owned by: Golden West Broadcasting Ltd.*
1704 Main St. North, Moose Jaw, SK S6J 1L4
Tel: 306-694-0800, *Toll-Free:* 800-820-1768
discovermoosejaw.com
Social Media: www.facebook.com/Country100, twitter.com/country100fm

***Moose Jaw:* CJAW-FM (Mix 103)** (Freq: 103.9)
Owned by: Golden West Broadcasting Ltd.*
1704 Main St. North, Moose Jaw, SK S6J 1L4
Tel: 306-694-0800, *Toll-Free:* 800-820-1768
discovermoosejaw.com
Social Media: www.facebook.com/mix103moosejaw, twitter.com/mix103

***Nipawin:* CJNE-FM** (Freq: 94.7)
PO Box 220, Nipawin, SK S0E 1E0
Tel: 306-862-9478, *Fax:* 306-862-2334
www.cjnefm.com
Social Media: twitter.com/CJNEFM
Norman Rudock, Owner, norm.cjne@sasktel.net

†*North Battleford:* CBKF-FM-5 (Freq: 96.9FM)
Détenteur: CBKF-FM (Première Chaîne)
North Battleford, SK

***North Battleford:* CJCQ-FM** (Freq: 97.9)
Owned by: Jim Pattison Broadcast Group*
PO Box 1460, North Battleford, SK S9A 2Z5
Tel: 306-445-2477
q98.ca
Social Media:
www.facebook.com/pages/Q98/330629900302824, twitter.com/q98radio
David Dekker, General Manager, ddekker@rawlco.com

***Prince Albert:* CFMM-FM** (Freq: 99.1)
Owned by: Jim Pattison Broadcast Group*
1316 Central Ave., Prince Albert, SK S6V 6P5
Tel: 306-763-7421
www.power99fm.com
Social Media: instagram.com/power99fm, www.facebook.com/175060595871715, twitter.com/Power99Fm
Karl Johnston, General Manager, kjohnston@rawlco.com

** For details on this company see listing in Major Broadcasting Companies section; † French language station*

***Prince Albert:* CHQX-FM** (Freq: 101.5)
Owned by: Jim Pattison Broadcast Group*
1316 Central Ave., Prince Albert, SK S6V 6P5
Tel: 306-763-7421
www.mix101fm.com
Social Media: www.facebook.com/pages/Mix-101/22694645377
Karl Johnston, General Manager, kjohnston@rawlco.com

***†Prince Albert:* CKSF-FM** (Freq: 90.1)
Détenteur: CBKF-FM (Première Chaîne)
Prince Albert, SK

***Regina:* CBK-FM** (Freq: 96.9)
Owned by: Canadian Broadcasting Corporation*
2440 Broad St., Regina, SK S4P 0A5
Tel: 306-347-9540
www.cbc.ca/sask
Social Media: www.facebook.com/cbcsask, twitter.com/cbcsask
Other information: Radio phone: 306-347-9692
Lenora Sturge, Communications Officer

***†Regina:* CBKF-FM (Première Chaîne)** (Freq: 97.7)
Détenteur: Canadian Broadcasting Corporation*
CP 540, 2440, rue Broad, Regina, SK S4P 4A1
Tél: 306-347-9540
saskatchewan@radio-canada.ca
www.radio-canada.ca/saskatchewan
Médias sociaux: www.facebook.com/radiocanadasaskatchewan, twitter.com/RC_Saskatchewan

***Regina:* CBK-FM** (Freq: CBC Radio 2; 96.9FM)
Owned by: Canadian Broadcasting Corporation*
2440 Broad St., Regina, SK S4P 0A5
Tel: 306-347-9540
www.cbc.ca/sask
Paul Dederick, Managing Editor, paul.dederick@cbc.ca

***Regina:* CFWF-FM** (Freq: 104.9)
Owned by: Harvard Broadcasting Inc.*
1900 Rose St., Regina, SK S4P 0A9
Tel: 306-546-6200
www.thewolfrocks.com
Social Media: www.youtube.com/user/1049thewolfrocks, www.facebook.com/thewolfrocks, twitter.com/thewolfrocks
Jason Huschi, General Manager, jasonh@harvardbroadcasting.com

***Regina:* CHBD-FM (Big Dog 92.7)** (Freq: 92.7)
Owned by: Bell Media Inc.*
#100, 4303 Albert St. South, Regina, SK S4S 3R6
Tel: 306-337-2850, *Fax:* 306-359-0931
www.bigdog927.com
Social Media: www.facebook.com/BigDogRegina, twitter.com/BigDog927regina
David Fisher, General Manager, david.fisher@bellmedia.ca

***Regina:* CHMX-FM** (Freq: 92.1)
Owned by: Harvard Broadcasting Inc.*
1900 Rose St., Regina, SK S4P 0A9
Tel: 306-936-6200
www.lite92fm.com
Social Media: www.youtube.com/channel/UCrRNalS0SnhqXmi9dZ-16CA, www.facebook.com/pages/My-921-Feel-Good-Now/249363191756352, twitter.com/my921feelgood
Jason Huschi, General Manager, jasonh@harvardbroadcasting.com

***Regina:* CIZL-FM** (Freq: 98.9)
Owned by: Rawlco Radio Ltd.*
#210, 2401 Saskatchewan Dr., Regina, SK S4P 4H8
Tel: 306-525-0000
onair@z99.com
www.z99.com
Social Media: www.youtube.com/user/z99Regina, www.facebook.com/Z99Regina, twitter.com/z99regina
Tom Newton, General Manager, tnewton@rawlco.com

***Regina:* CJTR-FM** (Freq: 91.3)
PO Box 334 Main, Regina, SK S4P 3A1
Tel: 306-525-7274, *Fax:* 306-525-9741
radius@cjtr.ca
www.cjtr.ca
Social Media: www.facebook.com/cjtrfm, twitter.com/CJTR_Radio
Karl Valiaho, President

***Regina:* CKCK-FM** (Freq: 94.5)
Owned by: Rawlco Radio Ltd.*
#210, 2401 Saskatchewan Dr., Regina, SK S4P 4H8
Tel: 306-525-0000, *Fax:* 306-547-8557
www.jackfmregina.com
Social Media: www.youtube.com/user/945jackfmregina, www.facebook.com/JackRegina, twitter.com/jackregina

***Rosetown:* CKVX-FM (Mix 104.9)** (Freq: 104.9)
Owned by: Golden West Broadcasting Ltd.*
PO Box 490, 208 Hwy. 4, Rosetown, SK S0L 2V0
Tel: 306-882-2686, *Toll-Free:* 800-667-5313
cjymnews@goldenwestradio.com
www.westcentralonline.com
Social Media: www.facebook.com/324448833194, twitter.com/Mix104FM

***Saskatoon:* CFCR-FM** (Freq: 90.5)
PO Box 7544, Saskatoon, SK S7K 4L4
Tel: 306-664-6678
cfcr@cfcr.ca
www.cfcr.ca
Social Media: www.youtube.com/CFCRSASKATOON, www.facebook.com/pages/CFCR-905-FM-Saskatoon-Community-Radio, twitter.com/CFCRSASKATOON
Neil Bergen, Station Manager, manager@cfcr.ca

***Saskatoon:* CFMC-FM** (Freq: 95.1)
Owned by: Rawlco Radio Ltd.*
715 Saskatchewan Cres. West, Saskatoon, SK S7M 5V7
Tel: 306-934-2222, *Fax:* 306-477-0002
www.c95.com
Social Media: www.facebook.com/pages/C95/1073093941 9, twitter.com/c95
Kristy Werner, General Manager, kwerner@rawlco.com

***Saskatoon:* CJDJ-FM** (Freq: 102.1)
Owned by: Rawlco Radio Ltd.*
715 Saskatchewan Cres. West, Saskatoon, SK S7M 5V7
Tel: 306-934-2222, *Fax:* 306-477-0002
www.rock102rocks.com
Social Media: www.youtube.com/rock102ube, www.facebook.com/rock102rocks, twitter.com/rock102twits

***Saskatoon:* CJMK-FM** (Freq: 98.3)
Owned by: Saskatoon Media Group*
366 - 3rd Ave. South, Saskatoon, SK S7K 1M5
Tel: 306-244-1975, *Fax:* 306-665-5501
cool@98cool.ca
www.98cool.ca
Social Media: www.facebook.com/98Cool, twitter.com/98COOLfm
Vic Dubois, General Manager

***Saskatoon:* CKBL-FM** (Freq: 92.9)
Owned by: Saskatoon Media Group*
366 - 3rd Ave. South, Saskatoon, SK S7K 1M5
Tel: 306-244-1975, *Fax:* 306-665-5501
thebull@929thebullrocks.com
www.929thebullrocks.com
Social Media: www.facebook.com/929theBULL, twitter.com/929TheBull
Vic Dubois, General Manager

***Swift Current:* CIMG-FM (The Eagle 94.1)** (Freq: 94.1)
Owned by: Golden West Broadcasting Ltd.*
134 Central Ave. North, Swift Current, SK S9H 0L1
Tel: 306-773-4605, *Toll-Free:* 800-821-8073
eaglecontrol@goldenwestradio.com
www.swiftcurrentonline.com
Social Media: www.facebook.com/164908956862679, twitter.com/theeagle94one

***Swift Current:* CKFI-FM (Magic 97.1)** (Freq: 97.1)
Owned by: Golden West Broadcasting Ltd.*
134 Central Ave. North, Swift Current, SK S9H 0L1
Tel: 306-773-4605, *Toll-Free:* 800-821-8073
www.swiftcurrentonline.com
Social Media: www.facebook.com/122248154511534, twitter.com/magic97sc

***Waskesiu:* CJVR-FM-2** (Freq: 106.3)
Owned by: CJVR-FM (CJVR Country)
Waskesiu, SK

***Weyburn:* CKRC-FM (Magic 103.5)** (Freq: 103.5)
Owned by: Golden West Broadcasting Ltd.*
305 Souris Ave., Weyburn, SK S4H 0C6
Tel: 306-848-1190, *Toll-Free:* 800-821-9642
discoverweyburn.com
Social Media: www.facebook.com/105410576167749, twitter.com/magic1035

***Yorkton:* CFGW-FM** (Freq: 94.1)
Owned by: Harvard Broadcasting Inc.*
120 Smith St. East, Yorkton, SK S3N 3V3
Tel: 306-782-9410, *Fax:* 306-783-4994
ykt-reception@harvardbroadcasting.com
www.941thefox.com
Social Media: www.youtube.com/user/foxfmyorkton, www.facebook.com/pages/Fox-FM/90324353077, twitter.com/MOREFOXFM
Angie Norton, General Manager, anorton@harvardbroadcasting.com

***†Zenon Park:* CBKF-FM-3** (Freq: 93.5FM)
Détenteur: CBKF-FM (Première Chaîne)
Zenon Park, SK

Yukon Territory

***Whitehorse:* CFWH-FM** (Freq: 94.5)
Owned by: Canadian Broadcasting Corporation*
3103 - 3rd Ave., Whitehorse, YT Y1A 2A2
Tel: 867-668-8400
cbcnorth@cbc.ca
www.cbc.ca/north
Kerry Fraser, Manager, Communications

***Whitehorse:* CHON-FM** (Freq: 98.1; 90.5)
#6, 4230A - 4 Ave., Whitehorse, YT Y1A 1K1
Tel: 867-668-6629, *Fax:* 867-668-6612
nnby@nnby.net
www.nnby.net
Social Media: www.facebook.com/pages/CHON-FM-Radio-981/366402063425924, twitter.com/CHONNews

***Whitehorse:* CIAY-FM** (Freq: 100.7)
91806 Alaska Hwy., Whitehorse, YT Y1A 5B7
Tel: 867-393-2429, *Fax:* 867-393-2439
info@lifewhitehorse.com
lifewhitehorse.com

***Whitehorse:* CKRW-FM (The Rush)** (Freq: 96.1)
Owned by: Klondike Broadcasting Ltd.*
#203, 4103 - 4th Ave., Whitehorse, YT Y1A 1H6
Tel: 867-668-6100, *Fax:* 867-668-4209
info@ckrw.com
www.ckrw.com

Television Stations

Alberta

***Athabasca:* CFRN-TV-12** (Channel: 13)
Owned by: CFRN-TV
Athabasca, AB

***Bonnyville:* CKSA-TV-2** (Channel: 9)
Owned by: CKSA-TV
Bonnyville, AB

***Calgary:* CBRT-DT** (Channel: 9; 21)
Owned by: Canadian Broadcasting Corporation*
PO Box 2640, Calgary, AB T2P 2M7
Tel: 403-521-6000, *Fax:* 403-521-6079
www.cbc.ca/calgary
Social Media: twitter.com/cbccalgary
Other information: Phone, TV Newsroom: 403-521-6055
Alan Thorgeirson, Director, Calgary Centre, 403-521-6252
Suzanne Waddell, Manager, Communications, 403-521-6207, suzanne.waddell@cbc.ca

***Calgary:* CFCN-DT** (Channel: 29)
Owned by: Bell Media TV*
80 Patina Rise SW, Calgary, AB T3H 2W4
Tel: 403-240-5600
calgarynews@ctv.ca
www.cfcn.ca

***Calgary:* CICT-TV** (Channel: 7)
Owned by: Global Television Network*
222 - 23 St. NE, Calgary, AB T2E 7N2
Tel: 403-235-7777
Calgary@globalnews.ca
www.globaltvcalgary.com
Social Media: instagram.com/globalcalgary, www.facebook.com/GlobalCalgary, twitter.com/GlobalCalgary

* For details on this company see listing in Major Broadcasting Companies section; † French language station

***Calgary:* CKAL-DT** (Channel: 5)
Owned by: Rogers Broadcasting Ltd.*
535 - 7th Ave. SW, Calgary, AB T2P 0Y4
Tel: 403-508-2222
www.citytv.com/calgary

***Calgary:* Shaw TV - Calgary** (Channel: 10)
Owned by: Shaw Media Inc.
2400 - 32nd Ave. NE, Calgary, AB T2E 9A7
Tel: 403-539-6711, *Fax:* 504-735-6100
shawtv.calgary@sjrb.ca
www.shaw.ca/ShawTV/Calgary
Social Media: www.facebook.com/ShawTVCalgary, twitter.com/ShawTVCalgary

***Drumheller:* CFCN-TV-1** (Channel: 12)
Calgary
Owned by: CFCN-TV
Drumheller, AB

†*Edmonton:* CBXFT-DT (Channel: 47)
Détenteur: Canadian Broadcasting Corporation*
CP 555, Edmonton, AB T5J 2P4
Tél: 780-468-7500, *Ligne sans frais:* 888-680-2432
nouvelles.alberta@radio-canada.ca
www.radio-canada.ca/alberta

***Edmonton:* CBXT-DT** (Channel: 42)
Owned by: Canadian Broadcasting Corporation*
PO Box 555, Edmonton, AB T5J 2P4
Tel: 780-468-7500
www.cbc.ca/edmonton
Social Media: www.facebook.com/cbcedmonton, twitter.com/CBCEdmonton
Neill Fitzpatrick, Executive Producer, 780-468-7527

***Edmonton:* CFRN-DT** (Channel: 12)
Owned by: Bell Media TV*
18520 Stony Plain Rd., Edmonton, AB T5S 1A8
Tel: 780-483-3311
edmonton.ctvnews.ca
Social Media: www.facebook.com/CTVEdmonton, twitter.com/ctvedmonton

***Edmonton:* CKEM-DT** (Channel: 57)
Owned by: Rogers Broadcasting Ltd.*
10212 Jasper Ave., Edmonton, AB T5J 5A3
Tel: 780-424-2222
www.citytv.com/edmonton

***Edmonton:* Shaw TV - Edmonton** (Channel: 10)
Owned by: Shaw Media Inc.
10450 - 178 St. NW, Edmonton, AB T5S 1S2
Tel: 780-490-3555, *Fax:* 780-490-3510
edmmc@sjrb.ca
www.shaw.ca/ShawTV/Edmonton
Social Media: www.facebook.com/ShawTvEdmonton, twitter.com/ShawTVEdm

***Fort McMurray:* Shaw TV - Fort McMurray** (Channel: 10)
Owned by: Shaw Media Inc.
#200, 208 Beaconhill Dr., Fort McMurray, AB T9H 2R1
Toll-Free: 888-472-2222
gowoodbuffalo@sjrb.ca
www.shaw.ca/ShawTV/FortMcMurray

***Jasper:* CFRN-TV-11** (Channel: 11)
Owned by: CFRN-TV
Jasper, AB

***Lac La Biche:* CFRN-TV-5** (Channel: 2)
Edmonton
Owned by: CFRN-TV
Lac La Biche, AB

***Lethbridge:* CFCN-DT** (Channel: 29)
Owned by: Bell Media TV*
640 - 13 St. North, Lethbridge, AB T1H 2S8
Tel: 403-329-3644, *Fax:* 403-317-2420
www.cfcn.ca

***Lethbridge:* CFCN-TV-5** (Channel: 13)
Owned by: CFCN-TV
Lethbridge, AB

***Lethbridge:* CISA-DT** (Channel: 7)
Owned by: Global Television Network*
1401 - 28 St. North, Lethbridge, AB T1H 6H9
Tel: 403-329-2903
lethbridge@globalnews.ca
www.globallethbridge.com
Social Media: www.facebook.com/globallethbridge, twitter.com/globalleth

***Lethbridge:* CJIL-TV** (Channel: 17)
450 - 31 St. North, Lethbridge, AB T1H 3Z3
Tel: 403-380-3399, *Fax:* 403-380-7490
info@miraclechannel.ca
www.miraclechannel.ca
Social Media: www.youtube.com/cjiltv, www.facebook.com/pages/Miracle-Channel/115781708437573, twitter.com/miraclechannel
Leon Fontaine, Chief Executive Officer

***Lethbridge:* CKAL-DT-1** (Channel: 46)
Owned by: CKAL-TV
Lethbridge, AB

***Lethbridge:* Shaw TV - Lethbridge** (Channel: 9)
Owned by: Shaw Media Inc.
1232 - 3 Ave. South, Lethbridge, AB T1J 0J9
Tel: 403-310-7429
shawtv.lethbridge@sjrb.ca
www.shaw.ca/ShawTV/Lethbridge

***Lloydminster:* CITL-TV (CTV)** (Channel: 4)
Owned by: Newcap Radio*
5026 - 50th St., Lloydminster, AB T9V 1P3
Tel: 780-875-3321, *Fax:* 780-875-4704
Toll-Free: 800-565-2572
tvag@newcap.ca
citltv.ca
Social Media: www.youtube.com/user/Newcaptv/videos, www.facebook.com/NewcapTelevision, twitter.com/NewcapTVNews
Chad Tabish, General Manager, ctabish@newcap.ca
Bob Cameron, Program Director, bcameron@newcap.ca

***Lloydminster:* CKSA-TV** (Channel: 2; CBC affiliate)
Owned by: Newcap Radio*
5026 - 50 St., Lloydminster, AB T9V 1P3
Tel: 780-875-3321, *Fax:* 780-875-4704
cksatv.ca
Social Media: www.youtube.com/user/Newcaptv, www.facebook.com/NewcapTelevision, twitter.com/NewcapTVNews
Chad Tabish, General Manager, ctabish@newcap.ca
Bob Cameron, Program Director, bcameron@newcap.ca

***Lougheed:* CFRN-TV-7** (Channel: 7)
Edmonton
Owned by: CFRN-TV
Lougheed, AB

***Medicine Hat:* CFCN-TV-8** (Channel: 8)
Calgary
Owned by: CFCN-TV
Medicine Hat, AB

***Medicine Hat:* Shaw TV - Medicine Hat** (Channel: 10)
Owned by: Shaw Media Inc.
954 Factory St. SE, Medicine Hat, AB T1A 8A5
Tel: 403-488-7077
shawtvmedicinehat@sjrb.ca
www.shaw.ca/shawtv/medicinehat

***Peace River:* CFRN-TV-2** (Channel: 3)
Edmonton
Owned by: CFRN-TV
Peace River, AB

***Red Deer:* CFRN-TV-6** (Channel: 8)
Edmonton
Owned by: CFRN-TV
Red Deer, AB

***Red Deer:* CKEM-DT-1** (Channel: 4)
Owned by: CKEM-TV
Red Deer, AB

***Red Deer:* Shaw TV - Central Alberta** (Channel: 10)
Owned by: Shaw Media Inc.
4761 - 62 St., Red Deer, AB T4N 2R4
Tel: 403-340-6435, *Fax:* 403-340-6414
gocentral@sjrb.ca
www.shaw.ca/ShawTV/RedDeer
Social Media: www.facebook.com/ShawTVRedDeer, twitter.com/ShawTVRedDeer

***Redcliff:* CHAT-TV** (Channel: 6)
Owned by: The Jim Pattison Broadcast Group*
10 Boundary Rd. SE, Redcliff, AB T0J 2P0
Tel: 403-548-8282, *Fax:* 403-548-8270
chatnews@jpbg.ca
chattelevision.ca
Social Media: instagram.com/chattvnews, www.facebook.com/CHATTV, twitter.com/chattelevision

***Rocky Mountain House:* CFRN-TV-10** (Channel: 12)
Edmonton
Owned by: CFRN-TV
Rocky Mountain House, AB

***Waterton Park:* CFCN-TV-17** (Channel: 6)
Calgary
Owned by: CFCN-TV
Waterton Park, AB

***Wetaskiwin:* EastLink TV - Wetaskiwin** (Channel: 10)
Owned by: EastLink TV*
Wetaskiwin, AB
eastlinktvgp@eastlink.ca
eastlinktv.com

***Whitecourt:* CFRN-TV-3** (Channel: 12)
Edmonton
Owned by: CFRN-TV
Whitecourt, AB

British Columbia

***100 Mile House:* CFJC-TV-6** (Channel: 5)
Kamloops
Owned by: CFJC-TV
100 Mile House, BC

***100 Mile House:* CITM-TV** (Channel: 3)
Owned by: CHAN-DT
100 Mile House, BC

***Apex Mountain:* CHNJ-TV-1** (Channel: 11)
Vancouver
Owned by: CHAN-DT
Apex Mountain, BC

***Blue River:* CH2531** (Channel: 13)
Owned by: CHAN-DT
Blue River, BC

***Burnaby:* CHAN-DT** (Channel: 8; 22)
Owned by: Global Television Network*
7850 Enterprise St., Burnaby, BC V58 1V7
Tel: 604-420-2288, *Fax:* 604-422-6466
tips@globaltvbc.com
www.globalnews.ca/bc
Social Media: www.facebook.com/GlobalBC, twitter.com/GlobalBC

***Burnaby:* KVOS-TV** (Channel: 12)
#218, 4259 Canada Way, Burnaby, BC V5G 1H3
Tel: 604-681-1212, *Fax:* 604-736-4510
metvnetwork.com
Social Media: www.facebook.com/KVOSTV
Jacky Nelson, Contact, jnelson@kvos.com

***Campbell River:* Shaw TV - Campbell River** (Channel: 4)
North Island & Powell River
Owned by: Shaw Media Inc.
500 Robron Rd., Campbell River, BC V9W 5Z2
Tel: 250-923-8821, *Fax:* 250-923-7796
campbellriver.shawtv@sjrb.ca
www.shaw.ca/ShawTV/Comox
Social Media: www.youtube.com/ShawTVNorthIsland, www.facebook.com/shawtvnviandpr, twitter.com/ShawTV_NVIPR

** For details on this company see listing in Major Broadcasting Companies section; † French language station*

***Castlegar:* Shaw TV - Castlegar** (Channel: 10)
Owned by: Shaw Media Inc.
1951 Columbia Ave., Castlegar, BC V2N 2W8
Tel: 250-365-3711, *Fax:* 250-365-2676
go_kootenays@sjrb.ca
www.shaw.ca/ShawTV/Cranbrook

***Celista:* CHBC-TV-6** (Channel: 3)
Kelowna
Owned by: CHBC-TV
Celista, BC

***Chase:* CFJC-TV-8** (Channel: 11)
Kamloops
Owned by: CFJC-TV
Chase, BC

***Chilliwack:* CHAN-TV-1** (Channel: 11)
Vancouver
Owned by: CHAN-DT
Chilliwack, BC

***Chilliwack:* Shaw TV - Chilliwack** (Channel: 4)
Owned by: Shaw Media Inc.
9275 Nowell St., Chilliwack, BC V2P 7G7
Tel: 604-792-8182, *Fax:* 604-792-0966
go_fraservalley@shaw.ca
www.shaw.ca/ShawTV/Chilliwack

***Clinton:* CFJC-TV-4** (Channel: 9)
Kamloops
Owned by: CFJC-TV
Clinton, BC

***Courtenay:* CHAN-TV-4** (Channel: 13)
Vancouver
Owned by: CHAN-DT
Courtenay, BC

***Courtenay:* Shaw TV - Comox Valley** (Channel: 4)
North Island & Powell River
Owned by: Shaw Media Inc.
1591 McPhee Ave., Courtenay, BC V9N 3A6
Tel: 250-898-2563, *Fax:* 250-334-3640
comoxvalleytv@shaw.ca
www.shaw.ca/ShawTV/Comox
Social Media: www.youtube.com/ShawTVNorthIsland, www.facebook.com/shawtvnviandpr, twitter.com/ShawTV_NVIPR

***Cranbrook:* Shaw TV - Cranbrook** (Channel: 10)
Kootenays
Owned by: Shaw Media Inc.
720 Kootenay St. North, Cranbrook, BC V1C 3V2
Tel: 250-417-3884, *Fax:* 250-417-3899
go_kootenays@sjrb.ca
www.shaw.ca/ShawTV/Cranbrook

***Creston:* CKTN-TV-4** (Channel: 12)
Vancouver
Owned by: CHAN-DT
Creston, BC

***Dawson Creek:* CJDC-TV** (Channel: 5; CBC affiliate)
Owned by: Bell Media Inc.*
901 - 102 Ave., Dawson Creek, BC V1G 2B6
Tel: 250-782-3341, *Fax:* 250-782-3154
www.cjdctv.com
Social Media: www.facebook.com/CJDCTVDawsonCreek, twitter.com/cjdctv
Terry Shepherd, General Manager, terry.shepherd@bellmedia.ca

***Enderby:* CHBC-TV-5** (Channel: 4)
Kelowna
Owned by: CHBC-TV
Enderby, BC

***Fort St John:* Shaw TV - Fort St John & Dawson Creek** (Channel: 10)
Northern BC
Owned by: Shaw Media Inc.
#204, 9817 - 100 Ave., Fort St John, BC V1J 1Y4
Tel: 250-785-9296, *Fax:* 250-785-9777
go_peacecountry@shaw.ca
www.shaw.ca/ShawTV/PrinceGeorge
Social Media: www.facebook.com/ShawTVNorthBC, twitter.com/shawtvnorthbc

***Grand Forks:* CISR-TV-1** (Channel: 7)
Vancouver
Owned by: CHAN-DT
Grand Forks, BC

***Granisle:* CH2798** (Channel: 7)
Vancouver
Owned by: CHAN-DT
Granisle, BC

***Hixon:* CKPG-TV-1** (Channel: 10)
Prince George
Owned by: CKPG-TV
Hixon, BC

***Houston:* CFHO-TV** (Channel: 8)
Vancouver
Owned by: CHAN-DT
Houston, BC

***Hudson's Hope:* CJDC-TV-1** (Channel: 11)
Dawson Creek
Owned by: CJDC-TV
Hudson's Hope, BC

***Kamloops:* CFJC-TV** (Channel: 4)
Owned by: The Jim Pattison Broadcast Group*
460 Pemberton Terrace, Kamloops, BC V2C 1T5
Tel: 250-372-3322, *Fax:* 250-374-0445
www.cfjctv.com
Social Media: www.facebook.com/CFJCnews, twitter.com/cfjc_news

***Kamloops:* CHKM-TV** (Channel: 6)
Vancouver
Owned by: CHAN-DT
Kamloops, BC

***Kamloops:* Shaw TV - Kamloops** (Channel: 10)
Owned by: Shaw Media Inc.
180 Briar Ave., Kamloops, BC V2B 1C1
Tel: 250-376-8888
go_kamloops@shaw.ca
www.shaw.ca/ShawTV/Kamloops
Social Media: www.youtube.com/ShawTVKamloops, www.facebook.com/ShawTVKamloops, twitter.com/ShawTVKamloops

***Kelowna:* CHBC-DT** (Channel: 27)
Owned by: Global Television Network*
342 Leon Ave., Kelowna, BC V1Y 6J2
Tel: 250-762-4535
okanagan@globalnews.ca
globalnews.ca/okanagan
Social Media: www.facebook.com/chbcglobalokanagan, twitter.com/GlobalOkanagan

***Kelowna:* CHKL-DT** (Channel: 24)
Vancouver
Owned by: CHAN-DT
Kelowna, BC

***Kelowna:* Shaw TV - Okanagan** (Channel: 11)
Owned by: Shaw Media Inc.
#106, 1223 Water St., Kelowna, BC V1Y 9V1
Tel: 250-979-6540, *Fax:* 250-979-6550
go_okanagan@shaw.ca
www.shaw.ca/ShawTV/Kelowna
Social Media: www.youtube.com/user/ShawTVOkanagan, www.facebook.com/ShawTVOk, twitter.com/ShawTVOkanagan
Tim Morton, Senior Producer

***Lillooet:* CFDF-TV-2** (Channel: 13)
Vancouver
Owned by: CHAN-DT
Lillooet, BC

***Logan Lake:* CH2518** (Channel: 18)
Vancouver
Owned by: CHAN-DT
Logan Lake, BC

***Lytton:* CILY-TV-2** (Channel: 8)
Vancouver
Owned by: CHAN-DT
Lytton, BC

***Mackenzie:* CIMK-TV-1** (Channel: 9)
Vancouver
Owned by: CHAN-DT
Mackenzie, BC

***Mackenzie:* CKPG-TV-4** (Channel: 6)
Prince George
Owned by: CKPG-TV
Mackenzie, BC

***Malakwa:* CFFI-TV-2** (Channel: 11)
Vancouver
Owned by: CHAN-DT
Malakwa, BC

***McBride:* CH2013** (Channel: 4)
Owned by: CHAN-DT
McBride, BC

***Merritt:* CFJC-TV-3** (Channel: 8)
Kamloops
Owned by: CFJC-TV
Merritt, BC

***Merritt:* Shaw TV - Merritt** (Channel: 10)
Owned by: Shaw Media Inc.
Merritt, BC
Tel: 250-378-4919, *Fax:* 250-378-5233
go_merritt@shaw.ca
www.shaw.ca/ShawTV/Merritt
Social Media: www.youtube.com/user/ShawTVMerritt, www.facebook.com/ShawTVMerritt

***Nakusp:* CJNP-TV-3** (Channel: 7)
Vancouver
Owned by: CHAN-DT
Nakusp, BC

***Nanaimo:* Shaw TV - Nanaimo** (Channel: 4)
Central Island
Owned by: Shaw Media Inc.
4316 Boban Dr., Nanaimo, BC V9T 6A7
Tel: 250-760-1974, *Fax:* 250-760-1998
nanaimotv@shaw.ca
www.shaw.ca/ShawTV/Nanaimo
Social Media: www.youtube.com/ShawTVCentralVI, www.facebook.com/ShawTV.CVI, twitter.com/ShawTV_CVI

***Nanaimo:* Shaw TV - Parksville** (Channel: 4)
Central Island
Owned by: Shaw Media Inc.
4316 Boban Dr., Nanaimo, BC V9T 6A7
Tel: 250-248-3141, *Fax:* 866-861-3662
parksvilletv@shaw.ca
www.shaw.ca/ShawTV/Nanaimo

***Nelson:* CKTN-TV-3** (Channel: 3)
Vancouver
Owned by: CHAN-DT
Nelson, BC

***New Denver:* CH5668 / CH5669** (Channel: 3; 6)
Vancouver
Owned by: CHAN-DT
New Denver, BC

***Nicola Valley:* CFJC-TV-12** (Channel: 10)
Kamloops
Owned by: CFJC-TV
Nicola Valley, BC

***Olalla:* CHKC-TV-5** (Channel: 11)
Vancouver
Owned by: CHAN-DT
Olalla, BC

***Oliver:* CKKM-TV** (Channel: 3)
Owned by: CHAN-DT
Oliver, BC

***Peachland:* CIPL-TV** (Channel: 9)
Vancouver
Owned by: CHAN-DT
Peachland, BC

***Penticton:* CHBC-TV-7** (Channel: 7)
Kelowna
Owned by: CHBC-TV
Penticton, BC

***Penticton:* CHKL-DT-1** (Channel: 30)
Vancouver
Owned by: CHAN-DT
Penticton, BC

** For details on this company see listing in Major Broadcasting Companies section; † French language station*

***Port Alberni:* CHEK-TV-3** (Channel: 11)
Victoria
Owned by: CHEK-TV
Port Alberni, BC

***Port Alberni:* Shaw TV - Port Alberni** (Channel: 4)
Central Island
Owned by: Shaw Media Inc.
4278 - 8 Ave., Port Alberni, BC V9Y 7S8
Tel: 250-723-7042, *Fax:* 250-723-4024
portalbernitv@shaw.ca
www.shaw.ca/ShawTV/Nanaimo
Social Media: www.youtube.com/user/ShawTVPA, www.facebook.com/ShawTVPA, twitter.com/ShawTV_PA

***Powell River:* Shaw TV - Powell River** (Channel: 4)
North Island & Powell River
Owned by: Shaw Media Inc.
4706 Ewing Pl., Powell River, BC V8A 2N5
Tel: 604-485-4647
powellrivertv@shaw.ca
www.shaw.ca/ShawTV/Comox
Social Media: www.youtube.com/ShawTVNorthIsland, www.facebook.com/shawtvnviandpr, twitter.com/ShawTV_NVIPR

***Prince George:* CIFG-TV** (Channel: 12)
Vancouver
Owned by: CHAN-DT
Prince George, BC

***Prince George:* CKPG-TV** (Channel: 2)
Owned by: The Jim Pattison Broadcast Group*
1810 - 3rd Ave., 2nd Fl., Prince George, BC V2M 1G4
Tel: 250-564-8861, *Fax:* 250-562-8768
ckpg.com
Social Media: www.youtube.com/user/CKPGTV, www.facebook.com/ckpgnews, twitter.com/ckpgnews
Mike Clotildes, General Manager, mclotildes@ckpg.com

***Prince George:* Shaw TV - Prince George** (Channel: 10)
Northern BC
Owned by: Shaw Media Inc.
2519 Queensway St., Prince George, BC V2L 1N1
Tel: 250-614-7325, *Fax:* 250-614-7347
go_princegeorge@shaw.ca
www.shaw.ca/ShawTV/PrinceGeorge
Social Media: www.facebook.com/ShawTVNorthBC, twitter.com/shawtvnorthbc

***Prince Rupert:* CFTK-TV-1** (Channel: 6)
Terrace
Owned by: CFTK-TV
Prince Rupert, BC

***Pritchard:* CFJC-TV-19** (Channel: 2)
Kamloops
Owned by: CFJC-TV
Pritchard, BC

***Pritchard:* CHKM-TV-1** (Channel: 9)
Vancouver
Owned by: CHAN-DT
Pritchard, BC

***Quesnel:* CFJC-TV-11** (Channel: 7)
Kamloops
Owned by: CFJC-TV
Quesnel, BC

***Quesnel:* CITM-TV-2** (Channel: 8)
Vancouver
Owned by: CHAN-DT
Quesnel, BC

***Quesnel:* CKPG-TV-5** (Channel: 13)
Prince George
Owned by: CKPG-TV
Quesnel, BC

***Quesnel:* Shaw TV - Quesnel** (Channel: 10)
Northern BC
Owned by: Shaw Media Inc.
156 Front St., Quesnel, BC V2J 2K1
Tel: 250-992-8363
go_quesnel@shaw.ca
www.shaw.ca/ShawTV/PrinceGeorge

***Revelstoke:* CHKL-TV-3** (Channel: 7)
Vancouver
Owned by: CHAN-DT
Revelstoke, BC

***Rimrock:* CKRR-TV-2** (Channel: 11)
Vancouver
Owned by: CHAN-DT
Rimrock, BC

***Salmon Arm:* CFSA-TV-1** (Channel: 13)
Vancouver
Owned by: CHAN-DT
Salmon Arm, BC

***Salmon Arm:* CHBC-TV-4** (Channel: 9)
Kelowna
Owned by: CHBC-TV
Salmon Arm, BC

***Santa Rosa:* CISR-TV** (Channel: 68)
Vancouver
Owned by: CHAN-DT
Santa Rosa, BC

***Savona:* CFSC-TV-1** (Channel: 13)
Vancouver
Owned by: CHAN-DT
Savona, BC

***Smithers:* CFHO-TV-1** (Channel: 13)
Vancouver
Owned by: CHAN-DT
Smithers, BC

***Spences Bridge:* CJNA-TV-2** (Channel: 7)
Vancouver
Owned by: CHAN-DT
Spences Bridge, BC

***Squamish:* CHAN-TV-3** (Channel: 7)
Vancouver
Owned by: CHAN-DT
Squamish, BC

***Squamish:* Shaw TV - Sea to Sky** (Channel: 4)
Owned by: Shaw Media Inc.
1103 Magee St., Squamish, BC V8B 0E8
Tel: 604-567-1112
www.shaw.ca/ShawTV/Whistler

***Surrey:* CHNU-DT** (Channel: 66)
Owned by: ZoomerMedia*
#204, 5668 - 192 St., Surrey, BC V3S 2V7
Tel: 604-576-6880, *Fax:* 604-576-6895
audience@joytv10.ca
www.joytv.ca
Social Media: www.facebook.com/JoytvBC, twitter.com/Joytv10BC
Duane Parks, Contact, duane.parks@zoomermedia.ca

***Taghum:* CKTN-TV-2** (Channel: 23)
Vancouver
Owned by: CHAN-DT
Taghum, BC

***Terrace:* CFTK-TV** (Channel: 3; CBC affiliate)
Owned by: Bell Media Inc.*
4625 Lazelle Ave., Terrace, BC V8G 1S4
Tel: 250-635-6316, *Fax:* 250-638-6320
www.cftktv.com
Social Media: www.facebook.com/230113003717168
Brian Langston, General Manager, brian.langston@bellmedia.ca

***Terrace:* Community Channel 10 (CityWest TV-10)** (Channel: 10)
Owned by: CityWest
2709 Kalum St., Terrace, BC V8G 2M4
Tel: 778-634-9712, *Fax:* 250-635-8214
communitychannel10@citywest.ca
www.citywest.ca/tv/community-tv

***Trail:* CKTN-TV** (Channel: 8)
Vancouver
Owned by: CHAN-DT
Trail, BC

†*Vancouver:* CBUFT-DT (Channel: 26)
Détenteur: Canadian Broadcasting Corporation*
CP 4600, Vancouver, BC V6B 2R5
Tél: 604-662-6000, *Téléc:* 604-662-6161
www.radio-canada.ca/colombie-britannique-et-yukon

***Vancouver:* CBUT-DT** (Channel: 2)
Owned by: Canadian Broadcasting Corporation*
PO Box 4600, Vancouver, BC V6B 4A2
Tel: 604-662-6000
www.cbc.ca/bc

***Vancouver:* CIVT-DT** (Channel: 32)
Owned by: Bell Media TV*
#500, 969 Robson St., Vancouver, BC V6Z 1X5
Tel: 604-608-2868, *Fax:* 604-608-2868
bccomments@ctv.ca
bc.ctvnews.ca
Social Media: www.facebook.com/CTVBCNews, twitter.com/CTVBC

***Vancouver:* CKVU-TV** (Channel: 10)
Owned by: Rogers Broadcasting Ltd.*
180 West 2nd St., Vancouver, BC V5Y 3T9
Tel: 604-876-1344, *Toll-Free:* 888-336-9978
www.citytv.com/vancouver
Social Media: www.facebook.com/Citytv, twitter.com/city_tv
Kirsten Robertson, Contact, Programming, kirsten.robertson@rci.rogers.com

***Vancouver:* Novus TV (NVTV 4)** (Channel: 4)
Owned by: Novus Entertainment Inc.
#300, 112 East 3rd Ave., Vancouver, BC V5T 1C8
Tel: 778-724-1371, *Fax:* 604-685-7832
communitychannel@novusnow.ca
www.novuscommunitytv.ca
Social Media: www.youtube.com/user/NovusTV, www.facebook.com/NVTV4, twitter.com/novustv

***Vancouver:* Shaw TV - Vancouver & Area** (Channel: 4)
Owned by: Shaw Media Inc.
#900, 1067 West Cordova St., Vancouver, BC V6C 3T5
Tel: 604-629-4274, *Fax:* 604-629-4231
ShawTVVancouver@sjrb.ca
www.shaw.ca/ShawTV/Vancouver
Social Media: www.youtube.com/Shawtvvancouver, www.facebook.com/ShawTvVancouver, twitter.com/ShawTVVancouver

***Vavenby:* CKVA-TV-1** (Channel: 8)
Vancouver
Owned by: CHAN-DT
Vavenby, BC

***Vernon:* CHBC-DT-2** (Channel: 20)
Kelowna
Owned by: CHBC-TV
Vernon, BC

***Vernon:* CHKL-DT-2** (Channel: 22)
Vancouver
Owned by: CHAN-DT
Vernon, BC

***Victoria:* CHEK-TV** (Channel: 6)
780 Kings Rd., Victoria, BC V8T 5A2
Tel: 250-383-2435, *Fax:* 250-384-7766
info@cheknews.ca
www.cheknews.ca
Social Media: www.facebook.com/cheknews, twitter.com/CHEK_News

***Victoria:* Shaw TV - Vancouver Island** (Channel: 4)
Owned by: Shaw Media Inc.
Save on Foods Memorial Centre, #111, 1925 Blanshard St., Victoria, BC V8T 4J2
Tel: 250-475-7202
go_islandsouth@shaw.ca
www.shaw.ca/ShawTV/Victoria
Social Media: www.youtube.com/ShawTVSouthVI, www.facebook.com/goislandsouth, twitter.com/ShawTV_SVI

***Williams Lake:* CFJC-TV-5** (Channel: 8)
Kamloops
Owned by: CFJC-TV
Williams Lake, BC

***Williams Lake:* CITM-TV-1** (Channel: 13)
Vancouver
Owned by: CHAN-DT
Williams Lake, BC

** For details on this company see listing in Major Broadcasting Companies section; † French language station*

Williams Lake: Shaw TV - Williams Lake (Channel: 10)
Northern BC
Owned by: Shaw Media Inc.
1290 Borland Rd., Williams Lake, BC V2L 4V1
Tel: 250-392-3911
go_williamslake@shaw.ca
www.shaw.ca/ShawTV/PrinceGeorge
Social Media: www.facebook.com/ShawTVNorthBC,
twitter.com/shawtvnorthbc

Manitoba

Flin Flon: CKYF-TV (Channel: 13)
Owned by: CKY-DT
Flin Flon, MB

McCreary: CKX-TV-3 (Channel: 11)
Owned by: CKX-TV
McCreary, MB

The Pas: CKYP-TV (Channel: 12)
Owned by: CKY-DT
The Pas, MB

Thompson: CKYT-TV (Channel: 9)
Owned by: CKY-DT
Thompson, MB

Thompson: Shaw TV - Thompson (Channel: 11)
Owned by: Shaw Media Inc.
50 Selkirk Ave., Thompson, MB R8N 0M7
Tel: 204-778-8949
shawcable11@yahoo.ca
www.shaw.ca/ShawTV/Thompson
Social Media: www.youtube.com/ShawTVThompson,
www.facebook.com/pages/Shaw-TV-Thompson,
twitter.com/ShawTVThompson

†Winnipeg: CBWFT-TV (Channel: 51)
Détenteur: Canadian Broadcasting Corporation*
541, rue Portage, Winnipeg, MB R3C 2H1
Tél: 204-788-3262, *Téléc:* 204-788-3245
manitoba@radio-canada.ca
www.radio-canada.ca/manitoba

Winnipeg: CBWT-DT (Channel: 27)
Owned by: Canadian Broadcasting Corporation*
541 Portage Ave., Winnipeg, MB R3B 2H1
Tel: 204-788-3222
www.cbc.ca/manitoba
Other information: TTY: 1-866-220-6045
John Bertrand, Director, Manitoba Centre

Winnipeg: CHMI-DT (Channel: 57)
Owned by: Rogers Broadcasting Ltd.*
8 Forks Market Rd., Winnipeg, MB R3C 4Y3
Tel: 204-947-9613
www.citytv.com/winnipeg

Winnipeg: CKND-DT (Channel: 2)
Owned by: Global Television Network*
201 Portage Ave., 30th Fl., Winnipeg, MB R3C 1A7
Tel: 204-235-8545
winnipeg@globalnews.ca
globalwinnipeg.com
Social Media: www.facebook.com/globalwinnipeg,
twitter.com/GlobalWinnipeg

Winnipeg: CKY-DT (Channel: 5)
Owned by: Bell Media TV*
#400, 345 Graham Ave., Winnipeg, MB R3C 5S6
Tel: 204-788-3300, *Fax:* 204-788-3399
winnipegnews@ctv.ca
winnipeg.ctvnews.ca
Social Media: twitter.com/ctvwinnipeg
Karen Mitchell, News Director, karen.mitchell@bellmedia.ca
Tara Vosbourgh, Human Resources Manager, tara.vosbourgh@bellmedia.ca

Winnipeg: Shaw TV - Winnipeg (Channel: 9)
Owned by: Shaw Media Inc.
Winnipeg, MB
Tel: 204-480-3500
shawtvwinnipeg@shaw.ca
www.shaw.ca/ShawTV/Winnipeg
Social Media: www.youtube.com/WinnipegShawTV,
www.facebook.com/GoWinnipegonShaw,
twitter.com/ShawTVWinnipeg

New Brunswick

†Beresford: Rogers TV - Bathurst (Français) (Channel: 9)
Détenteur: Rogers Broadcasting Ltd.*
1247, rue Principale, Beresford, NB E8K 1A1
Tél: 506-549-6657, *Téléc:* 506-546-8886
Ligne sans frais: 888-307-8862
www.rogerstv.com
Renelle LeBlanc, Superviseure de la programmation, 506-549-6676

Boiestown: CKLT-TV-2 (Channel: 7)
Owned by: CKLT-DT
Boiestown, NB

†Caraquet: Rogers TV - Péninsule acadienne (Channel: 10)
Détenteur: Rogers Broadcasting Ltd.*
220, boul St-Pierre ouest, Caraquet, NB E1W 1A5
Tél: 506-726-6262, *Ligne sans frais:* 888-307-8862
www.rogerstv.com
Renelle LeBlanc, Superviseure de la programmation, 506-549-6676

Chatham: CKAM-TV-2 (Channel: 10)
Moncton
Owned by: CKCW-TV
Chatham, NB

Doaktown: CKAM-TV-4 (Channel: 10)
Moncton
Owned by: CKCW-TV
Doaktown, NB

†Edmundston: CIMT-DT-1 (Channel: 4)
Détenteur: CIMT-DT
121, rue de l'Église, Edmundston, NB E3V 1J9
Tél: 506-353-0237
cimt.teleinterrives.com

Edmunston: CFTF-DT-1 (Channel: 42)
Owned by: CFTF-DT
Edmunston, NB
www.cftf.ca

†Edmunston: Rogers TV - Edmunston (Channel: 10)
Détenteur: Rogers Broadcasting Ltd.*
35, rue Court, Edmunston, NB E3V 1S4
Tél: 506-739-4533, *Téléc:* 506-735-1801
Ligne sans frais: 888-307-8862
www.rogerstv.com
Renelle LeBlanc, Superviseure de la programmation, 506-549-6676

Fredericton: CBAT-DT (Channel: 31)
Owned by: Canadian Broadcasting Corporation*
1160 Regent St., Fredericton, NB E3B 5G4
Tel: 506-451-4000, *Toll-Free:* 866-306-4636
www.cbc.ca/nb
Other information: Phone, CBC News: 506-451-4044
Denise Wilson, Senior Managing Director, Atlantic Canada
Nadine Antle, Regional Manager, Communications, Marketing & Brand, 902-420-4223
Mary-Pat Schutta, Senior Manager, New Brunswick Programs

Fredericton: CHNB-DT-1 (Channel: 44)
Owned by: CHNB-DT
Fredericton, NB

Fredericton: Rogers TV - Fredericton (Channel: 10)
Owned by: Rogers Broadcasting Ltd.*
377 York St., Fredericton, NB E3B 3P6
Tel: 506-462-3642, *Fax:* 506-452-2846
www.rogerstv.com
Terri Willis, Supervising Producer, 506-462-3659

†Kedgwick: CHAU-DT-11 (Channel: 27)
Détenteur: CHAU-DT
Kedgwick, NB

Miramichi: CHNB-TV-13 (Channel: 40)
Owned by: CHNB-DT
Miramichi, NB

Miramichi: Rogers TV - Miramichi (Channel: 10)
Owned by: Rogers Broadcasting Ltd.*
454 King George Hwy., Miramichi, NB E1V 1M1
Tel: 506-778-3009, *Fax:* 506-778-3035
Toll-Free: 888-307-8862
www.rogerstv.com
Terri Willis, Supervising Producer, 506-462-3659

†Moncton: CBAFT-DT (Channel: 11)
Détenteur: Canadian Broadcasting Corporation*
#15, 165, rue Main, Moncton, NB E1C 1B8
Tél: 506-853-6666, *Ligne sans frais:* 800-561-7010
www.radio-canada.ca/acadie
Richard Simoens, Directeur

Moncton: CHNB-DT-3 (Channel: 27)
Owned by: CHNB-DT
Moncton, NB

Moncton: CKCW-DT (Channel: 29)
Owned by: Bell Media TV*
Moncton, NB
atlantic.ctvnews.ca

Moncton: Rogers TV - Moncton (Channel: 10)
Owned by: Rogers Broadcasting Ltd.*
70 Assomption Blvd., Moncton, NB E1C 1A1
Tel: 506-388-8405, *Fax:* 506-388-8622
Toll-Free: 888-307-8862
www.rogerstv.com
Charles Oslcamp, Supervising Producer, 506-388-8671

Newcastle: CKAM-TV-1 (Channel: 10)
Moncton
Owned by: CKCW-TV
Newcastle, NB

Saint John: CHNB-DT (Channel: 12)
Owned by: Global Television Network*
#A500B, 1 Germain St., Saint John, NB E2L 4V1
Tel: 506-642-6488, *Fax:* 506-652-5965
newbrunswick@globalnews.ca
globalnews.ca/new-brunswick
Social Media: www.facebook.com/GlobalNB,
twitter.com/global_nb
Richard Dooley, Contact, richard.dooley@globalnews.ca

Saint John: CKLT-DT (Channel: 9)
Owned by: Bell Media TV
Red Rose Tea Building, #3, 12 Smythe St., Saint John, NB E2L 5G5
Tel: 506-658-1010, *Fax:* 506-658-1208
atlanticnews@bellmedia.ca
atlantic.ctvnews.ca

Saint John: Rogers TV - Saint John (Channel: 10)
Owned by: Rogers Broadcasting Ltd.*
55 Waterloo St., Saint John, NB E2L 4V9
Tel: 506-657-8862, *Fax:* 506-646-5116
Toll-Free: 888-307-8862
www.rogerstv.com
Terri Willis, Supervising Producer, 506-462-3659

†Saint-Quentin: CHAU-DT-2 (Channel: 31)
Détenteur: CHAU-DT
Saint-Quentin, NB

St Stephen: CHNB-TV-12 (Channel: 21)
Owned by: CHNB-DT
St Stephen, NB

St. John's: Rogers TV - St. John's (Channel: 9)
Owned by: Rogers Broadcasting Ltd.*
58 Kenmount Rd., St. John's, NB A1B 1W2
Tel: 709-753-7175, *Fax:* 709-753-7541
www.rogerstv.com
Linda Lambe, Regional Station Manager, 709-753-7349

Woodstock: CHNB-TV-11 (Channel: 38)
Owned by: CHNB-DT
Woodstock, NB

Newfoundland & Labrador

Corner Brook: Rogers TV - Corner Brook (Channel: 9)
Owned by: Rogers Broadcasting Ltd.*
4 Mt. Bernard Ave., Corner Brook, NL A2H 6T2
Tel: 709-634-0525, *Fax:* 709-639-1890
www.rogerstv.com
Wendy Woodland, Regional Station Manager, 709-634-7932

Gander: Rogers TV - Gander (Channel: 9)
Owned by: Rogers Broadcasting Ltd.*
141 Airport Blvd., Gander, NL A1V 1T5
Tel: 709-651-2652, *Fax:* 709-256-2797
www.rogerstv.com
Roger Robinson, Station Manager, roger.robinson@rci.rogers.com

** For details on this company see listing in Major Broadcasting Companies section; † French language station*

***Grand Falls-Windsor:* Rogers TV - Grand Falls-Windsor** (Channel: 9)
Owned by: Rogers Broadcasting Ltd.*
9 Hardy Ave., Grand Falls-Windsor, NL A2A 2K2
Tel: 709-489-3346, *Fax:* 709-489-1030
www.rogerstv.com
Roger Robinson, Regional Station Manager, 709-651-2652

***St. John's:* CBNT-DT** (Channel: 8)
Owned by: Canadian Broadcasting Corporation*
PO Box 12010 A, St. John's, NL A1B 3T8
Tel: 709-576-5000
www.cbc.ca/nl
Social Media: www.facebook.com/cbcnl, twitter.com/cbcnl
Denise Wilson, Senior Managing Director, Atlantic Canada, denise.wilson@cbc.ca
Nadine Antle, Regional Manager, Communications, Marketing & Brand, 902-420-4223, Nadine.Antle@cbc.ca

***St. John's:* CJON-TV** (Channel: 6)
Owned by: Newfoundland Broadcasting Co. Ltd.*
PO Box 2020, St. John's, NL A1C 5S2
Tel: 709-722-5015, *Fax:* 709-726-5107
greetings@ntv.ca
www.ntv.ca
Social Media: www.facebook.com/NTVNewsNL, twitter.com/ntvnewsnl

Northwest Territories

***Yellowknife:* CFYK-DT** (Channel: 8)
Owned by: Canadian Broadcasting Corporation*
PO Box 160, Yellowknife, NT X1A 2N2
Tel: 867-920-5400
www.cbc.ca/north

Nova Scotia

***Amherst:* EastLink TV - Amherst** (Channel: 10)
Owned by: EastLink TV*
PO Box 99 Main, 289 Willow St., Amherst, NS B4H 3Y6
Tel: 902-660-3588, *Toll-Free:* 902-667-0344
eastlinktv.com

***Antigonish:* CIHF-TV-15** (Channel: 21)
Owned by: CIHF-TV
Antigonish, NS

***Antigonish:* EastLink TV - Antigonish** (Channel: 5)
Owned by: EastLink TV*
4038 Old River Rd., Antigonish, NS B2G 2H6
Tel: 902-735-3588, *Toll-Free:* 902-863-5442
eastlinktv.com

***Aylesford:* EastLink TV - Aylesford** (Channel: 13)
Owned by: EastLink TV*
PO Box 217, 1257 Victoria Rd., Aylesford, NS B0P 1C0
Tel: 902-847-3404, *Fax:* 902-847-1808
eastlinktv.com

***Blockhouse:* EastLink TV - Bridgewater** (Channel: 10)
Owned by: EastLink TV*
PO Box 62, 140 Cornwall Rd., Blockhouse, NS B0J 1E0
Tel: 902-530-3588, *Fax:* 902-624-6194
eastlinktv.com

***Bridgewater:* CIHF-TV-6** (Channel: 9)
Owned by: CIHF-DT
Bridgewater, NS

***Dingwall:* CJCB-TV-3** (Channel: 9) **Sydney**
Owned by: CJCB-TV
Dingwall, NS

***Halifax:* CBHT-DT** (Channel: 39)
Owned by: Canadian Broadcasting Corporation*
#100, 7067 Chebucto Rd., Halifax, NS B3L 4R5
Tel: 902-420-8311, *Toll-Free:* 866-306-4636
www.cbc.ca/ns
Social Media: www.facebook.com/CBCNovaScotia, twitter.com/cbcns
Andrew Cochran, Managing Director, Maritimes
Kathy Large, Program Manager, Nova Scotia
Chantal Bernard, Senior Communications Officer, 902-420-4306

***Halifax:* CIHF-DT** (Channel: 8)
Owned by: Global Television Network*
2110 Gottingen St., Halifax, NS B3K 3B3
Tel: 902-481-7400, *Toll-Free:* 800-733-0592
www.globalhalifax.com
Social Media: www.facebook.com/globalhalifax, twitter.com/globalhalifax

***Halifax:* CJCH-DT** (Channel: 9)
Owned by: Bell Media TV*
PO Box 1653, Halifax, NS B3J 2Z4
Tel: 902-453-4000
atlanticnews@bellmedia.ca
atlantic.ctvnews.ca
Social Media: www.facebook.com/ctvnewsatlantic, twitter.com/CTVAtlantic

***Halifax:* Coast TV**
Owned by: Coast Cable
PO Box 8660 A, Halifax, NS B3K 5M3
Tel: 604-886-8565, *Fax:* 604-886-8936
coasttv@coastcable.com
www.coastcable.com/CoastTV.aspx

***Inverness:* CJCB-TV-1** (Channel: 6) **Sydney**
Owned by: CJCB-TV
Inverness, NS

***Liverpool:* EastLink TV - Liverpool** (Channel: 8)
Owned by: EastLink TV*
PO Box 449, 4130 Highway #3, Liverpool, NS B0T 1K0
Tel: 902-356-3588, *Toll-Free:* 902-354-2246
eastlinktv.com

***Lower Sackville:* EastLink TV** (Channel: 10) **Halifax Region**
Owned by: EastLink TV*
367 Sackville Dr., Lower Sackville, NS B4C 2R7
Tel: 902-446-3588, *Fax:* 902-453-5714
eastlinktv.com
Rhonda Ann MacDonald, Manager, 902-252-1052

***Mulgrave:* CIHF-TV-16** (Channel: 28)
Owned by: CIHF-TV
Mulgrave, NS

***New Glasgow:* CIHF-TV-8** (Channel: 34)
Owned by: CIHF-TV
New Glasgow, NS

***New Glasgow:* EastLink TV - New Glasgow** (Channel: 10)
Owned by: EastLink TV*
PO Box 157, 111 Park St., New Glasgow, NS B2H 5B7
Tel: 902-695-3588, *Toll-Free:* 902-695-3021
eastlinktv.com

***New Minas:* EastLink TV - New Minas** (Channel: 5)
Owned by: EastLink TV*
PO Box 4000, 1001 How Ave., New Minas, NS B4N 4S8
Tel: 902-681-0027, *Fax:* 902-681-6470
eastlinktv.com

***Sheet Harbour:* CJCH-TV-5** (Channel: 2) **Halifax**
Owned by: CJCH-TV
Sheet Harbour, NS

***Shelburne:* CIHF-TV-9** (Channel: 10)
Owned by: CIHF-TV
Shelburne, NS

***Shelburne:* EastLink TV - Shelburne** (Channel: 8)
Owned by: EastLink TV*
PO Box 1090, 1530 Jordan Branch Rd., Shelburne, NS B0T 1W0
Tel: 902-875-1267, *Fax:* 902-875-4219
eastlinktv.com

***Sydney:* CIHF-TV-7** (Channel: 11)
Owned by: CIHF-TV
Sydney, NS

***Sydney:* CJCB-TV** (Channel: 4)
Owned by: Bell Media TV*
1283 George St., Sydney, NS B1P 1N7
Tel: 902-562-5511, *Fax:* 902-562-9714
www.ctv.ca

***Sydney:* EastLink TV - Sydney** (Channel: 10)
Owned by: EastLink TV*
61 Melody Lane, Sydney, NS B1P 3K4
Tel: 902-539-9611, *Fax:* 866-976-7727
eastlinktv.com

***Truro:* CIHF-TV-4** (Channel: 18)
Owned by: CIHF-TV
Truro, NS

***Truro:* EastLink TV - Truro** (Channel: 4)
Owned by: EastLink TV*
69 Walker St., Truro, NS B2N 4A8
Tel: 902-843-3588, *Toll-Free:* 902-843-3067
eastlinktv.com

***Windsor:* EastLink TV - Windsor** (Channel: 8)
Owned by: EastLink TV*
PO Box 640, 19 Sanford Dr., Windsor, NS B0N 2T0
Tel: 902-798-8315, *Fax:* 902-798-0327
eastlinktv.com

***Wolfville:* CIHF-TV-5** (Channel: 20)
Owned by: CIHF-TV
Wolfville, NS

***Yarmouth:* CIHF-TV-10** (Channel: 45)
Owned by: CIHF-TV
Yarmouth, NS

***Yarmouth:* CJCH-TV-7** (Channel: 40) **Halifax**
Owned by: CJCH-TV
Yarmouth, NS

***Yarmouth:* EastLink TV - Yarmouth** (Channel: 5)
Owned by: EastLink TV*
25 Shaw Ave., Yarmouth, NS B5A 4C4
Tel: 902-881-3588, *Fax:* 902-742-6259
eastlinktv.com

Ontario

***Barrie:* CKVR-DT** (Channel: 10)
Owned by: Bell Media TV*
33 Beacon Rd., Barrie, ON L4M 4T9
Tel: 705-734-3300, *Fax:* 705-733-0302
Toll-Free: 800-461-5820
barrieinbox@ctv.ca
ctvbarrie.ca
Social Media: www.facebook.com/ctvbarrie, twitter.com/ctvbarrienews
Other information: TTY: 800-721-9110
Ruth Anderson, News Director, ruth.anderson@bellmedia.ca

***Barrie:* Rogers TV - Barrie** (Channel: 10)
Owned by: Rogers Broadcasting Ltd.*
1 Sperling Dr., Barrie, ON L4M 6B8
Tel: 705-737-4660, *Fax:* 705-737-0778
Toll-Free: 866-615-5527
www.rogerstv.com
Kevin Kelly, Supervising Producer, 705-737-4660

***Belleville:* CICO-DT-53** (Channel: 26)
Owned by: TVOntario*
Belleville, ON
tvo.org

***Belleville:* CogecoTV - Belleville** (Channel: 4; HD 700)
Owned by: Cogeco Inc.*
297 Front St., Belleville, ON K8N 4Z9
Tel: 613-967-6171, *Fax:* 613-966-0791
www.tvcogeco.com/belleville
Social Media: www.facebook.com/onTVCOGECO, twitter.com/onTVCOGECO
Scott Meyers, Manager, Programming & Community Relations, scott.meyers@cogeco.com

***Borden:* Rogers TV - Borden & Alliston** (Channel: 65)
Owned by: Rogers Broadcasting Ltd.*
Borden, ON
Tel: 705-737-4660
www.rogerstv.com
Kevin Kelly, Supervising Producer, 705-737-4660

***Brampton:* Rogers TV - Brampton** (Channel: 10)
Owned by: Rogers Broadcasting Ltd.*
8200 Dixie Rd., Brampton, ON L6T 0C1
Tel: 905-270-2124, *Fax:* 905-848-2831
www.rogerstv.com
Social Media: www.facebook.com/RTVPeel
Jake Dheer, Station Manager, 905-897-3928

** For details on this company see listing in Major Broadcasting Companies section; † French language station*

***Brantford:* Rogers TV - Brantford** (Channel: 20)
Owned by: Rogers Broadcasting Ltd.*
23 Harris Ave., Brantford, ON N3R 7W5
Tel: 519-759-7711, *Fax:* 519-759-2629
Toll-Free: 888-410-2020
www.rogerstv.com
Jeremy Cook, Supervising Producer, 519-894-8160

***Brockville:* CogecoTV - Brockville/Prescott** (Channel: 10)
Owned by: Cogeco Inc.*
#13A, 333 California Ave., Brockville, ON K6V 5W1
Tel: 613-342-7414, *Fax:* 613-342-6521
www.tvcogeco.com/brockville
Social Media: www.facebook.com/onTVCOGECO, twitter.com/onTVCOGECO
Ron Harrison, Production Manager, 613-205-0460, Fax: 613-283-1526, Ron.Harrison@cogeco.com

***Burlington:* CogecoTV - Burlington/Oakville** (Channel: 23; HD 700)
Owned by: Cogeco Inc.*
950 Syscon Rd., Burlington, ON L7R 4S6
Tel: 289-337-7000, *Fax:* 905-333-3394
www.tvcogeco.com/burlington-oakville
Social Media: www.facebook.com/onTVCOGECO, twitter.com/onTVCOGECO
Ben Lyman, Manager, Programming & Community Relations, 289-891-6702, ben.lyman@cogeco.com

***Chapleau:* CITO-TV-4** (Channel: 9)
Owned by: CITO-TV
Chapleau, ON

***Chatham:* CogecoTV - Chatham** (Channel: 11)
Owned by: Cogeco Inc.*
491 Richmond St., Chatham, ON N7M 1R2
Tel: 519-352-5241, *Fax:* 519-352-8274
www.tvcogeco.com/chatham
Social Media: www.facebook.com/onTVCOGECO, twitter.com/onTVCOGECO
Pete Martin, Manager, Programming & Community Relations, 519-352-5241, pete.martin@cogeco.com

***Cloyne:* CICO-DT-92** (Channel: 44)
Owned by: TVOntario*
Cloyne, ON
tvo.org

***Cobourg:* CogecoTV - Cobourg/Port Hope** (Channel: 10; HD 700)
Owned by: Cogeco Inc.*
259 Division St., #F, Cobourg, ON K9A 3P9
Fax: 866-859-9903
Toll-Free: 866-483-7878
feedback@cogeco.com
www.tvcogeco.com/cobourg-port-hope
Social Media: www.facebook.com/onTVCOGECO, twitter.com/onTVCOGECO
David Feeley, Senior Manager, Programming & Community Relations, 705-743-8602, david.feeley@cogeco.com

***Collingwood:* Rogers TV - Collingwood** (Channel: 53)
Owned by: Rogers Broadcasting Ltd.*
4 Sandford Fleming Dr., Collingwood, ON L9Y 4V9
Tel: 705-445-2120, *Fax:* 705-445-9949
Toll-Free: 866-615-5527
www.rogerstv.com
Kevin Kelly, Supervising Producer, 705-737-4600

***Cornwall:* CJOH-TV-8** (Channel: 8)
Owned by: CJOH-DT
Cornwall, ON

***Cornwall:* CogecoTV - Cornwall** (Channel: 11)
Owned by: Cogeco Inc.*
517 Pitt St., Cornwall, ON K6J 3R4
Tel: 613-937-2506, *Fax:* 613-932-3176
www.tvcogeco.com/cornwall
Social Media: www.facebook.com/onTVCOGECO, twitter.com/onTVCOGECO
Calvin Killoran, Manager, Programming & Community Relations, 613-937-2507, calvin.killoran@cogeco.com

***Deseronto:* CJOH-TV-6** (Channel: 6)
Owned by: CJOH-DT
Deseronto, ON

***Dryden:* Shaw TV - Dryden** (Channel: 10)
Owned by: Shaw Media Inc.
175 Queen St., Dryden, ON P8N 1A1
Tel: 807-221-2411
www.shaw.ca/ShawTV/Dryden
Tommy Johnson, Producer, tommy.johnson@sjrb.ca

***Elliot Lake:* CICI-TV-1** (Channel: 3)
Owned by: CICI-TV
Elliot Lake, ON

***Elliot Lake:* EastLink TV - Elliot Lake**
Owned by: EastLink TV*
Elliot Lake, ON
elliotlake@eastlinktv.com
eastlinktv.com

***Fergus:* CogecoTV - Fergus** (Channel: 14)
Owned by: Cogeco Inc.*
475 St. Patrick Street West, Fergus, ON N1M 1M2
Tel: 519-843-3700, *Fax:* 519-843-2312
www.tvcogeco.com/fergus
Social Media: www.facebook.com/onTVCOGECO, twitter.com/onTVCOGECO

***Georgina:* Rogers TV - Georgina** (Channel: 10)
Owned by: Rogers Broadcasting Ltd.*
Georgina, ON
www.rogerstv.com
Jim Anderson, Executive Producer, 905-476-1406

***Goderich:* EastLink TV - Goderich**
Owned by: EastLink TV*
Goderich, ON
eastlinktv.com

***Guelph:* Rogers TV - Guelph** (Channel: 20)
Owned by: Rogers Broadcasting Ltd.*
130 Silvercreek Pkwy., Guelph, ON N1H 7Y5
Tel: 519-824-1900, *Fax:* 519-824-4210
Toll-Free: 888-410-2020
www.rogerstv.com
Jeremy Cook, Supervisor Producer, 519-894-8160

***Halton Hills:* CogecoTV - Milton/Halton Hills** (Channel: 14; HD 700)
Owned by: Cogeco Inc.*
#1, 15 Brownridge Rd., Halton Hills, ON L7G 0C6
Tel: 289-891-6703, *Fax:* 289-891-7777
www.tvcogeco.com/milton
Social Media: www.facebook.com/onTVCOGECO, twitter.com/onTVCOGECO
Ben Lyman, Manager, Programming & Community Relations, 289-891-6702, Ben.Lyman@cogeco.com

***Hamilton:* Cable 14 (TV Hamilton Ltd.)** (Channel: 14)
Owned by: Cogeco Cable Inc.*
150 Dundurn St. South, Hamilton, ON L8P 4K3
Tel: 905-523-1414, *Fax:* 905-523-8141
www.cable14.com
Social Media: www.facebook.com/cable14hamilton, twitter.com/cable14
Brent Rickert, General Manager, 905-523-1414

***Hamilton:* CHCH-DT** (Channel: 11)
Owned by: Channel Zero Inc.*
PO Box 2230 A, 163 Jackson St. West, Hamilton, ON L8N 3A6
Tel: 905-522-1101, *Fax:* 905-523-8011
contact@chch.com
www.chch.com
Social Media: twitter.com/CHCHTV

***Hanover:* EastLink TV - Hanover**
Owned by: EastLink TV*
Hanover, ON
Fax: 519-291-5935
Toll-Free: 866-286-3484
midwest@eastlinktv.com
eastlinktv.com

***Hawkesbury:* CogecoTV - Hawkesbury** (Channel: 11)
Owned by: Cogeco Inc.*
1444 Aberdeen St., Hawkesbury, ON K6A 1K7
Tel: 613-632-2625, *Fax:* 613-632-8531
www.tvcogeco.com/hawkesbury-en
Social Media: www.facebook.com/onTVCOGECO, twitter.com/onTVCOGECO
Other information: French URL: www.tvcogeco.com/hawkesbury-fr
Ronald Handfield, Programming Supervisor, 613-632-2625, ronald.handfield@cogeco.com

***Hearst:* CITO-TV-3** (Channel: 4)
Owned by: CITO-TV
Hearst, ON

***Huntsville:* CogecoTV - Huntsville/Gravenhurst** (Channel: 10)
Owned by: Cogeco Inc.*
20 West St. South, Huntsville, ON P1H 1P2
Tel: 705-789-9801, *Fax:* 705-789-2331
www.tvcogeco.com/huntsville-gravenhurst
Social Media: www.facebook.com/onTVCOGECO, twitter.com/onTVCOGECO
Scott Acton, Manager, Programming & Community Relations, 705-789-9801, Scott.Acton@cogeco.com

***Kapuskasing:* CITO-TV-1** (Channel: 10)
Owned by: CITO-TV
Kapuskasing, ON

***Kapuskasing:* EastLink TV - Kapuskasing**
Owned by: EastLink TV*
Kapuskasing, ON
kapuskasing@eastlinktv.com
eastlinktv.com

***Kearns:* CITO-TV-2** (Channel: 11)
Owned by: CITO-TV
Kearns, ON

***Keewatin:* CJBN-TV** (Channel: 13)
Owned by: Shaw Media Inc.*
102 - 10th St., Keewatin, ON P0X 1C0
Tel: 809-547-2887, *Fax:* 807-547-2348
www.gokenora.com
Kyle Glieheisen, Station Manager, kyle.glieheisen@sjrb.ca

***Kenora:* Shaw TV - Kenora** (Channel: 10)
Owned by: Shaw Media Inc.
Kenora, ON
shawtvthunderbay@shaw.ca
www.shaw.ca/ShawTV/Kenora

***Kincardine:* Rogers TV - Kincardine** (Channel: 6)
Owned by: Rogers Broadcasting Ltd.*
Kincardine, ON
www.rogerstv.com
Matt Smith, Supervising Producer, 519-901-2911

***Kingston:* CKWS-TV** (Channel: 11; CBC affiliate)
Owned by: 591987 B.C. Ltd.*
170 Queen St., Kingston, ON K7K 1B2
Tel: 613-544-2340, *Fax:* 613-544-5508
newswatch@corusent.com
www.ckwstv.com
Social Media: www.facebook.com/CKWSTV, twitter.com/ckws_tv
Other information: News Phone: 613-542-9232; Sales Fax: 613-544-3587
Peter Mayhew, General Sales Manager, Sales, peter.mayhew@corusent.com
Jay Westman, Manager, News & TV Operations, jay.westman@corusent.com

***Kingston:* CogecoTV - Kingston** (Channel: 13; HD 700)
Owned by: Cogeco Inc.*
170 Colborne St., Kingston, ON K7L 5M7
Tel: 613-544-6311, *Fax:* 613-545-0169
www.tvcogeco.com/kingston
Social Media: www.facebook.com/onTVCOGECO, twitter.com/onTVCOGECO
Scott Meyers, Manager, Programming & Public Relations, scott.meyers@cogeco.com

***Kirkland Lake:* EastLink TV - Kirkland Lake**
Owned by: EastLink TV*
Kirkland Lake, ON
kirklandlake@eastlink.ca
eastlinktv.com

***Kitchener:* CICO-DT-28** (Channel: 28)
Owned by: TVOntario*
Kitchener, ON
tvo.org

***Kitchener:* CKCO-DT** (Channel: 13)
Owned by: Bell Media TV*
864 King St. West, Kitchener, ON N2G 1E8
Tel: 519-578-1314
viewermail@kitchener.ctv.ca
kitchener.ctvnews.ca
Social Media: www.facebook.com/ctvkitchener, twitter.com/CTVKitchener

** For details on this company see listing in Major Broadcasting Companies section; † French language station*

***Kitchener:* Rogers TV - Kitchener/Cambridge/Waterloo** (Channel: 20)
Owned by: Rogers Broadcasting Ltd.*
85 Grand Crest Pl., Kitchener, ON N2G 4A8
Tel: 519-893-4400, *Fax:* 519-893-5861
www.rogerstv.com
Jeremy Cook, Supervising Producer, 519-894-8160

***Listowel:* EastLink TV - Listowel**
Owned by: EastLink TV*
Listowel, ON
Fax: 519-291-5935
Toll-Free: 866-286-3484
midwest@eastlinktv.com
eastlinktv.com

***London:* Rogers TV - London** (Channel: 13)
Owned by: Rogers Broadcasting Ltd.*
800 York St., London, ON N6A 5B1
Tel: 519-675-1313, *Fax:* 519-660-7597
www.rogerstv.com
Social Media: twitter.com/RTVLondon
Bob Smith, Regional Station Manager, 519-660-7536

***London:* Rogers TV - St Thomas** (Channel: 13)
Owned by: Rogers Broadcasting Ltd.*
800 York St., London, ON N6A 5B1
Tel: 226-984-8186, *Fax:* 519-660-7597
www.rogerstv.com
Bob Smith, Regional Station Manager, 519-660-7536

***London:* Rogers TV - Strathroy-Caradoc** (Channel: 13)
Owned by: Rogers Broadcasting Ltd.*
800 York St., London, ON N6A 5B1
Tel: 519-675-1313
www.rogerstv.com
Bob Smith, Regional Station Manager, 519-660-7536

***Midland:* Rogers TV - Midland** (Channel: 53)
Owned by: Rogers Broadcasting Ltd.*
527 Len Self Blvd., Midland, ON L4R 5N6
Tel: 705-526-7905
www.rogerstv.com
Kevin Kelly, Supervising Producer, 705-737-4660

***Mississauga:* Rogers TV - Mississauga** (Channel: 10)
Owned by: Rogers Broadcasting Ltd.*
3573 Wolfedale Rd., Mississauga, ON L5C 3T6
Tel: 905-270-2124, *Fax:* 905-848-2831
www.rogerstv.com
Jake Dheer, Station Manager, 905-897-3928

***Newmarket:* Rogers TV - Newmarket/Aurora/Bradford/East Gwillimbury** (Channel: 10)
Owned by: Rogers Broadcasting Ltd.*
395-A Mulock Dr., Newmarket, ON L3Y 8P3
Tel: 905-780-7114, *Fax:* 905-898-7577
yorkregion@rci.rogers.com
www.rogerstv.com
David Blackwell, Executive Producer, 905-780-7137

***Niagara Falls:* CogecoTV - Niagara** (Channel: 10; HD 700)
Owned by: Cogeco Inc.*
7170 McLeod Rd., Niagara Falls, ON L2G 3H2
Tel: 905-374-2248, *Fax:* 800-807-8113
Toll-Free: 800-706-4221
www.tvcogeco.com/niagara
Social Media: www.facebook.com/onTVCOGECO, twitter.com/onTVCOGECO
Jack Custers, Manager, Programming & Community Relations, 800-706-4221, Jack.Custers@cogeco.com

***North Bay:* CKNY-TV** (Channel: 10)
Owned by: Bell Media TV*
245 Oak St. East, North Bay, ON P1B 8P8
Tel: 705-476-3111, *Fax:* 705-495-4474
Toll-Free: 877-303-6288
northernontario.ctvnews.ca
Social Media: www.facebook.com/ctvnorthernontario, twitter.com/CTVNorthernNews

***North Bay:* CogecoTV - North Bay** (Channel: 12; HD 700)
Owned by: Cogeco Inc.*
240 Fee St., North Bay, ON P1B 8G5
Tel: 705-472-9868, *Fax:* 705-472-7854
www.tvcogeco.com/north-bay
Social Media: www.facebook.com/onTVCOGECO, twitter.com/onTVCOGECO
Joey Roussy, Manager, Programming & Community Relations, 705-472-9868, joey.roussy@cogeco.com

***Oil Springs:* CKCO-TV-3** (Channel: 42)
Kitchener
Owned by: CKCO-TV
Oil Springs, ON

***Orangeville:* Rogers TV - Dufferin-Caledon** (Channel: 63)
Owned by: Rogers Broadcasting Ltd.*
70 C-Line, Orangeville, ON L9W 6E2
Fax: 519-941-6091
Toll-Free: 866-880-3994
www.rogerstv.com
Jake Dheer, Station Manager, 905-897-3928

***Orillia:* Rogers TV - Orillia** (Channel: 10)
Owned by: Rogers Broadcasting Ltd.*
#15, 425 West St. North, Orillia, ON L3V 7R2
Tel: 705-718-3632, *Toll-Free:* 866-615-5527
www.rogerstv.com
Kevin Kelly, Supervising Producer, 705-737-4660

***Oshawa:* CHEX-TV-2**
Owned by: 591987 B.C. Ltd.*
10 Simcoe St. North, Oshawa, ON L1G 4R8
Tel: 905-434-2421, *Fax:* 905-432-2315
www.channel12.ca
Social Media: www.youtube.com/user/channel12DOTca, www.facebook.com/channel12television, twitter.com/studio12news
Dave McCutcheon, General Manager, Dave.McCutcheon@corusent.com

***Oshawa:* Rogers TV - Durham Region** (Channel: 10; 63)
Owned by: Rogers Broadcasting Ltd.*
301 Marwood Dr., Oshawa, ON L1H 1J4
Tel: 905-436-4120, *Fax:* 905-579-5559
www.rogerstv.com
Patricia Raymond, Production Administrator, 905-780-7019

†*Ottawa:* CBOFT-DT (Channel: 9)
Détenteur: Canadian Broadcasting Corporation*
CP 3220 C, Ottawa, ON K1Y 1E4
Ligne sans frais: 866-306-4636
affairespubliques.ottawagatineau@radio-canada.ca
www.radio-canada.ca/ottawa-gatineau
Marco Dubé, Directeur, Marco.Dube@radio-canada.ca

***Ottawa:* CBOT-DT** (Channel: 25)
Owned by: Canadian Broadcasting Corporation*
PO Box 3220 C, Ottawa, ON K1Y 1E4
Tel: 613-288-6000
www.cbc.ca/ottawa

***Ottawa:* CICO-DT-24** (Channel: 24)
Owned by: TVOntario*
Ottawa, ON
tvo.org

***Ottawa:* CJOH-DT** (Channel: 13)
Owned by: Bell Media TV*
87 George St., Ottawa, ON K1N 9H7
Tel: 613-224-1313, *Fax:* 888-770-2192
ctvottawa@ctv.ca
ottawa.ctvnews.ca
Social Media: www.facebook.com/CTVNewsOttawa

***Ottawa:* Rogers TV - Ottawa** (Channel: 22)
Owned by: Rogers Broadcasting Ltd.*
475 Richmond Rd., Ottawa, ON K2A 3Y8
Tel: 613-728-2222, *Fax:* 613-728-9793
www.rogerstv.com
Gavin Lumsden, Supervising Producer, 613-759-8542

†*Ottawa:* Rogers TV - Ottawa (Français) (Channel: 23)
Détenteur: Rogers Broadcasting Ltd.*
475, ch Richmond, Ottawa, ON K2A 3Y8
Tél: 613-521-2323, *Téléc:* 613-521-2323
www.tvrogers.com
Médias sociaux: www.facebook.com/TVRogersOttawa, twitter.com/tvrogers
David Richard, Chef de station, 613-759-8602

***Owen Sound:* Rogers TV - Grey County** (Channel: 53)
Owned by: Rogers Broadcasting Ltd.*
1360 - 20th St. East, Owen Sound, ON N4K 5T7
Tel: 519-376-2832, *Fax:* 519-376-5216
Toll-Free: 866-615-5527
www.rogerstv.com
Mark Perry, Supervising Producer, 519-376-2832

***Pembroke:* CogecoTV - Ottawa Valley** (Channel: 12)
Owned by: Cogeco Inc.*
185 Lake St., Pembroke, ON K8A 5M1
Tel: 613-735-1228, *Fax:* 613-735-7134
www.tvcogeco.com/pembroke
Social Media: www.facebook.com/onTVCOGECO, twitter.com/onTVCOGECO
Michael Tharby, Program Manager, 613-735-2100, Michael.Tharby@cogeco.com

***Peterborough:* CHEX-DT** (Channel: 12)
Owned by: 591987 B.C. Ltd.*
743 Monaghan Rd., Peterborough, ON K9J 5K2
Tel: 705-742-0451, *Fax:* 705-742-7274
www.chextv.com
Social Media: www.facebook.com/CHEXTV, twitter.com/chextv
Other information: TTY: 705-749-2179
Dave McCutcheon, General Manager, Dave.McCutcheon@corusent.com
Jay Westman, Manager, News & TV Operations, 705-742-0451, Jay.Westman@corusent.ca

***Peterborough:* CogecoTV - Peterborough/Lindsay** (Channel: 10; HD 700)
Owned by: Cogeco Inc.*
1111 Goodfellow Rd., Peterborough, ON K9J 7X1
Tel: 705-743-8602, *Fax:* 705-742-3563
feedback@cogeco.com
www.tvcogeco.com/peterborough
Social Media: www.facebook.com/onTVCOGECO, twitter.com/onTVCOGECO
David Feeley, Manager, Programming & Community Relations, 705-743-8602, david.feeley@cogeco.com

***Port Elgin:* EastLink TV - Port Egin**
Owned by: EastLink TV*
Port Elgin, ON
Fax: 519-291-5935
Toll-Free: 866-286-3484
midwest@eastlinktv.com
eastlinktv.com

***Richmond Hill:* Rogers TV - Richmond Hill/King/Markham/Stouffville/Vaughan** (Channel: 63)
Owned by: Rogers Broadcasting Ltd.*
244 Newkirk Rd., Richmond Hill, ON L4C 3S5
Tel: 905-780-7060, *Fax:* 905-780-7072
www.rogerstv.com
David Blackwell, Executive Producer, 905-780-7137

***Sarnia:* CogecoTV - Sarnia** (Channel: 6; HD 700)
Owned by: Cogeco Inc.*
1421 Confederation St., Sarnia, ON N7S 5N9
Tel: 519-336-6200, *Fax:* 519-332-3952
www.tvcogeco.com/sarnia
Social Media: www.facebook.com/onTVCOGECO, twitter.com/onTVCOGECO
Terry Doyle, Manager, Programming & Community Relations, 519-336-6200, terry.doyle@cogeco.com

***Sault Ste Marie:* Shaw TV - Sault Ste Marie** (Channel: 10)
Owned by: Shaw Media Inc.
23 Manitou Dr., Sault Ste Marie, ON P6B 6GN
Tel: 705-541-7564, *Fax:* 705-541-7573
shawtvssm@shaw.ca
www.shaw.ca/ShawTV/saultstemarie

***Sault Ste. Marie:* CHBX-TV** (Channel: 2; 11)
Owned by: Bell Media TV
119 East St., Sault Ste. Marie, ON P6A 3C7
Tel: 705-759-8232, *Fax:* 705-759-7783
northernontario.ctvnews.ca

***Simcoe:* EastLink TV - Simcoe** (Channel: 5)
Owned by: EastLink TV*
21 Donly Dr., Simcoe, ON N3Y 4W3
Tel: 519-426-3090, *Fax:* 519-426-0162
simcoe@eastlinktv.com
eastlinktv.com

** For details on this company see listing in Major Broadcasting Companies section; † French language station*

***Smiths Falls:* CogecoTV - Smiths Falls/Perth/North Grenville** (Channel: 10)
Owned by: Cogeco Inc.*
270 Brockville St., #C, Smiths Falls, ON K7A 5L4
Tel: 613-283-8404, *Fax:* 613-283-1526
www.tvcogeco.com/smiths-falls
Social Media: www.facebook.com/onTVCOGECO, twitter.com/onTVCOGECO
Ron Harrison, Production Manager, 613-205-0460, Ron.Harrison@cogeco.com

***Straford:* Rogers TV - Stratford** (Channel: 20)
Owned by: Rogers Broadcasting Ltd.*
32 Erie St., Straford, ON N5A 2M4
Tel: 519-271-5202, *Fax:* 519-271-1787
Toll-Free: 888-410-2020
www.rogerstv.com
Jeremy Cook, Supervising Producer, 519-894-8160

***Sturgeon Falls:* EastLink TV - Sturgeon Falls**
Owned by: EastLink TV*
Sturgeon Falls, ON
sturgeonfalls@eastlinktv.com
eastlinktv.com

***Sudbury:* CICI-TV** (Channel: 5)
Owned by: Bell Media TV*
699 Frood Rd., Sudbury, ON P3C 5A3
Tel: 705-674-8301, *Fax:* 705-674-2706
Toll-Free: 866-389-6288
northernontario.ctvnews.ca/sudbury
Social Media: www.facebook.com/ctvnorthernontario, twitter.com/CTVNorthernNews

***Sudbury:* EastLink TV - Sudbury** (Channel: 10)
Owned by: EastLink TV*
PO Box 4500, #15, 500 Barrydowne Rd., Sudbury, ON P3A 5W1
Tel: 705-560-6397, *Fax:* 705-560-7891
sudbury@eastlinktv.com
eastlinktv.com

***Thunder Bay:* CHFD-TV** (Channel: 4)
87 North Hill St., Thunder Bay, ON P7A 5V6
Tel: 807-346-2600, *Fax:* 807-345-9923
www.ckprthunderbay.com
Social Media: www.facebook.com/CkprThunderBayTv, twitter.com/ckprthunderbay

***Thunder Bay:* CICO-DT-9** (Channel: 9)
Owned by: TVOntario*
Thunder Bay, ON
tvo.org

***Thunder Bay:* CKPR-DT** (Channel: 2; CBC affiliate)
87 North Hill St., Thunder Bay, ON P7A 5V6
Tel: 807-346-2600, *Fax:* 807-345-9923
www.ckprthunderbay.com

***Thunder Bay:* Shaw TV - Thunder Bay** (Channel: 10)
Owned by: Shaw Media Inc.
1635 Paquette Rd., Thunder Bay, ON P7G 2J2
Tel: 807-766-7010
shawtvthunderbay@shaw.ca
www.shaw.ca/ShawTV/Thunder-Bay

***Timmins:* CITO-TV** (Channel: 3)
Owned by: Bell Media TV*
681 Pine St. North, Timmins, ON P4N 7L6
Tel: 705-264-4211, *Fax:* 705-264-3266
Toll-Free: 800-797-6288
northernontario.ctvnews.ca

***Timmins:* EastLink TV - Timmins** (Channel: 3)
Owned by: EastLink TV*
PO Box 1429, 865 Mountjoy St. South, Timmins, ON P4N 7N2
Tel: 705-267-3000, *Fax:* 705-264-0121
timmins@eastlinktv.com
eastlinktv.com

***†Toronto:* CBLFT-DT** (Channel: 25)
Détenteur: Canadian Broadcasting Corporation*
Société Radio-Canada, CP 500 A, Toronto, ON M5W 1E6
Tél: 416-205-2887, *Ligne sans frais:* 800-551-2985
www.radio-canada.ca/ontario
Médias sociaux: twitter.com/RC_TV

***Toronto:* CBLT-DT** (Channel: 5)
Owned by: Canadian Broadcasting Corporation*
PO Box 500 A, Toronto, ON M5W 1E6
Tel: 416-205-3311
www.cbc.ca/toronto
Other information: Phone, Television Newsroom: 416-205-2500
Susan Marjetti, Managing Director, 416-205-5791
Don Ioi, Team Manager, Broadcast Sales, 416-205-2732

***Toronto:* CFMT-TV** (Channel: 47)
Owned by: Rogers Broadcasting Ltd.*
545 Lakeshore Blvd. West, Toronto, ON M5V 1A3
Tel: 416-260-0060, *Fax:* 416-764-3245
www.omnitv.ca

***Toronto:* CFTO-DT** (Channel: 9)
Owned by: Bell Media TV*
PO Box 9 O, Toronto, ON M4A 2M9
Tel: 416-384-5000, *Toll-Free:* 800-668-0060
www.ctv.ca
Social Media: www.facebook.com/ctv, twitter.com/CTV_Television
Other information: TTY: 1-800-461-1542

***Toronto:* CICA-DT** (Channel: 19)
Owned by: TVOntario*
PO Box 200 Q, Toronto, ON M4T 2T1
Tel: 416-484-2600, *Toll-Free:* 800-613-0513
ww3.tvo.org

***Toronto:* CITY-TV** (Channel: 57)
Owned by: Rogers Broadcasting Ltd.*
33 Dundas St. East, Toronto, ON M5B 1B8
Tel: 416-599-2489
www.citytv.com
Social Media: www.youtube.com/city, www.facebook.com/Citytv, twitter.com/city_tv

***Toronto:* CJMT-TV** (Channel: 44)
Owned by: Rogers Broadcasting Ltd.*
545 Lakeshore Blvd. West, Toronto, ON M5V 1A3
Tel: 416-260-0060, *Fax:* 416-764-3245
www.omnitv.ca

***Toronto:* Rogers TV - Toronto** (Channel: 10; 63)
Owned by: Rogers Broadcasting Ltd.*
855 York Mills Rd., Toronto, ON M3B 1Z1
Tel: 416-446-6500, *Fax:* 416-446-0901
www.rogerstv.com
Social Media: twitter.com/RogersTVToronto
Bryan Peters, Supervising Producer, 416-446-6516
Willy Jong, Supervising Producer, 416-446-6637

***†Toronto:* TFO**
CP 3005 F, Toronto, ON M4Y 2M5
Tél: 416-968-3536, *Téléc:* 416-968-8203
Ligne sans frais: 800-387-8435
vos_questions@tfo.org
www3.tfo.org
Médias sociaux: www.youtube.com/tfocanada, www.facebook.com/TFOCanada, twitter.com/TFOCanada
Glenn O'Farrell, Président et chef de la direction, gofarrell@tfo.org

***Uxbridge:* Rogers TV - Uxbridge/Scugog** (Channel: 10)
Owned by: Rogers Broadcasting Ltd.*
Uxbridge, ON
www.rogerstv.com
Patricia Raymond, Production Administrator, 905-780-7019

***Wawa:* CHBX-TV-1** (Channel: 7)
Owned by: CHBX-TV
Wawa, ON

***Windsor:* CBET-TV** (Channel: 9)
Owned by: Canadian Broadcasting Corporation*
825 Riverside Dr. West, Windsor, ON N9A 5K9
Tel: 519-255-3411, *Toll-Free:* 866-306-4636
www.cbc.ca/windsor
Other information: Phone, Windsor Newsroom: 519-255-3456
Shawna Kelly, Managing Director, 519-255-3563

***Windsor:* CICO-DT-32** (Channel: 32)
Owned by: TVOntario*
Windsor, ON
tvo.org

***Windsor:* CogecoTV - Windsor/Leamington** (Channel: 11; HD 700)
Owned by: Cogeco Inc.*
2525 Dougall Ave., Windsor, ON N8X 5A7
Tel: 519-972-4016, *Fax:* 519-972-6688
www.tvcogeco.com/windsor-leamington
Social Media: www.facebook.com/onTVCOGECO, twitter.com/onTVCOGECO
Robert Scussolin, Manager, Programming & Community Relations, robert.scussolin@cogeco.com

***Woodstock:* Rogers TV - Woodstock/Tillsonburg** (Channel: 13)
Owned by: Rogers Broadcasting Ltd.*
21 Ridgeway Circle, Woodstock, ON N4V 1C9
Tel: 519-533-5550, *Fax:* 519-533-5560
www.rogerstv.com
Bob Smith, Regional Station Manager, 519-660-7536

Prince Edward Island

***Charlottetown:* CBCT-DT** (Channel: 13)
Owned by: Canadian Broadcasting Corporation*
PO Box 2230, 430 University Ave., Charlottetown, PE C1A 8B9
Tel: 902-629-6400, *Toll-Free:* 866-306-4636
www.cbc.ca/pei
Social Media: www.facebook.com/142551811174
Other information: Phone, CBC News Compass: 902-629-6403; Toll-Free: 1-800-671-2228
Denise Wilson, Senior Managing Director, Atlantic Canada
Donna Allen, Executive Producer, News, Prince Edward Island
Nadine Antle, Regional Manager, Partnerships, Communications, Brand, & Promot, 902-420-4223

***Charlottetown:* CHNB-DT-14** (Channel: 42)
Owned by: CHNB-DT
Charlottetown, PE

***Charlottetown:* EastLink TV** (Channel: 10)
PEI Region
Owned by: EastLink TV*
100 Cable Ct., Charlottetown, PE C1B 1A9
Tel: 902-367-3588, *Toll-Free:* 902-569-4731
eastlinktv.com
Bruce MacLean, Regional Manager, 902-569-0115

Québec

***Alma:* CogecoTV - Alma** (Channel: 13; HD 555)
Owned by: Cogeco Inc.*
590, rue Collard ouest, Alma, QC G8B 1N2
Tel: 418-668-3310, *Fax:* 418-668-0938
commentaires.cogecotv@cogeco.com
www.tvcogeco.com/alma
Line Gaudreault, Directrice régionale, 418-668-3310, Line.gaudreault@cogeco.com

***Baie-Comeau:* CFTF-DT-5** (Channel: 9)
Owned by: CFTF-DT
Baie-Comeau, QC
www.cftf.ca

***†Baie-Comeau:* CogecoTV - Baie-Comeau** (Channel: 6; HD 555)
Détenteur: Cogeco Inc.*
323, boul Lasalle, Baie-Comeau, QC G4Z 2L5
Tél: 418-296-9505, *Téléc:* 418-296-6733
cogecotv.baie-comeau@cogeco.com
www.tvcogeco.com/baie-comeau
Patrick Delobel, Directeur régional, patrick.delobel@cogeco.com

***Baie-Saint-Paul:* CFTF-DT-10** (Channel: 26)
Owned by: CFTF-DT
Baie-Saint-Paul, QC
www.cftf.ca

***†Baie-Saint-Paul:* CIMT-DT-4** (Channel: 13)
Détenteur: CIMT-DT
Baie-Saint-Paul, QC
cimt.teleinterrives.com

***Baie-Saint-Paul:* CKRT-DT-1** (Channel: 36)
Owned by: CKRT-DT
Baie-Saint-Paul, QC
www.ckrt.ca

* *For details on this company see listing in Major Broadcasting Companies section; † French language station*

Baie-St-Paul: La Télévision de Charlevoix-Ouest
Owned by: DERYtelecom*
74, Ambroise-Fafard, Baie-St-Paul, QC G3Z 2J6
Tel: 418-435-5134, *Fax:* 418-435-6479
info@tvco.qc.ca
tvcotv.com

Cabano: CFTF-DT-3 (Channel: 12)
Owned by: CFTF-DT
Cabano, QC
www.cftf.ca

†_Cabano:_ CIMT-DT-8 (Channel: 23)
Détenteur: CIMT-DT
Cabano, QC
cimt.teleinterrives.com

Cabano: CKRT-DT-4 (Channel: 21)
Owned by: CKRT-DT
Cabano, QC
www.ckrt.ca

Carleton: CFTF-DT-11 (Channel: 44)
Owned by: CFTF-DT
Carleton, QC
www.cftf.ca

†_Carleton:_ CHAU-DT (Channel: 4)
Détenteur: Télé Inter-Rives ltée*
349, boul Perron, Carleton, QC G0C 1J0
Tél: 418-364-3344, *Téléc:* 418-364-7168
nousjoindre@chautva.com
www.chautva.com

†_Chandler:_ CHAU-DT-4 (Channel: 6)
Détenteur: CHAU-DT
Chandler, QC

†_Chicoutimi:_ CJPM-DT (Channel: 6)
Détenteur: Groupe TVA inc.
1, rue Mont Ste-Claire, Chicoutimi, QC G7H 5G3
Tél: 418-549-2576, *Téléc:* 418-549-1130
Ligne sans frais: 800-267-2576
tva.canoe.ca/stations/cjpm

†_Chicoutimi:_ CKTV-DT (Channel: 12)
Détenteur: Canadian Broadcasting Corporation*
500, rue des Saguenéens, Chicoutimi, QC G7H 6N4
Tél: 418-696-6600, *Ligne sans frais:* 800-463-9857
www.radio-canada.ca/saguenay-lac-saint-jean
Michel Gagné, Chef des services français, michel.gagne-SAG@radio-canada.ca

Chicoutimi: MAtv (Channel: 9; HD 609)
Owned by: Vidéotron ltée
1, rue de Mont Ste-Claire, Chicoutimi, QC G7H 5G3
Tel: 418-541-5920, *Fax:* 418-541-5939
saguenay@matv.ca
matv.ca
Social Media: www.facebook.com/matv, twitter.com/MAtv

†_Cloridorme:_ CHAU-DT-8 (Channel: 11)
Détenteur: CHAU-DT
Cloridorme, QC

Dégelis: CKRT-DT-2 (Channel: 25)
Owned by: CKRT-DT
Dégelis, QC
www.ckrt.ca

†_Drummondville:_ CogecoTV - Drummondville (Channel: 3; HD 555)
Détenteur: Cogeco Inc.*
1970, boul Lemire, Drummondville, QC J2B 6X5
Tél: 819-477-3978, *Téléc:* 819-474-5313
tvcogeco.drummondville@cgocable.ca
www.tvcogeco.com/drummondville
Reno Longpré, Directeur régional, 819-477-3978, reno.longpre@cogeco.com

Forestville: CFTF-DT-4 (Channel: 4)
Owned by: CFTF-DT
Forestville, QC
www.cftf.ca

Gaspé: CFTF-DT-9 (Channel: 30)
Owned by: CFTF-DT
Gaspé, QC
www.cftf.ca

†_Gaspé:_ CHAU-DT-6 (Channel: 7)
Détenteur: CHAU-DT
Gaspé, QC

Gatineau: CFGS-DT (V Gatineau-Ottawa) (Channel: 34)
Owned by: RNC MÉDIA, Inc.*
171-A, rue Jean-Proulx, Gatineau, QC J8Z 1W5
Tel: 819-770-1040, *Fax:* 819-770-0272
www.vgatineau.ca

†_Gatineau:_ CHOT-DT (TVA Gatineau-Ottawa) (Channel: 40)
Détenteur: RNC MÉDIA, Inc.*
171-A, rue Jean-Proulx, Gatineau, QC J8Z 1W5
Tél: 819-770-1040, *Téléc:* 819-770-0272
www.tvagatineau.ca
Médias sociaux: www.facebook.com/tvagatineauottawa, twitter.com/TVAgatineau

Gatineau: MAtv (Channel: 9; HD 609)
Owned by: Vidéotron ltée
190, rue d'Edmonton, Gatineau, QC J8Y 3S6
Tel: 819-771-7373, *Fax:* 819-771-7011
montreal@matv.ca
matv.ca
Social Media: www.facebook.com/matv, twitter.com/MAtv

Granby: MAtv (Channel: 9; HD 609)
Owned by: Vidéotron ltée
611, rue Cowie, Granby, QC J2G 3X4
Tel: 450-574-3252, *Fax:* 450-372-5464
granby@matv.ca
matv.ca
Social Media: www.facebook.com/matv, twitter.com/MAtv

†_Jonquière:_ CFRS-DT (V Saguenay) (Channel: 13)
Détenteur: V Interactions Inc.*
2303, rue Sir Wilfrid-Laurier, Jonquière, QC G7X 5Z2
Tél: 418-542-4551, *Téléc:* 418-542-7217
Ligne sans frais: 855-390-6100
vtele.ca

†_Jonquière:_ CIVV-TV (Channel: 8)
Détenteur: Télé-Québec*
Pavillon Joseph-Angers, 3788, rue de la Fabrique, Jonquière, QC G7X 3P4
Tél: 418-695-8152, *Téléc:* 418-695-8155
telequebec.tv
Jocelyn Robert, Coordonnatrice, jocelyn.robert@telequebec.tv

†_L'Anse-à-Valleau:_ CHAU-DT-9 (Channel: 12)
Détenteur: CHAU-DT
L'Anse-à-Valleau, QC

La Baie: Télévision DERYtélécom
Owned by: DERYtelecom*
PO Box 1154, La Baie, QC G7B 3P3
Tel: 418-544-0403
info@tvdl.tv
www.tvdl.tv
Social Media: www.youtube.com/user/TVDLDERY, www.facebook.com/tvdl.labaie

Lac-Mégantic: Télé locale Axion (Channel: 11; 111)
Owned by: Cable Axion inc.
4764, rue Laval, Lac-Mégantic, QC G6B 1C7
Fax: 418-387-6915
Toll-Free: 866-552-9466
cable11@axion.ca
www.axion.ca/communaute/presentation.php
Yannick Marceau, Coordinateur et journaliste

Les Escoumins: CFTF-DT-8 (Channel: 33)
Owned by: CFTF-DT
Les Escoumins, QC
www.cftf.ca

†_Les Escoumins:_ CIMT-DT-7 (Channel: 35)
Détenteur: CIMT-DT
Les Escoumins, QC
cimt.teleinterrives.com

†_Magog:_ CogecoTV - Magog (Channel: 3; HD 555)
Détenteur: Cogeco Inc.*
15, rue Saint-Patrice ouest, Magog, QC J1X 1V8
Tél: 819-843-3370, *Téléc:* 819-843-0698
commentaires.cogecotv@cogeco.com
www.tvcogeco.com/magog
Médias sociaux: www.facebook.com/CogecoQC, twitter.com/CogecoQC

Matane: CogecoTV - Matane (Channel: 4; HD 555)
Owned by: Cogeco Inc.*
63, rue Brillant, Matane, QC G4W 3P6
Tel: 418-562-4468, *Fax:* 418-562-9248
cogecotv.matane@cogeco.com
www.tvcogeco.com/matane
Michel Desrosiers, Directeur régional, 418-724-6058, michel.desrosiers@cogeco.com

†_Montmagny:_ CogecoTV - Montmagny (Channel: 6; HD 555)
Détenteur: Cogeco Inc.*
190, 6e av, Montmagny, QC G5V 0C3
Tél: 418-248-5698, *Téléc:* 418-248-4192
commentaires.cogecotv@cogeco.com
www.tvcogeco.com/montmagny
Médias sociaux: www.facebook.com/TVCogeco, twitter.com/TVCogeco
Suzy Walsh, Directrice de la programmation, 819-693-3561, suzy.walsh@cogeco.com

†_Montréal:_ CBFT-DT (Channel: 19)
Détenteur: Canadian Broadcasting Corporation*
Maison de Radio-Canada, CP 6000 Centre-ville, Montréal, QC H3C 3A8
Tél: 514-597-6000, *Téléc:* 514-597-5545
Ligne sans frais: 866-306-4636
www.radio-canada.ca/montreal
Médias sociaux: twitter.com/RC_TV
Autre information: Salle de nouvelles télévision: 514-597-6371; télécopier: 514-597-6354
Helen Evans, Directrice générale

Montréal: CBMT-DT (Channel: 21)
Owned by: Canadian Broadcasting Corporation*
PO Box 6000, Montréal, QC H3C 3A8
Tel: 514-597-6000, *Fax:* 514-597-6354
www.cbc.ca/montreal
Other information: Phone, CBC Montréal TV Newsroom: 514-597-6397
Shelagh Kinch, Managing Director, English Services, shelagh.kinch@cbc.ca

Montréal: CFJP-DT (V Montréal) (Channel: 35)
Owned by: V Interactions Inc.*
85, rue St-Paul ouest, Montréal, QC H2Y 3V4
Tel: 514-390-6100, *Fax:* 514-390-6056
vtele.ca

†_Montréal:_ CFTM-DT (Channel: 10)
Détenteur: Groupe TVA inc.*
1600 Est, boul de Maisonneuve, Montréal, QC H2L 4P2
Tél: 514-526-9251, *Téléc:* 514-599-5502
groupetva.ca
Médias sociaux: www.facebook.com/ReseauTVA, twitter.com/tvareseau

†_Montréal:_ CIVM-TV (Channel: 17)
Détenteur: Télé-Québec*
1000, rue Fullum, Montréal, QC H2K 3L7
Tél: 514-521-2424, *Téléc:* 514-864-1979
info@telequebec.tv
www.telequebec.tv
Médias sociaux: www.facebook.com/TeleQc, twitter.com/telequebec
Maryse Gagnon, Coordonnatrice, mgagnon@telequebec.tv

Montréal: CKMI-TV (Channel: 5)
Owned by: Global Television Network
1010 Saint Catherine St. West, Montréal, QC H3B 5L1
Tel: 514-521-4323
montreal@globalnews.ca
www.globalmontreal.com
Social Media: www.youtube.com/globalmontrealnews, www.facebook.com/globalmontreal, twitter.com/Global_Montreal

Montréal: MAtv (Channel: 9; HD 609)
Owned by: Vidéotron ltée
1475, rue Alexandre-DeSève, niveau 4D, Montréal, QC H2L 2V4
Tel: 514-985-8408, *Fax:* 514-985-8404
montreal@matv.ca
matv.ca
Social Media: www.facebook.com/matv, twitter.com/MAtv

†_Percé:_ CHAU-DT-5 (Channel: 13)
Détenteur: CHAU-DT
Percé, QC

** For details on this company see listing in Major Broadcasting Companies section; † French language station*

†*Plessisville:* CKYQ-FM (Channel: 95.7)
1646, av St-Laurent, Plessisville, QC G6L 2Y6
Tél: 819-362-3737, *Téléc:* 819-362-3414
Ligne sans frais: 800-839-9570
programmation@kyqfm.com
www.kyqfm.com
Médias sociaux: www.facebook.com/158724320809030
Stéphane Dion, Directeur général

†*Port-Daniel:* CHAU-DT-3 (Channel: 10)
Détenteur: CHAU-DT
Port-Daniel, QC

†*Québec:* CBVT-DT (Channel: 25)
Détenteur: Canadian Broadcasting Corporation*
CP 18800, Québec, QC G1K 9L4
Tél: 418-654-1341, *Ligne sans frais:* 866-954-1341
nouvelles.quebec@radio-canada.ca
www.radio-canada.ca/quebec
Jean François Rioux, Directeur région de Québec

†*Quebec:* CFAP-DT (V Québec) (Channel: 39)
Détenteur: V*
#335, 330, rue De St-Vallier est, Quebec, QC G9K 9C5
Tél: 418-624-2222, *Téléc:* 418-624-8930
Ligne sans frais: 855-390-6100
vtele.ca

***Québec:* MAtv** (Channel: 9; HD 609)
Owned by: Vidéotron ltée
#1200, 1000, av Myrand, Québec, QC G1V 2W3
Tel: 418-522-8289, *Fax:* 418-522-7237
quebec@matv.ca
matv.ca
Social Media: www.facebook.com/matv, twitter.com/MAtv

†*Rimouski:* CFER-TV (Channel: 5, 11)
Détenteur: Groupe TVA inc.*
465, boul Ste-Anne, Rimouski, QC G5M 1G1
Tél: 418-722-6011, *Téléc:* 418-723-0857
commentaires.suggestions@cfer.tva.ca
tva.canoe.ca/stations/cfer
Claude Auger, Directeur général, claude.auger@tva.ca

†*Rimouski:* CIVB-TV (Channel: 22)
Détenteur: Télé-Québec*
79, rue de l'Évêché Est, Rimouski, QC G5L 1X7
Tél: 418-727-3743, *Téléc:* 418-727-3814
bureau.rimouski@telequebec.tv
www.telequebec.tv

†*Rimouski:* CJBR-DT (Channel: 45)
Détenteur: Canadian Broadcasting Corporation*
185, boul René-Lepage est, Rimouski, QC G5L 1P2
Tél: 418-723-2217, *Téléc:* 418-723-6126
cjbr@radio-canada.ca
www.radio-canada.ca/est-du-quebec
Denis Langlois, Premier chef des services français, denis.langlois@radio-canada.ca

***Rimouski:* CJPC-DT** (Channel: 18)
Owned by: CFTF-DT
Rimouski, QC
www.cftf.ca

†*Rimouski:* CogecoTV - Rimouski (Channel: 4; HD 555)
Détenteur: Cogeco Inc.*
384, av de la Cathédrale, Rimouski, QC G5L 5L1
Tél: 418-724-5737, *Téléc:* 418-724-7167
commentaires.cogecotv@cogeco.com
www.tvcogeco.com/rimouski
Médias sociaux: www.facebook.com/tvCOGECO, twitter.com/tvCOGECO
Michel Desrosiers, Directeur régional, 418-724-6058, michel.desrosiers@cogeco.com

†*Rivière-au-Rénard:* CHAU-DT-7 (Channel: 4)
Détenteur: CHAU-DT
Rivière-au-Rénard, QC

†*Rivière-du-Loup:* CFTF-DT (Channel: 29; affiliated with V Interactions Inc.)
Détenteur: Télé Inter-Rives ltée*
103, rue des Équipements, Rivière-du-Loup, QC G5R 5W7
Tél: 418-862-2909, *Téléc:* 418-862-8147
nouvelles@cftf.ca
www.cftf.ca

***Rivière-du-Loup:* CFTF-DT-6** (Channel: 11)
Owned by: CFTF-DT
Rivière-du-Loup, QC
www.cftf.ca

†*Rivière-du-Loup:* CIMT-DT (Channel: 9)
Détenteur: Télé Inter-Rives ltée*
15, rue de la Chute, Rivière-du-Loup, QC G5R 5B7
Tél: 418-867-1341, *Téléc:* 418-867-4710
nousjoindre@cimt.ca
cimt.teleinterrives.com
Médias sociaux: www.facebook.com/176156409078792, twitter.com/cimt_nouvelles

†*Rivière-du-Loup:* CIMT-DT-6 (Channel: 41)
Détenteur: CIMT-DT
Rivière-du-Loup, QC
cimt.teleinterrives.com

†*Rivière-du-Loup:* CKRT-DT (Channel: 7; Radio-Canada owns part stake of the company)
Détenteur: Télé Inter-Rives ltée*
15, rue de la Chute, Rivière-du-Loup, QC G5R 5B7
Tél: 418-867-1341, *Téléc:* 418-867-4710
info@ckrt.ca
www.ckrt.ca

†*Rivière-du-Loup:* CKRT-DT (Channel: 7; possédé à Télé Inter-Rives ltée)
Détenteur: Canadian Broadcasting Corporation*
15, rue de la Chute, Rivière-du-Loup, QC G5R 5B7
Tél: 418-867-8080

***Rivière-du-Loup:* CKRT-DT-3** (Channel: 13)
Owned by: CKRT-DT
Rivière-du-Loup, QC
www.ckrt.ca

***Rivière-du-Loup:* MAtv** (Channel: 9; HD 609)
Owned by: Vidéotron ltée
55, rue de l'Hôtel-de-Ville, Rivière-du-Loup, QC G5R 1L4
Tel: 418-867-1479, *Fax:* 418-867-2829
riviereduloup@matv.ca
matv.ca
Social Media: www.facebook.com/matv, twitter.com/MAtv

†*Rouyn-Noranda:* CFEM-DT (TVA Abitibi-Témiscamingue) (Channel: 13)
Détenteur: RNC MÉDIA, Inc.*
380, av Murdoch, Rouyn-Noranda, QC J9X 1G5
Tél: 819-762-0741, *Téléc:* 819-762-6331
nouvelles@rncmedia.ca
www.tvaabitibi.ca
Médias sociaux: www.facebook.com/tvaabitibi, twitter.com/RNCNouvellesAT

***Rouyn-Noranda:* CFVS-DT (V Abitibi-Témiscamingue)** (Channel: 15)
Owned by: RNC MÉDIA, Inc.*
380, rue Murdoch, Rouyn-Noranda, QC J9X 1G5
Tel: 819-762-0741, *Fax:* 819-762-6331
nouvelles@rncmedia.ca
www.vabitibi.ca

†*Rouyn-Noranda:* CKRN-DT (Channel: 9)
Détenteur: RNC MÉDIA, Inc.*
380, av Murdoch, Rouyn-Noranda, QC J9X 1G5
Tél: 819-762-0741, *Téléc:* 819-762-6331
www.rncmedia.ca

***Rouyn-Noranda:* TVC9** (Channel: 9)
Owned by: Cablevision du Nord de Québec inc.
155, av du Portage, Rouyn-Noranda, QC J9X 7H3
Toll-Free: 800-567-6353
tvc9rn@cablevision.ca
tvc9.cablevision.qc.ca
Geneviève Bélisle, Directrice
Benoit Paquin, Coordinateur, TVC9 Rouyn-Noranda

***Saint-Georges:* CogecoTV - Saint-Georges** (Channel: 9; HD 555)
Owned by: Cogeco Inc.*
#150, 10, boul Lacroix, Saint-Georges, QC G5Y 1R7
Tel: 418-228-9828, *Fax:* 418-228-3015
commentaires@cogecotv@cogeco.com
www.tvcogeco.com/saint-georges
Paul Gauvin, Directeur régional, 418-218-1032, paul.gavin@cogeco.com

†*Saint-Hyacinthe:* CogecoTV - Saint-Hyacinthe (Channel: 3; HD 555)
Détenteur: Cogeco Inc.*
16900, av Bourdages sud, Saint-Hyacinthe, QC J2T 4P7
Tél: 450-774-1087, *Téléc:* 450-774-3373
cogecotv.st-hyacinthe@cogeco.com
www.tvcogeco.com/saint-hyacinthe
Médias sociaux: www.facebook.com/tvcogecosthyacinthe/, twitter.com/TVCStHyacinthe
Robert Desfonds, Directeur régional, 450-774-1087, robert.desfonds@cogeco.com

***Saint-Raymond:* CJSR La TVC Portneuvoise** (Channel: 3)
Owned by: DERYtelecom*
#131, 4, rue Saint-Joseph, Saint-Raymond, QC G3L 1H4
Tel: 418-337-4925, *Fax:* 418-337-4991
www.cjsr3.com
Social Media: www.facebook.com/cjsr.latvcportneuvoise

†*Saint-Urbain:* CIMT-DT-5 (Channel: 38)
Détenteur: CIMT-DT
Saint-Urbain, QC
cimt.teleinterrives.com

***Saint-Urbain:* CKRT-DT-5** (Channel: 35)
Owned by: CKRT-DT
Saint-Urbain, QC
www.ckrt.ca

†*Sainte-Adèle:* CogecoTV - Laurentides (Channel: 4; HD 555)
Détenteur: Cogeco Inc.*
421, boul Sainte-Adèle, Sainte-Adèle, QC J8B 2N1
Tél: 450-745-4003, *Téléc:* 450-229-7910
Ligne sans frais: 800-489-0129
cogecotv.laurentides@cogeco.com
www.tvcogeco.com/laurentides
Médias sociaux: www.facebook.com/tvCOGECO, twitter.com/tvCOGECO
Christian Fournier, Directeur de la programmation, 450-745-4003, christian.fournier@cogeco.com

†*Sainte-Foy:* CFCM-DT (Channel: 4)
Détenteur: Groupe TVA inc.*
1000, av Myrand, Sainte-Foy, QC G1V 2W3
Tél: 418-688-9330
administrationquebec@tva.ca
tva.canoe.ca
Nathalie Langevin, Directrice générale, nathalie.langevin@tva.ca

†*Sainte-Marguerite-Marie:* CHAU-DT-1 (Channel: 3)
Détenteur: CHAU-DT
Sainte-Marguerite-Marie, QC

***Sainte-Marie:* Télé locale Axion** (Channel: 11; 150)
Owned by: Cable Axion inc.
166, Notre-Dame nord, Sainte-Marie, QC G6E 3Z9
Fax: 418-387-6915
Toll-Free: 866-552-9466
cable11@axion.ca
www.axion.ca/communaute/presentation.php
Yannick Marceau, Coordinateur et journaliste

†*Salaberry-de-Valleyfield:* CogecoTV - Salaberry-de-Valleyfield (Channel: 13; HD 555)
Détenteur: Cogeco Inc.*
13, rue Saint-Urbain, Salaberry-de-Valleyfield, QC J6S 4M6
Tél: 450-377-1373, *Téléc:* 450-377-5632
cogecotv.valleyfield@cogeco.com
www.tvcogeco.com/salaberry-de-valleyfield
Nathalie Descôteaux, Directrice régionale, 450-377-1373, nathalie.descoteaux@cogeco.com

†*Sept-Iles:* CFER-TV-2 (Channel: 5)
Détenteur: CFER-TV
410, av Évangéline, Sept-Iles, QC G4R 2N5
Tél: 418-968-6011, *Téléc:* 418-968-5665
tva.canoe.ca/stations/cfer

***Sept-îles:* CFTF-DT-7** (Channel: 7)
Owned by: CFTF-DT
Sept-îles, QC
www.cftf.ca

†*Sept-îles:* CogecoTV - Sept-îles (Channel: 5; HD 555)
Détenteur: Cogeco Inc.*
410, rue Évangéline, Sept-îles, QC G4R 2N5
Tél: 418-962-3508, *Téléc:* 418-962-3531
cogecotv.sept-iles@cgocable.ca
www.tvcogeco.com/sept-iles

* *For details on this company see listing in Major Broadcasting Companies section; † French language station*

Patrick Delobel, Directeur régional, 418-962-3508, patrick.delobel@cogeco.com

***Sherbrooke:* CFKS-DT (V Estrie)** (Channel: 30)
Owned by: V*
3720, boul Industriel, Sherbrooke, QC J1L 1Z9
Tel: 819-565-9232, *Fax:* 819-822-4205
Toll-Free: 855-390-6100
vtele.ca

†*Sherbrooke:* CHLT-DT (Channel: 7)
Détenteur: Groupe TVA inc.*
3330, rue King Ouest, Sherbrooke, QC J1L 1C9
Tél: 819-565-7777, *Téléc:* 819-565-4650
tva.canoe.ca/stations/chlt
Médias sociaux: www.facebook.com/TVASherbrooke
Sarah Beaulieu, Directrice générale, sarah.beaulieu@quebecormedia.com

†*Sherbrooke:* CIVS-DT (Channel: 24)
Détenteur: Télé-Québec*
#1000, 3330, rue King Ouest, Sherbrooke, QC J1L 1C9
Tél: 819-820-3436, *Téléc:* 819-820-3449
bureau.sherbrooke@telequebec.tv
www.telequebec.tv
Pascal-Gilles Gervais, Coordonnateur

†*Sherbrooke:* CKSH-DT (Channel: 9)
Détenteur: Canadian Broadcasting Corporation*
#350, 1335, rue King ouest, Sherbrooke, QC J1J 2B8
Tél: 819-620-0000, *Téléc:* 819-823-0453
www.radio-canada.ca
Stéphane Laberge, Chef des services français, stephane.laberge@radio-canada.ca

***Sherbrooke:* MAtv** (Channel: 9; HD 609)
Owned by: Vidéotron ltée
#182, 3330, rue King Ouest, Sherbrooke, QC J1L 1C9
Tel: 819-820-7830, *Fax:* 819-820-7834
sherbrooke@matv.ca
matv.ca
Social Media: www.facebook.com/matv, twitter.com/MAtv

***Sorel-Tracy:* MAtv** (Channel: 9; HD 609)
Owned by: Vidéotron ltée
254, ch des Patriotes, Sorel-Tracy, QC J3P 6K7
Tel: 450-742-0113, *Fax:* 450-742-1018
soreltracy@matv.ca
matv.ca
Social Media: www.facebook.com/matv, twitter.com/MAtv

†*Thetford Mines:* CogecoTV - Thetford Mines (Channel: 9; HD 555)
Détenteur: Cogeco Inc.*
39 - 10e Rue Sud, Thetford Mines, QC G6G 7X6
Tél: 418-338-2079, *Téléc:* 418-335-9125
commentaires.cogecotv@cogeco.com
www.tvcogeco.com/thetford-mines
Médias sociaux: www.facebook.com/tvCOGECO, twitter.com/tvCOGECO

†*Tracadie:* CHAU-DT-10 (Channel: 9)
Détenteur: CHAU-DT
Tracadie, QC

***Trois Rivières:* CogecoTV - Mauricie** (Channel: 11; HD 555)
Owned by: Cogeco Inc.*
4141, boul Saint-Jean, Trois Rivières, QC G9B 2M8
Tel: 819-693-8353, *Fax:* 819-379-2232
Toll-Free: 800-667-8353
cogecotv.mauricie@cogeco.com
www.tvcogeco.com/mauricie
Suzy Walsh, Directrice de la programmation, 819-693-3561, suzy.walsh@cogeco.com

***Trois-Pistoles:* CFTF-DT-2** (Channel: 17)
Owned by: CFTF-DT
Trois-Pistoles, QC
www.cftf.ca

†*Trois-Pistoles:* CIMT-DT-2 (Channel: 13)
Détenteur: CIMT-DT
Trois-Pistoles, QC
cimt.teleinterrives.com

***Trois-Pistoles:* CKRT-DT-6** (Channel: 19)
Owned by: CKRT-DT
Trois-Pistoles, QC
www.ckrt.ca

***Trois-Rivière:* MAtv** (Channel: 9; HD 609)
Owned by: Vidéotron ltée
#101, 190, rue Fusey, Trois-Rivière, QC G8T 2V8
Tel: 819-375-9888, *Fax:* 819-375-8950
capdelamadeleine@matv.ca
matv.ca
Social Media: www.facebook.com/matv, twitter.com/MAtv

†*Trois-Rivières:* CFKM-DT (V Mauricie) (Channel: 34)
Détenteur: V*
926, rue Notre Dame Centre, Trois-Rivières, QC G9A 4W8
Tél: 819-377-6053, *Ligne sans frais:* 855-390-6100
vtele.ca

†*Trois-Rivières:* CHEM-DT (Channel: 8)
Détenteur: Groupe TVA inc.*
3625, boul Chanoine-Moreau, Trois-Rivières, QC G8Y 5N6
Tél: 819-376-8880, *Téléc:* 819-376-2906
administrationchem@tva.ca
tva.canoe.ca/stations/chem
Serge Buchanan, Directeur général, serge.buchanan@tva.ca

†*Trois-Rivières:* CIVC-DT (Channel: 45)
Détenteur: Télé-Québec*
#201, 1350, rue Royale, Trois-Rivières, QC G9A 4J4
Tél: 819-371-6752, *Téléc:* 819-371-6684
www.telequebec.tv
Marie-Josée Desjardins, Coordonnatrice, mjdesjardins@telequebec.tv

***Trois-Rivières:* CKTM-DT** (Channel: 28)
Owned by: Canadian Broadcasting Corporation*
#101, 225, rue des Forges, Trois-Rivières, QC G9A 2G7
Tel: 819-694-0114, *Toll-Free:* 877-695-6556
www.radio-canada.ca/mauricie
Nancy Sabourin, Chef des services français, Nancy.sabourin@radio-canada.ca

†*Val d'Or:* CIVA-TV (Channel: 12)
Détenteur: CIVM-TV*
#201, 689, 3e av, Val d'Or, QC J9P 1S7
Tél: 819-874-5132, *Téléc:* 819-824-2431
www.telequebec.tv
Josée Lacoste, Coordonnatrice, josee.lacoste@telequebec.tv

***Val-d'Or:* TVC9** (Channel: 9)
Owned by: Cablevision du Nord de Québec inc.
45, boul Hôtel de Ville, Val-d'Or, QC J9P 2M5
Toll-Free: 800-567-6353
tvc9.cablevision.qc.ca
Social Media: www.facebook.com/255688484493841
Geneviève Geneviève, Directrice
Pierre-Luc Létourneau, Coordinateur, TVC9 Val-d'Or, pletourneau@cablevision.ca

Saskatchewan

***Carlyle Lake:* CIEW-TV** (Channel: 7)
Owned by: CFQC-DT
Carlyle Lake, SK

***Colgate:* CKCK-TV-1** (Channel: 12)
Owned by: CKCK-TV
Colgate, SK

***Fort Qu'appelle:* CKCK-TV-7** (Channel: 7)
Owned by: CKCK-DT
Fort Qu'appelle, SK

***Golden Prairie:* CKMC-TV-1** (Channel: 10)
Owned by: CKCK-DT
Golden Prairie, SK

***Maple Creek:* CHAT-TV-2** (Channel: 6)
Medicine Hat
Owned by: CHAT-TV
Maple Creek, SK

***Meadow Lake:* CITL-TV-3** (Channel: 3)
Lloydminster
Owned by: CITL-TV
Meadow Lake, SK

***Moose Jaw:* CKMJ-TV** (Channel: 7)
Owned by: CKCK-DT
Moose Jaw, SK

***Moose Jaw:* Shaw TV - Moose Jaw** (Channel: 10)
Owned by: Shaw Media Inc.
201 Manitoba St. East, Moose Jaw, SK S6H 0A4
Tel: 306-691-7395
mjshawtv@shaw.ca
www.shaw.ca/ShawTV/Moosejaw

***North Battleford:* CFQC-TV-2** (Channel: 6)
Owned by: CFQC-DT
North Battleford, SK

***Pivot:* CHAT-TV-1** (Channel: 4)
Medicine Hat
Owned by: CHAT-TV
Pivot, SK

***Prince Albert:* CIPA-TV** (Channel: 9)
Owned by: Bell Media TV*
22 - 10 St. West, Prince Albert, SK S6V 3A5
Tel: 306-922-6066, *Fax:* 306-763-3041
cipa@ctv.ca
saskatoon.ctvnews.ca
Social Media: www.facebook.com/ctvsaskatoon, twitter.com/ctvsaskatoon

***Prince Albert:* Shaw TV - Prince Albert** (Channel: 10)
Owned by: Shaw Media Inc.
2990A - 2nd Ave. West, Prince Albert, SK S6V 7E9
Tel: 306-922-5622
www.shaw.ca/ShawTV/PrinceAlbert
Lisa Risom, Contact, lisa.risom@sjrb.ca

†*Regina:* CBKFT-DT (Channel: 13)
Détenteur: Canadian Broadcasting Corporation*
2440, rue Broad, Regina, SK S4P 4A1
Tél: 306-347-9540
saskatchewan@radio-canada.ca
www.radio-canada.ca/saskatchewan
Médias sociaux: www.facebook.com/cbcsask, twitter.com/cbcsask

***Regina:* CBKT-DT** (Channel: 9)
Owned by: Canadian Broadcasting Corporation*
2440 Broad St., Regina, SK S4P 4A1
Tel: 306-347-9540
www.cbc.ca/sask
Social Media: www.facebook.com/cbcsask, twitter.com/cbcsask

***Regina:* CFRE-TV** (Channel: 5)
Owned by: Global Television Network*
370 Hoffer Dr., Regina, SK S4N 7A4
Tel: 306-775-4000, *Fax:* 306-721-4817
regina@globalnews.ca
www.globalregina.com
Social Media: www.facebook.com/GlobalReginaNews, twitter.com/GlobalRegina

***Regina:* Citytv Saskatchewan**
Owned by: Rogers Broadcasting Ltd.*
PO Box 3464 Main, Regina, SK S4P 3J8
Tel: 306-779-2726
www.citytv.com/saskatchewan

***Regina:* CKCK-DT** (Channel: 2)
Owned by: Bell Media TV*
PO Box 2000, Regina, SK S4P 3E5
Tel: 306-569-2000, *Fax:* 306-522-0090
ckck@ctv.ca
regina.ctvnews.ca

***Saskatoon:* CFQC-DT** (Channel: 8)
Owned by: Bell Media TV*
216 - 1 Ave. North, Saskatoon, SK S7K 3W3
Tel: 306-665-8600, *Fax:* 306-665-0450
cfqcnews@ctv.ca
saskatoon.ctvnews.ca

***Saskatoon:* CFSK-DT** (Channel: 4)
Owned by: Global Television Network*
218 Robin Cres., Saskatoon, SK S7L 7C3
Tel: 306-665-6969, *Fax:* 306-665-6069
saskatoon@globalnews.ca
www.globalsaskatoon.com
Social Media: www.facebook.com/GlobalSaskatoon, twitter.com/GlobalSaskatoon

***Saskatoon:* Shaw TV - Saskatoon** (Channel: 10)
Owned by: Shaw Media Inc.
2326 Hanselman Ave., Saskatoon, SK S7L 5Z3
Tel: 306-665-3796
shawtv10@shaw.ca
www.shaw.ca/ShawTV/Saskatoon

** For details on this company see listing in Major Broadcasting Companies section; † French language station*

Stranraer: **CFQC-TV-1** (Channel: 3)
Owned by: CFQC-DT
Stranraer, SK

Swift Current: **CKMC-TV** (Channel: 12)
Owned by: CKCK-DT
Swift Current, SK

Swift Current: **Shaw TV - Swift Current** (Channel: 10)
Owned by: Shaw Media Inc.
15 Dufferin St. West, Swift Current, SK S9H 5A1
Tel: 306-973-3005
www.shaw.ca/ShawTV/SwiftCurrent
Juanita Tuntland, Contact, Juanita.tuntland@sjrb.ca

Willow Bunch: **CKCK-TV-2** (Channel: 6)
Owned by: CKCK-TV
Willow Bunch, SK

Wynyard: **CIWH-TV** (Channel: 12)
Owned by: CFQC-DT
Wynyard, SK

Cable Companies

Alberta

Calgary: **Seaview Communications Ltd.**
87 Woodbrook Rd. SW, Calgary, AB T2W 4M5
Tel: 403-238-4436
seaview@seaviewcable.net
seaviewcable.net
Val Weston, President
Leah Ungstad, Manager, Tofino Area, 250-725-2225

Calgary: **Shaw Direct**
Owned by: Shaw Communications Inc.*
c/o Shaw Communications Inc., #900, 630 - 3rd Ave. SW, Calgary, AB T2P 4L4
Toll-Free: 888-554-7827
www.shawdirect.ca
Social Media: www.youtube.com/user/ShawDirectProductTip, www.facebook.com/ShawDirectSatellite, twitter.com/shawdirect_news

Calgary: **Shaw Pay-Per-View Limited**
Owned by: Shaw Direct
c/o Shaw Communications Inc., #900, 630 - 3rd Ave. SW, Calgary, AB T2P 4L4
www.shawdirect.ca/english/ppv/default.asp
Social Media: www.youtube.com/user/ShawDirectProductTip, www.facebook.com/ShawDirectSatellite, twitter.com/shawdirect_news

Camrose: **Lynx Network**
4910 - 46 St., Camrose, AB T4V 1H1
Tel: 780-672-8839, *Fax:* 780-672-8830
hello@lynxnet.ca
www.cable-lynx.net

High Prairie: **KBS Cable**
5401 - 55th Ave., High Prairie, AB T0G 1E0
Tel: 780-523-3223
www.kbscable.com

Oyen: **Oyen Cable (Arts TV)**
212 Main St., Oyen, AB T0J 2J0
Tel: 403-664-3811
www.townofoyen.com/utilities.html
Art Berg, Owner/Operator

Rainbow Lake: **Rainbow Lake Cable TV**
PO Box 149, Rainbow Lake, AB T0H 2Y0
Tel: 780-956-3934, *Fax:* 780-956-3570
admin@rainbowlake.ca
www.rainbowlake.ca

Slave Lake: **Lynx Network Slave Lake**
PO Box 1008, Slave Lake, AB T0G 2A0
Tel: 403-849-5188, *Fax:* 403-849-6809
www.lynxnet.ca/slave

Veteran: **Veteran Television Society**
PO Box 470, Veteran, AB T0C 2S0
Tel: 403-575-3754

British Columbia

Ashcroft: **Copper Valley Cablevision Ltd.**
Owned by: YourLink Inc.*
PO Box 1120, Ashcroft, BC V0K 1A0
Tel: 250-453-2616
yourlink@coppervalley.bc.ca
www.coppervalley.ca

Brackendale: **Britannia Cablevision**
PO Box 461, Brackendale, BC V0N 1H0
Tel: 604-898-9767
Geoffrey Pickard, President

Campbell River: **Nimpkish Valley Communications Ltd.**
Campbell River, BC
Tel: 250-283-2521
tech@wosscable.com
www.wosscable.com

Clearwater: **Raftview Communications Ltd.**
50 Young Rd., Clearwater, BC V0E 1N2
Tel: 250-674-2555, *Fax:* 250-674-3950
Toll-Free: 800-661-1590
www.mercuryspeed.com
Paul Caissie, President

Delta: **Delta Cable**
Owned by: EastLink*
5381 Ladner Trunk Rd., Delta, BC V4K 1W7
Tel: 604-946-7676
www.deltacable.com
Social Media: www.facebook.com/DeltaCable
Other information: Business Services, Toll-Free: 1-877-813-1727

Fort St James: **Fort St. James TV & Radio Society**
PO Box 1536, Fort St James, BC
Tel: 250-996-2246
tv@fsjames.com
tv.fsjames.com
Dave Birdi, President
Bob Hughes, Secretary/Treasurer, 250-996-7251

Gold River: **Conuma Cable Systems**
475 Trumpeter Dr., Gold River, BC V0P 1G0
Tel: 250-283-2521
admin@conumacable.com
www.conumacable.com
Other information: Tahsis Phone: 250-283-2521

Hope: **Hope Cable Television**
PO Box 489, 360 Wallace St., Hope, BC V0X 1L0
Tel: 604-869-2616, *Toll-Free:* 800-663-5038
www.rainbowcountry.bc.ca/archive/hopecable

Logan Lake: **Logan Lake TV Society**
PO Box 56, Logan Lake, BC V0K 1W0
Tel: 250-523-6411
admin@LLTVS.com
www.lltvs.com

Masset: **Masset Haida Television Society**
PO Box 602, 1356 Main St., Masset, BC V0T 1M0
Tel: 250-626-3994, *Fax:* 250-626-3941
mhtv@mhtv.ca
masset.mhtv.ca
Alfred Brockley, President
Gerald Jennings, Vice-President

Nakusp: **Columbia Cable**
Owned by: YourLink Inc.*
PO Box 970, Nakusp, BC V0G 1R0
Tel: 250-265-3733
yourlink@nakusp.net
www.columbiacable.com

Port Alice: **Brooks Bay Cable Corporation**
1071 Marine Dr., Port Alice, BC V0N 2N0
Tel: 250-284-6622
brooksbay@cablerocket.com
www.brooksbaycable.com

Port Hardy: **Keta Cable**
7020 Market St., Port Hardy, BC V0N 2P0
Tel: 250-949-6109, *Fax:* 250-949-6566
ketacable@cablerocket.com
www.ketacable.com

Revelstoke: **Revelstoke Cable**
Owned by: YourLink Inc.*
PO Box 651, 416 - 2nd St. West, Revelstoke, BC V0E 2S0
Tel: 250-837-5246, *Fax:* 250-837-2900
rctv@rctvonline.net
www.revelstokecable.net

Riondel: **Riondel Cable Society**
PO Box 59, 232 Fowler Ave., Riondel, BC V0B 2B0
Tel: 250-225-3433, *Fax:* 250-225-3443
riondelcable@bluebell.ca
www.bluebell.ca

Salmon Arm: **Mascon Communications Corp.**
PO Box 3386, 4901 Auto Rd. SE, Salmon Arm, BC V1E 4S2
Tel: 250-832-6000, *Fax:* 250-832-5575
Toll-Free: 866-832-6020
info@masconcable.ca
www.masconcable.ca
Social Media: www.facebook.com/MasconCable, twitter.com/masconcable

Smithers: **CityWest Smithers Office**
3767 - 2nd Ave., Smithers, BC V0J 2N3
Fax: 866-387-7964
Toll-Free: 800-442-8664
citywest@cwct.ca
www.citywest.ca

Surrey: **Gulf Islands Cable**
Surrey, BC
Fax: 604-541-7620
Toll-Free: 877-666-8221
customerservice@gicable.com
www.gicable.com

Terrace: **CityWest Terrace Office**
2709 Kalum St., Terrace, BC V8G 2M4
Fax: 866-387-7964
Toll-Free: 800-442-8664
citywest@cwct.ca
www.citywest.ca

Ucluelet: **Ucluelet Video Services Ltd.**
1206 Eber St., Ucluelet, BC V0R 3A0
Tel: 250-726-7792
cs@ukeecable.net
www.ukeecable.net

Valemount: **Valemount Entertainment Society/CHVC-TV Community Television**
PO Box 922, Valemount, BC V0E 2Z0
Tel: 250-566-8288, *Fax:* 250-566-4645
tv@vctv.ca
www.vctv.ca
Social Media: www.youtube.com/user/ValemountCommunityTV
Andru McCracken, Station Manager
Barb Riswok, Vice-President
Penni Osadchuk, Station Manager

Vancouver: **Novus Entertainment Inc.**
#300, 112 East 3rd St., Vancouver, BC V5T 1C8
Tel: 604-642-6688, *Fax:* 604-685-7832
customerservice@novusnow.ca
www.novusnow.ca
Social Media: www.facebook.com/novusnow, twitter.com/Novusnow
Doug Holman, Co-President & CFO
Donna L. Robertson, Co-President & CLO

Vanderhoof: **Omineca Cable**
Owned by: YourLink Inc.*
PO Box 798, 2444 Burrard Ave., Vanderhoof, BC V0J 3A0
Fax: 250-567-8733
Toll-Free: 800-665-7599
yourlink@omineca.com
www.omineca.com
Other information: 24-hour Emergency Toll-Free Phone: 1-888-955-3122

Newfoundland & Labrador

Burgeo: **Burgeo Broadcasting System**
147 Reach Rd., Burgeo, NL A0M 1A0
Tel: 709-886-2935, *Fax:* 709-886-1243
www.bbsict.com/bbs/bbs.html
Claude Strickland, Operations Manager, claude@bbsict.ca
Marie Rose, Program Director

** For details on this company see listing in Major Broadcasting Companies section; † French language station*

***Labrador City:* Community Recreation Rebroadcasting Service Association/CRRS TV**
208 Amherst Ave., Labrador City, NL A2V 2Y5
Tel: 709-944-7676, *Fax:* 709-944-7675
info@crrstv.net
www.crrstv.net

***Ramea:* Ramea Broadcasting Co.**
PO Box 23, Ramea, NL A0M 1N0
Tel: 709-625-2618, *Fax:* 709-625-2048

Northwest Territories

***Deline:* Great Bear Co-operative**
PO Box 159, Deline, NT X0E 0G0
Tel: 867-589-3361, *Fax:* 867-589-4517
www.arcticco-op.com

***Fort McPherson:* Tetlit Service Co-operative**
General Delivery, Fort McPherson, NT X0E 0J0
Tel: 867-952-2417, *Fax:* 867-952-2602
manager.tetlit@ArcticCo-op.com
www.arcticco-op.com

***Fort Simpson:* HR Thomson Consultants**
PO Box 313, Fort Simpson, NT X0E 0N0
Tel: 867-695-3107, *Fax:* 867-695-2144
fortsim@cancom.net
Ivan Simons, Contact

Nova Scotia

***Canning:* Cross Country TV Ltd.**
PO Box 310, Canning, NS B0P 1H0
Tel: 902-678-2395, *Fax:* 902-678-2455
wireless@xcountry.tv
www.xcountry.tv

***Halifax:* Coast Cable**
Owned by:* EastLink
PO Box 8660 A, Halifax, NS B3K 5M3
Tel: 604-885-3224
www.coastcable.com
Other information: Business Services, Toll-Free: 1-877-813-1727

***Reserve Mines:* Seaside Communications**
PO Box 4558, Reserve Mines, NS B1E 1L2
Tel: 902-539-6250, *Fax:* 902-539-2597
Toll-Free: 866-872-2253
ads@seaside.ns.ca
www.seaside.ns.ca
Social Media: www.facebook.com/101027363320298
Mora MacDonald, Contact, moram@seaside.ns.ca

Nunavut

***Arctic Bay:* Taqqut Co-operative**
General Delivery, Arctic Bay, NU X0A 0A0
Tel: 867-439-9934, *Fax:* 867-439-8765
www.arcticco-op.com

***Arviat:* Padlei Co-operative Association**
PO Box 90, Arviat, NU X0C 0E0
Tel: 867-857-2933, *Fax:* 867-857-2762
www.arcticco-op.com

***Baker Lake:* Sanavik Co-op**
PO Box 69, Baker Lake, NU X0C 0A0
Tel: 867-793-2912, *Fax:* 867-793-2594
www.arcticco-op.com

***Cambridge Bay:* Ikaluktutiak Cooperative Limited**
PO Box 38, Cambridge Bay, NU X0B 0C0
Tel: 867-983-2201, *Fax:* 867-983-2085
manager.ikaluktutiak@ArcticCo-op.com
www.arcticco-op.com

***Chesterfield Inlet:* Pitsiulak Co-operative**
PO Box 500, Chesterfield Inlet, NU X0C 0B0
Tel: 867-898-9975, *Fax:* 867-898-9056
www.arcticco-op.com

***Coral Harbour:* Katudgevik Cooperative Association Ltd.**
General Delivery, Coral Harbour, NU X0C 0C0
Tel: 867-925-9969, *Fax:* 867-925-8308
www.arcticco-op.com/acl-keewatin-coral-habour.htm

***Gjoa Haven:* Qikiqtaq Co-operative Association Limited**
PO Box 120, Gjoa Haven, NU X0E 1J0
Tel: 867-360-7271, *Fax:* 867-360-6018
manager.qikiqtaq@ArcticCo-op.com
www.arcticco-op.com

***Kugluktuk:* Kugluktuk Co-operative**
PO Box 279, Kugluktuk, NU X0E 0E0
Tel: 867-982-4231, *Fax:* 867-982-3070
manager.kugluktuk@ArcticCo-op.com
www.arcticco-op.com

***Qikiqtarjuaq:* Tulugak Co-Op**
General Delivery, Qikiqtarjuaq, NU X0A 0B0
Tel: 867-927-8061, *Fax:* 867-927-8044
www.arcticco-op.com

***Rankin Inlet:* Kissarvik Co-Op**
PO Box 40, Rankin Inlet, NU X0C 0G0
Tel: 867-645-2801, *Fax:* 867-645-2280
www.arcticco-op.com

***Repulse Bay:* Naujat Co-operative**
General Delivery, Repulse Bay, NU X0C 0H0
Tel: 867-462-9943, *Fax:* 867-462-4152
www.arcticco-op.com/acl-keewatin-repulse-bay.htm

***Whale Cove:* Issatik Co-op Ltd.**
PO Box 60, Whale Cove, NU X0C 0J0
Tel: 867-896-9956, *Fax:* 867-896-9087
www.arcticco-op.com

Ontario

***Aurora:* Robust Computers**
#1, 15450 Yonge St., Aurora, ON L4G 0K1
Tel: 905-773-7046, *Toll-Free:* 877-976-2878
info@robustcomputers.com
www.robustcomputers.com
Social Media: twitter.com/RobustComputers
Other information: Aurora Internet URL: www.aurorainternet.ca

***Clifford:* Maitland Cable TV**
PO Box 70, Clifford, ON N0G 1M0
Tel: 519-327-8012, *Fax:* 519-327-8010
Toll-Free: 888-477-2177
questions@wightman.ca
www.wightman.ca
Social Media: www.youtube.com/wightmantel, www.facebook.com/wightmantelecom, twitter.com/wightmantel

***Dublin:* CABLE TV**
PO Box 118, 123 Ontario St., Dublin, ON N0K 1E0
Tel: 226-302-2341, *Fax:* 519-345-2873
cabletv@ezlink.ca
www.ezlink.ca

***Fenelon Falls:* Cable Cable Inc.**
16 Cable Rd., Fenelon Falls, ON K0M 1M0
Tel: 705-887-6433, *Fax:* 705-887-2580
Toll-Free: 866-887-6434
info@cablecable.net
www.cablecable.net
Social Media: pinterest.com/cablecable, www.facebook.com/cablecable, twitter.com/cablecableinc
Tony Fiorini, President, Tony@cablecable.net

***Hamilton:* Source Cable Ltd.**
1090 Upper Wellington St., Hamilton, ON L9A 3S6
Tel: 905-574-6464, *Fax:* 905-574-4909
Toll-Free: 866-785-7851
info@sourcecable.ca
www.sourcecable.ca
Social Media: www.youtube.com/user/SourceCableSecurity, www.facebook.com/SourceCableHamilton, twitter.com/sourcecable
Other information: Tech Support E-mail: techsupport@sourcecable.net

***Kakabeka Falls:* Fibre-Tel Enterprises**
1043 Gorham St., Kakabeka Falls, ON P7B 4A5
Tel: 807-622-0100, *Fax:* 807-626-8282

***Kincardine:* Kincardine Cable TV Ltd.**
223 Bruce Ave., Kincardine, ON N2Z 2P2
Tel: 519-396-8880, *Toll-Free:* 800-265-3064
kctv@tnt21.com
www.tnt21.com

***Markdale:* Markdale Cable TV**
PO Box 160, Markdale, ON N0C 1H0
Tel: 519-986-2262, *Fax:* 519-986-2612
Toll-Free: 866-686-2262
marcable@cablerocket.com
www.markdalecabletv.com

***Mississauga:* Shaw Broadcast Services**
Owned by:* Shaw Communications Inc.
2055 Flavelle Blvd., Mississauga, ON L5K 1Z8
Tel: 905-403-2020, *Fax:* 905-403-2022
Toll-Free: 800-268-2943
shawbroadcastsupport@sjrb.ca
www.shawbroadcast.com
Other information: Alternate Fax: 905-403-2662
Cam Kernahan, Group Vice-President, Shaw Satellite, cam.kernahan@sjrb.ca
Gary Pizante, Vice-President, Business Development/Satellite/SBS, gary.pizante@shawdirect.ca

***Moose Factory:* Mocreebec Council of the Cree Nation**
PO Box 4, Moose Factory, ON P0L 1W0
Tel: 705-658-5137, *Fax:* 705-658-5335
www.mocreebec.com
Michael Jolly, Director, Telecommunications & IT, michael.jolly@mocreebec.com

***Norwich:* Nor-Del Cablevision**
PO Box 340, Norwich, ON N0J 1P0
Tel: 519-879-6527, *Toll-Free:* 800-563-1954
nordel@nor-del.com
www.nor-del.com

***Toronto:* Academy of Canadian Cinema & Television**
#501, 49 Ontario St., Toronto, ON M5A 2V1
Tel: 416-366-2227, *Fax:* 416-366-8454
Toll-Free: 800-644-5194
communications@academy.ca
www.academy.ca
Social Media: www.youtube.com/academycan, www.facebook.com/acctv, twitter.com/Academy_NET
Martin Katz, Chair
Helga Stephenson, CEO

***Toronto:* Rogers Cable Inc.**
Owned by:* Rogers Communications Inc.
333 Bloor St. East, 10th Fl., Toronto, ON M4W 1G9
Toll-Free: 877-559-5202
www.rogers.com
Social Media: pinterest.com/rogerscanada, www.facebook.com/Rogers, twitter.com/rogersbuzz
Other information: TTY: 1-800-668-9286
Guy Laurence, President & CEO
Colette Watson, Vice-President, Rogers Cable

***Utica:* Compton Cable TV Ltd.**
631 RR#21, Utica, ON L9L 1B5
Tel: 905-985-8171, *Fax:* 905-985-0010
customerservice@compton.net
www.compton.net

Québec

†*Albanel:* Télé-câble Albanel inc.
227, rue Principale, Albanel, QC G8M 3K3
Tél: 418-279-5940
info@tcalbanel.com
www.tcalbanel.com

***Baie-Saint-Paul:* DERYtelecom - Charlevoix**
Owned by:* DERYtelecom
Centre commercial Le Village, #14B, 2, ch de l'Équerre, Baie-Saint-Paul, QC G3Z 2Y5
Fax: 418-435-4060
Toll-Free: 866-544-3358
servicecharlevoix@derytelecom.ca
www.derytele.com

†*Betsiamites:* Télécâble Pessamit
18, rue Messek, Betsiamites, QC G0H 1B0
Tél: 418-567-8863
www.pessamit.ca

†*Chisasibi:* Kinwapt Cable Inc.
CP 420, Chisasibi, QC J0M 1E0
Tél: 819-855-2191, *Téléc:* 819-855-3186

* *For details on this company see listing in Major Broadcasting Companies section; † French language station*

†*Fermont:* Coopérative de la télévision communautaire de Fermont / Diffusion Fermont
CP 1379, 20, place Daviault, Fermont, QC G0G 1J0
Tél: 418-287-5443, *Téléc:* 418-287-5776
www.diffusionfermont.ca
Autre information: Alt. Tel: 418-287-5147
Daniel Brouard, Président

†*Grande-Rivière-Ouest:* Briand et Moreau Câble inc.
CP 63, 205 B, rue du Parc, Grande-Rivière-Ouest, QC G0C 1W0
Tél: 418-385-2680, *Téléc:* 418-385-3705
bmcable@bmcable.ca
www.bmcable.ca

†*Havre-Saint-Pierre:* Radio Télévision Communautaire Hâvre-St-Pierre
992, rue du Bouleau, Havre-Saint-Pierre, QC G0G 1P0
Tél: 418-538-2451, *Téléc:* 418-538-3870
www.cilemf.com
Médias sociaux: www.facebook.com/143063915709007

†*La Malbaie:* Coopérative de câblodistribution de St-Fidèle
8, ch St-Paul, La Malbaie, QC G5A 2G6
Tél: 418-434-2486, *Téléc:* 418-434-1076
Marcel Couturier, Secrétaire

†*Labelle:* Teknocom Avantages Inc.
CP 630, 128, boul Curé-Labelle, Labelle, QC J0T 1H0
Tél: 819-686-2662, *Téléc:* 819-686-1284
Ligne sans frais: 800-293-8093
service@teknocom.ca
www.teknocom.ca

†*Lourdes-de-Blanc-Sablon:* Coopérative de câblodistribution de Brest
1147, boul Dr.-Camille-Marcoux, Lourdes-de-Blanc-Sablon, QC G0G 1W0
Tél: 418-461-2003, *Téléc:* 418-461-2703

†*Magog:* Cable Axion inc.
250, ch de l'Axion, Magog, QC J1X 6J2
Tél: 819-843-0611, *Téléc:* 819-868-4249
Ligne sans frais: 866-552-9466
info@axion.ca
www.axion.ca
Michel Laurent, Président
Rémi Tremblay, Directeur général

†*Matagami:* Cablevision Matagami
CP 519, 3, rue Vanier, Matagami, QC J0Y 2A0
Tél: 819-739-2148, *Téléc:* 819-739-2612
www.matagami.com/arrivants/communications.cfm

†*Matane:* Télécable Multivision inc.
655, ch de la Greve, Matane, QC G4W 7A1
Tél: 418-562-1950, *Ligne sans frais:* 888-562-1950
tmi@cgocable.ca
Raymond Vachon, Président

†*Montréal:* Vidéotron ltée
612, rue St-Jacques, Montréal, QC H3C 4M8
Tél: 514-281-1711, *Ligne sans frais:* 877-512-0911
www.videotron.com
Médias sociaux: www.youtube.com/user/Videotron, www.facebook.com/videotron, twitter.com/videotron
Robert Dépatie, Président et Chef de la direction, Québecor inc., Québecor Média et Vidéotron SE
Manon Brouillette, Président et chef de l'exploitation, Vidéotron

†*Percé:* Télédistribution de la Gaspésie Inc.
CP 234, 155, Place du Quai, Percé, QC G0C 2L0
Tél: 418-782-5355, *Téléc:* 418-782-5407
TDG01@bmcable.ca
www.bmcable.ca

†*Québec:* Coopérative de câblodistribution de l'arrière-pays
20850, boul Henri-Bourassa, Québec, QC G2N 1P7
Tél: 418-849-7125, *Téléc:* 418-849-7128
Ligne sans frais: 866-749-9125
info@ccapcable.com
www.ccapcable.com
Autre information: Support technique: support@ccapcable.com
Yvon Habel, Président, yhabel@ccapcable.com
Jacques Perron, Directeur général, perron@ccapcable.com
Stéphane Arseneau, Directeur, Service à la clientèle, sarseneau@ccapcable.com

†*Saint-Just-de-Bretenières:* Coopérative de câblodistribution de Saint-Just-de-Bretenières
11, rue du Couvent, Saint-Just-de-Bretenières, QC G0R 3H0
Tél: 418-244-3560, *Téléc:* 418-244-3560
cablo-st-just@sogetel.net
Lorraine Pelletier, Contact

***Saint-Raymond:* DERYtelecom - Portneuf**
Owned by: DERYtelecom*
131, rue Saint-Joseph, Saint-Raymond, QC G3L 1H4
Fax: 418-337-8983
Toll-Free: 866-544-3358
serviceportneuf@derytelecom.ca
www.derytele.com

***Sanikiluaq:* Mitiq Co-operative**
General Delivery, Sanikiluaq, QC X0A 0W0
Tel: 867-266-8860, *Fax:* 867-266-8844
www.arcticco-op.com/acl-baffin-region-sanikiluaq.htm

†*Shannon:* Shannon Vision inc.
#103, 438, boul. Jacques Cartier, Shannon, QC G0A 4N0
Tél: 418-844-3849, *Téléc:* 418-844-0347
gestion@cableshannon.com
www.cableshannon.com

†*Sherbrooke:* Groupe Transvision Réseau
#105, 175, rue Queen, Sherbrooke, QC J1M 1K1
Tél: 819-563-1001, *Téléc:* 819-563-3116
Ligne sans frais: 877-463-8738
support@gtvr.com
www.gtvr.com

†*St-Zacharie:* Cablovision ACL Enr
515, 9e av, St-Zacharie, QC G0M 2C0
Tél: 418-593-5262, *Téléc:* 418-593-3260

†*Ste-Catherine-de-la-Jacques-Cartier:* Coopérative de câblodistribution Ste-Catherine-Fossambault
130, rue Désiré-Juneau, Ste-Catherine-de-la-Jacques-Cartier, QC G3N 2X3
Tél: 418-875-1118, *Téléc:* 418-875-1971
gestion@coopcscf.com
www.coopcscf.com

†*Trois-Rivières:* Cogeco Câble inc. Québec
4141, boul. St-Jean, Trois-Rivières, QC G8B 2M8
Tél: 819-693-8353, *Téléc:* 819-379-2232
Ligne sans frais: 800-668-353
www.cogeco.ca
Martin Leuere, Responsable, mauricie.tvcogeco@cogeco.com

†*Val-D'Or:* Cablevision du Nord de Québec inc. une Division de Bell Aliant
45, boul de Hôtel de Ville, Val-D'Or, QC J9P 2M5
Tél: 819-825-5133, *Ligne sans frais:* 800-567-6353
www.cablevision.qc.ca
Bernard Gauthier, Président

†*Warwick:* Cablovision Warwick inc.
3, rue de l'Hôtel-de-ville, Warwick, QC J0A 1M0
Tél: 819-358-5858, *Téléc:* 819-358-5592
service@cablovision.com
www.cablovision.com

Saskatchewan

***Estevan:* Access Communications Co-operative Limited**
1126 - 6th St., Estevan, SK S4A 1A8
Tel: 306-634-7378, *Fax:* 306-634-9450
www.myaccess.ca

***Estevan:* SaskTel Max (maxTV)**
Estevan Shoppers Mall, 400 King St., Estevan, SK S4A 2B4
Toll-Free: 800-992-9912
www.sasktel.com

***Humboldt:* Access Communications Co-operative Limited**
645 Main St., Humboldt, SK S0K 2A0
Fax: 306-682-1823
Toll-Free: 866-363-2225
www.accesscomm.ca

***Ile-a-la-Crosse:* Ile a la Crosse Communications Society Inc.**
PO Box 480, Ile-a-la-Crosse, SK S0M 1C0
Tel: 306-833-2173, *Fax:* 306-833-2042
ilex@sasktel.net
Mike Bouvier, Chief Executive Officer

***Imperial:* Imperial Cable System**
310 Royal St., Imperial, SK S0G 2J0
Tel: 306-963-2220
www.imperial.ca/business.htm

***La Ronge:* Access Communications Co-operative Limited**
712 Finlayson St., La Ronge, SK S0J 1L0
Tel: 306-425-2276, *Fax:* 306-425-2042
www.myaccess.ca

***Limerick:* Village of Limerick**
PO Box 129, Limerick, SK S0H 2P0
Tel: 306-263-2020, *Fax:* 306-263-2013
rm73@sasktel.net
www.rmstonehenge.ca

***Melfort:* SaskTel Max (maxTV)**
109 McLeod Ave., Melfort, SK S03 1A0
Toll-Free: 800-992-9912
www.sasktel.com

***Moose Jaw:* SaskTel Max (maxTV)**
1250A Main St. North, Moose Jaw, SK S6H 3L1
Toll-Free: 800-992-9912
www.sasktel.com

***North Battleford:* Access Communications Co-operative Limited**
1192 - 99 St., North Battleford, SK S9A 0P3
Tel: 306-445-4045, *Fax:* 306-445-0755
Toll-Free: 866-363-2225
www.accesscomm.ca

***North Battleford:* SaskTel Max (maxTV)**
1201 - 100th St. North, North Battleford, SK S9A 3Z9
Toll-Free: 800-992-9912
www.sasktel.com

***Prince Albert:* SaskTel Max (maxTV)**
Gateway Mall, 1403 Central Ave., Prince Albert, SK S6V 7J4
Toll-Free: 800-992-9912
www.sasktel.com

***Regina:* SaskTel Max (maxTV)**
Cornwall Centre, 2121 Saskatchewan Dr., Regina, SK S4P 3Y2
Tel: 306-569-0062, *Toll-Free:* 800-992-9912
www.sasktel.com

***Rouleau:* Rouleau Cable TV**
PO Box 250, Rouleau, SK S0G 4H0
Tel: 306-776-2270, *Fax:* 306-776-2482
Shawn Duncan, President

***Saskatoon:* Askivision Systems Inc.**
826 - 57th St. East, Saskatoon, SK S7K 5Z1
Toll-Free: 800-819-9718
cs@aski.ca
www.aski.ca

***Saskatoon:* Image Wireless Communications - a division of YOURLINK Inc.**
204 Cardinal Cres., Saskatoon, SK S7L 6H8
Tel: 306-955-3122, *Fax:* 306-955-3148
Toll-Free: 888-671-5465
moreinfo@yourlink.ca
www.yourlink.ca

***Saskatoon:* SaskTel Max (maxTV)**
Scotia Centre, 123 - 2nd Ave. South, Saskatoon, SK S7K 5A6
Toll-Free: 800-992-9912
www.sasktel.com

***Saskatoon:* SaskTel Max (maxTV)**
Stonebridge, #110, 3055 Clarence Ave. South, Saskatoon, SK S7N 1H1
Toll-Free: 800-992-9912
www.sasktel.com

***Weyburn:* Access Communications Co-operative Limited**
120 - 10th Ave., Weyburn, SK S4H 2A1
Tel: 306-842-0320, *Fax:* 306-842-3465
Toll-Free: 866-363-2225
www.accesscomm.ca

***Weyburn:* SaskTel Max (maxTV)**
314 Coteau Ave., Weyburn, SK S4H 0G6
Toll-Free: 800-992-9912
www.sasktel.com

** For details on this company see listing in Major Broadcasting Companies section; † French language station*

Yorkton: Access Communications Co-operative Limited
22 - 6th Ave. North, Yorkton, SK S3N 0X5
Tel: 306-783-1566, *Fax:* 306-782-1952
www.myaccess.ca

Yorkton: SaskTel Max (maxTV)
275 Broadway St. East, #M, Yorkton, SK S3N 3G7
Toll-Free: 800-992-9912
www.sasktel.com

Young: Village of Young
PO Box 359, Young, SK S0K 4Y0
Tel: 306-259-2242, *Fax:* 306-259-2247
villageoffice@young.ca
www.young.ca
Belinda Rowan, Administrator

Yukon Territory

Dawson City: Dawson City Cable
c/o City Office, PO Box 308, 1336 Front St., Dawson City, YT Y0B 1G0
Tel: 867-993-7400, *Fax:* 867-993-7434
cityofdawson.ca/dawson-city-tv

Whitehorse: Northwestel Cable Inc.
PO Box 2727, Whitehorse, YT Y1A 4Y4
Tel: 867-668-5300, *Fax:* 867-668-7079
www.nwtel.ca
Social Media: www.facebook.com/Northwestel, twitter.com/northwestel
Paul Flaherty, President & CEO

Specialty Broadcasters

Action
Owned by: Corus Entertainment Inc.*
Toll-Free: 866-977-3663
feedback@showcase.ca
www.action-tv.ca

BBC Canada
Owned by: Corus Entertainment Inc.*
Toll-Free: 866-447-8353
bbccanada@corusent.com
www.bbccanada.com

CMT Music Fest
Owned by: Country Music Television Inc.
Tel: 416-479-7000
inquiries@cmtmusicfest.com
cmtmusicfest.com
Social Media: www.youtube.com/c/cmtmusicfestvideo, www.facebook.com/cmtmusicfest, twitter.com/cmtmusicfest

Country Music Television Inc.
Owned by: Corus Entertainment Inc.*
Tel: 416-479-7000, *Fax:* 416-479-7006
www.cmt.ca
Social Media: www.youtube.com/user/OfficialCMTCanada, facebook.com/CMTCanada, twitter.com/CMTCanada

Crime + Investigation
Owned by: Corus Entertainment Inc.*
Toll-Free: 866-977-3663
feedback@crimeandinvestigation.ca
www.crimeandinvestigation.ca
Social Media: twitter.com/ci

DejaView
Owned by: Corus Entertainment Inc.*
Toll-Free: 866-977-3663
feedback@dejaviewtv.ca
www.dejaviewtv.ca

DIY Network Canada
Owned by: Shaw Media Inc.*
Toll-Free: 866-967-4488
feedback@diy.ca
www.diy.ca

DTOUR
Owned by: Corus Entertainment Inc.*
feedback@dtourtv.com
www.dtourtv.com
Social Media: www.youtube.com/user/DTourChannel

Food Network Canada
Owned by: Corus Entertainment Inc.*
feedback@foodnetwork.ca
www.foodnetwork.ca
Social Media: www.youtube.com/user/foodnetworkcanada, www.facebook.com/foodnetworkcanada, twitter.com/foodnetworkca

FYI
Owned by: Corus Entertainment Inc.*
Tel: 416-967-3246
feedback@fyitv.ca
www.fyitv.ca
Social Media: www.facebook.com/FYI, twitter.com/FYI

History
Owned by: Corus Entertainment Inc.*
www.history.ca
Social Media: plus.google.com/+historychannelcanada/posts, www.facebook.com/HistoryCanada, twitter.com/HistoryTVCanada

Home & Garden Television Canada
Owned by: Corus Entertainment Inc.*
www.hgtv.ca
Social Media: www.youtube.com/user/hgtvcanada, www.facebook.com/hgtv.ca, twitter.com/hgtvcanada

The Independent Film Channel
Owned by: Corus Entertainment Inc.*
Toll-Free: 866-977-3663
IFCCanada@shawmedia.ca
www.ifctv.ca
Social Media: www.youtube.com/user/ifc, www.facebook.com/IFC, twitter.com/IFC

Lifetime
Owned by: Corus Entertainment Inc.*
Toll-Free: 866-967-4488
feedback@mylifetimetv.ca
www.mylifetimetv.ca

MovieTime
Owned by: Corus Entertainment Inc.*
www.movietimetv.ca
Social Media: twitter.com/MovieTimeTV

Nat Geo Wild
Owned by: National Geographic Channel
Toll-Free: 866-447-8353
feedback@nationalgeographic.ca
www.natgeotv.com/ca/wild
Social Media: www.facebook.com/natgeowild, twitter.com/NatGeo

National Geographic Channel
Owned by: Corus Entertainment Inc.*
Toll-Free: 866-447-8353
feedback@nationalgeographic.ca
natgeotv.com/ca
Social Media: www.facebook.com/natgeotvcanada

Showcase Television
Owned by: Corus Entertainment Inc.*
Toll-Free: 866-977-3663
feedback@showcase.ca
www.showcase.ca
Social Media: www.youtube.com/c/showcaseca, www.facebook.com/showcasedotca, twitter.com/showcasedotca

Slice
Owned by: Corus Entertainment Inc.*
info@slice.ca
www.slice.ca
Social Media: plus.google.com/+slicetv/posts, www.facebook.com/Slice, twitter.com/slice_tv

Sundance Channel
Owned by: Corus Entertainment Inc.*
info@sundancechannel.ca
www.sundancechannel.ca
Social Media: twitter.com/sundancecanada
Other information: TTY: 416-214-0110

Treehouse TV
Owned by: Corus Entertainment Inc.*
info@treehousetv.com
www.treehousetv.com

W Network Inc.
Owned by: Corus Entertainment Inc.*
www.wnetwork.com
Social Media: www.pinterest.com/wnetworkcanada, www.facebook.com/wnetwork, twitter.com/w_network

British Columbia

Burnaby: BBC Kids
Owned by: Knowledge Network Corporation
c/o Knowledge Network Corporation, 4355 Mathissi Pl., Burnaby, BC V5G 4S8
Tel: 604-431-3222, *Fax:* 604-431-3387
Toll-Free: 877-456-6988
www.bbckids.ca
Social Media: www.youtube.com/user/BBCKidsCanada, www.facebook.com/bbckids, twitter.com/BBCKidsCanada

Burnaby: Knowledge Network Corporation
4355 Mathissi Pl., Burnaby, BC V5G 4S8
Tel: 604-431-3222, *Fax:* 604-431-3387
Toll-Free: 877-456-6988
info@knowledge.ca
www.knowledgenetwork.ca
Social Media: www.facebook.com/kpassiton, twitter.com/kpassiton

Richmond: Fairchild Television Ltd.
Owned by: Fairchild Media Group*
Aberdeen Centre, #3300, 4151 Hazelbridge Way, Richmond, BC V6X 4J7
Tel: 604-295-1313, *Fax:* 604-295-1300
info@fairchildtv.com
www.fairchildtv.com
Social Media: www.linkedin.com/company/2682323, www.facebook.com/fairchildtv
Thomas Fung, Chair & Founder, Fairchild Media Group

Richmond: Talentvision TV
Owned by: Fairchild Television Ltd.
Aberdeen Centre, #3300, 4151 Hazelbridge Way, Richmond, BC V6X 4J7
Tel: 604-295-1328, *Fax:* 604-295-1399
info@talentvisiontv.com
www.talentvisiontv.com

Vancouver: OUTtv
53 East 6th Ave., Vancouver, BC V5T 1J3
www.outtv.ca
Social Media: www.facebook.com/outtv, twitter.com/outtv

Vancouver: Shaw Multicultural Channel
Owned by: Shaw Media Inc.
Shaw Tower, #900, 1067 West Cordova St., Vancouver, BC V6C 3T5
Tel: 604-629-4270
smc@shaw.ca
www.shaw.ca/ShawTV/Multicultural
Social Media: www.youtube.com/shawmulticultural, www.facebook.com/ShawMulticulturalChannel, twitter.com/ShawMulChannel
Sandra Murphy, Supervisor Producer, 604-629-3109, sandra.murphy@sjrb.ca
Tim Tremain, Senior Producer, 604-629-3126

Manitoba

Winnipeg: Aboriginal Peoples Television Network
339 Portage Ave., Winnipeg, MB R3B 2C3
Tel: 204-947-9331, *Fax:* 204-947-9307
Toll-Free: 888-330-2786
info@aptn.ca
www.aptn.ca
Social Media: www.youtube.com/c/aptnca, www.facebook.com/88781789916, twitter.com/APTN

Newfoundland & Labrador

Nain: Okalakatiget Society Television
Owned by: Okalakatiget Society*
PO Box 160, Nain, NL A0P 1L0
Tel: 709-922-2187, *Fax:* 709-922-2293
oktv@oksociety.com
www.oksociety.com

** For details on this company see listing in Major Broadcasting Companies section; † French language station*

Northwest Territories

***Yellowknife:* CBC North**
5002 Forrest Dr., Yellowknife, NT X1A 2A9
Tel: 867-920-5400
cbcnorth@cbc.ca
www.cbc.ca/north
Social Media: www.facebook.com/CBCNorth, twitter.com/CBCNorth
Janice Stein, Managing Director, janice.stein@cbc.ca

Ontario

***Burlington:* Yes TV**
1295 North Service Rd., Burlington, ON L7R 4X5
Tel: 905-331-7333, *Fax:* 905-332-6005
contactus@yestv.com
www.yestv.com
Social Media: instagram.com/yestvcanada, www.facebook.com/sayyestv, twitter.com/yestvcanada

***Markham:* Asian Television Network Ltd.**
330 Cochrane Dr., Markham, ON L3R 8E4
Tel: 905-948-8199, *Fax:* 905-948-8108
atn@asiantelevision.com
www.asiantelevision.com
Shan Chandrasekar, President & CEO

***Mississauga:* The Shopping Channel**
Owned by: Rogers Communications Inc.*
59 Ambassador Dr., Mississauga, ON L5T 2P9
Fax: 877-202-0877
Toll-Free: 888-202-0888
www.theshoppingchannel.com
Social Media: www.youtube.com/user/TheShoppingChannel, www.facebook.com/TheShoppingChannel, twitter.com/theShoppingChan
Other information: TTY: 800-263-2900
Anne Martin-Vachon, President

***Oakville:* Distribution Access**
#216, 1540 Cornwall Rd., Oakville, ON L6J 7W5
Tel: 416-363-6765, *Fax:* 416-363-7834
sales@distributionaccess.com
www.distributionaccess.com
Social Media: plus.google.com/110927652164124717268, www.facebook.com/AccessLearning, twitter.com/AccessLearning
Doug Connolly, President, doug.connolly@distributionaccess.com

***Oakville:* The Weather Network**
2655 Bristol Circle, Oakville, ON L6H 7W1
Tel: 905-829-1159, *Toll-Free:* 877-666-6761
www.theweathernetwork.com
Social Media: plus.google.com/+weathernetwork, www.facebook.com/theweathernetworkCAN, twitter.com/weathernetwork

***Ottawa:* CPAC**
PO Box 81099, Ottawa, ON K1P 1B1
Fax: 613-567-2741
Toll-Free: 877-287-2722
www.cpac.ca
Social Media: www.youtube.com/user/cpac, www.facebook.com/CPACTV, twitter.com/cpac_tv

***Sioux Lookout:* Wawatay TV**
Owned by: Wawatay Native Communications Society*
PO Box 1180, 16 - 5th Ave., Sioux Lookout, ON P8T 1B7
Tel: 807-737-2951, *Fax:* 807-737-3224
Toll-Free: 800-243-9059
www.wawataynews.ca
Social Media: www.facebook.com/wawataynews, twitter.com/wawataynews
Michael Dube, Producer & Editor, michaeld@wawatay.on.ca
Victor Lyon, Producer & Editor, victorl@wawatay.on.ca

***Toronto:* ABC Spark**
Owned by: Corus Entertainment Inc.*
25 Dockside Dr., Toronto, ON M5A 0B5
Tel: 416-479-7000, *Fax:* 416-479-7006
info@abcsparkcanada.com
www.abcspark.ca
Social Media: www.instagram.com/abcsparkcanada, www.facebook.com/abcsparkcanada, twitter.com/ABCSparkCanada

***Toronto:* Adult Swim**
Owned by: TELETOON Canada Inc.*
c/o TELETOON Canada Inc., PO Box 787, 181 Bay St., Toronto, ON M5J 2T3
Tel: 416-956-2060, *Fax:* 416-956-2070
www.adultswim.ca
Social Media: www.facebook.com/AdultSwimCAN, twitter.com/AdultSwimCAN

***Toronto:* Animal Planet**
Owned by: Bell Media Inc.*
9 Channel Nine Ct., Toronto, ON M1S 4B5
www.animalplanet.ca
Social Media: twitter.com/animalplanetca

***Toronto:* Aux**
Owned by: Blue Ant Media*
130 Merton St., Toronto, ON M4S 1A4
www.aux.tv
Social Media: www.youtube.com/user/auxtelevision, www.facebook.com/auxtv, twitter.com/auxtv
Ryan Fuss, Vice-President, Digital Solutions, 416-440-7223, ryan.fuss@blueantsolutions.com

***Toronto:* BookTelevision**
Owned by: Bell Media Inc.*
299 Queen St. West, Toronto, ON M5V 2Z5
Tel: 416-384-8000, *Fax:* 416-591-5117
info@booktelevision.com
www.booktelevision.com

***Toronto:* bravo**
Owned by: Bell Media Inc.*
299 Queen St. West, Toronto, ON M5V 2Z5
bravomail@bravo.ca
www.bravo.ca
Social Media: www.facebook.com/bravoCanada

***Toronto:* Business News Network**
Owned by: Bell Media Inc.*
299 Queen St. West, Toronto, ON M5V 2Z5
Tel: 416-664-8000
info@bnn.ca
www.bnn.ca
Grant Ellis, General Manager, grant.ellis@bellmedia.ca

***Toronto:* CablePulse 24**
Owned by: Bell Media Inc.*
299 Queen St. West, Toronto, ON M5V 2Z5
Tel: 416-384-2700
now@cp24.com
www.cp24.com

***Toronto:* Cartoon Network**
Owned by: TELETOON Canada Inc.*
c/o TELETOON Canada Inc., PO Box 787, 181 Bay St., Toronto, ON M5J 2T3
Tel: 416-956-2060, *Fax:* 416-956-2070
www.cartoonnetwork.ca
Social Media: www.facebook.com/cartoonnetworkCAN

***Toronto:* CBC News Network**
Owned by: Canadian Broadcasting Corporation*
PO Box 500 A, Toronto, ON M5W 1E6
Tel: 416-205-2130, *Toll-Free:* 866-306-4636
www.cbc.ca/news
Social Media: www.facebook.com/newscbc, twitter.com/cbcnews
Other information: TTY: 1-866-220-6045

***Toronto:* Cinelatino**
Owned by: Telelatino Network Inc.*
5125 Steeles Ave. West, Toronto, ON M9L 1R5
Tel: 416-744-8200, *Fax:* 416-744-0966
Toll-Free: 800-551-8401
info@tlntv.com
tlntv.com/digital-channels/CineLatino

***Toronto:* Comedy Gold**
Owned by: Bell Media Inc.*
299 Queen St. West, Toronto, ON M5V 2Z5
comedygoldfeedback@bellmedia.ca
www.comedygold.ca
Social Media: twitter.com/comedygoldtv

***Toronto:* The Comedy Network**
Owned by: Bell Media Inc.*
299 Queen St. West, Toronto, ON M5V 2Z5
mail@thecomendynetwork.ca
www.thecomedynetwork.ca
Social Media: www.facebook.com/comedynetwork, twitter.com/comedynetwork

***Toronto:* Cosmopolitan Television Canada Company**
Owned by: Corus Entertainment Inc.*
Corus Quay, 25 Dockside Dr., Toronto, ON M5A 0B5
Tel: 416-479-7000, *Fax:* 416-479-7006
info@cosmotv.ca
www.cosmotv.ca
Social Media: www.facebook.com/cosmotv, twitter.com/cosmotv

***Toronto:* CTV News Channel**
Owned by: Bell Media Inc.*
PO Box 9 O, Toronto, ON M4A 2M9
Tel: 416-384-5000
newschannel@ctv.ca
www.ctvnews.ca/ctv-news-channel
Social Media: www.facebook.com/CTVNewsExpress
Other information: Toll-Free TTY: 1-800-461-1542

***Toronto:* The Discovery Channel**
Owned by: Bell Media Inc.*
9 Channel Nine Ct., Toronto, ON M1S 4B5
discoverychannel.ca
Social Media: www.facebook.com/discoverycanada, twitter.com/discoverycanada

***Toronto:* Discovery Science**
Owned by: Bell Media Inc.*
9 Channel Nine Ct., Toronto, ON M1S 4B5
www.sciencechannel.ca
Social Media: plus.google.com/+discoverycanada, www.facebook.com/discoverycanada, twitter.com/discoverycanada

***Toronto:* Disney Junior**
Owned by: Corus Entertainment Inc.*
25 Dockside Dr, Toronto, ON M5A 0B5
Tel: 416-479-7000
info@disneyjunior.ca
www.disneyjunior.ca
Social Media: www.facebook.com/DisneyJuniorCanada, twitter.com/DisneyJunior

***Toronto:* Disney XD**
Owned by: Corus Entertainment Inc.*
Corus Quay, 25 Dockside Dr., Toronto, ON M5A 0B5
Tel: 416-479-7000, *Fax:* 416-479-7006
info@disneyxd.ca
www.disneyxd.ca
Social Media: www.facebook.com/disneyxdcanada, twitter.com/disneyxd
Other information: TTY: 1-888-835-7808

***Toronto:* documentary**
Owned by: Canadian Broadcasting Corporation*
PO Box 500 A, Toronto, ON M6W 1E6
Toll-Free: 866-306-4636
www.cbc.ca/documentarychannel
Social Media: twitter.com/cbcdocs
Other information: TTY: 1-866-220-6045

***Toronto:* E!**
Owned by: Bell Media Inc.*
299 Queen St. West, Toronto, ON M5V 2Z5
eonline@bellmedia.ca
ca.eonline.com
Social Media: twitter.com/EOnlineCanada

***Toronto:* Encore Avenue Ltd.**
Owned by: Corus Premium Television Ltd.*
Corus Quay, 25 Dockside Dr., Toronto, ON M5A 0B5
www.moviecentral.ca/encore-avenue

***Toronto:* ESPN Classic Canada**
Owned by: Bell Media Inc.*
9 Channel Nine Ct., Toronto, ON M1S 4B5
www.tsn.ca/classic

***Toronto:* EuroWorld Sport**
Owned by: Telelatino Network Inc.*
5125 Steeles Ave. West, Toronto, ON M9L 1R5
Tel: 416-744-8200, *Fax:* 416-744-0966
Toll-Free: 800-551-8401
info@tlntv.com
legacy.tlntv.com/Soccerspecials/EuroWorldSport

***Toronto:* The Family Channel Inc.**
Owned by: DHX Media Ltd.*
c/o DHX Television, Queen's Quay Terminal, #550, 207 Queen's Quay West, Toronto, ON M5J 1A7
info@family.ca
www.family.ca
Social Media: twitter.com/Family_Channel
Other information: TTY: 1-844-258-7458

** For details on this company see listing in Major Broadcasting Companies section; † French language station*

***Toronto:* Fashion Television**
Owned by: Bell Media Inc.*
299 Queen St. West, Toronto, ON M5V 2Z5
Tel: 416-384-8000
www.fashiontelevision.com

***Toronto:* G4**
545 Lakeshore Blvd. West, Toronto, ON M5V 1A3
Tel: 416-764-3004
www.g4tv.ca

***Toronto:* Global News**
Owned by: Global Television Network*
121 Bloor St. East, Toronto, ON M4S 3M5
viewercontact@globaltv.com
globalnews.ca
Social Media: www.facebook.com/GlobalNews, twitter.com/globaltvnews

***Toronto:* Grace TV**
190 Railside Rd., Toronto, ON M3A 1A3
Tel: 416-497-4940, *Fax:* 416-497-3987
gracetelevision.net

***Toronto:* H2**
Owned by: History
121 Bloor St. East, Toronto, ON M4S 3M5
Toll-Free: 866-447-8353
feedback@historytelevision.ca
www.history.ca
Social Media: www.facebook.com/More2History, twitter.com/More2History

***Toronto:* HIFI**
Owned by: Blue Ant Media*
#200, 130 Merton St., Toronto, ON M4S 1A4
Tel: 416-646-4434, *Fax:* 416-646-4444
feedback@blueantmedia.ca
www.hifi.ca
Social Media: www.youtube.com/user/TheHIFIchannel, www.facebook.com/HIFIchannel, twitter.com/hifichannel
Daniela Santia, Contact, Publicity/Media, daniela.santia@blueantmedia.ca

***Toronto:* HPItv Canada**
555 Rexdale Blvd., Toronto, ON M9W 5L2
Tel: 416-675-8886, *Fax:* 416-213-2130
Toll-Free: 888-675-8886
support@hpibet.com
www.hpibet.com/About/HPItv
Social Media: www.facebook.com/GetHPIbet, twitter.com/hpi

***Toronto:* HPItv International**
555 Rexdale Blvd., Toronto, ON M9W 5L2
Tel: 416-675-8886, *Fax:* 416-213-2130
Toll-Free: 888-675-8886
support@hpibet.com
www.hpibet.com/About/HPItv
Social Media: www.facebook.com/GetHPIbet, twitter.com/hpi

***Toronto:* HPItv Odds**
555 Rexdale Blvd., Toronto, ON M9W 5L2
Tel: 416-675-8886, *Fax:* 416-213-2130
Toll-Free: 888-675-8886
support@hpibet.com
www.hpibet.com/About/HPItv
Social Media: www.facebook.com/GetHPIbet, twitter.com/hpi

***Toronto:* HPItv West**
555 Rexdale Blvd., Toronto, ON M9W 5L2
Tel: 416-675-8886, *Fax:* 416-213-2130
Toll-Free: 888-675-8886
support@hpibet.com
www.hpibet.com/About/HPItv
Social Media: www.facebook.com/GetHPIbet, twitter.com/hpi

***Toronto:* Ichannel**
Stornoway Communications, #800, 105 Gordon Baker Rd., Toronto, ON M2H 3P8
www.ichannel.ca
Social Media: www.youtube.com/user/ichannelcanada, www.facebook.com/pages/ichannel/77254582010, twitter.com/ichanneltv
Sandy Baptist, Contact, Media, sbaptist@stornoway.com

***Toronto:* Investigation Discovery**
Owned by: Bell Media Inc.*
299 Queen St. West, Toronto, ON M5V 2Z5
comments@investigationdiscovery.ca
www.investigationdiscovery.ca
Social Media: plus.google.com/discoverycanada, www.facebook.com/discoverycanada, twitter.com/discoverycanada

***Toronto:* Leafs TV**
#500, 50 Bay St., Toronto, ON M5J 2L2
Tel: 416-815-5400, *Fax:* 416-851-6050
mapleleafs.nhl.com
Social Media: twitter.com/Leafs_TV

***Toronto:* Love Nature**
Owned by: Blue Ant Media*
130 Merton St., Toronto, ON M4S 1A4
Tel: 416-646-4431, *Fax:* 416-646-4444
feedback@blueantmedia.ca
tv.lovenature.com
Social Media: www.youtube.com/user/oasishdchannel, www.facebook.com/oasishdchannel, twitter.com/oasishd
Daniela Santia, Contact, Publicity/Media, daniela.santia@blueantmedia.ca

***Toronto:* M3**
Owned by: Bell Media Inc.*
299 Queen St. West, Toronto, ON M5V 2Z5
contact@m3tv.ca
www.m3tv.ca
Social Media: www.facebook.com/M3Television, twitter.com/m3tv

***Toronto:* Mediaset Italia**
Owned by: Telelatino Network Inc.*
5125 Steeles Ave. West, Toronto, ON M9L 1R5
Tel: 416-744-8200, *Fax:* 416-744-0966
Toll-Free: 800-551-8401
info@tlntv.com
legacy.tlntv.com/digitalchannels/mediaset2

***Toronto:* Movie Central**
Owned by: Corus Premium Television Ltd.*
Corus Quay, 25 Dockside Dr., Toronto, ON M5A 0B5
Tel: 416-479-6784
info@moviecentral.ca
www.moviecentral.ca
Social Media: www.facebook.com/moviecentral, twitter.com/moviecentral
Other information: TTY: 416-533-0955

***Toronto:* The Movie Network**
Owned by: Bell Media Inc.*
c/o Bell Media, 299 Queen St. West, Toronto, ON M5V 2Z5
Toll-Free: 800-565-6684
www.themovienetwork.ca
Social Media: instagram.com/themovienetwork, www.facebook.com/themovienetwork, twitter.com/themovienetwork

***Toronto:* The Movie Network Encore (TMN Encore)**
Owned by: Bell Media Inc.*
c/o Bell Media, 299 Queen St. West, Toronto, ON M5V 2Z5
Toll-Free: 800-565-6684
www.themovienetwork.ca
Social Media: instagram.com/themovienetwork, www.facebook.com/themovienetwork, twitter.com/themovienetwork

***Toronto:* The Movie Network Encore 2 (TMN Encore 2)**
Owned by: Bell Media Inc.*
c/o Bell Media, 299 Queen St. West, Toronto, ON M5V 2Z5
Toll-Free: 800-565-6684
www.themovienetwork.ca
Social Media: instagram.com/themovienetwork, www.facebook.com/themovienetwork, twitter.com/themovienetwork

***Toronto:* MTV Canada**
Owned by: Bell Media Inc.*
299 Queen St. West, Toronto, ON M5V 2Z5
www.mtv.ca
Social Media: www.facebook.com/MTVCanada, twitter.com/mtvcanada

***Toronto:* MTV2**
Owned by: Bell Media Inc.*
299 Queen St. West, Toronto, ON M5V 2Z5
www.mtv.ca/mtv2
Social Media: www.facebook.com/mtv2, twitter.com/MTV2

***Toronto:* MuchMusic**
Owned by: Bell Media Inc.*
299 Queen St. West, Toronto, ON M5V 2Z5
Fax: 416-384-6824
contactmuch@bellmedia.ca
www.much.com
Social Media: instagram.com/MuchMusic, facebook.com/MuchMusic, twitter.com/Much
Other information: TTY: 416-340-7207

***Toronto:* National Geographic Channel HD**
Owned by: National Geographic Channel
121 Bloor St. East, Toronto, ON M4S 3M5
Toll-Free: 866-447-8353
feedback@nationalgeographic.ca
natgeotv.com/ca/hd

***Toronto:* Nickelodeon**
Owned by: Corus Entertainment Inc.*
Corus Quay, 25 Dockside Dr., Toronto, ON M5A 0B5
Tel: 416-479-7000, *Fax:* 416-479-7006
www.nickcanada.com
Social Media: www.facebook.com/NickelodeonCanada, twitter.com/NickCanadaTV

***Toronto:* Odyssey**
#300, 437 Danforth Ave., Toronto, ON M4K 1P1
Tel: 416-462-1200, *Fax:* 416-462-1818
info@odysseytv.ca
www.odysseytv.ca

***Toronto:* OLN**
Owned by: Rogers Broadcasting Ltd.*
545 Lake Shore Blvd., Toronto, ON M5V 1A3
Tel: 416-260-0060
www.oln.ca
Social Media: www.facebook.com/OLNCanada, twitter.com/OLNCanada

***Toronto:* One**
Owned by: ZoomerMedia Limited*
c/o Zoomer Media, 70 Jefferson Ave., Toronto, ON M6K 1Y4
www.onetv.ca

***Toronto:* Ontario Legislature Broadcast & Recording Service**
Legislative Bldg., Queen's Park, #453, 111 Wellesley St. West, Toronto, ON M7A 1A2
Tel: 416-325-7900, *Fax:* 416-325-7916
www.ontla.on.ca

***Toronto:* Oprah Winfrey Network**
Owned by: Corus Entertainment Inc.*
Corus Quay, 25 Dockside Dr., Toronto, ON M5A 0B5
Tel: 416-479-7000, *Fax:* 416-479-7006
info@owntv.ca
www.owntv.ca
Social Media: www.facebook.com/OWNCanada, twitter.com/OWNCanada

***Toronto:* radX**
Owned by: Blue Ant Media*
#200, 130 Merton St., Toronto, ON M4S 1A4
Tel: 416-646-4434, *Fax:* 416-646-4444
feedback@blueantmedia.ca
radx.ca
Social Media: www.youtube.com/user/radxchannel, www.facebook.com/radxchannel, twitter.com/radXchannel
Daniela Santia, Contact, Publicity/Media, daniela.santia@blueantmedia.ca

***Toronto:* Raptors NBA TV**
#500, 50 Bay St., Toronto, ON M5J 2L2
Tel: 416-366-3865
www.nba.com/raptors

***Toronto:* Rewind**
Owned by: Channel Zero Inc.*
PO Box 6143 A, Toronto, ON M5W 1P6
Tel: 416-492-1595, *Fax:* 416-492-9539
Www.watchrewind.com
Social Media: Www.facebook.com/watchrewind, twitter.com/watchrewind

***Toronto:* The Score Television Network**
500 King St. West, 4th Fl., Toronto, ON M5V 1L9
Tel: 416-679-8812, *Fax:* 416-361-2045
hello@thescore.com
www.thescore.ca
Social Media: www.linkedin.com/company/thescore-inc-, www.facebook.com/thescore, twitter.com/theScore
Benjie Levy, President & COO

** For details on this company see listing in Major Broadcasting Companies section; † French language station*

***Toronto:* Silver Screen Classics**
Owned by: Channel Zero Inc.*
2844 Dundas St. West, Toronto, ON M6P 1Y7
Tel: 416-492-1595, *Fax:* 416-492-9539
info@silverscreenclassics.com
www.silverscreenclassics.com

***Toronto:* Sky TG24 Canada**
Owned by: Telelatino Network Inc.*
5125 Steeles Ave. West, Toronto, ON M9L 1R5
Tel: 416-744-8200, *Fax:* 416-744-0966
Toll-Free: 800-551-8401
info@tlntv.com
legacy.tlntv.com/tln_SkyTGEnglishAbout.aspx

***Toronto:* Smithsonian Channel**
Owned by: Blue Ant Media*
#200, 130 Merton St., Toronto, ON M4S 1A4
Tel: 416-646-4431, *Fax:* 416-646-4444
feedback@blueantmedia.ca
www.smithsonianchannel.ca
Social Media: www.youtube.com/user/smithsoniantvcanada, www.facebook.com/SmithsonianChannelCanada, twitter.com/smithsoniantvca
Daniela Santia, Contact, Publicity/Media, daniela.santia@blueantmedia.ca

***Toronto:* Space**
Owned by: Bell Media Inc.*
299 Queen St. West, Toronto, ON M5V 2Z5
space@space.ca
www.space.ca
Social Media: instagram.com/spacechannel, www.facebook.com/SPACEchannel, twitter.com/spacechannel

***Toronto:* The Sports Network**
Owned by: Bell Media Inc.*
9 Channel Nine Ct., Toronto, ON M1S 4B5
tsngo@bellmedia.ca
www.tsn.ca
Social Media: www.facebook.com/TSN, twitter.com/TSN_Sports

***Toronto:* Sportsnet**
1 Mount Pleasant Rd., Toronto, ON M4Y 3A1
Toll-Free: 888-451-6363
feedback@sportsnet.rogers.com
www.sportsnet.ca
Social Media: plus.google.com/+Sportsnet, www.facebook.com/sportsnet, twitter.com/sportsnet

***Toronto:* Telelatino**
Owned by: Telelatino Network Inc.*
5125 Steeles Ave. West, Toronto, ON M9L 1R5
Tel: 416-744-8200, *Fax:* 416-744-0966
Toll-Free: 800-551-8401
info@tlntv.com
www.tlntv.com

***Toronto:* TeleNiños**
Owned by: Telelatino Network Inc.*
5125 Steeles Ave. West, Toronto, ON M9L 1R5
Tel: 416-744-8200, *Fax:* 416-744-0966
Toll-Free: 800-551-8401
info@tlntv.com
legacy.tlntv.com/Teleninos

***Toronto:* Teletoon At Night**
Owned by: TELETOON Canada Inc.*
c/o TELETOON Canada Inc., PO Box 787, 181 Bay St., Toronto, ON M5J 2T3
Tel: 416-956-2060, *Fax:* 416-956-2070
teletoonatnight.com
Social Media: www.facebook.com/TeletoonAtNight, twitter.com/teletoonatnight

***Toronto:* Teletoon Retro**
Owned by: TELETOON Canada Inc.*
c/o TELETOON Canada Inc., PO Box 787, 181 Bay St., Toronto, ON M5J 2T3
Tel: 416-956-2060, *Fax:* 416-956-2070
www.teletoonretro.com
Social Media: www.facebook.com/TELETOONRetro, twitter.com/teletoonretro

†*Toronto:* Télétoon Rétro
Détenteur: TELETOON Canada Inc.*
c/o TELETOON Canada Inc., CP 787, 181 Bay St., Toronto, ON M5J 2T3
Tél: 416-956-2060, *Téléc:* 416-956-2070
www.teletoonretro.com/fr
Médias sociaux: www.facebook.com/teletoonretrofr, twitter.com/TeletoonRetroFR

***Toronto:* TLN en Español**
Owned by: Telelatino Network Inc.*
5125 Steeles Ave. West, Toronto, ON M9L 1R5
Tel: 416-744-8200, *Fax:* 416-744-0966
Toll-Free: 800-551-8401
info@tlntv.com
legacy.tlntv.com/TLNEspanol

***Toronto:* Travel + Escape**
Owned by: Blue Ant Media*
#200, 130 Merton St., Toronto, ON M4S 1A4
Tel: 416-646-4434, *Fax:* 416-646-4444
feedback@blueantmedia.ca
www.travelandescape.ca
Social Media: www.youtube.com/user/TravelAndEscapeTV, www.facebook.com/TravelAndEscapeTV, twitter.com/travelandescape
Daniela Santia, Contact, Publicity/Media, Daniela.Santia@blueantmedia.ca

***Toronto:* Viceland**
Owned by: Rogers Broadcasting Ltd.*
78 Mowat Ave., Toronto, ON M6K 3M1
inquiries@vice.com
www.video.vice.com
Social Media: www.facebook.com/VICELANDca, twitter.com/viceland_ca
Alyssa Mastromonaco, Chief Operating Officer, Vice Media

***Toronto:* Vision TV**
Owned by: ZoomerMedia Limited*
64 Jefferson Ave., Toronto, ON M6K 1Y4
Tel: 416-368-3194, *Fax:* 416-368-9774
Toll-Free: 888-321-2567
visiontv@visiontv.ca
www.visiontv.ca
Social Media: www.facebook.com/visiontelevision, twitter.com/visiontv
Other information: TTY: 416-216-6311

Québec

†*Longueuil:* Canal Evasion
619, rue Le Breton, Longueuil, QC J4G 1R9
Tél: 450-672-0052
info@groupeserdy.com
www.evasion.tv
Médias sociaux: instagram.com/evasion_tv, www.facebook.com/Evasion.tv, twitter.com/Evasion_tv
Pierre Bernatchez, Directeur général, pbernatchez@groupeserdy.com
Sébastien Arsenault, Président et chef de la direction, SArsenault@groupeserdy.com
Philippe Daigle, Chargé de production, 450-672-0052, pdaigle@groupeserdy.com

†*Montréal:* ARTV
Détenteur: Canadian Broadcasting Corporation*
#A41-4, 1400, boul René-Lévesque est, Montréal, QC H2L 2M2
Tél: 514-597-3636, *Téléc:* 514-597-3633
www.artv.ca
Médias sociaux: www.facebook.com/ARTV, twitter.com/artv
Gilbert Morin, Directeur général

†*Montréal:* Canal D
Détenteur: Bell Media Inc.*
1717, boul René-Lévesque est, Montréal, QC H2L 4T9
Tél: 514-983-3330, *Ligne sans frais:* 800-361-5194
www.canald.com
Médias sociaux: www.facebook.com/Canald

***Montréal:* Canal Indigo**
612, rue St-Jacques Ouest, 4e étage, Montréal, QC H3C 4M8.
info@canalindigo.com
www.canalindigo.com

†*Montréal:* Canal Savoir
Canal Savoir, 2200, rue Sainte-Catherine Est, 1e etage, Montréal, QC H2K 2J1
Tél: 514-509-2222, *Téléc:* 514-509-2299
Ligne sans frais: 888-640-2626
info@canalsavoir.tv
www.canalsavoir.tv
Médias sociaux: www.youtube.com/user/CanalSavoir, www.facebook.com/canal.savoir, twitter.com/canalsavoir
Sylvie Godbout, Directrice générale, sgodbout@canalsavoir.tv

†*Montréal:* Canal Vie
Détenteur: Bell Media Inc.*
1717, boul René-Lévesque est, Montréal, QC H2L 4T9
Tél: 514-938-3330, *Ligne sans frais:* 800-361-5194
www.canalvie.com
Médias sociaux: pinterest.com/canalvie, www.facebook.com/canalvie, twitter.com/CanalVie

†*Montréal:* Cinépop
Détenteur: Bell Media Inc.*
1717, boul René-Lévesque est, Montréal, QC H2L 4T9
Ligne sans frais: 800-317-2767
www.cinepop.ca

***Montréal:* Concert TV**
Owned by: Stingray Digital*
730, rue Wellington, Montréal, QC H3C 1T4
Tel: 514-664-1244, *Fax:* 514-664-1143
www.concerttv.com
Social Media: www.youtube.com/user/concerttvnews, www.facebook.com/ConcertTV.OnDemand, twitter.com/concerttv

†*Montréal:* Historia
Détenteur: Corus Entertainment Inc.*
#1000, 4200, boul. St-Laurent, Montréal, QC H2W 2R2
Tél: 514-904-4099, *Ligne sans frais:* 855-904-4091
auditoire@corusmedia.com
www.historiatv.com
Médias sociaux: www.facebook.com/historiatv, twitter.com/historiatv

***Montréal:* The Karaoke Channel**
Owned by: Stingray Digital*
730, rue Wellington, Montréal, QC H3C 1T4
info@thekaraokechannel.com
www.thekaraokechannel.com
Social Media: www.youtube.com/user/thekaraokechannel, www.facebook.com/TheKARAOKEChannel, twitter.com/karaokelounge
Other information: Sales, E-mail: sales@thekaraokechannel.com

†*Montréal:* MétéoMédia
1755, boul René-Lévesque est, Montréal, QC H2K 4P6
Tél: 514-597-0232, *Téléc:* 514-597-0426
www.meteomedia.com
Médias sociaux: plus.google.com/+meteomedia, www.facebook.com/meteomedia, twitter.com/meteomedia

***Montréal:* MusiMax**
MusiquePlus / MusiMax, 355, rue Ste-Catherine ouest, Montréal, QC H3B 1A5
Tel: 514-284-7587, *Fax:* 514-284-1889
auditoire@musimax.com
www.musimax.com
Social Media: www.youtube.com/user/MusiMaxTV, www.facebook.com/MusiMaxTV, twitter.com/musimax

†*Montréal:* MusiquePlus (M+)
MusiquePlus / MusiMax, 355, rue Ste-Catherine ouest, Montréal, QC H3B 1A5
Tél: 514-284-7587, *Téléc:* 514-284-1889
auditoire@musiqueplus.com
www.musiqueplus.com
Médias sociaux: www.youtube.com/user/musiqueplus, www.facebook.com/MusiquePlus, twitter.com/MusiquePlus

†*Montréal:* Quebecor Media inc.
612, rue St-Jacques, Montréal, QC H3C 4M8
Tél: 514-380-1999
www.quebecor.com
Pierre Dion, Président/Chef de la direction

†*Montréal:* RDI - Le réseau de l'information
Détenteur: Canadian Broadcasting Corporation*
CP 6000, Montréal, QC H3C 3A8
Tél: 514-597-5000
ici.radio-canada.ca/rdi
Médias sociaux: www.youtube.com/user/RadioCanadainfo, www.facebook.com/radiocanada.info, twitter.com/RadioCanadaInfo

†*Montréal:* Le Réseau des Sports
Détenteur: Bell Media Inc.*
#300, 1755, boul René-Lévesque est, Montréal, QC H2K 4P6
Tél: 514-599-2244, *Téléc:* 514-599-2299
Ligne sans frais: 888-737-6363
www.rds.ca
Médias sociaux: instagram.com/rds_ca, www.facebook.com/RDS, twitter.com/rdsca
Gerry Frappier, Président et directeur général

* *For details on this company see listing in Major Broadcasting Companies section; † French language station*

†*Montréal:* Séries+
Détenteur: Corus Entertainment Inc.*
#1000, 4200, boul. St-Laurent, Montréal, QC H2W 2R2
Tél: 514-904-4099, *Ligne sans frais:* 855-904-4099
auditoire@corusmedia.com
www.seriesplus.com
Médias sociaux: www.facebook.com/seriesplus, twitter.com/seriesplus

***Montréal:* Stingray Juicebox**
Owned by: Stingray Digital Group Inc.*
730, rue Wellington, Montréal, QC H3C 1T4
Tel: 514-664-124, *Fax:* 514-664-1143
info@stingray.com
www.stingray.com

***Montréal:* Stingray Loud**
Owned by: Stingray Digital Group Inc.*
730, rue Wellington, Montréal, QC H3C 1T4
Tel: 514-664-1244, *Fax:* 514-664-1143
info@stingray.com
www.stingray.com

***Montréal:* Stingray Music**
Owned by: Stingray Digital Group Inc.*
730, rue Wellington, Montréal, QC H3C 1T4
Tel: 514-664-1244, *Fax:* 514-664-1143
music.stingray.com
Social Media: twitter.com/Stingray_Music

***Montréal:* Stingray Retro**
Owned by: Stingray Digital Group Inc.*
730, rue Wellington, Montréal, QC H3C 1T4
Tel: 514-664-1244, *Fax:* 514-664-1143
info@stingray.com
www.stingray.com

***Montréal:* Stingray Vibe**
Owned by: Stingray Digital Group Inc.*
730, rue Wellington, Montréal, QC H3C 1T4
Tel: 514-664-1244, *Fax:* 514-664-1143
info@stingray.com
www.stingray.com

†*Montréal:* Super Écran
Détenteur: Bell Media Inc.*
1717, boul René-Lévesque est, Montréal, QC H2L 4T9
Ligne sans frais: 877-873-7327
www.superecran.com
Médias sociaux: twitter.com/superecran

†*Montréal:* TV5 Québec Canada
#101, 1755, boul René-Lévesque Est, Montréal, QC H2K 4P6
Tél: 514-522-5322, *Ligne sans frais:* 877-522-6660
www.tv5.ca
Médias sociaux: www.facebook.com/TV5.ca, twitter.com/TV5ca
Marie-Philippe Bouchard, Présidente/Directrice générale

†*Montréal:* TVA Nouvelles
Détenteur: Groupe TVA Inc.*
CP 170 C, Montréal, QC H2L 4P6
Tél: 514-598-2869, *Téléc:* 514-598-6073
tvanouvelles.ca
Médias sociaux: www.facebook.com/TVAnouvelles, www.twitter.com/tvanouvelles

***Montréal:* VRAK TV**
Owned by: Bell Media Inc.*
1717, boul René-Lévesque est, Montréal, QC H2L 4T9
www.vrak.tv
Social Media: instagram.com/vraktv, www.facebook.com/vraktv, twitter.com/vraktv

†*Montréal:* Ztélé
Détenteur: Bell Media Inc.*
1717, boul René-Lévesque Est, Montréal, QC H2L 4T9
Tél: 514-938-3330, *Ligne sans frais:* 800-361-5194
www.ztele.com
Médias sociaux: plus.google.com/+ZteleOfficiel, www.facebook.com/ztele, twitter.com/ztele

†*Québec:* Assemblée nationale du Québec - Canal de l'Assemblée
Édifice Jean-Antoine-Panet, 1020, rue des Parlementaires, Québec, QC G1A 1A3
Tél: 418-643-1992, *Téléc:* 418-644-3593
Ligne sans frais: 866-337-8837
diffusion.debats@assnat.qc.ca
www.assnat.qc.ca

** For details on this company see listing in Major Broadcasting Companies section; † French language station*

SECTION 5
BUSINESS & FINANCE

The listings in this section are arranged alphabetically unless otherwise indicated below.

Major Accounting Firms

BDO Canada LLP
#600, 36 Toronto St.
Toronto, ON M5C 2C5

Tel: 416-865-0111; *Fax:* 416-367-3912
national@bdo.ca
www.bdo.ca
Social Media: www.youtube.com/user/BDOCanada; www.facebook.com/BDOCanada; twitter.com/BDO_Canada; www.linkedin.com/company/bdo-canada

Former Name: BDO Dunwoody LLP
Ownership: Private. Member of BDO International Limited, UK.
Year Founded: 1921
Number of Employees: 3,000+
Revenues: $489,000,000 Year End: 20141231
Profile: One of Canada's largest accounting firms, concentrating on the special needs of independent business & community-based organizations. The firm provides a full range of comprehensive business advisory services.
Executives:
Pat Kramer, Chief Executive Officer
Offices:

Alexandria
55 Anik St.
Alexandria, ON K0C 1A0 Canada
Tel: 613-525-1585; *Fax:* 613-525-1436
alexandria@bdo.ca

Alliston
#13-14, 169 Dufferin St. South
Alliston, ON L9R 1E6 Canada
Tel: 705-435-5585; *Fax:* 705-435-5587
alliston@bdo.ca

Altona
#1, 45 - 4th Ave. NE
Altona, MB R0G 0B1 Canada
Tel: 204-324-8653; *Fax:* 204-324-1629
pembinavalley@bdo.ca

Athabasca
4917- 49 St.
Athabasca, AB T9S 1C5 Canada
Tel: 780-675-2397; *Fax:* 780-461-8800
athabasca@bdo.ca

Barrie
#201, 15 Sperling Dr.
Barrie, ON L4M 6K9 Canada
Tel: 705-797-3999
barriesred@bdo.ca

Barrie - Lakeshore Dr.
#300, 300 Lakeshore Dr.
Barrie, ON L4N 0B4 Canada
Tel: 705-726-6331; *Fax:* 705-722-6588
barrie@bdo.ca

Barrie - Sperling Dr.
#201, 15 Sperling Dr.
Barrie, ON L4M 6K9 Canada
Tel: 705-797-3999
barriesred@bdo.ca

Bedford
#101, 1496 Bedford Hwy.
Bedford, NS B4A 1E5 Canada
Tel: 902-444-5540; *Fax:* 902-444-5539
bedford@bdo.ca

Boissevain
PO Box 60
316 South Railway St.
Boissevain, MB R0K 0E0 Canada
Tel: 204-534-6040; *Fax:* 204-534-6042
boissevain@bdo.ca

Bracebridge
#1, 239 Manitoba St.
Bracebridge, ON P1L 1S2 Canada
Tel: 705-645-5215; *Fax:* 705-645-8125
bracebridge@bdo.ca

Brandon
148 - 10th St.
Brandon, MB R7A 4E6 Canada
Tel: 204-727-0671; *Fax:* 204-726-4580
brandon@bdo.ca

Brantford
#1, 505 Park Rd. North
Brantford, ON N3R 7K8 Canada
Tel: 519-759-8320; *Fax:* 519-759-8421
brantford@bdo.ca

Bridgewater
#102, 215 Dominion St.
Bridgewater, NS B4V 2K7 Canada
Tel: 902-543-7373; *Fax:* 902-543-9941
bridgewater@bdo.ca

Burlington
#400, 3115 Harvester Rd.
Burlington, ON L7N 3N8 Canada
Tel: 905-639-9500; *Fax:* 905-633-4939
burlington@bdo.ca

Calgary
#620, 903 - 8 Ave. SW
Calgary, AB T2P 0P7 Canada
Tel: 403-266-5608; *Fax:* 403-233-7833
calgary@bdo.ca

Cambridge
#107, 231 Shearson Cres.
Cambridge, ON N1T 1J5 Canada
Tel: 519-622-7676; *Fax:* 519-622-7870
cambridge@bdo.ca

Cardston
259 Main St.
Cardston, AB T0K OKO Canada
Tel: 403-653-4137
cardston@bdo.ca

Charlottetown
PO Box 2158
#200, 155 Belvedere Ave.
Charlottetown, PE C1A 8B9 Canada
Tel: 902-892-5365; *Fax:* 902-892-0383

Chatham
PO Box 1195
155 Thames St.
Chatham, ON N7M 5L8 Canada
Tel: 519-352-4130; *Fax:* 519-352-2744
chatham@bdo.ca

Cobourg
PO Box 627
204 Division St.
Cobourg, ON K9A 3P7 Canada
Tel: 905-372-6863; *Fax:* 905-372-6650
cobourg@bdo.ca

Collingwood
#100, 40 Huron St.
Collingwood, ON L9Y 4R3 Canada
Tel: 705-445-4421; *Fax:* 705-445-6691
collingwood@bdo.ca

Corner Brook
#300, 50 Main St.
Corner Brook, NL A2H 1C4 Canada
Tel: 709-634-1590; *Fax:* 709-634-1599
Cornerbrook@bdo.ca

Cornwall
PO Box 644
113 Second St. East
Cornwall, ON K6H 1Y5 Canada
Tel: 613-932-8691; *Fax:* 613-932-7591
cornwall@bdo.ca

Cranbrook
#200, 35 - 10 Ave. South
Cranbrook, BC V1C 2M9 Canada
Tel: 250-426-4285; *Fax:* 250-426-8886
cranbrook@bdo.ca

Dryden
PO Box 3010
37 King St.
Dryden, ON P8N 1B4 Canada
Tel: 807-223-5321; *Fax:* 807-223-2978
dryden@bdo.ca

Edmonton
9897 - 34th Ave. NW
Edmonton, AB T6E 5X9 Canada
Tel: 780-461-8000; *Fax:* 780-461-8000
edmonton@bdo.ca

Embrun
PO Box 128
991 Limoges Rd.
Embrun, ON K0A 1W0 Canada
Tel: 613-443-5201; *Fax:* 613-443-2538
embrun@bdo.ca

Erickson
PO Box 214
19 - 1st St. SW
Erickson, MB R0J 0P0 Canada
Tel: 204-636-2925; *Fax:* 204-636-7789
erickson@bdo.ca

Essex
180 Talbot St. South
Essex, ON N8M 1B6 Canada
Tel: 519-776-6488; *Fax:* 519-776-6090
essex@bdo.ca

Exeter
#2, 145 Thames Rd. West
Exeter, ON N0M 1S3 Canada
Tel: 519-235-0281; *Fax:* 519-235-3367
exeter@bdo.ca

Fort Frances
375 Scott St.
Fort Frances, ON P9A 1H1 Canada
Tel: 807-274-9848; *Fax:* 807-274-5142
fortfrances@bdo.ca

Fraser Valley
#303, 15127 - 100th Ave.
Fraser Valley, BC V3R 0N9 Canada
Tel: 604-496-5080; *Fax:* 604-496-5081
fraservalley@bdo.ca

Gatineau
#200, 160, boul de l'Hopital
Gatineau, QC J8T 8J1 Canada
Tel: 819-561-1422; *Fax:* 819-561-2415
gatineau@bdo.ca

Grande Prairie
#200, 9805 - 97th St.
Grande Prairie, AB T8V 8B9 Canada
Tel: 780-539-7075; *Fax:* 780-538-1890
grandeprairie@bdo.ca

Grenville
289, rue Principale
Grenville, QC J0V 1V0 Canada
Tel: 819-242-8157; *Fax:* 819-242-0535
grenville@bdo.ca

Guelph
512 Woolwich St.
Guelph, ON N1H 3X7 Canada
Tel: 519-824-5410; *Fax:* 519-824-5497
Toll-Free: 877-236-4835
guelph@bdo.ca

Hanover
485 - 10th St.
Hanover, ON N4N 1R2 Canada
Tel: 519-364-3790; *Fax:* 519-364-5334
hanover@bdo.ca

Harrow
37 King St. West
Harrow, ON N0R 1G0 Canada
Tel: 519-738-2236; *Fax:* 519-738-3326
harrow@bod.ca

Huntsville
4 Elm St.
Huntsville, ON P1H 1L1 Canada
Tel: 705-789-4469; *Fax:* 705-789-1079
huntsville@bdo.ca

Invermere
Bldg. 2
906 - 8th Ave., Lower Level
Invermere, BC V0A 1K0 Canada
Tel: 250-342-3383; *Fax:* 250-342-0248
invermere@bdo.ca

Kamloops
#300, 275 Landsdowne St.
Kamloops, BC V2C 6J3 Canada
Tel: 250-372-9505; *Fax:* 250-374-6323
kamloops@bdo.ca

Kelowna
#400, 1631 Dickson Ave.
Kelowna, BC V1Y 0B5 Canada
Tel: 250-763-6700; *Fax:* 250-763-4457
kelowna@bdo.ca

Kenora
#300, 301 First Ave. South
Kenora, ON P9N 4E9 Canada
Tel: 807-468-5531; *Fax:* 807-468-9774
kenora@bdo.ca

Kincardine
970 Queen St.
Kincardine, ON N2Z 2Y2 Canada
Tel: 519-396-3425; *Fax:* 519-396-9829
kincardine@bdo.ca

Kitchener
#201, 150 Caroline St. South
Kitchener, ON N2L 0A5 Canada
Tel: 519-576-5220; *Fax:* 519-576-5471
kitchenerwaterloo@bdo.ca

Lacombe
5820B Hwy. 2A
Lacombe, AB T4L 2G5 Canada
Tel: 780-782-3361; *Fax:* 780-782-3070
lacombe@bdo.ca

Langley
#220, 19916 - 64th Ave.
Langley, BC V2Y 1A2 Canada
Tel: 604-534-8691; *Fax:* 604-534-8900
langley@bdo.ca

Lethbridge
#600, 400 - 4th Ave. South
Lethbridge, AB T1J 4E1 Canada
Tel: 403-328-5292; *Fax:* 403-328-9534
lethbridge@bdo.ca

Lindsay
PO Box 358
165 Kent St. West
Lindsay, ON K9V 4S3 Canada
Tel: 705-324-3579; *Fax:* 705-324-0774
lindsay@bdo.ca
Liverpool
50 Water St.
Liverpool, NS B0T 1K0 Canada
Tel: 902-354-5706; *Fax:* 902-354-2467
liverpool@bdo.ca
London
#300, 633 Colborne St.
London, ON N6B 2V3 Canada
Tel: 519-672-8940; *Fax:* 519-672-5562
london@bdo.ca
MacGregor
78 Hampton St.
MacGregor, MB R0H 0R0 Canada
Tel: 204-685-2323; *Fax:* 204-685-2341
macgregor@bdo.ca
Manitou
330 Main St.
Manitou, MB R0G 1G0 Canada
pembinavalley@bdo.ca
Manotick
PO Box 978
5494 Manotick Main St.
Manotick, ON K4M 1A8 Canada
Tel: 613-692-3501; *Fax:* 613-692-2874
manotick@bdo.ca
Markham
#300, 60 Columbia Way
Markham, ON L3R 0C9 Canada
Tel: 905-946-1066; *Fax:* 905-946-9524
markham@bdo.ca
Marystown
PO Box 488
170 McGettigan Blvd.
Marystown, NL A0E 2M0 Canada
Tel: 709-279-7878; *Fax:* 709-279-7883
Marystown@bdo.ca
Minnedosa
39 Main St. South
Minnedosa, MB R0J 1E0 Canada
Tel: 204-867-2957; *Fax:* 204-867-5021
minnedosa@bdo.ca
Mississauga
#1700, 1 City Centre Dr.
Mississauga, ON L5B 1M2 Canada
Tel: 905-270-7700; *Fax:* 905-671-7915
mississauga@bdo.ca
Mitchell
PO Box 792
235 St. George St.
Mitchell, ON N0K 1N0 Canada
Tel: 519-348-8412; *Fax:* 519-348-4300
mitchell@bdo.ca
Montréal - Cremazie
#805, 110, boul Cremazie est
Montréal, QC H2P 2X2 Canada
Tel: 514-729-3221; *Fax:* 514-593-8711
northmontreal@bdo.ca
Montréal - Gauchetiere
#200, 1000, rue de la Gauchetiere ouest
Montréal, QC H3B 4W5 Canada
Tel: 514-931-0841; *Fax:* 514-931-9491
montreal@bdo.ca
Montréal - Sherbrooke
#2600, 1002, rue Sherbrooke
Montréal, QC H3A 3L6 Canada
Tel: 514-845-8657; *Fax:* 514-845-9985
Mount Forest
PO Box 418
191 Main St. South
Mount Forest, ON N0G 2L0 Canada
Tel: 519-323-2351; *Fax:* 519-323-3661
mountforest@bco.ca
Nakusp
PO Box 1078
87 - 3rd Ave.
Nakusp, BC V0G 1R0 Canada
Tel: 250-265-4750; *Fax:* 250-265-3220
nakusp@bdo.ca
Newmarket
Gates of York Plaza
#2, 17310 Yonge St.
Newmarket, ON L3Y 7R8 Canada
Tel: 905-898-1221; *Fax:* 905-898-0028
Toll-Free: 866-275-8836
newmarket@bdo.ca

North Bay
#301, 101 McIntyre St. West
North Bay, ON P1B 2Y5 Canada
Fax: 705-495-2001
Toll-Free: 800-461-6324
northbay@bdo.ca
Norwich
PO Box 190
8 Stover St. North
Norwich, ON N0J 1P0 Canada
Tel: 519-863-3126; *Fax:* 519-863-3756
norwich@bdo.ca
Orangeville
77 Broadway Ave.
Orangeville, ON L9W 1K1 Canada
Tel: 519-938-8630; *Fax:* 519-372-0189
orangeville@bdodebthelp.ca
Orillia
PO Box 670
19 Front St. North
Orillia, ON L3V 4R6 Canada
Tel: 705-325-1386; *Fax:* 705-325-6649
orillia@bdo.ca
Oshawa
Oshawa Executive Centre
#502, 419 King St. West
Oshawa, ON L1J 2K5 Canada
Tel: 905-576-3430; *Fax:* 905-436-9138
oshawa@bdo.ca
Ottawa - St. Laurent Blvd.
#100, 1730 St-Laurent Blvd.
Ottawa, ON K1G 5L1 Canada
Tel: 613-739-8221; *Fax:* 613-739-1517
ottawa@bdo.ca
Ottawa - Slater St.
275 Slater St., 20th Fl.
Ottawa, ON K1P 5H9 Canada
Tel: 613-237-9331; *Fax:* 613-237-9779
ottawagsl@bdo.ca
Owen Sound
PO Box 397
1717 - 2nd Ave. East
Owen Sound, ON N4K 6V4 Canada
Tel: 519-376-6110; *Fax:* 519-376-4741
owensound@bdo.ca
Pembina Valley
Stanley Business Centre
PO Box 1357
3-23111 PTH 14
Winkler, MB R6W 4B3 Canada
Tel: 204-325-4787; *Fax:* 204-325-8040
pembinavalley@bdo.ca
Penticton
#102, 100 Front St.
Penticton, BC V2A 1H1 Canada
Tel: 250-492-6020; *Fax:* 250-492-8110
penticton@bdo.ca
Peterborough
PO Box 1018
#202, 201 George St. North
Peterborough, ON K9J 7A5 Canada
Tel: 705-742-4271; *Fax:* 705-742-3420
Toll-Free: 888-369-6600
peterborough@bdo.ca
Petrolia
PO Box 869
4495 Petrolia Line
Petrolia, ON N0N 1R0 Canada
Tel: 519-882-3333; *Fax:* 519-882-2703
petrolia@bdo.ca
Picture Butte
325 Highway Ave.
Picture Butte, AB T0K 1V0 Canada
Tel: 403-732-4469; *Fax:* 403-732-5071
picturebutte@bdo.ca
Port Elgin
PO Box 1390
625 Mill St.
Port Elgin, ON N0H 2C0 Canada
Tel: 519-832-2049; *Fax:* 519-832-5659
portelgin@bdo.ca
Portage La Prairie
480 Saskatchewan Ave. West
Portage La Prairie, MB R1N 0M4 Canada
Tel: 204-857-2856; *Fax:* 204-239-1664
portagelaprairie@bdo.ca
Québec
Édifice Le Delta 3
#650, 2875, boul Laurier
Québec, QC G1V 2M2 Canada
Tel: 418-658-6915; *Fax:* 418-658-4008
quebecity@bdo.ca

Red Deer
Millenium Centre
#600, 4909 - 49th St.
Red Deer, AB T4N 1V1 Canada
Fax: 403-343-3070
Toll-Free: 800-661-1269
reddeer@bdo.ca
Red Lake
PO Box 234
#207, 14 Discovery Rd.
Red Lake, ON P0V 2M0 Canada
Tel: 807-727-3227; *Fax:* 807-727-1172
redlake@bdo.ca
Revelstoke
PO Box 2100
#202, 103 - 1st St. East
Revelstoke, BC V0E 2S0 Canada
Tel: 250-837-5225; *Fax:* 250-837-7170
revelstoke@bdo.ca
Ridgetown
211 Main St. East
Ridgetown, ON N0P 2C0 Canada
Tel: 519-674-5418; *Fax:* 519-674-5410
ridgetown@bdo.ca
Rimbey
PO Box 1080
5059 - 50th Ave.
Rimbey, AB T0C 2J0 Canada
Tel: 780-843-2208; *Fax:* 780-843-4611
rimbey@bdo.ca
Rockland
#5, 2784 Laurier St.
Rockland, ON K4K 1A2 Canada
Tel: 613-446-6497; *Fax:* 613-446-7117
rockland@bdo.ca
Saint-Claude
c/o Caisse Populaire St. Claude Ltée
76 First St.
St-Claude, MB R0G 1Z0 Canada
Tel: 204-379-2332; *Toll-Free:* 800-268-3337
stclaude@bdo.ca
St. John's
PO Box 8505
#200, 53 Bond St.
St. John's, NL A1B 3N9 Canada
Tel: 709-279-7878; *Fax:* 709-579-2120
stjohns@bdo.ca
Salmon Arm
#201, 571 - 6th St. NE
Salmon Arm, BC V1E 1R6 Canada
Tel: 250-832-7171; *Fax:* 250-832-2429
salmonarm@bdo.ca
Sarnia
Kenwick Place
PO Box 730
250 Christina St. North
Sarnia, ON N7T 7V3 Canada
Tel: 519-336-9900; *Fax:* 519-332-4828
sarnia@bdo.ca
Sault Ste Marie
PO Box 1109
747 Queen St. East
Sault Ste Marie, ON P6A 2A8 Canada
Tel: 705-945-0990; *Fax:* 705-942-7979
ssm@bdo.ca
Shediac
343 Main St., #B
Shediac, NB E4P 2B3 Canada
Tel: 506-533-9082; *Fax:* 506-532-9068
shediac@bdo.ca
Sherbrooke
2986, ch. Sainte-Catherine
Sherbrooke, QC J1N 3X9 Canada
Tel: 819-566-8064; *Fax:* 819-566-8020
Sioux Lookout
PO Box 1239
#1A, 76 1/2 Front St.
Sioux Lookout, ON P8T 1B8 Canada
Tel: 807-737-1500; *Fax:* 807-737-4443
siouxlookout@bdo.ca
Slave Lake
PO Box 297
#303, Lakeland Centre
Slave Lake, AB T0G 2A0 Canada
Tel: 780-849-3622; *Fax:* 780-849-3625
slavelake@bdo.ca
Squamish
PO Box 168
#202, 38147 Cleveland Ave.
Squamish, BC V8B 0A2 Canada
Tel: 604-892-9424; *Fax:* 604-892-9356
squamish@bdo.ca

Stratford
380 Hibernia St.
Stratford, ON N5A 5W3 Canada
Tel: 519-271-2491; *Fax:* 519-271-4013
stratford@bdo.ca
Strathroy
425 Caradoc St. South, #E
Strathroy, ON N7G 2P5 Canada
Tel: 519-245-1913; *Fax:* 519-245-5987
strathroy@bdo.ca
Sudbury
#4, 754 Falconbridge Rd.
Sudbury, ON P3A 5X5 Canada
Tel: 705-671-3336; *Fax:* 705-671-9552
Toll-Free: 877-820-0404
sudbury@bdo.ca
Summerside
PO Box 1347
107 Walker Ave.
Summerside, PE C1N 4K2 Canada
Tel: 902-436-2171; *Fax:* 902-436-0960
summerside@bdo.ca
Thunder Bay
1095 Barton St.
Thunder Bay, ON P7B 5N3 Canada
Tel: 807-625-4444; *Fax:* 807-623-8460
thunderbay@bdo.ca
Toronto - Wellington St. West
TD Bank Tower
PO Box 131
#3600, 66 Wellington St. West
Toronto, ON M5K 1H1 Canada
Tel: 416-865-0200; *Fax:* 416-865-0887
toronto@bdo.ca
Treherne
274 Railway Ave.
Treherne, MB R0G 2V0 Canada
Tel: 204-723-2454
treherne@bdo.ca
Uxbridge
#1, 1 Brock St. East
Uxbridge, ON L9P 1P6 Canada
Tel: 905-852-9714; *Fax:* 905-852-9898
uxbridge@bdo.ca
Vancouver
Cathedral Place
#600, 925 West Georgia St.
Vancouver, BC V6L 3L2 Canada
Tel: 604-688-5421; *Fax:* 604-688-5132
vancouver@bdo.ca
Vernon
#202, 2706 - 30th Ave.
Vernon, BC V1T 2B6 Canada
Tel: 250-545-2136; *Fax:* 250-545-3364
vernon@bdo.ca
Victoria
#500, 1803 Douglas St.
Victoria, BC V8T 5C3 Canada
Tel: 250-383-0426; *Fax:* 250-383-1091
victoria@bdo.ca
Virden
PO Box 1900
255 Wellington St. West
Virden, MB R0M 2C0 Canada
Tel: 204-748-1200; *Fax:* 204-748-1976
Toll-Free: 866-236-7656
virden@bdo.ca
Vulcan
122 Centre St.
Vulcan, AB T0L 2B0 Canada
Tel: 403-485-2923; *Fax:* 403-485-6098
vulcan@bdo.ca
Walkerton
PO Box 760
121 Jackson St.
Walkerton, ON N0G 2V0 Canada
Tel: 519-881-1211; *Fax:* 519-881-3530
walkerton@bdo.ca
Wetaskiwin
#103, 4725 - 56 St.
Wetaskiwin, AB T9A 3M2 Canada
Tel: 780-352-0808; *Fax:* 780-352-2970
wetaskiwin@bdo.ca
Whistler
#202, 1200 Alpha Lake Rd.
Whistler, BC V0N 1B1 Canada
Tel: 604-932-3799; *Fax:* 604-932-3764
whistler@bdo.ca
Whitehorse
202 - 9016 Quartz Rd.
Whitehorse, YT Y1A 2Z5 Canada
Tel: 867-667-7907; *Fax:* 867-668-3087
whitehorse@bdo.ca
Wiarton
PO Box 249
663 Berford St.
Wiarton, ON N0H 2T0 Canada
Tel: 519-534-1520; *Fax:* 519-534-3454
wiarton@bdo.ca
Windsor
Building 100
3630 Rhodes Dr.
Windsor, ON N8W 5A4 Canada
Tel: 519-944-6993; *Fax:* 519-944-6116
windsor@bdo.ca
Wingham
PO Box 1420
47 Alfred St. West
Wingham, ON N0G 2W0 Canada
Tel: 519-357-3231; *Fax:* 519-357-3230
wingham@bdo.ca
Winnipeg
Wawanesa Bldg.
#700, 200 Graham Ave.
Winnipeg, MB R3C 4L5 Canada
Tel: 204-956-7200; *Fax:* 204-926-7201
winnipeg@bdo.ca
Woodstock
94 Graham St.
Woodstock, ON N4S 6J7 Canada
Tel: 519-539-2081; *Fax:* 519-539-2571
woodstock@bdo.ca

Crowe MacKay LLP

#1100, 1177 West Hastings St.
Vancouver, BC V6E 4T5
Tel: 604-687-4511; *Fax:* 604-687-5805
Toll-Free: 800-351-0426
www.crowehorwath.net/mackay

Former Name: MacKay LLP
Ownership: An independent member of Crowe Horwath International, New York, USA
Year Founded: 1969
Profile: Services provided include bookkeeping, audit & accounting, taxation, corporate financing, executive financial planning, microcomputer support, management consulting, business investigation, valuation & litigation support, solvency & restructuring, & international affiliations. Affiliated with bankruptcy trustees Crowe MacKay & Company Ltd.
Executives:
Russell Law, CPA, CA, CIRP, CFE, President; russell.law@crowemackay.ca
Partners:
Stefan Ferris, CPA, CA, B.Comm, Managing Director, Vancouver & Surrey; stefan.ferris@crowemackay.ca
Craig Elliott, CPA, CGA, MBA; craig.elliott@crowemackay.ca
Keith Gagnon, CPA, CA, BBA; keith.gagnon@crowemackay.ca
Matthew So, CPA, CA, LIC Acct, BA, Tax Partner; matthew.so@crowemackay.ca
York Wong, CPA, CA, B.Comm; york.wong@crowemackay.ca
Affiliated Companies:
Crowe MacKay & Company Ltd.
Branches:
Calgary - 7th Ave.
Elveden House
#1700, 717 - 7 Ave. SW
Calgary, AB T2P 0Z3
Tel: 403-294-9292; *Fax:* 403-294-9262
Toll-Free: 866-599-9292
Edmonton
Highfield Place
#705, 10010 - 106th St.
Edmonton, AB T5J 3L8
Tel: 780-420-0626; *Fax:* 780-425-8780
Toll-Free: 800-622-5293
Kelowna
#500, 1620 Dickson Ave.
Kelowna, BC V1Y 9Y2
Tel: 250-763-5021; *Fax:* 250-763-3600
Toll-Free: 866-763-5021
Regina
#202, 2022 Cornwall St.
Regina, SK S4P 2K5
Tel: 306-347-2244
Surrey
#119, 7565 - 132nd St.
Surrey, BC V3W 1K5
Tel: 604-591-6181; *Fax:* 604-591-5676
Whitehorse
#200, 303 Strickland St.
Whitehorse, YT Y1A 2J9
Tel: 867-667-7651; *Fax:* 867-668-3797

Yellowknife
PO Box 727
5103 - 51st St.
Yellowknife, NT X1A 2N5
Tel: 867-920-4404; *Fax:* 867-920-4135
Toll-Free: 866-920-4404

Deloitte LLP

PO Box 8
#1200, 2 Queen St. East
Toronto, ON M5C 3G7
Tel: 416-874-3874; *Fax:* 416-874-3888
www.deloitte.ca
Social Media: www.youtube.com/deloittecanada; www.facebook.com/DeloitteCanada; twitter.com/deloittecanada; www.linkedin.com/company/1521182

Former Name: Deloitte & Touche LLP
Also Known As: Deloitte Canada
Ownership: Private partnership; Deloitte in Canada is a member firm of Deloitte Touche Tohmatsu.
Year Founded: 1861
Number of Employees: 8,397
Revenues: $1-10 billion
Profile: Deloitte LLP, an Ontario Limited Liability Partnership, is one of Canada's leading firms, providing a range of auditing, tax, financial advisory, & consulting services. Deloitte's offices in Québec operate under the corporate name Deloitte S.E.N.C.R.L./s.r.l., a Quebec limited liability partnership.
Executives:
Glenn Ives, Chair
Frank Vettese, FCA, MBA, CA.CBV, CA.IFA, CFE, ASA, Managing Partner & CEO
Pierre Laporte, President, Deloitte Québec
Branches:
Alma
Complexe Jacques Gagnon
#110, 100, rue St-Joseph sud
Alma, QC G8B 7A6 Canada
Tel: 418-669-6969; *Fax:* 418-668-2966
Amos
#200, 101, av 1re est
Amos, QC J9T 1H4 Canada
Tel: 819-732-8273; *Fax:* 819-732-9143
Bécancour
#107, 4825, rue Bouvet
Bécancour, QC G9H 1X5
Tel: 819-233-3355; *Fax:* 819-691-1213
Brossard
#200, 4605-A, boul Lapinière
Brossard, QC J4Z 3T5 Canada
Tel: 450-618-4270; *Fax:* 450-618-6420
Burlington
#202, 1005 Skyview Dr.
Burlington, ON L7P 5B1 Canada
Tel: 905-315-6770; *Fax:* 905-315-6700
Toll-Free: 866-836-6770
Calgary
#700, 850 - 2nd St. SW
Calgary, AB T2P 0R8 Canada
Tel: 403-267-1700; *Fax:* 403-264-2871
Chicoutimi
#400, 901, boul Talbot
Chicoutimi, QC G7H 0A1 Canada
Tel: 418-549-6650; *Fax:* 418-549-4694
Dolbeau-Mistassini
110, 8e av
Dolbeau-Mistassini, QC G8L 1Y9 Canada
Tel: 418-276-0133; *Fax:* 418-276-8559
Drummondville
212, rue Heriot
Drummondville, QC J2C 1J8 Canada
Tel: 819-477-6311; *Fax:* 819-477-9572
Edmonton
Manulife Place
#2000, 10180 - 101st St.
Edmonton, AB T5J 4E4 Canada
Tel: 780-421-3611; *Fax:* 780-421-3782
Farnham
149, rue Desjardins est
Farnham, QC J2N 2W6 Canada
Tel: 450-293-5327; *Fax:* 450-293-2817
Gatineau
#405, 200, rue Montcalm
Gatineau, QC JBY 3B5 Canada
Tel: 819-770-3221; *Fax:* 819-770-9662
Granby
190, rue Déragon
Granby, QC J2G 5H9 Canada
Tel: 450-372-3347; *Fax:* 450-372-8643

Grand-Mère
PO Box 10160
1671, 6e av
Grand-Mère, QC G9T 5K8 Canada
Tel: 819-538-1721; *Fax:* 819-538-1882
Halifax
Purdy's Wharf Tower II
#1500, 1569 Upper Water St.
Halifax, NS B3J 3R7 Canada
Tel: 902-422-8541; *Fax:* 902-423-5820
Hawkesbury
300, rue McGill
Hawkesbury, ON K6A 1P8 Canada
Tel: 613-632-4178; *Fax:* 613-632-7703
Jonquière
Complexe A E Fortin
2266, boul René-Lévesque
Jonquière, QC G7S 6C5 Canada
Tel: 418-542-9523; *Fax:* 418-542-8814
Kanata
#400, 515, ch Legget
Kanata, ON K2K 3G4 Canada
Tel: 613-254-6899; *Fax:* 613-599-4369
Kitchener
4210 King St. East
Kitchener, ON N2P 2G5 Canada
Tel: 519-650-7600; *Fax:* 519-650-7601
La Baie
365, rue Victoria
La Baie, QC G7B 3M5 Canada
Tel: 418-544-7313; *Fax:* 418-544-0275
La Sarre
226, 2e rue est
La Sarre, QC J9Z 2G9 Canada
Tel: 819-333-2392; *Fax:* 819-333-2517
Langley
#600, 8621 - 201 St.
Langley, BC V2Y 0G9
Tel: 604-534-7477; *Fax:* 604-534-4220
Laval
Les Tours Triomphe
#210, 2540, boul Daniel-Johnson
Laval, QC H7T 2S3 Canada
Tel: 514-978-3500; *Fax:* 514-382-4984
London
One London Place
#700, 255 Queen's Ave.
London, ON N6A 5R8 Canada
Tel: 519-679-1880; *Fax:* 519-640-4625
Matane
750, av du Phare ouest
Matane, QC G4W 3W8 Canada
Tel: 418-566-2637; *Fax:* 418-566-2839
Mississauga
#500, 1 City Centre Dr.
Mississauga, ON L5B 1M2
Tel: 905-601-6150; *Fax:* 819-732-9143
Montréal
#3000, 1, Place Ville-Marie
Montréal, QC H3B 4T9 Canada
Tel: 514-393-7115; *Fax:* 514-390-4100
Normandin
1131, rue St-Cyrille
Normandin, QC G8M 4J6 Canada
Tel: 418-274-2927; *Fax:* 418-274-5278
Ottawa
#800, 100 Queen St.
Ottawa, ON K1P 5T8 Canada
Tel: 613-236-2442; *Fax:* 613-236-2195
Prince Albert
#5, 77 - 15 St. East
Prince Albert, SK S6V 1E9
Tel: 306-763-7411; *Fax:* 306-763-0191
Prince George
#500, 299 Victoria St.
Prince George, BC V2L 5B8 Canada
Tel: 250-564-1111; *Fax:* 250-562-4950
Québec
#400, 925, Grande-Allée ouest
Québec, QC G1S 4Z4 Canada
Tel: 418-624-3333; *Fax:* 418-624-0414
Regina
Bank of Montreal Bldg.
#900, 2103 - 11th Ave.
Regina, SK S4P 3Z8 Canada
Tel: 306-585-5200; *Fax:* 306-757-4753
Rimouski
#402, 287, rue Pierre-Saindon
Rimouski, QC G5L 8V5 Canada
Tel: 418-724-4136; *Fax:* 418-724-3807
Roberval
713, boul St-Joseph
Roberval, QC G8H 2L3 Canada
Tel: 418-275-2111; *Fax:* 418-275-6398
Rouyn-Noranda
155, av Dallaire
Rouyn-Noranda, QC J9X 4T3 Canada
Tel: 819-762-5764; *Fax:* 819-797-1471
Saint John
Brunswick House
PO Box 6549
44 Chipman Hill, 7th Fl.
Saint John, NB E2L 4R9 Canada
Tel: 506-632-1080; *Fax:* 506-632-1210
St Catharines
25 Corporate Park Dr., 3rd Fl.
St Catharines, ON L2S 3W2 Canada
Tel: 905-323-6000; *Fax:* 905-323-6001
Saint-Hyacinthe
#100, 2200, av Pratte
Saint-Hyacinthe, QC J2S 4B6
Tel: 450-774-4000; *Fax:* 450-774-1709
St. John's
Fort William Bldg.
10 Factory Lane
St. John's, NL A1C 6H5 Canada
Tel: 709-576-8480; *Fax:* 709-576-8460
Saskatoon
PCS Tower
#400, 122 - 1st Ave.
Saskatoon, SK S7K 7E5 Canada
Tel: 306-343-4400; *Fax:* 306-343-4480
Sept-Iles
#200, 421, av Arnaud
Sept-Iles, QC G4R 3B3 Canada
Tel: 418-962-2513; *Fax:* 418-968-6422
Sherbrooke
#300, 1802, rue King ouest
Sherbrooke, QC J1J 0A4 Canada
Tel: 819-823-1616; *Fax:* 819-564-8078
St-Félicien
1180, boul Sacré-Cour
St-Félicien, QC G8K 0B5 Canada
Tel: 418-679-4711; *Fax:* 418-679-8723
Toronto - Bay St.
Brookfield Place, Bay Wellington Tower
#1400, 181 Bay St.
Toronto, ON M5J 2V1 Canada
Tel: 416-601-6150; *Fax:* 416-601-6151
Toronto - King St.
#300, 121 King St.
Toronto, ON M5H 3T9 Canada
Tel: 416-601-6150; *Fax:* 416-874-4401
Toronto - Simcoe St.
110 Simcoe St., 5th Fl.
Toronto, ON M5H 3G2 Canada
Tel: 416-408-4800; *Fax:* 416-408-4848
Toronto - Wellington St. West
PO Box 400
30 Wellington St. West
Toronto, ON M5L 1B1 Canada
Tel: 416-874-3874; *Fax:* 416-874-3888
Toronto - Yonge St. - North York
#1700, 5140 Yonge St.
Toronto, ON M2N 6L7 Canada
Tel: 416-601-6150; *Fax:* 416-229-2524
Toronto - Yonge St.
33 Yonge St., 2nd Fl.
Toronto, ON M5E 1G4 Canada
Tel: 416-601-6200; *Fax:* 416-601-6151
Trois-Pistoles
546a Jean Rioux
Trois-Pistoles, QC G0L 4K0 Canada
Tel: 418-851-2232; *Fax:* 418-851-4244
Trois-Rivières
PO Box 1600
1500, rue Royale
Trois-Rivières, QC G9A 5L9 Canada
Tel: 819-691-1212; *Fax:* 819-691-1217
Val-d'Or
#204, 450 - 3e av
Val-d'Or, QC J9P 1S2
Tel: 819-825-4101; *Fax:* 819-825-1155
Vancouver
4 Bentall Centre
#2800, 1055 Dunsmuir St.
Vancouver, BC V7X 1P4 Canada
Tel: 604-669-4466; *Fax:* 604-685-0395
Vaughan
#500, 400 Applewood Cres.
Vaughan, ON L4K 0C3 Canada
Tel: 416-601-6150; *Fax:* 416-601-6151
Victoria
St. Andrew Square
#300, 737 Yates St.
Victoria, BC V8W 1L6 Canada
Tel: 250-978-4403; *Fax:* 250-899-8432
Windsor
#200, 150 Ouellette Pl.
Windsor, ON N8X 1L9 Canada
Tel: 519-967-0388; *Fax:* 519-967-0324
Winnipeg
#2300, 360 Main St.
Winnipeg, MB R3C 3Z3 Canada
Tel: 204-942-0051; *Fax:* 204-947-9390

EPR Canada (EPR)

National Administration Office
PO Box 21148, Maple Ridge Square Stn. Maple Ridge Square
Maple Ridge, BC V2X 17P
Tel: 604-476-2009; *Fax:* 604-467-1219
eprnat@epr.ca
www.epr.ca

Former Name: Evancic Perrault Robertson
Profile: EPR Canada is a group of public accounting firms. Accounting, taxation, & management consulting services are provided. CPA-USA Network & IECnet are the organizations international affiliates.
Executives:
Paul Walker, Chair; pwalker@eprcga.com
Jeannine Brooks, MBA, CAE, FCPA, FCGA, GCBV, Executive Director; jbrooks@epr.ca
Verle Spindor, National Administrator; vspindor@eprcga.com
Branches:
Bathurst
1935 St. Peter Ave.
Bathurst, NB E2A 7J5
Tel: 506-548-1984; *Fax:* 506-548-0904
eprbath@eprbathurst.ca
Note: EPR Bathurst is a full-service management counsulting & accounting firm that focusses upon medium sized organizations in the professional, governmental, & non-profit sectors.
Calgary
#110, 7330 Fisher St. SE
Calgary, AB T2H 2H8
Tel: 403-278-5800; *Fax:* 403-253-9479
Note: Tax, accounting, audit & business advisory services are provided.
Caraquet
#13, 445, boul St-Pierre ouest
Caraquet, NB E1W 1B2
Tel: 506-727-2010; *Fax:* 506-727-2088
eprbath@eprbathurst.ca
Chatham
Centre Square
40 Centre St.
Chatham, ON N7M 5W3
Tel: 519-436-0556; *Fax:* 519-436-1291
Coquitlam
566 Lougheed Hwy., 2nd Fl.
Coquitlam, BC V3K 3S3
Tel: 604-936-4377; *Fax:* 604-936-8376
eprcoq@eprcoq.com
www.eprcoq.com
Note: Accounting & business advisory services are provided to the mid-market.
Devon
35 Athabasca Ave.
Devon, AB T9G 1G5
Tel: 780-987-2280; *Fax:* 780-987-2131
Dieppe
#301, 1040 Champlain St.
Dieppe, NB E1A 8L8
Tel: 506-855-3098; *Fax:* 506-855-3099
Note: EPR Dieppe offers accounting, auditing, tax, forecasting, business financing, & advisory services. It serves government & public agencies, as well as small & medium sized businesses.
Edmonton
#200, 17510 - 107 Ave.
Edmonton, AB T5S 1E9
Tel: 780-432-5262; *Fax:* 780-436-0115
Fredericton
#205, 206 Rookwood Ave.
Fredericton, NB E3B 2M2
Tel: 506-458-8620; *Fax:* 506-450-8286
eprfred@nbnet.nb.ca
Note: Clients include firms from the retail, agricultural, fishing, natural resources, manufacturing, financial, & transportation sectors, as well as municipal entities & not for profit enterprises.

Gatineau
128, boul Saint-Raymond
Gatineau, QC J8Y 1T2
Tel: 819-420-3512; *Toll-Free:* 888-404-9853
Note: The Quebec clientele consists of municipal & public organizations, non-profit organizations, the agricultural sector, the aviation industry, construction companies, & financial services.
Grand Falls
PO Box 7845
381, rue McCormick
Grand Falls, NB E3Z 3E8
Tel: 506-475-9440; *Fax:* 506-475-9449
Grande Prairie
#215, 10006 - 101st Ave.
Grande Prairie, AB T8V 0Y1
Tel: 780-539-3400; *Fax:* 780-538-1544
Hamilton
PO Box 30082
176 Rymal Rd. East
Hamilton, ON L9B 2Y5
Tel: 905-388-7453; *Fax:* 905-388-7397
ephamilton@iprimus.ca
Note: The Hamilton office provides accounting, income tax, & consulting services to a wide range of clients.
Langley
21542 - 48th Ave.
Langley, BC V3A 3M5
Tel: 604-534-1441; *Fax:* 604-534-1491
www.eprcga.com
Note: Clients in Langley include entertainment businesses, construction companies, franchisees, farming organizations, the equine industry, non-profit organizations, & associations.
London
#804, 150 Dufferin Ave.
London, ON N6A 5N6
Tel: 519-434-5847; *Fax:* 519-645-0727
Maple Ridge
22377 Dewdney Trunk Rd.
Maple Ridge, BC V2X 3J4
Tel: 604-467-5561; *Fax:* 604-467-1219
eprmr@eprcga.com
www.eprcga.com
Note: Maple Ridge's clientele includes professional services firms, construction companies, real estate developers, insurance agencies. social & correctional services providers, & non-profit organizations.
Moncton
84 Brandon St.
Moncton, NB E1C 7E9
Tel: 506-850-5045
North Vancouver
#102, 1975 Lonsdale Ave.
North Vancouver, BC V7M 2K3
Tel: 604-987-8101; *Fax:* 604-987-1794
cga@eprnv.ca
Note: Specialties include personal & small business services, such as general accounting, tax preparation, & management consulting.
Richmond
#230, 8833 Odlin Cres.
Richmond, BC V6X 3Z7
Tel: 604-270-9186; *Fax:* 604-270-6379
eprrmd@eprrmd.com
Saint-Hyacinthe
#200, 450 ave St-Joseph
Saint-Hyacinthe, QC J2S 8K5
Tel: 450-774-7165; *Fax:* 450-774-1589
reception.sthyacinthe@eprquebec.com
St. John's
74 O'Leary Ave.
St. John's, NL A1B 2C7
Tel: 709-726-0000; *Fax:* 709-726-2200
Note: Clients include nursing & personal care homes & construction companies.
Saskatoon
259 Robin Cres.
Saskatoon, SK S7L 6M8
Tel: 306-934-3944; *Fax:* 306-934-3409
www.eprsk.ca
Note: ERP Saskatoon's clients are mainly owner managed businesses that operate in all sectors of the economy. Specialties of this location include financial management & strategic financial consulting services.
Slave Lake
405 - 6th Ave. SW
Slave Lake, AB T0G 2A4
Tel: 780-849-4949; *Fax:* 780-849-3401
St-Jérôme
34, rue de Martigny ouest
Saint-Jérome, QC J7Y 2E9
Tel: 450-569-2641; *Fax:* 450-569-2647
Stonewall
Westside Plaza
PO Box 1038
333 Main St.
Stonewall, MB R0C 2Z0
Tel: 204-467-5566; *Fax:* 204-467-9133
eprstonewall@shawcable.com
Note: Specialties of EPR Stonewall are as follows: financial statements, personal & corporate taxation, business financing, farm accounting, estate planing, & computer consulting.
Terrebonne
3300, boul des Entreprises
Terrebonne, QC J6X 4J8
Tel: 450-477-0377; *Fax:* 450-477-4023
Tilbury
PO Box 130
40 Queen Sq.
Tilbury, ON N0P 2L0
Tel: 519-682-2300; *Fax:* 519-682-0705
reiger@ciaccess.com
Welland
250 Division St.
Welland, ON L3B 4A4
Tel: 905-735-7933; *Fax:* 905-735-2419
jks@bellnet.ca
White Rock
#104, 1656 Martin Dr.
White Rock, BC V4A 6E7
Tel: 604-536-7778; *Fax:* 604-536-7745
Whitecourt
PO Box 569
#101, 5011 - 51 Ave.
Whitecourt, AB T7S 1N6
Tel: 780-778-3981; *Fax:* 780-778-6226
Winnipeg
#1010, 1661 Portage Ave.
Winnipeg, MB R3J 3T7
Tel: 204-938-9696; *Fax:* 204-775-5609
eprwpg@mts.net

Ernst & Young LLP (EY)
Ernst & Young Tower, Toronto-Dominion Centre
PO Box 251
222 Bay St.
Toronto, ON M5K 1J7
Tel: 416-864-1234; *Fax:* 416-864-1174
www.ey.com/ca
Social Media: www.youtube.com/ernstandyoungglobal; www.pinterest.com/eycanada; www.facebook.com/195665063800329; twitter.com/EYCanada; www.linkedin.com/company/1073
Ownership: A division of Ernst & Young Global Limited, UK.
Year Founded: 1864
Number of Employees: 2,907
Profile: The following services are offered: assurance & advisory business services; corporate finance; tax; & other services. It is affiliated with Ernst & Young Orenda Corporate Finance Inc.
Executives:
Mark Weinberger, Global Chair & Chief Executive Officer
Carmine Di Sibio, Global Managing Partner, Client Service
Lou Pagnutti, Global Managing Partner, Business Enablement
Steve Howe, Managing Partner, Americas
Jay Nibbe, Vice-Chair, Tax
Affiliated Companies:
Ernst & Young Orenda Corporate Finance Inc.
Branches:
Calgary
Ernst & Young Tower
#1000, 440 - 2nd Ave. SW
Calgary, AB T2P 5E9
Tel: 403-290-4100; *Fax:* 403-290-4265
Dieppe
11 Englehart St.
Dieppe, NB E1A 7Y7
Tel: 506-853-3097; *Fax:* 506-859-7190
Note: The Dieppe office of the firm LeBlanc Nadeau Bujold merged with Ernst & Young in Sept., 2009.
Edmonton
EPCOR Tower
#1400, 10423 - 101st St.
Edmonton, AB T5H 0E7
Tel: 780-423-5811; *Fax:* 780-428-8977
Fredericton
#110, 527 Queen St.
Fredericton, NB E2B 3T2
Tel: 506-455-8181; *Fax:* 506-455-8141
Halifax
RBC Waterside Centre
#500, 1871 Hollis St.
Halifax, NS B3J 0C3
Tel: 902-420-1080; *Fax:* 902-420-0503
Kitchener
515 Riverbend Dr.
Kitchener, ON N2K 3S3
Tel: 519-744-1171; *Fax:* 519-744-9604
London
One London Place
#1800, 255 Queens Ave.
London, ON N6A 5S7
Tel: 519-672-6100; *Fax:* 519-438-5785
Montréal
#1900, 800, boul René-Lévesque ouest
Montréal, QC H3B 1X9
Tel: 514-875-6060; *Fax:* 514-879-2600
Ottawa
#1200, 99 Bank St.
Ottawa, ON K1P 6B9
Tel: 613-232-1511; *Fax:* 613-232-5324
Québec
Delta III
#410, 2875, boul Laurier
Québec, QC G1V 0C7
Tel: 418-524-5151; *Fax:* 418-524-0061
Saint John
Red Rose Tea Bldg.
12 Smythe St., 5th Fl.
Saint John, NB E2L 5G5
Tel: 506-634-7000; *Fax:* 506-634-2129
St. John's
Fortis Place
#800, 5 Springdale St.
St. John's, NL A1E 0E4
Tel: 709-726-2840; *Fax:* 709-726-0345
Saskatoon
#1200, 410 - 22nd St. East
Saskatoon, SK S7K 5T6
Tel: 306-934-8000; *Fax:* 306-653-5859
Toronto - King St. West
#1100, 200 King St. West
Toronto, ON M5H 3T4
Tel: 416-932-8000; *Fax:* 416-932-6200
Vancouver
Pacific Centre
700 West Georgia St.
Vancouver, BC V7Y 1C7
Tel: 604-891-8200; *Fax:* 604-643-5422
Winnipeg
Commodity Exchange Tower
#2700, 360 Main St.
Winnipeg, MB R3C 4G9
Tel: 204-947-6519; *Fax:* 204-956-0138

Grant Thornton LLP
50 Bay St., 12th Fl.
Toronto, ON M5J 2Z8
Tel: 416-366-4240; *Fax:* 416-360-4944
www.grantthornton.ca
Social Media: twitter.com/GrantThorntonCA; www.linkedin.com/company/grant-thornton-llp
Ownership: Private
Year Founded: 1939
Number of Employees: 1,172
Revenues: $100-500 million
Executives:
Kevin Ladner, CPA, CA, CBV, CEO, Executive Partner
Jim Copeland, CPA, CA, CMC, COO, Central Canada, Regional Managing Partner
Dave Peneycad, CPA, CA, CAO
Sharon Healy, Chief People & Culture Officer
Norm Raynard, CPA, CA, CBV, Regional Managing Partner, Western Canada
Michele Williams, FCPA, CBV, Regional Managing Partner, Atlantic Canada
Robin Cyna, Principal, National Office, Toronto
Linda Woo, Principal, National Office, Toronto
Affiliated Companies:
Grant Thornton Alger Inc.
Grant Thornton Poirier Limited
Green Hunt Wedlake Inc.
Raymond Chabot Grant Thornton LLP/RCGT
Branches:
Airdrie
225 - 1st Ave. NW
Airdrie, AB T4B 3H3
Toll-Free: 866-310-8888
Antigonish
#204, 220 Main St.
Antigonish, NS B2G 2C2 Canada
Tel: 902-863-4587; *Fax:* 902-863-0917
Barrie
#400, 85 Bayfield St.
Barrie, ON L4M 3A7 Canada
Tel: 705-728-3397; *Fax:* 705-728-2728

Bathurst - Douglas Ave. - Consumer Insolvency
Keystone Pl.
270 Douglas Ave., 1st Fl.
Bathurst, NB E2A 1M9 Canada
Tel: 506-546-9285; *Toll-Free:* 888-455-6060

Bathurst - Main St.
Harbourview Pl.
#500, 275 Main St.
Bathurst, NB E2A 3Z2 Canada
Tel: 506-546-6616; *Fax:* 506-548-5622

Beamsville
5026 King St.
Beamsville, ON L0R 1B0 Canada
Tel: 905-563-4528; *Fax:* 905-563-7780

Bridgewater
Dawson Centre
197 Dufferin St., 4th Fl.
Bridgewater, NS B4V 2G9 Canada
Tel: 902-543-8115; *Fax:* 902-543-7707

Burnaby
#102, 4664 Lougheed Hwy.
Burnaby, BC V5C 5T5

Calgary - 36th St. NE
Sunridge Professional Building
2675 - 36th St. NE
Calgary, AB T1Y 6H6

Calgary - 40th Ave. NW
Market Mall Professional Bldg.
#212, 4935 - 40th Ave. NW
Calgary, AB T3A 2N1

Calgary - 4th Ave. SW
#900, 833 - 4th Ave. SW
Calgary, AB T2P 3T5 Canada
Tel: 403-260-2500; *Fax:* 403-260-2571

Calgary - Macleod Trail South
Southcentre Executive Tower
#450, 11012 Macleod Trail South
Calgary, AB T2J 6A5

Camrose
#201, 4870 - 51 St.
Camrose, PE T4V 1S1
Tel: 780-672-9217; *Fax:* 780-672-9216

Charlottetown - Fitzroy St.
PO Box 187
#710, 98 Fitzroy St.
Charlottetown, PE C1A 7K4
Tel: 902-892-6547; *Fax:* 902-566-5358

Charlottetown - North River Rd. - Consumer Insolvency
557 North River Rd.
Charlottetown, PE C1E 1J7
Tel: 902-566-4381; *Toll-Free:* 888-455-6060

Corner Brook
#201, 4 Herald Ave.
Corner Brook, NL A2H 4B4
Tel: 709-634-4382; *Fax:* 709-634-9158

Digby
Basin Place
PO Box 848
68 Water St.
Digby, NS B0V 1A0 Canada
Tel: 902-245-2553; *Fax:* 902-245-6161

Edmonton - 137th Ave.
Northwoods Mall
9499 - 137th Ave.
Edmonton, AB T5E 5R8

Edmonton - 178th St.
Executive Business Centres Ltd.
#51, 10203 - 178th St.
Edmonton, AB T5S 1M3

Edmonton - 91st St.
Steppes Office Centre
1253 - 91st St.
Edmonton, AB T6X 1E9

Edmonton - Jasper Ave. NW
Scotia Place 2
#1401, 10060 Jasper Ave. NW
Edmonton, AB T5J 3R8 Canada
Tel: 780-422-7114; *Fax:* 780-426-3208

Edmunston - Consumer Insolvency
112 Church St.
Edmunston, NB E3V 1J8 Canada
Toll-Free: 888-455-6060

Fort Erie
#8, 450 Garrison Rd.
Fort Erie, ON L2A 1N2 Canada
Tel: 905-871-6620; *Fax:* 905-871-2544

Fort McMurray
8219 Fraser Ave.
Fort McMurray, AB T9H 0A2

Fredericton - Queen St.
PO Box 1054
570 Queen St., 4th Fl.
Fredericton, NB E3B 5C2 Canada
Tel: 506-458-8200; *Fax:* 506-453-7029

Fredericton - Smythe St. - Consumer Insolvency
#103, 1149 Smythe St.
Fredericton, NB E3B 3H4 Canada
Tel: 506-450-2288

Gander
PO Box 348
30 Roe Ave.
Gander, NL A1V 1W7 Canada
Tel: 709-651-4100; *Fax:* 709-256-2957

Georgetown
35 Main St. South
Georgetown, ON L7G 3G3 Canada
Tel: 905-877-5155; *Fax:* 905-877-5905
Toll-Free: 866-554-2030

Grand Falls - Broadway Blvd.
#205, 218 Broadway Blvd.
Grand Falls, NB E3Z 2J9 Canada
Tel: 506-473-5068; *Fax:* 506-473-7077

Grand Falls - McCormick St.
381 McCormick St.
Grand Falls, NB E3Z 3E8 Canada
Tel: 506-475-9440; *Fax:* 506-475-9449

Grand Falls - Windsor
PO Box 83
5B Harris Ave.
Grand Falls-Windsor, NL A2A 2J3 Canada
Tel: 709-489-6622; *Fax:* 709-489-6625

Halifax - Barrington St.
#1100, 2000 Barrington St.
Halifax, NS B3J 3K1 Canada
Tel: 902-421-1734; *Fax:* 902-420-1068

Halifax - Chebucto Rd.
#506, 7067 Chebucto Rd.
Halifax, NS B3L 4R5 Canada
Tel: 902-453-6600; *Fax:* 902-453-9257

Hamilton
33 Main St. East
Hamilton, ON L8N 4K5 Canada
Tel: 905-523-7732; *Fax:* 905-572-9333

Happy Valley-Goose Bay
PO Box 1029, B Sta. B
167 Hamilton River Rd.
Happy Valley-Goose Bay, NL A0P 1E0 Canada
Tel: 709-896-2691; *Fax:* 709-896-9160

Kelowna
#200, 1633 Ellis St.
Kelowna, BC V1Y 2A8 Canada
Tel: 250-712-6800; *Fax:* 250-712-6850

Kentville
15 Webster St.
Kentville, NS B4N 1H4 Canada
Tel: 902-678-7307; *Fax:* 902-679-1870

Kitchener
#230, 121 Charles St. West
Kitchener, ON N2G 1H6 Canada
Tel: 519-744-2474; *Fax:* 519-576-2425

Langley
#320, 8700 - 200th St.
Langley, BC V2Y 0G4 Canada
Tel: 604-455-2600; *Fax:* 604-455-2609

London
#406, 140 Fullarton St.
London, ON N6A 5P2 Canada
Tel: 519-672-2930; *Fax:* 519-672-6455

Markham
#200, 15 Allstate Pkwy.
Markham, ON L3R 5B4 Canada
Tel: 416-607-2656; *Fax:* 905-475-8906

Marystown
PO Box 518
2 Queen St.
Marystown, NL A0E 2M0 Canada
Tel: 709-279-2300; *Fax:* 709-279-2340

Miramichi
135 Henry St.
Miramichi, NB E1V 2N5 Canada
Tel: 506-622-0637; *Fax:* 506-622-5174

Mississauga
#501, 201 City Centre Dr.
Mississauga, ON L5B 2T4 Canada
Tel: 416-369-7076; *Fax:* 905-804-0509

Moncton - Main St.
PO Box 1005
#500, 633 Main St.
Moncton, NB E1C 8P2 Canada
Tel: 506-857-0100; *Fax:* 506-857-0105

Moncton - Mountain Rd. - Consumer Insolvency
#100, 1405 Mountain Rd.
Moncton, NB E1C 2T9 Canada
Tel: 506-382-2655; *Toll-Free:* 888-455-6060

Montague
PO Box 70
1 Bailey Dr.
Montague, PE C0A 1R0
Tel: 902-838-4121; *Fax:* 902-838-4802

New Glasgow
Aberdeen Business Centre
PO Box 427
#270, 610 East River Rd.
New Glasgow, NS B2H 5E5 Canada
Tel: 902-752-8393; *Fax:* 902-752-4009

New Liskeard
PO Box 2170
17 Wellington St.
New Liskeard, ON P0J 1P0 Canada
Tel: 705-647-8100; *Fax:* 705-647-7026

Niagara Falls
#7, 3930 Montrose Rd.
Niagara Falls, ON L2H 3C9 Canada
Tel: 905-358-5729; *Fax:* 905-358-7188

North Bay
#200, 222 McIntyre St. West
North Bay, ON P1B 2Y8 Canada
Tel: 705-472-6500; *Fax:* 705-472-7760

Orillia
#300, 6 West St. North
Orillia, ON L3V 5B8 Canada
Tel: 705-326-7605; *Fax:* 705-326-0837

Perth-Andover
#2, 15 Station St.
Perth-Andover, NB E7H 4Y2 Canada
Tel: 506-273-2276; *Fax:* 506-273-2033

Port Colborne
PO Box 336
222 Catharine St, #B
Port Colborne, ON L3K 5W1
Tel: 905-834-3651; *Fax:* 905-834-5095

Port Coquitlam
#2300, 2850 Shaughnessy St.
Port Coquitlam, BC V3C 6K5
Toll-Free: 310-8888

Port Hawkesbury
#2, 301 Pitt St.
Port Hawkesbury, NS B9A 2T6
Tel: 902-625-5383; *Fax:* 902-625-5242

Saint John - Canterbury St. - Consumer Insolvency
87 Canterbury St.
Saint John, NB E2L 2C7 Canada
Tel: 506-634-1202; *Fax:* 506-634-1205

Saint John - Germain St.
Brunswick Sq. Office Tower
#1100, 1 Germain St.
Saint John, NB E2L 4V1 Canada
Tel: 506-634-2900; *Fax:* 506-634-4569

St Catharines
#200, 80 King St.
St Catharines, ON L2R 7G1
Tel: 905-682-8363; *Fax:* 905-682-2191

St. John's
#300, 15 International Pl.
St. John's, NL A1A 0L4 Canada
Tel: 709-778-8800; *Fax:* 709-722-7892

Summerside
Royal Bank Bldg.
PO Box 1660
220 Water St.
Summerside, PE C1N 2V5 Canada
Tel: 902-436-9155; *Fax:* 902-436-6913

Sydney
George Place
#200, 500 George St.
Sydney, NS B1P 1K6 Canada
Tel: 902-562-5581; *Fax:* 902-562-0073

Thunder Bay
#300, 979 Alloy Dr.
Thunder Bay, ON P7B 5Z8 Canada
Tel: 807-345-6571; *Fax:* 807-345-0032

Toronto - King St. West
PO Box 11
200 King St. West, 11th Fl.
Toronto, ON M5H 3T4 Canada
Tel: 416-366-0100; *Fax:* 416-360-4949

Trail
1440 Bay Ave.
Trail, BC V1R 4B1
Tel: 250-368-6445; *Fax:* 250-368-8488
Truro - Commercial St. - Consumer Insolvency
#308, 35 Commercial St.
Truro, NS B2N 3H9 Canada
Tel: 902-897-2707; *Fax:* 902-897-2708
Truro - Prince St.
733 Prince St.
Truro, NS B2N 1G7 Canada
Tel: 902-893-1150; *Fax:* 902-893-9757
Vancouver
Grant Thornton Pl.
#1600, 333 Seymour St.
Vancouver, BC V6B 0A4 Canada
Tel: 604-687-2711; *Fax:* 604-685-6569
Victoria
888 Fort St., 3rd Fl.
Victoria, BC V8W 1H8 Canada
Tel: 250-383-4191; *Fax:* 250-381-4623
Wetaskiwin
5108 - 51st Ave.
Wetaskiwin, AB T9A 0V2 Canada
Tel: 780-352-1679; *Fax:* 780-352-2451
Winnipeg
94 Commerce Drive
Winnipeg, MB R3P 0Z3 Canada
Tel: 204-944-0100; *Fax:* 204-957-5442
Woodstock
#101, 318 Connell St.
Woodstock, NB E7M 5E2 Canada
Tel: 506-324-8040; *Fax:* 506-325-2262
Yarmouth
PO Box 297
328 Main St.
Yarmouth, NS B5A 4B2 Canada
Tel: 902-742-7842; *Fax:* 902-742-0224

KPMG

Bay Adelaide Centre
#4600, 333 Bay St.
Toronto, ON M5H 2S5

Tel: 416-777-8500; *Fax:* 416-777-8818
www.kpmg.ca
Social Media: www.youtube.com/kpmgcanada; plus.google.com/u/0/110080097037239039522; twitter.com/kpmg_canada; www.linkedin.com/company/kpmg-canada

Ownership: Private
Year Founded: 1860
Number of Employees: 5,000
Assets: $500m-1 billion
Revenues: $500m-1 billion
Executives:
Elio Luongo, Chief Executive Officer, Senior Partner; eluongo@kpmg.ca
Diane Jeffreys, Chief Financial Officer; djeffreys@kpmg.ca
Robert Brouwer, Canadian Managing Partner, Clients & Markets; rbrouwer@kpmg.ca
John A. Gordon, Canadian Managing Partner, Quality & Risk Management; johngordon@kpmg.ca
Mario Paron, Canadian Managing Partner, Enterprise; mparon@kpmg.ca
Austin Abas, Regional Managing Partner, Regions West; aabas@kpmg.ca
Grant McDonald, Regional Managing Partner, Regions East; gmcdonald@kpmg.ca
Branches:
Abbotsford
32575 Simon Ave.
Abbotsford, BC V2T 4W6 Canada
Tel: 604-854-2200; *Fax:* 604-853-2756
Calgary
#3100, 205 - 5th Ave. SW
Calgary, AB T2P 4B9 Canada
Tel: 403-691-8000; *Fax:* 403-691-8008
Chilliwack
#200, 9123 Mary St.
Chilliwack, BC V2P 4H7 Canada
Tel: 604-793-4700; *Fax:* 604-793-4747
Edmonton
Commerce Pl.
10125 - 102 St.
Edmonton, AB T5J 3V8 Canada
Tel: 780-429-7300; *Fax:* 780-429-7379
Fort St John
#102, 9705 - 100th Ave.
Fort St John, BC V1J 1Y2 Canada
Tel: 250-787-1989; *Fax:* 250-563-5693
Fredericton
Frederick Sq., TD Tower
#700, 77 Westmorland St.
Fredericton, NB E3B 6Z3 Canada
Tel: 506-452-8000; *Fax:* 506-450-0072
Halifax
Purdy's Wharf, Tower One
#1500, 1959 Upper Water St.
Halifax, NS B3J 3N2 Canada
Tel: 902-429-6000; *Fax:* 902-423-1307
Hamilton
Commerce Place
#700, 21 King St. West
Hamilton, ON L8P 4W7 Canada
Tel: 905-523-8200; *Fax:* 905-523-2222
Kamloops
#200, 206 Seymour St.
Kamloops, BC V2C 6P5 Canada
Tel: 250-372-5581; *Fax:* 250-828-2928
Kanata
#101, 750 Palladium Dr.
Kanata, ON K2V 1C7 Canada
Tel: 613-212-5764; *Fax:* 613-591-7607
Kelowna
#200, 3200 Richter St.
Kelowna, BC V1W 5K9 Canada
Tel: 250-979-7150; *Fax:* 250-763-0044
Kingston
#400, 863 Princess St.
Kingston, ON K7L 5C8 Canada
Tel: 613-549-1550; *Fax:* 613-549-6349
Langley
8506 - 200th St.
Langley, BC V2Y 0M1 Canada
Tel: 604-455-4000; *Fax:* 604-881-4988
Lethbridge
Lethbridge Centre Tower
#500, 400 - 4th Ave. South
Lethbridge, AB T1J 4E1 Canada
Tel: 403-380-5700; *Fax:* 403-380-5760
London
#1400, 140 Fullarton St.
London, ON N6A 5P2 Canada
Tel: 519-672-4880; *Fax:* 519-672-5684
Moncton
Place Marven's
One Factory Lane
Moncton, NB E1C 9M3 Canada
Tel: 506-856-4400; *Fax:* 506-856-4499
Montréal
#1500, 600 boul de Maisonneuve ouest
Montréal, QC H3A 0A3 Canada
Tel: 514-840-2100; *Fax:* 514-840-2187
North Bay
PO Box 990
#300, 925 Stockdale Rd.
North Bay, ON P1B 8K3 Canada
Tel: 705-472-5110; *Fax:* 705-472-1249
Ottawa
#1800, 150 Elgin Street
Ottawa, ON K2P 2P8 Canada
Tel: 613-212-5764; *Fax:* 613-212-2896
Prince George
#400, 177 Victoria St.
Prince George, BC V2L 5R8 Canada
Tel: 250-563-7151; *Fax:* 250-563-5693
Toll-Free: 888-665-5595
Québec
#600, 500, Grande-Allée est
Québec, QC G1R 2J7 Canada
Tel: 418-577-3400; *Fax:* 418-577-3440
Quesnel
#101, 455 McLean St.
Quesnel, BC V2J 2P3 Canada
Tel: 250-992-5547; *Fax:* 250-992-5372
Regina
McCallum Hill Centre, Tower II
1881 Scarth St., 20th Fl.
Regina, SK S4P 4K9 Canada
Tel: 306-791-1200; *Fax:* 306-757-4703
Saint John
Harbour Bldg.
PO Box 2388
#306, 133 Prince William St.
Saint John, NB E2L 3V6 Canada
Tel: 506-634-1000; *Fax:* 506-633-8828
St Catharines
#260, 80 King St.
St Catharines, ON L2R 7G1 Canada
Tel: 905-685-4811; *Fax:* 905-682-2008
St. John's
TD Place
#700, 140 Water St.
St. John's, NL A1C 6H6 Canada
Tel: 709-733-5000; *Fax:* 709-800-0929
Saskatoon
River Centre
#500, 475 - 2nd Ave. South
Saskatoon, SK S7K 1P4 Canada
Tel: 306-934-6200; *Fax:* 306-934-6233
Sault Ste Marie
#200, 111 Elgin St.
Sault Ste Marie, ON P6A 6L6 Canada
Tel: 705-949-5811; *Fax:* 705-949-0911
Sudbury
Claridge Executive Centre
144 Pine St.
Sudbury, ON P3C 1X3 Canada
Tel: 705-675-8500; *Fax:* 705-675-7586
Toronto
Yonge Corporate Centre
#200, 4100 Yonge St.
Toronto, ON M2P 2H3 Canada
Tel: 416-228-7000; *Fax:* 416-228-7123
Vancouver - Burnaby
#2400, 4710 Kingsway
Burnaby, BC V5H 4M2 Canada
Tel: 604-527-3600; *Fax:* 604-527-3636
Vancouver - Dunsmuir St.
777 Dunsmuir St.
Vancouver, BC V7Y 1K3 Canada
Tel: 604-691-3000; *Fax:* 604-691-3031
Vanderhoof
153 East Stewart St.
Vanderhoof, BC V0J 3A0 Canada
Tel: 250-567-5267; *Fax:* 250-567-5263
Vernon
Credit Union Bldg.
3205 - 32 St., 3rd Fl.
Vernon, BC V1T 9A2 Canada
Tel: 250-503-5300; *Fax:* 250-545-6440
Victoria
St. Andrew's Square II
800 - 730 View St.
Victoria, BC V8W 3Y7 Canada
Tel: 250-480-3500; *Fax:* 250-480-3539
Waterloo
115 King St. South
Waterloo, ON N2J 5A3 Canada
Tel: 519-747-8800; *Fax:* 519-747-8811
Windsor
Greenwood Centre
#618, 3200 Deziel Dr.
Windsor, ON N8W 5K8 Canada
Tel: 519-251-3500; *Fax:* 519-251-3530
Winnipeg
#2000, One Lombard Place
Winnipeg, MB R3B 0X3 Canada
Tel: 204-957-1770; *Fax:* 204-957-0808

MNP LLP

715 - 5th Ave. SW, 7th Fl.
Calgary, AB T2P 2X6

Tel: 403-444-0150; *Fax:* 403-444-0199
www.mnp.ca
Social Media: www.youtube.com/mnpllp; twitter.com/mnp_llp; www.linkedin.com/company/mnp

Former Name: Meyers Norris Penny
Year Founded: 1945
Number of Employees: 1300
Revenues: $100-500 million
Profile: MNP is a leading Western Canadian chartered accountancy & business advisory firm. In addition to traditional accounting services like taxation & assurance, MNP offers business services including corporate financing, human resource consulting, business & strategic planning, succession planning, valuations support, information technology consulting, self-employment training, & agricultural advisory services.
Directors:
Daryl Ritchie, FCPA, FCA, Chair; daryl.ritchie@mnp.ca
Executives:
Jason Tuffs, CPA, CA, Chief Executive Officer; jason.tuffs@mnp.ca
Kelly Bernakevitch, FCPA, FCA, Executive Vice-President, Operations & Finance; kelly.bernakevitch@mnp.ca
Jeremy Cole, CPA, CA, CBV, Executive Vice-President, Ontario & Québec; jeremy.cole@mnp.ca
Darren Turchansky, CPA, CA, Executive Vice-President, British Columbia; darren.turchansky@mnp.ca
Sean Wallace, CPA, CA, Executive Vice-President, Prairie Region; sean.wallace@mnp.ca
Laurel Wood, MBA, CMC, ICD.D, Executive Vice-President, Clients & Services; laurel.wood@mnp.ca

Affiliated Companies:
KNV Chartered Accountants LLP
MNP Corporate Finance Inc.
MNP Ltd
Branches:
Abbotsford
#300, 2975 Gladwin Rd.
Abbotsford, BC V2S 2A8
Tel: 604-853-9471; *Fax:* 604-850-3672
Toll-Free: 877-853-9471
Airdrie
#110A, 400 Main St. NE
Airdrie, AB T4B 2N1
Tel: 403-912-6235; *Fax:* 403-912-6332
Brandon
1401 Princess Ave.
Brandon, MB R7A 7L7
Tel: 204-727-0661; *Fax:* 204-726-1543
Toll-Free: 800-446-0890
Burlington
#602, 1122 International Blvd.
Burlington, ON L7L 6Z8
Tel: 905-333-9888; *Fax:* 905-333-9583
Calgary - 5th Ave. SW - Downtown
#1500, 640 - 5th Ave. SW
Calgary, AB T2P 3G4
Tel: 403-263-3385; *Fax:* 403-269-8450
Toll-Free: 877-500-0792
Cambridge
#600, 73 Water St. N.
Cambridge, ON N1R 7L6 Canada
Tel: 519-623-3820; *Fax:* 519-622-3144
Campbell River
#201, 990 Cedar St.
Campbell River, BC V9W 7Z8
Tel: 250-287-2131; *Fax:* 250-287-2134
Chilliwack
#1, 45780 Yale Rd.
Chilliwack, BC V2P 2N4
Tel: 604-792-1915; *Fax:* 604-795-6526
Toll-Free: 800-444-4070
Courtenay
467 Cumberland Rd.
Courtenay, BC V9N 2C5
Tel: 250-338-5464; *Fax:* 250-338-0609
Dauphin
PO Box 6000
32 - 2nd Ave. SW
Dauphin, MB R7N 2V5
Tel: 204-638-6767; *Fax:* 204-638-8634
Toll-Free: 877-500-0790
Deloraine
PO Box 528
130 Broadway St. North
Deloraine, MB R0M 0M0
Tel: 204-747-2842; *Fax:* 204-747-2956
Drumheller
PO Box 789
365 - 2nd St. East
Drumheller, AB T0J 0Y0
Tel: 403-823-7800; *Fax:* 403-823-8914
Toll-Free: 877-932-3387
Duncan
372 Coronation Ave.
Duncan, BC V9L 2T3
Tel: 250-748-3761; *Fax:* 250-746-1712
Edmonton - 103rd Ave. NW - City Centre
#400, 10104 - 103rd Ave. NW
Edmonton, AB T5J 0H8
Tel: 780-451-4406; *Fax:* 780-454-1908
Toll-Free: 800-661-7778
Edmonton - 51 Ave. NW - South
#201, 9426 - 51st Ave. NW
Edmonton, AB T6E 5A6
Tel: 780-462-8626; *Fax:* 780-462-8643
Estevan
#100, 1219 - 5th St.
Estevan, SK S4A 0Z5
Tel: 306-634-2603; *Fax:* 306-634-8706
Fort McMurray
9707 Main St.
Fort McMurray, AB T9H 1T5
Tel: 780-791-9000; *Fax:* 780-791-9047
Toll-Free: 866-465-1155
Fort St. John
10611 - 102nd St.
Fort St. John, BC V1J 5L3
Tel: 250-785-8166; *Fax:* 250-785-5660
Toll-Free: 877-898-2580
Grande Prairie
#700, 9909 - 102nd St.
Grande Prairie, AB T8V 2V4
Tel: 780-831-1700; *Fax:* 780-539-9600
Toll-Free: 888-831-2870
High Prairie
PO Box 360
4834 - 52nd Ave.
High Prairie, AB T0G 1E0
Tel: 780-523-4618; *Fax:* 780-523-5119
Humboldt
PO Box 2590
701 - 9th St.
Humboldt, SK S0K 2A0
Tel: 306-682-2673; *Fax:* 306-682-5910
Toll-Free: 877-500-0789
Kelowna
#600, 1628 Dickson Ave.
Kelowna, BC V1Y 9X1
Tel: 250-763-8919; *Fax:* 250-763-1121
Toll-Free: 877-766-9735
Kenora
315 Main St. South
Kenora, ON P9N 1T4
Tel: 807-468-3338; *Fax:* 807-468-1418
Toll-Free: 866-381-3338
Killarney
PO Box 550
501 Broadway Ave.
Killarney, MB R0K 1G0
Tel: 204-523-4633; *Fax:* 204-523-4538
Lacombe
#5, 5265 - 45th St.
Lacombe, AB T4L 2A2
Tel: 403-782-7790; *Fax:* 403-782-7703
Leduc
#200, 5019 - 49th Ave.
Leduc, AB T9E 6T5
Tel: 780-986-2626; *Fax:* 780-986-2621
Lethbridge
3425 - 2nd Ave. South
Lethbridge, AB T1J 4V1
Tel: 403-329-1552; *Fax:* 403-329-1540
Toll-Free: 800-661-8097
Lloydminster
2905 - 50th Ave.
Lloydminster, SK S9V 0N7
Tel: 306-825-9855; *Fax:* 306-825-9640
Maple Ridge
#201, 11939 - 224th St.
Maple Ridge, BC V2X 6B2
Tel: 604-463-8831; *Fax:* 604-463-0401
Markham
#700, 3100 Steeles Ave. East
Markham, ON L3R 8T3
Tel: 416-596-1711; *Fax:* 416-596-7894
Toll-Free: 877-251-2922
Medicine Hat
PO Box 580
666 - 4th St. SE
Medicine Hat, AB T1A 7G5
Tel: 403-527-4441; *Fax:* 403-526-6218
Toll-Free: 877-500-0786
Melfort
PO Box 2020
601 Main St.
Melfort, SK S0E 1A0
Tel: 306-752-5800; *Fax:* 306-752-5933
Mindemoya
PO Box 389
#3, 2134 Hwy. 551
Mindemoya, ON P0P 1S0
Tel: 705-377-5661; *Fax:* 705-377-5095
Toll-Free: 800-756-8303
Mississauga
#1, 75 Courtneypark Dr. West
Mississauga, ON L5W 0E3
Tel: 416-613-3100; *Fax:* 416-613-3101
Montréal
1155, boul René-Lévesque ouest, 19e étage
Montréal, QC H3B 2J8
Tel: 514-861-9724; *Fax:* 514-861-9446
Moosomin
PO Box 670
715 Main St.
Moosomin, SK S0G 3N0
Tel: 306-435-3347; *Fax:* 306-435-2494
Toll-Free: 877-500-0784
Nanaimo
96 Wallace St.
Nanaimo, BC V9R 0E2
Tel: 250-753-8251; *Fax:* 250-754-3999
Neepawa
PO Box 760
251 Davidson St.
Neepawa, MB R0J 1H0
Tel: 204-476-2326; *Fax:* 204-476-3663
Toll-Free: 877-500-0795
Peace River
9913 - 98th Ave.
Peace River, AB T8S 1J5
Tel: 780-624-3252; *Fax:* 780-624-8758
Port Moody
#601, 205 Newport Dr.
Port Moody, BC V3H 5C9
Tel: 604-949-2088; *Fax:* 604-949-0509
Portage La Prairie
780 Saskatchewan Ave. West
Portage La Prairie, MB R1N 0M7
Tel: 204-239-6117; *Fax:* 204-857-3972
Toll-Free: 866-939-6117
Red Deer
4922 - 53rd St.
Red Deer, AB T4N 2E9
Tel: 403-346-8878; *Fax:* 403-341-5599
Toll-Free: 877-500-0779
Red Lake
179 Howey St.
Red Lake, ON P0V 2M0
Tel: 807-727-1114
Regina
Royal Bank Bldg.
#900, 2010 - 11th Ave.
Regina, SK S4P 0J3
Tel: 306-790-7900; *Fax:* 306-790-7990
Toll-Free: 877-500-0780
Richmond
#201, 8360 Bridgeport Rd.
Richmond, BC V6X 3C7
Tel: 604-278-6468; *Fax:* 604-278-4669
Rimbey
PO Box 317
4714 - 50th Ave.
Rimbey, AB T0C 2J0
Tel: 403-843-4666; *Fax:* 403-843-4616
Saskatoon
#800, 119 - 4th Ave. South
Saskatoon, SK S7K 5X2
Tel: 306-665-6766; *Fax:* 306-665-9910
Toll-Free: 877-500-0778
Shaunavon
PO Box 897
424 Centre St.
Shaunavon, SK S0N 2M0
Tel: 306-297-3888; *Fax:* 306-297-2128
Souris
PO Box 927
25 Crescent Ave. West
Souris, MB R0K 2C0
Tel: 204-483-3903; *Fax:* 204-483-2489
Sudbury
1970 Paris St.
Sudbury, ON P3E 3C8
Tel: 705-523-0272; *Fax:* 705-523-8454
Toll-Free: 800-581-7510
Surrey
#316, 5455 - 152nd St.
Surrey, BC V3S 5A5
Tel: 604-574-7211; *Fax:* 778-571-3549
Toll-Free: 888-574-7211
Swift Current
50 - 1st Ave. NE
Swift Current, SK S9H 4W4
Tel: 306-773-8375; *Fax:* 306-773-7735
Toll-Free: 877-500-0762
Taber
4713 - 55th St.
Taber, AB T1G 1W6
Tel: 403-223-3581; *Fax:* 403-223-8695
Thunder Bay
#210, 1205 Amber Dr.
Thunder Bay, ON P7B 6M4
Tel: 807-623-2141; *Fax:* 807-622-1282
Toronto - Richmond Street
#300, 111 Richmond St. West
Toronto, ON M5H 2G4
Tel: 416-596-1711; *Fax:* 416-596-7894
Toll-Free: 877-251-2922
Toronto - Evans Ave.
701 Evans Ave., 8th Fl.
Toronto, ON M9C 1A3
Tel: 416-626-6000; *Fax:* 416-626-8650

Vancouver
PO Box 49148
#2300, 1055 Dunsmuir St.
Vancouver, BC V7X 1J1
Tel: 604-685-8408; *Fax:* 604-685-8594
Toll-Free: 877-688-8408
Vernon
#100, 2903 - 35th Ave.
Vernon, BC V1T 2S7
Tel: 778-475-5678; *Fax:* 778-475-5618
Toll-Free: 877-898-2580
Virden
PO Box 670
233 Queen St. West
Virden, MB R0M 2C0 Canada
Tel: 204-748-1340; *Fax:* 204-748-3294
Waterloo
554 Weber St. North
Waterloo, ON N2L 5C6
Tel: 519-725-7700; *Fax:* 519-725-7708
Toll-Free: 866-464-0740
Waterloo - Union St.
149 Union St. East
Waterloo, ON N2L 1C4
Tel: 519-746-3111; *Fax:* 519-746-8502
Toll-Free: 866-746-7465
Weyburn
#301, 117 - 3rd St. NE
Weyburn, SK S4H 0W3
Tel: 306-842-8915; *Fax:* 306-842-1966
Winnipeg
#2500, 201 Portage Ave.
Winnipeg, MB R3B 3K6
Tel: 204-336-6167; *Fax:* 204-772-9687
Toll-Free: 877-500-0795

Welch LLP
151 Slater St., 12th Fl.
Ottawa, ON K1P 5H3
Tel: 613-236-9191; *Fax:* 613-236-8258
www.welchllp.com
Social Media: www.youtube.com/user/WelchLLP; www.facebook.com/136200309743763; twitter.com/welchllp; www.linkedin.com/company/welch-llp
Former Name: Welch & Company LLP
Ownership: An independent member firm of BKR International, New York, USA
Year Founded: 1918
Number of Employees: 200
Profile: The firm serves business, government, & not-for-profit clients. Taxation, accounting, auditing, personal financial planning & wealth management services are provided.
Partners:
Micheal Burch, CPA, CA, CFP, Managing Partner, Ottawa; mburch@welchllp.com
Branches:
Belleville
525 Dundas St. East
Belleville, ON K8N 1G4
Tel: 613-966-2844; *Fax:* 613-966-2206
Campbellford
PO Box 1209
57 Bridge St. East
Campbellford, ON K0L 1L0
Tel: 705-653-3194; *Fax:* 705-653-1703
Cornwall
36 Second St. East
Cornwall, ON K6H 1Y3
Tel: 613-932-4953; *Fax:* 613-932-1731
Gatineau
101, 259, boul St-Joseph
Gatineau, QC J8Z 6T1
Tel: 819-771-7381; *Fax:* 819-771-3089
Napanee
36 Bridge St. East
Napanee, ON K7R 1J8
Tel: 613-354-2169; *Fax:* 613-354-2160
Pembroke
PO Box 757
270 Lake St.
Pembroke, ON K8A 6X9
Tel: 613-735-1021; *Fax:* 613-735-2071
Picton
290 Main St.
Picton, ON K0K 2T0
Tel: 613-476-3283; *Fax:* 613-476-1627
Renfrew
101 Raglan St. North
Renfrew, ON K7V 1N7
Tel: 613-432-8399; *Fax:* 613-432-9154
Toronto
#530, 36 Toronto St.
Toronto, ON M5C 2C5
Tel: 647-288-9200; *Fax:* 647-288-7600
Trenton
67 Ontario St.
Trenton, ON K8V 2G8
Tel: 613-392-1287; *Fax:* 613-392-5456
Tweed
PO Box 807
63 Victoria St. North
Tweed, ON K0K 3J0
Tel: 613-478-5051; *Fax:* 613-478-3069

Accounting Firms by Province

Alberta

Airdrie: **Padgett Business Services Airdrie**
#230, 52 Gateway Dr. NE
Airdrie, AB T4B 0J6
Tel: 403-948-7759
padgett.calgary@nucleus.com
www.padgettbusinesscalgary.ca

Calgary: **ALW Partners LLP Chartered Accountants**
#100, 129 - 17 Ave. NE
Calgary, AB T2E 1L7
Tel: 403-230-2454; *Fax:* 403-276-2815
www.alw.ca

Calgary: **Arthur O. Solheim, LLP**
#102, 811 Manning Rd. NE
Calgary, AB T2E 7L4
Tel: 403-235-2040; *Fax:* 403-272-8326
artsolheim@solheim.ca
www.solheim.ca

Calgary: **Bernard Martens Professional Corp.**
38 West Springs Gate SW
Calgary, AB T3H 4P5
Tel: 403-255-1262; *Fax:* 403-640-4652
Social Media: plus.google.com/115476666975210250093

Calgary: **Brander & Company**
5520 - 2nd Street SW
Calgary, AB T2H 0G9
Tel: 403-920-0467; *Fax:* 403-920-0383
www.branderco.ca
Other Contact Information: Alternate Phone: 403-247-0407

Calgary: **Brown Economic Consulting Inc.**
#216, 5718 - 1A St. SW
Calgary, AB T2H 0E8
Tel: 403-571-0115; *Fax:* 403-571-0932
Toll-Free: 800-301-8801
help@browneconomic.com
www.browneconomic.com
Other Contact Information: Help Line, Toll-Free Phone: 1-888-232-2778

Calgary: **Buchanan Barry LLP**
#800, 840 - 6th Ave. SW
Calgary, AB T2P 3E5
Tel: 403-262-2116; *Fax:* 403-265-0845
mailbox@buchananbarry.ca
www.buchananbarry.ca
Other Contact Information: Alternate E-mail: admin@buchananbarry.ca

Calgary: **Bultmann & Company**
#117, 5723 - 10th St. NE
Calgary, AB T2E 8W7
Tel: 403-250-8522; *Fax:* 403-250-8524
bultco.ca

Calgary: **Catalyst LLP**
#250, 200 Quarry Park Blvd. SE
Calgary, AB T2C 5E3
Tel: 403-296-0082; *Fax:* 403-296-0088
www.thecatalystgroup.ca
Social Media: www.facebook.com/183466335036020; twitter.com/Catalyst_yyc

Calgary: **Collins Barrow Calgary LLP**
First Alberta Place
#1400, 777 - 8th Ave. SW
Calgary, AB T2P 3R5
Tel: 403-298-1500; *Fax:* 403-298-5814
calgary@collinsbarrow.com
www.collinsbarrow.com/en/calgary-alberta

Calgary: **CompassTAX Chartered Accountants**
#510, 906 - 12th Ave. SW
Calgary, AB T2R 1K7
Tel: 403-531-2200; *Fax:* 403-263-1826
Toll-Free: 866-531-2281
www.compasstax.ca

Calgary: **Daunheimer Lynch Anderson LLP**
6620 Crowchild Trail SW
Calgary, AB T3E 5R8
Tel: 403-217-5925; *Fax:* 403-217-5934
Toll-Free: 888-452-5925
info@dlallp.com
www.dlallp.com

Calgary: **David Wallace Professional Corp.**
#205, 259 Midpark Way SE
Calgary, AB T2X 1M2
Tel: 403-254-0183
www.davidwallaceprofessionalcorp.ca

Calgary: **Don Akins Chartered Accountant**
431B - 41st Ave. NE
Calgary, AB T2E 2N4
Tel: 403-777-0858; *Fax:* 403-777-0385
da.ofc@donakinsca.com
www.donakinsca.com

Calgary: **Donald A. Mackay & Associates**
#203, 20 Sunpark Plaza SE
Calgary, AB T2X 3T2
Tel: 403-256-8118; *Fax:* 403-256-8103
www.donmackay.ca

Calgary: **D.W. Robart Professional Corporation**
#1800, 540 - 5th Ave. SW
Calgary, AB T2P 0M2
Tel: 403-266-2611; *Fax:* 403-265-8626

Calgary: **Flood & Associates Consulting Ltd.**
840 - 6 Ave. SW
Calgary, AB T2P 3E5
Tel: 403-263-1523; *Fax:* 403-263-1524

Calgary: **Garrett Gray Chartered Accountants**
Parkside Place
#920, 602 - 12 Ave. SW
Calgary, AB T2R 1J3
Tel: 403-806-2850; *Fax:* 403-806-2854
info@garrettgray.com
www.garrettgray.com

Calgary: **Grant Thornton Alger Inc.**
#900, 833 - 4th Ave. SW
Calgary, AB T2P 3T5
Tel: 403-310-8888; *Fax:* 403-260-2571
Toll-Free: 310-8888
www.alger.ca

Calgary: **Hamilton & Rosenthal Chartered Accountants**
Mission Square Building
#210, 2424 - 4 St. SW
Calgary, AB T2S 2T4
Tel: 403-266-2175; *Fax:* 403-514-2211
www.hamrose.com

Calgary: **James Yee & Company Certified General Accountant**
#10, 1015 Centre St. North
Calgary, AB T2E 2P8
Tel: 403-277-7172
info@jamesyee.ca
www.jamesyee.ca

Calgary: **John J. Geib, Chartered Accountant**
Southcentre Executive Tower
#405, 11012 Macleod Trail SE
Calgary, AB T2J 6A5
Tel: 403-259-4519; *Fax:* 403-255-0745
info@geibco.com
www.geibco.com

Calgary: **Kapasi & Associates Chartered Accountant**
#940, 396 - 11th Ave. SW
Calgary, AB T2R 0C5
Tel: 403-228-4974; *Fax:* 403-228-6823
www.kapasi.ca

***Calgary:* Kenway Mack Slusarchuk Stewart LLP (KMSS)**
#1500, 333 - 11 Ave. SW
Calgary, AB T2R 1L9
Tel: 403-233-7750; *Fax:* 403-266-5267
info@kmss.ca
www.kmss.ca

***Calgary:* Kirk Wormley Chartered Accountant**
#806, 7015 Macleod Trail SW
Calgary, AB T2H 2K6
Tel: 403-266-5607; *Fax:* 403-201-0248
www.kirkwormley.ca

***Calgary:* Masone & Company Ltd.**
111 - 22nd Ave. NE
Calgary, AB T2E 1T4
Tel: 403-204-1544
www.masoneandcompany.com
Social Media: www.facebook.com/masoneandcompany; twitter.com/Masoneandco

***Calgary:* The Matthews Group LLP**
#804, 322 - 11 Ave. SW
Calgary, AB T2R 0C5
Tel: 403-229-0066; *Fax:* 403-229-2817
info@matthewsgrp.com
www.matthewsgrp.com

***Calgary:* Mitchell-Jones Taxation Services Inc. (MJT)**
#350, 5010 Richard Rd. SW
Calgary, AB T3E 6L1
Tel: 403-265-8545; *Fax:* 403-265-8554
clientinfo@mjtaxation.com
www.mjtaxation.com

***Calgary:* PricewaterhouseCoopers LLP, Canada - Calgary**
Suncor Energy Centre, East Tower
#3100, 111 - 5th Ave. SW
Calgary, AB T2P 5L3
Tel: 403-509-7500; *Fax:* 403-781-1825
www.pwc.com/ca

***Calgary:* PROACT Chartered Accountants**
#408, 1324 - 17 Ave. SW
Calgary, AB T2T 5S8
Tel: 587-315-3887
www.businessaccountantcalgaryab.ca

***Calgary:* Prospera Chartered Accountants**
Willow Park Centre
#404, 10325 Bonaventure Dr. SE
Calgary, AB T2J 7E4
Tel: 403-252-5858; *Fax:* 403-259-8416
info@partnersinprosperity.ca
www.partnersinprosperity.ca

***Calgary:* Quadrant Chartered Accountants & Business Valuators**
816 - 13th Ave. SW
Calgary, AB T2R 0L2
Tel: 403-457-4477; *Fax:* 403-457-4059
info@quadrantaccounting.ca
quadrantaccounting.ca

***Calgary:* Quon & Associates, & Anchor Accounting Services Ltd.**
3700 - 19th St. NE, Bay 1
Calgary, AB T2E 6V2
Tel: 403-250-5111; *Fax:* 403-291-0412
service@quonassociates.com
www.quonassociates.com
Social Media: plus.google.com/+Quonassociates; www.facebook.com/QuonAssociates; twitter.com/QuonAssociates

***Calgary:* Roberts & Company Professional Accountants LLP**
#102, 2411 - 4th St. NW
Calgary, AB T2M 2Z8
Tel: 403-282-8889; *Fax:* 403-282-5880
www.robertsco.ca

***Calgary:* The Small Business Group of Companies**
60 High St. SE
Calgary, AB T2Z 3T8
Tel: 403-257-6235; *Fax:* 403-257-6258
Toll-Free: 855-489-3546
info@smallbusinesscompanies.ca
smallbusinesscompanies.ca
Social Media: www.youtube.com/user/smallbusinesscompany; www.facebook.com/smallbusinesscalgary

***Calgary:* Stephen R. Sefcik Professional Corp.**
#212, 20 Sunpark Plaza SE
Calgary, AB T2X 3T2
Tel: 403-255-6296
www.stephenrsefcik.ca

***Calgary:* Thompson Penner & Lo LLP**
#601, 2535 - 3 Ave. SE
Calgary, AB T2A 7W5
Tel: 403-283-1088; *Fax:* 403-283-1044
Toll-Free: 877-283-1088
tpl@thompsonpennerlo.com
thompsonpennerlo.com

***Calgary:* Vanessa A. Brown & Company**
#300, 508 - 24th Ave. SW
Calgary, AB T2S 0K4
Tel: 403-229-1996
info@vabrown.ca
www.vabrown.ca

***Calgary:* Vertefeuille Rempel Chartered Accountants**
#401, 304 - 8 Ave. SW
Calgary, AB T2P 1C2
Tel: 403-294-0733; *Fax:* 403-294-0734
Toll-Free: 877-794-0733
www.vertrempel.com

***Cochrane:* W. Callaway Professional Corporation**
PO Box 61
Site 5, RR#1
Cochrane, AB T4C 1A1
Tel: 403-932-5433; *Fax:* 403-932-5577
www.wcallaway.com

***Edmonton:* Bernhard Brinkmann Chartered Accountant**
PO Box 82090, Yellowbird Stn. Yellowbird
Edmonton, AB T6N 1B7
Tel: 780-244-3344
bhbrinkmann@brinkmann.ca
www.brinkmann.ca

***Edmonton:* Bryan Mason & Co.**
#200, 10004 - 79th Ave.
Edmonton, AB T6E 1R5
Tel: 780-463-8716; *Fax:* 780-463-7330
bryanmasonco.com

***Edmonton:* Collins Barrow Edmonton LLP**
Commerce Place
#2380, 10155 - 102 St. NW
Edmonton, AB T5J 4G8
Tel: 780-428-1522; *Fax:* 780-425-8189
edmonton@collinsbarrow.com
www.collinsbarrow.com/en/edmonton-alberta

***Edmonton:* Givens LLP**
West Chambers
#201, 12220 Stony Plain Rd.
Edmonton, AB T5N 3Y4
Tel: 780-482-7337; *Fax:* 780-482-7423
givens@porterhetu.com
www.givens.ca
Other Contact Information: Alternate E-mail: edmonton@givens.ca
Social Media: www.facebook.com/Givensaccounting

***Edmonton:* Hawkings Epp Dumont Chartered Accountants**
Mayfield Square I
10476 Mayfield Rd.
Edmonton, AB T5P 4P4
Tel: 780-489-9606; *Fax:* 780-484-9689
Toll-Free: 877-489-9606
www.hawkings.com

***Edmonton:* King & Company**
#1201, Energy Sq.
10109 - 106 St.
Edmonton, AB T5J 3L7
Tel: 780-423-2437; *Fax:* 780-426-5861
www.kingco.ca

***Edmonton:* Kingston Ross Pasnak LLP**
9Triple8 Jasper
#1500, 9888 Jasper Ave.
Edmonton, AB T5J 5C6
Tel: 780-424-3000; *Fax:* 780-429-4817
www.krpgroup.com

***Edmonton:* Koehli Wickenberg Chartered Accountants**
9771 - 54th Ave.
Edmonton, AB T6E 5J4
Tel: 780-466-6204; *Fax:* 780-466-6262
info@kwbllp.com
www.kwbllp.com
Social Media: www.facebook.com/KWBEdmonton; twitter.com/KWB_Edmonton

***Edmonton:* Liu & Associates LLP**
#300, 10534 - 124th St. NW
Edmonton, AB T5N 1S1
Tel: 780-429-1047; *Fax:* 780-423-5076
Toll-Free: 866-212-1318
liuandassociates.com
Other Contact Information: Calgary Fax: 403-261-6869
Social Media: www.facebook.com/liuandassociates; twitter.com/LiuLLP

***Edmonton:* Padgett Business Services Edmonton NW**
12203 - 107th Ave.
Edmonton, AB T5M 1Y9
Tel: 780-482-7297
padgettnw.com
Social Media: www.facebook.com/SmallBizProsCanada

***Edmonton:* Padgett Edmonton South**
3612 - 106th St. NW
Edmonton, AB T6J 1A4
Tel: 780-434-7146; *Fax:* 780-434-7697
padgettedmonton.ca

***Edmonton:* PricewaterhouseCoopers LLP, Canada - Edmonton**
Toronto-Dominion Tower, Edmonton City Centre
#1501, 10088 - 102 Ave. NW
Edmonton, AB T5J 3N5
Tel: 780-441-6700; *Fax:* 780-441-6776
www.pwc.com/ca

***Edmonton:* Romanovsky & Associates, Chartered Accountants**
10260 - 112 St.
Edmonton, AB T5K 1M4
Tel: 780-447-5830; *Fax:* 780-451-6291
Toll-Free: 800-861-5830
www.romanovsky.com

***Edmonton:* SVS Group LLP**
#100, 17010 - 103 Ave.
Edmonton, AB T5S 1K7
Tel: 780-486-3357; *Fax:* 780-486-3320
www.svsgroup.ca

***High River:* Muth & Company**
PO Box 5039
318 Centre St. SE
High River, AB T1V 1M3
Tel: 403-652-4272
muth_and_company@porterhetu.com
www.porterhetu.com

***Leduc:* Luchak Wright Wnuk Chartered Accountants**
4716 - 51 Ave.
Leduc, AB T9E 6Y8
Tel: 780-986-8383; *Fax:* 780-986-4499
Toll-Free: 888-986-8383
lww@lwwca.com
www.lwwca.com

***Lethbridge:* Blanchette Van Dyk Valgardson Logue (BVVL)**
#801B, 3 Ave. South
Lethbridge, AB T1J 0H8
Tel: 403-317-4500; *Fax:* 403-317-4501
admin@bvvl.ca
www.bvvl.ca

***Lethbridge:* Young Parkyn McNab LLP (YPM)**
#100, 530 - 8 St. South
Lethbridge, AB T1J 2J8
Tel: 403-382-6800; *Fax:* 403-327-8990
Toll-Free: 800-665-5034
www.ypm.ca
Social Media: twitter.com/ypmCAs

***Red Deer:* Collins Barrow Red Deer LLP**
Collins Barrow Centre
#300, 5010 - 43 St.
Red Deer, AB T4N 6H2
Tel: 403-342-5541; *Fax:* 403-347-3766
reddeer@collinsbarrow.com
www.collinsbarrow.com/en/red-deer-alberta

Red Deer: **Heywood Holmes & Partners LLP**
#500, 4911 - 51st St.
Red Deer, AB T4N 6V4
Tel: 403-347-2226; *Fax:* 403-343-6140
Toll-Free: 877-347-2226
office@hhpca.net
www.heywoodholmes.com
Social Media: twitter.com/HeywoodHolmes

Slave Lake: **Nash Giroux, LLP**
PO Box 129
4 Devonshire Rd. North
Slave Lake, AB T0G 2A0
Tel: 780-849-3977
nash_giroux@porterhetu.com
www.nashgirouxllp.com

St Paul: **Desjardins & Company**
PO Box 1600
4925 - 50 Ave.
St Paul, AB T0A 3A0
Tel: 780-645-5516; *Fax:* 780-645-6010
office@desjardins-co.com
www.desjardins-co.com

Stettler: **Gitzel & Company**
PO Box 460
4912 - 51 St.
Stettler, AB T0C 2L0
Tel: 403-742-4431; *Fax:* 403-742-1266
Toll-Free: 877-742-4431
gitzel.ca

Sundre: **Valerie L. Burrell Prof. Corp.**
PO Box 1963
#201, 101 - 6 St. SW
Sundre, AB T0M 1X0
Tel: 403-638-3116; *Fax:* 403-638-9166
info@valbpc.com
www.valbpc.com

Vegreville: **Wilde & Company Chartered Accountants**
PO Box 70
4902 - 50th St.
Vegreville, AB T9C 1R1
Tel: 780-632-3673; *Fax:* 780-632-6133
Toll-Free: 800-808-0998
office@wildeandco.com
www.wildeandco.com
Social Media: www.facebook.com/173231086093970

Wainwright: **Hall & Company**
219 - 10th St.
Wainwright, AB T9W 1N7
Tel: 780-842-6106; *Fax:* 780-842-5540
Toll-Free: 888-842-6106
www.hallco.ca

British Columbia

Burnaby: **Barkman & Tanaka**
Lougheed Plaza
#225, 9600 Cameron St.
Burnaby, BC V3J 7N3
Tel: 604-421-2591; *Fax:* 604-421-1171
barkman-tanaka.com

Burnaby: **Kanester Johal Chartered Accountants**
#208, 3993 Henning Dr.
Burnaby, BC V5C 6P7
Tel: 604-451-8300; *Fax:* 604-451-8301
info@kjca.com
www.kjca.com

Burnaby: **Kemp Harvey Goodison Hamilton Inc.**
#103, 4430 Halifax St.
Burnaby, BC V5C 5R4
Tel: 604-291-1470; *Fax:* 604-291-0264
Burnaby@khgcga.com
www.khgcga.com/index.php/offices/burnaby
Social Media: www.facebook.com/152379991466319; twitter.com/KempHarveyGroup

Burns Lake: **M. McPhail & Associates Inc.**
PO Box 597
Burns Lake, BC V0J 1E0
Tel: 250-692-7595; *Fax:* 250-692-3872
mcphail@mcphailcga.com
www.mcphailcga.com
Social Media: www.facebook.com/MMcPhailAssociatesInc

Campbell River: **Chase Sekulich Chartered Accountants**
#101, 400 Tenth Ave.
Campbell River, BC V9W 4E3
Tel: 250-287-8331; *Fax:* 250-287-7224
Toll-Free: 866-317-8331
office@chasesekulich.com
www.chasesekulich.com
Other Contact Information: Bankruptcy URL: www.bankruptcytrusteebc.ca

Campbell River: **Eidsvik & Co.**
#303, 1100 Island Hwy.
Campbell River, BC V9W 8C6
Tel: 250-286-6629; *Fax:* 250-286-6779

Castlegar: **Craig M. Gutwald Inc.**
880 Waterloo Rd.
Castlegar, BC V1N 4K8
Tel: 250-365-0434; *Fax:* 250-365-0469
www.gutwald.ca

Coquitlam: **Kemp Harvey Kok de Roca-Chan Inc.**
#210, 1140 Austin Ave.
Coquitlam, BC V3K 3P5
Tel: 604-937-3444; *Fax:* 604-937-3422
www.khgcga.com/index.php/offices/port-coquitlam
Social Media: www.facebook.com/152379991466319; twitter.com/KempHarveyGroup

Duncan: **Hayes Stewart Little & Co.**
823 Canada Ave.
Duncan, BC V9L 1V2
Tel: 250-746-4406; *Fax:* 250-746-1950
hslco@hslco.com
www.hslco.com

Duncan: **Palmer Leslie Chartered Professional Accountants**
#301, 394 Duncan St.
Duncan, BC V9L 3W4
Tel: 250-748-1426; *Fax:* 250-748-2805
Toll-Free: 800-818-5703
www.palmerleslie.ca

Grand Forks: **Kemp Harvey Burch Kientz Inc.**
PO Box 2020
619 Central Ave.
Grand Forks, BC V0H 1H0
Tel: 250-442-2121; *Fax:* 250-442-5825
GrandForks@khgcga.com
www.khgcga.com/index.php/offices/grand-forks
Social Media: www.facebook.com/152379991466319; twitter.com/KempHarveyGroup

Kelowna: **Chun & Company**
#202, 3320 Richter St.
Kelowna, BC V1W 4V5
Tel: 250-860-8687
www.chun.ca

Kelowna: **Wahl & Associates**
#203, 1441 Ellis St.
Kelowna, BC V1Y 2A3
Tel: 250-762-3362; *Fax:* 250-762-3409
info@wahlcga.com
www.wahlcga.com

Maple Ridge: **Choquette & Company Accounting Group**
10662 - 240A St.
Maple Ridge, BC V2W 2B1
Tel: 604-463-8202; *Fax:* 604-463-8210
Toll-Free: 800-667-9254
www.choquetteco.com
Social Media: plus.google.com/+AndreChoquette; www.facebook.com/ChoquetteCompany; twitter.com/ChoquetteCo

Nanaimo: **Church Pickard Chartered Accountants**
25 Cavan St.
Nanaimo, BC V9R 2T9
Tel: 250-754-6396; *Fax:* 250-754-8177
Toll-Free: 866-754-6396
mail@churchpickard.com
www.churchpickard.com

Nanaimo: **KMA Chartered Accountants Ltd.**
5107 Somerset Dr., #C
Nanaimo, BC V9T 2K5
Tel: 250-758-5557; *Fax:* 250-758-5720
www.kmacpa.ca

Nanaimo: **Robert F. Fischer & Company Inc., C.G.A.**
#13, 327 Prideaux St.
Nanaimo, BC V9R 2N4
Tel: 250-753-7287; *Fax:* 250-753-7453

Nelson: **Carmichael, Toews, Irving Inc.**
247 Baker St.
Nelson, BC V1L 4H4
Tel: 250-354-4451; *Fax:* 250-354-4427
admin@cti-cga.com
www.cti-cga.com

New Westminster: **McDonald & Co.**
631 Carnavon St.
New Westminster, BC V3M 1E3
Tel: 604-521-8885; *Fax:* 604-521-3611

North Vancouver: **Brager & Associates Certified General Accountant**
Griffin Centre
#210, 901 - 3rd St. West
North Vancouver, BC V7P 3P9
Tel: 604-998-4069; *Fax:* 604-243-6990
bragercga.com

North Vancouver: **Clearline Chartered Accountants**
#203, 1133 Lonsdale Ave.
North Vancouver, BC V7M 2H4
Tel: 604-639-0909; *Fax:* 778-375-3109
we_are@clearlineca.ca
www.clearlineca.ca
Social Media: twitter.com/ClearlineCA

North Vancouver: **Gray & Associates, Chartered Accountants**
#201, 1075 West 1st St.
North Vancouver, BC V7P 3T4
Tel: 604-990-0550; *Fax:* 604-990-0509
Toll-Free: 800-990-0550
info@grayandassociates.ca
grayandassociates.ca

North Vancouver: **J. Casperson & Associates Ltd.**
#117, 3721 Delbrook Ave.
North Vancouver, BC V7N 3Z4
Tel: 604-983-2113; *Fax:* 604-983-2114
jindra@jcasperson.com
www.jcasperson.com

Osoyoos: **Kemp Harvey Kemp - Osoyoos**
8901 Main St.
Osoyoos, BC V0H 1V0
Tel: 250-495-3223; *Fax:* 250-495-3559
Toll-Free: 888-9850-5595
Osoyoos@khgcga.com
www.khgcga.com/index.php/offices/osoyoos
Social Media: www.facebook.com/152379991466319; twitter.com/KempHarveyGroup

Penticton: **Harvey Lister & Webb Incorporated**
502 Ellis St.
Penticton, BC V2A 4M3
Tel: 250-492-8821; *Fax:* 250-492-8288
info@harveylisterwebb.com
www.harveylisterwebb.com

Penticton: **Kemp Harvey Kemp - Penticton**
445 Ellis St.
Penticton, BC V2A 4M1
Tel: 250-492-8800; *Fax:* 250-492-6921
Penticton@khgcga.com
www.khgcga.com/index.php/offices/penticton
Social Media: www.facebook.com/152379991466319; twitter.com/KempHarveyGroup

Penticton: **White Kennedy**
#201, 99 Padmore Ave. East
Penticton, BC V2A 7H7
Tel: 250-493-0600; *Fax:* 250-493-4709
penticton@whitekennedy.com
www.whitekennedy.com

Port Moody: **Gregory & Associates**
#402, 130 Brew St.
Port Moody, BC V3H 0E3
Tel: 604-939-2929; *Fax:* 604-936-4002
gregorywhittle.ca
Social Media: www.facebook.com/356687374350264

Prince George: **PricewaterhouseCoopers LLP, Canada - Prince George**
#10, 556 Nortn Nechako Rd.
Prince George, BC V2K 1A1
Tel: 250-564-2515; *Fax:* 250-562-8722
www.pwc.com/ca

***Prince George:* Terlesky Braithwaite Janzen LLP**
#300, 180 Victoria St.
Prince George, BC V2L 2J2
Tel: 250-564-2014; *Fax:* 250-564-5613
Toll-Free: 888-564-2014
tbjpg@tbjcga.com
www.tbjcga.com

***Revelstoke:* Collins Barrow Bow Valley LLP**
PO Box 2910
#201, 200 Campbell Ave.
Revelstoke, BC V0E 2S0
Tel: 250-837-4400; *Fax:*250-837-4494
revelstoke@collinsbarrow.com
www.collinsbarrow.com/en/cbi/contact-us/rev elstoke-british-columbia

***Richmond:* Bruce Dunn & Company Inc. Chartered Accountants**
#200, 5760 Minoru Blvd.
Richmond, BC V6X 2A9
Tel: 604-241-8824; *Fax:*604-241-8800
info@brucedunn.ca
wwwbrucedunn.ca

***Richmond:* Campbell Saunders, Ltd.**
Mazda Bldg.
#6080, 8171 Ackroyd Rd.
Richmond, BC V6X 3K1
Tel: 604-821-9882; *Fax* 604-821-9870
www.csvan.com

***Richmond:* Greig Sheppard Ltd.**
5090 - 8171 Ackroyd Rd.
Richmond, BC V6X 3K1
Tel: 604-270-7601; *Fax:* 604-270-3314
cga@greigsheppard.com
www.greigsheppard.com

***Richmond:* Jerry's Accounting Ltd.**
#530, 130 - 8191 Westminster Hwy.
Richmond, BC V6X 1A7
Tel: 604-273-7789
jerryky@shaw.ca
www.jerryaccounting.com

***Richmond:* Sunny Sun & Associates Inc.**
#708, 6081 No. 3 Rd.
Richmond, BC V6Y 2B2
Tel: 604-270-4610; *Fax:* 604-270-4618
info@bcsun.ca
www.sunnycga.com
Other Contact Information: Alternate Phone: 604-270-4613; 604-270-4688
Social Media: www.facebook.com/413258005410486

***Surrey:* Heming, Wyborn & Grewal**
#200, 17618 - 58th Ave.
Surrey, BC V3S 1L3
Tel: 604-576-9121; *Fax:* 604-576-2890
hwgca@hwgca.com
www.hwgca.com

***Surrey:* KNV Chartered Accountants LLP**
#200, 15300 Croydon Dr.
Surrey, BC V3S 0Z5
Tel: 604-536-7614; *Fax* 604-538-5356
Toll-Free: 800-761-7772
www.mnp.ca

***Surrey:* Luckett Wenman & Associates (LWA)**
#204, 10252 City Pkwy.
Surrey, BC V3T 4C2
Tel: 604-584-3566; *Fax:* 604-584-0629
Toll-Free: 866-584-3566
contact@lwatax.com
www.lwatax.com
Social Media: twitter.com/lwatax

***Surrey:* PricewaterhouseCoopers LLP, Canada - Surrey**
#1400, 13450 - 102nd Ave.
Surrey, BC V3T 5X3
Tel: 604-806-7000; *Fax:* 604-806-7806
www.pwc.com/ca

***Surrey:* Sharma & Associates**
#1, 13018 - 84th Ave.
Surrey, BC V3W 1L2
Tel: 604-597-5612; *Fax:* 604-590-5808
info@sharmacga.com
www.sharmacga.com

***Surrey:* Van Wensem & Associates**
#201, 19292 - 60th Ave.
Surrey, BC V3S 3M2
Tel: 604-510-4900
www.smallbiztax.ca

***Sydney:* Gary A Porter, CA**
10308 Bowerbank Rd.
Sydney, BC V8L 3L3
Tel: 613-918-0486
www.porterhetu.com

***Terrace:* Demers & Associates**
4734 Park Ave.
Terrace, BC V8G 1W1
Tel: 250-638-8705; *Fax:* 250-638-0600
demers@khgcga.com
www.demerscga.com

***Terrace:* Kemp Harvey Demers Inc.**
4734 Park Ave.
Terrace, BC V8G 1W1
Tel: 250-638-8705; *Fax:* 250-638-0600
Terrace@khgcga.com
www.khgcga.com/index.php/offices/terrace
Social Media: www.facebook.com/152379991466319; twitter.com/KempHarveyGroup

***Vancouver:* BBA Accounting Group Inc.**
PO Box 11554
#1760, 650 West Georgia St.
Vancouver, BC V6B 4N8
Tel: 604-685-9843; *Fax:* 604-685-9856
van@bbagroup.ca
www.bbagroup.ca

***Vancouver:* Bing C. Wong & Associates Ent. Ltd.**
124 East Pender St.
Vancouver, BC V6A 1T3
Tel: 604-682-7561; *Fax:* 604-682-7665
www.bcwaca.com

***Vancouver:* Brian C. Jang Inc.**
#300, 422 Richards St.
Vancouver, BC V6B 2Z4
Tel: 604-831-7893
bcj@brianjang.ca
brianjang.ca
Social Media: www.facebook.com/brianjangCA; twitter.com/brianjangCA

***Vancouver:* Buckley Dodds Parker LLP**
#1140, 1185 West Georgia St.
Vancouver, BC V6E 4E6
Tel: 604-688-7227; *Fax:* 604-681-7716
www.buckleydodds.com

***Vancouver:* Cawley, Curran, Wong & Associates**
601 West Broadway Ave., #M-9
Vancouver, BC V5Z 4C2
Tel: 604-731-1191; *Fax:* 604-731-3511
bcawley@cawley.ca
www.cawley.ca

***Vancouver:* Collins Barrow Vancouver**
Burrard Bldg.
#800, 1030 West Georgia St.
Vancouver, BC V6E 3B9
Tel: 604-685-0564; *Fax:* 604-685-2050
vancouver@collinsbarrow.com
www.collinsbarrow.com/en/vancouver-british-c olumbia

***Vancouver:* D+H Group LLP**
1333 West Broadway St., 10th Fl.
Vancouver, BC V6H 4C1
Tel: 604-731-5881; *Fax:* 604-731-9923
info@dhgroup.ca
www.dhgroup.ca
Social Media: www.facebook.com/37001994848; twitter.com/@dhgroup_recruit

***Vancouver:* Dale Matheson Carr-Hilton Labonte LLP**
#1500 & 1700, 1140 West Pender St.
Vancouver, BC V6E 4G1
Tel: 604-687-4747; *Fax:* 604-689-2778
www.dmcl.ca
Other Contact Information: 17th Floor, Fax: 604-687-4216
Social Media: www.facebook.com/118272074404

***Vancouver:* David Lin, Certified General Accountant**
5728 East Blvd.
Vancouver, BC V6M 4M4
Tel: 604-267-0381
www3.telus.net/davidlin

***Vancouver:* Davidson & Co.**
Pacific Centre
PO Box 10372
#1200, 609 Granville St.
Vancouver, BC V7Y 1G6
Tel: 604-687-0947; *Fax:* 607-687-6172
davidson@davidson-co.com
www.davidson-co.com
Social Media: www.facebook.com/DavidsonAndCompany

***Vancouver:* Desai & Associates**
#201, 5990 Fraser St.
Vancouver, BC V5W 2Z7
Tel: 604-321-9992; *Fax:* 604-321-9998
info@desaiassociates.ca
www.desaiassociates.ca

***Vancouver:* Equity Business Services Inc.**
#200, 1892 West Broadway
Vancouver, BC V6J 1Y9
Tel: 604-874-9080; *Fax:* 604-874-9080
www.equityinc.ca

***Vancouver:* Galloway Botteselle & Company (GBCO)**
Maple Place Professional Centre
#300, 2000 West 12th Ave.
Vancouver, BC V6J 2G2
Tel: 604-736-6581; *Fax:* 604-736-0152
vancouver@porterhetu.com
gbco.ca

***Vancouver:* Greenberg Associates**
North Office Tower, Oakridge Centre
#489, 650 West 41st Ave.
Vancouver, BC V5Z 2M9
Tel: 604-264-5170; *Fax:* 604-264-5101
admin@greenbergassociates.ca
greenbergassociates.ca

***Vancouver:* Horizon Chartered Accountants Ltd.**
#106, 1008 Beach Ave.
Vancouver, BC V6E 1T7
Tel: 604-697-7777; *Fax:* 604-697-7778
support@horizonca.ca
www.horizonca.ca
Other Contact Information: Alt. Phone: 778-654-6851; URL: www.vancouverprofessionalaccounting.ca

***Vancouver:* James Stafford Chartered Accountants**
#350, 1111 Melville St.
Vancouver, BC V6E 3V6
Tel: 604-669-0711; *Fax:* 604-669-0754
www.jamesstafford.ca

***Vancouver:* Lam Lo Nishio Chartered Accountants**
659-G Moberly Rd.
Vancouver, BC V5Z 4B2
Tel: 604-872-8883; *Fax:* 604-872-8889
info@lamlonishio.ca
www.lamlonishio.ca

***Vancouver:* Lancaster & David, Chartered Accountants**
PO Box 10122, Pacific Centre Stn. Pacific Centre
#510, 701 West Georgia St.
Vancouver, BC V7Y 1C6
Tel: 604-717-5526; *Fax:* 604-717-5560
Toll-Free: 877-668-5263
admin@lancasteranddavid.ca
www.lancasteranddavid.ca

***Vancouver:* Lohn Caulder LLP**
1500 West Georgia St., 3rd Fl.
Vancouver, BC V6G 2Z6
Tel: 604-687-5444; *Fax:* 604-688-7228
info@lohncaulder.com
www.lohncaulder.com
Social Media: www.facebook.com/LohnCaulderLLP; twitter.com/LohnCaulderLLP

***Vancouver:* Maharaj & Company Chartered Accountants**
#210, 1080 Mainland St.
Vancouver, BC V6B 2T4
Tel: 604-270-2703; *Fax:* 604-435-5329
www.mhrj.com
Social Media: www.facebook.com/maharajco; twitter.com/maharajco

Vancouver: **Manning Elliott**
1050 West Pender St., 11th Fl.
Vancouver, BC V6J 3S7
Tel: 604-714-3600; *Fax:* 604-714-3669
info@manningelliott.com
www.manningelliott.com
Social Media: plus.google.com/+Manningelliott; www.youtube.com/channel/UCuy1_ri_mjUxl4A-IwBPuqQ; www.facebook.com/ManningElliott; twitter.com/ManningElliott

Vancouver: **McLean Bartok Edwards**
#840, 475 West Georgia St.
Vancouver, BC V6B 4M9
Tel: 604-683-4533; *Fax:* 604-683-2585
info@mcleanbartok.ca
www.mcleanbartok.ca

Vancouver: **Mew & Company Chartered Accountants**
#418, 788 Beatty St.
Vancouver, BC V6B 2M1
Tel: 604-688-8189; *Fax:* 604-688-9192
www.mewco.ca
Social Media: www.facebook.com/170470313690; twitter.com/mewandco

Vancouver: **Midland Chartered Accountants**
#605, 815 Hornby St.
Vancouver, BC V6Z 2E6
Tel: 604-681-8835
info@midlandca.com
midlandca.com

Vancouver: **N.I. Cameron Inc.**
#303, 475 Howe St.
Vancouver, BC V6C 2B3
Tel: 604-669-9631; *Fax:* 604-669-1848
info@nicameroninc.com
www.nicameroninc.com

Vancouver: **NTA, Chartered Accountants**
#540, 475 West Georgia St.
Vancouver, BC V6B 4M9
Tel: 604-684-8221; *Fax:* 604-684-8299
ntacan.com

Vancouver: **PricewaterhouseCoopers LLP, Canada - Vancouver**
PricewaterhouseCoopers Place
#700, 250 Howe St.
Vancouver, BC V6C 3S7
Tel: 604-806-7000; *Fax:* 604-806-7806
www.pwc.com/ca

Vancouver: **Quantum Accounting Services Inc.**
#110, 828 West 8th Ave.
Vancouver, BC V5Z 1E2
Tel: 604-662-8985; *Fax:* 604-662-8986
www.qas.bc.ca

Vancouver: **Renaissance Group Chartered Accountants Ltd.**
#1460, 1075 West Georgia St.
Vancouver, BC V6E 3C9
Tel: 604-629-9600; *Fax:* 604-629-9601
info@rgroupca.com
www.rgroupca.com

Vancouver: **Rolfe, Benson LLP Chartered Accountants**
#1500, 1090 West Georgia St.
Vancouver, BC V6E 3V7
Tel: 604-684-1101; *Fax:* 604-684-7937
admin@rolfebenson.com
www.rolfebenson.com

Vancouver: **Sandhu & Company, CGA**
#202, 5128 Victoria Dr.
Vancouver, BC V5P 3V2
Tel: 604-322-7576
info@sandhutax.com
www.sandhutax.com
Other Contact Information: Alt. URL: www.vancouverbcaccountingfirm.ca

Vancouver: **Smythe Ratcliffe LLP**
#700, 355 Burrard St.
Vancouver, BC V6C 2G8
Tel: 604-687-1231; *Fax:* 604-688-4675
reception@smytheratcliffe.com
www.smytheratcliffe.com
Other Contact Information: Alternate E-mail: info@smytheratcliffe.com
Social Media: www.facebook.com/SmytheRatcliffeLLP; twitter.com/smytheratcliffe

Vancouver: **Stan W. Lee Chartered Accountant**
North Tower
#628, 650 West 41st Ave.
Vancouver, BC V5Z 2M9
Tel: 604-291-6016; *Fax:* 604-291-2018
stan@stanwleeca.com
www.stanwleeca.com

Vancouver: **Strategex Group**
#210, 1075 West Georgia St.
Vancouver, BC V6E 3C9
Tel: 604-688-2355; *Fax:* 604-688-2315
www.strategexgroup.ca

Vancouver: **Theresa Ko, Chartered Accountant**
2066 Qualicum Dr.
Vancouver, BC V5P 2M2
Tel: 604-327-2069; *Fax:* 604-324-1762
www3.telus.net/public/tkoinc

Vancouver: **Tompkins, Wozny, Miller & Co. Chartered Accountants**
#206, 698 Seymour St.
Vancouver, BC V6B 3K6
Tel: 604-681-7703; *Fax:* 604-681-7713
info@twmca.com
www.twmca.com

Vancouver: **Trout Lake Group**
Vancouver, BC
Tel: 604-569-4444; *Fax:* 604-569-5060
info@troutlakegroup.ca
troutlakegroup.com

Vancouver: **Vohora & Company Chartered Accountants LLP**
#1050, 777 Hornby St.
Vancouver, BC V6Z 1S4
Tel: 604-251-1535; *Fax:* 604-541-9845
Toll-Free: 800-281-5214
www.vohora.ca

Vancouver: **Watson Dauphinee & Masuch Chartered Accountants**
#420, 1501 West Broadway Ave.
Vancouver, BC V6J 4Z6
Tel: 604-734-3247; *Fax:* 604-734-4802
info@wdmca.com
www.wdmca.com

Vancouver: **Wolrige Mahon LLP**
400 Burrard St., 9th Fl.
Vancouver, BC V6C 3B7
Tel: 604-684-6212; *Fax:* 604-688-3497
info@wm.ca
www.wolrigemahon.com
Social Media: twitter.com/WolrigeMahonLLP

Vancouver: **Wong, Robinson & Co. Chartered Accountants**
1708 - West 6th Ave.
Vancouver, BC V6J 5E8
Tel: 604-739-9500; *Fax:* 604-739-9394
info@wongrobinson.com
www.wongrobinson.com

Vernon: **Clark Robinson**
3109 - 32nd Ave.
Vernon, BC V1T 2M2
Tel: 250-545-7264; *Fax:* 250-542-5116
clarkrobinson.com

Vernon: **Kemp Harvey Laidman-Betts Inc.**
#206, 3334 - 30th Ave.
Vernon, BC V1T 2C8
Tel: 250-545-1544; *Fax:* 250-260-3641
Toll-Free: 877-547-1544
Vernon@khgcga.com
www.khgcga.com/index.php/offices/vernon
Social Media: www.facebook.com/152379991466319; twitter.com/KempHarveyGroup

Vernon: **Willis Associates Insolvency Services Inc.**
#222, 10704 - 97th Ave.
Vernon, BC V1J 6L7
Tel: 250-787-7857

Victoria: **Burkett & Co. Chartered Accountants**
#200, 3561 Shelbourne St.
Victoria, BC V8P 4G8
Tel: 250-370-9718; *Fax:* 250-370-9179
accountants@burkett.ca
www.burkett.ca

Victoria: **Collins Barrow Victoria Ltd.**
#540, 645 Fort St.
Victoria, BC V8W 1G2
Tel: 250-386-0500; *Fax:* 250-386-6151
victoria@collinsbarrow.com
www.collinsbarrow.com/en/victoria-british-col umbia

Victoria: **Leslie Feil, CGA, Ltd.**
#200, 888 Fort St.
Victoria, BC V8W 1H8
Tel: 250-382-6177; *Fax:* 250-385-0154
email@feilnco.com
www.feilnco.com

Victoria: **MH Stimpson & Associates Ltd.**
Shamrock Professional Centre
#201, 830 Shamrock St.
Victoria, BC V8X 2V1
Tel: 250-475-0222; *Fax:* 250-475-0229
stimpsoncpa.ca

Victoria: **Padgett Business Services - Victoria Capital Region**
#5, 4011 Quadra St.
Victoria, BC V8X 1K1
Tel: 250-744-3854; *Fax:* 250-744-3856
www.countbeans.com
Other Contact Information: Paytrak Phone: 250-708-0070
Social Media: www.youtube.com/PadgettAccounting; plus.google.com/117269473140758938076; www.facebook.com/PadgettAccounting; twitter.com/PadgettBC

Victoria: **PricewaterhouseCoopers LLP, Canada - Victoria**
525 Fort St., 2nd Fl.
Victoria, BC V8W 1E8
Tel: 250-298-5260; *Fax:* 250-298-5265
www.pwc.com/ca

West Kelowna: **Expatax Services Ltd.**
1837 Olympus Way
West Kelowna, BC V1Z 3H9
Tel: 778-755-0754
www.expatax.ca

Whistler: **Gershon & Co. Accounting & Tax Ltd.**
#207A, 4368 Main St.
Whistler, BC V0N 1B0
Tel: 604-938-1892
info@gershonandco.com
gershonandco.com
Social Media: plus.google.com/101491658333864226202; www.facebook.com/whistler.accounting; twitter.com/Mark_Gershon

Whistler: **Gordon J. Wiber & Associates Inc.**
#22, 1212 Alpha Lake Rd.
Whistler, BC V0N 1B2
Tel: 604-935-1114; *Fax:* 604-935-1154
www.whistlerca.com

Whistler: **McMillan Thorn & Co. Ltd.**
#204, 1085 Millar Creek Rd.
Whistler, BC V0N 1B1
Tel: 604-938-1544; *Fax:* 604-938-1577
mail@mcmillanthorn.com
www.mcmillanthorn.com

Manitoba

Carman: **Nakonechny & Power Chartered Accountants Ltd.**
PO Box 880
31 Main St. South
Carman, MB R0G 0J0
Tel: 204-745-2061; *Fax:* 204-745-6322
admin@nakandpow.com
www.nakandpow.com

Flin Flon: **Kendall & Pandya**
#300, 29 Main St.
Flin Flon, MB R8A 1J5
Tel: 204-687-8211

Swan River: **Pacak Kowal Hardie & Company, Chartered Accountants**
PO Box 1660
100 - 4th Ave. North
Swan River, MB R0L 1Z0
Tel: 204-734-9331; *Fax:* 204-734-4785
Toll-Free: 800-743-8447
pkhl@pkhl.ca
www.pacakkowalhardie.com

Swan River: **Reimer & Company Inc.**
PO Box 146
359 Kelsey Trail
Swan River, MB R0L 1Z0
Tel: 204-734-2599; *Fax:* 204-734-3184
Toll-Free: 866-468-0259
info@reimerco.ca
www.reimerco.ca

Winnipeg: **A.L. Schellenberg, Chartered Accountant**
474 Panet Rd.
Winnipeg, MB R2C 3B9
Tel: 204-669-5143; *Fax:* 204-669-5145
leon@mts.net

Winnipeg: **Booke & Partners**
#500, 5 Donald St.
Winnipeg, MB R3L 2T4
Tel: 204-284-7060; *Fax:* 204-284-7105
www.bookeandpartners.ca

Winnipeg: **Chochinov Curry LLP**
#1250, 363 Broadway Ave.
Winnipeg, MB R3C 3N9
Tel: 204-957-7694
www.porterhetu.com

Winnipeg: **Collins Barrow HMA LLP**
#701, 330 Portage Ave.
Winnipeg, MB R3C 0C4
Tel: 204-989-2229; *Fax:* 204-944-9923
Toll-Free: 866-730-4777
winnipeg@collinsbarrow.com
www.collinsbarrow.com/en/winnipeg-manitoba

Winnipeg: **Craig & Ross Chartered Accountants**
#1515, 1 Lombard Place
Winnipeg, MB R3B 0X3
Tel: 204-956-9400; *Fax:* 204-956-9424
info@craigross.com
www.craigross.com

Winnipeg: **The Exchange Chartered Accountants LLP (ECA)**
#100, 123 Bannatyne Ave.
Winnipeg, MB R3B 0R3
Tel: 204-943-4584; *Fax:* 204-957-5195
info@exg.ca
www.exg.ca/ECA/about.asp

Winnipeg: **KWB Chartered Accountants Inc.**
#800, 125 Garry St.
Winnipeg, MB R3C 3P2
Tel: 204-982-3878; *Fax:* 204-982-3888
www.kwb.ca

Winnipeg: **Lazer Grant LLP Chartered Accountants & Business Advisors**
#300, 309 McDermot Ave.
Winnipeg, MB R3A 1T3
Tel: 204-942-0300; *Fax:* 204-957-5611
Toll-Free: 800-220-0005
lazergrant@lazergrant.ca
www.lazergrant.ca

Winnipeg: **M Group Chartered Accountants**
710 Corydon Ave.
Winnipeg, MB R3M 0X9
Tel: 204-992-7200; *Fax:* 204-992-7208
info@mgroup.ca
www.mgroup.ca
Social Media: www.facebook.com/122828771117017; twitter.com/Mgroupca

Winnipeg: **Magnus Chartered Accountants**
#430, 5 Donald St.
Winnipeg, MB R3L 2T4
Tel: 204-942-4441
BMM@MagnusLLP.ca
www.magnusllp.ca

Winnipeg: **Nachtigal Burgess LLP Certified General Accountants (NB)**
#222, 530 Kenaston Blvd.
Winnipeg, MB R3N 1Z4
Tel: 204-334-8972
www.nbllp.ca

Winnipeg: **Osborne Accounting Group LLP Certified General Accountants**
738 Osborne St.
Winnipeg, MB R3L 2C2
Tel: 204-489-2781; *Fax:* 204-452-5956
accountants.mb.ca

Winnipeg: **Peterson Group Chartered Accountants**
#209, 1661 Portage Ave.
Winnipeg, MB R3J 3T7
Tel: 204-594-7300; *Fax:* 204-594-7301
solutions@petersongroup.ca
www.petersongroup.ca

Winnipeg: **PKBW Group, Chartered Accountants & Business Advisors Inc.**
219 Fort St.
Winnipeg, MB R3C 1E2
Tel: 204-942-0861; *Fax:* 204-947-6834
www.pkbwgroup.ca

Winnipeg: **Pope & Brookes LLP**
#300, 530 Kenaston Blvd.
Winnipeg, MB R3N 1Z4
Tel: 204-487-7957; *Fax:* 204-487-1243
advice@popebrookes.ca
www.pb-dfk.com

Winnipeg: **PricewaterhouseCoopers LLP, Canada - Winnipeg**
Richardson Bldg.
#2300, 1 Lombard Pl.
Winnipeg, MB R3B 0X6
Tel: 204-926-2400; *Fax:* 204-994-1020
www.pwc.com/ca

Winnipeg: **RDK Chartered Accountant Ltd.**
5 Whitkirk Place
Winnipeg, MB R3R 2A2
Tel: 204-885-5280; *Fax:* 204-831-6670
rdkcharteredaccountant@shaw.ca
www.rdkcharteredaccountant.com

Winnipeg: **Scarrow & Donald LLP**
#100, 5 Donald St.
Winnipeg, MB R3L 2T4
Tel: 204-982-9800; *Fax:* 204-474-2886
sd@scarrowdonald.mb.ca
www.scarrowdonald.mb.ca

New Brunswick

Campbellton: **AC Allen, Paquet & Arseneau LLP**
PO Box 519
207 Roseberry St.
Campbellton, NB E3N 3G9
Tel: 506-789-0820; *Fax:* 506-759-7514
apa01@apa-ca.com
www.apa-ca.com

Dieppe: **Boudreau Porter Hétu**
#101, 654, boul Malenfant
Dieppe, NB E1A 5V8
Tél: 506-857-0262
boudreau_porter_hetu@porterhetu.com
www.porterhetu.com

Florenceville: **McCain & Company Chartered Accountants**
8688 Main St.
Florenceville, NB E7L 3G8
Tel: 506-392-5517

Fredericton: **AC Bringloe Feeney LLP**
#401, 212 Queen St.
Fredericton, NB E3B 1A8
Tel: 506-458-8326
www.acgca.ca

Fredericton: **Bringloe Feeney**
#401, 212 Queen St.
Fredericton, NB E3B 1A8
Tel: 506-458-8326; *Fax:* 506-458-9293

Moncton: **PricewaterhouseCoopers LLP, Canada - Moncton**
#450, 633 Main St.
Moncton, NB E1C 9X9
Tel: 506-859-8822; *Fax:* 506-859-8829
www.pwc.com/ca

Riverview: **AC Stevenson & Partners PC Inc.**
567 Coverdale Rd.
Riverview, NB E1B 3K7
Tel: 506-387-4044; *Fax:* 506-387-7270
sp@parternsnb.com
www.acgca.ca

Rothesay: **Steeves Porter Hétu**
Professional Centre
PO Box 4591
9 Scott Ave.
Rothesay, NB E2E 5X3
Tel: 506-847-7471; *Fax:* 506-847-3151
sph@porterhetu.com
www.steevesporterhetu.com

Saint John: **Beers Neal LLP**
#301, 53 King St.
Saint John, NB E2L 1G5
Tel: 506-632-9020
www.acgca.ca

Saint John: **Curry & Betts**
Admiral Beatty Building
PO Box 6789, A Stn. A
72 Charlotte St., 1st Fl.
Saint John, NB E2L 4S2
Tel: 506-635-8181; *Fax:* 506-633-5943
Toll-Free: 888-635-8181
www.currybetts.ca

Saint John: **Green Webber Company Chartered Accountants (GWC)**
#200, 53 King St.
Saint John, NB E2L 1G5
Tel: 506-632-3000
www.gcwco.ca

Saint John: **Padgett Business Services New Brunswick**
221 Loch Lomond Rd.
Saint John, NB E2J 1Y5
Tel: 506-642-4464; *Fax:* 506-652-2780
padgettnb@padgettnb.com
www.padgettnb.com

Saint John: **PricewaterhouseCoopers LLP, Canada - Saint John**
Brunswick House
PO Box 789
#300, 44 Chipman Hill
Saint John, NB E2L 4B9
Tel: 506-632-1810; *Fax:* 506-632-8997
www.pwc.com/ca

Saint John: **Teed Saunders Doyle & Co. Chartered Accountants**
39 Canterbury St.
Saint John, NB E2L 4S1
Tel: 506-636-9220; *Fax:* 506-634-8208
tsdsj@tsdca.com
www.teedsaundersdoyle.com

St. Stephen: **L K Toombs Chartered Accountants**
#207, 73 Milltown Blvd.
St. Stephen, NB E3L 1G5
Tel: 506-466-3291; *Fax:* 506-466-9825
lktpc@nb.aibn.com
www.acgca.ca

Sussex: **Turnbull & Kindred Certified General Accountants**
PO Box 4608
44 Moffett Ave.
Sussex, NB E4E 5L8
Tel: 506-433-4202; *Fax:* 506-432-6569
turnbull_kindred@porterhetu.com
tkcga.com
Social Media: www.youtube.com/TurnbullKindred; www.facebook.com/TurnbullKindred; twitter.com/TurnbullKindred

Tracadie-Sheila: **Mallet & Aubin CGA**
3653, rue Principale
Tracadie-Sheila, NB E1X 1E2
Tél: 506-395-1013; *Téléc:* 506-395-6911
info@malletaubin.ca
malletaubin.ca

Woodstock: **Lenehan McCain & Associates**
#1, 389 Connell St.
Woodstock, NB E7M 5G5
Tel: 506-325-3322

Newfoundland & Labrador

Corner Brook: **J. Pike & Company Ltd.**
PO Box 1031
98 Broadway
Corner Brook, NL A2H 6J3
Tel: 709-639-7774; *Fax:* 709-639-7775

***Corner Brook:* PricewaterhouseCoopers LLP, Canada - Corner Brook**
57 Park St.
Corner Brook, NL A2H 2X1
Tel: 709-634-8256; *Fax:* 709-639-1647
www.pwc.com/ca

***Marystown:* Jody Murphy, Chartered Accountant**
236 Ville Marie Dr.
Marystown, NL A0E 2M0
Tel: 709-279-1888; *Fax:* 709-279-1895

***Mount Pearl:* Feltham Attwood Certified General Accountants**
#202, 39 Commonwealth Ave.
Mount Pearl, NL A1N 1W7
Tel: 709-364-7300
accounting@feltham-attwood.ca
feltham-attwood.ca
Social Media: www.facebook.com/124975570879426; twitter.com/debrafelthamCGA

***St. John's:* Noseworthy Chapman Chartered Accountants**
#201, 516 Topsail Rd.
St. John's, NL A1E 2C5
Tel: 709-364-5600; *Fax:* 709-368-2146
info@noseworthychapman.ca
www.noseworthychapman.ca

***St. John's:* PricewaterhouseCoopers LLP, Canada - St. John's**
Atlantic Place
#200, 125 Kelsey Dr.
St. John's, NL A1B 0L2
Tel: 709-722-3883; *Fax:* 709-722-5874
www.pwc.com/ca

Northwest Territories

***Yellowknife:* Avery Cooper & Co.**
Laurentian Building
PO Box 1620
4918 - 50 St.
Yellowknife, NT X1A 2P2
Tel: 867-873-3441; *Fax:* 867-873-2353
Toll-Free: 800-661-0787
www.averycooper.com

Nova Scotia

***Amherst:* The AC Group of Independent Accounting Firms Limited**
c/o McIsaac Darragh Chartered Accountants
PO Box 217
11 Princess St.
Amherst, NS B4H 3Z2
Tel: 902-661-1027; *Fax:* 902-667-0884
Toll-Free: 877-282-6632
admin@acgca.ca
www.acgca.ca
Social Media: www.facebook.com/64587206840

***Amherst:* McIsaac Darragh Chartered Accountants**
PO Box 217
11 Princess St.
Amherst, NS B4H 3Z2
Tel: 902-661-1027; *Fax:* 902-667-0884
Toll-Free: 877-282-6632
contact@mcisaacdarragh.ca
www.acgca.ca

***Antigonish:* MacDonald & Murphy Inc.**
#101, 155 Main St.
Antigonish, NS B2G 2B6
Tel: 902-867-1820
www.acgca.ca

***Bedford:* Darrell B. Cochrane & Associates Inc.**
4 Sedgewick Pl.
Bedford, NS B4A 0G5
Tel: 902-430-4796
cochrane-and-associates@porterhetu.com
www.porterhetu.com

***Bedford:* Etter Macleod & Associates Inc.**
117 Brentwood Dr.
Bedford, NS B4A 3S3
Tel: 902-456-1031
www.porterhetu.com/ns_etter.html

***Bridgewater:* AC Belliveau Veinotte Inc.**
PO Box 29
11 Dominion St.
Bridgewater, NS B4V 2W6
Tel: 902-543-4278
office@bvca.ca
www.acgca.ca

***Cheticamp:* Harold Patrick Aucoin CGA, Inc.**
15262 Cabot Trail
Cheticamp, NS B0E 1H0
Tel: 902-224-3748
www.haroldaucoincga.com

***Dartmouth:* AC Hunter Tellier Belgrave Adamson**
#24, 260 Brownlow Ave.
Dartmouth, NS B3B 1V9
Tel: 902-468-1949
service@achtba.ca
www.acgca.ca

***Dartmouth:* Chassé & Associates Inc.**
344 Prince Albert Rd.
Dartmouth, NS B2Y 1N6
Tel: 902-468-0282

***Dartmouth:* Collins Barrow Nova Scotia Inc.**
#101, 120 Eileen Stubbs Ave.
Dartmouth, NS B3B 1Y1
Tel: 902-404-4000; *Fax:* 902-404-3099
infons@collinsbarrow.com
www.collinsbarrow.com/en/halifax-nova-scotia

***Dartmouth:* McNeil Porter Hétu**
344 Prince Albert Rd.
Dartmouth, NS B2Y 1N6
Tel: 902-464-9300
www.porterhetu.com

***Dartmouth:* WBLI Chartered Accountants**
#200, 100 Venture Run
Dartmouth, NS B3B 0H9
Tel: 902-835-7333; *Fax:* 902-835-5297
wbli.ca

***Halifax:* AC Horwich Rossiter**
#440, 36 Solutions Dr.
Halifax, NS B3S 1N2
Tel: 902-835-0232; *Fax:* 902-835-0060
www.acgca.ca

***Halifax:* Green Landers Limited**
#201, 273 Bedford Hwy.
Halifax, NS B3M 2K5
Tel: 902-481-8144
landerslimited.com

***Halifax:* Lyle Tilley Davidson Chartered Accountants**
#720, 1718 Argyle St.
Halifax, NS B3J 3N6
Tel: 902-423-7225; *Fax:* 902-422-3649
www.ltdca.com

***Halifax:* PricewaterhouseCoopers LLP, Canada - Halifax**
#400, 1601 Lower Water St.
Halifax, NS B3J 3P6
Tel: 903-491-7400; *Fax:* 903-422-1166
www.pwc.com/ca

***New Glasgow:* Kevin MacDonald & Associates Inc.**
635 East River Rd.
New Glasgow, NS B2H 3S4
Tel: 902-755-5890; *Fax:* 902-755-5888
www.acgca.ca

***Sydney:* MGM & Associates Chartered Accountants**
PO Box 1
Sydney, NS B1P 6G9
Tel: 902-539-3900; *Fax:* 902-564-6062
www.mgm.ca

***Sydney:* PricewaterhouseCoopers LLP, Canada - Sydney**
#220, 500 George St.
Sydney, NS B1P 1K6
Tel: 902-564-0802; *Fax:* 902-564-1470
www.pwc.com/ca

***Truro:* PricewaterhouseCoopers LLP, Canada - Truro**
PO Box 632, Prince Stn. Prince
710 Prince St.
Truro, NS B2N 5E5
Tel: 902-895-1641; *Fax:* 902-893-0460
www.pwc.com/ca

***Wolfville:* Bishop & Company Chartered Accountants Inc.**
189 Dykeland St.
Wolfville, NS B4P 1A3
Tel: 902-542-7665; *Fax:* 902-542-4554
www.acgca.ca

Ontario

***Almonte:* Colby McGeachy, PC**
PO Box 970
14 Mill St., 2nd Fl.
Almonte, ON K0A 1A0
Tel: 613-256-6415; *Fax:* 613-256-7569
Toll-Free: 866-259-2878
almonte@porterhetu.com
www.colbymcgeachy.com
Other Contact Information: www.linkedin.com/pub/colby-mcgeachy-pc-imf-porter-hetu-international/28/31 4/7a4
Social Media: www.youtube.com/user/colbymcgeachy; www.facebook.com/227623053961778; twitter.com/ColbyMcGeachyPC

***Ancaster:* Brownlow Partners Chartered Accountants**
259 Wilson St. East
Ancaster, ON L9G 2B8
Tel: 905-648-0404; *Fax:* 905-648-0403
Toll-Free: 888-648-0404
www.brownlowcas.com

***Arnprior:* Dave H. Laventure, Professional Corp.**
#203, 16 Edward St. South
Arnprior, ON K7S 3W4
Tel: 613-623-3181; *Fax:* 613-623-4299
davehlaventureaccounting.ca

***Aurora:* Morley, Sanderson, Millard & Foster PC**
#101, 15449 Yonge St.
Aurora, ON L4G 1P3
Tel: 905-727-1325; *Fax:* 905-727-1159
www.msmfca.ca

***Aylmer:* DenHarder McNames Button LLP**
174 Sydenham St. East
Aylmer, ON N5H 1L7
Tel: 519-773-5348; *Fax:* 519-773-7409

***Bancroft:* Dale Rose, CGA & Peter Stone, CA**
PO Box 1209
294 Hastings St. North
Bancroft, ON K0L 1C0
Tel: 613-332-0834; *Toll-Free:* 800-333-0834
dalerose_peterstone@porterhetu.com
www.porterhetu.com
Other Contact Information: Alternate Phone: 613-332-4154

***Barrie:* Powell Jones LLP Chartered Accountants**
121 Anne St. South
Barrie, ON L4N 7B6
Tel: 705-728-7461; *Fax:* 705-728-8317
Toll-Free: 888-828-7461
info@powelljones.ca
www.powelljones.ca

***Belleville:* Soden & Co.**
25 Campbell St.
Belleville, ON K8N 1S6
Tel: 613-968-3495

***Brampton:* Buttar & Associates Inc.**
Jaipur Chrysler Centre
#1, 470 Chrysler Dr.
Brampton, ON L6S 0C1
Tel: 905-866-6543; *Fax:* 905-866-6566
Toll-Free: 866-605-4430
accounting.buttar.ca

***Brampton:* Calvin G. Vickery, Chartered Accountant**
#100, 197 County Court Blvd.
Brampton, ON L6W 4K7
Tel: 289-807-0009
www.bramptonaccountantservices.ca

***Brampton:* Kenneth Bell CA Business Advisory Group**
#34, 18 Regan Rd.
Brampton, ON L7A 1C2
Tel: 905-453-0844; *Fax:* 905-453-1530
www.kenbell.ca

***Brampton:* M W Mirza, Chartered Accountant**
#404, 2250 Bovaird Dr. East
Brampton, ON L6R 0W3
Tel: 647-866-1285; *Fax:* 647-723-7516
info@mwmca.ca
mwmca.ca
Other Contact Information: Alternate URL: www.mkcas.ca

***Brampton:* SMCA Professional Corporation**
#201, 197 County Court Blvd.
Brampton, ON L6W 4P6
Tel: 905-451-4034; *Fax:* 905-451-7158
Toll-Free: 888-524-4844
www.smca.ca

***Brantford:* Millards**
PO Box 367
96 Nelson St.
Brantford, ON N3T 5N3
Tel: 519-759-3511; *Fax:* 519-759-7961
www.millards.com

***Brantford:* Susan L. Rice**
#B201, 325 West St.
Brantford, ON N3R 3V6
Tel: 519-752-8290; *Fax:* 519-752-9784
www.obwr.ca/Bios/susan.html
Social Media: plus.google.com/106927274067646281026

***Brockville:* George Caners Chartered Accountant**
#210, 9 Broad St.
Brockville, ON K6V 6Z4
Tel: 613-342-1555; *Fax:* 613-342-2845
Toll-Free: 888-829-9952
www.caners.com

***Burlington:* Bateman MacKay**
PO Box 5015
#200, 4200 South Service Rd.
Burlington, ON L7L 4X5
Tel: 905-632-6400; *Fax:* 905-639-2285
Toll-Free: 866-236-9585
www.batemanmackay.com

***Burlington:* Prapavessis Jasek**
#205, 3380 South Service Rd.
Burlington, ON L7N 3J5
Tel: 905-634-8999; *Fax:* 905-634-5057
www.pj.on.ca

***Burlington:* SB Partners LLP**
#301, 3600 Billings Ct.
Burlington, ON L7N 3N6
Tel: 905-632-5978; *Fax:* 905-632-9068
Toll-Free: 866-823-9990
www.sbpartners.ca
Social Media: www.facebook.com/SBPartners

***Burlington:* Scott, Pichelli & Easter Ltd.**
#109, 3600 Billings Ct.
Burlington, ON L7N 3N6
Tel: 905-632-5853; *Fax:* 905-632-6113
www.bankruptcy-trustees.ca
Social Media:
plus.google.com/+BankruptcytrusteesCanadaontario;
www.facebook.com/ScottAndPichelliLtd

***Burlington:* Steven J. Obranovich**
#6, 185 Plains Rd. East
Burlington, ON L7T 2C4
Tel: 905-632-8400; *Fax:* 905-632-9505
www.obwr.ca/Bios/steven.html

***Burlington:* Stevenson & Lehocki LLP Chartered Accountants**
310 Plains Rd. East
Burlington, ON L7T 4J2
Tel: 905-632-0640; *Fax:* 905-632-0645
www.stevensonlehocki.com

***Cambridge:* Graham Mathew Professional Corporation**
PO Box 880
150 Pinebush Rd.
Cambridge, ON N1R 5X9
Tel: 519-623-1870; *Fax:* 519-623-9490
www.gmpca.com

***Chatham:* Collins Barrow CK, LLP**
62 Keil Dr. South
Chatham, ON N7M 3G8
Tel: 519-351-2024; *Fax:* 519-351-8831
chatham@collinsbarrow.com
www.collinsbarrow.com/en/chatham-ontario

***Chatham:* Gilhula & Grant**
141 Grand Ave. East
Chatham, ON N7L 1W1
Tel: 519-352-3470
Social Media: plus.google.com/107205090490857502205

***Collingwood:* Collins Barrow SGB LLP**
PO Box 130
115 Hurontario St.
Collingwood, ON L9Y 3Z4
Tel: 705-445-2020; *Fax:* 705-444-5833
collingwood@collinsbarrow.com
www.collinsbarrow.com/en/collingwood-ontar io

***Concord:* Gary A. Freedman + Associates, Chartered Accountant**
#1, 70 Villarboit Cres.
Concord, ON L4K 4C7
Tel: 905-669-7950; *Fax:* 905-669-7951
info@freedmanca.com
www.freedmanca.com

***Concord:* Miller, Saperia & Company**
#418, 1600 Steeles Ave. West
Concord, ON L4K 4M2
Tel: 905-660-6840; *Fax:* 905-660-6729
www.millersaperia.com

***Concord:* PricewaterhouseCoopers LLP, Canada - Concord**
#100, 400 Bradwick Dr.
Concord, ON L4K 5V9
Tel: 905-326-6800; *Fax:* 905-326-5339
www.pwc.com/ca

***Concord:* Starkman, Salsberg & Feldberg Chartered Accountants**
#316, 1600 Steeles Ave. West
Concord, ON L4K 4M2
Tel: 905-669-9900; *Fax:* 905-669-9901
www.starkmansalsbergfeldberg.com

***Courtice:* Collins Barrow Durham LLP**
#200, 1748 Baseline Rd. West
Courtice, ON L1E 2T1
Tel: 905-579-5659; *Fax:* 905-579-8563
durham@collinsbarrow.com
www.collinsbarrow.com/en/courtice-ontario

***Elginburg:* Randy E. Brown CGA**
2908 Leeman Rd.
Elginburg, ON K0H 1M0
Tel: 613-542-0151; *Fax:* 613-549-1427
rbrown@porterhetu.com
www.porterhetu.com

***Elmvale:* Ian Vasey CGA**
42 Queen St.
Elmvale, ON L0L 1P0
Tel: 705-322-2440; *Fax:* 705-322-1462
www.ianvaseycga.ca

***Elora:* Collins Barrow Guelph Wellington Dufferin**
342 Gerrie Rd.
Elora, ON N0B 1S0
Tel: 519-846-5315; *Fax:* 519-846-9120
info@collinsbarrow.com
www.collinsbarrow.com/en/elora-ontario

***Fredericton:* Nicholson & Beaumont Chartered Accountants**
328 King St.
Fredericton, ON E3B 5C2
Tel: 506-458-9815; *Fax:* 506-459-7575
nicholson_beaumont@porterhetu.com
www.porterhetu.com
Other Contact Information: Alternate Phone: 506-459-7575

***Gananoque:* Collins Barrow Gananoque**
PO Box 704
82 King St. East
Gananoque, ON K7G 2V2
Tel: 613-382-4547; *Fax:* 613-382-4558
www.collinsbarrow.com/en/gananoque-ontario

***Grimsby:* Southcott Davoli Professional Corporation**
76 Main St. West
Grimsby, ON L3M 4G1
Tel: 905-945-4942; *Fax:* 905-945-0306

***Guelph:* Bairstow, Smart & Smith LLP**
100 Gordon St.
Guelph, ON N1H 4H6
Tel: 519-822-7670; *Fax:* 519-822-6997
bss@bssllp.ca
www.bssllp.ca

***Guelph:* Embree & Co. LLP**
#8, 350 Speedvale Ave. West
Guelph, ON N1H 7M7
Tel: 519-821-1555; *Fax:* 519-821-6168
Toll-Free: 866-531-1555
www.embreellp.ca

***Guelph:* Robinson, Lott & Brohman LLP**
#103, 197 Hanlon Creek Blvd.
Guelph, ON N1C 0A1
Tel: 519-822-9933; *Fax:* 519-822-9212
Toll-Free: 866-822-9992
info@rlb.ca
www.rlb.ca
Other Contact Information: Human Resources E-mail: hr@rlb.ca
Social Media: www.facebook.com/RLB.LLP; twitter.com/rlbllp

***Guelph:* Weiler & Company**
#3, 512 Woolwich St.
Guelph, ON N1H 3X7
Tel: 519-837-3111; *Fax:* 519-837-1049
Toll-Free: 888-239-3111
info@weiler.ca
www.weiler.ca

***Hamilton:* BC&C Professional Corporation**
1 Main St. East, 3rd Fl.
Hamilton, ON L8N 1E7
Tel: 905-570-1370; *Fax:* 905-570-1212
www.bccpc.ca

***Hamilton:* Padgett Business Services of Hamilton**
1051 Main St. East
Hamilton, ON L8M 1N5
Tel: 905-549-4418
info@padgetthamilton.com
www.padgetthamilton.com
Social Media: www.facebook.com/162791240399073

***Hamilton:* Taylor Leibow LLP, Accountants & Advisors**
105 Main St. East, 7th Fl.
Hamilton, ON L8N 1G6
Tel: 905-523-0000; *Fax:* 905-523-4681
hamilton@taylorleibow.com
www.taylorleibow.com
Social Media: www.youtube.com/user/taylorleibowllp;
www.facebook.com/taylorleibow/info; twitter.com/TaylorLeibow

***Hanover:* Padgett Business Services Mid-Western Ontario**
275 - 10th St.
Hanover, ON N4N 1P1
Tel: 519-506-4523; *Fax:* 519-881-4941
padgett@wightman.ca
www.biz-coach.ca
Other Contact Information: Alternate Phone: 519-881-4523; Cell Phone: 519-881-7498

***Jackson's Point:* Duncan W. Goodwin, Certified General Accountant**
#4, 915 Lake Dr.
Jackson's Point, ON L0E 1L0
Tel: 905-722-8587; *Fax:* 905-722-6519
info@dwgoodwincga.com
www.porterhetu.com
Other Contact Information: Alternate Phone: 289-470-5008; E-mail: duncan_goodwin@porterhetu.com

***Kanata:* Padgett Business Services - Ottawa**
#2D, 160 Terence Matthews Cres.
Kanata, ON K2M 0B2
Tel: 613-599-4224; *Fax:* 613-482-3737
info@smallbizottawa.ca
www.smallbizottawa.ca
Social Media: www.youtube.com/user/SmallbizProsOttawa;
www.facebook.com/131193766930669;
twitter.com/PadgettOttawa

Kapuskasing: **Collins Barrow Gagne Gagnon Bisson Hebert**
2 Ash St.
Kapuskasing, ON P5N 3H4
Tel: 705-337-6411; *Fax:* 705-335-6563
kapuskasing@collinsbarrow.com
www.collinsbarrow.com/en/kapuskasing-ontar io

Kelowna: **Kemp Harvey Hunt Ward Inc.**
#101, 1593 Sutherland Ave.
Kelowna, ON V1Y 5Y7
Tel: 250-763-8029; *Fax:* 250-763-5155
Kelowna@khgcga.com
www.khgcga.com/index.php/offices/kelowna
Social Media: www.facebook.com/152379991466319; twitter.com/KempHarveyGroup

Kenora: **Claudette M. Edie, CGA PC**
685 Lakeview Dr.
Kenora, ON P9N 3P6
Tel: 807-468-8899
claudette_edie@porterhetu.com
www.porterhetu.com
Other Contact Information: Alternate Phone: 807-468-6800

Kingston: **Collins Barrow SEO LLP**
#201, 1471 John Counter Blvd.
Kingston, ON K7M 8Z6
Tel: 613-544-2903; *Fax:* 613-544-6151
kingston@collinsbarrow.com
www.collinsbarrow.com/en/kingston-ontario

Kingston: **Davies & Wyngaarden Chartered Accountants**
Clock Tower Plaza
819 Norwest Rd.
Kingston, ON K7P 2N4
Tel: 613-389-8177; *Fax:* 613-389-7789
Toll-Free: 888-715-3555
acctg@dwca.com
www.dwca.com

Kitchener: **Collins Barrow National Cooperative Incorporated**
55 King St. West, 7th Fl.
Kitchener, ON N2G 4W1
Tel: 519-725-2539; *Fax:* 519-725-2539
info@collinsbarrow.com
www.collinsbarrow.com
Social Media: www.youtube.com/user/collinsbarrowca; www.facebook.com/CollinsBarrowa; twitter.com/collinsbarrow

Kitchener: **Dube & Cuttini Chartered Accountants LLP**
103 Queen St. South
Kitchener, ON N2G 1W1
Tel: 519-772-0990; *Fax:* 519-725-3567
Toll-Free: 877-475-3823
info@dubeaccountants.com
dubecuttini.com
Other Contact Information: Alternate Phone: 519-725-3566

Kitchener: **YNC LLP**
#300, 447 Frederick St.
Kitchener, ON N2H 2P4
Tel: 519-772-0125; *Fax:* 519-772-0428
info@yncllp.ca
www.yncllp.ca

Lakefield: **Dan Rosborough, CGA**
PO Box 368
35 Queen St.
Lakefield, ON K0L 2H0
Tel: 705-652-6347
dan_rosborough@porterhetu.com
www.porterhetu.com
Other Contact Information: Alternate Phone: 705-652-8891

Leamington: **Collins Barrow Leamington LLP**
203 Talbot St. West
Leamington, ON N8H 1N8
Tel: 519-326-2666; *Fax:* 519-326-7008
leamington@collinsbarrow.com
www.collinsbarrow.com/en/leamington-ontario

London: **Burghout Chartered Accountant**
932 Norton Cres.
London, ON N6J 2Y9
Tel: 519-852-2418

London: **Collins Barrow KMD LLP**
#700, 495 Richmond St.
London, ON N6A 5A9
Tel: 519-679-8550; *Fax:* 519-679-1812
london@collinsbarrow.com
www.collinsbarrow.com/en/london-ontario

London: **Davis Martindale LLP**
373 Commissioners Rd. West
London, ON N6J 1Y4
Tel: 519-673-3141; *Fax:* 519-645-1646
Toll-Free: 800-668-2167
info@davismartindale.com
www.davismartindale.com
Social Media: www.facebook.com/DavisMartindale; twitter.com/Davismartindale

London: **DFK Canada Inc.**
c/o Davis Martindale
373 Commissioners Rd. West
London, ON N6J 1Y4
Tel: 519-851-5158
www.dfk.ca

London: **MacNeill Edmundson**
82 Wellington St.
London, ON N6B 2K3
Tel: 519-660-6060; *Fax:* 519-672-6416
info@meb.on.ca
www.meb.on.ca

London: **Michael A. King, Chartered Accountant**
#502, 383 Richmond St.
London, ON N6A 3C4
Tel: 519-679-8391; *Fax:* 519-679-1446
www.michaelkingca.ca

London: **PricewaterhouseCoopers LLP, Canada - London**
#300, 465 Richmond St.
London, ON N6A 5P4
Tel: 519-640-8000; *Fax:* 519-640-8015
www.pwc.com/ca

Markham: **Applebaum, Commisso LLP Chartered Accountants (ACCA)**
#400, 2800 - 14th Ave.
Markham, ON L3R 0E4
Tel: 905-477-6996; *Fax:* 905-477-9381
info@applebaum-commisso.com
applebaum-commisso.com
Other Contact Information: Toronto, Phone: 416-494-4892

Markham: **Cooper Bick Chen LLP, Chartered Accountants (CBCCA)**
#202, 1001 Denison St.
Markham, ON L3R 2Z6
Tel: 905-475-6795; *Fax:* 905-475-1654
www.cbcca.ca

Markham: **Copland Chartered Accountant Professional Corporation**
#301, 325 Renfrew Dr.
Markham, ON L3R 9S8
Tel: 905-477-1300
enquire@copland-ca.com
www.copland-ca.com

Markham: **Eigenmacht Crackower Chartered Accountants Professional Corporation**
#202, 345 Renfrew Dr.
Markham, ON L3R 9S9
Tel: 905-305-9722; *Fax:* 905-305-9502
www.eigenmachtcrackower.com
Other Contact Information: Alt. Phones: 416-607-6468; 289-806-1130; Alt. URL: www.bramptonaccountantservices.ca

Markham: **Harris & Partners, LLP**
#300, 8920 Woodbine Ave.
Markham, ON L3R 9W9
Tel: 905-477-0363; *Fax:* 905-477-3735
Toll-Free: 877-401-8004
info@harrisandpartners.com
www.harrisandpartners.com

Markham: **HSM LLP Chartered Accountants**
West Tower
#200, 675 Cochrane Dr.
Markham, ON L3R 0B8
Tel: 905-470-7090; *Fax:* 905-470-7449
hsm@hsmllpcas.com
hsmllpcas.com

Markham: **Jack R. Cayne, CGA**
#303, 7321 Victoria Park Ave.
Markham, ON L3R 2Z8
Tel: 289-806-0054
www.markhamaccounting.ca

Markham: **Kestenberg, Rabinowicz & Partners LLP**
2797 John St.
Markham, ON L3R 2Y8
Tel: 905-946-1300; *Fax:* 905-946-9797
enquiries@krp.ca
www.krp.ca

Markham: **Kraft Berger LLP**
#300, 3160 Steeles Ave. East
Markham, ON L3R 3Y2
Tel: 905-475-2222; *Fax:* 905-475-9360
Toll-Free: 888-563-6868
accountants@kbllp.ca
www.kbllp.ca

Markham: **Kreston GTA LLP**
8953 Woodbine Ave.
Markham, ON L3R 0J9
Tel: 905-474-5593; *Fax:* 905-474-5591
info@krestongta.com
www.krestongta.com

Markham: **Larry Silverberg Chartered Accountant**
#226, 7181 Woodbine Ave.
Markham, ON L3R 1A3
Tel: 905-475-1000; *Fax:* 905-475-1001
www.larry.ca

Markham: **Mark Feldstein & Associates**
20 Crown Steel Dr.
Markham, ON L3R 9X9
Tel: 905-474-2442; *Fax:* 905-474-2441
toronto-accountant.ca
Other Contact Information: Alternate URL: fightbacktoday.ca
Social Media: www.facebook.com/markfeldsteintaxhelp; twitter.com/TorontoTax

Markham: **Rebecca Ling Chartered Accountant Professional Corporation**
#220, 3160 Steeles Ave. East
Markham, ON L3R 4G9
Tel: 905-305-9200; *Fax:* 905-305-9933
www.rebeccalingfca.com

Markham: **The Sheldon Group**
#220, 60 Renfrew Dr.
Markham, ON L3R 0E1
Tel: 905-475-5400; *Fax:* 905-475-4246
Toll-Free: 855-475-5400
letstalk@thesheldongroup.ca
www.thesheldongroup.ca
Social Media: www.youtube.com/SheldonGroupTaxFirms

Markham: **Valuation Support Partners Ltd.**
West Tower
#220, 675 Cochrane Dr.
Markham, ON L3R 0B8
Tel: 905-305-8775; *Fax:* 905-470-7449
vspltd.ca

Markham: **Wasserman Forensic Investigative Services Inc.**
Liberty Square, HSBC Tower
#1008, 3601 Hwy. #7
Markham, ON L3R 0M3
Tel: 905-948-8643; *Fax:* 905-948-8638
info@wassermaninvestigations.com
www.wassermaninvestigations.com

Markham: **Williams & Partners Chartered Accountants LLP**
East Tower
#505, 675 Cochrane Dr.
Markham, ON L3R 0B8
Toll-Free: 855-888-9913
www.williamsandpartners.com

Markham: **Williams & Partners Forensic Accountants Inc.**
East Tower
#505, 675 Cochrane Dr.
Markham, ON L3R 0B8
Toll-Free: 855-888-9913
www.wpforensicaccountants.com

Milton: **Bensen Industries Ltd.**
377 Scott Blvd.
Milton, ON L9T 0T1
Tel: 905-609-1047
www.bensenindustries.com

Milton: **Halton Tax & Accounting Services**
1171 Woodward Ave.
Milton, ON L9T 5Y5
Tel: 289-429-1278
info@haltontax.com
haltontax.com

Milton: **Mercer & Mercer**
245 Commercial St.
Milton, ON L9T 2J3
Tel: 905-876-1144; *Fax:* 905-876-4209
mail@mercerandmercer.com
www.mercerandmercer.com

Mississauga: **Aneja Professional Corporation Chartered Accountants**
#14, 6980 Maritz Dr.
Mississauga, ON L5W 1Z3
Tel: 905-564-9100; *Fax:* 905-874-8221
info@csaca.ca
www.csaca.ca

Mississauga: **Bimal Shah**
5484 Tomken Rd.
Mississauga, ON L4W 2Z6
Tel: 905-629-2653; *Fax:* 905-629-8701

Mississauga: **Bolton & Dignan, Chartered Accountants**
6509 Mississauga Rd., Unit D
Mississauga, ON L5N 1A6
Tel: 905-858-5006; *Fax:* 905-858-3392

Mississauga: **Clarkson Rouble LLP**
#102, 2576 Matheson Blvd. East
Mississauga, ON L4W 5H1
Tel: 905-629-4047; *Fax:* 905-629-3070
office@crllp.ca
ww.crllp.ca

Mississauga: **Doxsee & Co. Chartered Accountants**
#270, 2655 North Sheridan Way
Mississauga, ON L5K 2P8
Tel: 905-403-9001; *Fax:* 905-403-9002
info@dsaccountants.com
www.dsaccountants.com

Mississauga: **H&A Forensics**
#400, 2680 Matheson Blvd. East
Mississauga, ON L4W 0A5
Tel: 416-233-5577; *Fax:* 416-233-5578
Toll-Free: 866-233-5577
www.haforensics.com

Mississauga: **Hufton Valvano Grover Philipp LLP (HVGP)**
#100, 1599 Hurontario St.
Mississauga, ON L5G 4S1
Tel: 905-891-5339
www.hvgp.ca

Mississauga: **Kutum & Associates Inc.**
#A1, 5659 McAdam Rd.
Mississauga, ON L4Z 1N9
Tel: 905-276-1154; *Fax:* 905-276-2003
info@kutum.com
www.kutum.com

Mississauga: **Laurel L. Stultz (LLS)**
#211, 1425 Dundas St. East
Mississauga, ON L4X 2W4
Tel: 905-602-0001
info@certifiedgeneralaccountant.ca
www.certifiedgeneralaccountant.ca
Other Contact Information: Cell: 416-996-3919

Mississauga: **Les Lucyk Professional Corporation**
1617 Gallant Dr.
Mississauga, ON L5H 3S9
Tel: 905-271-9226; *Fax:* 905-271-8755
www.obwr.ca/Bios/les.html

Mississauga: **MacGillivray Partners, LLP**
#600, 6605 Hurontario St.
Mississauga, ON L5T 0A3
Tel: 905-696-0707; *Fax:* 905-453-3522
www.macgillivray.com

Mississauga: **MDP Chartered Accountants (MDP LLP)**
#200, 4230 Sherwoodtowne Blvd.
Mississauga, ON L4Z 2G6
Tel: 905-279-7500; *Fax:* 905-279-9300
mdp@mdp.on.ca
www.mdp.on.ca

Mississauga: **Padgett Business Services Mississauga**
#9, 6655 Kitimat Rd.
Mississauga, ON L5N 6J4
Tel: 905-858-9050
p_mineiro@smallbizpros.com
www.mississaugasmallbizpros.ca

Mississauga: **Padgett Business Services Mississauga South**
#208, 1077 North Service Rd.
Mississauga, ON L4Y 1A6
Tel: 905-949-4388; *Fax:* 905-949-9220
www.padgettmiss.ca

Mississauga: **Parker Simone LLP**
#201, 129 Lakeshore Rd. East
Mississauga, ON L5G 1E5
Tel: 905-271-7977; *Fax:* 905-271-7677
www.parker-simone.com

Mississauga: **S+C Partners LLP**
#204, 6465 Millcreek Dr.
Mississauga, ON L5N 5R3
Tel: 905-821-9215; *Fax:* 905-821-8212
Toll-Free: 866-965-1435
info@scpllp.com
scpllp.com

Mississauga: **SJ Chartered Accountants**
#4-101, 2600 Skymark Ave.
Mississauga, ON L4W 5B2
Tel: 905-625-1223; *Fax:* 905-625-1224
info@jainfinancial.com
www.jainfinancial.com

Mississauga: **Steve Manias, CPA, CA**
#103, 6711 Mississauga Rd.
Mississauga, ON L5N 2W3
Tel: 905-858-5559
www.stevemanias.ca
Other Contact Information: Alt. Phone: 289-277-0380; Alt. URL: www.accountingservicemississaugaon.ca

Mississauga: **Zaheda Dulai Certified General Accountant**
7341 Sandhurst Dr.
Mississauga, ON L5N 7G7
Tel: 416-912-7148
info@dulaicga.com
dulaicga.com

Nepean: **Jack R. Bowerman, CA - Professional Corporation**
#10, 28 Concourse Gate
Nepean, ON K2E 7T7
Tel: 613-723-8202; *Fax:* 613-723-1216
Toll-Free: 800-282-1879
info@jrbowerman.com
www.jrbowerman.com

Newmarket: **Padgett Newmarket**
#10, 171 Main St. South
Newmarket, ON L3Y 3Y9
Tel: 289-648-1880; *Fax:* 416-907-1132
save@padgettnewmarket.com
padgettnewmarket.com
Other Contact Information: York North, Phone: 289-366-0980; E-mail: yorknorth@padgettnewmarket.com; Durham North, Phone: 789-818-1859; E-mail: durhamnorth@padgettnewmarket.com
Social Media: www.facebook.com/SmallBizProsCanada; twitter.com/padgettnewmkt

Niagara Falls: **Padgett Niagara**
6260 Colborne St.
Niagara Falls, ON L2J 1E6
Tel: 905-374-6622
www.padgettniagara.com
Social Media: www.facebook.com/padgett.niagara; twitter.com/PadgettNiagara

Norland: **ABECK Accounting Tax & Computer Services Inc.**
PO Box 34
7524 Hwy. 35
Norland, ON K0M 2L0
Tel: 705-454-2418; *Fax:* 705-454-2422
info@abeckacctg.com
www.abeckacctg.com

Oakville: **Bazar McBean LLP**
440 Inglehart St. North
Oakville, ON L6J 3J6
Tel: 289-805-7148; *Fax:* 416-739-0538
Toll-Free: 866-480-0221
www.bazarmcbean.calls.net
Other Contact Information: Alt. URL: www.bazarmcbeanllpon.ca

Oakville: **CMR Wong Chartered Accountant**
#32, 1200 Speers Rd.
Oakville, ON L6L 2X4
Tel: 905-845-1408; *Fax:* 905-845-5931
cmrwong1@gmail.com
www.rickywong.ca

Oakville: **Glenn Graydon Wright LLP Chartered Accountants**
#310, 690 Dorval Dr.
Oakville, ON L6K 3W7
Tel: 289-805-6281
info@ggw.net
www.ggw.net
Other Contact Information: Alternate URL: www.oakvilleaccountingfirm.ca
Social Media: twitter.com/GGW_LLP

Oakville: **PricewaterhouseCoopers LLP, Canada - Oakville**
PwC Centre
#600, 354 Davis Rd.
Oakville, ON L6J 2X2
Tel: 905-815-6300; *Fax:* 905-816-6499
www.pwc.com/ca

Orléans: **Pyndus & Associates Ltd.**
1813 Woodhaven Heights
Orléans, ON K1E 2W3
Tel: 613-834-5054; *Fax:* 613-837-1591
pyndus.associates@sympatico.ca
www3.sympatico.ca/cpyndus

Ottawa: **Andrews & Co. Chartered Accountants**
540 Lacolle Way
Ottawa, ON K4A 0N9
Tel: 613-837-8282; *Fax:* 613-837-7482
website@andrews.ca
www.andrews.ca

Ottawa: **Charles Ghadban Accounting**
544 Bronson Ave.
Ottawa, ON K1R 6J9
Tel: 613-234-7856
info@ghadbanaccounting.com
www.ghadbanaccounting.com

Ottawa: **Collins Barrow Ottawa LLP**
#400, 301 Moodie Dr.
Ottawa, ON K2H 9C4
Tel: 613-820-8010; *Fax:* 613-820-0465
collinsbarrowottawa@collinsbarrow.com
www.collinsbarrowottawa.com
Social Media: plus.google.com/113532610412604008138

Ottawa: **David Ingram & Associates**
c/o Gro-Net
329 Waverly St.
Ottawa, ON K2P 0V9
Tel: 613-234-8023; *Fax:* 613-234-8925
www.gro-net.com

Ottawa: **Gary G. Timmons, Chartered Accountant**
#105, 2442 St. Joseph Blvd.
Ottawa, ON K1C 1G1
Tel: 613-830-0200; *Fax:* 613-830-8824
gtimmons@gtimmons.com
www.gtimmons.com

Ottawa: **Ginsberg Gluzman Fage & Levitz, LLP (GGFL)**
287 Richmond Rd.
Ottawa, ON K1Z 6X4
Tel: 613-728-5831; *Fax:* 613-728-8085
info@ggfl.ca
www.ggfl.ca
Social Media: plus.google.com/u/0/+GgflCa; www.facebook.com/194833287196455; twitter.com/GGFLca

Ottawa: **Gro-Net Financial Tax & Pension Planners Ltd.**
329 Waverly St.
Ottawa, ON K2P 0V9
Tel: 613-234-8023; *Fax:* 613-234-8925
www.gro-net.com

Ottawa: **Logan Katz LLP**
#105, 6 Gurdwara Rd.
Ottawa, ON K2E 8A3
Tel: 613-228-8282; *Fax:* 613-228-8284
reception@logankatz.com
www.logankatz.com
Social Media: www.facebook.com/140032509404120; twitter.com/LoganKatz_LLP

Ottawa: **McLarty & Co.**
#110, 495 Richmond Rd.
Ottawa, ON K2A 4B2
Tel: 613-726-1010; *Fax:* 613-726-9009
info@mclartyco.ca
www.mclartyco.ca
Social Media: www.facebook.com/McLartyCo

Ottawa: **Parker Prins Lebano Chartered Accountants**
1796 Courtwood Cres.
Ottawa, ON K2C 2B5
Tel: 613-727-7474; *Fax:* 613-727-3715
enquiries@ppl-ca.com
www.parkerprinslebano.com

Ottawa: **PricewaterhouseCoopers LLP, Canada - Ottawa**
#800, 99 Bank St.
Ottawa, ON K1P 1E4
Tel: 613-237-3702; *Fax:* 613-237-3963
www.pwc.com/ca

Ottawa: **Robertson Sharpe & Associates**
#2, 200 Colonnade Rd.
Ottawa, ON K2E 7M1
Tel: 613-727-3845
www.robertson-sharpe.com

Ottawa: **Rosalind Schlessinger Certified General Accountant**
332 Gilmour St.
Ottawa, ON K2P 0R3
Tel: 613-235-1807; *Fax:* 613-235-2253
Social Media: plus.google.com/117632251546964013165

Ottawa: **Surgeson Carson Associates Inc.**
#8, 99 Fifth Ave.
Ottawa, ON K1S 5K4
Tel: 613-567-6434; *Fax:* 613-567-0752
www.surgesoncarson.com
Social Media: plus.google.com/113394721190785718991; www.facebook.com/178127832227256; twitter.com/OttMoneyHelp

Ottawa: **Swindells & Company**
#101, 1700 Woodward Dr.
Ottawa, ON K2C 3R8
Tel: 613-230-1010; *Fax:* 613-230-1957
www.swindellsandwheatley.com

Ottawa: **Thomas R. West CGA Professional Corporation**
#209, 460 West Hunt Club Rd.
Ottawa, ON K2E 0B8
Tel: 613-825-8871; *Fax:* 613-825-4089
tom@thomasrwestcga.com
www.thomasrwestcga.com

Peterborough: **Collins Barrow Kawarthas LLP**
272 Charlotte St.
Peterborough, ON K9J 2V4
Tel: 705-742-3418; *Fax:* 705-742-9775
peterborough@collinsbarrow.com
www.collinsbarrow.com/en/peterborough-ont ario

Peterborough: **Jon S. Thornton, Chartered Accountant**
PO Box 2402
294 Rink St.
Peterborough, ON K9J 7Y8
Tel: 705-742-2308; *Fax:* 705-748-4824
www.thorntonca.com

Peterborough: **Robin E. Wrightly**
#203, 311 George St. North
Peterborough, ON K9J 3H3
Tel: 705-745-8643; *Fax:* 705-745-6358
www.obwr.ca/Bios/robin.html

Pickering: **Michael Evans, Chartered Accountant**
#6, 1730 McPherson Ct.
Pickering, ON L1W 3E6
Tel: 905-420-9637; *Fax:* 905-420-0910
info@gtaaccountant.com
www.gtaaccountant.com

Port Perry: **1st Financial Centre**
36 Water St.
Port Perry, ON L9L 1J2
Tel: 905-985-1926; *Toll-Free:* 877-775-3948
www.1fc.ca

Richmond Hill: **Bansal & Giga Chartered Accountants**
#303, 9011 Leslie St.
Richmond Hill, ON L4B 3B6
Tel: 289-807-1345
www.richmondhillonaccountant.ca

Richmond Hill: **Chan Yu Wong LLP**
#305, 350 Hwy. 7
Richmond Hill, ON L4B 3N2
Tel: 905-886-0203; *Fax:* 905-886-0201
www.cywca.com

Richmond Hill: **Chapman Matten Welton Winter LLP Chartered Accountants (CMWW)**
PO Box 79
#6010, 3080 Yonge St.
Richmond Hill, ON M4N 3N1
Tel: 905-882-0497; *Fax:* 905-882-0499
mail@cmww.ca
www.cmww.ca

Richmond Hill: **David Burkes - Chartered Accountant**
#201, 30 East Beaver Creek Rd.
Richmond Hill, ON L4B 1J2
Tel: 905-882-0497; *Fax:* 905-882-0499
www.dburkes.ca
Other Contact Information: Alternate Phone: 416-629-1469

Richmond Hill: **Edwin Law, CA, CFP, Licensed Public Accountant**
#17, 175 West Beaver Creek Rd.
Richmond Hill, ON L4B 3M1
Tel: 416-986-7700
taxdirector@edwinlaw.ca
www.edwinlaw.ca

Richmond Hill: **Hennick Herman, LLP**
100 York Boul.
Richmond Hill, ON L4B 1J8
Tel: 416-494-2606
www.hh-llp.ca

Richmond Hill: **inNumbers, Inc.**
65A West Beaver Creek Rd.
Richmond Hill, ON L4B 1K4
Tel: 905-882-3137; *Toll-Free:* 877-820-7313
info@innumbers.ca
innumbers.ca
Social Media: www.facebook.com/innumbers.ca; twitter.com/inNumbersInc

Richmond Hill: **MDS LLP Chartered Accountants**
#4, 30 Wertheim Ct.
Richmond Hill, ON L4B 1B9
Tel: 905-881-2244; *Fax:* 905-881-8006

Richmond Hill: **Ralph Lando Orvitz**
#6, 10 West Pearce St.
Richmond Hill, ON L4B 1B6
Tel: 905-889-1549; *Fax:* 905-889-2054
www.ralphlandoorvitz.ca

Richmond Hill: **Truster Zweig LLP**
500 Hwy. 7 East
Richmond Hill, ON L4B 1J1
Tel: 416-222-5555; *Fax:* 905-707-1322
www.trusterzweig.ca

Richmond Hill: **Willington Martin Professional Corporation**
#200, 30 Via Renzo Dr.
Richmond Hill, ON L4S 0B8
Tel: 416-848-1585
willington_martin@porterhetu.com
www.inbalance.org

Sarnia: **Collins Barrow Sarnia**
1350 L'Heritage Dr.
Sarnia, ON N7S 6H8
Tel: 519-542-7725; *Fax:* 519-542-8321
sarnia@collinsbarrow.com
www.collinsbarrow.com/en/sarnia-ontario

Sarnia: **Hazlitt Steeves Harris Dunn LLP**
301 Front St. North
Sarnia, ON N7T 5S6
Tel: 519-336-6133
www.hshd.ca

Sarnia: **TurnerMoore LLP, Certified General Accountants**
316 George St.
Sarnia, ON N7T 7H9
Tel: 519-344-1271; *Fax:* 519-344-1268
www.turnermoore.com

St Catharines: **Durward Jones Barkwell & Company LLP (DJB)**
#300, 20 Corporate Park Dr.
St Catharines, ON L2S 3W2
Tel: 905-684-9221; *Fax:* 905-684-0566
Toll-Free: 866-219-9431
stcath@djb.com
djb.com

St Catharines: **Finucci Watters LLP**
58 St. Paul St. West
St Catharines, ON L2S 2C5
Tel: 905-682-2406
finucciwatters.com

St Thomas: **Kee, Perry & DeVrieze**
15 Barrie Blvd.
St Thomas, ON N5P 4B9
Tel: 519-631-6360; *Fax:* 519-631-2198
info@kpl-accountants.ca
www.kpl-accountants.ca

Stouffville: **Joe Nemni Financial Services Inc.**
33 Katherine Cres.
Stouffville, ON L4A 1K4
Tel: 905-640-0065
www.joenemni.com

Sudbury: **Collins Barrow SNT LLP**
1174 St. Jerome St.
Sudbury, ON P3A 2V9
Tel: 705-560-5592; *Fax:* 705-560-8832
sudbury@cbsnt.ca
www.collinsbarrow.com/en/sudbury-ontario

Thornhill: **Brockman & Partners Forensic Accountants Inc.**
10 Maxwell Ct.
Thornhill, ON L4J 6Y3
Tel: 905-764-3851; *Fax:* 905-764-3537
www.brockmanandpartners.ca
Other Contact Information: Pager: 416-715-7147

Thornhill: **Ernest H. Wolkin, Chartered Accountant**
#500A, 300 John St.
Thornhill, ON L3T 5W4
Tel: 905-882-2100
info@wolkin.ca
www.wolkin.ca

Thornhill: **Herb Kokotow, Chartered Accountant**
3 German Mills Rd.
Thornhill, ON L3T 4H4
Tel: 905-764-6175
kokotow6175@rogers.com
www.charteredaccountantontario.ca

Thornhill: **Prasad Ghumman LLP**
7699 Yonge St.
Thornhill, ON L3T 1Z5
Tel: 416-226-9840; *Fax:* 416-226-9179
Toll-Free: 888-550-8227
firm@torontocasolutions.com
torontocasolutions.com

Toronto: **The Accounting Firm of D. Jae Gold, BA, CE CFE**
#806, 920 Yonge St.
Toronto, ON M4M 3C7
Tel: 416-944-3376; *Fax:* 416-944-3893
www.rocknrollaccountant.com

Toronto: Adams & Miles LLP Chartered Accountant
#501, 2550 Victoria Park Ave.
Toronto, ON M2J 5A9
Tel: 416-502-2201; *Fax:* 416-502-2210
solution@adamsmiles.com
www.adamsmiles.com
Social Media: www.facebook.com/359147854155757; twitter.com/AdamsMilesLLP

Toronto: Alan I. Stern, Chartered Accountant
#6, 4646 Dufferin St.
Toronto, ON M3H 5S4
Tel: 416-209-8318
info@sternca.com
www.sternca.com

Toronto: Albert L. Stal
#301, 1370 Don Mills Rd.
Toronto, ON M3B 3N7
Tel: 416-449-0130; *Fax:* 416-449-6694

Toronto: Allain, Isabella & McLean LLP
#205, 5401 Eglinton Ave. West
Toronto, ON M9C 5K6
Tel: 416-620-7740; *Fax:* 416-920-0023

Toronto: Allan W. Leppik, Chartered Accountant, Professional Corporation
260 Queen St. West, 4th Fl.
Toronto, ON M5V 1Z8
Tel: 416-822-6744; *Fax:* 416-850-5449
www.leppikaccounting.com

Toronto: Baratz Judelman Preisz Pajak, Chartered Accountants
4116 Bathurst St.
Toronto, ON M3H 3P2
Tel: 416-633-6061; *Fax:* 416-633-1653
www.baratzjudelman.com

Toronto: Bass & Murphy Chartered Accountants LLP
885 Progress Ave., #LPH1
Toronto, ON M1H 3G3
Tel: 416-431-3030; *Fax:* 416-431-3340
www.bassmurphy.com

Toronto: Bennett Gold LLP, Chartered Accountants
#900, 150 Ferrand Dr.
Toronto, ON M3C 3E5
Tel: 416-449-2249; *Fax:* 416-449-4133
www.bennettgold.ca

Toronto: Brian Borts, Chartered Accountant
892 Bathurst St.
Toronto, ON M5R 3G3
Tel: 416-588-4474; *Fax:* 416-588-8771
Toll-Free: 877-282-6274
tambriweb@interlog.com
www.brianborts.com

Toronto: Brief Rotfarb Wynberg Cappe LLP
#402, 3854 Bathurst St.
Toronto, ON M3H 3N2
Tel: 416-635-9080; *Fax:* 416-635-0462
info@brwc.com
www.brwc.com

Toronto: Brudner Herblum & McDougall LLP Chartered Accountants
#302, 4141 Yonge St.
Toronto, ON M2P 2A8
Tel: 416-250-7224; *Fax:* 416-733-4579
info@charteredaccountants.ca
www.charteredaccountants.ca

Toronto: CA4IT Inc.
478 Richmond St. West
Toronto, ON M5V 1Y2
Fax: 416-487-8045
Toll-Free: 800-465-7532
toronto@ca4it.com
www.ca4it.com
Other Contact Information: Local E-mails: edmonton@ca4it.com; ottawa@ca4it.com; calgary@ca4it.com; montreal@ca4it.com

Toronto: Cadesky & Associates LLP
Atria III
#1001, 2225 Sheppard Ave. East
Toronto, ON M2J 5C2
Tel: 416-498-9500; *Fax:* 416-498-9501
taxpros@cadesky.com
www.cadesky.com

Toronto: Campbell Valuation Partners Limited (CVPL)
#320, 70 University Ave.
Toronto, ON M5J 2M4
Tel: 416-597-1198
info@cvpl.com
www.cvpl.com

Toronto: Canham Rogers Chartered Accountants
#500, 2 Lansing Sq.
Toronto, ON M2J 4P8
Tel: 416-494-8000; *Fax:* 416-494-8032
info@canhamrogers.com
www.canhamrogers.com

Toronto: Chaplin & Burd Chartered Accountants, LLP
#501, 55 Town Centre Ct.
Toronto, ON M1P 4X4
Tel: 416-290-6455; *Fax:* 416-290-5190
chaplinburd.com

Toronto: Chaplin & Co. Chartered Accountants
#710, 1110 Finch Ave. West
Toronto, ON M3J 2T2
Tel: 416-667-7060; *Fax:* 416-663-3746
ca@chaplinco.com
www.chaplinco.com

Toronto: Cholkan & Stepczuk LLP
#300, 1 Eva Rd.
Toronto, ON M9C 4Z5
Tel: 416-695-9500; *Fax:* 416-695-3837
Toll-Free: 800-363-9500
info@c-s.ca
www.c-s.ca

Toronto: Clark & Horner LLP
Dynamic Funds Tower
PO Box 181
#2601, 1 Adelaide St. East
Toronto, ON M5C 2V9
Tel: 416-861-0431; *Fax:* 416-861-0587
info@clarkandhorner.com
www.clarkandhorner.com

Toronto: Clarke Henning LLP
#801, 10 Bay St.
Toronto, ON M5J 2R8
Tel: 416-364-4421; *Fax:* 416-367-8032
Toll-Free: 888-422-1241
ch@clarkehenning.com
www.clarkehenning.com

Toronto: Collins Barrow Toronto LLP
Collins Barrow Place
#700, 11 King St. West
Toronto, ON M5H 4C7
Tel: 416-480-0160; *Fax:* 416-480-2646
torontoinfo@collinsbarrow.com
www.collinsbarrow.com/en/toronto-ontario

Toronto: Cooper & Company Ltd.
#108, 1120 Finch Ave. West
Toronto, ON M3J 3H7
Tel: 416-665-3383; *Fax:* 416-665-0897
info@cooperco.ca
www.cooperco.ca

Toronto: Cooper, Green & Warren LLP
#100, 1370 Don Mills Rd.
Toronto, ON M3B 3N7
Tel: 416-510-1777; *Fax:* 416-510-1709
www.cgwca.com

Toronto: Craig & Company Chartered Accountant
#203, 5468 Dundas St. West
Toronto, ON M9B 6E3
Tel: 416-259-5161; *Fax:* 416-259-7224
www.craigco.ca

Toronto: Crowe Soberman LLP
#1100, 2 St. Clair Ave. East
Toronto, ON M4T 2T5
Tel: 416-964-7633; *Fax:* 416-964-6454
Toll-Free: 866-964-7633
info@crowesoberman.com
www.crowehorwath.net/soberman
Social Media: www.facebook.com/crowesoberman; twitter.com/CroweSoberman

Toronto: Cunningham LLP
#810, 2001 Sheppard Ave. East
Toronto, ON M2J 4Z8
Tel: 416-496-1051; *Fax:* 416-496-1546
Toll-Free: 800-461-4618
info@cunninghamca.com
www.cunninghamca.com
Social Media: twitter.com/CunninghamLLP

Toronto: Cusimano Professional Corporation, Chartered Accountant
#201, 185 Bridgeland Ave.
Toronto, ON M6A 1Y7
Tel: 416-849-4000; *Fax:* 416-849-0009
Toll-Free: 877-624-4001
www.cusimanopc.com
Social Media: twitter.com/@cusimanopc

Toronto: Darryl H. Hayashi, CA Professional Corporation
953 O'Connor Dr.
Toronto, ON M4B 2S7
Tel: 416-751-7653; *Fax:* 416-751-8032
www.darrylhayashi.com

Toronto: DCY Professional Corporation Chartered Accountants
50 Valleybrook Dr.
Toronto, ON M3B 2S9
Tel: 416-510-8888; *Fax:* 416-510-2699
dcy@dcy.ca
dcy.ca
Social Media: plus.google.com/116921024485656290576; www.facebook.com/DCYPCCA

Toronto: DNTW Toronto LLP
#703, 45 Sheppard Ave. East
Toronto, ON M2N 5W9
Tel: 416-638-2000; *Fax:* 416-638-6222
toronto.help@dntw.com
www.dntw.com

Toronto: Duff & Phelps Corp.
Bay Adelaide Centre
333 Bay St., 14th Fl.
Toronto, ON M5H 2R2
Tel: 416-364-9719; *Toll-Free:* 866-282-8258
www.duffandphelps.com/intl/en-ca

Toronto: Edmondson Ball Davies LLP, Chartered Accountants
#501, 10 Milner Business Ct.
Toronto, ON M1B 3C6
Tel: 416-293-5560; *Fax:* 416-293-5377
www.ebdcas.com

Toronto: Edward & Manning LLP
#200, 100 Consilium Pl.
Toronto, ON M1H 3E3
Tel: 416-621-9998
info@emllp.ca
emllp.ca

Toronto: Ernst & Young Orenda Corporate Finance Inc.
Ernst & Young Tower
PO Box 251
222 Bay St.
Toronto, ON M5K 1J7
Tel: 416-864-1234; *Fax:* 416-864-1174
www.ey.com/CA/en/Services/Transactions

Toronto: Fedder Gurau & Staniewski Chartered Accountants
5312 Yonge St.
Toronto, ON M2N 5P9
Tel: 416-222-3221; *Fax:* 416-222-2034
office@fgsaccountants.com
www.fgsaccountants.com

Toronto: Fruitman Kates LLP Chartered Accountants
1055 Eglinton Ave. West
Toronto, ON M6C 2C9
Tel: 416-920-3434; *Fax:* 416-920-7799
info@fruitman.ca
www.fruitman.ca

***Toronto:* Fuller Landau LLP**
151 Bloor St. West, 12th Fl.
Toronto, ON M5S 1S4
Tel: 416-645-6500; *Fax:* 416-645-6501
info.tor@fullerlandau.com
www.fullerllp.com
Social Media: www.facebook.com/FullerLandauLLP

***Toronto:* Galloway Consulting Group Inc.**
#703, 1200 Eglinton Ave. East
Toronto, ON M3C 1H9
Tel: 416-803-5638; *Fax:* 416-449-7342
info@gallowayconsulting.ca
www.gallowayconsulting.ca
Social Media: www.facebook.com/31042926672

***Toronto:* Gardner Zuk Dessen, Chartered Accountants**
#205, 265 Rimrock Rd.
Toronto, ON M3J 3C6
Tel: 416-631-9800; *Fax:* 416-631-9183
info@gzd.ca
www.gzd.ca

***Toronto:* Gary Booth Chartered Accountants**
#406, 555 Burnhamthorpe Rd.
Toronto, ON M9C 2Y3
Tel: 416-626-2727; *Fax:* 416-621-7136
admin@garybooth.com
www.garybooth.com

***Toronto:* Geoff Crewe, Chartered Professional Accountant**
#960, 200 Yorkland Blvd.
Toronto, ON M2J 5C1
Tel: 416-490-1042; *Fax:* 416-497-0120
info@gcrewe.com
www.gcrewe.com

***Toronto:* GO LLP Chartered Accountants**
#710, 200 Yorkland Blvd.
Toronto, ON M2J 5C1
Tel: 416-490-1600; *Fax:* 416-490-1606
info@gollp.com
www.gollp.com

***Toronto:* Goodman & Associates LLP**
#200, 45 St. Clair Ave. West
Toronto, ON M4V 1K6
Tel: 416-967-3444
www.sggg.com

***Toronto:* Granatstein Lusthouse Mar, LLP**
#940, 200 Yorkland Blvd.
Toronto, ON M2J 5C1
Tel: 416-499-9099; *Fax:* 416-499-9299
yourca.net

***Toronto:* Green Chencinski Starkman Eles LLP Chartered Accountants (GCSE)**
#1906, 4950 Yonge St.
Toronto, ON M2N 6K1
Tel: 416-512-6000; *Fax:* 416-512-9800
info@gcse-ca.com
www.gcse-ca.com

***Toronto:* Hasnain K. Panju, Chartered Accountant & Certified Management Consultant**
#102-103, 716 Gordon Baker Rd.
Toronto, ON M2H 3B4
Tel: 416-756-9562; *Fax:* 416-756-3118
www.hasnainkpanju.com
Social Media: www.facebook.com/1432655383624625

***Toronto:* Hema Murdock CPA, CA**
1312 Danforth Ave.
Toronto, ON M4J 1M9
Tel: 416-696-6653
hemamurdock.ca

***Toronto:* Hilborn LLP**
PO Box 49
#3100, 401 Bay St.
Toronto, ON M5H 2Y4
Tel: 416-364-1359; *Fax:* 416-364-9503
info@hilbornca.com
www.hilbornca.com

***Toronto:* Hogg, Shain & Scheck**
#404, 2255 Sheppard Ave. East
Toronto, ON M2J 4Y1
Tel: 416-499-3100; *Fax:* 416-499-4449
www.hss-ca.com
Social Media: plus.google.com/106775948331757072219; www.facebook.com/HoggShainScheck; twitter.com/HoggShainScheck

***Toronto:* Ilavsky Chartered Accountants**
943 Kingston Rd.
Toronto, ON M4E 1S8
Tel: 416-690-1597; *Fax:* 416-690-0617
contact@ilavskyaccounting.ca
www.ilavskyaccounting.ca
Social Media: www.facebook.com/149973658418286; twitter.com/ilavskyca

***Toronto:* Innes Robinson, Chartered Accountants Professional Corporation (ICRA)**
#100, 2005 Sheppard Ave. East
Toronto, ON M2J 5B4
Tel: 416-590-1728; *Fax:* 416-590-2576
innesrobinson.ca

***Toronto:* Jake Kuperhause - Chartered Accountant**
#504, 55 Eglinton Ave. East
Toronto, ON M4P 1G8
Tel: 416-932-2665; *Fax:* 416-932-9100
www.jakekuperhause.com

***Toronto:* John R. Motte, Chartered Accountant**
PO Box 2342
#1100, 2300 Yonge St.
Toronto, ON M4P 1E4
Tel: 416-487-7347; *Fax:* 416-486-6378
www.johnmott.com
Other Contact Information: Alternate Phone: 416-482-2478
Social Media: www.facebook.com/336939769680546; twitter.com/johnmottca

***Toronto:* Jones & Cosman Chartered Professional Accountants**
25 Laidlaw St.
Toronto, ON M6K 1X3
Tel: 647-495-9872
www.jonescosman.com
Other Contact Information: Alternate Phone: 416-629-1469

***Toronto:* JRPC Chartered Accountant Toronto**
#300, 261 Davenport Rd.
Toronto, ON M5R 1K3
Tel: 416-487-3000
www.professionalcorporation.ca
Other Contact Information: Alternate URL: www.jrpctaxes.com

***Toronto:* Kanish & Partners LLP**
#1203, 1200 Bay St.
Toronto, ON M5R 2A5
Tel: 416-975-9292; *Fax:* 416-975-9275
kp@kanish-partners.com
www.kanish-partners.com

***Toronto:* Kapadia LLP Chartered Accountants & Advisors**
#1, 265 Rimrock Rd.
Toronto, ON M3J 3C6
Tel: 416-635-8025; *Fax:* 416-638-6815
info@kapadiallp.com
www.kapadiallp.com

***Toronto:* Kay & Warburton Chartered Accountants (KWCA)**
#403, 225 Richmond St. West
Toronto, ON M5V 1W2
Tel: 416-977-2416; *Fax:* 416-977-8549
info@kwca.com
www.kwca.com

***Toronto:* Kelly Porter Hétu**
475 Queen St. East
Toronto, ON M5A 1T9
Tel: 416-955-0060; *Fax:* 416-955-0061
info@kellyporterhetu.com
kellyporterhetu.com

***Toronto:* Kenneth Michalak**
1576 Bloor St. West
Toronto, ON M6P 1A4
Tel: 416-588-2808; *Fax:* 416-588-3634
Toll-Free: 866-258-4788
www.kjmcga.com

***Toronto:* KJ Accounting Services**
1 Yonge St.
Toronto, ON M5E 1E5
www.kjaccounting.ca
Social Media: www.facebook.com/CanadaTax; twitter.com/canada_tax_info

***Toronto:* Klingbaum Barkin LLP**
The Madison Centre
#1906, 4950 Yonge St.
Toronto, ON M2N 6K1
Tel: 416-512-1221; *Fax:* 416-512-1284
mk@klingbaumbarkin.com
www.klingbaumbarkin.com

***Toronto:* Kopstick Osher Chartered Accountants, LLP**
#805, 970 Lawrence Ave. NW
Toronto, ON M6A 3B6
Tel: 416-256-7748
www.kopstick.ca

***Toronto:* Koster, Spinks & Koster LLP (KSK)**
4 Glengrove Ave. West
Toronto, ON M4R 1N4
Tel: 416-489-8100; *Fax:* 416-489-9194
info@ksk.ca
www.ksk.ca

***Toronto:* Kriens-LaRose, LLP**
37 Main St.
Toronto, ON M4E 2V5
Tel: 416-690-6800; *Fax:* 416-690-9919
www.krienslarose.com

***Toronto:* Kudlow & McCann Chartered Accountants**
#401, 21 St. Clair Ave.
Toronto, ON M4T 1L9
Tel: 416-924-4780; *Fax:* 416-924-5332
www.kudlowmccann.com

***Toronto:* Kwan Chan Law Chartered Accountants Professional Corporation**
#910, 4950 Yonge St.
Toronto, ON M2N 6K1
Tel: 416-226-6668; *Fax:* 416-226-6862

***Toronto:* Lior Zehtser, Chartered Accountant**
#408, 1183 Finch Ave. West
Toronto, ON M3J 2G2
Tel: 416-721-1651
www.zehtserca.com
Social Media: www.facebook.com/ZehtserCA; twitter.com/ZehtserCA

***Toronto:* Lipton LLP**
#600, 245 Fairview Mall Dr.
Toronto, ON M2J 4T1
Tel: 416-496-2900; *Fax:* 416-496-0559
Toll-Free: 877-869-2900
info@liptonllp.com
www.liptonllp.com
Social Media: www.facebook.com/268028273324135; twitter.com/LiptonLLP

***Toronto:* M. Schwab Accounting Services Ltd.**
#606, 94 Cumberland St.
Toronto, ON M5R 1A3
Tel: 416-324-9933

***Toronto:* Maureen Wei, CGA**
#1200, 251 Consumers Rd.
Toronto, ON M2J 4R3
Tel: 416-628-9423; *Fax:* 647-438-5835
Toll-Free: 855-986-0666
info@cancnaccounting.com
www.cancnaccounting.com
Social Media: www.facebook.com/246611085393446; twitter.com/cancncga

***Toronto:* McCarney Greenwood LLP**
#600, 10 Bay St.
Toronto, ON M5J 2R8
Tel: 416-362-0515; *Fax:* 416-362-0539
info@mgca.com
www.mgca.com

***Toronto:* McGovern, Hurley, Cunningham LLP**
#300, 2005 Sheppard Ave. East
Toronto, ON M2J 5B4
Tel: 416-496-1234; *Fax:* 416-496-0125
info@mhc-ca.com
www.mhc-ca.com

***Toronto:* Mehl & Reynolds LLP**
Yorkdale Pl.
#200, 1 Yorkdale Rd.
Toronto, ON M6A 3A1
Tel: 416-787-0681; *Fax:* 416-787-7630
webhome.idirect.com/~gmr

***Toronto:* Michael Argue Chartered Accountant**
#303, 150 Consumers Rd.
Toronto, ON M2J 1P2
Tel: 416-490-8544; *Fax:* 416-490-8096
www.argueca.com

***Toronto:* Michael Atlas, Chartered Accountant**
Richmond-Adelaide Centre
#2500, 120 Adelaide St. West
Toronto, ON M5H 1T1
Tel: 416-860-9175; *Fax:* 416-860-9189
matlas@taxca.com
www.taxca.com
Social Media: www.facebook.com/MichaelAtlasCPA; twitter.com/_matlas

***Toronto:* M.J. Zafar Chartered Accountant (MJZ)**
#201, 49 Elm St.
Toronto, ON M5G 1H1
Tel: 647-931-2425
info@mjzafar.com
mjzafar.com
Social Media: www.facebook.com/mjzafargroup; twitter.com/mjzafar

***Toronto:* MSI Spergel Inc.**
#200, 505 Consumers Rd.
Toronto, ON M2J 4V8
Tel: 416-497-1660; *Fax:* 416-494-7199
Toll-Free: 855-773-7435
www.spergel.ca
Social Media: www.youtube.com/user/msiSpergelinc; plus.google.com/107475087409077633516; www.facebook.com/250483285084239; twitter.com/msispergelinc

***Toronto:* Myers Tsiofas Norheim LLP**
#812, 330 Bay St.
Toronto, ON M5H 2S8
Tel: 416-868-9017; *Fax:* 416-868-9256
www.mtnllp.ca

***Toronto:* National Tax Service**
10 Four Seasons Pl., 10th Fl.
Toronto, ON M9B 6H7
Tel: 416-781-0829
admin@nationaltaxservice.ca
www.nationaltaxservice.ca
Other Contact Information: Alt. Phone: 647-493-7948; URL: www.etobicokeonaccountingservice.ca

***Toronto:* Nevcon Accounting Services**
PO Box 43541
1531 Bayview Ave.
Toronto, ON M4G 4G8
Tel: 416-487-7996; *Fax:* 416-946-1098
Toll-Free: 888-463-8366
info@nevcon.com
www.nevcon.com
Social Media: twitter.com/NevconAccount

***Toronto:* Nicholas Sider, Certified General Accountant**
#303, 344 Bloor St. West
Toronto, ON M5S 3A7
Tel: 416-913-9243; *Fax:* 416-406-4805
ns@torontotaxaccountant.com
www.taxaccountantnsider.com

***Toronto:* Norman A. Rothberg, Chartered Accountant**
#200, 1446 Don Mills Rd.
Toronto, ON M3B 3N3
Tel: 416-386-0388; *Fax:* 416-386-1823
enquiry@nrcatax.com
www.nrcatax.com

***Toronto:* Ozden & Cheung Chartered Accountants Professional Corporation**
431 Westmoreland Ave. North
Toronto, ON M6H 3A6
Tel: 416-799-0835; *Fax:* 647-776-7700
info@ozdencheung.com
www.charteredaccountantstoronto.ca

***Toronto:* Padgett Business Services Toronto**
#103, 38 Niagara St.
Toronto, ON M5V 3X1
Tel: 416-944-2746; *Fax:* 416-944-0957
info@padgetttoronto.com
www.padgetttoronto.com

***Toronto:* Pinto Professional Corporation**
#400, 1235 Bay St.
Toronto, ON M5R 3K4
Tel: 416-513-1012; *Fax:* 416-981-8625
contact@pintocpa.ca
www.pintocpa.ca

***Toronto:* PKF Kraft Berger Professional Corporation**
#1801, 1 Yonge St.
Toronto, ON M5E 1W7
Tel: 416-949-7311; *Fax:* 905-475-2260
Toll-Free: 888-563-6868
pkftoronto@pkfkb.ca
www.kbllp.ca

***Toronto:* PricewaterhouseCoopers LLP, Canada**
PwC Tower
#2600, 18 York St.
Toronto, ON M5J 0B2
Tel: 416-863-1133; *Fax:* 416-365-8178
www.pwc.com/ca
Social Media: www.youtube.com/user/PwCCanada; www.facebook.com/pwccanada; twitter.com/PwC_Canada_LLP

***Toronto:* Renée S. Karn, Certified General Accountant**
86 Acton Ave.
Toronto, ON M3H 4H1
Tel: 416-499-0012
info@reneekarn.com
www.porterhetu.com
Other Contact Information: Alternate Phone: 416-499-0194

***Toronto:* Ring Chartered Accountant**
443C Queen St. East
Toronto, ON M5A 1T6
Tel: 416-482-2477; *Fax:* 416-482-2752
www.ringca.ca
Other Contact Information: Alternate Phone: 416-482-2478

***Toronto:* Rita Zelikman Chartered Accountant Professional Corporation**
#301, 1137 Centre St.
Toronto, ON L4J 3M6
Tel: 416-644-4788; *Fax:* 416-644-4790
www.ritazelikman.com
Other Contact Information: Cell Phone: 416-271-2234

***Toronto:* Robin Taub Financial Consulting**
1210 Eglinton Ave. West
Toronto, ON M6C 2E3
Tel: 416-256-4498; *Fax:* 416-256-4604
robintaub.com

***Toronto:* Rosen & Associates Limited**
PO Box 101
#830, 121 King St. West
Toronto, ON M5H 3T9
Tel: 416-363-4515; *Fax:* 416-363-4849
j.cunningham@rosen-associates.com
www.rosen-associates.com

***Toronto:* Rosenberg Smith & Partners LLP**
#200, 2000 Steeles Ave. West
Toronto, ON L4K 3E9
Tel: 416-798-4997; *Fax:* 905-660-3064
rsp@rsp.ca
www.rsp.ca

***Toronto:* Rosenswig McRae Thorpe LLP**
#1101, 655 Bay St.
Toronto, ON M5G 2K4
Tel: 416-977-6600; *Fax:* 416-977-5874
info@rmtca.ca
www.rmtca.ca

***Toronto:* Rosenthal Zaretsky Niman & Co., LLP**
#625, 4211 Yonge St.
Toronto, ON M2P 2A9
Tel: 416-636-7500; *Fax:* 416-636-6545
Toll-Free: 877-871-4258
mail@rznaccountants.com
www.rznaccountants.com

***Toronto:* Roxana Rodriguez Tax & Accounting**
247 Westmount Ave.
Toronto, ON M6E 3M9
Tel: 647-495-9872
www.torontobusinessaccounting.ca

***Toronto:* Rumanek & Company Ltd.**
#714, 1280 Finch Ave. West
Toronto, ON M3J 3K6
Tel: 416-665-3328; *Fax:* 416-665-7634
www.rumanek.com
Other Contact Information: Alt. URL: www.trustee-in-bankruptcy.com
Social Media: rumanek.com/blog; www.youtube.com/user/trusteeinbankruptcy

***Toronto:* Sam Seidman, Chartered Accountant**
629 Sheppard Ave. West
Toronto, ON M3H 2S3
Tel: 416-398-1700; *Fax:* 416-398-6226
samseidman.com
Other Contact Information: Alternate URL: torontoaccountant.ca
Social Media: www.pinterest.com/torontoca; www.facebook.com/torontoaccountant; twitter.com/Sam_CA_Toronto

***Toronto:* Sandor M. Feld Chartered Accountant**
#319, 3089 Bathurst St.
Toronto, ON M6A 2A4
Tel: 416-789-4846; *Fax:* 416-789-5123
info@sfeldca.com
accountant-toronto.com

***Toronto:* Schwartz Levitsky Feldman Valuations Inc.**
RioCan Yonge Eglinton Centre
#1500, 2300 Yonge St.
Toronto, ON M4P 1E4
Tel: 416-785-5353; *Fax:* 416-785-5663
www.slf.ca/business_valuation.html

***Toronto:* Segal LLP**
#500, 2005 Sheppard Ave. East
Toronto, ON M2J 5B4
Tel: 416-391-4499; *Fax:* 416-391-3280
Toll-Free: 800-206-7307
www.segalllp.com
Social Media: www.facebook.com/SegalLLP

***Toronto:* Serbinski & Associates Inc.**
183 Sheppard Ave. West
Toronto, ON M2N 1M9
Tel: 416-733-0300; *Fax:* 416-352-6004
Toll-Free: 888-878-2937
mtscpa@serbinski.com
www.serbinski.com

***Toronto:* SF Partnership, LLP**
#400, 4950 Yonge St.
Toronto, ON M2N 6K1
Tel: 416-250-1212; *Fax:* 416-250-1225
general@sfgroup.ca
www.sfgroup.ca
Social Media: www.facebook.com/SFPartnership

***Toronto:* Shrigley Battrick Chartered Accountants**
#500, 34 King St. East
Toronto, ON M5C 2X8
Tel: 416-368-2834; *Fax:* 416-360-0278
shrigleybattrick.com

***Toronto:* Silver + Goren Chartered Accountants**
#107, 40 Wynford Dr.
Toronto, ON M3C 1J5
Tel: 416-385-1633; *Fax:* 416-385-2139
info@silvergoren.com
silvergoren.com

***Toronto:* Sims & Company Chartered Accountant Professional Corporation**
346 Forman Ave.
Toronto, ON M4S 2S7
Tel: 416-481-9101; *Fax:* 416-481-7693
www.simsandcompany.com

***Toronto:* Sloan Partners LLP**
#6, 4646 Dufferin St.
Toronto, ON M3H 5S4
Tel: 416-665-7735; *Fax:* 416-649-7725
info@sloangroup.ca
www.sloangroup.ca
Social Media: www.facebook.com/SloanGroup

***Toronto:* Sone & Rovet, LLP**
#406, 1200 Sheppard Ave. East
Toronto, ON M2K 2S5
Tel: 416-498-7200; *Fax:* 416-498-6877
www.sonerovet.com

***Toronto:* Sonny Jackson Chartered Accountant Professional Corporation**
Toronto, ON
Tel: 647-828-6652
contact@sonnyjackson.com
www.sonnyjackson.com

***Toronto:* Spergel Forster Silverberg & Gluckman LLP (SFSG)**
#200, 505 Consumers Rd.
Toronto, ON M2J 4V8
Tel: 416-497-1660; *Fax:* 416-494-7199
sfsg.ca

***Toronto:* SRJ Chartered Accountants Professional Corporation**
#1302A, 55 Queen St. East
Toronto, ON M5C 1R5
Tel: 647-725-2537
info@srjca.com
www.srjca.com
Other Contact Information: Mississauga Phone: 647-725-2537; Fax: 416-981-7979

***Toronto:* Stern Cohen LLP**
45 St. Clair Ave. West, 14th Fl.
Toronto, ON M4V 1L3
Tel: 416-967-5100; *Fax:* 416-967-4372
www.sterncohen.com

***Toronto:* Stewart & Kett Financial Advisors Inc.**
Citicorp Place
#911, 123 Front St. West
Toronto, ON M5J 2M2
Tel: 416-362-6322; *Fax:* 416-362-6302
mail@stewartkett.com
www.stewartkett.com

***Toronto:* Tator, Rose & Leong, Chartered Accountants**
#603, 160 Eglinton Ave. East
Toronto, ON M4P 3B5
Tel: 416-924-1404; *Fax:* 416-964-3383
email@tarole.ca
www.tarole.ca

***Toronto:* Trowbridge Professional Corporation**
#1400, 25 Adelaide St. East
Toronto, ON M5C 3A1
Tel: 416-214-7833; *Fax:* 416-214-1281
info@trowbridge.ca
www.trowbridge.ca

***Toronto:* V.B. Sharma Professional Corporation, Chartered Accountants**
#200, 3390 Midland Ave.
Toronto, ON M1V 5K3
Tel: 416-292-4431; *Fax:* 416-292-7247
info@vbsharma.ca
www.vbsharma.ca

***Toronto:* Vincent Zaffino Chartered Accountants**
#301, 155 University Ave.
Toronto, ON M5H 3B7
Tel: 416-363-3031
info@vzca.com
vzca.com
Other Contact Information: Alt. URL: www.accountingcompanytoronto.ca
Social Media: www.facebook.com/VincentZaffinoCA

***Toronto:* Walsh & Company**
#520, 1200 Sheppard Ave. East
Toronto, ON M2K 2S5
Tel: 416-494-3404; *Toll-Free:* 888-372-1210
www.walshco.ca

***Toronto:* Wealth Stewards Inc.**
#1000, 10 Four Season's Pl.
Toronto, ON M9B 6H7
Tel: 905-891-6052; *Fax:* 905-891-6052
info@wealthstewards.ca
wealthstewards.ca
Social Media: www.youtube.com/channel/UCJNnxVvctH_EFvcuJBUwYJQ; www.facebook.com/wealthstewards; twitter.com/Wealth_Stewards

***Toronto:* Yale & Partners LLP**
#400, 20 Holly St.
Toronto, ON M4S 3E8
Tel: 416-485-6000; *Fax:* 416-485-1105
office@yaleandpartners.ca
www.yaleandpartners.ca

***Toronto:* Young & Grunier Chartered Accountants**
945 Mt. Pleasant Rd.
Toronto, ON M4P 2L7
Tel: 416-484-4844; *Fax:* 416-484-3717
mail@ygca.com
www.ygca.com

***Toronto:* Zeifmans LLP**
201 Bridgeland Ave.
Toronto, ON M6A 1Y7
Tel: 416-256-4000; *Fax:* 416-256-4003
Toll-Free: 855-256-8500
info@zeifmans.ca
www.zeifmans.ca
Other Contact Information: Alternate Fax: 416-256-4001
Social Media: www.facebook.com/Zeifmans-156011321212569; twitter.com/zeifmansllp

***Trenton:* Wilkinson & Company LLP**
PO Box 400
71 Dundas St. West
Trenton, ON K8V 5R6
Tel: 613-392-2592; *Fax:* 613-392-8512
Toll-Free: 888-713-7283
www.wilkinson.net

***Trenton:* Wilkinson & Company LLP**
PO Box 400
71 Dundas St. West
Trenton, ON K8V 5R6
Tel: 613-392-2592; *Fax:* 613-392-8512
Toll-Free: 888-713-7283
www.wilkinson.net

***Unionville:* Jeffrey G. Greenfield & Associates Chartered Accountants**
#115, 4591 Hwy. 7 East
Unionville, ON L3R 1M6
Tel: 647-557-1903
www.accountingfirmtorontoon.ca

***Vaughan:* Collins Barrow Vaughan LLP**
#600, 3300 Hwy. 7 West
Vaughan, ON L4K 4M3
Tel: 416-213-2600; *Fax:* 905-669-8705
vaughan@collinsbarrow.com
www.collinsbarrow.com/en/vaughan-ontario

***Vaughan:* Domenic Galati, CGA**
#510, 3100 Steeles Ave. West
Vaughan, ON L4K 3R1
Tel: 416-745-0245
domenic_galati@porterhetu.com
www.porterhetu.com

***Vaughan:* Fazzari + Partners LLP Chartered Accountants**
#901, 3300 Hwy. 7
Vaughan, ON L4K 4M3
Tel: 905-738-5758; *Fax:* 905-660-7228
info@fazzaripartners.com
fazzaripartners.com

***Vaughan:* KT Partners LLP**
#13, 56 Pennsylvania Ave.
Vaughan, ON L4K 3V9
Tel: 416-642-2616; *Fax:* 416-642-2617
info@ktpartners.ca
www.ktpartners.ca
Other Contact Information: Montréal, Phone: 514-600-0015; Fax: 514-600-0016
Social Media: www.facebook.com/156012181131711; twitter.com/KTPartnersllp

***Waterloo:* Clarke Starke & Diegel LLP (CSD)**
7 Union St. East
Waterloo, ON N2J 1B5
Tel: 519-579-5520; *Fax:* 519-570-3611
www.csdca.com

***Waterloo:* PricewaterhouseCoopers LLP, Canada - Waterloo**
#201, 95 King St. South
Waterloo, ON N2J 5A2
Tel: 519-570-5700; *Fax:* 519-570-5730
www.pwc.com/ca

***Waterloo:* Transport Financial Services Ltd.**
105 Bauer Pl.
Waterloo, ON N2L 6B5
Tel: 519-886-8070; *Fax:* 519-886-5214
Toll-Free: 800-461-5970
www.tfsgroup.com

***Whitby:* Copetti & Co.**
601 Brock St.
Whitby, ON L1N 4L1
Tel: 905-666-2111; *Fax:* 905-666-7869
www.copetti.ca

***Winchester:* Collins Barrow WCM LLP**
PO Box 390
475 Main St.
Winchester, ON K0C 2K0
Tel: 613-744-2854; *Fax:* 613-744-2586
winchester@collinsbarrow.com
www.collinsbarrow.com/en/winchester-ontario

***Windsor:* Collins Barrow Windsor LLP**
3260 Devon Dr.
Windsor, ON N8X 4L4
Tel: 519-258-5800; *Fax:* 519-256-6152
windsor@collinsbarrow.com
www.collinsbarrow.com/en/windsor-ontario

***Windsor:* Hyatt Lassaline LLP**
#203, 2510 Ouellette Ave.
Windsor, ON N8X 1L4
Tel: 519-966-4626; *Fax:* 519-966-9206
Toll-Free: 855-614-6441
info@hyattlassaline.com
hyattlassaline.com

***Windsor:* mbsp LLP Chartered Accountants**
Chrysler Building
#301, 1 Riverside Dr. West
Windsor, ON N9A 5K3
Tel: 519-252-1163; *Fax:* 519-252-5893
www.mbsp.ca

***Windsor:* PricewaterhouseCoopers LLP, Canada - Windsor**
245 Ouellette Ave., 3rd Fl.
Windsor, ON N9A 7J4
Tel: 519-985-8900; *Fax:* 519-258-5457
www.pwc.com/ca

***Windsor:* Roth Mosey & Partners LLP**
#300, 3100 Temple Dr.
Windsor, ON N8W 5J6
Tel: 519-977-6410; *Fax:* 519-977-7083
info@roth-mosey.com
www.roth-mosey.com

***Woodbridge:* Rashid & Quinney Chartered Accountants**
#401, 216 Chrislea Rd.
Woodbridge, ON L4L 8S5
Tel: 905-856-2677; *Fax:* 905-856-2679

***Woodstock:* Thornton VanTassel Chartered Accountants**
#101, 318 Connell St.
Woodstock, ON E7M 6B7
Tel: 506-324-8040; *Fax:* 506-325-2262
www.thorntonvantassel.com

Prince Edward Island

***Bloomfield:* Sharon R. O'Halloran CGA Inc.**
Bloomfield Mall
PO Box 15
2238 O'Halloran Rd.
Bloomfield, PE C0B 1E0
Tel: 902-859-4430
www.porterhetu.com
Other Contact Information: Alternate Phone: 902-859-4426
Social Media: www.facebook.com/SharonOHalloranCGAInc

***Charlottetown:* Arsenault Best Cameron Ellis**
PO Box 455
80 Water St.
Charlottetown, PE C1A 7L1
Tel: 902-368-3100; *Fax:* 902-566-5074
office@abce.ca
www.acgca.ca

***Charlottetown:* MRSB Group**
PO Box 2679
139 Queen St.
Charlottetown, PE C1A 8C3
Tel: 902-368-2643; *Fax:* 902-566-5633
office@mrsbgroup.com
www.mrsbgroup.com
Social Media: www.facebook.com/mrsbgroup; twitter.com/mrsb_group

***Summerside:* Peter M. Baglole, Chartered Accountant**
PO Box 1373
#7, 293 Water St.
Summerside, PE C1N 4K2
Tel: 902-436-1663; *Fax:* 902-436-1604
www.baglole.ca

***Summerside:* Schurman Sudsbury & Associates Ltd.**
189 Water St.
Summerside, PE C1N 1B2
Tel: 902-436-2171; *Fax:* 902-436-0960
schurman-sudsbury@isn.net

Quebec

***Blainville:* LDL Lévesque Comptables Professionels Agréés inc.**
#204, 10, boul de la Seigneurie est
Blainville, QC J7C 3V5
Tél: 450-437-8969; *Téléc:* 450-437-8996
info@ldllevesque.com
ldllevesque.com

***Blainville:* MGPH International Inc.**
#200, 1340, boul Curé Labelle
Blainville, QC J7C 2P2
Tel: 450-430-7526; *Fax:* 450-430-6809
www.marcilgirard.com
Social Media: www.youtube.com/marcilgirard

***Brossard:* Lehoux Boivin Iannitello, CPA, LLP (LBI)**
#300, 4255, boul Lapiniere
Brossard, QC J4Z 0C7
Tél: 450-678-4255; *Téléc:* 450-678-1700
lbca@lehouxboivin.com
www.lehouxboivin.com/affiliations/lehoux-boivin-ia nnitello-cpa-llp.html

***Brossard:* Lehoux Boivin, LLP**
#300, 4255, boul Lapiniere
Brossard, QC J4Z 0C7
Tél: 450-678-4255; *Téléc:* 450-678-1700
lbca@lehouxboivin.com
www.lehouxboivin.com

***Brossard:* PricewaterhouseCoopers LLP, Canada - Brossard**
#300, 4255, boul Lapiniere
Brossard, QC J4Z 0C7
Tél: 450-678-4255; *Téléc:* 450-678-1700
www.pwc.com/ca
Other Contact Information: Alt. Phone: 514-875-4204; Alt. Fax: 514-866-1887

***Chicoutimi:* Tremblay Porter Hétu**
644, rue Albanel
Chicoutimi, QC G7J 1N8
Tél: 418-545-7343
tremblay_porter_hetu@porterhetu.com
www.porterhetu.com
Other Contact Information: Tél: 418-545-6441

***Gatineau:* Collins Barrow Gatineau Inc.**
#105, 290, boul St-Joseph
Gatineau, QC J8Y 3Y3
Tel: 819-770-0009; *Fax:* 819-965-0152
gatineau@collinsbarrow.com
www.collinsbarrow.com/en/gatineau-quebec

***Gatineau:* PricewaterhouseCoopers LLP, Canada - Gatineau**
#101, 900, boul de la Carrière
Gatineau, QC J8Y 6T5
Tel: 819-643-7476; *Fax:* 819-776-0347
Toll-Free: 888-643-7476
www.pwc.com/ca

***Joliette:* Martin, Boulard & Associés, sencrl**
37, Place Bourget sud
Joliette, QC J6E 5G1
Tél: 450-759-2825
info@martinboulard.com
www.mba.qc.ca

***Lachine:* Martin & Cie**
1100, rue Notre-Dame
Lachine, QC H8S 2C4
Tel: 514-637-7887; *Fax:* 514-637-3566
c.martin@martin-cie.com
www.martin-cie.com

***Longueuil:* Dubé & Tétreault, Comptables agréés, S.E.N.C.**
#200, 3065, ch de Chambly
Longueuil, QC J4L 1N3
Tél: 450-442-0944; *Téléc:* 450-442-2166
www.dube-tetreault.com

***Lévis:* Lemieux Nolet Comptables Agréés SENCRL**
#400, 1610, boul Alphonse-Desjardins
Lévis, QC G6V 0H1
Tél: 418-833-2114; *Téléc:* 418-833-9983
Ligne sans frais: 866-833-2114
courrier@lemieuxnolet.ca
lemieuxnoletsyndic.com

***Montréal:* A. Bertucci, Chartered Professional Accountant**
1445, rue Lambert Closse
Montréal, QC H3H 1Z5
Tel: 514-932-3229; *Fax:* 514-932-4634
www.abertucci.com

***Montréal:* Accountatax Inc./ Comptataxe inc.**
147, rue Spring Garden
Montréal, QC H9B 2T7
Tel: 514-685-7394; *Fax:* 514-685-7411
Toll-Free: 877-685-7394
accountatax@videotron.ca
www.accountatax.ca

***Montréal:* Accuracy Canada**
#2650, 630, boul René-Lévesque ouest
Montréal, QC H3B 1S6
Tel: 514-333-0633
accuracy.canada@accuracy.com
www.accuracy.com

***Montréal:* Beauchemin Trépanier Comptables professionnels agréés inc.**
69, rue Sherbrooke ouest
Montréal, QC H2X 1X2
Tel: 514-847-0182; *Fax:* 514-849-9082
info@bt-cpa.ca
www.bt-cpa.ca

***Montréal:* Bessner Gallay Kreisman LLP**
4150, rue Ste-Catherine Ouest, 6è étage
Montréal, QC H3Z 2Y5
Tel: 514-908-3600; *Fax:* 514-908-3630
admin@crowebgk.com
www.crowebgk.com
Social Media: www.facebook.com/crowebgk

***Montréal:* Brunet, Roy, Dubé, Comptables agrées**
#1200, 7100 rue Jean-Talon
Montréal, QC H1M 3S3
Tél: 514-255-1001; *Téléc:* 514-255-1002
info@brd-cpa.com
brd-cpa.com
Média social: plus.google.com/+Brd-cpa; www.facebook.com/118961208163437

***Montréal:* Collins Barrow Montréal S.E.N.C.R.L/LLP**
#200, 606, rue Cathcart
Montréal, QC H3B 1K9
Tel: 514-866-8553; *Fax:* 514-866-8469
montreal@collinsbarrow.com
www.collinsbarrow.com/fr/montreal-quebec

***Montréal:* DNTW Chartered Accountants, LLP**
#200, 4420, ch. de la Côte de Liesse
Montréal, QC H4N 2P7
Tel: 514-739-3606; *Fax:* 514-739-9226
montreal.help@dntw.com
www.dntw.com

***Montréal:* Fauteux, Bruno, Bussière, Leewarden CPA, s.e.n.c.r.l. (FBBL)**
#805, 1100, boul Crémazie est
Montréal, QC H2P 2X2
Tél: 514-729-3221; *Téléc:* 514-593-8711
info@fbbl.ca
fbbl.ca
Média social: www.youtube.com/ExperienceFBBL; www.facebook.com/103520489748577

***Montréal:* Fine et associés/ Fine & Associates**
5101, rue Buchan
Montréal, QC H4P 1S4
Tél: 514-731-0761; *Téléc:* 514-731-4639

***Montréal:* Fuller Landau SENCRL**
Place du Canada
200, 1010, rue de la Gauchetiere ouest
Montréal, QC H3B 2S1
Tél: 514-875-2865; *Téléc:* 514-866-0247
Ligne sans frais: 888-355-6697
www.flmontreal.com
Média social: www.youtube.com/user/FullerLandauLLP; www.facebook.com/fl.llp; twitter.com/fl_llp

***Montréal:* Gestion-Pro Molige**
6455, rue Christophe-Colomb
Montréal, QC H2S 2G5
Tel: 514-274-6831; *Fax:* 514-274-8128
info@gpmolige.com
www.gpmolige.com

***Montréal:* Goldsmith Hersh S.E.N.C.R.L.**
#190, 8200, boul Decarie
Montréal, QC H4P 2P5
Tel: 514-933-8611; *Fax:* 514-933-1142
Toll-Free: 866-933-8611
www.gmhca.com

***Montréal:* Gosselin & Associés inc.**
7930 - 20e av
Montréal, QC H1Z 3S7
Tél: 514-376-4090; *Téléc:* 514-376-4099
info@gosselin-ca.com
www.gosselin-ca.com

***Montréal:* Le Groupe Belzile Tremblay**
#610, 5650, rue d'Iberville
Montréal, QC H2G 2B3
Tel: 514-384-3620; *Fax:* 514-384-3710
nrosso@belziletremblay.ca
www.belziletremblay.ca

***Montréal:* Hardy, Normand & Associés, S.E.N.C.R.L.**
#200, 7875, boul Louis-H.-Lafontaine
Montréal, QC H1K 4E4
Tél: 514-355-1550; *Téléc:* 514-355-1559
hn@hardynormand.com
www.hardynormand.com
Média social: twitter.com/hardynormand

***Montréal:* Info Comptabilité Plus (ICP)**
#201, 2035, Côte de Liesse
Montréal, QC H4N 2M5
Tel: 514-337-2677; *Fax:* 514-337-1594
info@infocplus.com
infocplus.com

***Montréal:* James Kromida, Compatable Professionnel Agréé/ James Kromida, Chartered Professional Accountant**
750, av Sainte-Croix
Montréal, QC H4L 3Y2
Tel: 514-747-3413; *Fax:* 514-747-0799
www.kromida.com

***Montréal:* JDM Consultation Inc.**
#203, 759, carré Victoria
Montréal, QC H2Y 2J7
Tel: 514-844-4536; *Fax:* 514-849-8467
jimmy@menegakis.ca
www.menegakis.ca
Social Media: www.facebook.com/jimmy.menegakis; twitter.com/jimmy_CPA_CA

***Montréal:* Levy Pilotte S.E.N.C.R.L./ Levy Pilotte LLP**
#700, 5250, boul Décarie
Montréal, QC H3X 3Z6
Tél: 514-487-1566; *Téléc:* 514-488-5145
contact@levypilotte.com
www.levypilotte.com

Montréal: **Martel Desjardins**
Édifice de la Banque Nationale de Paris
#1440, 1981, av. McGill College
Montréal, QC H3A 2Y1
Tel: 514-849-2793; *Fax:* 514-849-7104
md@marteldesjardins.com
www.marteldesjardins.ca

Montréal: **Mazars Harel Drouin, LLP**
#1200, 215, rue Saint-Jacques
Montréal, QC H2Y 1M6
Tel: 514-845-9253; *Fax:* 514-845-3859
contact@mazars.ca
www.mazars.ca
Social Media: www.youtube.com/user/MazarsGroup; www.facebook.com/MazarsGroup; twitter.com/MazarsGroup

Montréal: **MCA Consulting Group**
5240-B, rue Saint Denis
Montréal, QC H2J 2M2
Tel: 514-277-8081; *Fax:* 514-276-9150
info@groupemca.com
www.groupemca.com

Montréal: **Padgett Business Service of Quebec Inc.**
#101, 3974, rue Notre Dame ouest
Montréal, QC H4C 1R1
Tel: 514-369-3868; *Fax:* 514-807-3528
info@padgett.org
www.padgett.org

Montréal: **Padgett Business Services (West Island - East)**
88, boul Brunswick
Montréal, QC H9B 2C5
Tel: 514-684-8086; *Fax:* 514-684-0884
www.padgettwestisland.com

Montréal: **Padgett Montréal**
#402, 1100, boul Crémazie est
Montréal, QC H2P 2X2
Tel: 514-324-5321; *Toll-Free:* 866-530-5321
padgettmontreal.com

Montréal: **Perreault, Wolman, Grzywacz & Co.**
#814, 5250, rue Ferrier
Montréal, QC H4P 2N7
Tél: 514-731-7987; *Téléc:* 514-731-8782
www.pwgca.com

Montréal: **Petrie Raymond LLP**
#1000, 255, boul Crémazie est
Montréal, QC H2M 1M2
Tél: 514-342-4740; *Téléc:* 514-737-4049
info@petrieraymond.qc.ca
www.petrieraymond.qc.ca

Montréal: **Porter Hétu International (Québec) inc. (PHIQ)**
#100, 790, boul Marcel-Laurin
Montréal, QC H4L 2M6
Tel: 514-744-1500
accueil@phiq.ca
phiq.ca
Social Media: www.facebook.com/porterhetuintqcinc; twitter.com/PhiqStLaurent

Montréal: **PricewaterhouseCoopers LLP, Canada - Montréal**
#2500, 1250, boul René-Lévesque ouest
Montréal, QC H3B 4Y1
Tel: 514-205-5000; *Fax:* 514-876-1502
www.pwc.com/ca

Montréal: **PSB Boisjoli Inc.**
#400, 3333, boul Graham
Montréal, QC H3R 3L5
Tél: 514-341-5511; *Téléc:* 514-342-0589
info@psbboisjoli.ca
www.psbboisjoli.ca
Média social: www.facebook.com/PSBBoisjoli

Montréal: **Richter**
1981 McGill College, 11th Fl.
Montréal, QC H3A 0G6
Tel: 514-934-3400; *Fax:* 514-934-3408
info@richter.ca
www.richter.ca
Social Media: www.facebook.com/Richtercanada; twitter.com/Richtercanada

Montréal: **RSW Accounting & Consulting/ RSW Comptabilité & Conseil**
Place du Parc
#1900, 300, rue Léo-Pariseau
Montréal, QC H2X 4B5
Tel: 514-842-3911; *Toll-Free:* 866-842-3911
www.rsw.com

Montréal: **Schwartz Levitsky Feldman LLP/SRL (SLF)**
1980, rue Sherbrooke ouest, 10e étage
Montréal, QC H3H 1E8
Tel: 514-937-6392; *Fax:* 514-933-9710
www.slf.ca

Montréal: **Stamos CPA Inc.**
800, av Ste. Croix
Montréal, QC H4L 3Y2
Tél: 514-744-1100
www.stamosporterhetu.com
Other Contact Information: Tél: 514-744-2200
Média social: plus.google.com/113176985427844297384/about

Montréal: **UHY Victor LLP**
#400, 759, carré Victoria
Montréal, QC H2Y 2J7
Tel: 514-282-1836; *Fax:* 514-282-6640
www.victorgold.com
Social Media: blog.uhyvictor.com; www.facebook.com/232042816878082; twitter.com/UHYVictorNews

Montréal: **WAKED**
#2825, 500, Place d'Armes
Montréal, QC H2Y 2W2
Tel: 514-875-6400; *Fax:* 514-861-6301
info@wakedcma.com
www.wakedcma.com/en-firm.htm

Montréal: **Xen Accounting/ Xen Comptabilité**
#B-533, 1001, rue Lenoir
Montréal, QC H4C 2Z6
Tel: 514-397-0215; *Toll-Free:* 855-692-4062
www.xenaccounting.com
Social Media: www.facebook.com/xenaccounting; twitter.com/XenAccounting

Québec: **Blouin, Julien, Potvin S.E.N.C.**
#300, 2795, boul Laurier
Québec, QC G1V 4M7
Tel: 418-651-0405; *Fax:* 418-651-0285
groupe@bjpcpa.ca
www.bjpcpa.ca

Québec: **Brassard Carrier, Comptables Agréés**
#200, 1651, ch Ste-Foy
Québec, QC G1S 2P1
Tel: 418-682-2929; *Fax:* 418-682-0282
info@groupebca.com
www.groupebca.com

Québec: **Cauchon Turcotte Thériault Latouche, comptables professionnels agréés, S.E.N.C.R.L.**
Place Iberville Un
#310, 1195, av Lavigerie
Québec, QC G1V 4N3
Tel: 418-658-8808; *Fax:* 418-658-3136
equipe@cttlca.com
www.cttlca.com

Québec: **Choquette Corriveau, Chartered Accountants**
Place Iberville I
#300, 1195, av Lavigerie
Québec, QC G1V 4N3
Tel: 418-658-5555; *Fax:* 418-658-1010
courrier@choquettecorriveau.com
choquettecorriveau.com

Québec: **Dallaire Forest Kirouac S.E.N.C.R.L. (DFK)**
#580, 1175, av Lavigerie
Québec, QC G1V 4P1
Tel: 418-650-2266; *Fax:* 418-650-2529
Toll-Free: 877-650-2266
www.dfk.qc.ca
Social Media: www.facebook.com/152895838063482

Québec: **Gariépy, Gravel, Larouche, Blouin comptables agréés S.E.N.C.R.L.**
#230A, 3333, rue du Carrefour
Québec, QC G1C 5R9
Tel: 418-666-3704; *Fax:* 418-666-6913
www.gglbca.com

Québec: **Laberge Lafleur Brown S.E.N.C.R.L.**
Place de la Cité
#1060, 2590, boul. Laurier
Québec, QC G1V 4M6
Tel: 418-659-7265; *Fax:* 418-659-5937
reception@llbca.com
www.llbca.com

Québec: **Malenfant Dallaire, S.E.N.C.R.L.**
Place de la Cité
#872, 2600, boul Laurier
Québec, QC G1V 4W2
Tel: 418-654-0636; *Fax:* 418-654-0639
maldal@malenfantdallaire.com
www.malenfantdallaire.com

Québec: **Mallette S.E.N.C.R.L.**
#200, 3075, ch des Quatre-Bourgeois
Québec, QC G1W 5C4
Tél: 418-653-4431; *Téléc:* 418-656-0800
info.quebec@mallette.ca
www.mallette.ca
Média social: www.facebook.com/mallette.ca

Québec: **Michel Bergeron, CA, Compatable agréé**
1780, Damiron
Québec, QC G2E 5S8
Tel: 418-877-8705; *Fax:* 418-877-0057
www.guideformationquickbooks.com

Québec: **PricewaterhouseCoopers LLP, Canada - Québec**
Place de la Cité, Tour Cominar
#1700, 2640, boul Laurier
Québec, QC G1V 5C2
Tel: 418-522-7001; *Fax:* 418-522-5663
www.pwc.com/ca

Québec: **RDL Légaré Mc Nicoll inc.**
1305, boul Lebourgneuf
Québec, QC G2K 2E4
Tel: 418-627-2050; *Fax:* 418-627-4193
info.quebec@grouperdl.ca
www.grouperdl.ca

Québec: **Roy, Labrecque, Busque, Blanchet CPA Inc.**
#160, 5055, boul Hamel ouest
Québec, QC G2E 2G6
Tel: 418-871-0013; *Fax:* 418-871-0162
rlb@roylabrecquebusque.com
www.roylabrecquebusque.com

Repentigny: **Villeneuve & Associés S.E.N.C.R.L.**
#200, 10, boul Brien
Repentigny, QC J6A 4R7
Tél: 450-585-5503; *Téléc:* 450-654-6414
vvrep@vvbkr.com
www.vvbkr.com

Saint-Hubert: **Hébert Turgeon CPA inc**
7695, ch de Chambly
Saint-Hubert, QC J3Y 5K2
Tel: 450-676-0624; *Fax:* 450-676-7677
info@htcga.qc.ca
www.htcga.qc.ca

Saint-Rémi: **Lefaivre Labrèche Gagné, sencrl**
151, rue Perras
Saint-Rémi, QC J0L 2L0
Tél: 450-454-3974; *Téléc:* 450-454-7320
info@lefaivre-labreche.com
www.lefaivre-labreche.com

Sainte-Émélie-de-l'Énergie: **Gestion Tellier St-Germain**
2801, ch des Sept-Chutes
Sainte-Émélie-de-l'Énergie, QC J0K 2K0
Tel: 450-886-3762
ghislaine@gestionrg.qc.ca

Shawville: **Smith Porter Hétu**
PO Box 896
389, rue Main
Shawville, QC J0X 2Y0
Tel: 819-647-2403; *Fax:* 819-647-3103
info@thetaxsmith.com
www.thetaxsmith.com
Social Media: www.facebook.com/TheTaxSmith-151121438267171; twitter.com/TheTaxSmith

Thetford Mines: RDL Lamontagne inc.
1031, rue Notre-Dame Est
Thetford Mines, QC G6G 2T4
Tel: 418-332-2288; *Fax:* 418-332-2207
info.thetford@grouperdl.ca
www.grouperdl.ca

Victoriaville: Groupe RDL
c/o Roy Desrochers Lambert SENCRL
450, boul des Bois-Francs nord
Victoriaville, QC G6P 1H3
Tel: 819-758-1544; *Fax:* 819-758-6467
info@grouperdl.ca
www.grouperdl.ca
Other Contact Information: Alternate Fax: 819-752-3836; Alternate E-mail: info.victo@grouperdl.ca; Human Resources, E-mail: rh@grouperdl.ca
Social Media: www.youtube.com/grouperdl; www.facebook.com/grouperdl

Victoriaville: Roy Desrochers Lambert SENCRL
450, boul des Bois-Francs nord
Victoriaville, QC G6P 1H3
Tel: 819-758-1544; *Fax:* 819-758-6467
info.victo@grouperdl.ca
www.grouperdl.ca
Other Contact Information: Alternate E-mail: info@grouperdl.ca

Saskatchewan

Esterhazy: Miller Moar Grodecki Kreklewich & Chorney, Chartered Professional Accountants
Bank of Montreal Bldg.
420 Main St.
Esterhazy, SK S0A 1X0
Tel: 306-745-6611; *Fax:* 306-745-2899
esterhazyoffice@millerandco.ca
millerandco.ca

Regina: PricewaterhouseCoopers LLP, Canada - Regina
#500, 2103 - 11th Ave.
Regina, SK S4P 3Z8
Tel: 306-564-4720
www.pwc.com/ca

Saskatoon: Byron J. Reynolds, Chartered Accountant
PO Box 32029, Erindale Stn. Erindale
Saskatoon, SK S7S 1N8
Tel: 306-384-1130; *Fax:* 306-373-6431
www.byronjreynolds.ca

Saskatoon: Collins Barrow PQ LLP
#201, 500 Spadina Cres.
Saskatoon, SK S7K 4H9
Tel: 306-242-4281; *Fax:* 306-242-4429
saskatoon@collinsbarrow.com
www.collinsbarrow.com/en/saskatoon-saskatche wan

Saskatoon: Diehl Accounting
611 - 47th St. East
Saskatoon, SK S7K 7V6
Tel: 306-384-5451; *Fax:* 306-384-5771
info@diehlaccounting.ca
www.diehlaccounting.ca

Saskatoon: DNTW Saskatoon
#104, 1640 Idylwyld Dr. North
Saskatoon, SK S7L 1B1
Tel: 306-242-5822; *Fax:* 306-242-5343
saskatoon.help@dntw.com
www.dntw.com

Saskatoon: Hounjet Tastad Harpham
#207, 2121 Airport Dr.
Saskatoon, SK S7L 6W5
Tel: 306-653-5100; *Fax:* 306-653-5141
www.hth-accountants.ca

Saskatoon: Lizée Gauthier, CGA
#202, 3550 Taylor St. East
Saskatoon, SK S7H 5H9
Tel: 306-653-5080; *Fax:* 306-663-3411
www.goguild.com/martensville/lizee-gauthier-cga

Saskatoon: PricewaterhouseCoopers LLP, Canada - Saskatoon
#600, 128 - 4th Ave. South
Saskatoon, SK S7K 1M8
Tel: 306-668-5900; *Fax:* 306-652-1315
www.pwc.com/ca

Saskatoon: Virtus Group
The King George Building
#200, 157 - 2nd Ave. North
Saskatoon, SK S7K 2A9
Tel: 306-653-6100; *Fax:* 306-653-4245
Toll-Free: 888-258-7677
virtus.saskatoon@virtusgroup.ca
www.virtusgroup.ca

Domestic Banks: Schedule I

See Index for Bank of Canada, and the Federal Business Development Bank, which are Crown Corporations, listed in the Government Section. *Chartered banks in Canada are incorporated by letters patent. They are governed by the Bank Act, which establishes the legislative framework for Canada's banking system. The Bank Act provides for the incorporation of banks. The Office of the Superintendent of Financial Institutions Canada regulates and supervises the Canadian financial system.*

Domestic banks are federally regulated Canadian banks. The subsidiaries of foreign banks are federally regulated foreign banks. Both domestic and foreign banks have the same powers, restrictions and obligations under the Bank Act.

Foreign bank representative offices are established by foreign banks in Canada. They act as a liaison between the foreign bank and its clients in Canada. These offices generally promote the services of the foreign bank, and do not accept deposits in Canada.

Foreign bank branches are federally regulated. They are permitted to establish specialized, commercially-focused branches in Canada, in accordance with the Bank Act. Full service branches generally are not permitted to accept deposits of less than $150,000.

ATB Financial exemplifies a savings bank in Canada. In Alberta, ATB Financial operates under the authority of the Alberta Treasury Branches Act Chapter A-37.9, 1997 and Treasury Branches Regulation 187/97.

B2B Bank
PO Box 279, Commerce Ct. Stn. Commerce Ct.
#600, 199 Bay St.
Toronto, ON M5L 0A2
Toll-Free: 800-263-8349
questions@b2bbank.com
b2bbank.com
Other Contact Information: GIC Deposits, Toll-Free Fax: 1-888-946-3448; Broker Mortgages, Toll-Free Fax: 1-877-812-8839
Social Media: twitter.com/b2b_bank
Former Name: Sun Life Trust Company; B2B Trust
Ownership: Private. Subsidiary of Laurentian Bank of Canada, Montréal, QC.
Year Founded: 1991
Assets: $39,659,504 Year End: 20151031
Revenues: $897,126,000 Year End: 20151031

The Bank of Nova Scotia (BNS)/ La Banque de Nouvelle-Écosse
Scotia Plaza
44 King St. West
Toronto, ON M5H 1H1
Tel: 416-701-7200; *Toll-Free:* 800-472-6842
email@scotiabank.com
www.scotiabank.com
Other Contact Information: 1-800-645-0288 (TTY Phone)
Social Media: plus.google.com/+scotiabank; www.youtube.com/user/Scotiabank; www.facebook.com/scotiabank; twitter.com/scotiabank
Also Known As: Scotiabank
Ownership: Public
Year Founded: 1832
Number of Employees: 86,932
Assets: $856,000,000,000 Year End: 20151231
Revenues: $24,000,000,000 Year End: 20151231

BMO Financial Group (BMO)
First Canadian Place
100 King St. West
Toronto, ON M5X 1B5
Toll-Free: 877-225-5266
feedback@bmo.com
www.bmo.com
Other Contact Information: 1-877-225-5266 (French); 1-800-665-8800 (Cantonese & Mandarin); 1-866 889-0889 (TTY service)
Social Media: www.youtube.com/bmocommunity; www.facebook.com/BMOcommunity; twitter.com/bmo
Also Known As: Bank of Montréal
Ownership: Public
Year Founded: 1817
Number of Employees: 46,000+
Assets: $642,000,000,000 Year End: 20151031

BMO Harris Private Banking
BMO Financial Group
119, rue St-Jacques ouest
Montréal, QC H2Y 1L6
Toll-Free: 855-834-2558
www.bmo.com/harrisprivatebanking
Other Contact Information: Toll-Free TTY: 1-866-889-0889
Ownership: Member of BMO Financial Group.

Bridgewater Bank
#150, 926 - 5th Ave. SW
Calgary, AB T2P 0N7
Toll-Free: 866-243-4301
customer.experience@bridgewaterbank.ca
www.bridgewaterbank.ca
Social Media: twitter.com/bridgewaterbank
Former Name: Bridgewater Financial Services Ltd.
Ownership: Private. Wholly owned subsidiary of Alberta Motor Association.
Year Founded: 1997
Number of Employees: 200+
Assets: $1-10 billion

Canadian Imperial Bank of Commerce (CIBC)/ Banque Canadienne Impériale de Commerce
Commerce Court
PO Box 1, Commerce Court Stn. Commerce Court
Toronto, ON M5L 1A2
Tel: 416-980-2211; *Fax:* 416-363-5347
Toll-Free: 800-465-2422
www.cibc.com
Other Contact Information: Client Care: 1-800-465-2255; Credit Cards: 1-800-465-4653; Mortgages: 1-888-264-6843; Communications & Public Affairs: 416-980-4523
Social Media: www.facebook.com/CIBC; twitter.com/cibc
Ownership: Public
Year Founded: 1867
Number of Employees: 44,000+
Assets: $414,903,000,000 Year End: 20151031
Revenues: $13,900,000,000 Year End: 20151031

Canadian Tire Bank
PO Box 3000
Welland, ON L3B 5S5
Toll-Free: 866-681-2837
www.myctfs.com
Ownership: Subsidiary of Canadian Tire Financial Services Ltd., which is a subsidiary of Canadian Tire Corporation Limited.

Canadian Western Bank (CWB)/ Banque Canadienne de l'Ouest
Canadian Western Bank Place
#3000, 10303 Jasper Ave.
Edmonton, AB T5J 3X6
Tel: 780-423-8888; *Fax:* 780-423-8897
comments@cwbank.com
www.cwbank.com
Other Contact Information: Investor Relations, E-mail: investorrelations@cwbank.com; Group URL: www.cwbankgroup.com
Social Media: www.facebook.com/cwbcommunity; twitter.com/CWBcommunity
Also Known As: Canada's Western Bank
Ownership: Widely held Canadian corporation. Part of the Canadian Western Bank Group.
Year Founded: 1984
Assets: $10-100 billion

Citizens Bank of Canada
#401, 815 West Hastings St.
Vancouver, BC V6C 1B4
Tel: 604-708-7800; *Fax:* 604-708-7858
Toll-Free: 888-708-7800
service@citizensbank.ca
www.citizensbank.ca
Other Contact Information: TTY: 1-888-702-7702; Alt. E-mails: visa_centre@vancity.com; prepaidvisa@citizensbank.ca
Ownership: Wholly-owned subsidiary of Vancouver City Savings Credit Union.
Year Founded: 1997

Continental Bank of Canada/ Banque Continentale du Canada
Ringwood Manor
1601 Hopkins St.
Whitby, ON L1N 9N1
Ownership: Owned and operated by Continental Currency Exchange Corporation.
Year Founded: 2013

CS Alterna Bank
319 McRae Ave., 2nd Fl.
Ottawa, ON K1Z 0B9
Tel: 613-560-0120; *Fax:* 613-560-0177
Toll-Free: 866-560-0120
www.alternabank.ca
Other Contact Information: 888-807-4101 (Lost or stolen card services)
Social Media: plus.google.com/+alternasavings; www.youtube.com/user/AlternaSavings; www.facebook.com/AlternaSavings; twitter.com/alternasavings
Also Known As: Alterna Bank
Ownership: Wholly owned subsidiary of Alterna Savings & Credit Union Limited, & part of the Alterna Financial Group.
Year Founded: 2000

DirectCash Bank
Bay 6
1420 - 28th St. NE
Calgary, AB T2A 7W6
Toll-Free: 888-466-4043
customersupport@directcashbank.com
www.dcbank.ca
Also Known As: DC Bank
Ownership: Private
Year Founded: 2007

Equitable Bank
#700, 30 St. Clair Ave. West
Toronto, ON M4V 3A1
Tel: 416-515-7000; *Fax:* 416-515-7001
Toll-Free: 866-407-0004
serviceclient@eqbank.ca
www.equitablebank.ca
Social Media: twitter.com/eqbank
Former Name: The Equitable Trust Company
Ownership: Wholly owned subsidiary of Equitable Group Inc.
Year Founded: 1970
Number of Employees: 300+

First Nations Bank of Canada
#406, 224 - 4th Ave. South
Saskatoon, SK S7K 5M5
Tel: 306-955-6739; *Fax:* 306-931-2409
Toll-Free: 888-454-3622
FNBC.service@fnbc.ca
www.fnbc.ca
Social Media: www.facebook.com/FNBC.Social; twitter.com/fnbc_bank
Ownership: Private. Over 80% Aboriginal owned & controlled.
Year Founded: 1996
Assets: $100-500 million
Revenues: $5-10 million

General Bank of Canada (GBC)
#006, 11523 - 100 Ave.
Edmonton, AB T5K 0J8
Fax: 780-443-5628
Toll-Free: 877-443-5620
info@generalbank.ca
www.generalbank.ca
Ownership: Parent company is Firstcan Management Inc.
Year Founded: 2005

Hollis Canadian Bank
44 King St. West
Toronto, ON M5H 1H1
Toll-Free: 866-884-3434
Former Name: Dundee Bank of Canada; Dundee Wealth Bank
Ownership: Subsidiary of The Bank of Nova Scotia.
Year Founded: 2006

Home Bank/ Banque Home
#2300, 145 King St. West
Toronto, ON M5H 1J8
Toll-Free: 855-263-2265
www.cffbank.ca
Other Contact Information: 855-767-3031 (Residential mortgage service); 844-233-2265 (Personal banking service)
Former Name: CFF Bank; MonCana Bank of Canada
Ownership: A wholly owned subsidiary of Home Trust Company. Home Bank & Home Trusy Company are both members of CIDC (Canada Deposit Insurance Corporation).
Year Founded: 2011

HomEquity Bank
#300, 1881 Yonge St.
Toronto, ON M4S 3C4
Tel: 416-925-4757; *Fax:* 416-925-9938
Toll-Free: 866-522-2447
www.homequitybank.ca
Social Media: www.youtube.com/channel/UCLfK9fatZpCAA6mPBXhSaGQ; plus.google.com/108902575883762034262; www.facebook.com/homequityb; twitter.com/HomEquityBank
Ownership: Wholly owned subsidiary of HOMEQ Corporation. Owned by Birch Hill Equity Partners Management Inc.
Year Founded: 2009

Laurentian Bank of Canada/ Banque Laurentienne du Canada
#1585, 1981, av McGill College
Montréal, QC H3A 3K3
Tel: 514-252-1846; *Toll-Free:* 800-252-1846
www.laurentianbank.ca
Other Contact Information: 1-866-262-2231 (TTY service); 514-284-4500, ext. 8232 (Media)
Ownership: Public
Year Founded: 1846
Number of Employees: 3,667
Assets: $39,659,504 Year End: 20151031
Revenues: $897,126,000 Year End: 20151031

Manulife Bank of Canada
PO Box 1602, Waterloo Stn. Waterloo
#500MA, 500 King St. North
Waterloo, ON N2J 4C6
Tel: 519-747-7000; *Toll-Free:* 877-765-2265
manulife_bank@manulife.com
www.manulifebank.ca
Other Contact Information: Advisor Support Centre, Toll-Free Phone: 1-800-567-9170; E-mail: advisorbank@manulife.com
Ownership: Private. Wholly-owned subsidiary of The Manufacturers Life Insurance Company.
Year Founded: 1993
Number of Employees: 200+
Assets: $1-10 billion

National Bank of Canada (NBC)/ Banque Nationale du Canada(BNC)
National Bank Tower
600, rue de La Gauchetière ouest
Montréal, QC H3B 4L2
Tél: 514-394-4494; *Ligne sans frais:* 844-394-4494
www.nbc.ca
Média social: www.youtube.com/nationalbanknetworks; www.facebook.com/nationalbanknetworks; twitter.com/nationalbank
Former Name: The Provincial Bank of Canada; The Mercantile Bank of Canada
Ownership: Public
Year Founded: 1859
Number of Employees: 20,000
Assets: $216,000,000,000 Year End: 20151031
Revenues: $5,746,000,000 Year End: 20151031

Pacific & Western Bank of Canada
#2002, 140 Fullarton St.
London, ON N6A 5P2
Tel: 519-645-1919; *Fax:* 519-645-2060
Toll-Free: 866-979-1919
www.pwbank.com
Ownership: Parent company is Pacific & Western Credit Corp., a public company.
Year Founded: 1979
Assets: $100-500 million
Revenues: $10-50 million

President's Choice Bank
PO Box 201
25 York St., 7th Fl.
Toronto, ON M5J 2V5
Toll-Free: 866-246-7262
www.pcfinancial.ca
Other Contact Information: TTY: 855-223-3499
Ownership: Owned & operated by President's Choice Financial, which is owned by Loblaw Companies Limited.

President's Choice Financial
PO Box 603, Agincourt Stn. Agincourt
Toronto, ON M1S 5K9
Toll-Free: 888-723-8881
www.pcfinancial.ca
Social Media: www.facebook.com/PCFinancial; twitter.com/pcfinancial
Also Known As: President's Choice Bank; PC Bank
Ownership: PC Financial is a joint venture between Loblaw Companies & CIBC.

Rogers Bank
350 Bloor St. East, 3rd Fl.
Toronto, ON M4W 1A9
Toll-Free: 855-775-2265
www.rogersbank.com
Ownership: Wholly owned subsidiary of Rogers Communications Inc.
Year Founded: 2013

Royal Bank of Canada (RBC)
South Tower
200 Bay St., 14th Fl.
Toronto, ON M5J 2S5
Tel: 416-955-7802; *Fax:* 416-955-7800
www.rbc.com
Social Media: plus.google.com/111348053817316580911; www.facebook.com/rbcroyalbank; twitter.com/RBC
Also Known As: RBC Financial Group
Year Founded: 1869
Number of Employees: 80,000
Revenues: $35,321,000,000 Year End: 20141031

Tangerine Bank
3389 Steeles Ave. East
Toronto, ON M2H 3S8
Tel: 416-756-2424; *Toll-Free:* 888-826-4374
clientservices@tangerine.ca
www.tangerine.ca
Other Contact Information: French Toll-Free Phone: 1-844-826-4374
Social Media: www.youtube.com/user/TangerineBank; www.facebook.com/TangerineBank; twitter.com/TangerineBank
Former Name: ING Bank of Canada; ING DIRECT Canada
Also Known As: Tangerine
Ownership: Subsidiary of The Bank of Nova Scotia.
Year Founded: 1997
Number of Employees: 900+
Assets: $10-100 billion

The Toronto-Dominion Bank
TD Centre
PO Box 1
Toronto, ON M5K 1A2
Tel: 416-982-8222; *Toll-Free:* 866-222-3456
www.td.com
Social Media: www.youtube.com/tdcanada; www.instagram.com/TD_Canada; www.facebook.com/TDCanada; twitter.com/td_canada
Also Known As: TD Bank; TD Canada Trust
Ownership: Public
Year Founded: 1855
Number of Employees: 85,000
Assets: $945,000,000,000 Year End: 20141031

Zag Bank
#120, 6807 Railway St. SE
Calgary, AB T2H 2V6
Toll-Free: 844-924-7253
clientservices@zagbank.ca
www.zagbank.ca
Social Media: www.facebook.com/zagbank; twitter.com/zagbank
Former Name: Bank West
Ownership: A subsidiary of the Desjardins Group.
Year Founded: 2002

Foreign Banks: Schedule II

Amex Bank of Canada
#100, 2225 Sheppard Ave. East
Toronto, ON M2J 5C2
Tel: 905-474-0870; *Toll-Free:* 800-869-3016
www.americanexpress.com/canada
Other Contact Information: Toll-Free TTY: 1-866-549-6426; Local TTY: 905-940-7702
Social Media: www.facebook.com/AmericanExpressCanada
Ownership: Wholly owned subsidiary of American Express Travel Related Services Company, Inc., New York, USA.
Year Founded: 1853
Number of Employees: 3,000

Bank of China (Canada)
#600, 50 Minthorn Blvd.
Markham, ON L3T 7X8
Tel: 905-771-6886; *Fax:* 905-771-8555
Toll-Free: 877-823-2288
boccanada@ca.bocusa.com
www.bankofchina.com/ca
Other Contact Information: VIP Customer Service: vsc@ca.bocusa.com
Ownership: Wholly owned subsidiary of the Bank of China Limited, Beijing, China.
Year Founded: 1992

Bank of Tokyo-Mitsubishi UFJ (Canada)
#1800, South Tower, Royal Bank Plaza
PO Box 42
Toronto, ON M5J 2J1
Tel: 416-865-0220; *Fax:* 416-865-0196
www.bk.mufg.jp/global
Ownership: Foreign. Part of The Bank of Tokyo-Mitsubishi UFJ, Ltd., Tokyo, Japan.
Year Founded: 1996

BNP Paribas (Canada)
1981, av McGill College
Montréal, QC H3A 2W8
Tél: 514-285-6000; *Téléc:* 514-285-6278
Ligne sans frais: 866-277-6100
contact@ca.bnpparibas.com
www.bnpparibas.ca
Former Name: Banque Nationale de Paris (Canada)
Ownership: Foreign. Wholly owned subsidiary of BNP Paribas, Paris, France
Year Founded: 1961
Assets: $1-10 billion

Citco Bank Canada
#2700, 2 Bloor St. East
Toronto, ON M4W 1A8
Tel: 416-966-9200; *Fax:* 647-426-5300
toronto-bank@citco.com
www.citco.com/divisions/banking-custody
Ownership: Part of the Citco Group of Companies.

Citibank Canada
Citigroup Place
#1900, 123 Front St. West
Toronto, ON M5J 2M3
Tel: 416-947-5500; *Fax:* 416-639-4878
Toll-Free: 888-834-2484
www.citibank.com/canada
Social Media: www.youtube.com/citi; www.facebook.com/citi; twitter.com/citi
Ownership: Subsidiary of Citigroup Inc., New York, NY, USA
Year Founded: 1982
Number of Employees: 5,000+

CTBC Bank Corp. (Canada)
1518 West Broadway
Vancouver, BC V6J 1W8
Tel: 604-683-3882; *Fax:* 604-683-3723
service@ctbcbank.ca
www.ctbcbank.ca
Former Name: CTC Bank of Canada
Ownership: Private. Subsidiary of CTBC Bank Co., Ltd., Taipei, Taiwan.

Habib Canadian Bank
#1B, 918 Dundas St. East
Mississauga, ON L4Y 4H9
Tel: 905-276-5300; *Fax:* 905-276-5400
Toll-Free: 855-824-2242
info@habibcanadian.com
www.habibcanadian.com
Ownership: Private. Foreign. Wholly owned by Habib Bank of AG Zurich, Switzerland.
Year Founded: 1967

HSBC Bank Canada
#300, 885 West Georgia St.
Vancouver, BC V6C 3E9
Tel: 604-525-4722; *Fax:* 604-641-1849
Toll-Free: 888-310-4722
info@hsbc.ca
www.hsbc.ca
Other Contact Information: Vancouver Media Contact, Phone: 604-641-2973
Social Media: www.youtube.com/user/HSBCCanada; twitter.com/HSBC_CA
Ownership: Subsidiary of HSBC Holdings plc, London, UK.
Year Founded: 1981
Number of Employees: 7,500
Assets: $94,000,000,000 Year End: 20151231

ICICI Bank Canada
PO Box 396
Toronto, ON M3C 2S7
Tel: 416-847-7979; *Toll-Free:* 888-424-2422
customercare.ca@icicibank.com
www.icicibank.ca
Other Contact Information: Mortgages, Toll-Free Phone: 1-866-726-0825; Toll-Free Fax: 1-866-399-3018; E-mail: icicibankmortgagecare@lenderservices.ca
Ownership: Wholly owned subsidiary of ICICI Bank Limited, Mumbai, India.

Industrial & Commercial Bank of China (Canada)
West Tower, Bay Adelaide Centre
#3710, 333 Bay St.
Toronto, ON M5H 2R2
Tel: 416-366-5588; *Fax:* 416-607-2030
Toll-Free: 877-779-5588
www.icbk.ca
Social Media: weibo.com/icbkmi; www.facebook.com/icbkcanada; twitter.com/ICBK_Canada
Former Name: The Bank of East Asia (Canada)
Ownership: Private. Parent is Industrial & Commercial Bank of China Limited, Beijing.
Year Founded: 1991

JPMorgan Chase Bank
South Tower, Royal Bank Plaza
PO Box 80
#1800, 200 Bay St.
Toronto, ON M5J 2J2
Tel: 416-981-9200
www.jpmorgan.com
Ownership: Branch of J.P. Morgan Chase & Co. Inc., Chicago, IL, USA.

KEB Hana Bank of Canada
Madison Centre
#103, 4950 Yonge St.
Toronto, ON M2N 6K1
Tel: 416-222-5200; *Fax:* 416-222-5822
www.kebcanada.com
Former Name: Korea Exchange Bank of Canada
Ownership: Wholly owned subsidiary of Hana Financial Group, Seoul, Republic of Korea.
Year Founded: 1981

Mega International Commercial Bank (Canada)
Madison Centre
#1002, 4950 Yonge St.
Toronto, ON M2N 6K1
Tel: 416-947-2800; *Fax:* 416-947-9964
icbcto@icbcca.com
www.megabank.com.tw/abroad/canada/canada01.asp
Former Name: International Commercial Bank of Cathay (Canada)
Ownership: Wholly owned subsidiary of Mega International Commercial Bank Co., Ltd., Taipei City, Taiwan.

Shinhan Bank Canada
#2300, 5140 Yonge St.
Toronto, ON M2N 6L7
Tel: 416-250-3500; *Fax:* 416-250-3507
www.shinhan.ca
Ownership: Wholly owned subsidiary of Shinhan Bank, Seoul, Korea.
Year Founded: 2009
Assets: $355,000,000 Year End: 20131231

Société Générale (Canada)
#1800, 1501, av McGill College
Montréal, QC H3A 3M8
Tél: 514-841-6000
ww2.sgcib.com/canada/default.rha
Média social: www.youtube.com/societegenerale; instagram.com/societegenerale; www.facebook.com/societegenerale; twitter.com/SocieteGenerale
Ownership: Wholly owned subsidiary of Société Générale Group, Paris, France.
Year Founded: 1974

State Bank of India (Canada) (SBIC)
Royal Bank Plaza, North Tower
PO Box 81, Royal Bank Stn. Royal Bank
#1600, 200 Bay St.
Toronto, ON M5J 2J2
Tel: 416-865-0414; *Fax:* 416-865-0324
Toll-Free: 800-668-8947
sbican@sbicanada.com
www.sbicanada.com
Ownership: Wholly owned subsidiary of State Bank of India.
Year Founded: 1982
Number of Employees: 45+
Assets: $100-500 million
Revenues: $1-5 million

Sumitomo Mitsui Banking Corporation of Canada (SMBC)
#1400, Ernst & Young Tower
PO Box 172, TD Centre Stn. TD Centre
Toronto, ON M5K 1H6
Tel: 416-368-4766; *Fax:* 416-367-3565
www.smbcgroup.com/americas/canada/smbcc/index
Former Name: Sakura Bank (Canada); The Sumitomo Bank of Canada
Ownership: Private. Foreign. Wholly owned subsidiary of Sumitomo Mitsui Banking Corporation, Tokyo, Japan.
Year Founded: 2001

UBS Bank (Canada)
#800, 154 University Ave.
Toronto, ON M5H 3Z4
Toll-Free: 800-268-9709
www.ubs.com/ca/en
Ownership: Foreign. Public. Subsidiary of UBS AG, Zürich, Switzerland.

Walmart Canada Bank (WMCB)/ La Banque Walmart du Canada
1940 Argentia Rd.
Mississauga, ON L5N 1P9
Toll-Free: 888-331-6133
www.walmartfinancialservices.ca
Other Contact Information: Fraud Department, Toll-Free Phone: 1-888-925-6218
Also Known As: Walmart Financial Services
Ownership: Owned by Walmart Canada Corp.

Foreign Banks: Schedule III

Bank of America, National Association (Canada Branch)
200 Front St. West
Toronto, ON M5V 3L2
Tel: 416-349-4100; *Toll-Free:* 800-387-1729
www.bankofamerica.com
Also Known As: Bank of America, N.A. (Canada Branch)

The Bank of New York Mellon, Toronto Branch
320 Bay St., 10th Fl.
Toronto, ON M5H 4A6
Tel: 416-643-3270
www.bnymellon.com/ca/en/
Former Name: Mellon Bank, N.A., Canada Branch
Also Known As: BNY Mellon
Ownership: Foreign. Branch of The Bank of New York Mellon Financial Corporation, New York City, New York.
Year Founded: 2007

Barclays Bank PLC, Canada Branch
Bay Adelaide Centre
333 Bay St., 49th Fl.
Toronto, ON M5H 2R2
Tel: 416-863-8902; *Fax:* 647-260-5076
corporatecommunicationsamericas@barclays.com
www.barclays.com/contact/ca .html
Ownership: Subsidiary of Barclays Bank PLC, London, UK.

BNP Paribas
1981, av McGill College
Montréal, QC H3A 2W8
Tél: 514-285-6000; *Téléc:* 514-285-6278
Ligne sans frais: 866-277-6100
contact@ca.bnpparibas.com
www.bnpparibas.ca
Ownership: Foreign. Branch of BNP Paribas, Paris, France

Capital One Bank (Canada Branch)
#1900, 5140 Yonge St.
Toronto, ON M2N 6L7
Toll-Free: 800-481-3239
ombudsman@capitalone.com
www.capitalone.ca
Other Contact Information: Customer Relations Address: PO Box 503, Stn. D, Toronto, ON M1R 5L1; Payment Address: PO Box 521, Stn. D, Toronto, ON M1R 5S4
Social Media: www.facebook.com/CapitalOneCanada; twitter.com/CapitalOneCA
Ownership: Foreign. Part of Capital One Services, Inc., McLean, VA, USA.

China Construction Bank Toronto Branch (MJ) (CCBTO)
#3650, 181 Bay St.
Toronto, ON M5J 2T3
Tel: 647-777-7700; *Fax:* 647-777-7739
enquiry@ca.ccb.com
ca.ccb.com/toronto/en/gywm.html
Ownership: Foreign. Branch of China Construction Bank, Beijing, China.
Year Founded: 2014

Citibank, N.A.
Citigroup Place
#1900, 123 Front St. West
Toronto, ON M5J 2M3
Tel: 416-947-5500
www.citibank.com/canada
Social Media: www.youtube.com/citi; www.facebook.com/citi; twitter.com/citi
Ownership: Branch of Citibank, New York, NY, USA

Comerica Bank - Canada Branch
South Tower, Royal Bank Plaza
PO Box 61
#2210, 200 Bay St.
Toronto, ON M5J 2J2
Tel: 416-367-3113
www.comerica.com
Ownership: Foreign. Branch of Comerica Bank, Detroit, Michigan, USA.

Credit Suisse Securities (Canada), Inc.
PO Box 301
#2900, 1 First Canadian Pl.
Toronto, ON M5X 1C9
Tel: 416-352-4500; *Fax:* 416-352-4680
www.credit-suisse.com/ca
Social Media: www.youtube.com/creditsuissevideo; www.flickr.com/photos/creditsuisse; www.facebook.com/creditsuisse; twitter.com/creditsuisse
Also Known As: Credit Suisse AG, Toronto Branch
Ownership: Part of Credit Suisse Group, Zurich, Switzerland.

Deutsche Bank AG, Canada Branch
Commerce Court West
PO Box 263
#4700, 199 Bay St.
Toronto, ON M5L 1E9
Tel: 416-682-8000; *Fax:* 416-682-8383
deutsche.bank@db.com
www.db.com/canada
Other Contact Information: Alternate Phone: 416-682-8400
Social Media: twitter.com/DeutscheBank
Ownership: Foreign. Branch of Deutsche Bank AG, Frankfurt, Germany.

Fifth Third Bank
#1253, 70 York St.
Toronto, ON M5J 1S9
Tel: 416-645-8373
www.53.com
Ownership: Foreign. Branch of Fifth Third Bank, Cincinnati, Ohio, USA

First Commercial Bank
#100, 5611 Cooney Rd.
Richmond, BC V6X 3J6
Tel: 604-207-9600; *Fax:* 604-207-9638
www.firstbank.com.tw
Ownership: Foreign. Branch of First Commercial Bank, Taiwan.

HSBC Bank USA, National Association
70 York St., 4th Fl.
Toronto, ON M5J 1S9
Tel: 416-868-8000
www.hsbc.ca
Other Contact Information: US Web Site: www.us.hsbc.com

JPMorgan Chase Bank, National Association
South Tower, Royal Bank Plaza
PO Box 80
#1800, 200 Bay St.
Toronto, ON M5J 2J2
Tel: 416-981-9200
www.chase.com/online/canada/canada-home-en.htm
Other Contact Information: Alternate URL: www.jpmorgan.com
Former Name: The Chase Manhattan Bank; Morgan Guaranty Trust Co. of New York; Sears Bank Canada
Ownership: Branch of J.P. Morgan Chase & Co. Inc., Chicago, IL, USA.

M&T Bank
TD Canada Trust Tower, Brookfield Place
PO Box 209
#2520, 161 Bay St.
Toronto, ON M5J 2S1
Tel: 416-214-2301; *Fax:* 416-363-0768
www.mtb.com/commercial/Pages/Canadian-Banking.aspx
Social Media: www.facebook.com/MandTBank; twitter.com/mandt_bank
Ownership: Subsidiary of M&T Bank, Buffalo, NY.

Maple Bank GmbH - Toronto Branch
c/o Maple Financial Group Inc., Maritime Life Tower, TD Centre
PO Box 328
#3500, 79 Wellington St. West
Toronto, ON M5K 1K7
Tel: 416-350-8200; *Fax:* 416-350-8226
info@maplefinancial.com
www.maplebank.com
Other Contact Information: Alternate URL: www.maplefinancial.com
Former Name: First Marathon Bank GmbH
Ownership: Subsidiary of Maple Financial Group Inc.

Merrill Lynch International Bank Limited, Canada Branch (MLIB)
Bay Wellington Tower, Brookfield Place
181 Bay St., 4th Fl.
Toronto, ON M5J 2V8
Tel: 416-369-7400
www.ml.com
Ownership: Branch of Merrill Lynch International Bank Limited, Dublin, Ireland
Revenues: $10-50 million

Mizuho Bank, Ltd., Canada Branch (MHCB)
PO Box 29
#1102, 100 Yonge St.
Toronto, ON M5C 2W1
Tel: 416-874-0222; *Toll-Free:* 800-668-5917
www.mizuhobank.com/americas/index.html
Former Name: Mizuho Corporate Bank (Canada); Mizuho Bank (Canada)
Ownership: Foreign. Branch of Mizuho Corporate Bank, Ltd., Tokyo, Japan.
Year Founded: 2000

The Northern Trust Company, Canada Branch
#1910, 145 King St. West
Toronto, ON M5H 1J8
Tel: 416-365-7161; *Fax:* 416-365-9484
www.northerntrust.com
Social Media: www.youtube.com/user/NorthernTrustVideos; www.facebook.com/ntcareers; twitter.com/NorthernTrust
Ownership: Part of Northern Trust Canada. Branch of Northern Trust Company, Chicago, USA

PNC Bank Canada Branch
The Exchange Tower
PO Box 462
#2140, 130 King St. West
Toronto, ON M5X 1E4
Tel: 416-361-1744
www1.pnc.com/businesscredit/ca/index.html
Former Name: National City Bank - Canada Branch
Also Known As: PNC Business Credit
Ownership: Owned by PNC Financial Services Group, Inc., Pittsburgh, Pennsylvania.
Year Founded: 1852

Rabobank Nederland Canada Branch
PO Box 57
#1830, 95 Wellington St.
Toronto, ON M5K 1E7
Tel: 647-258-2020; *Fax:* 416-941-9750
canada@rabobank.com
www.rabobank.com/en/locate-us/americas/canada.html
Former Name: Rabobank Canada
Ownership: Cooperative. Foreign. Branch of Rabobank Nederland, Netherlands
Year Founded: 1997

The Royal Bank of Scotland plc, Canada Branch
Toronto-Dominion Centre
#1610, 79 Wellington St. West
Toronto, ON M5K 1G8
Tel: 416-367-0850
canada.branch@rbs.com
cib.rbs.com/our-locations/americas/canada
Former Name: The Royal Bank of Scotland N.V. (Canada) Branch
Ownership: Branch of The Royal Bank of Scotland N.V.

Société Générale (Canada Branch)
#1800, 1501, av McGill College
Montréal, QC H3A 3M8
Tél: 514-841-6000
ww2.sgcib.com/canada/default.rha
Média social: www.youtube.com/societegenerale; instagram.com/societegenerale; www.facebook.com/societegenerale; twitter.com/SocieteGenerale
Ownership: Branch of Société Générale Group, Paris, France.

State Street Bank & Trust Company, Canada Branch
Also listed under: Trust Companies
#1100, 30 Adelaide St. East
Toronto, ON M5C 3G6
Tel: 416-362-1100; *Fax:* 416-956-2525
Toll-Free: 888-287-8639
www.statestreet.com/ca
Also Known As: State Street Trust Company Canada
Ownership: Part of State Street Corporation.
Year Founded: 1990
Number of Employees: 1,100
Assets: $100 billion +

UBS AG Canada Branch
Canada Trust Tower, Brookfield Place
#4100, 161 Bay St.
Toronto, ON M5J 2S1
Tel: 416-364-3293; *Fax:* 416-364-1976
www.ubs.com/ca
Ownership: Foreign. Public. Subsidiary of UBS AG, Zürich, Switzerland.

Union Bank, N.A., Canada Branch
#730, 440 - 2 Ave. SW
Calgary, AB T2P 5E9
Tel: 403-264-2700; *Fax:* 403-264-2770
www.uboc.com
Former Name: Union Bank of California, N.A.
Ownership: Subsidiary of Union BanCal Corporation, San Francisco, CA, USA.
Year Founded: 1864

United Overseas Bank Limited (UOB)
Vancouver Centre
#2400, 650 West Georgia St.
Vancouver, BC V6B 4N9
Tel: 604-662-7055; *Fax:* 604-662-3356
UOB.Vancouver@uobgroup.com
www.uobgroup.com
Also Known As: UOB Vancouver Branch
Ownership: Foreign. Branch of United Overseas Bank Limited, Singapore.
Year Founded: 1987

U.S. Bank National Association - Canada Branch
Adelaide Centre
#2300, 120 Adelaide St. West
Toronto, ON M5H 1T1
Toll-Free: 866-274-5898
intouchwithus@usbank.com
www.usbankcanada.com
Other Contact Information: Customer Service, Toll-Free Phone: 1-800-588-8065; E-mail: account.coordinators@usbank.com; Technical Help Desk, Toll-Free Phone: 1-877-332-7461
Ownership: Part of U.S. Bank, Minneapolis, MN, USA.
Year Founded: 2000

Wells Fargo Bank, National Association, Canadian Branch/ Société financière Wells Fargo Canada
#3200, 40 King St. West
Toronto, ON M5H 3Y2
Toll-Free: 866-997-9946
financial.wellsfargo.com/canada/en/index.html
Also Known As: Wells Fargo Financial Corporation Canada
Ownership: Branch of Wells Fargo & Company, San Francisco, CA, USA.

Foreign Banks Representative Offices

Agricultural Bank of China Limited (ABC)
#1260, 355 Burrard St.
Vancouver, BC V6C 2G8
Tel: 604-682-8468
www.abchina.com
Also Known As: ABC Vancouver Rep-Office
Ownership: Office of Agricultural Bank of China Limited, Beijing, China.

Banco Base, S.A., Institución de Banca Múltiple
#1502, 372 Bay St.
Toronto, ON M5H 2W9
Tel: 647-825-2273
www.bancobase.com
Social Media: www.youtube.com/user/BancoBASEoficial; twitter.com/banco_base
Also Known As: Banco BASE Representative Office
Ownership: Office of Banco Base, S.A., Madrid, Spain.

Banco BPI, SA
829 College St.
Toronto, ON M6G 1C9
Tel: 416-537-5400; *Fax:* 416-536-9635
www.bancobpi.pt

Ownership: Office of Banco Português de Investimento, Porto, Portugal.

Banco Espirito Santo, SA
860C College St.
Toronto, ON M6H 1A2

Tel: 416-530-1700
www.bes.pt
Former Name: Banco Espirito Santo e Comercial de Lisboa, SA
Ownership: Office of Novo Banco, formerly Banco Espírito Santo, Lisbon, Portugal.

Banco Santander Totta, SA
1110 Dundas St. West
Toronto, ON M6J 1X2

Tel: 416-538-7111
www.santandertotta.pt
Social Media: www.facebook.com/santandertotta.pt
Ownership: Office of Banco Santander Totta, SA, Lisbon, Portugal.

Banif - Banco Internacional do Funchal
836 Dundas St. West
Toronto, ON M6J 1V5

Tel: 416-603-0802; *Fax:* 416-603-8892
info@banif.ca
www.bca.pt
Former Name: Banco Comercial dos Açores
Ownership: Office of Banif Financial Group, Funchal, Portugal.

Bank Hapoalim B.M.
#2105, 4950 Yonge St.
Toronto, ON M2N 6K1

Tel: 416-398-4250; *Fax:* 416-398-4246
www.bankhapoalim.com
Ownership: Office of Bank Hapoalim, Tel Aviv, Israel.

Banque Centrale Populaire du Maroc
2208, boul René-Lévesque ouest
Montréal, QC H3H 1R6

Tel: 514-281-1855; *Fax:* 514-281-1974
www.gbp.ma
Ownership: Office of Banque Centrale Populaire du Maroc, Casablanca, Morocco.

Banque Marocaine du Commerce Extérieur S.A.
1241, rue Peel
Montréal, QC H3B 5L4

Tel: 514-875-4266; *Toll-Free:* 877-875-1118
www.bmcebank.ma
Also Known As: BMCE Bank
Ownership: Office of Banque Marocaine du Commerce Extérieur S.A., Casablanca, Morocco, in partnership with Desjardins Group, Montréal, QC.

Banque Transatlantique S.A.
#601, 1170, rue Peel
Montréal, QC H3B 4P2

Tel: 514-985-4137
btmontreal@banquetransatlantique.com
www.cic.fr
Ownership: Part of the Crédit Mutuel group (CIC), Paris, France.

Caixa Economica Montepio Geral
1286 Dundas St. West
Toronto, ON M6J 1X7

Tel: 416-588-7776; *Fax:* 416-588-0030
www.montepio.pt
Ownership: Part of the Montepio group, Lisbon, Portugal.

Caixa Geral de Depósitos, S.A.
#100, 425 University Ave.
Toronto, ON M5G 1T6

Tel: 416-260-2839; *Fax:* 416-260-1329
toronto@cgd.pt
www.cgd.pt
Ownership: Office of Caixa Geral de Depósitos, Lisbon, Portugal.

Crédit Agricole Corporate & Investment Bank
#1900, 2000, av McGill College
Montréal, QC H3A 3H3

Tel: 514-982-6200; *Fax:* 514-982-6298
info-ca@ca-cib.com
www.ca-cib.com/global-presence/canada.htm
Social Media: www.youtube.com/user/CreditAgricoleCIB; plus.google.com/114680630463718801620; facebook.com/CreditAgricoleCIB; twitter.com/CA_CIB_EN
Also Known As: Crédit Agricole CIB
Ownership: Office of Crédit Agricole Corporate & Investment Bank, Paris, France.

Crédit Foncier de France
Regus Montréal Le 1000
#2400, 1000, rue de la Gauchetière
Montréal, QC H3B 4W5

creditfoncier.fr
Ownership: Office of Crédit Foncier de France, Paris, France.

Crédit Industriel et Commercial S.A. (CIC)
#601, 1170, rue Peel
Montréal, QC H3B 4P2

Tel: 514-985-4137
btmontreal@banquetransatlantique.com
www.cic.fr
Ownership: Part of the Crédit Mutuel group (CIC), Paris, France.

Crédit Libanais S.A.L.
Place du Canada
#1325, 1010, rue de la Gauchetière ouest
Montréal, QC H3B 2N2

Tel: 514-866-6688; *Fax:* 514-866-6220
Toll-Free: 800-864-5512
info@creditlibanais.com
www.creditlibanais.com
Other Contact Information: Alternate E-mail: feedback@creditlibanais.com
Ownership: Office of Credit Libanais S.A.L., Beirut, Lebanon.

Doha Bank
First Canadian Place
#5600, 100 King St. West
Toronto, ON M5X 1C9

Tel: 647-255-3130; *Fax:* 647-255-3129
www.dohabank.com.qa
Social Media: www.facebook.com/Doha.Bank; twitter.com/DohaBankQatar
Ownership: Office of Doha Bank, Ad Dawha, Qatar.
Year Founded: 2013

Jamaica National Building Society
1390 Eglinton Ave. West
Toronto, ON M6C 2E4

Tel: 416-784-2074
info@jnocanada.com
www.jnbs.com/canada-page
Other Contact Information: Alternate Phone: 416-784-9611
Former Name: Jamaica National Overseas (Canada) Ltd.
Also Known As: JNBS Representative Office (Toronto)
Ownership: Office of Jamaica National Building Society, Kingston, Jamaica.

National Bank of Pakistan
#5600, 100 King St. West
Toronto, ON M5X 1C9

Tel: 416-644-5097; *Fax:* 416-644-8801
www.nbp.com.pk
Ownership: Office of National Bank of Pakistan, Karachi, Pakistan.

Natixis
#2811, 1800, av McGill College
Montréal, QC M3A 3J6

Tel: 438-333-0491; *Fax:* 438-333-0498
cib.natixis.com
Social Media: twitter.com/Natixis_com
Ownership: Office of Natixis, Paris, France.

Nedbank Limited
1400 Greendale Terrace
Oakville, ON L6M 1W6

Tel: 905-399-4760
www.nedbankgroup.co.za
Other Contact Information: Alternate URLs: www.nedbank.co.za; www.capital.nedbank.co.za
Ownership: Part of the Nedbank Group, Sandton, South Africa.

Standard Chartered Bank
#850, 36 Toronto St.
Toronto, ON M5C 2C5

www.sc.com/ca
Social Media: www.facebook.com/StandardChartered; twitter.com/stanchart
Ownership: Office of Standard Chartered Bank, London, UK.

Victoria Mutual Building Society (VMBS)
3117A Dufferin St.
Toronto, ON M6A 2S9

Tel: 416-783-8627; *Toll-Free:* 877-783-8627
www.vmbs.com
Social Media: www.facebook.com/VictoriaMutual; twitter.com/VictoriaMutual
Ownership: Office of Victoria Mutual Building Society, Kingston, Jamaica.

Savings Banks

AcceleRate Financial
PO Box 1860, Main Stn. Main
Winnipeg, MB R3C 3R1

Tel: 204-954-9543; *Fax:* 204-954-9805
Toll-Free: 888-954-9543
info@acceleratefinancial.ca
www.acceleratefinancial.ca
Other Contact Information: After Hours, Toll-Free Phone: 1-800-567-8111; Lost or Stolen Member Card, Phone: 905-764-3693; Toll-Free Phone: 1-877-764-3693
Ownership: A division of Crosstown Civic Credit Union.
Year Founded: 2010

Achieva Financial
PO Box 2729, Main Stn. Main
Winnipeg, MB R3C 4B3

Tel: 204-925-6824; *Fax:* 204-231-5096
Toll-Free: 877-224-4382
info@achieva.mb.ca
www.achieva.mb.ca
Other Contact Information: Lost or Stolen ATM Card, Toll-Free Phone: 1-888-277-1043
Ownership: A division of Cambrian Credit Union.
Year Founded: 1998

ATB Financial
#2100, 10020 - 100 St. NW
Edmonton, AB T5J 0N3

Toll-Free: 800-332-8383
atbinfo@atb.com
www.atb.com
Other Contact Information: Investor Services, Toll-Free Phone: 1-888-282-3863
Social Media: www.facebook.com/ATBFinancial; twitter.com/ATBFinancial
Former Name: Alberta Treasury Branches
Ownership: Crown. 100% owned by the Provincial Government of Alberta
Year Founded: 1938
Number of Employees: 5,000+
Assets: $43,074,923,000 Year End: 20150331
Revenues: $328,681,000 Year End: 20150331

Canadian Direct Financial (CDF)
#3000, 10303 Jasper Ave.
Edmonton, AB T5J 3X6

Toll-Free: 877-441-2249
cdfinfo@cwbank.com
www.canadiandirectfinancial.com
Ownership: A division of Canadian Western Bank. Part of the Canadian Western Bank Group.

EQ Bank
#700, 30 St. Clair Ave. West
Toronto, ON M4V 3A1

Toll-Free: 844-437-2265
contact@eqbank.ca
Other Contact Information: 844-235-2000 (Deposits Inquiries); 416-515-7000 (Investor Relations)
Social Media: www.facebook.com/EQBank; twitter.com/EQBank
Ownership: Wholly owned subsidiary of Equitable Bank, which is wholly owned by Equitable Group Inc.
Year Founded: 2016

Hubert Financial
233 Main St.
Selkirk, MB R1A 1S1

Toll-Free: 855-448-2378
hubert@happysavings.ca
www.happysavings.ca
Ownership: A division of Sunova Credit Union Ltd.

MAXA Financial
220 - 10th St., #C
Brandon, MB R7A 4E8

Tel: 204-571-6292; *Fax:* 204-571-2944
Toll-Free: 866-366-6292
info@maxafinancial.com
www.maxafinancial.com
Ownership: A division of Westoba Credit Union Limited.

Outlook Financial
PO Box 2, Main Stn. Main
Winnipeg, MB R3C 2G1

Tel: 204-958-8655; *Toll-Free:* 877-958-8655
save@outlookfinancial.com
www.outlookfinancial.com
Other Contact Information: Lost or Stolen Member Cards, Toll-Free Phone: 1-877-958-7333; After Hours Toll-Free Phone: 1-800-567-8111

Boards of Trade & Chambers of Commerce

International Chambers & Business Councils

Belgian Canadian Business Chamber (BCBC)
PO Box 508, 161 Bay St., 27th Fl., Toronto ON M5J 2S1
Tel: 416-816-9154
www.belgiumconnect.com
Dominiek Arnout, President & Chief Executive Officer
Christian Frayssignes, Vice-President & EUCCAN Representative
André van der Heyden, Vice-President & Chief Operating Officer
Grégory Oleffe, Treasurer & Chief Financial Officer
Idalia Obregón, Executive Director
Oliver Heijmans, Membership Secretary
Sébastien Dillien, Events Director

British Canadian Chamber of Trade & Commerce
Dominion Centre, Royal Trust Tower, 2401, 77 King St., Toronto ON M5K 1G8
Tel: 416-816-9154; *Fax:* 647-435-3436
central@bcctc.ca
www.bcctc.ca
Thomas O'Carroll, Vice-President, Central
Liam J. Hopkins, Vice President, Western
John Hoblyn, Contact, Eastern

Canada China Business Council (CCBC) / Conseil commercial Canada Chine
#1501, 330 Bay St., Toronto ON M5H 2S8
Tel: 416-954-3800; *Fax:* 416-954-3806
ccbc@ccbc.com
www.ccbc.com
Peter Kruyt, Chair
Sarah Kutulakos, Executive Director
#600, 890 West Pender St., Vancouver BC V6C 1J9
Tel: 604-281-8838; *Fax:* 604-281-8831
ccbcvan@ccbc.com
759, Square Victoria, Montréal QC H2Y 2K3
Tel: 514-880-3807; *Fax:* 514-846-3427
chenail@ccbc.com

Canada Czech Republic Chamber of Commerce (CNACC)
Stn. A, 115 George St, Oakville ON L6J 0A2
Tel: 905-845-9606
admin@ccrcc.net
www.ccrcc.net
Miroslav Princ, Chamber President

Canada Eurasia Russia Business Association (CERBA)
1 First Canadian Place, #1600, 100 King St. West, Toronto ON M5X 1G5
Tel: 416-862-4403; *Fax:* 416-862-7661
www.cerbanet.org
Lou Naumovski, National Chair
Katherine Balabanova, Regional Director, Toronto

Canada-Arab Business Council (CABC) / Conseil de commerce canado-arabe (CCCA)
#702, 116 Albert St., Toronto ON K1P 5G3
Tel: 613-680-3888; *Fax:* 613-565-3013
info@canada-arabbusiness.org
www.canada-arabbusiness.org
Affiliation(s): Canadian Chamber of Commerce
Hugh O'Donnell, Chairman & CEO

Canada-Finland Chamber of Commerce
c/o Finnish Credit Union, 191 Eglinton Ave. East, Toronto ON M4P 1K1
Tel: 416-486-1533; *Fax:* 416-486-1592
info@canadafinlandcc.com
www.canadafinlandcc.com
Lauri Asikainen, President

Canada-India Business Council (C-IBC) / Conseil de commerce Canada-Inde
#302, 1 St. Clair Ave. East, Toronto ON M4T 2V7
Tel: 416-214-5947; *Fax:* 416-214-9081
info@canada-indiabusiness.ca
www.canada-indiabusiness.ca
Don Stewart, Chair
Peter Sutherland, President & Executive Director

Canada-Poland Chamber of Commerce of Toronto
77 Stoneham Rd., Toronto ON M9C 4Y7
Tel: 416-621-2032; *Fax:* 416-621-2472
info@canada-poland.com
www.canada-poland.com
Jack Smagala, President

Canadian Council for the Americas (BCCC)
PO Box 1175, Stn. TD Centre, 77 King St. West, Toronto ON M5K 1P2
Tel: 416-367-4313; *Fax:* 416-595-8226
info@ccacanada.com
www.ccacanada.com
Social Media: www.youtube.com/user/CCATorontoOffice
Jonathan Hausman, Chair

Canadian Council for the Americas (CCA) / Conseil Canadien pour les Amériques
PO Box 48612, 595 Burrard St., Vancouver BC V7X 1A3
Tel: 604-868-8678; *Fax:* 604-806-6112
info@cca-bc.com
www.cca-bc.com
André Nudelman, Chair
Leon Teicher, Secretary

Canadian German Chamber of Industry & Commerce Inc. (CGCIC) / Deutsch-Kanadische Industrie- und Handelskammer
#1500, 480 University Ave., Toronto ON M5G 1V2
Tel: 416-598-3355; *Fax:* 416-598-1840
info@germanchamber.ca
kanada.ahk.de
Gerd U. Wengler, Chair
Thomas Beck, President & CEO

Canadian Slovenian Chamber of Commerce (CSCC)
747 Browns Line, Toronto ON M8W 3V7
Tel: 416-251-8456; *Fax:* 416-252-2092
info@canslo.com
www.canslo.com
Simon Pribac, Executive Director

Caribbean & African Chamber of Commerce of Ontario (CACCO)
PO Box 55328, Stn. Scarborough Town Centre, Toronto ON M1P 4Z7
Tel: 416-265-8603; *Fax:* 416-269-2081
www.cacco.ca
Affiliation(s): Ontario Chamber of Commerce; Board of Trade
Worrick Russel, Executive Chair

Chambre de commerce Canada-Pologne
5570 Waverly Rue, Montréal QC H2T 2Y1

Chambre de commerce Canado-Suisse (Québec) Inc. (SCCCQ) / Swiss Canadian Chamber of Commerce (Québec) Inc.
#152, 3450, rue Drummond, Montréal QC H3G 1Y4
Tél: 514-937-5822
www.cccsqc.ca
Christian G. Dubois, Président

Chambre de commerce Canado-Tunisienne (CCCT) / Tunisian Canadian Chamber of Commerce
#710, 276, rue Saint-Jacques, Montréal QC H2Y 1N3
Tél: 514-847-1281
info@cccantun.com
www.cccantun.ca

Chambre de commerce française au canada (CCFC) / French Chamber of Commerce
#202, 1819, boul René-Lévesque Ouest, Montréal QC H3H 2P5
Tél: 514-281-1246; *Téléc:* 514-289-9594
info@ccfcmtl.ca
www.ccfcmtl.ca
Véronique Loiseau, Directrice générale

Danish Canadian Chamber of Commerce (DCCC)
Tel: 416-923-1811; *Fax:* 416-962-3668
info@dccc.ca
www.dccc.ca
Anders Fisker, Chair

European Union Chamber of Commerce in Toronto (EUCOCIT)
#1500, 480 University Ave., Toronto ON M5G 1V2
Tel: 416-598-7087; *Fax:* 416-598-1840
info@eucocit.com
www.eucocit.com
Thomas Beck, President

Indo-Canada Chamber of Commerce (ICCC) / Chambre de commerce Indo-Canada
#940, 45 Sheppard Ave. East, Toronto ON M2N 5W9
Tel: 416-224-0090; *Fax:* 416-224-0089
iccc@iccc.org
www.iccc.org
Naval Bajaj, President
Puneet S. Kohli, Vice-President & Corp. Secretary
Mayank Bhatt, Contact

Indonesia Canada Chamber of Commerce (ICCC)
c/o Canadian Education International, Wisma Metropolitan I, 11th Fl., Jl. Jend. Sudirman kav 29-31, Jakarta 12920 Indonesia
secretariat@iccc.or.id
www.iccc.or.id
Karina Sherlen, Vice Executive Director

International Chamber of Commerce (ICC) / Chambre de Commerce Internationale
#33, 43, av du Président Wilson, Paris 75116 France
icc@iccwbo.org
www.iccwbo.org
Social Media: www.youtube.com/user/iccwbo1919
Affiliation(s): United Nations; World Trade Organization
John Danilovich, Secretary General
Harold McGraw, Chair

Ireland-Canada Chamber of Commerce (ICCC)
121 Decarie Circle, Toronto ON M9B 3J6
info@iccto.com
www.iccto.com
Matthew Cotter, President

Italian Chamber of Commerce of Ontario (ICCO)
201, 622 College St., Toronto ON M6G 1B6
Tel: 416-789-7169; *Fax:* 416-789-7160
info@italchambers.ca
www.italchambers.ca
George Visintin, President
Corrado Paina, Executive Director

Southeast Asia-Canada Business Council
5294 Imperial St., Burnaby BC V5J 1E4
Tel: 604-439-0779; *Fax:* 604-439-0284
info@aseancanada.com
www.aseancanada.com
Carmelita Salonga Tapia, President

The Swedish-Canadian Chamber of Commerce (SCCC)
#2109, 2 Bloor St. West, Toronto ON M4W 3E2
Tel: 416-925-8661
info@sccc.ca
www.sccc.ca
Marie Larsson, Contact

World Chambers Federation (WCF)
33-43, av du Président Wilson, Paris 75116 France
wcf@iccwbo.org
iccwbo.org/about-icc/organization/world-chambers-federation
Social Media: www.youtube.com/user/03WCF
Affiliation(s): Specialized div. of International Chamber of Commerce
Peter Mihok, Chair
Stephen Cartwright, Chief Executive Officer

Chambers of Mines

Alberta Chamber of Resources
Sun Life Place, 800, 10123 - 99 St. NW, Edmonton AB T5J 3H1
Tel: 780-420-1030; *Fax:* 780-425-4623
admin@acr-alberta.com
www.acr-alberta.com
Leon Zupan, President
Brad Anderson, Executive Director

Chamber of Mines of Eastern British Columbia
215 Hall St., Nelson BC V1L 5X4
Tel: 250-352-5242
chamberofmines@netidea.com
cmebc.com

East Kootenay Chamber of Mines
#201, 12 - 11th Ave. South, Cranbrook BC V1C 2P1
Tel: 250-489-2255; *Fax:* 250-426-8755
www.ekcm.org/chamber2
Ross Stanfield, President

Mining Association of Nova Scotia (MANS)
7744 St. Margaret's Bay Rd., Ingramport NS B3Z 3Z8
Tel: 902-820-2115
info@tmans.ca
tmans.ca
Affiliation(s): Mining Association of Canada
Sean Kirby, Executive Director

Northwest Territories & Nunavut Chamber of Mines
PO Box 2818, #103, 5102-50 Ave., Yellowknife NT X1A 2R1
Tel: 867-873-5281; *Fax:* 867-920-2145
info@miningnorth.com
www.miningnorth.com

Affiliation(s): Mining Association of Canada; Canadian Institute of Mining, Metallurgy & Petroleum
Tom Hoefer, Executive Director

Yukon Chamber of Mines (YCM)
3151B - 3rd Ave., Whitehorse YT Y1A 1G1
Tel: 867-667-2090; *Fax:* 867-668-7127
info@yukonminers.ca
www.yukonminers.ca
Affiliation(s): Mining Association of Canada
Mark Ayranto, President
Hugh Kitchen, Vice President

Provincial & Territorial Boards of Trade & Chambers of Commerce

Alberta Chambers of Commerce (ACC)
#1808, 10025 - 102A Ave., Edmonton AB T5J 2Z2
Tel: 780-425-4180; *Fax:* 780-429-1061
Toll-Free: 800-272-8854
www.abchamber.ca
Affiliation(s): Canadian Chamber of Commerce
Sean Ballard, Chair
Chris J. Dugan, Chair-Elect
Ken Kobly, President & CEO

Atlantic Chamber of Commerce (ACC) / Chambre de commerce de l'Atlantique
PO Box 2291, Windsor NS B0N 2T0
Tel: 902-698-0265; *Fax:* 902-678-7420
contact@apcc.ca
www.apcc.ca
Valerie Roy, Chief Executive Officer

British Columbia Chamber of Commerce
#1201, 750 West Pender St., Vancouver BC V6C 2T8
Tel: 604-683-0700; *Fax:* 604-683-0416
bccc@bcchamber.org
www.bcchamber.org
Social Media: www.youtube.com/user/bcchamberofcom
Patrick Giesbrecht, Chair
Maureen Kirkbride, Interim CEO

Chambre de Commerce française au Canada - Section Québec
#101, 300, rue Métivier, Québec QC G1M 3Y9
Tél: 418-522-3434; *Téléc:* 418-522-0045
info@ccfcquebec.ca
www.ccfcquebec.ca
Média social: ccfcquebec.wordpress.com
Maryse Grob, Présidente

Fédération des chambres de commerce du Québec (FCCQ)
#1100, 555, boul René-Lévesque ouest, Montréal QC H2Z 1B1
Tél: 514-844-9571; *Téléc:* 514-844-0226
Ligne sans frais: 800-361-5019
info@fccq.ca
www.fccq.ca
Françoise Bertand, Présidente-directrice générale

The Manitoba Chambers of Commerce
227 Portage Ave., Winnipeg MB R3B 2A6
Tel: 204-948-0100; *Fax:* 204-948-0110
Toll-Free: 877-444-5222
www.mbchamber.mb.ca
Chuck Davidson, President & CEO

Northwest Territories Chamber of Commerce
NWT Commerce Place, #13, 4802 - 50th Ave., Yellowknife NT X1A 1C4
Tel: 867-920-9505; *Fax:* 867-873-4174
admin@nwtchamber.com
www.nwtchamber.com
Richard Morland, President
Trevor Wever, First Vice-President
Bill Kellett, Second Vice-President
Jugjit More-Curran, Secretary-Treasurer

Ontario Chamber of Commerce (OCC)
#1500, 180 Dundas St. West, Toronto ON M5G 1Z8
Tel: 416-482-5222; *Fax:* 416-482-5879
info@occ.on.ca
www.occ.ca
Social Media: www.youtube.com/user/OntarioChamber
Allan O'Dette, President & CEO
Ali Mirza, Vice-President, Finance

Ontario Gay & Lesbian Chamber of Commerce
#1600, 401 Bay St., Toronto ON M5H 2Y4
info@oglcc.com
www.oglcc.com
Chris Matthews, President

Saskatchewan Chamber of Commerce
The Saskatchewan Chamber of Commerce, #1630, 1920 Broad St., Regina SK S4P 3V2
Tel: 306-352-2671; *Fax:* 306-781-7084
info@saskchamber.com
www.saskchamber.com
Social Media: www.youtube.com/user/SaskChamber
Steve McLellan, CEO

Swiss Canadian Chamber of Commerce (Ontario) Inc. (SCCC)
756 Royal York Rd., Toronto ON M8Y 2T6
Tel: 416-236-0039; *Fax:* 416-551-1011
sccc@swissbiz.ca
www.swissbiz.ca
Julien Favre, President

Yukon Chamber of Commerce (YCC)
#205, 2237 - 2 Ave., Whitehorse YT Y1A 0K7
Tel: 867-667-2000; *Fax:* 867-667-2001
office@yukonchamber.com
www.yukonchamber.com
Peter Turner, President

Alberta

Airdrie Chamber of Commerce
#102, 150 Edwards Way NW, Airdrie AB T4B 4B9
Tel: 403-948-4412; *Fax:* 403-948-3141
info@airdriechamber.ab.ca
www.airdriechamber.ab.ca
Hunt Lorna, Executive Director

Alberta Beach & District Chamber of Commerce
PO Box 280, Alberta Beach AB T0E 0A0
Tel: 780-924-3889; *Fax:* 780-924-3425
www.albertabeachchamber.com
Bert Pyper, President

Alix Chamber of Commerce
PO Box 145, Alix AB T0C 0B0
Tel: 403-747-2405; *Fax:* 403-747-2403
www.villageofalix.ca
Catherine Hepburn, President

Athabasca & District Chamber of Commerce (ADCofC)
PO Box 3074, Athabasca AB T9S 2B9
www.athabascachamber.org
Affiliation(s): Canadian Chambers of Commerce

Barrhead Chamber of Commerce
PO Box 4524, Barrhead AB T7N 1A4
admin@barrheadchamberofcommerce.com
barrheadchamberofcommerce.com

Bashaw Chamber of Commerce
PO Box 645, 5020 - 52nd St., Bashaw AB T0B 0H0
Tel: 780-372-3923
admin@enjoybashaw.com
enjoybashaw.com
Ryan Hewitt, President

Beaverlodge Chamber of Commerce
PO Box 303, Beaverlodge AB T0H 0C0
Tel: 780-354-8785
Judy Olson, Treasurer

Beiseker & District Chamber of Commerce
PO Box 277, Beiseker AB T0M 0G0
Iris Balson, Contact

Berwyn & District Chamber of Commerce
PO Box 144, Berwyn AB T0H 0E0
Tel: 780-338-3668; *Fax:* 780-336-2100
berwynchamber@gmail.com

Blackfalds & District Chamber of Commerce
PO Box 249, Blackfalds AB T0M 0J0
Tel: 403-885-2386; *Fax:* 403-885-2386
info@blackfaldslive.ca
www.blackfaldslive.ca
Shirley Johnson, President

Bluffton & District Chamber of Commerce
PO Box 38, Bluffton AB T0C 0M0
Tel: 403-843-6805; *Fax:* 403-843-3392
Peter Broere, Director

Bonnyville & District Chamber of Commerce
PO Box 6054, Hwy. 28 West, Bonnyville AB T9N 2G7
Tel: 780-826-3252; *Fax:* 780-826-4525
www.bonnyvillechamber.com
Megan Naylor, Contact

Bow Island / Burdett District Chamber of Commerce
PO Box 1001, Bow Island AB T0K 0G0
Tel: 403-545-6222; *Fax:* 403-545-6042
chamber@bowislandchamber.com
www.bowislandchamber.com
Bernice Deleenheer, President
Chandra Lane, Vice-President

Boyle & District Chamber of Commerce
PO Box 9, 5010, 3rd St., Boyle AB T0A 0M0
boylechamber@gmail.com
boylechamber.blogspot.ca
Bill Goodwin, President

Bragg Creek Chamber of Commerce
PO Box 216, Bragg Creek AB T0L 0K0
Tel: 403-949-0004
info@visitbraggcreek.com
visitbraggcreek.com
Louise-Marie Eager, President
Marcella Campbell, Secretary

Breton & District Chamber of Commerce
PO Box 364, Breton AB T0C 0P0
Tel: 780-696-2557; *Fax:* 780-696-2557
bretonchamber@gmail.com

Brooks & District Chamber of Commerce
PO Box 400, 403 - 2 Ave. West, Brooks AB T1R 1B4
Tel: 403-362-7641; *Fax:* 403-362-6893
manager@brookschamber.ab.ca
www.brookschamber.ab.ca
Karen Vogelaar, Executive Director
Michelle Gietz, President

Calgary Chamber of Commerce
#600, 237 - 8th Ave. SE, Calgary AB T2G 5C3
Tel: 403-750-0400
info@calgarychamber.com
www.calgarychamber.com
Rob Hawley, Chair
Adam Legge, President & CEO
Rebecca Wood, Director, Member Services

Camrose Chamber of Commerce
5402 - 48 Ave., Camrose AB T4V 0J7
Tel: 780-672-4217; *Fax:* 780-672-1059
www.camrosechamber.ca
Sharon Anderson, Executive Director
Tanya Fox, President

Cardston & District Chamber of Commerce
PO Box 1212, 490 Main St., Cardston AB T0K 0K0
Tel: 403-795-1032; *Fax:* 403-653-2644
Info@CardstonChamber.com
www.cardstonchamber.com/
Zenieth Gaynor, President
Jason Comin, Treasurer

Caroline & District Chamber of Commerce
PO Box 90, Caroline AB T0M 0M0
Tel: 403-722-4066; *Fax:* 403-722-4002
ccoc@telus.net
www.carolinechamber.ca
Shannon Fagnan, Manager

Carstairs Chamber of Commerce
PO Box 968, Carstairs AB T0M 0N0
Tel: 403-337-3710
carstairschamber@gmail.com
carstairs2020.ca/chamber/
Dennis Schmick, President
Karen Kneeland, Vice-President

Claresholm & District Chamber of Commerce
PO Box 1092, Claresholm AB T0L 0T0
Tel: 403-625-4229
info@claresholmchamber.com
www.claresholmchamber.com
Linda Petryshen, President

Coaldale & District Chamber of Commerce
PO Box 1117, 1401 - 20 Ave., Coaldale AB T1M 1M9
Tel: 403-345-2358; *Fax:* 403-345-2339
info@coaldalechamber.com
www.coaldalechamber.com
John Pollemans, President

Cochrane & District Chamber of Commerce
PO Box 996, Cochrane AB T4C 1B1
Tel: 403-932-0320; *Fax:* 403-541-0915
c.business@cochranechamber.ca
www.cochranechamber.ca

Cold Lake Regional Chamber of Commerce
PO Box 454, Cold Lake AB T9M 1P1
Tel: 780-594-4747; *Fax:* 780-594-3711
Toll-Free: 800-840-6140
info@coldlakechamber.ca
www.coldlakechamber.ca
Trevor Benoit, President
Sherri Bohme, Executive Director

Consort Chamber of Commerce
PO Box 490, 4901 - 50 Ave., Consort AB T0C 1B0
Tel: 403-577-3623; *Fax:* 403-577-2024
Peter G. Ringrose, Executive Director

Coronation Chamber of Commerce
PO Box 960, Coronation AB T0C 1C0
Tel: 403-578-4111
Jody Shipman, President

Cremona Water Valley & District Chamber of Commerce
PO Box 356, Cremona AB T0M 0R0
Tel: 403-637-2030
info@cremonawatervalley.com
www.cremonawatervalley.com
Linda Newsome, President

La Crete & Area Chamber of Commerce
PO Box 1088, 10406 - 100 St., La Crete AB T0H 2H0
Tel: 780-928-2278; *Fax:* 780-928-2234
admin@lacretechamber.com
lacretechamber.com
Larry Neufeld, Manager

Crossfield Chamber of Commerce
PO Box 1490, 1005 Ross St., Crossfield AB T0M 0S0
Tel: 403-813-5133; *Fax:* 403-946-0157
info@crossfieldchamber.ca
crossfieldchamber.org
Social Media: www.youtube.com/watch?v=z1ngfQV0fp8&feature=plcp
Karen Postill, President

Crowsnest Pass Chamber of Commerce
PO Box 706, 12707 - 20th Ave., Blairmore AB T0K 0E0
Tel: 403-562-7108; *Fax:* 403-562-7493
Toll-Free: 888-562-7108
office@crowsnestpasschamber.ca
www.crowsnestpasschamber.ca
Affiliation(s): Alberta Chamber of Commerce
Brian Gallant, President
Dawn Rigby, Treasurer

Delburne & District Chamber of Commerce
PO Box 341, Delburne AB T0M 0V0
Tel: 403-749-3606; *Fax:* 403-749-2800
www.delburne.ca
Brenda Smith, President

Devon & District Chamber of Commerce
#401, 32 Athabasca Ave., Devon AB T9G 1G2
Tel: 780-987-5177; *Fax:* 780-987-3303
devoncc@telus.net
www.devon.ca/Business/ChamberofCommerce.aspx
Jeff Millar, President
Barry Breau, Manager

Diamond Valley Chamber of Commerce
PO Box 61, Turner Valley AB T0L 2A0
Tel: 403-819-4994
info@diamondvalleychamber.ca
diamondvalleychamber.ca
Bev Geier, President

Didsbury Chamber of Commerce
PO Box 981, 1811 - 20 St., Didsbury AB T0M 0W0
Tel: 403-335-3265; *Fax:* 403-335-3267
info@didsburychamber.ca
www.didsburychamber.ca
Shelley Fakir, President

Drayton Valley & District Chamber of Commerce (DVDCC)
PO Box 5318, Drayton Valley AB T7A 1R5
Tel: 780-542-7578; *Fax:* 780-542-2688
www.dvchamber.com
Tom Campbell, President

Drumheller & District Chamber of Commerce (DDCC)
60 - 1st Ave. West, Drumheller AB T0J 0Y0
Tel: 403-823-8100; *Fax:* 403-823-4469
chamberinfo@drumhellerchamber.com
www.drumhellerchamber.com
Landon Bosch, President

Heather Bitz, Executive Director

Eckville & District Chamber of Commerce
PO Box 609, Eckville AB T0M 0X0
www.eckvillechamber.com

Edgerton & District Chamber of Commerce
PO Box 303, Edgerton AB T0B 1K0
Tel: 780-755-3933

Edmonton Chamber of Commerce
World Trade Centre, Sun Life Place, #700, 9990 Jasper Ave., Edmonton AB T5J 1P7
Tel: 780-426-4620; *Fax:* 780-424-7946
info@edmontonchamber.com
www.edmontonchamber.com
Social Media: www.youtube.com/edmontonchamber
James Cumming, President/CEO
Robin Bobocel, Vice President, Public Affairs

Edson & District Chamber of Commerce
221-55 St, Edson AB T7E 1L5
Tel: 780-723-4918; *Fax:* 780-723-5545
edsonchamber@gmail.com
www.edsonchamber.com
Wendy Holuboch, Executive Director

Elk Point Chamber of Commerce
PO Box 639, Elk Point AB T0A 1A0
Tel: 780-724-3810; *Fax:* 780-724-4087
www.elkpoint.ca/chamber-commerce.html
Lesia Porcina, Vice-President
Vicki Brooker, Secretary

Evansburg & Entwistle Chamber of Commerce
PO Box 598, Evansburg AB T0E 0T0
Tel: 780-727-3526
info@partnersonthepembina.com
www.partnersonthepembina.com
Eric Karlzen, President
Al Hagman, Vice-President

Fairview & District Chamber of Commerce
PO Box 1034, 10912 - 103 Ave., Fairview AB T0H 1L0
Tel: 780-835-5999; *Fax:* 780-835-5991
www.fairviewchamber.com
Sharon Noullett, President
Debie Knudsen, Executive Director

Falher Chamber of Commerce
PO Box 814, 11 Central Ave. SW, Falher AB T0H 1M0
Tel: 780-837-2364
Affiliation(s): Falher & Area Economic Development & Tourism

Foremost & District Chamber of Commerce
PO Box 272, Foremost AB T0K 0X0
Tel: 403-867-3077; *Fax:* 403-867-2700
cofc4mst@shockware.com
www.foremostalberta.com
Lorne Buis, President

Fort Macleod & District Chamber of Commerce
PO Box 178, Fort MacLeod AB T0L 0Z0
Tel: 403-553-3355
EDO@FortMacleod.com
www.fortmacleod.com/business/chamber_commerce.cfm
Emily McTighe, President

Fort McMurray Chamber of Commerce
#105, 9912 Franklin Ave., Fort McMurray AB T9H 2K5
Tel: 780-743-3100; *Fax:* 780-790-9757
www.fortmcmurraychamber.ca
Nick Sanders, President

Fort Saskatchewan Chamber of Commerce
PO Box 3072, 10030 - 99 Ave., Fort Saskatchewan AB T8L 2T1
Tel: 780-998-4355; *Fax:* 780-998-1515
chamber@fortsaskchamber.com
www.fortsaskchamber.com
Affiliation(s): Alberta Chamber of Commerce; Canadian Chamber of Commerce
Michelle Gamache, President
Conal MacMillan, Executive Director

Fort Vermilion & Area Board of Trade
PO Box 456, Fort Vermilion AB T0H 1N0
Tel: 780-927-3505

Fox Creek Chamber of Commerce
PO Box 774, Fox Creek AB T0H 1P0
Tel: 780-622-2670
admin@foxcreek.ca
www.foxcreek.ca/index.php/doing-business/chamber-of-commerce

Glendon & District Chamber
PO Box 300, Glendon AB T0A 1P0
Tel: 780-635-2557

Grande Cache Chamber of Commerce
PO Box 1342, 4600 Pine Plaza, Grande Cache AB T0E 0Y0
Tel: 780-827-0100
info@grandecachechamber.com
www.grandecachechamber.com
Affiliation(s): Alberta Chamber of Commerce; Canadian Chamber of Commerce
Susan Feddema-Leonard, President

Grande Prairie & District Chamber of Commerce
Centre 2000, #217, 11330 - 106 St., Grande Prairie AB T8V 7X9
Tel: 780-532-5340; *Fax:* 780-532-2926
info@gpchamber.com
www.grandeprairiechamber.com
Dan Pearcy, CEO

Grimshaw & District Chamber of Commerce
PO Box 919, Grimshaw AB T0H 1W0
Tel: 780-332-4370; *Fax:* 780-332-4375
www.grimshawchamber.com
Theresa Bruce, President
Jenny Borys, Secretary

Hanna & District Chamber of Commerce
PO Box 2248, Hanna AB T0J 1P0
Tel: 403-854-4004
info@hannachamber.ca
www.hannachamber.ca
Harlan Boss, President

High Level & District Chamber of Commerce
10803 - 96 St., High Level AB T0H 1Z0
Tel: 780-926-2470; *Fax:* 780-926-4017
hlchambr@incentre.net
highlevelchamber.com
Don Warman, President

High Prairie & Area Chamber of Commerce
PO Box 3600, High Prairie AB T0G 1E0
Tel: 780-507-1565
office@hpchamber.net
hpchamber.net
Affiliation(s): Alberta Chamber of Commerce; Canadian Chamber of Commerce
Gordon Olson, President

High River & District Chamber of Commerce
PO Box 5244, 149B Macleod Trail SW, High River AB T1V 1M4
Tel: 403-652-3336; *Fax:* 403-652-7660
hrdcc@telus.net
www.hrchamber.ca
Yousra Jomha, President
Lynette McCracken, Executive Director

Hinton & District Chamber of Commerce
309 Gregg Ave., Hinton AB T7V 2A7
Tel: 780-865-2777; *Fax:* 780-865-1062
info@hintonchamber.com
www.hintonchamber.com
Brian LeBerge, President
Natalie Charlton, Executive Director

Innisfail & District Chamber of Commerce
5031 - 40th St., Innisfail AB T4G 1H8
Tel: 403-227-1177; *Fax:* 403-227-6749
ichamber@telusplanet.net
www.innisfailchamber.ca
Doug Bos, President
Joelle Czuy, Secretary

Irma & District Chamber of Commerce
PO Box 284, Irma AB T0B 2H0
Tel: 780-754-3996
Claudia Williams, President

Jasper Park Chamber of Commerce
PO Box 98, Jasper AB T0B 1E0
Tel: 780-852-4621
admin@jpcc.ca
www.jaspercanadianrockies.com
Wayne Hnatyshin, President
Pattie Pavlov, General Manager

Kainai Chamber of Commerce
PO Box 350, Stand Off AB T0L 1Y0
Tel: 403-737-8124; *Fax:* 403-737-2116
chamber@bloodtribe.org

Killam & District Chamber of Commerce
PO Box 272, Killam AB T0B 2L0
Tel: 780-385-7052; *Fax:* 780-385-2413
Rob Hutchison, President
Chris Raab, Treasurer

Lac La Biche & District Chamber of Commerce
PO Box 804, Lac La Biche AB T0A 2C0
Tel: 780-623-2818; *Fax:* 780-623-7217
info@llbchamber.ca
www.llbchamber.ca
Affiliation(s): Alberta Chamber of Commerce
Reuel Thomas, President

Lacombe & District Chamber of Commerce
6005 - 50 Ave., Lacombe AB T4L 1K7
Tel: 403-782-4300; *Fax:* 403-782-4302
info@lacombechamber.ca
www.lacombechamber.ca
Keith Meyers, President

Langdon & District Chamber of Commerce
PO Box 18, Langdon AB T0J 1X0
Tel: 403-369-1590
membership@langdonchamber.ca
www.langdonchamber.ca
Affiliation(s): Alberta Chamber of Commerce; Canadian Chamber of Commerce
Gerard Lucyshyn, President

Leduc Regional Chamber of Commerce
6420 - 50 St., Leduc AB T9E 7K9
Tel: 780-986-5454; *Fax:* 780-986-8108
info@leduc-chamber.com
www.leduc-chamber.com
Social Media: www.youtube.com/user/LeducChamber
Shaun Green, Executive Director
Jessica Roth, Coordinator, Communications & Marketing

Legal & District Chamber of Commerce
PO Box 338, General Delivery, Legal AB T0G 1L0
Tel: 780-456-3424
www.legalchamberofcommerce.ca
Affiliation(s): Greater Edmonton Regional Chambers of Commerce
Ken Evans, President
Carol Tremblay, Secretary

Lethbridge Chamber of Commerce
#200, 529 - 6 St. South, Lethbridge AB T1J 2E1
Tel: 403-327-1586; *Fax:* 403-327-1001
office@lethbridgechamber.com
www.lethbridgechamber.com
Social Media: www.youtube.com/lethchamber
Karla Pyrch, Executive Director

Lloydminster Chamber of Commerce
4419 - 52 Ave., Lloydminster AB T9V 0Y8
Tel: 780-875-9013; *Fax:* 780-875-0755
contact_lcc@lloydminsterchamber.com
www.lloydminsterchamber.com
Social Media: www.youtube.com/user/LloydminsterChamber
Pat Tenney, Executive Director
Michael Holden, President

Magrath & District Chamber of Commerce
Magarath AB
www.magrathchamber.com
Affiliation(s): Alberta Chamber of Commerce; Canadian Chamber of Commerce
Jay Mackenzie, President

Mallaig Chamber of Commerce
PO Box 144, Mallaig AB T0A 2K0
Tel: 780-635-3952

Mannville & District Chamber of Commerce
PO Box 54, Mannville AB T0B 2W0
Tel: 780-763-2499; *Fax:* 780-763-2218
www.mannvillechamber.com
Verner Thompson, President

Marwayne & District Chamber of Commerce
PO Box 183, Marwayne AB T0B 2X0
Tel: 780-847-3784; *Fax:* 780-847-4144
www.village.marwayne.ab.ca
Sharon Kneen, President

McLennan Chamber of Commerce
PO Box 90, McLennan AB T0H 2L0
Tel: 780-324-2279
mclennanchamber@serbernet.com
mclennan.ca/town-a-government/businesses/chamber-of-commerce
Ray Johnson, President

Medicine Hat & District Chamber of Commerce
413 - 6th Ave. SE, Medicine Hat AB T1A 2S7
Tel: 403-527-5214; *Fax:* 403-527-5182
info@medicinehatchamber.com
www.medicinehatchamber.com
Affiliation(s): Alberta Chamber of Commerce; Canadian Chamber of Commerce
Khrista Vogt, President
Lisa Kowalchuk, Executive Director

Millet & District Chamber of Commerce
PO Box 389, Millet AB T0C 1Z0
Tel: 780-387-4554; *Fax:* 780-387-4459

Morinville & District Chamber of Commerce
10113 - 100 Ave., Morinville AB T8R 1P8
Tel: 780-939-9462
chamber@morinvillechamber.com
www.morinvillechamber.com
Heather Folkins, President

Nanton & District Chamber of Commerce
PO Box 711, Nanton AB T0L 1R0
Tel: 403-646-2111
www.nantonchamber.com
Pam Woodall, President

Okotoks & District Chamber of Commerce
PO Box 1053, 14 McRae St., Okotoks AB T1S 1B1
Tel: 403-938-2848; *Fax:* 403-938-6649
info@okotokschamber.ca
www.okotokschamber.ca
Cheryl Actemichuk, President

Olds & District Chamber of Commerce
PO Box 4210, Olds AB T4H 1P8
Tel: 403-556-7070; *Fax:* 403-556-1515
chamber@oldsalberta.com
www.oldsalberta.com
Doug Rieberger, President
Barb Babiak, Executive Director
Melanie Hepp, Vice-President

Onoway & District Chamber of Commerce
PO Box 723, Onoway AB T0E 1V0
Tel: 780-967-2550
info@onowaychamber.ca
business.onowaychamber.ca
Ed Gallagher, President

Oyen & District Chamber of Commerce
PO Box 420, Oyen AB T0J 2J0
Tel: 403-664-3622; *Fax:* 403-664-3622
oyenecho@telusplanet.net

Peace River & District Chamber of Commerce
PO Box 6599, 9309 - 100 St., Peace River AB T8S 1S4
Tel: 780-624-4166; *Fax:* 888-525-4423
www.peaceriverchamber.com
Social Media: www.instagram.com/pr_chamber
Shelly Shannon, President
George Brothers, General Manager

Picture Butte & District Chamber of Commerce
PO Box 517, Picture Butte AB T0K 1V0
Tel: 403-732-4302

Pigeon Lake Regional Chamber of Commerce (PLRCC)
#6B Village Dr., RR#2, Westerose AB T0C 2V0
Tel: 780-586-6263; *Fax:* 780-586-3667
info@pigeonlakechamber.ca
www.pigeonlakechamber.ca
Affiliation(s): Alberta Chambers of Commerce
Doug McKenzie, President
Sereda Bernadette, Manager

Pincher Creek & District Chamber of Commerce
Ranchland Mall, PO Box 2287, #4, 1300 Hewetson Ave., Pincher Creek AB T0K 1W0
Tel: 403-627-5199
www.pincher-creek.com

Ponoka & District Chamber of Commerce
PO Box 4188, 4900 Highway 2A, Ponoka AB T4J 1R6
Tel: 403-783-3888; *Fax:* 403-783-3888
info@ponokaLive.ca
www.ponokalive.ca
Greg Braat, President
Jim Hamilton, Vice-President

Provost & District Chamber of Commerce
PO Box 637, Provost AB T0B 3S0
Tel: 780-753-6643
provost.ca/economic-development/chamber-of-commerce

Raymond Chamber of Commerce
Raymond AB
Tel: 403-330-9057
Cory Rasmussen, President

Red Deer Chamber of Commerce
3017 Gaetz Ave., Red Deer AB T4N 5Y6
Tel: 403-347-4491; *Fax:* 403-343-6188
rdchamber@reddeerchamber.com
www.reddeerchamber.com
Bradley Williams, President
Tim Creedon, Executive Director

Redwater & District Chamber of Commerce
PO Box 322, Redwater AB T0A 2W0
Tel: 780-942-3519
Affiliation(s): Alberta Chamber of Commerce; Canadian Chamber of Commerce

Rimbey Chamber of Commerce
PO Box 87, Rimbey AB T0C 2J0
Tel: 403-843-2020; *Fax:* 403-843-2027
rimbeychamber@rimbey.com
www.rimbeylive.ca
Audreyann Bresnahan, President

Rocky Mountain House & District Chamber of Commerce
PO Box 1374, 5406 - 48 St., Rocky Mountain House AB T4T 1B1
Tel: 403-845-5450; *Fax:* 403-845-7764
Toll-Free: 800-565-3793
rmhcofc@rockychamber.org
www.rockychamber.org
Affiliation(s): AB Chamber of Commerce; Canadian Chamber of Commerce
Patrick Danis, President
Cindy Taschuk, Executive Director

St. Albert & District Chamber of Commerce
71 St. Albert Trail, St. Albert AB T8N 6L5
Tel: 780-458-2833; *Fax:* 780-458-6515
chamber@stalbertchamber.com
www.stalbertchamber.com
Barry Bailey, Chair
Lynda Moffat, President & CEO

St Paul & District Chamber of Commerce
PO Box 887, 4802 - 50 Ave., St Paul AB T0A 3A0
Tel: 780-645-5820; *Fax:* 780-645-5820
admin@stpaulchamber.ca
www.stpaulchamber.ca
Affiliation(s): Alberta Chambers of Commerce
Alice Herperger, President
Penny Fox, Executive Director

Sexsmith & District Chamber of Commerce
PO Box 146, Sexsmith AB T0H 3C0
info@sexsmithchamber.com
www.sexsmithchamber.com
Freda King, President

Sherwood Park & District Chamber of Commerce
100 Ordze Ave., Sherwood Park AB T8B 1M6
Tel: 780-464-0801; *Fax:* 780-449-3581
Toll-Free: 866-464-0801
www.sherwoodparkchamber.com
Todd Banks, Executive Director

Slave Lake & District Chamber of Commerce
PO Box 190, Slave Lake AB T0G 2A0
Tel: 780-849-3222; *Fax:* 780-849-6894
sldcc@telus.net
www.slavelake.ca
Laurie Renauer, Executive Director

Smoky Lake & District Chamber of Commerce
PO Box 654, Smoky Lake AB T0A 3C0
Tel: 780-656-4347
smokylakechamber@mcsnet.ca
Wayne Taylor, President

Smoky River Regional Chamber of Commerce
PO Box 814, 11 Centre Ave. SW, Falher AB T0H 1M0
Tel: 780-837-2188
office@smokyriverchamber.ca
www.smokyriverchamber.ca
Affiliation(s): Alberta Chamber of Commerce; Canadian Chamber of Commerce

Spruce Grove & District Chamber of Commerce
PO Box 4210, 99 Campsite Rd., Spruce Grove AB T7X 3B4
Tel: 780-962-2561; *Fax:* 780-962-4417
www.sprucegrovechamber.com
Michelle Thiebaud, President

Robin Grayston, 1st Vice-President

Stettler Regional Board of Trade & Community Development
6606 - 50th Ave., Stettler AB T0C 2L2
Tel: 403-742-3181; *Fax:* 403-742-3123
Toll-Free: 877-742-9499
info@stettlerboardoftrade.com
www.stettlerboardoftrade.com
Social Media: www.youtube.com/user/StettlerBoardofTrade
Matt Dorsett, President
Stacey Benjamin, Executive Director

Stony Plain & District Chamber of Commerce
4815 - 44 Ave., Stony Plain AB T7Z 1V5
Tel: 780-963-4545; *Fax:* 780-963-4542
info@stonyplainchamber.com
www.stonyplainchamber.ca
John Gilchrist, President
Doug Lovsin, 1st Vice President
Tyler Randolph, 2nd Vice President

Strathmore & District Chamber of Commerce
510 Hwy. 1, Bay A1, Strathmore AB T1P 1K2
Tel: 403-901-3175; *Fax:* 403-901-1785
contactus@strathmoredistrictchamber.com
strathmoredistrictchamber.com
Joyce Bazant, Acting President

Sundre Chamber of Commerce
PO Box 1085, Sundre AB T0M 1X0
Tel: 403-638-3245
info@sundrechamber.com
www.sundrechamber.com

Swan Hills Chamber of Commerce
PO Box 540, Swan Hills AB T0G 2C0
Tel: 780-333-4684
town@townofswanhills.com
www.townofswanhills.com
Rita Krawiec, Contact

Sylvan Lake Chamber of Commerce
PO Box 9119, Sylvan Lake AB T4S 1S6
Tel: 403-887-3048
info@sylvanlakechamber.com
www.sylvanlakechamber.com
Dwayne Stoesz, President

Taber & District Chamber of Commerce
4702 - 50 St., Taber AB T1G 2B6
Tel: 403-223-2265; *Fax:* 403-223-2291
tdcofc@telusplanet.net
www.taberchamber.com
Bruce Warkentin, President

Thorhild Chamber of Commerce
PO Box 384, 638 - 6th Ave., Thorhild AB T0A 3J0
Tel: 780-398-2575; *Fax:* 780-398-2010
thorhildchamber@telus.net
John Dickey, President
Ed Cowley, Secretary

Thorsby & District Chamber of Commerce
Thorsby AB
Mitch William, President

Three Hills & District Chamber of Commerce
PO Box 277, Three Hills AB T0M 2A0
Tel: 403-443-5570
3hillschamber@gmail.com
threehillschamber.ca
Ross Gaehring, Acting President

Tofield & District Chamber of Commerce
PO Box 967, Tofield AB T0B 4J0
www.tofieldalberta.ca/business/chamber-of-commerce
Affiliation(s): Alberta Chambers of Commerce
David Williamson, President
Greg Litwin, Vice-President
Calvin Andringa, Secretary
Janet Trotno, Treasurer

Trochu Chamber of Commerce
PO Box 771, Trochu AB T0M 2C0
Wanda Jones, Vice-President

Valleyview Chamber of Commerce
PO Box 1020, Valleyview AB T0H 3N0
Tel: 780-524-4535
info@valleyviewchamber.ca
www.valleyviewchamber.ca
Evan Heynemans, President

Vegreville & District Chamber of Commerce
PO Box 877, #106, 4925 - 50 Ave., Vegreville AB T9C 1R9
Tel: 780-632-2771; *Fax:* 780-632-6958
vegchamb@telus.net
www.vegrevillechamber.com
Darcie Sabados, President
Elaine Kucher, General Manager

Vermilion & District Chamber of Commerce
4606 - 52 St., Vermilion AB T9X 0A1
Tel: 780-853-6593; *Fax:* 780-853-1740
www.vermilionchamber.ca
Marlene Beattie, 1st Vice-President

Viking Economic Development Committee (VEDC)
PO Box 369, Viking AB T0B 4N0
Tel: 780-336-3466
info@viking.ca
www.townofviking.ca
Jackie Fenton, Chief Administrative Officer

Vilna & District Chamber of Commerce
PO Box 542, Vilna AB T0A 3L0
Tel: 780-636-3615
Affiliation(s): Alberta Chamber of Commerce; Canadian Chamber of Commerce

Vulcan & District Chamber of Commerce
Vulcan AB
info@vulcantourism.com
www.vulcanchamber.com
Dwayne Hill, President
Karen Currie, Vice-President

Wabamun District Chamber of Commerce Society
PO Box 29, Wabamun AB T0E 2K0
Tel: 780-892-4665
wabamun.chamber@xplornet.com
www.wabamunchamber.org
Vicki Specht, President

Wainwright & District Chamber of Commerce
PO Box 2997, #203, 1006 - 4th Ave., Wainwright AB T9W 1S9
Tel: 780-842-4910; *Fax:* 780-842-6061
exec@wdchamber.com
www.wdchamber.com
Sheri Ducolon, President
Shawna Batten, Executive Director

Waterton Park Chamber of Commerce & Visitors Association
PO Box 55, Waterton Lakes National Park AB T0K 2M0
Tel: 403-859-2224; *Fax:* 403-859-2650
waterton.info@pc.gc.ca
www.mywaterton.ca/community-chamber.cfm
Rod Kretz, President

Westlock & District Chamber of Commerce
PO Box 5917, Westlock AB T7P 2P7
Tel: 780-307-3251
Ben Kellert, President
John Bosman, Vice-President

Wetaskiwin Chamber of Commerce (WCC)
4910 - 55A St., Wetaskiwin AB T9A 2R7
Tel: 780-352-8003; *Fax:* 780-352-6226
www.wetaskiwinchamber.ca
Randy Plant, President
Alan Greene, Executive Director
Allan Halter, Secretary
Petra Erhardt, Treasurer

Whitecourt & District Chamber of Commerce
Synergy Business Centre, PO Box 1011, 4907 - 52 Ave., Whitecourt AB T7S 1N9
Tel: 780-778-5363; *Fax:* 780-778-2351
manager@whitecourtchamber.com
www.whitecourtchamber.com
Affiliation(s): Alberta Chamber of Commerce
Pat VanderBurg, General Manager
Neil Shewchuk, President

Worsley Chamber of Commerce
PO Box 181, Worsley AB T0H 3W0
Tel: 780-685-3943; *Fax:* 780-685-2115

British Columbia

Abbotsford Chamber of Commerce (ACOC)
207 - 32900 South Fraser Way, Abbotsford BC V2S 5A1
Tel: 604-859-9651; *Fax:* 604-850-6880
acoc@telus.net
www.abbotsfordchamber.com
Allan Asaph, Executive Director

Alberni Valley Chamber of Commerce
2533 Port Alberni Hwy., Port Alberni BC V9Y 8P2
Tel: 250-724-6535; *Fax:* 250-724-6560
office@avcoc.com
www.avcoc.com
Neil Malbon, President
Mike Carter, Executive Director

Armstrong-Spallumcheen Chamber of Commerce
PO Box 118, 3550 Bridge St., Armstrong BC V0E 1B0
Tel: 250-546-8155
manager@aschamber.com
aschamber.com
Social Media: pinterest.com/asvisitorcentre
Fran Stecyk, President

Ashcroft & District Chamber of Commerce
PO Box 741, Ashcroft BC V0R 1B0
ashcroftchamber@hotmail.com
www.ashcroftbc.ca/chamber_of_commerce

Bamfield Chamber of Commerce
Bamfield BC V0R 1B0
Tel: 250-728-3006
info@bamfieldchamber.com
www.bamfieldchamber.com
Affiliation(s): Pacific Rim Tourism Association

Barriere & District Chamber of Commerce
PO Box 1190, #3, 4353 Conner Rd., Barriere BC V0E 1E0
Tel: 250-672-9221
bcoc@telus.net
Affiliation(s): Canadian Chamber of Commerce
Scott Kershaw, President

Boundary Country Regional Chamber of Commerce
PO Box 2942, 1647 Central Ave., Grand Forks BC V0H 1H0
Tel: 250-442-2722; *Fax:* 250-442-5311
info@boundarychamber.com
www.boundarychamber.com
Todd Benson, President

Bowen Island Chamber of Commerce
PO Box 199, 432 Cardena Rd., Bowen Island BC V0N 1G0
Tel: 604-947-9024

Burnaby Board of Trade (BBOT)
#201, 4555 Kingsway, Burnaby BC V5H 4T8
Tel: 604-412-0100; *Fax:* 604-412-0102
admin@bbot.ca
www.bbot.ca
Social Media: www.youtube.com/user/burnabyboardoftrade
Paul Holden, CEO

Burns Lake & District Chamber of Commerce
Heritage Centre, PO Box 339, 540 Hwy. 16, Burns Lake BC V0J 1E0
Tel: 250-692-3773; *Fax:* 250-692-3701
info@burnslakechamber.com
burnslakechamber.com
Social Media: instagram.com/visitburnslake
Greg Brown, President

Cache Creek Chamber of Commerce
PO Box 460, Cache Creek BC V0K 1H0
Tel: 250-457-9668; *Fax:* 250-457-9669
Toll-Free: 888-457-7661
admin@cachecreek.info
www.cachecreekvillage.com
Gordon Daily, President

Campbell River & District Chamber of Commerce
900 Alder St., Campbell River BC V9W 2P6
Tel: 250-287-4636; *Fax:* 250-286-6490
admin@campbellriverchamber.ca
www.campbellriverchamber.ca
Social Media: www.youtube.com/user/CampbellRiverChamber
Colleen Evans, President & CEO

Castlegar & District Chamber of Commerce (CDCoC)
1995 - 6th Ave., Castlegar BC V1N 4B7
Tel: 250-365-6313; *Fax:* 250-365-5778
info@castlegar.com
www.castlegar.com
Jane Charest, President

Central Coast Chamber of Commerce (CCCC)
PO Box 40, Denny Island BC V0T 1B0
Tel: 250-957-2656; *Fax:* 250-957-2422
www.dennyislandbc.ca/chamber-of-commerce.php

Chambre de commerce francophone de Vancouver (CCFC)
1555, 7e av ouest, Vancouver BC V6J 1S1
Tél: 604-601-2124
info@ccfvancouver.com
ccfvancouver.com
Térence Doucet, Président

Chase & District Chamber of Commerce
PO Box 592, 400 Shuswap Ave., Chase BC V0E 1M0
Tel: 250-679-8432; *Fax:* 250-679-3120
admin@chasechamber.com
www.chasechamber.com
Carmen Miller, President

Chemainus & District Chamber of Commerce
PO Box 575, #102, 9799 Waterwheel Cres., Chemainus BC V0R 1K0
Tel: 250-246-3944; *Fax:* 250-246-3251
chamber@chemainus.bc.ca
www.chemainus.bc.ca
Jeanne Ross, Chamber Coordinator
Amy Fieldon, Coordinator, Visitor Centre

Chetwynd & District Chamber of Commerce
PO Box 870, 5217 North Access Rd., Chetwynd BC V0C 1J0
Tel: 250-788-3345; *Fax:* 250-788-3655
manager@chetwyndchamber.ca
www.chetwyndchamber.ca
Tonia Richter, Executive Director
Carmen Westgate, President

Chilliwack Chamber of Commerce
#201, 46093 Yale Rd., Chilliwack BC V2P 2L8
Tel: 604-793-4323
info@chilliwackchamber.com
www.chilliwackchamber.com
Social Media: www.youtube.com/user/ChilliwackChamber?ob=0
Kirk Dzaman, President
Fieny van den Boom, Executive Director

Christina Lake Chamber of Commerce
1675 Hwy. 3, Christina Lake BC V0H 1E2
Tel: 250-447-6161; *Fax:* 250-447-6161
info@christinalake.com
www.christinalake.com

Clearwater & District Chamber of Commerce
209 Dutch Lake Rd., Clearwater BC V0E 1N2
Tel: 250-674-2646; *Fax:* 250-674-3693
www.clearwaterbcchamber.com

Cloverdale & District Chamber of Commerce
#5748, 176 St., Cloverdale BC V3S 4C8
Tel: 604-574-9802; *Fax:* 604-574-9122
clovcham@axion.net
www.cloverdale.bc.ca
Brian Young, President
Bill Reid, Executive Director

Columbia Valley Chamber of Commerce (CVCC)
PO Box 1019, Invermere BC V0A 1K0
Tel: 250-342-2844; *Fax:* 250-342-3261
info@cvchamber.ca
www.cvchamber.ca
Affiliation(s): British Columbia Chamber of Commerce
Rose-Marie Regitnig, President
Susan E. Clovechok, Executive Director

Comox Valley Chamber of Commerce (CVCC)
2040 Cliffe Ave., Courtenay BC V9N 2L3
Tel: 250-334-3234; *Fax:* 250-334-4908
Toll-Free: 888-357-4471
admin@comoxvalleychamber.com
www.comoxvalleychamber.com
Tracey McGinnis, Chair
Dianne Hawkins, President & CEO

Cowichan Lake District Chamber of Commerce
PO Box 824, 125C South Shore Rd., Lake Cowichan BC V0R 2G0
Tel: 250-749-3244; *Fax:* 250-749-0187
info@cowichanlake.ca
www.cowichanlake.ca
Affiliation(s): Canadian Chamber of Commerce
Rita Dustow, President

Cranbrook & District Chamber of Commerce
Cranbrook & District Chamber of Commerce, PO Box 84, Cranbrook BC V1C 4H6
Tel: 250-426-5914; *Fax:* 250-426-3873
Toll-Free: 800-222-6174
info@cranbrookchamber.com
www.cranbrookchamber.com
David Struthers, President

David Hull, Executive Director

Creston Valley Chamber of Commerce
PO Box 268, 121 Northwest Blvd. (Hwy. 3), Creston BC V0B 1G0
Tel: 250-428-4342; *Fax:* 250-428-9411
Toll-Free: 866-528-4342
info@crestonvalleychamber.com
www.crestonvalleychamber.com
Rob Schepers, President
Jim Jacobsen, Executive Director

Cumberland Chamber of Commerce
PO Box 250, 2680 Dunsmuir Ave., Cumberland BC V0R 1S0
Tel: 250-336-8313; *Toll-Free:* 866-301-4636
chamber@cumberlandbc.org
cumberlandbc.org
Affiliation(s): North By Northwest Tourism Association of BC
Evan Loveless, President

Dawson Creek & District Chamber of Commerce
10201 - 10th St., Dawson Creek BC V1G 3T5
Tel: 250-782-4868; *Fax:* 250-782-2371
info@dawsoncreekchamber.ca
www.dawsoncreekchamber.ca
Affiliation(s): BC Chamber of Commerce
Anjula Benjamin, President
Kathleen Connolly, Executive Director

Dease Lake & District Chamber of Commerce
PO Box 338, Dease Lake BC V0C 1L0
Tel: 250-771-3900; *Fax:* 250-771-3900

Delta Chamber of Commerce
6201 - 60 Ave., Delta BC V4K 4E2
Tel: 604-946-4232; *Fax:* 604-946-5285
admin@deltachamber.ca
www.deltachamber.ca
Social Media: www.youtube.com/user/DeltaChamber
Ian Tait, Executive Director
Dave Hamilton, Chair

Discovery Islands Chamber of Commerce
PO Box 790, Quathiaski Cove BC V0P 1N0
chamber@discoveryislands.ca
www.discoveryislands.ca/chamber
Michael Lynch, President

Duncan-Cowichan Chamber of Commerce (DCCC)
381 Trans-Canada Hwy., Duncan BC V9L 3R5
Tel: 250-748-1111; *Fax:* 250-746-8222
chamber@duncancc.bc.ca
www.duncancc.bc.ca
Sonja Nagel, Executive Director

Elkford Chamber of Commerce
PO Box 220, 4A Front St., Elkford BC V0B 1H0
Tel: 250-425-5725
info@elkfordchamberofcommerce.com
www.elkfordchamberofcommerce.com

Enderby & District Chamber of Commerce
702 Railway St., Enderby BC V0E 1V0
Tel: 250-838-6727; *Fax:* 250-838-0123
Toll-Free: 877-213-6509
www.enderbychamber.com
Corinne Van De Crommenacker, General Manager
Lynne Holmes, President

Esquimalt Chamber of Commerce
PO Box 36019, 1153 Esquimalt Rd., Victoria BC V9A 7J5
Tel: 250-704-2525; *Fax:* 250-380-6932
admin@esquimaltchamber.ca
esquimaltchamber.ca
Chuck Palmer, President

Falkland Chamber of Commerce
PO Box 92, Hwy. 97, Falkland BC V0B 1M5
Tel: 250-379-2252
www.falklandbc.ca

Fernie Chamber of Commerce
102 Hwy. #3, Fernie BC V0B 1M5
Tel: 250-423-6868; *Fax:* 250-423-3811
Toll-Free: 877-433-7643
members@ferniechamber.com
www.ferniechamber.com
Affiliation(s): Economic Development Association of BC
Sheila Byers, President
Patty Vadnais, Executive Director

Fort Nelson & District Chamber of Commerce
PO Box 196, 5500 Alaska Hwy., Fort Nelson BC V0C 1R0
Tel: 250-774-2956; *Fax:* 250-774-2958
info@fortnelsonchamber.com
www.fortnelsonchamber.com

Jeremy Cote, President
Bev Vandersteen, Executive Director

Fort St. James Chamber of Commerce
PO Box 1164, 115 Douglas Ave., Fort St. James BC V0J 1P0
Tel: 250-996-7023; *Fax:* 250-996-7047
fsjchamb@fsjames.com
www.fortstjameschamber.ca

Fort St. John & District Chamber of Commerce
#100, 9907 - 99 Ave., Fort St John BC V1J 1V1
Tel: 250-785-6037; *Fax:* 250-785-6050
info@fsjchamber.com
www.fsjchamber.com
Lilia Hansen, Executive Director
Tony Zabinsky, President

Fraser Lake Chamber of Commerce
PO Box 1059, Fraser Lake BC V0J 1S0
Tel: 250-699-6605; *Fax:* 250-699-6469
www.fraserlake.ca
Maureen Olson, President

Gabriola Island Chamber of Commerce
PO Box 249, Gabriola BC V0R 1X0
Tel: 250-247-9332
giccmanager@shaw.ca
www.gabriolaisland.org
Affiliation(s): Tourism Association of Vancouver Island
Ken Gurr, President
Liz Rey, Manager

Galiano Island Chamber of Commerce
PO Box 73, Galiano BC V0N 1P0
Tel: 250-539-2233
info@galianoisland.com
www.galianoisland.com
Connie Nordin, President

Gibsons & District Chamber of Commerce
PO Box 1190, #21, 900 Gibsons Way, Gibsons BC V0N 1V0
Tel: 604-886-2325; *Fax:* 604-886-2379
www.gibsonschamber.com
Dean Walford, President
Donna McMahon, Executive Director

Gold River Chamber of Commerce
PO Box 39, Gold River BC V0P 1G0
Tel: 250-285-2724
goldriverchamber@gmail.com
www.goldriver.ca
Dawn Dakin, President
Norm Cowie, Vice-President

Greater Kamloops Chamber of Commerce
615 Victoria St., Kamloops BC V2C 2B3
Tel: 250-372-7722; *Fax:* 250-828-9500
mail@kamloopschamber.ca
www.kamloopschamber.ca
Social Media: www.youtube.com/watch?v=_55-O-Wp6Ko
Deb McClelland, Executive Director

Greater Langley Chamber of Commerce
#207, 8047 - 199 St., Langley BC V2Y 0E2
Tel: 604-371-3770; *Fax:* 604-371-3731
info@langleychamber.com
www.langleychamber.com
Scott Johnstone, President
Lynn Whitehouse, Executive Director

Greater Nanaimo Chamber of Commerce
2133 Bowen Rd., Nanaimo BC V9S 1H8
Tel: 250-756-1191; *Fax:* 250-756-1584
info@nanaimochamber.bc.ca
www.nanaimochamber.bc.ca
Kim Smythe, CEO
David Littlejohn, Chair
Justin Schley, Treasurer

Greater Vernon Chamber of Commerce (GVCC)
#102, 2901 - 32nd St., Vernon BC V1T 5M2
Tel: 250-545-0771; *Fax:* 250-545-3114
info@vernonchamber.ca
www.vernonchamber.ca
Affiliation(s): Canadian Chamber of Commerce
Dan Rogers, General Manager
Tracy Cobb-Reeves, President

Greater Victoria Chamber of Commerce (GVCC)
#100, 852 Fort St., Victoria BC V8W 1H8
Tel: 250-383-7191; *Fax:* 250-385-3552
chamber@victoriachamber.ca
www.victoriachamber.ca
Social Media: www.youtube.com/user/victoriachamber
Bruce Carter, CEO

Frank Bourree, Chair
Sang-Kiet Ly, Treasurer

Harrison Agassiz Chamber of Commerce
PO Box 429, Harrison Hot Springs BC V0M 1K0
info@harrison.ca
www.harrison.ca
Robert Reyerse, President

Hope & District Chamber of Commerce
PO Box 588, 519 - 6 Ave., #J, Hope BC V0X 1L0
Tel: 604-249-1246
info@hopechamber.net
hopechamber.net
Stephen Au-Yeung, President

Houston Chamber of Commerce
PO Box 396, 3289 Hwy. 16, Houston BC V0J 1Z0
Tel: 250-845-7640; *Fax:* 250-845-3682
info@houstonchamber.ca
www.houstonchamber.ca
Jean Marr, President

Kaslo & Area Chamber of Commerce
PO Box 329, Kaslo BC V0G 1M0
Toll-Free: 866-276-3212
thekaslochamber@gmail.com
www.kaslochamber.com
John Addison, President

Kelowna Chamber of Commerce
544 Harvey Ave., Kelowna BC V1Y 6C9
Tel: 250-861-3627; *Fax:* 250-861-3624
info@kelownachamber.org
www.kelownachamber.org
Affiliation(s): BC Chamber of Commerce
Dave Bond, President
Caroline Grover, Chief Executive Officer

Kicking Horse Country Chamber of Commerce (KHCCC)
PO Box 1320, #500, 10 North Ave., Golden BC V0A 1H0
Tel: 250-344-7125; *Fax:* 250-344-6688
Toll-Free: 800-622-4653
www.goldenchamber.bc.ca
Ruth Hamilton, Manager
Michele La Point, President

Kimberley Bavarian Society Chamber of Commerce (KBSCC)
270 Kimberley Ave., Kimberley BC V1A 3N3
Tel: 250-427-3666; *Toll-Free:* 866-913-3666
info@kimberleychamber.com
www.kimberleychamber.com
Darren Close, President

Kitimat Chamber of Commerce
PO Box 214, 2109 Forest Ave., Kitimat BC V8C 2G7
Tel: 250-632-6294; *Fax:* 250-632-4685
Toll-Free: 800-664-6554
info@kitimatchamber.ca
www.kitimatchamber.ca
Derick Stinson, President
Trish Parsons, Executive Director

Kitsilano Chamber of Commerce (KCC)
#400, 1681 Chestnut St., Vancouver BC V6J 4M6
Tel: 604-731-4454; *Fax:* 877-312-1898
office@kitsilanochamber.com
www.kitsilanochamber.com
Christian Johannsen, Chair
Cheryl Ziola, Executive Director

Kootenay Lake Chamber of Commerce
PO Box 120, Crawford Bay BC V0B 1E0
Tel: 250-227-9655
info@kootenaylake.bc.ca
www.kootenaylake.bc.ca
Jamie Cox, President
Lois Wakelin, Vice-President

Ladysmith Chamber of Commerce
441B - 1st Ave., Ladysmith BC V9G 1A4
Tel: 250-245-2112; *Fax:* 250-245-2124
info@ladysmithcofc.com
www.ladysmithcofc.com
Affiliation(s): Cowichan Regional Valley
Rob Waters, President

Lake Country Chamber of Commerce
Winfield Professional Building, #106, 3121 Hill Rd., Lake Country BC V4V Gg1
Tel: 250-766-5670; *Fax:* 250-766-0170
Toll-Free: 888-766-5670
manager@lakecountrychamber.com
www.lakecountrychamber.com
Garth McKay, President
Corrinne Cross, Manager

Likely & District Chamber of Commerce
PO Box 29, Likely BC V0L 1N0
Tel: 250-790-2127; *Fax:* 250-790-2323
chamber@likely-bc.ca
www.likely-bc.ca

Lillooet & District Chamber of Commerce
PO Box 650, Lillooet BC V0K 1V0
Tel: 250-256-3578; *Fax:* 250-256-4882
info@lillooetchamberofcommerce.com
www.lillooetchamberofcommerce.com
Scott Hutchinson, President

Lumby Chamber of Commerce
PO Box 534, 1882 Vernon St., Lumby BC V0E 2G0
Tel: 250-547-2300; *Fax:* 250-547-2300
lumbychamber@shaw.ca
www.monasheetourism.com
Stephanie Sexsmith, Manager
Bill Maltman, President

Lytton & District Chamber of Commerce
PO Box 460, 400 Fraser St., Lytton BC V0K 1Z0
Tel: 250-455-2523
info@lyttonchamber.com
lyttonchamber.com
Affiliation(s): Vancouver Coast & Mountains Tourism Region
Bernie Fandrich, President
Sheila Maguire, Secretary

Mackenzie Chamber of Commerce
PO Box 880, 88 Centennial Dr., Mackenzie BC V0J 2C0
Tel: 250-997-5459; *Fax:* 250-997-6117
office@mackenziechamber.bc.ca
www.mackenziechamber.bc.ca
Affiliation(s): Retail Merchants Association of BC
Peter McGaffin, President

Maple Ridge Pitt Meadows Chamber of Commerce
12492 Harris Rd., Pitt Meadows BC V3Y 2J4
Tel: 604-457-4599; *Fax:* 604-457-4598
info@ridgemeadowschamber.com
www.ridgemeadowschamber.com
Social Media: instagram.com/pmmrchamber
Affiliation(s): BC Chamber Executive; Canadian Chamber of Commerce; Southwestern BC Tourism
Andrea Madden, Executive Director

Mayne Island Community Chamber of Commerce (MICCC)
PO Box 2, Mayne Island BC V0N 2J0
executiveofficer@mayneislandchamber.ca
www.mayneislandchamber.ca
Millie Leathers, Chair
Lauren Underhill, Executive Officer

McBride & District Chamber of Commerce
PO Box 2, McBride BC V0J 2E0
Tel: 250-569-3366; *Fax:* 250-569-2376
Toll-Free: 866-569-3366
come2mcbride@telus.net
www.mcbridebc.info
Vincent de Niet, President

Merritt & District Chamber of Commerce
PO Box 1649, 2058B Granite Ave., Merritt BC V1K 1B8
Tel: 250-378-5634; *Fax:* 250-378-6561
manager@merrittchamber.com
www.merrittchamber.com

Mission Regional Chamber of Commerce
34033 Lougheed Hwy., Mission BC V2V 5X8
Tel: 604-826-6914; *Fax:* 604-826-5916
info@missionchamber.bc.ca
www.missionchamber.bc.ca
Social Media: www.youtube.com/TheMissionChamber
Sean Melia, President

Nakusp & District Chamber of Commerce
PO Box 387, 92 - 6th Ave. NW, Nakusp BC V0G 1R0
Tel: 250-265-4234; *Fax:* 250-265-3808
Toll-Free: 800-909-8819
nakusp@telus.net
www.nakusparrowlakes.com
Affiliation(s): Tourism British Columbia

Dawn Devlin, President

Nelson & District Chamber of Commerce
255 Hall St., Nelson BC V1L 5X4
Tel: 250-352-3433; *Fax:* 250-352-6355
Toll-Free: 877-663-5706
info@discovernelson.com
www.discovernelson.com
Affiliation(s): British Columbia Chamber of Commerce; Canadian Chamber of Commerce
Cal Renwick, President

New Westminster Chamber of Commerce
601 Queens Ave., New Westminster BC V3M 1L1
Tel: 604-521-7781; *Fax:* 604-521-0057
nwcc@newwestchamber.com
www.newwestchamber.com
Andrew Hopkins, President
Cori Lynn Germiquet, Executive Director

North Grenville Chamber of Commerce
PO Box 1047, 509 Kernahan St., Kemptville ON K0G 1J0
Tel: 613-258-4838
www.northgrenvillechamber.com
Mark Thornton, Chair

North Shuswap Chamber of Commerce
3871 Squilax-Anglemont Rd., #B, Scotch Creek BC V0E 1M5
Tel: 250-955-2113; *Toll-Free:* 888-955-1488
requests@northshuswapbc.com
northshuswapbc.com

North Vancouver Chamber of Commerce (NVCC)
1250 Lonsdale Ave., Vancouver BC V7M 2H6
Tel: 604-987-4488; *Fax:* 604-987-8272
www.nvchamber.ca
Social Media: www.instagram.com/nvchamber
Louise Ranger, Chief Executive Officer
Misha Wilson, Manager, Membership

Parksville & District Chamber of Commerce
PO Box 99, Parksville BC V9P 2G3
Tel: 250-248-3613; *Fax:* 250-248-5210
info@parksvillechamber.com
www.parksvillechamber.com
Social Media: www.youtube.com/user/ParksvilleChamber1
Kim Burden, Executive Director
Linda Tchorz, Manager, Member Services
Lynda Schneider, Bookkeeper
Patti Lee, Manager, Visitor Centre

Peachland Chamber of Commerce
5684 Beach Ave., Peachland BC V0H 1X6
Tel: 250-767-2422; *Fax:* 250-767-2420
peachlandchamber@gmail.com
www.peachlandchamber.bc.ca
Patrick Van Minsel, Executive Director

Pemberton & District Chamber of Commerce
PO Box 370, Pemberton BC V0N 2L0
Tel: 604-894-6477; *Fax:* 604-894-5571
info@pembertonchamber.com
www.pembertonchamber.com
Affiliation(s): Vancouver Board of Trade
Karen Ross, President
Shirley Henry, Secretary-Treasurer

Pender Harbour & Egmont Chamber of Commerce
Madeira Park, PO Box 265, Madeira Park BC V0N 2H0
Tel: 604-883-2561; *Fax:* 604-883-2561
Toll-Free: 877-873-6337
chamber@penderharbour.ca
www.penderharbour.ca
Kerry Milligan, Secretary
Dave Milligan, President

Pender Island Chamber of Commerce
PO Box 123, Pender Island BC V0N 2M0
Tel: 250-629-3988; *Toll-Free:* 866-468-7924
travel@penderislandchamber.com
www.penderislandchamber.com

Penticton & Wine Country Chamber of Commerce
553 Vees Dr., Penticton BC V2A 8S3
Tel: 250-492-4103
admin@penticton.org
www.penticton.org
Brandy Maslowski, Executive Director
Jason Cox, President

Port Hardy & District Chamber of Commerce
PO Box 249, 7250 Market St., Port Hardy BC V0N 2P0
Tel: 250-949-7622; *Fax:* 250-949-6653
Toll-Free: 866-427-3901
phccadm@cablerocket.com
www.porthardychamber.com
Social Media: statigr.am/visitporthardy
Todd Landon, President
Carly Pereboom, Executive Director

Port McNeill & District Chamber of Commerce
PO Box 129, 1594 Beach Dr., Port McNeill BC V0N 2R0
Tel: 250-956-3131; *Fax:* 250-956-3132
Toll-Free: 888-956-3131
pmccc@island.net
www.portmcneill.net
David Mitchell, President
Cheryl Jorgenson, Executive Director

Port Renfrew Chamber of Commerce
PO Box 39, Port Renfrew BC V0S 1K0
Tel: 250-858-7665
renfrewchamber@gmail.com
www.portrenfrewcommunity.com
Dan Hager, President

Powell River Chamber of Commerce
6807 Wharf St., Powell River BC V8A 2T9
Tel: 604-485-4051
office@powellriverchamber.com
www.powellriverchamber.com
Jack Barr, President
Kim Miller, General Manager

Prince George Chamber of Commerce (PGCOC)
890 Vancouver St., Prince George BC V2L 2P5
Tel: 250-562-2454; *Fax:* 250-562-6510
chamber@pgchamber.bc.ca
www.pgchamber.bc.ca
Jennifer Brandle-McCall, CEO

Prince Rupert & District Chamber of Commerce (PRDCC)
#170, 110 - 1st Ave., Prince Rupert BC V8J 1A8
Tel: 250-624-2296; *Fax:* 250-624-6105
www.princerupertchamber.ca
Social Media: www.youtube.com/user/princerupertchamber
Jason Scherr, President
John Farrell, 1st Vice-President
Carol Bulford, Chamber Manager

Princeton & District Chamber of Commerce
PO Box 540, 105 Hwy. 3 East, Princeton BC V0X 1W0
Tel: 250-295-3103; *Fax:* 250-295-3255

Qualicum Beach Chamber of Commerce
PO Box 159, 124 West 2nd Ave., Qualicum Beach BC V9K 1S7
Tel: 250-752-0960
chamber@qualicum.bc.ca
www.qualicum.bc.ca
Social Media: instagram.com/QualicumBeachVIC
Affiliation(s): Oceanside Tourism Association
Oura Giakoumakis, Chair
Evelyn Clark, CEO

Quesnel & District Chamber of Commerce
335 East Vaughan St., Quesnel BC V2J 2T1
Tel: 250-992-7262
qchamber@quesnelbc.com
quesnelchamber.com
William Lacy, President
Amber Gregg, Manager

Radium Hot Springs Chamber of Commerce
PO Box 225, Radium Hot Springs BC V0A 1M0
Tel: 250-347-9331; *Fax:* 250-347-9127
Toll-Free: 888-347-9331
info@RadiumHotSprings.com
www.RadiumHotSprings.com
Social Media: www.youtube.com/tourismradium

Revelstoke Chamber of Commerce
PO Box 490, 301 Victoria Rd. West, Revelstoke BC V0E 2S0
Tel: 250-837-5345; *Toll-Free:* 800-487-1493
revelstokechamber.com
Judy Goodman, Executive Director

Richmond Chamber of Commerce
North Tower, #202, 5811 Cooney Rd., Richmond BC V6X 3M1
Tel: 604-278-2822; *Fax:* 604-278-2972
rcc@richmondchamber.ca
www.richmondchamber.ca
Social Media: www.youtube.com/user/RichmondchamberBC
Affiliation(s): Tourism Richmond; Sister Chamber - Kent, Washington
Matt Pitcairn, President & CEO

Rossland Chamber of Commerce
PO Box 1385, #204, 2012 Washington St., Rossland BC V0G 1Y0
Tel: 250-362-5666; *Fax:* 250-362-5399
commerce@rossland.com
www.rossland.com/about
Paul Gluska, President
Renee Clark, Executive Director

Saanich Peninsula Chamber of Commerce (SPCOC)
#209, 2453 Beacon Ave., Sidney BC V8L 1X7
Tel: 250-656-3616; *Fax:* 250-656-7111
info@peninsulachamber.ca
www.peninsulachamber.ca
Social Media: www.youtube.com/sanpenchamber
Chris Fudge, Executive Director
Wendy Everson, President

Salmo & District Chamber of Commerce
PO Box 400, 100 - 4th St., Salmo BC V0G 1Z0
Tel: 250-357-2596
salmoch@telus.net
discoversalmo.ca/Chamber.aspx
Dave Reid, President

Salmon Arm & District Chamber of Commerce (SACC)
PO Box 999, #101, 20 Hudson Ave. NE, Salmon Arm BC V1E 4P2
Tel: 250-832-6247; *Fax:* 250-832-8382
admin@sachamber.bc.ca
www.sachamber.bc.ca
Jim Kimmerly, President
Corryn Grayston, General Manager

Salt Spring Island Chamber of Commerce (SSI Chamber)
121 Lower Ganges Rd., Salt Spring Island BC V8K 2T1
Tel: 250-537-4223; *Fax:* 250-537-4276
Toll-Free: 866-216-2936
chamber@saltspringchamber.com
www.saltspringchamber.com
Janet Clouston, General Manager

Sechelt & District Chamber of Commerce
PO Box 360, #102, 5700 Cowrie St., Sechelt BC V0N 3A0
Tel: 604-885-0662; *Fax:* 604-885-0691
sdcoc9@telus.net
www.secheltchamber.bc.ca
Kim Darwin, President
Colleen Clark, Executive Director

Seton Portage/Shalalth District Chamber of Commerce
PO Box 2067, Seton Portage BC V0N 3B0
Tel: 250-259-8268
Ray Klassen, Vice-President

Sicamous & District Chamber of Commerce
PO Box 346, 314A Finlayson St., Sicamous BC V0E 2V0
Tel: 250-836-0002; *Fax:* 250-836-4368
sicamouschamber@cablelan.net
www.sicamouschamber.bc.ca

Similkameen Chamber of Commerce
PO Box 490, Keremeos BC V0X 1N0
Tel: 250-499-5225

Slocan District Chamber of Commerce (SDCC)
PO Box 448, New Denver BC V0G 1S0
chamber@slocanlake.com
slocanlakechamber.com
Amanda Murphy, Manager
Nikita Boroumand, President

Smithers District Chamber of Commerce
PO Box 2379, Smithers BC V0J 2N0
Tel: 250-847-5072; *Fax:* 250-847-3337
Toll-Free: 800-542-6673
info@smitherschamber.com
www.smitherschamber.com
Affiliation(s): Northern BC Tourism Association
George Whitehead, President

Sooke Harbour Chamber of Commerce
PO Box 18, #301, 2015 Shields Rd., Sooke BC V9Z 0E4
Tel: 250-642-6112
info@sookeharbourchamber.com
www.sookeharbourchamber.com
Scott Gertsma, President

South Cariboo Chamber of Commerce
PO Box 2312, #2, 385 Birch Ave., 100 Mile House BC V0K 2E0
Tel: 250-395-6124
www.southcariboochamber.org
Affiliation(s): Canadian Chamber of Commerce
Tom Bachynski, President

South Cowichan Chamber of Commerce (SCCC)
#368, 2720 Mill Bay Rd., Mill Bay BC V0R 2P1
Tel: 250-743-3566; *Fax:* 250-743-5332
southcowichanchamber@shaw.ca
www.southcowichanchamber.org
Shauna Benson, Executive Director
Mike Hanson, President

South Okanagan Chamber Of Commerce
6431 Station St., Oliver BC V0H 1T0
Tel: 250-498-6321; *Fax:* 250-498-3156
www.sochamber.ca
Social Media: www.youtube.com/user/SouthOKChamber

South Shuswap Chamber of Commerce
PO Box 7, Blind Bay BC V0E 2W0
Tel: 250-675-3515; *Fax:* 250-675-3516
sorrentochamber@telus.net
www.southshuswapchamberofcommerce.org
Judy Smith, President
Nancy Kyle, Manager

South Surrey & White Rock Chamber of Commerce
#22, 1480 Foster St., White Rock BC V4B 3X7
Tel: 604-536-6844; *Fax:* 604-536-4994
admin@sswrchamber.ca
www.sswrchamberofcommerce.ca
Social Media: sswrchamber.tumblr.com
Affiliation(s): BC Tourism
Cliff Annable, Executive Director

Sparwood & District Chamber of Commerce
PO Box 1448, 141 Aspen Dr., Sparwood BC V0B 2G0
Tel: 250-425-2423; *Toll-Free:* 877-485-8185
administrator@sparwoodchamber.bc.ca
www.sparwoodchamber.bc.ca
Social Media:
www.youtube.com/channel/UCdVQtK--71Zi_qit0g3xqrQ
Marjorie Templin, President
Norma McDougall, Manager

Squamish Chamber of Commerce
Squamish Adventure Centre, #102, 38551 Loggers Lane, Squamish BC V8B 0H2
Tel: 604-815-4994; *Fax:* 604-815-4998
Toll-Free: 866-333-2010
info@squamishchamber.com
www.squamishchamber.com
Social Media: www.youtube.com/spiritofsquamish
Chris Pettingill, President

Stewart-Hyder International Chamber of Commerce
PO Box 306, Stewart BC V0T 1W0
Tel: 250-636-9224; *Fax:* 250-636-2199

Summerland Chamber of Commerce
PO Box 130, 15600 Hwy. 97, Summerland BC V0H 1Z0
Tel: 250-494-2686; *Fax:* 250-494-4039
membership@summerlandchamber.com
www.summerlandchamber.com
Social Media: www.youtube.com/user/scedt;
instagram.com/visit_summerland
Affiliation(s): Thompson/Okanagan Tourism Association; Penticton & Wine Country Chamber of Commerce; South Okanagan Chamber of Commerce
Kelly Marshall, President
Christine Petkau, Executive Director

Surrey Board of Trade (SBOT)
#101, 14439 - 104 Ave., Surrey BC V3R 1M1
Tel: 604-581-7130; *Fax:* 604-588-7549
Toll-Free: 866-848-7130
info@businessinsurrey.com
www.businessinsurrey.com
Anita Huberman, Chief Executive Officer
Bijoy Samuel, President
Gerard Breamault, Vice-President

Tahsis Chamber of Commerce
PO Box 278, 36 Rugged Mountain Rd., Tahsis BC V0P 1X0
Tel: 204-934-6425
info@tahsischamber.com
www.tahsischamber.com
Tony Ellis, President
Silvie Keene, Secretary/Treasurer

Terrace & District Chamber of Commerce
4511 Keith Ave., Terrace BC V8G 1K1
Tel: 250-635-2063; *Fax:* 250-635-2573
terracechamber@telus.net
www.terracechamber.com
Janice Shaben, President
Carol Fielding, Executive Director

Texada Island Chamber of Commerce
PO Box 249, Vananda BC V0N 3K0
Tel: 604-486-7597
Affiliation(s): British Columbia Chamber of Commerce; Canadian Chamber of Commerce
Mave Leclair, President

Tofino-Long Beach Chamber of Commerce
PO Box 249, 1426 Pacific Rim Hwy., Tofino BC V0R 2Z0
Tel: 250-725-3414; *Fax:* 250-725-3296
info@tofinochamber.org
www.tofinochamber.org
Don Travers, President
Gord Johns, Executive Director

Trail & District Chamber of Commerce
#200, 1199 Bay Ave., Trail BC V1R 4A4
Tel: 250-368-3144; *Fax:* 250-368-6427
tcocm@netidea.com
www.trailchamber.bc.ca
Lisa Gregorini, President
Norm Casler, Executive Director

Tri-Cities Chamber of Commerce Serving Coquitlam, Port Coquitlam & Port Moody
1209 Pinetree Way, Coquitlam BC V3B 7Y3
Tel: 604-464-2716
info@tricitieschamber.com
www.tricitieschamber.com
Michael Hind, Executive Director

Ucluelet Chamber of Commerce (UCOC)
PO Box 428, 200 Main St., Ucluelet BC V0R 3A0
Tel: 250-726-4641; *Fax:* 250-726-4611
info@uclueletinfo.com
www.uclueletinfo.com
Marny Saunders, General Manager

Valemount & Area Chamber of Commerce (VACC)
PO Box 690, Valemount BC V0E 2Z0
Tel: 250-566-0061; *Fax:* 250-566-0061
info@valemountchamber.com
www.valemountchamber.com
Christine Latimer, Chair

Vanderhoof Chamber of Commerce
PO Box 126, 2353 Burrard Ave., Vanderhoof BC V0J 3A0
Tel: 250-567-2124; *Fax:* 250-567-3316
Toll-Free: 800-752-4094
info@vanderhoofchamber.com
www.vanderhoofchamber.com
Affiliation(s): BC Chamber of Commerce
Joe Von Doellen, President
Spencer Siemens, Executive Director

Wells & District Chamber of Commerce
PO Box 123, Wells BC V0K 2R0
Tel: 250-994-2323; *Fax:* 250-994-3331
Toll-Free: 877-451-9355
wells.ca/profile/wells-district-chamber-commerce

West Shore Chamber of Commerce
2830 Aldwynd Rd., Victoria BC V9B 3S7
Tel: 250-478-1130; *Fax:* 250-478-1584
www.westshore.bc.ca
Julie Lawlor, Executive Director

West Vancouver Chamber of Commerce
2235 Marine Dr., West Vancouver BC V7V 1K5
Tel: 604-926-6614; *Fax:* 604-926-6647
info@westvanchamber.com
www.westvanchamber.com
Leagh Gabriel, Executive Director

Westbank & District Chamber of Commerce
2372 Dobbin Rd., Westbank BC V4T 2H9
Tel: 250-768-3378; *Fax:* 250-768-3465
Toll-Free: 866-768-3378
admin@westbankchamber.com
www.westbankchamber.com
Craig Brown, President
Karen Beaubier, Chamber Liaison Officer

Whistler Chamber of Commerce
#201, 4230 Gateway Dr., Whistler BC V0N 1B4
Tel: 604-932-5922; *Fax:* 604-932-3755
www.whistlerchamber.com
Social Media:
www.youtube.com/channel/UCphpSBZQmhRux_-jalEtcwQ
Val Litwin, Chief Executive Officer
Grant Cousar, Chair

Williams Lake & District Chamber of Commerce
1660 South Broadway, Williams Lake BC V2G 2W4
Tel: 250-392-5025; *Toll-Free:* 877-967-5253
info@williamslakechamber.com
www.williamslakechamber.com
Affiliation(s): BC Chamber of Commerce; Canadian Chamber of Commerce; Cariboo Chilcotin Coast Tourism Association
Angela Sommer, President
Claudia Blair, Executive Director

Zeballos Board of Trade
c/o Village of Zeballos, PO Box 127, Zeballos BC V0P 2A0
Tel: 250-761-4229; *Fax:* 250-761-4331
adminzeb@recn.ca
www.zeballos.com

Manitoba

Altona & District Chamber of Commerce
Altona Mall, PO Box 329, Altona MB R0G 0B0
Tel: 204-324-8793; *Fax:* 204-324-1314
chamber@shopaltona.com
www.shopaltona.com
Geoff Loewen, President
Becky Cianflone, Manager

Arborg Chamber of Commerce
PO Box 415, Arborg MB R0C 0A0
Tel: 204-376-2308
www.townofarborg.com
Ron Johnston, President

Ashern & District Chamber of Commerce
PO Box 582, Ashern MB R0C 0E0
info@ashern.ca
www.ashern.ca
Social Media:
www.youtube.com/channel/UCboTRxB0DQV43ZR4MNAsfzw

Assiniboia Chamber of Commerce (MB) (ACC)
PO Box 42122, Stn. Ferry Road, 1867 Portage Ave., Winnipeg MB R3J 3X7
Tel: 204-774-4154; *Fax:* 204-774-4201
info@assiniboiacc.mb.ca
www.assiniboiacc.mb.ca
Ernie Nairn, Executive Director

Beausejour & District Chamber of Commerce
PO Box 224, Beausejour MB R0E 0C0
Tel: 204-268-3502
beausejourchamber@ourhomeyourhome.ca
ourhomeyourhome.ca
Kerryleegh Hilderbandtt, President
Sherri Garrity, Executive Director

Birtle & District Chamber of Commerce
PO Box 278, Birtle MB R0M 0C0
Tel: 204-842-3234

Blue Water Chamber of Commerce
PO Box 204, St Georges MB R0E 1V0
Tel: 204-367-2762; *Fax:* 204-367-4030
bluewaterchamber@hotmail.com
Diane Dube, President

Boissevain & District Chamber of Commerce
c/o Municipal Office, PO Box 490, 420 South Railway St., Boissevain MB R0K 0E0
Tel: 204-534-2433; *Fax:* 204-534-3710
admin@boissevain.ca
www.boissevain.ca
Bill Dougall, President
Rhonda Coupland, Secretary

Brandon Chamber of Commerce
1043 Rosser Ave., Brandon MB R7A 0L5
Tel: 204-571-5340; *Fax:* 204-571-5347
info@brandonchamber.ca
brandonchamber.ca
Carolynn Cancade, General Manager

Carberry & District Chamber of Commerce
PO Box 101, Carberry MB R0K 0H0
Tel: 204-834-6616
edo@townofcarberry.ca
www.townofcarberry.ca

Christinia Steen, President
Lori Scott, Secretary

Carman & Community Chamber of Commerce
PO Box 249, Carman MB R0G 0J0
Tel: 204-750-3050
ccchamber@gmail.com
www.carmanchamberofcommerce.com
Affiliation(s): Manitoba Chamber of Commerce
Paul Clark, President
Nikki Bartley, Executive Director

Chambre de commerce de Notre Dame
PO Box 107, Notre Dame de Lourdes MB R0G 1M0
Tel: 204-248-2073; *Fax:* 204-248-2847
Lise Deleurme, President
Joey Dupasquler, Secretary

La chambre de commerce de Saint-Malo & District
CP 328, Saint-Malo MB R0A 1T0
Joël Fouasse, Co-président
Gilles Maynard, Co-président

Chambre de commerce francophone de Saint-Boniface (CCFSB) / St-Boniface chamber of Commerce
CP 204, #212, 383, boul. Provencher, Saint-Boniface MB R2H 3B4
Tél: 204-235-1406; *Téléc:* 204-233-1017
info@ccfsb.mb.ca
www.ccfsb.mb.ca
Paul Prenovault, Président

Churchill Chamber of Commerce
PO Box 176, Churchill MB R0B 0E0
Tel: 204-675-2022; *Fax:* 204-675-2021
Toll-Free: 888-389-2327
churchillchamber@mts.net
churchillchamberofcommerce.ca

Crystal City & District Chamber of Commerce
PO Box 56, Crystal City MB R0K 0N0
Tel: 204-873-2427; *Fax:* 204-873-2656
chamberofcommerce@crystalcitymb.ca
www.crystalcitymb.ca/organizations/chamber.html
Doug Rempel, Contact
Doug Treble, Contact

Cypress River Chamber of Commerce
PO Box 261, Cypress River MB R0K 0P0
Tel: 204-743-2119; *Fax:* 204-743-2339
www.cypressriver.ca
Jim Cassels, President

Dauphin & District Chamber of Commerce
100 Main St. South, Dauphin MB R7N 1K3
Tel: 204-622-3140; *Fax:* 204-622-3141
coordinator@dauphinchamber.ca
www.dauphinchamber.ca
Joanne Vandepoele, President

Deloraine & District Chamber of Commerce
PO Box 748, Deloraine MB R0M 0M0
Tel: 204-747-2655; *Fax:* 204-747-2927
deloraine.org/business/coc.html
Deb Calverley, President
Grant Cassils, Contact

Elie Chamber of Commerce
PO Box 175, Elie MB R0H 0H0
Tel: 204-353-2892; *Fax:* 204-353-2286
Bob Whitechurch, Chair, LUD of Elie

Elkhorn Chamber of Commerce
PO Box 418, Elkhorn MB R0M 0N0
www.elkhornchamberofcommerce.ca
Bob Nesbitt, Chamber Secretary
Tricia Forsythe, President

Eriksdale & District Chamber of Commerce
PO Box 434, Eriksdale MB R0C 0W0
Tel: 204-739-2606
www.eriksdale.com
Keith Lundale, President

Falcon, West Hawk & Caddy Lakes Chamber of Commerce (FWHLCC)
PO Box 187, Falcon Beach MB R0E 0N0
Tel: 204-349-3134; *Fax:* 204-349-3134
falconwesthawkchamber.com
Affiliation(s): Canadian Chamber of Commerce
Bob Harbottle, President

Fisher Branch & District Chamber of Commerce
PO Box 566, Fisher Branch MB R0C 0Z0
Tel: 204-372-8585; *Fax:* 204-372-6504
fisherchamber@gmail.com
Darcy Plett, President

Flin Flon & District Chamber of Commerce
#235, 35 Main St., Flin Flon MB R8A 1J7
Tel: 204-687-4518
flinflonchamber@mymts.net
www.flinflondistrictchamber.com
Dianne Russell, President
Karen MacKinnon, President Elect

Gilbert Plains & District Chamber of Commerce
PO Box 670, Gilbert Plains MB R0L 0X0
Tel: 204-548-2682; *Fax:* 204-548-2682
Brenda Kerns, President

Gillam Chamber of Commerce
PO Box 366, Gillam MB R0B 0L0
Tel: 204-652-5135; *Fax:* 204-652-5155
www.townofgillam.com
Ken Hill, President

Grahamdale Chamber of Commerce
R.M. Of Grahamdale Administration Office, PO Box 160, 23 Government Rd., Moosehorn MB R0C 2E0
Tel: 204-768-2858; *Fax:* 204-768-3374
info@grahamdale.ca
www.grahamdale.ca
Karen Bittner, President

Grandview & District Chamber of Commerce
PO Box 28, Grandview MB R0L 0Y0
Tel: 204-546-2501
www.grandviewmanitoba.com
Pierce Cairns, President
Robyn Dingwall, Secretary/Treasurer

Grunthal & District Chamber of Commerce
PO Box 451, Grunthal MB R0A 0R0
Tel: 204-434-6750
grunthal.ca/chamber.php
Leonard Hiebert, President

Hamiota Chamber of Commerce
PO Box 403, Hamiota MB R0J 1Z0
www.hamiota.com/business.html
Larry Oakden, President
Bonnie Michaudville, Secretary

Hartney & District Chamber of Commerce
PO Box 224, Hartney MB R0M 0X0

Headingley Chamber of Commerce
#1, 126 Bridge Rd., Headingley MB R4H 1G9
Tel: 204-837-5766; *Fax:* 204-831-7207
www.headingleychamber.ca
Affiliation(s): Central Plains Development Corporation; White Horse Plains Development Corporation; Headingley Heritage Centre
Jill Ruth, President
Barb McEachern, Secretary
Dave White, Executive Director

Killarney & District Chamber of Commerce
PO Box 809, Killarney MB R0K 1G0
Tel: 204-523-4202
killarneychamber@hotmail.com
Mark Witherspoon, Chair
Dale Banman, Executive Director

Lac du Bonnet & District Chamber of Commerce
PO Box 598, Lac du Bonnet MB R0E 1A0
Tel: 204-340-0497
ldbchamberofcommerce@gmail.com
www.lacdubonnetchamber.com
Affiliation(s): Manitoba Chambers of Commerce
Marie Hiebert, President
Jennifer Hudson Stewart, Administrator

Landmark & Community Chamber of Commerce
PO Box 469, Landmark MB R0A 0X0
Tel: 204-355-4035; *Fax:* 204-355-4800
office@landmarkonline.ca
Randy Wolgemuth, President

Leaf Rapids Chamber of Commerce
c/o Town of Leaf Rapids, Town Centre Mall, PO Box 340, Leaf Rapids MB R0B 1W0
Tel: 204-473-2436; *Fax:* 204-473-2566
www.townofleafrapids.ca
Lianna Anderson, Community Economic Development Officer

MacGregor Chamber of Commerce
PO Box 220, MacGregor MB R0H 0R0
Tel: 204-685-2390
Jason McKelvy, President

Melita & District Chamber of Commerce
PO Box 666, Melita MB R0M 1L0
Tel: 204-522-2490
www.melitamb.ca
Bill Warren, President

Minnedosa Chamber of Commerce
PO Box 857, Minnedosa MB R0J 1E0
Tel: 204-867-2951; *Fax:* 204-867-3641
minnedosachamber@gmail.com
www.discoverminnedosa.ca
Don Farr, President
Callie Mashtoler, Secretary

Morden & District Chamber of Commerce
#100, 379 Stephen St., Morden MB R6M 1V1
Tel: 204-822-5630
marketing@mordenchamber.com
www.mordenchamber.com
Ross Ariss, President
Pamela Hiebert, Director, Marketing & Promotions

Morris & District Chamber of Commerce
141 Main St. South, Morris MB R0G 1K0
Tel: 204-712-6162
info@morrischamberofcommerce.com
www.morrischamberofcommerce.com
Bruce Third, President
Andy Anderson, Secretary

Neepawa & District Chamber of Commerce
PO Box 726, 282 Hamilton St., Neepawa MB R0J 1H0
Tel: 204-476-5292; *Fax:* 204-476-5231
info@neepawachamber.com
www.neepawachamber.com

Niverville Chamber of Commerce
PO Box 157, Niverville MB R0A 1E0
Tel: 204-388-4600
chamber@niverville.com
www.niverville.com
Leighton Reimer, President

Oakville & District Chamber of Commerce
PO Box 263, Oakville MB R0H 0Y0
Tel: 204-267-2730; *Fax:* 888-552-9910
oakvillechamberoffice@gmail.com
Kam Blight, President
Barb Ingram, Contact

The Pas & District Chamber of Commerce
PO Box 996, The Pas MB R9A 1L1
Tel: 204-623-7256; *Fax:* 204-623-2589
tpchamber@mailme.ca
www.thepaschamber.com
James Berscheid, President

Pilot Mound & District Chamber of Commerce
Tel: 204-825-2587
chamberofcommerce@pilotmound.com
www.pilotmound.com

Pinawa Chamber of Commerce
PO Box 544, Pinawa MB R0E 1L0
www.pinawachamber.com
Jeff Simpson, President

Plum Coulee & District Chamber of Commerce
www.townofplumcoulee.com/chamber.html
Moira Porte, Contact

Portage la Prairie & District Chamber of Commerce
56 Royal Rd. North, Portage la Prairie MB R1N 1V1
Tel: 204-857-7778; *Fax:* 204-856-5001
info@portagechamber.com
www.portagechamber.com
Affiliation(s): Canadian Chamber of Commerce
Dave Omichinski, President
Cindy McDonald, Executive Director

Rivers & District Chamber of Commerce
PO Box 795, Rivers MB R0K 1X0
Tel: 204-328-7316; *Fax:* 204-328-5212
riverschamber@gmail.com
riversdaly.ca/chamber-of-commerce/
Melissa MacMillan, President
Jean Young, Sec./Tres.

Riverton & District Chamber of Commerce
PO Box 258, Riverton MB R0C 2R0
Tel: 204-378-2084; *Fax:* 204-378-2085
berniced@mts.net
www.rivertoncanada.com
Susie Eyolfson, Vice-Chair

Roblin & District Chamber of Commerce
PO Box 160, 147 Main St., Roblin MB R0L 1P0
Tel: 204-937-3194
rdcoc@mts.net
www.roblinmanitoba.com/index.php?pageid=BUSCOC
Norma Gaber, President

Rossburn & District Chamber of Commerce
PO Box 579, Rossburn MB R0J 1V0
Tel: 204-859-3334; *Fax:* 204-859-3313
rossburn.chamber@live.ca
Tony White, President
Myra Drul, Secretary

Russell & District Chamber of Commerce
PO Box 155, Russell MB R0J 1W0
Tel: 204-773-2456
chamber@russellmb.com
www.russellmb.com/chamber.html
Dale Wray, President

St. Pierre Chamber of Commerce
PO Box 71, St Pierre Jolys MB R0A 1V0
Tel: 204-377-4384
sundowng@mts.net
www.stpierrejolys.com
Robert Bruneau, President

La Salle & District Chamber of Commerce
PO Box 172, La Salle MB R0G 1B0
Fax: 866-234-6272
Toll-Free: 855-273-3278
info@lasalleonline.ca
lasalleonline.ca
Drew Howard, President
Jared Cormier, Treasurer

Selkirk & District Chamber of Commerce
City of Selkirk Bldg., 100 Eaton Ave., Selkirk MB R1A 0W6
Tel: 204-482-7176; *Fax:* 204-482-5448
info@selkirkanddistrictchamber.ca
www.selkirkanddistrictchamber.ca

Shoal Lake & District Chamber of Commerce
PO Box 176, Shoal Lake MB R0J 1Z0
Tel: 204-759-2215
pplace@mymts.net
Cory Luhowy, Manager
Tracey Myhill, President

Somerset & District Chamber of Commerce
PO Box 64, Somerset MB R0G 2L0
Tel: 204-744-2011; *Fax:* 204-744-2170
somcdc@mts.net
Affiliation(s): Manitoba Chamber of Commerce
Gilbert Mabon, President

Souris & Glenwood Chamber of Commerce
PO Box 939, Souris MB R0K 2C0
sourischamber@gmail.com
Affiliation(s): Manitoba Chamber of Commerce
Sande Denbow, President

Ste Rose & District Chamber of Commerce
PO Box 688, Ste Rose du Lac MB R0L 1S0
Tel: 204-447-2196; *Fax:* 204-447-2692
Trevor Gates, President
Monica Lambourne, Contact

Steinbach Chamber of Commerce
#D4, 225 Reimer Ave., Steinbach MB R5G 2J1
Tel: 204-326-9566; *Fax:* 204-346-6600
www.steinbachchamberofcommerce.com
Sjoerd Huese, President
Linda Peters, Executive Director

Stonewall & District Chamber of Commerce
PO Box 762, Stonewall MB R0C 2Z0
Tel: 204-467-8377
info@stonewallchamber.com
www.stonewallchamber.com
Stephanie Duncan, Director

Swan Valley Chamber of Commerce
PO Box 1540, Swan River MB R0L 1Z0
Tel: 204-734-3102; *Fax:* 204-734-4342
chamberofcommerce@chamber8.ca

Teulon Chamber of Commerce
PO Box 235, Teulon MB R0C 3B0
Tel: 204-294-6171; *Fax:* 204-886-3232
Jan Lambourne, Chair
Linda Lamoureux, Secretary

Thompson Chamber of Commerce
PO Box 363, 79 Selkirk Ave., Thompson MB R8N 1N2
Tel: 204-677-4155; *Toll-Free:* 888-307-0103
commerce@mts.net
www.thompsonchamber.ca
Linda Markus, President

Treherne Chamber of Commerce
c/o Town of Treherne / RM of South Norfolk, PO Box 30, 215 Broadway St., Treherne MB R0G 2V0
Tel: 204-723-2044; *Fax:* 204-723-2719
www.treherne.ca
Keith Sparling, President

Virden Community Chamber of Commerce
PO Box 899, 425 - 6th Ave. South, Virden MB R0M 2C0
Tel: 204-851-1551; *Fax:* 604-608-9110
info@virdenchamber.ca
www.virdenchamber.ca
Affiliation(s): Virden Wallace Community Development Corp.; Virden Employment Skills Centre Inc., Virden Agricultural Society; Virden Indoor Rodeo
Dave Wowk, President

Wasagaming Chamber of Commerce
PO Box 621, Onanole MB R0J 1N0
info@discoverclearlake.com
www.discoverclearlake.com
Scott Gowler, President
Bob Bickerton, Treasurer

Winkler & District Chamber of Commerce
185 Main St., Winkler MB R6W 1B4
Tel: 204-325-9758; *Fax:* 204-325-8290
www.winklerchamber.com
Ryan Hildebrand, President
Tanya Chateauneuf, Executive Director
Dianne Friesen, Manager

Winnipeg Chamber of Commerce (WCC) / Chambre de commerce de Winnipeg
#100, 259 Portage Ave., Winnipeg MB R3B 2A9
Tel: 204-944-8484; *Fax:* 204-944-8492
info@winnipeg-chamber.com
www.winnipeg-chamber.com
Social Media: www.youtube.com/wpgchamber; www.instagram.com/wpgchamber
Dave Angus, President & Chief Executive Officer
Maxine Kashton, Vice-President, Finance & Operations
Karen Weiss, Vice-President, Membership & Marketing

New Brunswick

Albert County Chamber of Commerce
PO Box 3051, Hillsborough NB E4H 4W5
Tel: 506-389-6002; *Fax:* 506-387-8331
accofc@gmail.com
www.albertcountychamber.com
Brian Keirstead, President
Kevin Snair, Secretary

Bouctouche Chamber of Commerce / Chambre de commerce de Bouctouche
PO Box 2104, Bouctouche NB E4S 2J2
Tel: 506-743-2411; *Fax:* 506-743-8991
chambouc@nb.aibn.com
www.bouctouche.ca/en/business/chamber-of-commerce

Campbellton Regional Chamber of Commerce / Chambre de commerce régional de Campbellton
41A Water St., Campbellton NB E3N 1A6
Tel: 506-759-7856
crcc@nbnet.nb.ca
Affiliation(s): NB Chamber of Commerce; Atlantic Chamber of Commerce

Central Carleton Chamber of Commerce
28 Palmer Rd., Waterville NB E7P 1B4
Tel: 506-375-4074
Dale Albright, President

Centreville Chamber of Commerce
836 Central St., Centreville NB E7K 2E7
Tel: 506-276-3674; *Fax:* 506-276-9891
Robert Taylor, President

Chambre de commerce de Cocagne, Notre-Dame et Grande-Digue
CP 166, 190 Cormier Cross Roads, Cocagne NB E4R 2J5
Tél: 506-576-6005; *Téléc:* 506-576-6073
cormier@carcajou.com

Chambre de commerce de Collette
11731, rte 126, Collette NB E4Y 1G4
Tél: 506-622-0752; *Téléc:* 506-622-0477
Maurice Desroches, Président

Chambre de commerce de la région d'Edmundston
1, ch Canada, Edmundston NB E3V 1T6
Tél: 506-737-1866; *Téléc:* 506-737-1862
info@ccedmundston.com
www.ccedmundston.com
Média social: www.flickr.com/photos/ccedmundston
Affiliation(s): Chambre de commerce du Nouveau-Brunswick; Chambre de commerce des Provinces Atlantiques; Chambre de commerce du Canada; Chambre de commerce Internationale
Gilles Daigle, Présidente
Marc Long, Directeur général

Chambre de commerce de Rogersville / Rogersville Chamber of Commerce
#5, 11101, rue Principale, Rogersville NB E4Y 2N2
www.rogersvillenb.com/la-fierte-acadienne/chambre-de-commerce

Chambre de Commerce de Saint Louis de Kent
83A rue Beauséjour, Saint-Louis-de-Kent NB E4X 1A6
Tel: 506-876-3475; *Fax:* 506-876-3477
René Côté, Présidente

Chambre de commerce de Shippagan inc.
227, boul J.D. Gauthier, Shippagan NB E8S 1N2
Tél: 506-336-3993
chambredecommercedeshippagan@nb.aibn.com
Shelley Robichaud, Présidente

Chambre de commerce des Iles Lamèque et Miscou inc.
CP 2075, Lamèque NB E8T 3N5
Tel: 506-344-3222; *Téléc:* 506-344-3266
cc.lamequemiscou@lameque.ca
www.lameque.ca
Jules Haché, Président

Chambre de commerce du Grand Caraquet Inc
39-1, boul St-Pierre ouest, Caraquet NB E1W 1B7
Tél: 506-727-2931; *Téléc:* 506-727-3191
chambre@nb.aira.com
www.chambregrandcaraquet.com
Normand Mourant, Présidente
Aline Landry, Directrice générale

Florenceville-Bristol Chamber of Commerce
#1, 8696 Main St., Florenceville-Bristol NB E7L 1Y7
Tel: 506-392-0900; *Fax:* 506-392-5211
chamber@florencevillebristol.ca
www.florencevillebristol.ca/html/chamber.html
Doug Thomson, Treasurer

Fredericton Chamber of Commerce / La Chambre de Commerce de Fredericton
PO Box 275, #200, 364 York St., Fredericton NB E3B 4Y9
Tel: 506-458-8006; *Fax:* 506-451-1119
fchamber@frederictonchamber.ca
www.frederictonchamber.ca
Stephen Hill, President
Krista Ross, Chief Executive Officer

Gagetown & Area Chamber of Commerce
c/o Village Office, 68 Babbit St., Gagetown NB E5M 1C8
Tel: 506-488-2020
Leone Pippard, President

Grand Manan Tourism Association & Chamber of Commerce
1141 Rte. 776, Grand Manan NB E5G 4K9
Tel: 506-662-3442; *Toll-Free:* 888-525-1655
info@grandmanannb.com
www.grandmanannb.com

Greater Bathurst Chamber of Commerce / Chambre de commerce du Grand Bathurst
Keystone Bldg., #101, 270 Douglas Ave., Bathurst NB E2A 1M9
Tel: 506-546-8100; *Fax:* 506-548-2200
info@bathurstchamber.ca
www.bathurstchamber.ca
Affiliation(s): Canadian Chamber of Commerce
Mitch Poirier, General Manager
Bernard Cormier, President
Linda Rogers, Treasurer

Greater Hillsborough Chamber of Commerce
PO Box 3051, Hillsborough NB E4H 4W5
Tel: 506-734-3773; *Fax:* 506-734-2244
Carole Coleman, Director

Greater Moncton Chamber of Commerce (GMCC) / Chambre de commerce du Grand Moncton
#200, 1273 Main St., Moncton NB E1C 0P4
Tel: 506-857-2883
info@gmcc.nb.ca
www.gmcc.nb.ca
Social Media: www.youtube.com/user/GreaterMonctonCham
Carol O'Reilly, CEO
Scott Lewis, Chair

Greater Sackville Chamber of Commerce (GSCC)
#87, 8 Main St., Sackville NB E4L 4A9
Tel: 506-364-8911; *Fax:* 506-364-8082
gscc@eastlink.ca
sackvillechamber.com
Laura Landriault, President
Lori Ann Roness, Executive Director
Susan Tower, Secretary

Greater Shediac Chamber of Commerce / Chambre de commerce du Grand Shediac
#302, 290 Main St., Shediac NB E4P 2E3
Tel: 506-532-7000; *Fax:* 506-532-6556
www.greatershediacchamber.com
Ronald Cormier, President

Greater Woodstock Chamber of Commerce
#2, 220 King St., Woodstock NB E7M 1Z8
Tel: 506-325-9049; *Fax:* 506-328-4683
info@gwcc.ca
www.gwcc.ca
Allison McLellan, President

Hampton Area Chamber of Commerce (HACC)
#7, 27 Centennial Rd., Hampton NB E5N 6N3
Tel: 506-832-2559; *Fax:* 506-832-2807
hacc@nbnet.nb.ca

Kennebecasis Valley Chamber of Commerce
PO Box 4455, 140L Hampton Rd., Rothesay NB E2E 5X2
Tel: 506-849-2860; *Fax:* 506-848-0121
kvchambr@nbnet.nb.ca
www.intellis.net/kvchamber
Michael F Cole, President
Catherine Selkirk, Executive Director

Kent Centre Chamber of Commerce
#1, 9235 rue Main, Richibucto NB E4W 4B4
Tel: 506-523-7870; *Fax:* 506-523-7850
www.kentcentre.com
Bobby Johnson, Président

Mactaquac County Chamber of Commerce
PO Box 1163, Nackawic NB E6G 2N1
Tel: 506-575-9622; *Fax:* 506-575-2035
mccc@mactaquaccountry.com
www.mactaquaccountry.com
Melanie Sloat, President
Dora Boudreau, Secretary

Miramichi Chamber of Commerce (MCC)
PO Box 342, #2, 120 Newcastle Blvd., Miramichi NB E1N 3A7
Tel: 506-622-5522; *Fax:* 506-622-5959
mirchamber@nb.aibn.com
www.miramichichamber.com
Social Media: instagram.com/miramichichamber
Affiliation(s): New Brunswick Chamber of Commerce; Atlantic Provinces Chamber of Commerce; Canadian Chamber of Commerce
Jason Harris, President
Joyce Buckley, Executive Director

Oromocto & Area Chamber of Commerce
Oromocto Mall, PO Box 20124, Oromocto NB E2V 2R6
Tel: 506-446-6043; *Fax:* 506-446-6925
oromoctochamber@nb.aibn.com

River Valley Chamber of Commerce (RVCC)
PO Box 3123, Grand Bay-Westfield NB E5K 4V4
Tel: 506-738-8666; *Fax:* 506-738-3697
www.rvchamber.ca
Social Media: www.youtube.com/rvchamberofcommerce
Danny Harrigan, President
Jim Balcomb, Vice-President/Treasurer

St. Andrews Chamber of Commerce
PO Box 3936, St Andrews NB E5B 3S7
stachamb@nbnet.nb.ca
www.standrewsbythesea.ca
Dave Bennett, President

Julie Crichton, Executive Director

St. Martins & District Chamber of Commerce
229 Main St., St Martins NB E5R 1B7
Tel: 506-833-2019; *Fax:* 506-833-2028
info@stmartinscanada.com
stmartinscanada.com
Kathy Miller-Zinn, President
Eric Bartlett, Secretary

St. Stephen Area Chamber of Commerce
73 Milltown Blvd., St Stephen NB E3L 1G5
Tel: 506-466-7703; *Fax:* 506-466-7753
chamber.ststephen@nb.aibn.com
www.ststephenchamber.com
Affiliation(s): Atlantic Chamber of Commerce; Canadian Chamber of Commerce
Dale Weeks, President

Sussex & District Chamber of Commerce
PO Box 4963, #2, 66 Broad St., Sussex NB E4E 5L2
Tel: 506-433-1845; *Fax:* 506-433-1886
sdcc@nb.aibn.com
sdccinc.org
Affiliation(s): Atlantic Provinces Chambers of Commerce
Greg Zed, President
Pam Kaye, Administrator

Valley Chamber of Commerce
#200, 131 Pleasant St., Grand Falls NB E3Y 1G6
Tel: 506-473-1905; *Fax:* 506-475-7779
gfcocgs@nbnet.nb.ca
www.grandfalls.com
Melanie Ouellette-Toner, Directrice générale
Mimi Rioux, Secrétaire

Washademoak Region Chamber of Commerce
Cambridge-Narrows NB
Tel: 506-488-8091
www.w-rcc.ca
David Craw, President
Vince Lalond, Vice-President

Newfoundland and Labrador

Baie Verte & Area Chamber of Commerce
PO Box 578, Baie Verte NL A0K 1B0
Tel: 709-532-4204; *Fax:* 709-532-4252
bvachamber@nf.aibn.com
www.bvachamber.com
Vacant, President
Celia Dicks, Chamber Coordinator

Bay St. George Chamber of Commerce
35 Carolina Ave., Stephenville NL A2N 3P8
Tel: 709-643-5854; *Fax:* 709-643-6398
www.bsgcc.org
Tom Rose, President

Bonavista Area Chamber of Commerce (BACC)
PO Box 280, Bonavista NL A0C 1B0
Fax: 709-468-2495
info@bacc.ca
www.bacc.ca
Diane Thorpe, Secretary

Burin Peninsula Chamber of Commerce
PO Box 728, Marystown NL A0E 2M0
Tel: 709-279-2080; *Fax:* 709-279-4492
administration@bpchamber.ca
burinpeninsulachamber.com
Don MacBeath, President
Lisa MacLeod, Business Manager

Channel Port Aux Basques & Area Chamber of Commerce
PO Box 1389, Channel-Port-aux-Basques NL A0M 1C0
Tel: 709-695-3688
pabchamber@nf.aibn.com

Clarenville Area Chamber of Commerce
#203, 293 Memorial Dr., Clarenville NL A5A 1R5
Tel: 709-466-5800; *Fax:* 709-466-5803
Toll-Free: 866-466-5800
info@clarenvilleareachamber.com
www.clarenvilleareachamber.com
Jason Strickland, President
Ina Marsh, Office Manager

Conception Bay Area Chamber of Commerce
#3, 702 Conception Bay Hwy., Conception Bay South NL A1X 3A5
Tel: 709-834-5670
info@cbachamber.com
www.conceptionbaysouth.ca/business/chamber-of-commerce

Deer Lake Chamber of Commerce
#3, 44 Trans Canada Hwy., Deer Lake NL A8A 2E4
Tel: 709-635-3260; *Fax:* 709-635-4077
info@deerlakechamber.com
www.deerlakechamber.com
Affiliation(s): Newfoundland Chambers of Commerce
Tina Barry-Keith, Treasurer
Roseann White, President

Exploits Regional Chamber of Commerce
PO Box 272, 2B Mill Rd., Grand Falls-Windsor NL A2A 2J7
Tel: 709-489-7512; *Fax:* 709-489-7532
info@exploitschamber.com
www.exploitschamber.com
Kris Spurrell, President

Gander & Area Chamber of Commerce (GACC)
109 Trans Canada Hwy., Gander NL A1V 1P6
Tel: 709-256-7110; *Fax:* 709-256-4794
ganderchamber@ganderchamber.nf.ca
www.ganderchamber.nf.ca
Darrin Murray, President
Hazel Bishop, Executive Director

Greater Corner Brook Board of Trade (GCBBT)
PO Box 475, 11 Confederation Dr., Corner Brook NL A2H 6E6
Tel: 709-634-5831; *Fax:* 709-639-9710
www.gcbbt.com
Chris Noseworthy, President

Irish Loop Chamber of Commerce
PO Box 139, Ferryland NL A0A 2H0
Tel: 709-432-3104; *Fax:* 709-432-3056
info@IrishLoopChamber.com
irishloopchamber.com
Jeff Marshall, President

Labrador North Chamber of Commerce (LNCC)
PO Box 460, Stn. B, 169 Hamilton River Rd., Happy Valley-Goose Bay NL A0P 1E0
Tel: 709-896-8787; *Fax:* 709-896-0585
Toll-Free: 877-920-8787
admin@chamberlabrador.com
www.chamberlabrador.com
Sterling Peyton, President
Brian Fowlow, Executive Director

Labrador Straits Chamber of Commerce
PO Box 179, Forteau NL A0K 2P0
Tel: 709-931-2073; *Fax:* 709-931-2073

Labrador West Chamber of Commerce
PO Box 273, 118 Humphrey Rd., Labrador City NL A2V 2K5
Tel: 709-944-3723; *Fax:* 709-944-4699
lwc@crrstv.net
www.labradorwestchamber.ca
Brian Brace, President
Patsy Ralph, Business Manager

Lewisporte & Area Chamber of Commerce
PO Box 953, Lewisporte NL A0G 3A0
Tel: 709-535-2500; *Fax:* 709-535-2482
lacc@superweb.ca
www.lewisporteareachamberofcommerce.ca
Cynthia Aylward, Executive Assistant

Mount Pearl Chamber of Commerce
39 Commonwealth Ave., Mount Pearl NL A1N 1W7
Tel: 709-364-8513; *Fax:* 709-364-8500
info@mtpearlparadisechamber.com
www.mtpearlchamber.com

Pasadena Chamber of Commerce
c/o Town of Pasadena, 18 Tenth Ave., Pasadena NL A0L 1K0
Tel: 709-686-2075; *Fax:* 709-686-2507
info@pasadena.ca
www.pasadena.ca/chamber.html

Placentia Area Chamber of Commerce (PACC)
1 O'Reilly St., Placentia NL A0B 2Y0
Tel: 709-227-0003
www.placentiachamber.ca
Gerry Sullivan, President
Eugene Collins, Executive Director

St Anthony & Area Chamber of Commerce
PO Box 650, St Anthony NL A0K 4S0
Tel: 709-454-6667
stanthonyandareachamber@yahoo.ca
www.town.stanthony.nf.ca/chamber.php
Maurice Simmonds, President
Agnes Patey, Coordinator

Springdale & Area Chamber of Commerce
PO Box 37, 393 Little Bay Rd., Springdale NL A0J 1T0
Tel: 709-673-3837
www.townofspringdale.ca
Cyril Pelley, President
Glenn Seabright, Secretary

Straits-St. Barbe Chamber of Commerce
PO Box 119, Flowers Cove NL A0K 2N0
Tel: 709-456-2592;

Northwest Territories

Fort Simpson Chamber of Commerce
PO Box 244, Fort Simpson NT X0E 0N0
Tel: 867-695-6538; *Fax:* 867-695-3551
fscofc@gmail.com
www.fortsimpsonchamber.ca
Social Media: www.youtube.com/user/FortSimpsonChamber
Angela Fiebelkorn, President

Fort Smith Chamber of Commerce
PO Box 121, Fort Smith NT X0E 0P0
Tel: 867-872-8400; *Fax:* 867-872-8401
www.fortsmith.ca/cms/webcontent/business-services

Hay River Chamber of Commerce
10K Gagnier St., Hay River NT X0E 1G1
Tel: 867-874-2565; *Fax:* 867-874-3631
www.hayriverchamber.com
Janet-Marie Fizer, President

Inuvik Chamber of Commerce
PO Box 3039, Inuvik NT X0E 0T0
inuvikchamber.com
Lee Smallwood, President

Norman Wells & District Chamber of Commerce
PO Box 400, Norman Wells NT X0E 0V0
Tel: 867-587-6609; *Fax:* 867-587-2865
info@normanwellschamber.com
www.normanwellschamber.com
Chris Buist, President

Yellowknife Chamber of Commerce
#21, 4802 - 50th Ave., Yellowknife NT X1A 1C4
Tel: 867-920-4944; *Fax:* 867-920-4640
admin@ykchamber.com
www.ykchamber.com
Daneen Everett, Executive Director

Nova Scotia

Amherst & Area Chamber of Commerce
PO Box 283, 35 Church St., Amherst NS B4H 3Z4
Tel: 902-667-8186; *Fax:* 902-667-2270
info@amherstchamber.ca
www.facebook.com/amherstchamber
David Mosley, President
Patti Colson, Executive Assistant

Annapolis Valley Chamber of Commerce (EKCC)
PO Box 314, 66 Cornwallis St., Kentville NS B4N 3X1
Tel: 902-678-4634
coordinator@annapolisvalleychamber.ca
annapolisvalleychamber.ca
Sue Hayes, President
Judy Rafuse, Executive Director

Antigonish Chamber of Commerce
21B James St. Plaza, Antigonish NS B2G 1R6
Tel: 902-863-6308; *Fax:* 902-863-2656
contact@antigonishchamber.com
www.antigonishchamber.com
Patrick Curry, President

Avon River Chamber of Commerce
PO Box 2188, Windsor NS B0N 2T0
Tel: 902-472-7200
info@whcc.ca
www.whcc.ca
Scott Geddes, President
Andrew Bauchman, Vice-President

Barrington & Area Chamber of Commerce
PO Box 110, Barrington NS B0W 1E0
Tel: 902-745-1655
barringtoncofc@eastlink.ca
www.barrington-chamberofcommerce.com
Gary Thomas, President
Bobbi Jo Symonds, Coordinator

Bridgetown & Area Chamber of Commerce (BACC)
PO Box 467, Bridgetown NS B0S 1C0
www.bridgetownareachamber.com

Jennifer D'Aubin, President
Gerry Bezanson, Secretary

Bridgewater & Area Chamber of Commerce (BACC)
373 King St., Bridgewater NS B4V 1B1
Tel: 902-543-4263; *Fax:* 902-527-1156
www.bridgewaterchamber.com
Ann O'Connell, Executive Director

Brier Island Chamber of Commerce
PO Box 74, Westport NS B0V 1H0
Tel: 902-839-2347; *Fax:* 902-839-2006
Harold Graham, President
Joan Riday, Secretary

Chambre de commerce de Clare / Clare Chamber of Commerce
CP 35, Pointe-de-l'Église NS B0W 1M0
Tél: 902-769-5312; *Téléc:* 902-769-5500
contact@commercedeclare.ca
www.commercedeclare.ca
Paul Emile LeBlanc, Président

Chester Municipal Chamber of Commerce
4171 Hwy. 3, RR#2, Chester NS B0J 1J0
Tel: 902-275-4709; *Fax:* 902-275-4629
Admin@ChesterAreaNS.ca
www.chesterns.com
Anthony Smith, Chair

East Hants & District Chamber of Commerce (EHDCC)
Parker Place Mall, Upper Level, 8 Old Enfield Rd., Enfield NS B2T 1C9
Tel: 902-883-1010; *Fax:* 902-883-7862
info@ehcc.ca
www.ehcc.ca
Pat Mills, President

Halifax Chamber of Commerce
#100, 32 Akerley Blvd., Dartmouth NS B3B 1N1
Tel: 902-468-7111; *Fax:* 902-468-7333
info@halifaxchamber.com
www.halifaxchamber.com
Valerie Payn, President & CEO

Mahone Bay & Area Chamber of Commerce
PO Box 59, Mahone Bay NS B0J 2E0
Tel: 902-624-6151; *Fax:* 902-624-6152
Toll-Free: 888-624-6151
info@mahonebay.com
www.mahonebay.com
Andrew Parrott, President
Ray Morin, Secretary
Marie Raymond, Staff

Northeast Highlands Chamber of Commerce
PO Box 125, Ingonish NS B0C 1L0
Tel: 902-285-2289; *Fax:* 902-285-2285
Walter Lauffer, President
Mary Sue Mackinnon, Staff
Ann Hussey, Secretary

Pictou County Chamber of Commerce
#3C, 115 MacLean St., New Glasgow NS B2H 4M5
Tel: 902-755-3463
info@pictouchamber.com
www.pictouchamber.com
Jack Kyte, Executive Director

Pugwash & Area Chamber of Commerce
PO Box 239, Pugwash NS B0K 1L0
Tel: 902-243-2606

Sheet Harbour & Area Chamber of Commerce & Civic Affairs
PO Box 239, Sheet Harbour NS B0J 3B0
sheetharbourchamber.com
Kent Smith, Acting President
Janice Christie, Secretary

Shelburne & Area Chamber of Commerce
PO Box 1150, Shelburne NS B0T 1W0
Tel: 902-875-0224; *Fax:* 902-875-3214
www.shelburnechamber.ca
Elizabeth Rhuland, President
Raymond Davis, Secretary

South Queens Chamber of Commerce
Tel: 902-350-1826
secretary@southqueenschamber.com
www.southqueenschamber.com
Barry Tomalin, President
Kevin Page, Treasurer
Monica Howard, Secretary

Springhill & Area Chamber of Commerce
PO Box 1030, Springhill NS B0M 1X0
Tel: 902-597-8462; *Fax:* 902-597-3839
audrey@surrette.com
www.springhillareachamber.com
Frank Likely, President
Marcie Meekins, Secretary

Strait Area Chamber of Commerce
#205, 609 Church St., Port Hawkesbury NS B9A 2X4
Tel: 902-625-1588; *Fax:* 902-625-5985
www.straitchamber.ca
Affiliation(s): Atlantic Provinces Chamber of Commerce
Shannon MacDougall, Executive Director
Parker Stone, President

Sydney & Area Chamber of Commerce (SACC)
275 Charlotte Street, Sydney NS B1P 1C6
Tel: 902-564-6453; *Fax:* 902-539-7487
www.sydneyareachamber.ca
Adrian White, Executive Director

Truro & Colchester Chamber of Commerce
605 Prince St., Truro NS B2N 1G2
Tel: 902-895-6328; *Fax:* 902-897-6641
oa@tcchamber.ca
www.trurocolchesterchamber.com
Sherry Martell, Executive Director
Trish Petrie, Office Administrator

Yarmouth & Area Chamber of Commerce (YCC)
PO Box 532, #1, 342 Main St., Yarmouth NS B5A 4B4
Tel: 902-742-3074; *Fax:* 902-749-1383
info@yarmouthchamberofcommerce.com
www.yarmouthchamberofcommerce.com
Dave Hall, President
Karen Churchill, 1st Vice-President
Mike Mercier, 2nd Vice-President

Nunavut

Baffin Regional Chamber of Commerce (BRCC)
Building 607, PO Box 59, Iqaluit NU X0A 0H0
Tel: 867-979-4654; *Fax:* 867-979-2929
www.baffinchamber.ca
Chris West, Executive Director
Ike Hauli, President

Iqaluit Chamber of Commerce
PO Box 1107, Iqaluit NU X0A 0H0
Tel: 867-979-4095; *Fax:* 867-979-2929

Kivalliq Chamber of Commerce
PO Box 819, Rankin Inlet NU X0C 0G0
Tel: 867-645-2823; *Fax:* 867-645-2082
Paul Delany, Contact

Kugluktuk Chamber of Commerce
PO Box 307, Kugluktuk NU X0B 0E0
Tel: 867-982-3232; *Fax:* 867-982-3229
Ken Brandly, Executive Director

Ontario

Aguasabon Chamber of Commerce
PO Box 695, Terrace Bay ON P0T 2W0
Tel: 807-825-4505; *Fax:* 807-825-9664
Toll-Free: 888-445-9999
jason.nesbitt@investorsgroup.com
www.noacc.ca
John Lubberdink, Chair
Robert Kirkpatrick, Director

Alexandria & District Chamber of Commerce
PO Box 1058, Alexandria ON K0C 1A0
Tel: 613-525-0588; *Fax:* 613-525-1232
info@alexandriachamber.ca
alexandriachamber.ca
Michael Madden, President

Alliston & District Chamber of Commerce
PO Box 32, 60B Victoria St. West, Alliston ON L9R 1T9
Tel: 705-435-7921; *Fax:* 705-435-0289
www.adcc.ca
Social Media: www.youtube.com/user/AllistonChamber
Crystal Kellard, Executive Director

Amherstburg Chamber of Commerce
PO Box 101, 268 Dalhousie St., Amherstburg ON N9V 2Z3
Tel: 519-736-2001; *Fax:* 519-736-9721
amherstburgchamber@gmail.com
www.amherstburgchamberofcommerce.ca
Scott Deslippe, President

Arthur & District Chamber of Commerce
PO Box 519, 146 George St., Arthur ON N0G 1A0
Tel: 519-848-5603; *Fax:* 519-848-4030
achamber@wightman.ca
www.arthurchamber.ca
Corey Bilton, President

Atikokan Chamber of Commerce
PO Box 997, 214 Main St. West, Atikokan ON P0T 1C0
Tel: 807-597-1599; *Fax:* 807-597-2726
Toll-Free: 888-334-2332
info@atikokanchamber.com
www.atikokanchamber.com
Affiliation(s): Canadian Chamber of Commerce
Michael McKinnon, President
Jolene Wood, Office Manager

Aurora Chamber of Commerce
#321, 6 - 14845 Yonge St., Aurora ON L4G 6H8
Tel: 905-727-7262; *Fax:* 905-841-6217
info@aurorachamber.on.ca
www.aurorachamber.on.ca
Social Media:
www.youtube.com/channel/UC0UDw3p5eidBgKjeTQJJnZA
Sandra Watson, Interim Manager

Bancroft & District Chamber of Commerce, Tourism & Information Centre
PO Box 539, 8 Hastings Heritage Way, Bancroft ON K0L 1C0
Tel: 613-332-1513; *Fax:* 613-332-2119
Toll-Free: 888-443-9999
chamber@bancroftdistrict.com
www.bancroftdistrict.com
Greg Webb, General Manager

Bayfield & Area Chamber of Commerce
PO Box 2065, Bayfield ON N0M 1G0
Tel: 519-565-2499; *Toll-Free:* 800-565-2499
info@villageofbayfield.com
cc.villageofbayfield.com
Janet Snider, President

Beaverton District Chamber of Commerce
PO Box 29, Beaverton ON L0K 1A0
Tel: 705-426-2051
chamber@beavertononlakesimcoe.com
www.beavertononlakesimcoe.com
Affiliation(s): Ontario Chamber of Commerce
Rossie Baillie, President

Belleville & District Chamber of Commerce (BCC)
5 Moira St., Belleville ON K8P 2S3
Tel: 613-962-4597; *Fax:* 613-962-3911
Toll-Free: 888-852-9992
info@bellevillechamber.ca
www.bellevillechamber.ca
Richard Davis, President
Bill Saunders, CEO

Black River-Matheson Chamber of Commerce
PO Box 518, Matheson ON P0K 1N0
chamber@brmchamberofcommerce.org
www.brmchamberofcommerce.org

Blenheim & District Chamber of Commerce
PO Box 1353, Blenheim ON N0P 1A0
Tel: 519-676-6555
blenheimontario.com/chamber-of-commerce
Frank Vercouteren, President
Betty Russell, Secretary

Blind River Chamber of Commerce (BRCC)
PO Box 998, 243 Causley St., Blind River ON P0R 1B0
Tel: 705-356-2555; *Fax:* 705-356-3911
Toll-Free: 800-563-8719
chamber@brchamber.ca
www.brchamber.ca
Affiliation(s): Algoma Kinniwabi Travel Association
Louise Demers, President
Betty-Ann Dunbar, Treasurer

Blue Mountains Chamber of Commerce
PO Box 477, Thornbury ON N0H 2P0
Tel: 519-599-1200; *Fax:* 519-599-2567
info@bluemountainschamber.ca
www.bluemountainschamber.ca
Jim Farmilo, President

Bobcaygeon & Area Chamber of Commerce
PO Box 388, 21 Canal St. East, Bobcaygeon ON K0M 1A0
Tel: 705-738-2202; *Fax:* 705-738-1534
Toll-Free: 800-318-6173
www.bobcaygeon.org
Affiliation(s): Kawartha Lakes Associated Chambers of Commerce

Kent Leckie, President

Bracebridge Chamber of Commerce
1 Manitoba St., 2nd Fl., Bracebridge ON P1L 1S4
Tel: 705-645-5231
chamber@bracebridgechamber.com
www.bracebridgechamber.com
Brenda Rhodes, Executive Director

Brighton & District Chamber of Commerce
PO Box 880, 74 Main Street, Brighton ON K0K 1H0
Tel: 613-475-2775; *Fax:* 613-475-3777
Toll-Free: 877-475-2775
info@brightonchamber.ca
www.brightonchamber.ca
Don Parks, President

Brockville & District Chamber of Commerce
#1, 3 Market St. West, Brockville ON K6V 7L2
Tel: 613-342-6553; *Fax:* 613-342-6849
info@brockvillechamber.com
www.brockvillechamber.com
Heather Halladay, President
Anne MacDonald, Executive Director

Burlington Chamber of Commerce
#201, 414 Locust St., Burlington ON L7S 1T7
Tel: 905-639-0174; *Fax:* 905-333-3956
info@burlingtonchamber.com
www.burlingtonchamber.com
Social Media: www.youtube.com/user/BurlingtonChamber
Bruce Nicholson, Chair
Keith Hoey, President

Caledon Chamber of Commerce
PO Box 626, 12598 Hwy. 50 South, Bolton ON L7E 5T5
Tel: 905-857-7393; *Fax:* 905-857-7405
info@caledonchamber.com
www.caledonchamber.com
Affiliation(s): Canadian Chamber of Commerce; Ontario Chamber of Commerce
Steve Owen, Chair
Kelly Darnley, President & CEO

Caledonia Regional Chamber of Commerce
PO Box 2035, 1 Grand Trunk Lane, Caledonia ON N3W 2G6
Tel: 905-765-0377
caledoniachamber@shaw.ca
www.caledonia-ontario.com
Suzanne Athanasiou, President
Barb Martindale, Executive Director

Carleton Place & District Chamber of Commerce & Visitor Centre
132 Coleman St., Carleton Place ON K7C 4M7
Tel: 613-257-1976; *Fax:* 613-257-4148
manager@cpchamber.com
www.cpchamber.com
Tracy Lamb, President

Cambridge Chamber of Commerce
750 Hespler Rd., Cambridge ON N3H 5L8
Tel: 519-622-2221; *Fax:* 519-622-0177
Toll-Free: 800-749-7560
cchamber@cambridgechamber.com
www.cambridgechamber.com
Social Media: www.youtube.com/thecambridgechamber
Greg Durocher, President & CEO

Cayuga & District Chamber of Commerce
PO Box 118, 6 Cayuga St. North, Cayuga ON N0A 1E0
Tel: 905-772-5954; *Fax:* 905-772-2680
info@cayugachamber.ca
cayugachamber.ca
John Edelman, President

Centre Wellington Chamber of Commerce
400 Tower St. South, Fergus ON N1M 2P7
Tel: 519-843-5140; *Fax:* 519-787-0983
chamber@cwchamber.ca
www.cwchamber.ca
Social Media: plus.google.com/107434428701192264584
Roberta Scarrow, General Manager

Chamber of Commerce Niagara Falls, Canada
4056 Dorchester Rd., Niagara Falls ON L2E 6M9
Tel: 905-374-3666; *Fax:* 905-374-2972
info@niagarafallschamber.com
www.niagarafallschamber.com
Social Media: www.youtube.com/user/NFChamber
Anna Pierce, Chair
Dolores Fabiano, Executive Director

Chamber of Commerce of Brantford & Brant (BRCC)
77 Charlotte St., Brantford ON N3T 2W8
Tel: 519-753-2617; *Fax:* 519-753-0921
www.brantfordbrantchamber.com
Cathy Oden, President
Charlene Nicholson, CEO

Chatham-Kent Chamber of Commerce
54 - 4th St., Chatham ON N7M 2G2
Tel: 519-352-7540
www.chatham-kentchamber.ca
G.A. (Gail) Antaya, President & CEO

Chesley & District Chamber of Commerce
PO Box 406, 106 - 1st Ave. South, Chesley ON N0G 1L0
Tel: 519-363-9837
townofchesley.com
Stacy Charlton, Treasurer

Collingwood Chamber of Commerce
#102, 115 Hurontario St., Collingwood ON L9Y 2L9
Tel: 705-445-0221
info@collingwoodchamber.com
www.collingwoodchamber.com
Affiliation(s): Canadian Chamber of Commerce; Ontario Chamber of Commerce
John Alsop, President
Trish Irwin, General Manager & CEO

Cornwall & Area Chamber of Commerce
#100, 113 - 2nd St. East, Cornwall ON K6J 1Y5
Tel: 613-933-4004
info@cornwallchamber.com
www.cornwallchamber.com
Denis Carr, President
Lezlie Strasser, Executive Manager

Dryden District Chamber of Commerce (DDCC)
284 Government St., Hwy. 17, Dryden ON P8N 2P3
Tel: 807-223-2622; *Fax:* 807-223-2626
Toll-Free: 800-667-0935
chamber@drytel.net
www.drydenchamber.ca
Affiliation(s): Sunset County Travel Association; Patricia Regional Tourist Council; Kenora District Camp Owners Association
Stafanie Armstrong, Chair
Gwen Kurz, Manager

Dufferin Board of Trade
246372 Hockley Rd., Mono ON L9W 6K4
Tel: 519-941-0490; *Fax:* 519-941-0492
office@dufferinbot.ca
dufferinbot.ca
Social Media: www.youtube.com/TheChamberGDACC
Affiliation(s): Ontario Chamber of Commerce; Canadian Chamber of Commerce
Ron Munro, CEO

Dunnville Chamber of Commerce
231 Chestnut St., Dunnville ON N1A 2H2
Tel: 905-774-3183; *Fax:* 905-774-9281
dunnvillecoc@rogers.com
www.dunnvillechamberofcommerce.ca
Sandy Passmore, Office Manager

East Gwillimbury Chamber of Commerce (EGCOC)
PO Box 199, 1590 Queensville Side Rd., Queensville ON L0G 1R0
Tel: 905-478-8447; *Fax:* 905-478-8786
www.egcoc.org
Kathy Scammell, Office Manager

Elliot Lake & District Chamber of Commerce
PO Box 81, Elliot Lake ON P5A 2J6
Tel: 705-848-3974; *Fax:* 705-848-7121
www.elliotlakechamber.com
Todd Stencill, General Manager

Emo Chamber of Commerce
c/o Township of Emo, PO Box 520, 39 Roy St., Emo ON P0W 1E0
Tel: 807-482-2378; *Fax:* 807-482-2741
www.twspemo.on.ca/chamberofcommerce.html
Dave Goodman, Vice-President
Mary Goodman, Treasurer

Englehart & District Chamber of Commerce
PO Box 171, Englehart ON P0J 1H0
englehartchamber.weebly.com
Stacey Borgford, President

Fenelon Falls & District Chamber of Commerce
PO Box 28, 15 Oak St., Fenelon Falls ON K0M 1N0
Tel: 705-887-3409; *Fax:* 705-887-6912
info@fenelonfallschamber.com
www.fenelonfallschamber.com
Social Media: www.youtube.com/channel/UCl3SxaMNk5V0hzAMYFuDlXg
Grant Allman, President

Flamborough Chamber of Commerce (FCC)
#227, 7 Innovation Dr., Flamborough ON L9H 7H9
Tel: 905-689-7650; *Fax:* 905-689-1313
admin@flamboroughchamber.ca
flamboroughchamber.ca
Affiliation(s): Ontario & Canadian Chamber of Commerce
Jason Small, President
Arend Kersten, Executive Director

Fort Frances Chamber of Commerce (FFCC)
#102, 240 - 1st St. East, Fort Frances ON P9A 1K5
Tel: 807-274-5773; *Fax:* 807-274-8706
Toll-Free: 800-820-3678
thefort@fortfranceschamber.com
www.fortfranceschamber.com
Affiliation(s): Ontario Chamber of Commerce; Canadian Chamber of Commerce
Jennifer Greenhalgh, President

Georgina Chamber of Commerce
430 The Queensway South, Keswick ON L4P 2E1
Tel: 905-476-7870; *Fax:* 905-476-6700
Toll-Free: 888-436-7446
admin@georginachamber.com
www.georginachamber.com
Christine Thomas, General Manager
Dan Fellini, President

Geraldton Chamber of Commerce
PO Box 128, Geraldton ON P0T 1M0
Tel: 807-854-0895
chamber@geraldtonchamber.com
www.geraldtonchamber.com

Gogama Chamber of Commerce
c/o Gogama CAP Committee, PO Box 116, Gogama ON P0M 1W0
Tel: 705-894-2111
gogamachamber@vianet.ca
www.gogama.ca/organizations.html#chamber

Grand Bend & Area Chamber of Commerce
PO Box 248, #1, 81 Crescent St., Grand Bend ON N0M 1T0
Tel: 519-238-2001; *Toll-Free:* 888-338-2001
info@grandbendchamber.ca
grandbendchamber.ca
Susan Mills, Manager

Gravenhurst Chamber of Commerce/Visitors Bureau
275 Muskoka Rd. South, Gravenhurst ON P1P 1J1
Tel: 705-687-4432; *Fax:* 705-687-4382
info@gravenhurstchamber.com
www.gravenhurstchamber.com
Bob Collins, President
Danielle Millar, Executive Director

Greater Arnprior Chamber of Commerce (GACC)
#111, 16 Edward St., Arnprior ON K7S 3W4
Tel: 613-623-6817; *Fax:* 613-623-6826
info@gacc.ca
www.gacc.ca
Cheryl Sparling, Administrative Assistant
Wes Schnob, President

Greater Barrie Chamber of Commerce
97 Toronto St., Barrie ON L4N 1V1
Tel: 705-721-5000; *Fax:* 705-726-0973
chadmin@barriechamber.com
barriechamber.com
Social Media: www.youtube.com/barriechamber
Sybil Goruk, Executive Director

Greater Fort Erie Chamber of Commerce
#1, 660 Garrison Rd., Fort Erie ON L2A 6E2
Tel: 905-871-3803; *Fax:* 905-871-1561
info@forteriechamber.com
www.forteriechamber.com
Rick Phibbs, President
Karen Audet, Operations Manager

Greater Innisfil Chamber of Commerce (GICC)
8034 Yonge St., #B, Innisfil ON L9S 1L6
Tel: 705-431-4199; *Fax:* 705-431-6628
info@innisfilchamber.com
www.innisfilchamber.com

Affiliation(s): Alcona Business Association; South Innisfil Business & Community Association; Cookstown Chamber of Commerce; 400 Industrial Group
Mary-Ellen Madeley, Manager
Shannon MacIntyre, President

Greater Kingston Chamber of Commerce (GKCC)
945 Princess St., Kingston ON K7L 3N6
Tel: 613-548-4453; *Fax:* 613-548-4743
info@kingstonchamber.on.ca
www.kingstonchamber.on.ca
Social Media: www.youtube.com/channel/UC1Pmf1i3uKXFF7PM_3_5cAA
Martin Sherris, CEO

Greater Kitchener & Waterloo Chamber of Commerce
PO Box 2367, 80 Queen St. North, Kitchener ON N2H 6L4
Tel: 519-576-5000; *Fax:* 519-742-4760
admin@greaterkwchamber.com
www.greaterkwchamber.com
Social Media: www.youtube.com/user/GreaterKWChamber
Ian McLean, President & CEO

Greater Nepean Chamber of Commerce
#1175, 2720 Queensview Dr., Ottawa ON K2B 1A5
Tel: 613-828-5556; *Fax:* 613-828-8022
gm@nepeanchamber.com
www.nepeanchamber.com
Virginia Boro, Chair

Greater Niagara Chamber of Commerce (GNCC)
PO Box 940, #103, 1 St. Paul St., St Catharines ON L2R 6Z4
Tel: 905-684-2361; *Fax:* 905-684-2100
info@gncc.ca
www.greaterniagarachamber.com
Kithio Mwanzia, Interim CEO
Walter Sendzik, CEO

Greater Oshawa Chamber of Commerce
#100, 44 Richmond St. West, Oshawa ON L1G 1C7
Tel: 905-728-1683; *Fax:* 905-432-1259
info@oshawachamber.com
www.oshawachamber.com
Social Media: www.youtube.com/oshawachamber
Affiliation(s): Ontario Chamber of Commerce; Canadian Chamber of Commerce
Dan Carter, President
Bob Malcolmson, CEO & General Manager

Greater Peterborough Chamber of Commerce (GPCC)
175 George St. North, Peterborough ON K9J 3G6
Tel: 705-748-9771; *Fax:* 705-743-2331
Toll-Free: 887-640-4037
info@peterboroughchamber.ca
www.peterboroughchamber.ca
Social Media: www.youtube.com/user/PeterboroughChamber
Stuart Harrison, President & CEO

Greater Sudbury Chamber of Commerce / Chambre de commerce du Grand Sudbury
#100, 40 Elm St., Sudbury ON P3C 1S8
Tel: 705-673-7133; *Fax:* 705-673-1951
cofc@sudburychamber.ca
www.sudburychamber.ca
Debbi Nicholson, President & Chief Executive Officer

Greater Summerside Chamber of Commerce (GSCC)
#10, 263 Heather Moyse Dr., Summerside PE C1N 5P1
Tel: 902-436-9651; *Fax:* 902-436-8320
info@summersidechamber.com
www.summersidechamber.com
Social Media: www.instagram.com/summersidechamber
Jan Sharpe, Executive Director

Grey Highlands Chamber of Commerce
PO Box 177, 19 Toronto St. North, Markdale ON N0C 1H0
Tel: 519-986-4612; *Toll-Free:* 888-986-4612
info@greyhighlandschamber.com
greyhighlandschamber.com
Doug Crawford, Co-President
David Turner, Co-President
Kate FitzPatrick, Office Administrator

Grimsby & District Chamber of Commerce
15 Main St. East, Grimsby ON L3M 1M7
Tel: 905-945-8319; *Fax:* 905-945-1615
info@grimsbychamber.com
www.grimsbychamber.com
Naomi Beirnes, President

Guelph Chamber of Commerce (GCC)
PO Box 1268, 111 Farquhar St., Guelph ON N1H 3N4
Tel: 519-822-8081; *Fax:* 519-822-8451
chamber@guelphchamber.com
www.guelphchamber.com
Social Media: www.youtube.com/user/GuelphChamberComerc1
Affiliation(s): Guelph Business Enterprise Centre; Guelph Partnership for Innovation
Kithio Mwanzia, President & CEO

Hagersville & District Chamber of Commerce
PO Box 1090, Hagersville ON N0A 1H0
Tel: 905-768-0422; *Fax:* 289-282-0105
Robert C. Phillips, President

Haliburton Highlands Chamber of Commerce (HHCofC)
PO Box 670, 195 Highland St., #L1, Haliburton ON K0M 1S0
Tel: 705-457-4700; *Fax:* 705-457-4702
Toll-Free: 877-811-6111
admin@haliburtonchamber.com
www.haliburtonchmaber.com
Eric Thompson, President
Jerry Walker, Vice-President
Rosemarie Jung, Chamber Manager

Halton Hills Chamber of Commerce
328 Guelph St., Halton Hills ON L7G 4B5
Tel: 905-877-7119
tourism@haltonhillschamber.on.ca
www.haltonhillschamber.on.ca
Kathleen Dills, General Manager

Hamilton Chamber of Commerce (HCC)
Plaza Level, #507, 120 King St. West, Hamilton ON L8P 4V2
Tel: 905-522-1151; *Fax:* 905-522-1154
hcc@hamiltonchamber.ca
www.hamiltonchamber.ca
Diane Stephenson, Manager, Advertising & Promotions

Hanover Chamber of Commerce
214 - 10th St., Hanover ON N4N 1N7
Tel: 519-364-5777; *Fax:* 519-364-6949
info@hanoverchamber.ca
www.hanoverchamber.ca
Michele Hettrick, President

Harrow & Colchester Chamber of Commerce
PO Box 888, Harrow ON N0R 1G0
Tel: 519-974-3200; *Fax:* 519-974-2222
www.harrowchamber.ca
Murdo Mclean, President

Havelock, Belmont, Methuen & District Chamber of Commerce
PO Box 779, Havelock ON K0L 1Z0
Tel: 705-778-2182; *Fax:* 866-822-2182
havelockchamber@hotmail.com
www.havelockchamber.com
Phil Higgins, President

Hawkesbury & Region Chamber of Commerce / Chambre de Commerce de Hawkesbury et région
PO Box 36, #5A, 151 Main St. East, Hawkesbury ON K6A 2R4
Tel: 613-632-8066
info@hawkesburychamberofcommerce.ca
www.hawkesburychamberofcommerce.ca
Yves Robert, President

Hearst, Mattice - Val Côté & Area Chamber of Commerce
PO Box 987, #60, 9th St., Hearst ON P0L 1N0
Tel: 705-362-5880
info@hearstcommerce.ca
hearstcommerce.ca
Lise Joanis, President

Huntsville, Lake of Bays Chamber of Commerce
8 West St. North, Huntsville ON P1H 2B6
Tel: 705-789-4771; *Fax:* 705-789-6191
chamber@huntsvillelakeofbays.on.ca
huntsvillelakeofbays.on.ca
Kelly Haywood, Executive Director

Huron Chamber of Commerce - Goderich, Central & North Huron
56 East St., Goderich ON N7A 1N3
Tel: 519-440-0176; *Fax:* 519-440-0305
Toll-Free: 855-440-0176
info@huronchamber.ca
www.huronchamber.ca
Social Media: instagram.com/huronchamber
Gerry Rogers, Chair
Heather Boa, Operations Manager

Huron East Chamber of Commerce
c/o Ralph Laviolette, PO Box 433, Seaforth ON N0K 1W0
Tel: 519-440-6206
www.huroneastcc.ca
Ralph Laviolette, Secretary

Ingersoll District Chamber of Commerce
132 Thames St. South, Ingersoll ON N5C 2T4
Tel: 519-485-7333; *Fax:* 519-485-6606
ingersollchamber.com
Robin Schultz, President
Ann Campbell, General Manager

Iroquois Falls & District Chamber of Commerce
727 Synagogue Ave., Iroquois Falls ON P0K 1G0
Tel: 705-232-4656; *Fax:* 705-232-4656
ifchamber@hotmail.com
www.iroquoisfallschamber.com
Dale Romain, President

Kapuskasing & District Chamber of Commerce
25 Millview St., Kapuskasing ON P5N 2X6
Tel: 705-335-2332
info@kapchamber.ca
www.kapchamber.ca
Martin Proulx, President
Jammy Pouliot, Contact, Administration

Kawartha Chamber of Commerce & Tourism
PO Box 537, 12 Queen St., Lakefield ON K0L 2H0
Tel: 705-652-6963; *Fax:* 705-652-9140
Toll-Free: 888-565-9140
info@kawarthachamber.ca
www.kawarthachamber.ca
Scott Davidson, President
Sherry Boyce-Found, General Manager

Kenora & District Chamber of Commerce (KDCC)
PO Box 471, Kenora ON P9N 3X5
Tel: 807-467-4646; *Fax:* 807-468-3056
kenorachamber@kmts.ca
www.kenorachamber.com
Carol Leduc, Chamber Manager

Kincardine & District Chamber of Commerce
PO Box 115, 717 Queen St., Kincardine ON N2Z 2Y6
Tel: 519-396-9333; *Fax:* 519-396-5529
www.kincardinechamber.com
Linda Bowers, President
Jackie Pawlikowski, Office Manager

King Chamber of Commerce
PO Box 381, Schomberg ON L0G 1T0
Tel: 905-717-7199; *Fax:* 416-981-7174
info@kingchamber.ca
kingchamber.ca
Lucy Belperio, President
Helen Neville, Administrator

Kirkland Lake District Chamber of Commerce (KLCC)
PO Box 966, 400 Government Rd. West, Kirkland Lake ON P2N 3N1
Tel: 705-567-5444; *Fax:* 705-567-1666
klcofc@ntl.sympatico.ca
www.kirklandlakechamberofcommerce.com
Affiliation(s): Ontario Chamber of Commerce
David Gorman, President
Jennifer Verge, Office Coordinator

LaCloche Foothills Chamber of Commerce
PO Box 5292, 133 Barber St., Espanola ON P5E 1S3
Tel: 705-869-7671
www.lacklochefoothillschamber.com
Cheryl Kay, President

Leamington District Chamber of Commerce
PO Box 321, Leamington ON N8H 3W3
Tel: 519-326-2721; *Fax:* 519-326-3204
www.leamingtonchamber.com
Wendy Parsons, General Manager

Lincoln Chamber of Commerce
PO Box 493, 4961 King St., #T2, Beamsville ON L0R 1B0
Tel: 905-563-5044; *Fax:* 905-563-7098
info@lincolnchamber.ca
www.lincolnchamber.ca
Cathy McNiven, Office Manager

Lindsay & District Chamber of Commerce
20 Lindsay St. South, Lindsay ON K9V 2L6
Tel: 705-324-2393; *Fax:* 705-324-2473
info@lindsaychamber.com
www.lindsaychamber.com
Ann Gibbons, President

Gayle Jones, General Manager

London Chamber of Commerce
#101, 244 Pall Mall St., London ON N6A 5P6
Tel: 519-432-7551; *Fax:* 519-432-8163
info@londonchamber.com
www.londonchamber.com
Gus Kotsiomitis, President
Gerry MacCartney, General Manager & CEO

Longlac Chamber of Commerce
PO Box 203, 110 Lake St., Longlac ON P0T 2A0
Tel: 807-876-4562
info@longlacchamber.com
Martin Boucher, Vice-President

Lucknow & District Chamber of Commerce
PO Box 313, Lucknow ON N0G 2H0
Tel: 519-357-8454
info@lucknowchamber.ca
www.lucknowchamber.ca
Morten Jokbsen, President

Lyndhurst Seeleys Bay & District Chamber of Commerce
PO Box 89, Lyndhurst ON K0E 1N0
Tel: 613-928-2382
info@lyndhurstseeleysbaychamber.com
www.lyndhurstseeleysbaychamber.com
John Sederis, Vice-President

Madoc & District Chamber of Commerce
PO Box 669, 20 Davidson St., Madoc ON K0K 2K0
Tel: 613-473-1616; *Fax:* 613-473-0860
cocmadoc@bellnet.ca
www.centrehastings.com/chamber_of_commerce.htm
Rob Price, President
Leigh Anne Lavender, Coordinator

Manitoulin Chamber of Commerce
PO Box 307, 6062 Hwy. 542, Mindemoya ON P0P 1S0
Tel: 705-377-7501; *Toll-Free:* 800-698-6681
office@manitoulinchamber.com
www.manitoulinchamber.com
Owen Legge, President

Manitouwadge Economic Development Corporation
c/o Township of Manitouwadge, 1 Mississauga Dr., Manitouwadge ON P0T 2C0
Tel: 807-826-3227; *Fax:* 807-826-4592
Toll-Free: 877-826-7529
www.manitouwadge.ca
Karen Robinson, Economic Development Assistant

Marathon Chamber of Commerce
PO Box 1439, Marathon ON P0T 2E0
Tel: 807-229-1340
marathonchamberofcommerce@gmail.com
www.marathon.ca
Affiliation(s): Northwestern Ontario Associated Chambers of Commerce
George Macey, President

Maxville & District Chamber of Commerce
PO Box 279, Maxville ON K0C 1T0
postmaster@maxvillechamber.ca
www.maxvillechamber.ca
Debbie Gaulin, President

Meaford Chamber of Commerce (MDCC)
#1, 16 Trowbridge St. West, Meaford ON N4L 1N2
Tel: 519-538-1640; *Fax:* 519-538-5493
Toll-Free: 888-632-3673
info@mcofc.ca
mcofc.ca
Shirley Keaveney, President
Donna Earl, Manager

Millbrook & District Chamber of Commerce
PO Box 271, 46 King St. East, Millbrook ON L0A 1G0
Tel: 705-932-7007
info@millbrook.ca
www.millbrook.ca
Angela Beal, President
Diane Moore, Office Manager

Milton Chamber of Commerce
#104, 251 Main St. East, Milton ON L9T 1P1
Tel: 905-878-0581; *Fax:* 905-878-4972
info@miltonchamber.ca
www.miltonchamber.ca
Social Media: www.youtube.com/miltonchamber
Sandy Martin, Executive Director

Minto Chamber of Commerce
PO Box 864, Harriston ON N0G 1Z0
Tel: 519-327-9619
info@mintochamber.on.ca
www.mintochamber.on.ca
John Mock, President

Mississippi Mills Chamber of Commerce
PO Box 1244, Almonte ON K0A 1A0
Tel: 613-256-7886
www.mississippimills.com

Mount Forest District Chamber of Commerce
514 Main St. North, Mount Forest ON N0G 2L0
Tel: 519-323-4480; *Fax:* 519-323-1557
chamber@mountforest.ca
www.mountforest.ca
David Ford, President

Muskoka Lakes Chamber of Commerce
PO Box 536, 3181 Muskoka Rd. 169, Bala ON P0C 1A0
Tel: 705-762-5663; *Fax:* 705-762-5664
info@muskokalakeschamber.com
www.muskokalakeschamber.com
Social Media: www.youtube.com/user/MuskokaLksCC; www.instagram.com/MuskokaLksCC
Jane Templeton, Manager

Napanee & District Chamber of Commerce
Napanee Business Centre, 47 Dundas St. East, Napanee ON K7R 1H7
Tel: 613-354-6601; *Toll-Free:* 877-354-6601
inquiry@napaneechamber.ca
www.napaneechamber.ca
Janet Flynn, President

New Clarence-Rockland Chamber of Commerce
#201, 8710 County Road 17, Rockland ON K4K 1T2
Tel: 613-761-1954; *Fax:* 866-648-2769
info@ccclarencerockland.com
ccclarencerockland.com
Martine Nolin-Simard, President

Newcastle & District Chamber of Commerce
PO Box 11, 20 King Ave. West, Newcastle ON L1B 1H7
www.newcastle.on.ca
Tom Ujfalussy, President

Newmarket Chamber of Commerce
470 Davis Dr., Newmarket ON L3Y 2P3
Tel: 905-898-5900; *Fax:* 905-853-7271
info@newmarketchamber.com
www.newmarketchamber.ca
Steve Hinder, Chair
Debra Scott, President & CEO

Niagara on the Lake Chamber of Commerce
PO Box 1043, 26 Queen St., Niagara-on-the-Lake ON L0S 1J0
Tel: 905-468-1950; *Fax:* 905-468-4930
tourism@niagaraonthelake.com
www.niagaraonthelake.com
Ray Guy, President
Janice Thomson, Executive Director

North Bay & District Chamber of Commerce
1375 Seymour St., North Bay ON P1B 9V6
Tel: 705-472-8480; *Fax:* 705-472-8027
Toll-Free: 888-249-8998
nbcc@northbaychamber.com
www.northbaychamber.com
Patti Carr, Executive Director

North Perth Chamber of Commerce
580 Main St., Listowel ON N4W 1A8
Tel: 519-291-1551; *Fax:* 519-291-4151
npchamber.com
Dan Proctor, President
Sharon DArcey, General Manager

Northumberland Central Chamber of Commerce
The Chamber Bldg., 278 George St., Cobourg ON K9A 3L8
Tel: 905-372-5831
nccofc.ca
Peter Dounoukos, Chair
Kevin Ward, President & CEO

Northwestern Ontario Associated Chambers of Commerce (NOACC)
#102, 200 Syndicate Ave. South, Thunder Bay ON P7E 1C9
Tel: 807-624-2626; *Fax:* 807-622-7752
www.noacc.ca
Affiliation(s): Ontario Chamber of Commerce
Nathan Lawrence, President

Oakville Chamber of Commerce
#200, 700 Kerr St., Oakville ON L6K 3W5
Tel: 905-845-6613; *Fax:* 905-845-6475
info@oakvillechamber.com
www.oakvillechamber.com
Social Media: instagram.com/oakvillechamber
Affiliation(s): Ontario Chamber of Commerce; Burlington Chamber of Commerce; Milton Chamber of Commerce; Halton Hills Chamber of Commerce; AmCham; Bronte Village Business Improvement Area; Downtown Oakville Business Improvement Area; Kerr Village Business Improvement Area
John Sawyer, President

1000 Islands Gananoque Chamber of Commerce
215 Stone St. South, Gananoque ON K7G 2A3
Tel: 613-382-7744; *Fax:* 613-382-1585
Toll-Free: 800-561-1595
info@1000islandsganchamber.com
www.1000islandsganchamber.com
Affiliation(s): Travel Media Association of Canada
Joe Baptista, President

Orillia & District Chamber of Commerce
150 Front St. South, Orillia ON L3V 4S7
Tel: 705-326-4424; *Fax:* 705-327-7841
www.orillia.com
Affiliation(s): Canadian Chamber of Commerce
Susan Lang, Managing Director

Orléans Chamber of Commerce / Chambre de commerce d'Orléans
880 Taylor Creek Dr., Orléans ON K1C 1T1
Tel: 613-824-9137; *Fax:* 613-824-0090
contact@orleanschamber.ca
www.orleanschamber.ca
Affiliation(s): National Capital Business Alliance
Jamie Kwong McDonald, Executive Director

Oro-Medonte Chamber of Commerce (OMCC)
PO Box 100, 148 Line 7 South, Oro ON L0L 2X0
Tel: 705-487-7337; *Fax:* 705-487-0133
info@oromedontecc.com
www.oromedontecc.com
Nadia Fitzgerald, Executive Director
Dave Dahinten, President
Lisa Groves, Secretary-Treasurer

Ottawa Chamber of Commerce (OCC)
328 Somerset St. West, Ottawa ON K2P 0J9
Tel: 613-236-3631; *Fax:* 613-236-7498
info@ottawachamber.ca
www.ottawachamber.ca
Alexa Ryan, Interim Executive Director
Laura Haber, Director, Events & Partnerships
Scott Williams, Director, Member Services
Kenny Leon, Manager, Communications

Otter Valley Chamber of Commerce
PO Box 36, Port Burwell ON N0J 1T0
Tel: 519-550-0088
ottervalleychamber.com
Val Donnell, President

Owen Sound & District Chamber of Commerce
PO Box 1028, 704 - 6th St. East, Owen Sound ON N4K 6K6
Tel: 519-376-6261; *Fax:* 519-376-5647
www.oschamber.com
Bert Loopstra, Manager

Paris & District Chamber of Commerce
PO Box 130, Paris ON N3L 3E1
Tel: 519-758-5095
www.pariscoc.ca
Leigha Oakes, President
Sue Swinton, Secretary

Parry Sound Area Chamber of Commerce
70 Church St., Parry Sound ON P2A 1Y9
Tel: 705-746-4213; *Toll-Free:* 800-461-4261
www.parrysoundchamber.ca
Andrew Ryeland, President
Perry S. Harris, CEO

Perth & District Chamber of Commerce
34 Herriott St., Perth ON K7H 1T2
Tel: 613-267-3200; *Fax:* 613-267-6797
Toll-Free: 888-319-3204
welcome@perthchamber.com
perthchamber.com
Affiliation(s): Canadian Chamber of Commerce; Ontario Chamber of Commerce
Pauline Fitchett, General Manager

Pointe-au-Baril Chamber of Commerce
PO Box 67, Pointe-au-Baril-Station ON P0G 1K0
Tel: 705-366-2331
Affiliation(s): Rainbow County Travel Association

Port Colborne-Wainfleet Chamber of Commerce
76 Main St. West, Port Colborne ON L3K 3V2
Tel: 905-834-9765; *Fax:* 905-834-1542
office@pcwchamber.com
www.pcwchamber.com

Port Hope & District Chamber of Commerce
58 Queen St., Port Hope ON L1A 3Z9
Tel: 905-885-5519; *Fax:* 905-885-1142
info@porthopechamber.com
www.porthopechamber.com
Doug Blundell, President
Bree Nixon, Manager

Port Sydney/Utterson & Area Chamber of Commerce
#4, 15 South Mary Lake Rd., Port Sydney ON P0B 1L0
Tel: 705-385-1117; *Fax:* 705-385-9753
info@portsydneycoc.com
www.portsydneycofc.com
Gordon Haig, President

Prescott & District Chamber of Commerce
950 Edward St. North, Prescott ON K0E 1T0
Tel: 613-925-2171; *Fax:* 613-925-4381
prescottchamberofcommerce@gmail.com
www.prescottanddistrictchamber.com
Dan Roddick, President

Prince Edward County Chamber of Tourism & Commerce (PECCTAC)
116 Main St., Picton ON K0K 2T0
Tel: 613-476-2421; *Fax:* 613-476-7461
Toll-Free: 800-640-4717
contactus@pecchamber.com
www.pecchamber.com
Mike McLeod, General Manager

Quinte West Chamber of Commerce (QWCC)
97 Front St., Trenton ON K8V 4N6
Tel: 613-392-7635; *Fax:* 613-392-8400
Toll-Free: 800-930-3255
info@quintewestchamber.ca
www.quintewestchamber.ca
Mike Cowan, President
Suzanne Andrews, Manager

Rainy River & District Chamber of Commerce
PO Box 458, Atwood Aee., Rainy River ON P0W 1L0
Tel: 807-852-3343
rrdcoc@gmail.com
rainyriverchamber.ca
Social Media: pinterest.com/singlepole
Richard Trenchard, President

Ramara & District Chamber of Commerce
PO Box 144, 2304 Hwy. 12, Brechin ON L0K 1B0
Tel: 705-484-2141; *Fax:* 705-484-0161
info@ramarachamber.com
www.ramarachamber.com
Walt Meyers, President

Red Lake Chamber of Commerce
PO Box 430, Red Lake ON P0V 2M0
Tel: 807-727-3722; *Fax:* 807-727-3285
redlakechamber@shaw.ca
Carol McPherson, President
Colin Knudsen, Vice President
Mark Vermette, Second Vice President
Yvonne Davis, Treasurer

Renfrew & Area Chamber of Commerce
161 Raglan St. South, Renfrew ON K7V 1R2
Tel: 613-432-7015; *Fax:* 613-432-8645
info@renfrewareachamber.ca
www.renfrewareachamber.ca
Rob Campbell, President

Richmond Hill Chamber of Commerce (RHCOC)
376 Church St. South, Richmond Hill ON L4C 9V8
Tel: 905-884-1961; *Fax:* 905-884-1962
info@rhcoc.com
www.rhcoc.com
Social Media: www.youtube.com/user/richmondhillchamber
Affiliation(s): Toronto Board of Trade
Bryon Wilfert, Chair
Elio Fulan, Executive Director

Rideau Chamber of Commerce
PO Box 247, Manotick ON K4M 1A3
Tel: 613-692-6262
rideauchamber.com
Affiliation(s): Ontario Chamber of Commerce
Salima Ismail, President

Ridgetown & South East Kent Chamber of Commerce
PO Box 522, Ridgetown ON N0P 2C0
Tel: 519-359-6597
ridgetownchamber@gmail.com
www.ridgetown.com
Charlie Mitton, President

Sarnia Lambton Chamber of Commerce
556 North Christina St., Sarnia ON N7T 5W6
Tel: 519-336-2400; *Fax:* 519-336-2085
info@sarnialambtonchamber.com
www.sarnialambtonchamber.com
Social Media: www.youtube.com/user/SarniaLambtonChamber
Mike Elliot, Chair
Rory Ring, President

Sauble Beach Chamber of Commerce
672 Main St., Sauble Beach ON N0H 2G0
Tel: 519-422-1262; *Fax:* 519-422-3198
www.saublebeach.com

Saugeen Shores Chamber Office
559 Goderich St., Port Elgin ON N0H 2C4
Tel: 519-832-2332; *Fax:* 519-389-3725
Toll-Free: 800-387-3456
portelgininfo@saugeenshores.ca
www.saugeenshores.ca/chamber/index.php
John Kirkham, President

Sault Ste Marie Chamber of Commerce (SSMCOC)
489 Bay St., Sault Ste Marie ON P6A 1X6
Tel: 705-949-7152; *Fax:* 705-759-8166
info@ssmcoc.com
www.ssmcoc.com
Robert W. Reid, President
Shelley Barich, General Manager

Scugog Chamber of Commerce
PO Box 1282, #G1, 181 Perry St., Port Perry ON L9L 1A7
Tel: 905-985-4971; *Fax:* 905-985-7698
Toll-Free: 877-820-3595
scugogchamber.ca
Affiliation(s): Joint Chambers of Durham Region; Durham Network for Excellence; Tourism Durham; Tourist Association of Durham Region; Durham Home & Small Business Association
Julie Curran, President

Simcoe & District Chamber of Commerce
Chamber Plaza, 95 Queensway West, Simcoe ON N3Y 2M8
Tel: 519-426-5867; *Fax:* 519-428-7718
www.simcoechamber.on.ca
Dave Churchill, President
Yvonne Di Pietro, General Manager

Sioux Lookout Chamber of Commerce
PO Box 577, 11 First Ave. South, Sioux Lookout ON P8T 1A8
Tel: 807-737-1937; *Fax:* 807-737-1778
chamber@siouxlookout.com
www.siouxlookout.com
Matt Cairns, President

Smiths Falls & District Chamber of Commerce
Town Hall, 77 Beckwith St. North, Smiths Falls ON K7A 2B8
Tel: 613-283-1334; *Fax:* 613-283-4764
info@smithsfallschamber.ca
www.smithsfallschamber.ca
Rebecca White, Marketing Coordinator
Ashley Lennox, Office Co-ordinator

Small Business Centre (SBC)
316 Rectory St., 3rd Fl., London ON N5W 3V9
Tel: 519-659-2882; *Fax:* 519-659-7050
info@sbcentre.ca
www.sbcentre.ca
Social Media: www.youtube.com/user/SBCLondon
Steve Pellarin, Executive Director

South Dundas Chamber of Commerce
PO Box 288, 91 Main St., Morrisburg ON K0C 1X0
Tel: 613-543-3982; *Fax:* 613-543-2971
managersdchamber@gmail.com
www.southdundaschamber.ca
Carl McIntyre, President

South Grenville Chamber of Commerce
950 Edward St. North, Prescott ON K0E 1T0
Tel: 613-213-1043
southgrenvillechamber@gmail.com
www.southgrenvillechamber.ca
Dan Roddick, President
Jerone Taylor, President-Elect

South Huron Chamber of Commerce
PO Box 550, 414 Main St. South, Exeter ON N0M 1S6
Tel: 226-423-3028; *Fax:* 519-235-3141
www.shcc.on.ca
Steve Boles, Interim President & Treasurer

South Stormont Chamber of Commerce
PO Box 489, Ingleside ON K0C 1M0
Tel: 613-537-8344; *Fax:* 613-537-9439
info@sscc.on.ca
www.sscc.on.ca
Donna Primeau, President

Southeast Georgian Bay Chamber of Commerce
PO Box 70, 99 Lone Pine Rd., Port Severn ON L0K 1S0
Tel: 705-756-4863; *Fax:* 705-756-4863
info@segbay.ca
www.segbay.ca
Marianne Braid, Manager

Southern Georgian Bay Chamber of Commerce / Chambre de Commerce de la Baie Georgienne Sud
208 King St., Midland ON L4R 3L9
Tel: 705-526-7884
info@sgbchamber.ca
southerngeorgianbay.on.ca
Denise Hayes, General Manager

Springwater Chamber of Commerce
2231 Nursery Rd., Minesing ON L0L 1Y2
Tel: 705-797-7500
info@springwaterchamber.ca
www.springwaterchamber.ca
Mike Guilbault, President

St Thomas & District Chamber of Commerce
#115, 300 South Edgeware Rd., St Thomas ON N5P 4L1
Tel: 519-631-1981; *Fax:* 519-631-0466
mail@stthomaschamber.on.ca
www.stthomaschamber.on.ca
Affiliation(s): Ontario Chamber of Commerce; Canadian Chamber of Commerce
Bob Hammersley, President & CEO

Stoney Creek Chamber of Commerce
21 Mountain Ave. South, Stoney Creek ON L8G 2V5
Tel: 905-664-4000; *Fax:* 905-664-7228
admin@chamberstoneycreek.com
www.chamberstoneycreek.com
Social Media: www.youtube.com/ChamberStoneyCreek
David Cage, Executive Director

Stratford & District Chamber of Commerce
55 Lorne Ave. East, Stratford ON N5A 6S4
Tel: 519-273-5250; *Fax:* 519-273-2229
info@stratfordchamber.com
www.stratfordchamber.com
Affiliation(s): Chamber of Commerce Executives of Canada
Garry Lobsinger, General Manager

Strathroy & District Chamber of Commerce
137 Frank St., Strathroy ON N7G 2R8
Tel: 519-245-7620; *Fax:* 519-245-9422
info@sdcc.on.ca
www.sdcc.on.ca
Shannon Churchill, General Manager

Tavistock Chamber of Commerce
PO Box 670, Tavistock ON N0B 2R0
Tel: 519-655-2700
www.tavistock.on.ca/chamber.html
Andrew Raymer, President

Temagami & District Chamber of Commerce
PO Box 57, Stn. T, 7 Lakeshore Dr., Temagami ON P0H 2H0
Tel: 705-569-3344; *Fax:* 705-569-3344
Toll-Free: 800-661-7609
info@temagamiinformation.com
temagamiinformation.com
Ann Richmond, Office Manager
Hendrika Krygsman, President

Temiskaming Shores & Area Chamber of Commerce (TSACC)
PO Box 811, 883356 Hwy. 65 East, New Liskeard ON P0J 1P0
Tel: 705-647-5771; *Fax:* 705-647-8633
Toll-Free: 866-947-5753
info@tsacc.ca
www.tsacc.ca
Lois Weston-Bernstein, Executive Director

Thunder Bay Chamber of Commerce (TBCC)
#102, 200 Syndicate Ave. South, Thunder Bay ON P7E 1C9
Tel: 807-624-2626; *Fax:* 807-622-7752
chamber@tbchamber.ca
www.tbchamber.ca
Affiliation(s): Northwestern Ontario Associated Chambers of Commerce; Ontario Chamber of Commerce; Canadian Chamber of Commerce
Charla Robinson, President

Tilbury & District Chamber of Commerce
PO Box 1299, 17 Superior St., Tilbury ON N0P 2L0
Tel: 519-682-3040
tbia.dcc@pppoe.ca
www.tilburyontario.com/Chamber
Kathy Cottingham, Chair
Natalie Whittal, Executive Director & Coordinator, Events

Tillsonburg District Chamber of Commerce
Tillsonburg ON
www.tillsonburgchamber.ca
Sheryl Williams, President
Suzanne Renken, General Manager

Timmins Chamber of Commerce / Chambre de commerce de Timmins
PO Box 985, 76 McIntyre Rd., Timmins ON P4N 7H6
Tel: 705-360-1900; *Fax:* 705-360-1193
info@timminschamber.on.ca
www.timminschamber.on.ca
Social Media: www.youtube.com/TimminsChamber
Kurt Bigeau, President
Keitha Robson, Chief Administrative Officer

Tobermory & District Chamber of Commerce
PO Box 250, Tobermory ON N0H 2R0
Tel: 519-596-2452; *Fax:* 519-596-2452
chamber@tobermory.org
www.tobermory.org
Affiliation(s): Central Bruce Peninsula Chamber of Commerce; South Bruce Peninsula Chamber of Commerce; Manitoulin Chamber of Commerce; Manitoulin Tourism Association; Sauble Beach Chamber of Commerce

Top of Lake Superior Chamber of Commerce
PO Box 402, Nipigon ON P0T 2P0
chamber@topoflakesuperior.com
www.topoflakesuperior.com
Brigitte Tremblay, Coordinator

Trent Hills & District Chamber of Commerce
PO Box 376, 51 Grand Rd., Campbellford ON K0L 1L0
Tel: 705-653-1551; *Fax:* 705-653-1629
Toll-Free: 888-653-1556
info@trenthillschamber.ca
www.trenthillschamber.ca
Nancy Allanson, Executive Director

Tweed Chamber of Commerce
PO Box 988, Tweed ON K0K 3J0
Tel: 613-813-2784
tweedcoc@yahoo.ca
www.tweed-chamber.ca
Richard Rashotte, President

Upper Ottawa Valley Chamber of Commerce
224 Pembroke St. West, Pembroke ON K8A 5N2
Tel: 613-732-1492
manager@uovchamber.com
www.upperottawavalleychamber.com
Social Media: www.youtube.com/user/UOVCC

Uxbridge Chamber of Commerce
PO Box 810, 2 Campbell Dr., Uxbridge ON L9P 0A3
Fax: 905-852-2632
info@uxcc.ca
www.uxcc.ca
Terry Barrett, President

Vaughan Chamber of Commerce (VCC)
#2, 25 Edilcan Dr., Vaughan ON L4K 3S4
Tel: 905-761-1366; *Fax:* 905-761-1918
info@vaughanchamber.ca
www.vaughanchamber.ca
Paula Curtis, President & CEO
Joanne Taibi, Accounting

Walkerton Business Improvement Area
PO Box 1344, 101 Durham St., Walkerton ON N0G 2V0
Tel: 519-881-3413; *Fax:* 519-881-4009
info@walkertonbia.ca
walkertonbia.ca
Affiliation(s): Ontario Chamber of Commerce
Christine Brandt, Chamber Manager
Dwayne Kaster, President
Trent Heipel, Vice-President

Wallaceburg & District Chamber of Commerce
152 Duncan St., Wallaceburg ON N8A 4E2
Tel: 519-627-1443; *Fax:* 519-627-1485
Toll-Free: 888-545-0558
info@wallaceburgchamber.com
www.wallaceburgchamber.com
Carmen McGregor, President
Tina Fraleigh, Office Administrator

Wasaga Beach Chamber of Commerce
PO Box 394, 550 River Rd. West, Wasaga Beach ON L9Z 1A4
Tel: 705-429-2247; *Fax:* 705-429-1407
Toll-Free: 866-292-7242
info@wasagainfo.com
www.wasagainfo.com
Affiliation(s): Canadian Chamber of Commerce; Ontario Chamber of Commerce
Trudie McCrea, Office Manager

The Welland/Pelham Chamber of Commerce / La Chambre de commerce de Welland/Pelham
32 East Main St., Welland ON L3B 3W3
Tel: 905-732-7515; *Fax:* 905-732-7175
www.wellandpelhamchamber.com
Verne Milot, President
Dolores Fabiano, Executive Director

Wellesley & District Board of Trade
c/o Wendy Sauder, Wellesley Service Centre, 1220 Queens Bush Rd., Wellesley ON N0B 2T0
Tel: 519-656-3494
wellesleyboardoftrade@gmail.com
wellesleyboardoftrade.com
Chris Franklin, President

West Elgin Chamber of Commerce
PO Box 276, Rodney ON N0L 2C0
secretary@westelginchamber.ca
www.westelginchamber.ca
Bill Denning, President

West Grey Chamber of Commerce
PO Box 800, 144 Garafraxa St. South, Durham ON N0G 1R0
Tel: 519-369-5750
westgreychamber@gmail.com
westgreychamber.ca
Affiliation(s): Durham Business Improvement Association
Maggie Harrison, President

West Lincoln Chamber of Commerce
PO Box 555, 288 Station St., Smithville ON L0R 2A0
Tel: 905-957-1606; *Fax:* 905-957-4628
www.westlincolnchamber.com
Ivan Carruthers, President
Pamela Haire, Administrator

West Nipissing Chamber of Commerce / Chambre de commerce de Nipissing Ouest
200 Main St., #B, Sturgeon Falls ON P2B 1P2
Tel: 705-753-5672; *Fax:* 705-580-5672
wnchamber@gmail.com
www.westnipissingchamber.ca
Greg Demers, President
Mike Bozzer, Project Manager

West Ottawa Board of Trade
#140, 555 Legget Dr., Kanata ON K2K 2X3
Tel: 613-592-8343; *Fax:* 613-592-1157
info@westottawabot.com
www.westottawabot.com
Social Media: www.youtube.com/user/KanataChamber
Rosemary Leu, Executive Director

Westport & Rideau Lakes Chamber of Commerce
PO Box 157, #2, 36 Main St., Westport ON K0G 1X0
Tel: 613-273-2929; *Fax:* 613-273-2929
wrlcc@rideau.net
www.westportrideaulakes.on.ca
Colin Horsfall, President

Whitby Chamber of Commerce (WCC)
128 Brock St. South, Whitby ON L1N 4J8
Tel: 905-668-4506; *Fax:* 905-668-1894
info@whitbychamber.org
www.whitbychamber.org
Tracy Hanson, Chief Executive Officer

Whitchurch-Stouffville Chamber of Commerce
PO Box 1500, 6176 Main St., Stouffville ON L4A 8A4
Tel: 905-642-4227; *Fax:* 905-642-8966
chamber@whitchurchstouffville.ca
www.whitchurchstouffville.ca
Penny Reid, Chair
Edward Nelles, Executive Director

Wiarton South Bruce Peninsula Chamber of Commerce
PO Box 68, #2, 402 William St., Wiarton ON N0H 2T0
Tel: 519-534-4545
info@wiartonchamber.ca
www.wiartonchamber.ca
Affiliation(s): Wiarton BIA
Paul Deacon, President

Windsor-Essex Regional Chamber of Commerce
2575 Ouellette Place, Windsor ON N8X 1L9
Tel: 519-966-3696
info@windsorchamber.org
www.windsorchamber.org
Carolyn Brown, Chair
Matt Marchand, President & CEO

Woodstock District Chamber of Commerce
476 Peel St., Woodstock ON N4S 1K1
Tel: 519-539-9411; *Fax:* 519-456-1611
info@woodstockchamber.ca
www.woodstockchamber.ca
Social Media: www.youtube.com/woodstockonchamber
Martha Dennis, General Manager

Zurich & District Chamber of Commerce
PO Box 189, Zurich ON N0M 2T0
zurichontario.com

Prince Edward Island

Chambre de commerce acadienne et francophone de l'Île-du-Prince-Édouard
CP 67, Wellington PE C0B 2E0
Tél: 902-854-3439; *Téléc:* 902-854-3099
Jeannette Arsenault, Contact

Eastern Prince Edward Island Chamber of Commerce
PO Box 1593, 540 Main St., Montague PE C0A 1R0
Tel: 902-838-4030; *Fax:* 902-838-4031
www.epeicc.ca
Chris Nicholson, President
Stella Jamieson, Executive Director

Greater Charlottetown & Area Chamber of Commerce
National Bank Tower, 134 Kent St., Charlottetown PE C1A 7K2
Tel: 902-628-2000; *Fax:* 902-368-3570
chamber@charlottetownchamber.com
www.charlottetownchamber.com
Affiliation(s): Atlantic Provinces Chamber of Commerce
Quentin Bevan, President
Kathy Hambly, Executive Director
Wendy Watts, Manager, Membership & Marketing Sales

Kensington & Area Chamber of Commerce
PO Box 234, Kensington PE C0B 1M0
Tel: 902-836-3209; *Fax:* 902-836-3206
kensingtonchamber.ca
Social Media: www.youtube.com/user/KtownChamber
Ryan Cochrane, President
Glenna Lohnes, Executive Director

South Shore Chamber of Commerce
PO Box 127, Crapaud PE C0A 1J0
Tel: 902-658-2738
Marion Miller, President

Québec

Chambre de commerce au Coeur de la Montérégie (CCCM)
#101, 2055, rue Du Pont, Marieville QC J3M 1J8
Tél: 450-460-4019; *Téléc:* 450-460-2362
info@coeurmonteregie.com
www.coeurmonteregie.com
Yanick Marchand, Président

Chambre de commerce Baie-des-Chaleurs
119, av Grand-Pré, Bonaventure QC G0C 1E0
Tél: 418-392-9832
www.ccmrcbonaventure.com

Maurice Quesnel, Directeur Général

Chambre de commerce Bellechasse-Etchemins
159-B, boul Bégin, Sainte-Clare QC G0R 2V0
Tél: 418-563-1131
ccb-e.ca
Yvon Laflamme, Président

Chambre de Commerce Bois-des-Filion - Lorraine
CP 72012, Bois-des-Filion QC J6Z 4N9
Tél: 450-818-3481
info@ccbdfl.com
www.ccbdfl.com
Michel Bourgeois, Co-Président
Michel Limoges, Co-Président

Chambre de Commerce d'industrie Les Moulins
#204, 760, montée Masson, Lachenaie QC J7K 3B6
Tél: 450-966-1536; *Téléc:* 450-966-1531
info@ccimoulins.com
www.ccimoulins.com
Affiliation(s): Chambre de commerce du Canada; Chambre de commerce du Québec; Chambre de commerce régionale de Lanaudière; Réseau canadien de centres de services aux entreprises; Centre local de développement économique des Moulins (CLDEM); Centre local d'emploi de Terrebonne; Société de développement touristique des Moulins; Conseil de développement bioalimentaire de Lanaudière.
Vicky Marchand, Directrice générale

Chambre de commerce de Beauceville
CP 5142, Beauceville QC G5X 2P5
Tél: 418-774-1020
info@chambredecommercedebeauceville.com
www.chambredecommercedebeauceville.com
Affiliation(s): Chambre de commerce du Québec; Chambre du commerce du Canada
Jacques Gagné, Président

Chambre de commerce de Brandon
151, rue Saint-Gabriel, Saint-Gabriel-de-Brandon QC J0K 2N0
Tél: 450-835-2105; *Téléc:* 450-835-2991
france.brisebois@qc.aira.com
Affiliation(s): Chambre de commerce du Québec
France Brisebois, Directrice générale

Chambre de Commerce de Cap-des-Rosiers
1127, boul de Cap-des-Rosiers, Cap-des-Rosiers QC G4X 6G3

Chambre de commerce de Carleton
629, boul Perron, Carleton QC G0C 1J0
Tél: 418-364-1004

Chambre de commerce de Causapscal
5, rue St-Jacques sud, Causapscal QC G0J 1J0
Tél: 418-756-6048

Chambre de commerce de Charlevoix
#209, 11, rue Saint-Jean-Baptiste, Baie-Saint-Paul QC G3Z 1M1
Tél: 418-760-8648
info@creezdesliens.com
www.creezdesliens.com
Johanne Côté, Coordonnatrice

Chambre de commerce de Chibougamau
#4, 600, 3e rue, Chibougamau QC G8P 1P1
Tél: 418-748-4827; *Téléc:* 418-748-6179
info@ccchibougamau.com
www.ccchibougamau.ca
Affiliation(s): Chambre de Commerce du Québec et du Canada
Alain Bradette, Président

Chambre de commerce de Clair
CP 1025, Clair NB E7B 2J5
Tél: 506-992-6030; *Téléc:* 506-992-6041
info@chambrecommerceclair.com
www.chambrecommerceclair.com
Marie-Josée Michaud, Responsable

Chambre de commerce de Cowansville et région
#150, 104, rue du Sud, Cowansville QC J2K 2X2
Tél: 450-266-1665; *Téléc:* 450-266-4117
cccr@chambre-cowansville.com
www.chambre-cowansville.com
Marc Blanchette, Président
Michel Fleury, Directeur général

Chambre de commerce de Danville-Shipton
CP 599, Danville QC J0A 1A0
Tél: 819-839-2742; *Téléc:* 819-839-2347
info@ccdanville.com
www.ccdanville.com
Isabelle Lodge, Présidente

Martine Satre, Vice-Présidente
Pierre Picard, Trésorier
Sylvie Beauchemin, Secrétaire

Chambre de commerce de Disraéli
CP 5008, Disraéli QC G0N 1E0
chambrecommercedisraeli@gmail.com
chambrecommercedisraeli.com
Catherine Morency, Présidente

Chambre de commerce de Dolbeau-Mistassini
#300, 1341, boul Wallberg, Dolbeau-Mistassini QC G8L 1H3
Tél: 418-276-6638; *Téléc:* 418-276-9518
info@cdcdm.com
Mélanie Robert, Directrice générale

Chambre de commerce de Ferme-Neuve
125, 12e rue, Ferme-Neuve QC J0W 1C0
Tél: 819-587-3882
ch.comm.fn@tlb.sympatico.ca
www.municipalite.ferme-neuve.qc.ca/Chambre_de_commerce.asp
Alexandre Sarrazin, Président

Chambre de Commerce de Fermont
CP 419, #6C, 299, Le Carrefour, Fermont QC G0G 1J0
Tél: 418-287-3000

Chambre de commerce de Fleurimont
924, rue King Est, Sherbrooke QC J1G 1L2
Tél: 819-565-7991; *Téléc:* 819-565-3160
info@ccfleurimont.com
icifleurimont.com/ccfleurimont
François Lemieux, Directeur général

Chambre de commerce de Forestville
40, route 138 Ouest, Forestville QC G0T 1E0
Tél: 418-587-1585
www.repertoire-chambres.fccq.ca

Chambre de commerce de Gatineau
#100, 45, rue de Villebois, Gatineau QC J8T 8J7
Tél: 819-243-2246; *Téléc:* 819-243-3346
ccgatineau@ccgatineau.ca
www.ccgatineau.ca
Karl Lavoie, Directeur général

Chambre de commerce de l'Est de la Beauce
Saint-Prosper QC
Tél: 418-594-1219
ccest.beauce@hotmail.com

Chambre de commerce de l'Est de Montréal
#100, 5600, rue Hochelaga, Montréal QC H1N 3L7
Tél: 514-354-5378; *Téléc:* 514-354-5340
info@ccemontreal.ca
www.ccemontreal.ca
Isabelle Foisy, Directrice générale

Chambre de commerce de l'Est de Portneuf
CP 4031, Pont-Rouge QC G3H 3R4
Tél: 418-873-4085; *Téléc:* 418-873-4599
ccep@globetrotter.net
www.portneufest.com
Karine Lacroix, Directrice

Chambre de commerce de l'Ile d'Orléans (CCIO)
490, côte du Pont, Saint-Pierre-Ile-d'Orléans QC G0A 4E0
Tél: 418-828-0880; *Téléc:* 418-828-2335
Ligne sans frais: 866-941-9411
ccio@videotron.ca
cciledorleans.com
Affiliation(s): Chambre de commerce de Québec
Sylvie Ann Tremblay, Directrice générale

Chambre de commerce de l'Ouest-de-l'Ile de Montréal / West Island Chamber of Commerce
#602, 1000, boul Saint-Jean, Pointe-Claire QC H9R 5P1
Tél: 514-697-4228; *Téléc:* 514-697-2562
info@wimcc.ca
www.ccoim.ca
Joseph Huza, Directeur exécutif

Chambre de commerce de la Haute-Gaspésie
96, boulevard Sainte-Anne ouest, Sainte-Anne-des-Monts QC G4V 1R3
Tél: 418-763-2200; *Téléc:* 418-763-3473
cchg@globetrotter.net
www.cchg.qc.ca
Hugo Caissy, LL.B, Président

Chambre de commerce de la Haute-Matawinie
521, rue Brassard, Saint-Michel-des-Saints QC J0K 3B0
Tél: 450-833-1334; *Téléc:* 450-833-1334
infocchm@satelcom.qc.ca
www.haute-matawinie.com

France Chapdelaine, Directrice générale

Chambre de Commerce de la Jacques-Cartier
4517, rte de Fossambault, RR#3, Ste-Catherine-de-la-J-Cartier QC G0A 3M0
Tél: 418-875-4103

Chambre de commerce de la MRC de L'Assomption
#100, 522, rue Notre-Dame, Repentigny QC J6A 2T8
Tél: 450-581-3010; *Téléc:* 450-581-5069
info@ccmrclassomption.ca
www.ccmrclassomption.ca
Peter Fogarty, Président
Linda Mallette, Directrice générale

Chambre de commerce de la MRC de la Matapédia
#403, 123, rue Desbiens, Amqui QC G5J 3S5
Tél: 418-629-5765; *Téléc:* 418-629-5530
information@ccmrcmatapedia.qc.ca
www.ccmrcmatapedia.qc.ca
Média social: plus.google.com/107383797735234822116
Affiliation(s): Fédération des Chambres de commerce du Québec
Chantal St-Pierre, Directrice générale

Chambre de commerce de la MRC de Rivière-du-Loup
298, boul. Armand-Thériault, Rivière-du-Loup QC G5R 4C2
Tél: 418-862-5243; *Téléc:* 418-862-5136
info@monreseaurdl.com
www.ccmrcrdl.com
Karine Malenfant, Directrice générale

Chambre de commerce de la région d'Acton
Édifice de la Gare, 980, rue Boulay, Acton Vale QC J0H 1A0
Tél: 450-546-0123; *Téléc:* 450-546-2709
ccracton@cooptel.qc.ca
www.chambredecommerce.info
Joanne Joannette, Directrice générale

Chambre de commerce de la région d'Asbestos
CP 34, Asbestos QC J1T 3M9
Tél: 819-300-1484
ccidessources@lives.ca
www.lccra.com
Denis Beaubien, Président

Chambre de commerce de la région de Berthier / D'Autray
960, av Gilles-Villeneuve, Berthierville QC J0K 1A0
Tél: 450-836-4689
www.ccberthier-dautray.com
Louis-Simon Lamontagne, Président

Chambre de commerce de la region de Cap-Pelé
CP 1219, Cap-Pelé NB E4N 3B1
Tél: 506-332-0118
chambredecommerce@yahoo.ca
www.cap-pele.com/chamber.cfm
Albert E. LeBlanc, Président
Gilles Haché, Secrétaire

Chambre de commerce de la région de Weedon
280, 9e av, Weedon QC J0B 3J0
Tél: 819-560-8555
admin@ccweedon.com
www.ccweedon.com
Affiliation(s): Chambre de Commerce du Québec

Chambre de commerce de Lac-Brome
CP 3654, #316, 1, rue Knowlton, Lac-Brome QC J0E 1V0
Tél: 450-242-2870
info@cclacbrome.com
www.cclacbrome.com
Suzanne Gregory, Directrice générale

Chambre de commerce de Lévis
#225, 5700, rue JB Michaud, Lévis QC G6V 0B1
Tél: 418-837-3411; *Téléc:* 418-837-8497
cclevis@cclevis.ca
www.cclevis.com
Stéphane Thériault, Directeur général

Chambre de commerce de Manicouagan
22, place la Salle, 2ème étage, Baie-Comeau QC G4Z 1K3
Tél: 418-296-2010; *Téléc:* 418-296-5397
info@ccmanic.qc.ca
www.ccmanic.qc.ca
Michel Truchon, Président

Chambre de commerce de Mascouche
#204, 760, Montée Masson, Mascouche QC J7K 3B6
Tél: 450-966-1536; *Téléc:* 450-966-1531
info@ccmascouche.com
www.ccmascouche.com

Vicky Marchand, Directrice générale

Chambre de commerce de Mont-Laurier
CP 64, Mont-Laurier QC J9L 3G9
Tél: 819-623-3642; *Téléc:* 819-623-5220
Ligne sans frais: 855-623-3642
info@ccmont-laurier.com
www.ccmont-laurier.com
Éric Tourangeau, Président
Jocelyn Girouard, Vice-Présidente
Audrey Lebel, Directrice générale

Chambre de commerce de Montmagny
#121, 6, rue St-Jean-Baptiste Est, Montmagny QC G5V 1J7
Tél: 418-248-3111; *Téléc:* 418-241-5779
www.ccmontmagny.com

Chambre de commerce de Mont-Tremblant
990, rue Lauzon, Mont-Tremblant QC J8E 3J5
Tél: 819-425-8441; *Téléc:* 819-425-7949
info@ccdemonttremblant.com
www.ccm-t.ca
Dominique Laverdure, Présidente
Françoise Tardif, Directrice générale

Chambre de commerce de Port-Cartier
CP 82, Port-Cartier QC G5B 2G7
Tél: 418-766-8047; *Téléc:* 418-766-6367
popco@globetrotter.net
Jean-Marie Potvin, Président

Chambre de commerce de Rawdon
3874, rue Queen, Rawdon QC J0K 1S0
Tél: 450-834-2282; *Téléc:* 450-834-3084
ccdr@bellnet.ca
www.chambrecommercerawdon.ca
Pénélope Lefebvre, Président

Chambre de commerce de Saint-Côme
1661A, rue Principale, Saint-Côme QC J0K 2B0
Tél: 450-883-2730
info@stcomelanaudiere.ca
www.stcomelanaudiere.com
Carole Lachance, Présidente

Chambre de commerce de Saint-Ephrem
CP 2015, Saint-Éphrem QC G0M 1R0
Tél: 418-484-2681
info@ccstephrem.com
www.ccstephrem.com
France St-Pierre, Présidente

Chambre de commerce de Saint-Quentin Inc.
144D, rue Canada, Saint-Quentin NB E8A 1G7
Tél: 506-235-3666; *Téléc:* 506-235-1804
Marc Beaulieu, Président
Pascale Bellavance, Secrétaire

Chambre de commerce de Sainte-Adèle
Promenades Sainte-Adèle, #134, 555, boul de St-Adèle, Sainte-Adèle QC J8B 1A7
Tél: 450-229-2644; *Téléc:* 450-229-1436
chambredecommerce@sainte-adele.net
www.sainte-adele.net
Guy Goyer, Directeur général

Chambre de commerce de Sept-Iles
#237, 700, boul Laure, Sept-Iles QC G4R 1Y1
Tél: 418-968-3488; *Téléc:* 418-968-3432
ccsi@globetrotter.net
www.ccseptiles.com
Emilie Paquet, Directrice générale

Chambre de commerce de Sherbrooke
#202, 9, rue Wellington Sud, Sherbrooke QC J1H 5C8
Tél: 819-822-6151; *Téléc:* 819-822-6156
info@ccsherbrooke.ca
www.ccsherbrooke.ca
Affiliation(s): La jeune chambre de commerce de Sherbrooke
Louise Bourgault, Directrice générale

Chambre de commerce de St-Côme-Linière (CCSCL)
1614, 6e rue, Saint-Côme-Linière QC G0M 1J0
Tél: 418-685-2630; *Téléc:* 418-685-2630
chambredecommerce@stcomeliniere.com
www.stcomeliniere.com/c_ccommerce.php
Sylvain Bourque, Président

Chambre de commerce de St-Donat
536A, rue Principale, Saint-Donat-de-Montcalm QC J0T 2C0
Tél: 819-424-2833
Diane Champagne, Agente de liaison

Chambre de commerce de St-Eugène-de-Guigues
CP 1013, 9, 1ere Avenue Ouest, Saint-Eugène-de-Guigues QC J0Z 3L0
Tél: 819-785-2057
Lillian Matteau, Secrétaire

Chambre de commerce de St-Frédéric
850, rue de l'Hôtel-de-Ville, Saint-Frédéric QC G0N 1P0
commerce@st-frederic.com
www.saint-frederic.com
Cathy Poulin, Directrice générale

Chambre de commerce de St-Georges
#310, 8585, boul Lacroix, Ville de Saint-Georges Beauce QC G5Y 5L6
Tél: 418-228-7879; *Téléc:* 418-228-8074
reception@ccstgeorges.com
www.ccstgeorges.com
Affiliation(s): Chambre de commerce du Québec; Chambre de commerce du Canada
Nathalie Roy, Directrice générale

Chambre de commerce de St-Jean-de-Dieu
32, rue Principale sud, Saint-Jean-de-Dieu QC G0L 3M0
Tél: 418-963-3529
chambredecommercestjean@outlook.com
Émilie Lebel, Directrice générale

Chambre de commerce de St-Jules-de-Beauce
CP 81, 169, Rang 3, Saint-Jules QC G0N 1R0
Tél: 418-397-1870
Sylvain Cloutier, Président

Chambre de commerce de St-Léonard
8370, boul. Lacordaire, Saint-Léonard QC H1R 3Y6
Tél: 514-325-4232; *Téléc:* 514-955-8544
info@saintleonardenaffaires.com
saintleonardenaffaires.com
Nick Fiasche, Président

Chambre de commerce de Ste-Julienne
1799, rte 125, Sainte-Julienne QC J0K 2T0
Tél: 819-831-3551; *Téléc:* 819-831-3551
Nicole Bourgie, Secrétaire

Chambre de commerce de Ste-Justine
167, rte 204, Sainte-Justine QC G0R 1Y0
Tél: 418-383-3207; *Téléc:* 418-383-3223
chambredecommercestejustine@sogetel.net
stejustine.net/chambre
Bruno Turcotte, Président

Chambre de commerce de Tring-Jonction
CP 1012, Tring-Jonction QC G0N 1X0
Tél: 418-426-1230
c_de_commerce_tring@hotmail.com
Marc Paré, Président

Chambre de commerce de Val-d'Or (CCVD)
#200, 921, 3e av, Val-d'Or QC J9P 1T4
Tél: 819-825-3703; *Téléc:* 819-825-8599
info@ccvd.qc.ca
www.ccvd.qc.ca
Média social: www.youtube.com/user/CCVDCom
Marcel H. Jolicoeur, Président
Hélène Paradis, Directrice générale

Chambre de commerce de Valcourt et Région
980, rue St-Joseph, Valcourt QC J0E 2L0
Tél: 450-532-3263; *Téléc:* 450-532-5855
info@valcourtregion.com
www.valcourtregion.com
Affiliation(s): Chambre de commerce régionale de l'Estrie
Sonia Gauthier, Présidente

Chambre de commerce des Iles-de-la-Madeleine (CCIM)
Édifice Fernand Cyr, #103, 735, ch Principal, Cap-aux-Meules QC G4T 1G8
Tél: 418-986-4111; *Téléc:* 418-986-4112
info@ccim.qc.ca
www.ccim.qc.ca
Gino Thorne, Président

Chambre de commerce du grand de Châteauguay
#100, 15, boul Maple, Châteauguay QC J6J 3P7
Tél: 450-698-0027; *Téléc:* 450-698-0088
info@ccgchateauguay.ca
www.ccgchateauguay.ca
Isabelle Poirier, Directrice générale par intérim

Chambre de commerce du Grand Joliette
500, boul. Dollard, Joliette QC J6E 4M4
Tél: 450-759-6363; *Téléc:* 450-759-5012
info@ccgj.qc.ca
www.ccgj.qc.ca
Média social: www.youtube.com/user/CCGJoliette
Pascale Lapointe-Manseau, Directrice générale

Chambre de commerce du Grand Tracadie-Sheila
#399, 124, rue de Couvent, Tracadie NB E1X 1E1
Tel: 506-394-4028; *Fax:* 506-394-4899
ccgtracadie-sheila@nb.aibn.com
Rebecca Preston, Directrice générale

Chambre de commerce du Haut-Richelieu
Centre Ernest-Thuot, 75, 5e av, Saint-Jean-sur-Richelieu QC J2X 1T1
Tél: 450-346-2544; *Téléc:* 450-346-3812
info@cchautrichelieu.qc.ca
www.cchautrichelieu.qc.ca
Claude Demers, Directeur général

Chambre de commerce du Haut-Saint-François
221, St-Jean Ouest, East Angus QC J0B 1R0
Tél: 819-832-4950; *Téléc:* 819-832-4950
info@chambredecommercehsf.com
www.chambredecommercehsf.com
Guy Boulanger, Président
Nancy Grenier, Directrice générale

Chambre de commerce du Montréal métropolitain / Board of Trade of Metropolitan Montréal
#6000, 380, rue Saint-Antoine ouest, Montréal QC H2Y 3X7
Tél: 514-871-4000; *Téléc:* 514-871-1255
info@ccmm.qc.ca
www.ccmm.qc.ca
Michel Leblanc, Président et chef de la direction
Guy Jobin, Vice-Président, Services aux entreprises

Chambre de commerce du Saguenay
194, rue Price ouest, Chicoutimi QC G7J 1H1
Tél: 418-543-5941; *Téléc:* 418-543-5576
info@ccsaguenay.ca
www.ccsaguenay.ca
Éric Dufour, Président
Marie-Josee Morency, Directrice générale

Chambre de commerce du Témiscouata
CP 147, 871 Commerciale, Notre-Dame-du-Lac QC G0L 1X0
Tél: 418-714-2735
info@temiscouata.cc
www.cctemiscouata.com
Michaël Lang, Président

Chambre de commerce du Transcontinental
CP 2004, Rivière-Bleue QC G0L 2B0
Tél: 418-893-5504; *Téléc:* 418-893-2889
cctrans@sympatico.ca
pages.globetrotter.net/cctrans
Sylvain Lafrance, Président

Chambre de commerce Duparquet
CP 369, Duparquet QC J0Z 1W0
Tél: 819-948-2030
Jasmine Therrien, Secrétaire

Chambre de commerce East Broughton
CP 916, East Broughton QC G0N 1G0
Tél: 418-351-0143
cceastbroughton@hotmail.com
cceastbroughton.com
Annie Roy, Secrétaire

Chambre de commerce et d'industrie Beauharnois-Valleyfield
#400, 100, rue Sainte-Cécile, Salaberry-de-Valleyfield QC J6T 1M1
Tél: 450-373-8789; *Téléc:* 450-373-8642
ccibv@rocler.com
www.ccibv.ca
Sylvie Villemure, Directrice générale

Chambre de commerce et d'industrie d'Abitibi-Ouest (CCAO)
364-A, rue Principale, La Sarre QC J9Z 1Z5
Tél: 819-333-9836; *Téléc:* 819-333-5737
ccao@ccao.qc.ca
www.ccao.qc.ca
Stéphanie Bédard, Directrice générale

Chambre de commerce et d'industrie d'Argenteuil
#225, 580, rue Principale, Lachute QC J8H 1Y7
Tél: 450-562-1947; *Téléc:* 450-562-1896
info@cciargenteuil.com
cciargenteuil.com/francais/Accueil.php

Mélanie Guérard, Directrice générale

Chambre de commerce et d'industrie de Drummond (CCID)
CP 188, 234, rue Saint-Marcel, Drummondville QC J2B 6V7
Tél: 819-477-7822
info@ccid.qc.ca
www.ccid.qc.ca
Média social: www.youtube.com/channel/UCoFAI0FERsHBU6CITMR1_Ug
Alain Côté, Directeur général

Chambre de commerce et d'industrie de la MRC de Maskinongé
396, Ste-Élisabeth, Louiseville QC J5V 1M8
Tél: 819-228-8582; *Téléc:* 819-228-8989
Ligne sans frais: 866-900-8582
servicemembres@cci-maskinonge.ca
www.ccimm.ca
Fannie Trudel, Coordonnatrice, service aux membres

Chambre de commerce et d'Industrie de la région de Coaticook (CCIRC)
150, rue Child, Coaticook QC J1A 2B3
Tél: 819-849-4733; *Téléc:* 819-849-6828
info@ccircoaticook.ca
www.ccircoaticook.ca
Dominic Arsenault, Présidente

Chambre de commerce et d'industrie de la région de Richmond
CP 3119, Richmond QC J0B 2H0
Tél: 819-826-5854
info@ccrichmond.com
www.ccrichmond.com
Hélène Tousignant, Présidente
Christian Bazinet, Vice-président
Rémi-Mario Mayette, Secrétaire
Ginette Coutu-Poirier, Trésorière

Chambre de commerce et d'industrie de la Rive-Sud
#101, 85, rue Saint-Charles ouest, Longueuil QC J4H 1C5
Tél: 450-463-2121; *Téléc:* 450-463-1858
info@ccirs.qc.ca
www.ccirs.qc.ca
Hélène Bergeron, Directrice générale

Chambre de commerce et d'industrie de la Vallée-du-Richelieu
#102, 230, rue Brébeuf, Beloeil QC J3G 5P3
Tél: 450-464-3733; *Téléc:* 450-446-4163
www.ccivr.com
Anne Durocher, Directrice générale

Chambre de commerce et d'industrie de Laval (CCIL)
#200, 1555, boul Chomedey, Laval QC H7V 3Z1
Tél: 450-682-5255; *Téléc:* 450-682-5735
info@ccilaval.qc.ca
www.ccilaval.qc.ca
Stéphane Corbeil, Président
Chantal Provost, Directrice générale

Chambre de commerce et d'industrie de Malartic (CCIM)
#160, 866, rue Royale, Malartic QC J0Y 1Z0
Tél: 819-757-3338
info@ccimalartic.com
www.ccimalartic.com
Claudette Jolin, Directrice

Chambre de commerce et d'industrie de Maniwaki & Vallée de la Gatineau (CCIM)
186, rue King, Maniwaki QC J9E 3N6
Tél: 819-449-6627; *Téléc:* 819-449-7667
Ligne sans frais: 866-449-6728
info@ccmvg.com
www.ccmvg.com
Kim Lafond, Administratrice

Chambre de commerce et d'industrie de Mirabel
#208, 13665, boul du Curé Labelle, Mirabel QC J7J 1L2
Tél: 450-433-1944
info@ccimirabel.com
www.ccimirabel.com
Thierry Lefebvre, Président

Chambre de commerce et d'industrie de Montréal-Nord (CRIMN)
#207, 5835, boul Léger, Montréal QC H1G 6E1
Tél: 514-329-4453; *Téléc:* 514-329-5318
www.ccimn.qc.ca
Palmina Panichella, Directrice générale

Chambre de commerce et d'industrie de Québec
17, rue St-Louis, Québec QC G1R 3Y8
Tél: 418-692-3853; *Téléc:* 418-694-2286
info@ccquebec.ca
www.ccquebec.ca
Affiliation(s): Chambre de commerce du Canada
Eric Lavoie, Président, Conseil d'administration
Alain Kirouac, Président et chef de la direction

Chambre de commerce et d'industrie de Roberval
CP 115, Roberval QC G8H 2N4
Tél: 418-275-3504; *Téléc:* 418-275-6895
info@ccroberval.ca
www.ccroberval.ca
Affiliation(s): Chambre de Commerce du Québec; Chambre de Commerce du Canada
Mélanie Paul, Coprésidente
Denis Taillon, Coprésident
Pascal Gagnon, Directeur général

Chambre de commerce et d'industrie de Rouyn-Noranda (CCIRN)
70, av du Lac, Rouyn-Noranda QC J9X 4N4
Tél: 819-797-2000; *Téléc:* 819-762-3091
reseau@ccirn.qc.ca
www.ccirn.qc.ca
Guy Veillet, Présidente

Chambre de commerce et d'industrie de Shawinigan
1635, 5e av, Shawinigan-Sud QC G9P 1M8
Tél: 819-536-0777; *Téléc:* 819-536-0039
info@ccishawinigan.ca
www.ccishawinigan.ca
Nancy Déziel, Présidente
Geneviève Bédard, Directrice générale

Chambre de commerce et d'industrie de St-Joseph-de-Beauce
CP 5042, Saint-Joseph-de-Beauce QC G0S 2V0
Tél: 418-397-5980
admin@ccstjoseph.com
ccstjoseph.com
Annie Thibeault, Coordonnatrice

Chambre de commerce et d'industrie de St-Laurent
#204, 935, Décarie, Saint-Laurent QC H4L 3M3
Tél: 514-333-5222; *Téléc:* 514-333-0937
info@ccstl.qc.ca
www.ccstl.qc.ca
Sylvie Séguin, Directrice générale

Chambre de commerce et d'industrie de Thetford Mines (CCITM)
81, rue Notre-Dame ouest, Thetford Mines QC G6G 1J4
Tél: 418-338-4551; *Téléc:* 418-335-2066
www.ccitm.com
Louis Thivierge, Directeur général

Chambre de commerce et d'industrie de Varennes (CCIV)
2368, boul Marie-Victorin, Varennes QC J3X 1R7
Tél: 450-652-4209; *Téléc:* 450-652-4244
info@cciv.ca
www.cciv.ca
Marie-Claude Lévesque, Coordonnatrice

Chambre de commerce et d'industrie des Bois-Francs et de l'Érable
122, rue de l'Acqueduc, Victoriaville QC G6P 1M3
Tél: 819-758-6371; *Téléc:* 819-758-4604
ccibf@ccibf.com
www.ccibf.qc.ca
Média social: www.youtube.com/ChambreCCIBFE
Josée Desharnais, Directrice générale

Chambre de commerce et d'industrie du bassin de Chambly (CCIB)
929, boul. de Périgny, Chambly QC J3L 5H5
Tél: 450-658-7598; *Téléc:* 450-658-3569
info@ccibc.qc.ca
www.ccibc.qc.ca
Pierre Cardinal, Président

Chambre de Commerce et d'Industrie du Centre-Abitibi
644, 1e av ouest, Amos QC J9T 1V3
Tél: 819-732-8100; *Téléc:* 819-732-8131
info@ccica.ca
ccica.ca
Joanne Breton, Directrice générale

Chambre de commerce et d'industrie du Coeur-du-Québec
1045, av Nicolas Perrot, Bécancour QC G9H 3B7
Tél: 819-294-6010; *Téléc:* 819-294-6020
Ligne sans frais: 877-994-6010
info@ccicq.ca
www.ccicq.ca
Jean-Denis Girard, Président

Chambre de commerce et d'industrie du Haut St-Laurent
CP 1914, 8, rue King, Huntingdon QC J0S 1H0
Tél: 450-264-5252; *Téléc:* 450-264-5111
cdechsl@suroit.com
www.cdechsl.com
Daniel Légaré, Président

Chambre de commerce et d'industrie du Haut St-Maurice
547-C, rue Commerciale, La Tuque QC G9X 3A7
Tél: 819-523-9933; *Téléc:* 819-523-9939
cchsm@lino.com
www.ccihsm.ca
Michael Scarpino, Président
Manon Côté, Directrice générale

Chambre de commerce et d'industrie du secteur Normandin
1048, rue St-Cyrille, Normandin QC G8M 4R9
Tél: 418-274-2004; *Téléc:* 418-274-7171
ccinormandin@hotmail.com
Sylvie Coulombe, Présidente
Nicole Bilodeau, Directrice générale

Chambre de commerce et d'industrie du Sud-Ouest de Montréal
#32, 410, av Lafleur, Montréal QC H8R 3H6
Tél: 514-365-4575; *Téléc:* 514-365-0487
info@ccisom.ca
www.ccisom.ca
Affiliation(s): Chambre de commerce du Canada; Fédération des Chambres de commerce du Québec

Chambre de commerce et d'industrie Lac-Saint-Jean-Est
640, rue Côté-Ouest, Alma QC G8B 7S8
Tél: 418-662-2734; *Téléc:* 418-669-2220
cci@ccilacsaintjeanest.com
www.ccilacsaintjeanest.com
Kathleen Voyer, Directrice générale

Chambre de commerce et d'industrie Les Maskoutains
780, av de L'Hôtel-de-ville, Saint-Hyacinthe QC J2S 5B2
Tél: 450-773-3474; *Téléc:* 450-773-9339
chambre@chambrecommerce.ca
www.chambrecommerce.ca
Claire Sarrasin, Directrice générale

Chambre de commerce et d'industrie Magog-Orford
355, rue Principale ouest, Magog QC J1X 2B1
Tél: 819-843-3494; *Téléc:* 819-769-0292
info@ccimo.qc.ca
www.ccimo.qc.ca
Robert Théorêt, Président
Jérémy Parent, Directeur général

Chambre de commerce et d'industrie MRC de Deux-Montagne (CCI2M)
67A, boul Industriel, Saint-Eustache QC J7R 5B9
Tél: 450-491-1991; *Téléc:* 450-491-1648
info@chambrecommerce.com
www.chambrecommerce.com
Affiliation(s): Chambre de Commerce du Québec
Michel Goyer, Directeur

Chambre de commerce et d'industrie Nouvelle-Beauce (CCINB)
700, rue Notre-Dame nord, #C, Sainte-Marie QC G6E 2K9
Tél: 418-387-2006; *Ligne sans frais:* 866-387-2006
info@ccinb.ca
www.ccinb.ca
Nancy Labbé, Directrice générale

Chambre de commerce et d'industrie régionale de Saint-Léonard-d'Aston
#1, 370, rue Principale, Saint-Léonard-d'Aston QC J0C 1M0
Tél: 819-399-2020

Chambre de commerce et d'industrie Rimouski-Neigette
#101, 125, rue de l'Évêché ouest, Rimouski QC G5L 4H4
Tél: 418-722-4494; *Téléc:* 418-722-4494
info@ccrimouski.com
www.ccrimouski.com
Chantal Pilon, Présidente

Chambre de commerce et d'industrie secteur Saint-Félicien inc.
CP 34, 1209, boul Sacré-Coeur, Saint-Félicien QC G8K 2P8
Tél: 418-679-2097; *Téléc:* 418-679-8183
sarah.michaud@chambre-sf.com
www.chambre-sf.com
Marie-Noël Gagnon, Présidente
Jean Tremblay, Directeur général

Chambre de commerce et d'industrie Sorel-Tracy métropolitain
#112, 67, rue George, Sorel-Tracy QC J3P 1C2
Tél: 450-742-0018; *Téléc:* 450-742-7442
info@ccstm.qc.ca
www.ccstm.qc.ca
Marcel Robert, Directeur général

Chambre de commerce et d'industrie St-Jérôme (CCISJ)
#20, 236, rue de Parent, Saint-Jérôme QC J7Z 1Z7
Tél: 450-431-4339; *Téléc:* 450-431-1677
www.ccisj.qc.ca
Raphaelle Prévost, Directrice, Développement des affaires et relations publiques

Chambre de commerce et d'industrie Thérèse-De Blainville (CCITB)
#202, 141, rue St-Charles, Ste-Thérèse QC J7E 2A9
Tél: 450-435-8228; *Téléc:* 450-435-0820
info@ccitb.ca
www.ccitb.ca
Média social: www.youtube.com/user/CCITB85
Samuel Bergeron, Président

Chambre de commerce et d'industrie Vaudreuil-Dorion
450, rue Aimé-Vincent, 2e étage, Vaudreuil-Dorion QC J7V 5V5
Tél: 450-424-6886
www.ccivs.ca
Nadine Lachance, Directrice générale

Chambre de commerce et d'industries de Trois-Rivières
CP 1045, #200, 225, rue des Forges, Trois-Rivières QC G9A 5K4
Tél: 819-375-9628; *Téléc:* 819-375-9083
info@ccitr.net
www.ccitr.net
Caroline Beaudry, Directrice générale

Chambre de commerce et de tourisme de Gaspé
27, boul de York Est, Gaspé QC G4X 2K9
Tél: 418-368-8525
info@cctgaspe.org
cctgaspe.org
Olivier Nolleau, Directeur général

Chambre de commerce et de tourisme de la Vallée de Saint-Sauveur/Piedmont
30, rue Filion, Saint-Sauveur QC J0R 1R0
Tél: 450-227-2564; *Téléc:* 450-227-6480
Ligne sans frais: 877-528-2553
info@valleesaintsauveur.com
www.valleesaintsauveur.com
Pierre Urquhart, Directeur général

Chambre de commerce et de tourisme de St-Adolphe-d'Howard
CP 326, Saint-Adolphe-d'Howard QC J0T 2B0
info@st-adolphe.com
www.st-adolphe.com
Michel Couture, Président

Chambre de commerce et industrie Mont-Joli-Mitis
CP 183, 1553, boul Jacques-Cartier, Mont-Joli QC G5H 3K9
Tél: 418-775-4366
info@ccimontjolimitis.com
www.ccimontjolimitis.com
Pierre-Luc Harrison, Président

Chambre de commerce gaie du Québec (CCGQ) / The Québec Gay Chamber of Commerce
#100, 1307 rue Ste-Catherine Est, Montréal QC H2L 2H4
Tél: 514-522-1885; *Ligne sans frais:* 888-647-2247
info@ccgq.ca
www.ccgq.ca
Marc-Antoine Saumier, Président

Chambre de commerce Haute-Yamaska et Région (CCHYR)
650, rue Principale, Granby QC J2G 8L4
Tél: 450-372-6100; *Téléc:* 450-696-1119
info@cchyr.com
www.cchyr.ca
Sylvain Perron, Président

Chambre de commerce Hemmingford—Napierville—Saint-Rémi
1009, rue Notre-Dame, Saint-Rémi QC J0L 2L0
Tél: 450-615-0512; *Téléc:* 450-615-0612
chambredecommercejardinsdenapierville.com
Karine Demers, Présidente

Chambre de commerce Kamouraska-L'Islet (CCKL)
#208, 1000, 6e av, La Pocatière QC G0R 1Z0
Tél: 418-856-6227; *Téléc:* 418-856-6462
Ligne sans frais: 877-856-6227
cckl@qc.aira.com
www.cckl.org
Gabriel Hudon, Président

Chambre de commerce Mont-Saint-Bruno (CCMSB)
CP 123, Saint-Bruno QC J3V 4P8
Tél: 450-653-0585; *Téléc:* 450-653-6967
info@ccstbruno.ca
www.ccstbruno.ca
Affiliation(s): Chambre de commerce du Québec; Chambre de commerce du Canada
Daniel Tousignant, CGA, Président
Jacques Laliberté, Directeur général

Chambre de commerce MRC du Rocher-Percé
#121-2, 129, boul René-Levesque Ouest, Chandler QC G0C 1K0
Tél: 418-689-6998
info@ccrocherperce.org
www.ccrocherperce.org
Roger Clavet, Directeur général

Chambre de commerce Notre-Dame-du-Nord
3, rue Principale sud, Notre-Dame-du-Nord QC J0Z 3B0
Tél: 819-723-2586
www.municipalite.notre-dame-du-nord.qc.ca
Ken Armitage, Président

Chambre de commerce région de Matane
CP 518, Matane QC G4W 3P5
Tél: 418-562-9344
info@ccmatane.com
www.ccmatane.com
Marc Charest, Président

Chambre de commerce région de Mégantic
4336, rue Laval, Lac-Mégantic QC G6B 1B8
Tél: 819-583-5392
www.ccrmeg.com
Pascal Hallé, Président
Isabelle Hallé, Directrice générale

Chambre de commerce régionale de St-Raymond (CCRSR)
#100, 1, av St-Jacques, Saint-Raymond QC G3L 3Y1
Tél: 418-337-4049; *Téléc:* 418-337-8017
ccrsr@cite.net
www.ccrsr.qc.ca
Hughes Genois, Président

Chambre de commerce régionale de Windsor
CP 115, Windsor QC J1S 2L7
Tél: 819-434-5936
www.ccrwindsor.com
Guillaumme Lussier, Président

Chambre de commerce Saint-Lin-Laurentides
#101, 704, rue St-Isidore, Saint-Lin-Laurentides QC J5M 2V2
Tél: 450-439-3704; *Téléc:* 450-439-2066
André Corbeil, Président

Chambre de commerce secteur ouest de Portneuf
#2, 295, rue Gauthier, Saint-Marc-des-Carrières QC G0A 4B0
Tél: 418-268-5447
ccsop@portneufouest.com
www.portneufouest.com
Guillaume Béliveau Côté, Chargé de projets

Chambre de commerce Ste-Émélie-de-l'Énergie
400, rue St-Michel, Sainte-Émélie-de-l'Énergie QC J0K 2K0
Tél: 450-886-1658

Chambre de commerce St-Félix de Valois
15, ch Joliette, Saint-Félix-de-Valois QC J0K 2M0
Tél: 450-889-8161; *Téléc:* 450-889-1590
ccst-fix@stfelixdevalois.qc.ca
www.stfelixdevalois.qc.ca
Johanne Dufresne, Directrice générale

Chambre de commerce St-Jean-de-Matha
204L, rue Principale, Saint-Jean-de-Matha QC J0K 2S0
Tél: 450-886-0599; *Téléc:* 450-886-3123
info@chambrematha.com
www.chambrematha.com
Sylvain Binette, Président
Sophie Moreau, Coordinatrice

Chambre de commerce St-Martin de Beauce
CP 2022, 131, 1e av Est, Saint-Martin QC G0M 1B0
Tél: 418-382-5549
chambre@st-martin.qc.ca
www.st-martin.qc.ca
Affiliation(s): Chambre de commerce du Québec; Chambre de commerce du Canada
Pascal Bergeron, Président

Chambre de commerce Témis-Accord
1E, rue Notre-Dame, Ville-Marie QC J9V 1W3
Tél: 819-629-2918
dg@temis-accord.com
www.temis-accord.com
Véronic Girard, Co-Présidente
Alexandre Touzin, Co-Président

Chambre de commerce Témiscaming-Kipawa (CCTK)
CP 442, 760, chemin Kipawa, Témiscaming QC J0Z 3R0
Tél: 819-627-6160; *Téléc:* 819-627-3390
cctk@temiscaming.net
www.temiscaming.net/chambre-commerce
Guylaine Létourneau, Présidente

Chambre de commerce Vallée de la Missisquoi
858, rte Missisquoi, Bolton Centre QC J0E 1G0
Tél: 450-292-4217; *Téléc:* 450-292-4224

Chambre de commerce Vallée de la Petite-Nation
185, rue Henri-Bourassa, Papineauville QC J0V 1R0
Tél: 819-427-8450
ccvpn@videotron.ca
www.ccvpn.org
Jean Careau, Directeur général

Jeune chambre de commerce de Montréal (JCCM)
#700, 1435, rue Saint-Alexandre, Montréal QC H3A 2G4
info@jccm.org
www.jccm.org
Sandrine Archambault, Directrice générale

Jeune chambre de commerce de Québec
#249, 4600, boul Henri-Bourassa, Québec QC G1H 3A5
Tél: 418-622-6937; *Téléc:* 418-628-7777
jccq@jccq.qc.ca
www.jccq.qc.ca
Média social: www.youtube.com/user/JeunechambredeQuebec
Marie-Eve Goulet, Présidente
Sophie Gingras, Directrice générale

Jewish Chamber of Commerce / Chambre de commerce juive
#400, 1 Cummings Square, Montréal QC H3W 1M6
Tel: 514-345-2645
info@jccmontreal.com
www.jccmontreal.com
Michel Ohayon, Co-president
Stacey Stivaletti, Co-president

Pontiac Chamber of Commerce
PO Box 119, Campbell's Bay QC J0X 1K0
Tel: 819-647-2312; *Toll-Free:* 855-647-2312
info@pontiacchamberofcommerce.ca
www.pontiacchamberofcommerce.ca
Jean-Claude Rivest, President

Regroupement des jeunes chambres de commerce du Québec (RJCCQ)
#1100, 555, 555 René-Lévesque ouest, 11e étage, Montréal QC H2Z 1B1
Tél: 514-933-7595
info@rjccq.com
www.rjccq.com
Média social: www.youtube.com/user/RJCCQ
Julie Labrecque, Présidente-directrice générale

Virginie Leblanc, Chargée de projets

West Island Chamber of Commerce
#602, 1000 St. Jean Blvd., Pointe-Claire QC H9R 5P1
Tel: 514-697-4228; *Fax:* 514-697-2562
info@wimcc.ca
ccoim.ca
Éric Léouzon, President
Joseph Huza, Executive Director

Saskatchewan

Assiniboia & District Chamber of Commerce (SK)
PO Box 1803, 110 - 4th Ave. West, Assiniboia SK S0H 0B0
Tel: 306-642-5553; *Fax:* 306-642-3529
www.assiniboia.net/business/chamber_of_commerce.html
Terry L. Sieffert, President
Sonia Dahlman, Treasurer
Bonnie Ruzicka, Executive Assistant

Battlefords Chamber of Commerce
PO Box 1000, Hwy. 16 & 40 East, North Battleford SK S9A 3E6
Tel: 306-445-6226; *Fax:* 306-446-0188
b.chamber@sasktel.net
www.battlefordschamber.com
Affiliation(s): Institution of Association Executives; Tourism Industry Association of Saskatchewan
Brendon Bootman, President
Linda Machniak, Executive Director

Big River Chamber of Commerce
PO Box 159, Big River SK S0J 0E0
Tel: 306-469-2124; *Fax:* 306-469-4409

Biggar & District Chamber of Commerce
PO Box 327, Biggar SK S0K 0M0
Tel: 306-948-2295; *Fax:* 306-948-5050
townofbiggar.com

Blaine Lake & District Chamber of Commerce
PO Box 178, Blaine Lake SK S0J 0J0
Tel: 306-226-4646; *Fax:* 306-497-2402
blainelakecofc@sasktel.net
www.blainelake.ca/business/chamber.html
Vivian Nemish, President

Buffalo Narrows Chamber of Commerce
PO Box 504, Buffalo Narrows SK S0M 0J0
Tel: 306-235-4485; *Fax:* 306-235-4416

Choiceland & District Chamber of Commerce
c/o Town of Choiceland, PO Box 279, 115 - 1st St. East, Choiceland SK S0J 0M0
Tel: 306-428-2070; *Fax:* 306-428-2071
Frank H. Bond, President
Colleen F Digness, Secretary

Coronach Community Chamber of Commerce
PO Box 577, Coronach SK S0H 0Z0
Tel: 306-267-2077; *Fax:* 306-267-2047
Affiliation(s): Saskatchewan Chamber of Commerce
J. Marshall, President
S. Nelson, Secretary

Cut Knife Chamber of Commerce
PO Box 504, Cut Knife SK S0M 0N0
Tel: 306-398-2060; *Fax:* 306-398-2062

Debden & District Chamber of Commerce
PO Box 91, Debden SK S0J 0S0
Tel: 306-724-2020; *Fax:* 306-724-2220
Rhonda Peterson, President
Amelie Patrick, Secretary

Eastend & District Chamber of Commerce
PO Box 534, Eastend SK S0N 0T0
Tel: 306-295-4070; *Fax:* 306-295-3571
Bonnie Gleim, President
Stephanie Morris, Secretary

Eatonia & District Chamber of Commerce
PO Box 370, Eatonia SK S0L 0Y0
Tel: 306-967-2506; *Fax:* 306-967-2267

Esterhazy & District Chamber of Commerce
PO Box 778, Esterhazy SK S0A 0X0
Tel: 306-745-5405; *Fax:* 306-745-6797
esterhazy.ed@sasktel.net

Estevan Chamber of Commerce
#2, 322 - 4th St., Estevan SK S4A 0T8
Tel: 306-634-2828; *Fax:* 306-634-6729
admin@estevanchamber.ca
www.estevanchamber.ca
Ken Rowan, President

Michel Cyrenne, Executive Director
Rebecca Howie, Marketing & Events Coordinator
Manpreet Sangha, Economic Development Officer

Foam Lake & District Chamber of Commerce
PO Box 238, Foam Lake SK S0A 1A0
Tel: 306-272-4578

Fort Qu'Appelle & District Chamber of Commerce
PO Box 1273, Fort Qu'Appelle SK S0G 1S0
Tel: 306-332-5717; *Fax:* 306-332-1287
FQChamber@hotmail.com
Kelly Nattern, Contact

Fox Valley Chamber of Commerce
PO Box 133, Fox Valley SK S0N 0V0
Tel: 306-666-4447; *Fax:* 306-666-4448
Lester N Lodoen, President
Delia E. Hughes, Secretary

Goodsoil & District Chamber of Commerce
PO Box 88, Goodsoil SK S0M 1A0
Tel: 306-238-2033; *Fax:* 306-238-4441

Gravelbourg Chamber of Commerce
PO Box 85, Gravelbourg SK S0H 1X0
Tel: 306-648-3182; *Fax:* 306-648-2311
Maria Lepage, Contact
Cees Brouwer, President

Greater Saskatoon Chamber of Commerce
#104, 202 - 4th Ave. North, Saskatoon SK S7K 0K1
Tel: 306-244-2151; *Fax:* 306-244-8366
chamber@saskatoonchamber.com
www.saskatoonchamber.com
Affiliation(s): Enterprise Centre; Leadership Saskatoon; Raj Manek Mentorship Program; Saskatchewan Agrivision Corporation; Saskatchewan Economic Development Authority; Saskatchewan Young Professionals & Entrepreneurs; Saskatoon Aboriginal Employment & Business Opportunities Inc., Saskatoon Air Services; Saskatoon Regional Economic Development Authority; Tourism Saskatoon; United Way of Saskatoon; Vision 2000
Kent Smith-Windsor, Executive Director

Herbert & District Chamber of Commerce
PO Box 700, Herbert SK S0H 2A0
Tel: 306-784-3475

Hudson Bay Chamber of Commerce
PO Box 730, Hudson Bay SK S0E 0Y0
Tel: 306-865-2288; *Fax:* 306-865-2177
www.townofhudsonbay.com
Corinne Reine, President
Janice Dyck, Secretary

Humboldt & District Chamber of Commerce
PO Box 1440, Humboldt SK S0K 2A0
Tel: 306-682-4990; *Fax:* 306-682-5203
admin@humboldtchamber.ca
www.humboldtchamber.ca
Social Media: www.youtube.com/user/humboldtchamber
Debra Nyczai, Executive Director

Kamsack & District Chamber of Commerce
PO Box 817, Kamsack SK S0A 1S0
Tel: 306-542-3553; *Fax:* 306-542-3553

Kenaston & District Chamber of Commerce
PO Box 70, Kenaston SK S0G 2N0
www.kenaston.ca/pages/chamber.htm
Susan Anbolt, Sec.-Treas.
Mary Lou Whittles, President

Kerrobert Chamber of Commerce
433 Manitoba Ave., Kerrobert SK S0L 1R0
Tel: 306-834-5423
kerrobertchamber@sasktel.net
www.kerrobertsk.com
Darryl Morris, President

Kindersley Chamber of Commerce
PO Box 1537, 605 Main St., Kindersley SK S0L 1S0
Tel: 306-463-2320; *Fax:* 306-463-2312
kindersleychamber@sasktel.net
www.kindersleychamber.com
Tolanda Baker, President

Kinistino & District Chamber of Commerce
PO Box 803, Kinistino SK S0J 1H0
Tel: 306-864-2244; *Fax:* 306-864-2244

Kipling Chamber of Commerce
PO Box 700, Kipling SK S0G 2S0
Tel: 306-736-9065; *Fax:* 306-736-2962
www.townofkipling.ca/business/chamber-of-commerce

Buck Bright, Secretary
Tammy Frater, Chair

Landis & District Chamber of Commerce
PO Box 400, Landis SK S0K 2K0
Tel: 306-658-2100; *Fax:* 306-658-4455

Langenburg & District Chamber of Commerce
PO Box 610, Langenburg SK S0A 2A0
Tel: 306-743-2231; *Fax:* 306-743-2873

Lumsden & District Chamber of Commerce
PO Box 114, Lumsden SK S0G 3C0
Tel: 306-731-2862
info@lumsdenchamber.ca
www.lumsdenchamber.ca
Wendy Joorisity, President

Macklin Chamber of Commerce
PO Box 642, Macklin SK S0L 2C0
Tel: 306-753-2221; *Fax:* 306-753-3585

Maidstone & District Chamber of Commerce
PO Box 300, Maidstone SK S0M 1M0
Tel: 306-893-2461; *Fax:* 306-893-4222

Maple Creek Chamber of Commerce
Tel: 306-662-4005
info@maplecreekchamber.ca
www.maplecreekchamber.ca
Tina Cresswell, President
Wayne Litke, Secretary

Meadow Lake & District Chamber of Commerce
PO Box 847, Meadow Lake SK S9X 1Y6
Tel: 306-236-4061
mlchamberofcommerce@sasktel.net
www.meadowchamber.com
Affiliation(s): Northwest Regional Economic Development Authority

Melfort & District Chamber of Commerce
PO Box 2002, 102 Spruce Haven Rd., Melfort SK S0E 1A0
Tel: 306-752-4636; *Fax:* 306-752-9505
melfortchamber@sasktel.net
www.melfortchamber.com
Grant Schutte, President
Nicole Gagné, Executive Director

Melville & District Chamber of Commerce
PO Box 429, 430 Main St., Melville SK S0A 2P0
Tel: 306-728-4177
melvillechamber@sasktel.net
www.melvillechamber.com
Ron Walton, Executive Director
Terry Sieffert, President

Moose Jaw & District Chamber of Commerce
88 Saskatchewan St. East, Moose Jaw SK S6H 0V4
Tel: 306-692-6414
www.mjchamber.com
Chris Aparicio, President
Brian Martynook, CEO

Moosomin Chamber of Commerce
Moosomin SK S0G 3N0
Tel: 306-435-2445
world_spectator@sasktel.net
www.moosomin.com/chamber
Ed Hildebrandt, President
Kevin Weedmark, Treasurer

Nipawin & District Chamber of Commerce
PO Box 177, Nipawin SK S0E 1E0
Tel: 306-862-5252; *Fax:* 306-862-5350
info@nipawinchamber.ca
www.nipawinchamber.ca
Linda Swehla, President

Norquay & District Chamber of Commerce
PO Box 457, Norquay SK S0A 2V0
Tel: 306-594-2248; *Fax:* 306-594-2347

Outlook & District Chamber of Commerce
PO Box 431, Outlook SK S0L 2N0
Tel: 306-867-9580; *Fax:* 306-867-9559
outlookchamber@gmail.com
outlookchamber.webs.com
Justin Turton, Executive President
Ken Fehr, Executive Treasurer

Paradise Hill Chamber of Commerce
PO Box 118, Paradise Hill SK S0M 2G0
Tel: 306-344-2123
George H Palen, President
Sheila M Phillips, Secretary

Prince Albert Chamber of Commerce
3700 - 2nd Ave. West, Prince Albert SK S6W 1A2
Tel: 306-764-6222; *Fax:* 306-922-4727
pachamber@sasktel.net
www.princealbertchamber.com
Affiliation(s): Canadian Chamber of Commerce; Saskatchewan Chamber of Commerce
Mike Mitchell, Chair
Merle Lacert, CEO

Radisson & District Chamber of Commerce
PO Box 397, Radisson SK S0K 3L0
Tel: 306-827-4801; *Fax:* 306-827-2336
www.radisson.ca/business/chamber-of-commerce
Tina Hamel, President

Radville Chamber of Commerce
PO Box 799, Radville SK S0C 2G0
Tel: 306-869-2610

Redvers Chamber of Commerce
PO Box 249, Redvers SK S0C 2H0
Tel: 306-452-3155; *Fax:* 306-452-3155
rdaycare@sasktel.net
Tricia Martel, President
Tanis Chalmers, Director

Regina & District Chamber of Commerce
2145 Albert St., Regina SK S4P 2V1
Tel: 306-757-4658; *Fax:* 306-757-4668
info@reginachamber.com
www.reginachamber.com
Social Media: www.youtube.com/ReginaChamber
Affiliation(s): Canadian Chamber of Commerce; Saskatchewan Chamber of Commerce
John Hopkins, CEO
Nadia Williamson, Chair

La Ronge & District Chamber of Commerce
PO Box 1046, La Ronge SK S0J 1L0
chamber@laclarongechamber.ca
www.laclarongechamber.ca
Clarence Neault, President
Victoria Magee, Secretary

Rosetown & District Chamber of Commerce
PO Box 744, Rosetown SK S0L 2V0
Tel: 306-882-1300; *Fax:* 306-882-1310
www.rosetown.ca
Gerry Clark, Chair
Shirley Helgason, Executive Director

St. Walburg Chamber of Commerce
PO Box 501, St Walburg SK S0M 2T0
Tel: 306-248-3269
townofstwalburg@sasktel.net
www.stwalburg.com
Ali Schmidt, Contact

Shaunavon Chamber of Commerce
PO Box 1048, 410 Centre St., Shaunavon SK S0N 2M0
Tel: 306-297-2671; *Fax:* 306-297-3051
shaunavonchamber@hotmail.com
www.shaunavon.com/?p=980
Joanne Gregoire, President
Debbie Widmer, Secretary

Spiritwood Chamber of Commerce
PO Box 267, Spiritwood SK S0J 2M0
Tel: 306-883-2426

Swift Current Chamber of Commerce
145 - 1st Ave. NE, Swift Current SK S9H 2B1
Tel: 306-773-7268; *Fax:* 306-773-5686
info@swiftcurrentchamber.ca
www.swiftcurrentchamber.ca
Affiliation(s): Saskatchewan Chamber of Commerce; Canadian Chamber of Commerce
Trevor Koot, Chair

Tisdale & District Chamber of Commerce
PO Box 219, Tisdale SK S0E 1T0
Tel: 306-873-4257; *Fax:* 306-873-4241

Unity & District Chamber of Commerce
PO Box 834, Unity SK S0K 4L0
Tel: 306-228-2688; *Fax:* 306-228-2185
www.townofunity.com
Helena Long, President
Kristine Moon, Treasurer

Vonda Chamber of Commerce
c/o Vonda Hometown Insurance Brokers, PO Box 285, Vonda SK S0K 4N0
Tel: 306-221-0559

Waskesiu Chamber of Commerce
PO Box 216, Waskesiu Lake SK S0J 2Y0
Tel: 306-663-5140; *Fax:* 306-663-5448
wakesiuchamber@sasktel.net
www.waskesiulake.ca
George Wilson, Manager

Watrous & District Chamber of Commerce
PO Box 906, Watrous SK S0K 4T0
Tel: 306-946-3353; *Fax:* 306-946-3966

Watson & District Chamber of Commerce
PO Box 686, Watson SK S0K 4V0
Tel: 306-287-3659; *Fax:* 306-287-3601

Weyburn Chamber of Commerce
11 - 3rd St. NE, Weyburn SK S4H 0W5
Tel: 306-842-4738; *Fax:* 306-842-0520
www.weyburnchamber.com
Affiliation(s): Saskatchewan Chamber of Commerce
Rodney Gill, President

Wynyard & District Chamber of Commerce
PO Box 508, Wynyard SK S0A 4T0
Tel: 306-554-3363; *Fax:* 306-554-3851

Yorkton Chamber of Commerce
PO Box 1051, Yorkton SK S3N 2X3
Tel: 306-783-4368; *Fax:* 306-786-6978
info@yorktonchamber.com
www.chamber.yorkton.sk.ca
Affiliation(s): Saskatchewan Economic Developers Association
Joel Martinuk, President
Juanita Polegi, Executive Director

Yukon Territory

Dawson City Chamber of Commerce
PO Box 1006, Dawson City YT Y0B 1G0
Tel: 867-993-5274; *Fax:* 867-993-6817
office@dawsoncitychamberofcommerce.ca
www.dawsoncitychamberofcommerce.ca
Dina Grenon, President

St. Elias Chamber of Commerce
PO Box 5419, Haines Junction YT Y0B 1L0
Tel: 867-634-2916; *Fax:* 867-634-2034
kluaneridin@yknet.ca
Wade Istchenko, President

Silver Trail Chamber of Commerce
PO Box 268, Mayo YT Y0B 1M0
Tel: 867-332-1770
Nancy Hager, President

Teslin Regional Chamber of Commerce
PO Box 181, Teslin YT Y0A 1B0
Tel: 867-390-2521; *Fax:* 867-390-2687
Wes Wirth, President

Watson Lake Chamber of Commerce
c/o Town Office, PO Box 590, 710 Adela Trail, Watson Lake YT Y0A 1C0
Tel: 867-536-8000; *Fax:* 867-536-7522
twl@northwestel.net
www.watsonlake.ca/business-services/chamber-of-commerce

Whitehorse Chamber of Commerce (WCC)
#101, 302 Steele St., Whitehorse YT Y1A 2C5
Tel: 867-667-7545; *Fax:* 867-667-4507
business@whitehorsechamber.ca
www.whitehorsechamber.ca
Affiliation(s): Yukon Chamber of Commerce; Tourism Industry Association of Yukon
Rick Karp, President

Credit Unions/Caisses Populaires

Credit unions and caisses populaires are owned and controlled by their members. These cooperative financial institutions are regulated at the provincial level. Credit unions, in most provinces, must engage external auditors to prepare financial statements. An annual inspection of credit unions is conducted by their provincial regulatory body.

The national trade association and central finance facility for Canadian credit unions is Credit Union Central of Canada. It is regulated under the Cooperative Credit Associations Act. In Québec, Mouvement des caisses Desjardins du Québec consists of a network of caisses. Fédération des caisses Desjardins du Québec is a cooperative which supports Mouvement des caisses Desjardins du Québec.

1st Choice Savings & Credit Union Ltd.
1320 - 3 Ave. South
Lethbridge, AB T1J 0K5
Tel: 403-320-4600; *Fax:* 403-320-4608
Toll-Free: 866-803-0733
info@1stchoicesavings.ca
www.1stchoicesavings.ca
Social Media: www.instagram.com/1stchoicesavings; www.facebook.com/1stchoicesavings; twitter.com/1stchoiceCU
Former Name: St. Patrick's Credit Union Ltd.; Southland Credit Union
Ownership: Public
Year Founded: 2001
Assets: $100-500 million

Acadian Credit Union
PO Box 250
15089 Cabot Trail
Cheticamp, NS B0E 1H0
Tel: 902-224-2055; *Fax:* 902-224-3510
Toll-Free: 877-477-7724
www.acadiancreditu.ca
Social Media: www.facebook.com/AcadianCU; twitter.com/AcadianCU
Former Name: Cheticamp Credit Union
Ownership: Member-owned
Year Founded: 1936
Number of Employees: 21

Accent Credit Union Ltd.
PO Box 520
78 Main St.
Quill Lake, SK S0A 3E0
Tel: 306-382-4155; *Fax:* 306-383-2622
info@accentcu.ca
www.accentcu.ca
Year Founded: 2010

Access Credit Union
Stanley Business Centre
PO Box 1418
#2 - 23111 PTH #14
Winkler, MB R6W 4B4
Tel: 204-325-4351; *Toll-Free:* 800-264-2926
accesscu.ca
Year Founded: 1950

Adjala Credit Union Limited
7320 St. James Lane
Colgan, ON L0G 1W0
Tel: 905-936-2761
info@adjalacu.com
www.adjalacu.com
Year Founded: 1946

Advance Savings Credit Union (ASCU)
141 Weldon St.
Moncton, NB E1C 5W1
Tel: 506-853-8881
www.advancesavings.ca
Former Name: Rexton Credit Union; Royal Credit Union; Trico Credit Union
Ownership: Member-owned
Year Founded: 2006
Assets: $50-100 million

Advantage Credit Union
PO Box 1657
118 Main St.
Melfort, SK S0E 1A0
Tel: 306-752-2744; *Fax:* 306-752-3113
reachus@advantage.cu.sk.ca
www.advantagecu.com
Former Name: Melfort Credit Union Ltd.; Spalding Savings & Credit Union Ltd.
Ownership: Member-owned
Year Founded: 1943

Affinity Credit Union
130 - 1st Ave. North
Saskatoon, SK S7K 0G1
Tel: 306-934-4000; *Fax:* 306-934-5490
Toll-Free: 866-863-6237
questions@affinitycu.ca
www.affinitycu.ca
Social Media: www.youtube.com/channel/UCJ3_ejuWkVg5z_NfN4ujtEA; www.facebook.com/affinitycu; twitter.com/Affinity_CU
Former Name: St. Mary's Credit Union Limited
Ownership: Member-owned
Year Founded: 1949
Assets: $1-10 billion

Airline Financial Credit Union Limited
#310, 2720 Birtannia Rd. East
Mississauga, ON L4W 2P7
Tel: 905-673-7262; *Fax:* 905-676-8437
Toll-Free: 800-392-5005
info@airlinecreditunion.com
www.airlinecreditunion.ca
Former Name: Airline (Malton) Credit Union Limited
Ownership: Member-owned
Year Founded: 1950
Assets: $10-50 million

Aldergrove Credit Union
3661 - 248 St.
Aldergrove, BC V4W 2B5
Tel: 604-856-7012; *Fax:* 604-856-7719
www.aldergrovecu.ca
Former Name: Otter Farmers' Institute Credit Union
Year Founded: 1954

All Trans Financial Credit Union Limited
Administration Ctr.
#707, 3250 Bloor St. West
Toronto, ON M8X 2X9
Tel: 416-231-8400; *Fax:* 416-231-8296
www.alltrans.com
Year Founded: 1993
Number of Employees: 18

L'Alliance des caisses populaires de l'Ontario limitée
PO Box 3500
1870 Bond St.
North Bay, ON P1B 4V6
Tel: 705-474-5634; *Fax:* 705-474-5326
support@acpol.com
www.caissealliance.com
Social Media: www.facebook.com/174831179214242
Ownership: Member-owned.
Year Founded: 1979
Number of Employees: 240
Assets: $500m-1 billion
Revenues: $10-50 million

Alterna Savings & Credit Union Limited
319 McRae Ave., 1st Fl.
Ottawa, ON K1Z 0B9
Tel: 613-560-0100; *Toll-Free:* 877-560-0100
www.alterna.ca
Other Contact Information: Qtrade/Alterna Wealth Line, Toll-Free: 1-855-731-3901
Social Media: plus.google.com/+alternasavings; www.youtube.com/user/AlternaSavings; www.facebook.com/AlternaSavings; twitter.com/alternasavings
Former Name: Ottawa Women's Credit Union Limited; Civil Service Co-operative Credit Society Ltd.; Metro Credit Union
Also Known As: Alterna Savings
Ownership: Member-owned. Part of the Alterna Financial Group.
Year Founded: 2005
Number of Employees: 600+
Assets: $1-10 billion

Apex Credit Union Limited
151 Karl Clark Rd. NW
Edmonton, AB T6N 1H5
Tel: 403-496-2350; *Toll-Free:* 877-378-8728
www.apexcu.com
Other Contact Information: TeleService Edmonton: 780-496-2350
Ownership: Member-owned
Year Founded: 1940
Assets: $50-100 million

Assiniboine Credit Union Limited (ACU)
Corporate Office
PO Box 2, Main Stn. Main
200 Main St., 6th Fl.
Winnipeg, MB R3C 2G1
Tel: 204-958-8588; *Fax:* 204-958-7348
Toll-Free: 877-958-8588
cu@assiniboine.mb.ca
www.assiniboine.mb.ca
Other Contact Information: Lost or Stolen Debit Card, Phone: 204-958-8588; Toll-Free Phone: 1-877-958-8588; Lost or Stolen MasterCard & After Hours Toll-Free: 1-800-567-8111
Social Media: www.facebook.com/298221280375663; twitter.com/myassiniboine
Ownership: Member-owned
Year Founded: 1943
Number of Employees: 500
Assets: $1-10 billion

Austin Credit Union
PO Box 205
24 - 2nd Ave.
Austin, MB R0H 0H0
Tel: 204-385-6140; *Fax:* 204-637-2204
Toll-Free: 877-228-2636
www.austincreditunion.com
Year Founded: 1949

Auto Workers' Community Credit Union Limited
PO Box 158
322 King St. West
Oshawa, ON L1H 7L1
Tel: 905-728-5187; *Toll-Free:* 800-268-8771
www.awccu.com
Ownership: Private. Cooperative
Year Founded: 1938
Number of Employees: 70
Revenues: $100-500 million

Bay Credit Union Limited
142 South Algoma St.
Thunder Bay, ON P7B 3B8
Tel: 807-345-7612; *Fax:* 807-345-8939
Toll-Free: 877-249-7076
info@baycreditunion.com
baycreditunion.com
Other Contact Information: Telephone Banking: 807-346-5478
Social Media: twitter.com/baycreditunion
Former Name: Apple Community Credit Union
Ownership: Member-owned

Bay St Lawrence Credit Union
3019 Bay St. Lawrence Rd.
St Margaret Village, NS B0C 1R0
Tel: 902-383-2003; *Fax:* 902-383-4002
Ownership: Member-owned
Year Founded: 1937

Bayshore Credit Union Ltd.
PO Box 878
191 North Front St.
Belleville, ON K8N 5B5
Tel: 613-966-5550; *Fax:* 613-966-9523
www.bayshorecu.com
Social Media: www.facebook.com/BayshoreCU

Bayview Credit Union
#400, 57 King St.
Saint John, NB E2L 1G5
Tel: 506-634-1263; *Fax:* 506-634-1686
www.bayviewnb.com
Other Contact Information: BayLine Telephone Banking, Toll-Free Phone: 1-800-342-8255
Social Media: www.facebook.com/BayviewCU; twitter.com/bayviewcu
Ownership: Member-owned
Year Founded: 1938
Number of Employees: 115
Assets: $100-500 million

Beaubear Credit Union
PO Box 764
376 Water St.
Miramichi, NB E1V 3V4
Tel: 506-622-4532; *Fax:* 506-622-5008
www.beaubear.ca
Social Media: www.facebook.com/BeaubearCU
Ownership: Member-owned
Year Founded: 1938
Assets: $10-50 million

Beaumont Credit Union Limited
5007 - 50th Ave.
Beaumont, AB T4X 1E7
Tel: 780-929-8561; *Fax:* 780-929-2999
www.beaumontcu.com
Other Contact Information: 1-800-561-7849 (Credit Card Balances); 306-566-1276 (Outside Canada)
Former Name: St Vital & Beaumont Savings & Credit Union
Year Founded: 1946

Beautiful Plains Credit Union
PO Box 99
239 Hamilton St.
Neepawa, MB R0J 1H0
Tel: 204-476-3341; *Fax:* 204-476-3609
info@bpcu.mb.ca
www.bpcu.mb.ca
Year Founded: 1955
Number of Employees: 20

Belgian-Alliance Credit Union
1177 Portage Ave.
Winnipeg, MB R3G 0T2
Tel: 204-927-0460; *Fax:* 204-927-0461
info@belgianalliancecu.mb.ca
www.belgianalliancecu.mb.ca
Former Name: Alliance Credit Union; Adanac Credit Union Ltd; Communicators Credit Union; Progress Vera Credit Union
Year Founded: 2008

Bengough Credit Union Ltd.
260 Main St.
Bengough, SK S0C 0K0
Tel: 306-268-2930
bencuqlx.sasktelwebhosting.com
Year Founded: 1943

Biggar & District Credit Union Ltd.
PO Box 670
302 Main St.
Biggar, SK S0K 0M0
Tel: 306-948-3352; *Fax:* 306-948-2053
www.biggarcu.com
Social Media: www.facebook.com/BiggarCU
Ownership: Member-owned
Assets: $100-500 million

Blackville Credit Union
128 Main St.
Blackville, NB E9B 1P1
Tel: 506-843-2219; *Fax:* 506-843-6773
Ownership: Member-owned
Year Founded: 1936

Bow Valley Credit Union Limited
PO Box 876
212 - 5 Ave. West
Cochrane, AB T4C 1A9
Tel: 403-932-4693; *Fax:* 403-932-9865
www.bowvalleycu.com
Ownership: Member-owned

Bruno Savings & Credit Union Limited
PO Box 158
511 Main St.
Bruno, SK S0K 0S0
Tel: 306-369-2901; *Fax:* 306-369-2225
brunocu.com
Ownership: Member-owned

Buduchnist Credit Union (BCU)
2280 Bloor St. West
Toronto, ON M6S 1N9
Tel: 416-763-6883; *Fax:* 416-763-4512
Toll-Free: 800-461-5941
info@buduchnist.com; help@buduchnist.com (Help Desk)
www.buduchnist.com
Other Contact Information: link@buduchnist.com (BCU Link); privacyofficer@buduchnist.com (Privacy Officer)
Social Media: www.facebook.com/BCUFinancial
Ownership: Member-owned
Year Founded: 1952

Bulkley Valley Credit Union
PO Box 3637
3872 - 1st Ave.
Smithers, BC V0J 2N0
Tel: 250-847-3255; *Fax:* 250-847-3012
infoadmin@bvcu.com
www.bvcu.com

Caisse centrale Desjardins du Québec (CCD)
#600, 1170 rue Peel
Montréal, QC H3B 0B1
Tél: 514-281-7070; *Téléc:* 514-281-7083
www.desjardins.com/ccd
Ownership: Cooperatively owned by the Fédération des caisses Desjardins du Québec
Year Founded: 1979

Caisse Groupe Financier/ Caisse Financial Group
Corporate Office
#400, 205 Provencher Blvd.
Winnipeg, MB R2H 0G4
Tél: 204-237-8988; *Téléc:* 204-233-6405
Ligne sans frais: 866-926-0706
info@caisse.biz
www.caisse.biz
Former Name: Fédération des caisses populaires du Manitoba inc.
Ownership: Member-owned
Year Founded: 2010
Assets: $1-10 billion

Caisse populaire d'Alban limitée
PO Box 40
#21 Delamere Rd.
Alban, ON P0M 1A0
Tel: 705-857-2082; *Fax:* 705-857-3181
www.caissealliance.com/en/services/alban-caisse.php
Ownership: Member-owned

Caisse populaire de Bonfield limitée
230 Yonge St.
Bonfield, ON P0H 1E0
Tel: 705-776-2831; *Fax:* 705-776-1023
www.caissealliance.com/caisses/bonfield/en/index.php
Ownership: Member-owned
Number of Employees: 2

Caisse populaire de Clare
Administration Office
CP 99
1726, route 1
Church Point, NS B0W 1M0
Tél: 902-769-5312; *Téléc:* 902-769-5500
Ligne sans frais: 888-273-3488
cpcinfo@caissepopclare.com
www.caissepopclare.com
Média social: twitter.com/caissepopclare
Former Name: Caisse populaire de Saulnierville
Ownership: Member-owned
Assets: $50-100 million

Caisse populaire de Hearst limitée
PO Box 698
908 Prince St.
Hearst, ON P0L 1N0
Tel: 705-362-4308; *Fax:* 705-372-1987
www.caissealliance.com/caisses/hearst/en/index.php
Ownership: Member-owned
Number of Employees: 6

Caisse populaire de Mattawa limitée
PO Box 519
370 Main St.
Mattawa, ON P0H 1V0
Tel: 705-744-5561; *Fax:* 705-744-5168
www.caissealliance.com/en/services/mattawa-caisse.php
Ownership: Member-owned
Number of Employees: 2

Caisse populaire de Mattice limitée
PO Box 178
249 King St.
Mattice, ON P0L 1T0
Tel: 705-364-4441; *Fax:* 705-364-2013
www.caissealliance.com/en/services/mattice-caisse.php
Ownership: Member-owned
Number of Employees: 2

Caisse populaire de Noëlville limitée
87 David St. North
Noëlville, ON P0M 2N0
Tel: 705-898-2350; *Fax:* 705-898-3265
www.caissealliance.com/caisses/noelville/en/index.php
Ownership: Member-owned

Caisse populaire de Timmins limitée
45 Mountjoy St. North
Timmins, ON P4N 8H7
Tel: 705-268-9724; *Fax:* 705-268-6858
www.caissealliance.com/en/services/timmins-caisse.php
Social Media: www.facebook.com/caissetimmins
Ownership: Member-owned
Number of Employees: 2

Caisse populaire de Verner limitée
PO Box 119
1 Principale St. East
Verner, ON P0H 2M0
Tel: 705-594-2388; *Fax:* 705-594-9423
Toll-Free: 855-590-2388
www.caissealliance.com/caisses/verner/en/index.php
Ownership: Member-owned
Number of Employees: 2

Caisse populaire Kapuskasing limitée
Main Branch & Administration Office
36 Riverside Dr.
Kapuskasing, ON P5N 1A6
Tel: 705-335-6161; *Fax:* 705-335-2707
adjointe.cpkap@gmail.com
www.en.cpkap.com
Social Media: www.facebook.com/cpkap
Ownership: Member-owned
Number of Employees: 40

Caisse populaire North Bay limitée
630 Cassells St.
North Bay, ON P1B 4A2
Tel: 705-474-5650; *Fax:* 705-474-5687
www.caissealliance.com/en/services/northbay-caisse.php
Ownership: Member-owned
Number of Employees: 2

Caisse populaire St. Charles limitée
15 King St. East
St. Charles, ON P0M 2W0
Tel: 705-867-2002; *Fax:* 705-867-5710
www.caissealliance.com/en/services/stcharles-caisse.php
Ownership: Member-owned
Number of Employees: 2

Caisse populaire Sturgeon Falls limitée
241 King St.
Sturgeon Falls, ON P2B 1S1
Tel: 705-753-2970; *Fax:* 705-753-2986
www.caissealliance.com/en/services/sturgeon-caisse.php
Ownership: Member-owned
Number of Employees: 2

Cambrian Credit Union Ltd.
225 Broadway
Winnipeg, MB R3C 5R4
Tel: 204-925-2727; *Fax:* 204-231-1306
Toll-Free: 888-695-8900
ccuinfo@cambrian.mb.ca
www.cambrian.mb.ca
Other Contact Information: Lost or Stolen Member Cards, Phone: 306-566-127; Toll-Free Phone: 1-888-277-1043; Lost or Stolen MasterCards, Toll-Free Phone: 1-800-567-8111
Social Media: www.facebook.com/CambrianCreditUnion; twitter.com/CambrianCU
Ownership: Member-owned
Year Founded: 1959
Assets: $1-10 billion

Canada Safeway Limited Employees Savings & Credit Union
1822 - 10 Ave. SW
Calgary, AB T3C 0J8
Tel: 403-261-5681; *Fax:* 403-261-5748
Toll-Free: 877-723-2653
info@safewaycucalgary.com
safewaycucalgary.com
Ownership: Member-owned
Year Founded: 1952
Number of Employees: 10

Canadian Alternative Investment Cooperative
585 Dundas St. East, 3rd Fl.
Toronto, ON M4G 3V7
Tel: 416-467-7797
caic@caic.ca
www.caic.ca
Social Media: www.facebook.com/canadian.alternative
Year Founded: 1984

Canadian Credit Union Association (CCUA)(ACCF)
#1000, 151 Yonge St.
Toronto, ON M5C 2W7
Tel: 416-232-1262; *Fax:* 416-232-9196
Toll-Free: 800-649-0222
inquiries@ccua.com
www.cucentral.ca
Other Contact Information: Alt. E-mails: conferences@ccua.com; webinars@ccua.com
Social Media: www.facebook.com/CCUA.ACCF; twitter.com/CCUA_ACCF
Former Name: Credit Union Central of Canada
Ownership: Owned by the provincial credit union centrals
Year Founded: 1953
Number of Employees: 46

Carpathia Credit Union
952 Main St., 3rd Fl.
Winnipeg, MB R2W 3P4
Tel: 204-989-7400; *Fax:* 204-989-7715
info@carpathiacu.mb.ca
www.carpathiacu.mb.ca
Social Media: www.facebook.com/CarpathiaCU; twitter.com/CarpathiaCU
Ownership: Member-owned
Year Founded: 1940
Assets: $100-500 million

Casera Credit Union
1300 Plessis Rd.
Winnipeg, MB R2C 2Y6
Tel: 204-958-6300; *Fax:* 204-222-6766
Toll-Free: 866-211-9233
talktous@caseracu.ca
www.caseracu.ca
Also Known As: Transcona Credit Union
Ownership: Member-owned
Year Founded: 1951

Catalyst Credit Union
PO Box 340
505 Main St. North
Dauphin, MB R7N 2V2
Tel: 204-622-4500; *Fax:* 204-622-4530
Toll-Free: 888-273-3488
info@dpcu.ca
www.dpcu.ca
Other Contact Information: Lost credit cards: 1-800-567-8111
Former Name: Dauphin Plains Credit Union; Ethelbert Credit Union; Roblin Credit Union
Ownership: Member-owned
Year Founded: 1940

CCB Employees' Credit Union Limited
46 Overlea Blvd.
Toronto, ON M4H 1B6
Tel: 416-424-6280; *Fax:* 416-701-1944
Year Founded: 1973
Number of Employees: 2
Revenues: Under $1 million

CCEC Credit Union
2223 Commercial Dr.
Vancouver, BC V5N 4B6
Tel: 604-254-4100; *Fax:* 604-254-6558
Toll-Free: 866-254-4100
info@ccec.bc.ca
www.ccec.bc.ca
Ownership: Cooperative
Year Founded: 1976

Central 1 Credit Union - British Columbia Region
1441 Creekside Dr.
Vancouver, BC V6J 4S7
Tel: 604-734-2511; *Fax:* 604-734-5055
Toll-Free: 800-661-6813
info@central1.com
www.central1.com
Social Media: www.youtube.com/user/central1creditunion; www.facebook.com/Central1CreditUnion; twitter.com/Central1CU
Former Name: Credit Union Central of British Columbia
Ownership: Member credit unions
Year Founded: 1944
Number of Employees: 500
Assets: $10-100 billion
Revenues: $100-500 million

Central 1 Credit Union - Ontario Region
2810 Matheson Blvd. East
Mississauga, ON L4W 4X7
Tel: 905-238-9400; *Toll-Free:* 800-661-6813
communications@central1.com
www.central1.com
Other Contact Information: Direct Banking Toll-Free Phone: 888-889-7878
Social Media: www.youtube.com/user/central1creditunion; www.facebook.com/Central1CreditUnion; twitter.com/Central1CU
Former Name: Credit Union Central of Ontario
Number of Employees: 125
Assets: $10-100 billion
Revenues: $100-500 million

Chinook Financial
100 - 2nd Ave.
Strathmore, AB T1P 1K1
Tel: 403-394-3358; *Fax:* 403-394-5229
www.chinookfinancial.com
Social Media: www.facebook.com/ChinookFinancial; twitter.com/chinookcu
Ownership: Member-owned. A division of Connect First Credit Union

Church River Credit Union
305 Burnt Church Rd.
Burnt Church, NB E9G 4C8
Tel: 506-776-3247; *Fax:* 506-776-3247
Ownership: Member-owned

Churchbridge Credit Union
PO Box 260
103 Vincent Ave. East
Churchbridge, SK S0A 0M0
Tel: 306-896-2544; *Fax:* 306-896-2325
info@churchbridge.cu.sk.ca
www.churchbridgecu.ca
Year Founded: 1945

Citizens Credit Union
179 Sunbury Dr.
Fredericton Junction, NS E5L 1R5
Tel: 506-368-9000; *Fax:* 506-368-9003
Toll-Free: 800-963-4848
www.citizenscreditunion.com
Ownership: Member-owned
Year Founded: 1997

City Plus Credit Union Ltd.
800 MacLeod Trail SE, 5th Fl.
Calgary, AB T2P 2M5
Tel: 403-268-2626; *Fax:* 403-268-4886
main@cpcu.ca
www.cpcu.ca
Former Name: Calgary Civic Employees Credit Union Limited
Ownership: Private
Year Founded: 2005
Number of Employees: 5

City Savings Financial Services
6002 Yonge St.
Toronto, ON M2M 3V9
Tel: 416-225-7716; *Fax:* 416-225-7772
info@citysavingscu.com
www.citysavingscu.com
Other Contact Information: Alternate Phone: 416-225-3293
Social Media: www.facebook.com/citysavingscu
Former Name: City Savings & Credit Union Ltd.; The North York Municipal Employees' Credit Union
Also Known As: City Savings Financial Services Credit Union
Year Founded: 1950

CN (London) Credit Union Limited
#301, 205 York St.
London, ON N6A 1B1
Tel: 519-667-2326; *Fax:* 519-434-5687
www.cncu.ca
Year Founded: 1945

Coady Credit Union
135 Reserve St.
Glace Bay, NS B1A 4W3
Tel: 902-849-7610; *Fax:* 902-842-0911
Ownership: Member-owned
Year Founded: 1933

Coast Capital Savings Credit Union
Corporate Head Office
15117 - 101 Ave.
Surrey, BC V3R 8P7
Tel: 604-517-7000; *Toll-Free:* 888-517-7000
info@coastcapitalsavings.com
www.coastcapitalsavings.com
Other Contact Information: 604-517-7822 (Cantonese); 604-517-7823 (Mandarin); 604-517-7780 (Punjabi)
Ownership: Member-owned
Year Founded: 2000
Number of Employees: 2,000+

Coastal Community Credit Union
#1, 13 Victoria Cres.
Nanaimo, BC V9R 5B9
Toll-Free: 888-741-1010
www.cccu.ca
Other Contact Information: 1-888-741-4040 (Telephone Banking Toll-Free); 1-800-567-8111 (Lost Member Card, Canada & the USA); 1-800-567-8111 (Lost MasterCard, Canada & the USA)
Social Media: www.facebook.com/CoastalCommunityCU; twitter.com/cccu
Ownership: Member-owned
Year Founded: 1946
Number of Employees: 600+
Assets: $1-10 billion

Coastal Financial Credit Union
Administration Office
2 Collins St.
Yarmouth, NS B5A 3C3
Tel: 902-742-7322; *Fax:* 902-742-7476
www.coastalfinancial.ca
Social Media: www.facebook.com/252263821574742; twitter.com/coastalcu
Ownership: Member-owned
Year Founded: 2001

Number of Employees: 53
Assets: $50-100 million

Columbia Valley Credit Union
PO Box 720
511 Main St.
Golden, BC V0A 1H0
Tel: 250-344-2282; *Fax:* 250-344-2117
Toll-Free: 888-298-1777
www.cvcu.bc.ca
Other Contact Information: Telephone Banking: 1-844-344-7968; Loans Phone: 250-344-7024
Ownership: Member-owned
Year Founded: 1955
Assets: $100-500 million

Communication Technologies Credit Union Limited
Eaton Centre
PO Box 501
#102, 220 Yonge St.
Toronto, ON M5B 2H1
Tel: 416-598-1197; *Fax:* 416-598-0171
Toll-Free: 800-209-7444
member_services@comtechcu.com
www.comtechcu.com
Social Media: www.youtube.com/user/comtechcu; www.facebook.com/ComtechCU; twitter.com/comtechcu
Ownership: Member-owned
Year Founded: 1940
Number of Employees: 14
Assets: $50-100 million

Community Credit Union
150 McGettigan Blvd.
Marystown, NL A0E 2M0
Tel: 709-279-3510; *Fax:* 709-279-3721
admin@ccunl.ca
www.ccunl.ca
Ownership: Member-owned

Community Credit Union of Cumberland Colchester Limited
PO Box 578
33 Prince Arthur St.
Amherst, NS B4H 4B8
Tel: 902-667-7541; *Fax:* 902-667-1779
Toll-Free: 866-318-7541
www.communitycreditunion.ns.ca
Other Contact Information: MemberDirect Assistance, Toll-Free Phone: 1-888-273-3488
Social Media: www.facebook.com/CommunityCreditUnionOfCumberlandColchester
Former Name: Amherst Credit Union; Colchester Credit Union
Ownership: Member-owned
Year Founded: 1999
Assets: $50-100 million

Community First Credit Union Limited
289 Bay St.
Sault Ste. Marie, ON P6A 1W7
Tel: 705-942-1000; *Fax:* 705-946-2363
Toll-Free: 866-942-2328
www.communityfirst-cu.com
Social Media: www.youtube.com/user/morethanbanking
Year Founded: 1948

Community Savings Credit Union
Central City Tower
#1600, 13450 - 102nd Ave.
Surrey, BC V3T 5X3
Tel: 604-654-2000; *Fax:* 604-586-5156
Toll-Free: 888-963-2000
www.comsavings.com
Former Name: IWA & Community Credit Union
Year Founded: 1944
Number of Employees: 500

Concentra Financial
333 - 3rd Ave. North
Saskatoon, SK S7K 2M2
Toll-Free: 800-788-6311
clientsupport@concentrafinancial.ca
www.concentrafinancial.ca
Other Contact Information: Mortgage Servicing Toll Free Phone: 1-855-795-4489
Social Media: twitter.com/concentrafin
Former Name: Concentra Financial Corporate Banking; CUCORP Financial Services
Ownership: Private
Year Founded: 1997
Number of Employees: 287
Assets: $10-100 billion
Revenues: $10-50 million

Conexus Credit Union
PO Box 1960, Main Stn. Main
Regina, SK S4P 4M1
Toll-Free: 800-667-7477
www.conexus.ca
Social Media: www.youtube.com/user/ConexusCU; www.facebook.com/conexuscu; twitter.com/Conexus_CU
Former Name: Assiniboia Credit Union Ltd.
Number of Employees: 1,000

Connect First Credit Union
#200, 510 - 16 Ave. NE
Calgary, AB T2E 1K4
Tel: 403-736-4000
www.connectfirstcu.com
Ownership: Member-owned
Year Founded: 2014
Assets: $1-10 billion Year End: 20151031

Consolidated Credit Union Ltd.
305 Water St.
Summerside, PE C1N 1C1
Tel: 902-436-9218; *Fax:* 902-436-7979
shickey@consolidated.creditu.net
www.consolidatedcreditu.com
Social Media: www.facebook.com/685747588159293; twitter.com/consolidatedcu
Ownership: Member-owned
Assets: $100-500 million

Copperfin Credit Union Ltd.
346 - 2nd St. South
Kenora, ON P9N 1G5
Tel: 807-467-4400; *Fax:* 807-468-3500
Toll-Free: 888-710-6664
kenora@copperfin.ca
www.copperfin.ca
Social Media: www.facebook.com/CopperfinCreditUnion; twitter.com/CopperfinCU
Former Name: Superior Credit Union Limited; Lakewood Credit Union Ltd.
Ownership: Member-owned
Year Founded: 1954

Cornerstone Credit Union Ltd.
PO Box 455
1202 - 100 St.
Tisdale, SK S0E 1T0
Tel: 306-873-2616; *Fax:* 306-873-4322
Toll-Free: 855-875-2255
connect@cornerstonecu.com
www.cornerstonecu.com
Other Contact Information: Cornerstone Connect Telephone Assistance Toll Free Phone: 1-855-875-2255
Social Media: www.youtube.com/user/CornerstoneCUSK; www.facebook.com/cornerstonecusk; twitter.com/CornerstoneCUSK
Former Name: Tisdale Credit Union Ltd.
Ownership: Private. Member-owned
Year Founded: 1943
Assets: $100-500 million
Revenues: $1-5 million

The Credit Union
422 William St.
Dalhousie, NB E8C 2X2
Tel: 506-684-5697; *Fax:* 506-684-2438
www.thecreditu.ca
Former Name: Dalhousie Industrial Credit Union
Ownership: Member-owned

Credit Union Atlantic (CUA)
#350, 7105 Chebucto Rd.
Halifax, NS B3L 4W8
Tel: 902-492-6500; *Fax:* 902-492-6501
Toll-Free: 800-474-4282
www.cua.com
Other Contact Information: Teleservice: 902-493-4800; TeleService Toll-Free: 1-800-963-4848; MasterCard Inquiries: 1-800-561-7849; Lost MasterCards: 1-800-567-8111
Social Media: www.facebook.com/creditunionatlantic; twitter.com/cuatlantic
Ownership: Member-owned
Year Founded: 1948
Assets: $100-500 million

Credit Union Central Alberta Limited
#350N, 8500 Macleod Trail South
Calgary, AB T2H 2N1
Tel: 403-258-5900; *Fax:* 403-253-7720
email@albertacentral.com
www.albertacentral.com
Social Media: www.youtube.com/user/AlbertaCreditUnions; www.facebook.com/346088465461276; www.albertacentral.com

Ownership: Owned by the credit unions of Alberta
Number of Employees: 230
Assets: $1-10 billion

Credit Unions of Atlantic Canada
Halifax Office
PO Box 9200
6074 Lady Hammond Rd.
Halifax, NS B3K 5N3
Tel: 902-453-0680; *Fax:* 902-455-2437
Toll-Free: 800-668-2879
atlanticcreditunions.ca
Social Media: twitter.com/AtlCreditUnions
Former Name: Credit Union Central of New Brunswick; Credit Union Central of Prince Edward Island; Credit Union Central of Nova Scotia
Also Known As: Atlantic Central; Atlantic Credit Unions
Ownership: Member-owned
Year Founded: 2011
Number of Employees: 1,587
Assets: $1-10 billion

Creston & District Credit Union
PO Box 215
140 - 11th Ave. North
Creston, BC V0B 1G0
Tel: 250-428-5351; *Fax:* 250-428-5302
Toll-Free: 866-857-2802
cdcu@cdcu.com
www.cdcu.com
Ownership: Credit Union Central, BC
Year Founded: 1951

Crocus Credit Union
1016 Rosser Ave.
Brandon, MB R7A 0L6
Tel: 204-729-4800; *Fax:* 204-729-4818
Toll-Free: 877-523-1949
info@crocuscu.mb.ca
www.crocuscu.mb.ca
Other Contact Information: 1-800-567-8111 (Lost ATM Cards)
Former Name: Brandon Terminal Credit Union Society Limited
Ownership: Member-owned
Year Founded: 1952

Crossroads Credit Union Ltd.
PO Box 2006
113 - 2nd Ave. East
Canora, SK S0A 0L0
Tel: 306-563-5641; *Toll-Free:* 877-535-1299
reception@crossroadscu.ca
www.crossroadscu.ca
Other Contact Information: TeleService Toll Free Phone: 877-535-1299
Social Media: www.facebook.com/CrossroadsCU; twitter.com/CrossroadsCU
Former Name: Canora Credit Union
Ownership: Member-owned
Year Founded: 1959
Assets: $100-500 million

Crosstown Civic Credit Union
171 Donald St.
Winnipeg, MB R3C 1M4
Tel: 204-947-1243; *Fax:* 204-954-9826
171donald@crosstowncivic.mb.ca
www.crosstowncivic.mb.ca
Other Contact Information: 1-877-764-3693 (Lost ATM & Member Cards); 204-949-1048 (ExpressLine TeleService)
Former Name: Crosstown Credit Union; Civic Credit Union
Ownership: Member-owned
Year Founded: 2007
Assets: $1,800,000,000 Year End: 20131231

Cypress Credit Union Ltd.
PO Box 1060
115 Jasper St.
Maple Creek, SK S0N 1N0
Tel: 306-662-2683; *Fax:* 306-662-3859
Toll-Free: 877-353-6311
www.cypresscu.sk.ca
Number of Employees: 56

Debden Credit Union Ltd.
PO Box 100
324 Main St.
Debden, SK S0J 0S0
Tel: 306-724-8370; *Fax:* 306-724-2129
info@debden.cu.sk.ca
www.debdencu.com
Ownership: Member-owned
Number of Employees: 16
Assets: $50-100 million

Desjardins Gestion d'actifs/ Desjardins Asset Management
Tour Sud
CP 153, Desjardins Stn. Desjardins
1, complexe Desjardins
Montréal, QC H5B 1B3
Tél: 514-350-8686; *Téléc:* 514-285-3120
Ligne sans frais: 877-353-8686
info@desjardinsgestiondactifs.com
www.desjardinsgestiondactifs.com
Ownership: A subsidiary of the Desjardins Group.

Diamond North Credit Union
PO Box 2074
100 - 1 St. West
Nipawin, SK S0E 1E0
Tel: 306-862-4651; *Fax:* 306-862-9611
www.diamondnorthcu.com
Social Media: www.facebook.com/DiamondNorthCreditUnion; twitter.com/diamondnorth
Former Name: Arctic Credit Union Ltd.
Ownership: Member-owned
Year Founded: 2006
Assets: $100-500 million

Dodsland & District Credit Union Ltd.
PO Box 129
201 - 2 Ave.
Dodsland, SK S0L 0V0
Tel: 306-356-2155; *Fax:* 306-356-2202
infodesk@dodslandcreditunion.com
www.dodslandcreditunion.com
Year Founded: 1961
Number of Employees: 10

Dominion Credit Union
94 Commercial St.
Dominion, NS B1G 1B4
Tel: 902-849-8648; *Fax:* 902-842-0273
dominioncreditunion.ca
Social Media: www.facebook.com/DominionCU
Ownership: Member-owned
Year Founded: 1934

DUCA Financial Services Credit Union Ltd.
Corporate Office
5290 Yonge St.
Toronto, ON M2N 5P9
Tel: 416-223-8838; *Fax:* 416-223-2575
Toll-Free: 866-900-3822
duca.info@duca.com
duca.com
Social Media: www.youtube.com/user/DUCAFSCU; www.facebook.com/DUCACU; twitter.com/DUCACU
Former Name: Virtual One Credit Union; Duca Community Credit Union; Canadian General Tower Employees (Galt) Credit Union
Ownership: Member-owned
Year Founded: 1954
Number of Employees: 100
Assets: $500m-1 billion
Revenues: $10-50 million

Dundalk District Credit Union Limited
PO Box 340
79 Proton St. North
Dundalk, ON N0C 1B0
Tel: 519-923-2400; *Fax:* 519-923-2950
www.dundalkdistrictcreditunion.ca
Year Founded: 1943
Assets: $10-50 million
Revenues: Under $1 million

Dunnville & District Credit Union Ltd.
208 Broad St. East
Dunnville, ON N1A 1G2
Tel: 905-774-7559; *Fax:* 905-774-4662
www.ddcu.com
Ownership: Member-owned
Number of Employees: 4

Eagle River Credit Union
Head Office / L'Anse au Loup Branch
PO Box 29
8 Branch Rd.
L'Anse au Loup, NL A0K 3L0
Tel: 709-927-5524; *Fax:* 709-927-5759
Toll-Free: 877-377-3728
erinfo@ercu.ca
www.eaglerivercu.com
Ownership: Member-owned
Year Founded: 1984
Number of Employees: 40
Assets: $10-50 million
Revenues: Under $1 million

East Coast Credit Union
Administrative Office
155 Ochterloney St., 3rd & 4th Fl.
Dartmouth, NS B2Y 1C9
Tel: 902-464-7100; *Fax:* 902-464-7123
info@eastcoastcu.ca
www.eastcoastcu.ca
Other Contact Information: Port Hawkesbury Admin. Office, Phone: 902-625-5610
Social Media: www.youtube.com/channel/UCWhiQN1qpEFQvJboaMMM76Q; www.facebook.com/EastCoastCU; twitter.com/EastCoastCU
Former Name: Bergengren Credit Union
Ownership: Member-owned
Year Founded: 2003
Assets: $100-500 million

East Kootenay Community Credit Union
920 Baker St.
Cranbrook, BC V1C 1A5
Tel: 250-426-6666; *Fax:* 250-426-7370
Toll-Free: 866-960-6666
www.ekccu.com
Number of Employees: 30

EasternEdge Credit Union
31 Corey King Dr.
Mount Pearl, NL A1N 0A5
Tel: 709-739-2920; *Fax:* 709-739-3728
Toll-Free: 800-716-7283
www.easternedgecu.com
Former Name: NewTel Credit Union
Ownership: Member-owned
Year Founded: 1976
Assets: $10-50 million

Eckville District Savings & Credit Union Ltd.
PO Box 278
Eckville, AB T0M 0X0
Tel: 403-746-2288; *Fax:* 403-746-3737
info@eckvillecu.com
www.eckvillecu.com
Social Media: pinterest.com/EckvilleCU; www.youtube.com/EckvilleCU; www.facebook.com/EckvilleCU; twitter.com/EckvilleCU
Ownership: Private
Year Founded: 1943
Number of Employees: 9

Edson Credit Union
PO Box 6118
4912 - 2nd Ave.
Edson, AB T7E 1T6
Tel: 780-723-4468; *Fax:* 780-723-7973
communicate@edsoncu.com
www.edsoncu.com
Year Founded: 1943
Number of Employees: 11

Electragas Credit Union
#202, 3600 Kempt Rd.
Halifax, NS B3K 4X8
Tel: 902-454-6843; *Fax:* 902-453-5161
Ownership: Member-owned

Electric Employees Credit Union
10 Lanceleve Cres.
Albert Bridge, NS B1K 3J3
Tel: 902-564-9707; *Fax:* 902-564-0956
Ownership: Member-owned

Encompass Credit Union
Administration Office
502 - 10th St.
Wainwright, AB T9W 1P4
Tel: 780-842-3391; *Fax:* 780-842-2855
Toll-Free: 877-842-1774
askus@encompasscu.ca
www.encompasscu.ca
Social Media: www.facebook.com/175075265854665; twitter.com/EncompassCU
Former Name: Wainwright Credit Union Ltd.; Wetaskiwin Credit Union
Ownership: Member-owned
Year Founded: 2015
Number of Employees: 95
Assets: $100-500 million
Revenues: $10-50 million

Enderby & District Financial
PO Box 670
703 Mill Ave.
Enderby, BC V0E 1V0
Tel: 250-838-6841; *Fax:* 250-838-9756
www.enderbyfinancial.com
Social Media: www.facebook.com/EnderbyDistrictFinancial
Ownership: Member-owned. A division of First West Credit Union

The Energy Credit Union
#810, 2 Carlton St.
Toronto, ON M5B 1J3
Tel: 416-238-5606; *Fax:* 647-689-3065
Toll-Free: 888-942-2522
theenergycu.com
www.theenergycu.com
Other Contact Information: Telephone Banking: 416-465-8251 (Toronto area); 866-222-0630 (Toll-Free)
Former Name: The Toronto Electrical Utilities Credit Union Limited
Ownership: Member-owned
Year Founded: 1941
Number of Employees: 8

The Energy Credit Union (TECU)
14 Carlton St.
Toronto, ON M5B 1K5
Tel: 416-542-2522; *Fax:* 416-542-2735
Toll-Free: 888-942-2522
www.theenergycu.com
Former Name: Lasco Employees' Credit Union; Southlake Regional Health Centre Employees' Credit Union; Canadian Transportation Employees' Credit Union
Ownership: Member-owned
Year Founded: 1939

Entegra Credit Union
Corporate Head Office
1335 Jefferson Ave.
Winnipeg, MB R2P 1S7
Tel: 204-949-7744; *Fax:* 204-949-5865
info@entegra.ca
www.entegra.ca
Other Contact Information: Lost or Stolen MasterCard Toll Free Phone: 1-800-567-8111
Former Name: Holy Spirit Credit Union
Year Founded: 1960
Number of Employees: 47
Assets: $100-500 million

Envision Credit Union
6470 - 201st St.
Langley, BC V2Y 2X4
Tel: 604-539-7300
communications@envisionfinancial.ca
www.envisionfinancial.ca
Social Media: www.flickr.com/photos/83890812@N06/; www.youtube.com/user/envisionfinancial; www.facebook.com/envisionfinancial.ca; twitter.com/EnvisionFin
Also Known As: Envision Financial
Ownership: Member-owned. A division of First West Credit Union
Year Founded: 1946
Number of Employees: 779
Assets: $1-10 billion
Revenues: $100-500 million

Equity Credit Union
Whitetail Centre
#1, 299 Kingston Rd.
Ajax, ON L1Z 0K5
Tel: 905-426-1389; *Fax:* 905-428-1590
Toll-Free: 800-263-9793
info@equitycu.com
www.equitycu.com
Social Media: www.facebook.com/EquityCU; twitter.com/EquityCU
Former Name: Equity Financial Services; Unilever Employees Credit Union Limited
Ownership: Member-owned

Erickson Credit Union Limited
PO Box 100
24 Main St. West
Erickson, MB R0J 0P0
Tel: 204-636-7771; *Fax:* 204-636-6199
Toll-Free: 866-922-7771
info@ericksoncu.mb.ca
www.ericksoncu.mb.ca
Ownership: Member-owned
Year Founded: 1952
Number of Employees: 8

Estonian (Toronto) Credit Union Limited
#305, 958 Broadview Ave.
Toronto, ON M4K 2R6
Tel: 416-465-4659; *Fax:* 416-465-8442
Toll-Free: 866-844-3828
info@estoniancu.com
www.estoniancu.com
Social Media: www.facebook.com/114919828530607
Year Founded: 1954

Évangéline-Central Credit Union
PO Box 130
37 Mill Rd.
Wellington, PE C0B 2E0
Tel: 902-854-2595; *Fax:* 902-854-3210
evangeline@eccu.ca
www.eccu.ca
Former Name: Evangeline Credit Union; Central Credit Union Limited
Ownership: Member-owned
Year Founded: 2012
Number of Employees: 35
Assets: $100-500 million

Fédération des caisses Desjardins du Québec
100, av des Commandeurs
Lévis, QC G6V 7N5
Tél: 418-835-8444; *Ligne sans frais:* 866-835-8444
www.desjardins.com
Former Name: Fédération des Caisses Populaires Desjardins du Québec

Fédération des caisses populaires acadiennes ltée
Édifice Martin-J.-Légère
CP 5554
295, boul St-Pierre ouest
Caraquet, NB E1W 1B7
Tél: 506-726-4000; *Téléc:* 506-726-4001
www.acadie.com
Média social: www.youtube.com/user/caissespopulaires; www.instagram.com/cpacadiennes; www.facebook.com/caissespopulairesacadiennes; twitter.com/CPAcadiennes
Ownership: A subsidiary of the Desjardins Group.
Year Founded: 1946
Number of Employees: 227

Fédération des caisses populaires de l'Ontario
214 Montreal Rd.
Ottawa, ON K1L 8L8
Tél: 613-746-3276; *Ligne sans frais:* 800-423-3276
www.desjardins.com/en/votre_caisse/ontario.jsp
Ownership: A subsidiary of the Desjardins Group.
Year Founded: 1946

Fire Services Credit Union Ltd.
1997 Avenue Rd.
Toronto, ON M5M 4A3
Tel: 416-440-1294; *Fax:* 416-440-4271
Toll-Free: 866-833-3285
memberservices@firecreditunion.ca
www.firecreditunion.ca
Other Contact Information: Lost or Stolen MasterCard: 1-800-567-8111
Social Media: www.facebook.com/firecreditunion
Former Name: The Fire Department Employees Credit Union Limited
Ownership: Member-owned
Year Founded: 1941

First Calgary Financial
#200, 510 - 16th Ave. NE
Calgary, AB T2E 1K4
Tel: 403-736-4220; *Fax:* 403-276-5299
www.firstcalgary.com
Other Contact Information: Client Contact Centre Toll-Free Phone: 1-866-923-4778
Social Media: www.facebook.com/firstcalgary; twitter.com/FirstCalgary
Former Name: First Calgary Savings & Credit Union Limited
Ownership: Member-owned. A division of Connect First Credit Union
Year Founded: 1987

First Credit Union
4448A Marine Ave.
Powell River, BC V8A 2K2
Tel: 604-485-6206; *Fax:* 604-485-7112
Toll-Free: 800-393-6733
info@firstcu.ca
www.firstcu.ca
Other Contact Information: Member Services E-mail: memberservice@firstcu.ca; Lending E-mail: lending@firstcu.ca; Wealth Management E-mail: wealth @firstcu.ca
Social Media: www.facebook.com/firstcugroup; twitter.com/firstcugroup
Former Name: Powell River Credit Union Financial Group
Also Known As: First Credit Union & Insurance
Year Founded: 1939
Number of Employees: 46
Assets: $100-500 million
Revenues: $5-10 million

First West Credit Union
6470 - 201 St.
Langley, BC V2Y 2X4
Tel: 604-501-4260
communications@firstwestcu.ca
www.firstwestcu.ca
Social Media: www.flickr.com/photos/62967987@N02; twitter.com/firstwestcu
Ownership: Member-owned
Year Founded: 2010

FirstOntario Credit Union Limited
688 Queensdale Ave. East
Hamilton, ON L8V 1M1
Tel: 905-387-0770; *Toll-Free:* 800-616-8878
www.firstontariocu.com
Former Name: Rochdale Credit Union Limited; Avestel Family Savings Credit Union Limited; Family Savings & Credit Union Limited
Ownership: Member-owned
Year Founded: 1940
Number of Employees: 300
Assets: $500m-1 billion

Flin Flon Credit Union
36 Main St.
Flin Flon, MB R8A 1J6
Tel: 204-687-6620; *Fax:* 204-687-5613
Toll-Free: 888-949-0226
www.flinfloncu.mb.ca
Former Name: Alpha Credit Union Society Limited
Year Founded: 1940

Foam Lake Credit Union Ltd.
PO Box 160
402 Main St.
Foam Lake, SK S0A 1A0
Tel: 306-272-3385; *Fax:* 306-272-4948
Toll-Free: 877-722-3528
info@foamlake.cu.sk.ca
www.foamlake.cu.sk.ca
Year Founded: 1941

Forget Credit Union Ltd.
General Delivery
Stoughton, SK S0C 0X0
Tel: 306-457-2747
Year Founded: 1950

Fort York Community Credit Union Limited
Sunnyside East Wing
#207, 30 The Queensway
Toronto, ON M6R 1B5
Tel: 416-530-6474; *Fax:* 416-530-6763
fyinfo@fortyork.com
www.fortyork.com
Year Founded: 1950

Frontline Credit Union
365 Richmond Rd.
Ottawa, ON K2A 0E7
Tel: 613-729-4312; *Fax:* 613-729-5075
Toll-Free: 877-542-9249
www.frontlinecu.com
Former Name: Ottawa Fire Fighters' Credit Union Ltd.
Year Founded: 1948

G&F Financial Group
7375 Kingsway
Burnaby, BC V3N 3B5
Tel: 604-517-5100; *Fax:* 604-659-4025
inquiry@gffg.com
www.gffg.com
Social Media: www.facebook.com/GFFGcu; twitter.com/gffg
Also Known As: Gulf & Fraser Fishermen's Credit Union

Ownership: Member-owned
Year Founded: 1941
Number of Employees: 175
Assets: $1-10 billion

Ganaraska Financial Credit Union
17 Queen St.
Port Hope, ON L1A 2Y8
Tel: 905-885-8134; *Fax:* 905-885-8298
info@ganaraskacu.com
www.ganaraskacu.com
Social Media: twitter.com/ganaraskacu
Former Name: Ganaraska Credit Union
Year Founded: 1945

Glace Bay Central Credit Union
598 Main St.
Glace Bay, NS B1A 4X8
Tel: 902-849-7512; *Fax:* 902-842-9201
gbccu.ca
Social Media: www.facebook.com/GlaceBayCentralCreditUnion; twitter.com/GBCentralCU
Ownership: Member-owned
Year Founded: 1932

Goodsoil Credit Union Limited
PO Box 88
Goodsoil, SK S0M 1A0
Tel: 306-238-2033; *Fax:* 306-238-4441
info@goodsoil.cu.sk.ca
www.goodsoilcu.com
Ownership: Member-owned
Year Founded: 1946
Number of Employees: 7
Assets: $10-50 million
Revenues: Under $1 million

Govan Credit Union Ltd.
PO Box 280
125 Elgin St.
Govan, SK S0G 1Z0
Tel: 306-484-2177; *Fax:* 306-484-4333
Toll-Free: 866-298-1336
govancreditunion@govan.cu.sk.ca
govancreditunion.ca
Year Founded: 1941

Grand Forks Credit Union
PO Box 2500
447 Market Ave.
Grand Forks, BC V0H 1H0
Tel: 250-442-5511; *Fax:* 250-442-5644
Toll-Free: 866-442-5511
info@gfdscu.com
www.gfdscu.com
Year Founded: 1949

Grandview Credit Union
PO Box 159
405 Main St.
Grandview, MB R0L 0Y0
Tel: 204-546-5200; *Fax:* 204-546-5219
info@grandviewcu.mb.ca
www.grandviewcu.mb.ca

Greater Vancouver Community Credit Union
1801 Willingdon Ave.
Burnaby, BC V5C 5R3
Tel: 604-298-3344; *Fax:* 604-421-8949
info@gvccu.com
www.gvccu.com

Hamilton Sound Credit Union
PO Box 272
Carmanville, NL A0G 1N0
Tel: 709-534-2224; *Fax:* 709-534-2227
www.hscunl.ca
Social Media: www.facebook.com/141787892554975; twitter.com/HSCUNL
Ownership: Member-owned
Year Founded: 1991
Number of Employees: 20
Assets: $50-100 million

Health Care Credit Union Ltd.
PO Box 5010, B Stn. B
800 Commissioners Rd. East
London, ON N6A 5W9
Tel: 519-685-8353; *Fax:* 519-685-8153
info@healthcarecu.ca
www.healthcarecu.ca
Year Founded: 1949

Healthcare & Municipal Employees Credit Union (HMECU)
209 Limeridge Rd. East
Hamilton, ON L9A 2S6
Tel: 905-575-8888; *Fax:* 905-575-3104
Toll-Free: 866-808-2888
www.hmecu.com

Heritage Credit Union
#100, 630 - 17th St.
Castlegar, BC V1N 4G7
Tel: 250-365-7232; *Fax:* 250-365-2913
hcu@heritagecu.ca
www.heritagecu.ca
Former Name: Castlegar Savings Credit Union
Ownership: Member-owned
Year Founded: 1948
Assets: $50-100 million

Heritage Savings & Credit Union Inc. (HSCU)
318 Merritt Ave.
Chatham, ON N7M 3G1
Tel: 519-351-0600; *Fax:* 519-351-0660
www.heritagecreditunion.ca
Former Name: Municipal Employees (Chatham) Credit Union Ltd.
Ownership: Member-owned
Year Founded: 1952

Horizon Credit Union
PO Box 1900
136 - 3rd Ave. East
Melville, SK S0A 2P0
Tel: 306-728-5425; *Fax:* 306-728-4520
info@horizoncu.ca
horizoncu.ca
Former Name: Melville District Credit Union Ltd.; Aspen Prairie Credit Union Ltd.
Ownership: Co-operative. Member-owned
Year Founded: 1949
Number of Employees: 49

Hudson Bay Credit Union Ltd.
PO Box 538
208 Churchill St.
Hudson Bay, SK S0E 0Y0
Tel: 306-865-2209; *Fax:* 306-865-2381
Toll-Free: 888-368-8808
info@hudsonbay.cu.sk.ca
www.hudsonbaycu.com
Social Media: www.facebook.com/144172915642765
Year Founded: 1954
Number of Employees: 17
Assets: $10-50 million
Revenues: $1-5 million

Inglewood Savings & Credit Union
1328 - 9 Ave. SE
Calgary, AB T2G 0T3
Tel: 403-265-5396; *Fax:* 403-265-1326
manager@inglewoodcu.com
www.inglewoodcu.com
Ownership: Member-owned
Year Founded: 1938
Assets: $10-50 million

Innovation Credit Union
PO Box 638
1202 - 102nd St.
North Battleford, SK S9A 2Y7
Tel: 306-446-7000; *Fax:* 306-445-6086
Toll-Free: 866-446-7001
www.innovationcu.ca
Social Media: www.youtube.com/user/innovationfatcat; www.facebook.com/134152873262765; twitter.com/InnovationCU
Ownership: Member-owned
Year Founded: 2007

iNova Credit Union
6175 Almon St.
Halifax, NS B3K 1T8
Tel: 902-453-1145; *Fax:* 902-453-0370
Toll-Free: 800-665-1145
www.inovacreditunion.coop
Social Media: twitter.com/inovacu
Former Name: Nova Scotia Postal Employees Credit Union
Ownership: Member-owned

Integris Credit Union
1598 - 6th Ave.
Prince George, BC V2L 3N4
Tel: 250-612-3456; *Fax:* 250-612-3450
www.integriscu.ca
Former Name: Prince George Savings Credit Union; Nechako Valley Credit Union; Quesnel & District Credit Union
Year Founded: 2004

Interior Savings Credit Union
#300, 678 Bernard Ave.
Kelowna, BC V1Y 6P3
Tel: 250-869-8200; *Fax:* 250-762-9581
info@interiorsavings.com
www.interiorsavings.com
Other Contact Information: Member Service Centre Toll-Free Phone: 1-855-220-2580
Social Media: www.youtube.com/user/interiorsavingscu; www.facebook.com/InteriorSavings; twitter.com/interiorsavings
Ownership: Member-owned
Assets: $1-10 billion

Island Savings Credit Union
#300, 499 Canada Ave.
Duncan, BC V9L 1T7
Tel: 250-748-4728; *Fax:* 250-748-8831
info@iscu.com
www.iscu.com
Social Media: www.youtube.com/user/IslandSavingsBank; www.facebook.com/IslandSavings; twitter.com/Island_Savings
Ownership: Member-owned. A division of First West Credit Union.
Year Founded: 1951
Number of Employees: 300
Assets: $500m-1 billion

Kawartha Credit Union Limited
PO Box 116
1054 Monaghan Rd.
Peterborough, ON K9J 6Y5
Tel: 705-743-3643; *Fax:* 705-749-1890
Toll-Free: 855-670-0510
info@kawarthacu.com
www.kawarthacu.com
Former Name: Pedeco (Brockville) Credit Union Limited; Unity Savings & Credit Union Limited
Ownership: Member-owned
Year Founded: 1952

Kerrobert Credit Union Ltd.
PO Box 140
437 Pacific Ave.
Kerrobert, SK S0L 1R0
Tel: 306-834-2611
www.kerrobertcreditunion.ca
Year Founded: 1963

Khalsa Credit Union (Alberta) Limited
#604, 4656 Westwinds Dr. NE
Calgary, AB T3J 3Z5
Tel: 403-285-0707; *Fax:* 403-285-0771
info@kcufinancial.com
www.kcufinancial.com
Year Founded: 1995
Number of Employees: 4
Assets: $1-5 million
Revenues: $1-5 million

Kingston Community Credit Union Ltd. (KCCU)
18 Market St.
Kingston, ON K7L 1W8
Tel: 613-549-3901; *Fax:* 613-549-6593
kccu@kccu.ca
www.kccu.ca
Social Media: www.youtube.com/user/KingstonCCU; www.facebook.com/116645398353538; twitter.com/KingstonCCU
Ownership: Member-owned
Assets: $100-500 million

Kootenay Savings Credit Union
1101 Dewdney Ave.
Trail, BC V1R 4T1
Fax: 250-368-5203
Toll-Free: 888-368-5728
www.kscu.com
Other Contact Information: Collections Department Toll-Free Phone: 1-866-540-8210
Social Media: www.youtube.com/channel/UCKp-D9fk-RZU6seG3ZEcn-w; www.facebook.com/KootenaySavings; twitter.com/KootenaySavings
Ownership: Member-owned
Year Founded: 1969
Assets: $500m-1 billion

Korean (Toronto) Credit Union Limited
#202, 721 Bloor St. West
Toronto, ON M6G 1L5
Tel: 416-535-4511; *Fax:* 416-535-9323
info@koreancu.com
www.koreancu.com
Ownership: Member-owned
Year Founded: 1976

Korean Catholic Church Credit Union Limited
849 Don Mills Rd., 2nd Fl.
Toronto, ON M3C 1W1
Tel: 416-447-7788; *Fax:* 416-447-5297
kcccu@on.aibn.com
Ownership: Member-owned

Ladysmith & District Credit Union
PO Box 430
330 First Ave.
Ladysmith, BC V9G 1A3
Tel: 250-245-2247; *Fax:* 250-245-5913
Toll-Free: 888-899-2247
info@ldcu.ca
www.ldcu.ca
Year Founded: 1944

LaFleche Credit Union Ltd.
PO Box 429
105 Main St.
Lafleche, SK S0H 2K0
Tel: 306-472-5215; *Fax:* 306-472-5545
www.laflechecu.com
Ownership: Member-owned
Year Founded: 1938
Number of Employees: 12
Assets: $10-50 million

LaHave River Credit Union
29 North St.
Bridgewater, NS B4V 2V7
Tel: 902-543-3921; *Fax:* 902-543-3947
lahaverivercreditunion.ca
Social Media: www.facebook.com/LahaveRiverCreditUnion
Ownership: Member-owned

Lake View Credit Union
800 - 102nd Ave.
Dawson Creek, BC V1G 2B2
Tel: 250-782-4871; *Fax:* 250-782-5828
lakeviewcreditunion.com
Ownership: Private

Lakeland Credit Union
PO Box 8057
5016 - 50 Ave.
Bonnyville, AB T9N 2J3
Tel: 780-826-3377; *Fax:* 780-826-6322
admin@lakelandcreditunion.com
www.lakelandcreditunion.com

Landis Credit Union Ltd.
Main St.
Landis, SK S0K 2K0
Tel: 306-658-2152
www.landis.cu.sk.ca
Ownership: Member-owned
Year Founded: 1942
Number of Employees: 4
Assets: $5-10 million
Revenues: Under $1 million

Latvian Credit Union
4 Credit Union Dr.
Toronto, ON M4A 2N8
Tel: 416-922-2551; *Fax:* 416-922-2758
www.kredsab.ca
Ownership: Member-owned
Number of Employees: 7

Leading Edge Credit Union
Corporate Office
27 Grand Bay Rd., 2nd Fl.
Grand Bay East, NL A0N 1K0
Tel: 709-695-7065; *Fax:* 709-695-7078
www.lecu.ca
Social Media: www.facebook.com/LeadingEdgeCU;
twitter.com/Leadingedgecu
Former Name: Codroy Valley Credit Union; Brook Street Credit Union
Ownership: Member-owned
Assets: $50-100 million

Legacy Savings & Credit Union Ltd.
1940 - 9 Ave. SE
Calgary, AB T2G 0V2
Tel: 403-265-6050; *Fax:* 403-265-8010
admin@legacysavings.com
legacysavings.com
Social Media: www.facebook.com/399866520087378
Number of Employees: 4

Lethbridge Legion Savings & Credit Union Ltd.
324 Mayor Magrath Dr.
Lethbridge, AB T1J 3L7
Tel: 403-327-6417; *Fax:* 403-317-0122
Year Founded: 1958

Libro Credit Union Limited
217 York St., 4th Fl.
London, ON N6A 5P9
Tel: 519-672-0130; *Fax:* 519-672-7831
Toll-Free: 800-265-5935
www.libro.ca
Other Contact Information: Lost or Stolen Cards Toll-Free Phone: 800-567-8111
Social Media: www.youtube.com/user/LibroMarketing;
plus.google.com/+LibroCreditUnion;
www.facebook.com/librocreditunion; twitter.com/LibroCU
Former Name: Libro Financial Group; United Communities CU; Kellogg Employees CU; St. Willibrod CU; St. Willibrod Community CU; Hald-Nor Community CU
Ownership: Member-owned
Year Founded: 1951
Number of Employees: 625
Assets: $1-10 billion
Revenues: $500m-1 billion

LIUNA Local 183 Credit Union Limited
#108, 1263 Wilson Ave.
Toronto, ON M3M 3G2
Tel: 416-242-6643; *Fax:* 416-242-7852
info@local183cu.ca
www.local183cu.ca
Year Founded: 1978

London Fire Fighters' Credit Union Limited
400 Horton St. East
London, ON N6B 1L7
Tel: 519-661-5635; *Fax:* 519-661-5635
www.lffcu.ca
Ownership: Private
Year Founded: 1947

Luminus Financial Services & Credit Union Limited
Corporate Office
1 Yonge St.
Toronto, ON M5E 1E5
Tel: 416-366-5534; *Fax:* 416-366-6225
Toll-Free: 877-782-7639
inquiries@luminusfinancial.com
www.luminusfinancial.com
Social Media:
www.youtube.com/channel/UCyawKQZaorY45nib81sYgFQ;
www.facebook.com/ClearlyLuminus; twitter.com/clearlyLuminus
Former Name: Starnews Credit Union
Also Known As: Luminus Financial
Ownership: Member-owned
Year Founded: 2011
Assets: $50-100 million

Macklin Credit Union Ltd.
PO Box 326
4809 Herald St.
Macklin, SK S0L 2C0
Tel: 306-753-2333; *Fax:* 306-753-2676
info@macklin.cu.sk.ca
www.macklincreditunion.com
Number of Employees: 13

Mainstreet Credit Union Limited
40 Keil Dr. South
Chatham, ON N7M 3G8
Tel: 519-436-4590; *Fax:* 519-436-5451
Toll-Free: 800-592-9592
www.mainstreetcu.ca
Social Media: www.facebook.com/MainstreetCreditUnion;
twitter.com/MainSt_CUCA
Former Name: Lambton Financial CU; Unigasco CU; Sydenham Community CU; Goderich Community CU
Ownership: Member-owned
Year Founded: 1952

Malpeque Bay Credit Union
1 Commercial St.
Kensington, PE C0B 1M0
Tel: 902-836-3030; *Fax:* 902-836-5659
www.malpequebaycreditu.com
Ownership: Member-owned

Me-Dian Credit Union
303 Selkirk Ave.
Winnipeg, MB R2W 2L8
Tel: 204-943-9111; *Fax:* 204-942-3698
info@mediancu.mb.ca
www.me-diancu.mb.ca
Number of Employees: 3

Member Savings Credit Union
55 Lakeshore Blvd. East
Toronto, ON M5E 1A4
Tel: 416-864-2461; *Fax:* 416-864-6858
Toll-Free: 888-560-2218
betterbanking@membersavings.ca
membersavings.ca
Other Contact Information: Telephone Teller: 416-640-0686 or 1-888-560-2218
Year Founded: 1949
Number of Employees: 12
Assets: $50-100 million

MemberOne Credit Union Ltd.
PO Box 35
200 Front St. West, Concourse Level
Toronto, ON M5V 3K2
Tel: 416-344-4070; *Fax:* 416-344-4069
Toll-Free: 866-696-8533
info@memberone.ca
www.memberone.ca
Former Name: WCB Credit Union Limited

Mendham-Burstall Credit Union
400 Martin St.
Mendham, SK S0N 1H0
Tel: 306-679-2280
Ownership: Member-owned

Mennonite Savings & Credit Union (Ontario) Limited
1265 Strasburg Rd.
Kitchener, ON N2R 1S6
Tel: 519-746-1010; *Fax:* 519-746-1045
Toll-Free: 888-672-6728
info@mscu.com
www.mscu.com
Other Contact Information: Telephone Banking: 844-320-5380
Social Media: www.facebook.com/9958613438
Also Known As: Mennonite Savings & Credit Union
Ownership: Member-owned
Year Founded: 1964
Number of Employees: 145
Assets: $500m-1 billion
Revenues: $50-100 million

Meridian Credit Union
Centre Tower
#2700, 3300 Bloor St. West
Toronto, ON M8X 2X3
Tel: 416-597-4400; *Toll-Free:* 866-592-2226
www.meridiancu.ca
Social Media: www.youtube.com/user/MeridianBanking;
www.facebook.com/MeridianCreditUnion;
twitter.com/MeridianCU
Former Name: Desjardins Credit Union; HEPCOE Credit Union Limited; NIAGARA Credit Union
Ownership: Member-owned
Year Founded: 2005
Number of Employees: 1,100
Assets: $1-10 billion

Minnedosa Credit Union
PO Box 459
60 Main St.
Minnedosa, MB R0J 1E0
Tel: 204-867-6350; *Fax:* 204-867-6391
Toll-Free: 877-663-7228
info@minnedosacu.mb.ca
www.minnedosacu.mb.ca
Year Founded: 1947
Number of Employees: 20

Momentum Credit Union
698 King St. East
Hamilton, ON L8M 1A3
Tel: 905-529-9445; *Fax:* 905-529-9016
king@momentumcu.ca
www.momentumcu.ca

Former Name: Hamilton Community Credit Union Limited; Twin Oak Credit Union Limited
Ownership: Member-owned
Number of Employees: 15

Morell Credit Union
29 Park St.
Morell, PE C0A 1S0
Tel: 902-961-2735
www.morellcreditu.com
Ownership: Member-owned
Assets: $10-50 million

Motor City Community Credit Union Limited
6701 Tecumseh Rd. East
Windsor, ON N8T 1E8
Tel: 519-944-7455; *Fax:* 519-944-1322
info@mcccu.com
www.mcccu.com
Social Media: www.facebook.com/MotorCityCommunityCU; twitter.com/MotorCityCCU
Ownership: Member-owned
Assets: $100-500 million

Mount Lehman Credit Union
5889 Mount Lehman Rd.
Mount Lehman, BC V4X 1V7
Tel: 604-856-7761; *Fax:* 604-856-1429
www.mtlehman.com
Year Founded: 1942
Number of Employees: 12

Mountain View Credit Union Ltd.
#401, 6501 - 51 St.
Olds, AB T4H 1Y6
Tel: 403-556-3306; *Fax:* 403-556-1050
mvcu@mvcu.ca
www.mvcu.ca
Ownership: Member-owned
Year Founded: 1977
Number of Employees: 1977
Assets: $100-500 million

Mouvement des caisses Desjardins du Québec/ Desjardins Group
Also listed under: *Insurance Companies*
100, av des Commandeurs
Lévis, QC G6V 7N5
Tél: 418-835-8444; *Ligne sans frais:* 866-835-8444
www.desjardins.com
Média social: www.youtube.com/user/mouvementdesjardins; www.instagram.com/mouvementdesjardins; www.facebook.com/desjardins; twitter.com/mvtdesjardins
Ownership: Private
Year Founded: 1901
Number of Employees: 45,900
Assets: $100 billion +
Revenues: $1-10 billion

Moya Financial Credit Union Limited
747 Browns Line
Toronto, ON M8W 3V7
Tel: 416-252-6527; *Fax:* 416-252-2092
Ownership: Private
Year Founded: 2016

Nelson & District Credit Union
PO Box 350
501 Vernon St.
Nelson, BC V1L 5R2
Tel: 250-352-7207; *Fax:* 250-352-9663
Toll-Free: 877-352-7207
www.nelsoncu.com
Number of Employees: 50

New Brunswick Teachers' Association Credit Union
PO Box 752
650 Montgomery St.
Fredericton, NB E3B 5R6
Tel: 506-452-1724; *Fax:* 506-452-1732
Toll-Free: 800-565-5626
nbtacu@nbtacu.nb.ca
www.nbtacu.nb.ca
Other Contact Information: Lost or Stolen Cards, Toll-Free Phone: 1-800-567-8111
Social Media: twitter.com/NBTACreditUnion
Also Known As: NBTA Credit Union
Ownership: Member-owned
Year Founded: 1971
Number of Employees: 12
Assets: $10-50 million

New Community Credit Union
321 - 20th St. West
Saskatoon, SK S7M 0X1
Tel: 306-653-1300; *Fax:* 306-653-4711
info@newcommunity.cu.sk.ca
www.newcommunitycu.com
Former Name: New Community Savings & Credit Union Ltd.
Year Founded: 1939

New Ross Credit Union
PO Box 32
56 Forties Rd.
New Ross, NS B0J 2M0
Tel: 902-689-2949; *Fax:* 902-689-2597
www.newrosscreditunion.ca
Social Media: www.facebook.com/NewRossCreditUnionLtd
Ownership: Member-owned
Year Founded: 1956

New Waterford Credit Union
3462 Plummer Ave.
New Waterford, NS B1H 1Z6
Tel: 902-862-6453; *Fax:* 902-862-9206
www.newwaterfordcreditunion.com
Social Media: www.facebook.com/newwaterfordcreditunion
Ownership: Member-owned
Year Founded: 1934
Number of Employees: 14
Assets: $10-50 million

Nexus Community Credit Union Limited
PO Box 876
97 Duke St.
Dryden, ON P8N 2Z5
Tel: 807-223-5358; *Fax:* 807-223-5576
Toll-Free: 800-465-7225
www.nlcu.on.ca
Year Founded: 2016

Niverville Credit Union
PO Box 430
62 Main St.
Niverville, MB R0A 1E0
Tel: 204-388-4747; *Fax:* 204-388-9970
info@nivervillecu.mb.ca
www.nivervillecu.mb.ca
Year Founded: 1949

North Peace Savings & Credit Union
10344 - 100th St.
Fort St. John, BC V1J 3Z1
Tel: 250-787-0361; *Fax:* 250-787-9704
www.npscu.ca
Ownership: Private
Number of Employees: 53

North Shore Credit Union
1112 Lonsdale Ave., 3rd Fl.
North Vancouver, BC V7M 2H2
Tel: 604-983-4000; *Fax:* 604-985-6810
Toll-Free: 888-713-6728
www.nscu.com
Social Media: www.youtube.com/nscu; www.facebook.com/5624269726; twitter.com/nscu
Year Founded: 1941

North Sydney Credit Union
97 King St.
North Sydney, NS B2A 3S1
Tel: 902-794-2535; *Fax:* 902-794-9888
www.northsydneycreditunion.com
Other Contact Information: Alternate Phone: 902-794-2536
Social Media: www.facebook.com/NorthSydneyCreditUnion
Ownership: Member-owned
Assets: $10-50 million

North Valley Credit Union Limited
PO Box 1389
516 Main St.
Esterhazy, SK S0A 0X0
Tel: 306-745-6615; *Fax:* 306-745-2858
Toll-Free: 866-533-6828
www.northvalleycu.com
Former Name: Esterhazy Credit Union Limited
Ownership: Member-owned
Year Founded: 1998
Number of Employees: 13

Northern Credit Union Limited
PO Box 2200
280 McNabb St.
Sault Ste. Marie, ON P6A 5N9
Tel: 705-253-9868; *Toll-Free:* 866-413-7071
www.northerncu.com
Social Media: www.youtube.com/northerncreditunion; www.facebook.com/NorthernCreditUnion; twitter.com/northerncu
Former Name: Espanola & District Credit Union Limited; Saugeen Community Credit Union Limited
Ownership: Member-owned
Year Founded: 1957
Assets: $500m-1 billion

Northern Savings Credit Union
138 Third Ave. West
Prince Rupert, BC V8J 1K8
Tel: 250-627-3600; *Fax:* 250-627-3602
Toll-Free: 800-330-9916
info@northsave.com
www.northsave.com
Ownership: Member-owned

Noventis Credit Union Limited
PO Box 99, Railway Stn. Railway
Eriksdale, MB R0C 0W0
Tel: 204-739-2137; *Fax:* 204-739-5409
noventis.ca
Former Name: Eriksdale Credit Union Limited
Ownership: Member-owned
Year Founded: 1972
Number of Employees: 29

Oak Bank Credit Union
PO Box 217
686 Main St.
Oakbank, MB R0E 1J0
Tel: 204-444-7200; *Fax:* 204-444-3513
info@oakbankcu.mb.ca
www.oakbankcu.mb.ca
Year Founded: 1946

OMISTA Credit Union
151 Cornhill St.
Moncton, NB E1C 6L3
Tel: 506-857-3222; *Fax:* 506-857-2235
cornhillstreet@omista.com
www.omista.com
Social Media: www.facebook.com/OMISTACU; twitter.com/omistacu
Ownership: Member-owned

Ontario Educational Credit Union Limited
PO Box 360
#101, 6435 Edwards Blvd.
Mississauga, ON L5T 2P7
Tel: 905-795-1637; *Fax:* 905-795-0625
Toll-Free: 800-463-3602
www.oecu.on.ca
Year Founded: 1962
Number of Employees: 8

Ontario Provincial Police Association Credit Union Limited
123 Ferris Lane
Barrie, ON L4M 2Y1
Tel: 705-726-5656; *Fax:* 705-726-1449
Toll-Free: 800-461-4288
gd@oppacu.com
www.oppacu.com
Also Known As: O.P.P.A Credit Union
Year Founded: 1971

Osoyoos Credit Union
PO Box 360
8312 Main St.
Osoyoos, BC V0H 1V0
Tel: 250-495-6522; *Fax:* 250-495-3363
Toll-Free: 800-882-1966
contact@ocubc.com
www.osoyooscreditunion.com
Ownership: Member-owned
Year Founded: 1946

Ottawa Police Credit Union Limited
#206, 474 Elgin St.
Ottawa, ON K2P 2J6
Tel: 613-236-1222; *Fax:* 613-567-3760
www.opcu.com
Other Contact Information: Telephone Banking: 613-567-6911
Former Name: Ottawa-Carleton Police Credit Union Limited
Ownership: Private.
Year Founded: 1955
Number of Employees: 5

Revenues: $10-50 million

PACE Savings & Credit Union Limited (PCU)
#1, 8111 Jane St.
Vaughan, ON L4K 4L7
Tel: 905-738-8900; *Fax:* 905-738-8283
Toll-Free: 800-433-9122
pace.info@pacecu.com
pacecu.ca
Other Contact Information:
www.youtube.com/user/PACECreditUnion
Social Media: www.facebook.com/148726618511433; twitter.com/PACECU
Former Name: ETCU Financial Credit Union; Peoples Credit Union; McMaster Savings & Credit Union; North York Community Credit Union
Ownership: Member-owned
Year Founded: 1984
Assets: $50-100 million
Revenues: $5-10 million

Parama Lithuanian Credit Union Limited
Lithuanian House
1573 Bloor St. West
Toronto, ON M6P 1A6
Tel: 416-532-1149; *Fax:* 416-532-5595
info@parama.ca
www.parama.ca
Social Media: www.facebook.com/ParamaCreditUnion; twitter.com/paramacu
Year Founded: 1952
Number of Employees: 30
Assets: $100-500 million

PenFinancial Credit Union Limited
247 East Main St.
Welland, ON L3B 3X1
Tel: 905-735-4801; *Fax:* 905-735-2983
Toll-Free: 866-272-4275
www.penfinancial.com
Other Contact Information: Telephone Banking: 1-877-282-4226
Social Media: www.youtube.com/user/penfinancialcu; www.facebook.com/PenFinancial; twitter.com/PenFinancial
Former Name: Fort Erie Community Credit Union Limited; Cataract Savings & Credit Union; St Catharines Civic Employees' Credit Union
Ownership: Member-owned
Year Founded: 1951
Assets: $100-500 million

Peterborough Community Savings
PO Box 1600
167 Brock St.
Peterborough, ON K9J 7S4
Tel: 705-748-4481; *Fax:* 705-748-5520
www.pboccu.com
Social Media: www.facebook.com/54357791226
Former Name: Peterborough Community Credit Union Limited
Ownership: A division of Alterna Savings & Credit Union Limited
Year Founded: 1939

Pierceland Credit Union Ltd.
PO Box 10
181 Main St.
Pierceland, SK S0M 2K0
Tel: 306-839-2071; *Fax:* 306-839-2292
info@pierceland.cu.sk.ca
piercelandcu.ca
Year Founded: 1941
Number of Employees: 8

Pincher Creek Credit Union Ltd.
PO Box 1660
750 Kettles St.
Pincher Creek, AB T0K 1W0
Tel: 403-627-4431; *Fax:* 403-627-5331
www.pinchercreek-creditunion.com
Ownership: Member-owned
Year Founded: 1944
Number of Employees: 5

Plainsview Credit Union
PO Box 150
600 Main St.
Kipling, SK S0G 2S0
Tel: 306-736-2813; *Fax:* 306-736-8290
Toll-Free: 877-472-5222
info@plainsview.cu.sk.ca
www.plainsview.com

The Police Credit Union Ltd.
#103, 3650 Victoria Park Ave.
Toronto, ON M2H 3P7
Tel: 416-226-3353; *Fax:* 416-226-1565
Toll-Free: 800-561-2557
callcentre@tpcu.on.ca
www.tpcu.on.ca
Ownership: Member-owned
Year Founded: 1946
Number of Employees: 23

Porcupine Credit Union Ltd.
PO Box 189
150 McAllister Ave.
Porcupine Plain, SK S0E 1H0
Tel: 306-278-2181; *Fax:* 306-278-2944
info@porcupinecu.ca
www.porcupinecu.ca
Year Founded: 1946

Prairie Centre Credit Union
PO Box 940
Rosetown, SK S0L 2V0
Tel: 306-882-2693; *Fax:* 306-882-3326
rosetown@pccu.ca
www.pccu.ca
Ownership: Member-owned
Year Founded: 1993
Number of Employees: 75
Assets: $547,126,700 Year End: 20141231
Revenues: $40,557,498 Year End: 20141231

Prairie Pride Credit Union
PO Box 37
Alameda, SK S0C 0A0
Tel: 306-489-2131; *Fax:* 306-489-2188
info@prairiepride.cu.sk.ca
www.prairiepridecu.com
Former Name: Gainsborough Credit Union Ltd.
Year Founded: 2001
Number of Employees: 9

Princess Credit Union
22 Fraser Ave.
Sydney Mines, NS B1V 2B7
Tel: 902-736-9204; *Fax:* 902-736-2887
princesscreditunion.ca
Ownership: Member-owned
Year Founded: 1934

Progressive Credit Union
Fredericton Branch
30 Hughes St.
Fredericton, NB E3A 2W3
Tel: 506-458-9145; *Fax:* 506-459-0106
www.progressivecu.nb.ca
Social Media: www.facebook.com/ProgressiveCU; twitter.com/progressivecu
Former Name: Capital Credit Union; Carleton Pioneer Credit Union
Ownership: Member-owned
Year Founded: 1949

Provincial Credit Union Ltd.
Main Branch
281 University Ave.
Charlottetown, PE C1A 4M3
Tel: 902-892-4107; *Fax:* 902-368-3567
www.provincialcu.com
Former Name: Metro Credit Union Ltd.; Montague Credit Union; Stella Maris Credit Union
Ownership: Member-owned
Year Founded: 1968
Assets: $100-500 million

Provincial Government Employees Credit Union
1724 Granville St.
Halifax, NS B3J 1X5
Tel: 902-424-5712; *Fax:* 902-424-3662
Toll-Free: 888-484-0880
info@provincialemployees.com
www.provincialemployees.com
Other Contact Information: Lost or Stolen Cards, Toll-Free: 1-800-561-7849
Social Media: www.facebook.com/provincehouse; twitter.com/PHCU2
Former Name: Province House Credit Union Ltd.
Ownership: Member-owned

Public Service Commission Employees Credit Union
450 Cowie Hill Rd.
Halifax, NS B3K 5M1
Tel: 902-490-4813; *Fax:* 902-490-4808
Ownership: Member-owned

Public Service Credit Union Ltd.
403 Empire Ave.
St. John's, NL A1E 1W6
Tel: 709-579-8210; *Fax:* 709-579-8233
Toll-Free: 800-563-6755
pscuadmin@pscu.ca
www.pscu.ca
Other Contact Information: Loan Inquiries E-mail: loans@pscu.ca; Account Clearing E-mail: ac@pscu.ca
Ownership: Member-owned
Year Founded: 1936
Number of Employees: 18
Assets: $10-50 million
Revenues: $1-5 million

QuintEssential Credit Union Limited
293 Sidney St.
Belleville, ON K8P 3Z4
Tel: 613-966-4111; *Fax:* 613-966-8909
info@qcu.ca
www.qcu.ca

Radius Credit Union
PO Box 339
Ogema, SK S0C 1Y0
Tel: 306-459-2266; *Fax:* 306-459-2950
info@radius.cu.sk.ca
www.radiuscu.com
Year Founded: 1950

Rapport Credit Union
#1, 18 Grenville St.
Toronto, ON M4Y 3B3
Tel: 416-314-6772; *Fax:* 416-314-7805
Toll-Free: 888-516-6664
www.partneringforstrength.ca
Former Name: Ontario Civil Service Credit Union Limited; Provincial Alliance Credit Union Limited
Ownership: Cooperative
Year Founded: 2014
Assets: $100-500 million

Raymore Credit Union Ltd.
PO Box 460
121 Main St.
Raymore, SK S0A 3J0
Tel: 306-746-2160; *Fax:* 306-746-5811
Toll-Free: 866-612-2300
www.raymorecu.com
Former Name: Dysart Credit Union Ltd.
Ownership: Member-owned
Year Founded: 1949

Reddy Kilowatt Credit Union Ltd.
PO Box 126
885 Topsail Rd.
Mount Pearl, NL A1N 2C2
Tel: 709-737-5624; *Fax:* 709-737-2937
Toll-Free: 800-409-2887
rkcu@reddyk.net
www.reddyk.net
Other Contact Information: TeleService: 1-800-963-4848; Lost or Stolen Cards, Toll-Free Phone: 1-800-567-8111
Ownership: Member-owned
Year Founded: 1956

Resurrection Credit Union Limited
3 Resurrection Rd.
Toronto, ON M9A 5G1
Tel: 416-532-3400; *Fax:* 416-532-4816
Toll-Free: 877-525-7285
rpcul@rpcul.com
www.rpcul.com
Social Media:
www.facebook.com/RCULithuanianResurrectionCreditUnion
Former Name: Resurrection Parish (Toronto) Credit Union Limited
Number of Employees: 13

River City Credit Union Ltd.
11715A - 108 Ave.
Edmonton, AB T5H 1B8
Tel: 780-496-3482; *Fax:* 780-496-3477
rivercity@alberta-cu.com
www.river-citycu.com
Former Name: Edmonton Civic Employees Credit Union Ltd.
Ownership: Member-owned

Rocky Credit Union Ltd.
PO Box 1420
5035 - 49 St.
Rocky Mountain House, AB T4T 1B1
Tel: 403-845-2861; *Fax:* 403-845-7295
info@rockycu.com
www.rockycreditunion.com
Other Contact Information: Loans Department Fax: 403-845-7441; Lost or Stolen Debit Card Phone: 403-845-2861; Lost or Stolen MasterCard Toll-Free Phone: 1-800-561-7849
Social Media: www.youtube.com/user/myrockycu; www.facebook.com/rockycu
Ownership: Public
Year Founded: 1944
Number of Employees: 45
Assets: $100-500 million
Revenues: $1-5 million

Rorketon & District Credit Union
PO Box 10
691 Main St.
Rorketon, MB R0L 1R0
Tel: 204-732-2448; *Fax:* 204-732-2275
rorkinfo@rorketoncu.mb.ca
www.rorketoncu.mb.ca
Year Founded: 1961

Rosenort Credit Union Limited
PO Box 339
23 Main St.
Rosenort, MB R0G 1W0
Tel: 204-746-2355; *Fax:* 204-746-2541
Toll-Free: 800-265-7925
www.rcu.ca
Year Founded: 1940
Assets: $50-100 million

St Gregor Credit Union Ltd.
PO Box 128
119 Main St.
St Gregor, SK S0K 3X0
Tel: 306-366-2116; *Fax:* 306-366-2032
www.stgregorcu.com

St. Joseph's Credit Union
PO Box 159
3552 Hwy. 206
Petit de Grat, NS B0E 2L0
Tel: 902-226-2288; *Fax:* 902-226-9855
www.stjosephscreditu.ca
Social Media: www.facebook.com/stjosephscreditu
Ownership: Member-owned
Year Founded: 1936
Number of Employees: 12
Assets: $50-100 million

St. Stanislaus & St. Casimir's Polish Parishes Credit Union Ltd.
220 Roncesvalles Ave.
Toronto, ON M6R 2L7
Tel: 416-537-2181; *Fax:* 416-537-5022
Toll-Free: 855-765-2822
info@polcu.com
www.polcu.com
Social Media: plus.google.com/u/0/113121739802892362251; www.youtube.com/PolishCU; www.facebook.com/PolishCreditUnion; twitter.com/PolishCU
Former Name: Polish (St Catharines) Credit Union Limited
Year Founded: 1945

Sandhills Credit Union
PO Box 249
202 - 1st Ave. West
Leader, SK S0N 1H0
Tel: 306-628-3687; *Fax:* 306-628-3674
info@sandhills.cu.sk.ca
www.sandhillscu.com
Ownership: Member-owned

Sandy Lake Credit Union
PO Box 129
102 Main St.
Sandy Lake, MB R0J 1X0
Tel: 204-585-2609; *Fax:* 204-585-2163
slcunion@slcu.mb.ca
www.slcu.mb.ca

Saskatoon City Employees Credit Union
City Hall
222 - 3 Ave. North
Saskatoon, SK S7K 0J5
Tel: 306-975-3280; *Fax:* 306-975-7806
www.scecu.com
Social Media: twitter.com/scecu
Former Name: Saskatoon City Employee Credit Union Ltd.
Year Founded: 1947
Number of Employees: 9
Assets: $10-50 million
Revenues: $1-5 million

SaskCentral
PO Box 3030
2055 Albert St.
Regina, SK S4P 3G8
Tel: 306-566-1200; *Fax:* 306-566-1372
Toll-Free: 866-403-7499
www.saskcentral.com
Other Contact Information: Media Inquiries Phone: 306-566-1314
Social Media: twitter.com/saskcentral
Ownership: Owned by Saskatchewan credit unions
Assets: $1-10 billion

Servus Credit Union
151 Karl Clark Rd. NW
Edmonton, AB T6N 1H5
Tel: 780-496-2350; *Toll-Free:* 877-378-8728
contact_us@servus.ca
www.servus.ca
Other Contact Information: askafinancialplanner@servuscu.ca (Financial Planning); 780-450-9647 (TTY for the hearing impaired)
Social Media: www.instagram.com/servusalberta; www.facebook.com/ServusCU; twitter.com/servuscu
Ownership: Member-owned
Year Founded: 1938
Assets: $1-10 billion

Sharons Credit Union
Administration Office & Main Branch
1055 Kingsway
Vancouver, BC V5V 3C7
Tel: 604-873-6490; *Fax:* 604-873-6498
info@sharonscu.ca
www.sharons.ca
Year Founded: 1988
Number of Employees: 30
Assets: $100-500 million

Shaunavon Credit Union
399 Centre St.
Shaunavon, SK S0N 2N0
Tel: 306-297-2635; *Fax:* 306-297-3137
Toll-Free: 800-667-0068
contactus@myscu.ca
www.myscu.ca
Also Known As: mySCU
Ownership: Member-owned
Year Founded: 1944

Shell Employees Credit Union Limited
#117, 400 - 4 Ave. SW
Calgary, AB T2P 2H5
Tel: 403-718-7770; *Fax:* 403-262-4009
shellcu@shellcu.com
www.shellcu.com
Other Contact Information: Toll Free: 1-877-582-6222 (AB only)
Ownership: Member-owned
Year Founded: 1953

Smiths Falls Community Credit Union Limited
1 Beckwith St. North
Smiths Falls, ON K7A 2B2
Tel: 613-283-3835
Ownership: Member-owned
Year Founded: 1951

Souris Credit Union
PO Box 159
129 Main St.
Souris, PE C0A 2B0
Tel: 902-687-2721; *Fax:* 902-687-3510
www.souriscreditu.com
Ownership: Member-owned
Assets: $10-50 million

Southwest Regional Credit Union
1205 Exmouth St.
Sarnia, ON N7S 1W7
Tel: 519-383-8001; *Fax:* 519-383-8841
info@southwestcu.com
www.southwestcu.com
Year Founded: 1939
Number of Employees: 30

Spiritwood Credit Union Ltd.
PO Box 129
Spiritwood, SK S0J 2M0
Tel: 306-883-2250; *Fax:* 306-883-2223
Toll-Free: 877-288-1414
contactus@spiritwood.cu.sk.ca
www.spiritwoodcu.com
Ownership: Member-owned
Year Founded: 1938

Spruce Credit Union
879 Victoria St.
Prince George, BC V2L 2K7
Tel: 250-562-5415; *Fax:* 250-564-9977
Toll-Free: 866-562-5411
sprucecu@cucbc.com
www.sprucecu.bc.ca
Assets: $50-100 million

Squamish Savings
PO Box 1940
Squamish, BC V8B 0B4
Tel: 604-892-8350
www.vancity.com/Squamish
Other Contact Information: Telephone Banking: 604-892-8350; Squamish Insurance Phone: 604-992-8363; Member Services Toll-Free Phone: 1-888-826-2489
Former Name: Squamish Credit Union
Ownership: Private. A division of VanCity.
Number of Employees: 3

Stanco Credit Union Ltd.
Chevron Plaza, Room 759
500 - 5 Ave. SW
Calgary, AB T2P 0L7
Tel: 403-234-5300; *Fax:* 403-234-5823
info@stancocu.com
www.stancocu.com
Number of Employees: 1
Assets: $1-5 million
Revenues: Under $1 million

Starbuck Credit Union
16 Main St.
Starbuck, MB R0G 2P0
Tel: 204-735-2394; *Fax:* 204-735-4020
Toll-Free: 866-398-9642
info@starbuckcreditunion.com
www.starbuckcreditunion.com
Year Founded: 1940
Assets: $50-100 million

Steel Centre Credit Union
340 Prince St.
Sydney, NS B1P 5K9
Tel: 902-562-5559; *Fax:* 902-539-6024
www.steelcentrecreditunion.ca
Social Media: www.facebook.com/SteelCentreCreditUnion
Ownership: Member-owned
Year Founded: 1993

Steinbach Credit Union (SCU)
305 Main St.
Steinbach, MB R5G 1B1
Tel: 204-326-3495; *Fax:* 204-326-5093
Toll-Free: 800-728-6440
scu@scu.mb.ca
www.scu.mb.ca
Other Contact Information: CUbyPhone: 204-326-4310
Ownership: Member-owned
Year Founded: 1941
Assets: $1-10 billion
Revenues: $50-100 million

Stoughton Credit Union Ltd.
PO Box 420
Stoughton, SK S0G 4T0
Tel: 306-457-2443; *Fax:* 306-457-2511
info@stoughton.cu.sk.ca
www.stoughtoncu.com
Year Founded: 1960
Number of Employees: 9
Assets: $10-50 million
Revenues: $1-5 million

Strathclair Credit Union
PO Box 246
Strathclair, MB R0J 2C0
Toll-Free: 877-365-4700
www.strathclaircu.mb.ca
Assets: $500m-1 billion

Sudbury Credit Union Limited
Corporate Office
PO Box 662
1 Gribble St.
Copper Cliff, ON P0M 1N0
Tel: 705-682-0645; *Fax:* 705-682-1348
Toll-Free: 855-869-2196
info@sudburycu.com
www.sudburycu.com
Former Name: Northridge Savings & Credit Union; Sudbury Regional Credit Union; Community Saving & Credit Union
Ownership: Member-owned
Year Founded: 1951
Assets: $100-500 million

Summerland & District Credit Union
PO Box 750
13601 Victoria Rd. North
Summerland, BC V0H 1Z0
Tel: 250-494-7181; *Fax:* 250-494-4261
sdcu@sdcu.com
www.sdcu.com
Ownership: Member-owned
Year Founded: 1944
Number of Employees: 39

Sunova Credit Union Ltd.
233 Main St.
Selkirk, MB R1A 1S1
Tel: 204-785-7625; *Fax:* 204-785-7649
www.sicu.mb.ca
Social Media: www.instagram.com/sunovacu; www.facebook.com/sunovacu; twitter.com/SunovaCU
Former Name: South Interlake Credit Union Ltd.
Ownership: Member-owned
Year Founded: 1944
Assets: $1-10 billion

Sunrise Credit Union Ltd.
2305 Victoria Ave., 2nd Fl.
Brandon, MB R7B 4H7
Tel: 204-726-2030; *Fax:* 204-726-3637
info@sunrisecu.mb.ca
www.sunrisecu.mb.ca
Other Contact Information: Lost or Stolen Card: 1-800-567-8111; MasterCard: 1-800-561-7849; Telephone Banking: 1-888-748-2907
Social Media: www.youtube.com/user/Sunrisecumarketing; www.facebook.com/SunriseCreditUnion; twitter.com/sunrisecu
Former Name: Cypress River Credit Union; Hartney Credit Union; Tiger Hills Credit Union; Turtle Mountain Credit Union; Virden Credit Union
Ownership: Member-owned
Year Founded: 2008
Assets: $500m-1 billion

Sunshine Coast Credit Union
985 Gibsons Way
Gibsons, BC V0N 1V0
Tel: 604-886-2122; *Fax:* 604-886-0797
Toll-Free: 866-886-2132
inquiries@sunshineccu.net
www.sunshineccu.com
Other Contact Information: Lost or Stolen CU MasterCard or Member Debit Card Toll Free Phone: 1-800-561-7849; Telephone Banking Toll Free Phone: 1-855-590-1136
Social Media: www.facebook.com/sunshinecoastcreditunion; twitter.com/SunshineCoastCU
Ownership: Member-owned
Year Founded: 1941
Number of Employees: 83
Assets: $482,046,458 Year End: 20151231
Revenues: $100-500 million Year End: 20151231

Sydney Credit Union
PO Box 1386
95 Townsend St.
Sydney, NS B1P 6K3
Tel: 902-562-5593; *Fax:* 902-539-8448
sydney@sydneycreditunion.com
www.sydneycreditunion.com
Social Media: www.youtube.com/user/CreditUnionSydney; www.instagram.com/sydneycreditunion; www.facebook.com/SydneyCreditUnion; twitter.com/SydCreditUnion
Ownership: Member-owned
Year Founded: 1935
Assets: $100-500 million

Taiwanese - Canadian Toronto Credit Union Limited
Metro Square
#305, 3636 Steeles Ave. East
Markham, ON L3R 1K9
Tel: 905-944-0981; *Fax:* 905-944-0982
Toll-Free: 866-889-8893
tcu@on.aibn.com
www.tctcu.com
Ownership: Member-owned
Year Founded: 1978
Assets: $5-10 million
Revenues: Under $1 million

Talka Lithuanian Credit Union Limited
830 Main St. East
Hamilton, ON L8M 1L6
Tel: 905-544-7125; *Fax:* 905-544-7126
talkacu@talka.ca
www.talka.ca
Former Name: Talka Hamilton Credit Union
Year Founded: 1955

Tandem Financial Credit Union
44 Main St. East
Milton, ON L9T 1N3
Fax: 905-662-8135
Toll-Free: 800-598-2891
www.tandia.com
Other Contact Information: After-hours Online Banking Assistance: 1-877-251-5229; Board of Directors, E-mail: boardofdirectors@tandia.com
Social Media: www.facebook.com/TandiaCooperativeBanking; twitter.com/tandiatweets
Former Name: Hamilton Teachers' Credit Union Limited; Prosperity One Credit Union Limited; Halton Community Credit Union
Also Known As: Tandia
Ownership: Member-owned
Year Founded: 1957
Assets: $50-100 million

TCU Financial Group
2615 Quance St., #E
Regina, SK S4V 3B7
Tel: 306-546-7800; *Fax:* 306-525-5019
tcu@tcu.sk.ca
www.tcufinancialgroup.com
Other Contact Information: TeleService Toll-Free Phone: 844-753-4270; Lost or Stolen Member Card or Debit Card Toll-Free Phone: 877-828-4343
Ownership: Member-owned
Assets: 20141231

Teachers Plus Credit Union
#16, 36 Brookshire Ct.
Bedford, NS B4A 4E9
Tel: 902-477-5664; *Fax:* 902-477-4108
Toll-Free: 800-565-3103
www.teachersplus.ca
Former Name: Nova Scotia Teachers Credit Union
Ownership: Member-owned
Year Founded: 1956
Assets: $10-50 million

Thorold Community Credit Union
63 Front St. South
Thorold, ON L2V 0A7
Tel: 905-227-1106; *Fax:* 905-227-1109
www.thoroldcu.com
Social Media: www.facebook.com/349116621855654
Number of Employees: 7

Tignish Credit Union Ltd.
284 Business St.
Tignish, PE C0B 2B0
Tel: 902-882-2303; *Fax:* 902-882-3733
www.tignishcreditu.com
Ownership: Member-owned
Number of Employees: 37
Assets: $100-500 million

Toronto Catholic School Board Employees' Credit Union Ltd.
80 Sheppard Ave. East
Toronto, ON M2N 6E8
Tel: 416-229-5315; *Fax:* 416-512-3427
tcsbe-info@teacherscu.on.ca
www.tcsbecu.com
Former Name: Metropolitan Separate School Board Employees Credit Union Limited
Ownership: Private
Year Founded: 1972
Assets: $10-50 million

Toronto Municipal Employees' Credit Union Limited
City Hall
PO Box 30
100 Queen St. West, Main Fl.
Toronto, ON M5H 2N2
Tel: 416-392-6868; *Fax:* 416-392-6895
www.tmecu.com
Other Contact Information: Telephone Banking: 1-866-863-9119
Year Founded: 1940

TransCanada Credit Union
450 - 1st St. SW
Calgary, AB T2P 5H1
Tel: 403-920-2664; *Fax:* 403-920-2445
credit_union@transcanada.com
www.transcanadacreditunion.com
Ownership: Member-owned

Turtleford Credit Union Ltd.
PO Box 370
208 Main St.
Turtleford, SK S0M 2Y0
Tel: 306-845-2105; *Fax:* 306-845-3035
info@turtleford.cu.sk.ca
turtleford.cu.sk.ca

Ukrainian Credit Union Limited (UCU)
#300, 145 Evans Ave.
Toronto, ON M8Z 5X8
Tel: 416-922-4407; *Fax:* 416-762-1803
Toll-Free: 800-461-0777
ucucentre@ukrainiancu.com
www.ukrainiancu.com
Social Media: www.youtube.com/user/ucuykc; ucu-building-community.blogspot.ca; www.facebook.com/ucuykc; twitter.com/UCUYKC
Former Name: United Ukrainian Credit Union Limited
Ownership: Member-owned
Year Founded: 2013

Union Bay Credit Union
PO Box 158
313 McLeod Rd.
Union Bay, BC V0R 3B0
Tel: 250-335-2122; *Fax:* 250-335-2131
www.unionbaycreditunion.com
Ownership: Member-owned
Year Founded: 1944

United Employees Credit Union Limited
964 Eastern Ave.
Toronto, ON M4L 1A6
Tel: 416-461-9257; *Fax:* 416-461-8141
Toll-Free: 800-894-7644
infounited@unitedcu.com
www.unitedcu.com
Year Founded: 1944

Unity Credit Union Ltd.
PO Box 370
120 - 2nd Ave. East
Unity, SK S0K 4L0
Tel: 306-228-2688; *Fax:* 306-228-2185
www.unitycu.ca
Year Founded: 1941
Number of Employees: 31
Assets: $50-100 million
Revenues: $1-5 million

Utilities Employees' (Windsor) Credit Union Limited
4545 Rhodes Dr.
Windsor, ON N8W 5T1
Tel: 519-945-5141
Ownership: Member-owned

Valley Credit Union
5680 Hwy. #1
Waterville, NS B0P 1V0
Tel: 902-538-4510; *Fax:* 902-538-4529
www.valleycreditunion.com
Social Media: www.facebook.com/valleycreditunion; twitter.com/valleycu
Ownership: Member-owned
Year Founded: 1994
Assets: $100-500 million

Valley First Credit Union
184 Main St., 3rd Fl.
Penticton, BC V2A 8G7
Tel: 250-490-2720
info@valleyfirst.com
www.valleyfirst.com
Other Contact Information: Telephone Banking Toll-Free Phone: 1-800-667-8328; Lost or Stolen MasterCard Toll-Free Phone: 1-800-567-8111
Social Media: www.youtube.com/user/FirstWestCU; www.facebook.com/valley.first; twitter.com/Valley_First
Former Name: Valley Field Credit Union
Also Known As: Valley First Financial Group
Ownership: A division of First West Credit Union
Year Founded: 2001
Assets: $1-10 billion

Vancouver City Savings Credit Union
PO Box 2120, Terminal Stn. Terminal
183 Terminal Ave.
Vancouver, BC V6B 5R8
Tel: 604-877-7000; *Fax:* 604-877-7639
Toll-Free: 888-826-2489
www.vancity.com
Other Contact Information: Governance Practice Inquiries, E-mail: board_governance@vancity.com
Social Media: www.youtube.com/vancitycu; www.instagram.com/vancitycu; www.facebook.com/Vancity; twitter.com/Vancity
Also Known As: VanCity Credit Union
Year Founded: 1946
Assets: $1-10 billion

Vanguard Credit Union
PO Box 430
44 Maple Ave. East
Hamiota, MB R0M 0T0
Tel: 204-764-6200; *Fax:* 204-764-6250
Toll-Free: 877-226-7957
vipconnect@vanguardcu.mb.ca
www.vanguardcu.mb.ca
Social Media: www.facebook.com/VanguardCU; twitter.com/vanguardcu
Ownership: Member-owned
Year Founded: 1987
Assets: $100-500 million
Revenues: $5-10 million

VantageOne Credit Union
Main Branch
3108 - 33rd Ave.
Vernon, BC V1T 2N7
Tel: 250-545-9251; *Fax:* 250-545-1957
Toll-Free: 888-339-8328
www.vantageone.net
Other Contact Information: Memberlink Toll-Free Phone: 1-855-393-2030
Social Media: www.facebook.com/VantageOne; twitter.com/VantageOneCU
Former Name: Vernon & District Credit Union
Ownership: Co-operative. Member-owned.
Year Founded: 1944
Number of Employees: 45
Assets: $100-500 million
Revenues: $10-50 million

Venture Credit Union Limited
Administrative Offices & Eastport Branch
38 Church St.
Eastport, NL A0G 1Z0
Tel: 709-677-2849; *Fax:* 709-677-2058
www.venturecu.ca
Former Name: First Coastal Credit Union Limited; Tri-Island Credit Union Limited
Ownership: Member-owned
Assets: $10-50 million

Vermilion Credit Union Ltd.
5019 - 50 Ave.
Vermilion, AB T9X 1A7
Tel: 780-853-2822; *Fax:* 780-853-4361
www.vermilioncreditunion.com

Victory Community Credit Union
#102, 2100 Lawrence Ave. West
Toronto, ON M9N 3W3
Tel: 416-243-0686; *Fax:* 416-243-9614
creditunion@vccu.com
www.vccu.com
Year Founded: 1948
Revenues: $5-10 million

Victory Credit Union
PO Box 340
41 Gerrish St.
Windsor, NS B0N 2T0
Tel: 902-798-1820; *Fax:* 902-798-1255
www.victorycreditunion.ca
Social Media: twitter.com/VictoryCU
Ownership: Member-owned
Revenues: $10-50 million

Vision Credit Union Ltd.
5030 - 51 St.
Camrose, AB T4V 1S5
Tel: 780-672-9221; *Fax:* 780-672-9230
www.visioncu.ca
Former Name: Battle River Credit Union Ltd.; Horizon Credit Union Ltd.
Ownership: Member-owned
Year Founded: 2014
Assets: $500m-1 billion

Westminster Savings Credit Union
Corporate Centre
#108, 960 Quayside Dr.
New Westminster, BC V3M 6G2
Tel: 604-517-0100; *Fax:* 604-528-3812
Toll-Free: 877-506-0100
www.wscu.com
Other Contact Information: TelExpress Telephone Banking Toll-Free Phone: 1-877-506-0100
Social Media: www.instagram.com/westminstersavings; www.facebook.com/westminstersavings; twitter.com/wscu
Ownership: Member-owned
Year Founded: 1944
Number of Employees: 357
Assets: $1-10 billion
Revenues: $50-100 million

Westoba Credit Union Limited
220 - 10th St., #C
Brandon, MB R7A 4E8
Tel: 204-729-2050; *Fax:* 204-729-8852
Toll-Free: 877-937-8622
www.westoba.com
Social Media: www.facebook.com/WestobaCU; twitter.com/WestobaCU
Ownership: Member-owned
Year Founded: 1963
Number of Employees: 200
Assets: $500m-1 billion
Revenues: $10-50 million

Weyburn Credit Union Limited
PO Box 1117
205 Coteau Ave.
Weyburn, SK S4H 2L3
Tel: 306-842-6641; *Fax:* 306-842-6620
Toll-Free: 800-667-8842
info@weyburn.cu.sk.ca
www.weyburncu.ca
Other Contact Information: Touch Tone TeleService: 306-842-1200; Lost or stolen MemberCard or Credit Union MasterCard: 1-800-567-8111 (within Canada or Continental USA)
Ownership: Member-owned
Year Founded: 1944
Assets: $50-100 million
Revenues: $50-100 million

Weymouth Credit Union
PO Box 411
4569 Hwy. #1
Weymouth, NS B0W 3T0
Tel: 902-837-4089; *Fax:* 902-837-4094
Ownership: Member-owned

Williams Lake & District Credit Union
139 North 3rd Ave.
Williams Lake, BC V2G 2A5
Tel: 250-392-4135; *Fax:* 250-392-4361
info@wldcu.com
www.wldcu.com
Year Founded: 1952

Windsor Family Credit Union Limited
2800 Tecumseth Rd East
Windsor, ON N8W 1G4
Tel: 519-974-3100; *Fax:* 519-974-4077
www.wfcu.ca
Social Media: www.youtube.com/user/WindsorFamilyCU; www.facebook.com/WindsorFamilyCreditUnion; twitter.com/WindsorFamilyCU
Former Name: Hir-Walk Employees' (Windsor) Credit Union

Winnipeg Police Credit Union Ltd.
300 William Ave.
Winnipeg, MB R3A 1P9
Tel: 204-944-1033; *Fax:* 204-949-0821
Toll-Free: 866-491-7122
info@wpcu.ca
wpcu.ca
Year Founded: 1949

Your Credit Union Limited
14 Chamberlain Ave
Ottawa, ON K1S 1V9
Tel: 613-238-8025; *Toll-Free:* 800-379-7757
info@yourcu.com
www.yourcu.com
Ownership: Member-owned

Your Neighbourhood Credit Union Ltd.
5415 Tecumseh Rd. East
Windsor, ON N8T 1C5
Tel: 519-258-3890; *Fax:* 519-945-5933
info@yncu.com
www.yncu.com
Other Contact Information: windsor@yncu.com
Social Media: www.facebook.com/YourNCU; twitter.com/YourNCU
Former Name: boomerang CREDIT UNION Limited; Windsor & Essex Educational Credit Union
Ownership: Member-owned
Year Founded: 1953

Insurance Companies

Insurance companies are registered to conduct business under the federal Insurance Companies Act and/or corresponding provincial legislation. Life insurance companies are registered to underwrite life insurance, accident and sickness insurance and annuity business. Property and casualty insurance companies are registered to underwrite insurance other than life insurance.

Included in these listings are federally and provincially incorporated insurance companies, reinsurance companies, fraternal benefit societies and reciprocal exchanges, with the classes of insurance they offer.

*Companies marked with an * are provincially incorporated. For provincially incorporated companies not listed below, contact the government agency for each province. For further information, please see the "Government Quick Reference" guide at the beginning of Section 7, and check under "Insurance."*

Classes of insurance listed below include: Accident, Auto, Aircraft, Boiler & Machinery, Credit, Fidelity, Fire, Hail & Crop, Legal Expense, Liability, Life, Marine, Personal Accident & Sickness, Property, Reinsurance, Surety, and Theft.

Insurance Class Index

Accident
ACE INA Insurance
American Bankers Life Assurance Company of Florida
Assumption Mutual Life Insurance Company
AssurePro Insurance Company
Ayr Farmers Mutual Insurance Company
Caisse Centrale de Réassurance
The Canada Life Assurance Company
Canadian Professional Sales Association
CIGNA Life Insurance Company of Canada
Connecticut General Life Insurance Co.
Continental Casualty Company
CUMIS Life Insurance Company
Desjardins Sécurité financière
Echelon Insurance
Empire Life Insurance Company
FaithLife Financial
Federated Insurance Company of Canada
Federation Insurance Company of Canada
The Guarantee Company of North America
Innovative Insurance Agencies
Life Insurance Company of North America
Noble Insurance
The Nordic Insurance Company of Canada
Northbridge Insurance
OdysseyRe - Canadian Branch
Old Republic Insurance Company of Canada
Optimum Réassurance inc.
Pacific Blue Cross
Peace Hills General Insurance Company
Promutuel Réassurance
Promutuel Vie inc
Québec Blue Cross
SGI CANADA Consolidated
Société de l'assurance automobile du Québec

South Easthope Mutual Insurance Co.
SSQ, Société d'assurances générales inc.
SSQ, Société d'assurance-vie inc.
Tradition Mutual Insurance Company
Trillium Mutual Insurance Company
Western Financial Group Inc.
Zurich Canada

Aircraft

ACE INA Insurance
AIG Insurance Company of Canada
Allianz Global Risks US Insurance Company
Aviation & General Insurance Company Limited
Aviva Canada Inc.
Berkley Canada
Caisse Centrale de Réassurance
Canadian Universities Reciprocal Insurance Exchange
Chubb Insurance Company of Canada
Continental Casualty Company
Co-operators General Insurance Company
Elite Insurance Company
Everest Insurance Company of Canada
Everest Reinsurance Company
General Reinsurance Corporation
Great American Insurance Company
Hannover Rück SE Canadian Branch
Hartford Fire Insurance Company
Heartland Farm Mutual Insurance Company
Henderson Insurance Inc.
Johnston Meier Insurance Agencies Group
Liberty Mutual Insurance Company
Lloyd's Underwriters
Mitsui Sumitomo Insurance Co., Limited.
OdysseyRe - Canadian Branch
Old Republic Insurance Company of Canada
Omega General Insurance Company
Peace Hills General Insurance Company
The Personal Insurance Company
SGI CANADA Consolidated
State Farm Canada
TD General Insurance Company
Travelers Canada
Wedgwood Insurance Limited
Western Assurance Company
Westport Insurance Corporation
XL Reinsurance America Inc.

Auto

ACE INA Insurance
AIG Insurance Company of Canada
Alberta Motor Association Insurance Co.
Algoma Mutual Insurance Co.
Alliance Assurance
Allianz Global Risks US Insurance Company
Allstate Insurance Company of Canada
L'ALPHA, compagnie d'assurances inc.
Alpine Insurance & Financial Inc.
The American Road Insurance Company
Astro Insurance 1000 Inc.
Atlantic Insurance Company Limited
Aviva Canada Inc.
A-WIN Insurance Network
Ayr Farmers Mutual Insurance Company
Bay of Quinte Mutual Insurance Co.
Belair Insurance Company Inc.
Berkley Canada
Bertie & Clinton Mutual Insurance Company
Brant Mutual Insurance Company
British Columbia Automobile Association Insurance Agency
Butler Byers Insurance Ltd.
CAA Insurance Company (Ontario)
Caisse Centrale de Réassurance
Canadian Northern Shield Insurance Company
Canadian Professional Sales Association
La Capitale assurances générales inc.
Caradoc Delaware Mutual Fire Insurance Company
Carleton Mutual Insurance Company
Certas Direct Insurance Company
Chubb Insurance Company of Canada
Coachman Insurance Company
Coastal Community Insurance Services (2007) Ltd.
The Commonwell Mutual Insurance Group
La Compagnie d'Assurance Missisquoi
Continental Casualty Company
Co-operators General Insurance Company
CorePointe Insurance Company
COSECO Insurance Company
Crowsnest Insurance Agencies Ltd.
CUMIS General Insurance Company
The CUMIS Group Limited
CUMIS Life Insurance Company
Desjardins assurances générales inc
Desjardins Groupe d'assurances générales inc
Dufferin Mutual Insurance Company
Dumfries Mutual Insurance Company
Ecclesiastical Insurance Office plc
Echelon Insurance
Economical Mutual Insurance Company
Edge Mutual Insurance Company
Elite Insurance Company
Energy Insurance Group Ltd.
Erie Mutual Insurance Company
Everest Insurance Company of Canada
Everest Reinsurance Company
Federal Insurance Company
Federated Insurance Company of Canada
Federation Insurance Company of Canada
Fenchurch General Insurance Company
First North American Insurance Company
Fundy Mutual Insurance Company
General Reinsurance Corporation
Gibb's Agencies (1997) Ltd.
Gore Mutual Insurance Company
Great American Insurance Company
Grenville Mutual Insurance Company
Le Groupe Estrie-Richelieu, compagnie d'assurance
Groupe Promutuel, Fédération de sociétés mutuelles d'assurance générale
The Guarantee Company of North America
Halwell Mutual Insurance Company
Hannover Rück SE Canadian Branch
Hartford Fire Insurance Company
Hay Mutual Insurance Company
Heartland Farm Mutual Insurance Company
Henderson Insurance Inc.
Howard Mutual Insurance Co.
Howick Mutual Insurance Company
HTM Insurance Company
HUB International Barton Insurance Brokers
HUB International Ontario
HUB International Québec
HUB International TOS
iA Financial Group
Industrial Alliance Auto & Home Insurance
Insurance Company of Prince Edward Island
Insurance Corporation of British Columbia
Intact Insurance Company of Canada
Jevco Insurance Company
Johnston Meier Insurance Agencies Group
Kent & Essex Mutual Insurance Company
Key West Insurance Services Ltd.
Kirkham Insurance
Lambton Mutual Insurance Company
Lennox & Addington Mutual Insurance Company
Liberty Mutual Insurance Company
Lloyd's Underwriters
Manitoba Public Insurance
McFarlane & Company Financial Group Limited
McKillop Mutual Insurance Company
Meloche Monnex Inc.
Mennonite Mutual Insurance Co. (Alberta) Ltd.
Middlesex Mutual Insurance Co.
Millennium Insurance Corporation
Mitsui Sumitomo Insurance Co., Limited.
Morgex Insurance
Motors Insurance Corporation
Munich Reinsurance Company of Canada
New Diamond Insurance Services Ltd.
Noble Insurance
The Nordic Insurance Company of Canada
Norfolk Mutual Insurance Company
North Blenheim Mutual Insurance Company
North Kent Mutual Fire Insurance Company
Northbridge Insurance
Northern Savings Insurance Agency Ltd.
Novex Group Insurance
Nunavut Insurance Brokers Ltd.
OdysseyRe - Canadian Branch
Old Republic Insurance Company of Canada
Ontario Mutual Insurance Association
Ontario School Boards' Insurance Exchange
Optimum Assurance Agricole inc.
Optimum Général inc.
Optimum Société d'Assurance inc.
Optimum West Insurance Company Inc.
Pafco Insurance Company
Paragon Insurance Agencies Ltd.
PartnerRe SA
PC Financial Insurance Brokers Inc.
Peace Hills General Insurance Company
Peel Mutual Insurance Company
Pembridge Insurance Company
The Personal General Insurance Inc.
The Personal Insurance Company
Perth Insurance Company
Pilot Insurance Company
The Portage La Prairie Mutual Insurance Company
Primmum Insurance Company
Québec Blue Cross
RBC General Insurance Company
RBC Insurance
Royal & Sun Alliance Insurance Company of Canada
S&Y Insurance Company
Saskatchewan Auto Fund
Saskatchewan Mutual Insurance Company
Scottish & York Insurance Co. Limited
Security National Insurance Company
Servus Insurance Services - Home & Auto
SGI CANADA Consolidated
SGI CANADA Insurance Services Ltd. Alberta
SGI CANADA Insurance Services Ltd. British Columbia
SGI CANADA Insurance Services Ltd. Manitoba
Sirius America Insurance Company
Société de l'assurance automobile du Québec
South Easthope Mutual Insurance Co.
SSQ, Société d'assurance inc.
SSQ, Société d'assurances générales inc.
SSQ, Société d'assurance-vie inc.
Stanley Mutual Insurance Company
State Farm Canada
Suecia Reinsurance Company
TD General Insurance Company
TD Home & Auto Insurance Company
Thistle Underwriting Services
Thomson Jemmett Vogelzang
Thomson-Schindle-Green Insurance & Financial Services Ltd.
The Tokio Marine & Nichido Fire Insurance Co., Ltd.
Town & Country Mutual Insurance
Townsend Farmers' Mutual Fire Insurance Company
Traders General Insurance Company
Tradition Mutual Insurance Company
Trafalgar Insurance Company of Canada
Travelers Canada
Trillium Mutual Insurance Company
Unica Insurance Inc.
Unifund Assurance Company
United General Insurance Corporation
Usborne & Hibbert Mutual Fire Insurance Company
Virginia Surety Company, Inc.
Wabisa Mutual Insurance Company
Waterloo Insurance Company
The Wawanesa Mutual Insurance Company
Wedgwood Insurance Limited
West Elgin Mutual Insurance Company
West Wawanosh Mutual Insurance Company
Western Assurance Company
Western Financial Group Inc.
Westland Insurance
Westminster Mutual Insurance Company
Westport Insurance Corporation
XL Catlin Canada Inc.
XL Reinsurance America Inc.
Yarmouth Mutual Fire Insurance Company
Zenith Insurance Company
Zurich Canada

Boiler & Machinery

ACE INA Insurance
Affiliated FM Insurance Company
AIG Insurance Company of Canada
Allianz Global Risks US Insurance Company
Allstate Insurance Company of Canada
The American Road Insurance Company
L'Assurance Mutuelle des Fabriques de Montréal
Atlantic Insurance Company Limited
Aviva Canada Inc.
Ayr Farmers Mutual Insurance Company
Bay of Quinte Mutual Insurance Co.
Belair Insurance Company Inc.
Berkley Canada
Bertie & Clinton Mutual Insurance Company
Brant Mutual Insurance Company
Caisse Centrale de Réassurance
Canadian Farm Insurance Corp.
Caradoc Delaware Mutual Fire Insurance Company
Chubb Insurance Company of Canada
The Commonwell Mutual Insurance Group
La Compagnie d'Assurance Missisquoi
Continental Casualty Company
Co-operators General Insurance Company
CUMIS General Insurance Company
Desjardins assurances générales inc

Dufferin Mutual Insurance Company
Dumfries Mutual Insurance Company
Ecclesiastical Insurance Office plc
Economical Mutual Insurance Company
Edge Mutual Insurance Company
Elite Insurance Company
Energy Insurance Group Ltd.
Erie Mutual Insurance Company
Everest Insurance Company of Canada
Everest Reinsurance Company
Federal Insurance Company
Federated Insurance Company of Canada
Federation Insurance Company of Canada
Fenchurch General Insurance Company
FM Global
Fundy Mutual Insurance Company
General Reinsurance Corporation
Great American Insurance Company
Grenville Mutual Insurance Company
Le Groupe Estrie-Richelieu, compagnie d'assurance
The Guarantee Company of North America
Halwell Mutual Insurance Company
Hannover Rück SE Canadian Branch
Hartford Fire Insurance Company
Heartland Farm Mutual Insurance Company
Howick Mutual Insurance Company
HSB BI&I
HUB International Atlantic Limited
Kent & Essex Mutual Insurance Company
Lambton Mutual Insurance Company
Liberty Mutual Insurance Company
Lloyd's Underwriters
MAX Canada Insurance Company
McKillop Mutual Insurance Company
Mennonite Mutual Fire Insurance Company
Mitsui Sumitomo Insurance Co., Limited.
Motors Insurance Corporation
The Nordic Insurance Company of Canada
Novex Group Insurance
OdysseyRe - Canadian Branch
Omega General Insurance Company
Ontario School Boards' Insurance Exchange
Peace Hills General Insurance Company
Peel Mutual Insurance Company
The Personal General Insurance Inc.
The Personal Insurance Company
Promutuel Réassurance
Red River Valley Mutual Insurance Co.
Saskatchewan Mutual Insurance Company
Scottish & York Insurance Co. Limited
SGI CANADA Consolidated
South Easthope Mutual Insurance Co.
Southeastern Mutual Insurance Company
Stanley Mutual Insurance Company
State Farm Canada
TD General Insurance Company
Temple Insurance Company
Town & Country Mutual Insurance
Townsend Farmers' Mutual Fire Insurance Company
Tradition Mutual Insurance Company
Travelers Canada
Trillium Mutual Insurance Company
Usborne & Hibbert Mutual Fire Insurance Company
Virginia Surety Company, Inc.
The Wawanesa Mutual Insurance Company
West Wawanosh Mutual Insurance Company
Western Assurance Company
Western Financial Group Inc.
Westport Insurance Corporation
Wynward Insurance Group
XL Catlin Canada Inc.
XL Reinsurance America Inc.
Zurich Canada

Credit

ACE INA Insurance
AIG Insurance Company of Canada
The American Road Insurance Company
Assurance-Vie Banque Nationale
Assurant Solutions Canada
Berkley Canada
The Canada Life Assurance Company
Canadian Premier Life Insurance Company
CIGNA Life Insurance Company of Canada
Continental Casualty Company
CUMIS Life Insurance Company
Euler Hermes Canada
Everest Insurance Company of Canada
Everest Reinsurance Company
General Reinsurance Corporation
The Guarantee Company of North America
Novex Group Insurance
Omega General Insurance Company
Peace Hills General Insurance Company
SSQ, Société d'assurance inc.
Transatlantic Reinsurance Company
Westport Insurance Corporation
Zurich Canada

Fidelity

ACE INA Insurance
Affiliated FM Insurance Company
AIG Insurance Company of Canada
Allstate Insurance Company of Canada
ATB Financial
Atlantic Insurance Company Limited
Aviva Canada Inc.
Ayr Farmers Mutual Insurance Company
Bay of Quinte Mutual Insurance Co.
Belair Insurance Company Inc.
Berkley Canada
Bertie & Clinton Mutual Insurance Company
Brant Mutual Insurance Company
Caisse Centrale de Réassurance
Canadian Farm Insurance Corp.
Chubb Insurance Company of Canada
La Compagnie d'Assurance Missisquoi
Continental Casualty Company
Co-operators General Insurance Company
CUMIS General Insurance Company
CUMIS Life Insurance Company
Dufferin Mutual Insurance Company
Ecclesiastical Insurance Office plc
Echelon Insurance
Edge Mutual Insurance Company
Elite Insurance Company
Erie Mutual Insurance Company
Everest Reinsurance Company
Federal Insurance Company
Federated Insurance Company of Canada
Federation Insurance Company of Canada
General Reinsurance Corporation
Great American Insurance Company
Grenville Mutual Insurance Company
The Guarantee Company of North America
Halwell Mutual Insurance Company
Hannover Rück SE Canadian Branch
Hartford Fire Insurance Company
Heartland Farm Mutual Insurance Company
Howard Mutual Insurance Co.
Kent & Essex Mutual Insurance Company
Lambton Mutual Insurance Company
Liberty Mutual Insurance Company
Lloyd's Underwriters
MAX Canada Insurance Company
McKillop Mutual Insurance Company
Mitsui Sumitomo Insurance Co., Limited.
The Nordic Insurance Company of Canada
Novex Group Insurance
Omega General Insurance Company
Peace Hills General Insurance Company
Peel Mutual Insurance Company
The Personal Insurance Company
Red River Valley Mutual Insurance Co.
Saskatchewan Mutual Insurance Company
Scottish & York Insurance Co. Limited
SGI CANADA Consolidated
Sirius America Insurance Company
State Farm Canada
Suecia Reinsurance Company
Swiss Reinsurance Company Canada
TD General Insurance Company
Town & Country Mutual Insurance
Tradition Mutual Insurance Company
Travelers Canada
Trillium Mutual Insurance Company
Wabisa Mutual Insurance Company
West Elgin Mutual Insurance Company
West Wawanosh Mutual Insurance Company
Western Assurance Company
Western Financial Group Inc.
Western Surety Company
Westport Insurance Corporation
Wynward Insurance Group
XL Reinsurance America Inc.
Zurich Canada

Fire

ACE INA Insurance
Affiliated FM Insurance Company
Alberta Motor Association Insurance Co.
Antigonish Farmers' Mutual Insurance Company
L'Assurance Mutuelle des Fabriques de Montréal
British Columbia Automobile Association Insurance Agency
Caisse Centrale de Réassurance
Carleton Mutual Insurance Company
Clare Mutual Insurance Company
La Compagnie d'Assurance Missisquoi
Co-operators General Insurance Company
CUMIS General Insurance Company
CUMIS Life Insurance Company
Echelon Insurance
Federated Insurance Company of Canada
Federation Insurance Company of Canada
Germania Mutual Insurance Company
Gore Mutual Insurance Company
Le Groupe Estrie-Richelieu, compagnie d'assurance
The Guarantee Company of North America
Hartford Fire Insurance Company
HTM Insurance Company
The Kings Mutual Insurance Company
Lloyd's Underwriters
Mennonite Mutual Fire Insurance Company
Mennonite Mutual Insurance Co. (Alberta) Ltd.
The Mutual Fire Insurance Company of British Columbia
Noble Insurance
Norfolk Mutual Insurance Company
North Kent Mutual Fire Insurance Company
OdysseyRe - Canadian Branch
Ontario School Boards' Insurance Exchange
Optimum Assurance Agricole inc.
Peace Hills General Insurance Company
Prince Edward Island Mutual Insurance Company
Promutuel Réassurance
RBC General Insurance Company
Red River Valley Mutual Insurance Co.
Security National Insurance Company
Southeastern Mutual Insurance Company
SSQ, Société d'assurances générales inc.
SSQ, Société d'assurance-vie inc.
State Farm Canada
The Tokio Marine & Nichido Fire Insurance Co., Ltd.
Travelers Canada
The Wawanesa Mutual Insurance Company
Western Financial Group Inc.
Wynward Insurance Group
Zurich Canada

Hail & Crop

ACE INA Insurance
Agriculture Financial Services Corporation
AIG Insurance Company of Canada
Allianz Global Risks US Insurance Company
Astro Insurance 1000 Inc.
Aviva Canada Inc.
Ayr Farmers Mutual Insurance Company
Berkley Canada
Brant Mutual Insurance Company
Butler Byers Hail Insurance Ltd.
Clare Mutual Insurance Company
The Commonwell Mutual Insurance Group
Continental Casualty Company
Co-operative Hail Insurance Company Ltd.
Co-operators General Insurance Company
Dumfries Mutual Insurance Company
Everest Insurance Company of Canada
Everest Reinsurance Company
Federation Insurance Company of Canada
General Reinsurance Corporation
Great American Insurance Company
The Guarantee Company of North America
Hannover Rück SE Canadian Branch
Hartford Fire Insurance Company
Hay Mutual Insurance Company
Heartland Farm Mutual Insurance Company
Henderson Insurance Inc.
Howard Mutual Insurance Co.
Lambton Mutual Insurance Company
Manitoba Agricultural Services Corporation
McFarlane & Company Financial Group Limited
North Kent Mutual Fire Insurance Company
Northbridge Insurance
OdysseyRe - Canadian Branch
Optimum West Insurance Company Inc.
Palliser Insurance Company Limited
Rain & Hail Insurance Corporation
Saskatchewan Crop Insurance Corporation
Saskatchewan Municipal Hail Insurance Association
SGI CANADA Insurance Services Ltd. Alberta
SGI CANADA Insurance Services Ltd. British Columbia
SGI CANADA Insurance Services Ltd. Manitoba
Sirius America Insurance Company
Suecia Reinsurance Company

Thomson-Schindle-Green Insurance & Financial Services Ltd.
Town & Country Mutual Insurance
Townsend Farmers' Mutual Fire Insurance Company
Tradition Mutual Insurance Company
Trillium Mutual Insurance Company
West Elgin Mutual Insurance Company
Western Financial Group Inc.
Westport Insurance Corporation
XL Reinsurance America Inc.
Yarmouth Mutual Fire Insurance Company

Legal Expense

Allstate Insurance Company of Canada
Aviva Canada Inc.
Belair Insurance Company Inc.
Berkley Canada
CAA Insurance Company (Ontario)
Caisse Centrale de Réassurance
La Compagnie d'Assurance Missisquoi
Echelon Insurance
Federation Insurance Company of Canada
The Guarantee Company of North America
Lloyd's Underwriters
The Nordic Insurance Company of Canada
Novex Group Insurance
Omega General Insurance Company
The Portage La Prairie Mutual Insurance Company
Scottish & York Insurance Co. Limited

Liability

ACE INA Insurance
ACE INA Life Insurance
Affiliated FM Insurance Company
AIG Insurance Company of Canada
Alliance Assurance
Allianz Global Risks US Insurance Company
Allstate Insurance Company of Canada
Alpine Insurance & Financial Inc.
The American Road Insurance Company
Amherst Island Mutual Insurance Company
L'Assurance Mutuelle des Fabriques de Montréal
Astro Insurance 1000 Inc.
Atlantic Insurance Company Limited
Aviation & General Insurance Company Limited
Aviva Canada Inc.
A-WIN Insurance Network
Ayr Farmers Mutual Insurance Company
Bay of Quinte Mutual Insurance Co.
Belair Insurance Company Inc.
Berkley Canada
Bertie & Clinton Mutual Insurance Company
Brant Mutual Insurance Company
CAA Insurance Company (Ontario)
Caisse Centrale de Réassurance
Canadian Direct Insurance Incorporated
Canadian Farm Insurance Corp.
Canadian Northern Shield Insurance Company
Canadian Universities Reciprocal Insurance Exchange
Canassurance Insurance Company
Caradoc Delaware Mutual Fire Insurance Company
Certas Direct Insurance Company
Chubb Insurance Company of Canada
The Commonwell Mutual Insurance Group
La Compagnie d'Assurance Missisquoi
Continental Casualty Company
CorePointe Insurance Company
Crowsnest Insurance Agencies Ltd.
Desjardins assurances générales inc
Dufferin Mutual Insurance Company
Dumfries Mutual Insurance Company
Ecclesiastical Insurance Office plc
Echelon Insurance
Edge Mutual Insurance Company
Elite Insurance Company
Energy Insurance Group Ltd.
Erie Mutual Insurance Company
Everest Insurance Company of Canada
Everest Reinsurance Company
Federal Insurance Company
Federated Insurance Company of Canada
Federation Insurance Company of Canada
Fenchurch General Insurance Company
Fundy Mutual Insurance Company
General Reinsurance Corporation
Germania Mutual Insurance Company
Gore Mutual Insurance Company
Great American Insurance Company
Grenville Mutual Insurance Company
Le Groupe Estrie-Richelieu, compagnie d'assurance
The Guarantee Company of North America
Halwell Mutual Insurance Company
Hannover Rück SE Canadian Branch
Hartford Fire Insurance Company
Hay Mutual Insurance Company
Heartland Farm Mutual Insurance Company
Henderson Insurance Inc.
Howard Mutual Insurance Co.
Howick Mutual Insurance Company
HSB BI&I
HUB International Atlantic Limited
HUB International Horizon Insurance
Kent & Essex Mutual Insurance Company
The Kings Mutual Insurance Company
Lambton Mutual Insurance Company
Lawyers' Professional Indemnity Company
Legacy General Insurance Company
Lennox & Addington Mutual Insurance Company
Liberty Mutual Insurance Company
Lloyd's Underwriters
MAX Canada Insurance Company
McFarlane & Company Financial Group Limited
McKillop Mutual Insurance Company
Mennonite Mutual Insurance Co. (Alberta) Ltd.
Middlesex Mutual Insurance Co.
Mitsui Sumitomo Insurance Co., Limited.
Motors Insurance Corporation
Munich Reinsurance Company of Canada
Municipal Insurance Association of British Columbia
MUNIX Reciprocal
The Nordic Insurance Company of Canada
North Blenheim Mutual Insurance Company
North Kent Mutual Fire Insurance Company
Northbridge Insurance
Novex Group Insurance
OdysseyRe - Canadian Branch
Old Republic Insurance Company of Canada
Omega General Insurance Company
Ontario School Boards' Insurance Exchange
Optimum Général inc.
Optimum Société d'Assurance inc.
Pafco Insurance Company
Peace Hills General Insurance Company
Peel Mutual Insurance Company
The Personal General Insurance Inc.
The Personal Insurance Company
The Portage La Prairie Mutual Insurance Company
Prince Edward Island Mutual Insurance Company
Promutuel Réassurance
Québec Blue Cross
RBC General Insurance Company
Real Estate Insurance Exchange
Red River Valley Mutual Insurance Co.
Saskatchewan Mutual Insurance Company
Scottish & York Insurance Co. Limited
SGI CANADA Consolidated
Sirius America Insurance Company
Southeastern Mutual Insurance Company
SSQ, Société d'assurances générales inc.
SSQ, Société d'assurance-vie inc.
Stanley Mutual Insurance Company
State Farm Canada
Suecia Reinsurance Company
TD General Insurance Company
TD Home & Auto Insurance Company
Thomson Jemmett Vogelzang
Thomson-Schindle-Green Insurance & Financial Services Ltd.
Town & Country Mutual Insurance
Townsend Farmers' Mutual Fire Insurance Company
Tradition Mutual Insurance Company
Trans Global Insurance Company
Travelers Canada
Trillium Mutual Insurance Company
Trisura Guarantee Insurance Company
Unica Insurance Inc.
Usborne & Hibbert Mutual Fire Insurance Company
Virginia Surety Company, Inc.
Wabisa Mutual Insurance Company
The Wawanesa Mutual Insurance Company
West Elgin Mutual Insurance Company
West Wawanosh Mutual Insurance Company
Western Assurance Company
Western Financial Group Inc.
Westland Insurance
Westminster Mutual Insurance Company
Westport Insurance Corporation
Wynward Insurance Group
XL Catlin Canada Inc.
XL Reinsurance America Inc.
Yarmouth Mutual Fire Insurance Company
Zenith Insurance Company
Zurich Canada

Life

ACTRA Fraternal Benefit Society
Alberta Motor Association Insurance Co.
Allianz Life Insurance Company of North America
Alpine Insurance & Financial Inc.
American Bankers Life Assurance Company of Florida
American Health & Life Insurance Company
American Income Life Insurance Company
AMEX Assurance Company
Assumption Mutual Life Insurance Company
Assurance-Vie Banque Nationale
AVie, Financial Security Advisors
AXA Equitable Life Insurance Company
BMO Life Assurance Company of Canada
British Columbia Automobile Association Insurance Agency
British Columbia Life & Casualty Company
Butler Byers Insurance Ltd.
C Finance Inc.
CAA Insurance Company (Ontario)
Canadian Premier Life Insurance Company
Canadian Professional Sales Association
Canassurance Insurance Company
La Capitale assurances et gestion du patrimoine
La Capitale assureur de l'administration publique inc.
La Capitale Financial Security Insurance Company
CIBC Life Insurance Company Limited
CIGNA Life Insurance Company of Canada
Combined Insurance Company of America
Connecticut General Life Insurance Co.
Co-operators General Insurance Company
Co-operators Life Insurance Company
Croatian Fraternal Union of America
The CUMIS Group Limited
CUMIS Life Insurance Company
Dave P. Financial Corp.
Desjardins Sécurité financière
DPB Insurance & Financial Services
Empire Life Insurance Company
The Equitable Life Insurance Company of Canada
Excellence Life Insurance Company
FaithLife Financial
Foresters Life Insurance Company
GAN Assurances Vie Compagnie française d'assurances vie mixte
General American Life Insurance Company
Gerber Life Insurance Company
Giraffe & Friends Life Insurance Company
The Grand Orange Lodge of British America Benefit Fund
The Great-West Life Assurance Company
HollisWealth Insurance Agency Ltd.
HUB International HKMB
HUB International Horizon Insurance
Humania Assurance Inc.
iA Financial Group
Independent Order of Foresters
Insurance Company of Prince Edward Island
ivari
Johnston Meier Insurance Agencies Group
Knights of Columbus Insurance
Life Insurance Company of North America
London Life Insurance Company
Manitoba Blue Cross
Manufacturers Life Insurance Company
Manulife Canada Ltd.
Manulife Financial
McFarlane & Company Financial Group Limited
MD Insurance Agency Limited
MD Life Insurance Company
Medavie Blue Cross
Munich Reinsurance Company Canada Branch (Life)
New Diamond Insurance Services Ltd.
Nunavut Insurance Brokers Ltd.
Optimum Réassurance inc.
The Order of United Commercial Travelers of America
Pacific Blue Cross
PartnerRe SA
PC Financial Insurance Brokers Inc.
PPI
PPI Advisory
Primerica Life Insurance Company of Canada
Principal Life Insurance Company
Promutuel Vie inc
Québec Blue Cross
RBC Insurance
RBC Life Insurance Company
RBC Travel Insurance Company
Reliable Life Insurance Company
Saskatchewan Blue Cross
SCOR Global Life SE, Canada Branch
Scotia Life Insurance Company

Solicour Inc.
Sons of Scotland Benevolent Association
SSQ, Société d'assurance inc.
SSQ, Société d'assurance-vie inc.
The Standard Life Assurance Company of Canada
Sun Life Assurance Company of Canada
Sun Life Financial Inc.
Supreme Council of the Royal Arcanum
TD Life Insurance Company
Thomson-Schindle-Green Insurance & Financial Services Ltd.
TK Insurance
Trans Global Life Insurance Company
Ukrainian Fraternal Society of Canada
Ukrainian National Association
L'Union-Vie, compagnie mutuelle d'assurance
United American Insurance Company
Uv Mutuelle
Vancity Life Insurance Services Ltd.
The Wawanesa Life Insurance Company
Wedgwood Insurance Limited
Western Financial Group Inc.
Western Life Assurance Company

Marine

ACE INA Insurance
AIG Insurance Company of Canada
Allianz Global Risks US Insurance Company
Antigonish Farmers' Mutual Insurance Company
Aviva Canada Inc.
Belair Insurance Company Inc.
Butler Byers Insurance Ltd.
CAA Insurance Company (Ontario)
Canadian Universities Reciprocal Insurance Exchange
Chubb Insurance Company of Canada
Coast Underwriters Limited
Ecclesiastical Insurance Office plc
Elite Insurance Company
Everest Insurance Company of Canada
Federal Insurance Company
Great American Insurance Company
Henderson Insurance Inc.
HUB International Barton Insurance Brokers
Johnston Meier Insurance Agencies Group
Key West Insurance Services Ltd.
Lennox & Addington Mutual Insurance Company
MAX Canada Insurance Company
Northbridge Insurance
Northern Savings Insurance Agency Ltd.
Pacific Coast Fishermen's Mutual Marine Insurance Company
Paragon Insurance Agencies Ltd.
Peace Hills General Insurance Company
Sunderland Marine Insurance Company Ltd.
Swiss Reinsurance Company Canada
The Tokio Marine & Nichido Fire Insurance Co., Ltd.
Travelers Canada
Trillium Mutual Insurance Company
Wedgwood Insurance Limited
Western Assurance Company
Zurich Canada

Personal Accident & Sickness

ACE INA Life Insurance
ACTRA Fraternal Benefit Society
AIG Insurance Company of Canada
Alberta Blue Cross
Alberta Motor Association Insurance Co.
Allianz Global Risks US Insurance Company
Allianz Life Insurance Company of North America
Allstate Insurance Company of Canada
American Bankers Life Assurance Company of Florida
American Income Life Insurance Company
AMEX Assurance Company
Amherst Island Mutual Insurance Company
Assumption Mutual Life Insurance Company
Assurance-Vie Banque Nationale
AVie, Financial Security Advisors
Aviva Canada Inc.
AXA Equitable Life Insurance Company
Ayr Farmers Mutual Insurance Company
Bay of Quinte Mutual Insurance Co.
Belair Insurance Company Inc.
Berkley Canada
Bertie & Clinton Mutual Insurance Company
BMO Life Assurance Company of Canada
Brant Mutual Insurance Company
British Columbia Automobile Association Insurance Agency
British Columbia Life & Casualty Company
Butler Byers Insurance Ltd.
C Finance Inc.
CAA Insurance Company (Ontario)
The Canada Life Assurance Company
Canadian Direct Insurance Incorporated
Canadian Farm Insurance Corp.
Canadian Premier Life Insurance Company
Canadian Professional Sales Association
Canassurance Insurance Company
La Capitale assurances et gestion du patrimoine
La Capitale Financial Security Insurance Company
Caradoc Delaware Mutual Fire Insurance Company
Chubb Insurance Company of Canada
CIBC Life Insurance Company Limited
CIGNA Life Insurance Company of Canada
Combined Insurance Company of America
Connecticut General Life Insurance Co.
Continental Casualty Company
Co-operators General Insurance Company
Co-operators Life Insurance Company
Croatian Fraternal Union of America
The CUMIS Group Limited
CUMIS Life Insurance Company
Dave P. Financial Corp.
Desjardins Sécurité financière
DPB Insurance & Financial Services
Dufferin Mutual Insurance Company
Echelon Insurance
The Economical Insurance Group
Edge Mutual Insurance Company
Elite Insurance Company
Empire Life Insurance Company
Erie Mutual Insurance Company
Everest Reinsurance Company
Excellence Life Insurance Company
FaithLife Financial
Federal Insurance Company
Fenchurch General Insurance Company
First North American Insurance Company
Foresters Life Insurance Company
General Reinsurance Corporation
Gore Mutual Insurance Company
Great American Insurance Company
The Great-West Life Assurance Company
Green Shield Canada
Grenville Mutual Insurance Company
The Guarantee Company of North America
Hannover Rück SE Canadian Branch
Hartford Fire Insurance Company
Heartland Farm Mutual Insurance Company
Howard Mutual Insurance Co.
Howick Mutual Insurance Company
HUB International HKMB
HUB International Ontario
Humania Assurance Inc.
iA Financial Group
Independent Order of Foresters
Innovative Insurance Agencies
Intact Financial Corporation
ivari
Kent & Essex Mutual Insurance Company
Lambton Mutual Insurance Company
Legacy General Insurance Company
Lennox & Addington Mutual Insurance Company
Liberty Mutual Insurance Company
Life Insurance Company of North America
Lloyd's Underwriters
London Life Insurance Company
Manitoba Blue Cross
Manufacturers Life Insurance Company
McKillop Mutual Insurance Company
Medavie Blue Cross
Mitsui Sumitomo Insurance Co., Limited.
Munich Reinsurance Company Canada Branch (Life)
New Diamond Insurance Services Ltd.
Novex Group Insurance
Omega General Insurance Company
Ontario Blue Cross
Ontario Mutual Insurance Association
Optimum Réassurance inc.
The Order of United Commercial Travelers of America
Pacific Blue Cross
Pafco Insurance Company
PartnerRe SA
The Personal Insurance Company
Petsecure Pet Health Insurance
Primerica Life Insurance Company of Canada
Principal Life Insurance Company
Promutuel Vie inc
Québec Blue Cross
RBC General Insurance Company
RBC Insurance
RBC Life Insurance Company
RBC Travel Insurance Company
Reliable Life Insurance Company
Royal & Sun Alliance Insurance Company of Canada
Saskatchewan Blue Cross
SCOR Global Life SE, Canada Branch
Scotia Life Insurance Company
Security National Insurance Company
Solicour Inc.
The Sovereign General Insurance Company
SSQ, Société d'assurance inc.
SSQ, Société d'assurance-vie inc.
The Standard Life Assurance Company of Canada
Suecia Reinsurance Company
Sun Life Assurance Company of Canada
Supreme Council of the Royal Arcanum
TD General Insurance Company
TD Life Insurance Company
TK Insurance
Town & Country Mutual Insurance
Townsend Farmers' Mutual Fire Insurance Company
Trans Global Insurance Company
Trans Global Life Insurance Company
Transatlantic Reinsurance Company
Ukrainian National Association
L'Union-Vie, compagnie mutuelle d'assurance
United American Insurance Company
Usborne & Hibbert Mutual Fire Insurance Company
Uv Mutuelle
Vancity Life Insurance Services Ltd.
Wabisa Mutual Insurance Company
The Wawanesa Life Insurance Company
West Elgin Mutual Insurance Company
West Wawanosh Mutual Insurance Company
Western Assurance Company
Western Financial Group Inc.
Western Financial Insurance Company
Western Life Assurance Company
Westport Insurance Corporation
XL Catlin Canada Inc.
XL Reinsurance America Inc.
Zenith Insurance Company
Zurich Canada

Property

ACE INA Insurance
Affiliated FM Insurance Company
AIG Insurance Company of Canada
Alberta Motor Association Insurance Co.
Algoma Mutual Insurance Co.
Alliance Assurance
Allianz Global Risks US Insurance Company
Allstate Insurance Company of Canada
L'ALPHA, compagnie d'assurances inc.
Alpine Insurance & Financial Inc.
The American Road Insurance Company
Amherst Island Mutual Insurance Company
Antigonish Farmers' Mutual Insurance Company
L'Assurance Mutuelle des Fabriques de Montréal
Astro Insurance 1000 Inc.
Atlantic Insurance Company Limited
Aviva Canada Inc.
A-WIN Insurance Network
AXA Art Insurance Corporation
Ayr Farmers Mutual Insurance Company
Bay of Quinte Mutual Insurance Co.
Belair Insurance Company Inc.
Berkley Canada
Bertie & Clinton Mutual Insurance Company
Brant Mutual Insurance Company
British Columbia Automobile Association Insurance Agency
Butler Byers Insurance Ltd.
CAA Insurance Company (Ontario)
Caisse Centrale de Réassurance
Canada Guaranty Mortgage Insurance Company
Canadian Direct Insurance Incorporated
Canadian Farm Insurance Corp.
Canadian Northern Shield Insurance Company
Canadian Professional Sales Association
Canadian Universities Reciprocal Insurance Exchange
Canassurance Insurance Company
La Capitale assurances générales inc.
Caradoc Delaware Mutual Fire Insurance Company
Carleton Mutual Insurance Company
Certas Direct Insurance Company
Chicago Title Insurance Company Canada
Chubb Insurance Company of Canada
Clare Mutual Insurance Company
Coastal Community Insurance Services (2007) Ltd.
The Commonwell Mutual Insurance Group
La Compagnie d'Assurance Missisquoi
Continental Casualty Company
Co-operators General Insurance Company

Co-operators Life Insurance Company
CorePointe Insurance Company
COSECO Insurance Company
Crowsnest Insurance Agencies Ltd.
CUMIS General Insurance Company
The CUMIS Group Limited
CUMIS Life Insurance Company
Desjardins assurances générales inc
Desjardins Groupe d'assurances générales inc
Dufferin Mutual Insurance Company
Dumfries Mutual Insurance Company
Ecclesiastical Insurance Office plc
Echelon Insurance
The Economical Insurance Group
Economical Mutual Insurance Company
Edge Mutual Insurance Company
Elite Insurance Company
Energy Insurance Group Ltd.
Erie Mutual Insurance Company
Everest Insurance Company of Canada
Everest Reinsurance Company
Federal Insurance Company
Federated Insurance Company of Canada
Federation Insurance Company of Canada
Fenchurch General Insurance Company
First Canadian Title
First North American Insurance Company
FM Global
FNF Canada
Fundy Mutual Insurance Company
General Reinsurance Corporation
Genworth Financial Mortgage Insurance Company Canada
Germania Mutual Insurance Company
Gibb's Agencies (1997) Ltd.
Gore Mutual Insurance Company
Great American Insurance Company
Grenville Mutual Insurance Company
Le Groupe Estrie-Richelieu, compagnie d'assurance
Groupe Promutuel, Fédération de sociétés mutuelles d'assurance générale
The Guarantee Company of North America
Halwell Mutual Insurance Company
Hannover Rück SE Canadian Branch
Hartford Fire Insurance Company
Hay Mutual Insurance Company
Heartland Farm Mutual Insurance Company
Henderson Insurance Inc.
Howard Mutual Insurance Co.
Howick Mutual Insurance Company
HSB BI&I
HTM Insurance Company
HUB International Atlantic Limited
HUB International Barton Insurance Brokers
HUB International HKMB
HUB International Horizon Insurance
HUB International Ontario
HUB International TOS
iA Financial Group
Industrial Alliance Auto & Home Insurance
Insurance Company of Prince Edward Island
Intact Financial Corporation
Intact Insurance Company of Canada
Jevco Insurance Company
Kent & Essex Mutual Insurance Company
The Kings Mutual Insurance Company
Kirkham Insurance
Lambton Mutual Insurance Company
Legacy General Insurance Company
Lennox & Addington Mutual Insurance Company
Liberty Mutual Insurance Company
Lloyd's Underwriters
MAX Canada Insurance Company
McFarlane & Company Financial Group Limited
McKillop Mutual Insurance Company
Meloche Monnex Inc.
Mennonite Mutual Fire Insurance Company
Mennonite Mutual Insurance Co. (Alberta) Ltd.
Middlesex Mutual Insurance Co.
Millennium Insurance Corporation
Mitsui Sumitomo Insurance Co., Limited.
Morgex Insurance
Munich Reinsurance Company of Canada
MUNIX Reciprocal
The Mutual Fire Insurance Company of British Columbia
New Diamond Insurance Services Ltd.
Noble Insurance
The Nordic Insurance Company of Canada
Norfolk Mutual Insurance Company
North Blenheim Mutual Insurance Company
North Kent Mutual Fire Insurance Company
Northbridge Insurance
Northern Savings Insurance Agency Ltd.
Novex Group Insurance
Nunavut Insurance Brokers Ltd.
OdysseyRe - Canadian Branch
Old Republic Insurance Company of Canada
Omega General Insurance Company
Ontario Mutual Insurance Association
Ontario School Boards' Insurance Exchange
Optimum Assurance Agricole inc.
Optimum Général inc.
Optimum Société d'Assurance inc.
Optimum West Insurance Company Inc.
Pafco Insurance Company
PartnerRe SA
PC Financial Insurance Brokers Inc.
Peace Hills General Insurance Company
Peel Mutual Insurance Company
Pembridge Insurance Company
The Personal General Insurance Inc.
The Personal Insurance Company
Perth Insurance Company
Pets Plus Us
Pilot Insurance Company
The Portage La Prairie Mutual Insurance Company
Primmum Insurance Company
Prince Edward Island Mutual Insurance Company
Promutuel Réassurance
RBC General Insurance Company
RBC Insurance
Red River Valley Mutual Insurance Co.
Royal & Sun Alliance Insurance Company of Canada
Saskatchewan Mutual Insurance Company
Scottish & York Insurance Co. Limited
Security National Insurance Company
Servus Insurance Services - Home & Auto
SGI CANADA Consolidated
SGI CANADA Insurance Services Ltd. Alberta
SGI CANADA Insurance Services Ltd. British Columbia
SGI CANADA Insurance Services Ltd. Manitoba
Sirius America Insurance Company
South Easthope Mutual Insurance Co.
Southeastern Mutual Insurance Company
The Sovereign General Insurance Company
SSQ, Société d'assurance inc.
SSQ, Société d'assurances générales inc.
SSQ, Société d'assurance-vie inc.
Stanley Mutual Insurance Company
State Farm Canada
Stewart Title Guaranty Company
Suecia Reinsurance Company
Swiss Reinsurance Company Canada
TD General Insurance Company
TD Home & Auto Insurance Company
Temple Insurance Company
Thistle Home
Thistle Underwriting Services
Thomson Jemmett Vogelzang
Thomson-Schindle-Green Insurance & Financial Services Ltd.
The Tokio Marine & Nichido Fire Insurance Co., Ltd.
Town & Country Mutual Insurance
Townsend Farmers' Mutual Fire Insurance Company
Traders General Insurance Company
Tradition Mutual Insurance Company
Trafalgar Insurance Company of Canada
Trans Global Insurance Company
Transatlantic Reinsurance Company
Travelers Canada
Trillium Mutual Insurance Company
Unica Insurance Inc.
Unifund Assurance Company
Usborne & Hibbert Mutual Fire Insurance Company
Virginia Surety Company, Inc.
Wabisa Mutual Insurance Company
Waterloo Insurance Company
The Wawanesa Mutual Insurance Company
Wedgwood Insurance Limited
West Elgin Mutual Insurance Company
West Wawanosh Mutual Insurance Company
Western Assurance Company
Western Financial Group Inc.
Westland Insurance
Westminster Mutual Insurance Company
Westport Insurance Corporation
Wynward Insurance Group
XL Catlin Canada Inc.
XL Reinsurance America Inc.
Yarmouth Mutual Fire Insurance Company
Zenith Insurance Company
Zurich Canada

Reinsurance

Aurigen Reinsurance Company
General American Life Insurance Company
HUB International HKMB
Key West Insurance Services Ltd.
Lloyd's Underwriters
London Life Insurance Company
Munich Reinsurance Company Canada Branch (Life)
OdysseyRe - Canadian Branch
Old Republic Insurance Company of Canada
Optimum Re inc.
Optimum Réassurance inc.
Paragon Insurance Agencies Ltd.
Promutuel Réassurance
RGA Life Reinsurance Company of Canada
SCOR Canada Reinsurance Company
SGI CANADA Consolidated
Suecia Reinsurance Company
Swiss Reinsurance Company Canada
The Toa Reinsurance Company of America (Canada Branch)
Transatlantic Reinsurance Company
Travelers Canada
L'Union-Vie, compagnie mutuelle d'assurance

Surety

ACE INA Insurance
Affiliated FM Insurance Company
AIG Insurance Company of Canada
Allianz Global Risks US Insurance Company
Allstate Insurance Company of Canada
L'ALPHA, compagnie d'assurances inc.
The American Road Insurance Company
Atlantic Insurance Company Limited
Aviva Canada Inc.
Belair Insurance Company Inc.
Berkley Canada
CAA Insurance Company (Ontario)
Caisse Centrale de Réassurance
Canadian Farm Insurance Corp.
Certas Direct Insurance Company
Chicago Title Insurance Company Canada
Chubb Insurance Company of Canada
La Compagnie d'Assurance Missisquoi
Continental Casualty Company
Co-operators General Insurance Company
CorePointe Insurance Company
Desjardins assurances générales inc
Echelon Insurance
Economical Mutual Insurance Company
Elite Insurance Company
Everest Insurance Company of Canada
Everest Reinsurance Company
Federal Insurance Company
Federated Insurance Company of Canada
Federation Insurance Company of Canada
Fenchurch General Insurance Company
General Reinsurance Corporation
Great American Insurance Company
The Guarantee Company of North America
Hannover Rück SE Canadian Branch
Hartford Fire Insurance Company
Johnston Meier Insurance Agencies Group
Liberty Mutual Insurance Company
Lloyd's Underwriters
McFarlane & Company Financial Group Limited
Mitsui Sumitomo Insurance Co., Limited.
The Nordic Insurance Company of Canada
Novex Group Insurance
OdysseyRe - Canadian Branch
Omega General Insurance Company
Peace Hills General Insurance Company
The Personal General Insurance Inc.
The Personal Insurance Company
Promutuel Réassurance
Red River Valley Mutual Insurance Co.
Scottish & York Insurance Co. Limited
SGI CANADA Consolidated
SGI CANADA Insurance Services Ltd. Alberta
SGI CANADA Insurance Services Ltd. British Columbia
SGI CANADA Insurance Services Ltd. Manitoba
Sirius America Insurance Company
State Farm Canada
Swiss Reinsurance Company Canada
TD General Insurance Company
Transatlantic Reinsurance Company
Travelers Canada
Trisura Guarantee Insurance Company
The Wawanesa Mutual Insurance Company
Western Assurance Company
Western Financial Group Inc.
Western Surety Company

Westport Insurance Corporation
Wynward Insurance Group
XL Catlin Canada Inc.
XL Reinsurance America Inc.
Zurich Canada

Theft
L'Assurance Mutuelle des Fabriques de Montréal
The Commonwell Mutual Insurance Group
La Compagnie d'Assurance Missisquoi
Co-operators General Insurance Company
CUMIS General Insurance Company
CUMIS Life Insurance Company
Federated Insurance Company of Canada
Germania Mutual Insurance Company
Gore Mutual Insurance Company
The Guarantee Company of North America
Hartford Fire Insurance Company
Mennonite Mutual Fire Insurance Company
Munich Reinsurance Company of Canada
North Kent Mutual Fire Insurance Company
Peace Hills General Insurance Company
Prince Edward Island Mutual Insurance Company
Promutuel Réassurance
RBC General Insurance Company
Red River Valley Mutual Insurance Co.
SSQ, Société d'assurances générales inc.
Trafalgar Insurance Company of Canada
The Wawanesa Mutual Insurance Company
Western Financial Group Inc.
Wynward Insurance Group
Zurich Canada

Federal and Provincial Insurance Companies

***ACE INA Insurance**
#1400, 25 York St.
Toronto, ON M5J 2V5
Tel: 416-368-2911; *Fax:* 416-594-2600
www.acegroup.com/ca-en
Classes of Insurance: Accident, Aircraft, Auto, Liability, Boiler & Machinery, Credit, Marine, Fidelity, Property, Fire, Surety, Hail & Crop

***ACE INA Life Insurance/ Assurance-vie ACE INA**
#1400, 25 York St.
Toronto, ON M5J 2V5
Tel: 416-368-2911; *Fax:* 416-594-2600
www.acegroup.com/ca-en
Classes of Insurance: Personal Accident & Sickness, Liability

ACTRA Fraternal Benefit Society (AFBS)
1000 Yonge St.
Toronto, ON M4W 2K2
Tel: 416-967-6600; *Fax:* 416-967-4744
Toll-Free: 800-387-8897
info@afbs.ca
www.afbs.ca
Classes of Insurance: Personal Accident & Sickness, Life

Affiliated FM Insurance Company
#500, 165 Commerce Valley Dr. West
Thornhill, ON L3T 7V8
Tel: 905-763-5555; *Fax:* 905-763-5556
www.affiliatedfm.ca
Classes of Insurance: Liability, Boiler & Machinery, Fidelity, Property, Fire, Surety

***Agriculture Financial Services Corporation (AFSC)**
5718 - 56 Ave.
Lacombe, AB T4L 1B1
Toll-Free: 877-899-2372
www.afsc.ca
Classes of Insurance: Hail & Crop

AIG Insurance Company of Canada
145 Wellington St. West
Toronto, ON M5J 1H8
Tel: 416-596-3000; *Toll-Free:* 800-387-4481
askaigcanada@aig.com
www.aig.ca
Other Contact Information: Claims E-mail: can.claims@aig.com
Classes of Insurance: Personal Accident & Sickness, Aircraft, Auto, Liability, Boiler & Machinery, Credit, Marine, Fidelity, Property, Surety, Hail & Crop

***Alberta Blue Cross**
Blue Cross Place
10009 - 108th St. NW
Edmonton, AB T5J 3C5
Tel: 780-498-8000; *Fax:* 780-425-4627
Toll-Free: 800-661-6995
www.ab.bluecross.ca
Other Contact Information: Travel Plans: 1-800-661-6995; Individual Health & Dental Plans: 1-800-394-1965; Group Sales: 780-498-8500; Switchboard: 780-498-8100
Social Media: vimeo.com/albertabluecross; www.facebook.com/AlbertaBlueCross; twitter.com/ABBluecross
Classes of Insurance: Personal Accident & Sickness

***Alberta Motor Association Insurance Co.**
PO Box 8180, South Stn. South
Edmonton, AB T6H 5X9
Tel: 780-430-5555; *Toll-Free:* 800-222-6400
www.ama.ab.ca
Other Contact Information: Insurance Toll-Free Phone: 1-800-615-5987; Insurance Claims Toll-Free Phone: 1-888-426-2444
Social Media: www.youtube.com/user/ExperienceAMA; www.instagram.com/albertamotorassociation; www.facebook.com/AlbertaMotorAssociation
Classes of Insurance: Personal Accident & Sickness, Auto, Life, Property, Fire

***Algoma Mutual Insurance Co.**
131 Main St.
Thessalon, ON P0R 1L0
Tel: 705-842-3345; *Fax:* 705-842-3500
www.amico.ca
Classes of Insurance: Auto, Property

***Alliance Assurance**
PO Box 7064
#200, 166 Broadway Blvd.
Grand Falls, NB E3Z 2J9
Fax: 506-473-9401
Toll-Free: 800-939-9400
info@alliance-assurance.com
www.alliance-assurance.com
Classes of Insurance: Auto, Liability, Property

Allianz Global Risks US Insurance Company
#1600, 130 Adelaide St. West
Toronto, ON M5H 3P5
Tel: 416-915-4247; *Fax:* 416-961-5442
AGCSCommunication@agcs.allianz.com
www.agcs.allianz.com/global-offices/c anada
Classes of Insurance: Personal Accident & Sickness, Aircraft, Auto, Liability, Boiler & Machinery, Marine, Property, Surety, Hail & Crop

Allianz Life Insurance Company of North America
#700, 2005 Sheppard Ave. East
Toronto, ON M2J 5B4
Tel: 416-502-2500; *Fax:* 416-502-2555
www.allianzlife.com
Classes of Insurance: Personal Accident & Sickness, Life

Allstate Insurance Company of Canada/ Allstate du Canada, Compagnie d'assurance
#100, 27 Allstate Pkwy.
Markham, ON L3R 5P8
Tel: 905-477-6900; *Toll-Free:* 800-255-7828
www.allstate.ca
Other Contact Information: Claims Toll-Free Numbers: 800-387-0462 (ON & USA); 800-661-1577 (BC, AB, SK, MB); 800-561-7222 (NS, NB, PE, NL); 800-463-2813 (QC)
Social Media: www.facebook.com/AllstateCanada; twitter.com/allstate
Classes of Insurance: Personal Accident & Sickness, Legal Expense, Auto, Liability, Boiler & Machinery, Fidelity, Property, Surety

***L'ALPHA, compagnie d'assurances inc.**
#119, 430, rue Saint-Georges
Drummondville, QC J2C 4H4
Tel: 819-474-7958; *Fax:* 819-477-6139
Toll-Free: 888-525-7428
drummond@assurance-alpha.com
www.alphaassurances.com
Social Media: www.youtube.com/user/AlphaAssurances; twitter.com/Alphaassurances
Classes of Insurance: Auto, Property, Surety

***Alpine Insurance & Financial Inc.**
#300, 5824 - 2nd St., SW
Calgary, AB T2H 0H2
Tel: 403-270-8822; *Fax:* 403-270-0201
Toll-Free: 877-770-8822
info.calgary@alpineinsurance.ca
www.alpineinsurance.ca
Social Media: www.youtube.com/user/AlpineInsuranceAB; plus.google.com/112617199727327791130; www.facebook.com/AlpineInsuranceAlberta; twitter.com/AlpineInsures
Classes of Insurance: Auto, Liability, Life, Property

American Bankers Life Assurance Company of Florida/ American Bankers Compagnie d'Assurance Vie de la Floride
#2000, 5000 Yonge St., 20th Fl.
Toronto, ON M2N 7E9
Tel: 416-733-3360; *Fax:* 416-733-7826
Toll-Free: 800-561-3232
Classes of Insurance: Accident, Personal Accident & Sickness, Life

American Health & Life Insurance Company
355 Wellington St.
London, ON N6A 3N7
Toll-Free: 800-285-8623
Classes of Insurance: Life

American Income Life Insurance Company
c/o McLean & Kerr
#2800, 130 Adelaide West
Toronto, ON M5H 3P5
Tel: 416-364-5371; *Fax:* 416-366-8571
Classes of Insurance: Personal Accident & Sickness, Life

The American Road Insurance Company
c/o CAS Accounting
#2, 1145 Nicholson Rd.
Newmarket, ON L3Y 9C3
Tel: 905-853-0858
Classes of Insurance: Auto, Liability, Boiler & Machinery, Credit, Property, Surety

AMEX Assurance Company/ AMEX Compagnie d'Assurance
c/o Focus Group Inc.
#500, 36 King St. East
Toronto, ON M5C 1E5
Tel: 416-361-1728; *Fax:* 416-361-6113
Classes of Insurance: Personal Accident & Sickness, Life

***Amherst Island Mutual Insurance Company**
RR#1
Stella, ON K0H 2S0
Tel: 613-389-2012; *Fax:* 613-389-9986
Classes of Insurance: Personal Accident & Sickness, Liability, Property

Antigonish Farmers' Mutual Insurance Company
188 Main St.
Antigonish, NS B2G 2B9
Tel: 902-863-3544; *Fax:* 902-863-0664
Toll-Free: 800-565-3544
reception@antigonishfarmersmutual.com
www.antigonishfarmersmutual.ca
Classes of Insurance: Marine, Property, Fire

***Assumption Mutual Life Insurance Company/ Assomption Compagnie Mutuelle d'Assurance-Vie**
Assumption Place
PO Box 160
770 Main St.
Moncton, NB E1C 8L1
Tel: 506-853-6040; *Fax:* 506-853-5428
Toll-Free: 800-455-7337
comments@assumption.ca
www.assumption.ca
Other Contact Information: Group Insurance, Phone: 506-869-9797; Toll Free: 1-888-869-9797; Individual Insurance, Toll-Free: 1-800-343-5622; Mortgage Loans, Phone: 506-869-9755
Classes of Insurance: Accident, Personal Accident & Sickness, Life,

***L'Assurance Mutuelle des Fabriques de Montréal**
1071, rue de la Cathédrale
Montréal, QC H3B 2V4
Tel: 514-395-4969; *Fax:* 514-861-8921
Toll-Free: 800-567-6586
info.general@amf-mtl.com
Classes of Insurance: Liability, Boiler & Machinery, Property, Fire, Theft

** Indicates Provincially Incorporated Insurance Company*

***Assurance-Vie Banque Nationale/ National Bank Life Insurance Company**
1100, rue University, 11e étage
Montréal, QC H3B 2G7
Tél: 514-871-7500; *Téléc:* 514-394-6604
Ligne sans frais: 877-871-7500
assurances@nbc.ca
www.bncplus.ca/assurancepret/vie
Classes of Insurance: Personal Accident & Sickness, Life, Credit

Assurant Solutions Canada
#2000, 5000 Yonge St., 20th Fl.
Toronto, ON M2N 7E9
Tel: 416-733-3360; *Fax:* 416-733-7826
Toll-Free: 800-561-3232
www.assurantsolutions.com/canada
Classes of Insurance: Credit

***AssurePro Insurance Company**
200 Albert St. North
Regina, SK S4R 5E2
Tel: 306-791-4321; *Fax:* 306-949-4461
www.assurepro.ca
Classes of Insurance: Accident

***Astro Insurance 1000 Inc.**
#100, 542 - 7th St.
Lethbridge, AB T1J 2H1
Tel: 403-328-1000; *Fax:* 403-320-1962
Toll-Free: 800-465-5242
info@astro-insurance.com
www.astro-insurance.com
Social Media: www.facebook.com/503786389701449; twitter.com/Astro_Insurance
Classes of Insurance: Auto, Liability, Property, Hail & Crop

***Atlantic Insurance Company Limited**
64 Commonwealth Ave.
Mount Pearl, NL A1N 1W8
Tel: 709-364-5209; *Fax:* 709-364-5262
Classes of Insurance: Auto, Liability, Boiler & Machinery, Fidelity, Property, Surety

Aurigen Reinsurance Company
18 King St. East, 2nd Fl.
Toronto, ON M5C 1C4
Tel: 416-847-1570; *Fax:* 416-847-3670
info@aurigenre.com
www.aurigenre.com
Social Media: www.facebook.com/AurigenRe; twitter.com/AurigenRe
Classes of Insurance: Reinsurance

Aviation & General Insurance Company Limited
#201, 3650 Victoria Park Ave.
Toronto, ON M2H 3P7
Tel: 416-496-1148; *Fax:* 416-496-1089
Classes of Insurance: Aircraft, Liability

***AVie, Financial Security Advisors/ AVie, Cabinet de conseillers en sécurité financière**
Édifice Martin-J.-Légère
CP 5554
295, boul St-Pierre ouest
Caraquet, NB E1W 1B7
Tél: 506-726-4203; *Téléc:* 506-726-8204
Ligne sans frais: 888-822-2343
www.aviesecuritefinanciere.ca/index_eng.cfm
Classes of Insurance: Personal Accident & Sickness, Life

Aviva Canada Inc./ Aviva, Compagnie d'Assurance du Canada
2206 Eglinton Ave. East
Toronto, ON M1L 4S8
Tel: 416-288-1800; *Toll-Free:* 800-387-4518
www.avivacanada.com
Other Contact Information: Claims: 1-866-692-8482
Social Media: www.youtube.com/user/avivacanada; www.facebook.com/AvivaCanada; twitter.com/avivacanada
Classes of Insurance: Personal Accident & Sickness, Aircraft, Legal Expense, Auto, Liability, Boiler & Machinery, Marine, Fidelity, Property, Surety, Hail & Crop

***A-WIN Insurance Network**
Main Branch & Support Staff
#100, 10325 Bonaventure Dr.
Calgary, AB T2J 7E4
Tel: 403-278-1050
www.awinins.ca
Other Contact Information: RV Direct Insurance, Phone: 403-271-7831; South Entrepreneur, Phone: 403-255-2252
Social Media: www.facebook.com/AWINInsurance; twitter.com/AwinInsurance
Classes of Insurance: Auto, Liability, Property

AXA Art Insurance Corporation
500 King St. West, 3rd Fl.
Toronto, ON M5V 1L9
Toll-Free: 877-269-1993
www.axa-art.ca
Classes of Insurance: Property

AXA Equitable Life Insurance Company/ AXA Equitable assurance-vie
PO Box 15
#606, 55 Town Centre Ct.
Toronto, ON M1P 4X4
Toll-Free: 877-269-1993
us.axa.com
Classes of Insurance: Personal Accident & Sickness, Life

***Ayr Farmers Mutual Insurance Company**
1400 Northumberland St.
Ayr, ON N0B 1E0
Tel: 519-632-7413; *Fax:* 519-632-8908
Toll-Free: 800-265-8792
www.ayrmutual.com
Social Media: www.facebook.com/AyrMutual; twitter.com/AyrMutual
Classes of Insurance: Accident, Personal Accident & Sickness, Auto, Liability, Boiler & Machinery, Fidelity, Property, Hail & Crop

***Bay of Quinte Mutual Insurance Co.**
PO Box 6050
13379 Loyalist Pkwy.
Picton, ON K0K 2T0
Tel: 613-476-2145; *Fax:* 613-476-7503
Toll-Free: 800-267-2126
www.bayofquintemutual.com
Social Media: www.facebook.com/602366356481229; twitter.com/bayofqmutual
Classes of Insurance: Personal Accident & Sickness, Auto, Liability, Boiler & Machinery, Fidelity, Property

***Belair Insurance Company Inc./ La Compagnie d'Assurance Belair Inc.**
#300, 7101, rue Jean-Talon est
Montréal, QC H1M 3T6
Tel: 514-270-9111; *Toll-Free:* 888-270-9111
belairdirect@belairdirect.com
www.belairdirect.com
Other Contact Information: 888-280-8549, 888-270-9732 (Toll Free, Auto & Home); 1-877-874-5433 (Toll Free, Travel Insurance); 877-270-9124 (Toll Free, Claims Emergency)
Social Media: www.youtube.com/user/belairdirect; www.instagram.com/belairdirect; www.facebook.com/belairdirect; twitter.com/belairdirect
Classes of Insurance: Personal Accident & Sickness, Legal Expense, Auto, Liability, Boiler & Machinery, Marine, Fidelity, Property, Surety

Berkley Canada
#1000, 145 King St. West
Toronto, ON M5H 1J8
Tel: 416-304-1178; *Fax:* 416-304-4108
Toll-Free: 877-304-1178
info@berkleycanada.com
www.berkleycanada.com
Classes of Insurance: Personal Accident & Sickness, Aircraft, Legal Expense, Auto, Liability, Boiler & Machinery, Credit, Fidelity, Property, Surety, Hail & Crop

***Bertie & Clinton Mutual Insurance Company**
1789 Merrittville Hwy., RR#2
Welland, ON L3B 5N5
Tel: 905-892-0606; *Fax:* 905-892-0365
Toll-Free: 800-263-0494
mail@bertieandclinton.com
www.bertieandclinton.com
Classes of Insurance: Personal Accident & Sickness, Auto, Liability, Boiler & Machinery, Fidelity, Property

BMO Life Assurance Company of Canada
60 Yonge St.
Toronto, ON M5E 1H5
Tel: 416-596-3900; *Fax:* 416-596-4143
Toll-Free: 877-742-5244
www.bmo.com/insurance
Classes of Insurance: Personal Accident & Sickness, Life

***Brant Mutual Insurance Company**
20 Holiday Dr.
Brantford, ON N3R 7J4
Tel: 519-752-0088; *Fax:* 519-752-7917
Toll-Free: 800-461-2543
solutions@brantmutual.com
www.brantmutual.com
Social Media: www.facebook.com/465624223523040; twitter.com/brantmutualins
Classes of Insurance: Personal Accident & Sickness, Auto, Liability, Boiler & Machinery, Fidelity, Property, Hail & Crop

***British Columbia Automobile Association Insurance Agency**
4567 Canada Way
Burnaby, BC V5G 4T1
Tel: 604-268-5000; *Fax:* 604-268-5569
Toll-Free: 800-719-2224
www.bcaa.com
Other Contact Information: Claims: 604-268-5260; Toll Free, TeleCentre: 1-877-325-8888; Toll Free, BCAA Advantage Home Policy: 310-2345; Customer Contact Centre: 604-268-5555
Classes of Insurance: Personal Accident & Sickness, Auto, Life, Property, Fire

***British Columbia Life & Casualty Company**
PO Box 7000
Vancouver, BC V6B 4E1
Tel: 604-419-2000; *Fax:* 604-419-2990
Toll-Free: 888-275-4672
www.pbchbs.com
Social Media: www.facebook.com/pacificbluecross; twitter.com/@pacbluecross
Classes of Insurance: Personal Accident & Sickness, Life

***C Finance Inc.**
#200, 205 Provencher Blvd.
Winnipeg, MB R2H 0G4
Tel: 204-231-1170; *Fax:* 204-231-1445
Toll-Free: 866-741-6797
info@cfinance.biz
www.cfinance.biz
Classes of Insurance: Personal Accident & Sickness, Life

***CAA Insurance Company (Ontario)**
60 Commerce Valley Dr. East
Thornhill, ON L3T 7P9
Tel: 905-771-3000; *Fax:* 905-771-3101
Toll-Free: 866-988-8878
info@caasco.ca
www.caasco.com/insurance
Other Contact Information: 877-222-3939 (Auto & Property); 800-387-2656 (Claims); 866-999-4222 (Health & Dental); 877-942-4222 (Group Life)
Social Media: blog.caasco.com; www.facebook.com/CAASouthCentralON; twitter.com/caasco
Classes of Insurance: Personal Accident & Sickness, Legal Expense, Auto, Liability, Life, Marine, Property, Surety

Caisse Centrale de Réassurance (CCR)
#1010, 150 York St.
Toronto, ON M5H 3S5
Tel: 416-644-0821; *Fax:* 416-644-0822
info@ccr.fr
www.ccr.fr
Classes of Insurance: Accident, Aircraft, Legal Expense, Auto, Liability, Boiler & Machinery, Fidelity, Property, Fire, Surety

Canada Guaranty Mortgage Insurance Company
#400, 1 Toronto St.
Toronto, ON M5C 2V6
Tel: 416-640-8924; *Fax:* 416-640-8948
Toll-Free: 866-414-9109
www.canadaguaranty.ca
Other Contact Information: Underwriting inquiries, Toll-Free: 1-877-244-8422; Fax: 1-877-244-8448; E-mail: underwriting@canadaguaranty.ca
Classes of Insurance: Property

The Canada Life Assurance Company
330 University Ave.
Toronto, ON M5G 1R8
Tel: 416-597-6981; *Toll-Free:* 888-252-1847
www.canadalife.com

** Indicates Provincially Incorporated Insurance Company*

Classes of Insurance: Accident, Personal Accident & Sickness, Credit

Canadian Direct Insurance Incorporated
#600, 750 Cambie St.
Vancouver, BC V6B 0A2
Tel: 604-699-3838; *Fax:* 604-699-3860
Toll-Free: 888-225-5234
www.canadiandirect.com
Other Contact Information: Claims, Toll-Free Phone: 888-261-8888; Toll-Free Fax: 888-261-8880
Classes of Insurance: Personal Accident & Sickness, Liability, Property

***Canadian Farm Insurance Corp. (CFIC)**
#310, 13220 St. Albert Trail
Edmonton, AB T5L 4W1
Tel: 780-447-3276; *Fax:* 780-732-3607
info@cdnfarmins.com
www.cdnfarmins.com
Other Contact Information: 24-hour Livestock Claims Assistance, Phone: 780-733-7720; Fax: 780-733-7724
Classes of Insurance: Personal Accident & Sickness, Liability, Boiler & Machinery, Fidelity, Property, Surety

***Canadian Lawyers Insurance Association/ L'Association d'Assurance des Juristes Canadiens**
#510, 36 Toronto St.
Toronto, ON M5C 2C5
Tel: 416-408-3721
info@clia.ca
www.clia.ca

Canadian Northern Shield Insurance Company (CNS)
#1900, 555 Hastings St. West
Vancouver, BC V6B 4N6
Tel: 604-662-2900; *Fax:* 604-662-5698
Toll-Free: 800-663-1953
www.cns.ca
Classes of Insurance: Auto, Liability, Property

Canadian Premier Life Insurance Company
5000 Yonge St.
Toronto, ON M2N 7J8
Toll-Free: 800-667-2570
www.canadianpremier.ca
Other Contact Information: Toll-Free Phone: 1-800-763-1300 (Credit Unions); 1-800-598-6918 (Claims)
Classes of Insurance: Personal Accident & Sickness, Life, Credit

Canadian Professional Sales Association (CPSA)
#400, 655 Bay St.
Toronto, ON M5G 2K4
Tel: 416-408-2685; *Fax:* 416-408-2684
Toll-Free: 888-267-2772
www.cpsa.com
Social Media: plus.google.com/111402728219182257386; www.facebook.com/CanadianProfessionalSalesAssociation; twitter.com/cpsa
Classes of Insurance: Accident, Personal Accident & Sickness, Auto, Life, Property

***Canadian Universities Reciprocal Insurance Exchange (CURIE)**
#901, 5500 North Service Rd.
Burlington, ON L7L 6W6
Tel: 905-336-3366; *Fax:* 905-336-3373
Toll-Free: 888-462-8743
inquiry@curie.org
www.curie.org
Classes of Insurance: Aircraft, Liability, Marine, Property

***Canassurance Insurance Company**
c/o Québec Blue Cross
550 Sherbrooke St. West
Montréal, QC H3A 3S3
Tel: 514-286-8400
www.qc.croixbleue.ca
Classes of Insurance: Personal Accident & Sickness, Liability, Life, Property

***La Capitale assurances et gestion du patrimoine/ La Capitale Insurance & Financial Services**
CP 1500
625, rue Saint-Amable
Québec, QC G1K 8X9
Tél: 418-644-4200; *Téléc:* 418-644-5226
Ligne sans frais: 800-463-4856
www.lacapitale.com
Other Contact Information: Service des ventes, Tél: 418 644-4180; Téléc: 418-644-4352

Classes of Insurance: Personal Accident & Sickness, Life

***La Capitale assurances générales inc./ La Capitale General Insurance Inc.**
Édifice Hector-Fabre
CP 17100
525, boul René-Lévesque est
Québec, QC G1K 9E2
Ligne sans frais: 888-522-5260
www.lacapitale.com
Other Contact Information: Réclamation: 1-800-461-0770
Classes of Insurance: Auto, Property

***La Capitale assureur de l'administration publique inc./ La Capitale Civil Service Insurer Inc.**
625, rue Saint-Amable
Québec, QC G1R 2G5
Tél: 418-747-7600; *Ligne sans frais:* 800-463-5549
www.lacapitale.com
Classes of Insurance: Life

La Capitale Financial Security Insurance Company/ La Capitale sécurité financière
7150 Derrycrest Dr.
Mississauga, ON L5W 0E5
Fax: 905-795-2316
Toll-Free: 800-268-2835
cs@lacapitale.com
www.lacapitalefs.com
Classes of Insurance: Personal Accident & Sickness, Life

***Caradoc Delaware Mutual Fire Insurance Company**
PO Box 460
22508 Adelaide Rd.
Mount Brydges, ON N0L 1W0
Tel: 519-264-2298; *Fax:* 519-264-9101
Toll-Free: 877-707-2298
info@cdmins.com
www.cdmins.com
Classes of Insurance: Personal Accident & Sickness, Auto, Liability, Boiler & Machinery, Property

***Carleton Mutual Insurance Company**
8750 Main St.
Florenceville, NB E7L 3G5
Tel: 506-392-6041; *Fax:* 506-392-8243
Toll-Free: 800-561-1550
cmi@nb.aibn.com
www.carletonmutual.com
Classes of Insurance: Auto, Property, Fire

Certas Direct Insurance Company/ Certas Direct, compagnie d'assurances
#550, 3 Robert Speck Pkwy.
Mississauga, ON L4Z 2G5
Toll-Free: 877-818-8873
www.certas.ca
Classes of Insurance: Auto, Liability, Property, Surety

Chicago Title Insurance Company Canada (CTIC)
55 Superior Blvd.
Mississauga, ON L5T 2X9
Toll-Free: 888-868-4853
info@chicagotitle.ca
https://express.ctic.ca
Other Contact Information: Claims, E-mail: claims@ctic.ca
Classes of Insurance: Property, Surety

Chubb Insurance Company of Canada/ Chubb du Canada Compagnie d'Assurance
PO Box 139, Commerce Court Stn. Commerce Court
#2500, 199 Bay St.
Toronto, ON M5L 1E2
Tel: 416-863-0550; *Fax:* 416-863-5010
www.chubb.com/international/canada
Other Contact Information: Worldwide Claims, Toll-Free: 1-800-532-4822; Canadian Claims, E-mail: canadaclaims@chubb.com
Social Media: www.youtube.com/user/ChubbInsurance; www.pinterest.com/ChubbInsurance; www.facebook.com/ChubbInsurance; twitter.com/ChubbInsurance
Classes of Insurance: Personal Accident & Sickness, Aircraft, Auto, Liability, Boiler & Machinery, Marine, Fidelity, Property, Surety

CIBC Life Insurance Company Limited/ Compagnie d'Assurance-Vie CIBC Limitée
3 Robert Speck Pkwy., 9th Fl.
Mississauga, ON L4Z 2G5
Toll-Free: 888-393-1110
www.cibcinsurance.com
Other Contact Information: Other Toll-Free: 1-866-581-0320 (CIBC Term Life Protection Plan); 1-866-774-3353 (CIBC Hospital Cash Benefit Plan)
Classes of Insurance: Personal Accident & Sickness, Life

CIGNA Life Insurance Company of Canada
PO Box 14
#606, 55 Town Centre Ct.
Toronto, ON M1P 4X4
Tel: 416-290-6666; *Fax:* 416-290-0732
Toll-Free: 800-668-7029
www.cigna.com
Social Media: www.youtube.com/cigna; www.pinterest.com/cignatogether; www.facebook.com/CIGNA; twitter.com/cigna
Classes of Insurance: Accident, Personal Accident & Sickness, Life, Credit

Clare Mutual Insurance Company
3300 Hwy. 1
Belliveau Cove, NS B0W 1J0
Tel: 902-837-4597; *Fax:* 902-837-7745
Toll-Free: 877-818-0887
www.claremutual.com
Classes of Insurance: Property, Fire, Hail & Crop

***Coachman Insurance Company**
#200, 10 Four Seasons Place
Toronto, ON M9B 6H7
Tel: 416-255-3417; *Fax:* 416-255-3347
Toll-Free: 800-361-2622
inquiries@coachmaninsurance.ca
www.coachmaninsurance.ca
Social Media: www.youtube.com/SGIcommunications; instagram.com/sgiphotos; www.facebook.com/SGIcommunity; twitter.com/SGItweets
Classes of Insurance: Auto

Coast Underwriters Limited
PO Box 11519
#2690, 650 West Georgia St.
Vancouver, BC V6B 4N7
Tel: 604-683-5631; *Fax:* 604-683-8561
www.coastunderwriters.ca
Classes of Insurance: Marine

***Coastal Community Insurance Services (2007) Ltd.**
291 4th St
Courtenay, BC V9N 1G7
Tel: 250-703-4120; *Fax:* 250-703-4109
www.cccu.ca/Personal
Classes of Insurance: Auto, Property

Combined Insurance Company of America/ Compagnie d'assurance Combined d'Amérique
PO Box 3720, MIP Stn. MIP
7300 Warden Ave., 3rd. Fl.
Markham, ON L3R 0X3
Tel: 905-305-1922; *Fax:* 905-305-8600
Toll-Free: 888-234-4466
www.combined.ca
Classes of Insurance: Personal Accident & Sickness, Life

***The Commonwell Mutual Insurance Group**
PO Box 28
336 Angeline St. South
Lindsay, ON K9V 4R8
Tel: 705-234-2146; *Fax:* 705-324-3406
Toll-Free: 800-461-0310
www.thecommonwell.ca
Social Media: www.facebook.com/280185955466883
Classes of Insurance: Auto, Liability, Boiler & Machinery, Property, Hail & Crop, Theft

La Compagnie d'Assurance Missisquoi/ The Missisquoi Insurance Company
#1400, 1 Place Ville Marie
Montréal, QC H3B 2B2
Tél: 514-875-5790; *Téléc:* 514-875-4804
Ligne sans frais: 800-361-7573
www.economicalinsurance.com
Classes of Insurance: Legal Expense, Auto, Liability, Boiler & Machinery, Fidelity, Property, Fire, Surety, Theft

** Indicates Provincially Incorporated Insurance Company*

Connecticut General Life Insurance Co. (CGLIC)
c/o CIGNA Life Insurance Company of Canada
#606, 55 Town Centre Ct.
Toronto, ON M1P 4X4
Tel: 416-290-6666; *Fax:* 416-290-0732
Toll-Free: 800-668-7029
www.cigna.com
Classes of Insurance: Accident, Personal Accident & Sickness, Life

Continental Casualty Company
#3700, 66 Wellington St. West
Toronto, ON M5K 1J5
Tel: 416-542-7300; *Fax:* 416-542-7310
Toll-Free: 800-268-9399
www.cnacanada.ca
Other Contact Information: Claims Fax: 416-542-7410
Social Media: www.facebook.com/cnainsurance; twitter.com/cna_insurance
Classes of Insurance: Accident, Personal Accident & Sickness, Aircraft, Auto, Liability, Boiler & Machinery, Credit, Fidelity, Property, Surety, Hail & Crop

***Co-operative Hail Insurance Company Ltd.**
PO Box 777
2709 - 13th Ave.
Regina, SK S4P 3A8
Tel: 306-522-8891; *Fax:* 306-352-9130
info@coophail.com
www.coophail.com
Classes of Insurance: Hail & Crop

Co-operators General Insurance Company
130 Macdonell St.
Guelph, ON N1H 6P8
Tel: 519-824-4400; *Fax:* 519-823-9944
Toll-Free: 800-265-2662
service@cooperators.ca
www.cooperators.ca
Social Media: www.youtube.com/CooperatorsInsurance; www.facebook.com/TheCooperatorsInsurance; twitter.com/The_Cooperators
Classes of Insurance: Personal Accident & Sickness, Aircraft, Auto, Boiler & Machinery, Life, Fidelity, Property, Fire, Surety, Hail & Crop, Theft

Co-operators Life Insurance Company
1920 College Ave.
Regina, SK S4P 1C4
Fax: 306-347-6808
Toll-Free: 800-454-8061
service@cooperators.ca
www.cooperators.ca
Other Contact Information: Group Benefits, Toll Free: 1-800-667-8164; Fax: 306-761-7373; Travel, Toll Free: 1-800-869-6747; Wealth Management: wealth_mgmt@cooperators.ca
Social Media: www.youtube.com/CooperatorsInsurance; www.facebook.com/TheCooperatorsInsurance; twitter.com/The_Cooperators
Classes of Insurance: Personal Accident & Sickness, Life, Property

CorePointe Insurance Company (DCIC)
#2, 1145 Nicholson Rd.
Newmarket, ON L3Y 9C3
www.corepointeinsurance.com
Classes of Insurance: Auto, Liability, Property, Surety

COSECO Insurance Company
5600 Cancross Ct.
Mississauga, ON L5R 3E9
Toll-Free: 800-387-1963
www.coseco.ca
Classes of Insurance: Auto, Property

Croatian Fraternal Union of America
c/o Deloitte & Touche
#1400, 181 Bay St.
Toronto, ON M5J 2V1
Tel: 416-601-6150; *Fax:* 416-601-6590
www.croatianfraternalunion.org
Social Media: www.youtube.com/channel/UC7FrwBMwojQS8bAIOHKFB0w; www.facebook.com/croatianfraternalunion
Classes of Insurance: Personal Accident & Sickness, Life

***Crowsnest Insurance Agencies Ltd.**
PO Box 88
12731 - 20th Ave.
Blairmore, AB T0K 0E0
Tel: 403-562-8822; *Fax:* 403-562-8239
Toll-Free: 800-361-8658
info@crowsnestinsurance.com
crowsnestinsurance.com
Classes of Insurance: Auto, Liability, Property,

CUMIS General Insurance Company
PO Box 5065
151 North Service Rd.
Burlington, ON L7R 4C2
Tel: 905-632-1221; *Toll-Free:* 800-263-9120
www.cumis.com
Classes of Insurance: Auto, Boiler & Machinery, Fidelity, Property, Fire, Theft

The CUMIS Group Limited
PO Box 5065
151 North Service Rd.
Burlington, ON L7R 4C2
Tel: 905-632-1221; *Toll-Free:* 800-263-9120
www.cumis.com
Classes of Insurance: Personal Accident & Sickness, Auto, Life, Property

CUMIS Life Insurance Company
PO Box 5065
151 North Service Rd.
Burlington, ON L7R 4C2
Tel: 905-632-1221; *Toll-Free:* 800-263-9120
www.cumis.com
Classes of Insurance: Accident, Personal Accident & Sickness, Auto, Life, Credit, Fidelity, Property, Fire, Theft

***Desjardins assurances générales inc/ Desjardins General Insurance Inc.**
PO Box 3500
6300, boul Guillaume-Couture
Lévis, QC G6V 6P9
Tel: 418-835-4850; *Toll-Free:* 877-699-9923
www.desjardinsassurancesgenerales.com
Other Contact Information: Claims, Toll-Free Phone: 1-888-785-5502; Payment, Toll-Free Phone: 1-800-794-0008
Classes of Insurance: Auto, Liability, Boiler & Machinery, Property, Surety

***Desjardins Groupe d'assurances générales inc (DGAG)/ Desjardins General Insurance Group Inc.**
6300, boul Guillaume-Couture
Lévis, QC G6V 6P9
Ligne sans frais: 888-277-8726
www.desjardinsassurancesgenerales.com
Other Contact Information: Claims, Toll-Free Phone: 1-888-776-8343; Payment, Toll-Free Phone: 1-800-463-7282; Customer Relations Centre Toll-Free Phone: 1-866-835-8975
Classes of Insurance: Auto, Property

***Desjardins Sécurité financière (DFS)/ Desjardins Financial Security**
200, av des Commandeurs
Lévis, QC G6V 6R2
Ligne sans frais: 866-838-7553
www.desjardinsassurancevie.com
Classes of Insurance: Accident, Personal Accident & Sickness, Life

***DPB Insurance & Financial Services**
#3, 305 Lakeshore Rd. East
Oakville, ON L6J 1J3
Tel: 905-829-3019; *Fax:* 905-829-3088
Toll-Free: 866-811-2711
info@dpbinsurance.com
dpbinsurance.com
Social Media: www.facebook.com/247181488625549
Classes of Insurance: Personal Accident & Sickness, Life

***Dufferin Mutual Insurance Company**
712 Main St. East
Shelburne, ON L0N 1S0
Tel: 519-925-2026; *Fax:* 519-925-3357
Toll-Free: 800-265-9115
info@dufferinmutual.com
www.dufferinmutual.com
Social Media: twitter.com/dufferinmutual
Classes of Insurance: Personal Accident & Sickness, Auto, Liability, Boiler & Machinery, Fidelity, Property

***Dumfries Mutual Insurance Company**
12 Cambridge St.
Cambridge, ON N1R 3R7
Tel: 519-621-4660; *Fax:* 519-740-8732
Toll-Free: 800-265-3573
info@dumfriesmutual.com
www.dumfriesmutual.com
Social Media: www.facebook.com/DumfriesMutual; twitter.com/DumfriesMutual
Classes of Insurance: Auto, Liability, Boiler & Machinery, Property, Hail & Crop

Ecclesiastical Insurance Office plc/ Société des Assurances écclésiastiques
PO Box 2004
#2200, 20 Eglinton Ave. West
Toronto, ON M4R 1K8
Tel: 416-484-4555; *Fax:* 416-484-6352
www.ecclesiastical.ca, www.ecclesiastical.com
Other Contact Information: After-Hours Emergency Claims Toll-Free Phone: 1-888-693-2253
Classes of Insurance: Auto, Liability, Boiler & Machinery, Marine, Fidelity, Property

Echelon Insurance/ Echelon Compagnie d'Assurances Générale
#300, 2680 Matheson Blvd. East
Mississauga, ON L4W 0A5
Tel: 905-214-7880; *Fax:* 905-214-7893
Toll-Free: 800-324-3566
marketing@echeloninsurance.ca
www.echelon-insurance.ca
Classes of Insurance: Accident, Personal Accident & Sickness, Legal Expense, Auto, Liability, Fidelity, Property, Fire, Surety

The Economical Insurance Group
PO Box 2000
111 Westmount St. South
Waterloo, ON N2J 4S4
Tel: 519-570-8200; *Fax:* 519-570-8389
Toll-Free: 800-265-2180
www.economicalinsurance.com
Social Media: www.youtube.com/user/EconomicalInsurance
Classes of Insurance: Personal Accident & Sickness, Property

Economical Mutual Insurance Company
PO Box 2000
111 Westmount Rd. South
Waterloo, ON N2J 4S4
Tel: 519-570-8200; *Fax:* 519-570-8389
Toll-Free: 800-265-9996
www.economicalinsurance.com
Classes of Insurance: Auto, Boiler & Machinery, Property, Surety

***Edge Mutual Insurance Company**
PO Box 190
103 Wellington St.
Drayton, ON N0G 1P0
Tel: 519-638-3304; *Fax:* 519-638-3521
pmmutual@pmmutual.on.ca
www.edgemutual.com
Other Contact Information: After-Hours Emergency Claims Phone: 519-741-3084
Classes of Insurance: Personal Accident & Sickness, Auto, Liability, Boiler & Machinery, Fidelity, Property

Elite Insurance Company
2206 Eglinton Ave. East
Toronto, ON M1L 4S8
Tel: 416-288-1800; *Toll-Free:* 800-387-4518
www.avivacanada.com
Other Contact Information: Claims: 1-866-692-8482
Classes of Insurance: Personal Accident & Sickness, Aircraft, Auto, Liability, Boiler & Machinery, Marine, Fidelity, Property, Surety,

Empire Life Insurance Company/ Empire Vie
259 King St. East
Kingston, ON K7L 3A8
Tel: 613-548-1881; *Toll-Free:* 877-548-1881
info@empire.ca
www.empire.ca
Other Contact Information: Investment & Individual Insurance: 1-800-561-1268; Quebec: 1-888-469-0969; Group Products: 1-800-267-0215; E-mail: group.csu@empire.ca
Social Media: www.facebook.com/828071143879692
Classes of Insurance: Accident, Personal Accident & Sickness, Life

* Indicates Provincially Incorporated Insurance Company

***Energy Insurance Group Ltd. (EIG)**
Guiness House
#1500, 727 - 7th Ave. SW
Calgary, AB T2P 0Z5
Tel: 403-261-6061; *Fax:* 403-261-6068
insurance@eigltd.com
www.eigltd.com
Classes of Insurance: Auto, Liability, Boiler & Machinery, Property

The Equitable Life Insurance Company of Canada
PO Box 1603, Waterloo Stn. Waterloo
1 Westmount Rd. North
Waterloo, ON N2J 4C7
Tel: 519-886-5110; *Fax:* 519-883-7400
Toll-Free: 800-265-8878
corporatecommunications@equitable.ca
www.equitable.ca
Other Contact Information: Automated Switchboard: 1-800-722-6615; HR E-mail: hr@equitable.ca
Social Media: www.facebook.com/EquitableLife; twitter.com/equitablelife
Classes of Insurance: Life

***Erie Mutual Insurance Company**
711 Main St. East
Dunnville, ON N1A 2W5
Tel: 905-774-8566; *Fax:* 905-774-6468
Toll-Free: 800-263-6484
eriemutual@eriemutual.com
www.eriemutual.com
Social Media: www.facebook.com/ErieMutualInsurance; twitter.com/ErieMutual
Classes of Insurance: Personal Accident & Sickness, Auto, Liability, Boiler & Machinery, Fidelity, Property

Euler Hermes Canada
#2810, 1155, boul René-Lévesque ouest
Montréal, QC H3B 2L2
Tel: 514-876-9656; *Fax:* 514-876-9658
Toll-Free: 877-509-3224
www.eulerhermes.ca
Social Media: twitter.com/ehworldwide
Classes of Insurance: Credit

Everest Insurance Company of Canada/ La Compagnie d'assurance Everest du Canada
#602, 130 Bloor St. West
Toronto, ON M5S 1N5
Tel: 416-487-3900; *Fax:* 416-487-0311
Toll-Free: 877-691-1247
www.everestre.com
Other Contact Information: Vancouver, Phone: 604-362-2769
Classes of Insurance: Aircraft, Auto, Liability, Boiler & Machinery, Credit, Marine, Property, Surety, Hail & Crop

Everest Reinsurance Company
The Exchange Tower
#2520, 130 King St. West
Toronto, ON M5X 1E3
Tel: 416-862-1228; *Fax:* 416-366-5899
www.everestre.com
Classes of Insurance: Personal Accident & Sickness, Aircraft, Auto, Liability, Boiler & Machinery, Credit, Fidelity, Property, Surety, Hail & Crop

***Excellence Life Insurance Company/ L'Excellence, Compagnie d'assurance-vie**
#202, 5055, boul. Métropolitain est
Montréal, QC H1R 1Z7
Tél: 514-327-0020; *Téléc:* 514-327-6242
Ligne sans frais: 800-465-5818
customerservice@iaexcellence.com
www.iaexcellence.com
Other Contact Information: Representative Service: compensationservice@iaexcellence.com; Underwriting: underwritingservice@iaexcellence.com
Classes of Insurance: Personal Accident & Sickness, Life

FaithLife Financial
470 Weber St. North
Waterloo, ON N2J 4G4
Tel: 519-886-4610; *Fax:* 519-886-0350
Toll-Free: 800-563-6237
moreinfo@faithlifefinancial.ca
www.faithlifefinancial.ca
Social Media: www.facebook.com/FaithLifeFinancial; twitter.com/FaithLifeFin
Classes of Insurance: Accident, Personal Accident & Sickness, Life

Federal Insurance Company
PO Box 139, Commerce Court Stn. Commerce Court
#2500, 199 Bay St.
Toronto, ON M5L 1E2
Tel: 416-863-0550; *Fax:* 416-863-5010
www.chubb.com/international/canada
Classes of Insurance: Personal Accident & Sickness, Auto, Liability, Boiler & Machinery, Marine, Fidelity, Property, Surety

Federated Insurance Company of Canada
255 Commerce Dr.
Winnipeg, MB R3P 1B3
Tel: 204-786-6431; *Fax:* 204-783-4443
Toll-Free: 800-665-1934
www.federated.ca
Other Contact Information: Fax Numbers: 204-786-5707 (Claims); 204-784-6762 (Human Resources); 204-784-6755 (Finance)
Classes of Insurance: Accident, Auto, Liability, Boiler & Machinery, Fidelity, Property, Fire, Surety, Theft

Federation Insurance Company of Canada/ La Fédération Compagnie d'Assurances du Canada
#1400, 1 Place Ville Marie
Montréal, QC H3B 2B2
Tel: 514-875-5790; *Fax:* 514-875-4804
Toll-Free: 800-361-7573
www.economicalinsurance.com
Classes of Insurance: Accident, Legal Expense, Auto, Liability, Boiler & Machinery, Fidelity, Property, Fire, Surety, Hail & Crop

***Fenchurch General Insurance Company (FGIC)**
Promontory II
#115, 2655 North Sheridan Way
Mississauga, ON L5K 2P8
Tel: 905-822-2282; *Fax:* 905-822-1282
Toll-Free: 800-515-8908
info@fenchurchgeneral.com
www.fenchurchgeneral.com
Classes of Insurance: Personal Accident & Sickness, Auto, Liability, Boiler & Machinery, Property, Surety

First Canadian Title (FCT)
2235 Sheridan Garden Dr.
Oakville, ON L6J 7Y5
Tel: 905-287-1000; *Fax:* 905-287-2400
Toll-Free: 800-307-0370
fct.ca
Social Media: www.youtube.com/channel/UCQf6IAQO_UxD0wTSfU073vA; plus.google.com/u/0/b/109582260593795176395; twitter.com/FCT_Canada
Classes of Insurance: Property

First North American Insurance Company
PO Box 4213, A Stn. A
2 Queen St. East
Toronto, ON M5W 5M3
www.manulife.ca
Other Contact Information: Manulife Corporate Phone: 416-926-3000
Classes of Insurance: Personal Accident & Sickness, Auto, Property

FM Global
#500, 165 Commerce Valley Dr. West
Thornhill, ON L3T 7V8
Tel: 905-763-5555; *Fax:* 905-763-5556
Toll-Free: 800-955-3632
www.fmglobal.com
Social Media: www.facebook.com/InsurerFMGlobal; twitter.com/FMGlobal
Classes of Insurance: Boiler & Machinery, Property

FNF Canada
55 Superior Blvd.
Mississauga, ON L5T 2X9
Tel: 289-562-0088; *Fax:* 289-562-2494
Toll-Free: 877-526-3232
info@fnf.ca
www.fnf.ca
Other Contact Information: Accounting & Finance E-mail: finance@fnf.ca; Marketing E-mail: marketing@fnf.ca; Human Resources E-mail: hr@fnf.ca
Social Media: twitter.com/fnf_canada
Classes of Insurance: Property

***Fonds d'assurance responsabilité professionnelle de la Chambre des notaires du Québec**
#1500, 1200, av. McGill College
Montréal, QC H3B 4G7
Tel: 514-871-4999; *Fax:* 514-879-1781
Toll-Free: 800-465-6534
web@farpcnq.qc.ca
www.farpcnq.qc.ca

***Fonds d'assurance responsabilité professionnelle du Barreau du Québec**
#300, 445, boul Saint-Laurent
Montréal, QC H2Y 3T8
Tél: 514-954-3452; *Téléc:* 514-954-3454
assuranceresponsabilite@farpbq.ca
www.assurance-barreau.com
Other Contact Information: Télécopieur du contentieux: 514-954-3467

Foresters Life Insurance Company
789 Don Mills Rd.
Toronto, ON M3C 1T9
Toll-Free: 800-267-8777
clientservice@foresters.com
www.foresters.com
Social Media: www.youtube.com/user/foresters; plus.google.com/+foresters; www.facebook.com/Foresters; twitter.com/weareforesters
Classes of Insurance: Personal Accident & Sickness, Life

***Fundy Mutual Insurance Company**
1022 Main St.
Sussex, NB E4E 2M3
Tel: 506-432-1535; *Fax:* 506-433-6788
Toll-Free: 800-222-9550
info@fundymutual.com
www.fundymutual.com
Social Media: www.facebook.com/881422585274115; twitter.com/fundymutual
Classes of Insurance: Auto, Liability, Boiler & Machinery, Property

GAN Assurances Vie Compagnie française d'assurances vie mixte
c/o Eric L. Clark
#716, 1010, rue Sherbrooke ouest
Montréal, QC H3A 2R7
Tel: 514-286-9007; *Fax:* 514-286-0997
Classes of Insurance: Life

General American Life Insurance Company (GALIC)
c/o RGA Life Reinsurance Company of Canada
1981, av McGill College, 13e étage
Montréal, QC H3A 3A8
Tel: 514-985-5260; *Fax:* 514-985-3066
Toll-Free: 800-985-4326
Classes of Insurance: Life, Reinsurance

General Reinsurance Corporation
PO Box 471
#5705, 1 First Canadian Pl.
Toronto, ON M5X 1E4
Tel: 416-869-0490; *Fax:* 416-360-2020
AskGenRe@genre.com
www.genre.com
Social Media: www.youtube.com/user/GenRePerspective; twitter.com/Gen_Re
Classes of Insurance: Personal Accident & Sickness, Aircraft, Auto, Liability, Boiler & Machinery, Credit, Fidelity, Property, Surety, Hail & Crop

Genworth Financial Mortgage Insurance Company Canada
#300, 2060 Winston Park Dr.
Oakville, ON L6H 5R7
Toll-Free: 800-511-8888
mortgage.info@genworth.com
www.genworth.ca
Classes of Insurance: Property

Gerber Life Insurance Company
PO Box 986, F Stn. F
50 Charles St. East
Toronto, ON M4Y 2T2
Toll-Free: 800-518-8884
www.gerberlife.ca
Social Media: www.facebook.com/101436288940; twitter.com/gerberlife
Classes of Insurance: Life

** Indicates Provincially Incorporated Insurance Company*

***Germania Mutual Insurance Company**
PO Box 30
403 Mary St.
Ayton, ON N0G 1C0
Tel: 519-665-7715; *Fax:* 519-665-7558
Toll-Free: 888-418-7770
www.germaniamutual.com
Social Media: www.facebook.com/GermaniaMutual; twitter.com/germaniamutual
Classes of Insurance: Liability, Property, Fire, Theft

***Gibb's Agencies (1997) Ltd.**
Main St.
Barons, AB T0L 0G0
Tel: 403-757-3820; *Fax:* 403-757-2083
Toll-Free: 888-974-4227
info@gibbsagencies.ca
www.gibbsagencies.com
Classes of Insurance: Auto, Property

Giraffe & Friends Life Insurance Company
#200, 880 Laurentian Dr.
Burlington, ON LVN 3V6
Toll-Free: 844-694-2633
www.giraffeandfriends.com
Classes of Insurance: Life

Gore Mutual Insurance Company
PO Box 70
252 Dundas St. North
Cambridge, ON N1R 5T3
Tel: 519-623-1910; *Toll-Free:* 800-265-8600
www.goremutual.ca
Social Media: twitter.com/GoreMutual
Classes of Insurance: Personal Accident & Sickness, Auto, Liability, Property, Fire, Theft

The Grand Orange Lodge of British America Benefit Fund
94 Sheppard Ave. West
Toronto, ON M2N 1M5
Tel: 416-223-1690; *Fax:* 416-223-1324
Toll-Free: 800-565-6248
info@orange.ca
www.grandorangelodge.ca
Classes of Insurance: Life

Great American Insurance Company
#800, 330 Bay St.
Toronto, ON M5H 2S8
Tel: 416-368-8200
www.greatamericaninsurancegroup.com
Social Media: www.youtube.com/user/GAIGroup; www.facebook.com/GreatAmericanInsuranceGroup
Classes of Insurance: Personal Accident & Sickness, Aircraft, Auto, Liability, Boiler & Machinery, Marine, Fidelity, Property, Surety, Hail & Crop

The Great-West Life Assurance Company (GWL)/ Great-West, Compagnie d'Assurance Vie
100 Osborne St. North
Winnipeg, MB R3C 3A5
Tel: 204-946-1190
www.greatwestlife.com
Other Contact Information: TTY, Toll-Free: 1-800-990-6654; GRS Access URL: www.grsaccess.com
Social Media: plus.google.com/+greatwestlife; www.youtube.com/channel/UCHepU86SgVKvarMoZkWPwcw; www.facebook.com/GreatWestLife; twitter.com/greatwestlifeca
Classes of Insurance: Personal Accident & Sickness, Life

Green Shield Canada (GSC)
PO Box 1606
8677 Anchor Dr.
Windsor, ON N9A 6W1
Tel: 519-739-1133; *Fax:* 519-739-0200
Toll-Free: 800-265-5615
www.greenshield.ca
Other Contact Information: Customer Service, Toll-Free: 1-888-711-1119
Social Media: www.youtube.com/user/GreenShieldCanada; www.facebook.com/111841632260596; twitter.com/gsc_1957
Classes of Insurance: Personal Accident & Sickness

***Grenville Mutual Insurance Company**
380 Clonnade Dr.
Kemptville, ON K0G 1J0
Tel: 613-258-9988; *Fax:* 613-258-1142
mail@grenvillemutual.com
www.grenvillemutual.com
Other Contact Information: 24-Hour Emergency Claims Toll-Free Phone: 1-800-267-4400; Claims Fax: 613-258-1174
Social Media: plus.google.com/+GrenvilleMutual; www.facebook.com/GrenvilleMutual; twitter.com/GrenvilleMutual
Classes of Insurance: Personal Accident & Sickness, Auto, Liability, Boiler & Machinery, Fidelity, Property

***Le Groupe Estrie-Richelieu, compagnie d'assurance (GER)**
770, rue Principale
Granby, QC J2G 2Y7
Tél: 450-378-0101; *Téléc:* 450-378-5189
Ligne sans frais: 800-363-8971
info@estrierichelieu.com
www.estrierichelieu.com
Classes of Insurance: Auto, Liability, Boiler & Machinery, Property, Fire

***Groupe Promutuel, Fédération de sociétés mutuelles d'assurance générale**
#400, 2000, boul Lebourgneuf
Québec, QC G2K 0B6
Ligne sans frais: 866-999-2433
federation@promutuel.ca
www.promutuelassurance.ca
Média social: www.youtube.com/user/PromutuelAssurance; fr.pinterest.com/promutuel/; www.facebook.com/PromutuelAssurance; twitter.com/Promutuel
Classes of Insurance: Auto, Property

The Guarantee Company of North America/ La Garantie, Compagnie d'Assurance de l'Amérique du Nord
Madison Centre
#1400, 4950 Yonge St.
Toronto, ON M2N 6K1
Tel: 416-223-9580; *Fax:* 416-223-6577
Toll-Free: 800-260-6617
www.theguarantee.com
Social Media: twitter.com/TheGuaranteeCo
Classes of Insurance: Accident, Personal Accident & Sickness, Legal Expense, Auto, Liability, Boiler & Machinery, Credit, Fidelity, Property, Fire, Surety, Hail & Crop, Theft

***Halwell Mutual Insurance Company**
PO Box 60
812 Woolwich St.
Guelph, ON N1H 6J6
Tel: 519-836-2860; *Fax:* 519-836-2831
www.halwellmutual.com
Classes of Insurance: Auto, Liability, Boiler & Machinery, Fidelity, Property

Hannover Rück SE Canadian Branch
#400, 220 Bay St.
Toronto, ON M5J 2W4
Tel: 416-607-7828; *Fax:* 416-867-9728
www.hannover-rueck.de
Classes of Insurance: Personal Accident & Sickness, Aircraft, Auto, Liability, Boiler & Machinery, Fidelity, Property, Surety, Hail & Crop

Hartford Fire Insurance Company
PO Box 112
#1810, 121 King St. West
Toronto, ON M5H 3T9
Tel: 416-733-9265; *Fax:* 416-733-0510
Toll-Free: 888-898-8334
Classes of Insurance: Personal Accident & Sickness, Aircraft, Auto, Liability, Boiler & Machinery, Fidelity, Property, Fire, Surety, Hail & Crop, Theft

***Hay Mutual Insurance Company**
PO Box 130
37868 Zurich-Hensall Rd.
Zurich, ON N0M 2T0
Tel: 519-236-4381; *Fax:* 519-236-7681
Toll-Free: 877-807-3812
www.haymutual.on.ca
Other Contact Information: After-Hours Emergency Claims Toll-Free Phone: 1-866-778-3555
Social Media: www.facebook.com/1395214114058397
Classes of Insurance: Auto, Liability, Property, Hail & Crop

***Heartland Farm Mutual Insurance Company**
100 Erb St. East
Waterloo, ON N2J 1L9
Tel: 519-886-4530; *Fax:* 519-746-0222
Toll-Free: 800-265-8813
claims@oxfordmutual.com
www.heartlandfarmmutual.com
Other Contact Information: Claims Phone: 519-746-0805; 24 Hour Emergency Claims Toll-Free Phone: 1-800-265-8813, 1-888-224-5677 (U.S.A.); Payment Fax: 519-886-1630
Social Media: www.facebook.com/196407977125467; twitter.com/HeartlandMutual
Classes of Insurance: Personal Accident & Sickness, Aircraft, Auto, Liability, Boiler & Machinery, Fidelity, Property, Hail & Crop

***Henderson Insurance Inc.**
339 Main St. North
Moose Jaw, SK S6H 0W2
Tel: 306-694-5959; *Fax:* 306-693-0117
Toll-Free: 888-661-5959
HII@hendersoninsurance.ca
www.hendersoninsurance.ca
Social Media: plus.google.com/113141274081142829703; www.facebook.com/263941916988982; twitter.com/HIIInsurance
Classes of Insurance: Aircraft, Auto, Liability, Marine, Property, Hail & Crop

HollisWealth Insurance Agency Ltd.
1 Adelaide St. East, 27th Fl.
Toronto, ON M5C 2V9
Tel: 416-350-3250; *Toll-Free:* 888-292-3847
inquiries@holliswealth.com
www.holliswealth.com
Classes of Insurance: Life

***Howard Mutual Insurance Co.**
PO Box 395
20 Ebenezer St. West
Ridgetown, ON N0P 2C0
Tel: 519-674-5434; *Fax:* 519-674-2029
Toll-Free: 866-931-2809
howardmutual.com
Classes of Insurance: Personal Accident & Sickness, Auto, Liability, Fidelity, Property, Hail & Crop

***Howick Mutual Insurance Company**
PO Box 148
1091 Centre St.
Wroxeter, ON N0G 2X0
Tel: 519-335-3561; *Fax:* 519-335-6416
Toll-Free: 800-265-5522
info@howickmutual.com
howickmutual.com
Social Media: www.facebook.com/HowickMutualInsurance; twitter.com/HowickMutual
Classes of Insurance: Personal Accident & Sickness, Auto, Liability, Boiler & Machinery, Property

HSB BI&I
#3000, 250 Yonge St.
Toronto, ON M5B 2L7
Tel: 416-363-5491; *Fax:* 416-363-0538
corporate@biico.com
www.biico.com
Social Media: www.facebook.com/biicocan; twitter.com/biicocan
Classes of Insurance: Liability, Boiler & Machinery, Property

***HTM Insurance Company**
PO Box 201
1176 Division St.
Cobourg, ON K9A 4K5
Tel: 905-372-0186; *Fax:* 905-372-1364
Toll-Free: 800-263-3935
info@htminsurance.ca
www.htminsurance.ca
Classes of Insurance: Auto, Property, Fire

***HUB International Atlantic Limited**
29 Duke St.
Saint John, NB E2L 1M9
Tel: 506-635-0760; *Fax:* 506-634-5641
www.huestiscommercial.ca
Social Media: www.youtube.com/user/hubinternational; www.facebook.com/HUBInternationalLimited; twitter.com/HUBInsurance
Classes of Insurance: Liability, Boiler & Machinery, Property

** Indicates Provincially Incorporated Insurance Company*

***HUB International Barton Insurance Brokers**
45710 Airport Rd.
Chilliwack, BC V2P 1A2
Tel: 604-703-7070; *Toll-Free:* 800-668-2112
info@barton.ca
barton.hubinternational.com
Social Media: www.youtube.com/user/hubinternational; www.facebook.com/HUBInternationalLimited; twitter.com/HUBInsurance
Classes of Insurance: Auto, Marine, Property

HUB International HKMB
Head Office
#900, 595 Bay St.
Toronto, ON M5G 2E3
Tel: 416-597-0008; *Fax:* 416-597-2313
Toll-Free: 800-232-2024
hkmb@hubinternational.com
www.hkmb.com
Classes of Insurance: Personal Accident & Sickness, Life, Property, Reinsurance

***HUB International Horizon Insurance**
1661 Portage Ave., 5th Fl.
Winnipeg, MB R3J 3T7
Tel: 204-988-4800
info@horizoninsurance.ca
www.hubhorizon.ca
Social Media: www.facebook.com/HubHorizon; twitter.com/HUBHorizon
Classes of Insurance: Liability, Life, Property

***HUB International Ontario**
2265 Upper Middle Rd. East, 7th Fl.
Oakville, ON L6H 0G5
Tel: 905-847-5500
ontario.hubinternational.com
Social Media: www.youtube.com/user/hubinternational; www.facebook.com/HUBInternationalLimited; twitter.com/HUBInsurance
Classes of Insurance: Personal Accident & Sickness, Auto, Property

***HUB International Québec**
110, boul Cremazie, 8e étage
Montréal, QC H2P 1B9
Tél: 514-374-9600; *Téléc:* 514-374-8840
que.particulier@hubinternational.com
quebec.hubinternational.com
Média social: www.youtube.com/user/hubinternational; www.facebook.com/HUBInternationalLimited; twitter.com/HUBInsurance
Classes of Insurance: Auto

***HUB International TOS**
Head Office
3875 Henning Dr.
Burnaby, BC V5C 6N5
Tel: 604-293-1481
tos.hubinternational.com
Social Media: www.youtube.com/user/hubinternational; www.facebook.com/HUBInternationalLimited; twitter.com/HUBInsurance
Classes of Insurance: Auto, Property

***Humania Assurance Inc.**
CP 10 000
1555, rue Girouard ouest
Saint-Hyacinthe, QC J2S 7C8
Tél: 450-773-6051; *Téléc:* 450-773-6470
Ligne sans frais: 800-773-8404
info@humania.ca
www.humania.ca
Média social: twitter.com/humaniaassurinc
Classes of Insurance: Personal Accident & Sickness, Life

***iA Financial Group/ iA Groupe financier**
CP 1907, Terminus Stn. Terminus
1080, Grand Allée ouest
Québec, QC G1K 7M3
Tél: 418-684-5000; *Ligne sans frais:* 800-463-6236
info@inalco.com
www.inalco.com
Other Contact Information: Accident Insurance, Phone: 418-684-5405, Fax: 418-688-0705
Média social: www.youtube.com/user/IAquebec; www.facebook.com/iacanada; twitter.com/iacanada
Classes of Insurance: Personal Accident & Sickness, Auto, Life, Property

Independent Order of Foresters
789 Don Mills Rd.
Toronto, ON M3C 1T9
Tel: 416-429-3000; *Toll-Free:* 800-828-1540
service@foresters.com
www.foresters.biz
Other Contact Information: Member Benefits, Toll-Free Phone: 800-444-3043; Unity Life Policy Holders, E-mail: clientservice@unitylife.ca, Toll-Free Phone: 800-267-8777
Social Media: www.youtube.com/c/foresters; plus.google.com/+foresters; www.facebook.com/Foresters; twitter/com/weareforesters
Classes of Insurance: Personal Accident & Sickness, Life

***Industrial Alliance Auto & Home Insurance/ Industrielle Alliance, Assurance auto et habitation**
#230, 925, Grande Allée ouest
Québec, QC G1S 1C1
Tél: 418-650-4486; *Ligne sans frais:* 877-700-7778
www.industrielleallianceauto.com
Other Contact Information: Claims Toll-Free Phone: 1-800-481-2424
Classes of Insurance: Auto, Property

Innovative Insurance Agencies
6351 Rideau Valley Dr. North
Ottawa, ON K4M 1B3
Fax: 613-692-0338
Toll-Free: 800-265-4275
info@innovativeinsurance.ca
www.innovativeinsurance.ca
Classes of Insurance: Accident, Personal Accident & Sickness

***Insurance Company of Prince Edward Island (ICPEI)**
ICPEI Home Office
PO Box 1120
14 Great George St.
Charlottetown, PE C1A 7M8
Fax: 902-626-3529
Toll-Free: 866-404-2734
inquiries@icpei.ca
www.icpei.ca
Other Contact Information: Commercial Property, Toll-Free: 1-866-321-0010
Classes of Insurance: Auto, Life, Property

***Insurance Corporation of British Columbia (ICBC)**
151 West Esplanade
North Vancouver, BC V7M 3H9
Tel: 604-661-2800; *Fax:* 604-646-7400
Toll-Free: 800-663-3051
www.icbc.com
Social Media: www.youtube.com/user/icbc; www.facebook.com/theICBC; twitter.com/icbc
Classes of Insurance: Auto

Intact Financial Corporation
700 University Ave.
Toronto, ON M5G 0A1
Tel: 416-341-1464; *Fax:* 416-941-5320
Toll-Free: 877-341-1464
info@intact.net
www.intactfc.com
Classes of Insurance: Personal Accident & Sickness, Property

Intact Insurance Company of Canada
700 University Ave.
Toronto, ON M5G 0A1
Tel: 416-341-1464; *Fax:* 416-344-8030
Toll-Free: 877-341-1464
info@intact.net
www.intact.ca
Social Media: twitter.com/intactinsurance
Classes of Insurance: Auto, Property

ivari
#500, 5000 Yonge St.
Toronto, ON M2N 7J8
Tel: 416-883-5000; *Fax:* 416-883-5003
Toll-Free: 800-846-5970
conversation@ivari.ca
ivari.ca
Social Media: plus.google.com/115269393590192887557/about; www.instagram.com/ivari_canada; www.facebook.com/Ivari_canada-951785261537674; twitter.com/ivari_canada
Classes of Insurance: Personal Accident & Sickness, Life

Jevco Insurance Company/ La Compagnie d'Assurances Jevco
#100, 4 Robert Speck Pkwy.
Mississauga, ON L4Z 1S1
Tel: 905-227-9350; *Fax:* 905-277-5008
Toll-Free: 800-265-5458
info@jevco.ca
www.jevco.ca
Other Contact Information: 24-Hour Toll-Free Claims Line: 1-866-864-1112
Classes of Insurance: Auto, Property

***Johnston Meier Insurance Agencies Group**
22367 Dewdney Trunk Road
Maple Ridge, BC V2X 3J4
Tel: 604-467-4184; *Fax:* 604-467-9711
Toll-Free: 888-256-4564
info@jmins.com
www.jmins.com
Social Media: www.facebook.com/JohnstonMeierInsurance; twitter.com/JohnstonMeier
Classes of Insurance: Aircraft, Auto, Life, Marine, Surety

***Kent & Essex Mutual Insurance Company**
PO Box 356
10 Creek Rd.
Chatham, ON N7M 5K4
Tel: 519-352-3190; *Fax:* 519-352-5344
Toll-Free: 800-265-5206
info@kemutual.com
www.kemutual.com
Social Media: www.facebook.com/kemutual; twitter.com/kemutual
Classes of Insurance: Personal Accident & Sickness, Auto, Liability, Boiler & Machinery, Fidelity, Property

***Key West Insurance Services Ltd.**
106 Causeway St.
Queen Charlotte, BC V0T 1S0
Tel: 250-559-8426; *Fax:* 250-559-8059
Toll-Free: 886-559-9378
www.northsave.com/Personal/ProductsAndServices/Insurance
Classes of Insurance: Auto, Marine, Reinsurance

The Kings Mutual Insurance Company
220 Commercial St.
Berwick, NS B0P 1E0
Tel: 902-538-3187; *Fax:* 902-538-7271
Toll-Free: 800-565-7220
info@kingsmutual.ns.ca
www.kingsmutual.ns.ca
Classes of Insurance: Liability, Property, Fire

***Kirkham Insurance**
205 - 11th St. South
Lethbridge, AB T1J 4A6
Tel: 403-328-1228; *Fax:* 403-380-4051
Toll-Free: 800-256-2955
info@kirkhaminsurance.com
www.kirkhaminsurance.com
Classes of Insurance: Auto, Property

Knights of Columbus Insurance
c/o The Raymond Richer Agency
26 Davis Court
Hampton, ON L0B 1J0
Tel: 905-263-4212
www.kofc.org/un/en/insurance
Social Media: www.youtube.com/knightsofcolumbus; plus.google.com/106872034535735019930; www.facebook.com/KnightsofColumbus; twitter.com/kofc
Classes of Insurance: Life

***Lambton Mutual Insurance Company**
PO Box 520
7873 Confederation Line
Watford, ON N0M 2S0
Tel: 519-876-2304; *Fax:* 519-876-6626
Toll-Free: 800-561-4136
info@lambtonmutual.com
www.lambtonmutual.com
Other Contact Information: After Hours Emergency Claims Toll-Free Phone: 1-877-488-6642; Claims Fax: 519-876-3940
Social Media: www.facebook.com/LambtonMutual; twitter.com/lambtonmutual
Classes of Insurance: Personal Accident & Sickness, Auto, Liability, Boiler & Machinery, Fidelity, Property, Hail & Crop

* *Indicates Provincially Incorporated Insurance Company*

Lawyers' Professional Indemnity Company (LAWPRO)
PO Box 3
#3101, 250 Yonge St.
Toronto, ON M5B 2L7
Tel: 416-598-5800; *Fax:* 416-599-8341
Toll-Free: 800-410-1013
service@lawpro.ca
www.lawpro.ca
Social Media: www.facebook.com/LAWPROinsurance; twitter.com/LAWPRO
Classes of Insurance: Liability

Legacy General Insurance Company/ Compagnie d'Assurances Générales Legacy
5000 Yonge St.
Toronto, ON M2N 7J8
Toll-Free: 800-667-2570
www.canadianpremier.ca
Other Contact Information: Toll-Free Phone: 1-800-763-1300 (Credit Unions); 1-800-598-6918 (Claims)
Classes of Insurance: Personal Accident & Sickness, Liability, Property

***Lennox & Addington Mutual Insurance Company**
PO Box 174
32 Mill St.
Napanee, ON K7R 3M3
Tel: 613-354-4810; *Fax:* 613-354-7112
Toll-Free: 800-267-7812
www.l-amutual.com
Classes of Insurance: Personal Accident & Sickness, Auto, Liability, Marine, Property

Liberty Mutual Insurance Company/ La Compagnie d'Assurance Liberté Mutuelle
Brookfield Place
#1000, 181 Bay St.
Toronto, ON M5J 2T3
Tel: 416-307-4353; *Fax:* 416-365-7281
www.libertymutual.com
Social Media: www.facebook.com/libertymutual; twitter.com/libertymutual
Classes of Insurance: Personal Accident & Sickness, Aircraft, Auto, Liability, Boiler & Machinery, Fidelity, Property, Surety

Life Insurance Company of North America (LINA)
#301, 1 Consilium Place
Toronto, ON M1H 3E3
Tel: 416-296-2900
www.cigna.com
Classes of Insurance: Accident, Personal Accident & Sickness, Life

Lloyd's Underwriters
#2220, 1155, rue Metcalfe
Montréal, QC H3B 2V6
Tel: 514-861-8361; *Fax:* 514-861-0470
Toll-Free: 877-455-6937
info@lloyds.ca
www.lloyds.com/lloyds/offices/americas/canada
Other Contact Information: Commercial Inquiries, Phone: 514-864-5444
Classes of Insurance: Personal Accident & Sickness, Aircraft, Legal Expense, Auto, Liability, Boiler & Machinery, Fidelity, Property, Fire, Surety, Reinsurance

London Life Insurance Company/ London Life, Compagnie d'Assurance-Vie
255 Dufferin Ave.
London, ON N6A 4K1
Tel: 519-432-5281
www.londonlife.com
Other Contact Information: TTY: 1-800-990-6654
Classes of Insurance: Personal Accident & Sickness, Life, Reinsurance

***Manitoba Agricultural Services Corporation (MASC)**
Insurance Corporate Office
#400, 50 - 24th St. NW
Portage La Prairie, MB R1N 3V9
Tel: 204-239-3246; *Fax:* 204-239-3401
mailbox@masc.mb.ca
www.masc.mb.ca
Classes of Insurance: Hail & Crop

***Manitoba Blue Cross**
PO Box 1046, Main Stn. Main
599 Empress St.
Winnipeg, MB R3C 2X7
Tel: 204-775-0151; *Fax:* 204-786-5965
Toll-Free: 888-873-2583
www.mb.bluecross.ca
Other Contact Information: Canada Toll-Free: 1-888-596-1032; Claims Fax: 204-772-1231
Classes of Insurance: Personal Accident & Sickness, Life

***Manitoba Public Insurance**
PO Box 6300
Winnipeg, MB R3C 4A4
Tel: 204-985-7000; *Toll-Free:* 800-665-2410
www.mpi.mb.ca
Other Contact Information: TTY: 204-985-8832; Out of Province Claims, Toll-Free: 1-800-661-6051
Classes of Insurance: Auto

Manufacturers Life Insurance Company/ La Compagnie d'Assurance-Vie Manufacturers
PO Box 1669
500 King St. North
Waterloo, ON N2J 4Z6
Toll-Free: 888-626-8543
valued_customer_centre@manulife.com
www.manulife.ca
Other Contact Information: French Toll-Free: 1-888-626-8843; Mandarin or Cantonese Toll-Free: 1-866-542-4550 (East); 1-877-248-3778 (West)
Classes of Insurance: Personal Accident & Sickness, Life

Manulife Canada Ltd./ Manuvie Canada Ltée
PO Box 1602
500 King St. North
Waterloo, ON N2J 4Z6
Toll-Free: 888-626-8543
valued_customer_centre@manulife.com
www.manulife.ca
Classes of Insurance: Life

Manulife Financial
500 King St. North
Waterloo, ON N2J 4C6
Toll-Free: 888-626-8543
www.manulife.ca
Other Contact Information: Québec, Toll-Free: 1-888-626-8843
Social Media: www.youtube.com/user/ManulifeFinancial; www.facebook.com/ManulifeFinancial
Classes of Insurance: Life

MAX Canada Insurance Company
140 Foundry St.
Baden, ON N3A 2P7
Fax: 519-634-5159
Toll-Free: 877-770-7729
www.maxinsurance.com
Social Media: www.youtube.com/user/MAXWholeness; maxwholenessblog.com; www.facebook.com/maxwholeness; twitter.com/maxwholeness
Classes of Insurance: Liability, Boiler & Machinery, Marine, Fidelity, Property

***McFarlane & Company Financial Group Limited**
#430, 999 - 8th St. SW
Calgary, AB T2R 1J5
Tel: 403-229-0466; *Fax:* 403-228-9784
Toll-Free: 888-224-0466
info@mcfarlaneco.com
www.mcfarlaneco.com
Social Media: www.facebook.com/mcfarlanecfg; twitter.com/mcfarlanecfg
Classes of Insurance: Auto, Liability, Life, Property, Surety, Hail & Crop

***McKillop Mutual Insurance Company**
PO Box 819
91 Main St. South
Seaforth, ON N0K 1W0
Tel: 519-527-0400; *Fax:* 519-527-2777
Toll-Free: 800-463-9204
www.mckillopmutual.com
Classes of Insurance: Personal Accident & Sickness, Auto, Liability, Boiler & Machinery, Fidelity, Property

MD Insurance Agency Limited
1870 Alta Vista Dr.
Ottawa, ON K1G 6R7
Tel: 613-731-4552; *Toll-Free:* 800-267-4022
mdm.ca/wealth-management/insurance
Social Media: www.facebook.com/MDPhysicianServices
Classes of Insurance: Life

MD Life Insurance Company
1870 Alta Vista Dr.
Ottawa, ON K1G 6R7
Tel: 613-731-4552; *Toll-Free:* 800-267-4022
mdm.ca/wealth-management/insurance
Social Media: www.facebook.com/MDPhysicianServices
Classes of Insurance: Life

***Medavie Blue Cross**
PO Box 220
644 Main St.
Moncton, NB E1C 8L3
Tel: 506-853-1811; *Fax:* 506-867-4651
Toll-Free: 800-667-4511
www.medavie.bluecross.ca
Other Contact Information: Group Benefits, Atlantic Provinces & Ontario: 1-888-227-3400; Group Benefits, Québec: 1-888-588-1212
Social Media: www.youtube.com/user/MedavieBlueCross; medaviesmallsteps.com; www.facebook.com/MedavieBlueCross; twitter.com/MedavieBC
Classes of Insurance: Personal Accident & Sickness, Life

Meloche Monnex Inc.
2161 Yonge St.
Toronto, ON M4S 3A6
Toll-Free: 877-777-7136
www.melochemonnex.com
Other Contact Information: Claims, Toll-Free: 1-877-323-0343; Alt. URL: www.group.tdinsurance.com
Classes of Insurance: Auto, Property

***Mennonite Mutual Fire Insurance Company**
PO Box 190
Waldheim, SK S0K 4R0
Tel: 306-945-2239; *Fax:* 306-945-4666
equery@mmfi.com
www.mmfi.com
Classes of Insurance: Boiler & Machinery, Property, Fire, Theft

***Mennonite Mutual Insurance Co. (Alberta) Ltd. (MMI)**
#300, 2946 - 32nd St. NE
Calgary, AB T1Y 6J7
Tel: 403-275-6996; *Fax:* 403-291-6733
Toll-Free: 866-222-6996
office@mmiab.ca
www.mmiab.ca
Social Media: www.facebook.com/438246342964994
Classes of Insurance: Auto, Liability, Property, Fire

***Middlesex Mutual Insurance Co.**
PO Box 100
13271 Ilderton Rd.
Ilderton, ON N0M 2A0
Tel: 519-666-0075; *Fax:* 519-666-0079
Toll-Free: 800-851-4045
www.middlesexmutual.on.ca
Classes of Insurance: Auto, Liability, Property

***Millennium Insurance Corporation**
340 Sioux Rd.
Sherwood Park, AB T8A 3X6
Tel: 780-467-1500; *Fax:* 780-467-0004
Toll-Free: 866-467-1245
info@millenniuminsurance.ca
www.directinsure.net
Other Contact Information: Calgary Phone: 403-265-4576; Fax: 403-265-4578
Classes of Insurance: Auto, Property

Mitsui Sumitomo Insurance Co., Limited. (MS&AD)
c/o Chubb Insurance Company of Canada, Commerce Court West
PO Box 139, Commerce Court Stn. Commerce Court
#2500, 199 Bay St.
Toronto, ON M5L 1E2
Tel: 416-863-0550
www.ms-ins.com/english/company/network/area03.html#anc-02
Classes of Insurance: Personal Accident & Sickness, Aircraft, Auto, Liability, Boiler & Machinery, Fidelity, Property, Surety

Motors Insurance Corporation
#400, 8500 Leslie St.
Thornhill, ON L3T 7M8
Toll-Free: 800-387-8095
www.gm.ca/gm/english/services/insurance/quote
Classes of Insurance: Auto, Liability, Boiler & Machinery

** Indicates Provincially Incorporated Insurance Company*

***Mouvement des caisses Desjardins du Québec/ Desjardins Group**
100, av des Commandeurs
Lévis, QC G6V 7N5
Tél: 418-835-8444; *Ligne sans frais:* 866-835-8444
www.desjardins.com
Média social: www.youtube.com/user/mouvementdesjardins; www.instagram.com/mouvementdesjardins; www.facebook.com/desjardins; twitter.com/mvtdesjardins

Munich Reinsurance Company Canada Branch (Life)
Munich Re Centre
390 Bay St., 26th Fl.
Toronto, ON M5H 2Y2
Tel: 416-359-2200; *Fax:* 416-361-0305
generalenquiries@munichre.ca
www.munichre.com/ca/life
Social Media: www.facebook.com/112684192080056; twitter.com/munichre
Classes of Insurance: Personal Accident & Sickness, Life, Reinsurance

Munich Reinsurance Company of Canada
#2200, 390 Bay St.
Toronto, ON M5H 2Y2
Tel: 416-366-9206; *Fax:* 416-366-4330
Toll-Free: 800-444-5321
info@mroc.com
www.munichre.com/ca/non-life
Social Media: twitter.com/munichre
Classes of Insurance: Auto, Liability, Property, Theft

***Municipal Insurance Association of British Columbia (MIA)**
#200, 429 - West 2nd Ave.
Vancouver, BC V5Y 1E3
Tel: 604-683-6266; *Fax:* 604-683-6244
Toll-Free: 855-683-6266
info@miabc.org
www.miabc.org
Classes of Insurance: Liability

***MUNIX Reciprocal (MUNIX)**
300-8616 51 Ave.
Edmonton, AB T6E 6E6
Tel: 780-433-4431; *Fax:* 780-409-4314
www.auma.ca
Social Media: twitter.com/theauma
Classes of Insurance: Liability, Property

***The Mutual Fire Insurance Company of British Columbia**
#201, 9366 - 200A St.
Langley, BC V1M 4B3
Tel: 604-881-1250; *Fax:* 604-881-1440
Toll-Free: 866-417-2272
info@mutualfirebc.com
www.mutualfirebc.com
Classes of Insurance: Property, Fire

***La Mutuelle d'Église de l'Inter-ouest**
180, boul du Mont-Bleu
Gatineau, QC J8Z 3J5
Tel: 819-595-2678
Social Media: plus.google.com/107181638918471275763

***New Diamond Insurance Services Ltd.**
#128, 6061 No. 3 Rd.
Richmond, BC V6Y 2B2
Tel: 604-279-0888; *Fax:* 604-279-0616
info@newdiamondfinancial.com
www.newdiamondfinancial.com/insurance
Classes of Insurance: Personal Accident & Sickness, Auto, Life, Property

The Nordic Insurance Company of Canada
#1500A, 700 University Ave.
Toronto, ON M5G 0A1
Toll-Free: 866-302-5094
Classes of Insurance: Accident, Legal Expense, Auto, Liability, Boiler & Machinery, Fidelity, Property, Surety

***Norfolk Mutual Insurance Company**
PO Box 515
33 Park Rd.
Simcoe, ON N3Y 4L5
Tel: 519-426-1294; *Fax:* 519-426-7594
Toll-Free: 800-304-5573
info@norfolkmutual.com
www.norfolkmutual.com
Other Contact Information: Claims Toll-Free Fax: 1-866-730-6995
Social Media: www.facebook.com/459163060811698; twitter.com/NorfolkMutual
Classes of Insurance: Auto, Property, Fire

***North Blenheim Mutual Insurance Company**
11 Baird St. North
Bright, ON N0J 1B0
Tel: 519-454-8661; *Fax:* 519-454-8785
Toll-Free: 800-665-6888
info@northblenheim.com
www.northblenheim.ca
Classes of Insurance: Auto, Liability, Property

***North Kent Mutual Fire Insurance Company**
PO Box 478
29553 St. George St.
Dresden, ON N0P 1M0
Tel: 519-683-4484; *Fax:* 519-683-4509
Toll-Free: 888-736-4705
nkm@nkminsurance.com
www.nkminsurance.com
Other Contact Information: After-Hours Emergency Claims Toll-Free Phone: 1-888-736-4705; Claims Fax: 519-683-6666
Social Media: www.facebook.com/NKMInsurance; twitter.com/NKMInsurance
Classes of Insurance: Auto, Liability, Property, Fire, Hail & Crop, Theft

Northbridge Insurance
#700, 105 Adelaide St. West
Toronto, ON M5H 1P9
Tel: 416-350-4400; *Toll-Free:* 855-620-6262
info@nbfc.com
www.nbins.com
Social Media: www.youtube.com/channel/UCe7LOfPaBS0C064xxT69Egw; plus.google.com/110547895885210824963; twitter.com/northbridgeins
Classes of Insurance: Accident, Auto, Liability, Marine, Property, Hail & Crop

***Northern Savings Insurance Agency Ltd.**
138 - 3rd Ave. West
Prince Rupert, BC V8J 1K8
Tel: 250-627-1123; *Fax:* 250-624-6444
Toll-Free: 800-555-4093
www.northsave.com/Personal/ProductsAndServices/Insurance
Classes of Insurance: Auto, Marine, Property

Novex Group Insurance/ ING Novex Compagnie d'Assurance du Canada
700 University Ave., 15th Fl.
Toronto, ON M5G 0A1
Tel: 416-941-5221; *Toll-Free:* 877-341-1464
info@intact.net
www.intact.ca/group-insurance
Classes of Insurance: Personal Accident & Sickness, Legal Expense, Auto, Liability, Boiler & Machinery, Credit, Fidelity, Property, Surety,

***Nunavut Insurance Brokers Ltd.**
1661 Portage Ave., 5th Fl.
Winnipeg, MB R3J 3T7
Tel: 204-988-4691; *Fax:* 204-988-4692
Toll-Free: 866-259-6940
www.nunavutinsurance.ca
Social Media: www.facebook.com/NunavutInsurance; twitter.com/nunavut_ins
Classes of Insurance: Auto, Life, Property

OdysseyRe - Canadian Branch
#1600, 55 University Ave.
Toronto, ON M5J 2H7
Tel: 416-862-0162; *Fax:* 416-367-3248
www.odysseyre.com
Classes of Insurance: Accident, Aircraft, Auto, Liability, Boiler & Machinery, Property, Fire, Surety, Hail & Crop, Reinsurance

Old Republic Insurance Company of Canada/ L'Ancienne République, Compagnie d'Assurance du Ca
PO Box 557
100 King St. West
Hamilton, ON L8N 3K9
Tel: 905-523-5936; *Fax:* 905-523-1471
Toll-Free: 800-530-5446
service@orican.com
www.orican.com
Classes of Insurance: Accident, Aircraft, Auto, Liability, Property, Reinsurance

Omega General Insurance Company
#500, 36 King St. East
Toronto, ON
Tel: 416-361-1728; *Fax:* 416-361-6113
www.omegageneral.com
Classes of Insurance: Personal Accident & Sickness, Aircraft, Legal Expense, Liability, Boiler & Machinery, Credit, Fidelity, Property, Surety

***Ontario Blue Cross**
#610, 185 The West Mall
Toronto, ON M9C 5P1
Tel: 416-646-2585; *Toll-Free:* 866-732-2583
bco.indhealth@ont.bluecross.ca
www.useblue.com
Other Contact Information: Travel, E-mail: bco.travel@ont.bluecross.ca; Tech Support: 1-800-563-2538
Classes of Insurance: Personal Accident & Sickness

***Ontario Mutual Insurance Association**
350 Pinebush Rd.
Cambridge, ON N1T 1Z6
Tel: 519-622-9220; *Fax:* 519-622-9227
information@omia.com
www.omia.com
Classes of Insurance: Personal Accident & Sickness, Auto, Property

***Ontario School Boards' Insurance Exchange (OSBIE)**
91 Westmount Rd.
Guelph, ON N1H 5J2
Tel: 519-767-2182; *Fax:* 519-767-0281
Toll-Free: 800-668-6724
info@osbie.on.ca
www.osbie.on.ca
Other Contact Information: Member Services: memberservices@osbie.on.ca; Risk Management: rm@osbie.on.ca; Claims: claims@osbie.on.ca
Classes of Insurance: Auto, Liability, Boiler & Machinery, Property, Fire

***Optimum Assurance Agricole inc./ Optimum Farm Insurance Inc.**
#422, 25 rue des Forges
Trois-Rivières, QC G9A 6A7
Tél: 819-373-2040; *Téléc:* 819-373-2801
www.optimum-general.com
Classes of Insurance: Auto, Property, Fire

Optimum Général inc./ Optimum General Inc.
#1500, 425, boul de Maisonneuve ouest
Montréal, QC H3A 3G5
Tél: 514-288-8725; *Téléc:* 514-288-0760
www.optimum-general.com
Classes of Insurance: Auto, Liability, Property

Optimum Re inc./ Optimum Re Inc.
#1200, 425, boul de Maisonneuve ouest
Montréal, QC H3A 3G5
Tél: 514-288-1900
www.optimumre.ca
Classes of Insurance: Reinsurance

***Optimum Réassurance inc./ Optimum Reassurance Inc.**
#1200, 425, boul de Maisonneuve ouest
Montréal, QC H3A 3G5
Tél: 514-288-1900
www.optimumre.ca
Classes of Insurance: Accident, Personal Accident & Sickness, Life, Reinsurance

***Optimum Société d'Assurance inc. (OSA)/ Optimum Insurance Company Inc.**
#1500, 425, boul de Maisonneuve ouest
Montréal, QC H3A 3G5
Tél: 514-288-8711; *Téléc:* 514-288-8269
www.optimum-general.com
Classes of Insurance: Auto, Liability, Property

** Indicates Provincially Incorporated Insurance Company*

***Optimum West Insurance Company Inc.**
#600, 4211 Kingsway
Burnaby, BC V5H 1Z6
Tel: 604-688-1541; *Fax:* 604-688-1527
www.optimum-general.com
Classes of Insurance: Auto, Property, Hail & Crop

The Order of United Commercial Travelers of America (UCT)
#300, 901 Centre St. North
Calgary, AB T2E 2P6
Tel: 403-277-0745; *Fax:* 403-277-6662
Toll-Free: 800-267-2371
www.uct.org
Social Media: www.youtube.com/user/UCTinAction; www.flickr.com/photos/uctinaction; www.facebook.com/UCTinAction
Classes of Insurance: Personal Accident & Sickness, Life

***Ordre des Architectes du Québec**
#200, 420, rue McGill
Montréal, QC H2Y 2G1
Tel: 514-937-6168; *Fax:* 514-933-0242
Toll-Free: 800-599-6168
info@oaq.com
www.oaq.com
Social Media: vimeo.com/tag:oaq; www.facebook.com/133353596740232; twitter.com/OAQenbref

***Ordre des dentistes du Québec (ODQ)**
#1640, 800, boul René-Lévesque ouest
Montréal, QC H3B 1X9
Tel: 514-875-8511; *Fax:* 514-393-9248
Toll-Free: 800-361-4887
www.odq.qc.ca
Social Media: www.youtube.com/webmestreodq; www.facebook.com/102225303175310; twitter.com/ordredentistes

***Pacific Blue Cross**
PO Box 7000
4250 Canada Way
Vancouver, BC V6B 4E1
Tel: 604-419-2000; *Fax:* 604-419-2990
Toll-Free: 888-275-4672
www.pac.bluecross.ca
Other Contact Information: Corporate/Group: 1-877-275-4768; Individual Health & Dental: 1-800-873-2583; Travel: 1-800-873-2583; Fraud Report: 1-800-661-9675
Social Media: www.facebook.com/pacificbluecross; twitter.com/pacbluecross
Classes of Insurance: Accident, Personal Accident & Sickness, Life

***Pacific Coast Fishermen's Mutual Marine Insurance Company**
3757 Canada Way
Burnaby, BC V5G 1G5
Tel: 604-438-4240; *Fax:* 604-438-5756
Toll-Free: 888-438-4242
info@mutualmarine.bc.ca
www.mutualmarine.bc.ca
Other Contact Information: Toll Free (BC only): 1-888-438-4242
Classes of Insurance: Marine

Pafco Insurance Company
#100, 27 Allstate Pkwy.
Markham, ON L3R 5P8
Tel: 905-513-4000; *Fax:* 905-513-4026
Toll-Free: 877-216-6973
contactus@pafco.ca
www.pafco.ca
Classes of Insurance: Personal Accident & Sickness, Auto, Liability, Property

***Palliser Insurance Company Limited**
PO Box 1358
Saskatoon, SK S7H 3N9
Tel: 306-955-4814; *Fax:* 306-955-1317
info@palliserinsurance.com
www.palliserinsurance.com
Classes of Insurance: Hail & Crop

***Paragon Insurance Agencies Ltd.**
4660 Lazelle Ave.
Terrace, BC V8G 1S6
Tel: 250-635-6371; *Fax:* 250-635-4844
Toll-Free: 888-549-5552
www.northsave.com/Personal/ProductsAndServices/Insurance
Classes of Insurance: Auto, Marine, Reinsurance

PartnerRe SA
#909, 123 Front St. West
Toronto, ON M5J 2M2
Tel: 416-861-0033; *Fax:* 416-861-0200
contactus@partnerre.com
www.partnerre.com
Classes of Insurance: Personal Accident & Sickness, Auto, Life, Property

***Peace Hills General Insurance Company**
#300, 10709 Jasper Ave., 3rd Fl.
Edmonton, AB T5J 3N3
Tel: 780-424-3986; *Fax:* 780-424-0396
Toll-Free: 800-272-5614
phi@phgic.com
www.peacehillsinsurance.com
Other Contact Information: Emergency Claims Toll-Free Phone: 1-800-272-5614; Claims Fax: 780-241-0984; Claims Toll-Free Fax: 1-888-421-8188
Classes of Insurance: Accident, Aircraft, Auto, Liability, Boiler & Machinery, Credit, Marine, Fidelity, Property, Fire, Surety, Theft

***Peel Mutual Insurance Company**
103 Queen St. West
Brampton, ON L6Y 1M3
Tel: 905-451-2386; *Toll-Free:* 800-268-3069
www.peelmutual.com
Social Media: twitter.com/PeelMutual
Classes of Insurance: Auto, Liability, Boiler & Machinery, Fidelity, Property

Pembridge Insurance Company
#100, 27 Allstate Pkwy.
Markham, ON L3R 5P8
Tel: 905-513-4013; *Toll-Free:* 877-736-2743
websitecontactus@pembridge.com
www.pembridge.com
Classes of Insurance: Auto, Property

***The Personal General Insurance Inc./ La Personnelle, assurances générales inc.**
PO Box 3500
6300, boul Guillaume-Couture
Lévis, QC G6V 6P9
Toll-Free: 888-476-8737
www.lapersonnelle.com
Other Contact Information: Claims Toll-Free Phone: 1-888-785-5502; Payment Toll-Free Phone: 1-888-277-6481
Classes of Insurance: Auto, Liability, Boiler & Machinery, Property, Surety

The Personal Insurance Company/ La Personnelle, compagnie d'assurances
PO Box 3500
6300, boul Guillaume-Couture
Lévis, QC G6V 6P9
Toll-Free: 888-476-8737
www.thepersonal.com
Other Contact Information: 24/7 Claims Line, Toll-Free: 1-866-785-5502; Payment Toll-Free Phone: 1-888-277-6481
Classes of Insurance: Personal Accident & Sickness, Aircraft, Auto, Liability, Boiler & Machinery, Fidelity, Property, Surety

Perth Insurance Company
#1500, 5255 Yonge St.
Toronto, ON M2N 6P4
Tel: 416-590-0038; *Fax:* 416-590-0869
Toll-Free: 800-268-8801
www.economicalinsurance.com
Classes of Insurance: Auto, Property

Pets Plus Us
#2, 1115 North Service Rd. West
Oakville, ON L6M 2V9
Toll-Free: 800-364-8422
info@pesplusus.com
www.petsplusus.com
Other Contact Information: Claims Toll-Free Fax: 1-855-456-7387
Social Media: www.youtube.com/user/PetsPlusUsCA; plus.google.com/111932247748500684675; www.facebook.com/PetsPlusUsCa; twitter.com/PetsPlusUsCA
Classes of Insurance: Property

Petsecure Pet Health Insurance
#300, 600 Empress St.
Winnipeg, MB R3G 0R5
Toll-Free: 800-268-1169
www.petsecure.com
Other Contact Information: Claims, Toll-Free Fax: 1-866-501-5580; Veterinary Toll-Free Fax: 1-866-501-5581
Social Media: www.youtube.com/user/petsecure; plus.google.com/108154468377313956310/posts; www.facebook.com/petsecure; twitter.com/petsecure
Classes of Insurance: Personal Accident & Sickness

***Pilot Insurance Company**
2206 Eglinton Ave. East
Toronto, ON M1L 4S8
Tel: 416-288-1800; *Toll-Free:* 800-387-4518
www.avivacanada.com
Other Contact Information: Claims: 1-866-692-8482
Classes of Insurance: Auto, Property

The Portage La Prairie Mutual Insurance Company
PO Box 340
749 Saskatchewan Ave. East
Portage La Prairie, MB R1N 3B8
Tel: 204-857-3415; *Fax:* 204-239-6655
Toll-Free: 800-567-7721
info@portagemutual.com
www.portagemutual.com
Other Contact Information: Claims Toll-Free Fax: 1-866-345-1770
Classes of Insurance: Legal Expense, Auto, Liability, Property,

Primerica Life Insurance Company of Canada
Plaza 5
#300, 2000 Argentia Rd.
Mississauga, ON L5N 2R7
Tel: 905-812-2900; *Fax:* 905-813-5310
www.primericacanada.ca
Social Media: plus.google.com/109104859117861437180; www.youtube.com/primerica; www.facebook.com/Primerica; twitter.com/primerica
Classes of Insurance: Personal Accident & Sickness, Life

Primmum Insurance Company/ Primmum Compagnie D'Assurance
#600, 304 The East Mall
Toronto, ON M9B 6E2
Tel: 416-233-7590; *Fax:* 416-233-9171
Toll-Free: 866-466-5276
www.primmum.com
Other Contact Information: Toll-Free Phone, Quotes: 1-800-816-9618; Toll-Free Phone, Claims: 1-866-725-9722; Toll-Free Phone, Calgary, Edmonton, & Halifax: 1-800-268-8955
Classes of Insurance: Auto, Property

***Prince Edward Island Mutual Insurance Company**
116 Walker Ave.
Summerside, PE C1N 6V9
Tel: 902-436-2185; *Fax:* 902-436-0148
Toll-Free: 800-565-5441
protect@peimutual.com
www.peimutual.com
Classes of Insurance: Liability, Property, Fire, Theft

Principal Life Insurance Company/ Compagnie d'assurance-vie Principal
#2100, 40 King St. West
Toronto, ON M5H 3C2
www.principal.com
Social Media: www.youtube.com/user/PrincipalFinancial; www.facebook.com/PrincipalFinancial; twitter.com/ThePrincipal
Classes of Insurance: Personal Accident & Sickness, Life

***Promutuel Réassurance**
#400, 2000, boul Lebourgneuf
Québec, QC G2K 0B6
Toll-Free: 866-999-2433
federation@promutuel.ca
www.promutuel.ca
Social Media: www.youtube.com/user/PromutuelAssurance; fr.pinterest.com/promutuel; www.facebook.com/PromutuelAssurance; twitter.com/Promutuel
Classes of Insurance: Accident, Liability, Boiler & Machinery, Property, Fire, Surety, Theft, Reinsurance

***Promutuel Vie inc**
#400, 2000, boul Lebourgneuf
Québec, QC G2K 0B6
Toll-Free: 866-999-2433
federation@promutuel.ca
www.promutuel.ca
Social Media: www.facebook.com/PromutuelAssurance; twitter.com/Promutuel

Classes of Insurance: Accident, Personal Accident & Sickness, Life

*Québec Blue Cross/ Croix Bleue du Québec
#B9, 550, rue Sherbrooke ouest
Montréal, QC H3C 3S3
Tel: 514-286-7686; *Toll-Free:* 877-909-7686
info@qc.bluecross.ca
www.qc.croixbleue.ca
Other Contact Information: Tech Support: 1-800-563-2538
Classes of Insurance: Accident, Personal Accident & Sickness, Auto, Liability, Life

Rain & Hail Insurance Corporation
#200, 4303 Albert St.
Regina, SK S4S 3R6
Tel: 306-584-8844; *Fax:* 306-584-3466
Toll-Free: 800-667-8084
regina@rainhail.com
www.rainhail.com/about/canada.html
Classes of Insurance: Hail & Crop

RBC General Insurance Company/ Compagnie d'assurance generale RBC
6880 Financial Dr.
Mississauga, ON L5N 7Y5
Tel: 905-286-5099; *Toll-Free:* 800-769-2526
www.rbcinsurance.com
Classes of Insurance: Personal Accident & Sickness, Auto, Liability, Property, Fire, Theft

RBC Insurance
Tower 1
6880 Financial Dr.
Mississauga, ON L5N 7Y5
Toll-Free: 866-235-4332
src-nationaloffice@rbc.com
www.rbcinsurance.com
Social Media: www.facebook.com/RBCInsurance
Classes of Insurance: Personal Accident & Sickness, Auto, Life, Property

RBC Life Insurance Company
6880 Financial Dr.
Mississauga, ON L5N 7Y5
Tel: 905-286-5099; *Toll-Free:* 877-519-9501
www.rbcinsurance.com/lifeinsurance
Other Contact Information: 866-223-7113 (Toll Free, New Life Insurance Inquiries); 800-461-1413 (Toll Free, Existing Life Insurance Inquiries)
Classes of Insurance: Personal Accident & Sickness, Life

RBC Travel Insurance Company
6880 Financial Dr.
Mississauga, ON L5N 7Y5
Tel: 905-816-2561; *Fax:* 905-813-4719
www.rbcinsurance.com/travelinsurance/index.html
Other Contact Information: Toll Free, Trip Cancellation Insurance Claim: 800-263-8944
Classes of Insurance: Personal Accident & Sickness, Life

*Real Estate Insurance Exchange (REIX)
#205, 4954 Richard Rd. SW
Calgary, AB T3E 6L1
Tel: 403-228-2667; *Fax:* 403-229-3466
Toll-Free: 877-462-7349
info@reix.ca
www.reix.ca
Classes of Insurance: Liability

*Red River Valley Mutual Insurance Co.
PO Box 940
245 Centre Ave. East
Altona, MB R0G 0B0
Tel: 204-324-6434; *Fax:* 204-324-1316
Toll-Free: 800-370-2888
info@redrivermutual.com
www.redrivermutual.com
Social Media: www.youtube.com/user/redrivermutual; www.facebook.com/rrmlossprevention; twitter.com/RedRiverMutual
Classes of Insurance: Liability, Boiler & Machinery, Fidelity, Property, Fire, Surety, Theft

Reliable Life Insurance Company
PO Box 557
100 King St. West
Hamilton, ON L8N 3K9
Tel: 905-523-5587; *Fax:* 905-528-8338
Toll-Free: 800-465-0661
service@reliablelifeinsurance.com
www.reliablelifeinsurance.com
Classes of Insurance: Personal Accident & Sickness, Life

RGA Life Reinsurance Company of Canada/ RGA Compagnie de réassurance-vie du Canada
#1100, 55 University Ave.
Toronto, ON M5J 2H7
Tel: 416-682-0000; *Fax:* 416-777-9526
Toll-Free: 800-433-4326
www.rgare.com/offices/canada
Social Media: www.facebook.com/rgaglobal
Classes of Insurance: Reinsurance

Royal & Sun Alliance Insurance Company of Canada (RSA)
#800, 18 York St.
Toronto, ON M5E 1L5
Tel: 416-366-7511; *Fax:* 416-367-9869
Toll-Free: 800-268-8406
www.rsagroup.ca
Social Media: twitter.com/rsacanada
Classes of Insurance: Personal Accident & Sickness, Auto, Property

*S&Y Insurance Company
2206 Eglinton Ave. East
Toronto, ON M1L 4S8
Tel: 416-288-1800; *Toll-Free:* 800-387-4518
www.avivacanada.com
Other Contact Information: Claims: 1-866-692-8482
Classes of Insurance: Auto

*Saskatchewan Auto Fund
2260 - 11th Ave.
Regina, SK S4P 0J9
Tel: 306-751-1200; *Fax:* 306-565-8666
Toll-Free: 800-667-8015
sgiinquiries@sgi.sk.ca
www.sgi.sk.ca
Social Media: www.youtube.com/SGIcommunications; instagram.com/sgiphotos; www.facebook.com/SGIcommunity; twitter.com/SGItweets
Classes of Insurance: Auto

*Saskatchewan Blue Cross
PO Box 4030
516, 2nd Ave. North
Saskatoon, SK S7K 3T2
Tel: 306-244-1192; *Fax:* 306-652-5751
Toll-Free: 800-667-6853
www.sk.bluecross.ca
Social Media: www.facebook.com/sk.push2play; twitter.com/SKBlueCross
Classes of Insurance: Personal Accident & Sickness, Life

*Saskatchewan Crop Insurance Corporation (SCIC)
PO Box 3000
484 Prince William Dr.
Melville, SK S0A 2P0
Tel: 306-728-7200; *Fax:* 306-728-7202
Toll-Free: 888-935-0000
customer.service@scic.gov.sk.ca
www.saskcropinsurance.com
Classes of Insurance: Hail & Crop

*Saskatchewan Municipal Hail Insurance Association
2100 Cornwall St.
Regina, SK S4P 2K7
Tel: 306-569-1852; *Fax:* 306-522-3717
Toll-Free: 877-414-7644
smhi@smhi.ca
www.smhi.ca
Classes of Insurance: Hail & Crop

Saskatchewan Mutual Insurance Company (SMI)
279 - 3 Ave. North
Saskatoon, SK S7K 2H8
Tel: 306-653-4232; *Fax:* 306-664-1957
Toll-Free: 800-667-3067
headoffice@saskmutual.com
www.saskmutual.com
Classes of Insurance: Auto, Liability, Boiler & Machinery, Fidelity, Property

SCOR Canada Reinsurance Company/ SCOR Canada Compagnie de Réassurance
PO Box 329, Commerce Court Stn. Commerce Court
#2800, 199 Bay St.
Toronto, ON M5L 1G1
Tel: 416-869-3670; *Fax:* 416-365-9393
ca@scor.com
www.scor.com
Social Media: www.youtube.com/channel/UC22APNWCxjyPJvMaU5xb9xg; twitter.com/SCOR_SE
Classes of Insurance: Reinsurance

SCOR Global Life SE, Canada Branch/ SCOR Global Vie Canada
#4510, 1250, boul René Lévesque ouest
Montréal, QC H3B 4W8
Tel: 514-933-6994; *Fax:* 514-933-6435
life@scor.com
www.scor.com
Classes of Insurance: Personal Accident & Sickness, Life

Scotia Life Insurance Company/ Scotia-Vie Compagnie d'Assurance
#400, 100 Yonge St.
Toronto, ON M5H 1H1
Toll-Free: 800-387-9844
www.scotialifefinancial.com
Classes of Insurance: Personal Accident & Sickness, Life

*Scottish & York Insurance Co. Limited
2206 Eglinton Ave. East
Toronto, ON M1L 4S8
Tel: 416-288-1800; *Toll-Free:* 800-387-4518
www.avivacanada.com
Other Contact Information: Claims: 1-866-692-8482
Classes of Insurance: Legal Expense, Auto, Liability, Boiler & Machinery, Fidelity, Property, Surety

Security National Insurance Company/ Sécurité Nationale compagnie d'assurance
50, Place Crémazie, 12e étage
Montréal, QC H2P 1B6
Toll-Free: 800-361-3821
www.melochemonnex.com
Classes of Insurance: Personal Accident & Sickness, Auto, Property, Fire

Servus Insurance Services - Home & Auto
PO Box 12049
10 Factory Lane
St. John's, NL A1B 1R7
Tel: 709-737-1500; *Fax:* 709-737-1580
Toll-Free: 800-563-1650
headoffice@johnson.ca
www.johnson.ca/servus
Classes of Insurance: Auto, Property

*SGI CANADA Consolidated
2260 - 11th Ave.
Regina, SK S4P 0J9
Tel: 306-751-1200; *Fax:* 306-565-8666
Toll-Free: 844-855-2744
sgiinquiries@sgi.sk.ca
www.sgi.sk.ca
Social Media: www.youtube.com/SGIcommunications; instagram.com/sgiphotos; www.facebook.com/SGIcommunity; twitter.com/SGItweets
Classes of Insurance: Accident, Aircraft, Auto, Liability, Boiler & Machinery, Fidelity, Property, Surety, Reinsurance

*SGI CANADA Insurance Services Ltd. Alberta
#303, 4220 - 98th St. NW
Edmonton, AB T6E 6A1
Tel: 780-822-1228; *Fax:* 780-435-1489
Toll-Free: 877-435-1484
inquiries.ab@sgicanada.ca
www.sgicanada.ca/ab
Other Contact Information: After-hours Claims, Toll-Free: 1-800-647-6448
Social Media: www.youtube.com/SGIcommunications; instagram.com/sgiphotos; www.facebook.com/SGIcommunity; twitter.com/SGItweets
Classes of Insurance: Auto, Property, Surety, Hail & Crop

*SGI CANADA Insurance Services Ltd. British Columbia
c/o SGI CANADA Insurance Services Ltd. Alberta
#303, 4220 - 98 St. NW
Edmonton, AB T6E 6A1
Tel: 780-822-1228; *Fax:* 780-435-1489
Toll-Free: 877-435-1484
inquiries.bc@sgicanada.ca
www.sgicanada.ca/bc
Social Media: www.youtube.com/SGIcommunications; instagram.com/sgiphotos; www.facebook.com/SGIcommunity; twitter.com/SGItweets
Classes of Insurance: Auto, Property, Surety, Hail & Crop

***SGI CANADA Insurance Services Ltd. Manitoba**
1321 Kenaston Blvd.
Winnipeg, MB R3P 2P2
Tel: 204-925-9200; *Fax:* 204-925-9219
Toll-Free: 888-444-4114
inquiries.mb@sgicanada.ca
www.sgicanada.ca/mb
Social Media: www.youtube.com/SGIcommunications; instagram.com/sgiphotos; www.facebook.com/SGIcommunity; twitter.com/SGItweets
Classes of Insurance: Auto, Property, Surety, Hail & Crop

Sirius America Insurance Company
#1202, 80 Bloor St. West
Toronto, ON M5S 2V1
Tel: 416-928-2430; *Fax:* 416-928-2459
info@siriusamerica.com
www.siriusamerica.com
Classes of Insurance: Auto, Liability, Fidelity, Property, Surety, Hail & Crop

***Société de l'assurance automobile du Québec**
CP 19600, Terminus Stn. Terminus
333, boul. Jean-Lesage
Québec, QC G1K 8J6
Tél: 418-643-7620; *Ligne sans frais:* 800-361-7620
www.saaq.gouv.qc.ca
Other Contact Information: Montréal: 514/873-7620
Média social: www.youtube.com/user/saaq; www.facebook.com/SAAQQC; twitter.com/saaq
Classes of Insurance: Accident, Auto

***Solicour Inc.**
2954, boul Laurier
Québec, QC G1V 4T2
Tél: 418-650-2211; *Téléc:* 418-650-2244
Ligne sans frais: 888-852-4444
solicour-que@solicour.com
www.solicour.com
Classes of Insurance: Personal Accident & Sickness, Life

Sons of Scotland Benevolent Association
#801, 505 Consumers Rd.
Toronto, ON M2J 4V8
Tel: 416-482-1250; *Fax:* 416-482-9576
Toll-Free: 800-387-3382
info@sonsofscotland.com
www.sonsofscotland.com
Classes of Insurance: Life

***South Easthope Mutual Insurance Co.**
PO Box 33
62 Woodstock St.
Tavistock, ON N0B 2R0
Tel: 519-655-2011; *Fax:* 519-655-2021
Toll-Free: 800-263-9987
seins@seins.on.ca
www.seins.on.ca
Classes of Insurance: Accident, Auto, Boiler & Machinery, Property

***Southeastern Mutual Insurance Company**
663 Pinewood Rd.
Riverview, NB E1B 5R6
Tel: 506-386-9002; *Fax:* 506-386-3325
Toll-Free: 800-561-7223
www.semutual.nb.ca
Social Media: www.facebook.com/semutual
Classes of Insurance: Liability, Boiler & Machinery, Property, Fire

The Sovereign General Insurance Company
#140, 6700 Macleod Trail SE
Calgary, AB T2H 0L3
Tel: 403-298-4200; *Toll-Free:* 800-661-1652
www.sovereigngeneral.com
Classes of Insurance: Personal Accident & Sickness, Property

***SSQ, Société d'assurance inc./ SSQ Insurance Company Inc.**
#1800, 2020, rue Université
Montréal, QC H3A 2A5
Tel: 514-282-6064; *Toll-Free:* 855-233-7056
communications@ssq.ca
www.ssq.ca
Classes of Insurance: Personal Accident & Sickness, Auto, Life, Credit, Property

***SSQ, Société d'assurances générales inc./ SSQ General Insurance Company Inc.**
Édifice Le Delta II
CP 10530, Sainte-Foy Stn. Sainte-Foy
2515, boul Laurier
Québec, QC G1V 0A5
Tél: 418-683-0554; *Téléc:* 418-683-5603
Ligne sans frais: 866-777-2886
service@ssqauto.com
ssqauto.com
Other Contact Information: SSQ Corporate Communications: communications@ssq.ca
Classes of Insurance: Accident, Auto, Liability, Property, Fire, Theft

***SSQ, Société d'assurance-vie inc./ SSQ, Life Insurance Company Inc.**
CP 10500
2525, boul Laurier
Québec, QC G1V 4H6
Tél: 418-651-7000; *Ligne sans frais:* 888-900-3457
communications@ssq.ca
www.ssq.ca
Classes of Insurance: Accident, Personal Accident & Sickness, Auto, Liability, Life, Property, Fire

The Standard Life Assurance Company of Canada
PO Box 11601, Centre-Ville Stn. Centre-Ville
Montréal, QC H3C 5S9
Toll-Free: 888-841-6633
css@manulife.com
www.manulife.ca
Other Contact Information: Group Savings & Retirement Toll-Free Phone: 1-800-242-1704; Group Life & Health Toll-Free Phone: 1-800-499-4425
Classes of Insurance: Personal Accident & Sickness, Life

***Stanley Mutual Insurance Company**
32 Irishtown Rd.
Stanley, NB E6B 1B6
Tel: 506-367-2273; *Fax:* 506-367-3076
Toll-Free: 800-442-9714
info@stanleymutual.com
www.stanleymutual.com
Social Media: www.facebook.com/1618887341689782
Classes of Insurance: Auto, Liability, Boiler & Machinery, Property

State Farm Canada
333 First Commerce Dr.
Aurora, ON L4G 8A4
Tel: 905-750-4100
info@statefarm.com
www.statefarm.ca
Other Contact Information: Technical Help Toll-Free: 1-888-559-1922
Social Media: www.youtube.com/statefarm; www.flickr.com/photos/statefarm; www.facebook.com/statefarmcanada; twitter.com/statefarm
Classes of Insurance: Aircraft, Auto, Liability, Boiler & Machinery, Fidelity, Property, Fire, Surety

Stewart Title Guaranty Company
North Tower, Royal Bank Plaza
#2600, 200 Bay St.
Toronto, ON M5J 2J2
Tel: 416-307-3300; *Fax:* 416-307-3305
Toll-Free: 888-667-5151
inquirycda@stewart.com
www.stewart.ca
Classes of Insurance: Property

Suecia Reinsurance Company
763 Pape Ave.
Toronto, ON M4K 3T2
Tel: 416-361-0056
Classes of Insurance: Personal Accident & Sickness, Auto, Liability, Fidelity, Property, Hail & Crop, Reinsurance

Sun Life Assurance Company of Canada
Corporate Office
150 King St. West
Toronto, ON M5H 1J9
Tel: 416-979-9966; *Fax:* 416-979-4853
www.sunlife.ca
Classes of Insurance: Personal Accident & Sickness, Life

Sun Life Financial Inc.
Corporate Office
150 King St. West
Toronto, ON M5H 1J9
Tel: 416-979-9966; *Toll-Free:* 877-786-5433
service@sunlife.ca
www.sunlife.ca
Social Media: www.youtube.com/sunlifefinancial; www.facebook.com/SLFCanada; twitter.com/SunLifeCA
Classes of Insurance: Life

Sunderland Marine Insurance Company Ltd./ Société d'assurance maritime Sunderland Limitée
#160, 200 Waterfront Dr.
Bedford, NS B4A 4J4
Tel: 902-405-7773; *Fax:* 902-405-8338
canada@sunderlandmarine.com
sunderlandmarine.com
Classes of Insurance: Marine

Supreme Council of the Royal Arcanum
#200, 1 Hunter St. East
Hamilton, ON L8N 3R1
Tel: 905-528-8411; *Fax:* 905-528-9008
www.royalarcanum.com
Social Media: www.facebook.com/467987633318865
Classes of Insurance: Personal Accident & Sickness, Life

Swiss Reinsurance Company Canada
#2200, 150 King St. West
Toronto, ON M5H 1J9
Tel: 416-408-0272; *Fax:* 416-408-4222
Toll-Free: 800-268-7116
www.swissre.com
Classes of Insurance: Marine, Fidelity, Property, Surety, Reinsurance

TD General Insurance Company
c/o Meloche Monnex Inc.
50, Place Crémazie, 12e étage
Montréal, QC H2P 1B6
www.tdinsurance.com
Classes of Insurance: Personal Accident & Sickness, Aircraft, Auto, Liability, Boiler & Machinery, Fidelity, Property, Surety

TD Home & Auto Insurance Company/ Compagnie d'Assurance Habitation et Auto TD
#401, 2161 Yonge St.
Toronto, ON M4S 3A6
Toll-Free: 800-338-0218
www.tdinsurance.com
Other Contact Information: 866-361-2311 (Toll Free, Client Services); 866-848-9744 (Toll Free, Claims)
Classes of Insurance: Auto, Liability, Property,

TD Life Insurance Company/ TD, Compagnie d'assurance-vie
Richmond Adelaide Centre
120 Adelaide St. West, 2nd Fl.
Toronto, ON M5H 1T1
Toll-Free: 877-397-4187
www.tdinsurance.com
Classes of Insurance: Personal Accident & Sickness, Life

Temple Insurance Company
390 Bay St., 21st Fl.
Toronto, ON M5H 2Y2
Tel: 416-364-2851; *Fax:* 416-361-1163
Toll-Free: 877-364-2851
www.templeinsurance.ca
Classes of Insurance: Boiler & Machinery, Property

***Thistle Home**
PO Box 11086
#136, 1055 West Georgia St.
Vancouver, BC V6E 3P3
Tel: 604-629-1922; *Fax:* 604-685-2273
Toll-Free: 855-666-4576
www.thistlecanada.com
Classes of Insurance: Property

***Thistle Underwriting Services (TUS)**
#136, 1055 West Georgia St.
Vancouver, BC V63 3P3
Tel: 604-629-1922; *Fax:* 604-685-2273
Toll-Free: 855-666-4576
www.thistlecanada.com
Classes of Insurance: Auto, Property

***Thomson Jemmett Vogelzang**
321 Concession
Kingston, ON K7K 2B9
Tel: 613-544-5313; *Fax:* 613-542-6839
Toll-Free: 800-787-5006
kingston@johnson.ca
www.insurancecentre.com
Other Contact Information: Gananoque: 613-382-2111; 1-800-798-1524
Classes of Insurance: Auto, Liability, Property

***Thomson-Schindle-Green Insurance & Financial Services Ltd.**
Chinook Place
#100, 623 - 4th St. SE
Medicine Hat, AB T1A 0L1
Tel: 403-526-3283; *Fax:* 403-526-8082
Toll-Free: 800-830-9423
tsg@tsginsurance.com
www.tsginsurance.com
Other Contact Information: After Hours Claims, Toll-Free Phone: 1-888-224-5677
Classes of Insurance: Auto, Liability, Life, Property, Hail & Crop

The Toa Reinsurance Company of America (Canada Branch)
PO Box 53
#1700, 55 University Ave.
Toronto, ON M5J 2H7
Tel: 416-366-5888; *Fax:* 416-366-7444
info@toare.com
www.toare.com
Classes of Insurance: Reinsurance

The Tokio Marine & Nichido Fire Insurance Co., Ltd.
c/o Lombard Canada Ltd.
105 Adelaide St. West, 3rd Fl.
Toronto, ON M5H 1P9
Tel: 416-362-6584
www.tokiomarine-nichido.co.jp/en
Classes of Insurance: Auto, Marine, Property, Fire

***Town & Country Mutual Insurance**
79 Caradoc St. North
Strathroy, ON N7G 2M5
Tel: 519-246-1132; *Fax:* 519-246-1115
Toll-Free: 888-868-5064
info@town-country-ins.ca
www.town-country-ins.ca
Other Contact Information: Emergency After-Hours Claims Service Toll-Free Phone: 1-877-488-6642
Social Media: www.facebook.com/350137961781422; twitter.com/TCMutualInsures
Classes of Insurance: Personal Accident & Sickness, Auto, Liability, Boiler & Machinery, Fidelity, Property, Hail & Crop

***Townsend Farmers' Mutual Fire Insurance Company**
PO Box 1030
7800 Old Highway 24
Waterford, ON N0E 1Y0
Tel: 519-443-7231; *Fax:* 519-443-5198
Toll-Free: 888-302-6052
www.townsendfarmers.com
Classes of Insurance: Personal Accident & Sickness, Auto, Liability, Boiler & Machinery, Property, Hail & Crop

Traders General Insurance Company/ Compagnie d'Assurance Traders Générale
2206 Eglinton Ave. East
Toronto, ON M1L 4S8
Tel: 416-288-1800; *Toll-Free:* 800-387-4518
www.avivacanada.com
Other Contact Information: Claims: 1-866-692-8482
Classes of Insurance: Auto, Property

***Tradition Mutual Insurance Company**
PO Box 10
264 Huron Rd.
Sebringville, ON N0K 1X0
Tel: 519-393-6402; *Fax:* 519-393-5185
Toll-Free: 877-380-6402
www.traditionmutual.com
Social Media: www.youtube.com/user/ontariomutuals; www.facebook.com/164242353651450; twitter.com/traditionmutual
Classes of Insurance: Accident, Auto, Liability, Boiler & Machinery, Fidelity, Property, Hail & Crop

Trafalgar Insurance Company of Canada
#1500, 700 University Ave.
Toronto, ON M5G 0A1
www.belairdirect.com
Classes of Insurance: Auto, Property, Theft

***Trans Global Insurance Company (TGI)**
c/o Borden Ladner Gervais, Scotia Plaza
40 King St. West
Toronto, ON M5H 3Y4
Tel: 416-367-6121; *Fax:* 416-361-2468
Toll-Free: 888-226-7876
tgli@tgins.com
www.tgins.com
Classes of Insurance: Personal Accident & Sickness, Liability, Property

***Trans Global Life Insurance Company (TGLI)**
c/o Borden Ladner Gervais, Scotia Plaza
40 King St. West
Toronto, ON M5H 3Y4
Tel: 416-367-6121; *Fax:* 416-361-2468
Toll-Free: 888-226-7876
tgli@tgins.com
www.tgins.com
Classes of Insurance: Personal Accident & Sickness, Life

Transatlantic Reinsurance Company
PO Box 3
#1110, 145 Wellington St. West
Toronto, ON M5J 1H8
Tel: 416-649-5300; *Fax:* 416-971-8782
www.transre.com
Classes of Insurance: Personal Accident & Sickness, Credit, Property, Surety, Reinsurance,

Travelers Canada
PO Box 4
#200, 20 Queen St. West
Toronto, ON M5H 3R3
Tel: 416-360-8183; *Toll-Free:* 800-330-5033
www.travelerscanada.ca
Social Media: www.youtube.com/travelersinsurance; www.facebook.com/travelers; twitter.com/Travelers
Classes of Insurance: Aircraft, Auto, Liability, Boiler & Machinery, Marine, Fidelity, Property, Fire, Surety, Reinsurance

***Trillium Mutual Insurance Company**
495 Mitchell Road S
Listowel, ON N4W 0C8
Tel: 519-291-9300; *Fax:* 519-291-1800
Toll-Free: 800-265-3020
admin@trilliummutual.com
www.trilliummutual.com
Social Media: www.facebook.com/trilliummutual; twitter.com/TrilliumMutual
Classes of Insurance: Accident, Auto, Liability, Boiler & Machinery, Marine, Fidelity, Property, Hail & Crop

Trisura Guarantee Insurance Company
Bay Adelaide Centre
PO Box 22
#1610, 333 Bay St.
Toronto, ON M5H 2R2
Tel: 416-214-2555; *Fax:* 416-214-9597
info@trisura.com
www.trisura.com
Classes of Insurance: Liability, Surety

Ukrainian Fraternal Society of Canada
235 McGregor St.
Winnipeg, MB R2W 4W5
Tel: 204-586-4482; *Fax:* 204-589-6411
Toll-Free: 800-988-8372
ufsc.ca
Classes of Insurance: Life

Ukrainian National Association (UNA)
Toronto, ON
www.ukrainiannationalassociation.org
Classes of Insurance: Personal Accident & Sickness, Life

***Unica Insurance Inc./ Unica assurances**
7150 Derrycrest Drive
Mississauga, ON L5W 0E5
Tel: 905-677-9777; *Toll-Free:* 800-676-6967
claims@unicainsurance.com
www.unicainsurance.com
Other Contact Information: Alt. E-mails: accounts@unicainsurance.com; commercial@unicainsurance.com; underwriting@unicainsurance.com
Classes of Insurance: Auto, Liability, Property

Unifund Assurance Company
PO Box 12049
10 Factory Lane
St. John's, NL A1C 6H5
Tel: 709-737-1500; *Fax:* 709-737-1580
Toll-Free: 888-737-1689
unifund@unifund.ca
www.unifund.ca
Classes of Insurance: Auto, Property

***L'Union-Vie, compagnie mutuelle d'assurance/ The Union Life, Mutual Assurance Company**
CP 696
142, rue Hériot
Drummondville, QC J2B 6W9
Tél: 819-478-1315; *Téléc:* 819-474-1990
Ligne sans frais: 800-567-0988
www.uvmutuelle.ca
Classes of Insurance: Personal Accident & Sickness, Life, Reinsurance

United American Insurance Company (UA)
c/o McLean & Kerr LLP
#2800, 130 Adelaide St. West
Toronto, ON M5H 3P5
Tel: 416-369-6624; *Fax:* 416-366-8571
www.unitedamerican.com
Social Media: www.youtube.com/user/UnitedAmerican1; plus.google.com/114538900986229499933; www.facebook.com/UnitedAmerican; twitter.com/United_American
Classes of Insurance: Personal Accident & Sickness, Life

***United General Insurance Corporation**
860 Prospect St.
Fredericton, NB E3B 2T8
Tel: 506-459-5120; *Fax:* 506-453-0882
Classes of Insurance: Auto

***Usborne & Hibbert Mutual Fire Insurance Company**
507 Main St. South
Exeter, ON N0M 1S1
Tel: 519-235-0350; *Fax:* 519-235-3623
www.usborneandhibbert.ca
Classes of Insurance: Personal Accident & Sickness, Auto, Liability, Boiler & Machinery, Property

***Uv Mutuelle/ The International Life Insurance Company**
CP 696
142, rue Hériot
Montréal, QC J2B 6W9
Tél: 819-478-1315; *Téléc:* 819-474-1990
Ligne sans frais: 800-567-0988
www.uvmutuelle.ca
Classes of Insurance: Personal Accident & Sickness, Life

***Vancity Life Insurance Services Ltd.**
PO Box 2120, Terminal Stn. Terminal
Vancouver, BC V6B 5R8
www.vancityinsurance.com
Classes of Insurance: Personal Accident & Sickness, Life

Virginia Surety Company, Inc. (VCS)/ Compagnie de Sûreté Virginia Inc.
#1200, 34 King St. East
Toronto, ON M5C 2X8
www.thewarrantygroup.com
Classes of Insurance: Auto, Liability, Boiler & Machinery, Property

***Wabisa Mutual Insurance Company**
35 Talbot St. East
Jarvis, ON N0A 1J0
Tel: 519-587-4454; *Fax:* 519-587-5470
Toll-Free: 888-507-3973
customer.service@wabisamutual.com
www.wabisamutual.com
Social Media: www.facebook.com/1454454134881976
Classes of Insurance: Personal Accident & Sickness, Auto, Liability, Fidelity, Property

Waterloo Insurance Company
590 Riverbend Dr.
Kitchener, ON N2K 3S2
Tel: 519-570-8335; *Fax:* 519-570-8312
Toll-Free: 800-265-4562
www.economicalinsurance.com
Classes of Insurance: Auto, Property

The Wawanesa Life Insurance Company
#400, 200 Main St.
Winnipeg, MB R3C 1A8
Tel: 204-985-3940; *Toll-Free:* 888-997-9965
life@wawanesa.com
www.wawanesalife.com
Other Contact Information: Group Phone: 204-985-3806; Fax: 204-985-5781; Toll-Free: 1-800-665-7076; E-mail: groupcustomerservice@wawanesa.com
Classes of Insurance: Personal Accident & Sickness, Life,

The Wawanesa Mutual Insurance Company
#900, 191 Broadway
Winnipeg, MB R3C 3P1
Tel: 204-985-3923; *Fax:* 204-942-7724
www.wawanesa.com
Social Media: www.facebook.com/WawanesaIns; twitter.com/WawanesaCanada
Classes of Insurance: Auto, Liability, Boiler & Machinery, Property, Fire, Surety, Theft

***Wedgwood Insurance Limited**
85 Thorburn Rd.
St. John's, NL A1B 4B7
Tel: 709-753-3210; *Fax:* 709-753-8238
Toll-Free: 888-884-4253
info@wedgwoodinsurance.com
www.wedgwoodinsurance.com
Social Media: www.facebook.com/WedgwoodIns; twitter.com/wedgwoodins
Classes of Insurance: Aircraft, Auto, Life, Marine, Property

***West Elgin Mutual Insurance Company**
PO Box 130
274 Currie Rd.
Dutton, ON N0L 1J0
Tel: 519-762-3530; *Fax:* 519-762-3801
Toll-Free: 800-265-7635
www.westelgin.com
Classes of Insurance: Personal Accident & Sickness, Auto, Liability, Fidelity, Property, Hail & Crop

***West Wawanosh Mutual Insurance Company**
PO Box 130
81 Southampton St., RR#1
Dungannon, ON N0M 1R0
Tel: 519-529-7921; *Fax:* 519-529-3211
wawains@wwmic.com
www.wwmic.com
Classes of Insurance: Personal Accident & Sickness, Auto, Liability, Boiler & Machinery, Fidelity, Property

Western Assurance Company (WA)
Sheridan Insurance Centre
#1000, 2225 Erin Mills Pkwy.
Mississauga, ON L5K 2S9
Tel: 905-403-3318; *Fax:* 905-403-3319
Toll-Free: 877-263-4442
www.westernassurance.ca
Classes of Insurance: Personal Accident & Sickness, Aircraft, Auto, Liability, Boiler & Machinery, Marine, Fidelity, Property, Surety

***Western Financial Group Inc.**
1010 - 24 St. SE
High River, AB T1V 2A7
Tel: 403-652-2663; *Fax:* 403-652-2661
Toll-Free: 866-843-9378
info@westernfg.ca
www.westernfinancialgroup.ca
Social Media: www.youtube.com/user/WesternFinancial; plus.google.com/+WesternFinancialGroupCa; www.facebook.com/westernfinancialgroup; twitter.com/Western_FG
Classes of Insurance: Accident, Personal Accident & Sickness, Auto, Liability, Boiler & Machinery, Life, Fidelity, Property, Fire, Surety, Hail & Crop, Theft

Western Financial Insurance Company
#300, 600 Empress St.
Winnipeg, MB R3G 0R5
Toll-Free: 800-581-0580
info@westernfic.com
www.westernfic.com
Classes of Insurance: Personal Accident & Sickness

Western Life Assurance Company
1010 - 24th St. SE
High River, AB T1V 2A7
Tel: 403-652-4356; *Fax:* 403-652-2673
Toll-Free: 877-452-4356
info@westernlife.com
www.westernlifeassurance.net
Classes of Insurance: Personal Accident & Sickness, Life

Western Surety Company
PO Box 527
#2100, 1881 Scarth St.
Regina, SK S4P 2G8
Tel: 306-791-3735; *Fax:* 306-359-0929
Toll-Free: 800-475-4454
wscinfo@westernsurety.ca
www.westernsurety.ca
Social Media: www.facebook.com/westernsurety; twitter.com/WesternSurety
Classes of Insurance: Fidelity, Surety

***Westland Insurance**
#200, 2121 - 160th St.
Surrey, BC V3Z 9N6
Tel: 778-545-2100; *Toll-Free:* 800-899-3093
contactus@westlandinsurance.ca
www.westlandinsurance.ca
Other Contact Information: Claims Toll-Free Fax: 1-866-775-6861
Social Media: plus.google.com/+WestlandInsuranceGroupSurrey; www.facebook.com/westland.insurance.canada; twitter.com/WestlandIns
Classes of Insurance: Auto, Liability, Property

***Westminster Mutual Insurance Company**
14122 Belmont Rd.
Belmont, ON N0L 1B0
Tel: 519-644-1663; *Fax:* 519-644-0315
Toll-Free: 800-565-3523
www.westminstermutual.com
Classes of Insurance: Auto, Liability, Property

Westport Insurance Corporation
#2200, 150 King St. West
Toronto, ON M5H 1J9
Tel: 416-408-0272; *Toll-Free:* 800-268-7116
www.swissre.com
Classes of Insurance: Personal Accident & Sickness, Aircraft, Auto, Liability, Boiler & Machinery, Credit, Fidelity, Property, Surety, Hail & Crop

Wynward Insurance Group
#1240, 1 Lombard Pl.
Winnipeg, MB R3B 0V9
Tel: 204-943-0721; *Fax:* 204-943-6419
Toll-Free: 800-665-3351
info@wynward.com
wynward.com
Other Contact Information: infowinnipeg@wynward.com
Social Media: www.facebook.com/Wynward?fref=ts
Classes of Insurance: Liability, Boiler & Machinery, Fidelity, Property, Fire, Surety, Theft

XL Catlin Canada Inc.
First Canadian Place
#3020, 100 King St. West
Toronto, ON M5X 1C9
Tel: 416-644-3312
www.xlcatlin.com
Social Media: www.youtube.com/user/MakeYourWorldGo; twitter.com/xlcatlin
Classes of Insurance: Personal Accident & Sickness, Auto, Liability, Boiler & Machinery, Property, Surety

XL Reinsurance America Inc.
Scotia Plaza
#1702, 100 Yonge St.
Toronto, ON M5C 2W1
Tel: 416-598-1084; *Fax:* 416-598-1980
www.xlcatlin.com
Social Media: www.youtube.com/user/MakeYourWorldGo
Classes of Insurance: Personal Accident & Sickness, Aircraft, Auto, Liability, Boiler & Machinery, Fidelity, Property, Surety, Hail & Crop

***Yarmouth Mutual Fire Insurance Company**
1229 Talbot St. East
St Thomas, ON N5P 1G8
Tel: 519-631-1572; *Fax:* 519-631-6058
Toll-Free: 877-792-3693
office@yarmouthmutual.com
www.yarmouthmutual.com
Social Media: www.facebook.com/yarmouthmutualinsurance
Classes of Insurance: Auto, Liability, Property, Hail & Crop

Zenith Insurance Company/ Compagnie d'Assurance Zenith
c/o Northbridge Financial Corporation
#700, 105 Adelaide St. West
Toronto, ON M5H 1P9
Tel: 416-350-4400; *Toll-Free:* 888-440-4876
inquiries@zenithinsurance.ca
www.privilege50.com
Classes of Insurance: Personal Accident & Sickness, Auto, Liability, Property

Zurich Canada
First Canadian Place
100 King St. West
Toronto, ON M5X 1C9
Tel: 416-586-3000; *Fax:* 416-586-2525
Toll-Free: 800-387-5454
www.zurichcanada.com
Social Media: twitter.com/zurichcanada
Classes of Insurance: Accident, Personal Accident & Sickness, Auto, Liability, Boiler & Machinery, Credit, Marine, Fidelity, Property, Fire, Surety, Theft

Major Companies

Agriculture

AG Growth International (AGI)
198 Commerce Dr.
Winnipeg, MB R3P 0Z6
204-489-1855
Fax: 204-488-6929
sales@aggrowth.com
www.aggrowth.com
Social Media: twitter.com/AgGrowthIntl
www.linkedin.com/company/ag-growth-international-agi-
Company Type: Public
Ticker Symbol: AFN / TSX
Staff Size: 1,667
Profile: AG Growth International Inc. was created in 1996. The company is involved in the manufacturing of grain handling, conditioning, & storage equipment. Products include belt conveyors, augers, grain storage bins, & grain aeration equipment.
Tim Close, President & Chief Executive Officer
Steve Sommerfeld, Executive Vice-President & Chief Financial Officer
Daniel Donner, Senior Vice-President, Commercial

AGT Food & Ingredients
6200 East Primrose Green Dr.
Regina, SK S4V 3L7
306-525-4490
Fax: 306-525-4463
www.agtfoods.com
Social Media: www.facebook.com/AGTFoodsRetail
twitter.com/agtfoodsretail
Company Type: Public
Ticker Symbol: AGT / TSX
Staff Size: 1,550
Profile: AGT Food & Ingredients was created in 2007, when Agtech Income Fund, the predecessor to Alliance Grain Traders, acquired Saskcan Pulse Trading. The re-branded fund, Alliance Grain Traders Income Fund, converted to a dividend paying corporation in 2009. AGT Food & Ingredients is engaged in the purchase of lentils, peas, beans, & chickpeas from farmers & exporting them to more than 100 countreies.
Murad Al-Katib, President & Chief Executive Officer
Gaetan Bourassa, Chief Operating Officer
Lori Ireland, Chief Financial Officer

Bevo Agro Inc.
PO Box 73, 7170 Glover Rd.
Milner, BC V0X 1T0
604-888-0420
Fax: 604-888-8048
www.bevoagro.com
Company Type: Public
Ticker Symbol: BVO / TSX-V
Staff Size: 300
Profile: Bevo is a supplier of propagated plants in North America, providing greenhouses, field farms, nurseries, and wholesalers across the continent with healthy, vigorous, pest-and-disease-free plants.
Jack Benne, President & CEO
John Hoekstra, Chief Financial Officer

Buhler Industries Inc.
1260 Clarence Ave.
Winnipeg, MB R3T 1T2
204-661-8711
Fax: 204-654-2503
info@buhler.com
www.buhlerindustries.com
Company Type: Public
Ticker Symbol: BUI / TSX
Staff Size: 1,100
Profile: Buhler Industries Inc. was established in 1932. The company manufactures & distributes agricultural equipment, such as tractors, augers, front-end loaders, & compact implements. Brand names include Versatile, Allied, & Farm King.
Yury Ryazanov, Chief Executive Officer
Willy Janzen, Chief Financial Officer

Canopy Growth
1 Hershey Dr.
Smiths Falls, ON K7A 0A8
855-558-9333
invest@canopygrowth.com
canopygrowth.com
Company Type: Public
Ticker Symbol: CGC / TSX
Profile: A marijuana growth company.
Bruce Linton, Chief Executive Officer
Tim Saunders, CFO & Senior Vice-President
Mark Zekulin, President

Ceres Global Ag Corp.
1660 South Hwy. 100
St. Louis Park, MN 55416 USA
info@ceresglobalag.com
ceresglobalagcorp.com
Company Type: Public
Ticker Symbol: CRP / TSX
Profile: Ceres Global Ag Corp. provide investors with a direct and indirect exposure to global agricultural assets.
Robert Day, President & Interim CEO
Mark Kucala, Vice-President & CFO

Feronia Inc.
Bay Wellington Tower, Brookfield Place
#1800, 181 Bay St.
Toronto, ON M5J 2T9
info@feronia.com
www.feronia.com
Other Communications: Investor Relations, E-mail: investor.relations@feronia.com
Social Media: twitter.com/feroniainc
www.linkedin.com/company/feronia-inc
Company Type: Public
Ticker Symbol: FRN / TSX
Staff Size: 3,853
Profile: Feronia PHC has been in operation since 1911 and is one of the largest palm oil producers in Africa. Its operations span 107,892 hectares in the Democratic Republic of the Congo.
Xavier de Carniere, Chief Executive Officer
Raymond Bantanga, Chief Operating Officer
David Steel, Chief Financial Officer

Input Capital
#300, 1914 Hamilton St.
Regina, SK S4P 3N6
Fax: 306-352-4110
844-715-7355
info@inputcapital.com
inputcapital.com
Social Media: twitter.com/InputCapital
Company Type: Private
Ticker Symbol: INP / TSX
Profile: Input Capital purchases canola from farmers through multi-year contracts.
Doug Emsley, President & CEO
Brad Farquhar, Executive Vice-President & CFO
Gord Nystuen, Vice-President, Market Development

MBAC Fertilizer Corp.
#2500, 1 Dundas St. West
Toronto, ON M5G 1Z3
416-367-2200
Fax: 416-367-2244
investor@mbacfert.com
www.mbacfert.com
Company Type: Public
Ticker Symbol: MBC / TSX
Profile: MBAC Fertilizer Corp. is focused on the production of phosphate and potash fertilizers in the Brazilian and Latin American markets.
Cristiano Melcher, Chief Executive Officer
Nelson Canato Jr., Vice-President, Operations, Brazil

Village Farms International, Inc.
4700 - 80th St.
Delta, BC V4K 3N3
604-940-6012
Fax: 604-940-6312
www.villagefarms.com
Social Media: www.facebook.com/124382917984
twitter.com/villagefarms
www.linkedin.com/company/village-farms-international-inc-
Company Type: Public
Ticker Symbol: VFF / TSX
Staff Size: 1,200
Profile: Village Farms produces, markets, & distributes greenhouse-grown bell peppers, tomatoes, & cucumbers. Greenhouse facilities are situated in British Columbia & Texas. Products are distributed mainly to retail grocers & fresh food distributors in Canada & the United States.
Michael A. DeGiglio, President & CEO
Stephen C. Ruffini, Chief Financial Officer & Executive Vice-President

Business & Computer Services

Absolute Software Corporation
PO Box 49211, #1400, 1055 Dunsmuir St.
Vancouver, BC V7X 1K8
604-730-9851
Fax: 604-730-2621
800-220-0733
www.absolute.com
Other Communications: USA Headquarters, Austin, Texas, Phone: 512-600-7455
Social Media: www.facebook.com/absolutesoftware
twitter.com/absolutecorp
www.linkedin.com/company/absolute-software
Company Type: Public
Ticker Symbol: ABT / TSX
Staff Size: 444
Profile: Absolute Software Corporation provides endpoint security & management for computers & ultra-portable devices.
Geoff Haydon, Chief Executive Officer
Christopher Bolin, Chief Product Officer
Sean Maxwell, Chief Commercial Officer
Errol Olsen, Chief Financial Officer

AgJunction Inc.
2207 Iowa St.
Hiawatha, KS 66434 USA
785-742-2976
Fax: 785-742-4584
800-247-3808
CorporateCommunications@AgJunction.com
www.corp.agjunction.com
Other Communications: Canadian Sales, Phone: 204-888-4472
Company Type: Public
Ticker Symbol: AJX / TSX
Staff Size: 182
Profile: AgJunction develops hardware & software used for agriculture machinery. Its brands include Outback Guidance & Satloc. In 2015 the company merged with Novariant.
David Vaughn, President & CEO
Mike Manning, Vice-President & CFO

AlarmForce Industries
675 Garyray Dr.
Toronto, ON M9L 1R2
416-445-0425
800-267-2001
www.alarmforce.com
Social Media: www.facebook.com/alarmforce
twitter.com/AlarmForceInc
Company Type: Public
Ticker Symbol: AF / TSX
Staff Size: 172
Profile: AlarmForce is the manufacturer of Alarmvoice, AlarmPlus, AlarmCare & VideoRelay systems. They distributes, installs and services these systems throughout Canada and in the States.
Graham Badun, CEO
Chris Lynch, Chief Financial Officer

Axia NetMedia Corporation
Corporate Head Office
#110, 220 - 12 Ave. SW
Calgary, AB T2R 0E9
403-538-4000
Fax: 403-538-4100
866-773-3348
info@axia.com
www.axia.com
Other Communications: Investor Relations: ir@axia.com
Social Media: www.facebook.com/AxiaFibre
twitter.com/axianmc
www.linkedin.com/company/339327
Company Type: Public
Ticker Symbol: AXX / TSX
Staff Size: 160
Profile: The company sells services over fibre optic communications infrastructure in regions that have implemented the Axia NGN Solution. Axia's networks are in Alberta, Massachusetts, France, Spain, & Singapore.
Arthur R. Price, Chair & Chief Executive Officer
Robert Price, Vice-President, Enterprise & Residential
Alan Hartslief, Chief Financial Officer
Mark Blake, Vice-President, Government
Cameron Barrett, Vice-President, Carrier
Lindsay Skabar, Vice-President, Marketing & Communications

BSM Technologies Inc.
#100, 75 International Blvd.
Toronto, ON M9W 6L9
416-675-1201
Fax: 416-679-8992
866-768-4771
info@bsmwireless.com
www.bsmwireless.com
Social Media: www.facebook.com/bsmwirelessinc
twitter.com/bsmwireless
www.linkedin.com/company/bsm-wireless
Company Type: Public
Ticker Symbol: GPS / TSX.V
Staff Size: 255
Profile: BSM Technologies is the owner of BSM Wireless Inc., a company which developments telematics & location smart software.
Aly Rahemtulla, President & CEO
Louis De Jong, CFO & Corporate Secretary
Alban Hoxha, Chief Technology Officer

Computer Modelling Group Ltd.
#200, 1824 Crowchild Trail NW
Calgary, AB T2M 3Y7
403-531-1300
Fax: 403-289-8502
support@cmgl.ca
www.cmgl.ca
Company Type: Public
Ticker Symbol: CMG / TSX
Staff Size: 213
Profile: Computer Modelling Group Ltd. is a computer software engineering & consulting company. It serves the oil & gas industry. Sales & technical support services are situated in Calgary, Houston, London, Dubai, & Caracas.
Ken M. Dedeluk, President & Chief Executive Officer
Sandra Balic, CFO & Vice-President, Finance
James Erdle, Vice-President, USA & Latin America
Ryan Schneider, Chief Operating Officer

Constellation Software Inc.
#1200, 20 Adelaide St. East
Toronto, ON M5C 2T6
416-861-2279
Fax: 416-861-2287
info@csisoftware.com
www.csisoftware.com
Company Type: Public
Ticker Symbol: CSU / TSX
Staff Size: 12,225
Profile: Constellation Software's area of expertise is the acquisition & management of industry specific software businesses. Specialized software solutions are provided to customers in more than 30 countries.
Mark Leonard, President & Chair
Jamel Baksh, Chief Financial Officer
Bernard Anzarouth, Vice-President, Mergers & Acquisitions
Mark Miller, Chief Operating Officer

Critical Control Energy Services Corporation
#800, 140 - 10th Ave. SE
Calgary, AB T2G 0R1
403-705-7500
Fax: 403-705-7555
www.criticalcontrol.com
Social Media: www.linkedin.com/company/ccescanada
twitter.com/CCESCanada

Company Type: Public
Ticker Symbol: CCZ / TSX
Profile: Critical Control Energy Services provides cloud-based software for the oil & gas industry, including production data measurement & management solutions.
Alykhan Mamdani, B.Math, LLB, LLM, CMA, President & Chief Executive Officer
Brad Lepla, CA, Chief Financial Officer
Karim Punja, Vice-President, Operations

Data Communications Management Corp.
Head Office
9195 Torbram Rd.
Brampton, ON L6S 6H2

905-791-3151
Fax: 905-791-3277
800-268-0128
info@datacm.com
www.datacm.com
Other Communications: Customer Service, Phone: 877-644-5500
Social Media: twitter.com/data_cm
www.linkedin.com/company/the-data-group-of-companies

Company Type: Public
Ticker Symbol: DGI / TSX
Staff Size: 1,400
Profile: Document management & marketing solutions are services offered by Data Communicarions Management Corp. Sectors served include financial, manufacturing, energy, retail & consumer services, distribution, government & public services, health care, & not-for-profit. Data Communications Management offers eco-print solutions to ensure its business is conducted in an environmentally responsible manner.
Michael Sifton, President & CEO
James Lorimer, Chief Financial Officer
Alan Roberts, Senior Vice-President, Operations
Judy Holcomb-Williams, Vice-President, Human Resources

DataWind Inc.
#207, 7895 Tranmere Dr.
Mississauga, ON L5S 1V9

905-712-0505
Fax: 905-712-0506
www.datawind.com
Social Media: www.facebook.com/datawindcorp
twitter.com/Datawind
www.linkedin.com/company/datawind-ltd

Company Type: Public
Ticker Symbol: DW / TSX
Profile: An internet, tablet & smartphone provider.
Suneet Singh Tuli, President & CEO
Dan Hilton, Chief Financial Officer
Donald Gunn, Chief Operations Officer

Descartes Systems Group Inc.
120 Randall Dr.
Waterloo, ON N2V 1C6

519-746-8110
Fax: 519-747-0082
800-419-8495
info@descartes.com
www.descartes.com
Social Media: www.facebook.com/DescartesSystemsGroup
twitter.com/descartessg
www.linkedin.com/company/descartes-systems-group

Company Type: Public
Ticker Symbol: DSG / TSX; DSGX / NASDAQ
Staff Size: 877
Profile: The Descartes Systems Group provides logistics management solutions. Solutions are used by the transportation logistics, distribution, manufacturing, & retail sectors.
Edward Ryan, Chief Executive Officer
Allan Brett, CA, Chief Financial Officer
Chris Jones, Executive Vice-President, Marketing and Services
Raimond Diederik, Executive Vice-President, Information Services
J. Scott Pagan, President & COO

Enghouse Systems Limited
#800, 80 Tiverton Ct.
Markham, ON L3R 0G4

905-946-3200
Fax: 905-946-3201
info@enghouse.com
www.enghouse.com
Other Communications: Acquisitions, E-mail: acquire@enghouse.com

Company Type: Public
Ticker Symbol: ESL / TSX
Staff Size: 1,381
Profile: Founded in 1984, Enghouse Systems Limited provides enterprise software solutions. The company's divisions include Enghouse Interactive, Enghouse Networks, & Enghouse Transportation.

Stephen J. Sadler, Chair/CEO
Craig Wallace, Chief Operating Officer
Sam Anidjar, Vice-President, Corporate Development
Doug Bryson, Vice-President, Finance & Administration
Todd M. May, Vice-President & General Counsel

Firan Technology Group (FTG)
250 Finchdene Sq.
Toronto, ON M1X 1A5

416-299-4000
Fax: 416-292-4308
info@ftgcorp.com
www.ftgcorp.com

Company Type: Private
Ticker Symbol: FTG / TSX
Staff Size: 419
Profile: FTG is a printed circuit board & precision illuminated display systems manufacturer.
Brad Bourne, President & CEO
Joe Ricci, Vice-President & Chief Financial Officer

Halogen Software
#100, 495 March Rd.
Ottawa, ON K2K 3G1

866-566-7778
info@halogensoftware.com
www.halogensoftware.com
Social Media: www.facebook.com/halogensoftware
twitter.com/HalogenSoftware
www.linkedin.com/company/halogen-software

Company Type: Public
Ticker Symbol: HGN / TSX
Staff Size: 450
Les Rechan, President & CEO
Pete Low, Chief Financial Officer

Kinaxis Inc.
700 Silver Seven Rd.
Ottawa, ON K2V 1C3

613-592-5780
Fax: 613-592-0584
877-546-2947
info@kinaxis.com
www.kinaxis.com
Social Media: twitter.com/kinaxis

Company Type: Public
Ticker Symbol: KXS / TSX
Staff Size: 395
Profile: Kinaxis is a software company whose focus is on RapidResponse, technology that provides solutions for supply planning, inventory management, order fulfillment, capacity planning, master scheduling, or sales & operations planning.
John Sicard, President & CEO
Richard Monkman, Chief Financial Officer & Vice-President, Corporate Services
Jeff Johnson, Executive Vice-President, Field Operations
Sarah Sedgman, Chief Knowledge Officer
Ed Shepherdson, Executive Vice-President, Products & Services Operations

MDA Ltd.
Also Known As: MacDonald, Dettwiler & Associates Ltd.
13800 Commerce Pkwy.
Richmond, BC V6V 2J3

604-278-3411
Fax: 604-231-2750
info@mdacorporation.com
www.mdacorporation.com
Other Communications: Investors: invest@mdacorporation.com
Social Media: twitter.com/MDA_geospatial
www.linkedin.com/company/mdacorp

Company Type: Public
Ticker Symbol: MDA / TSX
Staff Size: 4,500
Profile: Incorporated in 1969, MacDonald, Dettwiler & Associates Ltd. offers advanced information solutions to capture & process great amounts of data for business & government organizations. Products include tailored information services, complex operational systems, & electronic information products.
Howard Lance, President & Chief Executive Officer
Anil Wirasekara, Chief Financial Officer & Executive Vice-President

Mediagrif Interactive Technologies Inc./ Technologies Interactives Mediagrif
Tour est
#255, 1111, rue St-Charles ouest
Longueuil, QC J4K 5G4

450-449-0102
Fax: 450-449-8725
877-677-9088
info@mediagrif.com
www.mediagrif.com
Other Communications: careers@mediagrif.com

Company Type: Public
Ticker Symbol: MDF / TSX
Profile: Established in 1996, Mediagrif Interactive Technologies Inc. delivers e-commerce solutions to businesses.
Claude Roy, President & Chief Executive Officer
Paul Bourque, Chief Financial Officer
Hélène Hallak, Vice-President & General Counsel
Stéphane Anglaret, Vice-President, Technology

Mitel Networks Corporation
Corporate Headquarters
350 Legget Dr.
Kanata, ON K2K 2W7

613-592-2122
Fax: 613-592-4784
www.mitel.com
Social Media: www.facebook.com/mitel.networks
www.twitter.com/mitel
www.linkedin.com/groups/Official-Mitel-Group-3614051

Company Type: Public
Ticker Symbol: MITL / NASDAQ
Staff Size: 4,500
Profile: The organization provides a broad range of communications solutions, from basic business communications to tailored applications. Mitel is present in more than ninety countries.
Richard McBee, President/Chief Executive Officer
Steve Spooner, Chief Financial Officer

NexJ Systems Inc.
#700, 10 York Mills Rd.
Toronto, ON M2P 2G4

416-222-5611
Fax: 416-222-8623
info@nexj.com
www.nexj.com
Other Communications: investor.relations@nexj.com
Social Media: www.facebook.com/nexjsystems
twitter.com/nexj
www.linkedin.com/company/nexj-systems

Company Type: Public
Ticker Symbol: NXJ / TSX
Staff Size: 182
Profile: NexJ is a provider of cloud-based software, delivering enterprise customer relationship management (CRM) solutions for financial services, insurance, and healthcare.
William M. Tatham, Founder & CEO
Errol C. Singer, Chief Financial Officer & Vice-President, Finance

Open Text Corporation
275 Frank Tompa Dr.
Waterloo, ON N2L 0A1

519-888-7111
Fax: 519-888-0677
800-499-6544
www.opentext.com
Other Communications: Investors: investors@opentext.com
Social Media: www.facebook.com/opentext
twitter.com/OpenText
www.linkedin.com/company/opentext

Company Type: Public
Ticker Symbol: OTC / TSX; OTEX / NASDAQ
Staff Size: 8,500
Profile: Founded in 1991, Open Text Corporation provides enterprise content management solutions to assist organizations manage their information assets.
Mark J. Barrenechea, President/CEO
John Doolittle, Chief Financial Officer & Exec. Vice-President
Lisa Zangari, Senior Vice-President, Human Resources
Adam Howatson, Chief Marketing Officer

Pivot Technology Solutions
#4420, 161 Bay St.
Toronto, ON M5J 2S1

647-778-2034
info@pivotts.com
pivotac.com
Other Communications: Investor Relations, E-mail: investors@pivotts.com

Company Type: Public
Ticker Symbol: PTG / TSX
Profile: Pivot provides technology solutions to companies,

helping them create IT strategies that will incorporate their objectives as a business.
Kevin Shank, President & Chief Executive Officer
Shaun Maine, Chief Operating Officer & Chief Technology Officer
Cory Reid, Chief Information Officer
John Flores, Vice-President, Marketing

RDM Corporation
619A Kumpf Dr.
Waterloo, ON N2V 1K8
519-746-8483
Fax: 519-746-3317
800-567-6227
www.rdmcorp.com
Other Communications: Sales: sales@rdmcorp.com
Social Media: ca.linkedin.com/company/rdm-corporation
Company Type: Public
Ticker Symbol: RC / TSX
Profile: RDM Corp. provides financial institutions with Remote Deposit Capture services. RDM equips these organizations with the software and hardware that allow their clients to make deposits to their financial accounts.
Randy Fowlie, President & CEO
Rui Malhinha, Chief Financial Officer
Mark Leonard, Vice-President, Development
Harry Rose, Vice-President, Sales

Redknee Solutions Inc.
Corporate Headquarters
#500, 2560 Matheson Blvd. East
Mississauga, ON L4W 4Y9
905-626-2622
Fax: 905-625-2773
contact@redknee.com
www.redknee.com
Other Communications: Investors: investor_relations@redknee.com
Social Media: www.facebook.com/pages/RedkneeRKN/153720457985750
twitter.com/redkneeRKN/
www.linkedin.com/company/redknee
Company Type: Public
Ticker Symbol: RKN / TSX
Profile: Redknee Solutions provides communication software products & services.
Lucas Skoczkowski, Chief Executive Officer
David Charron, Chief Financial Officer
Vishal Kothari, Chief Operating Officer
Nitin Singhal, Vice-President, Partner Alliances

Sandvine Corp.
408 Albert St.
Waterloo, ON N2L 3V3
519-880-2600
Fax: 519-884-9892
investor_relations@sandvine.com
www.sandvine.com
Social Media: www.facebook.com/sandvine
twitter.com/sandvine
www.linkedin.com/company/sandvine
Company Type: Public
Ticker Symbol: SVC / TSX, London-AIM
Staff Size: 729
Profile: Sandvine Corporation provides network policy control equipment & software. The company serves broadband & mobile data subscribers.
Dave Caputo, President & Chief Executive Officer
Scott Hamilton, Chief Financial Officer
Brad Siim, Chief Operating Officer
Don Bowman, Chief Technology Officer
Rick Wadsworth, Contact, Investor Relations

Solium Capital Inc.
Headquarters
#1500, 800 - 6th Ave. SW
Calgary, AB T2P 3G3
403-515-3910
Fax: 403-515-3919
www.solium.com
Other Communications: Investors: investorrelations@solium.com
Social Media: www.facebook.com/Solium
twitter.com/Solium
www.linkedin.com/company/85799
Company Type: Public
Ticker Symbol: SUM / TSX
Staff Size: 468
Profile: Solium Capital is an independent provider of stock plan administration software & services. The company's technology platforms include StockVantage, Shareworks, & Transcentive. Solium Capital's headquarters is in Calgary, with regional offices in Toronto, Montréal, Shelton, Connecticut, Tempe, Arizona, & London, United Kingdom.

Marcos Lopez, President & CEO
Jim Wulforst, President & USA Country Head
Scott Camobell, Executive Vice-President, Global Shared Services
Kelly Schmitt, Chief Fiancial Officer

Sylogist Inc.
#102, 5 Richard Way SW
Calgary, AB T3E 7M8
403-266-4808
Fax: 403-233-0845
info@sylogist.com
www.sylogist.com
Company Type: Public
Ticker Symbol: SYZ / TSX
Profile: Sylogist is a software & technology company that provides intellectual property solutions to the public & private sectors.
James Wilson, President & CEO
Brian Grassby, Chief Financial Officer & Vice-President, Finance
David Elder, Corporate Secretary & Vice-President, Corporate Development

Tecsys Inc.
#800, 1, Place Alexis Nihon
Montréal, QC H3Z 3B8
514-866-0001
Fax: 514-866-1805
800-922-8649
info@tecsys.com
www.tecsys.com
Other Communications: Investor Relations, E-mail: investor@tecsys.com
Social Media: www.linkedin.com/company/35372
Company Type: Public
Ticker Symbol: TCS / TSX
Staff Size: 350
Profile: Tecsys develops technology is order to create more efficiency within supply chain management.
Peter Brereton, President & CEO
Berty Ho-Wo-Cheong, Chief Financial Officer & Vice-President, Finance & Administration
Greg MacNeill, Senior Vice-President, World-wide Sales
Roberto Colosino, Vice-President, Marketing & Business Development
Patricia Barry, Vice-President, Human Resources

Tio Networks Corp.
#1550, 250 Howe St.
Vancouver, BC V6C 3R8
604-298-4636
Fax: 604-298-4216
www.tionetworks.com
Social Media: www.facebook.com/tionetworks
twitter.com/TIONetworks
Company Type: Public
Ticker Symbol: TNC / TSX.V
Profile: TIO is a bill payment processor, which serves telecom, wireless, cable & utility companies.
Hamed Shahbazi, Chief Executive Officer
Richard Cheung, Chief Financial Officer
Chris Ericksen, Chief Revenue Officer
Hessam Shahbazi, Executive Vice-President, ISO

Chemicals

5N Plus Inc.
Head Office
4385, rue Garand
Montréal, QC H4R 2B4
514-856-0644
Fax: 514-856-9611
info@5nplus.com
www.5nplus.com
Other Communications: Investor Relations, E-mail: invest@5nplus.com
Company Type: Public
Ticker Symbol: VNP / TSX
Staff Size: 691
Profile: 5N Plus Inc. produces specialty metal & chemical products. Examples of products include bismuth, indium, germanium, compound semiconductor wafers, & inorganic chemicals. Manufacturing facilities & sales offices are located in North America, South America, Europe, & Asia.
Arjang Roshan, President & Chief Executive Officer
Bertrand Lessard, Chief Operating Officer
Richard Perron, Chief Financial Officer
Nicholas Audet, Chief Commercial Officer

Agrium Inc.
13131 Lake Fraser Dr. SE
Calgary, AB T2J 7E8
Fax: 403-225-7609
877-247-4861
www.agrium.com
Social Media: www.facebook.com/agrium
twitter.com/agriuminc
www.linkedin.com/company/agrium
Company Type: Public
Ticker Symbol: AGU / TSX, NYSE
Staff Size: 15,200
Profile: Agrium Inc. produces & markets major agricultural nutrients throughout the world. The company also supplies specialty fertilizers across North America. In North & South America, Agrium is engaged in the retail supply of agricultural products & services.
In Sept. 2016 it was announced that Agrium would merge with Potash Corporation of Saskatchewan.
Charles V. Magro, President/CEO
Leslie O'Donoghue, Q.C., Chief Risk Officer & Executive Vice-President, Corporate Development & Strategy
Steve J. Douglas, Senior Vice-President & Chief Financial Officer
Henry (Harry) Deans, Senior Vice-President & President, Wholesale Business Unit
Stephen Dyer, Senior Vice-President & President, Retail Business Unit
Susan Jones, Senior Vice-President & Chief Legal Officer

Canexus Corporation
#2100, 144 - 4th Ave. SW
Calgary, AB T2P 3N4
403-571-7300
Fax: 403-571-7800
www.canexus.ca
Other Communications: Sao Paulo, Brazil, Business Dev. Office: (55) (11) 3443-7467
Company Type: Public
Ticker Symbol: CUS / TSX
Staff Size: 405
Profile: Canexus produces chlor-alkali & sodium chlorate products for the water treatment & pulp & paper industries. Plants are located in Canada & Brazil.
Doug Wonnacott, President & Chief Executive Officer
Dean Beacon, Chief Financial Officer & Senior Vice-President, Finance
Brian P. Bourgeois, Senior Vice-President, Sales & Marketing
Ross Wonnick, General Counsel, Corporate Secretary & Vice-President

Chemtrade Logistics Inc.
#300, 155 Gordon Baker Rd.
Toronto, ON M2H 3N5
416-496-5856
Fax: 416-496-9942
866-887-8805
www.chemtradelogistics.com
Social Media: www.linkedin.com/company/chemtrade-logistics
Company Type: Public
Ticker Symbol: CHE.UN / TSX
Profile: Chemtrade provides industrial chemicals & services to customers around the world. The company also offers industrial services, such as processing hydrogen sulphide & waste streams. In 2011, Chemtrade acquired all the businesses of Marsulex Inc.
Mark Davis, President & Chief Executive Officer
Rohit Bhardwaj, Chief Financial Officer & Vice-President, Finance

EcoSynthetix
3365 Mainway
Burlington, ON L7M 1A6
905-335-5669
Fax: 289-337-9780
www.ecosynthetix.com
Social Media: www.facebook.com/EcoSynthetix
www.twitter.com/ecosynthetixinc
www.linkedin.com/company/1252284
Company Type: Public
Ticker Symbol: ECO / TSX
Profile: EcoSynthetix is a renewable chemicals manufacturer of a family of bio-based products that are used globally as inputs in the commercial manufacture of a wide range of consumer and industrial goods.
Jeff MacDonald, Chief Executive Officer
Robert Haire, Chief Financial Officer
Ted van Egdom, Senior Vice-President, Market Realization & Product Manufacturing

Methanex Corporation
Waterfront Centre
#1800, 200 Burrard St.
Vancouver, BC V6C 3M1

604-661-2600
Fax: 604-661-2676
800-661-8851
invest@methanex.com
www.methanex.com
Other Communications: Government & Public Affairs: publicaffairs@methanex.com
Social Media: twitter.com/methanex
www.linkedin.com/company/methanex-corporation

Company Type: Public
Ticker Symbol: MX / TSX, NASDAQ
Staff Size: 1,295
Profile: Methanex Corporation is a producer & marketer of methanol. The company supplies major international markets.
John Floren, President & CEO
Ian Cameron, Chief Financial Officer & Senior Vice-President, Finance
Mike Herz, Senior Vice-President, Corporate Development
Vanessa James, Senior Vice-President, Global Marketing & Logistics
Wendy Bach, Senior Vice-President, Corporate Resources
Sandra Daycock, Director, Investor Relations
Fax: 604-661-2666

Migao Corporation
Dong Fang Yin Zuo Office Bldg.
#16A, 48 Dong Zhi Men Wai St.
Beijing, 100027 China

info@migaocorp.com
www.migaocorp.com
Other Communications: Phone: +86-10-8447-7526; Fax: +86-10-8447-7206

Company Type: Public
Ticker Symbol: MGO / TSX
Profile: Migao Corporation is the the owner & operator of fertilizer production plants. Plants are situated across China. Products are used by Chinese domestic agricultural markets.
Registrar & Transfer Agent Contact: #300, 200 University Ave., Toronto, ON M5H 4H1.
Liu Guocai, Chief Executive Officer
liu.guocai@migaocorp.com
Helen Lu, Chief Financial Officer
helen.lu@migaocorp.com

Nemaska Lithium Inc.
450, rue Gare-du-Palais
Québec, QC G1K 3X2

418-704-6038
Fax: 418-614-0627
877-704-6038
info@nemaskalithium.com
www.nemaskalithium.com

Company Type: Public
Ticker Symbol: NMX / TSX
Profile: A lithium hydroxide supplier & lithium carbonate supplier.
Guy Bourassa, President & CEO
Steve Nadeau, Chief Financial Officer

Neptune Technologies & Bioressources Inc.
Also Known As: Neptune Wellness Solutions
#100, 545 Promenade du Centropolis
Laval, QC H7T 0A3

450-687-2262
Fax: 450-687-2272
888-664-9166
neptunecorp.com
Social Media: www.facebook.com/NeptuneKrillOil
twitter.com/neptunekrilloil
linkedin.com/company/neptune-technologies-&-bioressources

Company Type: Public
Ticker Symbol: NTB / TSX
Profile: Neptune Technologies and Bioressources Inc. is involved in the innovation, production and formulation of science-based and clinically proven novel phospholipid products.
Jim Hamilton, President & CEO
Mario Paradis, Chief Financial Officer

PFB Corporation
#100, 2886 Sunridge Way NE
Calgary, AB T1Y 7H9

403-569-4300
Fax: 403-569-4075
mailbox@pfbcorp.com
www.pfbcorp.com
Social Media: www.facebook.com/pages/Plasti-Fab/141865299208561
twitter.com/PlastiFab
www.linkedin.com/company/263513

Company Type: Public
Ticker Symbol: PFB / TSX
Staff Size: 366
Profile: Through its wholly-owned subsidiaries, PFB Corporation manufactures insulating building products, based on expanded polystyrene technology. Brands of insulating building products include Plasti-Fab EPS Product Solutions, Riverbend Timber Framing, Insulspan Structural Insulating Panels Systems, Precision Craft, & Advantage ICF Systems. The company serves the construction, industrial, commercial, & residential markets throughout North America.
C. Alan Smith, President, Chief Executive Officer & Chair
Bruce Carruthers, Chief Operating Officer
William H. Smith, Q.C., Corporate Secretary

QLT Inc.
#250, 887 Great Northern Way
Vancouver, BC V5T 4T5

604-707-7000
Fax: 604-707-7001
877-764-3131
ir@qltinc.com
www.qltinc.com
Other Communications: hr@qltinc.com; medaff@qltinc.com

Company Type: Public
Ticker Symbol: QLT / TSX; QLTI / NASDAQ
Profile: QLT is a biotechnology company dedicated to the development and commercialization of innovative ocular products.
Geoffrey Cox, Interim CEO
Glen Ibbott, Senior Vice-President, Finance, & CFO

Communications

Cineplex Inc.
1303 Yonge St.
Toronto, ON M4T 2Y9

416-323-6600
Fax: 416-323-6683
www.cineplex.com
Social Media: www.facebook.com/Cineplex
twitter.com/cineplexmovies

Company Type: Public
Ticker Symbol: CGX / TSX
Profile: Cineplex Inc. is a large motion picture exhibitor in Canada. The company owns, leases, or has a joint-venture in 163 theatres from across Canada.
Ellis Jacob, President & Chief Executive Officer
Gord Nelson, Chief Financial Officer
Jeffrey Kent, Chief Technology Officer
Dan McGrath, Chief Operating Officer
Pat Marshall, Vice-President, Communications & Investor Relations
Heather Briant, Sr. Vice-President, Human Resources

Cogeco Communications Inc.
#1700, 5 Place Ville-Marie
Montréal, QC H3B 0B3

514-764-4700
corpo.cogeco.com
Social Media: www.facebook.com/CogecoQC
www.twitter.com/CogecoQC

Company Type: Public
Ticker Symbol: CCA / TSX
Staff Size: 4,000
Profile: The cable telecommunications company provides the following services: internet, telephony, audio, & analog & digital television.
Louis Audet, President & CEO
Patrice Ouimet, Chief Financial Officer & Senior Vice-President
René Guimond, Senior Vice-President, Public Affairs & Communications
Christian Jolivet, Chief Legal Officer, Secretary & Senior Vice-President, Corporate Affairs
Diane Nyisztor, Senior Vice-President, Corporate Human Resources

Cogeco Inc.
#1700, 5 Place Ville-Marie
Montréal, QC H3B 0B3

514-764-4700
carriere@cogeco.com
corpo.cogeco.com
Other Communications: media@cogeco.com
Social Media: www.facebook.com/CogecoQC
www.twitter.com/CogecoQC

Company Type: Public
Ticker Symbol: CGO / TSX
Staff Size: 4,500
Profile: Cogeco a diversified communications company that provides cable distribution and radio broadcasting. Cogeco Connexion is the cable subsidiary, builds on its cable distribution base by offering Analogue and Digital Television, High Speed Internet and Telephony services.
Louis Audet, President/CEO
Patrice Ouimet, Sr. Vice-President/CFO
Renée Guimond, Senior Vice-President, Public Affairs & Communications

Corus Entertainment Inc.
Corporate Executive Head Office
25 Dockside Dr.
Toronto, ON M5A 0B5

416-479-7000
Fax: 416-479-7006
866-537-2397
www.corusent.com
Other Communications: Calgary Office, Phone: 403-716-6500, Fax: 403-444-4240

Company Type: Public
Ticker Symbol: CJR.B / TSX
Staff Size: 1,900
Profile: The media & entertainment company is engaged in the following services: television broadcasting, specialty television, pay television, specialty radio, digital audio services, advertising, children's animation, & children's book publishing. Some of the companies & brands that comprise Corus Entertainment include the following: W Network, YTV, Treehouse, TELETOON, Nelvana, & Kids Can Press.
In April 2016, Corus Entertainment completed its acquisition of Shaw Communications' broadcasting subsidiary Shaw Media Inc.
Doug Murphy, President & CEO
Thomas C. Peddie, Executive Vice-President
Gary Maavara, Exec. Vice-President, General Counsel & Corporate Secretary

DHX Media Ltd.
1478 Queen St.
Halifax, NS B3J 2H7

902-423-0260
Fax: 902-422-0752
info@dhxmedia.com
www.dhxmedia.com
Other Communications: Locations: toronto@dhxmedia.com; vancouver@dhxmedia.com
Social Media: www.facebook.com/dhxmedia
twitter.com/dhxmedia
www.linkedin.com/company/dhx-media

Company Type: Public
Ticker Symbol: DHX / TSX
Staff Size: 365
Profile: DHX Media produces, distributes, & licenses children's entertainment. WILDBRAIN Entertainment is the company's subsidiary.
Steven Graham DeNure, President & COO
Keith Abriel, Chief Financial Officer
Mark Gregory Gosine, General Counsel, Corp. Secretary, & Executive Vice-President, Legal Affairs
David A. Regan, Executive Vice-President, Corporate Development & Investor Relations

Manitoba Telecom Services Inc. (MTS)
PO Box 6666, 333 Main St.
Winnipeg, MB R3C 3V6

204-225-5687
800-883-2054
www.mts.ca
Other Communications: French: 1-800-255-6687; TTY: 204-942-4942; Repair: 611
Social Media: www.facebook.com/talktoMTS
www.twitter.com/talktomts

Company Type: Public
Ticker Symbol: MBT / TSX
Staff Size: 2,360
Profile: Through its wholly-owned subsidiary MTS Allstream Inc., Manitoba Telecom Services Inc. provides television, voice, data, wireless, & wireline services. Both residential & business customers are served in Manitoba, while across Canada, business clients are served through a portfolio of information technology consulting & security services, as well as voice & data connectivity services.
Jay Forbes, Chief Executive Officer
Paul Cadieux, Chief Financial Officer

Mood Media Corporation
#600, 1703 West 5th St.
Austin, TX 78703 USA

512-380-8500
800-345-5000
info@moodmedia.com
www.moodmedia.com
Social Media: www.facebook.com/moodmedia
twitter.com/moodmedia
www.linkedin.com/company/mood-media

Company Type: Public
Ticker Symbol: MM / TSX
Staff Size: 2,000
Profile: Mood Media Corporation uses music, visual, & scent media to help its clients communicate to consumers. The company's principal divisions are Retail Point-of-Purchase & In-Store Media.
In 2012, Mood Media Corporation acquired DMX Holdings, Inc., a provider of multi-sensory branding services.
Steve Richard, President & CEO
Tom Garrett, Executive Vice-President & CFO
Michael Zendanein, Executive Vice-President, General Counsel & CAO

Newfoundland Capital Corporation Limited (NCC)
8 Basinview Dr.
Dartmouth, NS B3B 1G4

902-468-7557
Fax: 902-468-7558
ncc@ncc.ca
www.ncc.ca
Other Communications: Investor Relations: investorrelations@ncc.ca
Company Type: Public
Ticker Symbol: NCC.A, NCC.B / TSX
Staff Size: 1,000
Profile: Newfoundland Capital Corporation Limited is the owner & operator of radio stations throughout Canada. Newcap Radio is a wholly owned subsidiary of Newfoundland Capital Corporation Limited.
In addition to its involvement in radio broadcasting, Newfoundland Capital Corporation Limited also owns & operates the Glynmill Inn in Corner Brook, Newfoundland & Labrador.
Robert G. Steele, President & Chief Executive Officer
Scott G.M. Weatherby, Chief Financial Officer & Corporate Secretary
David Murray, Chief Operating Officer

Norsat International Inc.
#110, 4020 Viking Way
Richmond, BC V6V 2L4

604-821-2800
Fax: 604-821-2801
www.norsat.com
Social Media: twitter.com/Norsat
www.linkedin.com/company/norsat-international
Company Type: Public
Ticker Symbol: NII / TSX
Staff Size: 178
Profile: Norsat International Inc. provides innovative communication solutions that enable the transmission of data, audio and video for remote and challenging applications.
Amiee Chan, President/CEO
Arthur Chin, Chief Financial Officer

Redline Communications Group
302 Town Centre Blvd., 4th Fl.
Markham, ON L3R 0E8

905-479-8344
Fax: 905-479-5331
866-633-6669
info@rdlcom.com
www.rdlcom.com
Other Communications: media@rdlcom.com
Social Media: www.facebook.com/rdlcom
twitter.com/rdlcom
www.linkedin.com/company/redline-communications
Company Type: Public
Ticker Symbol: RDL / TSX
Staff Size: 118
Profile: Redline Communications is the creator of powerful wide-area wireless networks for challenging locations.
Robert Williams, Chief Executive Officer
Jane Todd, Chief Financial Officer & Chief Operating Officer

Rogers Communications Inc.
333 Bloor St. East, 7th Fl.
Toronto, ON M4W 1G9

888-764-3771
investor.relations@rci.rogers.com
www.rogers.com
Other Communications: TTY: 800-668-9286; Media: 416-764-2000
Social Media: www.facebook.com/Rogers
twitter.com/rogersbuzz
Company Type: Public
Ticker Symbol: RCI.B / TSX
Staff Size: 26,000
Profile: The diversified communications & media company provides wireless voice & data communications services, as well as cable television, high-speed Internet, & telephony services. Through Rogers Media, magazines & trade publications, sports entertainment, television & radio broadcasteing, & televised shopping are provided.
Alan D. Horn, Chairman
Guy Laurence, President/CEO
Jamie Williams, Chief Information Officer
Tony Staffieri, Chief Financial Officer

Shaw Communications Inc.
#900, 630 - 3rd Ave. SW
Calgary, AB T2P 4L4

403-750-4500
888-472-2222
www.shaw.ca
Social Media: www.facebook.com/shaw
twitter.com/shawinfo
Company Type: Public
Ticker Symbol: SJR.B / TSX; SJR / NYSE
Profile: Established in 1966, the communications company provides broadband cable television, internet, digital phone, telecommunications services, & satellite direct-to-home services.
In April 2016, Corus Entertainment completed its acquisition of the company's broadcasting subsidiary Shaw Media Inc.
J.R. Shaw, Chair
Bradley Shaw, Chief Executive Officer
Jay Mehr, President
Vito Culmone, Executive Vice-President/CFO

SiriusXM Canada Holdings
Also Known As: Canadian Satellite Radio Holdings Inc.
135 Liberty St., 4th Fl.
Toronto, ON M6K 1A7

416-408-6000
Fax: 416-408-6005
www.siriusxm.ca
Social Media: www.facebook.com/siriusxmcanada
twitter.com/siriusxmcanada
Company Type: Public
Ticker Symbol: XSR / TSX
Staff Size: 155
Profile: SiriusXM Canada is the country's leading audio entertainment company and broadcasts more than 120 satellite radio channels featuring premier sports, news, talk, entertainment and commercial-free music.
Mark Redmond, President & CEO
Jason Redman, Chief Financial Officer
Paul Cunningham, Senior Vice-President, Sales & Marketing
Oliver Jaakkola, Senior Vice-President & General Counsel

Symbility Solutions
#900, 111 Peter St.
Toronto, ON M5V 2H1

Fax: 416-359-1911
866-796-2454
info@symbilitysolutions.com
www.symbilitysolutions.com
Social Media: www.facebook.com/Symbility
twitter.com/symbility
www.linkedin.com/company/symbility-solutions
Company Type: Public
Ticker Symbol: SY / TSX.V
Staff Size: 141
Profile: Symbility Solutions is a global provider of cloud-based and smartphone/tablet-enabled claims technology for the property and casualty and health insurance industries.
James R. Swayze, Chief Executive Officer
Marc-Olivier Huynh, Chief Technology Officer & Founder

Tellza Communications Inc.
#3302, 190 Borough Dr.
Toronto, ON M1P 0B6

954-456-3191
tellza.com
Company Type: Public
Ticker Symbol: TEL / TSX
Profile: Tellza Communications Inc. is a global communications company operating under several brands including Route Dynamix, Phonetime, Tel3, GoLifeTel, and Tellza Technologies.
Mike Vazquez, CEO
Ali Guven Kivilcim, President & CTO

TELUS Corp.
510 West Georgia St., 23rd Fl.
Vancouver, BC V6B 0M3

Fax: 604-899-9228
800-667-4871
ir@telus.com
www.telus.com
Other Communications: TTY: 800-855-1155; TELUS Mobility: 866-558-2273; Repair: 611
Social Media: www.facebook.com/telus
twitter.com/telus
www.linkedin.com/company/telus
Company Type: Public
Ticker Symbol: T / TSX, NYSE
Profile: TELUS is a national telecommunications company. Their services include wireless, data, Internet protocol (IP), voice, television, entertainment and video.
Darren Entwistle, President/CEO
Doug French, Exec. Vice-President/CFO
Monique Mercier, Chief Legal Officer, Corporate Secretary & Exec. VP, Corporate Affairs
Eros Spadotto, Exec. Vice-President, Technology Strategy
Josh Blair, Exec. Vice-President, TELUS Health & TELUS International

TeraGo Inc.
Corporate Headquarters
#800, 55 Commerce Valley Dr. West
Toronto, ON L3T 7V9

Fax: 905-707-6212
866-837-2461
www.terago.ca
Other Communications: Technical Support: 866-837-2462
Social Media: www.facebook.com/TeraGo.Networks
twitter.com/Terago_networks
www.linkedin.com/company/terago-networks
Company Type: Public
Ticker Symbol: TGO / TSX
Staff Size: 188
Profile: TeraGo Networks provides the following services to businesses in Canada: voice services, high speed internet, data networking, & internet redundancy. TeraGo owns & operates its National Wireless Network.
Stewart Lyons, President & CEO
Joe Prodan, Chief Financial Officer
Ryan Lausman, COO
Jeffrey Yim, Vice-President, Corporate Development

theScore Inc.
500 King St. West, 4th Fl.
Toronto, ON M5V 1L9

416-479-8812
Fax: 416-361-2045
hello@thescore.com
thescore.com
Social Media: www.facebook.com/theScore
twitter.com/theScore
www.linkedin.com/company/thescore-inc-
Company Type: Public
Ticker Symbol: SCR / TSX.V
Staff Size: 210
Profile: theScore Inc. curates sports content for mobile users.
John Levy, Chief Executive Officer
Tom Hearne, Chief Financial Officer
Benjie Levy, President & COO

TVA Group Inc./ Groupe TVA
1600, boul de Maisonneuve est
Montréal, QC H2L 4P2

514-526-9251
Fax: 514-599-5502
www.tva.canoe.ca
Social Media: www.facebook.com/ReseauTVA
twitter.com/tvareseau
Company Type: Public
Ticker Symbol: TVA.B / TSX
Staff Size: 1,793
Profile: The integrated communications company provides the following services: broadcasting, publishing, producing, & distributing audiovisual products. TVA Group owns French-language television stations, plus a specialty channel. It also publishes French-language magazines. The TVA Films subsidiary serves both Canada's English & French-language markets.
Julie Tremblay, President & Chief Executive Officer
Denis Rozon, CA, Chief Financial Officer & Vice-President

UrtheCast
#33, 1055 Canada Place
Vancouver, BC V6C 0C3

604-669-1788
844-265-6266
www.urthecast.com
Social Media: www.facebook.com/UrtheCast
twitter.com/UrtheCast
www.linkedin.com/company/urthecast
Company Type: Public
Ticker Symbol: UR / TSX
Staff Size: 225
Profile: UrtheCast is developing the world's first Ultra HD Earth video, streamed from the International Space Station (ISS) in full color.
Wade Larson, President & CEO
Issa Nakhleh, Chief Financial Officer

ViXS Systems Inc
#800, 1210 Sheppard Ave. East
Toronto, ON M2K 1E3
416-646-2000
Fax: 416-646-1042
ir@vixs.com
www.vixs.com
Social Media: twitter.com/ViXSSystems
Company Type: Public
Ticker Symbol: VXS / TSX
Staff Size: 127
Profile: ViXS Systems Inc. is a multimedia solutions innovator providing technologies for processing, managing, securing and distributing high quality video and audio.
Michael Michalyshyn, Executive Vice-President & General Counsel
Charlie Glavin, Chief Financial Officer
Sohail Khan, President & CEO

Construction

Aecon Group Inc.
Aecon East Headquarters
#800, 20 Carlson Ct.
Toronto, ON M9W 7K6
416-293-7004
877-232-2677
aecon@aecon.com
www.aecon.com
Other Communications: West Headquarters, Phone: 403-695-3085
Social Media: twitter.com/AeconGroup
www.linkedin.com/company/aecon
Company Type: Public
Ticker Symbol: ARE / TSX
Profile: Aecon Group is a construction & infrastructure development company. It serves both public & private sector clients through the provision of engineering, financing, procurement, construction, & project management services.
Teri McKibbon, President & CEO
Paula Palma, Executive Vice-President & Chief People & Information Officer
David Smales, Executive Vice-President & Chief Financial Officer
L. Brian Swartz, Corporate Secretary & Executive Vice-President, Legal & Commercial Services
Mike Archambault, Senior Vice-President & Chief Safety Officer
Roger Howarth, Senior Vice-President, Project Controls
Mathew Kattapuram, Senior Vice-President, Strategic Business Development
Alistair MacCallum, Senior Vice-President, Finance

Badger Daylighting Ltd.
#1000, 635 - 8th Ave. SW
Calgary, AB T2P 3M3
403-264-8500
Fax: 403-228-9773
corporate@badgerinc.com
www.badgerinc.com
Other Communications: Canada Contracts, E-mail: canadacontracts@badgerinc.com
Social Media: www.facebook.com/Badger-Daylighting-Corp-301969623293533
twitter.com/BadgerCorp
www.linkedin.com/company/badger-daylighting-inc
Company Type: Public
Ticker Symbol: BAD / TSX
Staff Size: 1,655
Profile: Badger Daylighting Ltd. provides non-destructive excavating services. The company has more than 400 hydrovac units that operate from over 80 field offices throughout Canada & the United States. Badger is employed by contractors & facility owners in the petroleum, construction, transportation, engineering, industrial, & utility industries.
Tor Wilson, President & Chief Executive Officer
Gerald Schiefelbein, Chief Financial Officer & Vice-President
John G. Kelly, Chief Operating Officer

Bird Construction Inc.
#400, 5700 Explorer Dr.
Mississauga, ON L4W 0C6
905-602-4122
www.bird.ca
Company Type: Public
Ticker Symbol: BDT / TSX
Staff Size: 837
Profile: The organization is a national general contractor in the residential, institutional, & industrial markets.
Ian Boyd, P.Eng., President & CEO
Wayne Gingrich, CA, Chief Financial Officer
Ken McClure, Vice-President, Commercial

Boyuan Construction Group Inc.
Boyuan Building No. 6
East Rd., Jiaxing Port
Jiaxing, Zhejiang, 314201 China
www.boyuangroup.com
Social Media: twitter.com/boyuangroup
www.linkedin.com/company/boyuan-construction-group-inc-
Company Type: Public
Ticker Symbol: BOY / TSX
Staff Size: 400
Profile: The construction company is engaged in residential, commercial, & municipal infrastructure projects. Boyuan Construction Group focuses on projects in Hainan Province, Shandong Province, & the Yangtze River Delta region of China.
Cai Liang Shou, Founder & Chair
Paul Law, CA, MBA, Chief Financial Officer
Ren Shu, Corporate Secretary

Dirtt Environmental Solutions
7303 - 30th St. SE
Calgary, AB T2C 1N6
403-723-5000
Fax: 403-723-6644
info@dirtt.net
www.dirtt.net
Social Media: www.facebook.com/DIRTTwalls
twitter.com/DIRTT
Company Type: Public
Ticker Symbol: DRT / TSX
Profile: DIRTT - Doing It Right This Time - creates customizable, sustainable architectural interiors.
Mogens Smed, Chief Executive Officer
Scott Jenkins, President
Derek Payne, Chief Financial Officer & Corporate Secretary

Enterprise Group, Inc.
#2, 64 Riel Dr.
St. Albert, AB T8N 4A4
780-418-4400
contact@enterprisegrp.ca
www.enterprisegrp.ca
Social Media: www.facebook.com/EnterpriseGroupINC
twitter.com/EnterpriseGrp
www.linkedin.com/company/enterprise-group-inc-
Company Type: Public
Ticker Symbol: E / TSX
Staff Size: 300
Profile: Enterprise Group, Inc. is a consolidator of construction services companies operating in the energy, utility and transportation infrastructure industries. Recently acquired companies include Artic Therm International Ltd., Calgary Tunnelling & Horizontal Augering Ltd., and Hart Oilfield Rentals Ltd.
Leonard D. Jaroszuk, Chairman, Chief Executive Officer & President
Warren Cabral, Chief Financial Officer
Richard Hoffart, Chief Operating Officer

Finning International Inc.
Park Pl.
#1000, 666 Burrard St.
Vancouver, BC V6C 2X8
604-691-6444
Fax: 604-691-6440
investor_relations@finning.ca
www.finning.com
Company Type: Public
Ticker Symbol: FTT / TSX
Staff Size: 13,000
Profile: The company sells, rents, & offers customer service for Caterpillar equipment. Business is conducted in Canada, South America, & the United Kingdom.
L. Scott Thomson, President & Chief Executive Officer
Juan Carlos Villegas, COO, Finning International Inc. & President, Finning Canada
Steven Nielsen, Executive Vice-President & Chief Financial Officer
David W. Cummings, Chief Information Officer

Stuart Olson
#600, 4820 Richard Rd. SW
Calgary, AB T3E 6L1
403-685-7777
info@stuartolson.com
www.stuartolson.com
Other Communications: Alternate E-mail: media@stuartolson.com
Company Type: Public
Ticker Symbol: SOX / TSX
Staff Size: 3,352
Profile: Stuart Olson is a provider of building construction, industrial construction, & related maintenance services. It operates in western Canada. Stuart Olson's business segments are as follows: Canem Systems Ltd., Stuart Olson Dominion Construction Ltd., Broda Construction Inc., Laird Electric Inc., Laird Constructors Inc., Fuller Austin (an insulation company), & Northern Industrial (an insulation company).
The company has policies, procedures, training programs, & compliance procedures in place to manage environmental issues & comply with legislation & regulations.
David Lemay, President & Chief Executive Officer
Daryl E. Sands, B.Comm, CA, Chief Financial Officer & Executive Vice-President

Distribution & Retail

Alimentation Couche-Tard inc
4204 Industriel Blvd.
Laval, QC H7L 0E3
450-662-6632
Fax: 450-662-6633
800-361-2612
www.couche-tard.com
Social Media: www.facebook.com/CoucheTardQc
Company Type: Public
Ticker Symbol: ATD.B / TSX
Staff Size: 80,000
Profile: In eastern, central, & western Canada, as well as in the United States, Alimentation Couche-Tard operates convenience stores. Some of these stores include motor fuel dispensing. In Canada, the businesses operate under the brands Couche-Tard & Mac's.
Brian Hannasch, President/CEO
Darrell Davis, Senior Vice-President, Operations
Geoffrey Haxel, Senior Vice-President, Operations
Dennis Tewll, Senior Vice-President, Operations
Claude Tessier, CFO

Birks Group Inc.
1240, carré Phillips
Montréal, QC H3B 3H4
514-397-2511
www.birksgroup.com
Other Communications: www.maisonbirks.com
Social Media: www.facebook.com/MaisonBirks
twitter.com/Maisonbirks
Company Type: Public
Ticker Symbol: BMJ / AMEX
Profile: Birks Group Inc. designs, manufactures, & retails fine jewellery, silverware, timepieces, & giftware. Brand names include Birks, Brinkhaus, & Mayors. Retail stores are located in Canada & the United States.
Jean-Christopher Bédos, President/CEO
Pasquale Di Lillo, Vice-President, CFO & CAO
Eva Hartling, Vice-President, Marketing & Communications
Miranda Melfi, Corporate Secretary & Vice-President, Legal Affairs
Marco Pasteris, Vice-President, Business Development & Support

BMTC Group Inc.
8500, Place Marien
Montréal, QC H1B 5W8
514-648-5757
Fax: 514-881-4056
Company Type: Public
Ticker Symbol: GBT / TSX
Staff Size: 2,187
Profile: BMTC Group is a holding company. Its subsidiaries include Ameublements Tanguay Inc. & Brault et Martineau Inc. These subsidiaries are engaged in the retail sale of furniture, electronic goods, & household appliances in Québec.
Yves Des Groseillers, Chair, President & Chief Executive Officer

Canadian Tire Corporation, Limited
PO Box 770 Stn. K, 2180 Yonge St.
Toronto, ON M4P 2V8
416-480-3000
www.canadiantire.ca
Other Communications: Corporate Customer Relations: 800-387-8803
Social Media: www.facebook.com/Canadiantire
twitter.com/canadiantire
Company Type: Public
Ticker Symbol: CTC, CTC.A / TSX
Staff Size: 28,000
Profile: Founded in 1922, Canadian Tire Corporation, Limited is engaged in retail, petroleum, & financial services. Canadian Tire has over 487 retail locations across Canada.
Stephen Wetmore, President & Chief Executive Officer
Mary Turner, President & CEO, Canadian Tire Bank
Jim Christie, Executive Vice-President, Canadian Tire Corporation, Ltd.
Rick White, President, Mark's Work Wearhouse, Ltd.
Dean McCann, CFO & Exec. Vice-President
Eugene Roman, Sr. Vice-President & Chief Technology Officer
Robyn Collver, Sr. Vice-President, Risk & Regulatory Affairs

Olga Giovanniello, Sr. Vice-President, Human Resources
Doug Nathanson, General Counsel & Corporate Secretary

CanWel Building Materials Group Ltd.
Corporate Office
#1100, 1055 West Georgia St.
Vancouver, BC V6E 3P3
604-432-1400
Fax: 604-436-6670
www.canwel.com

Company Type: Public
Ticker Symbol: CWX / TSX
Staff Size: 700
Profile: CanWel Building Materials Group is involved in the distribution of building materials & related products across Canada. Its divisions are CanWelBroadLeaf & Surewood Forest Products.
Marc Séguin, President
Amar S. Doman, Chair & Chief Executive Officer
James Code, Chief Financial Officer
Julie Wong, Director, Human Resources

Cervus Equipment Corporation
Harvest Hills Business Park
#5201, 333 - 96 Ave. NE
Calgary, AB T3K OS3
403-567-0339
Fax: 403-567-0309
www.cervuscorp.com

Company Type: Public
Ticker Symbol: CVL / TSX
Staff Size: 1,646
Profile: Cervus Equipment Corporation acquires & manages authorized agricultural, commercial, industrial, & transportation equipment dealerships. Business is conducted in Alberta, Saskatchewan, & Manitoba. The corporation also has an investment partnership with a New Zealand based company named Agriturf Limited.
Graham Drake, Chief Executive Officer
gdrake@cervuscorp.com
Randall Muth, Chief Financial Officer
rmuth@cervuscorp.com

Colabor Group Inc./ Groupe Colabor Inc.
1620, boul de Montarville
Boucherville, QC J4B 8P4
450-449-4911
Fax: 450-449-6180
info@colabor.com
www.colabor.com

Company Type: Public
Ticker Symbol: GCL / TSX
Staff Size: 1,598
Profile: In 2009, Colabor Group Inc. completed the conversion of Colabor Income Fund to a corporation. The corporation is engaged in the distribution of confectionery products, refrigerated products, frozen foods, food-related products, dry goods, & beauty & care products. Products are marketed & distributed to retail & foodservice markets.
Claude Gariépy, President & Chief Executive Officer
Jack Battersby, President, Summit Food Service (Ontario Division)
Jean-François Neault, Chief Financial Officer & Vice-President
Michel Delisle, Vice-President, Information Technology
Denis Desaulniers, Corporate Vice-President, Human Resources & Communications
Marko Potvin, Vice-President, Corporate Purchasing

Dollarama Inc.
5905 Royalmount Ave.
Montréal, QC H4P 0A1
514-737-1006
contactus@dollarama.com
www.dollarama.com

Company Type: Public
Ticker Symbol: DOL / TSX
Staff Size: 20,000
Profile: Dollarama Inc. was founded in 1992. It sells general merchandise & seasonal products for $3 or less in 900 locations in ten Canadian provinces.
Larry Rossy, Chair & Chief Executive Officer
Michael Ross, Chief Financial Officer
Johanne Choinière, Chief Operating Officer
Neil Rossy, Chief Merchandising Officer
Geoffrey Robillard, Senior Vice-President, Import Division

Dominion Diamond Corporation
#1102, 4920 - 52nd St.
Yellowknife, NT X1A 3T1
867-669-6100
Fax: 867-669-9293
ddc@ddcorp.ca
www.ddcorp.ca
Other Communications: Investor Relations, E-mail: investor@ddcorp.ca

Company Type: Public
Ticker Symbol: DDC / TSX; DDC / NYSE
Staff Size: 1,631
Profile: Dominion Diamond Corporation owns 40% interest in the Diavik Diamond Mine in the Northwest Territories. Rough diamonds are supplied to an international market.
The specialist diamond enterprise also supplies rough diamonds to the global market through its sorting and selling operations in Canada, Belgium and India.
James K. Gowans, Chair
Brendan Bell, Chief Executive Officer
Cara Allaway, Acting Chief Financial Officer
James R.W. Pounds, Exec. Vice-President, Diamonds
Kelley Stamm, Manager, Investor Relations
416-205-4380

goeasy Ltd.
#510, 33 City Centre Dr.
Mississauga, ON L5B 2N5
905-272-2788
Fax: 905-272-9886
888-528-3279
goeasy.ca
Social Media: www.facebook.com/easyhomeCA
twitter.com/goeasyltd

Company Type: Public
Ticker Symbol: GSY / TSX
Staff Size: 1,600
Profile: goeasy Ltd. is a merchandise lease company. The company rents products, such as household furnishings, home entertainment products, electronics, appliances & computers. Customers may have the option to purchase products.
David Ingram, President & Chief Executive Officer
Steve Goertz, Chief Financial Officer & Executive Vice-President
Andrea Fiederer, Executve Vice-President & Chief Marketing Officer

Hudson's Bay Co.
8925 Torbram Rd.
Brampton, ON L6T 461
800-521-2364
www.hbc.com

Company Type: Public
Ticker Symbol: HBC / TSX
Staff Size: 3,150
Profile: HBC offers customers a range of retailing categories and shopping experiences primarily in the United States and Canada.
Gerald Storch, Chief Executive Officer
Paul Beesley, Chief Financial Officer

Indigo Books & Music Inc.
#500, 468 King St. West
Toronto, ON M5V 1L8
416-364-4499
InvestorRelations@indigo.ca
www.chapters.indigo.ca
Other Communications: Corporate & Education: cisales@indigo.ca
Social Media: www.facebook.com/ChaptersIndigo
twitter.com/chaptersindigo

Company Type: Public
Ticker Symbol: IDG / TSX
Staff Size: 6,200
Profile: Indigo Books & Music Inc. is a Canadian retailer of books, gifts, & specialty toys. The company is the majority shareholder of the eReading service, Kobo Inc. Stores include Indigo Books & Music, Indigo Books, Gifts, Kids, IndigoSpirit, Chapters, Coles, & The World's Biggest Bookstore. The company's online channel is indigo.ca. Indigo Books & Music also founded the Indigo Love of Reading Foundation.
Heather Reisman, Chief Executive Officer
Laura Carr, Executive Vice-President & Chief Financial Officer
Bo Parizadeh, Chief Technology Officer & Executive Vice-President, Loyalty
Katie Gregory, Manager, Public Relations
kgregory@indigo.ca
Gil Dennis, Executive Vice-President, Human Resources & Retail

Jean Coutu Group (PJC) Inc.
245 Jean Coutu St.
Varennes, QC J3X 0E1
450-646-9760
Fax: 450-646-0550
www.jeancoutu.com
Social Media: www.facebook.com/JeanCoutu
twitter.com/JeanCoutu

Company Type: Public
Ticker Symbol: PJC.A /TSX
Staff Size: 1,229
Profile: The Jean Coutu Group is engaged in pharmacy retailing. It has 396 franchised stores in Ontario, Québec, & New Brunswick. Banners include PJC Clinique, PJC Jean Coutu, PJC Santé, & PJC Santé Beauté.
François J Coutu, President & Chief Executive Officer
André Belzile, Executive Vice-President, Finance & Corporate Affairs
Hélène Bisson, Vice-President, Communications
Marie-Chantal Lamothe, Vice-President, Human Resources

Le Château Inc.
105 Marcel-Laurin Blvd.
Montréal, QC H4N 2M3
514-738-7000
Fax: 514-738-3670
www.lechateau.com
Social Media: twitter.com/LeChateauStyle

Company Type: Public
Ticker Symbol: CTU.A / TSX
Staff Size: 2,418
Profile: Le Château was formed in 1987. It manufactures & retails fashion apparel, accessories, & footwear for women & men. The company has more than 240 stores in Canada, two stores in the United States, plus seven stores under license in the Middle East.
Jane Silverstone Segal, Chair & Chief Executive Officer
Emilia Di Raddo, CA, President
Johnny Del Ciancio, Secretary & Vice-President, Finance

Leon's Furniture Limited
45 Gordon Mackay Rd.
Toronto, ON M9N 3X3
416-243-7880
Fax: 416-243-7890
www.leons.ca
Social Media: www.facebook.com/leonsfurniture
twitter.com/leonsfurniture

Company Type: Public
Ticker Symbol: LNF / TSX
Staff Size: 8,380
Profile: The A. Leon Company was founded in 1909 as a general merchandise store. Today, through a chain of retail facilities & franchises across Canada, Leon's Furniture Limited is engaged in the sale of home furnishings, electronics, & appliances.
Terrence T. Leon, President & Chief Executive Officer
Dominic Scarangella, Chief Financial Officer & Vice-President

Ovivo Inc.
#117, 48 Alliance Blvd.
Barrie, ON L4M 5K3
705-735-6655
855-466-8486
rebuilds@ovivowater.com
www.ovivowater.com
Social Media: www.facebook.com/ovivo
twitter.com/ovivo
www.linkedin.com/company/ovivo

Company Type: Public
Ticker Symbol: OVI.A / TSX
Profile: Ovivo develops solutions for the treatment & recycling of municipal & industrial wastewater.
Marc Barbeau, President & Chief Executive Officer
France De Blois, Vice-President, Finance
Kaveh Someah, Vice-President, Global Energy

Parkland Fuel Corporation
#100, 4919 - 59th St.
Red Deer, AB T4N 6C9
403-357-6400
www.parkland.ca

Company Type: Public
Ticker Symbol: PKI / TSX
Profile: Parkland Fuel is engaged in the marketing & distributing of petroleum products. The company serves wholesale, retail, commercial, & home heating fuel customers. Brands include the following: Fas Gas Plus, Race Trac Gas, Bluewave Energy, Great Northern Oil, United Petroleum Products, Columbia Fuels, Neufeld Petroleum & Propane, & Island Petroleum.
Parkland Fuel has a Health, Safety, & Enviroment Department as well as HSE committees, & it developed risk mitigation programs & emergency response procedures for the handling of

transportation fuels in a manner that is safe & healthy for employees & the environment.
Robert Espey, President & Chief Executive Officer
Mike McMillan, Chief Financial Officer
Pierre Magnan, Vice-President, General Counsel & Corporate Secretary

Reitmans (Canada) Limited
250, rue Sauvé ouest
Montréal, QC H3L 1Z2
514-384-1140
www.reitmanscanadalimited.com
Social Media: www.facebook.com/Reitmans.en
www.linkedin.com/company/reitmans
Company Type: Public
Ticker Symbol: RET.A / TSX
Profile: Reitmans (Canada) Ltd. is the operator of clothing stores, which specialize in women's fashions & accessories. Stores are operated under the following names: Reitmans, RW & Co., Smart Set, Pennington Superstores, Addition-Elle, & Thyme Maternity. There are 800 stores across Canada.
Jeremy H. Reitman, Chair/Chief Executive Officer
Stephen F. Reitman, President
Michael Strachan, President, Reitmans
Lora Tisi, President, RW & Co.
Jonathan Plens, President, Thyme Maternity
Isabelle Oliva, Vice-President, Human Resources
Janice LeClerc, President, Addition Elle
Eric Williams, CA, CFO & Vice-President, Finance
Walter Lamothe, COO & President, Retail
Allen F. Rubin, Vice-President, Operations
Carl Janzen, President, Penningtons

Richelieu Hardware Ltd.
7900, boul Henri-Bourassa ouest
Montréal, QC H4S 1V4
514-336-4144
Fax: 514-336-9431
800-361-6000
www.richelieu.com
Company Type: Public
Ticker Symbol: RCH / TSX
Staff Size: 1,900
Profile: Richelieu Hardware manufactures, imports, & distributes specialty hardware & complementary products. The company serves manufacturers & retailers throughout North America.
Richard Lord, President & Chief Executive Officer
Antoine Auclair, Chief Financial Officer & Vice-President
Christian Dion, Manager, Human Resources

Rocky Mountain Dealerships Inc.
#301, 3345 - 8th St. SE
Calgary, AB T2G 3A4
403-265-7364
www.rockymtn.com
Social Media: www.facebook.com/RockyMountainEquipment
twitter.com/RMEHQ
www.linkedin.com/company/rocky-mountain-dealerships-inc
Company Type: Public
Ticker Symbol: RME / TSX
Staff Size: 860
Profile: Rocky Mountain Dealerships Inc. has a network of full-service dealership branches that sell, rent, & lease new & used agriculture & construction equipment. Examples of brands include New Holland, Case Construction, & Case IH Agriculture. Rocky Mountain Dealerships Inc. also provides repair & maintenance services, as well as third-party finance products. Stores are located in British Columbia, Alberta, Saskatchewan, Manitoba, & the Northwest Territories.
Garret Ganden, President & CEO
David Ascott, Chief Financial Officer

RONA Inc.
220, ch du Tremblay
Boucherville, QC J4B 8H7
514-599-5900
Fax: 514-599-5927
866-599-5900
www.rona.ca
Social Media: www.facebook.com/ronainc
twitter.com/ronainc
www.linkedin.com/company/rona
Company Type: Public
Ticker Symbol: RON / TSX
Profile: Hardware, home renovation, & gardening products are distributed & retailed by RONA inc. The company has over 950 franchise, corporate, & affiliate stores. The company was acquired by Lowes in February 2016.
Robert Niblock, Chair, President & CEO
Marshall Croom, Chief Risk Officer
Rick Damron, Chief Operating Officer
Robert Hull, Jr., Chief Financial Officer
Richard Maltsbarger, Chief Development Officer & President, International

Sears Canada Inc.
Headquarters Bldg.
#700, 290 Yonge St.
Toronto, ON M5B 2C3
416-362-1711
888-932-1015
www.sears.ca
Other Communications: National Customer Service Centre, Phone: 888-473-2772
Social Media: www.facebook.com/SearsCanada
twitter.com/searsca
Company Type: Public
Ticker Symbol: SCC / TSX
Profile: Sears Canada Inc. is a general merchandise retailer, home-service provider, as well as a catalogue publisher.
Carrie Kirkman, President & Chief Merchant
Billy Wong, Interim CFO
Becky Penrice, Executive Vice-President & Chief Operating Officer

Shopify Inc.
150 Elgin St., 8th Fl.
Ottawa, ON K2P 1L4
613-241-2828
www.shopify.ca
Social Media: www.facebook.com/shopify
twitter.com/shopify
www.linkedin.com/company/shopify
Company Type: Public
Ticker Symbol: SH / TSX
Profile: An online market place.
Tobi Lütke, Chief Executive Officer
Harley Finkelstein, Chief Operating Officer
Russ Jones, Chief Financial Officer

Sleep Country Canada Holdings
#1, 140 Wendell Ave.
Toronto, ON M9N 3R2
416-242-4774
Fax: 416-242-8722
www.sleepcountry.ca
Social Media: www.facebook.com/SleepCountryCanada
twitter.com/SleepCountryCan
Company Type: Public
Ticker Symbol: ZZZ / TSX
Profile: A mattress retailer.
David Friesema, Chief Executive Officer
Robert Masson, Chief Financial Officer

SunOpta Inc.
#401, 2233 Argentia Rd.
Mississauga, ON L5N 2X7
905-821-9669
Fax: 905-819-7971
info@sunopta.com
www.sunopta.com
Social Media: www.facebook.com/pages/Sunrich/100511224059
twitter.com/SunOpta
www.linkedin.com/company/sunopta
Company Type: Public
Ticker Symbol: SOY / TSX, NASDAQ
Staff Size: 1,754
Profile: SunOpta Inc. is focused upon sourcing, processing, & distributing healthy, environmentally responsible products. Products include natural, organic, & specialty foods. The company's SunOpta Foods is made up of the Grains & Foods Group, the Ingredients Group, the Consumer Products Group, & the International Foods Group. SunOpta Inc. has a 66.2% ownership in Opta Minerals Inc., plus a minority ownership in Mascoma Corporation.
Rik Jacobs, President & Chief Executive Officer
Robert McKeracher, Vice-President & Chief Financial Officer
Mike Thyken, Chief Information Officer

Uni-Sélect Inc.
170, boul Industriel
Boucherville, QC J4B 2X3
450-641-2440
Fax: 450-449-4908
questions@uni-select.com
www.uni-select.com
Other Communications: Investors: investorrelations@uniselect.com
Social Media: www.facebook.com/Uni-Select-inc-184068105287875
twitter.com/Uni_Select_inc
www.linkedin.com/company/uni-select-inc-
Company Type: Public
Ticker Symbol: UNS / TSX
Staff Size: 2,700
Profile: Uni-Sélect Inc. was founded in 1968. It is a wholesale distributor & marketer of heavy duty tools, equipment, replacement parts, & accessories. The company serves the North American automotive industry.
Henry Buckley, President & CEO
Gary O'Connor, President/Chief Operating Officer, Canadian Automotive
Steve Arndt, President & COO, FinishMaster Inc.
Eric Bussières, Chief Financial Officer, Finance
Annie Hotte, Chief People Officer
Louis Juneau, Chief Legal Officer & Corporate Secretary

Wajax Corporation
3280 Wharton Way
Mississauga, ON L4X 2C5
905-212-3300
Fax: 905-212-3350
www.wajax.com
Company Type: Public
Ticker Symbol: WJX / TSX
Profile: Through its subsidiaries, Wajax is involved in the sale & parts & service support of power systems, mobile equipment, & industrial components. Wajax serves the manufacturing, natural resources, utilities, construction, & industrial processing sectors. Branches are located throughout Canada.
Mark Foote, President/CEO
John J. Hamilton, Sr. Vice-President/CFO
Kathleen Hunter, Sr. Vice-President, Human Resources
Andrew Tam, General Counsel & Secretary

Electronics & Electrical Equipment

Amaya Gaming Group Inc.
7600 Trans Canada Hwy.
Pointe-Claire, QC H9R 1C8
514-744-3122
www.amayagaming.com
Other Communications: press@amaya.com
Social Media: www.facebook.com/AmayaGaming
twitter.com/Amayaonline
www.linkedin.com/company/amaya
Company Type: Public
Ticker Symbol: AYA / TSX
Staff Size: 1,991
Profile: Amaya provides a full suite of gaming products and services including casino, poker, sportsbook, platform, lotteries and slot machines.
Rafi Ashkenazi, Chief Executive Officer
Daniel Sebag, Chief Financial Officer

Avigilon
PO Box 378, #101, 1001 West Broadway
Vancouver, BC V6H 4E4
888-281-5182
investors@avigilon.com
avigilon.com
Other Communications: media@avigilon.com
Social Media: www.facebook.com/avigiloncorporation
twitter.com/avigilon
www.linkedin.com/company/avigilon
Company Type: Public
Ticker Symbol: AVO / TSX
Staff Size: 1,043
Profile: Avigilon designs and manufactures high-definition surveillance solutions.
Alexander Fernandes, President & CEO
Ric Leong, Chief Financial Officer & Senior Vice-President

Ballard Power Systems Inc.
9000 Glenlyon Pkwy.
Burnaby, BC V5J 5J8
604-454-0900
marketing@ballard.com
www.ballard.com
Other Communications: Customer Service, E-mail: bps.service@ballard.com
Social Media: www.facebook.com/pages/Ballard-Power-Systems/205546066131866
twitter.com/BallardPwr
www.linkedin.com/company/ballard-power-systems
Company Type: Public
Ticker Symbol: BLD / TSX, NASDAQ
Staff Size: 410
Profile: Ballard Power Systems, Inc provides clean energy fuel cell products for a range of applications.
Randall MacEwen, President/CEO
Tony Guglielmin, Vice-President/CFO
Kevin Cowlbow, Vice-President, Technology & Product Development
David Whyte, Vice-President, Operations

Baylin Technologies
PO Box 6210 Stn. A, 4711 Yonge St.
Toronto, ON M5W 1P6
www.baylintech.com
Social Media:
www.facebook.com/Baylin-Technologies-696388690441418
twitter.com/baylintech
www.linkedin.com/company/baylin-technologies-inc-
Company Type: Public
Ticker Symbol: BYL / TSX
Profile: A wireless techonology company.
Randy Dewey, President & CEO
James Newell, Chief Financial Officer

BlackBerry
2200 University Ave. East
Waterloo, ON N2K 0A7
519-888-7465
Fax: 519-888-7884
ca.blackberry.com
Other Communications: investor_relations@blackberry.com
Social Media: www.facebook.com/BlackBerryNA
twitter.com/BlackBerry
Company Type: Public
Ticker Symbol: BB / TSX; BBRY / NASDAQ
Staff Size: 4,534
Profile: BlackBerry was originally established as Research in Motion Limited in 1984. It changed its name in January 2013 to coincide with the release of the BlackBerry 10 device. The company designs, manufactures, & markets wireless solutions for the mobile communications market.
John Chen, Chief Executive Officer
James Yersh, Chief Financial Officer
Marty Beard, Chief Operating Officer
James Mackey, Executive Vice-President, Corporate Development & Strategic Planning
Steven E. Zipperstein, Chief Legal Officer

Celestica Inc.
844 Don Mills Rd.
Toronto, ON M3C 1V7
416-448-5800
Fax: 416-448-4810
888-899-9998
www.celestica.com
Social Media: www.facebook.com/CelesticaInc
twitter.com/Celestica_Inc
www.linkedin.com/company/celestica
Company Type: Public
Ticker Symbol: CLS / TSX, NYSE
Staff Size: 26,700
Profile: Clestica Inc delivers end-to-end product lifecycle solutions. The company specializes in electronics manufacturing, engineering, & supply chain management services.
Rob Mionis, President & Chief Executive Officer
Glen McIntosh, Executive Vice-President, Global Operations & Supply Chain Management
Betty DelBianco, Chief Legal Officer & Chief Administrative Officer
Darren Myers, Chief Financial Officer

DMD Digital Health Connections Group Inc
#206, 2, Place du Commerce
Montréal, QC H3E 1A1
514-769-5858
Fax: 514-844-8267
www.dmdconnects.com
Company Type: Public
Ticker Symbol: DMG.H / TSX
Profile: The company creates healthcare communications solutions to connect pharmaceutical companies with doctors & health care professionals.
Roger Korman, Chair & CEO
Andre Charron, Chief Financial Officer & Vice-President, Finance

DragonWave Inc.
#600, 411 Legget Dr.
Ottawa, ON K2K 3C9
613-599-9991
Fax: 613-599-4225
www.dragonwaveinc.com
Other Communications: Technical Support: 613-271-7010
Social Media:
www.facebook.com/pages/Dragonwave-Inc/121291504739541
twitter.com/DragonWave
www.linkedin.com/company/dragonwave-inc.
Company Type: Public
Ticker Symbol: DWI / TSX; DRWI / NASDAQ
Staff Size: 268
Profile: DragonWave Inc. supplies packet microwave radio systems for mobile & access networks. The systems transmit broadband voice, data, & video. The company's corporate headquarters is situated in Ottawa, with sales sites in North America, Europe, Asia, & the Middle East.
Peter Allen, President & Chief Executive Officer
Patrick Houston, Chief Financial Officer
Dave Farrar, Vice-President, Operations
Greg Friesen, Vice-President, Product Management

Electrovaya
2645 Royal Windsor Dr.
Mississauga, ON L5J 1K9
905-855-4610
sales@electrovaya.com
www.firstminingfinance.com
Social Media: www.facebook.com/Electrovaya-177374711463
twitter.com/electrovaya
www.linkedin.com/company/electrovaya
Company Type: Public
Ticker Symbol: EFL / TSX
Profile: A lithium ion battery supplier & manufacturer.
Sankar Das Gupta, CEO
Richard Halka, CFO
Gitanjali Das Gupta, Vice-President, Operations

Evertz Technologies Limited
5292 John Lucas Dr.
Burlington, ON L7L 5Z9
905-335-3700
Fax: 905-335-3573
877-995-3700
www.evertz.com
Other Communications: Customer Service: service@evertz.com; sales@evertz.com
Social Media: twitter.com/EvertzTV
www.linkedin.com/company/evertz
Company Type: Public
Ticker Symbol: ET / TSX
Profile: Evertz Technologies Limited is a high-technology company. It is engaged in the designing, manufacturing, & marketing of film production, post production, & broadcast equipment. This equipment is used in the film & television broadcast industry.
Romolo Magarelli, President/CEO
Douglas A DeBruin, CA, Chair
Anthony Gridley, CA, Chief Financial Officer
905-335-7580

exactEarth Ltd.
60 Struck Ct.
Cambridge, ON N1R 8L2
519-622-4445
Fax: 519-623-8575
info@exactearth.com
www.exactearth.com
Company Type: Public
Ticker Symbol: XCT / TSX
Profile: The company manufactures Satellite AIS data services for boats.
Peter Mabson, President & Chief Executive Officer
Sean Maybee, CA, Chief Financial Officer
Philip Miller, Vice-President, Operations & Engineering

EXFO Inc.
400, av Godin
Québec, QC G1M 2K2
418-683-0211
Fax: 418-683-2170
800-663-3936
www.exfo.com
Social Media:
www.facebook.com/pages/EXFO-Inc/253435391363396
twitter.com/EXFO
www.linkedin.com/company/exfo
Company Type: Public
Ticker Symbol: EXF / TSX; EXFO, NASDAQ
Staff Size: 1,500
Profile: Test, measurement, & monitoring products are designed & manufactured by EXFO Inc. The company's test & service assurance solutions are used by the global telecommunications industry.
Germain Lamonde, Chief Executive Officer & Chair
Pierre Plamondon, CA, Chief Financial Officer & Vice-President, Finance
Stephen Bull, Vice-President, Research & Development
Luc Gagnon, Vice-President, Manufacturing Operations & Customer Service

Frankly Inc.
#502, 1 - 27th St.
New York, NY 11101 USA
212-931-1200
franklyinc.com
Social Media: www.facebook.com/FranklyChat
twitter.com/Frankly_Inc
www.linkedin.com/company/franklyinc
Company Type: Public
Ticker Symbol: TLK / TSX.V
Profile: An online broadcast platform.
Steve Chung, Chief Executive Officer
Lou Schwartz, COO & CFO

Hammond Power Solutions Inc. (HPS)
595 Southgate Dr.
Guelph, ON N1G 3W6
519-822-2441
Fax: 519-822-9701
888-798-8882
www.hammondpowersolutions.com
Social Media: www.facebook.com/HammondPowerSolutions
twitter.com/HPSTransformers
www.linkedin.com/company/hammond-power-solutions
Company Type: Public
Ticker Symbol: HPS.A / TSX
Staff Size: 1,300
Profile: Established in 1917, Hammond Power Solutions Inc. engineers & manufactures custom & standard dry-type transformers & related magnetic products. The company's products are used by the global electrical industry.
W.G. (Bill) Hammond, Chair/CEO
Chris R. Huether, Chief Financial Officer & Corporate Secretary
Dawn Henderson, Manager, Investor Relations
ir@hammondpowersolutions.com

Nanotech Security Corp.
#505, 3292 Production Way
Burnaby, BC V5A 4R4
604-678-5775
Fax: 604-678-5780
www.nanosecurity.ca
Social Media:
www.facebook.com/pages/NanoTech-Security-Corp/1818675952 1833
twitter.com/NTS_Corp
www.linkedin.com/company/1033616
Company Type: Public
Ticker Symbol: NTS / TSX.V
Profile: A security technology development company.
Doug Blakeway, Chief Executive Officer
Troy Bullock, Chief Financial Officer
Ron Ridley, Vice-President, Operations

Nightingale Informatix
#200, 55 Renfrew Dr.
Markham, ON L3R 8H3
905-943-2600
Fax: 905-415-8780
support@nightingalemd.com
www.nightingalemd.com
Company Type: Public
Ticker Symbol: NGH / TSX
Profile: An electronic health record company.
Sam Chebib, President & Chief Executive Officer
David Toews, Chief Financial Officer
Mark Crerar, Chief Commercial Officer

Novadaq Technologies Inc.
#202, 5090 Explorer Dr.
Mississauga, ON L4W 4T9
905-629-3822
Fax: 905-247-0656
www.novadaq.com
Other Communications: Customer Service:
CustomerService@novadaq.com
Company Type: Public
Ticker Symbol: NDQ / TSX; NVDQ / NASDAQ
Staff Size: 215
Profile: Novadaq provides SPY fluorescence imaging technology for the healthcare industry.
Rick Mangat, President & Chief Executive Officer
Roger Deck, Chief Financial Officer
Lori Swalm, Vice-President, Marketing

Novanta Inc.
125 Middlesex Turnpike
Bedford, MA 01730 USA
781-266-5700
Fax: 781-266-5114
800-342-3757
www.novanta.com
Company Type: Public
Ticker Symbol: NOVT / NASDAQ
Staff Size: 1,355
Profile: Novanta supplies laser scanning devices & precision motion & optical control technologies. The company serves the medical, scientific, electronics, & industrial markets.
John A. Roush, Chief Executive Officer
Peter Chang, Vice-President, Corp. Controller & Chief Accounting Officer
Robert J. Buckley, Chief Financial Officer

Matthijs Glastra, Chief Operating Officer

Pacific Insight Electronics Corp.
Canada Operations Centre
1155 Insight Dr.
Nelson, BC V1L 5P5
250-354-1155
800-995-1155
info@pacificinsight.com
www.pacificinsight.com
Social Media: www.linkedin.com/company/419122
Company Type: Public
Ticker Symbol: PIH / TSX
Staff Size: 900
Profile: Pacific Insight Electronics Corp. designs, manufactures and delivers electronic products and full-service solutions to the automotive, commercial vehicle, off-road, and specialty markets.
Stuart D. Ross, Chief Executive Officer
Jonathan Fogg, Chief Financial Officer
Daryl Chappell, Director, Human Resources
Mike Medvec, Director, Engineering

Sangoma Technologies
#100, 100 Renfrew Dr.
Markham, ON L3R 9R6
905-474-1990
Fax: 905-474-9223
800-388-2475
info@sangoma.com
www.sangoma.com
Social Media: www.facebook.com/Sangoma
twitter.com/Sangoma
www.linkedin.com/company/106543
Company Type: Public
Ticker Symbol: STC / TSX
Profile: A hardware & software company that works with voice, data & video applications.
William Wignall, President & CEO
David Moore, Chief Financial Officer
Nenad Corbic, Vice-President, Software & Hardware Engineering

Sierra Wireless, Inc.
13811 Wireless Way
Richmond, BC V6V 3A4
604-231-1100
Fax: 604-231-1109
www.sierrawireless.com
Social Media: twitter.com/sierrawireless
Company Type: Public
Ticker Symbol: SW / TSX; SWIR / NASDAQ
Staff Size: 1,089
Profile: Sierra Wireless, Inc. specializes in wireless solutions. It provides professional services to clients who require expertise in wireless design, integration, & carrier certification.
Jason Cohenour, Chief Executive Officer
David G. McLennan, Chief Financial Officer
Philippe Guillemette, Chief Technology Officer
Bill Seefeldt, Sr. Vice-President, Engineering
Bill Dodson, Sr. Vice-President, Operations

Smart Technologies
3636 Research Rd. NW
Calgary, AB T2L 1Y1
403-245-0333
Fax: 403-228-2500
888-427-6278
smarttech.com
Social Media: www.facebook.com/SMARTforBusiness
twitter.com/SMARTCollab
ca.linkedin.com/company/smart-technologies
Company Type: Public
Ticker Symbol: SMA / TSX; SMT / NYSE
Staff Size: 795
Profile: SMART is a technology company serving the education, higher education, business, government and military communities.
Neil Gaydon, President/CEO
Greg Estell, President, Solutions
Warren Barkley, Chief Technology Officer
Nicholas Svensson, Vice-President, Operations

Vecima Networks Inc.
Corporate Headquarters
771 Vanalman Ave.
Victoria, BC V8Z 3B8
250-881-1982
Fax: 250-881-1974
www.vecima.com
Other Communications: Saskatoon Facility, Phone: 306-955-7075
Company Type: Public
Ticker Symbol: VCM / TSX
Profile: Vecima Networks Inc. is a designer, manufacturer, & distributor of hardware products with embedded software that supports broadband access to cable, wireless, & telephony networks. Principal markets include Broadband Wireless & Converged Wired Solutions. Vecima Networks has ISO 9001:2000 certified manufacturing operations in Saskatoon, Saskatchewan.
Sumit Kumar, President and Chief Executive Officer
John Hanna, Chief Financial Officer
Marshall Sali, Senior Vice-President, Operations
Mark Briggs, Senior Vice-President, Cable Sales

WiLAN Inc.
#300, 303 Terry Fox Dr.
Ottawa, ON K2K 3J1
613-688-4900
Fax: 613-688-4894
info@wilan.com
www.wi-lan.com
Other Communications: media@wilan.com; ir@wilan.com; hr@wilan.com
Company Type: Public
Ticker Symbol: WIN / TSX; WILN / NASDAQ
Staff Size: 47
Profile: The company is a technology innovation & licensing company. WiLAN Inc.'s patent portfolio applies to products in the communications & consumer electronics markets.
Jim Skippen, President/CEO
Michael B. Vladescu, Chief Operating Officer
Shaun McEwan, Chief Financial Officer
Ken Standwood, Chief Technology Officer
Andrew Parolin, Sr. Vice-President
Prashant Watchmaker, Senior Vice-President, General Corporate Counsel & Secretary

Engineering & Management

Calian Group Ltd.
#101, 340 Legget Dr.
Ottawa, ON K2K 1Y6
613-599-8600
Fax: 613-599-8650
877-225-4264
info@calian.com
www.calian.com
Other Communications: Investor Relations, E-mail: ir@calian.com
Social Media: twitter.com/CalianLtd
www.linkedin.com/company/calian
Company Type: Public
Ticker Symbol: CTY / TSX
Staff Size: 2,500
Profile: Calian Group Ltd. is a consulting firm, focusing on the areas of IT, training, health & systems engineering & manufacturing services.
Kevin Ford, President & CEO
Jacqueline Gauthier, Vice-President, Chief Financial Officer & Corporate Secretary

CGI Group Inc.
1350 René-Lévesque Blvd. West, 5th Fl.
Montréal, QC H3G 1T4
514-841-3200
Fax: 514-841-3299
www.cgi.com
Social Media: www.facebook.com/cgigroup
twitter.com/CGI_Global
www.linkedin.com/company/cgi
Company Type: Public
Ticker Symbol: GIB.A / TSX; GIB / NYSE
Staff Size: 65,000
Profile: The information technology & business process services firm is engaged in the integration & customization of technologies & software applications, as well as the management of business processes & transactions.
Michael E. Roach, President/CEO
Mark Boyajian, President, Canadian Operations
François Boulanger, Executive Vice-President & Chief Financial Officer
Benoit Dubé, Executive Vice-President, Chief Legal Officer & Secretary
Julie Godin, Executive Vice-President, Global Human Resources & Strategic Planning
Claude Séguin, Senior Vice-President, Corporate Development & Strategic Investments

Gemini Corp.
#400, 839 - 5th Ave. SW
Calgary, AB T2P 3C8
403-255-2006
Fax: 403-640-0401
contact@geminicorp.ca
www.geminicorp.ca
Other Communications: Investor Relations, E-mail: investor@geminicorp.ca
Company Type: Public
Ticker Symbol: GKX / TSX-V
Staff Size: 650
Profile: Gemini provides multi-disciplined engineering and field solutions for energy and industrial facilities.
Peter Sametz, President & CEO
Chris Podolsky, Chief Financial Officer
Terry Martin, Chief Operating Officer
Roger Harripersad, Vice-President, Human Resources

Linamar Corporation
287 Speedvale Ave. West
Guelph, ON N1H 1C5
519-836-7550
Fax: 519-824-8479
www.linamar.com
Company Type: Public
Ticker Symbol: LNR / TSX
Staff Size: 19,600
Profile: Highly engineered products are developed, designed, & produced by thie manufacturing company. Linamar Corporation's operating groups are as follows: Industrial, Commercial & Energy; Manufacturing; Skyjack; & Driveline Systems. The company supplies the global vehicle & mobile industrial equipment markets.
Linda Hasenfratz, Chief Executive Officer
Jim Jarrell, President & Chief Operating Officer
Mark Stoddart, Chief Technology Officer & Executive Vice-President, Sales & Marketing
Roger Fulton, General Counsel, Corporate Secretary, & Exec. Vice-President, Human Resources
Dale Schneider, Chief Financial Officer

SNC-Lavalin Group Inc.
455, boul René-Lévesque ouest
Montréal, QC H2Z 1Z3
514-393-1000
Fax: 514-866-0795
www.snclavalin.com
Social Media: www.facebook.com/snclavalin
twitter.com/snclavalin
www.linkedin.com/company/snc-lavalin_2
Company Type: Public
Ticker Symbol: SNC / TSX
Staff Size: 36,754
Profile: The international engineering & construction organization owns infrastructure, & is engaged in the provision of operation & maintenance services. Examples of services include project financing, project management, procurement, engineering, & construction. The group is involved in sectors such as pharmaceuticals, petroleum, agrifood, the environment, transit, power, & mining.
Neil Bruce, President & CEO
Sylvain Girard, Executive Vice-President/CFO
Marie-Claude Dumas, Executive Vice-President, Human Resources
Hartland J.A. Paterson, Executive Vice-President & General Counsel
Erik Ryan, Executive Vice-President, Marketing, Strategy & External Relations

Stantec Inc.
10160 - 112th St.
Edmonton, AB T5K 2L6
780-917-7000
866-782-6832
askstantec@stantec.com
www.stantec.com
Other Communications: Investor Relations, E-mail: investor.relations@stantec.com
Social Media: www.facebook.com/StantecInc
twitter.com/stantec
www.linkedin.com/company/stantec
Company Type: Public
Ticker Symbol: STN / TSX, NYSE
Staff Size: 15,200
Profile: Stantec Inc. offers professional consulting services for infrastructure & facilities projects. The following services are provided: planning, project management, project economics, surveying & geomatics, engineering, architecture, landscape architecture, environmental science, & interior design.
Robert J. Gomes, President & Chief Executive Officer
Dan Lefaivre, Executive Vice-President & Chief Financial Officer

Scott Murray, Executive Vice-President & Chief Operating Officer

WSP Global Inc.
1600 René Lévesque Blvd. West, 16th Fl.
Montréal, QC H3H 1P9

514-340-0046
Fax: 514-340-1337
www.wsp-pb.com/en/WSP-Canada
Social Media: www.facebook.com/WSPinCanada
twitter.com/WSPCanada
www.linkedin.com/company/wsp-in-canada

Company Type: Public
Ticker Symbol: WSP / TSX
Staff Size: 34,000
Profile: WSP is a large engineering company that provides a full range of consulting services. Market segments include energy, environmental, municipal infrastructure, transportation, industrial, & building.
Pierre Shoiry, President & Chief Executive Officer, WSP Global Inc.
Hugo Blasutta, President & CEO, Canada
Tony Veilleux, Chief Financial Officer, Canada

Finance

49 North Resources Inc.
#602, 224 - 4 Ave. South
Saskatoon, SK S7K 0C5

306-653-2692
Fax: 306-664-4483
www.fnr.ca

Company Type: Public
Ticker Symbol: FNR / TSX.V
Profile: A resource investment company, whose portfolio includes oil & gas, potash, uranium, diamonds, coal, base & precious metals & rare earth elements.
Tom MacNeill, President & CEO
Andrew Davidson, Chief Financial Officer

Accord Financial Corp.
77 Bloor St. West, 18th Fl.
Toronto, ON M5S 1M2

416-961-0007
Fax: 416-961-9443
800-231-2977
www.accordfinancial.com
Other Communications: Receivables Management: 800-967-0015

Company Type: Public
Ticker Symbol: ACD / TSX
Staff Size: 93
Profile: Through its subsidiaries, Accord Financial provides the following financial services to small & medium-sized businesses: record-keeping, financing, credit investigation, collection services, & guarantees.
Tom Henderson, President & Chief Executive Officer, Accord Financial Corp.
Fred Moss, President, Accord Financial Inc. Canada

AGF Management Limited
Toronto Dominion Bank Tower
66 Wellington St. West, 31st Fl.
Toronto, ON M5K 1E9

905-214-8203
Fax: 905-214-8243
800-268-8583
www.agf.com
Other Communications: Toll-Free Fax: 1-888-329-4243
Social Media: www.facebook.com/followagf

Company Type: Public
Ticker Symbol: AGF.B / TSX
Staff Size: 494
Profile: The independent investment management firm offers products such as mutual funds, pooled funds, & mutual fun wrap programs. Assets are managed on behalf of institutional investors & private clients.
AGF Trust is a complementary business. It provides mortgages, loans & GICs through mortgage brokers & financial advisors.
Blake C. Goldring, CFA, Chair & Chief Executive Officer
Robert J. Bogart, Executive Vice-President & Head, Corporate Development
Kevin McCreadie, President & Chief Investment Officer

Alaris Royalty Corp.
#250, 333 - 24th Ave. SW
Calgary, AB T2S 3E6

403-228-0873
Fax: 403-228-0906
www.alarisroyalty.com
Social Media: www.linkedin.com/company/alaris-royalty-corp

Company Type: Public
Ticker Symbol: AD / TSX
Staff Size: 13
Profile: Alaris Royalty provides alternative financing for private businesses in North America, in exchange for royalties or distributions from Private Company Partners.
Stephen King, CFA, President & Chief Executive Officer
Darren Driscoll, CA, Chief Financial Officer
Rachel Colabella, BComm, LLB, Chief Legal Officer & Corporate Secretary
Curtis Krawetz, Vice-President, Investments & Investor Relations

Allbanc Split Corp. II
Scotia Plaza
PO Box 4085 Stn. A, 40 King St. West
Toronto, ON M5W 2X6

416-863-5930
Fax: 416-863-7425
mc.allbanc2@scotiabank.com

Company Type: Public
Ticker Symbol: ALB / TSX
Profile: The company holds a portfolio of common shares of the Bank of Montreal, CIBC, National Bank of Canada, Bank of Nova Scotia, RBC & Toronto-Dominion Bank.
Brian D. McChesney, President & CEO
Stephen Pearce, Chief Financial Officer

Aston Hill Financial
Toronto-Dominion Centre
PO Box 92, #2110, 77 King St. West
Toronto, ON M5K 1G8

416-583-2300
Fax: 877-374-7952
800-513-3868
astonhill.ca
Other Communications: Investment email: funds@astonhill.ca

Company Type: Public
Ticker Symbol: AHF / TSX
Profile: Aston Hill Financial is a publicly traded asset management firm with offices in Calgary & Toronto.
James Werry, President & Chief Executive Officer
Ben Cheng, Chief Investment Officer
Derek Slemko, Chief Operating Officer & Chief Financial Officer

Bank of Nova Scotia
Also Known As: Scotiabank
Scotia Plaza
40 King St. West
Toronto, ON M5H 1H1

416-866-6161
Fax: 416-866-3750
800-472-6842
www.scotiabank.com
Other Communications: Hearing Impaired Services: 1-800-645-0288
Social Media: www.facebook.com/scotiabank
twitter.com/scotiabankhelps
www.linkedin.com/company/scotiabank

Company Type: Public
Ticker Symbol: BNS / TSX, NYSE
Staff Size: 89,214
Profile: Scotiabank's range of services includes personal & commercial banking, corporate & investment banking services & products, as well as wealth management services. Scotiabank has approximately 23 million customers in over 55 countries.
Brian J. Porter, President & Chief Executive Officer
Barbara Mason, Group Head & Chief Human Resources Officer
Sean D. McGuckin, Group Head & Chief Financial Officer
Deborah M. Alexander, Executive Vice-President & General Counsel
Andrew Branion, Executive Vice-President & Group Treasurer

BMO Financial Group (BMO)
Also Known As: Bank of Montreal
First Canadian Place
100 King St. West, 18th Fl.
Toronto, ON M5X 1A1

416-867-6656
Fax: 416-867-3367
877-225-5266
feedback@bmo.com
www.bmo.com
Other Communications: TTY: 1-866-889-0889; Cantonese/Mandarin: 1-800-665-8800
Social Media: www.facebook.com/BMOcommunity
twitter.com/bmo
www.linkedin.com/company/bank-of-montreal

Company Type: Public
Ticker Symbol: BMO / TSX
Staff Size: 53,585
Profile: Established in 1817 as Bank of Montreal, BMO Financial Group offers a wide range of financial products & services, including retail banking, investment banking, & wealth management.
William Downe, Chief Executive Officer
Thomas E. Flynn, Chief Financial Officer
Surjit Rajpal, Chief Risk Officer
Simon A. Fish, General Counsel
Richard Rudderham, Chief Human Resources Officer
Frank Techar, Chief Operating Officer

Builders Capital Mortgage
#405, 1210 - 8th St. SW
Calgary, AB T2R 1L3

403-685-9888
Fax: 403-225-9470
info@builderscapital.ca
builderscapital.ca

Company Type: Public
Ticker Symbol: BCF / TSX
Profile: A mortgage investment firm.
Sandy Loutitt, President & CEO
John Strangway, Chief Financial Officer

Callidus Capital Corporation
Bay Wellington Tower, Brookfield Place
PO Box 792, #4620, 181 Bay St.
Toronto, ON M5J 2T3

416-945-3222
www.calliduscapital.ca

Company Type: Public
Ticker Symbol: CBL / TSX
Staff Size: 33
Profile: Callidus Capital is a lending partner, with offices located in Toront0, Seattle & Montreal.
David Reese, President & COO
416-945-3016, dreese@calliduscapital.ca
Dan Nohdomi, Vice-President & CFO
416-945-3014, dnohdomi@calliduscapital.ca
Chris Dangerfield, Vice-President, Operations
416-945-3215, cdangerfield@calliduscapital.ca

Canaccord Genuity Group Inc.
Pacific Centre
PO Box 10337, #2200, 609 Granville St.
Vancouver, BC V7Y 1H2

604-643-7300
800-382-9280
www.canaccordgenuity.com

Company Type: Public
Ticker Symbol: CF / TSX; CF. / LSE
Staff Size: 1,928
Profile: Canaccord Genuity Group Inc. was established in 1950. It is an independent, full-service financial services firm. Through its subsidiaries, Canaccord Financial conducts operations in the areas of wealth management & global capital markets. There are over sixty Canaccord offices throughout the world.
Daniel Daviau, President & Chief Executive Officer
Brad Kotush, CA, Chief Financial Officer & Risk Officer
Dvai Ghose, Global Head, Equity Research

Canadian Imperial Bank of Commerce (CIBC)
Commerce Court
199 Bay St., B-2, Securities Level
Toronto, ON M5L 1A2

416-980-2211
800-465-2422
www.cibc.com
Other Communications: French: 888-337-2422; Telex: 065-24116
Social Media: www.facebook.com/CIBC
twitter.com/cibc
ca.linkedin.com/company/cibc

Company Type: Public
Ticker Symbol: CM / TSX
Staff Size: 44,201
Profile: The Canadian Imperial Bank of Commerce was formed in 1961. CIBC provides financial products & services through its three business units: Retail and Business Banking, Wealth Management and Wholesale Banking. Customers include individuals & small business clients, plus corporate & institutional clients. CIBC has 1,129 branches throughout Canada.
Victor Dodig, President & CEO
Kevin Glass, Senior Executive Vice-President & CFO
Steve Geist, Senior Executive Vice-President & Group Head, Wealth Management
Kevin Patterson, Senior Executive Vice-President, Technology & Operations
Michael G. Capatides, CAO, General Counsel & Senior Exec. Vice-President
Laura Dottori-Attanasio, Senior Executive Vice-President & Chief Risk Officer

Canadian Western Bank Group (CWB)
Corporate Office, Canadian Western Bank Place
#3000, 10303 Jasper Ave.
Edmonton, AB T5J 3X6

780-423-8888
Fax: 780-969-8326
800-836-1886
comments@cwbank.com
www.cwbankgroup.com
Other Communications: communications@cwbank.com; InvestorRelations@cwbank.com
Social Media: www.facebook.com/cwbcommunity
www.twitter.com/CWBcommunity
www.linkedin.com/company/canadian-western-bank
Company Type: Public
Ticker Symbol: CWB / TSX
Staff Size: 2,062
Profile: The federally chartered, Schedule I bank provides personal & commercial banking services across western Canada. Subsidiaries of Canadian Western Bank include Valiant Trust Company & Canadian Western Trust. These subsidiaries offer both personal & corporate trust services. Canadian Direct Insurance Inc., another of Canadian Western Bank's subsidiaries, is engaged in the provision of personal home & automobile insurance.
Chris H. Fowler, President & Chief Executive Officer
Carolyn Graham, FCA, Executive Vice-President & Chief Financial Officer
Bogie Ozdemir, Executive Vice-President & Chief Risk Officer
Glen Eastwood, Executive Vice-President, Business Transformation
Stephen Murphy, Executive Vice-President, Banking

Chesswood Group Limited
#15, 156 Duncan Mill Rd.
Toronto, ON M3B 3N2

416-386-3099
Fax: 416-386-3085
info@chesswoodgroup.com
www.chesswoodgroup.com
Other Communications: Investors: investorrelations@chesswoodgroup.com
Company Type: Public
Ticker Symbol: CHW / TSX
Staff Size: 100
Profile: The financial services company has operating businesses in Canada & the United States.
Barry W. Shafran, B.A., CA, President & Chief Executive Officer
Lisa Stevenson, MBA, CA, Director, Finance

CI Financial Corp.
2 Queen St. East, 20th Fl.
Toronto, ON M5C 3G7

416-364-1145
800-268-9374
www.cifinancial.com
Company Type: Public
Ticker Symbol: CIX / TSX
Staff Size: 1,546
Profile: CI Financial Corp. is a diversified wealth management firm & investment fund company. CI operates primarily through Assante Wealth Management (Canada) Ltd. & CI Investments Inc.
Peter W. Anderson, Chief Executive Officer
Douglas J. Jamieson, Chief Financial Officer & Executive Vice-President
David C. Pauli, Chief Operating Officer & Executive Vice-President
Sheila A. Murray, President, General Counsel, & Secretary

Clairvest Group Inc.
Also Known As: Clairvest
#1700, 22 St. Clair Ave. East
Toronto, ON M4T 2S3

416-925-9270
Fax: 416-925-5753
www.clairvest.com

Company Type: Public
Ticker Symbol: CVG / TSX
Profile: Clairvest Group Inc. is a private equity management firm. The group invests its own capital & that of third parties in businesses with the potential to generate superior returns.
Jeff Parr, Co-Chief Executive Officer
Ken Rotman, Co-Chief Executive Officer
Daniel Cheng, Chief Financial Officer
Maria Klyuev, Director, Investor Relations & Marketing 416-413-6008

Clarke Inc.
6009 Quinpool Rd., 9th Fl.
Halifax, NS B3K 5J7

902-442-3000
Fax: 902-442-0187
www.clarkeinc.com
Company Type: Public
Ticker Symbol: CKI / TSX
Profile: Clarke Inc. is an activist catalyst investment company, with several wholly-owned operating companies & divisions. The company has a diversified portfolio of investments, with operating subsidiaries as follows: Clarke Transport Inc., Clarke Road Transport Inc., Clarke IT Solutions Inc., La Traverse Rivière-du-Loup - St. Siméon Ltée., CIS Shipping International Inc., & Granby Industries.
Michael Rapps, President & CEO
Dustin Haw, Vice-President, Investments
Kim Langille, Vice-President, Taxation

Crosswinds Holdings Inc.
#400, 365 Bay St.
Toronto, ON M5H 2V1

800-439-5136
info@crosswindsinc.com
www.crosswindsinc.com
Company Type: Public
Ticker Symbol: CWI / TSX
Profile: A private equity firm & asset management company.
Colin King, Chief Executive Officer
Susan McCormich, Interim Chief Financial Officer
Helen Martin, Chief Operating Officer

Dealnet Capital
#300, 325 Milner Ave.
Toronto, ON M1B 5N1

855-912-3444
info@dealnetcapital.com
www.dealnetcapital.com
Social Media: www.facebook.com/dealnetcapitalcorp
twitter.com/dealnetcapital
www.linkedin.com/company/3192667
Company Type: Public
Ticker Symbol: DLS / TSX
Profile: A consumer loan provider.
Michael Hilmer, Chief Executive Officer
Paul Leonard, Chief Financial Officer

DH Corporation
Also Known As: D+H
Global Headquarters
120 Bremner Blvd., 30th Fl.
Toronto, ON M5J 0A8

416-696-7700
888-850-6656
investorrelations@dh.com
www.dh.com
Social Media: www.facebook.com/DHCorpCanada
twitter.com/DHCorpCanada
www.linkedin.com/company/d-h
Company Type: Public
Ticker Symbol: DH / TSX
Staff Size: 4,000
Profile: Founded in 1875, the organization supplies financial services to financial organizations, including mortgage lenders/brokers, insurance companies, governments, & regional banks.
Gerrard Schmid, Chief Executive Officer
Karen Weaver, Chief Financial Officer
William Neville, Chief Operating Officer
Edward Ho, Presdient, Global Payments Solutions

Difference Capital Financial
#1010, 130 Adelaide St. West
Toronto, ON M5H 3P5

416-649-5088
info@differencecapital.com
www.differencecapital.com
Social Media: twitter.com/diffcap
www.linkedin.com/company/difference-capital-funding-inc-
Company Type: Public
Ticker Symbol: DCF / TSX
Profile: Difference Capital Financial Inc. is a publicly listed specialty finance company focused on debt and equity growth capital to technology, media, and healthcare-related companies.
Henry Kneis, Chief Executive Officer
Tom Astle, Chief Investment Officer
Victor Duong, Chief Financial Officer

DirectCash Payments Inc.
Head Office
#6, 1420 - 28th St. NE
Calgary, AB T2A 7W6

888-414-3733
investorrelations@directcash.net
www.directcash.net
Other Communications: Customer Support: customersupport@directcash.net
Social Media: www.facebook.com/DCPayments
twitter.com/dcpayments
www.linkedin.com/company/directcash-management-inc-
Company Type: Public
Ticker Symbol: DCI / TSX
Staff Size: 392
Profile: DirectCash provides debit terminals, ATMS, prepaid phone cards, & prepaid cash cards in Canada.
Jeffrey J. Smith, President & Chief Executive Officer
Patrick Moriarty, Chief Financial Officer
Todd Schneider, Chief Operations Officer
Natalie Ng, Chief Technology Officer

Diversified Royalty Corp.
#902, 510 Burrard St.
Vancouver, BC V6C 3A8

604-235-3146
Fax: 604-685-9970
diversifiedroyaltycorp.com
Company Type: Public
Ticker Symbol: DIV / TSX
Profile: Diversified Royalty Corp. acquires royalties from businesses & franchisors in North America.
Sean Morrison, President & CEO
Greg Gutmanis, Chief Financial Officer & Vice-President, Acquisitions

Element Financial Corporation
#3600, 161 Bay St.
Toronto, ON M5J 2S1

416-386-1067
Fax: 888-772-8129
877-534-0019
www.elementfinancial.ca
Company Type: Public
Ticker Symbol: EFN / TSX
Staff Size: 1,700
Profile: Element Financial Corporation is an independent equipment finance company specializing in providing equipment financing solutions for the end-users, distributors and manufacturers of a wide variety of capital equipment.
Steven Hudson, Chief Executive Officer
Bradley Nullmeyer, President
Dan Jauernig, Chief Operating Officer
Michel Beland, Chief Financial Officer & Chief Administrative Officer

Equitable Group Inc.
Corporate Office
#700, 30 St. Clair Ave. West
Toronto, ON M4V 3A1

416-515-7000
Fax: 416-515-7001
866-407-0004
serviceclient@eqbank.ca
www.equitabletrust.com
Other Communications: Investors: investor_enquiry@equitablegroupinc.com
Company Type: Public
Ticker Symbol: EQB / TSX
Staff Size: 495
Profile: Through its wholly-owned subsidiary, The Equitable Trust Company, Equitable Group Inc. offers first mortgage financing & Guaranteed Investment Certificates to depositors. The Equitable Trust Company is a federally incorporated trust company.
Andrew Moor, President & Chief Executive Officer
Tim Wilson, Chief Financial Officer & Vice-President

Fiera Capital Inc.
#800, 1501, av McGill College
Montréal, QC H3A 3M8

514-954-3300
Fax: 514-954-5098
800-361-3499
info@fieracapital.com
www.fieracapital.com

Company Type: Public
Ticker Symbol: FSZ / TSX
Staff Size: 459
Profile: Fiera Sceptre is an independent, full-service, multi-product investment firm.
Sylvain Brosseau, President & COO
Jean-Guy Desjardins, Chief Executive Officer & Chair
John Valentini, Executive Vice-President & CFO

Firm Capital Mortgage Investment Corp.
163 Cartwright Ave.
Toronto, ON M6A 1V5

416-635-0221
Fax: 416-635-1713
info@firmcapital.com
www.firmcapital.com
Social Media: www.linkedin.com/company/firm-capital-corporation
Company Type: Public
Ticker Symbol: FC / TSX

Profile: Through its mortgage banker, Firm Capital Corporation, Firm Capital Mortgage Investment Trust is a non-bank lender. It provides residential & commercial real estate financing
Eli Dadouch, President & Chief Executive Officer
Jonathan Mair, CA, Senior Vice-President & Chief Financial Officer
Sandy Poklar, Chief Operating Officer

First National Financial LP
North Tower
#700, 100 University Ave.
Toronto, ON M5J 1V6

416-593-1100
Fax: 416-593-1900
800-465-0039
customer@firstnational.ca
www.firstnational.ca
Other Communications: Toll-Free Fax: 800-463-9584

Company Type: Public
Ticker Symbol: FN / TSX
Staff Size: 915
Profile: First National Financial LP is a non-bank mortgage originator that provides single-family & multi-unit residential & commercial mortgage solutions.
Stephen Smith, Chair, CEO & Co-Founder, First National Financial
Rob Inglis, Chief Financial Officer, First National Financial Corporation
Jason Ellis, Managing Director, Capital Markets
Jeremy Wedgbury, Managing Director, Commercial Mortgage Origination
Moray Tawse, Executive Vice-President & Co-Founder
Scott McKenzie, Senior Vice-President, Residential Mortgages
Lisa White, Vice-President, Mortgage Operations
Hilda Wong, General Counsel & Vice-President

Gluskin Sheff + Associates Inc.
Bay Adelaide Centre
#5100, 333 Bay St.
Toronto, ON M5H 2R2

416-681-6000
Fax: 416-681-6060
866-681-6001
questions@gluskinsheff.com
www.gluskinsheff.com
Other Communications: Calgary Office, Phone: 403-202-6483; media@gluskinsheff.com
Social Media: twitter.com/gluskinsheffinc
www.linkedin.com/company/gluskin-sheff---associates

Company Type: Public
Ticker Symbol: GS / TSX
Staff Size: 142
Profile: Gluskin Sheff + Associates Inc. was formed in 1984. The independent, wealth management firm serves institutional investors & private clients of high net worth.
Thomas MacMillan, President & Chief Executive Officer
Jim Bantis, Executive Vice-President, Client Wealth Management
Peter Mann, Executive Vice-President, Co-Chief Investment Officer, & Head of Equities
Peter Zaltz, Executive Vice-President, Co-Chief Investment Officer, & Head of Fixed Income

GMP Capital Inc.
#300, 145 King St. West
Toronto, ON M5H 1J8

416-367-8600
Fax: 416-367-8164
888-301-3244
www.gmpcapital.com
Other Communications: Investors: investorrelations@gmpcapital.com

Company Type: Public
Ticker Symbol: GMP / TSX
Staff Size: 313
Profile: GMP Capital Inc. is a Canadian independent investment dealer. Through its subsidiaries, GMP Capital is involved in the following investment areas: alternative investments, capital markets, & wealth management. Individual, corporate, & institutional investor clients are served.
Harris A. Fricker, MA, President & CEO
Doug Bell, Vice-Chair, Investment Banking
Chris Bond, Vice-Chair & Co-Head, Institutional Trading

Grenville Strategic Royalty Corp.
#550, 220 Bay St.
Toronto, ON M5J 2W4

416-777-0383
info@GrenvilleSRC.com
www.grenvillesrc.com

Company Type: Public
Ticker Symbol: GRC / TSX.V
Profile: Grenville provides financing to businesses in North America.

Steve Parry, CEO
Donnacha Rahill, Chief Financial Officer
Kevin Jarret, Vice-President, Investments
Darlene Deruchie, Financial Controller

Guardian Capital Group Limited
Commerce Court West
PO Box 201, #3100, 199 Bay St.
Toronto, ON M5L 1E8

416-364-8341
Fax: 416-364-2067
800-253-9181
info@guardiancapital.com
www.guardiancapital.com

Company Type: Public
Ticker Symbol: GCG.A / TSX
Staff Size: 320
Profile: Guardian Capital Group Limited is a diversified financial services company that was established in 1962. Through its businesses, Guardian Capital Group Limited is involved in the distribution of mutual funds, institutional & high net worth investment management, as well as other financial services.
George Mavroudis, Chief Executive Officer & President
Donald Yi, Chief Financial Officer

Home Capital Group Inc.
#2300, 145 King St. West
Toronto, ON M5H 1J8

416-360-4663
Fax: 416-363-7611
800-990-7881
inquiry.homecapitalgroup@hometrust.ca
www.homecapital.com

Company Type: Public
Ticker Symbol: HCG / TSX
Profile: Home Capital Group Inc. is a holding Company and operates through its principal subsidiary, Home Trust Company. Home Trust offers deposit, mortgage lending, retail credit and credit card issuing services.
Gerald M. Soloway, Chief Executive Officer
Martin K. Reid, President
Robert L. Morton, CFO/Exec. Vice-President
Fariba Rawhani, Exec. Vice-President & Chief Information Officer

HSBC Bank Canada
#300, 885 West Georgia St.
Vancouver, BC V6C 3E9

604-685-1000
Fax: 604-641-2506
888-310-4722
info@hsbc.ca
www.hsbc.ca
Other Communications: Business: 866-808-4722; Internet Banking: 877-621-8811
Social Media: twitter.com/HSBC_CA
www.linkedin.com/company/hsbc

Company Type: Public
Ticker Symbol: HSB.PR.C / TSX
Staff Size: 6,150
Profile: The chartered bank was established in 1981. It carries on business uner the provisions of the Bank Act.
Sandra Stuart, President & Chief Executive Officer
Jacques Fleurant, Chief Financial Officer
Linda Seymour, Executive Vice-President & Country Head, Commercial Banking
Betty Miao, Executive Vice-President & Head, Retail Banking & Wealth Management
Gail St. Germain, Executive Vice-President & Head, Human Resources

IGM Financial Inc.
One Canada Centre
447 Portage Ave.
Winnipeg, MB R3B 3H5

204-943-0361
Fax: 204-947-1659
www.igmfinancial.com

Company Type: Public
Ticker Symbol: IGM / TSX
Staff Size: 3,028
Profile: IGM Financial Inc. is a managed asset, mutual fund, & personal financial services company. Its operating units include Investment Planning Counsel Inc., Mackenzie Financial Corporation, & Investors Group. IGM is a member of the Power Financial Corporation group.
Jeffrey R. Carney, President & CEO
Kevin E. Regan, Exec. VP & CFO
Donald MacDonald, Sr. VP, General Counsel & Secretary

IOU Financial
#100, 600 TownPark Lane
Kennesaw, GA 30144

866-217-8564
ioufinancial.com
Social Media: www.facebook.com/ioufinancial
twitter.com/ioufinancial
www.linkedin.com/company/iou-financial-inc-

Company Type: Public
Ticker Symbol: IOU / TSX.V
Profile: A money lending company.
Phil Marleau, President/CEO
David Kennedy, Chief Financial Officer

Laurentian Bank of Canada/ Banque Laurentienne du Canada
Tour Banque Laurentienne
#1660, 1981, av McGill College
Montréal, QC H3A 3K3

514-252-1846
800-525-1846
www.laurentianbank.com
Other Communications: TTY: 1-866-262-2231; Media: 514-284-4500, ext. 8232
Social Media: www.facebook.com/BLaurentienne
twitter.com/BLaurentienne
www.linkedin.com/company/12074

Company Type: Public
Ticker Symbol: LB / TSX
Staff Size: 3,700
Profile: Founded in 1846, Laurentian Bank of Canada has operations across Canada today. It serves both individuals & small & medium-sized businesses. The bank also offers services to independent financial intermediaries through B2B Trust. Laurentian Bank Securities provides full-service brokerage solutions.
François Desjardins, President & Chief Executive Officer
Susan Kudzman, Exec. Vice-President & Chief Risk & Corporate Affairs Officer
François Laurin, Exec. Vice-President & Chief Financial Officer
Stéphane Therrien, Exec. Vice-President, Personal & Commercial Banking

MCAN Mortgage Corporation
#600, 200 King St. West
Toronto, ON M5H 3T4

416-572-4880
Fax: 416-598-4142
855-213-6226
mcanexecutive@mcanmortgage.com
www.mcanmortgage.com

Company Type: Public
Ticker Symbol: MKP / TSX
Profile: MCAN Mortgage is a mortgage investment corporation. Funds are invested in a portfolio of mortgages, as well as other types of loans & investments, real estate, & marketable securities.
William Jandrisits, President & Chief Executive Officer
Jeffrey Bouganim, Chief Financial Officer & Vice-President

Mogo Finance Technology Inc.
#2100, 401 West Georgia St.
Vancouver, BC V6B 5A1

604-659-4380
Fax: 604-733-4944
investors@mogo.ca
mogo.ca
Social Media: www.facebook.com/mogomoney
twitter.com/mogomoney

Company Type: Public
Ticker Symbol: GO / TSX
Profile: A technological lending company.
David Feller, Chief Executive Officer
Gregory Feller, Chief Financial Officer

Mosaic Capital Corporation
#400, 2424 - 4th St. SW
Calgary, AB T2S 2T4

403-218-6500
info@mosaiccapitalcorp.com
www.mosaiccapitalcorp.com

Company Type: Public
Ticker Symbol: M / TSX.V
Staff Size: 541
Profile: Mosaic Capital was formed in May 2011 through a merger with Mosaic Diversified Income Fund and First West Properties Ltd. Mosaic Capital Corporation is a Calgary-based investment company that owns a portfolio of established businesses.
Harold Kunik, President
Mark Gardhouse, Chief Executive Officer
Allan Fowler, Chief Financial Officer
Troy Pearce, Chief Operating Officer

National Bank Financial Group
Also Known As: National Bank of Canada
Tour de la Banque Nationale
600, rue de la Gauchetière ouest
Montréal, QC H3B 4L2
514-394-5555
888-483-5628
investorrelations@nbc.ca
www.nbc.ca
Social Media: www.facebook.com/nationalbanknetworks
twitter.com/nationalbank/
www.linkedin.com/company/national-bank-of-canada/
Company Type: Public
Ticker Symbol: NA / TSX
Staff Size: 19,696
Profile: Chartered under the Bank Act of Canada, the National Bank provides comprehensive financial services, including retail, commercial, corporate, international, & treasury banking services. Through its subsidiaries, National Bank Financial Group also offers security brokerage, insurance, wealth management, & mutual fund & retirement plan management. There are over 452 branches across Canada.
Louis Vachon, President & Chief Executive Officer
Ghislain Parent, Chief Financial Officer & Executive Vice-President, Finance & Treasury
Dominique Fagnoule, Exec. Vice-President, Information Technology
Karen Leggett, Chief Marketing Officer & Exec. Vice-President, Corporate Development
Lynn Jeanniot, Exec. Vice-President, Human Resources & Corporate Affairs

New Pacific Holdings Corp.
#1378, 200 Granville St.
Vancouver, BC V6C 1S4
604-633-1368
Fax: 604-669-9387
info@newpacificholdings.ca
www.newpacificmetals.com
Company Type: Public
Ticker Symbol: NUX / TSX.V
Profile: The company was formerly a precious metals exploration firm. It is now an investment issuer.
Rui Feng, Chief Executive Officer
Hongen Ma, President
Jalen Yuan, Chief Financial Officer

Pacific & Western Bank of Canada
Also Known As: P&W Bank of Canada
#2002, 140 Fullarton St.
London, ON N6A 5P2
519-645-1919
Fax: 519-645-2060
866-979-1919
www.pwbank.com
Company Type: Public
Ticker Symbol: PWB / TSX
Staff Size: 79
David R. Taylor, President & Chief Executive Officer
Shawn Clarke, Chief Operating Officer
Barry D. Walter, Senior Vice President & Chief Financial Officer
Jonathan F.P. Taylor, Sr. Vice President, Deposit Services & Human Resources

Partners Value Investments Inc.
Brookfield Place
#300, 181 Bay St.
Toronto, ON M5J 2T3
416-369-2512
Fax: 416-365-9642
Company Type: Public
Ticker Symbol: PVF / TSX.V
Profile: Partners Value Investments Inc. is a investment holding company. Its primary investment is with Brookfield Asset Management Inc.
George Myhal, President & CEO
Allen Taylor, Chief Financial Officer

Pinetree Capital Ltd.
#1100, 34 King St. East
Toronto, ON M5C 2X8
416-941-9600
www.pinetreecapital.com
Social Media: twitter.com/pinetreecapital
Company Type: Public
Ticker Symbol: PNP / TSX
Profile: The financial advisory, investment, & venture capital firm is focused on the small cap market. Investments are mainly in the resources sector.
Peter Tolnai, Chief Executive Officer

Power Financial Corporation
751 Victoria Sq.
Montréal, QC H2Y 2J3
514-286-7430
800-890-7440
www.powerfinancial.com
Social Media:
www.linkedin.com/company/power-financial-corporation
Company Type: Public
Ticker Symbol: PWF / TSX
Staff Size: 32,899
Profile: The diversified holding & management company was founded in 1940. It includes the following subsidiaries: IGM Financial Inc., Great-West Lifeco Inc., & Pargesa.
R. Jeffrey Orr, President/CEO
Gregory D. Tretiak, Exec. Vice-President/CFO
Claude Généreux, Exec. Vice-President
Stéphane Lemay, Vice-President, General Counsel & Secretary

Primewest Mortgage Investment Corporation
#700, 750 Spadina Cres. East
Saskatoon, SK S7K 3H3
306-955-1002
Fax: 306-955-9511
888-955-1002
www.primewest.ca
Social Media: www.facebook.com/primewest
twitter.com/Prime_West
Company Type: Public
Ticker Symbol: PRI / TSX
Profile: A company that offers mortgages to individuals & businesses aren't able to acquire one from other institutions.
Brad Penno, Chief Executive Officer
Marlene Kaminsky, Chief Financial Officer

PWC Capital Inc. (PWC)
140 Fullarton St., 20th Fl.
London, ON N6A 5P2
519-488-1280
Fax: 519-488-1298
866-792-8104
www.pwccapital.com
Company Type: Public
Ticker Symbol: PWC / TSX
Profile: Pacific & Western Credit Corp.'s wholly owned subsidiary is the Pacific & Western Bank of Canada. Pacific & Western Bank is a Schedule I chartered bank that offers financing to corporate & government entities.
David R. Taylor, President & Chief Executive Officer
Barry D. Walter, Chief Financial Officer
Cameron Mitchell, Vice-President, General Counsel & Corporate Secretary

RIFCO Inc.
#500, 5000 Gaetz Ave.
Red Deer, AB T4N 6C2
403-314-1288
Fax: 403-314-1132
888-303-2001
info@RIFCO.net
www.rifco.net
Social Media: www.facebook.com/377705218961796
twitter.com/rifconation
Company Type: Public
Ticker Symbol: RFC / TSX
Profile: RIFCO is an auto purchase finance company providing motorists with non-traditional financing operating in all provinces except Saskatchewan and Quebec.
Bill Graham, President & CEO
Monte Coates, Vice-President & COO
Doug Decksheimer, Vice-President & Chief Marketing Officer
Lance Kadatz, Vice-President & CFO

Royal Bank of Canada (RBC)
Royal Bank Plaza
PO Box 1, 200 Bay St.
Toronto, ON M5J 2J5
416-974-5151
Fax: 416-955-7800
www.rbc.com
Social Media: www.facebook.com/rbc
twitter.com/RBC
www.linkedin.com/company/rbc
Company Type: Public
Ticker Symbol: RY / TSX, NYSE
Staff Size: 72,839
Profile: The Royal Bank of Canada is engaged in the following services: personal & commercial banking; corporate & investment banking; insurance; wealth management; & transaction processing services. Offices are located in Canada, the United States, & 51 other countries.
David I. McKay, President & CEO
Janice Fukakusa, CFO & Chief Administrative Officer
Zabeen Hirji, Chief Human Resources Officer

Mark Hughes, Chief Risk Officer

Sprott Inc.
South Tower, Royal Bank Plaza
PO Box 27, #2700, 200 Bay St.
Toronto, ON M5J 2J1
416-362-7172
ir@sprott.com
www.sprottinc.com
Social Media: twitter.com/sprott
Company Type: Public
Ticker Symbol: SII / TSX
Staff Size: 194
Profile: Sprott Inc. is an independent asset management firm operating through its four business units: Sprott Asset Managemen L.P., Sprott Private Wealth L.P., Sprott Consulting L.P., & Sprott U.S. Holdings Inc..
Peter Grosskopf, Chief Executive Officer
James Fox, President
Kevin Hibbert, CPA, CA, Chief Financial Officer & Corporate Secretary

Street Capital Group Inc.
PO Box 3, #700, 1 Toronto St.
Toronto, ON M5C 2V6
647-259-7873
877-416-7873
investorinfo@streetcapital.ca
www.counselcorp.com
Company Type: Public
Ticker Symbol: SCB / TSX
Staff Size: 213
Profile: Founded in 1979, Street Capital Group is a financial services company. Through its businesses, the corporation is engaged in private equity investment, residental mortgage lending, real estate finance, & distressed & surplus capital asset transactions,.
W. Ed Gettings, Chief Executive Officer
Lazaro DaRocha, President
Marissa Lauder, Chief Financial Officer

Timbercreek Financial Corporation
25 Price St.
Toronto, ON M4W 1Z1
416-923-9967
844-304-9967
info@timbercreek.com
www.timbercreekfinancial.com
Company Type: Public
Ticker Symbol: TF / TSX
Profile: Timbercreek Financial is a commercial real estate lendor.
Andrew Jones, Chief Executive Officer
Craig Geier, Chief Financial Officer

TMX Group Inc.
Registered Office & Head Office, The Exchange Towe
130 King St. West
Toronto, ON M5X 1J2
416-947-4670
Fax: 416-947-4662
888-873-8392
info@tmx.com
www.tmx.com
Other Communications: Investor Relations: 416-947-4277
Social Media: www.facebook.com/tmxmoney
twitter.com/tmxgroup
www.linkedin.com/company/tmx-group
Company Type: Public
Ticker Symbol: X / TSX
Profile: TMX Group is headquartered in Toronto. The Group also has offices in the following cities: Montréal, Calgary, Vancouver, New York, London, Singapore & Beijing.
The following are key TMX Group companies: Toronto Stock Exchange, TSX Venture Exchange, TMX Select, Montreal Exchange, Canadian Derivatives Clearing Corporation, Natural Gas Exchange, Boston Options Exchange, Shorcan, Shorcan Energy Brokers, & Equicom. These companies offer listing markets, trading markets, clearing facilities, data products, plus other services to the financial sector around the globe.
Lou Eccleston, Chief Executive Officer
Mary Lou Hukezalie, Senior Vice-President & Group Head, Human Resources
James Oosterbaan, President, NGX
Luc Fortin, Interim President & Chief Executive Officer, Montreal Exchange
Eric Sinclair, President, TMX Datalinx, & Group Head, Information Services
John McKenzie, Chief Financial Officer, TMX Group
Cheryl Graden, Senior Vice-President & Group Head, Legal & Business Affairs
Paul Malcolmson, Director, Investor Relations
416-947-4277, TMXshareholder@tmx.com

Toronto-Dominion Bank
Also Known As: TD Bank Group
PO Box 1, 66 Wellington St. West
Toronto, ON M5K 1A2

416-944-6367
800-430-6095
tdshinfo@td.com
www.td.com
Other Communications: Shareholder Relations, Toll-Free: 866-756-8936
Social Media: facebook.com/tdbankgroup/
twitter.com/td_canada
www.linkedin.com/company/td

Company Type: Public
Ticker Symbol: TD / TSX
Staff Size: 81,483
Profile: The Toronto-Dominion Bank & its subsidiaries are known collectively as TD Bank Group. The Group's four key businesses are as follows: Canadian Personal & Commercial Banking; Wealth & Insurance; U.S. Personal & Commercial Banking; & Wholesale Banking. TD has over 24 million customers worldwide.
Bharat Masrani, Group President & CEO
Riaz Ahmed, Group Head & Chief Financial Officer
Norie Campbell, Group Head & General Counsel
Mark Chauvin, Group Head & Chief Risk Officer
Terri Currie, Group Head, Canadian Personal Banking
Sue Cummings, Executive Vice-President, Human Resources

Tricon Capital Group Inc.
1067 Yonge St.
Toronto, ON M4W 2L2

416-925-7228
Fax: 416-925-5022
www.triconcapital.com

Company Type: Public
Ticker Symbol: TCN / TSX
Staff Size: 230
Profile: Tricon Capital Group Inc. was founded in 1988. It is a residential real estate investment company. Financing is provided to operators or developers in markets in Canada & the United States.
Gary Berman, President & CEO
David Veneziano, Vice-President & General Counsel
Wissam Francis, Chief Financial Officer

Wilmington Capital Management Inc.
#700, 505 - 3rd St. SW
Calgary, AB T2P 3E6

403-705-8038
Fax: 403-705-8035
www.wilmingtoncapital.com

Company Type: Public
Ticker Symbol: WCM.A / TSX
Profile: The Canadian investment company holds cash & marketable securities. Wilmington Capital Management also owns land lease properties.
Joseph F. Killi, President & Chief Executive Officer
Christopher Killi, Vice-President, Finance
Alex Powell, Corporate Secretary

Food, Beverages & Tobacco

A&W Revenue Royalties Income Fund
#300, 171 Esplanade West
North Vancouver, BC V7M 3K9

604-988-2141
investorrelations@aw.ca
www.awincomefund.ca

Company Type: Public
Ticker Symbol: AW.UN / TSX
Profile: A&W Revenue Royalties Income Fund is a limited purpose trust. It invests in A&W Trade Marks Inc., which owns the trade-marks used in the A&W restaurant business in Canada. Through its subsidiary, A&W Trade Marks Inc., A&W Revenue Royalties licences trade-marks for royalty income.
Paul F.B. Hollands, Chair & Chief Executive Officer, A&W Food Services Management
Donald T. Leslie, Chief Financial Officer
Susan Senecal, President & COO

Andrew Peller Limited/ Andrew Peller Limitée
697 South Service Rd.
Grimsby, ON L3M 4E8

905-643-4131
Fax: 905-643-4944
info@andrewpeller.com
www.andrewpeller.com

Company Type: Public
Ticker Symbol: ADW.A, ADW.B / TSX
Staff Size: 1,121
Profile: Andrew Peller Limited has wineries in Nova Scotia, Ontario, & British Columbia. Wines are also imported from wine regions around the world. The company's wine agencies are Grady Wine Marketing Inc. in British Columbia, & The Small Winemaker's Collection Inc. in Ontario. Andrew Peller also owns & operates more than 100 retail locations. Store names include Aisle 43, WineCountry Vintners, & Vineyards Estate Wines. Through its wholly owned subsidiary, Global Vintners Inc., Andrew Peller also produces & markets personal winemaking products.
John E. Peller, President & Chief Executive Officer
Brian D. Athaide, Chief Financial Officer & Executive Vice-President, Human Resources & IT
Anthony M. Bristow, Chief Operating Officer
Shari A. Niles, Executive Vice-President, Marketing

Big Rock Brewery Inc.
5555 - 76th Ave. SE
Calgary, AB T2C 4L8

403-720-3239
Fax: 403-236-7523
800-242-3107
reception@bigrockbeer.com
www.bigrockbeer.com
Social Media: www.facebook.com/BigRockBrewery
twitter.com/bigrockbrewery

Company Type: Public
Ticker Symbol: BR / TSX
Staff Size: 133
Profile: Big Rock Brewery is a brewer whose products are marketed throughout Canada (excluding Quebec).
Robert Sartor, President & CEO

BioNeutra North America Inc.
9608 - 25 Ave. NW
Edmonton, AB T6N 1J4

780-466-1481
Fax: 780-801-0036
bioneutra.ca
Social Media: witter.com/bioneutra
www.linkedin.com/company/bioneutra

Company Type: Public
Ticker Symbol: BGA / TSX
Profile: BioNeutra is a prebiotic & fiber ingredient manufacturer.
Jianhua Zhu, President & CEO
Raymond Yong, Chief Finance Officer

Boston Pizza Royalties Income Fund
#100, 10760 Shellbridge Way
Richmond, BC V6X 3H1

604-303-6083
Fax: 604-270-4168
investorrelations@bostonpizza.com
www.bpincomefund.com

Company Type: Public
Ticker Symbol: BPF.UN / TSX
Staff Size: 183
Profile: Boston Pizza Royalties Income Fund is a limited purpose open-ended trust. There are over 370 stores in the Royalty Pool. Units are traded on the Toronto Stock Exchange. Boston Pizza Royalties Income Fund pays unitholders a monthly distribution.
Mark Pacinda, President & CEO
Wes Bews, Chief Financial Officer
Jordan Holm, Vice-President, Investor Relations
604-303-6083, Fax: 604-270-4168

Brick Brewing Co.
400 Bingemans Centre Dr.
Kitchener, ON N2B 3X9

519-742-2732
Fax: 519-742-9874
info@brickbeer.com
www.brickbeer.com
Social Media: www.facebook.com/WaterlooBrewing
twitter.com/waterloobrewing

Company Type: Public
Ticker Symbol: BRB / TSX
Staff Size: 115
Profile: Brick Brewing Co., founded in 1984, is an Ontario craft brewery.
George H. Croft, President/CEO
Sean Byrne, Chief Financial Officer
seanb@brickbeer.com
Russell Tabata, Chief Operating Officer

Cara Operations Ltd.
199 Four Valley Dr.
Vaughan, ON L4K 0B8

905-760-2244
www.cara.com
Other Communications: Investor relations: investorrelations@cara.com

Company Type: Public
Ticker Symbol: CAO / TSX
Staff Size: 5,700
Profile: Cara is the parent company of Swiss Chalet, East Side Mario's, Milestones, Casey's, Montana's, Bier Markt, Kelsey's, Prime Pubs & Harvey's. It is Canada's oldest & largest restaurant company.
William Gregson, Chief Executive Officer

Clearwater Seafoods Incorporated
757 Bedford Hwy.
Bedford, NS B4A 3Z7

902-443-0550
Fax: 902-443-8365
www.clearwater.ca
Social Media: www.facebook.com/Clearwaterseafood
twitter.com/Clearwatersea
www.linkedin.com/company/clearwater-seafoods-lp

Company Type: Public
Ticker Symbol: CLR / TSX
Staff Size: 1,400
Profile: Clearwater Seafoods Incorporated supplies wild, eco-labelled seafood, including lobster, clams, scallops, crab, groundfish, & coldwater shrimp. Biologists are employed to ensure innovative & sustainable fishing practices. The company has been in business since 1976.
Ian Smith, Chief Executive Officer
Teresa Fortney, Chief Financial Officer & Vice-President, Finance
Christine Penney, Vice-President, Sustainability & Public Affairs

Corby Spirit & Wine Limited
#1100, 225 King St. West
Toronto, ON M5V 3M2

416-479-2400
info.corby@pernod-ricard.com
www.corby.ca
Other Communications: investors.corby@pernod-ricard.com
Social Media: twitter.com/CorbySW
www.linkedin.com/company/corby-distilleries-limited

Company Type: Public
Ticker Symbol: CSW.A / TSX
Staff Size: 172
Profile: Corby Distilleries is a marketer of distilled spirits, whiskies, & liqueurs produced in Canada. In addition, imported wines, gin, cognac, scotch, & liqueurs are marketed by the organization. Its owned brands include Wiser's Canadian whiskies & Seagram Coolers. Corby Distilleries represents international brands, such as Jameson Irish whiskey & Wyndham Estate wines, through its affiliation with Pernod Ricard.
Sales offices are located in Halifax, NS (902-445-0705), Montréal, QC (514-856-4320), Toronto, ON (416-369-1859), Edmonton, AB (780-442-9000), Regina, SK (306-586-6546), & Richmond, BC (604-276-8121).
Patrick O'Driscoll, President & Chief Executive Officer
Antonio Sanchez Villarreal, Chief Financial Officer & Vice-President
Marc Valencia, General Counsel, Corporate Secretary, & Vice-President, Public Affairs
Maxime Kouchnir, Vice-President, Marketing
Stéphane Côté, Vice-President, Sales
Jim Stanski, Vice-President, Production

Cott Corporation
6525 Viscount Rd.
Mississauga, ON L4V 1H6

905-672-1900
888-260-3776
info@cott.com
www.cott.com
Other Communications: Investor Relations, E-mail: investorrelations@cott.com

Company Type: Public
Ticker Symbol: BCB / TSX; COT / NYSE
Staff Size: 9,500
Profile: The beverage company focuses upon private-label products & contract manufacturing.
Jerry Fowden, Chief Executive Officer
Jay Wells, Chief Financial Officer
Michael Creamer, Vice-President, Corporate Human Resources

Diamond Estates Wines & Spirits
1067 Niagara Stone Rd.
Niagara on the Lake, ON L0S 1J0

905-641-1042
www.diamondestates.ca
Social Media: www.facebook.com/diamondestates
twitter.com/DiamondEstates

Company Type: Private
Ticker Symbol: DWS / TSX.V
Staff Size: 113
Profile: Diamond Estates produces VQA Ontario wines under the brands Lakeview Cellars, EastDell Estates, 20 Bees, FRESH wines & 1914 wines. The vineyard is located in Niagara-on-the-Lake, Ontario.
J. Murray Souter, President & CEO

Alan Stratton, Chief Financial Officer
Thomas Green, Vice-President, Winemaking & Winery Operations

Empire Company Limited
115 King St.
Stellarton, NS B0K 1S0

902-755-4440
Fax: 902-755-6477
www.empireco.ca

Company Type: Public
Ticker Symbol: EMP.A / TSX
Staff Size: 65,000
Profile: The Empire Company Limited is engaged in food retailing, through its majority ownership of Sobeys Inc. Through wholly-owned companies, Empire Company is also involved in real estate.
François Vimard, Interim President & CEO
Clinton Keay, Interim Chief Financial Officer
Karin McCaskill, Senior Vice-President, General Counsel & Secretary

George Weston Limited
Corporate Office
22 St. Clair Ave. East
Toronto, ON M4T 2S7

416-922-2500
Fax: 416-922-4395
investor@weston.ca
www.weston.ca
Other Communications: Loblaw Companies: 905-459-2500; Norse Dairy: 614-294-4931

Company Type: Public
Ticker Symbol: WN / TSX
Staff Size: 196,000
Profile: George Weston Limited consists of Weston Foods & Loblaws.
Weston Foods is involved in the baking & dairy industries. Operated by Loblaw Companies Limited, Loblaws is engaged in food distribution. Loblaws also offers drug store merchandise & general merchandise, as well as financial products & services.
W. Galen Weston, O.C., B.A., LL.D., Executive Chair
Pavi Binning, President & CEO
Richard Dufresne, Exec. Vice-President & Chief Financial Officer
Gordon A.M. Currie, Exec. Vice-President & Chief Legal Officer
Khush Dadyburjor, Chief Strategy Officer
Robert Balcom, Senior Vice-President & General Counsel
Geoffrey H. Wilson, Sr. Vice-President, Investor Relations, Business Intelligence & Communications
Allison Doner, Group Controller
David Farnfield, Vice-President, Commodities

GLG Life Tech Corporation
Corporate Headquarters
#100, 10271 Shellbridge Way
Richmond, BC V6X 2W8

604-669-2602
Fax: 604-285-2606
855-454-7587
info@glglifetech
www.glglifetech.com
Other Communications: Investor Relations, E-mail: ir@glglifetech.com
Social Media: www.facebook.com/glglifetech
twitter.com/GLGLifeTech
www.linkedin.com/company/1912570

Company Type: Public
Ticker Symbol: GLG / TSX; GLGL / NASDAQ
Staff Size: 299
Profile: GLG Life Tech Corporation is a supplier of stevia extracts, a sweetener used in food & beverages. Through its subsidiary, ANOC, GLG Life Tech Corporation markets stevia sweetened beverages & foods to serve the Chinese market.
Luke Zhang, Chair & Chief Executive Officer

High Liner Foods Incorporated
PO Box 910, 100 Battery Point
Lunenburg, NS B0J 2C0

902-634-8811
Fax: 902-634-6228
info@highlinerfoods.com
www.highlinerfoods.com
Other Communications: Investor Relations: investor@highlinerfoods.com
Social Media: www.linkedin.com/company/high-liner-foods

Company Type: Public
Ticker Symbol: HLF / TSX
Staff Size: 1,416
Profile: High Liner Foods Incorporated specializes in processing & marketing prepared, frozen seafood products. Products are marketed under the following brands: High Liner, Sea Cuisine, Fisher Boy, Royal Sea, & Mirabel.
High Liner also sells FPI, Icelandic Seafood, Viking, Samband of Iceland, Seaside, & Seastar products to restaurants & institutions. In 2010, the company purchased the American based assets of Viking Seafoods, Inc., & in 2011 Icelandic USA, Inc. & subsidiaries of Icelandic Group hf were also purchased. High Liner Foods Incorporated serves the retail & food service markets throughout Canada, the United States, & Mexico.
Keith A. Decker, President & CEO
Jeff O'Neill, President & COO, Canadian Operations
Paul Jewer, FCA, Chief Financial Officer & Executive Vice-President
Tim Rorabeck, General Counsel & Executive Vice-President, Corporate Affairs
Paul Snow, Executive Vice-President, Global Procurement

Immunotec Inc.
300, rue Joseph Carrier
Vaudreuil-Doron, QC J7V 5V5

450-424-9992
info@immunotec.com
www.immunotec.com
Social Media: www.facebook.com/Immunotec
twitter.com/immunotec_hq
www.linkedin.com/company/1813270

Company Type: Public
Ticker Symbol: IMM / TSX
Profile: Imminotec is a nutrional supplements manufacturer.
Charles Orr, Chief Executive Officer
Patrick Montpetit, Vice-President & CFO
Robert Felton, Chief Operating Officer
John Molson, Vice-President, Research & Development

Imperial Ginseng Products
#310, 650 Georgia St. West
Vancouver, BC V6B 4N9

604-689-8863
Fax: 604-428-8470
www.imperialginseng.com

Company Type: Public
Ticker Symbol: IGP / TSX.V
Profile: The company grows ginseng in Ontario, & sells its product to Asian & North American distributors.
Hugh Cartwright, President
Stephen McCoach, Chief Executive Officer
Amelia Yeo, Chief Financial Officer
Maurice Levesque, Executive Vice-President

Imvescor Restaurant Group Inc.
#310, 8250 Decarie Blvd.
Montréal, QC H4P 2P5

514-341-5544
info@imvescor.ca
www.imvescor.ca

Company Type: Public
Ticker Symbol: IRG / TSX
Staff Size: 263
Profile: Imvescor Restaurant Group owns franchised & corporate restaurants across Canada. Brands include Pizza Delight, Mikes, Scores, & Bâton Rouge.
Frank Hennessey, President & CEO
Tania Clarke, Chief Financial Officer
Isabelle Breton, General Counsel & Corporate Secretary

Keg Royalties Income Fund
10100 Shellbridge Way
Richmond, BC V6X 2W7

604-821-6416
Fax: 604-276-2681
info@kegincomefund.com
www.kegincomefund.com
Social Media: www.facebook.com/thekegsteakhouseandbar
twitter.com/TheKeg
www.linkedin.com/company/the-keg-steakhouse-and-bar

Company Type: Public
Ticker Symbol: KEG.UN / TSX
Profile: The Keg Royalties Income Fund is an unincorporated open-ended, limited purpose trust. The Fund is the owner of The Keg Rights LP, which owns the trademarks, names, & other intellectual property used by The Keg restaurants. The Keg Royalties Income Fund licenses Keg Restaurants Ltd. to use these rights.
David Aisenstat, President & Chief Executive Officer, Keg Restaurants. Ltd.
Neil Maclean, Chief Financial Officer & Executive Vice-President, Keg Restaurants Ltd.
Doug Smith, Chief Operating Officer & Executive Vice-President, Keg Restaurants Ltd.
Ryan Bullock, Manager, Investor Relations
416-646-4517, Fax: 416-695-2401

Lassonde Industries Inc./ Industries Lassonde inc.
755, rue Principale
Rougemont, QC J0L 1M0

866-552-7643
www.lassonde.com
Social Media: twitter.com/lassondeinc
www.linkedin.com/company/lassonde

Company Type: Public
Ticker Symbol: LAS.A / TSX
Staff Size: 2,100
Profile: Through its subsidiaries, Lassonde Industries develops, manufactures, packages, & markets food products. The following products are manufactured: fruit juices, fruit beverages, canned corn, baked beans, barbecue sauces, dipping sauces, pasta sauces, meat marinades, bruschetta topping, tapenades, & fondue bouillon.
Pierre-Paul Lassonde, Chair & Chief Executive Officer
Jean Gattuso, President & Chief Operating Officer
Guy Blanchette, Executive Vice-President, Chief Financial Officer
Caroline Lemoine, Vice-President, General Counsel & Secretary

Liquor Stores N.A. Ltd.
#300, 10508 - 82 Ave.
Edmonton, AB T6E 2A4

780-944-9994
customerfeedback@lsgp.ca
www.liquorstoresgp.ca
Other Communications: investor@lsgp.ca
Social Media: www.facebook.com/liquordepotBC
twitter.com/liquordepotab

Company Type: Public
Ticker Symbol: LIQ / TSX
Staff Size: 2,250
Profile: Liquor Stores N.A. Ltd. is involved in the retail liquor industry. In 2010, the organization converted from an income trust to a dividend-paying corporation. The corporation has approximately 240 stores in Canada & the United States. Brand names include the Liquor Barn, Liquor Barn The Ultimate Party Source, Liqor Barn Express, the Liquor Depot, & Brown Jug
Stephen Bebis, President & Chief Executive Officer
David Gordey, Executive Vice-President & COO

Loblaw Companies Limited
National Head Office & Store Support Centre
1 President's Choice Circle
Brampton, ON L6Y 5S5

905-459-2500
Fax: 905-861-2387
888-495-5111
www.loblaw.ca
Other Communications: Media Relations, E-mail: pr@loblaw.ca
Social Media: www.facebook.com/LoblawCompaniesLimited
twitter.com/loblawco
ca.linkedin.com/company/loblaw-companies-limited

Company Type: Public
Ticker Symbol: L / TSX
Staff Size: 196,000
Profile: Formed in 1956, Loblaw Companies Limited is a food distributor, as well as a provider of general merchandise & drug store & financial products & services. The company operates the following grocery stores: Loblaws, The Real Canadian Superstore, Atlantic Superstore, Extra Foods, Independent, No Frills, Valu-mart, Provigo, Wholesale Club, Zehrs, Club Entrepôt, Cash & Carry, & Maxi. As of March 2014, Shoppers Drug Mart is an operating division of Loblaw.
Galen G. Weston, Executive Chairman & President
Sarah R. Davis, Chief Administrative Officer
Richard Dufresne, Chief Financial Officer
Grant Forese, Chief Operating Officer
Mark Wilson, Executive Vice-President, Human Resources & Labour Relations

Maple Leaf Foods Inc.
6897 Financial Dr.
Missisauga, ON L5N 0A8

800-268-3708
www.mapleleaffoods.com

Company Type: Public
Ticker Symbol: MFI / TSX
Staff Size: 11,500
Profile: Maple Leaf Foods' products include fresh & prepared meats, poultry, seafood, fresh & frozen bakery goods, & animal feed. Brands include Maple Leaf, Maple Leaf Prime Naturally, Schneiders, Olivieri, POM, Shopsy's, Mitchell's Gourmet Foods, Ben's, Bon Matin, Burns, Hygrade, Chevalier, New York Bakery, & Dempsters. Products are sold to wholesale, retail, & industrial customers around the world. Maple Leaf Foods has operations in Canada, the United States, Mexico, the United Kingdom, & Asia.
Michael H. McCain, President & Chief Executive Officer
Rory McAlpine, Senior Vice-President, Government & Industry Relations

Ben Brooks, Senior Vice-President & General Manager, Poultry
Iain Stewart, Senior Vice-President & General Manager, Fresh Pork
Richard Young, Senior Vice-President, Supply Chain & Purchasing
Debbie Simpson, Chief Financial Officer
Andreas Liris, Chief Information Officer
Randall Huffman, Chief Food Safety Officer & Senior Vice-President, Operations
Lynda Kuhn, Senior Vice-President, Sustainability & Public Affairs

Metro Inc.
11011, boul Maurice-Duplessis
Montréal, QC H1C 1V6

514-643-1000
800-361-4681
www.metro.ca
Social Media: www.linkedin.com/company/metro-inc.

Company Type: Public
Ticker Symbol: MRU / TSX
Staff Size: 65,000
Profile: Metro Inc. operates food retail stores in Ontario & Québec, under the following names: Metro, Super C, A&P, Loeb, Food Basics, Marché Richelieu, AMI, Les 5 Saisons, & GEM. The company also distributes pharmaceutical products under the following banners: Brunet, Clini-Plus, The Pharmacy, & Drug Basics.
Eric R. La Flèche, President/CEO
François Thibault, Executive Vice-President/CFO & Treasurer
Simon Rivet, Vice-President, General Counsel & Corporate Secretary
Frédéric Legault, Vice-President, Information Systems
Martin Allaire, Vice-President, Real Estate & Engineering
Geneviève Bich, Vice-President, Human Resources

MTY Food Group Inc./ Le Groupe MTY
#200, 8150 Transcanada Hwy.
Montréal, QC H4S 1M5

514-336-8885
Fax: 514-336-9222
866-891-6633
info@mtygroup.com
www.mtygroup.com

Company Type: Public
Ticker Symbol: MTY.TO / TSX
Staff Size: 435
Profile: MTY Food Group is an operator & franchisor of quick service restaurants. Examples of brands include Cultures, Country Style, Jugo Juice, Mr. Sub, Vanellis, Thai Express, & Yogen Früz Canada.
Stanley Ma, Chair & Chief Executive Officer
Eric Lefebvre, Chief Financial Officer

North West Company Inc.
77 Main St.
Winnipeg, MB R3C 1A3

204-943-0881
800-782-0391
nwc@northwest.ca
www.northwest.ca
Other Communications: Community Support, E-mail: communitysupport@northwest.ca
Social Media: www.facebook.com/TheNorthWestCompany
twitter.com/North_West_Co
www.linkedin.com/company/45623

Company Type: Public
Ticker Symbol: NWC / TSX
Staff Size: 7,378
Profile: Through its subsidiaries, The North West Company is engaged in the retail of food & daily products & services to rual communities & urban neighbourhoods. Areas of operations include Canada, Alaska, the Caribbean, & the South Pacific.
Edward S. Kennedy, President & Chief Executive Officer
Christie Frazier-Coleman, Executive Vice-President & Chief Merchandising Officer
Craig Gilpin, Executive Vice-President & Chief Operating Officer
John King, Executive Vice-President & Chief Financial Officer
Daniel McConnell, Executive Vice-President & Chief Development Officer

Pizza Pizza Royalty Corp. (PPRC)
500 Kipling Ave.
Toronto, ON M8Z 5E5

416-967-1010
Fax: 416-967-9865
feedback@pizzapizza.ca
www.pizzapizza.ca
Social Media: www.facebook.com/PizzaPizzaCanada
twitter.com/pizzapizzaltd

Company Type: Public
Ticker Symbol: PZA / TSX
Profile: Established in 2005, Pizza Pizza Royalty Corp. (formerly Pizza Pizza Royalty Income Fund) is a limited purpose, open-ended trust. The Fund acquired trademarks & trade names used by Pizza Pizza Limited in its restaurants. The trademarks are licensed to Pizza Pizza. There are 736 Pizza Pizza & Pizza 73 restaurants in the royalty pool.
Paul Goddard, Chief Executive Officer
Curt Feltner, Chief Financial Officer & Vice-President, Finance

Premium Brands Holdings Corporation
#100, 10991 Shellbridge Way
Richmond, BC V6X 3C6

604-656-3100
Fax: 604-656-3170
855-756-3100
investor@premiumbrandsgroup.com
www.premiumbrandsholdings.com

Company Type: Public
Ticker Symbol: PBH / TSX
Staff Size: 4,507
Profile: Premium Brands Holdings Corporation owns specialty food businesses with manufacturing & distribution facilities. The corporation also owns proprietary food distribution & wholesale networks. Facilities are located in Quebec, Ontario, Manitoba, Saskatchewan, Alberta, British Columbia, & Washington.
The following are some examples of Premium Brands' businesses: B&C Foods, Maximum Seafood, Direct Plus, Noble House Foods, Bread Garden Express, Kids Eat, Gloria's Catering, McSweeney's, Hempler's, Creekside Custom Foods, Quality Fast Foods, Harvest Meats, Grimm's Fine Fooks, SK Food Group, South Seas Meats, Deli Chef, & Multi-National Foods.
George Paleologou, CA, President & Chief Executive Officer
Will Kalutycz, CA, Chief Financial Officer

Restaurant Brands International Inc.
226 Wyecroft Rd.
Oakville, ON L6K 3X7

905-845-6511
rbi.com

Company Type: Public
Ticker Symbol: QSR / TSX
Staff Size: 4,300
Profile: Restaurant Brands International was created in 2014, after the merger between Tim Hortons & Burger King. The company operats over 19,000 restaurants in 100 countries. Tim Hortons & Burger King continue to operate independently.
Daniel Schwartz, Chief Executive Officer
José E. Cil, Executive Vice-President & President, Burger King Brand
Elias Diaz Sese, Executive Vice-President & President, Tim Hortons Brand
Jill Granat, Executive Vice-President & General Counsel
Joshua Kobza, Executive Vice-President & Chief Financial Officer

Rogers Sugar Inc. (RSI)
Administrative Office
4126, rue Notre-Dame est
Montréal, QC H1W 2K3

514-527-8686
Fax: 514-527-1610
888-526-8421
csr@lantic.ca
www.rogerssugar.com

Company Type: Public
Ticker Symbol: RSI / TSX
Profile: In 2008, Rogers Sugar Ltd. merged with Lantic Sugar Limited to create Lantic Inc.
In 2011, Rogers Sugar Income Fund converted into a conventional corporation named Rogers Sugar Inc.. The successor to Rogers Sugar Income Fund now owns all of the outstanding shares of Lantic Inc., plus the subordinated Lantic notes.
Lantic Inc. uses both the Lantic & Rogers trademarks. Lantic Inc. is engaged in the refining, processing, distributing, & marketing of sugar products, such as granulated sugar, sugar cubes, icing sugar, yellow & brown sugars, liquid sugars, specialty sugars, & syrups.
John Holliday, President & CEO, Lantic Inc.

Saputo Inc.
6869, boul Métropolitain est
Montréal, QC H1P 1X8

514-328-6662
Fax: 514-328-3364
www.saputo.com

Company Type: Public
Ticker Symbol: SAP / TSX
Staff Size: 11,700
Profile: Saputo Inc. is engaged in the production, commercialization, & distribution of dairy products & grocery products. The company's brands include the following: Saputo, Dairyland De Lucia, Frigo, Stella, HOP&GO!, Rondeau, Alexis de Portneuf, DuVillage de Warwick, La Paulina, Treasure Cave, Armstrong, Nutrilait, Vachon, Ricrem & Scotsburn. Production facilities are situated in five countries.
Lino A. Saputo, Jr., CEO
Dino Dello Sbarba, President & COO
Louis-Philippe Carrière, Chief Financial Officer
Gaétane Wagner, Chief Human Resources Officer

Second Cup Ltd.
6303 Airport Rd., 2nd Fl.
Mississauga, ON L4V 1R8

905-362-1818
Fax: 905-362-1121
877-212-1818
investor@secondcup.com
www.secondcup.com
Other Communications: marketing@secondcup.com; secondcupcustomercare@secondcup.com
Social Media: www.facebook.com/secondcup
twitter.com/secondcup

Company Type: Public
Ticker Symbol: SCU / TSX
Profile: In 2011, the Second Cup Income Fund converted from an income trust structure to a public corporation. Second Cup Ltd. is a large specialty coffee franchisor. It operates 345 cafés throughout Canada.
Alix Box, President & CEO
Barbara Mallon, CFO

SIR Royalty Income Fund
#200, 5360 South Service Rd.
Burlington, ON L7L 5L1

905-681-2997
Fax: 905-681-0394
info@sircorp.com
www.sircorp.com
Social Media: www.linkedin.com/company/sir-corp

Company Type: Public
Ticker Symbol: SRV.UN / TSX
Staff Size: 5,000
Profile: Trademarks related to SIR Corp.'s restaurant brands are used under a license agreement with SIR Royalty Limited Partnership. A royalty is paid by SIR Corp. to SIR Royalty Limited Partnership. SIR Royalty Income Fund has an investment in SIR Royalty Limited Partnership. The Fund receives distribution income from this investment. Distributions are paid to unitholders by the Fund on a monthly basis.
SIR Corp.'s restaurant brands include Alice Fazooli's, Jack Astor's Bar & Grill, Canyon Creek Chop House, Far Niente / Four / Petit Four, & Loose Moose Tap & Grill.
Peter Fowler, Chief Executive Officer
Jeff Good, Chief Financial Officer

Sportscene Group Inc./ Groupe Sportscene inc.
#102, 1180, Place Nobel
Boucherville, QC J4B 5L2

450-641-3011
Fax: 450-641-9742
800-413-2243
sports@cage.ca
www.cage.ca
Social Media: www.facebook.com/lacagebrasseriesportive
twitter.com/_lacage

Company Type: Public
Ticker Symbol: SPS.A / TSX Venture
Staff Size: 2,500
Profile: Sportscene Group Inc. has been in business since 1984. The company operates the chain of sports-themed resto-bars in Québec, known as La Cage aux Sport.
Sportscene is also involved in complementary activities, such as managing real estate holdings, constructing & renovating, & organizing sports-related activities.
Jean Bédard, President & CEO

Ten Peaks Coffee Company
3131 Lake City Way
Burnaby, BC V5A 3A3

604-420-4050
www.tenpeakscoffee.ca

Company Type: Public
Ticker Symbol: TPK / TSX
Profile: Ten Peaks Coffee owns two subsidiaries: the Swiss Water Decaffeinated Coffee Company Inc. & Seaforth Supply Chain Solutions Inc. Swiss Water is a cofee decaffeinator located in Burnaby, BC. Seaforth is a coffee handling & storage business, located in Vancouver, BC.
Frank Dennis, President & CEO
Sherry Tryssenaar, Chief Financial Officer

Forestry & Paper

Acadian Timber Corp.
PO Box 11179 Stn. Royal Centre, #1800, 1055 West Georgia St.
Vancouver, BC V6E 3R5

604-661-9143
Fax: 604-687-3419
www.acadiantimber.com

Company Type: Public
Ticker Symbol: ADN / TSX
Profile: The timberland operator supplies primary forest products. Areas of activity are eastern Canada & the northeastern United States.
Acadian Timber complies with environmental legislation & regulations & works with government, regulators, communities, & stakeholders. The company reports regularly on its environmental performance.
Mark Bishop, President & Chief Executive Officer
Wyatt Hartley, Senior Vice-President & Chief Financial Officer

Canfor Corporation
#100, 1700 West 75th Ave.
Vancouver, BC V6P 6G2

604-661-5241
Fax: 604-661-5253
info@canfor.com
www.canfor.com
Other Communications: Media Inquiries, E-mail: communications@canfor.com
Social Media: twitter.com/CanforCorp

Company Type: Public
Ticker Symbol: CFP / TSX
Staff Size: 6,047
Profile: Formed in 1966, Canfor Corporation is an integrated forest products company. Operations are carried out in British Columbia, Alberta, Quebec, Washington state, & North & South Carolina.
Don Kayne, President & Chief Executive Officer
Alan Nicholl, Chief Financial Officer & Senior Vice-President, Finance
David Calabrigo, Corporate Secretary & Senior Vice-President, Corporate Development & Legal Affairs
Mark Feldinger, Senior Vice-President, Environment, Energy, Transportation & Sourcing
Wayne Guthrie, Senior Vice-President, Sales & Marketing
Stephen Mackie, Senior Vice-President, Canadian Operations

Canfor Pulp Products Inc. (CPPI)
#100, 1700 West 75th Ave.
Vancouver, BC V6P 6G2

604-661-5241
Fax: 604-661-5235
info@canfor.ca
www.canfor.com

Company Type: Public
Ticker Symbol: CFX / TSX
Staff Size: 1,278
Profile: In 2011, Canfor Pulp Income Fund converted from an income trust structure to a corporate structure. Canfor Pulp Products Inc. is a producer of northern softwood kraft pulp & kraft paper.
Don Kayne, Chief Executive Officer
Alan Nicholl, Chief Financial Officer & Sr. Vice-President, Finance
Mark Feldinger, Sr. Vice-President, Environment, Energy, Transportation & Sourcing

Cascades Inc.
404, boul Marie-Victorin
Kingsey Falls, QC J0A 1B0

819-363-5100
Fax: 819-363-5155
info@cascades.com
www.cascades.com
Other Communications: Investor Relations, E-mail: investor@cascades.com
Social Media: www.facebook.com/cascades
twitter.com/CascadesSD
www.linkedin.com/company/cascades

Company Type: Public
Ticker Symbol: CAS / TSX
Staff Size: 10,700
Profile: Cascades Inc. was founded in 1964. The company is engaged in the production, transformation, & marketing of packaging & tissue products. Products are composed mainly of recycled fibres. Cascades operates throughout North America & Europe.
Mario Plourde, President & Chief Executive Officer
Jean Jobin, President & Chief Executive Officer, Cascades Tissue Group
Luc Langevin, President & Chief Operating Officer, Cascades Specialty Products Group
Charles Malo, President & Chief Operating Officer, Cascades Containerboard Packaging
Allan Hogg, Vice-President & Chief Financial Officer
Pascal Aguettaz, Vice-President, Corporate Services
Léon Marineau, Vice-President, Environment
Hugo D'Amours, Vice-President, Communications & Public Affairs

Catalyst Paper Corporation
3600 Lysander Lane, 2nd Fl.
Richmond, BC V7B 1C3

604-247-4400
Fax: 604-247-0512
www.catalystpaper.com
Social Media: www.linkedin.com/company/catalyst-paper

Company Type: Public
Ticker Symbol: CYT / TSX
Staff Size: 2,625
Profile: Catalyst Paper Corp. manufactures diverse specialty mechanical printing papers, newsprint and pulp.
Joe Nemeth, President & CEO
Frank De Costanzo, Senior Vice-President/CFO
Greg Maule, Senior Vice-President, Operations
Len Posyniak, Senior Vice-President, Human Resources & Corporate Services

Conifex Timber Inc.
Corporate Office
PO Box 10070, #980, 700 West Georgia St.
Vancouver, BC V7Y 1B6

604-216-2949
866-301-2949
www.conifex.com
Other Communications: Prince George: 250-561-2970; Fort St. James: 250-996-8241

Company Type: Public
Ticker Symbol: CFF / TSX Venture
Staff Size: 560
Profile: Conifex Timber Inc. & its subsidiaries are involved in the following activities: timber harvesting, reforestation, forest management, sawmilling logs into lumber & wood chips, & lumber finishing. Conifex is committed to responsible stewardship, & its work is guided by an environmental policy. The company's markets are in Canada, the United States, China, & Japan.
Ken Shields, Chief Executive Officer
ken.shields@conifex.com
Yuri Lewis, Chief Financial Officer
yuri.lewis@conifex.com
Tony Madia, Senior Vice-President, Operations
tony.madia@conifex.com

Fortress Paper Ltd.
157 Chadwick Ct., 2nd Fl.
North Vancouver, BC V7M 3K2

604-904-2328
888-820-3888
info@fortresspaper.com
www.fortresspaper.com

Company Type: Public
Ticker Symbol: FTP / TSX
Staff Size: 585
Profile: Established in 2006, Fortress Paper is engaged in the production of security & other specialty papers. It operates the following business segments: Pulp Segment; Security & Specialty Papers Segment; & Wallpaper Base Segment. The company's Fortress Specialty Cellulose mill is constructing a cogeneration facility, in order to expand into the renewable energy generation sector.
Yvon Pelletier, President & Chief Executive Officer
Kurt Loewen, Chief Financial Officer
Dan Buckle, Corporate Secretary & Director, Finance

Goodfellow Inc.
225, rue Goodfellow
Delson, QC J5B 1V5

450-635-6511
Fax: 450-635-3729
800-361-6503
info@goodfellowinc.com
www.goodfellowinc.com
Other Communications: USA, Toll-Free Phone: 800-361-0625
Social Media: www.facebook.com/goodfellowinc

Company Type: Public
Ticker Symbol: GDL / TSX
Staff Size: 877
Profile: Goodfellow Inc. re-manufactures, wholesales, & distributes wood & wood by-products, such as the following: dressed & rough lumber, sawn timber, composite & veneer based wood panel products, & prefinished & unfinished flooring. Customers are served in Canada & internationally.
Goodfellow Inc. has implemented an environmental policy to conduct its business in an environmentally responsible manner.
Denis Fraser, President & Chief Executive Officer
Pierre Lemoine, CMA, Vice-President/CFO
Nick Reonegro, Vice-President, Operations

Hardwoods Distribution Inc. (HDI)
#306, 9440 - 202 St.
Langley, BC V1M 4A6

604-881-1988
Fax: 604-881-1995
www.hardwoods-inc.com

Company Type: Public
Ticker Symbol: HWD / TSX
Staff Size: 494
Profile: In 2011, the Hardwoods Distribution Income Fund was converted to a corporation by way of a plan of arrangement. Hardwoods Distribution Inc. has a 100% ownership interest in Hardwoods Specialty Products LP & Hardwoods Specialty Products US LP. Every distribution centre of Hardwoods Specialty Products has been certified by the Forestry Stewardship Council for Chain of Custody. Hardwoods Distribution Inc. is also a member of the Canadian Green Building Council & the US Green Building Council in support of green building initiatives.
Rob Brown, President & Chief Financial Officer
Faiz Karmally, Chief Financial Officer & Vice-President
Lance Blanco, Senior Vice-President, Corporate Development

International Forest Products Limited
Also Known As: Interfor
Corporate Office
PO Box 49114, #3500, 1055 Dunsmuir St.
Vancouver, BC V7X 1H7

604-689-6800
Fax: 604-688-0313
info@interfor.com
www.interfor.com

Company Type: Public
Ticker Symbol: IFP / TSX
Staff Size: 1,162
Profile: International Forest Products Limited supplies lumber products. Operations are located in British Columbia, Washington, & Oregon.
Duncan K. Davies, President & Chief Executive Officer
John A. Horning, Chief Financial Officer & Executive Vice-President
Martin Juravsky, Senior Vice-President, Corporate Development & Strategy
Ian Fillinger, Senior Vice-President & Head, Operations
Mark Stock, Senior Vice-President, Human Resources

Norbord Inc.
#600, 1 Toronto St.
Toronto, ON M5C 2W4

416-365-0705
Fax: 416-777-4419
info@norbord.com
www.norbord.com
Other Communications: Sales & Product Information, E-mail: sales@norbord.com

Company Type: Public
Ticker Symbol: OSB / TSX
Staff Size: 2,600
Profile: Norbord Inc. produces wood-based panels & related products. The company has 13 operations in Canada, the United States, & Europe.
Peter C. Wijnbergen, President & Chief Executive Officer
Robin E. Lampard, Chief Financial Officer & Senior Vice-President
Karl R. Morris, Senior Vice-President, European Operations
Nigel Banks, Senior Vice-President, Corporate Services
Michael J. Dawson, Senior Vice-President, Sales, Marketing, & Logistics

Stella-Jones Inc.
#300, 3100 boul de la Côte-Vertu
Montréal, QC H4R 2J8

514-934-8666
Fax: 514-934-5327
ir@stella-jones.com
www.stella-jones.com
Other Communications: Human Resources, E-mail: hr@stella-jones.com

Company Type: Public
Ticker Symbol: SJ / TSX
Staff Size: 1757
Profile: Stella-Jones specializes in the production & marketing of industrial treated wood products. Products include the following: treated wood for bridges; pressure treated railway ties; marine & foundation pilings; construction timbers; highway guardrail posts; & wood poles for electrical utilities & telecommunications companies.
Brian McManus, President & Chief Executive Officer
Éric Vachon, Senior Vice-President & Chief Financial Officer
Marla Eichenbaum, Vice-President, General Counsel & Secretary

Supremex Inc.
Head Office
7213, rue Cordner
LaSalle, QC H8N 2J7
800-361-6659
info@supremex.com
www.supremex.com
Social Media: www.facebook.com/SupremeXInc
twitter.com/supremexinc
www.linkedin.com/company/supremex-inc.
Company Type: Public
Ticker Symbol: SXP / TSX
Staff Size: 650
Profile: Supremex specializes in manufacturing & marketing stock & custom envelopes & related products.
The company has an Enviro-logiX Program, which includes environmentally friendly bubble mailers, among other products.
Stewart Emerson, CEO & General Manager, Central Region
Benoit Crowe, Vice-President, Finance
Suzie Gaudreault, General Manager, Québec & Maritimes/Corporate IT Manager
Edward Gauer, General Manager, Western Region

Taiga Building Products Ltd.
#800, 4710 Kingsway
Burnaby, BC V5H 3X6
604-438-1471
Fax: 604-439-4242
800-663-1470
www.taigabuilding.com
Other Communications: Investor Relations, E-mail: i.relations@taigabuilding.com
Social Media:
www.linkedin.com/company/taiga-building-products
Company Type: Public
Ticker Symbol: TBL / TSX
Staff Size: 501
Profile: Taiga Building Products Ltd. distributes building products, such as lumber, engineered wood, mouldings, siding, flooring, & polyethylene sheeting. It is also involved in the production of treated wood, which reduces the use of timber resources. The company's customers are most often industrial manufacturers & building supply dealers.
Trent Balog, President & CEO
Russ Permann, Chief Operating Officer & Vice-President, Operations
Mark Schneidereit-Hsu, Chief Financial Officer & Vice-President, Finance & Administration
Grant Sali, Chief People Officer & Executive Vice-President, Supply Management

Tembec Inc.
Head Office
#1050, 800, boul Réne-Lévesque ouest
Montréal, QC H3B 1X9
514-871-0137
Fax: 514-397-0896
info@tembec.com
www.tembec.com
Company Type: Public
Ticker Symbol: TMB / TSX
Staff Size: 3,250
Profile: Tembec manufactures forest products such as pulp, paper, lumber, & specialty cellulose. Main operations take place in Canada & France. The company is engaged in sustainable forest management practices.
James Lopez, President & Chief Executive Officer
Chris Black, Executive Vice-President, Forest Products, Pulp & Paper
Michel J. Dumas, Chief Financial Officer & Executive Vice-President, Finance
Linda Coates, Vice-President, Human Resources & Corporate Affairs
Paul Dottori, Vice-President, Energy, Environment, & Procurement
Patrick LeBel, Vice-President, General Counsel, & Corporate Secretary

West Fraser Timber Co. Ltd.
#501, 858 Beatty St.
Vancouver, BC V6B 1C1
604-895-2700
Fax: 604-681-6061
shareholder@westfraser.com
www.westfraser.com
Other Communications: Environmental Inquiries, E-mail: trees@westfraser.com
Social Media:
www.linkedin.com/company/west-fraser-timber-co-ltd
Company Type: Public
Ticker Symbol: WFT / TSX
Staff Size: 7,560
Profile: West Fraser Timber Co. Ltd. is an integrated wood products company. From facilities in Canada & the United States, the company produces the following products: plywood, lumber, wood chips, LVL, MDF, pulp, & newsprint.
Henry H. Ketcham, Chair
Edward (Ted) Seraphim, President & Chief Executive Officer
Raymond Ferris, Chief Operating Officer & Executive Vice-President
Larry Hughes, Chief Financial Officer & Vice-President, Finance

Western Forest Products Inc. (WFP)
Royal Centre Bldg.
PO Box 11122, #800, 1055 West Georgia St.
Vancouver, BC V6E 3P3
604-648-4500
Fax: 604-681-9584
lumbersales@westernforest.com
www.westernforest.com
Company Type: Public
Ticker Symbol: WEF / TSX
Staff Size: 2,230
Profile: Western Forest Products is a large woodland operator & lumber producer in the coastal region of British Columbia. Activities include timber harvesting, sawmilling logs into lumber & wood chips, value-added remanufacturing, & reforestation. Customers are served in North America & around the world.
Don Demens, President & Chief Executive Officer
Stephen Williams, CFO, Senior Vice-President & Corporate Secretary
Shannon Janzen, Vice-President & Chief Forester

Holding & Other Investment

Aimia
Also Known As: Groupe Aeroplan Inc.
Tour Aimia
#1000, 525, av Viger ouest
Montréal, QC H2Z 0B2
514-897-6800
www.aimia.com
Social Media: www.facebook.com/AimiaInc
twitter.com/AimiaInc
www.linkedin.com/company/2353423
Company Type: Public
Ticker Symbol: AIM / TSX
Profile: The loyalty program, Aeroplan, is owned by Groupe Aeroplan Inc.. Members of the program earn Aeroplan Miles through the company's partners in the retail, travel, & financial sectors.
Robert Duchesne, Group Chief Executive
Tor Lonnum, Chief Financial Officer
Vince Timpano, President, Americas Coalitions

Brookfield Asset Management Inc.
Brookfield Place
#300, 181 Bay St.
Toronto, ON M5J 2T3
416-363-9491
Fax: 416-365-9642
www.brookfield.com
Company Type: Public
Ticker Symbol: BAM.A / TSX
Staff Size: 55,000
Profile: Brookfield Asset Management Inc. was formed in 1997. The global asset manager concentrates on property, infrastructure, & renewable power assets. The company offers clients an array of real estate advisory, property, & investment services. Brookfield Asset Management is listed on the TSX, NYSE, & Euronext Amsterdam.
Bruce Flatt, CEO
Brian D. Lawson, Senior Managing Partner & Chief Financial Officer
Suzanne Fleming, Sr. Vice-President, Branding & Communications
A.J. Silber, Corporate Secretary & Vice-President, Legal Affairs

Canadian Real Estate Investment Trust (CREIT)
#500, 175 Bloor St. East
Toronto, ON M4W 3R8
416-628-7771
Fax: 416-628-7777
info@creit.ca
www.creit.ca
Company Type: Public
Ticker Symbol: REF.UN / TSX
Profile: Canadian Real Estate Investment Trust is the owner of a portfolio of retail, office, & industrial properties. The trust delivers the benefits of real estates ownership to unitholders
Stephen E. Johnson, Chief Executive Officer
Rael L. Diamond, President & COO
Mario Barrafato, Exec. Vice-President & CFO

Capstone Infrastructure Corporation
#2930, 155 Wellington St. West
Toronto, ON M5V 3H1
416-649-1300
Fax: 416-649-1335
info@capstoneinfra.com
www.capstoneinfrastructure.com
Social Media: twitter.com/CapstoneCSE
www.linkedin.com/company/capstone-infrastructure-corporation
Company Type: Public
Ticker Symbol: CSE / TSX
Staff Size: 640
Profile: Capstone Infrastructure Corporation has a portfolio of infrastructure businesses in Canada & around the world. Investments include the following: hydro, wind, biomas, & solar power generating facilities; a 50% interest in a regulated water utility in the United Kingdom; & a 33.3% interest in a heating business in Sweden.
Michael Smerdon, Chief Financial Officer & Executive Vice-President
Jack Bittan, Executive Vice-President, Business Development
Jens Ehlers, Senior Vice-President, Finance
Aileen Gien, General Counsel & Corporate Secretary

Dundee Corporation
#2100, 1 Adelaide St. East
Toronto, ON M5C 2V9
416-350-3388
info@dundeecorporation.com
www.dundeecorporation.com
Company Type: Public
Ticker Symbol: DC.A / TSX
Staff Size: 108
Profile: The asset management company is engaged in real estate & resources. Subsidiaries include Dundee Realty Corporation, Dundee Resources Limited, & Dundee Real Estate Asset Management.
David Goodman, President & CEO
Lucie Presot, Chief Financial Officer & Executive Vice-President

Equity Financial Holdings Inc.
#400, 200 University Ave.
Toronto, ON M5H 4H1
416-361-0152
Fax: 416-342-0590
855-272-0050
inquiries@equityfinancialtrust.com
equityfinancialtrust.com
Social Media: twitter.com/EquityFinancial
www.linkedin.com/company/equity-financial-trust-company
Company Type: Public
Ticker Symbol: EQI / TSX
Profile: Equity Financial Holdings Inc. is a Canadian financial services company that serves corporate, institutional and retail clients.
Michael Jones, President & CEO
Josh Reusing, Chief Financial Officer
Paul Bowers, Chief Risk Officer

Exchange Income Corporation
1067 Sherwin Rd.
Winnipeg, MB R3H 0T8
204-982-1857
Fax: 204-982-1855
www.eiif.ca
Company Type: Public
Ticker Symbol: EIF / TSX
Staff Size: 3,161
Profile: Exchange Income Corporation was established to invest in profitable companies in Canada & the United States. Cash dividends are distributed each month to shareholders. Exchange Income Corporation owns subsidiaries in the business segments of specialty manufacturing & aviation.
Carmele Peter, President
cpeter@eig.ca
Michael Pyle, Chief Executive Officer
mpyle@eig.ca
Darwin Sparrow, Chief Operating Officer
dsparrow@eig.ca
Gary Beaurivage, Vice-President & Chief Operating Officer, Aviation
gbeaurivage@eig.ca
Michael Swistun, Director, Acquisitions
mswistun@eig.ca

Fairfax Financial Holdings Limited
#800, 95 Wellington St. West
Toronto, ON M5J 2N7
416-367-4941
Fax: 416-367-4946
www.fairfax.ca
Company Type: Public
Ticker Symbol: FFH / TSX
Staff Size: 23,576

Profile: Through its subsidiaries, the financial services holding company is involved in insurance claims management, property & casualty insurance & reinsurance, & investment management. Subsidiaries include Northbridge Financial, Crum & Forster, Falcon Insurance, First Capital, OdysseyRe, Group Re, Hamblin Watsa Investment Counsel, & MFXchange.
In 2012, 7948883 Canada Inc., a wholly owned subsidiary of Fairfax Financial Holdings Limited, acquired all the issued & outstanding shares of Prime Restaurants Inc.. Prime Restaurants' brands include Casey's, East Side Mario's, Fionn MacCool's, the Bier Markt, D'Arcy McGee's, & Paddy Flaherty's.
V. Prem Watsa, Chair/CEO
Paul Rivett, President
Ronald Schokking, Vice-President & Treasurer
David Bonham, Vice-President & CFO
Bradley Martin, Vice-President, Strategic Investments
Peter Clarke, Vice-President & Chief Risk Officer

Founders Advantage Capital
Also Known As: FA Capital
#232, 2031 - 33 Ave. SW
Calgary, AB T2T 1Z5
403-455-9660
Fax: 403-455-9659
advantagecapital.ca
Company Type: Public
Ticker Symbol: FCF / TSX.V
Profile: Founders Advantage Capital is an investment company dealing in equity, debt & other securities of public & private companies.
Stephen Reid, President & CEO
sreid@advantagecapital.ca
Darren Prins, Chief Financial Officer
dprins@advantagecapital.ca
Amar Leekha, Senior Vice-President, Capital Markets & Investments
aleekha@advantagecapital.ca
Allan Bezanson, Executive Vice-President, Capital Markets

Freehold Royalties Ltd.
#400, 144 - 4th Ave. SW
Calgary, AB T2P 3N4
403-221-0802
Fax: 403-221-0888
888-257-1873
www.freeholdroyalties.com
Company Type: Public
Ticker Symbol: FRU / TSX
Profile: Freehold Royalties acquires & manages a portfolio of non-Crown oil & gas royalties in Canada.
Thomas J. Mullane, President & Chief Executive Officer
Darren G. Gunderson, Chief Financial Officer & Vice-President, Finance
Michael J. Stone, Vice-President, Land

Gendis Inc.
1370 Sony Pl.
Winnipeg, MB R3T 1N5
204-474-5200
Fax: 204-474-5201
finance@gendis.ca
www.gendis.ca
Company Type: Public
Ticker Symbol: GDS / TSX
Profile: Gendis' principal assets include investments in Veresen Inc., Osum Oilsands Corp., & real estate for lease.
James E. Cohen, President & Chief Executive Officer
Ernest B. Reinfort, Chief Financial Officer
N. Paul Cloutier, Corporate Secretary

Gravitas Financial Inc.
Bay-Adelaide Centre
#650, 333 Bay St.
Toronto, ON M5H 2R2
647-252-1674
Fax: 416-646-1942
info@gravitasfinancial.com
www.gravitasfinancial.com
Company Type: Public
Ticker Symbol: GFI / CSE
Profile: The financial advisory firm is the parent to three subsidiaries: Gravitas Financial Services Holdings Inc., Gravitas Corp. Services Inc. & Gravitas Ventures Inc.
Vikas Ranjan, President
Rishi Tibriwal, CA, MBA, CFA, Chief Financial Officer

H&R Real Estate Investment Trust
#500, 3625 Dufferin St.
Toronto, ON M3K 1N4
416-635-7520
Fax: 416-398-0040
888-635-7717
info@hr-reit.com
www.hr-reit.com
Company Type: Public
Ticker Symbol: HR.UN / TSX
Profile: The organization is an open-ended real estate investment trust. Its portfolio include retail properties, office properties, single tenant industrial properties, & development projects.
Thomas J. Hofstedter, President & Chief Executive Officer
Larry Froom, Chief Financial Officer
Nathan Uhr, Chief Operating Officer

IBI Group Inc.
55 St. Clair Ave. West, 7th Fl.
Toronto, ON M4V 2Y7
416-596-1930
Fax: 416-596-0644
TO_General@ibigroup.com
www.ibigroup.com
Social Media: www.facebook.com/ibigroup
twitter.com/ibigroup
www.linkedin.com/companies/ibi-group_2
Company Type: Public
Ticker Symbol: IBG / TSX
Profile: IBI Group provides planning, design, & other consulting services related to the development of urban land, building facilities, transportation networks, & systems technology.
Scott Stewart, Chief Executive Officer
David Thom, President
Stephen Taylor, Chief Financial Officer
Steven Kresak, General Counsel

KP Tissue Inc.
#200, 1900 Minnesota Ct.
Mississauga, ON L5N 1P8
905-812-6900
Fax: 905-812-6910
www.kptissueinc.com
Company Type: Public
Ticker Symbol: KPT / TSX
Staff Size: 2,500
Profile: KP Tissue Inc. a holding company with a limited partnership interest in KPLP (Kruger Products L.P.), a leading tissue products supplier.
Mario Gosselin, Chief Executive Officer
Mark Holbrook, Chief Financial Officer

Labrador Iron Ore Royalty Corporation (LIORC)
Scotia Plaza
PO Box 4085 Stn. A, 40 King St. West, 26th Fl.
Toronto, ON M5W 2X6
416-863-7133
Fax: 416-863-7425
investor.relations@labradorironore.com
www.labradorironore.com
Company Type: Public
Ticker Symbol: LIF / TSX
Profile: In 2010, the Labrador Iron Ore Royalty Income Fund converted to the Labrador Iron Ore Royalty Corporatio. The Canadian corporation holds an equity interest in Iron Ore Company of Canada, directly & through its wholly-woned subsidiary, Hollinger-Hanna Limited.
Bruce C. Bone, President & Chief Executive Officer
Alan R. Thomas, Chief Financial Officer
James C. McCartney, Executive Vice-President & Secretary

Morguard North American Residential Real Estate Inves
#800, 55 City Centre Dr.
Mississauga, ON L5B 1M3
905-281-3800
800-928-6255
info@morguard.com
www.morguard.com
Social Media: www.linkedin.com/company/morguard
Company Type: Public
Ticker Symbol: MRG.UN / TSX
Profile: Morguard North American Residential REIT is a publicly traded open-ended real estate investment trust, created in April 2012. The company owns multi-unit residential rental properties across Canada and the United States.
K. Rai Sahi, Chairman & CEO
rsahi@morguard.com
Paul Miatello, Chief Financial Officer
pmiatello@morguard.com
Robert Wright, Vice-President
bwright@morguard.com
Beverly G. Flynn, General Counsel & Secretary
bflynn@morguard.com

Morguard Real Estate Investment Trust
#800, 55 City Centre Dr.
Mississauga, ON L5B 1M3
905-281-3800
800-928-6255
info@morguard.com
www.morguardreit.com
Social Media: www.linkedin.com/company/morguard
Company Type: Public
Ticker Symbol: MRT.UN / TSX
Staff Size: 12
Profile: The organization is an unincorporated, closed-end investment trust that was created in 1997. The Morguard Real Estate Investment Trust has a diversified portfolio of industrial, retail, & office properties across Canada.
Rai Sahi, Chief Executive Officer & Chair
rsahi@morguard.com
Paul Miatello, Chief Financial Officer
pmiatello@morguard.com
Beverley G. Flynn, General Counsel & Secretary
bflynn@morguard.com

Northfield Capital Corporation
#301, 141 Adelaide St. West
Toronto, ON M5H 3L5
416-628-5901
Fax: 416-628-5911
info@northfieldcapital.com
www.northfieldcapital.com
Company Type: Public
Ticker Symbol: NFD.A / TSX Venture
Profile: Formed in 1981, the investment company owns interests in diverse business activities. Major oil, gas, & mining holdings include GoldCorp Inc., Osisko Mining Corp., Canada Lithium Corp. & Trimac Transportation Ltd.
Robert D. Cudney, President & Founder
Brent J. Peters, Vice-President, Finance

Onex Corporation
PO Box 700, 161 Bay St.
Toronto, ON M5J 2S1
416-362-7711
Fax: 416-362-5765
investor@onex.com
www.onex.com
Company Type: Public
Ticker Symbol: OCX / TSX
Staff Size: 144,000
Profile: Through Onex Partners & ONCAP families of funds, Onex Corporation makes private equity investments. The company is also engaged in the management of alternative asset platforms, which focuses on real estate & distressed credit.
Gerald W. Schwartz, Chair, President & CEO
Christopher Govan, Chief Financial Officer
Emma Thompson, Managing Director, Investor Relations

Power Corporation of Canada
751 Victoria Sq.
Montréal, QC H2Y 2J3
514-286-7400
800-890-7440
www.powercorporation.com
Social Media:
www.linkedin.com/company/power-corporation-of-canada
Company Type: Public
Ticker Symbol: POW / TSX
Staff Size: 34,359
Profile: Power Corporation of Canada was formed in 1925. The main subsidiary of this diversified international management & holding company is Power Financial Corp.
Paul Desmarais Jr., O.C., Chair/Co-CEO
André Desmarais, O.C., President/Co-CEO & Deputy Chair
Michel Plessis-Bélair, FCA, Vice-Chair
John A. Rae, Exec. Vice-President
Gregory D. Tretiak, CFO & Executive Vice-President

Richards Packaging Income Fund
6095 Ordan Dr.
Mississauga, ON L5T 2M7
905-670-7760
Fax: 905-670-1961
www.richardspackaging.com
Company Type: Public
Ticker Symbol: RPI.UN / TSX
Staff Size: 485
Profile: Richards Packaging Income Fund is an indirect owner of securities of Richards Packaging Inc. Richards Packaging is a plastic & glass container manufacturer & distributor. The company also distributes metal & plastic closures, as well as injection molded containers & packaging systems.
David Prupas, President & COO
president@richardspackaging.com

Enzio DiGennaro, Chief Financial Officer
edigennaro@richardspackaging.com

Senvest Capital Inc.
#2400, 1000, rue Sherbrooke ouest
Montréal, QC H3A 3G4
514-281-8082
Fax: 514-281-0166
SenvestCapitalInquiries@senvest.com
www.senvest.com

Company Type: Public
Ticker Symbol: SEC / TSX
Profile: Senvest Capital Inc.'s subsidiaries are involved in the following sectors: asset management, merchant banking, real estate, & electronic security.
Victor Mashaal, President

Sonor Investments Limited
#2120, 130 Adelaide St. West
Toronto, ON M5H 3P5
416-369-1499
Fax: 416-369-0280

Company Type: Public
Ticker Symbol: SNI.PR.A / TSX Venture
Profile: Sonor Investments Limited makes portfolio investments in both public & private equity & fixed income securities. Sonor's wholly owned subsidiary is Toddle Opportunities Corporation.
Michael R. Gardiner, Chief Executive Officer

TerraVest Capital Inc.
4901 Bruce Rd.
Vegreville, AB T9C 1C3
780-632-2040
Fax: 780-632-7694
www.terravestcapital.com

Company Type: Public
Ticker Symbol: TVK / TSX
Staff Size: 422
Profile: The fund has investments in RJV Gas Field Services & Diamond Energy Services.
Paul A. Casey, Chief Financial Officer
pcasey@terravestcapital.com
Mitchell Gilbert, Chief Investment Officer
mitchell.gilbert@terravestcapital.com

Tuckamore Capital Management Inc.
Exchange Tower
#2950, 130 King St. West
Toronto, ON M5X 1B1
416-775-3790
irinfo@tuckamore.ca
www.tuckamore.ca

Company Type: Public
Ticker Symbol: TX / TSX
Profile: In 2011, shareholders of Newport Inc. approved a name change for the organization to Tuckamore Capital Management Inc.. Tuckamore Capital Management Inc. is a diversified fund that invests in Canadian private businesses.
Dean MacDonald, Executive Chair
Keith Halbert, Chief Financial Officer

Uranium Participation Corporation (UPC)
#1100, 40 University Ave.
Toronto, ON M5J 1T1
416-979-1991
info@uraniumparticipation.com
www.uraniumparticipation.com

Company Type: Public
Ticker Symbol: U / TSX
Profile: Uranium Participation Corporation was established in 2005. The investment holding company invests in uranium, either in the form of uranium oxide in concentrates or uranium hexafluoride. The manager of Uranium Participation Corporation is Denison Mines Inc.
David Cates, President & CEO
Mac McDonald, Chief Financial Officer
Scott Melbye, Vice-President, Commercial
Amanda Willett, Corporate Secretary

Westaim Corporation
#1700, 70 York St.
Toronto, ON M5J 1S9
416-969-3333
Fax: 416-969-3334
info@westaim.com
www.westaim.com

Company Type: Public
Ticker Symbol: WED / TSX
Profile: Westaim invests, directly and indirectly, through acquisitions, joint ventures and other arrangements.
J. Cameron MacDonald, President & CEO
Robert T. Kittel, Chief Operating Officer
Glenn MacNeil, Chief Financial Officer

WesternOne Inc.
Head Office
#910, 925 West Georgia St.
Vancouver, BC V6C 3L2
604-678-4042
Fax: 604-681-5969
877-278-4042
info@weq.ca
www.weq.ca

Company Type: Public
Ticker Symbol: WEQ / TSX
Staff Size: 487
Profile: WesternOne Inc. seeks to acquire private businesses that acquire and grow businesses in the sector of construction and infrastructure services.
Peter Blake, Chief Executive Officer
Geoff Shorten, President & COO, WesternOne Infrastructure Services
Carlos Yam, Chief Financial Officer
Andrew Greig, Manager, Investor Relations
agreig@weq.ca

Westshore Terminals Investment Corporation
1 Roberts Bank
Delta, BC V4M 4G5
604-646-4491
info@westshore.com
www.westshore.com

Company Type: Public
Ticker Symbol: WTE / TSX
Staff Size: 247
Profile: Westshore Terminals Investment Corporation's wholly-owned subsidiary is Westshore Terminals Holdings Ltd.. Westshore Investment & Westshore Holdings derive their cash inflows from their investment in Westshore Terminals Limited Partnership. Westshore Terminals Limited Partnership operates a coal storage & loading terminal in British Columbia.
William Stinson, CEO
Dallas Ross, Chief Financial Officer

Whistler Blackcomb Holdings Inc.
4545 Blackcomb Way
Whistler, BC V0N 1B4
604-967-8950
800-766-0449
www.whistlerblackcombholdings.com
Social Media: www.facebook.com/whistlerblackcomb
twitter.com/whistlerblckcmb

Company Type: Public
Ticker Symbol: WB / TSX
Staff Size: 500
Profile: Whistler Blackcomb Holdings Inc. owns a 75% interest in each of Whistler Mountain Resort Limited Partnership and Blackcomb Skiing Enterprises Limited Partnership.
Dave Brownlie, President & Chief Executive Officer
Jeremy Black, Senior Vice President & Chief Financial Officer
Stuart Rempel, Senior Vice President, Marketing & Sales

Insurance

Co-operators General Insurance Company
Service Quality Department
130 MacDonell St.
Guelph, ON N1H 6P8
Fax: 519-823-9944
800-265-2662
www.cooperators.ca
Other Communications: Quebec Clients, Toll-Free Phone: 1-866-731-2667
Social Media: www.facebook.com/TheCooperatorsInsurance
twitter.com/The_Cooperators
www.linkedin.com/company/the-co-operators

Company Type: Public
Ticker Symbol: CCS.PR.C / TSX
Staff Size: 2,505
Profile: Co-operators General Insurance Company provides home, automobile, farm, & commercial insurance services throughout Canada.
Kathy Bardswick, President/CEO
P. Bruce West, Executive Vice-President/CFO
Carol Poulsen, Executive Vice-President & Chief Information Officer
Rick McCombie, Executive Vice-President & Chief Client Officer

E-L Financial Corporation Limited
165 University Ave., 10th Fl.
Toronto, ON M5H 3B8
416-947-2578
Fax: 416-362-2592

Company Type: Public
Ticker Symbol: ELF / TSX
Staff Size: 13
Profile: The investment & insurance holding company was incorporated in 1968. E-L Financial Corporation consists of the following subsidiaries: E-L Financial Services Ltd., The Dominion of Canada General Insurance Company, & The Empire Life Insurance Company.
Duncan N.R. Jackman, Chairman, President & CEO
Mark M. Taylor, Chief Financial Officer & Executive Vice-President

Echelon Financial Holdings
#300, 2680 Matheson Blvd. East
Mississauga, ON L4W 0A5
905-214-7880
Fax: 905-214-7893
800-324-3566
marketing@echeloninsurance.ca
echeloninsurance.ca

Company Type: Public
Ticker Symbol: EFH / TSX
Staff Size: 169
Profile: Echelon Financial Holdings is a provider of specialized insurance operating in Canada & Europe.
Serge Lavoie, Chief Executive Officer
Alvin Sharma, Chief Financial Officer

Genworth MI Canada Inc.
Also Known As: The Homeownership Company
National Underwriting Centre
#300, 2060 Winston Park Dr.
Oakville, ON L6H 5R7
800-511-8888
mortgage.info@genworth.com
www.genworth.ca
Social Media: www.facebook.com/134979489900988

Company Type: Public
Ticker Symbol: MIC / TSX
Staff Size: 2,442
Profile: Genworth MI Canada Inc. provides mortgage default insurance in Canada through its subsidiary, Genworth Financial Mortgage Insurance Company Canada. Commonly known as Genworth Financial Canada, The Homeownership Company.
Stuart Levings, President & CEO
Winsor Macdonell, Senior Vice-President, General Counsel & Secretary
Philip Mayers, Senior Vice-President & Chief Financial Officer
Debbie McPherson, Senior Vice-President, Sales & Marketing
Craig Sweeney, Senior Vice-President & Chief Risk Officer

Great-West Lifeco Inc.
100 Osborne St. North
Winnipeg, MB R3C 1V3
204-946-1190
www.greatwestlifeco.com

Company Type: Public
Ticker Symbol: GWO / TSX
Staff Size: 22,470
Profile: The international financial services holding company has interests in life insurance, health insurance, reinsurance, asset management, retirement, & investment services. Great-West Lifeco's companies include The Great-West Life Assurance Company, Great-West Life & Anuity Insurance Company, The Canada Life Assurance Compnay, London Life Insurance Company, & Putnam Investments. Great-West Lifeco & its companies are members of the Power Financial Corporation group of companies.
Paul Mahon, President & CEO
Stefan Kristjanson, President & COO, Canada
Garry MacNicholas, Exec. Vice-President/CFO
S. Mark Corbett, Executive Vice-President & Global Chief Investment Officer

iA Financial Group
PO Box 1907 Stn. Terminus, 1080, Grande Allée ouest
Québec, QC G1K 7M3
418-684-5000
800-463-6236
www.ia.ca
Social Media:
www.facebook.com/pages/Industrial-Alliance/142299078460574
2
twitter.com/iacanada
www.linkedin.com/company/industrielle_alliance

Company Type: Public
Ticker Symbol: IAG / TSX
Staff Size: 5,148
Profile: iA Financial Group provides a great range of financial & insurance products & services, including life & health insurance, automobile & home insurance, RRSPs, savings & retirement plans, securities, mutual & segregated funds, & mortgage loans.
Yvon Charest, President/CEO
René Chabot, Executive Vice-President/CFO & Head, Information Technology & Legal Services

Intact Financial Corporation
700 University Ave.
Toronto, ON M5G 0A1
416-341-1464
Fax: 416-941-5320
877-341-1464
info@intact.net
www.intactfc.com
Other Communications: Toll-Free Fax: 866-933-7916
Social Media: www.linkedin.com/company/intact
Company Type: Public
Ticker Symbol: IFC / TSX
Profile: Intact Financial Corporation provides property & casualty insurance in Canada. Products & services are marketed & distributed through Intact Insurance, belairdirect, & Grey Power.
Charles Brindamour, Chief Executive Officer
Martin Beaulieu, Senior Vice-President & COO
Jean-François Blais, President, Intact Insurance
Louis Gagnon, President, Service & Distribution
Benoit Morissette, Chief Risk Officer
Louis Marcotte, Chief Financial Officer & Senior Vice-President, Finance
Jack Ott, Senior Vice-President, Innovation Partnerships
Anne Fortin, Senior Vice-President, Sales & Marketing
Françoise Guénette, Senior Vice-President, Legal Services

Kingsway Financial Services Inc.
#400, 45 St. Clair Ave. West
Toronto, ON M4V 1K9
416-848-1171
Fax: 416-850-5439
ir@kingsway-financial.com
www.kingsway-financial.com
Company Type: Public
Ticker Symbol: KFS / TSX, NYSE
Staff Size: 305
Profile: Kingsway is a holding company functioning as a merchant bank with a focus on long-term value-creation.
Larry Swets, President & CEO
William Hickey, CFO, COO & Executive Vice-President

Manulife Financial Corporation
Also Known As: Manufacturers Life Insurance Company
North Tower 7
200 Bloor St. East
Toronto, ON M4W 1E5
416-926-3000
www.manulife.com
Social Media: www.facebook.com/ManulifeFinancial
Company Type: Public
Ticker Symbol: MFC / TSX, NYSE
Staff Size: 33,000
Profile: Manulife Financial provides financial protection services & wealth management products with operations in Asia, Canada and the United States. In the United States, Manulife Financial operates as John Hancock.
Donald A. Guloien, President & Chief Executive Officer
Marianne Harrison, President & CEO, Manulife Canada
Paul L. Rooney, Senior Executive Vice-President & Chief Operating Officer
Stephen P. Sigurdson, Executive Vice-President/General Counsel
Stephani Kingsmill, Executive Vice-President, Human Resources

People Corp.
#1800, 360 Main St.
Winnipeg, MB R3C 3Z3
204-940-3933
Fax: 204-940-3903
www.peoplecorporation.com
Company Type: Public
Ticker Symbol: PEO / TSX.V
Staff Size: 363
Profile: People Corp. is a national provider of group benefits, group retirement and human resources services.
Laurie Goldberg, CEO
Bonnie Chwartacki, President
Dennis Stewner, Chief Financial Officer & Chief Operating Officer

Sun Life Financial Inc.
Sun Life Centre
150 King St. West
Toronto, ON M5H 1J9
416-979-9966
877-786-5433
service@sunlife.ca
www.sunlife.com
Other Communications: Investors: investor.relations@sunlife.com
Social Media: www.facebook.com/SLFCanada
twitter.com/brighterlifeCA
www.linkedin.com/company/sun-life-financial
Company Type: Public
Ticker Symbol: SLF / TSX
Staff Size: 18,330
Profile: Sun Life Financial serves both individuals & corporate customers. It offers customers a broad range of protection & wealth management products & services.
Kevin Dougherty, President, Sun Life Financial Canada
Rick Headrick, President, Sun Life Global Investments (Canada) Inc.
Isabelle Hudon, Senior Vice-President, Client Solutions
Chris Denys, Senior Vice-President & CFO
Rocco Taglioni, Sr. Vice-President, Distribution, Individual Insurance & Wealth
Sandy Delamere, Vice-President, Human Resources

Machinery

Exco Technologies Limited
Corporate Office
130 Spy Ct.
Markham, ON L3R 5H6
905-477-3065
www.excocorp.com
Company Type: Public
Ticker Symbol: XTC / TSX
Staff Size: 730
Profile: Exco Technologies Limited serves the automotive, die-cast, & extrusion industries by providing innovative technologies.
Brian Robbins, President & Chief Executive Officer
Paul Riganelli, Chief Operating Officer & Senior Vice-President

Logan International Inc.
Canadian Headquarters
#850, 635 - 8th Ave. SW
Calgary, AB T2P 3M3
403-930-6810
Fax: 403-930-6811
info@loganinternationalinc.com
www.loganinternationalinc.com
Social Media: www.facebook.com/LoganInternational
twitter.com/loganinternat
www.linkedin.com/company/logan-international-inc
Company Type: Public
Ticker Symbol: LII / TSX
Staff Size: 361
Profile: In 2010, Destiny Resource Services Corp. & Logan Holdings, Inc. merged. During the same year, Source Energy Tool Services Inc. & Complete Oil Tools Inc. were purchased. In 2011, Logan International Inc. purchased Scope Production Development & Kline Oilfield Services, Inc.
Logan International's Canadian business consists of Scope Production Development, Xtend Energy Services, & Logan Completion Systems. The company provides the following products: proprietary & patented products & services for production optimization in heavy oil wells; tools for horizontal drilling; & multi-zonal completion technology & conventional completion products.
David MacNeill, President/Chief Executive Officer
Lawrence D. Keister, CFO, Corporate Secretary & Vice-President, Finance

Ritchie Bros. Auctioneers
9500 Glenlyon Pkwy.
Burnaby, BC V5J 0C6
778-331-5500
Fax: 778-331-5501
800-663-1739
www.rbauction.com
Other Communications: USA, Toll-Free Phone: 800-663-8457
Social Media: www.facebook.com/ritchiebros
twitter.com/ritchiebros
www.linkedin.com/company/18317
Company Type: Public
Ticker Symbol: RBA / TSX
Staff Size: 1,522
Profile: Ritchie Bros. is an industrial auctioneer serving equipment buyers and sellers all over the world. They conduct live, unreserved public auctions with both on-site and online bidding, selling a wide range of used and unused equipment for Construction, Mining, Transportation, Agriculture, Oil & Gas, Lifting & material handling, Forestry & other industries.
Ravi Saligram, Chief Executive Officer
Randy Wall, President, Canada
Sharon Driscoll, Chief Financial Officer

Strongco Corporation
1640 Enterprise Rd.
Mississauga, ON L4W 4L4
905-670-5100
Fax: 905-670-7869
800-268-7004
www.strongco.com
Company Type: Public
Ticker Symbol: SQP / TSX
Profile: The large multiline mobile equipment dealer sells, rents, & services equipment. Equipment is used in the following sectors: mining, oil & gas, forestry, construction, municipal, & waste management. Operations take place in Canada & the United States.
Robert Beutel, Executive Chair
J. David Wood, Vice-President & Chief Financial Officer
Christopher D. Forbes, Vice-President & Chief Human Resources Officer

Tesco Corporation
Corporate Headquarters
#350, 11330 Clay Rd.
Houston, TX 77041 USA
713-359-7000
877-837-2677
contact@tescocorp.com
www.tescocorp.com
Social Media: www.linkedin.com/company/tesco-corporation
Company Type: Public
Ticker Symbol: TESO / NASDAQ
Staff Size: 1,594
Profile: Tesco Corporation specializes in the design, manufacture, & service of technology. The company's technology based solutions are used in the upstream energy industry.
Fernando Assing, President & CEO
Chris Boone, Chief Financial Officer & Senior Vice-President

Toromont Industries Ltd.
Executive Offices
PO Box 5511, 3131 Hwy. 7 West
Concord, ON L4K 1B7
416-667-5511
Fax: 416-667-5555
www.toromont.com
Company Type: Public
Ticker Symbol: TIH / TSX
Staff Size: 3,336
Profile: The company is engaged in the design, engineering, & sale of specialized equipment & other heavy equipment. Its business segments are the Equipment Group & CIMCO. The Equipment Group include rental operations. CIMCO is engaged in the engineering & installation of industrial & recreational refrigeration systems.
Toromont Industries has implemented environmental practices, such as technology to recycle energy, reduce greenhouse gas emissions, & cleanse oil of contaminants.
Scott Medhurst, President & CEO
Paul R. Jewer, CFO & Executive Vice-President
Michael P. Cuddy, Vice-President & Chief Information Officer
David C. Wetherald, Vice-President, Human Resources & Legal

Westport Innovations Inc.
#101, 1750 West 75th Ave.
Vancouver, BC V6P 6G2
604-718-2000
www.westport.com
Social Media: www.facebook.com/WestportDotCom
twitter.com/WestportDotCom
Company Type: Public
Ticker Symbol: WPT / TSX, NASDAQ
Staff Size: 725
Profile: Westport Innovations Inc. is a leading global supplier of proprietary solutions that allow engines to operate on clean-burning fuels such as compressed natural gas (CNG), liquefied natural gas (LNG), hydrogen, and renewable natural gas (RNG) and help reduce greenhouse gas gas emissions (GHG).
Nancy Gougarty, Chief Executive Officer
Ashoka Achuthan, Chief Financial Officer
Salman Manki, Chief Legal Officer & Corporate Secretary

Manufacturing, Miscellaneous

AirBoss of America Corp.
16441 Yonge St.
Newmarket, ON L3X 2G8
905-751-1188
Fax: 905-751-1101
www.airbossofamerica.com

Company Type: Public
Ticker Symbol: BOS / TSX
Staff Size: 1,037
Profile: The company is a developer, manufacturer, & seller of rubber compounds & specialty rubber moulded products. Products are used in the industrial, transportation, & defense industries.
Gren Schoch, Chief Executive Officer
Lisa Swartzman, President
Daniel Gagnon, Chief Financial Officer

ATS Automation Tooling Systems Inc.
Bldg. 2
730 Fountain St. North
Cambridge, ON N3H 4R7
519-653-6500
Fax: 519-650-6545
www.atsautomation.com
Other Communications: Investor Relations, E-mail: investor@atsautomation.com
Social Media: www.facebook.com/atsfactoryautomation
twitter.com/atsautomation
www.linkedin.com/company/atsautomation

Company Type: Public
Ticker Symbol: ATA / TSX
Profile: Established in 1978, ATS Automation Tooling Systems serves the automation systems needs of companies throughout the world. ATS Automation is also involved in the solar energy industry, through its solar business in Ontario. Manufacturing takes place in Canada, the United States, Europe, southeast Asia, & China.
Anthony Caputo, Chief Executive Officer

Avcorp Industries Inc.
10025 River Way
Delta, BC V4G 1M7
604-582-6677
www.avcorp.com

Company Type: Public
Ticker Symbol: AVP / TSX
Staff Size: 776
Profile: Avcorp Industries is a designer & builder for aircraft companies. The company specializes in custom solutions for airframe structures.
Peter George, Chief Executive Officer

Brampton Brick Limited
225 Wanless Dr.
Brampton, ON L7A 1E9
905-840-1011
Fax: 905-840-1535
www.bramptonbrick.com
Other Communications: Sales, Fax: 905-840-6461
Social Media: www.linkedin.com/company/brampton-brick-limited
Company Type: Public
Ticker Symbol: BBL.A / TSX
Staff Size: 269
Profile: Brampton Brick Limited manufactures clay brick, concrete masonry products, concrete interlocking paving stones, retaining walls, & enviro products. Products are used for residential construction & industrial & institutional building projects. Markets served include Ontario, Québec, & the northeastern & midwestern United States.
Universal Resource Recovery operates a waste composting facility in Welland, Ontario.
Jeffrey G. Kerbel, President & Chief Executive Officer
Trevor M. Sandler, Chief Financial Officer & Vice-President, Finance
David R. Carter, Chief Operating Officer
Brad Duke, Senior Vice-President, Manufacturing
George Housh, Vice-President, Manufacturing, Concrete Products
Marilia Macias, Controller

Carmanah Technologies Corp.
250 Bay St.
Victoria, BC V9A 3K5
250-380-0052
877-722-8877
carmanah.com
Social Media: twitter.com/CarmanahTech
www.linkedin.com/company/carmanah-technologies
Company Type: Public
Ticker Symbol: CMH / TSX
Staff Size: 150
Profile: Carmanah Technologies is a manufacturer of solar LED lights & solar power systems.
John Simmons, Chief Executive Officer
Evan Brown, Chief Financial Officer & Corporate Secretary

CCL Industries Inc.
#500, 105 Gordon Baker Rd.
Toronto, ON M2H 3P8
416-756-8500
ccl@cclind.com
www.cclind.com
Company Type: Public
Ticker Symbol: CCL.B / TSX
Staff Size: 13,800
Profile: CCL Industries Inc. is engaged in the development & provision of specialty packaging for producers of consumer brands. Products include labelling, plastic tubes, & aluminum containers. CCL serves customers in Canada, the United States, & Mexico.
Geoffrey T. Martin, President & Chief Executive Officer
Sean Washcuk, Chief Financial Officer & Senior Vice-President
Mark McClendon, Vice-President & General Counsel
Lalitha Vaidyanathan, Senior Vice-President, Finance, Information Technology, & Human Resources

China Keli Electric Company Ltd.
#210, 10451 Shellbridge Way
Richmond, BC V6X 2W8
604-270-2345
Fax: 604-270-9691
www.zkl.cc
Company Type: Public
Ticker Symbol: ZKL / TSX
Profile: The company owns & operates Zhuhai Keli Electric Co., Ltd. which manufactures & designs high-voltage switches, breakers, auto-control equipments, high voltage complete electric sets and high-power resistors.
Lou Meng Cheong, CEO
Philip Lo Fung, CFO

CRH Medical Corp.
World Trade Centre
#578, 999 Canada Pl.
Vancouver, BC V6C 3E1
800-660-2153
crhsystem.com
Company Type: Public
Ticker Symbol: CRH / TSX
Profile: CRH Medical focuses on promoting the CRH O'Regan system as a treatment for hemorrhoids.
Edward Wright, Chief Executive Officer
Richard Bear, Chief Financial Officer
Mitchel Guttenplan, Medical Director

D-Box Technologies Inc.
2172, rue de la Province
Longueuil, QC J4G 1R7
450-442-3003
888-442-3269
www.d-box.com
Company Type: Public
Ticker Symbol: DBO.A / TSX
Profile: A company that manufactures motion systems technology.
Claude McMaster, President & CEO
Luc Audet, Chief Financial Officer

Dorel Industries Inc.
#300, 1255, av Greene
Montréal, QC H3Z 2A4
514-934-3034
www.dorel.com
Company Type: Public
Ticker Symbol: DII.A, DII.B / TSX
Staff Size: 10,450
Profile: Established in 1962, Dorel Industries Inc. designs, manufactures, & markets juvenile products, bicycles, & home furnishings. The company has facilities in seventeen countries, & sells its products throughout the world.
Martin Schwartz, President/CEO
Norman Braunstein, Group President/CEO, Home Furnishings
Jean-Claude Jacomin, Group President/CEO, Juvenile
Peter Woods, Group President/CEO, Recreational/Leisure
Jeffrey Schwartz, Executive Vice-President, Chief Financial Officer & Secretary
Alan Schwartz, Executive Vice-President, Operations

Empire Industries Ltd.
717 Jarvis Ave.
Winnipeg, MB R2W 3B4
204-589-9300
Fax: 204-582-8057
www.empind.com
Social Media: twitter.com/empireind
Company Type: Public
Ticker Symbol: EIL / TSX.V
Staff Size: 400
Profile: Empire Industries Ltd. is a company involved in the design, engineering, and manufacture of complex engineered products. Empire produces marquee theme park rides, complex mechancial and structural installations, hydrovac excavation trucks, and other complex industrial equipment.
Guy Nelson, President & Chief Executive Officer
Allan Francis, Vice-President, Corporate Affairs & Administration
Michael Martin, Chief Financial Officer

Hammond Manufacturing Company Limited
394 Edinburgh Rd. North
Guelph, ON N1H 1E5
519-822-2960
Fax: 519-822-0715
www.hammondmfg.com
Other Communications: Datacom Sales: 877-535-3282; Electronic Sales: 519-886-7170
Social Media: www.facebook.com/hammondmfg
www.twitter.com/hammondmfg
www.linkedin.com/companies/448448
Company Type: Public
Ticker Symbol: HMM.A / TSX
Staff Size: 659
Profile: Hammond Manufacturing Company Limited was established in 1917. Products are manufactured for the electronic & electrical products industry. Examples of products manufactured by Hammond Manufacturing include small cases, racks, outlet strips, metallic & non-metallic enclosures, electronic transformers, & surge suppressors. Facilities are located in Canada, the United States & Europe.
Robert F. Hammond, Chair & Chief Executive Officer
Alexander Stirling, Chief Financial Officer
Ray Shatzel, Vice-President, Electronic Sales

Hanwei Energy Services Corp.
#902, 595 Howe St.
Vancouver, BC V6C 2T5
604-685-2239
Fax: 604-677-5579
info@hanweienergy.com
www.hanweienergy.com
Company Type: Public
Ticker Symbol: HE / TSX
Staff Size: 210
Profile: Hanwei Energy Services develops, manufactures, & sells high pressure fiberglass reinforced plastic products. Products are used mainly in the global energy sector. The company owns interest in Daqing Harvest Longwall High Pressure Pipe Co. Ltd. in China.
Fulai Lang, President/CEO
Yucai (Rick) Huang, Chief Financial Officer
Graham R. Kwan, Corporate Secretary & Exec. Vice-President, Strategic Development & Corporate Affairs

Héroux-Devtek Inc.
Tour est
#658, 1111, rue Saint-Charles ouest
Longueuil, QC J4K 5G4
450-679-3330
www.herouxdevtek.com
Company Type: Public
Ticker Symbol: HRX / TSX
Staff Size: 1,397
Profile: Héroux-Devtek Inc. develops, designs, manufactures, repairs, & overhauls systems & components. The company has three divisions: The Landing Gear Division; The Aerostructure Division; & The Industrial Division. Products are used in the aerospace market in both the commercial & military sectors, & in the industrial market for power generation & other machinery applications.
Héroux-Devtek requires management & employees to commit to a structured Environmental Management System.
Gilles Labbé, President & Chief Executive Officer
Stéphane Arsenault, Chief Financial Officer
Michel Robillard, Vice-President, Corporate Controller
Martin Brassard, COO & Vice-President, Landing Gear
Réal Bélanger, Executive Vice-President, Business Development & Special Projects

Imaflex Inc.
5710, rue Notre Dame ouest
Montréal, QC H4C 1V2
514-935-5710
Fax: 514-935-0264
www.imaflex.com
Company Type: Public
Ticker Symbol: IFX / TSX.V
Profile: Imaflex Inc. manufactures and sells polyethylene films.
Joseph Abbandonato, President & Chief Executive Officer

INSCAPE Corporation
Corporate Headquarters
67 Toll Rd.
Holland Landing, ON L9N 1H2
905-836-7676
Fax: 905-836-6000
www.inscapesolutions.com
Social Media: www.facebook.com/InscapeCorporation
twitter.com/InscapeCorp
www.linkedin.com/companies/inscape
Company Type: Public
Ticker Symbol: INQ / TSX
Staff Size: 385
Profile: INSCAPE Corporation designs, manufactures, & markets office systems & storage & wall solutions for commercial workplaces. Office & production facilities are located in Canada & the United States. INSCAPE Corporation is an ISO 9001 registered company.
Jim Stelter, Chief Executive Officer
John Gols, Executive Vice-President, Sales & Distribution

Lumenpulse Inc.
#1505, 1751, rue Richardson
Montréal, QC H3K 1G6
514-937-3003
Fax: 514-937-6289
877-937-3003
info@lumenpulse.com
www.lumenpulse.com
Other Communications: Media Inquiries, E-mail: press@lumenpulse.com
Social Media: twitter.com/Lumenpulse
www.linkedin.com/company/998167
Company Type: Public
Ticker Symbol: LMP / TSX
Staff Size: 446
Profile: Lumenpulse manufactures LED lighting fixtures.
François-Xavier Souvay, President & CEO
Peter Timotheatos, Executive Vice-President & CFO
Nicolas Vanasse, Executive Vice-President, Chief Legal Officer & Secretary

Magna International Inc.
337 Magna Dr.
Aurora, ON L4G 7K1
905-726-2462
www.magna.com
Social Media: www.facebook.com/MagnaInternational
twitter.com/MagnaInt
www.linkedin.com/company/magna-international
Company Type: Public
Ticker Symbol: MG / TSX; MGA / NYSE
Staff Size: 147,000
Profile: The diversified automotive supplier designs, develops, & manufactures automotive systems, assemblies, modules, & components. Magna also engineers & assembles complete vehicles to sell to original equipment manufacturers of cars & trucks. The company's geographic segments are North America, Europe, Asia, South America, & Africa.
Donald J. Walker, CEO
Vincent J. Galifi, Exec. Vice-President/CFO
Tom J. Skudutis, Chief Operating Officer, Exteriors, Interiors, Seating, Mirrors & Closures
Marc Neeb, Exec. Vice-President & Chief Human Resources Officer
Swamy Kotagiri, Exec. Vice-President/Chief Technology Officer & President, Magna Electronics
Jeffrey O. Palmer, Exec. Vice-President & Chief Legal Officer

McCoy Global Inc.
14755 - 121A Ave. NW
Edmonton, AB T5L 2T2
780-453-3277
Fax: 780-455-2432
www.mccoyglobal.com
Company Type: Public
Ticker Symbol: MCB / TSX
Staff Size: 220
Profile: McCoy Global serves the energy industry. The company's two business segments are Energy Products & Services & Mobile Solutions. Operations are based in western Canada & the United States Gulf Coast.
Jim Rakievich, President & CEO
Jacob Coonan, Chief Financial Officer
Kenneth Watt, Senior Vice-President, McCoy Global

NAPEC Inc.
1975, rue Jean-Bérimens Michaud
Drummondville, QC J2C 0H2
819-479-7771
Fax: 819-479-8887
info@napec.ca
www.napec.ca
Company Type: Public
Ticker Symbol: NPC / TSX
Staff Size: 1,169
Profile: Through its subsidiaries, NAPEC designs, manufactures, & sells continuously variable power transmission systems. Thirau Ltd., one of the company's subsidiaries, is a general contracting firm that specializes in the maintenance of transmission & distribution lines, electrical power houses, & substations.
Pierre Gauthier, President & CEO
Mario Trahan, Chief Financial Officer, C.M.A.
Emilie Duguay, General Counsel & Corporate Secretary
Pierre Joubert, Vice-President, Human Resources

Neovasc Inc.
#5138, 13562 Maycrest Way
Richmond, BC V6V 2J7
604-270-4344
Fax: 604-270-4384
info@neovasc.com
www.neovasc.com
Company Type: Public
Ticker Symbol: NVC / TSX
Profile: A medical device company that develops technology to treat mitral valve disease.
Alexei Marko, Chief Executive Officer
Christopher Clark, Chief Financial Officer
Brian McPherson, Chief Operating Officer

Omni Lite Industries Canada Inc.
17210 Edwards Rd.
Cerritos, CA 90703 USA
562-404-8510
Fax: 562-926-6913
800-577-6664
www.omni-lite.com
Social Media: www.facebook.com/Omni-Lite-Industries-116025328433222
twitter.com/OmniLiteInd
Company Type: Public
Ticker Symbol: OML / TSX.V
Profile: A research & development company that manufactures parts used in cars and aircrafts.
David Grant, Chief Executive Officer
Tim Leybold, Chief Financial Officer

Pearl River Holdings
#502, 383 Richmond St.
London, ON N6A 3C4
519-645-0267
Company Type: Public
Ticker Symbol: PRH / TSX.V
Profile: A plastic products manufacturer with distribution in China, Australia & the United States.

Photon Control
#200, 8363 Lougheed Hwy.
Burnaby, BC V5A 1X3
604-422-8861
Fax: 604-622-8418
855-574-6866
info@photon-control.com
www.photon-control.com
Social Media: www.facebook.com/pages/Photon-Control-Inc/216559795021765
twitter.com/PhotonControl
www.linkedin.com/company/photon-control-inc.
Company Type: Public
Ticker Symbol: PHO / TSX
Profile: Photon Control, founded in 1988, is a measurement tool manufacturing company.
Michael Goldstein, Acting CEO
Gerald Adams, Chief Financial Officer

Prism Medical Ltd.
#2, 485 Millway Ave.
Concord, ON L4K 3V4
416-260-2145
Fax: 416-260-9195
877-304-5438
info@prismmedicalltd.com
www.prismmedicalltd.com
Other Communications: USA Office, Phone: 314-692-9135
Company Type: Public
Ticker Symbol: PM / TSX Venture
Profile: Prism Medical Ltd. manufactures & supplies medical equipment & related services for mobility challenged persons. Customers are in Canada, the United States, & the United Kingdom.
Ross Scavuzzo, Chief Executive Officer
Bill Edwards, Chief Financial Officer

Reko International Group Inc.
469 Silver Creek Industrial Dr.
Lakeshore, ON N8N 4W2
519-727-3287
Fax: 519-727-6681
www.rekointl.com
Social Media: www.facebook.com/RekoInternationalGroup
Company Type: Public
Ticker Symbol: REK / TSX Venture
Profile: In business since 1976, Reko International Group Inc. is a designer & manufacturer of customized engineering solutions. The company serves the automotive, rail, military, mining, & oil & gas sectors. Business units include Reko Manufacturing Group & Concorde Machine Tool.
Diane Reko, Chief Executive Officer

Savaria Corporation
Corporate Office
4350 Hwy. 13
Laval, QC H7R 6E9
450-681-5655
Fax: 450-628-4500
800-931-5655
www.savaria.com
Other Communications: Elevators & Lifts: 800-661-5112; Vehicles: 800-668-8705
Social Media: www.facebook.com/savariabettermobility
twitter.com/Mobilityforlife
www.linkedin.com/company/savaria-inc
Company Type: Public
Ticker Symbol: SIS / TSX
Staff Size: 376
Profile: Savaria Corporation is a designer, manufacturer, & distributor of elevators, starlifts, & vertical & inclined platform lifts for residential & commercial use. The company also specializes in the conversion & adaptation of wheelchair accessible automotive vehicles. Scooters & motorized wheelchairs are also offered by Savaria.
The company's head office is located in Laval Québec, with plants in Montréal Québec, Brampton & London Ontario, Calgary Alberta, & Huizhou, China.
Marcel Bourassa, President & CEO
Jean-Marie Bourassa, Chief Financial Officer
Hélène Bernier, CA, Vice-President, Finance
Bill Richardson, Vice-Presidemt, Research & Development
Alison Harper, Vice-President, Business Development
Robert Berthiaume, Vice-Presidemt, Engineering

Sigma Industries
55 Route 271 South
Saint-Éphrem-de-Beauce, QC G0M 1R0
418-484-5285
Fax: 418-484-5294
www.sigmaindustries.ca
Company Type: Public
Ticker Symbol: SSG / TSX
Profile: The company manufactures parts for trucks, buses, light rail, construction, agriculture, military & recreational vehicles.
Denis Bertrand, President & CEO
Pierre Massicotte, Chief Financial Officer
Bruno Doyon, Vice-President, Sales
Jean-François Doré, Vice-President, Operations, Logistics & Supply chain

Winpak Ltd.
Corporate Office
100 Saulteaux Cres.
Winnipeg, MB R3J 3T3
204-889-1015
Fax: 204-888-7806
info@winpak.com
www.winpak.com
Company Type: Public
Ticker Symbol: WPK / TSX
Staff Size: 2,283
Profile: Manufacturing & distributing packaging materials & related packaging machines are the chief activities of Winpak Ltd. Products are used to protect perishable foods & beverages, as well as in health care applications. The company's facilities are located in Canada & the United States. Its services are offered in North America, Latin America, the Pacific Rim countries, & Europe.
B.J. Berry, President & Chief Executive Officer
K.P. Kuchma, Chief Financial Officer & Vice-President
O.Y. Muggli, Vice-President, Technology

Mining

Abacus Mining & Exploration Corp.
800 West Pender St., 6th Fl.
Vancouver, BC V6C 2V6
604-682-0301
Fax: 604-682-0307
866-834-0301
www.amemining.com
Company Type: Public
Ticker Symbol: AME / TSX Venture
Profile: Abacus Mining is a mineral exploration and mine development company with an interest in the Ajax Mining Camp in Kamloops, BC.
Michael McInnis, President & CEO
Jeannine Webb, Chief Financial Officer

Aberdeen International Inc.
PO Box 75, #815, 65 Queen St. West
Toronto, ON M5H 2M5
416-861-5812
www.aberdeeninternational.ca
Social Media: www.facebook.com/AberdeenAAB
twitter.com/AberdeenAAB
Company Type: Public
Ticker Symbol: AAB / TSX
Profile: Aberdeen International is a resource investment corporation & merchant bank. Aberdeen focuses on private, small-cap resource companies.
David Stein, President & Chief Executive Officer
dstein@aberdeeninternational.ca
Ryan Ptolemy, CGA, CFA, Chief Financial Officer

Abitibi Royalties
2864, ch Sullivan
Val-d'Or, QC J9P 0B9
819-824-2808
Fax: 819-824-3379
info@abitibiroyalties.com
www.abitibiroyalties.com
Company Type: Public
Ticker Symbol: RZZ / TSX.V
Profile: The company owns mines in Malartic, QC & in the Ring of Fire, in Ontario.
Ian Ball, President & CEO
Daniel Poisson, Chief Financial Officer

Adriana Resources Inc.
Corporate Office
#420, 141 Adelaide St. West
Toronto, ON M5H 3L5
416-363-2200
Fax: 416-363-2202
info@adrianaresources.com
www.adrianaresources.com
Company Type: Public
Ticker Symbol: ADI / TSX Venture
Profile: Adriana Resources Inc. is focused upon its Lac Otelnuk iron ore deposit, which is situated in the Labrador Trough, Nunavik, Québec.
Michael Harrison, Chief Executive Officer & President
Carlos Pinglo, Chief Financial Officer

African Gold Group
Yonge & Richmond Center
151 Yonge Street, 11th Fl.
Toronto, ON M5C 2W7
647-775-8538
Fax: 647-775-8301
www.africangoldgroup.com
Company Type: Public
Ticker Symbol: AGG / TSX
Profile: African Gold Group holds interests in mines based in Ghana & Mali.
Declan Franzmann, President & CEO

Africo Resources Ltd.
#520, 800 West Pender St.
Vancouver, BC V6C 2V6
604-646-3225
Fax: 604-646-3226
Company Type: Public
Ticker Symbol: ARL / TSX
Profile: Africo Resources Ltd. is engaged in the development of it Kalukundi cobalt-copper deposit in the Democratic Republic of the Congo. The Kalukundi Project developed an Environmental Management System, as part of the Health, Safety, Environment, & Community Management System, compliant with ISO 14001 standards. In May 2016 Africo was acquired by Camrose Resources Ltd.
Chris Theodoropoulos, Chair
Larry Okada, Chief Financial Officer

Agnico Eagle Mines Limited
Executive & Registered Office
#400, 145 King St. East
Toronto, ON M5C 2Y7
416-947-1212
Fax: 416-367-4681
888-822-6714
www.agnicoeagle.com
Social Media: www.facebook.com/AgnicoEagle
twitter.com/agnicoeagle
Company Type: Public
Ticker Symbol: AEM / TSX, NYSE
Staff Size: 7,821
Profile: Agnico Eagle Mines Limited is an international gold production company, which carries out exploration & development activities. Operations are conducted in Canada, the United States, Mexico, & Finland.
Sean Boyd, CA, Vice-Chair/CEO
Anmar Al-Joundi, President
David Smith, C.A., ICD.D, CFO & Sr. Vice-President, Finance
Yvon Sylvestre, Sr. Vice-President, Canadian & European Operations
Jean Robitaille, Sr. Vice-President, Business Strategy & Technical Services

Alacer Gold Corp.
#300, 9635 Maroon Circle
Englewood, CO 80112 USA
303-292-1299
Fax: 303-297-0538
info@alacergold.com
www.alacergold.com
Other Communications: Turkey Office, Phone: +90-312-472-8051
Company Type: Public
Ticker Symbol: ASR / TSX; AQG / ASX
Staff Size: 420
Profile: The intermediate gold company is active in Turkey, where it has interests in gold mines & possession of a portfolio of gold & copper exploration properties. In Turkey, Alacer Gold Corp.'s operating gold mine is known as Çöpler.
Rodney P. Antal, President & CEO
Robert D. Benbow, Senior Vice-President, Strategic Projects
Mark E. Murchison, Chief Financial Officer
Roy Kim, Vice-President, Corporate Development & Investor Relations
John LeRoux, Senior Vice-President & Country Manager, Turkish Business Unit

Alamos Gold Inc.
Brookfield Pl.
#3910, 181 Bay St.
Toronto, ON M5J 2T3
416-368-9932
Fax: 416-368-2934
866-788-8801
info@alamosgold.com
www.alamosgold.com
Company Type: Public
Ticker Symbol: AGI / TSX; AGI / NYSE
Profile: The Canadian-based gold producer owns & operates a mine in Mexico. The mining company also has exploration & development activities in Mexico & Turkey. In April 2015, Alamos merged AuRico Gold, a mining company whose main asset is located in Sonora, Mexico.
John A. McCluskey, President & Chief Executive Officer
Jamie Porter, Chief Financial Officer
Peter MacPhail, Chief Operating Officer & Vice-President
Aoife McGrath, Vice-President, Exploration

Alderon Iron Ore Corp.
#1240, 1140 West Pender St.
Vancouver, BC V6E 4G1
604-681-8030
Fax: 604-681-8039
info@alderonironore.com
www.alderonironore.com
Social Media: www.facebook.com/152692908106247
twitter.com/alderonironore
Company Type: Public
Ticker Symbol: ADV / TSX; AXX / NYSE
Profile: Alderon is a development company with an iron ore project located next to mining towns of Wabush and Labrador City in Western Labrador, Canada.
Mark J. Morabito, Chair & Chief Executive Officer
Kate-Lynn Genzel, Chief Financial Officer

Aldridge Minerals Inc.
#300, 10 King St. East
Toronto, ON M5C 1C3
416-477-6980
www.aldridge.com.tr
Company Type: Public
Ticker Symbol: AGM / TSX.V
Profile: The mining company is focused in Turkey & works to develop polymetallic VMS deposits.
Han Ilhan, President & CEO
Jim O'Neill, Chief Financial Officer
Serdar Akca, Vice-President, Country Manager

Alexandria Minerals
#201, 1 Toronto St.
Toronto, ON M5C 2V6
416-363-9372
info@azx.ca
www.azx.ca
Company Type: Public
Ticker Symbol: AZX / TSX.V
Profile: A gold mining company with projects in Ontario, Quebec & Manitoba.
Eric Owern, President & CEO
Mario Miranda, Chief Financial Officer

Alexco Resource Corp.
Two Bentall Centre
PO Box 216, 555 Burrard St.
Vancouver, BC V7X 1M9
604-633-4888
Fax: 604-633-4887
info@alexcoresource.com
www.alexcoresource.com
Other Communications: Whitehorse, YT Office, Phone: 867-633-4881
Company Type: Public
Ticker Symbol: AXR / TSX; AXU / NYSE
Profile: Alexco Resource Corp. holds several mineral properties, including the Bellekeno silver mine in the Keno Hill Silver District of the Yukon Territory. Through the company's wholly owned envrionmental services division, the Alexco Environmental Group, environmental services for mines are also offered. Services provided include remediation, reclamation, & mine closure.
Clynton R. Nauman, President & Chief Executive Officer
Brad A. Thrall, Chief Operating Officer, Executive Vice-President & President, Alexco Envrionmental Group
Alan McOnie, Vice-President, Exploration
Michael Clark, CA, Chief Financial Officer & Company Ethics Officer

Alloycorp Mining Inc.
#602, 67 Yonge St.
Toronto, ON M5E 1J8
416-847-0376
Fax: 604-620-9858
www.alloycorp.com
Company Type: Public
Ticker Symbol: AVT / TSX Venture
Profile: Alloycorp is the parent company of Avanti Mining Inc., an exploration and development company with its primary project in northern British Columbia, Canada. Its goal is to become the unique supplier of steel alloy metals.
Graham du Preez, Chief Financial Officer

Almaden Minerals Ltd.
#310, 1385 West 8th Ave.
Vancouver, BC V6H 3V9
604-689-7644
Fax: 604-689-7645
info@almadenminerals.com
www.almadenminerals.com
Company Type: Public
Ticker Symbol: AMM / TSX; AAU / NYSE
Profile: Almaden Minerals is an exploration company specializing in the generation of new mineral prospects.
Morgan Poliquin, President & CEO
Korm Trieu, Chief Financial Officer

Almonty Industries
#5700, 100 King St. West
Toronto, ON M5X 1C7
647-438-9766
Fax: 416-628-2516
info@almonty.com
www.almonty.com
Company Type: Public
Ticker Symbol: AII / TSX.V
Staff Size: 132
Profile: Almonty is focused on acquiring distressed and underperforming operations and assets in Tungsten markets.
Lewis Black, President & Chief Executive Officer
Dennis Logan, Chief Financial Officer

Alphamin Resources
No 372/10, Avenue du Lac, Quatier Himbi
Commune de Goma, RCCM:14-B-0095 Congo
230-269-4166
alphaminresources.com

Company Type: Public
Ticker Symbol: AFM / TSX-V
Boris Kamstra, CEO
Eoin O'Driscoll, CFO

Altius Minerals Corporation
Kenmount Business Center
#202, 66 Kenmount Rd.
St. John's, NL A1B 3V7

709-576-3440
Fax: 709-576-3441
877-576-2209
info@altiusminerals.com
www.altiusminerals.com
Social Media: twitter.com/AltiusMinerals

Company Type: Public
Ticker Symbol: ALS / TSX
Profile: Altius Minerals Corporation is a natural resource project generation & royalty business. The company has royalty interest or equity stakes in several natural resource projects.
Brian F. Dalton, President & Chief Executive Officer
Ben Lewis, B.Comm., C.A., Chief Financial Officer
Lawrence Winter, Ph.D., P.Geo., Vice-President, Exploration
Chad S. Wells, B.Sc. (Honours), Corporate Secretary & Vice-President, Corporate Development
Rod Churchill, M.Sc., P.Geo., Manager, Lands & Operations

Alvopetro Energy Ltd.
#1175, 332 - 6th Ave. SW
Calgary, AB T2P 0B2

587-794-4224
Fax: 587-747-7497
info@alvopetro.com
www.alvopetro.com

Company Type: Public
Ticker Symbol: ALV / TSX
Corey Ruttan, President & CEO
Alison Howard, Chief Financial Officer

Amarillo Gold Corp.
#1400, 1111 West Georgia St.
Vancouver, BC V6E 4M3

604-689-1799
Fax: 604-689-8199
info@amarillogold.com
www.amarillogold.com
Social Media: facebook.com/pages/Amarillo-Gold-Corp/170734576273879
twitter.com/amarillogold

Company Type: Public
Ticker Symbol: AGC / TSX.V
Profile: The company is a gold exploration organization, whose main project is in central Brazil.
Buddy Doyle, President & CEO
Scott Eldrige, Chief Financial Officer

Americas Silver Corporation
#2870, 145 King St. West
Toronto, ON M5H 1J8

416-848-9503
Fax: 866-401-3069
info@americassilvercorp.com
www.scorpiomining.com

Company Type: Public
Ticker Symbol: SPM / TSX
Staff Size: 503
Profile: Americas Silver Corporation is a silver producer. Exploring & mining activities are conducted in Mexico.
Darren Blasutti, President & CEO
Warren Varga, Chief Financial Officer
James M. Stonehouse, MA (Geology), Vice-President, Exploration
Peter McRae, Senior Vice-President, Corporate Affairs & General Counse

Amerigo Resources Ltd.
Commerce Pl.
#1260, 355 Burrard St.
Vancouver, BC V6C 2G8

604-681-2802
Fax: 604-682-2802
info@amerigoresources.com
www.amerigoresources.com

Company Type: Public
Ticker Symbol: ARG / TSX
Staff Size: 315
Profile: Amerigo Resources Ltd.'s wholly owned subsidiary is Minera Valle Central. The company specializes in the production of copper & molybdenum concentrates from tailings from an underground copper mine, known as Codelco's El Teniente mine.
Rob Henderson, President & Chief Executive Officer
Aurora G. Davidson, Executive Vice-President & Chief Financial Officer
Christian Cáceres, General Manager, Minera Valle Central Operations
Kimberly Thomas, Corporate Secretary

Anaconda Mining Inc.
#410, 150 York St.
Toronto, ON M5H 3S5

416-304-6622
Fax: 416-363-4567
info@anacondamining.com
www.anacondamining.com
Social Media: www.facebook.com/AnacondaMining
twitter.com/Anaconda_Mining
www.linkedin.com/company/anaconda-mining-inc-anx-

Company Type: Public
Ticker Symbol: ANX / TSX
Profile: Anaconda is a gold mining & exploration company, whose main project in located in Baie Verte, Newfoundland. Its ultimate goal is the raise annual production to 100,000 ounces.
Dustin Angelo, President & CEO
Errol Farr, Chief Financial Officer
Paul McNeill, Vice-President, Exploration

AQM Copper Inc.
205 Dunn Ave.
Toronto, ON M6K 2S1

info@aqmcopper.com
www.aqmcopper.com
Other Communications: Investors: investorinfo@pinnaclecapitalmarkets.ca

Company Type: Public
Ticker Symbol: AQM / TSX.V
Profile: AQM Copper Inc. is a Canadian-based mining company, exploring and developing copper deposits in South America.
Bruce L. Turner, President & CEO
Erick Underwood, Chief Financial Officer

Aquila Resources
#520, 141 Adelaide St. West
Toronto, ON M5H 3L5

647-943-5672
info@aquilaresources.com
www.aquilaresources.com
Social Media: www.facebook.com/AquilaResources
twitter.com/aquilaresources
www.linkedin.com/company/aquila-resources-inc.

Company Type: Public
Ticker Symbol: AQA / TSX
Profile: A mining company that owns a gold & zinc mine in Michigan.
Barry Hildred, Chief Executive Officer
Stephanie Malec, Chief Financial Officer
Tom Quigley, Vice-President, Exploration

Archon Minerals Ltd.
#2801, 323 Jervis St.
Vancouver, BC V6C 3P8

604-682-3303

Company Type: Public
Ticker Symbol: ACS / TSX.V
Profile: Archon Mines focuses on the exploration of minerals in the Northwest Territories.
Stewart Blusson, President & CEO

Argonaut Gold Inc.
9600 Prototype Ct.
Reno, NV 89521 USA

775-284-4422
Fax: 775-284-4426
info@argonautgold.com
www.argonautgold.com

Company Type: Public
Ticker Symbol: AR / TSX
Staff Size: 638
Profile: Argonaut Gold Inc is a mining company that engages in the exploration, development, and production of gold in Mexico.
Peter C. Dougherty, President/Chief Executive Officer
Richard Rhoades, Chief Operating Officer
David A. Ponczoch, Chief Financial Officer
Curtis Turner, Corporate Development Officer

Arianne Phosphate
#200, 393 rue Racine est
Chicoutimi, QC G7H 1T2

418-549-7316
Fax: 418-549-5750
855-549-7316
info@arianne-inc.com
www.arianne-inc.com
Social Media: twitter.com/arianne_dan
ca.linkedin.com/company/arianne-phosphate-inc-tsx-v-dan

Company Type: Public
Ticker Symbol: DAN / TSX.V
Profile: Une compagnie canadienne qui se consacre aujourd'hui au développement de son projet minier du Lac à Paul.
Brian Ostroff, Chef de la direction
James Cowley, Chef de la direction financière
Daniel Boulianne, Vice-président, Exploration

Arziona Mining Inc.
#555, 999 Canada Pl.
Vancouver, BC V6C 3E1

604-687-1717
Fax: 604-687-1715
info@azmininginc.com
www.azmininginc.com

Company Type: Public
Ticker Symbol: AZ / TSX
Profile: Arizona Mining Inc. is a mineral exploration company. The company has 80% ownership of a silver project located in Santa Cruz County, Arizona.
James Gowans, President & CEO
Donald R. Taylor, Chief Operating Officer
Paul J. Ireland, Chief Financial Officer
Purni Parikh, Vice-President & Corporate Secretary
Gregory F. Lucero, Vice-President, Community & Government Affairs

Asanko Gold Inc.
#680, 1066 West Hastings St.
Vancouver, BC V6E 3X2

604-683-8193
Fax: 604-683-8194
855-246-7341
info@asanko.com
www.asanko.com

Company Type: Public
Ticker Symbol: AKG / TSX, NYSE
Staff Size: 380
Profile: Asanko is a mineral exploration company focused on exploring and developing two gold properties in Ghana, West Africa; the Esaase Gold Property and the Asumura Gold Property.
Peter Breese, President & CEO
Greg McCunn, Chief Financial Officer

Ascot Resources Ltd.
#202, 15388 - 24 Ave.
Surrey, BC V4A 2J2

604-379-1170
Fax: 604-535-9946
www.ascotresources.ca

Company Type: Public
Ticker Symbol: AOT / TSX.V
Profile: The mining company focuses on developing gold in BC.
John Toffan, CEO
Bob Evans, Chief Financial Officer

Asian Mineral Resources Limited (AMR)
#2500, 120 Adelaide St. West
Toronto, ON M5H 1T1

416-360-3412
Fax: 416-367-1954
asianmineralres.com
Other Communications: Hanoi, Vietnam Office, Phone: + 84 4 3 773 7997

Company Type: Public
Ticker Symbol: ASN / TSX Venture
Staff Size: 406
Profile: Asian Mineral Resources Limited has a 90% interest in the Ban Phuc Nickel / Copper Project, which is located in northwestern Vietnam. Asian Mineral Resources also has a 90% ownership in the project company, Ban Phuc Nickel Mines LLC.
Evan Spencer, President & CEO
Sean Duffy, Chief Financial Officer
Tim Ashworth, General Manager, Operations
Dinh Huu Minh, Dip Geol/Eng, PhD, MAusIMM, Exploration Manager & Deputy General Director, BPNM
Paula Kember, Corporate Secretary

ATAC Resources Ltd.
#1016, 510 West Hastings St.
Vancouver, BC V6B 1L8

604-687-2522
info@atacresources.com
www.atacresources.com

Company Type: Public
Ticker Symbol: ATC / TSX Venture
Profile: The exploration company is developing its 100% owned Rackla Gold Project in the Yukon. The project contains Canada's only Carlin-Type gold discoveries. For its environmental standards, ATAC Resources has been the recipient of the Robert E. Leckie Award for Outstanding Reclamation Practices in Quartz Exploration & Mining by the Yukon Government.
Graham Downs, President & CEO
Julia Lane, Vice-President, Exploration
Larry Donaldson, Chief Financial Officer

Ian J. Talbot, Chief Operating Officer
Glenn R. Yeadon, B.Comm., LLB., Secretary

Atacama Pacific Gold Corporation
#1900, 25 Adelaide St. East
Toronto, ON M5C 3A1

647-560-9873
Fax: 844-964-7320
www.atacamapacific.com

Company Type: Public
Ticker Symbol: ATM / TSX.V
Profile: Atacama Pacific is a Chilean-focused precious metals company focused on developing its 100% owned Cerro Maricunga Oxide Gold Deposit, which is one of the largest undeveloped oxide gold deposits in the world.
Carl Hansen, President & Chief Executive Officer
Thomas Pladsen, Chief Financial Officer & Secretary

Athabasca Minerals Inc.
1319 - 91st St. SW
Edmonton, AB T6X 1H1

780-465-5696
Fax: 780-430-9865
info@athabascaminerals.com
www.athabascaminerals.com

Company Type: Public
Ticker Symbol: ABM / TSX.V
Profile: Athabasca Minerals Inc. is a Canadian management and exploration company specializing in developing and exploring for aggregates and industrial minerals in Alberta.
Don Paulencu, Interim Chief Executive Officer
William Woods, Chief Financial Officer

Atico Mining
#501, 543 Granville St.
Vancouver, BC V6C 1X8

604-633-9022
www.aticomining.com

Company Type: Public
Ticker Symbol: ATY / TSX.V
Profile: A copper-gold mining company with projects in South America. Its main location is the El Roble mine in Colombia.
Fernando Ganoza, Chief Executive Officer
Jorge Ganoza, President
Thomas Kelly, Chief Operating Officer

Atlanta Gold Inc.
First Canadian Pl.
#5600, 100 King St. West
Toronto, ON M5X 1C9

416-777-0013
Fax: 416-777-0014
info@atgoldinc.com
www.atgoldinc.com

Company Type: Public
Ticker Symbol: ATG / TSX Venture
Profile: Through its subsidiary, Atlanta Gold Corporation, Atlanta Gold Inc. has leases, options, or ownership interests in properties located in Idaho.
William Ernest Simmons, President & Chief Executive Officer

Atlantic Gold Corp.
Three Bentall Centre
PO Box 49298, #3083, 595 Burrard St.
Vancouver, BC V7X 1L3

604-689-5564
Fax: 604-566-9050
877-689-5599
www.atlanticgoldcorporation.com

Company Type: Public
Ticker Symbol: AGB / TSX.V
Profile: The mining company owns four projects in Nova Scotia.
Steven Dean, CEO
Maryse Belanger, Chief Operating Officer
Chris Batalha, Chief Financial Officer

Atlatsa Resources Corpoartion
PO Box 782103, Sandton, 2146 South Africa

info@atlatsa.com
www.atlatsaresources.co.za
Other Communications: Phone: +27 11 779 6800; Fax: +27 11 883 0863

Company Type: Public
Ticker Symbol: ATL / TSX.V, NYSE, JSE
Profile: Atlatsa Resources is a platinum group metals (PGM) mining, exploration and development company, with assets located on the Bushveld Igneous Complex of South Africa.
Harold Motaung, Chief Executive Officer
Joel Kesler, Chief Commercial Officer

Aura Minerals Inc.
#1240, 155 University Ave.
Toronto, ON M5H 3B7

416-649-1033
Fax: 416-649-1044
info@auraminerals.com
www.auraminerals.com

Company Type: Public
Ticker Symbol: ORA / TSX
Staff Size: 1,268
Profile: Aura Minerals Inc. is a Canadian mid-tier gold and copper production company focused on the development and operation of gold and base metal projects in the Americas.
Jim Bannantine, President & CEO
Rory Taylor, Chief Financial Officer
Ryan Goodman, Vice-President, Legal Affairs & Business Development

Aurcana Corporation
#850, 789 West Pender St.
Vancouver, BC V6C 1H2

604-331-9333
Fax: 604-633-9179
866-532-9333
info@aurcana.com
www.aurcana.com

Company Type: Public
Ticker Symbol: AUN / TSX Venture
Profile: Aurcana Corporation is a public, junior mining company, which is listed on the TSX Venture Exchange & the OTCQX. The company owns 100% of the Shafter silver mine in Presidio County, Texas. Aurcana also has a 92% interest in the La Negra silver, copper, lead, & zinc mine, which is located in Queretaro State, Mexico.
Kevin Drover, President & CEO
Salvador Huerta, BA, Accounting & Administration, Chief Financial Officer
Donna Moroney, Corporate Secretary

Aureus Mining Inc.
South Tower, Royal Bank Plaza
#3800, 200 Bay St.
Toronto, ON M5J 2Z4

aureus-mining.com
Other Communications: London, UK Office, Phone: +44-207-010-7690

Company Type: Public
Ticker Symbol: AUE / TSX
Staff Size: 108
Profile: Aureus Mining Inc. is engaged in the exploration and development of gold deposits in highly prospective and under-explored areas of Liberia and Cameroon.
Serhan Umurhan, Chief Executive Officer

Aurico Metals Inc.
#1601, 110 Yonge St.
Toronto, ON M5C 1T4

416-216-2780
Fax: 416-216-2781
info@auricometals.ca
www.auricometals.ca

Company Type: Public
Ticker Symbol: AMI / TSX
Profile: A precious metals mining company.
Chris Richter, President & CEO
John Fitzgerald, Chief Operating Officer

Avalon Advanced Materials Inc.
Corporate Headquarters
#1901, 130 Adelaide St. West
Toronto, ON M5H 3P5

416-364-4938
Fax: 416-364-5162
office@avalonAM.com
www.avalonadvancedmaterials.com
Social Media: www.facebook.com/AvalonAdvancedMaterials
twitter.com/AvalonAdvanced

Company Type: Public
Ticker Symbol: AVL / TSX, NYSE
Profile: The mineral development company is focused upon rare metals deposits in Canada. The Nechalacho Deposit, situated in the Northwest Territories, is Avalon Rare Metals' flagship project. Heavy rare earth elements are important for enabling advances in green energy technology.
Donald S. Bubar, M.Sc., P.Geo., President & Chief Executive Officer
R.J. Andersen, CA, CFP, CPA, Chief Financial Officer, Corporate Secretary & Vice-President, Finance
Mark Wiseman, Vice-President, Sustainability
William Mercer, Ph.D., P.Geo., Vice-President, Exploration
Melanie Smith, Senior Legal Counsel
Pierre Neatby, Vice-President, Sales & Marketing
Ron Malashewski, P.Eng., Manager, Investor Relations
ir@avalonAM.com

Avino Silver & Gold Mines Ltd.
#900, 570 Granville St.
Vancouver, BC V6C 3P1

604-682-3701
Fax: 604-682-3600
ir@avino.com
www.avino.com
Social Media: twitter.com/Avino_ASM

Company Type: Public
Ticker Symbol: ASM / TSX.V; MKT / NYSE
Profile: Avino is a junior mining company with interests in Mexico.
David Wolfin, President & CEO
Malcolm Davidson, CFO

Azarga Uranium Corp.
#140, 5575 DTC Pkwy.
Greenwood Village, CO 80111 USA

303-790-7528
info@azargauranium.com
azargauranium.com
Social Media: twitter.com/AzargaUranium

Company Type: Public
Ticker Symbol: AZZ / TSX
Profile: Azarga Uranium is a uranium development company. It owns uranium deposits in Colorado, Wyoming & Kyrgyzstan. It is the majority shareholder of Anatolia Energy & Black Range Minerals, both of which are listed on the ASX.
Richard Clement, Chair & Interim Chief Executive Officer
Blake Steele, President/Chief Financial Officer & Corporate Secretary
John Mays, Chief Operating Officer
Curtis Church, Vice-President, International Operations

B2Gold Corp.
PO Box 49143, #3100, 595 Burrard St.
Vancouver, BC V7X 1J1

604-681-8371
Fax: 604-681-6209
800-316-8855
investor@b2gold.com
www.b2gold.com
Social Media: twitter.com/B2GoldCorp

Company Type: Public
Ticker Symbol: BTO / TSX
Staff Size: 1,298
Profile: Founded in 2007, B2Gold Corp. is an international gold producer that has mines in Nicaragua, plus exploration & development assets in Columbia, Uruguay, & Nicaragua. The company trades on the Toronto Stock Exchange under the symbol BTO, as well as on the OTCXQ under the symbol BGLPF.
B2Gold Corp. employs a Vice-President who specializes in offering operational health & safety, plus environmental & social assistance during all phases of mining.
Clive T. Johnson, President, Chief Executive Officer & Director
Roger T. Richer, Executive Vice-President, General Counsel & Secretary
Mike Cinnamond, Chief Financial Officer & Senior Vice-President, Finance
Tom Garagan, Senior Vice-President, Exploration
Dale Craig, Vice-President, Operations
Dennis Stansbury, Senior Vice-President, Engineering & Product Evaluations

Bacanora Minerals
2204 - 6 Ave. NW
Calgary, AB T2N 0W9

403-237-6122
Fax: 403-237-6144
info@bacanoraminerals.com
www.bacanoraminerals.com

Company Type: Public
Ticker Symbol: BCN / TSX.V
Profile: A lithium mining company.
Peter Secker, Chief Executive Officer
Derek Batorowsky, Chief Financial Officer
Martin Vidal Torres, President

Baja Mining Corp.
#600, 890 West Pender St.
Vancouver, BC V6C 1J9

604-685-2323
info@bajamining.com
bajamining.com

Company Type: Public
Ticker Symbol: BAJ / TSX.V
Profile: Baja owns a 10% interest in the Boleo copper-cobalt-zinc-manganese project in Mexico.
C. Thomas Ogryzlo, Interim CEO
Nigel Kirkwood, Chief Financial Officer

Balmoral Resources
#1750, 700 West Pender St.
Vancouver, BC V6E 2K3
604-638-3664
Fax: 604-648-8809
877-838-3664
www.balmoralresources.com
Social Media:
www.facebook.com/pages/Balmoral-Resources-Ltd/3557371844
81200
twitter.com/balmoralgold
www.linkedin.com/company/2796299
Company Type: Public
Ticker Symbol: BAR / TSX
Profile: Founded in 2010, Balmoral Resources is a gold exploration and development company focused in the major gold districts of North America.
Darin Wagner, President/CEO
Peggy Wu, Chief Financial Officer
John Foulkes, Vice-President, Corporate Development

Banro Corporation
First Canadian Place
#7070, 100 King St. West
Toronto, ON M5X 1E3
416-366-2221
800-714-7938
info@banro.com
www.banro.com
Other Communications: Investor Relations, E-mail:
ir@banro.com
Social Media:
www.facebook.com/Banro-Foundation-123995677734860
twitter.com/banrocorp
linkedin.com/company/banro-corp
Company Type: Public
Ticker Symbol: BAA / TSX, NYSE
Staff Size: 1,496
Profile: Banro is a Canadian gold company with production from its first gold project, Twangiza, which is located in the Democratic Republic of the Congo.
John Clarke, President & CEO
Kevin Jennings, Senior Vice-President & Chief Financial Officer
Arnold Kondrat, Executive Vice-President

Barkerville Gold Mines
1111 Melville St., 11th Fl.
Vancouver, BC V6E 3V6
604-661-4100
Fax: 604-661-4101
888-222-1442
info@barkervillegold.com
www.barkervillegold.com
Company Type: Public
Ticker Symbol: BGM / TSX.V
Chris Lodder, President & CEO
Luc Lessard, COO
Andres Tinajero, Chief Financial Officer

Barrick Gold Corporation
TD Canada Trust Tower, Brookfield Place
PO Box 212, #3700, 161 Bay St.
Toronto, ON M5J 2S1
416-861-9911
Fax: 416-861-2492
800-720-7415
Investor Relations E-mail: investor@barri
www.barrick.com
Social Media: www.facebook.com/barrick.gold.corporation
twitter.com/BarrickGold
Company Type: Public
Ticker Symbol: ABX / TSX
Staff Size: 21,135
Profile: The gold mining company explores, develops, & operates mines in five continents. It trades on the Toronto & New York stock exchanges under the symbol ABX.
Kelvin Dushnisky, President
Kevin Thomson, Senior Executive Vice-President, Strategic Matters
Catherine Raw, Executive Vice-President & CFO
Richard Williams, Chief Operating Officer
Kathy Sipos, Chief of Staff

Bear Creek Mining Corporation
Corporate Head Office
#1400, 400 Burrard St.
Vancouver, BC V6C 3A6
604-685-6269
Fax: 604-685-6268
info@bearcreekmining.com
www.bearcreekmining.com
Other Communications: Lima Operations Office, Phone: (511)
222-0922
Company Type: Public
Ticker Symbol: BCM / TSX Venture
Profile: Formed in 2000, Bear Creek Mining Corporation explores for mineral deposits. The company's focus is in Peru, where projects include Corani & Santa Ana. These projects contain silver & by-product base metals.
Andrew T. Swarthout, President & Chief Executive Officer
Steven Krause, Chief Financial Officer
Corey M. Dean, Vice-President, Legal

Bellhaven Copper & Gold Inc.
#408, 837 Hastings St. West
Vancouver, BC V6C 2X1
604-684-6264
Fax: 604-684-6242
www.bellhavencg.com
Company Type: Public
Ticker Symbol: BHV / TSX
Profile: A gold & copper mining company with projects in Colombia.
Maria Milagros Paredes, President & CFO

Cabo Drilling Corp.
20 - 6th St.
New Westminster, BC V3L 2Y8
604-527-4201
Fax: 604-527-9126
info@cabo.ca
www.cabo.ca
Other Communications: Sales, E-mail: sales@cabo.ca
Company Type: Public
Ticker Symbol: CBE / TSX.V
Profile: Cabo Drilling Corp. is an international mineral and specialty drilling services provider serving the mining and exploration industries from Canada, Albania, Panama, Colombia and the USA.
John A. Versfelt, President & CEO
Calvin Lucyshyn, Controller & Chief Financial Officer
James Goodwin, Coordinator, Human Resources & Safety

Cameco Corporation
2121 - 11 St. West
Saskatoon, SK S7M 1J3
306-956-6200
Fax: 306-956-6201
www.cameco.com
Other Communications: Investor Inquiries, Phone: 306-956-6340
Social Media: www.facebook.com/Cameco.Careers
twitter.com/cameconews
www.linkedin.com/company/cameco-corporation
Company Type: Public
Ticker Symbol: CCO / TSX; CCJ / NYSE
Staff Size: 3,365
Profile: Cameco is engaged in the production of uranium to generate electricity in nuclear energy plants throughout the world.
Tim S. Gitzel, President & Chief Executive Officer
Grant E. Isaac, Chief Financial Officer & Senior Vice-President
Sean Quinn, Chief Legal Officer, Corporate Secretary & Sr. Vice-President
Alice Wong, Senior Vice-President & Chief Corporate Officer

Canada Zinc Metals Corp.
PO Box 11121 Stn. Royal Centre, #2050, 1055 West Georgia St.
Vancouver, BC V6E 3P3
604-684-2181
Fax: 604-682-4768
855-684-2181
info@canadazincmetals.com
www.canadazincmetals.com
Company Type: Public
Ticker Symbol: CZX / TSX Venture
Profile: The mineral exploration company conducts operations in British Columbia. Canada Zinc Metals Corp. holds the mineral belt known as the Kechika Trough. The Kechika Region hosts base metal resources.
Peeyush Varshney, LL.B., Chair, Chief Executive Officer & President
Praveen Varshney, FCPA, FCA, Chief Financial Officer
Ken MacDonald, P.Geo., Vice-President, Exploration

Candente Copper Corp.
#1100, 1111 Melville St.
Vancouver, BC V6E 3V6
604-689-1957
Fax: 604-484-7143
877-689-1964
info@candentecopper.com
www.candentecopper.com
Company Type: Public
Ticker Symbol: DNT / TSX, BVL
Profile: Candente Copper Corp. owns 100% of the Cañariaco Norte Copper Project in northern Peru. The company undertakes exploration in accordance with the Peruvian Ministry of Energy & Mines' General Mining Law & regulations.
Joanne C. Freeze, P.Geo., Chair & Chief Executive Officer
Sean I. Waller, P.Eng., President
Faisel Hussein, Executive Vice-President & Acting CFO

Capstone Mining Corp.
#2100, 510 West Georgia St.
Vancouver, BC V6B 0M3
604-684-8894
Fax: 604-688-2180
866-684-8894
info@capstonemining.com
www.capstonemining.com
Company Type: Public
Ticker Symbol: CS / TSX
Staff Size: 1,658
Profile: Capstone Mining Corp. operates a copper-silver-zinc-lead mine located in Mexico & a copper-gold-silver mine in the Yukon. Development projects are underway in British Columbia, Chile, & Australia.
In 2011, Capstone Mining acquired Far West Mining Ltd., a company engaged in the acquisition & exploration of mineral properties in Chile & Australia.
Darren M. Pylot, President & Chief Executive Officer
D. James Slattery, Chief Financial Officer & Senior Vice-President
Gregg B. Bush, Senior Vice-President/COO
Brad Mercer, Senior Vice-President, Exploration
Cindy Burnett, Vice-President, Investor Relations & Communications
Gillian McCombie, Vice-President, Human Resources

Castle Resources Inc.
TD Tower South
PO Box 139, #2100, 79 Wellington St. West
Toronto, ON M5K 1H1
403-593-8300
Fax: 416-366-4101
www.castleresources.com
Company Type: Public
Ticker Symbol: CRI / CSE
Profile: Castle Resources Inc. is focused on the acquisition, exploration, and development of mineral properties.
Tim Mann, Interim President & CEO
Jennifer Ta, CFO

Centerra Gold Inc.
#1500, 1 University Ave.
Toronto, ON M5J 2P1
416-204-1953
Fax: 416-204-1954
info@centerragold.com
www.centerragold.com
Company Type: Public
Ticker Symbol: CG / TSX
Staff Size: 2,803
Profile: Centerra Gold Inc. is engaged in the acquisition, exploration, development, & operation of gold properties in Central Asia, the former Soviet Union, & other emerging markets.
Frank Herbert, President
Scott Perry, CEO
Darren Millman, Vice-President & CFO

Century Global Commodities Corporation
#1301, 200 University Ave.
Toronto, ON M5H 3C6
416-977-3188
Fax: 416-977-8002
contact@centuryglobal.ca
www.centuryglobal.ca
Social Media: www.facebook.com/CenturyIronMines
Company Type: Public
Ticker Symbol: CNT.T / TSX
Profile: Century Iron Mines Corporation is a mining company with mineral exploration and development activities focused on iron ore.
Sandy Chim, President & Chief Executive Officer
Rebecca Ng, Chief Financial Officer
Robin Cook, Director, Corporate Development & Investor Relations
robin.cook@centuryglobal.ca

Chesapeake Gold Corp.
#201, 1512 Yew St.
Vancouver, BC V6K 3E4
604-731-1094
Fax: 604-731-0209
chesapeake@shaw.ca
www.chesapeakegold.com
Social Media: www.facebook.com/ChesapeakeGold
twitter.com/Chesapeake_Gold
www.linkedin.com/company/chesapeake-gold-corp-

Company Type: Public
Ticker Symbol: CKG / TSX Venture
Profile: Chesapeake Gold Corp. explores for & develops precious metals projects. The company's focus is upon its 100% owned Metates gold deposit in Durango state, Mexico.
P. Randy Reifel, President & Director
Gerald L. Sneddon, Executive Vice-President, Operations
Alberto Galicia, Vice-President, Exploration
Gary A. Parkison, Vice-President, Development
Bernard Poznanski, Corporate Secretary

Chieftain Metals Corp.
#2510, 2 Bloor St. West
Toronto, ON M4W 3E2
416-479-5410
Fax: 416-479-5420
www.chieftainmetals.com

Company Type: Public
Ticker Symbol: CFB / TSX.V
Profile: The mining company's main focus is the Tulsequah Project in northwestern British Columbia.
Victor Wyprysky, President & CEO
Pompeyo Gallardo, Chief Financial Officer
Keith Boyle, Chief Operating Officer
Peter Chodos, Executive Vice-President, Corporate Development

China Gold International Resources Corp. Ltd.
One Bentall Centre
PO Box 27, #660, 505 Burrard St.
Vancouver, BC V7X 1M5
604-609-0598
Fax: 604-688-0598
info@chinagoldintl.com
www.chinagoldintl.com
Other Communications: Investor Relations, Phone: 604-695-5031

Company Type: Public
Ticker Symbol: CGG / TSX
Staff Size: 1,664
Profile: China Gold International Resources Corp. Ltd. is a mineral development company that operates the CSH Gold Mine, located in Inner Mongolia, as well as the Jiama Copper-Polymetallic Mine, situated in the Tibet Autonomous Region of China. The company's aim is to explore, acquire, & develop new projects in China & elsewhere.
China Gold International Resources Corp. Ltd. is listed on the Toronto Stock Exchange, under the symbol CGG, & on the Board of the Stock Exchange of Hong Kong Limited, under the symbol HKSE:2099.
Bing Liu, Chief Executive Officer
Derrick Zhang, Chief Financial Officer
Jerry Xie, Executive Vice-President & Corporate Secretary
Xiangdong Jiang, Vice-President, Production
Songlin Zhang, Vice-President & Chief Engineer

Colt Resources
#1800, 500, Place D'Armes
Montréal, QC H2Y 2W2
438-259-3315
www.coltresources.com
Social Media: info@coltresources.com
www.linkedin.com/company/548157

Company Type: Public
Ticker Symbol: GTP / TSX Venture
Profile: Colt Resources is a mining exploration and development company focused on 100% owned advanced-stage high-grade gold and tungsten projects in Portugal.
Nikolas Perrault, President & CEO
Jorge Valente, Vice-President, Engineering & Development
Shahab Jaffrey, Chief Financial Officer
Filipe Faria, Vice-President, Exploration

Columbus Gold Corporation
1090 Hamilton St.
Vancouver, BC V6B 2R9
604-634-0970
Fax: 604-634-0971
888-818-1364
info@columbusgoldcorp.com
www.columbusgoldcorp.com
Social Media: www.facebook.com/columbusgoldcorp
twitter.com/columbusgoldcgt

Company Type: Public
Ticker Symbol: CGT / TSX
Profile: Columbus Gold Corporation is a gold exploration and development company operating principally in Nevada.
Robert Giustra, Chief Executive Officer
Rock Lefrançois, Chief Operating Officer
Andrew Yau, Chief Financial Officer
Jenna Virk, Vice-President, Legal & Corporate Secretary

Commerce Resources Corp.
#1450, 789 West Pender St.
Vancouver, BC V6C 1H2
604-484-2700
Fax: 604-681-8240
866-484-2700
info@commerceresources.com
www.commerceresources.com
Social Media: www.facebook.com/commerceresourcesfan
twitter.com/commercerescce
www.linkedin.com/company/1119844

Company Type: Public
Ticker Symbol: CCE / TSX Venture
Profile: The exploration & development company's focus is upon British Columbia's Upper Fir Tantalum & Niobium Deposit & Québec's Eldor Rare Earth Project.
David Hodge, CEO
Jody Dahrouge, Vice-President, Exploration

Copper Fox Metals Inc.
#650, 340 - 12th Ave. SW
Calgary, AB T2R 1L5
403-264-2820
Fax: 403-264-2920
info@copperfoxmetals.com
www.copperfoxmetals.com

Company Type: Public
Ticker Symbol: CUU / TSX.V
Profile: Copper Fox is a Canadian-based resource development company with a 25% interest in a Joint Venture on the Schaft Creek Project in Northern British Columbia.
Elmer B. Stewart, President and CEO
Braden Jensen, Chief Financial Officer

Copper Mountain Mining Corporation
#1700, 700 West Pender St.
Vancouver, BC V6C 1G8
604-682-2992
Fax: 604-682-2993
877-451-2662
www.cumtn.com
Other Communications: Copper Mountain Mine Site, Phone: 250-295-0123

Company Type: Public
Ticker Symbol: CUM / TSX
Staff Size: 425
Profile: The resource company owns 75% of the Copper Mountain Mine, which is located south of Princeton, British Columbia.
James C. O'Rourke, P.Eng., President & Chief Executive Officer
jim@CuMtn.com
Rodney A. Shier, CA, Chief Financial Officer
rod@CuMtn.com
Peter Holbek, B.Sc., M.Sc., P.Geo., Vice-President, Exploration

Cordoba Minerals Corp.
#1413, 181 University Ave.
Toronto, ON M5H 3M7
416-862-5253
info@cordobamineralscorp.com
www.cordobaminerals.com
Social Media: www.facebook.com/cordobaminerals
twitter.com/CordobaMinerals
www.linkedin.com/company/5204583

Company Type: Public
Ticker Symbol: CDB / TSX.V
Profile: A mineral exploration company with projects in Colombia.
Mario Stifano, President & CEO
Cybill Tsung, Chief Financial Officer
Chris Grainger, Vice-President, Exploration

Corsa Coal Corp.
#100, 125 Technology Dr.
Canonsburg, PA 15317 USA
724-754-0028
communication@corsacoal.com
www.corsacoal.com

Company Type: Public
Ticker Symbol: CSO / TSX Venture
Staff Size: 418
Profile: Corsa Coal Corp. mines, processes, & sells metallurgical coal. The company is active in the Northern Appalachia.
George G. Dethlefsen, Chief Executive Officer
Kevin Harrigan, Chief Financial Officer & Corporate Secretary
Kai Xia, Vice-President, Corporate Development

Crystal Peak Minerals Inc.
#200, 2180 South 1300 East
Salt Lake City, UT 84106 USA
801-485-0223
info@crystalpeakminerals.com
crystalpeakminerals.com

Company Type: Public
Ticker Symbol: CPM/TSX.V; CPMMF/OTCQX
Profile: Crystal Peak Minerals Inc. is an exploration-stage pre-revenue potash development company.
Lance D'Ambrosio, Chief Executive Officer
Thomas Pladsen, Chief Financial Officer

Cub Energy Inc.
#3300, 205 - 5 Ave. SW
Calgary, AB T2P 2V7
www.cubenergyinc.com
Other Communications: Houston Office: 713-677-0439

Company Type: Public
Ticker Symbol: KUB / TSX.V
Profile: Cub Energy Inc. is an upstream oil and gas company with 132,500 net acres in the Ukraine.
Mikhail Afendikov, Chief Executive Officer/Chair
Patrick McGrath, Chief Financial Officer

Dalradian Resources Inc.
Queen's Quay Terminal
#416, 207 Queen's Quay West
Toronto, ON M5J 1A7
416-583-5600
info@dalradian.com
www.dalradian.com
Other Communications: Omagh, Northern Ireland Office, Phone: +44 (0) 2882 246289
Social Media: twitter.com/DNA_CEO

Company Type: Public
Ticker Symbol: DNA / TSX; DALR / AIM
Profile: Dalradian Resources is engaged in the acquisition, exploration, & development of mineral properties. The company's wholly owned subsidiary is Dalradian Gold Limited, which has interests in Tyrone & Londonderry counties in Northern Ireland. In addition to its operations in Northern Ireland, Dalradian also hold minerals rights to land in Norway.
Patrick F.N. Anderson, Chief Executive Officer
Keith McKay, Chief Financial Officer
Eric Tremblay, Chief Operating Officer
Marla Gale, Vice-President, Communications

Denison Mines Corp.
#1100, 40 University Ave.
Toronto, ON M5J 1T1
416-979-1991
Fax: 416-979-5893
www.denisonmines.com
Social Media: www.facebook.com/denisonmines
twitter.com/DenisonMinesCo
www.linkedin.com/company/denison-mines-usa-corp-

Company Type: Public
Ticker Symbol: DML / TSX; DNN / NYSE
Profile: Denison Mines Corp. is a uranium exploration & production company. Its active uranium mines are located in Canada & the United States. Denison Environmental Services (DES) was established to provide mine decommissioning, long-term care, & maintenance services to closed mining facilities.
David D. Cates, President & Chief Executive Officer
Mac McDonald, Chief Financial Officer & Vice-President, Finance
Dale Verran, Vice-President, Exploration
Amanda Willett, Corporate Counsel & Corporate Secretary

Detour Gold Corporation
Commerce Court West
PO Box 121, #4100, 199 Bay St.
Toronto, ON M5L 1E2
416-304-0800
Fax: 416-304-0184
info@detourgold.com
www.detourgold.com

Company Type: Public
Ticker Symbol: DGC / TSX
Staff Size: 830
Profile: Detour Gold Corporation is a Canadian gold mining company with assets in the Detour Lake Mine in northeastern Ontario.
Paul Martin, President & CEO
James Mavor, Chief Financial Officer
Pierre Beaudoin, Chief Operating Officer
Laurie Gaborit, Director, Investor Relations

Dundee Precious Metals Inc.
Dundee Place
PO Box 195, #500, 1 Adelaide St. East
Toronto, ON M5C 2V9
416-365-5191
Fax: 416-365-9080
info@dundeeprecious.com
www.dundeeprecious.com

Company Type: Public
Ticker Symbol: DPM / TSX

Staff Size: 2,694
Profile: Dundee Precious Metals Inc. acquires, explores, develops, & mines precious metals properties. The company is active in Armenia, Bulgaria, Serbia, & Namibia.
Rick Howes, President/CEO
Hume Kyle, Exec. Vice-President/CFO
David Rae, Executive Vice-President & COO
Lori E. Beak, Senior Vice-President, Governance & Corporate Secretary
Richard Gosse, Senior Vice-President, Exploration

Dynacor Gold Mines Inc.
#1105, 625, boul René-Lévesque ouest
Montreal, QC H3B 1R2
514-393-9000
Fax: 514-393-9002
dyn@dynacor.com
www.dynacor.com
Other Communications: Investor Relations : 604-492-0099
Social Media: www.facebook.com/DynacorGoldMines
twitter.com/DynacorGold
Company Type: Public
Ticker Symbol: DNG / TSX
Staff Size: 366
Profile: The company operates a gold processing plant in Peru.
Jean Martineau, President & CEO
Leonard Teoli, Vice-President & Chief Financial Officer

Dynasty Metals & Mining Inc.
#270, 666 Burrard St.
Vancouver, BC V6C 2X8
604-687-7810
Fax: 604-687-0885
info@dynastymining.com
www.dynastymining.com
Social Media: twitter.com/dynastymining
Company Type: Public
Ticker Symbol: DMM / TSX
Staff Size: 513
Profile: The mining company is active in Ecuador, where it is engaged in the exploration & development of mineral properties. Dynasty Metals & Mining's projects include the Zaruma Gold Project, the Dynasty Copper-Gold Belt, & the Jerusalem Project.
Robert Washer, President & Chief Executive Officer

East Africa Metals Inc.
#700, 1055 West Georgia St.
Vancouver, BC V6E 3P3
604-488-0822
Fax: 604-899-1240
866-488-0822
investors@eastafricametals.com
www.eastafricametals.com
Company Type: Public
Ticker Symbol: EAM / TSX.V
Profile: The mining company has projects in Ethiopia & Tanzania.
Andrew Lee Smith, President & CEO
Peter Granata, Chief Financial Officer
Jeff Heidema, Vice-President, Exploration
Denis Dillip, President, Canaco Tanzania

Eastern Platinum Limited
#501, 837 West Hastings St.
Vancouver, BC V6C 2X1
647-345-3146
Fax: 604-685-6493
www.eastplats.com
Company Type: Public
Ticker Symbol: ELR / TSX
Profile: Eastern Platinum Limited was established in 2003. The metals mining company has acquired platinum & rhodium deposits in South Africa.
Diana Hu, President & Chief Executive Officer
David Li, Interim Chief Financial Officer

Eastmain Resources Inc.
#1000, 36 Toronto St.
Toronto, ON M5C 2C5
info@eastmain.com
www.eastmain.com
Other Communications: Exploration Office, Mono, ON: 519-940-4870
Company Type: Public
Ticker Symbol: ER / TSX
Profile: Eastmain Resources Inc. is a gold exploration company. The company's area of operation is the Eastmain River area, in northern Québec's James Bay District. Eastmain Resources owns 100% of the Eau Clair gold deposit. Exploration projects include the Éléonore & Éléonore South properties.
Claude Lemasson, P.Eng., MBA, President & Chief Executive Officer
George Duguay, Corporate Secretary

Eco Oro Minerals Corp.
#300, 1055 West Hastings St.
Vancouver, BC V6E 2E9
604-682-8212
Fax: 604-682-3708
contact@eco-oro.com
www.eco-oro.com
Company Type: Public
Ticker Symbol: EOM / TSX
Profile: A precious metals exploration company with projects in Colombia.
Mark Moseley-Williams, President & CEO
Paul Robertson, Chief Financial Officer

Ecuador Gold & Copper Corp.
#1128, 789 West Pender St.
Vancouver, BC V6C 1H2
604-687-2038
Fax: 604-687-3141
info@ecuadorgoldandcopper.com
www.ecuadorgoldandcopper.com
Company Type: Public
Ticker Symbol: EGX / TSX.V
Profile: The company owns the Condor Project, located in Ecuador.
Heye Daun, President & Chief Executive Officer
Mit Tilkov, Vice-President, Exploration

Eldorado Gold Corporation
Five Bentall Centre
#1188, 550 Burrard St.
Vancouver, BC V6C 2B5
604-687-4018
Fax: 604-687-4026
888-353-8166
www.eldoradogold.com
Social Media: www.facebook.com/EldoradoGoldCorp
www.linkedin.com/company/eldorado-gold-corporation
Company Type: Public
Ticker Symbol: ELD / TSX; EGO / NYSE
Staff Size: 7,300
Profile: Eldorado Gold Corporation is an international company that specializes in the exploration & development of gold properties. In 2012, Eldorado Gold Corporation acquired all the issued & outstanding securities of European Goldfields Limited, a company with gold reserves in the European Union.
The gold producer now has properties in Brazil, Greece, Turkey, China, & Romania. Industry best practices are implemented in each region in an effort to minimize environmental impacts.
Paul N. Wright, president & Chief Executive Officer
Fabiana Chubbs, Chief Financial Officer
Paul J. Skayman, Chief Operating Officer
Dawn L. Moss, Corporate Secretary & Exec. Vice-President, Administration

Encanto Potash
PO Box 6, #450, 800 West Pender St.
Vancouver, BC V6C 2V6
604-683-2402
www.encantopotash.com
Company Type: Public
Ticker Symbol: EPO / TSX.V
Jim Walchuck, CEO
Rob McMorran, CFO
Stavros Daskos, President

Endeavour Silver Corp.
#301, 700 West Pender St.
Vancouver, BC V6C 1G8
604-685-9775
Fax: 604-685-9744
877-685-9775
info@edrsilver.com
www.edrsilver.com
Social Media: twitter.com/EDRSilverCorp
Company Type: Public
Ticker Symbol: EDR / TSX; EXK / NYSE
Profile: The mid-cap silver mining company has resources in Mexico.
Bradford Cooke, M.Sc., P.Geo., Chief Executive Officer
Godfrey Walton, M.Sc., P.Geo., President & Chief Operating Officer
Dan Dickson, B.Comm., CA, Chief Financial Officer
Meghan Brown, Director, Investor Relations

Energold Drilling Corp.
#1100, 543 Granville St.
Vancouver, BC V6C 1X8
604-681-9501
Fax: 604-681-6813
info@energold.com
www.energold.com
Social Media: twitter.com/EnergoldEGD
Company Type: Public
Ticker Symbol: EGD / TSX Venture
Profile: The energy drilling company serves the international mining sector. The driller strives to operate in an environmentally & socially sensitive manner. Canada's E3 Environmental Excellence in Exploration chose one of Energold's drill programs as a case study.
Frederick W. Davidson, President & Chief Executive Officer
Steven Gold, Chief Financial Officer
Jerry Huang, Manager, Investor Relations

Energy Fuels Inc.
Victory Bldg.
80 Richmond St. West, 18th Fl.
Toronto, ON M5H 2A4
888-864-2125
info@energyfuels.com
www.energyfuels.com
Social Media: twitter.com/energy_fuels
www.linkedin.com/company/energy-fuels-resources
Company Type: Public
Ticker Symbol: EFR / TSX
Staff Size: 194
Profile: Energy Fuels focuses upon the development & expansion of uranium & vanadium assets in the United States. The company also has exploration properties in the Athabasca Basin of Saskatchewan.
In 2013, Energy Fuels acquired Strathmore Minerals.
Stephen P. Antony, MBA, President & Chief Executive Officer
Daniel Zang, Chief Financial Officer
David Frydenlund, Senior Vice-President, General Counsel & Corporate Secretary
Harold Roberts, Executive Vice-President, Conventional Operations

Entree Gold Inc.
#1201, 1166 Alberni St.
Vancouver, BC V6E 3Z3
604-687-4777
Fax: 604-687-4770
www.entreegold.com
Social Media: www.facebook.com/EntreeGold
twitter.com/entreegold
Company Type: Public
Ticker Symbol: ETG/TSX, AMEX, Frankfurt
Profile: Entrée Gold Inc. is a Canadian mineral exploration company focused on the worldwide discovery and development of copper and gold prospects.
Stephen Scott, President & CEO
Duane Lo, Interim Chief Financial Officer
Robert Cinits, Vice-President, Corporate Development

Eurasian Minerals
#501, 543 Granville St.
Vancouver, BC V6C 1X8
604-688-6390
Fax: 604-688-1157
www.eurasianminerals.com
Company Type: Public
Ticker Symbol: EMX / TSX.V
Profile: Eurasian Minerals Inc. is engaged in the exploration of precious metals in Serbia, Turkey and the Kyrgyz Republic.
David M. Cole, President & CEO
Christina Cepeliauskas, Chief Financial Officer

Euro Sun Mining
Corporate Office
#65, 800 Queen St. West
Toronto, ON M5H 2M5
416-309-4299
info@eurosunmining.com
www.carpathiangold.com
Social Media: www.facebook.com/EuroSunMining
twitter.com/EuroSunMining
Company Type: Public
Ticker Symbol: CPN.CN / TSX
Profile: Euro Sun Mining owns 100% of the Riacho dos Machados Gold Project in Brazil. The exploration & development company is also active in Romania, where it owns 100% of the Rovina Valley Au-Cu Project.
G. Scott Moore, President & CEO
Les Kwasik, Chief Operating Officer
Paul Bozoki, Chief Financial Officer

Excelsior Mining Corp.
#1240, 1140 West Pender St.
Vancouver, BC V6E 4G1
604-681-8030
Fax: 604-681-8039
866-683-8030
info@excelsiormining.com
www.excelsiormining.com
Company Type: Public
Ticker Symbol: MIN / TSX.V

Profile: A copper mining company currently developing a project in Arizona.
Stephen Twyerould, President & CEO
Mark Distler, Chief Financial Officer
Roland Goodgame, Executive Vice-President

First Majestic Silver Corp.
#1805, 925 West Georgia St.
Vancouver, BC V6C 3L2
604-688-3033
Fax: 604-639-8873
866-529-2807
info@firstmajestic.com
www.firstmajestic.com
Other Communications: sales@firstmajestic.com
Social Media: twitter.com/fmsilvercorp
Company Type: Public
Ticker Symbol: FR / TSX; AG / NYSE
Staff Size: 3,738
Profile: The silver company is focused on production in Mexico. In 2012, First Majestic Silver Corp. acquired all the issued & outstanding common share of Silvermex Resources Inc., a mining company with a portfolio of exploration & production projects in Mexico.
Keith Neumeyer, President & CEO
Raymond L. Polman, B.Sc (Econ), CA, Chief Financial Officer
Salvador Garcia, Chief Operating Officer
Martin Palacios, MBA, CMC, Chief Information Officer

First Quantum Minerals Ltd.
543 Granville St., 14th Fl.
Vancouver, BC V6C 1X8
604-688-6577
Fax: 604-688-3818
888-688-6577
info@fqml.com
www.first-quantum.com
Company Type: Public
Ticker Symbol: FM / TSX; FQM / LSE
Staff Size: 14,600
Profile: Operations of the mining & metals company include mineral exploration, development, mining, smelting, & refining. First Quantum Minerals is engaged in copper & cobalt mining in Africa. The company also has interest in gold & cobalt production.
Philip K.R. Pascall, Chair/CEO
Clive Newall, President/Director
Hannes Meyer, Chief Financial Officer
Christopher Lemon, General Counsel & Corporate Secretary

Fission Uranium Corp.
#700, 1620 Dickson Ave.
Kelowna, BC V1Y 9Y2
250-868-8140
Fax: 250-868-8493
877-868-8140
info@fissionuranium.com
fissionuranium.com
Other Communications: Investor Relations, E-mail: ir@fissionuranium.com
Social Media: twitter.com/FissionUranium
www.linkedin.com/company/fission-energy-corp
Company Type: Public
Ticker Symbol: FCU / TSX
Profile: The company mines & develops uranium in the Athabasca Basin in northern Saskatchewan.
Dev Randhawa, Chief Executive Officer
Paul Charlish, Chief Financial Officer
Ross McElroy, President & COO

Focus Graphite
PO Box 116, 945 Princess St.
Kingston, ON K7L 0E9
613-241-4040
Fax: 613-241-8632
info@focusgraphite.com
www.focusgraphite.com
Social Media: www.facebook.com/focusgraphite
twitter.com/focusgraphite
www.linkedin.com/groups/Focus-Graphite-3930058
Company Type: Public
Ticker Symbol: FMS / TSX.V
Profile: Focus Graphite Inc. is a mid-tier junior mining development company with our attention geared toward high purity graphite.
Gary Economo, President & CEO
Judith T. Mazvihwa-MacLean, CFO

Foran Mining Corporation
PO Box 26028, RPO Lawson Heights
Saskatoon, SK S7K 8C1
604-488-0008
ir@foranmining.com
www.foranmining.com
Social Media: twitter.com/foranmining
Company Type: Public
Ticker Symbol: FOM / TSX.V
Patrick Soares, President & CEO
Tim Thiessen, Chief Financial Officer
Dave Fleming, Vice-President, Exploration

Formation Metals Inc.
Head Office
#1810, 999 West Hastings St.
Vancouver, BC V6C 2W2
604-682-6229
Fax: 604-682-6205
inform@formationmetals.com
www.formationmetals.com
Other Communications: Investor Relations, Phone: 604-682-6229, ext. 228
Social Media: www.facebook.com/formationmetals
twitter.com/formationmetals
Company Type: Public
Ticker Symbol: FCO / TSX
Profile: Formation Metals Inc.'s area of expertise is mineral exploration, mine development, & refining. The company owns 100% of the Idaho Cobalt Project & the Big Creek Hydrometallurgical Complex, also located in Idaho. Through its wholly owned subsidiaries, Formation Metals also has interests in base, precious metal, & uranium projects. Areas of activity are Canada, the United States, & Mexico.
J. Paul Farquharson, President & CEO
Marc Tran, Chief Financial Officer & Corporate Secretary
E.R. (Rick) Honsinger, P.Geo., Senior Vice-President

Forsys Metals Corp.
Corporate Office
PO Box 909, #200, 20 Adelaide St. East
Toronto, ON M5V 2T6
416-361-1333
info@forsysmetals.com
www.forsysmetals.com
Other Communications: Namibian Office, Phone: +264 (0)64 402 772
Company Type: Public
Ticker Symbol: FSY / TSX
Profile: Forsys Metals Corp. is a uranium producer. The company owns 100% of the Namibplaas Uranium Project & the Valencia Uranium Project, which are both located in Namibia, Africa.
Marcel Hilmer, Chief Executive Officer
Rowen Colman, Chief Financial Officer
Mark Frewin, Vice-President, Legal Affairs

Fortuna Silver Mines Inc.
#650, 200 Burrard St.
Vancouver, BC V6C 3L6
604-484-4085
Fax: 604-662-8829
info@fortunasilver.com
www.fortunasilver.com
Company Type: Public
Ticker Symbol: FVI / TSX; FSM / NYSE
Staff Size: 686
Profile: Fortuna is a silver & base metal producer. Areas of operation are southern Peru & Mexico. In 2016 they acquired Goldrock Mines Corp.
Jorge Ganoza, President & Chief Executive Officer
Luis Dario Ganoza, B.Sc. Engineering, MBA, M.Sc., Chief Financial Officer & Chief Compliance Officer
Manuel Ruiz-Canejo, Vice-President, Operations
David Volkert, Vice-President, Exploration

Fortune Minerals Limited
#1600, 148 Fullarton St.
London, ON N6A 5P3
519-858-8188
Fax: 519-858-8155
info@fortuneminerals.com
www.fortuneminerals.com
Company Type: Public
Ticker Symbol: FT / TSX
Profile: The diversified resource company has mineral deposits & exploration projects located in Canada. Projects include the Mount Klappan anthracite metallurgical coal deposit in British Columbia, & the NICO gold, colbalt, bismuth, copper deposit in the Northwest Territories.
Robin Ellis Goad, M.Sc., P.Geo., President & Chief Executive Officer
Mahendra Naik, C.A., Interim CFO

Richard P. Schryer, M.Sc., Ph.D., Director, Regulatory & Envrionmental Affairs
Troy D. Nazarewicz, CIM, FCSI, Manager, Investor Relations

Franco-Nevada Corporation
PO Box 285 Stn. Commerce Cour, #2000, 199 Bay St.
Toronto, ON M5L 1G9
416-306-6300
info@franco-nevada.com
www.franco-nevada.com
Company Type: Public
Ticker Symbol: FNV / TSX, NYSE
Staff Size: 34
Profile: Franco-Nevada Corporation has interests in large gold development & exploration projects.
David Harquail, President & Chief Executive Officer
Sandip Rana, Chief Financial Officer

Freegold Ventures
PO Box 10351, #888, 700 West Georgia St.
Vancouver, BC V7Y 1G5
604-662-7307
Fax: 604-662-3791
ask@freegoldventures.com
www.freegoldventures.com
Company Type: Public
Ticker Symbol: FVL / TSX
Profile: Freegold is focussed on the exploration and development of Alaskan gold assets.
Kristina Walcott, President & CEO
Gordon Steblin, Chief Financial Officer

Gabriel Resources Ltd.
25 Southampton Bldgs.
London, WC2A 1AL UK
ir@gabrielresources.com
www.gabrielresources.com
Company Type: Public
Ticker Symbol: GBU / TSX
Profile: Gabriel Resources Ltd. is a resource company focused on permitting and developing its world class Rosia Montana gold and silver project.
Jonathan Henry, President/CEO
Richard Brown, Chief Commercial Officer
Max Vaughan, Chief Financial Officer
Horea Avram, Vice-President, Environment

Galane Gold Ltd.
Brookfield Place
PO Box 754, #1800, 181 Bay St.
Toronto, ON M5J 2T9
www.galanegold.com
Company Type: Public
Ticker Symbol: GG / TSX
Profile: Galane Gold Ltd. is an unhedged gold producer and explorer with mining operations and exploration tenements in the Republic of Botswana.
Nicholas Brodie, CEO
Bradshaw Zinyemba, Interim CFO

GB Minerals Ltd.
#1500, 701 West Georgia St.
Vancouver, BC V7Y 1C6
604-569-0721
Fax: 604-601-3443
855-569-0721
inquire@gbminerals.com
www.gbminerals.com
Company Type: Public
Ticker Symbol: GBL / TSX.V
Profile: GB Minerals Ltd. is a Canadian mining exploration and development company that is focused on developing the Farim Phosphate Project located in Guinea-Bissau, West Africa.
Luis G. Cabrita da Silva, President & CEO
Angel Law, Chief Financial Officer & Corporate Secretary

Geologix Exploration
#501, 570 Granville St.
Vancouver, BC V6C 3P1
604-694-1742
Fax: 604-694-1744
888-694-1742
ir@geologix.ca
www.geologix.ca
Company Type: Public
Ticker Symbol: GIX / TSX
Profile: The company owns 100% of the Tepal Copper-Gold Porphyry Project in Michoacán State, Mexico.
Kiran Patanker, President & CEO
Evelyn Abbott, Chief Financial Officer

GobiMin Inc.
#2110, 120 Adelaide St. West
Toronto, ON M5H 1T1
416-915-0133
Fax: 416-363-2908
info@gobimin.com
www.gobimin.com
Company Type: Public
Ticker Symbol: GMN / TSX.V
Profile: GobiMin Inc. is engaged in the development and exploration of mineral properties, mainly in the Xinjiang Uygur Autonomous Region of China.
Felipe Tan, President & CEO
Joyce Ko, CFO, Secretary, & Vice-President, Corporate Affairs

GoGold Resources Inc.
#1301, 2000 Barrington St.
Halifax, NS B3J 3K1
902-482-1998
Fax: 902-442-1898
www.gogoldresources.com
Social Media: www.facebook.com/pages/GoGold-Resources-Inc/194248863926608
twitter.com/GoGoldResources
linkedin.com/company/gogold-resources-inc-
Company Type: Public
Ticker Symbol: GGD / TSX
Profile: GoGold Resources Inc. is a mineral resource company with active development and exploration properties in Mexico.
Bradley Langille, President/CEO
Dana M. Hatfield, Chief Financial Officer
Anis Nehme, Chief Operating Officer

Gold Mountain Mining Corp.
#1700, 700 West Pender St.
Vancouver, BC V6C 1G8
604-558-4653
Fax: 604-682-2993
www.aumtn.com
Company Type: Public
Ticker Symbol: GUM / TSX.V
Profile: Gold Mountain Mining's main focus is the Elk Gold Project, located in southern British Columbia.
Chris McLeod, President & CEO
Rodney Shier, Chief Financial Officer

Gold Standard Ventures Corp.
#610, 815 West Hastings St.
Vancouver, BC V6C 1B4
604-669-5702
Fax: 604-687-3567
info@goldstandardv.com
goldstandardv.com
Company Type: Public
Ticker Symbol: GSV / TSX.V, NYSE
Profile: Gold Standard Ventures is an advanced stage precious metals exploration company focused on Nevada.
Jonathan Awde, President & CEO
Michael N. Waldkirch, Chief Financial Officer

Goldcorp Inc.
Park Place
#3400, 666 Burrard St.
Vancouver, BC V6C 2X8
604-696-3000
Fax: 604-696-3001
info@goldcorp.com
www.goldcorp.com
Company Type: Public
Ticker Symbol: G / TSX; GG / NYSE
Staff Size: 10,652
Profile: The mining company is engaged in the acquisition & exploration of gold properties in Mexico, as well as other areas in Central & South America. In May 2016, it was announced that Goldcorp would purchase Kaminak Gold Corporation, based in Dawson City, Yukon.
David Garofalo, President & CEO
George R. Burns, Executive Vice-President & Chief Operating Officer
Russell Ball, Executive Vice-President & CFO, Corporate Development
Charlene Ripley, Executive Vice-President & General Counsel

Golden Queen Mining Co. Ltd.
#2300, 1066 West Hastings St.
Vancouver, BC V6E 3X2
778-373-1557
www.goldenqueen.com
Company Type: Public
Ticker Symbol: GQM / TSX
Staff Size: 130
Profile: The gold company has assets & operations in the Soledad Mountains, in California.
Thomas Clay, Chair & CEO
Andrée St. Germain, Chief Financial Officer & Vice-President, Finance
Robert Walish, Chief Operating Officer

Golden Reign Resources Ltd.
#501, 595 Howe St.
Vancouver, BC V6C 2T5
604-685-4655
Fax: 604-685-4675
888-685-4655
info@goldenreign.com
goldenreignresources.com
Company Type: Public
Ticker Symbol: GRR / TSX.V
Profile: A gold mining company whose main project is San Albino Gold, located in Nicaragua.
Kim Evans, President
Kevin Bullock, Chief Executive Officer
Zoran Pudar, Vice-President, Exploration

Golden Star Resources Ltd.
Sun Life Financial Tower
#1200, 150 King St. West
Toronto, ON M5H 1J9
416-583-3800
corporate@gsr.com
www.gsr.com
Other Communications: Alternate E-mail: investor@gsr.com
Company Type: Public
Ticker Symbol: GSC / TSX; GSS / AMEX
Staff Size: 1,257
Profile: The gold mining company has two operating mines located on the Ashanti Gold Belt of Ghana, West Africa. Golden Star Resources conducts its activities with a long-term commitment to the environment, health, & education. Golden Star Resources Ltd. is listed on the following stock exchanges: Toronto Stock Exchange, NYSE Amex Stock Exchange, & the Ghana Stock Exchange.
Sam Coetzer, President & Chief Executive Officer
André van Niekerk, Executive Vice-President & Chief Financial Officer
Bruce Higson-Smith, Senior Vice-President, Corporate Strategy

Golden Valley Mines Ltd.
152, ch de la Mine École
Val-d'Or, QC J9P 7B6
819-824-2808
Fax: 819-824-3379
info@goldenvalleymines.com
www.goldenvalleymines.com
Company Type: Public
Ticker Symbol: GZZ / TSX.V
Profile: Golden Valley owns gold, base-metal & energy mineral projects in Québec, Ontario & Saskatchewan.
Glen Mullan, President & CEO
Annie Karahissarian, Chief Financial Officer
Michael Rosatelli, Vice-President, Exploration

Goldgroup Mining Inc.
#1502, 1166 Alberni St.
Vancouver, BC V6E 3Z3
604-682-1943
Fax: 604-682-5596
877-655-6928
info@goldgroupmining.com
www.goldgroupmining.com
Social Media: www.facebook.com/GoldgroupMining
twitter.com/GoldgroupMining
linkedin.com/company/goldgroup-mining-inc-
Company Type: Public
Ticker Symbol: GGA / TSX
Profile: Goldgroup Mining Inc. is a gold production, development and exploration company with a portfolio of projects in Mexico.
Keith Piggott, President & Chief Executive Officer
Sam Wong, Chief Financial Officer

GoviEx Uranium Inc.
#654, 999 Canada Place
Vancouver, BC V6C 3E1
604-681-5529
info@goviex.com
www.goviex.com
Company Type: Public
Ticker Symbol: GXU / CSE
Profile: GoviEx focuses on the development & mining of uranium. It fully owns the Madaouela Project, located in north central Niger.
Daniel Major, Chief Executive Officer
Lei Wang, CFO

Gran Colombia Gold
Head Office
#1100, 333 Bay St.
Toronto, ON M5H 2R2
416-360-4653
Fax: 416-360-7783
investorrelations@grancolombiagold.com
www.grancolombiagold.com
Other Communications: Colombia Office, Phone: 57-4-448-5220
Social Media: twitter.com/GCMGold
www.linkedin.com/company/1376887
Company Type: Public
Ticker Symbol: GCM / TSX
Staff Size: 2,098
Profile: The company is focused upon gold & silver exploration, development, & production in Colombia.
Lombardo Paredes Arenas, Chief Executive Officer
Michael Davies, Chief Financial Officer
Alessandro Cecchi, Vice-President, Exploration
Jose Ignacio Noguera, Vice-President, Corporate Affairs
Peter Volk, General Counsel & Secretary

Great Panther Silver Limited
#1330, 200 Granville St.
Vancouver, BC V6C 1S4
604-608-1766
888-355-1766
info@greatpanther.com
www.greatpanther.com
Social Media: www.facebook.com/GreatPantherSilver
twitter.com/Gr8_Panther
Company Type: Public
Ticker Symbol: GPR/TSX; GPL/NYSE Amex
Profile: The silver mining & exploration company has wholly-owned operating mines in Mexico. Great Panther Silver Limited is also pursuing opportunities in Latin America.
Robert A. Archer, P.Geo., President & Chief Executive Officer
Ali Soltani, Chief Operating Officer
Jim Zadra, Chief Financial Officer
Robert Brown, Vice-President, Exploration

Guyana Goldfields Inc.
#1608, 141 Adelaide St. West
Toronto, ON M5H 3L5
416-628-5936
Fax: 416-628-5935
info@guygold.com
www.guygold.com
Company Type: Public
Ticker Symbol: GUY / TSX
Staff Size: 705
Profile: Guyana Goldfields Inc. explores & develops gold deposits in Guyana, South America.
Scott A. Caldwell, Chief Executive Officer & President
Paul J. Murphy, B.Comm., CA, Chief Financial Officer & Executive Vice-President, Finance
Dan Noone, BApSci(Geol), MBA, Vice-President, Explorations
Jacqueline Wagenaar, B.MOS, Vice-President, Investor Relations & Corporate Communications

Harte Gold
#1700, 8 King St. East
Toronto, ON M5C 1B5
416-368-0999
Fax: 416-368-5146
www.hartegold.com
Company Type: Public
Ticker Symbol: HRT / TSX
Profile: The company owns the Sugar Zone mine in northern Ontario.
Stephen Roman, President & CEO
Rain Lehari, Chief Financial Officer

Highland Copper Company Inc.
Tour Ouest
#101, 1111, rue St-Charles ouest
Longueuil, QC J4K 5G4
450-677-2455
Fax: 450-677-2601
855-677-4826
info@highlandcopper.com
www.highlandcopper.com
Company Type: Public
Ticker Symbol: HI / TSX.V
Profile: The mining company is focused on the development of copper within the Upper Peninsula in Michigan.
David Fennell, Executive Chair & Interim President & CEO
Alain Krushnisky, Chief Financial Officer
Carole Plante, Corporate Secretary & Corporate Counsel

Horizon North Logistics Inc.
#1600, 505 - 3rd St. SW
Calgary, AB T2P 3E6
866-305-6565
www.horizonnorth.ca
Social Media: www.facebook.com/WeAreHNL
twitter.com/wearehnl
Company Type: Public
Ticker Symbol: HNL / TSX
Staff Size: 1,402
Profile: Horizon North Logistics Inc.'s services include northern marine transportation & logistics, mobile structures, matting solutions, & camp management & catering. Services are provided to natural resource development projects in Canada's western provinces & northern territories. Horizon North Logistics strives to conduct its business in a responsible manner that is compatible to the environment & communities where it operates.
Rod Graham, President & CEO
Scott Matson, Chief Financial Officer & Vice-President, Finance
William H. Anderson, Vice-President, Quality, Health & Safety Environment
Lyle Guard, General Counsel & Vice-President, Legal

HudBay Minerals Inc.
#800, 25 York St.
Toronto, ON M5J 2V5
416-362-8181
Fax: 416-362-7844
info@hudbayminerals.com
www.hudbayminerals.com
Other Communications: Investors: investor.relations@hudbayminerals.com
Company Type: Public
Ticker Symbol: HBM / TSX
Staff Size: 1,797
Profile: HudBay Minerals Inc. specializes in the discovery, production, & marketing of base & precious metals. Assets are located in North & South America.
In 2011, HudBay Minerals Inc. acquired Norsemont Mining Inc.. Norsemont was advancing the Constancia Copper Project in southern Peru.
Alan Hair, President & Chief Executive Officer
David S. Bryson, CFA, Chief Financial Officer & Senior Vice-President
Patrick Donnelly, Vice-President & General Counsel
Candace Brûlé, Director, Investor Relations
416-814-4387

IAMGOLD Corporation
PO Box 153, #3200, 401 Bay St.
Toronto, ON M5H 2Y4
416-360-4710
888-464-9999
info@iamgold.com
www.iamgold.com
Social Media: www.linkedin.com/company/iamgold-corporation
Company Type: Public
Ticker Symbol: IMG / TSX, NYSE
Staff Size: 4,900
Profile: The mid-tier mining company produces gold from mines on three continents. IAMGOLD also operates Niobec Inc., which produces niobium, plus development & exploration projects.
Stephen J.J. Letwin, President & Chief Executive Officer
Carol T. Banducci, Chief Financial Officer & Executive Vice-President
Benjamin Little, Senior Vice-President, Corporate Affairs, HSS & People
Craig MacDougall, Senior Vice-President, Exploration

IC Potash Corp.
600 West Bender Blvd.
Hobbs, NM 88240
575-942-2799
www.icpotash.com
Company Type: Public
Ticker Symbol: ICP / TSX
Profile: IC Potash Corp. produces Sulphate of Potash and Sulphate of Potash Magnesia by mining its 100%-owned Ochoa property in southeast New Mexico.
Mehdi Azodi, President & CEO
Ken Kramer, Chief Financial Officer

IMPACT Silver Corp.
#1100, 543 Granville St.
Vancouver, BC V6C 1X8
604-681-0172
Fax: 604-681-6813
inquiries@impactsilver.com
www.impactsilver.com
Social Media: twitter.com/IMPACT_Silver
ca.linkedin.com/pub/impact-silver-corp/4b/a31/957
Company Type: Public
Ticker Symbol: IPT / TSX Venture
Staff Size: 275
Profile: The exploration & mining company focuses on silver. Activities take place in Mexico.
Frederick W. Davidson, CA, President & CEO
Tiffany Dang, Chief Financial Officer
George Gorzynski, Vice-President, Exploration
Jerry Huang, Manager, Investor Relations

Imperial Metals Corporation
#200, 580 Hornby St.
Vancouver, BC V6C 3B6
604-669-8959
inquiries@imperialmetals.com
www.imperialmetals.com
Other Communications: Investor Relations E-mail: investor@imperialmetals.com
Company Type: Public
Ticker Symbol: III / TSX
Staff Size: 733
Profile: Imperial Metals Corporation explores, develops, operates, & maintains mine properties. The company's main properties are the The Mount Polley copper, gold mine & the Huckleberry copper, molybdenum mine, which are both open pit mines in British Columbia. The Red Chris copper, gold property in British Columbia & the Sterling gold property in Nevada are under development.
Brian Kynoch, President
Andre Deepwell, Chief Financial Officer & Corporate Secretary
Don Parsons, Chief Operating Officer
Steve Robertson, Vice-President, Corporate Affairs

Integra Gold Corp.
PO Box 11144 Stn. Royal Centre, #2270, 1055 West Georgia St.
Vancouver, BC V6E 3P3
604-629-0891
Fax: 604-229-1055
info@integragold.com
www.integragold.com
Social Media: twitter.com/integragoldcorp
Company Type: Public
Ticker Symbol: ICG / TSX.V
Profile: The company's main project is a gold mine in Val-d'Or, Québec.
Stephen de Jong, President & CEO
Langis St-Pierre, Chief Operating Officer
Travis Gingras, Chief Financial Officer

International Tower Hill Mines Ltd. (ITH)
#2300, 1177 West Hastings St.
Vancouver, BC V6E 2K3
604-683-6332
Fax: 604-408-7499
855-428-2825
www.ithmines.com
Other Communications: Fairbanks, AK Office, Phone: 907-328-2800
Company Type: Public
Ticker Symbol: ITH / TSX; THM / NYSE
Profile: International Tower Hill Mines Ltd. is active in Alaska, where it has a 100% interest in the Livengood Gold Project, situated north of Fairbanks. International Tower Hill Mines Ltd.'s indirect subsidiary is Tower Hill Mines (US) LLC, which manages exploration & project reviews.
Thomas Irwin, President & CEO
David Cross, Chief Financial Officer
Karl Hanneman, Chief Operating Officer
Marla K. Ritchie, Corporate Secretary

INV Metals
#700, 55 University Ave.
Toronto, ON M5J 2H7
416-703-8416
Fax: 416-703-8299
questions@invmetals.com
www.invmetals.com
Company Type: Public
Ticker Symbol: INV / TSX
Profile: The international mineral resource company is engaged in exploration, acquisition, & development. INV Metals has base & precious metal projects in Canada, Namibia, & Brazil.
Candace MacGibbon, Chief Executive Officer
Kevin Canario, Chief Financial Officer
Gabriel Vinas, Corporate Controller

Ivanhoe Mines Ltd.
World Trade Centre
#654, 999 Canada Pl.
Vancouver, BC V6C 3E1
604-688-6630
info@ivanhoemines.com
www.ivanhoemines.com
Company Type: Public
Ticker Symbol: IVN / TSX, NYSE, NASDAQ
Staff Size: 670
Profile: Ivanhoe Mines, exploring in Africa since 1994, now has discoveries and development projects covering copper and zinc-copper in the Central African Copperbelt in the Democratic Republic of Congo and platinum-group metals, gold, nickel and copper in South Africa Bushveld Complex.
Lars-Eric Johansson, President/CEO
Marna Cloete, Chief Financial Officer
Mark Farren, Executive Vice-President, Operations

Jaguar Mining Inc.
#1203, 67 Yonge St.
Toronto, ON M5E 1J8
416-628-9601
www.jaguarmining.com
Company Type: Public
Ticker Symbol: JAG / TSX, NYSE
Profile: Jaguar Mining Inc. is a gold producer in Brazil with operations in a prolific greenstone belt in the state of Minas Gerais.
Rodney Lamond, CEO
Hashim Ahmed, Chief Financial Officer
Jean-Marc Lopez, Vice-President, Geology & Exploration

Karnalyte Resources Inc.
3150B Faithfull Ave.
Saskatoon, SK S7K 8H3
306-986-1486
Fax: 306-986-1487
info@karnalyte.com
www.karnalyte.com
Social Media: www.facebook.com/KarnalyteResources
twitter.com/Karnalyte
Company Type: Public
Ticker Symbol: KRN / TSX
Profile: Karnalyte Resources explores for & develops agricultural & industrial potash & magnesium products. The company's region of activity is near Wynyard, Saskatchewan.
Robin L. Phinney, P.Eng., President
Quentin Plester, Executive Vice-President & Corporate Counsel
Siu Ma, MBA, P.Eng, Executive Vice-President & COO

KazaX Minerals Inc.
Arman Business Center
#630, 6 Saryarka Ave.
Astana, 010000 Kazakhstan
info@kazaxmineralsinc.com
www.kazaxmineralsinc.com
Other Communications: Phone: +011 7 717 279 0395
Company Type: Public
Ticker Symbol: KZX / TSX.V
Profile: KazarX Minerals focuses on the development & exploration of iron ore. Their main mining site is in northwestern Kazakhstan.
Mohamad Chafic, President & CEO
Nuriya Kamaledinova, Interim CFO

Kinross Gold Corporation
25 York St., 17th Fl.
Toronto, ON M5J 2V5
416-365-5123
Fax: 416-363-6622
866-561-3636
info@kinross.com
www.kinross.com
Social Media: www.facebook.com/pages/Kinross-Gold/164891496883427
twitter.com/kinrossgold
www.linkedin.com/company/kinross-gold-corporation
Company Type: Public
Ticker Symbol: K / TSX; KGC / NYSE
Profile: Formed in 1993, Kinross Gold Corporation explores, acquires, mines, & processes gold & silver ore in North & South America.
The company aims to minimize its environmental footprint through its Guiding Principles for Corporate Responsibility & its corporate Environmental Policy.
J. Paul Rollinson, President & CEO
Tony S. Giardini, Exec. Vice-President & Chief Financial Officer
Warwick Morley-Jepson, Executive Vice-President & Chief Operating Officer
Tom Elliott, Senior Vice-President, Investor Relations & Corporate Development

Kirkland Lake Gold Inc.
#1430, 95 Wellington St. West
Toronto, ON M5J 2N7
416-840-7884
866-384-2924
info@klgold.com
www.klgold.com
Social Media: www.linkedin.com/company/kirkland-lake-gold
Company Type: Public
Ticker Symbol: KGI / TSX, AIM
Staff Size: 1,389

Profile: Kirkland Lake Gold Inc. is an operating and exploration gold company located in Kirkland Lake, ON in the Southern Abitibi gold belt. In 2016, Kirkland Lake Gold Inc. acquired St. Andrew Goldfields Ltd.
Tony Makuch, President/CEO
Perry Ing, Chief Financial Officer
Chris Stewart, Vice-President, Operations
Suzette Ramcharan, Director, Investor Relations

Kivalliq Energy Corporation
#1020, 800 West Pender St.
Vancouver, BC V6C 2V6

604-646-4527
Fax: 604-646-4526
888-331-2269
info@kivalliqenergy.com
www.kivalliqenergy.com

Company Type: Public
Ticker Symbol: KIV / TSX
Profile: Kivalliq Energy Corporation is a uranium exploration company advancing the highest grade uranium deposit, outside of Saskatchewan's Athabasca Basin.
Jim Paterson, Chief Executive Officer
Michelle Yeung, Chief Financial Officer
Andrew Berry, Chief Operating Officer

Klondex Mines Ltd.
#2200, 1055 West Hastings St.
Vancouver, BC V6E 2E9

www.klondexmines.com
Social Media: twitter.com/KlondexIR

Company Type: Public
Ticker Symbol: KDX / TSX; KLNDF / OTCQX
Profile: Klondex Mines Ltd. is primarily engaged in the surface and underground exploration and development of its 100% owned Fire Creek gold property in North Central Nevada.
Paul Andre Huet, President & CEO
Barry Dahl, Chief Financial Officer

Kobex Capital Corp.
Also Known As: Kobex
Three Bentall Centre
PO Box 49131, #1703, 595 Burrard St.
Vancouver, BC V7X 1J1

647-818-2920
Fax: 604-681-4692
investor@kobex-capital.com
kobex-capital.com

Company Type: Public
Ticker Symbol: KXM / TSX.V
Philip du Toit, President and CEO
John Downes, Chief Financial Officer

Kootenay Silver
#1820, 1055 West Hastings St.
Vancouver, BC V6E 2E9

604-601-5650
Fax: 604-683-2249
888-601-5650
investor@kootenaysilver.com
www.kootenaysilver.com
Social Media: twitter.com/KootenaySilver

Company Type: Public
Ticker Symbol: KTN / TSX.V
James M. McDonald, President & CEO
Rajwant Kang, Chief Financial Officer

KWG Resources Inc.
#2750, 600, boul de Maisonneuve ouest
Montréal, QC H3A 3J2

416-646-1374
Fax: 416-644-0592
888-644-1374
info@kwgresources.com
www.kwgresources.com
Social Media:
www.facebook.com/pages/KWG-Resources/133274640872
twitter.com/kwgresources

Company Type: Public
Ticker Symbol: KWG / CSE
Profile: KWG Resources Inc is an exploration stage company that is participating in the discovery, delineation and development of chromite deposits in the James Bay Lowlands of Northern Ontario.
Frank C. Smeenk, President & Chief Executive Officer
Thomas E. (Ted) Masters, Chief Financial Officer
M.J. (Moe) Lavigne, Vice-President, Exploration & Development

Laramide Resources Ltd.
The Exchange Tower
PO Box 99, #3680, 130 King St. West
Toronto, ON M5X 1B1

416-599-7363
Fax: 416-599-4959
www.laramide.com

Company Type: Public
Ticker Symbol: LAM / TSX, ASX
Profile: Laramide Resources Ltd. explores for & develops uranium assets. Wholly owned uranium assets are located in the United States & Australia. The company's flagship project is Westmoreland in Queensland, Australia.
Marc Henderson, President & Chief Executive Officer
Dennis Gibson, Chief Financial Officer
Greg Ferron, Vice-President, Corporate Development & Investor Relations
Bryn Jones, Chief Operating Officer

Largo Resources Ltd.
Corporate Headquarters
#1101, 55 University Ave.
Toronto, ON M5J 2H7

416-861-9797
info@largoresources.com
www.largoresources.com
Social Media:
www.facebook.com/pages/Largo-Resources/232451330133020
twitter.com/LargoResources1
www.linkedin.com/company/largo-resources-ltd-

Company Type: Public
Ticker Symbol: LGO / TSX Venture
Profile: The mineral resource exploration & development company holds 100% interest in the following projects: the Currais Novos Tungsten Tailing Project in Brazil, the Campo Alegre de Lourdes Iron-Vanadium Project in Brazil, & the Northern Dancer Tungsten-Molybdenum property in the Yukon Territory. Largo Resources Ltd. also has a 90% interest in the Maracás Vanadium Project, which is located in Brazil.
Mark Smith, President & CEO
Ernest Cleave, Chief Financial Officer
Andy Campbell, Vice-President, Exploration

LEADFX Inc.
#3001, 1 Adelaide St. East
Toronto, ON M5C 2V9

416-867-9298
info@leadfxinc.com
www.leadfxinc.com
Other Communications: Australian Office, Phone: 61 (8) 9267 7000

Company Type: Public
Ticker Symbol: IVW / TSX
Profile: The international metals mining compnay is engaged in exploration & development. LEADFX owns the Magellan Mine in western Australia. The company also has an earn-in agreement on the Prairie Downs Project, which is situated north of the Magellan Mine.
Rob Scargill, President & Chief Executive Officer
Lincoln Greenridge, Chief Financial Officer
D'Arcy Doherty, Vice-President, Legal & General Counsel

Levon Resources Ltd.
#500, 666 Burrard St.
Vancouver, BC V6C 2X8

778-379-0040
ir@levon.com
www.levon.com

Company Type: Public
Ticker Symbol: LVN / TSX
Profile: Levon Resources is exploring one of the world's largest silver resources at the company's 100%-owned Cordero Project in northwest Mexico.
Ron Tremblay, President/CEO
Nigel Kirkwood, Chief Financial Officer
Vic Chevillon, Vice-President, Exploration

Lexam VG Gold Inc.
PO Box 24, #2800, 150 King St. West
Toronto, ON M5H 1J9

647-258-0395
Fax: 647-258-0408
866-441-0690
info@lexamvggold.com
www.lexamvggold.com

Company Type: Public
Ticker Symbol: LEX / TSX; LEXVF / OTCQX
Profile: Lexam VG Gold has four gold deposits located in Timmins, Ontario.
Andrew Iaboni, Chief Financial Officer
Ken Guy, Manager, Exploration
Gerry McDonald, Manager, Operations

Lion One Metals Ltd.
311 West 1st St.
North Vancouver, BC V7M 1B5

604-998-1250
Fax: 604-998-1253
855-805-1250
www.liononemetals.com
Social Media: twitter.com/liononemetals

Company Type: Public
Ticker Symbol: LIO / TSX.V
Profile: Lion One Metals Limited is based in North Vancouver, BC, and is focused on the acquisition, exploration and development of mineral projects.
Walter H. Berukoff, Chief Executive Officer
Samantha Shorter, Chief Financial Officer
Stephen Mann, Managing Director

Lithium Americas
#1100, 355 Burrard St.
Vancouver, BC V6C 2G8

778-656-5820
info@lithiumamericas.com
lithiumamericas.com
Social Media: twitter.com/lithiumamericas

Company Type: Public
Ticker Symbol: LAC / TSX
Profile: A lithium mining company.
Tom Hodgson, Chief Executive Officer
John Kanellitsas, President
Myron Manternach, Executive Vice-President, Finance

Loncor Resources Inc.
First Canadian Pl.
#7070, 100 King St. West
Toronto, ON M5X 1E3

416-366-2221
Fax: 416-366-7722
info@loncor.com
www.loncor.com

Company Type: Public
Ticker Symbol: LN / TSX; LON / NYSE
Profile: Loncor Resources Inc. is a gold exploration company focused on the Democratic Republic of the Congo (DRC).
Arnold Kondrat, President & CEO
Donat Madilo, Chief Financial Officer

Los Andes Copper Ltd.
Marine Bldg.
#1260, 355 Burrard St.
Vancouver, BC V6C 2G8

604-681-2802
Fax: 604-682-2802
info@losandescopper.com
www.losandescopper.com

Company Type: Public
Ticker Symbol: LA / TSX Venture
Profile: Los Andes Copper Ltd. is an exploration & development company. It holds an interest in a copper-molybdenum deposit in Chile.
Antony Amberg, President & CEO
Aurora Davidson, Chief Financial Officer

Lucara Diamond Corp.
#2000, 885 West Georgia St.
Vancouver, BC V6C 3E8

604-689-7842
Fax: 604-689-4250
www.lucaradiamond.com
Social Media: www.facebook.com/LucaraDiamondCorporation
twitter.com/LucaraDiamond
www.linkedin.com/company/lucara-diamond-corp-

Company Type: Public
Ticker Symbol: LUC / TSX
Profile: Lucara Diamond Corp. is a new diamond producer. It's two key assets are the Karowe mine in Botswana and the Mothae project in Lesotho.
William Lamb, President/CEO
Paul Day, Chief Operating Officer
Glenn Kondo, Chief Financial Officer

Luna Gold Corp.
#1400, 400 Burrard St.
Vancouver, BC V6C 3A6

604-558-0560
Fax: 604-558-0561
info@lunagold.com
www.lunagold.com
Other Communications: Investor Relations E-mail: ir@lunagold.com
Social Media: twitter.com/LunaGoldCorp
www.linkedin.com/company/luna-gold-corp-

Company Type: Public
Ticker Symbol: LGC / TSX
Staff Size: 174

Profile: Luna Gold Corp. is in the business of producing, expanding, developing and exploring gold assets in Brazil.
Christian Milau, CEO
Peter Hardie, Chief Financial Officer

Lundin Gold Inc.
#2000, 885 West Georgia St.
Vancouver, BC V6C 3E8

604-689-7842
Fax: 604-689-4250
888-689-7842
info@lundingold.com
www.lundingold.com
Social Media: www.facebook.com/LundinGold
twitter.com/LundinGoldEC

Company Type: Public
Ticker Symbol: LUG / TSX
Profile: Lundin Gold's main project is Fruta del Norte in Ecuador.
Ron F. Hochstein, President & CEO
Alessandro Bitelli, Executive Vice-President & CFO
Sheila Colman, Corporate Secretary & Vice-President, Legal
Nicholas Teasdale, Vice-President, Exploration
Anthony George, Vice-President, Operational Development

Lundin Mining Corporation
Corporate Head Office
PO Box 38, #1500, 150 King St. West
Toronto, ON M5H 1J9

416-342-5560
Fax: 416-348-0303
info@lundinmining.com
www.lundinmining.com
Other Communications: Operations Office in UK, Phone: +44 1444 411 900

Company Type: Public
Ticker Symbol: LUN / TSX; LUMI / OMX
Staff Size: 7,900
Profile: Lundin Mining Corporation was formed in 1994. The corporation is engaged in the exploration, mining, & production of base metal mineral resources, such as copper, nickel, zinc, & lead. Operations are located in Spain, Portugal, & Sweden. The corporation also holds a development project pipeline & an equity stake in a copper & cobalt project in the Democratic Republic of Congo.
Paul Conibear, President & Chief Executive Officer
Julie Lee Harrs, Senior Vice-President, Corporate Development
Marie Inkster, Senior Vice-President/Chief Financial Officer
Neil O'Brien, Senior Vice-President, Exploration & New Business Development
Sue Boxall, Vice-President, Human Resources

Lupaka Gold Corp.
#220, 800 West Pender St.
Vancouver, BC V6C 2V6

604-681-5900
Fax: 604-637-8794
info@lupakagold.com
www.lupakagold.com

Company Type: Public
Ticker Symbol: LPK / TSX.V
Profile: Lupaka Gold Corp. is a gold explorer with geographic diversification and balance through its asset-based resource projects spread across three regions of Peru.
Gordon Ellis, Chair/CEO
Darryl F. Jones, CFO

MAG Silver Corp.
#770, 800 West Pender St.
Vancouver, BC V6C 2V6

604-630-1399
Fax: 604-681-0894
info@magsilver.com
www.magsilver.com
Social Media: www.facebook.com/Magsilverc
twitter.com/magsilvercorp

Company Type: Public
Ticker Symbol: MAG / TSX; MVG / NYSE.A
Profile: MAG Silver Corp. is focused on advancing two significant projects located within the Mexican Silver Belt.
George Paspalas, President & CEO
Larry Taddei, Chief Financial Officer
Michael Curlook, Vice-President, Investor Relations & Communications

Majestic Gold Corp.
#306, 1688 - 152 St.
Surrey, BC V4A 4N2

604-560-9060
Fax: 604-560-9062
info@majesticgold.com
www.majesticgold.com

Company Type: Public
Ticker Symbol: MJS / TSX.V
Profile: Majestic Gold Corp. is an emerging gold producer in Shandong Province, China.
Stephen Kenwood, President & CEO
James Mackie, CFO & Corporate Secretary

Major Drilling Group International Inc.
Corporate Office
#200, 111 St George St.
Moncton, NB E1C 1T7

506-857-8636
Fax: 506-857-9211
866-264-3986
info@majordrilling.com
www.majordrilling.com
Other Communications: Investors: if@majordrilling.com; HR: hr@majordrilling.com

Company Type: Public
Ticker Symbol: MDI / TSX
Profile: Major Drilling Group International's drilling operations are carried out in the following areas: Canada, the United States, Central America, South America, Africa, Armenia, Indonesia, & Australia. Drilling services include geotechnical, environmental drilling, surface & underground coring, reverse circulation, water-well, shallow gas, & coal-bed methane. The company primarily serves the mining industry.
Denis Larocque, President & Chief Executive Officer
David Balser, Chief Financial Officer
Kelly Johnson, Vice-President, Latin American & West African Operations
Larry Pisto, Vice-President, North American Operations

Mandalay Resources Corporation
#330, 76 Richmond St. East
Toronto, ON M5C 1P1

647-260-1566
www.mandalayresources.com
Social Media: twitter.com/MandalayAuAg

Company Type: Public
Ticker Symbol: MND / TSX
Staff Size: 764
Profile: Mandalay Resources is a mineral exploration company focused on copper-silver prospects in northern Chile.
Mark Sander, President & Chief Executive Officer
Sanjay Swarup, Chief Financial Officer
Toni Streczynski, Vice-President, Processing & Metallurgy

Manitok Energy Inc.
#2600, 585 - 8th Ave. SW
Calgary, AB T2P 1G1

403-984-1750
Fax: 403-984-1749
www.manitokenergy.com

Company Type: Public
Ticker Symbol: MEI / TSX Venture
Profile: The oil & gas exploration & development company concentrates on conventional oil & gas reservoirs. Manitok's Energy's area of operation is the Canadian foothills.
Massimo M. Geremia, President & CEO
Cameron Vouri, Chief Operating Officer
Robert Dion, CA, Chief Financial Officer & Vice-President, Finance
Tim Jerhoff, Vice-President, Production & Engineering
Robert Brown, Senior Manager, Business Development

Marathon Gold
#501, 10 King St. East
Toronto, ON M5C 1C3

416-987-2366
www.marathon-gold.com

Company Type: Public
Ticker Symbol: MOZ / TSX
Profile: Marathon Gold is a gold resource development company, with projects located in Newfoundland and Labrador, Idaho and Oregon.
Phillip C. Walford, President & CEO
Jim Kirke, CFO, Corporate Secretary & Vice-President, Finance
Sherry M. Dunsworth, Vice-President, Exploration
Christopher Haldane, Manager, Investor Relations
chaldane@marathon-gold.com

Marlin Gold Mining Ltd.
#250, 1199 West Hastings St.
Vancouver, BC V6E 3T5

604-646-1580
Fax: 604-642-2411
info@marlingold.com
www.marlingold.com

Company Type: Public
Ticker Symbol: MLN / TSX.V
Staff Size: 148
Profile: The gold & silver mining company has properties in Mexico & Arizona. It is the parent company of Sailfish Royalty Corp.
Akiba Leisman, Interim CEO
Jesse Muñoz, Interim COO
Scott Kelly, Chief Financial Officer

Mason Graphite
#600, 3030 Le Carrefour Blvd.
Laval, QC H7T 2P5

514-289-3580
www.masongraphite.com
Social Media:
facebook.com/pages/Mason-Graphite-Inc/494698070611249
twitter.com/MasonGraphite

Company Type: Public
Ticker Symbol: LLG / TSX.V
Profile: A mining & mineral processing company.
Benoît Gascon, Chief Executive Officer
Luc Veilleux, Executive Vice-President, Chief Financial Officer & Corporate Secretary

Maya Gold & Silver
#207, 10 de la Seigneurie Blvd. East
Blainville, QC J7C 3V5

450-435-0700
Fax: 450-435-0705
mayagoldsilver.com
Social Media: www.facebook.com/MayaGoldSilver
twitter.com/MayaGoldSilver

Company Type: Public
Ticker Symbol: MYA / TSX.v
Profile: A mining company whose main assets are in Morocco.
Guy Goulet, Chief Executive Officer
Noureddine Mokaddem, President
Alain Lévesque, Chief Financial Officer

Meadow Bay Gold Corp.
#210, 905 West Pender St.
Vancouver, BC V6C 1L6

604-641-4450
Fax: 855-557-4622
855-777-4622
info@meadowbaygold.com
meadowbaygold.com
Social Media:
www.facebook.com/Meadow-Bay-Gold-Corp-197526263680250
twitter.com/MeadowBay_Gold

Company Type: Public
Ticker Symbol: MAY / TSX
Profile: The company owns the Atlanta Gold Mine Project in Lincoln County, Nevada.
Christopher Crupi, Chief Executive Officer
Keith Margetson, Chief Financial Officer

Mega Uranium Ltd.
#502, 211 Yonge St.
Toronto, ON M5B 1M4

416-643-7630
Fax: 416-941-1090
info@megauranium.com
www.megauranium.com
Other Communications: Alternate E-mail: ir@megauranium.com
Company Type: Public
Ticker Symbol: MGA / TSX
Profile: Mega Uranium is a producer of uranium through the development of its advanced Lake Maitland Project in Western Australia.
Richard Patricio, President & CEO
Carmelo Marrelli, Chief Financial Officer

Melior Resources Inc.
#2500, 120 Adelaide St. West
Toronto, ON M5H 1T1

416-644-1217
www.meliorresources.com

Company Type: Public
Ticker Symbol: MLR / TSX.V
Profile: The company's main project in the Goondicum Ilmenite & Apatite Mine in Australia.
Mark McCauley, Chief Executive Officer
Thomas Masney, Chief Financial Officer

Merrex Gold
Sun Tower
#802, 1550 Bedford Hwy.
Bedford, NS B4A 1E6

902-832-5555
info@merrexgold.com
www.merrexgold.com

Company Type: Public
Ticker Symbol: MXI / TSX.V
Profile: A gold mining company who has projects in Mali & Guinea.
Gregory Isenor, President & CEO
John Cumming, Chief Financial Officer

Metalo
#1600, 141 Adelaide St. West
Toronto, ON M5H 3L5
902-233-7255
Fax: 902-835-0585
info@metalo.ca
www.metalo.ca
Company Type: Public
Ticker Symbol: MMI / CSE
Profile: Muskrat is a mineral exploration firm.
Francis MacKenzie, President
C. H. (Bert) Loveless, COO
Lorne S. MacFarlane, CFO

Metanor Resources Inc.
#2, 2872, ch Sullivan
Val-d'Or, QC J9P 0B9
819-825-8678
Fax: 819-825-8224
info@metanor.ca
www.metanor.ca
Social Media:
www.facebook.com/Ressources-Métanor-175943052541375
www.linkedin.com/company/6278179
Company Type: Public
Ticker Symbol: MTO / TSX Venture
Staff Size: 250
Profile: Metanor Resources Inc. is a gold mining company, with operations in Québec.
Ghislain Morin, President & CEO
Claudine Lévesque, Chief Financial Officer
Pascal Hamelin, Vice-President, Operations
Anik Gendron, Corporate Secretary

Midland Exploration
#4000, 1, Place Ville Marie
Montréal, QC H3B 4M4
450-420-5977
Fax: 450-420-5978
info@midlandexploration.com
www.midlandexploration.com
Company Type: Public
Ticker Symbol: MD / TSX.V
Profile: A gold & mineral mining company.
Gino Roger, President & CEO
Ingrid Martin, Chief Financial Officer

Minco Silver Corporation
PO Box 11176, #2772, 1055 West Georgia St.
Vancouver, BC V6E 3R5
604-688-8002
Fax: 604-688-8030
888-288-8288
pr@mincosilver.ca
www.mincosilver.ca
Other Communications: Beijing Office: 86-10-5957-5377
Company Type: Public
Ticker Symbol: MSV / TSX
Profile: Minco Silver Corporation acquires & develops silver projects. The company owns a 90% interest in the Fuwan Silver Deposit, which is located in Guangdong China.
Ken Z. Cai, Chair & Chief Executive Officer
Jennifer Trevitt, Corporate Secretary

Mirasol Resources Ltd.
#910, 850 West Hastings St.
Vancouver, BC V6C 1E1
604-602-9989
Fax: 604-609-9946
844-695-1177
contact@mirasolresources.com
www.mirasolresources.com
Company Type: Public
Ticker Symbol: MRZ / TSX.V
Profile: Mirasol Resources is a premier prospect generator engaged in exploration and discovery in emerging areas in the Americas.
Stephen C. Nano, President & CEO
Mahesh Liyanage, Chief Financial Officer
Timothy W. Heenan, Exploration Manager

Monument Mining Limited
#1580, 1100 Melville St.
Vancouver, BC V6E 4A6
604-638-1661
Fax: 604-638-1663
www.monumentmining.com
Company Type: Public
Ticker Symbol: MMY / TSX Venture
Staff Size: 260
Profile: Monument Mining is a Canadian-based gold producer with gold production, gold development stage properties, exploration properties, and land positions in Malaysia.
Robert F. Baldock, CA(M), FCPA, FCMC, President & Chief Executive Officer
Cathy Zhai, B.Sc., CGA, Chief Financial Officer & Corporate Secretary
Zaidi Harun, B.Sc., Vice-President, Business Development

Mountain Province Diamonds Inc.
PO Box 216, #2315, 161 Bay St.
Toronto, ON M5J 2S1
416-361-3562
Fax: 416-603-8565
www.mountainprovince.com
Company Type: Public
Ticker Symbol: MPV / TSX; MDM / NASDAQ
Profile: Mountain Province Diamonds Inc. is engaged in diamond exploration & development. The Kennady Lake diamond project in the Northwest Territories is being developed by the company, in partnership with De Beers Canada.
Patrick Evans, B.A., B.Sc., President, Chief Executive Officer, & Director
Bruce C. Ramsden, Chief Financial Officer & Vice-President, Finance

Mustang Minerals Corp.
#305, 3335 Yonge St.
Toronto, ON M4N 2M1
416-955-4773
info@mustangminerals.com
www.mustangminerals.com
Company Type: Public
Ticker Symbol: MUM / TSX.V
Profile: Mustang Minerals is focused on the development of nickel, copper & platinum metals. The company's project is located in southeast Manitoba.
Robin Dunbar, President
Rodger Roden, CA, Chief Financial Officer
Carey Galeschuk, P.Geo, Vice-President, Exploration
David Black, Vice-President, Investor Relations

Nautilus Minerals Inc.
#1702, 141 Adelaide St. West
Toronto, ON M5H 3L5
416-551-1100
Fax: 416-703-5246
investor@nautilusminerals.com
www.nautilusminerals.com
Other Communications: hr@nautilusminerals.com
Company Type: Public
Ticker Symbol: NUS / TSX; NUSMF / OCTQX
Profile: Nautilus Minerals Inc is leading exploration of the seafloor for high grade copper, gold silver and zinc.
Michael Johnston, President & CEO
Shontel Norgate, Chief Financial Officer

Nevada Copper Corp.
#1238, 200 Granville St.
Vancouver, BC V6C 1S4
604-683-8992
Fax: 604-681-0122
877-648-8266
info@nevadacopper.com
www.nevadacopper.com
Other Communications: Yerington, Nevada Office, Phone: 885-463-3510
Company Type: Public
Ticker Symbol: NCU / TSX
Profile: Nevada Copper Corp. owns 100% of a development property in the Walker Lane mineralized belt situated in western Nevada.
Giulio Bonifacio, President & Chief Executive Officer
Robert McKnight, Chief Financial Officer & Executive Vice-President
Eugene Toffolo, Vice-President, Investor Relations & Communications
Timothy M. Dyhr, Vice-President, Environment & External Relations
Greg French, CPG, M.Sc., Vice-President, Exploration & Project Development
Catherine Tanaka, Corporate Secretary

Nevsun Resources Ltd.
#760, 669 Howe St.
Vancouver, BC V6C 0B4
604-623-4700
Fax: 604-623-4701
888-600-2200
ir@nevsun.com
www.nevsun.com
Social Media: twitter.com/NevsunNSU
www.linkedin.com/company/nevsun-resources
Company Type: Public
Ticker Symbol: NSU / TSX, NYSE
Staff Size: 1,230
Profile: Nevsun Resources handles the production of high-grade, low-cost gold, copper, silver, and zinc. Nevsun Resources is operator of the Bisha Mine in Eritrea (East Africa).
Cliff T. Davis, Chief Executive Officer
Frazer Bourchier, Chief Operating Officer
Tom Whelan, Chief Financial Officer

New Gold Inc.
Brookfield Place
#3510, 181 Bay St.
Toronto, ON M5J 2T3
416-324-6000
Fax: 416-324-9494
888-315-9715
info@newgold.com
www.newgold.com
Social Media: twitter.com/NewGoldInc
Company Type: Public
Ticker Symbol: NGD / TSX, AMEX
Profile: The intermediate gold mining company has assets in Canada, the United States, Mexico, Australia, & Chile.
Brian Penny, Exec. Vice-President/CFO
David Schummer, Executive Vice-President & COO

New Millennium Iron Corp.
Executive Office
1303, av Greene, 2e étage
Montréal, QC H3Z 2A7
514-935-3204
Fax: 514-935-9650
info@nmliron.com
www.nmliron.com
Other Communications: Calgary, AB: 403-296-4470; St. John's NL: 709-722-5714
Company Type: Public
Ticker Symbol: NML / TSX
Profile: New Millennium Iron Corp. controls the Millennium Iron Range, which is located in the provinces of Newfoundland & Labrador & Québec. The corporation & Tata Steel Limited are working together to advance the DSO Project in the same region.
Robert Patzelt, President & CEO
Mark Freedman, Chief Financial Officer
Stephen Fontanals, Vice-President, Adminstration
Ernest Dempsey, Vice-President, Marketing & Corporate Affairs

Newmarket Gold Corp.
#1680, 200 Burrard St.
Vancouver, BC V6C 3L6
604-559-8040
Fax: 604-681-6112
www.newmarketgoldinc.com
Company Type: Public
Ticker Symbol: NMI / TSX
Staff Size: 562
Profile: Newmarket owns three mines across Australia. In July 2015, Newmarket merged with Crocodile Gold, to become a top 20 Canadian listed gold mining company.
Douglas Forster, President & CEO
Robert Dufour, Chief Financial Officer
Darren Hall, Chief Operating Officer
Blayne Johnson, Executive Vice-President
Douglas Hurst, Vice-President, Corporate Development

NexGen Energy Ltd.
#3150, 1021 West Hastings St.
Vancouver, BC V6E 0C3
604-428-4112
Fax: 604-428-4113
www.nexgenenergy.ca
Company Type: Public
Ticker Symbol: NXE / TSX.V
Profile: The company explores & develops uranium in the Athabasca Basin, located in Saskatchewan.
Leigh Curyer, Chief Executive Officer
Grace Marosits, Chief Financial Officer
Garrett Ainsworth, Vice-President, Exploration & Development
Travis McPherson, Corporate Development Manager

Nighthawk Gold Corp.
#301, 141 Adelaide St. West
Toronto, ON M5H 3L5
416-628-5940
Fax: 416-628-5911
info@nighthawkgold.com
www.nighthawkgold.com
Company Type: Public
Ticker Symbol: NHK / TSX.V
Profile: Nighthawk is a Canadian-based exploration company focused on acquiring and developing gold mineral properties in the Northwest Territories.
Michael Byron, President/CEO & Chief Geologist
Michael Leskovec, Chief Financial Officer

Niocorp Developments
#115, 7000 South Yosemite St.
Centennial, CO 80112 USA

720-639-4647
niocorp.com

Company Type: Public
Ticker Symbol: NB / TSX
Profile: The company is currently developing a niobium/scandium/titanium project in Elk Creek, Nebraska.
Mark Smith, President & CEO
Neal Shah, Chief Financial Officer
John Ashburn, Vice-President & General Counsel

Noranda Income Fund
First Canadian Place
PO Box 403, #6900, 100 King St. West
Toronto, ON M5X 1E3

info@norandaincomefund.com
www.norandaincomefund.com

Company Type: Public
Ticker Symbol: NIF.UN / TSX
Staff Size: 574
Profile: The Fund's main asset is CEZinc, a zinc processing facility in Salaberry-de-Valleyfield, Québec. Canadian Electrolytic Zinc Limited operates & manages the CEZ processing facility. The facility has obtained ISO 9001 & ISO 14001 certification to cover all environmental processes at the plant.
Eva Carissimi, President/Chief Executive Officer
Michael Boone, Chief Financial Officer & Vice-President
416-775-1561

North American Nickel Inc.
PO Box 63623 Stn. Capilano, Vancouver, BC V7P 3P1

604-770-4334
Fax: 604-770-0334
866-816-0118
info@northamericannickel.com
www.northamericannickel.com
Social Media: twitter.com/namericannickel
www.linkedin.com/company/north-american-nickel

Company Type: Public
Ticker Symbol: NAN / TSX
Profile: A nickel mining company.
Keith Morrison, Chief Executive Officer
Mark Fedikow, President
Cheryl Messier, Chief Financial Officer

North American Palladium Ltd. (NAP)
#402, 1 University Ave.
Toronto, ON M5J 2J2

416-360-7590
Fax: 416-360-7709
info@nap.com
www.napalladium.com
Other Communications: Investor Relations E-mail: ir@nap.com

Company Type: Public
Ticker Symbol: PDL / TSX
Staff Size: 447
Profile: NAP is an established precious metals producer that has been operating its flagship Lac des Iles mine (LDI) located in Ontario.
Jim Gallagher, President/CEO
Timothy Hill, CFO/Vice-President, Finance
David Peck, Vice-President, Exploration

Northcliff Resources Ltd.
1040 West Georgia St., 15th Fl.
Vancouver, BC V6E 4H1

604-684-6365
Fax: 604-684-8092
800-667-2114
info@hdimining.com
www.northcliffresources.com
Social Media: www.facebook.com/482066445142167
twitter.com/HDI_Northcliff

Company Type: Public
Ticker Symbol: NCF / TSX
Profile: The company owns the Sisson Tungsten-Molybdenum Project, which has a tungsten-molybdenum deposit.
Christopher Zahovskis, President & CEO
Bryce Hamming, Chief Financial Officer

Northern Dynasty Minerals Ltd.
1040 West Georgia St., 15th Fl.
Vancouver, BC V6E 4H1

604-684-6365
Fax: 604-684-8092
800-667-2114
info@northerndynasty.com
www.northerndynastyminerals.com

Company Type: Public
Ticker Symbol: NDM / TSX; NAK / NYSE
Profile: Northern Dynasty Minerals Ltd. is a mineral exploration company focused on the Pebble gold-copper-molybdenum project in Alaska.
Ronald Thiessen, President & CEO
Marchand Snyman, Chief Financial Officer

Northern Vertex Mining Corp.
#1820, 1055 West Hastings St.
Vancouver, BC V6E 2E9

604-601-3656
855-633-8798
info@northernvertex.com
www.northernvertex.com
Social Media: twitter.com/Northern_Vertex

Company Type: Public
Ticker Symbol: NEE / TSX.V
Profile: A mining company that owns 100% of the Moss Mine Gold-Silver Project in Arizona.
J.R.H. Whittington, President & CEO
Ed J. Duda, Chief Financial Officer

NovaCopper Inc.
#1950, 777 Dunsmuir St.
Vancouver, BC V7Y 1K4

604-638-8088
Fax: 604-638-0644
855-638-8088
info@novacopper.com
www.novacopper.com
Other Communications: Employment Inquiries, E-mail: careers@novacopper.com
Social Media: www.facebook.com/novacopper

Company Type: Public
Ticker Symbol: NCQ / TSX, NYSE-MKT
Profile: NovaCopper Inc. is dedicated to advancing exploration at the Upper Kobuk Mineral Projects ("UKMP"), high-grade copper-zinc-lead-gold-silver properties in Northwest Alaska.
Rick Van Nieuwenhuyse, President & CEO
Elaine M. Sanders, Chief Financial Officer & Corporate Secretary

NovaGold Resources Inc.
PO Box 24, #720, 789 West Pender St.
Vancouver, BC V6C 1H2

604-669-6227
Fax: 604-669-6272
866-669-6227
info@novagold.net
www.novagold.com
Social Media: www.facebook.com/NovaGold
twitter.com/novagold
www.linkedin.com/company/novagold

Company Type: Public
Ticker Symbol: NG / TSX, AMEX
Profile: Novagold is focused on permitting and developing its 50%-owned flagship property, Donlin Gold, one of the world's largest known undeveloped gold deposits. Novagold also owns Galore Creek copper-gold-silver project BC.
Gregory A. Lang, President/CEO
David Ottewell, CFO & Vice-President
Mélanie Hennessey, Vice-President, Corporate Communications

OceanaGold Corp.
#1910, 777 Hornby St.
Vancouver, BC V6Z 1S4

604-235-3360
info@oceanagold.com
www.oceanagold.com
Social Media: twitter.com/OceanaGold
www.linkedin.com/company/oceana-gold

Company Type: Public
Ticker Symbol: OGC / TSX, ASX, NZX
Staff Size: 1,551
Profile: The gold producer has a portfolio of exploration, development, & operating assets in the Asia Pacific region.
Michael Wilkes, Chief Executive Officer
Mark Chamberlain, Executive Vice-President & Chief Financial Officer
Michael Holmes, Executive Vice-President & Chief Operating Officer
Mark Cadzow, Executive Vice-President & Chief Development Officer

Oceanic Iron Ore Corp.
Three Bentall Centre
#3083, 595 Burrard St.
Vancouver, BC V7X 1L3

604-566-9080
Fax: 604-566-9081
www.oceanicironore.com

Company Type: Public
Ticker Symbol: FEO / TSX.V
Profile: Oceanic is focused on the development of the Ungava Bay iron properties.
Alan Gorman, President & CEO
Chris Batalha, CFO & Corporate Secretary

Orbit Garant Drilling Inc.
3200, boul Jean-Jacques Cossette
Val-d'Or, QC J9P 6Y6

Fax: 819-824-2195
866-824-2707
www.orbitgarant.com

Company Type: Public
Ticker Symbol: OGD / TSX
Staff Size: 850
Profile: The mineral drilling compnay provides both underground & surface drilling services. Operations are carried out in Canada & internationally.
Éric Alexandre, CNA, President & CEO
Alain Laplante, FCGA, Chief Financial Officer & Vice-President
Michel Mathieu, Vice-President
Serge Turgeon, Vice-President, Human Resources
Daniel Maheu, Corporate Controller

Orbite Technologies Inc.
#610, 6505, rte Transcanadienne
Saint-Laurent, QC H4T 1S3

514-744-6264
Fax: 514-744-4193
info@orbitetech.com
www.orbitetech.com

Company Type: Public
Ticker Symbol: ORT / TSX
Profile: Orbite Technologies Inc. is a Canadian cleantech company whose technolgies enable environmentally-neutral extraction of smelter-grade alumina (SGA), high-purity alumina (HPA) and high-value elements, including rare earths and rare metals.
Glenn R. Kelly, President & CEO
Jacques Bédard, Chief Financial Officer & Vice-President, Finance
Denis Arguin, Vice-President, Engineering & Operations
Yves Noël, Vice-President, Business Development

Orosur Mining Inc.
#105, 1667 Costa Rica
Montevideo, 11500 Uruguay

info@orosur.ca
www.orosur.ca
Other Communications: Phone: 598-2-601-6354; Fax: 598-2-600-6232

Company Type: Public
Ticker Symbol: OMI / TSX
Staff Size: 426
Profile: The exploration company & gold producer is active in Latin America. Orosur Mining's exploration portfolio includes assets in Chile & Uruguay. It also operates a producing gold mine in Uruguay.
Ignacio Salazar, Chief Executive Officer
Ryan Cohen, Vice-President, Planning & Corporate Development
Alejandra López, Interim Chief Financial Officer

Orvana Minerals Corp.
#900, 170 University Ave.
Toronto, ON M5H 3B3

416-369-1629
Fax: 416-369-1402
www.orvana.com

Company Type: Public
Ticker Symbol: ORV / TSX
Profile: The Canadian gold & copper mining & exploration company evaluates, develops, & mines precious & base metals deposits. Orvana Minerals is the owner & operator of the Don Mario gold mine in eastern Bolivia. Through its wholly owned subsidiary, Kinbauri España S.L.U., Orvana Minerals also operates the El Valle-Boinás/Carlés copper & gold mine in northern Spain. Another Orvana asset is the Cooperwood copper project, situated in Michigan's Upper Peninsula.
Jeffrey Hills, Chief Financial Officer
James Gilbert, Chief Executive Officer
Joanne Jobin, Officer, Investor Relations
jjobin@orvana.com

Osisko Gold Royalties
PO Box 211, #300, 1100, av des Canadiens-de-Montréal
Montréal, QC H3B 2S2

514-940-0670
Fax: 514-940-0669
info@osiskogr.com
osiskogr.com

Company Type: Public
Ticker Symbol: OR / TSX
Profile: The company owns a 5% stake in a gold mine in Malartic, QC, as well as a 2% royalty in 3 gold mines in Ontario.
Sean Roosen, Chief Executive Officer
Bryan Coates, President
Elif Lévesque, Chief Financial Officer & Vice-President, Finance

Osisko Mining
#1440, 155 University Ave.
Toronto, ON M5H 3B7
416-848-9504
Fax: 416-363-9813
info@osiskomining.com
www.osiskomining.com
Company Type: Public
Ticker Symbol: OSK / TSX
Profile: A gold mining company whose main project is in Québec.
John Burzynski, President & CEO
Blair Zaritsky, Chief Financial Officer

Pacific Booker Minerals Inc.
#1103, 1166 Alberni St.
Vancouver, BC V6E 3Z3
604-681-8556
Fax: 604-687-5995
800-747-9911
info@pacificbooker.bc.ca
www.pacificbooker.com
Company Type: Public
Ticker Symbol: BKM / TSX
Profile: The company owns the Morrison property, a copper/gold/molybdenum mine.
John Plourde, President & CEO
Ruth Swan, Chief Financial Officer
Erik Tornquist, Chief Operating Officer

Pan American Silver Corp.
#1440, 625 Howe St.
Vancouver, BC V6C 2T6
604-684-1175
Fax: 604-684-0147
info@panamericansilver.com
www.panamericansilver.com
Social Media: www.facebook.com/panamericansilver
www.linkedin.com/company/311801
Company Type: Public
Ticker Symbol: PAA / TSX; PAAS / NASDAQ
Staff Size: 4,100
Profile: The silver producer was founded in 1994. Pan American Silver conducts its mining & exploration activities in Mexico, Bolivia, Peru, & Argentina.
Michael Steinmann, President & Chief Executive Officer
Steve Busby, Chief Operating Officer
Rob Doyle, Chief Financial Officer
Keenan Kohol, General Counsel

Panoro Minerals Ltd.
#1610, 700 West Pender St.
Vancouver, BC V6C 1G8
604-684-4246
Fax: 604-684-4200
info@panoro.com
www.panoro.com
Other Communications: Peru Office, Phone: +51 1 628 5978
Company Type: Public
Ticker Symbol: PML / TSX Venture, BVL
Profile: Panoro Minerals Ltd. has a portfolio of mineral properties situated in southeastern Peru. The region is known for its copper & gold deposits.
Luquman Shaheen, M.B.A., P.Eng., P.E., President & Chief Executive Officer
Bill Boden, Chair & Interim CFO
Yves Barsimantov, General Manager, Peru, & Vice-President, Operations
Luis Vela, Vice-President, Exploration

Parex Resources Inc.
Eight Avenue Place, West Tower
#2700, 585 - 8 Ave. SW
Calgary, AB T2P 1G1
403-265-4800
Fax: 403-265-8216
info@parexresources.com
www.parexresources.com
Other Communications: Colombia: +(571) 629-1716
Company Type: Public
Ticker Symbol: PXT / TSX
Staff Size: 279
Profile: Oil & natural gas exploration & production are conducted in the Caribbean area & South America. Parex Resources has holdings onshore Trinidad & in Colombia's Llanos Basin.
Wayne K. Foo, Chief Executive Officer
David Taylor, President
Kenneth G. Pinsky, Chief Financial Officer
Stuart Davie, Vice-President, Corporate Services

Pershimco Resources Inc.
11, rue Perreault est
Rouyn-Noranda, QC J9X 3C1
819-797-2180
Fax: 819-797-9617
info@pershimco.ca
www.pershimco.ca
Company Type: Public
Ticker Symbol: PRO / TSX.V
Profile: Pershimco Resources is a junior mineral exploration company which operations include the acquisition, exploration, mineral deposit evaluation, development and, where possible, the operating of mining properties.
Alain Bureau, President & CEO
Pierre Monet, Chief Financial Officer & Vice-President, Finance

Pilot Gold
#1900, 1055 West Hastings St.
Vancouver, BC V6E 2E9
604-632-4677
Fax: 604-632-4678
877-632-4677
info@pilotgold.com
www.pilotgold.com
Company Type: Public
Ticker Symbol: PLG / TSX
Profile: Pilot Gold is a gold discovery company.
Cal Everett, President/CEO
John Wenger, Chief Financial Officer & Corporate Secretary
Moira Smith, Vice-President, Exploration & Geoscience

Plateau Uranium Inc.
#1200, 141 Adelaide St. West
Toronto, ON M5H 3L5
416-628-9600
Fax: 416-360-3415
info@plateauuranium.com
plateauuranium.com
Company Type: Public
Ticker Symbol: PLU / TSX.V
Profile: The company's main project is located in south-eastern Peru.
Ted O'Connor, Chief Executive Officer
Laurence Stefan, President & COO

Platinum Group Metals
Bentall Tower 5
#788, 550 Burrard St.
Vancouver, BC V6C 2B5
604-899-5450
Fax: 604-484-4710
866-899-5450
info@platinumgroupmetals.net
www.platinumgroupmetals.net
Other Communications: South Africa Office Phone: +27 (11) 782-2186
Company Type: Public
Ticker Symbol: PTM / TSX; PLG / NYSE
Staff Size: 279
Profile: Formed in 2000, & based in Vancouver, British Columbia & Johannesburg, South Africa, Platinum Group Metals Ltd. is engaged in the exploration, construction, & operation of mines. The company holds mineral rights in the Bushveld Igneous Complex of South Africa, in addition to two joint ventures with the government of Japan. Platinum Group Metals Ltd.'s focus is upon the development of platinum operations.
R. Michael Jones, B.A.SC., P.Eng, President, CEO & Co-Founder
Peter C. Busse, P.Eng, Chief Operating Officer
Frank Hallam, B.B.A., C.A., Chief Financial Officer, Corporate Secretary, & Director
Kris Begic, Vice-President, Corporate Development

Polaris Materials Corporation
PO Box 11175, #2740, 1055 West Georgia St.
Vancouver, BC V6E 3R5
604-915-5000
Fax: 604-915-5001
info@polarismaterials.com
www.polarismaterials.com
Company Type: Public
Ticker Symbol: PLS / TSX
Profile: Polaris Materials Corporation is a supplier of high quality construction aggregates to major coastal city markets in California, Hawaii and British Columbia.
Kenneth Palko, President & CEO
Darren McDonald, CFO & Vice-President, Finance

Polymet Mining Corp.
First Canadian Place
#5700, 100 King St. West
Toronto, ON M5X 1C7
416-915-4149
www.polymetmining.com
Other Communications: St. Paul, MN, USA Office, Phone: 651-389-4100
Social Media: www.facebook.com/PolyMet
twitter.com/PolyMetMining
www.linkedin.com/company/1002716
Company Type: Public
Ticker Symbol: POM / TSX; PLM / NYSE
Profile: PolyMet Mining Corp. is a mine development company. It controls 100% of the NorthMet copper, nickel, precious metals, ore project, which is located on the Mesabi Range of northeastern Minnesota. The company also owns 100% of a nearby processing facility, known as Erie Plant.
Jon Cherry, President & Chief Executive Officer
Douglas J. Newby, Chief Financial Officer
Brad Moore, Executive Vice-President, Environmental & Governmental Affairs
Bruce Richardson, Vice-President, Corporate Communications & External Affairs

Potash Corporation of Saskatchewan, Inc.
#500, 122 - 1st Ave. South
Saskatoon, SK S7K 7G3
306-933-8500
800-667-0403
www.potashcorp.com
Social Media: www.facebook.com/potashcorp
twitter.com/potashcorp
www.linkedin.com/companies/37849
Company Type: Public
Ticker Symbol: POT / TSX
Staff Size: 5,395
Profile: Potash Corporation of Saskatchewan was created in 1975 as a Crown Corporation by the Saskatchewan government. The fertilizer enterprise produces the following plant nutrients: potash, nitrogen, & phosphate. Potash Corporation of Saskatchewan supplies the agriculture, animal nutrition, & industrial chemical markets. The company is now listed on the Toronto & New York stock exchanges under the symbol POT. In Sept. 2016 it was announced that Potash Corporation of Saskatchewan would merge with Calgary-based Agrium.
Jochen Tilk, President/CEO
Mark Fracchia, President, PCS Potash
Raef Sully, President, PCS Nitrogen & PCS Phosphate
Wayne Brownlee, Exec. Vice-President & CFO
Lee M. Knafelc, Senior Vice-President, Human Resources & Administration
Denita C. Stann, Senior Vice-President, Investor & Public Relations

Potash Ridge
#1000, 36 Toronto St.
Toronto, ON M5C 2C5
416-362-8640
www.potashridge.com
Social Media: twitter.com/PotashRidge
Company Type: Public
Ticker Symbol: PRK / TSX
Profile: The company is a fertilizer producer with projects in Quebec & Utah.
Guy Bentinck, President & CEO

Premier Gold Mines Limited
#200, 1100 Russell St.
Thunder Bay, ON P7B 5N2
807-346-1390
888-346-1390
info@premiergoldmines.com
www.premiergoldmines.com
Social Media: www.facebook.com/436163563157462
twitter.com/PremierGoldMine
linkedin.com/company/premier-gold-mines-limited
Company Type: Public
Ticker Symbol: PG / TSX
Staff Size: 17
Profile: The exploration company is active in Canada & the United States. Premier Gold Mines Limited's major assets are located in Ontario's Geraldton, Red Lake, & Musselwhite regions, & also in the Carlin Trend of Nevada.
In 2011, Premier Gold Mines Limited acquired ownership & control of common shares of Goldstone Resources Inc.
Ewan S. Downie, President & Chief Executive Officer
Steve Filipovic, Chief Financial Officer
Stephen McGibbon, Executive Vice-President, Corporate & Project Development

Pretium Resources Inc.
Four Bentall Centre
PO Box 49334, #2300, 1055 Dunsmuir St.
Vancouver, BC V7X 1L4
604-558-1784
invest@pretivm.com
www.pretivm.com
Company Type: Public
Ticker Symbol: PVG / TSX
Profile: Pretivm is involved in the development of the Brucejack Project, a high-grade undeveloped gold project in northern British Columbia.
Robert A. Quartermain, Chief Executive Officer
Joseph J. Ovsenek, President
Kenneth C. McNaughton, Chief Exploration Officer
Tom Yip, Chief Financial Officer
Michelle Romero, Vice-President, Corporate

Primero Mining Corp.
TD Tower South
PO Box 139, #2100, 79 Wellington St. West
Toronto, ON M5K 1H1
416-814-3160
Fax: 416-814-3170
877-619-3160
info@primeromining.com
www.primeromining.com
Social Media:
www.facebook.com/pages/Primero-Mining/123193107782411
twitter.com/PrimeroMiningCo
www.linkedin.com/company/primero-mining-corp
Company Type: Public
Ticker Symbol: P / TSX; PPP / NYSE
Staff Size: 1,817
Profile: Primero Mining Corp. is a Canadian-based precious metals producer with operations in Mexico.
Ernest Mast, President & Chief Executive Officer
Wendy Kaufman, Chief Financial Officer
H. Maura Lendon, Chief General Counsel & Corporate Secretary
Louis Toner, Vice-President, Project Development & Construction

Prophecy Development Corp.
#1610, 409 Granville St.
Vancouver, BC V6C 1T2
604-569-3661
info@prophecydev.com
www.prophecydev.com
Company Type: Public
Ticker Symbol: PCY / TSX
Profile: A mining company with projects in Mongolia, Bolivia & Canada.
John Lee, Chief Executive Officer
Irina Plavutska, Chief Financial Officer
Bekzod Kasimov, Vice-President, Operations

Pure Gold Mining
#1900, 1055 West Hastings St.
Vancouver, BC V6E 2E9
604-646-8000
info@puregoldmining.ca
puregoldmining.ca
Company Type: Public
Ticker Symbol: PGM / TSX
Profile: A gold mining company with projects in northwestern Ontario.
Darin Labrenz, President & CEO
Sean Tetzlaff, Chief Financial Officer

QMX Gold Corporation
PO Box 75, #815, 65 Queen St. West
Toronto, ON M5H 2M5
416-861-5899
Fax: 416-861-8165
877-717-3027
info@qmxgold.ca
www.alexisminerals.com
Social Media: twitter.com/QMX_Gold
Company Type: Public
Ticker Symbol: QMX / TSX
Profile: QMX Gold Corporation is a mining company operating in Val-d'Or, Quebec and Snow Lake, Manitoba.
David Rigg, Interim President & CEO
Deborah Battiston, Chief Financial Officer

Quaterra Resources Inc.
Head Office
#1100, 1199 West Hastings St.
Vancouver, BC V6E 3T5
604-681-9059
Fax: 604-641-2740
855-681-9059
info@quaterra.com
www.quaterra.com
Company Type: Public
Ticker Symbol: QTA / TSX Venture
Profile: The junior mineral exploration company conducts operations in North America.
Thomas Patton, B.Sc., M.Sc., Ph.D., Chair & Chief Executive Officer
Gerald Prosalendis, President & COO
Lei Wang, CPA, CGA, BSE, CFO

Redhawk Resources
One Bentall Centre
#1560, 505 Burrard St.
Vancouver, BC V7X 1M5
604-633-5088
redhawkresources.com
Social Media: twitter.com/redhawkcopper
Company Type: Public
Ticker Symbol: RDK / TSX
Profile: Redhawk Resources is a Canadian-based resource exploration and development company with primary focus on the accelerated development of its advanced stage Copper Creek copper-molybdenum project in San Manuel, Arizona.
R. Joe Sandberg, President & CEO
Alec Peck, CFO

Regulus Resources
#2300, 1177 West Hastings St.
Vancouver, BC V6E 2K3
604-685-6800
info@regulusresources.com
www.regulusresources.com
Company Type: Public
Ticker Symbol: REG / TSX.V
Profile: A mining company whose main project is the Rio Grande porphyry Cu-Au mine located in Argentina.
John Black, Chief Executive Officer
Fernando Pickmann, President & COO
Mark Wayne, Chief Financial Officer

Reservoir Minerals
#760, 669 Howe St.
Vancouver, BC V6C 0B4
604-623-4700
Fax: 604-623-4701
888-600-2200
www.reservoirminerals.com
Company Type: Public
Ticker Symbol: RMC / TSX.V
Profile: Reservoir Minerals is an exploration company, that holds licenses in Serbia to mine for gold, silver, copper, lead & zinc.
Cliff Davis, Chief Executive Officer
Tom Whelan, Chief Financial Officer
Frazer Bourchier, Chief Operating Officer
Peter Manojlovic, Vice-President, Exploration

Richmont Mines Inc.
161, av Principale
Rouyn-Noranda, QC J9X 4P6
819-797-2465
Fax: 819-797-0166
info@richmont-mines.com
www.richmont-mines.com
Other Communications: Toronto Corporate Office, Phone: 416-368-0291
Social Media: www.facebook.com/RichmontMines/
twitter.com/RichmontMines
linkedin.com/company/mines-richmont-inc
Company Type: Public
Ticker Symbol: RIC / TSX, AMEX
Staff Size: 435
Profile: Richmont Mines Inc. specializes in gold exploration, development, & mining. Operations take place in Ontario, Quebec, & Newfoundland & Labrador.
Renaud Adams, President & Chief Executive Officer
Nicole Veilleux, Vice-President, Finance
Steve Burleton, Vice-President, Business Development
Daniel Adam, Vice-President, Exploration
Maxime Grondin, Chief Director, Human Resources
Anne Day, Vice-President, Investor Relations
aday@richmont-mines.com

Robex Resources
#100, 437, Grande Allée est
Québec, QC G1R 2J5
581-741-7421
Fax: 581-742-7241
info@robexgold.com
robexgold.com
Social Media: twitter.com/Relation_Robex
www.linkedin.com/company/ressources-robex-inc-
Company Type: Public
Ticker Symbol: RBX / TSX-V
Profile: Robex is a junior Canadian mining exploration & development company.
Georges Cohen, CEO
Augustin Rousselet, Vice-President, Finance & Chief Operating Officer

Rockwell Diamonds Inc.
PO Box 251, Barkly West, 8375 South Africa
info@rockwelldiamonds.com
www.rockwelldiamonds.com
Other Communications: Phone: +27(0)11-484-0830; Fax: +27(0)86-501-6328
Social Media: www.facebook.com/groups/RockwellSparkle
twitter.com/RockwellDiamond
www.linkedin.com/company/2311472
Company Type: Public
Ticker Symbol: RDI / TSX; RDIAF / OTCBB
Staff Size: 528
Profile: Rockwell Diamonds develops & operates alluvial diamond deposits. The compnay has an interest in properties in southern Africa.
James Campbell, President & Chief Executive Officer
John Shelton, Chief Financial Officer

Roxgold Inc.
#500, 360 Bay St.
Toronto, ON M5H 2V6
416-203-6401
Fax: 416-203-0341
info@roxgold.com
www.roxgold.com
Company Type: Public
Ticker Symbol: ROG / TSX Venture
Profile: Roxgold Inc. is a gold exploration company currently investigating three exploration permits in mineral rich Burkina Faso, West Africa.
John Dorward, President & Chief Executive Officer
Natacha Garoute, Chief Financial Officer & Corporate Secretary
Paul Criddle, Chief Operating Officer

Royal Nickel Corporation (RNC)
#1200, 220 Bay St.
Toronto, ON M5J 2W4
416-363-0649
www.royalnickel.com
Other Communications: Amos, QC Regional Office, Phone: 819-727-3777
Company Type: Public
Ticker Symbol: RNX / TSX
Profile: Royal Nickel Corporation acquires, explores, & develops base metal & platinum group metal properties. The company owns 100% of the Dumont Nickel Project, situated in the Abitibi Mining Camp near Amos, Québec.
Mark Selby, President & CEO
Tim Hollaar, Chief Financial Officer
Christian Brousseau, Project Director
Alger St-Jean, Vice-President, Exploration
Johnna Muinonen, Vice-President, Operations
Pierre-Philippe Dupont, Manager, Sustainable Development
Rob Buchanan, Director, Investor Relations
rbuchanan@royalnickel.com

Rubicon Minerals Corporation
#400, 44 Victoria St.
Toronto, ON M5C 1Y2
416-766-2804
Fax: 416-642-2299
www.rubiconminerals.com
Social Media: twitter.com/RubiconMinerals
Company Type: Public
Ticker Symbol: RMX / TSX; RBY / NYSE
Profile: Rubicon Minerals Corporation is an advanced stage gold development company, focused on the responsible and environmentally sustainable development of its high-grade Phoenix Gold Project.
Julien Kemp, Interim President & CEO
Nicholas Nikolakakis, Chief Financial Officer
Allan Candelario, Vice-President, Investor Relations

Sabina Gold & Silver Corp.
PO Box 200, #375, 555 Burrard St.
Vancouver, BC V7X 1M7
604-998-4175
Fax: 604-998-1051
888-648-4218
info@sabinagoldsilver.com
www.sabinagoldsilver.com
Company Type: Public
Ticker Symbol: SBB / TSX
Profile: The precious metals company has flagship projects in Nunavut. Primary assets include the following: the Back River Gold Project; a royalty on the Hackett River silver & zinc property; & the Wishbone greenstone belt & its potential for gold discoveries.

Bruce McLeod, President & Chief Executive Officer
Elaine Bennett, Chief Financial Officer & Vice-President, Finance
Wes Carson, Vice-President, Project Development
Angus Campbell, Vice-President, Exploration

Sandspring Resources Ltd.
#180, 9137 East Mineral Cirlce
Centennial, CO 80112 USA
780-854-0104
info@sandspringresources.com
www.sandspringresources.com
Company Type: Public
Ticker Symbol: SSP / TSX.V
Profile: A mining company with projects in South America.
Rich Munson, Chief Executive Officer
Harpreet Dhaliwal, Chief Financial Officer

Sandstorm Gold Ltd.
#1400, 400 Burrard St.
Vancouver, BC V6C 3A6
604-689-0234
Fax: 604-689-7317
866-584-0234
info@sandstormLTD.com
www.sandstormgold.com
Social Media: twitter.com/sandstormSSL
Company Type: Public
Ticker Symbol: SSL / TSX
Profile: Sandstorm Gold Ltd. is a commodity streaming company that provides upfront financing to resource companies.
Nolan Watson, President & CEO
Erfan Kazemi, Chief Financial Officer

Santacruz Silver Mining Ltd.
#880, 580 Hornby St.
Vancouver, BC V6C 3B6
604-569-1609
www.santacruzsilver.com
Social Media: www.facebook.com/SantacruzSilver
twitter.com/SantacruzSilver
www.linkedin.com/company/santacruz-silver-mining
Company Type: Public
Ticker Symbol: SCZ / TSX.V
Profile: The company owns four silver mines in Mexico.
Arturo Préstamo Elizondo, President & CEO
Robert McMorran, Chief Financial Officer
Cesar Maldonado, Chief Operating Officer

Sarama Resources Ltd.
HSBC Bldg.
#2200, 885 West Georgia St.
Vancouver, BC V6C 3E8
info@saramaresources.com
www.saramaresources.com
Other Communications: Australian Office, Phone: +61-8-9363-7600
Social Media: twitter.com/SaramaResources
www.linkedin.com/company/3146261
Company Type: Public
Ticker Symbol: SWA / TSX.V
Profile: The company's main focus is the development & exploration of gold. Its main focus is in Burkina Faso, & also has interests in Liberia & Mali.
John (Jack) Hamilton, Founder & Vice-President, Exploration
Nicholas Longmire, Chief Financial Officer
Paul Schmiede, Vice-President, Corporate Development

Scorpio Gold Corp.
#206, 595 Howe St.
Vancouver, BC V6C 2T5
604-678-9639
Fax: 604-558-1136
scorpio@scorpiogold.com
www.scorpiogold.com
Company Type: Public
Ticker Symbol: SGN / TSX.V
Profile: The precious metals company owns 70% of the Mineral Ridge mine in Esmeralda County, Nevada. It is the full owner of the Goldwedge property in Manhattan, Nevada.
Peter J. Hawley, CEO
Gilbert Comtois, Chief Financial Officer
Chris Zerga, President

Seabridge Gold Inc.
#400, 106 Front St. East
Toronto, ON M5A 1E1
416-367-9292
Fax: 416-367-2711
info@seabridgegold.net
www.seabridgegold.net
Company Type: Public
Ticker Symbol: SEA / TSX; SA / NYSE
Profile: Seabridge Gold's principal assets are the 100% owned Courageous Lake gold project in the Northwest Territories & the 100% owned KSM property near Stewart, British Columbia.
Rudi P. Fronk, Chief Executive Officer
Jay S. Layman, President & Chief Operating Officer
Christopher J. Reynolds, Chief Financial Officer & Vice-President, Finance
R. Brent Murphy, Vice-President, Environmental Affairs

SEMAFO Inc.
100, boul Alexis-Nihon, 7e étage
Montréal, QC H4M 2P3
514-744-4408
Fax: 514-744-2291
888-744-4408
info@semafo.com
www.semafo.com
Social Media: www.linkedin.com/company/899081
Company Type: Public
Ticker Symbol: SMF / TSX, OMX
Staff Size: 993
Profile: SEMAFO is a mining & gold production company. It operates gold mines in Burkina Faso, Guinea, & Niger. Exploration activities take place in West Africa.
Benoit Desormeaux, President & Chief Executive Officer
Martin Milette, Chief Financial Officer
Michel Crevier, Vice-President, Exploration & Mining Geology

Sherritt International Corporation
Brookfield Pl.
181 Bay St., 26th Fl.
Toronto, ON M5J 2T3
416-924-4551
Fax: 416-924-5015
800-704-6698
info@sherritt.com
www.sherritt.com
Other Communications: Investor Relations E-mail: investor@sherritt.com
Company Type: Public
Ticker Symbol: S / TSX
Profile: Sherrit International Corporation has interests in a nickel & cobalt metals business, thermal coal production, electricity generation, & oil & gas exploration, development, & production. The company conducts its operations in Canada & internationally.
David V. Pathe, President/CEO
Dean Chambers, Executive Vice-President/CFO

Sierra Metals Inc.
TD Tower South
PO Box 157, #2100, 79 Wellington St. West
Toronto, ON M5K 1H1
416-366-7777
866-493-9646
info@sierrametals.ca
www.sierrametals.com
Social Media: www.facebook.com/SierraMetalsInc
twitter.com/SierraMetals
www.linkedin.com/company/sierra-metals-inc-
Company Type: Public
Ticker Symbol: SMT / TSX
Staff Size: 1,026
Profile: Sierra Metals Inc. is a mid-tier precious and base metals producer in Latin America.
Mark Brennan, President & CEO
Ed Guimaraes, Chief Financial Officer
Herbert Fiedler, Chief Commercial Officer

Silver Standard Resources Inc.
PO Box 49088, #800, 1055 Dunsmuir St.
Vancouver, BC V7X 1G4
604-689-3846
Fax: 604-689-3847
888-338-0046
invest@silverstandard.com
www.silverstandard.com
Company Type: Public
Ticker Symbol: SSO / TSX
Staff Size: 1,139
Profile: Silver Standard Resources explores & operates precious metals projects. Operations take place in Canada, the United States, Mexico, Argentina, Peru, & Chile. Shares are listed on the Toronto Stock Exchange under the symbol SSO & on the Nasdaq Global Market under the symbol SSRI. In 2016 Silver Standard acquired Canadian mining company Claude Resources, including its Seabee gold mine in Saskatchewan.
Paul Benson, President & CEO
Gregory J. Martin, Sr. Vice-President/Chief Financial Officer
Nadine Block, Vice-President, Human Resources

Silver Wheaton Corp.
#3500, 1021 West Hastings St.
Vancouver, BC V6E 0C3
604-684-9648
Fax: 604-684-3123
800-380-8687
info@silverwheaton.com
www.silverwheaton.com
Social Media: www.facebook.com/SilverWheatonCorp
twitter.com/silver_wheaton
www.linkedin.com/company/silver-wheaton
Company Type: Public
Ticker Symbol: SLW / TSX, NYSE
Profile: Silver Wheaton Corp. is engaged in silver production. The company purchases silver production from mines in Canada, the United States, Mexico, Peru, Chile, Portugal, Sweden, & Greece.
Randy Smallwood, President & CEO
Gary Brown, Senior Vice-President/Chief Financial Officer
Haytham Hodaly, Senior Vice-President, Corporate Development

Silvercorp Metals Inc.
#1378, 200 Granville St.
Vancouver, BC V6C 1S4
604-669-9397
Fax: 604-669-9387
888-224-1881
investor@silvercorp.ca
www.silvercorp.ca
Other Communications: China Head Office, Phone: 8610-8587-1130
Company Type: Public
Ticker Symbol: SVM / TSX, NYSE
Staff Size: 826
Profile: Silvercorp Metals acquires, explores, & mines silver-related properties located in Canada & China. The company has implemented a range of employee safety measures & environmental protection measures.
Rui Feng, Ph.D., Chair/CEO
Lorne Waldman, Senior Vice-President
Derek Liu, Chief Financial Officer
Luke Liu, Vice-President, China Operations
Alex Zhang, Vice-President, Exploration

SouthGobi Resources Ltd.
#1100, 355 Burrard St.
Vancouver, BC V6C 2G8
604-681-6799
info@southgobi.com
www.southgobi.com
Other Communications: SouthGobi Resources (Hong Kong) Limited; +852-2156-1438
Company Type: Public
Ticker Symbol: SGQ / TSX, Hong Kong
Staff Size: 354
Profile: SouthGobi Resources has metallurgical & thermal coal deposits in the South Gobi Region of Mongolia. The company's flagship coal mine is known as Ovoot Tolgoi. Coal is produced & sold to customers in China.
Mr. Aminbuhe, Chief Executive Officer
Yulan (Allen) Guo, Chief Financial Officer
Allison Snetsinger, Corporate Secretary

Spanish Mountain Gold Ltd.
Head Office
#1120, 1095 West Pender St.
Vancouver, BC V6E 2M6
604-601-3651
Fax: 604-681-6866
855-772-6397
info@spanishmountaingold.com
www.spanishmountaingold.com
Social Media: www.facebook.com/spanishmountaingold
twitter.com/SpMtnGold
Company Type: Public
Ticker Symbol: SPA / TSX.V; S3Y / FSE
Profile: Spanish Mountain Gold's flagship project is located in south central British Columbia.
Larry Yau, Chief Financial Officer & Interim CEO
Judy Stoeterau, Vice-President, Geology

Sprott Resource Corp.
Royal Bank Plaza, South Tower
PO Box 90, #2750, 200 Bay St.
Toronto, ON M5J 2J2
416-977-7333
Fax: 416-977-7555
info@sprottresource.com
www.sprottresource.com
Social Media: twitter.com/SprottResource
www.linkedin.com/company/sprott-resource-corp-
Company Type: Public
Ticker Symbol: SCP / TSX

Profile: Sprott Resource Corp. invests and operates through its subsidiaries in the natural resource sector. Sprott's investments include operations in oil and gas, energy, agriculture and agricultural nutrients, as well as a large position in physical gold bullion.
Steve Yuzpe, President & CEO
Michael Staresinic, Chief Financial Officer
Arthur Einav, General Counsel & Corporate Secretary

Starcore International Mines Ltd.
PO Box 113, #750, 580 Hornby St.
Vancouver, BC V6C 3B6

604-602-4935
866-602-4935
www.starcore.com
Social Media: twitter.com/StarcoreIR
www.linkedin.com/company/999500

Company Type: Public
Ticker Symbol: SAM / TSX
Staff Size: 313
Profile: The mining company acquires & develops gold & silver properties. Starcore International Mines is active in Mexico.
Robert Eadie, President & Chief Executive Officer
Gary Arca, CA, Chief Financial Officer
David Gunning, P.Eng., Chief Operating Officer
Cory Kent, LLB, Corporate Secretary

Stonegate Agricom Ltd.
20 Adelaide St. East, 13th Fl.
Toronto, ON M5C 2T6

416-864-0303
Fax: 416-860-0813
www.stonegateagricom.com

Company Type: Public
Ticker Symbol: ST / TSX
Profile: Stonegate Agricom Ltd. acquires & develops agricultural nutrient projects. Projects include the Mantaro Phosphate Project in Peru & the Paris Hills Phosphate Project in Idaho.
Ian McDonald, Chief Executive Officer
Germaine Coombs, Chief Financial Officer & Vice-President
Lorna D. MacGillivray, LL.B., Vice-President, Secretary, & General Counsel

Stornoway Diamond Corp.
Tour ouest
#400, 1111, rue St-Charles ouest
Longueuil, QC J4K 5G4

450-616-5555
Fax: 450-674-2012
www.stornowaydiamonds.com
Social Media: www.facebook.com/313277295359632
www.twitter.com/SWYDiamonds
www.linkedin.com/company/2476947

Company Type: Public
Ticker Symbol: SWY / TSX
Staff Size: 320
Profile: Stornoway is a leading Canadian diamond exploration and development company with 100% ownership of the Renard Diamond Project in Quebec.
Matt Manson, President & CEO
Robert Chausse, Chief Financial Officer
Patrick Godin, Chief Operating Officer

Strategic Metals Ltd.
#1016, 510 West Hastings St.
Vancouver, BC V6B 1L8

604-687-2522
Fax: 604-688-2578
888-688-2522
www.strategicmetalsltd.com
Social Media: www.facebook.com/StrategicMetals
twitter.com/tsxvsmd

Company Type: Public
Ticker Symbol: SMD / TSX Venture
Profile: Strategic Metals Ltd. is an exploration company, with properties & royalty interests in the Yukon. The company also owns shares of the following resource companies: Silver Range Resources, ATAC Resources Ltd., Wolverine Minerals Corp., & Rockhaven Resources Ltd.
W. Douglas Eaton, President & CEO
Larry B. Donaldson, Chief Financial Officer
Ian J. Talbot, B.Sc., LL.B, Chief Operating Officer

Sutter Gold Mining
2414 Garland St.
Lakewood, CO 80215 USA

303-238-1438
info@suttergoldmining.com
www.suttergoldmining.com

Company Type: Public
Ticker Symbol: SGM / TSX.V
Profile: A gold mining company with projects in California & Mexico.
Richard Winers, President & CEO
Amanda Miller, Chief Financial Officer

Tahoe Resources Inc.
#1500, 1055 West Georgia St.
Vancouver, BC V6E 4N7

investors@tahoeresourcesinc.com
www.tahoeresourcesinc.com
Other Communications: Human Resources, E-mail: jobs@tahoeresourcesinc.com
Social Media: www.facebook.com/154605538947778
www.linkedin.com/company/tahoe-resources-inc.

Company Type: Public
Ticker Symbol: THO.CA / TSX; TAHO / NYSE
Staff Size: 2,025
Profile: Tahoe Resources Inc. is a mining company of precious metals in the Americas.
Ron Clayton, President & Chief Operating Officer
Mark Sadler, Vice-President, Projects Development
Brian Bodsky, Vice-President, Exploration
Tom Fudge, Vice-President, Operations

Tanzanian Royalty Exploration Corporation
Scotia Plaza
#4400, 40 King St. West
Toronto, ON M5H 3Y4

844-364-1830
investors@tanzanianroyaltyexploration.com
www.tanzanianroyalty.com
Social Media: www.facebook.com/tanzanianroyalty

Company Type: Public
Ticker Symbol: TNX / TSX
Profile: Tanzanian Royalty Exploration Corporation is engaged in the exploration of mineral properties in Tanzania.
Jim Sinclair, President/CEO
Marco Guidi, Chief Financial Officer

Taseko Mines Limited
1040 West Georgia St., 15th Fl.
Vancouver, BC V6E 4H1

778-373-4533
Fax: 778-373-4534
877-441-4533
investor@tasekomines.com
www.tasekomines.com
Social Media: www.facebook.com/TasekoMines
twitter.com/tasekomines

Company Type: Public
Ticker Symbol: TKO / TSX
Staff Size: 172
Profile: Taseko Mines Limited is a mineral exploration & mining company. The company is engaged in the following main projects in British Columbia: the New Prosperity gold-copper project; the Gibraltar open pit copper mine; the wholly owned Aley niobium project; & the Harmony gold prospect.
Russell Hallbauer, President/Chief Executive Officer & Director
Stuart McDonald, Chief Financial Officer
John McManus, Chief Operating Officer
Brian Battison, Vice-President, Corporate Affairs

Teck Resources Limited
Five Bentall Centre
#3300, 550 Burrard St.
Vancouver, BC V6C 0B3

604-699-4000
Fax: 604-699-4750
www.teck.com
Social Media: www.facebook.com/TeckResourcesLtd
twitter.com/teckresources
www.linkedin.com/company/teck-resources-limited

Company Type: Public
Ticker Symbol: TCK.A / TSX; TCK / NYSE
Staff Size: 10,000
Profile: The resource company has business units focused on zinc, copper, stealmaking coal, & energy. Teck is building parnerships to confront sustainability challenges in the regions where it operates & globally. The company is committed to increasing awareness of the global health issue of zinc deficiency. Shares are listed on the Toronto & New York stock exchanges.
Donald R. Lindsay, President/CEO
Ronald A. Millos, CA, CFO & Sr. Vice-President, Finance
Peter C. Rozee, Sr. Vice-President, Commercial & Legal Affairs
Dean Winsor, Vice-President, Human Resources

Teranga Gold Corporation
#2600, 121 King St. West
Toronto, ON M5H 3T9

416-594-0000
Fax: 416-594-0088
investor@terangagold.com
www.terangagold.com
Social Media:
www.linkedin.com/company/teranga-gold-corporation

Company Type: Public
Ticker Symbol: TGZ / TSX
Staff Size: 1,194
Profile: Teranga is a Canadian-based gold company which operates the Sabodala gold mine in Senegal.
Richard S. Young, President/Chief Executive Officer
Navin Dyal, Chief Financial Officer

Teras Resources
#206, 6025 - 12 St. SE
Calgary, AB T2H 2K1

403-262-8411
Fax: 403-269-3290
info@teras.ca
www.teras.ca

Company Type: Public
Ticker Symbol: TRA / TSX
Profile: A gold mining company with projects in Montana & Nevada.
Peter Leger, President
Kuldip Baid, Chief Financial Officer

Terraco Gold Corp.
#2390, 1055 West Hastings St.
Vancouver, BC V6E 2E9

604-443-3830
Fax: 604-682-3860
877-792-6688
info@terracogold.com
www.terracogold.com

Company Type: Public
Ticker Symbol: TEN / TSX.V
Profile: A gold royalty company whose portfolio is on the Spring Valley Gold Project in Nevada.
Todd Hilditch, President & Chief Executive Officer
Bryan McKenzie, Chief Financial Officer

THEMAC Resources Group Ltd
#488, 625 Howe St.
Vancouver, BC V6C 2T6

info@themacresourcesgroup.com
www.themacresourcesgroup.com
Other Communications: Investor Relations E-mail: investor@themacresourcesgroup.com
Social Media: www.facebook.com/themacresourcesgroup
www.linkedin.com/company/themac-resources-group

Company Type: Public
Ticker Symbol: MAC / TSX
Profile: THEMAC Resources Group Ltd is a Canadian-based resource company focused on acquiring, exploring and developing natural resource properties, bringing innovation and sustainable approaches to mine development, production and reclamation processes.
Jeffrey Smith, Chief Operating Officer
Mark McIntosh, Chief Financial Officer

Thompson Creek Metals Company Inc.
#810, 26 West Dry Creek Circle
Littleton, CO 80120 USA

303-761-8801
Fax: 303-761-7420
info@tcrk.com
www.thompsoncreekmetals.com
Social Media: twitter.com/TC_Metals
www.linkedin.com/company/thompson-creek-metals-company

Company Type: Public
Ticker Symbol: TCM / TSX; TC / NYSE
Staff Size: 700
Profile: The molybdenum producer owns the Thompson Creek open-pit molybdenum mine & mill in Idaho, a metallurgical roasting facility in Pennsylvania, as well as 75% of northern British Columbia's Endako open-pit mine, mill, & roasting facility. Thompson Creek Metals Company is exploring on properties in northern British Columbia, the Yukon, & Nunavut.
Jacques Perron, President & CEO
Pamela L. Saxton, Chief Financial Officer & Executive Vice-President
Mark Wilson, Executive Vice-President & Chief Commercial Officer

Timmins Gold Corp.
#615, 700 West Pender St.
Vancouver, BC V6C 1G8

604-682-4002
Fax: 604-682-4003
info@timminsgold.com
www.timminsgold.com

Company Type: Public
Ticker Symbol: TMM / TSX; TGD / NYSE
Profile: Timmins Gold Corp.'s wholly owned San Francisco Gold Mine is situated in Sonora, Mexico.
Mark Backens, Interim Chief Executive Officer & Director

Tinka Resources Ltd.
#1305, 1090 West Georgia St.
Vancouver, BC V6E 3V7
info@tinkaresources.com
www.purenickel.com
Social Media: www.facebook.com/561690623848382
twitter.com/tinkaresources
linkedin.com/company/tinka-resources
Company Type: Public
Ticker Symbol: TK / TSX.V
Profile: A junior mining company with projects in Peru.
Graham Carman, President & Chief Executive Officer
Nick DeMare, Chief Financial Officer
Alvaro Fernandez-Baca, Vice-President, Exploration

TMAC Resources Inc.
PO Box 44, #1010, 95 Wellington St. West
Toronto, ON M5J 2N7
416-628-0216
info@tmacresources.com
www.tmacresources.com
Social Media: www.facebook.com/tmacresources
www.linkedin.com/company/3553570
Company Type: Public
Ticker Symbol: TMR / TSX
Profile: The company's main project is the Hope Bay Project in Nunavut.
Catharine Farrow, Chief Executive Officer
Ronald Gagel, Chief Financial Officer
Gordon Morrison, President & Chief Technology Officer

Torex Gold Resources Inc.
The Exchange Tower
#740, 130 King St. West
Toronto, ON M5X 2A2
647-260-1500
Fax: 416-640-2011
www.torexgold.com
Company Type: Public
Ticker Symbol: TXG / TSX
Profile: The mining company explores for precious metal resources, especially gold. Torex Gold Resources Inc. owns 100% of the Morelos Gold Project, which is situated in the Morelos Gold Belt near Mexico City.
Fred Stanford, P.Eng., President & Chief Executive Officer
Jeff Swinoga, CPA, CA, MBA, Chief Financial Officer
Gabriela Sanchez, MBA, Vice-President, Investor Relations

Treasury Metals Incorporated
The Exchange Tower
PO Box 99, #3680, 130 King St. West
Toronto, ON M5X 1B1
416-214-4654
Fax: 416-599-4959
info@treasurymetals.com
www.treasurymetals.com
Social Media: twitter.com/TreasuryMetals
www.linkedin.com/company/treasury-metals-inc.
Company Type: Public
Ticker Symbol: TML / TSX
Profile: The mineral exploration & development company is focused on the acquisition of gold projects in the Americas. Treasury Metals' main asset is the Goliath Gold Project, which is situated in the Kenora Mining District near Dryden, Ontario. Another of the company's operations is the Goldcliff Project, which is located in the Manitou Straits Fault Zone, south of Dryden, Ontario.
Dennis Gibson, CGA, Chief Financial Officer
Norm Bush, B.Sc. Mech Eng., Vice-President, Goliath Gold Project
Greg Ferron, B.Com., Vice-President, Corporate Development & Investment Relations
Mark Wheeler, Director, Projects

Trevali Mining Corporation
#2300, 1177 West Hastings St.
Vancouver, BC V6E 2K3
604-488-1661
Fax: 604-408-7499
info@trevali.com
www.trevali.com
Other Communications: hrstaffing@trevali.com
Social Media: www.facebook.com/TrevaliMiningCorporation
twitter.com/TrevaliMining
www.linkedin.com/company/trevali-mining-corporation
Company Type: Public
Ticker Symbol: TV / TSX, Frankfurt
Staff Size: 626
Profile: Trevali Mining Corporation has two zinc, lead, silver, & copper deposits in northern New Brunswick & in Peru. Through its wholly owned subsidary, Trevali Renewable Energy Inc., the Trevali Mining Corporation is upgrading its hydroelectric generating facility & transmission lines, in order to supply power to mining operations & sell surplus power to the Peruvian National Energy Grid.
Mark Cruise, President & Chief Executive Officer
Anna Ladd, Chief Financial Officer
Paul Keller, P.Eng., Chief Operating Officer
Steve Stakiw, Vice-President, Investor Relations & Corporate Communications

TriMetals Mining Inc.
#880, 580 Hornby St.
Vancouver, BC V6C 3B6
604-639-4523
Fax: 604-684-0642
www.trimetalsmining.com
Social Media: www.facebook.com/241865769349624
twitter.com/TriMetalsMining
www.linkedin.com/company/south-american-silver-corp
Company Type: Public
Ticker Symbol: TMI, TMI.B / TSX
Profile: TriMetals Mining Inc. is a mineral exploration company involved in the development of the large scale Escalones copper-gold project located in Chile.
Ralph Fitch, President & CEO
Matias Herrero, Chief Financial Officer
Felipe Malbran, Vice-President, Exploration, South America
Randall Moore, Vice-President, Exploration, North America

True North Gems Inc.
PO Box 11108, #700, 1055 West Georgia St.
Vancouver, BC V6E 3P3
604-687-8055
Fax: 604-889-1240
info@truenorthgems.com
www.truenorthgems.com
Social Media: www.facebook.com/1512608292325835
twitter.com/true_north_gems
Company Type: Public
Ticker Symbol: TGX / TSX.V
Profile: True North Gems mines is involved with the acquisition & exploration of minerals. Their focus is on the Aappaluttoq Ruby and Pink Sapphire Project, in Greenland.
Nicholas Houghton, President & CEO
Christopher Richards, Chief Financial Officer
Hayley Henning, Vice-President, Sales & Marketing Development

Turquoise Hill Resources
#354, 200 Granville St.
Vancouver, BC V6C 1S4
604-688-5755
888-273-9999
info@turquoisehill.com
www.turquoisehill.com
Social Media: twitter.com/TurquoiseHillRe
Company Type: Public
Ticker Symbol: TRQ / TSX, NYSE
Staff Size: 2,678
Profile: Turquoise Hill Resources is an international mining company focused on copper, gold and coal mines in the Asia Pacific region.
Jeffrey Tygesen, Chief Executive Officer
Steeve Thibeault, Chief Financial Officer

Ucore Rare Metals Inc.
#106, 210 Waterfront Dr.
Bedford, NS B4A 0H3
902-482-5214
Fax: 902-492-0197
info@ucore.com
ucore.com
Social Media: www.facebook.com/UcoreRareMetals
twitter.com/ucore
Company Type: Public
Ticker Symbol: UCU / TSX.V
Profile: The mining company focuses on developing technology metals.
Jim McKenzie, President & CEO
Peter Manuel, CFO, Vice-President & Corporate Secretary

UEX Corporation
#1700, 750 West Pender St.
Vancouver, BC V6C 2T8
604-669-2349
www.uex-corporation.com
Social Media: www.facebook.com/uexcorporation
twitter.com/uexcorporation
linkedin.com/company/uex-corporation
Company Type: Public
Ticker Symbol: UEX / TSX
Profile: Formed in 2002, UEX Corporation is engaged in uranium exploration & development. The company is active in northern Saskatchewan's Athabasca Basin.
Roger Lemaitre, President & Chief Executive Officer
Ed Boney, CA, Chief Financial Officer
Nan H. Lee, M.Sc., P.Eng., Vice-President, Project Development

Unigold Inc.
PO Box 936 Stn. Adelaide, Toronto, ON M5C 2K3
416-866-8157
unigold@unigoldinc.com
www.unigoldinc.com
Company Type: Public
Ticker Symbol: UGD / TSX.V
Profile: Unigold Inc. is a junior natural resource company focused on exploring and developing its gold projects in the Dominican Republic.
Joe Del Campo, Interim President & CEO
John Green, Chief Financial Officer

Ur-Energy Inc.
#200, 10758 West Centennial Rd.
Littleton, CO 80127 USA
720-981-4588
Fax: 720-981-5643
866-981-4588
www.ur-energy.com
Company Type: Public
Ticker Symbol: URE / TSX; URG / NYSE
Staff Size: 81
Profile: Ur-Energy is a dynamic junior mining company operating the Lost Creek in-situ recovery (ISR) uranium facility in south-central Wyoming.
Jeffrey Klenda, Executive Director & Acting CEO

Victoria Gold Corp.
Corporate Office
#303, 80 Richmond St. West
Toronto, ON M5H 2A4
416-866-8800
Fax: 416-866-8801
www.vitgoldcorp.com
Other Communications: Vancouver: 604-682-5122; Whitehorse: 867-393-4653
Company Type: Public
Ticker Symbol: VIT / TSX Venture
Profile: The gold company is engaged in acquisitions, exploration, & project development. Victoria Gold Corp.'s flagship project is the Eagle Gold Deposit, which is located on the Dublin Gulch property in the Yukon. The company continues to explore in the Yukon & Nevada.
John McConnell, President & Chief Executive Officer
Marty Rendall, Chief Financial Officer
Mark Ayranto, Executive Vice-President

Victory Nickel Inc.
Victory Building
80 Richmond St. West, 18th Fl.
Toronto, ON M5H 2A4
416-363-8527
Fax: 416-626-0890
admin@victorynickel.ca
www.victorynickel.ca
Company Type: Public
Ticker Symbol: NI / TSX
Profile: Victory Nickel Inc. is a nickel producer, with properties in Manitoba & northwestern Québec. The company also owns shares in Prophecy Coal Corp., Prophecy Platinum Corp., Wallbridge Mining Company Limited, & Miocene Metals Limited.
René Galipeau, CGA, Vice-Chair & Chief Executive Officer
David Mchaina, Ph.D., P.Eng., Vice-President, Environment & Sustainable Development
Sean Stokes, Corporate Secretary & Vice-President, Public Affairs

Vista Gold Corp.
#5, 7961 Shaffer Pkwy.
Littleton, CO 80127 USA
720-981-1185
Fax: 720-981-1186
866-981-1185
www.vistagold.com
Company Type: Public
Ticker Symbol: VGZ / TSX, NYSE
Profile: Vista is focused on the development of the Mt. Todd gold project in Northern Territory, Australia.
Frederick H. Earnest, President/CEO
John F. (Jack) Engele, Chief Financial Officer & Senior Vice-President
John W. Rozelle, Senior Vice-President

Wellgreen Platinum Ltd.
#915, 700 West Pender St.
Vancouver, BC V6C 1G8
604-569-3690
Fax: 604-428-7528
888-715-7528
info@wellgreenplatinum.com
www.wellgreenplatinum.com
Other Communications: Media Inquiries, E-mail: media@wellgreenplatinum.com
Company Type: Public
Ticker Symbol: WG / TSX
Profile: Wellgreen Platinum is a Canadian mining company focused on the acquisition and development of platinum group metals.
Diane Garrett, President & CEO
Joe Romagnolo, Senior Vice-President & Chief Financial Officer
John Sagman, Senior Vice-President & Chief Operating Officer

Wesdome Gold Mines Ltd.
Head Office
#811, 8 King St. East
Toronto, ON M5C 1B5
416-360-3743
Fax: 416-360-7620
info@wesdome.com
www.wesdome.com
Company Type: Public
Ticker Symbol: WDO / TSX
Staff Size: 243
Profile: Wesdome Gold Mines Ltd. is the owner of the Mishi & Eagle River gold mining operations in Wawa, Ontario & the Kiena mining complex, situated in Val d-Or, Québec.
Duncan Middlemiss, President & Chief Executive Officer
Philip Ng, Chief Operating Officer
Hemdat Sawh, Chief Financial Officer
George Mannard, Vice-President, Exploration

West Kirkland Mining Inc.
Five Bentall Centre
#788, 550 Burrard St.
Vancouver, BC V6C 2B5
604-685-8311
Fax: 604-484-4710
info@wkmining.com
www.wkmining.com
Company Type: Public
Ticker Symbol: WKM / TSX.V
Profile: West Kirkland Mining focuses on exploring & developing gold in Nevada & Utah.
R. Michael Jones, President & CEO
Frank Hallam, CFO & Corporate Secretary
Sandy McVey, Chief Operating Officer

Western Copper & Gold Corporation
Corporate Head Office
1040 West Georgia St., 15th Fl.
Vancouver, BC V6E 4H1
604-684-9497
Fax: 604-669-2926
888-966-9995
info@westerncopperandgold.com
www.westerncopperandgold.com
Social Media: www.facebook.com/WesternCopperandGold
twitter.com/westernCuandAu
www.linkedin.com/company/western-copper-and-gold
Company Type: Public
Ticker Symbol: WRN / TSX
Profile: The exploration & development company has gold, copper, & molybdenum resources & reserves. The company is active in the Yukon, where it owns 100% of the Casino Project.
Dale Corman, B.Sc., P.Eng., Executive Chair
Paul West-Sells, Ph.D., President & Chief Executive Officer
Julien François, CPA, CA, Chief Financial Officer & Vice-President, Finance
Cameron Brown, Vice-President, Engineering

Western Potash Corp.
#1400, 1111 West Georgia St.
Vancouver, BC V6E 4M3
604-689-9378
Fax: 604-689-8199
866-689-9378
info@westernpotash.com
www.westernpotash.com
Other Communications: Regina, SK: 306-924-9378
Company Type: Public
Ticker Symbol: WPX / TSX
Profile: Western Potash Corp. is engaged in the development of its potash mineral properties in western Canada.
Xue (Bill) Wenye, President
Troy Nikolai, CFO
David Thornley-Hall, Executive Vice-President & Corporate Secretary

WesternZagros Resources Ltd.
Head Office
#600, 440 - 2nd Ave. SW
Calgary, AB T2P 5E9
403-693-7001
Fax: 403-263-0616
www.westernzagros.com
Company Type: Public
Ticker Symbol: WZR / TSX Venture
Staff Size: 147
Profile: The natural resources company is engaged in the acquisition of properties to explore for, develop, & produce crude oil & natural gas. WesternZagros Resources is active in Iraq.
Simon Hatfield, Chief Executive Officer
Lance Berg, Vice-President, Engineering & Operatins
Tony Kraljic, Senior Vice-President, Finance

Whitecap Resources Inc.
#3800, 525 - 8th Ave. SW
Calgary, AB T2P 1G1
403-266-0767
Fax: 403-266-6975
info@wcap.ca
www.wcap.ca
Other Communications: Emergency Phone: 1-866-590-5289
Company Type: Public
Ticker Symbol: WCP / TSX
Staff Size: 107
Profile: The oil company's core operating areas include the Valhalla North Property in Alberta, the Pembina Property in Alberta, the Fosterton Property in Saskatchewan, & the West Central Sask Property.
Grant Fagerheim, President & Chief Executive Officer
Thanh Kang, Chief Financial Officer
Joel Armstrong, Vice-President, Production & Operations
Darin Dunlop, Vice-President, Engineering
Gary Lebsack, Vice-President, Land
Dave Mombourquette, Vice-President, Business Development

Yamana Gold Inc.
North Tower, Royal Bank Plaza
#2200, 200 Bay St.
Toronto, ON M5J 2J3
416-815-0220
Fax: 416-815-0021
888-809-0925
investor@yamana.com
www.yamana.com
Social Media: www.facebook.com/pages/Yamana-Gold/150944298311295
twitter.com/YamanaGoldInc
Company Type: Public
Ticker Symbol: YRI / TSX; AUY / NYSE
Staff Size: 12,372
Profile: Yamana Gold Inc. began operations in 2003. It is engaged in the exploration & production of gold, copper, & other precious metals. Development projects & operating mines are located in Mexico, Central America, Brazil, & Argentina.
Peter Marrone, Chair/CEO
Charles Main, CFO & Executive Vice-President, Finance
Richard C. Campbell, Sr. Vice-President, Human Resources
Barry Murphy, Sr. Vice-President, Technical Services
Sofia Tsakos, Senior Vice-President, General Counsel & Corporate Secretary

Yangarra Resources Ltd. (YGR)
#1530, 715 - 5th Ave. SW
Calgary, AB T2P 2X6
403-262-9558
Fax: 403-262-8281
info@yangarra.ca
www.yangarra.ca
Company Type: Public
Ticker Symbol: YGR / TSX Venture
Profile: The junior oil & gas company is engaged in exploration, development, & production in central Alberta.
Jim Evaskevich, President & Chief Executive Officer
James Glessing, CA, Chief Financial Officer
Lorne Simpson, B.Sc., C.E.T., Vice-President, Operations
Randall Faminow, Vice-President, Land

Oil & Gas

Advantage Oil & Gas Ltd.
E&Y Tower
#300, 440 - 2 Ave. SW
Calgary, AB T2P 5E9
403-718-8000
Fax: 403-718-8332
866-393-0393
ir@advantageog.com
www.advantageog.com
Company Type: Public
Ticker Symbol: AAV / TSX, NYSE
Staff Size: 26
Profile: The intermediate oil & natural gas corporation has properties in western Canada, including the Montney natural gas resource at Glacier, Alberta.
Andy J. Mah, President & Chief Executive Officer
Craig Blackwood, Chief Financial Officer & Vice-President, Finance
Neil Bokenfohr, Senior Vice-President

Africa Oil Corp.
#2000, 885 West Georgia St.
Vancouver, BC V6C 3E8
604-689-7842
Fax: 604-689-4250
africaoilcorp@namdo.com
www.africaoilcorp.com
Company Type: Public
Ticker Symbol: AOI / TSX Venture
Profile: The oil & gas company has assets in Ethiopia, Kenya, & Mail. Through its equity interest in Horn Petroleum Corporation, Africa Oil Corp. also has assets in Somalia.
Keith C. Hill, President & Chief Executive Officer
Ian Gibbs, Chief Financial Officer
Tim Thomas, Chief Operating Officer
Mark Dingley, Vice-President, Operations

Akita Drilling Ltd.
#1000, 333 - 7 Ave. SW
Calgary, AB T2P 2Z1
403-292-7979
Fax: 403-292-7990
akitainfo@akita-drilling.com
www.akita-drilling.com
Company Type: Public
Ticker Symbol: AKT.A / TSX
Profile: Akita Drilling Ltd. serves the oil & gas industry by providing contract drilling services. Western Canada, Canada's northern territories, & Alaska are the principal areas of activity.
Karl A. Ruud, President & Chief Executive Officer
Darcy Reynolds, Vice-President, Finance
Raymond Coleman, Senior Vice-President
Colin Dease, Corporate Secretary

Alberta Oilsands
#600, 815 - 8 Ave. SW
Calgary, AB T2P 3P2
403-263-6700
Fax: 416-907-1788
bvu@aboilsands.ca
www.aboilsands.ca
Company Type: Public
Ticker Symbol: AOS / TSX.V
Profile: Alberta Oilsands develops oil sands in the Athabasca region of Alberta as well as in Eastern Africa.
Binh Vu, Interim Chief Executive Officer
Michael Galloro, Chief Financial Officer

Altura Energy Inc.
PO Box 858 Stn. Main, Calgary, AB T2P 2J6
403-984-5197
Fax: 844-269-8922
info@alturaenergy.ca
www.alturaenergy.ca
Company Type: Public
Ticker Symbol: ATU.VN / TSX
Profile: An oil & gas producer.
David Burghardt, President & CEO
Tavis Carlson, Vice-President, Finance & CFO

Anderson Energy Ltd.
Selkirk
#1000, 555 - 4th Ave. SW
Calgary, AB T2P 3E7
403-262-6307
Fax: 403-261-2792
info@andersonenergy.ca
www.andersonenergy.ca
Company Type: Public
Ticker Symbol: AXL / TSX
Profile: Anderson Energy Ltd. is a resource-based oil and gas development company with property in central Alberta around the Sylvan Lake and Pembina fields.
Brian H. Dau, President & CEO
M. Darlene Wong, Vice-President & CFO, Finance
Sandra M. Drinnan, Vice-President, Land

ARC Resources Ltd.
#1200, 308 - 4th Ave. SW
Calgary, AB T2P 0H7
403-503-8600
Fax: 403-509-6427
888-272-4900
www.arcresources.com
Social Media: www.facebook.com/arcresources
twitter.com/arcresources
www.linkedin.com/company/61848
Company Type: Public
Ticker Symbol: ARX / TSX
Staff Size: 560
Profile: ARC resources is a conventional oil & gas company focused in Western Canada. ARC was formed in 1996.
Myron M. Stadnyk, President/Chief Executive Officer
Terry Anderson, Chief Operating Officer & Senior Vice-President
Van Dafoe, Chief Financial Officer & Senior Vice-President
Sean Calder, Vice-President, Production
Bevin Wirzba, Senior Vice-President, Business Development & Capital Markets

Arsenal Energy Inc.
#1900, 639 - 5th Ave. SW
Calgary, AB T2P 0M9
403-262-4854
Fax: 403-265-6877
info@arsenalenergy.com
www.arsenalenergy.com
Other Communications: Investor Relations E-mail: ir@arsenalenergy.com
Company Type: Public
Ticker Symbol: AEI / TSX
Profile: The energy exploration & production company has properties in Canada & the United States.
Tony van Winkoop, President & Chief Executive Officer
J. Paul Lawrence, Chief Financial Officer & Vice-President, Finance
Ron Forth, P.Eng., Vice-President, Engineering
Gjoa Taylor, Vice-President, Land

Athabasca Oil Corp. (AOC)
#1200, 215 - 9th Ave. SW
Calgary, AB T2P 1K3
403-237-8227
info@atha.com
www.atha.com
Other Communications: 24-Hour Emergency Toll-Free Phone: 1-877-235-9233
Company Type: Public
Ticker Symbol: ATH / TSX
Staff Size: 167
Profile: Athabasca Oil Sands Corp. was incorporated in 2006. The oil company is engaged in the development of oilsands resources in northern Alberta's Athabasca region.
The company promotes sustainable development through applying in situ technologies.
Rob Broen, President & Chief Executive Officer
Kim Anderson, Chief Financial Officer
Matt Taylor, Vice-President, Capital Markets & Communications

Bankers Petroleum Ltd.
#800, 777 - 8th Ave. SW
Calgary, AB T2P 3R5
403-513-2699
Fax: 403-228-9506
888-797-7170
info@bankerspetroleum.com
www.bankerspetroleum.com
Other Communications: Investor Relations Phone: 403-513-3428
Company Type: Public
Ticker Symbol: BNK / TSX; BNK / AIM
Staff Size: 580
Profile: The company focuses on oil & gas exploration & production in Albania.
David French, President & Chief Executive Officer
Douglas C. Urch, B.Comm., CMA, Chief Financial Officer & Executive Vice-President, Finance
Suneel Gupta, Exec. Vice-President & Chief Operating Officer
Robert Carss, Vice-President, Health, Safety, Social and Environment

Baytex Energy Corp.
East Tower, Centennial Place
#2800, 520 - 3rd Ave. SW
Calgary, AB T2P 0R3
587-952-3000
Fax: 587-952-3029
800-524-5521
investor@baytexenergy.com
www.baytexenergy.com
Other Communications: 24 Hour Emergency Phone: 403-250-0086
Social Media: twitter.com/BaytexEnergy
Company Type: Public
Ticker Symbol: BTE / TSX, NYSE
Profile: Baytex Energy specializes in the acquisition, development, & production of oil & natural gas. The area of operation is the Western Canadian Sedimentary Basin, in addition to a growing presence in the United States.
James L. Bowzer, Chief Executive Officer
Rodney D. Gray, Chief Financial Officer
Richard Ramsay, Chief Operating Officer
Cameron Hercus, Vice-President, Corporate Development
Kendall D. Arthur, Vice-President, Lloydminster Business Unit
Brian G. Ector, Senior Vice-President, Capital Markets & Public Affairs
Greg A. Sawchenko, Vice-President, Land
Ryan M. Johnson, Vice-President, Central Business Unit

Bellatrix Exploration Ltd.
#1920, 800 - 5th Ave. SW
Calgary, AB T2P 3T6
403-266-8670
Fax: 403-264-8163
www.bellatrixexploration.com
Other Communications: Investor Relations, Phone: 1-800-663-8072
Company Type: Public
Ticker Symbol: BXE / TSX
Staff Size: 188
Profile: The oil & gas company operates in British Columbia, Alberta, & Saskatchewan.
Raymond G. Smith, P.Eng., President & Chief Executive Officer
Edward J. Brown, C.A., Chief Financial Officer & Executive Vice-President, Finance
Brent Eshleman, P.Eng., Chief Operating Officer & Executive Vice-President
Tim A. Blair, Vice-President, Land
Russell G. Oicle, P. Geol., Vice-President, Exploration
Garrett K. Ulmer, P.Eng.., Vice-President, Engineering

Bengal Energy Ltd.
#1810, 801 - 6th Ave. SW
Calgary, AB T2P 3W2
403-205-2526
Fax: 403-263-3168
info@bengalenergy.ca
www.bengalenergy.ca
Other Communications: investor.relations@bengalenergy.ca
Company Type: Public
Ticker Symbol: BNG / TSX.V
Profile: Bengal Energy is an international oil and gas exploration and production company with an active inventory of highly prospective international opportunities in India and Australia.
Chayan Chakrabarty, President/CEO
Jerrad Blanchard, Chief Financial Officer
Gordon MacMahon, Vice-President, Exploration

Birchcliff Energy Ltd.
#500, 630 - 4th Ave. SW
Calgary, AB T2P 0J9
403-261-6401
Fax: 403-261-6424
866-566-2923
info@birchcliffenergy.com
www.birchcliffenergy.com
Social Media: ca.linkedin.com/company/birchcliff-energy
Company Type: Public
Ticker Symbol: BIR / TSX
Staff Size: 162
Profile: The intermediate oil & gas company is involved in exploration, development, & production.
A. Jeffery Tonken, President & Chief Executive Officer
Myles R. Bosman, Chief Operating Officer & Vice-President, Exploration
Bruno P. Geremia, Chief Financial Officer & Vice-President

Blackbird Energy Inc.
#400, 444 - 5 Ave. SW
Calgary, AB T2P 2T8
403-699-9929
www.blackbirdenergyinc.com
Social Media: twitter.com/blackbirdenergy
linkedin.com/company/blackbird-energy-inc-
Company Type: Public
Ticker Symbol: BBI / TSX.V
Profile: An oil & gas exploration company whose main project is in Alberta.
Garth Braun, President & CEO
Jeffrey Swainson, Chief Financial Officer
Don Noakes, Vice-President, Operations

BlackPearl Resources Inc.
#700, 444 - 7th Ave. SW
Calgary, AB T2P 0X8
403-215-8313
Fax: 403-262-5123
info@pxx.ca
www.blackpearlresources.ca
Company Type: Public
Ticker Symbol: PXX / TSX
Profile: BlackPearl Resources Inc. operates in western Canada, where it has heavy oil & oil sands assets.
John Festival, President & CEO
Don Cook, Chief Financial Officer
Chris Hogue, Vice-President, Operations
Ed Sobel, Vice-President, Exploration

BNK Petroleum Inc.
#350, 760 Paseo Camarillo
Camarillo, CA 93010
805-484-3613
Fax: 805-484-9649
www.bnkpetroleum.com
Company Type: Public
Ticker Symbol: BKX.TO / TSX
Profile: The company is focused on the exploration for & production of oil & gas. Through its subsidiaries & affiliates, BNK Petroleum Inc. is the owner & operator of shale gas properties located in the United States, Spain, Poland, & Germany.
Wolf E. Regener, President & CEO
Gary W. Johnson, Chief Financial Officer & Vice-President
Ray Payne, Vice-President, US Operations
Steven M. Warshauer, Ph.D., Vice-President, Exploration

Bonavista Energy Corporation
#1500, 525 - 8th Ave. SW
Calgary, AB T2P 1G1
403-213-4300
Fax: 403-262-5184
www.bonavistaenergy.com
Social Media: twitter.com/bonavistaenergy
www.linkedin.com/company/bonavista-energy-corporation
Company Type: Public
Ticker Symbol: BNP / TSX
Profile: Bonavista Energy is an oil & gas company, formed in 1997, that focuses on select multi-zone regions of Western Canada.
Bruce Jensen, Chief Operating Officer
Jason E. Skehar, President & Chief Executive Officer
Dean Kobelka, Chief Financial Officer & Vice-President, Finance
Scott Shimek, Vice-President, Operations
Colin Ranger, Vice-President, Production

Bonterra Energy Corp.
#901, 1015 - 4th St. SW
Calgary, AB T2R 1J4
403-262-5307
Fax: 403-265-7488
info@bonterraenergy.com
www.bonterraenergy.com
Company Type: Public
Ticker Symbol: BNE / TSX
Profile: Bonterra Energy Corp. is engaged in acquiring, exploring, & developing oil & natural gas properties. Activities are conducted in Saskatchewan, Alberta, & British Columbia.
George F. Fink, Chair & Chief Executive Officer
Robb D. Thompson, Chief Financial Officer & Corporate Secretary
Adrian Neumann, Chief Operating Officer

Boulder Energy
#540, 222 - 3rd Ave. SW
Calgary, AB T2P 0B4
403-767-3060
info@boulderenergy.ca
www.boulderenergy.ca
Company Type: Public
Ticker Symbol: BXO / TSX
Profile: An oil & gas company whose main project in located in Alberta.
Martin Cheyne, Chief Executive Officer
Clayton Thatcher, President
Robin Bieraugle, Chief Operating Officer
Casey Paulhus, Chief Financial Officer

Calfrac Well Services Ltd.
Corporate Headquarters
411 - 8th Ave. SW
Calgary, AB T2P 1E3
403-266-6000
866-770-3722
www.calfrac.com
Company Type: Public
Ticker Symbol: CFW / TSX
Staff Size: 2,600

Profile: Calfrac Well Services Ltd. is engaged in the provision of oilfield services, such as cementing, fracturing, & well stimulation services. Operations are situated in western Canada, the United States, Mexico, Argentina, & Russia.
Fernando Aguilar, President & CEO
Lindsay Link, Chief Operating Officer
Michael Olinek, Vice-President, Finance & Interim CFO

Canacol Energy Ltd.
Eighth Avenue Pl.
#4500, 525 - 8th Ave. SW
Calgary, AB T2P 1G1

403-561-1648
www.canacolenergy.com
Other Communications: Colombia Office: +571-621-1747; Texas Office: 713-595-3000

Company Type: Public
Ticker Symbol: CNE / TSX; CNE.C / BVC
Staff Size: 246
Profile: The oil & gas company has operations in Colombia & Ecuador.
Charle Gamba, President & Chief Executive Officer
Jason Bednar, Chief Financial Officer
Ravi Sharma, Chief Operating Officer
Mark Teare, Vice-President, Exploration
Anthony Zaidi, General Counsel & Vice-President, Business Development
Felix Betancourt, Country Manager, Colombia

Canadian Energy Services & Technology Corp. (CESTC)
#1400, 700 - 4th Ave. SW
Calgary, AB T2P 3J4

403-269-2800
Fax: 403-266-5708
888-785-6695
www.canadianenergyservices.com

Company Type: Public
Ticker Symbol: CEU / TSX
Staff Size: 1,417
Profile: Canadian Energy Services & Technology Corp. is involved in the design & implementation of drilling fluid systems. The company serves the oil & natural gas industry in western Canada & in the United States through its subsidiary, AES Drilling Fluids, LLC.
Thomas Simons, President & Chief Executive Officer

Canadian Natural Resources Limited
#2100, 855 - 2nd St. SW
Calgary, AB T2P 4J8

403-517-6700
Fax: 403-517-7350
www.cnrl.com
Other Communications: Investor Relations, Phone: 403-514-7777
Social Media: twitter.com/cnrlcareers
www.linkedin.com/company/cnrl

Company Type: Public
Ticker Symbol: CNQ / TSX
Staff Size: 7,568
Profile: Canadian Natural Resources Limited is an independent oil & natural gas producer. It is engaged in the exploration, development, & production of oil & natural gas. Operations are carried out in western Canada, the North Sea, & offshore west Africa.
Steve W. Laut, President
Corey B. Bieber, CFO & Senior Vice-President, Finance
Tim S. McKay, Chief Operating Officer
William R. Clapperton, Vice-President, Regulatory, Stakeholder & Environmental Affairs
Réal M. Cusson, Sr. Vice-President, Marketing
Ronald Laing, Sr. Vice-President, Corporate Development & Land

Canadian Overseas Petroleum
#3200, 715 - 5 Ave. SW
Calgary, AB T2P 2X6

403-262-5114
Fax: 403-263-3251
www.canoverseas.com
Social Media: twitter.com/COPLinvestor

Company Type: Public
Ticker Symbol: XOP / TSX.V
Profile: An oil & gas company with projects in Sub-Saharan African.
Arthur Millholland, President & CEO

Canadian Spirit Resources Inc. (CSRI)
First Alberta Place
#1520, 777 - 8th Ave. SW
Calgary, AB T2P 3R5

403-539-5005
info@csri.ca
www.csri.ca

Company Type: Public
Ticker Symbol: SPI / TSX Venture
Profile: The natural resources company focuses on opportunities in the unconventional gas sector.
J. Richard Couillard, President & CEO
Dean G. Hill, BComm, CA, Chief Financial Officer & Vice-President, Finance
Paul A. Smolarchuk, B.Sc., P.Eng., Vice-President, Engineering & Operations

Canyon Services Group Inc.
Bow Valley III
#2900, 255 - 5th Ave. SW
Calgary, AB T2P 3G6

403-355-2300
Fax: 403-355-2211
877-350-3722
www.canyontech.ca
Social Media: www.facebook.com/CanyonTechnicalServices
twitter.com/canyon_tech

Company Type: Public
Ticker Symbol: FRC / TSX
Staff Size: 990
Profile: Fracturing & chemical stimulation services are provided to oil & natural gas exploration & production companies throughout the Western Canadian Sedimentary Basin. Canyon Services Group Inc.'s wholly owned subsidiary is Canyon Technical Services Ltd.
Brad Fedora, President & Chief Executive Officer
Barry O'Brien, Chief Financial Officer & Vice-President, Finance
Todd Thue, Chief Operating Officer
Chuck Vozniak, Vice-President, Technical Services

Cathedral Energy Services Ltd.
Head Office (Drilling & Completions)
6030 - 3rd St. SE
Calgary, AB T2H 1K2

Fax: 403-262-4682
866-276-8201
info@cathedralenergyservices.com
www.cathedralenergyservices.com
Social Media: www.facebook.com/Cathedral-Energy-Services-1452838224971022
www.linkedin.com/company/cathedral-energy-services

Company Type: Public
Ticker Symbol: CET / TSX
Staff Size: 356
Profile: Cathedral Energy Services provides drilling & completions services. The company employs more than 850 people. Cathedral Energy works to meet its social, environmental, & ethical responsibilities.
P. Scott MacFarlane, President & Chief Executive Officer
Michael Hill, Chief Financial Officer
Randy Pustanyk, Executive Vice-President & COO

Caza Oil & Gas, Inc.
#200, 10077 Grogan's Mill Rd.
The Woodlands, TX 77380

281-363-4442
Fax: 281-363-4454
www.cazapetro.com

Company Type: Public
Ticker Symbol: CAZ / TSX, AIM
Profile: Caza Oil & Gas, Inc. is an exploration, appraisal, development, & production company. Through its subsidiary, Caza Petroleum, Inc., Caza Oil & Gas is active in the Texas & Louisiana Gulf Coast & in Permian Basin of western Texas & southeastern New Mexico.
W. Michael Ford, President & CEO
James Michael Markgraf, Chief Financial Officer & Vice-President, Finance
Richard Ronald Albro, Secretary & Vice-President, Land
Anthony Bryan Sam, Vice-President, Operations

Cenovus Energy Inc.
PO Box 766, 500 Centre St. SE
Calgary, AB T2P 0M5

403-766-2000
Fax: 403-766-7600
877-766-2066
questions&comments@cenovus.com
www.cenovus.com
Social Media: www.facebook.com/Cenovus
twitter.com/cenovus
www.linkedin.com/company/cenovus-energy

Company Type: Public
Ticker Symbol: CVE / TSX, NYSE
Staff Size: 3,600
Profile: Cenovus Energy oversees the following operations: a natural gas & oil production situated in southern Alberta & across Alberta; & an oil sands projects located in northern Alberta. Cenovus also has 50 percent ownership in two refineries in Roxana, Illinois & Borger, Texas. Cenovus Energy employs environmental specialists to analyze land for drilling activities & to develop a plan to reclaim the land.
Brian Ferguson, President & CEO
Ivor Ruste, Executive Vice-President & Chief Financial Officer

Cequence Energy Ltd.
#3100, 525 - 8th Ave. SW
Calgary, AB T2P 1G1

403-229-3050
Fax: 403-229-0603
info@cequence-energy.com
www.cequence-energy.com

Company Type: Public
Ticker Symbol: CQE / TSX
Profile: In western Canada, Cequence Energy Ltd. is engaged in the acquisition, exploration, development, & production of natural gas & crude oil.
Todd Brown, Chief Executive Officer

CGX Energy Inc.
#1100, 333 Bay St.
Toronto, ON M5H 2R2

416-364-5569
Fax: 416-360-7783
info@cgxenergy.com
www.cgxenergy.ca

Company Type: Public
Ticker Symbol: OYL / TSX Venture
Profile: The oil & gas exploration company is active in the Guyana - Suriname Basin. CGX Energy is also pursuing the Equatorial Atlantic Margin Play.
Dewi Jones, Chief Executive Officer
Tralisa Maraj, Chief Financial Officer
Michael Galego, General Counsel & Secretary

Chinook Energy Inc.
#1000, 517 - 10 Ave. SW
Calgary, AB T2R 0A8

403-261-6883
Fax: 403-266-1814
info1@chinookenergyinc.com
www.chinookenergyinc.com

Company Type: Public
Ticker Symbol: CKE / TSX
Profile: Chinook Energy Inc. is an oil & gas exploration & development company. It has assets in western Canada as well as onshore & offshore Tunisia in North Africa.
Walter Vrataric, President & CEO
Jason Dranchuk, Chief Financial Officer & Vice-President, Finance
Tim Halpen, Chief Operating Officer
Brent Dube, Vice-President, Production
Darrel Zacharias, Vice-President, Exploration

Condor Petroleum Inc.
#2400, 144 - 4th Ave. SW
Calgary, AB T2P 3N4

403-201-9694
Fax: 403-201-9607
contactus@condorpetroleum.com
www.condorpetroleum.com

Company Type: Public
Ticker Symbol: CPI / TSX
Profile: Condor Petroleum Inc. is an international oil and gas company that is engaged in exploration, development and production of oil, natural gas and NGLs in Kazakhstan.
Don Streu, President & Chief Executive Officer
Sandy Quilty, Vice-President & Chief Financial Officer
William Hatcher, Chief Operating Officer

Connacher Oil & Gas Limited
#1040, 640 - 5th Ave. SW
Calgary, AB T2P 3G4

403-538-6201
Fax: 403-538-6225
inquiries@connacheroil.com
www.connacheroil.com

Company Type: Public
Ticker Symbol: CLC / TSX
Staff Size: 124
Profile: Connacher Oil & Gas Limited is involved in the exploration, development, & production of oil & natural gas. The company's operations are carried out in western Canada, where its principal asset is oil sands leases in the Great Divide & Halfway Creek regions near Fort McMurray, Alberta. It is also the owner & operator of a refinery in Montana.
Merle D. Johnson, Chief Executive Officer
Jeff Beeston, Vice-President, Finance & Interim CFO
Suzanne Loov, General Counsel & Corporate Secretary

Corridor Resources Inc.
Head Office
#301, 5475 Spring Garden Rd.
Halifax, NS B3J 3T2
902-429-4511
Fax: 902-429-0209
888-429-4511
info@corridor.ca
www.corridor.ca
Other Communications: Penobsquis, New Brunswick, Field Office, Phone: 506-433-3066
Company Type: Public
Ticker Symbol: CDH / TSX
Profile: Corridor Resources Inc. is a junior resource company, which is engaged in the exploration & development of oil & gas properties. Activities are carried out onshore in Prince Edward Island, New Brunswick, & Québec, & offshore in the Gulf of St. Lawrence.
Steve Moran, President & CEO
Lisette F. Hachey, Chief Financial Officer
Tom Martel, Chief Geologist

Crescent Point Energy Corp.
#2000, 585 - 8th Ave. SW
Calgary, AB T2P 1G1
403-693-0020
Fax: 403-693-0070
888-693-0020
www.crescentpointenergy.com
Other Communications: Investor Relations, Toll-Free Phone: 855-767-6923
Social Media: twitter.com/cpg_corp
www.linkedin.com/company/crescent-point-energy
Company Type: Public
Ticker Symbol: CPG / TSX, NYSE
Staff Size: 491
Profile: Formed in 1994, Crescent Point Energy Corp. is an oil & gas producer. The company is engaged in the acquisition of reserves & production in western Canada. On June 30, 2015, Crescent Point Energy completed the acquisition of Legacy Oil + Gas, an energy production company whose assets lie primarily in Saskatchewan.
Scott Saxberg, President & Chief Executive Officer
Ken Lamont, Chief Financial Officer
C. Neil Smith, Chief Operating Officer
Tamara MacDonald, Senior Vice-President, Corporate & Business Development
Trent Stangl, Senior Vice-President, Investor Relations & Communications
Derek Christie, Vice-President, Exploration & Geosciences
Mark Eade, Vice-President, General Counsel & Corporate Secretary

Crew Energy Inc.
#800, 250 - 5th St. SW
Calgary, AB T2P 0R4
403-266-2088
Fax: 403-266-6259
investor@crewenergy.com
www.crewenergy.com
Company Type: Public
Ticker Symbol: CR / TSX
Profile: The junior oil & natural gas producer carries out its activities in northeastern British Columbia & central Alberta.
Dale O. Shwed, President/CEO
John G. Leach, CFO & Sr. Vice-President, Finance
Rob Morgan, Sr. Vice-President/Chief Operating Officer
Shawn Van Spankeren, Vice-President, Finance & Administration
Ken Truscott, Senior Vice-President, Business Development & Land
Jamie Bowman, Vice-President, Marketing

Crown Point Energy
#1600, 700 - 6th Ave. SW
Calgary, AB T2P 0T8
403-232-1150
Fax: 403-232-1158
info@crownpointenergy.com
www.crownpointenergy.com
Company Type: Public
Ticker Symbol: CWV / TSX.V
Profile: Crown Point Energy Inc. is a junior international oil and gas company with a base in the three largest producing basins in Argentina.
Murray D. McCartney, President & CEO
Brian J. Moss, Executive Vice-President/COO
Marisa Tormakh, Chief Financial Officer & Vice-President, Finance

CWC Energy Services Corp.
Bow Valley Square II
#610, 205 - 5th Ave. SW
Calgary, AB T2P 2V7
403-264-2177
Fax: 403-264-2842
info@cwcenergyservices.com
www.cwcenergyservices.com
Social Media: www.facebook.com/122409711146882
www.linkedin.com/company/1613347
Company Type: Public
Ticker Symbol: CWC / TSX Venture
Staff Size: 366
Profile: CWC operates in the Western Canadian Sedimentary Basin. Services include coil tubing, well testing, & snubbing. Operations centers are located in Red Deer, Grande Prairie, Lloydminster, Provost, Brooks, & Weyburn.
Duncan Au, CA, CFA, President & Chief Executive Officer
Craig Flint, Chief Financial Officer
Paul Donohue, Vice-President, Drilling Operations
Darwin McIntyre, Vice-President, Well Services Operations

Dalmac Energy Inc.
4934 - 89 St.
Edmonton, AB T6E 5K1
403-988-8510
Fax: 403-988-8512
888-632-5622
info@dalmacenergy.com
www.dalmacenergy.com
Company Type: Public
Ticker Symbol: DAL / TSX.V
Staff Size: 160
Profile: Dalmac provides fluid management services, such as hot oiling, frac heating, well acidizing and fluid transfers. It also supplies glycol & methanol products to energy companies.
John Babic, President
jbabic@dalmacenergy.com
Jonathan Gallo, Chief Financial Officer
jgallo@dalmac.ca
Tim Sturko, Vice-President, Operations
tsutrko@dalmac.ca

Delphi Energy Corp.
Head Office
#300, 500 - 4th Ave. SW
Calgary, AB T2P 2V6
403-265-6171
Fax: 403-265-6207
info@delphienergy.ca
www.delphienergy.ca
Company Type: Public
Ticker Symbol: DEE / TSX
Profile: Delphi Energy is engaged in the exploration for & the development & production of oil & natural gas. Operations take place in western Canada.
David J. Reid, President & Chief Executive Officer
Brian P. Kohlhammer, Chief Financial Officer & Senior Vice-President
Rob Hume, P.Eng., Senior Vice-President, Engineering
Hugo Batteke, P.Eng., Vice-President, Operations

Divestco Inc.
#300, 520 - 3rd Ave. SW
Calgary, AB T2P 0R3
587-952-8000
Fax: 587-952-8370
888-294-0081
info@divestco.com
www.divestco.com
Social Media: www.facebook.com/Divestco
Company Type: Public
Ticker Symbol: DVT / TSX
Profile: Divestco is an exploration services company dedicated to providing a focused offering of products and services to the oil and gas industry worldwide.
Stephen Popadynetz, President & CEO
Danny Chiarastella, Chief Financial Officer
Steve Sinclair-Smith, Chief Operating Officer

Dundee Energy Limited
Dundee Pl.
#2100, 1 Adelaide St. East
Toronto, ON M5C 2V9
416-863-6990
Fax: 416-363-4536
dundee-energy@dundee-energy.com
www.dundee-energy.com
Other Communications: London Office, Phone: 519-433-7710, Fax: 519-433-7588
Company Type: Public
Ticker Symbol: DEN / TSX
Profile: The oil & natural gas company is engaged in exploration, development, production & marketing. Dundee Energy Limited has interests in Ontario & Spain. Through a preferred share investment, the company also has exploration & evaluation programs for oil & natural gas offshore Tunisia.
Bruce Sherley, President & CEO
David Bhumgara, CA, CA-IT, Chief Financial Officer
Lucie Presot, CMA, Vice-President

DXI Energy Inc.
#598, 999 Canada Pl.
Vancouver, BC V6C 3E1
604-638-5050
Fax: 604-638-5051
www.dxienergy.com
Social Media: www.facebook.com/dxienergy
twitter.com/DXIEnergy
Company Type: Public
Ticker Symbol: DXI / TSX
Profile: The company own oil & gas projects in Colorado & British Columbia.
Robert Hodgkinson, Chief Executive Officer
David Matheson, Chief Financial Officer

Eagle Energy Inc.
#2710, 500 - 4th Ave. SW
Calgary, AB T2P 2V6
403-531-1575
Fax: 403-508-9840
855-531-1575
info@eagleenergy.com
www.eagleenergytrust.com
Other Communications: Houston, TX, Office, Phone: 713-300-3245
Company Type: Public
Ticker Symbol: EGL.UN / TSX
Profile: Eagle Energy is an oil and natural gas producer.
Richard W. Clark, Chief Executive Officer
Kelly A. Tomyn, Chief Financial Officer
Wayne Wisniewski, President & COO

Enbridge Inc.
Fifth Avenue Pl.
#200, 425 - 1st St. SW
Calgary, AB T2P 3L8
403-231-3900
Fax: 403-231-3920
webmaster-corp@enbridge.com
www.enbridge.com
Other Communications: Investor Relations, E-mail: investor.relations@enbridge.com
Social Media: www.facebook.com/enbridge
twitter.com/enbridge
www.linkedin.com/company/enbridge
Company Type: Public
Ticker Symbol: ENB / TSX, NYSE
Staff Size: 8,652
Profile: Enbridge Inc. is engaged in the following businesses: natural gas pipelines, crude oil & liquids pipelines, & natural gas distribution. The company's pipeline system is located in Canada & the United States. International activity includes energy projects & renewable energy.
In 2011, Enbridge, through Canadain Acquireco, acquired all the outstanding common shares of Tonbridge Power Inc.
In 2016, it was announced that Enbridge would be acquiring Houston-based Spectra Energy Corp. The new combined company would continue to be known as Enbridge Inc.
Al Monaco, President/CEO
John Whelen, Executive Vice-President/CFO
Leon Zupan, President & COO, Liquids Pipelines
David T. Robottom, Executive Vice-President & Chief Legal Officer
Karen Radford, Executive Vice-President & Chief Transformation Officer

Encana Corporation
PO Box 2850, 500 Centre St. SE
Calgary, AB T2P 2S5
403-645-2000
Fax: 403-645-3400
888-568-6322
general.inquiries@encana.com
www.encana.com
Other Communications: Investor Relations, E-mail: investor.relations@encana.com
Social Media: www.facebook.com/Encana
twitter.com/encanacorp
www.linkedin.com/company/encana-corporation
Company Type: Public
Ticker Symbol: ECA / TSX
Staff Size: 2,726
Profile: The company is engaged in producing natural gas, oil, & natural gas liquids. Common shares trade on the Toronto & New York stock exchanges under the symbol ECA.
Doug Suttles, President & Chief Executive Officer
Sherri Brillon, Executive Vice-President & Chief Financial Officer

Mike Williams, Executive Vice-President, Corporate Services

Enerflex Ltd.
#904, 1331 Macleod Trail SE
Calgary, AB T2G 0K3
403-387-6377
800-242-3178
info@enerflex.com
www.enerflex.com
Social Media:
www.facebook.com/pages/Enerflex-Ltd/161910453868539
twitter.com/enerflexltd
www.linkedin.com/company/enerflex-ltd-
Company Type: Public
Ticker Symbol: EFX / TSX
Staff Size: 1,900
Profile: Enerflex is the single-source supplier for natural gas compression, oil and gas processing, refrigeration systems and power generation equipment - plus in-house engineering and mechanical services expertise.
Blair Goertzen, President/Chief Executive Officer
James Harbilas, Executive Vice-President & Chief Financial Officer
Jamie Plosz, Director, Marketing & Public Relations

Enerplus Corp.
The Dome Tower
#3000, 333 - 7th Ave. SW
Calgary, AB T2P 2Z1
403-298-2200
Fax: 403-298-2211
www.enerplus.com
Other Communications: investorrelations@enerplus.com
Social Media: twitter.com/EnerplusCorp
www.linkedin.com/company/enerplus
Company Type: Public
Ticker Symbol: ERF / TSX
Staff Size: 588
Profile: Enerplus Resources Fund has a portfolio of oil & natural gas producing properties. Properties are situated in western Canada & the United States.
Ian C. Dundas, President/CEO
Jodine Jenson Labrie, B.Comm., CA, CBV, Sr. Vice-President/CFO
Raymond (Ray) J. Daniels, Senior Vice-President, Operations
Lisa M. Ower, Vice-President, People & Culture

Enhanced Oil Resources, Inc.
#150, 777 North Eldridge Pkwy.
Houston, TX 77079 USA
832-485-8500
info@enhancedoilres.com
www.enhancedoilres.com
Other Communications: Investor Relations E-mail: IR@enhancedoilres.com
Company Type: Public
Ticker Symbol: EOR / TSX.V
Profile: Through enhanced oil recovery & infill drilling projects, it is the goal of Enhanced Oil Resources Inc. to increase crude oil & natural gas production.
Andrew Hromyk, President & CEO
Rick Powers, Chief Financial Officer, Treasurer & Vice-President

Ensign Energy Services Inc.
#1000, 400 - 5th Ave. SW
Calgary, AB T2P 0L6
403-262-1361
Fax: 403-262-8215
www.ensignenergy.com
Social Media:
www.facebook.com/pages/Ensign-Energy/45665635750
www.linkedin.com/company/ensign-energy-services
Company Type: Public
Ticker Symbol: ESI / TSX
Staff Size: 4,404
Profile: Ensign Energy Services Inc. is a service contractor that provides oilfield services throughout the world to the oil & natural gas industry. Some of Ensign Energy Services's principal operating subsidiaries include Arctic Ensign Drilling Ltd., Big Sky Drilling Inc., Encore Coring & Drilling Inc., Opsco Energy Industries Ltd., Rockwell Servicing Inc., & Gwich'in Ensign Oilfield Services Inc.
Robert H. Geddes, President & Chief Operating Officer
Timothy Lemke, Vice-President & Chief Financial Officer
Ed Kautz, President, United States Operations
Brage Johannessen, Executive Vice-President, International

Epsilon Energy Ltd.
Centennial Place, West Tower
#2110, 250 - 5 St. SW
Calgary, AB T2P 0R4
281-670-0002
Fax: 281-668-0985
www.epsilonenergyltd.com
Company Type: Public
Ticker Symbol: EPS.TO, EPS.DB / TSX
Profile: Established in 2005, Epsilon Energy Ltd. is involved in the exploration & production of natural gas reserves. The company has participating interests & production sharing agreements in North America & Africa.
Michael Raleigh, Chief Executive Officer
B. Lane Bond, Chief Financial Officer

Essential Energy Services Ltd.
Livingston Placw West
#1100, 250 - 2nd St. SW
Calgary, AB T2P 0C1
403-263-6778
service@essentialenergy.ca
www.essentialenergy.ca
Other Communications: Investor Relations: 403-513-7272
Company Type: Public
Ticker Symbol: ESN / TSX
Staff Size: 588
Profile: Essential Energy Services Ltd. offers oilfield services to oil & gas producers in western Canada. In 2011, Essential Energy Services acquired Technicoil Corporation to strengthen the company's position as a coil tubing well service provider.
Garnet K. Amundson, President & Chief Executive Officer
Allan Mowbray, Chief Financial Officer

Estrella International Energy Services Ltd.
Cerrito 1136, 9th Fl.
Buenos Aires, C1010AAX Argentina
info@estrellaies.com
www.estrellaies.com
Other Communications: +54-11-5217-5250; Fax: +54-11-5217-5280
Company Type: Public
Ticker Symbol: EEN / TSX
Profile: Estrella provides drilling and workover services to the natural resource sector in Latin America.

Explor Resources Inc.
#204, 15 Gamble St. East
Rouyn Noranda, QC J9X 3B6
819-797-4630
Fax: 819-797-6050
800-388-8668
info@explorresources.com
www.explorresources.com
Company Type: Public
Ticker Symbol: EXS / TSX.V
Profile: Explor Resources is a junior gold and base metals exploration company with mineral holdings in Ontario, Quebec and Saskatchewan.
Chris Dupont, President

Falcon Oil & Gas Ltd.
68 Merrion Sq. South
Dublin, 2 Ireland
info@falconoilandgas.com
www.falconoilandgas.com
Other Communications: Phone: +353-1-676-8702
Company Type: Public
Ticker Symbol: FO / TSX.V
Profile: Falcon Oil & Gas Ltd. is a global energy company that is focused on acquiring, exploring and developing large acreage positions of unconventional and conventional oil and gas resources.
Philip O'Quigley, Chief Executive Officer
Michael Gallagher, Chief Financial Officer

Gastar Exploration Ltd.
#650, 1331 Lamar St.
Houston, TX 77010 USA
713-739-1800
Fax: 713-739-0458
ir@gastar.com
www.gastar.com
Company Type: Public
Ticker Symbol: GST / AMEX, NYSE
Profile: Gastar Exploration Ltd. is engaged in the exploration, development and production of natural gas, natural gas liquids, oil and condensate in the United States.
J. Russell Porter, President & CEO
Michael Gerlich, Chief Financial Officer

Gear Energy
#2600, 240 - 4th Ave. SW
Calgary, AB T2P 4H4
403-538-8435
Fax: 403-705-2660
info@gearenergy.com
www.gearenergy.com
Company Type: Public
Ticker Symbol: GXE / TSX
Profile: Gear Energy is an exploration and production company focused on heavy oil. In 2016 Gear Energy merged with Striker Exploration.
Ingram B. Gillmore, President & Chief Executive Officer
David Hwang, Vice President, Finance & Chief Financial Officer

Gibson Energy Inc.
Also Known As: Gibsons
Head Office
#1700, 440 - 2nd Ave. SW
Calgary, AB T2P 5E9
403-206-4000
Fax: 403-206-4001
www.gibsons.com
Company Type: Public
Ticker Symbol: GEI / TSX
Staff Size: 2,700
Profile: Gibson Energy Inc. is a midstream energy company that is engaged in the following activities: crude oil transportation; blending & processing hydrocarbons; marketing & distributing crude oil & refined products; & providing water disposal & oilfield waste management services.
In 2011, Gibson Energy Inc. & Palko Environmental Ltd. entered into an arrangement agreement, providing for the acquisition by Gibson of all the issued & outstanding common shares of Palko.
Stew Hanlon, President & Chief Executive Officer
Sean Brown, Chief Financial Officer
Doug Wilkins, Chief Commercial Officer
Richard M. Wise, Chief Operating Officer
Brian Recatto, President, US Operations
Sean Duffee, Senior Vice-President, Marketing & Commercial Development

Gordon Creek Energy
#1350, 734 - 7 Ave. SW
Calgary, AB T2P 3P8
403-453-1608
Fax: 403-453-1609
www.atna.com
Company Type: Public
Ticker Symbol: GDN / TSX.V
Profile: The company acquires and develops natural gas projects in the United States.
Rupert Evans, President & Chief Executive Officer
John Bell, Chief Financial Officer
Barry Brumwell, Vice-President, Operations

Granite Oil Corp.
#432, 222 - 3rd Ave. SW
Calgary, AB T2P 0B4
587-349-9113
info@graniteoil.ca
www.graniteoil.ca
Company Type: Public
Ticker Symbol: GXO / TSX
Staff Size: 16
Profile: The company focuses on oil and natural gas exploration in western Canada.
Michael Kabanuk, President & CEO
Gail Hannon, Chief Financial Officer
Jonathan Fleming, Executive Vice-President

GrowMax Resources Corp.
#203, 602 - 11th Ave. SW
Calgary, AB T2R 1J8
587-390-7015
info@growmaxcorp.com
www.growmaxcorp.com
Social Media: www.linkedin.com/company/317699
Company Type: Public
Ticker Symbol: GRO / TSX Venture
Profile: GrowMax Resources Corp. has both conventional & unconventional shale oil & gas & tight sands oil & gas interests. The company is active in Argentina's Neuquen Basin.
Abdel (Abby) Badwi, Executive Chair
Douglas Yee, Chief Financial Officer

Hawk Exploration Ltd.
#1320, 396 - 11th Ave. SW
Calgary, AB T2R 0C5
403-264-0191
Fax: 403-263-9076
info@hawkexploration.ca
www.hawkexploration.ca
Company Type: Public
Ticker Symbol: HWK.A / TSX.V
Steve Fitzmaurice, President, CEO & Chairman
Dennis Jamieson, Chief Financial Officer

Hemisphere Energy Corp.
#2000, 1055 West Hastings St.
Vancouver, BC V6E 2E9
604-685-9255
Fax: 604-685-9676
info@hemisphereenergy.ca
www.hemisphereenergy.ca
Company Type: Public
Ticker Symbol: HME / TSX.V
Profile: Hemisphere Energy is an oil & gas company whose main projects are in southeast Alberta near Jenner & Atlee Buffalo.
Don Simmons, President & CEO
Dorlyn Evancic, Chief Financial Officer
Ian Duncan, Chief Operating Officer
Andrew Arthur, Vice-President, Exploration
Ashley Ramsden-Wood, Vice-President, Engineering

High Arctic Energy Services Inc.
#2010, 444 - 5 Ave. SW
Calgary, AB T2P 2T8
403-508-7836
Fax: 403-362-5176
800-668-7143
info@haes.ca
www.haes.ca
Social Media: www.facebook.com/pages/High-Arctic-Energy-Services/255987967732
www.linkedin.com/company/high-arctic-energy-services
Company Type: Public
Ticker Symbol: HWO / TSX
Staff Size: 497
Profile: Through its subsidiaries, High Arctic Energy Services specializes in providing oilfield equipment & services. Operations are carried out in western Canada & in Papua New Guinea.
Tim Braun, Chief Executive Officer
Brian Peters, Chief Financial Officer
Dan Beaulieu, Chief Operating Officer, Canada
Mike Maguire, Vice-President, International Operations

Husky Energy Inc.
PO Box 6525 Stn. D, Calgary, AB T2P 3G7
403-298-6111
Fax: 403-298-7464
www.huskyenergy.com
Other Communications: 24-Hour Emergency Toll-Free Phone: 1-877-262-2111
Company Type: Public
Ticker Symbol: HSE / TSX
Staff Size: 5,552
Profile: Husky Energy Inc. is engaged in the exploration & development of crude oil & natural gas, as well as the production, transportation & marketing of petroleum products. The company has upstream, midstream, & downstream business segments, & operates globally. Husky Energy works to meet & exceed regulatory requirements to reduce its impact to land, habitat, air, & water.
Asim Ghosh, President & CEO
Jonathan McKenzie, Chief Financial Officer
Robert Peabody, Chief Operating Officer
Edward Connolly, Senior Vice-President, Heavy Oil
David Gardner, Senior Vice-President, Business Development
James Girgulis, Senior Vice-President, General Counsel & Secretary

Hyduke Energy Services Inc.
Head Office
2707 - 6 St.
Nisku, AB T9E 7X8
780-955-0360
Fax: 780-955-0367
www.hyduke.com
Company Type: Public
Ticker Symbol: HYD / TSX
Staff Size: 121
Profile: The oilfield services company specializes in the manufacture, repair, & distribution of oilfield equipment & supplies. Drilling rigs & well service equipment are also inspected & certified. Hyduke Energy Services serves the drilling & well service industries in Canada & internationally.
Patrick F. Ross, Chief Executive Officer
Veronica Dutchak, CA, Chief Financial Officer

Ikkuma Resources Corp.
#2700, 605 - 5th Ave. SW
Calgary, AB T2P 3H5
403-261-5900
Fax: 403-261-5902
mailbox@ikkumarescorp.com
www.ikkumarescorp.com
Social Media: www.linkedin.com/company/ikkuma-resources-corp-canada
Company Type: Public
Ticker Symbol: IKM / TSX.V
Profile: The junior oil company carries out its operations in western Canada.
Tim de Freitas, President & CEO
Carrie Yuill, Chief Financial Officer & Vice-President, Finance
Dorothy Else, Executive Vice-President
Yvonne McLeod, Senior Vice-President, Engineering
Greg Feltham, Vice-President, Exploration
Kavanagh Mannas, Vice-President, Operations

Imperial Oil Limited
505 Quarry Park Blvd.
Calgary, AB T2C 4K8
Fax: 800-367-0585
800-567-3776
rccr.essoweb@exxonmobil.com
www.imperialoil.ca
Other Communications: Customer Help Centre, Toll-Free Phone: 1-877-359-9792
Social Media: twitter.com/imperialoil
linkedin.com/company/imperial-oil
Company Type: Public
Ticker Symbol: IMO / TSX
Staff Size: 4,800
Profile: The company is a producer of crude oil & natural gas. Imperial Oil also refines & markets petroleum products. The company aims to minimize its impact on the air, land, & water by investing in research & technology & adhering to detailed management systems.
Rich Kruger, President/CEO & Chair
Beverley Babcock, Controller & Senior Vice-President, Finance & Administration
W.J. (Bill) Hartnett, Vice-President & General Counsel
B.P. (Bart) Cahir, Senior Vice-President, Upstream

Inter Pipeline Ltd.
#3200, 215 - 2nd St.
Calgary, AB T2P 1M4
403-290-6000
Fax: 403-290-6090
866-716-7473
investorrelations@interpipeline.com
www.interpipeline.com
Other Communications: Media Relations, E-mail: mediarelations@interpipeline.com
Social Media: twitter.com/inter_pipeline
www.linkedin.com/company/inter-pipeline
Company Type: Public
Ticker Symbol: IPL / TSX
Profile: Inter Pipeline Fund was created in 1997. It is involved in natural gas liquids extraction, petroleum storage, & transportation.
Christian Bayle, President & CEO
Brent Heagy, CFO
James Madro, Senior Vice-President, Operations

InterOil Corp.
#23A, 1330 Avenue of the Americas
New York, NY 10019 USA
212-653-9778
www.interoil.com
Company Type: Public
Ticker Symbol: IOC / NYSE
Staff Size: 220
Profile: InterOil Corporation is an integrated oil and gas company that produces jet fuel, diesel and gasoline for the domestic market and light naphtha and mixed naphtha for international markets.
Michael Hession, Chief Executive Officer
Jon Ozturgut, Chief Commercial Officer
Donald Spector, Chief Financial Officer
Sheree Ford, General Counsel & Corporate Secretary

Ithaca Energy Inc.
8 Rubislaw Terrace
Aberdeen, AB10 1XE UK
www.ithacaenergy.com
Other Communications: Phone: +44-(0)-1224-638-582; Fax: +44-(0)-1224-635-795
Company Type: Public
Ticker Symbol: IAE / TSX
Profile: Ithaca Energy is involved in the exploration, development, & production of oil & gas. The company is active in the United Kingdom's Continental Shelf.
Les Thomas, Chief Executive Officer
Roy Buchan, Chief Operations Officer
Graham Forbes, Chief Financial Officer

Journey Energy Inc.
#700, 517 - 10th Ave. SW
Calgary, AB T2R 0A8
403-294-1635
Fax: 403-232-1317
888-294-1635
info@journeyenergy.ca
www.journeyenergy.ca
Company Type: Public
Ticker Symbol: JOY / TSX
Profile: An oil & gas producer working in Western Canada.
Alex Verge, President & CEO
Gerald Gilewicz, Chief Financial Officer

Junex Inc.
#200, 2795, boul Laurier
Québec, QC G1V 4M7
418-654-9661
Fax: 418-654-9662
junex@junex.ca
www.junex.ca
Company Type: Public
Ticker Symbol: JNX / TSX Venture
Profile: Founded in 1999, Junex is engaged in oil & gas exploration in Québec. The junior oil & gas company holds exploration rights on lands in the Appalachian basin, the St. Lawrence lowlands, & on Anticosti Island.
Jean-Yves Lavoie, Eng., Chairman & Co-Founder
Peter Dorrins, Eng., President & CEO
Dave Pépin, MBA, Chief Financial Officer & Vice-President, Corporate Affairs
Mathieu Lavoie, Eng., Vice-President, Operations
Jean-Sébastien Marcil, Eng., Manager, Exploration

Jura Energy Corporation
#5100, 150 - 6th Ave. SW
Calgary, AB T2P 3Y7
403-266-6364
info@juraenergy.com
www.juraenergy.com
Company Type: Public
Ticker Symbol: JEC / TSX
Profile: Jura Energy Corporation is an international independent upstream oil & gas company.
Shahid Hameed, Interim CEO & President
Nadeem Farooq, Chief Financial Officer

Kelt Exploration
East Tower
#300, 311 - 6th Ave. SW
Calgary, AB T2P 3H2
403-294-0154
Fax: 403-291-0155
www.keltexploration.com
Company Type: Public
Ticker Symbol: KEL / TSX
Profile: Kelt Exploration is an oil & gas company. It specializes in the exploration, development & production of crude oil & natural gas resources.
David Wilson, President & CEO
Sadiq Lalani, Chief Financial Officer & Vice-President, Finance
Douglas MacArthur, Vice-President, Operations
Douglas Errico, Vice-President, Land
Alan Franks, Vice-President, Production

Leucrotta Exploration Inc.
#700, 639 - 5th Ave. SW
Calgary, AB T2P 0M9
403-705-4525
Fax: 403-705-4526
info@leucrotta.ca
www.leucrotta.ca
Company Type: Public
Ticker Symbol: LXE / TSX.V
Profile: Luecrotta's main project is located in the Dawson-Sunrise area, in Northeast British Columbia.
Robert J. Zakresky, President & Chief Executive Officer
Nolan Chicoine, Chief Financial Officer & Vice-President, Finance
Terry Trudeau, Chief Operating Officer & Vice-President, Operations

LGX Oil + Gas
c/o Ernst & Young
#2200, 215 - 2nd St. SW
Calgary, AB T2P 1M4
403-206-5035
www.lgxoil.com
Company Type: Public
Ticker Symbol: OIL / TSX.V
Profile: LGX Oil + Gas Inc. is a Calgary-based junior oil and natural gas company engaged in the exploration and development of resource-type oil and natural gas opportunities primarily focused in southern Alberta.

Duncan MacRae, Contact
Duncan.MacRae@ca.ey.com
Curt Ziemer, CFO & Vice-President, Finance
Dale C.J. Mennis, Vice-President, Land
Mark Oliver, Vice-President, Exploration

Lightstream Resources Ltd.
#2800, 525 - 8th Ave. SW
Calgary, AB T2P 1G1
403-268-7800
Fax: 403-218-6075
ir@lightstreamres.com
www.lightstreamresources.com

Company Type: Public
Ticker Symbol: LTS / TSX
Staff Size: 301
Profile: Lightstream Resources Ltd was established in 2009. During the same year, it acquired TriStar Oil & Gas Ltd.
The oil exploration & production company has light oil assests in southeast Saskatchewan, as well as Cardium potential in central Alberta. The company is also exploring natural gas development opportunities in the Horn River & Montney regions of northeastern British Columbia.
John D. Wright, President & Chief Executive Officer
Peter D. Scott, Chief Financial Officer & Senior Vice-President
Rene LaPrade, Chief Operating Officer & Senior Vice-President
Lawrence Fisher, Vice-President, Land
Peter Hawkes, Vice-President, Geoscience
Mary Bulmer, Vice-President, Corporate Services

Lonestar West Inc.
Site 5, RR#1, Box 1
Sylvan Lake, AB T4S 1X6
403-887-2074
info@lonestarwest.com
lonestarwest.com
Social Media: www.facebook.com/Lonestarwest
www.linkedin.com/company/lonestar-west-service-llc

Company Type: Public
Ticker Symbol: LSI / TSX.V
Staff Size: 327
Profile: Lonestar West provides oil & gas companies with equipment & drilling services in western Canada, California, Oklahoma & Texas.
James Horvath, President & CEO
Delanie Hill, Chief Financial Officer
Chris Anderson, Executive Vice-President
Kristin York, Director, Operations

Long Run Exploration
Livingston Place, West Tower
#400, 250 - 2 St. SW
Calgary, AB T2P 0C1
403-261-6012
Fax: 403-262-5561
888-598-1330
information@longrunexploration.com
www.longrunexploration.com

Company Type: Public
Ticker Symbol: LRE / TSX
Staff Size: 227
Profile: Long Run Exploration is a midcap Canadian Oil and Gas company focused on the Western Canadian Sedimentary Basin.
William E. Andrew, Chair & Chief Executive Officer
Dale A. Miller, President & COO
Corine Bushfield, Senior Vice-President & CFO
Dale Orton, Senior Vice-President, Development

Macro Enterprises Inc.
PO Box 6781, Fort St John, BC V1J 4J2
250-785-0033
Fax: 250-785-0073
office@macroindustries.ca
www.macroenterprises.ca

Company Type: Public
Ticker Symbol: MCR / TSX.V
Staff Size: 230
Profile: Macro Industries specializes in construction and maintenance of small- to mid-inch pipelines, facilities and gathering systems.
Frank Miles, President & CEO
frank@macroindustries.ca
Jeff Redmond, Chief Financial Officer
jredmond@macroindustries.ca

Madalena Energy Inc.
#3200, 500 - 4th Ave. SW
Calgary, AB T2P 2V6
403-262-1901
Fax: 403-262-1905
www.madalenaenergy.com

Company Type: Public
Ticker Symbol: MVN / TSX.V
Profile: Madalena is an independent, Canadian-based, domestic and international upstream oil and gas company whose main business activities include exploration, development and production of crude oil, natural gas liquids and natural gas.
Steven Sharpe, Interim President & Chief Executive Officer
Thomas Love, Chief Financial Officer & Vice-President, Finance
Steve Dabner, Vice-President, Exploration & New Ventures

Marquee Energy Ltd.
#1700, 500 - 4th Ave. SW
Calgary, AB T2P 2V6
403-384-0000
Fax: 403-265-0073
www.marquee-energy.com
Other Communications: Accounts Payable, E-mail: ap@marquee-energy.com

Company Type: Public
Ticker Symbol: MQL / TSX.V
Profile: Marquee Energy focuses predominately on light oil and liquids-rich gas opportunities in Alberta.
Richard Thompson, President & CEO
Dan Toews, Chief Financial Officer & Vice-President, Finance
Steve Bradford, Vice-President, Land & Investor Relations
Dave Washenfelder, Vice-President, Exploration

MEG Energy Corp. (MEG)
520 - 3rd Ave. SW, 15th Fl.
Calgary, AB T2P 0R3
403-770-0446
Fax: 403-264-1711
www.megenergy.com
Other Communications: Media, E-mail: media@megenergy.com; invest@megenergy.com

Company Type: Public
Ticker Symbol: MEG / TSX
Staff Size: 627
Profile: The Canadian oil sands company focuses upon sustainable in situ development & production. The area of activity is Alberta's Southern Athabasca oil sands region. MEG Energy Corp. also owns interests in Stonefell Terminal & Access Pipeline.
The company strives to meet environmental regulations & look beyond compliance, by implementing technology & environmental programs to mitigate impacts on land, air, water, & wildlife.
William McCaffrey, President, Chief Executive Officer, & Director
Eric Toews, Chief Financial Officer
Grant Boyd, Senior Vice-President, Resource Management - Growth Properties
Jamey Fitzgibbon, Senior Vice-President, Resource Management - Christina Lake & Special Projects
Richard Sendall, Senior Vice-President, Strategy & Government Relations
Chi-Tak Yee, Senior Vice-President, Reservoir & Geosciences
John Rogers, Vice-President, Investor Relations
Don Sutherland, Vice-President, Regulatory & Community Relations

Midas Gold Corp.
#1250, 999 West Hastings St.
Vancouver, BC V6C 2W2
778-724-4700
Fax: 604-558-4700
info@midasgoldcorp.com
www.midasgoldcorp.com
Social Media: www.facebook.com/MidasGoldIdaho
twitter.com/MidasIdaho
www.linkedin.com/company/2252374

Company Type: Public
Ticker Symbol: MAX / TSX
Profile: Midas Gold Corp. is a junior natural resource / mining company.
Stephen Quin, President & Chief Executive Officer
Bob Barnes, Chief Operating Officer
Darren Morgans, Chief Financial Officer
Liz Monger, Corporate Secretary & Manager, Investor Relations

New Zealand Energy Corp. (NZEC)
PO Box 24, #86, 96 Victoria St., Level 2
Wellington, 147 New Zealand
info@newzealandenergy.com
www.newzealandenergy.com
Other Communications: +64-6-757-4470
Social Media: www.facebook.com/216889475024871
twitter.com/NZEnergy

Company Type: Public
Ticker Symbol: NZ / TSX.V
Profile: New Zealand Energy Corp. is focused on the production, development and exploration of oil and natural gas prospects in New Zealand.
Michael Adams, Chief Executive Officer
Derek Gardiner, Chief Financial Officer
Mike Oakes, General Manager, Operations

Niko Resources Ltd.
#510, 800 - 6th Ave. SW
Calgary, AB T2P 3G3
403-262-1020
Fax: 403-263-2686
niko@nikoresources.com
www.nikoresources.com

Company Type: Public
Ticker Symbol: NKO / TSX
Profile: Niko Resources Ltd. is engaged in the exploration for & production of oil & natural gas. Operations are conducted in Bangladesh, India, Kurdistan Iraq, Indonesia, Pakistan, Madagascar, & Trinidad.
Robert S. Ellsworth Jr., Interim Chief Executive Officer
William T. Hornaday, Chief Operating Officer
Glen Valk, Chief Financial Officer & Vice-President, Finance

North American Energy Partners Inc. (NAEP)
#300, 18817 Stony Plain Rd.
Edmonton, AB T5S 0C2
780-960-7171
Fax: 780-969-5599
www.nacg.ca

Company Type: Public
Ticker Symbol: NOA / TSX, NYSE
Staff Size: 1,000
Profile: North American Energy Partners Inc. is the corporate parent of North American Construction Group Inc. The following services are provided by North American Energy Partners Inc.: pipeline, piling, heavy construction, & mining. Large oil, natural gas, & resource companies are the main recipients of these services. The principal area of activity is the Canadian oil sands.
Martin Ferron, President & Chief Executive Officer
Barry Palmer, Vice-President, Heavy Construction & Mining
Joe Lambert, Chief Operating Officer

Northern Blizzard Resources Inc.
TD Canada Trust Tower
#1900, 421 - 7th Ave. SW
Calgary, AB T2P 4K9
403-930-3000
877-316-6006
info@northernblizzard.com
www.northernblizzard.com

Company Type: Public
Ticker Symbol: NBZ / TSX
Staff Size: 260
Profile: Northern Blizzard is an oil production company, whose operations are focused in Kerrobert & Lloydminster, Saskatchewan.
John Rooney, Chair & Chief Executive Officer
Jim Artindale, President & COO
Michael Makinson, Chief Financial Officer & Vice-President, Finance
Cindi McKenna, Vice-President, Land Contracts
Larry Pewar, Vice-President, Engineering

NuVista Energy Ltd.
#3500, 700 - 2nd St. SW
Calgary, AB T2P 2W2
403-538-8500
Fax: 403-538-8505
investor.relations@nuvistaenergy.com
www.nuvistaenergy.com
Other Communications: Accounts Payable E-mail: ap@nvaenergy.com

Company Type: Public
Ticker Symbol: NVA / TSX
Profile: Nuvista Energy is a Canadian oil & gas company, which acquires, explores, & develops oil & gas properties. The company is active in the Western Canadian Sedimentary Basin.
Jonathan A. Wright, President/CEO
Ross L. Andreachuk, CFO & Vice-President, Finance
D. Chris McDavid, Vice-President, Operations

Oando Energy Resources
Sun Life Plaza
#1230, 112 - 4th Ave. SW
Calgary, AB T2P 0H3
403-719-9152
info@oandoenergyresources.com
www.oandoenergyresources.com
Social Media: www.facebook.com/oandoplc
twitter.com/Oando_PLC

Company Type: Public
Ticker Symbol: OER / TSX
Profile: Oando Energy Resources is an African upstream oil and gas exploration and production company.
Olapade Durotoye, Chief Executive Officer
Deola Ogunsemi, Chief Financial Officer
Tokunbo Akindele, Head, Investor Relations & Corporate Development

Oryx Petroleum Corp
First Canadian Centre
#3400, 350 - 7 Ave. SW
Calgary, AB T2P 3N9

info@oryxpetroleum.com
www.oryxpetroleum.com
Social Media:
www.facebook.com/pages/Oryx-Petroleum/174532429386561
twitter.com/Oryxinfo
www.linkedin.com/company/1370104

Company Type: Public
Ticker Symbol: OXC / TSX
Staff Size: 169
Vance Querio, Chief Executive Officer

Pacific Exploration & Production
Canada Office
#1100, 333 Bay St.
Toronto, ON M5H 2R2

416-362-7735
Fax: 416-360-7783
www.pacific.energy/en
Other Communications: Columbia Corporate Office, Phone: +57 1 511-2000
Social Media: es-es.facebook.com/PacificRubiales
twitter.com/pacificep

Company Type: Public
Ticker Symbol: PRE / TSX
Staff Size: 2,525
Profile: Pacific Rubiales Energy is engaged in oil & gas exploration. It owns 100% of Pacific Stratus & Meta Petroleum Limited, which are Colombian oil & gas operators.
Ronald Pantin, Chief Executive Officer
Miguel de la Campa, Co-Chair & Executive Director
Serafino Iacono, Co-Chair & Executive Director
Carlos Perez, Chief Financial Officer
Luis Andres Rojas, Chief Operating Officer

Painted Pony Petroleum Ltd.
#1800, 736 - 6th Ave. SW
Calgary, AB T2P 3T7

403-475-0440
Fax: 403-238-1487
866-975-0440
info@paintedpony.ca
www.paintedpony.ca

Company Type: Public
Ticker Symbol: PPY / TSX
Profile: The public resource company is engaged in exploration, drilling, & production in western Canada.
Patrick R. Ward, P.Geol., President & Chief Executive Officer
John H. Van de Pol, Chief Financial Officer & Senior Vice-President
Edwin Hanbury, Senior Vice-President, Engineering
Bruce G. Hall, Vice-President, Land

Pan Orient Energy Corp.
#1505, 505 - 3rd St. SW
Calgary, AB T2P 3E6

403-294-1770
Fax: 403-294-1780
www.panorient.ca

Company Type: Public
Ticker Symbol: POE / TSX-V
Staff Size: 4,597
Profile: The junior oil & natural gas company has principal properties located in the following regions: on-shore Thailand; onshore Indonesia; & the Canadian oil sands.
Jeff Chisholm, B.Sc, Chief Executive Officer & Director
Bill Ostlund, CA, Chief Financial Officer & Corporate Secretary

Paramount Resources Ltd.
#4700, 888 - 3rd St. SW
Calgary, AB T2P 5C5

403-290-3600
www.paramountres.com

Company Type: Public
Ticker Symbol: POU / TSX
Staff Size: 196
Profile: The oil & natural gas exploration, development, & production company carries out its operations in western Canada. In 2011, Paramount Resources Ltd. completed the acquisition of ProspEx Resources Ltd.
James Riddell, President & CEO
Paul Kinvig, Controller & Vice-President, Finance
Bernard Lee, Chief Financial Officer
Phil Tahmazian, Vice-President, Midstream
Mitch Shier, General Counsel, Corporate Secretary & Manager, Land

Pason Systems Corp.
6130 - 3 St. SE
Calgary, AB T2H 1K4

403-301-3400
Fax: 403-301-3499
canada@pason.com
www.pason.com
Other Communications: Investor Relations, E-mail: investorrelations@pason.com
Social Media: www.linkedin.com/company/pason-systems

Company Type: Public
Ticker Symbol: PSI / TSX
Staff Size: 707
Profile: Pason Systems Inc. specializes in the design & manufacture of data management systems. These systems are used by the oilfield industry on land based & offshore drilling & service rigs. Operations are located in Canada, the United States, Mexico, South America, & Australia.
Marcel Kessler, President/Chief Executive Officer
Jon Faber, Chief Financial Officer
Ronald Dudar, Vice-President, People & Culture
Kevin Lo, Vice-President, New Ventures
Russell Smith, Vice-President, International Operations

Pembina Pipeline Corporation
#4000, 585 - 8th Ave. SW
Calgary, AB T2P 1G1

403-231-7500
Fax: 403-237-0254
888-428-3222
investor-relations@pembina.com
www.pembina.com

Company Type: Public
Ticker Symbol: PPL / TSX
Staff Size: 1,274
Profile: In 2010, Pembina converted from an income trust to a corporation. Pembina Pipeline Corporation is an energy transportation & service provider that has over 9,100 kilometres of pipeline. Areas of activity are British Columbia & Alberta
Michael (Mick) Dilger, President & Chief Executive Officer
Scott Burrows, Chief Financial Officer & Vice-President, Finance
Paul Murphy, Senior Vice-President, Pipeline & Crude Oil Facilities
Stuart (Stu) Taylor, Senior Vice-President, NGL & Natural Gas Facilities
Harry Andersen, General Counsel & Vice-President, Legal
Andrew (Andy) G. Gruszecki, Vice-President, Oil Sands & Heavy Oil
Brad Smith, Vice-President, Operating Services
Debbie Sulkers, Vice-President, Corporate Services

Pengrowth Energy Corporation
#2100, 222 - 3rd Ave. SW
Calgary, AB T2P 0B4

403-233-0224
Fax: 403-265-6251
800-223-4122
investorrelations@pengrowth.com
www.pengrowth.com
Other Communications: Investor Relations, Toll-Free Phone: 855-336-8814
Social Media: twitter.com/Pengrowth
www.linkedin.com/company/pengrowth-energy-corporation

Company Type: Public
Ticker Symbol: PGF / TSX; PGH / NYSE
Staff Size: 449
Profile: The corporation is an intermediate producer of oil & natural gas. Pengrowth's main area of activity is the Western Canadian Sedimentary Basin.
In 2012, Pengrowth Energy Corporation & NAL Energy Corporation entered into an arrangement agreement that provides for the strategic combination of Pengrowth & NAL.
Derek Evans, President & Chief Executive Officer
Christopher Webster, Chief Financial Officer
Andrew Grasby, Senior Vice-President, General Counsel & Corporate Secretary
Steve De Maio, Senior Vice-President, Thermal Operations
Randy Steele, Senior Vice-President, Conventional Operations

Penn West Petroleum Ltd.
Also Known As: Penn West Exploration
Penn West Plaza
#200, 207 - 9th Ave. SW
Calgary, AB T2P 1K3

403-777-2500
866-693-2707
investor_relations@pennwest.com
www.pennwest.com
Other Communications: Investor Relations, Toll-Free Phone: 888-770-2633

Company Type: Public
Ticker Symbol: PWT / TSX; PWE / NYSE
Staff Size: 718
Profile: Penn West is engaged in the production of oil & natural gas. Operations are conducted in western Canada.
David E. Roberts, President & Chief Executive Officer
David Dyck, Chief Financial Officer & Senior Vice-President
Gregg Gegunde, Senior Vice-President, Exploitation, Production & Delivery

Perpetual Energy Inc.
#3200, 605 - 5th Ave. SW
Calgary, AB T2P 3H5

403-269-4400
Fax: 403-269-4444
800-811-5522
www.perpetualenergyinc.com
Other Communications: Human Resources, E-mail: careers@perpetualenergyinc.com

Company Type: Public
Ticker Symbol: PMT / TSX
Staff Size: 210
Profile: Established in 2010, Perpetual Energy Inc. operates as an independent natural gas company. Perpetual Energy's field offices are located in Athabasca, Alberta (780-675-9252), Mannville, Alberta (780-763-3544), & Edson, Alberta (780-723-4708).
Susan L. Riddell Rose, President & Chief Executive Officer
Cameron R. Sebastian, Chief Financial Officer & Vice-President, Finance
Jeffrey R. Green, Vice-President, Corporate & Engineering Services
Gary C. Jackson, Vice-President, Land & Divestitures
Linda L. McKean, Vice-President, Exploitation
Vicki L. Benoit, Vice-President, Production Operations

Petrocapita Income Trust
#1400, 717 - 7 Ave. SW
Calgary, AB T2P 0Z3

587-393-3450
www.petrocapita.com
Social Media: corporate@petrocapita.com

Company Type: Public
Ticker Symbol: PCE.UN / TSX
Alex Lemmens, President & CEO
Richard Mellis, Vice-President, Land & Environment

Petrodorado Energy Ltd.
#1500, 850 - 2nd St. SW
Calgary, AB T2P 0R8

403-800-9240
Fax: 403-800-9241
info@petrodorado.com
www.petrodorado.com

Company Type: Public
Ticker Symbol: PDQ / TSX.V
Profile: Petrodorado Energy Ltd. is an international oil exploration company with oil operations in South America.
Chris Reid, President & CEO
Lynn Chapman, CA, Vice-President, Finance & CFO

Petrolia Inc.
304, 511, rue Saint-Joseph
Québec, QC G1K 3B7

418-657-1966
Fax: 418-657-1880
855-657-1966
info@petrolia-inc.com
www.petrolia-inc.com

Company Type: Public
Ticker Symbol: PEA / TSX.V
Profile: Petrolia Inc. is a Canada-based is a junior oil exploration company, engaged in the exploration and development of oil and gas properties.
Alexandre Gagnon, President & CEO
Mario Racicot, Chief Financial Officer & Corporate Secretary

Petroshale Inc.
#3900, 350 - 7th Ave. SW
Calgary, AB T2P 3N9

403-266-1717
info@petroshaleinc.com
www.petroshaleinc.com

Company Type: Public
Ticker Symbol: PSH / TSX.V
Profile: The oil & gas exploration company focuses on exploration in the North Dakota Bakken/Three Forks.
Bruce Chernoff, Chief Executive Officer
David Rain, Chief Financial Officer
Tony Izzo, Vice-President, Business Development
Dominic Pallone, Vice-President, Land & Acquisitions

Petrowest Corporation
Head Office
#800, 407 - 2 St. SW
Calgary, AB T2P 2Y3
403-237-0881
info@petro-west.com
www.petrowestcorp.com
Other Communications: Investor Relations E-mail: investorrelations@petro-west.com
Social Media: twitter.com/Petrowest1
www.linkedin.com/company/petrowest-corporation
Company Type: Public
Ticker Symbol: PRW / TSX
Staff Size: 534
Profile: Pre-drilling & post-completion services are provided by Petrowest Corporation. The company works in the northern area of the Western Canadian Sedimentary Basin.
Rick Quigley, Chief Executive Officer
Roy Larson, Chief Operating Officer
Lloyd A. Wiggins, CA, Chief Financial Officer

Petrus Resources Ltd.
#2400, 240 - 4th Ave. SW
Calgary, AB T2P 4H4
416-984-4014
Fax: 416-984-2717
www.petrusresources.com
Company Type: Public
Ticker Symbol: PRQ / TSX
Profile: An oil & gas company with developments in Alberta.
Kevin Adair, President & CEO

PEYTO Exploration & Development Corp.
#300, 600 - 3rd Ave. SW
Calgary, AB T2P 0G5
403-261-6081
Fax: 403-451-4100
www.peyto.com
Company Type: Public
Ticker Symbol: PEY / TSX
Profile: PEYTO Exploration & Development is engaged in the exploration for & the production of unconventional natural gas in Alberta's Deep Basin.
Darren Gee, President & Chief Executive Officer
Scott Robinson, Chief Operating Officer & Executive Vice-President
Kathy Turgeon, Chief Financial Officer & Vice-President
Tim Louie, Vice-President, Land
David Thomas, Vice-President, Exploration

PHX Energy Services Corp.
#1400, 250 - 2nd St. SW
Calgary, AB T2P 0C1
403-543-4466
Fax: 403-543-4485
investor@phxtech.com
www.phxtech.com
Company Type: Public
Ticker Symbol: PHX / TSX
Staff Size: 906
Profile: PHX Energy Services' Canadian operations are carried out through Phoenix Technology Service LP. American operations are conducted through PHX Energy Services' wholly owned subsidiary, Phoenix Technology Services USA Inc.. PHX Energy Services also has sales offices in Peru, Colombia, Albania, & Russia.
John M. Hooks, Chair & Chief Executive Officer
Mike Buker, President
Cameron M. Ritchie, CA, Chief Financial Officer & Senior Vice-President, Finance
Craig Brown, Senior Vice-President, International Operations & Technology

Pine Cliff Energy
#850, 1015 - 4th St. SW
Calgary, AB T2R 1J4
403-269-2289
Fax: 403-265-7488
info@pinecliffenergy.com
www.pinecliffenergy.com
Other Communications: 24-Hour Emergency Toll-Free Phone: 1-877-486-0470
Company Type: Public
Ticker Symbol: PNE / TSX.V
Profile: Pine Cliff Energy Ltd. is a company engaged in the exploration, development and production of natural gas, crude oil and natural gas liquids.
Philip B. Hodge, President & Chief Executive Officer
Kristi L. Kunec, Chief Financial Officer & Corporate Secretary
Terry L. McNeill, Chief Operating Officer

PrairieSky Royalty Ltd.
PO Box 780 Stn. M, Calgary, AB T2P 2J6
587-293-4000
Fax: 587-293-4001
General.inquiries@prairiesky.com
www.prairiesky.com
Other Communications: Investor Relations: Investor.relations@prairiesky.com
Company Type: Public
Ticker Symbol: PSK / TSX
Profile: Prairiesky Royalty is a company that buys & sells fee simple mineral title & gross overriding royalty lands in Western Canada.
Andrew Phillips, President & CEO
Cameron Proctor, Chief Operating Officer
Pamela Kazeil, CFO & Vice-President, Finance
Michelle Radomski, Vice-President, Land

Precision Drilling Corporation
#800, 525 - 8th Ave. SW
Calgary, AB T2P 1G1
403-716-4500
info@precisiondrilling.com
www.precisiondrilling.com
Social Media: www.facebook.com/Precisiondrilling
www.linkedin.com/company/precision-drilling
Company Type: Public
Ticker Symbol: PD / TSX; PDS / NYSE
Staff Size: 4,337
Profile: The oilfield services company provides drilling, well servicing, & strategic support services to customers.
Kevin A. Neveu, President & CEO
Gene C. Stahl, President, Drilling Operations
Carey T. Ford, Senior Vice-President/CFO
Darren Ruhr, Senior Vice-President, Corporate Services

Questerre Energy Corporation
#1650, 801 - 6th Ave. SW
Calgary, AB T2P 3W2
403-777-1185
Fax: 403-777-1578
info@questerre.com
www.questerre.com
Social Media: www.facebook.com/Questerre
twitter.com/Questerre_Utica
Company Type: Public
Ticker Symbol: QEC / TSX
Profile: Questerre Energy Corporation is an independent energy company focused on unconventional oil and gas projects.
Michael R. Binnion, President & CEO
Jason D'Silva, Chief Financial Officer
Peter Coldham, Vice-President, Engineering
John Brodylo, Vice-President, Exploration

Questfire Energy Corp.
#1100, 350 - 7th Ave. SW
Calgary, AB T2P 3N9
403-263-6688
Fax: 403-263-6683
www.questfire.ca
Company Type: Public
Ticker Symbol: Q.A / TSX.V
Profile: The junior oil & natural gas company is engaged in exploration, acquisition, development, & production activities in western Canada.
Richard Dahl, President & CEO
rdahl@questfire.ca
Ronald Williams, Chief Financial Officer & Vice-President, Finance
rwilliams@questfire.ca

Raging River Exploration Inc.
605 - 5th Ave. SW, 17th Fl.
Calgary, AB T2P 3H5
403-387-2950
Fax: 403-387-2951
www.rrexploration.com
Company Type: Public
Ticker Symbol: RRX / TSX
Staff Size: 35
Profile: Raging River Exploration Inc. is a junior oil and gas producer currently focused in the Kindersley area of Saskatchewan.
Neil Roszell, President & CEO
Jerry Sapieha, Chief Financial Officer & Vice-President, Finance

Range Energy Resources
#1128, 789 West Pender St.
Vancouver, BC V6C 1H2
604-688-9600
Fax: 604-687-3141
range@rangeenergyresources.com
www.rangeenergyresources.com

Company Type: Public
Ticker Symbol: RGO / CSE
Toufic Chahine, Interim President & Chief Executive Officer

Renaissance Oil Corp.
Three Bentall Centre
PO Box 49139, #3123, 595 Burrard St.
Vancouver, BC V7X 1J1
604-536-3637
Fax: 604-536-3621
www.renaissanceoil.com
Company Type: Public
Ticker Symbol: ROE / TSX
Profile: An oil & shale development company, whose main project is in Mexico.
Rob Harris, Chief Executive Officer
Carol Law, Chief Operating Officer
Harpeet Dhaliwhal, Chief Financial Officer

RMP Energy Inc.
Head Office
#1200, 500 - 4th Ave. SW
Calgary, AB T2P 2V6
403-930-6300
Fax: 403-930-6301
ir@rmpenergyinc.com
www.rmpenergyinc.com
Other Communications: Investors: 403-930-6304; Stettler Field Office: 403-742-5200
Company Type: Public
Ticker Symbol: RMP / TSX
Profile: The junior, upstream oil & gas company has assets in the Big Muddy area of southeastern Saskatchewan & in the Pine Creek, Waskahigan, & Kaybob regions of west central Alberta.
John W. Ferguson, President & Chief Executive Officer
Dean J.W. Bernhard, Chief Financial Officer & Vice-President, Finance
Brent W. DesBrisay, Vice-President, Geosciences
Jonathan L. Grimwood, Vice-President, Exploration
Greg T. Kubat, Vice-President, Engineering
R. Bruce McFarlane, Vice-President, Business Development

Rock Energy Inc.
c/o Raging River Exploration
605 - 5th Ave. SW, 17th Fl.
Calgary, AB T2P 3H5
403-387-2950
Fax: 403-387-2951
www.rockenergy.ca
Company Type: Public
Ticker Symbol: RE / TSX
Profile: Rock Energy Inc. is focused upon heavy oil exploration & development in its Plains & southwest Saskatchewan regions. The company is a member of the Canadian Association of Petroleum Producers & is committed to the association's Steward of Excellence Program. In May 2016 the company was acquired by Raging River Exploration, an oil & gas producer.
Neil Roszell, President & Chief Executive Officer
Jerry Sapieha, Vice-President & Chief Financial Officer
Jason Jaskela, Chief Operating Officer & Vice-President, Production

Rooster Energy Ltd.
#120, 16285 Park Ten Place
Houston, TX 77084 USA
832-772-6313
Fax: 832-772-6314
info@roosterpetroleum.com
www.roosterenergyltd.com
Company Type: Public
Ticker Symbol: COQ / TSX.V
Profile: Rooster Energy Ltd. is an independent oil and gas exploration and production company.
Robert P. Murphy, Chief Executive Officer & President
Gary Nuschler, Jr., Chief Financial Officer
Tod Darcey, Sr. Vice-President, Operations

Savanna Energy Services Corp.
#800, 311 - 6th Ave. SW
Calgary, AB T2P 3H2
403-503-9990
Fax: 403-503-0654
www.savannaenergy.com
Social Media: www.facebook.com/SavannaEnergy
twitter.com/SavannaEnergy
www.linkedin.com/companies/savanna-energy-services-corp
Company Type: Public
Ticker Symbol: SVY / TSX
Staff Size: 1,433
Profile: Drilling & well servicing are provided by Savanna Energy Services. Operations take place in Canada, the United States, & Australia.
Christopher Strong, President & Chief Executive Officer

Dwayne LaMontagne, Chief Financial Officer & Executive Vice-President

Secure Energy Services Inc.
Bow Valley Square II
#3600, 205 - 5th Ave. SW
Calgary, AB T2P 2V7
403-984-6100
Fax: 403-984-6101
www.secure-energy.ca
Social Media: www.facebook.com/139211619450029
twitter.com/secure_ses
www.linkedin.com/company/secure-energy-services-inc-
Company Type: Public
Ticker Symbol: SES / TSX
Staff Size: 1,250
Profile: The energy services company provides specialized services to upstream oil & natural gas compnaies. Secure Energy Services' two divisions are the Processing, Recovery & Disposal Division & the Drilling Division. Operations are carried out in the Western Canadian Sedimentary Basin.
Rene Amirault, President & CEO
George Wadsworth, Exec. Vice-President, Drilling & Productuin Services Division
Allen Gransch, Chief Financial Officer & Exec. Vice-President
David Mattinson, Executive Vice-President, On Site Services
Dan Steinke, Exec. Vice-President, Processing, Recovery & Disposal
Brian McGurk, Exec. Vice-President, Human Resources & Strategy

Serinus Energy
#1500, 700 - 4th Ave. SW
Calgary, AB T2P 3J4
403-264-8877
Fax: 403-264-8861
info@serinusenergy.com
www.serinusenergy.com
Company Type: Public
Ticker Symbol: SEN / TSX
Profile: Serinus Energy is an international oil and gas exploration and production company.
Timothy M. Elliott, President & Chief Executive Officer
Tracy Heck, Chief Financial Officer

Seven Generations Energy Ltd.
#300, 140 - 8 Ave. SW
Calgary, AB T2P 1B3
403-718-0700
www.7genergy.com
Company Type: Public
Ticker Symbol: VII / TSX
Profile: Seven Generations Energy is a petroleum company. Its current project is located in Kakwa River in northwestern Alberta.
Marty Proctor, President & COO
Patrick Carlson, Chief Executive Officer
Christopher Law, Chief Financial Officer

ShaMaran Petroleum Corp.
#2000, 885 West Georgia St.
Vancouver, BC V6C 3E8
604-689-7842
Fax: 604-689-4250
www.shamaranpetroleum.com
Company Type: Public
Ticker Symbol: SNM / TSX Venture
Profile: The oil exploration & development company is focused upon projects in Kurdistan. The Canadian oil & gas company is listed on the TSX Venture Exchange & on the NASDAQ OMX First North.
Chris Bruijnzeels, President & CEO
Brenden Johnstone, Chief Financial Officer

ShawCor Ltd.
25 Bethridge Rd.
Toronto, ON M9W 1M7
416-743-7111
Fax: 416-743-7199
www.shawcor.com
Social Media: www.linkedin.com/company/433763
Company Type: Public
Ticker Symbol: SCL / TSX
Staff Size: 5,919
Profile: ShawCor Ltd. is a provider of technology-based products & services for the pipeline & pipe services market, as well as the petrochemical & industrial market. Facilities are located in over twenty countries.
S.M. Orr, President & CEO
Gary S. Love, Chief Financial Officer & Vice-President, Finance
D.R. Ewert, Secretary & Vice-President, Corporate Affairs

Spartan Energy
#500, 850 - 2nd St. SW
Calgary, AB T2P 0R8
403-355-8920
Fax: 403-410-3378
info@spartanenergy.ca
www.spartanenergy.ca
Company Type: Public
Ticker Symbol: SPE / TSX
Profile: Spartan Energy Corp. is an oil and gas company based in Calgary, Alberta.
Richard McHardy, President & CEO
Adam MacDonald, Interim CFO

Sterling Resources Ltd.
Bankers Hall West
#4300, 888 - 3rd St. SW
Calgary, AB T2P 5C5
403-237-9256
info@sterling-resources.com
www.sterling-resources.com
Company Type: Public
Ticker Symbol: SLG / TSX Venture
Profile: The oil & gas company has assets in the United Kingdom, France, the Netherlands, & Romania.
Jacob S. Ulrich, Chair
David Blewden, Chief Financial Officer
John Rapach, CEO & COO

Storm Resources Ltd.
PO Box 1420 Stn. M, Calgary, AB T2P 2L6
403-817-6145
Fax: 403-817-6146
info@stormresourcesltd.com
www.stormresourcesltd.com
Company Type: Public
Ticker Symbol: SRX / TSX Venture
Profile: Storm Resources Ltd. is a junior exploration & production company that commenced operations in 2010. The company focuses upon exploring for, acquiring, & developing oil & natural gas reserves in the Grande Prairie region of northwestern Alberta & the Horn River Basin & Umbach areas of northeastern British Columbia. In 2012, Storm Resources Ltd. acquired Bellamont Exploration Ltd..
Brian Lavergne, President & Chief Executive Officer
Donald G. McLean, Chief Financial Officer
Robert S. Tiberio, Chief Operating Officer

Strad Energy Services Ltd.
#1200, 440 - 2nd Ave. SW
Calgary, AB T2P 5E9
403-232-6900
Fax: 403-232-6901
866-778-2552
www.stradenergy.com
Other Communications: Denver, CO Office, Toll-Free Phone: 877-337-8723
Social Media: www.linkedin.com/company/strad-energy-services-ltd.
Company Type: Public
Ticker Symbol: SDY / TSX
Staff Size: 139
Profile: The energy services company provides oilfield solutions to the natural gas & oil industry. An example of Strad Energy Services' work is the provision of drilling related oilfield equipment.
Andy Pernal, President/Chief Executive Officer
Michael Donovan, Chief Financial Officer
Shane Hopkie, Chief Operating Officer

Strategic Oil & Gas Ltd.
#1100, 645 - 7 Ave. SW
Calgary, AB T2P 4G8
403-767-9000
Fax: 403-767-9122
855-525-2900
www.sogoil.com
Company Type: Public
Ticker Symbol: SOG / TSX
Profile: Strategic Oil & Gas Ltd. is an emerging junior oil and gas company focused on upstream oil and gas exploitation and development.
Gurpreet Sawhney, President & Chief Executive Officer
Cody Smith, Chief Operating Officer
Aaron Thompson, Chief Financial Officer

Suncor Energy Inc.
PO Box 2844, 150 - 6 Ave. SW
Calgary, AB T2P 3E3
403-269-8000
Fax: 403-269-3030
866-786-2671
www.suncor.com
Other Communications: Investor Relations: invest@suncor.com
Social Media: www.facebook.com/suncorenergy
twitter.com/suncorenergy
www.linkedin.com/company/suncor-energy
Company Type: Public
Ticker Symbol: SU / TSX
Staff Size: 13,190
Profile: Suncor Energy Inc. is engaged in natural gas production in western Canada, with a focus on the oil sands. Refinement & marketing operations are carried out in Ontario & Colorado. The company also invests in renewable energy, especially ethanol production & wind power.In March 2016, Suncor completed its acquisition of Canadian Oil Sands, increasing Suncor's stake in the Syncrude project.
Steve Williams, President/CEO
Alister Cowan, CFO & Exec. VP
Eric Axford, Exec. Vice-President, Business Services
Paul Gardner, Sr. Vice-Presidemt, Human Resources
Janice Odegaard, General Counsel & Sr. Vice-President, Legal
Mark Little, Exec. Vice-President, Upstream
Mike MacSween, Exec. Vice-President, Major Projects
Steve Reynish, Exec. Vice-President, Strategy & Corporate Development
Kris Smith, Exec. Vice-President, Downstream

Surge Energy Inc.
#2100, 635 - 8th Ave. SW
Calgary, AB T2P 3M3
403-930-1010
Fax: 403-930-1011
info@surgeenergy.ca
www.surgeenergy.ca
Other Communications: Investor Relations E-mail: invest@surgeenergy.ca
Company Type: Public
Ticker Symbol: SGY / TSX
Profile: The oil & gas company conducts operations in Manitoba, Alberta, & North Dakota.
Paul Colborne, President & Chief Executive Officer
Dan Brown, Chief Operating Officer
Paul Ferguson, Chief Financial Officer
Murray Bye, Vice-President, Production
Margaret Elekes, Vice-President, Land

TAG Oil Ltd.
#2040, 885 West Georgia St.
Vancouver, BC V6C 3E8
604-682-6496
Fax: 604-682-1174
info@tagoil.com
www.tagoil.com
Other Communications: New Plymouth, NZ, Technical Office, Phone: 06-759-4019
Company Type: Public
Ticker Symbol: TAO / TSX; TAOIF / OTCQX
Profile: Tag Oil is involved in international oil and gas exploration, development and production.
Toby Pierce, Chief Executive Officer
Henrik Lundin, Chief Operating Officer
Barry MacNeil, Chief Financial Officer

Tamarack Valley Energy Ltd.
Fifth Avenue Place - East Tower
#600, 425 - 1st St. SW
Calgary, AB T2P 3L8
403-263-4440
Fax: 403-263-5551
operations@tamarackvalley.ca
www.tamarackvalley.ca
Other Communications: Investors: investorrelations@tamarackvalley.ca
Company Type: Public
Ticker Symbol: TVE / TSX.V
Profile: Tamarack Valley Energy Ltd. is an oil & gas company with operations in the Western Canadian Sedimentary Basin. Assets are located in the following places: the Garrington/Harmattan, Buck Lake, Lochend, Foley Lake, & the Quaich areas of Alberta; Wilder in northeastern British Columbia; southeast of Lloydminster in Saskatchewan.
Brian Schmidt, President & Chief Executive Officer
Ron Hozjan, Chief Financial Officer & Vice-President, Finance
Ken Cruikshank, Vice-President, Land
Dave Christensen, Vice-President, Engineering
Kevin Screen, Vice-President, Production & Operations

Terrace Energy Corp.
PO Box 21546, 1424 Commercial Dr.
Vancouver, BC V5L 5G2

604-282-7897
Fax: 604-629-0418
terrace@terraceenergy.net
www.terraceenergy.net

Company Type: Public
Ticker Symbol: TZR / TSX.V
Profile: An oil & gas company with projects in the United States.
Dave Gibbs, President & CEO
George Morris, Chief Operating Officer

Tesla Exploration Ltd.
4500 - 8A St. NE
Calgary, AB T2E 4J7

403-216-0999
Fax: 403-216-0989
emailus@teslaexploration.com
www.teslaexploration.com
Other Communications: Safety:
safetydept@teslaexploration.com
Social Media: www.facebook.com/teslaexplorationltd
twitter.com/TeslaExp
www.linkedin.com/company/1734104

Company Type: Public
Ticker Symbol: TXL / TSX
Staff Size: 200
Profile: Established in 2000, Telsa Exploration Ltd. serves the oil & gas exploration industry. Tesla Exploration Ltd. is engaged in geophysical & related services in Canada. The company also provides these services internationally, through the following wholly owned subsidiaries: Tesla Exploration International Ltd.; Tesla Exploration Trinidad Ltd.; Tesla Exploration Inc. in the United States & Tesla Offshore LLC, which is also in the United States.
Richard Habiak, President
Graham Reid, Vice-President, Finance
Milt Tetzlaff, Senior Vice-President, Canadian Operations
tetzlaffm@teslaexploration.com

TORC Oil & Gas Ltd.
Eighth Avenue Place
#1800, 525 - 8th Ave. SW
Calgary, AB T2P 1G1

403-930-4120
Fax: 403-930-4159
torcoil.com

Company Type: Public
Ticker Symbol: TOG / TSX
Profile: TORC Oil & Gas Ltd. is an oil and gas exploration and production company.
Brett Herman, President & CEO
Jason Zabinsky, Vice-President & Chief Financial Officer, Finance
Eric Strachan, Vice-President, Exploration
Jeremy Wallis, Vice-President, Land

Toro Oil & Gas Ltd.
#2200, 250 - 5th St. SW
Calgary, AB T2P 0R4

403-237-9996
Fax: 403-264-0416
admin@torooil.com
www.torooil.com

Company Type: Public
Ticker Symbol: TOO / TSX.V
Profile: Toro works to acquire light oil & liquids-rich natural gas in central Alberta & southern Saskatchewan.
Barry Olson, President & CEO
Don Sabo, Executive Vice-President
Greg Phaneuf, Chief Financial Officer & Vice-President, Finance
Elizabeth More, Vice-President, Exploration & Geology
Neil Wilson, COO & Vice-President, Engineering
Kellie D'Hondt, Vice-President, Land & Business Development

Toscana Energy Income Corporation
#3410, 421 - 7th Ave. SW
Calgary, AB T2P 4K9

403-410-6790
info@sprotttoscana.com
sprott-toscana.com

Company Type: Public
Ticker Symbol: TEI / TSX
Profile: Toscana Energy Income Corporation is a publicly-listed company that invests in medium to long-life oil and natural gas assets, unitized production, and royalties for yield and capital appreciation. Toscana Energy Income is owned by Sprott Toscana, a Calgary-based energy finance company.
Joseph S. Durante, Chief Executive Officer
Glen Tanaka, President, Toscana Energy Income Corporation

Total Energy Services Inc.
#2550, 300 - 5th Ave. SW
Calgary, AB T2P 3C4

Fax: 403-234-8731
877-818-6825
general@totalenergy.ca
www.totalenergy.ca
Other Communications: Investor Relations, E-mail:
investorrelations@totalenergy.ca

Company Type: Public
Ticker Symbol: TOT, TOT-DB / TSX
Profile: Total Energy Services Inc. is an energy services company based in Calgary, Albert with drilling services, rentals and transportation services, the fabrication, sale, rental and servicing of new and used equipment for both oil and gas processing, and gas compression.
Daniel Halyk, President & Chief Executive Officer
Yuliya Gorbach, Chief Financial Officer & Vice-President, Finance
Brad Macson, Vice-President, Operations

Touchstone Exploration Inc.
#1100, 332 - 6 Ave. SW
Calgary, AB T2P 0B2

403-750-4400
Fax: 403-266-5794
866-677-7411
info@touchstoneexploration.com
www.touchstoneexploration.com
Social Media: www.facebook.com/TouchstoneExploration
twitter.com/TouchstoneOil
www.linkedin.com/company/touchstone-exploration-inc-

Company Type: Public
Ticker Symbol: TXP / TSX
Profile: Established in 2010, Touchstone Exploration Inc. is a junior, international oil company focused primarily on the Country of Trinidad.
Paul Baay, President & CEO
Scott Budau, Chief Financial Officer
James Shipka, Chief Operating Officer

Tourmaline Oil Corp.
#3700, 250 - 6th Ave. SW
Calgary, AB T2P 3H7

403-266-5992
Fax: 403-266-5952
info@tourmalineoil.com
www.tourmalineoil.com

Company Type: Public
Ticker Symbol: TOU / TSX
Staff Size: 186
Profile: Formed in 2008, Tourmaline Oil Corp. is an intermediate crude oil & natural gas exploration & production company. The company's operations are conducted in the Western Canadian Sedimentary Basin.
In 2011, Tourmaline Oil Corp. acquired Cinch Energy Corp.
Michael L. Rose, President & Chief Executive Officer
Brian G. Robinson, Chief Financial Officer & Vice-President, Finance
Ronald Hill, Vice-President, Exploration
Drew E. Tumbach, Vice-President, Land & Contracts
W. Scott Kirker, General Counsel & Secretary

TransGlobe Energy Corporation
Head Office
#2300, 250 - 5th Ave. SW
Calgary, AB T2P OR4

403-264-9888
Fax: 403-770-8855
www.trans-globe.com
Other Communications: Investors:
investor.relations@trans-globe.com

Company Type: Public
Ticker Symbol: TGL / TSX; TGA / NASDAQ
Profile: TransGlobe Energy acquires, explores, & develops oil & gas properties. The Alberta-based oil & gas exploration & development company focuses its production activities in Egypt & Yemen.
Ross G. Clarkson, P.Geol., ICD.D, President & Chief Executive Officer
Randall C. Neely, CA., CFA, Chief Financial Officer & Vice-President, Finance
Lloyd W. Herrick, P.Eng, ICD.D, Chief Operating Officer & Vice-President
Albert E. Gress, CPA, Vice-President, Business Development
Steve Langmaid, Contact, Investor Relations
403-444-4787

Traverse Energy Ltd.
#780, 839 - 5th Ave. SW
Calgary, AB T2P 3C8

403-264-9223
Fax: 403-264-9558
www.traverseenergy.com

Company Type: Public
Ticker Symbol: TVL / TSX.V
Profile: The company is involved with the development & production of petroleum & natural gas in Alberta.
Laurie Smith, President & Chief Executive Officer
David Erickson, Chief Operating Officer & Vice-President
Sharon Supple, Chief Financial Officer
Daniel Kolibar, Corporate Secretary

Trican Well Service Ltd.
#2900, 645 - 7th Ave. SW
Calgary, AB T2P 4G8

403-266-0202
info@trican.ca
www.trican.ca
Other Communications: Investor Inquiries, Phone: 403-476-6767
Social Media: twitter.com/TricanWS
www.linkedin.com/company/trican-well-service-ltd-

Company Type: Public
Ticker Symbol: TCW / TSX
Staff Size: 2,454
Profile: Trican Well Service Ltd. is an international pressure pumping company. It provides products, equipment, & services, which are employed in the exploration & development of oil & gas reserves. The company conducts its operations in Canada, the United States, Russia, Kazakhstan, & Algeria.
Dale Dusterhoft, Chief Executive Officer
Michael Baldwin, Chief Financial Officer & Senior Vice-President, Finance
Robert Cox, Vice-President, Canadian Geographic Region
David J. Girard, Vice-President, Human Resources

Trilogy Energy Corp.
#1400, 332 - 6th Ave. SW
Calgary, AB T2P 0B2

403-290-2900
Fax: 403-263-8915
info_@trilogyenergy.com
www.trilogyenergy.com

Company Type: Public
Ticker Symbol: TET / TSX
Staff Size: 220
Profile: In 2010, Trilogy converted from an income trust to a corporate structure. The Canadian energy corporation is engaged in the development & production of crude oil, natural gas, & natural gas liquids.
James H.T. Riddell, Chief Executive Officer
John B. Williams, President & Chief Operating Officer
Michael Kohut, Chief Financial Officer

Trinidad Drilling Ltd.
#1000, 585 - 8th Ave. SW
Calgary, AB T2P 1G1

403-265-6525
Fax: 403-265-4168
www.trinidaddrilling.com
Other Communications: Investor Relations E-mail:
investors@trinidaddrilling.com
Social Media: www.facebook.com/TrinidadTDG
twitter.com/TrinidadTDG
www.linkedin.com/company/trinidad-drilling-lp

Company Type: Public
Ticker Symbol: TDG / TSX
Staff Size: 1,599
Profile: Trinidad Drilling provides services to the oil & gas industry. Drilling takes place in the Western Canadian Sedimentary Basin, the Permian Basin in western Texas, North Dakota, & the Ebano-Panuco-Cacalilao field near Tampico, Mexico. In 2012, the company entered into an amalgamation agreement to acquire all the issued & outstanding securities of CanGas Solutions Ltd.
Brent Conway, President
Lyle Whitmarsh, Chief Executive Officer
Lesley Bolster, Chief Financial Officer
Adrian Lachance, Chief Operating Officer, USA & International Operations
Randy Hawkings, Executive Vice-President, Canada & Mexico

Tuscany Energy
#1800, 633 - 6th Ave. SW
Calgary, AB T2P 2Y5

403-269-9889
Fax: 403-269-9890
IR@tuscanyenergy.com
www.tuscanyenergy.com

Company Type: Public
Ticker Symbol: TUS / TSX.V
Robert W. Lamond, CEO
Charles A. Teare, Executive Vice-President & CFO

Twin Butte Energy Ltd.
#410, 396 - 11 Ave. SW
Calgary, AB T2R 0C5
403-215-2045
Fax: 403-215-2055
www.twinbutteenergy.com
Company Type: Public
Ticker Symbol: TBE / TSX
Profile: Twin Butte Energy is a junior oil & gas company. The company is active in the greater Lloydminster area of Alberta & Saskatchewan.
Rob Wollmann, President & Chief Executive Officer
Dave Middleton, Chief Operating Officer
Alan Steele, Chief Financial Officer & Vice-President, Finance
Gordon Howe, Vice-President, Land

Ultra Petroleum Corp.
#1200, 400 North Sam Houston Pkwy. East
Houston, TX 77060 USA
281-876-0120
Fax: 281-876-2831
www.ultrapetroleum.com
Company Type: Public
Ticker Symbol: UPL / NYSE
Staff Size: 167
Profile: Incorporated in British Columbia in 1979, Ultra Petroleum Corp. is engaged in the exploration & development of oil & gas properties in the Green River Basin of Wyoming. The company's registrar & transfer agent is Computershare Investor Services Inc. in Vancouver (service@computershare.com).
Michael D. Watford, President/CEO & Chair
Garland Shaw, Senior Vice-President & Chief Financial Officer
Brad Johnson, Senior Vice-President, Operations
Sandi Kraemer, Manager, Investor Relations
skraemer@ultrapetroleum.com

Union Gas Limited
PO Box 2001, Chatham, ON N7M 5M1
519-352-3100
800-265-5230
www.uniongas.com
Social Media: www.facebook.com/uniongas
twitter.com/uniongas
www.linkedin.com/company/union-gas
Company Type: Public
Ticker Symbol: UNG.PR.C / TSX
Staff Size: 2,283
Profile: The natural gas storage, transmission, & distribution company provides services in northern, southwestern, & eastern Ontario to commercial, industrial, & residential customers. In Quebec, Ontario, & the United States, Union Gas Limited also offers natural gas storage & transportation services to other utilities.
Stephen W. Baker, President

US Oil Sands Inc.
#1600, 521 - 3rd Ave. SW
Calgary, AB T2P 3T3
403-233-9366
Fax: 587-353-5373
info@usoilsandsinc.com
www.usoilsandsinc.com
Company Type: Public
Ticker Symbol: USO / TSX.V
Profile: US Oil Sands is company focused on environmentally sustainable heavy oil (bitumen) production of oil sands.
Cameron M. Todd, Chief Executive Officer
D. Glen Snarr, President & Chief Financial Officer

Valener Inc.
1717, rue du Havre
Montréal, QC H2K 2X3
514-598-6220
Fax: 514-521-8168
888-598-6220
investors@valener.com
www.valener.com
Other Communications: Media Relations E-mail: communications@valener.com
Company Type: Public
Ticker Symbol: VNR / TSX
Profile: Valener is engaged in the production, storage, transportation, & distribution of energy. It owns an economic interest in Gaz Métro.
The company favours clean energy sources. It owns a stake in the Seigneurie de Beaupré wind power projects, situated northeast of Québec City.
Sophie Brochu, Acting Manager
Pierre Despars, Acting Manager

Valeura Energy Inc.
Bow Valley Square I
#1200, 202 - 6th Ave. SW
Calgary, AB T2P 2R9
403-237-7102
www.valeuraenergy.com
Company Type: Public
Ticker Symbol: VLE / TSX
Profile: Valeura Energy Inc. is an explorer, developer, & producer of petroleum & natural gas. Operations take place in western Canada & Turkey.
Jim McFarland, B.Sc., M.Sc., P.Eng., President & Chief Executive Officer
Steve Bjornson, B.Comm., CA, Chief Financial Officer
Lyle Martinson, B.Sc., P.Eng., Vice-Preident, Operations
Donald Shepherd, B.Sc., P.Eng., Vice-President, Engineering

Veresen Inc.
Livingston Place, South Tower
#900, 222 - 3rd Ave. SW
Calgary, AB T2P 0B4
403-296-0140
Fax: 403-213-3648
investor-relations@vereseninc.com
www.vereseninc.com
Other Communications: Investors, Phone: 403-213-3633
Social Media: www.linkedin.com/company/veresen-inc-
Company Type: Public
Ticker Symbol: VSN / TSX
Staff Size: 259
Profile: Veresen Inc. is engaged in the following businesses: a pipeline business, with interests in the Alliance Pipeline & the Alberta Ethane Gathering System; a midstream business, with interest in an extraction facility near Chicago, Illinois; & a power business, with renewable & gas-fired facilities & development projects as well as district energy systems & waste heat power facilities.
Don L. Althoff, Chief Executive Officer & President
Theresa Jang, Chief Financial Officer & Senior Vice-President, Finance
Kevan S. King, Senior Vice-President, General Counsel & Secretary
Pam Ramotowski, Vice-President, Human Resources & Administration

Vermilion Energy Inc.
#3500, 520 - 3rd Ave. SW
Calgary, AB T2P 0R3
403-269-4884
Fax: 403-476-8100
866-895-8101
investor_relations@vermilionenergy.com
www.vermilionenergy.com
Other Communications: Community Investment, E-mail: community@vermilionenergy.com
Social Media: twitter.com/vermilionenergy
www.linkedin.com/company/vermilion-energy
Company Type: Public
Ticker Symbol: VET / TSX, NYSE
Staff Size: 516
Profile: Vermilion Energy Inc. specializes in the acquisition, exploration, development & optimization of oil & natural gas producing properties. Activities take place in western Canada, western Europe, & Australia.
Anthony Marino, P.Eng., President & Chief Executive Officer
Curtis W. Hicks, CA, Chief Financial Officer & Executive Vice-President
Michael Kaluza, Chief Operating Officer & Executive Vice-President
John Donovan, FCA, Executive Vice-President, Business Development
Mona Jasinski, MBA, ICD.D., C.H.R.P., Executive Vice-President, People & Culture

Virginia Energy Resources Inc.
#650, 1021 West Hastings St.
Vancouver, BC V6E 0C3
434-432-1065
Fax: 604-558-7695
info@virginiaenergyresources.com
www.virginiaenergyresources.com
Company Type: Public
Ticker Symbol: VUI / TSX.V
Profile: Virginia Energy is a uranium development & exploration company. Its main site is in Virginia, USA.
Walter Coles Sr., Chair & CEO
Karen Allan, Chief Financial Officer
Walter Coles Jr., Executive Vice-President
Neal Keesee, Senior Legal Counsel

Virginia Hills Oil Corp.
Bow Valley Square I
#1500, 202 - 6th Ave. SW
Calgary, AB T2P 2R9
403-817-2550
info@virginiahillsoil.com
www.virginiahillsoil.com
Company Type: Public
Ticker Symbol: VHO / TSX Venture
Profile: Virginia Hills Oil is a Calgary-based junior oil and gas exploration company focused on exploring and developing light oil reserves.
Colin Witwer, President & Chief Executive Officer
Brent Conrad, Chief Operating Officer & Vice-President, Engineering
Adeline Martin, Chief Financial Officer & Vice-President, Finance

Westcoast Energy Inc.
#1100, 1055 West Georgia St.
Vancouver, BC V6E 3P3
604-691-5500
noms.wei-pipeline.com
Company Type: Public
Ticker Symbol: W.PR.H / TSX
Staff Size: 3,654
Profile: Westcoast is an indirect subsidiary of Spectra Energy Corp. Spectra Energy Corp. is a natural gas infrastructure company engaged in gathering & processing, transmission & storage, & distribution.
R. Mark Fiedorek, President

Western Energy Service Corp.
#1700, 215 - 9th Ave. SW
Calgary, AB T2P 1K3
403-984-5916
Fax: 403-984-5917
info@wesc.ca
www.wesc.ca
Other Communications: Investor Relations E-mail: ir@wesc.ca
Company Type: Public
Ticker Symbol: WRG / TSX
Staff Size: 632
Profile: Western Energy Services Corp. provides contract drilling services & well servicing for oil companies. In 2011, Western Energy Services Corp. acquired Stoneham Drilling Trust. Stoneham Drilling Corporation is now a Western company that provides drilling services in the United States. Western Energy Services' wholly owned subsidiary, Horizon Drilling Inc. offers services in Canada. Well servicing is handled by another of Western Energy Services' wholly owned subsidiaries, Matrix Well Servicing Inc.
Alex Macausland, President & CEO
Jeffrey K. Bowers, Chief Financial Officer & Senior Vice-President, Finance

Xtreme Drilling & Coil Services Corp.
#770, 340 - 12th Ave. SW
Calgary, AB T2R 1L5
403-262-9500
Fax: 403-262-9522
ir@xtremecoil.com
www.xtremecoil.com
Social Media: www.facebook.com/XtremeDrillCoilSvces
www.linkedin.com/company/xtreme-drilling-and-coil-services
Company Type: Public
Ticker Symbol: XDC / TSX
Staff Size: 269
Profile: Xtreme Drilling & Coil Services is the brand name for Xtreme Coil Drilling Corp. & its subsidiaries. The company designs, builds, & operates coiled tubing well service units & drilling rigs.
Matt Porter, President & CEO
Martin Ramirez, Vice-President, Finance & Coporate Development

Yoho Resources Inc.
#500, 521 - 3rd Ave. SW
Calgary, AB T2P 3T3
403-537-1771
Fax: 403-537-1775
info@yohoresources.ca
www.yohoresources.ca
Company Type: Public
Ticker Symbol: YO / TSX Venture
Profile: The junior oil & natural gas company has operations in the Western Canadian Sedimentary Basin. Core areas of activity include the Peace River Arch region of northern Alberta, west central Alberta, & northeastern British Columbia.
Brian A. McLachlan, President & Chief Executive Officer
Barry Stobo, Chief Operating Officer & Vice-President, Engineering
Wendy Woolsey, Chief Financial Officer & Vice-President, Finance
Clark Drader, Vice-President, Land

Zargon Oil & Gas Ltd.
Corporate Office
#700, 333 - 5th Ave. SW
Calgary, AB T2P 3B6
403-264-9992
Fax: 403-265-3026
www.zargon.ca
Other Communications: Investor Relations, E-mail: investor-relations@zargon.ca
Company Type: Public
Ticker Symbol: ZAR / TSX
Profile: Zargon is involved in oil & natural gas exploration, development, & production. The organization is active in the western Canadian & Williston sedimentary basins.
Craig H. Hansen, President & Chief Executive Officer
Jeffrey Post, Chief Financial Officer
Randolph Doetzel, Vice-President, Operations
Brian Kergan, Vice-President, Corporate Development
Robert T. Moriyama, Vice-President, Enhanced Recovery

ZCL Composites Inc.
1420 Parson Rd. SW
Edmonton, AB T6X 1M5
780-466-6648
Fax: 780-466-6126
800-661-8265
www.zcl.com
Company Type: Public
Ticker Symbol: ZCL / TSX
Staff Size: 685
Profile: ZCL Composites Inc. designs, manufactures & distributes fiberglass tank systems. The environmentally friendly liquid handling solutions are used by the petroleum industry.
Ronald (Ron) M. Bachmeier, President/Chief Executive Officer
ron.bachmeier@zcl.com
Kathy Demuth, Chief Financial Officer
kathy.demuth@zcl.com

Pharmaceuticals

Acasti Pharma Inc.
#100, 545 Promenade du Centropolis
Laval, QC H7T 0A3
450-686-4555
Fax: 450-686-2505
info@acastipharma.com
www.acastipharma.com
Company Type: Public
Ticker Symbol: APO / TSX.V
Profile: The company does research & development of active pharmaceutical ingredients used in cardiometabolic medication.
Jan D'Alvise, Chief Executive Officer
Laurent Harvey, Vice-President, Clinical & non-clinical affairs
Pierre Lemieux, Chief Operating Officer

Acerus Pharmaceuticals Corporation
2486 Dunwin Dr.
Mississauga, ON L5L 1J9
416-679-0771
Investor Relations: IR@aceruspharma.com
trimelpharmaceuticals.com
Social Media: twitter.com/aceruspharma
www.linkedin.com/company/acerus-pharma
Company Type: Public
Ticker Symbol: ASP / TSX
Profile: The pharmaceutical company develops & markets specific drugs that use a bioadhesive intranasal gel delivery technology. It also owns the dry powder inhaler/nasal dispersion system TriVair.
Tom Rossi, President & CEO
Philippe Savard, Corporate Secretary & Vice-President, Legal Affairs
Nathan Bryson, Vice-President, Scientific Affairs

AEterna Zentaris Inc.
#2500, 1 Place Marie
Montréal, QC H3B 1R1
514-847-4516
www.aezsinc.com
Company Type: Public
Ticker Symbol: AEZ / TSX; AEZS / NASDAQ
Profile: Aeterna Zentaris Inc. is a specialty biopharmaceutical company engaged in developing novel treatments in oncology and endocrinology.
David A. Dodd, President & CEO
Genevieve Lemaire, Chief Accounting Officer & Interim Vice President, Finance

Aurinia Pharmaceuticals Inc.
#1203, 4464 Markham St.
Victoria, BC V8Z 7X8
250-708-4272
Fax: 250-744-2498
www.auriniapharma.com
Company Type: Public
Ticker Symbol: AUP / TSX
Profile: A pharmaceutical development company.
Charles Rowland, Chief Executive Officer
Dennis Bourgeault, Chief Financial Officer
Michael Martin, Chief Operating Officer

Cardiome Pharma Corp.
1441 Creekside Dr., 6th Fl.
Vancouver, BC V6J 4S7
604-677-6905
Fax: 604-677-6915
800-330-9928
ir@cardiome.com
www.cardiome.com
Other Communications: Business Development, E-mail: bus-dev@cardiome.com
Company Type: Public
Ticker Symbol: COM / TSX; CRME / NASDAQ
Profile: The biopharmaceutical company is committed to the discovery, development, & commercialization of therapies to improve health.
William Hunter, Chief Executive Officer
Jennifer Archibald, Chief Financial Officer
Sheila Grant, Chief Operating Officer

Cipher Pharmaceuticals
#100A, 2345 Argentia Rd.
Mississauga, ON L5N 8K4
905-602-5840
www.cipherpharma.com
Company Type: Public
Ticker Symbol: CPH / TSX
Profile: Cipher is a specialty pharmaceutical company that develops improved formulations of existing drugs.
Shawn Patrick O'Brien, President & CEO
Norman Evans, Chief Financial Officer
Joan Chypyha, President & General Manager, Canada

Concordia Healthcare Corp.
#302, 277 Lakeshore Rd. East
Oakville, ON L6H 1J9
905-842-5150
Fax: 905-842-5154
info@concordiarx.com
concordiarx.com
Company Type: Public
Ticker Symbol: CXR / TSX
Staff Size: 476
Profile: Concordia develops & acquires pharmaceutical products.
Mark Thompson, Chief Executive Officer
Edward Borkowski, Chief Financial Officer
Wayne Kreppner, President & COO

Cynapsus Therapeutics Inc.
828 Richmond St. West
Toronto, ON M6J 1C9
416-703-2449
Fax: 416-703-8752
info@cynapsus.ca
www.cynapsus.ca
Company Type: Public
Ticker Symbol: CTH / TSX
Profile: The pharmaceutical company develops drugs that treat Parkinsons Disease.
Anthony Giovinazzo, President & CEO
Andrew Williams, Chief Operating Officer & Chief Financial Officer

Merus Labs International Inc.
PO Box 151, #2110, 100 Wellington St. West
Toronto, ON M5K 1H1
800-287-7686
www.meruslabs.com
Company Type: Public
Ticker Symbol: MSL / TSX; MSLI / NASDAQ
Profile: Merus is a specialty pharmaceutical company that acquires prescription medicines.
Barry Fishman, Chief Executive Officer
Michael Burnby, Chief Financial Officer
Geoff Morrow, Vice-President, Business Development

Nuvo Pharmaceuticals Inc.
#10, 7560 Airport Rd.
Mississauga, ON L4T 4H4
905-673-6980
Fax: 905-673-1842
888-398-3463
www.nuvoresearch.com
Company Type: Public
Ticker Symbol: NRI / TSX
Profile: Nuvo is a pharmaceutical company, which operations the Topical Products & Technology Gropu & the Immunology Group.
John London, President & Chief Executive Officer
Stephen Lemieux, Vice-President & Chief Financial Officer
Tina Loucaides, Vice-President, Secretary & General Counsel

Oncolytics Biotech Inc.
#210, 1167 Kensington Cres. NW
Calgary, AB T2N 1X7
403-670-7377
Fax: 403-283-0858
info@oncolyticsbiotech.com
www.oncolyticsbiotech.com
Social Media: www.facebook.com/Oncolytics.Biotech.Inc
twitter.com/oncolytics
www.linkedin.com/company/oncolytics-biotech-inc.
Company Type: Public
Ticker Symbol: ONC / TSX
Profile: The company develops oncolytic viruses to help with cancer treatments.
Brad Thompson, President & CEO
Matt Coffey, Chief Operating Officer
Kirk Look, Chief Financial Officer

ProMetic Life Sciences
#300, 440 boul Armand-Frappier
Laval, QC H7V 4B4
450-781-0115
Fax: 450-781-4477
info@prometic.com
www.prometic.com
Other Communications: hr@prometic.com
Company Type: Public
Ticker Symbol: PLI / TSX
Staff Size: 276
Profile: ProMetic offers its technologies for large-scale purification of biologics, drug development, proteomics and the elimination of pathogens to a growing base of industry leaders.
Pierre Laurin, President & Chief Executive Officer
Bruce Pritchard, Chief Financial Officer & Chief Operating Officer

QHR Corporation
#300, 1620 Dickson Ave.
Kelowna, BC V1Y 9Y2
855-550-5004
inquiry@QHRtechnologies.com
www.qhrtechnologies.com
Social Media: www.facebook.com/QHRTechnologies
twitter.com/QHRTechnologies
www.linkedin.com/company/608834
Company Type: Public
Ticker Symbol: QHR / TSX.V
Staff Size: 200
Profile: QHR creates and delivers applications for use in physician's medical offices through software licensing and hosted services to enhance the delivery of healthcare.
Michael Checkley, President & CEO
Jerry Diener, Vice President & Chief Financial Officer

Resverlogix Corp.
#300, 4820 Richard Rd. SW
Calgary, AB T3E 6L1
403-254-9252
Fax: 403-256-8495
info@resverlogix.com
www.resverlogix.com
Company Type: Public
Ticker Symbol: RVX / TSX
Profile: A pharmaceutical development company.
Donald McCaffrey, President & CEO

Theratechnologies Inc.
2015 Peel St., 5th Fl.
Montréal, QC H3A 1T8
514-336-7800
Fax: 514-331-9691
communications@theratech.com
theratech.com
Company Type: Public
Ticker Symbol: TH.T / TSX
Profile: The pharmaceutical comany focuses on promoting drugs that treat metabolic disorders.
Luc Tanguay, President & CEO

Marie-Noël Colussi, Vice-President, Finance
Lyne Fortin, Senior Vice-President & Chief Commercial Officer
Jocelyn Lafond, Corporate Secertary & Vice-President, Legal Affairs
Christian Marsolais, Senior Vice-President & Chief Medical Officer

Transition Therapeutics Inc.
#220, 101 College St.
Toronto, ON M5G 1L7
416-260-7770
info@transitiontherapeutics.com
www.transitiontherapeutics.com
Company Type: Public
Ticker Symbol: TTH / TSX
Profile: Transition is a biopharmaceutical company, developing novel therapeutics for disease indications with large markets.
Tony Cruz, Chief Executive Officer
Nicole Rusaw, Chief Financial Officer
Carl Damiani, President & COO

Trillium Therapeutics Inc.
2488 Dunwin Dr.
Mississauga, ON L5L 1J9
416-595-0627
info@trilliumtherapeutics.com
trilliumtherapeutics.com
Company Type: Public
Ticker Symbol: TR / TSX
Profile: The company develops cancer treatment therapies.
Niclas Stiernholm, President & CEO
James Parsons, Chief Financial Officer

Valeant Pharmaceuticals International, Inc.
2150 St. Elzéar Blvd. West
Laval, QC H7L 4A8
514-744-6792
Fax: 514-744-6272
800-361-1448
www.valeant.com
Other Communications: Human Resources: recruiting@valeant.com
Company Type: Public
Ticker Symbol: VRX / TSX, NYSE
Staff Size: 48,202
Profile: The specialty pharmaceutical company develops, manufactures, & markets pharmaceutical products. Valeant Pharmaceuticals specializes in the areas of neurology & dermatology. Products are sold in North America, Brazil, central Europe, & Australia.
Joseph C. Papa, Chair & Chief Executive Officer
Pavel Mirovsky, President & General Manager, Europe
Ari Kellen, Executive Vice-President
Paul Herendeen, Chief Financial Officer & Executive Vice-President
Christina Ackermann, Exec. Vice-President & General Counsel
Anne Whitaker, Executive Vice-President

VBI Vaccines Inc.
#2241, 222 - 3rd St.
Cambridge, MA 02142 USA
617-830-3031
info@vbivaccines.com
www.vbivaccines.com
Social Media: www.facebook.com/vbivaccines
twitter.com/vbivaccines
www.linkedin.com/company/1484859
Company Type: Public
Ticker Symbol: VBV / TSX
Profile: A vaccine development company.

Printing & Publishing

Glacier Media Inc.
2188 Yukon St.
Vancouver, BC V5Y 3P1
604-872-8565
Fax: 604-638-2453
info@glaciermedia.ca
www.glaciermedia.ca
Other Communications: Investor Relations: investors@glaciermedia.ca
Company Type: Public
Ticker Symbol: GVC / TSX
Staff Size: 479
Profile: Glacier Media Inc. provides information & related services through print, electronic, & online media.
The Business & Professional Information Group consists of organizations such as CD-Pharma, Eco Log, Specialty Technical Publishers, & Fundata.
The Newspaper & Trade Information Group is comprised of newspapers such as the Prince George Citizen, The Kamloops Daily News, & the Estevan Mercury. Trade information group publications include The Western Producer, The Daily Oil Bulletin, New Technology Magazine, Business in Vancouver, Canadian Cattlemen, & The Northern Miner.
Jonathon J.L. Kennedy, President & Chief Executive Officer
Orest Smysniuk, Chief Financial Officer

GVIC Communications Corp.
389 West 6th Ave.
Vancouver, BC V5Y 1L1
604-708-3264
Fax: 604-879-1483
Company Type: Public
Ticker Symbol: GCT / TSX
Staff Size: 479
Profile: GVIC Communications is an information communications company. Information is provided through print, electronic, & online media. The company's core businesses are local newspapers, trade information, & business & porfessional information markets.
In 2011, GVIC Communications Corp., through its affiliates, completed the acquisition of Postmedia Network Inc.'s community newspapers in British Columbia, the Times Colonist, related digital media assets, plus certain real estate assets.
Jonathon J.L. Kennedy, President & CEO
Orest Smysniuk, CA, Chief Financial Officer

MDC Partners
33 Draper St.
Toronto, ON M5V 2M3
416-960-9000
www.mdc-partners.com
Social Media: twitter.com/mdcpartners
www.linkedin.com/company/mdc-partners
Company Type: Public
Ticker Symbol: MDZ.A / TSX
Staff Size: 5,690
Profile: MDC Partners Inc. provides marketing communication services and secure transaction products and services in North America, Europe, Australia and Latin America.
Scott Kauffman, CEO/Chair
David Doft, Chief Financial Officer

Pollard Banknote Limited (PBL)
140 Otter St.
Winnipeg, MB R3T 0M8
204-474-2323
Fax: 204-453-1375
winnipeg@pollardbanknote.com
www.pollardbanknote.com
Other Communications: humanresources@pollardbanknote.com
Company Type: Public
Ticker Symbol: PBL / TSX
Staff Size: 1,168
Profile: Pollard Banknote Limited is a lottery vendor & supplier to the charitable gaming industry. The company manufactures instant tickets, pull tab tickets, & bingo paper. Other activities include warehousing, distributing, & marketing.
Douglas Pollard, Co-Chief Executive Officer
John Pollard, Co-Chief Executive Officer
Riva Richard, General Counsel & Executive Vice-President, Legal Affairs
Robert Rose, CFO & Executive Vice-President, Finance
Robert Young, Executive Vice-President, Operations
Jennifer Westbury, Executive Vice-President, Sales & Customer Development

Postmedia Network Canada Corp.
365 Bloor St. East
Toronto, ON M4W 3L4
416-383-2300
www.postmedia.com
Social Media: www.facebook.com/Postmedia
www.twitter.com/postmedianet
www.linkedin.com/company/1191505
Company Type: Public
Ticker Symbol: PNC.A / TSX
Staff Size: 4,733
Profile: Postmedia Network Canada Corp. is a communications & media publishing & printing company.
Rod Phillips, Chair
Paul Godfrey, President & Chief Executive Officer
Doug Lamb, Executive Vice-President & Chief Financial Officer
Andrew MacLeod, Executive Vice-President & Chief Commercial Officer

Quebecor Inc.
612, rue Saint-Jacques
Montréal, QC H3C 4M8
514-380-1999
www.quebecor.com
Company Type: Public
Ticker Symbol: QBR.A, QBR.B / TSX
Profile: Quebecor Inc. is a holding company that has a 81.07% interest in Quebecor Media Inc. Quebecor Media is a large media group with close to 11,000 employees.
Pierre Dion, President & Chief Executive Officer
Jean-François Pruneau, Chief Financial Officer & Senior Vice-President
Brian Mulroney, Chairman of the Board

Thomson Reuters Corp.
3 Times Sq.
New York, NY 10036 USA
646-223-4000
thomsonreuters.com
Other Communications: Canadian Phone: 416-360-8700
Social Media: www.facebook.com/thomsonreuters
twitter.com/thomsonreuters
www.linkedin.com/company/thomson-reuters_1400
Company Type: Public
Ticker Symbol: TRI / TSX
Staff Size: 52,000
Profile: Thomson Reuters is a Mass Media company, which provides organizations with information pertaining to finance, governance, intellectual property, legality, tax & accounting.
James C. Smith, President & CEO
Stephane Bello, Executive Vice-President & CFO
Gus Carlson, Executive Vice-President & Chief Communications Officer

Torstar Corporation
Corporate Office
1 Yonge St.
Toronto, ON M5E 1P9
416-869-4010
Fax: 416-869-4183
www.torstar.com
Company Type: Public
Ticker Symbol: TS.B / TSX
Profile: The media & book publishing company includes the following businesses: Star Media Group, which features the Toronto Star & digital properties such as toronto.com & thestar.com & Metroland Media Group, which publishes community & daily newspapers throughout Ontario.
David Holland, President & Chief Executive Officer
Jennifer Barber, Senior Vice-President, Finance
Ian Oliver, President, Metroland Media Group Ltd.
Chris Goodridge, Senior Vice-President, Digital Ventures
Lorenzo DeMarchi, Chief Financial Officer & Executive Vice-President
Marie Beyette, Senior Vice-President, General Counsel & Corporate Secretary

Transcontinental Inc.
#3315, 1, Place Ville Marie
Montréal, QC H3B 3N2
514-954-4000
Fax: 514-954-4016
www.transcontinental.com
Social Media: twitter.com/TCTranscontinen
www.linkedin.com/company/tc-transcontinental
Company Type: Public
Ticker Symbol: TCL.A / TSX
Profile: The company is engaged in the printing & publishing of consumer magazines & community newspapers, as well as direct marketing, & distribution of advertising material.
Transcontinental Inc. has worked to address environmental issues, by programs such as the implementation of the Transcontinental Paper Purchasing Policy.
François Olivier, President & Chief Executive Officer
Brian Reid, President, Transcontinental Printing & Transcontinental Packaging
Nelson Gentiletti, Chief Financial & Development Officer
Christine Desaulniers, Chief Legal Officer & Corporate Secretary
Jennifer F. McCaughey, Vice-President, Communications
jennifer.mccaughey@tc.tc

Yellow Pages Inc.
Ile des Soeurs
16, Place du Commerce
Montréal, QC H3E 2A5
514-934-2611
800-361-6010
www.ypg.com
Other Communications: Customer Accounts: 877-909-9356
Social Media: www.facebook.com/yellowpagesgroup
twitter.com/yellowpages_ca
Company Type: Public
Ticker Symbol: Y / TSX
Staff Size: 3,500
Profile: Yellow Pages owns & operates properties & publications such as the Yellow Pages print directories, YellowPages.ca, Canada411.ca, & RedFlagDeals.com. The company is also involved in digital advertising through Mediative.
Julien Billot, President & CEO
Ginette Maillé, Chief Financial Officer & Senior Vice-President
François D. Ramsay, General Counsel & Senior Vice-President, Corporate Affairs
Dany Paradis, Vice-President & Chief Human Resources Officer

ZoomerMedia Limited
70 Jefferson Ave.
Toronto, ON M6K 1Y4
416-368-3194
Fax: 416-368-9774
www.zoomermedia.ca

Company Type: Public
Ticker Symbol: ZUM / TSX Venture
Profile: Formed in 1991, ZoomerMedia Limited is a multimedia company that serves the interests of persons 45 years of age & older. The company offers the following services: television, radio, magazines, internet, & trade shows. Examples of ZoomerMedia's television properties include Vision TV, ONE, & Joytv. Radio properties include CFMZ-FM Toronto, CFMX-FM Cobourg, & CFZM-AM 740 Toronto. ZoomerMedia also publishes Zoomer Magazine. An example of the company's online content is www.50plus.com. ZoomerMedia's trade show division produces the Zoomer Show.
Moses Znaimer, President & CEO
MosesAssistant@Zoomer.ca
George Kempff, Chief Financial Officer & Vice-President
g.kempff@zoomermedia.ca
Leanne Wright, Vice-President, Communications
leanne@zoomer.ca

Real Estate

Agellan Commercial Real Estate Investment Trust
#303, 156 Front St. West
Toronto, ON M5J 2L6
416-593-6800
Fax: 416-593-6700
www.agellanreit.com
Social Media: twitter.com/AgellanREIT

Company Type: Public
Ticker Symbol: ACR.UN / TSX
Staff Size: 47
Profile: Agellan Commercial REIT is involved in the acquisition & ownership of properties located in Texas, Ontario & the mid-western United States.
Frank Camenzulli, Chief Executive Officer
Daniel Millett, Chief Financial Officer

Allied Properties Real Estate Investment Trust
#1700, 134 Peter St.
Toronto, ON M5V 2H2
416-977-9002
Fax: 416-977-9053
info@alliedreit.com
alliedreit.com
Social Media: twitter.com/AlliedREIT
www.linkedin.com/company/allied-properties

Company Type: Public
Ticker Symbol: AP.UN / TSX
Profile: Allied Properties Real Estate Investment Trust is the owner of urban office properties. The organization plans to continue the acquisition of Class I & other office properties. Target markets are in Victoria, Vancouver, Edmonton, Calgary, Winnipeg, Kitchener, Toronto, Ottawa, Montréal, & Québec.
Michael R. Emory, President & Chief Executive Officer
Thomas G. Burns, Chief Operating Officer & Executive Vice-President
Cecilia C. Williams, Chief Financial Officer & Vice-President
Tyrone Bowers, Vice-President, Acquisitions
Jennifer L. Irwin, Vice-President, Human Resources & Communications

Altus Group Limited
Head Office
#500, 33 Yonge St.
Toronto, ON M5E 1G4
416-641-9500
Fax: 416-641-9501
877-953-9948
info@altusgroup.com
www.altusgroup.com
Social Media: www.facebook.com/AltusGroup
twitter.com/Altus_Group
www.linkedin.com/company/altus-group

Company Type: Public
Ticker Symbol: AIF / TSX
Staff Size: 2,300
Profile: Altus Group offers real estate consulting & advisory services. The organization's business units are as follows: Research, Valuation, & Advisory; Realty Tax Consulting; Cost Consulting & Project Management; ARGUS Software; & Geomatics.
Robert Courteau, Chief Executive Officer
Angelo Bartolini, Chief Financial Officer

American Hotel Income Properties REIT
#1660, 401 West Georgia St.
Vancouver, BC V6B 5A1
604-630-3134
Fax: 604-629-0790
info@ahipreit.com
www.ahipreit.com

Company Type: Public
Ticker Symbol: HOT.UN / TSX
Profile: American Hotel Income Properties REIT LP has been formed to indirectly own and acquire hotel properties in the United States.
Robert O'Neill, Chief Executive Officer
Azim Lalani, Chief Financial Officer

Artis Real Estate Investment Trust
#300, 360 Main St.
Winnipeg, MB R3C 3Z3
204-947-1250
Fax: 204-947-0453
www.artisreit.com
Social Media: www.facebook.com/ArtisREIT
twitter.com/ArtisREIT
www.linkedin.com/company/artis-real-estate-investment-trust

Company Type: Public
Ticker Symbol: AX.UN / TSX
Profile: Artis REIT is an unincorporated closed-ended real estate investment trust whose portfolio is comprised of industrial, retail, and office space in Canada and the United States.
Armin Martens, President/Chief Executive Officer
Jim Green, Chief Financial Officer
Frank Sherlock, Executive Vice-President, Property Management

Atrium Mortgage Investment Corporation
#900, 20 Adelaide St. East
Toronto, ON M5C 2T6
416-867-1053
Fax: 416-867-1303
info@atriummic.com
www.atriummic.com
Social Media: www.facebook.com/AtriumMIC
twitter.com/AtriumMIC
linkedin.com/company/atrium-mortgage-investment-corporation

Company Type: Public
Ticker Symbol: AI / TSX
Staff Size: 25
Profile: Atrium Mortgage Investment Corp. is a Canadian non-bank lender that provides financial solutions in both the commercial and residential real estate sectors.
Robert Goodall, President & CEO
Jeffrey D. Sherman, Chief Financial Officer

Becker Milk Co. Ltd.
393 Eglinton Ave. East, 2nd Fl.
Toronto, ON M4P 1M6
416-698-2591

Company Type: Public
Ticker Symbol: BEK.B / TSX
Profile: The Becker Milk Company Limited, is engaged in the ownership and management of retail commercial properties, mainly in Ontario.
Geoffrey Pottow, President & Chief Executive Officer
Brian Rattenbury, Chief Financial Officer

Boardwalk Real Estate Income Trust
#200, 1501 - 1st St. SW
Calgary, AB T2R 0W1
403-531-9255
www.boardwalkreit.com
Social Media: www.facebook.com/BoardwalkRentalCommunities
twitter.com/bwalkcommunity

Company Type: Public
Ticker Symbol: BEI.UN / TSX
Staff Size: 1,400
Profile: The open-ended real estate investment trust owns & operates multi-family communities. Boardwalk REIT's portfolio is concentrated in British Columbia, Alberta, Saskatchewan, Ontario, & Quebec.
Sam Kolias, Chair & Chief Executive Officer
403-206-6789
William Wong, Chief Financial Officer, Finance
William Zigomanis, Vice-President, Investments
Roberto Geremia, President

Brookfield Canada Office Properties
Brookfield Place
PO Box 770, #330, 181 Bay St.
Toronto, ON M5J 2T3
416-359-8555
Fax: 416-359-8596
www.brookfieldofficepropertiescanada.com

Company Type: Public
Ticker Symbol: BOX.UN / TSX; BOXC / NYSE
Profile: The corporation owns, develops, & manages office properties in Toronto, Ottawa, Calgary and Vancouver.
Jan Sucharda, President/Chief Executive Officer
Bryan Davis, Chief Financial Officer
T. Nga Gilgan, Senior Vice-President, Investments

Brookfield Real Estate Services Inc.
39 Wynford Dr.
Toronto, ON M3C 3K5
416-510-5800
info@brookfieldresinc.com
www.brookfieldresinc.com

Company Type: Public
Ticker Symbol: BRE / TSX
Profile: Brookfield Real Estate Services is involved in the provision of services to residential real estate brokers & their realtors. Cash flow is generated from franchise royalties & service fees from brokers & agents who operate under the following brand names: Johnston & Daniel; Royal LePage; & Via Capitale Real Estate Network.
Philip Soper, President & Chief Executive
416-386-6000, philsoper@brookfieldres.com
Glen McMillan, Chief Financial Officer
416-510-5605, Glen.McMillan@brookfieldres.com

BTB Real Estate Investment Trust/ Fonds de placement immobilier BTB
Also Known As: BTB REIT
2155, rue Crescent
Montréal, QC H3G 2C1
514-286-0188
Fax: 514-286-0011
www.btbreit.com
Social Media: twitter.com/btbreit

Company Type: Public
Ticker Symbol: BTB.UN / TSX Venture
Staff Size: 60
Profile: The real estate investment trust invests in a portfolio of industrial, commercial, office & retail properties. BTB Real Estate Investment Trust's properties are located predominantly in Québec.
Michael Léonard, Chief Executive Officer & President
mleonard@btbreit.com
Benoit Cyr, Chief Financial Officer & Vice-President
bcyr@btbreit.com
Dominic Gilbert, Vice-President, Leasing
dgilbert@btbreit.com
Sylvie Laporte, Vice-President, Property Management
slaporte@btbreit.com

Canadian Apartment Properties REIT (CAP REIT)
Also Known As: Canadian Apartment Properties Real Estate Investment Trust
#401, 11 Church St.
Toronto, ON M5E 1W1
416-861-9404
Fax: 416-861-9209
IR@capreit.net
www.caprent.com
Social Media: www.facebook.com/caprent
twitter.com/caprent

Company Type: Public
Ticker Symbol: CAR.UN / TSX
Staff Size: 937
Profile: Canadian Apartment Properties Real Estate Investment Trust is an investment trust that owns freehold interests in multi-unit residential properties, such as townhouses & apartment buildings. Properties are situated in or near major Canadian urban centres.
Thomas Schwartz, President & CEO
Scott Cryer, Chief Financial Officer
Mark Kenney, Chief Operating Officer
Roberto Israel, Chief Information Officer
Trish MacPherson, Executive Vice-President, Operations
Corinne Pruzanski, General Counsel & Corporate Secretary

Chartwell Retirement Residence
#700, 100 Milverton Dr.
Mississauga, ON L5R 4H1
905-501-9219
Fax: 905-501-0813
855-461-0685
www.chartwell.com
Social Media: www.facebook.com/chartwellretirement
www.linkedin.com/company/chartwell-retirement-residences

Company Type: Public
Ticker Symbol: CSH.UN / TSX
Staff Size: 13,500
Profile: Chartwell Retirement Residences owns and manages senior housing properties through its indirect subsidiary Chartwell Master Care LP.
Brent Binions, President & Chief Executive Officer

Vlad Volodarski, Chief Financial Officer & Chief Investment Officer
Karen Sullivan, Chief Operating Officer

CHC Student Housing
53 Yonge St., 5th Fl.
Toronto, ON M5E 1J3

416-504-9380
info@chcrealty.ca
chcstudenthousing.com
Social Media: www.facebook.com/CHCRealtyCapitalCorp
twitter.com/chcrealty
www.linkedin.com/company/chc-realty-capital-capital-corp

Company Type: Public
Ticker Symbol: CHC / TSX.V
Profile: The company owns student housing complexes.
Mark Hansen, President & CEO
Bradley Williams, Vice-President, Operations

Choice Properties Real Estate Investment Trust
#500, 22 St. Clair Ave. East
Toronto, ON M4T 2S5

416-324-7840
Fax: 416-324-7845
855-322-2122
www.choicereit.ca
Other Communications: Investor Relations, E-mail: investor@choicereit.ca

Company Type: Public
Ticker Symbol: CHP.UN / TSX
Staff Size: 115
Profile: Choice Properties REIT is an owner & developer of retail & commercial real estate in Canada. Loblaw Companies Ltd. is Choice Properties' principal tenant.
John Morrison, President & CEO
Bart Munn, Executive Vice-President & CFO

Colliers International Canada
200 Granville St., 19th Fl.
Vancouver, BC V6C 2R6

604-681-4111
www.collierscanada.com
Social Media: www.facebook.com/collierscanada
twitter.com/collierscanada
www.linkedin.com/company/colliers-international-canada

Company Type: Public
Ticker Symbol: CIG / TSX
Staff Size: 16,000
Profile: Colliers International is a commercial real estate company. They are involved with real estate management, valuation, consulting, project management, project marketing & research.
David Bowden, Chief Executive Officer
Scott Addison, President, Canadian Brokerage Services
Antoinette Tummillo, Executive Vice-President, Real Estate Management Services

Cominar Real Estate Investment Trust
Complexe Jules-Dallaire
#850, 2820 boul Laurier
Québec, QC G1V 0C1

418-681-8151
Fax: 418-681-2946
866-266-4627
info@cominar.com
www.cominar.com

Company Type: Public
Ticker Symbol: CUF.UN / TSX
Staff Size: 709
Profile: Cominar is a large, diversified real estate investment trust. It ownscommercial property in Québec. The real estate investment trust also has a portfolio of properties in the Atlantic provinces, Ontario, & western Canada.
Michel Dallaire, CEO & Chairman
Gilles Hamel, CA, Chief Financial Officer & Executive Vice-President
Sylvain Cossette, President & COO
Manon Deslauriers, Corporate Secretary & Vice-President, Legal Affairs
Guy Charron, Executive Vice-President, Retail Operations
Todd Bechard, Executive Vice-President, Acquisitions

Consolidated HCI Holdings Corporation
#3, 100 Strada Dr.
Woodbridge, ON L4L 5V7

905-851-7741
Fax: 416-253-5074

Company Type: Public
Ticker Symbol: CXA.B / TSX
Profile: Consolidated HCI Holdings Corporation is an Ontario-based real estate & development company.
Stanley Goldfarb, President & CEO
Arnold J. Resnick, Chief Financial Officer

Crombie Real Estate Investment Trust
#200, 610 East River Rd.
New Glasgow, NS B2H 3S2

902-755-8100
www.crombiereit.ca

Company Type: Public
Ticker Symbol: CRR.UN / TSX
Profile: Crombie REIT is an open-ended real estate investment trust. It owns & manages properties in eight provinces. Crombie's portfolio consists of retail, office, & mixed-use properties.
Donald E. Clow, President & Chief Executive Officer
Glenn R. Hynes, Executive Vice-President, Chief Fiancial Officer & Secretary
Scott R. MacLean, Regional Vice-President, Atlantic Region

Dream Global Real Estate Investment Trust
Also Known As: Dream Global REIT
#301, 30 Adelaide St. East
Toronto, ON M5C 3H1

416-365-3535
Fax: 416-365-6565
globalinfo@dream.ca
www.dream.ca/global
Social Media: twitter.com/DreamUltd

Company Type: Public
Ticker Symbol: DRG.UN / TSX
Staff Size: 60
Profile: Dream Global REIT is a Canadian real estate investment trust that provides investors with the opportunity to invest in commercial real estate outside of the country.
Jane Gavan, President & CEO
Tamara Lawson, Chief Financial Officer

Dream Industrial REIT
#301, 30 Adelaide St. East
Toronto, ON M5C 3H1

416-365-3535
Fax: 416-365-6565
industrialinfo@dream.ca
dream.ca/industrial
Social Media: twitter.com/DreamUltd

Company Type: Public
Ticker Symbol: DIR.UN / TSX
Profile: Dream Industrial REIT is a national pure-play industrial REIT primarily made up of high-quality light industrial properties.
Brent Chapman, Chief Executive Officer
Lenis Quan, Chief Financial Officer
Joe Iadeluca, Sr. Vice-President, Portfolio Management
David McLean, Vice-President, Portfolio Management
Ashley Phillips, Vice-President, Portfolio Management
Nick Stryland, Vice-President, Portfolio Management

Dream Office Real Estate Investment Trust
Also Known As: Dream Office REIT
#301, 30 Adelaide St. East
Toronto, ON M5C 3H1

416-365-3535
Fax: 416-365-6565
officeinfo@dream.ca
www.dream.ca/office

Company Type: Public
Ticker Symbol: D.UN / TSX
Staff Size: 602
Profile: Dream Office REIT is an unincorporated, open-ended real estate investment trust. It owns industrial & office assets throughout Canada.
In 2012, Dream Office (formerly Dundee REIT) acquired Whiterock Real Estate Investment Trust, a provider of office, retail & industrial properties in Canada.
Jane Gavan, Chief Executive Officer
Andrew Reial, Senior Vice-President, Portfolio Management
Paul Skeans, Senior Vice-President, Portfolio Management
Kevin Hardy, Senior Vice-President, Portfolio Management

Dream Unlimited
#301, 30 Adelaide St. East
Toronto, ON M5C 3H1

416-365-3535
Fax: 416-365-6565
info@dream.ca
dream.ca

Company Type: Public
Ticker Symbol: DRM / TSX
Staff Size: 228
Profile: Dream was founded in 1994 and is now the largest residential developer in Western Canada. The company owns and operates Homes by Dream, Dream Development, and three TSX-listed REITs: Dream Office REIT, Dream Industrial REIT, and Dream Global REIT.
Michael J. Cooper, President & Chief Executive Officer
Pauline Alimchandani, Chief Financial Officer
Daniel Marinovic, Sr. Vice President, Land & Housing
Jason Lester, Sr. Vice President, Urban Development

Edgefront Real Estate Investment Trust
#4050, 525 - 8th Ave. SW
Calgary, AB T2P 1G1

403-817-9496
info@edgefrontrealty.com
edgefrontreit.com

Company Type: Private
Ticker Symbol: ED.UN / TSX.V
Profile: Edgefront REIT develops & owns commercial real estate.
Kelly C. Hanczyk, President & CEO
Robert Chiasson, CFO & Corporate Secretary

Firm Capital American Realty Partners Corp.
163 Cartwright Ave.
Toronto, ON M6A 1V5

416-635-0021
Fax: 416-635-1713
info@firmcapital.com
firmcapital.com
Social Media: www.linkedin.com/company/firm-capital-corporation

Company Type: Public
Ticker Symbol: FCA / TSX.V
Profile: A private equity real estate firm.
Eli Dadouch, President & CEO
Jonathan Mair, Senior Vice-President & CFO
Sandy Poklar, Chief Operating Officer

Firm Capital Property Trust
163 Cartwright Ave.
Toronto, ON M6A 1V5

416-635-0221
Fax: 416-635-1713
info@firmcapital.com
www.firmcapital.com
Social Media: www.linkedin.com/company/firm-capital-corporation

Company Type: Public
Ticker Symbol: FCD.UN / TSX.V
Profile: Firm Capital REIT is a real estate investment & development company.
Bob McKee, President & CEO
rmckee@firmcapital.com

First Capital Realty Inc.
#400, 85 Hanna Ave.
Toronto, ON M6K 3S3

416-504-4114
Fax: 416-941-1655
investor.relations@firstcapitalrealty.ca
www.firstcapitalrealty.ca
Other Communications: HR Inquiries, E-mail: HumanResources@firstcapitalrealty.ca
Social Media: www.facebook.com/FirstCapitalRealtyInc

Company Type: Public
Ticker Symbol: FCR / TSX
Staff Size: 351
Profile: First Capital Realty Inc. owns, develops, & operates shopping centres, anchored by supermarkets & drug stores. Properties are located mainly in metropolitan areas.
Adam E. Paul, President & Chief Executive Officer
Kay Brekken, Chief Financial Officer & Executive Vice-President
Maryanne McDougald, LEED AP, Senior Vice-President, Operations

FirstService Corporation
FirstService Building
#4000, 1140 Bay St.
Toronto, ON M5S 2B4

416-960-9500
Fax: 416-960-5333
www.firstservice.com

Company Type: Public
Ticker Symbol: FSV / TSX, NASDAQ
Staff Size: 16,000
Profile: FirstService Corporation is involved in residential property management, property improvement services, & commerical real estate.
Jay S. Hennick, Founder & Chair
D. Scott Patterson, Chief Executive Officer
Jeremy Rakusin, Chief Financial Officer
Alex Nguyen, Vice-President, Strategy & Corporate Development
Douglas G. Cooke, Vice-President, Corporate Controller, & Secretary

Fronsac REIT
#200, 90 rue Morgan
Baie d'Urfé, QC H9X 3A8
450-536-5328
Fax: 416-457-0220
www.en.fronsacreit.com
Company Type: Public
Ticker Symbol: GAZ.UN / TSX.V
Profile: A commercial real estate company.
Michel Lassonde, President & Chair
Jason Parravano, Chief Financial Officer

Genesis Land Development Corp.
7315 - 8 St. NE
Calgary, AB T2E 8A2
403-265-8079
Fax: 403-266-0746
info@genesisland.com
www.genesisland.com
Social Media: www.facebook.com/GenesisBuilds
twitter.com/genesis_builds
www.linkedin.com/company/genesis-land-developments
Company Type: Public
Ticker Symbol: GDC / TSX
Staff Size: 80
Profile: The community development company operates in British Columbia & Alberta. Most of the land is situated in & around Calgary. Activities include land development, single-family & multi-family home building, & commercial development & leasing.
Bruce Rudichuk, President & Chief Executive Officer

Granite Real Estate Investment Trust
Toronto-Dominion Centre
PO Box 159, #4010, 77 King St. West
Toronto, ON M5K 1H1
647-925-7500
ir@granitereit.com
www.granitereit.com
Company Type: Public
Ticker Symbol: GRT.UN/TSX; GRP.U/NYSE
Staff Size: 54
Profile: Granite REIT is involved in the acquisition, development, selective construction, leasing, management and ownership of a predominantly industrial global rental portfolio of properties in North America and Europe.
Michael Forsayeth, Chief Executive Officer & Chief Financial Officer

Gulf & Pacific Equities Corp.
#300, 1300 Bay St.
Toronto, ON M5R 3K8
416-968-3337
Fax: 416-968-3339
info@gpequities.com
www.gpequities.com
Company Type: Public
Ticker Symbol: GUF / TSX.V
Profile: Gulf & Pacific Equities Corp. is focused on the acquisition, management and development of grocery store anchored shopping centres in Western Canada.
Anthony Cohen, President & CEO
Greg K.W. Wong, CFO

Halmont Properties Corporation
#400, 51 Yonge St.
Toronto, ON M5E 1J1
416-956-5140
Fax: 416-203-9931
Company Type: Public
Ticker Symbol: HMT / TSX Venture
Profile: Halmont Properties Corporation invests directly in real estate & securities of companies with real estate interests.
Edward C. Kress, President
Anthony E. Rubin, Vice-President

Holloway Lodging Corp.
6009 Quinpool Rd., 10th Fl.
Halifax, NS B3K 5J7
902-404-3499
Fax: 902-423-4001
investorrelations@hlcorp.ca
www.hlcorp.ca
Company Type: Public
Ticker Symbol: HLC / TSX
Profile: Holloway Lodging Corporation is a corporation focused on select and limited service hotels in tertiary and suburban markets.
Felix Seiler, Chief Operating Officer
Jane Rafuse, CFO

Imperial Equities Inc.
Scotia Pl.
#2151, 10060 Jasper Ave.
Edmonton, AB T5J 3R8
780-424-7227
Fax: 780-425-6379
www.imperialequities.com
Social Media:
www.facebook.com/Imperial-Equities-Inc-165258513892172
Company Type: Public
Ticker Symbol: IEI / TSX Venture
Profile: Imperial Equities Inc. is an indsutrial landlord focusing on the acquisition, development & re-development of real estate assets.
Sine Chadi, President & Chief Executive Officer
sine@imperialequities.com
Wendy Fair, CMA, Chief Financial Officer
wendyf@imperialequities.com

InnVest Real Estate Investment Trust
Also Known As: InnVest REIT
Royal Bank Plaza, South Tower
PO Box 126, #2200, 200 Bay St.
Toronto, ON M5J 2J1
416-607-7100
Fax: 416-607-2353
877-209-3429
investor@innvestreit.com
www.innvestreit.com
Company Type: Public
Ticker Symbol: INN.UN / TSX
Staff Size: 8,100
Profile: InnVest Real Estate Investment Trust holds a portfolio of hotels. InnVest's hotels are managed by the following companies; Delta Hotels Limited, Westmont Hospitality Management Canada Limited, Hilton Canada Co., & Fairmont Hotels & Resorts.
InVest also owns retail & office real estate, plus a retirement home. These interests are adjacent to owned hotels.
Anthony Coles, President/CEO
George Koszíwka, Chief Financial Officer

InterRent Real Estate Investment Trust
Also Known As: InterRent REIT
#207, 485 Bank St.
Ottawa, ON K2P 1Z2
613-569-5699
Fax: 888-696-5698
www.interrentreit.com
Other Communications: investorinfo@interrentreit.com
Company Type: Public
Ticker Symbol: IIP.UN / TSX
Staff Size: 222
Profile: InterRent Real Estate Investment Trust works to increase unitholder value by acquiring & owning multi-residential properties.
Mike McGahan, Chief Executive Officer
Curt Millar, CA, Chief Financial Officer

Killam Apartment Real Estate Investment Trust
#100, 3700 Kempt Rd.
Halifax, NS B3K 4X8
902-453-9000
Fax: 902-455-4525
866-453-8900
leasing@killamproperties.com
www.killamproperties.com
Social Media: www.facebook.com/killamproperties
twitter.com/KillamTweets
Company Type: Public
Ticker Symbol: KMP.UN / TSX
Staff Size: 549
Profile: Killam Properties Inc. is a large residential landlord. The company owns, develops, & operates multi-family apartments & manufactured home communities.
Environmental intiatives at Killam's properties include the increasing use of solar power, reducing heating costs with outdoor controllers, & reducing water consumption with water saving kits.
Philip D. Fraser, President & Chief Executive Officer
Robert Richardson, Chief Financial Officer & Executive Vice-President
Ruth Buckle, Vice-President, Property Management
Erin Cleveland, Vice-President, Finance
Michael McLean, Vice-President, Development
Dale Noseworthy, Vice-President, Investor Relations & Corporate Planning

King George Financial Corp.
#750, 510 Burrard St.
Vancouver, BC V6C 3A8
604-687-8882
Fax: 604-687-1476
Company Type: Public
Ticker Symbol: KGF / TSX.V
Profile: A commercial & residential real estate firm.
Dennis Ng, President & CEO
Tim Koo, Chief Financial Officer

Lakeview Hotel Investment Corp.
Also Known As: Lakeview Hotel REIT
#600, 185 Carlton St.
Winnipeg, MB R3C 3J1
204-947-1161
Fax: 204-957-1697
info@lakeviewhotels.com
www.lakeviewhotels.com
Social Media: www.facebook.com/LakeviewHotelsAndResorts
twitter.com/lakeviewhotels1
Company Type: Public
Ticker Symbol: LHR.DB.C / TSX Venture
Profile: Lakeview Hotel Investment owns and co-manages the Lakeview Inn & Suites and has licensing income from five other hotels through its 49% interest in the "Lakeview Flag".
Keith Levit, President & CEO
Avrum Senensky, Executive Vice-President

Lanesborough Real Estate Investment Trust (LREIT)
Also Known As: Lanesborough REIT
c/o Shelter Canadian Properties Limited
#2600, 7 Evergreen Pl.
Winnipeg, MB R3L 2T3
204-475-9090
Fax: 204-452-5505
info@lreit.com
www.lreit.com
Company Type: Public
Ticker Symbol: LRT.UN / TSX
Profile: Lanesborough Real Estate Investment Trust aims to provide unitholders with stable cash distributions by investing in a diversified portfolio of real estate properties.
Arni C. Thorsteinson, President & CEO
Gary Benjaminson, Chief Financial Officer & Secretary

Madison Pacific Properties Inc.
389 - 6th Ave. West
Vancouver, BC V5Y 1L1
604-732-6540
info@madisonpacific.ca
www.madisonpacific.ca
Company Type: Public
Ticker Symbol: MPC / TSX
Staff Size: 10
Profile: Madison Pacific Properties Inc. is a real estate investment & development company. Its properties include rentable industrial & commercial space.
In 2011, Madison Pacific Properties Inc. acquired the shares of MP Western Properties Inc.. The shares were acquired for investment purposes.
Marvin Haasen, President & CEO
Dino Di Marco, Chief Financial Officer
Rob Hackett, Vice-President, Property Management

Mainstreet Equity Corp.
305 - 10 Ave. SE
Calgary, AB T2G OW2
403-215-6060
Fax: 403-266-8867
mainstreet@mainst.biz
www.mainst.biz
Social Media: www.facebook.com/MainstreetEquity
twitter.com/mainst_apts
Company Type: Public
Ticker Symbol: MEQ / TSX
Staff Size: 300
Profile: Mainstreet Equity is engaged in the acquisition & renting of apartments. Business is conducted in Abootsford & Surrey British Columbia, Calgary & Edmonton Alberta, Saskatoon Saskatchewan, & Toronto & Mississauga Ontario.
Bob Dhillon, President & Chief Executive Officer
Johnny Lam, Chief Financial Officer & Chief Operating Officer
Sheena Keslick, Vice-President, Operations
Trina Cui, Vice-President, Coporate Finance

Melcor Developments Ltd.
#900, 10310 Jasper Ave. NW
Edmonton, AB T5J 1N8
780-423-6931
Fax: 780-426-1796
info@melcor.ca
www.melcor.ca
Other Communications: Investor Relations, E-mail: ir@melcor.ca
Social Media: twitter.com/melcordev
www.linkedin.com/company/melcor-developments-ltd
Company Type: Public
Ticker Symbol: MRD / TSX
Staff Size: 140

Profile: Melcor Developments Ltd. is a real estate development company that was established in 1923. It acquires land to develop & sell for multi-family sites, residential communities, & commercial sites. The organization is also the owner, developer, & manager of commercial income properties & golf courses.
Brian Baker, President & CEO
Jonathan Chia, CA, Chief Financial Officer

Melcor Real Estate Investment Trust
#900, 10310 Jasper Ave.
Edmonton, AB T5J 1Y8

780-423-6931
866-635-2671
info@Melcorreit.ca
www.melcorreit.ca

Company Type: Public
Ticker Symbol: MR.UN / TSX
Profile: The corporation owns, develops, & manages commercial properties in western Canada.
Darin Rayburn, Chief Executive Officer
Jonathan Chia, Chief Financial Officer

Milestone Apartments Real Estate Investment Trust
#800, 5429 LBJ Freeway
Dallas, TX 75240 USA

214-561-1200
Fax: 214-561-1290
investor-relations@milestonereit.com
www.milestonereit.com
Other Communications: Toronto phone: 647-496-7856

Company Type: Public
Ticker Symbol: MST.UN / TSX
Staff Size: 1,510
Profile: Milestone manages apartment communities in the southeast & southwest United States. It is the largest real estate investment trust focused on the US multifamily sector listed on the TSX.
Robert P. Landin, Chief Executive Officer
Ryan Newberry, Chief Financial Officer
Steve Lamberti, Chief Operating Officer

Mongolia Growth Group Ltd.
First Canadian Place
#5600, 100 King St. West
Toronto, ON M5X 1C9

289-848-2035
Fax: 866-468-9119
877-644-1186
info@mongoliagrowthgroup.com
mongoliagrowthgroup.com
Social Media: twitter.com/MongoliaGG
www.linkedin.com/company/mongolia-growth-group-ltd

Company Type: Public
Ticker Symbol: YAK / TSX.V
Profile: Mongolia Growth Group Ltd. is a real estate and financial services conglomerate focusing its operations on Mongolia.
Harris Kupperman, Chief Executive Officer
Genevieve Walkden, Corporate Secretary, Interim CFO & Senior Vice-President, Finance

Morguard Corporation
#800, 55 City Centre Dr.
Mississauga, ON L5B 1M3

905-281-3800
800-928-6255
info@morguard.com
www.morguard.com
Social Media: www.linkedin.com/company/morguard

Company Type: Public
Ticker Symbol: MRC / TSX
Staff Size: 1,500
Profile: Morguard Corporation is a real estate & property management company. Through its investment in Morguard REIT, the corporation has a diversified portfolio of residential, office, retail, & industrial properties owned or under management. Through Morguard Investments Limited & Morguard Residential, management services to institutional & other investors for residential & commercial real estate are offered.
K. Rai Sahi, Chair & CEO
rsahi@morguard.com
Paul Miatello, Chief Financial Officer
pmiatello@morguard.com
Beverley G. Flynn, General Counsel & Secretary
bflynn@morguard.com
Brian Athey, Vice-President, Development
bathey@morguard.com

Mountain China Resorts (Holding) Limited (MCR)
No. 54 Lishi Hutong
Beijing
Other Communications: Phone: +86 10 66420868; Fax: +86 10 66420288

Company Type: Public
Ticker Symbol: MCG / TSX.V
Profile: Mountain China Resorts (Holding) Limited develops ski resorts in China.
Gang Han, Chief Executive Officer
Yang Shi, Chief Financial Officer

Northview Apartment Real Estate Investment Trust Also Known As: Northview Apartment REIT
6131 - 6 St. SE
Calgary, AB T2H 1L9

403-531-0720
www.northviewreit.com
Social Media: www.facebook.com/NorthviewREIT
twitter.com/northviewREIT

Company Type: Public
Ticker Symbol: NVU.UN / TSX
Profile: In 2015, Northern Property REIT acquired True North Apartment REIT and became Northview Apartment REIT. The company is a multi-family REIT that also owns & manages executive suites & hotels.
Todd Cook, President & Chief Executive Officer
Leslie Veiner, Chief Operating Officer
Travis Beatty, Chief Financial Officer

OneREIT
#300, 700 Applewood Cres.
Vaughan, ON L4K 5X3

416-741-7999
Fax: 416-741-7993
info@onereit.ca
www.onereit.ca

Company Type: Public
Ticker Symbol: ONR.UN / TSX
Staff Size: 100
Profile: OneREIT, created in 2004, focuses on owning and acquiring retail properties across Canada.
Richard Michaeloff, Chief Executive Officer
rmichaeloff@onereit.ca
Tom Wenner, Chief Financial Officer
twenner@onereit.ca

Partners Real Estate Investment Trust Also Known As: Partners REIT
#3, 249 Saunders Rd.
Barrie, ON L4N 9A3

705-725-6020
Fax: 705-725-8026
844-474-9620
info@partnersreit.com
www.partnersreit.com

Company Type: Public
Ticker Symbol: PAR.UN / TSX Venture
Profile: Partners REIT is an open-end real estate investment trust. The real estate investment trust owns retail properties situated in British Columbia, Alberta, Manitoba, Ontario, & Québec.
Jane Domenico, President & CEO
Derrick West, Chief Financial Officer & Corporate Secretary

Plaza Retail REIT
Head Office
98 Main St.
Fredericton, NB E3A 9N6

506-451-1826
Fax: 506-451-1802
info@plaza.ca
www.plaza.ca
Other Communications: Montréal Office: 514-457-7007; Halifax Office: 902-468-8688

Company Type: Public
Ticker Symbol: PLZ.UN / TSX Venture
Staff Size: 88
Profile: Plaza Retail REIT is engaged in the acquisition, development, & re-development of enclosed mall shopping centres & strip plazas. Operations take place in Ontario, Québec, & Atlantic Canada.
Michael Zakuta, President & Chief Executive Officer
Floriana Cipollone, Chief Financial Officer
Jamie Petrie, Executive Vice-President & COO

Pro Real Estate Investment Trust
#920, 2000 Manfield St.
Montréal, QC H3A 2Z6

514-933-9552
proreit.com

Company Type: Public
Ticker Symbol: PRV.UN / TSX.V
Profile: Pro REIT owns commercial real estate in Québec, Atlantic Canada, Alberta, British Columbia & Ontario.
James Beckerleg, President & CEO
Gordon Lawlor, Chief Financial Officer

Pure Industrial Real Estate Trust
#910, 925 West Georgia St.
Vancouver, BC V6C 3L6

604-398-2836
Fax: 604-681-5969
888-681-5959
info@piret.ca
www.piret.ca

Company Type: Public
Ticker Symbol: AAR.UN / TSX Venture
Staff Size: 40
Profile: Pure Industrial Real Estate Trust is an open-ended, unincorporated trust. Its purpose is to acquire, own, & operate a portfolio of income producing industrial properties throughout Canada.
Kevan Gorrie, President & CEO
Francis Tam, Chief Financial Officer
Allan T. Saito, Vice-President, Property Management & Leasing

Pure Multi-Family REIT
#910, 925 West Georgia St.
Vancouver, BC V6C 3L6

604-681-5959
Fax: 604-681-5969
888-681-5959
info@puremultifamily.com
www.puremultifamily.com

Company Type: Public
Ticker Symbol: RUF.U / TSX.V
Staff Size: 118
Profile: Pure Multi is a Canadian-based company which allows Canadian investors the opportunity to buy into under-valued American hard assets while the Canadian dollar trades.
Stephen Evans, Chief Executive Officer
Scott Shillington, Chief Financial Officer

RioCan Real Estate Investment Trust
RioCan Yonge Eglinton Centre
PO Box 2386, #500, 2300 Yonge St.
Toronto, ON M4P 1E4

416-866-3033
Fax: 416-866-3020
800-465-2733
inquiries@riocan.com
www.riocan.com
Other Communications: HR: recruiting@riocan.com; Investors: ir@riocan.com

Company Type: Public
Ticker Symbol: REI.UN / TSX
Staff Size: 727
Profile: The Trust owns a portfolio of retail properties throughout Canada. RioCan manages neighbourhood shopping centres that are anchored by supermarkets.
Edward Sonshine, Q.C., Chief Executive Officer
Raghunath Davloor, President & COO
Cynthia Devine, Executive Vice-President & CFO
Michael Connolly, Senior Vice-President, Construction
Stuart Baum, Vice-President, Human Resources

Slate Retail REIT
#200, 121 King St. West
Toronto, ON M5H 3T9

416-644-4264
Fax: 416-947-9366
info@slateam.com
www.slateam.com

Company Type: Public
Ticker Symbol: SRT.UN / TSX
Profile: Slate Retail REIT provides investors with direct exposure to the recovery in grocery-anchored retail properties in strategic markets across the U.S.
Greg Stevenson, CEO
Robert Armstrong, CFO

SmartREIT
#200, 700 Applewood Cres.
Vaughan, ON L4K 5X3

905-326-6400
Fax: 905-326-0783
info@smartreit.com
www.smartreit.com

Company Type: Public
Ticker Symbol: SRU.UN / TSX
Staff Size: 308
Profile: In 2015, Calloway REIT acquired the SmartCentre platform, and changed their name to SmartREIT. The company is an unincorporated, open-ended real estate investment trust that provides planning, develoment, leasing, operations & construction.
Huw Thomas, President & Chief Executive Officer
hthomas@smartreit.com
Peter E. Sweeney, Chief Financial Officer
Rudy Gobin, Exec. Vice-President, Portfolio Management & Investments

Summit Industrial Income Real Estate Investment Trust
Also Known As: Summit II
#1, 294 Walker Dr.
Brampton, ON L6T 4Z2

905-791-1181
info@summitiireit.com
www.summitiireit.com

Company Type: Public
Ticker Symbol: SMU.UN / TSX
Staff Size: 950
Profile: Summit Industrial Income REIT is an open ended mutual fund trust focused on growing and managing a portfolio of light industrial properties across Canada.
Paul Dykeman, CA, Chief Executive Officer
Ross Drake, CA, Chief Financial Officer

Temple Hotels Inc.
c/o Morguard Corporation
#1000, 55 City Centre Dr.
Mississauga, ON L5B 1M3

905-281-4800
Fax: 905-281-5890
info@morguard.com
www.templehotels.ca

Company Type: Public
Ticker Symbol: TPH / TSX
Profile: Temple Hotels invests in a portfolio of hotel properties & related assets in order to provide unitholders with stable cash distributions.
K. Rai Sahi, Chief Executive Officer
Paul Miatello, Chief Financial Officer

Terra Firma Capital Corporation
#200, 22 St. Clair Ave. East
Toronto, ON M4T 2S3

416-792-4700
Fax: 416-792-4711
investorrelations@tfcc.ca
tfcc.ca
Social Media: twitter.com/TerraFirmaCap
www.linkedin.com/company/terra-firma-capital-corporation

Company Type: Public
Ticker Symbol: TII / TSX-V
Profile: Terra Firma Capital Corporation is a boutique real estate finance company that provides customized debt and equity solutions to the real estate industry.
Glenn Watchorn, President & CEO
gwatchorn@tfcc.ca
Mano Thiyagarajah, CFO & Corporate Secretary
mthiyagarajah@tfcc.ca
Seth Greenspan, Vice-President
sgreenspan@tfcc.ca

True North Commercial REIT
West Tower
#1801, 3300 Bloor St. West
Toronto, ON M8X 2X2

416-234-8444
ircommercial@truenorthreit.com
commercial.truenorthreit.com

Company Type: Public
Ticker Symbol: TNT.UN / TSX
Profile: True North Commercial Real Estate Investment Trust is an owner and acquirer of Canadian commercial real estate properties.
Daniel Drimmer, President & Chief Executive Officer
Tracy C. Sherren, Chief Financial Officer

Urbanfund Corp.
35 Lesmill Rd.
Toronto, ON M3B 2T3

416-703-1877
Fax: 416-504-9216

Company Type: Public
Ticker Symbol: UFC / TSX.V
Profile: Urbanfund Corp. engages in the development and operation of real estate properties in Canada.
Mitchell Cohen, President & Chief Executive Officer
Victor Safirstein, CFO

Wall Financial Corporation
#3502, 1088 Burrard St.
Vancouver, BC V6Z 2R9

604-893-7131
Fax: 604-893-7179

Company Type: Public
Ticker Symbol: WFC / TSX
Staff Size: 502
Profile: The corporation is engaged in the following activities: real estate development; investment in properties; management of residential rental apartments & hotel properties; & development & construction of residential housing for resale.
Bruno Wall, President
Darcee Wise, Executive Vice-President & Secretary
Joanne Liu, Vice-President, Finance

WPT Industrial Real Estate Investment Fund
#4000, 199 Bay St.
Toronto, ON M5L 1A9

info@wptreit.com
www.wptreit.com

Company Type: Public
Ticker Symbol: WIR.U / TSX
Profile: WPT Industrial REIT is focused on the aquisition & sale of warehouse & distribution properties in the United States.
Scott T. Frederiksen, CCIM, SIOR, Chief Executive Officer
stf@wptreit.com
Dennis Heieie, CPA, Chief Financial Officer
dheieie@wptreit.com
Matthew Cimino, General Counsel & Secretary
mcimino@wptreit.com

Services, Miscellaneous

Axios Mobile Assets Corp.
#7, 30 Topflight Dr.
Mississauga, ON L5S 0A8

877-762-9467
axiosma.com

Company Type: Private
Ticker Symbol: AXA / TSX
Richard MacDonald, President & CEO
Michael Cook, Chief Financial Officer

Black Diamond Group Limited
#2000, 715 - 5th Ave. SW
Calgary, AB T2P 2X6

403-206-4747
Fax: 403-264-9281
888-569-4880
investor@blackdiamondgroup.com
www.blackdiamondlimited.com
Other Communications: Media Relations, E-mail: media@blackdiamondgroup.com
Social Media: www.linkedin.com/company/black-diamond-limited

Company Type: Public
Ticker Symbol: BDI / TSX
Staff Size: 274
Profile: Black Diamond Group was founded in 2003. The corporation provides modular buildings, workforce accommodations, & energy services. The three operating divisions are Black Diamond Camps & Logistics, Black Diamond Energy Services, & BOXX Modular.
Trevor Haynes, President & Chief Executive Officer
Toby Labrie, Chief Financial Officer & Executive Vice-President
Troy Cleland, Chief Operating Officer & Executive Vice-President, North America
Harry Klukas, Executive Vice-President, International

Boyd Group Income Fund
3570 Portage Ave.
Winnipeg, MB R3K 0Z8

204-895-1244
Fax: 204-895-1283
info@boydgroup.com
www.boydgroup.com

Company Type: Public
Ticker Symbol: BYD.UN / TSX
Staff Size: 5,922
Profile: The Boyd Group Income Fund is an unincorporated, open-ended mutual fund trust. It was formed to acquire & hold investments, including a majority interest in The Boyd Group Inc. & its subsidiaries. Boyd Group Inc. operates collision repair centres throughout North America. Boyd Group Income Fund pays monthly distributions to unitholders of record on or around the last business day of the month.
Brock Bulbuck, President & Chief Executive Officer
bulbuck@boydgroup.com
Pat Pathipati, Executive Vice-President & CFO
pat.pathipati@boydgroup.com

Brightpath Early Learning & Child Care
#201, 200 Rivercrest Dr. SE
Calgary, AB T2C 2X5

403-705-0362
888-808-2252
info@brightpathkids.com
brightpathkids.com
Social Media: facebook.com/brightpathkidscanada
twitter.com/brightpathkids_

Company Type: Public
Ticker Symbol: BPE / TSX
Staff Size: 1,400
Profile: BrightPath is an innovative provider of early education and provides families with care, programs and child development services.
Mary Ann Curran, Chief Executive Officer
Dale Kearns, President & Chief Financial Officer

Caldwell Partners International
#600, 165 Avenue Rd.
Toronto, ON M5R 3S4

416-920-7702
Fax: 416-922-8646
888-366-3827
www.caldwellpartners.com
Social Media: twitter.com/CaldwellPtners
www.linkedin.com/company/33585

Company Type: Public
Ticker Symbol: CWL / TSX
Staff Size: 117
Profile: Caldwell Partners is a staffing company, with a focus on finding senior executives & directors.
John N. Wallace, President & CEO
C. Christopher Beck, CFO & Corporate Secretary

Canlan Ice Sports Corp.
Western Corporate office
6501 Sprott St.
Burnaby, BC V5B 3B8

604-736-9152
www.canlanicesports.com
Other Communications: Eastern Corporate Office (Toronto), Phone: 416-661-4423

Company Type: Public
Ticker Symbol: ICE / TSX
Staff Size: 1,100
Profile: Canlan Ice Sports develops, owns, & operates multi-purpose recreation & entertainment facilities in Canada & the United States. The company's flagship facility is Canlan Ice Sports - Burnaby 8 Rinks, located in Burnaby, British Columbia. Canlan Ice Sports also offers programs such as Canlan Sports Camps, Hockey Academy, Canlan Classic Tournaments, & Skating Academy.
Joey St-Aubin, President & Chief Executive Officer
Michael F. Gellard, Chief Financial Officer & Senior Vice-President
Paul Dillon, Vice-President, Sales, Marketing, & Service
Mark Faubert, Senior Vice-President, Operations
Mark Reynolds, Vice-President, Human Resources

Centric Health Corporation
#2100, 20 Eglinton Ave. West
Toronto, ON M4R 1K8

416-927-8400
Fax: 416-927-8405
800-265-9197
www.centrichealth.ca

Company Type: Public
Ticker Symbol: CHH / TSX
Staff Size: 501
Profile: Centric Health Corporation is a diversified healthcare services company. Operations include medical assessments, specialty pharmacy services, surgical centres, physiotherapy, rehabilitation & disability management, homecare, & the provision of home medical equipment.
David Cutler, President & Chief Executive Officer
Diane Mason, Chief Human Resources Officer

CERF Inc.
Calgary Place 1
#2440, 330 - 5 Ave. SW
Calgary, AB T2P 0L3

403-930-5430
Fax: 403-460-6216
Info@Cerfcorp.Com
cerfcorp.com
Social Media: www.linkedin.com/company/3745596

Company Type: Public
Ticker Symbol: CFL / TSX.V
Profile: CERF Inc. provides construction equipment rental, sales and service, oilfeild rental equipment,sale and service as well as waste management and environmental services.
Artie Kos, Chair & Chief Executive Officer
Austin Fraser, President
Ken Olson, Chief Financial Officer

CIBT Education Group Inc.
International Head Office
#1200, 777 West Broadway
Vancouver, BC V5Z 4J7

604-871-9909
Fax: 604-871-9919
888-865-0901
info@cibt.net
www.cibt.net

Company Type: Public
Ticker Symbol: MBA / TSX; MBAIF / OTCQX
Staff Size: 311
Profile: The education management company is the owner & operator of language, business, & technical colleges. CIBT

Education Group's subsidiaries include Sprott-Shaw Degree College, Sprott-Shaw Community College, King George International College, & the CIBT School of Business China. These subsidiaries enable the CIT Education Group to offer Western & Chinese accredited business & management degrees, plus programs in college preparation, information technology, English language training, English teacher certification, automotive maintenance, hotel management, & tourism.
Toby Chu, Chair, President & CEO
Dennis Huang, Chief Financial Officer & Exec. Vice-President

Ergoresearch Ltd.
#200, 2101, boul de Carrefour
Laval, QC H7S 2J7

450-973-6700
info@ergoresearch.com
www.ergoresearch.com
Social Media: www.linkedin.com/company/ergoresearch
Company Type: Public
Ticker Symbol: ERG / TSX.V
Profile: Ergoresearch develops orthopedic productions that help patients deal with pain management.
Sylvain Boucher, President & CEO
Danielle Boucher, Vice-President
Frederic Petit, Vice-President, Operations
Louis Desrosiers, Vice-President, Research & Development

Espial Group Inc.
#1000, 200 Elgin St.
Ottawa, ON K2P 1L5

613-230-4770
Fax: 613-230-8498
888-437-7425
espial.com
Social Media: www.facebook.com/EspialGroup
twitter.com/espial
www.linkedin.com/company/espial
Company Type: Public
Ticker Symbol: ESP / TSX
Profile: The company designs software used for Internet protocol television, allowing users to connect to the internet via their televion.
Jaison Dolvane, President & CEO
Carl Smith, Chief Financial Officer
Kumanan Yogaratnam, Chief Technical Officer

Evergreen Gaming
8200 Tacoma Mall Blvd.
Lakewood, WA 98499 USA

206-258-3250
Fax: 425-282-4172
info@evergreengaming.com
www.evergreengaming.com
Company Type: Public
Ticker Symbol: TNA / TSX.V
Profile: Evergreen own four card rooms in Washington State.
Monty Harmon, Executive Officer & President
Kathy Dirks, Chief Financial Officer

Extendicare Inc.
#103, 3000 Steeles Ave. East
Markham, ON L3R 9W2

905-470-4000
communications@extendicare.com
www.extendicare.com
Social Media: twitter.com/extendicare
Company Type: Public
Ticker Symbol: EXE / TSX
Staff Size: 16,800
Profile: Extendicare Inc. operates senior care facilities. Through its ParaMed Home Health Care division, home health care services are also provided.
Timothy L. Lukenda, President/Chief Executive Officer
Elaine Everson, Vice-President/Chief Financial Officer
Jillian Fountain, Corporate Secretary

Gamehost Inc.
#104, 548 Laura Ave.
Red Deer, AB T4E 0A5

403-346-4545
Fax: 403-340-0683
877-703-4545
www.gamehost.ca
Company Type: Public
Ticker Symbol: GH, GH.DB / TSX
Staff Size: 800
Profile: The corporation was established under the laws of the Province of Alberta. Gamehost Inc. is involved in the hotel & gaming business. Operations include the Great Northern Casino, Boomtown Casino, & Service Plus Inns & Suites hotel in Alberta. The company also has a 91% controlling interest in Deerfoot Inn & Casino in Calgary.
David J. Will, President & CEO
Darcy J. Will, Vice-President & Secretary
Craig M. Thomas, CMA, Chief Financial Officer
Elston J. Noren, Chief Operations Officer

Grand Power Logistics Group Inc.
#2806, 505 - 6th St. SW
Calgary, AB T2P 1X5

403-237-8211
Fax: 403-228-3013
www.grandpowerlogistics.com
Company Type: Public
Ticker Symbol: GPW / TSX.V
Profile: Grand Power Logistics Group Inc. is a provider of logistics and related services in the global market.
Ricky Chiu, President & Chief Executive Officer
Alan Chan, Chief Financial Officer & Secretary-Treasurer

Great Canadian Gaming Corporation
95 Schooner St.
Coquitlam, BC V3K 7A8

604-303-1000
Fax: 604-516-7155
www.gcgaming.com
Other Communications: ir@gcgaming.com
Social Media:
www.linkedin.com/company/great-canadian-gaming-corporation
Company Type: Public
Ticker Symbol: GC / TSX
Staff Size: 4,900
Profile: Great Canadian Gaming Corporation is a gaming & entertainment operator. Operations include entertainment facilities, such as casinos, racetracks, & show theatres. Business is conducted in Nova Scotia, Ontario, British Columbia, & Washington State.
Rod N. Baker, President & CEO
Terrance Doyle, Chief Operating Officer
Chuck Keeling, Vice-President, Stakeholder Relations & Responsible Gaming
Vic Poleschuk, Executive Vice-President, Operations - East

Information Services Corporation
#300, 10 Research Dr.
Regina, SK S4S 7J7

306-787-8179
866-275-4721
ask@isc.ca
www.isc.ca
Company Type: Public
Ticker Symbol: ISV / TSX
Staff Size: 304
Profile: Information Services Corporation is responsible for the development, management and administration of: registries - land titles, personal property, corporate and survey registries; geographic information; and access to government services for people and business.
Jeff Stusek, President & Chief Executive Officer
Shawn B. Peters, Chief Financial Officer & Vice-President, Finance & Technology
Kathy Hillman-Weir, Q.C., Chief Privacy Officer, General Counsel & Vice-President, Corporate Affairs
Kenneth W. Budzak, Vice-President, Operations & Customer Experience

Innova Gaming Group
9340 Penfield Ave.
Chatsworth, CA 91311 USA

818-727-1690
877-727-1690
www.innovagaminggroup.com
Company Type: Private
Ticker Symbol: IGG / TSX
Richard Weil, CEO

Intertain Group Ltd.
24 Duncan St., 2nd Fl.
Toronto, ON M5V 2B8

416-207-3307
info@intertain.com
intertain.com
Company Type: Public
Ticker Symbol: IT / TSX
Staff Size: 182
Profile: Intertain Group is an online gaming company. Its websites include Costa Bingo, InterCasino, Vera&John, Vera&Juan, Vera&John Social, Jackpotjoy, Starspins & Botemania.
Andrew McIver, Chief Executive Officer
Keith Laslop, Chief Financial Officer

K-Bro Linen Inc.
14903 - 137 Ave. NW
Edmonton, AB T5V 1R9

780-453-5218
Fax: 780-455-6676
www.k-brolinen.com
Company Type: Public
Ticker Symbol: KBL / TSX
Staff Size: 1,870
Profile: K-Bro Linen Inc. is involved in the operation of laundry & linen processing facilities. It serves industrial & commercial sectors, such as hospitality & healthcare. Processing facilities are located in Montréal, Québec, Toronto, Calgary, Edmonton, Vancouver, & Victoria. Brands include Les Buanderies Dextraze, Buanderie HMR, & K-Bro Linen Systems Inc.
Linda McCurdy, President & Chief Executive Officer
Kristie Plaquin, Chief Financial Officer

Lions Gate Entertainment Corp.
#5000, 2700 Colorado Ave.
Santa Monica, CA 90404 USA

310-449-9200
investorrelations@lionsgate.com
www.lionsgate.com
Company Type: Public
Ticker Symbol: LGF / NYSE
Staff Size: 719
Profile: Lions Gate Entertainment Corp. is a developer, producer, & distributor of television, motion picture, family entertainment, home entertainment, video-on-demand, & digitally delivered content. The company is made up of the following operating divisions: Motion Pictures, Television, Animation, & Studio Facilities.
Jon Feltheimer, CEO
Steve Beeks, Co-COO & President, Motion Picture Group
Brian Goldsmith, Co-COO
James Barge, Chief Financial Officer
Wayne Levin, General Counsel & Chief Strategy Officer
Peter D. Wilkes, Sr. Vice-President, Investor Relations & Executive Communications

Medical Facilities Corporation (MFC)
#200, 45 St. Clair Ave. West
Toronto, ON M4V 1K6

416-848-7380
877-402-7162
medicalfacilitiescorp.ca
Company Type: Public
Ticker Symbol: DR / TSX
Staff Size: 1,254
Profile: Medical Facilities Corporation owns controlling interests in four specialty surgical hospitals in Oklahoma & South Dakota. The corporation also owns interests in an ambulatory surgery center, located in California. The specialty surgical hospitals derive revenue from fees charged for use of the facilities.
Britt Reynolds, Chief Executive Officer
Michael Salter, CA, CPA, Chief Financial Officer

MFC Bancorp Ltd.
#1860, 400 Burrard St.
Vancouver, BC V6C 3A6

604-683-8286
www.mfcbancorpltd.com
Company Type: Public
Ticker Symbol: MIL / NYSE
Staff Size: 651
Profile: In 2011, Terra Nova Royalty Corporation changed its name to MFC Industrial Ltd.. The global commodity supply chain company sources & delivers materials & commodities to clients. MFC Industrial Ltd. specializes in the financing & risk management business areas.
Gerardo Cortina, President & CEO
Samuel Morrow, Chief Financial Officer

Morneau Shepell Ltd.
Tower One
#700, 895 Don Mills Rd.
Toronto, ON M3C 1W3

416-445-2700
Fax: 416-445-7989
www.morneaushepell.com
Other Communications: Media: media@morneaushepell.com
Social Media: twitter.com/Morneau_Shepell
www.linkedin.com/company/morneau-shepell
Company Type: Public
Ticker Symbol: MSI / TSX
Staff Size: 4,000
Profile: Morneau Shepell offers human resource consulting & outsourcing services. The company provides services to organizations in Canada & around the world.
Alan Torrie, President & Chief Executive Officer
René Beaudoin, Chief Technology Officer & Executive Vice-President, U.S. Region

Pierre Chamberland, Chief Operating Officer & Executive Vice-President, Administrative Solutions
Scott Milligan, Chief Financial Officer & Executive Vice-President
Hazel Claxton, Executive Vice-President & Chief Human Resources Officer
Randal Phillips, Executive Vice-President & Chief Client Officer
Susan Marsh, General Counsel & Corporate Secretary

New Look Eyewear Inc./ Lunetterie New Look
#100, 1100 Bouvier St.
Québec, QC G2K 1L9
Fax: 418-624-4040
800-463-5665
www.newlook.ca
Social Media: www.facebook.com/NewLook.ca
Company Type: Public
Ticker Symbol: BCI / TSX
Staff Size: 1,464
Profile: In 2010, Benvest New Look Income Fund was converted into a corporation named New Look Eyewear Inc.. The eye care organization operates laboratories & stores in eastern Canada.
Martial Gagné, President
Marie-Josée Mercier, Vice-President, Sales & Operations

Newalta Corporation
211 - 11th Ave. SW
Calgary, AB T2R 0C6
403-806-7000
Fax: 403-806-7348
800-774-8466
www.newalta.com
Social Media: www.linkedin.com/company/newalta
Company Type: Public
Ticker Symbol: NAL / TSX
Staff Size: 900
Profile: Newalta Corporation is involved in the product recovery business in order to reduce the environmental impact of industrial waste. The corporation has 85 facilities throughout Canada.
John Barkhouse, President & CEO
Michael Borys, Chief Financial Officer & Executive Vice-President
Took Whiteley, General Counsel & Senior Vice-President, Corporate Development

Nobilis Health
#300, 11700 Katy Freeway
Houston, TX 77079 USA
713-355-8614
Fax: 713-355-8615
www.nobilishealth.com
Company Type: Public
Ticker Symbol: NHC / TSX
Staff Size: 715
Profile: Nobilis Health is a healthcare development & management company. It manages over 100 surgical centres. The company is also involved with marketing, finance & legal aspects of the centres.
Harry Fleming, Chief Executive Officer
Kenny Klein, Chief Financial Officer
Michael Nelson, Vice-President, Operations

Noble Iron
505 Rankin Rd.
Houston, TX 77073 USA
855-767-4424
www.nobleiron.com
Social Media: www.facebook.com/NobleIronInc
www.linkedin.com/company/2752572
Company Type: Public
Ticker Symbol: NIR / TSX.V
Profile: Noble Iron offers equipment for rent, equipment for sale, & software applications for the construction & industrial equipment industry.
Nabil Kassam, Founder, Chairman & CEO
Vahid Hassanpour, General Manager & Director, Equipment Operations

Oneroof Energy Group
#240, 4445 Eastgate Mall Rd.
San Diego, CA 92121 USA
858-458-0533
info@oneroofenergy.com
www.oneroofenergy.com
Social Media: www.facebook.com/oneroofenergy
twitter.com/OneRoofEnergy
www.linkedin.com/company/917218
Company Type: Public
Ticker Symbol: ON / TSX
Profile: A residential solar energy company.
David Field, President & CEO

Park Lawn Corporation
#400, 2323 Yonge St.
Toronto, ON M4P 2C9
416-231-1462
parklawncorp.com
Social Media: www.facebook.com/ParkLawnLP
twitter.com/Park_Lawn_LP
www.linkedin.com/company/park-lawn-limited-partnership
Company Type: Public
Ticker Symbol: PLC / TSX Venture
Profile: In 2011, Park Lawn Income Trust converted from an income trust to a corporation. Park Lawn Corporation indirectly holds six cemeteries in the Greater Toronto Area of Ontario, plus Services Memorables Harmonia Inc. located in Quebec City. The corporation also has an interest in Bloorpark Developments Inc.
Andrew Clark, Chief Executive Officer
Joseph Leeder, Chief Financial Officer

Patient Home Monitoring Corp.
#1250, 14724 Ventura Blvd.
Sherman Oaks, CA 91403 USA
323-253-3055
Fax: 415-693-9694
phmhometesting.com
Company Type: Private
Ticker Symbol: PHM / TSX.V
Profile: PHM provides home solutions to people who have heart disease & health conditions.
Casey Hoyt, Chief Executive Officer
Steve Lazarus, Chief Financial Officer
Mike Moore, Managing Director, Disease Management

Points International Ltd.
171 John St.
Toronto, ON M5T 1X3
416-595-0000
Fax: 416-595-6444
www.points.com
Social Media: www.facebook.com/pointsfans
twitter.com/pointsadvisor
www.linkedin.com/companies/points
Company Type: Public
Ticker Symbol: PTS / TSX
Staff Size: 181
Profile: Points International Ltd. owns & operates the loyalty reward management program platform, www.Points.com. The platform permits users to redeem, exchange, & trade miles & rewards.
Christopher Barnard, President
Michael D'Amico, Chief Financial Officer

Poydras Gaming Finance
#800, 789 Pender St.
Vancouver, BC V6C 1H2
604-683-8393
Fax: 604-648-8350
info@poydrasgaming.com
www.poydrasgaming.com
Company Type: P
Ticker Symbol: PYD / TSX.V
Profile: An equipment & finance provider for casinos.
Daniel Davila, President
Adam Kniec, Chief Financial Officer
Peter Macy, Chief Executive Officer

Progressive Waste Solutions Ltd.
Corporate Office
400 Applewood Cres., 2nd Fl.
Vaughan, ON L4K 0C3
905-532-7510
Fax: 905-532-7576
corporate.communications@progressivewaste
www.progressivewaste.com
Social Media: www.facebook.com/506993962699534
twitter.com/ProgressiveWste
www.linkedin.com/company/progressive-waste-solutions
Company Type: Public
Ticker Symbol: BIN / TSX, NYSE
Staff Size: 7,900
Profile: Progressive Waste Solutions Ltd. is a full-service waste management company. It offers non-hazardous solid waste collection & landfill disposal services. The company serves residential, municipal, commercial, & industrial customers located in six Canadian provinces & the District of Columbia in the United States. Brand BFI Canada, Waste Services, & IESI.
Dan Pio, Chief Executive Officer
William Herman, Executive Vice-President & Interim CFO
Izzie Abrams, Vice-President, Corporate Development & Government Relations
Chaya Cooperberg, Vice-President, Investor Relations & Corporate Communications

Pulse Seismic Inc.
Head Office
#2400, 639 - 5th Ave. SW
Calgary, AB T2P 0M9
403-237-5559
Fax: 403-531-0688
877-460-5559
www.pulseseismic.com
Social Media: www.linkedin.com/company/pulse-seismic-inc.
Company Type: Public
Ticker Symbol: PSD / TSX
Profile: Pulse Seismic Inc. is engaged in the acquisition, marketing, & licensing of 2D & 3D seismic data. The company's data library covers key areas in the Northwest Territories, Yukon, northeastern British Columbia, Alberta, Saskatchewan, Manitoba, & Montana. Pulse Seismic serves the western Canadian energy sector.
Neal Coleman, President & Chief Executive Officer
Pamela Wicks, Chief Financial Officer & Vice-President, Finance

Pure Technologies Ltd.
#300, 705 - 11th Ave. SW
Calgary, AB T2R 0E3
403-266-6794
Fax: 403-266-6570
855-280-7873
www.puretechltd.com
Other Communications: Investor Relations, Phone: 403-266-6794
Social Media: www.facebook.com/puretechnologies
twitter.com/PTLNews
www.linkedin.com/company/pure-technologies
Company Type: Public
Ticker Symbol: PUR / TSX
Staff Size: 500
Profile: The asset management technology & service company developed technologies for inspecting, monitoring, & managing critical infrastructure throughout the world. Physical infratructure include buildings, bridges, & water & hydrocarbon pipelines.
John F. Elliott, President & CEO
Mark W. Holley, Executive Vice-President & Chief Operating Officer
Geoffrey Krause, Vice-President & Chief Financial Officer

Rainmaker Entertainment Inc.
#200, 2025 West Broadway
Vancouver, BC V6J 1Z6
604-714-2600
Fax: 604-714-2641
www.rainmaker.com
Social Media: www.facebook.com/RainmakerEnt
twitter.com/rainmakerent
www.linkedin.com/company/4579
Company Type: Public
Ticker Symbol: RNK / TSX.V
Staff Size: 238
Profile: Rainmaker Entertainment is an animation production company that is responsible for the creation of feature films, shorts & direct to DVD movies.
Craig Graham, Chief Executive Officer
Michael Hefferon, President & Chief Creative Officer
Bryant Pike, Chief Financial Officer
Kim Dent Wilder, Senior Vice-President, Production & Operations
Tara Kemes, Vice-President, Culture & Talent

Sienna Senior Living
#300, 302 Town Centre Blvd.
Markham, ON L3R 0E8
905-477-4006
Fax: 905-415-7623
info@siennaliving.ca
siennaliving.ca
Social Media: www.facebook.com/siennaliving
www.linkedin.com/company/333290
Company Type: Public
Ticker Symbol: SIA / TSX
Staff Size: 8,170
Profile: Sienna Senior Living is a licensed long-term care provider, with operations in Ontario. The corporation owns 54 seniors' residences. Subsidiaries include Ontario Long Term Care & Preferred Health Care Services
Lois Cormack, President & CEO
Nitin Jain, Executive Vice-President & Chief Financial Officer
Joanne Dykeman, Executive Vice-President, Operations
Michael Annable, Chief Administrative Office & Executive Vice-President, People
Cristina Alaimo, Vice-President & General Counsel

Spin Master
450 Front St. West
Toronto, ON M5V 1B6
416-364-6002
Fax: 416-364-5097
customercare@spinmaster.com
www.loyalistgroup.com
Social Media: www.facebook.com/SpinMaster
twitter.com/spinmaster
www.linkedin.com/company/29884
Company Type: Public
Ticker Symbol: TOY / TSX
Staff Size: 985
Profile: Spin Master is a toy manufacturer, founded in 1994. It is the owner of the Air Hoggs brand, Zoobles & Bakugan. It has also launched 2 children's programs, PAW Patrol & Little Charmers.
Anton Rabie, Chair & Co-Chief Executive Officer
Ronnen Harary, Co-Chief Executive Officer
Ben Gadbois, Chief Operating Officer
Mark Segal, Executive Vice-President & Chief Financial Officer

StorageVault Canada
PO Box 32062, Regina, SK S4N 7L2
306-775-3383
storagevaultcanada.com
Social Media:
www.facebook.com/pages/StorageVault-Canada-Inc/177734989015919
twitter.com/StorageVaultInc
Company Type: Public
Ticker Symbol: SVI / TSX.V
Profile: A self storage centre company.
Steven Scott, Chief Executive Officer
Iqbal Khan, Chief Financial Officer

Superior Plus Corp.
#401, 200 Wellington St. West
Toronto, ON M5V 3C7
416-346-8050
Fax: 416-340-6030
866-490-7587
info@superiorplus.com
www.superiorplus.com
Company Type: Public
Ticker Symbol: SPB / TSX
Staff Size: 4,277
Profile: Superior Plus Corp. consists of the following businesses: Specialty Chemical, including manufacturing & selling; Energy Services, involving the distribution of propane & distillates; & Construction Products Distribution.
Luc Desjardins, President & Chief Executive Officer
Ed Bechberger, President, Specialty Chemicals
Greg McCamus, President, Energy Services & Superior Propane
Keith Wrisley, President, US Refined Fuels
Shawn Vammen, Senior Vice-President, Superior Gas Liquids
John Engelen, Vice-President, Mergers & Acquisitions
Beth Summers, Vice-President & Chief Financial Officer

TSO3 Inc.
2505, av Dalton
Québec, QC G1P 3S5
418-651-0003
Fax: 418-653-5726
866-715-0003
info@tso3.com
www.glentel.com
Company Type: Public
Ticker Symbol: TOS / TSX
Profile: The company is the developer of a medical instrument sterilization system, called the Sterizone sterilizer.
Ric Rumble, Chief Executive Officer
Glen Kayll, Chief Financial Officer

TWC Enterprises Ltd.
55 City Centre Dr.
Mississauga, ON L5B 1M3
905-281-3800
Fax: 905-281-5890
www.twcenterprises.ca
Company Type: Public
Ticker Symbol: TWC / TSX
Staff Size: 550
Profile: TWC owns & operates the ClubLink golf clubs & resorts.
K. Rai Sahi, Chief Executive Officer
Andrew Tamlin, Chief Financial Officer

Steel & Metal

ADF Group Inc.
300, rue Henry-Bessemer
Terrebonne, QC J6Y 1T3
450-965-1911
Fax: 450-965-8558
800-263-7560
infos@adfgroup.com
www.adfgroup.com
Company Type: Public
Ticker Symbol: DRX / TSX
Staff Size: 571
Profile: ADF Group Inc. specializes in the design, engineering, fabrication, & installation of steel superstructures, architectural, & miscellaneous metals. The company serves the non-residential construction market.
Jean Paschini, Co-Chair & Chief Executive Officer
Pierre Paschini, P.Eng., President & Chief Operating Officer
Jean-François Boursier, Chief Financial Officer

Bri-Chem Corp.
#15, 53016 Hwy. 60
Acheson, AB T7X 5A7
780-962-9490
Fax: 780-962-9875
info@brichem.com
www.brichem.com
Company Type: Public
Ticker Symbol: BRY / TSX
Profile: Bri-Chem Corp. was formed in 1985. Its divisions are the Drilling Fluid Division & the Steel Pipe Division. The Drilling Fluid Division supplies drilling fluids to the oil & gas industry, while the Steel Pipe Division manufactures & provides steel pipe for the energy industry.
Don Caron, Chief Executive Officer
Trent Abraham, President, Fluids Division
Jason Theiss, CA, Chief Financial Officer

Canam Group Inc.
#500, 11535 - 1st Ave.
Saint-Georges, QC G5Y 7H5
418-228-8031
877-499-6049
www.groupecanam.com
Social Media: www.facebook.com/groupecanam
twitter.com/GroupeCanam
www.linkedin.com/company/66983
Company Type: Public
Ticker Symbol: CAM / TSX
Staff Size: 4,269
Profile: Canam Group Inc. is engaged in the design & fabrication of construction products & solutions. The company operates over twenty-five engineering offices & manufacturing plants in Canada, the United States, Romania, India, & China.
Marc Dutil, President & Chief Executive Officer
Kurt Langsenkamp, President, Canam Steel Corporation
Mario Bernard, Chief Manufacturing Officer & Executive Vice-President
René Guizzetti, Chief Financial Officer & Vice-President

Excellon Resources Inc.
#900, 20 Victoria St.
Toronto, ON M5C 2N8
416-364-1130
Fax: 416-324-6745
info@excellonresources.com
www.excellonresources.com
Social Media: twitter.com/EXN_Resources
www.linkedin.com/company/ecellon-resources-inc.
Company Type: Public
Ticker Symbol: EXN / TSX
Staff Size: 254
Profile: Excellon Resources, is a mining company operating in Durango and Zacatecas States, Mexico, and Ontario and Quebec, Canada.
Brendan Cahill, President & Chief Executive Officer
Rupy Dhadwar, Chief Financial Officer

Kincora Copper Limited
#800, 1199 West Hastings St.
Vancouver, BC V6E 3T5
604-283-1722
888-241-5996
enquiries@kincoracopper.com
www.kincoracopper.com
Company Type: Public
Ticker Symbol: KCC / TSX.V
Profile: Kincora Copper Limited mining exploration and development company with a focus in Mongolia.
Jonathan (Sam) Spring, President & CEO
Anthony Jackson, Chief Financial Officer

Martinrea International Inc.
3210 Langstaff Rd.
Vaughan, ON L4K 5B2
416-749-0314
www.martinrea.com
Other Communications: Investor Information, E-mail: Investor@martinrea.com
Company Type: Public
Ticker Symbol: MRE / TSX
Staff Size: 12,000
Profile: Martinrea International Inc. specializes in the production of metal parts, assemblies & modules, & fluid management systems. The company supplies the automotive industry & other industrial sectors. Divisions are located in Canada, the United States, Mexico, & Europe.
Pat D'Eramo, President & CEO

Russel Metals Inc.
6600 Financial Dr.
Mississauga, ON L5N 7J6
905-819-7777
Fax: 905-819-7409
800-268-0750
info@russelmetals.com
www.russelmetals.com
Other Communications: Investor Relations, Phone: 905-816-5178
Company Type: Public
Ticker Symbol: RUS / TSX
Staff Size: 3,000
Profile: The metal processor & distributor operates in North America. The company implemented environmental standards & an ongoing audit process.
Brian R. Hedges, Chief Executive Officer
John G. Reid, President & COO
Marion E. Britton, Executive Vice-President & Chief Financial Officer

Tree Island Steel Ltd.
3933 Boundary Rd.
Richmond, BC V6V 1T8
604-524-3744
Fax: 604-524-2362
800-663-0955
www.treeisland.com
Social Media:
www.facebook.com/pages/Tree-Island-Steel-Ltd/256804541095369
www.linkedin.com/company/96869
Company Type: Public
Ticker Symbol: TSL / TSX
Staff Size: 600
Profile: Tree Island manufacturers wire and wire products.
Dale R. MacLean, President & Chief Executive Officer
Nancy Davies, Vice-President/CFO, Finance

Velan Inc.
7007, ch de la Côte-de-Liesse
Montréal, QC H4T 1G2
514-748-7743
Fax: 514-748-8635
sales@velan.com
www.velan.com
Company Type: Public
Ticker Symbol: VLN / TSX
Staff Size: 1,953
Profile: Velan Inc. manufactures industrial steel valves. Manufacturing plants are located in Canada, the United States, Europe, & Asia. Velan valves are used in numerous industries, such as oil & gas, chemical & petrochemical, pulp & paper, mining, & power generation. The company also offers aftermarket services.
Tom Velan, Chair & Chief Executive Officer
John Ball, Chief Financial Officer

Textiles, Apparel & Leather

Gildan Activewear Inc.
600, boul de Maisonneuve ouest, 33rd Fl.
Montréal, QC H3A 3J2
514-735-2023
Fax: 514-735-6810
866-755-2023
info@gildan.com
www.gildan.com
Other Communications: Customer Service, Toll-Free: 800-668-8337, ext. 4115
Social Media: www.facebook.com/GildanOnline
Company Type: Public
Ticker Symbol: GIL / TSX, NYSE
Staff Size: 42,000
Profile: Gildan Activewear manufactures & markets activewear,

athletic socks, & underwear. The company serves both North American & international markets.
Glenn J. Chamandy, President & Chief Executive Officer
Michael R. Hoffman, President, Printwear
Rhodri Harries, Exec. Vice-President, CFO & Administrative Officer
Benito Masi, Executive Vice-President, Manufacturing
Eric Lehman, President, Branded Apparel

Intertape Polymer Group Inc. (IPG)
#200, 9999, boul Cavendish
Montréal, QC H4M 2X5
514-731-7591
info@itape.com
www.intertapepolymer.com
Other Communications: itp$info@itape.com; Lrequest@itape.com
Social Media: www.facebook.com/intertape
www.twitter.com/IPGtape
www.linkedin.com/company/intertape-polymer-group
Company Type: Public
Ticker Symbol: ITP / TSX
Staff Size: 1,900
Profile: Intertape Polymer Group Inc. develops, manufactures and markets a variety of specialized polyolefin plastic packaging products and systems for industrial and retail use.
Gregory Yull, President & CEO
Shawn Nelson, Senior Vice-President, Sales
Jeffrey Crystal, CFO
Douglas Nalette, Senior Vice-President, Operations

Performance Sports Group Ltd.
100 Domain Dr.
Exter, NH 03833
603-610-5805
Fax: 603-292-1505
investor@performancesportsgroup.com
www.performancesportsgroup.com
Other Communications: Media Inquiries: media@performancesportsgroup.com
Company Type: Public
Ticker Symbol: PSG / TSX, NYSE
Staff Size: 872
Profile: Performance Sports Group develops & manufactures ice hockey, roller hockey, & lacrosse equipment, plus related apparel. Brands include Bauer Hockey, Mission Roller Hockey & Maverik Lacrosse.
Harlan Kent, Chief Executive Officer
Mark Vendetti, Chief Financial Officer
Paul Gibson, Executive Vice-President & Chief Supply Chain Officer
Paul Dachsteiner, Vice-President, Information Services

Unisync Corp.
#508, 333 Seymour St.
Vancouver, BC V6B 5A6
778-370-1725
Fax: 604-370-1726
www.unisyncgroup.com
Company Type: Public
Ticker Symbol: UNI / TSX
Profile: A uniform designer.
Douglas Good, President & CEO
Richard Smith, Chief Financial Officer
James Bottoms, Chief Operating Officer

Transportation & Travel

Air Canada
7373, boul Côte-Vertu ouest
Montréal, QC H4S 1Z3
514-393-3333
866-584-0380
shareholders.actionnaires@aircanada.ca
www.aircanada.com
Other Communications: Investors, E-mail: investors.investisseurs@aircanada.ca
Social Media: www.facebook.com/aircanada
twitter.com/aircanada
Company Type: Public
Ticker Symbol: AC / TSX
Staff Size: 25,000
Profile: The Canadian-based international air carrier provides scheduled & chartered air transportation for both passengers & cargo. Air Canada serves over 180 destinations on five continents. Air Canada is a founding member of the Star Alliance air transportation network.
Calin Rovinescu, President/CEO
Benjamin A. Smith, President, Passenger Airlines
Klaus Goersch, Executive Vice-President & Chief Operating Officer
Michael Rousseau, Executive Vice-President & Chief Financial Officer
Lise Fournel, Senior Vice-President & Chief Information Officer
David Shapiro, Senior Vice-President & Chief Legal Officer
Ed Doyle, Vice-President, Flight Operations
Chris Isford, Vice-President & Controller

Algoma Central Corporation
Executive Office
#600, 63 Church St.
St Catharines, ON L2R 3C4
905-687-7888
Fax: 905-687-7840
Inquiry@algonet.com
www.algonet.com
Social Media: twitter.com/algomacentral
Company Type: Public
Ticker Symbol: ALC / TSX
Staff Size: 2,000
Profile: Algoma Central Corporation is a Canadian-flag ship owner on the Great Lakes - St. Lawrence Waterway. The company owns both dry-bulk carriers & product tankers. As well as the operation of vessels, ship & diesel engine repair & fabrication are part of Algoma Central's operations. In addition to shipping, Algoma Central Corporation also owns Algoma Central Hotels & Algoma Central Properties Inc. These businesses own & manage commercial real estate properties in St Catharines, Waterloo, & Sault Ste. Marie.
Ken Bloch Soerensen, FCA, President & CEO
Peter D. Winkley, CA, Chief Financial Officer & Vice-President, Finance
Al J. Vanagas, C.E.T., Sr. Vice-President, Technical
Wayne A. Smith, Sr. Vice-President, Commercial
J. Wesley Newton, Secretary & General Counsel

AutoCanada Inc.
#200, 15511 - 123rd Ave. West
Edmonton, AB T5V 0C3
Fax: 780-447-0651
888-717-3558
www.autocan.ca
Social Media: www.facebook.com/autocan
twitter.com/autocanada
Company Type: Public
Ticker Symbol: ACQ / TSX
Staff Size: 4,000
Profile: AutoCanada is an automobile dealership group. It operates franchised dealerships in Nova Scotia, New Brunswick, Ontario, Manitoba, Alberta, & British Columbia.
Tom Orysiuk, President
Steven Landry, Chief Executive Officer
Steve Rose, Chief Operating Officer
Christopher Burrows, Chief Financial Officer

Aveda Transportation & Energy Services
#300, 435 - 4th Ave. SW
Calgary, AB T2P 3A8
403-264-4950
Fax: 403-262-9195
888-829-1370
info@avedaenergy.com
www.avedaenergy.com
Company Type: Public
Ticker Symbol: AVE / TSX.V
Staff Size: 433
Profile: Aveda Transportation and Energy Services is an oilfield hauling and rentals company serving North America.
Ronnie Witherspoon, President & Chief Executive Officer
Bharat Mahajan, Vice-President, Finance & Chief Financial Officer
Paula Breeze, Vice-President, Human Resources

Bombardier Inc.
800, boul René-Lévesque ouest
Montréal, QC H3B 1Y8
514-861-9481
Fax: 514-861-2420
www.bombardier.com
Social Media: twitter.com/Bombardier
www.linkedin.com/company/bombardier
Company Type: Public
Ticker Symbol: BBD.A, BBD.B / TSX
Staff Size: 70,900
Profile: Bombardier Inc. manufactures transportation solutions, such as rail equipment & commercial aircraft. Bombardier is listed as an index component to the Dow Jones Sustainability World & North America indexes.
Alain Bellemare, President & Chief Executive Officer
David Coleal, President, Business Aircraft
Fred Cromer, President, Commercial Aircraft
Jean Séguin, President, Aerostructures & Engineering Services
Laurent Troger, President, Transportation
John Di Bert, Senior Vice-President & Chief Financial Officer
Daniel Desjardins, Senior Vice-President, General Counsel & Corporate Secretary

BRP Inc.
565, rue de la Montagne
Valcourt, QC J0E 2L0
450-532-2211
Fax: 450-532-5133
www.brp.com
Social Media: twitter.com/BRPnews
www.linkedin.com/company/brp
Company Type: Public
Ticker Symbol: DOO / TSX
Staff Size: 7,900
Profile: BRP designs, manufactures, distributes, and markets motorized recreational vehicles and powersports engines.
José Boisjoli, President & CEO
Sébastien Martel, Chief Financial Officer
Martin Langelier, General Counsel & Vice-President, Public Affairs

CAE Inc.
8585, ch de Côte-de-Liesse
Montréal, QC H4T 1G6
514-341-6780
Fax: 514-341-7699
800-564-6253
investor.relations@cae.com
www.cae.com
Social Media: twitter.com/CAE_Inc
www.linkedin.com/company/cae
Company Type: Public
Ticker Symbol: CAE / TSX, NYSE
Profile: CAE Inc. serves the civil aviation & defense forces, through the provision of simulation & modelling technologies, as well as integrated training solutions. The company's civil aviation & military training centres are located throughout the world. CAE Inc. has been granted the BOMA Go Green plan certification, & has implemented environmental programs such as the management of residual materials, recycling, pollution prevention, & residue exchange.
Marc Parent, President & Chief Executive Officer
Gene Colabatistto, Group President, Defense & Security
Nick Leontidis, Group President, Civil Aviation Training Solutions
Sonya Branco, Chief Financial Officer & Vice-President, Finance
Andrew Arnovitz, Vice-President, Strategy & Investor Relations
Hélène Gagnon, Vice-President, Public Affairs & Global Communications
514-340-5536, Media.Relations@cae.com

Canadian National Railway Company (CN)
935 de La Gauchetière St. West
Montréal, QC H3B 2M9
888-888-5909
www.cn.ca
Social Media: www.facebook.com/CNrail
twitter.com/shipCN
www.linkedin.com/company/cn
Company Type: Public
Ticker Symbol: CNR / TSX; CNI / NYSE
Staff Size: 23,172
Profile: Crossing the North American continent with ovver 21,000 route miles of track, the Canadian National Railway Company serves ports on the Atlantic, Pacific, & Gulf coasts.
Luc Jobin, President & CEO
Ghislain Houle, Exec. Vice-President/CFO
Sean Finn, Chief Legal Officers & Exec. Vice-President, Corporate Services
Serge Leduc, Vice-President & Chief Information Officer
Janet Drysdale, Vice-President, Corporate Development
Mack Barker, Vice-President, Network Operations & Planning

Canadian Pacific Railway Limited (CP)
7550 Ogden Dale Rd. SE
Calgary, AB T2C 4X9
888-333-6370
www.cpr.ca
Other Communications: Carload Sales Inquiries & Rates, Phone: 1-877-277-7283
Social Media: www.facebook.com/canadian.pacific
twitter.com/CanadianPacific
www.linkedin.com/company/canadian-pacific-railway
Company Type: Public
Ticker Symbol: CP / TSX, NYSE
Staff Size: 12,500
Profile: The transcontinental carrier operates in North America. Canadian Pacific provides freight transportation services, supply chain expertise, & logistics solutions. The company incorporates technology & environmental practices for safety & efficiency.
Andrew Reardon, Chair
E. Hunter Harrison, Chief Executive Officer
Keith Creel, President & Chief Operating Officer
Mark Erceg, Executive Vice-President & Chief Financial Officer
Robert Johnson, Executive Vice-President, Operations
Peter Edwards, Vice-President, Human Resources & Labour Relations

Laird Pitz, Vice-President, Chief Risk Officer
Michael Redeker, Vice-President, Chief Information Officer

CanaDream Corporation
292154 Crosspointe Dr.
Rocky View County, AB T4A 0V2

888-480-9726
www.canadream.com
Social Media: www.facebook.com/CanaDreamRV
twitter.com/CanaDreamRV

Company Type: Public
Ticker Symbol: CDN / TSX.V
Profile: CanaDream Corporation is an international tourism business that provides Recreational Vehicles ("RVs") in Canada.
Brian Gronberg, President
brian@canadream.com

Cargojet Inc.
#5&6, 350 Britannia Rd. East
Mississauga, ON L4Z 1X9

905-501-7373
866-551-5529
www.cargojet.com

Company Type: Public
Ticker Symbol: CJT / TSX
Staff Size: 667
Profile: Cargojet provides overnight air cargo services across North America.
Ajay K. Virmani, President & Chief Executive Officer
Jamie Porteous, Executive Vice-President & Chief Commercial Officer

Chorus Aviation Inc.
3 Spectacle Lake Dr.
Dartmouth, NS B3B 1W8

902-873-5000
investorsinfo@chorusaviation.ca
www.chorusaviation.ca

Company Type: Public
Ticker Symbol: CHR.A, CHR.B / TSX
Staff Size: 4,400
Profile: Incorporated in September 2010, Chorus Aviation is the successor to Jazz Air Income Fund. Jazz Aviation LP is wholly owned by Chorus Aviation.
Joseph D. Randell, Chief Executive Officer & President
Rick Flynn, Exec. Vice-President & Chief Corporate Development Officer
Jolene Mahody, Exec. Vice-President & Chief Financial Officer
Dennis Lopes, Senior Vice-President, General Counsel & Corporate Secretary
Scott Tapson, Vice-President, Corporate & Commercial Development

Discovery Air Inc.
#370, 170 Attwell Dr.
Toronto, ON M9W 5Z5

416-246-2684
www.discoveryair.com
Other Communications: London, ON, Office, Phone: 519-660-4247
Social Media: www.facebook.com/pages/Discovery-Air/325565460607
twitter.com/DiscoveryAirInc

Company Type: Public
Ticker Symbol: DA.A / TSX
Profile: Incorporated in 2004, Discovery Air Inc. created an alliance of aviation companies to provide safe, professional air transportation in selected niche markets. The following are Discovery Air's subsidiaries: Discovery Air Technical Services, Great Slave Helicopters Ltd., Discovery Mining Services, Air Tindi, Discovery Air Fire Services, Top Aces, & Discovery Air Innovation.
Jacob (Koby) Shavit, Chief Executive Officer
Paul Bernards, Chief Financial Officer
David Kleiman, Vice-President, General Counsel & Corporate Secretary
Sheila Venman, Vice-President, Human Resources & Communications

ENTREC Corporation
26420 Township Rd. 531A
Acheson, AB T7X 5A3

780-962-1600
Fax: 780-962-1722
888-962-1600
www.entrec.com
Social Media: www.facebook.com/EntrecCorporation
twitter.com/entreccorp
www.linkedin.com/company/2428543

Company Type: Public
Ticker Symbol: ENT / TSX
Staff Size: 550
Profile: ENTREC is a provider of heavy lift and heavy haul services with offerings encompassing crane services, heavy haul transportation, engineering, logistics and support.
John Stevens, President & CEO
Glen Fleming, Executive Vice-President, Operations
Jason Vandenberg, Chief Financial Officer

HNZ Group Inc.
1215, montee Pilon
Les Cèdres, QC J7T 1G1

450-452-3000
800-303-7148
info@hnz.com
www.hnz.com
Other Communications: Investor Relations, E-mail: investor@hnz.com

Company Type: Public
Ticker Symbol: HNZ.A, HNZ.B / TSX
Staff Size: 628
Profile: HNZ is an international provider of helicopter transportation and related support services with operations in Canada, Australia, New Zealand, Afghanistan, Antarctica and southeast Asia.
Don Wall, President/Chief Executive Officer
Matthew Wright, Vice-President & Chief Financial Officer

International Road Dynamics Inc. (IRD)
702 - 43 St. East
Saskatoon, SK S7K 3T9

306-653-6600
Fax: 306-242-5599
info@irdinc.com
www.irdinc.com
Social Media: www.facebook.com/InternationalRoadDynamics
twitter.com/IRDInc1
www.linkedin.com/company/ird_3

Company Type: Private
Ticker Symbol: IRD / TSX
Staff Size: 286
Profile: IRD creates technology for transportation companies. These markets include HTMS/traffic safety systems, commercial vehicle enforcement/operations, highway toll collection systems, border & security systems & Weigh-In-Motion (WIM) scales & sensors.
Terry Bergan, President & CEO
Randy Hanson, Executive Vice-President & Chief Operating Officer
David Cortens, Chief Financial Officer
Sharon Parker, Vice-President, Corporate Resources

Logistec Corporation
#1500, 360, rue Saint-Jacques
Montréal, QC H2Y 1P5

514-844-9381
info@logistec.com
www.logistec.com

Company Type: Public
Ticker Symbol: LGT.B / TSX
Staff Size: 1,600
Profile: Logistec Corporation & its subsidiaries serve the marine & industrial sectors. Cargo-handling services are offered at port terminals situated in eastern Canada & the United States, & on the Great Lakes. Other services include agency services to foreign ship-owners & operators at Canadian ports, marine transportation services, & on-site decontamination services.
Madeleine Paquin, President & Chief Executive Officer
Jean-Claude Dugas, CA, Vice-President, Finance
Ingrid Stefancic, LL.B., Vice-President, Corporate & Legal Services

Magellan Aerospace Corporation
3160 Derry Rd. East
Mississauga, ON L4T 1A9

905-677-1889
Fax: 905-677-5658
magellan.corporate@magellan.aero
www.magellanaerospace.com
Social Media: www.linkedin.com/company/magellan-aerospace

Company Type: Public
Ticker Symbol: MAL / TSX
Staff Size: 3,800
Profile: Magellan is engaged in designing, engineering, & manufacturing aeroengine & aerostructure assemblies & components. The company serves the aerospace & military markets. Operating units are located in Canada, the United States, & the United Kingdom.
Phillip Underwood, President & CEO
Elena Milantoni, Chief Financial Officer & Corporate Secretary

Mullen Group
#121A, 31 Southridge Dr.
Okotoks, AB T1S 2N3

403-995-5200
Fax: 403-995-5296
866-995-7711
IR@mullen-group.com
www.mullen-group.com

Company Type: Public
Ticker Symbol: MTL / TSX
Staff Size: 6,200
Profile: Mullen Group serves western Canada's oil & natural gas industry by providing specialized transportation & related services. The company also provides management & financial services as well as technology & systems support to the independently operated businesses that it owns.
Murray K. Mullen, Chair, President & CEO
Richard Maloney, Senior Vice-President
P. Stephen Clark, Chief Financial Officer

New Flyer Industries Inc.
711 Kernaghan Ave.
Winnipeg, MB R2C 3T4

204-224-1251
www.newflyer.com

Company Type: Public
Ticker Symbol: NFI / TSX
Profile: The company manufactures heavy-duty transit vehicles. New Flyer Industries' operations are located in Winnipeg Manitoba, Crookston Minnesota, & St. Cloud Minnesota. All facilities are ISO 9001, ISO 14001, & OHSAS 18001 certified.
Paul Soubry, President & Chief Executive Officer
Glenn Asham, Chief Financial Officer
Paul Smith, Executive Vice-President, Sales & Marketing
Janice Harper, Vice-President, Human Resources

Student Transportation Inc. (STI)
#6, 160 Saunders Rd.
Barrie, ON L4N 9A4

705-721-2626
Fax: 705-721-2627
888-942-2250
www.ridesta.com
Other Communications: Investor Relations, E-mail: Invest@ridestbus.com
Social Media: www.facebook.com/studenttransportation
twitter.com/RideSTBus

Company Type: Public
Ticker Symbol: STB / TSX
Staff Size: 3,300
Profile: Founded in 1997, Student Transportation Inc. is a provider of school bus transportation services. The company operates over 8,500 vehicles throughoutCanada & the United States.
Denis J. Gallagher, Founder, Chair & Chief Executive Officer
Patrick Vaughan, Chief Operating Officer
Patrick J. Walker, Chief Financial Officer & Executive Vice-President
Christopher J. Harwood, President, Student Transportation of Canada
Keith P. Engelbert, Chief Technology Officer

Titanium Transportation Group
#4, 400 Zenway Blvd.
Woodbridge, ON L4H 0S7

905-851-1688
Fax: 905-851-1180
800-785-4369
www.ttgi.com

Company Type: Public
Ticker Symbol: TTR / TSX
Profile: Titanium Transportation is a trucking, transportation logistics & warehouse company.
Ted Daniel, President & CEO
Kasia Malz, Chief Financial Offier
Marilyn Daniel, Vice-President, Operations

Transat A.T. Inc.
#500, 300, rue Léo-Pariseau
Montréal, QC H2X 4C2

Fax: 800-387-2672
800-387-2672
customerrelations@transat.com
www.transat.com
Social Media: www.facebook.com/AirTransatCanada
twitter.com/AirTransat
www.linkedin.com/company/air-transat

Company Type: Public
Ticker Symbol: TRZ.B / TSX
Staff Size: 5,500
Profile: Transat A.T. is an integrated tour operator, which organizes & markets holiday travel. Tour operators are based in Canada & France.
Jean-Marc Eustache, Chair, President & Chief Executive Officer

Patrice Caradec, President & General Manager, Transat France
André De Montigny, President, Transat International
Michel Bellefeuille, Vice-President & Chief Information Officer
Denis Pétrin, Chief Financial Officer & Vice-President, Finance & Administration

TransForce Inc.
#500, 8801, rte Transcanadienne
Montréal, QC H4S 1Z6
514-331-4000
Fax: 514-337-4200
www.transforcecompany.com
Company Type: Public
Ticker Symbol: TFI / TSX
Staff Size: 16,050
Profile: TransForce provides trucking & transportation logistics services. The company operates across Canada & the United States.
Alain Bédard, Chair, President & Chief Executive Officer
Greg Rumble, Executive Vice-President & CFO
Johanne Dean, Vice-President, Marketing & Communications
Chantal Martel, LL.B., Vice-President, Insurance & Compliance
Josiane-M. Langlois, LL.M., Corporate Secretary & Vice-President, Legal Affairs
Sylvain Desaulniers, Vice-President, Human Resources

Trimac Transportation Ltd.
Head Office
3215 - 12 St. NE
Calgary, AB T2E 7S9
403-298-5100
Fax: 403-298-5258
www.trimac.com
Social Media:
facebook.com/pages/Trimac-Transportation/139837889392249
www.linkedin.com/company/trimac-transportation
Company Type: Public
Ticker Symbol: TMA / TSX
Staff Size: 2,110
Profile: Trimac Transportation was extablished in 1945. The company provides bulk trucking service throughout Canada. Through its National Tank Services division, Trimac is involved in repairing, maintaining, & cleaning the Trimac fleet & the fleets of commercial customers. Bulk Plus Logistics is Trimac's wholly owned subsidiary. It provides third party transportation logistics services. Areas of operation are Canada & the United States. Trimac's Environmental Protection Policy has been in place since 1990 & is reviewed annually.
Mathieu Faure, Chief Executive Officer

WestJet Airlines Ltd.
22 Aerial Pl. NE
Calgary, AB T2E 3J1
403-539-7594
Fax: 403-444-2604
888-937-8538
investor_relations@westjet.com
www.westjet.com
Other Communications: TTY: 877-952-0100; Invest: 877-493-7853
Social Media: www.facebook.com/westjet
www.twitter.com/westjet
www.linkedin.com/company/westjet
Company Type: Public
Ticker Symbol: WJA / TSX
Staff Size: 9,211
Profile: Westjet Airlines provides scheduled passenger airline transportation to cities in North America & the Caribbean.
Gregg Saretsky, President/CEO
Rocky Wiggins, Exec. Vice-President/Chief Information Officer
Harry Taylor, Exec. Vice-President, Finance/CFO
Bob Cummings, Exec. Vice-President, Commercial WestJet Airlines

Utilities

Algonquin Power & Utilities Corp.
354 Davis Rd.
Oakville, ON L6J 2X1
905-465-4500
Fax: 905-465-4514
www.algonquinpower.com
Social Media: twitter.com/AQN_Utilities
www.linkedin.com/company/algonquin-power-&-utilities-corp
Company Type: Public
Ticker Symbol: AQN / TSX
Staff Size: 1,466
Profile: Algonquin Power & Utilities Corp. is a renewable energy & regulated utility company. Its operating subsidiaries are Algonquin Power Company & Liberty Utilities. Through these subsidiaries, Algonquin Power & Utilities Corp. invests in sustainable utility distribution businesses as well as hydroelectric, wind, & solar power facilities.
Ian Robertson, Chief Executive Officer
David Pasieka, President, Liberty Utilities
Mike Snow, President, Algonquin Power Company
David Bronicheski, Chief Financial Officer
Linda Beairsto, General Counsel & Corporate Secretary

AltaGas Ltd.
#1700, 355 - 4th Ave. SW
Calgary, AB T2P 0J1
403-691-7575
Fax: 403-691-7576
888-890-2715
www.altagas.ca
Other Communications: Vancouver, BC, Office, Phone: 604-623-4750
Company Type: Public
Ticker Symbol: ALA / TSX
Profile: AltaGas is a business involved in power, natural gas, & regulated utilities. It will focus on renewable energy sources.
David Harris, President & CEO
Tim Watson, Executive Vice President & Chief Financial Officer
Brad Grant, Vice-President & General Counsel

Alterra Power Corp.
#600, 888 Dunsmuir St.
Vancouver, BC V6C 3K4
604-669-4999
Fax: 604-682-3727
877-669-4999
info@alterrapower.ca
www.alterrapower.ca
Social Media: www.facebook.com/alterrapower
twitter.com/Alterra_Power
www.linkedin.com/company/alterra-power-corp-
Company Type: Public
Ticker Symbol: AXY / TSX
Staff Size: 126
Profile: In 2011, Magma Energy Corp. & Plutonic Power Corp. merged to create Alterra Power Corp.. The renewable energy company operates power plants & projects in British Columbia, Nevada, Chile, Peru, Iceland, & Italy. In British Columbia, Alterra Power has a wind farm & run of river hydro facilities.
John Carson, Chief Executive Officer
Lynda Freeman, Chief Financial Officer
Murray Kroeker, Vice-President, Solar Power & Engineering
Paul Rapp, Vice-President, Wind & Geothermal Power
Jonathan Schintler, Vice-President, Project Finance/Mergers & Acquisitions
Jay Sutton, Vice-President, Hydro Power
Shannon D. Webber, General Counsel

ATCO Ltd.
#700, 909 - 11th Ave. SW
Calgary, AB T2R 1N6
403-292-7500
Fax: 403-292-7532
investorrelations@atco.com
www.atco.ca
Other Communications: Media Relations, E-mail: mediarelations@atco.com
Social Media: www.facebook.com/ATCOGroup
twitter.com/ATCO
www.linkedin.com/company/atco-group
Company Type: Public
Ticker Symbol: ACO.X / TSX
Staff Size: 8,000
Profile: ATCO Ltd. delivers business solutions with companies engaged in the following: utilities, including natural gas & electricity transmission & distribution; energy, including power generation & liquids extraction; logistics & structures, included manufacturing & noise abatement; & technologies.
Nancy C. Southern, President & Chief Executive Officer
Brian R. Bale, Chief Financial Officer & Senior Vice-Presidnent
Siegfried W. Kiefer, President & COO, Canadian Utilities Limited
Alan M. Skiffington, Chief Information Officer & Vice-President
Carson J. Ackroyd, Vice-President, Marketing & Communications
Clinton Warkentin, Vice-President, Finance & Risk

Atlantic Power Corporation
#220, 3 Allied Dr.
Dedham, MA 02026 USA
617-977-2400
855-280-4737
info@atlanticpower.com
www.atlanticpower.com
Company Type: Public
Ticker Symbol: ATP / TSX
Staff Size: 285
Profile: Atlantic Power Corporation is a power & infrastructure company that trades on the TSX under the symbol ATP, & on the New York Stock Exchange, under the symbol AT. The company's portfolio of assets are located in Canada & the United States. Electricity from Atlantic Power's generation projects are sold to utilities & commercial customers.
In 2011, Atlantic Power acquired Capital Power Income L.P.
James J. Moore, President & CEO
Terrence Ronan, Executive Vice-President & Chief Financial Officer

BCE Inc.
Also Known As: Bell Canada
Bldg. A
1, carrefour Alexander-Graham-Bell
Montréal, QC H3B 3B3
Fax: 514-766-5735
888-932-6666
bcecomms@bce.ca
www.bce.ca
Other Communications: Investor Relations, E-mail: investor.relations@bell.ca
Company Type: Public
Ticker Symbol: BCE / TSX, NYSE
Staff Size: 49,968
Profile: Formed in 1970, BCE Inc. is a communications company that provides broadband wireless & wireline communication services. Clients include both residents & businesses across Canada.
Bell Media is a multimedia company, with assets in television, radio, & digital media. Bell Media purchased Astral in July 2013.
George Cope, President & CEO
Mary Ann Turcke, President, Bell Media
Charles Brown, President, The Source
Tom Little, President, Bell Business Markets
Blaik Kirby, President, Bell Mobility
Michael Cole, Exec. Vice-President & Chief Information Officer
Glen LeBlanc, Exec. Vice-President & Chief Financial Officer

BIOX Corporation
585 Wentworth St. North
Hamilton, ON L8L 5X5
905-521-8205
info@bioxcorp.com
www.bioxcorp.com
Company Type: Public
Ticker Symbol: BX / TSX
Profile: BIOX Corporation is a renewable energy company that designed, built, owns and operates a 67 million litre per annum nameplate capacity biodiesel production facility in Hamilton, Ontario Canada.
Alan Rickard, Chief Executive Officer
Scott Lewis, Executive Vice-President, Commercial Operations & Growth
Nakyun G. Paik, Vice-President, Operations

Boralex Inc.
36, rue Lajeunesse
Kingsey Falls, QC J0A 1B0
819-363-6363
Fax: 819-363-6399
info@boralex.com
www.boralex.com
Other Communications: Communications Dept., Phone: 514-985-1360, Fax: 514-284-9895
Social Media: www.facebook.com/BoralexInc
twitter.com/boralexinc
www.linkedin.com/company/boralex
Company Type: Public
Ticker Symbol: BLX, BLX.DB / TSX
Profile: Boralex Inc. is a power producer. It focuses on the following power generation types: hydroelectric, thermal, wind, & solar. The company has more than 200 employees.
Patrick Lemaire, President & Chief Executive Officer
Jean-François Thibodeau, Chief Financial Officer & Vice-President
Sylvain Aird, Chief Legal Officer & Vice-President, Europe
Marie-Josée Arsenault, Corporate Director, Human Resources
Denis Aubut, General Manager, Operations

Canadian Utilities Limited
#700, 909 - 11th Ave. SW
Calgary, AB T2R 1N6
403-292-7500
Fax: 403-292-7532
investorrelations@atco.com
www.canadian-utilities.com
Company Type: Public
Ticker Symbol: CU / TSX
Staff Size: 5,500
Profile: Part of the ATCO Group of Companies, Canadian Utilities Limited is engaged in natural gas & electricity transmission & distribution, as well as technology, logistics, & energy services.
Siegfried W. Kiefer, President & Chief Operating Officer
Nancy C. Southern, Chair & CEO
Brian R. Bale, Sr. Vice-President/CFO
Erhard M. Kiefer, Senior Vice-President & Chief Administration Officer

Capital Power Corporation
Corporate Head Office
#1200, 10423 - 101 St. NW
Edmonton, AB T5H 0E9
780-392-5100
info@capitalpower.com
www.capitalpower.com
Social Media: www.facebook.com/capitalpowercommunity
twitter.com/capitalpower
www.linkedin.com/company/capital-power-corporation
Company Type: Public
Ticker Symbol: CPX / TSX
Staff Size: 714
Profile: Capital Power Corporation is a power producer. The company has sixteen facilities throughout North America. Capital Power is also developing wind generation projects in Ontario, Alberta, & British Columbia.
Brian Vaasjo, President & Chief Executive Officer
Bryan DeNeve, Senior Vice-President, Commercial Services
Kate Chisholm, Q.C., Senior Vice-President, Legal & External Relations
Darcy Trufyn, Senior Vice-President, Construction & Engineering

Ceiba Energy Services
#910, 521 - 3rd Ave. SW
Calgary, AB T2P 3T3
403-262-2783
Fax: 403-263-0603
info@ceibaenergy.com
www.ceibaenergy.com
Other Communications: 24-Hour Emergency Toll-Free Phone: 855-222-6236
Social Media:
www.linkedin.com/company/cancen-oil-canada-inc-
Company Type: Private
Ticker Symbol: CEB / TSX.V
Profile: Ceiba Energy manufactures & installs facilities that treat crude oil emulsion & dispose production water.
Ian Simister, President
Richard Lane, Chief Operating Officer
Peter Cheung, Chief Financial Officer & Corporate Secretary

Changfeng Energy Inc.
#306, 650 Hwy. 7 East
Richmond Hill, ON L4B 2N7
416-362-5032
Fax: 416-362-2393
info@changfengenergy.com
www.changfengenergy.com
Company Type: Private
Ticker Symbol: CFY / TSX.V
Profile: Changfeng Energy distributes natural gas in China.
Huajun Lin, Chair, President & CEO
Yan Zhao, Chief Financial Officer
Ann Lin, Vice-President, Corporate Development

CU Inc.
Corporate Head Office
#700, 909 - 11 Ave. SW
Calgary, AB T2R 1N6
403-292-7500
Fax: 403-292-7523
www.canadian-utilities.com
Company Type: Public
Ticker Symbol: CIU.PR.A / TSX
Staff Size: 5,460
Profile: A wholly owned subsidiary of Canadian Utilities Ltd., CU Inc. is involved in natural gas & electricity transmission & distribution, as well as power generation.
Nancy C. Southern, Chair & Chief Executive Officer
Siegfried W. Kiefer, President & COO
Brian R. Bale, Chief Financial Officer & Senior Vice-President

Emera Inc.
1223 Lower Water St.
Halifax, NS B3J 3S8
902-450-0507
Fax: 902-428-6112
888-450-0507
investors@emera.com
www.emera.com
Other Communications: Investor Services, Toll-Free Phone: 800-358-1995
Company Type: Public
Ticker Symbol: EMA / TSX
Staff Size: 3,452
Profile: The holding company is involved in the energy sector. Emera Inc.'s investments include Bangor Hydro-Electric Company, Nova Scotia Power Inc., Emera Energy, Emera Utility Services, Bayside Power, Maritimes & Northeast Pipeline, ATlantic Hydrogen Inc., Emera New Brunswick, Emera Newfoundland & Labrador, Barbados Light & Power Co., & Grand Bahama Power Ltd.
Christopher Huskilson, President/Chief Executive Officer
Scott Balfour, Chief Operating Officer
Greg Blunden, Chief Financial Officer
Bruce Marchand, Chief Legal & Compliance Officer

Enbridge Income Fund Holdings Inc.
Fifth Ave. Pl.
#200, 425 - 1st St. SW
Calgary, AB T2P 3L8
403-231-3900
Fax: 403-231-3920
www.enbridgeincomefund.com
Company Type: Public
Ticker Symbol: ENF / TSX
Profile: Through its investment in Enbridge Income Fund, Enbridge Income Fund Holdings Inc. holds energy infrastructure assets. These assets include the following: a 100% interest in the pipelines that comprise the Saskatchewan System; a 50% interest in the Canadian segment of the Alliance Pipeline; & interests in renewable & alternative power generation capacity. The manager of Enbridge Income Fund Holdings Inc. is Enbridge Management Services Inc.
Perry F. Schuldhaus, President
Wanda Opheim, Chief Financial Officer

EnerCare Inc.
4000 Victoria Park Ave.
Toronto, ON M2H 3P4
416-649-1900
855-255-5458
www.enercare.ca
Other Communications: Investor Relations: investor.relations@enercare.ca
Social Media: www.facebook.com/EnercareInc
www.linkedin.com/company/enercare-inc-
Company Type: Public
Ticker Symbol: ECI / TSX
Staff Size: 924
Profile: EnerCare Inc. is the owner of approximately 1.2 million installed water heaters & other assets, which are rented mainly to residential customers in Ontario. The company also owns EnerCare Connections, a sub-metering company. EnerCare Connections has metering contracts for apartment & condominium suites, primarily in Ontario & Alberta.
John MacDonald, President & Chief Executive Officer
Evelyn Sutherland, Chief Financial Officer
John Toffoletto, Senior Vice-President, Chief Legal Officer & Secretary
John Piercy, Senior Vice-President & General Manager

Etrion Corporation
PH-1, 40 Southwest 13 St.
Miami, FL 33130 USA
786-636-6449
info@etrion.com
www.etrion.com
Company Type: Public
Ticker Symbol: ETX / TSX
Profile: Etrion Corporation is an independent power producer that owns and operates renewable assets.
Marco A. Northland, Chief Executive Officer
Paul Rapisarda, Chief Financial Officer

Fortis Inc.
Fortis Pl.
PO Box 8837, #1100, 5 Springdale St.
St. John's, NL A1B 3T2
709-737-2800
Fax: 709-737-5307
investorrelations@fortisinc.com
www.fortisinc.com
Company Type: Public
Ticker Symbol: FTS / TSX
Staff Size: 7,700
Profile: Fortis Inc. is an international distribution utility holding company, which serves gas & electricity customers. The company sold its property division (which included hotels & commercial real estate in Canada) in January 2015.
Barry V. Perry, President/CEO
Karl W. Smith, Executive Vice-President & Chief Financial Officer
David Bennett, Vice-President, Chief Legal Officer & Corporate Secretary

Global Water Resources (GWR)
#220, 21410 North 19th Ave.
Phoenix, AZ 85027 USA
480-360-7775
Fax: 623-518-4100
866-940-1102
www.gwresources.com
Company Type: Public
Ticker Symbol: GWR / TSX
Staff Size: 49
Profile: The company owns & operates regulated water & wastewater utilities.
Ron L. Fleming, Chief Executive Officer
Mike Liebman, Senior Vice-President & Chief Financial Officer

H2O Innovation Inc.
#340, 330, rue St-Vallier Est
Québec, QC G1K 9C5
418-688-0170
Fax: 418-688-9259
888-688-0170
info@h2oinnovation.com
www.h2oinnovation.com
Social Media: twitter.com/H2O_Innovation
www.linkedin.com/company/h2o-innovation
Company Type: Public
Ticker Symbol: HEO / TSX.V
Profile: H2O Innovation is a developer of water treatment solutions. Its clients include municipalities, as well as energy & mining companies.
Frédéric Dugré, President & CEO

HTC Purenergy Inc.
#002, 2305 Victoria Ave.
Regina, SK S4P 0S7
306-352-6132
Fax: 306-545-3262
info@kerrmines.com
www.htcenergy.com
Company Type: Public
Ticker Symbol: HTC / TSX
Profile: An energy & fertilizer company.
Lionel Kambeitz, President & CEO
Jeff Allison, Senior Vice-President
Ahmed Ahboudheir, Chief Technology Officer

Hydro One
South Tower
483 Bay St., 8th Fl.
Toronto, ON M5G 2P5
416-345-5000
877-955-1155
CustomerCommunications@hydroone.com
www.spackmanequities.com
Other Communications: Investor Relations: investor.relations@HydroOne.com
Social Media: twitter.com/HydroOne
Company Type: Public
Ticker Symbol: H / TSX
Profile: Hydro One is the providor of power to the province of Ontario.
Mayo Schmidt, President & CEO
Michael Vels, Chief Financial Officer

Hydrogenics Corp.
220 Admiral Blvd.
Mississauga, ON L5T 2N6
905-361-3638
Fax: 905-361-3626
investors@hydrogenics.com
www.hydrogenics.com
Social Media: twitter.com/hydrogenics
www.linkedin.com/company/hydrogenics
Company Type: Public
Ticker Symbol: HYG / TSX; HYGS / NYSE
Profile: Hydrogenics provides new technologies and applications for industrial and commercial hydrogen systems.
Daryl Wilson, Chief Executive Officer
Joseph Cargnelli, Chief Technology Officer
Bob Motz, Chief Financial Officer

Innergex Renewable Energy Inc.
Tour est
#1255, 1111, rue Saint-Charles ouest
Longueuil, QC J4K 5G4
450-928-2550
Fax: 450-928-2544
info@innergex.com
www.innergex.com
Other Communications: Vancouver Office, Phone: 604-633-9990, Fax: 604-633-9991
Social Media: twitter.com/innergex_ine
Company Type: Public
Ticker Symbol: INE / TSX
Staff Size: 145
Profile: Innergex Renewable Energy develops & operates renewable power generating facilities. Operations are carried out in British Columbia, Ontario, Québec, & Idaho, USA. The company focuses upon the wind power, solar power, & hydroelectric sectors.
Michel Letellier, MBA, President & Chief Executive Officer
Jean Perron, Chief Financial Officer
jperron@innergex.com

Nathalie Théberge, Secretary & Vice-President, Corporate Legal Affairs
Peter Grover, Vice-President, Wind & Solar Project Management
Matt Kennedy, Vice-President, Environment

Just Energy
#200, 6345 Dixie Rd.
Mississauga, ON L5T 2E6
905-670-4440
info@justenergy.com
www.justenergy.com
Other Communications: Investors, Phone: 905-795-3560
Social Media: www.facebook.com/justenergygroup
twitter.com/JustEnergyGroup
www.linkedin.com/company/just-energy_2
Company Type: Public
Ticker Symbol: JE / TSX
Staff Size: 1,220
Profile: The independent energy supplier sells electricity & natural gas to residential & commercial customers throughout Canada & the United States. Through National Home Services, high efficiency & tankless water heaters, furnaces, & air conditioners are sold & rented. Wheat-based ethanol is produced & sold through Terra Grain Fuels. Green products are offered through Just Energy's JustGreen & JustClean programs. JustGreen products are sourced from renewable sources such as wind, biomass, or run of the river hydro. JustClean products allow some customers to offset their carbon footprint.
James Lewis, Co-Chief Executive Officer
Deb Merril, Co-Chief Executive Officer
Pat McCullough, Chief Financial Officer
Jonah Davids, Executive Vice-President & General Counsel

Keyera Corp.
Sun Life Plaza, West Tower
144 - 4 Ave. SW, 2nd Fl.
Calgary, AB T2P 3N4
403-205-8300
Fax: 403-205-8318
888-699-4853
ir@keyera.com
www.keyera.com
Other Communications: Human Resources Department, E-mail: hr@keyera.com
Company Type: Public
Ticker Symbol: KEY / TSX
Staff Size: 985
Profile: Keyera is engaged in natural gas gathering & processing. The company also transports, stores, & markets natural gas liquids. Activities are conducted in the Western Canada Sedimentary Basin.
David Smith, President & CEO
Steven B. Kroeker, Chief Financial Officer & Senior Vice-President
Rick Koshman, Vice-President, Engineering
Lavonne Zdunich, Contact, Investor Relations
403-205-7670

MAXIM Power Corp.
Also Known As: MAXIM
#1210, 715 - 5th Ave. SW
Calgary, AB T2P 2X6
403-263-3021
Fax: 403-263-9125
maxim@maximpowercorp.com
www.maximpowercorp.com
Other Communications: Investor Relations, E-mail: investors@maximpowercorp.com
Company Type: Public
Ticker Symbol: MXG / TSX
Profile: MAXIM Power Corp. is an independent power producer. The company is involved in the acquisition, development, ownership, & operation of environmentally responsible power projects. Its assets include coal & natural gas powered generators in western Canada, the United States, & France.
Bruce Chernoff, Chair & Interim CEO
Michael R. Mayder, Chief Financial Officer & Senior Vice-President, Finance
Jim Pollock, Vice-President, Corporate Development

Northland Power Inc.
30 St. Clair Ave. West, 12th Fl.
Toronto, ON M4V 3A1
416-962-6262
investorrelations@northlandpower.ca
www.northlandpower.ca
Company Type: Public
Ticker Symbol: NPI / TSX
Profile: Northland Power Inc. is engaged in the development of wind, solar, run-of-river hydro projects, & additional power generation opportunities. The company's assets include facilities that produce electricity form natural gas & renewable resources such as biomass, solar, & wind.
John W. Brace, Chief Executive Officer

Paul J. Bradley, Chief Financial Officer
Barb Bokla, Manager, Investor Relations
647-288-1438

ONEnergy Inc.
#301, 155 Gordon Baker Rd.
Toronto, ON M2H 3N5
Fax: 647-253-2525
855-753-2525
customercare@onenergyinc.com
www.onenergyinc.com
Other Communications: Investor & Media Relations, E-mail: irinfo@onenergyinc.com
Social Media: twitter.com/onenergyinc
www.linkedin.com/company/onenergy-inc
Company Type: Public
Ticker Symbol: OEG / TSX.V
Profile: ONEnergy supplies energy products & services to residential & commercial customers.
Stephen J.J. Letwin, Chair
Ray de Ocampo, Chief Financial Officer
Robert Weir, Chief Operating Officer

Polaris Infrastructure Inc.
#2700, 2 Bloor St. West
Toronto, ON M4W 3E2
416-849-2587
info@polarisinfrastructure.com
www.polarisinfrastructure.com
Company Type: Public
Ticker Symbol: PIF / TSX
Profile: Polaris Infrastructure Inc. is a renewable energy company acquires, explores, develops, & operates geothermal properties in Latin America.
Marc Murnaghan, Chief Executive Officer
Shane Downey, Chief Financial Officer

Synex International Inc.
Head Office
1444 Alberni St., 4th Fl.
Vancouver, BC V6G 2Z4
604-688-8271
Fax: 604-688-1286
www.synex.com
Company Type: Public
Ticker Symbol: SXI / TSX
Profile: Synex International Inc. has two wholly owned subsidiary companies: Synex Energy Resources Ltd and Sigma Engineering Ltd.
Alan W. Stephens, Chair & Secretary
Gregory J. Sunell, President

TransAlta Corporation
PO Box 1900 Stn. M, 110 - 12 Ave. SW
Calgary, AB T2P 2M1
403-267-7110
www.transalta.com
Other Communications: Investor Relations, Toll-Free Phone: 800-387-3598
Social Media: www.facebook.com/transalta
twitter.com/transalta
ca.linkedin.com/company/transalta
Company Type: Public
Ticker Symbol: TA.TO / TSX
Staff Size: 2,380
Profile: TransAlta Corporation is engaged in coal & gas-fired generation. The company carries out its activities in Canada, the United States, Mexico, & Australia.
The company works to limit environmental impact by focusing growth on renewable generation methods. It meets ISO 14001 standards.
Dawn Farrell, President/CEO
Donald Tremblay, Chief Financial Officer
Wayne Collins, Executive Vice-President, Coal & Mining Operations
Cynthia Johnston, Executive Vice-President, Gas, Renewables & Operations Services

TransAlta Renewables
PO Box 1900 Stn. M, 110 - 12 Ave. SW
Calgary, AB T2P 2M1
403-267-2520
Investor_Relations@transalta.com
www.transaltarenewables.com
Other Communications: Investor Relations, Toll-Free Phone: 800-387-3598
Company Type: Public
Ticker Symbol: RNW / TSX
Profile: TransAlta Renewables is a section of TransAlta Corporation, a coal & gas-fired generation provider. The company specializes in renewable power generation facilities.
Brett M. Gellner, President & Chief Executive Officer
Cynthia Johnston, Chief Operating Officer
Donald Tremblay, Chief Financial Officer

TransCanada Corporation
450 - 1 St. SW
Calgary, AB T2P 5H1
403-920-2000
Fax: 403-920-2200
800-661-3805
communications@transcanada.com
www.transcanada.com
Other Communications: Communications/Media, E-mail: communications@transcanada.com
Social Media: twitter.com/transcanada
www.linkedin.com/company/transcanada
Company Type: Public
Ticker Symbol: TRP / TSX
Profile: TransCanada is engaged in the development & operation of energy infrastructure, including natural gas & oil pipelines, power generation, & gas storage facilities in North America. Common shares trade on the Toronto & New York stock exchanges.
Russell Girling, President & Chief Executive Officer
Alexander Pourbaix, Chief Operating Officer
Karl Johannson, Executive Vice-President & President, Natural Gas Pipelines
Paul Miller, Executive Vice-President & President, Liquids Pipelines
William (Bill) Taylor, Executive Vice-President & President, Energy
Donald R. Marchand, Executive Vice-President, Corporate Development & CFO

Stock Exchanges

Aequitas NEO Exchange Inc.
#400, 155 University Ave.
Toronto, ON M5H 3B7
Tel: 416-933-5900
info@aequin.com
aequitasneoexchange.com
Other Contact Information: Listing Inquiries: listings@aequin.com; Trading Inquiries: 416-933-5950, neotradingservices@aequin.com; Media Inquiries: media@aequin.com
Social Media: www.youtube.com/user/AequitasInnovations; plus.google.com/+Aequitasinnovations; www.facebook.com/AequitasNEOExchange; twitter.com/Aequitas_NEO
Ownership: Subsidiary of Aequitas Innovations Inc., Toronto, ON
Year Founded: 2014

Alpha Exchange Inc.
c/o TMX Group, The Exhange Tower
130 King St. West
Toronto, ON M5X 1J2
Tel: 647-259-0405; *Toll-Free:* 888-873-8392
www.tsx.com/trading/tsx-alpha-exchange
Other Contact Information: Alternate E-mails: businessdevelopment@tsx.com; trading_sales@tsx.com
Also Known As: TSX Alpha Exchange
Ownership: Subsidiary of Alpha Trading Systems Limited Partnership, a limited partner of TMX Group Limited, Toronto, ON.

Alpha Trading Systems Limited Partnership
c/o TMX Group, The Exhange Tower
130 King St. West
Toronto, ON M5X 1J2
Tel: 647-259-0405; *Toll-Free:* 888-873-8392
www.tsx.com/trading/tsx-alpha-exchange
Other Contact Information: Alternate E-mails: businessdevelopment@tsx.com; trading_sales@tsx.com; marketdata@tmx.com
Also Known As: Alpha Group; Alpha
Ownership: Limited partner of TMX Group Limited, Toronto, ON.

Canadian Securities Exchange (CSE)
220 Bay St., 9th Fl.
Toronto, ON M5J 2W4
Tel: 416-572-2000; *Fax:* 416-572-4160
info@thecse.com
www.thecse.com
Other Contact Information: Alternate E-mails: listings@thecse.com; trading@thecse.com
Social Media: twitter.com/CSE_News
Former Name: Canadian National Stock Exchange; Canadian Trading & Quotation System Inc.
Ownership: Owned & operated by CNSX Markets Inc.
Year Founded: 2004

Canadian Unlisted Board Inc.
Toronto Stock Exchange, The Exchange Tower, c/o Trading Services
130 King St. West
Toronto, ON M5X 1J2
Tel: 416-947-4705; *Fax:* 416-947-4280
cubadmin@cub.ca
www.cub.ca
Also Known As: CUB
Year Founded: 2000

CanDeal.ca, Inc.
#400, 152 King St. East
Toronto, ON M5A 1J3
Tel: 416-814-7831; *Fax:* 416-814-7840
Toll-Free: 866-422-6332
sales@candeal.com
www.candeal.ca
Other Contact Information: US Inquiries: 314-854-1324; E-mail: ekenny@candeal.com; European Inquiries: 00 800 0422 6332; E-mail: jbartello@candeal.com
Social Media: twitter.com/CanDeal
Ownership: 47% owned by TMX Group Limited, Toronto, ON.

ICE Futures Canada, Inc.
850A Pembina Hwy.
Winnipeg, MB R3M 2M7
Tel: 204-925-5000; *Fax:* 204-943-5448
compliance-canada@theice.com
www.theice.com/futures-canada
Other Contact Information: ICE Clear Canada, Phone: 204-925-5017; Market Supervision, US & Canada, Phone: 212-748-3949, ext. 1; E-mail: MarketSupervision-US@theice.com
Social Media: twitter.com/ICE_Markets
Former Name: Winnipeg Commodity Exchange Inc.; Winnipeg Grains & Produce Exchange
Ownership: Wholly owned subsidiary of IntercontinentalExchange (ICE), Atlanta, GA, USA
Year Founded: 1887

Montréal Exchange Inc. (MX)/ Bourse de Montréal Inc.
Tour de la Bourse
CP 61
800, carré Victoria
Montréal, QC H4Z 1A9
Tél: 514-871-2424; *Téléc:* 514-871-3514
Ligne sans frais: 800-361-5353
info@tmx.com
www.m-x.ca
Other Contact Information: Alternate E-mails: samsupport@m-x.ca; finances@m-x.ca; marketdata@tmx.com; reg@m-x.ca; legal@m-x.ca
Média social: www.facebook.com/montrealexchange; twitter.com/MtlExchange
Also Known As: MX
Ownership: Subsidiary of TMX Group Limited, Toronto, ON.
Year Founded: 1874

Natural Gas Exchange Inc. (NGX)
300 - 5th Ave. SW, 10th Fl.
Calgary, AB T2P 3C4
Tel: 403-974-1700; *Fax:* 403-974-1719
Clearing@ngx.com
www.ngx.com
Other Contact Information: NGX Help Desk & Operations, E-mail: Marketing@ngx.com; Ops@ngx.com
Ownership: Wholly owned by TMX Group Limited, Toronto, ON.
Year Founded: 1994

NEX
Filing Office
#2700, 650 West Georgia St.
Vancouver, BC V6B 4N9
Tel: 604-689-3334; *Fax:* 604-844-7502
Toll-Free: 866-344-5639
nex@tsx.com
apps.tmx.com/en/nex
Former Name: NEX Board
Ownership: Owned by TMX Group Limited, Toronto, ON.
Year Founded: 2003

TMX Group Limited
The Exchange Tower
130 King St. West, 3rd Fl.
Toronto, ON M5X 1J2
Tel: 416-947-4670; *Fax:* 416-947-4662
Toll-Free: 888-873-8392
info@tmx.com
www.tmx.com
Other Contact Information: Couriered deliveries to TMX Group Inc.: c/o Plus One Inc., First Canadian Place, 77 Adelaide St. West, Toronto, ON, M5X 1A4
Social Media: www.facebook.com/tmxmoney; twitter.com/TMXGroup
Former Name: TSX Group Inc.; Maple Group Acquisition Corporation

TMX Select Inc.
The Exchange Tower
130 King St. West
Toronto, ON M5X 1J2
Tel: 416-947-4670; *Fax:* 416-947-4662
Toll-Free: 877-421-2369
trading_sales@tmx.com
apps.tmx.com/en/tmxselect/index.html
Other Contact Information: General Inquiries: businessdevelopment@tsx.com
Social Media: www.youtube.com/tmxgroup; www.facebook.com/tmxmoney; twitter.com/TMXGroup
Ownership: Wholly owned by TMX Group Limited, Toronto, ON.

The Toronto Stock Exchange (TSX)
The Exchange Tower
PO Box 450
130 King St. West , 3rd Fl.
Toronto, ON M5X 1J2
Tel: 416-947-4670; *Fax:* 416-947-4770
Toll-Free: 888-873-8392
info@tsx.com
www.tsx.com
Other Contact Information: Alternate E-mails: businessdevelopment@tsx.com; trading_sales@tsx.com; marketdata@tmx.com
Social Media: www.facebook.com/tmxmoney; twitter.com/TMXGroup
Also Known As: TSX
Ownership: Subsidiary of TMX Group Limited, Toronto, ON.
Year Founded: 1861

TSX Venture Exchange
Head Office
300 - 5th Ave. SW
Calgary, AB T2P 3C4
Tel: 403-218-2800; *Fax:* 403-237-0450
Toll-Free: 888-873-8392
businessdevelopment@tsx.com
www.tsx.com
Other Contact Information: TMX Equity Trading Account Management: trading_sales@tsx.com; Compliance & Disclosure General Email: complianceanddisclosure@tsxventure.com
Social Media: www.facebook.com/tmxmoney; twitter.com/TMXGroup
Former Name: Canadian Venture Exchange
Ownership: Subsidiary of TMX Group Limited, Toronto, ON.

Trust Companies

Trust companies are regulated under the federal Trust and Loan Companies Act and operate under either provincial or federal legislation. The business of trust companies include activities like those of a bank, plus fiduciary functions.

All Nations Trust Company (ANTCO)
520 Chief Eli LaRue Way
Kamloops, BC V2H 1H1
Tel: 778-471-4110; *Fax:* 250-372-2585
Toll-Free: 800-663-2959
antco@antco.bc.ca
www.antco.bc.ca
Ownership: Private. Aboriginal-owned.
Year Founded: 1984
Number of Employees: 13

The Bank of Nova Scotia Trust Company
Scotia Plaza
44 King St. West
Toronto, ON M5H 1H1
Tel: 416-866-6161; *Fax:* 416-866-3750
email@scotiabank.com
www.gbm.scotiabank.com
Ownership: Private. Subsidiary of Bank of Nova Scotia
Year Founded: 1993

BMO Trust Company
302 Bay St., 7th Fl.
Toronto, ON M5X 1A1
Toll-Free: 877-469-2020
advisorsadvantagetrust@bmo.com
www.advisorsadvantagetr ust.com
Other Contact Information: Dealer Services, Toll-Free Fax: 1-866-801-7499; BMO Estate & Trust Services, URL: www.bmo.com/estate
Former Name: The Trust Company of Bank of Montréal
Also Known As: Advisor's Advantage Trust (AAT)
Ownership: Wholly owned subsidiary of Bank of Montreal. Member of BMO Financial Group.

BNY Trust Company of Canada
320 Bay St., 11th Fl.
Toronto, ON M5H 4A6
Tel: 416-933-8500
www.bnymellon.com/ca
Ownership: Foreign. Wholly owned subsidiary of The Bank of New York Mellon Financial Corporation, New York City, New York.
Year Founded: 2001

Caledon Trust Company
#2401, 20 Queen St. West
Toronto, ON M5H 3R3
Tel: 416-361-4561
www.commonwealthfundservices.com/about/caledon-trust-company
Ownership: Private

The Canada Trust Company
Toronto Dominion Centre
PO Box 1, TD Centre Stn. TD Centre
55 King St. West
Toronto, ON M5K 1A2
Tel: 416-216-6868; *Toll-Free:* 888-222-3456
www.tdcanadatrust.com
Social Media: www.youtube.com/tdcanada; www.facebook.com/TDCanada?brand_redir=1; twitter.com/td_canada
Year Founded: 1855

Canadian Stock Transfer & Trust Company
320 Bay St., 3rd Fl.
Toronto, ON M5H 4A6
Toll-Free: 800-387-0825
www.canstockta.com
Ownership: Part of the North American division of the Link Group.
Year Founded: 2011

Canadian Western Trust Co. (CWT)
#600, 750 Cambie St.
Vancouver, BC V6B 0A2
Tel: 604-685-2081; *Fax:* 604-669-6069
Toll-Free: 800-663-1124
informationservices@cwt.ca
www.cwt.ca
Ownership: A division of Canadian Western Bank. Part of the Canadian Western Bank Group.

Central 1 Trust Company
c/o Central 1 Credit Union
1441 Creekside Dr.
Vancouver, BC V6J 4S7
Tel: 604-734-2511; *Toll-Free:* 800-661-6813
communications@central1.com
www.central1.com/trust
Ownership: Subsidiary of Central 1 Credit Union.
Assets: $1-10 billion

CIBC Mellon Trust Company
PO Box 1
320 Bay St., 4th Fl.
Toronto, ON M5H 4A6
Tel: 416-643-5000; *Fax:* 416-643-6409
www.cibcmellon.com
Social Media: twitter.com/cibcmellon
Ownership: Parent companies are Canadian Imperial Bank of Commerce & Mellon Financial Corporation
Year Founded: 1978
Number of Employees: 350
Assets: $500m-1 billion

CIBC Trust Corporation
#900, 55 Yonge St.
Toronto, ON M5E 1J4
www.cibc.com/ca/pwm/financial-services/trust.html

Citco (Canada) Inc.
5151 George St.
Halifax, NS B3J 1M5
Tel: 902-442-4242; *Fax:* 902-442-4258
halifax-fund@citco.com
www.citco.com/divisions/corporate-trust
Ownership: Part of the Citco Group of Companies.

Citi Trust Company Canada/ La Compagnie de Fiducie Citi Canada
2920 Matheson Blvd.
Mississauga, ON L4W 5J4
Toll-Free: 800-648-1977
Ownership: Subsidiary of Citibank Canada.
Year Founded: 2008

Citizens Trust Company
#401, 815 West Hastings St.
Vancouver, BC V6C 1B4
www.citizensbank.ca
Ownership: Subsidiary of Citizens Bank of Canada.

Community Trust Company
2325 Skymark Ave.
Mississauga, ON L4W 5A9
Tel: 416-763-2291; *Fax:* 416-763-2444
info@communitytrust.ca
www.communitytrust.ca
Ownership: Private
Year Founded: 1975

Computershare Canada
100 University Ave., 8th Fl.
Toronto, ON M5J 2Y1
Tél: 416-263-9200
www.computershare.com
Média social: www.youtube.com/user/COMPUTERSHARE; www.facebook.com/ComputershareCPU; twitter.com/computershare
Former Name: Montreal Trust
Ownership: Public. Owned by Computershare Limited, listed on the Australian Stock Exchange
Year Founded: 2000
Number of Employees: 1,400
Revenues: $1-5 million

Computershare Trust Company of Canada
100 University Ave., 11th Fl.
Toronto, ON M5J 2Y1
Tel: 416-263-9445
computershare.com/ca/en/business/corporate-trust-services
Other Contact Information: Oil Royalties Unitholder Inquiries, Phone: 403-267-6502; E-mail: oilroyalties@computershare.com
Ownership: Subsidiary of Computershare Canada.

Concentra Trust
2055 Albert St.
Regina, SK S4P 3G8
Tel: 306-956-5100; *Toll-Free:* 800-788-6311
www.concentrafinancial.ca
Ownership: Wholly owned subsidiary of Concentra Financial.
Assets: $1-10 billion

The Effort Trust Company
240 Main St. East
Hamilton, ON L8N 1H5
Tel: 905-528-8956; *Fax:* 905-528-8182
www.efforttrust.ca
Ownership: Private. Wholly owned subsidiary of Effort Corporation.
Year Founded: 1978
Number of Employees: 100
Assets: $100-500 million
Revenues: $10-50 million

Fiduciary Trust Company of Canada
#3000, 350 Seventh Ave. SW
Calgary, AB T2P 3N9
Tel: 403-215-5373; *Fax:* 403-543-3955
Toll-Free: 800-574-3822
www.fiduciarytrust.ca
Former Name: Bissett & Associates Investment Management Ltd.
Ownership: A member of the Franklin Templeton Investments family of companies.
Year Founded: 1982

Fiducie Desjardins inc/ Desjardins Trust Inc.
CP 34, Desjardins Stn. Desjardins
1, complexe Desjardins
Montréal, QC H5B 1E4
Tél: 514-286-9441; *Ligne sans frais:* 800-361-6840
www.fiduciedesjardins.com
Other Contact Information: Programme Immigrants Investisseurs, Phone: 514-499-8440; Toll-Free: 1 800-363-3915; info@immigrantinvestor.com
Ownership: A subsidiary of the Desjardins Group.
Year Founded: 2005

Georgeson Inc.
100 University Ave., 8th Fl.
Toronto, ON M5J 2Y1
Tel: 514-982-2390; *Fax:* 416-981-9663
Toll-Free: 800-890-1037
inquiries@georgeson.com
www.georgeson.com
Ownership: Private. A Computershare company.

Gestion privée Desjardins
Tour est
CP 991, Desjardins Stn. Desjardins
2, complexe Desjardins
Montréal, QC H5B 1C1
Tél: 514-286-3180; *Téléc:* 514-286-3145
Ligne sans frais: 877-286-3180
gestionprivee@desjardins.com
www.gestionpriveedesjardins.com
Other Contact Information: Télé: 514-843-9157
Ownership: Subsidiary of Fiducie Desjardins inc

Home Trust Company
#2300, 145 King St. West
Toronto, ON M5H 1J8
Tel: 416-360-4663; *Fax:* 416-363-7611
Toll-Free: 877-903-2133
inquiry.htc@hometrust.ca
www.hometrust.ca
Other Contact Information: Alternate E-mail: torontobranch@hometrust.ca
Ownership: Wholly owned subsidiary of Home Capital Group Inc.
Year Founded: 1977
Number of Employees: 296
Assets: $1-10 billion
Revenues: $100-500 million

Household Trust Company
#300, 3381 Steeles Ave. East
Toronto, ON M2H 3S7
Toll-Free: 800-489-4501
Ownership: Subsidiary of HSBC Bank Canada.

HSBC Trust Company (Canada)
885 West Georgia St. 3rd Fl.
Vancouver, BC V6C 3E9
Tel: 604-641-1122; *Fax:* 604-641-1138
Toll-Free: 888-887-3388
www.hsbc.ca
Ownership: Private. Wholly owned subsidiary of HSBC Bank Canada
Year Founded: 1972
Number of Employees: 28

Industrial Alliance Trust Inc.
CP 1907, Terminus Stn. Terminus
1080, Grande Allée ouest
Québec, QC G1K 7M3
Téléc: 418-684-5161
Ligne sans frais: 844-744-4272
savings@iatrust.ca
www.iatrust.ca
Former Name: Industrial-Alliance Trust Company
Ownership: Wholly owned subsidiary of iA Financial Group, Québec, QC.
Year Founded: 2000
Assets: $1-10 billion

Investors Group Trust Co. Ltd./ La Compagnie de Fiducie du Groupe Investors Ltée
One Canada Centre
447 Portage Ave.
Winnipeg, MB R3C 3B6
Tel: 204-943-3385; *Toll-Free:* 888-746-6344
www.investorsgroup.com
Other Contact Information: Toll-Free, Quebec: 1-800-661-4578; TTY: 1-866-844-5909
Social Media: www.youtube.com/investorsgroupcanada; www.facebook.com/InvestorsGroup; twitter.com/Valueoftheplan
Ownership: Subsidiary of Investors Group Inc.
Year Founded: 1968

Laurentian Trust of Canada Inc.
#1660, 1981, av. McGill College
Montréal, QC H3A 3K3
Tel: 514-284-4500
www.laurentianbank.com
Ownership: Private. Wholly owned subsidiary of the Laurentian Bank of Canada.
Year Founded: 1939
Assets: $500m-1 billion
Revenues: $10-50 million

LBC Trust
1981 McGill College Ave., 20th Fl.
Montréal, QC H3A 3K3
Toll-Free: 800-522-1846
www.laurentianbank.ca
Ownership: Wholly owned subsidiary of Laurentian Bank

Legacy Private Trust
PO Box 1
#800, 1 Toronto St.
Toronto, ON M5C 2V6
Tel: 416-868-0001; *Fax:* 416-868-6541
mbl@legacyprivatetrust.com
legacyprivatetrust.com
Ownership: Private
Year Founded: 2002

Manulife Trust Company
500 King St. North
Waterloo, ON N2J 4C6
Toll-Free: 877-765-2265
manulife_bank@manulife.com
www.manulifebank.ca
Ownership: Wholly owned subsidiary of Manulife Bank of Canada.

MD Private Trust Company
1870 Alta Vista Dr.
Ottawa, ON K1G 6R7
Toll-Free: 800-267-4022
mdm.ca/wealth-management/estate-and-trust
Social Media: www.facebook.com/MDPhysicianServices
Ownership: Private. Subsidiary of MD Physician Services Inc., part of the CMA Group of Companies.

Mennonite Trust Limited
PO Box 40
3005 Central Ave.
Waldheim, SK S0K 4R0
Tel: 306-945-2080; *Fax:* 306-945-2225
mtl@sasktel.ca
mennonitetrust.com
Year Founded: 1917

Montreal Trust Company of Canada/ Montreal Trust Company
44 King St. West
Toronto, ON M5H 1H1
www.scotiabank.com
Ownership: Owned by The Bank of Nova Scotia.
Year Founded: 1889

Natcan Trust Company
National Bank
1100, rue University, 12e étage
Montréal, QC H3B 2G7
Tel: 514-871-7633; *Fax:* 514-871-7580
Toll-Free: 800-235-5566
Ownership: Wholly owned by National Bank Acquisition Holding Inc.

National Bank Trust Inc./ Trust Banque National
1100, rue University, 12e étage
Montréal, QC H3B 2G7
Tel: 514-871-7240; *Toll-Free:* 800-463-6643
www.nbc.ca
Ownership: Wholly owned subsidiary of National Bank of Canada

National Trust Company
44 King St. West
Toronto, ON M5H 1H1
www.scotiabank.com
Ownership: Owned by The Bank of Nova Scotia.

The Northern Trust Company, Canada
#1910, 145 King St. West
Toronto, ON M5H 1J8
Tel: 416-365-7161; *Fax:* 416-365-9484
www.northerntrust.com
Other Contact Information: Client Services Phone: 1-312-630-0779
Social Media: www.youtube.com/user/NorthernTrustVideos; twitter.com/NorthernTrust

Ownership: Part of Northern Trust Canada. Subsidiary of The Northern Trust Company, Canada Branch, which is a branch of The Northern Trust Company, Chicago

Oak Trust Company
One London Place
#1770, 255 Queens Ave.
London, ON N6A 5R8

Tel: 519-433-6629; *Fax:* 519-433-6652
Toll-Free: 866-973-6631
www.oaktrust.ca

Year Founded: 2004

Olympia Trust Company
#2300, 125 - 9th Ave. SW
Calgary, AB T2G 0P6

Tel: 403-261-0900; *Fax:* 403-265-1455
Toll-Free: 800-727-4493
info@olympiatrust.com
www.olympiatrust.com
Social Media: twitter.com/olyrsp; twitter.com/olyfx

Ownership: Wholly owned subsidiary of Olympia Financial Group Inc.

Peace Hills Trust Company
Corporate Office
10011 - 109 St., 10th Fl.
Edmonton, AB T5J 3S8

Tel: 780-421-1606; *Fax:* 780-426-6568
pht@peacehills.com
www.peacehills.com

Ownership: Private
Year Founded: 1981
Number of Employees: 120
Assets: $100-500 million
Revenues: $10-50 million

Peoples Trust Company
888 Dunsmuir St., 14th Fl.
Vancouver, BC V6C 3K4

Tel: 604-683-2881; *Fax:* 604-331-3469
people@peoplestrust.com
www.peoplestrust.com
Other Contact Information: Alternate URL: www.peoplescardservices.com

Ownership: Private
Year Founded: 1985

RBC Investor Services Trust
155 Wellington St. West, 2nd Fl.
Toronto, ON M5V 3L3

Tel: 416-955-6251
generalinquiries@rbc.com
rbcis.com

Former Name: RBC Dexia Investor Services Trust
Also Known As: RBC Investor & Treasury Services (RBC I&TS)
Ownership: Wholly owned subsidiary of Royal Bank of Canada

Rothschild Trust
15 Queen St.
Charlottetown, PE C1A 7K7

contact@rothschildtrust.com
wealthmanagementandtrust.rothschild.com

Ownership: Private. Part of the Rothschilds Group.

The Royal Trust Company
Royal Bank
#600, 1, Place Ville-Marie
Montréal, QC H3B 2B2

Tel: 514-876-2525; *Fax:* 514-876-2421
www.rbc.com

Ownership: Part of RBC Financial Group.
Year Founded: 1899

Royal Trust Corporation of Canada
155 Wellington St. West, 17th Fl.
Toronto, ON M5V 3K7

www.rbc.com

Ownership: Part of RBC Financial Group.

State Street Bank & Trust Company, Canada Branch
***Also listed under:** Foreign Banks: Schedule III*
#1100, 30 Adelaide St. East
Toronto, ON M5C 3G6

Tel: 416-362-1100; *Fax:* 416-956-2525
Toll-Free: 888-287-8639
www.statestreet.com/ca

Also Known As: State Street Trust Company Canada
Ownership: Part of State Street Corporation.
Year Founded: 1990
Number of Employees: 1,100
Assets: $100 billion +

Sun Life Financial Trust Inc.
PO Box 1601, Waterloo Stn. Waterloo
227 King St. South
Waterloo, ON N2J 4C5

Toll-Free: 877-786-5433
service@sunlife.ca
www.sunlifefinancialtrust.ca

Year Founded: 1865

Valiant Trust Company
#600, 750 Cambie St.
Vancouver, BC V6B 0A2

Tel: 604-699-4880; *Fax:* 604-681-3067
Toll-Free: 866-313-1872
inquiries@valianttrust.com
www.valianttrust.com

Ownership: A division of Canadian Western Bank. Part of the Canadian Western Bank Group.

Western Pacific Trust Company
#920, 789 West Pender St.
Vancouver, BC V6C 1H2

Tel: 604-683-0455; *Fax:* 604-669-6978
Toll-Free: 800-663-9536
www.westernpacifictrust.com

Ownership: Public
Year Founded: 1964

SECTION 6
EDUCATION

Arranged by province, and each province includes the following categories. Each category is further arrangd by specific subcategories, as applicable to each province.

Government Agencies

School Boards/Districts/Divisions
Public; Faith-Based; Catholic; French; School Authorities

Schools: Specialized
Charter; First Nations; Hearing Impaired; Distance Education; Special Education

Schools: Independent & Private

Universities & Colleges

Post Secondary/Technical

Alberta

Government Agencies

Edmonton: Alberta Ministry of Advanced Education
Commerce Place
10155 - 102 St., 6th Fl., Edmonton, AB T5J 4L5, Canada
Tel: 780-422-5400; *Toll-Free:* 310-0000
www.iae.alberta.ca
Hon. Marlin Schmidt, Minister of Advanced Education

School Boards/Districts/Divisions

Public

Airdrie: Rocky View School Division #41
2651 Chinook Winds Dr., Airdrie, AB T4B 0B4, Canada
Tel: 403-945-4000; *Fax:* 403-945-4001
www.rockyview.ab.ca
www.facebook.com/166268840087518
twitter.com/rvsed
Number of Schools: 48; *Grades:* K - 12; *Enrollment:* 16000
Sylvia Eggerer, Chair
seggerer@rockyview.ab.ca
Don Hoium, Superintendent of Schools, 403-945-4002
kdolynny@rockyview.ab.ca
Darrell Couture, Associate Superintendent of Business and Operations, 403-945-4009
lcastle@rockyview.ab.ca
Murray Besenski, Associate Superintendent of Schools, 403-945-4016
vwoodman@rockyview.ab.ca
Dave Morris, Associate Superintendent of Learning, 403-945-4031
lshemko@rockyview.ab.ca
Susan Williams, Associate Superintendent of Human Resources, 403-945-4017
kdolynny@rockyview.ab.ca
Mabel Pugh, Manager of Supply Management, 403-945-4098
mpugh@rockyview.ab.ca

Athabasca: Aspen View Regional Division #19
3600 - 48 Ave., Athabasca, AB T9S 1M8, Canada
Tel: 780-675-7080; *Fax:* 780-675-3660
Toll-Free: 888-488-0288
info@aspenview.org
www.aspenview.org
Number of Schools: 13; *Grades:* K - 12
Brian Bifforf, Board Chair, 780-675-5553
brian.bittorf@aspenview.org
Brian LeMessurier, Superintendent, Schools
brian.lemessurier@aspenview.org
Derm Madden, Associate Superintendent
derm.madden@aspenview.org
Mark Francis, Associate Superintendent
mark.francis@aspenview.org
Donna Wesley, Director, Innovation
donna.wesley@aspenview.org
Rodney Boyko, Director, Business Services
rodney.boyko@aspenview.org

Barrhead: Pembina Hills Regional Division #7
5310 - 49 St., Barrhead, AB T7N 1P3, Canada
Tel: 780-674-8500; *Fax:* 780-674-3262
Toll-Free: 1-877-693-1333
info@phrd.ab.ca
www.phrd.ab.ca
Number of Schools: 14 schools; 2 outreach; 2 colony; *Grades:* 1 - 12; Adult Ed.
Colleen Symyrozum-Watt, Superintendent
Wendy Scinski, Assistant Superintendent, Employee Services & Facilities
Mark Thiesen, Assistant Superintendent of Education Services
Cam Oulton, Assistant Superintendent of ADLC
Tracy Meunier, Secretary Treasurer
Rob McGarva, Director of Student Services

Bonnyville: Northern Lights School Division #69 (NLSD)
6005 - 50 Ave., Bonnyville, AB T9N 2L4, Canada
Tel: 780-826-3145; *Fax:* 780-826-4600
www.nlsd.ab.ca
www.facebook.com/NLSD69
twitter.com/nlsd69
www.youtube.com/user/NLSDTV
Number of Schools: 26; *Grades:* K-12; *Enrollment:* 5885; *Note:* This division is an amalgamation of the Lac La Biche School Division and the Lakeland Public School District.
Roger Nippard, Superintendent, Schools
roger.nippard@nlsd.ab.ca
Ron Taylor, Associate Superintendent, Human Resources
roy.ripkens@nlsd.ab.ca
Paula Elock, Secretary-Treasurer
paula.elock@nlsd.ab.ca
Carolyn Kellett, Director of Business Services
carolyn.kellett@nlsd.ab.ca
Lou Macaulay, Purchasing Agent
lou.macaulay@nlsd.ab.ca

Brooks: Grasslands Regional Division #6
Also known as: **Grasslands Public Schools**
745 - 2nd Ave. East, Brooks, AB T1R 1L2, Canada
Tel: 403-793-6700; *Fax:* 403-362-8225
info@grasslands.ab.ca
www.grasslands.ab.ca
Number of Schools: 13 schools; 7 Hutterian Brethren Colony Schools; *Grades:* K - 12; Alternative Ed.
David Steele, Superintendent
Scott Brandt, Deputy Superintendent
Rhian Schroeder, Associate Superintendent, Business Services
Kathleen Jensen, Assistant Superintendent
Shane Harahus, Director, Finance
Michael Nielsen, Director, Technology
Alan Kloepper, Manager, Facilities & Maintenance

Calgary: Calgary Board of Education
Also known as: **Calgary School District No. 19**
1221 - 8 St. SW, Calgary, AB T2R 0L4, Canada
Tel: 403-817-4000
cbecommunications@cbe.ab.ca
www.cbe.ab.ca
Other Information: 403-817-7955; Trustees: 403-294-8487; Aboriginal Education: 403-777-8970
Number of Schools: 132 elem; 34 elem/mid/high; 20 junior high; 7 junior/senior high; 17 senior high; 15 unique settings; *Grades:* K - 12; Continuing Ed.; *Enrollment:* 107104
Naomi Johnson, Chief Superintendent, Schools, 403-817-7900
chiefsuperintendent@cbe.ab.ca
David Stevenson, Deputy Chief Superintendent, Schools, 403-817-7901
Brad Grundy, Superintendent, CFO, Corporate Treasurer, Finance and Supply, 403-817-7400
Frank Coppinger, Superintendent, Facilities & Environment Servicess, 403-214-1119
Cathy Faber, Superintendent, Learning Innovation, 403-817-7555
cfaber@cbe.ab.ca
Cheryl Oishi, Superintendent, Human Resources, 403-817-7300
Dennis Parsons, Superintendent, Learning, 403-817-7600
Joy Bowen-Eyre, Director, Ward 1 & 2
Lynn Ferguson, Director, Area 3 & 4
Pamela King, Director, Area 5 & 6
George Lane, Director, Area 6 & 7
Pat Cochrane, Director, Area 11 & 13

Camrose: Battle River Regional Division #31
5402 - 48A Ave., Camrose, AB T4V 0L3, Canada
Tel: 780-672-6131; *Fax:* 780-672-6137
Toll-Free: 1-800-262-4869
www.brrd.ab.ca
Number of Schools: 35; *Grades:* K - 12; *Enrollment:* 6700
Cheryl Smith, Board Chair, 780-678-3265
csmith@brsd.ab.ca
Dr. Larry Payne, Superintendent, Schools, 780-672-4718, ext. 5227
LPayne@brsd.ab.ca
Ray Bosh, Assistant Superintendent, Student Services, 780-672-4718, ext. 5011
RBosh@brsd.ab.ca
Rick Jarret, Assistant Superintendent, Instruction, 780-672-4718, ext. 5238
RJarrett@brsd.ab.ca
Imogene Walsh, Assistant Superintendent, Business, 780-672-4718, ext. 5235
IWalsh@brsd.ab.ca
Greg Friend, Director, Personnel, 780-672-4718, ext. 5247
GFriend@brsd.ab.ca
Brenda Johnson, Director, Transportation, 780-672-4718, ext. 5245
BJohnson@brsd.ab.ca
Maureen Parker, Director, Curriculum, 780-672-4718, ext. 5223
MParker@brsd.ab.ca
Percy Roberts, Director, Maintenance & Operations, 780-672-4718, ext. 5246
PRoberts@brsd.ab.ca
Diane Hutchinson, Coordinator, Communications, 780-672-4718, ext. 5248
DHutchinson@brsd.ab.ca
Loretta Foshaug, Coordinator, Instructional Media, 780-672-4718, ext. 5241
LFoshaug@brsd.ab.ca

Canmore: Canadian Rockies Public Schools
Also known as: **Canadian Rockies Regional Division No. 12**
618 - 7th St., Canmore, AB T1W 2H5, Canada
Tel: 403-609-6072; *Fax:* 403-609-6071
www.crps.ca
www.facebook.com/219467748215165
twitter.com/mountainedu
Number of Schools: 6; *Grades:* K - 12; *Enrollment:* 1975
Christopher MacPhee, Superintendent, Schools, 403-609-6070
Kate Bedford, Assistant Superintendent, Student Services, 403-678-1677
Darren Dick, Director of Learning and Innovation, 403-763-7164
Dave MacKenzie, Secretary-Treasurer, 403-679-2242

Cardston: Westwind School Division #74
P.O. Box 10
445 Main St., Cardston, AB T0K 0K0, Canada
Tel: 403-653-4991; *Fax:* 403-653-4641
Toll-Free: 800-655-4991
www.youtube.com/channel/UC2goWB3izHuZ54Re1S0HglA
www.westwind.ab.ca
www.facebook.com/westwindschool
twitter.com/wwsd74
Number of Schools: 14; *Grades:* Pre-K.-12; *Enrollment:* 4249
Ken Summerfeldt, Superintendent
Dexter Durfey, Associate Superintendent, Business Services/Sec.-Treas.
Lance Miller, Chair, 403-634-4770

Claresholm: Livingstone Range School Division #68
P.O. Box 69
5202 - 5 St. East, Claresholm, AB T0L 0T0, Canada
Tel: 403-625-3356; *Fax:* 403-325-2424
Toll-Free: 800-310-6579
centraloffice@lrsd.ab.ca
www.lrsd.ab.ca
Number of Schools: 15 schools; 4 outreach/friendship centres; *Grades:* Pre.-12; *Enrollment:* 3845
Dave Driscoll, Superintendent of Schools, 800-310-6579, ext. 235
driscolld@lrsd.ab.ca
Kathy Olmstead, Associate Superintendent, Learning Services, 800-310-6579, ext. 241
olmsteadk@lrsd.ab.ca
Jeff Perry, Associate Superintendent, Business Services, 800-310-6579, ext. 227
perryj@lrsd.ab.ca
Darryl Seguin, Associate Superintendent, Administrative Services, 800-310-6579, ext. 230
seguind@lrsd.ab.ca

Dunmore: Prairie Rose Regional Division #8 (PRRD)
P.O. Box 204
918 - 2 Ave., Dunmore, AB T0J 1A0, Canada
Tel: 403-527-5516; *Fax:* 403-528-2264
prrd@prrd.ab.ca
www.prrd.ab.ca
www.youtube.com/user/PrairieRoseSD8
Number of Schools: 17 public schools, 15 colony schools, 1 outreach; 1 Mennonite Alternative; *Grades:* JK-12; *Enrollment:* 3380; *Number of Employees:* 645
Brian Andjelic, Superintendent of Schools
Brad Volkman, Deputy Superintendent
Kal Koch, Assistant Superintendent
Patricia Cocks, Secretary-Treasurer
Camille Quinton, Director of Inclusion
Kerry Watson, Coordination of Student Service
Val Miller, Transportation Supervisor
Lyle Roberts, Director of Technology
Brian Frey, Maintenance Supervisor

Edmonton: Edmonton School District #7
Centre for Education
One Kingsway Ave., Edmonton, AB T5H 4G9, Canada
Tel: 780-429-8000; *Fax:* 780-429-8318
info@epsb.ca
www.epsb.ca
www.facebook.com/EdmontonPublicSchools
twitter.com/EPSBNews
www.linkedin.com/company/edmonton-public-schools
www.YouTube.com/EdPublicSchools
Number of Schools: 202; *Enrollment:* 86543; *Number of Employees:* 7,482 full-time employees
Darrel Robertson, Superintendent, Schools, 780-429-8010
darrel.robertson@epsb.ca
Diana Bolan, Assistant Superintendent, Schools, 780-429-8267
diana.bolan@epsb.ca
Mark Liguori, Assistant Superintendent, Schools, 780-429-8177
mark.liguori@epsb.ca

Kathy Muhlethaler, Assistant Superintendent, Schools, 780-429-8011
kathy.muhlethaler@epsb.ca
Ron MacNeil, Assistant Superintendent, Schools, 780-429-8374
ron.macneil@epsb.ca
David Fraser, Executive Director, Corporate Services, 780-429-8262
david.fraser@epsb.ca

Edson: Grande Yellowhead Public School Division No. 77
3656 - 1st Ave., Edson, AB T7E 1S8, Canada
Tel: 780-723-2414; *Fax:* 780-723-2414
Toll-Free: 1-800-723-2564
escgyrd@gyrd.ab.ca
www.gyrd.ab.ca
facebook.com/gypsd

Number of Schools: 20; *Grades:* Elementary - Secondary; *Enrollment:* 5000; *Number of Employees:* 800
Cory Gray, Superintendent, Schools, 780-723-4471, ext. 103
Ewen Murray, Deputy Superintendent, Leadership & Human Resources, 780-723-4471, ext. 106
Ed Latka, Assistant Superintendent, Business Services, 780-723-4471, ext. 102
edlatk@gyrd.ab.ca
Leslee Jodry, Assistant Superintendent, Learning Services, 780-723-4471, ext. 116
Nancy Spencer Poitras, Assistant Superintendent, Research and Planning, 780-728-8269
Ken Baluch, Director, Facility Services, 780-723-4471, ext. 119
kenbalu@gyrd.ab.ca
Gail Prokopchuk, Director, Transportation Services, 780-723-4471, ext. 121
Tracy Goertzen, Director, Financial Services, 780-723-4471, ext. 112
Nikki Gilks, Manager, Communications, 780-723-4471, ext. 142
nikkgilk@gyrd.ab.ca
Jody Beck, Supervisor, Learning Services - Student Programs, 780-723-4471
jodybeck@gyrd.ab.ca
Kurt Scobie, Supervisor, Learning Services - Technology, 780-865-5692
kurtscob@gyrd.ab.ca
Sandy Axmann, Supervisor, Learning Services - Curriculum & Instruction, 780-723-4471

Fort McMurray: Fort McMurray Public School District #2833
Clearwater Public Education Centre
231 Hardin St., Fort McMurray, AB T9H 2G2, Canada
Tel: 780-799-7900; *Fax:* 780-743-2655
fmpsdschools.ca
www.facebook.com/fmpsd
twitter.com/fmpsd
www.youtube.com/user/fmpsd2833

Number of Schools: 9 elementary schools; 4 high schools; *Grades:* ECS - 12
Jeff Thompson, Board Chair, 780-799-5568
jeff.thompson@fmpsd.ab.ca
Doug Nicholls, Superintendent, Schools, 780-799-7903
douglas.nicholls@fmpsd.ab.ca
Allan Kallal, Associate Superintendent, Business & Finance, 780-799-7908
Allan.Kallal@fmpsd.ab.ca
Dr. Brenda Sautner, Associate Superintendent, Education & Administration, 780-792-5656
brenda.sautner@fmpsd.ab.ca
Phil Meagher, Associate Superintendent, Human Resources & Administration, 780-799-9970
phil.meagher@fmpsd.ab.ca
Leslie Ann Booker, Coordinator, Early Childhood Programs, 780-799-7928
Leslie.Booker@fmpsd.ab.ca
Ram Etwaroo, Coordinator, Student Information Systems, 780-799-7907
ram.etwaroo@fmpsd.ab.ca
Myrna Matheson, Coordinator, Literacy, 780-799-7906
Myrna.Matheson@fmpsd.ab.ca
Nancy Gauthier, Coordinator, Communications, 780-788-8009
nancy.gauthier@fmpsd.ab.ca
Miguel Borges, Coordinator, Educational Technology, 780-799-8004
miguel.borges@fmpsd.ab.ca

Fort Vermilion: Fort Vermilion School Division No. 52 (FVSD)
P.O. Box 1
5213 River Rd., Fort Vermilion, AB T0H 1N0, Canada
Tel: 780-927-3766; *Fax:* 780-927-4625
fvsd_52@fvsd.ab.ca
www.fvsd.ab.ca

Number of Schools: 15 & 4 Learning Stores; *Grades:* Kindergarten - 12; *Enrollment:* 3045; *Number of Employees:* 500
Roger Clarke, Superintendent, Schools, 780-927-3766
rogerc@fvsd.ab.ca
Rick Cusson, Assistant Superintendent, Operations, 780-927-3766
rickc@fvsd.ab.ca
Kathryn Kirby, Assistant Superintendent, Teaching & Learning, 780-927-3766
kathrynk@fvsd.ab.ca
Bill Driedger, Assistant Superintendent, Teaching & Learning, 780-927-3766
billd@fvsd.ab.ca
Dan Dyck, Manager, Maintenance, 780-928-3013
dand@fvsd.ab.ca
Peter Braun, Manager, Transportation & Safety, 780-928-3860
peterb@fvsd.ab.ca
Norman Buhler, Secretary-Treasurer, 780-927-3766
normanb@fvsd.ab.ca

Grande Prairie: Grande Prairie School District
10213 - 99 St., Grande Prairie, AB T8V 2H3, Canada
Tel: 780-532-4491; *Fax:* 780-539-4265
www.gppsd.ab.ca
www.facebook.com/162375753809463
www.youtube.com/user/GPPSDVC/videos?view=0

Number of Schools: 15; *Grades:* K - 12; *Enrollment:* 8000
Karen Prokopowich, Chair, 780-532-1575
Karen.Prokopowich@gppsd.ab.ca
Carol Ann MacDonald, Superintendent
carolann.macdonald@gppsd.ab.ca
Alexander McDonald, Assistant Superintendent, Human Resources & Technology
sandy.mcdonald@gppsd.ab.ca
Nick Radujko, Assistant Superintendent, Curriculum
nick.radujko@gppsd.ab.ca
James Robinson, Assistant Superintendent, Student Services
james.robinson@gppsd.ab.ca
Geoff Barron, Director, Operations
geoff.barron@gppsd.ab.ca
Angela DesBarres, Director, Instruction
angela.desbarres@gppsd.ab.ca
Kimberly Frykas, Director, Education Technology
kimberly.frykas@gppsd.ab.ca
Justin Vickers, Director, Information Technology
justin.vickers@gppsd.ab.ca
Wade Webb, Director, Finance
wade.webb@gppsd.ab.ca
Lorna Nordhagen, Manager, Human Resources
lorna.nordhagen@gppsd.ab.ca

Grande Prairie: Peace Wapiti Public School Division #76
8611A - 108 St., Grande Prairie, AB T8V 4C5, Canada
Tel: 780-532-8133; *Fax:* 780-532-4234
www.pwsd76.ab.ca
www.facebook.com/129272180467814
twitter.com/pwsd76

Number of Schools: 32; *Grades:* K - 12; *Enrollment:* 5600; *Number of Employees:* 345 teachers; 600 non-teaching staff
Sheldon Rowe, Superintendent
Mark Davidson, Deputy Superintendent
Ralph Paquin, Secretary Treasurer
Susan Karpisek, Human Resources & Labour Relations Director

Hanna: Prairie Land Regional Division #25 (PLRD)
P.O. Box 670
101 Palliser Trail, Hanna, AB T0J 1P0, Canada
Tel: 403-854-4481; *Fax:* 403-854-2803
Toll-Free: 800-601-3898
www.plrd.ab.ca
www.facebook.com/plrd25
twitter.com/plrd25

Number of Schools: 9 schools; 9 colony schools; *Grades:* K-12; *Enrollment:* 1712
Wes Neumeier, Superintendent, 403-854-4481, ext. 701
wes.neumeier@plrd.ab.ca
Cam McKeage, Chief Deputy Superintendent, 403-854-4481, ext. 702
cam.mckeage@plrd.ab.ca
Sharon Orum, Secretary-Treasurer, 403-854-4481, ext. 717
sharon.orum@plrd.ab.ca

High Prairie: High Prairie School Division #48 (HPSD)
P.O. Box 870
4806 - 53 Ave., High Prairie, AB T0G 1E0, Canada
Tel: 780-523-3337; *Fax:* 780-523-4639
Toll-Free: 877-523-3337
www.hpsd48.ab.ca
www.facebook.com/HPSD48
twitter.com/hpsd48

Number of Schools: 13; *Grades:* K - 12; *Enrollment:* 3000; *Number of Employees:* 220 school-based teachers; 170 full & part-time supprt staff
Laura Poloz, Superintendent, 780-523-3337
lpoloz@hpsd48.ab.ca
Margaret Hartman, Deputy Superintendent, 780-523-3337
mhartman@hpsd48.ab.ca
Raymonde Lussier, Assistant Superintendent, Business, 780-523-3337
rlussier@hpsd48.ab.ca
Brenda Stafford, Assistant Superintendent, Human Resources, 780-523-3337
bstafford@hpsd48.ab.ca
Paul Burrows, Assistant Superintendent, Finances, 780-523-3337
pburrows@hpsd48.ab.ca
Evan Dearden, Assistant Superintendent, Curriculm, 780-523-3337
edearden@hpsd48.ab.ca
Brian Bliss, Supervisor of Purchasing & Custodial Services, 780-523-4557
bbliss@hpsd48.ab.ca

High River: Foothills School Division
P.O. Box 5700
120 - 5th Ave. West, High River, AB T1V 1M7, Canada
Tel: 403-652-3001; *Fax:* 403-938-4410
www.fsd38.ab.ca
Other Information: Alternate Phone: 403-938-6436
facebook.com/pages/Foothills-School-Division-38/24586167549 9080
twitter.com/FSD38

Number of Schools: 19 public schools; 3 open campus locations; 3 Hutterite Colony schools; *Grades:* Pre K - 12; French Immersion; *Enrollment:* 7750; *Number of Employees:* 800
Diana Froc, Chair, 403-995-6551
frocd@fsd38.ab.ca
Del Litke, Acting Superintendent, Schools, 403-652-6501
litked@fsd38.ab.ca
Todd Schmekel, Assistant Superintendent, Learning Services, 403-652-6501
schmekelt@fsd38.ab.ca
Allen Davidson, Assistant Superintendent, Employee Services, 403-652-6501
davidsona@fsd38.ab.ca
Drew Chipman, Assistant Superintendent, Corporate Services, 403-652-6501
chipmand@fsd38.ab.ca
Denise Gow, Director of Financial Services, 403-652-6503
gowd@fsd38.ab.ca
Deborah Spence, Manager, Communications & Events, 403-652-6502
spenced@fsd38.ab.ca

Innisfail: Chinook's Edge School Division #73
4904 - 50 St., Innisfail, AB T4G 1W4, Canada
Tel: 403-227-7070; *Fax:* 403-227-3652
Toll-Free: 800-561-9229
division.office@chinooksedge.ab.ca
www.chinooksedge.ab.ca

Number of Schools: 43; *Enrollment:* 10800; *Number of Employees:* 1,300
Kurt Sacher, Superintendent of Schools, 403-227-7054
ksacher@chinooksedge.ab.ca
Shawn Russell, Associate Superintendent, People Services, 403-227-7075
srussell@chinooksedge.ab.ca
Allan Tarnoczi, Associate Superintendent, Corporate Services, 403-227-7056
atarnoczi@chinooksedge.ab.ca
Lissa Steele, Associate Superintendent, Learning Services, 403-227-7060
lsteele@chinooksedge.ab.ca
Wanda Christensen, Associate Superintendent, Student Services, 403-227-7088
wchristensen@chinooksedge.ab.ca
Sandy Bexon, Communications Officer, 403-227-7085
sbexon@chinooksedge.ab.ca
Marjorie Jantzen, Library Technician
mjantzen@chinooksedge.ab.ca

Lethbridge: Lethbridge School District #51
433 - 15 St. South, Lethbridge, AB T1J 2Z5, Canada
Tel: 403-380-5300
lethsdweb.lethsd.ab.ca

Number of Schools: 12 elementary schools; 4 middle schools; 10 secondary schools; *Grades:* K-12; *Enrollment:* 9000; *Number of Employees:* 531 teachers; 477 support staff
Mich Forster, Chair, 403-381-8720
mich.forster@lethsd.ab.ca
Cheryl Gilmore, Superintendent, Schools, 403-380-5301
cheryl.gilmore@lethsd.ab.ca

Don Lussier, Associate Superintendent, Business Affairs, 403-380-5303
don.lussier@lethsd.ab.ca
Wendy Fox, Associate Superintendent, Instruction, 403-380-5318
wendy.fox@lethsd.ab.ca
Sharon Mezei, Associate Superintendent, Human Resources, 403-380-5321
sharon.mezei@lethsd.ab.ca
Joe Perry, Purchasing Coordinator, 403-382-2160
joe.perry@lethsd.ab.ca

Lethbridge: Palliser Regional Division #26
#101, 3305 - 18 Ave. North, Lethbridge, AB T1H 5S1, Canada
Tel: 403-328-4111; *Fax:* 403-380-6890
Toll-Free: 877-667-1234
www.pallisersd.ab.ca
twitter.com/PalliserSchools
Number of Schools: 15 community; 17 Hutterian colony; 10 Christian alternative; 4 outreach; 1 online; 2 alternative; *Grades:* Pre - 12; *Enrollment:* 7200
Kevin Gietz, Superintendent
Dale Backlin, Associate Superintendent, Education Services
Pat Rivard, Associate Superintendent, Education Services
Kevin C. Garinger, Associate Superintendent, Human Resources
Dan Ryder, Director of Learning, Leadership/School Development
Amber Darroch, Director of Learning, Technology, Counselling, Crisis Respons
Laurie Wilson, Director of Learning, Inclusive Education, Wrap-Around

Lloydminster: Lloydminster Public School Division (LPSD)
5017 - 46 St., Lloydminster, AB T9V 1R4, Canada
Tel: 780-875-5541; *Fax:* 780-875-7829
contact@lpsd.ca
www.lpsd.ca
twitter.com/LloydPublic
Number of Schools: 6 elementary schools; 2 middle schools; 1 secondary school; 1 outreach school; *Grades:* Pre - 12; *Enrollment:* 3945; *Number of Employees:* 507
Dr. Michael Diachuk, Director, Education, 780-808-2520
michael.diachuk@lpsd.ca
Collin Adams, Superintendent of Administration, 780-808-2523
collin.adams@lpsd.ca
Scott Wouters, Superintendent of Human Resources, 780-808-2538
scott.wouters@lpsd.ca
Lois Hardy, Superintendent of Student Services, 780-808-2533
lois.hardy@lpsd.ca
Trisha Rawlake, Superintendent of Learning and Instruction, 780-808-2522
trisha.rawlake@lpsd.ca

Medicine Hat: Medicine Hat School District #76
601 - 1 Ave. SW, Medicine Hat, AB T1A 4Y7, Canada
Tel: 403-528-6700; *Fax:* 403-529-5339
www.sd76.ab.ca
Number of Schools: 11 elementary schools; 4 secondary schools; 1 elementary/middle school; *Grades:* K.-12; *Enrollment:* 7000
Dr. Grant Henderson, Superintendent, Schools, 403-528-6701
grant.henderson@sd76.ab.ca
Terry Riley, Chair, 403-528-3726
Lyle Cunningham, Associate Superintendent, Human Resources, 403-528-6734
lyle.cunningham@sd76.ab.ca
Jerry Labossiere, Secretary-Treasurer, 403-528-6728
jerry.labossiere@sd76.ab.ca
Sherrill Fedor, Associate Superintendent, Student Services, 403-528-6718
sherrill.fedor@sd76.ab.ca

Morinville: Sturgeon School Division #24 (SSD)
9820 - 104 St., Morinville, AB T8R 1L8, Canada
Tel: 780-939-4341; *Fax:* 780-939-5520
Toll-Free: 888-459-4062
info@sturgeon.ab.ca
www.sturgeon.ab.ca
Number of Schools: 16; *Grades:* K - 12; *Enrollment:* 5000
Dr. Michèle Dick, Superintendent, 780-939-4341
mdick@sturgeon.ab.ca
Gerry Schick, Deputy Superintendent
Iva Paulik, Secretary Treasurer
Dave Johnson, Associate Superintendent, Human Resources
Wolfgang Jeske, Director, Curriculum & Instruction

Nisku: Black Gold Regional Division #18
1101 - 5 St., 3rd Fl., Nisku, AB T9E 7N3, Canada
Tel: 780-955-6025; *Fax:* 780-955-6050
www.blackgold.ab.ca
Number of Schools: 27; *Grades:* JK - 12; *Enrollment:* 9200; *Number of Employees:* 460 teachers; 200 secretaries, library clerks, and educational assistants
Barb Martinson, Chair, Board of Education
barb.martinson@blackgold.ca
Dr. Norman Yanitski, Superintendent
Neil Fenske, Associate Superintendent, 780-955-6028
neil.fenske@blackgold.ca
Dennis Nosyk, Associate Superintendent, 780-955-6032
dennis.nosyk@blackgold.ca
Calvin Monty, Associate Superintendent, Human Resources & Administration, 780-955-6032
calvin.monty@blackgold.ca
Dianne Butler, Director, Student Services, 780-955-6037
dianne.butler@blackgold.ca
Peter Balding, Administrator, Division Technology, 780-955-6037
dianne.butler@blackgold.ca
Dan Borys, Manager, Operations & Maintenance, 780-955-6068
dan.borys@blackgold.ca
Laurel Kvarnberg, Director, Finance, 780-955-6059
laurel.kvarnberg@blackgold.ca
Sue Timmermans, Manager, Transportation, 780-955-6034
sue.timmermans@blackgold.ca
Warren Watson, Manager, Projects, 780-955-6062
warren.watson@blackgold.ca

Peace River: Northland School Division #61
P.O. Box 1400
9809 - 77 Ave., Peace River, AB T8S 1V2, Canada
Tel: 780-624-2060; *Fax:* 780-624-5914
Toll-Free: 800-362-1360
centralofficestaff@nsd61.ca
www.northland61.ab.ca
www.facebook.com/NorthlandSchoolDivisionNo61
twitter.com/northland61
Number of Schools: 23; *Grades:* K.-12
Donna Barrett, Superintendent, Schools, 780-624-2060, ext. 6102
Donna.Barrett@nsd61.ca
Dennis Walsh, Secretary-Treasurer, 780-624-2060, ext. 6141
Dennis.Walsh@nsd61.ca
Dr. Don Tessier, Associate Superintendent, 780-331-3774, ext. 3007
Don.Tessier@nsd61.ca
Wes Oginski, Director of Human Resources, 780-624-2060, ext. 6157
Wesley.Oginski@nsd61.ca
Patty Johnson, Purchasing Clerk, 780-624-2060, ext. 6146
Patty.Johnson@nsd61.ca
Delores Pruden, Director, First Nations, Métis Programs, 780-624-2060, ext. 6161
Delores.Pruden@nsd61.ca

Peace River: Peace River School Division #10 (PRSD)
10018 - 101 St., Peace River, AB T8S 2A5, Canada
Tel: 780-624-3601; *Fax:* 780-624-5941
peaceriversd@prsd.ab.ca
www.prsd.ab.ca
www.facebook.com/116920318387092
twitter.com/prsd10
google.prsd.ab.ca
Number of Schools: 20; *Grades:* K-12; *Enrollment:* 3160
Darren Kuester, Chair, 780-971-2465
Paul Bennett, Superintendent, 780-624-3650, ext. 102
Karen Penney, Deputy Superintendent, 780-624-3650, ext. 10115
Sharon Darrah, Instructional Materials Center Supervisor, 780-624-3650, ext. 10120

Ponoka: Wolf Creek School Division #72
6000 Hwy. 2A, Ponoka, AB T4J 1P6, Canada
Tel: 403-783-5441; *Fax:* 403-783-3483
info@wolfcreek.ab.ca
www.wolfcreek.ab.ca
www.facebook.com/336597836437398
twitter.com/WCPS72
wolftube.mediacore.tv
Number of Schools: 26 schools; 5 colony schools; *Grades:* K.-12; Special Education
Larry Jacobs, Superintendent
ljacobs@wolfcreek.ab.ca
Joe Henderson, Secretary-Treasurer
jhenderson@wolfcreek.ab.ca
Trudy Bratland, Chair
tbratland@wolfcreek.ab.ca
Amber Hester, Assistant Superintendent, Inclusive Learning Services
ahester@wolfcreek.ab.ca
Gerry Varty, Assistant Superintendent, Learning Support
gvarty@wolfcreek.ab.ca
Jayson Lovell, Assistant Superintendent, People Support
jlovell@wolfcreek.ab.ca

Red Deer: Red Deer School District #104
4747 - 53 St., Red Deer, AB T4N 2E6, Canada
Tel: 403-343-1405; *Fax:* 403-347-8190
info@rdpsd.ab.ca
www.rdpsd.ab.ca
twitter.com/rdpschools
Number of Schools: 24; *Grades:* K-12; *Enrollment:* 10000; *Number of Employees:* 550 teachers; 385 classified staff; 112 caretakers and maintenance staff
Bev Manning, Chair, 403-343-6292
beverly.manning@rdpsd.ab.ca
Pieter Langstraat, Superintendent, 403-342-3710
piet.langstraat@rdpsd.ab.ca
Stu Henry, Deputy Superintendent, 403-342-3711
stu.henry@rdpsd.ab.ca
Brian Bieber, Associate Superintendent, Human Resources, Payroll, Benefits, 403-342-3720
brian.bieber@rdpsd.ab.ca
Cody McClintock, Associate Superintendent, Business Services, 403-342-3702
cody.mcclintock@rdpsd.ab.ca
Ron Eberts, Associate Superintendent, Learning Services, 403-342-3700
Ron.Eberts@rdpsd.ab.ca
Jodi Goodrick, Associate Superintendent, Student Services, 403-342-3715
jodi.goodrick@rdpsd.ab.ca
Robin Lane, Purchasing Clerk, 403-342-3718
robin.lane@rdpsd.ab.ca

Rocky Mountain House: Wild Rose School Division #66 (WRSD)
4912 - 43 St., Rocky Mountain House, AB T4T 1P4, Canada
Tel: 403-845-3376; *Fax:* 403-845-3850
www.wrsd.ca
Number of Schools: 17 schools; 3 alternative programs; *Grades:* K-12; *Enrollment:* 5100; *Number of Employees:* 319 teachers; 350 non-teaching
Brian Celli, Superintendent of Schools
brian.celli@wrsd.ca
Greg Wedman, Associate Superintendent, Central Services
Gord Atkinson, Associate Superintendent, Learning Services
Gordon Majeran, Associate Superintendent, Corporate Services

Sherwood Park: Elk Island Public Schools Regional Division #14 (EIPS)
Central Administration Building
683 Wye Rd., Sherwood Park, AB T8B 1N2, Canada
Tel: 780-464-3477; *Fax:* 780-417-8181
Toll-Free: 800-905-3477
communications@ei.educ.ab.ca
www.ei.educ.ab.ca
twitter.com/eips
Number of Schools: 42; *Enrollment:* 16600; *Number of Employees:* 890 full-time equivalent teaching staff; 515 full-time equivalent non-teaching staff
Bruce Beliveau, Superintendent of Schools, 780-417-8203
bruce.beliveau@eips.ca
Karen Sand, Director, Communication Services, 780-417-8204
karen.sand@eips.ca

St Albert: St. Albert Public School District #5565
60 Sir Winston Churchill Ave., St Albert, AB T8N 0G4, Canada
Tel: 780-460-3712; *Fax:* 780-460-7686
info@spschools.org
www.spschools.org
www.facebook.com/pages/St-Albert-Public-Schools/201395229889976
twitter.com/StAlbertPublic
Number of Schools: 8 elementary; 4 junior high; 4 high school; *Grades:* K - 12; *Enrollment:* 7000
Barry Wowk, Superintendent of Schools
wowkb@spschools.org
Doug McDavid, Deputy Superintendent
doug.mcdavid@spschools.org
Krimsen Sumners, Associate Superintendent, Program & Planning
sumnersk@spschools.org
Michael Brenneis, Associate Superintendent, Finance/Secretary-Treasurer
brenneism@spschools.org

St Paul: St. Paul Education Regional Division #1
4313 - 48th Ave., St Paul, AB T0A 3A3, Canada
Tel: 780-645-3323; *Fax:* 780-645-5789
www.stpauleducation.ab.ca
www.facebook.com/109991642493405

Number of Schools: 18 (including 5 K-12 schools, 2 Hutterite colonies, 2 outreach schools); *Grades:* K - 12; *Enrollment:* 3988; *Number of Employees:* 270 teaching staff; 346 support staff
Heather Starosielski, Chair, 780-726-2289
Glen Brodziak, Superintendent, 780-645-3323
Patricia Gervais, Assistant Superintendent, 780-645-3323
Dalane Imeson, Assistant Superintendent, 780-645-3323
Glenda Bristow, Program Coordinator, 780-645-3323
Sha Tichkowsky, District Consultant of Student Supports, 780-645-3323
Jean Champagne, Secretary-Treasurer, 780-645-3323

***Stettler:* Clearview School Division #71**
P.O. Box 1720
5031 - 50 St., Stettler, AB T0C 2L0, Canada
Tel: 403-742-3331; *Fax:* 403-742-1388
www.clearview.ab.ca
www.facebook.com/CPS71
twitter.com/csd71
Number of Schools: 14; *Grades:* K - 12; *Enrollment:* 2462
John Bailey, Superintendent, Schools
jbailey@clearview.ab.ca
Eileen Johnstone, Director of Student Services
ejohnstone@clearview.ab.ca
Steve Meyer, Director of Technology
smeyer@clearview.ab.ca
Cheryl Cysouw, Director of Human Resources/Payroll Administrator
ccysouw@clearview.ab.ca
Maryann Wingie, Director of Transportation
mwingie@clearview.ab.ca
Susan Hernando, Director of Finance
shernando@clearview.ab.ca
Rob Rathwell, Coordinator of Administrative and Instructional Support
rrathwell@clearview.ab.ca

***Stony Plain:* Parkland School Division #70**
Centre for Education
4603 - 48 St., Stony Plain, AB T7Z 2A8, Canada
Tel: 780-963-4010; *Fax:* 780-963-4169
Toll-Free: 800-282-3997
DivisionOffice@psd70.ab.ca
www.psd70.ab.ca
Number of Schools: 21; *Enrollment:* 9454; *Number of Employees:* 590 teaching staff; 469 support staff
Tim Monds, Superintendent of Schools, 780-963-8404
TMonds@psd70.ab.ca
Kelly Wilkins, Deputy Superintendent, 780-963-8404
KDWilkins@psd70.ab.ca
Claire Jonsson, Associate Superintendent, Business and Finance, 780-963-8411
CJonsson@psd70.ab.ca
Emilie Keane, Associate Superintendent, 780-963-8471
EKeane@psd70.ab.ca
Dianne McConnell, Associate Superintendent, 780-963-8422
EKeane@psd70.ab.ca

***Strathmore:* Golden Hills School Division #75**
435A Hwy. #1, Strathmore, AB T1P 1J4, Canada
Tel: 403-934-5121; *Fax:* 403-934-5125
Toll-Free: 1-800-320-3739
www.ghsd75.ca
www.facebook.com/247661348609708
twitter.com/ghsd75
Number of Schools: 17 regular; 18 Hutterite colonies; 2 Christian, 2 Virtual; 4 outreach; 1 international program; *Grades:* ECS - 12; *Enrollment:* 6000; *Number of Employees:* 361 teachering staff; 273 non-teaching staff
Dave Price, Chair, 403-651-5317
Bevan Daverne, Superintendent, Schools
Wes Miskiman, Associate Superintendent, Human Resources
Dr. Kandace Jordan, Deputy Superintendent of Schools / Director of International
Michael Kuystermans, Manager, Financial Services, 403-934-5121, ext. 2022
Don Hartman, Manager, Facilities & Maintenance, 403-934-5121, ext. 2053
Ken MacLean, Supervisor, Transportation, 877-442-4340
Patty MacDonald, Library Technician, 403-934-5121, ext. 2067

***Taber:* Horizon School Division #67**
6302 - 56 St., Taber, AB T1G 1Z9, Canada
Tel: 403-223-3547; *Fax:* 403-223-2999
www.horizon.ab.ca
www.facebook.com/HSD67
twitter.com/horizonsd67
Number of Schools: 16 schools; 18 Hutterian Brethren schools; *Enrollment:* 3550
Marie Logan, Chair, 403-792-3696
marie@wheatcrest.ca
Wilco Tymensen, Superintendent
Clark Bosch, Associate Superintendent, Programs and Services
Erin Hurkett, Associate Superintendent, Curriculum and Instruction
John Rakai, Associate Superintendent, Finance and Operations
Dorthea Mills, Communications and Information Coordinator
Philip Johansen, Finance Director
Deanna Killinger, Human Resource Coordinator

***Wainwright:* Buffalo Trail Public Schools Regional Division No. 28**
Central Office
1041 - 10A St., Wainwright, AB T9W 2R4, Canada
Tel: 780-842-6144; *Fax:* 780-842-3255
central_office@btps.ca
www.btps.ca
Number of Schools: 27; *Grades:* K - 12; *Enrollment:* 4200; *Number of Employees:* 575 full and part time teachers and support staff
Darcy Eddleston, Chair, 780-745-2370
darcy.eddleston@btps.ca
Bob Allen, Superintendent, Schools, 780-842-6144
superintendent@btps.ca
Brad Romanchuk, Assistant Superintendent, Human Resources, 780-842-6144
brad.romanchuk@btps.ca
Lisa Blackstock, Assistant Superintendent, Learning Services, 780-842-6144
lisa.blackstock@btps.ca
Bob Brown, Secretary-Treasurer, 780-806-2050
bob.brown@btps.ca
Daryl Hoey, Director, Technology, 780-806-2065
daryl.hoey@btps.ca
Randy Huxley, Director, Facilities, 780-806-2064
randy.huxley@btps.ca
Chrysti Mannix, Director, Transportation, 780-806-2051
chrysti.mannix@btps.ca
Shannon Melin, Director, Human Resources, 780-806-2062
shannon.melin@btps.ca
Crystal Tower, Director, Student Services, 780-806-2056
crystal.tower@btps.ca
Hugh Forrester, Curriculum Lead, 780-872-1885
hugh.forrester@btps.ca

***Wetaskiwin:* Wetaskiwin Regional Division #11**
***Also known as:* Wetaskiwin Regional Public Schools**
5515 - 47A Ave., Wetaskiwin, AB T9A 3S3, Canada
Tel: 780-352-6018; *Fax:* 780-352-7886
Toll-Free: 877-352-8078
wrps@wrps.ab.ca
www.wrps.ab.ca
www.facebook.com/wrps11
twitter.com/WRPS11
Number of Schools: 17 schools; 2 off-campus programs; 1 early education and family wellness centre; *Grades:* Pre-K.-12; *Enrollment:* 3936
Terry Pearson, Superintendent of Schools, 780-352-6018
pearsont@wrps.ab.ca
Sherri Senger, Associate Superintendent, Business, 780-352-6018
sengers@wrps.ab.ca
Randy Risto, Associate Superintendent, Personnel, 780-352-6018
ristor@wrps.ab.ca
Brian Taje, Associate Superintendent, Instruction, 780-352-6018
tajeb@wrps.ab.ca

***Whitecourt:* Northern Gateway Regional Division #10**
P.O. Box 840
4816 - 49 Ave., Whitecourt, AB T7S 1N8, Canada
Tel: 780-778-2800; *Fax:* 780-778-6719
Toll-Free: 800-262-8674
www.ngps.ca
www.facebook.com/northerngatewaypublicschools
twitter.com/ngrdschools
Number of Schools: 18 schools; 4 outreach schools; *Grades:* K.-12; *Enrollment:* 5300
Kevin Andrea, Superintendent
kevin.andrea@ngps.ca
Mike Gramatovich, Secretary-Treasurer
mgramatovich@ngrd.ca
Michelle Brennick, Deputy Superintendent
michelle.brennick@ngrd.ca
Roger Lacey, Director of Learning Services
roger.lacey@ngrd.ca
Lisa Bakos, Communications Officer
lisa.bakos@ngrd.ca

Catholic

***Bonnyville:* Lakeland Roman Catholic Separate School District #150**
Catholic Education Centre
4810 - 46 St., Bonnyville, AB T9N 1B5, Canada
Tel: 780-826-3764; *Fax:* 780-826-7576
www.lcsd150.ab.ca
twitter.com/LCSD_150
Number of Schools: 7; *Enrollment:* 2000; *Number of Employees:* 196
Joe Arruda, Superintendent
Diane Bauer, Associate Superintendent of Personnel and Corporate Services
Glenn Nowosad, Associate Superintendent of Technology & Student Learning
Sylvia Slowski, Secretary Treasurer
Clayton Brown, Communications Officer

***Calgary:* Calgary Catholic School District**
Catholic School Centre
1000 - 5th Ave. SW, Calgary, AB T2P 4T9, Canada
Tel: 403-500-2000
communications@cssd.ab.ca
www.cssd.ab.ca
Other Information: Communications: 403-500-2763; Trustees: 403-500-2761
www.facebook.com/CalgaryCatholicSchoolDistrict
www.twitter.com/CCSD_edu
Number of Schools: 50 elem.; 36 elem/jun. high; 2 jun./sen; 9 sen. high; 6 junior high; 2 congregated special education; *Grades:* K - 12; *Enrollment:* 51047; *Number of Employees:* 3,264 instructional staff; 1,340 support staff; 323 caretaking staff; 147 exempt staff; 9 senior off
Gary Strother, Chief Superintendent, 403-500-2783
John Deausy, Superintendent, Finance & Business, & Secretary-Treasurer, 403-500-2779
Craig Foley, Superintendent, Human Resources, 403-500-2429
Mark Rawlek, Superintendent, Support Services, 403-500-2433
Richard Svoboda, Superintendent, Area A Schools, 403-500-2606
Luba Diduch, Superintendent, Area B Schools, 403-500-2431
Judy MacKay, Superintendent, Area C Schools, 403-500-2600
Michael Ross, Superintendent, Area D Schools, 403-500-2430
Dr. Andra McGinn, Superintendent, Specialized Program Schools, 403-500-2419
Jamie Dobbin, Manager, Supply Management, 403-500-2804
james.dobbin@cssd.ab.ca

***Edmonton:* Edmonton Catholic School District #7**
9807 - 106 St., Edmonton, AB T5K 1C2, Canada
Tel: 780-441-6000; *Fax:* 780-425-8759
Toll-Free: 888-441-6010
info@ecsd.net
www.ecsd.net
www.facebook.com/EdmontonCatholicSchoolDistrict
twitter.com/EdmCathSchools
www.youtube.com/user/EdmontonCatholic?feature=mhee#p/u
Number of Schools: 88 schools; 11 outreach programs; *Grades:* K - 12; *Enrollment:* 37427; *Number of Employees:* 3005
Joan Carr, Superintendent, 780-441-6000

***Fort McMurray:* Fort McMurray Roman Catholic Separate School District #32 (FMCS)**
Fort McMurray Catholic Education Centre
9809 Main St., Fort McMurray, AB T9H 1T7, Canada
Tel: 780-799-5700; *Fax:* 780-799-5706
district@fmcsd.ab.ca
www.fmcsd.ab.ca
Other Information: Service Support Centre, Phone: 780-799-5714
www.facebook.com/166299413409478?fref=ts
twitter.com/fmcsd
Number of Schools: 9; *Grades:* K - 12; French Immersion; *Enrollment:* 5500; *Number of Employees:* 260 teachers; 160 support staff
Geraldine Carbery, Chair
George McGuigan, Superintendent, Schools, 780-799-5799, ext. 5001
gmcguigan@fmcsd.ab.ca
Monica Mankowski, Deputy Superintendent, 780-799-5799, ext. 5020
Francois Gagnon, Associate Superintendent, Business & Finance, 780-799-5700
fgagnon@fmcsd.ab.ca
Norena Hart, Director, Facilities, 780-799-5714
NHart@fmcsd.ab.ca
Monica Mankowski, Director, Student Services, 780-799-5799, ext. 5041
mmankowski@fmcsd.ab.ca

Kathleen Murray House, Director, School Based Administration, & Mentor Principal, 780-799-5799, ext. 5001
kmurphy@fmcsd.ab.ca
Betty-Lou Cahill, Coordinator, Human Resources, 780-799-5799, ext. 5021
BCahill@fmcsd.ab.ca

Grande Prairie: Grande Prairie Roman Catholic Separate School District #28
Catholic Education Centre
9902 - 101 St., Grande Prairie, AB T8V 2P4, Canada
Tel: 780-532-3013; *Fax:* 780-532-3430
Toll-Free: 1-800-661-2568
cec@gpcsd.ca
www.gpcsd.ca
Other Information: Transportation & Maintenance, Phone: 780-513-1220
www.facebook.com/128702977199090
twitter.com/KarlGermann
Number of Schools: 12; *Grades:* JK - 12; French Immersion; Outreach; *Enrollment:* 4350; *Number of Employees:* 500
Karl Germann, Superintendent, Schools, 780-532-3013
Greg Miller, Assistant Superintendent, Human Resources, 780-532-3013, ext. 121
Jessie Shirley, Assistant Superintendent, Teaching & Learning, 780-532-3013, ext. 122
Bryan Turner, Associate Superintendent, Business Operations, 780-532-3013, ext. 123
Pauline Ruel-Wyant, Director, Student Services, 780-532-3013, ext. 403
Clint Carrell, Administrator, Information Systems, 780-532-3013, ext. 300
John Dooley, Supervisor, Maintenance, 780-513-1220
Randy Lester, Supervisor, Transportation & Custodians, 780-513-1220

Leduc: St. Thomas Aquinas Roman Catholic Separate Regional Division #38
Also known as: STAR Catholic Schools
4906 - 50th Ave., Leduc, AB T9E 6W9, Canada
Tel: 780-986-2500; *Fax:* 780-986-8620
Toll-Free: 1-800-583-0688
feedback@starcatholic.ab.ca
www.starcatholic.ab.ca
www.facebook.com/starcatholic?fref=ts
twitter.com/STARCatholic
www.youtube.com/user/starcatholic
Number of Schools: 9 schools; 1 outreach centre; *Grades:* Pre-K - 12; *Enrollment:* 3300; *Number of Employees:* 350
Troy A. Davies, Superintendent, Schools
troy.davies@starcatholic.ab.ca
Kevin Booth, Assistant Superintendent
kevin.booth@starcatholic.ab.ca
Charlie Bouchard, Assistant Superintendent
charlie.bouchard@starcatholic.ab.ca
Jeanne Fontaine, Secretary-Treasurer
jeanne.fontaine@starcatholic.ab.ca
Amanda Villetard, Director of Finance and Business Administration
amanda.villetard@starcatholic.ab.ca
Wanda Lehman, Director of Faith Life and Religious Education
wanda.lehman@starcatholic.ab.ca
Dallas Zielke, Director of Facilities
dallas.zielke@starcatholic.ab.ca
Pius MacLean, Director of Curriculum and Instruction
pius.maclean@starcatholic.ab.ca
Marilyn Kunitz, Director of Student Services
marilyn.kunitz@starcatholic.ab.ca
Susan Baudin, Officer, Human Resouces & Payroll
susan.baudin@starcatholic.ab.ca
Kent Dixon, Manager of Communications
kent.dixon@starcatholic.ab.ca

Lethbridge: Holy Spirit Roman Catholic Separate Regional Division #4
620 - 12B St. North, Lethbridge, AB T1H 2L7, Canada
Tel: 403-327-9555; *Fax:* 403-327-9595
www.holyspirit.ab.ca
www.facebook.com/116136991799341
twitter.com/HolySpiritCSD
www.youtube.com/user/HolySpiritSchools1?feature=mhee
Number of Schools: 13; *Grades:* K - 12; *Enrollment:* 4232; *Number of Employees:* 257 teachers; 259 support staff
Christopher Smeaton, Superintendent
Brian Macauley, Deputy Superintendent
Lisa Palmarin, Secretary-Treasurer
Ken Sampson, Director of Student Services
Lorelie Lenaour, Director of Learning
Amanda Lindemann, Director of Finance

Lloydminster: Lloydminster Roman Catholic School Division (LCSD)
6611B - 39th St., Lloydminster, AB T9V 2Z4, Canada
Tel: 780-808-8585; *Fax:* 780-808-8787
information@lcsd.ca
www.lcsd.ca
www.facebook.com/lcsd89
twitter.com/LloydCatholic
www.flickr.com/photos/67057495@N06
Number of Schools: 6; *Grades:* K.-12
Doug Robertson, Director, Education
Tom Schinold, Superintendent of Administration
tschinold@lcsd.ca
Aubrey Patterson, Superintendent of Instruction
Kevin Kusch, Superintendent of Student Services
JoAnn Lider, Human Resources/Payroll Manager
Cheryl Sikora, Learning Resources Coordinator

Medicine Hat: Medicine Hat Catholic Separate Regional Division #20
1251 - 1 Ave. SW, Medicine Hat, AB T1A 8B4, Canada
Tel: 403-527-2292; *Fax:* 403-529-0917
Toll-Free: 866-864-0013
www.mhcbe.ab.ca
Grades: Pre-K.-12; *Enrollment:* 2800
David Leahy, Supt. of Schools

Okotoks: Christ the Redeemer Catholic Separate Regional Division #3 (CRCS)
1 McRae St., Okotoks, AB T1S 1B3, Canada
Tel: 403-938-2659; *Fax:* 403-938-4575
Toll-Free: 800-737-9383
info@redeemer.ab.ca
www.redeemer.ab.ca
www.facebook.com/crcsrd3
twitter.com/ChristRedeemer1
Number of Schools: 17; *Grades:* K - 12; *Enrollment:* 6200
Mary Stengler, Chair, 403-362-4040
mstengler@redeemer.ab.ca
Scott Morrison, Superintendent, 403-938-8069
smorrison@redeemer.ab.ca
Gary Chiste, Chief Deputy Superintendent, 403-938-8795
gchiste@redeemer.ab.ca
Bonnie Annicchiarico, Associate Superintendent, 403-995-4841
bannicchiarico@redeemer.ab.ca
Michael Kilcommons, Director of Curriculum & Instruction Secondary, 403-995-4829
mkilcommons@redeemer.ab.ca
Kathi Lalonde, Director of Curriculum and Instruction Elementary, 403-995-3047
klalonde@redeemer.ab.ca
Dennis Schneider, Secretary-Treasurer, 403-938-8071
dschneider@redeemer.ab.ca

Peace River: Holy Family Catholic Regional Division #37 (HFCRD)
10307 - 99 St., Peace River, AB T8S 1R5, Canada
Tel: 780-624-3956; *Fax:* 780-624-1154
Toll-Free: 800-285-8712
www.hfcrd.ab.ca
www.facebook.com/295804927180125
twitter.com/HFCRD37
Number of Schools: 9; *Enrollment:* 2000
Betty Turpin, Superintendent
betty.turpin@hfcrd.ab.ca
Jim Taplin, Assistant Superintendent of Inclusion and Student Support
jim.taplin@hfcrd.ab.ca
Cora Ostermeier, Assistant Superintendent of Human Resources and Learning
Cora.Ostermeier@hfcrd.ab.ca
Helen Diaz, Secretary-Treasurer
helen.diaz@hfcrd.ab.ca
Yvonne Dollevoet, Contact, Payroll and Human Resources
yvonne.dollevoet@hfcrd.ab.ca

Red Deer: Red Deer Catholic Regional Division #39
Montfort Centre
5210 - 61 St., Red Deer, AB T4N 6N8, Canada
Tel: 403-343-1055; *Fax:* 403-347-6410
info@rdcrs.ca
www.rdcrd.ab.ca
www.facebook.com/317027491725647
twitter.com/RDCatholic
Number of Schools: 18; *Enrollment:* 7500; *Number of Employees:* 350 teachers; 350 support staff
V. Paul Mason, Superintendent of Schools
Paul.Mason@rdcrs.ca
Dr. Paul Stewart, Associate Superintendent, Personnel
Paul.Stewart@rdcrs.ca
Ryan Ledene, Associate Superintendent, Faith Development & Division Supp.
Ryan.Ledene@rdcrs.ca
Kathleen Finnigan, Associate Superintendent, Inclusive Learning
Kathleen.Finnigan@rdcrs.ca
Dave Khatib, Division Principal of Inclusive Service
Dave.Khatib@rdcrs.ca
Ken Jaeger, Supervisor of Support Services
Ken.Jaeger@rdcrs.ca
Roderic M. Steeves, Secretary-Treasurer
Rod.Steeves@rdcrs.ca

Sherwood Park: Elk Island Catholic Separate Regional Division #41 (EICS)
160 Festival Way, Sherwood Park, AB T8A 5Z2, Canada
Tel: 780-467-8896; *Fax:* 780-467-5469
eics@eics.ab.ca
www.eics.ab.ca
Number of Schools: 16; *Grades:* K - 12; *Enrollment:* 5700
Shawn Haggarty, Acting Superintendent, Schools, 780-449-6444
Robert Simonowits, Assistant Superintendent, Learning Services, 780-449-6445
Hedi Klassen, Director of Financial Services, 780-449-6457
Brian Mittelsteadt, Acting Director, Human Resources, 780-449-6451
Bev Olexson, Learning Services Librarian, 780-449-7487

Spruce Grove: Evergreen Catholic Separate Regional Division No. 2
#110, 381 Grove Dr., Spruce Grove, AB T7X 2Y9, Canada
Tel: 780-962-5627; *Fax:* 780-962-4664
Toll-Free: 1-800-825-7152
www.ecsrd.ca
Number of Schools: 9; *Grades:* ECS - 12; *Enrollment:* 3412
Gerald Bernakevitch, Board Chair
Dr. Cindi Vaselenak, Superintendent
Michael Hauptman, Deputy Superintendent
Sime Fatovic, Director, Facilities & Technology
Sheila Shumate, Director, Student Services
Karen Koester, Coordinator, Religious Education
Jackie Gilbert, Secretary Treasurer

St Albert: Greater St. Albert Roman Catholic Separate School District #734
6 St. Vital Ave., St Albert, AB T8N 1K2, Canada
Tel: 780-459-7711; *Fax:* 780-458-3213
www.gsacrd.ab.ca
Number of Schools: 16 schools; 1 outreach location; *Grades:* K - 12; *Enrollment:* 6200; *Number of Employees:* 575 staff in schools; 31 staff in division operations
Rosaleen McEvoy, Chair
rmcevoy@gsacrd.ab.ca
Joan Crockett, Vice-Chair
jcrockett@gsacrd.ab.ca
David Keohane, Superintendent
dkeohane@gsacrd.ab.ca
Steve Bayus, Deputy Superintendent
sbayus@gsacrd.ab.ca
David Quick, Assistant Superintendent, Learning Services
dquick@gsacrd.ab.ca
Colleen McClure, Interim Associate Superintendent, Student Services
cmcclure@gsacrd.ab.ca
Calvin Wait, Director, Facilities
cwait@gsacrd.ab.ca
Lydia Yeomans, District Principal
lyeomans@gsacrd.ab.ca
Deb Schlag, Secretary-Treasurer
dschlag@gsacrd.ab.ca

Wainwright: East Central Alberta Catholic Separate School Regional Division #16
1018 - 1st Ave., Wainwright, AB T9W 1G9, Canada
Tel: 780-842-3992; *Fax:* 780-842-5322
reception@ecacs16.ab.ca
www.ecacs16.ab.ca
Number of Schools: 8; *Grades:* K - 12; *Enrollment:* 3000
Charles McCormack, Superintendent, Schools

Whitecourt: Living Waters Catholic Regional Division #42
P.O. Box 1949
4204 Kepler St., Whitecourt, AB T7S 1P6, Canada
Tel: 780-778-5666; *Fax:* 780-778-2727
Toll-Free: 888-434-7348
www.livingwaters.ab.ca
Number of Schools: 5; *Grades:* Pre.-12; *Enrollment:* 1800
Carol Lemay, Superintendent
Jo-Anne Lanctot, Deputy Superintendent

French

Calgary: Conseil scolaire du Sud de l'Alberta (CSSA)
Southern Francophone Education Region #4
Également connu sous le nom de: Conseil scolaire FrancoSud
Old Name: Conseil scolaire du Sud de l'Alberta
#230, rue 6940 Fisher SE, Calgary, AB T2H 0W3, Canada
Tél: 403-686-6998; *Téléc:* 403-686-2914
Ligne sans frais: 1-877-245-7686
infoconseil@csud.ca
www.conseildusud.ab.ca
Number of Schools: 9; *Grades:* K - 12; *Enrollment:* 2008
Jacqueline Lessard, Directrice générale, 403-686-6998
jacqueline.lessard@csud.ca
Éliane Collin, Directrice générale adjointe, ressources humaines, catholicit, 403-686-6998
eliane.collin@csud.ca
Daniel Therrien, Directeur général adjoint, services éducatifs, 403-686-6998
daniel.therrien@csud.ca
Christian Roux, Directeur des services éducatifs, 403-686-6998
christian.roux@csud.ca
Karina Labelle, Directrice des services financiers, 403-692-2029
karina.labelle@csud.ca

Edmonton: Conseil scolaire Centre-Nord
Greater North Central Francophone Education Region #2
#322, 8627, rue Marie-Anne-Gaboury (91 St.), Edmonton, AB T6C 3N1, Canada
Tél: 780-468-6440; *Téléc:* 780-440-1631
Ligne sans frais: 1-800-248-6886
conseil@centrenord.ab.ca
www.centrenord.ab.ca
www.facebook.com/conseil.centrenord
twitter.com/CSCNInfo
Number of Schools: 14; *Grades:* K - 12; *Enrollment:* 2800; *Number of Employees:* 350
Karen Doucet, Présidente
kdoucet@centrenord.ab.ca
Henrie Lemire, Directeur général
hlemire@centrenord.ab.ca
Nicole Bugeaud, Directrice générale adjointe
nbugeaud@centrenord.ab.ca
Josée Devaney, Secrétaire-trésorière
jdevaney@centrenord.ab.ca
Nathalie Gosselin, Préposée à la paie et aux finances
ngosselin@centrenord.ab.ca
Martine Ruest, Préposée aux ressources humaines
mruest@centrenord.ab.ca
Denise Lavallée, Coordonnatrice des communications
dlavallee@centrenord.ab.ca
Suzanne Amyotte, Préposée aux comptes payables / recevables
samyotte@centrenord.ab.ca

St Isidore: Conseil scolaire du Nord-Ouest #1
Northwest Francophone Education Region #1
P.O. Box 1220
#23, 3 av des Compagnons, St Isidore, AB T0H 3B0, Canada
Tél: 780-624-8855; *Téléc:* 780-624-8554
Ligne sans frais: 866-624-8855
conseil@csno.ab.ca
www.csno.ab.ca
www.facebook.com/367025016718824
twitter.com/CSNO
Number of Schools: 3; *Grades:* K - 12; *Enrollment:* 279
Marcel Lizotte, Directeur général
marcellizotte@csno.ab.ca
Brigitte Kropielnicki, Directrice générale adjointe
brigittekropielnicki@csno.ab.ca
Paulette Carrier, Trésorière générale/Entretien Santé et sécurité au travail
paulettecarrier@csno.ab.ca
Rachelle Bergeron, Coordonnatrice des communications et du marketing
rachellebergeron@csno.ab.ca
Madeleine Fortin-Bergeron, Secrétaire à la direction / Ressources humaines
madeleinefortin@csno.ab.ca
Lise St-Laurent, Préposée aux finances
lisestlaurent@csno.ab.ca
Claudette Boisvert, Technicienne en informatique
claudetteboisvert@csno.ab.ca

St-Paul: Conseil scolaire Centre-Est
East Central Francophone Education Region #3
P.O. Box 249
4617 - 50 Ave., St-Paul, AB T0A 3A0, Canada
Tél: 780-645-3888; *Téléc:* 780-645-2045
Ligne sans frais: 866-645-9556
centreest@centreest.ca
www.centreest.ca
Number of Schools: 5; *Grades:* Pre-12; *Enrollment:* 493
Marc Dumont, Directeur général
Josée Verreault, Directrice des services pédagogiques
Marc Labonté, Secrétaire-trésorier

First Nations

Brocket: Peigan Board of Education
P.O. Box 130
Brocket, AB T0K 0H0, Canada
Tel: 403-965-3910; *Fax:* 403-965-3713
Toll-Free: 877-965-3910
info@piikani.ca
www.piikani.ca
Grades: K - 12
Ruth Bellegarde, Director of Education
Director@piikani.ca
Casey Provost, Financial Administrator
Finance@piikani.ca

Brownvale: Duncan's First Nation Education
P.O. Box 148
Brownvale, AB T0H 0L0, Canada
Tel: 780-597-3777; *Fax:* 780-597-3920
Note: Duncan's First Nation is a small band situated southwest of Peace River, Alberta. A Child Development Centre offers daycare & a head start program. The head start program, for children from age three to five, includes a Cree language & cultural program. School buses transport Duncan's First Nation students to Berwyn, Grimshaw, & Peace River to enter a public school system.
Don Testawich, Chief, Duncan's First Nation

Chard: Chipewyan Prairie Dene First Nation Education Authority
General Delivery, Chard, AB T0P 1G0, Canada
Tel: 780-559-2259; *Fax:* 780-559-2213
cpdhs1@hughes.net
Number of Schools: 1; *Note:* Chipewyan Prairie First Nation operates the Chipewyan Prairie Dene High School.

Chateh: Dene Tha' First Nation Education Department
P.O. Box 120
Chateh, AB T0H 0S0, Canada
Tel: 780-321-3775; *Fax:* 780-321-3886
Toll-Free: 877-336-3842
www.denetha.ca/education/
Number of Schools: 1; *Grades:* KJ - 12; Dene language; *Enrollment:* 450; *Note:* The Dene Tha' First Nation Education Department oversees education, counselling, transportation, & accommodation for Dene Tha' First Nation band members. They operate the Dene Tha' Community School.
Jim Brown, Principal, 780-321-3940
jamesb@chateh-education.net
Virginia Alarcon, Vice-Prinicpal (Jr. High), 780-321-3940

Driftpile: Driftpile Band Education Authority
P.O. Box 240
Driftpile, AB T0G 0V0
Tel: 780-355-3615
www.driftpilecreenation.com
Note: The Driftpile Band operates the Driftpile First Nation Community School.

Duffield: Paul Band Education Authority
P.O. Box 89
Duffield, AB T0E 0N0, Canada
Tel: 780-892-2025; *Fax:* 780-892-2019
directorrbird@pfneducation.ca
www.paulfirstnation.com
Grades: K-12; *Note:* Paul Band Education Authority operates the Paul Band First Nation School.

Enoch: Kitaskinaw Education Authority
P.O. Box 90
Enoch, AB T7X 3Y3, Canada
Tel: 780-470-5657
Number of Schools: 1; *Grades:* Nursery - 9; *Note:* The Kitaskinaw Education Authority oversees education for the Enoch Cree Nation and operates the Kitaskinaw School.

Fort Vermilion: Tallcree Band Education Authority
P.O. Box 310
Fort Vermilion, AB T0H 1N0, Canada
Tel: 780-927-3803
www.tallcreefirstnation.ca
Number of Schools: 2; *Grades:* K - 6; *Enrollment:* 100; *Note:* Chief Tallcree North School & Chief Tallcree South School
Vic Dikaitis, Director, Education

Glenevis: Alexis Band Education Authority
P.O. Box 27
Glenevis, AB T0E 0X0, Canada
Tel: 780-967-5919
www.alexised.ca
Grades: Elementary - Junior Secondary; *Note:* The Alexis Band operates the Alexis Elementary Junior Senior High School and the Nikoodi Upgrading School.
Gloria Potts, Education Portfolio Holder / Chairwoman, 780-967-2225
gloria.potts@alexised.ca
Loretta Mustus-Duncan, Principal / Education Leader, 780-967-5919
loretta.mustus-duncan@alexised.ca
Elizabeth Letendre, Director of Heritage & Language, 780-967-4878
l.letendre@alexised.ca

Goodfish Lake: Whitefish Lake Education Authority
P.O. Box 271
Goodfish Lake, AB T0A 1R0, Canada
Tel: 780-636-7000; *Fax:* 780-636-3101
www.wfl128.ca/dept14.html
Grades: K-9
Ed Cardinal, Chair

Hobbema: Kisipatnahk School Society
P.O. Box 1290
Hobbema, AB T0C 1N0, Canada
Tel: 780-585-3978; *Fax:* 780-585-3799
Number of Schools: 1; *Grades:* Pre.-6; *Enrollment:* 177
Charmaine Roasting, Director of Education

Hobbema: Miyo Wahkohtowin Community Education Authority (MWE)
P.O. Box 248
Hobbema, AB T0C 1N0, Canada
Tel: 780-585-2118; *Fax:* 780-585-2116
www.miyo.ca
Number of Schools: 3; *Grades:* Pre.-9; *Note:* A First Nations-managed education system that operates three schools: Ermineskin Elementary, Junior Senior High, & Ehpewapahk schools for the Ermineskin Cree Nation in Alberta.
Brian Wildcat, Director, Education
brian_wildcat@miyo.ca
Sanila Mehal, Director, Student Services
sanila_mehal@miyo.ca
Peter Kerr, Financial Controller
peter_kerr@miyo.ca

Hobbema: Nipisihkopahk Education Authority (NEA)
P.O. Box 658
Hobbema, AB T0C 1N0, Canada
Tel: 780-585-2211; *Fax:* 780-585-3857
Toll-Free: 800-843-7359
www.scnea.com
www.facebook.com/groups/nea.info/
Number of Schools: 5; *Grades:* 1-12; *Enrollment:* 1000
Kevin Wells, Superintendent

Hythe: Horse Lake First Nation Education Authority
P.O. Box 303
Hythe, AB T0H 2C0
Tel: 780-356-2248; *Fax:* 780-356-3666
Note: Horse Lake First Nation operates the Horse Lake School.

John D'Or Prairie: Little Red River Board of Education
P.O. Box 30
John D'Or Prairie, AB T0H 3X0, Canada
Tel: 780-759-3912; *Fax:* 780-759-3780
www.lrrcn.ab.ca
Number of Schools: 3; *Grades:* Kindergarten - 12; Special Ed.; *Enrollment:* 1050; *Note:* The Little Red River Board of Education administers the provision of educational programming for First Nation students of the Little Red River Cree Nation. Cultural programming is part of the students' education. The Board also offers adult upgrading & trades training.
Gloria Cardinal, Director, Education
glocardinal@gmail.com
Leah Blesse, Financial Controller

Kehewin: **Kehewin Band Education Department**
P.O. Box 220
Kehewin, AB T0A 1C0
Tel: 780-826-3333; *Fax:* 780-826-2355
kehewincreenation.ca
Number of Schools: 2; *Note:* The Kehewin Band operates the Kehewin Community Education Centre.
Victor John, Education Manager
victor.john@kehewin.ca

Kinuso: **Swan River First Nation Education Authority**
P.O. Box 270
Kinuso, AB T0G 1K0
Tel: 780-775-3536; *Fax:* 780-775-3796
www.swanriverfirstnation.org
Number of Schools: 1
Yvonne Sound, Education Director

Lac La Biche: **Beaver Lake Education Authority**
P.O. Box 5000
Lac La Biche, AB T0A 2C0, Canada
Tel: 780-623-4549; *Fax:* 780-623-4523
amiskcommunityschool@yahoo.ca
www.beaverlakecreenation.ca
Other Information: Amisk Community School, Phone: 780-623-4548; Fax: 780-623-4659
Number of Schools: 1; *Grades:* Early Childhood Svs.-Jr. Secondary; *Note:* The Beaver Lake Education Authority operates the Amisk Community School. The school is led by a nine member management team which is supervised by the Beaver Lake Cree Nation Band Council Education Portfolio Holder.
Councillor Germaine Anderson, Beaver Lake Cree Nation Council Education Portfolio Holder

Lac La Biche: **Heart Lake Band #469 Education Authority**
P.O. Box 447
Lac La Biche, AB T0A 2C0
Tel: 780-623-2130; *Fax:* 780-623-3505
Note: Heart Lake Band #469 operates the Heart Lake Kohls School.

Morinville: **Alexander First Nation Education Authority**
P.O. Box 3449
Morinville, AB T8R 1S3, Canada
Tel: 780-939-3551; *Fax:* 780-939-3523
education@alexanderfn.com
alexanderfn.com/index.php/departments/education
Note: The Alexander First Nation Education Authority operates the Kipohtakaw Education Centre.
Jody Kootenay, Director of Education, 780-939-3551, ext. 265
jodyarcand@gmail.com
Verna Arcand, Assistant Director of Education, 780-939-3551, ext. 261
vbarcand@hotmail.com

Morley: **Stoney Education Authority**
P.O. Box 238
Morley, AB T0L 1N0, Canada
Tel: 403-881-2743; *Fax:* 403-881-4252
sites.google.com/a/stoneyeducation.ca/schools/
Number of Schools: 3; *Grades:* K - 12; Stoney language; *Enrollment:* 1100; *Note:* The Stoney Education Authority, located west of Calgary, Alberta, provides education to members of the Stoney Nakoda First Nation. Education includes cultural programs.
Nadeem Altaf, Administrator, Education, 403-881-2776

Red Earth Creek: **Loon River First Nation Education Authority**
P.O. Box 189
Red Earth Creek, AB T0G 1X0
Tel: 780-649-3883; *Fax:* 780-649-3873
www.loonriver.net/education.html
Note: The Loon River First Nation operates the Clarence Jaycox School.

Rocky Mountain House: **Sunchild First Nation Band Education Authority**
P.O. Box 1149
Rocky Mountain House, AB T4T 1A8, Canada
Tel: 403-989-3476
Number of Schools: 1; *Grades:* K - 12
Caroline Bigchild, Director, Education
girly_bigchild@yahoo.ca

Saddle Lake: **Saddle Lake Education Authority**
P.O. Box 130
Saddle Lake, AB T0A 3T0, Canada
Tel: 780-726-7609; *Fax:* 780-726-4069
Toll-Free: 800-668-0243
www.saddlelake.ca
Number of Schools: 4; *Grades:* 1-12
Debra Cardinal, Superintendent of Schools
dcardinal@saddlelake.ca

Siksika: **Siksika Board of Education**
P.O. Box 1099
Siksika, AB T0J 3W0, Canada
Tel: 403-734-5220; *Fax:* 403-734-2505
siksikaeducation.ca
Number of Schools: 4; *Grades:* K - 12
Daphne McHugh, Superintendent
daphnem@siksikaeducation.ca
Esther Healy, Assistant Superintendent
estherh@siksikaeducation.ca
Darren Pietrobono, Treasurer, 403-734-4027
pietrobonod@siksikaboardofeducation.com

Stand Off: **Kainai Board of Education**
P.O. Box 240
Stand Off, AB T0L 1Y0, Canada
Tel: 403-737-3966; *Fax:* 403-737-2361
kainaied.ca
Number of Schools: 5; *Grades:* 7-12
Richard Fox, Superintendent
Dr. Morris Many Fingers, Deputy Superintendent (Finance/Human Resources)

Tsuu T'ina Sarcee: **Tsuu T'ina Nation Board of Education**
#250, 9911 Chiila Blvd. SW, Tsuu T'ina Sarcee, AB T2W 6H6, Canada
Tel: 403-238-5484
www.tsuutina.ca
Number of Schools: 3; *Grades:* K4 - 12; Adult Upgrading; *Enrollment:* 299; *Note:* (Chiila Elementary School; Tsuu T'ina Junior Senior High School; & Tsuu T'ina Bullhead Adult Education Centre)

Valleyview: **Sturgeon Lake First Nation, Band #154, Education Authority**
P.O. Box 5
Valleyview, AB T0H 3N0, Canada
Tel: 780-524-4590
Number of Schools: 1; *Grades:* K - 12; *Note:* Sturgeon Lake First Nation Band #154 operates the Sturgeon Lake School.

Wabasca: **Bigstone Education Authority Society**
P.O. Box 870
Wabasca, AB T0G 2K0, Canada
Tel: 780-891-3825; *Toll-Free:* 1-877-458-2447
www.bigstone.ca/content/bigstone-education
Number of Schools: 1; *Grades:* Elementary; *Enrollment:* 247; *Note:* Bigstone Education Authority Society operates the Bigstone Community School.
P. Ray Peters, Director, Education
ray.peters@bigstone.ca
Priscilla Auger, Counsellor, Post-Secondary Education, 877-458-2447
priscilla.auger@bigstone.ca

Schools: Specialized

Charter

Androssan: **New Horizons School**
53145 Range Rd., Androssan, AB T8E 2M8, Canada
Tel: 780-467-6409; *Fax:* 780-417-1786
administration@newhorizons.ab.ca
www.newhorizons.ab.ca
Grades: K - 9; *Enrollment:* 200
Don Falk, Superintendent

Calgary: **Almadina Language Charter Academy (ALCA)**
#210, 1829 - 54 St. SE, Calgary, AB T2B 1N5, Canada
Tel: 403-543-5078; *Fax:* 403-543-5079
www.esl-almadina.com
Number of Schools: 2; *Grades:* ECS - 9; *Enrollment:* 600
Haytham Ghouriri, Board Chair
hghouriri@esl-almadina.com
Yvonne DePeel, Superintendent, 403-543-5078
ydepeel@esl-almadina.com
Suzanne Bedard, Secretary Treasurer, 403-543-5078

Calgary: **Calgary Arts Academy Society (CAA)**
4931 Grove Hill Rd. SW, Calgary, AB T3E 4G4, Canada
Tel: 403-532-3020; *Fax:* 403-217-0965
info@calgaryartsacademy.com
www.calgaryartsacademy.com
www.facebook.com/20345525638
Number of Schools: 2; *Grades:* K - 9; *Enrollment:* 279
Dale Erickson, Superintendent
derickson@calgaryartsacademy.com
Jan Jordan, Secretary-Treasurer
jjordan@calgaryartsacademy.com
Kevin Loftus, Communications / Registrar
kloftus@calgaryartsacademy.com

Calgary: **Calgary Girls' School (CGS)**
#203, 610 - 70th Ave. SE, Calgary, AB T2H 2J6, Canada
Tel: 403-252-0702; *Fax:* 403-252-0717
www.calgarygirlsschool.com
twitter.com/CalGirlsSchool
Number of Schools: 2; *Grades:* 4-9; *Enrollment:* 600
Dianne McBeth, Superintendent
dianne.mcbeth@calgarygirlsschool.com
Wendy Juergens, Secretary Treasurer
Wendy.Juergens@calgarygirlsschool.com
Debbie Malone, Library Technologist
Debbie.Malone@calgarygirlsschool.com

Calgary: **Connect Charter School (CCS)**
5915 Lewis Dr. SW, Calgary, AB T3E 5Z4
Tel: 403-282-2890; *Fax:* 403-282-2896
www.connectcharter.ca
www.facebook.com/connectcharter
twitter.com/connectcharter
www.youtube.com/channel/UCPNG2xEVeXrAqPpiuTFKCGQ
Grades: 4-9; *Enrollment:* 600; *Number of Employees:* 34 teaching staff
Garry McKinnon, Superintendent, 403-282-2890, ext. 232
garry.m@connectcharter.ca
Darrell Lonsberry, Principal, 403-282-2890, ext. 122
darrell.l@connectcharter.ca
Phil Butterfield, Assistant Principal, 403-282-2890, ext. 116
phil.b@connectcharter.ca
Scott Petronech, Assistant Principal & Educational Technologist
scott.p@connectcharter.ca
Myra Penberthy, Secretary-Treasurer
myra.p@connectcharter.ca
Michelle Hodgson, Library Assistant and Outdoor Education Coordinator
michelle.h@connectcharter.ca

Calgary: **Foundations for the Future Charter Academy (FFCA)**
FFCA Central Office
#240, 688 Heritage Dr. SE, Calgary, AB T2H 1M6
Tel: 403-520-3206; *Fax:* 403-520-3209
board@ffca-calgary.com
www.ffca-calgary.com
Number of Schools: 7; *Grades:* K - 12
Jay Pritchard, Superintendent
Rick Byers, Director, Facilities, 403-520-3206, ext. 157
Judy Gray, Coordinator, School Improvement, 403-520-3206, ext. 152
John Deines, Coordinator, Instruction, 403-520-3206, ext. 162

Calgary: **Westmount Charter School Society**
728 - 32 St. NW, Calgary, AB T2N 2V9, Canada
Tel: 403-217-3707; *Fax:* 403-249-3422
admin@westmountcharter.com
www.westmountcharter.com
Number of Schools: 2; *Grades:* K-12; *Enrollment:* 880
Joe Frank, Superintendent, 403-217-3707, ext. 1023
joe.frank@westmountcharter.com
Johnathan Liu, Secretary-Treasurer, 403-217-3707, ext. 1020
johnathan.liu@westmountcharter.com

Edmonton: **Aurora Charter School**
12245 - 131 St., Edmonton, AB T5L 1M8
Tel: 780-454-1855; *Fax:* 780-454-8104
aurorasc@auroraschool.com
www.auroraschool.com
Grades: K - 9; *Enrollment:* 600
Don Wilson, Board Chair
Dale Bischoff, Superintendent
dbischoff@auroraschool.com
Ian Gray, Principal
igray@auroraschool.com
Janet Rockwood, Assistant Principal
jrockwood@auroraschool.com
Georgia Foster, Registrar
gfoster@auroraschool.com
Kathy Holubitsky, Learning Resources
kholubitsky@auroraschool.com

Edmonton: Boyle Street Education Centre (BSEC)
10312 - 105 Ave., Edmonton, AB T5J 1E6, Canada
Tel: 780-428-1420; *Fax:* 780-429-1428
info@bsec.ab.ca
www.bsec.ab.ca
www.facebook.com/BoyleStreedEducationCentre
twitter.com/BoyleStreetEd
www.youtube.com/user/BoyleStreetEd
Grades: 7-12; *Enrollment:* 105

Edmonton: Suzuki Charter School Society
10720 - 54 St., Edmonton, AB T6A 2H9
Tel: 780-468-2598; *Fax:* 780-463-8630
www.suzukischool.ca
Grades: Preschool - 6; *Note:* The charter school provides academics, enriched with music based on the Suzuki Approach.
Lee Lucente, Superintendent
lucentel@suzukischool.ca
Karen Spencer, Principal
spencerk@suzukischool.ca
Dale Szalacsi, Assistant Principal
szalacsid@suzukischool.ca
Heather Christison, Secretary-Treasurer
christison@suzukischool.ca
Allison Elsdon, Library Technician

Medicine Hat: Centre for Academic & Personal Excellence Institute (CAPE)
830A Balmoral St. SE, Medicine Hat, AB T1A 0W9, Canada
Tel: 403-528-2983; *Fax:* 403-528-3048
tdininno@capeisgreat.org
www.capeisgreat.org
www.facebook.com/107913172565986
Grades: K - 8; *Enrollment:* 135
Teresa Di Ninno, Superintendant, 403-528-2983
Riaan Swiegers, Chair

Stony Plain: Mother Earth's Children's Charter School Society (MECCS)
P.O. Box 11
Site 504, RR#5, Stony Plain, AB T7Z 1X5, Canada
Tel: 780-892-7531; *Fax:* 780-848-2395
admin@meccs.org
www.meccs.org
Grades: K - 9
Ed Wittchen, Superintendent
ed.wittchen@telus.net
Anita LeMoignan, Secretary/Treasurer
alemoignan@meccs.org

Valhalla Centre: Valhalla School Foundation
Also known as: Valhalla Community School
P.O. Box 148
9702 - 100 Ave., Valhalla Centre, AB T0H 3M0, Canada
Tel: 780-356-2370; *Fax:* 780-356-2789
info@valhallacommunityschool.ca
www.valhallacommunityschool.ca
Grades: K - 9

First Nations

Atikameg: Whitefish Lake First Nation School
General Delivery, Atikameg, AB T0G 0C0
Tel: 780-767-3797

Brocket: Napi's Playground Elementary School (NPES)
P.O. Box 10
Brocket, AB T0K 0H0
Tel: 403-965-2121; *Fax:* 403-965-2054
www.piikani.ca
Grades: K - 6; *Number of Employees:* 15
Rudy Schuh, Principal
Principal@piikani.ca

Brocket: Piikani Nation Secondary School
P.O. Box 10
Brocket, AB T0K 0H0
Tel: 403-965-2121; *Fax:* 403-965-2054
www.piikani.ca
Grades: 7 - 12
Rudy Schuh, Principal
Principal@piikani.ca

Cadotte Lake: Woodland Cree First Nation Cadotte Lake School
General Delivery, Cadotte Lake, AB T0H 0N0
Tel: 780-629-3767
Grades: K - 12

Cardston: Kainai High School
P.O. Box 2640
Cardston, AB T0K 0K0
Tel: 403-737-3963; *Fax:* 403-737-2100
khs.kainaied.ca
Annette Bruised Head, Principal

Cardston: Tatsikiisaapo'p Middle School
P.O. Box 250
Cardston, AB T0K OKO
Tel: 403-737-2846
tms.kainaied.ca
Grades: 6 - 8
Ramona Big Head, Principal

Chard: Chipewyan Prairie Dene High School
General Delivery, Chard, AB T0P 1G0
Tel: 780-559-2478

Chateh: Dene Tha' Community School (DTCS)
P.O. Box 30
Chateh, AB T0H 0S0
Tel: 780-321-3940; *Fax:* 780-321-3800
Toll-Free: 877-336-3842
reception@chateh-education.net
www.denetha.ca/education/dtcs/
Grades: K - 10; Dene language; *Enrollment:* 150; *Note:* Dene Tha' Community School provides education that follows Alberta's kindergarten to grade 10 curriculum, as well as programs such as an early literacy program, a special education program, & Dene language & culture programs.
Jim Brown, Principal, 780-321-3940
jamesb@chateh-education.net
Virginia Alarcon, Vice-Principal, Junior High, 780-321-3940

Cold Lake: LeGeoff School
P.O. Box 1769
Cold Lake, AB T9M 1P4
Tel: 780-594-7183; *Fax:* 780-594-3577
clfns.com
Grades: K-9; *Enrollment:* 96; *Number of Employees:* 13; *Note:* LeGeoff School is federally administered & funded by the Department of Indian Affairs. The school employs seven federally funded teachers & six Cold Lake First Nations funded positions.
Maryanne Bushore, Principal, 780-594-3733
maryannebushore@kinusoo.ca

Driftpile: Driftpile Community School
P.O. Box 240
Driftpile, AB T0G 0V0, Canada
Tel: 780-355-3615; *Fax:* 780-355-2135
www.driftpilecreenation.com
Grades: K - 8; Cree language; *Enrollment:* 75; *Note:* Driftpile Community School offers a full academic program, as well as a Cree language & cultural program with traditional music, folklore, & crafts.
Daisy McGee, Principal
Josephine Willier, Secretary
Janice Chalifoux, Family School Wellness Worker
Leonard Isadore, Contact, Cultural Appreciation

Duffield: Paul Band First Nation School
P.O. Box 63
Duffield, AB T0E 0N0
Tel: 780-892-2675
www.paulfirstnation.com
Ruby Bird, Principal, 780-892-2025
rubybird@paulfirstnation.com

Enilda: Sucker Creek K4-K5 School
P.O. Box 65
Enilda, AB T0G 0W0
Tel: 780-523-5593

Enoch: Kitaskinaw School
P.O. Box 90
Enoch, AB T7X 3Y3
Tel: 780-470-5657; *Fax:* 780-470-5687
www.kitaskinaw.com
Grades: Nursery - 9; *Note:* Kitaskinaw School is part of the Kitaskinaw Education Authority. The school educates members of the Enoch Cree Nation.
Phyllis Cardinal, Principal
phyllis.cardinal@kitaskinaw.com

Fort Vermillion: Chief Tallcree School North
P.O. Box 310
Fort Vermillion, AB T0H 1N0
Tel: 780-927-4381

Fort Vermillion: Chief Tallcree School South
P.O. Box 310
Fort Vermillion, AB T0H 1N0
Tel: 780-927-3803

Fox Lake: Jean Baptiste Sewepagaham School
P.O. Box 270
Fox Lake, AB TOH 1R0
Tel: 780-659-3820
Grades: K - 12; Cree language; *Enrollment:* 600; *Note:* Jean Baptiste Sewepagaham School is one of three schools in the Little Red River Board of Education. The school serves members of the Little Red River Cree Nation, located approximately 125 kilometres east of High Level, Alberta.

Frog Lake: Chief Napeweaw Comprehensive School
General Delivery, Frog Lake, AB T0A 1M0, Canada
Tel: 780-943-3918; *Fax:* 780-943-2336
www.froglake.ca/education_authority.html
Grades: K - 12; *Enrollment:* 300
Sherri O'Dell, Principal
sherriodell@froglake.ca

Garden River: Sister Gloria School
P.O. Box 90
Garden River, AB T0H 4G0
Tel: 780-659-3644; *Fax:* 780-659-3890
Note: The Little Red River Board of Education consists of three schools, including Sister Gloria School. Sister Gloria School provides education to First Nation students of the Little Red River Cree Nation. The Alberta community is situated approximately 125 kilometres east of High Level.
Garry Wilson, Principal
wilson_garry@hotmail.com

Glenevis: Alexis Elementary Junior Senior High School
P.O. Box 27
Glenevis, AB T0E 0X0
Tel: 780-967-5919; *Fax:* 780-967-2671
www.alexised.ca/alexis-school-%28es-jr-sr%29.aspx
Loretta Mustus-Duncan, Principal

Glenevis: Nikoodi Upgrading School
P.O. Box 135
Glenevis, AB T0E 0X0
Tel: 780-967-4878; *Fax:* 780-967-4999

Goodfish Lake: Pakan Elementary and Junior High School
P.O. Box 274
Goodfish Lake, AB T0A 1R0
Tel: 780-636-2525
www.wfl128.ca
Grades: K - 9
Duane Manderscheid, Principal

Hobbema: Kisipatnahk School
P.O. Box 1290
Hobbema, AB T0C 1N0
Tel: 780-585-0035; *Fax:* 780-585-0039
school@lbschool.com
lbschool.com
www.facebook.com/kisipatnahkschool.louisbull
Grades: K - 9; *Enrollment:* 212; *Number of Employees:* 28; *Note:* The School is a Cree Cultural School offering instruction in Maskwacis Cree language.
Patricia Marshall, Principal

Hobbema: Maskwacis Outreach School
P.O. Box 658
Hobbema, AB T0C 1N0
Tel: 780-585-3076; *Fax:* 780-585-3792
www2.scnea.com/academy/
Enrollment: 139; *Note:* This four nations joint initiative is being co-administered by Samson Cree Nation (NEA) and Ermineskin Cree Nation (MWE) on behalf of the four Hobbema communities.
Sharon Seright, Principal, 780-585-3076
sseright@scnea.com

Hobbema: Meskanahk Ka-Nipa-Wit School
Also known as: Montana School
P.O. Box 129
Hobbema, AB T0C 1N0, Canada
Tel: 780-585-2799; *Fax:* 780-585-2264
www.montana-education.ca
Grades: K-9; *Enrollment:* 100
Butch French, Principal
butch@montana-education.ab.ca

Hythe: Horse Lake School
P.O. Box 303
Hythe, AB T0H 2C0
Tel: 780-356-3151

John D'Or Prairie: **John D'Or Prairie School**
P.O. Box 120
John D'Or Prairie, AB T0H 3X0
Tel: 780-759-3772
Note: John D'Or Prairie School is part of the Little Red River Board of Education. Education is provided to the Little Red River Cree Nation, located approximately 865 kilometres north of Edmonton, Alberta.

Kehewin: **Kehewin Community Education Centre**
P.O. Box 30
Kehewin, AB T0A 1C0, Canada
Tel: 780-826-6200; *Fax:* 780-826-5919
kehewincreenation.ca
Grades: K-12
Linda Gadwa, Principal
lrgadwa@yahoo.ca

Kinuso: **Swan River First Nation School**
P.O. Box 120
Kinuso, AB T0G 1K0
Tel: 780-775-2177; *Fax:* 780-775-2155
www.swanriverfirstnation.org
Grades: 7 - 12; *Enrollment:* 40; *Number of Employees:* 7; *Note:* The Swan River First Nation School operates on the Swan River First Nation Reserve in Kinuso, Alberta.

Lac La Biche: **Amisk Community School**
P.O. Box 5000
Lac La Biche, AB T0A 2C0
Tel: 780-623-4548; *Fax:* 780-623-4659
www.beaverlakecreenation.ca
Grades: Early Childhood Svs.-Jr. Secondary; *Note:* Operated by the Beaver Lake Education Authority, the Amisk Community School provides education to the Beaver Lake Cree Nation.

Lac La Biche: **Heart Lake Kohls School**
P.O. Box 447
Lac La Biche, AB T0A 2C0, Canada
Tel: 780-623-2330; *Fax:* 780-623-3505
Grades: Pre.K-12
David Keffer, Principal
david.keffer@hlks.org

Longview: **Chief Jacob Bearspaw School**
P.O. Box 116
100 Center St. SW, Longview, AB T0L 1H0
Tel: 403-558-2480; *Fax:* 403-558-3618
Note: Chief Jacob Bearspaw School, located on the Eden Valley Reserve in Alberta, is part of the Stoney Education Authority.
Bill Shade, Principal

Mameo Beach: **Mimiw-Sakahikan School**
P.O. Box 154
Mameo Beach, AB T0C 1X0
Tel: 780-586-3808; *Fax:* 780-586-3809
www.scnea.com/MSS/
Grades: K - 6
Dianne Crane, Principal

Maskwacis: **Ermineskin Ehpewapahk Alternate School**
P.O. Box 360
Maskwacis, AB T0C 1N0
Tel: 780-585-2202; *Fax:* 780-585-2204
www.miyo.ca/alternate/
Grades: 13-19 yrs old
Wendy Solland, Principal

Maskwacis: **Ermineskin Elementary School**
P.O. Box 420
Maskwacis, AB T0C 1N0
Tel: 780-585-3760; *Fax:* 780-585-2001
www.miyo.ca/elementary/
www.facebook.com/ermineskinelementaryschool/
Grades: K - 6
Debbie Stockdale, Principal
debbie_stockdale@miyo.ca

Maskwacis: **Ermineskin Junior Senior High School**
P.O. Box 249
Maskwacis, AB T0C 1N0
Tel: 780-585-3931; *Fax:* 780-585-2023
www.miyo.ca/juniorhigh/
Grades: 7 - 12; *Enrollment:* 318; *Number of Employees:* 45
Keith MacQuarrie, Principal
Keith_Macquarrie@miyo.ca

Maskwacis: **Nipishkopahk Primary School**
P.O. Box 1350
Maskwacis, AB T0C 1N0
Tel: 780-585-2075; *Fax:* 780-585-2028
www.scnea.com/NPS/
Grades: K - 2
Kathy Kiss, Principal

Maskwacis: **Nipisihkopahk Elementary School**
P.O. Box 369
Maskwacis, AB T0C 1N0
Tel: 780-585-2244; *Fax:* 780-585-2084
www.scnea.com/NES/
Grades: 3 - 7; *Enrollment:* 247
Tracy Larocque, Principal
tlarocque@scnea.com

Maskwacis: **Nipisihkopahk Secondary School**
P.O. Box 990
Maskwacis, AB T0C 1N0
Tel: 780-585-4449; *Fax:* 780-585-2259
www.scnea.com/NSS/
Grades: 8 - 12

Morinville: **Kipohtakaw Education Centre (KEC)**
P.O. Box 3449
Morinville, AB T8R 1S3
Tel: 780-939-3868; *Fax:* 780-939-3991
Grades: K5 - 12
Gloria Cardinal, Principal

Morley: **Morley Community School**
P.O. Box 238
Morley, Morley, AB T0L 1N0
Tel: 403-881-2755; *Fax:* 403-881-2793
sites.google.com/a/stoneyeducation.ca/morley-community-school
Grades: 6 - 12; *Note:* The Stoney Education Authority oversees the Morley Community School. The First Nations school serves members of the Nakoda First Nation, situated west of Calgary, Alberta.

Red Earth Creek: **Clarence Jaycox School**
Bag #4, Red Earth Creek, AB T0G 1X0
Tel: 780-649-2942; *Fax:* 780-649-2714
www.clarencejaycoxschool.com
Grades: K - 12
LaVina Gillespie, Principal

Rocky Mountain House: **O'Chiese Education Authority**
P.O. Box 337
Rocky Mountain House, AB T4T 1A3, Canada
Tel: 403-989-3911; *Fax:* 403-989-2122
ochiese.ca/education/education
Grades: K-12
Lara Jollymore, Principal
lara.jollymore@ochieseeducation.ca

Rocky Mountain House: **O'Chiese First Nation School**
P.O. Box 337
Rocky Mountain House, AB T4T 1A3
Tel: 403-989-3911; *Fax:* 403-989-2122
www.ochiese.ca/Education/Education/
Kathy Breaker, Principal

Rocky Mountain House: **Sunchild First Nation School**
P.O. Box 1149
Rocky Mountain House, AB T4T 1A8
Tel: 403-989-3476; *Fax:* 403-989-3614
www.sunchildschool.com
Grades: K - 12; *Enrollment:* 400; *Number of Employees:* 50; *Note:* The Sunchild First Nation School is part of the Sunchild First Nation Band Education Authority.
Susan Collicutt, Principal
collicutts@yahoo.ca
David Malthouse, Vice-Principal
malthoused@sunchildschool.com

Saddle Lake: **Kehew Asiniy School**
P.O. Box 159
Saddle Lake, AB T0A 3T0, Canada
Tel: 780-726-2000; *Fax:* 780-726-2002
www.saddlelake.ca
Florence Quinn, Principal

Saddle Lake: **Onchaminahos School**
P.O. Box 70
Saddle Lake, AB T0A 3T0
Tel: 780-726-3730; *Fax:* 780-726-4141
www.saddlelake.ca
Enrollment: 358; *Number of Employees:* 42
Gloria McGilvery, Principal

Siksika: **Chief Old Sun Elementary School**
P.O. Box 1070
Siksika, AB T0J 3W0
Tel: 403-734-5300; *Fax:* 403-734-3529
coss@siksikaeducation.org
www.siksikaboardofeducation.com

Siksika: **Crowfoot School**
P.O. Box 1280
Siksika, AB T0J 3W0
Tel: 403-734-5320
www.siksikaboardofeducation.com
Enrollment: 180; *Number of Employees:* 26
Geraldine Red Gun, Principal

Siksika: **Siksika Nation High School**
P.O. Box 1220
Siksika, AB T0J 3W0
Tel: 403-734-5400
www.siksikaboardofeducation.com

Stand Off: **Aahsaopi Elementary School**
P.O. Box 240
Stand Off, AB T0L 1Y0
Tel: 403-737-3808
aes.kainaied.ca
Grades: K - 5; *Number of Employees:* 28
Lauretta Many Bears, Principal, 403-737-3808
Billy Yellow Horn, Librarian

Stand Off: **Blood Tribe Youth Ranch Alternate High School**
P.O. Box 240
Stand Off, AB T0L 1Y0
Tel: 403-737-2257; *Fax:* 403-737-3520

Stand Off: **Kainai Adolescent Treatment Center**
P.O. Box 120
Stand Off, AB T0L 1Y0
Tel: 403-653-3315; *Fax:* 403-653-3338
www.katcenter.ca
Grades: 12-17 yrs

Stand Off: **Kainai Alternate Academy**
P.O. Box 419
Stand Off, AB T0L 1Y0
Tel: 403-737-3288
kaa.kainaied.ca
Eric Spencer, Principal, 403-737-3288

Stand Off: **Saipoyi Community School**
General Delivery, Stand Off, AB T0L 1Y0
Tel: 403-737-3772
scs.kainaied.ca
Grades: K - 5
Marie Shade, Principal

Tsuu T'ina: **Tsuu T'ina Bullhead Adult Education Centre (BAEC)**
#250 - 9911 Chilla Blvd., Tsuu T'ina, AB T2W 6H6
Tel: 403-974-1400; *Fax:* 409-974-1449
www.tsuutina.ca

Tsuu T'ina Sarcee: **Chiila Elementary School**
#250, 991 Chiila Blvd. SW, Tsuu T'ina Sarcee, AB T2W 6H6
Tel: 403-238-5484
www.tsuutina.ca
Grades: K4 - 5; *Note:* Chiila Elementary School is part of the Tsuu T'ina Nation Board of Education.

Tsuu T'ina Sarcee: **Tsuu T'ina Junior Senior High School**
#250, 991 Chiila Blvd. SW, Tsuu T'ina Sarcee, AB T2W 6H6
Tel: 403-251-9555; *Fax:* 403-251-9833
www.tsuutina.ca
Grades: 6 - 12; *Note:* The Tsuu T'ina Nation Board of Education oversees the operations of the Tsuu T'ina Junior Senior High School.

Valleyview: **Sturgeon Lake School**
Bag 5, Valleyview, AB T0H 3N0
Tel: 780-524-4590; *Fax:* 780-524-3696
www.sturgeonlake.ca/sturgeon_lake_school.html
Grades: K - 12; *Enrollment:* 230; *Note:* The Sturgeon Lake School is part of the Sturgeon Lake First Nation, Band #154, Education Authority. The First Nation school serves the Sturgeon Lake Cree Nation.

Wabasca: **Bigstone Cree Nation Community School Oski Pasikoniwew Kamik**
P.O. Box 930
Wabasca, AB T0G 2K0
Tel: 780-891-3830; *Fax:* 780-891-3831
www.bigstone.ca/content/oski-pasikoniwew-kamik-school

Grades: Preschool - 6; *Enrollment:* 247; *Note:* The Bigstone Community School operates under the direction of the Bigstone Cree Nation Education Authority. The school strives to maintain traditional values as its educational foundation.

Hearing Impaired

Edmonton: **Alberta School for the Deaf (ASD)**
6240 - 113 St., Edmonton, AB T6H 3L2
Fax: 780-436-0385
abschdeaf@epsb.ca
asd.epsb.ca
TTY: 780-439-3323
Grades: 1-12; *Note:* Serves Deaf and Hard of Hearing students of Edmonton Public Schools, across Alberta and beyond.
Joanne Aldridge, Principal
Sandra Mason, Supervisor
Sherry Cote, Business Manager

Distance Education

Didsbury: **Northstar Academy Canada**
P.O. Box 2220
#103, 1001- 20th Ave., Didsbury, AB T0M 0W0
Tel: 403-335-9587; *Fax:* 403-335-9513
Toll-Free: 877-335-1171
office@nsaschool.ca
www.northstaracademycanada.org
Grades: Secondary; *Note:* NorthStar Academy Canada is a Canadian Evangelical Christian community of learners working and studying in an online context.

Schools: Independent & Private

Public

Edmonton: **Kate Chegwin School**
3119 - 48 St., Edmonton, AB T6L 6P5
Tel: 780-469-0470; *Fax:* 780-463-7844
kchegwin@epsb.ca
katechegwin.epsb.ca
Grades: Jr. High
John Holmes, Principal
john.holmes@epsb.ca

Faith-Based

Airdrie: **Airdrie Koinonia Christian School (AKCS)**
77 Gateway Dr., Airdrie, AB T4B 0J6, Canada
Tel: 403-948-5100; *Fax:* 403-948-5563
www.akcs.com
Grades: K-12; *Enrollment:* 300; *Number of Employees:* 36
Earl Driedger, Principal
Dave Kenney, Business Administrator

Bow Island: **Cherry Coulee Christian Academy (CCCA)**
P.O. Box 10370
Bow Island, AB T0K 0G0, Canada
Tel: 403-545-2107; *Fax:* 403-545-2944
cherrycoulee@shaw.ca
www.cherrycoulee.ca
Grades: K-9
Mike Daniels, Principal

Brant: **Brant Christian School**
P.O. Box 130
Brant, AB T0L 0L0, Canada
Tel: 403-684-3752; *Fax:* 403-684-3894
brantchristianschool.ca
Grades: K - 12
Rob Cowie, Principal
Susan McLean, Librarian

Brooks: **Newell Christian School (NCS)**
P.O. Box 100
Hwy. 544, Junction #36, Brooks, AB T1R 1B2, Canada
Tel: 403-378-4448; *Fax:* 403-378-3991
ncsadmin@newellchristianschool.com
www.newellchristianschool.com
Grades: K - 9; *Note:* The Alberta curriculum is taught from a Christian perspective.
Theresa Nagal, Principal

Calgary: **Bearspaw Christian School (BCS)**
15001 - 69 St. NW, Calgary, AB T3R 1C5, Canada
Tel: 403-295-2566; *Fax:* 403-275-8170
info@bearspawschool.com
www.bearspawschool.com
www.facebook.com/BearspawChristianSchool
twitter.com/BearspawCSchool
Grades: JK - 12; *Enrollment:* 600; *Number of Employees:* 90
Kelly Blake, President & CEO
kblake@bearspawschool.com
Judy Huffman, Principal
jhuffman@bearspawschool.com
Jennifer Lockhart, Vice Principal, Elementary
jlockhart@bearspawschool.com
Lara Melashenko, Vice Principal, Secondary
lmelashenko@bearspawschool.com

Calgary: **Bethel Christian Academy**
2220 - 39th Ave. NE, Calgary, AB T2E 5T4, Canada
Tel: 403-735-3335
tbetts@encountergod.org
www.encountergod.org
Grades: Kindergarten - 12
Terry Denney, Principal

Calgary: **Calgary Christian School (CCS)**
North Bldg.
5029 - 26th Ave. SW, Calgary, AB T3E 0R5, Canada
Tel: 403-242-2896; *Fax:* 403-242-6682
CalgaryChristianSchool@csce.net
www.calgarychristianschool.com
www.facebook.com/calgarychristianschool
Grades: Preschool - 12; *Enrollment:* 825; *Note:* Calgary Christian School has an elementary campus & a secondary campus.
Doug MacLachlan, Interim Executive Director
Harry Fritschy, Principal, Elementary
Jason Kupery, Principal, Secondary
Monique Wagner, Vice Principal, Elementary
Shannon Dean, Vice Principal, Secondary

Calgary: **Eastside Christian Academy (ECA)**
1320 Abbeydale Dr. SE, Calgary, AB T2A 7L8
Tel: 403-569-1003; *Fax:* 403-569-7557
admin@ecaab.ca
eastsidechristianacademy.ca
www.facebook.com/122526574470804
Number of Schools: 1; *Grades:* K - 9
Frank Moody, Principal
drmoody52@hotmail.com
Marie Poulin, Career Counsellor
mpoulin@shaw.ca

Calgary: **Glenmore Christian Academy (GCA)**
16520 - 24th St., Calgary, AB T2Y 4W2, Canada
Tel: 403-254-9050; *Fax:* 403-256-9695
www.gcaschool.ca
www.facebook.com/glenmorechristianacademyalumnae
twitter.com/gcacalgary
Grades: Pre.-9; Special Ed.
Derrick Mohamed, Principal, Junior High
Gwen Uittenbosch, Principal, Elementary

Calgary: **Heritage Christian Academy**
2003 McKnight Blvd. NE, Calgary, AB T2E 6L2, Canada
Tel: 403-219-3201; *Fax:* 403-219-3210
ibelong@hcacalgary.com
www.hcacalgary.com
www.facebook.com/109224936589
twitter.com/HCA_Calgary
Grades: K-12; *Enrollment:* 500
Sharon Fuchs, Executive Director
Ryan Brennan, Principal
ryan.brennan@pallisersd.ab.ca

Calgary: **Master's Academy & College**
4414 Crowchild Trail SW, Calgary, AB T2T 5J4
Tel: 403-242-7034
Academy@masters.ab.ca
Other Information: Academy (K-6): 403-242-7034, ext. 200; College (7-12): ext. 260
www.facebook.com/MastersAcademyCollege
Grades: K - 12; *Note:* Master's Academy & College, established in 1997, is known as a school of Profound Learning. Instruction & guidance is provided from a Christian perspective. Master's Academy features Kindergarten to grade 6, & Master's College includes grades 7 to 12.
Tom Rudmik, Founder & Chief Executive Officer
Paul Graham, Chief Operating Officer
Lynda Dyck, Academy Principal
Peter Muller, College Principal
Susan McAllister, College Vice-Principal
Doreen Grey, Coordinator, Research & Development

Calgary: **Menno Simons Christian School**
7000 Elkton Dr. SW, Calgary, AB T3H 4Y7, Canada
Tel: 403-531-0745; *Fax:* 403-531-0747
office@mennosimons.ab.ca
www.mennosimonschristianschool.ca
Grades: Pre.-9
Byron Thiessen, Principal

Calgary: **Trinity Christian School (TCS)**
#100, 295 Midpark Way SE, Calgary, AB T2X 2A8, Canada
Tel: 403-254-6682; *Fax:* 403-254-9843
trinity@tcskids.com
www.tcskids.com
Other Information: 403-254-6716 (Phone, Business Office)
Grades: K - 9
Stan Hielema, Principal
stan.hielema@pallisersd.ab.ca
Michelle Duimel, Vice Principal
michelle.duimel@pallisersd.ab.ca
John Unrau, Business Manager
john.unrau@pallisersd.ab.ca
Carol Nudd, Librarian
carol.nudd@pallisersd.ab.ca

Calgary: **Tyndale Christian School**
18 Hart Estates Blvd., Calgary, AB T2P 2G7
Tel: 403-590-5881
tcs@tyndalecalgary.ca

Champion: **Hope Christian School (HSC)**
P.O. Box 235
320 - 3rd Ave. North, Champion, AB T0L 0R0
Tel: 403-897-3019; *Toll-Free:* 1-877-897-3131
secretary@hopechristianschool.ca
www.hopechristianschool.ca
Other Information: Home School Office, Phone: 403-897-3799
Grades: 1-12; *Note:* Hope Christian School was established in 1981. It is owned & operated by the Evangelical Free Church of Champion, Alberta. The school offers day school on campus, home education, & HSC online learning.
Dale Anger, Principal & Administrator
Mayruth Guenter, Manager, Day School Office
Sherrill Losey, Manager, Homeschool Office

Coaldale: **Coaldale Christian School**
2008 - 8 St., Coaldale, AB T1M 1L1, Canada
Tel: 403-345-4055; *Fax:* 403-345-6436
ccsoffic@telusplanet.net
www.coaldalechristianschool.com
Grades: Pre.-12; Special Ed.
Joop Harthoorn, Principal

Coalhurst: **Calvin Christian School**
P.O. Box 26
Coalhurst, AB T0L 0V0, Canada
Tel: 403-381-3030; *Fax:* 403-381-3051
office@ccschool.ca
www.ccschool.ca

Cochrane: **Canadian Southern Baptist Seminary & College**
200 Seminary View, Cochrane, AB T4C 2G1
Tel: 403-932-6622; *Fax:* 403-932-7049
www.csbs.edu
Rob Blackaby, President, 403-932-6622
Rob.Blackaby@csbs.ca
Barry Nelson, Director of Development, 403-932-6622, ext. 264
Barry.Nelson@csbs.ca
Kathleen McNaughton, Registrar, 403-932-6622, ext. 221
Kathleen.McNaughton@csbs.ca

Cold Lake: **Lakeland Christian Academy**
P.O. Box 8397
Cold Lake, AB T9M 1N2
Tel: 780-639-2077; *Fax:* 780-639-4151
lca@hlvc.org
Grades: K - 12; *Note:* The school offers an individualized academic program & an emphasis on moral values.
Allan Amesman, Contact

Cold Lake: **Trinity Christian School**
5731 - 50th Ave., Cold Lake, AB T9M 1T1, Canada
Tel: 780-594-2205
trinity@cablerocket.com
www.trinitychristian.ca
Grades: 1 - 12
Richard Schienbein, Principal

Devon: **Devon Christian School**
205 Miquelon Ave. West, Devon, AB T9G 1Y1, Canada
Tel: 780-987-4157; *Fax:* 780-987-4156
dcs@devonchristianschool.ca
www.devonchristianschool.ca
Grades: Pre.-9; *Enrollment:* 90
Rhonda Bray, Principal

Didsbury: **Koinonia Christian Schools**
c/o Koinonia Christian Education Society
P.O. Box 1405
#107, 1001 - 20th Ave., Didsbury, AB T0M 0W0, Canada
Tel: 403-335-9587; *Fax:* 403-335-9513
kces@koinoniaschools.com
www.koinoniaschools.com
Number of Schools: 9; *Grades:* Pre-12; *Enrollment:* 785; *Note:* Koinona Christian Schools is a system of 9 evangelical, non-denominational schools in Alberta.
Vern Rand, Superintendent
vern.rand@koinonia.ca
Garry Anderson, Associate Superintendent
garryka@gmail.com
Judy Nelson, Business Administrator
jnelson@koinoniaschools.com

Edmonton: **Edmonton Bible Heritage Christian School**
13054 - 112 St. NW, Edmonton, AB T5E 6E6
Tel: 780-454-3672; *Fax:* 780-488-3672
Grades: 1-9; *Note:* The school offers a home education program & a home education blended program.

Edmonton: **Edmonton Christian Schools**
Northeast School
5940 - 159 Ave., Edmonton, AB T5Y 0J5
Tel: 780-408-7942; *Fax:* 780-478-1728
ecsne@epsb.ca
www.edmchristian.org
Number of Schools: 3
Lori Price-Wagner, Principal
Lori.price-wagner@epsb.ca

Campuses
Edmonton Christian West School
14345 McQueen Rd., Edmonton, AB T5N 3L5
Tel: 780-408-7948; *Fax:* 780-452-5669
ecswest@epsb.ca
www.edmchristian.org
Mike Suderman, Principal
Mike.Suderman@epsb.ca
Edmonton Christian High School
14304 - 109 Ave., Edmonton, AB T5N 1H6
Tel: 780-408-7945; *Fax:* 780-454-0793
echs@epsb.ca
www.edmchristian.org
Mike Suderman, Principal
mike.suderman@epsb.ca

Edmonton: **Meadowlark Christian School**
9825 - 158 St., Edmonton, AB T5P 2X4, Canada
Tel: 780-483-6476; *Fax:* 780-487-8992
meadowlarkChristian@epsb.ca
www.k-9christian.com
Grades: K - 9
Darren Sweeney, Principal

Edmonton: **Parkland Immanuel Christian School**
21304 - 35 Ave. NW, Edmonton, AB T6M 2P6, Canada
Tel: 780-444-6443; *Fax:* 780-444-6448
info@parklandimmanuel.ca
www.parklandimmanuel.ca
Grades: Pre.-12
John Jagersma, Principal
jjagersma@parklandimmanuel.ca

Edmonton: **Victory Christian School (VCS)**
820 Saddleback Rd., Edmonton, AB T6J 4W4, Canada
Tel: 780-988-5433; *Fax:* 780-988-6323
info@victorychristianschool.ca
www.victorychristianschool.ca
Grades: Preschool - 12; *Enrollment:* 120; *Note:* Victory Christian School's preschool offers curriculum suited to the developmental stages of four year old children.

Edson: **Yellowhead Koinonia Christian School**
430 - 72 St., Edson, AB T7E 1N3
Tel: 780-723-3850; *Fax:* 780-723-7566
office@ykcschool.com
www.ykcschool.com
Grades: Pre-kindergarten - 12; *Note:* The independent Christian school serves Edson & the surrounding area.
Jason Rand, Principal, 780-693-3775
Glenda Ferguson, Home School Coordinator (West)
Bobbie Luymeson, Home School Coordinator (East)

Fort McMurray: **Fort McMurray Christian School**
190 Tamarack Way, Fort McMurray, AB T9K 1A1
Tel: 780-743-1079; *Fax:* 780-743-1379
christian.fmpsdschools.ca
www.facebook.com/143827752310999
www.twitter.com/fmpsd
Grades: K - 8; *Note:* The Fort McMurray Christian School is an interdenominational Christian school that is affiliated with the Association of Independent Schools & Colleges in Alberta as well as Christian Schools International.
Joseph Champion, Principal

Grande Prairie: **Grande Prairie Christian School**
8202 - 110 St., Grande Prairie, AB T8W 1M3, Canada
Tel: 780-539-4566; *Fax:* 780-539-4748
www.gppsd.ab.ca/school/gpchristian
Grades: Pre.-12; *Enrollment:* 220
Travis Fehler, Principal

Grande Prairie: **Hillcrest Christian School**
10306 - 102 St., Grande Prairie, AB T8V 2W3, Canada
Tel: 780-539-9161; *Fax:* 780-532-6932
hcsadmin@hcsgp.ca
Grades: Pre.-12

High Level: **High Level Christian Academy**
P.O. Box 1100
10701 - 100 Ave., High Level, AB T0H 1Z0, Canada
Tel: 780-926-2360; *Fax:* 780-926-3245
www.highlevelchristianacademy.ca
Grades: Pre.-12
Mark Pelley, Principal

Kingman: **Cornerstone Christian Academy**
P.O. Box 63
Kingman, AB T0B 2MO, Canada
Tel: 780-672-7197; *Fax:* 780-608-1420
www.brsd.ab.ca/school/cornerstonekingman
Grades: Pre.-12; Special Ed.; *Note:* Core subjects are taught; Bible Studies.
Steve Ioanidis, Principal
sioanidis@brsd.ab.ca

Lacombe: **Central Alberta Christian High School (CACHS)**
22 Eagle Rd., Lacombe, AB T4L 1G7, Canada
Tel: 403-782-4535; *Fax:* 403-782-5425
office@cachs.ca
www.cachs.ca
www.facebook.com/167864616645517
Grades: 10-12; *Enrollment:* 105; *Number of Employees:* 8 teaching staff; 7 support staff
Beatrice Vriend, Development Director
bvriend@cachs.ca
Mel Brandsma, Principal
mbrandsma@cachs.ca
Wendy Barnes, Business Administrator
wbarnes@cachs.ca
Peter Hoekstra, Vice Principal
phoekstra@cachs.ca

Lacombe: **College Heights Christian School (CHCS)**
5201 College Ave., Lacombe, AB T4L 1Z6
Tel: 403-782-6212
office@collegeheightschristianschool.ca
www.collegeheightschristianschool.ca
Grades: Early chilhood services - 9; *Note:* Operated by the Seventh-day Adventist Church, the College Heights Christian School offers a spiritually oriented education.
Reo Ganson, Principal
Pastor Myles, Chaplain & Bible Teacher

Lacombe: **Lacombe Christian School**
5206 - 58 St., Lacombe, AB T4L 1G9, Canada
Tel: 403-782-6531; *Fax:* 403-782-5760
office@lacs.ca
www.lacs.ca
Grades: Pre.-9
M. Folkerts, Principal
mfolkerts@lacs.ca

Lacombe: **Parkview Adventist Academy**
5505 College Ave., Lacombe, AB T4L 2E7, Canada
Tel: 403-782-3381; *Fax:* 403-782-7308
office@paa.ca
www.paa.ca
www.facebook.com/ParkviewAdventistAcademy
www.youtube.com/user/ParkviewAA
Grades: 10-12; *Note:* Christian boarding school affiliated with Canadian University College

Leduc: **Covenant Christian School (CCS)**
P.O. Box 3827
Leduc, AB T9E 6M7, Canada
Tel: 780-986-8353; *Fax:* 780-986-8360
www.covenantchristian.ca
Grades: K-9; Special Ed.; *Enrollment:* 165; *Note:* Christ-centered education within a curriculum of core subjects.
Gayle Monsma, Principal
gayle.monsma@blackgold.ca

Lethbridge: **Immanuel Christian Schools**
Elementary Campus
2010 - 5 Ave. North, Lethbridge, AB T1H 0N5, Canada
Tel: 403-317-7860; *Fax:* 403-317-7862
icesoffice@gmail.com
ices.icssa.ca
www.facebook.com/108903105879650?ref=ts&fref=ts
Grades: Pre.-6
Jay Visser, Principal
jvisser@immanuelcs.ca
Annie Kooiker, Business Office Manager, 403-327-4223

Campuses
High School Campus
802 - 6 Ave. North, Lethbridge, AB T1H 0S1, Canada
Tel: 403-328-4783; *Fax:* 403-327-6333
ichs.icssa.ca
www.facebook.com/120978791290008
twitter.com/ICHS_RVS
Grades: 7-12
Rob van Spronsen, Principal
rob.vanspronsen@gmail.com

Linden: **Kneehill Christian School**
P.O. Box 370
Linden, AB T0M 1J0
Tel: 403-546-3781; *Fax:* 403-546-3181
Grades: 1-9

Medicine Hat: **Cornerstone Christian School**
2566 Southview Dr. SE, Medicine Hat, AB T1B 1R2
Tel: 403-529-6169; *Fax:* 403-529-6165
www.cornerstonechristianschool.ca
www.facebook.com/293343004056497
twitter.com/CCSMedHat
Grades: K - 9
Sandy Sergeant, Principal

Medicine Hat: **Higher Ground Christian School**
1 Shirley St. SE, Medicine Hat, AB T1A 8N5
Tel: 403-527-2714
www.highergroundchristianschool.ca
Grades: 1 - 9; ESL

Medicine Hat: **Medicine Hat Christian School**
68 Rice Dr. SE, Medicine Hat, AB T1B 3X2, Canada
Tel: 403-526-3246; *Fax:* 403-528-9048
mhcs@sd76.ab.ca
www.medhatchristianschool.com
twitter.com/medhatchristian
Grades: K-9; *Enrollment:* 195
Shade Holmes, Principal, 403-526-3246, ext. 5102

Mirror: **Living Truth Christian School**
P.O. Box 89
4803 - 49 Ave., Mirror, AB T0B 3C0
Tel: 403-788-2444; *Fax:* 403-788-2445
ltcs@abchristianschools.ca
www.livingtruthchristian.ca
Grades: 1 - 12

Monarch: **Providence Christian School**
P.O. Box 240
615 Queen Ave., Monarch, AB T0L 1M0, Canada
Tel: 403-381-4418; *Fax:* 403-381-4428
admin@pcsmonarch.com
www.pcsmonarch.com
www.facebook.com/256229551179711
Grades: K - 12
Hugo VanderHoek, Principal
Ash Diek, Vice Principal

Morinville: **Morinville Christian School**
10515 - 100 Ave., Morinville, AB T8R 1A2, Canada
Tel: 780-939-2987; *Fax:* 780-939-6646
www.mcfchurch.net/mcs
Grades: 1 - 12
Lou Brunelle, Director, School

Olds: **Olds Koinonia Christian School**
P.O. Box 4039
Olds, AB T4H 1P7, Canada
Tel: 403-556-4038; *Fax:* 403-556-8770
www.oldskoinonia.com
Grades: K-12; *Enrollment:* 300
Dwayne Brown, Administrator/Principal
dwaynebrown@chinooksedge.ab.ca

Ponoka: **Ponoka Christian School (PCS)**
6300 - 50 St., Ponoka, AB T4J 1V3, Canada
Tel: 403-783-6563; *Fax:* 403-783-6687
office@ponokachristianschool.com
www.ponokachristianschool.com
Grades: Pre.-9

Robert Morris, Principal
bob.morris@ponokachristianschool.com

Purple Springs: Tween Valley Christian School
P.O. Box 96
Purple Springs, AB T0K 1X0, Canada
Tel: 403-223-9571
tvcs.principal@hotmail.com
www.tweenvalleychristianschool.com
Grades: 1 - 12
Dennis Dyck, Principal

Red Deer: Destiny Christian School
P.O. Box 30
Site 4, RR#4, Red Deer, AB T4N 5E4, Canada
Tel: 403-343-6510; *Fax:* 403-343-1963
info@destinyschool.ca
www.destinyschool.ca
Grades: Pre.-9
Glenn Mullen, Principal
Marjorie Mullen, Principal

Red Deer: Koinonia Christian School of Red Deer
6014 - 57 Ave., Red Deer, AB T4N 4S9, Canada
Tel: 403-346-1818; *Fax:* 403-347-3013
accounts@koinonia.ca
www.koinonia.ca
Grades: Pre.-12
Vern Rand, Principal

Red Deer: South Side Christian School
P.O. Box 219
Red Deer, AB T4N 5E8, Canada
Tel: 403-886-2266; *Fax:* 403-886-5026
www.southsidechristianschool.ca
www.facebook.com/140592702777091?ref=ts&fref=ts
Grades: Pre.-10; *Note:* Affiliated with the Seventh-day Adventist Church

Rimbey: Rimbey Christian School
P.O. Box 90
4522 - 54th Ave., Rimbey, AB T0C 2J0, Canada
Tel: 403-843-4790; *Fax:* 403-843-3904
office@rimbeychristianschool.com
www.rimbeychristianschool.com
Grades: K - 9; *Enrollment:* 84; *Note:* The Alberta Provincial Program of Studies is taught from a Christian perspective.
Edith Dening, Principal, 403-843-4790
principal@rimbeychristianschool.com

Rocky Mountain House: Rocky Christian School (RCS)
5204 - 54 Ave., Rocky Mountain House, AB T4T 1S5, Canada
Tel: 403-845-3516; *Fax:* 403-845-4370
rocky-christian@wrsd.ca
www.rockycs.com
Grades: K - 9; *Enrollment:* 105; *Note:* The interdenominational school provides a Biblically based curriculum, which reflects Alberta Learning requirements.
Robert Duiker, Principal

Slave Lake: Slave Lake Koinonia Christian
P.O. Box 1548
328 - 2 St. NE, Slave Lake, AB T0G 2A0, Canada
Tel: 780-849-5400; *Fax:* 780-849-5460
admin@slkcs.com
www.slkcs.com
Grades: 1-12
Theresa Nagel, Principal
principal@slkcs.com

Spruce Grove: Living Waters Christian Academy (LWCA)
5 Grove Dr. West, Spruce Grove, AB T7X 3X8, Canada
Tel: 780-962-3331; *Fax:* 780-962-3958
www.lwca.ab.ca
www.facebook.com/lwca.ab.ca
Grades: Pre.-12
Keith Penner, Principal
kpenner@lwca.ab.ca
Savaya Hofsink, Community Resource Director
savaya.hofsink@lwca.ab.ca

Sundre: Olds Mountain View Christian School
Box 2, Site 8, RR#2, Sundre, AB T4H 1P3, Canada
Tel: 403-556-1551; *Fax:* 403-556-5936
principal@omvcs.ca
www.omvcs.ca
Grades: K-12

Sylvan Lake: Lighthouse Christian School (LCA)
PO Box 1078, RR#1, Sylvan Lake, AB T4S 1X6
Tel: 403-887-2166; *Fax:* 403-887-5729
www.lighthousechristianacademy.com
www.facebook.com/group.php?gid=133384233375987
Grades: Kindergarten - 12; *Note:* Private education is offered in a Christian community setting.
Evan McKay, Board Chair
Leland Makaroff, Principal, 250-474-5311
info@lighthousechristianacademy.com
Sharon Ocello, Vice-Principal

Taber: Taber Christian School
Taber, AB
Tel: 403-223-4550
taberchristian.horizon.ab.ca
www.facebook.com/HSD67
twitter.com/horizonsd67
Grades: K - 9
John Bronsema, Principal

Three Hills: Prairie Bible Institute (PBI)
P.O. Box 4000
330 - 5th Ave. Northeast, Three Hills, AB T0M 2N0
Tel: 403-443-5511; *Fax:* 403-443-5540
presidentsoffice@prairie.edu
www.prairie.edu
www.facebook.com/PrairieColleges
twitter.com/prairiecolleges
www.youtube.com/user/PrairieColleges
Number of Employees: 45 employees
Mark Maxwell, President
mark.maxwell@prairie.edu
Peter Mal, Dean, 4034435511, ext. 3054
Peter.Mal@prairie.edu

Schools
Prairie Christian Academy (PCA) Elementary School
P.O. Box 68
1025 - 4th St. N, Three Hills, AB T0M 2A0
Tel: 403-443-4210
pcainfo@ghsd75.ca
www.pca3hills.ca
www.facebook.com/group.php?gid=2260682242
twitter.com/pca3hills
Grades: K.-6; *Enrollment:* 300; *Note:* Prairie Christian Academy (PCA) is a non-denominational, Christian school for Preschool to Grade 6 students.

Prairie Christian Academy (PCA) Secondary School
P.O. Box 68
Three Hills, AB T0M 2A0, Canada
Tel: 403-443-4220
pcainfo@ghsd75.ca
pca.ghsd75.ca
Grades: 7-12

Catholic

Calgary: Clear Water Academy
2521 Dieppe Ave. SW, Calgary, AB T3E 7J9, Canada
Tel: 403-217-8448; *Fax:* 403-217-8043
administration@clearwateracademy.com
www.clearwateracademy.com
www.facebook.com/147970885245245?v=wall
Grades: Pre.-12; *Note:* An independent Catholic school.
Darren Forrester, Principal, 403-240-7912
dforrester@clearwateracademy.com
Bill Tomiak, Executive Director, 403-240-7911
btomiak@clearwateracademy.com

First Nations

Ponoka: Mamawi Atosketan Native School
RR#2, Ponoka, AB T4J 1R2
Tel: 403-783-4362; *Fax:* 403-783-3839
mamawiatosketan@xplornet.com
an6440.adventistschoolconnect.org
Grades: K - 12

Special Education

Calgary: Calgary Quest School
c/o Spruce Cliff Elementary
3405 Spruce Dr. SW, Calgary, AB T3C 0A5, Canada
Tel: 403-253-0003; *Fax:* 403-253-0025
info@calgaryquestschool.com
www.calgaryquestschool.com
www.facebook.com/CalgaryQuestSchool
twitter.com/CalgaryQuest
Grades: Pre. - 12; *Note:* Calgary Quest School offers a program for children with special challenges.

Angela Rooke, Executive Director

Calgary: Foothills Academy
745 - 37 St. NW, Calgary, AB T2N 4T1, Canada
Tel: 403-270-9400; *Fax:* 403-270-9438
info@foothillsacademy.org
www.foothillsacademy.org
www.facebook.com/pages/Foothills-Academy/333239973359586
twitter.com/FoothillsAC
www.linkedin.com/groups?gid=3112702&trk=hb_side_g
Grades: 1-12; Special Ed.
Gordon M. Bullivant, Executive Director

Calgary: Janus Academy
2223 Spiller Rd. SE, Calgary, AB T2G 4G9
Tel: 403-262-3333
contact@janusacademy.org
www.janusacademy.org
Other Information: Jr. High & High School Site, Phone: 403-228-5559
Grades: 1-12; Special Education; *Enrollment:* 44; *Note:* Janus Academy strives to enhance the lives of children with autism. The program is accredited by both Alberta Education & The Association of Independent Schools & Colleges. Janus Academy is a registered charity.
Stacey Oliver, Principal
Paige McNeill, Program Director, Elementary School
Koren Trnka, Program Director, Junior & Senior High School

Calgary: New Heights School & Learning Services
4041 Breskens Dr. SW, Calgary, AB T3E 7M1
Tel: 403-240-1312; *Fax:* 403-769-0633
info@newheightscalgary.com
www.newheightscalgary.com
Grades: Pre. - 12
Katie Blasetti, Principal

Edmonton: Columbus Academy
6770 - 129 Ave., Edmonton, AB T5C 1V7
Tel: 780-440-0708; *Fax:* 780-440-0760
www.boscohomes.ca
Grades: 7-12; *Note:* The school is a special education, private school in Alberta. Students are referred from social service agencies, surrounding school jurisdictions, & parents.

Edmonton: Edmonton Academy
10231 - 120 St., Edmonton, AB T5K 2A4, Canada
Tel: 780-482-5449; *Fax:* 780-482-0902
www.edmontonacademy.com
Grades: 7-12; *Note:* Provides specialized teaching for students with learning disabilities.
Liz Richards, Executive Director, 780-482-5449
lizrich@telusplanet.net

Edmonton: Elves Child Development Centre
Elves Special Needs Society
10825 - 142 St., Edmonton, AB T5N 3Y7, Canada
Tel: 780-454-5310; *Fax:* 780-454-5889
info@elves-society.com
www.elves-society.com
Grades: Pre.-12; *Note:* The Elves Special Needs Society offers programs for pre-school and older children, youth and adults who are severely developmentally delayed and/or medically fragile, as well as outreach to students unable to attend school for extended periods of time.
Cristina Molina, Executive Director

Edmonton: John Howard Society of Edmonton Alternative Learning Program
10523 - 100 Ave., 2nd Fl., Edmonton, AB T5J 0A8, Canada
Tel: 780-423-4878; *Fax:* 780-425-0008
info@johnhoward.ab.ca
www.johnhoward.ab.ca
www.facebook.com/JohnHowardSocietyOfAlberta
twitter.com/johnhowardab
Grades: To Gr. 9; *Note:* The Edmonton John Howard Society's Adult Transition Learning Centre offers courses to clients at every stage of learning, including: literacy, GED & college preparation, language arts, math & computer basics, personal development, & life skills (addictions, anger management, mental health; all aspects of employment preparation). The Centre is located at 10010 105th St., Suite 401, in Edmonton.

Edmonton: Thomas More Academy
Edmonton, AB
Tel: 780-440-0708
abh_admin@boscohomes.ca
www.boscohomes.ca
Grades: K - 12

Independent & Private Schools

Calgary: Akiva Academy
140 Haddon Rd. SW, Calgary, AB T2V 2Y3, Canada
Tel: 403-258-1312; *Fax:* 403-258-3812
office@akiva.ca
www.akiva.ca
Grades: Pre.-6
John Hadden, Principal
johnhadden@akiva.ca
Rabbi Chaim Greenwald, Director of Judaic Studies
rabbigreenwald@akiva.ca

Calgary: Asasa Academy
Northmount Campus
599 Northmount Dr. NW, Calgary, AB T2K 3J6
Tel: 403-285-5677; *Fax:* 403-457-5289
contact@asasa.ca
www.asasa.ca
Grades: JK - 9
Amber St Pierre, Principal
Campuses
Pinetown Campus
119 Pinetown Place NE, Calgary, AB T1Y 5J1
Tel: 403-285-9277; *Fax:* 403-457-5289
contact@asasa.ca
Grades: JK

Calgary: Banbury Crossroads Private School
#201, 2451 Dieppe Ave. SW, Calgary, AB T3E 7K1, Canada
Tel: 403-270-7787; *Fax:* 403-270-7486
general@banburycrossroads.com
www.banburycrossroads.com
Note: Banbury Crossroads Private School offers education to children aged 3 to 18.
Diane Swiatek, Director

Calgary: Calgary Academy
1677 - 93th Ave. SW, Calgary, AB T3H 0R3, Canada
Tel: 403-686-6444
info@calgaryacademy.com
www.calgaryacademy.com
Grades: 2 - 12; *Enrollment:* 625
Dana Braunberger, Principal, Grades 2-8
dbraunberger@calgaryacademy.com
Kim McLean, Principal, Grades 9-12
kmclean@calgaryacademy.com

Calgary: Calgary Chinese Alliance School
Calgary Chinese Alliance Church
150 Beddington Blvd. NE, Calgary, AB T3K 2E2, Canada
Tel: 403-274-7046; *Fax:* 403-275-7799
chineseschool@calgarychinesealliance.org
calgarychinesealliance.org
Grades: 1 - 12; *Enrollment:* 500
Alex Hung, President
Mimi Fong, Principal
mimiefong@hotmail.com

Calgary: Calgary Chinese Private School
128 - 2 Ave SW, Calgary, AB T2P 0B9, Canada
Tel: 403-264-2233; *Fax:* 403-282-9854
www.calgarychineseschool.com
www.facebook.com/CalgaryChinesePrivateSchool
Grades: K - 12; *Note:* The Calgary Chinese Private School works to maintain Chinese heritage & culture in the community.
Henry Chan, President
Constance Chan, Vice President
Shirley Leung, Treasurer
Annie Lam, Secretary

Calgary: Calgary French & International School (CFIS)
700 - 77th St. SW, Calgary, AB T3H 5R1, Canada
Tel: 403-240-1500; *Fax:* 403-249-5899
inquiries@cfis.com
www.cfis.com
Grades: Preschool - 12; *Enrollment:* 700; *Number of Employees:* 80; *Note:* Calgary French & International School offers French Immersion education.
Joanne Weninger, Chair
societyboard@cfis.com
Margaret Dorrance, Head of School, 403-240-1500, ext. 130
mdorrance@cfis.com
Karen MacPherson, Director of Admissions, 403-240-1500, ext. 329
kmacpherson@cfis.com
Amy Murray, Director of Early Childhood Education, 403-240-1500, ext. 113
amurray@cfis.com
Robert Ward, Principal of Elementary Education (4-6), 403-240-1500, ext. 229
rward@cfis.com
Janet Crofton, Director of Finance and Business Operations, 403-240-1500, ext. 135
jcrofton@cfis.com
Nicola (Nikki) Abrioux-Camirand, Principal of Primary Education (PreK-3), 403-240-1500, ext. 210
ncamirand@cfis.com
Ahmed Amrouche, Principal of Secondary Education (7-12), 403-240-1500, ext. 156
aamrouche@cfis.com

Calgary: Calgary Islamic School (CIS)
Akram Joma'a Campus
2612 - 37th Ave. NE, Calgary, AB T1Y 5L2, Canada
Tel: 403-248-2773; *Fax:* 403-569-6654
info@cislive.ca
www.calgaryislamicschool.com
Grades: K - 9; *Enrollment:* 490; *Note:* Calgary Islamic School offers the regular curriculum, as well as a Quran recitation & memorization curriculum, an Arabic language curriculum, an Islamic Studies curriculum.
Moussa Ouarou, Principal
Campuses
Omar Ibn Alkattab Campus
225 - 28 St. SE, Calgary, AB T2A 5K4, Canada
Tel: 587-353-8900; *Fax:* 587-353-8999
info.omar@cislive.ca
Adam Browning, Principal

Calgary: Calgary Italian School
Centro Linguistico e culturale italiano di Calgar
416 - 1st Ave. NE, Calgary, AB T2E 0B4, Canada
Tel: 403-264-6349
clcic@shaw.ca
italianschoolcalgary.com
Grades: K-12; *Enrollment:* 196; *Number of Employees:* 12 teachers; *Note:* A total of 13 courses (9 courses for children and 4 for adults).

Calgary: Calgary Jewish Academy (CJA)
6700 Kootenay St. SW, Calgary, AB T2V 1P7, Canada
Tel: 403-253-3992; *Fax:* 403-255-0842
info@cja.ab.ca
www.cja.ab.ca
Grades: Preschool - 9
Reva Faber, Interim Principal
faberr@cja.ab.ca
Shoshana Kirmayer, Associate Principal
kirmayers@cja.ab.ca
Deborah Sherwood, Office Manager
sherwoodd@cja.ab.ca

Calgary: Calgary Waldorf School
515 Cougar Ridge Dr. SW, Calgary, AB T3H 5G9, Canada
Tel: 403-287-1868; *Fax:* 403-287-3414
info@calgarywaldorf.org
www.calgarywaldorf.org
Grades: Pre. - 9; *Note:* Calgary Waldorf School offers a Parent-and-Tot program.
Laureen Loree, Principal
Anna Driehuyzen, Pedagogical Administrator
Dinah Clark, Financial Administrator
Cathie Foote, School Administrator
Sandra Langlois, Manager, Admissions & Facility
Barbara Hergert, Library Coordinator

Calgary: The Chinese Academy
John G. Diefenbaker Senior High School
6620 - 4th St. NW, Calgary, AB T2K 1C2, Canada
Tel: 403-777-7663; *Fax:* 403-777-7669
thechineseacademy@gmail.com
www.chineseacademy.ca
Grades: K - 12; *Enrollment:* 1925; *Note:* Kindergarten, Level 1, begins for children aged 3.5 years at the Sir John A. Macdonald Junior High School, 6600 - 4th St. NW in Calgary. The goal of the school is to promote Chinese language & culture. Cantonese & Mandarin classes, as well as Chinese as a Second Language for beginners in Cantonese & Mandarin.
Elaine Chan, Principal

Calgary: Chinook Winds Adventist Academy (CWAA)
10101 - 2nd Ave. SW, Calgary, AB T3B 5T2, Canada
Tel: 403-286-5686; *Fax:* 403-247-1623
www.cwaa.net
www.facebook.com/ChinookWindsAdventistAcademy
twitter.com/cwaa_academy
Grades: K - 12; *Note:* The Seventh-day Adventist school also features music, outdoor education, Bible instruction, & mission trips for senior high students.
Lara Melashenko, Principal
lmelashenko@cwaa.net
David Elias, Vice Principal
delias@cwaa.net
Brent Wilson, Chaplain
bwilson@cwaa.net
Katie Crews, Librarian
kcrews@cwaa.net

Calgary: Community Connections School
225 - 37 St. NW, Calgary, AB T2N 4N6, Canada
Tel: 403-283-6361; *Fax:* 403-283-5741
Grades: 1-12

Calgary: Delta West Academy
414 - 11A St. NE, Calgary, AB T2E 4P3, Canada
Tel: 403-290-0767; *Fax:* 403-290-0768
info@deltawestacademy.ca
www.deltawestacademy.ca
twitter.com/DWACalgary
Grades: Pre.-12; Special Ed.
Denise Dutchuk-Smith, B.A., B.Ed., Head of School
ddutchuk-smith@deltawestacademy.ca
C. Tiltmann, Principal, Academic Head
ctiltmann@deltawestacademy.ca

Calgary: Edge School for Athletes
33055 Township Rd. 250, Calgary, AB T3Z 1L4
Tel: 403-246-6432; *Fax:* 403-217-8463
info@edgeschool.com
www.edgeschool.com
www.facebook.com/edgeschool
twitter.com/edgeschool
Grades: 5-12; *Note:* The school prepares student-athletes for university.
Cameron Hodgson, Chief Executive Officer & Principal, 403-246-6432, ext. 105
chodgson@edgeschool.com
Dale Unruh, Chief Operating Officer
Anne McCaffrey, Director, Admissions, 403-246-6432, ext. 111
amccaffrey@edgeschool.com
Lauren Ritchie, Director, Marketing & Communications, 403-246-6432, ext. 439
lritchie@edgeschool.com
Jaques Ferguson, Director, Sport, 403-246-6432, ext. 447
jferguson@edgeschool.com
Keith Taylor, Principal, 403-246-6432, ext. 110
ktaylor@edgeschool.com

Calgary: Educere International College
#1500, 910 - 7 Ave. SW, Calgary, AB T2P 3N8, Canada
Tel: 403-232-8551
Note: Founded in 1962, the school offers the opportunity to acquire English & learn about business & culture in North America.

Calgary: Equilibrium International Educational Institute
707 - 14 St. NW, Calgary, AB T2N 2A4, Canada
Tel: 403-283-1111; *Fax:* 403-270-7786
school@equilibrium.ab.ca
www.equilibrium.ab.ca
Grades: 10-12

Calgary: German Language School
German Canadian Club
#204, 2333 18 Ave NE, Calgary, AB T2E 8T6, Canada
Tel: 403-288-2255; *Fax:* 403-286-8457
info@germancanadianclub.com
www.germancanadianclub.com

Calgary: Greek Community School
1 Tamarac Cres. SW, Calgary, AB T3C 3B7, Canada
Tel: 403-246-4553; *Fax:* 403-246-8191
school@calgaryhellenic.com
calgaryhellenic.com/our-school/
Grades: Pre. - 6
Yvonne Paschalis, Principal
greekschoolofcalgaryprincipal@gmail.com

Calgary: Green Learning Academy (GLA)
#150, 7260 - 12 St. SE, Calgary, AB T2H 2S5
Tel: 403-873-1966; *Fax:* 403-873-1967
glainformation@greenlearning.com
www.greenlearning.com
Grades: Pre. - 9

Calgary: International School of Excellence (ISE)
3915 - 34th St. NE, Calgary, AB T1Y 6Z8
Tel: 403-234-0453; *Fax:* 403-250-2401
isoe@telus.net
www.isoe-online.com
Grades: Early Childhood Services - 12; *Note:* The International School of Excellence was incorporated in 2002. The private

school serves a diverse community & follows the Alberta curriculum.
Jean Fevry, Founder
Kassem Hammoud, Vice-Principal & Head, Arabic Language Department
Jennifer Berriault, Head, Junior & Senior High Schools
Jean Reimer, Head, Elementary School

Calgary: Khalsa School Calgary
P.O. Box 2
#RR6 Site 1, Calgary, AB T2M 4L5
Tel: 403-293-7712; *Fax:* 403-293-2245
info@khalsaschoolcalgary.ca
www.khalsaschoolcalgary.ca
Grades: 1 - 9
Beverly Hammond, Principal
beverly.hammond@khalsaschoolcalgary.ca

Calgary: Lycée Louis Pasteur
4099, boul Garrison sud-ouest, Calgary, AB T2T 6G2, Canada
Tél: 403-243-5420; *Téléc:* 403-287-2245
bureau@lycee.ca
www.lycee.ca
www.facebook.com/lycee.ca
twitter.com/LyceeLP
Grades: Pre.-12; *Note:* The Lycée Louis Pasteur is accredited by both the French Ministry of Education and Alberta Education.
Hervé Gagliardi, Chef d'établissement

Calgary: Maria Montessori Education Centre of Calgary
Building B4
#003, 2452 Battleford Ave. SW, Calgary, AB T3E 7K9
Tel: 403-668-8538; *Fax:* 403-685-2048
mmec.ca
Grades: Toddler - Elem.
Amanda Kershaw, Principal
amanda@mmec.ca

Calgary: Montessori School of Calgary
2201 Cliff St. SW, Calgary, AB T2S 2G4, Canada
Tel: 403-229-1011; *Fax:* 403-229-4474
admissions@msofc.ca
www.montessorischoolofcalgary.com
Grades: Pre. - Elem.; *Enrollment:* 100; *Note:* The children at the Montessori School of Calgary range in age from 2.5 to 12. Both the Montessori program & the Alberta Programme of Studies are followed.
Sandy Moser, Principal
sandy.moser@msofc.ca

Calgary: Mountain View Academy (MVA)
#B4, 2452 Battleford Ave. SW, Calgary, AB T3E 7K9, Canada
Tel: 403-217-4346; *Fax:* 403-249-4312
www.mountainviewacademy.ca
www.facebook.com/mtnviewacademy
twitter.com/mtviewacademy
Grades: Preschool - 12
Lenka Popplestone, Principal
lpopplestone@mountainviewacademy.ca
Colleen Ryan, Vice Principal
cryan@mountainviewacademy.ca
Jane Lizotte, Assistant Principal
jlizotte@mountainviewacademy.ca

Calgary: Phoenix Foundation
320 - 19 St. SE, Calgary, AB T2E 6J6
Tel: 403-265-7701; *Fax:* 403-275-7715
info@phoenixfoundation.ca
phoenixfoundation.ca
Note: Phoenix is a non-profit private school that specializes in homeschooling.

Calgary: Prince of Peace Lutheran School
243209 Garden Rd. NE, Calgary, AB T1X 1E1
Tel: 403-285-2288; *Fax:* 403-285-2855
school@princeofpeace.ca
ppeace.rockyview.ab.ca
Grades: K - 9; *Enrollment:* 395; *Note:* Prince of Peace Lutheran School is affiliated with Lutheran Church-Canada.
Todd Hennig, Principal

Calgary: The Renert School
14 Royal Vista Link NW, Calgary, AB T3R 0K4
Tel: 587-353-1053
info@renertschool.ca
renertschool.ca
Grades: 1 - 12

Calgary: Renfrew Educational Services
Main School & Administrative Centre
2050 - 21st St. NE, Calgary, AB T2E 6S5, Canada
Tel: 403-291-5038; *Fax:* 403-291-2499
renfrew@renfreweducation.org
www.renfreweducation.org
www.facebook.com/62176705325
Grades: Preschool - Elementary; *Enrollment:* 650; *Note:* Renfrew Educational Services offers specialized educational programs for preschool & elementary students. The not-for-profit society also develops programs for children with special needs.
Tom Buchanan, Chair
Janice McTighe, Executive Director
Kim LaCourse, Associate Executive Director
Cathy Gable, Director, Community Services
Mary lou Hill, Director, Education
Bruce Monnery, Director, Finance & Administration

Calgary: River Valley School (RVS)
3127 Bowwood Dr. NW, Calgary, AB T3B 2E7
Tel: 403-246-2275; *Fax:* 403-686-7631
info@rivervalleyschool.ca
www.rivervalleyschool.ca
www.facebook.com/287475947950915
twitter.com/rvssocial
www.linkedin.com/pub/erin-corbett/42/655/4b0
www.flickr.com/photos/69513039@N07
Grades: JK-6; *Enrollment:* 200
Erin Corbett, Head of School

Calgary: Rundle College Society
4411 Manitoba Rd. SE, Calgary, AB T2G 4B9
Tel: 403-291-3866; *Fax:* 403-291-5458
www.rundle.ab.ca
Grades: Pre. - 12
Dave Hauk, Superintendent/Headmaster
hauk@rundle.ab.ca
Doug Hodgins, Director of Finance, Business Manager, 403-214-3703
hodgins@rundle.ab.ca
Nicola Spencer, Director of Admissions, 403-214-3700
spencer@rundle.ab.ca

Campuses
Rundle College Elementary School
2634 - 12 Ave. NW, Calgary, AB T2N 1K6, Canada
Tel: 403-282-8411; *Fax:* 403-282-4460
www.rundle.ab.ca/elementary
Grades: 4 - 6

Rundle College Junior/Senior High School
7375 - 17 Ave. SW, Calgary, AB T3H 3W5, Canada
Tel: 403-250-7180; *Fax:* 403-250-7184
www.rundle.ab.ca/high/
Grades: 7-12
Wayne Schneider, Principal
schneider@rundle.ab.ca

Rundle College Academy
4330 - 16 St. SW, Calgary, AB T2T 4H9
Tel: 403-250-2965; *Fax:* 403-250-2914
www.rundle.ab.ca/academy
twitter.com/rundleacademy
Grades: 4-12; *Note:* Rundle College Academy offers a program for students with learning disabilities.
Jason Rogers, Contact
rogers@rundle.ab.ca

Rundle College Primary School
2445 - 23rd Ave. SW, Calgary, AB T2T 0W3, Canada
Tel: 403-229-0386
www.rundle.ab.ca/primary
Grades: Pre. - 3

Calgary: St. John Bosco Private School
712 Fortalice Cres. SE, Calgary, AB T2A 2E1, Canada
Tel: 403-248-3664; *Fax:* 403-273-8012
school.stdennis.ca
Grades: Pre.-9
Dr. Carol Donaldson, Principal

Calgary: The School of Alberta Ballet
West Annex
906 - 12 Ave. SW, 2nd Fl., Calgary, AB T2R 1K7
Tel: 403-245-2274; *Fax:* 403-245-2293
calgarystudios@albertaballet.com
www.schoolofalbertaballet.com
Other Information: Edmonton Studio: 780-702-4725; edmontonstudios@albertaballet.com
Grades: 7 - 12
Chris George, Managing Director, 403-245-2274, ext. 559
chrisg@albertaballet.com
Edmund Stripe, Artistic Director, 403-245-2274, ext. 731
edmunds@albertaballet.com
Jane Roberts, Academic Principal, 403-245-2274, ext. 711
janer@albertaballet.com

Calgary: Tanbridge Academy
P.O. Box 4
Site 22, #RR 8, Calgary, AB T2J 2T9
Tel: 403-259-3443; *Fax:* 403-259-3432
info@tanbridge.com
www.tanbridge.com
Grades: 4 - 9
Linda Choy, Principal

Calgary: Third Academy
North Campus
510 - 77th Ave. SE, Calgary, AB T2H 1C3, Canada
Tel: 403-288-5335; *Fax:* 403-288-5804
info@thirdacademy.com
www.thirdacademy.com
Grades: 1 - 12; *Note:* The Third Academy offers an Individualized Program Plan for students with special needs to remediate or compensate for their learning disorder. There is a Calgary North location, a Calgary South location, & a Red Deer location.
Joe Smith, Principal
Dr. S. Lal Mattu, CEO & Founder
Sunil Mattu, LLB (Hons) Law, BEd, Chief Operating Officer
David Lambe, Vice President, Business & Community Relations.
Kathleen Colmant, Coordinator, Special Events

Campuses
South Campus
P.O. Box 4
Site 22, RR#8, Calgary, AB T2J 2T9, Canada
Tel: 403-201-6335; *Fax:* 403-201-2036

Calgary: Truth Academy
615 Northmount Dr. NW, Calgary, AB T2K 3J6, Canada
Tel: 403-282-0238
Grades: Preschool - 12

Calgary: Webber Academy
1515 - 93rd St. SW, Calgary, AB T3H 4A8, Canada
Tel: 403-277-4700; *Fax:* 403-277-2770
www.webberacademy.ca
Grades: JK - 12; *Note:* Webber Academy is a coeducational, non-denominational university preparatory school.
Dr. Neil Webber, President and Chairman, 403-277-4700, ext. 222
nwebber@webberacademy.ca
Barbara Webber, Vice-President, Administration, 403-277-4700, ext. 223
bwebber@webberacademy.ca
Dianne Lever, Contact, Admissions, 403-277-4700, ext. 225
admissions@webberacademy.ca

Calgary: West Island College (WIC)
7410 Blackfoot Trail SE, Calgary, AB T2H 1M5, Canada
Tel: 403-255-5300; *Fax:* 403-252-1434
office@westislandcollege.ab.ca
www.westislandcollege.ab.ca
Other Information: admissions@westislandcollege.ab.ca (E-mail, Admissions)
Grades: 7 - 12; *Note:* West Island College provides pre-university training. Programs include English & French communication skills & the arts.
Carol Grant-Watt, Head of School, 403-255-5300, ext. 238
CarolGrant-Watt@westislandcollege.ab.ca
Gord Goodwin, Principal
GordGoodwin@westislandcollege.ab.ca
Claire Allen, Director, International Studies, 403-255-5300, ext. 302
ClaireAllen@westislandcollege.ab.ca
Scott Bennett, Director, Business Studies, 403-255-5300, ext. 501
scottbennett@westislandcollege.ab.ca
Nicole Tremblay, Director, Professional Development
NicoleTremblay@westislandcollege.ab.ca
Todd Larsen, Director, Co-Curricular Programmes, 403-255-5300, ext. 231
ToddLarsen@westislandcollege.ab.ca
Nicole Bernard, Director, Admissions
NicoleBernard@westislandcollege.ab.ca
Malcolm Rennie, Director, Post-Secondary Placement, 403-255-5300, ext. 286
MalcolmRennie@westislandcollege.ab.ca
John Ralph, Librarian
JohnRalph@westislandcollege.ab.ca

Canmore: Mountain Gate Community School
P.O. Box 8287
Canmore, AB T1W 2V1, Canada
Tel: 403-609-2105
Grades: 1 - 6

Cold Lake: Art Smith Aviation Academy
Acadèmie de l'Aviation Art Smith
Cold Lake, AB
Tel: 780-594-1404; Fax: 780-594-1406
artsmithaviationacademy.ca
Grades: K-4 French Immersion; K-8 English
R. Young, Principal
ryoung@artsmithaviationacademy.ca

Edmonton: Alberta International College (AIC)
#307, 10621 - 100 Ave. NW, Edmonton, AB T5H 3A3
Tel: 587-524-5644
info@albertainternationalcollege.ca
www.albertainternationalcollege.ca
Grades: 9 - 12

Edmonton: Concordia University College of Alberta University & College Entrance Program
7128 Ada Blvd., Edmonton, AB T5B 4E4, Canada
Tel: 780-479-8481; Fax: 780-378-8460
Toll-Free: 866-479-5200
ucep@concordia.ab.ca
concordia.ab.ca/academic-upgrading
www.facebook.com/Concordia.University.College
twitter.com/cuca_edmonton
www.youtube.com/user/ConcordiaEdmonton
Grades: 10-12

Edmonton: Coralwood Adventist Academy
12218 - 135 St. NW, Edmonton, AB T5L 1X1, Canada
Tel: 780-454-2173; Fax: 780-455-6946
office@coralwood.org
www.coralwood.org
Grades: K - 12
Michelle Northam, Principal
principal@coralwood.org

Edmonton: Dante Alighieri Society School of Italian Language and Culture
c/o Archbishop O'Leary High School
8760 - 132 Ave., Edmonton, AB T5E 0X8, Canada
Tel: 780-474-1787; Fax: 780-451-0669
aristidem@shaw.ca
www.ladanteedmonton.org
Enrollment: 192; Number of Employees: 13 teachers; Note: Courses are offered for both children and adults.
Aristide Melchionna, Principal

Edmonton: Edmonton Islamic Academy
14525 - 127 St., Edmonton, AB T6V 0B3, Canada
Tel: 780-454-4573; Fax: 780-454-3498
eia@islamicschool.ca
www.islamicacademy.ca
Grades: K.-9; Enrollment: 700
Jawdah Jorf, Principal

Edmonton: Edmonton Khalsa School
4504 Millwoods Rd. South, Edmonton, AB T6L 6Y8
edkhalsa@telus.net
www.ihla.ca/IHLA
Grades: K - 6; Enrollment: 160

Edmonton: Edmonton Menorah Academy
10735 McQueen Rd. NW, Edmonton, AB T5N 3L1, Canada
Tel: 780-451-1848; Fax: 780-451-2254
menorahacademy.org
www.facebook.com/menorahacademy
Grades: Pre.-9
Rabbi Rafi Draiman, Head of School
rabbidraiman@menorahacademy.org
Bobbi Scheelar, Director of Communications
bobbi@menorahacademy.org

Edmonton: Faith Lutheran School
11515 - 36 St., Edmonton, AB T5W 2A9, Canada
Tel: 780-496-9302; Fax: 780-496-3556
Grades: Pre.-9

Edmonton: German Language School Society of Edmonton
c/o Rio Terrace School
7608 - 154 St., Edmonton, AB T5R 1R7, Canada
Tel: 780-435-7540
kerstin.buelow@shaw.ca
www.germanschooledmonton.org
Grades: Pre. - 12
Kerstin Buelow, School Director
kerstin.buelow@shaw.ca
Judith Meyers, Administrator
judith.meyers@gmx.de

Edmonton: Gil Vicente Portuguese School
Escola Gil Vicente
St. Cecilia Junior High School
8830 - 132 Ave., Edmonton, AB T5E 0X8, Canada
Tel: 780-966-1189
www.gilvicenteedmonton.ca
www.facebook.com/167591875959?ref=mf
Grades: Pre-K-12; Adult; Number of Employees: 12
Cindy Pereira, Principal, 780-966-1189
cindy.pereira@gilvicenteedmonton.ca

Edmonton: Headway School Society of Alberta
3530 - 91 St., Edmonton, AB T6E 6P1, Canada
Tel: 780-466-7733; Fax: 780-461-7683
headway@telus.net
www.headwayschool.ca
Grades: K - 12
Jagwinder Singh Sidhu, Principal
headman@telus.net

Edmonton: Inner City High School
11205 - 101 St., Edmonton, AB T5G 2A5
Tel: 780-424-9425; Fax: 780-426-3386
info@innercity.ca
innercity.ca
Grades: 9 - 12; Note: Senior academic and arts based high school. Inner City High School is accredited by Alberta Education

Edmonton: Ivan Franko School of Ukrainian Studies (IFSUS)
10611 - 110 Ave., Edmonton, AB T5H 2W9
Tel: 780-439-2320; Fax: 780-439-0989
Note: The school teaches Ukrainian courses.
Liliya Sukhy, Director, 780-476-7529
lsukhy@hotmail.com

Edmonton: MAC Islamic School
11342 - 127th St., Edmonton, AB T5M 0T8
Tel: 780-453-2220; Fax: 780-453-2233
office@macislamicschool.com
www.macislamicschool.com
www.facebook.com/MacIslamicSchool
Grades: K - 5
Raiha Idrees Ali, Principal

Edmonton: Newman Theological College
10012 - 84 St., Edmonton, AB T6A 0B2
Tel: 780-392-2450; Fax: 780-462-4013
www.newman.edu
www.facebook.com/NewmanTheologicalCollege
Dr. Jason West, President/Academic Dean

Edmonton: Phoenix Academy
6770 - 129 Ave., Edmonton, AB T5C 1V7, Canada
Tel: 780-440-0708; Fax: 780-440-0760
www.boscohomes.ca
Grades: K-12; Note: School for students who struggle with behavioural disorders and learning disabilities

Edmonton: Progressive Academy
13212 - 106 Ave., Edmonton, AB T5N 1A3, Canada
Tel: 780-455-8344; Fax: 780-455-1425
info@progressiveacademy.ca
www.progressiveacademy.ca
www.facebook.com/pages/Progressive-Academy/178409648877068
Grades: K - 12; Note: The school offers small classes & the flexibility for students to progress through grades at an irregular pace. Progressive Academy is licensed by Applied Scholastics International & accredited by Alberta Education.

Edmonton: St. George's Hellenic Language School
10831 - 124 St., Edmonton, AB T5M 0H4, Canada
Tel: 780-452-1455; Fax: 780-452-1455
st.georgesgreekschool@gmail.com
www.gocedm.com/greek-school/
Grades: 10-12
Maria Carrozza, Principal

Edmonton: Solomon College
#228, 10621 - 100 Ave., Edmonton, AB T5J 0B3, Canada
Tel: 780-431-1515; Fax: 780-431-1644
info@solomoncollege.ca
www.solomoncollege.ca
Grades: 10-12; Enrollment: 1000
Ping Ping Lee, Principal

Edmonton: Tempo School
5603 - 148 St., Edmonton, AB T6H 4T7, Canada
Tel: 780-434-1190; Fax: 780-430-6209
admin@temposchool.org
www.temposchool.org
Grades: Pre.-12; Enrollment: 380

B. Michael, Head, Lower School
R. Slevinsky, Head, Upper School

Edmonton: Waldorf Independent School of Edmonton
7114 - 98 St., Edmonton, AB T6E 3M1
Tel: 780-466-3312
info@wese.ca
www.thewise.ca
Grades: K - 4
Mandie Abrams, President
mandie@wese.ca

Neerlandia: Covenant Canadian Reformed School
P.O. Box 67
Neerlandia, AB T0G 1R0, Canada
Tel: 780-674-4774; Fax: 780-401-3295
ccrs.office@gmail.com
covenantschool.ca
Grades: K - 12; Special Ed.; Enrollment: 170; Note: Students are members of the Canadian Reformed or United Reformed churchesLocation: 3030 Township Rd. 615A, Neerlandia.
J. Meinen, Principal
principal@covenantschool.ca

Okotoks: Edison School
Box 2, Site 11, RR#2, Okotoks, AB T1S 1A2
Tel: 403-938-7670; Fax: 403-938-7224
office@edisonschool.ca
www.edisonschool.ca
Grades: K - 12; Enrollment: 185; Note: Edison School is a fully accredited private school.

Okotoks: Strathcona-Tweedsmuir School
RR#2, Okotoks, AB T1S 1A2, Canada
Tel: 403-938-4431; Fax: 403-938-4492
advancement@sts.ab.ca
www.sts.ab.ca
www.facebook.com/StrathconaTweedsmuirSchool
twitter.com/STSConnections
www.linkedin.com/groups?gid=3237845
www.youtube.com/user/STSConnections
Grades: 1-12
William Jones, Head of School
wagerj@sts.ab.ca

Ponoka: Woodlands Adventist School
P.O. Box 16
Site 2, RR#3, Ponoka, AB T4J 1R3, Canada
Tel: 403-783-2640; Fax: 403-783-2878
woodlands22.adventistschoolconnect.org
Grades: 1 - 8
Andrea Gray, Principal
andrea.a.gray@gmail.com

Red Deer: Parkland School
6016 - 45 Ave., Red Deer, AB T4N 3M4, Canada
Tel: 403-347-3911; Fax: 403-342-2677
prkland@shaw.ca
www.parklandschool.org
Grades: 4 - 19 yrs old; Special Ed.; Number of Employees: 45
Trudy Lewis, Chief of Educational Services

Spirit River: Northern Lights School
Box 19, Site 4, RR#1, Spirit River, AB T0H 3G0, Canada
Tel: 780-351-2242; Fax: 780-351-2280
Grades: 1 - 9; Note: The Northern Lights Church of God in Christ Mennonite congregation operates the Northern Lights School.

St Paul: Blue Quills First Nations College (BQFNC)
P.O. Box 279
3 Airport Rd. North, St Paul, AB T0A 3A0, Canada
Tel: 780-645-4455; Fax: 780-645-5215
Toll-Free: 1-888-645-4455
www.bluequills.ca
www.facebook.com/179353185415252
Dr. Leona Makokis, BAdm, BEd, MA, EdD, President
Bernadine Houle-Steinhauer, BA, PRdip, Director, Special Projects
Dr. Patricia Makokis, EdD, Director, Curriculum Development
Dr. Halia Boychuk, BEd, MA, PhD, Coordinator, University Transfer
Sherri Chisan, BMgmt, MA, Coordinator, Leadership & Management
Sharon Steinhauer, BSW, RSW, Coordinator, Social Work Diploma
Lena Lapatrack, Registrar
registrar@bluequills.ca

Stony Plain: St. Matthew Lutheran School
5014 - 53 Ave., Stony Plain, AB T7Z 1R8, Canada
Tel: 780-963-2715; Fax: 780-963-7324
school@st-matthew.com
www.stmatthewschool.ca

Grades: Pre.-9
Rev. Mark Dressler, Principal

Sylvan Lake: Sylvan Meadows Adventist School
P.O. Box 1006B
Sylvan Lake, AB T4S 1X6
Tel: 403-887-5766; *Fax:* 403-887-5766
www.sylvanmeadows.org

Wetaskiwin: Peace Hills Adventist School
RR#3, Stn Main, Wetaskiwin, AB T9A 1X1
Tel: 780-352-8555
peacehillsschool@gmail.com
peace23.adventistschoolconnect.org

Universities & Colleges

First Nations

Edmonton: Yellowhead Tribal College
Also known as: Yellowhead Tribal Education Centre
#304, 17304 - 105 Ave., Edmonton, AB T5S 1G4, Canada
Tel: 780-484-0303; *Fax:* 780-481-7275
ytced.ab.ca
www.facebook.com/389508347728000
twitter.com/YTCLibrary
www.youtube.com/user/YTCollege
Note: Academic environment that nurtures First Nations cultures & traditions.
Sam Shaw, President & Chief Academic Officer
Dawn Arcand, Registrar

Maskwacis: Maskwacis Cultural College
P.O. Box 960
Maskwacis, AB T0C 1N0
Tel: 780-585-3925; *Fax:* 780-585-2080
info@mccedu.ca
www.mccedu.ca
www.facebook.com/maskwacisculturalcollege
maskwacisculturalcollege.wordpress.com
Note: An Indigenous People's cultural college

Distance Education

Athabasca: Athabasca University (AU)
1 University Dr., Athabasca, AB T9S 3A3, Canada
Tel: 780-675-6782; *Fax:* 780-675-6450
Toll-Free: 800-788-9041
www.athabascau.ca
www.facebook.com/Athabasca.University
twitter.com/AUAnnounce
www.athabascau.ca/contact/social/index.php
www.youtube.com/user/AthabascaUniversity
Full Time Equivalency: 30660; *Note:* An open university offering any student access to university-level study.
Mark Fabbro, Registrar, 780-675-6165
markf@athabascau.ca
Dr Frits Pannekoek, President
Dr Margaret Haughey, Vice-Pres., Academic
mhaughey@athabascau.ca
Dr Ray Block, Vice-Pres., Finance/Admin.
Lori Van Rooijen, Vice-Pres., Advancement
Brian Stewart, Chief Information Officer
brians@athabascau.ca
Greg Wiens, Dir., Facilities/Services
gregw@athabascau.ca
David Hrenewich, Dir., Computing Services
daveh@athabascau.ca
Elizabeth Munroe, Assoc. Dir., Human Resources
Elaine Fabbro, Acting Dir., Library Services

Faculties

Faculty of Business
Tel: 780-675-6189; *Toll-Free:* 800-468-6531
business@athabascau.ca
business.athabascau.ca
www.facebook.com/athabascau.business
twitter.com/AU_Business
www.youtube.com/channel/UCjBH3ZlWtTfvzqYPB0yAEGg
Deborah Hurst, Dean, Faculty of Business (Acting)
deborah.hurst@fb.athabascau.ca

Faculty of Health Disciplines
Toll-Free: 800-788-9041
fhdcontact@athabascau.ca
ovpa.athabascau.ca/faculties/fhd/
Margaret Edwards, Acting Dean, Faculty of Health Disciplines

Faculty of Humanities & Social Sciences
Tel: 780-675-6564
fhss.athabascau.ca
Dr. Veronica Thompson, Dean, Faculty of Humanities & Social Sciences

Faculty of Science & Technology
Toll-Free: 855-362-2870
fst_success@athabascau.ca
fst.athabascau.ca
www.facebook.com/athabascau.ScienceTech
twitter.com/AthaU_ScTech
Dr. Lisa Carter, Dean, Faculty of Science and Technology
lisac@athabascau.ca

Faculty of Graduate Studies
Tel: 780-418-7536; *Fax:* 780-459-2093
Toll-Free: 800-561-4650
fgs@athabascau.ca
fgs.athabascau.ca
Dr. Pamela Hawranik, Dean, Faculty of Graduate Studies
phawranik@athabascau.ca
Dr. Shawn Fraser, Acting Dean, Faculty of Graduate Studies, 780-430-0590
sfraser@athabascau.ca

Centres/Institutes

Centre for Learning Design and Development
Fax: 780-675-6144
Toll-Free: 800-788-9041
cldd.athabascau.ca
Cindy Ives, Director, 780-675-6957
cindyi@athabascau.ca

Centre for Distance Education
Tel: 780-675-6179; *Fax:* 780-675-6170
Toll-Free: 800-788-9041
mde@athabascau.ca
cde.athabascau.ca
Marti Cleveland-Innes, Chair
martic@athabascau.ca

Research Centre
Fax: 780-675-6722
Toll-Free: 800-788-9041
research@athabascau.ca
research.athabascau.ca
Rebecca Heartt, Manager, Research Services, 780-675-6275
rebeccah@athabascau.ca

Centre for Learning Accreditation
Tel: 780-675-6348; *Fax:* 780-675-6431
Toll-Free: 800-788-9041
plar@athabascau.ca
prior-learning.athabascau.ca
Dr Dianne Conrad, Director
diannec@athabascau.ca

Centre for World Indigenous Knowledge & Research
Tel: 780-428-2064
indigenous@athabascau.ca
indigenous.athabascau.ca
Dr Tracey Lindberg, Director
traceyl@athabascau.ca

Universities

Calgary: University of Calgary
2500 University Dr. NW, Calgary, AB T2N 1N4, Canada
Tel: 403-220-5110
www.ucalgary.ca
www.facebook.com/97582259854
twitter.com/UCalgary
www.linkedin.com/company/university-of-calgary
Full Time Equivalency: 31495; *Number of Employees:* 1800 faculty; 3000 staff
Elizabeth Cannon, B.Sc., M.Sc., Ph.D., President & Vice-Chancellor
Susan Belcher, Secretary
Nuvyn L. Peters, Vice-President, Development
Linda Dalgetty, Vice-President, Finance & Services
Bart Becker, Vice-President, Facilities
Karen Jackson, General Counsel
Diane Kenyon, Vice-President, University Relations
Dru Marshall, Vice-President Academic & Provost
Ed McCauley, Vice-President, Research

Education
Tel: 403-220-6794; *Fax:* 403-282-5849
educ.ucalgary.ca
twitter.com/UCalgaryEduc
Dr. Dennis Sumara, B.Ed., M.Ed., Ph.D., Dean

Schulich School of Engineering
Tel: 403-284-3697; *Fax:* 403-220-5738
schulich.ucalgary.ca
twitter.com/SchulichENGG
M. Elizabeth Cannon, P.Eng, FCAE, FRSC, Dean

Environmental Design
Tel: 403-220-6601; *Fax:* 403-284-4399
evdsinfo@ucalgary.ca
evds.ucalgary.ca
www.facebook.com/pages/EVDS/89197466145?sk=wall
Prof. Loraine Fowlow, Dean

Arts
Tel: 403-220-3580
arts@ucalgary.ca
arts.ucalgary.ca
twitter.com/UCalgary_Arts
Ann E. Calvert, B.A., Dip.Ed., M.Ed., Ph., Dean

Graduate Studies
Tel: 403-220-4938; *Fax:* 403-220-5417
graduate@ucalgary.ca
grad.ucalgary.ca
Dr. Fred Hall, Ph.D., Dean

Law
Tel: 403-220-7115
lawdean@ucalgary.ca
www.ucalgary.ca/law
www.facebook.com/UCalgaryLaw
twitter.com/UCalgaryLaw
Alastair R. Lucas, Q.C., Dean

Medicine
Foothills Campus
3330 Hospital Dr. NW, Calgary, AB T2N 4N1
Tel: 403-220-6842
medicine.ucalgary.ca
www.facebook.com/ucalgarymedicine
twitter.com/UofCMedicine
www.youtube.com/UCalgaryMedicine
Dr. Jon Meddings, Dean
meddings@ucalgary.ca

Nursing
Tel: 403-220-6262
nursing.ucalgary.ca
twitter.com/ucalgarynursing
www.youtube.com/ucalgarynursing
Dianne Tapp, M.N., Ph.D., Dean

Kinesiology
Tel: 403-220-3407
www.ucalgary.ca/knes
www.facebook.com/UofCKinesiology
twitter.com/uofcknes
Penny Werthner, Dean

Science
Tel: 403-220-5516; *Fax:* 403-282-9154
scidean@ucalgary.ca
science.ucalgary.ca
www.facebook.com/UofCFacultyofScience?ref=nf
twitter.com/UofC_Science
ca.linkedin.com/company/university-of-calgary?trk=ppro_cprof
Dr. J.S. Murphree, B.Sc., Ph.D., Dean

Social Work
Tel: 403-220-5942; *Fax:* 403-282-7269
socialwk@ucalgary.ca
fsw.ucalgary.ca
twitter.com/FSWServices
Gayla Rogers, B.A., B.SW., R.SW., Ph.D., Dean

Haskayne School of Business
Tel: 403-220-5685
haskayne.ucalgary.ca
www.facebook.com/uofchaskayne
twitter.com/haskayneschool
Leonard Waverman, Dean

Edmonton: University of Alberta
116 St. & 85 Ave., Edmonton, AB T6G 2R3
Tel: 780-492-3111
chat@ualberta.ca
www.ualberta.ca
www.facebook.com/ualberta
twitter.com/ualberta
www.youtube.com/user/UniversityofAlberta
Full Time Equivalency: 37830
Ralph Young, Chancellor
David H. Turpin, CM, PhD, LLD, FRSC, President, 780-492-3212
Dew Steve, PhD, Provost & Vice-President, Academic
provost@ualberta.ca
Phyllis Clark, Vice-President, Finance & Administration, 780-492-2657
Don Hickey, PEng, Vice-President, Facilities
Lorne Babiuk, Vice-President, Research, 780-492-5353
lorne.babiuk@ualberta.ca

Debra Pozega Osburn, PhD, Vice-President, University Relations, 780-492-1583
debra.osburn@ualberta.ca
Heather McCaw, Vice-President, Advancement Services, 780-492-7400
giving@ualberta.ca

Faculties

Faculty of Agriculture, Life & Environmental Sciences (ALES)
2-14 Agriculture Forestry Centre, University of A
Edmonton, AB T6G 2P5
Tel: 780-492-4931; *Fax:* 780-492-8524
questions.ales@ualberta.ca
www.ales.ualberta.ca
Stan Blade, Dean
stan.blade@ualberta.ca

Faculty of Business
2-20 Business Building, University of Alberta
Edmonton, AB T6G 2R6
Tel: 780-492-5773; *Fax:* 780-492-5863
Toll-Free: 866-492-7676
bcominfo@ualberta.ca
www.business.ualberta.ca/BCom
www.facebook.com/UofASoB
twitter.com/UofAABFI
www.youtube.com/user/abbusinessschool
Joseph Doucet, Ph.D., Dean

Faculty of Education
Faculty of Education, University of Alberta
11210 - 87 Ave., Edmonton, AB T6G 2G5
Tel: 780-492-3659
educ.info@ualberta.ca
www.education.ualberta.ca
www.facebook.com/UofAEducation
twitter.com/Education_UofA
www.youtube.com/user/EducationUofA
Fern Snart, Ph.D., Dean

Faculty of Engineering
E6-050 Engineering Teaching & Learning Complex
Edmonton, AB T6G 2V4
Tel: 780-492-3320; *Fax:* 780-492-0500
Toll-Free: 800-407-8354
www.engineering.ualberta.ca
David Lynch, Ph.D., Dean
david.lynch@ualberta.ca

Faculty of Extension
10230 Jasper Ave., Edmonton, AB T5J 4P6
Tel: 780-492-3116; *Fax:* 780-492-0627
extnregistration@ualberta.ca
www.extension.ualberta.ca
www.facebook.com/uaextension
twitter.com/uaextension
extensionnews.tumblr.com
Bill Connor, Acting Dean
bill.connor@ualberta.ca

Faculty of Graduate Studies & Research
2-29 Triffo Hall, Killam Centre for Advanced Stud
Edmonton, AB T6G 2E1
Tel: 780-492-3499; *Fax:* 780-492-0692
Toll-Free: 800-758-7136
grad.mail@ualberta.ca
www.gradstudies.ualberta.ca
twitter.com/UAGradStudies
Mazi Shirvani, Ph.D., Dean
grad.dean@ualberta.ca

Faculty of Law
111 - 89 Ave., Edmonton, AB T6G 2H5
Tel: 780-492-3115; *Fax:* 780-492-4924
lawschool.ualberta.ca
www.facebook.com/facultyoflaw.universityofalberta
twitter.com/UofALawFaculty
www.youtube.com/user/UofALaw1
Paul Paton, B.A., LL.B., M.Phil, JSM,, Dean

Faculty of Medicine & Dentistry
Walter C. Mackenzie Health Sciences Centre
9440 - 112 St. NW, Edmonton, AB T6G 2R7
Tel: 780-492-6621; *Fax:* 780-492-7303
meddent@ualberta.ca
www.med.ualberta.ca
www.facebook.com/UofAMedicineDentistry
twitter.com/UAlberta_FoMD
www.youtube.com/user/FoMDcommsteam
Doug Miller, Dean

Faculty of Nursing
Level 3, Edmonton Clinic Health Academy
11405 - 87 Ave., Edmonton, AB T6G 1C9
Fax: 780-492-2551
Toll-Free: 888-492-8089
undergraduate@nurs.ualberta.ca
www.nursing.ualberta.ca
www.facebook.com/UofANursing
Dr. Anita Molzahn, Ph.D., Dean

Faculty of Pharmacy & Pharmaceutical Sciences
2-55 Medical Sciences
8613 - 114 St., Edmonton, AB T6G 2H1
Tel: 780-492-3362
studentservices-pharmacy@ualberta.ca
www.pharm.ualberta.ca
James Kehrer, Ph.D., Dean
phdean@ualberta.ca

Faculty of Physical Education & Recreation
W1-34 Van Vliet Centre, University of Alberta
Edmonton, AB W1-34 Van V
Tel: 780-492-5604
www.physedandrec.ualberta.ca
www.facebook.com/physedandrec
Kerry Mummery, Dean

Faculty of Rehabilitation Medicine
3-48 Corbett Hall
8205 - 114 St., Edmonton, AB T6G 2G4
Tel: 780-492-2903; *Fax:* 780-492-1626
info@rehabmed.ualberta.ca
www.rehabilitation.ualberta.ca
www.facebook.com/UofARehabMedicine
twitter.com/UofARehabMed
www.youtube.com/user/RehabMedicineUofA
Bob Haennel, Ph.D., Dean

Faculty of Native Studies
2-31 Pembina Hall, University of Alberta
Edmonton, AB T6G 2H8
Tel: 780-492-2991; *Fax:* 780-492-0527
nativestudies@ualberta.ca
nativestudies.ualberta.ca
www.facebook.com/nativestudies
twitter.com/nativefaculty
Brendan Hokowhitu, Ph.D., Dean
nsdean@ualberta.ca

Faculty of Science
1-001 CCIS, University of Alberta
Edmonton, AB T6G 2E9
Tel: 780-492-4758; *Fax:* 780-492-7033
Toll-Free: 800-358-8314
www.science.ualberta.ca
www.facebook.com/UofAScience
twitter.com/ualbertascience
instagram.com/ualbertascience
Jonathan Schaeffer, Ph.D., Dean

Campus Saint-Jean
8406, rue Marie-Anne-Gaboury, Edmonton, AB T6C 4G9
Tél: 780-465-8700; *Téléc:* 780-465-8760
Ligne sans frais: 800-537-2509
saintjean@ualberta.ca
www.csj.ualberta.ca
www.facebook.com/UofACSJ
twitter.com/CSJ_Rec
www.youtube.com/user/LeCampusSaintJean
Pierre-Yves Mocquais, Ph.D., Doyen

Faculty of Arts
6-33 Humanities Centre
Edmonton, AB T6G 2E5
Tel: 780-492-2787; *Fax:* 780-492-7251
artsdean@ualberta.ca
www.foa.ualberta.ca
www.facebook.com/UofAArts
twitter.com/UofA_Arts
www.youtube.com/user/UofAlbertaArts
Lesley Cormack, Ph.D., Dean
artsdean@ualberta.ca
Lise Gotell, Ph.D., Vice-Dean
lise.gotell@ualberta.ca

Schools

School of Public Health
3-300 Edmonton Clinic Health Academy
11405 - 87 Ave., Edmonton, AB T6G 1C9
Tel: 780-492-9954; *Fax:* 780-492-0364
school.publichealth@ualberta.ca
www.publichealth.ualberta.ca
twitter.com/UofAPublicHlth
ca.linkedin.com/pub/school-of-public-health-ualberta/49/a41/507
www.youtube.com/user/SPHUofA
Kue Young, Dean
kue.young@ualberta.ca

School of Library & Information Studies
3-20 Rutherford South
Edmonton, AB T6G 2J4
Tel: 780-492-4578; *Fax:* 780-492-2430
slis@ualberta.ca
www.slis.ualberta.ca
www.facebook.com/UAlbertaSLIS
Sophia Sherman, Senior Administrator, 780-492-0373
slis@ualberta.ca

Campuses

Augustana Faculty
4901 - 46 Ave., Camrose, AB T4V 2R3
Tel: 780-679-1100; *Fax:* 780-679-1129
info@augustana.ca
www.augustana.ualberta.ca
www.facebook.com/UofAAugustana
twitter.com/UofA_Augustana
www.youtube.com/user/AugustanaCampus
Allen Berger, Dean & Executive Officer
allen.berger@ualberta.ca

St. Joseph's College
University of Alberta
11325 - 89 Ave., Edmonton, AB T6G 2J5
Tel: 780-492-7681; *Fax:* 780-492-8145
sjcdev@ualberta.ca
stjosephs.ualberta.ca
www.facebook.com/stjoesuofa
twitter.com/sjc_edmonton
Note: The College, located at the University of Alberta, was established by the Roman Catholic Archdiocese of Edmonton. It offers courses in Christian theology & philosophy.
Fr. Terry Kersch, President
kersch@ualberta.ca
Brian Maraj, Academic Dean
bmaraj@ualberta.ca

St. Stephen's College
University of Alberta Campus
8810 - 112 St., Edmonton, AB T6G 1J6
Tel: 780-439-7311; *Fax:* 780-433-8875
Toll-Free: 1-800-661-4956
ststephens@ualberta.ca
www.ualberta.ca/st.stephens/
www.facebook.com/pages/St-Stephens-College/301735949851204
Note: A graduate studies college at the University of Alberta whose program areas include Theology, Counselling, Art Therapy & Ministry
Earle Sharam, Dean
Shelley Westermann, Director, Academic/Administrative Services
westerma@ualberta.ca

Centres/Institutes

Alberta Centre for Sustainable Rural Communities (ACSRC)
Augustana Campus
4901 - 46 Ave., Camrose, AB T4V 2R3
Tel: 780-679-1672
www.augustana.ualberta.ca/research/centres/acsrc
www.facebook.com/UofA.ACSRC
twitter.com/ACSRC
www.youtube.com/user/AdminACSRC
Lars K. Hallström, Director
lars.hallstrom@ualberta.ca

Alberta Institute for Human Nutrition (AIHN)
4-126 Li Ka Shing Centre
Edmonton, AB T6G 2E1
Tel: 780-492-6668
www.ales.ualberta.ca/FacultyResearch/AlbertaInstituteHumanNutrition

Poultry Research Centre
F83 Edmonton Research Station
Edmonton, AB T6G 2E1
Tel: 780-492-6221; *Fax:* 780-492-4346
prc@ualberta.ca
www.poultry.ales.ualberta.ca
Martin Zuidhof, Academic Leader
martin.zuidhof@ualberta.ca

Dairy Research & Technology Centre (DRTC)
F-30 Edmonton Research Station, South Campus
Edmonton, AB T6H 2V5
Tel: 780-492-9003; *Fax:* 780-492-8580
drtc.ales.ualberta.ca

Canadian Centre for Corporate Social Responsibility (CCCSR)
Alberta School of Business
Edmonton, AB T6G 2R6
Tel: 780-492-2386; *Fax:* 780-492-3325
cccsr@ualberta.ca
business.ualberta.ca/centres/corporate-social-responsibility
Roy Suddaby, Academic Director
roy.suddaby@ualberta.ca

Canadian Corporate Governance Institute
4-20K Business Building
Edmonton, AB T6G 2R6
Tel: 780-492-2457; *Fax:* 780-492-9924
ccgi@ualberta.ca
business.ualberta.ca/centres/corporate-governance

Centre for Applied Business Research in Energy & the Environment
3-23 Alberta School of Business
Edmonton, AB T6G 2R6
Tel: 780-248-1650
business.ualberta.ca/centres/applied-research-energy-and-environment
Richard Dixon, Executive Director
rjdixon@ualberta.ca

Centre for Entrepreneurship & Family Enterprise
4-20B Business Building
Edmonton, AB T6G 2R6
Tel: 780-492-5876; *Fax:* 780-492-2519
cefe@ualberta.ca
business.ualberta.ca/centres/family-entrepreneurship
Llpud Steier, Vice Dean

Centre for International Business Studies
3-23 Alberta School of Business
Edmonton, AB T6G 2R6
Fax: 780-492-4631
Toll-Free: 866-492-7676
cibs@ualberta.ca
business.ualberta.ca/centres/international-business-studies
Edy Wong, Director
edy@ualberta.ca

Technology Commercialization Centre
4-21F Alberta School of Business
Edmonton, AB T6G 2R6
Tel: 780-492-3054; *Fax:* 780-492-3325
tcc@ualberta.ca
business.ualberta.ca/centres/technology-commercialization
Mike Lounsbury, Director
ml37@ualberta.ca

***Lethbridge:* University of Lethbridge**
4401 University Dr., Lethbridge, AB T1K 3M4, Canada
Tel: 403-329-2111
www.uleth.ca
www.facebook.com/ulethbridge
twitter.com/ulethbridge
www.linkedin.com/company/university-of-lethbridge
www.youtube.com/user/ulethbridge
Full Time Equivalency: 8212; *Number of Employees:* 1157
Mike Mahon, Ph.D., President & Vice-Chancellor
president@uleth.ca
Lesley Brown, Vice-President, Research
l.brown@uleth.ca
Andrew Hakin, Vice-President, Academic & Provost
hakin@uleth.ca
Nancy Walker, Vice-President, Finance & Administration
nancy.walker@uleth.ca

Faculties

Faculty of Arts & Science
Tel: 403-329-5101
www.uleth.ca/artsci
Chris Nicol, Dean

Faculty of Education
Tel: 403-329-2254; *Fax:* 403-329-2372
edu.sps@uleth.ca
www.uleth.ca/education
twitter.com/ULethbridgeEdu
Jane O'Dea, Dean

Faculty of Fine Arts
Tel: 403-329-2126; *Fax:* 403-382-7127
finearts@uleth.ca
www.uleth.ca/finearts
Dr. Desmond Rochfort, Dean

Faculty of Management
Tel: 403-329-2153
undergrad.management@uleth.ca
www.uleth.ca/management
www.facebook.com/232080066811333
Murray Lindsay, Dean

Faculty of Health Sciences
Tel: 403-329-2699
health.sciences@uleth.ca
www.uleth.ca/healthsciences
Christopher Hosgood, Dean

Schools

School of Graduate Studies
Tel: 403-329-5194; *Fax:* 403-332-5239
sgsinquiries@uleth.ca
www.uleth.ca/graduatestudies
www.facebook.com/105561602818712
twitter.com/UofLGradStudies
uoflgradprogram.blogspot.ca
Dr. Jo-Anne Fiske, Dean

Colleges

***Calgary:* Alberta College of Art & Design (ACAD)**
1407 - 14 Ave. NW, Calgary, AB T2N 4R3, Canada
Tel: 403-284-7600
registrar@acad.ca
www.acad.ca
www.facebook.com/AlbertaCollegeofArtandDesign
twitter.com/acadonline
www.youtube.com/acadonline
Full Time Equivalency: 1115
Dr. Daniel Doz, President & CEO
Donald Dart, Senior Vice-President, Finance & Corporate Service
Alison Miyauchi, Associate Vice-President, Research & Academic Affairs

***Calgary:* Ambrose University College**
150 Ambrose Circle SW, Calgary, AB T3H 0L5, Canada
Tel: 403-410-2000; *Fax:* 403-571-2556
reception@ambrose.edu
ambrose.edu
facebook.com/ambroseuc
twitter.com/ambroseuc
www.youtube.com/AmbroseUniversity
Full Time Equivalency: 700; *Note:* Formerly Alliance University College/Nazarene University College
Dr. Gordon T. Smith, President
Riley Coulter, Chancellor

***Calgary:* Bow Valley College**
345 - 6 Ave. SE, Calgary, AB T2G 4V1, Canada
Tel: 403-410-1400; *Fax:* 403-297-4887
Toll-Free: 866-428-2669
info@bowvalleycollege.ca
www.bowvalleycollege.ca
TTY: 403-410-1505
www.facebook.com/bowvalleycollege
twitter.com/BowValley
www.flickr.com/photos/bowvalleycollege
Full Time Equivalency: 13000
Sharon Carry, President & CEO
Anna Kae Todd, Vice-President, Academic & Chief Learning Officer, 403-410-1442
Gayle Burnett, Vice-President, College Services & Chief Financial Officer, 403-410-1445
David J. Michell, Vice-President, College Advancement & External Relations, 403-410-1760
Catherine Koch, Vice-President, Learner Services & Student Services, 403-410-1445

***Calgary:* St. Mary's University College**
14500 Bannister Rd. SE, Calgary, AB T2X 1Z4, Canada
Tel: 403-531-9130; *Fax:* 403-531-9136
admissions@stmu.ca
www.stmu.ab.ca
twitter.com/StMarysUC
Full Time Equivalency: 700; *Note:* The post-secondary institution operates in the tradition of Catholic scholarship in Canada. Liberal arts & sciences are taught.
Most Rev. Frederick Henry, DD, Chancellor
Dr. Gerry Turcotte, Vice-Chancellor & President, 403-254-3701
Dr. Tara Hyland-Russell, Vice-President, Academic & Dean, 403-254-3771
Bob Hann, Vice-President, Student Services, 403-254-3772
Debra Osiowy, Vice-President, Business & Finance, 403-254-3702
Thérèse Takacs, Vice-President, Advancement, 403-254-3702

***Edmonton:* Concordia University of Edmonton**
7128 Ada Blvd. NW, Edmonton, AB T5B 4E4, Canada
Tel: 780-479-8481; *Fax:* 780-477-1033
Toll-Free: 866-479-5200
info@concordia.ab.ca
concordia.ab.ca
www.facebook.com/Concordia.University.College
twitter.com/CUCA_Edmonton
www.youtube.com/user/ConcordiaEdmonton
Full Time Equivalency: 1420
Dr. Gerald Krispin, President & Vice-Chancellor
gerald.krispin@concordia.ab.ca
Judy Kruse, Director, Policy & Records Management, 780-479-9253
judy.kruse@concordia.ab.ca

***Edmonton:* Grant MacEwan Community College**
P.O. Box 1796
Edmonton, AB T5J 2P2
Tel: 780-497-5040; *Fax:* 780-497-5001
Toll-Free: 1-888-497-4622
info@macewan.ca
www.gmcc.ab.ca
www.facebook.com/GrantMacEwanUniversity
twitter.com/macewanu
www.youtube.com/macewanchannel
Note: Enrolment figure includes full-time & part-time students
Dr. David Atkinson, President

***Edmonton:* The King's University College**
9125 - 50 St., Edmonton, AB T6B 2H3
Tel: 780-465-3500; *Fax:* 780-465-3534
Toll-Free: 800-661-8582
www.kingsu.ca
www.facebook.com/TheKingsUniversityCollege
twitter.com/TheKingsUC/
www.linkedin.com/company/746587?trk=tyah
www.youtube.com/user/TheKingsUC
Full Time Equivalency: 690
Dr. Melanie Humphreys, President

***Edmonton:* NorQuest College**
Downtown Campus, Main Bldg.
10215 - 108 St. NW, Edmonton, AB T5J 1L6
Tel: 780-644-6000; *Fax:* 780-644-6013
Toll-Free: 866-534-7218
info@norquest.ca
www.norquest.ca
www.facebook.com/pages/NorQuest-College/144418728949989
twitter.com/NorQuest
www.linkedin.com/company/36492
www.youtube.com/NorQuestVids
Jodi Abbott, President & CEO

***Edmonton:* Taylor College & Seminary**
11525 - 23 Ave. NW, Edmonton, AB T6J 4T3
Tel: 780-431-5200; *Fax:* 780-436-9416
Toll-Free: 800-567-4988
info@taylor-edu.ca
www.taylor-edu.ca
www.facebook.com/TaylorUpdates
David Williams, President
Su Jin Chong, Registrar
Eric Ohlmann, Academic Dean

***Fort McMurray:* Keyano College**
8115 Franklin Ave., Fort McMurray, AB T9H 2H7
Tel: 780-791-4800; *Toll-Free:* 800-251-1408
www.keyanoc.ab.ca
www.facebook.com/keyanocollege
www.twitter.com/keyanocollege
www.linkedin.com/company/keyano-college
www.youtube.com/user/keyanocollege
Kevin F. Nagel, President
Dwayne Hart, Vice-President, Finance & Administration
Catherine Koch, Vice-President, Academic

Campuses

Janvier Learning Center
P.O. Box 85
Janvier, AB T0P 1G0
Tel: 780-559-2047; *Fax:* 780-559-2999

Gregoire Lake Learning Centre
General Delivery, Arzac, AB, Canada
Tel: 780-334-2559; *Fax:* 780-334-2559

Conklin Learning Centre
245 Northland Dr., Conklin, AB T0P 1H1, Canada
Tel: 780-559-2434

Fort McKay Learning Centre
General Delivery, Fort McKay, AB T0P 1C0
Tel: 780-828-4433; *Fax:* 780-828-4434

***Grande Prairie:* Grande Prairie Regional College (GPRC)**
10726 - 106 Ave., Grande Prairie, AB T8V 4C4, Canada
Tel: 780-539-2944; *Fax:* 780-539-2832
Toll-Free: 888-539-4772
studentinfo@gprc.ab.ca
www.gprc.ab.ca
www.facebook.com/441390429205593
twitter.com/GPRC_AB
www.youtube.com/user/GPRCab
Full Time Equivalency: 2000
Don Gnatiuk, President & CEO
dgnatiuk@gprc.ab.ca
Susan Bansgrove, Vice-President, Academics & Research
sbansgrove@gprc.ab.ca

Campuses
Fairview Campus
P.O. Box 3000
11235 - 98 Ave., Fairview, AB T0H 1L0, Canada
Tel: 780-835-6600; *Fax:* 780-835-6788
Toll-Free: 888-999-7882
Marg McCuaig-Boyd, Vice President
mmccuaig-boyd@gprc.ab.ca

***Lac La Biche:* Portage College**
P.O. Box 417
Lac La Biche, AB T0A 2C0, Canada
Tel: 780-623-5580; *Fax:* 780-623-5519
Toll-Free: 866-623-5551
info@portagecollege.ca
www.portagecollege.ca
www.facebook.com/PortageCollege
twitter.com/PortageCollege
www.linkedin.com/company/portage-college
www.flickr.com/photos/portagetrail
Note: Business Career; Human Services; Native Arts & Culture; Health & Wellness; Trades & Technical; Academic Upgrading programs
Ray Danyluk, Chair
Trent Keough, President

Campuses
Cold Lake Campus
Cold Lake Energy Centre
#101, 7825 - 51 St., Cold Lake, AB T9M 0B6
Tel: 780-639-0030; *Fax:* 780-639-2330
Toll-Free: 866-623-5551
www.portagecollege.ca/Campus_Locations/Cold_Lake.htm
Note: Also provides administrative & support services for the school's Bonnyville & Frog Lake campuses.

St. Paul Campus
P.O. Box 1471
5205 - 50 Ave., St Paul, AB T0A 3A0
Tel: 780-645-5223; *Fax:* 780-645-5162
Toll-Free: 866-623-5551
www.portagecollege.ca/Campus_Locations/St_Paul.htm
Note: Also provides administrative & support services for the school's Saddle Lake & Whitefish Lake campuses.

***Lacombe:* Burman University**
6730 University Dr., Lacombe, AB T4L 2E5
Tel: 403-782-3381; *Toll-Free:* 800-661-8129
info@burmanu.ca
www.burmanu.ca
www.facebook.com/burmanuniversity
www.youtube.com/cucvideos
Mark Haynal, President, 403-782-3381, ext. 4147
mhaynal@burmanu.ca

***Lethbridge:* Lethbridge College**
3000 College Dr. South, Lethbridge, AB T1K 1L6
Tel: 403-320-3200; *Toll-Free:* 800-572-0103
info@lethbridgecollege.ca
www.lethbridgecollege.ca
www.facebook.com/LethbridgeCollege
www.twitter.com/LethCollege
www.youtube.com/lethbridgecollege
Paula Burns, President, 403-320-3209
president@lethbridgecollege.ca

Campuses
Claresholm Campus
P.O. Box 2049
Claresholm, AB T0L 0T0
Tel: 403-625-4231; *Fax:* 403-625-4266
claresholm@lethbridgecollege.ca

Crowsnest Pass Campus
P.O. Box 1349
Blairmore, AB T0K 0E0, Canada
Tel: 403-562-2853; *Fax:* 403-562-8045
crowsnestpass@lethbridgecollege.ca

Vulcan County Campus
110 - 1 Ave. South, Lethbridge, AB T0L 2B0
Tel: 403-485-4100; *Fax:* 403-485-3143
vulcancounty@lethbridgecollege.ca

***Olds:* Olds College**
4500 - 50th St., Olds, AB T4H 1R6, Canada
Tel: 403-556-8281; *Fax:* 403-556-4711
Toll-Free: 1-800-661-6537
info@oldscollege.ca
www.oldscollege.ca
Other Information: Continuing Education: 403-507-7956; Registrar: 403-556-8281
www.facebook.com/olds.college
www.twitter.com/oldscollege
www.youtube.com/user/OldsCollegeComm
Full Time Equivalency: 1309; *Note:* Olds College features the following areas of study: Agriculture; Animal Sciences; Business; Fashion; Horticulture; Land & Environment; School of Trades; & Continuing Education.
Robert C. Clark, Chair
H.J. (Tom) Thompson, President & CEO

Campuses
Calgary Campus
345 - 6th Ave. SE, Calgary, AB T2G 4V1
Tel: 403-697-6130; *Fax:* 403-697-6131

***Siksika:* Old Sun Community College**
P.O. Box 1250
Siksika, AB T0J 3W0, Canada
Tel: 403-734-3862; *Fax:* 403-734-5363
Toll-Free: 888-734-3862
admin@oldsuncollege.net
www.oldsuncollege.net
Amelia Clark, President/Post-Secondary Director, 403-734-3862, ext. 222
amelia@oldsuncollege.net

***Slave Lake:* Northern Lakes College**
1201 Main St. SE, Slave Lake, AB T0G 2A3
Tel: 780-849-8600; *Fax:* 780-849-2570
Toll-Free: 1-866-652-3456
info@northernlakescollege.ca
www.northernlakescollege.ca
Other Information: Grouard Phone: 780-751-3200; Library (Slave Lake): 780-849-8670
www.facebook.com/NorthernLakesCollege
www.twitter.com/Your_Future
Note: Distance learning is an important part of the college education. Northern Lakes College reaches full-time & part-time students in 30 rural communities in north central Alberta.
Archie Cunningham, Chair
Ann Everatt, President/CEO, 780-751-3260

Campuses
Grouard Campus
P.O. Box 3000
Grouard, AB T0G 1C0, Canada
Tel: 780-849-8600; *Fax:* 780-751-3355

***Vermilion:* Lakeland College**
Also known as: Alberta/Saskatchewan Interprovincial Coll.
Vermillion Campus
5707 College Dr., Vermilion, AB T9X 1K5
Tel: 780-853-8400; *Toll-Free:* 800-661-6490
livethelearning@lakelandcollege.ca
www.lakelandcollege.ca
www.facebook.com/pages/Lakeland-College-Canada/31034183894
twitter.com/LakelandCollege
www.linkedin.com/company/lakeland-college-canada
www.youtube.com/user/LakelandCollegeAB
Tracy Edwards, President & CEO

Campuses
Lloyminster Campus
2602 - 59 Ave., Lloydminster, AB T9V 3N7
Tel: 780-871-5700; *Toll-Free:* 800-661-6490

Emergency Training Centre
5704 College Dr., Vermilion, AB T9X 1K4
Tel: 780-853-5800;

Post Secondary/Technical

First Nations

***Cardston:* Red Crow Community College (RCCC)**
P.O. Box 1258
Cardston, AB T0K 0K0, Canada
Tel: 403-737-2400; *Fax:* 403-737-2101
Toll-Free: 866-937-2400
webmaster@redcrowcollege.com
www.redcrowcollege.com
Note: Mi'Kai'sto Red Crow Community College is a post-secondary institution whcih offers Diploma, Degree and Masters programs. The College partners with Mount Royal, Lethbridge Community College, SAIT, the University of Lethbridge, & the University of Calgary.
Dr. Marie Smallface-Marule, President

Distance Education

***Barrhead:* Alberta Distance Learning Centre (ADLC)**
P.O. Box 4000
4601 - 63 Ave., Barrhead, AB T7N 1P4
Tel: 780-674-5333; *Fax:* 780-674-7593
Toll-Free: 866-774-5333
information@adlc.ca
www.adlc.ca
Note: ADLC is a provincially-funded school serving students and schools throughout Alberta, the Northwest Territories, and Nunavut.

Colleges

***Calgary:* Mount Royal University**
Lincoln Park Campus
4825 Mount Royal Gate SW, Calgary, AB T3E 6K6, Canada
Tel: 403-440-6111; *Fax:* 403-440-5938
Toll-Free: 1-877-440-5001
externalrelations@mtroyal.ca
www.mtroyal.ca
www.facebook.com/MountRoyal4U
twitter.com/mountroyal4u
www.youtube.com/user/MountRoyal4U
Enrollment: 11890; *Note:* Sixty-eight credit programs are offered by the college.
Bryan Pinney, Chair
Dr. David Docherty, Ph.D., President, 403-440-6393
president@mtroyal.ca
Dr. Kathryn Shailer, Ph.D., Provost & Vice-President, Academic

Campuses
Sprinkbank Campus
143 MacLaurin Dr., Springbank, AB
Tel: 403-288-9551
Paul Tigchelaar, Principal
Grace Lo-Voo, Vice Principal
Dan Dowber, Director, Development

***Edmonton:* Grant MacEwan University**
P.O. Box 1796
Edmonton, AB T5J 2P2, Canada
Toll-Free: 888-497-4622
info@macewan.ca
www.macewan.ca
www.facebook.com/GrantMacEwanUniversity
twitter.com/macewanu
www.linkedin.com/edu/school?id=21055
www.youtube.com/macewanchannel
Dr. David Atkinson, President

Campuses
Alberta College Campus
10050 MacDonald Dr., Edmonton, AB T5J 0S3, Canada
Tel: 780-497-5040

Centre for the Arts and Communications
10045 - 156 St., Edmonton, AB T5P 2P7
Tel: 780-497-4340

City Centre Campus
10700 - 104 Ave., Edmonton, AB T5J 4S2, Canada
Tel: 780-497-4037; *Fax:* 780-497-5001

South Campus
7319 - 29 Ave., Edmonton, AB T6K 2P1, Canada
Tel: 780-497-4040

***Fort McMurray:* Keyano College**
8115 Franklin Ave., Fort McMurray, AB T9H 2H7, Canada
Tel: 780-791-4800; *Fax:* 780-791-1555
Toll-Free: 1-800-251-1408
registrar@keyano.ca
www.keyano.ca
www.facebook.com/keyanocollege
www.twitter.com/keyanocollege
www.youtube.com/user/keyanocollege
Dr. Kevin Nagel, President

***Medicine Hat:* Medicine Hat College**
299 College Dr. SE, Medicine Hat, AB T1A 3Y6, Canada
Tel: 403-529-3811; *Fax:* 403-504-3517
Toll-Free: 866-282-8394
info@mhc.ab.ca
www.mhc.ab.ca
www.facebook.com/MHCollege
twitter.com/mhcollege
www.youtube.com/mhcca
Ralph Weeks, Ph.D., President
weeks@mhc.ab.ca

Campuses
Brooks Campus
200 Horticultural Rd. East, Brooks, AB T1R 1E5, Canada
Tel: 403-362-1677; *Fax:* 403-362-1474
brooksinfo@mhc.ab.ca
www.mhc.ab.ca/BrooksCampus
Other Information: Academic Advising: 403-362-1682

***Red Deer:* Red Deer College**
P.O. Box 5005
100 College Blvd., Red Deer, AB T4N 5H5, Canada
Tel: 403-342-3300; *Fax:* 403-340-8940
inquire@rdc.ab.ca
www.rdc.ab.ca
www.facebook.com/RedDeerCollege?sk=app_21310458208813
6
www.twitter.com/RedDeerCollege
Joel Ward, President

Post Secondary/Technical

***Banff:* The Banff Centre**
P.O. Box 1020
107 Tunnel Mountain Dr., Banff, AB T1L 1H5, Canada
Tel: 403-762-6100; *Fax:* 403-762-6444
www.banffcentre.ca
Other Information: Telex: Artsbanff 03-826657
www.facebook.com/thebanffcentre
www.twitter.com/thebanffcentre
www.youtube.com/thebanffcentre
Janice Price, President & CEO

***Calgary:* ABM College**
#200, 3880 - 29 St. NE, Calgary, AB T1Y 6B6
Tel: 403-719-4300; *Fax:* 403-910-4300
info@ABMCollege.com
www.abmcollege.com
Note: Health and Technology College.

Campuses
ABM College - Toronto Campus
#205, 705 Lawrence Ave. West, Toronto, ON M6A 1B4
Tel: 416-913-4700; *Fax:* 416-913-3335
info@ABMCollege.com
www.abmcollege.com
Note: Health and Technology College.

***Calgary:* Alberta Business & Educational Services (ABES)**
2910 - 3 Ave. NE, Calgary, AB T2A 6T7
Tel: 403-232-8758; *Fax:* 403-265-9368
recruiter@abes.ca
www.abes.ca
twitter.com/ABESCalgary
Note: Healthcare and medical service training.

***Calgary:* Alberta College of Acupuncture & Traditional Chinese Medicine**
#125, 4935 - 40th Ave. NW, Calgary, AB T3A 2N1
Tel: 403-286-8788; *Toll-Free:* 888-789-9984
info@acatcm.com
www.acatcm.com
Dr. Dennis Lee, Co-President
Dr. Colton Oswald, Co-President

***Calgary:* Alberta Health & Safety Training Institute (AHSTI)**
#125, 3510 - 29th St. NE, Calgary, AB T1Y 7E5
Tel: 403-670-5406; *Fax:* 866-202-1822
Toll-Free: 888-670-5406
info@safetyed.ca
www.safetyed.ca

***Calgary:* Alberta Professional Driving School**
#22, 3434 - 34 Ave. NE, Calgary, AB T1Y-6X3
Tel: 403-250-8800; *Fax:* 403-250-8911
salena_grewal@hotmail.com
www.albertaprodrivingschool.com
Note: Class 1,3 and 5 training, Defensive Driving Course (DDC) and insurance reduction courses.

***Calgary:* Artists With Makeup Academy**
#306, 822 - 11th Ave. SW, Calgary, AB T2R 0E5
Tel: 403-208-0034
info@artistswithin.com
www.artistswithin.com
www.facebook.com/125396134349
twitter.com/artistswithin
ca.linkedin.com/pub/artists-within/21/908/292

***Calgary:* Breden Institute - Centre for Learning**
#500, 744 - 4th Ave. SW, Calgary, AB T2P 3T4
Tel: 403-261-5775; *Fax:* 403-264-9736
pharmacycal@bredin.ca
www.bredin.ca
www.facebook.com/162888623758374
twitter.com/BredinInstitute
Note: Building Information Modelling (BIM) Program; International Pharmacy Bridge Program

Campuses
Breden Institute - Centre for Learning - Edmonton
#500, Capital Place, Edmonton, AB T5K 2L9
Tel: 780-425-3730; *Fax:* 780-426-3709
pharmacyedm@bredin.ca
www.bredin.ca
www.facebook.com/162888623758374
twitter.com/BredinInstitute
Note: International Pharmacy Bridge Program.

***Calgary:* Calgary College of Traditional Medicine and Acupuncture**
#107/217, 4014 Macleod Trail, Calgary, AB T2G 2R7
Tel: 403-287-8688; *Fax:* 403-287-8660
Toll-Free: 866-676-8688
info@cctcma.com
www.cctcma.com
www.facebook.com/156679827719322?fref=ts
Dr. Frank H. Du, President

***Calgary:* Cambrooks College**
#202, 4015 - 17 Ave. SE, Calgary, AB T2A 0S8
Tel: 403-452-3694; *Fax:* 403-452-6111
info@cambrooks.ca
www.cambrooks.ca
www.facebook.com/pages/Cambrooks-College-Calgary/1482426
12041392
Note: Programs in Information Technology, Business, Health, Academic Upgrading, or English as a Second Language.

***Calgary:* Canadian Institute of Traditional Chinese Medicine (CITCM)**
138 - 17th Ave. NE, Calgary, AB T2E 1L6
Tel: 403-520-5258; *Fax:* 866-428-2909
Toll-Free: 888-859-8686
www.citcm.com/college
www.facebook.com/CITCM
Note: CITCM offers programs including an Acupuncture Diploma program, a fully funded Double Major Acupuncture/Doctor of Traditional Chinese Medicine diploma program and a Bachelor of Traditional Chinese Medicine degree.

***Calgary:* Canadian School of Natural Nutrition - Calgary**
1415 - 28 St. NE, Calgary, AB T2A 2P6
Tel: 403-276-1551
info@csnncal.ca
www.csnn.ca/calgary

Campuses
Canadian School of Natural Nutrition - Edmonton
#200, 9413 - 45th Ave., Edmonton, AB T6E 6B9
Tel: 780-437-3933; *Fax:* 780-437-3905
info@csnnedm.ca
www.csnn.ca/edmonton

Canadian School of Natural Nutrition - Halifax
#205, 800 Windmill Rd., Dartmouth, NS B3B 1L1
Tel: 902-425-0895; *Fax:* 902-425-0592
halifax@csnn.ca
www.csnn.ca/halifax
www.facebook.com/110296279072783
twitter.com/CSNNHalifax

Canadian School of Natural Nutrition - Kelowna
#102, 1626 Richter St., Kelowna, BC V1Y 2M3
Tel: 250-862-2766
kelowna@csnn.ca
www.csnn.ca/kelowna

Canadian School of Natural Nutrition - London
#108, 747 Hyde Park Rd., London, ON N6H 3S3
Tel: 519-936-1610; *Fax:* 519-936-1809
london@csnn.ca
www.csnn.ca/london
www.facebook.com/joni.yungblut.CSNN.London
twitter.com/CSNN_London

Canadian School of Natural Nutrition - Mississauga
#205, 1107 Lorne Park Rd., Mississauga, ON L5H 3A1
Tel: 905-891-0024
mississauga@csnn.ca
www.csnn.ca/mississauga
www.facebook.com/joni.yungblut.CSNN.London
twitter.com/CSNN_London

Canadian School of Natural Nutrition - Moncton
#205, 1201 Mountain Rd., Moncton, NB E1C 2T4
Tel: 506-384-2700
moncton@csnn.ca
www.csnn.ca/moncton

Canadian School of Natural Nutrition - Nanaimo
70 Church St., Nanaimo, BC V9R 5H4
Tel: 250-741-4805
nanaimo@csnn.ca
www.csnn.ca/nanaimo

Canadian School of Natural Nutrition - Ottawa
#204, 2148 Carling Ave., Ottawa, ON K2A 1H1
Tel: 613-728-2485; *Fax:* 613-728-3397
ottawa@csnn.ca
www.csnn.ca/ottawa

Canadian School of Natural Nutrition - Richmond Hill
#220, 10720 Yonge St., Richmond Hill, ON L4C 3C9
Tel: 905-737-0284
richmondhill@csnn.ca
www.csnn.ca/richmondhill

Canadian School of Natural Nutrition - Toronto
#305, 2221 Yonge St., Toronto, ON M4S 2B4
Tel: 416-482-3772
info@csnntoronto.ca
www.csnntoronto.ca

Canadian School of Natural Nutrition - Toronto East
#210, 150 Consumers Rd., Toronto, ON M2J 1P9
Tel: 416-497-4111
torontoeast@csnn.ca
csnntorontoeast.com

Canadian School of Natural Nutrition - Vancouver
#100, 2245 West Broadway, Vancouver, BC V6K 2E4
Tel: 604-730-5611
van@csnn.ca
www.csnn.ca/vancouver

***Calgary:* Canadian Sport Institute**
Olympic Oval
#125, 2500 University Dr. NW, Calgary, AB T2N 1N4
Tel: 403-220-4405; *Fax:* 403-282-6972
CSCC@csicalgary.ca
csicalgary.ca/en/
www.facebook.com/CSIalgary
twitter.com/CSICalgary
www.linkedin.com/company/274917
www.youtube.com/user/CSCCalgary?feature=mhum
Note: Offers The National Coaching Certification Program (NCCP).

***Calgary:* Columbia College**
802 Manning Rd. NE, Calgary, AB T2E 7N8, Canada
Tel: 403-235-9300; *Fax:* 403-272-3805
columbia@columbia.ab.ca
www.columbia.ab.ca
Note: Adult education & continuing education. Professional programmes (business management, dental assisting, paramedic, health care aide, practical nurse); ESL; bridging programmes/university preparation; academic upgrading. ISO 9001:2000 certified.

Calgary: DelMar College of Hair and Esthetics
1520 - 4th St. SW, 2nd Fl., Calgary, AB T2R 1H5
Tel: 403-264-8055; Fax: 403-264-8050
Toll-Free: 888-264-2422
www.delmarcollege.com
www.facebook.com/DelmarCollegeSchool
twitter.com/delmarcollegeAB
www.youtube.com/user/TheDelmarCollege

Calgary: École Holt Couture; School of Sewing and Design
2227 - 20 Ave. SW, Calgary, AB T2T 0M4
Tel: 403-244-5460; Fax: 403-228-1416
info@ecoleholtcouture.com
www.ecoleholtcouture.com
www.facebook.com/ecoleholtcouture
twitter.com/EHCSchool
www.youtube.com/user/ecoleholtcouture

Calgary: Elevated Learning Academy Inc. - Calgary
6115 - 10th St. SE, 2nd Fl., Calgary, AB T2H 2Z9
Tel: 403-802-0933; Toll-Free: 888-544-5573
info@elevatedlearningacademy.com
elevatedlearningacademy.com
www.facebook.com/elevatedlearningacademy
twitter.com/ElevateLearn
Note: Personal Fitness Training.
Campuses
Elevated Learning Academy Inc. - Edmonton
World Health at City Centre Mall
#220, 10205 - 101 St. NW, Edmonton, AB T5J 4Y9
Tel: 780-425-0933; Toll-Free: 888-544-5573
info@elevatedlearningacademy.com
elevatedlearningacademy.com
www.facebook.com/elevatedlearningacademy
twitter.com/ElevateLearn
Note: Personal Fitness Training.

Calgary: Enform
5055 - 11 St. NE, Calgary, AB T2E 8N4, Canada
Tel: 403-516-8000; Fax: 403-516-8166
Toll-Free: 800-667-5557
customerservice@enform.ca
www.enform.ca
Note: Enform provides training for the oil and gas industry.
Cameron MacGillvray, President/CEO
Campuses
Fort St. John Campus
#2060, 9600 - 93rd Ave., Fort St. John, BC V1J 5Z2
Tel: 250-794-1000; Fax: 250-785-6013
Toll-Free: 855-436-3676
Genessee Campus
Genessee, AB
Nisku Campus
1803 - 11 St., Nisku, AB T9E 1A8
Tel: 780-955-7770; Fax: 780-955-2454
Toll-Free: 800-667-5557
Weyburn Campus
#208, 117 - 3 St. NE, Weyburn SK S4H 0W3
Tel: 306-842-9822Toll-Free: 877-336-3676

Calgary: Fleet Safety International (FSI)
#119, 4999 - 43rd St. SE, Calgary, AB T2B 3N4
Tel: 403-283-0077; Toll-Free: 866-432-5076
info@fleetsafetyinternational.com
www.fleetsafetyinternational.com
Note: Driver training.

Calgary: KDM Dental College International Inc.
#520, 940 - 6th Ave. SW, Calgary, AB T2P 3T1
Tel: 403-264-2744; Fax: 403-264-2757
Toll-Free: 800-463-9201
www.kdmdental.com
Campuses
KDM Dental College International Inc. - Edmonton
#2101, 10104 - 103rd Ave., Edmonton, AB T5J 0H8
Tel: 780-423-6863; Fax: 780-423-6892
Toll-Free: 800-463-9201
www.kdmdental.com

Calgary: L R Helicopters Inc.
Springbank Airport
135 MacLaurin Dr., Calgary, AB T3Z 3S4
Tel: 403-286-4601; Fax: 403-286-4602
Toll-Free: 877-286-4601
info@lrhelicopters.ca
lrhelicopters.ca

Calgary: Medical Reception College Ltd.
Ford Tower
#410, 633 - 3rd Ave. SW, Calgary, AB T2P 2Y5
Fax: 587-363-3633
Toll-Free: 877-622-2672
www.medicalreceptioncollegeltd.com

Calgary: Mountain View Helicopters
402 A Otter Bay, Calgary, AB T3Z 3S6
Tel: 403-286-7186; Fax: 403-286-7161
training@mvheli.com
www.mvheli.com
www.facebook.com/170315746357459
Note: Helicopter training.

Calgary: MTG Healthcare Academy
#403 4655 - 54 Ave. NE, Calgary, AB T3J 3Z4
Tel: 403-264-2009; Fax: 403-264-2049
mlbadillo@MTGhealthcare.com
mtghealthcare.com

Calgary: National Institute of Wellness & Esthetics
#200, 2748 - 37th Ave. NE, Calgary, AB T1Y 5L2
Tel: 587-351-9024
support@niwe.ca
niwe.ca

Calgary: The Southern Alberta Institute of Technology (SAIT)
1301 - 16th Ave. NW, Calgary, AB T2M 0L4, Canada
Tel: 403-284-7248; Fax: 403-284-7112
Toll-Free: 1-877-284-7248
advising@sait.ca
www.sait.ca
www.facebook.com/SAITPolytechnic
twitter.com/saitpolytechnic
Note: Canada's premier technical institute by 2010
Irene Lewis, President & CEO

Calgary: Springbank Air Training College
132 Maclaurin Dr., Calgary, AB T3Z 3S4
Tel: 403-288-7700; Fax: 403-288-7990
info@springbankair.com
www.springbankair.com

Camrose: High Velocity Equipment Training
#201 - 5061 - 50th St., Camrose, AB T4V 1R3
Fax: 780-678-2274
Toll-Free: 866-963-4766
info@heavymetaltraining.com
www.heavymetaltraining.com
www.facebook.com/HighVelocityEquipmentTraining
www.twitter.com/HVETtraining
www.youtube.com/user/HVETCamrose
Note: Heavy machinery training school.

Clairmont: About Town Driver Education Ltd.
P.O. Box 1069
Clairmont, AB T0H 0W0
Tel: 780-567-4608; Toll-Free: 888-418-6579
dispatch@abouttowndriver.com
www.abouttowndriver.com/en/
www.facebook.com/107181669314433

Condor: Total Health School of Nutrition
P.O. Box 17
Condor, AB T0M 0P0
Tel: 403-746-5388; Fax: 403-746-5377
rdblaney@harewaves.net
www.totalhealthschoolofnutrition.com

Drumheller: Hope College
#420 - 12 St. East, Drumheller, AB T0J 0Y5
Tel: 403-856-8108
info@hopecollege.ca
www.hopecollege.ca
www.facebook.com/pages/Hope-College/193154790715280
www.twitter.com/Hope_College
Jon Ohlhauser, President

Edmonton: A & J Driving School
17527 - 100 Ave., Edmonton, AB T5S 2B8
Tel: 780-486-5090; Fax: 780-443-2592
info@aj-drivingschool.com
aj-drivingschool.com

Edmonton: Airbrake Academy of Alberta Ltd.
15845 - 112 Ave. NW, Edmonton, AB T5M 2V9
Tel: 780-752-7253; Toll-Free: 855-682-8996
infoairbrake@shaw.ca
www.airbrakeacademyofalberta.ca
Note: Driving School.

Edmonton: Alberta Academy of Aesthetics
West Edmonton Mall
#2926, 8882 - 170 St., Edmonton, AB T5T 3J7
Tel: 780-486-7201; Fax: 780-486-7504
Toll-Free: 800-661-4675
www.academyofaesthetics.com
www.facebook.com/261875777174989

Edmonton: Alberta Caregiving Institute
#205, 2920 Calgary Trail, Edmonton, AB T6J 2G8
Tel: 780-761-2234; Fax: 780-328-6470
admin@albertacaregivinginstitute.com
albertacaregivinginstitute.com
www.facebook.com/135077749864773

Edmonton: Alberta Transport Training Academy
12019 - 160 St., Edmonton, AB T5V 1G7
Tel: 780-454-2856; Fax: 780-482-7424
Toll-Free: 877-454-2856
atta@telusplanet.net
www.a-t-t-a.ca
Campuses
Alberta Transport Training Academy - Edson
5101 - 3 Ave., Edson, AB T7E 1B2
Tel: 780-732-2860; Fax: 780-732-2870
Toll-Free: 877-454-2856
atta@telusplanet.net
www.a-t-t-a.ca

Edmonton: Auctioneering College of Canada
11635 - 145 St., Edmonton, AB T5M 1V9
Tel: 780-453-6964; Fax: 780-447-7307
Toll-Free: 888-453-6964
auction@compusmart.ab.ca
www.auctioneeringcollege.com

Edmonton: Big Rig Driver Education
Also known as: Big Valley Driver Education
12350 Fort Rd., Edmonton, AB T5B 4H5
Tel: 780-468-1185; Fax: 780-476-1962
sales@bigrigdrivereducation.com
www.bigrigdrivereducation.com

Edmonton: Campbell College
Stanley Building #2
#101, 11748 Kingsway Ave., Edmonton, AB T5G 0X5
Tel: 780-448-1850; Fax: 780-447-5902
info@campbellcollege.ca
campbellcollege.ca
Note: Administrative Professional Diploma Program.

Edmonton: Centennial Flight Centre
Building 15
25 Airport Rd., Edmonton, AB T5G 0W6
Tel: 780-451-7676; Fax: 780-452-3575
info@centennial.ca
www.centennial.ca
Note: Flight training school located at the City Centre Airport in Edmonton, Alberta offering training in Recreational Pilot Permit (RPP), Private Pilot Licence (PPL), Commercial Pilot Licence (CPL), Multi-Engine (ME) and Instrument Rating (IFR).

Edmonton: CLI College of Business, Health & Technology
#1, 10575 - 114th St., Edmonton, AB T5H 3J6
Tel: 780-421-0224; Toll-Free: 855-421-0224
admin@clicollege.ca
www.clicollege.ca
Campuses
CLI College of Business, Health & Technology - Toronto Campus
#1, 10575 - 114th St., Edmonton, AB T5H 3J6
Tel: 780-421-0224; Toll-Free: 855-421-0224
admin@clicollege.ca
www.clicollege.ca

Edmonton: Digital School
#304, 10205 - 101 St., Edmonton, AB T5J 4H5
Tel: 780-414-0200; Fax: 780-414-0201
Toll-Free: 877-414-0200
learn@digitalschool.ca
www.digitalschool.ca
www.facebook.com/digitalschool.ca
www.youtube.com/user/digitalschoolchannel
Note: Digital School is a private vocational career college specializing in computer-aided drafting and design training.

Edmonton: Edmonton Public Schools Metro Continuing Education
8205 90 Ave. NW, Edmonton, AB T6C 1N8
Tel: 780-428-1111; *Fax:* 780-428-1112
Toll-Free: 877-202-2003
metro@epsb.ca
www.metrocontinuingeducation.ca
www.facebook.com/163127883715678
twitter.com/MetroConEd
pinterest.com/metroconed/
Note: Edmonton Public Schools Metro Continuing Education offers courses in English as a Second Language, academics, business, computers and personal interest.

Edmonton: Est-elle Academy of Hair Design
8004 Gateway Blvd., Edmonton, AB T6E 6A2
Tel: 780-432-7577; *Fax:* 780-433-4799
Toll-Free: 888-432-8828
info@est-elle.ab.ca
www.est-elle.ab.ca
www.facebook.com/114408491925065
www.twitter.com/estelleacademy

Edmonton: European School of Esthetics MediSpa & Laser Training Centre
6724 - 75 St., Edmonton, AB T6E 6T9, Canada
Tel: 780-466-5271; *Toll-Free:* 877-422-5271
info@dreamcareer.ca
www.dreamcareer.ca
www.facebook.com/EIEMediSpa
twitter.com/EIEMediSpa
Note: Esthetics
Linda Malito, General Manager

Edmonton: EvelineCharles Academy
#301, 10205 - 101 St., Edmonton, AB T5J 4H5
Toll-Free: 877-709-5672
admissions@ecacademy.com
www.evelinecharles.com/beauty-school
www.facebook.com/ECAcademy
twitter.com/ECAcademy
www.youtube.com/user/EvelineCharles

Campuses
EvelineCharles Academy - Calgary
#404, 510 - 8th Ave. SW, Calgary, AB T2P 4H9
Toll-Free: 877-709-5672
admissions@ecacademy.com
www.evelinecharles.com/beauty-school
www.facebook.com/ECAcademy
twitter.com/ECAcademy
www.youtube.com/user/EvelineCharles

Edmonton: Excel Academy
10766 - 97 St., Edmonton, AB T5H 4R2
Tel: 780-411-7999
info@excelacademy.ca
excelacademy.ca
www.facebook.com/Excel.Academy.Edmonton
twitter.com/ExcelAcademy_
Note: The Excel Academy offers the Health Care Aide and Community Support Worker Certificate Programs, as well as other Professional Development courses related to the human services industry.

Edmonton: E-Z Air Helicopter Training Inc.
Building 19, City Centre Airport
#203, 63 Airport Rd., Edmonton, AB T5G 0W6
Tel: 780-453-2085; *Fax:* 780-453-2080
admin@e-zair.com
www.e-zair.com

Edmonton: Gennaro Transport Training
15430 - 131 Ave., Edmonton, AB T5V 0A1
Tel: 780-451-0111; *Fax:* 780-488-3115
info@gennaro.ca
www.gennaro.ca
Note: Professional truck driver training.

Edmonton: GRB College of Welding
9712 - 54 Ave., Edmonton, AB T6E 0A9
Tel: 780-436-7342
www.grbwelding.com
www.twitter.com/GRB_Enterprises

Edmonton: Guru Digital Arts College
Mercer Warehouse
#204, 10359 - 104 St. NW, Edmonton, AB T5J 1B9
Tel: 780-429-4878
info@gurudigitalarts.com
www.gurudigitalarts.com
www.facebook.com/GuruDigitalArtsCollege
twitter.com/gurudigi
www.linkedin.com/company/guru-digital-arts-college
www.youtube.com/user/gurudigi?sub_confirmation=1
Owen Brierley, Executive Director

Edmonton: MaKami College
Capilano Mall
#205A, 5004 - 98 Ave., Edmonton, AB T6A 0A1
Tel: 780-468-3454; *Fax:* 780-485-6081
info@makamicollege.com
makamicollege.com
www.facebook.com/pages/Makami-College/188108847893360
twitter.com/MaKamiCollege
www.youtube.com/user/MaKamiCollege1
Note: Massage Therapy Courses.

Campuses
MaKami College - Calgary
9618 Horton Rd. SW, Calgary, AB
Tel: 403-474-0772; *Fax:* 780-485-6081
info@makamicollege.com
makamicollege.com
www.facebook.com/pages/Makami-College/188108847893360
twitter.com/MaKamiCollege
www.youtube.com/user/MaKamiCollege1
Note: Massage Therapy Courses.

Edmonton: MC College
Also known as: Marvel College
Corporate Office
10541 - 106 St., Edmonton, AB T5H 2X5
www.mccollege.ca
www.facebook.com/mccollegegroup
twitter.com/mccollegegroup
www.youtube.com/user/MCCollegeCanada
Note: MC College offers courses in Fashion, Hairstyling, and Esthetics.
Joe Cairo, President, 780-497-3163
joe@mccollege.ca
Anna Gemellaro, Director of Education, 780-497-3155
anna@mccollege.ca

Campuses
MC College - Calgary
1023 - 7th Ave. SW, Calgary, AB T2P 1A8
Tel: 403-290-0051; *Fax:* 403-269-3359
info-cal@mccollege.ca

MC College - Edmonton
10018 - 106 St., Edmonton, AB T5J 1G1
Tel: 780-429-4407; *Fax:* 780-424-9588
info-ed@mccollege.ca

MC College - Kelowna
#100, 1875 Spall Rd., Kelowna, BC V1Y 4R2
Tel: 250-861-5828; *Fax:* 250-763-1747
info-kel@mccollege.ca

MC College - Red Deer
5008 Ross St., Red Deer, AB T4N 1Y3
Tel: 403-342-1110; *Fax:* 403-342-5210
info-rd@mccollege.ca

MC College - Saskatoon
#228, 21 St. East, Saskatoon, SK S7K 0B9
Tel: 306-664-2474; *Fax:* 306-653-6883
info-sk@mccollege.ca

MC College - Vernon
3409 - 31st Ave., Vernon, BC V1T 2H6
Tel: 250-542-8393; *Fax:* 250-542-1109
info-ver@mccollege.ca

MC College - Winnipeg
575 Wall St., Winnipeg, MB V1T 2H6
Tel: 204-786-5081; *Fax:* 204-783-7342
info-win@mccollege.ca

Edmonton: McBride Career Group Inc.
#801, 10242 - 105 St., Edmonton, AB T5J 3L5
Tel: 780-448-1380; *Fax:* 780-448-1392
mcge@mcbridecareers.com
www.mcbridecareergroup.com

Campuses
McBride Career Group Inc. - Calgary - Parkside Place
602 - 12 Ave. SW, 4th Fl., Calgary, AB T2R 1J3
Tel: 403-777-5633; *Fax:* 403-777-5655
mcge@mcbridecareers.com
www.mcbridecareergroup.com

McBride Career Group Inc. - Calgary - Petrowest Plaza
#220, 1210 - 8 St. SW, Calgary, AB T2R 1L3
Tel: 403-290-1000; *Fax:* 403-234-7206
wt@mcbridecareergroup.com
www.mcbridecareergroup.com

McBride Career Group Inc. - Red Deer
Central Block
#304, 5000 Gaetz Ave., Red Deer, AB T4N 6C2
Tel: 403-346-8599; *Fax:* 403-340-0220
rdmcg@mcbridecareergroup.com
www.mcbridecareergroup.com

McBride Career Group Inc. - Okotoks
Bay 3
P.O. Box 1216
87 Elizabeth St., Okotoks, AB T1S 1B2
Tel: 403-995-4377; *Fax:* 403-995-3616
okotoks@mcbridecareergroup.com
www.mcbridecareergroup.com

McBride Career Group Inc. - High River
#6, 28 - 12 Ave. SE, 2nd Fl., High River, AB T1V 1T2
Tel: 403-601-2660; *Fax:* 403-601-2627
highriver@mcbridecareergroup.com
www.mcbridecareergroup.com

McBride Career Group Inc. - Strathmore
#103, 227 - 3rd Ave., Strathmore, AB T1P 1N7
Tel: 403-934-4305
strathmore@mcbridecareergroup.com
www.mcbridecareergroup.com

McBride Career Group Inc. - Three Hills
160 - 3rd Ave. South, Three Hills, AB T0M 2A0
Toll-Free: 877-934-4305
threehills@mcbridecareergroup.com
www.mcbridecareergroup.com

Edmonton: MH Vicars School of Massage Therapy
2828 Calgary Trail, Edmonton, AB T6J 6V7
Tel: 780-491-0574; *Fax:* 780-432-7034
Toll-Free: 866-491-0574
info@mhvicarsschool.com
www.mhvicarsschool.com
www.facebook.com/109536523050
www.twitter.com/MHVicarsSchool
Roberta Brosseau, Executive Director

Campuses
MH Vicars School of Massage Therapy - Calgary
101 200 Country Hills Landing NW, Calgary, AB T3K 5P3
Fax: 780-432-7034
Toll-Free: 866-491-0574
info@mhvicarsschool.com
www.mhvicarsschool.com
www.facebook.com/109536523050
www.twitter.com/MHVicarsSchool

Edmonton: Nightingale Academy of Health Services Inc.
Venta Care Centre
13525 - 102 St., Edmonton, AB T5E 4K3
Tel: 780-478-5267; *Fax:* 780-478-5284
info@nightingaleacademy.com
www.nightingaleacademy.com

Edmonton: The Northern Alberta Institute of Technology
11762 - 106 St. NW, Edmonton, AB T5G 2R1, Canada
Tel: 780-471-6248; *Fax:* 780-471-8583
Toll-Free: 877-333-6248
AskNAIT@nait.ca
www.nait.ca
www.facebook.com/NAIT
twitter.com/nait
www.linkedin.com/company/nait
www.linkedin.com/company/nait

Patricia Campus
12204 - 149 St. NW, Edmonton, AB T5V 1A2, Canada

Souch Campus
7110 Gateway Blvd., Edmonton, AB T6E 0E6, Canada

Aviation Training Centre
11311 - 120 St. NW, Edmonton, AB T5G 2Y1, Canada

St. Albert Campus
506B St. Albert Rd., St Albert, AB T8N 5Z1, Canada
Tel: 780-378-2899

Edmonton: Numa International Institute of Makeup and Design
9902 - 109 St., Edmonton, AB T5K-1H5
Tel: 780-437-6862
info@niimd.com
niimd.com
www.facebook.com/numa.makeup
twitter.com/NiiMDmakeup

Campuses
Numa International Institute of Makeup and Design - Calgary
6402 - 1A St. SW, Calgary, AB T2H 0G6
Tel: 403-455-6862; *Fax:* 866-686-2857
info@niimd.com
niimd.com
www.facebook.com/numa.makeup
twitter.com/NiiMDmakeup

Edmonton: Pixel Blue College
Empire Building
#200, 10080 Jasper Ave., Edmonton, AB T5J 1V9
Tel: 780-756-3990; *Fax:* 780-756-3992
info@pixelbluecollege.com
www.pixelblue.ca
www.facebook.com/PixelBlueCollege
twitter.com/PixelBlueFx
www.linkedin.com/company/pixel-blue-college
instagram.com/pixelbluecollege
Note: Diploma programs offered in art and design, including graphic design, 3D animation and audio production.
Curtis Greenland, Director of Education

Edmonton: Reeves College
#620, 10310 Jasper Ave, Edmonton, AB T5J 2W4
Toll-Free: 1-800-670-4512
www.reevescollege.ca
www.facebook.com/ReevesCollege
twitter.com/ReevesCollege
www.youtube.com/ReevesCollege
Note: Reeves College delivers vocational training licensed under the Private Vocational Schools Act. Programs are offered in the areas of business, legal, health care, & art & design. The college has five campus locations across Alberta.

Campuses
Calgary City Centre Campus
#1500, 910 - 7th Ave. SW, Calgary, AB T2P 3N8
Toll-Free: 1-800-670-4512
www.reevescollege.ca
www.facebook.com/ReevesCollege
twitter.com/ReevesCollege
www.youtube.com/ReevesCollege
Note: Reeves College delivers vocational training licensed under the Private Vocational Schools Act. Programs are offered in the areas of business, legal, health care, & art & design. The college has five campus locations across Alberta.

Calgary North Campus
#111, 2323 - 32nd Ave. NE, Calgary, AB T2E 6Z3
Toll-Free: 1-800-670-4512
www.reevescollege.ca
www.facebook.com/ReevesCollege
twitter.com/ReevesCollege
www.youtube.com/ReevesCollege
Note: Reeves College delivers vocational training licensed under the Private Vocational Schools Act. Programs are offered in the areas of business, legal, health care, & art & design. The college has five campus locations across Alberta.

Lethbridge Campus
435 - 5th St. South, Lethbridge, AB T1J 2B6
Toll-Free: 1-800-670-4512
www.reevescollege.ca
www.facebook.com/ReevesCollege
twitter.com/ReevesCollege
www.youtube.com/ReevesCollege
Note: Reeves College delivers vocational training licensed under the Private Vocational Schools Act. Programs are offered in the areas of business, legal, health care, & art & design. The college has five campus locations across Alberta.

Lloydminster Campus
#103, 5704 - 44th St., Lloydminster, AB T9V 2A1
Toll-Free: 1-800-670-4512
www.reevescollege.ca
www.facebook.com/ReevesCollege
twitter.com/ReevesCollege
www.youtube.com/ReevesCollege
Note: Reeves College delivers vocational training licensed under the Private Vocational Schools Act. Programs are offered in the areas of business, legal, health care, & art & design. The college has five campus locations across Alberta.

Edmonton: Wholistic Health Training & Research Centre
5626 - 72 St., 2nd Fl., Edmonton, AB T6B 3J4
Tel: 780-461-6708; *Fax:* 780-450-2912
Toll-Free: 866-463-6390
ikanji@wholistictraining.com
www.wholistictraining.com

Fort McMurray: McMurray Aviation
Site 1 Box 5 RR1, Fort McMurray, AB T9H 5B4
Tel: 780-791-2182; *Fax:* 780-790-2364
info@mcmurrayaviation.com
www.mcmurrayaviation.com
www.facebook.com/mcmurrayaviation
www.twitter.com/MAviation
www.youtube.com/mcmurrayaviation
Note: Flight Training.

Grande Prairie: Adventure Aviation Inc.
7117 - 102 St., Grande Prairie, AB T8W 2R8
www.adventureaviation.ca
www.facebook.com/groups/173523792673050
twitter.com/#!/pilotexaminer
Note: Flight training.

Grande Prairie: Alberta Massage Training
#211, 11402 - 100th St., Grande Prairie, AB T8V 2N5
Tel: 780-402-7735; *Fax:* 780-513-1362
Toll-Free: 877-768-8400
www.albertamassagetraining.com
www.facebook.com/pages/Alberta-Massage-Training/177235915636149
ca.linkedin.com/pub/alberta-massage-training/29/231/576

Campuses
Alberta Massage Training - Calgary
St. Mary's University College
14500 Bannister Rd. SE, Calgary, AB T2X 1Z4
Tel: 403-263-2075
www.albertamassagetraining.com
www.facebook.com/pages/Alberta-Massage-Training/177235915636149
ca.linkedin.com/pub/alberta-massage-training/29/231/576

Alberta Massage Training - Edmonton
Lister Centre, University of Alberta
11515 Sask Dr., Edmonton, AB T6G 2C4
Tel: 780-470-3366
www.albertamassagetraining.com
www.facebook.com/pages/Alberta-Massage-Training/177235915636149
ca.linkedin.com/pub/alberta-massage-training/29/231/576

Alberta Massage Training - Lloydminster
#2602, 59 Ave., Lloydminster, AB
Tel: 780-874-9075
www.albertamassagetraining.com
www.facebook.com/pages/Alberta-Massage-Training/177235915636149
ca.linkedin.com/pub/alberta-massage-training/29/231/576

Alberta Massage Training - Fort McMurray
Keyano College
8115 Franklin Ave., Fort McMurray, AB T9H 2H7
Tel: 780-743-1467
www.albertamassagetraining.com
www.facebook.com/pages/Alberta-Massage-Training/177235915636149
ca.linkedin.com/pub/alberta-massage-training/29/231/576

Grande Prairie: Hi-Volt Safety
9645 - 116 St., Grande Prairie, AB T8V 5W3
Tel: 780-539-5353; *Fax:* 780-539-5351
www.hivoltsafety.ca

Grande Prairie: Mar-don Academy of Hair Design
#209, 10001 - 101st Ave., Grande Prairie, AB T8V 0X9
Tel: 780-532-4443
www.mar-don.com

Grande Prairie: Mayfair College
#305, 9804 - 100 Ave., Grande Prairie, AB T8V 0T8, Canada
Tel: 780-539-5090; *Fax:* 780-539-7089
www.mayfaircareers.com
Note: Computer training.

Leduc: Alberta School of Dog Grooming
5009 - 50th Ave., Leduc, AB T9E 6V9
Tel: 780-980-5327
info@albertaschoolofdoggrooming.com
www.albertaschoolofdoggrooming.com

Lethbridge: Excel Flight Training Inc.
#201, 421 Stubb Ross Rd., Lethbridge, AB T1K 7N3
Tel: 403-329-4887; *Fax:* 403-329-4872
excelflt@telus.net
flywithexcel.com
Roland Morton, President

Lethbridge: Gateway Safety Services Ltd.
3804 - 18 Ave. North, Lethbridge, AB T1H 5G3
Tel: 403-328-8496; *Fax:* 403-320-8446
Toll-Free: 866-922-4283
info@gatewaysafety.ca
www.gatewaysafety.ca
Note: Certified Business & Driver Safety Training.

Lethbridge: Purely Inspired Academy of Beauty
1239 - 2nd Ave. South, Lethbridge, AB T1J 0E5
Tel: 403-394-7884; *Fax:* 403-394-7894
info@purelyinspired.ca
www.purelyinspired.ca
www.facebook.com/150388661647911
twitter.com/purely_inspired

Campuses
Purely Inspired Academy of Beauty - Medicine Hat
634 - 2 St. South East, Medicine Hat, AB T1A 0C9
Tel: 403-527-6822; *Fax:* 403-527-4151
info@purelyinspired.ca
www.purelyinspired.ca
www.facebook.com/150388661647911
twitter.com/purely_inspired

Lethbridge: Southern Alberta Institute of Massage
534 - 18 St. South, Lethbridge, AB T1J 3G7
Tel: 403-331-5657
info@southernalbertainstituteofmassage.com
www.southernalbertainstituteofmassage.com

Campuses
Medicine Hat Office
P.O. Box 577
Medicine Hat, AB T1A 7G5
Tel: 403-526-5922
info@southernalbertainstituteofmassage.com
www.southernalbertainstituteofmassage.com

Lethbridge: Training Inc.
444 - 5th Ave. South, Lethbridge, AB
Tel: 403-320-5100; *Fax:* 403-320-0567
Toll-Free: 866-380-3480
www.traininginc.ca
Note: Occupational training in Oilfield Occupational Training and Community Disability Support Worker.

Lloydminster: 3A Academy & Consulting Ltd.
#101, 5012 - 46th St., Lloydminster, AB T9V 0C5
Tel: 780-808-2258; *Fax:* 780-808-2268
marlene@3aacademy.com
www.3aacademy.com
Note: Workplace training services and computer training services.

Lloydminster: Border City Aviation
P.O. Box 10963
7054 - 83rd Ave., Lloydminster, AB T9V 3B3
Tel: 780-875-5834; *Fax:* 780-875-5871
info@bordercityaviation.com
www.bordercityaviation.com
Note: Flight training.

Medicine Hat: Cypress College
#3 - 7 St. SE, Medicine Hat, AB T1A 1J2
Tel: 403-527-4382; *Fax:* 403-526-4388
Toll-Free: 888-636-7926
admissions@cypresscollege.ca
www.cypresscollege.ca
www.facebook.com/pages/Cypress-College/182441864008
www.twitter.com/CypressCollege1
Note: Training for computer, business, and employment-related skills.

Medicine Hat: Super T Aviation Academy
#11, 49 Viscount Ave. SW, Medicine Hat, AB T1A 5G4
Tel: 403-548-6636; *Fax:* 403-548-6687
www.supertaviation.ca

Olds: Calgary Flight Training Centre (CFTC)
P.O. Box 15
RR 4 Site 4, Olds, AB T4H 1T8
Tel: 403-335-4892; *Fax:* 403-678-6525
info@calgaryflight.com
www.calgaryflight.com
Tom McCordic, Chief Flight Instructor
cfi@calgaryflight.com

Penhold: Sky Wings Aviation Academy
Hangar 13, Red Deer Industrial Airport
P.O. Box 190
Penhold, AB T0M 1R0
Tel: 403-886-5191; *Fax:* 403-886-4279
Toll-Free: 800-315-8097
info@skywings.com
www.skywings.com
www.facebook.com/104334069643608

Red Deer: AB RoadSafe
Bay 1, 7611 - 49 Ave., Red Deer, AB
Tel: 403-348-0079
www.abroadsafe.com
Note: AB RoadSafe offers Class 1 and Class 3 truck training, safety training, and online training.

Red Deer: Academy of Professional Hair Design (APHD)
4929 - 49 St., Red Deer, AB T4N 1Z1, Canada
Tel: 403-347-2018; *Fax:* 403-342-4244
aphd@telus.net
www.academyofprofessionalhairdesign.com
www.facebook.com/AcademyofProfessionalHairDesign
Note: Esthetics, hair design.

Red Deer: Alberta Institute of Massage
#4, 7710 Gaetz Ave., Red Deer, AB T4P 2A5
Tel: 403-346-1018; *Fax:* 403-346-0606
info@AlbertaInstituteOfMassage.com
www.albertainstituteofmassage.com

Red Deer: The Health Care Aide Academy
4929 - 49 St., Red Deer, AB T4N-1V1
Tel: 403-347-4233; *Fax:* 403-342-4244
info@healthcareaideacademy.com
www.healthcareaideacademy.com
www.facebook.com/444391692246701
twitter.com/HCAAcademy

Red Deer: Medi Aesthetics Institute of Canada
4601 - 50th Ave., Red Deer, AB
Tel: 403-347-2900; *Fax:* 403-346-4303
Toll-Free: 877-347-3901
info@mediinstitute.ca
mediinstitute.ca
www.facebook.com/MediAestheticsInstituteOfCanada
twitter.com/MediInstitute

Red Deer: Northern Institute of Massage Therapy Inc
#115 - 5301 - 43rd St., Red Deer, AB T4N 1C8
Fax: 403-517-7675
Toll-Free: 888-261-8999
info@nimt.ca
www.nimt.ca
www.facebook.com/177521155621742

Sexsmith: Peace River Bible Institute
P.O. Box 99
Sexsmith, AB T0H 3C0
Tel: 780-568-3962; *Fax:* 780-568-4431
Toll-Free: 800-959-7724
prbi@prbi.edu
www.prbi.edu
Note: Interdenominational school that focuses on the basics of evangelical Christianity.

Sherwood Park: Emergency Services Academy (ESA)
161 Broadway Blvd., 2nd Fl., Sherwood Park, AB T8H 2A8
Tel: 780-416-8822; *Fax:* 780-449-4787
info@esacanada.com
www.esacanada.com
www.facebook.com/161540340536925
twitter.com/ESAready
Note: Fully-accredited programs for Emergency Medical Responder, Emergency Medical Technician/Primary Care Paramedic and Professional Fire Fighter.

Sherwood Park: International Academy of Esthetics (IAE)
#122, 150 Chippewa Rd., Sherwood Park, AB T8A 6A2
Tel: 780-449-1225; *Fax:* 780-467-1481
Toll-Free: 800-352-4383
nuoxygen@shaw.ca
www.iaesthetics.com
www.facebook.com/iaesthetics
www.twitter.com/splaserclinic

Wetaskiwin: Wetaskiwin Air Services
6301 - 47 Ave., Wetaskiwin, AB T9A 3S1
Tel: 780-352-5643; *Fax:* 780-352-7148
WASL1@telus.net
www.absoluteaviation.ca
www.facebook.com/pages/Absolute-Aviation/85639311498
www.twitter.com/absoavia
Note: Flight training.

Whitecourt: Rotoworks Inc.
P.O. Box 86
Whitecourt, AB T7S 1N3
Tel: 780-778-6600; *Fax:* 780-648-2029
jhofland@rotorworks.com
www.rotorworks.com
www.facebook.com/215780135110534
Note: Helicopter Flight Training.

British Columbia

Government Agencies

Victoria: British Columbia Ministry of Advanced Education
P.O. Box 9884 Prov Govt
Victoria, BC V8W 9T6, Canada
Tel: 250-952-6400; *Fax:* 250-356-6942
AVED.GeneralInquiries@gov.bc.ca
www.gov.bc.ca/aved
TTY: 604-775-0303
Hon. Andrew Williamson, Minister of Advanced Education
AVED.Minister@gov.bc.ca

Victoria: British Columbia Ministry of Education (BCED)
Ministry of Education
P.O. Box 9150 Prov Govt
Victoria, BC V8W 9H1
Tel: 250-356-5963; *Fax:* 250-356-5945
Toll-Free: 800-663-7867
EDUC.Correspondence@gov.bc.ca
www.gov.bc.ca/bced
TTY: 604-775-0303
Hon. Mike Bernier, Minister of Education, 250-387-1977
minister.educ@gov.bc.ca

School Boards/Districts/Divisions

Public

Abbotsford: Abbotsford School District #34
2790 Tims St., Abbotsford, BC V2T 4M7
Tel: 604-859-4891; *Fax:* 604-852-8587
info@sd34.bc.ca
www.sd34.bc.ca
Other Information: Facilities, Phone: 604-852-9494; Fax: 604-852-4876
www.facebook.com/AbbotsfordSchoolDistrict
twitter.com/AbbotsfordSD34
Number of Schools: 30 elementary; 8 middle; 1 middle-secondary; 7 secondary; *Grades:* K-12; *Enrollment:* 18500; *Number of Employees:* approx. 2,100; *Note:* Also has a virtual school, an Aboriginal education centre, an annual summer school, continuing education courses, and an International student program.
Kevin Godden, Superintendent
Ray Velestuk, Secretary-Treasurer
Linda Peters, Director, Finance, 604-859-4891, ext. 1287
linda_peters@sd34.bc.ca
Marnie Wright, Assistant Superintendent, Human Resources, 604.859.4891, ext. 1249
marnie_wright@sd34.bc.ca
Dave Stephen, Manager, Communications, 604-859-4891, ext. 1206
dave_stephen@sd34.bc.ca
Derrin Demaer, Manager, Purchasing Services, 604-859-4891, ext. 1242
derrin_demaer@sd34.bc.ca
Corissa St. George, Executive Assistant to Kevin Godden, 604-859-4891, ext. 1230
Corissa_Stgeorge@sd34.bc.ca
Cheryl McLeod, Executive Assistant to Ray Velestuk, 604-859-4891, ext. 1241
cheryl_mcleod@sd34.bc.ca

Ashcroft: Gold Trail School District #74
P.O. Box 250
400 Hollis Rd., Ashcroft, BC V0K 1A0, Canada
Tel: 250-453-9101; *Fax:* 250-453-2425
Toll-Free: 855-453-910
www.sd74.bc.ca
Number of Schools: 4 elementary; 2 secondary; 3 K-12; 1 rural; *Grades:* K - 12; *Enrollment:* 1800; *Number of Employees:* 150 teachers & support staff; *Note:* The rural school is a one-room schoolhouse.
Valerie Adrian, Chair, 250-452-9151, ext. 201
vadrian@sd74.bc.ca
Teresa Downs, Superintendent of Schools, 250-453-9101, ext. 208
tdowns@sd74.bc.ca
Tamara Mountain, District Principal of Aboriginal Education, 250-453-9101, ext. 215
tmountain@sd74.bc.ca
Steven Steeves, Information Technology Manager, 250-453-9101, ext. 222
ssteeves@sd74.bc.ca
Diana Hillocks, Human Resources Manager, 250-453-9101, ext. 211
dhillocks@sd74.bc.ca
Lynda Minnabarriet, Secretary-Treasurer, 250-453-9101, ext. 200
lminnabarriet@sd74.bc.ca

Burnaby: Burnaby School District #41
5325 Kincaid St., Burnaby, BC V5G 1W2
Tel: 604-296-6300; *Fax:* 604-296-6910
www.sd41.bc.ca
twitter.com/studyinburnaby
Number of Schools: 41 elementary; 7 community; 8 secondary; *Grades:* K - 12; Continuing Ed.; *Enrollment:* 24000; *Number of Employees:* 4,000
Ron Burton, Chair, 604-290-3740
Gina Niccoli-Moen, Superintendent of Schools & CEO, 604-296-6900, ext. 661001
Gina.Niccoli-Moen@sd41.bc.ca
Heather Hart, Assistant Superintendent, 604-296-6900, ext. 661007
heather.hart@sd41.bc.ca
Roberto Bombelli, Assistant Superintendent, 604-296-6900, ext. 661008
roberto.bombelli@sd41.bc.ca
Wanda Mitchell, Assistant Superintendent, 604-296-6900, ext. 661008
wanda.mitchell@sd41.bc.ca
Greg Frank, Secretary-Treasurer, 604-296-6900, ext. 661003
Greg.Frank@sd41.bc.ca

Campbell River: Campbell River School District #72
425 Pinecrest Rd., Campbell River, BC V9W 3P2
Tel: 250-830-2300
info@sd72.bc.ca
www.sd72.bc.ca
www.facebook.com/190414822472
twitter.com/CRSD72
www.youtube.com/user/schooldistrict72
Number of Schools: 14 elementary; 2 middle; 2 secondary; 3 specialized; *Grades:* K-12; Continuing Ed; ESL; *Enrollment:* 5240; *Number of Employees:* 750
Michele Babchuk, Chair
michele.babchuk@sd72.bc.ca
Tom Longridge, Superintendent, Schools, 250-830-2398
tom.longridge@sd72.bc.ca
Nevenka Fair, Assistant Superintendent, Schools, 250-830-2398
nevenka.fair@sd72.bc.ca
Kevin Patrick, Secretary-Treasurer, 250-830-2302
kevin.patrick@sd72.bc.ca
Greg Johnson, District Principal of Aboriginal Education, 250-923-4918
greg.johnson@sd72.bc.ca
Yves Vachon, Director of Human Resources, 250-830-2310
yves.vachon@sd72.bc.ca
Ruth Kine, District Teacher Librarian, 250-830-2322
ruth.kine@sd72.bc.ca

Chilliwack: Chilliwack School District #33
8430 Cessna Dr., Chilliwack, BC V2P 7K4
Tel: 604-792-1321; *Fax:* 604-792-9665
www.sd33.bc.ca
Number of Schools: 20 elementary; 6 middle; 3 secondary; 4 alternative; *Grades:* K.-12; Adult Ed.; *Enrollment:* 14000; *Number of Employees:* 1800; *Note:* Offers continuing and distance education programs.
Silvia Dyck, Chair

Evelyn Novak, Superintendent
Evelyn_Novak@sd33.bc.ca
Gerry Slykhuis, Secretary-Treasurer
Gerry_Slykhuis@sd33.bc.ca
Rohan Arul-Pragasam, Assistant Superintendent of Schools
rohan_arul@sd33.bc.ca
Janet Hall, Director of Instruction
Janet_Hall@sd33.bc.ca
Kirk Savage, Director of Instruction
kirk_savage@sd33.bc.ca
Maureen Carradice, Director of Human Resources
maureen_carradice@sd33.bc.ca
Kevin Josephson, Manager of Finance
kevin_josephson@sd33.ba.ca

Coquitlam: Coquitlam School District #43
550 Poirier St., Coquitlam, BC V3J 6A7
Tel: 604-939-9201; *Fax:* 604-939-7828
information@sd43.bc.ca
www.sd43.bc.ca
www.facebook.com/sd43bc
twitter.com/sd43bc
Number of Schools: 45 elementary; 14 middle; 11 secondary; 3 alternative; *Grades:* K-12; *Enrollment:* 33131
Judy Shirra, Board Chair
JShirra@sd43.bc.ca
Patricia Gartland, CEO/Superintendent of Schools
pgartland@sd43.ba.ca
Mark Ferrari, Secretary-Treasurer

Courtenay: Comox Valley School District #71
607 Cumberland Rd., Courtenay, BC V9N 7G5
Tel: 250-334-5500; *Fax:* 250-334-4472
info@sd71.bc.ca
www.sd71.bc.ca
www.facebook.com/SchoolDistrict71
twitter.com/ComoxValleySD71
plus.google.com/112750829425460904312
Number of Schools: 15 elementary; 7 secondary; *Grades:* K-12; *Enrollment:* 9959; *Note:* Also offer an Aboriginal Education Centre, a Learning Resources Centre, a Nala'atsi Program, an International Student Program, an outdoor education centre, continuing education classes, and a Teddies'n'Toddlers program.
Tom Weber, Board Chair, 250-218-4036
Tom.Weber@sd71.bc.ca
Tom Demeo, Acting Superintendent
Tom.Demeo@sd71.bc.ca
Lynda-Marie Handfield, Director of Human Resources
Lynda-Marie.Handfield@sd71.bc.ca
Sheldon Lee, Acting Secretary-Treasurer
Sheldon.Lee@sd71.bc.ca
Bruce Carlos, District Principal, Aboriginal Education
Bruce.Carlos@sd71.bc.ca

Cranbrook: Southeast Kootenay School District #5
#1, 940 Industrial Rd., Cranbrook, BC V1C 4C6
Tel: 250-426-4201; *Fax:* 250-489-5460
www.sd5.bc.ca
Number of Schools: 10 elementary; 7 secondary; 2 alternative; *Grades:* K - 12; Adult Ed.; *Enrollment:* 5485; *Number of Employees:* 600
Lynn Hauptman, Superintendent/CEO, 250-417-2079
lynn.hauptman@sd5.bc.ca
Robert Norum, Secretary-Treasurer, 250-417-2054
rob.norum@sd5.bc.ca
Diane Casault, Director of Student Learning & Innovation, 250-417-2053
diane.casault@sd5.bc.ca

Dawson Creek: Peace River South School District #59
11600 - 7 St., Dawson Creek, BC V1G 4R8, Canada
Tel: 250-782-8571; *Fax:* 250-782-3204
SBO_Reception@sd59.bc.ca
www.sd59.bc.ca
www.facebook.com/SchoolDistrict59
www.twitter.com/sd59prs
Number of Schools: 14 elementary; 4 secondary; 1 Montessori; 2 alternative; *Grades:* K - 12; *Enrollment:* 4855
Tamara Zeimer, Board Chair
tamara_zeimer@sd59.bc.cac.ca
Leslie Lambie, Superintendent of Schools
leslie_lambie@sd59.bc.cac.ca
Melissa Panoulias, Secretary-Treasurer
melissa_panoylias@sd59.bc.ca
Keith Maurer, Director of Instruction
keith_maurer@sd59.bc.ca
Kim Maurer, Director of Human Resources
kim_maurer@sd59.bc.ca

Dease Lake: Stikine School District #87
P.O. Box 190
5 Commerical Dr., Dease Lake, BC V0C 1L0, Canada
Tel: 250-771-4440; *Fax:* 250-771-4441
www.sd87.bc.ca
Number of Schools: 1 K-7; 2 K-9; 1 K-12; *Grades:* K - 12; Alternative Ed.; *Enrollment:* 260; *Number of Employees:* 71
Yvonne Tashoots, Board Chair (Acting)
yvonne.tashoots@sd87.bc.ca
Mike Gordon, Superintendent, Schools
mgordon@sd87.bc.ca
Ken Mackie, Secretary-Treasurer
kmackie@sd87.bc.ca
Gerry Brennan, Director of Instruction - Literacy Contact
gbrennan@sd87.bc.ca

Delta: Delta School District #37
4585 Harvest Dr., Delta, BC V4K 5B4
Tel: 604-946-4101; *Fax:* 604-952-5375
webmaster@deltasd.bc.ca
web.deltasd.bc.ca
twitter.com/deltasd37
Number of Schools: 24 elementary; 7 secondary; *Grades:* K.-12; Adult Ed.; *Enrollment:* 15800; *Note:* Also offers the Delta Manor Education Centre, Delta Community College, & Home Quest alternative education centre.
Laura Dixon, Chairperson, 604-999-2053
ldixon@deltasd.bc.ca
Diane Turner, Superintendent, 604-952-5340
dturner@deltasd.bc.ca
Nancy Gordon, Assistant Superintendent, 604-952-5345
ngordon@deltasd.bc.ca
Doug Sheppard, Assistant Superintendent, 604-952-5346
dsheppard@deltasd.bc.ca
Joe Strain, Secretary Treasurer, 604-952-5354
jstrain@deltasd.bc.ca
Nicola Christ, Director of Finance and Management, 604-952-5334
nchrist@deltasd.bc.ca
Jennifer Hill, Communications & Marketing Manager, 604-952-5397
jhill@deltasd.bc.ca
Donna Stevens, Library Clerk, 604-952-5063
dgstevens@deltasd.bc.ca

Duncan: Cowichan Valley School District #79
2557 Beverly St., Duncan, BC V9L 2X3
Tel: 250-748-0321; *Fax:* 250-748-6591
info@sd79.bc.ca
www.sd79.bc.ca
twitter.com/TransportSD79
Number of Schools: 16 elementary; 4 secondary; 3 alternative; *Grades:* K - 12; *Enrollment:* 9801
Rod Allen, Superintendent, 250-748-0321, ext. 215
rallen@sd79.bc.ca
Jason Sandquist, Secretary-Treasurer, 250-748-0321, ext. 208
jsandqui@sd79.bc.ca
Denise Augustine, District Principal of Aboriginal Education, 250-748-0321, ext. 241
daugusti@sd79.bc.ca
Roma Medves, Human Resources Manager, 250-748-0321, ext. 221
rmedves@sd79.bc.ca
Patti Doege, Supervisor of Purchasing, 250-748-0321, ext. 229
purchasing@sd79.ba.ca

Fort Nelson: Fort Nelson School District #81
P.O. Box 87
5104 Airport Dr., Fort Nelson, BC V0C 1R0
Tel: 250-774-2591; *Fax:* 250-774-2598
www.sd81.bc.ca
Number of Schools: 2 primary; 1 elementary; 1 secondary; 1 K-12; *Grades:* K - 12; *Enrollment:* 871; *Number of Employees:* 100
Linda Dolen, Chair
ldolen@sd81.bc.ca
Diana Samchuck, Superintendent
dsamchuck@sd81.bc.ca
Margaret-Anne Hall, Secretary-Treasurer
mhall@sd81.bc.ca
Darryl Low, Supervisor, Maintenance
dlow@sd81.bc.ca
David Johnstone, District Technology Coordinator
djohnstone@sd81.bc.ca

Fort St John: Peace River North School District #60
10112 - 105 Ave., Fort St John, BC V1J 4S4, Canada
Tel: 250-262-6000; *Fax:* 250-262-6048
www.prn.bc.ca
www.facebook.com/SD60PRN
twitter.com/sd60
Number of Schools: 9 elementary; 2 middle; 1 secondary; 4 K-12; 3 rural; 2 alternative; *Grades:* K - 12; *Enrollment:* 5792
Dave Sloan, Superintendent, 250-262-6017
dsloan@prn.bc.ca
Doug Boyd, Secretary-Treasurer, 250-262-6006
dboyd@prn.bc.ca
Cindy Byrd, Human Resources Manager, 250-262-6016
cbyrd@prn.bc.ca
Stephen Petrucci, Assistant Superintendent of Schools, 250-262-6019
spetrucci@prn.bc.ca

Gibsons: Sunshine Coast School District #46
P.O. Box 220
494 South Fletcher Rd., Gibsons, BC V0N 1V0, Canada
Tel: 604-886-8811; *Fax:* 604-886-4652
Toll-Free: 877-886-8811
questions@sd46.bc.ca
www.sd46.bc.ca
www.facebook.com/116283995054194
twitter.com/SSCschools
Number of Schools: 10 elementary; 3 secondary; 2 alternative; *Grades:* K - 12; Alternative Ed.; *Enrollment:* 3043
Betty Baxter, Board Chair, 604-885-8839
bettybaxter@dccnet.com
Patrick Bocking, Superintendent of Schools, 604-886-4489
pbocking@sd46.bc.ca
Greg Kitchen, Assistant Superintendent, 604-886-4487
gkitchen@sd46.bc.ca
Rob Collison, Manager of Facilities & Transportation, 604-886-9870
rcollison@sd46.bc.ca
Nicholas Weswick, Secretary-Treasurer, 604-886-4484
nweswick@sd46.bc.ca
Tara Sweet, Human Resources Manager
tsweet@sd46.bc.ca

Gold River: Vancouver Island West School District #84
P.O. Box 100
2 Hwy. 28, Gold River, BC V0P 1G0, Canada
Tel: 250-283-2241; *Fax:* 250-283-7352
www.sd84.bc.ca
Number of Schools: 4 elementary; 1 secondary; *Grades:* K - 12; *Enrollment:* 466; *Note:* Also offers continuing education classes.
Kathy Kennedy, Chairperson, 250-283-2585
kkennedy@viw.sd84.bc.ca
Lawrence Tarasoff, Superintendent of Schools & Secretary-Treasurer, 250-283-2241, ext. 225
ltarasoff@viw.sd84.bc.ca
Annie James, Human Resources Administrator, 250-283-2241, ext. 224
ajames@viw.sd84.bc.ca
Peter Skilton, Operations Supervisor, 250-283-2241, ext. 230
pskilton@viw.sd84.bc.ca

Grand Forks: Boundary School District #51
P.O. Box 640
1021 Central Ave., Grand Forks, BC V0H 1H0
Tel: 250-442-8258; *Fax:* 250-442-8800
info@sd51.bc.ca
www.sd51.bc.ca
www.facebook.com/SD51Boundary
www.youtube.com/channel/UCxX7jRPt61DN5E3RpStyQjg
Number of Schools: 7 elementary; 2 secondary; 1 K-12; 1 alternative education; *Grades:* K - 12; Alternate Ed.
Teresa Rezansoff, Board Chair, 250-442-2240
teresa.rezansoff@sd51.bc.ca
Kevin Argue, Superintendent of Schools
kevin.argue@sd51.bc.ca
Jeanette Hanlon, Secretary-Treasurer
jeanette.hanlon@sd51.bc.ca
Doug Lacey, Director of Learning
doug.lacey@sd51.bc.ca
Dean Higashi, Operations Manager
dean.higashi@sd51.bc.ca
John Popoff, Technology Manager
john.popoff@sd51.bc.ca

Hagensborg: Central Coast School District #49
P.O. Box 130
Hagensborg, BC V0T 1H0
Tel: 250-982-2691; *Fax:* 250-982-2319
contact@sd49.bc.ca
www.sd49.bc.ca
Number of Schools: 5; *Grades:* K - 12; *Enrollment:* 200
Nicola Koroluk, Chair
nkoroluk@sd49.bc.ca
Norma Hart, CEO, Superintendent of Schools, & Secretary-Treasurer
nhart@sd49.bc.ca
Sheldon Lee, CMA, Director, Business Operations
slee@sd49.bc.ca

Lela Walkus, Coordinator, Aboriginal Studies
lwalkus@sd49.bc.ca
John Breffitt, Director of Information Technology
itadmin@sd49.bc.ca

Hope: Fraser Cascade School District #78
650 Kawkawa Lake Rd., Hope, BC V0X 1L4
Tel: 604-869-2411; *Fax:* 604-869-7400
info@sd78.bc.ca
www.sd78.bc.ca
Other Information: Agassiz Phone: 604-796-2225
Number of Schools: 4 elementary; 3 elementary-secondary; 1 secondary; 2 alternative; *Grades:* K - 12
Linda Kerr, Chairperson
linda.kerr@sd78.bc.ca
Dr. Karen Nelson, Superintendent of Schools
Natalie Lowe, CA, Secretary-Treasurer
Dan Landrath, Supervisor of Transportation, 604-796-1024
Mike Repstock, Supervisor of Operations, 604-869-5848
Rod Peters, District Aboriginal Education Coordinator, 604-869-2842

Invermere: Rocky Mountain School District #6
P.O. Box 430
620 - 4th St., Invermere, BC V0A 1K0, Canada
Tel: 250-342-9243; *Fax:* 250-342-6966
www.sd6.bc.ca
twitter.com/RMSD6
Number of Schools: 1 primary; 11 elementary; 3 secondary; 4 alternative; *Grades:* JK - 12; *Enrollment:* 3119
Paul Carriere, Superintendent of Schools, 250-342-9243, ext. 4671
Paul.Carriere@sd6.bc.ca
Cheryl Lenardon, Assistant Superintendent of Schools - Literacy Contact, 250-342-9243, ext. 4673
cheryl.lenardon@sd6.bc.ca
Jennifer Turner, Assistant Superintendent of Schools - Special Needs Contact, 250-342-9243, ext. 4674
jennifer.turner@sd6.bc.ca
Dale Culler, Secretary-Treasurer, 250-342-9243, ext. 4672
dale.culler@sd6.bc.ca

Kamloops: Kamloops-Thompson School District #73
1383 - 9th Ave., Kamloops, BC V2C 3X7
Tel: 250-374-0679; *Fax:* 250-372-1183
www.sd73.bc.ca
Number of Schools: 33 elementary; 1 middle; 10 secondary; 3 alternative; *Grades:* K - 12; Continuing Ed.; *Enrollment:* 14675; *Number of Employees:* 1,113 full time, part time, and relief educators; 759 support staff
Karl de Bruijn, Superintendent of Schools
kdebruijn@sd73.bc.ca
Kelvin Stretch, Secretary-Treasurer
Cheryl Sebastian, District Principal - Aboriginal Education
John Churchley, Assistant Superintendent - Early Learning/Literacy
Raymond Miller, SCMP, Purchasing Manager, 250-377-2565

Kelowna: Central Okanagan School District #23
1940 Underhill St., Kelowna, BC V1X 5X7
Tel: 250-860-8888; *Fax:* 250-860-9799
SchoolBoard.Office@sd23.bc.ca
www.sd23.bc.ca
Number of Schools: 31 elementary; 6 middle; 5 secondary; 1 alternative; *Grades:* K - 12; Alternate Ed.; *Enrollment:* 22230
Moyra Baxter, Chair, 250-470-3216
board@sd23.bc.ca
Kevin Kaardal, Superintendent, 250-470-3256
Kevin.Kaardal@sd23.bc.ca
Terry Lee Beaudry, Assistant Superintendent, 250-470-3225
Terry.Beaudry@sd23.bc.ca
Jim Colquhoun, Director, Labour Relations, 250-470-3237
Jim.Colquhoun@sd23.bc.ca
Mitch Van Aller, Director, Operations, 250-870-5150
Yvonne.Brown@sd23.bc.ca
Lloyd Pendleton, Purchasing Manager, 250-870-5152
po@sd23.bc.ca
Peter Molloy, PhD, Director, Student Support Services, 250-470-3267
Lee.Erikson@sd23.bc.ca
Eileen Sadlowski, Director, Finance, 250-470-3224
Eileen.Sadlowski@sd23.bc.ca
John Simonson, Director, Instruction - Human Resources, 250-860-8888
john.simonson@sd23.bc.ca
Vianne Kintzinger, Co-Director, Instruction K-12, 250-470-3271
Yvonne.Hildebrandt@sd23.bc.ca
Rick Oliver, Co-Director, Instruction K-12, 250-470-3210
Jan.Nicholls@sd23.bc.ca
Rhonda Ovelson, Co-Director, Instruction K-12, 250-470-3227
Linda.Paziuk@sd23.bc.ca
Jon Rever, Co-Director, Instruction K-12, 250-470-3288

Langley: Langley School District #35
4875 - 222 St., Langley, BC V3A 3Z7
Tel: 604-534-7891; *Fax:* 604-533-1115
www.sd35.bc.ca
www.facebook.com/LangleySchoolDistrict
twitter.com/langleyschools
Number of Schools: 29 elementary; 3 middle; 8 secondary; 2 k-12; 1 middle-secondary; *Grades:* K - 12; *Enrollment:* 18000; *Number of Employees:* 2,500
Robert McFarlane, Board Chair, 604-530-8263
rmcfarlane@sd35.bc.ca
Gordon Stewart, Acting Superintendent, 604-534-7891
gstewart@sd35.bc.ca
David Green, Secretary-Treasurer, 604-532-1477
dgreen@sd35.bc.ca
Michael Morgan, District Principal - Aboriginal Contact, 604-534-7891, ext. 231
mmorgan@sd35.bc.ca

Maple Ridge: Maple Ridge-Pitt Meadows School District #42
22225 Brown Ave., Maple Ridge, BC V2X 8N6
Tel: 604-463-4200; *Fax:* 604-463-4181
www.sd42.ca
www.facebook.com/MapleRidgePittMeadowsSchoolSD42?ref=hl
twitter.com/sd42news
Number of Schools: 21 elementary; 6 secondary; *Grades:* K-12; *Enrollment:* 14754; *Note:* Also offers continuing education at Riverside Centre and higher education qualifications at Ridge Meadows College.
Mike Murray, Board Chair, 604-626-5193
mike_murray@sd42.ca
Sylvia Russell, Superintendent of Schools, 604-463-4200
sylvia_russell@sd42.ca
Flavia Coughlan, Secretary Treasurer, 604-463-4200
flavia_coughlan@sd42.ca
Ron Lanzarotta, Principal - Aboriginal Contact, 604-466-6265
ron_lanzarotta@sd42.ca
Dana Sirsiris, Director of Human Resources, 604-463-4200
Dana_Sirsiris@sd42.ca
Jennifer Hendricks, Director of Finance, 604-466-6281
jennifer_hendricks@sd42.ca
Paul Harrison, Manager of Purchasing and Transportation, 604-466-6236
Paul_Harrison@sd42.ca

Merritt: Nicola-Similkameen School District #58
P.O. Box 4100 Main
1550 Chapman St., Merritt, BC V1K 1B8
Tel: 250-378-5161; *Fax:* 250-378-6263
Toll-Free: 800-778-3208
www.sd58.bc.ca
Number of Schools: 7 elementary; 2 secondary; 4 alternative; *Grades:* K-12; *Enrollment:* 2500
Gordon Comeau, Board Chair, 250-295-8802
gcomeau@sd58.bc.ca
Stephen McNiven, Superintendent of Schools
smcniven@sd58.bc.ca
Kevin Black, Secretary-Treasurer, 250-315-1105
kblack@sd58.bc.ca
Shelley Oppenheim-Lacerte, Principal, Aboriginal Education, 250-378-5161, ext. 1111
so-lacerte@sd58.bc.ca

Mission: Mission School District #75
33046 - 4 Ave., Mission, BC V2V 1S5
Tel: 604-826-6286; *Fax:* 604-826-4517
www.mpsd.ca
www.twitter.com/mpsd75
www.youtube.com/missionpublicschools
Number of Schools: 12 elementary; 2 middle; 1 secondary; 1 alternative; *Grades:* Pre-K.-12; *Enrollment:* 6311; *Note:* Also provides apprenticeship programs & high education training at Riverside College.
Angus Wilson, Superintendent of Schools
angus.wilson@mpsd.ca
Corien Becker, Secretary-Treasurer
corien.becker@mpsd.ca
Joseph Heslip, Acting District Principal - Aboriginal Contact, 604-826-3103
joseph.heslip@mpsd.ca

Nakusp: Arrow Lakes School District #10
P.O. Box 340
98 - 6th Ave. NW, Nakusp, BC V0G 1R0
Tel: 250-265-3638
sd10.bc.ca
Number of Schools: 6; *Grades:* K - 12; *Enrollment:* 479
Terry Taylor, Superintendent & Secretary-Treasurer
terry.taylor@sd10.bc.ca
Heather Dennill, Director of Learning
heather.dennill@sd10.bc.ca

Nanaimo: Nanaimo-Ladysmith School District #68
395 Wakesiah Ave., Nanaimo, BC V9R 3K6
Tel: 250-754-5521; *Fax:* 250-741-5248
info@sd68.bc.ca
www.sd68.bc.ca
facebook.com/pages/Nanaimo-Ladysmith-School-District/259438914072
twitter.com/sd68bc
Number of Schools: 30 elementary; 7 secondary; 2 secondary alternative; *Grades:* Pre-K.-12; *Enrollment:* 13000; *Number of Employees:* 2,000
Steve Rae, Board Chair, 250-741-5231
steve.rae@sd68.bc.ca
John Blain, Superintendent of Schools/CEO, 250-741-5231
jblain@sd68.bc.ca
Graham Roberts, Secretary-Treasurer, 250-741-5240
graham.roberts@sd68.bc.ca
Laura Tait, Director of Instruction - Aboriginal Contact, 250-741-5318
ltait@sd68.bc.ca
Wendy Addison, Executive Assistant - Human Resources
wendy.addison@sd68.bc.ca

Nelson: Kootenay Lake School District #8
570 Johnstone Rd., Nelson, BC V1L 6J2
Tel: 250-352-6681; *Fax:* 250-352-6686
www.sd8.bc.ca
twitter.com/SD8KootenayLk
Number of Schools: 14 elementary; 4 secondary; 1 elementary-secondary; 1 middle; *Grades:* K-12; *Enrollment:* 5248; *Note:* Also offers 3 alternative schools.
Lenora Trenaman, Board Chair, 250-229-4633
ltrenaman@sd8.bc.ca
Jeff Jones, Superintendent, 250-505-7046
jjones@sd8.bc.ca
Kim Morris, Secretary-Treasurer, 250-505-7039
kmorris@sd8.bc.ca
Deanna Holitzki, Director of Human Resources, 250-505-7012
dholitzki@sd8.bc.ca
Ben Eaton, Director, Independent Learning Services, 250-505-7053
beaton@sd8.bc.ca

New Aiyansh: Nisga'a School District #92
P.O. Box 240
5201 Tait Ave., New Aiyansh, BC V0J 1A0
Tel: 250-633-2228; *Fax:* 250-633-2401
www.nisgaa.bc.ca
www.facebook.com/sd92nisgaa
twitter.com/sd92nisgaa
Number of Schools: 3 elementary; 1 secondary; *Grades:* K.-12; *Enrollment:* 480
Peter Leeson, Board Chair, 250-621-3313
pleeson@nisgaa.bc.ca
Nancy Wells, Superintendent of Schools, 250-633-2228, ext. 1102
nwells@nisgaa.bc.ca
Alanna Cameron, Secretary-Treasurer, 250-633-2228, ext. 1104
acameron@nisgaa.bc.ca
Dave Griffin, Director of Instruction - Aboriginal Contact, 250-633-2228, ext. 1112
dgriffin@nisgaa.bc.ca

New Westminster: New Westminster School District #40
1001 Columbia St., 2nd Fl., New Westminster, BC V3M 1C4
Tel: 604-517-6240; *Fax:* 604-517-6390
district.sd40.bc.ca
Number of Schools: 8 elementary; 3 middle; 1 secondary; 4 alternative; *Grades:* K.-12; *Enrollment:* 6095
Jonina Campbell, Board Chair, 604-517-6328
pduncan@sd40.bc.ca
Pat Duncan, Superintendent/CEO of Schools, 604-517-6328
pduncan@sd40.bc.ca
Kevin Lorenz, Secretary Treasurer, 604-517-6312
klorenz@sd40.bc.ca
Robert Weston, Director, Human Resources, 604-517-6346
rweston@sd40.bc.ca
Chris Nicholson, District Vice Principal - Student Services, 604-517-6369
cnicholson@sd40.bc.ca

North Vancouver: North Vancouver School District #44
2121 Lonsdale Ave., North Vancouver, BC V7M 2K6, Canada
Tel: 604-903-3444; *Fax:* 604-903-3445
info@sd44.ca
www.nvsd44.bc.ca
www.facebook.com/nvsd44
twitter.com/NVSD44
www.youtube.com/user/NVSDChannel

Number of Schools: 25 elemetnary; 8 secondary; *Grades:* K-12; *Enrollment:* 15762; *Number of Employees:* 2,363; *Note:* Also offers 7 StrongStart centres & an outdoor school.
Christie Sacre, Board Chair, 604-999-2894
csacre@sd44.ca
Mark Pearmain, Superintendent of Schools, 604-903-3449
mpearmain@sd44.ca
Georgia Allison, Secretary-Treasurer, 604-903-3470
gallison@sd44.ca
Brad Baker, District Principal - Aboriginal Contact, 904-903-3452
bbaker@sd44.ca

Oliver: Okanagan Similkameen School District #53
P.O. Box 1770
6161 Okanagan St., Oliver, BC V0H 1T0, Canada
Tel: 250-498-3481; *Fax:* 250-498-4070
general@sd53.bc.ca
www.sd53.bc.ca
Number of Schools: 5 elementary; 3 secondary; 1 alternative; *Grades:* K - 12; Continuing Education; *Enrollment:* 2500
Marieze Tarr, Board Chair, 250-498-1333
mtarr@sd53.bc.ca
Beverly Young, Superintendent of Schools, 250-498-3481, ext. 115
byoung@sd53.bc.ca
Lynda Minnabarriet, Secretary-Treasurer, 250-498-3481, ext. 114
lminnaba@sd53.bc.ca
Debby Sansome, Director of Facilities, 250-498-9090
dsansome@sd53.bc.ca
Susan Trower, Manager of Human Resources, 250-498-3481, ext. 102
strower@sd53.bc.ca

Parksville: Qualicum School District #69
P.O. Box 430
100 East Jensen Ave., Parksville, BC V9P 2G5, Canada
Tel: 250-248-4241; *Fax:* 250-248-5767
www.sd69.bc.ca
Number of Schools: 8 elementary; 2 secondary; 3 alternative; *Grades:* K - 12; *Enrollment:* 5322
Eve Flynn, Board Chair, 250-240-2845
eflynn@sd69.bc.ca
Rollie Koop, Superintendent of Schools, 250-248-4241
rkoop@sd69.bc.ca
Ron Amos, Secretary-Treasurer, 250-248-4241
ramos@sd69.bc.ca
Rosie McLeod-Shannon, District Principal, First Nations, 250-752-2834
rmcleods@sd69.bc.ca
JoAnne Shepherd, Director of Human Resources, 250-248-4241

Penticton: Okanagan Skaha School District #67
425 Jermyn Ave., Penticton, BC V2A 1Z4, Canada
Tel: 250-770-7700; *Fax:* 250-770-7730
sd67@summer.com
www.sd67.bc.ca
Number of Schools: 11 elementary; 4 middle; 3 secondary; 6 alternative; *Grades:* K-12; *Enrollment:* 5989; *Number of Employees:* 800
Linda Van Alphen, Board Chair, 250-494-9204
lvanalphen@summer.com
Wendy Hyer, Superintendent, 250-770-7700, ext. 6182
whyer@summer.com
Bonnie Roller-Routley, Secretary-Treasurer, 250-770-7700, ext. 6104
broller-routley@summer.com
Dave Burgoyne, Assistant Superintendent, 250-770-7700, ext. 6189
dburgoyne@summer.com
Maureen Maywood, Director of Finance, 250-770-7700, ext. 6484
mmaywood@summer.com
Don MacIntyre, Director of Instruction - Curriculum, 250-770-7700, ext. 6025
dmacintyre@summer.com

Port Alberni: Alberni School District #70
4690 Roger St., Port Alberni, BC V9Y 3Z4
Tel: 250-723-3565; *Fax:* 250-723-0318
www.sd70.bc.ca
Number of Schools: 13; *Grades:* K - 12
Greg Smyth, Superintendent, 250-720-2770
gsmyth@sd70.bc.ca
Lindsay Cheetham, Secretary-Treasurer, 250-720-2756
lcheetham@sd70.bc.ca
Jack Hitchings, Director of Instruction - Learning Services, 250-720-2779
jhitchings@sd70.bc.ca
Vera Kaiser, Director of Instruction - Student Services, 250-720-2764
vkaiser@sd70.bc.ca
Peter Klaver, Director of Instruction - Human Resources, 250-720-2757
pklaver@sd70.bc.ca

Port Hardy: Vancouver Island North School District #85
P.O. Box 90
6975 Rupert St., Port Hardy, BC V0N 2P0, Canada
Tel: 250-949-6618; *Fax:* 250-949-8792
www.sd85.bc.ca
Number of Schools: 8 elementary; 4 secondary; *Grades:* K - 12; *Enrollment:* 1335; *Number of Employees:* 194
Leightan Wishart, Board Chair, 250-949-8431
lwishart@telus.net
Scott Benwell, PhD, Superintendent of Schools & CEO, 250-949-6618, ext. 2236
sbenwell@sd85.bc.ca
John Martin, Secretary-Treasurer, 250-949-6618, ext. 2222
jmartin@sd85.bc.ca
Kaleb Child, Director of Instruction, First Nation Programs, 250-949-6618, ext. 2233
kchild@sd85.bc.ca
Darby Gildersleeve, Manager of Operations & Maintenance, 250-949-8155, ext. 222
dgildersleeve@sd85.bc.ca

Powell River: Powell River School District #47
4351 Ontario Ave., Powell River, BC V8A 1V3, Canada
Tel: 604-485-6271; *Fax:* 604-485-6435
info@sd47.bc.ca
www.sd47.bc.ca
Number of Schools: 6 elementary; 2 secondary; 4 alternative; *Grades:* K - 12; *Enrollment:* 2121; *Note:* Also offer an Eco/Sustainability Program, an Outdoor Learning Centre, an early years centre, and a distributed learning centre called Partners in Education.
Doug Skinner, Board Chair, 604-485-7531
doug.skinner@sd47.bc.ca
Jay Yule, Superintendent of Schools, 604-414-2600
jay.yule@sd47.bc.ca
Steve Hopkins, Secretary-Treasurer, 604-485-6271
steve.hopkins@sd47.bc.ca
Colleen Hallis, Human Resources Manager, 604-414-2603
colleen.hallis@sd47.bc.ca

Prince George: Prince George School District #57
2100 Ferry Ave., Prince George, BC V2L 4R5, Canada
Tel: 250-561-6800; *Fax:* 250-561-6801
sd57@sd57.bc.ca
www.sd57.bc.ca
Number of Schools: 31 elementary; 8 secondary; 1 Centre for Learning Alternatives; *Grades:* K - 12; *Enrollment:* 14239; *Number of Employees:* 2,100; *Note:* The Centre for Learning Alternatives includes continuing education, distance education, and community alternate programs.
Tony Cable, Board Chair, 250-962-9349
tonycable@sd57.bc.ca
Sharon Cairns, Superintendent of Schools, 250-561-6800, ext. 302
scairns@sd57.bc.ca
Allan Reed, Secretary-Treasurer, 250-561-6800, ext. 246
areed@sd57.bc.ca
Victor Jim, District Principal, Aboriginal Education
vjim@sd57.bc.ca
Rob Prideaux, Manager, Supply & Fleet Management, 250-561-6812
Tom Paterson, Director of Human Resources, 250-561-6800, ext. 232
tpaterson@sd57.bc.ca
Darleen Patterson, Director of Finance, 250-561-6800, ext. 247
dpatterson@sd57.bc.ca

Prince Rupert: Prince Rupert School District #52
634 - 6th Ave. East, Prince Rupert, BC V8J 1X1, Canada
Tel: 250-624-6717; *Fax:* 250-624-6517
www.sd52.bc.ca
Number of Schools: 9; *Grades:* K - 12; *Enrollment:* 2937
Tina Last, Chair, 250-627-7260
tlast@sd52.bc.ca
Sandra Jones, Superintendent of Schools, 250-627-0772
sjones@sd52.bc.ca
Cam McIntyre, Secretary-Treasurer, 250-627-0774
cmcintyre@sd52.bc.ca
Roberta Edzerza, District Principal - Aboriginal Education, 250-627-1536
redzerza@sd52.bc.ca
Dave Garcia, Director of Operations, 250-624-4841
dgarcia@sd52.bc.ca
Peter Edwards, Director of Finance, 250-627-0775
PEdwards@sd52.bc.ca
Kathy Gomez, Director, Human Resources, 250-627-0771
kgomez@sd52.bc.ca
Andrew Samoil, Director of Instruction/Information Technology, 250-600-3770
asamoil@sd52.bc.ca

Queen Charlotte: Haida Gwaii School District #50
P.O. Box 69
107 - 3rd Ave., Queen Charlotte, BC V0T 1S0, Canada
Tel: 250-559-8471; *Fax:* 250-559-8849
Toll-Free: 1-888-771-3131
trustees@sd50.bc.ca
sd50.bc.ca
www.facebook.com/201312166556584
Number of Schools: 4 elementary; 2 secondary; *Grades:* Elem.-Sec.; Aboriginal Ed
Elizabeth Condrotte, Board Chair, 250-557-4323
econdrotte@sd50.bc.ca
Angus Wilson, Superintendent of Schools, 250-559-8471, ext. 104
awilson@sd50.bc.ca
Shelley Sansome, Secretary-Treasurer, 250-559-8471, ext. 103
ssansome@sd50.bc.ca
Joanne Yovanovich, Principal of Aboiginal Education, 250-559-8471, ext. 31
jyovanovich@sd50.bc.ca

Quesnel: Quesnel School District #28
401 North Star Rd., Quesnel, BC V2J 5K2, Canada
Tel: 250-992-8802; *Fax:* 250-992-7652
www.sd28.bc.ca
Number of Schools: 14 elementary; 4 secondary; 1 continuing education; *Grades:* K - 12; *Enrollment:* 4360
Sue-Ellen Miller, Superintendent
sueellenmiller@sd28.bc.ca
Bettina Ketcham, Secretary-Treasurer
bettinaketcham@sd28.bc.ca
Cynthia Bernier, Director of Instruction - Early Learning Contact
cynthiabernier@sd28.bc.ca
Randy Curr, Director of Instruction - Human Resources
RandyCurr@sd28.bc.ca
Alison Dodge, District Literacy Resource Teacher, 250-992-0416
AlisonDodge@sd28.bc.ca

Revelstoke: Revelstoke School District #19
P.O. Box Bag 5800
501 - 11 St., Revelstoke, BC V0E 2S0, Canada
Tel: 250-837-2101; *Fax:* 250-837-9335
www.sd19.bc.ca
Number of Schools: 3 elementary; 1 secondary; *Grades:* K - 12; *Enrollment:* 960
Bill MacFarlane, Board Chair, 250-837-6449
bmacfarlane07@hotmail.com
Mike Hookers, Superintendent of Schools, 250-837-2101
mhooker@sd19.bc.ca
Bruce Tisdale, Secretary-Treasurer, 250-837-2101
btisdale@sd19.bc.ca
Ariel McDowell, District Principal - Aboriginal Contact, 250-837-4744
amcdowell@sd19.bc.ca

Richmond: Richmond School District #38
7811 Granville Ave., Richmond, BC V6Y 3E3, Canada
Tel: 604-668-6000; *Fax:* 604-233-0150
www.sd38.bc.ca
www.facebook.com/RichmondSD38
twitter.com/RichmondSD38
www.youtube.com/user/RichmondSD38
Number of Schools: 38 elementary; 11 secondary; 1 alternative; *Grades:* K - 12; *Enrollment:* 22208
Sherry Elwood, Superintendent of Schools, 604-668-6081
selwood@sd38.bc.ca
Mark De Mello, Secretary-Treasurer, 604-668-6012
mdemello@sd38.bc.ca
Richard Steward, Director of Instruction, Learning Services, 604-668-6093
Ray Jung, Director of Instruction, Technology & Communications Services, 604-668-6406
Michael Khoo, Director of Instruction, Continuing Education, 604-668-6111
Laura Buchanan, Director of Human Resources, 604-668-6085
Richard Hudson, Director of International Student Programs, 604-668-6092
Clive Mason, Director of Facility Planning, 604-668-6000, ext. 6127

Saanichton: Saanich School District #63
2125 Keating Cross Rd., Saanichton, BC V8M 2A5, Canada
Tel: 250-652-7300; *Fax:* 250-652-6421
inquiries@sd63.bc.ca
www.sd63.bc.ca
Number of Schools: 4 middle; 9 elementary; 6 secondary; 3 alternative; *Grades:* JK - 12; *Enrollment:* 6000
Victoria Martin, Board Chair, 250-652-7326
board_trustees@sd63.bc.ca

Keven Elder, CEO & Superintendent of Schools, 250-652-7332
kelder@sd63.bc.ca
Jason Reid, Secretary-Treasurer, 250-652-7326
jreid@sd63.bc.ca
Scott Stinson, Assistant Superintendent - Learning Services, 250-652-7322
sstinson@sd63.bc.ca
Mark Fraser, Assistant Superintendent - Instructional Services, 250-652-7330
mfraser@sd63.bc.ca
Paul Standring, Director of Human Resources, 250-652-7333
pstandring@sd63.bc.ca

Salmon Arm: North Okanagan-Shuswap School District #83
P.O. Box 129
220 Shuswap St. NE, Salmon Arm, BC V1E 4N2, Canada
Tel: 250-832-2157; *Fax:* 250-832-9428
www.sd83.bc.ca
Number of Schools: 16 elementary; 3 middle; 5 secondary; *Grades:* K-12; *Enrollment:* 6723
Mike McKay, Board Chair
trusteefeedback@sd83.bc.ca
Glenn Borthistle, Superintendent, 250-832-2157
gborthis@sd83.bc.ca
Nicole Bittante, Secretary Treasurer, 250-804-7830
nbittante@sd83.bc.ca
Carl Cooper, Director of Instruction, Elementary, 250-804-7826
ccooper@sd83.bc.ca
Morag Asquith, Director of Instruction, Student Services, 250-804-7828
masquith@sd83.bc.ca
Kyle Cormier, Director of Human Resources, 250-804-7841
kcormier@sd83.bc.ca
Gary Greenhough, Director of Finance, 250-804-7832
ggreenho@sd83.bc.ca

Salt Spring Island: Gulf Islands School District #64
112 Rainbow Rd., Salt Spring Island, BC V8K 2K3
Tel: 250-537-5548; *Fax:* 250-537-4200
giss@gulfislandssecondary.ca
www.sd64.bc.ca
www.facebook.com/GulfIslandsSecondary
twitter.com/GISecondary
gulfislandssecondaryschoolnews.blogspot.ca
Number of Schools: 1 primary; 3 elementary; 1 secondary; 5 K-12; 1 alternative; *Grades:* K-12
May McKenzie, Chair, 250-539-2530
mayonmayne@shaw.ca
Lisa Halstead, Superintendent
lhalstead@sd64.bc.ca
Doug Livingston, Director of Instruction, Learning Services
dlivingston@sd64.bc.ca
Linda Underwood, Director of Instruction, Human Resources
lunderwood@sd64.bc.ca
Rob Scotvold, Secretary-Treasurer
rscotvold@sd64.bc.ca

Smithers: Bulkley Valley School District #54
P.O. Box 758
1235 Montreal St., Smithers, BC V0J 2N0
Tel: 250-877-6820; *Fax:* 250-877-6835
contact-sd54@sd54.bc.ca
www.sd54.bc.ca
Number of Schools: 6 elementary; 2 secondary; *Grades:* K - 12; *Note:* Also offers the Bulkley Valley Learning Centre (BVLC) at Northwest Community College (250-877-3218) and Bulkley Valley Education Connection, a combined elementary and secondary home school distributed leraning program tailored to individual students (250-877-6834).
Les Kearns, Board Chair, 250-845-7859
Chris van der Mark, Superintendent, Schools
Mike McDiarmid, Assistant Superintendent
Dave Margerm, Secretary-Treasurer
Ed Hildebrandt, Director of Facilities & Maintenance

Squamish: Sea to Sky School District #48
P.O. Box 250
37866 Second Ave., Squamish, BC V8B 0A2
Tel: 604-892-5228; *Fax:* 604-892-1038
sd48seatosky.org
twitter.com/SeatoSkySD48
Number of Schools: 10 elementary; 4 secondary; *Grades:* K - 12; *Enrollment:* 4593
Lisa McCullough, Superintendent, 604-892-5228, ext. 113
lmccullough@sd48.bc.ca
Shehzad Somji, Secretary Treasurer, 604-892-5228, ext. 104
ssomji@sd48.bc.ca
Susan Leslie, District Principal, Aboriginal Education, 604-892-5228, ext. 123
sleslie@sd48.bc.ca
Louise Harris, Human Resources Assistant, 604-892-5228, ext. 106
lharris@sd48.bc.ca

Surrey: Surrey School District #36
14033 - 92nd Ave., Surrey, BC V3V 0B7, Canada
Tel: 604-596-7733; *Fax:* 604-596-4197
www.surreyschools.ca
Number of Schools: 102 elementary schools; 25 secondary schools; 5 student learning centres; 4 adult education centres; *Grades:* K - 12; Adult Education; *Enrollment:* 69696; *Number of Employees:* 9,000; *Note:* Also offers Aboriginal and online/distace programs, preschool programs, special needs support, trades/career courses, and choice programs.
Shawn Wilson, Board Chair, 604-583-0634
wilson_shawn@surreyschools.ca
Jordan Tinney, PhD, Superintendent of Schools & CEO, 604-595-6308
tinney_j@surreyschools.ca
Rick Ryan, Deputy Superintendent
ryan_r@surreyschools.ca
Christy Northway, Assistant Superintendent, West
northway_c@surreyschools.ca
Andrew Holland, Assistant Superintendent, East
holland_a@surreyschools.ca
Yrsa Jensen, Assistant Superintendent, North
jensen_y@surreyschools.ca
Lynda Reeve, Assistant Superintendent, South
reeve_l@surreyschools.ca

Terrace: Coast Mountains School District #82
3211 Kenney St., Terrace, BC V8G 3E9
Tel: 250-635-4931; *Fax:* 888-290-4786
Toll-Free: 855-635-4931
cmsd.bc.ca
Number of Schools: 1 primary; 10 elementary; 1 middle; 1 middle/secondary; 2 secondary; 1 K-12; 4 alternative; *Grades:* K.-12; Adult Ed.; *Enrollment:* 5050; *Number of Employees:* 299 teachers
Shar McCrory, Board Chair, 250-842-6065
shar.mccrory@cmsd.bc.ca
Katherine McIntosh, Superintendent of Schools, 250-638-4407
katherine.mcintosh@cmsd.bc.ca
Alanna Cameron, Secretary-Treasurer, 250-638-4434
alanna.cameron@cmsd.bc.ca
Cameron MacKay, Director of Human Resource, 250-638-4441
cam.mackay@cmsd.bc.ca

Trail: Kootenay-Columbia School District #20
2001 - 3rd Ave., Trail, BC V1R 1R6, Canada
Tel: 250-368-6434; *Fax:* 250-364-2470
Toll-Free: 888-316-3338
www.sd20.bc.ca
Number of Schools: 7 elementary; 2 elementary/secondary; 2 secondary; 1 alternative; *Grades:* K - 12; *Enrollment:* 3741; *Note:* Also offers 3 Early Learning schools in Blueberry Creek, Fruitvale, and Rossland
Teri Ferworn, Board Chair, 250-365-3026
tferworn@sd20.bc.ca
Greg Luterbach, Superintendent of Schools, 250-368-2224
gluterbach@sd20.bc.ca
Natalie Verigin, Secretary-Treasurer, 250-368-2223
natalieverigin@sd20.bc.ca
Bonnie Vickers, Cultural Coordinator, 250-364-3997
Bill Ford, Assistant Superintendent, 250-368-2230
bford@sd20.bc.ca
Marcy VanKoughnett, Director of Human Resources, 250-368-2227
mvankoughnett@sd20.bc.ca

Vancouver: Vancouver School District #39
1580 West Broadway Ave., Vancouver, BC V6J 5K8, Canada
Tel: 604-713-5000; *Fax:* 604-713-5049
info@vsb.bc.ca
www.vsb.bc.ca
www.facebook.com/VancouverSchoolBoard
twitter.com/VSB39
www.youtube.com/VanSchoolBoard
Number of Schools: 75 elementary; 18 secondary; 22 alternative; 3 adult education; *Grades:* K-12; Continuing Ed.; *Enrollment:* 54000
Mike Lombardi, Trustee, 604-306-6948
mike.lombardi@vsb.bc.ca
Scott Robinson, Superintendent of Schools, 604-713-5100
smrobinson@vsb.bc.ca
Russell Horswill, Secretary-Treasurer, 604-713-5080
rhorswill@vsb.bc.ca
Catherine Jamieson, Director of Instruction for Learning Services, 604-713-5180
Lisa Landry, Director of Finance, 604-713-5015
llandry@vsb.bc.ca
Don Fiddler, District Principal Aboriginal Education, 604-713-5682
dfiddler@vsb.bc.ca

Vanderhoof: Nechako Lakes School District #91
P.O. Box 129
153 East Connaught St., Vanderhoof, BC V0J 3A0
Tel: 250-567-2284; *Fax:* 250-567-4639
www.sd91.bc.ca
www.facebook.com/286157811451886
twitter.com/sd91bc
Number of Schools: 9 elementary; 3 secondary; 3 elementary-secondary; 4 alternative; *Grades:* K-12; *Enrollment:* 5500
Nadine Frenkel, Board Chair, 250-567-2284
nfrenkel@mail.sd91.bc.ca
Charlene Seguin, Superintendent
cseguin@mail.sd91.bc.ca
Darlene Turner, Secretary-Treasurer, 250-567-2284
dturner@mail.sd91.bc.ca
Calvin Desmarais, District Principal, Aboriginal Education, 250-567-2284
cdesmarais@mail.sd91.bc.ca
Debbie Simrose, District Principal of Human Resources/Leadership Development
dsimrose@sd91.bc.ca

Vernon: Vernon School District #22
1401 - 15 St., Vernon, BC V1T 8S8, Canada
Tel: 250-542-3331; *Fax:* 250-549-9200
district_web@sd22.bc.ca
www.sd22.bc.ca
www.facebook.com/pages/Vernon-School-District-22/397149120325675
twitter.com/SD22Vernon
Number of Schools: 14 elementary; 5 secondary; *Grades:* Pre-K.-12; *Enrollment:* 9047; *Note:* Also offers alternative education, international, and Aboriginal programs.
Kelly Smith, Board Chair
kellysmith@sd22.bc.ca
Joe Rogers, Superintendent of Schools
jrogers@sd22.bc.ca
Sterling Olson, Secretary-Treasurer
solson@sd22.bc.ca
Gerry William, PhD, Director of Aboriginal Programs, 250-549-9291
gwilliam@sd22.bc.ca

Victoria: Greater Victoria School District #61
556 Boleskine Rd., Victoria, BC V8Z 1E8
Tel: 250-475-3212; *Fax:* 250-475-6161
Trustees@sd61.bc.ca
www.sd61.bc.ca
Other Information: Alternative Ed., Phone: 250-360-4321; Continuing Ed: 250-360-4332
Number of Schools: 27 elementary; 10 middle; 7 secondary; 5 alternative; *Grades:* K - 12; Continuing Ed.; *Enrollment:* 20000
Edith Loring-Kuhanga, Board Chair, 250-889-0689
eloring@sd61.bc.ca
Piet Langstraat, Superintendent of Schools, 250-475-4126
plangstraat@sd61.bc.ca
Shelley Green, Deputy Superintendent, 250-475-4117
sgreen@sd61.bc.ca
Greg Kitchen, Associate Superintendent, 250-475-4133
gkitchen@sd61.bc.ca
Deb Whitten, Associate Superintendent, 250-475-4220
dwhitten@sd61.ba.ca
Janine Roy, District Principal of Learning Initiatives, 250-475-4156
jroy@sd61.bc.ca
Ted Pennell, Director of Information Technology
tpennell@sd61.bc.ca
Mark Walsh, Secretary-Treasurer, 250-475-4106
mwalsh@sd61.bc.ca

Victoria: Sooke School District #62
3143 Jacklin Rd., Victoria, BC V9B 5R1, Canada
Tel: 250-474-9800; *Fax:* 250-474-9825
info@sd62.bc.ca
www.sd62.bc.ca
Number of Schools: 18 elementary; 4 middle; 3 secondary; 1 alternative; *Grades:* K - 12; Alternative Learning; *Enrollment:* 8500
Bob Phillips, Board Chair, 250-642-3297
bother@telus.net
Jim Cambridge, Superintendent of Schools & CEO, 250-474-9807
jcambridge@sd62.bc.ca
Harold Cull, Secretary-Treasurer, 250-474-9804
hcull@sd62.bc.ca
Dawn Kardos, Director of Finance, 250-474-9881
dkardos@sd62.bc.ca

Dan Haley, Executive Director of Human Resources, 250-474-9802
dhaley@sd62.bc.ca

West Vancouver: **West Vancouver School District #45**
1075 - 21st St., West Vancouver, BC V7V 4A9, Canada
Tel: 604-981-1000; *Fax:* 604-981-1001
info@wvschools.ca
www.sd45.bc.ca
www.facebook.com/103459136305
twitter.com/WestVanSchools
www.youtube.com/user/1AMPWilson
Number of Schools: 3 primary; 14 elementary; 3 secondary; *Grades:* K-12; *Enrollment:* 7210
Carolyn Broady, Board Chair, 604-981-1000
cbroady@wvschools.ca
Chris Kennedy, Superintendent/CEO, 604-981-1031
ckennedy@wvschools.ca
Julia Leiterman, Secretary-Treasurer, 604-981-1033
jleiterman@wvschools.ca
Stephanie Mascoe, Manager of Human Resources, 604-981-1044
smascoe@wvschools.ca
Lynne Tomlinson, Director of Instruction - Learning & Innovation, 604-981-1087
ltomlinson@wvschools.ca
Sean Nosek, Director of Instruction - Learning & Innovation, 604-981-1341
snosek@wvschools.ca
Sonya Margolles, Manager of Purchasing & Transportation, 604-981-1022
smargolles@wvschools.ca

Williams Lake: **Cariboo-Chilcotin School District #27**
School Administration Office
350 - 2nd Ave. North, Williams Lake, BC V2G 1Z9
Tel: 250-398-3800; *Fax:* 250-392-3600
info@SD27.bc.ca
www.sd27.bc.ca
www.facebook.com/136197719789468
Number of Schools: 15 elementary; 6 combined elementary-junior secondary; 2 secondary; *Grades:* K - 12; Adult Education; *Enrollment:* 5200; *Number of Employees:* 1000+; *Note:* Also provide the Graduate Routes Other Ways (GROW) Centre offering adult continuing education, Skyline alternate programs for grades 8-12, distance education for grades K-12, and cross-enrolled courses for grades 10-12.
Tanya Guenther, Board Chair, 250-305-4366
tanya.guenther@sd27.bc.ca
Mark Thiessen, Superintendent of Schools, 250-398-3824
shannon.augustine@sd27.bc.ca
Kevin Futcher, Secretary-Treasurer, 250-398-3833
kevin.futcher@sd27.bc.ca
Jerome Beauchamp, Director of Instruction - Education Services, 250-398-3811
jerome.beauchamp@sd27.bc.ca

Catholic

Victoria: **Island Catholic Schools**
#1, 4044 Nelthorpe St., Victoria, BC V8X 2A1
Tel: 250-727-6893; *Fax:* 250-727-6879
info@cisdv.bc.ca
www.cisdv.bc.ca
Number of Schools: 7; *Grades:* K - 12
Joe Colistro, Superintendent of Schools
mcarmichael@cisdv.bc.ca
Char Deslippe, Director, Office of Religious Education
cdeslippe@cisdv.bc.ca
Susie Nute, Contact, Media Resource Center
snute@cisdv.bc.ca

French

Richmond: **Conseil scolaire francophone de la C.-B. (S.D. #93) (CSF)**
French Education Authority of British Columbia
#180, 10200 Shellbridge Way, Richmond, BC V6X 2W7, Canada
Tél: 604-214-2600; *Téléc:* 604-214-9881
Ligne sans frais: 888-715-2200
info@csf.bc.ca
www.csf.bc.ca
Number of Schools: 28 écoles primaires; 16 écoles secondaires; *Enrollment:* 4703; *Number of Employees:* 260 enseignants du primaire; 100 enseignants du secondaire
Mario Cyr, Directeur général, 604-214-2601
dg@csf.bc.ca
Bertrand Dupain, Directeur général adjoint, 604-214-2603
dga@csf.bc.ca
Sylvain Allison, Secrétaire trésorier, 604-214-2606
sylvain_allison@csf.bc.ca
Johanne Ross, Coordonnatrice aux achats, installations et transport, 604-214-2634
jross@csf.bc.ca
Pierre Claveau, Directeur, Relations publiques, 604-214-2617
pierre_claveau@csf.bc.ca
Nathalie Labrie, Directrice, Ressources humaines, 604-214-2626
nathalie_labrie@csf.bc.ca

First Nations

Chase: **Neskonlith Education Center**
P.O. Box 608
Chase, BC V0E 1M0
Tel: 250-679-2963; *Fax:* 250-679-2968
neskonlith.org
www.facebook.com/profile.php?id=100001272488826

Kamloops: **Secwepemc Cultural Education Society**
274A Halston Connector Rd., Kamloops, BC V2H 1J9
Tel: 778-471-5789; *Fax:* 778-471-5792
info@secwepemc.org
www.secwepemc.org

Savona: **Skeetchestn Indian Band Education**
P.O. Box 178
Savona, BC V0K 2J0
Tel: 250-373-2493; *Fax:* 250-373-2494
education@skeetchestn.ca
www.skeetchestn.ca/education

Schools: Specialized

First Nations

Bella Coola: **Acwsalcta Band School**
P.O. Box 778
834 Four Mile Subdivision, Bella Coola, BC V0T 1C0, Canada
Tel: 250-799-5911; *Fax:* 250-799-5576
www.acwsalcta.ca
twitter.com/Acwsalcta
Grades: K-12; *Enrollment:* 136; *Note:* Acwsalcta School promotes the teaching of Nuxalk cultural skills and values, and promote the use of twenty-first-century technology.
Barry Prong, Principal, 250-799-5911, ext. 201
principal@acwsalcta.ca
Theresa Brook (Qway), Acting Director of Education, 250-799-5911, ext. 209
theresabrook@acwsalcta.ca

Merritt: **Lower Nicola Band School**
181 Nawishaskin Ln., Merritt, BC V1K 1N2, Canada
Tel: 250-378-5157; *Fax:* 250-378-6188
reception@lnib.net
www.lnib.net
Grades: K-6; *Enrollment:* 34; *Note:* As an independent school, the Band School follows the BC Curriculum. Their teachers not only have their BC Teaching Certificates, but have knowledge and deep appreciation of First Nations cultures.
Angie Sterling, Principal
asterling@lnib.net

Hearing Impaired

Burnaby: **BC Provincial School for the Deaf**
c/o Burnaby South Secondary School
5455 Rumble St., Burnaby, BC V5J 2B7, Canada
Tel: 604-664-8560; *Fax:* 604-664-8561
www.sd41.bc.ca/programs/school_for_the_deaf.htm
TTY: 604-664-8563
Grades: K - 12; *Enrollment:* 75
M. Henderson, Principal

Special Education

North Vancouver: **Kenneth Gordon Maplewood School**
420 Seymour River Place, North Vancouver, BC V7H 1S8
Tel: 604-985-5224; *Fax:* 604-985-4562
www.kgms.ca
www.facebook.com/KennethGordonMaplewoodSchool
twitter.com/JimRChristopher
Grades: 2-9; *Note:* School for children with language-based learning disabilities
Dr. James Christopher, Head of School
jchristopher@kgms.ca

Richmond: **Glen Eden Multimodal Centre**
#190, 13151 Vanier Place, Richmond, BC V6V 2J1
Tel: 604-821-1457; *Fax:* 604-821-1527
glenedenschool@gleneden.org
www.gleneden.org
Grades: K - 12; *Note:* Teaches children and adolescents who, because of unique combinations of medical, psychiatric, and developmental problems, are not functioning adequately and have not shown improvement in school based special service programs.

Vancouver: **Avenir School**
#207, 877 East Hastings St., Vancouver, BC V6A 3Y1
avenirschool.ca
www.facebook.com/AvenirSchool
twitter.com/AvenirSchoolBC
www.youtube.com/AvenirSchoolBC
Grades: 5 - 12
Martin Hamm, Principal, 604-569-2222
mhamm@avenirschool.ca

Distance Education

Chilliwack: **Fraser Valley Distance Education School (FVDES)**
46361 Yale Rd., Chilliwack, BC V2P 2P8, Canada
Tel: 604-701-4910; *Fax:* 604-701-4970
Toll-Free: 800-663-3381
www.fvdes.com
www.twitter.com/fvdes_news
Grades: K - 12; Adult; *Enrollment:* 3000
David Manuel, Principal, 604-701-4915
dmanuel@k12connect.ca
Gordon Bridge, Business Manager, 604-701-4918
gbridge@k12connect.ca

Courtenay: **North Island Distance Education School**
2505 Smith Rd., Courtenay, BC V9J 1T6, Canada
Tel: 250-898-8999; *Fax:* 250-898-8883
Toll-Free: 800-663-7925
principal@nides.bc.ca
www.nides.bc.ca
www.facebook.com/NavigateNIDES
twitter.com/navigatenides
www.youtube.com/user/navigatenides
Grades: K-12; Adult; *Enrollment:* 466
Jeff Stewart, Principal
jeff.stewart@sd71.bc.ca

Fort St John: **Northern BC Distance Education School**
10511 - 99 Ave., Fort St John, BC V1J 1V6, Canada
Tel: 250-261-5660; *Fax:* 250-785-1188
Toll-Free: 800-663-9511
info@nbcdes.com
nbcdes.com
www.facebook.com/186605384690919
twitter.com/nbcdes
Grades: K-12; *Enrollment:* 228
Randy Pauls, Principal

Grindrod: **Christian Homelearner's eStreams (CHeS)**
P.O. Box 162
Grindrod, BC V0E 1Y0, Canada
Tel: 877-777-1547; *Fax:* 877-777-1547
info@estreams.ca
www.estreams.ca
Grades: K-12
H. Hunt, Principal

Kelowna: **Heritage Christian Online School**
905 Badke Rd., Kelowna, BC V1X 5Z5, Canada
Tel: 250-862-2376; *Fax:* 250-762-9277
Toll-Free: 877-862-2375
info@onlineschool.ca
www.onlineschool.ca
Grades: K-12; *Enrollment:* 864
Greg Bitgood, Superintendent
gbitgood@onlineschool.ca
Janet Rainbow, Director of Individualized Education
jrainbow@onlineschool.ca
Ted Gerk, Director of Operations
tgerk@onlineschool.ca
Gordon Robideau, Director of Development, Heritage Christian Schools
grobideau@onlineschool.ca
Delayne Cama Moroka, Assistant Director of BC Online School
dcmoroka@bconlineschool.ca

Merritt: South Central Interior Distance Education School (SCIDES)
P.O. Box 4700 Main
2475 Merritt Ave., Merritt, BC V1K 1B8, Canada
Tel: 250-378-4245; *Fax:* 250-378-1447
Toll-Free: 800-663-3536
www.scides.com
Grades: K-12; *Enrollment:* 137
Al Mackay-Smith, Principal, 800-663-3536, ext. 1200
amackay@scides.ca

Nelson: Distance Education School of the Kootenays (DESK)
811 Stanley St., Nelson, BC V1L 1N8, Canada
Tel: 250-354-4311; *Fax:* 250-505-7007
Toll-Free: 800-663-4614
www.desk.bc.ca
Grades: K-12
Tim Huttemann, Principal
thuttemann@sd8.bc.ca
Ron Kilgour, Vice Principal
rkilgour@sd8.bc.ca

Prince George: Central Interior Distance Education (CIDES)
3400 Westwood Dr., Prince George, BC V2N 1S1, Canada
Tel: 250-564-6574; *Fax:* 250-563-5487
Toll-Free: 800-661-7515
www.cides.sd57.bc.ca
Grades: K-12; *Enrollment:* 188
Chris Molcak, Principal, 250-564-6574, ext. 2003
Joyce Chow, Business Manager, 250-564-6574, ext. 2005

Salmon Arm: Anchor Academy Distributed Learning
P.O. Box 3015
7201 Hurst Rd., Salmon Arm, BC V1E 4R8, Canada
Tel: 250-832-2754; *Fax:* 250-832-4379
Toll-Free: 888-917-3783
anchor@ark.net
www.ark.net
www.facebook.com/pages/Anchor-Academy/180829665299141
Grades: K-12; *Enrollment:* 595
Melanie Bartusek, Acting Principal
melanie@ark.net

Surrey: Traditional Learning Academy (DL) (TLA)
#103, 17688 - 66th Ave., Surrey, BC V3S 7X1, Canada
Tel: 604-575-8596; *Fax:* 604-575-8565
Toll-Free: 800-745-1320
info@schoolathome.ca
www.schoolathome.ca
Grades: K-12; *Enrollment:* 334; *Note:* Christian school.
Karen Gledhill, Principal

Terrace: North Coast Distance Education (NCDES)
#2, 3211 Kenney St., Terrace, BC V8G 3E9, Canada
Tel: 250-635-7944; *Fax:* 888-546-0027
Toll-Free: 800-663-3865
www.ncdes.ca
www.facebook.com/165376870170928
www.youtube.com/channel/UCq522BKANJk95EB2bPniH6w
Grades: K-12; *Enrollment:* 220
Cindy Sousa, Principal, 250-638-4467
Cindy.Sousa@cmsd.bc.ca
Rob Wahl, Vice-Principal, 250-638-4478
Rob.Wahl@ncdes.ca

Vancouver: SelfDesign Learning Community
PO Box 74560 RPO Kitsilano, Vancouver, BC V6K 4P4, Canada
Tel: 604-224-3640; *Fax:* 604-224-3662
Toll-Free: 877-353-3374
info@selfdesign.org
www.selfdesign.org
www.facebook.com/SelfDesignLearningCommunity
twitter.com/SelfDesignHigh
Grades: K - 12; *Enrollment:* 652
Brent Cameron, Principal
brentcameron@selfdesign.org

Vancouver: Vancouver Learning Network (VLN)
Also known as: Greater Vancouver Distance Education
530 East 41st Ave., Vancouver, BC V5W 1P3, Canada
Tel: 604-713-5520; *Fax:* 604-713-5528
vln@vsb.bc.ca
vlns.ca
www.facebook.com/pages/Vancouver-Learning-Network/297010393309
vlnbuzz.wordpress.com/
Grades: K-12; *Enrollment:* 578
Pedro Da Silva, Principal, 604-713-5520
pdasilva@vsb.bc.ca
Jim DStassinopoulos, Vice Principal, 604-713-5534
jstassinop@vsb.bc.ca

Victoria: South Island Distance Education (SIDES)
4575 Wilkinson Rd., Victoria, BC V8Z 7E8, Canada
Tel: 250-704-4979; *Fax:* 250-479-9870
Toll-Free: 800-663-7610
sides@sides.ca
www.sides.sd63.bc.ca
www.facebook.com/311415469129
twitter.com/SIDESBC
www.linkedin.com/company/930424
www.youtube.com/user/SIDESTV
Grades: K-12; *Enrollment:* 626
Kevin White, Principal, 250-704-4962
kwhite@sides.ca

Schools: Independent & Private

Public

Summerland: Glenfir School
P.O. Box 1800
7808 Pierre Drive, Summerland, BC V0H 1Z0
Tel: 250-494-0004; *Fax:* 250-494-0058
Toll-Free: 1-866-494-0005
mtaylor@glenfir.com
www.glenfir.com
Grades: JK-12
Daphne O'Sullivan, Principal
dducharme@glenfir.com

Faith-Based

Abbotsford: Abbotsford Christian School (ACS)
35011 Old Clayburn Rd., Abbotsford, BC V2S 7L7, Canada
Tel: 604-755-1891; *Fax:* 604-850-6978
administration@abbotsfordchristian.com
www.abbotsfordchristian.com
www.facebook.com/myacs
www.pinterest.com/AbbyChristianS/
Grades: Pre-School - 12; *Enrollment:* 1000
Julius Siebenga, Executive Director
jsiebenga@abbotsfordchristian.com
Alvin Scholing, Director of Development
ascholing@abbotsfordchristian.com
Lorraine Child, Financial Administrator
lchild@abbotsfordchristian.com
Roy Van Eerden, Principal, Elementary
rvaneerden@abbotsfordchristian.com
Tym Berger, Principal, Middle School
tberger@abbotsfordchristian.com
Gerry Goertzen, Principal, Secondary
ggoertzen@abbotsfordchristian.com

Abbotsford: Cornerstone Christian School
P.O. Box 520 Main
3970 Gladwin Rd., Abbotsford, BC V2T 6Z7, Canada
Tel: 604-859-7867; *Fax:* 604-859-7860
admin@cornerstoneschool.ca
www.cornerstoneschool.ca
Grades: K.-12; *Enrollment:* 176
M. Dana, Principal

Abbotsford: Mennonite Educational Institute (MEI)
4081 Clearbrook Rd., Abbotsford, BC V4X 2M8, Canada
Tel: 604-859-3700; *Fax:* 604-859-9206
infod@meischools.com
www.meisoc.com
www.facebook.com/pages/MEI-Schools/121446387975066
twitter.com/meischools
Grades: Pre. - 12; *Enrollment:* 1774; *Note:* The British Columbia curriculum is taught from a Biblical perspective.
Tim Regehr, President
Peter Froese, Superintendent
Ernest Janzen, Principal, Elementary
Dave Loewen, Principal, Chilliwack
David Neufeld, Principal, Secondary
dneufeld@meisoc.com
Heather Smith, Principal, Middle
Jeff Gamache, Vice Principal, Elementary
Rick Thiessen, Vice Principal, Secondary
rthiessen@meisoc.com
Grant Wardle, Vice Principal, Middle
Mr. M. Friesen, Business Adminstrator

Agassiz: Agassiz Christian School
7571 Morrow Rd., Agassiz, BC V0M 1A2, Canada
Tel: 604-796-9310; *Fax:* 604-796-9519
office@agassizchristianschool.com
www.agassizchristianschool.com
Grades: K.-7; *Enrollment:* 58
J. Zuidhof, Principal

Burnaby: Carver Christian High School
7650 Sapperton Ave., Burnaby, BC V3N 4E1
Tel: 604-523-1580; *Fax:* 604-523-9646
office@carverchristian.org
carverchristian.org
facebook.com/carverchristian
twitter.com/carverchristian
Grades: 9 - 12

Burnaby: John Knox Christian School
8260 - 13 Ave., Burnaby, BC V3N 2G5, Canada
Tel: 604-522-1410; *Fax:* 604-522-4606
admin@johnknoxbc.org
johnknoxbc.org
Grades: K.-7; *Enrollment:* 310
A. Ferguson, Principal

Campbell River: Campbell River Christian School (CRCS)
250 South Dogwood St., Campbell River, BC V9W 6Y7, Canada
Tel: 250-287-4266; *Fax:* 250-287-3130
office@crcs.bc.ca
www.crcs.bc.ca
www.facebook.com/crcs.bc.ca
Grades: K - 12
Neil Steinke, Principal
ns-admin-crcs@uniserve.com

Chetwynd: Peace Christian School
P.O. Box 2050
6189 Dokkie School Rd., Chetwynd, BC V0C 1J0, Canada
Tel: 250-788-2044; *Fax:* 888-615-9510
peacechristianschool@gmail.com
peacechristianschool.ca
facebook.com/groups/Peacechristian/?fref=ts
www.youtube.com/user/peacechristian
Grades: K-10; *Enrollment:* 74
S. Lee, Principal

Chilliwack: Cascade Christian School
46420 Brooks Ave., Chilliwack, BC V2P 1C5
Tel: 604-793-7997; *Fax:* 604-793-7991
office@cascadechristian.ca
www.cascadechristian.ca
www.facebook.com/290056471071316
Grades: K - 9; EU
Ryan Morrow, Principal
rmorrow@cascadechristian.ca

Chilliwack: Mount Cheam Christian School (MCCS)
48988 Yale Rd. East, Chilliwack, BC V2P 6H4, Canada
Tel: 604-794-3072; *Fax:* 604-794-3078
office@mccs.ca
www.mccs.ca
Grades: K - 12; *Enrollment:* 360
Jan Neels, Principal
jneels@mccs.ca
Marianne Luteyn, Elementary Coordinator / Special Needs & Learning Assistance
mluteyn@mccs.ca
Stephan Hoogendijk, Middle School Coordinator
shoogendijk@mccs.ca
Jaap Ter Haar, Secondary Coordinator
jterhaar@mccs.ca
Marry Kardux, Librarian
mkardux@mccs.ca

Chilliwack: Timothy Christian School
50420 Castleman Rd., Chilliwack, BC V2P 6H4, Canada
Tel: 604-794-7114; *Fax:* 604-794-7114
office@timothychristian.ca
www.timothychristian.ca
Grades: Pre. - 12; *Enrollment:* 367
Doug Stam, Principal

Chilliwack: Unity Christian School (UCS)
P.O. Box 371
50950 Hack Brown Rd., Chilliwack, BC V4Z 1K9, Canada
Tel: 604-794-7797; *Fax:* 604-794-7667
general@unitychristian.ca
www.unitychristian.ca
www.facebook.com/289932854352155
twitter.com/UnityChristian1
Grades: Pre. - 12; *Note:* A Christ-centered education is provided by Unity Christian School.
Mike Campbell, Principal
mcampbell@unitychristian.ca
Jeanette Berkenbosch, Vice Principal
jberkenbosch@unitychristian.ca

Cranbrook: Kootenay Christian Academy (KCA)
1200 Kootenay St. North, Cranbrook, BC V1C 5X1
Tel: 250-426-0166; *Fax:* 250-426-0186
office@kcacademy.ca
www.kcacademy.ca
Other Information: KCA Preschool, Phone: 250-489-3426
Grades: Preschool - 9; Special Education; *Note:* The Kootenay Christian Academy is an independent, non-denominational school. Operated by the Cranbrook Christian Society, the school offers a biblically directed education. Kootenay Christian Academy is accredited by the British Columbia Ministry of Education, & it follows British Columbia's curriculum guidelines.
Dave Heidt, Chair
Larry Schalk, Secretary
Bob Conroy, Treasurer

Dawson Creek: Mountain Christian School (MCS)
9700 - 5th St., Dawson Creek, BC V1G 3L4, Canada
Tel: 250-782-9528; *Fax:* 250-782-3888
info@mcsed.ca
www.mcsed.ca
www.facebook.com/MountainChristianSchool
Grades: K - 12; *Enrollment:* 94
Eva Hutchinson, Principal
principal@mcsed.ca

Dawson Creek: Ron Pettigrew Christian School
1761 - 110th Ave., Dawson Creek, BC V1G 4X4
Tel: 250-782-4580; *Fax:* 250-782-9805
rpcs@pris.ca
www.rpschool.ca
Grades: K - 12; *Enrollment:* 75
Phyllis Roch, Principal

Delta: Delta Christian School
4789 - 53 St., Delta, BC V4K 2Y9, Canada
Tel: 604-946-2514; *Fax:* 604-946-2589
Info@deltachristianschool.org
deltachristianschool.org
Grades: K.-7; *Enrollment:* 169
G. de Vos, Principal

Duncan: Duncan Christian School
495 Beech Ave., Duncan, BC V9L 3J8, Canada
Tel: 250-746-3654; *Fax:* 250-746-3615
office@duncanchristianschool.ca
www.duncanchristianschool.ca
www.facebook.com/duncanchristianschool/
twitter.com/@duncancschool
Grades: K-12; *Enrollment:* 276
Jeremy Tinsley, Principal

Fort St John: Christian Life School
8923 - 112th Ave., Fort St John, BC V1J 5H8
Tel: 250-785-1437; *Fax:* 250-785-4852
office@christianlifeschool.ca
www.christianlifeschool.ca
Grades: Kindergarten - 12; *Number of Employees:* 17
Justin Sewell, Chairman
jsewell@christianlifeschool.ca

Fort St John: Maccabee Christian School
P.O. Box 6051 Main
Fort St John, BC V1J 4H6, Canada
Tel: 250-772-5010
mcbschool95@yahoo.ca
Rudolf Walter, Principal

Grindrod: Christian Homelearners eStreams
P.O. Box 162
Grindrod, BC V0E 1Y0
Fax: 877-777-1547
Toll-Free: 877-777-1547
info@estreams.ca
www.estreams.ca
Grades: K - 12; *Note:* Christian Homelearners eStreams is an independent, faith-based community dedicated to providing personalized, educational support.

Houston: Houston Christian School
P.O. Box 237
2161 Caledonia Ave., Houston, BC V0J 1Z0
Tel: 250-845-7736; *Fax:* 250-845-7738
hcschool@houstonchristianschool.ca
www.houstonchristianschool.ca
Grades: K.-12; *Enrollment:* 131
John Siebenga, Principal

Kamloops: Kamloops Christian School
750 Cottonwood Ave., Kamloops, BC V2B 3X2
Tel: 250-376-6900; *Fax:* 250-376-6904
www.kamcs.org
www.facebook.com/KamloopsChristianSchool
twitter.com/KCS_Kamloops
Grades: K-12
Gordon Hohensee, Principal
gordonh@kamcs.org

Kamloops: Our Lady of Perpetual Help School
235 Poplar St., Kamloops, BC V2B 4B9
Tel: 250-376-2343; *Fax:* 250-376-2361
rose@olphschool.ca
www.olphschool.ca
Grades: K.-7; *Enrollment:* 181
Rose Nowicki, Principal
rose@olphschool.ca

Kelowna: First Lutheran Christian School
4091 Lakeshore Rd., Kelowna, BC V1W 1V7, Canada
Tel: 250-764-3111; *Fax:* 250-764-3129
school@firstlutheran.ca
Grades: K.-6; *Enrollment:* 64
T. Hennig, Principal
thennig@firstlutheran.ca

Kelowna: Heritage Christian School (HCS)
907 Badke Rd., Kelowna, BC V1X 5Z5
Tel: 250-862-2377; *Fax:* 250-862-4943
office@heritagechristian.ca
www.heritagechristian.ca
www.facebook.com/heritagechristianschool
Grades: K-12; *Enrollment:* 308
Greg Bitgood, Superintendent
gbitgood@heritagechristian.ca
Paul Kelly, Principal, Secondary
pkelly@heritagechristian.ca
Steve Cox, Principal, Elementary
scox@heritagechristian.ca

Kelowna: Kelowna Christian School
2870 Benvoulin Rd., Kelowna, BC V1W 2E3
Tel: 250-861-3238; *Fax:* 250-861-4844
info@kelownachristian.ca
kcschool.ca
www.facebook.com/KCSchool
twitter.com/kcslatest
Grades: 7-12; *Enrollment:* 802
Tyler Bishop, Principal, Middle/High School, 250-861-3238, ext. 302
Scott Campbell, Principal, Elementary School, 250-861-5432
Darren Lewis, Vice-Principal, Middle/High School, 250-861-3238, ext. 308

Kelowna: Kelowna Christian School
2870 Benvoulin Rd., Kelowna, BC V1W 2E3, Canada
Tel: 250-861-3238; *Fax:* 250-861-4844
kcschool.ca
Grades: K.-9; *Enrollment:* 195
Dave Shinness, Head of School, 250-861-3238
dave.shinness@kelownachristian.ca

Kelowna: Okanagan Adventist Academy
1035 Hollywood Rd. South, Kelowna, BC V1X 4N3
Tel: 250-860-5305; *Fax:* 250-868-9703
www.okaa.ca
Grades: JK-12; *Enrollment:* 135; *Note:* Operated by the Seventh-day Adventist Church.
Don Straub, Principal

Langley: Aldergrove Christian Academy
4057 - 248 St., Langley, BC V4W 1E3, Canada
Tel: 604-856-2577
academy@rosbc.com
www.rosbc.com/christianschool.html
Grades: K - 12; Religious ed.
David Strauss, Principal

Langley: Credo Christian Schools
21846 - 52 Ave., Langley, BC V2Y 2M7, Canada
Tel: 604-530-5396; *Fax:* 604-530-8965
office@credochs.com
www.credochs.com
Grades: K-12; *Enrollment:* 470
H. Moes, Principal, 604-530-1941
h.moes@credochs.com

Langley: Langley Christian School
22702 48th Ave., Langley, BC V2Z 2T6, Canada
Tel: 604-533-2222; *Fax:* 604-533-7276
elem@langleychristian.com
www.langleychristian.com
www.facebook.com/143371662374567
ca.linkedin.com/company/langley-christian-school
plus.google.com/108969825945184160157/about
Grades: K-12; *Enrollment:* 813
Henry Vanderveen, Superintendent
superintendent@langleychristian.com

Maple Ridge: Maple Ridge Christian School
12140 - 203 St., Maple Ridge, BC V2X 2S5, Canada
Tel: 604-465-4442; *Fax:* 604-465-1685
www.mrcs.ca
www.facebook.com/MapleRidgeChristianSchool
twitter.com/MRCSCommunity
Grades: Pre.-12; *Enrollment:* 322
R. Roxburgh, Principal

Mission: Valley Christian School (VCS)
8955 Cedar St., Mission, BC V4S 1A3, Canada
Tel: 604-826-1388; *Fax:* 604-826-2744
info@valleychristianschool.ca
www.valleychristianschool.ca
www.facebook.com/VCSMission
Grades: K - 12
Ken Keis, Chair, Board of Directors
Bill Humphreys, Principal
Bob Barclay, Business Administrator

Nanaimo: Nanaimo Christian School (NCS)
198 Holland Rd., Nanaimo, BC V9R 6W2, Canada
Tel: 250-754-4512; *Fax:* 250-754-4271
admin.ncs@shaw.ca
www.ncsnanaimo.com
www.facebook.com/#!/groups/2250494826/?bookmark_t=group
Grades: Pre. - 12
James Sijpheer, Executive Principal
Shelley Yates, Preschool Director

Nanoose Bay: Beacon Christian School
2210 Morello Rd., Nanoose Bay, BC V9P 9A9, Canada
Tel: 250-468-9433
Grades: K - 8; *Enrollment:* 12

North Vancouver: Lions Gate Christian Academy (LGCA)
925 Harbourside Dr., North Vancouver, BC V7P 3S1
Tel: 604-984-8226; *Fax:* 604-984-8254
lgca@lionsgateca.org
www.lionsgateca.org
Grades: Kindergarten - 12; *Enrollment:* 250; *Note:* Established in 1994, the school offers Christian education for students on the North Shore of British Columbia. The British Columbia curriculum of the Ministry of Education is provided by the Lions Gate Christian Academy.
Terry Kooy, Principal
tkooy@lionsgateca.org

Penticton: Penticton Community Christian School
#102, 96 Edmonton Ave., Penticton, BC V2A 2G8, Canada
Tel: 250-493-5233; *Fax:* 250-276-4124
office@pentictonchristianschool.ca
www.pentictonchristianschool.ca
Grades: K-12; *Enrollment:* 54
K. Boehmer, Principal
kboehmer@pentictonchristianschool.ca

Port Alberni: Port Alberni Christian School (PACS)
6211 Cherry Creek Rd., Port Alberni, BC V9Y 8S9, Canada
Tel: 250-723-2700; *Fax:* 250-723-5799
office@portalbernichristianschool.ca
www.portalbernichristianschool.ca
Grades: K-8; *Enrollment:* 36
Mary Walker, Acting Principal

Port Coquitlam: British Columbia Christian Academy (BCCA)
1019 Fernwood Ave., Port Coquitlam, BC V3B 5A8, Canada
Tel: 604-941-8426; *Fax:* 604-945-6455
admissions@bcchristianacademy.ca
www.bcchristianacademy.ca
www.facebook.com/pages/BC-Christian-Academy/10359398302 6791
twitter.com/BCCASchool
Grades: JK - 12; *Note:* British Columbia Christian Academy is an interdenominational Christian school.
Ian Jarvie, Head Principal
ijarvie@bcchristianacademy.ca
Beth Peters, Elementary Principal
Theresa Lee, Director, Pre-School, Daycare
kidsclub@bcchristianacademy.ca
Doug Dowell, Director, Development & Sports
ddowell@bcchristianacademy.ca
Tracy Tko, Librarian
tko@bcchristianacademy.ca

Prince George: Cedars Christian School
701 North Nechako Rd., Prince George, BC V2K 1A2
Tel: 250-564-0707; *Fax:* 250-564-0729
www.cedars.bc.ca
Grades: Preschool - 12; *Note:* Cedars Christian School is a non-denominational school.

Curtis Tuininga, Principal

***Prince George:* Immaculate Conception School**
3285 Cathedral Ave., Prince George, BC V2N 5R2
Tel: 250-964-4362; *Fax:* 250-964-9465
iconceptoffice@shawcable.com
www.icschool.ca

Grades: K.-7
Donncha O'Callaghan, Principal

***Quesnel:* North Cariboo Christian School (NCCS)**
2876 Red Bluff Rd., Quesnel, BC V2J 6C7
Tel: 250-747-4417; *Fax:* 250-747-4410
office@nccschool.ca
www.nccschool.ca
www.youtube.com/user/NCCSchoolify
Grades: K - 9; *Enrollment:* 63; *Note:* The North Cariboo Christian School is a non-denominational school.
John Hengen, Principal

***Richmond:* Cornerstone Christian Academy**
7890 No. 5 Rd., Richmond, BC V6Y 2V2
Tel: 604-303-9181; *Fax:* 604-303-9187
cca@cebccanada.com
cornerstonechristianacademy.ca
Grades: Pre. K-7; *Enrollment:* 141; *Note:* Associated with the Cornerstone Evangelical Baptist Church located on the same property.
W. Kushnir, Principal

***Richmond:* Richmond Christian School (RCS)**
Elementary School Campus
5240 Woodwards Rd., Richmond, BC V7E 1H1, Canada
Tel: 604-272-5720; *Fax:* 604-272-7370
ec@richmondchristian.ca
www.richmondchristian.ca
Grades: Pre. - 5; *Enrollment:* 400; *Note:* The Richmond Christian Elementary School is an independent school, which offers a Christ-centered curriculum.
Roger Grose, Superintendent
rgrose@richmondchristian.ca
Darlene Neufield, Principal, Elementary Campus
dneufeld@richmondchristian.ca
Aza Nakagawa, Business Manager
anakagawa@richmondchristian.ca

Campuses
Middle School Campus
10200 No. 5 Rd., Richmond, BC V7A 4E5
Tel: 604-274-1122; *Fax:* 604-274-1128
mc@richmondchristian.ca
www.richmondchristian.ca
Grades: 6 - 8; *Enrollment:* 200
E. Walker, Principal, Middle Campus
ewalker@richmondchristian.ca

Secondary School Campus
10260 No. 5 Rd., Richmond, BC V7A 4E5
Tel: 604-274-1122; *Fax:* 604-274-1128
sc@richmondchristian.ca
www.richmondchristian.ca
Grades: 9 - 12; *Enrollment:* 233

***Salmon Arm:* King's Christian School**
350B - 30th St. NE, Salmon Arm, BC V1E 1J2, Canada
Tel: 250-832-5200; *Fax:* 250-832-5201
info@kingschristianschool.com
www.kingschristianschool.com
www.facebook.com/KCSOkanagan
twitter.com/KCSOkanagan
kcsnews.wordpress.com
Grades: K-12; *Enrollment:* 214
Dan Demeter, Principal

***Sechelt:* Gibsons Christian School**
5078 Davis Bay Rd., Sechelt, BC V0N 3A2
Tel: 604-885-3628; *Fax:* 604-885-3625
gcs@dccnet.com
www.gibsonschristian.org
Deborah Levy, Principal
gcsprincipal@dccnet.com

***Smithers:* Bulkley Valley Christian School (BVCS)**
P.O. Box 3635
3575 - 14th Ave., Smithers, BC V0J 2N0
Tel: 250-847-4238; *Fax:* 250-847-3564
www.bvcs.ca
Other Information: 250-857-9833 (Elementary); 250-847-4238 (Distributed Learning)
Grades: Elementary / Secondary; *Note:* Bulkley Valley Christian School offers an program for international students.
Klaas Kort, Principal
Hugo VanderHoek, Vice Principal
Glenda Posthuma, Business Adminstrator, 250-847-4238

John Buikema, Director, Development

***Surrey:* Bibleway Christian Academy (BCA)**
18603 - 60th Ave., Surrey, BC V3S 7P4, Canada
Tel: 604-576-8188; *Fax:* 604-576-1370
www.biblewayacademy.org
Grades: K - 9
Kim Dingwall, President
Terry Tekatch, Principal

***Surrey:* Pacific Academy**
10238 - 168 St., Surrey, BC V4N 1Z4, Canada
Tel: 604-581-5353; *Fax:* 604-581-0087
contact@pacificacademy.net
www.pacificacademy.net
www.facebook.com/groups/154091321343008/
Grades: K-12; *Enrollment:* 1450; *Note:* Private Christian School
Paul Horban, Head of School

***Surrey:* Regent Christian Academy (RCA)**
15100 - 66A Ave., Surrey, BC V3S 2A6, Canada
Tel: 604-599-8171; *Fax:* 604-599-8175
www.regent.bc.ca
www.facebook.com/RegentCA
Grades: Preschool - 13; *Enrollment:* 550; *Note:* Regent Christian Academy is a coeducational school, which offers primary, middle, high school, English as a Second Language, & international programs.
Paul Johnson, Principal
pjohnson@regent.bc.ca
Linda Barber, Administrator, Middle Division
lbarber@regent.bc.ca
Allan Visser, Administrator, International Division
avisser@regent.bc.ca
Maureen Sayler, Registrar & Secretary
msayler@regent.bc.ca

***Surrey:* Surrey Christian School**
8930 - 162 St., Surrey, BC V4N 3G1, Canada
Tel: 604-498-3233; *Fax:* 604-581-3520
info@surreychristian.com
www.surreychristian.com
www.facebook.com/SurreyChristianSchool
twitter.com/surreychristian
www.youtube.com/user/SurreyChristianFilms
Grades: K - 12; *Enrollment:* 608
A. Stegeman, Principal

***Surrey:* White Rock Christian Academy**
2265 - 152 St., Surrey, BC V4A 4P1, Canada
Tel: 604-531-9186; *Fax:* 604-531-1727
Toll-Free: 888-531-9186
wrca@wrca.bc.ca
wrca.bc.ca
www.facebook.com/WhiteRockChristianAcademy
twitter.com/w_r_c_a
www.linkedin.com/company/white-rock-christian-academy
Grades: K-12; *Enrollment:* 308
Stephen Hardy, Principal

***Surrey:* William of Orange Christian School**
P.O. Box 34090
17790 Hwy. 10, Surrey, BC V3S 8C4, Canada
Tel: 604-576-2144; *Fax:* 604-576-0975
admin@wofo.org
www.credochs.com/wohome.cfm
Grades: K-7; *Enrollment:* 106
J. Siebenga, Principal

***Surrey:* Zion Lutheran Christian Church & School**
***Also known as:* Cloverdale Christian School**
5950 - 179 St., Surrey, BC V3S 4J9, Canada
Tel: 604-576-6313; *Fax:* 604-576-1399
www.cloverdalechristianschool.ca/school
Grades: K.-9; *Enrollment:* 162
D. Davis, Principal

***Terrace:* Centennial Christian School**
3608 Sparks St., Terrace, BC V8G 2V6
Tel: 250-635-6173; *Fax:* 250-635-9385
office@centennialchristian.ca
www.centennialchristian.ca
Grades: K - 12
Edgars Veldman, Principal
Mrs. Petras, Vice Principal

***Terrace:* Mountain View Christian Academy**
4506 Lakelse Ave., Terrace, BC V8G 1P4
Tel: 250-635-5518; *Fax:* 250-635-5528
mvcacademy@yahoo.ca
www.mountainviewchristianacademy.net
Grades: K - 12
Gunther Rauschenberger, Principal

***Vancouver:* Vancouver Christian School (VCS)**
3496 Mons Dr., Vancouver, BC V5M 3E6, Canada
Tel: 604-435-3113; *Fax:* 604-430-1591
office@vancouverchristian.org
www.vancouverchristian.org
Other Information: 604-523-1580 (Phone, Carver Christian High School)
Grades: K - 12; *Note:* Vancouver Christian School is an independent, interdenominational school. Grades nine to twelve are offered at Carver Christian High School.
Ellen Freestone, Principal
Andrea Wiebe, Vice Principal, Kindergarten - Grade 5
Mrs. Con, Vice Principal, Grades 6 to 8

***Vancouver:* West Coast Christian School (WCCS)**
15 North Renfrew St., Vancouver, BC V5K 3N6, Canada
Tel: 604-255-2990; *Fax:* 604-255-2103
office@westcoastchristianschool.ca
www.westcoastchristianschool.ca
Grades: K - 12; *Enrollment:* 100; *Note:* The school is a ministry of West Coast Christian Fellowship. It offers a Christian approach to learning.
David Ferguson, Principal
Julie Shettler, Administrative Assistant

***Vanderhoof:* Northside Christian School**
3337 Voth Rd., Vanderhoof, BC V0J 3A2
Tel: 250-567-9335; *Fax:* 250-567-9332
info@thenorthsideschool.ca
www.thenorthsideschool.ca
www.twitter.com/NCS_Vanderhoo
Grades: 1 - 12; *Enrollment:* 67
Michael Shenk, Principal

***Vernon:* Pleasant Valley Christian Academy**
1802 - 45th Ave., Vernon, BC V1T 3M7
Tel: 250-545-7852; *Fax:* 250-545-9230
admin@pleasantvalleychristian.com
Grades: K.-9; *Enrollment:* 30; *Note:* Affiliated with the Seventh-day Adventist Church
Melanie Kartik, Principal

***Vernon:* Vernon Christian School**
Elementary Campus
6890 Pleasant Valley Rd., Vernon, BC V1B 3R5
Tel: 250-545-7345
info@vcs.ca
www.vcs.ca
www.facebook.com/pages/Vernon-Christian-School/1723235761 27694
twitter.com/myvcs
www.youtube.com/user/vernonchristian
Grades: Kindergarten - 12; *Enrollment:* 350; *Note:* Vernon Christian School is an interdenominational school. The school's secondary campus is located at 6920 Pleasant Valley Road.
Karen Wiseman, Chair
kwiseman@vcs.ca
Steve Onsorge, Lead Principal / Principal Elementary Campus
sonsorge@vcs.ca
Matt Driediger, Principal, Secondary Campus
mdriediger@vcs.ca
Andy Overend, Vice-Principal, Elementary Campus
aoverend@vcs.ca
Brad Martens, Vice-Principal, Secondary Campus
bmartens@vcs.ca

***Victoria:* Lakeview Christian School**
729 Cordova Bay Rd., Victoria, BC V8Y 1P7
Tel: 250-658-5082; *Fax:* 250-658-5072
www.lakeviewchristianschool.ca
Grades: Preschool - 9; *Note:* The Lakeview Christian School is affiliated with other Seventh-day Adventist Christian schools to provide Christian education.
Erin Sutherland, Board Chair
Agnes Oosterhof, Principal

***Victoria:* Lighthouse Christian Academy**
1289 Parkdale Dr., Victoria, BC V9B 4G9, Canada
Tel: 250-474-5311; *Fax:* 250-474-5021
info@lighthousechristianacademy.com
www.lighthousechristianacademy.com
www.facebook.com/133384233375987
Grades: K-9; *Enrollment:* 70
Leland Makaroff, Principal

***Victoria:* Pacific Christian School (PCS)**
654 Agnes St., Victoria, BC V8Z 2E7, Canada
Tel: 250-479-4532; *Fax:* 250-479-3511
www.pacificchristian.ca
www.facebook.com/yourPCS
twitter.com/pcsvictoria
pinterest.com/yourpcs
Grades: K-12; *Enrollment:* 900

B. Helmus, Principal
bhelmus@pacificchristian.ca

Williams Lake: Cariboo Adventist Academy
1405 South Lakeside Dr., Williams Lake, BC V2G 3A7
Tel: 250-392-4741
cacademy@yahoo.com
an681g.adventistschoolconnect.org
Grades: Kindergarten - 12; Note: The Cariboo Adventist Academy is operated by the Seventh-day Adventist Church.

Williams Lake: Maranatha Christian School
1278 Lakeview Cres., Williams Lake, BC V2G 1A3, Canada
Tel: 250-392-7410; Fax: 250-392-7409
maranatha@wlefc.org
www.wlmcs.org
Grades: K-12; Enrollment: 155
C. Klaue, Principal

Catholic

Abbotsford: St. James School
2767 Townline Rd., Abbotsford, BC V2T 5E1, Canada
Tel: 604-852-1788; Fax: 604-850-5376
www.stjameselementary.ca
Grades: K-7; Enrollment: 219
Terri Sask, Principal

Abbotsford: St. John Brebeuf
2747 Townline Rd., Abbotsford, BC V2T 5E1, Canada
Tel: 604-855-0571; Fax: 604-855-0572
www.stjohnbrebeuf.ca
Grades: 8-12; Enrollment: 347
Ted Brennan, Principal
tbrennan@stjohnbrebeuf.ca

Burnaby: Holy Cross Elementary
1450 Delta Ave., Burnaby, BC V5B 3G2, Canada
Tel: 604-299-3530; Fax: 604-299-3534
hcoffice@telus.net
www.holycrosselementary.ca
Grades: K-7; Enrollment: 224
Dino Alberti, Principal
dinohc@telus.net

Burnaby: Our Lady of Mercy School
7481 - 10 Ave., Burnaby, BC V3N 2S1, Canada
Tel: 604-526-7121; Fax: 604-520-3194
office@ourladyofmercy.ca
www.ourladyofmercy.ca
Grades: K-7; Enrollment: 240
Neva Grout, Principal

Burnaby: St. Francis de Sales School
6656 Balmoral St., Burnaby, BC V5E 1J1, Canada
Tel: 604-435-5311; Fax: 604-434-4798
office@sfdsschool.ca
www.sfdsschool.ca
www.facebook.com/sfdsflames
twitter.com/sfdsflames
instagram.com/sfdsflames
Grades: K.-7; Enrollment: 217; Note: St. Francis de Sales is a Catholic school located in the Highgate region of South Burnaby.
Irene Wihak, Principal

Burnaby: St. Helen's School
3894 Triumph St., Burnaby, BC V5C 1Y7, Canada
Tel: 604-299-2234; Fax: 604-299-3565
school.sthelensparish.ca
Grades: K-7; Enrollment: 352
Waldemar Sambor, Principal
wsambor@cisva.bc.ca

Burnaby: St. Michael's School
9387 Holmes St., Burnaby, BC V3N 4C3, Canada
Tel: 604-526-9768; Fax: 604-540-9799
school@stmichaelsparish.ca
www.stmichaelschool.ca
Grades: K-7; Enrollment: 216
C. Kennedy, Principal

Burnaby: St. Thomas More Collegiate (STMC)
7450 - 12 Ave., Burnaby, BC V3N 2K1, Canada
Tel: 604-521-1801; Fax: 604-520-0725
info@stmc.bc.ca
www.stmc.bc.ca
Grades: 8-12; Enrollment: 675; Number of Employees: 55
Michel DesLauriers, Principal
mdeslauriers@stmc.bc.ca

Chemainus: St. Joseph's Elementary School
9735 Elm St., Chemainus, BC V0R 1K0, Canada
Tel: 250-246-3191; Fax: 250-246-2921
sjc@cisdv.bc.ca
www.stjosephselem.ca
Grades: K-7; Enrollment: 115
Bern Muller, Principal
bmuller@cisdv.bc.ca

Chilliwack: St. Mary's Catholic School
8909 Mary St., Chilliwack, BC V2P 4J4, Canada
Tel: 604-792-7715; Fax: 604-792-7031
www.stmarysschoolchwk.com
Grades: K-7; Enrollment: 183
M. McDermott, Principal

Coquitlam: Our Lady of Fatima School
315 Walker St., Coquitlam, BC V3K 4C7, Canada
Tel: 604-936-4228; Fax: 604-936-4403
info@fatimaschool.ca
www.fatimaschool.ca
Grades: K-7; Enrollment: 388; Note: Independent, English and French Immersion School accredited in British Columbia under the terms of the Independent School Act.
Maria Katsionis, Principal

Coquitlam: Queen of All Saints Elementary School (QAS)
1405 Como Lake Ave., Coquitlam, BC V3J 3P4, Canada
Tel: 604-931-9071; Fax: 604-931-9089
queenofallsaintsschool@shawcable.com
www.queenofallsaintsschool.ca
Grades: K - 7; Note: Queen of All Saints Elementary School was established by the Roman Catholic Archdiocese of Vancouver. The school belongs to All Saints Parish.
Joan Sandberg, Principal

Coquitlam: Traditional Learning Academy (TLA)
1189 Rochester Ave., Coquitlam, BC V3K 2X3, Canada
Tel: 604-931-7265; Fax: 604-931-3432
tlaoffice@traditionallearning.com
www.traditionallearning.com
Other Information: tlaprincipal@traditionallearning.com (E-mail, Principal)
Grades: K - 12; Note: Traditional Learning Academy encourages students to know the Catholic faith.
Allan Garneau, Administrator

Cranbrook: St. Mary's Catholic Independent School
1701 - 5 St. South, Cranbrook, BC V1C 1K1
Tel: 250-426-5017; Fax: 250-426-5076
jmacneil@cintek.com
Grades: K.-6; Enrollment: 143
J. Macneil, Principal

Dawson Creek: Notre Dame School
925 - 104th Ave., Dawson Creek, BC V1G 2H8
Tel: 250-782-4923; Fax: 250-782-4388
www.notredamedc.org/notre-dame-school
Grades: K.- 7; Enrollment: 150
Mrs. Terri Haynal, Principal
Kathy Lear, Principal

Delta: Immaculate Conception School
8840 - 119 St., Delta, BC V4C 6M4, Canada
Tel: 604-596-6116; Fax: 604-596-4338
immaculate_conception_school@hotmail.com
www.icdelta.com
Grades: K-7; Enrollment: 473
Maurice Jacob, Principal
Fr. Patrick Tepoorten, Pastor

Delta: Sacred Heart School
P.O. Box 10 Main
3900 Arthur Dr., Delta, BC V4K 3N5, Canada
Tel: 604-946-2611; Fax: 604-946-0598
office@shsdelta.org
www.shsdelta.net
Grades: K-7; Enrollment: 400
Wendell MacCormack, Principal

Duncan: Queen of Angels Catholic School
2085 Maple Bay Rd., Duncan, BC V9L 5L9, Canada
Tel: 250-746-5919; Fax: 250-746-8689
qa@cisdv.bc.ca
www.queenofangels.ca
Grades: Pre-K - 9
Tina Campagne, Chair, Local School Council
Art Therrien, Principal
Ciaran McLaverty, Vice Principal
Lana Durand, Coordinator, Special Education
Denika Osmond, Secretary

Kelowna: Immaculata Catholic Regional High School
1493 K.L.O. Rd., Kelowna, BC V1W 3N8
Tel: 250-762-2730; Fax: 250-861-3028
secretary@immaculatakelowna.ca
www.immaculatakelowna.ca
twitter.com/IRHS_Athletics
Grades: Secondary; Religious Education; Enrollment: 350; Number of Employees: 26 (14 teachers)
Rob Plaxton, B.Ed. M.Ed., Principal
Lois Ehman, B.Ed. M.Ed., Vice-Principal
lehman@immaculatakelowna.ca
Fr. Pat Monette, Chaplain
Mary Gallagher, B.Ed, Coordinator, Religious Education
mgallagher@immaculatakelowna.ca
Chris Schmidt, B.Ed., Librarian
cschmidt@immaculatakelowna.ca
Nadine Casorso, Librarian
ncasorso@immaculatakelowna.ca

Langley: St. Catherines School
20244 - 32 Ave., Langley, BC V2Z 2E1, Canada
Tel: 604-534-6564; Fax: 604-534-4871
lfa@lfabc.org
www.stcatherines.ca
Grades: K-7; Enrollment: 229
Diane Little, Principal

Maple Ridge: St. Patrick's School
22589 - 121 Ave., Maple Ridge, BC V2X 3T5, Canada
Tel: 604-467-1571; Fax: 604-467-2686
school@stpatsschool.org
www.stpatsschool.org
twitter.com/stpatsmr
Grades: K-7; Enrollment: 214
Clive Heah, Principal

North Vancouver: Holy Trinity Elementary School
128 - West 27 St., North Vancouver, BC V7N 2H1, Canada
Tel: 604-987-4454
holyt@telus.net
www.holytrinityschool.ca
Grades: K-7; Enrollment: 233
Kevin Smith, Principal
ksmith@cisva.bc.ca

North Vancouver: St. Edmund's School
535 Mahon Ave., North Vancouver, BC V7M 2R7, Canada
Tel: 604-988-7364; Fax: 604-988-7350
office@stedmunds.ca
www.stedmunds.ca
Grades: K-7; Enrollment: 204
Michael Field, Principal
mfield@stedmunds.ca

North Vancouver: St. Pius X Elementary School
1150 Mount Seymour Rd., North Vancouver, BC V7G 1R6, Canada
Tel: 604-929-0345; Fax: 604-929-5051
www.saintpius.ca
Grades: K-7; Enrollment: 227
Fabio Battisti, Principal

North Vancouver: St. Thomas Aquinas Regional Secondary School
541 Keith Rd. West, North Vancouver, BC V7M 1M5, Canada
Tel: 604-987-4431; Fax: 604-987-7816
office@aquinas.org
www.aquinas.org
Grades: 8-12; Enrollment: 601
John Campbell, Principal
jcampbell@aquinas.org

Penticton: Holy Cross Elementary School
1298 Main St., Penticton, BC V2A 5G2, Canada
Tel: 250-492-4480; Fax: 250-490-4602
www.holyc.com
Grades: K.-7; Enrollment: 145
Jeff Brophy, Principal

Port Coquitlam: Archbishop Carney Regional Secondary School (ACRSS)
1335 Dominion Ave., Port Coquitlam, BC V3B 8G7, Canada
Tel: 604-942-7465; Fax: 604-942-5289
office@acrss.org
www.acrss.org
Grades: 8-12; Enrollment: 720
Lorraine Paruzzolo, Principal, 604-942-7465, ext. 2
paruzzol@acrss.org

Port Coquitlam: Our Lady of the Assumption School
2255 Fraser Ave., Port Coquitlam, BC V3B 6G8, Canada
Tel: 604-942-5522; Fax: 604-942-8313
info@assumptionschool.com
www.assumptionschool.com
Grades: K-7; Enrollment: 244
Rosaleen Heffernan, Principal

Powell River: Assumption Catholic School
7091 Glacier St., Powell River, BC V8A 1R8, Canada
Tel: 604-485-9894; Fax: 604-485-7984
assump.office@shaw.ca
www.assumpschool.com
Grades: K.-9; Enrollment: 186; Note: Accredited by the B.C. Min. of Education. Curriculum includes math, sciences, social studies, physical education, languages, music, art, drama, & relgion.
Mimi Richardson, Principal

Richmond: St. Joseph the Worker School
4451 Williams Rd., Richmond, BC V7E 1J7, Canada
Tel: 604-277-1115; Fax: 604-272-5214
office.sjosw@cisva.bc.ca
stjosephtheworker.ca
Grades: K-7; Enrollment: 222
Paul Fraser, Principal
paulfraser.stjo@gmail.com

Richmond: St. Paul's School
8251 St. Alban's Rd., Richmond, BC V6Y 2L2, Canada
Tel: 604-277-4487; Fax: 604-277-1810
office@stpaulschool.ca
www.stpaulschool.ca
Grades: K-7; Enrollment: 241
Nicole Regush, Principal

Surrey: Cloverdale Catholic School
17511 - 59th Ave., Surrey, BC V3S 1P3, Canada
Tel: 604-574-5151; Fax: 604-574-5160
office@ccsunited.ca
ccsunited.ca
www.facebook.com/204955139548051
www.twitter.com/ClovCatholicSch
Grades: Preschool; K.-7; Enrollment: 245
Jason Borkowski, Principal
jborkowski@cisva.bc.ca
Janet Mahussier, Librarian
jmahussier@ccsunited.ca

Surrey: Holy Cross Regional High School
16193 - 88 Ave., Surrey, BC V4N 1G3, Canada
Tel: 604-581-3023; Fax: 604-583-4795
office@holycross.bc.ca
www.holycross.bc.ca
www.facebook.com/holycrossregionalhighschool
twitter.com/dailycrusader
www.flickr.com/photos/holycrossregionalsecondary
Grades: 8-12; Enrollment: 797
Chris Blesch, Principal

Surrey: Our Lady of Good Counsel School
10504 - 139 St., Surrey, BC V3T 4L5, Canada
Tel: 604-581-3154; Fax: 604-588-1633
olgcprincipal@shaw.ca
www.olgcschool.ca
Grades: K-7; Enrollment: 245
Gerard Wright, Principal

Surrey: St. Bernadette School
13130 - 65B Ave., Surrey, BC V3W 9M1, Canada
Tel: 604-596-1101; Fax: 604-596-1550
www.stbernadetteschool.ca
Grades: K-7; Enrollment: 227
Kelly Kozack, Principal

Surrey: St. Matthew's Elementary
16065 - 88th Ave., Surrey, BC V4N 1G3
Tel: 604-589-7545
office@stmatthewselementary.ca
www.stmatthewselementary.ca
Grades: K - 3
Deborah Welsh, Principal
welsh@stmatthewselementary.ca

Surrey: Star of the Sea School
15024 - 24 Ave., Surrey, BC V4A 2H8, Canada
Tel: 604-531-6316; Fax: 604-531-0171
school@starofthesea.ca
www.staroftheseaschool.ca
twitter.com/StaroftheSeaBC
Grades: K-7; Enrollment: 316
Lesya Balsevich, Principal
lbalsevich@starofthesea.bc.ca

Terrace: Veritas Catholic School
4836 Straume Ave., Terrace, BC V8G 4G3
Tel: 250-635-3035; Fax: 250-635-7588
veritas.class@telus.net
www.veritascatholicschool.com
Grades: Kindergarten - 7; Enrollment: 200
Colleen LeBlanc, Chair
Glen Palahicky, Principal
veritas.principal@telus.net
Isabel DeMedeiros, Secretary

Trail: St. Michael's Catholic School
1329 - 4 Ave., Trail, BC V1R 1S3
Tel: 250-368-6151; Fax: 250-368-9962
www.smces.ca
Grades: K.-7; Enrollment: 179
Julia Mason, Principal

Vancouver: Blessed Sacrament School
École Saint Sacrement
3020 Heather St., Vancouver, BC V5Z 3K3, Canada
Tel: 604-876-7211; Fax: 604-876-7280
admin@ess.vancouver.bc.ca
ess.vancouver.bc.ca/moodle
Grades: K - 7

Vancouver: Corpus Christi School
6344 Nanaimo St., Vancouver, BC V5P 4K7, Canada
Tel: 604-321-1117; Fax: 604-321-1410
officecc@telus.net
www.corpuschristi-school.ca
Grades: K-7; Enrollment: 241
Rosa Natola, Principal

Vancouver: Immaculate Conception School Vancouver
3745 - 28 Ave. West, Vancouver, BC V6S 1S6, Canada
Tel: 604-224-5012; Fax: 604-224-3721
www.icschoolvancouver.com
Grades: K-7; Enrollment: 200
Colette Foran, Principal

Vancouver: Little Flower Academy (LFA)
4195 Alexandra St., Vancouver, BC V6J 4C6, Canada
Tel: 604-738-9016; Fax: 604-738-5749
lfa@lfabc.com
www.lfabc.org
Grades: 8-12; Enrollment: 469
M. DeFreitas, Principal

Vancouver: Notre Dame Regional Secondary School
2880 Venables St., Vancouver, BC V5K 4Z6, Canada
Tel: 604-255-5454; Fax: 604-255-2115
scirillo@ndrs.org
www.ndrs.ca
Grades: 8 - 12; Enrollment: 620; Note: Notre Dame Regional Secondary School is a Catholic school.
Roger DesLauriers, Principal, 604-255-5454
rdeslauriers@ndrs.org
George Oswald, Vice Principal, 604-255-5454
goswald@ndrs.org
Andrew McCracken, Librarian
amccracken@ndrs.org
Maureen Grant, Manager, Office, 604-255-5454
mgrant@ndrs.org

Vancouver: Our Lady of Perpetual Help School
2550 Camosun St., Vancouver, BC V6R 3W6, Canada
Tel: 604-228-8811; Fax: 604-224-6822
office@olphbc.ca
www.olphbc.ca
Grades: K-7; Enrollment: 406
Lora Clarke, Principal

Vancouver: Our Lady of Sorrows School
575 Slocan St., Vancouver, BC V5K 3X5, Canada
Tel: 604-253-2434; Fax: 604-253-1523
ourladyofsorrows1@telus.net
www.ourladyofsorrows.ca
Grades: K-7; Enrollment: 231
P. Balletta, Principal

Vancouver: Saint Patrick Elementary School
2850 Quebec St., Vancouver, BC V5T 3A9, Canada
Tel: 604-879-4411; Fax: 604-879-3737
www.spev.ca
Grades: K-7; Enrollment: 249
M. Boreham, Principal
mboreham@spev.ca

Vancouver: Saint Patrick Regional Secondary School
115 - 11 Ave. East, Vancouver, BC V5T 2C1, Canada
Tel: 604-874-6422; Fax: 604-874-5176
administration@stpats.bc.ca
www.stpats.bc.ca
www.facebook.com/129972273748715
twitter.com/StPatsSecVanBC
www.youtube.com/STPCouncil
Grades: 8-12; Enrollment: 501
Ralph Gabriele, Principal

Vancouver: St. Andrew's School
450 - 47th Ave. East, Vancouver, BC V5W 2B4, Canada
Tel: 604-325-6317; Fax: 604-325-0920
principal@standrewsschool.ca
standrewsschool.ca/wordpress/
Grades: K-7; Enrollment: 227
Marian Mailley, Principal

Vancouver: St. Anthony of Padua
1370 - 73rd Ave. West, Vancouver, BC V6P 3E8, Canada
Tel: 604-261-4043; Fax: 604-261-4036
office@stanthonyofpaduaschool.ca
www.stanthonyofpaduaschool.ca
Grades: K-7; Enrollment: 209
Oscar Pozzolo, Principal

Vancouver: St. Augustine's School
2145 - 8 Ave. West, Vancouver, BC V6K 2A5, Canada
Tel: 604-731-8024; Fax: 604-739-1712
info@faithandfoundation.com
www.faithandfoundation.com
Grades: K-7; Enrollment: 224
Catherine Oberndorf, Principal

Vancouver: St. Francis of Assisi School
870 Victoria Dr., Vancouver, BC V5L 4E7, Canada
Tel: 604-253-7311; Fax: 604-253-7375
sfaoffice@telus.net
www.sfaschool.ca
Grades: K-7; Enrollment: 191
Joan Sandberg, Principal

Vancouver: St. Francis Xavier School
428 Great Northern Way, Vancouver, BC V5T 4S5, Canada
Tel: 604-254-2714; Fax: 604-254-2514
admin@sfxschool.ca
www.sfxschool.ca
Grades: K-7; Enrollment: 327
B. Krivuzoff, Principal

Vancouver: St. Joseph's School
3261 Fleming St., Vancouver, BC V5N 3V6, Canada
Tel: 604-872-5715; Fax: 604-872-5700
stjosephsvancouver@telus.net
www.stjoesschool-vancouver.org
Grades: K-7; Enrollment: 210
Dierdre O'Callaghan, Principal

Vancouver: St. Jude's School
2953 - 15 Ave. East, Vancouver, BC V5M 2K7, Canada
Tel: 604-434-1633; Fax: 604-434-8677
stjude@shawcable.com
stjude.ca
twitter.com/stjudevan
Grades: K-7; Enrollment: 221
M. Perry, Principal

Vancouver: St. Mary's School
5239 Joyce St., Vancouver, BC V5R 4G8, Canada
Tel: 604-437-1312; Fax: 604-437-1193
www.stmary.bc.ca
twitter.com/SMSaints604
instagram.com/smsaints604?ref=badge
Grades: K-7; Enrollment: 230
Brenda Krivuzoff, Principal

Vancouver: Vancouver College
5400 Cartier St., Vancouver, BC V6M 3A5, Canada
Tel: 604-261-4285
info@vc.bc.ca
www.vc.bc.ca
Grades: K - 12; Enrollment: 1000; Note: Vancouver College consists of an elementary school, a middle school, & a senior school.
John McFarland, Principal
jmcfarland@vc.bc.ca
Kelly Lattimer, Business Manager
klattimer@vc.bc.ca
Ronith Cogswell, Director, Advancement
rcogswell@vc.bc.ca
Margaret Vossen, Registrar
mvossen@vc.bc.ca

Victoria: St. Andrew's Regional High School
880 Mckenzie Ave., Victoria, BC V8X 3G5, Canada
Tel: 250-479-1414; *Fax:* 250-479-5356
sarhs@cisdv.bc.ca
www.standrewshigh.ca
Grades: 8-12; *Enrollment:* 469
Andrew Keleher, Principal
akeleher@cisdv.bc.ca

Victoria: St. Joseph's Victoria Elementary School
757 Burnside Rd. West, Victoria, BC V8Z 1M9, Canada
Tel: 250-479-1232; *Fax:* 250-479-1907
sjv@cisdv.bc.ca
www.stjosephschool.ca
Grades: K-7; *Enrollment:* 203
Simon Di Castri, Co-Principal
Keefer Pollard, Co-Principal

Victoria: St. Patrick's Elementary School
2368 Trent St., Victoria, BC V8R 4Z3, Canada
Tel: 250-592-6713; *Fax:* 250-592-6717
sp@cisdv.bc.ca
www.stpatrickselem.ca
Grades: K-7; *Enrollment:* 355
Deanne Paulson, Principal

West Vancouver: St. Anthony's School
595 Keith Rd., West Vancouver, BC V7T 1L8, Canada
Tel: 604-922-0011; *Fax:* 604-922-3196
office@saswv.ca
www.saswv.ca
Grades: K-7; *Enrollment:* 204
Laila Maravillas, Principal
principal@saswv.ca

Williams Lake: Sacred Heart Catholic School
455 Pigeon Ave., Williams Lake, BC V2G 4R5, Canada
Tel: 250-398-7770; *Fax:* 250-398-7725
admin@sacredheartwl.com
sacredheartwl.com
Grades: Pre. K - 7; *Enrollment:* 84
Nicholas Iachetta, Principal
principal@sacredheartwl.com

French

Vancouver: L'Ecole Française Internationale de Vancouver
French International School of Vancouver
3657, rue Fromme, Vancouver, BC V7K 2E6
Tél: 604-924-2457; *Téléc:* 604-924-4483
info@efiv.org
www.efiv.org
twitter.com/EFIVANCOUVER
www.flickr.com/photos/efivancouver
Grades: Pre.-8; *Enrollment:* 143
Gérard Martinez, Principal
principal@efiv.org

First Nations

Iskut: Klappan Independent Day School
P.O. Box 30
Iskut, BC V0J 1K0
Tel: 250-234-3561; *Fax:* 250-234-3563
www.bced.gov.bc.ca
Grades: K.-9; *Note:* Serving students of Iskut First Nation.
Shelley Jones, Principal
principal@iskut.org

Merritt: Coldwater Band School
P.O. Box 4600
2249 Quilchena Ave., Merritt, BC V1K 1B8
Tel: 250-378-9261; *Fax:* 250-378-9212
Grades: K - 12

Merritt: N'Kwala School (Upper Nicola Band)
P.O. Box 3700
Merritt, BC V1K 1J5
Tel: 250-350-3370; *Fax:* 250-350-3319

Port Hardy: Gwa'sala-'Nakwaxda'xw School
P.O. Box 1799
Port Hardy, BC V0N 2P0, Canada
Tel: 250-949-7743; *Fax:* 250-949-7402
www.gwanak.info
Enrollment: 82; *Note:* Independent First Nation's school
Grace Smith, Education Coordinator
grace.smith176@gmail.com

Special Education

Kelowna: Venture Academy
#101, 1865 Dilworth Dr., Kelowna, BC V1Y 9T1
Tel: 250-491-4593; *Fax:* 250-491-0251
Toll-Free: 866-762-2211
info@ventureacademy.ca
www.ventureacademy.ca
Grades: 7-12; *Note:* A therapeutic program & boarding school for troubled teens; also has locations in Alberta & Ontario
Gordon Hay, B.G.S., Executive Director & Founder
Louise Beard, Executive Director

Maple Ridge: James Cameron School
P.O. Box 157 Del Ctr.
20245 Dewdney Trunk Rd., Maple Ridge, BC V2X 7G1, Canada
Tel: 604-465-8444; *Fax:* 604-465-4561
jcsadmin@jcs.bc.ca
www.jcs.bc.ca
www.facebook.com/pages/James-Cameron-School/285177034850085
Grades: 2-7; *Enrollment:* 54
Olive Wagstaff, Principal

Vancouver: Eaton Arrowsmith School
#204, 6190 Agronomy Rd., Vancouver, BC V6T 1Z3
Tel: 604-264-8327; *Fax:* 604-222-8327
info@eatonarrowsmithschool.com
www.eatonarrowsmithschool.com
www.facebook.com/eatonarrowsmithschool
twitter.com/eatonarrowsmith
Grades: K-12; *Enrollment:* 100
Howard Eaton, Director
Simon Hayes, Principal
Campuses
Victoria Campus
#200, 3200 Shelbourne St., Victoria, BC V8P 5G8
Tel: 250-370-0046; *Fax:* 250-370-0034
victoria@eatonarrowsmithschool.com
Jason Cruickshank, Principal
Surrey/White Rock Campus
1538 Foster St., 3rd Fl., White Rock, BC V4B 3X7
Tel: 604-264-8327; *Fax:* 604-222-8327
info@eatonarrowsmithschool.com
Luciana Holmes, Principal

Vancouver: PALS Autism School
Also known as: Phoenix Academy of Learning
2409 East Pender St., Vancouver, BC V5K 2B2
Tel: 604-251-7257; *Fax:* 604-251-1627
info@palsautismschool.ca
palsautismschool.ca
Grades: 3 - 12; Adult
Andrea Kasunic, Head of School

Distance Education

Victoria: Regent Christian Online Academy (RCOA)
#105, 4475 Viewmont Ave., Victoria, BC V8Z 6L8
Tel: 250-592-1759; *Fax:* 250-721-0036
Toll-Free: 866-877-1737
regentonline.ca
Grades: K - 12; *Enrollment:* 1100; *Number of Employees:* 85 teachers
Mark Langley, Principal
Carolyn Langley, Business Administrator

Independent & Private Schools

Abbotsford: Dasmesh Punjabi School
33094 South Fraser Way, Abbotsford, BC V2S 2A9, Canada
Tel: 604-852-8986; *Fax:* 604-852-8924
www.dasmeshschool.com
Grades: K.-10; *Enrollment:* 397
Dalip Singh Gill, Principal

Agassiz: Seabird College
P.O. Box 650
2895 Chowat Rd., Agassiz, BC V0M 1A0, Canada
Tel: 604-796-6896; *Fax:* 604-796-3729
www.seabirdisland.ca/page/seabird-college
www.facebook.com/pages/Seabird-Island-Band/147393798735724
twitter.com/SeabirdIsland
Grades: K - 12; *Enrollment:* 162
Dianne Parkinson, Contact
dianneparkinson@seabirdisland.ca

Ahousat: Maaqtusiis School
General Delivery, Ahousat, BC V0R 1A0, Canada
Tel: 250-670-9555; *Fax:* 250-670-9543
maaqtusiis.wordpress.com
Grades: 1-12; *Enrollment:* 217
Rebecca Atleo, Principal

Aldergrove: Fraser Valley Adventist Academy (FVAA)
26026 - 48th Ave., Aldergrove, BC V4W 1J2, Canada
Tel: 604-607-3822; *Fax:* 604-856-1002
fvaa@fvaa.net
www.fvaa.ca
www.facebook.com/FVAAeducation
www.twitter.com/fvaaeducation
Grades: K-12; *Enrollment:* 173; *Note:* Seventh-day Adventist college preparatory secondary & elementary school.
Karen Wallace, Principal, 604-607-3822, ext. 315
principal@fvaa.ca
Colleen Russell, Business Manager, 604-607-3822, ext. 341
business@fvaa.ca
Joan Septembre, Secretary, Librarian, 604-607-3822, ext. 301
info@fvaa.ca

Alert Bay: T'lisalagi'lakw School
P.O. Box 50
Alert Bay, BC V0N 1A0, Canada
Tel: 250-974-5591; *Fax:* 250-974-2475
WayneP@namgis.bc.ca
Grades: K.-11; *Enrollment:* 66
G. Alfred, Principal

Armstrong: North Okanagan Junior Academy (NOJA)
4699 South Grandview Flats Rd., Armstrong, BC V0E 1B5, Canada
Tel: 250-546-8330; *Fax:* 250-546-8343
info@noja.ca
www.noja.ca
www.facebook.com/.../north-okanagan-junior-academy/
Note: The Academy is operated by the Seventh-day Adventist Church.
Marilyn Ilchuk, Principal
marilynilchuk@aol.com
Sharon Trussell, Vice Principal
shrbet@shaw.ca

Bowen Island: Island Pacific School
P.O. Box 128
671 Carter Rd., Bowen Island, BC V0N 1G0, Canada
Tel: 604-947-9311; *Fax:* 604-947-9366
info@go.islandpacific.org
www.islandpacific.org
www.facebook.com/islandpacificschool
www.facebook.com/islandpacificschool
www.youtube.com/user/islandpacificschool
Grades: 6-9; *Enrollment:* 52; *Note:* Core program elements include inquiry-based learning within the IB Middle Years Program; special classes in reasoning, philosophy and ethics; hiking, sailing and kayaking expeditions; a grade 9 Masterworks program that requires student to complete, (and publicly defend), a 15-30 page independent research project; monthly community service activities; and a House system that requires, among other things, that students clean the school.
Dr. Ted Spear, Principal

Burnaby: Deer Lake SDA School
5550 Gilpin St., Burnaby, BC V5G 2H6, Canada
Tel: 604-434-5844; *Fax:* 604-434-5845
office@deerlakeschool.ca
www.deerlakeschool.ca
Grades: K-12; *Enrollment:* 278
Caren Erickson, Principal

Chilliwack: Highroad Academy
46641 Chilliwack Central Rd., Chilliwack, BC V2P 1K3, Canada
Tel: 604-792-4680; *Fax:* 604-792-2465
info@highroadacademy.com
www.highroadacademy.com
www.facebook.com/pages/Highroad-Academy/173722670118
Grades: K-12; *Enrollment:* 430
Dave Shinness, Principal
dshinness@highroadacademy.com

Chilliwack: John Calvin School
4268 Stewart Rd., Chilliwack, BC V2R 5G3, Canada
Tel: 604-823-6814; *Fax:* 604-823-6791
office@jcss.ca
www.jcss.ca
Grades: K-7; *Enrollment:* 170
Pieter H. Torenvliet, Principal, 604-823-6814

Cobble Hill: Evergreen Independent School
P.O. Box 166
3515 Watson Ave., Cobble Hill, BC V0R 1L0, Canada
Tel: 250-743-2433; Fax: 250-743-2570
evergreen@evergreenbc.net
www.evergreenbc.net
Grades: K.-6; Enrollment: 63
J. Ovans, Principal

Comox: Phil & Jennie Gaglardi Academy
1475 Noel Ave., Comox, BC V9M 4H8, Canada
Tel: 250-339-1200; Fax: 250-339-1215
office@cvchristian.com
www.pjgaglardiacademy.ca
www.facebook.com/GatewayAcademyComox
Grades: K-9; Enrollment: 112
R. Janzen, Principal

Coquitlam: Coquitlam College
516 Brookmere Ave., Coquitlam, BC V3J 1W9, Canada
Tel: 604-939-6633; Fax: 604-939-0336
admiss@coquitlamcollege.com
www.coquitlamcollege.com
www.facebook.com/coquitlamcollege
www.youtube.com/user/ccoquitlam
Grades: 11-12; Enrollment: 85
Tom Tait, President
Will Eckford, Principal

Coquitlam: Eagle Ridge Montessori Elementary
2541 Quay Pl., Coquitlam, BC V3S 3H7, Canada
Tel: 604-461-1223; Fax: 604-461-1228
info@childrenofintegrity.com
www.childrenofintegrity.com
Grades: K.-6; Enrollment: 38
V. Lawrie, Principal

Coquitlam: Mediated Learning Academy
550 Thompson Ave., Coquitlam, BC V3J 3Z8, Canada
Tel: 604-937-3641; Fax: 604-931-5155
info@mediatedlearningacademy.org
www.mediatedlearningacademy.org
Grades: K-12; Enrollment: 84; Note: The Mediated Learning Academy is an educational facility for children to learn through Mediated Learning Experience and "brain-based" teaching.
Kathleen Jeffrey, Principal

Courtenay: Saltwater School
2311 Rosewall Cres., Courtenay, BC V9N 8R9
Tel: 250-871-7777
info@saltwaterschool.com
www.saltwaterschool.com
www.facebook.com/278554592436?ref=ts&sk=wall
Grades: Pre. - 6
Rebecca Watkin, Pedagogical Coordinator

Duncan: Island Oak High School
P.O. Box 873 Main
5814 Banks Rd., Duncan, BC V9L 3Y2, Canada
Tel: 250-701-0400; Fax: 250-701-0410
mail@islandoak.org
islandoak.org
www.tumblr.com/register/follow/islandoak
Grades: 9-12; Enrollment: 36
Gary Ward, Principal

Duncan: Queen Margaret's School (QMS)
660 Brownsey Ave., Duncan, BC V9L 1C2, Canada
Tel: 250-746-4185; Fax: 250-746-4187
admissions@qms.bc.ca
www.qms.bc.ca
www.facebook.com/240936919190
twitter.com/QMSDuncan
Grades: JK - 12; Enrollment: 325; Number of Employees: 115; Note: Queen Margaret's School consists of a coeducational junior school for students from junior kindergarten to grade seven. The school also consists of an All-Girls High School, which offers a university preparatory program. An English as a Second Language Program is available for beginner & advanced students.
Leigh Taylor, Chair
Wilma Jamieson, Head of School
wjamieson@qms.bc.ca
Sharon Klein, Deputy Head, Education & Senior School Principal
sklein@qms.bc.ca
Susan Cruikshank, Junior School Principal
scruikshank@qms.bc.ca
Celina Mason, Director, Residential Life & Student Support
cmason@qms.bc.ca
Julie Scurr, Director, Finance & Privacy Officer
jascurr@qms.bc.ca
Courtney Gillan, Executive Director, Admissions & Advancement
cgillan@qms.bc.ca

Duncan: Sunrise Waldorf School (SWS)
2148 Lakeside Rd., Duncan, BC V9L 6M3, Canada
Tel: 250-743-7253; Fax: 250-743-7245
mail@sunrisewaldorfschool.org
www.sunrisewaldorfschool.org
www.facebook.com/sunrisewaldorf
Grades: K-8; Enrollment: 162
J. Canty, Principal

Fernie: Fernie Academy
P.O. Box 2677
451 - 2nd Ave., 2nd Fl., Fernie, BC V0B 1M0, Canada
Tel: 250-423-0212; Fax: 250-423-4799
office@theferneacademy.ca
www.thefernieacademy.ca
Grades: K-12; Enrollment: 97
J. Sombrowski, Principal
jsombrowski@fernieacademy.com

Fort Nelson: Chalo School
Mile 293, RR#1, Fort Nelson, BC V0C 1R0, Canada
Tel: 250-774-7651; Fax: 250-774-7655
chaloschool@gmail.com
www.chaloschool.bc.ca
Grades: Preschool - 12; Enrollment: 200; Note: Fort Nelson First Nation owns & operates Chalo School.
Colette Duperreault-Young, Principal
chaloschool@gmail.com

Fort St James: Nak'albun Elementary School
P.O. Box 1390
Fort St James, BC V0J 1P0, Canada
Tel: 250-996-8441; Fax: 250-996-2229
nkbprincipal@hotmail.ca
www.nakalbun.com
Grades: K - 7; Enrollment: 60; Note: The elementary school is operated under the jurisdiction of Nak'azdli Band.
Rick Aucoin, Principal
nkbprincipal@fsjames.com

Fort Ware: Aatse Davie School
P.O. Box 79
Fort Ware, BC V0J 3B0, Canada
Tel: 250-471-2002; Fax: 250-471-2080
aatse@pris.bc.ca
www.kwadacha.com
www.facebook.com/pages/Aatse-Davie-School/138180549552045
Grades: K.-12; Enrollment: 84; Note: The school serves the Kwadacha First Nation. In addition to the standard humanities & sciences curriculum, classes in the Tsek'ene language are taught. Governed by the Kwadacha Education Society.
Andreas Rohrbach, Principal

Kamloops: St. Ann's Academy
205 Columbia St., Kamloops, BC V2C 2S7
Tel: 250-372-5452; Fax: 250-372-5257
admin@st-anns.ca
st-anns.ca
Grades: K.-12; Enrollment: 480
S. Chisholm, Principal
principal@stannsacademy.bc.ca

Kelowna: Aberdeen Hall Preparatory School
950 Academy Way, Kelowna, BC V1V 3A4
Tel: 250-491-1270; Fax: 250-491-1289
info@aberdeenhall.com
www.aberdeenhall.com
www.facebook.com/AberdeenHallPS
twitter.com/aberdeenhallPS
Grades: Pre.-12; Enrollment: 320
Christopher H. Grieve, Head of School

Kelowna: Kelowna Waldorf School
429 Collett Rd., Kelowna, BC V1W 1K6
Tel: 250-764-4130; Fax: 250-764-4139
info@kelownawaldorf.org
www.kelownawaldorf.org
www.youtube.com/user/TheMarinWaldorf
Grades: K.-7
Cindy Taylor, Principal
cindy.taylor@kelownawaldorf.org

Kelowna: St. Joseph Elementary School
839 Sutherland Ave., Kelowna, BC V1Y 5X4
Tel: 250-763-3371; Fax: 250-763-2740
school@stjosephkelowna.ca
www.stjosephkelowna.ca
www.facebook.com/SaintJosephCatholicElementarySchool
Grades: K.-7; Enrollment: 316
R. Smith, Principal

Kelowna: Studio 9 Independent School of the Arts
1180 Houghton Rd., Kelowna, BC V1X 2C9, Canada
Tel: 250-868-8816; Fax: 250-868-8836
www.studio9.ca
www.facebook.com/pages/Studio-9/185017564940417?sk=info
twitter.com/Studio9Kelowna
Grades: K - 12
C. Belliveau, Principal

Kispiox: Kispiox Elementary-Junior Secondary School
1439 Mary Blackwater Dr., Kispiox, BC V0J 1Y4
Tel: 250-842-6148; Fax: 250-842-5799
rsteinbeisser@kispioxschool.ca
Grades: K.-7; Enrollment: 85

Kitimat: St. Anthony's School
1750 Nalabila Blvd., Kitimat, BC V8C 1E6
Tel: 250-632-6313; Fax: 250-632-6317
stanthonys@citywest.ca
www.stanthonysschoolkitimat.com
www.facebook.com/groups/151699398219872
Grades: K.-7; Enrollment: 150; Number of Employees: 13 teachers
Katja Groves, Principal

Ladysmith: Stu"ate Lelum Secondary School
P.O. Box 730
Ladysmith, BC V9G 1A5, Canada
Tel: 250-245-3522; Fax: 250-245-8263
www.facebook.com/140555322648015
Enrollment: 100
L. Merriman, Principal

Langley: Global Montessori School
19785 - 55A Ave., Langley, BC V3A 3X1
Tel: 604-534-1556; Fax: 604-532-4358
info@globalmontessorischool.com
globalmontessorischool.com
Grades: K - 8
Andrea Riegert, Head of School
andrear@globalmontessorischool.com
Karun Kumar, Director of Operations
karunk@globalmontessorischool.com

Langley: King's School
The King's Centre
P.O. Box 28
21783 - 76B Ave., Langley, BC V0X 1T0, Canada
Tel: 604-888-0969; Fax: 604-888-0977
school@tkc.com
www.thekingsschool.org
Grades: K-12; Enrollment: 141
P. Thomas, Principal

Langley: Langley Montessori School
21488 Old Yale Rd., Langley, BC V3A 4M8
Tel: 604-532-5667; Fax: 604-532-5634
info@langleymontessorischool.com
www.langleymontessorischool.com
Other Information: Early Learning Centre Phone: 604-533-5664
www.facebook.com/LangleyMontessoriSchool
Grades: Preschool-7
Ursula Hodgson, Principal
admin@langleymontessorischool.com

Langley: Whytecliff Agile Learning Centres
Langley School
20561 Logan Ave., Langley, BC V3A 7R3, Canada
Tel: 604-532-1268; Fax: 604-532-1269
whytecliflangley@focusbc.org
www.focusbc.org
www.facebook.com/focusfoundationBC
Grades: 8-11; Enrollment: 49; Note: Whytecliff Agile Learning Centres are provincially accredited, independent schools for boys and girls, aged 12-19, who face personal or behavioural challenges. Many of the students have dropped out of school, been excluded or expelled.
A. Butler, Principal
abutler@focusbc.org

Campuses
Whytecliff Agile Learning Centre - Burnaby
3450 Boundary Rd., Burnaby, BC V5M 4A5
Tel: 604-438-4451; Fax: 604-438-5572
whytecliffburnaby@focusbc.org
Grades: 8-11

Lantzville: Aspengrove School
7660 Clark Dr., Lantzville, BC V0R 2H0, Canada
Tel: 250-390-2201; *Fax:* 250-390-2281
cgrunlund@aspengroveschool.ca
aspengroveschool.ca
www.facebook.com/AspengroveSchool
www.twitter.com/aspengrovenews
www.youtube.com/AspengroveSchool
Grades: JK-12; *Enrollment:* 190; *Note:* Accredited International Baccalaureate programs for primary and middle years; core academic subjects, as well as performing arts, physical and outdoor education, community service.
Zinda Fitzgerald, Head of School

Lax Kw'Alaams: Coast Tsimshian Academy
11 Legaic St., Lax Kw'Alaams, BC V0V 1H0, Canada
Tel: 604-625-3207; *Fax:* 604-625-3425
ctahome@tsimshianacademy.com
www.tsimshianacademy.com
Grades: K-12; *Enrollment:* 152
S. Campbell, Principal

Lillooet: Fountainview Academy
P.O. Box 500
7615 Lytton-Lillooet Hwy., Lillooet, BC V0K 1V0, Canada
Tel: 250-256-5400; *Fax:* 250-256-5499
info@fountainview.ca
fountainviewacademy.ca
www.facebook.com/pages/Fountainview-Academy/23591277644
2
www.youtube.com/user/fountainviewacademy
Grades: 10-12; *Enrollment:* 87; *Number of Employees:* 9 administrators; 9 teachers; 10 student life; 3 industry; 4 maintenance; 2 cafeteria; 5 media dept.
Baird Corrigan, Principal
bcorrigan@fountainview.ca

Lytton: Stein Valley Nlakapamux School
P.O. Box 300
Lytton, BC V0K 1Z0, Canada
Tel: 250-455-2522; *Fax:* 250-455-2512
Grades: K-12; *Enrollment:* 109
C. Holmes, Principal

Mansons Landing: Linnaea School
P.O. Box 98
Mansons Landing, BC V0P 1K0, Canada
Tel: 250-935-6747; *Fax:* 250-935-6413
Grades: K.-8; *Enrollment:* 60

Maple Ridge: Meadowridge School
12224 - 240th St., Maple Ridge, BC V4R 1N1, Canada
Tel: 604-467-4444; *Fax:* 604-467-4989
www.meadowridge.bc.ca
www.facebook.com/meadowridge
twitter.com/Meadowridge
www.linkedin.com/pub/meadowridge-school/2a/6a7/316
Grades: JK - 12; *Enrollment:* 450
H. Burke, Principal
hburke@meadowridge.bc.ca

Mill Bay: Brentwood College School (BCS)
2735 Mount Baker Rd., Mill Bay, BC V0R 2P1, Canada
Tel: 250-743-5521; *Fax:* 250-743-2911
admissions@brentwood.bc.ca
www.brentwood.bc.ca
www.facebook.com/pages/Brentwood-College-School/34438070
228
twitter.com/BrentwoodNews/everything-brentwood-2
www.linkedin.com/groups?gid=2561828
Grades: 9 - 12; *Enrollment:* 480; *Number of Employees:* 200; *Note:* Brentwood College School is a co-educational university prep school.
Bud Patel, Head of School
David Burton, Director of Finance

Mission: Seminary of Christ the King
General Delivery, Mission, BC V2V 4J2
Tel: 604-820-9969; *Fax:* 604-826-8725
frpeterosb@gmail.com
www.sck.ca
Grades: 8 - 12

Nanaimo: Discover Montessori School
4355 Jingle Pot Rd., Nanaimo, BC V9T 5P4
Tel: 250-760-0615
office@dm-school.ca
www.dm-school.ca
Grades: K - 8
Diana Chalmers, Principal

Campuses
Parksville Campus
1223 Smithers Rd., Parksville, BC V9P 2C1
Tel: 250-760-0615
office@dm-school.ca
www.dm-school.ca

Nanaimo: The High School at Vancouver Island University
Also known as: Malaspina International High School
900 Fifth St., Nanaimo, BC V9R 5S5, Canada
Tel: 250-740-6317; *Fax:* 250-740-6470
highschool@viu.ca
www2.viu.ca/highschool
www.facebook.com/144549182292155
twitter.com/MHS_at_VIU
www.flickr.com/photos/vancouverislanduniversity/
Grades: 10-12; *Enrollment:* 121
T. Lewis, Principal

Nelson: Nelson Waldorf School
P.O. Box 165 Main
Nelson, BC V1L 5P9
Tel: 250-352-6919; *Fax:* 250-352-6887
info@nelsonwaldorf.org
www.nelsonwaldorf.org
www.facebook.com/pages/Nelson-Waldorf-School
Grades: Kindergarten - 8; *Note:* The school offers Waldorf education to children in the West Kootenay area.
Beverley Barcham, General Administrator & Principal
Lisa Bramson, Coordinator, Special Needs
Diana Finley, Coordinator, Social Inclusion
Andromeda Drake, Bookkeeper

Nelson: St. Joseph's School
523 Mill St., Nelson, BC V1L 4S2
Tel: 250-352-3041; *Fax:* 250-352-9188
office@stjosephnelson.ca
www.stjosephnelson.ca
Grades: K.-6; *Enrollment:* 122
Marlene Suter, Principal
MarleneSuter@stjosephnelson.ca

New Westminster: Purpose Independent Secondary School
Also known as: Purpose Young Adult Learning Centre
40 Begbie St., New Westminster, BC V3M 3L9, Canada
Tel: 604-526-2522; *Fax:* 604-526-6546
info@purposesociety.org
purposesecondary.org
Grades: 10 - 12; *Note:* The program at The Purpose School is designed for students, aged fifteen to nineteen, who are unable to succeed in the traditional school system. A Purpose Secondary School education leads to a Standard Dogwood Diploma.
Phill Esau, Principal
phill.esau@purposesociety.org
Jacquie Robertson, Student Services\Child Care Worker
jacquie.robertson@purposesociety.org

New Westminster: Urban Academy
101 Third St., New Westminster, BC V3L 2P9
Tel: 604-524-2211; *Fax:* 604-524-2711
admin@urbanacademy.ca
www.urbanacademy.ca
www.facebook.com/278963742167615
Grades: JK-12; *Enrollment:* 115
Michael Bouchard, B.A., M.A., Head of School

North Vancouver: Bodwell High School
955 Harbourside Dr., North Vancouver, BC V7P 3S4, Canada
Tel: 604-924-5056; *Fax:* 604-924-5058
onlineinquiry@bodwell.edu
www.bodwell.edu/highschool
www.facebook.com/bodwell.highschool
www.flickr.com/photos/bodwellcollege/collections
Grades: 8 - 12; *Enrollment:* 450; *Note:* Bodwell High School is a co-educational day & boarding school.
Mark Lewis, B.Ed., M.A., Principal
Cathy Lee, B.S.Sc., M.S.W., Director, Admissions
Stephen Goobie, BSc.(Hons.), B.Ed., M.Ed., Director, Residence

North Vancouver: Brockton School
3467 Duval Rd., North Vancouver, BC V7J 3E8
Tel: 604-929-9201; *Fax:* 604-929-9501
info@brocktonschool.com
www.brocktonschool.com
Grades: K.-11; *Enrollment:* 140
Alison Wall, B.A. (Hons.), M.Sc., Head of School

North Vancouver: L'École française internationale de Vancouver
French International School of Vancouver
3657 Fromme Rd., North Vancouver, BC V7K 2E6, Canada
Tél: 604-924-2457
www.efiv.org
Grades: Pre - 12; *Note:* Programme du Ministère de l'Éducation Nationale Français, enrichi par des cours d'histoire, de géographie et des cultures du Canada.
Gérard Martinez, Directeur

North Vancouver: North Star Montessori Elementary School
1325 East Keith Rd., North Vancouver, BC V7J 1J3
Tel: 604-980-1205; *Fax:* 604-980-1805
admin@northstarmontessori.ca
northstarmontessori.ca
Grades: Pre. - 8

North Vancouver: Vancouver Waldorf School (VWS)
2725 St. Christophers Rd. North, North Vancouver, BC V7K 2B6, Canada
Tel: 604-985-7435; *Fax:* 604-985-4948
reception@vws.ca
www.vws.ca
Other Information: board@vws.ca (E-mail, Board of Trustees)
www.facebook.com/vancouverwaldorfschool/
twitter.com/vws_waldorf
google.com/+VwsCa
Grades: Preschool - 12; *Note:* Vancouver Waldorf School integrates the movement arts & artistic activities throughout the curriculum.
Brian Gohlke, Business Manager
Jeffrey Onans, Pedagogical Manager
Feza Sanigok, Development Manager
Fiona Thatcher, Admissions Manager, 604-985-7435, ext. 200
admissions@vws.ca

Oliver: Sen Pok Chin School
1006 McKinney Rd., Oliver, BC V0H 1T8, Canada
Tel: 250-498-2019; *Fax:* 250-498-3096
office@senpokchin.com
www.senpokchin.com
Grades: JK-7; *Enrollment:* 85
R. Laurie, Principal
principal@senpokchin.com

Port Alberni: Haahuupayak School
6000 Santu Dr., Port Alberni, BC V9Y 7M2, Canada
Tel: 250-724-5542; *Fax:* 250-724-7335
ha-ak-sap@hotmail.com
www.haahuupayak.com
Grades: K-6; *Enrollment:* 79
Tricia McAuley, Principal

Port Coquitlam: Hope Lutheran Elementary
3151 York St., Port Coquitlam, BC V3B 4A7, Canada
Tel: 604-942-5322; *Fax:* 604-942-5311
info@hopelcs.ca
www.hopelcs.ca
www.facebook.com/hopelcs
twitter.com/hopelcs
Grades: K.-11; *Enrollment:* 190
Mike Schiemann, Principal

Port Hardy: Avalon Adventist Junior Academy
P.O. Box 974
Port Hardy, BC V0N 2P0, Canada
Tel: 250-949-8243; *Fax:* 250-949-6770
avalonacad@hotmail.com
www.aaja.ca
Grades: K - 10
Clifford Wood, Principal
wagonwoody2003@yahoo.ca

Prince George: Sacred Heart School
785 Patricia Blvd., Prince George, BC V2L 3V5
Tel: 250-563-5201; *Fax:* 250-563-5201
shspg@netbistro.com
www.shspg.com
www.facebook.com/127658757272916
Grades: K.-7; *Enrollment:* 104; *Number of Employees:* 9
Rebecca Gilbert, Principal
principal@shspg.com

Prince George: St. Mary's School
1088 Gillett St., Prince George, BC V2M 2V3
Tel: 250-563-7502; *Fax:* 250-563-7818
coachbrent@stmaryspg.org
www.stmaryspg.org
Grades: K.-7; *Enrollment:* 199
Brent Arsenault, Principal
coachbrent@stmaryspg.org

***Prince George:* Westside Academy**
3791 Hwy. 16 West, Prince George, BC V2N 5P8
Tel: 250-964-9600
office@westsideacademy.ca
www.westsideacademy.ca
Grades: K - 12; *Note:* Westside Academy is a ministry of Westside Family Fellowship.
Donna Rosenbaum, High School Principal
drosenbaum@westsideacademy.ca
Sherry Breck, Elementary Principal
sbreck@westsideacademy.ca

***Prince Rupert:* Annunciation School**
627 - 5 Ave. West, Prince Rupert, BC V8J 1V1
Tel: 250-624-5873; *Fax:* 250-627-4486
www.annunciationpr.ca
Grades: K.-7
Laura Lowther, Principal

***Quesnel:* St. Ann's School**
150 Sutherland Ave., Quesnel, BC V2J 2J5
Tel: 250-992-6237; *Fax:* 250-992-6234
office.stanns@shawcable.com
www.stannsschool.ca
Grades: K.-7; *Enrollment:* 71
R. Nieman, Principal
principal.stanns@shawcable.com

***Richmond:* BC Muslim School**
12300 Blundell Rd., Richmond, BC V6W 1B3, Canada
Tel: 604-270-2511; *Fax:* 604-270-2679
admin@bcmuslimschool.ca
www.bcmuslimschool.ca
Grades: K - 7; *Note:* BC Muslim School offers an accredited Arabic program.
Farida Wahab, Principal

***Richmond:* Choice School**
Main Campus
20451 Westminster Hwy. North, Richmond, BC V6V 1B3, Canada
Tel: 604-273-2418; *Fax:* 604-273-2419
info@choiceschool.org
www.choiceschool.org
www.facebook.com/pages/Choice-School/157302764416275
twitter.com/RayProbyn
Grades: Pre-K. - 8; *Note:* Choice School offers gifted education to talented & gifted children.
Ray Probyn, Principal

***Richmond:* Richmond Jewish Day School (RJDS)**
8760 No. 5 Rd., Richmond, BC V6Y 2V4, Canada
Tel: 604-275-3393; *Fax:* 604-275-9322
info@rjds.ca
www.rjds.ca
www.facebook.com/pages/Richmond-Jewish-Day-School/12185 4451208916
twitter.com/myrjds
Grades: Preschool - 7; *Note:* Richmond Jewish Day School incorporates Hebrew & Judaic studies with the British Columbia curriculum.
Abba Brodt, Principal
abrodt@rjds.ca
Mary Jane Brown, Business Manager
mjbrown@rjds.ca

***Roberts Creek:* Sun Haven Waldorf School**
1341 Margaret Rd., Roberts Creek, BC V0N 2W2
Tel: 604-741-0949
office@sunhavenschool.ca
www.sunhaven.ca
www.facebook.com/sunhavenwaldorfschool
Grades: Pre. - 8
Catherine Solomon, School Administrator

***Shawnigan Lake:* Dwight International School**
2371 Shawnigan Lake Rd., Shawnigan Lake, BC V0R 2W5
Tel: 250-929-0506
admissions@dwightcanada.org
dwightinternational.com
www.facebook.com/dwightcanada
twitter.com/dwightcanada
www.linkedin.com/company/dwight-school-canada
Grades: 6-12
Jerry Salvador, Head of School
Christine Bater, Contact, Admissions Office

***Shawnigan Lake:* Shawnigan Lake School**
1975 Renfrew Rd., Shawnigan Lake, BC V0R 2W0, Canada
Tel: 250-743-5516; *Fax:* 250-743-6200
info@sls.bc.ca
www.shawnigan.ca
www.facebook.com/shawnigan
www.twitter.com/shawnigan
www.linkedin.com/groups?gid=830377&trk=myg_ugrp_ovr
www.youtube.com/user/shawnigantube
Grades: 8-12; *Enrollment:* 454
Sara Blair, Headmaster
sblair@shawnigan.ca

***Smithers:* Ebenezer Canadian Reformed School**
P.O. Box 3700
1685 Viewmount Rd. North, Smithers, BC V0J 2N0, Canada
Tel: 250-847-3492; *Fax:* 250-847-3912
office@ebenezerschool.com
www.ebenezerschool.com
Grades: K-12; *Enrollment:* 133
D. Stoffels, Principal

***Smithers:* Moricetown Elementary School**
#2 - 205 Beaver Rd., Smithers, BC V0J 2N1
Tel: 250-847-3166; *Fax:* 250-877-5092
school@moricetown.ca
www.moricetown.ca
Grades: Elementary; *Enrollment:* 49

***Smithers:* St. Joseph's School**
P.O. Box 454
4054 Broadway Ave., Smithers, BC V0J 2N0
Tel: 250-847-9414; *Fax:* 250-847-9402
stjosephs@telus.net
Grades: K.-7; *Enrollment:* 191
S. Forbrigger, Principal

***South Hazelton:* Gitsegukla Elementary School**
21 Seymour Ave., RR#1, South Hazelton, BC V0J 2R0, Canada
Tel: 250-849-5739; *Fax:* 250-849-5276
www.gitsegukla.org
Grades: K-7; *Enrollment:* 60
Tuskasa Sakata, Principal

***Squamish:* Cedar Valley Waldorf School**
P.O. Box 5356
38265 Westway Ave., Squamish, BC V8B 0C2
Tel: 604-898-3287
info@cedarvalleyschool.com
www.cedarvalleyschool.com
facebook.com/pages/Cedar-Valley-Waldorf-School/14217126246 5059
Grades: Elem.

***Surrey:* Cornerstone Montessori School**
14724 - 84 Ave., Surrey, BC V3S 2M5, Canada
Tel: 604-599-9918; *Fax:* 604-597-0468
corstone@telus.net
cornerstone-montessori.ca
Grades: K-7; *Enrollment:* 121
Rita Gausman, Principal

***Surrey:* Dogwood School**
10752 - 157 St., Surrey, BC V4N 1K6
Tel: 604-581-8111; *Fax:* 604-581-8219
dogwood@SurreySchools.ca
www.surreyschools.ca
www.twitter.com/@Dogwood159
Grades: 3 - 12
Lys Paredes, Principal
Paredes_l@surreyschools.ca

***Surrey:* Iqra School**
14590 - 116A Ave., Surrey, BC V3R 2V1
Tel: 604-583-7530; *Fax:* 604-583-7510
info@iqraschool.com
www.iqraschool.com
Grades: K.-8; *Enrollment:* 340
Faisal Ali, Principal

***Surrey:* Khalsa School (Surrey)**
6933 - 124th St., Surrey, BC V3W 3W6, Canada
Tel: 604-591-2248; *Fax:* 604-591-3396
kssinfo@khalsaschool.ca
www.khalsaschoolcanada.com
Grades: K.-10; *Enrollment:* 1468
J. Bhatia, Principal
jsbhatia@khalsaschool.ca

***Surrey:* Relevant Schools' Society**
Relevant High School
18620 Hwy. #10, Surrey, BC V3S 1G1, Canada
Tel: 604-574-4736; *Fax:* 604-574-9831
relevantschool@shawlink.ca
www.relevanthighschool.ca
Number of Schools: 2; *Grades:* 8 - 12; *Note:* Relevant High School is coeducational, non-denominational secondary school.

Schools

Diamond Elementary
18620, Hwy. 10, Surrey, BC V3S 1G1, Canada
Tel: 604-576-1146; *Fax:* 604-574-9831
diamondschool@shawlink.ca
www.relevanthighschool.ca
Grades: K-7; *Enrollment:* 159
Douglas Smith, Principal

***Surrey:* Roots & Wings Montessori Place**
15250 - 54A Ave., Surrey, BC V3S 5J9, Canada
Tel: 604-574-5399; *Fax:* 604-574-5319
info@rootsandwingsbc.com
www.rootsandwingsbc.com
www.facebook.com/127080180684668
twitter.com/RWMontessori
www.youtube.com/user/rootsandwingsbc
Number of Schools: 4; *Grades:* Pres - 9; *Note:* Primary Montessori programs are offered for children between the ages of 2.5 & 5. The senior program at the school is designed for students from age 9 to 12.
Daryl Marples, Chair
dmarples1@yahoo.com
Kristin Cassie, Principal
Veronique Bodart, Vice Principal

***Surrey:* Southridge School**
2656 - 160 St., Surrey, BC V3S 0B7, Canada
Tel: 604-535-5056; *Fax:* 604-535-3676
www.southridge.bc.ca
www.facebook.com/336018147405
twitter.com/SouthridgeNews
Grades: 8-12; *Enrollment:* 680; *Number of Employees:* 103
M. Ayotte, Head of Senior School
mayotte@southridge.bc.ca

***Surrey:* Surrey Muslim School**
#119, 7475 - 135 St., Surrey, BC V3W 0M8
Tel: 604-599-6608; *Fax:* 604-599-6790
administration@surreymuslimschool.ca
www.surreymuslimschool.ca
Grades: K - 7
Ebrahim Bawa, Acting Principal
vp.surreymuslimschool@gmail.com

***Tsawwassen:* Southpointe Academy**
1900 - 56 St., Tsawwassen, BC V4L 2B1, Canada
Tel: 604-948-8826; *Fax:* 604-948-8853
info@spacademy.ca
www.southpointeacademy.ca
www.facebook.com/SouthpointeAcademy
Grades: K-12; *Enrollment:* 425
Bruce Griffioen, Headmaster
bruce.griffioen@spacademy.ca

***Vancouver:* Canadian College**
#200, 1050 Alberni St., Vancouver, BC V6E 1A3, Canada
Tel: 604-688-9366
www.canadiancollege.com
Enrollment: 300
Jim Clark, Chair & Owner
jim.clark@canadiancollege.com
Jay Ariken, Director, Academic & COO
Lane Clark, CEO

***Vancouver:* Century High School (CHS)**
#200, 1788 West Broadway, Vancouver, BC V6J 1Y1, Canada
Tel: 604-730-8138; *Fax:* 604-731-9542
admission@centuryhighschool.ca
www.centuryhighschool.ca
www.facebook.com/pages/Century-High-School/1133006622135 29
Grades: 8 - 12

***Vancouver:* Columbia College**
438 Terminal Ave., Vancouver, BC V6A 0C1, Canada
Tel: 604-683-8360; *Fax:* 604-682-7191
admin@columbiacollege.ca
www.columbiacollege.ca
www.facebook.com/cc.vancouver.bc
twitter.com/ccvancouver
www.youtube.com/user/ColumbiaCollegeTV
Enrollment: 57; *Note:* A liberal arts college offering 1st & 2nd year university transfer courses, associate degrees, university

preparation programmes, adult secondary school completion, & English language instruction geared to international students.
Dr. Trevor Toone, Principal

Vancouver: Core Education & Fine Arts (CEFA)
2946 Commercial Dr., Vancouver, BC V5N 4C9
Tel: 604-879-2332; *Fax:* 604-879-2330
vancouver@cefa.ca
www.cefa.ca
www.facebook.com/167143796669678
twitter.com/cefakids
cefakids.wordpress.com
Grades: Pre.-K.
Natacha V. Beim, Founder

Campuses
Abbotsford Campus
1785 Clearbrook Rd., Abbotsford, BC V2T 5X5
Tel: 604-853-2332; *Fax:* 604-608-3585
abbotsford@cefa.ca
cefaabbotsford.wordpress.com

Burnaby - Canada Way Campus
4970 Canada Way, Burnaby, BC V5G 1M4
Tel: 604-299-2373; *Fax:* 604-299-2378
canadaway@cefa.ca

Burnaby - Kingsway Campus
4021 Kingsway, Burnaby, BC V5H 1Y9
Tel: 604-568-8808
kingsway@cefa.ca

Calgary - Chinook Campus
5728 - 1 St. SW, Calgary, AB T2H 0E2
Tel: 403-319-2332
calgary-chinook@cefa.ca

Coquitlam Campus
3380 David Ave., Coquitlam, BC V3E 3G8
Tel: 604-315-6020
coquitlam@cefa.ca

Langley Campus
#100, 19950 - 88th Ave. East, Langley, BC V1M 0A5
Tel: 604-881-2332; *Fax:* 604-881-2338
langley@cefa.ca

New Westminster Campus
725 Carnarvon St., New Westminster, BC V3M 1E6
Tel: 604-777-0053
newwestminster@cefa.ca

North Vancouver Campus
#402, 935 Marine Dr., North Vancouver, BC V7P 1S3
Tel: 604-929-2332; *Fax:* 604-929-2303
newwestminster@cefa.ca

Richmond Campus
#160, 10811 No. 4 Rd., Richmond, BC V7A 2Z5
Tel: 604-275-2332; *Fax:* 604-288-5065

West Vancouver Campus
2008 Park Royal South, West Vancouver, BC V7T 2W4
Tel: 604-913-7713; *Fax:* 604-913-7714

White Rock Campus
15300 Croydon Dr., South Surrey, BC V3S 0Z5
Tel: 778-294-2646; *Fax:* 604-608-2585
cefawhiterock.wordpress.com

Vancouver: Crofton House School
3200 - 41 Ave. West, Vancouver, BC V6N 3E1, Canada
Tel: 604-263-3255; *Fax:* 604-263-4941
www.croftonhouse.ca
Grades: Elem./Sec.; girls; *Enrollment:* 667
Patricia J. Dawson, Head of School
pdawson@croftonhouse.ca
Susan Mueller, Director of Business Administration
Bill McCracken, Director of Admissions
Patricia Vasseur, Director of Advancement
Ryan Melsom, Director of Communications & Marketing

Vancouver: Fraser Academy
2294 - 10 Ave. West, Vancouver, BC V6K 2H8, Canada
Tel: 604-736-5575; *Fax:* 604-736-5578
info@fraseracademy.ca
www.fraseracademy.ca
www.facebook.com/fraseracademy
www.twitter.com/fraseracademy
www.youtube.com/fraseracademyschool
Grades: 1-12; *Enrollment:* 188
Maureen Steltman, Head of School
msteltman@fraseracademy.ca
Frans Ang, Business Manager
fang@fraseracademy.ca

Vancouver: Khalsa School (Vancouver)
5987 Prince Albert St., Vancouver, BC V5W 3E2, Canada
Tel: 604-321-1226; *Fax:* 604-321-2709
Toll-Free: 866-933-2248
Grades: K.-7; *Enrollment:* 207
Amar Dhaliwal, Principal

Vancouver: King David High School
5718 Willow St., Vancouver, BC V5Z 4S9, Canada
Tel: 604-263-9700; *Fax:* 604-263-4848
kdhs.org
www.facebook.com/kdhsvancouver
twitter.com/KDHSVancouver
Grades: 8-12; *Enrollment:* 140; *Note:* King David High School (KDHS) is a pluralistic, community, co-educational, Jewish high school in the Oakridge district of Vancouver.
Russ Klein, Head of School
rklein@kdhs.org

Toronto: Language Studies Canada Toronto (LSC)
#400, 124 Eglinton Ave. West, Toronto, ON M4R 2G8, Canada
Tel: 416-488-2200; *Fax:* 416-488-2225
toronto@lsc-canada.com
www.lsc-canada.com
www.facebook.com/ec.english.language.centres
twitter.com/ecenglish
www.youtube.com/user/ecwebteam
David S. Diplock, Director

Vancouver: LSC Vancouver
#200, 570 Dusmuir St., Vancouver, BC V6B 1Y1, Canada
Tel: 604-683-1199; *Fax:* 604-683-6088
vancouver@lsc-canada.com

LSC Montréal
#401, 1610 St. Catherine West., Montréal, QC H3H 2S2, Canada
Tel: 514-939-9911; *Fax:* 514-939-2223
montreal@lsc-canada.com

Vancouver: Madrona School Society
2050 West 10th Ave., Vancouver, BC V6J 2B3
Tel: 604-732-9965
www.madronaschool.com
Grades: 1-9; *Enrollment:* 25
Eric D'Donnell, Director, 778-991-5545
eric@madronaschool.com
Judy O'Donnell, Principal
judy@madronaschool.com

Vancouver: Pacific Spirit School (PSS)
12620 Westminster Hwy., Vancouver, BC V6V 1A1, Canada
Tel: 604-222-1900; *Fax:* 604-222-1934
info@pacificspiritschool.org
www.pacificspiritschool.org
www.facebook.com/Pacificspiritschool
Grades: K-7; *Enrollment:* 227; *Note:* Pacific Spirit School is the flagship for the New Learning Society, which promotes and supports the growth of the whole child.
Ingrid Price, Ph.D., Executive Director
Ann-Marie Gasher, B.GS., Business Manager

Vancouver: Pacific Torah Institute
5750 Oak St., 4th Fl., Vancouver, BC V6M 2V9
Tel: 604-261-1502
office@ptibc.org
www.ptibc.org
Grades: 8 - 12

Vancouver: Pattison High School
981 Nelson St., Vancouver, BC V6Z 3B6
Tel: 604-608-8788; *Fax:* 604-608-8789
info@pattisonhighschool.ca
www.pattisonhighschool.ca
www.facebook.com/pattison.high
twitter.com/pattisonhigh
www.youtube.com/user/pattisonhigh
www.youtube.com/user/pattisonhigh
Grades: 8-12; *Enrollment:* 170
Daniel Chowne, Principal
principal@pattisonhighschool.ca

Vancouver: Royal Canadian College
8610 Ash St., Vancouver, BC V6P 3M2, Canada
Tel: 604-738-2221; *Fax:* 604-738-2282
info@royalcanadiancollege.com
www.royalcanadiancollege.com
Grades: 8-12; *Enrollment:* 52
Leon King, President

Vancouver: St. George's School
4175 - 29 Ave. West, Vancouver, BC V6S 1V1, Canada
Tel: 604-224-1304; *Fax:* 604-224-7066
info@stgeorges.bc.ca
www.stgeorges.bc.ca
facebook.com/pages/St-Georges-School-Vancouver/154294807937533
www.twitter.com/saintsbc
www.youtube.com/saintscommunications
Grades: 1-12; *Enrollment:* 1150; *Note:* Day and boarding school for boys
Dr. Tom Matthews, Headmaster
tmatthews@stgeorges.bc.ca
Greg Devenish, Principal - Junior School, 604-222-5892
gdevenish@stgeorges.bc.ca
Shawn Lawrence, Principal - Senior School, 604-221-3618
slawrence@stgeorges.bc.ca
Barry Mitchell, Director of Finance, 604-221-3886
bmitchell@stgeorges.bc.ca

Vancouver: St. John's International
1885 West Broadway, Vancouver, BC V6J 1Y5, Canada
Tel: 604-683-4572; *Fax:* 604-683-4679
info@stjohnsis.com
www.stjohnsis.com
Grades: 8-12; *Enrollment:* 76

Vancouver: St. John's School
2215 - 10 Ave. West, Vancouver, BC V6K 2J1, Canada
Tel: 604-732-4434; *Fax:* 604-732-1074
admissions@stjohns.bc.ca
www.stjohns.bc.ca
www.facebook.com/StJohnsSchoolVancouver
twitter.com/stjohnssociety
Grades: JK - 12; *Enrollment:* 342; *Note:* University prep school
Stephen L.M. Hutchison, Head of School
shutchison@stjohns.bc.ca

Vancouver: Stratford Hall
3000 Commercial Dr., Vancouver, BC V5N 4E2, Canada
Tel: 604-436-0608; *Fax:* 604-436-0616
info@stratfordhall.ca
www.stratfordhall.ca
twitter.com/Stratford_Hall
Grades: K-12; *Enrollment:* 370
J. McConnell, Principal

Vancouver: Torah High School - Vancouver
Schara Tzedeck Synagogue
3476 Oak St., Vancouver, BC V6H 2L8
Tel: 604-736-7607; *Fax:* 604-730-1621
info@vncsy.com
vancouver.torahhigh.ca
Grades: 8-12; *Note:* Torah High offers courses in Religious Studies, Hebrew Language, Philosophy, Political Science, Nutrition, Arts & Interdisciplinary Studies for students attending public or private secondary schools. Classes take place on Monday nights in King David High School.
Rabbi Stephen Berger, Director, Education
rabbiberger@vncsy.com

Vancouver: Vancouver Hebrew Academy (VHA)
1545 West 62nd Ave., Vancouver, BC V6P 2E8, Canada
Tel: 604-266-1245; *Fax:* 604-264-0648
vha@vhebrewacademy.com
www.vhebrewacademy.com
Grades: Preschool - 10; *Note:* Vancouver Hebrew Academy is an Orthodox Jewish school which offers Judaic & general studies.
Rabbi Don Pacht, Head of School
dpacht@vhebrewacademy.com
Alaina Smith, Principal, General Studies
asmith@vhebrewacademy.com
Rabbi Eleazar Durden, Principal, Judaic Studies
ejdurden@vhebrewacademy.com
Nancy Scambler, Administrative Secretary

Vancouver: Vancouver Montessori School
8650 Barnard St., Vancouver, BC V6P 5G5, Canada
Tel: 604-261-0315
www.vancouvermontessorischool.com
Grades: Preschool - Elementary; *Note:* Preschool (Casa) programs are available for three to six year old children. Elementary classes are offered for children from age six to twelve.
Prasannata Runkel, Principal
Roni (Bamendine) Jones, Administrator, School Operations
Chrystle Williams, Registrar & Administration Assistant

Vancouver: Vancouver Talmud Torah School (VTT)
998 West 26th Ave., Vancouver, BC V5Z 2G1, Canada
Tel: 604-736-7307; Fax: 604-736-9754
info@talmudtorah.com
www.talmudtorah.com
Grades: Preschool - 7; Enrollment: 500; Note: Vancouver Talmud Torah School is a Jewish day school.
Cathy Lowenstein, Head of School
Leigh Ariel, Principal of Primary Grades
Rabbi Matthew Bellas, Principal of Judaic Studies/School Rabbi
Candice Gartry, Chief Financial Officer
Gaby Lutrin, Director, Preschool
Jessica Neville, Senior Principal, Intermediate Grades & Student Services
Jennifer Shecter-Balin, Director, Admissions & Communications

Vancouver: West Point Grey Academy (WPGA)
4125 West 8th Ave., Vancouver, BC V6R 4P9, Canada
Tel: 604-222-8750; Fax: 604-222-8756
info@wpga.ca
www.wpga.ca
Other Information: 604-224-1332 (Phone, Senior School)
www.facebook.com/pages/West-Point-Grey-Academy/170329919655197
twitter.com/wpgadotca
www.linkedin.com/company/2390550?trk=tyah
www.youtube.com/
Grades: Pre. - 12; Enrollment: 905; Note: West Point Grey Academy demonstrates a belief in Humanism in its community of Renaissance learners. The pre-kindergarten class is for four year old children.
Robert Standerwick, Chair
boardchair@wpga.ca
Clive S.K. Austin, Headmaster
headmaster@wpga.ca
Stephen Anthony, Head, Senior School
headmaster@wpga.ca

Vancouver: Westside Montessori Academy
3075 Slocan St., Vancouver, BC V5M 3E4
Tel: 604-434-9611
info@westsidemontessoriacademy.ca
www.westsidemontessoriacademy.ca
Grades: Pre.-4; Enrollment: 85
Sarah Gatiss, Principal, Preschool/Director, Administration
Andrea Nardi, Principal, Elementary

Vancouver: The Westside School
788 Beatty St., Vancouver, BC V6B 2M1
Tel: 604-687-8021; Fax: 604-687-8024
www.thewestsideschools.ca
Grades: K - 12
Graham Baldwin, President & Chief Executive Officer

Vancouver: York House School
4176 Alexandra St., Vancouver, BC V6J 2V6, Canada
Tel: 604-736-6551
webmaster@yorkhouse.ca
www.yorkhouse.ca
www.facebook.com/yorkhouseschool
twitter.com/yorkhouseschool
www.youtube.com/yorkhousedotca
Grades: K-12; Enrollment: 598
Shelley Lammie, Principal
slammie@yorkhouse.ca

Vanderhoof: St. Joseph's School
P.O. Box 1429
Vanderhoof, BC V0J 3A0
Tel: 250-567-2794; Fax: 250-567-2333
Grades: K.-7; Enrollment: 92
G. Gillis, Principal

Vernon: St. James School
2700 - 28 Ave., Vernon, BC V1T 1V7
Tel: 250-542-4081; Fax: 250-542-5696
principalsjs@shaw.ca
www.stjamesvernon.com
Grades: K.-7; Enrollment: 106
Gordon Higginson, Principal

Victoria: Artemis Place Secondary
#103, 2610 Douglas St., Victoria, BC V8T 4M1
artemisplace.org/PlaceForGirls/secondary-school
Grades: 9 - 12

Victoria: Christ Church Cathedral School (CCCS)
Cathedral Memorial Hall
912 Vancouver St., Victoria, BC V8V 3V7, Canada
Tel: 250-383-5125
cathedralschool@cathedralschool.ca (office)
cathedralschool.ca
www.facebook.com/293192810724819
vimeo.com/cccathedralschool
Grades: Kindergarten - 8; Enrollment: 155; Note: Christ Church Cathedral School is an Anglican school attached to a cathedral.
Bruce McKinnon, President
Stuart Hall, Head of School
head@cathedralschool.ca
Marylee McKeown, Assistant Head, Middle & Intermediate Grades & Teacher

Victoria: Discovery School
4052 Wilkinson Rd., Victoria, BC V8Z 5A5
Tel: 250-595-7765; Fax: 250-595-7712
principal@discoveryschool.ca
www.discoveryschool.ca
Grades: 1 - 12

Victoria: Glenlyon Norfolk School (GNS)
801 Bank St., Victoria, BC V8S 4A8, Canada
Tel: 250-370-6800; Fax: 250-370-6840
gns@mygns.ca
www.mygns.ca
www.facebook.com/mygns
twitter.com/glenlyonnorfolk
www.youtube.com/user/glenlyonnorfolk/feed?filter=2
Grades: K-12; Enrollment: 643
Simon Bruce-Lockhart, Head of School

Victoria: Maria Montessori Academy
1841 Fairburn Dr., Victoria, BC V8N 1P8, Canada
Tel: 250-479-4746; Fax: 250-744-1925
mma@montessori.bc.ca
www.montessori.bc.ca
Grades: K.-7; Enrollment: 95
B. McDermitt, Principal

Victoria: Oak and Orca Bioregional School
2738 Higgins St., Victoria, BC V8T 3N1
Tel: 250-383-6609; Fax: 877-544-3427
yj383@victoria.tc.ca
oakandorca.ca
Grades: Pre. - 10

Victoria: St. Margaret's School (SMS)
1080 Lucas Ave., Victoria, BC V8X 3P7, Canada
Tel: 250-479-7171; Fax: 250-479-8976
info@stmarg.ca
www.stmarg.ca
www.facebook.com/saintmargarets
twitter.com/st_margarets/
www.flickr.com/photos/st_margarets
Grades: K-12; Enrollment: 379; Note: An independent, all-girls school
Cathy Thornicroft, Head of School, 250-479-7171
mcameron@stmarg.ca
Megan Hedderick, Principal, Foundation and Middle Years, 250-479-7171, ext. 2228
mhedderick@stmarg.ca
Robert Ducharme, Principal, Senior Years / Director of Instruction, 250-479-7171, ext. 2126
Elaine Bell, Director of Finance and Corporate Relations, 250-479-7171, ext. 2537

Victoria: St. Michael's University School
3400 Richmond Rd., Victoria, BC V8P 4P5, Canada
Tel: 250-592-2411; Fax: 250-592-2812
info@smus.ca
www.smus.ca
www.facebook.com/yoursmus
twitter.com/gosmus
Number of Schools: 3; Grades: 9-12; Enrollment: 923
Bob Snowden, Head of School
bob.snowden@smus.ca

Victoria: Selkirk Montessori School
2970 Jutland Rd., Victoria, BC V8T 5K2, Canada
Tel: 250-384-3414; Fax: 250-384-3449
office@selkirkmontessori.ca
www.selkirkmontessori.ca
www.facebook.com/159664350728103
Grades: K - 8; Enrollment: 202
G. Henry, Interim Academic Head

Victoria: West-Mont Montessori School
4075 Metchosin Rd., Victoria, BC V9C 4A4, Canada
Tel: 250-474-2626; Fax: 250-478-8944
info@west-mont.ca
www.west-mont.ca
www.facebook.com/westmontschool
twitter.com/west_mont
www.pinterest.com/westmontschool/
Grades: Preschool - 8; Note: West-Mont School provides a Montessori preschool to grade three. For students in grades four to seven, an enriched British Columbia curriculum is offered. The school is operated by the Western Communities Montessori Society.
Magnus Hanton, Principal
principal@west-mont.ca
Jason Bowers, Assistant Principal
jasonb@west-mont.ca
Barbara Kennelly, Manager, Business
bkennelly@west-mont.ca
Barb Lewis, Head, Admissions
barbl@west-mont.ca

Waglisla: Bella Bella Community School (BBCS)
General Delivery, Waglisla, BC V0T 1Z0, Canada
Tel: 250-957-2391; Fax: 250-957-2691
Brendah@bellabella.net
www.bellabella.ca
www.facebook.com/bbcsbellabellacommunityschool
Grades: K - 12
Jan Gladish, Principal
Jason Cobey, Vice Principal
Frances Brown, Head, Heiltsuk Language Program

West Vancouver: The Anna Wyman School of Dance Arts
1457 Marine Dr., West Vancouver, BC V7T 1B8
Tel: 604-926-6535; Fax: 604-926-6912
info@annawyman.com
www.annawyman.com
Enrollment: 300; Number of Employees: 12 faculty members; Note: The school of dance features two large studios.
Anna Wyman, Founder & Artistic Director
Neil Wortley, Founder, Co-Director, & Stage Manager

West Vancouver: Collingwood School
Morven Campus
70 Morven Dr., West Vancouver, BC V7S 1B2, Canada
Tel: 604-925-3331; Fax: 604-925-3862
jonna.mcguinness@collingwood.org
www.collingwood.org
www.facebook.com/pages/Collingwood-School/153302904721667?sk=wall
twitter.com/#!/collingwoodcavs
www.linkedin.com/groups?home=&gid=3706309&trk=anet_ug_hm
Grades: K-12; Enrollment: 1200
Rodger Wright, Headmaster, 604-925-3331, ext. 2295
rodger.wright@collingwood.org

West Vancouver: Mulgrave School
2330 Cypress Lane, West Vancouver, BC V7S 3H9, Canada
Tel: 604-922-3223; Fax: 604-922-3328
admissions@mulgrave.com
www.mulgrave.com
www.facebook.com/90857640164
twitter.com/MulgraveSchool
Grades: K - 12; Note: The coeducational, non-denominational school is an IB World School.
Harry Wierenga, Chair
John Wray, Head of School
jwray@mulgrave.com
Gordon MacIntyre, Deputy Head of School
gmacintyre@mulgrave.com
Martin Jones, Principal, Middle School
mjones@mulgrave.com
Karyn Mitchell, Principal, Junior School
kmitchell@mulgrave.com
Lesley Tetiker, Principal, Early Learnng Centre
ltetiker@mulgrave.com
Isobel Willard, Principal, Senior School
iwillard@mulgrave.com
Linda Ash, Director, Admissions
lash@mulgrave.com
Christine Bridge, Director, Communications & Marketing
cbridge@mulgrave.com
Kelly Chow, Director, Business, Finance & Operations
kchow@mulgrave.com
Nicola Ferguson, Director, Summer Programme
nferguson@mulgrave.com
Graham Gilley, Director, Risk & Safety / First Aid Attendant
ggilley@mulgrave.com

Luke Lawson, Director, University Counseling
llawson@mulgrave.com
Claire Lynch, Director, Advancement
clynch@mulgrave.com
Brad Ovenell-Carter, Director, Educational Technology
Bovenell-carter@mulgrave.com
Mark Steffens, Director, Community Development
msteffens@mulgrave.com

Westbank: Our Lady of Lourdes Elementary School
2547 Hebert Rd., Westbank, BC V4T 2J6, Canada
Tel: 250-768-9008; *Fax:* 250-768-0168
adminolol@telus.net
www.olol-bc.com/olol-bc/
Grades: K-7; *Enrollment:* 132
Diane Letendre, Principal

Westbank: Sensisyusten House of Learning
1920 Quail Lane, Westbank, BC V4T 2H3
Tel: 250-768-2802; *Fax:* 250-768-5462
school@wfn.ca
Grades: K.-6; *Enrollment:* 36
R. Howardson, Principal

Whistler: Whistler Secondary Community School
8000 Alpine Way, Whistler, BC V0N 1B8
Tel: 604-905-2581; *Fax:* 604-905-2583
www.whistlersecondary.bc.ca
Grades: Secondary
Bev Oakley, Principal
boakley@sd48.bc.ca

Whistler: Whistler Waldorf School
P.O. Box 1501
7324 Kirkpatrick Way, Whistler, BC V0N 1B0
Tel: 604-932-1885
info@whistlerwaldorf.com
www.whistlerwaldorf.com
www.facebook.com/WhistlerWaldorf
Grades: Pre. K - 8
Aegir Morgan, Principal

Winlaw: The Whole School
P.O. Box 240
5614 Highway #6, Winlaw, BC V0G 2J0
Tel: 250-226-7737
wholeschool@gmail.com
www.wholeschool.ca
Grades: K - 7

Universities & Colleges

Independent & Private Schools

Vancouver: Fairleigh Dickinson University - Vancouver (FDU)
842 Cambie St., Vancouver, BC V6B 2P6
Tel: 604-682-8112; *Fax:* 604-682-8132
Toll-Free: 877-338-8002
vancouver@fdu.edu
view.fdu.edu
www.facebook.com/fairleighdickinsonuniversity
twitter.com/FDUWhatsNew
instagram.com/fduwhatsnew
Note: Fairleigh Dickinson University is an independent university founded in 1942. FDU has campuses in Teaneck, New Jersey, Madison, New Jersey, Wroxton, England, and downtown Vancouver, Canada.
Cecil A. Abrahams, PhD, Campus Provost

Universities

Abbotsford: Summit Pacific College
P.O. Box 1700
35235 Straiton Rd., Abbotsford, BC V2S 7E7, Canada
Tel: 604-853-7491; *Fax:* 604-853-8951
Toll-Free: 1-800-976-8388
pr@summitpacific.ca
www.summitpacific.ca
www.facebook.com/summitpc
www.twitter.com/summitpc
www.youtube.com/user/SPCcollege
Note: Formerly Western Pentecostal Bible College; Canada Post does not deliver to this address

Abbotsford: University of the Fraser Valley
33844 King Rd., Abbotsford, BC V2S 7M8, Canada
Tel: 604-504-7441; *Fax:* 604-855-7614
Toll-Free: 888-504-7441
info@ufv.ca
www.ucfv.ca
www.facebook.com/goUFV
www.twitter.com/goUFV
www.linkedin.com/company/university-of-the-fraser-valley_2
www.youtube.com/user/goUFV
Full Time Equivalency: 8350
Dr Brian Minter, Chancellor
Dr Mark Evered, President & Vice-Chancellor, 604-864-4608
jill.smith@ufv.ca
Dr Brian Minter, Chancellor
Dr Eric Davis, Provost & Vice-Pres., Academic, 604-864-4642
eric.davis@ufv.ca
Eleanor Busse-Klassen, Exec. Ass't to Vice-Pres., Administration
eleanor.busse@ufv.ca
Bill Cooke, Registrar, ext. 2820
bill.cooke@ufv.ca

Faculties

College of Arts
Tel: 604-851-6351; *Fax:* 604-859-6653
www.ufv.ca/arts/
Dr Jacqueline Nolte, Dean of Arts, 604-864-4632
jacqueline.nolte@ufv.ca

Faculty of Science
www.ufv.ca/faculty_of_science/
Dr. Lucy Lee, Dean, Faculty of Science, 604-851-6346
lucy.lee@ufv.ca

Faculty of Professional Studies
www.ufv.ca/ps/
Dr Rosetta Khalideen, Dean, Faculty of Professional Studies, 604-851-6341
Rosetta.Khalideen@ufv.ca

Faculty of Applied & Technical Studies
trades@ufv.ca
www.ufv.ca/trades/
John English, Dean, Faculty of Applied & Technical Studies, 604-847-5700
john.english@ufv.ca

Faculty of Access & Continuing Studies
www.ufv.ca/faos/
Dr Sue Brigden, Dean, Faculty of Access & Open Studies, 604-504-7441, ext. 4643
sue.brigden@ufv.ca

Faculty of Health Sciences
www.ufv.ca/health/
Joanne MacLean, Dean, Faculty of Health Sciences, 604-795-2816

Schools

Graduate Studies
www.ufv.ca/graduate_studies
Adrienne Chan, Assc. Vice-President, Research, Engagement & Graduate Studies, 604-557-4074
adrienne.chan@ufv.ca

Campuses

Chilliwack Campus
45635 Yale Rd., Chilliwack, BC V2P 6T4, Canada
Tel: 604-792-0025; *Fax:* 604-792-2388

Chilliwack, Trades & Tech Centre
Canada Education Park
5579 Tyson Rd., Chilliwack, BC V2R 0H9, Canada
Tel: 604-792-0025; *Fax:* 604-824-7931
Toll-Free: 888-504-7441

UFV Aerospace Centre
Abbotsford Airport
30645 Firecat Ave., Abbotsford, BC V2T 6H5, Canada
Fax: 604-852-7399
Toll-Free: 888-504-7441
aerospace@ufv.ca

Hope Centre
1250 7th Ave., Hope, BC V0X 1L4, Canada
Tel: 604-869-9991; *Fax:* 604-869-7431

Mission Campus
Heritage Park Centre
33700 Prentis Ave., Mission, BC V2V 7B1, Canada
Tel: 604-557-7603; *Fax:* 604-826-0681

Clearbrook Centre
32355 Veterans Way, Abbotsford, BC V2T 0B3
Tel: 604-851-6324

UFV India Office
SD College Chandigarh (SDCC)
Sector 32C, Chandigarth, UT, India
ufv.india@ufv.ca
www.ufv.ca/chandigarh
Other Information: +91 (0) 172-499-2400

Burnaby: Simon Fraser University
8888 University Dr., Burnaby, BC V5A 1S6, Canada
Tel: 604-291-3111
www.sfu.ca
Other Information: Student Services: 778-782-6930
www.facebook.com/simonfraseruniversity
twitter.com/sfu
www.linkedin.com/company/simon-fraser-university
www.youtube.com/user/SFUNews
Full Time Equivalency: 35398
Anne E. Giardini, Chancellor
Andrew Petter, President & Vice-Chancellor
Dr. Jon Driver, Vice-President, Academic
Philip Steenkamp, Vice-President, External Relations
Pat Hibbitts, Vice-President, Finance & Administration
Judith Osborne, Vice-President, Legal Affairs & University Secretary
Mark Walker, Registrar
Gwen Bird, University Librarian & Dean
Joy Johnson, Vice-President, Research
Cathy Daminato, Vice-President, Advancement & Alumni Engagement

Faculties

Faculty of Applied Sciences
Tel: 778-782-4724; *Fax:* 778-782-5802
fasgen@sfu.ca
www.sfu.ca/fas.html
Brian Lewis, B.A., M.A., Ph.D., Dean

School for Contemporary Arts (SCA)
Tel: 778-782-3363; *Fax:* 778-782-5907
ca@sfu.ca
www.sfu.ca/sca
www.facebook.com/SFUContemporaryArts
twitter.com/SFUContmpryArts
John T. Pierce, B.A., M.A., Ph.D., Dean

Continuing Studies
Tel: 778-782-8000; *Fax:* 778-782-5238
csreg@sfu.ca
www.sfu.ca/cs
www.facebook.com/sfucontinuingstudies
twitter.com/CS_SFU
www.linkedin.com/company/sfu-continuing-studies
www.youtube.com/sfucontinuingstudies
John Labrie, Ph.D., Dean

Faculty of Education
Tel: 778-782-3395; *Fax:* 778-782-4203
www.sfu.ca/education.html
Paul Shaker, B.A., M.A., Ph.D., Dean

Graduate Studies & Postdoctoral Fellows
Tel: 778-782-3042; *Fax:* 778-782-3080
gradstudies@sfu.ca
www.sfu.ca/dean-gradstudies.html
Wade Parkhouse, B.P.E., M.P.E., Ph.D., Dean

Health Sciences
Tel: 778-782-4821; *Fax:* 778-782-5927
fhs@sfu.ca
www.sfu.ca/fhs.html
John O'Neil, Dean

Centres/Institutes

Centre for Experimental & Constructive Mathematics
Shrum Science Building P8495
8888 University Dr., Burnaby, BC V5A 1S6
Tel: 778-782-5617; *Fax:* 778-782-5614
www.cecm.sfu.ca

Centre for Natural Hazard Research
Department of Earth Sciences
8888 University Dr., Burnaby, BC V5A 1S6
Tel: 778-782-4924; *Fax:* 778-782-4198
www.cecm.sfu.ca
John Clague, Director
jclague@sfu.ca

Centre for Wildlife Ecology
Department of Biological Sciences
8888 University Dr., Burnaby, BC V5A 1S6
Tel: 778-782-5958; *Fax:* 778-782-3496
www.sfu.ca/biology/wildberg
Ron Ydenberg, Director
ydenberg@sfu.ca

Institute of Micromachine & Microfabrication Research
School of Engineering Science
8888 University Dr., Burnaby, BC V5A 1S6
Tel: 778-782-4971; *Fax:* 778-782-4951
www.sfu.ca/biology/wildberg
Ash Parameswaran, Director
paramesw@sfu.ca

Centre for Coastal Science & Management
622 Strand Hall Annex, Faculty of Environment
8888 University Dr., Burnaby, BC V5A 1S6
Tel: 778-782-9235
www.sfu.ca/coastal
Patricia Gallaugher, Director
pgallaug@sfu.ca

Centre for Sustainable Community Development
TASC2 8800
8888 University Dr., Burnaby, BC V5A 1S6
Tel: 778-782-8787; *Fax:* 778-782-8788
scdadmin@sfu.ca
www.sfu.ca/cscd
Stevie Benisch, Academic Program Coordinator

Centre for Tourism Policy & Research
TASC1
8888 University Dr., Burnaby, BC V5A 1S6
Tel: 778-782-3074; *Fax:* 778-782-4968
www.rem.sfu.ca/tourism
Peter Williams, Director
peter_williams@sfu.ca

Cooperative Resource Management Institute
School of Resource and Environmental Management
8888 University Dr., Burnaby, BC V5A 1S6
Tel: 778-782-5778; *Fax:* 778-782-4968
www.rem.sfu.ca/crmi
Sean Cox, Director

Kamloops: Thompson Rivers University
P.O. Box 3010
900 McGill Rd., Kamloops, BC V2C 5N3, Canada
Tel: 250-828-5000; *Fax:* 250-828-5086
Toll-Free: 800-663-1663
admissions@tru.ca
www.tru.ca
www.facebook.com/tru.kamloops/posts/10152239676539616
www.twitter.com/myTRU
www.youtube.com/watch?v=8oks8FkixjU&feature=you
Full Time Equivalency: 13170; *Number of Employees:* 1,693 staff; 425 faculty; *Note:* With distance-learning, enrolment figures swell to over 25,000 students.
The Hon Nancy Greene Raine, Chancellor
Dr Alan Shaver, President & Vice-Chancellor, 250-828-5001
president@tru.ca
Dr Ulrich Scheck, Provost & Vice-Pres., Academic, 250-377-6126
uscheck@tru.ca
Matt Milovick, Vice-Pres., Admin. & Finance, 250-828-5012
Christopher Seguin, Vice-Pres., Advancement, 250-574-0474
cseguin@tru.ca
Gordon Tarzwell, Vice-Pres., Open Learning, 250-828-5007
Nathan Matthew, Executive Director of Aboriginal Education

Faculties
Faculty of Adventure, Culinary Arts & Tourism
Tel: 250-371-5566; *Fax:* 250-371-5510
baadvising@tru.ca
Harold Richins, Dean, 250-852-7138
hrichins@tru.ca

Faculty of Arts
Tel: 250-371-5566; *Fax:* 250-371-5510
baadvising@tru.ca
Dr Jim Gaisford, Dean, 250-828-5170
jgaisford@tru.ca

Faculty of Science
Dr Tom Dickinson, Dean, 250-852-7137
tdickinson@tru.ca

Faculty of Human, Social & Educational Development
Dr. Patricia Neufeld, Interim Dean, 250-828-5249
DeanHSED@tru.ca

Faculty of Law
Tel: 250-852-7699
lawadmissions@tru.ca
Anne N. Pappas, Interim Dean, 250-852-7268
apappas@tru.ca

Faculty of Student Development

Schools
School of Business & Economics (SoBE)
www.facebook.com/203791719633560
www.twitter.com/TRUBusinessEcon
flickr.com/photos/54437427@N07
Russell Currie, Dean, 250-828-5217
rcurrie@tru.ca

School of Nursing
Tel: 250-377-6169; *Fax:* 250-371-5909
Donna Murnaghan, Dean
dmurnaghan@tru.ca

School of Trades & Technology
Lindsay Langill, Dean, 250-828-5110
lblangill@tru.ca

Campuses
100 Mile House Training & Education Centre
P.O. Box 2109
485 South Birch Ave., 100 Mile House, BC V0K 2E0, Canada
Tel: 250-395-3115; *Fax:* 250-395-2894
Robin Bercowski, Coordinator
rbercowski@tru.ca

Ashcroft & Cache Creek Centre
P.O. Box 1419
310 Railway Ave., Ashcroft, BC V0K 1A0, Canada
Tel: 250-453-9999; *Fax:* 250-453-2518
Sloane Hammond, Coordinator
shammond@tru.ca

Barriere Centre
629 Barriere Town Rd., Barriere, BC V0E 1E0, Canada
Tel: 250-672-9875; *Fax:* 250-672-9875
Susan Ross, Coordinator
sross@tru.ca

Clearwater Centre
Also known as: North Thompson Community Skills Centre
751 Clearwater Village Rd., RR#1, Clearwater, BC V0E 1N0, Canada
Tel: 250-674-3530; *Fax:* 250-674-3540
Sylvia Arduini, Coordinator
sarduini@tru.ca

Lillooet Training & Education Centre
P.O. Box 339
#10, 155 Main St., Lillooet, BC V0K 1V0, Canada
Tel: 250-256-4296; *Fax:* 250-256-4278
Jane Bryson, Coordinator
jbryson@tru.ca

Williams Lake Campus
1250 Western Ave., Williams Lake, BC V2G 1H7, Canada
Tel: 250-392-8000; *Fax:* 250-392-4984
Toll-Free: 800-663-4936
wlmain@tru.ca
www.tru.ca/williamslake.html

Open Learning Division
P.O. Box 3010
900 McGill Rd., Kamloops, BC V2C 5N3, Canada
Tel: 250-852-7000; *Fax:* 250-852-6405
Toll-Free: 1-800-663-1663
student@tru.ca

Open Learning Division
Vancouver Centre
#233 - 1030 West Georgia St., Vancouver, BC V6E 2Y3, Canada
Tel: 604-568-6438; *Fax:* 604-568-6439
student@tru.ca

Langley: The Associated Canadian Theological Schools of Trinity Western University (ACTS)
7600 Glover Rd., Langley, BC V2Y 1Y1, Canada
Tel: 604-888-6045; *Fax:* 604-513-2045
acts@twu.ca
acts.twu.ca

Langley: Canadian Pentecostal Seminary
Fosmark Centre, Trinity Western University
7600 Glover Rd., Langley, BC V2Y 1Y1, Canada
Tel: 604-513-2161; *Fax:* 604-513-2078
cps@twu.ca
canadianpentecostalseminary.ca
Note: This institution is in partnership with Trinity Western University, and with five other denominations, to form ACTS, the Associated Canadian Theological Schools. It is located on the Trinity Western U. campus.

Langley: Mennonite Brethren Biblical Seminary - BC
Also known as: MB Biblical Seminary
7600 Glover Rd., Langley, BC V2Y 1Y1
Tel: 604-513-2133; *Toll-Free:* 855-252-3293
langley@mbseminary.ca
www.mbseminary.ca
www.facebook.com/mbbscanada
twitter.com/MBBSCanada
www.youtube.com/mbseminary
Bruce L. Guenther, President

Campuses
Mennonite Brethren Biblical Seminary - MB
Also known as: MB Biblical Seminary
500 Shaftesbury Blvd., Winnipeg, BC R3P 2N2
Tel: 204-487-3300; *Toll-Free:* 877-231-4570
winnipeg@mbseminary.ca

Langley: Trinity Western University
7600 Glover Rd., Langley, BC V2Y 1Y1, Canada
Tel: 604-888-7511; *Fax:* 604-513-2061
admissions@twu.ca
www.twu.ca
www.facebook.com/trinitywestern
twitter.com/TrinityWestern
instagram.com/twuem
Full Time Equivalency: 4000
Bob Kuhn, President, 604-888-7511
president@twu.ca
Paul Weme, Vice-Pres., Strategic Advancement
paul.weme@twu.ca
David Coons, Vice-Pres., Developemnt
Jim Poulsen, Vice-Pres., Finance
poulsen@twu.ca
Joan van Dyck, Vice-Pres., University Communications
joan.vandyck@twu.ca
Alma Barranco-Mendoza, Exec. Dir., Information Technology
alma.barranco@twu.ca
Janis Ryder, Exec. Dir., Human Resources
janis.ryder@twu.ca
Scott Henderson, Dir., University Enterprises
scott.henderson@twu.ca
Grant McMillan, Registrar, 604-513-2070
registrar@twu.ca

Faculties
Faculty of Natural and Applied Sciences
twu.ca/academics/science/
Dr Ka Yin Leung, Dean
kayin.leung@twu.ca

Faculty of Humanities and Social Sciences
twu.ca/academics/fhss/
Dr Robert K. Burkinshaw, Dean
burkinsh@twu.ca

School of the Arts, Media & Culture
twu.ca/academics/samc
Dr. David Squires, Dean
david.squires@twu.ca

School of Business
twu.ca/academics/business
Darlene Hahn, Program Operations Coordinator
darlene.hahn@twu.ca

School of Education
twu.ca/academics/school-of-education
Dr Kimberly Franklin, Dean, 604-513-2105
kimberly.franklin@twu.ca

School of Human Kinetics, Sport & Leisure Management
Tel: 604-513-2162
www.twu.ca/academics/school-of-human-kinetics
www.facebook.com/trinity.hkin
Dr Blair Whitmarsh, Dean, 604-513-2114
whitmars@twu.ca

School of Nursing
Tel: 604-513-2050; *Fax:* 604-513-2012
twu.ca/academics/school-of-nursing
Dr Sonya Grypma, Dean, 604-513-2121
dean.nursing@twu.ca

School of Graduate Studies
fgs@twu.ca
www.twu.ca/research-and-graduate-studies
Eve Stringham, Vice Provost of Research and Graduate Studies
stringha@twu.ca

Campuses
Bellingham Campus
143 West Kellogg Rd., Bellingham, WA
Tel: 360-527-0222
info@twubellingham.com
www.twubellingham.com

Richmond Campus
Minoru Boulevard & Firbridge Way, Richmond, BC
Tel: 360-527-0222
Phil Laird, Contact
laird@twu.ca

Affiliations

Associated Canadian Theological Seminaries of Trinity Western University (ACTS)
Also known as: ACTS Seminaries
7600 Glover Rd., Langley, BC V2Y 1Y1, Canada
Tel: 604-513-2044
acts@twu.ca
acts.twu.ca
Dr. Kenton C. Anderson, President & Dean, Northwest Baptist Seminary
kenta@twu.ca
Dr. John Auxier, Dean, Trinity Western Seminary & Associate Professor
auxier@twu.ca

Canadian Baptist Seminary
7600 Glover Rd., Langley, BC V2Y 1Y1, Canada
Tel: 604-513-2015
canbapseminary@twu.ca
canadianbaptistseminary.com
Dr Ed Stuckey, Associate Professor
estuckey@journeycentre.ca
Dr. Cal Netterfield, Acting President & Associate Professor
cal.netterfield@twu.ca
Dr Daryl Busby, Associate Professor
daryl@twu.ca
Wendell Phillips, Registrar, ext. 3807
phillips@twu.ca

Canadian Pentecostal Seminary
Fosmark Centre, Trinity Western University
7600 Glover Rd., Langley, BC V2Y 1Y1, Canada
Tel: 604-513-2161
cps@twu.ca
canadianpentecostalseminary.ca
Dr. Jim Lucas, President
jim@clcc.ca
Dr. Michael Wilkinson, Dean

Northwest Baptist Seminary
7600 Glover Rd., Langley, BC V2Y 1Y1, Canada
Tel: 604-888-7592; *Fax:* 604-637-3212
www.nbseminary.ca
www.facebook.com/nbseminary
twitter.com/nbseminary
Kent Anderson, President/Academic Dean
Loren Warkentin, Registrar

Trinity Western Seminary
7600 Glover Rd., Langley, BC V2Y 1Y1, Canada
Tel: 604-513-2044; *Fax:* 604-513-2078
Dr John Auxier, Acting President

Summit Pacific College
P.O. Box 1700
35235 Straiton Rd., Abbotsford, BC V2S 7E7, Canada
Tel: 604-853-7491; *Fax:* 604-853-8951
Toll-Free: 800-976-8388
pr@summitpacific.ca
www.summitpacific.ca
www.facebook.com/summitpc
www.twitter.com/summitpc
www.youtube.com/user/SPCcollege
Note: Formerly Western Pentecostal Bible College
Dr. Dave Demchuk, President
ddemchuk@summitpacific.ca
Melody Deeley, Registrar, 604-851-7225
registrar@summitpacific.ca
Mark Hawkes, Dean of Students, 604-851-7213
deanofstudents@summitpacific.ca
Dr. Wilf Hildebrandt, Dean of Education, 604-851-7235
interculturalstudies@summitpacific.ca
Joanne Knight, Dean of Women, 604-851-7217
deanofwomen@summitpacific.ca
Laurie Van Kleek, Librarian, 604-851-7230
librarian@summitpacific.ca

Nanaimo: Vancouver Island University (VIU)

Nanaimo Campus
900 - 5th St., Nanaimo, BC V9R 5S5
Tel: 250-753-3245; *Toll-Free:* 888-920-2221
info@viu.ca
www.viu.ca
www.facebook.com/LoveWhereYouLearn
twitter.com/VIUniversity
www.linkedin.com/companies/vancouver-island-university
www.youtube.com/user/viuchannel
Full Time Equivalency: 6856
Dr. Ralph Nilson, President

Campuses

Cowichan Campus
2011 University Way, Duncan, BC V9L 0C7
Tel: 250-746-3500
www.cc.viu.ca

Parksville-Qualicum Campus
100 Jensen Ave. East, Parksville, BC V9P 2G3
Tel: 250-248-2096; *Fax:* 250-248-9792
pqcampus@viu.ca
www.viu.ca/parksville

Powell River Campus
#100, 7085 Nootka St., Powell River, BC V8A 3C6
Tel: 604-485-2878; *Fax:* 604-485-2868
Toll-Free: 877-888-8890
pr.viu.ca

North Vancouver: Capilano University

North Vancouver Campus
2055 Purcell Way, North Vancouver, BC V7J 3H5, Canada
Tel: 604-986-1911; *Fax:* 604-984-4985
www.capilanou.ca
TTY: 604-990-7848
www.facebook.com/capilanou
www.twitter.com/capilanou
www.youtube.com/user/CapilanoUniversity
Full Time Equivalency: 14500
Peter Ufford, Chancellor
Dr. Kris Bulcroft, President/Vice-Chancellor, 604-984-4925
kbulcrof@capilanou.ca
Cindy Turner, VP, Finance & Administration, 604-984-4937
cturner@capilanou.ca
Dr Jacalyn Snodgrass, VP, Education - Academic & Arts Programs, 604-984-1740
jsnodgra@capilanou.ca
Catherine Vertesi, VP, Education - Mgmt. & International Programs, 604-990-7894
cvertesi@capilanou.ca
Dr Patrick Donahoe, VP, Student and Institutional Support, 604-984-4975
pdonahoe@capilanou.ca
Mike Arbogast, VP, Human Resources, 604-984-4991
marbogas@capilanou.ca
Karen McCredie, Registrar, 604-984-4912, ext. 4912
kmccredi@capilanou.ca
Paul Gruber, Manager, Purchasing, 604-990-7967, ext. 7967
pgruber@capilanou.ca

Faculties

Faculty of Arts and Sciences
Julia Denholm, Dean, 604-984-4976
juliadenholm@capilanou.ca

Faculty of Business and Professional Studies
Graham Fane, Dean, 604-984-4988
gfane@capilanou.ca

Faculty of Fine and Applied Arts
Jennifer Moore, Dean, 604-990-7801
jmoore2@capilanou.ca

Faculty of Education, Health & Human Development
Jean Bennett, Dean, 604-990-7982
jbennett@capilanou.ca

Faculty of Global & Community Studies
Dr Chris Bottrill, Dean, 604-983-7586
cbottril@capilanou.ca

Campuses

Squamish Campus
P.O. Box 1538
1150 Carson Pl., Squamish, BC V8B 0B1, Canada
Tel: 604-892-5322; *Fax:* 604-892-9274
squamish@capilanou.ca

Sunshine Coast Campus
P.O. Box 1609
5627 Inlet Ave., Sechelt, BC V0N 3A0, Canada
Tel: 604-885-9310; *Fax:* 604-885-9350

Prince George: University of Northern British Columbia (UNBC)

3333 University Way, Prince George, BC V2N 4Z9, Canada
Tel: 250-960-5555; *Fax:* 250-960-5794
www.unbc.ca
www.facebook.com/UNBC
twitter.com/UNBC
www.youtube.com/UNBCnews
Full Time Equivalency: 4152; *Number of Employees:* 194 Full-time faculty; 204 Part-time faculty; 389 Non-academic staff
John MacDonald, Chancellor
Mark Dale, Interim President
John Young, Vice-President Academic and Provost
Ranjana Bird, Vice-President, Research
Eileen Bray, Vice-President, Administration
Robert Van Adrichem, Vice-President, External Relations
Shelley Rennick, Director, Facilities Management, 250-960-6413
Colleen Smith, Director, Finance and Budgets, 250-960-5510, ext. 5519
colleen.smith@unbc.ca
Sheila Page, Director, Human Resources, 250-960-5534
sheila.page@unbc.ca
Greg Condon, Chief Information Officer, 250-960-5289
greg.condon@unbc.ca
Sheila Keith, Director, Purchasing, Contract & Risk Management, 250-960-5502
sheila.keith@unbc.ca

Faculties

Arts, Social & Health Sciences
Dr. John Young, Acting Dean

Graduate Programs
Dr. Ian Hartley, Dean

Science & Management
Dr. William McGill, Dean

Campuses

Northwest Campus (Terrace)
4837 Keith Ave., Terrace, BC V8G 1K7
Fax: 250-615-5478
Toll-Free: 800-697-7388
nw-info@unbc.ca

Northwest Campus (Prince Rupert)
353 - 5th St., Prince Rupert, BC V8J 3L5
Tel: 250-624-2862; *Fax:* 250-624-9703
Toll-Free: 888-554-6554
nw-info@unbc.ca

Peace River-Liard Campus (Fort St John)
P.O. Box 1000
9820 - 120th Ave., Fort St John, BC V1J 6K1
Tel: 250-787-6220; *Fax:* 250-758-9665
Toll-Free: 800-935-2270
prl-info@unbc.ca

South-Central Campus (Quesnel)
#S100, 100 Campus Way, Quesnel, BC V2J 7K1
Tel: 250-991-7540; *Fax:* 250-997-7528
Toll-Free: 800-627-9931
sc-info@unbc.ca

Wilp Wilxo'oskwhl Nisga-a (Affiliate Campus)
P.O. Box 70
3001 Ts'oohl Ts'ap Ave., Gitwinksihlkw, BC V0J 3T0
Tel: 250-633-2292; *Fax:* 250-633-2463
Toll-Free: 800-980-8838

Vancouver: University Canada West (UCW)

#100, 626 West Pender Street, Vancouver, BC V6B 1V9
Tel: 800-288-9502; *Fax:* 604-915-9607
Toll-Free: 877-431-6887
info@ucanwest.ca
www.ucanwest.ca
www.facebook.com/UniversityCanadaWest
www.twitter.com/UCANedu
www.youtube.com/CanadaUniversity
Full Time Equivalency: 800; *Note:* University Canada West (UCW) is an independent university established in 2004. UCW offers programs at their Vancouver campus and Online.
Dr. Arthur Coren, President & Vice-Chancellor
John Winter, Chancellor

Vancouver: University of British Columbia (UBC)

2329 West Mall, Vancouver, BC V6T 1Z4, Canada
Tel: 604-822-2211
www.ubc.ca
Other Information: Telex: 04-51233
www.facebook.com/universityofbc?fref=ts
twitter.com/ubcaplaceofmind
www.linkedin.com/company/4373?trk=NUS_CMPY_TWIT
www.youtube.com/user/ubc
Full Time Equivalency: 58284; *Number of Employees:* 15,171 faculty and staff
Stuart Belkin, Chair
Lindsay Gordon, Chancellor
Santa J. Ono, President, 604-822-8300
presidents.office@ubc.ca
A. Simpson, Vice-President Finance, 604-822-2823
kirin.jeffrey@ubc.ca
Barbara Miles, Vice-President, Development & Alumni Engagement, 604-822-1585
barbara.miles@ubc.ca
Philip Steenkamp, Vice-President, External, Legal & Community Relations, 604-822-5017
Professor Helen M. Burt, Interim Vice-President, Research & International, 604-822-1467
helen.burt@ubc.ca

Louise Cowin, Vice President, Students
vpstudents@exchange.ubc.ca
Kate Ross, Assocate Vice-President, Enrolment Services & Registrar, 604-822-2951
kate.ross@ubc.ca

Faculties

Faculty of Applied Science
www.apsc.ubc.ca
Dr Tyseer Aboulnasr, Dean, 604-822-6413
info@apsc.ubc.ca

Faculty of Arts
www.arts.ubc.ca
Dr Gage Averill, Dean, 604-822-3751
mtw@mail.arts.ubc.ca

Faculty of Dentistry
www.dentistry.ubc.ca
Dr Charles Shuler, Dean, 604-822-0738
foddo@interchange.ubc.ca

Faculty of Education
www.educ.ubc.ca
Dr Jon shapiro, Interim Dean, 604-822-5214
jon.shapiro@ubc.ca

Faculty of Forestry
www.forestry.ubc.ca
Dr John Innes, Dean, 604-822-3542
john.innes@ubc.ca

Faculty of Graduate & Postdoctoral Studies
www.grad.ubc.ca
Barbara Evans, Dean, 604-827-5547
barbara.evans@ubc.ca

Faculty of Land & Food Systems
www.landfood.ubc.ca
Murray B. Isman, Dean, 604-822-1219
dean.landfood@ubc.ca

Faculty of Law
www.law.ubc.ca
Mary Ann Bobinski, Dean, 604-822-6335
deansoffice@law.ubc.ca

Faculty of Medicine
www.med.ubc.ca
Dr Gavin Stuart, Dean, 604-822-2421
fomdo_reception@medd.med.ubc.ca

Faculty of Pharmaceutical Sciences
www.pharmacy.ubc.ca
Robert Sindelar, Dean, 604-822-2343
sindelar@interchange. ubc.ca

Faculty of Sciences
www.science.ubc.ca
Dr Simon Peacock, Dean, 604-822-3336
scidean@science.ubc.ca

Schools

School of Architecture & Landscape Architecture
Tel: 604-822-2779; *Fax:* 604-822-3808
arch1@interchange.ubc.ca
www.sala.ubc.ca
Leslie Van Duzer, Director
vanduzer@interchange.ubc.ca

School of Audiology & Speech Sciences
Tel: 604-822-5591; *Fax:* 604-822-6569
inquiry@audiospeech.ubc.ca
www.audiospeech.ubc.ca
Valter Ciocca, Director
director@audiospeech.ubc.ca

School of Community & Regional Planning
Tel: 604-822-3276; *Fax:* 604-822-3787
www.scarp.ubc.ca
Dr Penny Gurstein, Director
gurstein@interchange.ubc.ca

School of Continuing Studies
Tel: 604-822-1444; *Fax:* 604-822-1599
www.cstudies.ubc.ca
Dr Judith Plessis, Executive Director

School of Kinesiology
Tel: 604-822-3838; *Fax:* 604-822-6842
www.hkin.educ.ubc.ca
Dr Robert E.C. Sparks, Director
robert.sparks@ubc.ca

School of Library, Archival & Information Studies
Tel: 604-822-2404; *Fax:* 604-822-6006
slais@interchange.ubc.ca
www.slais.ubc.ca
Terry Eastwood, Interim Director
eastwood@interchange.ubc.ca

School of Music
Tel: 604-822-3113; *Fax:* 604-822-4884
www.music.ubc.ca
Dr Richard Kurth, Director
richard.kurth@ubc.ca

School of Nursing
Tel: 604-822-7417; *Fax:* 604-822-7466
www.nursing.ubc.ca
Dr Sally Thorne, Director
sally.thorne@nursing.ubc.ca

School of Population & Public Health
Tel: 604-822-2772; *Fax:* 604-822-4994
www.spph.ubc.ca
Dr Martin Schechter, Director
martin.schechter@ubc.ca

School of Journalism
Tel: 604-822-6688; *Fax:* 604-822-6707
journal@interchange.ubc.ca
www.journalism.ubc.ca
Dr Mary Lynn Young, Director

School of Social Work
Tel: 604-822-2255; *Fax:* 604-822-8656
www.socialwork.ubc.ca
Dr Kwong-leung Tang, Director
kltang@interchange.ubc.ca

Sauder School of Business
Tel: 604-822-8868; *Fax:* 604-822-8468
www.sauder.ubc.ca
Dr Daniel Muzyka, Dean
daniel.muzyka@sauder.ubc.ca

School of Environmental Health
Tel: 604-822-9595; *Fax:* 604-822-9588
soeh@interchange.ubc.ca
www.soeh.ubc.ca
Christie Hurrell, Executive Director
hurrell@interchange.ubc.ca

College of Health Disciplines
Tel: 604-822-5571; *Fax:* 604-822-2495
chd@interchange.ubc.ca
www.health-disciplines.ubc.ca
Louise Nasmith, Principal
louise.nasmith@ubc.ca

College of Interdisciplinary Studies
www.cfis.ubc.ca
Michael Burgess, Principal, 604-827-5262
cfis.principal@ubc.ca

Campuses

UBC Okanagan Campus
3333 University Way, Kelowna, BC V1V 1V7, Canada
Tel: 250-807-8000; *Toll-Free:* 866-596-0767
askme@ubc
www.ubc.ca/okanagan

UBC Robson Square Campus
800 Robson St., Vancouver, BC V6Z 3B7
Tel: 604-822-3333; *Fax:* 604-822-0070
robson.info@ubc.ca
www.robsonsquare.ubc.ca
www.facebook.com/pages/UBC-Robson-Square/160283167345709?v=wall
twitter.com/UBCRobsonSquare
pinterest.com/ubcrobsonsquare/

Great Northern Way Campus (GNW)
577 Great Northern Way, Vancouver, BC V5T 1E1
Tel: 778-370-1005; *Fax:* 778-370-1045
admin@gnwc.ca
www.gnwc.ca
Note: Great Northern Way Campus Trust is jointly owned by UBC, SFU, BCIT and Emily Carr University. This campus operates The Centre for Digital Media.

UBC Vantage College
CK Choi Building
1855 West Mall, 1st Fl., Vancouver, BC V6T 1Z2
Tel: 604-827-0337
info@vantagecollege.ubc.ca
www.vantagecollege.ubc.ca
James Ridge, Principal, 604-822-9485
james.ridge@vantagecollege.ubc.ca
Susanne Schmiesing, Director, Business Development & Operations, 604-822-5212
susanne.schmiesing@vantagecollege.ubc.ca

Affiliations

Regent College
5800 University Blvd., Vancouver, BC V6T 2E4, Canada
Tel: 604-224-3245; *Fax:* 604-224-3097
Toll-Free: 1-800-663-8664
registrar@regent-college.edu
www.regent-college.edu
Other Information: Regent Bookstore, Toll Free: 1-800-334-3279
www.facebook.com/regentcollege
twitter.com/regentcollege
www.linkedin.com/company/regent-college
www.youtube.com/user/underthegreenroof
Dr Rod J.K. Wilson, President
presidentsoffice@regent-college.edu

St. Mark's College
5935 Iona Dr., Vancouver, BC V6T 1J7, Canada
Tel: 604-822-4463; *Fax:* 604-822-4659
info@stmarkscollege.ca
www.stmarkscollege.ca
Paul C. Burns, Interim Principal
Dr. Marjorie Budnikas, Registrar
registrar@stmarkscollege.ca

Carey Theological College
5920 Iona Dr., Vancouver, BC V6T 1J6
Tel: 604-224-4308; *Fax:* 604-224-5014
info@careytheologicalcollege.ca
www.careycentre.com

Vancouver School of Theology
6000 Iona Dr., Vancouver, BC V6T 1L4
Tel: 604-822-0824; *Fax:* 604-822-9212
possibilities@vst.edu
www.vst.edu
www.facebook.com/107758090070?ref=ss
twitter.com/vst_vancouver
www.youtube.com/user/VSTVancouver
Richard Topping, Principal, 604-822-9813
rtopping@standrews.edu
Pat Dutcher-Walls, Dean, 604-822-9804
patdw@vst.edu

Victoria: Royal Roads University

2005 Sooke Rd., Victoria, BC V9B 5Y2, Canada
Tel: 250-391-2511; *Fax:* 250-391-2500
Toll-Free: 1-800-788-8028
www.royalroads.ca
www.facebook.com/royalroadsu
twitter.com/royalroads
www.linkedin.com/company/19123
www.youtube.com/user/RoyalRoadsUni
Full Time Equivalency: 4640; *Note:* Royal Roads University offers: Doctoral degrees in Social Sciences; Masters degrees in Arts, Business Admin., Science; Bachelor degrees in Arts, Commerce, Science; Graduate Certificates; Graduate Diplomas.
Wayne Standlund, Chair & Chancellor
Dr Allan Cahoon, President & Vice-Chancellor
Dr. Stephen Grundy, Vice-President, Academic & Provost, 250-391-2545

Victoria: University of Victoria

3800 Finnerty Rd., Victoria, BC V8P 5C2, Canada
Tel: 250-721-7211; *Fax:* 250-721-7212
Toll-Free: 888-721-8620
www.uvic.ca
Other Information: 250-721-7599
www.facebook.com/universityofvictoria
twitter.com/uvic
www.linkedin.com/company/university-of-victoria
www.youtube.com/UVic
Full Time Equivalency: 20330
Shelagh Rogers, Chancellor
Jamie Cassels, Q.C., President
pres@uvic.ca
David Castle, PhD, Vice-President, Research
vpr@uvic.ca
Carmen Charette, Vice-President, External Relations
ncernoia@uvic.ca
Gayle Gorrill, B.B.A., C.A., C.B.V., Vice-President, Finance & Operations
vpfo@uvic.ca
Valerie Kuehne, B.Sc.N., M.Ed., M.A., Ph., Vice-President, Academic & Provost (Acting)
provost@uvic.ca
Julia Eastman, B.A., M.A., Ph.D., University Secretary
usec@uvic.ca

Faculties
Gustavon School of Business
Also known as: Gustavon
P.O. Box 1700 CSC
Victoria, BC V8W 2Y2
Tel: 250-472-4139; *Fax:* 250-721-6613
gustavson@uvic.ca
www.uvic.ca/gustavson
www.facebook.com/GustavsonUVic
twitter.com/GustavsonUVic
www.linkedin.com/groups?home=&gid=154136
Ali Dastmalchian, B.Sc., M.Sc., Ph.D., Dean
University of Victoria Continuing Studies (UVCS)
Tel: 250-472-4747; *Fax:* 250-721-8774
register@uvcs.uvic.ca
www.uvcs.uvic.ca
Maureen MacDonald, B.A., LL.B., M.B.A., D.Ph, Dean
Faculty of Education
Tel: 250-721-7877
adve@uvic.ca
www.uvic.ca/education
www.facebook.com/UVicEducation
twitter.com/UVicEducation
Ted Riecken, B.A., M.Ed., Ph.D., Dean
Faculty of Engineering
P.O. Box 3055
Victoria, BC
Tel: 250-472-5322; *Fax:* 250-472-5323
engr@uvic.ca
www.uvic.ca/engineering
www.facebook.com/engr.undergrad
twitter.com/UVicEngineering
Thomas Tiedje, B.Sc., M.Sc., Ph.D., Dean
Fine Arts
finearts@uvic.ca
finearts.uvic.ca
www.facebook.com/183745571661580
twitter.com/uvic_finearts
www.youtube.com/user/UVicFineArts
Sarah Blackstone, B.A., M.A., Ph.D., Dean
Graduate Studies
P.O. Box 3025 CSC
Victoria, BC V8W 3P2
Tel: 250-472-4657; *Fax:* 250-472-5420
garo@uvic.ca
www.uvic.ca/graduatestudies
Aaron H. Devor, B.A., M.A., Ph.D., Dean
Human & Social Development (HSD)
P.O. Box 1700 CSC
Victoria, BC V8W 2Y2
Tel: 250-853-3213
hsdinfo@uvic.ca
www.uvic.ca/hsd
www.facebook.com/UVicHSD
twitter.com/UVicHSD
Mary Ellen Purkis, B.S.N., M.Sc., Ph.D., Dean
Humanities
Fax: 250-721-7059
humsoff@uvic.ca
web.uvic.ca/humanities
twitter.com/UVicHumanities
www.youtube.com/user/HumanitiesUVic
Andrew Rippin, B.A., M.A., Ph.D., Dean
Faculty of Law
Tel: 250-721-8150; *Fax:* 250-721-6390
www.uvic.ca/law
twitter.com/UVicLaw
Donna Greschner, B.Comm., LL.B., Dean
Faculty of Science
Fax: 250-472-5012
sciadmin@uvic.ca
www.uvic.ca/science
Tom Pedersen, B.Sc., Ph.D., Dean
Faculty of Social Sciences
Tel: 250-472-4496
soscadmn@uvic.ca
www.uvic.ca/socialsciences
www.facebook.com/133010843398365
twitter.com/UVicSocialSci
www.youtube.com/user/facultysocialscience
Peter Keller, B.A., M.A., Ph.D., Dean

Centres/Institutes
Centre for Aboriginal Health Research
P.O. Box 1700 CSC
Victoria, BC V8W 2Y2
Tel: 250-472-5456; *Fax:* 250-472-5450
cahr@uvic.ca
www.uvic.ca/research/centres/cahr
www.facebook.com/172450862782198
twitter.com/CAHR_UVic
www.linkedin.com/groups/Centre-Aboriginal-Health-Research-5068403
Charlotte Reading, Director
Centre for Addictions Research BC (CARBC)
P.O. Box 1700 CSC
Victoria, BC V8W 2Y2
Tel: 250-472-5445; *Fax:* 250-472-5321
carbc@uvic.ca
www.carbc.ca
www.facebook.com/CARBC.UVic
twitter.com/CARBC_Uvic
www.youtube.com/user/CARBCUVic
Tim Stockwell, Director
timstock@uvic.ca
Centre for Advanced Materials & Related Technology (CAMTEC)
P.O. Box 3055 CSC
Victoria, BC V8W 3P6
Tel: 250-721-7736
camtec@uvic.ca
www.camtec.uvic.ca
B.C. Choi, Director
bchoi@uvic.ca
Centre for Asia-Pacific Initiatives
P.O. Box 1700 CSC
Victoria, BC V8W 2Y2
Tel: 250-721-7020; *Fax:* 250-721-3107
capi@uvic.ca
www.uvic.ca/research/centres/capi
www.facebook.com/uviccapi
twitter.com/CAPIUVic
www.youtube.com/uviccapi
Helen Lansdowne, Associate Director
lansdown@uvic.ca
Centre for Biomedical Research
P.O. Box 3020 CSC
Victoria, BC V8W 3N5
Tel: 250-472-4067; *Fax:* 250-472-4075
cfbr@uvic.ca
cbr.uvic.ca
Paul Zehr, Director
Centre for Co-operative & Community-Based Economy
University House 2
3800 Finnerty Rd., Victoria, BC V8P 5C2
Tel: 250-472-5227
cccbe@uvic.ca
www.uvic.ca/research/centres/cccbe
www.facebook.com/CentreForCoOperativeAndCommunityBasedEconomy
twitter.com/UVICcccbe
Ana Maria Peredo, Director
aperedo@uvic.ca

Colleges

Castlegar: Selkirk College
Castlegar Campus
301 Frank Beinder Way, Castlegar, BC V1N 4L3
Tel: 250-365-7292; *Fax:* 250-365-6568
Toll-Free: 1-888-953-1133
www.selkirk.ca
www.facebook.com/SelkirkCollege
twitter.com/FrankenSmarter
www.youtube.com/selkirkcollege
Note: The regional community college consists of the following schools: Kootenay School of the Arts; School of Adult Basic Education & Transitional Training; School of Business & Aviation; School of Digital Media & Music; School of Health & Human Services; School of Hospitality & Tourism; School of Industry & Trades Training; School of Renewable Resources; School of University Arts & Sciences & Selkirk International.
Bruce Morrison, Chair
Angus Graeme, President

Campuses
Grand Forks Campus
P.O. Box 968
486 - 72nd Ave., Grand Forks, BC V0H 1H0, Canada
Tel: 250-442-2704; *Fax:* 250-442-2877
Kaslo Centre
P.O. Box 1149
421 Front St., Kaslo, BC V0G 1M0, Canada
Tel: 250-353-2618; *Fax:* 250-353-7121
Kootenay School of the Arts (KSA) Campus
606 Victoria St., Nelson, BC V1L 4K9
Tel: 250-352-2821; *Fax:* 250-352-1625
Toll-Free: 1-877-552-2821
Nakusp Centre
P.O. Box 720
311 Broadway, Nakusp, BC V0H 1R0, Canada
Tel: 250-265-4077; *Fax:* 250-265-3195
Other Information: Adult Basic Education: 250-265-3640
Silver King Campus
2001 Silver King Rd., Nelson, BC V1L 1C8, Canada
Tel: 250-352-6601; *Fax:* 250-352-3180
Toll-Free: 1-866-301-6601
Tenth Street Campus
820 Tenth St., Nelson, BC V1L 3C7, Canada
Tel: 250-352-6601; *Fax:* 250-352-5716
Toll-Free: 1-866-301-6601
Trail Campus
900 Helena St., Trail, BC V1R 4S6, Canada
Tel: 250-368-5236; *Fax:* 250-368-4983

Courtenay: North Island College
Comox Valley Campus
2300 Ryan Rd., Courtenay, BC V9N 8N6
Tel: 250-334-5000; *Fax:* 250-334-5018
Toll-Free: 800-715-0914
questions@nic.bc.ca
www.northislandcollege.ca
www.facebook.com/pages/North-Island-College/327464742944
John Bowman, President

Campuses
Campbell River Campus
1685 South Dogwood St., Campbell River, BC V9W 8C1
Tel: 250-923-9700; *Fax:* 250-923-9703
Port Alberni Campus
3699 Roger St., Port Alberni, BC V9Y 8E3
Tel: 250-724-8711; *Fax:* 250-724-8700
Mount Waddington Regional Campus
P.O. Box 901
9300 Trustee Rd., Port Hardy, BC V0N 2P0
Tel: 250-949-7912; *Fax:* 250-949-2617
Vigar Vocational Centre
2780 Vigar Rd., Campbell River, BC V9W 6A3
Tel: 250-923-9794; *Fax:* 250-830-0816
Tebo Vocational Centre
4781 Tebo Ave., Port Alberni, BC V9Y 6X7
Tel: 250-724-8738; *Fax:* 250-723-4573
Ucluelet Centre
P.O. Box 198
#10, 1636 Penninsula Rd., Ucluelet, BC V0R 3A0
Tel: 250-726-2697; *Fax:* 250-726-2698

Cranbrook: College of the Rockies
P.O. Box 8500
2700 College Way, Cranbrook, BC V1C 5L7
Tel: 250-489-2751; *Fax:* 250-489-1790
Toll-Free: 877-489-2687
info@cotr.bc.ca
www.cotr.bc.ca
www.facebook.com/COTR1
twitter.com/cotr_updates
www.linkedin.com/company/561622
www.youtube.com/cotr1
David Walls, President & CEO

Campuses
Creston Campus
P.O. Box 1978
Creston, BC V0B 1G0
Tel: 250-428-5332; *Fax:* 250-428-4314
creston@cotr.bc.ca
www.cotr.bc.ca/creston/
Kerry Hobbs, Campus Manager
khobbs@cotr.bc.ca
Invermere Campus
#2, 1535 - 14th St., RR#4, Invermere, BC V0A 1K4
Tel: 250-342-3210; *Fax:* 250-342-9221
invermere@cotr.bc.ca
www.cotr.bc.ca/invermere/
www.facebook.com/168647829825291
twitter.com/COTRinvermere

Doug Clovechok, Campus Manager

Fernie Campus
P.O. Box 1770
Fernie, BC V0B 1M0
Tel: 250-423-4691; *Fax:* 250-423-3932
Toll-Free: 866-423-4691
fernie@cotr.bc.ca
www.cotr.bc.ca/fernie/

Golden Campus
P.O. Box 376
Golden, BC V0A 1H0
Tel: 250-344-5901; *Fax:* 250-344-5745
golden@cotr.bc.ca
www.cotr.bc.ca/golden/
www.facebook.com/cotrgolden
twitter.com/COTR_Golden

Kimberley Campus
1850 Warren Ave., Kimberley, BC V1A 1S1
Tel: 250-427-7116; *Fax:* 250-427-3034
kimberley@cotr.bc.ca
www.cotr.bc.ca/kimberley
www.facebook.com/COTRConEd

Dawson Creek: Northern Lights College

Regional Administration
11401 - 8th St., Dawson Creek, BC V1G 4G2
Tel: 250-782-5251; *Fax:* 250-784-7563
Toll-Free: 866-463-6652
appinfo@nlc.bc.ca
www.nlc.bc.ca
www.facebook.com/NLCollege
twitter.com/NLCinthenews
www.youtube.com/user/NLCdotBCdotCA
Karen Simpson, Board Chair
Laurie Rancourt, CEO

Campuses

Atlin Campus
Also known as: Atlin Learning Centre
P.O. Box 29
Atlin, BC V0W 1A0
Tel: 250-651-7762; *Fax:* 250-651-7730
Toll-Free: 866-463-6652
Note: The campus offers continuing education in academic & pre-professional studies, development & upgrading, distance education, & industrial & workforce training.

Chetwynd Campus
P.O. Box 1180
5132 - 50th St., Chetwynd, BC V0C 1J0
Tel: 250-788-2248; *Fax:* 250-788-9706
Toll-Free: 866-463-6652
Note: Programs offered include applied business technology, teacher assistant training, social services worker training, forestry, hospitality & tourism operations, continuing education, adult basic education, university transfer, & adult special education.
Donna Merry, Campus Administrator
dmerry@nlc.bc.ca

Dawson Creek Campus
11401 - 8 St., Dawson Creek, BC V1G 4G2
Tel: 250-782-5251; *Fax:* 250-784-7563
Toll-Free: 866-463-6652
Note: The campus features technical, academic, trades, & vocational programs.
Lorelee Friesen, Dean of Student Services

Dease Lake Campus
P.O. Box 220
Commercial Dr., Lot 10, Dease Lake, BC V0C 1L0
Tel: 250-771-5500; *Fax:* 250-771-5510
Toll-Free: 866-463-6652
Note: The campus serves full-time & part-time vocational and continuing education students in Atlin, Telegraph Creek, Lower Post, Iskut, & Good Hope Lake.

Fort Nelson Campus
P.O. Box 860
5201 Simpson Trail, Fort Nelson, BC V0C 1R0
Tel: 250-774-2741; *Fax:* 250-774-2750
Toll-Free: 1-866-463-6652
Note: Continuing education programs are provided.
Laurie Dolan, Campus Administrator
ldolan@nlc.bc.ca

Fort St. John Campus
P.O. Box 1000
9820 - 120 Ave., Fort St John, BC V1J 6K1
Tel: 250-785-6981; *Fax:* 250-785-1294
Toll-Free: 866-463-6652
Note: Academic, apprenticeship, career/technical, vocational, & international students students are served by the Fort St. John campus.
Kathy Handley, Campus Administrator
khandley@nlc.bc.ca

Tumbler Ridge Campus
P.O. Box 180
180 Southgate Dr., Tumbler Ridge, BC V0C 2W0
Tel: 250-242-5591; *Fax:* 250-242-3109
Toll-Free: 866-463-6652
Note: Adult basic education is offered in Tumbler Ridge.
Donna Merry, Administrator
dmerry@nlc.bc.ca

Kelowna: Okanagan University College

Kelowna Campus
1000 KLO Rd., Kelowna, BC V1V 1V7
Tel: 250-762-5445; *Toll-Free:* 877-755-2266
www.okanagan.bc.ca
www.facebook.com/okanagancollege.ca
twitter.com/OkanaganCollege
www.youtube.com/user/OkanaganCollege
Jim Hamilton, President, 250-862-5628
jhamilton@okanagan.bc.ca

Campuses

Salmon Arm Campus
2552 Trans Canada Hwy. NE, Salmon Arm, BC V1E 4N3
Tel: 250-832-2126; *Toll-Free:* 888-831-0341

Vernon Campus
7000 College Way, Vernon, BC V1B 2N5, Canada
Tel: 250-545-7291; *Toll-Free:* 800-289-8993

Penticton Campus
583 Duncan Ave. West, Penticton, BC V2A 8E1
Tel: 250-492-4305; *Toll-Free:* 866-510-8899

Langley: Trinity Western Seminary

7600 Glover Rd., Langley, BC V2Y 1Y1, Canada
Tel: 604-513-2019; *Fax:* 604-513-2045
Toll-Free: 888-468-6898
acts@twu.ca
www.acts.twu.ca
www.facebook.com/trinitywestern
twitter.com/TrinityWestern
www.linkedin.com/company/trinity-western-university

Prince George: College of New Caledonia

3330 - 22nd Ave., Prince George, BC V2N 1P8, Canada
Tel: 250-562-2131; *Fax:* 250-561-5816
Toll-Free: 1-800-371-811
askcnc@cnc.bc.ca
www.cnc.bc.ca
www.facebook.com/CollegeOfNewCaledonia
twitter.com/cnc_bc_ca
www.linkedin.com/edu/school?id=42168
www.youtube.com/user/CaledoniaCollege
Full Time Equivalency: 5250
M. Bryn Kulmatycki, Interim President
kulmatyckib@cnc.bc.ca
Patricia Covington, Acting Vice President, Academic
covington@cnc.bc.ca
Penny Fahlman, Vice President - Finance/Admin/ Bursar
fahlman@cnc.bc.ca
Marlene Erickson, Acting Director, Aboriginal Education
erickson@cnc.bc.ca

Campuses

Nicholson Campus
2211 Nicholson Ave. South, Prince George, BC V2N 1P8, Canada
Tel: 250-562-2131; *Toll-Free:* 800-371-8111

Lakes District Campus
Also known as: Burns Lake
P.O. Box 5000
545 Hwy. 16 West, Burns Lake, BC V0J 1E0, Canada
Tel: 250-692-1715; *Fax:* 250-692-1750
Toll-Free: 866-692-1943
lksdist@cnc.bc.ca
Joan Ragsdale, Director, 250-692-1715
ragsdale@cnc.bc.ca

Mackenzie Campus
P.O. Box 2110
540 Mackenzie Blvd., Mackenzie, BC V0J 2C0, Canada
Tel: 250-997-7200; *Fax:* 250-997-3779
Toll-Free: 877-997-4333
cncmackenzie@cnc.bc.ca
Shannon Bezo, Director, 250-997-7203
sbezo@cnc.bc.ca

Quesnel Campus
100 Campus Way, Quesnel, BC V2J 7K1, Canada
Tel: 250-991-7500; *Fax:* 250-991-7502
Toll-Free: 866-680-7523
quesnel@cnc.bc.ca
Doug Larsen, Director, 250-991-7622
larsend@cnc.bc.ca

Nechako Campus
3231 Hospital Rd., Vanderhoof, BC V0J 3A2, Canada
Tel: 250-567-3200; *Fax:* 250-567-3217
nechako@cnc.bc.ca
Maureen Mallais, Director, 250-567-3200
mallais@cnc.bc.ca

Fort St. James Campus
P.O. Box 1557
179 Douglas St., Fort St. James, BC V0J 1P0
Tel: 250-996-7019; *Fax:* 250-996-7014
cncfsj@cnc.bc.ca
Maureen Mallais, Director

Centres/Institutes

Fraser Lake Learning Centre
298 McMillan Ave., Fraser Lake, BC V0J 1S0
Tel: 250-699-6249; *Fax:* 250-699-6269
cncfl@cnc.bc.ca
Maureen Mallais, Director

John A. Brink Trades & Technology Centre
1727 W. Central, Prince George, BC V2N 1P6
Tel: 250-561-5804

Surrey: Kwantlen Polytechnic University

12666 - 72nd Ave., Surrey, BC V3W 2M8, Canada
Tel: 604-599-2100; *Fax:* 604-599-2068
inquiries@kwantlen.ca
www.kwantlen.ca
www.facebook.com/kwantlenU
twitter.com/kwantlenu
Full Time Equivalency: 11660
Alan R. Davis, President & Vice Chancellor, 604-599-2078
Arvinder Singh Bubber, Chancellor
Salvador Ferreras, Provost & Vice President Academic
Dr. Robert Hensley, Registrar, 604-599-2018
robert.hensley@kpu.ca
Scott Gowen, Director, Supply & Business Services, 604-599-2134
supply@kwantlen.ca

Faculties

Faculty of Arts
Tel: 604-599-3068; *Fax:* 604-599-2966
arts@kpu.ca
Dr Diane Purvey, Dean, 604-599-2052

Faculty of Science and Horticulture
www.facebook.com/1402998016610195
twitter.com/kpusciencehort
Dr Elizabeth Worobec, Dean, 604-599-2244
elizabeth.worobec@kpu.ca

Faculty of Health
Dr. Tru Freeman, Dean, 604-599-2263
tru.freeman@kpu.ca

Faculty of Academic and Career Advancement
www.facebook.com/kwantlenU/photos_albums
Dr Kathleen Haggith, Associate Dean, Faculty of Academic and Career Advancement

Faculty of Trades and Technology
Henry Reiser, Dean, 604-598-6101
Henry.Reiser@kpu.ca

Schools

School of Business
Tel: 604-599-3251; *Fax:* 604-599-3242
business@kpu.ca
www.facebook.com/223929307620683
twitter.com/KPU_business
Wayne Tebb, Dean, 604-599-3252
wayne.tebb@kpu.ca

Chip and Shannon Wilson School of Design
Carolyn Robertson, Dean pro tem, 604-599-2673
carolyn.robertson@kpu.ca

Campuses

Surrey Campus
12666 - 72 Ave., Surrey, BC V3T 5H8, Canada
Fax: 604-599-2068

Richmond Campus
8771 Lansdowne Rd., Richmond, BC V6X 3V8, Canada
Fax: 604-599-2578

Cloverdale Campus
Also known as: Tech Campus
5500 - 180 St., Surrey, BC V3S 4K5, Canada
Tel: 604-599-2000

Langley Campus
20901 Langley Bypass, Langley, BC V3A 8G9, Canada
Fax: 604-599-3242

Terrace: Northwest Community College
College Services
5331 McConnell Ave., Terrace, BC V8G 4X2, Canada
Tel: 250-635-6511; *Fax:* 250-635-5432
Toll-Free: 1-877-277-2288
www.nwcc.bc.ca
www.facebook.com/NWCCBC
twitter.com/nwccbc/
www.youtube.com/NWCCBC
Stephanie Forsyth, President

Campuses
Hazelton Campus
P.O. Box 338
4815 Swannell Dr., Hazelton, BC V0J 1Y0, Canada
Tel: 250-842-5291; *Fax:* 250-842-5813
Houston Campus
P.O. Box 1277
3221 - 14 St. West, Houston, BC V0J 1Z0, Canada
Tel: 250-845-7266; *Fax:* 250-845-5629
Kitimat Campus
606 Mountainview Sq., Kitimat, BC V8C 2N2, Canada
Tel: 250-632-4766; *Fax:* 250-632-5069
Prince Rupert Campus
353 - 5th St., Prince Rupert, BC V8J 3L6, Canada
Tel: 250-624-6054; *Fax:* 250-624-3923
Queen Charlotte Campus
P.O. Box 67
138 Bay St., Queen Charlotte Village, BC V0T 1S0, Canada
Tel: 250-559-8222; *Fax:* 250-559-8219
Smithers Campus
P.O. Box 3606
3966 - 2nd Ave., Smithers, BC V0J 2N0, Canada
Tel: 250-847-4461; *Fax:* 250-847-4568
Kaay Llnagaay (Skidegate)
P.O. Box 1523
2 Second Beach Rd., Skidegate, BC V0T 1S0, Canada
Tel: 250-559-7885; *Fax:* 250-559-4782
Terrace Campus
5331 McConnell Ave., Terrace, BC V8G 4X2, Canada
Tel: 250-635-6511; *Fax:* 250-638-5432
Masset Campus
P.O. Box 559
2151 Tahayghen, Masset, BC V0T 1M0, Canada
Tel: 250-626-3670; *Fax:* 250-626-3680

Victoria: Camosun College
Lansdowne Campus
3100 Foul Bay Rd., Victoria, BC V8P 5J2
Tel: 250-370-3550; *Toll-Free:* 877-554-7555
www.camosun.bc.ca
www.facebook.com/CamosunCollege
twitter.com/camosun
youtube.com/user/mycamosun
Full Time Equivalency: 18500; *Number of Employees:* 900
Kathryn Laurin, President

Campuses
Interurban Campus
Liz Ashton Campus Centre
#226, 4461 Interurban Rd., Victoria, BC V9E 2C1

Victoria: Lester B. Pearson United World College of the Pacific
Also known as: Pearson College UWC
Old Name: Lester B. Pearson College of the Pacific
650 Pearson College Dr., Victoria, BC V9C 4H7
Tel: 250-391-2411
www.pearsoncollege.ca
www.facebook.com/PearsonUWC
twitter.com/PCUWC
www.linkedin.com/groups?gid=49277
www.youtube.com/user/PearsonUWC
Full Time Equivalency: 200
Désirée McGraw, President

Post Secondary/Technical

Colleges

Kelowna: Okanagan College
1000 KLO Rd., Kelowna, BC V1Y 4X8, Canada
Tel: 250-762-5445; *Toll-Free:* 877-755-2266
acoyle@okanagan.bc.ca
www.okanagan.bc.ca
www.facebook.com/okanagancollege.ca
twitter.com/OkanaganCollege
www.linkedin.com/company/okanagan-college
www.youtube.com/user/OkanaganCollege
Enrollment: 4850
Jim Hamilton, President

Campuses
Penticton Campus
583 Duncan Ave. West, Penticton, BC V2A 8E1, Canada
Tel: 250-492-4305; *Fax:* 250-492-3950
Toll-Free: 866-510-8899
penticton@okanagan.bc.ca
www.okanagan.bc.ca/southokanagan
www.facebook.com/OCPen
Donna Lomas, Regional Dean
Salmon Arm Campus
P.O. Box 189
Salmon Arm, BC V1E 4N3, Canada
Tel: 250-832-2126; *Fax:* 250-804-8850
Toll-Free: 888-831-0341
Lynda Wilson, Regional Dean
Vernon Campus
7000 College Way, Vernon, BC V1B 2N5, Canada
Tel: 250-545-7291; *Fax:* 250-545-3277
Tony Sellars, Regional Dean

New Westminster: Douglas College
P.O. Box 2503
700 Royal Ave., New Westminster, BC V3M 2Z4, Canada
Tel: 604-527-5400; *Fax:* 604-527-5095
ce-tg_registration@douglascollege.ca
www.douglas.bc.ca
www.facebook.com/douglascollege
twitter.com/douglascollege/
www.linkedin.com/company/douglas-college
www.youtube.com/user/DouglasCollegeVideo
Enrollment: 7000
Susan R. Witter, President

Campuses
David Lam Campus
1250 Pinetree Way, Coquitlam, BC V3B 7X3, Canada

North Vancouver: Capilano University
2055 Purcell Way, North Vancouver, BC V7J 3H5, Canada
Tel: 604-986-1911; *Fax:* 604-984-4985
www.capilanou.ca
TTY: 604-990-7848
www.facebook.com/capilanou
twitter.com/CapilanoU
www.linkedin.com/company/capilano-university
www.youtube.com/user/CapilanoUniversity
Enrollment: 7500
Dr. Kris Bulcroft, President, Vice-Chancellor

Vancouver: Langara College
100 West 49th Ave., Vancouver, BC V5Y 2Z6, Canada
Tel: 604-323-5511; *Fax:* 604-323-5555
geninfo@langara.bc.ca
www.langara.bc.ca
Enrollment: 12218
Korena Jang, Manager, Executive & Board Operations

Vancouver: Vancouver Community College
1155 East Broadway, Vancouver, BC V5T 4V5, Canada
Tel: 604-871-7000; *Fax:* 604-871-7100
www.vcc.ca
www.facebook.com/vcc
twitter.com/myVCC
www.linkedin.com/company/vancouver-community-college
www.youtube.com/user/myVCC
Dale Dorn, President
L. Martin, Vice-President
Alan Davis, Vice-President
Peter Legg, Interim Vice-President

Campuses
City Centre Campus
250 West Pender St., Vancouver, BC V6B 1S9, Canada
Fax: 604-443-8588

Victoria: Camosun College
Lansdowne Campus
3100 Foul Bay Rd., Victoria, BC V8P 5J2, Canada
Tel: 250-370-3000; *Fax:* 250-370-3551
Toll-Free: 877-554-7555
camosun.ca
www.facebook.com/CamosunCollege
twitter.com/camosun
www.linkedin.com/company/camosun-college
youtube.com/user/mycamosun
Kathryn Laurin, President, 250-370-3410

Campuses
Interurban Campus
4461 Interurban Rd., RR#3, Victoria, BC V9E 2C1, Canada
Fax: 250-370-3750

Post Secondary/Technical

Abbotsford: BC Helicopters
1404 Townline Rd., Abbotsford, BC V2T 6E1
Tel: 604-639-9090; *Fax:* 604-639-9091
www.bchelicopters.com
www.facebook.com/lists/2437092329522
twitter.com/bchelicopters
Mischa Gelb, Chief Flight Instructor
mischa@bchelicopters.com

Burnaby: BC Institute of Technology
3700 Willingdon Ave., Burnaby, BC V5G 3H2, Canada
Tel: 604-434-1610; *Fax:* 604-431-6917
Toll-Free: 866-434-1610
www.bcit.ca
www.facebook.com/bcit.ca
twitter.com/bcit
www.linkedin.com/company/bcit
www.youtube.com/bcit
Dr. Tony Knowles, President
Marshall Heinekey, Acting Vice President
Dr. Verna Magee-Shepherd, Vice President

Burnaby: Brighton College
#305, 4538 Kingsway, Burnaby, BC V5H 4T9
Tel: 604-430-5608; *Fax:* 604-430-5638
study@brightoncollege.com
brightoncollege.com
www.facebook.com/brightoncollege
twitter.com/BrightonCol
www.linkedin.com/company/brighton-career-college
goo.gl/fcg4m
Patrick Zhao, Acting President

Burnaby: Cambridge College
#454, 4800 Kingsway, Burnaby, BC V5H 4J2
Tel: 604-438-7246; *Fax:* 604-438-2667
info@cambridgecollege.ca
www.cambridgecollege.ca

Burnaby: CDI College of Business, Technology, & Health Care (CDI)
Collège CDI de la Technologie et de la Santé
Headquarters
#500, 5021 Kingsway, Burnaby, BC V5H 4A5
Toll-Free: 1-800-675-4392
www.cdicollege.com
www.facebook.com/CDICollege
twitter.com/CDICollege
www.youtube.com/CDICareerCollege
Note: Graduates of the college are trained to work in the business, technology, & healthcare sectors.
Bohdan J. Bilan, Vice-President, Academics

Campuses
Victoria Campus
950 Kings Rd., Victoria, BC V8T 1W6
Vancouver Campus
#200, 789 Pender St., Vancouver, BC V6C 1H2
Burnaby Campus
#500, 5021 Kingsway, Burnaby, BC V5H 4M4
Surrey Campus
#100, 11125 - 124th St., Surrey, BC V3V 4V2
Tel: 604-585-8585
Abbotsford Campus
31838 Fraser Way South, Abbotsford, BC V2T 1V3
Richmond Campus
#100, 4351 No 3 Rd., Richmond, BC V6X 3A7
Calgary City Centre Campus
Trimac House
#100, 800 - 5th Ave. SW, Calgary, AB T2P 3T6
Tel: 888-707-0573

Calgary North Campus
#100, 403 - 33rd St. NE, Calgary, AB T2A 1X5

Calgary South Campus
Midnapore Mall
#200, 240 Midpark Way SE, Calgary, AB T2X 1N4

Edmonton City Centre Campus
P.O. Box 30
9939 Jasper Ave., Edmonton, AB T5J 2W8

Edmonton North Campus
#104, 9450 - 137th Ave., Edmonton, AB T5E 6C2

Edmonton South Campus
#2, 810 Saddleback Rd. NW, Edmonton, AB T6J 4W4

Edmonton West Campus
176 Mayfield Common, Edmonton, AB T5P 4B3

Winnipeg Campus
280 Main St., Winnipeg, MB R3C 1A9

Scarborough Campus
2131 Lawrence Ave. East, 3rd Fl., Toronto, ON M1R 3A3

Mississauga Campus
#280, 33 City Centre Dr., Mississauga, ON L5B 2N5

Hamilton Campus
#104, 14 Hughson St. South, Hamilton, ON L8N 2A1

North York Campus
#33, 4950 Yonge St., North York, ON M2N 6K1

Ajax Campus
#E100, 100 Westney Rd. South, Ajax, ON L1S 7H3

Toronto Campus
2 Bloor St. East, 16th Fl., Toronto, ON M4W 1A1
Bohdan J. Bilan, Vice-President, Academics

Montréal Campus
#700, 416, boul de Maisonneuve ouest, Montréal, QC H3A 1L2

Laval Campus
#400, 3, place Laval, Laval, QC H7N 1A2, Canada
Martin Gascon, Directeur

Québec City Campus
#20, 905, av Honore-Mercier, Quebec, QC G1R 5M6

Pointe-Claire Campus
1000, boul Saint-Jean, Pointe-Claire, QC H9R 5P1

Longueuil Campus
Complexe St-Charles
#120, 1111, rue St-Charles ouest, Longueuil, QC J4K 5G4

Burnaby: Jennings Institute for Performing Artists Inc.
1870 Sperling Ave., Burnaby, BC V5B 4K5
Tel: 604-420-3213; *Fax:* 604-420-3210
forperfomingartists@hotmail.com
Note: Established in 1974, the institute is a not-for-profit college engaged in training artists of all ages.

Burnaby: Nicola Valley Institute of Technology - Vancouver Campus (NVIT)
#200, 4355 Mathissi Place, Burnaby, BC V5G 4S8, Canada
Tel: 604-602-9555; *Fax:* 604-602-3400
info@nvit.bc.ca
www.nvit.bc.ca

Burnaby: Pacific Vocational College (PVC)
4064 McConnell Dr., Burnaby, BC V5A 3A8
Tel: 604-421-5255; *Fax:* 604-421-7445
admin@pacificvocationalcollege.ca
www.pacificvocationalcollege.ca
Note: Technical training is offered through the following programs: plumbing, sprinklerfitting, steamfitting, gasfitting, & cross connection control.
Robert F. Bradbury, President

Burnaby: ProCare Institute Inc.
#240, 4411 Hastings St., Burnaby, BC V5C 2K1
Tel: 604-291-0030; *Fax:* 604-291-0003
Toll-Free: 1-800-282-0030
procare@telus.net
www.procare.ca
Note: ProCare Institute is a private post-secondary education institution that was founded in 1987. It is registered with & accredited by the Private Career Training Institutions Agency of British Columbia. The institute offers the Health Care Assistant program, which prepares students for work in the long-term care sector.

Burnaby: Winston College
4277 Kingsway, #M11, Burnaby, BC V5H 3Z2
Tel: 604-630-2069; *Fax:* 604-630-2068
info@winstoncollege.com
www.winstoncollege.com
www.facebook.com/WinstonCollege.Burnaby

Campbell River: Canadian Outdoor Leadership Training (COLT)
Km 44, Hwy. 28 West, Campbell River, BC V9W 5C5
Tel: 250-286-3122; *Fax:* 250-286-6010
info@colt.bc.ca
www.colt.bc.ca
www.facebook.com/23897848816
www.youtube.com/user/COLTprogram

Campbell River: Discovery Community College - Campbell River Spirit Square
1130 Shoppers Row, Campbell River, BC V9W 2C8
Tel: 250-287-9850
discoverycommunitycollege.com
www.facebook.com/123788041025880
twitter.com/disccommcollege
www.youtube.com/user/DiscCommCollege

Campuses

Discovery Community College - Campbell River Robron Centre
740 Robron Rd., Campbell River, BC V9W 6J7
Tel: 250-297-9898
discoverycommunitycollege.com
www.facebook.com/123788041025880
twitter.com/disccommcollege
www.youtube.com/user/DiscCommCollege

Discovery Community College - Parksville
#201, 160 Cornfield St. South, Parksville, BC V9P 2H5
Tel: 250-468-7777
discoverycommunitycollege.com
www.facebook.com/123788041025880
twitter.com/disccommcollege
www.youtube.com/user/DiscCommCollege

Discovery Community College - Nanaimo
1713 Bowen Rd., #A-B, Nanaimo, BC V9S 1G8
Tel: 250-740-0110
discoverycommunitycollege.com
www.facebook.com/123788041025880
twitter.com/disccommcollege
www.youtube.com/user/DiscCommCollege

Discovery Community College - Selby
420 Selby St., Nanaimo, BC V9R 2R7
Tel: 250-740-0110
discoverycommunitycollege.com
www.facebook.com/123788041025880
twitter.com/disccommcollege
www.youtube.com/user/DiscCommCollege

Discovery Community College - Surrey
10040 King George Blvd., Surrey, BC V3T 2W4
Tel: 604-930-9908
discoverycommunitycollege.com
www.facebook.com/123788041025880
twitter.com/disccommcollege
www.youtube.com/user/DiscCommCollege

Discovery Community College - Maple Ridge
22141 119 Ave., Maple Ridge, BC V2X 2Y7
Tel: 604-463-1174
discoverycommunitycollege.com
www.facebook.com/123788041025880
twitter.com/disccommcollege
www.youtube.com/user/DiscCommCollege

Courtenay: Comox Valley Beauty School
911 McPhee Ave., Courtenay, BC V9N 3A1
Tel: 250-338-9982;

Kelowna: Fine-Art Bartending School - Kelowna
Invue Building
#202, 2040 Springfield Rd., Kelowna, BC V1Y 9N7
Tel: 250-863-6392
www.fineartbartending.com
Note: Since 1973, Fine Art Bartending has provided bartending training & certification. Subjects include mixology, beer & wine service, responsible alcohol service, & customer service. Fine Art Bartending is a Registered Private Trade School with Human Resources & Skills Development Canada.

Kelowna: Kelowna College of Professional Counselling (KCPC)
#101, 251 Lawrence Ave., Kelowna, BC V1Y 6L2
Tel: 250-717-0412; *Fax:* 250-717-0427
Toll-Free: 1-855-888-5272
www.counsellortraining.com
Note: The Kelowna College of Professional Counselling is accrdited by the Private Career Training Institutions Agency. Students may earn a Diploma of Applied Psychology & Counselling.
Phillip R. Hay, Executive Director & Registrar
Tristyn Hay, Director, Student Services
Libby Stowers, Ph.D., Director, Program
Ilona Sobczak, Financial Officer

Langley: New Directions - Langley
#5566, 204 St., Langley, BC V3A 1Z5
Tel: 604-530-0535; *Fax:* 604-532-0561
newdir_elsa@telus.net
www.elsanet.org
Note: New Directions in Langley, British Columbia is an English Language Services for Adults (ELSA) school.
Kate Collins, Coordinator, ELSA

Langley: RCABC (Roofing Contractors Association of British Columbia) Roofing Institute
9734 - 201st St., Langley, BC V1M 3E8
Tel: 604-882-9734; *Fax:* 604-882-9684
www.rcabc.org
Note: Instruction is delivered to the roofing & construction-related industries of British Columbia. Apprenticeship training is provided in the architectural sheet metal & the roof, damp, & waterproofing sectors.
Ivan van Spronsen, Executive. Vice-President
Barbara Porth, Manager, Administrative Services

Maple Creek: RSH International College of Cosmetology
11922 - 227th St., Maple Creek, BC V2X-6J2, Canada
Tel: 604-467-0222
www.hairdressing.ca
www.facebook.com/groups/4792886444
twitter.com/instructor6
Note: Hairstyling courses

Maple Ridge: Ridge Meadows College
20575 Thorne Ave., Maple Ridge, BC V2X 9A6
Tel: 604-466-6555; *Fax:* 604-463-5437
rmc@sd42.ca
www.rmcollege.ca
Note: The fully accredited private college offers certificate programs. General interest courses are available, as well as trades programs, such as Forklift Operator & Building Service Worker.

Merritt: Nicola Valley Institute of Technology
4155 Belshaw St., Merritt, BC V1K 1R1, Canada
Tel: 250-378-3300; *Fax:* 250-378-3332
Toll-Free: 1-877-682-330
info@nvit.bc.ca
www.nvit.bc.ca
Enrollment: 800; *Note:* Certificate & diploma programs, adult basic education, collaborative degrees & on-campus, in-community & online delivery
Ken Tourand, Director
ktourand@nvit.bc.ca
John Chenoweth, MA, Dean of Community Education & Applied Programs
jchenoweth@nvit.bc.ca

Nelson: Academy of Classical Oriental Sciences (ACOS)
303 Vernon St., Nelson, BC V1L 4E3
Tel: 250-352-5887; *Toll-Free:* 888-333-8868
registrar@acos.org
www.acos.org
Note: The Academy of Classical Oriental Sciences (ACOS) is a fully-accredited TCM and acupuncture school, founded in 1996.

New Westminster: Boucher Institute of Naturopathic Medicine
#200, 435 Columbia St., New Westminster, BC V3L 5N8
Tel: 604-777-9981; *Fax:* 604-777-9982
info@binm.org
www.binm.org
www.facebook.com/220620474675439
twitter.com/BoucherInst
www.youtube.com/BoucherInstitute

New Westminster: Central College
55 - 8th St., New Westminster, BC V3M 1N9
Tel: 604-523-2388; *Fax:* 604-523-2389
contact@centralcollege.ca
centralcollege.ca
www.facebook.com/pages/Central-College/236071536416675

New Westminster: Hilltop Academy
#440, 604 Columbia St., New Westminster, BC V3M 1A5
Tel: 604-553-0505; *Fax:* 604-357-1133
info@hilltopacademy.ca
www.hilltopacademy.ca
Note: The academy offers a fitness leadership diploma program. Graduates become BC Recreation & Park Association registered weight trainers, personal trainers, & group fitness instructors. The academy is a partner of the American Council on Exercise, so students are able to become ACE certified personal trainers.

New Westminster: Justice Institute of B.C.
715 McBride Blvd., New Westminster, BC V3L 5T4, Canada
Tel: 604-525-5422; *Fax:* 604-528-5518
Toll-Free: 1-88-865-7764
infodesk@jibc.ca
www.jibc.ca
www.facebook.com/justiceinstitute
twitter.com/JIBCnews
www.linkedin.com/company/justice-institute-of-british-columbia
www.youtube.com/user/JusticeInstitute
Michel Tarko, President
mtarko@jibc.ca
Janet Haberfield, Assistant
jhaberfield@jibc.ca

Campuses

Chilliwack Campus
5470 Dieppe St., Chilliwack, BC V2R 5Y8, Canada
Tel: 604-847-0881; *Fax:* 604-847-0134

Vancouver
555 Great Northern WayFl., Vancouver, BC V5T 1E2, Canada
Tel: 604-528-5801; *Fax:* 604-638-0137

Maple Ridge Campus
13500 - 256 St., Maple Ridge, BC V4R 1C9, Canada
Tel: 604-462-1000; *Fax:* 604-462-9149
Toll-Free: 1-888-844-0445

Okanagan Campus
825 Walrod St., Kelowna, BC V1Y 2S4, Canada
Tel: 250-469-6020; *Fax:* 250-469-6022

Victoria Campus
810 Fort St., Victoria, BC V8W 1H8, Canada
Tel: 250-405-3500; *Fax:* 250-405-3505

Fire & Safety Training Centre
13500 - 256 St., Maple Ridge, BC V4R 1C9, Canada
Tel: 604-462-1000; *Fax:* 604-462-9149
Toll-Free: 1-888-844-0445
fire@jibc.ca
www.facebook.com/JIBC.FSD
Note: Courses offered on marine & industrial firefighting, emergency response to incidents involving hazardous materials, fire service training from recruit to chief officer.
Dan Murphy, Manager

New Westminster: West Coast College of Massage Therapy - New Westminster Campus (WCCMT)
613 Columbia St., New Westminster, BC V3M 1A7
Tel: 604-520-1844
admissions@collegeofmassage.com
collegeofmassage.com
www.facebook.com/MassageTherapyColleges

Campuses

West Coast College of Massage Therapy - Victoria Campus (WCCMT)
#101 - 637 Bay St., Victoria, BC V8T 5L2
Tel: 250-381-9800; *Fax:* 250-381-9801
vicadmissions@collegeofmassage.com

Canadian College of Massage & Hydrotherapy - Toronto Campus (CCMH)
250 Davisville Ave., Toronto, ON M4S 1H2
Tel: 416-736-4576; *Fax:* 416-736-9382
Toll-Free: 877-748-7800
susyg@collegeofmassage.com

Canadian College of Massage & Hydrotherapy - Cambridge Campus (CCMH)
#4, 405 Maple Grove Rd., Cambridge, ON N3E 1B6
Tel: 519-650-5533; *Fax:* 519-650-5507
davidm@collegeofmassage.com

Canadian College of Massage & Hydrotherapy - Halifax Campus (CCMH)
Mumford Professional Centre
#180, 6960 Mumford Rd., Halifax, NS B3L 4P1
Tel: 902-484-0158; *Fax:* 902-832-1077
sheric@nscollegeofmassage.com

North Vancouver: Vogue Esthetics College
#201/229, 1433 Lonsdale Ave., North Vancouver, BC V7M 2H9
Tel: 604-983-9900; *Fax:* 604-986-4645
info@voguecollege.com
www.voguecollege.com
www.facebook.com/110443645675605
www.twitter.com/voguec

Port Coquitlam: All Body Laser Corp. Training Institute
#140, 2627 Shaughnessy St., Port Coquitlam, BC V3C 0E1
Tel: 604-773-7515; *Fax:* 778-285-1519
marina@allbodylaser.com
www.allbodylaser.com/training
Note: Specialized training institute in the area of cosmetic medical laser technology and advanced skin care.

Port Coquitlam: Sprott-Shaw Community College
#200, 1405 Broadway St., Port Coquitlam, BC V3C 6L6
Tel: 604-552-9711
www.sprottshaw.com
www.facebook.com/sprottshaw
twitter.com/sprottshaw
www.flickr.com/photos/sprottshaw/collections
Note: Trades programs are offered at the Port Coquitlam location.

Port Moody: Western Montessori Teachers' College
#108, 135 Balmoral Dr., Port Moody, BC V3H 1X7, Canada
Tel: 604-461-7132; *Toll-Free:* 1-888-832-4030
wmtcbc@telus.net
www.westernmontessori.ca

Campuses

AB Office
P.O. Box 1120
Bragg Creek, AB T0L 0K0, Canada
Tel: 403-949-2238; *Fax:* 403-949-2238
WMTCab@telus.net

Prince George: ABC Safety & First Aid Training Services
#215, 1990 Ogilvie St., Prince George, BC V2N 6C5
Tel: 250-960-1112
www.abcsoffirstaid.ca
Note: Training is provided in all areas of first aid training & safety. Instructors for ABC Safety & First Aid Training Services are certified by WorkSafe BC & EMP Canada.
Robbin Worthington, Manager
Melanie Funk, Evaluator & Instructor
Christine Hale, Evaluator & Instructor

Revelstoke: Canadian Avalanche Association
P.O. Box 2759
110 MacKenzie Ave., Revelstoke, BC V0E 2S0
Tel: 250-837-2141; *Fax:* 250-366-2094
canav@avalanche.ca
www.avalanche.ca
Note: The Canadian Avalanche Association offers an Industry Training Program for avalanche workers. The Industry Training Program is a fully bonded, private, post-secondary educational institution that teaches over 500 student each year across Canada.
Joe Obad, Executive Director, 250-837-2435
jobad@avalanche.ca
Bridget Daughney, Manager, Industry Training Program, 250-837-2435, ext. 223
itpadmin@avalanche.ca

Surrey: BC College of Optics
#208, 10070 King George Blvd., Surrey, BC V3T 2W4
Tel: 604-581-0101; *Fax:* 604-581-0107
Toll-Free: 877-581-0106
tmorse@uniserve.com
www.bccollegeofoptics.ca
Note: Private post-secondary training facility teaching opticianry and contact lens fitting.

Surrey: Stenberg College
#750, 13450 - 102nd Ave., Surrey, BC V3T 5X3, Canada
Tel: 604-580-2772; *Fax:* 604-580-2774
Toll-Free: 1-866-580-2772
www.stenbergcollege.com
Note: Resident care attendant; community support worker; nursing unit clerk, medical office assistant; institutional aid; veterinary assistant; practical nursing program; automotive technician
Jeremy Sabell, President

Surrey: West Coast College of Health Care
#204, 9648 - 128 St., Surrey, BC V3T 2X9
Tel: 604-951-6644; *Toll-Free:* 1-800-807-8558
admin@westcoastcollege.com
www.westcoastcollege.com
www.facebook.com/pages/West-Coast-College/173782172655449
Note: West Coast College of Health Care provides health & human services training. Programs include instruction to become a medical laboratory assistant, a pharmacy technician, & a veterinary assistant. The college is accredited by the Private Career Training Institutions Agency of British Columbia.
Jill Arnold, Director

Vancouver: Ashton College
1190 Melville St., Vancouver, BC V6E 3W1
Tel: 604-899-0803; *Fax:* 604-899-0830
Toll-Free: 866-759-6006
info@ashtoncollege.com
www.ashtoncollege.com
Other Information: Toll Free Fax: 866-759-6009
www.facebook.com/AshtonCollege
twitter.com/AshtonCollege
www.youtube.com/user/AshtonCommunications

Schools

School of Business

School of Part-Time Studies

School of Continuing Education

Vancouver: Blanche Macdonald Centre
City Square
#100, 555 West 12th Ave., Vancouver, BC V5Z 3X7
Tel: 604-685-0347
info@blanchemacdonald.com
www.blanchemacdonald.com
www.facebook.com/blanchemacdonaldcentre/
twitter.com/blancheworld/
www.pinterest.com/blancheworld/
Note: Since 1960, the Blanche Macdonald Centre has provided training in the areas of fashion design & merchandising, makeup artistry, hair design, nail technology, & spa therapy.
Lise Graham, Managing Director
lise@blanchemacdonald.com
Barbara Johnston, Managing Director
barb@blanchemacdonald.com
Jaye Wong Klippenstein, Director, International Marketing
jaye@blanchemacdonald.com

Vancouver: BM Chan International Cosmetology College
3012 Kingsway, Vancouver, BC V5R 5J7
Tel: 604-437-3109
info@bmchan.com
www.bmchan.com
Note: Established in 1985, the accredited cosmetology college provides training & diploma courses in hair design, medical esthetics, & nail technology.
Monita Chan, Founder & Managing Director

Vancouver: Body Glamour Institute of Beauty by Anita Inc.
1919 Lonsdale Ave., Vancouver, BC V7M-2K3
Tel: 604-904-4111; *Fax:* 604-980-5744
anitaamini@hotmail.com
www.bodyglamourinc.com
www.facebook.com/195386870484936

Vancouver: Cambridge Western Academy (CWA)
473 West Hastings St., Vancouver, BC V6B 1L4
Tel: 604-622-4446; *Fax:* 604-909-4850
info@cwacanada.com
www.cwacanada.com
www.facebook.com/136613179692048
Note: Cambridge Western Academy is associated with Cambridge International College (CIC) in Australia. They provide English language courses.
Roger Ferrett, Principal & CEO

Vancouver: Canadian College of English Language
#450, 1050 Alberni St., Vancouver, BC V6E 1A3
Tel: 604-688-9366
www.canada-english.com
Note: An English certificate & diploma are offered, as well as English for business lessons, & English tutoring.
Jim Clark, Chair & Owner
Lane Clark, Chief Executive Officer
Jay Ariken, Chief Operating Officer & Academic Director
Jeremy Clark, Chief Information Officer

***Vancouver:* Canadian College of Shiatsu Therapy (CCST)**
142 Lonsdale Ave., Vancouver, BC V7M 2E8
Tel: 604-904-4187; *Fax:* 604-904-4183
school@oyayubi.com
www.shiatsuvancouver.ca
www.facebook.com/160433124015383
twitter.com/ShiatsuCollege

***Vancouver:* Canadian Electrolysis College Ltd. (CEC)**
#265, 1651 Commercial Dr., Vancouver, BC V5L 3Y3
Tel: 604-319-2515
info@canadianelectrolysiscollege.ca
www.canadianelectrolysiscollege.ca
Note: Opened in 1986, the Canadian Electrolysis College provides state of the art training for professional electrologists, featuring both theory & practical instruction. Graduates receive a diploma & are able to apply for membership uin The Association of Professional Electrologists of BC & the Federation of Canadian Electrolysis Associations.
Athena Martins, RE, CCE, CPE, Contact

***Vancouver:* Canadian Institute of Gemmology (CIG)**
P.O. Box 57010
Vancouver, BC V5K 5G6
Tel: 604-530-8569; *Toll-Free:* 1-800-294-2211
info@cigem.ca
www.cigem.ca
Note: The institute provides the opportunity to learn about gems, diamonds, & jewellery. Examples of courses include introductory gemmology, advanced gemmology, & appraisal.

***Vancouver:* Canadian Tourism College (CTC)**
#501, 1755 West Broadway, Vancouver, BC V6J 4S5
Tel: 604-736-8000; *Fax:* 604-731-9819
Toll-Free: 1-877-731-9810
www.tourismcollege.com
www.facebook.com/ctcfans
twitter.com/tourismcollege1
www.youtube.com/user/tourismcollegeCTC
Note: The Canadian Tourism College was established in 1980 to offer hospitality & tourism education in British Columbia. The college is fully accredited college by the Private Career Training Institutions Agency of British Columbia.

***Vancouver:* Dorset College**
1885 West Broadway, Vancouver, BC V6J 1Y5
Tel: 604-879-8686; *Fax:* 604-874-8686
Toll-Free: 888-272-3333
info@dorsetcollege.bc.ca
www.dorsetcollege.bc.ca

***Vancouver:* Emily Carr Institute of Art & Design**
1399 Johnston St., Vancouver, BC V6H 3R9, Canada
Tel: 604-844-3800; *Fax:* 604-844-3801
Toll-Free: 1-800-832-7788
www.eciad.ca
Enrollment: 1880
Dr. Ronald Burnett, President

***Vancouver:* Erickson College International**
2021 Columbia St., Vancouver, BC V5Y 3C9
Tel: 604-879-5600; *Fax:* 604-879-7234
Toll-Free: 1-800-665-6949
info@erickson.edu
www.erickson.edu
Note: Erickson College offers certified professional coach training.
Lawrence McGinnis, LLB, Executive Director
corporate@erickson.edu
Talyaa Vardar, Head, Corporate Development
talyaa@erickson.edu

***Vancouver:* Eurocentres Vancouver**
#250, 815 West Hastings St., Vancouver, BC V6C 1B4
Tel: 604-688-7942; *Fax:* 604-688-7985
info@languagecanada.com
www.languagecanada.com
www.facebook.com/eurocentres.canada.schools
twitter.com/eurocentrescan
www.flickr.com/people/eurocentrescanada
Note: Eurocentres Vancouver provides instruction in English as a Second Language to international students.

***Vancouver:* Gateway College**
395 West Broadway, Vancouver, BC V5Y 1A7
Tel: 604-738-0285; *Fax:* 604-738-0994
info@gwcollege.ca
www.gwcollege.ca
Other Information: Admissions Office, Phone: 604-738-0994
Note: Founded in 1986, the college offers programs that lead to careers such as a health care assistant, a long-term care aide, a nursing assistant, & a dementia professional. Red Cross emergency first aid training is also available.
Gateway College is a member of the following organizations: Private Career Training Institutes Agency, British Columbia Career Colleges Association, British Columbia Education Quality Assurance, National Association of Career Colleges, BC Care, & the Better Business Bureau.

***Vancouver:* Granville Business College**
#725, 570 Dunsmuir St., Vancouver, BC V6B 1Y1
Tel: 604-683-8850; *Fax:* 604-682-7115
Toll-Free: 1-800-661-9885
vetassistant@telus.net
www.vet-assistant.com
Note: Granville Business College is accredited by the Private Career Training Institutions Agency. Since 1993, the college has prepared students to work as veterinary office assistants in the animal health care sector.

***Vancouver:* MTI Community College - Vancouver**
541 Seymour St., Vancouver, BC V6B 3K3, Canada
Tel: 604-682-6020; *Fax:* 604-682-6468
Toll-Free: 1-866-682-6020
vancouver@mticc.com
www.metrocollege.net
www.facebook.com/mticc
www.twitter.com/MTI_College
ca.linkedin.com/in/mticareercollege
Note: ECCE; Residential Care; Long Term Care Aide; Community Support Worker; Internet Development; MCSE

Campuses

Surrey Campus
10072 King George Blvd., Surrey, BC V3T 2W4, Canada
Tel: 604-583-6020; *Fax:* 604-583-6019
surrey@mticc.com

Coquitlam Campus
#405, 2963 Glen Dr., Coquitlam, BC V3B 2P7, Canada
Tel: 604-464-8718; *Fax:* 604-942-6355
coquitlam@mticc.com

Burnaby Campus
#200, 4980 Kingsway, Burnaby, BC V5H 4K7, Canada
Tel: 604-437-6030; *Fax:* 604-437-6036
burnaby@mticc.com

Chilliwack Campus
#107, 7491 Vedder Rd., Chilliwack, BC V2R 4E7, Canada
Tel: 604-824-6081; *Fax:* 604-824-6084
chilliwack@mticc.com

Abbotsford Campus
#308, 2777 Gladwin Rd., Abbotsford, BC V2T 4V1, Canada
Tel: 604-864-8920; *Fax:* 604-864-8947
abbotsford@mticc.com

***Vancouver:* Native Education College (NEC)**
285 East 5th Ave., Vancouver, BC V5T 1H2
Tel: 604-873-3772; *Fax:* 604-873-9152
Info@NECVancouver.org
www.necvancouver.org
Note: The college opened in 1967 to offer developmental, vocational, & applied academic programs to Aboriginal adult students. The non-profit society is governed by a Board of Directors.
Keith Henry, Chair

***Vancouver:* Pacific Gateway International College (PGIC)**
1155 Robson St., 3rd Fl., Vancouver, BC V6E 1B5, Canada
Tel: 604-687-3595; *Fax:* 604-687-3586
info@pgicvancouver.com
pgic.ca
www.facebook.com/pages/PGIC-Vancouver/181044735269225

Toronto Campus
2040 Yonge St., 3rd Fl., Toronto, ON M4S 1Z9, Canada
Tel: 416-977-9800; *Fax:* 416-977-9801
info@pgicvancouver.com

***Vancouver:* Rhodes Wellness College**
#280, 1125 Howe St., Vancouver, BC V6Z 2K8
Tel: 604-708-4416; *Fax:* 604-708-4418
Toll-Free: 1-877-708-4416
admin@rhodescollege.ca
www.rhodescollege.ca
Note: Since 1996, Rhodes Wellness College has offered coaching, counselling, & wellness training to certify professional life coaches & counsellors.
Bea Rhodes, B.A., M.Ed., Founder & President, 604-708-4416, ext. 26
bea@rhodescollege.ca
Brendan Stitchman, R.P.C., Director, Training, 604-708-4416, ext. 31
brendan@rhodescollege.ca
Denise Stroude, R.P.C., Director, Admissions, 604-708-4416, ext. 23
denise@rhodescollege.ca
Kim Waters, Office Manager
kim@rhodescollege.ca

***Vancouver:* Vancouver School of Theology**
6000 Iona Dr., Vancouver, BC V6T 1L4, Canada
Tel: 604-822-9031; *Fax:* 604-822-9212
Toll-Free: 1-866-822-9031
possibilities@vst.edu
www.vst.edu
Note: Multi-denominational graduate school educating leaders for the church, service agencies & businesses
Rev. Dr. Wendy Fletcher, Principal

***Vancouver:* Western Imperial College of Canada**
#201, 2460 Commercial Dr., Vancouver, BC V5N 4B9
Tel: 604-872-1236
wiccbc.tripod.com
Note: The college was established by ESL International in association with Aspen University. Western Imperial College of Canada offers Masters programs in Business Management & Information Technology. Imperial College is registered with the Private Post-Secondary Education Commission of British Columbia.
Jay Ariken, Dean

***Victoria:* Academy of Excellence Hair Design & Aesthetics Ltd.**
303 Goldstream Ave., Victoria, BC V9B 2W4
Tel: 250-386-7843; *Fax:* 250-386-0090
excellence@telus.net
www.academyofexcellencevictoria.com
Note: Established in 1963, the Academy of Excellence offers career training in hair design & spa therapy.
Lorie Chadsey, Director & Esthetic / Spa Therapy Instructor
Tina Kelly, Registrar
Danielle St. Jacques Rand, Registrar
Greg Abbott, Manager, Hair Design Education

***Victoria:* Aveda Institute - Victoria**
1400 Douglas St., Victoria, BC V8W 2G1
Tel: 250-386-7985; *Fax:* 250-386-7945
Toll-Free: 1-800-391-7873
info@avedainstitutevictoria.ca
www.avedainstitutevictoria.ca
www.facebook.com/178218612191241?ref=ts&sk=wall
Note: Founded in 1978, the Aveda Institute offers Private Career Training Institutions Agency accredited programs leading to careers in hair styling or cosmetology.
Paul Da Costa, Founder, Aveda Institute Victoria
Roxana Barlow, Director

Campuses

Aveda Institute - Calgary
225 - 8th Ave. SW, Calgary, AB T2P 1B7
Tel: 403-264-5070; *Fax:* 403-264-5065
Toll-Free: 1-800-391-7873
Calgary@avedainstitute.ca
www.avedainstitutevictoria.ca
www.facebook.com/AvedaInstituteCalgary
twitter.com/Aveda604
Note: Founded in 1978, the Aveda Institute offers Private Career Training Institutions Agency accredited programs leading to careers in hair styling or cosmetology.

Aveda Institute - Edmonton
10632 - 82nd Ave., Edmonton, AB T6E 2A7
Tel: 780-433-7115; *Fax:* 780-433-7241
Toll-Free: 1-800-391-7873
Edmonton@avedainstitute.ca
www.avedainstitutevictoria.ca
Note: Founded in 1978, the Aveda Institute offers Private Career Training Institutions Agency accredited programs leading to careers in hair styling or cosmetology.

Aveda Institute - Winnipeg
80 Rorie St., Winnipeg, MB R3B 3L6
Tel: 204-452-7380; *Fax:* 204-284-1355
Toll-Free: 1-800-391-7873
winnipeg@avedainstitute.ca
www.avedainstitutevictoria.ca
www.facebook.com/AvedaInstituteWinnipeg
twitter.com/Aveda204
Note: Founded in 1978, the Aveda Institute offers Private Career Training Institutions Agency accredited programs leading to careers in hair styling or cosmetology.

Aveda Institute - Montréal
3613, boul St-Laurent, Montréal, QC H2X 2V5
Tel: 514-499-9494; *Fax:* 514-499-1566
Toll-Free: 1-800-391-7873
Montreal@avedainstitute.ca
www.avedainstitutevictoria.ca
www.facebook.com/avedamontreallifestyle
twitter.com/AvedaMontreal
Note: Founded in 1978, the Aveda Institute offers Private Career Training Institutions Agency accredited programs leading to careers in hair styling or cosmetology.

Aveda Institute - Toronto
125 King St. East, Toronto, ON M5C 1G6
Tel: 416-921-2961; *Fax:* 416-941-9526
Toll-Free: 1-800-391-7873
Toronto@avedainstitute.ca
www.avedainstitutevictoria.ca
www.facebook.com/AvedaInstituteToronto
twitter.com/Aveda416
Note: Founded in 1978, the Aveda Institute offers Private Career Training Institutions Agency accredited programs leading to careers in hair styling or cosmetology.

Aveda Institute - Vancouver
#101, 111 Water St., Vancouver, BC V6B 1A7
Tel: 604-669-6992; *Fax:* 604-669-6982
Toll-Free: 1-800-391-7873
Vancouver@avedainstitute.ca
www.avedainstitutevictoria.ca
www.facebook.com/AvedaInstituteVancouver
twitter.com/Aveda604
Note: Founded in 1978, the Aveda Institute offers Private Career Training Institutions Agency accredited programs leading to careers in hair styling or cosmetology.

Victoria: BC School of Art Therapy
125 Skinner St., Victoria, BC V9A 6X4
Tel: 250-598-6434; *Fax:* 250-598-6449
info@bcsat.com
www.bcsat.com
Note: The School of Art Therapy offers a post-master's certifcate & a post-bachelor's diploma. The organization is a registered charity.
Barbara M. Klassen, President
Lucille Proulx, Executive Director
Michelle Winkel, Registrar & Practicum Coordinator

Victoria: Canadian Acupressure College
256 Linden Ave., Victoria, BC V8V 4E5
Tel: 250-388-7475; *Fax:* 250-388-7498
Toll-Free: 1-877-909-2244
cai@islandnet.com
www.acupressureshiatsuschool.com
Note: The Canadian Acupressure College is a member of the Health Action Network Society, Association of Holistic Practitioners, & Natural Health Practitioners of Canada. The college is registered by the Private Career Training Institutions Agency of British Columbia.
Since 1994, the Canadian Acupressure College has developed health practitioners who use acupressure for human & social change.
Kathy de Bucy, Founder, Administrator & Director

Victoria: Canadian College of Performing Arts
1701 Elgin Rd., Victoria, BC V8R 5L7, Canada
Tel: 250-595-9970; *Fax:* 250-595-0779
admin@ccpacanada.com
www.ccpacanada.com
www.facebook.com/144880562234742
twitter.com/CCPACanada
Enrollment: 84; *Note:* Two, 1-year extensive training programs in acting, voice, dance & career management
Steven Seltzer, Contact, 250-545-9970
communications@ccpacanada.com

Victoria: Canadian Onsite Wastewater Institute
P.O. Box 44121
2947 Tillicum Rd., Victoria, BC V9A 7K1
Tel: 250-590-2514
info@canowi.com
www.canowi.com

Campuses
Canadian Onsite Wastewater Institute - Ontario & Eastern Canada
P.O. Box 831
Cobourg, ON K9A 4S3
Tel: 905-372-2722; *Fax:* 905-372-0322
Info-cowi@cogeco.ca
www.canowi.com

Victoria: Lester B. Pearson United World College
650 Pearson College Dr., Victoria, BC V9C 4H7, Canada
Tel: 250-391-2411; *Fax:* 250-391-2412
www.pearsoncollege.ca
www.facebook.com/PearsonUWC
twitter.com/PCUWC
www.youtube.com/user/PearsonUWC
David Hawley, Director
dhawley@pearsoncollege.ca

Victoria: Waterworks Technology School
#101, 2610 Douglas St., Victoria, BC V8T 4M1
Tel: 250-385-5407; *Fax:* 250-385-5409
Toll-Free: 888-685-2288
wnowlan@wtechs.ca
www.waterworks-tech.com

Victoria: Western Academy of Photography
755A Queens Ave., Victoria, BC V8T 1M2
Tel: 250-383-1522; *Fax:* 250-383-1534
Toll-Free: 1-866-889-1235
infowaop@shaw.ca
www.westernacademyofphotography.com
www.facebook.com/group.php?gid=123708291001707
Note: Western Academy of Photography offers training in professional photography, photojournalism, & journalism.

West Vancouver: Vancouver Art Therapy Institute
#350, 1425 Marine Dr., West Vancouver, BC V7T 1B9, Canada
Tel: 604-681-8284; *Fax:* 604-926-5728
vatimail@telus.net
www.vati.bc.ca

Westminster: Canadian Health Care Academy
93 Sixth St., Westminster, BC V3L 2Z8
Tel: 604-540-2421; *Fax:* 604-540-8550
info@chcabc.com
www.chcabc.com
www.facebook.com/223861147627540
twitter.com/CanHealthCareAc

Winfield: Interior Heavy Equipment Operator School
Also known as: IHE School
#2 - 10058 Hwy. 97 North, Winfield, BC V4V 1P8
Tel: 250-766-3853; *Fax:* 877-347-6384
Toll-Free: 866-399-3853
info@iheschool.com
www.iheschool.com
www.facebook.com/iheschool?sk=wall
twitter.com/IHESchool

Campuses
Interior Heavy Equipment Operator School - Alberta Campus
Also known as: IHE School
36040 Range Road 284A, Innisfail, AB T4G 1T8
Tel: 250-766-3853; *Fax:* 877-347-6384
Toll-Free: 866-399-3853
info@iheschool.com
www.iheschool.com
www.facebook.com/iheschool?sk=wall
twitter.com/IHESchool

Manitoba

Government Agencies

Winnipeg: Manitoba Ministry of Education & Training
#168, 450 Broadway, Winnipeg, MB R3C 0Y8, Canada
Tel: 204-945-3720; *Fax:* 204-945-1291
minedu@leg.gov.mb.ca
www.edu.gov.mb.ca
Other Information: Facebook by Region: www.gov.mb.ca/socialmedia/facebook/index.html
Hon. Ian Wishart, Minister of Education & Advanced Learning, 204-945-3720
minedu@leg.gov.mb.ca

School Boards/Districts/Divisions

Public

Altona: Border Land School Division
P.O. Box 390
120 - 9th St. NW, Altona, MB R0G 0B0, Canada
Tel: 204-324-6491; *Fax:* 204-324-1664
Toll-Free: 1-866-324-6491
blsd@blsd.ca
www.blsd.ca
Other Information: Transportation Office: 204-427-2091; Maintenance: 204-324-9536
Number of Schools: 17; *Grades:* K - 12; French Immersion
Craig Smiley, Board Chair, 204-324-5352
Krista Curry, CEO/Superintendent, 204-324-6491, ext. 1010
Carol Braun, Assistant Superintendent, 204-324-6491, ext. 1011
Rachel Geirnaert, Secretary-Treasurer, 204-324-6491, ext. 1012
Shauna Hamm, Student Services Manager, 204-324-6491, ext. 1013

Beausejour: Sunrise School Division
Sunrise Education Center
P.O. Box 1206
344 - 2nd St. N, Beausejour, MB R0E 0C0, Canada
Tel: 204-268-6500; *Fax:* 204-268-6545
Toll-Free: 1-866-444-5559
www.sunrisesd.ca
Other Information: Transportation, Phone: 204-444-2498; Business, Fax: 204-268-4149
Number of Schools: 24; *Grades:* K - 12; Adult Education
Lynne Champagne, Chair, 204-268-4239
trustee.champagne@sunrisesd.ca
Barb Isaak, Superintendent/CEO, 204-268-6500
bisaak@sunrisesd.ca
Paul Barnard, Assistant Superintendent of Student Support Services, 204-268-6535
leblietrudel@sunrisesd.ca
Cathy Tymko, Assistant Superintendent of Student Learning & Instruction, 204-268-6543
ctymko@sunrisesd.ca
Elise Downey, Secretary-Treasurer, 204-268-6514
edowney@sunrisesd.ca

Birtle: Park West School Division
P.O. Box 68
1126 St. Claire St., Birtle, MB R0M 0C0, Canada
Tel: 204-842-2100; *Fax:* 204-842-2110
Toll-Free: 877-418-5320
www.pwsd.ca
Number of Schools: 7 elementary; 1 middle-secondary; 2 secondary; 4 K-12; *Grades:* K - 12; *Enrollment:* 1800; *Number of Employees:* 196 teaching; 214 non-teaching
Darren Naherniak, Chair
dnaherniak@pwsd.ca
Tim Mendel, CEO/Superintendent, 204-842-2100
tmendel@pwsd.ca
Gerald Puhach, Secretary-Treasurer, 204-842-2112
gpuhach@pwsd.ca
Colleen Clearsky, Director of Aboriginal Education, 204-859-2777
cclearsky@pwsd.ca
Rick Hrycak, Transportation Supervisor
rhrycak@pwsd.ca

Brandon: Brandon School Division
1031 - 6th St., Brandon, MB R7A 4K5, Canada
Tel: 204-729-3100; *Fax:* 204-727-2217
info@bsd.ca
www.bsd.ca
twitter.com/BrandonMBSD
Number of Schools: 18 elementary; 3 secondary; 1 alternative; *Grades:* K.-12; French Immersion; *Enrollment:* 8284
George Buri, Chair, 204-727-3156
buri.george@brandonsd.mb.ca
Donna Michaels, PhD, Superintendent of Schools/CEO
michaels.donna@brandonsd.mb.ca
Greg Malazdrewicz, Assistant Superintendent
malazdrewicz.greg@brandonsd.mb.ca
Denis Labossiere, Secretary-Treasurer
labossiere.denis@bsd.ca
Becky Switzer, Director of Human Resources
switzer.becky@bsd.ca
Brent Ewasiuk, Director of Management of Information Systems Technology
ewasiuk.brent@bsd.ca
Mel Clark, Director of Facilities and Transportation
clark.mel@bsd.ca
Ron Harkness, Transportation Supervisor, 204-729-3976
harkness.ron@bsd.ca

Carman: **Prairie Rose School Division**
P.O. Box 1510
45 Main St. South, Carman, MB R0G 0J0, Canada
Tel: 204-745-2003; *Fax:* 204-745-3699
Toll-Free: 866-745-3699
prsd@prsdmb.ca
www.prsdmb.ca
Number of Schools: 11; *Grades:* K - 12; *Enrollment:* 2278
Terry Osiowy, Superintendent
Ron Sugden, Assistant Superintendent
Agnes Gaultier, Secretary Treasurer
Wilma Ritzer, Director of Student Services
Kevin Affleck, Operations Supervisor

Dauphin: **Mountain View School Division**
P.O. Box 715
Dauphin, MB R7N 3B3, Canada
Tel: 204-638-3001; *Fax:* 204-638-7250
www.mvsd.ca
Number of Schools: 9 elementary; 1 middle; 4 secondary; 2 K-12; *Grades:* K-12; *Enrollment:* 3300
Della Perih, Chairperson
DPerih@mvsd.ca
Donna Davidson, Superintendent & CEO
ddavidson@mvsd.ca
Bart Michaleski, Secretary-Treasurer
michale@mvsd.ca
Dan Ward, Assistant Superintendent, Programs and Planning
dward@mvsd.ca
Ernest Karpiak, Transportation Supervisor, 204-638-2268
ekarpiak@mvsd.ca

Eriksdale: **Lakeshore School Division**
P.O. Box 100
23 - 2nd Ave., Eriksdale, MB R0C 0W0, Canada
Tel: 204-739-2101; *Fax:* 204-739-2145
admin@lakeshoresd.mb.ca
www.lakeshoresd.mb.ca
twitter.com/LakeshoreSD
Number of Schools: 11; *Enrollment:* 1226; *Number of Employees:* 270
Jim Cooper, Board Chair, 204-739-5469
cooperj@lakeshoresd.mb.ca
Janet Martell, Superintendent, 204-739-2101, ext. 1223
martelj@lakeshoresd.mb.ca
Leanne Peters, Assistant Superintendent, 204-739-2101, ext. 1240
petersl@lakeshoresd.mb.ca
Marlene Michno, Secretary Treasurer, 204-739-2101, ext. 1222
michnom@lakeshoresd.mb.ca
Brett Sander, Director, Technology & Information Systems, 204-739-2101, ext. 1225
sanderb@lakeshoresd.mb.ca
Curtis Basso, Director, Operations & Infrastructure, 204-739-2101, ext. 1227
bassoc@lakeshoresd.mb.ca

Flin Flon: **Flin Flon School Division**
9 Terrace Ave., Flin Flon, MB R8A 1S2, Canada
Tel: 204-681-3413; *Fax:* 204-681-3417
www.ffsd.mb.ca
twitter.com/MBSchoolBoards
Number of Schools: 1 elementary community 1 elementary dual track; 1 secondary; 1 alternative; *Grades:* K - 12; Alternative Ed.; *Enrollment:* 1000
Murray Skeavington, Chair
mskeavington@ffsd.mb.ca
Blaine Veitch, Superintendent
bveitch@ffsd.mb.ca
Dean Grove, Assistant Superintendent
dgrove@ffsd.mb.ca
Heather Fleming, Secretary-Treasurer
hfleming@ffsd.mb.ca
Brent Osika, Transportation Supervisor
bosika@ffsd.mb.ca

Gimli: **Evergreen School Division**
P.O. Box 1200
140 Centre Ave. West, Gimli, MB R0C 1B0, Canada
Tel: 204-642-6260; *Fax:* 204-642-7273
info@esd.ca
www.esd.mb.ca
Number of Schools: 1 primary; 4 elementary-middle; 3 secondary; *Grades:* K - 12; Continuing Ed.; *Enrollment:* 1550; *Number of Employees:* 273
Ruth Ann Furgala, Board Chair, 204-378-2901
ruthann.furgala@esd.ca
Roza Gray, Superintendent & CEO, 204-642-6267
roza.gray@esd.ca
Scott Hill, Assistant Superintendent, 204-642-6278
scott.hill@esd.ca
Gary Thompson, Manager of Operations, 204-642-6269
gary.thompson@esd.ca
Fay Cassidy, Student Services Coordinator, 204-642-6279
fay.cassidy@esd.ca
Sandra Ferguson, Safety Officer, 204-641-1365
sandra.ferguson@esd.ca
Charlie Grieve, Secretary-Treasurer, 204-642-6266
charlie.grieve@esd.ca

Gladstone: **Pine Creek School Division**
P.O. Box 420
25 Brown St., Gladstone, MB R0J 0T0, Canada
Tel: 204-385-2216; *Fax:* 204-385-2825
pcsddo@pinecreeksd.mb.ca
www.pinecreeksd.mb.ca
Number of Schools: 5 elementary; 2 senior high; 7 Hutterite Colony; *Grades:* K - 12; *Enrollment:* 1100
Diedrich Toews, Board Chair
dtoews@pinecreeksd.mb.ca
Brian Gouriluk, Superintendent
bgouriluk@pinecreeksd.mb.ca
Robyn Winters, Secretary Treasurer
rwinters@pinecreeksd.mb.ca
Michelle Marriott, Student Services Coordinator
mmarriott@pinecreeksd.mb.ca

Killarney: **Turtle Mountain School Division**
P.O. Box 280
435 Williams Ave., Killarney, MB R0K 1G0, Canada
Tel: 204-523-7531; *Fax:* 204-523-7269
dbo@tmsd.mb.ca
www.tmsd.mb.ca
Number of Schools: 1 elementary / middle school; 2 K - 12 schools; 2 adult ed; 4 Hutterite colony; *Grades:* K - 12; Continuing Ed.
Tim De Ruyck, Superintendent/CEO
tderuyck@tmsd.mb.ca
Tanya Edgar, Assistant Superintendent of Student Services
tedgar@tmsd.mb.ca
Kathy Siatecki, Secretary-Treasurer
ksiatecki@tmsd.mb.ca

Lorette: **Seine River School Division (SRSD)**
475-A Senez St., Lorette, MB R0A 0Y0, Canada
Tel: 204-878-4713; *Fax:* 204-878-4717
esummers@srsd.ca
www.srsd.mb.ca
Number of Schools: 16; *Grades:* K - 12; *Note:* Also offers adult learning programs.
Wendy Bloomfield, Chairperson
wbloomfield@srsd.ca
Michael Borgfjord, Superintendent/CEO
mborgfjord@srsd.ca
Paul Ilchena, Secretary-Treasurer, 204-878-4713
pilchena@srsd.ca
Elaine Lochhead, Assistant Superintendent, Student Services
elochhead@srsd.ca
Monica Biggar, Assistant Superintendent, Curriculum & Instruction
mbiggar@srsd.ca

McCreary: **Turtle River School Division**
P.O. Box 309
808 Burrows Rd., McCreary, MB R0J 1B0, Canada
Tel: 204-835-2067; *Fax:* 204-835-2426
trsd32.mb.ca
Number of Schools: 7; *Grades:* K - 12; *Enrollment:* 771; *Number of Employees:* 63 teachers; 52 support staff
Gwen McLean, Board Chair
gmclean@trsd32.mb.ca
Bev Szymesko, Superintendent/Student Services
bevs@trsd32.mb.ca
Shannon Desjardins, Secretary-Treasurer
shannon@trsd32.mb.ca
Dean Bluhm, Transportation & Maintenance Supervisor
deanb@trsd32.mb.ca
Nicole Wareham, Accountant
nicole@trsd32.mb.ca
Eric Rochon, Information & Communication Technology Technician
eric@trsd32.mb.ca

Minnedosa: **Rolling River School Division**
P.O. Box 1170
Minnedosa, MB R0J 1E0, Canada
Tel: 204-867-2754; *Fax:* 204-867-2037
rrsd@rrsd.mb.ca
www.rrsd.mb.ca
Number of Schools: 8 elementary; 4 secondary; 4 Hutterite Colony; *Grades:* K - 12
Victoria Blackbird, Board Chair
vblackbird@rrsd.mb.ca
Mary-Anne Ploshynsky, Superintendent, 204-867-2754, ext. 222
mploshynsky@rrsd.mb.ca
Marg Janssen, Assistant Superintendent
mjanssen@rrsd.mb.ca
Kathlyn McNabb, Secretary-Treasurer, 204-867-2754, ext. 226
kmcnabb@rrsd.mb.ca

Morden: **Western School Division**
#4, 75 Thornhill St., Morden, MB R6M 1P2, Canada
Tel: 204-822-4448; *Fax:* 204-822-4262
divoff@westernsd.mb.ca
www.westernsd.mb.ca
Number of Schools: 5; *Grades:* K.-12
Robyn Wiebe, Chairperson, 204-822-1458
rwiebe@westernsd.mb.ca
Stephen Ross, Superintendent of Schools/CEO
sross@westernsd.mb.ca
Carl Pedersen, Secretary-Treasurer
cpedersen@westernsd.mb.ca
Cyndy Kutzner, Assistant Superintendent
ckutzner@westernsd.mb.ca
Allan Toews, Supervisor of Operations
atoews@westernsd.mb.ca

Morris: **Red River Valley School Division**
P.O. Box 400
233 Main St., Morris, MB R0G 1K0, Canada
Tel: 204-746-2317; *Fax:* 204-746-2785
rrvsd@rrvsd.ca
www.rrvsd.ca
Number of Schools: 15; *Grades:* K - 12; *Enrollment:* 2196
Shelley Syrota, Chair
ssyrota@rrsvd.ca
Pauline Lafond-Bouchard, Superintendent & CEO, 204-746-2317, ext. 2225
plbouchard@rrsvd.ca
Darren Skog, Assistant Superintendent, 204-746-2317, ext. 2223
dskog@rrvsd.ca
Alma Mitchell, Secretary Treasurer, 204-746-2317, ext. 2226
amitchell@rrvsd.ca
Darren Cameron, Transportation Supervisor, 204-746-2317, ext. 2229
dcameron@rrvsd.ca

Neepawa: **Beautiful Plains School Division**
P.O. Box 700
213 Mountain Ave., Neepawa, MB R0J 1H0, Canada
Tel: 204-476-2387; *Fax:* 204-476-3606
bpsd@bpsd.mb.ca
www.bpsd.mb.ca
www.facebook.com/166870530146015?fref=ts
twitter.com/beautifulplains
Number of Schools: 14; *Grades:* K-12; Special Ed.; *Enrollment:* 1529; *Number of Employees:* 171 instructional staff; 45 non-teaching staff
John McNeily, Chairperson
jmcneily@bpsd.mb.ca
Jason Young, Superintendent
jyoung@bpsd.mb.ca
Gord Olmstead, Secretary-Treasurer
golmstead@bpsd.mb.ca
Rhonda Dickenson, Student Services Coordinator
rdickenson@bpsd.mb.ca
Royce Hollier, Technology Coordinator
rhollier@bpsd.mb.ca
Warren Rainka, Transportation Supervisor
wrainka@bpsd.mb.ca

Pinawa: **Whiteshell School District**
P.O. Box 130
20 Vanier Dr., Pinawa, MB R0E 1L0, Canada
Tel: 204-753-8366; *Fax:* 204-753-2237
tstef@sdwhiteshell.mb.ca
www.sdwhiteshell.mb.ca
www.facebook.com/wix
www.twitter.com/wix
Number of Schools: 1 elementary; 1 secondary; *Grades:* K-12; *Enrollment:* 206
Tim Stefanishyn, Superintendent
tstef@sdwhiteshell.mb.ca
Brian Wilcox, Board Chair
wilcoxb@sdwhiteshell.mb.ca

Portage la Prairie: **Portage la Prairie School Division**
535 - 3 St. NW, Portage la Prairie, MB R1N 2C4, Canada
Tel: 204-857-8756; *Fax:* 204-239-5998
www.plpsd.mb.ca
Number of Schools: 9; *Grades:* K - 12; *Enrollment:* 3300
Dave Citulsky, Board Chair
dave_citulsky@plpsd.mb.ca
Hazen Barrett, Superintendent
hbarrett@plpsd.mb.ca

Mike Mauws, Assistant Superintendent
Judy Smith, Manager of Business and Finance, 204-857-8756
Rochelle Rands, Director of Student Services, 204-857-8756
Tom Henry, Transportation Supervisor
thenry@plpsd.mb.ca

Selkirk: Lord Selkirk School Division (LSSD)
205 Mercy St., Selkirk, MB R1A 2C8, Canada
Tel: 204-482-5942; *Fax:* 204-482-3000
Toll-Free: 866-433-5942
lssd.boardoffice@lssd.ca
www.lssd.ca
twitter.com/lordselkirk_sd
Number of Schools: 17; *Grades:* K-12; *Enrollment:* 5000; *Note:* The schools celebrate the heritage and culture of the region - including the Brokenhead Ojibway Nation, the Scottish pioneers, the French Canadian voyageurs and the Ukrainian settlers. Also offer an adult learning programs.
Jean Oliver, Board Chair
jeanoliver@lssd.ca
Scott Kwasnitza, Superintendent/CEO
skwasnitza@lssd.ca
Brian Spurrill, Secretary Treasurer
bspurril@lssd.ca
Angie Munch, Director of Human Resources

Souris: Southwest Horizon School Division Education & Operations
P.O. Box 820
67 Willow Ave. E, Souris, MB R0K 2C0, Canada
Tel: 204-483-5533; *Fax:* 204-483-5535
www.shmb.ca
Number of Schools: 12; *Grades:* K - 12; *Enrollment:* 1793
Scott Perkin, Board Chair
scottp@shmb.ca
Carolyn Cory, Superintendent, 204-483-6248
carolync@shmb.ca
Kevin Zabowski, Secretary-Treasurer, 204-483-6261
kevinz@shmb.ca
Robin Brigden, Curriculum/SYAO Coordinator, 204-483-6234
robinb@shmb.ca

Affiliations
Melita
Finance & Payroll
P.O. Box 370
165 North St., Melita, MB R0M 1L0, Canada
www.shmb.ca

Steinbach: Hanover School Division
5 Chrysler Gate, Steinbach, MB R5G 0E2, Canada
Tel: 204-326-6471; *Fax:* 204-326-9901
info@hsd.ca
www.hsd.ca
Number of Schools: 6 elementary; 3 elementary-middle; 2 middle; 3 middle-secondary; 1 secondary; 1 K-12; *Enrollment:* 7700; *Number of Employees:* 1100
Ron Falk, Board Chair
rfalk@hsd.ca
Randy Dueck, Superintendent/CEO
rdueck@hsd.ca
Chris Gudziunas, Assistant Superintendent
cgudziunas@hsd.ca
Rick Ardies, Assistant Superintendent
rardies@hsd.ca
Geri Harder-Robson, Assistant Superintendent of Student Services
grobson@hsd.ca
Kevin Heide, Secretary-Treasurer
kheide@hsd.ca
Scott Bestvater, Business Services Manager
scottb@hsd.ca
Dave Rushforth, Human Resources Manager
drushforth@hsd.ca

Stonewall: Interlake School Division
192 - 2nd Ave. North, Stonewall, MB R0C 2Z0, Canada
Tel: 204-467-5100; *Fax:* 204-467-8334
www.isd21.mb.ca
Number of Schools: 2 elementary; 6 elementary/middle; 2 middle; 3 secondary; 9 K-12; *Grades:* K - 12; Continuing Ed.; *Enrollment:* 2796; *Number of Employees:* 229 FTE teachers; 275 support staff
Alan Campbell, Chairperson, 204-467-9626
acampbell@isd21.mb.ca
Christine Penner, Superintendent/CEO, 204-467-5100, ext. 226
cpenner@isd21.mb.ca
Margaret Ward, Assistant Superintendent, 204-467-5100, ext. 232
mward@isd21.mb.ca
Allen Leiman, Secretary/Treasurer, 204-467-5100, ext. 222
aleiman@isd21.mb.ca

Swan Lake: Prairie Spirit School Division
P.O. Box 130
15 Lorne Ave., Swan Lake, MB R0G 2S0, Canada
Tel: 204-836-2147; *Fax:* 204-825-2725
prspirit@mts.net
www.prairiespirit.mb.ca
Number of Schools: 15 schools; 14 Hutterite Colony; *Grades:* K - 12; *Enrollment:* 2479
Jan McIntyre, Board Chair
j.mcintyre@prspirit.org
Keith Murray, Superintendent of Schools
kmurray@prspirit.org
Jody Parsonage, Secretary-Treasurer
jparsonage@prspirit.org
Darryl Mason, Transportation Supervisor
dmason@prspirit.org

Swan River: Swan Valley School Division
John Kastrukoff Building
1481 - 3rd St. North, Swan River, MB R0L 1Z0, Canada
Tel: 204-734-4531
www.svsd.ca
Number of Schools: 2 elementary; 5 elementary-middle; 1 middle; 1 secondary; *Grades:* JK - 12; French Immersion
William (Bill) Schaffer, Chair
wschaffer@svsd.ca
Marilyn Marquis-Forster, Superintendent
mmarquis@svsd.ca
Brent Rausch, Secretary-Treasurer
brausch@svsd.ca
Doug Coulthart, Transportation Supervisor, 204-734-3415
dcoulthart@svsd.ca
Deborah Burnside, Coordinator of Student Services

The Pas: Kelsey School Division
P.O. Box 4700
322 Edwards Ave., The Pas, MB R9A 1R4, Canada
Tel: 204-623-6421; *Fax:* 204-623-7704
www.ksd.mb.ca
Number of Schools: 5; *Grades:* K - 12; *Enrollment:* 1733
Doug Long, Superintendent
douglong@ksd.mb.ca
Jeannette Freese, Secretary Treasurer
jfreese@ksd.mb.ca
Linda Markus, Student Services Coordinator
lindamarkus@ksd.mb.ca

Thompson: Mystery Lake School District
408 Thompson Dr. North, Thompson, MB R8N 0C5, Canada
Tel: 204-677-6150; *Fax:* 204-677-9528
sdml@mysterynet.mb.ca
www.mysterynet.mb.ca
Number of Schools: 6 elementary; 1 secondary; *Grades:* K-12; *Enrollment:* 3036; *Number of Employees:* 207 teaching staff; 94 non-teaching staff
Lorie Henderson, Superintendent of Educational Services & Programming
lhenderson@mysterynet.mb.ca
Leslie Tucker, Chair
ltucker@mysterynet.mb.ca
Kelly Knott, Secretary-Treasurer
kknott@mysterynet.mb.ca

Virden: Fort La Bosse School Division
P.O. Box 1420
523 - 9th Ave. South, Virden, MB R0M 2C0, Canada
Tel: 204-748-2692; *Fax:* 204-748-2436
flbsd@flbsd.mb.ca
www.flbsd.mb.ca
Number of Schools: 10; *Grades:* K - 12; *Enrollment:* 1400
Gary E. Draper, Chair
gdraper@flbsd.mb.ca
Barry Pitz, Superintendent
bpitz@flbsd.mb.ca
Vaughn Wilson, Supervisor of Operations
vwilson@flbsd.mb.ca
Kent Reid, Secretary-Treasurer
kreid@flbsd.mb.ca
Judy Dandridge, Coordinator of Student Services
jdandridge@flbsd.mb.ca

Winkler: Garden Valley School Division
P.O. Box 1330
750 Triple E Blvd., Winkler, MB R6W 4B3, Canada
Tel: 204-325-8335; *Fax:* 204-325-4132
gvsd@gvsd.ca
www.gvsd.ca
Number of Schools: 4 elementary; 4 elementary-middle; 2 middle; 2 secondary; 1 K-12; *Grades:* K - 12; *Enrollment:* 4374
Laurie Dyck, Board Chair
Laurie.Dyck@gvsd.ca
Vern Reimer, Superintendent/CEO
vem.reimer@gvsd.ca

Todd Monster, Assistant Superintendent
Doreen Prazak, Assistant Superintendent, Student Services
Shayne Thomson, Human Resource Manager
Ken Bergen, Supervisor of Operations
Abe Wiebe, Capital Projects Supervisor
Angela Plett, Trasportation Supervisor
angela.plett@gvsd.ca
Terry Penner, Secretary-Treasurer
terry.penner@gvsd.ca

Winnipeg: Frontier School Division
30 Speers Rd., Winnipeg, MB R2J 1L9, Canada
Tel: 204-775-9741; *Fax:* 204-775-9940
frontier@frontiersd.mb.ca
www.frontiersd.mb.ca
Number of Schools: 42; *Grades:* K - 12; *Enrollment:* 6869; *Number of Employees:* 50 support staff
Linda Ballantyne, Chairperson
lballa@frontiersd.mb.ca
Reg Klassen, Chief Superintendent
reg.klassen@frontiersd.mb.ca
Bradley Hampson, Assistant Superintendent, Technology & Library Services
Tyson MacGillivray, Assistant Superintendent, High School & Careers Program
Gerald Cattani, Secretary-Treasurer
gcatta@frontiersb.mb.ca

Winnipeg: Louis Riel School Division
900 St. Mary's Rd., Winnipeg, MB R2M 3R3, Canada
Tel: 204-257-7827; *Fax:* 204-256-8553
www.lrsd.net
www.facebook.com/LouisRielSchoolDivision
twitter.com/louis_riel_sd
Number of Schools: 31 elementary; 7 high schools; 1 technical & vocational training; 1 learning centre; *Grades:* K-12; *Enrollment:* 14216; *Number of Employees:* 1,900; *Note:* The is an amalgamation of the St. Boniface and St. Vital School Divisions.
Duane Brothers, Superintendent of Schools
duane.brothers@lrsd.net
Brad Fulton, Secretary-Treasurer
brad.fulton@lrsd.net
Louise Johnston, Chair
Louise.johnston@lrsd.net
Burke Okrainec, Transportation Supervisor
Burke.okrainec@lrsd.net
Denis Granger, Director of Student Services
Peter Kolba, Director of Facilities

Winnipeg: Pembina Trails School Division
181 Henlow Bay, Winnipeg, MB R3Y 1M7, Canada
Tel: 204-488-1757; *Fax:* 204-487-3667
ptsdwebinfo@pembinatrails.ca
www.pembinatrails.ca
www.facebook.com/157088451003481
twitter.com/PembinaTrails
Number of Schools: 18 elementary; 5 elementary-middle; 6 middle; 4 secondary; 2 alternative; *Grades:* K - 12; *Enrollment:* 13385
Tim Johnson, Chair of the Board
timjohnson@pembinatrails.ca
Ted Fransen, Superintendent of Education
tfransen@pembinatrails.ca
Craig Stahlke, Secretary Treasurer
cstahlke@pembinatrails.ca
Steve Hazelwood, Transportation Supervisor
shazelwood@pembinatrails.ca

Winnipeg: River East Transcona School Division
589 Roch St., Winnipeg, MB R2K 2P7, Canada
Tel: 204-667-7130; *Fax:* 204-661-5618
www.retsd.mb.ca
Number of Schools: 36 elementary & middle; 6 secondary; 2 learning centres; *Enrollment:* 16300; *Number of Employees:* 2,900
Colleen Carswell, Chair
ccarswell@retsd.mb.ca
Kelly Barkman, Superintendent/CEO
Joan Trubyk, Assistant Superintendent of Student Services
Jason Drysdale, Assistant Superintendent - Educational Services & Planning
Vince Mariani, Secretary-Treasurer/CFO

Winnipeg: St. James-Assiniboia School Division
2574 Portage Ave., Winnipeg, MB R3J 0H8, Canada
Tel: 204-888-7951; *Fax:* 204-831-0859
inquiries@sjsd.net
www.sjsd.net
Other Information: Continuing Ed., Phone: 204-832-9637; Intl. Program: 204-837-1331
Number of Schools: 15 early years; 6 middle years; 5 senior years; *Grades:* K - 12

Craig McGregor, Board Chair
cmcgregor@sjsd.net
Brett Lough, Chief Superintendent
blough@sjsd.net
Michael J. Friesen, Secretary-Treasurer/CFO
mfriesen@sjsd.net
Mike Wake, Acting Assistant Superintendent, Administration
Michelle Clarke, Acting Assistant Superintendent, Education & Program
Randy Calvert, Manager, Facilities & Maintenance
Carrol A. Harvey, Manager, Human Resources (Professional Staff)
Cindy Labaty, Manager, Human Resources (CUPE & MANTE)

***Winnipeg:* Seven Oaks School Division**
830 Powers St., Winnipeg, MB R2V 4E7, Canada
Tel: 204-586-8061; *Fax:* 204-589-2504
www.7oaks.org
www.facebook.com/510220119018091
twitter.com/7oaksschooldiv
Number of Schools: 23; *Grades:* K - 12
Claudia Sarbit, Chairperson, 204-339-8758
Claudia.sarbit@7oaks.org
Brian O'Leary, Superintendent
brian.oleary@7oaks.org
Verland Force, Assistant Superintendent - Student Services
verland.force@7oaks.org
Lydia Hedrich, Assistant Superintendent - Curriculum
lydia.hedrich@7oaks.org
Gwen Birse, Assistant Superintendent - Personnel
gwen.birse@7oaks.org
Wayne Shimizu, Secretary Treasurer
wayne.shimizu@7oaks.org

***Winnipeg:* Winnipeg School Division**
1577 Wall St. East, Winnipeg, MB R3E 2S5, Canada
Tel: 204-775-0231; *Fax:* 204-772-6464
WSD@wsd1.org
www.winnipegsd.ca
twitter.com/WinnipegSD
Number of Schools: 78; *Grades:* Pre-K.-12; *Enrollment:* 32000
Mark Wasyliw, Board Chair
mwasyliw@wsd1.org
Pauline Clarke, Chief Superintendent
pclarke@wsd1.org
Tom Bobby, Interim Secretary-Treasurer
tbobby@wsd1.org

Catholic

***Winnipeg:* Archdiocese of Winnipeg Catholic Schools**
1495 Pembina Hwy., Winnipeg, MB R3T 2C6
Tel: 204-452-2227; *Fax:* 204-453-8236
awcs@archwinnipeg.ca
www.archwinnipeg.ca/catholic_schools.php
Number of Schools: 11; *Grades:* K - 12; University
Robert Praznik, Director of Catholic Education
Gail Gel, Administrative Coordinator to Catholic Schools

French

***Lorette:* Division scolaire franco-manitobaine (DSFM)**
P.O. Box 204
1263, ch Dawson, Lorette, MB R0A 0Y0
Tél: 204-878-9399; *Téléc:* 204-878-9407
Ligne sans frais: 800-699-3736
dsfm@dsfm.mb.ca
www.dsfm.mb.ca
Number of Schools: 21 élémentaires; 15 secondaires; 1 autre; *Grades:* K-12
Bernard Lesage, Président
bernard.lesage@atrium.ca
Alain Laberge, Directeur général, 204 878-4424, ext. 211
alain.laberge@dsfm.mb.ca
Louise Gauthier, Directrice des ressources humaines, 204-878-9399, ext. 244
ressources.humaines@dsfm.mb.ca
Serge Bisson, Secrétaire-trésorier, 204-878-4424, ext. 214
serge.bisson@dsfm.mb.ca

First Nations

***Birch River:* Wuskwi Sipihk Education Authority**
P.O. Box 307
Birch River, MB R0L 0E0
Tel: 204-236-4783; *Fax:* 204-236-4779
Number of Schools: 1; *Note:* Wuskwi Sipihk Education Authority operates the Chief Charles Audy Memorial School.
Bob McKenzie, Education Director
bmckenzie60@hotmail.com

***Bloodvein:* Miskooseepi Education Authority Inc.**
General Delivery, Bloodvein, MB R0C 0J0
Tel: 204-395-2148; *Fax:* 204-395-2189
Stella Keller, Education Director

***Crane River:* O-Chi-Chak-Ko-Sipi First Nation Education Authority**
P.O. Box 91
Crane River, MB R0L OMO
Tel: 204-732-2548; *Fax:* 204-732-2753
Note: The O-Chi-Chak-Ko-Sipi First Nation operates the Donald Ahmo School.
Peter McKay, Education Director
mckay-pj@hotmail.com

***Cross Lake:* Cross Lake Education Authority (CLEA)**
P.O. Box 370
Cross Lake, MB R0B 0J0
Tel: 204-676-2917; *Fax:* 204-676-2087
crosslakeeducation.homestead.com
Number of Schools: 2
Greg Halcrow, Director Of Education
ghalcrow@clea.mb.ca

***Easterville:* Chemawawin Education Authority**
P.O. Box 174
Easterville, MB R0C 0V0
Tel: 204-329-2161; *Fax:* 204-329-2214
Chief Clarence Easter, Education Director

***Ebb & Flow:* Ebb & Flow Eduction Authority**
P.O. Box 160
Ebb & Flow, MB R0L 0R0
Tel: 204-448-2438; *Fax:* 204-448-2393
eandf@mts.net
Number of Schools: 1; *Grades:* Elementary - Secondary; *Enrollment:* 426; *Note:* Ebb & Flow School. The Ebb & Flow Eduction Authority serves the Ebb & Flow First Nation in Manitoba
Arlene Mousseau, Director, Education

***Edwin:* Dakota Plains Education Authority**
General Delivery, Edwin, MB R0H 0G0
Tel: 204-252-2895; *Fax:* 204-252-2188

***Elphinstone:* Keeseekoowenin Education Authority**
P.O. Box 250
Elphinstone, MB R0J 0N0
Tel: 204-625-2028; *Fax:* 204-625-2693
www.keeseekoowenin.com/education.html
Note: Keeseekoowenin Education Authority operates the Keeseekoowenin School.
Barry Bone, Education Director
bonebl@mymts.net

***Erickson:* Rolling River First Nation**
P.O. Box 606
Erickson, MB R0J 0P0
Tel: 204-636-2983; *Fax:* 204-636-2545
Note: Rolling River First Nation operates the Wapi-Penace School.
Charles Gaywish, Education Director

***Fairford:* Pinaymootang First Nation Education Authority**
General Delivery, Fairford, MB R0C 0X0
Tel: 204-659-5705; *Fax:* 204-659-2068
Note: Pinaymootang First Nation operates the Pinaymootang School.

***Fisher River:* Fisher River Cree Nation Board of Education**
P.O. Box 368
Fisher River, MB R0C 1S0
Tel: 204-645-2283; *Fax:* 204-645-2788
www.fisherriver.com/fisher-river-board-of-education/
Note: The Fisher River Cree Nation Board of Education operates the Charles Sinclair School.
Nora Murdock, Education Director
nora@csschool.mb.ca

***Garden Hill:* Garden Hill Education Authority**
General Delivery, Garden Hill, MB R0B 0T0
Tel: 204-456-2880; *Fax:* 204-456-2129
Number of Schools: 2; *Grades:* Pre. - 12
David Flett, Education Director

***Gillam:* Fox Lake First Nation Education Authority**
P.O. Box 379
Gillam, MB R0B 0L0
Tel: 204-486-2307; *Fax:* 204-486-2606
www.foxlakecreenation.com

***Ginew:* Roseau River Anishinabe First Nation**
P.O. Box 10
Ginew, MB R0A 2R0
Tel: 204-427-2490; *Fax:* 204-427-2398
Note: Roseau River Anishinabe First Nation operates the Ginew School.
Marlene Starr, Education Director
mstarr10@hotmail.com

***God's Lake Narrows:* God's Lake First Nation Education Authority**
P.O. Box 284
God's Lake Narrows, MB R0B 0N0
Tel: 204-335-2499; *Fax:* 204-335-2019
Note: God's Lake First Nation Education Authority operates the God's Lake Narrows First Nation School.

***God's River:* Amos Okemow Memorial Education Authority**
P.O. Box 103
God's River, MB R0B 0N0, Canada
Tel: 204-366-2312; *Fax:* 204-366-2569
Number of Schools: 1; *Grades:* Pre - 11; *Enrollment:* 250; *Note:* The Amos Okemow Memorial Education Authority serves the Manto Sipi Cree Nation through operation of the Amos Okemow Memorial School. To continue their secondary school education, students must leave the community.
Rebecca Ross, Director, Education

***Griswold:* Sioux Valley Education Authority**
P.O. Box 99
Griswold, MB R0M 0S0
Tel: 204-855-2536; *Fax:* 204-855-2023
Number of Schools: 2; *Note:* Sioux Valley Education Authority operates the Sioux Valley High School.
Kevin Nabess, Education Director
kcnabess@hotmail.com

***Gypsumville:* Dauphin River Education Authority**
P.O. Box 140
Gypsumville, MB R0C 1J0
Tel: 204-659-5268; *Fax:* 204-659-5790
Note: Dauphin River Education Authority operates the Dauphin River School.

***Gypsumville:* Little Saskatchewan Education Authority**
P.O. Box 5050
Gypsumville, MB R0C 1J0
Tel: 204-659-2672; *Fax:* 204-659-5763
Note: The Little Saskatchewan Education Authority operates the Little Saskatchewan H.A.G.M.E. School.
Jerry Sumner, Education Director

***Gypsumville:* Narrows Education Authority**
P.O. Box 2020
Gypsumville, MB R0C 1J0
Tel: 204-659-2699; *Fax:* 204-659-5739
narrowsed@xplornet.ca
Note: The Narrows Education Authority operates the Lake St. Martin School.
Allan Moar, Education Director

***Hodgson:* Kinonjeoshtegon Education Authority**
P.O. Box 359
Hodgson, MB R0C 1N0
Tel: 204-394-2429; *Fax:* 204-394-2431
Note: The Kinonjeoshtegon Education Authorityoperates the Lawrence Sinclair Memorial School.
Adeline Travers, Education Director

***Lac Brochet:* Northlands Dene Education Authority**
General Delivery, Lac Brochet, MB R0B 2E0
Tel: 204-367-2278; *Fax:* 204-337-2078
Note: The Northlands Dene Education Authority operates the Petit Casimir Memorial School.
Gerard Butt, Education Director

***Marius:* Sandy Bay Education Foundation**
P.O. Box 108
Marius, MB R0H 0T0
Tel: 204-843-2431; *Fax:* 204-843-2269
Note: Sandy Bay Education Foundation operates the Isaac Beaulieu Memorial School.
George Beaulieu, Education Director
george_beaulieu@msn.com

***Nelson House:* Nelson House Education Authority**
General Delivery, Nelson House, MB R0B 1A0
Tel: 204-484-2095; *Fax:* 204-484-2257
www.nhea.info
Number of Schools: 2; *Note:* Nelson House Education Authority operates Nisichawayasihk Neyo Ohtinwak Collegiate and Otetiskiwin Kiskinwamahtowekamik.

Paul Bonner, CEO
Elvis Thomas, Director of Education
wethomas@shaw.ca

Opaskwayak: Opaskwayak Educational Authority Inc.
P.O. Box 10370
Opaskwayak, MB R0B 2J0
Tel: 204-623-7431; Fax: 204-623-2870
oca@mts.net
www.opased.com
Note: Opaskwayak Educational Authority Inc. operates the Oscar Lathlin Collegiate and the Joe A. Ross School.
Beverly Fontaine, Education Director

Oxford House: Oxford House First Nation Board of Education
General Delivery, Oxford House, MB R0B 1C0
Tel: 204-538-2051; Fax: 204-538-2013
Number of Schools: 2; Grades: Elementary - S4; Enrollment: 675; Note: Oxford House Elementary School & 1972 Memorial High School. The Oxford House First Nation Board of Education serves the Bunibonibee Cree Nation of Oxford House, which is situated 600 km north of Winnipeg, Manitoba.
Alvin Grieves, Director, Education
argrieves@hotmail.com

Peguis: Peguis First Nation School Board
P.O. Box 190
Peguis, MB R0C 3J0
Tel: 204-645-2648; Fax: 204-645-2730
Note: Peguis First Nation School Board operates the Peguis Central School.
Sherri Sutherland, Education Director

Pelican Rapids: Sapotaweyak Education Authority
General Delivery, Pelican Rapids, MB R0L 1L0
Tel: 204-587-2115; Fax: 204-587-2123
Number of Schools: 1; Grades: Nursery - 12; Number of Employees: 50; Note: Neil Dennis Kematch Memorial School. The Sapotaweyak Education Authority is responsible for the provision of education for the Sapotaweyak Cree Nation, near the towns of Swan River & The Pas in Manitoba.
Margaret Leask, Director, Education

Pine Falls: Sagkeeng Education Authority
P.O. Box 1610
Pine Falls, MB R0E 0P0, Canada
Tel: 204-367-2287; Fax: 204-367-4315
Toll-Free: 1-866-878-2911
www.sagkeeng.ca
Number of Schools: 3; Grades: Elementary - Secondary; Note: Anicinabe Community School; Sagkeeng Junior High School; & Sagkeeng Anicinabe High School
Eva Courchene, Education Director
ecourchene@sfnedu.org

Pipestone: Canupawakpa Dakota Nation Education Authority
P.O. Box 146
Pipestone, MB R0M 1T0
Tel: 204-854-2959; Fax: 204-854-2525

Poplar River: Poplar River First Nation Education
P.O. Box 90
Poplar River, MB R0B 0Z0
Tel: 204-244-2267; Fax: 204-244-2690

Portage La Prairie: Long Plain First Nation Education Board
P.O. Box 430
Portage La Prairie, MB R1N 3B7
Tel: 294-252-2081; Fax: 204-252-2421
Note: The Long Plain First Nation Education Board operates the Long Plain School.
Liz Merrick, Education Director

Pukatawagan: Pukatawagan Education Authority
P.O. Box 318
Pukatawagan, MB R0B 1G0
Tel: 204-553-2089; Fax: 204-553-2419
Note: The Pukatawagan Education Authority operates the Sakastew School.
Jackie Ferland, Education Director
ferlandjackie@hotmail.com

Red Sucker Lake: Red Sucker Lake Education Authority
General Delivery, Red Sucker Lake, MB R0B 1H0
Tel: 204-469-5039; Fax: 204-469-5206
Leonard McDougall, Education Director

Scanterbury: Brokenhead Education Authority
P.O. Box 179
Scanterbury, MB R0E 1W0
Tel: 204-766-2636; Fax: 204-766-2809
Wendell Sinclair, Education Director
wsinclair@stpschool.ca

Shamattawa: Shamattawa Education Authority
General Delivery, Shamattawa, MB R0B 1K0
Tel: 204-565-2320; Fax: 204-565-2320
Note: Shamattawa Education Authority operates the Abraham Beardy Memorial School.
Roy Miles, Education Director

Shortdale: Tooinaowaziibeeng Education Authority
General Delivery, Shortdale, MB R0L 1W0
Tel: 204-546-2641; Fax: 204-546-3120
Note: Tooinaowaziibeeng Education Authority operates the Chief Clifford Lynxleg Anishinabe School.
Dan Furman, Education Director

Split Lake: Tataskweyak Education Authority
General Delivery, Split Lake, MB R0B 1P0
Tel: 294-342-2148; Fax: 204-342-2240
teduauthority@mts.net
Note: Tataskweyak Education Authority operates the Chief Sam Cook Mahmuwee Education Centre.
Alfred Beardy, Education Director

St. Theresa Point: St. Theresa Point Education Authority
P.O. Box 520
St. Theresa Point, MB R0B 1J0
Tel: 204-462-2131; Fax: 204-462-2552
Number of Schools: 3; Note: St. Theresa Point Education Authority operates the St. Theresa Point Elementary School, the St. Theresa Point High School and the St. Theresa Point Middle School.
Charles Monias, Education Director

Swan Lake: Swan Lake First Nation Education Authority
P.O. Box 145
Swan Lake, MB R0G 2S0
Tel: 204-836-2332; Fax: 204-836-2317
Note: Swan Lake First Nation operates the Indian Springs School.
Donovan Mann, Education Director

Tadoule Lake: Sayisi Dene First Nation Education Authority
General Delivery, Tadoule Lake, MB R0B 2C0
Tel: 204-684-2014; Fax: 204-684-2187
Note: Sayisi Dene First Nation operates the Peter Yassie Memorial School.
Betty Bickell, Education Director

Vogar: Lake Manitoba Education Authority
P.O. Box 1249
Vogar, MB R0C 3K0
Tel: 204-768-2728; Fax: 204-768-2194
Note: The Lake Manitoba Education Authority operates the Lake Manitoba School.

Wasagamack: Wasagamack Education Authority
P.O. Box 55
Wasagamack, MB R0B 1Z0
Tel: 204-457-2225; Fax: 204-457-2413
Note: Wasagamack Education Authority operates the George Knott School.
Percy Harper, Education Director

Winnipeg: Little Grand Rapids Educational Authority Inc.
360 Broadway St., 6th Fl., Winnipeg, MB R3C 0T6
Tel: 204-956-7500; Fax: 204-956-7382
Note: The Little Grand Rapids Educational Authority Inc. operates the Abbalak Thunderswift Memorial School.
Margaret Simmons, Education Director

York Landing: York Factory First Nation Education
General Delivery, York Landing, MB R0B 2B0
Tel: 204-341-2180; Fax: 204-341-2322

Schools: Specialized

First Nations

Beulah: Chan Kagha Otina Dakota Wayawa Tipi School
P.O. Box 40
Beulah, MB R0M 0B0, Canada
Tel: 204-568-4757
www.frontiersd.mb.ca
Enrollment: 130; Note: The Chan Kagha Otina Dakota Wayawa Tipi School serves the Birdtail Sioux Dakota Nation. It is part of Manitoba's Frontier School Division.
Karen Crozier, Superintendent, Frontier School Division (Dauphin Area), 204-638-6839

Birch River: Chief Charles Thomas Audy Memorial School
P.O. Box 307
Birch River, MB R0L 0E0, Canada
Tel: 204-236-4783; Fax: 204-236-4779
wuskwisipihkschool@gmail.com
Grades: Nursery - 8; Enrollment: 37; Note: Chief Charles Thomas Audy Memorial School serves the Wuskwi Sipihk First Nation.

Black River: Little Black River School
P.O. Box 260
Black River, MB, Canada
Tel: 204-367-4411; Fax: 204-367-1414
www.black-river.ca
Note: Members of the Little Black River First Nation are educated at the Little Black River School in O'Hanley, Manitoba. The First Nation community is situated approximately 150 kilometres north of Winnipeg.
Jack Johnson, Program Manager, Special Projects and Alternative Education

Bloodvein: Miskooseepi School
General Delivery, Bloodvein, MB R0C 0J0
Tel: 204-395-2012; Fax: 204-395-2189
Grades: Pre.-9; Enrollment: 163
Irene Rupp, Principal

Brandon: Sioux Valley High School
2320 Louis Ave., Brandon, MB R7B 2C6, Canada
Tel: 204-729-2770; Fax: 204-727-2054
kcnabess@hotmail.com
Grades: 7 - 12; Enrollment: 136
Kevin Nabess, Principal
kcnabess@hotmail.com

Camperville: Pine Creek Indian Day School
P.O. Box 130
973 Duck Bay Rd., Camperville, MB R0L 0J0
Tel: 204-524-2318; Fax: 204-524-2177
Grades: K-11

Crane River: Donald Ahmo School
P.O. Box 91
Crane River, MB R0L 0M0, Canada
Tel: 204-732-2548; Fax: 204-732-2753
Grades: K - 8; Enrollment: 109; Note: The Donald Ahmo School is a band-operated First Nation school which serves the O-Chi-Chak-Ko-Sipi First Nation in Crane River, Manitoba.
Andrew Spence, Principal
bigandy4@hotmail.com

Cross Lake: Mikisew Middle School
P.O. Box 128
Cross Lake, MB R0B 0J0, Canada
Tel: 204-676-3030; Fax: 204-676-2798
crosslakeeducation.homestead.com/MIKISEW.html
Grades: K, 5-8
Connie McIvor, Principal
cmcivor@clea.mb.ca

Cross Lake: Otter Nelson River School
P.O. Box 370
Cross Lake, MB R0B 0J0
Tel: 204-676-2050; Fax: 204-676-2464
crosslakeeducation.homestead.com/ONR.html
Grades: Pre.-12; Enrollment: 1200; Number of Employees: 50 teachers
Irvin Spence, Principal
ispence@clea.mb.ca

Dakota Tipi: Dakota Tipi School
2000A Dakota Dr., Dakota Tipi, MB R1N 3P1, Canada
Tel: 204-857-7190
Enrollment: 60; Note: Located outside the city of Portage La Prairie, Manitoba, the Dakota Tipi School is a First Nations band operated school. The school serves the Dakota Tipi First Nation.

***Dominion City:* Ginew School**
P.O. Box 10
Dominion City, MB R0A 2R0
Tel: 204-427-2490; *Fax:* 204-427-2398
Grades: Pre.-8; *Enrollment:* 126
Teresa Anderson, Principal
ltandersonbrowning@gmail.com

***Easterville:* Chemawawin School**
P.O. Box 10
Easterville, MB R0C 0V0, Canada
Tel: 204-329-2115; *Fax:* 204-329-2214
Grades: JK - 12; *Enrollment:* 512; *Note:* Located on the southern shore of Cedar Lake, 300 kilometres north of Winnipeg, Manitoba, the Chemawawin School provides education to the Chemawawin Cree Nation.
Rachel Clarke, Principal
Sandra Lavallee, Vice Principal

***Ebb & Flow:* Ebb & Flow School**
P.O. Box 160
Ebb & Flow, MB R0L 0R0, Canada
Tel: 204-448-2012; *Fax:* 204-448-2393
Grades: Pre. - 12; *Enrollment:* 611; *Note:* The Ebb & Flow School is a band-operated school in Manitoba which provides education to the Ebb & Flow First Nation.
Paul Monchka, Principal

***Edwin:* Dakota Plains School**
P.O. Box 100
Edwin, MB R0H 0G0, Canada
Tel: 204-252-2895; *Fax:* 204-252-2188
Grades: K - 8; *Enrollment:* 63; *Note:* The Dakota Plains School serves the Dakota Plains Wahpeton Nation.
Jannita Emerson, Principal

***Elphinstone:* Keeseekoowenin School**
P.O. Box 129
Elphinstone, MB R0J 0N0
Tel: 204-625-2062; *Fax:* 204-625-2418
keesee@mts.net
keeseekoowenin.wix.com/school
Grades: Pre.-8; *Enrollment:* 57
Audrey Blackbird, Principal
audreyblackbird@keeseekoowenin.com

***Erickson:* Wapi-Penace School**
P.O. Box 588 Erickson, MB
Erickson, MB R0J 0P0
Tel: 204-636-7894; *Fax:* 204-636-2545
Grades: Pre. K; *Enrollment:* 10
Angeline McKay, Principal

***Fairford:* Pinaymootang School**
General Delivery, Fairford, MB R0C 0X0, Canada
Tel: 204-659-2045; *Fax:* 204-659-2270
pinayschoolprin@yahoo.com
kinaabik.tripod.com
Grades: Pre.-12; *Enrollment:* 280
Moti Patram, Principal

***Fisher River:* Charles Sinclair School**
P.O. Box 109
Fisher River, MB R0C 1S0, Canada
Tel: 204-645-2206; *Fax:* 204-645-2614
www.csschool.mb.ca
www.facebook.com/pages/Charles-Sinclair-School/16143565071 4825#
Grades: Pre - 12; *Enrollment:* 442; *Note:* Part of the Fisher River Board of Education, Charles Sinclair School provides education to the Fisher River Cree Nation.
Delores Bouchey, Principal, 204-645-2206
Warren Woodhouse, Vice-Principal

***Fort Alexander:* Sagkeeng Consolidated School**
P.O. Box 5
Fort Alexander, MB R0E 0P0
Tel: 204-367-2588; *Fax:* 204-367-9231
www.sagkeengeducation.org
Grades: K, 4 - 8; *Enrollment:* 347; *Note:* The school operates under the Sagkeeng Education Authority.
Garry Swampy, Principal
garryswampy@yahoo.ca

***Garden Lake:* Kistiganwacheeng Elementary School**
General Delivery, Garden Lake, MB R0B 0T0, Canada
Tel: 204-456-2391; *Fax:* 204-456-2350
kistiganwacheengelementaryschool@knet.ca
Grades: K-6; *Enrollment:* 665
Madeline Little, Principal
madlittle194@yahoo.ca

***Gillam:* Fox Lake School**
P.O. Box 379
Gillam, MB R0B 0L0
Tel: 204-486-2307; *Fax:* 204-486-2606
Grades: K.-9; *Enrollment:* 32
Russell Sinclair, Principal
r.sinclair@foxlakecreenation.com

***God's Lake Narrows:* God's Lake Narrows First Nation School**
P.O. Box 284
God's Lake Narrows, MB R0B 0M0
Tel: 204-335-2003; *Fax:* 204-335-2440
www.glns.ca
Grades: Pre.-9; *Enrollment:* 400
Peter Andrews, Principal
pandrews@glns.ca

***God's River:* Amos Okemow Memorial School**
General Delivery, God's River, MB R0B 0N0
Tel: 204-366-2070; *Fax:* 204-366-2105
www.mantosipi.com
Grades: K - 11; *Enrollment:* 229; *Note:* Under the direction of the Amos Okemow Memorial Education Authority, the Amos Okemow Memorial School serves the Manto Sipi Cree Nation. Students must leave the community to continue their secondary school education.
Arthur MacDonald, Principal

***Griswold:* Sioux Valley School**
P.O. Box 99
Griswold, MB R0M 0S0
Tel: 204-855-2536; *Fax:* 204-855-3204
svschool@dakotaoyate.com
Grades: Pre. - 6; *Enrollment:* 192
Bernice Ledoux, Principal

***Gypsumville:* Little Saskatchewan H.A.G.M.E. School**
P.O. Box 5050
Gypsumville, MB R0C 1J0, Canada
Tel: 204-659-2672; *Fax:* 204-659-5763
saskatchewanlittle@yahoo.ca
Grades: JK-9; *Enrollment:* 36
Patrick Anderson, Principal
patpinay@yahoo.ca

***Hodgson:* Lawrence Sinclair Memorial School**
P.O. Box 359
Hodgson, MB R0C 1N0, Canada
Tel: 204-394-2429; *Fax:* 204-394-2431
Grades: Nursery - 10; *Enrollment:* 51; *Note:* Lawrence Sinclair Memorial School is a band operated school which serves members of the Kinonjeoshtegon First Nation.
Adeline Traverse, Principal
adelinetravers@kinonjeo.com

***Island Lake:* Garden Hill First Nations High School**
General Delivery, Island Lake, MB R0B 0T0, Canada
Tel: 204-456-2886; *Fax:* 204-456-2894
Grades: 7-12; *Enrollment:* 472
Wilfred Fiddler, Principal

***Lac Brochet:* Petit Casimir Memorial School**
P.O. Box 60
Lac Brochet, MB R0B 2E0
Tel: 204-337-2278; *Fax:* 204-337-2078
pcms@gmail.com
www.pcmschool.ca
Grades: K - 8; *Enrollment:* 248; *Note:* Petit Casimir Memorial School is a Northlands Dene First Nation School. The Dene culture, heritage, & language are integrated in education.
Gerard Butt, Principal
Gerard.butt@gmail.com
Pierre Bernier, Vice-Principal

***Lake Manitoba First Nation:* Lake Manitoba School**
P.O. Box 1249
Lake Manitoba First Nation, MB R0C 3K0, Canada
Tel: 204-768-2728; *Fax:* 204-768-2194
Grades: Pre - 8; *Enrollment:* 218; *Note:* Lake Manitoba School provides education to the Lake Manitoba First Nation.
Freda Missayabit, Principal
fmissyabit@hotmail.ca

***Little Grand Rapids:* Abbalak Thunderswift Memorial School**
P.O. Box 160
Little Grand Rapids, MB R0B 0V0
Tel: 204-397-2199; *Fax:* 204-397-2102
Grades: Pre. - 10; *Enrollment:* 207
Clarence Greene, Principal
cjgreene2003@yahoo.com

***Marius:* Isaac Beaulieu Memorial School**
P.O. Box 108
Marius, MB R0H 0T0
Tel: 204-843-2407; *Fax:* 204-843-2269
Grades: Pre.-12; *Enrollment:* 975
Colleen West, Principal
colleenwest@live.ca

***Nelson House:* Nisichawayasihk Neyo Ohtinwak Collegiate**
1A School Rd., Nelson House, MB R0B 1A0, Canada
Tel: 204-484-2602; *Fax:* 204-484-2612
www.nhea.info/schools.html
Grades: 9-12; *Enrollment:* 220
Lillian Gail Gossfeld McDonald, Principal
gailm@nhea.info

***Nelson House:* Otetiskiwin Kiskinwamahtowekamik**
1 School Dr., Nelson House, MB R0B 1A0, Canada
Tel: 204-484-2242; *Fax:* 204-484-2002
www.nhea.info
Grades: Pre.-8; *Enrollment:* 718
Natalie Tays, Principal
nataliet@nhea.info

***Opaskwayak:* Joe A. Ross School**
P.O. Box 10160
136 Waller Rd., Opaskwayak, MB R0B 2J0
Tel: 204-623-4286; *Fax:* 204-623-4442
www.joeaross-school.ca
Grades: Pre.-6
Karon McGillivary, Principal
karon.mcgillivary@opased.com

***Opaskwayak:* Oscar Lathlin Collegiate**
P.O. Box 10160
Opaskwayak, MB R0B 2J0
Tel: 204-623-5259; *Fax:* 204-623-5361
www.oscarlathlincollegiate.ca
Grades: 7 - 12; *Enrollment:* 452
Ronald E. Constant, Principal
ron.constant@opased.com

***Oxford House:* 1972 Memorial High School**
General Delivery, Oxford House, MB R0B 1C0, Canada
Tel: 204-538-2020; *Fax:* 204-538-2075
Toll-Free: 1-888-377-8520
Grades: 7 - 13; *Enrollment:* 310; *Note:* Under the Oxford House First Nation Board of Education, the 1972 Memorial High School serves the Bunibonibee Cree Nation of Oxford House.
James Forward, Principal
jforwardmusic@yahoo.ca

***Oxford House:* Oxford House Elementary School**
General Delivery, Oxford House, MB R0B 1C0, Canada
Tel: 204-538-2389; *Fax:* 204-538-5023
Grades: Pre - 6; *Enrollment:* 453; *Note:* Under the Oxford House First Nation Board of Education, the Oxford House Elementary School serves the Bunibonibee Cree Nation of Oxford House.
Wilfred Wood, Principal
wilnaniwood_25@yahoo.ca

***Pauingassi:* Omiishosh Memorial School**
P.O. Box 31
Pauingassi, MB R0B 2G0
Tel: 204-397-2219; *Fax:* 204-397-2379
Grades: Pre. K - 9; *Enrollment:* 75
Roddy Owens, Education Portfolio
Byron Murdock, Principal
byronmurdock@gmail.com

***Peguis First Nation:* Peguis Central School**
P.O. Box 670
Peguis First Nation, MB R0C 3J0, Canada
Tel: 204-645-2164; *Fax:* 204-645-2270
www.peguiscentralschool.ca
Grades: Pre - 12; *Enrollment:* 820; *Number of Employees:* 82
Jean Malcolm, Principal
jeanmalcolm@peguiscentralschool.ca

***Pelican Rapids:* Neil Dennis Kematch Memorial School (NDKMS)**
General Delivery, Pelican Rapids, MB R0L 1L0, Canada
Tel: 204-587-2045; *Fax:* 204-587-2341
school@ndkms.com
www.ndkms.com
Grades: Nursery - 12; *Enrollment:* 392; *Note:* The Neil Dennis Kematch Memorial School serves the citizens of Sapotaweyak Cree First Nation in a community located approximately 120 kilometres north of Swan River, Manitoba. The school is administered by the Sapotaweyak Education Authority.
Cora Campeau, Principal
coracook@ndkms.com

Pine Falls: Anicinabe Community School
P.O. Box 219
Pine Falls, MB R0E 1M0
Tel: 204-367-2285; *Fax:* 204-367-9231
Grades: Nursery - 3; *Enrollment:* 250; *Note:* Anicinabe Community School serves the Sagkeeng First Nation. It operates under the direction of the Sagkeeng Education Authority.
Rick Fewchuck, Principal
rfewchuck@sagkeengeducation.com

Pine Falls: Sagkeeng Anicinabe High School
P.O. Box 1610
Pine Falls, MB R0E 1M0
Tel: 204-367-2243; *Fax:* 204-367-4566
www.sagkeengeducation.org
Grades: 8 - 12; *Enrollment:* 215; *Note:* The Sagkeeng Education Authority operates the Sagkeeng Anicinabe High School, which educates secondary school students of the Sagkeeng First Nation.
Claude Guimond, Principal
cgmojo@hotmail.com

Pipestone: Wambdi Iyotaka School
P.O. Box 146
Pipestone, MB R0M 1T0, Canada
Tel: 204-854-2975; *Fax:* 204-854-2933
Grades: Pre.- K; *Enrollment:* 15; *Note:* The Wambdi Iyotaka School serves members of the Canupawakpa Dakota Nation in Manitoba.
Laura Ellen Elliot, Principal
Wis.cdn.lee@gmail.com

Poplar River: Poplar River School
P.O. Box 120
Poplar River, MB R0B 0Z0
Tel: 204-244-2113; *Fax:* 204-244-2259
Grades: Pre. K - 9; *Enrollment:* 254
Roy Hammond, Principal
roy_hammond@hotmail.com

Portage la Prairie: Long Plain School
P.O. Box 430
Portage la Prairie, MB R1N 3B7
Tel: 204-252-2326; *Fax:* 204-252-2786
Grades: Pre.-9; *Enrollment:* 267
Isaac Edwards, Principal
ijedw@hotmail.com

Pukatawagan: Sakastew School
P.O. Box 319
Pukatawagan, MB R0B 1G0, Canada
Tel: 204-553-2163; *Fax:* 204-553-2225
Grades: K-12; *Enrollment:* 602
Melvin George, Principal
Melvin_george@hotmail.com

Red Sucker Lake: Red Sucker Lake School
General Delivery, Red Sucker Lake, MB R0B 1H0
Tel: 204-469-5302; *Fax:* 204-469-5436
redsuckerlakeschool@gmail.com
Grades: Pre.-12; *Enrollment:* 341
Wesley Harper, Principal

Scanterbury: Sergeant Tommy Prince School
P.O. Box 179
Scanterbury, MB R0E 1W0
Tel: 204-766-2636; *Fax:* 204-766-2809
Grades: K-12
Robert Moore, Principal
principal@stpschool.ca

Shamattawa: Abraham Beardy Memorial School
General Delivery, Shamattawa, MB R0B 1K0, Canada
Tel: 204-565-2022; *Fax:* 204-565-2122
Grades: K - 10; *Enrollment:* 327; *Note:* Abraham Beardy Memorial School serves the Cree First Nation of Shamattawa.
Lawrence W. Einarsson, Principal
l.einarsson@hotmail.com
Rebecca McCaffery, Vice Principal

Shortdale: Chief Clifford Lynxleg Anishinabe School
General Delivery, Shortdale, MB R0L 1W0, Canada
Tel: 204-546-2641; *Fax:* 204-546-3120
Grades: Pre. - 7; *Enrollment:* 63; *Number of Employees:* 13; *Note:* Chief Clifford Lynxleg Anishinabe School is located on the Tootinawaziibeeng (Valley River) Reserve, where it provides education to the Tootinaowaziibeeng First Nation.
Donna Dudek, Principal
donnacatagas@yahoo.ca

Split Lake: Chief Sam Cook Mahmuwee Education Centre
P.O. Box 100
Split Lake, MB R0B 1P0, Canada
Tel: 204-342-2134; *Fax:* 204-342-2139
Grades: Nursery - 12; *Enrollment:* 713; *Note:* Chief Sam Cook Mahmuwee Education Centre serves the Tataskweyak Cree Nation. The Tataskweyak reserve is located approximately 150 kilometres northeast of Thompson, Manitoba.
Caroline Flett, Principal, Elementary
flettcaroline@live.com
Thelma Spence, Principal, High School
thelmaspence@hotmail.com

St Theresa Point: St. Theresa Point School
P.O. Box 520
St Theresa Point, MB R0B 1J0, Canada
Tel: 204-462-9179; *Fax:* 204-462-2341
Grades: Pre - 4; *Enrollment:* 565
Giselle McDougall, Principal
Gisellemcd2012@yahoo.com

St. Theresa Point: St. Theresa Point High School
P.O. Box 670
St. Theresa Point, MB R0B 1J0
Tel: 204-462-2600; *Fax:* 204-462-2341
Grades: 5 - 12; *Enrollment:* 537
Raymond Flett, Principal
raymondflett@hotmail.com

St. Theresa Point: St. Theresa Point Middle School
P.O. Box 350
St. Theresa Point, MB R0B 1J0
Tel: 204-462-2420; *Fax:* 204-462-2793
Grades: 5 - 8; *Enrollment:* 327
Roy A. Mason, Principal
Ramason.ca@yahoo.com

Swan Lake: Indian Springs School
P.O. Box 145
Swan Lake, MB R0G 2S0
Tel: 204-836-2332; *Fax:* 204-836-2317
Toll-Free: 866-786-7841
lssprincipal@mts.net
www.swanlakefirstnation.ca/iss.html
Grades: K - 8; *Enrollment:* 68
Donovan Mann, Principal

Tadoule Lake: Peter Yassie Memorial School
P.O. Box 77
Tadoule Lake, MB R0B 2C0
Tel: 204-684-2279; *Fax:* 204-684-2130
Grades: Pre. - 8; *Enrollment:* 64; *Note:* Peter Yassie Memorial School is a Sayisi Dene First Nation school.
Geoffrey Ndibali, Principal
gndibali@yahoo.ca

Wasagamack: George Knott School
P.O. Box 82
Wasagamack, MB R0B 1Z0
Tel: 204-457-2485; *Fax:* 204-457-2273
Grades: Pre.-12; *Enrollment:* 575
Randy Harper, Principal
R_harper@live.ca

Waywayseecappo: Waywayseecappo Community School
P.O. Box 9
Waywayseecappo, MB R0J 1S0, Canada
Tel: 204-859-2811; *Fax:* 204-859-2992
waywayeducation@inetbiz.ca
Grades: Nursery - 8; *Enrollment:* 340; *Note:* The Waywayseecappo Community School is a band operated elementary school, which provides education to members of Manitoba's Waywayseecappo First Nation. The First Nation community is situated approximately thirty-four kilometres east of Russell. Secondary school students from Waywayseecappo First Nation are transported to Russell's Major Pratt School.
Troy Luhowy, Principal

Winnipeg: Lake St. Martin School
1970 Ness Ave., Winnipeg, MB R3J 0Y9, Canada
Tel: 204-942-2270; *Fax:* 204-942-6759
www.facebook.com/168797906499673
Grades: Nursery - 9; *Enrollment:* 109; *Note:* The Lake St. Martin School provides elementary education to the Lake St. Martin First Nation in Manitoba's Interlake Region.
C. Allan Moar, Principal
c.allanmoar@yahoo.ca

Winnipeg: Southeast Collegiate
1301 Lee Blvd., Winnipeg, MB R3T 5W8, Canada
Tel: 204-261-3551; *Fax:* 204-269-7880
secinfo@secollege.ca
www.secollege.ca
Grades: 10-12; *Enrollment:* 163
Sheryl McCorrister, Principal

York Landing: George Saunders Memorial School
General Delivery, York Landing, MB R0B 2B0, Canada
Tel: 204-341-2118; *Fax:* 204-341-2235
gsmschool@hotmail.com
Grades: K-8; *Enrollment:* 99
Lloyd Chubb, Principal

Hearing Impaired

Winnipeg: Manitoba School for the Deaf (MSD)
242 Stradford St., Winnipeg, MB R2Y 2C9
Tel: 204-945-8934; *Fax:* 204-945-1767
principal@msd.ca
www.msd.ca
TTY: 204-945-8934
Grades: JK-12
Kathy Melnyk, Principal
kmelnyk@msd.ca

Special Education

Brandon: Child & Adolescent Treatment Centre (CATC)
1240 - 10th St., Brandon, MB R7A 7L6
Tel: 204-727-3445; *Fax:* 204-727-3451
Toll-Free: 866-403-5459
www.brandonrha.mb.ca/en/Mental_Health/CATC
Other Information: After Hours Phone: 204-571-7278
Grades: 4-12; *Note:* The CATC provides mental health services to children, including a day program, Crisis Stabilization Unit, Early Intervention Services, & educational services
Brian Schoonbaert, CEO, Brandon Regional Health Authority, 204-578-2301
schoonbaertb@brandonrha.mb.ca
Jayne Troop, VP, Community Services & Long-Term Care, 204-578-2304
troopj@brandonrha.mb.ca
Elizabeth McLeod, Program Manager, 204-571-7255

Portage la Prairie: Gladys Cook Educational Centre
P.O. Box 1342
2 River Rd., Portage la Prairie, MB R1N 3A9
Tel: 204-239-3029; *Fax:* 204-239-3025
Grades: 1-12

St Norbert: Behavioural Health Foundation
P.O. Box 250
35 av de la Digue, St Norbert, MB R3V 1L6, Canada
Tel: 204-269-3430; *Fax:* 204-269-8049
info@bhf.ca
www.bhf.ca
Note: The Behavioural Health Foundation provides long term residential addictions treatment programming for men, women, teens and family units experiencing a variety of addiction problems and co-occurring mental health concerns.
Maureena Downing, Contact, 204-269-3430
maureenad@bhf.ca

Winnipeg: Marymound School
442 Scotia St., Winnipeg, MB R2V 1X4, Canada
Tel: 204-336-5285; *Fax:* 204-338-4690
school@marymound.com
www.marymound.com/main/education/
www.facebook.com/marymoundwpg
twitter.com/marymound
Grades: Elem.-11
Mark Miles, Principal

Winnipeg: St. Amant School
440 River Rd., Winnipeg, MB R2M 3Z9, Canada
Tel: 204-256-4301; *Fax:* 204-257-4349
inquiries@stamant.ca
www.stamant.mb.ca
www.facebook.com/pages/St-Amant/123434846345
twitter.com/StAmantMB
www.linkedin.com/company/st-amant
www.youtube.com/user/StAmantMB
Grades: K.-12
John Leggat, President & CEO

Distance Education

Winnipeg: Wapaskwa Virtual Collegiate
#200, 1090 Waverley St., Winnipeg, MB R3T 0P4
Tel: 204-594-1290; *Fax:* 204-477-4314
www.wapaskwa.ca
Note: Wapaskwa Virtual Collegiate is under the leadership of the Manitoba First Nations Education Resource Centre (MFNERC). They help First Nation students in Manitoba access new sources of education and learning opportunities to meet all of their graduation or post-secondary requirements.
Allison McDonald, Principal

Schools: Independent & Private

Faith-Based

Altona: Sunflower Valley Christian School
P.O. Box 2484
Altona, MB R0G 0B0, Canada
Tel: 204-324-1564; *Fax:* 204-327-5505
Grades: 1-9

Arborg: Interlake Mennonite Fellowship School
P.O. Box 388
Arborg, MB R0C 0A0, Canada
Tel: 204-364-2328
Grades: 1-12

Arborg: Lake Center Mennonite Fellowship School
P.O. Box 838
Arborg, MB R0C 0A0, Canada
Tel: 204-364-2201; *Fax:* 204-364-2272
Grades: K-9

Arborg: Morweena Christian School (MCS)
P.O. Box 1030
Arborg, MB R0C 0A0, Canada
Tel: 204-364-2466; *Fax:* 204-364-3117
info@morweenaschool.org
www.morweenaschool.org
Grades: K - 12; *Enrollment:* 135
Tim Reimer, Principal

Austin: Austin Christian Academy
P.O. Box 460
Austin, MB R0H 0C0, Canada
Tel: 204-637-2303; *Fax:* 204-637-2529
Grades: Kindergarten - 12; *Enrollment:* 50

Austin: Austin Mennonite School
P.O. Box 267
Austin, MB R0H 0C0, Canada
Tel: 204-637-2008
Grades: 1 - 12

Austin: Edrans Christian School
P.O. Box 1
RR #1, Austin, MB R0H 0C0, Canada
Tel: 204-466-2865; *Fax:* 204-466-2994
www.echurchnet.ca/christian-school/
Grades: K-12

Birnie: Shady Oak Christian School
P.O. Box 14
Birnie, MB R0J 0J0, Canada
Tel: 204-966-3477; *Fax:* 204-966-3479
www.shadyoak.net
www.facebook.com/shady.oak.3
Grades: 1-9
Joyce Trigger, Director

Brandon: Christian Heritage School
Heritage Campus
2025 - 26 St., Brandon, MB R7B 3Y2
Tel: 204-725-3209; *Fax:* 204-728-9641
office@chsbrandon.ca
www.chsbrandon.ca
Grades: K.-8; *Enrollment:* 135
Gerry Groening, President, Christian Heritage School Society
Bryan Schroeder, Principal
principal@chsbrandon.ca

Carman: Dufferin Christian School
P.O. Box 1450
Carman, MB R0G 0J0
Tel: 204-745-2278; *Fax:* 204-745-3441
office@dufferinchristian.ca
www.dufferinchristian.ca
Grades: K.-12
Arie Veenendaal, Chair
arieveenendaal@dufferinchristian.ca
Andy Huisman, Principal
andyhuisman@dufferinchristian.ca

Elie: Huron Christian Academy
Elie, MB R0H 0H0, Canada
Tel: 204-353-4120
Grades: 1-12

Fairford: Interlake Christian Academy
Fairford, MB R0C 0X0, Canada
Tel: 204-659-5359
Grades: 1-10

Gretna: Mennonite Collegiate Institute
P.O. Box 250
466 Mary St., Gretna, MB R0G 0V0
Tel: 204-327-5891; *Fax:* 204-327-5872
Toll-Free: 877-624-2583
info@mciblues.net
www.mciblues.net
www.facebook.com/156227284431207
Grades: 7-12; *Enrollment:* 140
Darryl Loewen, Principal
darrylloewen@mciblues.net

Grunthal: Mennonite Christian Academy
P.O. Box 149
Grunthal, MB R0A 0R0
Tel: 204-434-9315
Grades: K-12

Hodgson: Hodgson Christian Academy
P.O. Box 220
Hodgson, MB R0C 1N0, Canada
Tel: 204-372-8483
Grades: 1-12

Horndean: Horndean Christian Day School
P.O. Box 79
Horndean, MB R0G 0Z0, Canada
Tel: 204-829-3354
Grades: 1-10

Kane: Kane Christian Academy
P.O. Box 51
RR#1, Lowe Farm, Kane, MB R0G 1E0
Tel: 204-343-2526
Grades: 2 - 8

Killarney: Lakeside Christian School
P.O. Box 894
Killarney, MB R0K 1G0
Tel: 204-523-8240; *Fax:* 204-523-8351
ics@mts.net
www.facebook.com/lcskillarney
Grades: K.-10
Nancy Reimer, Principal

Kleefeld: New Hope Christian School
P.O. Box 120
Kleefeld, MB R0A 0V0, Canada
Tel: 204-377-4204
Grades: 1 - 12

Lorette: Daystar Christian Academy
PO Box 5, Group 100, RR#2, Lorette, MB R0A 0Y0
Tel: 204-878-3044
Grades: 1-12

Pine Falls: Christian Faith Academy
P.O. Box 130
Pine Falls, MB R0E 1M0, Canada
Tel: 204-367-2056
Grades: 1 - 12

Plum Coulee: Christ Full Gospel Academy
P.O. Box 107
75 Elm St., Plum Coulee, MB R0G 1R0, Canada
Tel: 204-829-3576
www.christfullgospel.org
www.facebook.com/christfullgospel
twitter.com/ChristFullGF
Grades: K - 12; *Note:* Christ Full Gospel Academy uses the Accelerated Christian Education curriculum.

Plum Coulee: Prairie Mennonite School
P.O. Box 50
Plum Coulee, MB R0G 1R0
Tel: 204-829-3336
Grades: K-12

Portage La Prairie: Solid Rock Ministries Christian School
124 4th Ave. NE, Portage La Prairie, MB R1N 0E9, Canada
Tel: 204-239-6785; *Fax:* 204-239-6785
Grades: 1 - 10

Portage la Prairie: Lighthouse Christian Academy
P.O. Box 1360
Portage la Prairie, MB R1N 3N9, Canada
Tel: 204-428-5332; *Fax:* 204-428-5386
Grades: K-12

Roblin: Parkland Christian School
P.O. Box 480
Roblin, MB R0L 1P0, Canada
Tel: 204-937-2870
Grades: 1-9

Steinbach: Steinbach Christian High School
50 Pth 12 North, Steinbach, MB R5G 1T4, Canada
Tel: 204-326-3537; *Fax:* 204-326-5164
info@schs.ca
www.schs.ca
Grades: K-12; *Enrollment:* 161; *Note:* Christian High School with Mennonite affiliation

Stonewall: Faith Academy - Stonewall Campus
New Life Church
P.O. Box 1669
539 - 4th Ave. South, Stonewall, MB R0C 2Z0, Canada
Tel: 204-467-5833
www.faithacademy.ca
Grades: K. - 8
Trevor Warkentin, Principal
trevor.warkentin@faithacademy.ca

Stuartburn: Border View Christian Day School
P.O. Box 103
Stuartburn, MB R0A 2B0, Canada
Tel: 204-427-2932
Grades: 1-10

Swan River: Community Bible Fellowship Christian School (CBFCS)
P.O. Box 1630
Hwy. #834 South, Swan River, MB R0L 1Z0, Canada
Tel: 204-734-2174; *Fax:* 204-734-5706
cbfchristianschool@gmail.com
www.cbfchristianschool.ca
Grades: JK - 8
Jocelyn Beehler, Principal

Winkler: Grace Valley Mennonite Academy
P.O. Box 839
Winkler, MB R6W 4A9, Canada
Tel: 204-829-3301; *Fax:* 204-829-3038
Grades: K-12

Winkler: Valley Mennonite Academy
P.O. Box 139
Grp. 7, R.R.#1, Winkler, MB R6W 4A1, Canada
Tel: 204-325-8172; *Fax:* 204-331-3199
Number of Schools: 2; *Grades:* K - 12; *Enrollment:* 134

Winnipeg: Calvin Christian School
Collegiate Campus
706 Day St., Winnipeg, MB R2C 1B6, Canada
Tel: 204-222-7910; *Fax:* 204-222-8511
calvinchristian.mb.ca
Other Information: 204-338-7981 (Elementary phone); 204-339-3280 (Elementary fax)
twitter.com/ccselementary
Grades: Kindergarten - 12
David Taylor, Principal, Collegiate Campus
Hank Vande Kraats, Principal, Elementary Campus

Winnipeg: Christ the King School
12 Lennox Ave., Winnipeg, MB R2M 1A6, Canada
Tel: 204-257-0027; *Fax:* 204-257-2129
admin@ctkschool.ca
www.ctkschool.ca
Grades: Junior Kindergarten - 8
Anita Wilson, Chair
Susan Enns, Principal

Winnipeg: Faith Academy - Elementary School
437 Matheson Ave., Winnipeg, MB R2W 0E1, Canada
Tel: 204-582-3400; *Fax:* 204-582-2616
www.faithacademy.ca
Grades: K.- 4; *Enrollment:* 182; *Note:* Faith Academy is a conservative, evangelical, Christian, revival-based educational institution open to any Manitoba student willing and able to follow the established school guide. Winnipeg Middle School located at 600 Jefferson Ave., (204) 338-6150; Pritchard Campus located at 220 Pritchard Ave., (204) 589-6885.
Trevor Warkentin, Principal
trevor.warkentin@faithacademy.ca

***Winnipeg:* Hosanna Christian School**
129 Dagmar St., Winnipeg, MB R3A 0Z3
Tel: 204-944-8237
Grades: N-12

***Winnipeg:* Immaculate Heart of Mary School**
650 Flora Ave., Winnipeg, MB R2W 2S5
Tel: 204-582-5698; *Fax:* 204-586-6698
ihms.mb.ca
Other Information: Alternate Phone: 204-589-2709
www.facebook.com/immaculateheartofmary
twitter.com/ihms_winnipeg
Grades: JK-8
Sr. Anne Pidskalny, S.S.M.I., School Director
Rod Picklyk, Principal

***Winnipeg:* Immanuel Christian School**
215 Rougeau Ave., Winnipeg, MB R2C 3Z9
Tel: 204-661-8937; *Fax:* 204-669-7013
office@immanuelchristian.ca
www.immanuelchristian.ca
Grades: K.-12; *Enrollment:* 181
Rob Dewitt, Chair
Peter Veenendaal, Principal

***Winnipeg:* The King's School**
851 Panet Rd., Winnipeg, MB R2K 4C9, Canada
Tel: 204-989-6581; *Fax:* 204-989-6584
www.thekingsschool.ca
Grades: Kindergarten - 12; *Enrollment:* 250; *Note:* The King's School is a co-educational school, which is a ministry of Gateway Christian Community Church.
Andrew Micklefield, Principal

***Winnipeg:* Linden Christian School**
877 Wilkes Ave., Winnipeg, MB R3P 1B8
Tel: 204-989-6730; *Fax:* 204-487-7068
www.lindenchristian.org
www.facebook.com/LindenChristianSchool
instagram.com/lindenchristianschool
Grades: K.-12; *Enrollment:* 800
Garry Nickel, Chair
Robert Charach, Principal
rcharach@lindenchristian.org

***Winnipeg:* Mennonite Brethren Collegiate Institute (BMCI)**
173 Talbot Ave., Winnipeg, MB R2L 0P6
Tel: 204-667-8210; *Fax:* 204-661-5091
mbci.mb.ca
Grades: 6-12
Fred Pauls, Principal

***Winnipeg:* St. Aidan's Christian School**
Aberdeen Campus
418 Aberdeen Ave., Winnipeg, MB R2W 1V7, Canada
Tel: 204-586-6792; *Fax:* 204-582-4729
staidanschool@mts.net
staidansschool.ca
Grades: K-8; *Enrollment:* 30
Peter Lurvey, Principal

Campuses
Calvary Temple Campus
400 Hargrave St., Winnipeg, MB, Canada
Tel: 204-944-9674

***Winnipeg:* Springs Christian Academy**
261 Youville St., Winnipeg, MB R2H 2S7, Canada
Tel: 204-331-3640; *Fax:* 204-257-1286
www.springschurch.com/sca
instagram.com/springschristianacademy
Grades: K.-12; *Enrollment:* 689; *Note:* Affiliated with Springs Church
Darcy Bayne, Principal
dbayne@springs.ca

***Winnipeg:* Westgate Mennonite Collegiate**
86 West Gate, Winnipeg, MB R3C 2E1, Canada
Tel: 204-775-7111; *Fax:* 204-786-1651
www.westgatemennonite.ca
Grades: 7 - 12; *Enrollment:* 315; *Note:* The Christian school is based upon the Anabaptist Mennonite tradition.
Bob Hummelt, Principal

***Winnipeg:* Winnipeg Mennonite Elementary & Middle School**
Bedson Campus
250 Bedson St., Winnipeg, MB R3K 1R7
Tel: 204-885-1032; *Fax:* 204-897-4068
wmems@wmems.ca
www.wmems.ca
www.facebook.com/pages/WMEMS/337515113011622
Grades: K.-8; *Enrollment:* 400
John Sawatzky, Principal
john.sawatzky@wmems.ca

Schools
Winnipeg Mennonite Elementary School - Katherine Friesen Campus
26 Agassiz Dr., Winnipeg, MB R3T 2K7
Tel: 204-261-9637; *Fax:* 204-275-5181
agassiz.office@wmems.ca
Grades: K.-6
David Stoesz, Principal
david.stoesz@wmems.ca

Catholic

***Winnipeg:* Holy Cross School**
300 Dubuc St., Winnipeg, MB R2H 1E4, Canada
Tel: 204-237-4936; *Fax:* 204-237-7433
www.holycrossschoool.mb.ca
Grades: K.-8; *Enrollment:* 311; *Number of Employees:* 30
Alexander Cap, Principal, 204-273-4936
acap@holycrossschool.mb.ca

***Winnipeg:* Our Lady of Victory School**
249 Arnold Ave., Winnipeg, MB R3L 0W4, Canada
Tel: 204-452-7632; *Fax:* 204-453-3081
olv@shawbiz.ca
www.victoryedu.com
twitter.com/olv_school
Grades: Pre K.-8; *Enrollment:* 117
A. Cap, Principal

Independent & Private Schools

***Austin:* Pine Creek Colony School**
P.O. Box 370
Austin, MB R0H 0C0, Canada
Tel: 204-466-2925; *Fax:* 204-466-2698
Grades: K.-12

***Austin:* Pine Creek School**
P.O. Box 219
Austin, MB ROH OCO, Canada
Tel: 204-385-3025
Grades: K-10

***Beausejour:* Willow Grove School**
P.O. Box 59
Beausejour, MB R0E 0C0
Tel: 204-268-4035; *Fax:* 204-268-9452
Grades: 1-9

***Cartwright:* Cartwright Community Independent School (CCIS)**
P.O. Box 419
Cartwright, MB R0K 0L0, Canada
Tel: 204-529-2357; *Fax:* 204-529-2455
Grades: 12 (Senior 4)

***Cartwright:* Rock Lake School**
P.O. Box 69
Cartwright, MB R0K 0L0, Canada
Tel: 204-529-2349; *Fax:* 204-529-2184
Grades: 1 - 9; *Note:* Rock Lake School is a private school established by the Church of God in Christ, Mennonite.

***Elie:* Milltown Academy**
P.O. Box 250
Elie, MB R0H 0H0, Canada
Tel: 204-353-4111; *Fax:* 204-353-2729
Grades: K - 12

***Elm Creek:* Wingham HB School**
P.O. Box 45
RR #1, Elm Creek, MB R0G 0N0, Canada
Tel: 204-436-3231; *Fax:* 204-436-3230
winghamhbschool.com
Grades: K.-12
James Waldner, Principal
james@winghamhbschool.com

***Elma:* Riverside School**
P.O. Box 136
Elma, MB R0E 0Z0, Canada
Tel: 204-348-2686; *Fax:* 204-348-7181
Grades: 1 - 9

***Elma:* Twin Rivers Country School**
P.O. Box 30
Elma, MB R0E 0Z0, Canada
Tel: 204-426-5611; *Fax:* 204-426-5611
Grades: K - 8

***Gladstone:* Prairie View Amish School**
General Delivery, Gladstone, MB R0J 0T0
Grades: 1 - 9

***Grandview:* Poplar Grove School**
P.O. Box 70
Grandview, MB R0L 0Y0, Canada
Tel: 204-546-2691
Grades: 1-9

***Kenville:* Riverdale School**
RR#1, Kenville, MB R0L 0Z0, Canada
Tel: 204-539-2660; *Fax:* 204-539-2480
Grades: 1 - 9

***Kleefeld:* Wild Rose School**
P.O. Box 167
Kleefeld, MB R0A 0V0
Tel: 204-377-4778; *Fax:* 204-377-4778
Grades: 1-9

***Kola:* Kola Community School**
P.O. Box 312
Kola, MB R0M 1B0, Canada
Tel: 204-556-2347; *Fax:* 204-556-2425
kola.flbsd.mb.ca
Grades: K.-9; *Number of Employees:* 4 teachers; 3 administrative; 2 custodial; 1 bus driver; *Note:* Kola School is a Grade One to Grade Nine School within Fort La Bosse School Division. They offer complete programming in 3 combined classrooms with the following divisions: Grade One to Grade Three, Grade Four to Grade Six, and Grade Seven to Grade Nine.
Lance Barrate, Principal, 204-748-1605

***MacGregor:* H.B. Community Baker Colony School**
P.O. Box 40
MacGregor, MB R0H 0R0, Canada
Tel: 204-252-2178; *Fax:* 204-252-2381
Grades: K-12

***Neepawa:* Living Hope School**
P.O. Box 2158
Neepawa, MB R0J 1H0, Canada
Tel: 204-966-3274
Grades: 3-12

***Pine River:* Pine River Country School**
P.O. Box 242
Pine River, MB R0L 1M0
Tel: 204-263-2001
Grades: 1 - 8

***Portage la Prairie:* Airport Colony School**
P.O. Box 967
Portage la Prairie, MB R1N 3C4, Canada
Tel: 204-274-2412
Grades: K-12; *Note:* Location: NE 2-13-8 W, MacDonald, MB.

***Portage la Prairie:* Westpark School**
P.O. Box 91
2375 Saskatchewan Ave. West, Portage la Prairie, MB R1N 3B2, Canada
Tel: 204-857-3726
office@westparkschool.com
www.westparkschool.com
www.facebook.com/westparkschool
Grades: K.-12 (Senior 1 - 4); *Enrollment:* 220; *Note:* The school is a ministry of Portage Alliance Church.
Lydia Stoesz, B.Ed., M.Div, Principal

***Rosenort:* Prairie View School**
P.O. Box 117
112 River Rd. North, Rosenort, MB R0G 1W0, Canada
Tel: 204-746-8837
Grades: 1 - 9

***Sinclair:* Stony Creek School**
P.O. Box 5
Sinclair, MB R0M 2A0, Canada
Tel: 204-662-4431; *Fax:* 204-662-4539
Grades: 1-9

***Sperling:* Silverwinds School**
P.O. Box 130
Sperling, MB R0G 2M0, Canada
Tel: 204-626-3378; *Fax:* 204-626-3397
Grades: K-12

***Ste. Anne:* Greenland School**
P.O. Box 22
Grp. 15, RR#1, Ste. Anne, MB R5H 1R1, Canada
Tel: 204-355-4922; *Fax:* 204-355-9280
Grades: K-9

***Steinbach:* Church of God Sunrise Academy**
P.O. Box 3368
Steinbach, MB R5G 1P6, Canada
Tel: 204-434-6643; *Fax:* 204-326-6681
Grades: K-12

***Steinbach:* Countryview School**
P.O. Box 3910
Steinbach, MB R5G 1P9, Canada
Tel: 204-326-1481; *Fax:* 204-326-4788
Number of Schools: 1; *Grades:* 2-9; *Enrollment:* 22; *Number of Employees:* 2
Phyllis Wohlgemuth, Principal, 306-326-4968
Tim Wiebe, Vice-Principal, 306-326-1413

***Steinbach:* VCFG School**
P.O. Box 3160
Steinbach, MB R5G 1P5
Tel: 204-320-2716; *Fax:* 204-320-2716
Grades: K - 10

***Winkler:* New Life Fellowship**
P.O. Box 41
Winkler, MB R6W 4A7
Tel: 204-331-1689
Grades: 1 - 10

***Winnipeg:* Al-Hijra Islamic School (AOS)**
410 Desalaberry Ave., Winnipeg, MB R2L 0Y7
Tel: 204-489-1300; *Fax:* 204-489-1323
ais123@mts.net
www.alhijra.ca
Grades: Kindergarten - 9; *Enrollment:* 185; *Note:* Established in 1996, teaching at Al-Hijra Islamic School includes Arabic, Quranic, & Islamic studies.
Abdo El-Tassi, Board Chair
Abed Moussa, Principal
Khadijah Abdulkader, Arabid & Islam Teacher
Fouad Elmazini, Arabid & Islam Teacher

***Winnipeg:* Balmoral Hall School**
630 Westminster Ave., Winnipeg, MB R3C 3S1, Canada
Tel: 204-784-1600
www.balmoralhall.com
TTY: 1-866-373-2611
www.facebook.com/balmoralhall
twitter.com/balmoralhall
www.youtube.com/user/BalmoralHallWinnipeg
Grades: Nursery - 5; *Note:* Balmoral Hall School specializes in education for girls. It also offers a child care program for girls, aged 2 & 3.
Jim Perchaluk, Chair
Joanne Kamins, Head of School
Geneviève Delaquis, Director, Advancement, 204-784-1615
Bin Dong Jiang, Administrator, Day Admissions, 204-784-1608

***Winnipeg:* Beautiful Savior Lutheran School (BSLS)**
52 Birchdale Ave., Winnipeg, MB R2H 1R9, Canada
Tel: 204-984-9600; *Fax:* 204-984-9607
admin@bsls.ca
www.bsls.ca
Grades: Nursery - 8; *Note:* Beautiful Savior Lutheran School also offers a daycare program & before & after school care.
Jennifer McCrea, Principal
principal@bsls.ca
Heather Burnett, Director, Child Care Services

***Winnipeg:* Casa Montessori and Orff**
1055 Wilkes Ave., Winnipeg, MB R3P 2L7
Tel: 204-487-6167; *Fax:* 204-487-2944
montessoriandorff.ca
Number of Schools: 2; *Grades:* Pre.-6
Fay Sequeira, Co-Founder/Director
Lorraine Barnett, Co-Founder/Director

***Winnipeg:* The Collegiate at the University of Winnipeg**
515 Portage Ave., Winnipeg, MB R3B 2E9, Canada
Tel: 204-786-9221; *Fax:* 204-775-1942
collegiate@uwinnipeg.ca
www.uwinnipeg.ca/index/collegiate-index
Grades: 9 - 12; *Note:* The independent secondary school is a division of The University of Winnipeg.
Robert Bend, Dean, 204-988-7583
r.bend@uwinnipeg.ca
Richard Martin, Associate Dean, 204-786-9843
rc.martin@uwinnipeg.ca
Carole Anderson, Registrar & Office Manager, 204-786-9901
c.anderson@uwinnipeg.ca

***Winnipeg:* Gray Academy of Jewish Education**
A100, 123 Doncaster St., Winnipeg, MB R3N 2B4, Canada
Tel: 204-477-7410; *Fax:* 204-477-7474
info@grayacademy.ca
www.grayacademy.ca
www.facebook.com/MyGrayAcademy
www.twitter.com/MyGrayAcademy
Grades: JK-12; *Note:* The largest independent Jewish day school in Western Canada. Co-educational. General subjects & Jewish studies programmes.
Rory Paul, Head of School & CEO, 204-477-7425
Dr. Ruth Ashrafi, Director of Judaic Studies, 204-477-7483
Jack Cipilinski, Chief Financial Officer, 204-477-7402
Ashley Morgan, Coordinator of Marketing & Communications, 204-477-7489

***Winnipeg:* Holy Ghost School**
319 Selkirk Ave., Winnipeg, MB R2W 2L8
Tel: 204-582-1053; *Fax:* 204-582-4870
schooloffice@holyghost.ca
www.holyghostschool.ca
Grades: K.-8
Fr. Alfred Grzempa, Pastor
J. Siska, Principal

***Winnipeg:* Islamic Academy of Manitoba**
Académie islamique du Manitoba
1188 Dakota St., Winnipeg, MB R2N 3H4, Canada
Tel: 204-231-4441
islamic-academy@mts.net
ecolesofiyaschool.weebly.com
Grades: K.-6; *Note:* Program & instruction Arabic, English & French. Daily Qur'an studies.
Dr. Taib Soufi, Principal

***Winnipeg:* The Laureate Academy**
100 Villa Maria Pl., Winnipeg, MB R3V 1A9
Tel: 204-831-7107; *Fax:* 204-885-3217
frontdesk@laureateacademy.com
www.laureateacademy.com
www.facebook.com/16844073327162O
Grades: 1 - 12
Edward T. Scully, President & Co-Founder
Barbara E. Butler, Vice-President & Co-Founder

***Winnipeg:* Montessori Learning Centre (MLC)**
170 Ashland Ave., Winnipeg, MB R3L 1L1, Canada
Tel: 204-475-1039; *Fax:* 204-452-4643
mlcmont@mts.net
www.mlcwinnipeg.ca
Grades: Preschool - Kindergarten; *Note:* The Centre's preschool program is designed for children from age 3 to 5.
Lucille Labassiere, Principal & Director

***Winnipeg:* Oholei Torah School**
1845 Mathers Ave., Winnipeg, MB R3N 0N2, Canada
Tel: 204-339-8737; *Fax:* 204-586-0487
rabbialtein@chabadwinnipeg.org
Grades: Gr. N.-8; *Enrollment:* 13

***Winnipeg:* Ohr Hatorah School**
620 Brock St., Winnipeg, MB R3N 0Z4, Canada
Tel: 204-489-1147; *Fax:* 204-489-5899
principal@ohrhatorah.ca
Grades: N.-4

***Winnipeg:* Paradise Montessori School**
1341 Kenaston Blvd., Winnipeg, MB R3P 2P2
Tel: 204-832-0866; *Fax:* 204-487-3469
www.paradisemontessori.ca
Grades: N-K
Lileena Mendis, Director
lileena@paradisemontessori.ca

***Winnipeg:* Red River Valley Junior Academy (RRVJA)**
56 Grey St., Winnipeg, MB R2L 1V3, Canada
Tel: 204-661-2408; *Fax:* 204-667-1396
mail@rrvja.ca
www.rrvja.ca
Other Information: Admissions: 204-667-2383
www.facebook.com/groups/117850445470
Grades: Junior Kindergarten - 10; *Note:* Red River Valley Junior Academy is owned & operated by the Seventh Day Adventist Church.
Ian Mighty, M.A., B.Ed., PBCE, Admin., Principal
imight@rrvja.ca
Daniel NcGuire, B.Ed., Vice Principal & Middle Years Specialist
dmcguire@rrvja.ca
Evelyn Mallorca, Administrative Assistant
emallorca@rrvja.ca

***Winnipeg:* St. Alphonsus School**
343 Munroe Ave., Winnipeg, MB R2K 1H2, Canada
Tel: 204-667-6271; *Fax:* 204-663-4187
info@stalphonsusschool.ca
www.stalphonsusschool.ca
www.facebook.com/stalphonsusschool1
twitter.com/stalphonsus1
Grades: K.-8; *Enrollment:* 230
Christine McInnis, Principal
christine.mcinnis@stalphonsusschool.ca

***Winnipeg:* St. Boniface Diocesan High School**
282 Dubuc St., Winnipeg, MB R2H 1E4, Canada
Tel: 204-987-1560; *Fax:* 204-237-9891
admin@sbdhs.net
www.sbdhs.net
Grades: 9 - 12; *Enrollment:* 150
Erik Persson, Principal

***Winnipeg:* St. Charles Interparochial School**
331 St. Charles St., Winnipeg, MB R3K 1T6, Canada
Tel: 204-837-1520; *Fax:* 204-837-2326
sec@stccs.ca
www.stccs.ca
Grades: K.-8; *Enrollment:* 206; *Number of Employees:* 32
Dr. Anne Penny, Principal
dr_penny@stccs.ca

***Winnipeg:* St. Edward's School**
836 Arlington St., Winnipeg, MB R3E 2E4, Canada
Tel: 204-774-8773; *Fax:* 204-775-0011
www.stedwards.ca
Grades: K.-6; *Enrollment:* 191
Linda Doyle, Principal
lindadoyle@mts.net

***Winnipeg:* St. Emile School**
552 St. Anne's Rd., Winnipeg, MB R2M 3G4, Canada
Tel: 204-989-5020
admin@stemileschool.ca
www.stemileschool.ca
Grades: Pre - 8
Luca Macchia, President

***Winnipeg:* St. Gerard School**
40 Foster St., Winnipeg, MB R2L 1V7, Canada
Tel: 204-667-4862; *Fax:* 204-668-7932
stgerard@shaw.ca
www.stgerardschool.net
Grades: Pre-8
Jean Gilbert, Principal
jgilbert.stgerard@shaw.ca

***Winnipeg:* St. Ignatius School**
239 Harrow St., Winnipeg, MB R3M 2Y3, Canada
Tel: 204-475-1386
www.stignatius.mb.ca
Grades: 1-8
Michael Crooks, Principal

***Winnipeg:* St. John Brebeuf School**
605 Renfrew St., Winnipeg, MB R3N 1J8, Canada
Tel: 204-489-2115; *Fax:* 204-928-7455
schooloffice@sjbcommunity.ca
www.sjbschool.ca
Grades: K.-8; *Enrollment:* 221
Father Mark A. Tarrant, Pastor
matarrant@sjbcommunity.ca
Ms. Carreiro, Principal
carreiro@sjbcommunity.ca

***Winnipeg:* St. John's-Ravenscourt School**
400 South Dr., Winnipeg, MB R3T 3K5, Canada
Tel: 204-477-2485; *Fax:* 204-477-2429
info@sjr.mb.ca
www.sjr.mb.ca
www.facebook.com/196987707625
www.twitter.com/@SJR_School
www.linkedin.com/company/st-john%27s-ravenscourt-school
Grades: K.-12; *Enrollment:* 780
Sean Lawton, Chair

***Winnipeg:* St. Joseph the Worker School**
505 Brewster St., Winnipeg, MB R2C 2W6, Canada
Tel: 204-222-1841; *Fax:* 204-222-1769
stjoesch@mymts.net
sjtwschool.ca
Grades: K.-6; *Enrollment:* 129
Judi Pacheco, Principal

Winnipeg: St. Mary's Academy
550 Wellington Cres., Winnipeg, MB R3M 0C1, Canada
Tel: 204-477-0244; *Fax:* 204-453-2417
www.stmarysacademy.mb.ca
www.facebook.com/smawinnipeg
twitter.com/SMAwpg
www.linkedin.com/company/st-mary%27s-academy---winnipeg-mb
www.youtube.com/user/SMAWinnipeg
Grades: 7-12; *Enrollment:* 550
Mark Dufresne, Chair

Winnipeg: St. Maurice School
1639 Pembina Hwy., Winnipeg, MB R3T 2G6, Canada
Tel: 204-453-4020; *Fax:* 204-452-4050
admin@stmaurice.mb.ca
www.stmaurice.mb.ca
Grades: K.-12; *Enrollment:* 585
B. Doiron, Principal
bdoiron@stmaurice.mb.ca

Winnipeg: St. Paul's High School
2200 Grant Ave., Winnipeg, MB R3P 0P8, Canada
Tel: 204-831-2300; *Fax:* 204-831-2340
contact-us@stpauls.mb.ca
www.stpauls.mb.ca
www.facebook.com/stpaulshigh
twitter.com/stpauls
www.linkedin.com/groups?home=&gid=6717518&trk=anet_ug_hm
Grades: 9-12; *Enrollment:* 582; *Note:* Jesuit University prep school for boys
Tom Lussier, Principal
Fr. Len Altilia, President

Winnipeg: St. Vital Montessori School
613 St Mary's Rd., Winnipeg, MB R3M 3L8, Canada
Tel: 204-255-0209
stvms@hotmail.ca
www.stvitalmontessori.ca
Grades: Pre.

Winnipeg: Twelve Tribes School
90 East Gate, Winnipeg, MB R3C 2C3, Canada
Tel: 204-779-1118
Grades: K - 10

Winnipeg: Winnipeg Montessori School Inc.
1525 Willson Pl., Winnipeg, MB R3T 4H1, Canada
Tel: 204-452-3315; *Fax:* 204-452-3315
wpgmont@winnipegmontessori.com
www.winnipegmontessori.com
Grades: K
Dana Downey, Chair

Winnipeg: Winnipeg South Academy
870 Scotland Ave., Winnipeg, MB R3M 1X8
Tel: 204-452-6547
info@kiddiekampus.ca
www.kiddiekampus.ca
Grades: Junior Kindergarten - 3; *Note:* Founded in 1990, Winnipeg South Academy is a private school that offers an extension of the Montessori philosophy.
Gayle Lavigne, Founder
Susan Kiburn, Head of School
Suzanne Van Cauwenberghe, Principal

Universities & Colleges

Universities

Brandon: Brandon University
270 - 18th St., Brandon, MB R7A 6A9, Canada
Tel: 204-728-9520; *Fax:* 204-726-4573
www.brandonu.ca
www.facebook.com/brandonu.ca
twitter.com/brandonunews
www.linkedin.com/company/51014?trk=tyah
Full Time Equivalency: 2940
Dr. Gervan Fearon, President & Vice-Chancellor
president@brandonu.ca
Scott J.B. Lamont, Vice-President, Administration & Finance
lamont@brandonu.ca
Dr. Heather Duncan, Acting Vice-President, Academic & Provost
duncanh@brandonu.ca
Steve Robinson, Acting Dean, Arts
artsdean@brandonu.ca
Dr Heather Duncan, Dean, Education
deanofed@brandonu.ca
Dr W. Dean Care, Dean, Health Studies
cared@brandonu.ca
Dr Andrew Egan, Dean, Science
egana@brandonu.ca
Kim Fallis, Registrar, 204-727-9751
fallis@brandonu.ca

Faculties
Faculty of Arts
Tel: 204-727-9780; *Fax:* 204-726-0473
artsdean@brandonu.ca
www.brandonu.ca/arts
S. Grills, Dean

Faculty of Education
Tel: 204-727-9626
facultyed@brandonu.ca
www.brandonu.ca/education
www.facebook.com/BUeducation
twitter.com/BU_Faculty_Ed
bu-facultyofed.ning.com
Jerrie Storie, Acting Dean

Faculty of Science
Tel: 204-727-9624; *Fax:* 204-728-7346
science@brandonu.ca
www.brandonu.ca/science
Dr. Austin Gulliver, Acting Dean

Schools
Faculty of Health Studies
Tel: 204-727-7409; *Fax:* 204-571-8568
healthstudies@brandonu.ca
www.brandonu.ca/health-studies
W. Dean Care, Dean

School of Music
Tel: 204-727-7388; *Fax:* 204-728-6839
www.brandonu.ca/music
G. Carruthers, Dean

Winnipeg: Booth University College
447 Webb Pl., Winnipeg, MB R3B 2P2, Canada
Tel: 204-947-6701; *Fax:* 204-942-3856
Toll-Free: 877-942-6684
admissions@boothuc.ca
www.boothuc.ca
www.facebook.com/BoothUniversityCollege
www.twitter.com/boothuc
Donald E Burke, President, 204-924-4871
donald_burke@boothuc.ca
Marjory Kerr, Dean & VP Academic, 204-924-4863
majory_kerr@boothuc.ca
Karen Ng, Dean of Students, 204-924-4876
karen_ng@boothuc.ca
Anita Ratnam, Registrar, 204-924-4861
anita_ratnam@boothuc.ca

Winnipeg: Canadian Mennonite University
500 Shaftesbury Blvd., Winnipeg, MB R3P 2N2, Canada
Tel: 204-487-3300; *Fax:* 204-487-3858
Toll-Free: 877-231-4570
info@cmu.ca
www.cmu.ca
www.facebook.com/CMUwinnipeg
www.twitter.com/CMUwpg
www.youtube.com/cmumedia
Full Time Equivalency: 610
Cheryl Pauls, President
Earl Davey, Vice-Pres., Academic
edavey@cmu.ca
Wesley Toews, Registrar & Assistant VP
wtoews@cmu.ca
John Unger, Vice-President Administration & Finance
Ruth Taronno, Assoc. Vice-Pres., MSC
rtaronno@cmu.ca

Schools
Redekop School of Business
Ray Vander Zaag, Director, 204-487-3300, ext. 643
rvanderzaag@cmu.ca

Canadian School of Peacebuilding
500 Shaftesbury Blvd., Winnipeg, MB R3P 2N2
Tel: 204-487-3300; *Fax:* 204-837-7415
csop@cmu.ca
csop.cmu.ca
www.facebook.com/128875250034
twitter.com/cmu_csop
www.youtube.com/cmumedia
Jarem Sawatsky, Co-Director
Valerie Smith, Co-Director

Community School of Music & the Arts
500 Shaftesbury Blvd., Winnipeg, MB R3P 2N2
Tel: 204-487-3300; *Fax:* 204-487-3858
Toll-Free: 877-231-4570
Verna Wiebe, Director, 204-837-4870
vwiebe@cmu.ca

Graduate School of Theology & Ministry
Karl Koop, Director, 204-487-3300, ext. 630
kkoop@cmu.ca

School of Music
Janet Brenneman, Dean, School of Music, 204-487-3300, ext. 682
jbrenneman@cmu.ca

Winnipeg: Prairie Theatre School
300-393 Portage Ave., #Y, Winnipeg, MB R3B 2H6, Canada
Tel: 204-942-7291; *Fax:* 204-942-1774
education@pte.mb.ca
www.pte.mb.ca/school/about.htm
www.facebook.com/pages/PTE-School/152388992656?ref=hl

Winnipeg: University of Manitoba
66 Chancellors Circle, Winnipeg, MB R3T 2N2
Tel: 204-474-8880; *Toll-Free:* 800-432-1960
www.umanitoba.ca
www.facebook.com/umanitoba
twitter.com/umanitoba
www.linkedin.com/company/university-of-manitoba
www.youtube.com/user/YouManitoba
Full Time Equivalency: 29150
Harvey Secter, Chancellor
Dr. David T. Barnard, B.Sc., M.Sc., Ph.D., Dip., President & Vice-Chancellor
John Kearsey, Vice-President, External
Digvir Jayas, Ph.D., Vice-President, Research & International
Joanne C. Keselman, B.A., M.A., Ph.D., Vice-President, Academic & Provost
Paul Kochan, Vice-President, Administration
Janice Ristock, Vice-Provost, Academic Affairs
David Collins, Vice-Provost, Integrated Planning & Academic Programs
Susan Gottheil, Vice-Provost, Students
Jay Doering, Vice-Provost, Graduate Education
Jeffrey M. Leclerc, B.Ed., University Secretary

Faculties
Faculty of Agricultural & Food Sciences (AFS)
256 Agriculture Building
66 Dafoe Rd., Winnipeg, MB R3T 2N2
Tel: 204-474-6026; *Fax:* 204-474-7525
agfoodsci@umanitoba.ca
umanitoba.ca/afs
Karin Wittenberg, Dean
agdean@umanitoba.ca

Faculty of Architecture
201 Russell Building
84 Curry Pl., Winnipeg, MB R3T 2N2
Tel: 204-474-6433; *Fax:* 204-474-7532
umanitoba.ca/faculties/architecture
Ralph Stern, Dean

Faculty of Arts
Fletcher Argue Building, 3rd Fl.
Winnipeg, MB R3T 2N2
Tel: 204-474-9100; *Fax:* 204-474-7590
Toll-Free: 800-432-1960
arts-inquiry@lists.umanitoba.ca
umanitoba.ca/faculties/arts
www.facebook.com/UManitobaArtsFaculty
twitter.com/UM_Arts_Advisor
Jeffrey Taylor, Dean

Continuing Education
166 Extended Education Complex
Winnipeg, MB R3T 2N2
Tel: 204-474-9921; *Fax:* 204-474-7661
Toll-Free: 888-216-7011
extended@umanitoba.ca
umanitoba.ca/faculties/con_ed
Gary Hepburn, Dean

Faculty of Dentistry
#D212, 780 Bannatyne Ave., Winnipeg, MB R3T 2N2
Tel: 204-789-3631; *Fax:* 204-789-3912
info_dent@umanitoba.ca
umanitoba.ca/faculties/dentistry
Anthony Iacopino, Dean

Faculty of Education
203 Education Bldg.
Winnipeg, MB R3T 2N2
Tel: 204-474-9004; *Fax:* 204-474-7551
Toll-Free: 800-432-1960
education@umanitoba.ca
umanitoba.ca/faculties/education
David Mandzuk, Dean

Faculty of Engineering
E2-290 Engineering & Information Technology Compl
Winnipeg, MB R3T 5V6
Tel: 204-474-9809; *Fax:* 204-275-3773
dean_engineering@umanitoba.ca
umanitoba.ca/faculties/engineering

Jonathan Beddoes, Dean
dean_engineering@umanitoba.ca

Clayton H. Riddell Faculty of Environment, Earth & Resources
440 Wallace Bldg.
Winnipeg, MB R3T 2N2
Tel: 204-474-7252; *Fax:* 204-275-3147
Riddell.Faculty@UManitoba.ca
umanitoba.ca/faculties/environment
www.facebook.com/UManitobaRiddellFaculty
twitter.com/riddellfaculty

Norman Halden, Dean
nm_halden@umanitoba.ca

Faculty of Graduate Studies
500 University Centre
65 Chancellors Circle, Winnipeg, MB R3T 2N2
Tel: 204-474-9377; *Fax:* 204-474-7553
graduate_studies@umanitoba.ca
umanitoba.ca/faculties/graduate_studies
www.facebook.com/umgradstudies
twitter.com/umgradstudies

Jay Doering, Dean

Human Ecology
209 Human Ecology Bldg.
Winnipeg, MB R3T 2N2
Tel: 204-474-8508; *Fax:* 204-474-7592
umanitoba.ca/faculties/human_ecology

Harvy Frankel, Acting Dean

Asper School of Business
Drake Centre
181 Freedman Cres., Winnipeg, MB R3T 5V4
Tel: 204-474-9353; *Fax:* 204-474-7544
ASB_Info@UManitoba.ca
umanitoba.ca/faculties/management
www.youtube.com/user/aspermedia

Michael Benarroch, Dean
m.benarroch@ad.umanitoba.ca

Robson Hall, Faculty of Law
224 Dysart Rd., Winnipeg, MB R3T 2N2
Tel: 204-474-6130; *Fax:* 204-474-7580
lawinfo@umanitoba.ca
law.robsonhall.ca
www.facebook.com/umanitoba.law
twitter.com/robsonhall
www.youtube.com/user/robsonhallvideo

Lorna Turnbull, Dean
Lorna.Turnbull@umanitoba.ca

Faculty of Medicine
260 Brodie Centre
727 McDermot Ave., Winnipeg, MB R3E 3P5
Tel: 204-789-3557; *Fax:* 204-789-3928
communications@med.umanitoba.ca
umanitoba.ca/faculties/medicine
www.facebook.com/139137906136021
twitter.com/um_medicine
instagram.com/um_medicine

Brian Postl, Dean

Marcel A. Desautels Faculty of Music
65 Dafoe Rd., Winnipeg, MB R3T 2N2
Tel: 204-474-9310; *Fax:* 204-474-7546
music@umanitoba.ca
umanitoba.ca/faculties/music
www.facebook.com/Marcel.A.Desautels.FacultyofMusic
twitter.com/facultyofmusic
www.youtube.com/UofMFacultyofMusic

Edmund Dawe, Dean

Faculty of Nursing
Helen Glass Centre for Nursing
89 Curry Pl., Winnipeg, MB R3T 2N2
Tel: 204-474-7452; *Fax:* 204-474-7682
Toll-Free: 800-432-1960
nursing@umanitoba.ca
umanitoba.ca/faculties/nursing
www.facebook.com/NursingatUofM

Beverly O'Connell, Dean

Faculty of Pharmacy
Apotex Centre
750 McDermot Ave., Winnipeg, MB R3E 0T5
Tel: 204-474-9603; *Fax:* 204-789-3738
pharmacy@umanitoba.ca
umanitoba.ca/faculties/pharmacy

Neal Davies, Dean

Students Association for Health, Physical Education & Recreation Studies
194 Extended Education Complex
Winnipeg, MB R3T 2N2
Tel: 204-474-8892
sahpercouncil@gmail.com
umanitoba.ca/faculties/kinrec/undergrad/sahper
www.facebook.com/sahper.council
twitter.com/sahpercouncil

Chris Thiessen, President

Faculty of Science
239 Machray Hall
186 Dysart Rd., Winnipeg, MB R3T 2N2
Tel: 204-474-8256; *Fax:* 204-474-7618
science_advisor@umanitoba.ca
umanitoba.ca/faculties/science
www.facebook.com/umanitobafacultyofscience
twitter.com/UManitobaSciAdv

Mark Whitmore, Dean

Faculty of Social Work
521 Tier Building
Winnipeg, MB R3T 2N2
Tel: 204-474-7050; *Fax:* 204-474-7594
socialwk@umanitoba.ca
umanitoba.ca/faculties/social_work
www.facebook.com/umsocialwork

James Mulvale, Dean

Affiliations

St. John's College
92 Dysart Rd., Winnipeg, MB R3T 2M5
Tel: 204-474-8531; *Fax:* 204-474-7610
Toll-Free: 1-800-432-1960
umanitoba.ca/colleges/st_johns
Note: Affiliated with the Anglican Church of Canada, St. John's College is located on the University of Manitoba campus.
Dr. Chris Trott, Warden & Vice-Chancellor
Christopher.trott@ad.umanitoba.ca
Sherry Peters, Registrar
sherry.peters@ad.umanitoba.ca

St. Paul's College
70 Dysart Rd., Winnipeg, MB R3T 2M6
Tel: 204-474-8575; *Fax:* 204-474-7620
stpaulscollege@umanitoba.ca
www.umanitoba.ca/stpauls
www.facebook.com/pages/St-Pauls-College-U-of-M/188780044507028
www.youtube.com/user/stpaulscollegeuofm
Note: The Roman Catholic College is located on the University of Manitoba campus.
Christopher Adams, Rector
rector_stpaulscollege@umanitoba.ca
Moti Shojania, Dean of Studies
Mohtaram.Shojania@umanitoba.ca

University College
University of Manitoba
#203, 220 Dysart Rd., Winnipeg, MB R3T 2N2
Tel: 204-474-6839; *Fax:* 204-261-0021
Toll-Free: 800-432-1960
umanitoba.ca/colleges/uc

Prairie Theatre Exchange
#Y300, 393 Portage Ave., Winnipeg, MB R3B 2H6
Tel: 204-942-7291; *Fax:* 204-942-1774
education@pte.mb.ca
www.pte.mb.ca
www.facebook.com/pages/Prairie-Theatre-Exchange/423687680006
twitter.com/PrairieTheatre
www.youtube.com/user/PTEtv

John B. Lowe, School Director, 204-925-5252

Winnipeg: University of Winnipeg

515 Portage Ave., Winnipeg, MB R3B 2E9, Canada
Tel: 204-786-7811; *Fax:* 204-783-4996
www.uwinnipeg.ca
www.facebook.com/uwinnipeg
twitter.com/UWinnipeg
www.linkedin.com/edu/school?id=10811
www.youtube.com/user/uwinnipeg
Full Time Equivalency: 10106
Robert Silver, Chancellor
Annette Trimbee, President & Vice-Chancellor, 204-786-9214
president@uwinnipeg.ca
Neil Besner, Vice-Pres., Academic & Provost, 204-988-7104
n.besner@uwinnipeg.ca
Bill Balan, Vice-Pres., Finance & Administration, 204-786-9229
b.balan@uwinnipeg.ca
Laurel Repski, Vice-Pres., Human Resources, 204-789-1451
l.repski@uwinnipeg.ca
Sherman Kreiner, Vice-Pres., Student Life, 204-988-7116
s.kreiner@uwinnipeg.ca

Faculties

Faculty of Arts
arts@uwinnipeg.ca
uwinnipeg.ca/arts
www.facebook.com/309764740634
twitter.com/UWFacultyofArts

Glenn Moulaison, Dean of Arts, 204-786-9942
g.moulaison@uwinnipeg.ca

Faculty of Business & Economics
uwinnipeg.ca/fbe
www.facebook.com/239496476077267
twitter.com/UWFBE

Dr. Sylvie Albert, Dean, Business and Economics, 204-786-9990
s.albert@uwinnipeg.ca

Faculty of Education
Tel: 204-786-9491
education@uwinnipeg.ca

Ken Mccluskey, Dean, Faculty of Education, 204-786-9470
k.mccluskey@uwinnipeg.ca

Faculty of Graduate Studies
Tel: 204-779-8946
gradstudies@uwinnipeg.ca
uwinnipeg.ca/graduate-studies
www.facebook.com/271256406461
twitter.com/UWGradStudies
www.flickr.com/photos/104575821@N02/

Michael Weinrath, Acting Dean of Graduate Studies, 204-988-7625
m.reimer@uwinnipeg.ca

Gupta Faculty of Kinesiology & Applied Health
Fax: 204-783-7866
kinesiology@uwinnipeg.ca
uwinnipeg.ca/kinesiology

David Fitzpatrick, Dean of Kinesiology, 204-786-9943
d.fitzpatrick@uwinnipeg.ca

Faculty of Science
sciences@uwinnipeg.ca
www.facebook.com/129478117154189
twitter.com/uwsciences

Danny Blair, Acting Dean of Science, 204-786-9236
d.blair@uwinnipeg.ca

Schools

The United Centre for Theological Studies (UCTS)
515 Portage Ave., Winnipeg, MB R3B 2E9
Tel: 204-786-9320
www.uwinnipeg.ca/index/theology-index

Chris Wells, Director of Studies, 204-988-7685
ch.wells@uwinnipeg.ca

Global College
520 Portage Ave., Winnipeg, MB R3B 2E9
Tel: 204-988-7105
global.college@uwinnipeg.ca
www.uwinnipeg.ca/index/global-college-index

Dean Peachey, Executive Director, 204-988-7106
d.peachey@uwinnipeg.ca

Richardson College for the Environment
599 Portage Ave., Winnipeg, MB R3B 2E9
Tel: 204-786-9236; *Fax:* 204-783-7981
www.uwinnipeg.ca/index/richardson-college-index

Danny Blair, Principal, the Richardson College for the Environment
d.blair@uwinnipeg.ca

Affiliations

Menno Simons College
520 Portage Ave., Winnipeg, MB R3C 0G2, Canada
Tel: 204-953-3855; *Fax:* 204-783-3699
msc@uwinnipeg.ca
mscollege.ca
www.facebook.com/mennosimonscollege
twitter.com/MSCwpg
www.youtube.com/user/cmumedia
Note: A college of the Canadian Mennonite University, maintaining an affiliation with the University of Winnipeg. It is located on the campus of the U. of W.
Gordon Zerbe, Vice-President, Academic (CMU), 204-487-3300, ext. 637
gzerbe@cmu.ca
Jerry Buckland, PhD, Academic Dean & Professor, 204-953-3859
j.buckland@uwinnipeg.ca

Colleges

Brandon: Assiniboine Community College
1430 Victoria Ave. East, Brandon, MB R7A 2A9
Tel: 204-725-8700; *Fax:* 204-725-8740
Toll-Free: 800-862-6307
info@assiniboine.net
www.assiniboine.net
facebook.com/accmanitoba
twitter.com/accmb
youtube.com/user/accmanitoba
Number of Employees: 500
Mark Frison, President & CEO

Campuses
Parkland Campus
520 Whitmore Ave. East, Dauphin, MB R7N 2V5
Tel: 204-622-2222; *Fax:* 800-482-2933
parklandinfo@assiniboine.net
Victoria Avenue East Campus
1430 Victoria Ave. East, Brandon, MB R7A 2A9
Tel: 204-725-8700; *Fax:* 204-725-8740
Toll-Free: 1-800-862-6307
info@assiniboine.net
North Hill Campus
1035 - 1st St. North, Brandon, MB R7A 2Y1
Fax: 204-725-8740
Adult Collegiate
725 Rosser Ave., Brandon, MB R7A 0K8
Tel: 204-725-8735; *Fax:* 204-725-8740
adultcollegiate@assiniboine.net

Brandon: Manitoba Emergency Services College
1601 Van Horne Ave. East, Brandon, MB R7A 7K2, Canada
Tel: 204-726-6855; *Toll-Free:* 1-888-253-1488
firecomm@gov.mb.ca
www.firecomm.gov.mb.ca/mesc.html
Note: The college is a broad-based emergency services training organization which offers a full-time program for those interested in a career in the EMS field.
Brenda D. Popko, Director
brenda.popko@gov.mb.ca

The Pas: University College of the North (UCN)
P.O. Box 3000
436 - 7 St. East, The Pas, MB R9A 1M7, Canada
Tel: 204-627-8500; *Fax:* 204-623-7316
Toll-Free: 866-627-8500
admissions@ucn.ca
www.ucn.ca
www.facebook.com/345539599541
www.linkedin.com/company/university-college-of-the-north
www.youtube.com/user/UCNTube
Full Time Equivalency: 3500
Konrad Jonasson, President & Vice-Chancellor
Florence Watson, Dean of Student Development & Registrar, 204-627-8553
fwatson@ucn.ca

Campuses
Thompson Campus (UCN)
55 UCN Dr., The Pas, MB R8N 1L7, Canada
Tel: 204-677-6450; *Toll-Free:* 866-677-6450

Winnipeg: Red River College (RRC)
2055 Notre Dame Ave., Winnipeg, MB R3H 0J9, Canada
Tel: 204-632-3960; *Toll-Free:* 1-888-515-7722
register@rrc.mb.ca
www.rrc.mb.ca
www.facebook.com/redrivercollege
twitter.com/rrc
www.linkedin.com/company/red-river-college
www.youtube.com/redrivercollege
Full Time Equivalency: 32000
Lloyd Schreyer, Chair
Paul Vogt, President & CEO, 204-632-2360
pevogt@rrc.ca

Campuses
Interlake Campus
P.O. Box 304
825 Manitoba Ave., Selkirk, MB R1A 1T0
Tel: 204-785-5328; *Fax:* 204-482-7082
Toll-Free: 866-946-3241
interlake@rrc.ca
www.rrc.ca/index.php?pid=408
Peguis-Fisher River Campus
P.O. Box 304
Selkirk, MB R1A 1T0
Tel: 204-785-5328; *Fax:* 204-482-7082
interlake@rrc.ca
www.rrc.ca/peguis
Portage Campus
32 - 5th St. SE, Portage la Prairie, MB R1N 1J2
Tel: 204-856-1914; *Fax:* 204-856-1915
portage@rrc.mb.ca
www.rrc.ca/index.php?pid=410
Steinbach Campus
#2, 385 Loewen Blvd., Steinbach, MB R5G 0B3
Tel: 204-320-2500; *Fax:* 204-346-0178
mshukla@rrc.ca
www.rrc.ca/index.php?pid=416
Note: The Steinbach Campus has community learning centres in Steinbach (204-320-2500) and in St. Pierre (204-433-7404).
Winkler Campus
#100, 561 Main St., Winkler, MB R6W 1E8
Tel: 204-325-9672; *Fax:* 204-325-4947
winkler@rrc.ca
www.rrc.ca/index.php?pid=414
Other Information: Winkler Community Learning Centre, Phone: 204-325-4997

Winnipeg: St. Andrew's College
29 Dysart Rd., Winnipeg, MB R3T 2M7
Tel: 204-474-8895; *Fax:* 204-474-7624
st_andrews@umanitoba.ca
www.umanitoba.ca/colleges/st_andrews
Note: Affiliated with the University of Manitoba, St. Andrew's College is an institution of the Ukrainian Orthodox Church of Canada. It works to promote spiritual, academic, cultural, & moral leadership.
V. Rev. Fr. Roman Bozyk, Dean, Theology

Winnipeg: Université de Saint-Boniface
200, av de la Cathédrale, Winnipeg, MB R2H 0H7, Canada
Tél: 204-233-0210; *Téléc:* 204-237-3240
Ligne sans frais: 1-888-233-5112
info@ustboniface.mb.ca
www.ustboniface.mb.ca
www.facebook.com/ustboniface
www.twitter.com/ustboniface
www.youtube.com/ustboniface
Full Time Equivalency: 1260
Raymonde Gagné, B.A., Cert.Ed., M.B.A., Présidente, 204-233-0210, ext. 318
André Samson, Doyen des arts et des sciences
Stéfan Delaquis, Doyen de l'éducation et des études professionnelles

Faculties
Faculté des arts
Alexandre Brassard, Dean
Faculté des sciences
École de service social
École technique et professionnelle
Charlotte Walkty
Faculté d'éducation
Stéfan Delaquis, Dean

Post Secondary/Technical

Blumenort: Free Eagle Driver Education Ltd.
P.O. Box 542
30 Penner Dr., Blumenort, MB R0A 0C0
Tel: 204-326-2878; *Fax:* 204-346-1490
Toll-Free: 866-766-0667
bernie@freeeagle.ca
www.freeeagle.ca
Note: Free Eagle is a Transport Driver Training School.

Brandon: Advanced School of Hairstyling & Nail Technology
603 Princess Ave., Brandon, MB R7A 0P2
Tel: 204-727-0358; *Fax:* 204-728-0085
www.advancedschoolofhairstyling.ca

Brandon: Systems Beauty College (SBC)
763 - 13th St., Brandon, MB R7A 4R6
Tel: 204-728-8843; *Toll-Free:* 877-536-7655
systems@hotmail.ca
www.systemsbeautycollege.ca
Number of Employees: 3

Dauphin: Academy of Learning College
Village Mall
P.O. Box 603
1430 Main St. South, Dauphin, MB R7N 2V4, Canada
Tel: 204-622-9999; *Fax:* 204-622-9998
academyoflearning@wcgwave.ca
www.academyoflearning.com
www.facebook.com/academyoflearning
twitter.com/AcademyLearning
www.linkedin.com/company/201041?trk=tyah
www.youtube.com/user/AcademyofLearning09
Note: Computer & business training; Students can choose from over 30 diploma and certificate programs.

Campuses
Academy of Learning College - Airdrie
#201, 2002 Luxstone Blvd., Airdrie, AB T4B 3K8, Canada
Tel: 403-912-3430; *Fax:* 403-912-3433
airdrie@airdrieacademyoflearning.com
Academy of Learning College - Brooks
#2, 715 - 2 St. West, Brooks, AB T1R 1A9, Canada
Tel: 403-793-2294; *Fax:* 403-793-7925
aol.brooks@gmail.com
Academy of Learning College - Calgary North East
#260, 495 - 36th St. NE, Calgary, AB T2A 6K3, Canada
Tel: 403-569-8973; *Fax:* 403-569-1085
calgaryne@academyoflearning.ab.ca
Academy of Learning College - Calgary South
#220, 8228 Macleod Trail South, Calgary, AB T2H 2B8, Canada
Tel: 403-252-8973; *Fax:* 403-252-8993
calgarys@academyoflearning.ab.ca
Academy of Learning College - Edmonton Downtown
Edmonton City Centre East
#326, 10205 - 101st St., Edmonton, AB T5J 4H5, Canada
Tel: 780-424-1144; *Fax:* 780-423-8962
edmdtn@academyoflearning.ab.ca
Academy of Learning College - Edmonton South
5650 - 23 Ave., Edmonton, AB T6L 6N2, Canada
Tel: 780-433-7284; *Fax:* 780-435-6656
edmsouth@academyoflearning.ab.ca
Academy of Learning College - High River
#2, 28 - 12 Ave. SE, High River, AB T1V 1T2, Canada
Tel: 403-652-2116; *Fax:* 403-652-1492
academyoflearning@highriver.net
Academy of Learning College - Medicine Hat
#115, 3030 - 13th Ave. SE, Medicine Hat, AB T1B 1E3, Canada
Tel: 403-526-5833; *Fax:* 403-526-4376
medicinehat@academyoflearning.ab.ca
Academy of Learning College - Red Deer
2965 Bremner Ave., Red Deer, AB T4R 1S2, Canada
Tel: 403-347-6676; *Fax:* 403-347-9097
reddeer@academyoflearning.ab.ca
Academy of Learning College - West Edmonton Mall
West Edmonton Mall
#1434, 8882 - 170th St., Edmonton, AB T5T 4M2, Canada
Tel: 780-496-9428; *Fax:* 780-944-9341
westedm@academyoflearning.ab.ca
Academy of Learning College - Abbotsford
#103, 32883 South Fraser Way, Abbotsford, BC V2S 2A6, Canada
Tel: 604-855-3315; *Fax:* 604-855-3365
admissionsabbotsford@telus.net
Academy of Learning College - Kamloops
699 Victoria St., Kamloops, BC V2C 2B3, Canada
Tel: 250-372-5429; *Fax:* 250-372-5462
Kamloops@310jobs.ca
Academy of Learning College - Kelowna
#101, 1740 Gordon Dr., Kelowna, BC V1Y 3H2, Canada
Tel: 250-868-3688; *Fax:* 250-868-3511
Kelowna@310jobs.ca
Academy of Learning College - Langley
5722 Glover Rd., Langley, BC V3A 4H8, Canada
Tel: 604-532-4040; *Fax:* 604-532-4001
admissionslangley@telus.net
Academy of Learning College - Nanaimo
#7, 1551 Estevan Rd., Nanaimo, BC V9S 3Y3, Canada
Tel: 250-753-4220; *Fax:* 250-753-4295
Nanaimo@310jobs.ca
Academy of Learning College - Richmond
6513 Buswell St., Richmond, BC V6Y 2G9, Canada
Tel: 604-270-3907; *Fax:* 604-270-6109
admissionsrichmond@telus.net

Academy of Learning College - Surrey
#102, 13753 - 72nd Ave., Surrey, BC V3W 2P2, Canada
Tel: 604-598-3555; *Fax:* 604-549-1234
joep@bcaol.com

Academy of Learning College - Vancouver
#302, 2555 Commercial Dr., Vancouver, BC V5N 4C1, Canada
Tel: 604-876-8600; *Fax:* 604-876-4333
DominicaV@bcaol.com

Academy of Learning College - Victoria Downtown
#204, 1111 Blanshard St., Victoria, BC V8W 2H7, Canada
Tel: 250-385-1333; *Fax:* 250-385-0100
Victoria@310jobs.ca

Academy of Learning College - Westshore
#206, 2780 Veterans Memorial Pkwy., Victoria, BC V9B 3S6, Canada
Tel: 250-391-6020; *Fax:* 250-391-6021
WestShore@310jobs.ca

Academy of Learning College - Selkirk
389 Eveline St., Selkirk, MB R1A 1N7, Canada
Tel: 204-785-8223; *Fax:* 204-785-8016
aolwpg@mts.net

Academy of Learning College - Steinbach
248 Lumber Ave., Steinbach, MB R5G 0T6, Canada
Tel: 204-326-4188; *Fax:* 204-326-3480
aol@trainingsolutionsmanitoba.ca

Academy of Learning College - Swan River
P.O. Box 667
129 - 4th Ave. South, Swan River, MB R0L 1Z0, Canada
Tel: 204-734-9900; *Fax:* 204-734-3238
aolswan@gmail.com

Academy of Learning College - Winnipeg North
77 Redwood Ave., 2nd Fl., Winnipeg, MB R2W 5J5, Canada
Tel: 204-582-9400; *Fax:* 204-582-8444
aolwpg@mts.net

Academy of Learning College - Winnipeg South
297 St. Mary's Rd., Winnipeg, MB R2H 1J5, Canada
Fax: 204-478-5020

Academy of Learning College - Bathurst
#13, 219 Main St., Bathurst, NB E2A 1A9, Canada
Tel: 506-546-7441; *Fax:* 506-546-7441
aolbathurst@nb.aibn.com

Academy of Learning College - Miramichi
208 McCallum St., Miramichi, NB E1V 2A1, Canada
Tel: 506-622-8935; *Fax:* 506-622-8909
academyoflearning@nb.aibn.com

Academy of Learning College - Dartmouth
Cambridge Tower 1
#206, 202 Brownlow Ave., Dartmouth, NS B3B 1T5, Canada
Tel: 902-469-8973; *Fax:* 902-461-4331
learn@aolhrm.com

Academy of Learning College - Halifax
Mumford Professional Centre
#155, 6960 Mumford Rd., Halifax, NS B3L 4P1, Canada
Tel: 902-455-3395; *Fax:* 902-461-4331
learn@aolhrm.com

Academy of Learning College - Barrie
#3, 18 Cundles Rd. East, Barrie, ON L4M 2Z5, Canada
Tel: 705-719-9494; *Fax:* 705-719-7174
parry.aolbarrie@rogers.com

Academy of Learning College - Belleville
Bay View Mall
#16, 470 Dundas St. East, Belleville, ON K8N 1G1, Canada
Tel: 613-967-8973; *Fax:* 613-967-4642
academyoflearning1@cogeco.net

Academy of Learning College - Cornwall
225 Pitt St., Cornwall, ON K6J 3P8, Canada
Tel: 613-936-8973; *Fax:* 613-936-6685
Administration@CornwallCareerCollege.ca

Academy of Learning College - Guelph
#9, 226 Speedvale Ave. West, Guelph, ON N1H 1C4, Canada
Tel: 519-824-9431; *Fax:* 519-824-8306
aolguelph@sentex.net

Academy of Learning College - Hamilton
401 Main St. East, Hamilton, ON L8N 1J7, Canada
Tel: 905-777-8553; *Fax:* 905-777-0103
academy@cogeco.net

Academy of Learning College - Kingston
1469 Princess St., Kingston, ON K7M 3E9, Canada
Tel: 613-544-8973
admissions@aolkingston.com

Academy of Learning College - Mississauga East
#205, 1310 Dundas St. East, Mississauga, ON L4Y 2C1, Canada
Tel: 905-273-6788; *Fax:* 905-273-3114
admin@aolmississauga.com

Academy of Learning College - Niagara / St. Catharines
50 Niagara St., St Catharines, ON L2R 4K9, Canada
Tel: 905-641-0835; *Fax:* 905-641-2752
aolniagara@on.aibn.com

Academy of Learning College - Ottawa West
#217, 1600 Merivale Rd., Ottawa, ON K2G 5J8, Canada
Tel: 613-224-8973; *Fax:* 613-224-2669
aolnepean@on.aibn.com

Academy of Learning College - Owen Sound
1077 - 2nd Ave. East, 2nd Fl., Owen Sound, ON N4K 2H8, Canada
Tel: 519-371-6188; *Fax:* 519-376-1737
info@academytraining.ca

Academy of Learning College - Richmond Hill
10235 Yonge St., Richmond Hill, ON L4C 3B4, Canada
Tel: 905-508-5791; *Fax:* 905-508-9409
aolrichmondhill1@rogers.com

Academy of Learning College - Thunder Bay
101 Syndicate Ave. North, #B, Thunder Bay, ON P7C 3V4, Canada
Tel: 807-624-2380; *Fax:* 807-476-1894
calli.academyoflearning@shaw.ca

Academy of Learning College - Toronto - Albion & Islington
#201, 1123 Albion Rd., Toronto, ON M9V 1A9, Canada
Tel: 416-746-3333; *Fax:* 416-746-3330
training@academyolrexdale.com

Academy of Learning College - Toronto - Bay & Bloor
1255 Bay St., 6th Fl., Toronto, ON M5R 2A9, Canada
Tel: 416-969-8845
info@aoltoronto.com

Academy of Learning College - Toronto - Downsview
#112, 1280 Finch Ave. West, Toronto, ON M3J 3K6, Canada
Tel: 416-767-7679; *Fax:* 416-767-3770
training@academyolrexdale.com

Academy of Learning College - Toronto - Downtown East
702 Pape Ave., Toronto, ON M4K 3S7, Canada
Tel: 416-422-5627
info@collegeaol.com

Academy of Learning College - Toronto - Lawrence
3585 Lawrence Ave. East, Toronto, ON M1G 1P4, Canada
Tel: 416-499-7994; *Fax:* 416-499-3060
aollawrence@aolctoronto.com

Academy of Learning College - Toronto - Warden & Sheppard
2190 Warden Ave., Toronto, ON M1T 1V6, Canada
Tel: 416-754-4456
info@aolscarborough.com
www.aolscarborough.com
www.facebook.com/aol.scarborough
twitter.com/AOLScarborough

Academy of Learning College - Charlottetown
55 Grafton St., Charlottetown, PE C1A 1K8, Canada
Tel: 902-894-8973; *Toll-Free:* 888-328-8973
info@aolpei.ca

Academy of Learning College - Summerside
10 Slemon Park Dr., Summerside, PE C0B 2B0, Canada
Tel: 902-436-9889; *Toll-Free:* 888-328-8973
info@aolpei.ca

Academy of Learning College - North Battleford
1492 - 105th St., North Battleford, SK S9A 1T3, Canada
Tel: 306-445-8188; *Fax:* 306-445-9133
Admissions@aolbattlefords.com

Academy of Learning College - Prince Albert
14 - 13th St. West, Prince Albert, SK S6V 3E8, Canada
Tel: 306-763-8551; *Fax:* 306-764-1744
aolpa@shaw.ca

Academy of Learning College - Saskatoon
1202A Quebec Ave., Saskatoon, SK S7K 1V2, Canada
Tel: 306-373-8700; *Fax:* 306-373-8708
academysk@shaw.ca

Otterburne: Providence University College
10 College Cres., Otterburne, MB R0A 1G0, Canada
Tel: 204-433-7488; *Fax:* 204-433-7158
Toll-Free: 800-668-7768
www.prov.ca
www.facebook.com/ProvManitoba
twitter.com/ProvManitoba
Note: Institution for Christian higher education
David H. Johnson, President

Steinbach: United Transportation Driver Training (UTDT)
P.O. Box 5223
21 Clearsprings Rd., Steinbach, MB R5G 1V2
Tel: 204-326-4200; *Fax:* 204-320-1989
www.uniteddrivertraining.ca

Campuses
United Transportation Driver Training - Winkler (UTDT)
425 George Ave., Winkler, MB R6W 4A1
Tel: 204-332-2223; *Fax:* 204-325-1020

Winnipeg: Anokiiwin Training Institute
105-260 St. Mary Ave., Winnipeg, MB R3C 0M6, Canada
Tel: 204-925-2790; *Fax:* 204-943-0023
learn@anokiiwin.com
www.anokiiwin.com
Note: Aboriginally owned and operated training company committed to providing culturally sensitive, high quality training to First Nation communinities.

Campuses
Thompson Campus
79 Selkirk Ave., Thompson, MB R8N 0M5, Canada
Tel: 204-778-5937; *Fax:* 204-677-5813
learn@anokiiwin.com
www.anokiiwin.com/learn
Note: Aboriginally owned and operated training company committed to providing culturally sensitive, high quality training to First Nation communinities.

Winnipeg: Applied Schooling and Professional Training Ltd. (ASAP)
1061 Autumnwood Dr., Winnipeg, MB R2J 1C6
Tel: 204-231-1414; *Fax:* 204-231-1428
infoasap@asaptraining.ca
www.asaptraining.ca
www.facebook.com/196902657015799
twitter.com/ASAP_training
ca.linkedin.com/pub/lorie-gregorchuk/23/488/623

Winnipeg: Arnold Bros. Transportation Academy
739 Lagimodiere Blvd., Winnipeg, MB R2J 0T8
Tel: 204-231-1183; *Fax:* 204-256-7762
bweimer@arnoldbrosacademy.com
www.arnoldbrosacademy.com

Winnipeg: Canadian School of Floral Art
569 St. Mary's Rd., Winnipeg, MB R2M 3L6, Canada
Tel: 204-233-2426; *Fax:* 204-237-7301

Winnipeg: Criti Care EMS
191 River Ave., Winnipeg, MB R3C 3R6
Tel: 204-989-3671; *Fax:* 204-989-3678
Toll-Free: 888-292-3671
Info@criticareems.com
www.criticareems.com
Note: Paramedic and Fire training academy.
William M. Sommers, Chief Operating Officer, 204-989-3672
Bill@criticareems.com
Mike Mason, Vice President, Professional Education, 204-989-3679
Mike@criticareems.com

Winnipeg: European School of Esthetics (ESE)
241 Vaughan St., 2nd Fl., Winnipeg, MB R3C 1T6
Tel: 204-943-3440
info@europeanschoolofesthetics.ca
www.europeanschoolofesthetics.ca/en/

Winnipeg: First Class Training Centre Inc.
325 Eagle Dr., Winnipeg, MB R2R 1V4
Tel: 204-632-5302; *Fax:* 204-632-5329
Toll-Free: 855-632-5302
www.firstclasstrainingcentre.com
www.facebook.com/FirstClassTrainingCentre
twitter.com/FCTCTraining
www.youtube.com/user/FirstClassTrainingMB
Note: First Class is a private training institute for the truck transport industry.

Winnipeg: G & T Class 1 Training Ltd.
2040 Logan Ave., Winnipeg, MB R2R 0H9
Tel: 204-633-5222; *Fax:* 204-633-6334
www.gtclass1.com
Note: Truck driver training.

Campuses
Winkler Campus
124 Roblin Blvd. East, Winkler, MB
Tel: 204-325-1244; *Fax:* 204-633-6334
Toll-Free: 866-490-9960

Note: Truck driver training.

***Winnipeg:* Hua Xia Acupuncture & Herb College of Canada**
2810 Pembina Hwy., #A, Winnipeg, MB R3T 2H8
Tel: 204-452-3654; *Fax:* 204-275-3273
yujingqiu56@gmail.com
www.mbacuschool.com
Note: The Hua Xia Acupucture and Herb College of Canada offers courses in Traditional Chinese Medicine.

***Winnipeg:* Ideal Driver Training**
1180 Fife St., Winnipeg, MB R2X 2N6
Tel: 204-786-4705; *Fax:* 204-786-4706
Toll-Free: 888-999-9082
info@idealdt.ca
www.idealdt.ca

***Winnipeg:* Law Enforcement & Security Training Academy of Canada**
987 Portage Ave., Winnipeg, MB R3G 0R7
Tel: 204-982-6840; *Toll-Free:* 866-982-6840
admin@lestac.ca
www.lestac.ca

***Winnipeg:* Massage Therapy College of Manitoba (MTCM)**
691 Wolseley Ave., 2nd Fl., Winnipeg, MB R3G 1C3
Tel: 204-772-8999; *Fax:* 204-772-5090
www.massagetherapycollege.com
www.facebook.com/massagetherapycollege

***Winnipeg:* Mid-Ocean School of Media Arts (MOSMA)**
1588 Erin St., Winnipeg, MB R3E 2T1, Canada
Tel: 204-775-3308; *Fax:* 204-775-9231
info@midoceanschool.ca
www.midoceanschool.ca
Note: Audio engineer, audio in media

***Winnipeg:* National Screen Institute**
#400, 141 Bannatyne Ave., Winnipeg, MB R3B 0R3, Canada
Tel: 204-956-7800; *Fax:* 204-956-5811
Toll-Free: 800-952-9307
info@nsi-canada.ca
www.nsi-canada.ca
Note: Professional training & development for Canadian film & television writers, directors & producers
Susan Millican, CEO
Glynis Corkal, Manager
Paul Moreau, Director

***Winnipeg:* Neeginan College of Applied Technology**
#403, 181 Higgins Ave., Winnipeg, MB R3B 3G1
Tel: 204-989-6249; *Fax:* 204-989-8870
www.cahrd.org
Note: Neeginan Institute of Applied Technology is the post-secondary, training division of CAHRD. It administers post-secondary programs and training, and partners with industry and trades.

***Winnipeg:* Northwest Law Enforcement Academy**
#200, 1821 Wellington Ave., Winnipeg, MB R3H 0G4
Fax: 204-953-8309
Study@NorthWestLaw.ca
www.northwestlaw.ca

***Winnipeg:* Operating Engineers Training Institute of Manitoba Inc. (OETIM)**
244 Cree Cres., Winnipeg, MB R3J 3W1
Tel: 204-775-7059; *Fax:* 204-772-6041
Toll-Free: 866-949-0333
www.oetim.com

***Winnipeg:* Panache Model & Talent Management & School**
#106, 897 Corydon Ave., Winnipeg, MB R3M 0W7, Canada
Tel: 204-982-6150; *Fax:* 204-474-2687
www.panachemanagement.com
Note: Models training

***Winnipeg:* Patal Vocational School**
264 Portage Ave., Winnipeg, MB R3C 0B6
Tel: 204-944-8202; *Fax:* 204-944-8207
Toll-Free: 1-877-829-8071
www.patalvoc.com
Note: Patal Vocational School has operated since 1986 as a registered private vocational school. Patal delivers diploma programs to students in areas such as culinary arts, network management, & office assistance.
Amelia Knoedler, Contact
aknoedler@patalvocational.mb.ca

***Winnipeg:* PrairieView School of Photography**
#200, 464 Hargrave St., Winnipeg, MB
Tel: 204-956-4708; *Fax:* 204-947-9881
Toll-Free: 866-579-4154
info@prairieview.ca
www.prairieview.ca
www.facebook.com/158680287519602
twitter.com/pvschool

***Winnipeg:* Professional Transport Driver Training School**
300 Oak Point Hwy., Winnipeg, MB R2R 1V1, Canada
Tel: 204-925-1580; *Fax:* 204-925-1587
Toll-Free: 1-888-883-7483
learn@transportdriver.com
www.transportdriver.com
Note: Class 1 air brake licence training
Tim McArthur, General Manager
tim@transportdriver.com

Campuses
Brandon Branch
1731 B Middleton Ave., Brandon, MB R7A 1A7, Canada
Tel: 204-729-0240; *Toll-Free:* 1-888-883-7483
Darrell Wonnick, Manager

***Winnipeg:* Reimer Express Driver Training Institute Inc.**
50 Milner St., Winnipeg, MB R2X 2X3, Canada
Tel: 204-958-5100; *Fax:* 204-958-3034
wayne.hartle@reimerexpress.com
Note: Class 1S driver training.
Wayne Hartle, Manager

***Winnipeg:* Robertson College**
265 Notre Dame Ave., Winnipeg, MB R3B 1N9, Canada
Tel: 204-800-7919; *Fax:* 204-926-8320
Toll-Free: 1-877-880-8789
info@robertsoncollege.com
www.robertsoncollege.com
www.facebook.com/OfficialRobertsonCollege
www.twitter.com/RobertsonColleg
www.youtube.com/RobertsonCollege
Wayne Palendat, Registrar

Campuses
Calgary Campus
#300, 417 - 14th St. NW, Calgary, AB T2N 2A1, Canada
Tel: 403-331-8233; *Fax:* 403-263-8176
Toll-Free: 1-866-920-0070
CalgaryInfo@RobertsonCollege.com

Brandon Campus
Town Centre
800 Rosser Ave., Brandon, MB R7A 6N5, Canada
Tel: 204-725-7200; *Fax:* 204-725-7218
Toll-Free: 1-877-757-7575
Info@RobertsonCollegeBrandon.com

***Winnipeg:* The Salon Professional Academy (TSPA)**
#260, 1395 Ellice Ave., Winnipeg, MB R3G 3P2
Tel: 204-772-TSPA
admissions@tspawinnipeg.com
www.tspawinnipeg.com
www.facebook.com/tspawinnipeg
Note: Courses offered in Hairstyling, Esthetics, and Make-up Artistry.

***Winnipeg:* Southern Manitoba Academy for Response Training**
#13, 854 Marion St., Winnipeg, MB
Tel: 204-453-4412
info@smartems.net
www.smartems.net
Note: Firefighter & EMS Training.

***Winnipeg:* Wellington College of Remedial Massage Therapies Inc.**
435 Berry St., Winnipeg, MB R3J 1N6
Tel: 204-957-2402; *Fax:* 204-957-1578
Toll-Free: 888-957-2402
info@wellingtoncollege.com
www.wellingtoncollege.com
www.facebook.com/wcrmt
twitter.com/wcrmt

***Winnipeg:* Winnipeg Technical College**
130 Henlow Bay, Winnipeg, MB R3Y 1G4, Canada
Tel: 204-989-6500; *Fax:* 204-488-4152
www.wtc.mb.ca
www.facebook.com/winnipegtechnicalcollege?ref=ts
twitter.com/@WpgTechCollege
Enrollment: 1200
Dave Thorlakson, Director

New Brunswick

Government Agencies

***Fredericton:* New Brunswick Department of Education & Early Childhood Development**
P.O. Box 6000
Place 2000, Fredericton, NB E3B 5H1
Tel: 506-453-3678; *Fax:* 506-457-4810
edcommunication@gnb.ca
www2.gnb.ca/content/gnb/biling/eecd-edpe.html
Hon. Brian Kenny, Minister of Education & Early Childhood Development

***Fredericton:* New Brunswick Department of Post-Secondary Education, Training & Labour**
Chestnut Complex
P.O. Box 6000
Fredericton, NB E3B 5H1, Canada
Tel: 506-453-2597; *Fax:* 506-453-3618
dpetlinfo@gnb.ca
www.gnb.ca/post-secondary
Hon. Donald Arseneault, Minister of Post-Secondary Education, Training & Labour

School Boards/Districts/Divisions

Public

***Fredericton:* Anglophone West School District**
P.O. Box 10
1135 Prospect St., Fredericton, NB E3B 4Y4, Canada
Tel: 506-453-5454; *Fax:* 506-444-5264
asdwinfo@nbed.nb.ca
web1.nbed.nb.ca/sites/asd-w
twitter.com/ASD_West
Number of Schools: 73; *Grades:* K - 12; *Enrollment:* 24114; *Number of Employees:* 2958
David McTimoney, Superintendent, 506-444-4034
david.mctimoney@gnb.ca
Dianne Kay, Director of Curriculum and Instruction, 506-444-4035
dianne.kay@gnb.ca
Catherine Blaney, Director of Education Support Services, 506-462-5180
catherine.blaney@gnb.ca
Susan Haanstra, Human Resources Officer (Wellness Coordinator), 506-453-8343
susan.haanstra@gnb.ca
Shawn Tracey, Director of Finance and Administration, 506-325-4744
shawn.tracey@gnb.ca

***Miramichi:* Anglophone North School District**
78 Henderson St., Miramichi, NB E1N 2R7, Canada
Tel: 506-778-6075; *Fax:* 506-778-6090
asd-n.nbed.nb.ca
twitter.com/asdnnb
Number of Schools: 1 primary; 17 elementary; 8 elementary-middle; 6 middle; 1 middle-secondary; 7 secondary; 1 K-12; *Grades:* K - 12; *Enrollment:* 8100
Micheal Mortlock, District Education Council Chair
Beth Stymiest, Superintendent, 506-778-6301
Elizabeth.Stymiest@gnb.ca
Anne Heckbert, Director of Human Resources, 506-778-6314
anne.heckbert@gnb.ca
Joan MacMillan, Director of Curriculum and Instruction, 506-549-5123
joan.macmillan@nbed.nb.ca
Lynn Orser, Director of Education Support Services, 506-778-6312
lynn.orser@nbed.nb.ca
Tim Dunn, Director of Finance and Administration, 506-778-6710
tim.dunn@gnb.ca

***Moncton:* Anglophone East School District**
1077 St. George Blvd., Moncton, NB E1E 4C9, Canada
Tel: 506-856-3222; *Fax:* 506-856-3224
web1.nbed.nb.ca/sites/ASD-E
www.facebook.com/anglophoneeast
twitter.com/anglophoneeast
Number of Schools: 12 elementary; 12 elementary-middle; 4 middle; 2 middle-secondary; 5 secondary; 2 K-12; *Enrollment:* 15600; *Number of Employees:* 2500
Gregg Ingersoll, Superintendent
Gregg.Ingersoll@gnb.ca
Todd Silliphant, Director of Human Resources, 506-856-3222
todd.silliphant@gnb.ca

***Saint John:* Anglophone South School District**
490 Woodward Ave., Saint John, NB E2K 5N3, Canada
Tel: 506-658-5300; *Fax:* 506-658-5399
web1.nbed.nb.ca/sites/ASD-S
twitter.com/ASD_South
Number of Schools: 74; *Grades:* K - 12
Zoë Watson, Superintendent, 506-658-5301
zoe.watson@gnb.ca
Kathryn McLellan, Director, Education Support Services, 506-658-5303
kathryn.mclellan@gnb.ca
John MacDonald, Director of Finance & Administration, 506-643-7313
John.MacDonald@gnb.ca
Stewart Stanger, Director of Human Resources, 506-643-5628
stewart.stanger@gnb.ca
Suzanne LeBlanc-Healey, Director of Curriculum & Instruction (Acting), 506-658-5633
suzanne.leblanc-healey@gnb.ca

French

***Dieppe:* District scolaire francophone Sud**
425, rue Champlain, Dieppe, NB E1A 1P2
Tél: 506-856-3333; *Téléc:* 506-856-3254
Ligne sans frais: 888-268-9088
francophonesud.nbed.nb.ca
www.facebook.com/francophonesud
twitter.com/francophonesud
Number of Schools: 36 écoles; *Enrollment:* 13300; *Number of Employees:* 1800
Gérard McKen, Président
gerard.mcken@nbed.nb.ca
Monique Boudreau, Directrice générale, 506-856-3225
monique.boudreau2@gnb.ca
Isabelle Savoie, Directrice exécutive de l'apprentissage (par intérim), 506-533-3630
isabelle.savoie2@gnb.ca
Nathalie Kerry, Directrice exécutive de l'apprentissage, 506-856-3081
nathalie.kerry@nbed.nb.ca
David Després, Directeur des ressources humaines, 506-856-3250
david.despres@gnb.ca
Luc Lajoie, Directeur des services administratifs et financiers, 506-856-3225
luc.lajoie@gnb.ca

***Edmundston:* District scolaire francophone Nord-Ouest (DSFNO)**
298, rue Martin, Edmundston, NB E3V 5E5, Canada
Tél: 506-737-4567; *Téléc:* 506-737-4568
info@dsfno.ca
www.dsfno.ca
www.facebook.com/DistrictScolaireFrancophoneDuNordOuest
twitter.com/District_sc3
Number of Schools: 19; *Enrollment:* 7676; *Number of Employees:* 850
Luc Caron, Directeur général
luc.caron@gnb.ca
Chantal Thériault-Horth, Directrice exécutive de l'apprentissage
Dany Desjardins, Directrice des services de soutien à l'apprentissage
Danielle Gauthier St-Onge, Directrice des services à la petite enfance
Yvan Guérette, Directeur des services administratifs

***Tracadie-Sheila:* District scolaire francophone Nord-Est**
P.O. Box 3668
3376, rue Principale, Tracadie-Sheila, NB E1X 1G5
Tél: 506-394-3400; *Téléc:* 506-394-3455
web1.nbed.nb.ca/sites/dsne
Number of Schools: 31 primaries; 6 secondaries; 1 m-12; *Grades:* K - 12; *Enrollment:* 10142; *Number of Employees:* 815 Enseignants; 771 Non-enseignants
Pierre Lavoie, Directeur général & secrétaire du Conseil
pierre.lavoie@nbed.nb.ca
Carole Raymond, Directrice des ressources humaines
carole.raymond@gnb.ca
Eloi Doucet, Directeur des services administratifs et financiers
eloi.doucet@gnb.ca

Schools: Specialized

First Nations

***Eel Ground:* Eel Ground First Nation School**
55 Church Rd., Eel Ground, NB E1V 4E6, Canada
Tel: 506-627-4615
www.eelgroundschool.ca
Grades: Kindergarten - 8; Mi'kmaq Language; *Note:* Eel Ground First Nation School operates as part of School District #16 in Miramichi, New Brunswick. The school provides education to the Eel Ground First Nation, a Mi'kmaq community in northeastern New Brunswick.
Helen Bernard-Ward, Principal

***Eel River Bar:* Eel River Bar First Nation Pre-School**
Eel River Bar First Nation
P.O. Box 4007
#201, 11 Main St., Eel River Bar, NB E8C 1A1, Canada
Tel: 506-684-1196; *Fax:* 506-684-6282
Grades: Pre-School (K4); *Note:* Eel River Bar First Nation Pre-School is a First Nations band operated school in a Mi'kmaq village on New Brunswick's north shore.
Daniele Vautour, Principal

***Elsipogtog:* Elsipogotg School**
356 Big Cove Rd., Elsipogtog, NB E4W 2S6, Canada
Tel: 506-523-8240; *Fax:* 506-523-8235
www.elsipogtogschool.ca
Grades: Pre. - 8; *Note:* Part of Miramichi, New Brunswick's School District #16, the Elsipogtog School provides education to the Elsipogtog First Nation.
Nancy Boucher, Superintendent
nancy.boucher@gnb.ca
Ivan Augustine, Principal

***Esgenoopetitj:* Esgenoôpetitj School**
603 Bayview Dr., Esgenoopetitj, NB E9G 2A5, Canada
Tel: 506-776-1206; *Fax:* 506-776-1226
burntchurchschool.ca
Grades: Kindergarten - 8; *Enrollment:* 120; *Note:* The Esgenoopetitj School, located northeast of the City of Miramichi, is part of School District #16. The school serves the Burnt Church First Nation.
Larry Flanagan, Principal
larry.flanagan@nbed.nb.ca

***Fredericton:* Chief Harold Sappier Memorial Elementary School (CHSMES)**
***c/o* St. Mary's Maliseet First Nation**
305 Maliseet Dr., Fredericton, NB E3A 5R8, Canada
Tel: 506-462-9683; *Fax:* 506-462-9686
chsmes.ca
Grades: K4 - K5; 1 - 5; Maliseet Language; *Note:* In addition to providing elementary education beginning with kindergarten, the Chief Harold Sappier Memorial Elementary School provides education about the Maliseet language & culture.
Allison Brooks, Principal
allison.brooks@nb.aibn.com
Judith Fullarton, Administrative Assistant
chsmesjf@nb.aibn.com

***Fredericton:* Wulastukw Elementary School**
Kingsclear First Nation
712 Church St., Fredericton, NB E3E 1K8
Tel: 506-363-3019; *Fax:* 506-363-4051
www.firstnationhelp.com/wulastukw
Grades: K4; 1-5
Sarah Sacobie, Contact
sacobie_sarah@hotmail.com

***Red Bank:* Metepenagiag - Red Bank School**
1926 MicMac Rd., Red Bank, NB E9E 1B3, Canada
Tel: 506-836-6160; *Fax:* 506-836-2787
metdu@nbnet.nb.ca
metepenagiagschool.ca
twitter.com/met_school
Grades: K4; 1-6
Lori Gillham, Principal
lgillham@metepenagiagschool.ca
Mindy Ward-Wayne, Administrative Assistant

***Tobique First Nation:* Mah-Sos School**
270 Main St., Tobique First Nation, NB E7H 2Y8
Tel: 506-273-5407; *Fax:* 506-273-5436
w8liftr@hotmail.com
firstnationhelp.com/mahsos/
Grades: K4; 1-5
Paula Pirie, Principal

***Woodstock First Nation:* Woodstock First Nation Pre-School**
6 Eagles Nest Dr., Woodstock First Nation, NB E7M 4J3
Tel: 506-328-4332; *Fax:* 506-328-2420
www.woodstockfirstnation.com/services/child-development-centre/
Number of Schools: 1; *Grades:* K-12; *Note:* The school serves Woodstock First Nation.
Lisat Sappier, Coordinator, 506-328-4332
Jennifer Pitts, Child & Family Services Director, 506-324-6253

Schools: Independent & Private

Faith-Based

***Fredericton:* Fredericton Christian Academy**
778 MacLaren Ave., Fredericton, NB E3A 3L7
Tel: 506-458-9379; *Fax:* 506-459-6148
office@fcae.ca
www.fcae.ca
www.facebook.com/Frederictonchristianacademy
twitter.com/MeetFCA
Grades: K.-12; *Enrollment:* 180
Jonathan McAloon, Principal
j.mcaloon@dpcs.ca

***Moncton:* Moncton Christian Academy (MCA)**
945 St. George Blvd., Moncton, NB E1E 2C9, Canada
Tel: 506-855-5403; *Fax:* 506-857-9016
monctonca.ipower.com
Grades: Kindergarten - 12; *Enrollment:* 120; *Number of Employees:* 20 full & part-time; *Note:* Moncton Christian Academy is an interdenominational school.

***Plaster Rock:* Apostolic Christian School**
123 Main St., Plaster Rock, NB E7G 2H2
Tel: 506-356-8690; *Fax:* 506-356-9996
Grades: K.-12
Sanford Goodine, Principal

***Rothesay:* Valley Christian Academy (VCA)**
P.O. Box 4722
30 Vincent Rd., Rothesay, NB E2E 5X4, Canada
Tel: 506-848-6373; *Fax:* 506-848-6379
vca@nbnet.nb.ca
www.valleychristianacademy.com
www.facebook.com/valleychristianacademynb?ref=ts&fref=ts
Grades: K - 8; *Note:* Valley Christian Academy is a ministry of Rothesay Baptist Church. The preschool accepts children as young as three years of age.
Barry Todd, Principal
principal@bellaliant.com
Linda Hallahan, Vice Principal
principal@bellaliant.com

***Somerville:* Somerville Christian Academy (SCA)**
2608 Hwy 103, Somerville, NB E7P 3A9, Canada
Tel: 506-375-4327; *Fax:* 506-375-4406
somervillechristian.ca
Grades: K-5; *Enrollment:* 63
Angela Mabey, Principal

***Sussex:* Sussex Christian School**
45 Chapman Dr., Sussex, NB E4E 1M4, Canada
Tel: 506-433-4005; *Fax:* 506-433-3402
info@sussexchristianschool.ca
www.sussexchristianschool.ca
Grades: Jr. K.-12; *Enrollment:* 67
Marsha Boyd-Mitchell, Principal

Independent & Private Schools

***Rothesay:* Rothesay Netherwood School (RNS)**
40 College Hill Rd., Rothesay, NB E2E 5H1, Canada
Tel: 506-847-8224; *Fax:* 506-848-0851
education@rns.cc
www.rns.cc
www.facebook.com/RothNeth
twitter.com/rothnetherwood
www.linkedin.com/groups/Rothesay-Netherwood-School-2665809
Grades: 6 - 12; *Enrollment:* 270; *Note:* Rothesay Netherwood School is a day & boarding school.
Dr. David Marr, Chair
Paul G. Kitchen, Head of School, 506-848-0863
paul.kitchen@rns.cc
Paul McLellan, Director, Senior School & Assistant Head of School, 506-848-0864
paul.mclellan@rns.cc
Dean Van Doleweerd, Director, Middle School & Assistant Head of School, 506-847-8224
dean.vandoleweerd@rns.cc
Jayne Fillman Murray, Director, Admission, 506-848-0859
jayne.murray@rns.cc
Tanya Moran, Director, Finance & Operations, 506-848-0855
tanya.moran@rns.cc
Geoffrey McCullogh, Director, Athletics, 506-848-0852
geoffrey.mccullogh@rns.cc
Brian Murray, Director, Student Life, 506-848-0876
brian.murray@rns.cc
Tammy Earle, Director, Information & IB Coordinator, 506-848-1739
tammy.earle@rns.cc

***Rothesay:* Touchstone Community School**
68A Hampton Rd., Rothesay, NB E2E 5L5
Tel: 506-847-2673; *Fax:* 506-849-9582
info@tcsweb.ca
www.touchstonecommunityschool.ca
Grades: Pre.-5; *Enrollment:* 80
Jeff McAloon, Principal
Angela Prosser, Head, Academics

Universities & Colleges

Universities

***Fredericton:* St. Thomas University**
51 Dineen Dr., Fredericton, NB E3B 5G3, Canada
Tel: 506-452-0640; *Fax:* 506-450-9615
Toll-Free: 877-788-4443
admissions@stu.ca
www.stu.ca
www.facebook.com/StThomasUCanada
twitter.com/StThomasU
www.youtube.com/user/UStThomas
Full Time Equivalency: 2500
Robert Harris, Chancellor
Dawn Russell, President & Vice-Chancellor, 506-452-0537
president@stu.ca
Kim Fenwick, Vice-President, Academic & Research, 506-452-0531
vpacademic@stu.ca
Lily Fraser, Vice-President, Finance & Administration, 506-452-0533
vpfa@stu.ca
Jeff Wright, Vice-President, Advancement & Alumni, 506-452-0521
wrightj@stu.ca
Karen Preston, Registrar, 506-452-0400
preston@stu.ca
Kathryn Monti, Director of Admissions, 506-452-0603
monti@stu.ca
Wanda Bearresto, Alumni Affairs Officer, 506-452-0521
wbearresto@stu.ca
Fr. Don Savoie, Chaplain, 506-452-0643

***Fredericton:* University of New Brunswick**
P.O. Box 4400
Fredericton, NB E3B 5A3
Tel: 506-453-4666
www.unb.ca
www.facebook.com/uofnb
twitter.com/unb
www.youtube.com/unbtube
Full Time Equivalency: 10510
Dr. H.E.A. (Eddy) Campbell, President & Vice-Chancellor
Dr. Anthony (Tony) Secco, Vice-President, Academic
Bob Skillen, Vice-President, Advancement
Dr. David Burns, Vice-President, Research
Sara Strople, University Secretary
sjd@unb.ca
Daniel Murray, Vice-President, Finance & Administration

Faculties

Faculty of Arts
P.O. Box 4400
Fredericton, NB E3B 5A3
Tel: 506-453-4655; *Fax:* 506-453-5102
ARTS@unb.ca
www.unb.ca/arts
George MacLean, Ph.D., Dean
George.MacLean@unb.ca

Arts (Saint John)
P.O. Box 5050
Saint John, NB E2L 4L5
Tel: 506-648-5560; *Fax:* 506-648-5947
www.unb.ca/saintjohn/arts

Faculty of Business (Saint John)
P.O. Box 5050
Saint John, NB E2L 4L5
Tel: 506-648-5570; *Fax:* 506-648-5574
Toll-Free: 800-508-6275
BUSINESS@unbsj.ca
www.unb.ca/saintjohn/business
Fazley Siddiq, Dean

Faculty of Business Administration
255 Singer Hall
7 Macauley Lane, Fredericton, NB E3B 5A3
Tel: 506-453-4869; *Fax:* 506-453-3561
fba@unb.ca
www.unb.ca/fredericton/business
Devashis Mitra, Dean
dmitra@unb.ca

Faculty of Computer Science
Information Technology Centre
P.O. Box 4400
#C314, 550 Windsor St., Fredericton, NB E3B 5A3
Tel: 506-453-4566; *Fax:* 506-453-3566
fcs@unb.ca
www.cs.unb.ca
www.facebook.com/UNBCS
www.youtube.com/unbcs
Ali A. Ghorbani, Dean

Faculty of Education
Marshall d'Avray Hall
#327, 10 MacKay Dr., Fredericton, MB E3B 5A3
Tel: 506-453-3508; *Fax:* 506-453-3569
www.unb.ca/fredericton/education
Ann Sherman, Dean

Faculty of Engineering
P.O. Box 4400
Fredericton, NB E3B 5A3
Tel: 506-453-4570; *Fax:* 506-453-4569
engineer@unb.ca
www.unb.ca/fredericton/engineering
David Coleman, B.Sc.E., Ph.D., P.Eng., M, Dean

Faculty of Forestry & Environmental Management
P.O. Box 4400
Fredericton, NB E3B 5A3
Tel: 506-453-4501; *Fax:* 506-453-3538
www.unb.ca/fredericton/forestry
Van Lantz, Dean

Faculty of Kinesiology
P.O. Box 4400
Fredericton, NB E3B 5A3
Tel: 506-453-4575; *Fax:* 506-453-3511
kin@unb.ca
www.unb.ca/fredericton/kinesiology
Wayne Albert, Dean

Faculty of Law
41 Dineen Dr., Fredericton, NB E3B 5A3
Tel: 506-453-4669; *Fax:* 506-453-4548
LAWGEN@unb.ca
www.unb.ca/fredericton/law
Jeremy Levitt, Dean
Jeremy.Levitt@unb.ca

Faculty of Nursing
P.O. Box 4400
Fredericton, NB E3B 5A3
Tel: 506-458-7670; *Fax:* 506-453-3512
registrar@unb.ca
www.unb.ca/fredericton/nursing
Gail Storr, Dean

School of Graduate Studies
Sir Howard Douglass Hall
P.O. Box 4400
Fredericton, NB E3B 5A3
Tel: 506-453-4673; *Fax:* 506-453-4817
gradschl@unb.ca
www.unb.ca/gradstudies
Demetres Tryphonopoulos, B.A., M.A., Ph.D., Acting Dean

Faculty of Science
P.O. Box 4400
Fredericton, NB E3B 5A3
Tel: 506-453-4586; *Fax:* 506-453-3570
science@unb.ca
www.unb.ca/fredericton/science
Stephen Heard, B.Sc., Ph.D., Acting Dean

Faculty of Science, Applied Science & Engineering (Saint John)
P.O. Box 5050
Saint John, NB E2L 4L5
Tel: 506-648-5615; *Fax:* 506-648-5650
SCI-ENG@unbsj.ca
www.unb.ca/saintjohn/sase

Campuses

Renaissance College
P.O. Box 4400
Fredericton, NB E3B 5A3
Tel: 506-447-3092; *Fax:* 506-447-3224
RC@unb.ca
www.unb.ca/fredericton/renaissance
www.facebook.com/RenaissanceCollege
Cynthia Stacey, Dean

Saint John Campus
P.O. Box 5050
Saint John, NB E2L 4L5
Tel: 506-648-5500; *Fax:* 506-648-5691
unbsjreg@unbsj.ca
Peter McGill, Director
pmcgill@unb.ca

Affiliations

Maritime College of Forest Technology
1350 Regent St., Fredericton, NB E3C 2G6
Tel: 506-458-0199; *Fax:* 506-458-0679
info@mcft.ca
www.mcft.ca
www.facebook.com/268728173163393
twitter.com/MCFTfredericton
www.youtube.com/user/MCFTVIDEOS
Loretta Phillips, Contact
lphillips@mcft.ca

***Fredericton:* Yorkville University**
#102, 100 Woodside Lane, Fredericton, NB E3C 2R9
Fax: 506-454-1221
Toll-Free: 866-838-6542
www.yorkvilleu.ca
www.facebook.com/YorkvilleUniversity
twitter.com/YorkvilleU
www.youtube.com/user/YorkvilleUniversity
Rick Davey, President

Faculties

Education
Rita Kop, Ph.D, Dean

Behavioural Sciences
Helen Massfeller, Dean

Business
Jana Comeau, Dean

***Moncton:* Crandall University**
P.O. Box 6004
333 Gorge Rd., Moncton, NB E1C 9L7
Tel: 506-858-8970; *Fax:* 506-863-6460
Toll-Free: 888-968-6228
www.crandallu.ca
www.facebook.com/CrandallUniversity
twitter.com/CrandallU
www.youtube.com/user/CrandallUniversity
Full Time Equivalency: 900; *Note:* Crandall University is an independent Christian university founded in 1949. They offer multiple bachelor degrees and professional education and certificate programs.
Dr. Bruce G. Fawcett, President & Vice-Chancellor
Donald Simmons, Chancellor

***Moncton:* Université de Moncton**
Campus de Moncton
18, av Antonine-Maillet, Moncton, NB E1A 3E9
Tél: 506-858-4000; *Ligne sans frais:* 1-800-363-8336
info@umoncton.ca
www.umoncton.ca
www.facebook.com/umoncton
twitter.com/campus_moncton
www.youtube.com/UMoncton
Note: Une institution d'enseignement exclusivement de langue française; campus: Edmunston, Moncton et Shippagan
Raymond Théberge, Recteur et Vice-Chancelier
Lynne Castonguay, Secrétaire générale
Edgar Robichaud, Vice-recteur à l'administration et aux ressources humaines
Linda Schofield, Directrice générale des relations universitaires
Daniel Godbout, Directeur du Service des finances
daniel.godbout@umoncton.ca
Roger Boulay, Directeur des Services aux étudiantes et étudiants
Marthe Brideau, Bibliothécaire en chef
Janique Léger, Directrice du service des ressources matérielles
janique.leger@umoncton.ca
Gaston LeBlanc, Doyen
Isabelle McKee-Allain, Direrice par intérim, Institut d'études acadiennes
isabelle.mckee-allain@umoncton.ca
Francis LeBlanc, Doyen, faculté des sciences
Paul Chiasson, Doyen de la Faculté d'ingénierie
Natalie Carrier, Directrice de l'ÉSANEF
Sylvie Robichaud-Ekstrand, Vice-doyenne de la Faculté des sciences de la santé
Paul Bourque, Doyen de la Faculté des sciences de la santé
Jocelyne Roy-Vienneau, Vice-rectrice au Campus de Shippagan
Zénon Chiasson, Directeur, affaires professorales
zenon.chiasson@umoncton.ca
Terrance J. LeBlanc, Director, service des ressources humaines
terrance.leblanc@umoncton.ca
Marc Boudreau, Directeur, sports universitaires
marc.boudreau@umoncton.ca
André Samson, Vice-recteur à l'enseignement et à la recherche

Campuses
Campus d'Edmundston
165, boul Hébert, Edmundston, NB E3V 2S8
Tél: 506-737-5051; *Ligne sans frais:* 800-363-8336
info@umce.ca
www.umoncton.ca/umce
www.facebook.com/UdeMEdmundston

Campus de Shippagan
218, boul J.-D.-Gauthier, Shippagan, NB E8S 1P6
Tél: 506-336-3400; *Ligne sans frais:* 800-363-8336
www.umoncton.ca/umcs
info@umcs.ca
www.facebook.com/UdeMCampusdeShippagan
twitter.com/umcs_umoncton
www.youtube.com/user/campusdeshippagan

Sackville: Mount Allison University
62 York St., Sackville, NB E4L 1E2, Canada
Tel: 506-364-2269; *Fax:* 506-364-2263
regoffice@mta.ca
www.mta.ca
www.facebook.com/653821366.2440121137
www.twitter.com/mountallison
www.youtube.com/MountAllison
Full Time Equivalency: 2350; *Number of Employees:* 129
Peter Mansbridge, Chancellor
Robert M. Campbell, President & Vice-Chancellor, 506-364-2300
rcampbell@mta.ca
Brian G. Johnston, Chair
Jeff Ollerhead, Provost & Vice-President, Academic & Research, 506-364-2622
provost@mta.ca
Robert Inglis, Vice-President, Finance & Administration, 506-364-2630
Kim Meade, Vice-President, International & Student Affairs
Gloria Jollymore, Vice-President, University Advancement, 506-364-2261
Elizabeth Wells, Dean, Faculty of Arts
deanofarts@mta.ca
Amanda Cockshutt, Dean, Faculty of Science
deanofsocialsciences@mta.ca
Dr. Nauman Farooqi, Dean, Faculty of Social Sciences
deanofsocialsciences@mta.ca
Chris Parker, Registrar

St. Stephen: St. Stephen's University
8 Main St., St. Stephen, NB E3L 3E2
Tel: 506-466-1781; *Fax:* 855-466-1783
Toll-Free: 888-225-5778
ssu@ssu.ca
www.ssu.ca
Note: St. Stephen's is an independent Christian university.
Robert J. Cheatley, President
A. Gregg Finely, Dean of Arts, History & Registrar
Peter D. Fitch, Dean of Ministry Studies, Religious Studies

Colleges

Bathurst: Collège communautaire du Nouveau-Brunswick
P.O. Box 266
725, rue du Collège, Bathurst, NB E2A 3Z6, Canada
Tél: 506-547-2145; *Téléc:* 506-547-7674
Ligne sans frais: 800-552-5483
nbcc.admission.ccnb@gnb.ca
ccnb.nb.ca
www.facebook.com/CCNB.officielle
Liane Roy, Directrice générale, 506-547-2634
liane.roy@ccnb.ca

Campuses
Campus de Dieppe
505, rue de Collège, Dieppe, NB E1A 6X2, Canada
Tél: 506-856-2200; *Téléc:* 506-856-2847
Ligne sans frais: 1-800-561-7162
Full Time Equivalency: 840
Pauline Duguay, Directeur
pauline.duguay@ccnb.ca

Campus de Campbellton
P.O. Box 309
47, av du Village, Campbellton, NB E3N 3G7
Tél: 506-789-2377; *Téléc:* 506-789-2433
Ligne sans frais: 888-648-4111
Suzanne Beaudoin, Directrice
suzanne.beaudoin@ccnb.ca

Campus de Bathurst
P.O. Box 266
725, rue du Collège, Bathurst, NB E2A 3Z2
Tél: 506-547-2145; *Téléc:* 506-547-7674
Ligne sans frais: 800-552-5483
Paolo Fongemie, Directeur
paolo.fongemie@ccnb.ca

Campus d'Edmundston
P.O. Box 70
35, rue du 15-Août, Edmundston, NB E3V 3K7
Tél: 506-735-2500; *Téléc:* 506-735-2717
Ligne sans frais: 1-888-695-2262
Lise C. Ouellette, Directrice
lise.ouellette@ccnb.ca

Campus de la Péninsule acadienne
232A, av de l'Église, Shippagan, NB E8S 1J2
Tél: 506-336-3073; *Téléc:* 506-336-3075
Ligne sans frais: 866-299-9900
Alain Boisvert, Directeur
alain.boisvert@ccnb.ca

Post Secondary/Technical

Bathurst: Bathurst Hair Academy Inc. Académie La Coupe Plus
238, rue Cunard, Bathurst, NB E2A 5A2
Tel: 506-548-2526; *Fax:* 506-548-4492
info@bathursthairacademy.com
www.academielacoupeplusdebathurst.com

Dieppe: Chez Bernard Beauty Academy Inc.
106 Dieppe Blvd., Dieppe, NB E1A 6P8
Tel: 506-857-0192; *Fax:* 506-854-5403
academy@nb.aibn.com
www.chezbernardbeautyacademy.com

Dieppe: Medes College
#300, 1040 Champlain St., Dieppe, NB E1A 8L8
Tel: 506-384-3223; *Fax:* 506-853-3062
college@medes.ca
www.medes.ca
www.facebook.com/pages/College-Medes/162506230435172
www.youtube.com/collegemedes
Note: Programs offered in Esthetics, Nail Technology, Makeup, and Electrolysis.
France Bouchard-Michaud, Owner/President

Fredericton: Atlantic Business College (ABC)
1115 Regent St., Fredericton, NB E3B 3Z2, Canada
Tel: 506-450-1408; *Fax:* 506-450-8388
Toll-Free: 1-800-983-2929
atlantic@abc.nb.ca
www.abc.nb.ca
www.facebook.com/AtlanticBusinessCollege?ref=ts
twitter.com/ABCFredericton
Note: Day school programs, continuing education courses, corporate training; also in Moncton.
Jacqueline Devine, Principal

Fredericton: Atlantic College of Therapeutic Massage
Kings Place
440 King St., Fredericton, NB E3B 5H8
Tel: 506-451-8188; *Fax:* 506-451-8402
actmoffice@nb.aibn.com
www.actmonline.com
Candace Gilmore, Director
cgactm@nb.aibn.com
Lisa Ivany, Director
liactm@nb.aibn.com

Campuses
Collège Atlantique de Massage Thérapeutique
1040 Champlain St., Dieppe, NB E1A 8L8
Tél: 506-855-2286; *Téléc:* 506-855-9251
camt@nb.aibn.com
www.actmonline.com

Fredericton: Atlantic Hairstyling & Aesthetics Academy
440 Brunswick St., Fredericton, NB E3B 1H3
Tel: 506-453-9192; *Fax:* 506-459-1792
atlantichairstylingacademy@rogers.com
www.atlantichairstyling.com

Fredericton: East Coast Trades College Inc.
1080 Brookside Dr., Fredericton, NB E3G 8T8
Tel: 506-470-4565
Carman.Sangster@eastcoasttrades.com
www.eastcoasttrades.com

Fredericton: The Gaming & Animation Institute of Fredericton (GAIF)
#203, 348 King St., Fredericton, NB E3B 1E3
Tel: 506-450-4243
info@thegaif.com
www.thegaif.com

Fredericton: Majestany Institute - Fredericton Campus
120 Westmorland St., Fredericton, NB E3B 3L5
Tel: 506-458-8070; *Fax:* 506-457-1708
inquiry@majestany.ca
www.majestany.ca
www.facebook.com/majestany.saintjohn
Note: Programs offered in aesthetics, hairstyling and nail technology.

Campuses
Majestany Institute - Moncton Campus
51 Highfield St., Moncton, NB E1C 5N2
Tel: 506-857-8111; *Fax:* 506-860-3423
inquiry@majestany.ca
www.majestany.ca
www.facebook.com/majestany.saintjohn

Majestany Institute - Saint John Campus
30 Charlotte St., Saint John, NB E2L 2H4
Tel: 506-693-4125; *Fax:* 506-693-4126
inquiry@majestany.ca
www.majestany.ca
www.facebook.com/majestany.saintjohn

Fredericton: Maritime College of Forest Technology (MCFT)
1350 Regent St., Fredericton, NB E3C 2G6, Canada
Tel: 506-458-0199; *Fax:* 506-458-0652
hflinn@mcft.ca
mcft.ca
Note: Established 1946. Identical francophone program offered at the Bathurst, NB campus. A minimum 12-month pre-admission apprenticeship in woods work or forestry is required. In addition to course work, students are required to work a minimum 12-week practicum.
J.S. Hoyt, Director

Fredericton: New Brunswick Community Colleges Collèges communautaires du Nouveau-Brunswick
284 Smythe St., Fredericton, NB E3B 3C9, Canada
Tel: 506-462-5012; *Toll-Free:* 888-796-6222
collegeworks@nbcc.ca
www.nbcc.ca

Campuses
New Brunswick Community College (Bathurst)
Collège communautaire du Nouveau-Brunswick (Bathurst)
P.O. Box 266
725, rue du Collège, Bathurst, NB E2A 3Z2, Canada
Tél: 506-547-2145; *Téléc:* 506-547-7674
Ligne sans frais: 1-800-552-5483
Jeanne A. Comeau, Principal
jeanne.a.comeau@gnb.ca

New Brunswick Community College (Edmundston)
Collège communautaire du Nouveau-Brunswick (Edmundston)
P.O. Box 70
35, rue du 15-Août, Edmundston, NB E3V 3K7, Canada
Tel: 506-735-2500; *Fax:* 506-735-2717
Toll-Free: 1-888-695-2262
Richard Doiron, Principal
richard.doiron@gnb.ca

New Brunswick Community College (Miramichi)
Collège communautaire du Nouveau-Brunswick (Miramichi)
P.O. Box 1053
80 University Ave., Miramichi, NB E1N 3W4, Canada
Tel: 506-778-6000; *Fax:* 506-778-6001
Toll-Free: 877-773-6222
nbcc.miramichi@nbcc.ca
Karen White-O'Connell, Principal

New Brunswick Community College (Moncton)
Collège communautaire du Nouveau-Brunswick (Moncton)
1234 Mountain Rd., Moncton, NB E1C 8H9, Canada
Tel: 506-856-2220; *Fax:* 506-856-3288
Toll-Free: 1-888-664-1477
student.services@nbcc.ca
Full Time Equivalency: 3500
Darren Ros, Principal
darren.rose@gnb.ca

New Brunswick Community College (St. Andrews)
Collège communautaire du Nouveau-Brunswick (St. Andrews)
99 Augustus St., St Andrews, NB E5B 2E9, Canada
Tel: 506-529-5024; *Fax:* 506-529-5078
webinquiries@nbcc.ca
Diane Burt, Principal
diane.burt@gnb.ca

New Brunswick Community College (Saint John)
Collège communautaire du Nouveau-Brunswick (Saint John)
P.O. Box 2270
950 Grandview Ave., Saint John, NB E2L 3V1, Canada
Tel: 506-658-6600; *Fax:* 506-658-6792
Toll-Free: 800-416-4080
studentservices.nbccsj@nbcc.ca
Annette Albert, Principal
annette.albert@gnb.ca

New Brunswick Community College (Woodstock)
Collège communautaire du Nouveau-Brunswick (Woodstock)
100 Broadway St., Woodstock, NB E7M 5C5, Canada
Tel: 506-325-4400; *Fax:* 506-328-8426
studentservices.nbccwood@nbcc.ca
Joy Dion, Principal
joy.dion@gnb.ca

New Brunswick Community College (Péninsule acadienne)
Collège communautaire du Nouveau-Brunswick (Péninsule acad
232A, avenue de l'Église, Shippagan, NB E8S 1J2, Canada
Tél: 506-336-3073; *Téléc:* 506-336-3075
Ligne sans frais: 1-866-299-9900
Thérèse Finn-McGraw, Principal
therese.finn-mcgraw@gnb.ca

New Brunswick Community College (Fredericton)
Collège communautaire du Nouveau-Brunswick (Fredericton)
26 Duffie Dr., Fredericton, NB E3B 0R6, Canada
Tel: 506-453-3641; *Fax:* 506-453-7944
nbccfrederictoncampus@nbcc.ca
Bronwen Cunningham, Principal
bronwen.cunningham@gnb.ca

New Brunswick Community College (Campbellton)
Collège communautaire du Nouveau-Brunswick (Campbellton)
P.O. Box 309
47, avenue Village, Campbellton, NB E3N 3G7, Canada
Tél: 506-789-2377; *Téléc:* 506-789-2433
Ligne sans frais: 888-648-4110

New Brunswick Community College (Dieppe)
Collège communautaire du Nouveau-Brunswick (Dieppe)
505, rue du Collège, Dieppe, NB E1A 6X2, Canada
Tél: 506-856-2200; *Téléc:* 506-856-2847
Ligne sans frais: 800-561-7162

***Grand Falls:* École de coiffure LaFrance**
LaFrance School of Hair Design
P.O. Box 7428
514B, rue Chapel OW, Grand Falls, NB E3Z 2M8
Tel: 506-473-7212
www.lafrancehairdesign.com

***Grand Falls:* Grand Falls Academy of Esthetics**
192 Veteran St., Grand Falls, NB E3Y 1C8
Tel: 506-473-5039; *Fax:* 506-473-5039
giselepyne@nb.aibn.com
www.grandfallsacademyofesthetics.ca

***Miramichi:* Amoura Aesthetics**
205 Edward St., Miramichi, NB E1V 2Y7
Tel: 506-622-4331; *Fax:* 506-836-7969
amoura@nb.sympatico.ca
www.amouraaesthetics.com

***Miramichi:* Miramichi Health Training Centre**
P.O. Box 297
Miramichi, NB E1N 3A6
Tel: 506-773-7971; *Fax:* 506-773-6896
mhtcentre@nb.aibn.com
www.healthtrainingcentre.com

***Moncton:* BayTech College**
Also known as: BayTech Institute of Trades & Technology
120 English Dr., Moncton, NB E1E 4G7
Tel: 506-853-8883; *Fax:* 506-853-8740
info@baytechcollege.ca
www.baytechcollege.ca
www.facebook.com/BayTechCollege
Note: Private college offering courses in carpentry, electrician, plumbing, and welding.
Kevin Horsman, President
Linda Horsman, College Coordinator

***Moncton:* Brenda's Academy of Professional Dog Grooming**
18 Brandon St., Moncton, NB E1C 7E6
Tel: 506-858-9947; *Fax:* 506-382-2571
www.brendas.ca

***Moncton:* Elite Dog Grooming & Academy**
45 Colonial Dr., Moncton, NB E1G 2J1
Tel: 506-855-8808
www.elitedoggrooming.com

***Moncton:* L'Institut Jon rayMond**
21 Stone Ave., Moncton, NB E1A 3M3
Tel: 506-857-9840; *Fax:* 506-857-9844
Toll-Free: 877-857-9840
info@jonraymond.com
www.jonraymond.com
www.facebook.com/jonraymondnb
www.twitter.com/jonraymond
www.youtube.com/channel/jonraymond
Note: Bilingual Hairstyling & Aesthetics School.

***Moncton:* McKenzie College School of Art & Design**
100 Cameron St., Moncton, NB E1C 5Y6
Tel: 506-384-6460; *Fax:* 506-384-6224
info@mckenzie.edu
www.mckenzie.edu
www.facebook.com/mckenziecollegemoncton
www.twitter.com/mckenziecollege

***Moncton:* Medavie HealthEd - Moncton**
567 St. George Blvd., Moncton, NB E1E 2B9
Fax: 506-389-2198
Toll-Free: 888-798-3888
info@medaviehealthed.com
www.medaviehealthed.com
Note: Paramedicine training.

Campuses
Medavie HealthEd - Dartmouth
#33, 201 Brownlow Ave., Dartmouth, NS B3B 1W2
Fax: 902-434-2242
Toll-Free: 888-798-3888
info@medaviehealthed.com
www.medaviehealthed.com
Note: Paramedicine training.

***Moncton:* Oulton College**
4 Flanders Crt., Moncton, NB E1C 0K6
Fax: 506-858-8490
Toll-Free: 888-757-2020
info@oultoncollege.com
www.oultoncollege.com
www.facebook.com/CollegeOulton
twitter.com/OultonCollege
www.youtube.com/OultonCollege1956
Note: Health Sciences & Computer College.

Campuses
Oulton College - Dental Education Campus
5 Pacific Ave., Moncton, NB E1E 2G2
Fax: 506-858-8490
Toll-Free: 888-757-2020
info@oultoncollege.com
www.oultoncollege.com
www.facebook.com/CollegeOulton
twitter.com/OultonCollege
www.youtube.com/OultonCollege1956

***Moncton:* Pretty Pooch Dog Grooming**
316 Worthington, Moncton, NB E1C 0B7
Tel: 506-382-9393
www.atyp.com/prettypooch/

***Moncton:* Sharon's Grooming School**
65 Mapleton Rd., Moncton, NB E1C 7W6
Tel: 506-384-3647
sharonsgroomingshop@gmail.com
www.sharonsgroomingschool.com

***New Maryland:* Labourers' Training Institute of New Brunswick Inc.**
572-D New Maryland Hwy., New Maryland, NB E3C 1K1
Tel: 506-452-7643; *Fax:* 506-459-3974
Toll-Free: 800-332-3985
registrationdesk@ltinb.ca
www.ltinb.ca
Note: The Labourers' Training Institute serves the common interest of union members and union employers in the area of quality skills training and health and safety training in the province of New Brunswick.

***Newtown:* ECR Heavy Equipment & Construction Training**
65 Taylor Rd., Newtown, NB E4G 1N9
Tel: 506-434-4328
info@ecrheavyequipmenttraining.ca
www.ecrheavyequipmenttraining.ca
www.facebook.com/ECRSussex

***Saint John:* The Academy of Hair Design**
200 Union St., Saint John, NB E2L 1B1
Tel: 506-633-8292; *Fax:* 506-642-7551
www.hairnb.com
www.facebook.com/AcademyofHairDesign?sk=app_3801015922

***Saint John:* Atlantica Centre for the Arts**
45 Hanover St., Saint John, NB E2L 3G1
Tel: 506-672-7625; *Fax:* 506-642-5366
Toll-Free: 866-672-7656
www.atlanticacentre.com
www.facebook.com/atlanticacollege
twitter.com/AtlanticaCTR
www.youtube.com/atlanticaartscentre

***Saint John:* Care-Ed Learning Centre**
Also known as: Senior Watch
33 Hanover St., Saint John, NB E2L 3G1
Tel: 506-634-8906; *Toll-Free:* 800-561-2463
train@seniorwatch.com
www.seniorwatch.com/learning-centre.html
Note: Focus on the preparation of persons seeking a caregiving career as well as support for family caregivers.

***Saint John:* Carpenters Training Centre of New Brunswick Inc.**
P.O. Box 2181
120 Ashburn Rd., Saint John, NB E2L 3V1
Tel: 506-632-8840; *Toll-Free:* 888-753-7474
www.ctcnb.com

***Saint John:* Dental Assistants College of Saint John Inc.**
Saint John, NB
Tel: 506-696-2299; *Fax:* 506-696-2296
info@dacsj.com
www.dacsj.com

***Saint John:* Fundy Learning Center (FLC)**
142 Harrington St., Saint John, NB E2k 1Y2
Tel: 506-693-7688; *Fax:* 506-693-8431
info@fundyspeechpathology.com
www.fundyspeechpathology.com
www.facebook.com/158550674213160
twitter.com/FundyLearningCe
Note: Courses in preparation for working with children with autism.

***Saint John:* The Landscape Horticulture Training Institute**
P.O. Box 742
Saint John, NB E2L 4B3
Toll-Free: 866-752-6862
lnb@nbnet.nb.ca
www.landscapenbmember.com/lhti
www.facebook.com/Landscapenewbrunswick

***Saint John:* Ready Arc Welding (2000) Inc.**
600 Grandview Ave., Saint John, NB E2J 4M9
Tel: 506-696-8336
readyarcwelding@nb.aibn.com
www.readyarc.ca
Note: Private Welding School.

***Sussex:* Versatile Training Solutions**
P.O. Box 4591
Sussex, NB E4E 5L8
Tel: 506-433-5832; *Fax:* 506-433-5530
infovts@nb.aibn.com
versatiletrainingsolutions.com
Note: Training available in Emergency Services, Municipal Works Departments, Utility Companies, Construction and Transportation Industries.

***Woodstock:* Kreative Cosmetology Institute**
628 Main St., Woodstock, NB E7M 2C5
Tel: 506-328-8654; *Fax:* 506-328-4973
info@kreativecosmetology.com
www.kreativecosmetology.com
www.facebook.com/194793954016503?ref=hl

Newfoundland & Labrador

Government Agencies

St. John's: Newfoundland Department of Advanced Education & Skills
Confederation Building
P.O. Box 8700
3rd Fl., West Block, St. John's, NL A1B 4J6
Tel: 709-729-2729; Fax: 709-729-5878
Toll-Free: 877-771-3737
aesweb@gov.nl.ca
www.aes.gov.nl.ca
Hon. Gerry Byrne, Minister of Advanced Education & Skills
gerrybyrne@gov.nl.ca

St. John's: Newfoundland Department of Education & Early Childhood Development
Confederation Bldg., West Block
P.O. Box 8700
100 Prince Philip Dr., 3rd Fl., St. John's, NL A1B 4J6, Canada
Tel: 709-729-5097; Fax: 709-729-5896
education@gov.nl.ca
www.ed.gov.nl.ca/edu
Hon. Susan Sullivan, Minister of Education & Early Childhood Development, 709-729-5040
susansullivan@gov.nl.ca

School Boards/Districts/Divisions

Public

St. John's: Newfoundland & Labrador English School District
Atlantic Place
#601, 215 Water St., St. John's, NL A1C 6C9, Canada
Tel: 709-758-2372; Fax: 709-758-2706
www.nlesd.ca
Number of Schools: 261; Enrollment: 67000; Number of Employees: 8,000
Darrin Pike, CEO/Director of Education, 709-758-2381
dpike@esdnl.ca
Ken Morrissey, Director of Communications, 709-758-2371
kenmorrissey@esdnl.ca
Jeff Thompson, Associate Director of Education (Provincial), 709-757-4663
jeffthompson@esdnl.ca
Gerald Buffett, Assistant Director of Education (HR - Provincial), 709-758-2345
geraldbuffett@esdnl.ca
Lawrence Blanchard, Assistant Director of Education (Finance - Provincial), 709-758-2382
larryblanchard@esdnl.ca
Anthony Stack, Assistant Director of Education (Operations - Provincial), 709-758-2701
anthonystack@esdnl.ca

Faculties
Regional Office (Lab.West)
669 Tamarack Dr., Labrador City, NL A2V 2V2, Canada
Tel: 709-944-7628; Fax: 709-944-3480
sthibeau@lsb.ca
www.lsb.ca

Campuses
Labrador Regional Office
P.O. Box 1810 B
16 Strathcona St., Happy Valley-Goose Bay, NL A0P 1E0, Canada
Tel: 709-896-2431; Fax: 709-896-9638
Number of Schools: 15
Fiona Frawley, Assistant Director of Education, 709-896-2431, ext. 224
ffrawley@lsb.ca
Desmond Sellars, Senior Education Officer, 709-896-2431, ext. 233
dsellars@lsb.ca
Andrew Battcock, Senior Education Officer, 709-896-2431, ext. 231
abattcock@lsb.ca
George Michelau, Manager of Special Funding & Projects, 709-896-2431, ext. 223
gmichelau@lsb.ca

Western Regional Office
P.O. Box 368
10 Wellington St., Corner Brook, NL A2H 6G9, Canada
Tel: 709-637-4000; Fax: 709-634-1828
Number of Schools: 63
George Keeping, Assistant Director of Education, 709-637-4006
george.keeping@wnlsd.ca
Delores Clarke-Genge, Senior Education Officer, 709-637-4008
delores.clarkegenge@wnlsd.ca
Brian Feltham, Director of School Financial Support and Administration, 709-637-4013
brian.feltham@wnlsd.ca

Central Regional Office
203 Elizabeth Dr., Gander, NL A1V 1H6, Canada
Tel: 709-256-2547; Fax: 709-651-3044
Number of Schools: 65
Bronson Collins, Assistant Director of Education, 709-256-2547
bcollins@ncsd.ca
Elizabeth Green, Senior Education Officer, Human Resources, 709-256-2547, ext. 228
egreen@ncsd.ca
Amanda Broderick, Manager of Finance and Administration, 709-256-2547, ext. 225
amandabroderick@ncsd.ca

Eastern Regional Office
#601 Atlantic Place
P.O. Box 64-66
215 Water St., St. John's, NL A1C 6C9
Tel: 709-758-2372; Fax: 709-758-2706
Number of Schools: 119
Lucy Warren, Assistant Director of Education, 709-758-2341
lucywarren@esdnl.ca

French

St. Jean: Conseil scolaire francophone provincial de Terre-Neuve-et-Labrador (CSFP)
#212, 65, ch Ridge, St. Jean, NL A1B 4P5, Canada
Tél: 709-722-6324; Téléc: 709-722-6325
Ligne sans frais: 888-794-6324
conseil@csfp.nl.ca
www.csfp.nf.ca
Claude Giroux, Directeur général, 709-722-6324
cgiroux@csfp.nl.ca
Peter C. Smith, Directeur général adjoint, finances et administration, 709-722-6747
psmith@csfp.nl.ca
Patricia Greene, Directrice des services éducatifs, 709-757-2818
pgreene@csfp.nl.ca
Hermance Paulin, Comptable et agente aux ressources humaines, 709-722-6324, ext. 750
hpaulin@csfp.nl.ca

First Nations

Sheshatshiu: Innu School Board
Also known as: Mamu Tshishkutamashutau Innu Education
P.O. Box 539
Sheshatshiu, NL A0P 1M0
Tel: 709-497-8343
info@innueducation.ca
www.innueducation.ca
Number of Schools: 2 K-12; Note: Offers Aboriginal culture and language curriculum components.
Craig Benoit, Director of Education
cbenoit@setaneway.ca

Schools: Specialized

First Nations

Conne River: Se't A'newey Kina'magino'kuom School
Also known as: St. Anne's School
Miawpukek Mi'kamawey Mawi'omi
P.O. Box 100
Conne River, NL A0H 1J0
Tel: 709-882-2747; Fax: 709-882-2528
vpiercey@setaneway.ca
Grades: K-12; Note: The Miawpukek Mi'kmaw Mawi'omi of Conne River operate the Se't A'newey Kina'magino'kuom school. The curriculum, prescribed by the province of Newfoundland & Larador, is provided to members of the community from preschool children to elders. The school also offers a Mi'kmaq studies program that includes the language & spiritual & cultural teachings of the Mi'kmaq
Rod Jeddore, Director of Education

Natuashish: Mushuau Innu Natuashish
P.O. Box 189
Natuashish, NL A0P 1A0, Canada
Tel: 709-497-3664; Fax: 709-497-3678
info@innueducation.ca
www.innueducation.ca
Grades: K-12
Dave Jackman, Manager K-12
djackman@innueducation.ca

North West River: Sheshatshiu Innu Natuashish
P.O. Box 70
Mackenzie Dr., North West River, NL A0P 1M0, Canada
Tel: 709-497-3533; Fax: 709-497-3588
info@innueducation.ca
www.innueducation.ca
Grades: K-12
Clarence Davis, Manager K-12
cdavis@innueducation.ca

Schools: Independent & Private

Independent & Private Schools

Churchill Falls: Eric G. Lambert All-Grade School
P.O. Box 40
Churchill Falls, NL A0R 1A0, Canada
Tel: 709-925-3371; Fax: 709-925-3364
www.ericglambert.ca
Grades: K.-12; Enrollment: 156
Adrian Clarke, Principal
aclarke@nlh.nf.ca

St. John's: Lakecrest - St. John's Independent School
58 Patrick St., St. John's, NL A1E 2S7, Canada
Tel: 709-738-1212; Fax: 709-738-1701
rpittman@lakecrest.ca
www.lakecrest.ca
Grades: K.-9; Enrollment: 129
Ron Pellerin, Principal

St. John's: St. Bonaventure's College
2A Bonaventure Ave., St. John's, NL A1C 6B3, Canada
Tel: 709-726-0024; Fax: 709-726-0148
info@stbons.ca
www.stbonaventurescollege.ca
www.facebook.com/stbonaventures
twitter.com/StBonaventures
Grades: K-12; Enrollment: 325; Note: Catholic school in the Jesuit tradition
Cecil Critch, Principal
ccritch@stbonaventurescollege.ca

Universities & Colleges

Universities

St. John's: Memorial University of Newfoundland (MUN)
P.O. Box 4200
St. John's, NL A1C 5S7
Tel: 709-737-8000; Fax: 709-864-3514
www.mun.ca
www.facebook.com/MemorialUniversity
twitter.com/MemorialU
www.linkedin.com/company/memorial-university-of-newfoundland
www.youtube.com/user/MemorialUVideos
Full Time Equivalency: 18470
Susan Knight, Chancellor
smknight@mun.ca@mun.ca
Dr. Gary Kachanoski, President & Vice-Chancellor
Dr. Noreen Golfman, Provost & Vice-President, Academic
Kent Decker, Vice-President, Administration & Finance
Dr. Ray Gosine, Vice-President, Research
Sheila Singleton, Registrar
ssinglet@mun.ca

Faculties
Faculty of Arts
A-5015 Arts & Administration Building
St. John's, NL A1C 5S7
Tel: 709-864-8254; Fax: 709-864-2135
arts@mun.ca
www.mun.ca/arts
www.facebook.com/MemorialFacultyofArts
twitter.com/memorialarts
Dr. Lynne Phillips, Dean

Business Administration
Tel: 709-864-8512
busihelp@mun.ca
www.business.mun.ca
www.facebook.com/MUNBusiness
twitter.com/MUNBusiness
www.youtube.com/MUNBusiness
Dr. Wilfred Zerbe, Dean

Faculty of Education
Tel: 709-864-8553; *Fax:* 709-864-4379
gradeduc@mun.ca
www.mun.ca/educ
www.facebook.com/190728607604792
twitter.com/MUNEducation
Dr. Kirk Anderson, Dean

Engineering & Applied Science
Tel: 709-864-8810; *Fax:* 709-864-8975
www.engr.mun.ca
Dr. Greg Naterer, Dean

School of Graduate Studies
230 Elizabeth Ave., St. John's, NL A1C 5S7
Tel: 709-864-2445; *Fax:* 709-864-4702
sgs@mun.ca
www.mun.ca/sgs
www.facebook.com/mungradstudies
Dr. Fay Murrin, Dean

Faculty of Medicine
Tel: 709-864-6358; *Fax:* 709-864-6294
www.med.mun.ca
www.facebook.com/MUNMedicine
twitter.com/MUNMed
www.youtube.com/user/MUNmedicine
Dr. James Rourke, Dean

Faculty of Science
Tel: 709-864-8153; *Fax:* 809-864-3316
science@mun.ca
www.mun.ca/science
www.facebook.com/MUNScience
twitter.com/MUN_Science
Dr. Mark Abrahams, Dean

Schools
Distance Education, Learning & Teaching Support (DELTS)
Tel: 709-864-8700; *Toll-Free:* 866-435-1396
www.delts.mun.ca
www.facebook.com/delts.memorial
twitter.com/delts_memorial
Susan Cleyle, Director

School of Human Kinetics & Recreation
Tel: 709-864-8130; *Fax:* 709-864-3979
www.mun.ca/hkr
www.facebook.com/SchoolofHumanKineticsandRecreation
Dr. Heather Carnahan, Dean

School of Music
Tel: 709-864-7486; *Fax:* 709-864-2666
music@mun.ca
www.mun.ca/music
www.facebook.com/136323293083102
twitter.com/musicatmemorial
Dr. Ellen Waterman, Dean

School of Nursing
300 Prince Phillip Dr., St. John's, NL A1B 3V6
Tel: 709-777-2165
www.nurs.mun.ca
www.facebook.com/196576727034976
twitter.com/MUN_Nursing
Dr. Alice Gaudine, Dean

School of Pharmacy
Tel: 709-777-8300; *Fax:* 709-777-7044
pharminfo@mun.ca
www.mun.ca/pharmacy
www.facebook.com/schoolofpharmacy
twitter.com/SchoolofPharm
Dr. Carlo Marra, Dean

School of Social Work
P.O. Box 4200
323 Prince Phillip Dr., St. John, NL A1C 5S7
Tel: 709-864-8165; *Fax:* 709-864-2408
socialwork@mun.ca
www.mun.ca/socwrk
Dr. Donna Hardy Cox, Dean

Harlow Campus
The Maltings, St Johns Walk, Old Harlow
Essex, UK
harlow@mun.ca
www.mun.ca/harlow
Other Information: Phone: (0)1279-455900; Fax: (0)1279-455921
Sandra Wright, General Manager
sandra.wright@mun.ca

Queen's College
Faculty of Theology
#3000, 210 Prince Philip Dr., St. John's, NL A1B 3R6
Tel: 709-753-0116; *Toll-Free:* 877-753-0116
queens@mun.ca
www.mun.ca/queens
The Rev. Dr. Alex Faseruk, Interim Administrator

Sir Wilfred Grenfell College
P.O. Box 2000
20 University Dr., Corner Brook, NL A2H 6P9
Tel: 709-637-6200; *Toll-Free:* 866-381-7022
info@grenfell.mun.ca
www.swgc.mun.ca
www.facebook.com/grenfellcampus
twitter.com/grenfellcampus
www.youtube.com/grenfellcampus
Note: The College features the following divisions: Arts, Fine Arts, Science, & Social Science.
Mary Bluechardt, Vice-President, 709-637-6231
mbluechardt@grenfell.mun.ca

Centres/Institutes
Fisheries & Marine Institute of Memorial University of Newfoundland (MI)
Also known as: Marine Institute
P.O. Box 4920
St. John's, NL A1C 5R3
Tel: 709-778-0200; *Fax:* 709-778-0346
Toll-Free: 1-800-563-5799
www.mi.mun.ca
www.facebook.com/marine.institute
twitter.com/marineinstitute
www.linkedin.com/company/3338651
www.youtube.com/marineinstitutepr

Colleges

***Stephenville:* College of the North Atlantic (CNA)**
P.O. Box 5400
Stephenville, NL A2N 2Z6, Canada
Toll-Free: 888-982-2268
info@cna.nl.ca
www.cna.nl.ca
www.facebook.com/CNANewfoundlandLabrador
twitter.com/cna_news
www.youtube.com/user/CNamarketing
Full Time Equivalency: 25000
Bob Gardiner, Interim President & CEO
William Radford, Chief Learning Officer & Senior Vice-President, Academic, 709-643-7732
Elizabeth Kidd, COO & Vice-President, Corporate Services, 709-643-7704
Robin Walters, Vice-President, Industry & Community Engagement, 709-643-3012

Schools
School of Academics
Brenda Tobin, Dean, 709-292-5636
brenda.tobin@cna.nl.ca
Jason Rolls, Dean, Lang Studies & Academics (Qatar)
jason.rolls@cna-qatar.edu.qa

School of Applied Arts
Brenda Tobin, Dean, 709-292-5636
brenda.tobin@cna.nl.ca

School of Business
Mary Vaughan, Dean, 709-649-7970
mary.vaughan@cna.nl.ca
David King, Dean, Qatar
david.king@cna-qatar.edu.qa

School of Engineering Technology
Brent Howell, Dean, 709-637-8608
brent.howell@cna.nl.ca
Michael Walsh, Dean, Qatar
mike.walsh@cna-qatar.edu.qa

School of Health Sciences
Jane Gamberg, Dean, 709-758-7624
jane.gamberg@cna.nl.ca
Irene O'Brien, Dean, Qatar
irene.obrien@cna-qatar.edu.qa

School of Industrial Trades
Robin Walters, Dean, 709-744-3012
robin.walters@cna.nl.ca

School of Information Technology
Mary Vaughan, Dean, 709-649-7970
mary.vaughan@cna.nl.ca
Theodore Chiasson, Dean, Qatar
theodore.chiasson@cna-qatar.edu.qa

School of Natural Resources
Brent Howell, Dean, 709-637-8608
brent.howell@cna.nl.ca

School of Tourism
Brenda Tobin, Dean, 709-292-5636
brenda.tobin@cna.nl.ca

Campuses
Baie-Verte Campus
1 Terra Nova Rd., Baie Verte, NL A0K 1B0, Canada
Tel: 709-532-8066; *Fax:* 709-532-4624
Emily Foster, Campus Administrator, 709-532-8066
emily.foster@cna.nl.ca

Bay St. George Campus - Headquarters
DSB Fowlow Bldg.
P.O. Box 5400
432 Massachussetts Dr., Stephenville, NL A2N 2Z6, Canada
Tel: 709-643-7730; *Fax:* 709-643-7734
Chris Dohaney, Campus Administrator, 709-643-7916
chris.dohaney@cna.nl.ca

Bonavista Campus
P.O. Box 670
301 Confederation Dr., Bonavista, NL A0C 1B0, Canada
Tel: 709-468-1700; *Fax:* 709-468-2004

Burin Campus
P.O. Box 370
105 Main St., Burin Bay, NL A0E 1G0, Canada
Tel: 709-891-5600; *Fax:* 709-891-2256
Toll-Free: 800-838-0976
Stephen Warren, Campus Administrator, 709-891-5613

Carbonear Campus
P.O. Box 60
4 Pike's Lane, Carbonear, NL A1Y 1A7, Canada
Tel: 709-596-6139; *Fax:* 709-596-2688
Josiah Mullins, Campus Administrator, 709-596-8911
joe.mullins@cna.nl.ca

Clarenville Campus
P.O. Box 308
69 Pleasant St., Clarenville, NL A0E 1J0, Canada
Tel: 709-466-6900; *Fax:* 709-466-2771
Maisie Caines, Campus Administrator, 709-446-6931
maisie.caines@cna.nl.ca

Corner Brook Campus
P.O. Box 822
41 O'Connell Dr., Corner Brook, NL A2H 6H6, Canada
Tel: 709-637-8530; *Fax:* 709-634-2126
Chad Simms, Campus Administrator, 709-637-8549
chad.simms@cna.nl.ca

Gander Campus
P.O. Box 395
1 Magee Rd., Gander, NL A1V 1W8, Canada
Tel: 709-651-4800; *Fax:* 709-651-4854
Fergus O'Brien, Campus Administrator, 709-651-4821
fergus.obrien@cna.nl.ca

Grand Falls-Windsor Campus
P.O. Box 413
5 Cromer Ave., Grand Falls-Windsor, NL A2A 1X3, Canada
Tel: 709-292-5600; *Fax:* 709-489-4180
Joan Pynn, Campus Administrator, 709-292-5625
joan.pynn@cna.nl.ca

Happy Valley-Goose Bay Campus
P.O. Box 1720 B
219 Hamilton River Rd., Happy Valley-Goose Bay, NL A0P 1E0, Canada
Tel: 709-896-6300; *Fax:* 709-896-3733
Paul Motty, Campus Administrator, 709-896-6312
paul.motty@cna.nl.ca

Labrador West Campus
1600 Nichols-Adam Hwy, Labrador City, NL A2V 0B8, Canada
Tel: 709-944-7210; *Fax:* 709-944-6581
Richard Sawyer, Campus Administrator, 709-944-5895
richard.sawyer@cna.nl.ca

Placentia Campus
P.O. Box 190
1 Roosevelt Ave., Placentia, NL A0B 2Y0, Canada
Tel: 709-227-2037; *Fax:* 709-227-7185
Darrell Clarke, Campus Administrator, 709-227-2037
darrell.clarke@cna.nl.ca

Port-aux-Basques Campus
P.O. Box 760
59 Grand Bay Rd., Port-aux-Basques, NL A0M 1C0, Canada
Tel: 709-695-3343; *Fax:* 709-695-2963
Jan Peddle, Campus Administrator, 709-695-3343
jan.peddle@cna.nl.ca

Prince Philip Drive Campus - St. John's
P.O. Box 1693
1 Prince Philip Dr., St. John's, NL A1C 5P7, Canada
Tel: 709-758-7284; *Fax:* 709-758-7304
Trudy Barnes, Campus Administrator, 709-757-5187
trudy.barnes@cna.nl.ca

Ridge Road Campus
P.O. Box 1150
153 Ridge Rd., St. John's, NL A1C 6L8
Tel: 709-758-7000; *Fax:* 709-758-7304
Paul Forward, Campus Administrator, 709-793-3214
paul.forward@cna.nl.ca

Seal Cove Campus
P.O. Box 19003 Seal Cove
1670 Conception Bay Hwy., Conception Bay South, NL A1X 5C7, Canada
Tel: 709-744-2047; *Fax:* 709-744-3929
Chris Patey, Campus Administrator, 709-744-1041
chris.patey@cna.nl.ca

St. Anthony Campus
P.O. Box 550
83-93 East St., St Anthony, NL A0K 4S0, Canada
Tel: 709-454-3559; *Fax:* 709-454-8808
Cecil Roberts, Campus Administrator, 709-454-2884
cecil.roberts@cna.nl.ca

Qatar Campus
P.O. Box 24449
68 Al Tarafa, Duhail North, Doha, Qatar
Other Information: Int'l Phone: 974-4495-2222; Fax: 974-4495-2200
Shawn Brace, Vice-Pres., Finance & Administration
shawn.brace@cna-qatar.edu.qa

Post Secondary/Technical

Badger: Central Training Academy
P.O. Box 400
6 Third Ave., Badger, NL A0H 1A0
Tel: 709-539-5150; *Fax:* 709-539-5145
Toll-Free: 1-800-563-5153
www.centraltraining.ca
Note: The Academy has state-of-the-art heavy equipment for national accredited training. The hands-on program also provides instruction for excavating, land clearing, road, building, grading, & the maintenance of machinery.

Conception Bay South: Woodford Training Centre Inc.
P.O. Box 17145 Kelligrews
4 Woodgrove Acres, Conception Bay South, NL A1X 3H1, Canada
Tel: 709-834-7000; *Fax:* 709-834-9663
info@woodfordtraining.com
www.woodfordtraining.com
Note: Cosmetology & barbering
Sharon Woodford

Corner Brook: Academy Canada - Corner Brook Campus
2 University Dr., Corner Brook, NL A2H 5G4, Canada
Tel: 709-637-2100; *Fax:* 709-637-2123
Toll-Free: 1-800-561-8000
www.academycanada.com
www.facebook.com/AcademyCanada
www.twitter.com/academycanada
M.A.Ed. Michael Barrett, President

Campuses
St. John's Campus
#167, 169 Kenmount Rd., St. John's, NL A1B 3P9, Canada
Tel: 709-739-6767; *Fax:* 709-739-6797

Trades College
#37, 45 Harding Rd., St. John's, NL A1C 5R4, Canada
Tel: 709-722-9151; *Fax:* 709-722-9197

Gander: Gander Flight Training Aerospace
P.O. Box 355
70 C. L. Dobbin Dr., Gander, NL A1V 1W7, Canada
Tel: 709-256-7484; *Fax:* 709-256-7953
Toll-Free: 1-877-438-2359
admin@gft.ca
www.gft.ca
Patrick White, President & CEO

Grand Falls-Windsor: Corona Training Institute
Excite Building
32 Queensway Business Park, Grand Falls-Windsor, NL A2A 2J3, Canada
Tel: 709-489-7825; *Fax:* 709-489-5001
Toll-Free: 1-888-926-7662
admin@coronacollege.com
www.coronacollege.com
www.facebook.com/coronacollege
twitter.com/coronacollege
Number of Employees: 14
Bernice Walker, President & CEO
bwalker@coronacollege.com

Holyrood: Boilermakers Industrial Training Centre
P.O. Box 250
Holyrood, NL A0A 2R0, Canada
Tel: 709-229-7958; *Fax:* 709-229-7300
Tom Welsh

Holyrood: Operating Engineers College (OEC)
P.O. Box 389 Salmonier Line
Holyrood, NL A0A 2R0, Canada
Tel: 709-229-6464; *Fax:* 709-229-6469
Toll-Free: 888-229-6468
oec@oecollege.com
www.oecollege.com

Lewisporte: DieTrac Technical Institute
P.O. Box 970
82 Premier Dr., Lewisporte, NL A0G 3A0, Canada
Tel: 709-535-0550; *Fax:* 709-535-6101
studentservices@dietrac.com
www.dietrac.com

Mount Pearl: Iron Workers Education & Training Co. Inc.
Donavans Industrial Park
38 Sagona Ave., Mount Pearl, NL A1N 4R3, Canada
Tel: 709-747-2158; *Fax:* 709-747-1042
info@ironworkerslocal764.com
www.ironworkerslocal764.com
Note: This program follows the Provincial Plan of Training. The Ironworker Generalist Program offers the student both theory and practical exposure to all aspects of the Ironworker trade including structural erection and dismantling, reinforcing, post-tensioning, rigging, and cranes.
Lawrence R. Hawco, President, Training Coordinator

Paradise: Carpenters Millwrights College Inc.
P.O. Box 3040
89 McNamara Dr., Paradise, NL A1L 3W2, Canada
Tel: 709-364-5586; *Fax:* 709-364-5587
kpower@nlrc.ca
www.nlrc.ca

St. John's: Association for New Canadians (ANC)
P.O. Box 2031 C
St. John's, NL A1C 5R6
Tel: 709-726-6848; *Fax:* 709-726-6841
linc@nfld.net
www.ancnl.ca
Note: The Association for New Canadians is a non-profit organization that offers an ESL Training Centre to support the integration of immigrants & refugees.

St. John's: Graduate Centre of Applied Technology
P.O. Box 6345 C
275 Duckworth St., St. John's, NL A1C 6J9, Canada
Tel: 709-722-8580; *Fax:* 709-722-8318
Toll-Free: 1-800-563-1393
Cal Burton

St. John's: Judy Knee Dance Studio
27 Mayor Ave., St. John's, NL A1C 4N4, Canada
Tel: 709-579-3233
judy@judyknee.com
judyknee.com
Judy Knee, Owner

St. John's: Keyin College
303 Thorburn Rd., St. John's, NL A1B 4G3, Canada
Tel: 709-579-1061; *Fax:* 709-579-6002
Toll-Free: 1-800-563-8989
www.keyin.com
twitter.com/KeyinCollege
Note: Industry-directed education
Gwen Tucker, Founder

Campuses
Carbonear Campus
81 LeMarchant St., Carbonear, NL A1Y 1A9, Canada
Tel: 709-596-6472; *Fax:* 709-596-0217
Toll-Free: 800-563-8989
dpenney@keyin.ca
Ken Drover, Principal

Clarenville Campus
240A Memorial Dr., Clarenville, NL A5A 1N9, Canada
Tel: 709-466-7115; *Fax:* 709-466-1290
pdrover@keyin.ca
Paula Benson, Principal

Fortune Adult Learning Centre Campus
8 Benson St., Fortune, NL A0E 1P0, Canada
Tel: 709-279-5090; *Fax:* 709-279-5091
Toll-Free: 1-800-563-8989
wlewis@keyin.ca

Gander Campus
175 Airport Blvd., Gander, NL A1V 1K6, Canada
Tel: 709-651-8560; *Fax:* 709-651-8565
Toll-Free: 1-800-563-8989
thayden@keyincentral.nf.ca
Elise Babstock, Principal

Grand Falls-Windsor Campus
60 Hardy Ave., Grand Falls-Windsor, NL A2A 2P&, Canada
Tel: 709-489-8560; *Fax:* 709-489-8565
Toll-Free: 1-800-563-8989
thayden@keyincentral.nf.ca
Bill Hanlon, Principal

Lamaline Adult Learning Centre Campus
GLADA Bldg.
P.O. Box 39
Lamaline, NL A0E 2C0, Canada
Tel: 709-279-5090; *Fax:* 709-279-5091
Toll-Free: 1-800-563-8989
wlewis@keyin.ca

Lewisporte Adult Learning Centre Campus
139 Main St., Lewisporte, NL A0G 3A0, Canada
Tel: 709-535-3946; *Fax:* 709-535-3946
Toll-Free: 1-800-563-8989
thayden@keyincentral.nf.ca
Brian Caravan, Principal

Marystown Campus
P.O. Box 1327
814 Ville Marie Dr., Marystown, NL A0E 2M0, Canada
Tel: 709-279-8090; *Fax:* 709-279-5091
Toll-Free: 1-800-563-8989
wlewis@keyin.ca
Marc Coady, Principal

St. John's Campus
P.O. Box 13609 A
44 Austin St., St. John's, NL A1B 4G1, Canada
Tel: 709-579-1061; *Fax:* 709-579-6002
Toll-Free: 1-800-563-8989
jim@keyin.com

St. Lawrence Adult Learning Centre
P.O. Box 1327
414 Ville Marie Dr., Marystown, NL A0E 2M0, Canada
Tel: 709-279-5090; *Fax:* 709-279-5091
Toll-Free: 1-800-563-8989
wlewis@keyin.ca

Lawn Adult Learning Centre
P.O. Box 1327
414 Ville Marie Dr., Marystown, NL A0E 2M0, Canada
Tel: 709-279-5090; *Fax:* 709-279-5091
Toll-Free: 1-800-563-8989
wlewis@keyin.ca

St. John's: LeMoine's School of Hair Design
P.O. Box 5744
St. John's, NL A1C 5X3, Canada
Tel: 709-576-2148; *Fax:* 709-579-1134
lemoines@nl.rogers.com
www.lemoines.com
Note: Hair dressing and esthetics school.
Verna LeMoine, Executive Director

St. John's: T&R Goldshield Institute
300 Topsail Rd., St. John's, NL A1E 2B5, Canada
Tel: 709-697-2038
Don Ross

St.John's: **United Association of Journeymen & Apprentices of the Plumbing & Pipefitting (UA)**
P.O. Box 8583 A
48 Sagona Ave., St.John's, NL A1B 3P2, Canada
Tel: 709-747-0364; *Fax:* 709-747-2861
www.ualocal740.ca
Note: Official name: "United Association of Journeymen & Apprentices of the Plumbing and Pipefitting Industry of the United States and Canada".
Betty Shea, Organizer, 709-7472248
bshea@ualocal740.ca

Northwest Territories

Government Agencies

Yellowknife: **Northwest Territories Department of Education, Culture & Employment**
P.O. Box 1320
Yellowknife, NT X1A 2L9, Canada
Tel: 867-669-2344; *Fax:* 867-873-0481
ecepublicaffairs@gov.nt.ca
www.ece.gov.nt.ca
Hon. Jackson Lafferty, Minister of Education, Culture & Employment, 867-669-2344
jackson_lafferty@gov.nt.ca

School Boards/Districts/Divisions

Public

Fort Simpson: **Dehcho Divisional Education Council**
P.O. Box 276
Fort Simpson, NT X0E 0N0, Canada
Tel: 867-695-7300; *Fax:* 867-695-7348
www.dehcho.nt.ca
Number of Schools: 9; *Grades:* K - 12
Terry Jaffray, Superintendent

Fort Smith: **South Slave Divisional Education Council (SSDEC)**
P.O. Box 510
Fort Smith, NT X0E 0P0, Canada
Tel: 867-872-5701; *Fax:* 867-872-2150
slee@ssdec.nt.ca
www.ssdec.nt.ca
Number of Schools: 8; *Grades:* K - 12; *Enrollment:* 1500
Curtis Brown, Superintendent, 867-872-5701
cbrown@ssdec.nt.ca
Brent Kaulback, Assistant Superintendent, 867-872-5701
bkaulback@ssdec.nt.ca
Joan Duford, Finance Clerk, 867-872-5701
jduford@ssdec.nt.ca
Steven Lee, Public Affairs Coordinator, 867-872-5701
slee@ssdec.nt.ca

Inuvik: **Beaufort Delta Education Council (BDEC)**
c/o Bag Service No. 12, Inuvik, NT X0E 0T0, Canada
Tel: 867-777-7136
www.bdec.nt.ca
Number of Schools: 9; *Grades:* K - 12; *Enrollment:* 1800
Carolyn Lennie, Chair
Robert Charlie, Vice-Chair
Denise Kurszewski, Superintendent of Schools, 867-777-7176
denise_kurszewski@bdec.learnnet.nt.ca
Greta Sittichinli, Associate Assistant Superintendent, 807-777-7199
David Reid, Supervisor of Schools, 867-777-7131
david_reid@bdec.learnnet.nt.ca
Austin Abbott, Coordinator, Skills Programs, 867-777-7367
austin_abbott@bdec.learnnet.nt.ca
Crystal Lennie, Coordinator, Public Affairs, 867-777-7322
crystal_lennie@bdec.learnnet.nt.ca

Norman Wells: **Sahtu Divisional Education Council**
P.O. Box 64
Norman Wells, NT X0E 0V0, Canada
Tel: 867-587-3450; *Fax:* 867-587-2551
info@sahtudec.ca
www.sahtudec.ca
Number of Schools: 5; *Grades:* K - 12
Seamus Quigg, Superintendent
Renee Closs, Assistant Superintendent
Thomas Cabot, Finance Officer
Jessie Jane Campbell, Aboriginal Languages Consultant

Rae Edzo: **Tłı̨chǫ Community Services Agency**
Bag Service #5, Rae Edzo, NT X0E 0Y0, Canada
Tel: 867-392-3000; *Fax:* 867-392-3001
tcsa@tlicho.net
www.tlicho.ca
Number of Schools: 5
Lucy Lafferty, Superintendent

Yellowknife: **Yellowknife Catholic Schools**
P.O. Box 1830
5124 - 49 St., Yellowknife, NT X1A 2P4, Canada
Tel: 867-766-7400
Number of Schools: 3; *Grades:* K-12; *Enrollment:* 1320; *Number of Employees:* 110
Claudia Parker, Supt.
Mike Huvenaars, Asst. Supt., Business
Dianne Lafferty, Coordinator, Aboriginal Ed.

Yellowknife: **Yellowknife Education District #1**
P.O. Box 788
5402 - 50th Ave., Yellowknife, NT X1A 2N6, Canada
Tel: 867-766-5050; *Fax:* 867-873-5051
yk1@yk1.nt.ca
www.yk1.nt.ca
www.facebook.com/YK1District
Number of Schools: 8; *Grades:* K-12; *Enrollment:* 2000; *Number of Employees:* 250
Metro Huculak, Superintendent of Education, 867-766-5064
metro.huculak@yk1.nt.ca
Bernie Giacobbo, Assistant Superintendent of Education, 867-766-5057
bernie.giacobbo@yk1.nt.ca
Mattie McNeill, Aboriginal Education Coordinator, 867-766-5054
Stacey Scarf, Manager, Personnel Services, 867-766-5058
Tram Do, Director of Corporate Services, 867-766-5062
tram.do@yk1.nt.ca

French

Yellowknife: **Commission scolaire francophone des Territoires du Nord-Ouest**
Également connu sous le nom de: Commission scolaire francophone TNO
P.O. Box 1980
#207, 4915, rue 48, Yellowknife, NT X1A 2P5, Canada
Tél: 867-873-6555; *Téléc:* 867-873-5644
Ligne sans frais: 866-238-2733
csftno@gov.nt.ca
www.csftno.com
Number of Schools: 2; *Grades:* K-12
Marie LeBlanc-Warick, Directrice générale, 867-873-6555
Marie_LeBlanc-Warick@learnnet.nt.ca
Suzette Montreil, Présidente, 867-873-6555
Éric Frenette, Contrôleur financier, 867-873-6555
Eric_Frenette@gov.nt.ca

Schools: Independent & Private

Independent & Private Schools

Yellowknife: **Northwest Territories Montessori Society**
5212 - 52nd St., Yellowknife, NT X1A 1T9
Tel: 867-669-7987; *Fax:* 867-873-2526
montess@ssimicro.com
www.ykmontessori.ca
www.facebook.com/groups/48934094227/
Lynda Baillargeon, Executive Director

Universities & Colleges

Colleges

Inuvik: **Aurora College**
P.O. Box 1008
Inuvik, NT X0E 0P0
Tel: 867-287-2655; *Fax:* 867-777-7800
Toll-Free: 866-287-2655
www.auroracollege.nt.ca
www.facebook.com/131796776862510
www.flickr.com/photos/auroracollege
Jane Arychuk, President

Thebacha Campus
P.O. Box 600
50 Conibear Cres., Fort Smith, NT X0E 0P0
Tel: 867-872-7500; *Fax:* 867-872-4511
Toll-Free: 866-266-4966
Margaret Imrie, Director, Student Services

Yellowknife/North Shore Campus
P.O. Box 9700
5004 - 54th St., Yellowknife, NT X1A 2R3
Tel: 867-920-3030; *Fax:* 867-920-0333
Toll-Free: 866-291-4856
Heather McCagg-Nystrom, Vice-President, Community & Extensions

Nova Scotia

Government Agencies

Halifax: **Nova Scotia Department of Education & Early Childhood Development**
P.O. Box 578
2021 Brunswick St., Halifax, NS B3J 2S9, Canada
Tel: 902-424-5168; *Fax:* 902-424-0511
Toll-Free: 888-825-7770
Susan.McKeage@novascotia.ca
www.ednet.ns.ca
Hon. Karen Lynn Casey, Minister of Education & Early Childhood Development, 902-424-4236
educmin@gov.ns.ca

Halifax: **Nova Scotia Department of Labour & Advanced Education**
P.O. Box 697
5151 Terminal Rd., Halifax, NS B3J 2T8
Tel: 902-424-5301; *Fax:* 902-424-0575
MIN_LAE@novascotia.ca
novascotia.ca/lae
Hon. Kelly Regan, Minister of Labour & Advanced Education, 902-424-6647
kelly@kellyregan.ca

School Boards/Districts/Divisions

Public

Berwick: **Annapolis Valley Regional School Board (AVRSB)**
P.O. Box 340
121 Orchard St., Berwick, NS B0P 1E0, Canada
Tel: 902-538-4600; *Fax:* 902-538-4630
Toll-Free: 1-800-850-3887
www.avrsb.ca
twitter.com/avrsb
Number of Schools: 43; *Grades:* Pre - 12; adult educarion; *Enrollment:* 14000
Margo Tait, Superintendent, Schools, 902-538-4615
margo.tait@avrsb.ca
Stuart Jamieson, Director of Finance, 902-538-4607
stu.jamieson@avrsb.ca
Erica Weatherbie, Director of Human Resources, 902-538-4610
erica.weatherbie@avrsb.ca

Bridgewater: **South Shore Regional School Board (SSRSB)**
130 North Park St., Bridgewater, NS B4V 4G9, Canada
Tel: 902-543-2468; *Fax:* 902-541-3051
Toll-Free: 888-252-2217
tsmith@ssrsb.ca
www.ssrsb.ca
twitter.com/SouthShoreRSB
Number of Schools: 26 schools; 7 adult/alternate school programs; *Grades:* Pre-K - 12; *Enrollment:* 6917
Elliott Payzant, Chair
Geoff Cainen, Superintendent of Schools, 902-541-3002
gcainen@ssrsb.ca
Wade Tattrie, Director of Finance, 902-541-3032
wtattrie@ssrsb.ca
Clayton Smith, Procurement Analyst, 902-541-3006
csmith@ssrsb.ca
Tina Munro, Director of Human Resources, 902-521-2479
tmunro@ssrsb.ca
Jeff DeWolfe, Director of Programs and Student Services, 902-541-3045
jdewolfe@ssrsb.ca

Dartmouth: **Halifax Regional School Board**
33 Spectacle Lake Dr., Dartmouth, NS B2Y 4S8, Canada
Tel: 902-464-2000
www.hrsb.ns.ca
twitter.com/HRSB_Official
Number of Schools: 86 elementary schools; 28 junior high schools; 13 senior high schools; 9 K-9 schools;; *Grades:* Pre - 12; *Enrollment:* 49552; *Number of Employees:* 9,000
Gin Yee, Chair, 902-464-2000, ext. 4445
gyee@hrsb.ca
Elwin LeRoux, Superintendent, 902-464-2000, ext. 2312
Alison Leverman, Director, Program, 902-464-2000, ext. 2567
Mike Christie, Director, Human Resource Services, 902-464-2000, ext. 2210
Ron Heiman, Director, Operations Services, 902-464-2000, ext. 2144
Danielle McNeil-Hessian, Director, School Administration, 902-464-2000, ext. 2275
Terri Thompson, Director, Financial Services, 902-464-2000, ext. 2241

Kathryn Burlton, Manager, Accounting & Purchasing, 902-464-2000, ext. 2843

Port Hastings: Strait Regional School Board (SRSB)
16 Cemetery Rd., Port Hastings, NS B9A 1K6, Canada
Tel: 902-625-2191; *Fax:* 902-625-2281
Toll-Free: 1-800-650-4448
srsb@srsb.ca
srsb.ca
twitter.com/straitrsb
Number of Schools: 21; *Grades:* K - 12; *Enrollment:* 6633; *Number of Employees:* 976
Mary Jess MacDonald, Chair
Ford Rice, Superintendent, Schools, 902-625-7065
ford.rice@srsb.ca
William J. Cormier, Director, Finance, 902-625-7050
william.cormier@srsb.ca
Terry Doyle, Director, Operations, 902-747-3647
terry.doyle@srsb.ca
Sherman England, Director, Human Resources, 902-625-7081
Paul Landry, Director, Programs & Student Services, 902-625-7083
paul.landry@srsb.ca
Shirley Hart, Manager, Purchasing, 902-625-7050
shirley.hart@srsb.ca

Sydney: Cape Breton-Victoria Regional School Board
275 George St., Sydney, NS B1P 1J7, Canada
Tel: 902-564-8293; *Fax:* 902-564-0123
www.cbv.ns.ca
www.facebook.com/CapeBretonVictoriaRegionalSchoolBoard
twitter.com/CBVRSB
Number of Schools: 54; *Grades:* Elementary - Secondary; *Enrollment:* 13774; *Number of Employees:* 1067 teachers; 923 support staff; 29 administrators
Lorne Green, Chair
lgreen@cbvrsb.ca
Ambrose White, Superintendent, 902-564-8293
awhite@cbvrsb.ca
George Boudreau, Director, Financial Services, 902-562-6489
gboudreau@cbvrsb.ca
Susan Kelley, Director, Programs and Student Services, 902-562-6480
skelley@cbvrsb.ca
Beth MacIsaac, Director, Human Resources Services, 902-562-6486
bmacisaac@cbvrsb.ca

Truro: Chignecto-Central Regional School Board (CCRSB)
60 Lorne St., Truro, NS B2N 3K3, Canada
Tel: 902-897-8900; *Fax:* 902-897-8989
Toll-Free: 800-770-0008
www.ccrsb.ednet.ns.ca
www.facebook.com/ChignectoCRSB
twitter.com/ChignectoCRSB
Number of Schools: 77; *Grades:* K - 12; *Enrollment:* 25722
Gary G. Clarke, Superintendent, 902-897-8910
Scott Milner, Director of Education Services, 902-897-8950
Valerie Gauthier, Director of Financial Services, 902-897-8920
Valerie Tucker, Purchasing Manager, 902-897-8923
Allison McGrath, Director of Human Resources Services, 902-897-8940

Yarmouth: Tri-County Regional School Board (TCRSB)
79 Water St., Yarmouth, NS B5A 1L4
Tel: 902-749-5696; *Fax:* 902-749-5697
Toll-Free: 800-915-0113
www.tcrsb.ca
Number of Schools: 28; *Grades:* Primary - 12
Donna Tidd, Chair
Lisa Doucet, Superintendent, Schools, 902-749-5682
ldoucet@tcrsb.ca
Trevor Cunningham, Director, Programs & Student Services, 902-749-5675
tcunning@tcrsb.ca
Gerry Purdy, Director, Human Resources, 902-749-5684
gpurdy@tcrsb.ca
Steve Stoddart, Director, Operations, 902-749-5691
sstoddar@tcrsb.ca
Wade Tattrie, Director, Finance, 902-541-3009
wtattrie@ssrsb.ca

French

Saulnierville: Conseil scolaire acadien provincial
P.O. Box 88
Saulnierville, NS B0W 2Z0, Canada
Tél: 902-769-5458; *Téléc:* 902-769-5459
Ligne sans frais: 888-533-2727
csap.ednet.ns.ca
Number of Schools: 21; *Enrollment:* 4059; *Note:* Adresse civique: 9248, rte 1, La Butte, Meteghan River, N-É.
Darrell Samson, Directeur général, 902-769-5458
Michel Comeau, Directeur des services et programmes, 902-769-5475
Chantale Desbiens, Secrétaire de direction, 902-424-4183
Normand DeCelles, Directeur des ressources humaines, 902-226-5232
Janine Saulnier, Directrice des finances, 902-769-5464

First Nations

Eskasoni: Eskasoni First Nation School Board
P.O. Box 7959
4645 Shore Rd., Eskasoni, NS B1W 1B8
Tel: 902-379-2507; *Fax:* 902-379-2273
eskasoni@schoolbd.ca
www.eskasonischoolbd.com
Grades: Day Care - Secondary; Mi'kmaq; *Enrollment:* 1249; *Note:* Eskasoni Ksite'taqnk Day Care; Eskasoni Unama'ki Training & Education Centre; Eskasoni Elementary & Middle School, & Chief Allison Bernard Memorial High School. Number of Employees: 175. Situated on eastern Cape Breton Island, Eskasoni First Nation is a large Mi'kmaq community. Education in the community is directed by the Eskasoni First Nation School Board, which is overseen by the Eskasoni Band Council.
John F. Toney, Chair
Patricia Marshall, Director, Education, 902-379-2507
Patrick Johnson, Director, Mi'kmaq Student Services at Cape Breton University, 902-379-2507
Terry Lynn Marshall, Contact, Finance, 902-379-2507
terrylynnmarshall@schoolbd.ca
Barbara Sylliboy, Contact, Language, 902-379-2507
barbsylliboy@schoolbd.ca
Belinda Stevens, Clerk, Post-Secondary Program, 902-379-2507
belindastevens@schoolbd.ca

Schools: Specialized

First Nations

Chapel Island: Potlotelewey Kina'matmokuam
P.O. Box 538
RR#1, Richmond County, Chapel Island, NS B0E 3B0, Canada
Tel: 902-535-2307; *Fax:* 902-535-3428
Grades: K - 6; *Note:* The school serves the Chapel Island First Nation.
Shaunna Francis, Principal
sfrancis@potloek.ca

Eskasoni: Chief Allison Bernard Memorial High School
P.O. Box 7969
4673 Shore Rd., Eskasoni, NS B1W 1B8, Canada
Tel: 902-379-3000; *Fax:* 902-379-3011
www.eskasonischoolbd.com
Grades: 10 - 12; Mi'kmaq language & culture; *Enrollment:* 200; *Note:* Chief Allison Bernard Memorial High School operates under the direction of the Eskasoni First Nation School Board. The First Nation secondary school is situated in the Mi'kmaq community of Eskasoni in Cape Breton Island. Chief Allison Bernard Memorial High School follows the Nova Scotia Curriculum Guide & also offers Mi'kmaq studies.
Newell Johnson, Principal

Eskasoni: Eskasoni Elementary & Middle School
P.O. Box 7970
4675 Shore Rd., Eskasoni, NS B1W 1B8, Canada
Tel: 902-379-2825; *Fax:* 902-379-2886
eems@eskasonischool.ca
www.eskasonischool.ca
Grades: K - 9; Mi'kmaq language; *Note:* Eskasoni Elementary & Middle School is a Mi'kmaq First Nation school, which operates under the direction of the Eskasoni First Nation School Board. Mi'kmaq immersion classes are offered from kindergarten to grade 3.
Philomena Moore, Principal
philmoore46@hotmail.com
Cameron Frost, Vice-Principal

Eskasoni: Eskasoni Ksite'taqnk Day Care
c/o Eskasoni First Nation School Board
P.O. Box 7959
4645 Shore Rd., Eskasoni, NS B1W 1B8
Tel: 902-379-2017
www.eskasonischoolbd.com/id11.html
Grades: Pre-School; *Number of Employees:* 1 coordinator, 6 early childhood educators; 1 cook / day care worker; *Note:* The Eskasoni Ksite'taqnk Day Care operates under the administration of the Eskasoni First Nation School Board. The day care offers a Mi'kmaq educational program, taught in the Mi'kmaq language.
Miranda Bernard, Contact

Eskasoni: Unama'ki Training & Education Centre
P.O. Box 7010
Eskasoni, NS B1L 1A1, Canada
Tel: 902-379-2758; *Fax:* 902-379-2586
www.unamakitec.ca
Grades: 9 - 12; *Enrollment:* 75; *Number of Employees:* 1 principal; 1 teaching vice-principal; 5 teachers; 1 guidance counsellor; 1 secretary; *Note:* Activities of the Unama'ki Training & Education Centre are guided by the Eskasoni First Nation School Board.
Michelle Marshall-Johnson, Principal
Joanne MacDonald, Vice-Principal

Indian Brook: L'nu Sipu'k Kina'matnuokuom
579 Church St., Indian Brook, NS B0N 1W0
Tel: 902-236-3041; *Fax:* 902-236-3049
Grades: K - 12

Sydney: Membertou Elementary School
45 Maillard St., Sydney, NS B1S 2P5
Tel: 902-562-2205; *Fax:* 902-562-4561
www.membertouschool.ca
Grades: Primary - 6; *Note:* Membertou Elementary School's staff consists of a Mi'kmaw language teacher. The school follows the curriculum guidelines established by the Nova Scotia Department of Education.
Sharon Bernard, M.Ed, B.Ed, BACS, Principal
sbernard@membertouschool.ca
Lucy Joe, M.Ed, B.Ed, BA, Vice-Principal
ljoe@membertouschool.ca

Trenton: Pictou Landing First Nation School
P.O. Box 116
Site 6, RR#2, Trenton, NS B0K 1X0
Tel: 902-755-9954; *Fax:* 902-752-4916
schooladmin@pictoulandingschool.ca
www.pictoulandingschool.ca
Grades: K - 6; *Note:* The Pictou Landing First Nation School works in partnership with the Pictou Landing First Nation community, its Elders, & parents to provide an education that includes the Mi'kmaw language & culture.
Irene Endicott, Principal
iendicott@pchg.net

Wagmatcook: Wagmatcookewey School
P.O. Box 30018
Wagmatcook, NS B0E 3N0, Canada
Tel: 902-295-3491; *Fax:* 902-295-1091
wagmatcookeweyschool.ca
Grades: Primary - 12; Mi'kmaq Studies; *Note:* Located on the Wagmatcook First Nation Reserve in Cape Breton, Nova Scotia, the Wagmatcookewey School provides education to Mi'Kmaq First Nation students.
Marjorie Pierro, Principal
marjoriepierro@gmail.com

Whycocomagh: We'koqma'q Mikmaw School
P.O. Box 209
15 Reservation Rd., Whycocomagh, NS B0E 3M0, Canada
Tel: 902-756-9000; *Fax:* 902-756-2171
admin@wfns.ca
www.wfns.ca
Grades: K - 12
Joanne Alex, Principal
joanna@wfnes.ca

Special Education

Halifax: Atlantic Provinces Special Education Authority (APSEA)
5940 South St., Halifax, NS B3H 1S6, Canada
Tel: 902-424-8500; *Fax:* 902-424-0543
apsea@apsea.ca
www.apsea.ca
TTY: 902-424-8500
Note: The Atlantic Provinces Special Education Authority (APSEA) is an interprovincial cooperative agency established in 1975 by joint agreement among the Ministers of Education of New Brunswick, Newfoundland, Nova Scotia, and Prince Edward Island.
Bertram R. Tulk, Supt.

Schools: Independent & Private

Public

Oxford: Oxford Regional Education Centre
P.O. Box 340
249 Lower Main St., Oxford, NS B0M 1P0
Tel: 902-447-4513; *Fax:* 902-447-4517
www.goldenbears.ca
www.facebook.com/OxfordRegionalEducationCentreHomeSchool
Judy Davis, Principal
Carmen Buchanan-Baker, Acting Vice Principal

Faith-Based

Bedford: Sandy Lake Academy
435 Hammond's Plains Rd., Bedford, NS B4B 1Y2, Canada
Tel: 902-835-8548; *Fax:* 902-835-9752
principal@sandylakeacademy.ca
www.sandylakeacademy.ca
www.facebook.com/SandyLakeAcademy
twitter.com/SandyLakeAcdmy
Grades: Pre.-12; *Enrollment:* 76; *Note:* A Seventh-day Adventist Christian School
Chris Dupuis, Principal

Halifax: Halifax Christian Academy
114 Downs Ave., Halifax, NS B3N 1Y6, Canada
Tel: 902-475-1441; *Fax:* 902-477-4922
office@halifaxchristianacademy.ca
halifaxchristianacademy.ca
Grades: Pre.-12; *Number of Employees:* 35
Jessica Wilson, Principal
jwilson@halifaxchristianacademy.ca

Truro: Colchester Christian Academy
P.O. Box 403
Truro, NS B2N 5C5, Canada
Tel: 902-895-6520; *Fax:* 902-893-3727
cca@eastlink.ca
colchesterchristianacademy.ca
Grades: Pre.-12; *Enrollment:* 132
Steve Vanderkwaak, Principal

Tusket: Living Waters Christian Academy
P.O. Box 175
Tusket, NS B0W 3M0, Canada
Tel: 902-648-2676; *Fax:* 902-648-2676
Grades: Pre.-9; *Enrollment:* 44
Mardee Nickerson, Acting Principal

Independent & Private Schools

Blockhouse: South Shore Kindergarten
P.O. Box 177
64 School Rd., Blockhouse, NS B0J 1E0
Tel: 902-624-0874; *Fax:* 902-624-0874
sswaldorf@waldorfns.org
www.waldorfns.org
www.facebook.com/SouthShoreWaldorfSchool/
twitter.com/SSWaldorfSchool
www.youtube.com/channel/UCPe6r6QxSKIF18txXRiPS2A
Grades: Pre. K - K
Kirsty Cousins, Administrative Director & Enrollment Coordinator

Guysborough: Chedabucto Education Centre / Guysborough Academy
P.O. Box 19
27 Green St., Guysborough, NS B0H 1N0
Tel: 902-533-2288; *Fax:* 902-533-3554
cecga.srsb.ca
Other Information: Alternate Phone: 902-533-4006
Grades: K-12; *Enrollment:* 296
Paul Lang, Principal
paul.landry@srsb.ca

Halifax: Armbrae Academy
1400 Oxford St., Halifax, NS B3H 3Y8, Canada
Tel: 902-423-7920; *Fax:* 902-423-9731
office@armbrae.ns.ca
www.armbrae.ns.ca
Grades: Pre.-12; *Number of Employees:* 34 teachers; 4 support staff
Gary O'Meara, Headmaster
head@armbrae.ns.ca

Halifax: Halifax Grammar School
945 Tower Rd., Halifax, NS B3H 2Y2, Canada
Tel: 902-423-9312; *Fax:* 902-423-9315
reception@hgs.ns.ca
www.hgs.ns.ca
www.facebook.com/halifaxgrammarschool
twitter.com/halifaxgrammar
www.linkedin.com/company/halifax-grammar-school
www.youtube.com/halifaxgrammar
Grades: Pre.-12; *Enrollment:* 520
Blayne Addley, Headmaster
headmaster@hgs.ns.ca

Halifax: Maritime Muslim Academy
6225 Chebucto Rd., Halifax, NS B3L 1K7, Canada
Tel: 902-429-9067; *Fax:* 902-429-0136
www.maritimemuslimacademy.ca/
Grades: Pre.-12; Islamic studies; Arabic; *Enrollment:* 78
Dr. Hadi Salah, Principal

Halifax: Sacred Heart School of Halifax
5820 Spring Garden Rd., Halifax, NS B3H 1X8, Canada
Tel: 902-422-4459; *Fax:* 902-423-7691
admin@shsh.ca
www.sacredheartschool.ns.ca
www.facebook.com/SacredHeartHalifax
twitter.com/SacredHeartHfx
www.youtube.com/channel/UCXgY2VIKCHog2VCGCKxf7gg
Grades: Pre.-12
Anne Wachter, Headmistress
awachter@shsh.ca

Halifax: Shambhala School
5450 Russell St., Halifax, NS B3K 1W9, Canada
Tel: 902-454-6100; *Fax:* 902-454-6157
director@shambhalaschool.org
www.shambhalaschool.org
Grades: Preschool - 12; *Enrollment:* 160; *Note:* This is a non-denominational school, which offers an enriched curriculum.
Steve Mustain, Director

Lower Sackville: Newbridge Academy
409 Glendale Dr., Lower Sackville, NS B4C 2T6
Tel: 902-252-3339; *Fax:* 902-252-3108
info@newbridgeacademy.ca
www.newbridgeacademy.ca
Grades: Pre.-12; *Enrollment:* 140
Travor MacEachern, CEO/Chair
Jason Wolfe, Headmaster
jason.wolfe@newbridgeacademy.ca

Lunenburg: Class Afloat - West Island College International
P.O. Box 10
97 Kaulbach St., Lunenburg, NS B0J 2C0
Tel: 902-634-1895; *Fax:* 902-634-7155
info@classafloat.com
www.classafloat.com
www.facebook.com/classafloat
twitter.com/classafloat
Grades: 10-Univ.; *Enrollment:* 60; *Note:* Students at Class Afloat sail the world on a classic tall ship, which they themselves sail, while engaged in academic study. Courses are available at the following levels of study: grade 11, 12, & first-year university.
David Jones, President

Tantallon: Crossroads Academy
15 French Village Station Rd., Tantallon, NS B3Z 1H3, Canada
Tel: 902-826-1805
ca@crossroadsacademy.ca
www.crossroadsacademy.ca
Grades: Pre.-6
Sylvia Luffman, Principal

Windsor: King's-Edgehill School
33 King's-Edgehill Lane, Windsor, NS B0N 2T0, Canada
Tel: 902-798-2278; *Fax:* 902-798-2105
admissions@kes.ns.ca
www.kes.ns.ca
www.facebook.com/kingsedgehill
twitter.com/kingsedgehill
www.youtube.com/kingsedgehill
Grades: 1-12; *Enrollment:* 282
David R. Penaluna, Headmaster

Wolfville: Landmark East School
708 Main St., Wolfville, NS B4P 1G4
Tel: 902-542-2237; *Fax:* 902-542-4147
Toll-Free: 800-565-5887
admissions@landmarkeast.org
www.landmarkeast.org
twitter.com/landmarkeast
www.youtube.com/lmeschoolcanada
Grades: 3-12; *Enrollment:* 60; *Note:* The international school serves students with learning disabilities. Landmark East has an overall student-teacher ratio of 3:1.
Jim Sotvedt, Chair
Peter Coll, Headmaster
pcoll@landmarkeast.org
Glen Currie, Director, Students
gcurrie@landmarkeast.org

Universities & Colleges

Universities

Antigonish: St. Francis Xavier University
The Admissions Office
P.O. Box 5000
5005 Chapel Sq., Antigonish, NS B2G 2W5, Canada
Tel: 902-867-2219; *Fax:* 902-867-2329
admit@stfx.ca
www.stfx.ca
Other Information: Admissions: 902-867-2219
www.facebook.com/stfxuniversity
twitter.com/stfxuniversity
www.linkedin.com/company/st.-francis-xavier-university
www.youtube.com/user/stfxbox
Full Time Equivalency: 4200; *Note:* The university is primarily an undergraduate university, offering education in the arts, science, business & information systems, & applied programs.
Kent MacDonald, President, 902-867-2188
kdmacdon@stfx.ca
Dr. Kevin Wamsley, Vice-President, Academic & Provost
avp@stfx.ca
Murray Kyte, Vice-President, Advancement
Andrew Beckett, Vice-President, Finance & Administration
Fred Rosmanitz, Registrar, 902-867-2213
registr@stfx.ca
John Blackwell, Director, Research Grants, 902-867-3733
jblackwe@stfx.ca
Kris MacSween, Manager, Access Services, 902-867-4917
kmacswee@stfx.ca

Faculties

Faculty of Arts
www.stfx.ca/faculties/arts/
Dr. Steve Baldner, Dean

Faculty of Science
www.stfx.ca/faculties/science/
Dr. Petra Hauf, Dean

Schools

Coady International Institute
51 West St., Antigonish, NS B2G 2W5
Tel: 902-867-3960
coadyreg@stfx.ca
coady.stfx.ca
www.facebook.com/coady.institute
twitter.com/coadystfx
www.youtube.com/CoadyInstitute
Dr. Phil Davidson, Director

Halifax: Atlantic School of Theology
660 Francklyn St., Halifax, NS B3H 3B5, Canada
Tel: 902-423-6939; *Fax:* 902-492-4048
www.astheology.ns.ca
www.facebook.com/159377874139812
twitter.com/ASTComm
www.youtube.com/user/astheology
Full Time Equivalency: 150
The Rev. Canon Eric Beresford, President, 902-423-6801
eberesford@astheology.ns.ca
Rev. Dr. Jody clark, Academic Dean, 902-425-5315
jclarke@astheology.ns.ca
David Myatt, Chief Admin. Officer, 902-496-7946
dmyatt@astheology.ns.ca

Halifax: Dalhousie University
P.O. Box 15000
Halifax, NS B3H 4R2
Tel: 902-494-2211; *Fax:* 902-494-1630
communications.marketing@dal.ca
www.dal.ca
www.facebook.com/DalhousieUniversity
twitter.com/Dalnews
www.youtube.com/user/DalhousieU

Full Time Equivalency: 18650; *Note:* Dalhousie University is a comprehensive teaching & research university located in Atlantic Canada. Dalhousie places special emphasis on Ocean Studies & Health Studies & has a growing involvement in Advanced Technical Studies.
Dr Fred Fountain, Chancellor
Richard Florizone, Vice-Chancellor & President, 902-494-2511
richard.florizone@dal.ca
Dr Carolyn Watters, Vice-President, Academic & Provost, 902-494-2586
carolyn.watters@dal.ca
Ian Nason, Acting Vice-President, Finance & Admin., 902-494-3862
Ian.Nason@dal.ca
Floyd Dykeman, Vice-President, External, 902-494-7562
floyd.dykeman@dal.ca
Dr Anne Forrestall, Interim Senior Leader for Student Services, 902-494-8021
anne.forrestall@dal.ca
Dr Martha Crago, Vice-Pres., Research, 902-494-6513
martha.crago@dal.ca

Faculties

Faculty of Agriculture
P.O. Box 550
Truro, NS B2N 5E3
Tel: 902-893-6600
www.facebook.com/dalagriculture
Dr. David Gray, Dean, Faculty of Agriculture, 902-893-6720
dean.agriculture@dal.ca

Faculty of Architecture & Planning
P.O. Box 15000
5410 Spring Garden Rd., Halifax, NS B3H 4R2
Tel: 902-494-3971; *Fax:* 902-423-6672
arch.office@dal.ca
archplan.dal.ca
Christine Macy, Dean, 902-494-3210
christine.macy@dal.ca

Faculty of Arts & Social Sciences
Tel: 902-494-1440; *Fax:* 902-494-1957
fass@dal.ca
Dr Robert Summerby-Murray, Dean, 902-494-1439
fassdean@dal.ca

Faculty of Computer Science
Tel: 902-494-2093; *Fax:* 902-492-1517
inquiries@cs.dal.ca
www.facebook.com/dalfcs
Dr Michael Shephard, Dean, 902-494-1199
shepherd@cs.dal.ca

Faculty of Dentistry
P.O. Box 15000
5981 University Ave., Halifax, NS B3H 4R2
Tel: 902-494-2824; *Fax:* 902-494-2527
admissions.dentistry@dal.ca
www.facebook.com/daldentistry
Dr Thomas Boran, Dean, 902-494-2274
thomas.boran@dal.ca

Faculty of Engineering
#108, 5269 Morris St., Halifax, NS B3H 4R2
Tel: 902-494-2963; *Fax:* 902-492-0011
www.facebook.com/DalhousieEngineering
Dr J. Leon, Dean, 902-494-6217
joshua.leon@dal.ca

Faculty of Graduate Studies
Tel: 902-494-2485; *Fax:* 902-494-8797
graduate.studies@dal.ca
facebook.com/pages/Dalhousie-Grad-Studies-Team/1176506382 65857
twitter.com/dalgradstudies
Bernard P. Boudreau, Dean, Faculty of Graduate Studies, 902-494-6723
grad.dean@dal.ca

Faculty of Health Professions
Tel: 902-494-3327; *Fax:* 902-494-1966
Dr William G. Webster, Dean, 902-494-3856
will.webster@dal.ca

Faculty of Management
Tel: 902-494-2582; *Fax:* 902-494-1195
Peggy Cunningham, Dean, 902-494-7487
managementdean@dal.ca

Faculty of Medicine
Tel: 902-494-6592; *Fax:* 902-494-7119
Dr Thomas J. Marrie, Dean
dean.medicine@dal.ca

Faculty of Science
Tel: 902-494-3540; *Fax:* 902-494-1123
science@dal.ca
Chris Moore, Dean, 902-494-3540
chris.moore@dal.ca

Rowe School of Business
Kenneth C. Rowe Management Building
P.O. Box 15000
6100 University Ave., Halifax, NS B3H 4R2
Tel: 902-494-7080; *Fax:* 902-494-1107
Dr Greg Hebb, Director, 902-494-1802
gregory.hebb@dal.ca

College of Continuing Education
Tel: 902-494-2526; *Fax:* 902-494-3662
Toll-Free: 800-565-8867
ducceinf@dal.ca
Andrew Cochrane, Dean

College of Pharmacy
Tel: 902-494-2378; *Fax:* 902-494-1396
pharmacy@dal.ca
Rita Caldwell, Director, 902-494-2457
rita.caldwell@dal.ca

School of Health & Human Performance
Tel: 902-494-2152; *Fax:* 902-494-5120
hahp@dal.ca
Dr Fred McGinn, Interim Director

School of Health Administration
#700, 5161 George St., Halifax, NS B3H 4R2
Tel: 902-494-7097; *Fax:* 902-494-6849
healthadmin@dal.ca
Dr Joseph M. Byrne, Director

School of Human Communication Disorders
P.O. Box 15000
1256 Barrington St., Halifax, NS B3H 4R2
Tel: 902-494-7052; *Fax:* 902-494-5151
hucd@dal.ca
Joy Armson, Director, 902-494-5154
joy.armson@dal.ca

School of Information Management
Tel: 902-494-3656; *Fax:* 902-494-2451
sim@dal.ca
www.facebook.com/117354161707599
twitter.com/dalsimnews
www.linkedin.com/groups?gid=2360751&trk=hb_side_g
Louise Spiteri, Director, 902-494-2473
louise.spiteri@dal.ca

School of Nursing
Tel: 902-494-2535; *Fax:* 902-494-3487
son@dal.ca
Dr. Patricia Sullivan, Director

School of Occupational Therapy
Tel: 902-494-8804; *Fax:* 902-494-1229
occupational.therapy@dal.ca
www.facebook.com/160203867325613
Dr Fazley Siddiq, Director

School of Physiotherapy
Tel: 902-494-2524; *Fax:* 902-494-1941
physiotherapy@dal.ca
Dr Sandy Rennie, Director

School of Public Administration
Tel: 902-494-3742; *Fax:* 902-494-7023
dalmpa@dal.ca

School for Resource & Environmental Studies
Tel: 902-494-3632; *Fax:* 902-494-3728
sres@dal.ca
Dr. Peter Duinker, Director, 902-494-6517
peter.tyedmers@dal.ca

Schulich School of Law
Tel: 902-494-3495; *Fax:* 902-494-1316
lawinfo@dal.ca
www.facebook.com/SchulichSchoolofLaw
twitter.com/SchulichLaw
instagram.com/schulichlaw/
Kim R. Brooks, Dean, 902-494-2114
lawdean@dal.ca
Donna Beaver, Director of Finance & Administration, 902-494-2115
donna.beaver@dal.ca

School of Social Work
P.O. Box 15000
#3201, 1459 LeMarchant St., Halifax, NS B3H 4R2
Tel: 902-494-3760; *Fax:* 902-494-6709
social.work@dal.ca
Brenda Richard, Interim Director, 902-494-1356
brenda.richard@dal.ca

Centres/Institutes

Atlantic Health Promotion Research Centre (AHPRC)
City Centre Atlantic
#209, 1535 Dresden Row, Halifax, NS B3J 3T1
Tel: 902-494-2240; *Fax:* 902-494-3594
ahprc@dal.ca
www.ahprc.dal.ca
Sally Walker, Acting Managing Director, 902-494-2880
sally.walker@dal.ca
Lois Jackson, Scientific Director, 902-494-6316
lois.jackson@dal.ca

Centre for Foreign Policy Studies
6299 South St., Halifax, NS B3H 4R2
Tel: 902-494-3769; *Fax:* 902-494-3825
centre@dal.ca
Dr. David R. Black, Director, 902-494-6638
david.black@dal.ca

Neuroscience Institute
Tel: 902-494-1251; *Fax:* 902-494-2050
neurosci@dal.ca
neuroscience.dal.ca
Dr Alan Fine, Director, 902-494-1251
A.Fine@Dal.Ca

Halifax: NSCAD University (NSCAD)

Also known as: Nova Scotia College of Art & Design
5163 Duke St., Halifax, NS B3J 3J6, Canada
Tel: 902-444-9600; *Fax:* 902-425-2420
admiss@nscad.ca
www.nscad.ca
www.facebook.com/pages/NSCAD-University/115630861812958
twitter.com/NSCADUniversity
www.youtube.com/user/NSCADAdmissions
Full Time Equivalency: 1025
Dianne Taylor-Gearing, President
Kenn Gardner Honeychurch, Sr. Vice-President
Peter Flemming, Vice-President
Dr. Laurelle LeVert, Registrar & Director
Deborah Carver, Executive Director

Halifax: Saint Mary's University

923 Robie St., Halifax, NS B3H 3C3, Canada
Tel: 902-420-5400
helpdesk@smu.ca
www.smu.ca
Other Information: Students Closure/Cancellation Hotline: 902-491-6263
www.facebook.com/smuhalifax
twitter.com/SMUHalifaxNews
www.linkedin.com/company/saint-mary%27s-university
Full Time Equivalency: 8500; *Note:* Offers a wide range of both undergraduate & graduate programs.
Dr. Paul D. Sobey, Chancellor
Dr. Robert Summerby-Murray, President
Gabrielle Morrison, Vice-President, Finance & Administration
Dr. Esther E. Enns, Vice-President, Academic & Research, 902-496-8191
vpacademic@smu.ca

Faculties

Faculty of Arts
Tel: 902-420-5437; *Fax:* 902-491-5634
smarts@smu.ca
www.smu.ca/academics/faculty-of-arts.html
Dr. Margaret MacDonald, Dean of Arts

David Sobey School of Business
ssbcs.ca/
Patricia Bradshaw, PhD, Dean

Continuing Education
883 Robie St., , NS B3H 3C3
Tel: 902-491-6288
conted@smu.ca
www.smu.ca/conted
www.facebook.com/500446875528
twitter.com/elearn2advance
Betty MacDonald, Director
betty.macdonald@smu.ca

Graduate Studies & Research
Tel: 902-420-5089; *Fax:* 902-496-8772
fgsr@smu.ca
Dr. J. Kevin Vessey, Dean, 902-496-8169
kevin.vessey@smu.ca

Faculty of Science
Tel: 902-491-6446
science@smu.ca
Kathy Singfield, PhD, Acting Dean of Science - Curriculum, 902-420-5494
dean.science@smu.ca

Centres/Institutes
Centre for Environmental Analysis & Remediation (CEAR)
Science Building
#501, 923 Robie St., Halifax, NS B3H 3C3
Tel: 902-496-8798; *Fax:* 902-496-8104
cear@smu.ca
www.smu.ca/centres-and-institutes/cear
Patricia Granados, Research Instrument Technician, 902-420-5660
patricia.granados@smu.ca

Centre for Occupational Health & Safety
5960 Inglis St., Halifax, NS B3H 3C3
Tel: 902-491-6253; *Fax:* 902-496-8135
cncohs@smu.ca
www.smu.ca/centres-and-institutes/cncohs

Electron Microscopy Centre
Science Building
#422, 923 Robie St., Halifax, NS B3H 3C3
Tel: 902-420-5709; *Fax:* 902-496-8104
www.smu.ca/research/emc
Xiang Yang, Instrument Technician
xiang.yang@smu.ca

Institute for Computational Astrophysics
Department of Astronomy & Physics
Halifax, NS B3H 3C3
Tel: 902-420-5105; *Fax:* 902-496-8218
icaadmin@ap.smu.ca
www.smu.ca/centres-and-institutes/ica
Florence Woolaver, Contact

Maritime Provinces Spatial Analysis Research Centre (MP_SpARC)
Burke Building
#207B, 923 Robie St., Halifax, NS B3H 3C3
Tel: 902-420-5737
husky1.smu.ca/~dvanproo/Research_MP_SpARC
Greg Baker, Research Instrument Technician, 902-420-5472
mpsparc@smu.ca

Regional Analytical Facility
422 Science Building
923 Robie St., Halifax, NS B3H 3C3
Tel: 905-420-5709; *Fax:* 902-420-5261
www.smu.ca/research/rgc
Xiang Yang, Technician
xiang.yang@smu.ca

Halifax: University of King's College
6350 Coburg Rd., Halifax, NS B3H 2A1, Canada
Tel: 902-422-1271; *Fax:* 902-423-3357
registrar@ukings.ca
www.ukings.ca
www.facebook.com/300102340040911
twitter.com/ukings
www.youtube.com/kingscollegehfx
Full Time Equivalency: 1170
Hon. Kevin Lynch, Chancellor
William Lahey, President
Elizabeth Yeo, Registrar, 902-422-1271, ext. 122
elizabeth.yeo@ukings.ca

Pointe-de-L'Église: Université Sainte-Anne
1695, Rte 1, Pointe-de-L'Église, NS B0W 1M0
Tél: 902-769-2114; *Téléc:* 902-769-2930
Ligne sans frais: 888-338-8337
www.usainteanne.ca
facebook.com/usainteanne
twitter.com/usainteanne
www.youtube.com/user/usainteannecom/videos
Full Time Equivalency: 500; *Note:* La seule institution d'enseignement post-secondaire de langue française en Nouvelle-Écosse. Programmes: administration des affaires, éducation, sciences humaines, science pures, programmes professionnels. Campus: Pointe-de-L'Église, Halifax, Petit-de-Grat, Saint-Joseph-du Moine, et Tusket
Kenneth Deveau, Vice-recteur à l'enseignement et recherche
Allister Surette, Recteur et vice-chancelier
Éric Tufts, Vice-recteur (Administrations)
Hughie Batherson, Vice-recteur (Affaires étudiantes)

Campuses
Campus de Halifax
1589, rue Walnut, Halifax, NS B3H 3S1, Canada
Tel: 902-424-2630; *Fax:* 902-424-3607
Daniel Lamy, Directeur
Daniel.Lamy@usainteanne.ca

Campus de Petit-de-Grat
3433, rte 206, Petit-de-Grat, NS B0E 2L0, Canada
Tel: 902-226-3900; *Fax:* 902-226-3919
Philippe Haché, Directeur
philippe.hache@usainteanne.ca

Campus de Saint-Joseph-du-Moine
12521, Cabot Trail, St-Joseph-du-Moine, NS B0E 3A0, Canada
Tel: 902-244-4100; *Fax:* 902-224-4119
René Aucoin, Directeur
Rene.Aucoin@usainteanne.ca

Campus de Tusket
1 Slocumb Cres., Tusket, NS B0W 3M0, Canada
Tel: 902-648-3524; *Fax:* 902-648-3525
Marie-Germaine Chartrand, Directrice
mariegermaine.chartrand@usainteanne.ca

Sydney: Cape Breton University
P.O. Box 5300
1250 Grand Lake Rd., Sydney, NS B1P 6L2, Canada
Tel: 902-539-5300; *Fax:* 902-562-0119
Toll-Free: 888-959-9995
registrar@cbu.ca
www.cbu.ca
www.facebook.com/CapeBretonUniversity
twitter.com/cbuniversity
www.youtube.com/user/capebretonu
Full Time Equivalency: 3110; *Note:* The university is also home to Unama'ki College which offers Mi'kmaw programs and services, such as teacher training, court worker certification, business, Mi'kmaw language, health careers, and natural resources. Email: mci@cbu.ca
Annette Verschuren, Chancellor
David Wheeler, President & Vice-Chancellor, 902-563-1120
david_wheeler@cbu.ca
Gordon MacInnis, Vice-President, Finance & Operations, 902-563-1128
gordon_macinnis@cbu.ca
Dale Keefe, Vice-President, Academic & Provost, 902-563-1980
dale_keefe@cbu.ca
Keith Brown, Vice-President, External, 902-563-1859
keith_brown@cbu.ca
Debbie Rudderham, Chief Information Officer, 902-563-1446
debbie_rudderham@cbu.ca
Alexis Manley, Registrar & Vice-President of Student Services, 902-563-1650
registrar@cbu.ca

Faculties
School of Arts & Social Sciences
Tel: 902-563-1368; *Fax:* 902-563-1371
admissions@cbu.ca
Dr Roderick Nicholls, Dean, 902-563-1354
rod_nicholls@cbu.ca

School of Science & Technology
Tel: 902-563-1368
Dr Allen Britten, Dean, 902-563-1262
allen_britten@cbu.ca

Schools
Shannon School of Business
Tel: 902-563-1110
John MacKinnon, Dean, 902-563-1221
john_mackinnon@cbu.ca

School of Professional Studies
Tel: 902-563-1368
Robert Baily, Interim Dean, 902-563-1304
brenda_leloup@cbu.ca

Wolfville: Acadia University
15 University Ave., Wolfville, NS B4P 2R6, Canada
Tel: 902-542-2201; *Fax:* 902-585-1072
Toll-Free: 877-585-1121
agi@acadiau.ca
www.acadiau.ca
www.facebook.com/acadiauniversity
twitter.com/acadiau
www.youtube.com/user/AcadiaWebmaster
Full Time Equivalency: 3538
Ray Ivany, Pres./Vice-Chancellor, 902-585-1218
president@acadiau.ca
Dr. Tom Herman, Vice-Pres., Academic, ext. 1357
Dr Akivah Starkman, Vice-Pres., Admin.
Rosemary Jotcham, Registrar
Scott Roberts, Exec. Dir., Communications & Public Affairs, 902-585-1705

Faculties
Faculty of Arts
Tel: 902-585-1485; *Fax:* 902-585-1070
arts.acadiau.ca
Robert Perrins, Dean of Arts, 902-585-1485, ext. 1782
robert.perrins@acadiau.ca

Faculty of Professional Studies
P.O. Box 144
Wolfville, NS B4P 2R6
Tel: 902-585-1597; *Fax:* 902-585-1086
professionalstudies.acadiau.ca
Dr Heather Hemming, Dean, Faculty of Professional Studies

Faculty of Pure & Applied Science
Tel: 902-585-1472; *Fax:* 902-585-1637
dean.science@acadiau.ca
science.acadiau.ca
Dr Peter Williams, Dean of Pure and Applied Science, 902-585-1472, ext. 1472
peter.williams@acadiau.ca

Schools
Acadia Divinity College
38 Highland Ave., Wolfville, NS B4P 2R6, Canada
Tel: 902-585-2210; *Fax:* 902-585-2233
Toll-Free: 866-875-8975
adcinfo@acadiau.ca
adc.acadiau.ca
www.facebook.com/acadiadivinitycollege
www.twitter.com/acadiadiv
www.youtube.com/user/AcadiaDivCollege
Full Time Equivalency: 160
Dr Harry G. Gardner, President/Dean, Theology, 902-585-2212
harry.gardner@acadiau.ca
Anna M. Robbins, Academic Dean & Director of Doctoral Studies, 902-585-2251
anna.robbins@acadiau.ca
Shawna Peverill, Registrar, 902-585-2216
shawna.peverill@acadiau.ca

Colleges

Halifax: Nova Scotia Community College (NSCC)
NSCC Admissions
P.O. Box 220
Halifax, NS B3J 2M4, Canada
Tel: 902-491-4911; *Fax:* 902-491-3514
Toll-Free: 1-866-679-6722
admissions@nscc.ca
www.nscc.ca
Other Information: Toll Free Fax: 1-866-329-6722
TTY: 1-866-288-7034
twitter.com/NSCCNews
Full Time Equivalency: 1400; *Note:* The college has the following institutes: The Aviation Institute, located in the Halifax Regional Municipality at Shearwater, the Centre of Geographic Sciences in Lawrencetown, & the Nautical Institute in Port Hawkesbury & the School of Fisheries at Pictou.
David P. Saxton, Chair
Don Bureaux, President, 902-491-4898
Lucy Kanary, Dean, Trades & Technology, 902-491-2176
Greg Russell, Dean, Business, 902-491-2177
Marlene MacLellan, Dean, Health & Human Services, 902-491-6764
Kenda MacFadyen, Manager, Leadership & Management Development
Jill Provoe, Acting Dean, Access & Flexible Learning, 902-491-2605
Ian MacLeod, Dean, Applied Arts & New Media, 902-491-3007
Kathleen Allen, Dean, Student Services, 902-491-7334
Gary Elliott, Dean, Academic QA & Program Development, 902-491-2807

Campuses
Akerley Campus
21 Woodlawn Rd., Dartmouth, NS B3W 2R7
Tel: 902-491-4900; *Fax:* 902-491-4903
akerley.info@nscc.ca
Other Information: Student Services: 902-491-4908
Enrollment: 4000
Rosalind Penfound, Principal

Annapolis Valley Campus & Centre of Geographic Sciences (AVCCOGS)
RR#1, Elliott Rd., Lawrencetown, NS B0S 1M0
Tel: 902-825-3491; *Fax:* 902-825-2285
avc.info@nscc.ca
Other Information: Student Services: 902-825-2930

Burridge Campus
372 Pleasant St., Yarmouth, NS B5A 2L2
Tel: 902-749-3501; *Fax:* 902-749-2402
burridge.info@nscc.ca
Other Information: Student Services: 902-742-0760
Mary Thompson, Principal, 902-742-0642

Cumberland Campus
P.O. Box 550
1 Main St., Springhill, NS B0M 1X0
Tel: 902-597-3737; *Fax:* 902-597-8548
cumberland.info@nscc.ca
Other Information: Student Services: 902-597-4101
Donald McCormack, Principal, 902-597-4403

Aviation Institute - Dartmouth Gate
#100, 375 Pleasant St., Dartmouth, NS B2Y 4N4
Tel: 902-491-1100; *Fax:* 902-491-4989
Shelley Carter-Rose, Principal

Amherst Learning Centre
147 Albion St. South, Amherst, NS B4H 2X2
Tel: 902-661-3180; *Fax:* 902-661-3170

Institute of Technology Campus
P.O. Box 2210
5685 Leeds St., Halifax, NS B3J 3C4
Tel: 902-491-6722; *Fax:* 902-491-4800
it.info@nscc.ca
Other Information: Student Services: 902-491-4744
Enrollment: 5200

Kingstec Campus
236 Belcher St., Kentville, NS B4N 0A6
Tel: 902-678-7341; *Fax:* 902-679-4381
kingstec.info@nscc.ca
Other Information: Student Services: 902-679-7361
Enrollment: 1750
Jason Clark, Principal, Valley Region, 902-679-7350

Lunenburg Campus
75 High St., Bridgewater, NS B4V 1V8
Tel: 902-543-4608; *Fax:* 902-543-0190
lunenburg.info@nscc.ca
Other Information: Student Services: 902-543-2295
Craig Collins, Principal, 902-543-0846

Marconi Campus
P.O. Box 1042
1240 Grand Lake Rd., Sydney, NS B1P 6J7
Tel: 902-563-2450; *Fax:* 902-563-3440
marconi.info@nscc.ca
Other Information: Student Services: 902-563-2464
Fred Tilley, Principal, 902-563-2344

Nautical Institute
226 Reeves St., Port Hawkesbury, NS B9A 2A2
Tel: 902-625-4228; *Fax:* 902-625-0193

NSCC Online Learning
P.O. Box 1153
5685 Leeds St., Halifax, NS B3J 2X1
Tel: 902-491-6774; *Fax:* 902-491-4835
Toll-Free: 1-877-491-6774
online.learning@nscc.ca

Pictou Campus
P.O. Box 820
39 Acadia Ave., Stellarton, NS B0K 1S0
Tel: 902-752-2002; *Fax:* 902-752-5446
pictou.info@nscc.ca
Other Information: Student Services: 902-755-7299
Enrollment: 1675
Dave Freckelton, Principal, 902-755-7209

School of Fisheries
P.O. Box 700
Pictou, NS B0K 1H0
Tel: 902-485-8031; *Fax:* 902-485-7065
nssf@nscc.ca

Shelburne Campus
P.O. Box 760
1575 Lake Rd., Shelburne, NS B0T 1W0
Tel: 902-875-8640; *Fax:* 905-875-3797
shelburne.info@nscc.ca
Other Information: Student Services: 902-875-8640
Note: The Nautical Institute is located on the Strait Area Campus.

Strait Area Campus
226 Reeves St., Port Hawkesbury, NS B9A 2A2
Tel: 902-625-2380; *Fax:* 902-625-0193
strait.info@nscc.ca
Other Information: Student Services: 902-625-4017
Note: The Nautical Institute is located on the Strait Area Campus.

Truro Campus
36 Arthur St., Truro, NS B2N 1X5
Tel: 902-893-5385; *Fax:* 902-893-5610
truro.info@nscc.ca
www.truro.nscc.ca
Other Information: Student Services: 902-893-5346
Enrollment: 1300
Lech Krzywonos, Principal, 902-893-5368

Waterfront Campus
80 Mawiomi Pl., Dartmouth, NS B2Y 0A5
Tel: 902-491-1100; *Fax:* 902-491-1795
waterfront.info@nscc.ca
Other Information: Student Services: 902-491-1794
Enrollment: 4300
Paul Little, Principal, 902-491-7367

Post Secondary/Technical

Distance Education

***North Sydney:* Mactech Distance Education**
P.O. Box 457
North Sydney, NS B2A 3M3, Canada
Fax: 902-794-1414
Toll-Free: 1-888-622-8324
administration@HomeEd.com
www.homeed.com
www.facebook.com/group.php?gid=39322797586
twitter.com/Mactech_HomeEd
www.youtube.com/user/MactechDistanceEd
Note: Distance education
Heather Sophocleous, Vice-President of Operations
hsophocleous@HomeEd.com

***Sydney:* Centre for Distance Education**
Heritage Professional Centre
222 George St., #C, Sydney, NS B1P 1J3
Fax: 866-559-0131
Toll-Free: 866-446-5898
info@cd-ed.com
www.cd-ed.com
www.facebook.com/group.php?gid=14399795124
twitter.com/cd_ed
www.flickr.com/groups/darttinstitute/pool/
Note: Online program offerings in technology, media design, healthcare, and business.

Post Secondary/Technical

***Amherst:* Amherst Changes School of Hair Design**
8 Croft St., Amherst, NS B4H 2Z4
Tel: 902-667-3810
changesschool@bellaliant.com
www.changesschool.ca
Enrollment: 14
Brenda J. Chapman, Director of Education

***Bedford:* C.L. Douglas - Centre for Computer Studies**
1142 Bedford Hwy., Bedford, NS B4A 1B8, Canada
Tel: 902-835-8880; *Fax:* 902-835-6751
info@cldouglas.com
www.cldouglas.com
Note: Computer software, network management training.
Paul Cudmore

***Dartmouth:* The Academy of Cosmetology**
363 Windmill Rd., Dartmouth, NS B3A 1J2
Tel: 902-469-7788
academy@ns.sympatico.ca
www.academyofcosmetology.com
www.facebook.com/pages/Academy-Of-Cosmetology/123283184396385

***Dartmouth:* Atlantic Petroleum Training College**
Woodside Ocean Industries Park
40 Mount Hope Ave., Dartmouth, NS B2Y 4K9
Tel: 902-442-0119; *Fax:* 902-442-5271
Toll-Free: 888-442-0116
aptc@sstl.com
www.aptcollege.com
Note: Private career college to train for careers in the land based drilling and well servicing industry.

***Dartmouth:* Maritime Business College**
#100, 45 Alderney Dr., Dartmouth, NS B2Y 2N6
Tel: 902-463-6700; *Fax:* 902-469-4433
Toll-Free: 800-550-6516
www.maritimebusinesscollege.ca
www.facebook.com/132729526796030
twitter.com/MBC1899

***Dartmouth:* Operatng Engineers Training Institute of Nova Scotia (OETINS)**
#721, 251 Brownlow Ave., Dartmouth, NS B3B 2A9
Tel: 902-865-8844; *Fax:* 902-864-0676
iuoel721@ns.aliantzinc.ca
www.oetins.ca

***Halifax:* Atlantic Flight Attendant Academy Limited**
2586 Beech St., Halifax, NS B3L 2Y1
Tel: 902-422-0339; *Fax:* 902-444-5681
Toll-Free: 877-329-2699
cynthiasullivan@eastlink.ca
www.flightattend.com
Note: Flight Attendant Diploma Program.

***Halifax:* Centre for Arts & Technology - Halifax Campus (CAT)**
1577 Barrington St., Halifax, NS B3J 1Z7
Tel: 902-429-1847; *Fax:* 902-423-5414
Toll-Free: 866-429-1847
halifax@digitalartschool.com
www.digitalartschool.com
www.facebook.com/CentreforArtsandTech
twitter.com/digiarts_ca

Campuses

Centre for Arts & Technology - Kelowna Campus (CAT)
#100, 1632 Dickson Ave., Kelowna, BC V1Y 7T2
Tel: 250-860-2787; *Fax:* 250-712-1083
Toll-Free: 866-860-2787
kelowna@digitalartschool.com
www.digitalartschool.com
www.facebook.com/CentreforArtsandTech
twitter.com/digiarts_ca

Centre for Arts & Technology - Fredericton Campus (CAT)
130 Carleton St., Fredericton, NB E3B 3T4
Tel: 506-460-1280; *Fax:* 506-460-1289
Toll-Free: 877-369-1888
fredericton@digitalartschool.com
www.digitalartschool.com
www.facebook.com/CentreforArtsandTech
twitter.com/digiarts_ca

***Halifax:* Concepts Career College**
3660 Commission St., Halifax, NS B3K 0A5
Tel: 902-492-2444
info@conceptscollege.ca
conceptscollege.ca
www.facebook.com/ConceptsCareerCollege
Note: Private college offering programs in Esthetics, Hairstyling, and Makeup Artistry.

***Halifax:* Eastern College - Halifax**
Bay West Centre
7067 Chebucto Rd., Halifax, NS B3L 4R5
Toll-Free: 877-297-0777
easterncollege.ca
www.facebook.com/EasternCollege
twitter.com/easterncollege

Campuses

Eastern College - St. John's
22 Pearl Place, St. John's, NL A1E 4P3
Toll-Free: 877-297-0777
easterncollege.ca
www.facebook.com/EasternCollege
twitter.com/easterncollege

Eastern College - Charlottetown
134 Kent St., 3rd Fl., Charlottletown, PE C1A 7N4
Toll-Free: 877-297-0777
easterncollege.ca
www.facebook.com/EasternCollege
twitter.com/easterncollege

Eastern College - Moncton
1070 St. George Blvd., Moncton, NB E1E 4K7
Toll-Free: 877-297-0777
easterncollege.ca
www.facebook.com/EasternCollege
twitter.com/easterncollege

Eastern College - Fredericton
850 Prospect St., Fredericton, NB E3B 9M5
Toll-Free: 877-297-0777
easterncollege.ca
www.facebook.com/EasternCollege
twitter.com/easterncollege

Eastern College - Saint John
212 McAllister Dr., Saint John, NB E2J 2S5
Toll-Free: 877-297-0777
easterncollege.ca
www.facebook.com/EasternCollege
twitter.com/easterncollege

***Halifax:* Eastern Esthetics Career College**
Bayers Lake Business Park
19 Crane Lake Dr., Halifax, NS B3S 1B5
Tel: 902-450-2160; *Fax:* 902-450-2165
Toll-Free: 888-859-3434
lcneast.com

***Halifax:* The Hair Design Centre School of Cosmetology**
278 Lacewood Dr., Halifax, NS B3M 3N8
Tel: 902-455-0535; *Fax:* 902-422-6420
www.hairdesigncentre.com

***Halifax:* Maritime Conservatory of Performing Arts**
6199 Chebucto Rd., Halifax, NS B3L 1K7, Canada
Tel: 902-423-6995; *Fax:* 902-423-6029
admin@maritimeconservatory.com
www.maritimeconservatory.com
Cheryl McCarthy, Dean, School of Music
cheryl.mcpa@gmail.com
Barbara Dearborn, Dean, School of Dance
bjdearborn@hotmail.com

***Halifax:* Nova Scotia College of Early Childhood Education (NSCECE)**
6208 Quinpool Rd., 2nd Fl., Halifax, NS B3L 1A3
Tel: 902-423-7114; *Fax:* 902-423-3346
Toll-Free: 877-323-3382
info@nscece.ca
www.nscece.ca
www.facebook.com/nscece
twitter.com/Nscece/
www.youtube.com/user/nscece/
Note: NSCECE offers a two-year Early Childhood Education (ECE) diploma program.
Jane Crawley, Executive Director, 902-423-7114, ext. 222
janecawley@nscece.ca

***Halifax:* Ravensberg College**
5426 Portland Place, Halifax, NS B3K 1A1
Tel: 902-482-4704; *Fax:* 902-404-4225
firststep@ravensbergcollege.ca
www.ravensbergcollege.ca
www.facebook.com/ravensbergcollege.ca
Note: Ravensberg College offers a two-year Law Enforcement Foundations Diploma.

***Halifax:* Success College**
800 Sackville Dr., Halifax, NS B4E 1R8, Canada
Toll-Free: 1-800-352-0094
successcollege.ca
www.facebook.com/pages/Success-College/191535104191456
www.twitter.com/Success_NS
www.linkedin.com/company/1169863
www.youtube.com/user/SuccessCollegeNS
Note: Work-related programs.
Hazel Matthews

***Hubbards:* Atlantic Home Building & Renovation Sector Council**
P.O. Box 337
Hubbards, NS B0J 1T0
Toll-Free: 1-800-565-2151
info@ahbrsc.com
www.ahbrsc.com
Note: The Atlantic Home Building & Renovation Sector Council has provided courses to over 7,000 builders, carpenters, renovators, designers, inspectors, labourers, & sub-trade workers.
Michael Montgomery, Executive Director, 902-240-1133

***New Glasgow:* Paisley College**
46 Summit Ave., New Glasgow, NS B2H 3L2
Tel: 902-695-3235
www.paisleycollege.ca
www.facebook.com/paisleycollege
Note: Programs in hair styling, esthetics, and nails.

***North Sydney:* Hair Masters**
26 Archibald Ave., North Sydney, NS B2A 2W3
Tel: 902-794-2460
hairmasters2002@yahoo.ca
www.hairmasters-esthetics.com
Note: Offers courses in Esthetics / Nail Technology, Hair Dressing, and Cosmotology.

***North Sydney:* Maritime Drilling Schools**
Energy Training Center
P.O. Box 1916
150 Peppett St., North Sydney, NS B2A 3S9
Tel: 902-794-1132; *Fax:* 902-794-5138
Toll-Free: 866-807-3960
lw.mds@ns.sympatico.ca
mdslimited.ca
Note: Preparation courses for careers in the Oil & Gas industry.

***Sackville:* Carpenter Millwright Trades College (CMTC)**
1000 Sackville Dr., Sackville, NS B4E 0C2
Tel: 902-252-3553; *Fax:* 902-252-3554
admissions@cmtctradescollege.ca
www.cmtctradescollege.ca
www.facebook.com/190041386237?sk=wall
Bev Young, College Administrator
byoung@cmtctradescollege.ca

***St. Ann's:* The Gaelic College/Colaisde Na Gàidhlig**
P.O. Box 80
51779 Cabot Trail, St. Ann's, NS B0C 1H0, Canada
Tel: 902-295-3411; *Fax:* 902-295-2912
info@gaeliccollege.edu
www.gaeliccollege.edu
www.facebook.com/GaelicCollege
twitter.com/GaelicCollege
youtube.com/user/gaeliccollege
Number of Schools: 1

***Sydney:* Cape Breton Business College**
315 Jamieson St., Sydney, NS B1N 3B1
Tel: 902-564-2222; *Fax:* 902-539-8606
www.cbbc.ns.ca
www.facebook.com/TheBusinessCollege
www.twitter.com/CBBCollege

***Sydney:* Island Career Academy**
721 Alexandra St., Sydney, NS B1S 2H4
Tel: 902-564-6112; *Fax:* 902-562-6175
admissions@islandcareeracademy.ca
www.islandcareeracademy.ns.ca
www.facebook.com/islandcareeracademy

***Sydney:* Maritime Environmental Training Institute (METI)**
301 Alexandra St., Sydney, NS B1S 2E8
Tel: 902-539-9766; *Fax:* 902-567-1029
Toll-Free: 877-800-6384
training@metiatlantic.com
www.metiatlantic.com
www.facebook.com/metiatlantic

***Sydney:* McKenzie College - Sydney Campus**
74 Townsend St., Sydney, NS B1P 5C8
Tel: 902-562-8549; *Fax:* 902-567-2003
registrar@mckenziecollege.com
www.mckenziecollege.com
www.facebook.com/mckenziecollege
Note: McKenzie College offers Business, Arts and Technology and Driving and Transportation programs.

***Sydney:* New Dawn College**
P.O. Box 1055
106 Townsend St., Sydney, NS B1P 6J7
Tel: 902-270-3659; *Fax:* 902-270-3603
newdawncollege.ca
Note: New Dawn College is a registered Private Career College offering programs in Hospitality & Tourism, Esthetics and Management.
Boxer George, Director
boxer@newdawncollege.ca

***Truro:* Commercial Safety College (CSC)**
P.O. Box 848
Truro, NS B2N 5G6
Tel: 902-662-2190; *Fax:* 902-662-2657
csc@safetycollege.ca
safetycollege.ca
www.facebook.com/CommercialSafetyCollege
www.twitter.com/safety_college
Note: Private career college.

Campuses

Commercial Safety College - Masstown Campus (CSC)
11490 Hwy #2, Masstown, NS B0M 1G0
Tel: 902-662-2190; *Fax:* 902-662-2657
csc@safetycollege.ca
safetycollege.ca
Note: Private career college.

Commercial Safety College - Waverley Campus (CSC)
48 Powder Mill Rd., Waverley, NS B2R 1E9
Tel: 902-662-2190; *Fax:* 902-662-2657
csc@safetycollege.ca
safetycollege.ca
Note: Private career college.

***Truro:* Institute for Human Services Education (IHSE)**
#1, 60 Lorne St., 2nd Fl., Truro, NS B2N 3K3, Canada
Tel: 902-893-3342; *Fax:* 902-895-4487
admin@inst-hse.ca
www.inst-hse.ca
www.facebook.com/183944004972097
Note: Early Childhood Education Diploma, Public School Program Assistants Certificate, Special Education Diploma, Youth Worker Diploma
Kimberly Elliott, B.Comm., Executive Director
Anna MacDonell, CDSA IV, B.A., M.Ed., Program Director
Debbie Connolly, CDSA IV, BBA, Student Services Coordinator

***Truro:* Victoria Court Career College**
P.O. Box 161
14 Court St., Truro, NS B2N 3H7
info@victoriacourtcareercollege.ca
www.victoriacourtcareercollege.ca

***Waverley:* Nova Scotia Firefighters School (NSFS)**
48 Powder Mill Rd., Waverley, NS B2R 1E9
Tel: 902-861-3823; *Fax:* 902-860-0255
www.nsfs.ns.ca
www.facebook.com/home.php?sk=group_2603990340
www.youtube.com/user/nsfireschool

***Wentzells Lake:* Dogs Of Pride Grooming School**
487 Sarty Rd., Wentzells Lake, NS B4V 4J6
Tel: 902-298-0999; *Toll-Free:* 888-644-4364
info@dogsofpride.com
www.dogsofpride.com
www.facebook.com/243410538801
twitter.com/Dogs_of_Pride
pinterest.com/dogirl/

***Wolfville:* Acadia Centre for Social & Business Entrepreneurship**
Acadia University
P.O. Box 142
Wolfville, NS B4P 2R6
Tel: 902-585-1180; *Fax:* 902-585-1057
acsbe@acadiau.ca
www.acsbe.com
www.facebook.com/acsbe

Nunavut

Government Agencies

***Iqaluit:* Nunavut Department of Education**
Building 1107, 2nd Fl.
P.O. Box 1000 900
Iqaluit, NU X0A 0H0, Canada
Tel: 867-975-5600; *Fax:* 867-975-5605
info.edu@gov.nu.ca
www.edu.gov.nu.ca
Hon. Paul Aarulaaq Quassa, Minister of Education

School Boards/Districts/Divisions

Public

***Baker Lake:* Kivalliq School Operations**
P.O. Box 90
Baker Lake, NU X0C 0A0, Canada
Tel: 867-793-2803; *Fax:* 867-793-2996
kivalliq.edu.nu.ca
Number of Schools: 12

***Iqaluit:* Iqaluit District Education Authority**
P.O. Box 235
Iqaluit, NU X0A 0H0, Canada
Tel: 867-979-5314; *Fax:* 867-979-0330
IDEA_Office@qikiqtani.edu.nu.ca
iqaluitdistricteducationauthority.com
Sabrina Sherman, Administrator

***Kugluktuk:* Kitikmeot School Operations**
P.O. Box 287
Kugluktuk, NU X0B 0E0, Canada
Tel: 867-982-7422; *Fax:* 867-982-3054
kitikmeot.edu.nu.ca
Number of Schools: 8

***Pond Inlet:* Qikiqtani School Operations**
P.O. Box 429
Pond Inlet, NU X0A 0S0, Canada
Tel: 867-899-7350; *Fax:* 867-899-7334
qikiqtani.edu.nu.ca
Trudy Pettigrew, Executive Director

French

Iqaluit: La Commission scolaire francophone du Nunavut
P.O. Box 6030
Iqaluit, NU X0A 0H0, Canada
Tél: 867-979-5849; *Téléc:* 867-979-5878
3soleilssecretaire@qikiqtani.edu.nu.ca
www.trois-soleils.ca
Number of Schools: 1
Serge Gagnon, Directeur

Post Secondary/Technical

Arviat: Nunavut Arctic College
Head Office
P.O. Box 230
Arviat, NU X0C 0E0, Canada
Tel: 867-857-8608; *Fax:* 867-857-8623
Toll-Free: 866-988-4636
www.arcticcollege.ca
www.facebook.com/NunavutArcticCollege
twitter.com/NunavutCollege
Hon. Paul Quassa, Minister Responsible for Nunavut Arctic College
Joe Adla Kunuk, President
jkunuk@gov.nu.ca
Linda Pemik, Director, Academic Affairs, 867-857-8603
linda.pemik@arcticcollege.ca
Penny Dominix-Nadeau, Registrar, 866-979-7222
penny.dominix-nadeau@arcticcollege.ca

Campuses
Kitikmeot Campus - Cambridge Bay
P.O. Box 54
Cambridge Bay, NU X0B 0C0, Canada
Tel: 867-983-4111; *Fax:* 867-983-4106
Toll-Free: 866-383-4533
KitikmeotCampus@gov.nu.ca
Fiona Buchan-Corey, Director

Kivalliq Campus - Rankin Inlet
P.O. Box 002
Rankin Inlet, NU X0C 0G0, Canada
Tel: 867-645-5500; *Fax:* 867-645-2387
Toll-Free: 866-979-7222
kivalliq@arcticcollege.ca
Mike Shouldice, Director, 866-988-4636

Nunatta Campus - Iqaluit
P.O. Box 600
Iqaluit, NU X0A 0H0, Canada
Tel: 867-979-7222; *Fax:* 867-979-7102
Toll-Free: 866-979-7222
nunatta@arcticcollege.ca
Peesee Pitsiulak-Stephens, Director, 867-979-7216

Centres/Institutes
Nunavut Trades Training Centre
Rankin Inlet, NU
Tel: 867-645-4871; *Toll-Free:* 866-979-7222
kivalliq@arcticcollege.ca

Nunavut Research Institute
P.O. Box 1720
Iqaluit, NU XOA OHO
Tel: 867-979-7280; *Fax:* 867-979-7109
www.nri.nu.ca

Ontario

Government Agencies

Toronto: Ontario Ministry of Advanced Education & Skills Development
Mowat Block
900 Bay St. 14th Fl., Toronto, ON M7A 1N2, Canada
Tel: 416-325-2929; *Fax:* 416-325-6348
information.met@ontario.ca
www.tcu.gov.on.ca
TTY: 1-800-263-289
Hon. Deb Matthews, Minister of Advanced Education & Skills Development, 416-326-9500
dmatthews.mpp@liberal.ola.org

Toronto: Ontario Ministry of Education
Mowat Block, 14th Fl.
900 Bay St., Toronto, ON M7A 1L2
Tel: 416-325-2929; *Fax:* 416-325-6348
Toll-Free: 800-387-5514
information.met@ontario.ca
www.edu.gov.on.ca
TTY: 800-325-3408
twitter.com/OntarioEDU
www.youtube.com/user/OntarioEDU
Number of Employees: 1700
Hon. Mitzie Hunter, Minister of Education, 416-325-2600
mhunter.mpp.co@liberal.ola.org

London
#207, 217 York St., London, ON N6A 5P9, Canada
Tel: 519-667-1440; *Fax:* 519-667-9769
Toll-Free: 800-265-4221

North Bay/Sudbury
#211, 447 McKeown Ave., North Bay, ON P1B 9S9, Canada
Tel: 705-474-7210; *Fax:* 705-497-6896
Toll-Free: 800-461-9570

Ottawa
#504, 1580 Merivale Rd., Nepean, ON K2G 4B5, Canada
Tel: 613-225-9210; *Fax:* 613-225-2881
Toll-Free: 800-267-1067

Thunder Bay
#336, 435 James St. South, Thunder Bay, ON P7E 6S9, Canada
Tel: 807-475-1571; *Fax:* 807-475-1550
Toll-Free: 800-465-5020

Toronto & Area
880 Bay St., 2nd Fl., Toronto, ON M7A 1N3, Canada
Tel: 416-325-6870; *Fax:* 416-325-4190
Toll-Free: 800-268-5755

School Boards/Districts/Divisions

Public

Aurora: York Region District School Board
The Education Centre
P.O. Box 40
60 Wellington St. West, Aurora, ON L4G 3H2, Canada
Tel: 905-727-3141; *Fax:* 905-727-1931
feedback@yrdsb.edu.on.ca
www.yrdsb.edu.on.ca
twitter.com/yrdsb
Number of Schools: 172 elementary; 31 secondary; *Grades:* K-12; *Enrollment:* 120285; *Number of Employees:* 11,769
J. Philip Parappally, Director of Education, 905-727-3141, ext. 2278
director@yrdsb.edu.on.ca
Anna DeBartolo, Board Chair, 416-898-9653
anna.debartolo@yrdsb.ca
Denese Belchetz, PhD, Associate Director of Education - Leadership & Learning
denese.belchetz@yrdsb.ca
Margaret Roberts, Associate Director of Education - Corporate & School Services
margaret.roberts@yrdsb.ca
Leslie Johnstone, Associate Director of Education - School & Staff Resources
leslie.johnstone@yrdsb.ca

Belleville: Hastings & Prince Edward District School Board (HPEDSB)
156 Ann St., Belleville, ON K8N 3L3, Canada
Tel: 613-966-1170; *Fax:* 613-961-2003
Toll-Free: 800-267-4350
information@hpedsb.on.ca
www.hpedsb.on.ca
twitter.com/hpedsbschools
Number of Schools: 39 elementary; 8 secondary; *Grades:* JK-12; *Enrollment:* 15300; *Number of Employees:* 1700 teaching and support staff
Mandy Savery-Whiteway, Director of Education, 613-966-1170, ext. 2201
directors.office@hpedsb.on.ca
Dwayne Inch, Chair of the Board, 613-476-5174
dinch@hpedsb.on.ca
Colleen DeMille, Superintendent of Education, Special Education Services, 800-267-4350, ext. 2312
cdemille@hpedsb.on.ca
Trish FitzGibbon, Superintendent of Education, Human Resources Support Services, 800-267-4350, ext. 2203
tfitzgibbon@hpedsb.onca
Cathy Portt, Superintendent of Education, Curriculum Services, 800-267-4350, ext. 2210
cportt@hpedsb.on.ca
Mark Fisher, Superintendent of Education, School Climate & Well-being, 800-267-4350, ext. 2535
mfisher@hpedsb.on.ca
Leslie Miller, Superintendent of Business Services & Treasurer of the Board, 800-267-4350, ext. 2280
lmiller@hpedsb.on.ca
Andrea Pickett, Manager of Accounting & Procurement, 800-267-4350, ext. 2218
purchasing.services@hpedsb.on.ca

Brantford: Grand Erie District School Board
Education Centre
349 Erie Ave., Brantford, ON N3T 5V3, Canada
Tel: 519-756-6301; *Fax:* 519-756-9181
Toll-Free: 1-888-548-8878
info@granderie.ca
www.granderie.ca
www.facebook.com/310696652315484
twitter.com/GEDSB
Number of Schools: 60 elementary; 16 secondary; *Grades:* JK - 12; Special Ed; Continuing Ed.; *Enrollment:* 28226; *Number of Employees:* 1,835 Instructional; 956 Non-instructional
David Dean, Chair, 519-582-4969
david.dean@granderie.ca
Scott Sincerbox, Superintendent of Education
Jamie Gunn, Business Services

Brockville: Upper Canada District School Board (UCDSB)
225 Central Ave. West, Brockville, ON K6V 5X1, Canada
Tel: 613-342-0371; *Toll-Free:* 1-800-267-7131
inquiries@ucdsb.on.ca
www.ucdsb.on.ca
www.facebook.com/UCDSB
twitter.com/UCDSB
www.youtube.com/uppercanadadsb
Number of Schools: 86; *Grades:* K-12; *Enrollment:* 18000; *Number of Employees:* 4,000; *Note:* Also offers alternative and continuing education programs.
David K. Thomas, Director, Education, 613-342-0371, ext. 1234
david.thomas@ucdsb.on.ca
Ian Carswell, Associate Director, 613-342-0371, ext. 1397
ian.carswell@ucdsb.on.ca
Valerie Allen, Superintendent, School Effectiveness, 613-933-5256, ext. 4279
valerie.allen@ucdsb.on.ca
Susan Edwards, Superintendent, Student Engagement, 877-485-1211
susan.edwards@ucdsb.on.ca
Nancy Barkley, Superintendent, Business, 613-342-0371, ext. 1207
nancy.barkley@ucdsb.on.ca
David Coombs, Superintendent, School Operations, 613-258-9393, ext. 2551
david.coombs@ucdsb.on.ca
Victoria Hemming, Superintendent, School Effectiveness (Special Education), 613-342-0371, ext. 1146
victoria.hemming@ucdsb.on.ca
Charlotte Patterson, Superintendent, Human Resources, 613-342-0371, ext. 1240
charlotte.patterson@ucdsb.on.ca
Jeremy Hobbs, Chief Information & Facilities Officer, 613-342-0371, ext. 1126
jeremy.hobbs@ucdsb.on.ca
Terry Davies, Acting Manager of Communications, 613-342-0371, ext. 1119
terry.davies@ucdsb.on.ca

Burlington: Halton District School Board
J.W. Singleton Education Centre
P.O. Box 5005 LCD 1
2050 Guelph Line, Burlington, ON L7R 3Z2, Canada
Tel: 905-335-3663; *Fax:* 905-335-9802
Toll-Free: 877-618-3456
director@hdsb.ca
www.hdsb.ca
Other Information: New Street Education Centre: 905-631-6120
twitter.com/HaltonDSB
Number of Schools: 84 elementary; 21 secondary & alternative; *Grades:* K-12; *Enrollment:* 60000
Kelly Amos, Chair, 905-339-2870
amosk@hdsb.ca
Stuart Miller, Director of Education, 905-335-3663, ext. 3296
millers@hdsb.ca
Debra McFadden, Executive Officer of Human Resources, 905-335-3663, ext. 3272
mcfaddend@hdsb.ca
Bruce Smith, Chief Information Officer, 905-335-9802, ext. 3434
smithbru@hdsb.ca
Jack Blackwell, Associate Director of Education, 905-335-3663, ext. 3352
blackwellj@hdsb.ca

Marnie Denton, Manager, Communication Services, 905-335-3663, ext. 2227
dentonm@hdsb.ca
Gail Gortmaker, Manager, Director's Office, 905-335-3663, ext. 3296
gortmakerg@hdsb.ca
Jason Misner, Communications Officer, 905-335-3663, ext. 3387
misnerj@hdsb.ca
Lucy Veerman, Superintendent of Business Services, 905-315-8930, ext. 2217
veermanl@hdsb.ca
Brenda Blain, Manager of Purchasing & Risk Management, 905-335-3663, ext. 3226
blainb@hdsb.ca

Chesley: Bluewater District School Board
P.O. Box 190
351 - 1st Ave. North, Chesley, ON N0G 1L0, Canada
Tel: 519-363-2014; *Fax:* 519-370-2909
Toll-Free: 1-800-661-7509
communications@bwdsb.on.ca
www.bwdsb.on.ca
Other Information: Purchasing & Transportation Dept.: 519-364-0605
twitter.com/BluewaterDSB
Number of Schools: 41 elementary; 11 secondary; *Grades:* Elementary - Secondary; Special Ed.; *Enrollment:* 17175; *Number of Employees:* 3,000 permanent and casual
Ron Motz, Chair
ron_motz@bwdsb.on.ca
Jan Johnstone, Vice-Chair
Steve Blake, Director of Education
Alana Murray, Superintendent of Education
Lori Wilder, Superintendent of Education
Jean Stephenson, Superintendent of Education
Cynthia Lemon, Executive Officer of Human Resources Services

Dryden: Keewatin-Patricia District School Board (KPDSB)
79 Casimir Ave., Dryden, ON P8N 2H4, Canada
Tel: 807-468-5571; *Fax:* 807-468-3857
Toll-Free: 877-275-7771
www.kpdsb.on.ca
Number of Schools: 17 elementary; 6 secondary; *Grades:* K-12; *Enrollment:* 5180; *Number of Employees:* 722 permanent staff; 617 non-permanent staff
Sean Monteith, Director of Education, 807-468-5571, ext. 236
sean.monteith@kpdsb.on.ca
David Penney, Board Chair, 807-934-2757
david.penney@kpdsb.on.ca
Dean Carrie, Superintendent of Business, 807-468-5571, ext. 237
dean.carrie@kpdsb.on.ca
Joan Kantola, Superintendent of Education, 807-468-5571, ext. 225
joan.kantola@kpdsb.on.ca
Caryl Hron, Superintendent of Education, 807-223-5311, ext. 264
caryl.hron@kpdsb.on.ca
Kim Carlson, Facilities Manager, 807-468-5571, ext. 260
kim.carlson@kpdsb.on.ca
Kathleen O'Flaherty, Finance Manager, 807-468-5571, ext. 230
kathleen.oflaherty@kpdsb.on.ca
Arlene Szestopalow, Purchasing & Payables Officer, 807-468-5571, ext. 253
arlene.szestopalow@kpdsb.on.ca
Jocelyn Bullock, Human Resources Manager, 807-468-5571, ext. 267
jocelyn.bullock@kpdsb.on.ca

Fort Frances: Rainy River District School Board
522 Second St. East, Fort Frances, ON P9A 1N4, Canada
Tel: 807-274-9855; *Fax:* 807-274-5078
Toll-Free: 800-214-1753
www.rrdsb.com
www.facebook.com/192226297577677
Number of Schools: 10 elementary; 3 secondary; 1 alternative; *Grades:* JK - 12
Heather Campbell, Director of Education
heather.campbell@mail.rrdsb.com
Dianne McCormack, Chair, 807-852-1695
dianne.mccormack@mail.rrdsb.com
Donna Braun Chief, Aboriginal Education Leader
Laura Mills, Superintendent of Business, 807-274-9855, ext. 4991
laura.mills@mail.rrdsb.com
Casey Slack, Superintendent of Education
robert.slack@mail.rrdsb.com
Allan McManaman, Superintendent of Education
allan.mcmanaman@mail.rrdsb.com
Ann Cox, Manager, Human Resources
ann.cox@mail.rrdsb.com
Travis Enge, Manager, Plant Operations & Maintenance
travis.enge@mail.rrdsb.com
Stephen Danielson, Manager of Information Technology Services
stephen.danielson@mail.rrdsb.com
Lloyd Lovelace, Purchasing Clerk

Guelph: Upper Grand District School Board (UGDSB)
Main Office
500 Victoria Rd. North, Guelph, ON N1E 6K2
Tel: 519-822-4420; *Fax:* 519-822-4487
Toll-Free: 800-321-4025
inquiry@ugdsb.on.ca
www.ugdsb.on.ca
twitter.com/ugdsb
Number of Schools: 60 elementary schools; 11 secondary schools; *Grades:* K-12; Continuing Ed.; *Enrollment:* 32000
Mark Bailey, Chairperson, 519-822-4420, ext. 735
mark.bailey@ugdsb.on.ca
Martha Rogers, Director of Education, 519-822-4420, ext. 721
sue.krueger@ugdsb.on.ca
Tracey Lindsay, Superintendent of Program, 519-822-4420, ext. 254
donna.glodziak@ugdsb.on.ca
Doug Morrell, Superintendent of Education, 519-822-4420, ext. 749
krystyna.gazo@ugdsb.on.ca
Bonnie Talbot, Superintendent of Education, 519-822-4420, ext. 746
june.pollard@ugdsb.on.ca
Linda Benallick, Superintendent of Education, 519-822-4420, ext. 745
janice.stokman@ugdsb.on.ca
Brent McDonald, Superintendent of Education, 519-822-4420, ext. 741
lynne.mcinnis@ugdsb.on.ca
Gary Slater, Superintendent of Education, 519-822-4420, ext. 850
karen.zorzi@ugdsb.on.ca
Janice Wright, Superintendent of Finance, 519-822-4420, ext. 791
heather.fisher@ugdsb.on.ca
Lidia Halyk, Purchasing Manager, 519-822-4420, ext. 804
lidia.halyk@ugdsb.on.ca

Hamilton: Hamilton-Wentworth District School Board
P.O. Box 2558
20 Education Ct., Hamilton, ON L8N 3L1, Canada
Tel: 905-527-5092; *Fax:* 905-521-2544
info@hwdsb.on.ca
www.hwdsb.on.ca
twitter.com/hwdsb
www.youtube.com/user/HWDSBtv
Number of Schools: 95 elementary; 18 secondary; *Grades:* K-12
John Malloy, Director, Education, 905-527-5092, ext. 2297
pat.stones@hwdsb.on.ca
Jessica Brennan, Chair, 905-512-4599
jessica.brennan@hwdsb.on.ca
Mag Gardner, Superintendent of Student Achievement, 905-527-5092, ext. 2502
Krys Croxall, Superintendent of Student Achievement, 905-527-5092, ext. 2626
Laura Romano, Superintendent of Student Achievement, 905-527-5092, ext. 2361
Michael Prendergast, Superintendent of Student Achievement, 905-527-5092, ext. 2622
Peter Joshua, Superintendent of Student Achievement, 905-527-5092, ext. 2673
Peter Sovran, Superintendent of Student Achievement, 905-527-5092, ext. 2323
Stacey Zucker, Superintendent of Business Services, 905-527-5092, ext. 2500
Pat Rocco, Superintendent of Human Resources, 905-527-5092, ext. 2271
Vicki Corcoran, Superintendent of Leadership and Learning, 905-527-5092, ext. 2625
Sharon Stephanian, Superintendent of Leadership and Learning, 905-527-5092, ext. 2386
Jane Miceli, Manager, Purchasing, 905-527-5092, ext. 2528
jane.miceli@hwdsb.on.ca

Kingston: Limestone District School Board (LDSB)
P.O. Box Bag 610
220 Portsmouth Ave., Kingston, ON K7L 4X4, Canada
Tel: 613-544-6920; *Fax:* 613-544-6804
Toll-Free: 800-267-0935
inq@limestone.on.ca
www.limestone.on.ca
Other Information: Automated: 613-544-6925
TTY: 613-548-0279
twitter.com/LimestoneDSB
www.youtube.com/LimestoneDSB
Number of Schools: 51 elementary schools; 11 secondary schools & community education centres; *Grades:* K-12; *Enrollment:* 21000
Debra Rantz, Director of Education, 613-544-6925, ext. 235
rantzd@limestone.on.ca
Paula Murray, Chair, 613-544-6925, ext. 365
murrayp@limestone.on.ca
Paul Babin, Superintendent of Business Services, 613-544-6925, ext. 338
babinp@limestone.on.ca
Barbara Fraser-Stiff, Superintendent of Education - Elementary, 613-544-6925, ext. 218
fraserstifb@limestone.on.ca
Norah Marsh, Superintendent of Education - Secondary, 613-544-6925, ext. 229
marshn@limestone.on.ca
Andre Labrie, Superintendent of Human Resources, 613-544-6925, ext. 230
Patrick Fisher, Financial Supervisor, Procurement & Payments, 613-544-6925, ext. 291
fisherpa@limestone.on.ca

Kitchener: Waterloo Region District School Board (WRDSB)
51 Ardelt Ave., Kitchener, ON N2C 2R5, Canada
Tel: 519-570-0003; *Fax:* 519-742-1364
info@wrdsb.on.ca
www.wrdsb.ca
Number of Schools: 120; *Grades:* K-12; *Enrollment:* 63000
John Bryant, Director of Education & Secretary of the Board, 519-570-0003, ext. 4223
Kathleen Woodcock, Chairperson, 519-504-8940
Kathleen_Woodcock@wrdsb.on.ca
Matthew Gerard, Superintendent, Business Services & Treasurer of the Board, 519-570-0003, ext. 4322
matthew_gerard@wrdsb.on.ca
Mark W. Carbone, Chief Information Officer, 519-570-0003, ext. 4402
mark_carbone@wrdsb.on.ca
Mark Schinkel, Senior Superintendent, Student Achievement & Well-Being, 519-570-0003, ext. 4253
mark_schinkel@wrdsb.on.ca
Lila Read, Senior Superintendent, Student Achievement & Well-Being, 519-570-0003, ext. 4456
lila_read@wrdsb.on.ca
Michael R. Weinert, Superintendent, Human Resource Services, 519-570-0003, ext. 4284
michael_weinert@wrdsb.on.ca

Lindsay: Trillium Lakelands District School Board (TLDSB)
P.O. Box 420
300 County Rd. 36, Lindsay, ON K9V 4S4, Canada
Tel: 705-324-6776; *Fax:* 705-328-2036
Toll-Free: 1-888-526-5552
info@tldsb.on.ca
tldsb.ca
Other Information: Muskoka Office, Phone: 705-645-8704
twitter.com/TLDSB
Number of Schools: 41 elementary; 7 secondary; 7 education centres; *Grades:* K-12; French Immersion; Adult Ed.
Larry Hope, Director of Education, 888-526-5552, ext. 22104
Bruce Barrett, Superintendent - Lindsay Education Centre, 888-526-5552, ext. 22115
Katherine MacIver, Superintendent - Lindsay Education Centre, 888-526-5552, ext. 21253
Dianna Scates, SUperintendent - Lindsay Education Centre, 888-526-5552, ext. 22101
Andrea Gillespie, Superintendent - Muskoka Education Centre, 888-526-5552, ext. 21254
Bob Kaye, Superintendent of Business, 888-526-5552, ext. 22139
Earl Manners, Human Resources Administrator, 888-526-5552, ext. 22105
Dick Kearns, Purchasing Supervisor, 888-526-5552, ext. 22198

***London:* Thames Valley District School Board**
P.O. Box 5888
1250 Dundas St. East, London, ON N6A 5L1, Canada
Tel: 519-452-2000; *Fax:* 519-452-2395
contact@tvdsb.on.ca
www.tvdsb.ca
www.facebook.com/TVDSB
twitter.com/TVDSB
Number of Schools: 133 elementary schools; 28 secondary schools; 31 alternative schools; *Grades:* K-12; Adult Ed.; Alternative Ed.; *Enrollment:* 71000; *Number of Employees:* 7,200 teachers, principals and support staff
Laura Elliot, Director of Education & Secretary
Christine Beal, Superintendent of Business
Barb Sonier, Superintendent of Student Achievement - Human Resources
Karen Edgar, Superintendent of Student Achievement - Learning Support
Lynne Griffith-Jones, Superintendent of Student Achievement - Human Resources
Marion Moynihan, Superintendent of Student Achievement - IT Services, 519-452-2000, ext. 20075
m.moynihan@tvdsb.on.ca
Karen Dalton, Executive Superintendent - Operations Services
Riley Culhane, Superintendent of Student Achievement - Curriculum K-12
Jeff Pratt, Associate Director
Kevin Bushell, Executive Officer - Facility Services & Capital Planning, 519-452-2000, ext. 21025
k.bushell@tvdsb.on.ca
Karen Wilkinson, Superintendent of Student Achievement - Student Success, 519-452-2000, ext. 20501
k.wilkinson@tvdsb.on.ca
Gary Keathley, Supervisor, Purchasing, 519-452-2000, ext. 20466
g.keathley@tvdsb.on.ca

***Marathon:* Superior-Greenstone District School Board**
P.O. Box Bag A
12 Hemlo Dr., Marathon, ON P0T 2E0, Canada
Tel: 807-229-0436; *Fax:* 807-229-1471
boardoffice@sgdsb.on.ca
www.sgdsb.on.ca
twitter.com/SGDSBoard
www.youtube.com/user/SuperiorGreenstone
Number of Schools: 12 elementary; 5 secondary; *Grades:* K-12; *Enrollment:* 1583
David Tamblyn, Director of Education
dtamblyn@sgdsb.on.ca
Nicole Morden-Cormier, Superintendent of Education - Effectiveness & Early Years
nmorden-cormier@sgdsb.on.ca
Cathy Tsubouchi, Superintendent of Business
ctsubouchi@sgdsb.on.ca
Valerie Nakani, Human Resources Administrator
vnakani@sgdsb.on.ca
Nicole Richmond, Aboriginal Liaison
nrichmond@sgdsb.on.ca

***Midhurst:* Simcoe County District School Board (SCDSB)**
Education Centre
1170 Hwy. 26, Midhurst, ON L0L 1X0, Canada
Tel: 705-728-7570; *Fax:* 705-728-2265
Toll-Free: 1-877-728-1187
www.scdsb.on.ca
Other Information: 905 Calling: 905-729-2265 (Switchboard); 905-729-3600 (Auto)
www.facebook.com/SCDSB?ref=ts
twitter.com/SCDSB_Schools
Number of Schools: 87 elementary; 16 secondary; 6 Adult Learning Centres; *Grades:* K-12; Continuing Ed.; *Enrollment:* 50000; *Number of Employees:* 6,000 full-time and part-time staff
Kathi Wallace, Director of Education, 705-734-6363, ext. 11223
Peter Beacock, Chairperson, 705-734-6363, ext. 11007
pbeacock@trustee.scdsb.on.ca
Stuart Finlayson, Superintendent of Education, Area 1, 705-734-6363, ext. 11397
Paul Sloan, Superintendent of Education, Area 2, 705-734-6363, ext. 11208
Paula Murphy, Superintendent of Education, Area 3A, 705-734-6363, ext. 11811
Anita Simpson, Superintendent of Education, Area 3B, 705-734-6363, ext. 11357
Chris Sarnis, Superintendent of Education, Area 3C, 705-734-6363, ext. 11244
Daryl Halliday, Superintendent of Education, Area 4, 705-734-6363, ext. 11318
Jackie Kavanagh, Superintendent of Education, Area 5, 705-734-6363, ext. 11638
John Dance, Superintendent of Facility Services, 705-734-6363, ext. 11375
Brian Jeffs, Superintendent of Business Services, 705-734-6363, ext. 11259
Janis Medysky, Associate Director & Superintendent of HR Services, 705-734-6363, ext. 11304

***Mississauga:* Peel District School Board**
HJA Brown Education Centre
5650 Hurontario St., Mississauga, ON L5R 1C6, Canada
Tel: 905-890-1099; *Fax:* 905-890-6747
Toll-Free: 800-668-1146
communications@peelsb.com
www.peelschools.org
www.facebook.com/peelschools
twitter.com/peelschools
www.youtube.com/peelschools
Number of Schools: 205 elementary; 37 secondary; *Grades:* K-12; *Enrollment:* 152884; *Number of Employees:* 10,651 academic; 5,019 business
Tony Pontes, Director, Education, 905-890-1010, ext. 2006
Janet McDougald, Chair, 905-278-1402
janet.mcdougald@peelsb.com
Brian Woodland, Director of Communications & Community Relations, 905-890-1010, ext. 2812
brian.woodland@peelsb.com
Shawn Moynihan, Superintendent of Curriculum & Instruction Support Services, 905-890-1010, ext. 2343
Adam Hughes, Chief Information Officer, 905-890-1010, ext. 2478
Marlene McAlister, Manager of Purchasing, 905-890-1010, ext. 2127
marlene.mcalister@peelsb.com

***North Bay:* Near North District School Board**
P.O. Box 3110
963 Airport Rd., North Bay, ON P1B 8H1, Canada
Tel: 705-472-8170; *Fax:* 705-472-9927
Toll-Free: 800-278-4922
info@nearnorthschools.ca
www.nearnorthschools.ca
www.facebook.com/141124442647950
twitter.com/NearNorthSchool
Number of Schools: 35 elementary; 7 secondary; *Grades:* K.-12; *Enrollment:* 10500; *Note:* Also offers continuing education programs.
Jackie Young, Director, 705-472-8170, ext. 5012
jackie.Young@nearnorthschools.ca
David Thompson, Chair, 705-474-0442
david.thompson@nearnorthschools.ca
Liz Therrien, Superintendent of Business, 705-472-8170, ext. 5023
Liz.Therrien@nearnorthschools.ca
Jeff Hewitt, Superintendent of Support Services, 705-472-8170, ext. 5008
Jeffrey.Hewitt@nearnorthschools.ca
Craig Myles, Superintendent of Support Success, 705-472-8170, ext. 5002
Craig.Myles@nearnorthschools.ca
Roz Bowness, Superintendent of Schools, 705-472-8170, ext. 8256
Roslyn.Bowness@nearnorthschools.ca
Tim Graves, Superintendent of Schools and Programs, 705-472-8170, ext. 7031
Timothy.Graves@nearnorthschools.ca

***Ottawa:* Ottawa-Carleton District School Board (OCDSB)**
133 Greenbank Rd., Ottawa, ON K2H 6L3, Canada
Tel: 613-721-1820; *Fax:* 613-820-6968
communications@ocdsb.ca
www.ocdsb.ca
www.facebook.com/OCDSB
twitter.com/OCDSB
www.linkedin.com/company/25512
www.youtube.com/user/TheOCDSB
Number of Schools: 117 elementary; 27 secondary; 5 education centres; 7 alternative; *Grades:* JK - 12; Special Education; *Enrollment:* 72436; *Number of Employees:* 4,600
Shirley Seward, Chair
shirley.seward@ocdsb.ca
Jennifer Adams, PhD, Director of Education/Secretary of the Board, 613-596-8211, ext. 8490
Olga Grigoriev, Superintendent of Learning Support Services, 613-596-8211, ext. 8254
Pino Buffone, Superintendent of Curriculum Services, 613-596-8211, ext. 8573
Michael Clarke, Chief Financial Officer, 613-596-8211, ext. 8881
Mike Carson, Superintendent of Facilities, 613-596-8211, ext. 8818
Susan MacDonald, Executive Officer of Instruction, 613-596-8287
Janice McCoy, Superintendent of Human Resources, 613-596-8207
Sandra Lloyd, Manager of Risk & Supply Chain Management, 613-596-8762

***Pembroke:* Renfrew County District School Board (RCDSB)**
1270 Pembroke St. West, Pembroke, ON K8A 4G4, Canada
Tel: 613-735-0151; *Fax:* 613-735-6315
Toll-Free: 1-800-267-1098
www.rcdsb.on.ca
www.facebook.com/RCDSB
twitter.com/rcdsb
Number of Schools: 24 elementary; 7 secondary; 4 continuing education centres; *Grades:* K-8; *Enrollment:* 10000; *Note:* Also offers continuing education programs.
Roger Clarke, Director of Education, 613-735-0151
Dave Shields, Chair, 613-582-3483
shields@rcdsb.on.ca
Gayle Bishop, Superintendent of Education - Assessment and Evaluation, 613-735-0151
Dennis Jenkins, Superintendent of Education - Employee Services, 613-735-0151
Brent McIntyre, Superintendent of Education - Program Services, 613-735-0151
Lisa Schimmens, Superintendent of Corporate Services, 613-735-0151
Peggy Fiebig, Purchasing Agent, 613-735-0151, ext. 2237

***Peterborough:* Kawartha Pine Ridge District School Board**
Education Centre
P.O. Box 7190
1994 Fisher Dr., Peterborough, ON K9J 7A1, Canada
Tel: 705-742-9773; *Fax:* 705-742-7801
Toll-Free: 877-741-4577
kpr_info@kprdsb.ca
www.kprschools.ca
Number of Schools: 76 elementary schools; 17 secondary schools; 3 adult and alternative learning centres; *Enrollment:* 34053; *Number of Employees:* 2050 teachers; 1400 administrative staff
W.R. (Rusty) Hick, Director of Education & Secretary of the Board
Cathy Abraham, Chairperson of the Board
Deborah White-Hassell, Manager of Purchasing Services, 705-742-9773, ext. 2054

***Sarnia:* Lambton Kent District School Board (LKDSB)**
Sarnia Education Centre
P.O. Box 2019
200 Wellington St., Sarnia, ON N7T 7L2, Canada
Tel: 519-336-1500; *Fax:* 519-336-0992
Toll-Free: 800-754-7125
webmaster@lkdsb.net
www.lkdsb.net
Other Information: Purchasing Dept.: 519-336-1500
www.facebook.com/LKDSB
twitter.com/LKDSB
Number of Schools: 54 elementary schools; 13 secondary schools; *Grades:* JK - 12; *Enrollment:* 24000
Jim Costello, Director of Education, 519-336-1500, ext. 31297
Jim.Costello@lkdsb.net
Jane Bryce, Chair, 519-674-2331
Jane.Bryce@lkdsb.net
Brian McKay, Superintendent of Business, 519-336-1500, ext. 31480
Brian.Mckay@lkdsb.net
Joy Badder, Superintendent of Education - Leading & Learning, 519-336-1500, ext. 31263
Joy.Badder@lkdsb.net
Taf Lounsbury, Superintendent of Education - Early Years/Elementary, 519-336-1500, ext. 31570
Taf.Lounsbury@lkdsb.net
Phil Warner, Superintendent of Education - Human Resources, 519-336-1500, ext. 31464
Phil.Warner@lkdsb.net
Dave Doey, Superintendent of Education - Special Education, 519-336-1500, ext. 31303
David.Doey@lkdsb.net
Mike Gilfoyle, Superintendent of Education - Student Success/Secondary, 519-336-1500, ext. 31449
Mike.Gilfoyle@lkdsb.net
Chris Marvell, Manager of Information Technology, 519-354-3775, ext. 31314
Chris.Marvell@lkdsb.net

Campuses
Lambton Kent District School Board
Chatham Regional Education Centre
P.O. Box 1000
476 McNaughton Ave. East, Chatham, ON N7M 5L7, Canada
Tel: 519-354-3770; *Fax:* 519-354-0662
Toll-Free: 800-754-7125

Sault Ste Marie: Algoma District School Board
Central Board Office, Education Centre
644 Albert St. East, Sault Ste Marie, ON P6A 2K7, Canada
Tel: 705-945-7111; *Fax:* 705-942-2540
Toll-Free: 1-888-393-3639
Comments@adsb.on.ca
www.adsb.on.ca
Number of Schools: 38 elementary; 23 secondary & adult education centres; *Grades:* K-12; *Enrollment:* 11386; *Number of Employees:* 2100 permanent and casual; *Note:* Also offers continuing education programs.
Lucia Reece, Director of Education, 705-945-7234
Jennifer Sarlo, Chair
sarloj@trustee.adsb.on.ca
Brenda O'Neill, Superintendent of Education - Elementary Programs, 705-945-7235
Joe Santa Maria, Superintendent of Business, 705-945-7233
Joe Maurice, Superintendent of Education, 705-945-7235
Marcy Bell, Superintendent of Education, 705-945-7245
Brent Vallee, Superintendent of Education, 705-945-7297

Campuses
Algoma District School Board
Northern Area Office
36 McKinley Ave., Wawa, ON P0S 1K0, Canada
Tel: 705-856-2309; *Fax:* 705-856-4332
Matthew Morrison, Coordinator

Algoma District School Board
Eastern Area Office
50 Roman Ave., Elliot Lake, ON P5A 1R9, Canada
Tel: 705-848-3661; *Fax:* 705-848-9225
Ian Gauld, Coordinator

Algoma District School Board
Central Plant Office
190 Northern Ave. E., Sault Ste. Marie, ON P6B 4H6, Canada
Tel: 705-945-7308; *Fax:* 705-759-2811
David Steele, Manager

Seaforth: Avon Maitland District School Board
Education Centre
62 Chalk St. North, Seaforth, ON N0K 1W0, Canada
Tel: 519-527-0111; *Fax:* 519-527-0222
Toll-Free: 1-800-592-5437
info@fc.amdsb.ca
yourschools.ca
www.facebook.com/AvonMaitlandSchools
twitter.com/yourschools
Number of Schools: 48; *Grades:* JK - Secondary; Continuing Ed.; *Enrollment:* 16388
Colleen Schenk, Chair of the Board, 519-357-1066
collsche@fc.amdsb.ca
Ted Doherty, Director of Education & Secretary of the Board, 519-527-0111, ext. 106
teddohe@fc.amdsb.ca
Paul Langis, Superintendent of Education - School Operations, 519-527-0111, ext. 113
paullang@fc.amdsb.ca
Janet Baird-Jackson, Superintendent, Business & Treasurer, 519-527-0111, ext. 206
jbj@fc.amdsb.ca
Peggy Blair, Superintendent of Education - Learning Services, 519-527-0111, ext. 109
peggblai@fc.amdsb.ca
Jodie Baker, Superintendent, Education - Human Resources, 519-527-0111, ext. 208
jodibake@fc.amdsb.ca
Jane Morris, Superintendent of Education - Program, 519-527-0111, ext. 116
janemorr@fc.amdsb.ca
Brad Hill, Manager of Procurement Services, 519-527-0111, ext. 217
bradhill@fc.amdsb.ca
Jen Smith, Manager of IT, 519-482-5428, ext. 243
jensmit@fc.amdsb.ca

St. Catharines: District School Board of Niagara
191 Carleton St., St. Catharines, ON L2R 7P4
Tel: 905-641-1550
inquiries@dsbn.org
www.dsbn.edu.on.ca
Other Information: Free Local Phone: 905-563-0909
www.facebook.com/DSBNiagara
www.twitter.com/dsbn
Number of Schools: 88 elementary; 18 secondary; *Grades:* K-12; *Enrollment:* 36000; *Number of Employees:* 3,000 teachers; 1,300 support staff
Dale Robinson, Chair, 905-680-2427
dale.robinson@dsbn.org
Warren Hoshizaki, Director of Education & Secretary
Kim Yielding, Manager of Communications and Public Relations, 905-641-2929, ext. 54160
Kim.Yielding@dsbn.edu.on.ca
Colin Munro, Manager of Operations, 905-641-2929, ext. 54310
Bob Dunn, Manager of Projects & Maintenance, 905-641-2929, ext. 54305
Jim Morgan, Superintendent of Human Resources, 905-641-2929, ext. 54130
Jim.Morgan@dsbn.org
Glen MacMillan, Manager of Purchasing & Central Services, 905-641-2929, ext. 54240
Glen.MacMillan@dsbn.org

Sudbury: Rainbow District School Board
69 Young St., Sudbury, ON P3E 3G5, Canada
Tel: 705-674-3171; *Fax:* 705-674-3167
Toll-Free: 888-421-2661
info@rainbowschools.ca
www.rainbowschools.ca
Number of Schools: 35 elementary; 10 secondary; *Grades:* K-12; *Enrollment:* 13762
Norm Blaseg, Director of Education, 705-674-3171, ext. 7216
Doreen Dewar, Chair
Dennis Bazinet, Superintendent of Business, 705-674-3171, ext. 7216
Bruce Bourget, Superintendent of Schools, 705-674-3171, ext. 7236
Lesleigh Dye, Superintendent of Schools, 705-674-3171, ext. 7236
Judy Noble, Superintendent of Schools, 705-674-3171, ext. 7213
Kathy Wachnuk, Superintendent of Schools, 705-674-3171, ext. 7213

Thunder Bay: Lakehead District School Board
The Jim McCuaig Education Centre
2135 Sills St., Thunder Bay, ON P7E 5T2, Canada
Tel: 807-625-5100; *Fax:* 807-622-0961
Toll-Free: 888-565-1406
www.lakeheadschools.ca
twitter.com/LakeheadSchools
www.youtube.com/user/LakeheadSchools
Number of Schools: 25 elementary; 4 secondary; 1 adult education centre; *Grades:* K-12; *Enrollment:* 13000; *Number of Employees:* 840 teaching staff
Ian MacRae, Director of Education, 807-625-5131
simacrae@lakeheadschools.ca
Deborah Massaro, Chair, 807-767-3673
dmassaro@lakeheadschools.ca
Colleen Kappel, Superintendent of Education, 807-625-5126
colleen_kappel@lakeheadschools.ca
Sherri-Lynne Pharand, Superintendent of Education, 807-625-5158
spharand@lakeheadschools.ca
David Wright, Superintendent of Business, 807-625-5126
david_wright@lakeheadschools.ca
Gerrie Tennant, Supervisor of Purchasing, 807-625-5275
gtennant@lakeheadschools.ca
Wayne Bahlieda, Manager of Human Resources, 807-625-5171
wbahlieda@lakeheadschools.ca

Timmins: District School Board Ontario North East
P.O. Box 1020
383 Birch St. North, Timmins, ON P4N 7H7
Tel: 705-360-1151; *Fax:* 705-268-7100
Toll-Free: 800-381-7280
comments@dsb1.edu.on.ca
www.dsb1.ca
Number of Schools: 25 elementary; 9 secondary; 3 alternative; *Grades:* K.-Sec.; Adult Ed.; *Enrollment:* 8105
Doug Shearer, Chair, 705-679-5511
doug.shearer@dsb1.edu.on.ca
Linda Knight, Director, Education
Jim Rowe, Senior Manager of Human Resources
Pearl Fong-West, Superintendent of Business/Finance and Treasurer

Toronto: Toronto District School Board (TDSB)
5050 Yonge St., Toronto, ON M2N 5N8, Canada
Tel: 416-397-3000
communications@tdsb.on.ca
www.tdsb.on.ca
Other Information: Public Affairs, Phone: 416-395-2721
www.facebook.com/toronto.dsb?ref=ts
twitter.com/TDSB
www.youtube.com/user/TDSBOfficial
Number of Schools: 588; *Grades:* K-12; Adult Ed.; French Immersion; *Enrollment:* 405000; *Number of Employees:* 17,415 permanent teachers; 15,461 permanent support staff; 3,500 occasional staff
Robin Pilkey, Chair of the Board
John Malloy, Director of Education, 416-397-3190
Christopher Usih, Associate Director - Student Achievement, Well-being, 416-397-3187
Carla Kisko, Associate Director, Finance & Operations, 416-397-3188
Jim Clement, Manager, Purchasing Services, 416-395-8303
Dan Nortes, Registrar, 416-393-8939
registrar@tdsb.on.ca
Mary Jane McNamara, Superintendent, WR1, 416-394-2036
MaryJane.McNamara@tdsb.on.ca
Jacqueline Spence, Superintendent, Region WR02, 416-394-2034
Jacqueline.Spence@tdsb.on.ca
Peter Chang, Superintendent, Region WR03, 416-394-2032
P.Chang@tdsb.on.ca
Susan Winter, Superintendent, Region WR04, 416-394-2038
Susan.Winter@tdsb.on.ca
Glenford Duffus, Superintendent, Region WR05, 416-394-2030
Glenford.Duffus@tdsb.on.ca
Jane Phillips-Long, Superintendent, Region WR06, 416-394-2042
Jane.Phillips-Long@tdsb.on.ca
Curtis Ennis, Superintendent, Region WR07, 416-394-2044
Curtis.Ennis@tdsb.on.ca
Sandra Tondat, Superintendent, Region WR08, 416-394-2046
Sandra.Tondat@tdsb.on.ca
Louie Papathanasakis, Superintendent, Region WR09, 416-394-2050
Louie.Papathanasakis@tdsb.on.ca
Mike Gallagher, Superintendent, Region WR10, 416-394-2048
Mike.Gallagher@tdsb.on.ca
Lucy Giannotta, Superintendent, Region ER11, 416-396-9196
Lucy.Giannotta@tdsb.on.ca
Audley Salmon, Superintendent, Region ER12, 416-396-9186
Audley.Salmon@tdsb.on.ca
Kerry-Lynn Stadnyk, Superintendent, Region ER13, 416-396-9192
Stacey.MKerry-Lynn.Stadnyk@tdsb.on.ca
John Chasty, Superintendent, Region ER14, 416-396-9188
John.Chasty@tdsb.on.ca
Tracy Hayhurst, Superintendent, Region ER15, 416-396-9174
Tracy.Hayhurst@tdsb.on.ca
Kathleen Garner, Superintendent, Region ER16, 416-396-9182
Kathleen.Garner@tdsb.on.ca
Linda Curtis, Superintendent, Region ER17, 416-396-9172
Linda.Curtis@tdsb.on.ca
Beth Veale, Superintendent, Region ER18, 416-396-9180
Beth.Veale@tdsb.on.ca
Shirley Chan, Superintendent, Region ER19, 416-396-9178
Shirley.Chan@tdsb.on.ca
Nadira Persaud, Superintendent, Region ER20, 416-396-9190
Nadira.Persaud@tdsb.on.ca
Karen Falconer, Superintendent, 416-394-3155
Karen.Falconer@tdsb.on.ca

Whitby: Durham District School Board
400 Taunton Rd. E, Whitby, ON L1R 2K6, Canada
Tel: 905-666-5500; *Fax:* 905-666-6474
Toll-Free: 1-800-265-3968
General_Inquiry@durham.edu.on.ca
www.ddsb.ca
Other Information: Trustees' Administrative Assistant, Phone: 905-666-6363
TTY: 905-666-6943
www.facebook.com/447874875238636
twitter.com/durhamdsb
Number of Schools: 105 elementary; 24 secondary & learning centres; *Grades:* K - 12; Special Ed.; Continuing Ed.; *Enrollment:* 69823; *Number of Employees:* 7,000 teaching and educational services staff; *Note:* In addition to its teachers, the school board also employs 208 elementary administrators, 77 secondary administrators, & 2,665 educational services staff (including educational assistants, clerical, custodial, maintenance, & lunchroom supervisors).
Martyn Beckett, Director of Education, 905-666-5500
beckett_martyn@ddsb.ca
Luigia Ayotte, Superintendent of Education - Programs, 905-666-6356
ayotte_luigia@ddsb.ca
Richard Kennelly, Superintendent of Education - Special Education, 905-666-6371
richard.kennelly@ddsb.ca
Janet Edwards, Superintendent of Education - Employee Services, 905-666-6343
edwards_janet@ddsb.ca
David Visser, Associate Director/Business, 905-666-6459
david.visser@ddsb.ca

Lisa Millar, Superintendent of Education - Operations, 905-666-6351
lisa.millar@ddsb.ca
Lisa Miller, Superintendent of Education - Early Learning & Childcare, 905-666-6486
millar_lisa@ddsb.ca
David Visser, Associate Director/Facilities Services/Transportation, 905-666-6426
visser_david@ddsb.ca

Windsor: Greater Essex County District School Board
P.O. Box 210
451 Park St. West, Windsor, ON N9A 6K1, Canada
Tel: 519-255-3200
publicboard.ca
Other Information: Adult & Continuing Education, Phone: 519-253-5006

Number of Schools: 58 elementary; 17 secondary; 3 agency; 1 continuing education; *Grades:* K-12; Alternative Ed.; *Enrollment:* 34000; *Number of Employees:* 4,500
Erin Kelly, Director of Education, 519-255-3200, ext. 10259
Director@publicboard.ca
Cathy Lynd, Superintendent of Business & Treasurer, 519-255-3200, ext. 10210
cathy.lynd@publicboard.ca
Paul Antaya, Superintendent of Human Resources, 519-255-3200, ext. 10254
paul.antaya@publicboard.ca
Clara Howitt, PhD, Superintendent of Program & Professional Learning, 519-255-3200, ext. 10255
clara.howitt@publicboard.ca
John Howitt, Superintendent of Elementary Staffing & Information Technolog, 519-255-3200, ext. 10253
john.howitt@publicboard.ca
Lynn McLaughlin, Superintendent of Special Education, 519-255-3200, ext. 10335
lynn.mclaughlin@publicboard.ca
Terry Lyons, Superintendent of Secondary Staffing, 519-255-3200, ext. 10223
terry.lyons@publicboard.ca
Todd Awender, Superintendent of Accommodations, 519-255-3200, ext. 10394
todd.awender@publicboard.ca
Sharon Pyke, Superintendent of Health, Operations, Safe Schools & Equity, 519-255-3200, ext. 10222
sharon.pyke@publicboard.ca
Mary Guthrie, Chief Information Officer, 519-255-3200, ext. 10260
Dawn Lamontagne, Supervisor of Purchasing and Supply, 519-255-3200, ext. 10282

Catholic

Aurora: York Catholic District School Board
320 Bloomington Rd. West, Aurora, ON L4G 0M1, Canada
Tel: 905-713-1211; *Fax:* 905-713-1272
www.ycdsb.ca
Other Information: Alternate Phone: 416-221-5051
twitter.com/ycdsb
www.youtube.com/user/YorkCatholicDSB

Number of Schools: 88 elementary; 15 secondary; 1 alternative education; *Grades:* K-12; *Enrollment:* 55000; *Number of Employees:* 5000 teaching staff
Patricia Preston, Director
John Sabo, Associate Director, Corporate Services & Treasurer, 905-713-1211, ext. 12300
john.sabo@ycdsb.ca
Carol Cotton, Chair of the Board, 905-713-1211, ext. 17134
carol.cotton@ycdsb.ca
Diane Murgaski, Superintendent of Education: Curriculum & Assessment, 905-713-1211, ext. 13840
diane.murgaski@ycdsb.ca
Frances Bagley, Coordinating Superintendent (Director's Office), 905-713-1211, ext. 13860
frances.bagley@ycdsb.ca
Lynda Coulter, Superintendent of Human Resources, 905-713-1211, ext. 13850
lynda.coulter@ycdsb.ca
Michael Nasello, Superintendent of Education: School Leadership & Safe Schools, 905-713-1211, ext. 13663
michael.nasello@ycdsb.ca
Tina D'Acunto, Superintendent of Education: Exceptional Learners, 905-713-1211, ext. 11630
tina.dacunto@ycdsb.ca
Carol Recine, Manager of Purchasing Services, 905-713-1211, ext. 12470
carol.recine@ycdsb.ca
Mary Battista, Superintendent of Education: School Leadership, 905-713-1211, ext. 13656
mary.battista@ycdsb.ca
Ron Crocco, Superintendent of Education: School Leadership, 905-713-1211, ext. 13133
ron.crocco@ycdsb.ca
Nancy Di Nardo, Superintendent of Education: School Leadership, 905-713-1211, ext. 13123
nancy.dinardo@ycdsb.ca
Marianne Fedrigoni, Superintendent of Education: School Leadership, 905-713-1211, ext. 13625
marianne.fedrigoni@ycdsb.ca
Opiyo Oloya, Superintendent of Education: School Leadership, 905-713-1211, ext. 13130
opiyo.oloya@ycdsb.ca

Barrie: Simcoe Muskoka Catholic District School Board
46 Alliance Blvd., Barrie, ON L4M 5K3, Canada
Tel: 705-722-3555; *Fax:* 705-722-6534
www.smcdsb.on.ca

Number of Schools: 41 elementary; 9 secondary; *Grades:* K-12; *Enrollment:* 20000; *Number of Employees:* 4,000 permanent, part-time, and occasional
Brian Beal, Director of Education
directorofeducation@smcdsb.on.ca
Maria Hardie, Board Chair
mhardie@smcdsb.on.ca
Lonnie Bolton, Superintendent of Education, Secondary, 705-722-3555, ext. 228
Stephen Charbonneau, Superintendent of Education, Elementary, 705-722-3555, ext. 321
Ab Falconi, Superintendent of Education, Elementary, 705-722-3555, ext. 272
Jane Dillon-Leitch, Superintendent of Education, Elementary, 705-722-3555, ext. 247

Brantford: Brant Haldimand Norfolk Catholic District School Board (BHNCDSB)
Catholic Education Centre
P.O. Box 217
322 Fairview Dr., Brantford, ON N3T 5M8, Canada
Tel: 519-756-6505; *Fax:* 519-756-9913
info@bhncdsb.ca
www.bhncdsb.ca
Other Information: Purchasing: purchasing@bhncdsb.ca; 519-756-9913
www.facebook.com/260644804051272?sk=wall
twitter.com/bhncdsb
www.youtube.com/user/BHNCDSBvideo

Number of Schools: 30 elementary; 4 secondary; *Grades:* K-12; Special Ed.; *Enrollment:* 10000; *Number of Employees:* 700+ teachers; 300+ non-academic staff
June Szeman, Chair of the Board, 519-753-9198
jszeman@bhncdsb.ca
Chris Roehrig, Director of Education, 519.756.6505, ext. 223
aclement@bhncdsb.ca
Tom Grice, Superintendent of Business & Treasurer, 519-756-6505, ext. 272
lluciani@bhncdsb.ca
Patrick Daly, Superintendent of Education, 519-756-6505, ext. 0
pdaly@bhncdsb.ca
Michelle Shypula, Superintendent of Education, 519-756-6505, ext. 237
lnadeau@bhncdsb.ca
Leslie Telfer, Superintendent of Education, 519-756-6505, ext. 237
lnadeau@bhncdsb.ca
Paula Dunn, Manager, Human Resources, 519-756-6505, ext. 235
pdunn@bhncdsb.ca
Pat Petrella, Manager, Finance, 519-756-6505, ext. 228
ppetrella@bhncdsb.ca
Norm Cicci, Manager, Information Technology, 519-756-6505, ext. 317
ncicci@bhncdsb.ca
Tracey Austin, Manager, Communications & Community Relations, 519-756-6505, ext. 234
taustin@bhncdsb.ca

Burlington: Halton Catholic District School Board
Education Center
802 Drury Lane, Burlington, ON L7R 2Y2, Canada
Tel: 905-632-6300; *Fax:* 905-333-4661
Toll-Free: 1-800-741-8382
comments@hcdsb.org
www.hcdsb.org
Other Information: Special Education Services, E-mail: speced@hcdsb.org
www.facebook.com/HCDSB
twitter.com/HCDSB

Number of Schools: 43 elementary; 9 secondary; 3 continuing education centres; *Grades:* K-12; Continuing Ed; *Enrollment:* 29000
Paula Dawson, Director of Education, 905-632-6314, ext. 115
Erica van Roosmalen, Chief Officer, Research & Development Services, 905-632-6314, ext. 367
Giacomo Corbacio, Superintendent, Facility Management Services, 905-632-6314, ext. 171
Jack Nigro, Superintendent, Curriculum Services, 905-632-6314, ext. 122
Lorrie Naar, Superintendent, School Services, 905-632-6314, ext. 120
Camillo Cipriano, Superintendent, School Services, 905-632-6314, ext. 127
Colin McGillicuddy, Superintendent, School Services, 905-632-6314, ext. 181
Paul McMahon, Superintendent, Business Services, 905-632-6314, ext. 131
Brendan Browne, Superintendent, Special Education Services, 905-632-6314, ext. 125
Tim Overholt, Superintendent, Human Resources, 905-632-6314, ext. 129
Toni Pinelli, Superintendent, School Services, 905-632-6314, ext. 181
Wayne Elshof, Senior Administrator, Information Technology, 905-632-6314, ext. 550
Terrence Glover, Administrator, Planning Services, 905-632-6314, ext. 107
Lisa Stocco, Administrator, Communication Services, 905-632-6314, ext. 126
Pamela Harling, Manager, Purchasing Services, 905-632-6314, ext. 136

Burlington: Burlington - Resource Centre
2333 Headon Forest Dr., Burlington, ON L7M 3X6, Canada
Tel: 905-632-4814

Dublin: Huron-Perth Catholic District School Board
P.O. Box 70
87 Mill St., Dublin, ON N0K 1E0, Canada
Tel: 519-345-2440; *Fax:* 519-345-2449
www.huronperthcatholic.ca
www.facebook.com/hpcdsb
twitter.com/hpcdsb

Number of Schools: 16 elementary; 2 secondary; *Grades:* K-12; *Enrollment:* 4500; *Number of Employees:* 500
Vince MacDonald, Director of Education, 519-345-2440, ext. 310
vmacdonald@hpcdsb.ca
Jim McDade, Chair of the Board
jmcdade@hpcdsb.ca
Dawne Boersen, Superintendent of Education, 519-345-2440, ext. 307
dboersen@hpcdsb.ca
Gary O'Donnell, Superintendent of Education, 519-345-2440, ext. 309
godonnell@hpcdsb.ca
Chris Howarth, Superintendent of Business, 519-345-2440, ext. 330
chowarth@hpcdsb.ca
Karen McDowell, Executive Manager of Employee Relations, 519-345-2440, ext. 317
kmcdowell@hpcdsb.ca
Sean McDade, Coordinator of Information Technology, 519-345-2440, ext. 306
smcdade@hpcdsb.ca

Fort Frances: Northwest Catholic District School Board
555 Flinders Ave., Fort Frances, ON P9A 3L2, Canada
Tel: 807-274-2931; *Fax:* 807-274-8792
Toll-Free: 888-311-2931
www.tncdsb.on.ca

Number of Schools: 6; *Grades:* K-8

Dryden
Business Office
Suite B, 75 Van Horne Ave., Dryden, ON P8N 2B2, Canada
Tel: 807-223-4663; *Fax:* 807-223-4014
Toll-Free: 877-235-4663

Rick Boisvert, Director, Education, 807-274-2931, ext. 1222
Anne-Marie Fitzgerald, Chair
amfitzgerald@tncdsb.on.ca
Margot Saari, Superintendent of Education, 807-223-4663, ext. 1033
Chris Howarth, Superintendent of Business, 807-223-4663, ext. 1024
Natasha Getson, Curriculum Coordinator, 807-223-4663, ext. 1023
Seija Van Haesendonck, Manager of Finance, 807-223-4663, ext. 1031

Guelph: Wellington Catholic District School Board
75 Woolwich St., Guelph, ON N1H 6N6, Canada
Tel: 519-821-4600; *Fax:* 519-824-3088
generalinquiries@wellingtoncdsb.ca
www.wellingtoncssb.edu.on.ca

Number of Schools: 17 elementary; 3 secondary; 1 alternative; *Grades:* K-12; *Enrollment:* 8700
Tamara Nugent, Director of Education, 519-821-4640, ext. 214
tnugent@wellingtoncdsb.ca
Tracy McLennan, Superintendent of Corporate Services & Treasurer, 519-821-4640
tmclennan@wellingtoncdsb.ca
Brian Capovilla, Superintendent of Education, 519-821-4640, ext. 209
bcapovilla@wellingtoncdsb.ca
Mariano L. Gazzola, Chair, 226-979-2008
mgazzola@wellingtoncdsb.ca

Hamilton: Hamilton-Wentworth Catholic District School Board
Father Kyran Kennedy Catholic Education Centre
P.O. Box 2012
90 Mulberry St., Hamilton, ON L8N 3R9, Canada
Tel: 905-525-2930; *Fax:* 905-525-1724
www.hwcdsb.ca
Other Information: Summer fax: 905-525-2914; Emergency Phone: 905-522-6680
www.facebook.com/hwcdsb
twitter.com/HWCDSB
Number of Schools: 48 elementary; 7 secondary; 1 adult education centre; *Grades:* K-12; continuing education
D. Hansen, Director of Education, 905-525-2930, ext. 2181
P. Daly, Chairperson of the Board
J. LoPresti, Executive Officer of Human Resources

Hanover: Bruce-Grey Catholic District School Board
799 - 16th Ave., Hanover, ON N4N 3A1, Canada
Tel: 519-364-5820; *Fax:* 519-364-5882
bruce_grey@bgcdsb.org
www.bgcdsb.org
www.facebook.com/185958928107172
twitter.com/BGCDSB
www.youtube.com/user/BruceGreyCatholicDSB
Number of Schools: 13; *Grades:* K-12; Religious Ed.; ESL; *Enrollment:* 3600; *Number of Employees:* 400
Beverley Eckensweiler, Chairperson, 519-376-2770
bev_eckensweiler@bgcdsb.ca
Jamie McKinnon, Director of Education, 519-364-5820, ext. 224
Francine Pilon, Superintendent of Education, 519-364-5820, ext. 225
Michael Bethune, Superintendent of Education, 519-364-5820, ext. 231
Alecia Lantz, Superintendent of Business, 519-364-5820, ext. 223
Suzanne White, Superintendent of Human Resources, 519-364-5820
Nancy Fischer, Supervisor of Payroll Services, 519-364-5820, ext. 275
Jamie Carter, Supervisor of Financial Services, 519-364-5820, ext. 256
Derrick Farwell, Supervisor of Information & Communications Technology, 519-364-5820, ext. 253
Steve Lustig, General Manager of Purchasing & Transportation Consortium, 519-364-5820, ext. 227
Ann-Marie Deas, Mental Health Lead, 519-364-5820, ext. 242
Tracy Slater, Speech Language Pathologist, 519-364-5820, ext. 251
Jennifer Caldwell, Psychometrist, 519-364-5820, ext. 247
Doreen Schultz, Community Relations, Communications & Outreach Coordinator, 519-364-5820, ext. 268

Kemptville: Catholic District School Board of Eastern Ontario
c/o Kemptville Board Office
P.O. Box 2222
2755 Hwy. 43, Kemptville, ON K0G 1J0, Canada
Tel: 613-258-7757; *Fax:* 613-258-7134
Toll-Free: 1-800-443-4562
mail@cdsbeo.on.ca
www.cdsbeo.on.ca
Other Information: hr@cdsbeo.on.ca; religioused@cdsbeo.on.ca
www.facebook.com/CDSBEO
twitter.com/CDSBEO
Number of Schools: 31 elementary; 13 secondary; *Grades:* K-12; *Enrollment:* 13200; *Number of Employees:* 890 teachers; 535 support staff
Brent Laton, Chair, 613-925-3313
Brent.Laton@cdsbeo.on.ca
John Cameron, Supertintendent of School Effectiveness, 613-933-1720, ext. 371
John.Cameron@cdsbeo.on.ca
Natalie Cameron, Superintendent of School Effectiveness, 613-258-7757, ext. 236
Natalie.Cameron@cdsbeo.on.ca
Donaleen Hawes, Superintendent of School Effectiveness, 613-283-5007, ext. 234
Donaleen.Hawes@cdsbeo.on.ca
Tom Jordan, Superintendent of School Effectiveness, 613-258-7757, ext. 207
Tom.Jordan@cdsbeo.on.ca
WM. J. Gartland, Director of Education, 613-258-7757, ext. 204
director@cdsbeo.on.ca

Kenora: Kenora Catholic District School Board
Catholic Education Center
1292 Heenan Pl., Kenora, ON P9N 2Y8, Canada
Tel: 807-468-9851; *Fax:* 807-468-8094
info@kcdsb.on.ca
www.kcdsb.on.ca
www.facebook.com/KenoraCatholic
twitter.com/KCDSB
www.youtube.com/user/KenoraCatholicDSB
Number of Schools: 4 elementary; 1 secondary; *Grades:* K-12
Phyllis Eikre, Director of Education, 807-468-9851, ext. 239
peikre@kcdsb.on.ca
Frank Bastone, Chair
fbastone@kcdsb.on.ca
Trina Henley, Communications Officer, 807-468-9851, ext. 224
thenley@kcdsb.on.ca
Mary Cunningham, Superintendent of Instructional Services, 807-468-9851, ext. 233
mcunningham@kcdsb.on.ca
Tammy Bush, Curriculum Coordinator, 807-468-9851, ext. 234
tbush@kcdsb.on.ca
Tina Sinclair, Manager of Human Resource Services, 807-468-9851, ext. 232
tina.sinclair@kcdsb.on.ca

Kitchener: Waterloo Catholic District School Board (WCDSB)
P.O. Box 91116
#A, 35 Weber St. West, Kitchener, ON N2G 4G2, Canada
Tel: 519-578-3660; *Fax:* 519-578-5291
info@wcdsb.ca
www.wcdsb.ca
twitter.com/WCDSBNewswire
www.youtube.com/user/WCDSBVidLink
Number of Schools: 45 elementary; 5 secondary; *Grades:* K-12
Manuel da Silva, Chair, 519-622-3039
manuel.dasilva@wcdsb.ca
Loretta Notten, Director of Education & Secretary of the Board
laura.notten@wcdsb.ca
John Shewchuk, Chief Managing Officer
john.shewchuk@wcdsb.ca
Shesh Maharaj, Superintendent of Corporate Services, Treasurer, & CFO
shesh.maharaj@wcdsb.ca
Chris Demers, Chief Information Officer
chris.demers@wcdsb.ca
Gerry Clifford, Superintendent of Learning: Adult & Continuing Education
Gerry.Clifford@wcdsb.ca
David DeSantis, Superintendent of Learning: Student Success
Gerry.Clifford@wcdsb.ca
Derek Haime, Superintendent of Learning: Faith Development, Inclusions
derek.haime@wcdsb.ca
John Klein, Superintendent of Learning: Program Services
john.klein@wcdsb.ca
Laura Shoemaker, Superintendent of Learning: Special Education
Laura.Shoemake@wcdsb.ca
Jeff Admans, Manager of Purchasing Services, 519-578-3660, ext. 2323
Jeff.Admans@wcdsb.ca

L'Orignal: Conseil scolaire de district catholique de l'Est ontarien (CSDCEO)
875, ch de comté 17, L'Orignal, ON K0B 1K0, Canada
Tél: 613-675-4691; *Téléc:* 613-675-2921
Ligne sans frais: 800-204-4098
bur-central@csdceo.on.ca
www.csdceo.ca
twitter.com/CSDCEO
www.youtube.com/user/csdceo
Number of Schools: 34; *Grades:* Élém.-Sec.; *Enrollment:* 3718
François Turpin, Directrice de l'éducation/Sec., 613-675-4691
Martial Levac, Président du Conseil, 800-204-4098
France D. Lamarche, Surintendante de l'éducation, 800-204-4098, ext. 253
Martin Lavigne, Surintendant des affaires et trésorier, 800-204-4098, ext. 212
Alain Martel, Surintendant de l'éducation, 800-204-4098, ext. 255
Lyne Racine, Surintendant de l'éducation, 800-204-4098

London: London District Catholic School Board
5200 Wellington Rd. South, London, ON N6A 3X8, Canada
Tel: 519-663-2088; *Fax:* 519-663-9250
communications@ldcsb.on.ca
www.ldcsb.on.ca
Number of Schools: 46 elementary schools; 9 secondary schools; 1 continuing education centre; *Grades:* JK - 12; Continuing Ed; *Enrollment:* 18000
Bill Hall, Chair
Linda Staudt, Director of Education & Secretary, 519-663-2088, ext. 40002
Jacquie Davison, Superintendent of Business & Treasurer, 519-663-2088, ext. 43602
Ed Dedecker, Superintendent of Education, 519-663-2088, ext. 40011
Kathy Furlong, Superintendent of Education, 519-663-2088, ext. 40007
Kelly Holbrough, Superintendent of Education, 519-663-2088, ext. 42203
Sharon Wright-Evans, Superintendent of Education, 519-663-2088, ext. 40009
Jim Vair, Senior Manager - Human Resources Services, 519-663-2088, ext. 43403
Linda Wells, Supervisor of Library & Media Services, 519-663-2088, ext. 41018

Mississauga: Dufferin-Peel Catholic District School Board
40 Matheson Blvd. West, Mississauga, ON L5R 1C5
Tel: 905-890-1221; *Fax:* 905-890-7610
Toll-Free: 800-387-9501
www.dpcdsb.org
twitter.com/DPCDSBSchools
www.youtube.com/user/DPCDSBVideos?feature=watch
Number of Schools: 123 elementary; 26 secondary; *Grades:* K.-12; Adult Ed.; *Enrollment:* 83578; *Number of Employees:* 7,465 academic and 2,076 non-academic
Mario Pascucci, Chair
mario.pascucci@dpcdsb.org
Marianne Mazzorato, Director of Education, 905-890-0708, ext. 24201
John Hrajnik, Associate Director, Corporate Services & Chief Financial Off.
Clara Pitoscia, Superintendent - Human Resources & Employee Relations
Julie Cherepacha, Superintendent - Financial Services
Charles Blanchard, Supertintendent - Special Projects, Strategy & Policy
Daniel Del Blanco, Superintendent - Planning & Operations
Max Vecchiarino, Superintendent - Program
Shirley Kendrick, Superintendent - Special Education & Support Services

Napanee: Algonquin & Lakeshore Catholic District School Board
151 Dairy Ave., Napanee, ON K7R 4B2, Canada
Tel: 613-354-2255; *Toll-Free:* 1-800-581-1116
info@alcdsb.on.ca
www.alcdsb.on.ca
twitter.com/ALCDSB
www.youtube.com/user/ALCDSBvid
Number of Schools: 36 elementary; 5 secondary; 1 Adult learning centre; 2 outdoor education centres; *Grades:* Elementary - Secondary; *Enrollment:* 12800; *Number of Employees:* 1900
Jody DiRocco, Director of Education, 613-354-6257, ext. 448
dricco@alcdsb.on.ca
Bob Koubsky, Superintendent of Finance & Business Services, 613-354-6257, ext. 435
koubsky@alcdsb.on.ca
David Giroux, Superintendent of School Effectiveness, 613-354-6257, ext. 447
giroux@alcdsb.on.ca
Theresa Kennedy, Superintendent of School Effectiveness, 613-354-6257, ext. 439
kennedyt@alcdsb.on.ca
Karen Shannon, Superintendent of School Effectiveness, 613-354-6257, ext. 447
shannon@alcdsb.on.ca
Terri Slack, Superintendent of School Effectiveness, 613-354-6257, ext. 442
slacther@alcdsb.on.ca
Erin Walker, Assistant to the Director of Education, 613-354-6257, ext. 442
walker@alcdsb.on.ca
Lori Bryden, Coodinator of Student Services, 613-354-6257, ext. 434
bryden@alcdsb.on.ca
Ann Boniferro, Coodinator of Religous & Family Life Education, 613-354-6257, ext. 462
boniferr@alcdsb.on.ca

Erica Pennell, Manager - Financial Services, 613-354-6257, ext. 429
pennell@alcdsb.on.ca
Michelle Lamarche, Manager - Human Resources, 613-354-6257, ext. 415
lamarcmi@alcdsb.on.ca
Louise Lannan, Coodinator of Curriculum & Staff Development, 613-354-6257, ext. 402
lannan@alcdsb.on.ca

Nepean: Ottawa Catholic District School Board
570 West Hunt Club Rd., Nepean, ON K2G 3R4, Canada
Tel: 613-224-2222; *Fax:* 613-224-5063
info@ocsb.ca
www.ottawacatholicschools.ca
www.facebook.com/ottawacatholicschools
twitter.com/ottcatholicsb
www.youtube.com/user/OttawaCatholicSB
Number of Schools: 64 elementary; 2 intermediate; 15 secondary; 1 adult high; 4 continuing education centres; *Grades:* K-12; Continuing Education; *Enrollment:* 36500; *Number of Employees:* 3,910 full-time equivalent teaching and non-teaching staff
Denise Andre, Director of Education & Secretary-Treasurer, 613-224-4455, ext. 2272
Director@ocsb.ca
Elaine McMahon, Chairperson, 613-828-3573
Elaine.McMahon@ocsb.ca
Peter Atkinson, Superintendent of the Continuing and Community Education, 613-224-4455, ext. 2501
Peter.Atkinson@ocsb.ca
David Leach, Superintendent of the Finance & Administration, 613-224-4455, ext. 2281
David.Leach@ocsb.ca
Brenda Wilson, Superintendent of the Student Success (Learning Technologies), 613-224-4455, ext. 2303
Brenda.Wilson@ocsb.ca
Manon Séguin, Superintendent of Student Success (Intermediate/Secondary), 613-224-4455, ext. 2371
Manon.Seguin@ocsb.ca
Simone Oliver, Superintendent of the Student Success (Elementary), 613-224-4455, ext. 2345
Simone.Oliver@ocsb.ca
Steve McCabe, Superintendent of the Student Success (Leading & Learning), 613-224-4455, ext. 2345
Steve.McCabe@ocsb.ca
Cindy Owens, Superintendent of the Human Resources, 613-224-4455, ext. 2402
Cindy.Owens@ocsb.ca
Fred Chrystal, Superintendent of the Planning & Facilities, 613-224-4455, ext. 2322
Fred.Chrystal@ocsb.ca
Mary Donaghy, Superintendent of Special Education and Student Services, 613-224-4455, ext. 2351
Mary.Donaghy@ocsb.ca

North Bay: Conseil scolaire catholique Franco-Nord
681-C, rue Chippewa ouest, North Bay, ON P1B 6G8, Canada
Tél: 705-472-1702; *Téléc:* 705-474-3824
information@franco-nord.ca
www.franco-nord.edu.on.ca
Number of Schools: 14 écoles élémentaires, 3 écoles secondaires; *Grades:* Élem.-Sec.; *Enrollment:* 3400
Monica Ménard, Directrice de l'éducation, 705-472-1701, ext. 2360
menardm@franco-nord.ca
Ronald Demers, Président du Conseil
Éric Foisy, Surintendant de l'éducation, 705-472-1701, ext. 2350
foisye@franco-nord.ca
Michel Paulin, Surintendant des affaires, 705-472-1701, ext. 2300
paulinm@franco-nord.ca
Marc Cantin, Directeur du service de l'immobilisation, 705-472-1701, ext. 2030
cantinm@franco-nord.ca
Claire Riley, Directrice des ressources humaines, 705-472-1701, ext. 2470
rileyc@franco-nord.ca
Pierre Chaput, Chef des services financiers, 705-472-1701, ext. 2570
chaputp@franco-nord.ca
Daniel Gagné, Chef des services informatiques, 705-472-1701, ext. 2260
gagned@franco-nord.ca

North Bay: Nipissing-Parry Sound Catholic District School Board (NPSC)
1000 High St., North Bay, ON P1B 6S6, Canada
Tel: 705-472-1201; *Fax:* 705-472-0507
contact@npsc.ca
www.npsc.ca
twitter.com/npsc_schools
Number of Schools: 12 elementary; 1 secondary; 1 continuing ed
Barbara McCool, Chair
mccoolb@npsc.ca
Anna Marie Bitonti, Director of Education, 705-472-1201, ext. 2243
bitontia@npsc.ca
Paula Mann, Superintendent of Education, 705-472-1201, ext. 2242
mannp@npsc.ca
Paula Mann, Superintendent of Education, 705-472-1201, ext. 2242
mannp@npsc.ca
Grace Barnhardt, Superintendent of Business & Treasurer, 705-472-1201, ext. 2225
barnharg@npsc.ca
Connie Vander Wall, Senior Manager, Human Resources, 705-472-1201, ext. 2218
vanderwc@npsc.ca
Kate Bondett, Communications Officer, 705-472-1201, ext. 2229
bondettk@npsc.ca

Oshawa: Durham Catholic District School Board
650 Rossland Rd. West, Oshawa, ON L1J 7C4
Tel: 905-576-6150; *Fax:* 905-721-8239
Toll-Free: 877-482-0722
www.dcdsb.ca
www.facebook.com/124498987628845
twitter.com/DurhamCatholic
www.linkedin.com/company/dcdsb
www.youtube.com/user/DurhamCatholicDSB
Number of Schools: 39 elementary; 7 secondary; 6 alternative & continuing education; *Grades:* K-12; *Enrollment:* 21150
Theresa Corless, Chair of the Board, 905-441-1792
Theresa.Corless@dcdsb.ca
Anne O'Brien, Director of Education, 905-576-6150, ext. 2317
Ryan Putnam, Superintendent of Business & Chief Financial Officer, 905-576-6150, ext. 2244
Tracy Barill, Superintendent of Education, 905-576-6150, ext. 2121
Janine Bowyer, Superintendent of Education, 905-576-6150, ext. 2279
Bob Camozzi, Superintendent of Education, 905-576-6150, ext. 2353
Ronald Rodriguez, Chief Information Officer, 905-576-6150, ext. 2287

Ottawa: Conseil des écoles catholiques du Centre-Est (CECCE)
4000, rue Labelle, Ottawa, ON K1J 1A1, Canada
Tél: 613-744-2555; *Téléc:* 613-746-3081
Ligne sans frais: 888-230-5131
ecolecatholique@ecolecatholique.ca
www.cecce.edu.on.ca
www.facebook.com/ecolecatholique?ref=mf
twitter.com/ecolecatholique
Number of Schools: 39 écoles élémentaire; 10 écoles secondaire; *Grades:* JK-12; *Enrollment:* 20000
Diane Doré, Présidente du Conseil
Bernard Roy, Directeur de l'éducation/Sec.-trésorier
Sylvie Tremblay, Surintendante exécutive de l'éducation
Yvon Bellerose, Directeur exécutif des services administratifs
René Bordeleau, Directeur exécutif des ressources humainestifs
Roxanne Deevey, Directrice des communications, relations publiques

Pembroke: Renfrew County Catholic District School Board (RCCDSB)
499 Pembroke St. West, Pembroke, ON K8A 5P1, Canada
Tel: 613-735-1031; *Fax:* 613-735-2649
Toll-Free: 800-267-0191
www.rccdsb.edu.on.ca
twitter.com/RCCDSB
Number of Schools: 23 elementary; 6 secondary; *Grades:* K-12; *Enrollment:* 4600; *Number of Employees:* 525 permanent staff; 300 occaisional staff
Michele Arbour, Director of Education, 613-735-1031, ext. 201
marbour@rccdsb.edu.on.ca
Bob Michaud, Chairperson, 613-735-7387
bmichaud@rccdsb.edu.on.ca
Jaimie Perry, Superintendent of Educational Services, 613-735-1031, ext. 206
jperry@rccdsb.edu.on.ca
Peter Adam, Superintendent of Educational Services, 613-735-1031, ext. 205
padam@rccdsb.edu.on.ca
Mark Searson, Superintendent of Educational Services, 613-735-1031, ext. 271
msearson@rccdsb.edu.on.ca
Mary Lynn Schauer, Superintendent of Business Services, 613-735-1031, ext. 310
mschauer@rccdsb.edu.on.ca
Colleen Mirault, Supervisor for Purchasing Services, 613-735-1031, ext. 320
cmirault@rccdsb.edu.on.ca
Melanie Leclair, Manager of Human Resources Services, 613-735-1031, ext. 220
mleclair@rccdsb.edu.on.ca

Peterborough: Peterborough Victoria Northumberland & Clarington Catholic District School Board (PVNCCDSB)
1355 Lansdowne St. West, Peterborough, ON K9J 7M3, Canada
Tel: 705-748-4861; *Fax:* 705-748-9734
Toll-Free: 800-461-8009
www.pvnccdsb.on.ca
www.facebook.com/PVNCCDSB
twitter.com/pvnccdsb
www.youtube.com/pvncc
Number of Schools: 31 elementary; 6 secondary; *Grades:* K-12; *Enrollment:* 14465; *Number of Employees:* 897 academic; 344 occasional academic; 515 support staff; 97 administrative; 199 temporary
Barbara McMorrow, Director of Education & Secretary-Treasurer, 705-748-4861, ext. 247
bmcmorrow@pvnccdsb.on.ca
Michelle Griepsma, Board Chairperson, 705-928-4474
mgriepsma@pvnccdsb.on.ca
Galen Eagle, Communications Officer, 705-748-4861, ext. 245
geagle@pvnccdsb.on.ca
Isabel Grace, Supterintendent Business & Finance/Plant, 705-748-4861, ext. 246
igrace@pvnccdsb.on.ca
Dawn Michie, Superintendent of Learning/Leadership & HR Services, 705-748-4861, ext. 167
dmichie@pvnccdsb.on.ca
Timothy Moloney, Superintendent of Learning Services/Student Success (Sec.), 705-748-4861, ext. 230
tmoloney@pvnccdsb.on.ca
Deirdre Thomas, Superintendent of Schools
dthomas@pvnccdsb.on.ca
Joan Carragher, Superintendent of Schools, 705-748-4861, ext. 200
jcarragher@pvnccdsb.on.ca
Catherine Ciolko-Sutton, Supervisor of Purchasing and Administative Services, 705-748-4861, ext. 238

Sault Ste Marie: Huron-Superior Catholic District School Board (HSCDSB)
90 Ontario Ave., Sault Ste Marie, ON P6B 6G7, Canada
Tel: 705-945-5400; *Fax:* 705-945-5575
Toll-Free: 800-267-0754
frontdesk@hscdsb.on.ca
www.hscdsb.on.ca
www.youtube.com/user/HSCDSB1
Number of Schools: 19 elementary; 2 secondary; *Grades:* K-12; *Enrollment:* 5000; *Number of Employees:* 1,000+
John Stadnyk, Director of Education, 705-945-5600
john.stadnyk@hscdsb.on.ca
Leslie Cassidy-Amadio, Chair, 705-779-2836
leslie.cassidy-amadio@hscdsb.on.ca
Chris Spina, Superintendent of Business, 705-945-5624
chris.spina@hscdsb.on.ca
Janine Brodie, Purchase & Planning Officer, 705-945-5622
janine.brodie@hscdsb.on.ca
Marian Brooks, Manager of Human Resources, 705-945-5612
marian.brooks@hscdsb.on.ca

Sudbury: Conseil scolaire catholique du Nouvel-Ontario (CSCNO)
201, rue Jogues, Sudbury, ON P3C 5L7, Canada
Tél: 705-673-5626; *Téléc:* 705-669-1270
Ligne sans frais: 800-259-5567
info@nouvelon.ca
www.nouvelon.ca
www.facebook.com/540011212710119?fref=ts
Number of Schools: 27 écoles élémentaires, 9 écoles secondaires et 1 centre d'éducation aux adultes; *Enrollment:* 7000
Marcel Montpellier, Président du Conseil
Lyse-Anne Papineau, Directrice de l'éducation, 705-673-5626, ext. 274
Monique Chrétien, Surintendante de l'éducation, 705-673-5626, ext. 205

Robert Mayer, Surintendante de l'éducation, 705-673-5626, ext. 235
Cathy Modesto, Surintendante d'affaires et de finances, 705-673-5626, ext. 236
Nicole Sonier, Directrice exécutive de l'apprentissage, 705-673-5626, ext. 214
Maryse Barrette, Directrice du Service des finances et des achats, 705-673-5626, ext. 379
Cathy Charles, Directrice du Service des ressources humaines, 705-673-5626, ext. 214

Sudbury: Sudbury Catholic District School Board

Catholic Education Centre
165A D'Youville St., Sudbury, ON P3C 5E7, Canada
Tel: 705-673-5620; *Fax:* 705-673-6670
webmaster@scdsb.edu.on.ca
www.scdsb.edu.on.ca
www.facebook.com/sudburycatholicschools
twitter.com/SCDSB
vimeo.com/sudburycatholicschools
Number of Schools: 18 elementary; 5 secondary; *Grades:* K-12; French Immersion; Adult Ed
Joanne Bénard, Director of Education & CEO of the Board, 705-673-5620, ext. 238
Joanne.Bernard@sudburycatholicschools.ca
Rossella Bagnato, Superintendent of School Effectiveness, 705-673-5620, ext. 200
Rossella.Bagnato@sudburycatholicschools.ca
Cheryl Ann Corallo, Superintendent of Business & Finance, 705-673-5620, ext. 418
Terry Papineau, Superintendent of School Effectiveness, 705-673-5620, ext. 301
Terry.Papineau@sudburycatholicschools.ca
Nicole Snow, Superintendent of School Effectiveness, 705-673-5620, ext. 212
Nicole.Snow@sudburycatholicschools.ca
Michael Bellmore, Chairperson, 705-669-0166
bellmom@sudburycatholicschools.ca

Terrace Bay: Superior North Catholic District School Board (SNCDSB)

P.O. Box 610
21 Simcoe Plaza, Terrace Bay, ON P0T 2W0, Canada
Tel: 807-825-3209; *Fax:* 807-825-3885
BoardOffice@sncdsb.on.ca
www.sncdsb.on.ca
Number of Schools: 9 elementary; *Grades:* Elementary; Religious Program
Alexa McKinnon, Director of Education, 807-825-3209, ext. 24
amckinnon@sncdsb.on.ca
Tina Visintin, Superintendent of Education, 807-825-3209, ext. 28
tvisintin@sncdsb.on.ca
Scott Adams, Manager of Finance, 807-825-3209, ext. 23
sadams@sncdsb.on.ca
Laureen Kay, Payroll and Human Resources Officer, 807-825-3209, ext. 25
lkay@sncdsb.on.ca
Maria Lapenskie, Secretary & Transportation Officer, 807-825-3209, ext. 32
mlapenskie@sncdsb.on.ca
Velvet Bouchard, Accounts Payable & Purchasing Officer, 807-825-3209, ext. 29
Hugh McCorry, Chair of the Board, 807-876-4581

Thunder Bay: Conseil scolaire de district catholique des Aurores boréales

175, rue High nord, Thunder Bay, ON P7A 8C7, Canada
Tél: 807-344-2266; *Téléc:* 807-344-3734
Ligne sans frais: 800-367-0874
info@csdcab.on.ca
www.csdcab.on.ca
Number of Schools: 1 secondaires; 9 élémentaires; *Grades:* Élém-Sec.; *Enrollment:* 652
Sylvianne Mauro, Directrice de l'éducation, 807-343-4050
smauro@csdcab.on.ca
Angèle Brunelle, Présidente du Conseil
Carol-Ann van Rassel, Coordonnatrice des communications, 807-343-4089
cavanrassel@csdcab.on.ca
Roger Lepage, Directeur du Service des ressources humaines, 807-343-4072
rlepage@csdcab.on.ca
Yvon Bolduc, Directeur du Service des finances, 807-343-4063
ybolduc@csdcab.on.ca
Therese Dechene, Directrice des Services pédagogiques, 807-343-4073
tdechene@csdcab.on.ca
Lucie Allaire, Directrice des Services à l'élève, 807-343-4066
lallaire@csdcab.on.ca

Thunder Bay: Thunder Bay Catholic District School Board

Catholic Education Centre
459 Victoria Ave. West, Thunder Bay, ON P7C 0A4, Canada
Tel: 807-625-1555; *Fax:* 807-623-0431
www.tbcdsb.on.ca
Number of Schools: 15 elementary; 3 senior elementary; 2 secondary; 8 alternative; *Grades:* K-12; Alternative Ed
Pino Tassone, Director of Education, 807-625-1567
ptassone@tbcdsb.ca
Sheila Chiodo, Supertintendent of Business & Corporate Services, 807-625-1508
schiodo@tbcdsb.ca
Jean-Paul Tennier, Superintendent of Education (7 - 12 Schools), 807-625-1590
jptennier@tbcdsb.ca
Omer Belisle, Superintendent of Education (K - 6 Schools), 807-625-1573
obelisle@tbcdsb.ca
Nadia Marson, Education Officer, 807-625-1509
nmarson@tbcdsb.ca
Michael Thompson, Communications Officer, 807-625-1587
mthompson@tbcdsb.ca
Garry Grgurich, Manager, Employee Services, 807-625-1577
ggrguric@tbcdsb.ca
Vacant, Purchasing Officer, 807-625-1510
rloyer@tbcdsb.on.ca

Timmins: Conseil scolaire catholique de district des Grandes Rivières

896, promenade Riverside, Timmins, ON P4N 3W2, Canada
Tél: 705-267-1421; *Téléc:* 705-267-7247
Ligne sans frais: 800-465-9984
www.cscdgr.on.ca
www.facebook.com/187598094729525
Number of Schools: 8 Écoles secondaires; 12 Écoles pour adultes; 32 Écoles élémentaires; *Grades:* Élém-Sec. et adultes; *Enrollment:* 2668
Isabelle Charbonneau, Présidente du Conseil, 705-567-7086
charbonneau@cscdgr.on.ca
Lorraine Presley, Directrice de l'éducation, 800-465-9984, ext. 211
presleyl@cscdgr.on.ca
Richard Loiselle, Directeur de la Politique d'aménagement linguistique & comm., 800-465-9984, ext. 245
Colinda Morin-Secord, Chef des services en enfance en difficulté, 800-465-9984, ext. 244
Nathalie Grenier-Ducharme, Chef des services pédagogiques 7e - 12e, 705-628-3029
Vivian Girouard, Chef des services pédagogiques mat à 6e, 705-267-1421, ext. 261
Mario Filion, Gérant des services financiers, 705-267-1421, ext. 206
Julie Bisson, Gérante des ressources humaines et des services d'appui, 705-267-1421, ext. 203

Timmins: Northeastern Catholic District School Board (NCDSB)

101 Spruce St. North, Timmins, ON P4N 6M9, Canada
Tel: 705-268-7443; *Fax:* 705-267-3590
Toll-Free: 877-422-9322
www.ncdsb.on.ca
www.facebook.com/NCDSB
twitter.com/NCDSB
Number of Schools: 13 elementary; 1 secondary; *Grades:* K-12
Rick Brassard, Chair, 705-544-8055
rbrassard@ncdsb.on.ca
Glenn Sheculski, Director of Education, 705-268-7443
gsheculski@ncdsb.on.ca
Daphne Brumwell, Superintendent of Education, 705-268-7443
dbrumwell@ncdsb.on.ca
Tricia Stefanic Weltz, Superintendent of Education, 705-268-7443
tricia.weltz@ncdsb.on.ca
Erika Adam, Manager of Finance, 705-268-7443, ext. 3208
eadam@ncdsb.on.ca
Mélanie Bidal-Mainville, Manager of Human Resources, 705-268-7443, ext. 3204
mbidal@ncdsb.on.ca
Glen Nakashoji, Manager of Information Technology, 705-268-7443, ext. 3214
gnakashoji@ncdsb.on.ca

Toronto: Conseil scolaire de district catholique Centre-Sud

110, av Drewry, Toronto, ON M2M 1C8, Canada
Tél: 416-397-6564; *Téléc:* 416-397-6576
Ligne sans frais: 800-274-3764
commentaires@csdccs.edu.on.ca
www.csdccs.edu.on.ca
www.facebook.com/csdccs
www.twitter.com/csdccs
Number of Schools: 44 écoles élémentaire; 10 écoles secondaire; *Grades:* Élem.-Sec.; *Enrollment:* 15000
Réjean Sirois, Directeur de l'éducation/Sec.-trésorier, 416-397-6564, ext. 73100
rsirois@csdccs.edu.on.ca
Mikale-Andrée Joly, Directrice du Service des relations corporatives, 416-397-6564, ext. 73130
mjoly@csdccs.edu.on.ca
Sébastien Lacroix, Conseiller en gestion des affaires diocésaines et scolaires, 416-397-6564, ext. 72021
slacroix@csdccs.edu.on.ca
Robert Castel, Directeur du Service des ressources matérielles, 416-397-6564, ext. 73600
rcastel@csdccs.edu.on.ca
Dereck Chin, Directeur du Service des ressources financières, 416-397-6564, ext. 73500
dchin@csdccs.edu.on.ca
Réal Pilon, Directeur du Service des ressources informatiques, 416-397-6564, ext. 73700
rpilon@csdccs.edu.on.ca
Veronique-Anne Towner-Sarault, Directrice du Service des ressources humaines, 416-397-6564, ext. 73410
vtowner-sarault@csdccs.edu.on.ca

Toronto: Toronto Catholic District School Board (TCDSB)

80 Sheppard Ave. East, Toronto, ON M2N 6E8, Canada
Tel: 416-222-8282; *Fax:* 416-229-5345
webmaster@tcdsb.org
www.tcdsb.org
twitter.com/TCDSB
Number of Schools: 166 elementary; 31 secondary; 3 combined elementary & secondary; *Grades:* K-12; Adult Education; *Enrollment:* 92034; *Number of Employees:* 5,997 teachers; 2,806 support & academic staff; 356 principals & vps; 202 administrative personnel; *Note:* Also offer night school and summer school.
Angela Gauthier, Director of Education, 416-222-8282, ext. 2296
angela.gauthier@tcdsb.org
Adrian Della Mora, Superintendent, Schools - Area 1, 416-222-8282, ext. 2732
adrian.dellamora@tcdsb.org
Douglas Yack, Superintendent, Schools - Area 2, 416-222-8282, ext. 2596
douglas.yack@tcdsb.org
Michael Caccamo, Superintendent, Schools - Area 3, 416-222-8282, ext. 2267
michael.caccamo@tcdsb.org
Peter Aguiar, Superintendent, Schools - Area 4, 416-222-8282, ext. 2267
peter.aguiar@tcdsb.org
John Wujek, Superintendent, Schools - Area 5, 416-222-8282, ext. 5371
john.wujek@tcdsb.org
John Shanahan, Superintendent, Schools - Area 6, 416-222-8282, ext. 5371
john.shanahan@tcdsb.org
Kevin Malcolm, Superintendent, Schools - Area 7, 416-222-8282, ext. 2263
kevin.malcolm@tcdsb.org
Dan Koenig, Superintendent, Schools - Area 8, 416-222-8282, ext. 2263
dan.koenig@tcdsb.org
Cristina Fernandes, Superintendent of Education - Special Services, 416-222-8282, ext. 2486
cristina.fernandes@tcdsb.org
Gary Poole, Associate Director of Academic Services, 416-222-8282, ext. 2641
gary.poole@tcdsb.org
Carlene Jackson, Executive Superintendent, Business Services, CFO, & Treasurer, 416-222-8282, ext. 2288
carlene.jackson@tcdsb.org
Angelo Sangiorgio, Associate Director, Planning & Facilities, 416-222-8282, ext. 2349
angelo.sangiorgio@tcdsb.org
John Yan, Senior Coordinator, Communications, 416-222-8282, ext. 5331
john.yan@tcdsb.org
Martin Farrell, Coordinator, Materials Management, 416-222-8282, ext. 2213
martin.farrell@tcdsb.org
Angela Kennedy, Chair of the Board, 416-512-3411
angela.kennedy@tcdsb.org

Wallaceburg: **St. Clair Catholic District School Board**
Catholic Education Centre
420 Creek St., Wallaceburg, ON N8A 4C4, Canada
Tel: 519-627-6762; *Fax:* 519-627-8230
Toll-Free: 1-866-336-6139
media@st-clair.net
www.st-clair.net
www.facebook.com/1777877255893630
twitter.com/sccdsb
Number of Schools: 26 elementary; 2 secondary; *Grades:* K-12
Carol Bryden, Chair, 519-627-8976
Dan Parr, Director of Education, 519-627-6762, ext. 10241
dan.parr@st-clair.net
Jim McKenzie, Associate Director, Treasurer & Corporate Services, 519-627-6762, ext. 10325
jim.mckenzie@st-clair.net
Deb Crawford, Superintendent of Education, 519-627-6762, ext. 10227
deb.crawford@st-clair.net
Scott Johnson, Superintendent of Education, 519-627-6762, ext. 10282
scott.johnson@st-clair.net
Steven Mitchell, Chief Information Officer
Tony Prizio, Procurement Specialist, 519-627-6762, ext. 10256
tony.prizio@st-clair.net
Todd Lozon, Supervisor, Communications & Community Relations, 519-627-6762, ext. 10243
todd.lozon@st-clair.net

Welland: **Niagara Catholic District School Board**
427 Rice Rd., Welland, ON L3C 7C1, Canada
Tel: 905-735-0240; *Fax:* 905-734-8828
info@ncdsb.com
www.niagaracatholic.ca
www.facebook.com/153813052403
twitter.com/niagaracatholic
www.youtube.com/niagaracatholicdsb
Number of Schools: 51 elementary; 8 secondary; *Grades:* Pre-K-12; *Enrollment:* 22458; *Number of Employees:* 1422 teachers; 492 support staff; 81 principals & vice principals; 7 directors & superintendents
John Crocco, Director of Education & Secretary-Treasurer, 905-735-0240, ext. 220
john.crocco@ncdsb.com
Fr. Paul MacNeil, Chair of the Board, 905-358-7611
macneil65@gmail.com
Yolanda Baldasaro, Superintendent of Education, 905-735-0240, ext. 227
yolanda.baldasaro@ncdsb.com
Ted Farrell, Superintendent of Education, 905-735-0240, ext. 230
ted.farrell@ncdsb.com
Lee Ann Forsyth-Sells, Superintendent of Education, 905-735-0240, ext. 228
leeann.forsythsells@ncdsb.com
Frank Iannantuono, Superintendent of Education, 905-735-0240, ext. 228
frank.iannantuono@ncdsb.com
Mark Lefebvre, Superintendent of Education, 905-735-0240, ext. 231
mark.lefebvre@ncdsb.com
Giancarlo Vetrone, Superintendent of Business & Financial Services, 905-735-0240, ext. 232
giancarlo.vetrone@ncdsb.com

Windsor: **Conseil scolaire catholique Providence**
7515, promenade Forest Glade, Windsor, ON N8T 3P5, Canada
Tél: 519-948-9227; *Téléc:* 519-948-1091
Ligne sans frais: 888-768-2219
Question@CscProvidence.ca
CscProvidence.ca
www.facebook.com/CscProvidence
www.twitter.com/CscProvidence
Number of Schools: 23 écoles élémentaire; 7 écoles secondaire; 1 centre de formation continue; *Enrollment:* 8965; *Number of Employees:* 657 enseignants
Janine Griffore, Directrice générale
Céline Vachon, Présidente
Carolyn Bastien, Surintendante adjointe de l'education
Paul Levac, Surintendante de l'education
Joseph Picard, Surintendante de l'education
Céline Verville, Surintendante de l'education

Windsor: **Windsor-Essex Catholic District School Board (WECBSB)**
1325 California Ave., Windsor, ON N9B 3Y6, Canada
Tel: 519-253-2481; *Fax:* 519-253-8397
www.wecdsb.on.ca
www.facebook.com/WECDSB
twitter.com/wecdsb
www.youtube.com/user/WECDSBMedia
Number of Schools: 38 elementary; 10 secondary; *Grades:* K-12; *Enrollment:* 21751; *Number of Employees:* 1555 teaching staff; 570 non-teaching staff
Paul A. Picard, Director of Education, 519-253-2481, ext. 1201
director@wecdsb.on.ca
Penny King, Superintendent of Business, 519-253-2481, ext. 1211
penny_king@wecdsb.on.ca
Barbara Holland, Chair, 519-567-2305
barbara_holland@wecdsb.on.ca
Terry Lyons, Executive Superintendent of Human Resources, 519-253-2481, ext. 1286
supthr@wecdsb.on.ca
Jamie Bumbacco, Superintendent of Education - Student Achievement K-12, 519-253-2481, ext. 1524
jamie_bumbacco@wecdsb.on.ca
Emelda Byrne, Superintendent of Education - Student Achievement K-12, 519-253-2481, ext. 1526
emelda_byrne@wecdsb.on.ca
Rosemary Lo Faso, Superintendent of Education - Student Achievement K-12, 519-253-2481, ext. 1120
rosemary_lofaso@wecdsb.on.ca
Sharon O'Hagan-Wong, Superintendent of Education - Student Achievement K-12, 519-253-2481, ext. 1207
sharonohaganwong@wecdsb.on.ca
Mike Seguin, Superintendent of Education - Student Achievement K-12, 519-253-2481, ext. 1203
mike_seguin@wecdsb.on.ca
Shannon Ficon, Manager of Purchasing & Payroll, 519-253-2481, ext. 1217
shannon_ficon@wecdsb.on.ca

French

North Bay: **Conseil scolaire public du Nord-Est de l'Ontario**
P.O. Box 3600
820, promenade Lakeshore, North Bay, ON P1B 9T5, Canada
Tél: 705-472-3443; *Téléc:* 705-472-5757
Ligne sans frais: 888-591-5656
information@cspne.ca
www.cspne.ca
www.facebook.com/cspne.ca
twitter.com/cspne
Number of Schools: 20; *Grades:* M-12; *Note:* Timmins: 111, av Wilson, (705) 264-1119.
Simon Fecteau, Directeur de l'éducation par intérim, 705-264-1119
simon.fecteau@cspne.ca
Denis Labelle, Président du Conseil
denis.labelle@cspne.ca
Linda Lacroix, Surintendant de l'éducation, 705-472-3443, ext. 233
Linda.lacroix@cspne.ca
Tracy Dottori, Surintendante adjointe des affaires - ressources humaines
tracy.dottori@cspne.ca
Jamie Point, Gestionnaire des technologies de l'information & de la comm., 705-472-3443, ext. 229
jamie.point@cspne.ca

Ottawa: **Conseil des écoles publiques de l'Est de l'Ontario**
2445, boul Saint-Laurent, Ottawa, ON K1G 6C3, Canada
Tél: 613-742-8960; *Ligne sans frais:* 888-332-3736
www.cepeo.on.ca
www.facebook.com/cepeo
twitter.com/ottawacepeo
www.linkedin.com/company/cepeo
vimeo.com/cepeo
Number of Schools: 38; *Grades:* Mat-12è anées; écoles spécialisées; *Enrollment:* 13000
Denis Chartrand, Président du Conseil
denis.m.chartrand@cepeo.on.ca
Édith Dumont, Directrice de l'éducation et secrétaire-trésorière
edith.dumont@cepeo.on.ca
Rachid El Keurti, Directeur éxécutif
rachid.elkeurti@cepeo.on.ca
Christian-Charle Bouchard, Surintendant de l'éducation
charle.bouchard@cepeo.on.ca
Jean-Pierre Dufour, Surintendant de l'éducation
jean-pierre.dufour@cepeo.on.ca
Ann Mahoney, Surintendant de l'éducation
ann.mahoney@cepeo.on.ca
Matthieu Vachon, Surintendant de l'éducation
matthieu.vachon@cepeo.on.ca

Sudbury: **Conseil scolaire public du Grand Nord de l'Ontario (CSPGNO)**
296, rue Van Horne, Sudbury, ON P3B 1H9, Canada
Tél: 705-671-1533; *Téléc:* 705-671-1720
Ligne sans frais: 800-465-5993
information@cspgno.ca
www.cspgno.ca
www.facebook.com/CSPGNO
twitter.com/CSPGNO
Number of Schools: 11 écoles élémentaire; 8 écoles secondaire; *Grades:* JK-12; *Enrollment:* 2327; *Number of Employees:* 534
Marc Gauthier, Directeur de l'éducation, 705-671-1533, ext. 2202
marc.gauthier@cspgno.ca
Jean-Marc Aubin, Président
Alain Gélinas, Surintendant des Affaires, 705-671-9186, ext. 2245
alain.gelinas@cspgno.ca
Barbara Breault, Surintendant, 705-671-9235, ext. 2203
Barbara.Breault@cspgno.ca
Carole Audet, Directrice des Ressources humaines, 705-671-1794, ext. 2260
Carole.Audet@cspgno.ca
Carole Brouillard-Landry, Directrice des services pédagogiques, 705-671-9235, ext. 2230
Carole.Brouillard-Landry@cspgno.ca
Carole Dubé, Directrice des communications et agente de liaison, 705-671-1720, ext. 2233
Carole.Dube@cspgno.ca
Monique Dubreuil, Directrice - Services aux élèves, 705-671-2398, ext. 2229
monique.dubreuil@cspgno.ca

Toronto: **Conseil scolaire Viamonde**
116, Cornelius Pkwy., Toronto, ON M6L 2K5, Canada
Tél: 416-614-0844; *Téléc:* 416-397-2012
Ligne sans frais: 888-583-5383
csviamonde.ca
www.facebook.com/CSViamonde
twitter.com/CSViamonde
Number of Schools: 32 élémentaire; 13 secondaire; 1 élémentaire et secondaire; *Grades:* M-12; *Enrollment:* 10100; *Number of Employees:* 1,000+ (750 enseignants)
Martin Bertrand, Directeur de l'éducation, 416-614-5929
bertrandm@csviamonde.ca
Claire Francoeur, Directrice des communications et du marketing, 416-465-5772, ext. 1
francoeurc@csviamonde.ca
Françoise Fournier, Surintendante des affaires, 905-732-7809
fournierf@csviamonde.ca
Jo-Anne Doyon, Surintendante de l'éducation, 416-614-5913
doyonj@csviamonde.ca
Miguel Ladouceur, Dir. de l'immobilisation, de l'entretien, de la planification, 416-614-5917
adouceurm@csviamonde.ca
Marie-Eve Blais, Directrice des ressources humaines, 416-614-5895
blaism@csviamonde.ca

School Authorities

Moose Factory: **Moose Factory Island District School Area Board**
P.O. Box 160
Moose Factory, ON P0L 1W0, Canada
Tel: 705-658-4571; *Fax:* 705-658-4768
mfidsab.ca/mfidsab/
Grades: JK-8
Victor Weapenicappo, Chair
v.weap@mfidsab.ca
Lise Haman, Supervisory Officer
lise.haman@mfidsab.ca
Kathy Cheechoo, Business Administrator & Treasurer
kathy.cheechoo@mfidsab.ca

Moosonee: **James Bay Lowlands Secondary School Board (JBLSSB)**
P.O. Box 157
1 Pinew St., Moosonee, ON P0L 1Y0, Canada
Tel: 705-336-2903; *Fax:* 705-336-0234
jblssb.ca
Number of Schools: 1 secondary; *Grades:* 9-12; *Enrollment:* 179
Bill O'Hallarn, Superintendent of Education
Christina Nielsen, Chair
Brenda Chilton-Jeffries, Business Administrator/Treasurer
Val Hunter, Board Office Clerk

Moosonee: **Moosonee District School Area Board**
P.O. Box 250
22 2nd St., Moosonee, ON P0L 1Y0, Canada
Tel: 705-336-2300; *Fax:* 705-336-0334
Grades: K-8; *Enrollment:* 275

Kelly Reuben, Chair
Cheryl Wapachee, Secretary-Treasurer & Business Administrator

Oshawa: Campbell Children's School Authority
600 Townline Rd. South, Oshawa, ON L1H 7K6, Canada
Tel: 905-576-8403; *Fax:* 905-576-4414
Note: Hospital-based school authority that serves students from the local District School Boards with communication and/or multiple disabilities in specialized programs.
Lynda Schuler, Chair

Ottawa: Ottawa Children's Treatment Centre School Authority
395 Smyth Rd., Ottawa, ON K2H 8L2, Canada
Tel: 613-737-0871; *Fax:* 613-523-5167
www.octc.ca/school.php
Number of Schools: 1; *Grades:* JK - 3; *Enrollment:* 30; *Note:* The OCTC School provides full day educational instruction in both English and French to children who have a primary diagnosis of a physical disability and other associated complex needs.
Leslie Walker, Principal, 613-737-0871, ext. 4308
lwalker@octc.ca
Kathleen Stokely, CEO

Penetanguishene: The Protestant Separate School Board of the Town of Penetanguishene (PSSBP)
P.O. Box 107
2 Poyntz St., Penetanguishene, ON L9M 1M2, Canada
Tel: 705-549-6422; *Fax:* 705-549-2768
pssbp@bellnet.ca
pssbp.ca
www.facebook.com/144201435591912
Number of Schools: 1; *Grades:* JK-8; *Enrollment:* 234
Lynne Cousens, Chair
June Merkley, Supervisory Officer
jmerkley@pssbp.ca
Sean Turner, Manager of Finance and Treasurer
sturner@pssbp.ca

St Catharines: Niagara Peninsula Children's Centre School Authority
567 Glenridge Ave., St Catharines, ON L2T 4C2, Canada
Tel: 905-688-3550; *Fax:* 905-688-1055
Toll-Free: 800-896-5496
info@niagarachildrenscentre.com
niagarachildrenscentre.com/school
Number of Schools: 1; *Grades:* Special Education; *Enrollment:* 84; *Note:* The Niagara Children's Centre School Authority provides individualized education and therapeutic programming in small group settings to children and youth 4-21 years of age with communication and/or physical disabilities.
Maxine Gaylor, Chair
Oksana Fisher, CEO, 905-688-1890, ext. 102
Staci Whittle, Principal, 905-688-3550, ext. 230
staci.whittle@niagarachildrenscentre.com
Diane Hennessy, School Secretary, 905-688-3550, ext. 231
diane.hennessy@niagarachildrenscentre.com

Toronto: Bloorview School Authority
150 Kilgour Rd., Toronto, ON M4G 1R8, Canada
Tel: 416-424-3831; *Fax:* 416-425-2981
school@hollandbloorview.ca
www.bloorviewschool.ca
www.facebook.com/HBKRH
twitter.com/#!/bloorviewpr
www.linkedin.com/company/holland-bloorview
www.youtube.com/user/PRBloorview
Note: Bloorview School Authority provides school programs to children & youth with special needs.
Rachee Allen, Chair

Waterloo: KidsAbility School Authority Board
500 Hallmark Dr., Waterloo, ON N2K 3P5, Canada
Tel: 519-886-8886; *Fax:* 519-886-7291
Toll-Free: 1-888-372-2259
info@kidsability.ca
www.kidsability.ca/en/school
www.facebook.com/184568644892738
twitter.com/kidsability
www.youtube.com/user/KidsAbility1957#p/a
Number of Schools: 5; *Note:* KidsAbility School Authority Board serves children with a wide range of special needs. Programs & services include a kindergarten program, individual education plans, composite classes, communication classes, & language classes.
Deirdre Large, Chair - Advisory Council
Linda Rogers, Principal & Secretary to the Board, 519-886-8886, ext. 1225
lrogers@kidsability.ca
Joanne Cotter, Executive Assistant, 519-886-8886, ext. 1227
jcotter@kidsability.ca
Cynthia Davis, Chair - Authority Board
schoolauthoritychair@kidsability.ca

Windsor: John McGivney Children's Centre School Authority
John McGivney Children's Centre
3945 Matchette Rd., Windsor, ON N9C 4C2, Canada
Tel: 519-282-7281; *Fax:* 519-252-5873
school@jmccentre.ca
www.jmccentre.ca
www.facebook.com/243715438993933
Number of Schools: 1; *Note:* The John McGivney Children's Centre School Authority governs the John McGivney Children's Centre School, formerly known as the Children's Rehabilitation Centre School. The school provides a post trauma / post operative rehabilitation program for students from ages four to twenty-one, who live in Windsor / Essex County.
Grant Gagnon, Chair
Elaine Whitmore, CEO, 519-252-7281, ext. 221
Dr. Brenda Roberts-Santarossa, Secretary & Principal
Adelina Irvine, Treasurer

First Nations

Akwesasne: Ahkwesahsne Mohawk Board of Education (AMBE)
P.O. Box 819
169 International Rd., Akwesasne, ON K6H 5R7, Canada
Tel: 613-933-0409; *Fax:* 603-933-9262
www.ambe.ca
www.facebook.com/565932096829084
twitter.com/ambe_ca
Number of Schools: 3; *Grades:* K-8; Alternative Ed.; *Note:* The Ahkwesahsne Mohawk Board of Education operates three elementary schools. Since the Ahkwesahsne Mohawk Board of Education does not have a secondary school, there is an agreement with the Upper Canada Public School Board to provide secondary education.
Donna Wahienha:wi Lahache, Interim Director of Education
donna.lahache@ambe.ca
Deborah Terrance, Associate Director of Education
debbie.terrance@ambe.ca

Attawapiskat: Attawapiskat First Nation Education Authority
P.O. Box 247
General Delivery, Attawapiskat, ON P0L 1A0, Canada
Tel: 705-997-2114
reception.board@afnea.com
www.afnea.com
Number of Schools: 1 elementary; 1 secondary; *Grades:* JK - 12; Special Ed.; *Enrollment:* 800; *Note:* J.R. Nakogee School & Vezina Secondary School
John B. Nakogee, Director of Education
Travis Koostachin, Chair

Big Trout Lake: Kitchenuhmaykoosib Education Authority
General Delivery, Big Trout Lake, ON P0V 1G0, Canada
Tel: 807-537-2553; *Fax:* 807-537-2316
kifirstnation@knet.ca
www.bigtroutlake.firstnation.ca
Number of Schools: 1; *Grades:* JK-11; Special Ed.; *Enrollment:* 275; *Note:* Aglace Chapman Education Centre. The Kitchenuhmaykoosib Education Authority serves the Kitchenuhmaykoosib Inninnuwug First Nation, formerly known as Big Trout Lake First Nation, located north of Thunder Bay, Ontario. Secondary programs are also available through computer, radio, & television.

Christian Island: Beausoleil Education Department
Beausoleil Education Department
11 O'Gemaa Miikaan, Christian Island, ON L0K 0A9, Canada
Tel: 705-247-2051; *Fax:* 705-247-2239
n.assance@beausoleil-education.ca
www.beausoleil-education.ca
Number of Schools: 1 elementary; *Grades:* JK - 8; Special Ed; *Note:* The Beausoleil Education Department serves the Chippewas of the Beausoleil First Nation by operating the Christian Island Elementary School. For secondary education, students attend high schools in the Simcoe County District School Board or the Simcoe Muskoka Catholic School Board.
Nancy Assance, Acting Director, Education
n.assance@beausoleil-education.ca
Sarah Boyle, Adult Education Director
s.boyle@beausoleil-education.ca
Doug King, Native Language Director
d.king@beausoleil-education.ca

Constance Lake: Constance Lake First Nation Education Authority
P.O. Box 5000
Constance Lake, ON P0L 1B0, Canada
Tel: 705-463-1199; *Fax:* 705-463-2077
www.clfn.on.ca
Number of Schools: 1 K-12; *Grades:* JK-12; *Enrollment:* 257; *Note:* Mamawmatawa Holistic Education Center. Located in the District of Cochrane, the Constance Lake First Nation Education Authority provides education to community members of Cree & Ojibway ancestry. The Constance Lake First Nation Education Authority is supported by the Matawa Education Department in Thunder Bay, Ontario. Also offers day care services and adult education.
Lizzie Sutherland, Chairperson
lizzie.sutherland@clfn.on.ca
Bonnie John-George, Day Care Administrator, 705-463-1199, ext. 125
bonnie.joh-george@clfn.on.ca
Ken Neegan, Education Administrator, 705-463-1199, ext. 115
ken.neegan@clfn.on.ca

Deer Lake: Deer Lake Education Authority
P.O. Box 69
Deer Lake, ON P0V 1N0
Tel: 807-775-2055
TTY: 1-888-751-9225
Number of Schools: 1; *Grades:* K4 - K5; 1 - 9; Special Education; *Note:* Deer Lake School. The Deer Lake Education Authority oversees education for the Deer Lake First Nation, an Oji-Cree community situated about 180 kilometres north of Red Lake, Ontario. Deer Lake School provides education to grade nine. The Authority coordinates the enrollment & boarding for students who leave the reserve for schooling beyond ninth grade, in places such as Ear Falls, Sioux Lookout, Red Lake, Thunder Bay, & Winnipeg.
Leonard Mamakeesic, Director, Education

Dinorwic: Wabigoon Lake Ojibway Nation Education Authority
P.O. Box 24
Site 112, Dinorwic, ON P0V 1P0, Canada
Tel: 807-938-6684; *Fax:* 807-938-1166
Number of Schools: 1; *Grades:* JK-8; *Note:* Wabsnki-Penasi School. Elementary education is provided in a school operated by the Wabigoon Lake Ojibway Nation. Secondary school students are bused to nearby Dryden, Ontario.

Eabamet Lake: Eabametoong (Fort Hope) First Nation Education Authority
P.O. Box 294
Eabamet Lake, ON P0T 1L0, Canada
Tel: 807-242-1305; *Fax:* 807-242-1313
efnea64@gmail.com
www.eabametoong.firstnation.ca
Other Information: Education Coordinator, Phone: 807-242-1305, ext. 24
Number of Schools: 1; *Grades:* K - 10; Special Ed.; *Enrollment:* 380; *Note:* John C. Yesno Education Centre. Number of Employees: 25 teachers; 10 teaching assistants & tutor escorts; 3 counsellors. Eabametoong (Fort Hope) is a fly-in Ojibwe First Nations community located approximately 360 kilometres northeast of Thunder Bay, Ontario. The Eabametoong (Fort Hope) First Nation Education Authority consists of a Board of Directors & a head office staff. The Matawa Education Department in Thunder, Bay, Ontario supports the education authority.

Fort Albany: Mundo Peetabeck Education Authority
P.O. Box 31
Fort Albany, ON P0L 1H0, Canada
Tel: 705-278-3390; *Fax:* 705-278-1049
Number of Schools: 1 elementary; *Enrollment:* 150
Nicole Gillies, Education Director

Fort Severn: Wasaho Education Authority
P.O. Box 165
General Delivery, Fort Severn, ON P0V 1W0, Canada
Tel: 807-478-9548; *Fax:* 807-478-9546
Number of Schools: 1; *Note:* The Wasaho Education Authority provides education to members of the Fort Severn First Nation. The Fort Severn First Nation Reserve is situated in northern Ontario, near the mouth of the Severn River.
Moses Kakekaspan, Education Director
Sherri Curtis, Principal
Shirley Miles, Social Counsellor

Hudson: Lac Seul Education Authority
c/o LSEA
P.O. Box 319
Hudson, ON P0V 1X0, Canada
Tel: 807-582-3499; *Fax:* 807-582-3431
lacseul.firstnation.ca

Number of Schools: 3; *Grades:* K-12; *Enrollment:* 97
Jennifer Manitowabi, Education Director
jmanitowabi@lsfn.ca
Richard Morris, Dir.

Kasabonika: **Sineonokway Education Authority**
P.O. Box 33
Kasabonika, ON P0V 1Y0, Canada
Tel: 807-535-1117; *Fax:* 807-535-1152
Grades: K-12; *Enrollment:* 250
Josie Semple, Education Director
Ruby Anderson, Education Executive Secretary, 807-535-2547, ext. 245

Kashechewan: **Hishkoonikun Education Authority (HEA)**
P.O. Box 210
430 Riverside Rd., Kashechewan, ON P0L 1S0, Canada
Tel: 705-275-4538; *Fax:* 705-275-4515
Toll-Free: 1-800-433-4863
www.kashechewan.firstnation.ca/kfn/education
www.facebook.com/140558452626096
Number of Schools: 1 elementary; 1 secondary; *Grades:* JK-12; *Enrollment:* 580; *Number of Employees:* 77 employees
Leo Metatawabin, Chair

Keewaywin: **Keewaywin First Nation Education Authority**
P.O. Box 90
Keewaywin, ON P0V 3G0, Canada
Tel: 807-771-1210; *Fax:* 807-771-1053
Toll-Free: 866-437-9505
David Thompson, Chief
Chris Kakegamic, Director, Education

Kejick: **Shoal Lake #40 Education Authority**
Shoal Lake #40
General Delivery, Kejick, ON P0X 1E0, Canada
Tel: 807-733-2315; *Fax:* 807-733-3115
sl40secretary@hotmail.com
www.sl40.ca/contact.htm
Grades: Elementary; *Enrollment:* 50
Frances Green, Band Manager
frances.redsky@hotmail.com
Randy Paishk, Director of Education

Kenora: **Northwest Angle #33 Education Authority**
P.O. Box 1490
Kenora, ON P9N 3X7, Canada
Tel: 807-733-2200; *Fax:* 807-733-3148
www.akrc.on.ca
Grades: Elem.; *Enrollment:* 16
Josephine Sandy, Education Counsellor

Kingfisher: **Kingfisher Lake Education Authority**
P.O. Box 57
Kingfisher, ON P0V 1Z0, Canada
Tel: 807-532-2067; *Fax:* 807-532-2063
www.kingfisherlake.ca
Grades: Elementary; *Enrollment:* 100
Solomon Mamakwa, Director

Longlac: **Long Lake #58 & Ginoogaming First Nations Education Authority**
P.O. Box 89
Longlac, ON P0T 2A0
Tel: 807-876-4914
www.ginoogaming.ca
Number of Schools: 2; *Grades:* JK-12; Special Ed; Ojibway language; *Enrollment:* 173; *Note:* Migizsi Wazisin Elementary School & Nimiki Migizsi Secondary School. Number of Employees: 24 teachers, board administrative personnel, support staff, & custodial personnel. The Long Lake #58 & Ginoogaming First Nations Education Authority consists of three board members from Long Lake #58 First Nation & three board members from Ginoogaming First Nation (formerly the Long Lake #77 First Nation). Both First Nations are members of Matawa First Nations, so that educational support services for the Long Lake #58 & Ginoogaming First Nations Education Authority are provided by the Matawa Education Department in Thunder Bay, Ontario.
Georgette O'Nabigon, Contact
gonabigon@matawa.on.ca

M'Chigeeng: **West Bay Board of Education**
22 Bebonang St., M'Chigeeng, ON P0P 1G0, Canada
Tel: 705-377-5611; *Fax:* 705-377-5080
Grades: Elem.; *Enrollment:* 180
Melvina Corbiere, Education Coordinator

MacDiarmid: **Biinjitiwaabik Zaaging Anishnaabek Education Authority**
Also known as: Rocky Bay First Nation Education Authority
Rocky Bay Reserve
501 Spirit Bay Rd., MacDiarmid, ON P0T 2B0, Canada
Tel: 807-885-3401; *Fax:* 807-885-1218
www.rockybayfn.ca
Number of Schools: 2; *Grades:* Elem.; *Enrollment:* 41; *Note:* Biinjitiwaabik Zaaging Anishnaabek Education Authority operates the Rocky Bay Alternative High School and Biinjitiwaabik Zaaging Anishnaabek School (Rocky Bay).
Malvina Echum, Contact
mechum@rockybayfn.ca

Migisi Sahgaigan: **Eagle Lake First Nation Education Board**
P.O. Box 2086
Migisi Sahgaigan, ON P0V 3H0, Canada
Tel: 807-755-5350; *Fax:* 807-755-2086
www.eaglelakefirstnation.ca
Grades: Elem.; *Enrollment:* 44; *Note:* Eagle Lake First Nation Education Board operates the Migisi Sahgaigan School.
Andrew Kivell, Director of Education/Principal
principal@migisi.ca

Mishkeegogamang: **Mishkeegogamang Education Authority**
c/o Education Services
General Delivery, Mishkeegogamang, ON P0V 2H0
Tel: 807-928-2299; *Fax:* 807-928-2494
missabayschool@live.ca
www.mishkeegogamang.ca
Number of Schools: 3; *Grades:* K-8; *Enrollment:* 255
Ida Mackuck, Education Coordinator
Connie Gray McKay, Chief, 807-928-2414
conniegraymckay@knet.ca

Morson: **Big Grassy River (Mishkosiimiiniiziibig) Education Authority**
Pegamigaabo School
P.O. Box 453
513 Beach Rd., Morson, ON P0W 1J0, Canada
Tel: 807-488-5916; *Fax:* 807-488-5345
Toll-Free: 1-800-265-3379
school@biggrassy.ca
biggrassy.ca/education
Other Information: Alternate Phone: 807-488-5986
Number of Schools: 1 elementary; *Grades:* JK - 8; Special Ed.; *Enrollment:* 61

Muncey: **Chippewas of the Thames First Nation Board of Education**
330 Chippewa Rd., Muncey, ON N0L 1Y0, Canada
Tel: 519-289-0621; *Fax:* 519-289-0633
cottares.ca
www.facebook.com/124527361025016?ref=hl
Number of Schools: 1 elementary school; *Grades:* Elementary; *Note:* Chippewas of the Thames First Nation Board of Education operates the Antler River Elementary School.
JoAnn Henry, Principal
Starr McGahey-Albert, Education Coordinator
Jody Joseph, Secondary/ Post Sec. Counsellor, 519-289-0621
Tammy Deleary, Education Finance Secretary

Muskrat Dam: **Muskrat Dam First Nation Education Authority**
c/o Samson Beardy Memorial School
P.O. Box 140
Muskrat Dam, ON P0V 3B0, Canada
Tel: 807-471-2527; *Fax:* 807-471-2649
Other Information: Whasa Distant Education Centre, Phone: 807-471-2619
Number of Schools: 1; *Grades:* JK - 8; *Note:* Samson Beardy Memorial School. The Muskrat Dam First Nation community is situated approximately 370 kilometres north of Sioux Lookout. Oji-Cee & English are spoken. The community features an elementary school, plus the Wahsa Distance Education Centre to support secondary & post-secondary students attending schools in towns & cities.
Edith Thunder, Principal, 807-471-2524
Roy Morris, Education Director, 807-471-2573, ext. 211

Neyaashiinigmiing: **Chippewas of Nawash Unceded First Nation Board of Education**
6 Harbour Rd., Neyaashiinigmiing, ON N0H 2T0, Canada
Tel: 519-534-0882; *Fax:* 519-534-5138
www.nawash.ca/education/
Number of Schools: 1 elementary; *Grades:* JK-8; *Number of Employees:* 19; *Note:* The board of education serves the Chippewas of Nawash Unceded First Nation band members of the Neyaashiinigmiing Indian Reserve No. 27. The reserve is situated on the eastern shore of the Saugeen (Bruce) Peninsula in Ontario, approximately 26 kilometres from Wiarton. The Chippewas of Nawash Unceded First Nation Board of Education strives to offer a culturally & community based education, based upon traditional values.
Judy Nadjiwan, Education Administrator, 519-534-0882
nawashed.administrator@gbtel.ca
Jennifer Linklater, Coordinator, Nawash Post-Secondary Education Program
nawashed.postsec@gbtel.ca
Connie Salkey, Education Counsellor, Secondary Student Services Program
nawashed.edcounsellor@gbtel.ca
Vanessa M. Keeshig, Administrative Support
nawashed.vkeeshig@gbtel.ca

North Spirit Lake: **North Spirit Lake Education Authority**
General Delivery, North Spirit Lake, ON P0V 2G0, Canada
Tel: 807-776-0001; *Fax:* 807-776-0003
nsl.firstnation.ca
Number of Schools: 2; *Grades:* Elem.; *Enrollment:* 60
Troy Kakepetum, Education Director

Ogoki Post: **Marten Falls (Ogoki) First Nation Education Authority**
c/o Henry Coaster Memorial School
General Delivery, Ogoki Post, ON P0T 2L0, Canada
Tel: 807-349-2532; *Fax:* 807-349-2602
Number of Schools: 1; *Grades:* K-8; *Note:* The Marten Falls (Ogoki) First Nation Education Authority offers elementary education in the Cree-Ojibwe community. Members of the First Nation board in Thunder Bay, Ontario to attend secondary school. The Matawa Education Department provides educational support services to the Marten Falls (Ogoki) First Nation Education Authority.
Paul Sproat, Principal
Angela Wesley, Education Administrator, 807-349-2628

Pawitik: **Naotkamegwanning Northwest Angle Education Authority**
c/o Education Authority
1800 Pawitik St., Pawitik, ON P0X 1L0, Canada
Tel: 807-226-5411; *Fax:* 807-226-5389
Grades: K-12; *Enrollment:* 300
Loranda Kavanaugh, Executive Assistant
Donna Copenace, Acting Education Director

Peawanuck: **Weenusk First Nation Education Services**
P.O. Box 1
34 Main St., Peawanuck, ON P0L 2H0, Canada
Tel: 705-473-2554; *Fax:* 705-473-2503
Grades: Elementary; *Enrollment:* 60
Edmond Hunter, Chief

Pic River First Nation: **Pic River First Nation Education Authority**
Pic River Children & Family Learning Centre
P.O. Box 156
10 Lynx Rd., Pic River First Nation, ON P0T 1R0, Canada
Tel: 807-229-0198; *Fax:* 807-229-1944
www.picriver.com
Number of Schools: 1 elementary; 2 secondary; 1 early childhood education; *Grades:* K-12; *Enrollment:* 94
Lisa Michano-Courchene, Education Director
lisamichano@picriver.com

Pikangikum: **Pikangikum Education Authority**
c/o Eenchokay Birchstick School
General Delivery, Pikangikum First Nations, Pikangikum, ON P0V 2L0, Canada
Tel: 807-773-5561; *Fax:* 807-773-5958
www.ebs-school.org/pikangikum-education-authority.html
Number of Schools: 1; *Grades:* K-12; *Enrollment:* 520; *Number of Employees:* 60 teachers
Kyle Peters, Director of Education, 807-773-1093
Jimmy Keeper, Assistant Director of Education, 807-773-1093

Rama: **Chippewas of Rama First Nation Chief & Council**
#200, 5884 Rama Rd., Rama, ON L3V 6H6, Canada
Tel: 705-325-3611; *Fax:* 705-325-0879
Toll-Free: 866-854-2121
www.mnjikaning.ca
Note: The Chippewas of Rama First Nation Chief & Council are responsible for education & career planning.
Galen Plett, Contact, 705-325-3611, ext. 1436

***Sandy Lake:* Sandy Lake Board of Education**
P.O. Box 8
Sandy Lake, ON P0V 1V0, Canada
Tel: 807-774-1135; *Fax:* 807-774-1166
www.sandylake.firstnation.ca
Other Information: Alternate Phone: 807-774-1089
Number of Schools: 3; *Grades:* K-12; Adult Ed.; *Enrollment:* 514; *Note:* The Sandy Lake Board of Education oversees the management of schools which serve students of Sandy Lake First Nation.
Christine Meekis, Education Director
Troy Kakepetum, Assistant Director
Russell Kakepetum, Band Councillor - Education Portfolio
Florance Ballentyne, Finance Officer

***Sarnia:* Aamjiwnaang First Nation Education Administration**
978 Tashmoo Ave., Sarnia, ON N7T 7H5, Canada
Tel: 519-336-8410; *Fax:* 519-336-0382
www.aamjiwnaang.ca/education-department/
www.facebook.com/Aamjiwnaang-Education-113370038827438/
Number of Schools: 6; *Grades:* K-12; *Note:* Formerly Chippewas of Sarnia, the community of Aamjiwnaang First Nation is located in the city limits of Sarnia, Ontario.

***Sioux Lookout:* Windigo Education Authority**
P.O. Box 299
160 Alcona Dr., Sioux Lookout, ON P8T 1A3, Canada
Tel: 807-737-1064; *Fax:* 807-737-3452
wea@windigo.on.ca
www.windigoeducation.on.ca
Number of Schools: 4 elementary-middle; *Grades:* JK-8; *Enrollment:* 362; *Note:* Windigo Education Authority consists of the following First Nation members: Bearskin Lake First Nation, Cat Lake First Nation, Sachigo Lake First Nation, & Slate Falls Nation. The language of each First Nation community is Ojibway or Oji-Cree. Language and culture programs are offered by WEA.
Charles Meekis, Program Services Director
Brittany Jeffery, Financial Administrator
Rachelle Ningewance, Office Assistant

***Sioux Narrows:* Northwest Angle #37 Education Authority**
P.O. Box 267
Sioux Narrows, ON P0X 1N0, Canada
Tel: 807-226-5353; *Fax:* 807-226-1164

***Southwold:* Onyota'aka Kalthuny Nihtsla Tehatilihutakwas (OKT) Education Authority**
2315 Keystone Pl., Southwold, ON N0L 2G0, Canada
Tel: 519-652-1580; *Fax:* 519-652-3219
Grades: Elementary; *Enrollment:* 185
Neil Cornelius, Chair
Lynda Doxtator, Education Adm.

***Thunder Bay:* Matawa Education Department**
#500, 28 Cumberland St. N, Thunder Bay, ON P7A 4K9, Canada
Tel: 807-768-3300; *Fax:* 807-768-3301
Toll-Free: 1-800-283-9747
education@matawa.on.ca
education.matawa.on.ca
Number of Schools: 9; *Grades:* K-12; *Note:* The Matawa Education Department delivers educational support services to local education authorities. Education is provided at local Matawa First Nation schools in a culturally appropriate environment to meet the diverse needs of students. Post-secondary student support services, as well as alternative learning & adult education & training are also offered.
Brad Battiston, Principal
bbattiston@matawa.on.ca
Murray Waboose, Education Advisor
mwaboose@matawa.on.ca
Georgette O'Nabigon, Coordinator, Post Secondary Program
gonabigon@matawa.on.ca
Jordon Sturgeon, Systems Administrator
jsturgeon@matawa.on.ca

***Tyendinaga Mohawk Territory:* Tyendinaga Mohawk Education, Culture, & Language Department**
Administration Building
13 Old York Rd., Tyendinaga Mohawk Territory, ON K0K 1X0, Canada
Tel: 613-396-3424; *Fax:* 613-396-3627
www.mbq-tmt.org/
Number of Schools: 2; *Grades:* Pre-K-12; *Note:* Educational programs available for the Mohawks of the Bay of Quinte include the Eksa'okon:'a Child Care Centre, the Tahatikonhsotontie Head Start Program, a Post-Secondary Education Program, a Native Student Liaison Program, an Employment & Training Program, the Ka:nhiote Public Library, & Mohawk Bus Lines. Mohawk language & cultural instruction is part of Tahatikonhsotontie Head Start, an early childhood education program.
Diana Barlow, Good Minds Coordinator, 967-01226716, ext. 102
dianabg@mbq-tmt.org
Angela Maracle, Interim Eksa'okon Centre Manager, 613-967-4401
Mike Hill, Mohawk Bus Lines Manager, 613-396-2000
mbl@mbq.tmt.org
Karen Lewis, Kanhiote Librarian, 613-967-6264
kanhiote@gmail.com
Patti Brinklow, Post-Secondary Education Counsellor, 613-396-3424
pattig@mbq-tmt.org
Kerri Smart, Mohawk Language Teacher, 613-396-6716
kerris@mbq-tmt.org
Lynda Leweeп, Employment & Training Officer, 613-396-3424, ext. 101
lyndal@mbq-tmt.org

***Wallaceburg:* Walpole Island Elementary School**
RR#3, Wallaceburg, ON N8A 4K9, Canada
Tel: 519-627-0712; *Fax:* 519-627-8596
office@walpoleislandschool.org
Grades: JK-8; *Enrollment:* 450; *Note:* The Walpole Island Elementary School is a First Nation operated school which serves members of the Walpole Island First Nation community. School employees are required to have knowledge & understanding of the Anishinaabeg culture. The education program is administered by the Walpole Island First Nation Board of Education. For secondary education, students from Walpole Island First Nation are transported to the nearby communities of Sarnia, Chatham, & Wallaceburg.

***Wallaceburg:* Walpole Island First Nation Board of Education**
RR#3, Wallaceburg, ON N8A 4K9
Tel: 519-627-1481; *Fax:* 519-627-0440
Number of Schools: 1; *Grades:* JK - 8; *Note:* Walpole Island Elementary School. Secondary school students from the Walpole Island First Nation community are transported to Chatham, Sarnia, & Wallaceburg to attend school.
Joseph Gilbert, Chief
Bill Tooshkenig, Chair
Cynthia Williams, Officer, Human Resources
cynthia.williams@wifn.org

***Weagamow Lake:* North Caribou Lake First Nation Education Authority**
P.O. Box 155
Weagamow Lake, ON P0V 2Y0, Canada
Tel: 807-469-1254; *Fax:* 807-469-1351
northcariboulakefirstnation@knet.ca
Grades: Elem.; *Enrollment:* 136
Saul Williams, Education Director

***Webequie:* Webequie First Nation Education Authority**
P.O. Box 102
Webequie, ON P0T 3A0
Tel: 807-353-9942; *Fax:* 807-353-9966
webequieeducation@knet.ca
www.webequie.ca
Number of Schools: 1; *Grades:* K-10; Native Language; Special Ed.; *Enrollment:* 200; *Note:* Simon Jacob Memorial Education Centre. The Webequie First Nation Education Authority is located in a Oji-Cree community on the Winisk River in northern Ontario. The education authority receives educational support services from the Matawa Education Department in Thunder Bay, Ontario. Programs include special education, native education, distance education, & post-secondary education support services.
Ennis Jacob, Director, Education
ennisjacob@hotmail.com
Paul Quisses, Administrator, Finance

***Whitedog:* Wabaseemoong Education Authority**
General Delivery, Whitedog, ON P0X 1P0, Canada
Tel: 807-927-2062; *Fax:* 807-927-2176
Number of Schools: 1; *Grades:* JK - 12; *Enrollment:* 300; *Note:* Wabaseemoong School. The Wabaseemoong Education Authority oversees education in the Wabaseemoong First Nation community located approximately 100 kilometres northwest of Kenora, Ontario.

***Wikwemikong:* Wikwemikong Board of Education**
34 Henry St, Wikwemikong, ON P0P 2J0, Canada
Tel: 705-859-3834; *Fax:* 705-859-2407
info@wbe-education.ca
www.wbe-education.ca
Number of Schools: 7 schools; *Grades:* K-12; *Enrollment:* 486
Maureen Aiabens, Financial Controller/Manager, 705-859-3834, ext. 224
maiabens@wbe-education.ca
Dominic Beaudry, Education Director, 705-859-3834, ext. 229

***Wunnummin Lake:* Wunnumin Lake Education Authority**
P.O. Box 105
Wunnummin Lake, ON P0V 2Z0, Canada
Tel: 807-442-2559; *Fax:* 807-442-2627
www.wunnumin.ca
Grades: Elementary; *Enrollment:* 146
Sam Mamakwa, Director
samm@wunnumin.ca

Independent & Private Schools

***North York:* Toronto Adventist District School Board (TADSB)**
531 Finch Ave. West, North York, ON M2R 3X2
Tel: 416-633-0090
info@tadsb.com
crawford22.adventistschoolconnect.org
www.facebook.com/TADSB
twitter.com/TJACAAAlumni
Number of Schools: 4; *Grades:* K./Elem./Sec.; *Enrollment:* 850
Donald Maitland, Education Superintendent
Norman Brown, Supervising Principal, 416-633-0090, ext. 222
nbrown@tadsb.com

Schools: Specialized

First Nations

***Aroland:* Johnny Therriault Memorial School**
c/o Aroland First Nation
P.O. Box 40
Hwy 643, Aroland, ON P0T 1B0
Tel: 807-329-5470; *Fax:* 807-329-5472
arolandfirstnation@yahoo.ca
www.education.matawa.on.ca
Grades: K-9; *Enrollment:* 75; *Note:* The Johnny Therriault School serves the Aroland First Nation School, which is located approximately 350 kilometres northeast of Thunder Bay, Ontario. The school is supported by the Matawa Education Department. Tuition agreements are in place with the Superior-Greenstone District School Board, so that Aroland First Nation students can attend grades 10 to 12 in the communities of Nakina & Geraldton.
Sam Kashkeesh, Chief, Aroland First Nation
Patricia Magiskan, Member, Matawa Regional Committee on Education
Stephanie Ash, Communications Officer, Aroland First Nation, 807-767-4443

***Attawapiskat:* J.R. Nakogee Elementary School**
Also known as: Attawapiskat First Nation Elementary
P.O. Box 15
Attawapiskat, ON P0L 1A0
Tel: 705-997-2114; *Fax:* 705-997-2357
www.attawapiskat.org
Grades: JK - 8; Special Ed; *Note:* J.R. Nakogee Elementary School is located in the Ontario Cree fly-in only community of Attawapiskat. It is part of the Attawapiskat First Nation Education Authority.

***Attawapiskat:* Vezina Secondary School**
P.O. Box 15
Attawapiskat, ON P0L 1A0
Tel: 705-997-2117; *Fax:* 705-997-2357
Grades: 9 - 12; *Note:* Attawapiskat First Nation Education Authority operates the high school on the west coast of James Bay.

***Bearskin Lake:* Michikan Lake School**
c/o Michikan Lake School
P.O. Box 78
Bearskin Lake, ON P0V 1E0
Tel: 807-363-1011; *Fax:* 807-363-2519
www.windigoeducation.on.ca/schools/michikan-lake
Grades: JK-8; *Enrollment:* 100; *Note:* Operations of the Michikan Lake School are overseen by the Windigo Education Authority. The school provides elementary education to young people of the Bearskin Lake First Nation. The First Nation community is located about 425 kilometres north of Sioux Lookout, Ontario & offers classes on Aboriginal language and cultures.
Stephanie Petiquan, Principal, 807-363-2570
Jerry Mekanak, Education Director, 807-363-1011

***Big Trout Lake:* Aglace Chapman Education Centre**
P.O. Box 168
Big Trout Lake, ON P0V 1G0, Canada
Tel: 807-537-2264; *Fax:* 807-537-1067
Grades: JK-11; Special Ed.; *Enrollment:* 275; *Note:* The Kitchenuhmaykoosib Education Authority oversees operations of the Aglace Chapman Education Centre. The centre is located

about 270 air miles north of Sioux Lookout, Ontario, where it provides education to the Kitchenuhmaykoosib Inninnuwug First Nation.

Cat Lake: Lawrence Wesley Education Centre
c/o Education Authority
P.O. Box 80
122 Back Rd., Cat Lake, ON P0V 1J0
Tel: 807-347-2102; *Fax:* 807-347-2057
www.titotayschool.myknet.org
Grades: JK-8; *Enrollment:* 120; *Note:* The Titotay Memorial School is one of four schools within the Windigo Education Authority. The First Nation School provides elementary education to members of the Cat Lake First Nation. The school is situated about 180 kilometres north of Sioux Lookout, Ontario & offers classes on Aboriginal language & culture.
Ruby Keesiquayash, Principal, 807-347-2294, ext. 1000
Marie Stewart, Education Director

Christian Island: Christian Island Elementary School
67 Kate Kegwin St., Christian Island, ON L0K 1C0
Tel: 705-247-2011
www.beausoleil-education.ca
Grades: JK - 8; Special Ed; *Note:* Under the Beausoleil First Nation Education Authority, the Christian Island Elementary School provides education to the Chippewas of the Beausoleil First Nation.
Mike Lucas, Principal
m.lucas@beausoleil-education.ca
Sylvia Norton-Sutherland, Native Student Advisor

Constance Lake: Mamawmatawa Holistic Education Center
P.O. Box 4000
Constance Lake, ON P0L 1B0
Tel: 705-463-1199; *Fax:* 705-463-2077
www.clfn.on.ca
Grades: Daycare - JK - 12; Adult Education; *Enrollment:* 257; *Note:* The Mamawmatawa Holistic Education Center educates members of the Constance Lake First Nation, who live west of Hearst, Ontario. The school operates under the direction of the Constance Lake First Nation Education Authority.
Zandra Bear-Lowen, Principal
zandra.bear-lowen@clfn.on.ca

Deer Lake: Deer Lake School
P.O. Box 69
Deer Lake, ON P0V 1N0, Canada
Tel: 807-775-2055; *Fax:* 807-775-2148
Toll-Free: 1-888-751-9225
www.dls.firstnationschools.ca
Grades: K4 - K5; 1 - 9; Special Education; *Note:* The Deer Lake School also offers native language instruction.
Leonard Mamakeesic, Director, Education
Elizabeth Rae, Finance Officer
Loretta Cameron, Teacher, Special Education
Victoria Meekis, Senior Instructor, Native Language

Dinorwic: Wabsnki-Penasi School
P.O. Box 24
Site 112, Dinorwic, ON P0V 1P0
Tel: 807-938-6825; *Fax:* 807-938-1166
Grades: JK - 8; *Note:* The First Nation elementary school is part of the Wabigoon Lake Ojibway Nation Education Authority. For secondary school education, students are transported thirty kilometres west to Dryden, Ontario.

Fort Hope: John C. Yesno Education Centre
P.O. Box 297
Fort Hope, ON P0T 1L0, Canada
Tel: 807-242-8421; *Fax:* 807-242-1592
www.facebook.com/jcyschool
Grades: Kindergarten - 10; Special Ed.; *Note:* The John C. Yesno Education Centre serves the Eabametoong First Nation. The Ojibwe First Nations community is located on the north shore of northern Ontario's Eabamet Lake. Eabametoong First Nation students, continuing their education beyond tenth grade, attend schools in Thunder Bay, Sault Ste. Marie, & Sioux Lookout.
Nick Shaver, Principal

Fort Severn: Wasaho First Nations School
P.O. Box 165
Fort Severn, ON P0V 1W0
Tel: 807-478-9548
Enrollment: 120; *Note:* The Wasaho First Nations School is part of the Wasaho Education Authority. The school serves members of the Fort Severn First Nation in northern Ontario.

Landsdowne House: Neskantaga First Nation Education Centre
P.O. Box 106
Lansdowne House, ON P0T 1Z0
Tel: 807-479-1170; *Fax:* 807-479-1178
Grades: JK - 9; Native culture & language; *Note:* The Neskantaga First Nation Education Centre is situated in a community approximately 180 kilometres north of Pickle Lake in northern Ontario. The elementary school is a Matawa First Nations community school which receives educational support services from the Matawa Education Department.
Tony Sakanee, Education Director, 807-479-1024
tonysakanee@hotmail.com

Longlac: Migizi Wazisin Elementary School
P.O. Box 240
Martin Rd., Longlac, ON P0T 2A0
Tel: 807-876-4482; *Fax:* 807-876-4128
www.longlake58fn.ca
Grades: JK - 7; Special Ed; Native language; *Note:* The Migizi Wazisin Elementary School is located in Long Lake #58 First Nation, an Anishinaabe (Ojibway) First Nation near Geraldton, Ontario. It serves students from both the Long Lake #58 First Nation & the Ginoogaming First Nation. Operations of the elementary school are administered by the Long Lake #58 & Ginoogaming First Nations Education Authority.

Longlac: Nimiki Migizi Secondary School
P.O. Box 360
100 Balsam St., Longlac, ON P0T 2A0
Tel: 807-876-1270
www.education.matawa.on.ca
Grades: 8 - 12; Ojibway language; *Note:* The Nimiki Migizi Secondary School is located in the Ginoogaming First Nation, which is an Anishnawbe (Ojibway) First Nation near Geraldton, Ontario. The high school serves students from both the Ginoogaming First Nation & Long Lake #58 First Nation. Nimiki Migizi Secondary School operates with support from the Long Lake #58 & Ginoogaming First Nations Education Authority.

Mobert: Netamisakomik Education Centre
P.O. Box 615
Mobert, ON P0M 2J0, Canada
Tel: 807-822-2011; *Fax:* 807-822-2710
www.picmobert.ca
Grades: JK-8
Jacky Craig, Principal
principal@picmobert.ca

Muskrat Dam: Samson Beardy Memorial School
P.O. Box 43
Muskrat Dam, ON P0V 3B0
Tel: 807-471-2524; *Fax:* 807-471-2649
Grades: JK - 8; *Note:* The Samson Beardy Memorial School is a First Nation operated school administered by the Muskrat Dam First Nation Education Authority. Secondary & post-secondary students attend schools outside the remote First Nation community.

Nordegg: Taotha School
P.O. Box 39
Nordegg, ON T0M 2H0
Tel: 403-721-3989; *Fax:* 403-721-2174
Note: The Taotha School is part of the Stoney Education Authority. The school serves members of the Stoney Nakoda First Nation.

Ogoki Post: Henry Coaster Memorial School
General Delivery, Ogoki Post, ON P0T 2L0
Tel: 807-349-2509; *Fax:* 807-349-2511
Grades: JK - 8; *Enrollment:* 90; *Note:* Henry Coaster Memorial School is located in Marten Falls Nation, on the north side of the Albany River in northern Ontario. The First Nation school offers traditional culture & language programming. The elementary school operates with support from the Marten Falls (Ogoki) First Nation Education Authority.
Norma Achneepineskum, A/Education Administrator, 807-349-2628

Ohsweken: Six Nations of the Grand River
P.O. Box 5000
1695 Chiefswood Rd., Ohsweken, ON N0A 1M0, Canada
Tel: 519-445-2201; *Fax:* 519-445-4208
www.sixnations.ca
Number of Schools: 5; *Grades:* 3-8; *Enrollment:* 1328
Kathy Knott

Pikangikum: Eenchokay Birchstick School
General Delivery, Pikangikum, ON P0V 2L0, Canada
Tel: 807-773-5561; *Fax:* 807-773-5958
www.ebs-school.org
Grades: K./Elem./Sec.; *Note:* Serving students of the Pikangikum First Nation.

Melanie Doyle, Principal

Sachigo Lake: Martin McKay Memorial School
P.O. Box 51
Sachigo Lake, ON P0V 2P0, Canada
Tel: 807-595-2526; *Fax:* 807-595-1305
www.windigoeducation.on.ca/schools/martin-mckay-memorial
Grades: JK-8; Aboriginal language & culture; *Enrollment:* 100; *Note:* The Martin McKay Memorial School serves students of the Sachigo Lake First Nation. The First Nation community is situated approximately 150 kilometres west of Big Trout Lake, Ontario. Activities of the Sachigo Lake First Nation school are administerd by the Windigo Education Authority.
Robin Warner, Principal, 807-595-2526

Sarnia: Aamjiwnaang First Nation Junior Kindergarten
1900 Virgil Ave., Sarnia, ON N7T 8A7
Tel: 519-344-4132; *Fax:* 519-344-6956
Grades: JK; *Note:* Under the Aamjiwnaang First Nation Education Administration, education is offered to members of the Aamjiwnaang First Nation.
Kim Henry, Principal
Muriel Joseph-Plain, Supervisor, 519-344-5831

Sault St. Marie: Batchewana Learning Centre
15 Jean Ave., Sault St. Marie, ON P6B 4B1, Canada
Tel: 705-759-7285; *Fax:* 705-759-9982
Toll-Free: 1-866-339-3370
colleen@batchewana.ca
www.batchewana.ca
Elaine McDonagh, Education Director/Principal

Slate Falls: Bimaychikamah School
c/o Bimaychikamah School General Delivery
54 Lakeview Dr., Slate Falls, ON P0V 3C0
Tel: 807-737-5701; *Fax:* 888-431-5617
www.slatefalls.firstnation.ca
Grades: JK-8; Aboriginal language & culture; *Enrollment:* 42; *Note:* Education for members of the Slate Falls Nation is provided by the Bimaychikamah School. The elementary school is situated in the Slate Falls Nation community north of Sioux Lookout, Ontario. Operations of Bimaychikamah School are overseen by the Windigo Education Authority.
Danick Clavel, Principal, 807-737-5701
Chancillor Crane, Education Director

Summer Beaver: Nibinamik First Nation Education Centre
c/o Nibinamik Education Centre General Delivery
P.O. Box 117
Summer Beaver, ON P0T 3B0
Tel: 807-593-2195; *Fax:* 807-593-2198
www.nibinamikeducationcentre.firstnationschools.ca
Grades: K-9; *Enrollment:* 100; *Note:* The Nibinamik First Nation Education Centre is a Matawa First Nations community school which receives educational support services from the Matawa Education Department. The Nibinamik First Nation is located approximately 185 kilometres northwest of Pickle Lake in northern Ontario & offers classes in Native languages.
Kevin Booth, Principal
Doreen Beaver, Administrative Assistant
doreenbeaver@gmail.com

Whitedog: Mizhakiiwetung Memorial School
General Delivery, Whitedog, ON P0X 1P0, Canada
Tel: 807-927-2000; *Fax:* 807-927-2176
Grades: JK - 12; Alternative Education; *Enrollment:* 300; *Note:* Elementary & secondary education is provided to Wabaseemoong First Nation students living in a community situated about 100 kilometres northwest of Kenora, Ontario. The school focuses upon academics as well as cultural education. School activities are overseen by the Wabaseemoong Education Authority.
Ron R. McDonald, Principal, 807-927-2000, ext. 264

Wiarton: Cape Croker Elementary School
Also known as: Chippewas of Nawash Elementary School
17 School Rd., RR#5, Wiarton, ON N0H 2T0
Tel: 519-534-0719; *Fax:* 519-534-1592
www.nawash.ca/school/
Grades: Pre.- 8; *Note:* Part of the Chippewas of Nawash Unceded First Nation Board of Education, the Cape Croker Elementary School provides a culturally-based education, which includes the history of the Anishnabek, band sovereignty, & communication & language arts in Anishinaabemowin & English.
Judy Nadjiwan, Education Administrator, Board of Education, 519-534-0882
nawashed.administrator@gbtel.ca
Debra Chegahno, Principal, Cape Croker Elementary School, 519-534-0719
nawashed.principal@gbtel.ca

Chastity Jenner, Ojibway Language Resource Teacher
nawashed.nativelanguage@gbtel.ca

Hearing Impaired

Belleville: The Sir James Whitney School for the Deaf
350 Dundas St. West, Belleville, ON K8P 1B2
Tel: 613-967-2823; *Toll-Free:* 800-501-6240
www.psbnet.ca/eng/schools/sjw
TTY: 613-967-2823
Janice Drake, Principal

Brantford: The W. Ross Macdonald School for the Blind
350 Brant Ave., Brantford, ON N3T 3J9
Tel: 519-759-0730; *Toll-Free:* 866-618-9092
www.psbnet.ca/eng/schools/wross
Enrollment: 217
Donald Neale, Principal, Blind/Low Vision Program
Martha Martino, Principal, Deafblind Programs
Elizabeth Dunton, Principal, Resource Services

London: The Robarts School for the Deaf
1515 Cheapside St., London, ON N5V 3N9
Tel: 519-453-4400
www.psbnet.ca/eng/schools/robarts
TTY: 519-453-4400
John Barry, Principal

Milton: Ernest C. Drury School for the Deaf
255 Ontario St. South, Milton, ON L9T 2M5
Tel: 905-878-2851
www.psbnet.ca/eng/schools/ecd
TTY: 905-878-7195
Jeanne Leonard, Principal, Elementary Program
Antony McLetchie, Principal, Secondary Program

Special Education

Alliston: Above & Beyond Learning Experience
#19 Church St. North, Alliston, ON L9R 1L6
Tel: 705-796-2253; *Toll-Free:* 855-796-2253
able_info@ablearning.org
www.ablearning.org
Grades: 1 - 12
Mikki White, Principal / Curriculum Developer
Phil White, Principal / Cooperative & Outreach Education Director

Belleville: Sagonaska Demonstration School
350 Dundas St. West, Belleville, ON K8P 1B2
Tel: 613-967-2830
www.psbnet.ca/eng/schools/sagonaska
Enrollment: 120
Martin Smit, Principal

London: Amethyst Demonstration School
1515 Cheapside St., London, ON N5Y 4V9
Tel: 519-453-4400
www.psbnet.ca/eng/schools/amethyst
John Barry, Principal

Milton: Trillium Demonstration School
347 Ontario St. South, Milton, ON L9T 3X9
Tel: 905-878-2851
www.psbnet.ca/eng/schools/trillium
TTY: 905-878-7195
Enrollment: 120
Diane Johnstone, Principal

Mississauga: Kids CAN Social Centre Oakwood Academy
155 Queen St. East, Mississauga, ON L5G 1N2
Tel: 905-486-1035
info@kidscancentre.com
kidscancentre.com
www.facebook.com/kidscan.charity.9?fref=ts
twitter.com/KidsCANCharity
Grades: JK - 8; *Note:* Oakwood Academy is a special needs private school.
Michele Kane, Co-Founder & Director of Programming
Trillian Bateson, Co-Founder & Director of Programming

Oakville: Missing Links Academy
P.O. Box 60026
1515 Rebecca St., Oakville, ON L6L 6R4
Tel: 905-876-0055
info@missinglinks.ca
www.missinglinks.ca
Grades: Pre.-8; *Note:* Missing Links fills the gaps to Autism by delivering unique, individualized programming for the education and treatment of children with Autism Spectrum Disorder (ASD) and other exceptionalities.
Am Badwall, Clinical Director
Mike Daniels, Educational Consultant

Ottawa: Centre Jules-Léger
281, av Lanark, Ottawa, ON K1Z 6R8, Canada
Tél: 613-761-9300; *Téléc:* 613-761-9301
Ligne sans frais: 866-390-3670
www.centrejulesleger.com
Other Information: ATS: 613-761-9302
Note: Services aux enfants (et leurs familles) en difficultés d'apprentissage, avec ou sans déficit d'attention/hyperactivité, qui sont sourds ou malentendant, qui sont aveugles ou en basse vision, ou qui sont sourds et aveugles.
Marie-France Ricard, Surintendante, 613-761-9300
Marie-France.Ricard@Ontario.ca
André L. Duguay, Directeur des programmes, 613-761-1623
Andre.Duguay@Ontario.ca

Thornhill: Giant Steps Toronto Inc. School
35 Flowervale Rd., Thornhill, ON L3T 4J3
Tel: 905-881-3104; *Fax:* 905-881-4592
info@giantstepstoronto.ca
www.giantstepstoronto.ca
www.facebook.com/GiantStepsToronto#
Note: Giant Steps is a school and therapy centre for elementary school-aged children with Autism Spectrum Disorder (ASD)
Howat Noble, President

Toronto: The Dunblaine School
21 Deloraine Ave., Toronto, ON M5M 2A8
Tel: 416-483-9215; *Fax:* 416-483-0903
info@dunblaineschool.com
www.dunblaineschool.com
Grades: Elem.; *Note:* A specialized school for students with learning disabilities.
Charleen Pryke, Principal

Toronto: New Haven Learning Centre
301 Lanor Ave., Toronto, ON M8W 2R1
Tel: 416-259-4445; *Fax:* 416-259-2023
info@newhavencentre.com
www.newhavencentre.com
twitter.com/NewHavenCentre
www.linkedin.com/groups/New-Haven-Learning-Centre-3010708
www.youtube.com/user/NewHavenCentre
Note: Centre of Excellence in the treatment and education of children with autism.
Audrey Meissner, Executive Director, 416-259-4445, ext. 12
ameissner@newhavencentre.com

Toronto: Reach Toronto
#206, 2238 Dundas St. West, Toronto, ON M5R 3A9
Tel: 416-929-1670
www.reachtoronto.ca
www.facebook.com/ReachToronto
twitter.com/reachtoronto
Note: Reach Toronto is a not-for-profit organization, offering unique programs for adults and youth with ASD and Asperger's Syndrome.

Distance Education

Bayfield: Virtual High School (Ontario) (VHS)
P.O. Box 402
27 Main St. North, Bayfield, ON N0M 1G0
www.virtualhighschool.com
Stephen Baker, Principal, Founder and CEO
Principal@VirtualHighSchool.com
Kim Loebach, Director of Operations; Human Resources
Kimberley.Loebach@VirtualHighSchool.com
Ashley Homuth, School Administrative Head
Ashley.Homuth@VirtualHighSchool.com
Adam Wise, Registrar
Adam.Wise@VirtualHighSchool.com

Clinton: Avon Maitland Distance Education Centre (AMDEC)
P.O. Box 729
165 Princess St. East, Clinton, ON N0M 1L0
Tel: 519-482-5428; *Fax:* 519-482-8795
office@amdec.ca
www.amdec.ca
Other Information: principal@amdec.ca
Grades: Secondary; *Note:* The Avon Maitland District e-Learning Centre is a full distance, online secondary school course provider administered by the Avon Maitland District School Board.

Embrun: Ottawa Carleton E-School (OCES)
P.O. Box 277
#201, 993 Notre-Dame St., Embrun, ON K0A 1W0
Tel: 613-443-9522; *Fax:* 613-482-4504
info@ottawacarletone-school.ca
www.ottawacarletone-school.ca
www.facebook.com/myeschool
www.twitter.com/Canada_eSchool
ca.linkedin.com/in/canadaeschool/
myskype.info/myeschool
Grades: Secondary; *Note:* Accredited Internet high school offering Ontario Secondary School Diploma (OSSD).
Annette Levesque, Director
Carl J. Frizell, Principal

Lindsay: OpenSchool (OS)
230 Angeline St. South, Lindsay, ON K9V 4R2
Tel: 705-328-2925; *Fax:* 705-878-8891
office@openschoolontario.ca
www.openschoolontario.ca
Grades: Secondary; *Note:* OpenSchool is a continuous entry online school offering Ontario high school credits "on demand." They are part of the Adult and Continuing Education program with Trillium Lakelands District School Board.

Lindsay: Trillium Lakelands District School Board ~ Virtual Learning Centre (VLC)
230 Angeline St. South, Lindsay, ON K9V 4R2
Tel: 705-328-2925; *Fax:* 705-878-8891
www.virtuallearning.ca
twitter.com/tldsbvlc
Grades: Secondary; *Note:* Provides on-line secondary level credit courses that count towards the high school diploma.
Peter Warren, Principal, 705-328-2925
Kim Boldt, Manager/Registrar, 705-328-2925

Sioux Lookout: Wahsa Distance Education Centre
P.O. Box 1118
74 Front St., Sioux Lookout, ON P8T 1B7, Canada
Tel: 807-737-1488; *Fax:* 807-737-1732
Toll-Free: 800-667-3703
Grades: 9 - 12; *Enrollment:* 950; *Note:* The Wahsa Distance Education Centre allows students in northern Ontario communities across the Sioux Lookout District to complete their secondary school education at home. Courses & services are developed in consultation with First Nation communities. The Centre is operated by the Northern Nishnawbe Education Council.
Darrin Head, Principal
DHead@nnec.on.ca

Toronto: Granton Institute of Technology
263 Adelaide St. West, Toronto, ON M5H 9Z9
Tel: 416-977-3929; *Fax:* 416-977-5612
info@grantoninstitute.com
www.grantontech.com
www.facebook.com/264715466875614
Note: Offers learn-at-home Certificate and Diploma courses.

Toronto: Independent Learning Centre (ILC)
P.O. Box 200 Q
Toronto, ON M4T 2T1
Tel: 416-484-2704; *Fax:* 416-484-2722
Toll-Free: 800-387-5512
www.ilc.org
www.facebook.com/independentlearningcentre
twitter.com/ILC_CEI
Grades: 9 - 12; OSSD; GED: ESL; *Note:* The Independent Learning Centre (ILC) is Ontario's leading provider of accredited distance education and GED Testing.
Lise Leclair, Senior Information Officer, 416-484-2600, ext. 2144
lleclair@tvo.org
Sarah Irwin, Managing Director, 416-484-2600, ext. 2003
sirwin@tvo.org

Independent & Private Schools

Rockland: Canadian International Hockey Academy
8720 County Rd. 17, Rockland, ON K4K 1T2
Fax: 866-739-8652
Toll-Free: 877-244-9199
www.cihacademy.com
Grades: 9 - 12; *Enrollment:* 80; *Note:* Hockey boarding institution providing athletes a tailored education provided by the Upper Canada District School Board (UCDSB).
Randy Stevenson, Headmaster, 613-446-2212, ext. 222
rstevenson@cihacademy.com
Germain Laflèche, Director of Admissions, 613-446-2212, ext. 223
glafleche@cihacademy.com
Claudine Loiselle, Director of Finance, 613-446-2212, ext. 228
cloiselle@cihacademy.com

Schools: Independent & Private

Faith-Based

Ajax: Faithway Baptist Church School
1964 Salem Rd., Ajax, ON L1T 4V3, Canada
Tel: 905-686-0951; *Fax:* 905-686-1450
faithway@faithway.org
www.school.faithway.org
Grades: K./Elem./Sec.; *Enrollment:* 65
L. Homan

Ajax: Pickering Christian School
162 Rossland Rd. East, Ajax, ON L1T 4V2, Canada
Tel: 905-427-3120; *Fax:* 905-427-0211
office@pickeringcs.on.ca
www.pickeringcs.on.ca
www.facebook.com/PickeringCS
www.linkedin.com/company/pickering-christian-school
Grades: JK - 8; *Enrollment:* 219
Dr. Paul Douglas Ogborne, Principal

Alliston: Alliston Community Christian School (ACCS)
4428 Adjala-Tecumseth Townline, RR#4, Alliston, ON L9R 1V4, Canada
Tel: 705-434-2227; *Fax:* 705-435-0126
info@allistonccs.ca
www.allistonccs.ca
Grades: K./Elem.; *Enrollment:* 113
Lillian Parasol, Principal

Ancaster: Hamilton District Christian High
92 Glancaster Rd., Ancaster, ON L9G 3K9, Canada
Tel: 905-648-6655; *Fax:* 905-648-3139
info@hdch.org
hdch.org
www.facebook.com/HDCH.info
www.twitter.com/HDCH_Info
Grades: Sec.; *Enrollment:* 448; *Number of Employees:* 49
Nathan Siebenga, Principal

Aylmer: Immanuel Christian School Society
75 Caverly Rd., Aylmer, ON N5H 2P6
Tel: 519-773-8476; *Fax:* 519-773-8315
info@immanuelchristianschool.net
www.immanuelchristianschool.net
www.facebook.com/150239838428877
twitter.com/ICSAylmer
Grades: K./Elem.
Keith Cameron, Principal
k.cameron@immanuelchristianschool.net

Aylmer: Mount Salem Christian School (MSCS)
c/o Evangelical Mennonite Church
6576 Springfield Rd., RR#6, Aylmer, ON N5H 2R5, Canada
Tel: 519-765-3555; *Fax:* 519-765-3879
info@mtscs.ca
www.mountsalemchristianschool.ca
www.facebook.com/mountsalemchristianschool
Grades: Junior Kindergarten - 12; *Note:* Mount Salem Christian School is an interdenominational school, using a BEKA curriculum.
Lena Wall, Principal
Judy Wiebe, Vice Principal

Barrie: Heritage Christian Academy
79 Ardagh Rd., Barrie, ON L4N 9B6, Canada
Tel: 705-733-0112; *Fax:* 705-733-2054
Grades: JK.-12; *Enrollment:* 75
Pastor Brett Pennell, Principal

Barrie: Timothy Christian School
750 Essa Rd., Barrie, ON L4N 9E9, Canada
Tel: 705-726-6621
tcsgen@timothychristianschool.ca
www.timothychristianschool.ca
Grades: Junior Kindergarten - 8; *Note:* Timothy Christian School is an interdenominational school.
Steve Wood, Chair
Rod Berg, Principal
Brenda Goodnough, Vice Principal

Beamsville: Great Lakes Christian College
4875 King St., Beamsville, ON L0R 1B0, Canada
Tel: 905-563-5374; *Fax:* 905-563-0818
www.glchs.on.ca
www.facebook.com/294769903952932
twitter.com/glchs
Grades: Pre; 9-12
Don Rose, Chief Administrator
drose@glchs.on.ca

Belleville: Belleville District Christian School (BCS)
18 Christian School Rd., RR#5, Belleville, ON K8N 4Z5, Canada
Tel: 613-962-7849; *Fax:* 613-962-6440
office@bellevillechristianschool.ca
www.bellevillechristianschool.ca
www.facebook.com/BellevilleChristianSchool
Grades: Junior Kindergarten - 8
Jennifer Shoniker, Principal

Belleville: Quinte Christian High School (QCHS)
138 Wallbridge-Loyalist Rd., Belleville, ON K8N 4Z2, Canada
Tel: 613-968-7870; *Fax:* 613-968-7970
admin@qchs.ca
qchs.ca
www.facebook.com/QCHS.CA
twitter.com/quintechristian
www.youtube.com/user/QuinteChristian
Grades: Secondary
John Vanderwindt, Principal
principal@qchs.ca

Bloomingdale: Koinonia Christian Academy
850 Sawmill Rd., Bloomingdale, ON N0B 1K0, Canada
Tel: 519-744-7447; *Fax:* 519-744-6745
kcf@kcf.org
www.kcf.org
www.facebook.com/koinoniacf
www.twitter.com/kcf_org
Enrollment: 157
David J. Champion
dave.champion@kcf.org

Bowmanville: Durham Christian Academy
RR#3, Bowmanville, ON L1J 3K4
Tel: 905-697-2351; *Fax:* 905-697-6495
durhamca@rogers.com
www.durhamca.ca
Grades: JK-8
Carol Dempsey, Principal

Bowmanville: Durham Christian High School
340 West Scugog Lane, Bowmanville, ON L1C 3K2
Tel: 905-623-5940; *Fax:* 905-623-6258
office@dchs.com
www.dchs.com
www.facebook.com/185439688168242
Grades: Sec.
Fred Spoelstra, Principal
principal@dchs.com

Bowmanville: Knox Christian School
410 North Scugog Ct., Bowmanville, ON L1C 3K2
Tel: 905-623-5871
office@knoxchristian.com
www.knoxchristian.com
Grades: K./Elem.; *Enrollment:* 150
Terry Vanleeuwen, Principal
principal@knoxchristian.com

Brampton: Canada Christian Academy
22 Abbey Rd., Brampton, ON L6W 2T8, Canada
Tel: 905-789-5841; *Fax:* 905-789-0645
canadachristianacademy@gmail.com
canadachristianacademy.com
Grades: Junior Kindergarten - 12; *Enrollment:* 100
Deepa Patro, Principal

Brampton: John Knox Christian School
82 McLaughlin Rd. South, Brampton, ON L6Y 2C7
Tel: 905-451-3236; *Fax:* 905-451-3448
bramptonjkcs.org
Grades: JK-8; *Enrollment:* 300
Garry Zondervan, Principal
gzondervan@bramptonjkcs.org

Brantford: Brantford Christian Collegiate
Friendship House
P.O. Box 28116
452 Grey St., Brantford, ON N3R 7X5, Canada
Tel: 519-753-4900
Grades: 9 - 12
Jeff Gillmore, Principal
Rev. Ron Humphries, Faculty Member

Brantford: Brantford Christian School (BCS)
7 Calvin St., Brantford, ON N3S 3E4, Canada
Tel: 519-752-0433; *Fax:* 519-752-6088
bcsbrantford.ca
Grades: Junior Kindergarten - 8
Walter Hartholt, Principal
whartholt@bcsbrantford.ca
Heather Murray, Vice Principal
hmurray@bcsbrantford.ca
Francine Roth, Vice Principal
froth@bcsbrantford.ca

Brantford: Central Baptist Academy (CBA)
300 Fairview Dr., Brantford, ON N3R 2X6, Canada
Tel: 519-754-4806; *Fax:* 519-754-4201
cbaoffice@centralbaptistbrantford.com
cbabrantford.ca
Grades: Junior Kindergarten - 8
Rev. Minne Bouma, Principal

Breslau: Woodland Christian High School
1058 Spitzig Rd., Breslau, ON N0B 1M0
Tel: 519-648-2114; *Fax:* 519-648-3402
office@woodland.on.ca
www.woodland.on.ca
www.facebook.com/WoodlandCHS
twitter.com/@woodlandchs
www.linkedin.com/company/woodland-christian-high-school
www.youtube.com/user/WoodlandCHSVideos
Grades: Sec.; *Enrollment:* 194
John VanPelt, Principal

Burlington: Burlington Christian Academy (BCA)
521 North Service Rd. West, Burlington, ON L7P 5C3, Canada
Tel: 905-639-7364
office@onlyatbccs.com
onlyatbca.com
Grades: JK - 9; *Enrollment:* 160
Gord McNeice, Principal
gordm@onlyatbccs.com
Heather Crossing, Vice Principal
heather.crossing@onlyatbccs.com
Jessica Purdy, Vice Principal
jessica.purdy@onlyatbccs.com

Burlington: John Calvin Christian School
607 Dynes Rd., Burlington, ON L7N 2V4
Tel: 905-634-8015; *Fax:* 905-634-9772
jcss@on.aibn.com
Grades: K./Elem.; *Enrollment:* 72
Jason Heemskerk, Principal

Burlington: Trinity Christian School
2170 Itabashi Way, Burlington, ON L7M 5B3, Canada
Tel: 905-634-3052; *Fax:* 905-634-9382
trinity@tcsonline.ca
tcsonline.ca
www.facebook.com/TCSBurlington
Grades: Junior Kindergarten - 8
Rick Schenk, Principal
principal@tcsonline.ca

Caledon: Brampton Christian School (BCS)
12480 Hutchinson Farm Lane, Caledon, ON L7C 2B6, Canada
Tel: 905-846-3771; *Fax:* 905-843-2929
admin@bramptoncs.org
www.bramptoncs.org
www.facebook.com/bramptoncs
twitter.com/BramptonCS
Grades: JK - 12
A. Abdulnour, Principal
aabdulnour@bramptoncs.org
A. Cabral, Vice Princical, Senior High
afcabral@bramptoncs.org
C. Doggart, Vice Principal, Elementary
cdoggart@bramptoncs.org
J. Miller, Vice Principal, Junior High
jmiller@bramptoncs.org

Cambridge: Cambridge Christian School (CCS)
229 Myers Rd., Cambridge, ON N1R 7H3, Canada
Tel: 519-623-2261
info@cambridgechristianschool.com
www.cambridgechristianschool.com
www.facebook.com/CambridgeCS
Grades: Kindergarten - 8
Scott Beda, Principal & COO
sbeda@cambridgechristianschool.com

Cambridge: Temple Baptist Christian Academy (TBCA)
400 Holiday Inn Dr., Cambridge, ON N3C 3T1, Canada
Tel: 519-658-9001; *Fax:* 519-658-9821
academy@tbca.ca
tbca.ca
Grades: Jr. K-8; *Enrollment:* 267
Evelyn Hewitt, Principal

Chatham: Chatham Christian High School (CCHS)
475 Keil Dr. South, Chatham, ON N7M 6L8
Tel: 519-352-4980; *Fax:* 519-352-4041
office@chathamchristian.ca
www.chathamchristian.ca
www.facebook.com/pages/Chatham-Christian-School/473514572702801
twitter.com/CK_CCS
Grades: 9-12; *Enrollment:* 140
Marvin Bierling, Head Administrator

Chatham: Chatham Christian School
475 Keil Dr. South, Chatham, ON N7M 6L8
Tel: 519-352-4980
www.chathamchristian.ca
www.facebook.com/ChathamChristianSchool
twitter.com/CK_CCS
Grades: JK-12
Marvin Bierling, Head Administrator
marvinbierling@chathamchristian.ca

Chatham: Eben-Ezer Christian School
485 McNaughton Ave. East, Chatham, ON N7L 2H2
Tel: 519-354-1142; *Fax:* 519-354-2159
eecs@eecschatham.com
eecschatham.com
Grades: Elem.
R. Vanderveen, Chair
Carlos Bos, Principal

Clinton: Huron Christian School
87 Percival St., Clinton, ON N0M 1L0
Tel: 519-482-7851; *Fax:* 519-482-7448
office@huronchristianschool.ca
www.huronchristianschool.ca
Grades: JK.-8
Heather VanDorp, Chair
Nick Geleynse, Principal
principal@huronchristianschool.ca

Cobourg: Northumberland Christian School
8861 Danforth Rd., RR#5, Cobourg, ON K9A 4J8, Canada
Tel: 905-372-8766; *Fax:* 905-372-6299
ncsoffice@bellnet.ca
www.northumberlandchristianschool.com
Grades: Junior Kindergarten - 8; *Note:* Northumberland Christian School is an interdenominational school.

Copetown: Rehoboth Christian School (RCS)
P.O. Box 70
198 Inksetter Rd., Copetown, ON L0R 1J0, Canada
Tel: 905-627-5977; *Fax:* 905-628-4422
office@rehoboth.on.ca
www.rehoboth.on.ca
Grades: Kindergarten - 12; *Note:* Rehoboth Free Reformed Christian School Society of Copetown owns & operates the school. Education is provided with a Reformed Christian view.
Raymond Roth, Principal
principal@rehoboth.on.ca
Dick Naves, High School Vice Principal
dnaves@rehoboth.on.ca
Herman den Hollander, Elementary Vice Principal
hdenhollander@rehoboth.on.ca

Drayton: Community Christian School (CCS)
P.O. Box 141
35 High St., Drayton, ON N0G 1P0, Canada
Tel: 519-638-2935
ccsdray@bellnet.ca
www.ccsdrayton.org
Grades: Junior Kindergarten - 8; *Number of Employees:* 18
Paul Marcus, Principal & COO

Dundas: Providence Christian School
542 Ofield Rd. North, Dundas, ON L9H 5E2, Canada
Tel: 905-627-1411; *Fax:* 905-627-8004
office@dccs.ca
www.dccs.ca
twitter.com/DCCS_ca
Grades: Pre - 8; *Enrollment:* 180
Kevin Bouwers, Principal
kbouwers@dccs.ca
I. Vos, Coordinator, Curriculum & Resource
ivos@dccs.ca

Dunnville: Dunnville Christian School
37 Robinson Rd., RR#1, Dunnville, ON N1A 2W1, Canada
Tel: 905-774-5142; *Fax:* 905-774-5519
www.dunnvillechristianschool.ca
www.facebook.com/groups/2413644356
Grades: K./Elem.; *Enrollment:* 100
Ralph De Boer, Chair
info@dunnvillechristianschool.ca
Joyce Koornneef, Principal
principal@dunnvillechristianschool.ca

Etobicoke: Richmond Hill Christian Academy Administration
96 Antioch Dr., Etobicoke, ON M9B 5V4, Canada
Tel: 416-621-4100
rhca@rogers.com
rhcaweb.ca
Grades: Pre - 8; *Enrollment:* 339; *Note:* Richmond Hill Christian Academy is a non-denominational school, which is a member of the Association of Christian Schools International. The A Beka curriculum is used. Its campus is located at 9711 Bayview Avenue in Richmond Hill.
Brian R. Hayes, B.Com., C.F.A., Administrator
Madeline J. Hayes, B.A., M.Ed., Principal

Fergus: Emmanuel Christian High School
8037 Wellington Rd. 19, RR#3, Fergus, ON N1M 2W4
Tel: 519-843-3029; *Fax:* 519-843-4711
office@echs.ca
www.echs.ca
Grades: Elem./Sec.
Henk Nobel, Principal
henk_nobel@bellnet.ca

Fergus: Maranatha Christian School
8037 Wellington Rd. 19, RR#3 Garafraxia St., Fergus, ON N1M 2W4
Tel: 519-843-3029; *Fax:* 519-843-4711
info@mcsfergus.ca
mcsfergus.ca
Grades: Elem.; *Enrollment:* 175
R. Hoeksema, Principal

Fort Erie: Niagara Christian Community of Schools (NCC)
2619 Niagara Pkwy., Fort Erie, ON L2A 5M4, Canada
Tel: 905-871-6980; *Fax:* 905-871-9260
ncc@niagaracc.com
www.niagaracc.com
Grades: Junior Kindergarten - 12
Mark Thiessen, Principal
Chris Baird, Vice Principal

Georgetown: Halton Hills Christian School
11643 Trafalgar Rd., Georgetown, ON L7G 4S4, Canada
Tel: 905-877-4221; *Fax:* 905-877-1483
office@haltonhillschristianschool.org
www.haltonhillschristianschool.org
Grades: K./Elem.; *Enrollment:* 228; *Note:* Formerly known as Georgetown District Christian School
Marianne Vangoor, Principal

Guelph: Elora Road Christian School (ERCS)
5696 Wellington Rd.7, RR #5, Guelph, ON N1H 6J2, Canada
Tel: 519-824-1890; *Fax:* 519-821-3518
school@ercf.ca
www.eloraroad.ca
Grades: JK-8; *Enrollment:* 99
Amanda McAlpine, Vice Principal

Guelph: Guelph Community Christian School
195 College Ave. West, Guelph, ON N1G 1S6, Canada
Tel: 519-824-8860; *Fax:* 519-824-2105
info@guelphccs.ca
www.guelphccs.ca
Grades: K. - 8; *Enrollment:* 188
Bob Moore, M.Ed., Principal

Guelph: Resurrection Christian Academy
400 Speedvale Ave. East, Guelph, ON N1E 1N9
Tel: 519-836-5395
www.rcaflames.com
www.facebook.com/groups/139369669490620
Grades: K./Elem.
Sue Warren, Director & Co-Founder

Hamilton: Calvin Christian School (CCS)
547 West 5th St., Hamilton, ON L9C 3P7, Canada
Tel: 905-388-2645; *Fax:* 905-388-2769
ccshamilton.ca
Grades: Junior Kindergarten - 8; *Enrollment:* 420
Ted Postma, Principal

Hamilton: Guido de Bres Christian High School
420 Crerar Dr., Hamilton, ON L9A 5K3, Canada
Tel: 905-574-4011; *Fax:* 905-574-8662
office@guidodebres.org
www.guidodebres.org
Grades: Sec.; *Enrollment:* 400
R. Vanoostveen, Principal
principal@guidodebres.org

Hawkesville: Countryside Christian School
3745 Hergott Rd., Hawkesville, ON N0B 1X0, Canada
Tel: 519-699-5793; *Fax:* 519-699-4576
Grades: K./Elem./Sec.
Howard Lichty, Contact

Jarvis: Jarvis Community Christian School
149 Talbot St. East, Jarvis, ON N0A 1J0
Tel: 519-587-4444; *Fax:* 519-587-2985
info@jdcs.ca
www.jccs.ca
Grades: K.-8; *Enrollment:* 129
Doug Osborn, Principal
principal@jdcs.ca

Jordan: Heritage Christian School
P.O. Box 400
2850 Fourth Ave., Jordan, ON L0R 1S0, Canada
Tel: 905-562-7303; *Fax:* 905-562-0020
heritage@hcsjordan.ca
www.hcsjordan.ca
Grades: K - 12; *Enrollment:* 501
Ben Harsvoort, Principal

Jordan Station: Jordan Christian School
P.O. Box 69
4171 - 15 St. South, Jordan Station, ON L0R 1S0, Canada
Tel: 905-562-4023; *Fax:* 905-562-4024
jcsecr@talkwireless.ca
www.jordanchristianschool.ca
Enrollment: 132
Mark Fintelman

Kingston: Kingston Christian School
1212 Woodbine Rd., Kingston, ON K7L 4V2
Tel: 613-384-9572; *Fax:* 613-384-9580
kcs@kingston.jkl.net
www.kingstonchristianschool.ca
Grades: K./Elem.
Karl Reid, Contact

Kitchener: Fellowship Christian School
1780 Glasgow St., Kitchener, ON N2N 0A7
Tel: 519-746-0008; *Fax:* 519-746-4206
fcsprincipal@execulink.com
www.kwfcs.com
Grades: Elem.
Trevor Long, Principal

Kitchener: Laurentian Hills Christian School (LHCS)
11 Laurentian Dr., Kitchener, ON N2E 1C1
Tel: 519-576-6700; *Fax:* 519-576-2583
lhcs.ws
facebook.com/LaurentianHills
Grades: JK-8; *Enrollment:* 275
Ian Timmerman, Principal

Kitchener: Rockway Mennonite Collegiate Inc.
110 Doon Rd., Kitchener, ON N2G 3C8, Canada
Tel: 519-743-5209
rockway.ca
www.facebook.com/109708292388486
Grades: 7 - 12; *Enrollment:* 350; *Note:* Rockway Mennonite Collegiate is an inspected & accredited private school, with students from Mennonite congregations & Christian denominations.
Ann Schultz, Principal
Tom Bileski, Director, Community Relations
Bernie Burnett, Director, Development
Karen Martin Schiedel, Business Manager

Kleinburg: Kleinburg Christian Academy (KCA)
6950 Nashville Rd., Kleinburg, ON L0J 1C0, Canada
Tel: 905-893-7211
ccs.behosted.ca
Grades: Junior Kindergarten - 8
LeeAnn Major, Principal

Laurel: Dufferin Area Christian School
General Delivery, Laurel, ON L0N 1L0
Tel: 519-941-4368; *Fax:* 519-941-3748
dacs@on.aibn.com
Grades: Elem.
Nick Mans, Principal

Leamington: United Mennonite Educational Institute (UMEI)
614 Mersea Rd. 6, RR#5, Leamington, ON N8H 3V8, Canada
Tel: 519-326-7448; *Fax:* 519-326-0278
office@umei.on.ca
umei.ca
www.facebook.com/154197132033
twitter.com/schoolon6th
www.youtube.com/user/umeichristian

Grades: 9 - 12; *Note:* United Mennonite Educational Institute is a secondary school which provides an education that incorporates an Anabaptist / Mennonite world view.
Sonya Bedal, Principal
umeiadm@gmail.com

***Lindsay:* Heritage Christian School**
159 Colborne St. West, Lindsay, ON K9V 5Z8, Canada
Tel: 705-324-8363; *Fax:* 705-324-8372
hcs_office@bellnet.ca
www.myhcs.ca
www.facebook.com/279519142064875
Grades: K - 8; *Enrollment:* 102
Kim Bolton, Principal

***Listowel:* Listowel Christian School**
P.O. Box 151
6020 Line 87, Listowel, ON N4W 3H2
Tel: 519-291-3086; *Fax:* 519-291-3086
lcs@cyg.net
www.listowelchristianschool.ca
Grades: JK-8
Garth Bierma, Principal

***London:* Covenant Christian School**
7 Howard Ave., London, ON N6P 1B3
Tel: 519-203-0266
info@ccslondon.org
www.ccslondon.org
Grades: K.-8; *Enrollment:* 80
William Dokter, Chair
board@ccslondon.org
Shawn Wolski, Principal
principal@ccslondon.org

***London:* London Christian Academy (LCA)**
85 Charles St., London, ON N6H 1H1, Canada
Tel: 519-473-3332; *Fax:* 519-473-9843
www.londonchristianacademy.ca
www.facebook.com/londonchristianacademy
www.youtube.com/user/londoncatv
Grades: Junior Kindergarten - 8; *Note:* London Christian Academy is an interdenominational, Christian school.
Ron Hesman, Principal
principal@londonchristianacademy.ca
Steve Gaunt, Vice Principal
sgaunt@londonchristianacademy.ca

***London:* London Christian Elementary School**
202 Clarke Rd., London, ON N5W 5E4, Canada
Tel: 519-455-0360; *Fax:* 519-455-6717
info@londonchristian.ca
www.londonchristian.ca
Grades: JK-8; *Enrollment:* 200
Mary Haven, Principal
mhaven@londonchristian.ca

***London:* London District Christian Secondary School**
24 Braesyde Ave., London, ON N5W 1V3, Canada
Tel: 519-455-4360; *Fax:* 519-455-4364
office@ldcss.ca
www.ldcss.ca
Grades: Sec.; *Enrollment:* 360
Dwayne Bulthuis, Principal
dbulthuis@ldcss.ca

***Lucknow:* Lucknow & District Christian School**
37521 Amberley Rd., Lucknow, ON N0G 2H0
Tel: 519-528-2016; *Fax:* 519-528-2095
Grades: K./Elem.
Lawrence Uyl

***Markham:* Peoples Christian Academy (PCA)**
245 Renfrew Dr., Markham, ON L3R 6G3
Tel: 416-733-2010
info@pca.ca
www.pca.ca
www.facebook.com/181436515199705
Grades: Pre.-12; *Enrollment:* 350
Rev. Reg Andrews, B.A., B.Ed., M.A.

***Markham:* Wesley Christian Academy**
22 Heritage Rd., Markham, ON L3P 1M4, Canada
Tel: 905-201-8461; *Fax:* 905-201-6438
info@wesleyca.com
wesleyca.com
www.facebook.com/wca.elc
twitter.com/wca_elc
Grades: Senior Kindergarten - 8; *Note:* Wesley Christian Academy offers an academic program within the context of Christian principles.
M. Serio, Principal

***Metcalfe:* Community Christian School (CCS)**
2681 Glen St., Metcalfe, ON K0A 2P0, Canada
Tel: 613-821-3669; *Fax:* 613-821-6135
info@ccsmetcalfe.ca
www.ccsmetcalfe.ca
Grades: JK - 8; *Enrollment:* 65; *Number of Employees:* 11
Rick Dykstra, Principal
rick.dykstra@communitychristianschool.ca

***Millgrove:* Covenant Christian School**
P.O. Box 2
497 Millgrove Side Rd., Millgrove, ON L0R 1V0, Canada
Tel: 905-689-3191; *Fax:* 905-689-0191
covenantchristianschool@bellnet.ca
Grades: Elem.; *Enrollment:* 119
Tracy Jelsma, Principal

***Milverton:* Fair Haven Christian Day School**
4184 Line 61, RR#1, Milverton, ON N0K 1M0, Canada
Tel: 519-595-4568
Grades: K.-10
Howard Bean, Principal, 519-462-2220
Melvin Roes, Bishop, 519-273-1515

***Mississauga:* Mississauga Christian Academy (MCA)**
Gananoque Campus
2690 Gananoque Dr., Mississauga, ON L5N 2R2, Canada
Tel: 905-826-4114; *Fax:* 905-567-5874
info@mississaugachristianacademy.com
www.mississaugachristianacademy.com
Grades: Pre - 8; *Note:* The Mississauga Christian Academy also operates a licensed day care.
Daniel Jovin, Principal

***Mississauga:* Philopateer Christian College**
6341 Mississauga Rd., Mississauga, ON L5N 1A5
Tel: 905-814-5181
www.pccprivateschool.com
Grades: Pre.-12; *Enrollment:* 300
Mary Ashun, Principal

***Newmarket:* Holland Marsh District Christian School**
18955 Dufferin St., RR#2, Newmarket, ON L3Y 4V9
Tel: 905-775-3701; *Fax:* 905-775-2395
hmdcs@hmdcs.ca
www.hmdcs.ca
Grades: K./Elem.; *Enrollment:* 220
Rod Berg, Principal

***Newmarket:* Newmarket & District Christian Academy (NDCA)**
P.O. Box 297
221 Carlson Dr., Newmarket, ON L3Y 4X1, Canada
Tel: 905-895-1199; *Fax:* 905-895-4353
ndca@rogers.com
www.ndca.ca
Grades: Kindergarten - 8

***North York:* Signet Christian School**
95 Jonesville Cres., North York, ON M4A 1H2, Canada
Tel: 416-750-7515; *Fax:* 905-750-7720
info@signetschool.ca
www.signetschool.ca
www.facebook.com/124533100975300
Grades: K. - 12; *Enrollment:* 276

***Oakville:* John Knox Christian School**
2232 Sheridan Garden Dr., Oakville, ON L6J 7T1
Tel: 905-829-8048; *Fax:* 905-829-8056
info@jkcs-oakville.org
www.jkcs-oakville.org
Grades: Elem.; *Enrollment:* 395
George Petrusma, Principal
gpetrusma@jkcs-oakville.org

***Oakville:* King's Christian Collegiate**
528 Burnhamthorpe Rd. West, Oakville, ON L6M 4K6, Canada
Tel: 905-257-5464; *Fax:* 905-257-5463
office@kingschristian.net
www.kingschristian.net
Grades: 9-12; *Enrollment:* 470; *Note:* An independent government-inspected and approved Christian high school.
John De Boer, Principal, 905-257-5464, ext. 505
jdeboer@kingschristian.net

***Oakville:* Oakville Christian School (OCS)**
112 Third Line, Oakville, ON L6L 3Z6, Canada
Tel: 905-825-1247; *Fax:* 905-825-3398
ocsadmissions@ocsonline.org
www.ocsonline.org
Grades: Junior Kindergarten - 8; *Enrollment:* 245
Jeff Kennedy, Principal

***Orillia:* Orillia Christian School (OCS)**
P.O. Box 862
505 Gill St., Orillia, ON L3V 6K8, Canada
Tel: 705-326-0532; *Fax:* 705-327-9856
www.orilliachristianschool.com
Grades: JK - 8; *Enrollment:* 120
Donna Veenstra, Principal
principal@orilliachristianschool.com

***Oshawa:* Immanuel Christian School**
849 Rossland Rd. West, Oshawa, ON L1J 8R5
Tel: 905-728-9071; *Fax:* 905-728-0604
www.immanuelschool.ca
www.facebook.com/169017956538053
Grades: K./Elem.
Jasper Hoogendam, Principal

***Ottawa:* Life Christian Academy**
1080B St Pierre St., Ottawa, ON K1C 1L3
Tel: 613-834-6588; *Fax:* 613-834-6588
www.lifechristianacademy.ca
www.facebook.com/LifeChristianAcademy
twitter.com/LCA_AVC
Grades: Elem./Sec.
Mike Karpishka, Principal

***Ottawa:* Ottawa Christian School**
255 Tartan Dr., Ottawa, ON K2M 1N4, Canada
Tel: 613-825-3000; *Fax:* 613-825-4008
info@ocschool.org
www.ocschool.org
www.facebook.com/pages/Ottawa-Christian-School/123631987687122
Grades: K.-8; *Enrollment:* 194
Paul Triemstra, Principal

***Ottawa:* Redeemer Christian High School (RCHS)**
82 Colonnade Rd. North, Ottawa, ON K2E 7L2, Canada
Tel: 613-723-9262; *Fax:* 613-723-9321
info@rchs.on.ca
www.rchs.on.ca
www.facebook.com/RedeemerChristianHighSchool
Grades: 9 - 12; *Note:* Redeemer Christian High School offers a Christ-centered education. The school also provides programs for students with learning disabilities.
Chuck Schoenmaker, Principal
principal@rchs.on.ca
J. David Naftel, B.Ed., B.Sc., Vice Principal
dnaftel@rchs.on.ca

***Owen Sound:* Timothy Christian School (TCS)**
1735 - 4th Ave. West, Owen Sound, ON N4K 4X7, Canada
Tel: 519-371-9151; *Fax:* 519-371-8607
www.tcsowensound.com
Grades: Junior Kindergarten - 8
Matthew Bittel, Principal

***Peterborough:* Rhema Christian School**
29 County Rd. 4, Peterborough, ON K9L 1B8, Canada
Tel: 705-743-1400; *Fax:* 705-743-1415
office@rhema.ca
www.rhema.ca
Grades: JK - 8; *Note:* Rhema Christian School is a day school which offers a Christ-centered education.
Joel Slofstra, Principal
Joanne Brethour, Business Administrator

***Picton:* Sonrise Christian Academy**
P.O. Box 845
58 Johnson St., Picton, ON K0K 2T0, Canada
Tel: 613-476-7883
office@sonrisechristianacademy.com
www.sonrisechristianacademy.com
www.facebook.com/120078748064586
Grades: JK - 8; *Enrollment:* 62
Julie Scrivens, Principal

***Prince Albert:* Scugog Christian School**
P.O. Box 3308
14480 Old Simcoe Rd., Prince Albert, ON L9L 1C3, Canada
Tel: 905-985-3741; *Fax:* 905-985-7153
scugogchristianschool@powergate.ca
www.scugogchristianschool.com
Grades: K.-8; *Enrollment:* 53
Grace van Niejenhuis, Principal

***Rosslyn:* Thunder Bay Christian School (TBCS)**
37 Cooper Rd., Rosslyn, ON P7K 0E2, Canada
Tel: 807-939-1209; *Fax:* 807-939-2843
office@tbaychristianschool.ca
www.tbaychristianschool.ca
Grades: Junior Kindergarten - 10; *Enrollment:* 165; *Note:* Thunder Bay Christian School is an interdenominational school operated by parents.

Andy Alblas, Principal

Sarnia: Sarnia Christian School
1273 Exmouth St., Sarnia, ON N7S 1W9, Canada
Tel: 519-383-7750; *Fax:* 519-383-6304
info@sarniachristian.com
www.sarniachristian.com
www.facebook.com/SarniaChristian
Grades: K.-8; *Enrollment:* 164
Len Smit, Principal
len.smit@sarniachristian.com

Sarnia: Temple Christian Academy (TCA)
1410 Quinn Dr., Sarnia, ON N7T 7H4, Canada
Tel: 519-542-9563; *Fax:* 519-542-9889
office@templechristianacademy.ca
www.templechristianacademy.ca
Grades: Jr. K.-8; *Enrollment:* 84
Dave Lawrence, Acting Administrator
Joyce Baker, Principal

Smithville: Covenant Christian School
6470 Regional Rd. #14, Smithville, ON L0R 2A0, Canada
Tel: 905-957-7796; *Fax:* 905-957-7794
ccs@nace.ca
www.nace.ca
Grades: K - 8; *Enrollment:* 226; *Note:* The Niagara Ass'n for Christian Education (NACE).
Sid Bakker, Principal
sbakker@nace.ca

Smithville: Smithville Christian High School
P.O. Box 40
6488 Smithville Rd., Smithville, ON L0R 2A0, Canada
Tel: 905-957-3255; *Fax:* 905-957-3431
office@smithvillechristian.ca
www.smithvillechristian.ca
www.facebook.com/smithvillechristian
twitter.com/smthvllechrstn
www.smithvillechristian.blogspot.com
www.youtube.com/smithCHSchool
Grades: Sec.; *Enrollment:* 224
Ted Harris, Administrator
Marlene Bergsma, Contact

St Catharines: Beacon Christian School
300 Scott St., St Catharines, ON L2N 1J3
Tel: 905-937-7411
mail@beaconchristian.org
www.beaconchristian.org
www.facebook.com/pages/Beacon-Christian-School/139816026123900
twitter.com/BeaconChristian
Grades: JK-8; *Note:* Beacon Christian School is an independent, interdenominational school.
Ralph Pot, Principal
rpot@beaconchristian.org

St Thomas: Faith Christian Academy
345 Fairview Ave., St Thomas, ON N5R 6M7
Tel: 519-633-0943; *Fax:* 519-633-6848
www.faithchristianacademy.ca
Grades: JK-8
Barry E. Pearce, Principal
bpearce@path2faith.com

Stoney Creek: John Knox Christian School
795 Hwy. #8, Stoney Creek, ON L8E 5J3, Canada
Tel: 905-643-2460; *Fax:* 905-643-5875
www.nace.ca
Number of Schools: 2; *Grades:* K.-Elem.; *Enrollment:* 122; *Number of Employees:* 18; *Note:* The Niagara Ass'n for Christian Education (NACE).
Bonnie Desjardins, Principal
bdesjardins@nace.ca
Tony Kamphuisns, Executive Director
tkamphuis@nace.ca

Stouffville: Stouffville Christian School
3885 Stouffville Rd., 2nd Fl., Stouffville, ON L4A 7X5, Canada
Tel: 905-887-3330; *Fax:* 905-887-3355
info@stouffvillechristianschool.com
www.stouffvillechristianschool.com
Grades: Jr. K.-8
Dave Burns, Principal

Strathroy: Strathroy Community Christian School (SCCS)
7880 Walkers Dr., Strathroy, ON N7G 3H4, Canada
Tel: 519-245-1934; *Fax:* 519-245-4424
office@sccs.ca
www.sccs.ca
www.facebook.com/221558934557393
Grades: Jr. K.-8; *Enrollment:* 212; *Number of Employees:* 21
Ken VanMinnen, Principal
principal@sccs.ca

Thorold: Grand River Academy of Christian Education
29 Claremont St., Thorold, ON L2V 1R4, Canada
Tel: 905-227-7507
Grades: Elem./Sec.; *Enrollment:* 125
Terrence Edwards

Toronto: Alive Christian Academy International
20 Progress Ave., Toronto, ON M1H 2X3
Tel: 416-439-2480
aca@jciami.com
www.jciami.com/aca/
Grades: Pre.-12; *Note:* Established by Jesus Christ Is Alive Ministries International.
Elias Sebastian, Principal

Toronto: Cathedral Christian Academy
1111 Arrow Rd., Toronto, ON M9N 3B3, Canada
Tel: 416-747-2843; *Fax:* 416-241-4404
mail@ccaschool.ca
www.ccaschool.ca
Grades: JK - 12

Toronto: People's Christian Academy
374 Sheppard Ave. East, Toronto, ON M2N 3B6, Canada
Tel: 416-222-3341; *Fax:* 416-222-3344
info@pca.ca
www.pca.ca
www.facebook.com/pages/Peoples-Christian-Academy/181436515199705
Grades: Jr. K.-12; *Enrollment:* 808
Rev. Reg Andrews, Director, Operations & Ministry

Toronto: Signet Christian School
95 Jonesville Cres., Toronto, ON M4A 1H2
Tel: 416-750-7515; *Fax:* 416-750-7720
info@signetschool.ca
www.signetschool.ca
www.facebook.com/124533100975300
Grades: JK-12; *Enrollment:* 80
Martin D. Sandford, Principal

Toronto: Three Fishes Christian Elementary School
801 Progress Ave., Toronto, ON M1H 2X4, Canada
Tel: 416-284-9003
3fishes@threefishes.org
www.threefishes.org
Grades: JK - 8; *Note:* Three Fishes Christian Elementary School offers a Christ-centered & academically demanding program.
Laurel Ann Mirams, Principal
dmirams@sympatico.ca

Toronto: Timothy Christian School (Rexdale) (TCS)
28 Elmhurst Dr., Toronto, ON M9W 2J5, Canada
Tel: 416-741-5770; *Fax:* 416-741-3359
www.timothycs.com
www.facebook.com/TimothyChristianSchool
Grades: Junior Kindergarten - 8; *Enrollment:* 100; *Note:* Timothy Christian School in Rexdale offers a Christ-centred education.
Margareth Lise, Principal

Toronto: Whitefield Christian Schools
5808 Finch Ave. East, Toronto, ON M1B 4Y6
Tel: 416-297-1212; *Fax:* 416-291-4632
wcs@bellnet.ca
whitefieldchristianschools.ca
Grades: Elem.

Toronto: Willowdale Christian School
60 Hilda Ave., Toronto, ON M2M 1V5
Tel: 416-222-1711; *Fax:* 416-222-1939
office@willowdalechristianschool.org
www.willowdalechristianschool.org
Grades: K.-8
Justin De Moor, Principal

Toronto: The Yorkland School (TYS)
255 Yorkland Blvd., Toronto, ON M2J 1S3, Canada
Tel: 416-491-7667; *Fax:* 416-491-3806
admin@yorkland.on.ca
www.yorkland.on.ca
www.facebook.com/ntcschool
Grades: JK - 12; *Note:* The Yorkland School is the middle & upper school division of the North Toronto Christian School. The school is commited to Biblical principles & values.
Allen Schenk, Principal
aschenk@ntcs.on.ca
Lyne Gagné, Vice Principal
lgagne@ntcs.on.ca
Gordon Cooke, Administrator / Treasurer
gcooke@ntcs.on.ca

Trenton: Trenton Christian School
340 Second Dug Hill Rd., Trenton, ON K8V 5P7, Canada
Tel: 613-392-3600
office@trentonchristianschool.com
trentonchristianschool.com
Grades: Junior Kindergarten - 8
David Wikkerink, Chair
Allen Bron, Principal
principal@trentonchristianschool.com

Utterson: Muskoka Christian School
P.O. Box 150
2483 Old Muskoka Rd., Utterson, ON P0B 1M0, Canada
Tel: 705-385-2847; *Fax:* 705-385-1756
mcs@muskoka.com
www.muskokachristianschool.com
Grades: Junior Kindergarten - 8; *Note:* The school is owned and operated by the Muskoka Association for Christian Education.

Wallaceburg: Wallaceburg Christian Private School (WCS)
693 Albert St., Wallaceburg, ON N8A 1Y8, Canada
Tel: 519-627-6013; *Fax:* 519-627-5051
admin@wallaceburgchristianschool.com
www.wallaceburgchristianschool.com
Grades: Junior Kindergarten - 8; *Note:* The school is a member of the Ontario Alliance of Christian Schools & Christian Schools International. It is independent of the Ministry of Education, although the school is registerd with the Ministry.

Wheatley: Old Colony Christian Academy
21311 Campbell Rd., RR#1, Wheatley, ON N0P 2P0, Canada
Tel: 519-825-9188; *Fax:* 519-825-9122
Grades: Elem.; *Enrollment:* 252

Williamsburg: Timothy Christian School (TCS)
P.O. Box 179
12600 County Rd. 18, Williamsburg, ON K0C 2H0, Canada
Tel: 613-535-2687; *Fax:* 613-535-1074
office@tcswilliamsburg.ca
www.tcswilliamsburg.ca
www.facebook.com/104962496361440
Grades: JK - 8; *Enrollment:* 130
Gary Postma, Principal
Principal@tcswilliamsburg.ca

Windsor: First Lutheran Christian Academy
3850 Locke St., Windsor, ON N9G 1S1, Canada
Tel: 519-250-7888; *Fax:* 519-250-7715
flca@mnsi.net
www.flca.ca
Enrollment: 201
Suzanne Eberhard, Principal
Rev. Gilvan L.C. de Azevedo, Pastor

Windsor: Maranatha Christian Academy
939 Northwood St., Windsor, ON N9E 1A2
Tel: 519-966-7424; *Fax:* 519-966-9519
www.maranathachristian.ca
Grades: JK-12
Amy Kulik, Principal
akulik@maranathachristian.ca

Windsor: Windsor Christian Fellowship Academy
4490 - 7th Concession, RR#1, Windsor, ON N9A 6J3, Canada
Tel: 519-972-5977; *Fax:* 519-972-0075
www.wcf.ca
www.facebook.com/WindsorChristianFellowship
twitter.com/wincf/wcf-pastors
Grades: Elem.; *Enrollment:* 81
Patti Banks

Woodbridge: Credo Christian Private School
8260 Huntington Rd., RR#1, Woodbridge, ON L4L 1A5, Canada
Tel: 905-851-1620; *Fax:* 905-851-1620
office@credochristianschool.com
credochristianschool.com
Grades: K.-8
L.P. Maat, Principal
G. Vanluik, Principal's Relief

Woodbridge: Toronto District Christian High School
377 Woodbridge Ave., Woodbridge, ON L4L 2V7, Canada
Tel: 905-851-1772; *Fax:* 905-851-9992
info@tdchristian.ca
www.tdchristian.ca
Grades: Secondary
William Groot, Principal
principal@tdchristian.ca

Tim Bentum, Vice Principal, Admissions & Students
bentum@tdchristian.ca
Tim Buwalda, Coordinator, Communications
buwalda@tdchristian.ca
Meg Cate, Financial Administrator
cate@tdchristian.ca

Wyoming: John Knox Christian School of Wyoming
4738 Confederation Line, Wyoming, ON N0N 1T0
Tel: 519-845-3112; *Fax:* 519-845-1404
www.wyomingjkcs.com
Grades: K./Elem.
Ymko Boersma, Principal

Catholic

Mississauga: Holy Name of Mary College School
2241 Mississauga Rd., Mississauga, ON L5H 2K8
Tel: 905-891-1890; *Fax:* 905-891-2082
office@hnmcs.ca
www.holynameofmarycollegeschool.com
Grades: 5-12; Girls
Margaret DeCourcy, President
decourcy@hnmcs.ca
Marilena Tesoro, Principal
tesoro@hnmcs.ca

Mississauga: Lumen Veritatis Academy
225 Broadway St., Mississauga, ON L5M 1H9
Tel: 905-813-9215
lumenveritatis.ca
www.facebook.com/lumenveritatisacademy
twitter.com/lvablog
Grades: JK-8; *Enrollment:* 75
Greg La Chimea, Principal
Alma Grace Crowe, Vice-Principal, Streetsville Campus

Campuses
Thornhill Campus
191 Wade Gate, Thornhill, ON L4J 5Y4
Tel: 905-597-4933

Richmond Hill: Holy Trinity School
11300 Bayview Ave., Richmond Hill, ON L4S 1L4, Canada
Tel: 905-737-1114; *Fax:* 905-737-5187
www.hts.on.ca
www.facebook.com/HTSHolyTrinitySchool
twitter.com/HTSRichmondHill
Grades: JK - 12; *Enrollment:* 759
Barry Hughes, Head of School
HeadofSchool@hts.on.ca

Toronto: De La Salle College 'Oaklands' (DEL)
131 Farnham Ave., Toronto, ON M4V 1H7, Canada
Tel: 416-969-8771; *Fax:* 416-969-9175
info@delasalle.toronto.on.ca
www.delasalleoaklands.ca
www.facebook.com/398396406871450
Grades: Elem./Sec.; *Enrollment:* 578
Joseph Pupo, Principal, 416-969-8771, ext. 230
jpupo@delasalleoaklands.org

French

Mississauga: Mississauga Christian French School (MCFS)
1245 Eglinton Ave. West, Mississauga, ON L5V 2M4
Tel: 905-567-4032
principal@mcfschool.ca
www.mcfschool.ca
Grades: Pre.-8; *Enrollment:* 120
Sandra Gerges, Principal

Hearing Impaired

Toronto: Yeshivas Nefesh Dovid
77 Stormont Ave., Toronto, ON M5N 2C3
Tel: 416-630-6220
info@nefeshdovid.com
www.nefeshdovid.com
Grades: 9 - 12

Special Education

Brant: The Gregory School for Exceptional Learning
1249 Colborne St. West, Brant, ON N3T 5L7
Tel: 519-449-1650
info@gregoryschool.ca
www.gregoryschool.ca
Note: School for children with special needs that require special programming.
Angeline Savard, Principal

Burlington: Woodview Learning Centre
69 Flatt Rd., Burlington, ON L7R 3X5
Tel: 905-689-4727; *Fax:* 905-689-2474
wcc@woodview.ca
www.woodview.ca
www.facebook.com/225044664274074
twitter.com/WoodviewWLC
Grades: K.-9; *Enrollment:* 12; *Note:* The Learning Centre provides individualized learning strategies for students with Autism.
Cindy l'Anson, Executive Director

Campuses
Brantford Office
643 Park Rd. North, Brantford, ON N3T 5L8
Tel: 519-752-5308; *Fax:* 519-752-9102
general@woodview.ca

Hamilton Office
Also known as: Mischa Weisz Centre for Autism Services
1900 Main St. West, Hamilton, ON L8S 4R8
Tel: 905-527-9771; *Fax:* 905-522-4690
wcc@woodview.ca

Mississauga: Good Samaritan School for Exceptional Learners
Also known as: Good Samaritan Private School
6341 Mississauga Rd., Mississauga, ON L5N 1A7
Tel: 905-219-9969
Grades: JK-12; Adult Ed.

Ottawa: Académie de la Capitale
#200, 1010 Morrison Dr., Ottawa, ON K2H 8K7
Tel: 613-721-3872; *Fax:* 613-721-8189
info@acadecap.org
www.acadecap.org
www.facebook.com/175529857687
twitter.com/Acadecap
Grades: Pre.-12
Lucy Lalonde, Director

Ottawa: Astolot Educational Centre
#203, 1187 Bank St., Ottawa, ON K1S 3X7
Tel: 613-260-5996
astolot@rogers.com
www.astolot.com
Jennifer Cowan, M.Ed., Owner/Director

Peterborough: Arrowsmith School Peterborough
366 Parkhill Rd. East, Peterborough, ON K9L 1C3
Tel: 705-741-4800; *Fax:* 705-741-1832
peterborough@arrowsmithprogram.ca
www.arrowsmithschool.org/arrowsmithschool-peterborough
www.facebook.com/arrowsmithprogram
Grades: 1-12; *Enrollment:* 40
Jill Marcinkowski, Program Director

Richmond Hill: Academy for Gifted Children
Also known as: P.A.C.E.
12 Bond Cres., Richmond Hill, ON L4E 3K2, Canada
Tel: 905-773-0997; *Fax:* 905-773-4722
www.pace.on.ca
Grades: Elem./Sec.; *Enrollment:* 284; *Note:* P.A.C.E. - Programming for Academic & Creative Excellence. A non-denominational, co-ed, private day school, with programmes focussing on basic skills, with a strong emphasis on math & science, accelerated learning & individual instruction.
Barbara Rosenberg, Founder & Principal

Toronto: Arrowsmith School Toronto
245 St. Clair Ave. West, Toronto, ON M4V 1R3
Tel: 416-963-4962; *Fax:* 416-963-5017
reception@arrowsmithschool.org
www.arrowsmithschool.org
www.facebook.com/arrowsmithprogram
Grades: 1-12; *Enrollment:* 75
Barbara Arrowsmith Young, Director

Toronto: Brighton School
240 The Donway West, Toronto, ON M3B 2V8
Tel: 416-932-8273; *Fax:* 416-850-5493
contactus@brightonschool.ca
www.brightonschool.ca
twitter.com/brighton_school
Grades: 1-12; *Enrollment:* 60; *Note:* Brighton is a private school for students who learn best in small classes, are one or more years behind academically, have a learning disability or an uneven learning profile.
Kathy Lear, Principal & Executive Director

Toronto: Don Valley Academy
#408, 4576 Yonge St., Toronto, ON M2N 6N4
Tel: 416-223-7561; *Fax:* 416-223-0065
www.donvalleyacademy.com
www.facebook.com/donvalleyacademy
Grades: 9-12; *Enrollment:* 30; *Note:* Don Valley Academy provides personalized education for gifted students, as well as those with learning difficulties.
Alex J. Evans, Principal

Toronto: Finding The Way Learning Centre & Bright Start Academy (FTW)
#102 & 202, 2950 Keele St., Toronto, ON M3M 2H2
Tel: 647-347-6122; *Fax:* 647-347-6153
info@brightstartacademy.info
www.brightstartacademy.info
www.facebook.com/pages/Bright-Start-Academy/394124197310338
twitter.com/ftwlcautism
www.linkedin.com/pub/allie-offman/55/465/82?trk=tbr
Grades: Pre.-9; *Note:* The Academy offers a behaviour & education program for children with autism & learning difficulties.
Allie Offman, Executive Director

Toronto: Kohai Educational Centre
41 Roehampton Ave., Toronto, ON M4P 1P9
Tel: 416-489-3636; *Fax:* 416-489-3662
kohai@bellnet.ca
www.kohai.ca
www.facebook.com/pages/Kohai-Educational-Centre/509009145793089
www.twitter.com/Kohai41
Grades: Pre.-8; *Note:* Programs & education for students with genetic disorders, behaviour problems, & language disorders.
Barbara Brown, Principal

Toronto: Magnificent Minds
47 Glenbrook Ave., Lower Level, Toronto, ON M6B 2L7
Tel: 647-404-6349
MagnificentMindsToronto@Gmail.com
www.magnificentminds.ca
www.facebook.com/MagnificentMinds
twitter.com/MagMinds
www.pinterest.com/magnificentmind/
Grades: Pre-K-Elem.
Alley Dezenhouse, Principal, Director, Behaviour Therapist

Toronto: Merle Levine Academy
#318, 4630 Dufferin St., Toronto, ON M3H 5S4
Tel: 416-661-4141; *Fax:* 416-661-4143
merle@merlelevineacademy.com
www.merlelevineacademy.com
www.facebook.com/pages/Merle-Levine-Academy/286041258174405
twitter.com/MLevineAcademy
Grades: Elem.-Sec.; *Note:* Private school specializing in areas of learning disabilities, attentional problems (ADD-ADHD) and other disorders affecting academic achievement.
Merle Levine, BA, MEd, Director
merle@merlelevineacademy.com
Persaud Levine, MA, MEd, Director/Principal
yuwattee.persaud@merlelevineacademy.com

Toronto: Shoore Centre for Learning
801 Eglinton Ave. West, Toronto, ON M5N 1E3
Tel: 416-781-4754; *Fax:* 416-781-0163
info@shoorecentre.com
www.shoorecentre.com
www.facebook.com/222318484489159
twitter.com/ShooreCentre
www.youtube.com/user/ShooreCentre
Grades: 7 - 12
Michael I. Shoore, B.Sc., M.Ed., Director
michael@shoorecentre.com
Tamara Shoore, Principal
tammy@shoorecentre.com

Toronto: Tikvat Hayim School
c/o Beth Tikvah Synagogue
3080 Bayview Ave., Toronto, ON M2N 5L3
Tel: 416-221-3433
Note: The school offers programs every Sunday for children with learning disabilities, aged 5-12.
Dr. Zeev Greenberg, Principal

Toronto: The YMCA Academy
Also known as: The Academy
15 Breadalbane St., 3rd Fl., Toronto, ON M4Y 1C2
Tel: 416-928-0124; *Fax:* 416-928-0212
www.ymcaacademy.org
www.facebook.com/ymcaacademy
twitter.com/ymcaacademy
www.youtube.com/user/YMCAAcademy

Grades: Secondary; *Note:* The YMCA Academy is a high school for students with learning disabilities, located in downtown Toronto.
Don Adams, Head of School, 416-928-0124, ext. 31401
don.adams@ymcagta.org

***Toronto:* Zareinu Educational Centre of Metropolitan Toronto**
Administration Office
#301, 4630 Dufferin St., Toronto, ON M3H 5S4
Tel: 416-661-1800; *Fax:* 416-661-1801
info@zareinu.org
zareinu.org
www.facebook.com/ZareinuEducationalCentre
Grades: Pre.-12; *Note:* Zareinu Educational Centre is a treatment centre & Jewish day school for children with physical & developmental disabilities.
Dr. Mitchell Parker, Principal & Clinical Director

Campuses
School Office
#108, 7026 Bathurst St., Thornhill, ON L4J 8K3
Tel: 905-738-5542; *Fax:* 905-738-8047
Phyllis Resnick, Contact, School Administration
Sarah Weitz, Contact, School Administration

***Utopia:* Renaissance Academy**
8058 - 8th Line, Utopia, ON L0M 1T0
Tel: 705-423-9688; *Fax:* 705-423-9788
www.renaissanceacademy.ca
Grades: K-12; *Note:* Renaissance Academy offers residential and day programs, ranging from gifted to life skills.
Giancarlo Marchi, Head of School
gmarchi@renaissanceacademy.ca

Independent & Private Schools

***Ajax:* Avalon Private High School**
#204, 40 Old Kingston Rd., Ajax, ON L1T 2Z7
Tel: 905-683-5299
Grades: 9 - 12
Kathy Greenfield, Principal

***Ajax:* Jaamiah Aluloom Al-Islamyyah Institute of Islamic Learning**
2944 Audley Rd., Ajax, ON L1Z 1T7
Tel: 905-686-4003; *Fax:* 905-686-4428
info@jaamiahajax.com
www.jaamiahajax.com
Enrollment: 400

***Ajax:* Montessori Learning Centre of Ajax**
Also known as: 849179 Ontario Inc.
#17, 250 Bayly St. West, Ajax, ON L1S 3V4, Canada
Tel: 905-428-3122
info@mlcajax.com
www.mlcajax.com
Grades: Pre - 6; *Note:* Montessori Learning Centre of Ajax offers a toddler program for children from 18 months to 3 years, as well as a Casa program for 3 to 6 year old children. Elementary education is provided for children from age 6 to 12.

***Ajax:* Wasdell Centre for Innovative Learning**
85 Kings Cres., Ajax, ON L1S 2M4
Tel: 905-426-3241; *Fax:* 905-426-2921
Toll-Free: 888-525-2385
www.wasdellcentre.org
Grades: Pre.-12; *Enrollment:* 55
Elizabeth Moxley-Paquette, Principal/Director
e.moxley-paquette@wasdellcentre.org

***Amaranth:* The Maples Academy**
Also known as: The Maples Independent Country School
513047 2nd Line, Amaranth, ON L9W 0S3, Canada
Tel: 519-942-3310; *Fax:* 519-942-8041
info@TheMaplesSchool.com
www.themaplesschool.com
www.facebook.com/154097964653598
twitter.com/TheMaplesSchool
www.pinterest.com/themaplesschool/
Grades: Preschool - 8; *Enrollment:* 120
Greg Playford, Principal
greg.playford@themaplesschool.com

***Aurora:* Aurora Montessori School**
330 Industrial Pkwy. North, Aurora, ON L4G 4C3, Canada
Tel: 905-841-0065; *Fax:* 905-841-2022
info@auroramontessori.com
www.auroramontessori.com
Grades: Pre - 8; *Note:* Aurora Montessori School & Private School also offers a toddler program for children from ages 18 months to 3 years. Casa programs are for children from ages 2.5 to 6 years.
Brenda Glashan, Principal

***Aurora:* Foundations Private School**
81 Industrial Pkwy. North, Aurora, ON L4G 4C4, Canada
Tel: 905-713-1141; *Fax:* 905-713-6340
www.foundationsps.com
Grades: JK-8; *Enrollment:* 159
Ellen Powers, Principal
powers@greatschool.ca

***Aurora:* La Maison Montessori House**
14 Stone Rd., Aurora, ON L4G 6X9
Tel: 905-726-2110
info@lmmh.ca
www.lmmh.ca
Grades: Toddler - Pre.
Shelley Salisbury, Principal

Campuses
Newmarket Campus (Elementary)
1205 Stellar Dr., Newmarket, ON L3Y 7B8
Tel: 905-895-2110
elementary@lmmh.ca
Grades: Elem.
Anne Martin, Principal

***Aurora:* St. Andrew's College**
15800 Yonge St., Aurora, ON L4G 3H7, Canada
Tel: 905-727-3178; *Fax:* 905-841-6911
info@sac.on.ca
www.sac.on.ca
www.facebook.com/standrewscollege
twitter.com/StAndrews1899
www.youtube.com/StAndrews1899
Grades: 5-12; *Enrollment:* 614; *Note:* All-boys boarding and day school
Kevin McHenry, Headmaster, 905-727-3178, ext. 226
kevin.mchenry@sac.on.ca
Michael Paluch, Assistant Headmaster, Academics, 905-727-3178, ext. 285
michael.paluch@sac.on.ca
Greg L. Reid, Assistant Headmaster, School Life and Operations, 905-727-3178, ext. 258
greg.reid@sac.on.ca
Courtenay Shrimpton, Assistant Headmaster, Strategic Development and Student Life, 905-727-3178, ext. 307
courtenay.shrimpton@sac.on.ca
Sherrill Knight, Director of Human Resources, 905-727-2580, ext. 230
sherrill.knight@sac.on.ca

***Baden, Region of Waterloo:* Canadian Independent College (CIC)**
3601 Sandhills Rd., Baden, Region of Waterloo, ON N3A 3B9
Tel: 519-634-9255; *Fax:* 519-634-9355
info@cicbaden.ca
www.cicbaden.ca
Grades: 6-12; *Enrollment:* 115; *Note:* The CIC has a sister campus in Accra, Ghana.
Dr. Heather Bohez, B.Sc., N.D.

***Barrie:* Kempenfelt Bay School**
576 Bryne Dr., Barrie, ON L4N 9P6
Tel: 705-739-4731; *Fax:* 705-739-3678
www.kempenfeltbayschool.com
www.facebook.com/153567748086397
Grades: JK-8; *Enrollment:* 175
Graham Hookey, Head of School
Diane Fitzgerald, Director, Academics & School Life

***Belleville:* Albert College**
160 Dundas St. West, Belleville, ON K8P 1A6
Tel: 613-968-5726; *Fax:* 613-968-9651
Toll-Free: 1-800-952-5237
info@albertcollege.ca
www.albertcollege.ca
www.facebook.com/209735436302
twitter.com/AlbertCollege
www.youtube.com/user/AlbertSince1857
Grades: Elem./Sec.; *Enrollment:* 298
Heather Kidd, Director, Admission
hkidd@albertc.on.ca

***Bolton:* Countryside Montessori Private School**
1 Loring Dr., Bolton, ON L7E 1Y1, Canada
Tel: 905-951-3359; *Fax:* 905-951-3920
Enrollment: 257

***Brampton:* Academic Montessori**
#1-6, 333 Fairhill Ave., Brampton, ON L7A 3N9
Tel: 905-846-4611; *Fax:* 905-459-3800
www.academicmontessori.com
Grades: Elem.
Peter Sesek, Principal

***Brampton:* Al-Iman School**
#1-4, 253 Summerlea Rd., Brampton, ON L6T 5A8
Tel: 905-799-9231
islamicprivate@bellnet.ca
alimanschool.ca
Grades: JK - 8
Syyed Hamid Ali, Principal

***Brampton:* Brampton-Georgetown Montessori School (BGMS)**
1030 Queen St. West, Brampton, ON L6X 0B2, Canada
Tel: 905-457-2496
info@bgmschool.com
www.bgmschool.com
Grades: Toddler - Elem.; *Note:* Brampton-Georgetown Montessori School provides programs for children from ages 2.5 to 11.

***Brampton:* Har Tikvah Congregational School**
P.O. Box 36023
9893 Torbram Rd., Brampton, ON L6S 6A3
Tel: 905-792-7589; *Fax:* 905-792-7589
info@hartikvah.org
www.hartikvah.org

***Brampton:* Khalsa Community School**
69 Maitland St., Brampton, ON L6S 3B5, Canada
Tel: 905-791-1750; *Fax:* 905-458-9133
khalsacommunityschool@hotmail.com
www.khalsacommunityschool.com
Grades: K.-8; *Enrollment:* 187

***Brampton:* Khalsa Montessori School**
Also known as: KM School
#2, 4535 Ebenezer Rd., Brampton, ON L6P 2P7
Tel: 905-913-0801; *Fax:* 866-566-6069
info@kmschool.org
www.kmschool.org
www.facebook.com/theKMSchool
twitter.com/theKMSchool
Grades: Toddler - Elem.
Harpeet Singh, Principal

***Brampton:* Rowntree Montessori Schools - RMS Academy**
3 Sunforest Dr., Brampton, ON L6Z 2Z2
Tel: 905-790-3838; *Fax:* 905-790-5686
admin@rowntreemontessori.com
rowntreemontessori.com
Grades: K.-10; *Enrollment:* 100
J. Essaye, Managing Director
D. Zebeljan, Principal

Campuses
Bramalea Campus
93 Autumn Blvd., Brampton, ON L6T 2W1
Tel: 905-793-2196; *Fax:* 905-790-9083
rowntreemontessori.com/campuses/bramalea
Grades: Pre.-SK; Toddler
S. Verma, Principal

Central Park Campus
502 Central Park Dr., Brampton, ON L6S 2C8
Tel: 905-793-6231; *Fax:* 905-793-9020
rowntreemontessori.com/campuses/central-park
Grades: Pre.-SK; Toddler
M. Penrice, Principal

Downtown Campus
4 Elizabeth St. North, Brampton, ON L6X 1S2
Tel: 905-457-7439; *Fax:* 905-457-2518
rowntreemontessori.com/campuses/downtown
Grades: Pre.-SK; Toddler
T. Rivard, Principal

***Brampton:* Tall Pines School**
8525 Torbram Rd., Brampton, ON L6T 5K4, Canada
Tel: 905-458-6770; *Fax:* 905-458-7967
registrar@tallpinesschool.com
www.tallpinesschool.com
Number of Schools: Montessori programs, Traditional Private School; *Grades:* K.-9; *Enrollment:* 519; *Note:* Private Montessori and Progressive school
Elizabeth Szekeres, Registrar, 905-458-6770, ext. 228
eszekeres@insidetps.com

***Brantford:* Braemar House School**
36 Baxter St., Brantford, ON N3R 2V8, Canada
Tel: 519-753-2929; *Fax:* 519-753-1235
admin@braemarhouseschool.ca
www.braemarhouseschool.ca
www.facebook.com/BraemarHouseSchool
Grades: JK - 8; *Enrollment:* 92; *Note:* Braemar House School also offers a Montessori Casa program.

Annette Minutillo, Executive Director

***Brantford:* Montessori House of Children**
85 Charlotte St., Brantford, ON N3T 2X2, Canada
Tel: 519-759-7290; *Fax:* 519-759-6774
mails@montessorihouseofchildren.com
www.montessorihouseofchildren.com
Other Information: admissions@montessorihouseofchildren.com (Admission inquiries)
Note: Brantford's Montessori House of Children provides programs for children from 2.5 to 9 years of age.

***Breslau:* St. John's-Kilmarnock School**
P.O. Box 179
2201 Shantz Station Rd., Breslau, ON N0B 1M0, Canada
Tel: 519-648-2183; *Fax:* 519-648-2186
info@sjkschool.org
www.sjkschool.org
www.facebook.com/sjkschool
twitter.com/sjkschool
www.youtube.com/user/sjkschool
Grades: Jr. K.-12; *Enrollment:* 505
Norman Southward, Head of School
nsouthward@sjkschool.org

***Brockville:* Fulford Academy**
280 King St. East, Brockville, ON K6V 1E2
Tel: 613-341-9330; *Fax:* 613-341-9344
www.fulfordacademy.com
www.facebook.com/fulfordacademy
www.youtube.com/fulfordacademy
Grades: 7 - 10; *Enrollment:* 60; *Note:* Private international boarding school.
Dr. Thomas Steel, Head of School
tom.steel@fulfordacademy.com

***Burlington:* Fairview Glen Montessori**
3508 Commerce Ct., Burlington, ON L7N 3L7
Tel: 905-634-0781
info@fairviewglen.com
www.fairviewglen.com
Grades: Pre.-6; *Enrollment:* 125
Tammy-Leigh Sage, Director

***Burlington:* Halton Waldorf School (HWS)**
2193 Orchard Rd., Burlington, ON L7R 3X5, Canada
Tel: 905-331-4387; *Fax:* 905-331-3231
enrollment@haltonwaldorf.com
www.waldorfschool.net
Grades: Preschool - 8; *Enrollment:* 160; *Note:* The school provides Waldorf education.

***Burlington:* Niagara Montessori School**
3132 South Dr., Burlington, ON L7N 1H7, Canada
Tel: 905-632-2374
Grades: Preschool - Kindergarten; *Note:* The Montessori School offers programs for children from age 2.5 to 6.

***Caledon:* King's College School**
16379 The Gore Rd., Caledon, ON L7E 0X4
Tel: 905-880-7645; *Fax:* 905-880-9439
info@kingscollegeschool.ca
www.kingscollegeschool.ca
www.facebook.com/132101376817812
twitter.com/kingscollschool
Grades: 3-12; *Enrollment:* 36
Barbara H. Lord, Headmistress
Emily Lord, Contact, 905-880-7645
elord@kingscollegeschool.ca

***Cambridge:* Montessori School of Cambridge**
9 Roseview Ave., Cambridge, ON N1R 4A5
Tel: 519-622-1470; *Fax:* 519-622-4801
montessori@in.on.ca
montessoricambridge.com
www.facebook.com/MontessoriSchoolofCambridge
twitter.com/montessoricamb
Grades: Toddler - Pre.
Marilyn Herriot, Principal

***Campbellville:* Hitherfield Preparatory School**
2439 - 10th Side Rd., Campbellville, ON L0P 1B0, Canada
Tel: 905-854-0890; *Fax:* 905-854-3155
hitherfield.org/www/
twitter.com/HitherfieldInfo
Grades: Elem./Sec.; *Enrollment:* 115
Ann J. Scott, Principal, 9058540890, ext. 102

***Carp:* Venta Preparatory School**
2013 Old Carp Rd., Carp, ON K0A 1L0, Canada
Tel: 613-839-2175; *Fax:* 613-839-1956
info@ventaprep.com
www.ventapreparatoryschool.com
www.facebook.com/pages/Venta-Preparatory-School/311042463153
twitter.com/VentaSchool
www.pinterest.com/ventaprep/
Grades: JK - 10; *Note:* Venta Preparatory School is a day & boarding school. The maximum class size is twelve students.
Marilyn Mansfield, Principal, 613-839-2175, ext. 223
mmansfield@ventaprep.com
Sean Hopper, Executive Director, 613-839-2175, ext. 225
shopper@ventaprep.com
Shaun Quinn, Director, Studies, 613-839-2175, ext. 224
squinn@ventaprep.com
Tanya Kaye, Director, Marketing & Admissions, 613-839-2175, ext. 240

***Cookstown:* Thor College**
4073 - 4th Line Innisfil, Cookstown, ON L0L 1L0
Tel: 705-458-9705
info@thorcollege.ca
www.thorcollege.ca
www.facebook.com/213239166825
twitter.com/thorcollege
www.youtube.com/user/thorcollege1
Grades: JK - 8
Cherie Hughes, Head of School

***Cornwall:* Islamic Institute Al-Rashid**
18345 County Rd. 2, RR#1, Cornwall, ON K6H 5R5
Tel: 613-931-2895
contact@alrashid.ca
www.alrashid.ca
Grades: Elem./Sec.
M. Mazhar Alam, Principal

***Cornwall:* Ontario Hockey Academy**
1541 Vincent Massey Dr., Cornwall, ON K6H 5R6
Tel: 613-938-5009; *Fax:* 613-937-3422
OHA.admissions@gmail.com
www.ontariohockeyacademy.com
www.facebook.com/pages/Ontario-Hockey-Academy/108238760044?ref=hl
twitter.com/OHAMavericks
Grades: 9 - 12

***Deep River:* The Deep River Science Academy (DRSA)**
P.O. Box 600
20 Forest Ave., Deep River, ON K0J 1P0, Canada
Tel: 613-584-4541; *Fax:* 613-584-9597
info@drsa.ca
www.drsa.ca
www.facebook.com/DeepRiverScienceAcademy
twitter.com/DRSA_25
www.pinterest.com/drsa
Grades: 10 - 12; *Enrollment:* 25; *Number of Employees:* 3; *Note:* The Deep River Science Academy partners with Atomic Energy of Canada, Ltd. to offer science camps. Students must have completed a grade 10 or higher science high school credit. Hhigh school credits are awarded.
Shawna Miller, Executive Director
shawna.miller@drsa.ca
Margo Ingram, Principal

***Dundas:* Dundas Valley Montessori School**
14 Kemp Dr., Dundas, ON L9H 2M9
Tel: 905-627-1073; *Fax:* 289-494-0102
dvms.ca
www.facebook.com/DVMSbook
twitter.com/dvmstweets
Grades: Pre. - Jr. High
Tony Evans, Director
dvms@golden.net

***Durham:* Edge Hill Country School**
RR#1, Durham, ON N0G 1R0
Tel: 519-369-3195
info@edgehill-school.com
www.edgehill-school.com
www.facebook.com/pages/Edge-Hill-Country-School/141510425967319
Grades: K - 8
Lise Gunby, School Administrator

***Embrun:* Canada eSchool**
P.O. Box 277
921 Notre-Dame St., Embrun, ON K0A 1W0
Tel: 613-443-9522; *Fax:* 613-482-4504
info@myeschool.ca
www.canadaeschool.ca
www.facebook.com/142423952478564
twitter.com/Canada_eSchool
Grades: 9-12; *Enrollment:* 1340; *Note:* Canada eSchool supplements students' education with eLearning technology, accessible anywhere in the world.
Carl J. Frizell, Principal

***Etobicoke:* Al Azhar Islamic School**
2074 Kipling Ave., Etobicoke, ON M9W 4J4
Tel: 416-741-3420; *Fax:* 416-741-5143
contact@alazhar.ca
www.alazharacademy.com
www.facebook.com/alazharacademy
twitter.com/alazharacademy
www.youtube.com/alazharacademy

***Etobicoke:* Al-Ashraf Islamic School**
23 Brydon Dr., Etobicoke, ON M9W 4M7, Canada
Tel: 416-740-1495
Grades: Elem./Sec.; *Enrollment:* 157
Riyad Khan, Principal

***Etobicoke:* Alderwood Toronto Private School**
26 Fieldway Rd., Etobicoke, ON M8Z 3L2
Tel: 416-239-2100
info@alderwoodtoronto.ca
alderwoodtoronto.com
Grades: Pre.-8
Sheileen Krone, Principal

***Etobicoke:* Etobicoke Montessori School**
4 La Rose Ave., Etobicoke, ON M9P 1A5
Tel: 416-246-9896; *Fax:* 416-243-2999
info@etobicokemontessorischool.ca
www.etobicokemontessorischool.ca
Grades: Toddler - Pre.
Christina Zentena, Principal

***Etobicoke:* Kingsley Primary School**
516 The Kingsway, Etobicoke, ON M9A 3W6
Tel: 416-233-0150; *Fax:* 416-233-5971
kingsleyschool@bellnet.ca
www.kingsleyschool.ca
www.facebook.com/kingsleyprimaryschool
Grades: K./Elem.
Mark Huttram, Chair
Julie Middleton, Principal
Louisa Florio, Principal-Elect

***Etobicoke:* Kingsway College School**
4600 Dundas St. West, Etobicoke, ON M9A 1A5
Tel: 416-234-5073; *Fax:* 416-234-8386
office@kcs.on.ca
www.kcs.on.ca
www.facebook.com/KCSMatters
twitter.com/KCSMatters
www.linkedin.com/groups?home=&gid=4030878
www.youtube.com/KCSMatters
Grades: Elem.; *Enrollment:* 309
Derek Logan, Head of School

***Etobicoke:* Madresatul Banaat Almuslimaat Muslim Girl's School**
10 Vulcan St., Etobicoke, ON M9W 1L2
Tel: 416-244-8600; *Fax:* 416-244-0059
www.muslimgirlsschool.com
Grades: JK-12; Girls; *Enrollment:* 152; *Note:* Alhamdulillah, Madresatul Banaat Almuslimaat, the first Muslim girls school in Toronto, Ontario, Canada, is a registered, non-profit, charitable organization duly approved and accredited by the Ontario Ministry of Education and Waqf Lillahi Taala.
S. Ataullah Qadri, President/Principal

Schools

Madresatul Atfaal Almuslimeen Muslim Children's School
Grades: JK.-5; Boys and Girls; *Note:* The school now provides primary education from JK to grade 5, for boys and girls at the same location (under the same management) as Madresatul Banaat Almuslimaat's, at their junior school.

***Etobicoke:* Olivet New Church School**
279 Burnhamthorpe Rd., Etobicoke, ON M9B 1Z6
Tel: 416-239-3054; *Fax:* 416-239-4935
contact@olivetnewchurch.org
www.olivetnewchurch.org
Grades: JK-6; *Enrollment:* 50
Rev. James Cooper, Pastor

Fort Frances: **Lac La Croix Elementary & High School**
P.O. Box 640
Fort Frances, ON P9A 3M9
Tel: 807-485-2402; *Fax:* 807-485-2558
Grades: Elem./9-12

Fort Frances: **Seven Generations Education Institute School**
Nanicost Complex
P.O. Box 297
1455 Idylwild Dr., Fort Frances, ON P9A 3M6, Canada
Tel: 807-274-2796; *Fax:* 807-274-8761
www.7generations.org
www.facebook.com/115074575204883
Dan Bird

Guelph: **Montessori School of Wellington**
68 Suffolk St. West, Guelph, ON N1H 2J2
Tel: 519-821-5876; *Fax:* 519-821-3531
montessori.wellington@bellnet.ca
www.montessori-school.ca
Grades: Casa
Glynis Hamilton, Principal

Guelph: **Trillium Waldorf School**
540 Victoria Rd. North, Guelph, ON N1E 6Z4
Tel: 519-821-5140; *Fax:* 519-821-0453
info@trilliumwaldorfschool.com
www.trilliumwaldorfschool.com
Grades: Pre. K - 8

Haliburton: **St. Peter's ACHS College School**
#21, 4252 County Rd., Haliburton, ON K0M 1S0
Tel: 705-457-8887
achscanada@gmail.com
achscanada.com
Grades: 1-8; Boys
Peter Thyrring, Headmaster

Hamilton: **Columbia International College of Canada**
1003 Main St. West, Hamilton, ON L8S 4P3, Canada
Tel: 905-572-7883; *Fax:* 905-572-9332
columbia@cic-totalcare.com
www.cic-totalcare.com
www.facebook.com/53144393827
twitter.com/cic_totalcare
Grades: 7 - 12; *Enrollment:* 1700; *Note:* Private boarding and university preparatory school.
Ron Rambarran, Principal
principal@cic-totalcare.com

Hamilton: **Hamilton Hebrew Academy Zichron Meir School**
60 Dow Ave., Hamilton, ON L8S 1W4, Canada
Tel: 905-528-0330; *Fax:* 905-528-0544
school@hamiltonhebrewacademy.ca
www.hamiltonhebrewacademy.ca
Grades: Pre - 8
Daniel Green, Dean
dean@hamiltonhebrewacademy.ca
Joanne Mcintosh, Principal
jmcintosh@hamiltonhebrewacademy.ca

Hamilton: **Hamilton Hebrew High / Midrasha (H3)**
60 Dow Ave., Hamilton, ON L8S 1W4
Tel: 905-528-0039
info@hhhmidrasha.ca
hhhmidrasha.ca
Grades: 8-12; *Note:* Hamilton Hebrew High offers secondary school students extra Ontario Secondary School credits with a Jewish perspective.
Yaakov Morel, Director
yaakov@hhhmidrasha.ca
Gord Garshowitz, Educational Coordinator, 905-906-6900
gord@hhhmidrasha.ca

Hamilton: **Hillfield Strathallan College**
299 Fennell Ave. West, Hamilton, ON L9C 1G3
Tel: 905-389-1367; *Fax:* 905-389-6366
www.hsc.on.ca
www.facebook.com/hillfieldstrathallancollege
twitter.com/HillStrath
www.youtube.com/officialHSC
Grades: JK-12; *Enrollment:* 1000
Marc Ayotte, Head, College

Hamilton: **Islamic School of Hamilton (ISH)**
1545 Stonechurch Rd. East, Hamilton, ON L8W 3P8, Canada
Tel: 905-383-7786; *Fax:* 905-297-4420
info@ishcanada.com
www.ishcanada.com
Grades: Pre. - 8; *Enrollment:* 170; *Note:* The school also teaches the Arabic language, Quran, & Islam Studies.
Yousef Kfaween, Principal
principal@ishcanada.com

Hamilton: **Lyonsgate Montessori School**
86 Homewood Ave., Hamilton, ON L8P 2M4
Tel: 905-525-4283
info@lyonsgate.ca
www.lyonsgate.ca
Grades: Pre.
Rachel Lyons, Principal

Hamilton: **Southern Ontario College**
430 York Blvd., Hamilton, ON L8R 3K8, Canada
Tel: 905-546-1500; *Fax:* 905-538-5494
info@mysoc.ca
www.mysoc.ca
Other Information: Alternate Phone: 905-546-1501
Grades: Sec.; *Enrollment:* 181; *Note:* International Secondary School specializing in ESL and University prep.
Brian Inglis, Director, Finance & Operations

Hamilton: **Timothy Canadian Reformed School**
430 East 25th St., Hamilton, ON L8V 3B4, Canada
Tel: 905-385-3953; *Fax:* 905-385-8073
office@timothschool.org
Grades: Kindergarten - 8; *Note:* The school is affiliated with the Canadian Reformed Church.
Hendrik Plug, Principal

Hamilton: **Westdale Children's School**
2 Bond St. North, Hamilton, ON L8S 3W1
Tel: 905-529-4678
info@westdalechildrensschool.org
www.westdalechildrensschool.org
www.facebook.com/groups/472740230301/?fref=ts
Grades: K

Huntsville: **Muskoka Montessori School**
228 Chub Lake Rd., Huntsville, ON P1H 1S4
Tel: 705-788-3802
info@muskokamontessori.ca
www.muskokamontessori.ca
twitter.com/MiMSy_ca
Grades: Pre. - Jr. High
Timo Bijl, Principal

Kanata: **Kanata Montessori School**
355 Michael Cowpland Dr., Kanata, ON K2M 2C5
Tel: 613-592-2189; *Fax:* 613-592-3705
admin@kanata-montessori.com
www.kanatamontessori.com
www.facebook.com/kanatamontessori
twitter.com/KMSMontessori
Grades: Toddler - Jr. High
Jonathan Robinson, Principal
jonathan@kanata-montessori.com

Campuses
North Campus
1030 Riddell Dr., Kanata, ON K2K 1X7
Tel: 613-592-2189; *Fax:* 613-592-3705

King: **The Country Day School (CDS)**
13415 Dufferin St., King, ON L7B 1K5, Canada
Tel: 905-833-1220; *Fax:* 905-833-1350
questions@cds.on.ca
www.cds.on.ca
Grades: Junior Kindergarten - 12; *Note:* The co-educational school is non-denominational.
John Leggett, Head of School
David Huckvale, Director, Admission

King City: **Villanova College**
P.O. Box 133
2480 15th Sideroad, King City, ON L7B 1A4, Canada
Tel: 905-833-1909; *Fax:* 905-833-1915
info@villanovacollege.org
www.villanovacollege.net
www.facebook.com/VillanovaCollege
twitter.com/VC_Online
www.youtube.com/channel/UCGeUZLn6mmQcBpKh33fZ5UQ
Grades: 5-12; *Enrollment:* 450
Paul Paradiso

Kingston: **Mulberry Waldorf School**
25 Markland St., Kingston, ON K7K 1S2
Tel: 613-542-0669; *Fax:* 613-542-0667
administrator@mulberrywaldorfschool.ca
www.mulberrywaldorfschool.ca
www.facebook.com/MulberryWaldorfSchool
Grades: Elem.
Peelu Hira, Administrator

Kitchener: **Carmel New Church School**
40 Chapel Hill Dr., Kitchener, ON N2R 1N2
Tel: 519-748-5802
secretary@carmelnewchurch.org
www.carmelnewchurch.org/school.html
Grades: JK-10
Brad Heinrichs, Pastor/Principal
pastor@carmelnewchurch.org

Kitchener: **St. Jude's School Inc.**
888 Trillum Dr., Kitchener, ON N2R 1K4, Canada
Tel: 519-888-0807; *Fax:* 519-884-0316
www.stjudes.com
Grades: 1-12; *Enrollment:* 172; *Note:* Founded in 1980 for students with learning difficulties. Also offers an after-hours Tutoring School and Second Language School

Kitchener: **Scholar's Hall**
888 Trillium Dr., Kitchener, ON N2R 1K4
Tel: 519-888-6620; *Fax:* 519-884-0316
director@scholarshall.com
www.scholarshall.com
www.facebook.com/scholars.hall
Grades: K - 12

Kitchener: **Sunshine Montessori School Kitchener**
10 Boniface Ave., Kitchener, ON N2C 1L9, Canada
Tel: 519-744-1423; *Fax:* 519-744-9929
admin@sunshinemontessori.on.ca
www.sunshinemontessori.on.ca
Grades: Jr. K.-8; *Enrollment:* 209
C. Bradshaw, Principal

Kleinburg: **Montessori School of Kleinburg**
P.O. Box 445
10515 Hwy. 27, Kleinburg, ON L0J 1C0.
Tel: 905-893-0560; *Fax:* 905-893-8109
admin@msk2002.com
www.msk2002.com
Grades: Pre. - Elem.
Enza Pellegrini, Principal
e.pellegrini@msk2002.com
John Pellegrini, Director
j.pellegrini@msk2002.com

Lakefield: **Lakefield College School**
4391 County Rd. 29, Lakefield, ON K0L 2H0, Canada
Tel: 705-652-3324; *Fax:* 705-652-6320
www.lcs.on.ca
www.facebook.com/LakefieldCollege
twitter.com/LakefieldCS
www.linkedin.com/groups?gid=874867&trk=hb_side_g
www.youtube.com/LakefieldCollege
Grades: 9 - 12; *Enrollment:* 365; *Note:* Founded 1879; co-ed boarding and day school, for grades 9-12 and 7-12 respectively; core academics, athletics, and co-curricular arts programmes.
Struan Robertson, Head of School, 705-652-3324, ext. 327
srobertson@lcs.on.ca
John Runza, Assistant Head: School Life, 705-652-3324, ext. 353
jrunza@lcs.on.ca
Tim Rutherford, Chief Financial Officer, 705-652-3324, ext. 325
trutherford@lcs.on.ca

London: **Al-Taqwa Islamic Schools**
Elementary School
35 Jim Ashton St., London, ON N5V 3H4, Canada
Tel: 519-951-1414; *Fax:* 519-951-1092
Toll-Free: 866-812-9127
ischool@altaqwa.org
www.altaqwa.org
Grades: Elem./Sec.; *Enrollment:* 163; *Note:* The elementary school is located at 35 Jim Ashton St.; the secondary school is located at 1697 Trafalgar St., (519) 452-3366, secondary@altaqwa.org.
Siham Kaloti, Principal

London: **London Community Hebrew Day School**
536 Huron St., London, ON N6A 2M2
Tel: 519-439-8419; *Fax:* 519-439-0404
info@lchds.ca
www.lchds.ca
www.facebook.com/130138960416975
Grades: K./Elem.
Carol Marcus, Chair
Rachelle Frydman, Principal

London: **London International Academy (LIA)**
#361, 365 Richmond St., London, ON N6A 3C2
Tel: 519-433-3388; *Fax:* 519-433-3387
admissions@lia-edu.ca
lia-edu.ca
twitter.com/LondonIntlAcad
Grades: 9 - 12

London: **London Islamic School**
151 Oxford St. West, London, ON N6H 1S3, Canada
Tel: 519-679-9920; *Fax:* 519-679-6842
www.londonislamicschool.com
Grades: K.-8; *Enrollment:* 187
Patricia Zabian, Principal

London: **London Waldorf School**
7 Beaufort St., London, ON N6G 1A5
Tel: 519-858-8862
info@londonwaldorf.ca
www.londonwaldorf.ca
www.facebook.com/122238667810381
twitter.com/londonwaldorf
londonwaldorf.wordpress.com
Grades: Pre.-8; *Enrollment:* 109
Ruth Baer, Business Manager
Rebecca Soltan, Business Manager

London: **Matthews Hall Private School**
1370 Oxford St. West, London, ON N6H 1W2
Tel: 519-471-1506; *Fax:* 519-471-8647
matthewshall.on.ca
Grades: JK-8
Patricia A. Doig, Head of School
Janet Frame, Associate Head
frame.j@matthewshall.ca
Suzanne Fratschko Elliott, Director, Advancement
elliott.s@matthewshall.ca

London: **Montessori Academy of London**
711 Waterloo St., London, ON N6A 3W1
Tel: 519-433-9121; *Fax:* 519-433-8941
reception@montessori.on.ca
www.montessori.on.ca
www.facebook.com/MontessoriAcademyofLondon
twitter.com/MAofLondon
Grades: Pre.-8; *Enrollment:* 345; *Number of Employees:* 49 teachers; *Note:* The Montessori Academy of London also offers a toddler program for children from 18 to 30 months & a Casa program, for children from ages 2.5 to 6.
Margaret Whitley, Director
mwhitley@montessori.on.ca
Chandra Peretic, Coordinator, Communications & Administration
Kristen Crouse, Coordinator, Elementary & Junior High
kcrouse@montessori.on.ca
Marianne Rutledge, Coordinator, Admissions
registrar@montessori.on.ca
Kathy Work-Schlattman, Coordinator, Casa
kwork@montessori.on.ca
Shonagh Stevenson-Ramsay, Directress, Toddler Program
sstevenson@montessori.on.ca
Walter Iwanowski, Controller
wki@montessori.on.ca

Campuses
Oxford Central Campus
311 Oxford St. East, London, ON N6A 1V3
Tel: 519-433-1019; *Fax:* 519-433-5976

Westmount South Campus
362 Commissioners Rd. West, London, ON N6J 1Y3
Tel: 519-472-0930; *Fax:* 519-472-0847

Maple: **Maple Children's Montessori School**
#9, 10175 Keele St., Maple, ON L6A 3Y9
Tel: 905-832-6665
www.maplechildrensmontessori.com
Grades: Toddler - Pre.
Gary Carrera, Principal
Mr.carrera@maplechildrensmontessori.com

Markham: **Academic Vision**
Cosburn Plaza
#A, 6061 Hwy. 7 East, Markham, ON L3P 3B2
Tel: 905-471-6273
inquiries@academicvision.ca
academicvision.ca
www.facebook.com/pages/Academic-Vision/217811964912761
www.twitter.com/Academic_Vision
Jennifer Hou, Principal & Director

Markham: **Aspiration Academy**
60 Riviera Dr., Markham, ON L3R 5M1
Tel: 905-752-0988
info@AspirationandDiscoveries.com
aspirationacademy.com

Markham: **J. Addison School**
2 Valleywood Dr., Markham, ON L3R 8H3
Tel: 905-477-4999
info@addisonschool.com
www.addisonschool.com
www.facebook.com/150702185027644
twitter.com/JAddisonSchool
www.pinterest.com/jaddison2002/
Grades: 9 - 12; *Enrollment:* 100
Lee Venditti, Principal
lvenditti@addisonschool.com

Markham: **Learning Has No Limits (LHNL)**
#2669, 2 Bur Oak Ave., Markham, ON L6B 1K9
Tel: 905-265-7553
admin@learninghasnolimits.com
www.learninghasnolimits.com
Grades: 9-12

Campuses
Markham Campus
#2705, 2 Bur Oak Ave., Markham, ON L6B 1K9
Tel: 905-265-7553
Note: School located in the former Keen Minds Inc. building

Woodbridge Campus
7971 Kipling Ave., Woodbridge, ON L4L 1Z3
Tel: 905-265-7553
Note: School located inside the Faith Apostolic Church

Markham: **Marander Montessori School**
5906-16th Ave., Markham, ON L3P 3J3
Tel: 905-471-7118; *Fax:* 905-471-9338
marander@rogers.com
www.marandermontessori.com
www.facebook.com/149992325157734?ref=ts&fref=ts
Grades: Toddler - Pre.
Margaret Lee, Principal

Markham: **Merit College**
HSBC Tower
#808, 3601 Hwy. 7 East, Markham, ON L3R 0M3
Tel: 416-800-4168
info@meritedu.ca
www.meritedu.ca
www.facebook.com/MeritEducation
twitter.com/Merit_Education
www.youtube.com/user/MeritEducation/feed
Grades: 9 - 12
Joe Lu, Principal

Markham: **Queens Montessori Academy (QMA)**
1151 Denison St., Markham, ON L3R 3Y4
Tel: 905-944-0077; *Fax:* 905-944-0078
queensmontessori@brightpathkids.com
www.queensmontessori.com
Grades: Toddler - Pre.
Jan Sharma, Principal

Markham: **Royal Cachet Montessori School**
9921 Woodbine Ave., Markham, ON L6C 1H7
Tel: 905-888-7700; *Fax:* 905-888-6200
info@rcmschool.ca
www.rcmschool.ca
Grades: Pre.-3; *Enrollment:* 110
Kathy Bobotsis, Director

Markham: **Somerset Academy**
7700 Brimley Rd., Markham, ON L3R 0E5, Canada
Tel: 905-940-8990; *Fax:* 905-940-8992
administration@somersetacademy.ca
www.somersetacademy.ca
Grades: Jr. K.-8; *Enrollment:* 172
Cathy Barogianis, Principal

Markham: **Town Centre Montessori Private Schools (TCMPS)**
Main Campus
155 Clayton Dr., Markham, ON L3R 7P3, Canada
Tel: 905-470-1200; *Fax:* 905-470-0184
admin@tcmps.com
tcmps.com
Other Information: 905-474-3434 (Phone, Preschool & Grade 1)
Grades: Preschool - 8; *Note:* The preschool program accepts children as young as two years of age.
Marianne Vanderlugt, Principal

Markham: **Town Centre Private High School (TCPHS)**
155 Clayton Dr., Markham, ON L3R 7P3
Tel: 905-470-1200; *Fax:* 905-470-1721
www.tcphs.com
www.facebook.com/254938157912596
Grades: 9 - 12; *Note:* This is a coeducational school which provides university bound & advanced placement courses.

Markham: **Trillium School**
4277 - 14th Ave., Markham, ON L3R 0J2, Canada
Tel: 905-946-1181; *Fax:* 905-946-8267
info@trilliumschool.ca
www.trilliumschool.ca
Grades: Preschool - 8; *Note:* Trillium School is a coeducational, non-denominational school. It features a pre-Casa program for toddlers & a Casa program.
Lily Moon, Principal
lmoon@trilliumschool.ca

Markham: **Wishing Well Montessori School**
#30, 455 Cochrane Dr., Markham, ON L3R 9R4
Tel: 905-470-9751
www.wishingwellschools.com
www.facebook.com/207952285907957
Grades: K./Elem.
Anthony Mauriell, Principal

Merrickville: **Fulford Preparatory College**
P.O. Box 100
118 Main St. East, Merrickville, ON K0G 1N0
Tel: 613-269-2064
admissions@fulfordprep.com?
www.fulfordprep.com
www.facebook.com/344493712305585?ref=hl
instagram.com/fulfordpreparatory
Grades: 7 - 10; *Note:* Boarding school for students looking to complete their secondary school education, ESL skills, and to be prepared for university or college.
Don Rickers, Headmaster
donr@fulfordprep.com

Missisauga: **Elpis College**
Mississauga Campus
#6, 2145 Dunwin Dr., Missisauga, ON L5L 4L9
Tel: 905-607-7773
info@eduelpis.com
elpiscollege.com
www.facebook.com/ElpisGobalEducation
twitter.com/ElpisGlobalEdu/
Grades: 9 - 12
David Jinman Kim, Principal

Campuses
North York Campus
#205, 77 Finch Ave. West, Toronto, ON M2N 2H5
Tel: 416-228-8878
Elpiscollege@gmail.com
Grades: 9 - 12

Mississauga: **3sixty Education**
141 Brunel Rd., Mississauga, ON L4Z 1X3
Tel: 647-494-4340; *Fax:* 647-494-4341
Toll-Free: 866-360-2622
info@3sixtyeducation.ca
www.3sixtyeducation.ca
Grades: 9 - 12
Sangeeta Kumar, Principal

Mississauga: **ABC Montessori Elementary Campus**
305 Matheson Blvd. East, Mississauga, ON L4Z 1X8
Tel: 905-568-8989
abcmontessori@bellnet.ca
www.abcmontessori.com
Grades: Pre-5; *Enrollment:* 140
Raj Vekaria, Principal

Campuses
Cawthra Casa Campus
4300 Cawthra Rd., Mississauga, ON L4Z 1V8
Tel: 905-281-2595; *Fax:* 905-568-0958
Mari Ang, Principal

Matheson Casa & Toddler Campus
285 Matheson Blvd. East, Mississauga, ON L4Z 1X8
Tel: 905-568-1716; *Fax:* 905-568-0958
Rick Kordts, Campus Administrator

Mississauga: Applewood Rainbow Montessori School
24 Stavebank Rd., Mississauga, ON L5G 2T5
Tel: 905-274-2321; Fax: 905-829-0341
info@rainbowmontessori.ca
www.applewoodrainbowmontessori.com
Grades: Pre.-K
Razia Rangooni, Director

Mississauga: Bet Sefer Solel
2399 Folkway Dr., Mississauga, ON L5L 2M6
Tel: 905-820-5915
info@solel.ca
www.solel.ca/betsefersolel.html
Note: Bet Sefer Solel is a Reform Jewish school.
Rabbi Lawrence Englander
Ted Greenberg, President
Arliene Botnick, B.A., M.Ed., Director, Education
amora@solel.ca

Mississauga: Bright Scholars Academy - Cooksville
3180 Kirwin Ave., Mississauga, ON L5A 2K7
Tel: 905-896-4553
www.brightscholars.ca
Campuses
Bright Scholars Academy - Streetsville
24 Falconer Dr., Mississauga, ON L5N 1B1
Tel: 905-826-3595
www.brightscholars.ca
Heritage Montessori - Oakville
#20, 1289 Marlborough Ct., Oakville, ON L6H 2N7
Tel: 905-842-3061
www.brightscholars.ca
Bright Scholars Montessori - Meadowvale
5920 Montevideo Rd., Mississauga, ON L5N 3J5
Tel: 905-542-1895
www.brightscholars.ca

Mississauga: Bronte College
Senior School Campus
88 Bronte College Ct., Mississauga, ON L5B 1M9, Canada
Tel: 905-270-7788; Fax: 905-270-7828
info@brontecollege.ca
www.brontecollege.ca
www.facebook.com/brontecollege
twitter.com/brontecollege
www.youtube.com/user/brontecollege
Grades: Pre - 12; Enrollment: 550; Note: Bronte College of Canada is a co-educational, international day & boarding school. The school also offers University of Guelph & Bronte College first year university courses, an advanced placement program, & English as a Second Language (ESL).
Diane Finlay, Head of School
W. Johnson, Principal, Junior School

Mississauga: Dewey College
5889 Coopers Ave., Mississauga, ON L4Z 1P9
Tel: 905-897-6668; Fax: 905-897-6662
info@deweycollege.ca
deweycollege.ca
www.facebook.com/pages/Dewey-College/122655961211500
Grades: 9 - 12; Note: Offers courses from high School OSSD (9-12 Grades) program to Advanced Placement (AP) program to English as Second Language program.
Dr. Donna Zhang, Principal

Mississauga: Froebel Education Centre
1576 Dundas St. West, Mississauga, ON L5C 1E5, Canada
Tel: 905-277-9371
office@froebel.com
www.froebel.com
www.facebook.com/FroebelEducationCentre
twitter.com/froebelschool
www.youtube.com/froebeleducation
Grades: K.-8; Enrollment: 89; Note: Education based on the principle's of Friedrich Froebel: working in partnership with the child's family, tranformation of creative play into creative work, & making connections with others, the world & God.

Mississauga: Fun to Learn Montessori School
1840 Argentia Rd., Mississauga, ON L5N 1P9
Tel: 905-812-9606; Fax: 905-812-9606
info@funtolearn.org
www.funtolearn.org
www.facebook.com/474762045967575
Grades: Toddler - Pre.
Shahla Ambreen, Director

Mississauga: Golden Orchard Montessori School
1170 Tynegrove Rd., Mississauga, ON L4W 3B2
Tel: 905-629-7555; Fax: 905-507-3377
education@goldenorchardmontessori.com
www.goms.ca
Grades: Pre.
Virginia Rajakumar, Principal

Mississauga: Grade Learning
#20, 5225 Orbitor Dr., Mississauga, ON L4W 4Y8
Tel: 905-624-9661; Fax: 905-629-0079
Toll-Free: 800-208-3826
office@gradelearning.ca
gradelearning.ca
www.facebook.com/gradelearning
twitter.com/gradelearning
www.linkedin.com/company/grade-learning
www.youtube.com/gradelearning
Grades: 9-12
Margaret Prophet, Program Director
Campuses
Barrie Campus
#6, 250 Bayview Dr., Barrie, ON L4N 4Y8
Tel: 705-739-6619; Fax: 705-739-1236
barrie@gradelearning.ca
Brampton West Campus
#202, 37 George St. North, Brampton, ON L6X 1R5
Tel: 905-861-9554; Fax: 905-861-9797
bramptonwest@gradelearning.ca
Downsview Campus
#15, 1126 Finch Ave. West, Downsview, ON M3J 3J6
Tel: 416-667-1500; Fax: 416-667-1502
downsview@gradelearning.ca
Etobicoke Campus
#502, 1243 Islington Ave., Etobicoke, ON M8X 1Y9
Tel: 416-231-0333; Fax: 416-231-0023
etobicoke@gradelearning.ca
Kingston Campus
#200, 1020 Bayridge Dr., Kingston, ON K7P 2S2
Tel: 613-389-1361; Fax: 613-389-7571
kingston@gradelearning.ca
Kitchener Campus
1378 Weber St. East, Kitchener, ON N2A 1C4
Tel: 519-745-8798; Fax: 519-745-2720
kitchener@gradelearning.ca
Markham Campus
#100, 25 Royal Crest Ct., Markham, ON L3R 9X4
Tel: 905-471-9166; Fax: 905-474-2226
markham@gradelearning.ca
Mississauga West Campus
#101, 2227 South Millway, Mississauga, ON L5L 3R6
Tel: 905-821-0112; Fax: 905-821-0113
mississaugawest@gradelearning.ca
North York Campus
#7B, 3200 Dufferin St., Toronto, ON M6A 3B2
Tel: 416-781-7667; Fax: 416-781-3560
northyork@gradelearning.ca
Orangeville Campus
#100, 14 Stewart Ct., Orangeville, ON L9W 3Z9
Tel: 519-940-4498; Fax: 519-940-9628
orangeville@gradelearning.ca
Orillia Campus
#4B, 575 West St. South, Orillia, ON L4V 7N6
Tel: 705-327-3459; Fax: 705-327-2458
orillia@gradelearning.ca
Oshawa Campus
#1J, 57 Simcoe St. South, Oshawa, ON L1H 4G4
Tel: 905-433-1033; Fax: 866-817-2392
oshawa@gradelearning.ca
Ottawa Campus
#10-12, 1300 - 340 Albert St., Ottawa, ON K1R 7Y6
Tel: 613-721-6777; Fax: 800-410-2023
ottawa@gradelearning.ca
Owen Sound Campus
#1, 1450 - 1st Ave., Owen Sound, ON N4K 6W2
Tel: 519-371-2675; Fax: 519-371-2770
owensound@gradelearning.ca
Rexdale Campus
#109-110, 557 Dixon Rd., Toronto, ON M9W 6K1
Tel: 416-244-4433; Fax: 416-244-8076
rexdale@gradelearning.ca
Richmond Hill Campus
#13-14, 1455 - 16th Ave., Richmond Hill, ON L4B 4W5
Tel: 905-886-6500; Fax: 416-781-3560
richmondhill@gradelearning.ca
Scarborough East Campus
#207, 2425 Eglinton Ave. East, Toronto, ON M1K 5G8
Tel: 416-755-8547; Fax: 866-817-2392
scarborougheast@gradelearning.ca
Stoney Creek Campus
#303, 800 Queenston Rd., Stoney Creek, ON L8G 1A7
Tel: 905-662-5325; Fax: 905-662-3728
stoneycreek@gradelearning.ca
Sudbury Campus
Sudbury, ON
Tel: 705-524-1158; Fax: 800-410-2023
sudbury@gradelearning.ca
Note: Contact for location information.
Toronto Central Campus
#902, 2300 Yonge St., Toronto, ON M4P 2W6
Tel: 416-482-2272; Fax: 416-482-2270
torontocentral@gradelearning.ca
Weston Campus
#12, 2007 Lawrence Ave. West, Toronto, ON M9N 3V1
Tel: 416-243-2272; Fax: 416-243-2262
weston@gradelearning.ca
Windsor Campus
1215 Walker Rd., Windsor, ON N8Y 2N9
Tel: 519-968-1776; Fax: 519-419-3176
windsor@gradelearning.ca
Woodbridge Campus
#10, 4140 Steeles Ave., Woodbridge, ON L4L 4V3
Tel: 905-850-3719; Fax: 905-850-2981
woodbridge@gradelearning.ca

Mississauga: IQRA Islamic School
5751 Coopers Ave., Mississauga, ON L4Z 1R9, Canada
Tel: 905-507-6688; Fax: 905-507-9243
iqraislamicschool@gmail.com
www.iqraislamicschool.com
Grades: 1 - 8; Enrollment: 150

Mississauga: ISNA Elementary School
1525 Sherway Dr., Mississauga, ON L4X 1C5
Tel: 905-272-4303; Fax: 905-272-4311
elementary@isnaschools.com
elementary.isnaschools.com
Grades: K./Elem.
Obaid Yarkhan, Principal

Mississauga: ISNA High School
2200 South Sheridan Way, Mississauga, ON L5J 2M4
Tel: 905-403-8406; Fax: 905-403-8409
info@isnacanada.com
high.isnaschools.com
www.facebook.com/pages/Isna-High-School/147123958690080
twitter.com/ISNAHigh
ca.linkedin.com/pub/isna-high-school/61/a79/863
www.youtube.com/user/ISNAHighTube?feature=watch
Grades: 9-12
S.A. Rasoul, Principal

Mississauga: Kaban Montessori School
2449 Dunwin Dr., Mississauga, ON L5L 1T1
Tel: 905-569-3112
www.kabanmontessori.ca
Grades: Infant - Elem.
Karla Escobedo, Executive Director
karla@kabanmontessori.ca

Mississauga: Kendellhurst Academy
175 Queen St. South, Mississauga, ON L5M 1L2
Tel: 905-567-1070; Fax: 905-821-0891
info@kendellhurst.com
www.kendellhurst.com
Grades: Pre.-6; Enrollment: 150
Paula Carrasco, Director
Campuses
Oakville Campus
#11 & 12, 2460 Neyagawa Blvd., Oakville, ON L6H 7P4
Tel: 905-257-2030

Mississauga: Lakeside Montessori School
1079 Lakeshore Rd. East, Mississauga, ON L5E 1E8
Tel: 905-891-8332
schoolinfo@lakesidemontessorischool.com
www.lakesidemontessorischool.com
Grades: Toddler - Pre.
Carolyn Peto-De Khors, Director

Mississauga: Lynn-Rose Heights Private School
7215 Millcreek Dr., Mississauga, ON L5N 3R3
Tel: 905-567-3553; Fax: 905-567-5318
lynnroseinfo@lynnroseheights.net
www.lynnroseheights.net
Grades: Pre.-8; Enrollment: 300

Mississauga: Meadow Green Academy
649 Queensway West, Mississauga, ON L5B 1C2
Tel: 905-273-3344
mgainfo@meadowgreenacademy.ca
meadowgreenacademy.ca
www.facebook.com/MeadowGreenAcademy
twitter.com/MeadowGreenAc
Grades: Pre.-8; Enrollment: 150
Georganne M. MacKenzie, Director

Campuses
Senior Campus
1884 Lakeshore Rd. West, Mississauga, ON L5J 1J7
Tel: 905-273-3344
Grades: 4-8

Mississauga: Mentor College
Main Campus
40 Forest Ave., Mississauga, ON L5G 1L1, Canada
Tel: 905-271-3393; Fax: 905-271-8367
admissions@mentorcollege.edu
www.mentorcollege.edu
Other Information: 56cayuga@mentorcollege.edu (E-mail, Primary campus)
www.facebook.com/152322951530170
www.youtube.com/user/TEAMMentor
Grades: Junior Kindergarten - 12
Ken Philbrook, Director, Mentor College & TEAM School

Mississauga: Northstar Montessori Private School
4900 Tomken Rd., Mississauga, ON L4W 1J8, Canada
Tel: 905-890-7827; Fax: 905-890-6771
admin@northstarmontessori.com
www.northstarmontessori.com
www.facebook.com/NorthstarMontessoriPrivateSchool
www.twitter.com/NorthstarMontes
Grades: Preschool / Elementary; Note: Northstar Montessori offers the following programs: toddlers, pre-Casa, primary, & elementary. Ages of children range from 18 months to 12 years.
Virginia Ramirez, Principal
Sherry Gosal, Vice Principal
Rick Ramirez, Manager, Business
Rose Sta. Ana, Office Administrator

Mississauga: Olive Grove School (OGS)
2300 Speakman Dr., Mississauga, ON L5K 1B4
Tel: 905-855-8557; Fax: 905-855-7917
info@olivegroveschool.ca
www.olivegroveschool.ca
www.facebook.com/pages/Olive-Grove-School/189480721139381
Grades: Pre. - 8; Note: Olive Grove School is a private Islamic School registered by the Ontario Ministry of Education
Mr. Bakbak, Principal

Mississauga: Peel Montessori School
964 Meadow Wood Rd., Mississauga, ON L5J 2S6
Tel: 905-823-6522
info@peelmontessori.com
peelmontessori.com
Grades: JK-6; Enrollment: 100
Santina Cowdrey, Founding Principal

Mississauga: Royal School of Canada
#108, 1140 Burnhamthorpe Rd. West, Mississauga, ON L5C 4E9
Tel: 905-279-4567; Fax: 905-279-0969
admissions@royalschoolofcanada.com
royalschoolofcanada.com
Grades: 9 - 12
Scott Headrick, Principal

Mississauga: Safa & Marwa Islamic School
5550 McAdam Rd., Mississauga, ON L4Z 1P1
Tel: 905-566-8533; Fax: 905-823-3938
admin@safaandmarwa.ca
safaandmarwa.ca
Grades: K - 8

Mississauga: St. Jude's Academy
6670 Campobello Rd., Mississauga, ON L5N 2L8
Tel: 905-814-0202; Fax: 905-814-0299
info@stjudesacademy.com
www.stjudesacademy.com
Grades: Pre.-8; Enrollment: 115
Aaron Sawatsky, Head of School

Mississauga: Sherwood Heights School
Erin Mills Campus
3065 Glen Erin Dr., Mississauga, ON L5L 1J3, Canada
Tel: 905-569-8999; Fax: 905-569-9034
info@sherwoodheights.com
www.sherwoodheights.com
www.facebook.com/113774888639558
twitter.com/SherwoodHeights
Grades: Elem.; Enrollment: 206

Mississauga: Springfield Preparatory School
1444 Dundas Cres., Mississauga, ON L5C 1E9, Canada
Tel: 905-273-9717; Fax: 905-273-3735
admissions@springfieldprep.ca
www.springfieldprep.ca
Grades: Pre - 8
Janet Murphy, Principal
jmurphy@springfieldprep.ca

Mississauga: Star Academy
1587 Cormack Cres., Mississauga, ON L5E 2P8
Tel: 905-891-1555; Fax: 905-891-1696
info@staracademy.ca
www.staracademy.ca
twitter.com/myStarAcademy
Grades: JK-8; Enrollment: 95
Belinda Bernardo, Principal

Mississauga: TEAM School
Also known as: Tutorial & Educ. Assistance in Mississauga
275 Rudar Rd., Mississauga, ON L5A 1S2, Canada
Tel: 905-279-7200; Fax: 905-279-1561
www.teamschool.com
Grades: 1 - 12
Lillian Sawtschuk, TSS Principal

Mississauga: White Oaks Montessori School Ltd. (WOMS)
Vanier Campus
1200 Vanier Dr., Mississauga, ON L5H 4C7, Canada
Tel: 905-278-4454; Fax: 905-278-5184
admin@woms.ca
www.whiteoaksmontessori.com
Other Information: 905-855-2321 (Phone, Clarkson Campus)
Grades: Preschool - Elementary; Note: White Oaks Montessori School is a fully accredited Canadian Council of Montessori Administrators school. The youngest children are offered toddler programs. Casa programs are provided for children from age three to five. The Clarkson Campus is located at the following address: 1338 Clarkson Road North, Mississauga.
Barbara S. Ward, AMI, Founder & Chief Administrative Officer
Irene Stathoukos, BSc., AMI, Principal
Daniel Ward, Information Technologist

Mount Hope: Grandview Adventist Academy
3975 Hwy. 6, Mount Hope, ON L0R 1W0, Canada
Tel: 905-679-4492; Fax: 905-679-4492
info@grandviewschool.ca
www.grandviewschool.ca
twitter.com/GrandviewSDA
Grades: Elem./Sec.; Enrollment: 58
Lisa Clarke, Principal
principal@grandviewschool.ca

Nepean: Ottawa Islamic School
10 Coral Ave., Nepean, ON K2E 5Z6, Canada
Tel: 613-727-5066; Fax: 613-727-8486
info@ottawaislamicschool.org
www.ottawaislamicschool.org
Grades: JK-12; Enrollment: 246
Mohamed Sheik Ahmed (Dalmar, Principal

Nestor Falls: Mikinaak Onigaming School
P.O. Box 339
Nestor Falls, ON P0X 1K0, Canada
Tel: 807-484-2162; Fax: 807-484-1252
Grades: Junior Kindergarten - 12; Enrollment: 100; Note: Mikinaak Onigaming School is a band operated school, providing education for the Ojibways of Onigaming First Nation.
Owen Zoccole, Director, Education

New Hamburg: Our Lady of Mount Carmel Academy
2483 Bleams Rd. East, New Hamburg, ON N3A 3J2
Tel: 519-634-4932; Fax: 519-634-9395
olmc@sspx.ca
fsspx.com/olmc/
Grades: K - 12
Fr. David Sherry, Principal

Newmarket: Or Hadash Religious School
#5, 451 Botsford St., Newmarket, ON L3Y 1T2
Tel: 905-898-2220
info@orhadash.org
www.orhadash.org
Len Bates, President
len@orhadash.org
Mark Klady, Contact
markklady@rogers.com

Newmarket: Pickering College
16945 Bayview Ave., Newmarket, ON L3Y 4X2, Canada
Tel: 905-895-1700; Fax: 905-895-9076
Toll-Free: 877-895-1700
info@pickeringcollege.on.ca
www.pickeringcollege.on.ca
Grades: JK - 12; Enrollment: 400; Note: Day and Boarding School
Peter C. Sturrup, Headmaster
Maria Wolscht, Director of Junior School
Scott Hammell, Director of Senior School

Niagara Falls: Niagara Centre for the Arts Academy
4700 Epworth Circle, Niagara Falls, ON L2E 1C6
Tel: 905-513-1685; Fax: 905-339-2994
info@NiagaraCentreForTheArts.com
academy.niagaracentreforarts.com
Grades: 11-12; adult

Nobleton: The Montessori Country School
Nobleton Campus
P.O. Box 455
6185 - 15th Sideroad, Nobleton, ON L0G 1N0, Canada
Tel: 905-859-4739; Toll-Free: 1-866-557-2272
admin@mcs-nobleton.com
www.montessoricountryschool.ca
Grades: Pres - 8; Note: The Montessori Country School offers a toddler program, a Casa program, & an elementary program. Children range in age from 12 months to 12 years.
Sarah Enright, Princial
Joanne Hastie, Vice Principal

Oakville: Al-Falah Islamic School
391 Burnhamthorpe Rd. East, Oakville, ON L6H 7B4, Canada
Tel: 905-257-5782; Fax: 905-257-0848
office@al-falah.org
www.al-falah.org
twitter.com/Al_FalahSchool
Grades: Elem.; Enrollment: 215; Note: Accredited by the Ontario Min. of Education; curriculum also includes programmes in the arts, computers, physical education, Arabic language, & Quran studies.
Mohsin Chowdhury, Principal, 905-257-5782, ext. 252

Oakville: Appleby College
540 Lakeshore Rd. West, Oakville, ON L6K 3P1, Canada
Tel: 905-845-4681; Fax: 905-845-0617
info@appleby.on.ca
www.appleby.on.ca
www.facebook.com/applebycollege
twitter.com/applebycollege
www.youtube.com/applebycollege
Grades: 7 - 12; Enrollment: 740; Note: Independent, co-educational school for boarding & day students in Grandes 7 through 12.
Katrina Samson, Head of School
ksamson@appleby.on.ca
Innes van Nostrand, Principal
ivannostrand@appleby.on.ca
Val Cambre, Vice Principal & Chief Administration Officer
vcambre@appleby.on.ca

Oakville: Chisholm Educational Centre
Also known as: Chisholm Academy
1484 Cornwall Rd., Oakville, ON L6J 7W5, Canada
Tel: 905-844-3240; Fax: 905-844-7321
www.chisholmcentre.com
Grades: Secondary; Note: Chisholm Educational Centre consists of the Academy High School & the Collegiate.
Dr. Howard Bernstein, Executive Director
Dr. Shirley Bryntwick, Director, Professional Services
Sylvia Moyssakos, Head, Specialized Academic Services
C. David Jowett, M.Ed., Principal, Chisholm Academy
Adam Bernstein, Manager, Operations & Development
Jarvis Sheridan, Chair

Oakville: Clanmore Montessori School
2463 Lakeshore Rd. East, Oakville, ON L6J 1M7
Tel: 905-337-8283
info@clanmore.ca
www.clanmore.ca
www.facebook.com/Clanmore
twitter.com/ClanmoreMontess
foursquare.com/clanmoremontess
Grades: Pre.-8; *Enrollment:* 110
Elaine Delsnyder, Coordinator, Casa Program
Grace Kidney, Coordinator, Elementary Program
Cathy Sustronk, Coordinator, School & Education

Oakville: Dearcroft Montessori School & West Wind Montessori Jr. High
1167 Lakeshore Rd. East, Oakville, ON L6J 1L3
Tel: 905-844-2114; *Fax:* 905-844-3529
dearcroft@primus.ca
www.dearcroft.com
Grades: JK-8
Gordon Phippen, Principal/Director

Oakville: Fern Hill School
Oakville Campus
3300 Ninth Line Rd., Oakville, ON L6H 7A8, Canada
Tel: 905-257-0022
admissions@fernhillschool.com
oakville.fernhillschool.com
Grades: Elem.; *Note:* Co-educational.
Joanne McLean, Co-Director & Founder
Deb Bell, Head of School, Primary Division
Robin Grout Ogden, Head of School, Junior/Intermediate Division

Campuses
Burlington Campus
801 North Service Rd., Burlington, ON L7P 5B8
Tel: 905-634-8652
enrol@fernhillschool.com
burlington.fernhillschool.com
Grades: Pre.-8; *Enrollment:* 180
Derrick Muntwyler, Assistant Head of School
dmuntwyler@fernhillschool.com

Oakville: Glen Abbey Montessori School
1081 Glen Valley Rd., Oakville, ON L6M 3K4
Tel: 905-825-2121
info@glenabbeymontessori.com
www.glenabbeymontessori.com
Grades: Pre.
Mary Jesu, Director

Oakville: Glenburnie School
2035 Upper Middle Rd. East, Oakville, ON L6J 7G6, Canada
Tel: 905-338-6236; *Fax:* 905-338-2654
admin@glenburnieschool.com
www.glenburnieschool.com
www.facebook.com/GlenburnieSchool
twitter.com/GlenburnieSch
www.youtube.com/user/glenburnieschool
Grades: Pre - 8; *Enrollment:* 361
Melissa Leduc, Principal
mleduc@glenburnieschool.com

Oakville: MacLachlan College
337 Trafalgar Rd., Oakville, ON L6J 3H3
Tel: 905-844-0372; *Fax:* 905-844-9369
admissions@maclachlan.ca
www.maclachlan.ca
www.facebook.com/MacLachlanCollege
www.youtube.com/maclachlanc
Grades: Pre.-12; *Enrollment:* 300
Michael Piening, Head of School

Oakville: Rotherglen School
Oakville Primary Campus
2045 Sixth Line, Oakville, ON L6H 1X9
Tel: 905-338-3528
rotherglen.com
Grades: Preschool - 1; *Enrollment:* 1000; *Note:* The Casa program is designed for children as young as three years of age. The school includes students from age three to six.
Mary Williamson, Head of School

Campuses
Oakville Elementary Campus
2050 Neyagawa Blvd., Oakville, ON L6H 6R2, Canada
Tel: 905-849-1897; *Fax:* 905-849-1354
Grades: Pre - 8
Laura Crumb, Head of School
lcrumb@rotherglen.com

Erin Mills Campus
3553 South Common Ct., Mississauga, ON L5L 2B3
Tel: 905-820-9445; *Fax:* 905-569-1569
Grades: Preschool - 6; *Note:* The Erin Mills campus provides a Montessori program for its students, from Casa to grade six.

Meadowvale Elementary Campus
929 Old Derry Rd., Mississauga, ON L5W 1A1
Tel: 905-565-8707; *Fax:* 905-565-0485
Grades: Preschool - 8

Oakville: St. Mildred's-Lightbourn School
1080 Linbrook Rd., Oakville, ON L6J 2L1, Canada
Tel: 905-845-2386
info@smls.on.ca
www.smls.on.ca
Grades: Jr. K.-12; *Enrollment:* 600; *Note:* All-girls school
Dorothy Byers, Head of School
dbyers@smls.on.ca

Oakville: Shaarei-Beth El Religious School
186 Morrison Rd., Oakville, ON L6J 4J4
Tel: 905-849-6000; *Fax:* 905-849-1134
office@sbe.ca
www.sbe.ca
Grades: Pre.-12
Cheryl Wise, Educator, 905-849-6000, ext. 15
educator@sbe.ca

Oakville: Wildwood Academy
2250 Sheridan Garden Dr., Oakville, ON L6J 7T1
Tel: 905-829-4226; *Fax:* 905-829-2318
wildwoodadmin.wix.com/wildwood-academy
www.facebook.com/WildwoodAcademy
Grades: 2-8; *Enrollment:* 60
Kim Ewing, Co-Director
Michelle Quick, Co-Director

Orangeville: Hillcrest School
7A Little York St., Orangeville, ON L9W 1L8
Tel: 519-941-5591
Grades: K./Elem./Sec.
Gail P. Hooper, Principal

Oshawa: College Park Elementary School
220 Townline Rd. North, Oshawa, ON L1K 2J6, Canada
Tel: 905-723-0163; *Fax:* 905-723-2984
www.cpes.ca
Grades: K.-8; *Enrollment:* 200
Daniel Carley, Principal
dancarley@yahoo.com

Oshawa: Kingsway College
1200 Leland Rd., Oshawa, ON L1K 2H4
Tel: 905-433-1144; *Fax:* 905-433-1156
admissions@kingswaycollege.on.ca
www.kingswaycollege.on.ca
Other Information: Records Fax: 905-433-8078
www.facebook.com/groups/kingswaycollege
twitter.com/kingswayc
www.youtube.com/user/KingswayCollege
Grades: 9-12
Scott Bowes, President, 905-433-1144, ext. 217
bowess@kingswaycollege.on.ca
Jeremy O'Dell, Vice-President, Finance, 905-433-1144, ext. 214

Ottawa: Abraar School
70 Fieldrow St., Ottawa, ON K2G 2Y7, Canada
Tel: 613-226-1396; *Fax:* 613-820-1495
info@abraarschool.com
www.abraarschool.com
Grades: JK - 9; *Enrollment:* 212; *Note:* Islamic school. Location: 1085 Grenon Ave., Ottawa.
Mohammed Saleem, Principal

Ottawa: Ashbury College
362 Mariposa Ave., Ottawa, ON K1M 0T3
Tel: 613-749-5954; *Fax:* 613-749-9724
info@ashbury.ca
www.ashbury.ca
www.facebook.com/pages/Ashbury-College/9869212766
twitter.com/ashburycollege
www.linkedin.com/groups?gid=1353977
www.youtube.com/user/ashburycollege
Grades: 4-12; *Enrollment:* 680; *Note:* Boarding school.
Norman Southward, Head of School
Brian Storosko, Head, Junior School
Gary Godkin, Head, Senior School
Alex Milroy, Director of Finance and Operations
Bruce Mutch, Director of Admissions

Ottawa: Bishop Hamilton Montessori School
2199 Regency Terrace, Ottawa, ON K2C 1H2
Tel: 613-596-4013; *Fax:* 613-596-4971
info@bhms.ca
www.bhsmontessori.ca
Grades: Pre.-8; *Enrollment:* 222; *Note:* Bishop Hamilton School is a Christian Montessori school for children from ages 18 months to 14 years.
Heather Smith, Chair
Renette Sasouni, Director

Ottawa: Counterpoint Academy Inc.
149 King George St., Ottawa, ON K1K 1V2, Canada
Tel: 613-748-1052
www.counterpointacademy.com
Grades: K.-6; *Enrollment:* 163; *Note:* Enriched curriculum, including early literacy, spelling/phonics/grammar, writing skills, math, science, English & French language arts, public speaking, art, music, drama, computers, & physical education. Counterpoint Academy West: 35 Beaufort Dr., Kanata, (613) 271-6356 (Ms. C. Kim, B.A., B.Ed., Principal & Registrar). Day care centres at both locations.
Laura W. Tilson, B.A., B.Ed., M.Ed., Principal

Ottawa: Elmwood School
Rockcliffe Park
261 Buena Vista Rd., Ottawa, ON K1M 0V9
Tel: 613-749-6761
communications@elmwood.ca
www.elmwood.ca
www.facebook.com/ElmwoodSchool
twitter.com/ElmwoodDotCa
pinterest.com/elmwoodschool
Grades: JK-12; girls; *Enrollment:* 564
Cheryl Boughton, Headmistress

Ottawa: Fern Hill School (Ottawa) Inc.
50 Vaughan St., Ottawa, ON K1M 1X1, Canada
Tel: 613-746-0255; *Fax:* 613-746-7514
www.fernhillottawa.com
Grades: Pre - Elem.; *Enrollment:* 99; *Note:* Enriched academic programme; before/after school care & after school programmes; Extended French programme.
Deborah Gutierrez, Principal
principal@fernhillottawa.com

Ottawa: Joan of Arc Academy
2221 Elmira Dr., Ottawa, ON K2C 1H3
Tel: 613-728-6364; *Fax:* 613-728-2935
administration@joanofarcacademy.com
joanofarcacademy.com
www.facebook.com/pages/Joan-of-Arc-Academy/183912149161
twitter.com/JoAAcademy
Grades: K.-8; Girls

Ottawa: Lycée Claudel
1635, prom Riverside, Ottawa, ON K1G 0E5, Canada
Tél: 613-733-8522; *Téléc:* 613-733-3782
www.claudel.org
Grades: Mat - Terminale; *Enrollment:* 887
Bruno Bigi, Chef d'établissement

Ottawa: Ottawa Montessori School (OMS) L'École Montessori d'Ottawa
335 Lindsay St., Ottawa, ON K1G 0L6, Canada
Tel: 613-769-1443; *Fax:* 613-521-6796
communications@omsmontessori.com
www.omsmontessori.com
www.facebook.com/omsmontessori
twitter.com/OMSMontessori
www.linkedin.com/company/oms-montessori
Grades: Pre.-8; *Enrollment:* 300; *Number of Employees:* 50
Pat Gere, Director

Ottawa: Rambam Day School
31 Nadolny Sachs Private, Ottawa, ON K2A 1R9, Canada
Tel: 613-820-9484
info@rambam.ca
www.rambam.ca
Grades: Preschool - 8; *Note:* The RAMBAM Day School offers general & Judaic studies, in Hebrew, French, & English.
Chana Hayes, Principal & Head, Judaica
Shannon McIntyre, Vice Principal

Ottawa: St-Laurent Academy
Académie St-Laurent
641 Sladen Ave., Ottawa, ON K1K 2S8
Tel: 613-842-8047; *Fax:* 613-842-9956
admin@st-laurentacademy.com
www.st-laurentacademy.com
Grades: Pre.-8; *Enrollment:* 200
Susan Kelly, Principal
principal@st-laurentacademy.com

***Ottawa:* Torah High School - Ottawa**
21 Nadolny Sachs Private, Ottawa, ON K2A 1R9
Tel: 613-262-6279; *Fax:* 613-798-9839
torahhighottawa.weebly.com
www.facebook.com/TorahHighOttawa
Grades: 8-12; *Note:* Torah High offers courses in Religious Studies, Hebrew Language, Philosophy, Political Science, Nutrition, Arts & Interdisciplinary Studies for students attending public or private secondary schools. The school is located at 261 Centrepointe Dr., Ottawa, ON K2G 5Y6.
Rabbi Yehuda Simes, Dean & Co-Founder
Bram Bregman, Executive Director & Co-Founder
bram@ncsy.ca

***Ottawa:* Turnbull School**
1132 Fisher Ave., Ottawa, ON K1Z 6P7, Canada
Tel: 613-729-9940; *Fax:* 613-729-1636
info@turnbull.ca
turnbull.ca
Grades: Junior Kindergarten - 8
Gareth Reid, Director
Buddy Clinch, Principal, Junior School
Craig Dunn, Principal, Senior School
Liz Doran, Head, Academic Studies (Primary Division)
Christine Ferris, Head, Academic Studies (Senior Division)
Katie Horton, Head, Academic Studies (Junior Division)
Steve Fini, Head, Community Engagement
Joyce Walker-Steed, Registrar
jwalker-steed@turnbull.ca

***Ottawa:* Westboro Academy**
Académie Westboro
200 Brewer Way, Ottawa, ON K1S 5R2, Canada
Tel: 613-737-9543; *Fax:* 613-737-7716
Westboro@WestboroAcademy.com
www.westboroacademy.com
www.facebook.com//120750381288847?ref=ts
Grades: JK - 8; *Note:* Westboro Academy is a coeducational school, which offers an enriched bilingual education.
Marcel Papineau, Principal

***Owen Sound:* Riverforest Montessori School**
1595 - 3rd Ave. West, Owen Sound, ON N4K 4R2, Canada
Tel: 519-371-2313; *Fax:* 519-371-1178
riverforestmontessori@hotmail.com
www.riverforestmontessori.com
Grades: Preschool - 6; *Note:* The Casa program is offered for children from age 2.5 to 6.

***Pawitik:* Baibombeh Anishinabe School**
Whitefish Bay First Nation
General Delivery, Pawitik, ON P0X 1L0, Canada
Tel: 807-226-5698; *Fax:* 807-226-1089
Grades: Junior Kindergarten - 12; *Note:* Baibombeh Anishinabe School is a band operated Ojibway school.

***Peterborough:* Kawartha Montessori School**
580 Cameron St., Peterborough, ON K9J 3Z5
Tel: 705-748-5437; *Fax:* 705-748-6674
admin@kawarthamontessori.com
www.kawarthamontessori.com
Grades: Pre. - 8
Ugette Vanderpost, Principal
principal@kawarthamontessori.com

***Pickering:* Blaisdale Montessori School**
415 Toynevale Rd., Pickering, ON L1W 2G9, Canada
Tel: 905-509-5005; *Fax:* 905-509-1959
info@blaisdale.com
www.blaisdale.com
Grades: Toddler/Casa/Elementary/Renaissance; *Note:* Blaisdale Montessori School offers programs for ages 12 months to 14 years, including pre-toddler.
Heather Wilson, Principal & Administrator, 905-509-5005, ext. 107
hwilson@blaisdale.com

Campuses

Bowmanville Campus
80 Rhonda Blvd., Bowmanville, ON L1C 3Y9
Tel: 905-697-3064
www.blaisdale.com/bowmanville.html
Grades: 12 mo. - Gr. 6

Milner Campus
231 Milner Ave., Toronto, ON M1S 5E3
Tel: 416-289-2273
www.blaisdale.com/milner-scarb.html
Grades: 12 mo. - Gr. 3

Oshawa Campus
1037 Simcoe St. North, Oshawa, ON L1G 4W3
Tel: 905-721-1933
www.blaisdale.com/oshawa-ajax.html
Other Information: Alternate Phone: 416-607-6297
Grades: 12 mo. - Gr. 8

Rotherglen Campus
403 Kingston Rd., Ajax, ON L1S 6L7
Tel: 905-683-5005
www.blaisdale.com/rotherglen-ajax.html
Grades: 12 mo. - Gr. 8

Village Campus
56 Old Kingston Rd., Ajax, ON L1T 2Z7
Tel: 905-427-5006
www.blaisdale.com/viillage-ajax.html
Grades: 12 mo. - 9 yrs

Westney Campus
20 O'Brien Ct., Ajax, ON L1S 7J8
Tel: 905-426-5665
www.blaisdale.com/westney-ajax.html
Grades: 12 mo. - Gr. 8

Whitby Campus
200 Byron St. South, Ajax, ON L1N 4P6
Tel: 905-665-1516
www.blaisdale.com/whitby-whitby.html
Grades: 12 mo. - 6 yrs

Annex Campus
1340 Rougemount Dr., Pickering, ON L1V 1M9
Tel: 905-509-9989
www.blaisdale.com/rotherglen-ajax.html
Grades: 12 mo. - 6 yrs

***Pickering:* Montessori Learning Centre of Pickering (MLCP)**
401 Kingston Rd., Pickering, ON L1V 1A3, Canada
Tel: 905-509-1722; *Fax:* 905-509-8283
info@montessorilearningcentre.com
www.mlcp.ca
www.facebook.com/MontessoriLearningCentreOfPickering
www.youtube.com/channel/UCUgUxS2K-LQUMY3RVJNEa0Q
Grades: Preschool / Elementary; *Enrollment:* 240; *Note:* Montessori Learning Centre of Pickering provides the following programs: infants, pre-Casa, Casa, & elementary.

***Port Hope:* Trinity College School (TCS)**
55 Deblaquire St. North, Port Hope, ON L1A 4K7, Canada
Tel: 905-885-3217; *Fax:* 905-885-9690
info@tcs.on.ca
www.tcs.on.ca
www.facebook.com/TCSBears
twitter.com/tcsbears
www.youtube.com/user/TCSBears
Grades: 5 - 12; *Enrollment:* 600; *Note:* The school is a coeducational boarding / day school. The senior school has approximately 500 students. Over 100 students attend the junior school.
Stuart K.C. Grainger, Headmaster
sgrainger@tcs.on.ca

***Richmond Hill:* Beit Rayim Hebrew School**
Ross Doan Public School
101 Weldrick Rd. West, Richmond Hill, ON L4C 3T9
Tel: 905-889-0276; *Fax:* 905-889-4413
school@beitrayim.org
www.beitrayim.org
Note: Beit Rayim Hebrew School is an egalitarian Conservative Jewish school. Classes meet two days a week: Sunday mornings & Thursday afternoons. The school will soon be moving to the Joseph & Wolf Lebovic Jewish Community Campus.
Kevin Knopman, Principal
principalkevin@beitrayim.org
Steffi Goodfield, Director & Team Leader
Grace Tetelbaun, School Administrator

***Richmond Hill:* Century Montessori School**
Regent Campus
71 Regent St., Richmond Hill, ON L4C 9Y1, Canada
Tel: 905-737-9494
info@CenturyMontessori.com
www.centurymontessori.com
Grades: PresSchool - 1; *Note:* Century Montessori School offers education for children from age 2.5 to grade 8.

***Richmond Hill:* Chabad Romano Sunday Hebrew School**
Silver Pines Public School
112 Stave Cres., Richmond Hill, ON L4C 9J2
Tel: 905-303-1880; *Fax:* 905-303-1008
www.chabadrc.org
Rabbi Shlomo Vorovitch, Director, Education
sv@chabadrc.org

***Richmond Hill:* Children's Montessori Academy**
201 King Rd., Richmond Hill, ON L4E 2W2
Tel: 905-773-1234
montessorimagic@yahoo.ca
www.thechildrensmontessori.com
Lorraine Pinto, Owner

***Richmond Hill:* Discovery Academy**
10030 Yonge St., Richmond Hill, ON L4C 1T8
Tel: 416-302-4085; *Fax:* 888-778-0492
diacademyonline@gmail.com
www.diacademy.ca
Other Information: Dayschool Phone: 647-727-1737
Grades: 6-12
Marina Blumin, Ph.D., Headmistress

***Richmond Hill:* Richland Academy**
11570 Yonge St., Richmond Hill, ON L4E 3N7
Tel: 905-224-5600; *Fax:* 905-224-4080
info@richlandacademy.ca
www.richlandacademy.ca
www.facebook.com/500962613256697
twitter.com/richlandinquiry
www.linkedin.com/company/richland-academy
www.youtube.com/user/RichlandAcademyMedia
Grades: Pre.-6; *Enrollment:* 115
Marlina Oliveira, Head of School
moliveira@richlandacademy.ca

***Richmond Hill:* Richmond Hill Montessori & Elementary School (RHMS)**
189 Weldrick Rd. East, Richmond Hill, ON L4C 0A6, Canada
Tel: 905-508-2228; *Fax:* 905-508-2229
reception@rhms.ca
www.rhms.ca
Number of Schools: 1; *Grades:* Preschool - 8; *Number of Employees:* 75; *Note:* The school's preschool program is Montessori based. The junior program includes three & four year old children. The senior program is designed for children who are four & five year olds.
Walter Ribeiro, Director
w.ribeiro@rhms.ca
Janet Darbey, Registrar
jdarbey@rhms.ca
Dino D'Amato, Principal
ddamato@rhms.ca
Andrea Cudini, Human Resources Manager
hr@rhms.ca
Ashley Travassos, Contact, Marketing & Communications
atravassos@rhms.ca
Rose Chitiz, Administrator
reception@rhms.ca
Claude Rodrigues, Contact, Purchasing & Finance
crodrigues@rhms.ca

***Richmond Hill:* Toronto Montessori Schools (TMS)**
***Also known as:* TMS School**
8569 Bayview Ave., Richmond Hill, ON L4B 3M7
Tel: 905-889-6882
admissions@tmsschool.ca
www.tmsschool.ca
Other Information: tmshr@tmsschool.ca (E-mail, Human Resources)
Grades: Pre.-12; *Enrollment:* 750

Campuses

Toronto Montessori School (TMS)
Elgin Mills Campus
500 Elgin Mills Rd. East, Richmond Hill, ON L4C 5G1
Tel: 905-889-6882
admissions@tmsschool.ca
www.torontomontessori.ca

***Rosseau:* Rosseau Lake College (RLC)**
1967 Bright St., Rosseau, ON P0C 1J0, Canada
Tel: 705-732-4351; *Fax:* 705-732-6319
Toll-Free: 800-265-0569
school.office@rlc.on.ca
www.rosseaulakecollege.com
www.facebook.com/569881713028836
twitter.com/Rosseaulake
Grades: 7 - 12; *Enrollment:* 90; *Note:* Rosseau Lake College is a coeducational day & boarding school. The average class size is twelve.
Lance Postma, Head of School

Sandy Lake: Thomas Fiddler Memorial Elementary School
P.O. Box 8
Sandy Lake, ON P0V 1V0, Canada
Tel: 807-744-4491
www.sandylake.firstnation.ca
Grades: K - 6; Special Ed.; *Enrollment:* 390; *Number of Employees:* 53; *Note:* The Thomas Fiddler Memorial Elementary School is part of the Sandy Lake Board of Education. The elementary school educates members of Sandy Lake First Nation. From kindergarten to grade four, Thomas Fiddler Memorial Elementary School provides a native immersion program.

Sandy Lake: Thomas Fiddler Memorial High School
P.O. Box 8
Sandy Lake, ON P0V 1V0
Tel: 807-774-1229; *Fax:* 807-774-1228
www.sandylake.firstnation.ca
Grades: 7 - 10; *Enrollment:* 124; *Note:* The activities of Thomas Fiddler Memorial High School are overseen by the Sandy Lake Board of Education. The secondary school serves students of the Sandy Lake First Nation.

Scarborough: Islamic Foundation School
441 Nugget Ave., Scarborough, ON M1S 5E1, Canada
Tel: 416-754-7752
school@myifs.ca
myifs.ca
twitter.com/MYIFS
Grades: Elem.; *Enrollment:* 327
Yahya Qurechi, Principal, 416-754-7752, ext. 242

Schools

Full-Time Hifz School
441 Nugget Ave., Scarborough, ON M1V 5E1, Canada
Tel: 416-321-0909
www.islamicfoundation.ca
Grades: Religious Education
Quari Yunus Ingar, Principal
yingar@islamicfoundation.ca

Evening Madressah
441 Nugget Ave., Scarborough, ON M1V 5E1, Canada
Tel: 416-321-0909; *Fax:* 416-321-1995
yingar@islamicfoundation.ca
www.islamicfoundation.ca
Grades: Religious Education
Qani Yunus Ingar, Principal, 416-321-0909, ext. 226

Sunday School
Islamic Foundation
441 Nugget Ave., Scarborough, ON M1V 5E1, Canada
Tel: 416-321-0909; *Fax:* 416-321-1995
yingar@islamicfoundation.ca
www.islamicfoundation.ca
Grades: Religious Education

Summer Hifz & Summer School
Islamic Foundation
441 Nugget Ave., Scarborough, ON M1V 5E1, Canada
Tel: 416-321-0909; *Fax:* 416-321-1995
ukhan@islamicfoundation.ca
www.islamicfoundation.ca
Grades: Religious Education
Uzma Khan, Administrative Assistant, 416-321-3776, ext. 231
ukhan@islamicfoundation.ca

Scarborough: Madinatul-Uloom Academy
670 Progress Ave., Scarborough, ON M1H 3A4, Canada
Tel: 416-332-9428; *Fax:* 416-332-0470
info@mua.ca
www.mua.ca
Grades: Elem.-Sec.; *Enrollment:* 358
Nilofar Asif, Principal

Scarborough: NAMF Islamic Academy
4140 Finch Ave. East, Scarborough, ON M1S 3T9
Tel: 416-299-1969; *Fax:* 416-299-4890
www.namf.ca
Grades: K - 8

Scarborough: Ontario International Institute (OII)
#203, 1001 Sandhurst Circle, Scarborough, ON M1V 1Z6
Tel: 416-701-1763; *Fax:* 905-471-3586
info@oii-edu.ca
www.oii-edu.ca
Grades: 9 - 12; *Note:* A Government-inspected school, fully authorized by the Ministry of Education to award credits leading to the Ontario Secondary School Diploma (OSSD).
Sami Appadurai, Principal

Scarborough: Salaheddin Islamic School
741 Kennedy Rd., Scarborough, ON M1K 2C6, Canada
Tel: 416-264-9495; *Fax:* 416-264-3343
principal@salaheddin.org
www.salaheddin.org
Grades: Elem.; *Enrollment:* 185
Laila Maarouf

Scarborough: Tayyibah Islamic Academy (TIA)
#205, 100 McLevin Ave., Scarborough, ON M1B 2V5
Tel: 416-297-7336; *Fax:* 416-297-7930
theprincipal@tayyibahacademy.com
www.tayyibahacademy.com
Grades: K - 12

Sioux Lookout: Pelican Falls First Nation High School (PFFNHS)
P.O. Box 4127
Sioux Lookout, ON P8T 1J9, Canada
Tel: 807-737-1110; *Fax:* 807-737-1449
Toll-Free: 1-800-378-9111
www.nnec.on.ca/pffnhs/
Grades: Sec.; *Enrollment:* 143
Darryl Tinney, Principal

Smithville: John Calvin Private School
P.O. Box 280
320 Station St., Smithville, ON L0R 2A0, Canada
Tel: 905-957-2341; *Fax:* 905-957-2342
Grades: K./Elem.
Frank C. Ludwig, Principal

St Catharines: Beyond Montessori School
St. George's Anglican Church
P.O. Box 647
83 Church St., St Catharines, ON L0S 1E0
Tel: 905-937-0700
info@beyondmontessori.com
www.beyondmontessori.com
www.facebook.com/208151271840
twitter.com/BMontessoriStC
beyondmontessori.wordpress.com
Grades: Pre.-3; *Enrollment:* 50; *Number of Employees:* 12
Natasha Secord, Head of School

St Catharines: Nelephant Montessori School
134 Louth St., St Catharines, ON L2S 2T4
Tel: 905-704-1388; *Fax:* 905-704-4520
gcns@becon.org
www.nelephant.ca
Grades: Toddler - Casa
Nicole Boulet, Academic Supervisor

St Catharines: Ridley College
P.O. Box 3013
2 Ridley Rd., St Catharines, ON L2R 7C3, Canada
Tel: 905-684-1889; *Fax:* 905-684-8875
admission@ridleycollege.com
www.ridley.on.ca
www.facebook.com/pages/Ridley-College/145690058823243
twitter.com/Ridley_College
www.youtube.com/RidleyCollege1889
Grades: K - 12; *Enrollment:* 625; *Note:* Ridley College is a university preparatory school, which features both a lower school & an uppper school. Boarding is available. Over 30% of students are international students.
George C. Hendrie, President, Board Chair
Ed Kidd, Headmaster, 905-684-1889
ed_kidd@ridleycollege.com
Stephen Clarke, Deputy Headmaster, 905-684-1889, ext. 2205
stephen_clarke@ridleycollege.com
Jim Parke, Director, Finance & Operations
jim_parke@ridleycollege.com
Andrew T. Weller, Dean of Admissions, 905-684-1889, ext. 2298
andrew_t_weller@ridleycollege.com
Margaret Lech, Assistant Headmaster, Student Affairs
margaret_lech@ridleycollege.com
James Milligan, Assistant Head, Lower School, 905-684-1889, ext. 2296
jim_milligan@ridleycollege.com

St Catharines: Wheatley School of Montessori Education Inc.
497 Scott St., St Catharines, ON L2M 3X3, Canada
Tel: 905-641-3012; *Fax:* 905-641-1443
mail@wheatleyschool.com
www.wheatleyschool.com
Grades: Preschool - 8; *Note:* The coeducational, non-denominational school provides Montessori programs for children from preschool to grade four. The Wheatley School's preschool program accepts children as young as two years of age. For upper elementary students in grades five to eight, a traditional, enriched program is offered.
Eda Varalli, Head of School

St Thomas: St. Thomas Community School
77 Fairview Ave., St Thomas, ON N5R 4X7, Canada
Tel: 519-633-0690
info@stthomaschristian.org
www.stthomaschristian.org
Grades: Jr. K.-8; *Enrollment:* 789
Jason Schouten, Principal

Stittsville: Ottawa Waldorf School
1 Goulbourn St., Stittsville, ON K2S 1N9, Canada
Tel: 613-836-1547; *Fax:* 613-836-8372
ottawawaldorf@bellnet.ca
www.ottawawaldorf.ca
www.facebook.com/OttawaWaldorfSchool
twitter.com/OttawaWaldorf
Grades: K. - 8; *Enrollment:* 91

Stouffville: The Progressive Montessori Academy
6411 Main St., Stouffville, ON L4A 1G4
Tel: 416-220-8070
www.thepma.ca
Grades: Pre.-6; *Enrollment:* 40
Lubna Jaffer, Principal
ljaffer@thepma.ca

Stratford: Nancy Campbell Collegiate Institute
45 Waterloo St. South, Stratford, ON N5A 4A8
Tel: 519-272-1900; *Toll-Free:* 888-641-6224
info@nancycampbell.ca
www.nancycampbell.ca
Grades: K - 12; *Note:* Not-for-profit, private, residential and day school.

Thornhill: Associated Hebrew Schools of Toronto — The Kamin Education Centre
300 Atkinson Ave., Thornhill, ON L4J 8A2, Canada
Tel: 905-889-3998; *Fax:* 905-889-5183
www.associatedhebrewschools.com/branches/kamin
Grades: K./Elem.; *Enrollment:* 1415
Kathy Friedman, Principal
kfriedman@ahschools.com
Linda Kichler, Vice Principal
lkichler@ahschools.com
Bari Horowitz, Vice Principal
bhorowitz@ahschools.com

Thornhill: Central Montessori Schools (CMS)
72 Steels Ave. West, Thornhill, ON L4J 1A1, Canada
Tel: 416-889-0012; *Fax:* 905-889-0422
www.cmschool.net
Grades: Toddlers - 8; *Enrollment:* 900; *Note:* Central Montessori Schools are co-educational, non-denominational schools. The early childhood education program is designed for children from 18 months to 2.5 years.
Deborah Sharp, Principal

Campuses

Florence Campus
157 Florence Ave., Toronto, ON M2N 1G5
Tel: 416-222-5097; *Fax:* 416-222-0584

Sheppard Campus
200 Sheppard Ave. East, Toronto, ON M2N 3A9
Tel: 416-222-5940; *Fax:* 416-222-2546

Willowdale Campus
157 Willowdale Ave., Toronto, ON M2N 4Y3
Tel: 416-250-1022; *Fax:* 416-250-5191

York Mills Campus
18 Coldwater Rd., Toronto, ON M2N 1Y7
Tel: 416-510-1200; *Fax:* 416-510-1230

Maplehurst Campus
181 Maplehurst Ave., Toronto, ON M2N 3C1
Tel: 416-222-9207

Thornhill: Chabad of Markham Hebrew School
83 Green Lane, Thornhill, ON L3T 6K6
Tel: 905-886-0420
www.chabadmarkham.org
www.facebook.com/267334146633060
Grades: K.-9

Thornhill: Everest Academy
130 Racco Pkwy., Thornhill, ON L4J 8X9
Tel: 905-881-3335; *Fax:* 905-756-1111
info@everestacademies.com
www.everestacademies.com
Grades: 1-12
Tim Sim, Principal

***Thornhill:* Jewish Youth Network Hebrew School (JYN)**
#5, 8700 Bathurst St., Thornhill, ON L4J 9J8
Tel: 905-889-7582
www.jewishyouth.ca
www.facebook.com/JewishYouth

Grades: 1-7
Chani Nachlas, Director

***Thornhill:* Joe Dwek Ohr HaEmet Sephardic School**
7026 Bathurst St., Thornhill, ON L4J 8K3
Tel: 905-669-7653; *Fax:* 905-669-5138
www.orhaemet.com

Note: Orthodox & Sephardic Jewish education for children aged 4 & 5.
Sarah Wasserman, Principal
s.wasserman@ohrhaemet.com

***Thornhill:* The Leo Baeck Day School North Campus**
36 Atkinson Ave., Thornhill, ON L4J 8C9
Tel: 905-709-3636; *Fax:* 905-709-1999
info@leobaeck.ca
www.leobaeck.ca
www.facebook.com/leobaeckdayschool
twitter.com/LeoBaeckNorth

Grades: Preschool - 8; *Note:* The Leo Baeck Day School is a Reform Jewish day school. Students experience Judaism from a Reform perspective.
Laurie Davis, President
board@leobaeck.ca
Eric Petersiel, RJE, Head of School
epetersiel@leobaeck.ca
Robyn Buchmam, Director, Admission
rbuchman@leobaeck.ca
Yvette Burke, B.A., B.Ed., M.Ed., Principal
yburke@leobaeck.ca

Campuses
South Campus
1950 Bathurst St., Toronto, ON M5P 3K9
Tel: 416-787-9899; *Fax:* 416-787-9893
twitter.com/LeoBaeckSouth

Ron Mintz, Prinicpal
rmintz@leobaeck.ca

***Thornhill:* Ner Israel Yeshiva College**
250 Bathurst Glen Dr., Thornhill, ON L4J 8A7, Canada
Tel: 905-731-1224; *Fax:* 905-731-2104

Note: The college provides undergraduate & graduate religious degrees.

***Thornhill:* Netivot HaTorah Day School**
18 Atkinson Ave., Thornhill, ON L4J 8C8, Canada
Tel: 905-771-1234; *Fax:* 905-771-1807
www.netivot.com

Grades: Pre - 6; *Enrollment:* 600; *Note:* Netivot HaTorah is an orthodox Jewish school. Its program includes Judaic & general studies.
Dr. Reuven Stern, Head of School
rstern@netivothatorah.com

***Thornhill:* Northwood Academy Montessori Plus Centre St. Campus**
86 Centre St., Thornhill, ON L4J 1E9
Tel: 416-492-7812
info@northwoodmontessori.ca
www.northwoodmontessori.ca

Number of Schools: 6; *Grades:* Pre.-K.; *Enrollment:* 50
Heather Spear, Director

Campuses
Finch Campus
Tri-Congregational Church
1080 Finch Ave. East, Toronto, ON M2J 2X2
Tel: 416-492-7812; *Fax:* 905-881-8394

Gallanough Campus
Gallanough Resource Centre
1 Brooke St., Thornhill, ON L4J 2K2
Tel: 416-492-7812; *Fax:* 416-492-7812

Madawaska Campus
Newton Baptist Church
53 Madawaska Ave., Toronto, ON M2M 2R2
Tel: 416-492-7812; *Fax:* 416-492-7812

Markham Campus
Markham Community Church
9329 McCowan Rd., Markham, ON L3P 3J3
Tel: 416-492-7812; *Fax:* 416-492-7812

St. Agnes Campus
St. Agnes School
280 Otonabee Ave., Toronto, ON M2M 2T2
Tel: 416-492-7812; *Fax:* 416-492-7812

***Thornhill:* Temple Har Zion Religious School**
7360 Bayview Ave., Thornhill, ON L3T 2R7
Tel: 905-889-2252; *Fax:* 905-889-2258
information@templeharzion.com
www.templeharzion.com/education.html
www.facebook.com/templeharzion
twitter.com/templeharzion
www.youtube.com/user/TempleHarZion

Grades: K.-10
Susan Sermer, Director, Education
susansermer@templeharzion.com

***Thornhill:* Temple Kol Ami Religious School**
36 Atkinson Ave., Thornhill, ON L4J 8C9
Tel: 416-578-0809; *Fax:* 905-695-9232
templekolami.ca

Grades: Elem.
Judy Silver, Director, Education
educator@templekolami.ca
Brenda Gottlieb, Administrator
brenda@templekolami.ca

***Thornhill:* Torah 4 Teens**
#5, 8700 Bathurst St., Thornhill, ON L4J 9J8
Tel: 905-889-7582; *Fax:* 416-661-5477
www.jewishyouth.ca

Note: Torah 4 Teens offers secondary school students approved high school & pre-university courses about the Torah.

***Thornhill:* Toronto Waldorf School (TWS)**
#1, 9100 Bathurst St., Thornhill, ON L4J 8C7, Canada
Tel: 905-881-1611; *Fax:* 905-881-6710
www.torontowaldorfschool.com
www.facebook.com/TorontoWaldorfSchool
twitter.com/torontowaldorf
plus.google.com/109156546982795194219

Grades: Preschool - Secondary
Bill Harlow, Chair
Michèle Andrews, Administrative Director
Katharina Dannenberg, High School Administrator
Kristine Che, Financial Coordinator
Darlene Gregoire, Manager, Business
Paul Sheardown, Manager, Facilities
Aileen Stewart, High School Admissions

***Thunder Bay:* Little Lions Waldorf Daycare & Kindergarten**
211 Clarke St., Thunder Bay, ON P7A 2M1
Tel: 807-344-2283; *Fax:* 807-344-4252
llwaldorf@tbaytel.net
www.littlelionswaldorf.ca

Grades: Pre. K - K

***Toronto:* Abacus Montessori & Private School**
Eglinton Campus
1 Credit Union Dr., Toronto, ON M4A 2S6
Tel: 416-494-4650; *Fax:* 416-494-4650
info@abacusmontessori.ca
www.abacusmontessori.ca

Campuses
Don Mills Campus
1300 Don Mills Rd., Toronto, ON M3B 2W6
Tel: 416-331-8637; *Fax:* 416-331-8637
donmills@abacusmontessori.ca
www.abacusmontessori.ca

***Toronto:* The Abelard School**
203 College St., Toronto, ON M5T 1P9
Tel: 416-944-0661; *Fax:* 416-944-8902
info@abelardschool.org
www.abelardschool.org

Grades: 9-12; *Enrollment:* 55
Michelle White, Principal

***Toronto:* Acacia International High School**
#251, 385 The Westmall, Toronto, ON M9C1E
Tel: 416-712-8864
www.mytorontoschool.com

Grades: Sec.

***Toronto:* Academy c60**
1650 Ave. Rd, 2nd Fl., Toronto, ON M5M 2Y1
Tel: 647-352-6060
learn@academyc60.com
www.academyc60.com

Grades: 9-12
Leslie Zulauf, Founder & Executive Director

***Toronto:* Adath Israel Religious School**
37 Southbourne Ave., Toronto, ON M3H 1A4
Tel: 416-635-5340; *Fax:* 416-635-1629
info@adathisrael.com
www.adathisrael.com

Grades: Pre.-Sec.; Adult Ed.
Rabbi Steven Saltzman, Senior Rabbi, 416-635-5340, ext. 302
rabbi@adathisrael.com
Bernie Rabinovitch, Executive Director, 416-635-5340, ext. 317
bernie@adathisrael.com
Cantor A. Eliezer Kirshblum, M.Sc., Educational Director
Linda Schwartz, School Administrator, 416-635-5354
linda@adathisrael.com
Wendy Steinberg-Himmel, Director, Preschool Program
wendy@adathisrael.com

***Toronto:* Ahavat Yisrael Hebrew School**
54 Glen Park Ave., Toronto, ON M6B 2C2
Tel: 416-781-8088
contact@ahavatyisrael.ca
www.ahavatyisraelhebrewschool.com

Grades: JK-7; *Note:* Sunday morning classes for junior kindergarten-grade 7 are held in Ventura Park Middle School, Stephen Lewis Secondary School, & Bais Yaakov Elementary School, 10:00 am-12:30 pm. Tuesday evening classes for grades 1-6 are held in Stephen Lewis Secondary School, 6:00-7:30 pm.
Leslie Shapiro, Principal & Director, Education

***Toronto:* Alathena International Academy**
1065 McNicoll Ave., Toronto, ON M1W 3W6
Tel: 416-756-3338
alathena.com

Grades: 9-12
Simon Huynh, Director

Campuses
Richmond Hill Campus
#201, 650 Hwy. 7, Richmond Hill, ON L4B 1G7
Tel: 905-763-8788

North York Campus
1470 Don Mills Rd., 3rd Fl., Toronto, ON M3B 2X7
Tel: 416-510-8080

***Toronto:* Alpha International Academy**
3405 Kennedy Rd. 2nd Fl., Toronto, ON M1V 4Y3
Tel: 416-640-0161; *Fax:* 416-640-1330
info@slc-alpha.ca
slc-alpha.ca
www.facebook.com/pages/AIA-St-Lawrence-College/387829337955885
twitter.com/SLCAlpha

Grades: 9 - 12; *Note:* An affiliate of St. Lawrence College.

***Toronto:* Alpha Quality Education Inc**
#200, 6120A Yonge St., Toronto, ON M2M 3W7
Tel: 416-661-4446; *Fax:* 416-661-4301

Grades: 9 - 12
Izadpanah Zohreh, Principal

***Toronto:* ARS Armenian Private School**
45 Hallcrown Pl., Toronto, ON M2J 4Y4
Tel: 416-491-2675; *Fax:* 416-491-8559
www.arsdayschool.ca
www.facebook.com/arsarmenianschool

Grades: K.-12; *Enrollment:* 363
Armen Martirossian, Principal

***Toronto:* Associated Hebrew Schools of Toronto**
Hurwich Education Centre
252 Finch Ave. West, Toronto, ON M2R 1M9, Canada
Tel: 416-494-7666; *Fax:* 416-494-2925
www.associatedhebrewschools.com

Grades: K.-8; *Enrollment:* 1700; *Note:* A community day school with a focus on Torah-values & high academic standards. Locations in Toronto & Thornhill.
Dr. Mark Smiley, Director, Education
msmiley@ahschools.com

***Toronto:* Bais Chaya Mushka Preschool**
4375 Chesswood Dr., Toronto, ON M3J 2C2
Tel: 416-398-9532

Grades: Pre./Elem.; *Note:* Orthodox Jewish education for girls.
Rabbi Nochum Sosover, Director

***Toronto:* Bais Yaakov Elementary School**
15 Saranac Blvd., Toronto, ON M6A 2G4, Canada
Tel: 416-256-4436

Grades: Pre-school - 8; *Enrollment:* 400; *Note:* Bais Yaakov Elementary School is a school for girls.
Magda Simon, Principal, 416-783-6181
msimon@baisyaakov.ca
Devorah Drebin, Junior High Principal, 416-783-6181

***Toronto:* Bannockburn School**
12 Bannockburn Ave., Toronto, ON M5M 2M8, Canada
Tel: 416-789-7855; *Fax:* 416-789-7963
bannockburn@bannockburn.ca
www.bannockburn.ca
www.facebook.com/BannockburnSchool
plus.google.com/112293779478263620724
Grades: Toddler / Preschool / Elementary; *Note:* Bannockburn School offers Montessori education.
Adalove Gorrie, Principal, Toddler, Primary, and Elementary Programs, 416-789-7855, ext. 303
agorrie@bannockburn.ca
Isabella Foster, Librarian, 416-789-7855, ext. 307
library@bannockburn.ca
Terry Gorrie, Director, Business, 416-789-7855, ext. 302
tgorrie@bannockburn.ca

***Toronto:* Bayview Glen**
275 Duncan Mill Rd., Toronto, ON M3B 3H9, Canada
Tel: 416-443-1030; *Fax:* 416-443-1032
www.bayviewglen.ca
www.facebook.com/175696199146059
twitter.com/edaunt
Grades: Preschool - 12; *Enrollment:* 1011; *Note:* Preschool education at Bayview Glen starts at age 2. The school includes lower school, prep school, & upper school.
Eileen Daunt, Head of School
Vince Haines, Director, Finance
vhaines@bayviewglen.ca
Judy Maxwell, Director, Admissions
jmaxwell@bayviewglen.ca

***Toronto:* Beth Jacob High School**
410 Lawrence Ave. West, Toronto, ON M5M 1C2, Canada
Tel: 416-787-4949; *Fax:* 416-787-0453
Grades: Secondary; *Note:* Beth Jacob High School is a school for Orthodox Jewish girls.
Rabbi E. Brauner, Executive Director
ebrauner@byhs-toronto.com
Rabbi Moshe Silver, Principal
msilver@byhs-toronto.com

***Toronto:* Beth Radom Jumpin' for Judaism**
***Also known as:* J4J**
Beth Radom Congregation
18 Reiner Rd., Toronto, ON M3H 2K9
Tel: 416-636-3451; *Fax:* 416-636-1042
info@bethradomj4j.com
www.bethradomj4j.com
Note: Programs at J4J include small group turorials, classroom activities, & family education. Classes also meet at Toronto Waldorf School; please see website for more detials.

***Toronto:* Beth Sholom Hebrew School**
1445 Eglinton Ave. West, Toronto, ON M6C 2E6
Tel: 416-783-6103; *Fax:* 416-783-9923
www.bethsholom.net/hebrew-school.htm
Grades: JK-7
Karen L. Goodis, Principal, 416-783-6103, ext. 225
karen@bethsholom.net

***Toronto:* Beth Torah Hebrews' Cool**
47 Glenbrook Ave., Toronto, ON M6B 2L7
Tel: 416-782-4495
yourshul@bethtorah.ca
www.bethtorah.ca
www.facebook.com/bethtorah.ca
Grades: 1-6; *Note:* A one-day-a-week program teaching children about the Torah, Israel, Hebrew & Jewish tradition.

***Toronto:* Beth Tzedec Congregational School**
1700 Bathurst St., Toronto, ON M5P 3K3
Tel: 416-781-3514; *Fax:* 416-781-0150
www.beth-tzedec.org
Grades: JK-7; *Note:* Classes in Conservative Judaism are held on Sunday mornings & Wednesday evenings. For more information please see the website, or contact the school office.
Ron Polster, Contact, School Office
rpolster@beth-tzedec.org

***Toronto:* Bialik Hebrew Day School**
2760 Bathurst St., Toronto, ON M6B 3A1, Canada
Tel: 416-783-3346; *Fax:* 416-785-8287
communications@bialik.ca
www.bialik.ca
www.facebook.com/Bialik.Hebrew.Day.School
twitter.com/bialikhds
Grades: JK - 8; *Enrollment:* 800; *Note:* The Ben and Edith Himel Education Centre on the Joseph & Wolf Lebovic Jewish Community Campus is lcoated at 180 Ilan Ramon Blvd., Vaughan, ON L6A 4P6, Phone: 905-417-3737, Fax: 905-417-0606
Marlene Brickman, Executive Director
mbrickman@bialik.ca
Shana Harris, Head of School
sharris@bialik.ca
Benjamin Cohen, Principal, General Studies
bcohen@bialik.ca
Sabrina Barczynski, Registrar, 416.783.3346, ext. 207
sbarczynski@bialik.ca
Anita Eckhaus, Vice Principal, Elementary Division
aeckhaus@bialik.ca
Amy Platt, Vice Principal, Primary
aplatt@bialik.ca
Beverley Young, Vice Principal, Senior Division
beverley_young@bialik.on.ca

***Toronto:* Birmingham International College of Canada (BICC)**
#203, 2221 Yonge St., Toronto, ON M4S 2B4
Tel: 416-481-8866
info@bicc-edu.com
bicc-edu.com
twitter.com/BICC_EDU
Grades: 9 - 12; *Note:* An accredited, multi-cultural, university preparatory school.
Brian Israel, Principal, 416-481-8866, ext. 103

***Toronto:* The Bishop Strachan School (BSS)**
298 Lonsdale Rd., Toronto, ON M4V 1X2, Canada
Tel: 416-483-4325; *Fax:* 416-481-5632
info@bss.on.ca
bss.on.ca
www.facebook.com/thebishopstrachanschool
twitter.com/bss_bobcats
www.linkedin.com/company/the-bishop-strachan-school
vimeo.com/bssvideo
Grades: JK - 12; *Enrollment:* 900; *Note:* Independent school for girls.
Sarah Kavanagh, Chair
Deryn Lavell, Head of School
dlavell@bss.on.ca
Dr. Angela Terpstra, Principal, Middle and Senior School
aterpstra@bss.on.ca
Patti MacDonald, Principal, Junior School
pmacdonald@bss.on.ca

***Toronto:* Blyth Academy**
146 Yorkville Ave., Toronto, ON M5R 1C2
Tel: 416-960-3552; *Fax:* 416-960-9506
Toll-Free: 866-960-3552
info@blytheducation.com
www.blytheducation.com

Campuses
Barrie Campus
11 Victoria St., Barrie, ON L4N 6T3
Tel: 705-719-9595

Burlington Campus
952 Century Dr., Burlington, ON L7L 5P2
Tel: 905-637-0346
Alex MacKinnon, Principal

Lawrence Park Campus
3284 Yonge St., Toronto, ON M4N 3M7
Tel: 416-488-9301; *Fax:* 416-916-9060

Port Credit Campus
1470 Hurontario St., Mississauga, ON L5G 3G4
Tel: 905-990-2855; *Fax:* 905-990-3155

Thornhill Campus
300 John St., Toronto, ON L3T 5W4
Tel: 905-889-8081; *Fax:* 905-889-4797

Whitby Campus
209 Dundas St. East, Whitby, ON L1N 7H8
Tel: 905-666-3773

***Toronto:* Bnei Akiva Schools - Ulpanat Orot**
45 Canyon Ave., Toronto, ON M3H 3S4, Canada
Tel: 416-630-5434; *Fax:* 416-638-7905
www.bneiakivaschools.org
www.facebook.com/bneiakivaschoolstoronto
twitter.com/BneiAkivaSchool
Grades: 9-12; *Enrollment:* 210; *Note:* Bnei Akiva Schools serves the Jewish community.
Rabbi Seth Grauer, Head of School
rabbigrauer@bneiakivaschools.org
Mordechai Sabeti, Director of Education, General Studies
sabeti@bneiakivaschools.org
Yael Gelernter, Assistant Principal / Director of Admissions
ygelernter@bneiakivaschools.org
Sara Munk, Assistant Principal / Director of Jewish Studies
smunk@bneiakivaschools.org
Shari Weinberg, Assistant Principal
sweinberg@bneiakivaschools.org

Campuses
Bnei Akiva Schools - Yeshivat Or Chaim
159 Almore Ave., Toronto, ON M3H 2H9, Canada
Tel: 416-630-6772; *Fax:* 416-398-5711
www.bneiakivaschools.org
www.facebook.com/bneiakivaschoolstoronto
Grades: 9-12; *Enrollment:* 210; *Note:* Bnei Akiva Schools serves the Jewish community.
Rabbi Yair Spitz, Menahel
yspitz@bneiakivaschools.org
Nicky Kagan, Assistant Principal
nkagan@bneiakivaschools.org

***Toronto:* Boardwalk Montessori School**
1975 B. Queen St. East, Toronto, ON M4L 1J1
Tel: 416-691-6740; *Fax:* 416-691-9046
office@boardwalkmontessori.com
www.boardwalkmontessori.com
Grades: Toddler - Pre.
Joan Walder, Principal

***Toronto:* Bond Academy**
1500 Birchmount Rd., Toronto, ON M1P 2G5
Tel: 416-266-8878; *Fax:* 416-266-3898
www.bondacademy.ca
Grades: K./Elem./Sec.; *Enrollment:* 450
John Healey, Principal, Elementary
johnh@web.bondacademy.ca
Jeffrey Farber, Principal, Secondary
jfarber@web.bondacademy.ca

***Toronto:* Bond International College**
1500 Birchmount Rd., Toronto, ON M1P 2G5, Canada
Tel: 416-266-8878; *Fax:* 416-266-3898
info@bondcollege.com
www.bondcollege.com
Grades: Secondary; *Note:* Bond International College prepares international students for colleges & universities in Canada, the United States, the United Kingdom, & Australia.
Jeffrey Farber, Principal

***Toronto:* Braemar College**
229 College St., Toronto, ON M5T 1R4
Tel: 416-487-8138; *Fax:* 416-487-6165
info@braemarcollege.com
www.braemarcollege.com
Grades: 9 - 12

***Toronto:* Branksome Hall**
10 Elm Ave., Toronto, ON M4W 1N4, Canada
Tel: 416-920-9741; *Fax:* 416-920-5390
attendance@branksome.on.ca
www.branksome.on.ca
www.facebook.com/pages/Branksome-Hall-Toronto/95081778626
twitter.com/#!/branksomehall
www.linkedin.com/groups?home=&gid=3802471&trk=anet_ug_hm
Grades: JK - 12; *Enrollment:* 880; *Number of Employees:* 120 faculty; *Note:* Branksome Hall is an independent day & boarding school for girls & an International Baccalaureate (IB) World School.
Karen Jurjevich, Principal, 416-920-6265, ext. 208
Sarah Craig, Head, Junior School, 416-920-6265, ext. 105
scraig@branksome.on.ca
Amanda Kennedy, Head, Middle School, 416-920-6265, ext. 373
akennedy@branksome.on.ca
Joanne Colwell, Head, Senior School, 416-920-6265, ext. 271
jcolwell@branksome.on.ca
Denise Power, Director, Student Life, 416-920-6265, ext. 111
dpower@branksome.on.ca
Julia Drake, Executive Director, Communications & Marketing, 416-920-6265, ext. 103
jdrake@branksome.on.ca
Heather Friesen, Head, Academics, 416-920-6265, ext. 102
hfriesen@branksome.on.ca
Heidi Vesely, Executive Director, Finance & Administration, 416-920-6265, ext. 108
hvesely@branksome.on.ca
Kelly Longmore, Interim Director, Residence, 416-920-6265, ext. 162
klongmore@branksome.on.ca

***Toronto:* Canadian Montessori Teacher Education Institute**
#35546, 2528 Bayview Ave., Toronto, ON M2L 2Y4
Tel: 416-458-8970
www.montessori-institute.ca

Toronto: Casa Vera Montessori School
2000 Keele St., Toronto, ON M6M 3Y4
Tel: 416-850-9705; *Fax:* 416-850-9706
mail@casaverams.com
www.casaverams.com
Grades: Toddler - Casa
Viera Scurova, Principal

Toronto: Centre for Jewish Living & Learning Religious School
Also known as: Lomdim
120 Old Colony Rd., Toronto, ON M2I 2K2
Tel: 416-449-3880; *Fax:* 416-449-9831
reception@templeemanuel.ca
www.templeemanuel.ca
Note: The school offers progressive Jewish learning for children.
Robin Leszner, Director, Education
robin@templeemanuel.ca

Toronto: Children's Garden Junior School (CGS)
670 Eglinton Ave. East, Toronto, ON M4G 2K4, Canada
Tel: 416-423-5017; *Fax:* 416-423-0727
info@cgsschool.com
www.childrensgardenschool.com
Grades: Pre- K - 3
Marie Bates, Principal & Founder, 416-423-5017, ext. 24
marie@cgsschool.com
Zandee Toovey, Executive Assistant, 416-423-5017, ext. 44
ztoovey@cgsschool.com

Toronto: Children's Garden Nursery School
1847 Bayview Ave., Toronto, ON M4G 3E4
Tel: 416-488-4298; *Fax:* 416-488-6499
info@childrensgarden.ca
www.childrensgarden.ca
Grades: Pre-K.; *Enrollment:* 140
Pauline Foulkes, Director

Toronto: La Citadelle International Academy of Arts & Science
15 Mallow Rd., Toronto, ON M3B 1G2
Tel: 416-385-9685; *Fax:* 416-385-9685
info@lacitadelleacademy.com
www.lacitadelleacademy.com
www.facebook.com/la.citadelle.1
twitter.com/LaCitadelle1
www.youtube.com/channel/UCBAmw50YMGo3VVD-WeJS5bw
Grades: Pre.-12; *Enrollment:* 230
Alfred Abouchar, Headmaster
Faye Tabbara, Coordinator, Administration & Admission
admin@lacitadelleacademy.com

Toronto: City Academy
#1000, 3080 Yonge St., Toronto, ON M4N 3N1, Canada
Tel: 416-482-2521; *Fax:* 416-482-2496
info@cityacademy.ca
www.cityacademy.ca
Grades: Sec.; *Enrollment:* 230
Sheila Dever, Principal

Toronto: Community Hebrew Academy of Toronto (CHAT)
Also known as: TanenbaumCHAT
Wallenberg Campus
200 Wilmington Ave., Toronto, ON M3H 5J8, Canada
Tel: 416-636-5984
info@tanenbaumchat.org
tanenbaumchat.org
www.facebook.com/TanenbaumCHAT1
twitter.com/TanenbaumCHAT; twitter.com/TCWallenberg
Grades: Sec.; *Enrollment:* 800; *Note:* Co-educational high school of the Greater Toronto Jewish community. Campuses in Toronto & Vaughan. Programmes include core subjects & Jewish studies. The Wallenberg Campus is for students living south of Steeles Ave. in Toronto.
Bradley Mittelman, Dean of Students
Helen Fox, B.A., Principal
Rosemary Tile, Manager, Admissions & Recruitment
rtile@tanenbaumchat.org
Heather Weinstock, Dean of Students
Jory Vernon, Vice Principal, General Studies
Eli Mandel, Vice Principal, Jewish Studies
Ilana Shapira, Vice Principal, Ivrit

Campuses
Kimel Family Education Centre
Joseph & Wolf Lebovic Jewish Community Campus
9600 Bathurst St., Vaughan, ON L6A 3Z8
Tel: 905-787-8772; *Fax:* 905-787-8773
info@tanenbaumchat.org
tanenbaumchat.org/locations/kimel/
Enrollment: 1500; *Note:* The Kimel Family Education is for students living north of Steeles Ave. in Vaughan.
Jonathan Levy, Principal
Rosemary Tile, Director, Admissions, 416-636-5984, ext. 377
rtile@tanenbaumchat.org

Toronto: Cornerstone Montessori Prep School (CMPS)
177 Beverley St., Toronto, ON M5T 1Y7
Tel: 416-977-1204
www.cornerstoneprep.ca
Grades: Pre.-12; *Enrollment:* 130
Dr. Stephanie Ling, Ph.D., Principal

Campuses
Don Mills Campus
33 Mallard Rd., Toronto, ON M3B 1S4
Tel: 647-977-5584

Toronto: Crescent School
2365 Bayview Ave., Toronto, ON M2L 1A2, Canada
Tel: 416-449-2556
info@crescentschool.org
www.crescentschool.org
Grades: 3 - 12; *Note:* Crescent School is a day school for boys.
Geoff Roberts, Headmaster
Mark Hord, Head, Middle School
Ross MacDonald, Head, Lower School
Christopher White, Director, Admissions

Toronto: Crestwood Preparatory College
217 Brookbanks Dr., Toronto, ON M3A 2T7, Canada
Tel: 416-391-1441; *Fax:* 416-444-0949
www.crestwood.on.ca
www.facebook.com/pages/Crestwood-Preparatory-College/1091
25222250
Grades: Elem./Sec.; *Enrollment:* 391
Vince Pagano, Principal

Toronto: Crestwood School
411 Lawrence Ave. East, Toronto, ON M3C 1N9
Tel: 416-444-5858; *Fax:* 416-444-2127
Grades: Elem.
Dalia Eisen, Contact
dalia.eisen@crestwood.on.ca

Toronto: Danforth Jewish Circle Children's Jewish Studies Programme (DJC)
#125, 283 Danforth Ave., Toronto, ON M4K 1N2
Tel: 416-580-1233
info@djctoronto.com
djctoronto.com/explore/children.php
Grades: JK-7; *Note:* Jewish studies program emphasizing arts, music, culture, & film.

Toronto: Darchei Noam Hebrew School
864 Sheppard Ave. West, Toronto, ON M3H 2T5
Tel: 416-638-4783; *Fax:* 416-638-5852
caroldn@bellnet.ca
sites.google.com/site/youthandfamilyatdn
Grades: JK-6
Jennifer Katz, Director, Youth Education & Programming
educator.darcheinoam@gmail.com

Toronto: David & Esther Freiman Childhood Education Centre
4588 Bathurst St., Toronto, ON M2R 1W6
Tel: 416-638-1881; *Fax:* 416-636-5813
Note: Non-denominational education for children aged 18 months to 5 years.

Toronto: Discovering Minds Montessori Preschool
74 Bathurst St., Toronto, ON M5V 2P5
Tel: 416-504-0110; *Fax:* 416-731-7419
discovering@dmmps.com
www.dmmps.com
www.facebook.com/159824140742150
www.youtube.com/watch?v=S0HIl7dmOzU
Grades: Pre.
Guadalupe Rengifo, Director

Toronto: Downtown Jewish Community School (DJCS)
Miles Nadal Jewish Community Centre
750 Spadina Ave., Toronto, ON M5S 2J2
Tel: 416-924-6212; *Fax:* 416-924-0442
djcs.org
www.facebook.com/downtownjewishcommunityschool
Grades: JK-7
Naomi Azrieli, Chair
Joan Schoenfeld, Founder & Principal

Toronto: Downtown Montessori School
City Place Campus
335 Bremner Blvd., Toronto, ON M5V 3V4
Tel: 416-623-1738; *Fax:* 416-623-1742
downtownmontessori@rogers.com
www.downtownmontessori.ca
Grades: Toddler - Pre.
Liz Ferguson, Director, 416-698-0218

Campuses
Coatsworth Campus
11 Coatsworth Cres., Toronto, ON M4C 5P8
Tel: 416-694-9444; *Fax:* 416-694-9925

Infinity Place Campus
26 Grand Trunk Cres., Toronto, ON M5J 3A9
Tel: 416-849-3691

Simcoe Place Campus
200 Front St. West, Toronto, ON M5V 3J1
Tel: 416-340-8757

Toronto: Dr. Abraham Shore She'Arim Hebrew Day School
4588 Bathurst St., Toronto, ON M2R 1W6, Canada
Tel: 416-633-8247; *Fax:* 416-633-4783
info@shearim.ca
Grades: Elem./Spec. Ed.

Toronto: The Dragon Academy
35 Prince Arthur Ave., Toronto, ON M5R 1B2
Tel: 416-323-3243; *Fax:* 416-323-7780
info@dragonacademy.org
www.dragonacademy.org
www.facebook.com/151620228237983
twitter.com/dragonacademy
Grades: 7-12; *Enrollment:* 75
Meg Fox, Ph.D., Founding Principal

Toronto: Eastern Canada High School
36 Colville Rd., Toronto, ON M6M 2Yz
Tel: 416-567-4404; *Fax:* 416-551-7036
www.easterncanadahs.com
Grades: 9 - 12

Toronto: Eitz Chaim Schools - Administrative/Patricia Branch
475 Patricia Ave., Toronto, ON M2R 2N1
Tel: 416-225-1187; *Fax:* 416-225-3732
patricia@eitzchaim.com
Grades: 1-8; *Enrollment:* 800; *Note:* This branch houses the boys school & administrative offices.
Elias Levy, Executive Director
Rabbi Pliner, Dean

Campuses
Spring Farm Branch
80 York Hill Blvd., Thornhill, ON L4J 2P6
Tel: 905-764-6633; *Fax:* 905-764-9577
spring@eitzchaim.com
Grades: Pre.-8; *Note:* This branch houses the girls school.

Viewmount Branch
1 Viewmount Ave., Toronto, ON M5B 1T2
Tel: 416-789-4366; *Fax:* 416-785-1384
view@eitzchaim.com
Grades: Pre.-8; *Note:* This branch houses the girls school (grades 1-8); preschool, JK & SK are mixed

Toronto: Ellesmere Montessori School
37 Marchington Circle, Toronto, ON M1R 3M6
Tel: 416-447-1059; *Fax:* 416-447-1059
info@ellesmeremontessori.ca
www.ellesmeremontessori.ca
Grades: K./Elem.

Toronto: Ellington Montessori School
40 Cowdray Crt., Toronto, ON M1S 1A1
Tel: 416-759-8363; *Fax:* 416-759-2162
ellingtonmontessorischool@on.aibn.com
www.ellingtonmontessori.ca
Grades: Toddler - Middle; *Note:* Located in the lower level of Wexford United Church.
Deborah Renwick, Principal

Toronto: Fieldstone Day School
2999 Dufferin St., Toronto, ON M6B 3T4, Canada
Tel: 416-487-7381; *Fax:* 416-487-8190
admissions@fieldstonekcschool.org
www.fieldstonedayschool.org
www.facebook.com/138883499499203
Grades: JK - 12; *Enrollment:* 244; *Note:* Enriched curriculum.
Ginie Wong, Head of School, 416-487-1989, ext. 230
gwong@fieldstonekcschool.org

Lisa Akita, Librarian, 416-487-1989, ext. 221
lakita@fieldstonekcschool.org

Toronto: Forest Hill Montessori School
2 Wembley Rd., Toronto, ON M6C 2E9
Tel: 416-781-4449
info@foresthillmontessorischool.com
www.foresthillmontessorischool.com
www.facebook.com/ForestHillMontessoriSchool
twitter.com/fhms_toronto
Grades: Pre. - Elem.
Sandra Bosnar-Dale, Director

Campuses
North Toronto Campus
585 Cranbrooke Ave., Toronto, ON M6A 2X9
Tel: 416-781-5034

Toronto: FutureSkills High School
#204, 5635 Yonge St., Toronto, ON M2M 3S9
Tel: 416-227-1177; *Fax:* 416-227-0811
info@futureskills.com
www.futureskills.com
Grades: 9 - 12
Hassan Mirzai, Principal

Toronto: Gan Netivot
470 Glencairn Ave., Toronto, ON M5N 1V8
Tel: 416-789-3213
Grades: Pre.-JK; Orthodox

Toronto: German International School Toronto
960 Dufferin St., Toronto, ON M6H 4B4
Tel: 416-922-6413
www.gistonline.ca
www.facebook.com/175972742449216
www.linkedin.com/company/german-international-school-toronto
Grades: Pre.-8; *Enrollment:* 54; *Note:* German International School Toronto offers students a curriculum that blends German & Ontario educational standards.
Dr. Christian von Twickel, Chair & President
Arnd Rupp, Principal

Toronto: The Giles School
L'École Giles
80 Scarsdale Rd., Toronto, ON M3C 2C3, Canada
Tel: 416-446-0825; *Fax:* 416-446-0846
office@gilesschool.ca
www.gilesschool.ca
www.facebook.com/TheGilesSchool
Grades: Pre-K - 12; *Note:* The Giles School is a co-educational school which offers an enriched French immersion program. Students are introduced to a third language in grade one.
Kemp Rickett, Headmaster
kemp_rickett@gilesschool.ca
Caroline Bernaba, Principal
caroline_bernaba@gilesschool.ca
Rosine Dika Balotoken, Manager, Administration
rosine_dika@gilesschool.ca
Bob Spencer, Manager, Special Projects
rgspencer@rogers.com

Toronto: Gradale Academy
159 Roxborough Dr., Toronto, ON M4W 1X7
Tel: 416-923-9009
www.gradaleacademy.com
Grades: Pre.-3; *Enrollment:* 60; *Note:* Gradale Academy also offers classes outdoors at Evergreen Brick Works in Toronto.
Michelle Gradish, Founder & Head of School

Toronto: Great Lakes College of Toronto (GLCT)
323 Keele St., Toronto, ON M6P 2K6, Canada
Tel: 416-763-4121; *Fax:* 416-763-5225
query@glctschool.com
www.glctschool.com
Grades: 10 - 12; *Note:* The school is an international high school, which offers a pre-university program. English as a Second Language courses are also provided.
Tom Tidey, B.A., M.Ed., Principal

Campuses
The Canadian Trillium College - Quanzhou (CTC)
#7 High School, 46 Tian Hou Rd., Quanzhou City, China
www.ctc-school.com
Other Information: Tel: 011-86-595-2203068; Fax: 011-86-595-220-2528
Grades: 9 - 12; *Enrollment:* 150; *Note:* Ontario curriculum.

Toronto: Greenwood College School
443 Mount Pleasant Rd., Toronto, ON M4S 2L8
Tel: 416-482-9811; *Fax:* 416-482-9188
www.greenwoodcollege.com
www.facebook.com/138629896185229
twitter.com/chiefthegrizzly
www.linkedin.com/company/501131
www.youtube.com/user/greenwoodcollege
Richard Wernham, Chair
Allan Hardy, B.A., B.Ed., M.A.T., Principal
allan.hardy@greenwoodcollege.com

Toronto: Guildwood Village Montessori School (GVMS)
Montessori Village & Education Centre
297 Old Kingston Rd., Toronto, ON M1C 1B4
Tel: 416-266-0424
www.gvmontessori.ca
Grades: Pre.-8; *Enrollment:* 75
Elisa Bourdon, Principal
edeblasibourdon@rogers.com

Toronto: Haadi Elementary School
710 Progress Ave., Toronto, ON M1H-2X3
Tel: 416-628-6252; *Fax:* 416-490-0317
SchoolAdmin@Haadi.ca
school.haadi.ca
Grades: K - 12

Toronto: Hanson International Academy
#102A, 155 Consumers Rd., Toronto, ON M2J 0A3
Tel: 416-977-8188; *Fax:* 416-979-9880
info.toronto@CanadaHanson.com
www.canadahanson.com
www.facebook.com/212810255419249
twitter.com/HansonInt
www.youtube.com/user/ningxinzhou
Grades: 9 - 12

Campuses
Brampton Campus
#111, 44 Peel Centre Dr., Brampton, ON L6T 4B5
Tel: 905-791-7555; *Fax:* 905-791-5176
info.brampton@CanadaHanson.com
www.facebook.com/212810255419249

Vancouver Campus
#218, 810 Quayside Dr., New Westminster, BC V3M 6B9
Tel: 604-553-2835; *Fax:* 604-553-2835
info.vancouver@CanadaHanson.com
www.facebook.com/hansoninvernational.vancouver

Toronto: Havergal College
Senior School
1451 Avenue Rd., Toronto, ON M5N 2H9, Canada
Tel: 416-483-3843; *Fax:* 416-483-6796
info@havergal.on.ca
www.havergal.on.ca
www.facebook.com/HavergalCollege
twitter.com/HavergalCollege
www.youtube.com/user/HavergalCollege
Grades: JK - 12; *Enrollment:* 956; *Note:* University-preparatory day and boarding school for girls.
Lois Rowe, Acting Principal, 416-483-3843, ext. 4729
Leslie Anne Dexter, Head of the Junior School, 416-483-3843, ext. 4713

Toronto: Hawthorn School for Girls
101 Scarsdale Rd., Toronto, ON M3B 2R2, Canada
Tel: 416-444-3054; *Fax:* 416-449-2891
www.hawthornschool.com
www.facebook.com/HawthornSchool
twitter.com/hawthornschool
Grades: Pre - 12; *Enrollment:* 120
Eliza Trotter, School Head

Toronto: Head Start Montessori School
260 Yorkland Blvd., Toronto, ON M2J 1R7
Tel: 416-756-7300; *Fax:* 416-756-9019
ifo@headstartmontessori.ca
www.headstartmontessori.ca
Grades: Pre.
Naureen Shah, Principal

Toronto: High Park Day School
#202, 2150 Bloor St. West, Toronto, ON M6S 1M8
Tel: 416-762-4447
info@highparkdayschool.com
highparkdayschool.com
www.facebook.com/highpark.dayschool
twitter.com/HighParkDS
Grades: 1-8; *Enrollment:* 13
Amanda Dervaitis, Founder & Director
amanda@highparkdayschool.com
Aaron Downey, Teacher & Curriculum Coordinator
aaron@highparkdayschool.com

Toronto: High Park Gardens Montessori School
35 High Park Gdns., Toronto, ON M6R 1S8, Canada
Tel: 416-763-6097
admin@highparkgardensmontessori.com
www.mildenhallmontessori.com
Grades: Pre - 6
Lee Gair, Principal

Toronto: Hillside Montessori School
76 Anglesey Blvd., Toronto, ON M9A 3C1
Tel: 416-695-3466
www.hillsidemontessori.com
Grades: Pre.
Diana Pace-Asciak, Principal
dianapace@sympatico.ca

Toronto: Holy Blossom Preschool
Holy Blossom Temple
1950 Bathurst St., Toronto, ON M5V 2R3
Tel: 416-789-3291; *Fax:* 416-789-9697
templemail@holyblossom.org
www.holyblossom.org/study-limud/preschool
www.facebook.com/pages/Holy-Blossom-Temple/98017462501
twitter.com/holyblossom
www.linkedin.com/groups?gid=4507427
www.youtube.com/user/holyblossomtemple
Grades: Preschool
Pamela Hamovitch, Principal, Nursery School
phamovitch@holyblossom.org

Toronto: Horizons Secondary School (Toronto) (HSS)
#202, 4632 Yonge St., Toronto, ON M2N 5M1
Tel: 416-966-4009; *Fax:* 416-226-6888
canadahorizons.ca
Grades: 9 - 12
Dr. Martin Reinink, Principal

Toronto: Humberside Montessori School
121 Kennedy Ave., Toronto, ON M6S 2X8
Tel: 416-762-8888; *Fax:* 416-766-1211
www.humbersidemontessori.ca
Grades: Elem./Ungraded
Felix Bednarski, Principal
Molly Galle, Director & Owner

Toronto: Humbervale Montessori School Inc.
1447 Royal York Rd., Toronto, ON M9P 3V8
Tel: 416-244-4001
info@HumbervaleMontessori.ca
humbervalemontessori.ca
Grades: Pre.-JK; *Enrollment:* 85
Andrea Heitz, Principal

Toronto: Imperial College of Toronto
20 Queen Elizabeth Blvd., Toronto, ON M8Z 1L8
Tel: 416-251-4970; *Fax:* 416-251-0259
info@imperialcollege.org
www.imperialcollege.org
Grades: 9 - 12
Eileen Crichton, Principal

Toronto: The Japanese School of Toronto Shokokai Inc.
c/o McMurrich Junior Public Shool
115 Winnona Dr., Toronto, ON M6G 3S8, Canada
Tel: 416-656-4822; *Fax:* 416-658-8931
torohoshomu@bellnet.ca
www.torontohoshuko.ca
Note: This is a Japanese Saturday school

Toronto: The Jewish Heritage School at Congregation Habonim
5 Glen Park Ave., Toronto, ON M6B 4J2
Tel: 416-782-2682
info@jewishheritageschool.com
jewishheritageschool.wordpress.com
Grades: 1-6; *Note:* The school offers Judaic & Hebrew language studies, & Jewish music class.
Yodfat S. Mandil, Principal
habonimprincipal@gmail.com
Cathy Rechtshaffen, Registrar
habonimschool@gmail.com

Toronto: Junior Academy
2454 Bayview Ave., Toronto, ON M2L 1A6, Canada
Tel: 416-425-4567; *Fax:* 416-425-7379
www.junioracademy.com
www.facebook.com/465133306867808?fref=ts
Grades: JK - 8

Pat Kendall, Administrator
pk@junioracademy.com
Dianne Johnson, Principal
Julie Stewart, Vice Principal
Cathy Hibbert, Director, Physical Education
Susan Jones, Director, Middle School
Kris Potter, Director, Student Affairs

Toronto: Kesher School
729 St. Clair Ave. West, Toronto, ON M6C 1B2
Tel: 647-444-7291
kesher.school@gmail.com
kesherschool.weebly.com

Grades: JK-2
Mika Gang, Principal

Toronto: Kew Park Montessori Day School
79 Hiawatha Rd., Toronto, ON M4L 2X7
Tel: 416-694-6273; *Fax:* 416-694-9452
info@kewparkmontessori.com
www.kewparkmontessori.com

Grades: Pre. - Elem.
Tarynn Parry, Co-Principal
Tacha Pearce-Miller, Co-Principal

Toronto: Kiosk International College
#104, 40 Wellesley St. East, Toronto, ON M4Y 1G4
Tel: 416-545-1660
info@kiosk.on.ca
highschool.kiosk.on.ca
www.facebook.com/kiosklc
twitter.com/KioskLC

Grades: 9 - 12

Toronto: The Laurel School
44 Upjohn Rd., Toronto, ON M3B 2W1
Tel: 416-510-2500
info@laurelschool.ca
www.laurelschool.ca

Grades: Pre.-6; *Enrollment:* 70
Mary Kindos, Principal

Toronto: Leaside Children's House Montessori
839 Millwood Rd., Toronto, ON
Tel: 416-425-0101; *Fax:* 416-778-7753
info@leasidechildrenshouse.com
www.leasidechildrenshouse.com

Grades: Toddler - Pre.
Lillian Nimis, Director

Toronto: Leonardo Da Vinci Academy of Arts & Sciences
100 Allanhurst Dr., Toronto, ON M9A 4K4
Tel: 416-247-6137; *Fax:* 416-247-6138
Toll-Free: 877-218-0079
ldva@ldva.on.ca
www.ldva.on.ca

Grades: Pre.-8
Salvatore Ritacca, President & Co-Founder
sr@ldva.on.ca
Dom Tassielli, Treasurer & Co-Founder
dt@ldva.on.ca

Toronto: The Linden School
10 Rosehill Ave., Toronto, ON M4T 1G5, Canada
Tel: 416-966-4406
linden@lindenschool.ca
www.lindenschool.ca
twitter.com/TheLindenSchool

Grades: 1 - 12; *Enrollment:* 130; *Note:* The Linden School provides education for girls.
Mary Ladky, Principal
Tracey Addison, Head of Admissions and Development
Nancy Hurst, Business Manager

Toronto: Little Feet Little Faces
183 Avenue Rd., Toronto, ON M5R 2J2
Tel: 416-923-8882
arts@littlefeetlittlefaces.com
www.littlefeetlittlefaces.com

Grades: Pre.-SK; *Enrollment:* 55; *Note:* A private licensed daycare following the Ontario academic curriculum, with an emphasis on the arts.
Ingrid Rea, Creative Director

Toronto: Lycée Français de Toronto (LFT)
2327, rue Dufferin, Toronto, ON M6E 3S5, Canada
Tél: 416-924-1789; *Téléc:* 416-924-9078
admissions@lft.ca
www.lft.ca

Grades: Pre.-12; *Enrollment:* 450
M. Dominique Duthel, Proviseur

Toronto: The Mabin School
50 Poplar Plains Rd., Toronto, ON M4V 2M8, Canada
Tel: 416-964-9594; *Fax:* 416-964-3643
admissions@mabin.com
www.mabin.com
www.facebook.com/113792558651689

Grades: Junior Kindergarten - 6; *Note:* The Mabin School provides a full day, non-denominational program for girls & boys.
Kim McInnes, Principal

Toronto: Maria Montessori School
125 Brentcliffe Rd., Toronto, ON M4G 3Y7
Tel: 416-423-9123; *Fax:* 416-423-7819
www.mariamontessori.ca

Grades: Elem.
James Brand, Head of School

Toronto: McDonald International Academy
920 Yonge St., 2nd Fl., Toronto, ON M4W 3C7, Canada
Tel: 416-322-1502; *Fax:* 416-322-5775
mia@mcdonaldacademy.com
www.mcdonaldacademy.com

Enrollment: 753
Fraser Rose

Toronto: Metropolitan Preparatory Academy
49 Mobile Dr., Toronto, ON M4A 1H5, Canada
Tel: 416-285-0870; *Fax:* 416-285-0873
www.metroprep.com
twitter.com/MetroPrep
www.youtube.com/MetroPrepAcademy

Grades: 7 - 12; *Note:* Metropolitan Preparatory Academy offers a middle & high school program for university-oriented students.
William Wayne McKelvey, Principal
Debra McKelvey-Cleveland, Vice Principal & Head, Guidance
dmckelvey@MetroPrep.com
Jason Van Allen, Administrator, Information Technology
jvanallen@metroprep.com

Toronto: Miles Nadal Jewish Community Centre Nursery School
750 Spadina Ave., Toronto, ON M5S 2J2
Tel: 416-924-6211; *Fax:* 416-924-0442
mnjccnurseryschool.com

Grades: Preschool; *Note:* Non-denominational education for children aged 2 1/2 - 5 years.
Cathy Indig, Director, Early Childhood Education
cathyi@mnjcc.org

Toronto: Montcrest School
4 Montcrest Blvd., Toronto, ON M4K 1J7, Canada
Tel: 416-469-2008; *Fax:* 416-469-0934
office@montcrest.on.ca
www.montcrest.on.ca
twitter.com/montcrest

Grades: Junior Kindergarten - 8; *Enrollment:* 300; *Note:* Montcrest School is a co-educational, nondenominational school. The school also offers special education classes for students with learning disabilities.
David Thompson, Head of School

Toronto: Montessori Jewish Day School
55 Yeomans Rd., Toronto, ON M3H 3J7
Tel: 416-784-5071
adminmjds@mjds.ca
www.mjds.ca
www.facebook.com/133140750091854

Grades: Pre.-8; *Enrollment:* 115
Regina Lulka, Head of School
regina@mjds.ca
Matti Shorr, Director, Administration

Toronto: Morris Winchevsky School: Toronto's Secular Jewish Community School
The Winchevsky Centre
585 Cranbrooke Ave., Toronto, ON M6A 2X9
Tel: 416-789-5502; *Fax:* 416-789-5981
info@mwstoronto.org
www.mwstoronto.org
www.facebook.com/167027090018410

Grades: K.-8; *Note:* The school caters to secular, non-traditional, mixed culture, & unaffiliated families.
David Lipovitch, Director, Education
dllipovitch@tsjcs.com

Toronto: National Ballet School (NBS)
400 Jarvis St., Toronto, ON M4Y 2G6, Canada
Tel: 416-964-3780; *Fax:* 416-964-5133
Toll-Free: 1-800-387-0785
careers@nbs-enb.ca
www.nbs-enb.ca
www.facebook.com/NBSENB
twitter.com/NBS_ENB
www.youtube.com/nbsenb

Note: The school offers elite ballet training, academic instruction, & residential care.
Troy Maxwell, Chair
Grant Troop, Executive Director & Co-Chief Executive Officer
Mavis Staines, Artistic Director & Co-Chief Executive Officer

Toronto: New Oriental International College
#500, 3660 Midland Ave., Toronto, ON M1V 0B8
Tel: 416-291-8829; *Fax:* 416-291-8859
www.neworientalgroup.org

Note: University preparation courses for international students.

Toronto: Newton's Grove School
1 City View Dr., Toronto, ON M9W 5A5, Canada
Tel: 416-745-1328
info@newtonsgroveschool.com
www.newtonsgroveschool.com

Grades: Junior Kindergarten - 12; *Enrollment:* 350
Gabrielle Bush, Director

Toronto: Northern Lights Preparatory College
5075 Yonge St. 8th Fl., Toronto, ON M2N 6C6
Tel: 416-225-0057; *Fax:* 416-225-4727
info@northernlightscollege.ca
www.northernlightscollege.ca

Grades: K - 12
Robert Eckler, Principal
principal@northernlightscollege.ca

Toronto: Northmount School
26 Mallard Rd., Toronto, ON M3B 1S3, Canada
Tel: 416-449-8823; *Fax:* 416-449-1244
info@northmount.com
www.northmount.com

Grades: Junior Kindergarten - 8; *Note:* Northmount School specializes in the education of boys.
Glenn C. Domina, Headmaster

Toronto: Odyssey Montessori School
136 Sorauren Ave., Toronto, ON M6R 2E4
Tel: 416-535-9402; *Fax:* 647-477-6585
www.odysseymontessori.com

Grades: Casa
Mary Tomazos, Principal
mary@odysseymontessori.com

Toronto: Ontario International College Collège International de l'Ontario
#600, 4580 Dufferin St., Toronto, ON M3H 5Y2
Tel: 416-739-1888; *Fax:* 416-739-1884
adm@oicedu.ca
www.oicedu.ca
www.facebook.com/oicedu

Grades: 9 - 12
Ekaterina Agar, Vice Principal, 416-739-1888, ext. 1600
dean@oicedu.ca

Toronto: Oraynu Children's School
St. Andrews Junior High School
131 Fenn Ave., Toronto, ON M2P 1X7
Tel: 416-385-3910
info@oraynu.org
www.oraynu.org/school
www.facebook.com/Oraynu

Grades: K.-7; *Note:* The school is part of the Oraynu Congregation for Humanistic Judaism.
Steven Shabes, Director, Education
stevenshabes@yahoo.com
Roby Sadler, Contact

Toronto: P.T. Montessori School
280 Culford Rd., Toronto, ON M6L 2V3, Canada
Tel: 416-242-3725
Grades: Elem.; *Enrollment:* 51

Toronto: Petite Maison Montessori School
126 O'Connor Dr., Toronto, ON M4K 2K7
Tel: 416-429-0507; *Fax:* 416-429-0507
info@petitemaison.ca
www.petitemaison.ca

Grades: Casa - Elem.
Roula Patsavos, Principal

***Toronto:* Phoenix Montessori School**
19 Glen Agar Dr., Toronto, ON M9B 5L5
Tel: 416-695-1212; *Fax:* 416-695-1095
info@phoenixmontessori.ca
www.phoenixmontessori.ca
Grades: Toddler - Elem.
Lori Priolo, Principal
lpriolo@phoenixmontessori.ca

***Toronto:* The Prestige School**
44 Appian Dr., Toronto, ON M2J 2P9
Tel: 647-494-9977
www.prestigeprivateschool.ca
www.facebook.com/prestigeprivateschool
Grades: JK-12; *Enrollment:* 150
Olga Margold, Principal
Campuses
Richmond Hill Campus
11 Headdon Game, Richmond Hill, ON L4C 9W9
Tel: 905-780-6565
Grades: Pre.-6

***Toronto:* Prince Edward Montessori School**
2850 Bloor St. West, Toronto, ON M8X 1B2
Tel: 416-234-9127
info@princeedwardmontessori.com
www.princeedwardmontessori.com
Grades: Pre.-SK; *Enrollment:* 96
Bozena Nowicka-Lipa, Principal
Campuses
Mississauga Campus
12 Peter St. South, Mississauga, ON L5H 0A1
Tel: 905-891-6912

***Toronto:* Queen's Collegiate**
2 Gibbs Rd., Toronto, ON M9B 6L6
Tel: 416-231-9899; *Fax:* 416-231-3936
info@queenscollegiate.com
www.queenscollegiate.com
www.facebook.com/pages/Queens-Collegiate/110355299021172
Grades: K - 12
Dr. Jooyon Cho, Principal
jooyon.cho@queenscollegiate.com

***Toronto:* Robbins Hebrew Academy**
Administration Office
1700 Bathurst St., Toronto, ON M2N 5L3
Tel: 416-224-8737; *Fax:* 855-271-2236
info@rhacademy.ca
www.rhacademy.ca
www.facebook.com/RobbinsHebrewAcademy
twitter.com/RobbinsHebrew
Grades: JK - 8; *Enrollment:* 600; *Note:* Robbins Hebrew Academy is a Conservative Jewish day school.
Claire Sumerlus, Head of School
csumerlus@rhacademy.ca
Michele Viner, Director, Admissions
mviner@rhacademy.ca
Campuses
Bathurst Campus
1700 Bathurst St., Toronto, ON M5P 2K3
Tel: 416-781-5658; *Fax:* 416-787-9632
Valerie Turner, Principal
vturner@rhacademy.ca
Bayview Campus
3080 Bayview Ave., Toronto, ON M2N 5L3
Tel: 416-225-1143; *Fax:* 416-225-0659
Silvia Eilath, Principal
seilath@rhacademy.ca

***Toronto:* The Rosedale Day School**
#426, 131 Bloor St. West, Toronto, ON M5S 1R1
Tel: 416-923-4726; *Fax:* 416-923-7379
office@rds-on.com
www.rds-on.com
Grades: JK-8; *Enrollment:* 115
James Lee, Head of School

***Toronto:* Royal St. George's College**
120 Howland Ave., Toronto, ON M5R 3B5
Tel: 416-533-9481; *Fax:* 416-533-0028
contactus@rsgc.on.ca
www.rsgc.on.ca
www.facebook.com/RSGC1
twitter.com/RoyalSGC
www.youtube.com/user/royalsgc
Grades: Elem./Sec.; Boys; *Enrollment:* 426
Stephen Beatty, Headmaster
sbeatty@rsgc.on.ca
Paul O'Leary, Assistant Headmaster & Head of Senior School
poleary@rsgc.on.ca
Catherine Kirkland, Head of Junior School
ckirkland@rsgc.on.ca

***Toronto:* Sabouhi Academy Of Art & Design**
#6303, 6305 Yonge St., Toronto, ON M2M 3X7
Tel: 416-221-2111; *Fax:* 416-221-7274
Info@SabouhiAcademy.com
www.sabouhiacademy.com
www.facebook.com/pages/Sabouhi-Academy/264268530298940
www.youtube.com/user/SabouhiAcademy
Grades: 9 - 12

***Toronto:* St. Clement's School**
21 St. Clement's Ave., Toronto, ON M4R 1G8, Canada
Tel: 416-483-4835; *Fax:* 416-483-8242
admissions@scs.on.ca
www.scs.on.ca
www.facebook.com/StClementsSchoolToronto
twitter.com/SCS_Clementines
Grades: 1-12; *Enrollment:* 470; *Note:* All-girl's school affiliated with the Anglican church
Martha Perry, Principal

***Toronto:* St. Michael's College School**
1515 Bathurst St., Toronto, ON M5P 3H4, Canada
Tel: 416-653-3180; *Fax:* 416-653-7704
info@smcsmail.com
www.stmichaelscollegeschool.com
www.facebook.com/smcs1852
twitter.com/smcs1852
www.youtube.com/user/SMCS1852
Grades: 7-12; *Enrollment:* 1100; *Note:* St. Michael's College School provides Catholic, Liberal Arts educatioin for young men.
Fr. Richard Ranalletti, C.S.B., Chair, Board of Directors
Terence Sheridan, President & Principal
sheridan@smcsmail.com
Emile John, Vice-Principal, 416-653-3180, ext. 156
john@smcsmail.com
David Lee, Vice-Principal
lee@smcsmail.com
Michael De Pellegrin, Director, Communications, 416-653-3180, ext. 292
md@smcsmail.com
Fr. John Malo, C.S.B., Director, Pastoral Care, 416-653-3180, ext. 229
Greg Paolini, Director, Admissions, 416-653-3180, ext. 195
paolini@smcsmail.com
Fr. John Reddy, C.S.B., Chaplain, 416-653-3180, ext. 217
Gino Saccone, Corporate Controller, 416-653-3180, ext. 239
saccone@smcsmail.com

***Toronto:* Sathya Sai School of Canada**
#4, 505 Ellesmere Rd., Toronto, ON M1R 4E5
Tel: 416-297-7970; *Fax:* 416-297-0945
info@sathyasaischool.ca
www.sathyasaischool.ca
Grades: JK-6; *Enrollment:* 160; *Note:* Sathya Sai School seeks to promote the five human values of Truth, Right Conduct, Peace, Love, & Non-violence in students through education of character, along with academics.
Revathi Chennabathni, Ph.D., Principal
principal@sathyasaischool.ca

***Toronto:* Shmuel Zahavy Cheder Chabad of Toronto**
#203, 900 Alness St., Toronto, ON M3J 2H6, Canada
Tel: 416-663-1972; *Fax:* 416-650-9404
www.chederchabad.com
Note: Students at Shmuel Zahavy Cheder Chabad of Toronto also receive education in Torah scholarship & classic Jewish values.
Rabbi Yona Shur, Director
Rabbi Baruch Zaltzman, Principal

***Toronto:* Sidney Ledson School Ltd.**
#107, 220 Duncan Mill Rd., Toronto, ON M3B 3J5, Canada
Tel: 416-447-5355
sidney.ledson@bellnet.ca
www.sidneyledsoninstitute.net
Grades: Pre - 6; *Enrollment:* 50

***Toronto:* Sterling Hall School of Toronto (SHS)**
99 Cartwright Ave., Toronto, ON M6A 1V4, Canada
Tel: 416-785-3410; *Fax:* 416-785-6616
shsadmin@sterlinghall.com
www.sterlinghall.com
www.facebook.com/SterlingHallSchool
twitter.com/thesterlinginst
vimeo.com/user3297765
Grades: Junior Kindergarten - 8; *Enrollment:* 300; *Number of Employees:* 70; *Note:* Sterling Hall School of Toronto educates boys.
Rick Parsons, Principal, 416-785-3410
rparsons@sterlinghall.com
Kate Sherk, Director, Admissions, 416-785-3410
ksherk@sterlinghall.com

***Toronto:* Sunnybrook School (SBS)**
469 Merton St., Toronto, ON M4S 1B4, Canada
Tel: 416-487-5308; *Fax:* 416-487-5381
admissions@sunnybrookschool.ca
www.sunnybrookschool.com
www.facebook.com/154018124624187
Grades: JK.-6; *Enrollment:* 130; *Number of Employees:* 20
Dr. Irene Davy, Ph.D., Director & Principal

***Toronto:* SuOn International Academy**
70 Chartwell Rd., Toronto, ON M8Z 4G6
Tel: 416-255-8808
suon.admi@gmail.com
www.suon.ca
Grades: 9 - 12; *Note:* SuOn International Academy is a private secondary and university preparatory school.

***Toronto:* TAIE International Institute**
296 Parliament St., Toronto, ON M5A 3A4
Tel: 416-368-2882
taie.ca
www.facebook.com/taie.canada
twitter.com/TAIECanada
Grades: 9 - 12
Raymond Lee, Chief Director of Offices, 416-368-2882
raymondlee@taie.ca

***Toronto:* Temple Sinai Hebrew & Religious School**
210 Wilson Ave., Toronto, ON M5M 3B1
Tel: 416-487-3281; *Fax:* 416-487-5499
templesinai.net/study
Grades: Pre./Elem.; *Note:* The Temple Sinai Congregation of Toronto also offers a nursery program.
Ira Schweitzer, Director, Education
ira@templesinai.net
Charlotte Koven, Principal, Hebrew & Religious Schools
charlotte@templesinai.net
Bibi Golberg, Principal, Nursery
bibi@templesinai.net

***Toronto:* Tiferes Bais Yaakov**
***Also known as:* Daniel T. Gordon High School for Girls**
85 Stormont Ave., Toronto, ON M5N 2C3
Tel: 416-785-4044; *Fax:* 416-785-4046
secretary@tiferesbaisyaakov.com
tiferesbaisyaakov.com
Grades: Secondary; Girls; *Note:* Tiferes Bais Yaakov is an Orthodox Jewish high school for girls.
Rabbi Yitzchak Feigenbaum, Principal
rabbif@tiferesbaisyaakov.com
Malka Meckler, Principal, General Studies
Adina Ribacoff, Principal, Judaic Studies

***Toronto:* Torah High School - Toronto**
Sherman Campus
4600 Bathurst St., Toronto, ON M2R 3V2
Tel: 905-761-6279; *Toll-Free:* 1-866-867-2444
help@TorahHigh.org
torahhigh.org
www.facebook.com/TorahHigh
twitter.com/TorahHigh
www.youtube.com/ncsytube
Grades: 8-12; *Note:* Torah High offers courses in Religious Studies, Hebrew Language, Philosophy, Political Science, Nutrition, Arts & Interdisciplinary Studies for students attending public or private secondary schools. The school has seven locations in Toronto.

***Toronto:* Toronto Cheder School**
3995 Bathurst St., Toronto, ON M3H 5V3, Canada
Tel: 416-636-2987
thetorontocheder@bellnet.ca
Enrollment: 200; *Note:* Toronto Cheder School is an Orthodox school for boys.
Rabbi D. Engel, Principal

***Toronto:* Toronto Collegiate Institute**
#25, 50 Weybright Crt., Toronto, ON M1S 5A8
Tel: 416-289-0051; *Fax:* 866-810-7489
admin@torontoci.com
www.torontoci.com
Grades: 9 - 12

***Toronto:* Toronto Farsi School**
5527 Yonge St., Toronto, ON M2N 1A1
www.torontofarsischool.com
Grades: 9 - 12

***Toronto:* Toronto French Montessori**
432 Sheppard Ave. East, Toronto, ON M2N 3B7
Tel: 416-250-9952
info@torontofrenchmontessori.com
www.torontofrenchmontessori.com
www.facebook.com/119316424792686
Grades: Pre.-8; *Enrollment:* 90
Marie Mousa, Principal
principal@torontofrenchmontessori.com
Campuses
Cummer Campus
53 Cummer Ave., Toronto, ON M2M 2E5

***Toronto:* Toronto French School (TFS)**
Toronto Campus
306 Lawrence Ave. East, Toronto, ON M4N 1T7, Canada
Tel: 416-484-6533; *Fax:* 416-488-3090
admissions@tfs.ca
www.tfs.ca
www.facebook.com/TorontoFrenchSchoolFB
twitter.com/TFS_Toronto
www.youtube.com/user/torontofrenchschool
Grades: Preschool - 12; *Enrollment:* 1400; *Number of Employees:* 200; *Note:* Toronto French School is a co-educational, non-denominational school, which offers bilingual education.
Nathalie Mercure, Chair
board@tfs.ca
Mirna Hafez, Head of School
Alain Delaune, Principal, Mississauga School
Heidi Gollert, Principal, Senior School
Mirna Hafez, Principal, Junior School

***Toronto:* The Toronto Heschel School**
819 Sheppard Ave. West, Toronto, ON M3H 2T3, Canada
Tel: 416-635-1876; *Fax:* 416-635-1800
info@torontoheschel.org
www.torontoheschel.org
www.facebook.com/163617997000292
twitter.com/TorontoHeschel
Grades: Junior Kindergarten - 8; *Enrollment:* 300; *Note:* The Jewish day school combines the teaching of Judaism with a general studies curriculum.
Gail Baker, Head of School & Principal
head@torontoheschel.org
Mark Abramsohn, Director, Business Operations
admin@torontoheschel.org
Greg Beiles, Curriculum Consultant
curriculum@torontoheschel.org

***Toronto:* Toronto International College (TIC)**
Collège International de Toronto
***Also known as:* Toronto International College of Business**
#500, 3550 Victoria Park Ave., Toronto, ON M2H 2N5
Tel: 416-498-9299; *Fax:* 416-493-9166
www.ticedu.ca
Grades: 9 - 12
Yelena Mordovskaya, Dean, 416-498-9299, ext. 5192
dean@ticedu.ca

***Toronto:* Toronto New School**
519 Jarvis St., Toronto, ON M4Y 2H7
Tel: 416-960-1867
Grades: 9-12
Ewa Kasinska, Head of School

***Toronto:* Toronto Prep School**
#200, 250 Davisville Ave., Toronto, ON M4S 1H2
Tel: 416-545-1020; *Fax:* 416-545-1456
www.torontoprepschool.com
Grades: 7-12; *Enrollment:* 185
Steve Tsimikalis, B.A., B.Ed., M.E.S., Principal
stsimikalis@torontoprepschool.com

***Toronto:* University of Toronto Schools (UTS)**
371 Bloor St. West, Toronto, ON M5S 2R7, Canada
Tel: 416-978-3212; *Fax:* 416-978-6775
info@utschools.ca
www.utschools.ca
Other Information: 416-946-7995 (Phone, Admissions); 416-978-7325 (Student Services)
Grades: 7 - 12; *Enrollment:* 640; *Number of Employees:* 65; *Note:* UTS is a coeducational school, affiliated with the University of Toronto.
Jim Fleck, Board Chair
UTSBoard@utschools.ca
Rosemary Evans, Principal, 416-946-7936
revans@utschools.ca

***Toronto:* Upper Canada College (UCC)**
200 Lonsdale Rd., Toronto, ON M4V 1W6, Canada
Tel: 416-488-1125; *Fax:* 416-484-8611
administration@ucc.on.ca
www.ucc.on.ca
Other Information: 416-488-1125, ext. 2313 (Phone, Office of Advancement)
Grades: Senior Kindergarten - 12; *Note:* The Preparatory School has over 400 boys from Senior Kindergarten to grade seven. The Upper School offers a five year secondary education.
Andy Burgess, Chair, Board of Governors
andyburgess64@gmail.com
Jim Power, Principal, 416-488-1125, ext. 4010
Steve Griffin, Head, Upper School
David Matthews, Asst. Head, University Relations & Sec., Board of Governors, 416-488-1125, ext. 2260
dmatthews@ucc.on.ca
Andrea Aster, Associate Director, Marketing & Communications 416-488-1125, ext. 3355

***Toronto:* Upper Madison College (UMC)**
#500, 5075 Yonge St., 5th Fl., Toronto, ON M2N 7H3
Tel: 416-512-1026; *Fax:* 416-512-0024
info@umcollege.ca
www.umcollege.ca
www.facebook.com/pages/UMC-Upper-Madison-College/128445840591801
twitter.com/UMC
linkedin.com/UMC
www.youtube.com/user/UMC
Grades: 9 - 12
Campuses
Montréal Campus
360, rue Mayor, Montreal, QC H3A 1N7

***Toronto:* Voice Intermediate School**
50 Gristmill Lane, Toronto, ON M5A 3C4
Tel: 416-691-4639; *Fax:* 416-691-3722
vis@voiceintermediate.com
www.voiceintermediate.com
Grades: 4-8; *Enrollment:* 85
Marie Lardino, B.A., B.Ed., M.Ed., Founder & Principal

***Toronto:* Waldorf Academy**
250 Madison Ave., Toronto, ON M4V 2W6
Tel: 416-962-6447; *Fax:* 416-975-5513
info@waldorfacademy.org
waldorfacademy.org
www.facebook.com/121407927910549
twitter.com/WALDORFtoronto
Grades: Pre.-8; *Enrollment:* 240
Dean Husseini, Director
Sara Anderson, Enrollment
admissions@waldorfacademy.org

***Toronto:* Wales College**
#518, 4002 Sheppard Ave. East, Toronto, ON M1S 4R5
Tel: 416-299-9966; *Fax:* 416-299-1577
info@walescollege.ca
www.walescollege.ca
Grades: 9 - 12
Juan Federici, Principal

***Toronto:* William School**
#200, 3761 Victoria Park Ave., Toronto, ON M1W 3S3
Tel: 416-491-6888; *Fax:* 416-640-2000
wschool@rogers.com
www.williamschool.ca
Grades: 9 - 12

***Toronto:* WillowWood School**
55 Scarsdale Rd., Toronto, ON M3B 2R3
Tel: 416-444-7644; *Fax:* 416-444-1801
info@willowwoodschool.ca
www.willowwoodschool.ca
Grades: Elem./Sec./Spec. Ed.; *Enrollment:* 250
Joy Kurtz, Principal
joykurtz@willowwoodschool.ca

***Toronto:* Yeshiva Bnei Zion of Bobov**
44 Champlain Blvd., Toronto, ON M3H 2Z1, Canada
Tel: 416-633-6332; *Fax:* 416-633-6704
Grades: JK-8; Boys
Rabbi Shlomo Tzvi Frank, Director, Education
schloime.frank@gmail.com

***Toronto:* Yeshiva Darchei Torah**
18 Champlain Blvd., Toronto, ON M3H 2Z1
Tel: 416-782-7974; *Fax:* 416-782-7811
darchei.ca
Grades: Secondary; *Note:* Yeshiva Darchei Torah is an Orthodox Jewish high school for boys, with Jewish & secular programs.
Rabbi Eliezer Breitowitz, Rosh Yeshiva
breitowitz@darchei.ca
Ron Roberto, English Principal
ronrob17@yahoo.com
Jeff Toledano, Executive Director
toledano@darchei.ca

***Toronto:* Yeshiva Yesodei Hatorah**
77 Glen Rush Blvd., Toronto, ON M5N 2T8
Tel: 416-787-1101; *Fax:* 416-787-9044
yesodeihat@gmail.com
Grades: Pre.-8; Boys; *Enrollment:* 450
Rabbi M. Bornstein, Principal

***Toronto:* Yeshivas Nachalas Zvi**
475 Lawrence Ave. West, Toronto, ON M5M 1C6, Canada
Tel: 416-782-8912; *Fax:* 416-782-8517
Grades: 8-12; Religious Orthodox, Boys; *Enrollment:* 75
Bruce Graham

***Toronto:* The York School**
1320 Yonge St., Toronto, ON M4T 1X2, Canada
Tel: 416-926-1325; *Fax:* 416-926-9592
info@yorkschool.com
www.yorkschool.com
Other Information: 416-646-5275 (Phone, Admissions)
www.facebook.com/pages/The-York-School/144875382199807
twitter.com/theyorkschool
www.linkedin.com/company/the-york-school
Grades: JK - 12; *Enrollment:* 593; *Note:* The York School is co-educational & non-denominational. It is an International Baccalaureate World School, which offers PYP, MYP, & Diploma programs.
Jason Hanson, Chair
Conor Jones, Head of School, 416-646-5271
Susan Charron, Principal, Lower School, 416-646-5273
susan_charron@tys.on.ca
David Hamilton, Principal, Upper School, 416-646-5272
david_hamilton@tys.on.ca
Helen Gin, Principal, Middle School
Conor Jones, Director, Admission
Robin Kester, Director, Advancement
Annette Whiteley, Director, Business & Finance

***Unionville:* Montessori North School**
4561 Highway 7 East, Unionville, ON L3R 1M4
Tel: 905-475-9341; *Fax:* 416-953-0391
info@montessorinorth.ca
www.montessorinorth.ca
Grades: Toddler - Pre.
Anahita Faroogh, Principal

***Unionville:* Unionville Montessori School (UMS)**
9302 Kennedy Rd., Unionville, ON L6C 1N6, Canada
Tel: 905-474-9888; *Fax:* 905-474-5767
office@unionvillemontessori.com
www.unionvillemontessori.com
Grades: Preschool - 8; *Note:* Unionville Montessori School is a coeducational, non-denominational school. The Casa program is available for children from age two to six.

***Unionville:* Yip's Music & Montessori Elementary School**
100 Lee Ave., Unionville, ON L3R 8G2
Tel: 905-948-9477
www.yips.com
Other Information: Administration Phone: 905-752-0275, ext. 2100
www.facebook.com/YipsCanada
twitter.com/YipsCanada
www.youtube.com/user/kenny72ca
Grades: Pre.-8
Katherine Kwok, Chief Administrator
katherine@yips.com
Christian Bayly, Principal, Unionville Campus
christian@yips.com
Campuses
Markham Campus
#19, 28 Crown Steel Dr., Markham, ON L3R 0A1
Tel: 905-513-0955
Elsa Lee, Principal
elsa@yips.com
Thornhill Campus
#8, 8100 Yonge St., Thornhill, ON L4J 1W3
Tel: 905-881-9333
Amy Or, Principal
amy.or@yips.com

***Vaughan:* Anne & Max Tanenbaum Community Hebrew Academy of Toronto**
Also known as: Community Hebrew Academy of Toronto
Kimel Family Education Centre
9600 Bathurst St., Vaughan, ON L4A 3Z8, Canada
Tel: 905-787-8772; *Fax:* 905-787-8773
info@tanenbaumchat.org
www.chat-edu.ca
www.facebook.com/pages/TanenbaumCHAT/119806924756219
www.twitter.com/TCWallenberg
Grades: Sec.; *Enrollment:* 600
Paul Shaviv, M.A., M.Phil., Director, Education
Frances Bigman, Director of Advancement, 416-636-5984, ext. 230
fbigman@tanenbaumchat.org
Laurie Wasser, Director of Development, 905-292-4381
lwasser@tanenbaumchat.org
Jonathan Levy, Principal

Campuses
Wallenberg Campus
200 Wilmington Ave., Toronto, ON M3H 5J8, Canada
Tel: 416-636-5984; *Fax:* 416-636-7717
www.facebook.com/pages/TanenbaumCHAT/119806924756219
www.twitter.com/TCWallenberg
Helen Fox, Principal
Zanele Minsker, Admissions Coordinator, 416-636-5984, ext. 292
zminsker@tanenbaumchat.org

***Vaughan:* Casa Dei Bambini Montessori School**
#4-6, 661 Chrislea Rd., Vaughan, ON L4L 8A3
Tel: 905-851-8837; *Fax:* 905-851-8839
info@casadeibambini.ca
www.casadeibambini.ca
www.facebook.com/191392617592230
Grades: Pre.-1; *Enrollment:* 75
Francesca Davide, Director

***Vaughan:* The Hill Academy**
2600 Rutherford Rd., Vaughan, ON L4K 5R1
Tel: 905-303-4530; *Fax:* 905-303-2201
admissions@thehillacademy.com
www.thehillacademy.com
Grades: K - 12
Peter Merrill, Founder & CEO
peter.merrill@thehillacademy.com
Wally Tymkiv, Principal
wtymkiv@thehillacademy.com

***Vaughan:* Kachol Lavan - The Centre for Hebrew & Israel Studies Administration**
Schwartz/Reisman Centre
#240, 9600 Bathurst St., Vaughan, ON L6A 3Z8
Tel: 905-303-5025
info@kachol-lavan.com
www.kachol-lavan.com
Note: Kachol-Lavan holds classes at the following schools: Leo Baek School, Thornhill Woods Public School, Bialik Hebrew Day School, & the University of Toronto. Please see website for more details.
Ariel Zaltzman, Director, Education
ariel@kachol-lavan.com

***Vaughan:* RoyalCrest Academy**
9500 Dufferin St., Vaughan, ON L6A 1S2
Tel: 905-303-7557
info@royalcrestacademy.com
www.royalcrestacademy.com
Grades: Pre.-8; *Enrollment:* 250
Michelle Johnson, Director, Admissions & Student Services
Sandy Palombo, Head of Curriculum

***Vaughan:* Victoria International Ballet Academy**
7 Bradwick Dr., Vaughan, ON L4K 2T4
Tel: 905-707-7580
info@victoriaballet.com
www.victoriaballet.com
www.facebook.com/VictoriaBalletAcademy
twitter.com/VictoriaBalletA
www.youtube.com/user/victoriaballet1
Grades: 9 - 12

***Vaughn:* As-Sadiq Islamic School**
9000 Bathurst St., Vaughn, ON L4J 8A7, Canada
Tel: 905-695-1588; *Fax:* 905-695-1590
www.as-sadiqschool.com
Grades: Toddler - 8; *Enrollment:* 165
Fernanda Pires, Principal

***Vineland:* Niagara Academy**
3373 First Ave., Vineland, ON L0R 2E0
Tel: 905-562-0683
www.niagaraacademy.ca
www.facebook.com/group.php?gid=34689612376
Grades: K - 12

***Waterloo:* Kitchener Waterloo Bilingual School**
600 Erb St. West, Waterloo, ON N2L 2Z4
Tel: 519-886-6510
kitchenerwaterloobilingualschool.org
Grades: JK-8
Michel Poinot
mpoinot@kitchenerwaterloobilingualschool.org

***Waterloo:* Kitchener-Waterloo Montessori School**
194 Allen St. East, Waterloo, ON N2J 1K1
Tel: 519-742-1051; *Fax:* 519-742-1051
mont.k-w@sympatico.ca
www.kwmontessorischool.com
Grades: K./Elem.

Campuses
Bridgeport (Kitchener) Campus
527 Bridgeport Rd. East, Kitchener, ON N2K 1N6
Tel: 519-579-2157; *Fax:* 519-742-1051
Grades: K./Elem.

***Webequie:* Simon Jacob Memorial Education Centre**
P.O. Box 265
Webequie, ON P0T 3A0, Canada
Tel: 807-353-6491; *Fax:* 807-353-1306
www.webequie.ca/article/education-136.asp
Grades: K-10; Native Language; Special Ed.; *Note:* The Simon Jacob Memorial Education Centre is operated by the Webequie First Nation Education Authority.
Mary Gardiner, Principal
Stephanie Jones, Teacher, Special Education
Lois Whitehead, Instuctor, Native Language

***Wellandport:* Robert Land Academy (RLA)**
6727 South Chippawa Rd., Wellandport, ON L0R 2J0, Canada
Tel: 905-386-6203; *Fax:* 905-386-6607
www.robertlandacademy.com
www.facebook.com/robertlandacademy
www.youtube.com/user/robertlandacademy1
Grades: 6 - 12; *Enrollment:* 125; *Note:* Robert Land Academy is a highly structured military boarding school, which provides education for previously under-achieving boys with potential.
Major (retired) G. Scott Bowman, Founder & Headmaster

***Whitby:* Kendalwood Montessori School**
104 Consumers Dr., Whitby, ON L1N 5T3
Tel: 905-665-4766
admin@kendalwoodmontessori.com
www.kendalwoodmontessori.com
www.facebook.com/228602640484301
twitter.com/KendalwoodMont
Grades: Toddler - Elem.
Lisa Jobe, Principal

***Whitby:* Trafalgar Castle School**
401 Reynolds St., Whitby, ON L1N 3W9, Canada
Tel: 905-668-3358; *Fax:* 905-668-4136
www.trafalgarcastle.ca
www.facebook.com/Trafalgarcastle
twitter.com/trafalgarcastle
Grades: 5 - 12; *Note:* The day & boarding school educates young women.
Adam De Pencier, Head of School
depencier.adam@trafalgarcastle.ca
Gillian Martin, Vice Principal, School Life, 905-668-3358, ext. 228
martin.gillian@trafalgarcastle.ca
Tim Southwell, Vice Principal, Academics, 905-668-3358, ext. 229
southwell.tim@trafalgarcastle.ca
Marguerita Dykstra, Director, Finance, 905-668-3358, ext. 232
dykstra.marguerita@trafalgarcastle.ca
Sharon Magor, Director, Marketing & Development
magor.sharon@trafalgarcastle.ca

***Whitby:* Whitby Montessori & Elementary School**
95 Taunton Rd., Whitby, ON L1R 3L3, Canada
Tel: 905-430-8201
WelcomeCentre@whitbymontessori.ca
www.whitbymontessori.ca
Grades: Preschool - Elementary; *Note:* Whitby Montessori & Elementary School educates children from age thirteen months to fourteen years.
Cathy Barber, Principal
cathy@whitbymontessori.ca

***Willowdale:* Montessori Education Centre**
80 George Henry Blvd., Willowdale, ON M2J 1E7
Tel: 416-502-1769; *Fax:* 416-502-1769
www.montessoried.ca
Grades: Casa
Imanthi Nanayakkara, Principal
imanthi86@gmail.com

***Windsor:* A21 Academy**
8787 McHugh St., Windsor, ON N8S 0A1
Tel: 519-900-6021
info@a21academy.com
www.axxiacademy.com
twitter.com/a21academy
Grades: Elem.
Kristi Spidalieri, Principal

***Windsor:* Académie Ste. Cécile International School**
925 Cousineau Rd., Windsor, ON N9G 1V8, Canada
Tél: 519-969-1291; *Téléc:* 519-969-7953
info@stececile.ca
www.stececile.ca
twitter.com/@OnlyatASCIS
Grades: Pre./Elem./Sec.; *Enrollment:* 250; *Note:* Affiliated with the Univ. of Windsor. Programmes include the Ontario Sec. School Programme, the International Bacc. Programme, Advanced Placement; emphasis on music, dance, art, & performing arts, as well as programmes in technology; ESL, FSL & TOEFL courses; summer school.
Thérèse H. Gadoury, Directrice

Campuses
Ste Cécile Child Enrichment Centre
12021 Tecumseh Rd. East, Tecumseh, ON N8N 1M1, Canada
Tél: 519-735-7575
swchildcare_asc@bellnet.ca
www.stececile.ca

Dance Studio of Académie Ste Cécile
2676 Grand Marais Rd. West, Windsor, ON N9E 1G2, Canada
Tél: 519-966-7755
dancestudio@stececile.ca
www.stececile.ca

***Windsor:* An-Noor Private School**
1480 Janette Ave., Windsor, ON N8X 1Z4, Canada
Tel: 519-966-4422; *Fax:* 519-966-5233
www.wiao.org
www.facebook.com/windsormosque
Grades: JK-8; *Enrollment:* 158; *Note:* Provides students with an academic and Islamic education.
Amney Behiry, Principal
amneybehiry@cogeco.ca

***Woodbridge:* King Heights Academy**
28 Roytec Rd., Woodbridge, ON L4L 8E4
Tel: 905-652-1234; *Fax:* 905-652-9000
info@kingheightsacademy.com
kingheightsacademy.com
Grades: JK-6; *Enrollment:* 150
Elsa Norberto, Director

***Woodbridge:* Maple Leaf Montessori Schools Inc.**
8286 Islington Ave., Woodbridge, ON L4L 1W8, Canada
Tel: 905-856-3359
mmad1@hotmail.com
www.mlmontessori.org
Grades: Pre - 6
Johanna Madeley, Administrator & Co-founder
Michael Madeley, Elementary Principal

Campuses
Kipling Campus
8066 Kipling Ave., Woodbridge, ON L4L 2A1, Canada
Tel: 905-856-3359

***Wunnummin Lake:* Lydia Lois Beardy Memorial School**
P.O. Box 108
General Delivery, Wunnummin Lake, ON P0V 2Z0
Tel: 807-442-2575; *Fax:* 807-442-2640
llbms.firstnationschools.ca
Grades: Elem./Sec.

Universities & Colleges

Universities

Guelph: University of Guelph
50 Stone Rd. East, Guelph, ON N1G 2W1, Canada
Tel: 519-824-4120; *Fax:* 519-767-1693
www.uoguelph.ca
www.facebook.com/uofguelph
twitter.com/uofg
www.linkedin.com/company/university-of-guelph
www.youtube.com/uofguelph
Full Time Equivalency: 27040
Pamela Wallin, O.C., S.O.M., Chancellor
chancellor@uoguelph.ca
Franco Vaccarino, President & Vice-Chancellor
president@uoguelph.ca
Maureen Mancuso, Provost & Vice-President (Academic)
Don O'Leary, Vice-President (Finance & Administration)
Martha Harley, Asst. Vice-President (Human Resources)
Brenda Whiteside, Assoc. Vice-President (Student Affairs)
Serge Desmarais, Assoc. Vice-President (Academic)
Michael Ridley, Chief Librarian & Chief Information Officer

Faculties

College of Arts
MacKinnon Bldg.
87 Trent Lane, Guelph, ON N1G 1Y4
www.uoguelph.ca/arts
Donald Bruce, Dean

College of Biological Science (CBS)
www.uoguelph.ca/cbs
Dr. Michael J. Emes, Dean

Office of Graduate Studies
www.uoguelph.ca/graduatestudies
Isobel Heathcote, Dean

College of Management & Economics
www.uoguelph.ca/cme
twitter.com/CMEGuelph
www.linkedin.com/groups?home=&gid=3719672&trk=anet_ug_hm
www.youtube.com/user/cmeguelph
Julia Christensen Hughes, Dean

Ontario Agricultural College (OAC)
www.uoguelph.ca/oac
twitter.com/UofGuelphOAC
www.linkedin.com/3708372
www.youtube.com/user/UofGuelphOAC
Robert J. Gordon, Dean

Ontario Veterinary College (OVC)
www.ovc.uoguelph.ca
www.facebook.com/ontariovetcollege
twitter.com/OntVetCollege
www.youtube.com/user/OntarioVetCollege
Dr. Elizabeth Stone, Dean

Physical & Engineering Science
Anthony Vannelli, Dean

College of Social & Applied Human Sciences (CSAHS)
Tel: 519-824-4120; *Fax:* 519-766-4797
csahs@uoguelph.ca
www.uoguelph.ca/csahs
www.facebook.com/195767463900558
twitter.com/CSAHS_UoG
www.youtube.com/user/CSAHSUofG
John Smithers, Interim Dean
csahsdean@uoguelph.ca

Schools

Campus d'Alfred
P.O. Box 580
31 rue St-Paul, Alfred, ON K0B 1A0
Tél: 613-679-2218
www.alfredc.uoguelph.ca
Marcel Couture, Acting Director

School of Environmental Design & Rural Development
www.uoguelph.ca/sedrd
Robert Brown, Acting Director

School of Fine Arts & Music (SOFAM)
www.uoguelph.ca/sofam
John Kissick, Director

Kemptville Campus
P.O. Box 2003
830 Prescott St., Kemptville, ON K0G 1J0
Tel: 613-258-8336; *Fax:* 613-258-8384
kcampus@uoguelph.ca
www.kemptvillec.uoguelph.ca
Michael Goss, Director

Ridgetown Campus
120 Main St. East, Ridgetown, ON N0P 2C0
Tel: 519-674-1500
www.ridgetownc.uoguelph.ca
Ron Pitblado, Acting Director

School of English & Theatre Studies (SETS)
www.uoguelph.ca/sets/www.uoguelph.ca/sets
David Murray, Acting Director

Centres/Institutes

Advanced Analysis Centre (AAC)
50 Stone Rd. East, Guelph, ON N1G 2W1
Tel: 519-824-4120
aac@uoguelph.ca
www.uoguelph.ca/aac
Debbie Chan, Manager

Hamilton: McMaster University
1280 Main St. West, Hamilton, ON L8S 4L8, Canada
Tel: 905-525-9140
www.mcmaster.ca
www.facebook.com/mcmasteruniversity
twitter.com/mcmasteru
www.linkedin.com/company/mcmaster-university
www.youtube.com/mcmastertv
Full Time Equivalency: 29411
Suzanne Labarge, Chancellor, 905-525-9140, ext. 24340
Patrick Deane, President & Vice-Chancellor, 905-525-9140, ext. 24340

Engineering
delsey@mcmaster.ca
www.eng.mcmaster.ca
www.facebook.com/103372759743308
twitter.com/McMasterEng
www.youtube.com/user/McMasterEngineering
David S. Wilkinson, Dean

Graduate Studies
askgrad@mcmaster.ca
graduate.mcmaster.ca
www.facebook.com/177435845612000
twitter.com/mcmastersgs
F.L. Hall, Dean

Faculty of Humanities
www.humanities.mcmaster.ca
www.facebook.com/mcmaster.humanities
twitter.com/mcmasterhum
www.youtube.com/user/mcmasterhumanities
Suzanne Crosta, Dean

Faculty of Science
www.science.mcmaster.ca
John P. Capone, Dean

Faculty of Social Sciences
www.socsci.mcmaster.ca
www.facebook.com/McMasterSocialSciences
twitter.com/McMasterSocSci
www.youtube.com/user/McMasterSocSci?feature=mhee
Charlotte A.B. Yates, Dean

Schools

DeGroote School of Business
www.degroote.mcmaster.ca
www.facebook.com/degrootebiz?v=wall&ref=ts
twitter.com/DeGrooteBiz
Paul Bates, Dean

Arts & Science Program
artsci.os.mcmaster.ca
Gary Warner, Director

Indigenous Studies Program
www.indigenous.mcmaster.ca
Dawn Martin-Hill, Director

Institute on Globalization & the Human Condition
globalization.mcmaster.ca
Robert O'Brien, Director

Affiliations

McMaster Divinity College (MDC)
1280 Main St. West, Hamilton, ON L8S 4K1
Tel: 905-525-9140; *Fax:* 090-577-4782
divinity@mcmaster.ca
www.mcmasterdivinity.ca
www.facebook.com/pages/McMaster-Divinity-College/121294174658731
twitter.com/McMasterDiv
instagram.com/mcmasterdiv
Stanley E. Porter, President & Dean
Bill Marshall, Director, Finance, 905-525-9140, ext. 24685
marshaw@mcmaster.ca
Dr. Phil Zylla, Academic Dean, 905-525-9140, ext. 20104
zyllap@mcmaster.ca

Centres/Institutes

AllerGen
Michael DeGroote Centre for Learning & Discovery
#3120, 1280 Main St. West, Hamilton, ON L8S 4K1
Tel: 905-525-9140; *Fax:* 905-524-0611
info@allergen-nce.ca
www.allergen-nce.ca
Note: Research network focused on allergic disease.
Judah Denburg, Scientific Director & CEO

Biointerfaces Institute
1280 Main St. West, #ETB416, Hamilton, ON L8S 4K1
Tel: 905-525-9140
biointerfaces@mcmaster.ca
biointerfaces.mcmaster.ca
John Brennan, Institute Director
brennanj@mcmaster.ca

Bertrand Russell Research Centre
Mills Memorial Library
1280 Main St. West, #L108, Hamilton, ON L8S 4K1
Tel: 905-525-9140; *Fax:* 905-522-1277
www.humanities.mcmaster.ca/~russell
Arlene Duncan, Contact
duncana@mcmaster.ca

Canadian Centre For Electron Microscopy (CCEM)
A. N. Bourns Building
1280 Main St. West, #B161, Hamilton, ON L8S 4K1
Tel: 905-525-9140; *Fax:* 905-521-2773
ccem.mcmaster.ca
Glynis de Silveira, Analytical Facilities Manager
desilgl@mcmaster.ca

CanChild Centre for Childhood Disability Research
Institute for Applied Health Sciences
#408, 1400 Main St. West, Hamilton, ON L8S 1C7
Tel: 905-525-9140; *Fax:* 905-524-0069
canchild@mcmaster.ca
www.canchild.ca
www.facebook.com/canchild.ca
twitter.com/canchild_ca
Jan Willem Gorter, Director

Centre for Advanced Polymer Processing & Design
John Hodgins Engineering Building
1280 Main St. West, Hamilton, ON L8S 4L7
Tel: 905-525-9140; *Fax:* 905-521-1350
mmri.mcmaster.ca/cappa-d
Elizabeth Takacs, Lab Manager
etakacs@mcmaster.ca

Centre for Emerging Device Technologies (CEDT)
1280 Main St. West, Hamilton, ON L8S 4L7
Tel: 905-525-9140; *Fax:* 905-528-5406
CEMD@mcmaster.ca
www.eng.mcmaster.ca/cedt
Rafael Kleinman, Director

Centre for Evaluation of Medicines (CEM)
Centre for Evaluation of Medicines
#2000, 25 Main St. West, Hamilton, ON L8P 1H1
Tel: 905-523-7284; *Fax:* 905-523-9222
www.thecem.net
Mitchell Levine, Director
levinem@mcmaster.ca

Centre for Functional Genomics
Michael G. DeGroote Centre for Learning & Discove
1280 Main St. West, Hamilton, ON L8S 4K1
Tel: 905-525-9140; *Fax:* 905-522-6750
www.fhs.mcmaster.ca/cfg
John Hassell, Director
hassell@mcmaster.ca

Centre for Health Economics & Policy Analysis (CHEPA)
CRL Building
#282, 1280 Main St. West, Hamilton, ON L8S 4K1
Tel: 905-525-9140; *Fax:* 905-546-5211
chepa@mcmaster.ca
www.chepa.org
Michel Grignon, Director
grignon@mcmaster.ca

Centre for Microbial Chemical Biology (CMCB)
#2325, 1200 Main St. West, Hamilton, ON L8S 4K1
Tel: 905-525-9140; *Fax:* 905-528-5330
fhs.mcmaster.ca/cmcb
Tracey Campbell, Research Manager
campbtl@mcmaster.ca

Centre for Minimal Access Surgery (CMAS)
50 Charlton Ave. East, #T2141, Hamilton, ON L8N 4A6
Tel: 905-522-1155; *Fax:* 905-521-6194
info@cmas.ca
www.cmas.ca
www.facebook.com/CMASHamilton
twitter.com/cmashamilton
Marie Fairgrieve, Manager
mfairgri@stjosham.on.ca

Centre for Peace Studies
Togo Salmon Hall
#308, 1280 Main St. West, Hamilton, ON L8S 4M2
Tel: 905-525-9140; *Fax:* 905-570-1167
peace@mcmaster.ca
www.humanities.mcmaster.ca/~peace
Anna Moro, Acting Director
adeanhum@mcmaster.ca

Centre for Probe Development & Commercialization
Nuclear Research Building
1280 Main St. West, Hamilton, ON L8S 4K1
Tel: 905-525-9140
cpdc@imagingprobes.ca
www.imagingprobes.ca
John Valliant, CEO & Scientific Director

Centre for Spatial Analysis (CSPA)
Burke Science Building
#342, 1280 Main St. West, Hamilton, ON L8S 4M1
Tel: 905-525-9140; *Fax:* 905-546-0463
www.science.mcmaster.ca/cspa
Laura Labate, Contact
labatel@mcmaster.ca

Centre for Surgical Invention & Innovation (CSII)
39 Charlton Ave. East, Hamilton, ON L8N 1Y3
Tel: 905-522-1155
www.csii.ca
www.facebook.com/174502995911995
twitter.com/CSiiCECR
Elizabeth Ewinger, Director, Clinical Operations
ewinger@stjosham.on.ca

Centre for Sustainable Archaeology
175 Longwood Rd. South, #B22, Hamilton, ON L8P 0A1
Tel: 905-525-9140
Aubrey Cannon, Principal Investigator
cannona@mcmaster.ca

Centre for Effective Design of Structures
John Hodgins Engineering Building
#301, 1280 Main St. West, Hamilton, ON L8S 4L7
Tel: 905-525-9140; *Fax:* 905-529-9688
www.eng.mcmaster.ca/civil/ceds
Wael El-Dakhakhni, Chair, Effective Design of Structures
eldak@mcmaster.ca

Farncombe Family Digestive Health Research Institute
Heath Sciences Centre
1280 Main St. West, #3N4, Hamilton, ON L8S 4K1
Tel: 905-525-9140; *Fax:* 905-522-3454
farncombe.mcmaster.ca
Paul Moayyedi, Acting Director

Firestone Institute for Respiratory Health
St. Joseph's Healthcare
50 Charlton Ave. East, Hamilton, ON L8N 4A6
Tel: 905-522-1155
www.fhs.mcmaster.ca/firh
Paul O'Byrne, Executive Director

Gilbrea Centre for Studies in Aging
Kenneth Taylor Hall
#204, 1280 Main St. West, Hamilton, ON L8S 4M4
Tel: 905-525-9140; *Fax:* 905-525-4198
gilbrea@mcmaster.ca
www.aging.mcmaster.ca
Amanada Grenier, Director
grenier@mcmaster.ca

Institute on Globalization & the Human Condition
Kenneth Taylor Hall
#220, 1280 Main St. West, Hamilton, ON L8S 4M4
Tel: 905-525-9140; *Fax:* 905-527-3071
globalhc@mcmaster.ca
socialsciences.mcmaster.ca
Donald Goellnicht, Director
goellnic@mcmaster.ca

McMaster Ancient DNA Centre
Chester New Hall
#524, 1280 Main St. West, Hamilton, ON L8S 4L9
socserv.mcmaster.ca/adna
Hendrik Poinar, Principal Investigator

McMaster Centre for Scholarship in the Public Interest (MCSPI)
Chester New Hall
#231, 1280 Main St. West, Hamilton, ON L8S 4L9
Tel: 905-525-9140
info@mcspi.ca
mcspi.ca
twitter.com/PublicIntellec
www.youtube.com/user/PublicIntellec
Jennifer Fisher, Project Director

McMaster Centre for Software Certification
Information Technology Building
#101, 1280 Main St. West, Hamilton, ON L8S 4K1
Tel: 905-525-9140; *Fax:* 905-524-0340
mcscert@cas.mcmaster.ca
www.mcscert.ca
Alan Wassyng, Director
wassyng@mcmaster.ca

McMaster Centre for Climate Change
Burke Science Building
#318, 1280 Main St. West, Hamilton, ON L8S 4K1
Tel: 905-525-9140; *Fax:* 905-546-0463
climate@mcmaster.ca
climate.mcmaster.ca
www.facebook.com/McMasterClimateCentre
twitter.com/MAC_Climate
Altaf Arain, Director
arainm@mcmaster.ca

McMaster eBusiness Research Centre
DeGroote School of Business
1280 Main St. West, #A203, Hamilton, ON L8S 4M4
Tel: 905-525-9140
merc.mcmaster.ca
Khaled Hassanein, Director
hassank@mcmaster.ca

McMaster Immunology Research Centre
MDCL
#4010, 1280 Main St. West, Hamilton, ON L8S 4K1
Tel: 905-525-9140; *Fax:* 905-522-6750
mirc.mcmaster.ca
www.facebook.com/169351976425223
www.youtube.com/user/immunologyresearch
Jonathan Bramson, Director
bramsonj@mcmaster.ca

McMaster Institute of Applied Radiation Sciences (McIARS)
1280 Main St. West, Hamilton, ON L8S 4L8
Tel: 905-525-9140
www.science.mcmaster.ca/mciars
Karen Carter, Administrator

McMaster Institute for Automotive Research and Technology (MacAUTO)
1280 Main St. West, Hamilton, ON L8S 4L7
Tel: 905-525-9140; *Fax:* 905-528-9295
macauto@mcmaster.ca
macauto.mcmaster.ca

McMaster Institute for Energy Studies (MIES)
John Hodgins Engineering Building
1280 Main St. West, #A216, Hamilton, ON L8S 4L7
Tel: 905-525-9140
energy.mcmaster.ca
David Novog, Director
novog@mcmaster.ca

McMaster Institute for Innovation & Excellence in Teaching & Learning (MIIETL)
Mills Library
1280 Main St. West, #L504, Hamilton, ON L8S 4K1
Tel: 905-525-9140
support.avenue@cll.mcmaster.ca
miietl.mcmaster.ca
twitter.com/McMaster_MIIETL
www.youtube.com/channel/UCZbOqWQbPCrad757DmX2blg
Sylvia Avery, Executive Administrator
riselays@mcmaster.ca

McMaster Institute for Molecular Biology & Medicine (MOBIX)
Life Sciences Bldg.
1280 Main St. West, #B123, Hamilton, ON L8S 4K1
Tel: 905-525-9140; *Fax:* 905-526-1427
mobixlab@mcmaster.ca
www.science.mcmaster.ca/mobixlab
Galina Kataeva, Manager

McMaster Institute for Music & the Mind (MIMM)
1280 Main St. West, Hamilton, ON L8S 4L7
Tel: 905-525-9140; *Fax:* 905-529-6225
mimm.mcmaster.ca
Laurel Trainor, Director

McMaster Institute for Polymer Production Technology (MIPPT)
1280 Main St. West, Hamilton, ON L8S 4L7
Tel: 905-525-9140
chemeng.mcmaster.ca/emeritus-faculty/archie-hamielec
Archie Hamielec, Director
hamielec@mcmaster.ca

McMaster Institute for Transportation & Logistics (MITL)
General Science Building
#206, 1280 Main St. West, Hamilton, ON L8S 4K1
Tel: 905-525-9140; *Fax:* 905-546-0463
mitl@mcmaster.ca
mitl.mcmaster.ca
Pavlos Kanaroglou, Director
pavlos@mcmaster.ca

McMaster Institute of Environment & Health (MIEH)
Burke Science Building
#333, 1280 Main St. West, Hamilton, ON L8S 4K1
Tel: 905-525-9140
www.mcmaster.ca/mieh
Jim Dunn, Director

McMaster Manufacturing Research Institute (MMRI)
John Hodgins Engineering Building
#316, 1280 Main St. West, Hamilton, ON L8S 4L7
Tel: 905-525-9140
mmri-admin@mcmaster.ca
mmri.mcmaster.ca
Stephen Veldhuis, Director
veldhu@mcmaster.ca

Stem Cell & Cancer Research Institute (SCC-RI)
Michael DeGroote Centre for Learning & Discovery
1280 Main St. West, Hamilton, ON L8S 4K1
Tel: 905-525-9140
sccri@mcmaster.ca
sccri.mcmaster.ca
Mick Bhatia, Scientific Director

Medical Imagining Informatics Research Centre at McMaster (MIIRC@M)
1280 Main St. West, Hamilton, ON L8S 4K1
Tel: 905-667-1418
www.miircam.ca
Jane Castelli, Project Manager
jane.castelli@miircam.ca

Michael G. DeGroote Institute for Infectious Disease Research
MDCL
#2301, 1280 Main St. West, Hamilton, ON L8S 4K1
Tel: 905-525-9140; *Fax:* 905-528-5330
iidr.mcmaster.ca
www.facebook.com/161236873937262
twitter.com/McMasterIIDR
www.youtube.com/user/McMasterIIDR
Gina Mannen, Manager, Administration
manneng@mcmaster.ca

Michael G. DeGroote Institute for Pain Research & Care
MDCL
#2101, 1280 Main St. West, Hamilton, ON L8S 4K1
Tel: 905-525-9140; *Fax:* 905-523-1224
npc@mcmaster.ca
fhs.mcmaster.ca/paininstitute
Norm Buckley, Acting Scientific Director
buckleyn@mcmaster.ca

Offord Centre for Child Studies
Patterson Bldg., Hamilton Health Sciences
#2, 566 Sanatorium Rd., Hamilton, ON L9C 7V6
Tel: 905-521-2100; *Fax:* 905-574-6665
Toll-Free: 888-541-5437
info@offordcentre.com
www.offordcentre.com
Harruet MacMillan, Interim Director

Origins Institute (OI)
Arthur Bourns Building
#241, 1280 Main St. West, Hamilton, ON L8S 4M1
Tel: 905-525-9140; *Fax:* 905-546-1252
origins@mcmaster.ca
origins.mcmaster.ca
Mara Esposto, Administrator
esposto@mcmaster.ca

Population Health Research Institute (PHRI)
Hamilton Health Sciences
237 Barton St., East, Hamilton, ON L8L 2X2
Tel: 905-521-2100
information@phri.ca
www.phri.ca
Salim Yusuf, Executive Director

Lewis & Ruth Sherman Centre for Digital Scholarship
Mills Memorial Library
1280 Main St. West, Hamilton, ON L8S 4L8
Tel: 905-525-9140
scds.ca
Sandra Lapointe, Academic Director
lapoint@mcmaster.ca

Statistics Canada Research Data Centre
Mills Memorial Library
#217, 1280 Main St. West, Hamilton, ON L8S 4L6
Tel: 905-525-9140
rdc@mcmaster.ca
socserv.socsci.mcmaster.ca/rdc
Byron Spencer, Director
spencer@mcmaster.ca

Steel Research Centre (SRC)
John Hodgins Engineering Building
1280 Main St. West, #213D, Hamilton, ON L8S 4L8
Tel: 905-525-9140; *Fax:* 905-526-8404
mcmasteel.mcmaster.ca
Ken Coley, Director
coleyk@mcmaster.ca

Surgical Outcomes Research Centre (SOURCE)
#202, 39 Charlton Ave. East, Hamilton, ON L8N 1Y3
Tel: 905-523-0019; *Fax:* 905-523-0229
www.fhs.mcmaster.ca/source
Achilleas Thoma, Director
athoma@mcmaster.ca

Thrombosis & Atherosclerosis Research Institute (TaARI)
David Braley Research Institute
237 Bartin St. East, #C5-121, Hamilton, ON L8L 2X2
Tel: 905-521-2100; *Fax:* 905-575-2646
info@taari.ca
www.taari.ca
Annette Rosati, Administrator
annette.rosati@taari.ca

McMaster University Chaplaincy Centre
MUSC
#231, 1280 Main St. West, Hamilton, ON L8S 4L8
Tel: 905-525-9140; *Fax:* 905-524-1111
chaplain@mcmaster.ca
www.mcmaster.ca/chaplain

McMaster University Centre for Continuing Education
Also known as: McMaster CCE
50 Main St. East, 2nd Fl., Hamilton, ON L8N 1E9
Tel: 905-525-9140; *Fax:* 905-546-1690
Toll-Free: 800-463-6223
conted@mcmaster.ca
www.mcmastercce.ca
www.facebook.com/McMaster.Continuing.Education
twitter.com/McMasterContEd
www.linkedin.com/groups/McMaster-University-Centre-162178
www.youtube.com/user/McMasterContEd

McMaster Automotive Resource Center (MARC)
McMaster Innovation Park
#105, 175 Longwood Rd. South, Hamilton, ON L8P 0A1
Tel: 905-667-5500; *Fax:* 905-667-5501
mcmasterinnovationpark.ca

Hearst: Université de Hearst
P.O. Box 580
60, 9e Rue, Hearst, ON P0L 1N0, Canada
Tél: 705-372-1781; *Ligne sans frais:* 1-800-887-1781
www.uhearst.ca
www.facebook.com/uhearst
twitter.com/udehearst
www.youtube.com/user/UHearst
Pierre Ouellette, B.A., M.A., Recteur
Sophie Dallaire, B.A.A, M.Sc., Vice-rectrice
Manon Cyr, B.A.A, Secrétaire générale

Campuses
Kapuskasing
7, av Aurora, Kapuskasing, ON P5N 1J6, Canada
Tél: 705-335-8561; *Ligne sans frais:* 1-866-335-8561

Timmins
395, boul Thériault, Timmins, ON P4N 0A8, Canada
Tél: 705-267-2144; *Ligne sans frais:* 1-866-467-2144

Centres/Institutes
Centre d'archives de la Grande Zone
60, 9e rue, Hearst, ON P0L 1N0
Tél: 705-372-1781
www.uhearst.ca/archives
Danielle Coulombe, Responsable
danielle_coulombe@uhearst.ca

Kingston: Queen's University
99 University Ave., Kingston, ON K7L 3N6, Canada
Tel: 613-533-2000
admission@queensu.ca
www.queensu.ca
www.facebook.com/queensuniversity
twitter.com/queensu
www.linkedin.com/company/queen's-university
www.youtube.com/QueensUCanada
Full Time Equivalency: 24582
Jim Leech, Chancellor
Dr. Daniel Woolf, Principal & Vice-Chancellor
Mike Young, Rector
Alan Harrison, Vice-Principal Academic & Provost
Thomas Harris, Vice-Principal Advancement
John Metcalfe, University Registrar
Lon Knox, Secretary of the Senate, University & Board
Caroline Davis, Vice-Principal Finance & Administration
Dr. Steven Liss, Vice-Principal, Research
Michael Fraser, Vice-Principal University Relations

Faculties
Faculty of Engineering & Applied Science
45 Union St., Kingston, ON K7L 3N6
Tel: 613-533-2055; *Fax:* 613-533-6500
reception@appsci.queensu.ca
engineering.queensu.ca
Dr. K. Woodhouse, Ph.D., P.Eng., Dean

Faculty of Arts & Science
Tel: 613-533-2470; *Fax:* 613-533-2467
www.queensu.ca/artsci
Dr. A. MacLean, Ph.D., C.Psych., Dean

Faculty of Education
education.registrar@queensu.ca
educ.queensu.ca
www.facebook.com/QueensEduc
twitter.com/QueensEduc
Dr. Rosa Bruno-Jofré, Ph.D., Dean

Faculty of Health Sciences
Decanal Office
18 Barrie St., Kingston, ON K7L 3N6
Tel: 613-533-2544
healthsci.queensu.ca
Dr. Richard Reznick, Dean
deanfhs@queensu.ca

Faculty of Law
Macdonald Hall
128 Union St., Kingston, ON K7L 3N6
Tel: 613-533-2220; *Fax:* 613-533-8509
law.queensu.ca/index.html
William F. Flanagan, J.D., D.E.A., LL.M., Dean

Schools
School of Business
Goodes Hall
143 Union St., Kingston, ON K7L 3N6
Toll-Free: 877-533-2330
business.queensu.ca
Dr. David Saunders, Ph.D., Dean

Queen's School of English (QSOE)
96 Albert St., Kingston, ON K7L 3N6
Tel: 613-533-2472; *Fax:* 613-533-6809
soe@queensu.ca
www.queensu.ca/qsoe
www.facebook.com/qsoecanada
twitter.com/Queens_SoE
www.youtube.com/user/QSOECanada
Amanda Marshall, Acting Co-Chair
Barbara Yates, Acting Co-Chair

School of Graduate Studies (SGS)
Gordon Hall Rm. 45
74 Union St., Kingston, ON K7L 3N6
Tel: 613-533-6100; *Fax:* 613-533-6015
grad.studies@queensu.ca
www.queensu.ca/sgs/index.html
www.facebook.com/queensugradstudy
twitter.com/queensgradstudy
www.linkedin.com/groups/Queens-School-Graduate-Studies
Dr. J. Deakin, Ph.D., Dean

School of Music
www.queensu.ca/music
www.facebook.com/queensschoolofmusic
Gordon E. Smith, A.R.C.T., B.A., M.A., Ph., Director

School of Nursing (SON)
Cataraqui Bldg.
92 Barrie St., Kingston, ON K7L 3N6
Tel: 613-533-2668; *Fax:* 613-533-6770
nursing@queensu.ca
nursing.queensu.ca
www.facebook.com/Queensu.SON
twitter.com/QueensuSON
www.linkedin.com/groups/Queens-University-School-Nursing-8189529
instagram.com/queensnursing
Jennifer Medves, Director

School of Kinesiology & Health Sciences (SKHS)
SKHS Bldg.
28 Division St., Kingston, ON K7L 3N6
Tel: 613-533-2666; *Fax:* 613-533-2009
www.queensu.ca/skhs
www.facebook.com/SchoolOfKinesiologyAndHealthStudies
Jean Côté, Director

School of Policy Studies (SPS)
#217 Robert Sutherland Hall
138 Union St., Kingston, ON K7L 3N6
Tel: 613-533-3020; *Fax:* 613-533-2135
www.queensu.ca/sps/index.html
Arthur Sweetman, B.Eng., M.A., Ph.D., Director

School of Rehabilitation Therapy
Louise D. Action Bldg.
31 George St., Kingston, ON K7L 3N6
Tel: 613-533-6103; *Fax:* 613-533-6776
rehab@queensu.ca
www.rehab.queensu.ca
www.facebook.com/QueensSRT
twitter.com/QueensSRT
Richard Reznick, Director

School of Religion
Tel: 613-533-2110; *Fax:* 613-533-6879
www.queensu.ca/religion/index.html
Jean Stairs, Mus.Bac., M.Div., D.Min., Principal

School of Urban & Regional Planning (SURP)
#539 Robert Sutherland Hall
138 Union St., Kingston, ON K7L 3N6
Tel: 613-533-2188; *Fax:* 613-533-6905
rudachuk@queensu.ca
www.queensu.ca/surp
twitter.com/QueensSURP
Hok-Lin Leung, B.Arch., M.C.P., M.Sc., P., Director

Queen's School of Computing
Tel: 613-533-6050; *Fax:* 613-533-6513
www.cs.queensu.ca
James Cordy, B.Sc., M.Sc., Ph.D., P.En, Director

Centres/Institutes
Centre for International & Defence Policy (CIDP)
#403 Robert Sutherland Hall
138 Union St., Kingston, ON K7L 3N6
Tel: 613-533-2381; *Fax:* 613-533-6885
cidp@queensu.ca
www.queensu.ca/cidp/index.html
Charles Pentland, B.A., M.A., Ph.D., Director

Canadian Institute for Military & Veteran Health Research
111 Botterell Hall, Kingston, ON K7L 3N6
Tel: 613-533-3329; *Fax:* 613-533-3405
communications@cimvhr.ca
www.cimvhr.ca
www.facebook.com/1430071567228983
twitter.com/CIMVHR_ICRSMV
Alice Aiken, Director
Lauren Hanlon, Communications Coordinator
lauren.hanlon@queensu.ca

Institute of Intergovernmental Relations (IIGR)
#301 Robert Sutherland Hall
138 Union St., Kingston, ON K7L 3N6
Tel: 613-533-2080; *Fax:* 613-533-6868
iigr@queensu.ca
www.queensu.ca/iigr/index.html
twitter.com/IIGR_QueensU
Sean Conway, Director

Queen's Cancer Research Institute (QCRI)
#300, 10 Stuart St., Kingston, ON K7L 3N6
Tel: 613-533-6627; *Fax:* 613-533-2139
qcri.queensu.ca
Roger Deeley, Director
deeleyr@post.queensu.ca

Queen's Centre for Energy and Power Electronics Research
Also known as: ePOWER
Walter Light Hall
19 Union St., Kingston, ON K7L 3N6
Tel: 613-533-6829
www.queensu.ca/epower
Praveen Jain, Director
praveen.jain@queensu.ca

Centre for Health Services & Policy Research
Abramsky Hall
21 Arch St., 3rd. Fl, Kingston, ON K7L 3N6
Tel: 613-533-6387; *Fax:* 613-533-6353
chspr@queensu.ca
healthsci.queensu.ca/research/chspr
Michael Green, Director
michael.green@dfm.queensu.ca

Centre for Law in the Contemporary Workplace (CLCW)
Macdonald Hall
128 Union St., #C521, Kingston, ON K7L 3N6
Tel: 613-533-6000
clcw@queensu.ca
www.queensu.ca/clcw
twitter.com/QueensCLCW
www.youtube.com/QueensCLCW
Kevin Banks, Director
banksk@queensu.ca

Centre for Neuroscience Studies (CNS)
Botterell Hall
18 Stuart St., Kingston, ON K7L 3N6
Tel: 613-533-6360; *Fax:* 613-533-6840
www.queensu.ca/neuroscience
Doug Munoz, Director
doug.munoz@queensu.ca

Centre for Studies in Primary Care (CSPC)
P.O. Box 8888
Kingston, ON K7L 5E9
Tel: 613-533-9300; *Fax:* 613-533-9302
Toll-Free: 866-599-8090
www.queensu.ca/cspc
Richard Birtwhistle, Director
richard.birtwhistle@dfm.queensu.ca

Queen's - RMC Fuel Cell Research Centre (FCRC)
Queen's Innovation Park
945 Princess St., 2nd Fl., Kingston, ON K7L 3N6
Tel: 613-547-6700; *Fax:* 613-547-8125
www.fcrc.ca
J.G. Pharoah, Director
pharoah@me.queensu.ca

GeoEngineering Centre
101 Ellis Hall
Kingston, ON K7L 3N6
Tel: 613-533-6370; *Fax:* 613-533-2128
www.geoeng.ca
Ian D. Moore, Director
moore@civil.queensu.ca

High Performance Computing Virtual Laboratory (HPCVL)
#115, 993 Princess St., Kingston, ON K7L 1H3
Tel: 613-533-2561; *Fax:* 613-533-2015
www.hpcvl.org
Ken Edgecombe, Executive Director
ken.edgecombe@queensu.ca

John Deutsch Institute for the Study of Economic Policy (JDI)
Dunning Hall
Kingston, ON K7L 3N6
Tel: 613-533-2294; *Fax:* 613-533-6025
jdi@econ.queensu.ca
jdi.econ.queensu.ca
Christopher Ferrall, Director

Monieson Centre for Business Research in Healthcare
Also known as: Monieson Centre
Goodes Hall
Kingston, ON K7L 3N6
Tel: 613-533-3318
monieson@business.queensu.ca
www.moniesoncentre.com
www.facebook.com/MoniesonCentre
twitter.com/moniesonhealth
www.youtube.com/moniesonhealth
A. Scott Carson, Director
scarson@business.queensu.ca

Southern African Research Centre (SARC)
152 Albert St., Kingston, ON K7L 3N6
Tel: 613-533-6964; *Fax:* 613-533-2171
www.queensu.ca/sarc
Jonathan Crush, Director
crushj@post.queensu.ca

Surveillance Studies Centre
Department of Sociology
Kingston, ON K7L 3N6
www.sscqueens.org
twitter.com/sscqueens
David Lyon, Director

Sudbury Neutrino Observatory Laboratory (SNOLAB)
Institute Project Office
99 University Ave., Kingston, ON K7L 2N6
Tel: 613-533-2702; *Fax:* 613-533-6813
info@snolab.ca
www.snolab.ca

Queen's University International Centre (QUIC)
John Deutsch University Centre
87 Union St., Kingston, ON K7L 3N6
Tel: 613-533-2604; *Fax:* 613-533-3159
quic.queensu.ca
www.facebook.com/quic.queensu.ca
twitter.com/quic
www.youtube.com/user/quicatqueens
Susan Anderson, Director
susan.anderson@queensu.ca

Centre for Teaching & Learning
B176 Mackintosh-Corry Hall
Kingston, ON K7L 3N6
Tel: 613-533-6428; *Fax:* 613-533-6735
ctl@queensu.ca
www.queensu.ca/ctl
Denise Stockley, Interim Director
stockley@queensu.ca

Francophone Centre
195 University Ave., Kingston, ON K7L 3P5
Tel: 613-533-2086; *Fax:* 613-533-6522
centre.francophone@queensu.ca
www.queensu.ca/french/frenchcentre

Human Mobility Research Centre (HMRC)
Kingston General Hospital
76 Stuart St., Kingston, ON K7L 2V7
Tel: 613-548-2430; *Fax:* 613-549-2529
hmrc@queensu.ca
hmrc.engineering.queensu.ca
James Stewart, Director

Industrial Relations Centre (IRC)
Robert Sutherland Hall
138 Union St., 1st Fl., Kingston, ON K7L 2P1
Tel: 613-533-6628; *Toll-Free:* 888-858-7838
irc@QueensU.ca
irc.queensu.ca
www.facebook.com/pages/Queens-IRC/8158714372
twitter.com/QueensIRC
www.linkedin.com/company/541934
www.youtube.com/user/QueensIRC
Paul Juniper, Director
Paul.Juniper@QueensU.ca

Bader International Study Centre
Herstmonceux Castle
Hailsham, East Sussex BN27 1RN, UK
biscadmin@bisc.queensu.ac.uk
queensu.ca/bisc
Other Information: Phone: 44-1323-834444; Fax: 44-1323-834499
www.facebook.com/BaderISC
twitter.com/_thecastle
www.youtube.com/BISCtv
Kutay Ulkuer, Manager, 613-533-6000, ext. 75665
kutay.ulkuer@queensu.ca

Community Outreach Centre
A342 Duncan McArthur Hall
Kingston, ON K7M 5R7
Tel: 613-533-6000
www.educ.queensu.ca/coc
Lynda Colgan, Contact
lynda.colgan@queensu.ca

Ban Righ Centre
32 Bader Lane, Kingston, ON K7L 3N8
Tel: 613-533-2976
banrighcentre.queensu.ca
www.facebook.com/pages/Ban-Righ-Centre/85116218998
Carole Morrison, Director
carole.morrison@queensu.ca

Kingston: Royal Military College of Canada (RMCC)
Collège militaire royal du Canada
P.O. Box 17000 Forces
Kingston, ON K7K 7B4
Tel: 613-541-6000; *Fax:* 613-542-3565
Toll-Free: 1-866-762-2672
liaison@rmc.ca
www.rmc.ca
twitter.com/CanadianForces
www.youtube.com/user/CanadianForcesVideos
Full Time Equivalency: 2180; *Note:* Individuals must be a Canadian citizen in possession of the necessary academic qualifications. Applicants must also be one of the following: an MOC ((Military Occupation Classification) qualified member of the Canadian Forces; an applicant for the Regular Officer Training Plan (ROTP) or the Reserve Entry Training Plan (RETP); an employee of the Department of National Defence; or the spouse of a member of the Canadian Forces.
Dr. H.J. Kowal, Principal
principals.office@rmc.ca
BGen Don Macnamara, Chair
MGen Pierre Forgues, Vice-Chair
Raymond Stouffer, PhD, Registrar, 613-541-6000, ext. 6302

Faculties

Arts
J.J. Sokolsky, BA, MA, PhD, Dean
sokolsky-j@rmc.ca

Continuing Studies
M.A. Hennessy, BA, MA, PhD., Dean
hennessy-m@rmc.ca

Engineering
Dr. John A. Stewart, Dean
stewart_j@rmc.ca

Graduate Studies & Research
Dr. B.J. Fugère, Dean
fugere-j@rmc.ca

Science
Dr. Richard Marsden, Dean
marsden-r@rmc.ca

London: Brescia University College
1285 Western Rd., London, ON N6G 1H2, Canada
Tel: 519-432-8353; *Fax:* 519-858-5137
brescia@uwo.ca
www.brescia.uwo.ca
www.facebook.com/BresciaUniversityCollege
twitter.com/bresciauc
www.linkedin.com/company/brescia-university-college
www.youtube.com/user/Bresciauniversityc
Note: A women's university affiliated with the University of Western Ontario

London: Western University
Also known as: University of Western Ontario
1151 Richmond St., London, ON N6A 3K7, Canada
Tel: 519-661-2111
media@uwo.ca
www.uwo.ca
www.facebook.com/WesternUniversity
twitter.com/westernu
www.linkedin.com/company/westernuniversity
www.youtube.com/user/WesternUniversity
Full Time Equivalency: 28386; *Number of Employees:* 3,868
Dr. Amit Chakma, President & Vice-Chancellor, 519-661-3106
achakma@uwo.ca
Janice Deakin, Provost & Vice-President, 519-661-3110
provostvpa@uwo.ca
Gitta Kulczycki, Vice-President, Resources & Operations, 519-661-3114
gitta@uwo.ca
John Capone, Vice-President, Research, 519-661-3812
vpr@uwo.ca
Kelly Cole, Vice-President, External, 519-661-4120
kelly.cole@uwo.ca
Jennifer Meister, Ombudsperson, 519-661-3573, ext. 82602
jmeiste@uwo.ca
Irene Birrell, Secretary, 519-661-2056
ibirrell@uwo.ca
Lynn Logan, Associate Vice-President, Financial Services, 519-661-2111, ext. 85416
llogan2@uwo.ca
Elizabeth Krische, Director of Purchasing, 519-661-2038, ext. 84576
ekrische@uwo.ca
Debbie Jones, Director, Information Technology Services, 519-850-2470, ext. 82470
debbie@uwo.ca

Helen Connell, Associate Vice-President, Communications & Public Affairs, 519-850-2446, ext. 85469
hconnell@uwo.ca
Susan Grindrod, Associate Vice-President, Housing & Ancillary Services, 519-661-3549
grindrod@housing.uwo.ca

Faculties

Faculty of Arts & Humanities
Tel: 519-661-2111
arts@uwo.ca
www.uwo.ca/arts
www.facebook.com/167996849913934
twitter.com/uwo_arts
www.youtube.com/user/ArtsUWO
Michael Milde, Dean, Faculty of Arts & Humanities
Andrea Purvis, Director of Administration, 519-661-2111, ext. 84530
ajpurvis@uwo.ca

Faculty of Education
John George Althouse Building
1137 Western Rd., London, ON N6G 1G7
Tel: 519-661-3182; *Fax:* 519-661-3833
foe.feedback@uwo.ca
www.edu.uwo.ca
www.facebook.com/360244505069
twitter.com/western_fac_ed
www.linkedin.com/groups?gid=4413033
Dr. Vicki Schwean, Dean, Faculty of Education, 519-661-2080, ext. 82080
vschwean@uwo.ca
Dr. Stephen Bird, Associate Dean, Research, 519-661-2111, ext. 88694
sbird23@uwo.ca
Dr. Pamela Bishop, Associate Dean, Graduate Programs, 519-661-2111, ext. 88879
pbishop@uwo.ca

Faculty of Engineering
Spencer Engineering Bldg., Room 2008
London, ON N6A 5B9
Tel: 519-661-2128; *Fax:* 519-661-3808
contactWE@eng.uwo.ca
www.eng.uwo.ca
twitter.com/WesternEng
Andrew N. Hrymak, Dean, Western Engineering

Faculty of Health Sciences
200 Arthur and Sonia Labatt Health Sciences Bldg.
London, ON N6A 5B9
Tel: 519-661-2111
www.uwo.ca/fhs
www.facebook.com/fhswestern
twitter.com/westernuFHS
instagram.com/westernufhs
Jim Weese, Dean, Faculty of Health Sciences, 519-661-2111, ext. 84239
jweese1@uwo.ca
Krys Chelchowski, Director of Administration, 519-661-2111, ext. 86695
kchelcho@uwo.ca

Faculty of Information & Media Studies
240 North Campus Bldg.
London, ON N6A 5B7
Tel: 519-661-3720; *Fax:* 519-661-3506
mit@uwo.ca
www.fims.uwo.ca
Other Information: 519-661-3542; Graduate Student Services: 519-661-4017
www.facebook.com/westernuFIMS
twitter.com/FIMS_GRC
Dr. Thomas Carmichael, Dean, Faculty of Information & Media Studies, 519-661-2111, ext. 84235
fimsdean@uwo.ca
Joanna Asuncion, Director, Administration, 519-661-2111, ext. 88474
jasuncio@uwo.ca

Faculty of Law
1151 Richmond St., London, ON N6A 3K7
Tel: 519-661-3346
www.law.uwo.ca
www.facebook.com/UWOLaw
twitter.com/UWOLaw
vimeo.com/uwolaw
W. Iain Scott, Dean, Faculty of Law, 519-661-2111, ext. 84002
iain.scott@uwo.ca

Don Wright Faculty of Music
210 Talbot College
London, ON N6A 3K7
Tel: 519-661-2111
music@uwo.ca
www.music.uwo.ca
www.facebook.com/westernuMusic
twitter.com/westernuMusic
Dr. Betty Anne Younker, Dean, Don Wright Faculty of Music, 519-661-4008, ext. 84008
byounker@uwo.ca

Faculty of Science
191 Western Science Centre
London, ON N6A 5B7
Tel: 519-661-2111; *Fax:* 519-661-3703
science@uwo.ca
www.uwo.ca/sci
www.facebook.com/scibmsac
twitter.com/westernuScience
www.youtube.com/user/westernuscience
Charmaine Dean, Dean

Faculty of Social Science
Social Science Centre
London, ON N6A 5C2
Tel: 519-661-2053
social-science@uwo.ca
www.ssc.uwo.ca
www.facebook.com/westernussaco
twitter.com/westernuSocSci
www.youtube.com/user/SSUWO1
Brian Timney, Dean

Schools

School of Graduate & Postdoctoral Studies
1151 Richmond St., London, ON N6A 3K7
Tel: 519-661-2102
grad.uwo.ca
Enrollment: 5000
Linda Miller, Vice-Provost
grad-vp@uwo.ca
Ron Wagler, Director of Administration
ron.wagler@uwo.ca

Schulich School of Medicine & Dentistry
Clinical Skills Building
London, ON N6A 5C1
Tel: 519-661-3459
www.schulich.uwo.ca
www.facebook.com/SchulichMedicineAndDentistry
twitter.com/SchulichMedDent
Dr. Michael J. Strong, Dean, Schulich School of Medicine & Dentistry

Ivey Business School
1255 Western Rd., London, ON N6G 0N1
Tel: 519-661-3206; *Fax:* 519-661-3485
www.ivey.ca
twitter.com/iveybusiness
Robert (Bob) Kennedy, Dean, Ivey Business School, 519-661-3285
rkennedy@ivey.uwo.ca
John Irwin, CFO, CIO, Director of Facilities, 519-661-3728
jirwin@ivey.uwo.ca

Western Continuing Studies (WCO)
Citi Plaza
London, ON
Tel: 519-661-3658
cstudies@uwo.ca
wcs.uwo.ca
www.facebook.com/153147848037846
twitter.com/westernucs
www.linkedin.com/groups/Western-Continuing-Studies
pinterest.com/cstudies
Carolyn Young, Director

Affiliations

Brescia University College
1285 Western Rd., London, ON N6G 1H2
Tel: 519-432-8353; *Fax:* 519-858-5137
brescia@uwo.ca
www.brescia.uwo.ca
www.facebook.com/BresciaUniversityCollege
twitter.com/bresciauc
www.linkedin.com/company/brescia-university-college
www.youtube.com/bresciauc
Dr. Susan Mumm, Principal, 519-432-8353, ext. 28263
bucprincipal@uwo.ca
Donna M. Rogers, Vice-Principal & Academic Dean, 519-432-8353, ext. 28263
donna.rogers@uwo.ca

Huron University College
1349 Western Rd., London, ON N6G 1H3
Tel: 519-438-7224; *Fax:* 519-438-3938
huron@uwo.ca
www.huronuc.on.ca
www.facebook.com/101245552822
twitter.com/huronatwestern
www.linkedin.com/groups/Huron-University-College-125520
www.youtube.com/user/HuronUC
Dr. Stephen McClatchie, Principal
smcclatchie@huron.uwo.ca

King's University College
266 Epworth Ave., London, ON N6A 2M3
Tel: 519-433-3491; *Toll-Free:* 800-265-4406
kings@uwo.ca
www.kings.uwo.ca
www.facebook.com/kingsatwestern
twitter.com/kucatuwo
www.youtube.com/kingsatuwo
Full Time Equivalency: 3800

Centres/Institutes

Applied Electrostatics Research Centre (AERC)
www.eng.uwo.ca/research/aerc
Ion Inculet, Director

Alan G. Davenport Wind Engineering Group (BLWTL)
Faculty of Engineering
London, ON N6A 5B9
Tel: 519-661-3338; *Fax:* 519-661-3889
info@blwtl.uwo.ca
www.blwtl.uwo.ca

Canadian Centre for Activity & Aging
CCAA
1490 Richmond St., London, ON N6G 2M3
Tel: 519-661-1603; *Fax:* 519-661-1612
Toll-Free: 866-661-1603
ccaa@uwo.ca
www.uwo.ca/actage
www.facebook.com/actage
www.youtube.com/user/CCAAUWO
Clara Fitzgerald, Program Director

Canadian Research Centre on Inclusive Education
1137 Western Rd., London, ON N6G 1G7
Tel: 519-661-2111
www.inclusiveeducationresearch.ca

Centre for the Study of International Economic Relations (CSIER)
economics.uwo.ca/csier
Jing Wang, Contact
jwang624@uwo.ca

Centre for the Study of Theory & Criticism
#2345A Somerville House
London, ON N6A 3K7
Tel: 519-661-3442; *Fax:* 519-850-2927
theory@uwo.ca
www.uwo.ca/theory
www.facebook.com/theoryandcriticism
Tilottama Rajan, Director
trajan@uwo.ca

Chemical Reactor Engineering Centre (CREC)
London, ON N6A 5B9
Tel: 519-661-2144; *Fax:* 519-850-2931
www.eng.uwo.ca/crec
Hugo de Lasa, Director
hdelasa@eng.uwo.ca

Geotechnical Research Centre
#3010C Spencer Engineering Bldg.
1151 Richmond St. North, Toronto, ON N6A 5B9
Tel: 519-661-3344
www.eng.uwo.ca/grc
Cynthia Quintus, Coordinator
cquintus@eng.uwo.ca

International Centre for Olympic Studies (ICOS)
317 Sciences Bldg.
London, ON
Tel: 519-661-4113
www.uwo.ca/olympic
Janice Forsyth, Director

Robarts Imaging
Imaging Research Laboratories
1151 Richmond St. North, London, ON N6A 5B7
Tel: 519-931-5777; *Fax:* 519-931-5713
www.imaging.robarts.ca

Museum of Ontario Archaeology
1600 Attawandaron Rd., London, ON N6G 3M6
Tel: 519-473-1360; *Fax:* 519-850-2363
www.archaeologymuseum.ca
www.facebook.com/ArchaeologyMuseum
twitter.com/MuseOntArch
Joan Kanigan, Executive Director

Lawrence Centre
Ivey Business School
1255 Western Rd., London, ON N6G 0N1
Tel: 519-661-4253; *Fax:* 519-661-4297
lawrence@ivey.ca
www.ivey.uwo.ca/lawrencecentre
twitter.com/lawrencecentre
www.linkedin.com/groups?home=&gid=5134867
Paul Boothe, Director

Centre for Population, Aging & Health
#5230 Social Science Centre
London, ON N6A 5C2
Fax: 519-661-3220
cpah@uwo.ca
sociology.uwo.ca/cpah

Surface Science Western
P.O. Box 12
#LL31, 999 Collip Circle, London, ON N6G 0J3
Tel: 519-661-2173; *Fax:* 519-661-3709
info@surfacesciencewestern.com
www.surfacesciencewestern.com
www.facebook.com/190702930970998
twitter.com/SurfSciWestern
www.linkedin.com/company/surface-science-western
www.youtube.com/user/ssw
David Shoesmith, Director

North Bay: Nipissing University
P.O. Box 5002
100 College Dr., North Bay, ON P1B 8L7, Canada
Tel: 705-474-3450; *Fax:* 705-474-1947
nuinfo@nipissingu.ca
www.nipissingu.ca
TTY: 877-688-5507
www.facebook.com/NipissingU
twitter.com/NipissingU
www.youtube.com/user/nipissinguniversity
Jon S. Dellandrea, Chancellor
Mike DeGagné, President & Vice-Chancellor
Dr. Sharon Rich, Associate Vice-President, Academic
Richard Onley, Vice-Pres., Finance & Administration
Dr. Harley d'Entremont, Vice-Pres., Academic & Research
Bob Keech, Vice-Pres., Operations
Laurie McLaren, Exec. Dir., Aboriginal Initiatives
Jamie Graham, Asst. VP, Institutional Planning and Quality Assurance
Karen Charles, Manager, Accounting & Purchasing Services, ext. 4435
karench@nipissingu.ca

Faculty of Arts & Science
Dr. Ann-Barbara Graff, Dean (Interim), Faculty of Arts & Science, ext. 4290
annbg@nipissingu.ca

Faculty of Applied and Professional Studies
Dr. Rick Vanderlee, Dean, Faculty of Applied and Professional Studies, ext. 4666
rickv@nipissingu.ca

Schools

School of Graduate Studies
Dr. Murat Tuncali, Assistant Vice President, Research & Graduate Studies, ext. 4565
muratt@nipissingu.ca

Schulich School of Education
Dr. Carole Richardson, Dean of Education (Interim), ext. 4268
caroler@nipissingu.ca
Jessica McMillan, Administrator, ext. 4264
jessicam@nipissingu.ca

Campuses

Brantford Campus
50 Wellington St., Brantford, ON N3T 2L6
Tel: 519-752-1524; *Fax:* 519-752-8372
brant@nipissingu.ca
Darius Sookram, Campus Administrator, ext. 7501
dariuss@nipissingu.ca

Muskoka Campus
125 Wellington St., Bracebridge, ON P1L 1E2
Tel: 705-645-2921; *Fax:* 705-645-2922
muskoka@nipissingu.ca
Jan Lucy, Campus Administrator, ext. 7202
janl@nipissingu.ca

Oshawa: University of Ontario Institute of Technology (UOIT)
2000 Simcoe St. North, Oshawa, ON L1H 7K4, Canada
Tel: 905-721-8668; *Fax:* 905-721-3178
admissions@uoit.ca
www.uoit.ca
facebook.com/myuoit
twitter.com/uoit
www.linkedin.com/company/uoit
www.youtube.com/uoit

Full Time Equivalency: 9990
Hon. Perrin Beatty, B.A., Chancellor
Tim McTiernan, President & Vice-Chancellor
Deborah Saucier, Provost & Vice-President, Academic
provost@uoit.ca
Susan McGovern, Vice-President, External Relations, 905-721-8668, ext. 3135
susan.mcgovern@uoit.ca
Murray Lapp, Vice-President, Human Resources & Services, 905-721-8668, ext. 5666
murray.lapp@uoit.ca
Michael Owen, Vice-President, Research, Innovation & International, 905-721-8668, ext. 5661
michael.owen@uoit.ca
Pamela Drayson, B.A., M.A., Ph.D., Chief Librarian, 905-721-8668, ext. 2348
pamela.drayson@uoit.ca
Brad MacIsaac, Registrar, 905-721-8668, ext. 5688
brad.macisaac@uoit.ca

Faculties

Business & Information Technology
fbit@uoit.ca
www.businessandit.uoit.ca
Pamela Ritchie, B.A., M.Sc., Ph.D., Dean, 905-721-8668, ext. 3160
pamela.ritchie@uoit.ca

Social Sciences & Humanities
SSH@uoit.ca
www.socialscienceandhumanities.uoit.ca
Nawal Ammar, B.Sc. (Hons.), M.Sc., Ph., Dean, 905-721-8668, ext. 3159
nawal.ammar@uoit.ca

Education
faculty-of-education@uoit.ca
education.uoit.ca
Jim Greenlaw, B.A., B.Ed., M.A.(T), Ph., Dean, 905.721.8668, ext. 3158
jim.greenlaw@uoit.ca

Energy Systems & Nuclear Science
admissions@uoit.ca
nuclear.uoit.ca
George Bereznai, B.Eng., M.Eng., Ph.D., Dean, 905-721-8668, ext. 3142
george.bereznai@uoit.ca

Engineering & Applied Science
engineering@uoit.ca
www.engineering.uoit.ca
George Bereznai, B.Eng., M.Eng., Ph.D., Dean, 905-721-8668, ext. 3142
george.bereznai@uoit.ca

Health Sciences
Tel: 905-721-3166; *Fax:* 905-721-3179
healthsciences@uoit.ca
www.healthsciences.uoit.ca
Ellen Vogel, R.D., F.D.C., Ph.D., Dean, 905-721-8668, ext. 2518
ellen.vogel@uoit.ca

Science
facultyofscience@uoit.ca
www.science.uoit.ca
Deborah Saucier, Ph.D., Dean, 905-721-8668, ext. 3235
deborah.saucier@uoit.ca

Office of Graduate Studies
gradstudies@uoit.ca
gradstudies.uoit.ca
Brian Campbell, Dean, 905-721-8668, ext. 2650
brian.campbell@uoit.ca

Ottawa: Carleton University
1125 Colonel By Dr., Ottawa, ON K1S 5B6, Canada
Tel: 613-520-7400; *Fax:* 613-520-7858
info@carleton.ca
www.carleton.ca
www.facebook.com/carletonuniversity
twitter.com/@Carleton_U
www.youtube.com/user/carletonuvideos

Full Time Equivalency: 27771; *Number of Employees:* 859 academic staff; 1090 management & support staff; 664 contract instructors; 1745 TAs
Charles Chi, Chancellor
Dr. Roseann O'Reilly Runte, President & Vice-Chancellor, 613-520-3801
presidents_office@carleton.ca
Peter Ricketts, Provost & Vice-President, 613-520-3884
provost@carleton.ca
Duncan Watt, Vice-Pres., Finance & Administration, 613-520-3804
duncan_watt@carleton.ca
Kimberly Matheson, Vice-Pres., Research & International, 613-520-3570
vpri@carleton.ca
Ron Jackson, Chair
Suzanne Blanchard, Registrar, 613-520-3500
registrar@carleton.ca

Faculties

Arts & Social Sciences
Paterson Hall
#330, 1125 Colonel By Dr., Ottawa, ON K1S 5B6
Tel: 613-520-2355; *Fax:* 613-520-4481
fassod@carleton.ca
www.carleton.ca/fass/
Enrollment: 6888; *Number of Employees:* 318 faculty and 68 administrative staff; *Note:* Bachelor of Arts, Bachelor of Music, Bachelor of Humanities, Bachelor of Arts Honours, Bachelor of Arts Combined Honours, 14master's and nine doctoral programs.
John Osborne, Dean, 613-520-2355
fassod@carleton.ca

Engineering & Design
The Minto Centre
#3010, 1125 Colonel By Dr., Ottawa, ON K1S 5B6
Tel: 613-520-5790; *Fax:* 613-520-7481
info_engdesign@carleton.ca
carleton.ca/engineering-design/
Note: Bachelor of Engineering, Bachelor of Architectural Studies, Bachelor of Industrial Design and Bachelor of Information Technology degrees.
Dr Rafik Goubran, Dean, 613-520-5790
info_engdesign@carleton.ca

Graduate & Postdoctoral Affairs
Tory Building
#512, 1125 Colonel By Dr., Ottawa, ON K1S 5B6
Tel: 613-520-2525; *Fax:* 613-520-4049
graduate_studies@carleton.ca
gradstudents.carleton.ca
www.twitter.com/CUGradStudies
Wallace Clement, Dean, 613-520-2518
wallace.clement@carleton.ca

Public Affairs
Loeb Building
#D391, 1125 Colonel By Dr., Ottawa, ON K1S 5B6
Tel: 613-520-3741; *Fax:* 613-520-3742
odfpa@carleton.ca
www.carleton.ca/fpa/
www.facebook.com/cufpa
www.twitter.com/@fpacarleton
Number of Employees: 200 faculty members; *Note:* Bachelor of Journalism, Bachelor of Social Work, Bachelor of Public Affairs and Policy Management, and, run in tandem with the Faculty of Arts and Social Sciences, the Bachelor of Arts; as well as an array of MA and PhD programs, a Master of Journalism, a Master of Social Work, and the Clayton H. Riddell Graduate Program in Political Management.
André Plourde, Dean, 613-520-3741

Science
3230 Herzberg Laboratories, Carleton University
1125 Colonel By Dr., Ottawa, ON K1S 5B6
Tel: 613-520-4388; *Fax:* 613-520-4389
odscience@carleton.ca
science.carleton.ca
twitter.com/carletonscience
Enrollment: 3793; *Note:* Bachelor of Science - variety of programs, Bachelor of Computer Science - variety of streams, Bachelor of Health Sciences, Bachelor of Mathematics - variety of programs, Master of Science , Master of Computer Science, Master of Health: Science, Technology and Policy, Ph.D. in Biology, Chemistry, Computer Science, Earth Sciences, Mathematics, Neuroscience, or Phyiscs.
Malcolm Butler, Dean, 613-520-4388
odscience@carleton.ca

Schools
Azrieli School of Architecture & Urbanism
202 Architecture Building
1125 Colonel By Dr., Ottawa, ON K1S 5B6
Tel: 613-520-2855; *Fax:* 613-520-2849
architecture@carleton.ca
carleton.ca/architecture/
Sheryl Boyle, Interim Director, 613-520-2855
architecture@carleton.ca

School for Studies in Art & Culture (SSAC)
423 St. Patrick's Building, Carleton University
1125 Colonel By Dr., Ottawa, ON K1S 5B6
Tel: 613-520-2342; *Fax:* 613-520-3575
ssac@carleton.ca
www.carleton.ca/ssac/
Note: Departments of Art History, Film Studies, and Music joined together to form the School for Studies in Art and Culture.
Brian Foss, Director, 613-520-2600, ext. 3791
brian_foss@carleton.ca

School of Linguistics & Language Studies
236 Paterson Hall, Carleton University
1125 Colonel By Dr., Ottawa, ON K1S 5B6
Tel: 613-520-2802; *Fax:* 613-520-6641
linguistics@carleton.ca
www.carleton.ca/slals/
Lynne Young, Acting Director, 613-520-6612
slals@carleton.ca

Sprott School of Business
810 Dunton Tower, Carleton University
1125 Colonel By Dr., Ottawa, ON K1S 5B6
Tel: 613-520-2388; *Fax:* 613-520-2532
info@sprott.carleton.ca
sprott.carleton.ca
www.facebook.com/sprott.careercentre
twitter.com/SprottSchool
www.youtube.com/user/SprottSchoolCarleton
Enrollment: 2242; *Number of Employees:* 56 faculty members; 29 staff; *Note:* Bachelor of Commerce, Bachelor of International Business, Sprott MBA, PhD in Management, Professional Programs
Dr. Jerry Tomberlin, Dean, 613-520-2600, ext. 8848
jerry_tomberlin@carleton.ca

School of Canadian Studies
1206 Dunton Tower, Carleton University
1125 Colonel By Dr., Ottawa, ON K1S 5B6
Tel: 613-520-2366; *Fax:* 613-520-3903
carleton.ca/canadianstudies/
Note: BA degree in Canadian Studies; MA program or Ph.D. program that is run jointly with Trent University.

School of Computer Science
5302 Herzberg Building, Carleton University
1125 Colonel By Dr., Ottawa, ON K1S 5B6
Tel: 613-520-4333; *Fax:* 613-520-4334
www.scs.carleton.ca
Note: Undergraduate Programs, Master's degree in Computer Science (MCS), and Doctor in Philosophy (Ph.D) in Computer Science.
Michel Barbeau, Interim Director, 613-520-2600, ext. 4330
director@scs.carleton.ca

Technology, Society, Environment Studies
2240 Herzberg Laboratories
1125 Colonel By Dr., Ottawa, ON K1S 5B6
Tel: 613-520-2600; *Fax:* 613-520-3422
tse.carleton.ca
Dr. John Buschek, Director, 613-520-4483
john_buschek@carleton.ca

School of Industrial Design
3470 Mackenzie Building, Carleton University
1125 Colonel By Dr., Ottawa, ON K1S 5B6
Tel: 613-520-5672; *Fax:* 613-520-4465
www.id.carleton.ca
Note: Bachelor of Industrial Design, Master of Design
Thomas Garvey, Director, 613-520-5672

School of Information Technology
Carleton University
1125 Colonel By Dr., Ottawa, ON K1S 5B6
Tel: 613-520-5644; *Fax:* 613-520-6623
info@csit.carleton.ca
www.csit.carleton.ca
Dr Anthony Whitehead, Director, 613-520-2600, ext. 1696
anthony_whitehead@carleton.ca

School of Journalism & Communication
4309 River Building, Carleton University
1125 Colonel By Dr., Ottawa, ON K1S 5B6
Tel: 613-520-7404; *Fax:* 613-520-6690
journalism@carleton.ca
carleton.ca/sjc
Enrollment: 1500; *Note:* Bachelor of Journalism and Bachelor of Arts in Communication Studies, Master of Journalism, Master of Arts in Communication, and PhD in Communication.
Christopher Waddell, Director, 613-520-2600, ext. 8495
chris_waddell@carleton.ca

Norman Paterson School of International Affairs
5306 River Building, Carleton University
1125 Colonel By Dr., Ottawa, ON K1S 5B6
Tel: 613-520-6655; *Fax:* 613-520-2889
international.affairs@carleton.ca
www.carleton.ca/npsia
Note: Master of Arts in International Affairs and Juris Doctor degree (M.A./JD)., Ph.D. Program, Master of Infrastructure Protection and International Security (MIPIS)
Dane Rowlands, Director, 613-520-2600, ext. 8884
dane.rowlands@carleton.ca

School of Public Policy & Administration (SPPA)
5224, River Building, Carleton University
1125 Colonel By Dr., Ottawa, ON K1S 5B6
Tel: 613-520-2547; *Fax:* 613-520-2551
sppa@carleton.ca
carleton.ca/sppa
Note: Doctoral degree in Public Policy and masters degree programs in Public Administration, Sustainable Energy Policy, and Philanthropy and Nonprofit Leadership
Dr. Susan Phillips, Director, 613-520-2600, ext. 2633
susan_phillips@carleton.ca

School of Social Work
509 Dunton Tower, Carleton University
1125 Colonel By Dr., Ottawa, ON K1S 5B6
Tel: 613-520-5601; *Fax:* 613-520-7496
carleton.ca/socialwork
Hugh Shewell, Director, 613-520-2600, ext. 5717
hugh_shewell@carleton.ca

School of Mathematics & Statistics
4302 Herzberg Laboratories, Carleton University
1125 Colonel By Dr., Ottawa, ON K1S 5B6
Tel: 613-520-2152
mathstat@carleton.ca
www.carleton.ca/math
Note: Joint graduate program with the University of Ottawa.
Patrick Farrell, Director, 613-520-2152
ms-dir@math.carleton.ca

Institute for Comparative Studies in Literature, Art & Culture
201 St. Patrick's Building, Carleton University
1125 Colonel By Dr., Ottawa, ON K1S 5B6
Tel: 613-520-2177; *Fax:* 613-520-2564
icslac@carleton.ca
www.carleton.ca/icslac
Mitchell Frank, Director, 613 520-2607, ext. 6045
mitchell_frank@carleton.ca

Institute of African Studies
439 Paterson Hall, Carleton University
1125 Colonel By Dr., Ottawa, ON K1S 5B6
Tel: 613-520-2600; *Fax:* 613-520-2363
african_studies@carleton.ca
www.carleton.ca/africanstudies/
Blair Rutherford, Director, 613-520-2600, ext. 2422
blair_rutherford@carleton.ca
Chris Brown, Interim Director, 613-520-2600, ext. 2422
chris_brown@carleton.ca

Institute of Cognitive Science
2201, Dunton Tower, Carleton University
1125 Colonel By Dr., Ottawa, ON K1S 5B6
Tel: 613-520-2368; *Fax:* 613-520-3985
www.carleton.ca/ics
Dr Jo-Anne Lefevre, Director, 613-520-2600, ext. 2693
jo-anne_lefevre@carleton.ca

Institute of Interdisciplinary Studies
2201 Dunton Tower, Carleton University
1125 Colonel By Dr., Ottawa, ON K1S 5B6
Tel: 613-520-2368; *Fax:* 613-520-3985
iis@carleton.ca
www.carleton.ca/iis
Patrizia Gentile, Director, 613-520-2600, ext. 1456
patrizia.gentile@carleton.ca
Peter Hodgins, Acting Director, 613-520-2600, ext. 1107
Peter.Hodgins@carleton.ca

Pauline Jewett Institute of Women's & Gender Studies
1401 Dunton Tower, Carleton University
125 Colonel By Dr., Ottawa, ON K1S 5B6
Tel: 613-520-6645; *Fax:* 613-520-2622
womens_studies@carleton.ca
www.carleton.ca/womensstudies
Katharine Kelly, Director, 613-520-2600, ext. 6643
katharine.kelly@carleton.ca

Institute of Criminology & Criminal Justice
C562 Loeb Building, Carleton University
1125 Colonel By Dr., Ottawa, ON K1S 5B6
Tel: 613-520-2588
criminology@carleton.ca
www.carleton.ca/criminology
Note: Undergraduate degree in Criminology and Criminal Justice
Peter Swan, Director, 613-520-2600, ext. 1412
peter.swan@carleton.ca

Institute of European, Russian & Eurasian Studies
3304, River Bldg., Carleton University
1125 Colonel By Dr., Ottawa, ON K1S 5B6
Tel: 613-520-2888; *Fax:* 613-520-7501
www.carleton.ca/eurus
Dr Jeff Sahadeo, Director, 613-520-2888
jeff_sahadeo@carleton.ca

Institute of Political Economy
1501 Dunton Tower, Carleton University
1125 Colonel By Dr., Ottawa, ON K1S 5B6
Tel: 613-520-7414
political_economy@carleton.ca
carleton.ca/politicaleconomy
Laura Macdonald, Director
Laura.Macdonald@carleton.ca

Institute of Biochemistry
209 Nesbitt Biology Building, Carleton University
1125 Colonel By Dr., Ottawa, ON K1S 5B6
Tel: 613-520-2478; *Fax:* 613-520-3539
biochem@carleton.ca
www.carleton.ca/biochem
Enrollment: 200; *Number of Employees:* 20 faculty members
Anatoli Ianoul, Director, 613-520-2600, ext. 6043
anatoli_ianoul@carleton.ca

Institute of Environmental Science
2240 Herzberg Building, Carleton University
1125 Colonel By Dr., Ottawa, ON K1S 5B6
Tel: 613-520-4461; *Fax:* 613-520-3422
EnvironmentalScience@carleton.ca
envirosci.carleton.ca
Brian Burns, Director, 613-520-2600, ext. 4401
brian_burns@carleton.ca

Integrated Science Institute
2240 Herzberg Laboratories, Carleton University
1125 Colonel By Dr., Ottawa, ON K1S 5B6
Tel: 613-520-2600; *Fax:* 613-520-3422
IntegratedScience@carleton.ca
isi.carleton.ca
Pam Wolff, Director, 613-520-2600, ext. 2259
pamela_wolff@carleton.ca

Centres/Institutes
Carleton Centre for Community Innovation
Dunton Tower
#2104, 1125 Colonel By Dr., Ottawa, ON M2J 2X5
Tel: 613-520-5792
ccci@carleton.ca
www.carleton.ca/3ci
Tessa Hebb, Director
thebb@attglobal.net

Carleton Centre for Public History
pubhist@gmail.com
ccph.carleton.ca
James Opp, Co-Director

Carleton Immersive Media Studio (CIMS)
Visualization & Simulation Building
1125 Colonel By Dr., 4th Fl., Ottawa, ON K1S 5B6
Tel: 613-520-2600; *Fax:* 613-520-7841
info@cims.carleton.ca
www.cims.carleton.ca
Johan Voordouw, Contact

Carleton Research Unit on Innovation, Science & Environment (CRUISE)
www.carleton.ca/cruise

Carleton Sustainable Energy Research Centre (CSERC)
Tel: 613-520-2600
www.carleton.ca/cserc
James Meadowcroft, Contact
james.meadowcroft@carleton.ca

Centre for Conflict Education & Research (CCER)
Loeb Bldg.
1125 Colonel By Dr., #D498, Ottawa, ON K1S 5B6
Tel: 613-520-2600
www.carleton.ca/ccer
Neil Sargent, Director

Centre for European Studies (CES)
Dunton Tower
#1103, 1125 Colonel By Dr., Ottawa, ON K1S 5B6
Tel: 613-520-2600; *Fax:* 613-520-7483
ces@carleton.ca
www.carleton.ca/ces
Joan DeBardeleben, Director
joan_debardeleben@carleton.ca

Centre for Indigenous Research, Culture, Language & Education (CIRCLE)
circle@carleton.ca
carleton.ca/circle
John Kelly, Co-Director
john.kelly@carleton.ca
Anna Hoefnagels, Co-Director
anna.hoefnagels@carleton.ca

Centre for International Migration & Settlement Studies (CIMSS)
Dunton Tower
#2106, 1125 Colonel By Dr., Ottawa, ON K1S 5B6
Tel: 613-520-2717; *Fax:* 613-520-3476
cimss@carleton.ca
www.carleton.ca/cimss
Adnan Türegün, Executive Director

Centre for Research & Education on Women & Work (CREWW)
Dunton Tower
#702, 1125 Colonel By Dr., Ottawa, ON K1S 5B6
Tel: 613-520-2717
creww@sprott.carleton.ca
sprott.carleton.ca
Merridee Bujaki, Director
merridee.bujaki@carleton.ca

Centre for Trade Policy & Law (CTPL)
Dunton Tower
1125 Colonel By Dr., 21st Fl., Ottawa, ON K1S 5B6
Tel: 613-520-6696; *Fax:* 613-520-3981
ctpl@carleton.ca
www.ctpl.ca
Phil Rourke, Executive Director
phil_rourke@carleton.ca

Centre for Transnational Cultural Analysis (CTCA)
Dunton Tower
#1801, 1125 Colonel By Dr., Ottawa, ON K1S 5B6
Tel: 613-520-2600
www.carleton.ca/ctca
Sarah Casteel, Contact
sarah_casteel@carleton.ca

Centre on Values and Ethics (COVE)
1125 Colonel By Dr., Ottawa, ON K1S 5B6
www.carleton.ca/cove
Stephen Maguire, Director
stephen.maguire@carleton.ca

Geomatics and Cartographic Research Centre (GCRC)
1125 Colonel By Dr., Ottawa, ON K1S 5B6
Tel: 613-520-2600
gcrc.carleton.ca
Fraser Taylor, Director
fraser_taylor@carleton.ca

Max & Tessie Zelikovitz Centre for Jewish Studies
Paterson Hall
1125 Colonel By Dr., #2A49, Ottawa, ON K1S 5B6
Tel: 613-520-2600
jewish_studies@carleton.ca
www.carleton.ca/jewishstudies
Deidre Butler, Director
deidre_butler@carleton.ca

Ottawa Medical Physics Institute (OMPI)
ompi_ao@physics.carleton.ca
www.physics.carleton.ca/ompi
Malcolm McEwan, Director

Ottawa-Carleton Bridge Research Institute (OCBRI)
Tel: 613-520-2600

Centre for Research on Health: Science, Technology & Policy
Tel: 613-520-2600
Karen Schwartz, Contact
karen_schwartz@carleton.ca

Visualization and Simulation Centre (VSIM)
1125 Colonel By Dr., Ottawa, ON K1S 5B6
www.carleton.ca/vsim

Center for Applied Cognitive Research (CACR)
Loeb Bldg.
1125 Colonel By Dr., #B550, Ottawa, ON K1S 5B6
Tel: 613-520-2600; *Fax:* 613-520-3515
www.carleton.ca/vsim
Jo-Anne Lefevre, Director
jlefevre@connect.carleton.ca

Centre for Aboriginal Culture & Education (CACE)
Robertson Hall
#503, 1125 Colonel By Dr., Ottawa, ON K1S 5B6
Tel: 613-520-5622; *Fax:* 613-520-4037
cace@carleton.ca
www.carleton.ca/aboriginal
Mallory Whiteduck, Aboriginal Cultural Liaison Officer
mallory_whiteduck@carleton.ca

Centre for European Studies
Dunton Tower
#1103, 1125 Colonel By Dr., Ottawa, ON K1S 5B6
Tel: 613-520-2600; *Fax:* 613-520-7501
ces@carleton.ca
www.carleton.ca/aboriginal
twitter.com/Cen4EUStudies
Joan DeBardeleben, Director
joan_debardeleben@carleton.ca

Discovery Centre
MacOdrum Library, 4th Fl.
Ottawa, ON K1S 5B6
Tel: 613-520-2600; *Fax:* 613-520-2600
discovery.centre@carleton.ca
carleton.ca/discoverycentre
www.facebook.com/CarletonUniversityDiscoveryCentre
twitter.com/CU_Discovery
www.tumblr.com/blog/carletondiscoverycentre
Alan Steele, Director

Carleton Technology & Training Centre

Minto Centre for Advanced Studies in Engineering

Educational Development Centre (EDC)
Dunton Tower
#410, 1125 Colonel By Dr., Ottawa, ON K1S 5B6
Tel: 613-520-4433; *Fax:* 613-520-4456
edc@carleton.ca
carleton.ca/edc
Patrick Lyons, Director
patrick.lyons@carleton.ca

Centre for Initiatives in Education (CIE)
Dunton Tower
#1516, 1125 Colonel By Dr., Ottawa, ON K1S 5B6
Tel: 613-520-6624; *Fax:* 613-520-2515
cie@carleton.ca
www.carleton.ca/cie
Timothy Pychyl, Director
Tim.Pychyl@carleton.ca

National Wildlife Research Centre

Canada-India Centre for Excellence in Science, Technology, Trade & Policy
River Building
1125 Colonel By Dr., #1401R-F, Ottawa, ON K1S 5B6
Tel: 613-520-7873
india@carleton.ca
www.carleton.ca/india
twitter.com/cice_carleton
Jaswinder Kaur, Manager
jaswinder.kaur@carleton.ca

Ottawa: Dominican University College
Collège Universitaire Dominicain
Also known as: Dominican College of Philosophy & Theology
96 Empress Ave., Ottawa, ON K1R 7G3, Canada
Tel: 613-233-5696
info@dominicancollege.ca
www.collegedominicain.ca
www.facebook.com/63353836890
twitter.com/DUCOttawa
Full Time Equivalency: 160
Ousmane Diallo, Academic Services Manager
Maxime Allard, President & Regent of Studies
maxime.allard@udominicaine.ca
Peter Foy, Vice-President, Finance & Admin, & Secretary-Treasurer
peter.foy@dominicanu.ca
Jean-Francois Méthot, Vice-President of Studies, 613-233-5696, ext. 323
jf.methot@dominicanu.ca
Francis Peddle, Vice-President of Academic Affairs & Registrar
francis.peddle@dominicanu.ca
Eduardo Andujar, Dean, Faculty of Philosophy
eduardo.andujar@dominicanu.ca
Hervé Tremblay, Dean, Faculty of Theology
herve.tremblay@udominicaine.ca

Ottawa: Saint Paul University
Université Saint-Paul
223 Main St., Ottawa, ON K1S 1C4, Canada
Tel: 613-236-1393; *Fax:* 613-782-3005
Toll-Free: 1-800-637-6859
www.ustpaul.ca
www.facebook.com/143697609023948
twitter.com/ustpaul_ca
www.linkedin.com/company/saint-paul-university
www.youtube.com/user/uspottawa
Full Time Equivalency: 820
Chantal Beauvais, Rector
rectrice-rector@ustpaul.ca
Jean-Marc Barrette, Vice-Rector, Academic & Research
Normand Beaulieu, Vice-Rector, Administration
Yvan Mathieu, Dean, Faculty of Theology

Faculties

Canon Law
ustpaul.ca/canon-law
Anne Asselin, Dean

Faculty of Human Sciences
Tel: 613-236-1393; *Toll-Free:* 800-637-6859
humansciences@ustpaul.ca
Manal Guirguis-Younger, Dean

Public Ethics & Philosophy
ustpaul.ca/ethics-philosophy

Theology
ustpaul.ca/theology
Andrea Spatafora, Dean

Centre for Women & Christian Traditions
223 Main St., Ottawa, ON K1S 1C4
Tel: 613-236-1393
ustpaul.ca/en/centre-for-women-and-christian-traditions

Research Centre for the Religious History of Canada
223 Main St., Ottawa, ON K1S 1C4
Tel: 613-236-1393
ustpaul.ca/en/research-centre-for-religious-history-of-canada

Ottawa: University of Ottawa
Université d'Ottawa
Also known as: uOttawa
75 Laurier Ave. East, Ottawa, ON K1N 6N5, Canada
Tel: 613-562-5700; *Fax:* 613-562-5103
Toll-Free: 1-877-868-8292
www.uottawa.ca
www.facebook.com/uottawa
twitter.com/uottawa
www.linkedin.com/edu/school?id=10858
www.youtube.com/uOttawa
Full Time Equivalency: 42700; *Number of Employees:* 5,000
Calin Rovinescu, Chancellor
Jacques Frémont, President & Vice-Chancellor
Michel Laurier, Vice-President, Academic & Provost, 613-562-5737
vpacademic@uOttawa.ca
Mona Nemer, Vice-President, Research
Louis de Melo, Vice-President, External Relations
Marc Joyal, Vice-President, Resources
Diane Davidson, Vice-President, Governance

Faculties

Arts
Antoni Lewkowicz, B.A., M.A., Ph.D., Dean

Civil Law
Sébastien Grammond, Dean

Common Law
Nathalie Des Rosiers, Dean

Education
Michel Laurier, Dean

Engineering
Claude Lagué, Dean

Graduate & Postdoctoral Studies
Ross Hastings, Interim Dean

Health Sciences
Hélène Perrault, Dean

Medicine
Jacques Bradwejn, Dean

Science
Steve F. Perry, Dean

Social Sciences
Marcel Mérette, Dean

Schools
Official Languages and Bilingualism Institute (OLBI)
#130, 70 Laurier Ave. East, Ottawa, ON K1N 6N5
Tel: 613-562-5743; *Fax:* 613-562-5126
olbi@uOttawa.ca
www.olbi.uottawa.ca

Telfer School of Management
55 Laurier Ave. East, Ottawa, ON K1N 6N5
Tel: 613-562-5731
info@telfer.uOttawa.ca
www.telfer.uottawa.ca
www.facebook.com/Telfer.uOttawa
www.twitter.com/Telfer_uOttawa
www.youtube.com/TelferSchool
Enrollment: 4200; *Number of Employees:* 200; *Note:* Degree programs in business and healthcare management.
François Julien, Dean, 613-562-5800, ext. 5815
julien@telfer.uOttawa.ca

Peterborough: Trent University
1600 West Bank Dr., Peterborough, ON K9J 7B8, Canada
Tel: 705-748-1011; *Toll-Free:* 1-855-698-7368
communications@trentu.ca
www.trentu.ca
www.facebook.com/trentuniversity
twitter.com/TrentUniversity
www.linkedin.com/company/trent-university
www.youtube.com/user/trentUniversity
Full Time Equivalency: 8006
Bryan P. Davies, Chair
Don Tapscott, Chancellor
Leo Groarke, President
Gary Boire, Vice-President Academic & Provost
Steven Pillar, Vice-President Administration
Tracy Al-Idrissi, Registrar
Deb deBruijn, University Secretary
Bruce Cater, Dean of Arts & Science - Social Science
Hugh Elton, Dean of Arts & Science - Humanities
Holger Hintelmann, Dean of Arts & Science - Science

Frost Centre fo Canadian Studies & Indigenous Studies
103 Kerr House, Trail College
266 Dublin St., Peterborough, ON K9H 7P4
Tel: 705-748-1750; *Fax:* 705-748-1801
www.trentu.ca/frostcentre
www.facebook.com/frostcentre
twitter.com/TrentFrostCtr
John Milloy, Director
jmilloy@trentu.ca

Water Quality Centre (WQC)
Department of Environmental & Resource Studies
Peterborough, ON K9J 7B8
Tel: 708-748-1011
www.trentu.ca/wqc
Dirk Wallschläger, Director
dwallsch@trentu.ca

Trent University Archaeological Research Centre (TUARC)
c/o Department of Anthropology & Archaeology
1600 West Bank Dr., Peterborough, ON K9J 7B8
Tel: 708-748-1011; *Fax:* 705-748-1913
tuarc@trentu.ca
www.trentu.ca/tuarc
Jocelyn Williams, Director
jocelynwilliams@trentu.ca

St Catharines: Brock University
500 Glenridge Ave., St Catharines, ON L2S 3A1, Canada
Tel: 905-688-5550; *Fax:* 905-688-2789
www.brocku.ca
www.facebook.com/brockuniversity
twitter.com/brockuniversity
www.linkedin.com/companies/brock-university
www.youtube.com/brockuvideo
Full Time Equivalency: 18688; *Number of Employees:* 597 faculty
Dr Ned Goodman, Chancellor
Dr Jack N. Lightstone, President & Vice-Chancellor, 905-688-5550, ext. 3322
Neil McCartney, Provost/Vice-Pres., Academic
Brian Hutchings, Vice-Pres., Finance/Admin.
Gary Libben, Vice-Pres., Research
Barb Anderson, Registrar, ext. 3566
bdavis@brocku.ca
Chuck MacLean, Manager Purchasing Services, ext. 3746
cmaclean@brocku.ca

Faculty of Education
www.facebook.com/144363215666128
www.twitter.com/brockeducation
Fiona Blaikie, Dean, 905-688-5550, ext. 3712
fblaikie@brocku.ca

Faculty of Humanities
Douglas Kneale, Dean
jdkneale@brocku.ca

Faculty of Social Sciences
Ingrid Makus, Acting Dean, 905-688-5550, ext. 4077
imakus@brocku.ca

Faculty of Mathematics & Sciences
Ejaz Ahmed, Dean, ext. 3421
dean.fms@brocku.ca

Faculty of Applied Health Sciences
facebook.com/brockfahs
twitter.com/brockfahs
www.youtube.com/user/brockappliedhealthsc
James Mandigo, Interim Dean, 905-688-5550, ext. 4789
jmandigo@brocku.ca

Faculty of Graduate Studies
Tel: 905-688-5550; *Fax:* 905-688-0748
gradadmissions@brocku.ca
www.facebook.com/BrockGradStudies
twitter.com/BrockGradStudy
Michael Plyley, Dean
mplyley@brocku.ca

Schools
Goodman School of Business
facebook.com/GoodmanSchool
twitter.com/GoodmanSchool
www.linkedin.com/company/goodman-school-of-business
instagram.com/GoodmanSchool
Don Cyr, Dean, Goodman School of Business, 905-688-5550, ext. 4006
dcyr@brocku.ca

Campuses
Hamilton Campus
1842 King St. East, Hamilton, ON L8K 1V7
Tel: 905-547-3555

Sudbury: Huntington University
935 Ramsey Lake Rd., Sudbury, ON P3E 2C6, Canada
Tel: 705-673-4126; *Fax:* 705-673-6917
Toll-Free: 800-461-6366
info@huntingtonuniversity.com
huntingtonu.ca
www.facebook.com/pages/Huntington-University/162876393781377
twitter.com/HuntingtonUni
instagram.com/huntingtonuniversity
Note: Liberal Arts University specializing in Communication Studies, Ethics, Gerontology, Religious studies and Theology.

Centres/Institutes
Centre for Holistic Health
935 Ramsey Lake Rd., Sudbury, ON P3E 2C6
huntingtonu.ca/centres/centre-for-holistic-health

Canadian Institute for Studies in Aging (CISA)
935 Ramsey Lake Rd., Sudbury, ON P3E 2C6
huntingtonu.ca/centres/canadian-institute-for-studies-in-aging-cisa
Krishnan Venkataraman, Director
kvenkataraman@huntingtonu.ca

Lougheed Teaching & Learning Centre of Excellence
935 Ramsey Lake Rd., Sudbury, ON P3E 2C6
huntingtonu.ca/centres/the-lougheed-teaching-and-learning-centre
Lorraine Mercer, Director
lmercer@huntingtonu.ca

Sudbury: Laurentian University (Sudbury) (LU) Université Laurentienne (Sudbury)
935 Ramsey Lake Rd., Sudbury, ON P3E 2C6, Canada
Tel: 705-675-1151; *Toll-Free:* 800-461-4030
explore@laurentian.ca
www.laurentian.ca
www.facebook.com/laurentian
twitter.com/laurentianu
www.linkedin.com/company/laurentian-university
www.youtube.com/laurentianuniversity
Full Time Equivalency: 9515; *Note:* Teaching is in French & English. Certain faculties offer parallel programs in both languages.
Dominic Giroux, MBA, President
Robert Kerr, Vice-President & Provost
Carol McAulay, Vice-President
Rui Wang, Vice-President
Terez Klotz, Execurive Director, Human Resources & Org Dev
Serge Demers, Registrar
Chris Mercer, Executive Director, Student Life
Sara Kunto, University Secretary & General Counsel

Faculties
Social Work

Faculty of Professional Schools

Earth & Forensic Science

Schools
Commerce

Education, English Concurrent
Roger Couture, Dean

Éducation (Français)

Engineering
Note: Includes Natural Resource, Chemical, Mining & Mineral Resource Engineering
Osman Abou-Rabia, Dean

Alumni Association
Tel: 705-675-4818; *Fax:* 705-671-3825
alumni@laurentian.ca
laurentian.ca/alumni
www.facebook.com/laurentian.alumni
Diane Mihalek, President

Human Kinetics
Céline Boudreau-Larivière, Director

Nursing
nursing@laurentian.ca
Sylvie Laroque, Director

Sports Administration
Anthony Church, Director
AChurch@laurentian.ca

Affiliations
University of Sudbury
Université de Sudbury
935 Ramsey Lake Rd., Sudbury, ON P3E 2C6, Canada
Tel: 705-673-5661
usudburyalumni@usudbury.ca
usudbury.ca
www.facebook.com/260336550720945
twitter.com/UofSudbury
Note: Founded in 1913 as Collège du Sacré-Coeur, the University of Sudbury operates in the Jesuit tradition. The bilingual university is committed to the English, French, & First Nations cultures. Courses include Religious Studies, Philosophy, Communications, French-Canadian Folklore, & Native Studies.
Gérald Michel, Chancellor
Josée Forest-Niesing, Chair, Board of Regents
Dr. Pierre Zundel, Ph.D., President & Vice-Chancellor
presidentrecteur@usudbury.ca
Sylvie Renault, H.B.Com., Registrar & Director, Recruitment & Communications
srenault@usudbury.ca
Shelley R. Machum, B.Com., C.A., Treasurer & Director, Administrative Services
smachum@usudbury.ca
David Shulist, Director, Spiritual Services
dshulist@usudbury.ca
Paul Laverdure, Ph.D., Director, Library Services
plaverdure@usudbury.ca

Huntington University
935 Ramsey Lake Rd., Sudbury, ON P3E 2C6
Tel: 705-673-4126; *Fax:* 705-673-6917
Toll-Free: 800-461-6366
huntingtonu.ca
www.facebook.com/pages/Huntington-University/162876393781377
twitter.com/HuntingtonUni
www.pinterest.com/huniversity
Dr. Kevin McCormick, President & Vice-Chancellor

Thorneloe University at Laurentian University
935 Ramsey Lake Rd., Sudbury, ON P3E 2C6, Canada
Tel: 705-673-1730; *Fax:* 705-673-4979
Toll-Free: 1-866-846-7635
info@thorneloe.ca
www.thorneloe.ca
www.facebook.com/ThorneloeUni
twitter.com/ThorneloeUni
Note: Affiliated with the Anglican Church, Thorneloe University features the departments of Religious Studies, Classical Studies, Theatre Arts, & Women's Studies.
Robert Derrenbacker, President

Centres/Institutes
Centre for Evolutionary Ecology & Ethical Conservation
935 Ramsey Lake Rd., Sudbury, ON P3E 2C6
laurentian.ca/centre-evolutionary-ecology-and-ethical-conservation

Centre for Humanities Research & Creativity
L-707 R.D. Parker Building
935 Ramsey Lake Rd., Sudbury, ON P3E 2C6
Tel: 705-675-1151
laurentian.ca/centre-humanities-research-and-creativity
Gillian Crozier, Director
gcrozier@laurentian.ca

Centre for Mining Materials Research
935 Ramsey Lake Rd., Sudbury, ON P3E 2C6
laurentian.ca/centre-mining-materials-research
Louis Mercier, Director

Centre for Research in Human Development
935 Ramsey Lake Rd., Sudbury, ON P3E 2C6
laurentian.ca/centre-research-human-development

Centre for Research in Occupational Safety & Health
935 Ramsey Lake Rd., Sudbury, ON P3E 2C6
laurentian.ca/centre-research-occupational-safety-and-health
Tammy Eger, Director
teger@laurentian.ca

Centre for Research in Social Justice & Policy
935 Ramsey Lake Rd., Sudbury, ON P3E 2C6
laurentian.ca/centre-research-social-justice-and-policy

Centre for Rural & Northern Health Research
935 Ramsey Lake Rd., Sudbury, ON P3E 2C6
laurentian.ca/centre-rural-and-northern-health-research

Cooperative Freshwater Ecology Unit
935 Ramsey Lake Rd., Sudbury, ON P3E 2C6
laurentian.ca/cooperative-freshwater-ecology-unit

Evaluating Children's Health Outcomes Research Centre
935 Ramsey Lake Rd., Sudbury, ON P3E 2C6
laurentian.ca/node/378
Nancy Young, Director

Mining Innovation, Rehabilitation & Applied Research Corporation (MIRARCO)
935 Ramsey Lake Rd., Sudbury, ON P3E 2C6
laurentian.ca/mirarco

International Centre for Interdisciplinary Research in the Human Sciences
935 Ramsey Lake Rd., Sudbury, ON P3E 2C6
laurentian.ca/ICIRHS

Institut Franco-Ontarien
935 Ramsey Lake Rd., Sudbury, ON P3E 2C6
laurentian.ca/institut-franco-ontarien

Institute for Northern Ontario Research & Development
935 Ramsey Lake Rd., Sudbury, ON P3E 2C6
laurentian.ca/institute-northern-ontario-research-and-developme nt
David Robinson, Director

Institute for Sports Marketing
935 Ramsey Lake Rd., Sudbury, ON P3E 2C6
laurentian.ca/institute-sports-marketing
Ann Pegoraro, Director

International Economic Policy Institute
935 Ramsey Lake Rd., Sudbury, ON P3E 2C6
laurentian.ca/international-economic-policy-institute
Louis-Phillipe Rochon, Director

International Centre for Interdisciplinary Research in Law
935 Ramsey Lake Rd., Sudbury, ON P3E 2C6
laurentian.ca/international-centre-interdisciplinary-research-law
Henri Pallard, Director

Mineral Exploration Research Centre (MERC)
935 Ramsey Lake Rd., Sudbury, ON P3E 2C6
merc.laurentian.ca

Sudbury Neutrino Observation Laboratory (SNOLAB)
935 Ramsey Lake Rd., Sudbury, ON P3E 2C6
laurentian.ca/snolab
Nigel Smith, Director

Sudbury: Thorneloe University
935 Ramsey Lake Rd., Sudbury, ON P3E 2C6
Tel: 705-673-1730; *Fax:* 705-673-4979
Toll-Free: 866-846-7635
info@thorneloe.ca
www.thorneloe.ca
www.facebook.com/ThorneloeUni
twitter.com/ThorneloeUni
Note: Thorneloe offers diploma, certificates & bachelor degree. The University is partners with Laurentian University & Cambrian College.

Sudbury: University of Sudbury
935 Ramsey Lake Rd., Sudbury, ON P3E 2C6, Canada
Tel: 705-673-5661
usudburyalumni@usudbury.ca
www.usudbury.ca
www.facebook.com/260336550720945
twitter.com/UofSudbury
www.linkedin.com/groups?gid=4419839

Faculties
Folklore et ethnologie
Études journalistiques
Indigenous Studies
Philosophy
Religious Studies

Thunder Bay: Lakehead University
955 Oliver Rd., Thunder Bay, ON P7B 5E1, Canada
Tel: 807-343-8110; *Fax:* 807-343-8023
www.lakeheadu.ca
www.facebook.com/lakeheaduniversity
twitter.com/mylakehead
www.linkedin.com/company/lakehead-university
www.youtube.com/lakeheaduniversity
Full Time Equivalency: 7848; *Number of Employees:* 2567
Derek Burney, Chancellor
Brian Stevenson, President & Vice-Chancellor
Andrea Tarsitano, Registrar
Anne Deighton, University Librarian
Rita Blais, Associate Vice-President, Financial Services
Kathy Pozihun, Vice-President, Administration & Finance
Moira McPherson, Provost & Vice-President, Academic
Andrew Dean, Vice-President, Research, Economic Development & Innovation
Kerrie-Lee Clarke, Vice-Provost
Deb Comuzzi, Vice-President, External Relations

Faculties
Business Administration
Bahram Dadgostar, Dean
Education
John O'Meara, Dean
Engineering
David Barnett, Dean
Natural Resources Management
Ulf Runesson, Dean
Graduate & International Studies
Christine Gottardo, Interim Dean
Northern Ontario School of Medicine
www.nosm.ca
Roger Strasser, Dean
Science & Environmental Studies
Todd Randall, Acting Dean
Bora Laskin Faculty of Law
Angelique EagleWoman, Dean

Schools
Kinesiology
Joey Farrell, Director
Nursing
Karen Poole, Director
Outdoor Recreation, Parks & Tourism
Rhonda Koster, Director
Social Work
Margaret McKee, Director

Centres/Institutes
Lakehead University's Centre for Analytical Services (LUCAS)
Balmoral Bldg.
#1012, 955 Oliver Rd., Thunder Bay, ON P7B 5E1
Tel: 807-343-8590
lucas.lakeheadu.ca
Francis Appoh, Director

Centre for Education and Research on Aging & Health
955 Oliver Rd., Thunder Bay, ON P7B 5E1
Tel: 807-766-7271; *Fax:* 807-766-7222
cerah@lakeheadu.ca
cerah.lakeheadu.ca
Ian Newhouse, Director
ian.newhouse@lakeheadu.ca

Centre of Excellence for Sustainable Mining & Exploration
955 Oliver Rd., Thunder Bay, ON P7B 5E1
Tel: 807-343-8329; *Fax:* 807-346-7853
cesme.lakeheadu.ca
Pete Hollings, Director

Instructional Development Centre
955 Oliver Rd., Thunder Bay, ON P7B 5E1
Tel: 807-343-8059
idc.lakeheadu.ca
Jane Nicholas, Director
jnichola@lakeheadu.ca

Centre for Place and Sustainability Studies
955 Oliver Rd., Thunder Bay, ON P7B 5E1
Tel: 807-766-7193
www.placecentre.org
David Greenwood, Director
david.greenwood@lakeheadu.ca

Centre of Education and Research on Positive Youth Development
955 Oliver Rd., Thunder Bay, ON P7B 5E1
Tel: 807-343-8196; *Fax:* 807-346-7991
childrenandadolescents.lakeheadu.ca
Andrew Friesen, Grant Facilitator

Centre for Research on Safe Driving
#BB1043, 955 Oliver Rd., Thunder Bay, ON P7B 5E1
Tel: 807-766-7256; *Fax:* 807-346-7707
crsd@lakeheadu.ca
crsd.lakeheadu.ca
Hillary Maxwell, Research Coordinator
hmaxwell@lakeheadu.ca

Toronto: Innis College
2 Sussex Ave., Toronto, ON M5S 1J6, Canada
Tel: 416-978-2513; *Fax:* 416-978-5503
registrar.innis@utoronto.ca
www.utoronto.ca/innis
www.facebook.com/innisregistrar
twitter.com/innisregistrar
Full Time Equivalency: 1480; *Note:* Constituent college of the University of Toronto
Charlie Keil, Principal, 416-978-2510
principal.innis@utoronto.ca
Donald Boere, Assistant Principal & Registrar, 416-978-2513
donald.boere@utoronto.ca

Toronto: Knox College
59 St. George St., Toronto, ON M5S 2E6, Canada
Tel: 416-978-4500; *Fax:* 416-971-2133
knox.college@utoronto.ca
www.knox.utoronto.ca
www.facebook.com/KnoxCollege.CA
twitter.com/knox_college
Note: Theological college at the University of Toronto affiliated with the Presbyterian Church in Canada

Toronto: Massey College
4 Devonshire Pl., Toronto, ON M5S 2E1, Canada
Tel: 416-978-2895
porter@masseycollege.ca
masseycollege.ca
www.facebook.com/MasseyCollege
twitter.com/MasseyCollege
www.youtube.com/MasseyCollege
Note: A graduate students' residence associated with the University of Toronto.

Toronto: OCAD University (OCAD)
Also known as: Ontario College of Art & Design
100 McCaul St., Toronto, ON M5T 1W1, Canada
Tel: 416-977-6000; *Fax:* 416-977-0235
general@ocad.ca
www.ocad.ca
www.facebook.com/ocaduniversity
twitter.com/OCAD
Full Time Equivalency: 4560
Sara Diamond, President
Christine Bovis-Cnossen, Vice-President, Academic
cboviscnossen@ocadu.ca
Jill Birch, Vice-President, Development & Alumni Relations, 416-977-6000, ext. 4887
jbirch@ocadu.ca
Helmut Reichenbächer, Associate Vice-President, Research, 416-977-6000, ext. 464
hreichenbacher@ocadu.ca
Peter Fraser, Director, Finance
Nicky Davis, Director, Human Resources
Geeta Sharma, Director, Safety & Risk Management

Faculties
Faculty of Art
Dr. Vladimir Spicanovic, Dean
Faculty of Design
Dr. Gayle Nicoll, Dean

Faculty of Liberal Arts & Sciences
Langill Caroline, Interim Dean

Graduate Studies
Helmut Reichenbächer, Dean, 416-977-6000, ext. 464
hreichenbacher@ocadu.ca

Toronto: Ontario Institute for Studies in Education
252 Bloor St. West, Toronto, ON M5S 1V6
Tel: 416-978-1110; *Fax:* 416-926-4725
www.oise.utoronto.ca
www.facebook.com/OISEUofT
twitter.com/OISENews
Julia O'Sullivan, Dean

Toronto: Ryerson University
350 Victoria St., Toronto, ON M5B 2K3, Canada
Tel: 416-979-5000
inquire@ryerson.ca
www.ryerson.ca
www.facebook.com/ryersonu
twitter.com/ryersonu
www.linkedin.com/company/ryerson-university
www.youtube.com/user/RyersonUTube
Full Time Equivalency: 36970
Janice Fukakusa, Chair
Lawrence S. Bloomberg, Chancellor
Sheldon Levy, President & Vice-Chancellor
Sheldon Levy, Provost & Vice-President
Michael Dewson, Vice-Provost
Dr. Linda Grayson, Vice-President
Keith Alnwick, Registrar
Janice Winton, Executive Director
Marion Creery, Sr. Director
Renée Lemieux, Sr. Director
Shirley Lewchuk, Secretary of the Board of Governors
Ian Marlatt, Sr. Director
Peter Lukasiewicz, Vice-Chair
Dr. Anastasios (Tas) Venetsanopoulos, Vice-President
Judith Sandys, Assoc. Vice-President

Faculties
Faculty of Arts
help@arts.ryerson.ca
www.ryerson.ca/arts
Dr. Carla Cassidy, Dean

Ted Rogers School of Management
tedrogersschool.ca
www.facebook.com/TedRogersSchool
twitter.com/TRSMRyersonU
Note: Programs include Business Management; Technology Management; Hospitality & Tourism Management; Retail Management & Graduate Programs
Dr. Ken Jones, Ph.D., Dean

Faculty of Communication & Design (FCAD)
R.C.C. 320 - 80 Gould St.
Tel: 416-979-5348; *Fax:* 416-979-5285
www.ryerson.ca/fcad
Dr. Daniel Doz, Dean

Faculty of Community Services (FCS)
Tel: 416-979-5034
ugeorge@ryerson.ca
www.ryerson.ca/fcs
Dr. Usha George, Ph.D., Dean

Faculty of Engineering & Architectural Science (FEAS)
245 Church St.
www.ryerson.ca/feas
Dr. Mohamed Lachemi, Interim Dean

Research & Innovation
#1 Dundas St. West, Toronto, ON M5G 1Z3
Tel: 416-797-5042; *Fax:* 416-797-5336
www.ryerson.ca/research
twitter.com/Ryersonresearch
linkedin.com/company/ryerson-university-research-and-innovation
Steven Liss, Assoc. Dean

Faculty of Science
Tel: 416-979-5251
www.ryerson.ca/science
Zouheir Fawaz, Assoc. Dean

The G. Raymond Chang School of Continuing Education
Also known as: The Chang School
Tel: 416-979-5035
ce@ryerson.ca
ce-online.ryerson.ca/ce
Enrollment: 70000
Anita Shilton, Dean

Graduate Studies
www.ryerson.ca/graduate

Centres/Institutes
Ryerson Centre for Immigration & Settlement (RCIS)
Jorgenson Hall
#620, 350 Victoria St., Toronto, ON M5B 2K3
rcis@ryerson.ca
www.ryerson.ca/rcis
twitter.com/rc1s
www.youtube.com/user/rcis01
Herald Bauder, Academic Director
hbauder@ryerson.ca

Centre for Labour Management Relations (CLMR)
Ted Rogers School of Management
#2-027, 55 Dundas St. West, Toronto, ON M5G 2C5
Tel: 416-979-5000
clmr@ryerson.ca
www.ryerson.ca/clmr
twitter.com/RyersonCLMR
Buzz Hargrove, Executive Director
buzzhargrove@rogers.com

Centre for the Study of Commercial Activity (CSCA)
350 Victoria St., Toronto, ON M5B 2K3
Tel: 416-979-5000
www.csca.ryerson.ca
Tony Hernandez, Director
thernand@research.ryerson.ca

Ryerson Law Research Centre
350 Victoria St., Toronto, ON M5B 2K3
Tel: 416-979-5000
lawcentre@ryerson.ca
www.ryerson.ca/lawcentre
twitter.com/LawCentreRye
Avner Levin, Academic Director

Ryerson Centre for Cloud and Context-Aware Computing (RC4)
#1000, 10 Dundas St. East, Toronto, ON M5B 2K3
Tel: 416-979-5000
rc4@ryerson.ca
rc4.ryerson.ca
www.facebook.com/RyersonRC4
twitter.com/RyersonRC4
www.youtube.com/user/RC4Ryerson

Ryerson University Analytical Centre (RUAC)
350 Victoria St., Toronto, ON M5B 2K3
Tel: 416-979-5000; *Fax:* 416-979-5044
www.ryerson.ca/ruac
Steve Wylie, Director

Toronto: University of Guelph Humber
207 Humber College Blvd., Toronto, ON M9W 5L7
Tel: 416-798-1331; *Fax:* 416-798-3606
info@guelphhumber.ca
www.guelphhumber.ca
www.facebook.com/uoguelphhumber
twitter.com/guelphhumber
www.youtube.com/chooseguelphhumber
Dr. John Walsh, Vice-Provost, Chief Academic & Executive Officer
Nancy Birch, Department Head, Library Services
Grant Kerr, Registrar
Gabrielle Bernardi-Dengo, Department Head, Finance & Administration Services

Toronto: University of Toronto
Also known as: U of T
Old Name: King's College
563 Spadina Cres., Toronto, ON M5S 2J7
Tel: 416-978-2011
www.utoronto.ca
Other Information: 416-978-7669
www.facebook.com/universitytoronto
twitter.com/uoft
www.linkedin.com/company/university-of-toronto
www.youtube.com/user/universitytoronto
Full Time Equivalency: 83012; *Note:* Founded in 1827, the University of Toronto has over 700 undergraduate programs across three campuses in the Greater Toronto Area, & offers the most courses of any University in Canada. The University contributes to the country's research landscape in both the scientific & medical fields. The library network is the largest collection in the country. U of T is home to more students & faculty than any other in Canada.
The Hon. Michael Wilson, Chancellor
Meric S. Gertler, President
Cheryl Regehr, Vice-President & Provost
Sioban Nelson, Vice-Provost, Academic Programs
Jill Matus, Vice-Provost, Students & First-Entry Divisions
Locke Rowe, Vice-Provost, Graduate Research & Education
Catharine Whiteside, Vice-Provost, Relations with Health Care Institutions
Scott Mabury, Vice-President, University Operations
Lucy Fromowitz, Assistant Vice-President, Student Life
Sally Garner, Executive Director, Planning & Budget
Joan E. Foley, University Ombudsperson
Bryn MacPherson, Assistant Vice-President
Shirley Hoy, Chair of the Governing Council
Sheila Brown, CFO
Judith Wolfson, Vice-President, University Relations

Faculties
Faculty of Applied Science & Engineering
35 St. George St., Toronto, ON M5S 1A4
Tel: 416-978-5896
engineering@ecf.utoronto.ca
www.engineering.utoronto.ca
www.facebook.com/uoftengineering
twitter.com/uoftengineering
vimeo.com/uoftengineering
Prof. Cristina Amon, Dean

John H. Daniels Faculty of Architecture, Landscape & Design
230 College St., Toronto, ON M5T 1R2
Tel: 416-978-5038
enquiry@daniels.utoronto.ca
www.daniels.utoronto.ca
www.facebook.com/UofTDaniels
twitter.com/UofTDaniels
www.youtube.com/uoftdaniels
Richard M. Sommer, Dean

Faculty of Arts & Science
Sidney Smith Hall
100 St. George St., Toronto, ON M5S 3G3
Tel: 416-978-3384
ask@artsci.utoronto.ca
www.artsci.utoronto.ca
David Cameron, Dean

Faculty of Dentistry
124 Edward St., Toronto, ON M5G 1G6
Tel: 416-979-4900; *Fax:* 416-979-4936
www.dentistry.utoronto.ca
www.facebook.com/UofTDentistry
twitter.com/UofTDentistry
Daniel Haas, Dean

Faculty of Forestry
33 Willcrocks St., Toronto, ON M5S 3B3
Tel: 416-978-5751
www.forestry.utoronto.ca
Mohini M. Sain, Dean

Faculty of Information
Claude Bissell Building
140 St. George St., Tornto, ON M5S 3G6
Tel: 416-978-3264; *Fax:* 416-978-5762
inquire.ischool@utoronto.ca
www.ischool.utoronto.ca
www.facebook.com/171445139536113
twitter.com/ischool_TO
www.youtube.com/user/iSchoolUofT
Dr. Ross Seamus, Dean

Faculty of Law
84 Queen's Park, Toronto, ON M5S 2C5
Tel: 416-978-0210; *Fax:* 416-978-7899
www.law.utoronto.ca
twitter.com/utlaw
www.linkedin.com/company/university-of-toronto-faculty-of-law
www.youtube.com/user/UTorontoLaw
Jutta Brunnée, Interim Dean

Rotman School of Management
105 St. George St., Toronto, ON M5S 3E6
Tel: 416-978-5703; *Fax:* 416-978-5433
www.rotman.utoronto.ca
www.facebook.com/RotmanSchoolOfManagement
twitter.com/rotmanschool
www.linkedin.com/groups?home=&gid=2631
www.youtube.com/user/RotmanSchool
Tiff Macklem, Dean
Peter H. Pauly, Vice-Dean
pauly@rotman.utoronto.ca
Kenneth Corts, Associate Dean, Undergraduate Education
kenneth.corts@rotman.utoronto.ca
Joel Baum, Associate Dean, Faculty
jbaum@rotman.utoronto.ca
Beatrix Dart, Associate Dean, Executive Programs
bdart@rotman.utoronto.ca
Anita McGahan, Associate Dean, Research
anita.mcgahan@rotman.utoronto.ca
Mihnea Moldoveanu, Associate Dean, Full-Time MBA
micamo@rotman.utoronto.ca

Faculty of Medicine
Medical Sciences Bldg.
#2109, 1 King's College Circle, Toronto, ON M5S 1A8
Tel: 416-978-6585
discovery.commons@utoronto.ca.
www.facmed.utoronto.ca
www.facebook.com/UofTMedicine
twitter.com/uoftmedicine
www.youtube.com/user/UofTMed
Catharine Whiteside, MD, PhD, FRCP (C), Dean

Faculty of Music
Edward Johnson Bldg.
80 Queen's Park, Toronto, ON M5S 3C5
Tel: 416-978-3750; *Fax:* 416-976-3353
www.music.utoronto.ca
www.facebook.com/UofTMusic
notes.music@utoronto.ca
Don McLean, Dean
dean.music@utoronto.ca

Lawrence S. Bloomberg Faculty of Nursing
#130, 155 College St., Toronto, ON M5T 1P8
Tel: 416-978-2392
communications.nursing@utoronto.ca
bloomberg.nursing.utoronto.ca
www.facebook.com/UofTNursing
twitter.com/UofTNursing
www.youtube.com/user/uoftnursing
Linda Johnston, Dean

Ontario Institute for Studies in Education (OISE)
Also known as: Faculty of Education
252 Bloor St. West, Toronto, ON M5S 1V6
Tel: 416-978-1628; *Fax:* 416-323-9964
communications@oise.utoronto.ca
www.oise.utoronto.ca
www.facebook.com/OISEUofT
twitter.com/OISENews
Julia O'Sullivan, Dean

Leslie Dan Faculty of Pharmacy
144 College St., Toronto, ON M5S 3M2
Tel: 416-978-2889; *Fax:* 416-978-8511
adm.phm@utoronto.ca
www.pharmacy.utoronto.ca
www.facebook.com/LeslieDanFacultyOfPharmacy
twitter.com/UofTPharmacy
Heather Boon, Dean

Faculty of Kinesiology & Phisical Education
#102, 55 Harbord St., Toronto, ON M5S 2W6
Tel: 416-978-4796; *Fax:* 416-971-2118
www.physical.utoronto.ca
twitter.com/UofTKPE
Ira Jacobs, Dean

School of Graduate Studies (SGS)
63 St. George St., Toronto, ON M5S 2Z9
Tel: 416-978-6614
graduate.information@utoronto.ca
www.sgs.utoronto.ca
www.facebook.com/GradlifeUofT
twitter.com/UofTGradlife
Locke Rowe, Dean

Factor-Inwentash Faculty of Social Work
246 Bloor St. West, Toronto, ON M5S 1V4
Tel: 416-978-6314; *Fax:* 416-978-7072
fifsw.phdsa@utoronto.ca
socialwork.utoronto.ca
www.facebook.com/PhDSAFIFSW
Faye Wishna, Dean

Munk School of Global Affairs
Also known as: Munk
315 Bloor St. West, Toronto, ON M5S 1A3
Tel: 416-946-8900
munkschool@utoronto.ca
munkschool.utoronto.ca
www.facebook.com/munkschool
twitter.com/munkschool
vimeo.com/munkschool
Prof. Janice Gross Stein, Director

Transitional Year Program
123 St. George St., Toronto, ON M5S 2E8
Tel: 416-978-6832; *Fax:* 416-971-1397
typ.info@utoronto.ca
www.utoronto.ca/typ
Note: Sold to Metrus Development in 2008, operated by The Royal Astronomical Society of Canada
Francis Ahia, Director

Affiliations

University of Toronto Mississauga (UTM)
Also known as: Erindale College
3359 Mississauga Rd., Mississauga, ON L5L 1C6, Canada
Tel: 905-569-4455
news.utm@utoronto.ca
www.utm.utoronto.ca
Other Information: Admissions, Phone: 905-828-5400; Public Affairs: 905-828-5214
www.facebook.com/UTMississauga
twitter.com/UofTMississauga
www.linkedin.com/groups?gid=135733
www.youtube.com/user/UTMississauga
Full Time Equivalency: 13900; *Number of Employees:* 2000
Deep Saini, Vice-President & Principal, 905-828-5211
principal.utm@utoronto.ca
Amrita Daniere, Vice-Principal, Academic & Dean, 905-828-3719
vpdean.utm@utoronto.ca
Diane Crocker, Registrar & Director of Enrolment Management
Lynda Collins, Director, Human Resources, 905-828-5210
lynda.collins@utoronto.ca

Massey College
4 Devonshire Pl., Toronto, ON M5S 2E1, Canada
Tel: 416-978-2895
porter@masseycollege.ca
www.masseycollege.ca
www.facebook.com/MasseyCollege
twitter.com/MasseyCollege
www.youtube.com/MasseyCollege
Hugh Segal, Master
Amela Marin, Registrar, 416-978-2891
amarin@masseycollege.ca
Anna Luengo, Administrator, 416-978-6606
annaluengo@masseycollege.ca

New College
300 Huron St., Toronto, ON M5S 2Z3
Tel: 416-978-2460; *Fax:* 416-978-0554
newcollege.registrar@utoronto.ca
www.newcollege.utoronto.ca
www.facebook.com/192175714169723
www.twitter.com/newcollegeUofT
Prof. Yves Roberge, Principal, 416-978-2461
yves.roberge@utoronto.ca
Kerri Huffman, Assistant Principal & Registrar, 416-978-2460
kerri.huffman@utoronto.ca

University of Toronto Scarborough
1265 Military Trail, Toronto, ON M1C 1A4
Tel: 416-287-8872; *Fax:* 416-287-7528
www.utsc.utoronto.ca
www.facebook.com/utsc1
twitter.com/utsc
www.linkedin.com/edu/school?id=10861
www.youtube.com/user/uoftscarborough
Note: Number of Programs: 242
Bruce Kidd, Principal, U of T Scarborough
Professor Rick Halpern, Dean & Vice-Principal, Academic
Heinz-Bernhard Kraatz, Vice-Principal, Research
vpresearch@utsc.utoronto.ca
Desmond Pouyat, Dean, Student Affairs, 416-208-4760
stuaff@utsc.utoronto.ca
Andrew Arifuzzaman, Chief Administrative Officer, 416-208-5103
cao@utsc.utoronto.ca
Georgette Zinaty, Executive Director, Development & Alumni Relations, 416-208-5104
gzinaty@utsc.utoronto.ca
Heather Black, Director, Human Resource Services, 416-287-7077
heather.black@utoronto.ca
Curtis Cole, Registrar & Assistant Dean, Enrolment Management, 416-287-7527
cole@utsc.utoronto.ca
George Cree, Chair, Department of Psychology
gcree@utsc.utoronto.ca
Professor William Bowen, Assoc. Prof. & Chair, Department of Arts, Culture & Media, 416-208-5116
bowen@utsc.utoronto.ca
Professor George Arhonditsis, Chair, Department of Physical & Environmental Sciences, 416-208-4858
georgea@utsc.utoronto.ca
Professor David Fleet, Chair, Department of Computer & Mathematical Sciences, 416-287-7201
fleet@utsc.utoronto.ca
Professor David Zweig, Associate Professor & Chair, Department of Management, 416-208-5188
mgmtchair@utsc.utoronto.ca
Professor Andre Sorensen, Associate Professor & Chair, Department of Human Geography, 416-287-5607
sorensen@utsc.utoronto.ca
Professor Andrew Mason, Chair, Department of Biological Sciences, 416-287-7433, ext. 7431
biochair@utsc.utoronto.ca

University College
15 King's College Circle, Toronto, ON M5S 3H7
Tel: 416-978-3170; *Fax:* 416-978-6019
uc.registrar@utoronto.ca
www.uc.utoronto.ca
Donald Ainslie, Principal

Woodsworth College
119 St. George St., Toronto, ON M5S 1A9
Tel: 416-978-4444; *Fax:* 416-978-6111
wdwregistrar@utoronto.ca
www.wdw.utoronto.ca
www.facebook.com/WoodsworthCollege
twitter.com/WWCollege
Carol Chin, Acting Principal
principal.woodsworth@utoronto.ca
Roger Bulgin, Chief Administrative Officer
Cheryl Shook, Assistant Principal & Registrar

St. Michael's College
81 St. Mary St., Toronto, ON M4S 1J4
Tel: 416-926-1300
stmikes.utoronto.ca
Full Time Equivalency: 4893; *Note:* Fully federated with the University of Toronto, St. Michael's College has a large Faculty of Theology. It also features the Canadian Catholic Bioethics Institute & the Pontifical Institute of Mediaeval Studies.
Anne Anderson, President
Domenico Pietropaolo, Principal

Trinity College in the University of Toronto
6 Hoskin Ave., Toronto, ON M5S 1H8
Tel: 416-978-2522; *Fax:* 416-978-2797
registrar@trinity.utoronto.ca
www.trinity.utoronto.ca
Other Information: Bursar's Office, E-mail: fees@trinity.utoronto.ca
twitter.com/trinregistrar
www.linkedin.com/groups?home=&gid=59623
Full Time Equivalency: 1700; *Note:* Founded in 1851, it is Canada's oldest Anglican theological school.
The Hon. William C. Graham, Chancellor
Nelson De Melo, Registrar, 416-946-7614
demelo@trinity.utoronto.ca
Linda W. Corman, A.B. (Vassar), M.A. (Chi., College Librarian, 416-978-4398
linda.corman@utoronto.ca

Victoria University
73 Queen's Park Cres., Toronto, ON M5S 1K7
Tel: 416-585-4508; *Fax:* 416-585-4459
vic.registrar@utoronto.ca
www.vicu.utoronto.ca
www.facebook.com/vicu.utoronto
twitter.com/VicCollege_UofT
William Robins, President & Vice-Chancellor, 416-585-4511
vic.president@utoronto.ca
Yvette Ali, Registrar - Office of the Registrar, 416-585-4405
wanda.chin@utoronto.ca
Wanda Chin, Registrar - Office of the Principal, 416-585-4538
wanda.chin@utoronto.ca
Kelly Castle, Dean of Students, 416-585-4495
vic.dean@utoronto.ca

Knox College
59 St. George St., Toronto, ON M5S 2E6
Tel: 416-978-4500; *Fax:* 416-971-2133
knox.college@utoronto.ca
www.knox.utoronto.ca
www.facebook.com/knoxcollege.ca
twitter.com/knoxcollegeca
www.youtube.com/user/KnoxCollegeCA
Rev. Dr. J. Dorcas Gordon, Principal, 416-978-4503
jd.gordon@utoronto.ca
Rev. Dr. John Vissers, Director, Academic Programs, 416-978-2791
john.vissers@utoronto.ca

Wycliffe College
5 Hoskin Ave., Toronto, ON M5S 1H7
Tel: 416-979-3535
www.wycliffecollege.ca
Rt. Rev. Dr. Stephen Andrews, Principal
stephen.andrews@wycliffe.utoronto.ca

Regis College
100 Wellesley St. West, Toronto, ON M5S 2Z5
Tel: 416-922-5474; *Fax:* 416-922-2898
inquiries@regiscollege.ca
www.regiscollege.ca
ca.linkedin.com/edu/university-of-toronto—regis-college-10866

Note: Regis is a Roman Catholic college in the Jesuit tradition. It is a federated college of the University of Toronto.
John COstello, S.J., President

Elliott Allen Institute for Theology & Ecology
81 St. Mary's St., Toronto, ON M5S 1J4
Tel: 416-926-1300; *Fax:* 416-926-7294
eaite.contact@utoronto.ca
stmikes.utoronto.ca/theology/eaite
Dr. Dennis Patrick O'Hara, Director, 416-926-1300, ext. 3408

Innis College
2 Sussex Ave., Toronto, ON M5S 1J5
Tel: 416-978-2513; *Fax:* 416-978-5503
registrar.innis@utoronto.ca
innis.utoronto.ca
www.facebook.com/innisregistrar
twitter.com/innisregistrar
www.youtube.com/user/InnisCollegeVideo
Janet Paterson, Principal
principal.innis@utoronto.ca

Centres/Institutes

Asian Institute
1 Devonshire Pl., Toronto, ON M5S 3K7
Tel: 416-946-8900; *Fax:* 416-946-8915
asian.institute@utoronto.ca
www.munk.utoronto.ca/ai
www.facebook.com/contemporaryasianstudies
twitter.com/ai_uoft
www.youtube.com/user/AsianInstituteUofT
Joshua Barker, Director
ai.director@utoronto.ca

Canadian Institute for Theoretical Astrophysics (CITA)
60 St. George St., 14th Fl., Toronto, ON M5S 3H8
Tel: 416-978-6879; *Fax:* 416-978-3921
office@cita.utoronto.ca
www.cita.utoronto.ca
eww.facebook.com/CanadianInstituteforTheoreticalAstrophysics
Norm Murray, Director

Centre for Comparative Literature
c/o Isabel Bader Theatre, 3rd Fl.
93 Charles St. West, Toronto, ON M5S 1K9
Tel: 416-813-4041; *Fax:* 416-813-4040
complit.utoronto.ca
Neil ten Kortenaar, Director

Centre for Environmental Studies
#1016V, 33 Willcocks St., Toronto, ON M5S 3E8
Tel: 416-978-3475; *Fax:* 416-978-3884
environment@utoronto.ca
www.environment.utoronto.ca
www.facebook.com/252688278178579
twitter.com/UofTEnvironment
Kimberly Strong, Director

Centre for European, Russian, & Eurasian Studies
Monk School of Global Affairs
1 Devonshire Pl., Toronto, ON M5S 3K7
Tel: 416-946-8938; *Fax:* 416-946-8915
munkschool.utoronto.ca/ceres
Note: Part of the Munk School of Global Affairs
Randall Hansen, Director
r.hansen@utoronto.ca
Jana Oldfield, Business Officer
jana.oldfield@utoronto.ca

Centre for Industrial Relations & Human Resources
121 St. George St., Toronto, ON M5S 2Z9
Tel: 416-978-2927; *Fax:* 416-978-5696
cir.info@utoronto.ca
www.cirhr.utoronto.ca
Anil Verma, Director

Centre for Medieval Studies (CMS)
125 Queen's Park, 3rd Fl., Toronto, ON M5S 2C7
Tel: 416-978-4884
medieval.studies@utoronto.ca
medieval.utoronto.ca
Suzanne Akbari, Director
director.medieval@utoronto.ca

Centre for Reformation & Renaissance Studies (CRRS)
71 Queen's Park Cres. East, Toronto, ON M5S 1K7
Tel: 416-585-4468; *Fax:* 416-585-4430
info@vicu.utoronto.ca
crrs.ca
twitter.com/CRRS_Toronto
www.flickr.com/people/crrs
Ethan Kavaler, Interim Director
crrs.director@utoronto.ca

Centre for South Asian Studies
1 Devonshire Pl., Toronto, ON M5S 2K7
Tel: 416-946-8979
csas.assist@utoronto.ca
www.utoronto.ca/csas
www.facebook.com/csasut
twitter.com/CSASToronto
Rita Birla, Director

Centre for the Study of Pain
#300, 155 College St., Toronto, ON M5T 1P8
Tel: 416-946-8270
www.utoronto.ca/pain
twitter.com/UofT_Pain
Sara Promislow, Coordinator

Centre for Urban & Community Studies (CUCS)
Cities Centre
#400, 455 Spadina Ave., Toronto, ON M5S 2G8
Tel: 416-978-2072; *Fax:* 416-978-7162
urban.centre@utoronto.ca
www.urbancenter.utoronto.ca

Centre for Criminology & Sociolegal Studies
14 Queen's Park Cres. West, Toronto, ON M5S 3K9
Tel: 416-978-7124; *Fax:* 416-978-4195
criminology.utoronto.ca
Kelly Hannah-Moffat, Director
hannah.moffat@utoronto.ca

Computing in the Humanities & Social Sciences
Robarts Library
130 St. George St., 14th Fl., Toronto, ON M5S 3H1
Tel: 416-978-2535; *Fax:* 416-978-6519
support@chass.utoronto.ca
www.chass.utoronto.ca

Fields Institute for Research in Mathematical Sciences
222 College St., Toronto, ON M5T 3J1
Tel: 416-348-9710; *Fax:* 416-348-9714
inquiries@fields.utoronto.ca
www.fields.utoronto.ca
Walter Craig, Director
director@fields.utoronto.ca

Centre for Drama, Theatre & Performance Studies (CDTPS)
Also known as: Drama Centre
214 College St., 3rd Fl., Toronto, ON M5T 2Z9
Tel: 416-978-7980; *Fax:* 416-971-1378
graduate.drama@utoronto.ca
dramacentre.utoronto.ca
www.facebook.com/pages/UC-Drama-Program/128904873845506
twitter.com/DramaCentre
Stephen Johnson, Director, 416-978-7982
director.graddrama@utoronto.ca

University of Toronto Institute for Aerospace Studies (UTIAS)
4925 Dufferin St., Toronto, ON M3H 5T6
Tel: 416-667-7700; *Fax:* 416-667-7799
www.utias.utoronto.ca
David Zingg, Director
dwz@oddjob.utias.utoronto.ca

Institute for History & Philosophy of Science & Technology (IHPST)
Victoria College
#316, 91 Charles St. West, Toronto, ON M5S 1K7
Tel: 416-978-5397; *Fax:* 416-978-3003
ihpst.info@utoronto.ca
www.hps.utoronto.ca
Craig Fraser, Director
director.ihpst@utoronto.ca

Institute for Life Course & Aging
#328, 263 McCaul St., Toronto, ON M5T 1W7
Tel: 416-978-0377; *Fax:* 416-798-4771
aging@utoronto.ca
www.aging.utoronto.ca
www.facebook.com/events/144927762276522/
twitter.com/lifecourseUofT
www.youtube.com/watch?v=eXtnm4sxV9A
Dr. Lynn McDonald, Director

Women & Gender Studies Institute (WGSI)
Wilson Hall, New College
40 Willcocks St., Toronto, ON M5S 1C6
Tel: 416-946-5383
wgsi.director@utoronto.ca
www.wgsi.utoronto.ca
www.facebook.com/wgsiuoft
twitter.com/wgsi
Rinaldo Walcott, Director

Institute of Biomaterials & Biomedical Engineering
Rosebrugh Bldg.
#407, 164 College St., Toronto, ON M5S 3E2
Tel: 416-946-8258
www.ibbme.utoronto.ca
www.twitter.com/IBBME_UofT
Christopher Yip, Director

Institute of Medical Science (IMS)
#2374, 1 King's College Circle, Toronto, ON M5S 1A8
Tel: 416-946-8286; *Fax:* 416-971-2253
dir.medscience@utoronto.ca
www.ims.utoronto.ca
Allan S. Kaplan, Director

Knowledge Media Design Institute (KMDI)
Robarts Library
#1153 & #1155, 130 St. George St., Toronto, ON M5S 1A5
Tel: 416-978-5634
www.kmdi.utoronto.ca
www.facebook.com/pages/KMDI-Toronto/144338295610580
twitter.com/kmdi
www.youtube.com/channel/UCoAWoYkU6OeIH0JmI_x3MTg
Mark Chignell, Director

McLuhan Program in Culture & Technology
Also known as: The Coach House Institute
39A Queen's Park Cres. East, Toronto, ON M5S 2C3
Tel: 416-978-7026
mcluhan.program@utoronto.ca
mcluhan.ischool.utoronto.ca
www.facebook.com/mcluhan.ischool.utoronto
twitter.com/McLuhan100
vimeo.com/mcluhan100/videos
Dr. Dominique Scheffel-Dunand, Director

Dr. Eric Jackman Institute of Child Study
45 Walmer Rd., Toronto, ON M5R 2X2
Tel: 416-934-4526; *Fax:* 416-934-4565
www.oise.utoronto.ca/ics/
Joan Peskin, Director, 416-934-4555
j.peskin@utoronto.ca
Elizabeth Morley, Principal, 416-934-4509
elizabeth.morley@utoronto.ca

Centre for Aboriginal Initiatives
North Borden Bldg.
#222, 563 Spadina Ave., Toronto, ON M5S 2J7
Tel: 416-978-2233
aboriginal.studies@utoronto.ca
aboriginalstudies.utoronto.ca
www.facebook.com/433190543428601
twitter.com/UofTABS
www.youtube.com/channel/UC__vuJH9x3YX7b_z5FepP8A
Alana Johns, Director
director.aboriginal@utoronto.ca

Academic Retiree Centre (ARC)
#412, 256 McCaul St., Toronto, ON M5T 1W5
Tel: 416-978-7553
academic.retiree@utoronto.ca
www.faculty.utoronto.ca/arc
Vennese Croasdaile, Administrator

Joint Centre for Bioethics (JCB)
#754, 155 Collge St., Toronto, ON M5T 1P8
Tel: 416-978-2709; *Fax:* 416-978-1911
jcb.info@utoronto.ca
jointcentreforbioethics.ca
www.facebook.com/164894946861612
twitter.com/utjcb
Julie Weston, Associate Director
julie.weston@utoronto.ca

Institute for Canadian Music
Edward Johnson Bldg.
80 Queen's Park, Toronto, ON M5S 2C5
Tel: 416-946-8622; *Fax:* 416-946-3353
chalmerschair@yahoo.ca
www.utoronto.ca/icm
Robin Elliot, Director

Terrence Donnelly Centre for Cellular and Biomolecular Research
#230, 160 College St., Toronto, ON M5S 3E1
Tel: 416-978-8861; *Fax:* 416-978-8287
www.thedonnellycentre.utoronto.ca
Brenda Andrews, Director
brenda.andrews@utoronto.ca

Cinema Studies Institute
Innis College
2 Sussex Ave., Toronto, ON M5S 1J5
Tel: 416-978-5809; *Fax:* 416-946-0168
sites.utoronto.ca/cinema

Corinn Columpar, Director
corinn.columpar@utoronto.ca

Institute of Communication, Culture, Information & Technology (ICCIT)
University of Toronto Mississauga
3359 Mississauga Rd., Toronto, ON L5L 1C6
Tel: 905-569-4489
www.utm.utoronto.ca/iccit
www.facebook.com/ICCITUTM
twitter.com/iccitutm

Anthony Wensley, Director

Dental Research Institute
124 Edward St., Toronto, ON M5G 1G6
Tel: 416-979-4900
www.dentistry.utoronto.ca/research

Dennis Cvitkovitch, Director
d.cvitkovitch@dentistry.utoronto.ca

Centre for Diaspora & Transnational Studies
#230, 170 St. George St., Toronto, ON M5R 2M8
Tel: 416-946-8464; *Fax:* 416-978-7045
cdts@utoronto.ca
sites.utoronto.ca/cdts

Ato Quayson, Director
a.quayson@utoronto.ca

Toronto Nanofabrication Centre (TNFC)
Sandford Fleming Building
10 King's College Rd., #B540, Toronto, ON M5S 3G4
Tel: 416-946-5176
tnfc@utoronto.ca
tnfc.utoronto.ca

Wai Tung Ng, Director

Centre for Ethics
6 Hoskin Ave., Toronto, ON M5S 1H8
Tel: 416-978-6288; *Fax:* 416-946-8069
ethics@utoronto.ca
ethics.utoronto.ca

Simone Chambers, Director
schamber@chass.utoronto.ca

Centre for Forensic Science & Medicine
Medical Science Bldg.
#6231, 1 King's College Cirlce, Toronto, ON M5S 1A8
Tel: 416-946-0136
www.forensics.utoronto.ca

Michael Pollanen, Director

Centre for the Study of France and the Francophone World
Centre des Études de la France et du Monde Francophone
1 Devonshire Pl., Toronto, ON M5S 3K7
Tel: 416-585-4431
cefmf.utoronto.ca

Eric Jennings, Director
eric.jennings@utoronto.ca

Centre for Global Change Science
60 St. George St., Toronto, ON M5S 1A7
Tel: 416-978-2933; *Fax:* 416-978-8905
www.cgcs.utoronto.ca

Ana Sousa, Contact
ana@atmosp.physics.utoronto.ca

Institute of Health Policy, Management & Evaluation
#425, 155 College St., Toronto, ON M5T 3M6
Tel: 416-978-4326; *Fax:* 416-978-7350
ihpme@utoronto.ca
ihpme.utoronto.ca
twitter.com/IHPMEGSU
www.linkedin.com/groups?home=&gid=228973

Adalsteinn Brown, Director
adalsteinn.brown@utoronto.ca

Jackman Humanities Institute
Jackman Humanities Bldg.
170 St. George St., 10th Fl., Toronto, ON M5R 2M8
Tel: 416-978-7415; *Fax:* 416-946-7434
www.humanities.utoronto.ca

Robert Gibbs, Director

Centre for Innovation Law & Policy
78 Queen's Park, Toronto, ON M5S 2C5
Tel: 416-946-7549
centre.ilp@utoronto.ca
innovationlaw.org

Elizabeth Chien-Hale, Associate Director
e.chien.hale@utoronto.ca

Lassonde Institute
Mining Bldg.
170 College St., Toronto, ON M5S 3E3
Tel: 416-946-4095
www.lassondeinstitute.utoronto.ca

Brent Sleep, Acting Director

McLaughlin Centre for Molecular Medicine
Peter Gilgan Centre for Research & Learning
686 Bay St., 13th Fl., Toronto, ON M5G 0A4
Tel: 416-813-7654
www.mclaughlin.utoronto.ca

Stephen Scherer, Director
stephen.scherer@sickkids.ca

Institute for Optical Sciences (IOS)
#331, 60 St. George St., Toronto, ON M5S 1A7
Tel: 416-978-1457; *Fax:* 416-978-3936
www.optics.utoronto.ca

Cynthia Goh, Director

Trudeau Centre for Peace, Conflict & Justice
1 Devonshire Pl., Toronto, ON M5S 3K7
Tel: 416-946-0326
munkschool.utoronto.ca/trudeaucentre

Reina Shishikura, Program Administrator
pcj.programme@utoronto.ca
Wendy Wong, Director

Pulp & Paper Centre
#420, 200 College St., Toronto, ON M5S 3E5
Tel: 416-978-3062; *Fax:* 416-971-2106
paper@chem-eng.utoronto.ca
www.pulpandpaper.utoronto.ca

Honghi Tran, Director

Centre for Quantum Information & Quantum Control
cqiqc@physics.utoronto.ca
cqiqc.physics.utoronto.ca

Amr Helmy, Director
a.helmy@utoronto.ca

Tanz Centre for Research in Neurodegenerative Diseases
Krembil Discovery Tower
60 Leonard Ave., #4KD481, Toronto, ON M5T 2S8
Tel: 416-507-6838; *Fax:* 416-507-6435
crnd.admin@utoronto.ca
tanz.med.utoronto.ca

Peter St. George-Hyslop, Director
Brian Bachand, Associate Director
brian.bachand@utoronto.ca

Rotman Institute for International Business (RIIB)
www.rotman.utoronto.ca

Wendy Dobson, Co-Director
dobson@rotman.utoronto.ca
Ig Horstman, Co-Director
Ihorstmann@rotman.utoronto.ca

Bonham Centre for Sexual Diversity Studies
University College
15 King's College Circle, Toronto, ON M5S 3H7
Tel: 416-819-1921; *Fax:* 416-971-2027
www.uc.utoronto.ca/sexualdiversity

Brenda Cossman, Director
b.cossman@utoronto.ca

Centre for the Study of the United States
Munk School of Global Affairs
1 Devonshire Pl., #327N, Toronto, ON M5S 3K7
Tel: 416-946-8972
csus@utoronto.ca
sites.utoronto.ca/csus
www.facebook.com/csus.utoronto

Peter Loewn, Director
csus.director@utoronto.ca

Centre for Urban Health Initiatives
University College
#259, 15 King's College Circle, Toronto, ON M5S 3H7
Tel: 416-978-7223; *Fax:* 416-946-0669
cuhi.admin@utoronto.ca
sites.utoronto.ca/cuhi

John Myles, Principal Investigator

Centre for Urban Schooling (CUS)
Ontario Institute for Studies in Education
252 Bloor St. West, 10th Fl., Toronto, ON M5S 1V6
Tel: 416-978-0146
cusinquiries@utoronto.ca
cus.oise.utoronto.ca
www.facebook.com/CUSatOISE
twitter.com/CUS_OISE

Tara Goldstein, Contact

Wilson Centre
200 Elizabeth St., #1ES-565, Toronto, ON M5G 2C4
Tel: 416-340-3646; *Fax:* 416-340-3792
www.thewilsoncentre.ca

Neil P. Byrne, Program Coordinator
niall.byrne@utoronto.ca

Centre for Women's Studies in Education (CWSE)
OISE
#2-225, 252 Bloor St. West, Toronto, ON M5S 1V6
cwse@utoronto.ca
www.oise.utoronto.ca/cwse
www.facebook.com/cwse.oise
twitter.com/cwseoise

Angela Miles, Head

Toronto: Victoria University
#106, 73 Queen's Park Cres., Toronto, ON M5S 1K7, Canada
Tel: 416-585-4508; *Fax:* 416-585-4459
vic.registrar@utoronto.ca
www.vicu.utoronto.ca
www.facebook.com/vicu.utoronto
twitter.com/VicCollege_UofT

Note: Although the university is located within the University of Toronto campus, it has its own independent administration, faculty and governing body.

Emmanuel College
#102, Queen's Park Cres., Toronto, ON M5S 1K7, Canada
Tel: 416-585-4539; *Fax:* 416-585-4516
ec.office@utoronto.ca
www.emmanuel.utoronto.ca

Note: Theological college affiliated with the United Church of Canada
Rev. Ralph Carl Wushke, Chaplain, 416-813-4099

Toronto: Woodsworth College
119 Saint George St., Toronto, ON M5S 1A9, Canada
Tel: 416-978-4444; *Fax:* 416-978-6111
wdwregistrar@utoronto.ca
wdw.utoronto.ca

Full Time Equivalency: 6000

Toronto: Wycliffe College
5 Hoskin Ave., Toronto, ON M5S 1H7, Canada
Tel: 416-979-3535; *Fax:* 416-946-3545
www.wycliffecollege.ca

Note: Seminary at the University of Toronto affiliated with the Anglican Church of Canada

Toronto: York University
4700 Keele St., Toronto, ON M3J 1P3, Canada
Tel: 416-736-2100
www.yorku.ca
www.facebook.com/yorkuniversityhome
twitter.com/YorkUnews
www.linkedin.com/company/york-university
www.youtube.com/user/YorkUniversity

Full Time Equivalency: 55000; *Number of Employees:* 7000 administrative staff
Rick E. Waugh, Chair of the Board
Gregory Sorbara, Chancellor
Mahmoud Shoukri, B.Sc., M.Eng., Ph.D., President & Vice-Chancellor
Rhonda Lenton, Vice-President & Academic Provost
Jeff O'Hagan, Vice-President Advancement
Gary Brewer, Vice-President Finance & Administration
Robert Haché, Vice-President Research & Innovation
Maureen Armstron, University Secretary & General Counsel
Janet Morrison, Vice-Provost, Students
Trudy Pound-Curtis, BCom., FCA, CFO & Assistant Vice-President Finance
Bob Gagne, Chief Information Officer, 416-736-5818
bgagne@yorku.ca
Carol Altilia, Registrar, 416-736-2100, ext. 55262
roinfo@yorku.ca

Faculties

Faculty of Fine Arts
Tel: 416-736-5888
finearts@yorku.ca
finearts.yorku.ca
twitter.com/YorkUFineArts
www.youtube.com/user/YorkUFineArts

Bob Drummond, Dean

Faculty of Education
135 Winters College, Toronto, ON M3J 1P3
Tel: 416-736-5001; *Fax:* 416-736-5409
osp@edu.yorku.ca
edu.yorku.ca
www.facebook.com/YorkUeducation
twitter.com/yorkueducation
www.youtube.com/yorkueducation

Paul Axelrod, Dean

Faculty of Environmental Studies (FES)
Tel: 416-736-5252; *Fax:* 416-736-5679
esrecept@yorku.ca
fes.yorku.ca

David Morley, Dean

Glendon College
2275 Bayview Ave., Toronto, ON M4N 3M6
Tel: 416-487-6710
liaison@glendon.yorku.ca
www.glendon.yorku.ca
Enrollment: 2700
K. McRoberts, B.A., M.A., Ph.D., Principal

Faculty of Health
Tel: 416-736-5124; *Fax:* 416-736-5760
healthdn@yorku.ca
health.info.yorku.ca
www.facebook.com/yorkuniversityfacultyofhealth
twitter.com/YorkUHealth
www.youtube.com/user/FacultyofHealth
Harvey Skinner, Dean

Faculty of Science
Tel: 416-736-5085; *Fax:* 416-736-5804
sciquest@yorku.ca
science.yorku.ca
Nick Cercone, Dean

Schools

Osgoode Hall Law School
Tel: 416-736-5712
admissions@osgoode.yorku.ca
www.osgoode.yorku.ca
www.facebook.com/Osgoode
twitter.com/osgoodenews
www.linkedin.com/company/osgoode-hall-law-school
www.youtube.com/user/OsgoodeHallLawSchool
Number of Employees: 59 full-time faculty; 150 adjunct faculty
Lorne Sossin, Dean, 416-736-5199
lawdean@osgoode.yorku.ca

Schulich School of Business
Tel: 416-736-5060; *Fax:* 416-650-8174
admissions@schulich.yorku.ca
www.schulich.yorku.ca
Other Information: International Students: 416-736-5059
Dezső J. Horvath, Dean

School of Public Policy & Administration (SPPA)
Tel: 416-736-5384; *Fax:* 416-736-5382
lapssppa@yorku.ca
www.yorku.ca/laps/sppa
twitter.com/YorkUSPPA
Bruce Ryder, Director

Lassonde School of Engineering
Tel: 416-736-5484
ask@lassonde.yorku.ca
lassonde.yorku.ca
facebook.com/lassondeschool
twitter.com/lassondeschool
www.linkedin.com/company/lassonde-school-of-engineering
Enrollment: 2000; *Number of Employees:* 200
G.G. Shepherd, B.Sc., M.Sc., Ph.D., F.R., Director

Centres/Institutes

Canadian Centre for German & European Studies (CCGES)
ccges@yorku.ca
ccges.apps01.yorku.ca
Kurt Huebner, Acting Director

Centre for Atmospheric Chemistry
Tel: 416-736-5410; *Fax:* 416-736-5411
cac@yorku.ca
www.cac.yorku.ca
G.W. Harris, B.Sc., Ph.D., Director

Israel & Golda Koschitzky Centre for Jewish Studies
cjs@yorku.ca
cjs.blog.yorku.ca
M. Lockshin, Director

York Collegium for Practical Ethics (YCPE)
Fax: 416-736-5436
ycpe@yorku.ca
www.yorku.ca/ycpe
Shirley Katz, Acting Director

Centre for Refugee Studies (CRS)
Tel: 416-736-5663; *Fax:* 416-736-5688
crs@yorku.ca
crs.yorku.ca
Susan McGrath, Director

Centre for Research in Mass Spectrometry
Tel: 416-736-5752
www.chem.yorku.ca/CRMS
M. Siu, Director

Centre for Research on Latin America & the Caribbean
Tel: 416-736-5237; *Fax:* 416-736-5688
cerlac@yorku.ca
www.yorku.ca/cerlac
Viviana Patroni, Director

Centre for Research on Work & Society (CRWS)
Tel: 416-736-5612; *Fax:* 416-736-5916
crws@yorku.ca
www.yorku.ca/crws
N. Pupo, Director

The Centre for Vision Research (CVR)
Tel: 416-736-5659; *Fax:* 416-736-5857
manini@cvr.yorku.ca
www.cvr.yorku.ca
Laurence Harris, Director & Professor

Institute for Research & Innovation in Sustainability (IRIS)
Tel: 416-736-5784
irisinfo[@]yorku.ca
www.irisyorku.ca
www.facebook.com/irisyorku
twitter.com/irisyorku
David Wheeler, Director

Institute for Research on Learning Technologies (IRLT)
Tel: 416-736-5019
irlt.yorku.ca
Ron Owston, Director

Institute for Social Research (IRS)
Tel: 416-736-5061; *Fax:* 416-736-5749
Toll-Free: 888-847-0148
isrnews@yorku.ca
www.isr.yorku.ca
M.D. Ornstein, B.Sc., Ph.D., Director

Jack & Mae Nathanson Centre on Transnational Human Rights, Crime & Security
Also known as: Jack & Mae Nathanson Centre
Old Name: Jack & Mae Nathanson Centre for the Study of Organized Crime & Corruption
Tel: 416-736-5030
nathansoncentre@osgoode.yorku.ca
nathanson.osgoode.yorku.ca
twitter.com/NathansonCentre
www.youtube.com/user/nathansoncentre
M. Beare, B.A., M.A., M.P.H.L., Ph., Director

LaMarsh Centre for Child & Youth Research
Also known as: LaMarsh
www.yorku.ca/lamarsh
Anne Marie Wall, Acting Director

Robarts Centre for Canadian Studies
Tel: 416-736-5499; *Fax:* 416-650-8069
robarts.info.yorku.ca
S. Feldman, Director

York Centre for Asian Research
Tel: 416-736-2100; *Fax:* 416-736-5688
ycar@yorku.ca
www.yorku.ca/ycar
P. Vandergeest, Director

Centre for Feminist Research (CFR)
Tel: 416-736-5915
cfr@yorku.ca
cfr.info.yorku.ca
V. Agnew, Director

York Institute for Health Research
Tel: 416-736-5941; *Fax:* 416-736-5986
yihr@yorku.ca
www.yorku.ca/yihr
www.facebook.com/102017273196330
twitter.com/York_YIHR
Jianhong Wu, Director

York University English Language Institute (YUELI)
035 Founders College, Keele Campus, York Universi
4700 Keele St., Toronto, ON M3J 1P3
Tel: 416-736-5353; *Fax:* 416-736-5908
yueli@yorku.ca
yueli.yorku.ca
www.facebook.com/pages/Yueli/250727951649094
www.twitter.com/YORKUYueli
Calum MacKechnie, Director

Waterloo: Conrad Grebel University College
140 Westmount Rd. North, Waterloo, ON N2L 3G6, Canada
Tel: 519-885-0220; *Fax:* 519-885-0014
congreb@uwaterloo.ca
grebel.uwaterloo.ca
www.facebook.com/ConradGrebel
twitter.com/Conrad_Grebel
www.youtube.com/user/ConradGrebelUC

Waterloo: University of Waterloo
200 University Ave. West, Waterloo, ON N2L 3G1, Canada
Tel: 519-888-4567
www.uwaterloo.ca
Other Information: 519-888-4911
www.facebook.com/university.waterloo
twitter.com/uWaterloo
www.linkedin.com/company/university-of-waterloo
www.youtube.com/uwaterloo
Full Time Equivalency: 31362
V. Prem Watsa, Chancellor
Kevin Lynch, Chair
Feridun Hamdullahpur, C.C., A.B., L.L.B., President & Vice-Chancellor
Ian Orchard, Vice-President Academic & Provost
George Dixon, Vice-President University Research
Chris Read, Associate Provost, Students
Kenneth McGillivray, Vice-President Advancement
Jim Frank, Interim Associate Provost, Graduate Studies
Logan Atkinson, University Secretary & General Counsel
Nello Angerilli, Associate Vice-President, International
Ray Darling, Registrar

Faculties

Faculty of Applied Health Sciences
Tel: 519-888-4567; *Fax:* 519-746-6776
ahsrecep@uwaterloo.ca
uwaterloo.ca/applied-health-sciences
www.facebook.com/waterloo.appliedhealthsciences
twitter.com/ahswaterloo
instagram.com/uwaterlooahs
James Rush, Interim Dean
jwerush@uwaterloo.ca

Faculty of Arts
arts@uwaterloo.ca
www.arts.uwaterloo.ca
www.facebook.com/waterlooarts
twitter.com/uwaterlooARTS
www.youtube.com/user/artsfaculty
Ken Coates, Dean

Faculty of Engineering
www.engineering.uwaterloo.ca
www.facebook.com/uWaterlooEngineering
twitter.com/waterlooENG
A.S. Sedra, B.Sc., M.A.Sc., Ph.D., Dean

Faculty of Environmental Studies
Jean Andrey, Dean

Faculty of Graduate Studies
uwaterloo.ca/graduate-studies
R. Bird, B.Sc., M.Sc., Ph.D., Dean

Faculty of Mathematics
uwaterloo.ca/math
www.facebook.com/waterloo.math
twitter.com/WaterlooMath
www.youtube.com/playlist?list=PL4C021AAAD2BD8126
Enrollment: 7000; *Number of Employees:* 200
T.F. Coleman, Ph.D., Dean

Faculty of Science
science@uwaterloo.ca
uwaterloo.ca/science
www.facebook.com/WaterlooScience
twitter.com/waterloosci
Terry McMahon, Dean

Affiliations

Conrad Grebel University College
140 Westmount Rd. North, Waterloo, ON N2L 3G6, Canada
Tel: 519-885-0220; *Fax:* 519-885-0014
congreb@uwaterloo.ca
uwaterloo.ca/grebel
facebook.com/ConradGrebel
twitter.com/Conrad_Grebel
www.linkedin.com/groups?home=&gid=1582077
www.youtube.com/user/ConradGrebelUC
Susan Schultz Huxman, President, 519-885-0220, ext. 24237
E. Paul Penner, Director of Operations, 519-885-0220, ext. 24231
eppenner@uwaterloo.ca
Marlene Epp, Interim Dean, 519-885-0220, ext. 24257
mgepp@uwaterloo.ca

Renison University College
240 Westmount Rd. North, Waterloo, ON N2L 3G4, Canada
Tel: 519-884-4404; *Fax:* 519-884-5135
uwaterloo.ca/renison
www.facebook.com/RenisonUniversityCollege
twitter.com/renisoncollege
www.youtube.com/user/renisonvideo
Note: College programs lead to a Bachelor of Arts or an Honours Bachelor of Social Work degree of the University of Waterloo.

Wendy Fletcher, Principal

St. Jerome's University
290 Westmount Rd. North, Waterloo, ON N2L 3G3
Tel: 519-884-8110; *Fax:* 519-884-5759
www.sju.ca
www.facebook.com/stjeromesuniversity?ref=ts
twitter.com/StJeromesUni
www.linkedin.com/groups?home=&gid=2548753
www.youtube.com/sjuwaterloo
Note: Federated with the University of Waterloo, St. Jerome's University is a public Catholic university. Education in the Arts & Mathematics is provided.
Jim Beingessner, Chancellor
Dr. Katherine Bergman, President & Vice-Chancellor

St. Paul's United College
University of Waterloo
190 Westmount Rd. North, Waterloo, ON N2L 3G5, Canada
Tel: 519-885-1460
stpauls@uwaterloo.ca
uwaterloo.ca/stpauls
www.facebook.com/StPaulsUniversityCollege
twitter.com/UWStPauls
www.linkedin.com/edu/10879
www.youtube.com/uwstpauls
Note: The residential teaching institution is affiliated with the University of Waterloo. It features the international development program.
Rod Barr, Chair
Graham Brown, Principal
ggbrown@uwaterloo.ca
Peter Frick, Academic Dean
pfrick@uwaterloo.ca

Centres/Institutes

Centre for Extended Learning
200 University Ave. West, Waterloo, ON N2L 3G1
Tel: 519-888-4050; *Fax:* 519-746-4607
extendedlearning@uwaterloo.ca
de.uwaterloo.ca
Cathy Newell Kelly, Director
cnkelly@uwaterloo.ca

Centre for Teaching Excellence
325 Environment 1
200 University Ave. West, Waterloo, ON N2L 3G1
Tel: 519-888-4567; *Fax:* 519-888-9806
cte@uwaterloo.ca
uwaterloo.ca/centre-for-teaching-excellence
www.facebook.com/Centre.for.Teaching.Excellence
twitter.com/uwcte
Donna Ellis, Director

Waterloo Aboriginal Education Centre
St. Paul's University College
190 Westmount Rd. North, Waterloo, ON N2L 3G5
Tel: 519-885-1460
uwaterloo.ca/stpauls/waterloo-aboriginal-education-centre
www.facebook.com/WaterlooAboriginalEducationCentre
twitter.com/UWAboriginal
Jo-Anne Absolon, Coordinator
abserv@uwaterloo.ca

Women's Centre
2101 Student Life Centre
200 University Ave., Waterloo, ON N2L 3G1
Tel: 519-888-4567
womenscentre@feds.ca
women.feds.ca
www.facebook.com/pages/UW-Womens-Centre/120165958098427
twitter.com/uwwomenscentre

Waterloo: Wilfrid Laurier University
75 University Ave. West, Waterloo, ON N2L 3C5, Canada
Tel: 519-884-0710
chooselaurier@wlu.ca
www.wlu.ca
www.facebook.com/LaurierNow
twitter.com/LaurierNews
www.linkedin.com/company/wilfrid-laurier-university
www.youtube.com/lauriervideo
Full Time Equivalency: 18541
Dr. Max Blouw, President & Vice-Chancellor
Dr. Deborah MacLatchy, Vice-President Academic & Provost
Jim Butler, Vice-President Finance & Administration
Ruth MacNeil, Acting Registrar
Robert Donelson, Vice-President Development & Alumni Relations
David McMurray, Vice-President Student Affairs

Faculties

Faculty of Arts
artsadvising@wlu.ca
www.facebook.com/WLUArts
twitter.com/LaurierArts
Dr. David Docherty, Dean

Brantford Campus
73 George St., Brantford, ON N3T 2Y3, Canada
Tel: 519-756-8228; *Fax:* 519-759-2172
servicelaurierbrantford@wlu.ca
Dr. Bruce Arai, Dean
barai@wlu.ca

Faculty of Graduate & Postdoctoral Studies
Fax: 519-884-1020
fgps@wlu.ca
www.wlu.ca/gradstudies
www.facebook.com/342693802429736
twitter.com/Lauriergrad
www.youtube.com/lauriervideo
Dr. Joan Norris, Dean

Faculty of Music
Fax: 519-884-5285
choosemusic@wlu.ca
www.wlu.ca/music
www.facebook.com/LaurierMusic
twitter.com/LaurierMusic
Charles Morrison, Dean
cdmorris@wlv.ca

School of Business & Economics (SBE)
Fax: 519-884-0201
sbenews@wlu.ca
www.wlu.ca/sbe
www.facebook.com/LaurierSBE
twitter.com/LaurierSBE
lauriersbe.tumblr.com
Enrollment: 5500
Ginny Dybenko, Dean
gdybenko@wlv.ca

Faculty of Science
Fax: 519-884-0464
scienceinquiries@wlu.ca
www.wlu.ca/science
Dr. Peter Tiidus, Acting Dean
ptiidus@wlv.ca

Lyle S. Hallman Faculty of Social Work
120 Duke St. West, Kitchener, ON N2H 3W8, Canada
Fax: 519-888-9732
socialwork@wlu.ca
www.wlu.ca/socialwork
Lesley Cooper, Dean

Waterloo Lutheran Seminary
Fax: 519-725-2434
www.seminary.wlu.ca
www.facebook.com/69250265745
Dr. David Pfrimmer, Principal-Dean
dpfrimmer@wlu.ca

Centre for Teaching Innovation & Excellence
75 University Ave. West, Waterloo, ON N2L 3C5
Tel: 519-884-0710
www.wlu.ca/ctie
Sandy Hughes, Director
shughes@wlu.ca

Windsor: Iona College
208 Sunset Ave., Windsor, ON N9B 3A7, Canada
Tel: 519-253-3000; *Fax:* 519-973-7050
office@ionacollege.edu
www.ionacollege.edu
Note: Affiliate College to the University of Windsor, affiliated with the United Church of Canada designed to promote theological educaion, social justice and Chaplaincy.
Rev. Dr. BoJeong Kim, Principal & Chaplain Emeritus, 519-253-3000, ext. 3440
principal@ionacollege.edu
Rev. Dr. Lloyd Smith, Chancellor
Dr. Norman King, Director, School of Theology, 519-253-3000, ext. 3443
theology@ionacollege.edu

Windsor: University of Windsor
401 Sunset Ave., Windsor, ON N9B 3P4, Canada
Tel: 519-253-3000; *Fax:* 519-973-7050
www.uwindsor.ca
www.facebook.com/uwindsor
www.twitter.com/uwindsor
www.linkedin.com/groups?gid=38761
www.youtube.com/uwindsor
Full Time Equivalency: 16500
Dr. Alan Wildeman, President & Vice-Chancellor
Edward Lumley, Chancellor

Faculties

Faculty of Arts & Social Sciences
Chrysler Hall Tower
#101, 401 Sunset Ave., Windsor, ON N9B 3P4
Tel: 519-253-3000
www1.uwindsor.ca/fahss
Dr. Nancy E. Wright, Dean

Faculty of Education & Academic Development
Tel: 519-253-3000
educ@uwindsor.ca
www1.uwindsor.ca/education
Dr. Alan Wright, Acting Dean

Faculty of Engineering
www.uwindsor.ca/engineering
Dr. Mehrdad Saif, Dean

Faculty of Graduate Studies
401 Sunset Ave., Windsor, ON N9B 3P4
Tel: 519-253-3000
gradst@uwindsor.ca
www1.uwindsor.ca/graduate
Dr. Patricia Weir, Dean

Faculty of Human Kinetics
www1.uwindsor.ca/hk
Dr. Michael A. Khan, Dean

Faculty of Law
401 Sunset Ave., Windsor, ON N9B 3P4
Tel: 519-253-3000
www.uwindsor.ca/law
Camilla Cameron, Dean

Faculty of Nursing
Toldo Health Education Centre
#336, 401 Sunset Ave., Windsor, ON N9B 3P4
Tel: 519-253-3000; *Fax:* 519-973-7084
nurse@uwindsor.ca
www1.uwindsor.ca/nursing
twitter.com/UWinNursing
Dr. Linda Patrick, RN, BScN, MA, MSc, PhD, Dean

Odette School of Business
www1.uwindsor.ca/odette
Dr. Allan Conway, Dean

Faculty of Science
Essex Hall
#242, 401 Sunset Ave., Windsor, ON N9B 3P4
Tel: 519-253-3000; *Fax:* 519-973-7068
science@uwindsor.ca.
www1.uwindsor.ca/science
Dr. Marlys Koschinsky, Dean

Schools

Athletics & Recreation
www.uwindsor.ca/recreation-and-fitness

Biological Sciences
Biology Bldg.
#119, 401 Sunset Ave., Windsor, ON N9B 3P4
Tel: 519-253-3000; *Fax:* 519-971-3609
biosci@uwindsor.ca
www1.uwindsor.ca/biology

Chemistry & Biochemistry
www1.uwindsor.ca/chemistry
Bulent Mutus, Head

Civil & Environmental Engineering
401 Sunset Ave., Windsor, ON N9B 3P4
Tel: 519-253-3000; *Fax:* 519-971-3686
www1.uwindsor.ca/civil
Faouzi Ghrib, B.A.Sc., M.Sc., Ph.D., Head

Department of Languages, Literatures & Cultures
www1.uwindsor.ca/languages

Department of Communication, Media & Film
www1.uwindsor.ca/communications
Valerie Scatamburlo, Head

School of Dramatic Art
www1.uwindsor.ca/drama
Tina Pugliese, Director

Earth & Environmental Sciences
Fax: 519-973-7081
earth@uwindsor.ca
www1.uwindsor.ca/ees
www.facebook.com/EESWindsor
Iain Samson, Head

Electrical & Computer Engineering
Fax: 519-971-3695
ece@uwindsor.ca
www1.uwindsor.ca/engineering/electrical
Maher Sid-Ahmed, Head

Department of History
www1.uwindsor.ca/history
Miriam Wright, Head

Industrial & Manufacturing Systems Engineering (IMSE)
www1.uwindsor.ca/imse
Waguih El Maraghy, Head

Intelligent Manufacturing Systems (IMS)
Centre for Engineering Innovation
401 Sunset Ave., Windsor, ON N9B 3P4
Tel: 519-253-3000
imscadmin@uwindsor.ca
www1.uwindsor.ca/imsc
Hoda ElMaraghy, B.Eng., M.Eng., Ph.D., Head
Waguih ElMaraghy, B.Eng., M.Eng., Ph.D., Director

Mechanical, Automotive & Materials Engineering (MAME)
Fax: 519-973-7007
www.uwindsor.ca/engineering/mame
Andrzej Sobiesiak, Head

Philosophy
www1.uwindsor.ca/philosophy
Marcello Guarini, Head

Department of Physics
physics@uwindsor.cas
www1.uwindsor.ca/physics
Chitra Rangan, Head

Political Science
www1.uwindsor.ca/polsci
John Sutcliffe, Head

Department of Psychology
Fax: 519-973-7021
psychology@uwindsor.ca
www1.uwindsor.ca/psychology
Greg Chung-Yan, Head

School of Social Work
Fax: 519-973-7036
socwork@uwindsor.ca
www1.uwindsor.ca/socialwork
Patrick Selmi, Acting Director

Sociology, Anthropology & Criminology
www1.uwindsor.ca/criminology
Janice Drakich, Head

Visual Arts
Fax: 519-971-3647
art@uwindsor.ca
www1.uwindsor.ca/visualarts
Karen Engle, Director

Women's Studies
womenst@uwindsor.ca
www1.uwindsor.ca/womensstudies
Anne Forrest, Head

Affiliations

Assumption University
Assumption Hall
400 Huron Church Rd., 2nd Fl., Windsor, ON N9C 2J9, Canada
Tel: 519-973-7033; *Fax:* 519-973-7089
assumptionu.ca
twitter.com/WindsorCM
www.youtube.com/user/cvalka1
Most Rev. Ronald P. Fabbro, C.S.B., D.D.Bishop of Lon, Chancellor
Rev. Dr. Thomas Rosica, C.S.B., Pres./Vice-Chancellor
Dr J. Norman King, Chair, Centre for Religion & Culture

Canterbury College
2500 University Ave. West, Windsor, ON N9B 3Y1, Canada
Tel: 519-971-3646; *Fax:* 519-971-3645
canter@uwindsor.ca
www.uwindsor.ca/canterbury
Note: Canterbury College offers the following courses: Doctor of Ministry Degree (in affiliation with Ashland Theological Seminary at Ashland University); certificate courses for the Anglican Community of Deacons & interested lay people; & professional courses for the community.
Dr. Gordon W.F. Drake, Principal
gdrake@uwindsor.ca
Janet Harris, General Manager
harrisja@uwindsor.ca
Brenda Smith, Coordinator, Residence Admissions
brsmith@uwindsor.ca

Iona College
208 Sunset Ave., Windsor, ON N9B 3A7, Canada
Tel: 519-253-3000; *Fax:* 519-973-7050
office@ionacollege.edu
ionacollege.edu
Dr. Bo Jeong Kim, Principal & Chaplain Emeritus
principal@ionacollege.edu
Dr. Norman King, Director, School of Theology
theology@ionacollege.edu
Marilyn Farough, Chair

Colleges

Barrie: Georgian College
1 Georgian Dr., Barrie, ON L4M 3X9, Canada
Tel: 705-728-1968; *Fax:* 705-722-5123
inquire@georgianc.on.ca
www.georgianc.on.ca
www.facebook.com/georgiancollege
www.twitter.com/georgiancollege
www.georgianc.on.ca/linkedin
www.youtube.com/user/georgianvideos
Full Time Equivalency: 9000
MaryLynn West-Moynes, President & CEO

Midland Campus
649 Prospect Blvd., Midland, ON L4R 4L3, Canada
Tel: 705-526-3666; *Fax:* 705-526-5124
midland@georgiancollege.ca

Muskoka Campus
111 Wellington St., Bracebridge, ON P1L 1E2, Canada
Tel: 705-646-7629; *Fax:* 705-646-2120
muskoka@georgiancollege.ca

Orangeville Campus
22 Centennial Rd., Orangeville, ON L9W 1P8, Canada
Tel: 519-940-0331; *Fax:* 519-941-0905
orangeville@georgiancollege.ca

Orillia Campus
P.O. Box 2316
825 Memorial Ave., Orillia, ON L3V 6S2, Canada
Tel: 705-325-2740; *Fax:* 705-325-3690
orillia@georgiancollege.ca

Owen Sound Campus
1450 - 8th St. East, Owen Sound, ON N4K 5R4, Canada
Tel: 519-376-0840; *Fax:* 519-376-5395
owensound.inquire@georgiancollege.ca

South Georgian Bay Campus
499 Raglan St., Collingwood, ON L9Y 3Z1, Canada
Tel: 705-445-2961; *Fax:* 705-445-1218
southgeorgianbay@georgiancollege.ca

Belleville: Loyalist College of Applied Arts & Technology
P.O. Box 4200
Belleville, ON K8N 5B9
Tel: 613-969-1913; *Fax:* 613-962-1376
Toll-Free: 888-569-2547
info@loyalistcollege.com
www.loyalistcollege.com
www.facebook.com/loyalistcollege
twitter.com/loyalistcollege
www.linkedin.com/company/loyalist-college
www.youtube.com/user/goloyalist
Laura Naumann, Registrar, 613-969-1913, ext. 2366
lnaumann@Loyalistc.on.ca

Hamilton: Mohawk College
Fennell Campus
P.O. Box 2034
135 Fennell Ave. West, Hamilton, ON L8N 3T2, Canada
Tel: 905-575-1212; *Fax:* 905-575-2378
www.mohawkcollege.ca
www.facebook.com/mohawkcollege
www.mohawkcollege.ca/social-media/twitter.html
www.linkedin.com/company/20545
www.youtube.com/mohawkcollege
Full Time Equivalency: 13000
Ron McKerlie, President, 905-575-1212
Dr. Christine Bradaric-Baus, Vice-President, Academic
Kim Watkins, Chief Financial Officer

Wentworth Campus
196 Wentworth St. North, Hamilton, ON L8L 5V7, Canada
Tel: 905-575-2424; *Fax:* 905-523-8504

Centre for Teaching & Learning
#A227, 135 Fennell Ave. West, Hamilton, ON L9C 1E9
Tel: 905-575-1212
www.mohawkcollege.ca/about/TeachingLearningQuality/CTL.html
Nadine Ogborn, Manager
nadine.ogborn@mohawkcollege.ca

Mohawk - McMaster Institute for Applied Health Sciences
1400 Main St. West, Hamilton, ON L8S 1C7, Canada
Tel: 905-540-4247; *Fax:* 905-528-8242

Skilled Trades & Apprenticeship Research, Resources & Training (STARRT)
481 Barton St. East, Stoney Creek, ON L8E 2L7, Canada
Tel: 905-575-1212; *Fax:* 905-575-2549

Kingston: St. Lawrence College
Also known as: Collège Saint-Laurent
Kingston Campus
100 Portsmouth Ave., Kingston, ON K7L 5A6, Canada
Tel: 613-544-5400; *Fax:* 613-545-3923
Toll-Free: 800-463-0752
dreamit@sl.on.ca
www.stlawrencecollege.ca
www.facebook.com/stlawrencecollege.ca
www.twitter.com/whatsinsidesIc
www.youtube.com/aboutslc
Full Time Equivalency: 26500; *Number of Employees:* 418 full-time employees; 938 part-time employees
Glenn Vollebregt, President & CEO
Janet Greer, Director of Finance, 613-345-0660, ext. 3128
Gordon C. MacDougall, Sr. Vice-President, Advancement, Student External Affairs, 613-544-5400, ext. 1298
Lorraine Carter, Sr. Vice-President, Academic, 613-544-5400, ext. 1446

Campuses

Brockville Campus
2288 Parkedale Ave., Brockville, ON K6V 5X3, Canada
Tel: 613-345-0660; *Fax:* 613-345-2231
Toll-Free: 888-622-8880
Beverlie Dietze, Campus Dean, ext. 3260
bdietze@sl.on.ca

Cornwall Campus
2 St. Lawrence Dr., Cornwall, ON K6H 4Z1, Canada
Tel: 613-933-6080; *Fax:* 613-937-1523
Don Fairweather, Campus Dean, ext. 2223
dfairweather@sl.on.ca

Kitchener: Conestoga College Institute of Technology & Advanced Learning
299 Doon Valley Dr., Kitchener, ON N2G 4M4, Canada
Tel: 519-748-5220; *Fax:* 519-748-3505
www.conestogac.on.ca/
TTY: 1-866-463-4484
www.facebook.com/ConnectWithConestoga
www.twitter.com/ConestogaC
www.youtube.com/user/conestogapolytechnic
Full Time Equivalency: 6900
Dr. John W. Tibbits, President
jtibbits@conestogac.on.ca

Campuses

Cambridge Campus
850 Fountain St. South, Cambridge, ON N3H 0A8, Canada
Tel: 519-748-5220
Note: School of Engineering Technology & Trades; Institute of Food Processing Technology

Cambridge Downtown Campus
#402, 150 Main St., Cambridge, ON N1R 6P9, Canada
Tel: 519-623-4890
Note: Language Instruction for Newcomers to Canada

Guelph Campus
460 Speedvale Ave. West, Guelph, ON N1H 6N6, Canada
Tel: 519-824-9390
Note: Business Foundations, General Business & Office Administration

Stratford Campus
130 Youngs St., Stratford, ON N5A 1J7, Canada
Tel: 519-271-5700
Note: Continuing education & acdemic upgrading

Waterloo Campus
108 University Ave. East, Waterloo, ON N2J 2W2, Canada
Tel: 519-885-0300
Note: Skilled trades & culinary arts training; English studies; Roofing Skills Training Centre & Heating, Refrigeration & Air Conditioning Training Centre; Masonry Centre

Ingersoll Skills Training Centre
420 Thomas St., Ingersoll, ON N5C 3J7
Tel: 519-485-5666
www.conestogac.on.ca/campuses/ingersoll

***London:* Fanshawe College**
P.O. Box 7005
1001 Fanshawe College Blvd., London, ON N5Y 5R6, Canada
Tel: 519-452-4430; *Fax:* 519-452-4420
www.fanshawec.ca
www.facebook.com/fanshaweapplicants
www.twitter.com/fanshawecollege
www.linkedin.com/company/fanshawe-college
www.youtube.com/myfanshawe
Full Time Equivalency: 15000
Peter Devlin, President

Downtown London Campus
Citi Plaza Mall
#114, 355 Wellington St., London, ON N6A 3N7, Canada
Tel: 519-667-2392

James N. Allan Campus (Simcoe)
P.O. Box 10
634 Ireland Rd., Simcoe, ON N3Y 4K8, Canada
Tel: 519-426-8260; *Fax:* 519-428-3112

St. Thomas/Elgin Campus
120 Bill Martyn Pkwy., St Thomas, ON N5R 6A7, Canada
Tel: 519-633-2030; *Fax:* 519-633-0043

Woodstock Campus
369 Finkle St., Woodstock, ON N4V 1A3, Canada
Tel: 519-421-0144; *Fax:* 519-539-3870

Centres/Institutes

Centre for Applied Transportation Technology
Z Bldg.
1764 Oxford St., London, ON N5V 5R6, Canada
Tel: 519-452-4430; *Fax:* 519-452-4420

Centre for Digital & Performance Arts
137 Dundas St., London, ON N6A 1E9
Tel: 519-452-4430

Centre for Sustainable Energy & Environments
1001 Fanshawe College Blvd., #T3010, London, ON N5Y 5R6
Tel: 519-452-4430;
Dan Douglas, Dean
ddouglas@fanshawec.ca

***North Bay:* Canadore College of Applied Arts & Technology**
P.O. Box 5001
100 College Dr., North Bay, ON P1B 8K9, Canada
Tel: 705-474-7600; *Toll-Free:* 855-495-7915
info@canadorec.on.ca
www.canadorec.on.ca
www.facebook.com/canadorecollege
twitter.com/canadorecollege
www.youtube.com/user/CanadoreLiaison
Full Time Equivalency: 3500
George Burton, President
george.burton@canadorecollege.ca
Shawn Chorney, Vice President, Student Services & Recruitment
shawn.chorney@canadorecollege.ca
Marguerite Donohue, Vice President, Academic
marguerite.donohue@canadorecollege.ca
Richard Peters, Vice President, Finance & Corporate Services
richard.peters@canadorecollege.ca

Campuses

Commerce Court Campus
60 Commerce Cres., North Bay, ON, Canada
Tel: 705-474-7600

Aviation Campus
55 Aviation Ave., North Bay, ON, Canada
Tel: 705-474-7600; *Fax:* 705-474-2384

West Parry Sound Campus
1 College Dr., Parry Sound, ON P2A 0A9, Canada
Tel: 705-746-9222

***Oakville:* Sheridan College Institute of Technology & Advanced Learning**
1430 Trafalgar Rd., Oakville, ON L6H 2L1
Tel: 905-845-9430
infosheridan@sheridancollege.ca
www.sheridancollege.ca
www.facebook.com/sheridaninstitute
twitter.com/sheridancollege
www.youtube.com/user/SheridanInstitute
Full Time Equivalency: 53000; *Note:* The polytechnic institute offers pre-apprenticeship & apprenticeship training, one-year certificate & graduate certificates, two & three-year diplomas, & Bachelor's degrees in applied areas of study. Collaborative degree progrmas are provided through partnerships with the following universities: Brock University, University of Toronto at Mississauga, & York University.
Dr. Jeff Zabudsky, President/CEO

Davis Campus
7899 McLaughlin Rd., Brampton, ON L6V 5H9, Canada
Tel: 905-459-7533

Hazel McCallum (Mississauga) Campus
4180 Duke of York Blvd., Mississauga, ON L5B 0G5, Canada
Tel: 905-845-9430

***Oshawa:* Durham College**
P.O. Box 385
2000 Simcoe St. North, Oshawa, ON L1H 7L7, Canada
Tel: 905-721-2000; *Fax:* 905-721-3113
registrarsoffice@durhamcollege.ca
www.durhamcollege.ca
www.facebook.com/durhamcollege
twitter.com/durhamcollege
www.linkedin.com/company/durham-college
Full Time Equivalency: 6000; *Number of Employees:* 715 full-time; 400 part-time
Don Lovisa, President
Pat Ferren, Manager of Operations, Facilities & Ancillary
patrick.ferren@durhamcollege.ca
Linda Marco, President, Foundation & Associate Vice-President, Development, 905-721-5000, ext. 3138
linda.marco@durhamcollege.ca
Elaine Popp, Vice-President, Academic
Meri Kim Oliver, Vice-President, Student Affairs
Carol Beam, Executive Director, Communications & Marketing
Scott Blakey, Vice-President, Human Resources
Gerry Pinkney, Vice-President, Information Technology Services

Campuses

Whitby Campus
1610 Champlain Ave., Whitby, ON L1N 6A7, Canada
Tel: 905-721-3300
whitbyregistrarsoffice@durhamcollege.ca

***Ottawa:* Algonquin College of Applied Arts & Technology**
1385 Woodroffe Ave., Ottawa, ON K2G 1V8, Canada
Tel: 613-727-4723
www.algonquincollege.com
www.facebook.com/algonquincollege
twitter.com/AlgonquinColleg
www.linkedin.com/company/14808
www.youtube.com/user/algonquinvideos
Full Time Equivalency: 19000
Cheryl Jensen, President

Faculties

School of Advanced Technology (SAT)
www3.algonquincollege.com/sat
Chris Janzen, Dean

School of Health & Community Studies
Tel: 613-727-4723
www3.algonquincollege.com/healthandcommunity
twitter.com/AChealthstudies
Barbara Foulds, Dean

School of Media & Design
www3.algonquincollege.com/mediaanddesign
Russell Mills, Dean

School of Business
www3.algonquincollege.com/business
Karen Davies, Dean

School of Hospitality & Tourism
www3.algonquincollege.com/hospitalityandtourism
Michel Savard, Dean

Algonquin Centre for Construction Excellence (ACCE)
www3.algonquincollege.com/acce
Linda Rees, Dean

Campuses

Perth Campus
7 Craig St., Perth, ON K7H 1X7, Canada
Tel: 613-267-2859

Pembroke Campus
315 Pembroke St. East, Pembroke, ON K8A 3K2, Canada
Tel: 613-735-4700

Mamidosewin Centre
1385 Woodroffe Ave., #E122, Ottawa, ON K2G 1V8
Tel: 613-727-4723; *Fax:* 613-727-7829
www.algonquincollege.com/mamidosewin
www.facebook.com/mamidosewin.centre
Jeffrey Agate, Manager
agatej@algonquincollege.com

***Peterborough:* Sir Sandford Fleming College**
***Also known as:* Fleming College**
Sutherland Campus
599 Brealey Dr., Peterborough, ON K9J 7B1
Tel: 705-749-5530; *Fax:* 705-749-5507
Toll-Free: 866-353-6464
info@flemingcollege.ca
flemingcollege.ca
facebook.com/flemingcollege
twitter.com/flemingcollege
www.linkedin.com/company/323364
www.youtube.com/flemingcollege
Full Time Equivalency: 16000; *Note:* The College consists of the following schools: School of Business & Technology; School of Environmental & Natural Resource Sciences; School of Health & Wellness; School of Interdisciplinary Studies; School of Law, Justice & Community Services; School of Continuing Education & Skilled Trades; & the Haliburton School of The Arts.
Peter McLean, Chair
Tony Tilly, PhD, President

Campuses

Cobourg Campus
1005 Elgin St. West, Cobourg, ON K9A 5J4
Tel: 905-372-6865; *Fax:* 905-372-8570
Note: The Cobourg Campus offers academic upgrading & part time studies, as well as esthetician studies.

Frost Campus
P.O. Box 8000
200 Albert St. South, Lindsay, ON K9V 5E6, Canada
Tel: 705-324-9144; *Fax:* 705-878-9312
Note: The Frost Campus features Fleming College's School of Environmental & Natural Resource Sciences, The Centre for Alternative Wastewater Treatment, The Centre for Heavy Equipment Technology, & The Geomatics Institute.

Haliburton Campus
P.O. Box 839
297 College Dr., Haliburton, ON K0M 1S0, Canada
Tel: 705-457-1680; *Fax:* 705-457-2255
Note: The Haliburton Campus features the Haliburton School of The Arts & Fleming's Ecotourism & Adventure Tourism Management program.

McRae Campus
P.O. Box 4350
555 Bonnacord St., Peterborough, ON K9J 7B1
Tel: 705-749-5530; *Fax:* 705-741-3279
Note: This campus offers specialized programs in skilled trades, apprenticeships, & several part-time studies.
Dr. Glenn Zederayko, Head of Schools

***Sarnia:* Lambton College of Applied Arts & Technology**
South Building - Main Campus
1457 London Rd., Sarnia, ON N7S 6K4, Canada
Tel: 519-542-7751; *Fax:* 519-541-2418
info@lambtoncollege.ca
www.lambton.on.ca
www.facebook.com/lambtoncollege.ca?v=wall
twitter.com/lambtoncollege
www.linkedin.com/company/lambton-college-sarnia
Full Time Equivalency: 2500
Patrick Bennett, Registrar, 519-542-7751, ext. 3310
Patrick.Bennett@lambtoncollege.ca
Judith Morris, President & CEO, 519-542-7751, ext. 2410
judy.morris@lambtoncollege.ca

Campuses

Toronto Campus
400 - 265 Yorkland Blvd., Sarnia, ON M2J 1S5, Canada
Tel: 416-485-2098; *Fax:* 416-485-3505
toronto@lambtoncollege.ca
www.lambton.on.ca/Toronto

***Sault Ste Marie:* Sault College of Applied Arts & Technology**
443 Northern Ave., Sault Ste Marie, ON P6A 5L3
Tel: 705-759-2554; *Fax:* 705-759-3273
Toll-Free: 1-800-461-2260
registrar@saultcollege.ca
www.saultcollege.ca
www.facebook.com/SaultCollege
twitter.com/SaultCollege
www.youtube.com/thesaultcollege
Full Time Equivalency: 4500; *Note:* The College offers education & training to full-time & part-time students in post-secondary, apprenticeship, adult retraining, continuing education, & contract training programs. Specializes in Environmental Studies, Nursing & Aviation.
Peter Berlingieri, Chair
Dr. Ron Common, President

***Sault Ste. Marie:* Algoma University**
1520 Queen St. East, Sault Ste. Marie, ON P6A 2G4, Canada
Tel: 705-949-2301; *Fax:* 705-949-6583
Toll-Free: 888-254-6628
info@algomau.ca
www.algomau.ca
www.facebook.com/algomau
www.twitter.com/algomau
www.linkedin.com/company/algoma-university
www.youtube.com/user/algomauniversity
Full Time Equivalency: 1300
Dr Richard Myers, President
Richard McCutcheon, Academic Dean
dean@algomau.ca
David Marasco, Registrar
registrar@algomau.ca

Campuses
Brampton Campus
#102/103, 24 Queen St. East, Brampton, ON L6V 1A3, Canada
Tel: 905-451-0100; *Fax:* 905-451-0102
brampton@algomau.ca

Timmins Campus
4715 Hwy. 101 East, South Porcupine, ON P0N 1H0, Canada
Tel: 705-235-2311
timmins@algomau.ca

St. Thomas Campus
50 Wellington St., St Thomas, ON N5R 2P8, Canada
Tel: 519-633-6501
info@algomau.ca

***Sudbury:* Cambrian College of Applied Arts & Technology**
1400 Barrydowne Rd., Sudbury, ON P3A 3V8, Canada
Tel: 705-566-8101; *Fax:* 705-524-7334
Toll-Free: 800-461-7145
info@cambriancollege.ca
www.cambriancollege.ca
www.facebook.com/cambriancollege
www.twitter.com/CambrianCollege
www.linkedin.com/company/cambrian-college
www.youtube.com/user/CambrianCollege?gl=CA&hl=en
Full Time Equivalency: 4500
Bill Best, President

Campuses
Manitoulin Campus
7 Water St., Little Current, ON POP 1KO, Canada
Tel: 705-368-3194; *Fax:* 705-368-3496

Espanola Campus
#101, 91 Tudhope St., Espanola, ON P5E 1S6, Canada
Tel: 705-869-4113; *Fax:* 705-869-3071

***Sudbury:* Collège Boréal**
21, boul Lasalle, Sudbury, ON P3A 6B1
Tél: 705-560-6673; *Ligne sans frais:* 800-361-6673
info@collegeboreal.ca
www.collegeboreal.ca
www.facebook.com/pages/Sudbury-ON/College-Boreal/5656218
5756
twitter.com/borealAPP
www.youtube.com/collegeboreal
Note: Le Collège Boréal est un francophone Collège des Arts et des technologies appliquées. Son campus principal est à Sudbury, en Ontario, avec six autres campus situés à Toronto, Timmins, Nipissing Ouest, Hearst, Kapuskasing, et New Liskeard.
Pierre Ropel, Président
Daniel Giroux, Vice-président

***Thunder Bay:* Confederation College**
P.O. Box 398
1450 Nakina Dr., Thunder Bay, ON P7C 4W1, Canada
Tel: 807-475-6110; *Fax:* 807-473-3727
Toll-Free: 800-465-5493
www.confederationc.on.ca
www.facebook.com/confederation
www.twitter.com/confederation
www.youtube.com/confederationcollege
Full Time Equivalency: 3200
Jim Madder, President, 807-475-6350
madder@confederationc.on.ca

Campuses
Dryden Campus
100 Casimir Ave., Dryden, ON P8N 3L4, Canada
Tel: 807-223-3035; *Fax:* 807-223-5460
drydencampus@confederationc.on.ca
www.confederationc.on.ca/dryden
Angelina Anderson, Director
angelina@confederationc.on.ca

Greenstone Campus (Geraldton)
P.O. Box 368
500 - 2nd St. West, Geraldton, ON P0T 1M0, Canada
Tel: 807-854-0652; *Fax:* 807-854-0809
www.confederationc.on.ca/geraldton
Nicole Richmond, Director
nicole.richmond@confederationc.on.ca

Lake of the Woods Campus (Kenora)
P.O. Box 1370
900 Golf Course Rd., Kenora, ON P9N 3X7, Canada
Tel: 807-468-3121; *Fax:* 807-468-3601
kenoracampus@confederationc.on.ca
www.confederationc.on.ca/kenora
Laura Christie, Director

Northshore Campus (Marathon)
P.O. Box 520
14 Hemio Dr., Marathon, ON P0T 2E0, Canada
Tel: 807-229-2464; *Fax:* 807-229-3393
northshorecampus@confederationc.on.ca
www.confederationc.on.ca/marathon
Nicole Richmond, Director
nrichmon@confederationc.on.ca

Rainy River District Campus (Fort Frances)
440 McIrvine Rd., Fort Frances, ON P9A 3T8, Canada
Tel: 807-274-5395; *Fax:* 807-274-2462
fortfrancescampus@confederationc.on.ca
www.confederationc.on.ca/fortfrances
Anne Renaud, Director
arenaud@confederationc.on.ca

Red Lake Campus
P.O. Box 328
60B Hwy. 105, Red Lake, ON P0V 2M0, Canada
Tel: 807-727-2604; *Fax:* 807-727-2144
redlakecampus@confederationc.on.ca
www.confederationc.on.ca/redlake
Angelina Anderson, Director
angelina@confederationc.on.ca

Sioux Lookout Campus
70 Wellington St., Sioux Lookout, ON P8T 1B1, Canada
Tel: 807-737-2851; *Fax:* 807-737-2436
siouxlookoutcampus@confederationc.on.ca
www.confederationc.on.ca/siouxlookout
Angelina Anderson, Director
angelina@conferationc.on.ca

Wawa Campus
3 Maple St., Wawa, ON P0S 1K0, Canada
Tel: 705-856-0713; *Fax:* 705-856-0443
wawacampus@confederationc.on.ca
www.confederationc.on.ca/wawa
Nicole Richmond, Director
nrichmon@confederationc.on.ca

Aviation Centre of Excellence
2003 Derek Burney Dr., Thunder Bay, ON P7K 1J4
Tel: 807-474-2013
www.confederationc.on.ca/aviation

Confederation Natural Resources Centre (CNRC)
398
Thunder Bay, ON P7C 4W1
Tel: 807-475-6651; *Fax:* 807-475-6636
naturalresourcescentre@confederationc.on.ca
www.confederationc.on.ca/naturalresourcescentre
Brian Kirkka, General Manager

***Toronto:* Centennial College of Applied Arts & Technology**
Centennial College
P.O. Box 631 A
Toronto, ON M1K 5E9, Canada
Tel: 416-289-5000; *Fax:* 416-439-7358
Toll-Free: 800-268-4419
success@centennialcollege.ca
www.centennialcollege.ca
www.facebook.com/centennialcollege
www.twitter.com/centennialc
ca.linkedin.com/company/centennial-college?trk=ppro_cprof
www.youtube.com/centennialcollege
Full Time Equivalency: 40000
Ann Buller, President
abuller@centennialcollege.ca

Ashtonbee Campus
75 Ashtonbee Rd., Toronto, ON M1L 4N4, Canada
Note: Home of School of Transportation & largest automotive & aircraft technology training centres in Canada

Midland Campus
1450 Midland Ave., Scarborough, ON M1P 4Z8, Canada
Note: Home of Job Connect, which helps people in the community find work

Morningside Campus
755 Morningside Ave., Toronto, ON M1C 5J9, Canada
Note: School of Health Studies, Engineering Technology & Applied Science

Pickering Learning Site
1340 Pickering Pkwy., Pickering, ON L1V 4E2, Canada
Note: Post-graduate programs

Progress Campus
941 Progress Ave., Toronto, ON M1G 3T8, Canada
Note: Houses Business & Hospitality, Tourism & Culture, Advanced Manufacturing & Automation Engineering Technology, as well as Child Studies & Community Service

Centres/Institutes
Applied Research & Innovation Centre (ARIC)
P.O. Box 631 A
Room D2-04, 941 Progress Ave., Toronto, ON M1K 5E9
Tel: 416-289-5000; *Fax:* 416-289-5070
research@centennialcollege.ca
twitter.com/CentennialARIC
Deepak Grupta, Director

Centennial Energy Institute (CEI)
P.O. Box 631 A
Toronto, ON M1K 5E9
Tel: 416-289-5000
cei@centennialcollege.ca

Institute for Global Citizenship & Equity
P.O. Box 631 A
Room B2-12, 941 Progress Ave., Toronto, ON M1K 5E9
Tel: 416-289-5000
igce@centennialcollege.ca

Residence and Conference Centre
940 Progress Ave., Toronto, ON M1G 3T8, Canada
Note: School of Hospitality, Tourism & Culture

Story Arts Centre
951 Carlaw Ave., Toronto, ON M4K 3M2, Canada
Note: Houses School of Communications, Media & Design

***Toronto:* George Brown College**
St. James Campus
P.O. Box 1015 B
200 King St. East, Toronto, ON M5T 2T9, Canada
Tel: 416-415-2000; *Fax:* 416-415-4641
Toll-Free: 800-265-2002
info@georgebrown.ca
www.georgebrown.ca
TTY: 1-877-515-5559
www.facebook.com/georgebrowncollege
twitter.com/GBCollege
www.linkedin.com/company/george-brown-college
Full Time Equivalency: 15000
Laurae Jo-Gunter, Senior Vice-President, Academic
ljogunter@georgebrown.ca
Anne Sado, President
asado@georgebrown.ca

Campuses
Casa Loma Campus
160 Kendal Ave., Toronto, ON M5R 1M3, Canada
Tel: 416-415-2000

School of Design
230 Richmond St. East, Toronto, ON M5A 1P4, Canada

Waterfront Campus
51 Dockside Dr., Toronto, ON M5A 0B6, Canada

Affiliations
Ryerson University
99 Gerrard St. East, Toronto, ON M5B 2K8, Canada

Centre for Hospitality & Culinary Arts
300 Adelaide St. East, Toronto, ON M5A 1N1, Canada

Centre for Preparatory and Liberal Studies
160 Kendall Ave., Toronto, ON M5R 1M3
Tel: 416-415-5000
liberalarts@georgebrown.ca

Centre for Health Sciences
160 Kendall Ave., Toronto, ON M5R 1M3
Tel: 416-415-5000

Centre for Business
200 King St. East, #313A, Toronto, ON M5A 1N1
Tel: 416-415-5000; *Toll-Free:* 800-265-2002
business@georgebrown.ca

Centre for Arts & Design
160 Kendall Ave., Toronto, ON M5R 1M3
Tel: 416-415-5000

Centre for Construction & Engineering Technologies
160 Kendall Ave., Toronto, ON M5R 1M3
Tel: 416-415-5000

Young Centre for the Performing Arts
50 Tankhouse Lane, Toronto, ON M5A 3C4, Canada

Toronto: Humber Institute of Technology & Advanced Learning

North Campus
205 Humber College Blvd., Toronto, ON M9W 5L7, Canada
Tel: 416-675-3111; *Fax:* 416-675-2427
enquiry@humber.ca
www.humber.ca
www.facebook.com/humbercollege
twitter.com/humbercollege
www.linkedin.com/company/humber-college
youtube.com/humberlive

Full Time Equivalency: 15000
Laurie Rancourt, Senior Vice-President, Academic
laurie.rancourt@humber.ca
Rani Dhaliwal, Senior Vice-President, Planning & Corporate Services, CEO, ext. 5041
rani.daliwal@humber.ca
Tracy Fattore, Vice-President, Finance & Administrative Services
tracy.fattore@humber.ca
Chris Whitaker, President & CEO, ext. 5070

Campuses

Lakeshore Campus
3199 Lakeshore Blvd. West, Toronto, ON M8V 1K8, Canada
Fax: 416-252-8842
Enrollment: 7800

Orangeville Campus
Alder Street Recreation Complex
275 Alder St., Orangeville, ON L9W 5A9, Canada
Fax: 416-798-0307
Enrollment: 200

Centres/Institutes

Sailing & Powerboating Centre (SPC)
Humber Bay Park Rd. West, Toronto, ON M8V 3X7, Canada
Tel: 416-252-7291; *Fax:* 416-252-5393
sailing@humber.ca
www.humber.ca/sailing

Transportation Training Centre (TTC)
55 Woodbine Downs Blvd., Toronto, ON M9W 6N5, Canada
Tel: 416-798-0300; *Fax:* 416-798-0307
humber.ca/trucking

Toronto: New College

Wilson Hall
40 Willcocks St., Toronto, ON M5S 1C6, Canada
Tel: 416-978-2460; *Fax:* 416-978-0554
newcollege.registrar@utoronto.ca
www.newcollege.utoronto.ca

Toronto: Seneca College of Applied Arts & Technology

Newnham Campus
1750 Finch Ave. East, Toronto, ON M2J 2X5
Tel: 416-491-5050; *Fax:* 416-493-3958
admissions@senecac.on.ca
www.senecac.on.ca
www.facebook.com/senecacollege
twitter.com/Seneca_College
www.youtube.com/user/VideoSeneca

Note: The polytechnic educational institution consists of the following faculties: Faculty of Applied Arts & Health Sciences; Faculty of Applied Science & Engineering Technology; Faculty of Business; Faculty of Information Arts & Technology; Faculty of Continuing Education & Training; & Faculty of Workforce Skills Development
Colleen Fleming, B.A., MBA, Chair
David Agnew, President
president@senecacollege.ca

Campuses

Peterborough Aviation Campus
#925, 580 Aiport Rd., Peterborough, ON K9J 0E7
Tel: 416-491-5050
Other Information: 705-775-2376

Jane Campus
21 Beverley Hills Dr., Toronto, ON M3L 1A2
Tel: 416-491-5050; *Fax:* 416-235-0462

King Campus
13990 Dufferin St., King City, ON L7B 1B3
Tel: 416-491-5050

Markham Campus
8 The Seneca Way, Markham, ON L3R 5Y1
Tel: 416-491-5050

Seneca @ York Campus
70 The Pond Rd., Toronto, ON M3J 3M6
Tel: 416-491-5050

Newmarket Campus
Weston Produce Plaza
#3, 16655 Yonge St., Newmarket, ON L3X 1V6
Tel: 905-898-6199

Yorkgate Campus
1 York Gate Blvd., Toronto, ON M3N 3A1
Tel: 416-491-5050

Scarborough Campus
3660 Midland Ave., 2nd Fl., Toronto, ON M1V 0B8
Tel: 416-293-3722

Vaughan Campus
1490 Major Mackenzie Dr. West, #D5, Vaughan, ON L6A 4H6
Tel: 905-417-1781

Centre for Advanced Technologies
1750 Finch Ave. East, Toronto, ON M2J 2X5
Tel: 416-491-5050
www.senecacollege.ca/school/centreadvtech

Centre for Financial Services
1750 Finch Ave. East, Toronto, ON M2J 2X5
Tel: 416-491-5050
www.senecacollege.ca/school/cfs

Centre for Human Resources
1750 Finch Ave. East, Toronto, ON M2J 2X5
Tel: 416-491-5050
www.senecac.on.ca/chr
www.facebook.com/pages/Seneca-CHR/110955898980691

Centre for the Built Environment
1750 Finch Ave. East, Toronto, ON M2J 2X5
Tel: 416-491-5050
www.senecacollege.ca/school/centreforthebuiltenvironment

Welland: Niagara College

Welland Campus
300 Woodlawn Rd., Welland, ON L3C 7L3
Tel: 905-735-2211; *Fax:* 902-736-6000
info@niagaracollege.ca
www.niagaracollege.ca
Other Information: Grimsby Phone: 905-563-3254
www.facebook.com/niagaracollege
twitter.com/Niagara_College
www.youtube.com/user/niagaracollegecanada

Full Time Equivalency: 24000; *Note:* Niagara College offers over 90 post-secondary diploma & graduate certificate programs, skills & apprenticeship training programs, plus two bachelor degree programs.
Allan Schmidt, Chair
Dan Patterson, President, 905-641-2252, ext. 4040
dpatterson@niagaracollege.ca

Campuses

Maid of the Mist Campus
Also known as: Tourism Industry Development Centre
5881 Dunn St., Niagara Falls, ON L2G 2N9, Canada
Tel: 905-374-7454

Niagara-on-the-Lake Campus
135 Taylor Rd., Niagara-on-the-Lake, ON L0S 1J0, Canada
Tel: 905-641-2252

Centres/Institutes

Centre for Students with Disabilities
300 Woodlawn Rd., #SE102, Welland, ON L3C 7L3
Tel: 905-735-2211; *Fax:* 905-736-6008
www.niagaracollege.ca/content/CentreforStudentswithDisabilities CSWD

Windsor: St. Clair College

South Campus
2000 Talbot Rd. West, Windsor, ON N9A 6S4
Tel: 519-966-1656; *Fax:* 519-972-3811
Toll-Free: 1-800-387-0524
info@stclaircollege.ca
www.stclaircollege.ca
www.facebook.com/StClairCollege
www.twitter.com/stclaircollege
www.youtube.com/stclairmarketing

Full Time Equivalency: 8300; *Note:* The College consists of the following schools of specialization: School of Liberal Arts & Sciences; School of Business & Information Technology; School of Academic Studies; School of Community Studies; School of Media, Art & Design; School of Engineering Technologies; School of Health Sciences; & School of Skilled Trades.
Vince Marcotte, Chair
John A. Strasser, Ph.D., President, 519-972-2701
jstrasser@stclaircollege.ca
Mike Silvaggi, Registrar, 519-972-2727, ext. 4260
msilvaggi@stclaircollege.ca

Campuses

Thames Campus
1001 Grand Ave. West, Chatham, ON N7M 5W4, Canada
Tel: 519-354-9100; *Fax:* 519-354-6941
Note: The campus provides specialized training from the Schools of Business & Technology, & Health & Community Studies.

Wallaceburg Campus - James A. Burgess Skills Centre
920 Elgin St., Wallaceburg, ON N9A 3E1, Canada
Tel: 519-627-8336; *Fax:* 519-627-5950
Note: The campus features the Technical Industry Education Partnership.

Centres/Institutes

Centre For Applied Health Sciences
2000 Talbot Rd. West, Windsor, ON N9A 6S4
www.stclaircollege.ca/healthsciences

Ford Centre for Excellence in Manufacturing
2000 Talbot Rd. West, Windsor, ON N9A 6S4
www.stclaircollege.ca/fcem

St. Clair Centre for the Arts
201 Riverside Dr. West, Windsor, ON N9A 5K4
Tel: 519-252-8311; *Fax:* 519-973-4976
Enrollment: 500; *Note:* The campus features the School of Media, Art & Design.
Ed Noot, Principal
Mike Campbell, Vice Principal & Counsellor

Post Secondary/Technical

Independent & Private Schools

Toronto: Outward Bound Canada

Centre for Green Cities
#404, 550 Bayview Ave., Toronto, ON M4W 3X8, Canada
Tel: 705-382-5454; *Fax:* 705-382-5959
Toll-Free: 1-888-688-9273
info@outwardbound.ca
www.outwardbound.ca
www.facebook.com/outwardboundcanada?ref=ts
twitter.com/OutwardBoundCan
www.linkedin.com/company/outward-bound-canada
www.youtube.com/user/OutwardBoundCanada

Enrollment: 440
Sarah Wiley, Executive Director
sarah_wiley@outwardbound.ca

Post Secondary/Technical

Alfred: Collège d'Alfred de l'Université de Guelph

31, rue St-Paul, CP 580, Alfred, ON K0B 1A0, Canada
Tél: 613-679-2218; *Téléc:* 613-679-2423
www.alfredc.uoguelph.ca

Note: Agriculture, horticulture, techniques de diététique, développement international, techniques soins vétérinaires
Dr. Renée Bergeron, Ph.D., Directrice

Ancaster: Redeemer University College

777 Garner Rd. East, Ancaster, ON L9K 1J4, Canada
Tel: 905-648-2131; *Fax:* 905-648-2134
communications@redeemer.ca
www.redeemer.ca
www.facebook.com/redeemer
twitter.com/RedeemerUC
www.youtube.com/redeemeruc#p/a/u/1/U073KL05ktI

Enrollment: 910; *Number of Employees:* 150
Justin D. Cooper, Ph.D., President
Jacob P. Ellens, Ph.D., Vice-President
William van Staalduinen, M.A., Vice-President
Ineke VanBruinessen, C.G.A., Senior Director
Marian Ryks-Szelekovszky, M.Ed., Senior Director, Admissions & Student Services
Mark Van Beveren, M.B.A., Media & Public Relations Director
Doug Loney, Ph.D., Dean
Doug Needham, Ph.D., Dean

Belleville: Loyalist College
P.O. Box 4200
376 Wallbridge-Loyalist Rd., Belleville, ON K8N 5B9, Canada
Tel: 613-969-1913; *Fax:* 613-962-1376
Toll-Free: 888-569-2547
liaison@loyalistc.on.ca
www.loyalistcollege.com
TTY: 613-962-0633
www.facebook.com/loyalistcollege
twitter.com/loyalistcollege
www.linkedin.com/company/loyalist-college
Douglas A.L. Auld, President
Centres/Institutes
Loyalist Training & Knowledge Centre
284B Wallbridge-Loyalist Rd., Belleville, ON K8N 5B9
Tel: 613-966-8121; *Toll-Free:* 877-887-8223
ltkc@loyalistc.on.ca
www.loyalisttraining.com

Belleville: Quinte Ballet School of Canada (QBSC)
196 Palmer Rd., Belleville, ON K8P 4E1
Tel: 613-962-9274; *Fax:* 613-962-9275
Toll-Free: 866-962-9274
info@qbsc.ca
www.quinteballetschool.com
www.facebook.com/133112012368
twitter.com/QuinteBallet
Note: Full-time professional ballet school.
Marilyn Lawrie, Executive Director
executivedirector@qbsc.ca
Catherine Taylor, Artistic Director
artisticdirector@qbsc.ca

Brampton: Brampton College of Health, Business and Technology
#206-208, 7956 Torbram Rd., Brampton, ON L6T 5A2
Tel: 905-790-3940; *Fax:* 905-790-9377
info@bramptoncollege.ca
www.bramptoncollege.ca

Brantford: Medical Radiation Technology
c/o Ontario Association of Medical Radiation Tech
P.O. Box 1054
Brantford, ON N3T 5S7, Canada
Tel: 519-753-6037; *Fax:* 519-753-6408
Toll-Free: 1-800-387-467
inquiries@oamrt.on.ca
www.oamrt.on.ca

Burlington: Business Education College (BEC)
#207, 2289 Fairview St., Burlington, ON
Tel: 905-631-1206
info@beduc.com
beduc.com
Campuses
Business Education College - Mississauga (BEC)
#404, 151 City Centre Dr., Mississauga, ON
Tel: 905-270-2730
info@beduc.com
beduc.com

Burlington: Charles Sturt University, Ontario
Bay Area Learning Centre
860 Harrington Ct., Burlington, ON L7N 3N4, Canada
Tel: 905-333-4955; *Fax:* 905-333-6562
canada@csu.edu.au
www.charlessturt.ca
Number of Employees: 20 academic staff; 8 faculty advisors; 2 adminsitrative staff; *Note:* 1-year teacher education program
Dr. Will Letts, Head of School, 905-333-4955, ext. 55105
wletts@csu.edu.au

Burlington: HBI College (HBI)
#26, 460 Brant St., Burlington, ON L7R 4B6, Canada
Tel: 905-637-3415; *Fax:* 905-637-2843
Toll-Free: 1-855-949-9909
info@hbicollege.com
www.hbicollege.com
Note: Administrative & computer programs.
Campuses
Brampton Campus (HBI)
#314, 7700 Hurontario St., Brampton, ON L6Y 4M3, Canada
Toll-Free: 1-855-949-9909

Concord: RCC College of Technology
2000 Steeles Ave. West, Concord, ON L4K 4N1, Canada
Tel: 905-669-0544; *Fax:* 905-669-0551
Toll-Free: 1-800-83865428
www.rcc.on.ca
Note: Electronics & computer networks engineering technology training & programs
Dr. Rick Davey, President
Schools
School of Engineering Technology & Computing
2000 Steeles Ave. West, Concord, ON L4K 4N1, Canada
Fax: 905-695-1389
Toll-Free: 866-838-6542
www.rccsetc.ca
www.facebook.com/SETCCanada
twitter.com/SETCCanada
www.youtube.com/user/rccit?feature=mhum
Rick Davey, President
Academy of Design
2000 Steeles Ave. West, Concord, ON L4K 4N1, Canada
Tel: 905-669-0544; *Fax:* 905-669-0551
Toll-Free: 1-866-838-6542
www.aodt.ca
www.facebook.com/AcademyOfDesignToronto
twitter.com/TorontoAOD
www.youtube.com/user/AcademyToronto
Note: Fashion design, fashion marketing, interior design, graphic media.
Toronto Film School
2000 Steeles Ave. West, Concord, ON L4K 4N1, Canada
Tel: 905-669-0544; *Fax:* 905-669-0551
Toll-Free: 1-800-83865428
www.torontofilmschool.ca
www.facebook.com/TorontoFilmSchool
twitter.com/TorontoFilmS
www.youtube.com/user/TorontoFilmS1
Campuses
Davisville Campus
1835 Yonge St., 2nd Fl., Toronto, ON M4S 1X8, Canada
Tel: 905-669-0544; *Fax:* 905-669-0551
Dundas Campus
#704, 10 Dundas St. East, Toronto, ON M5B 2G9, Canada
Tel: 647-288-8496; *Fax:* 647-644-1903

Dundas: Dundas Valley School of Art (DVSA)
21 Ogilvie St., Dundas, ON L9H 2S1, Canada
Tel: 905-628-6357; *Fax:* 905-628-1087
dvsa@cogeco.net
www.dvsa.ca
Arthur Greenblatt, Director

Guelph: Ontario Agricultural College
OAC Dean's Office, Univ. of Guelph
103 Johnston Hall, Guelph, ON N1G 2W1, Canada
Tel: 519-824-4120; *Fax:* 519-766-1423
oacinfo@uoguelph.ca
www.oac.uoguelph.ca
Heather Renwick, Executive Assistant, 519-824-4120, ext. 56513
hrenwick@oac.uoguelph.ca
Dr. Craig J. Pearson, Dean, 519-824-4120, ext. 52285
cpearson@uoguelph.ca

Hamilton: Canadian Institute for NDE
135 Fennell Ave. West, Hamilton, ON L8N 3T2, Canada
Tel: 905-387-1655; *Fax:* 905-574-6080
info@cinde.ca
www.cinde.ca
Note: Nondestructive testing/nondestructive examination
Douglas Marshall, Managing Director

Hamilton: Grand Health Academy
760 King St. East, Hamilton, ON L8M 1A6
Tel: 905-577-7707; *Fax:* 905-577-7738
www.grandhealthacademy.com
www.facebook.com/grandhealthacademy
twitter.com/GHA_school
Note: Established in 1992, Grand Health Academy offers programs that prepare students to become personal support workers, food service workers, pharmacy assistants, & rehabilitation assistants.

Hamilton: Luba Mera School of Aesthetics & Cosmetology
370 Main St. East, Hamilton, ON L8N 1J6, Canada
Tel: 905-522-3883; *Toll-Free:* 1-888-809-5559
institute@lubamera.com
www.lubamera.com
www.facebook.com/LubaMeraInstitute
Note: Aesthetics training.

Hamilton: Medical Laboratory Technology
The Canadian Society for Medical Laboratory Scien
P.O. Box 2830
Hamilton, ON L8N 3N8, Canada
Tel: 905-528-8642; *Fax:* 905-528-4968
kurtd@csmls.org
www.csmls.org
Kurt H. Davis, Executive Director

London: AlphaLogic Career College
280 King Edward Ave., London, ON N5Z 3V3
Tel: 519-858-0010; *Fax:* 519-858-0089
info@alphalogic.net
www.alphalogic.net
Note: Since 1995, the private career college has offered diploma programs, industry standard certifications, & courses in the areas of customer service, network administration, desktop support, & medical office & automotive specialties.
Jerry S. Vandergoot, President
Kerry Cruickshank, Director, Student Services

London: Elegance Schools Inc.
219 Oxford St. West, London, ON N6H 1S5, Canada
Tel: 519-434-1181; *Fax:* 519-434-1182
www.eleganceschools.on.ca
Note: Esthetics & electrolysis.
Lisa Hakim, Director

London: St. Peter's Seminary
1040 Waterloo St. North, London, ON N6A 3Y1, Canada
Tel: 519-432-1824; *Fax:* 519-432-0964
stpeters@uwo.ca
www.stpetersseminary.ca
Rev. W.T. McGrattan, B.E.Sc., M.Div., S.T.L., Rector
Rev. T.F. O'Connor, M.A., M.T.S., M.Th., Spiritual Director
Rev. Brian Dunn, Dean
Rev. John Comiskey, B.A., M.Div., H.E.L., H.E, Vice Rector & Registrar
Gabriella Catolino, D.M.C., M.Div., Executive Director

London: Westervelt College
1060 Wellington Rd., London, ON N6E 3W5
Tel: 226-289-2108; *Toll-Free:* 1-877-668-2001
Info@WesterveltCollege.com
www.westervelt.ca
Note: Westervelt College opened in 1885. The college has faculties of healthcare, business, law, service, & technology.

Mississauga: BizTech College
#205, 5170 Dixie Rd., Mississauga, ON L4W 1E3
Toll-Free: 866-328-6687
info@biztechcollege.com
www.biztechcollege.com
www.facebook.com/BiztechCollege
twitter.com/Biztechcollege
ca.linkedin.com/pub/biztechcollege-ontario/63/442/bb6

Mississauga: Credit Institute of Canada
#216C, 219 Dufferin St., Mississauga, ON M6K 3J1, Canada
Tel: 905-572-2615; *Fax:* 905-572-2619
www.creditedu.org
E. Keith Devolin, President & Dean
Geoff Wilkinson, General Manager

Mississauga: The Investment Funds Institute of Canada (IFSE)
#601, 50 Burnhamthorpe Rd. West, Mississauga, ON L5B 3C2, Canada
Tel: 416-865-1237; *Toll-Free:* 1-888-865-2437
ifse@ifse.ca
www.ifse.ca
Keith Costello, Managing Director
Campuses
Québec Branch
#1800, 1010, rue Sherbrooke ouest, Montréal, QC H3A 2R7, Canada
Fax: 514-985-5113

Mississauga: triOS College
#103, 6755 Mississauga Rd., Mississauga, ON L5N 7Y2
Tel: 905-814-7212; *Fax:* 905-813-8250
Toll-Free: 888-958-7467
www.trios.com
www.facebook.com/groups/trioscollege
www.twitter.com/trioscollegeBTH
www.linkedin.com/company/trios-college
www.youtube.com/user/triosTV
Note: triOS is a private career college offering numerous career-focused diploma programs.
Frank Gerencser, Chief Executive Officer
Stuart Bentley, President & Chief Operating Officer

Campuses
Windsor Campus
7610 Tecumseh Rd. East, Windsor, ON N8T 1E9
Tel: 519-945-0770; *Fax:* 519-945-3662
Toll-Free: 888-958-7467

London Campus
520 First St., London, ON N5V 3C6
Tel: 519-455-0551; *Fax:* 519-455-0090
Toll-Free: 888-958-7467

Kitchener Campus
110 King St. East, Kitchener, ON N2G 0A5
Tel: 519-578-0838; *Fax:* 519-578-8081
Toll-Free: 866-348-7467

Hamilton Campus
4 Hughson St. South, Hamilton, ON L8N 3Z1
Tel: 905-528-8972; *Fax:* 905-528-9608
Toll-Free: 866-348-7467

Mississauga Campus
55 City Centre Dr., 2nd Fl., Mississauga, ON L5B 1M3
Tel: 905-949-4955; *Fax:* 905-897-9755
Toll-Free: 866-348-7467

Brampton Campus
252 Queen St. East, Brampton, ON L6V 1C1
Tel: 905-450-2230; *Fax:* 905-450-3041
Toll-Free: 866-348-7467

Toronto Campus
#200, 425 Bloor St. East, Toronto, ON M4W 3R4
Tel: 416-922-4250; *Fax:* 416-413-0862
Toll-Free: 877-798-7467

Toronto Campus
#3128, 4438 Sheppard Ave. East, 3rd Fl., Toronto, ON M1S 5V9
Tel: 416-646-1222; *Fax:* 416-646-1232
Toll-Free: 866-339-8276

Oshawa Campus
#C5, 200 John St. West, Oshawa, ON L1J 2B4
Tel: 905-435-9911; *Fax:* 905-435-9985
Toll-Free: 888-718-7467

Niagara Falls: Niagara Parks School of Horticulture
P.O. Box 150
2565 Niagara Pkwy., Niagara Falls, ON L2E 6T2, Canada
Tel: 905-356-8554; *Fax:* 905-356-5488
schoolofhorticulture@niagaraparks.com
www.niagaraparks.com/school-of-horticulture
Enrollment: 30; *Number of Employees:* 15
R. Stoner, Contact, 905-356-8554, ext. 226
rstoner@niagaraparks.com

North Bay: Canadore College of Applied Arts & Technology
P.O. Box 5001
100 College Dr., North Bay, ON P1B 8K9, Canada
Tel: 705-474-7600; *Toll-Free:* 855-495-7915
info@canadorec.on.ca
www.canadorec.on.ca
www.facebook.com/canadorecollege
twitter.com/canadorecollege
www.youtube.com/canadoreliaison
Enrollment: 2977
George Burton, President

North York: Bryan College of Applied Health & Business Science
1200 Lawrence Ave. West, North York, ON M6A 1E3
Tel: 416-630-6300; *Fax:* 416-630-9066
Toll-Free: 888-641-6300
admissions@bryancollege.ca
bryancollege.ca
www.facebook.com/pages/Bryan-College-Toronto/304323792989579
Adriana Costenaro, Campus Director

Norwood: Eastern Ontario Fire Academy
P.O. Box 460
36 Industrial Dr., Norwood, ON K0L 2V0
Tel: 705-639-2121; *Fax:* 905-426-3032
eofa@oafc.on.ca
www.eofa.ca

Ohsweken: Six Nations Polytechnic
P.O. Box 700
Ohsweken, ON N0A 1M0, Canada
Tel: 519-445-0023; *Fax:* 519-445-4416
president@snpolytechnic.com
www.snpolytechnic.com
Rebecca Jamieson, President

Ottawa: Algonquin Careers Academy
1830 Bank St., Ottawa, ON K1V 7Y6
Tel: 613-722-7811; *Fax:* 613-722-4494
Toll-Free: 1-888-722-7818
www.algonquinacademy.com
www.facebook.com/AlgonquinCareersAcademy?sk=wall
Note: Since 1981, the Algonquin Careers Academy has offered programs in areas such as travel counselling, personal support work, medical lab assistance, medical office assistance, health & fitness promotion, & accounting.

Ottawa: Canadian Police College (CPC) Collège canadien de police
P.O. Box 8900
1 Sandridge Rd., Ottawa, ON K1G 3J2, Canada
Tel: 613-993-9500; *Fax:* 613-990-9738
cpc-ccp@rcmp-grc.gc.ca
www.cpc.gc.ca
www.facebook.com/262605970429119
twitter.com/cpc1976ccp
www.youtube.com/user/CanPoliceCollege?feature=mhee
Cal Corley, Director general
cal.corley@rcmp-grc.gc.ca

Campuses
Canadian Police College West
Collège canadien de police
1101 Calais Cres., Chilliwack, BC V2R 5S7, Canada
Tel: 604-703-7500; *Fax:* 604-703-2517
Number of Employees: 300 instructors
Sue Gadsby, Contact
susan.gadsby@rcmp-grc.gc.ca

Ottawa: La Cité collégiale
801, promenade de l'Aviation, Ottawa, ON K1K 4R3, Canada
Tél: 613-742-2483; *Téléc:* 613-742-2481
Ligne sans frais: 1-800-267-2483
info@lacitec.on.ca
www.lacitecollegiale.com
www.facebook.com/lacitecollegiale.on
twitter.com/citecollegiale
www.youtube.com/user/LaCitecollegiale
Enrollment: 3500
Andrée Lortie, Président

Campuses
Campus Alphonse-Desjardins
Centre des métiers Minto
8865, North Service Rd., Orléans, ON, Canada
Ligne sans frais: 1-800-267-2483

Campus de Hawkesbury
570, rue Kitchener, Hawkesbury, ON K6A 2P3, Canada
Ligne sans frais: 1-800-267-2483

Campus de Pembroke
412, rue Pembroke ouest, Pembroke, ON K8A 5N6, Canada
Ligne sans frais: 1-800-267-2483

Ottawa: Ican College of Computers and Healthcare
1825 Woodward Dr., Ottawa, ON K2C 0P9, Canada
Tel: 613-519-0703
www.icancollegeottawa.ca

Ottawa: International Academy Health Education Centre
380 Forest St., Ottawa, ON K2B 8E6, Canada
Tel: 613-820-0318; *Fax:* 613-820-7478
Toll-Free: 800-267-8732
info@intlacademy.com
www.intlacademy.com
www.facebook.com/internationalacademyhealtheducation
www.youtube.com/channel/UCCzjnU6PgSoZwvIKjIC1hhg
Note: Nutrition; herbs; iridology; reflexology; aromatherapy; homeopathy; shiatsu/accupressure; massage
Dorothy Marshall, Ph.D., N.D., C.H.H.P., N., Executive Director

Ottawa: International Academy of Natural Health Sciences
380 Forest St., Ottawa, ON K2B 8E6, Canada
Tel: 613-820-0318; *Fax:* 613-820-7478
Toll-Free: 1-800-267-8732
naturalhealth@intlacademy.com
www.intlacademy.com
Note: Nutrition; herbs; iridology; reflexology
Paul Raven, Principal
Tanya Sparkes, Program Director

Ottawa: Ottawa School of Art
35 George St., Ottawa, ON K1N 8W5, Canada
Tel: 613-241-7471; *Fax:* 613-241-4391
info@artottawa.ca
www.artottawa.ca
Note: Fine arts training.
Jeff Stellick, Executive Director

Ottawa: Pères Montfortains (Residence des étudiants)
463 Riverdale Ave., Ottawa, ON K1S 1S1, Canada
Tél: 613-731-2271
Cor Kauffman, s.m.m., Superior

Ottawa: Versailles Academy of Make-Up Arts, Esthetics, Hair
#1, 1930 Bank St., Ottawa, ON K1V 7Z8
Tel: 613-521-4155; *Fax:* 613-521-6945
info@versaillesacademy.com
www.versaillesacademy.com
Note: Since 1981, the private career college has trained students for work in the cosmetic, hairstyling, & esthetic fields.

Ottawa: Willis College of Business & Technology
85 O'Connor St., Ottawa, ON K1P 5M6, Canada
Tel: 613-233-1128; *Fax:* 613-233-9286
Toll-Free: 877-233-1128
inquiries@ottawa.williscollege.com
www.williscollege.com
www.facebook.com/pages/Willis-College/161733597204726
www.twitter.com/williscollege
www.youtube.com/williscollege
Note: E-business & IT training.
Rima Aristocrat, President/CEO

Campuses
Smith Falls Campus
25 William St. West, Smith Falls, ON K7A 1N2, Canada
Tel: 613-283-1905; *Fax:* 613-283-1333
inquires@smithsfalls.williscollege.com

Cobourg Campus
1111 Elgin St. West, Cobourg, ON K9A 5H7, Canada
Tel: 905-372-8978; *Fax:* 905-372-5189
Toll-Free: 877-762-9979

Owen Sound: Creative Career Systems Academy
114 Drive-In Cres., RR#5, Owen Sound, ON N4K 5N7, Canada
Tel: 519-376-7396; *Fax:* 519-376-6772
info@CCSAcademy.com
www.ccsacademy.com
www.twitter.com/ccsacademy
Note: Health care aide program.

Ridgetown: University of Guelph Ridgetown Campus
120 Main. St. East, Ridgetown, ON N0P 2C0, Canada
Tel: 519-674-1500; *Fax:* 519-674-1515
www.ridgetownc.uoguelph.ca
Ken McEwan, Interim Director
J.M. Brooks, Executive Officer
jbrooks@ridgetownc.uoguelph.ca

Scarborough: Durham Business & Computer College
#216, 1457 McCowan Rd., Scarborough, ON M1E 2S2, Canada
Tel: 416-724-1053; *Fax:* 416-724-5258
Toll-Free: 1-866-427-3010
geninfo@staff.dbcc.on.ca
www.dbcc.on.ca
Note: Business; Information Technology; Health Care; Corporate Training

Campuses
Oshawa Campus
#111, 50 Richmond St., Oshawa, ON L1G 7C7, Canada
Tel: 905-443-3010; *Fax:* 905-443-3011
Note: Business; Information Technology; Health Care; Corporate Training

Pickering Campus
#220, 1099 Kingston Rd., Pickering, ON L1V 1B5, Canada
Tel: 905-427-3010; *Fax:* 905-420-6752
Note: Business; Information Technology; Health Care; Corporate Training
Farid Jenabieh, President

Scarborough: St. Augustine's Seminary of Toronto
2661 Kingston Rd., Scarborough, ON M1M 1M3, Canada
Tel: 416-261-7207; *Fax:* 416-261-2529
tehil@web.net
www.staugustines.on.ca
Enrollment: 95
Rev. Msgr. A. Robert Nusca, B.A., M.Div., S.T.B., S.S, Rector
Rev. Robert J. Barringer, C.S.B., Dean

***Sudbury:* Transport Canada Training Institute**
2565 Kingsway Blvd., Sudbury, ON P3B 2G1, Canada
Tel: 705-521-1157; *Fax:* 705-521-1156
Toll-Free: 1-800-805-0662
headoffice@ttcc.ca
www.ttcc.ca
www.facebook.com/transporttraining
Note: 23 locations around Ontario, Nova Scotia and New Brunswick.

***Thunder Bay:* Northern Ontario School of Medicine (NOSM)**
West Campus, Lakehead University
955 Oliver Rd., Thunder Bay, ON P7B 5E1, Canada
Tel: 807-766-7300; *Fax:* 807-766-7370
Toll-Free: 1-800-461-8777
communications@nosm.ca
www.nosm.ca
www.facebook.com/thenosm
twitter.com/nosmtweets
www.youtube.com/user/NOSMtv
Note: 4-year MD program
Moira McPherson, Chair
Roger Strasser, Dean & CEO

Campuses
East Campus (NORMED)
935 Ramsey Lake Rd., Sudbury, ON P3E 2C6, Canada
Tel: 705-675-4883; *Fax:* 705-675-4858
Note: Associated with Laurentian University.
West Campus (NORMED)
955 Oliver Rd., Thunder Bay, ON P7B 5E1, Canada
Tel: 807-766-7300; *Fax:* 807-766-7370
Note: Associated with Lakehead University.

***Timmins:* Northern College**
P.O. Box 3211
Timmins, ON P4N 8R6
Tel: 705-235-3211; *Fax:* 705-235-7279
info@northern.on.ca
www.northernc.on.ca
www.facebook.com/northernc
twitter.com/northernc_on_ca
Enrollment: 2300
Fred Gibbons, President
Don Wyatt, Chair

Campuses
Haileybury Campus
P.O. Box 2060
640 Latchford St., Haileybury, ON P0J 1K0
Tel: 705-672-3376;
Kirkland Lake Campus
140 Government Rd. East, Kirkland Lake, ON P2N 3L8, Canada
Tel: 705-567-9291; *Fax:* 705-568-8186
Timmins Campus
4715 Highway 101 East, South Porcupine, ON P0N 1H0, Canada
Tel: 705-235-3211; *Fax:* 705-235-7279
Moosonee Campus
P.O. Box 130
Moosonee, ON P0L 1Y0
Tel: 705-336-2913

***Toronto:* APLUS Institute**
Madison Centre
4950 Yonge St., Toronto, ON M2N 6K1
Tel: 416-222-0500
info@aplusinstitute.com
aplusinstitute.ca
www.facebook.com/aplusdentalhygiene
twitter.com/aplusik
ca.linkedin.com/
www.youtube.com/watch?v=rliykPuNZGo
Note: Dental Hygiene Programs.

***Toronto:* Automotive Training Centres - Toronto Centre**
152 Norseman St., Toronto, ON M8Z 2R4, Canada
Tel: 416-231-7227; *Fax:* 416-231-2753
Toll-Free: 1-800-458-7473
toronto@autotrainingcentre.com
www.autotrainingcentre.com
Note: Private college specializing in automotive training

Campuses
Montreal Campus
7555, boul Henri-Bourassa, Montréal, QC H1E 1N9, Canada
Tel: 514-725-6026; *Fax:* 514-725-1630
Toll-Free: 1-877-725-6026
Montreal@AutoTrailingCentre.com
Surrey Campus
12160 - 88th Ave., Surrey, BC V3W 3J2, Canada
Tel: 604-635-2222; *Fax:* 604-635-2223
Toll-Free: 1-888-546-2886
Surry@AutoTrainingCentre.com

***Toronto:* BBT Computer Training Centre**
#210, 3790 Victoria Park Ave., Toronto, ON M2H 3H7
Tel: 416-323-3398; *Fax:* 416-323-1689
bbt@bbtcollege.com
www.bbtcollege.com

***Toronto:* Business & Technical Training College (BIT)**
***Also known as:* BTT College**
#402, 150 Eglinton Ave. East, Toronto, ON M4P 1E8
Tel: 416-483-3567; *Fax:* 416-483-7567
admin@bttcollege.com
www.bttcollege.com
www.facebook.com/bttcollege
Number of Employees: 20

***Toronto:* Canadian Academy of Floral Art (CAFA) L'Académie canadienne d'art floral**
72 Northdale Rd., Toronto, ON M2L 2M1
Tel: 519-836-5495; *Fax:* 519-836-7529
Toll-Free: 800-698-0113
www.cafachat.com
www.cafachat.com
www.facebook.com/group.php?gid=113431802003393
Note: Floral designers who become members of the Canadian Academy of Floral Art are permitted to add the initials CAFA after their name.

***Toronto:* Canadian Business College**
Head Office
2 Bloor St. West, 22nd Fl., Toronto, ON M4W 3E2
Tel: 416-925-9929; *Fax:* 416-925-9220
www.cbstraining.com
www.facebook.com/cbstraining
twitter.com/cbstraining
www.youtube.com/watch?v=ylidYvYAVxc
Note: Courses are offered in the areas of business, information technology, digital media, law, health, community service, & child care. The Canadian Business College is registered with the Government of Canada's Human Resources Development Canada.

***Toronto:* Canadian Churches' Forum for Global Ministries**
Toronto School of Theology
47 Queen's Park Cres. East, Toronto, ON M5S 2C3, Canada
Tel: 416-924-9351; *Fax:* 416-978-7821
director@ccforum.ca
www.ccforum.ca
Note: Cross cultural orientation programs for church related personnel & volunteers involved in global mission & ministry

***Toronto:* The Canadian College of Naturopathic Medicine**
1255 Sheppard Ave. East, Toronto, ON M2K 1E2, Canada
Tel: 416-498-1255; *Toll-Free:* 1-866-241-2266
www.ccnm.edu
www.facebook.com/myccnm
twitter.com/myccnm
www.youtube.com/myccnm
Enrollment: 600; *Number of Employees:* 100 full time; 100 part time; *Note:* Naturopathic medical education, research & clinical practice; 4,500+ hours of classroom & clinical training
Nicholas De Groot, Dean
Bob Bernhardt, President & CEO

***Toronto:* Canadian Jewellers Association (CJA)**
#600, 27 Queen St. East, Toronto, ON M5C 2M6, Canada
Tel: 416-368-7616; *Fax:* 416-368-1986
Toll-Free: 1-800-580-0942
www.canadianjewellers.com
Note: Programs include Jewellery Education Training System (JETS), and the Accredited Appraiser Program.
Maria Garcia, Manager, Education Services

***Toronto:* Canadian Law Enforcement Training College**
#2, 4646 Dufferin St., Toronto, ON M3H 5S4, Canada
Tel: 416-480-1545
info@policefoundations.org
www.policefoundations.org
twitter.com/cdnlawenforce
Note: Police & law enforcement courses

***Toronto:* Canadian Memorial Chiropractic College**
6100 Leslie St., Toronto, ON M2H 3J1, Canada
Tel: 416-482-2340; *Fax:* 416-482-9745
Toll-Free: 800-463-2923
communications@cmcc.ca
www.cmcc.ca
Note: Undergraduate and graduate Chiropratic College.
Jean A. Moss, D.C., M.B.A., President
president@cmcc.ca

***Toronto:* Canadian School of Private Investigation & Security Ltd.**
2828 Dufferin St., Toronto, ON M6B 3S3, Canada
Tel: 416-785-5701; *Fax:* 416-785-6064
efranco@CSPIS.com
www.cspis.com
Note: Private investigation, paralegal, security, law enforcement & police foundations training.
Carl Franco, President & Founder

***Toronto:* Canadian Securities Institute (CSI)**
200 Wellington St. West, 15th Fl., Toronto, ON M5V 3C7, Canada
Tel: 416-364-9130; *Fax:* 866-866-2660
Toll-Free: 1-866-866-2601
customer_support@csi.ca
www.csi.ca
www.facebook.com/csiglobal
twitter.com/CSIGlobalEd
www.linkedin.com/groups?gid=3720042
csiblog.csi.ca

Campuses
Montréal Office
#400, 625, boul René-Lévesque ouest, Montréal, QC H3B 1R2, Canada
Fax: 866-866-2660
Toll-Free: 1-866-866-2601

***Toronto:* The Certified General Accountants Association of Ontario**
240 Eglinton Ave. East, Toronto, ON M4P 1K8, Canada
Tel: 416-322-6520; *Fax:* 416-322-5594
Toll-Free: 1-800-668-1454
info@cga-ontario.org
www.cga-ontario.org/
www.facebook.com/cga
twitter.com/CGA_Ontario
www.linkedin.com/company/cga-ontario

***Toronto:* CJ Health Care College - Scarborough Campus**
#401, 1371 Neilson Rd., Toronto, ON M1B 4Z8, Canada
Tel: 416-283-8252; *Fax:* 416-283-3796
admin.scar@cjcollege.com
www.cjcollege.com
Note: Health care related program.
Altheia Jordan, Manager

Campuses
Toronto Campus
#L101, 1123 Albion Rd., Toronto, ON M9V 1A9, Canada
Tel: 416-422-5900; *Fax:* 416-422-5628

***Toronto:* CMS Training**
205 Richmond St. West, Toronto, ON M5V 1V3, Canada
Tel: 416-971-4267; *Fax:* 416-971-6750
info@cms.ca
www.cmstraining.ca
Note: Home study in computer programming

***Toronto:* Complections College of Makeup Art & Design**
110 Lombard St., Toronto, ON M5C 1M3
Tel: 416-968-6739; *Fax:* 416-968-7340
www.complectionsmake-up.com
www.facebook.com/ComplectionsMakeup?sid=a
twitter.com/Complections
www.youtube.com/user/ComplectionsMakeup
Note: Complections, the International Academy of Make-up Artistry offers instruction that leads to a career in makeup artistry.
Pamela Earle, President, Complections International Academy

***Toronto:* Frontier College**
35 Jackes Ave., Toronto, ON M4T 1E2, Canada
Fax: 416-323-3522
Toll-Free: 1-800-555-6523
information@frontiercollege.ca
www.frontiercollege.ca
www.facebook.com/137772832974312
twitter.com/FrontierCollege
www.youtube.com/user/frontiercollege
Note: Volunteer-based, literacy organization.

Sherry Campbell, President & CEO

Toronto: The Glenn Gould School of the Royal Conservatory of Music
90 Croatia St., Toronto, ON M6H 1K9, Canada
Tel: 416-408-2824; *Fax:* 416-408-3096
glenngouldschool@rcmusic.ca
rcmusic.ca/glenn-gould-school
Enrollment: 130; *Note:* Professional training in music performance & pedagogy at the bachelor & graduate levels
Rennie Regehr, Dean

Toronto: Global Village - Toronto
#202, 180 Bloor St. West, Toronto, ON M5S 2V6, Canada
Tel: 416-968-1405; *Fax:* 416-968-6667
toronto@gvenglish.com
www.gvenglish.com
www.facebook.com/GlobalVillageToronto
twitter.com/GVECMarketing
www.youtube.com/user/readyforielts
www.flickr.com/photos/gvenglish
Geneviève Bouchard, Director
Chris Pink, Contact
cpink@gvenglish@com

Campuses
Global Village - Calgary
North-West Travellers Building
#200, 515 - 1st Str. SE, Calgary, AB T2G 2G6, Canada
Tel: 403-543-7300; *Fax:* 403-543-7309
calgary@gvenglish.com
www.facebook.com/GlobalVillageCalgary

Global Village - Vancouver
888 Cambie St., Vancouver, BC V6B 2P6, Canada
Tel: 604-684-2112; *Fax:* 604-684-2124
vancouver@gvenglish.com
www.facebook.com/GlobalVillageVancouver
www.gvenglish.com/videos/gvvancouver01.html
Paul Maher, President/CEO

Global Village - Victoria
#200, 1290 Broad St., Victoria, BC V8W 2A5, Canada
Tel: 250-384-2199; *Fax:* 250-384-2123
victoria@gvenglish.com
www.facebook.com/gvvictoria
www.youtube.com/gvvictoria

Toronto: Herzing College
Toronto, ON
www.herzing.ca
Note: Information technology programs (programming, networking, database management & microprocessor technology), healthcare & legal.

Campuses
Montréal Campus
1616, boul René-Lévesque ouest, Montréal, QC H3H 1P8
Tél: 450-686-7494; *Téléc:* 450-933-6182
Ligne sans frais: 800-818-9688
info@mtl.herzing.edu
www.herzing.ca/montreal
www.facebook.com/herzingmontreal
Note: Founded in 1968, Herzing College Montreal prepares studens for careers in business, technology, & design.
Hayat Telmat Drinali, Campus President

Ottawa Campus
P.O. Box 225
1200. boul St. Laurent, Ottawa, ON K1K 3B8
Tel: 613-742-8099; *Fax:* 613-742-8336
info@otw.herzing.edu
www.facebook.com/herzingottawa
Michael McAllister, Campus President

Toronto Campus
Eaton Centre Galleria Offices
#202, 220 Yonge St., Toronto, ON M5B 2H1, Canada
Tel: 416-599-6996; *Fax:* 416-599-0192
info@tor.herzing.edu
www.facebook.com/herzingtoronto
George Hood, Campus President

Winnipeg Campus
723 Portage Ave., Winnipeg, MB R3G 0M8, Canada
Tel: 204-775-8175; *Fax:* 204-783-8107
info@wpg.herzing.edu
Bill Riches, President

Toronto: ICT Schools - ICT Kikkawa College
2340 Dundas St. West, Toronto, ON M6P 4A9
Tel: 416-762-4857; *Fax:* 416-762-5733
Toll-Free: 888-890-5888
kcregistrar@ictschools.com
www.ictschools.com
Note: Massage therapy course instruction.

Campuses
ICT Schools - ICT Northumberland College
1888 Brunswick St., 5th Fl., Halifax, NS B3J 3J8
Tel: 902-425-2869; *Fax:* 902-425-2858
Toll-Free: 888-862-2230
ncregistrar@ictschools.com
www.ictschools.com
Note: Massage therapy course instruction.

ICT Schools - ICT Moncton College
80 Driscoll Cres., Moncton, NB E1E 3R8
Tel: 506-872-4255; *Fax:* 506-872-4255
Toll-Free: 888-862-2230
nbadmissions@ictschools.com
www.ictschools.com
Note: Massage therapy course instruction.

Toronto: Institute of Technical Trades Ltd.
749 Warden Ave., Toronto, ON M1L 4A8, Canada
Tel: 416-750-1950; *Fax:* 416-750-4702
Toll-Free: 1-800-461-4981
info@instituteoftechnicaltrades.com
www.instituteoftechnicaltrades.com
Note: Welding & CNC machine setup operation.

Toronto: International Institute of Travel (iitravel)
Admissions & Registration
#402, 120 Carlton St., Toronto, ON M5A 4K2, Canada
Tel: 416-924-2271; *Fax:* 416-924-9632
www.iitravel.com
Note: Travel & tourism training including "Learning at Seas Seminars".

Toronto: Marvel Beauty Schools
25 Yorkville Ave., 2nd Fl., Toronto, ON M4W 1L1, Canada
Tel: 416-923-0993; *Fax:* 416-640-4490
Toll-Free: 1-800-661-6096
info@marvelschools.com
www.marvelschools.com
www.facebook.com/pages/Marvel-Beauty-Schools/13867192281 9589
Note: Skin care & hairstyling

Schools
The School of Make-Up Art
25 Yorkville Ave., 3rd Fl., Toronto, ON M4W 1L1, Canada
Tel: 416-340-1300; *Fax:* 416-640-4491
info@schoolofmakeupart.com

Pebec School of Esthetics
496 Dundas St., London, ON N6B 1W6, Canada
Tel: 519-432-7162; *Fax:* 416-640-5950
info@pebec.com

Toronto: Medix School - Toronto Campus
Head Office
#300, 700 Lawrence Ave. West, Toronto, ON M6A 3B4, Canada
Tel: 866-981-0683; *Fax:* 416-630-9790
Toll-Free: 1-866-962-7685
www.medixschool.ca
Note: Health care programs
Randy Henry, President

Campuses
Brantford Campus
39 King George Rd., Brantford, ON N3R 5K2, Canada
Tel: 519-752-4859; *Fax:* 519-752-2217

Kitchener Campus
#14, 248 Stirling Ave., Kitchener, ON N2G 4L1, Canada
Tel: 519-895-0013; *Fax:* 519-772-0107
Toll-Free: 800-695-2414

London Campus
1299 Oxford St. East, London, ON N5Y 4W5, Canada
Tel: 519-659-4822; *Fax:* 519-659-2516
Toll-Free: 800-695-2414

Scarborough Campus
#205, 2130 Lawrence Avenue East, Scarborough, ON M1R 3A6, Canada
Tel: 866-981-0684; *Fax:* 416-701-0855
Toll-Free: 866-981-0684

Brampton Campus
13 Queen St. East, Brampton, ON L6W 2A7, Canada
Fax: 905-487-1162
Toll-Free: 866-981-3295

Toronto: Mothercraft College
646 St. Clair Ave. West, Toronto, ON M6C 1A9
Tel: 416-483-0511; *Fax:* 416-483-0119
college@mothercraft.org
www.mothercraft.ca
Note: Specialized training programs for child care providers and other professionals. Offers a Diploma in Early Childhood Education.
Michele Lupa, Executive Director, 416-483-0511
michele.lupa@mothercraft.org

Toronto: National Institute of Broadcasting (NIB)
1498 Yonge St., Toronto, ON M4T 1Z6, Canada
Tel: 416-922-2556; *Fax:* 416-922-5470
Toll-Free: 1-800-216-6247
www.nibbroadcasttraining.com
Note: Radio & television broadcast training.
Mona Matteo, President

Toronto: New Skills College of Health, Business, & Technology
1500 Birchmount Rd., Toronto, ON M1P 2G5
Tel: 416-269-8878; *Fax:* 416-266-3898
www.newskillscollege.ca
Note: The New Skills College is a member of the Ontario Association of Career Colleges. The college provides training for health care personnel. Examples of programs include training for food handlers, personal attendants, & medical office assistants.
Julia Li, President, 416-266-8878
Paul Preikschas, Program Manager, 416-269-2666, ext. 221

Toronto: The RCM Community School at The Royal Conservatory of Music
90 Croatia St., Toronto, ON M6H 1K9, Canada
Tel: 416-408-2825; *Fax:* 416-408-3096
communityschool@rcmusic.ca
www.rcmusic.ca
Enrollment: 6000; *Note:* Music lessons for people of all ages & levels of ability; recognized for its Early Childhood Education programs & its commitment to life-long learning

Toronto: Regency Dental Hygiene Academy Inc.
#400, 481 University Ave., Toronto, ON M5G 2E9, Canada
Tel: 416-341-0100; *Fax:* 416-341-0747
Toll-Free: 1-866-666-0481
info@regencydha.ca
www.regencydha.com
www.facebook.com/121627584576269
twitter.com/#%21/RegencyDHA

Toronto: Rets PLC Training
2084 Danforth Ave., Toronto, ON M4C 1J9, Canada
Tel: 416-698-5287; *Fax:* 416-689-5288
Note: PLC automation; engineering technology; government regulated & approved.

Toronto: The Royal Conservatory of Music
McMaster Hall
273 Bloor St. West, Toronto, ON M5S 1W2
Tel: 416-408-2825; *Fax:* 866-263-4447
Toll-Free: 1-800-461-6058
conservatoryschool@rcmusic.ca
www.rcmusic.ca
Other Information: TELUS Centre for Performance & Learning, Phone: 416-408-0208
www.facebook.com/theroyalconservatory
twitter.com/the_rcm
www.youtube.com/rcmusic
Note: The Royal Conservatory was founded in 1886. The Conservatory's core programs are as follows: The Royal Conservatory School; The Glenn Gould School; the Young Artists Performance Academy; Learning Through the Arts; The Frederick Harris Music Co., Limited; & Examinations. Every year, approximately 600,000 people from across Canada participate in music education programs offered by The Royal Conservatory.
Michael Foulkes, Chair
Michael M. Koerner, Chancellor
Peter Simon, President
Tony Flynn, Chief Administrative Officer
Krista O'Donnell, Chief Development Officer
Mervon Mehta, Executive Director, Performing Arts
Angela Elster, Vice-President, Academic
Karen Leiter, Vice-President, Marketing & Communication

Toronto: Shiatsu School of Canada Inc.
547 College St., Toronto, ON M6G 1A9, Canada
Tel: 416-323-1818; *Fax:* 416-323-1681
Toll-Free: 1-800-263-1703
info@shiatsucanada.com
www.shiatsucanada.com
Note: 2,200-hour program has the highest standard in the world outside of Japan
Enza Ierullo, Director

Toronto: The Society of Management Accountants of Ontario
#1100, 25 York St., Toronto, ON M5J 2V5, Canada
Tel: 416-977-7741; *Fax:* 416-977-6079
Toll-Free: 1-800-387-299
info@cmaontario.org
www.cma-canada.org/ontario/default.asp
Merv Hillier, FCMA, C. Dir., President & CEO

Toronto: Sutherland Chan School & Teaching Clinic
#400, 330 Dupont St., Toronto, ON M5R 1V9, Canada
Tel: 416-924-1107; *Fax:* 416-924-9413
admissions@sutherland-chan.com
www.sutherland-chan.com
www.facebook.com/127460549809
twitter.com/SutherlandChan
Note: Massage therapy.
Grace Chan, President
Carol Oya, Admissions & Student Services Coordinator

Toronto: Toronto Art Therapy Institute
#103, 66 Portland St., Toronto, ON M5V 2M6, Canada
Tel: 416-924-6221
www.tati.on.ca
Regina Cowan, Chair

Toronto: Toronto Baptist Seminary & Bible College
130 Gerrard St. East, Toronto, ON M5A 3T4, Canada
Tel: 416-925-3263; *Fax:* 416-925-8305
www.tbs.edu
www.facebook.com/pages/Toronto-Baptist-Seminary/176191542436733
twitter.com/tbsedu
Dr. Glendon G. Thompson, President

Toronto: Toronto Institute of Pharmaceutical Technology
#800, 55 Town Centre Ct., Toronto, ON M1P 4X4, Canada
Tel: 416-296-8860; *Fax:* 416-296-7077
info@tipt.com
www.tipt.com
www.facebook.com/TIPTechnology
www.twitter.com/TIPTechnology
Alexander MacGregor, President & Dean

Toronto: Townshend College of Business & Computers Inc.
#714, Victoria St., Toronto, ON M5C 1Y2
Tel: 416-642-0567; *Fax:* 416-642-0567
canada@kkjgroup.ca
www.townshendcollege.com
Note: Founded in 1992, Townshend College provides courses in computerized accounting, e-commerce design & development, computer programming, business, office administration, & technology.

Toronto: Travel Training Career Centre Ltd.
#201, 16 Spadina Rd., Toronto, ON M5R 2S7, Canada
Tel: 416-481-2265; *Fax:* 416-487-5428
info@travelcollege.ca
www.travelcollege.ca
www.facebook.com/TravelCollegeCanada
Note: Travel & tourism industry courses, customer service.
Louise Blazik, Founder & Director

Toronto: Tyndale University College & Seminary
25 Ballyconnor Ct., Toronto, ON M2M 4B3, Canada
Tel: 416-226-6380; *Fax:* 416-226-6746
Toll-Free: 1-877-896-3253
contact@tyndale.ca
www.tyndale.ca
Note: A Christian College and Seminary whose mission is to educate and equip Christians to serve the world with passion for Jesus Christ.
Archie McLean, Chair
Dr. Brian C. Stiller, President
The Hon. Jake Epp, Chancellor

Waterloo: Shad International
8 Young St. East, Waterloo, ON N2J 2L3, Canada
Tel: 519-884-8844; *Fax:* 519-884-8191
info@shad.ca
www.shad.ca
Grades: 10-12; *Note:* Four week summer enrichment program for students in grades 11 or 12, secondaire V or CEGEP I for Quebec students, or the international equivalent. The program includes the sciences, technology, and entrepreneurship. Shad Valley is held on campus at 10 leading universities across Canada. Students live in residence at each university for the month of July.
Barry Bisson, President
barry@shad.ca
Mary Dever, National Director of Development
mary@shad.ca

Prince Edward Island

Government Agencies

Charlottetown: Prince Edward Island Department of Innovation & Advanced Learning
Shaw Building
P.O. Box 2000
105 Rochford St., 5th Fl., Charlottetown, PE C1A 7N8
Tel: 902-368-5956; *Fax:* 902-368-5277
www.gov.pe.ca/ial
Hon. Richard E. Brown, Minister of Innovation & Advanced Learning
rebrown@gov.pe.ca

Summerside: Prince Edward Island Department of Education & Early Childhood Development
Holman Centre
#101, 250 Water St., Summerside, PE C1N 1B6, Canada
Tel: 902-438-4130; *Fax:* 902-438-4062
registrar@edu.pe.ca
www.gov.pe.ca/eecd
Other Information: Charlottetown Phone: 902-368-4600
Hon. Doug Currie, Minister of Education & Early Childhood Development
katiemacdonald@gov.pe.ca

School Boards/Districts/Divisions

Public

Summerside: English Language School Board of Prince Edward Island (ELSB)
Stratford Office
P.O. Box 8600
234 Shakespeare Dr., Summerside, PE C1A 8V7, Canada
Tel: 902-368-6990; *Fax:* 902-368-6960
Toll-Free: 800-280-7965
www.gov.pe.ca/edu/elsb/
twitter.com/elsbpei
Number of Schools: 57; *Grades:* K-12; *Enrollment:* 19000
Cynthia Fleet, Superintendent of Education, 902-368-6850
John Cummings, Director, Corporate Services, 902-368-6845
jacummings@edu.pe.ca
Becky Chaisson, Coordinator, Financial Services
blchaisson@edu.pe.ca
Sandra Callbeck, Contact, Purchasing
sscallbeck@edu.pe.ca
Doug MacDougall, Director, Curriculum Delivery, 902-432-2781
dmmacdougall@gov.pe.ca
Wayne Noseworthy, Director, Human Resources, 902-368-6819
wgnoseworthy@gov.pe.ca
Bob Andrews, Director, School Effectiveness, 902-368-6823
rgandrews@edu.pe.ca
Julia Gaudet, Director, Student Services, 902-368-6832
jlgaudet@gov.pe.ca

Campuses
Summerside Office
288 MacEwen Rd., Summerside, PE C1N 0J1, Canada
Tel: 902-888-8400; *Fax:* 902-888-8449
Toll-Free: 800-280-7965
Cindy MacLean, Superintendent
cjmaclean@edu.pe.ca
Ronald Lee, Vice-Chair
John Cummings, Director, Corporate Services
jacummings@edu.pe.ca
Bob Andrews, Director, School Development
rgandrews@edu.pe.ca
David MacDonald, Secretary

French

Abram Village: La Commission scolaire de langue française de l'Ie-du-Prince-Édouard (CSLF)
P.O. Box 124
1596 rte. 124, Abram Village, PE C0B 2E0, Canada
Tel: 902-854-2975; *Fax:* 902-854-2981
cslf@edu.pe.ca
www.edu.pe.ca/cslf
www.facebook.com/158736104225285
Number of Schools: 6; *Grades:* 1 - 12
Anne Bernard-Bourgeois, Directrice générale
abernardbourgeois@gov.pe.ca
Rachelle Arsenault, Secrétaire administrative
raarsenault@edu.pe.ca
Paul Cyr, Directeur de l'instruction
pacyr@edu.pe.ca
Brad Samson, Directeur des services administratifs et financiers
blsamson@edu.pe.ca
Nathalie Malo, Gestionnaire des ressources humaines et du transport scolaire
nmalo@edu.pe.ca

Schools: Specialized

First Nations

Lennox Island: John J. Sark Memorial School
24 Eagle Feather Trl., Lennox Island, PE C0B 1P0, Canada
Tel: 902-831-2777; *Fax:* 902-831-3065
www.johnjsark.wordpress.com/contact/
www.facebook.com/johnj.sarkmemorial
Grades: K.-6; *Enrollment:* 50; *Number of Employees:* 10; *Note:* Curriculum includes Mi'kmaq language & culture.
Neil Forbes, Education Director
neil.forbes@lennoxisland.com

Schools: Independent & Private

Faith-Based

Charlottetown: Grace Christian School
50 Kirkdale Rd., Charlottetown, PE C1E 1N6, Canada
Tel: 902-628-1668; *Fax:* 902-628-1668
gbc@gracechristianschool.ca
www.gracechristianschool.ca
Grades: K.-12; *Note:* A ministry of Grace Baptist Church
Jason Biech, Principal
principal@gracechristianschool.ca

Charlottetown: Immanuel Christian School
7 Trafalgar St., Charlottetown, PE C1A 3Z2, Canada
Tel: 902-628-6465; *Fax:* 902-628-1831
icsprincipal@eastlink.ca
www.immanuelchristianschool.ca
Grades: K-9; *Enrollment:* 28
Matthew Mann, Principal

Independent & Private Schools

Charlottetown: Fair Isle Adventist School
20 Lapthorne Ave., Charlottetown, PE C1A 2M2, Canada
Tel: 902-894-9301
Grades: 1-9; Seventh-day Adventist; *Enrollment:* 7
Deanna Fall, Principal

Charlottetown: Full Circle Co-operative
219 Kent St., Charlottetown, PE C1A 1P1, Canada
Tel: 902-628-6174
principal@fullcircleschoolonline.net
Grades: 5-12; *Enrollment:* 15
Scott Davidson, B.A., B.Ed., Principal

Universities & Colleges

Universities

Charlottetown: University of Prince Edward Island
550 University Ave., Charlottetown, PE C1A 4P3, Canada
Tel: 902-566-0439; *Fax:* 902-566-0420
home.upei.ca
www.facebook.com/UniversityofPEI
twitter.com/upei
www.youtube.com/UofPEI
Full Time Equivalency: 3500
Tom Cullen, Chair of the Board
Don McDougall, Chancellor
Alaa Abd-El-Aziz, President & Vice-Chancellor
presidentea@upei.ca
Robert Gilmour, Vice-President, Research & Graduate Studies
research@upei.ca
Christian Lacroix, Vice-President, Academic
ecardy@upei.ca
Jackie Podger, Vice-President, Administration & Finance
kharrison@upei.ca
Dana Sanderson, Chief Information Officer
dsanderson@upei.ca
Kathleen Kielly, Registrar & Director, Enrolment Services
kkielly@upei.ca
Mark Leggott, University Librarian
mleggott@upei.ca
Roger Cook, Procurement Services Manager
rcook@upei.ca

Faculties
Faculty of Arts
Tel: 902-566-0307
arts@upei.ca
arts.upei.ca

Richard Kurial, B.A., M.A., Ph.D., Dean

School of Business Administration
Tel: 902-566-0626; *Fax:* 902-628-4302
business.upei.ca
Other Information: 902-566-0564
Roberta MacDonald, B.A., Dean

Faculty of Education
Tel: 902-620-5154
education@upei.ca
ww.upei.ca/education
J. Tim Goddard, Ph.D., Dean

School of Nursing
Tel: 902-566-0733
nursing@upei.ca
nursing.upei.ca
Dr. Rosemary Herbert, Dean

Faculty of Science
Tel: 902-566-0382
science@upei.ca
www.upei.ca/science
Christian Lacroix, B.Sc., M.Sc., Dean

Atlantic Veterinary College (AVC)
Tel: 902-566-0882
avc@upei.ca
avc.upei.ca
Dr. Donald L. Reynolds, Dean

Post Secondary/Technical

***Charlottetown:* Holland College of Applied Arts & Technology**
140 Weymouth St., Charlottetown, PE C1A 4Z1, Canada
Tel: 902-629-4217; *Fax:* 902-629-4239
Toll-Free: 800-446-5265
info@hollandcollege.com
www.hollandc.pe.ca
www.facebook.com/HollandCollege
twitter.com/hollandcollege
ca.linkedin.com/company/holland-college
www.youtube.com/hollandhurricanes
Dr. Brian McMillan, President

Campuses
Atlantic Police Academy
P.O. Box 156
66 Argus St., Slemon Park, PE C0A 2A0, Canada
Tel: 902-888-6700; *Fax:* 902-888-6725

Marine Training Centre
100 Water St., Summerside, PE C1N 1A9, Canada
Tel: 902-888-6485; *Fax:* 902-888-6404

Royalty Centre
40 Enman Cres., Charlottetown, PE C1E 1E6, Canada
Tel: 902-566-9628; *Fax:* 902-566-6988

Souris Centre
Main St. Plaza
P.O. Box 429
Souris, PE C0B 2B0, Canada
Tel: 902-687-2447; *Fax:* 902-687-3543

East Prince Centre
223 Water St., Summerside, PE C1N 1B4, Canada
Tel: 902-888-6495; *Fax:* 902-888-6402

Montague Centre
P.O. Box 939
544 Main St., Montague, PE C0A 1R0, Canada
Tel: 902-838-4026; *Fax:* 902-838-3518

Tourism & Culinary Centre
4 Sydney St., Charlottetown, PE C1A 1E9, Canada
Tel: 902-894-6805; *Fax:* 902-894-6801
Toll-Free: 877-475-2844
www.facebook.com/CulinaryInstituteofCanada

Georgetown Centre
117 Kent St., Georgetown, PE C0A 1L0, Canada
Tel: 902-652-2055; *Fax:* 902-652-2424

***Summerside:* The College of Piping & Celtic Performing Arts of Canada**
619 Water St. East, Summerside, PE C1N 4H8, Canada
Tel: 902-436-5377; *Fax:* 902-436-4930
Toll-Free: 1-877-224-7473
info@collegeofpiping.com
www.collegeofpiping.com
Scott MacAulay, Director

Québec

Government Agencies

***Québec:* Ministère de l'Éducation et de l'Enseignement supérieur et de la Recherche**
Renseignement generaux
1035, rue De La Chevrotière, 28e étage, Québec, QC G1R 5A5, Canada
Tél: 418-643-7095; *Téléc:* 418-646-6561
Ligne sans frais: 866-747-6626
www.mels.gouv.qc.ca
L'hon. Sébastien Proulx, Ministre de l'Éducation, du Loisir et du Sport, 416-644-0664
ministre@mels.gouv.qc.ca
L'hon. Hélène David, Ministre responsable de l'Enseignement supérieur, 418-644-0664
ministre@mels.gouv.qc.ca

School Boards/Districts/Divisions

Public

***Aylmer:* Western Québec School Board**
Commission scolaire Western Québec
15, rue Katimavik, Aylmer, QC J9J 0E9, Canada
Tel: 819-684-2336; *Fax:* 819-684-1328
Toll-Free: 800-363-9111
wqsb@wqsb.qc.ca
www.wqsb.qc.ca
Number of Schools: 18 primary; 6 secondary; *Grades:* Prim - Sec
Paul Lamoureux, Directeur général, 819-684-2336, ext. 1149
plamoureux@wqsb.qc.ca
Ruth Ahern, Assistant Director General, 819-684-2336, ext. 1153
rahern@wqsb.qc.ca
Richard Vézina, Secretary General, 819-684-2336, ext. 1152
rvezina@wqsb.qc.ca
Sandra Cox, Coordinator, Finance, 819-684-2336, ext. 1156
scox@wqsb.qc.ca
Mike Dubeau, Director of Human Resources, 819-684-2336, ext. 1143
mdubeau@wqsb.qc.ca

***Châteauguay:* New Frontiers School Board**
Commission scolaire New Frontiers
219, rue McLeod, Châteauguay, QC J6J 2H4, Canada
Tel: 450-691-1440; *Fax:* 450-699-8327
info@nfsb.qc.ca
www.nfsb.qc.ca
www.facebook.com/nfschoolboard
Number of Schools: 15; *Grades:* K - 12; Audlt Ed.
Wayne Goldthorp, Directeur général

***Dorval:* Lester B. Pearson School Board**
Commission scolaire Lester-B.-Pearson
1925, av Brookdale, Dorval, QC H9P 2Y7, Canada
Tel: 514-422-3000
www.lbpsb.qc.ca
Number of Schools: 39 primary; 13 secondary; *Grades:* Pre - Sec; Adult Ed.
Robert T. Mills, Director General

***Magog:* Eastern Townships School Board**
Commission scolaire Eastern Townships
340, rue Saint-Jean-Bosco, Magog, QC J1X 1K9, Canada
Tel: 819-868-3100; *Fax:* 819-868-2286
priests@etsb.qc.ca
www.etsb.qc.ca
www.facebook.com/ETSB2
Number of Schools: 20 écoles primaires; 4 écoles secondaires; *Grades:* Prim - Sec
André Turcotte, Director General, 819-868-3100, ext. 55005
dg@etsb.qc.ca
Kandy Mackey, Assistant Director General, 819-868-3100, ext. 55015
mackeyk@etsb.qc.ca
Sophie Leduc, Director, Financial Services, 819-868-3100, ext. 55050
leducs@etsb.qc.ca
Jeff Pauw, Director, Human Resources, 819-868-3100, ext. 55045
pauwj@etsb.qc.ca
Éric Campbell, Secretary General, 819-868-3100, ext. 55025
campbelle@etsb.qc.ca

***Montréal:* English Montréal School Board (EMSB)**
Commission scolaire English-Montréal
6000, av Fielding, Montréal, QC H3X 1T4, Canada
Tel: 514-483-7200
www.emsb.qc.ca
www.facebook.com/EMSB1
twitter.com/englishmtl
vimeo.com/emsb
Number of Schools: 35 écoles primaires; 18 écoles secondaires; 9 écoles innovatrices; 12 centres de formation générale; *Grades:* Pre - Sec
Robert Stocker, Director General, 514-483-7200, ext. 7262
rstocker@emsb.qc.ca
Angelo Marino, Deputy Director General, Administration, 514-483-7200, ext. 7227
amarino@emsb.qc.ca
Roma Medwid, Deputy Director General, Education Division 2, 514-483-7200, ext. 7266
rmedwid@emsb.qc.ca
Paola Miniaci, Deputy Director General, Education Division 1, 514-483-7200, ext. 7264
pminiaci@emsb.qc.ca
Joanne Bisbikos, Secretary General, 514-483-7200, ext. 7228
jbisbikos@emsb.qc.ca
Livia Nassivera, Director of Finance, 514-483-7200, ext. 7485
lharvey@emsb.qc.ca
Christine Dénommée, Director of Human Resources, 514-483-7200, ext. 7279
Cdenommee@emsb.qc.ca

***New Carlisle:* Eastern Shores School Board (ESSB)**
Commission scolaire Eastern Shores
40, rue Mount Sorrel, New Carlisle, QC G0C 1Z0, Canada
Tel: 418-752-2247; *Fax:* 418-752-6447
info@essb.qc.ca
www.essb.qc.ca
Number of Schools: 14 elementary schools; 8 secondary schools; 6 adult education centers; *Grades:* Pre - Sec; *Enrollment:* 1700
Howard Miller, Director General, 419-752-2247, ext. 250
howard.miller@essb.qc.ca
Suzanne West, Assistant Director General, 419-752-2247, ext. 243
suzanne.ward@essb.qc.ca
Nancy Doddridge, Director of Human Resources, 419-752-2247, ext. 228
nancy.doddridge@essb.qc.ca
Lisa Mosher, Director of Educational Services, 419-752-2247, ext. 226
lisa.mosher@essb.qc.ca
Suzanne Ward, Director of Finance, 419-752-2247, ext. 243
suzanne.ward@essb.qc.ca

***Québec:* Central Québec School Board (CQSB)**
Commission scolaire Central Québec
2046, ch Saint-Louis, Québec, QC G1T 1P4, Canada
Tel: 418-688-8730; *Fax:* 418-682-5891
Toll-Free: 800-249-5573
cqsb@cqsb.qc.ca
www.cqsb.qc.ca
Number of Schools: 19; *Grades:* K - 12; Adult Ed.; *Enrollment:* 4324; *Number of Employees:* 85
Stephen Pigeon, Directeur général, 418-688-8730, ext. 3011
Stephen.Pigeon@cqsb.qc.ca
Pierrette Laliberté, Assistant Director General / Director of Human Resources, 418-688-8730, ext. 3111
Pierrette.Laliberte@cqsb.qc.ca
Patti Moore, Secretary General, 418-688-8730, ext. 3021
moorep@cqsb.qc.ca
Laurent Després, Director of Financial Services, 418-688-8730, ext. 3031
despresl1@cqsb.qc.ca
Sally Coleman, Buyer, 418-688-8730, ext. 3051
colemans@cqsb.qc.ca
Pierrette Laliberté, Director of Human Resources, 418-688-8730, ext. 3061
lalibertep@cqsb.qc.ca

***Rosemère:* Sir Wilfrid Laurier School Board**
Commission scolaire Sir-Wilfrid-Laurier
235, montée Lesage, Rosemère, QC J7A 4Y6, Canada
Tel: 450-621-5600; *Fax:* 450-621-7929
Toll-Free: 866-621-5600
www.swlauriersb.qc.ca
www.facebook.com/SWLSB
twitter.com/swlsb
Number of Schools: 26 écoles primaires; 10 écoles secondaires; *Grades:* Prim - Sec; *Enrollment:* 15000
Stephanie Vucko, Directrice générale
svucko@swlauriersb.qc.ca
Johanne Brabant, Secretary General
jbrabant@swlauriersb.qc.ca

Jérôme Dionne, Director, Material Resources
jedionne@swlauriersb.qc.ca
Richard Greschner, Director, Human Resources
rgreschner@swlauriersb.qc.ca

Saint-Hubert: Commission scolaire Riverside Riverside School Board
7525, ch de Chambly, Saint-Hubert, QC J3Y 5K2, Canada
Tel: 450-672-4010; *Fax:* 450-465-8809
rsb@rsb.qc.ca
www.rsb.qc.ca
Number of Schools: 19 écoles primaires; 6 écoles secondaires; *Grades:* Prim - Sec
Sylvain Racette, Directeur général, 450-672-4010, ext. 5040
sracette@rsb.qc.ca
Michel Bergeron, Directeur, Ressources financières, 450-672-4010, ext. 5260
michel.bergeron@rsb.qc.ca
Mary Williams, Directrice des Services éducatifs, 450-672-4010, ext. 5347
mwilliams@rsb.qc.ca
Wendy Bernier, Directrice intérimaire, Ressources humaines, 450-672-4010, ext. 5250
wbernier@rsb.qc.ca
Pierre Farmer, Directeur gén. adj. et Directeur des ressources matérielles, 450-672-4010, ext. 5275
pfarmer@rsb.qc.ca
Denise Paulson, Secrétaire générale, 450-672-4010, ext. 5242
dpaulson@rsb.qc.ca

French

Alma: Commission scolaire du Lac-Saint-Jean
350, boul Champlain sud, Alma, QC G8B 5W2, Canada
Tél: 418-669-6000; *Téléc:* 418-669-6351
php.cslsj.qc.ca
Number of Schools: 20 écoles primaires; 4 écoles secondaires; 3 centres d'éducation des adultes; *Grades:* Prim - Sec; *Enrollment:* 8842; *Number of Employees:* 1 000
Christine Fortin, Directrice générale, 418-669-6000, ext. 5100
Christine Flaherty, Directrice générale adjointe, 418-669-6000, ext. 5200
Marc-Pascal Harvey, Directeur, Services éducatifs (jeunes et adultes), 418-669-6000, ext. 5301
Jacinthe Girard, Directeur, Service des ressources humaines, 418-669-6000, ext. 5501
Maryse Pilote, Directrice, Service des ressources financières & informatique, 418-669-6000, ext. 5601
Lise Simard, Directrice, Service des ressources matérielles, 418-669-6000, ext. 5701

Amos: Commission scolaire Harricana
341, rue Principale nord, Amos, QC J9T 2L8, Canada
Tél: 819-732-6561; *Téléc:* 819-732-1623
communications@csharricana.qc.ca
www.csharricana.qc.ca
Number of Schools: 20 écoles primaires; 3 écoles secondaires; *Grades:* Prim - Sec; éducation des adultes
Yannick Roy, Directeur général
Pascal Germain, Directeur, Ressources financières
Hélène Turcotte, Directrice, Ressources humaines
Johanne Godbout, Secrétaire générale, 819-732-6561, ext. 2268
Francis Audet, Directeur, Ressources matérielles

Amqui: Commission scolaire des Monts-et-Marées
93, rue du Parc, Amqui, QC G5J 2L8, Canada
Tél: 418-629-6200
www.csmm.qc.ca
Number of Schools: 17 écoles préscolaires; 19 écoles primaires; 9 écoles secondaires; 2 centres d'éducation des adultes; *Grades:* Pre - Sec; d'éducation des adultes; *Enrollment:* 7450; *Note:* Centre de services de Matane: 530, av Saint-Jérôme, 418-566-2500.
France Gagnon, Directrice générale
Marie-Pierre Guenette, Directrice, Service des ressources humaines
Pierre Berthelet, Secrétaire général
Geneviève Corbin, Directrice, Ressources financières

Baie-Comeau: Commission scolaire de l'Estuaire
771, boul Joliet, Baie-Comeau, QC G5C 1P3, Canada
Tél: 418-589-0806; *Téléc:* 418-589-2711
Ligne sans frais: 877-589-0806
www.csestuaire.qc.ca
Number of Schools: 20 écoles primaires; 1 école primaire et secondaire; 4 écoles secondaires; *Grades:* Prim - Sec; *Number of Employees:* 530 personnel enseignant; 355 personnel de soutien
Alain Ouellet, Directeur général, 418-589-0806, ext. 4813
Chantal Gagnon, Directrice des ressources financières, 418-589-0806, ext. 4832
chantal.gagnon@csestuaire.qc.ca
Nadine Desrosiers, Directrice des ressources humaines et matérielles, 418-589-0806, ext. 4823
nadine.desrosiers@csestuaire.qc.ca
Suzie Roy, Directrice du Service ressources informatiques, 418-589-0806, ext. 4851
suzie.roy@csestuaire.qc.ca

Beauharnois: Commission scolaire de la Vallée-des-Tisserands
630, rue Ellice, Beauharnois, QC J6N 3S1, Canada
Tél: 450-225-2788; *Téléc:* 450-225-0691
Ligne sans frais: 877-225-2788
info@csvt.qc.ca
www.csvt.qc.ca
Number of Schools: 26 écoles primaires; 6 écoles secondaires; 3 centres intégrés du Nouvel-Envol; *Grades:* Pre - Sec; *Enrollment:* 8259; *Number of Employees:* 1 700
Carole Houle, Directrice générale, 450-225-2788, ext. 6319
dg@csvt.qc.ca
Jean-François Primeau, Dir., Services du secrétariat général et des communications, 450-225-2788, ext. 6314
Richard Carrière, Directeur, Services éducatifs aux jeunes, 450-225-2788, ext. 6385
sec-sej@csvt.qc.ca
Denis Ménard, Directeur, Services éducatifs aux adultes, 450-225-2788, ext. 6390
seafp@csvt.qc.ca
Jean-François Lavertu, Directeur, Services des ressources humaines, 450-225-2788, ext. 6337
humaines@csvt.qc.ca
Danielle Dupuy, Directrice, Services des ressources financières, 450-225-2788, ext. 6325
finances@csvt.qc.ca
Jean-Sirice Loisel, Directeur, Services des ressources matérielles, 450-225-2788, ext. 6359
materiellesr@csvt.qc.ca

Beauport: Commission scolaire des Premières-Seigneuries
643, av du Cénacle, Beauport, QC G1E 1B3, Canada
Tél: 418-666-4666; *Téléc:* 418-666-9783
sic@csdps.qc.ca
www.csdps.qc.ca
www.facebook.com/136523216368423
Number of Schools: 36 écoles primaires; 7 écoles secondaires; *Grades:* Prim.-Sec.; *Enrollment:* 19000
Serge Pelletier, Directeur général
dg@csdps.qc.ca
Marie-Claude Asselin, Directrice générale adjointe aux affaires administratives
dg@csdps.qc.ca
Line Beaulieu, Directrice générale adjointe aux affaires éducatives
dg@csdps.qc.ca
Jean-François Parent, Secrétaire général
secgen@csdps.qc.ca
Martine Chouinard, Directrice, Ressources humaines
martine.chouinard@csdps.qc.ca
Louis Dandurand, Directeur, Ressources financières, 418-666-4666, ext. 1217
srf@csdps.qc.ca
Jean-Marc Drolet, Directeur, Ressources matérielles, 418-666-4666, ext. 8471
srm@csdps.qc.ca

Bonaventure: Commission scolaire René-Lévesque
145, av Louisbourg, Bonaventure, QC G0C 1E0, Canada
Tél: 418-534-3003; *Téléc:* 418-534-3220
www.csrl.qc.ca
Number of Schools: 23 écoles primaires; 5 écoles secondaires; 2 écoles primaires-secondaires; *Grades:* Prim - Sec; éducation des adultes; *Enrollment:* 7300
Chantal Bourdages, Directrice générale, 418-534-3003, ext. 6007
dg@csrl.net
Gilles Cavanagh, Secrétaire général, 418-534-3003, ext. 6010
sg@csrl.net
Richard Litalien, Directeur, Ressources financières, 418-534-3003, ext. 6012
richard.litalien@csrl.net
Denis Gauthier, Directeur, Service des ressources humaines, 418-534-3003, ext. 6019
drh@csrl.net

Chibougamau: Commission scolaire de la Baie-James
596, 4e rue, Chibougamau, QC G8P 1S3, Canada
Tél: 418-748-7621; *Téléc:* 418-748-2440
www.csbj.qc.ca
Number of Schools: 8 écoles primaires; 5 écoles secondaires; *Grades:* Prim - Sec
Michèle Perron, Directrice générale, 418-748-7621, ext. 2223

Chicoutimi: Commission scolaire des Rives-du-Saguenay
36, rue Jacques-Cartier est, Chicoutimi, QC G7H 1W2, Canada
Tél: 418-698-5000; *Téléc:* 418-698-5262
info@csrsaguenay.qc.ca
www.csrsaguenay.qc.ca
www.facebook.com/119771281400622
www.youtube.com/user/csrsaguenay
Number of Schools: 31 écoles primaires; 6 écoles secondaires; *Grades:* Prim - Sec; *Note:* Centre de services La Baie: 3111, rue Mgr Dufour, La Baie, 418-544-3307. Service informatique: 475, rue Lafontaine, Chicoutimi, 418-541-7799.
Christine Tremblay, Directrice générale, 418-698-5000, ext. 5207
christine.t@csrsaguenay.qc.ca
Gilles Routhier, Directeur général adjoint
dga@csrsaguenay.qc.ca
Sarah Tremblay, Secrétaire générale, 418-698-5000, ext. 5207
sarah.tremblay2@csrsaguenay.qc.ca
Josée Gaudreault, Directrice des Services éducatifs jeunes, 418-698-5000, ext. 5413
Jean Blackburn, Directrice, Services éducatifs adultes, 418-698-5000, ext. 5213
Jocelyn Ouellet, Directeur, Ressources humaines, 418-698-5000, ext. 5213
Michel Simard, Directeur, Services des ressources financières, 418-698-5000
Martin Deschênes, Directeur, Service des ressources matérielles, 418-698-5000, ext. 5210
Paul Lalancette, Directeur, Service informatique, 418-698-5000, ext. 5100
paul.lalancette@csrsaguenay.qc.ca

Donnacona: Commission scolaire de Portneuf
310, rue de l'Église, Donnacona, QC G3M 1Z8, Canada
Tél: 418-285-2600; *Téléc:* 418-285-2738
www.csportneuf.qc.ca
Number of Schools: 15 écoles primaires; 3 écoles secondaires; *Grades:* Pre - Sec
Jean-Pierre Soucy, Directeur général, 418-285-2600, ext. 5063
jeanpsoucy@csdp.qc.ca
Monique Delisle, Directrice des services du sécrétariat général, 418-285-2600, ext. 5027
moniqued@csdp.qc.ca
Éric Bouchard, Directeur, Service des ressources humaines, 418-285-2600, ext. 5006
ebouchard@csdp.qc.ca
Jean-François Lussier, Directeur, Service des ressources matérielles et financières, 418-285-2600, ext. 5008
jflussier@csdp.qc.ca

Drummondville: Commission scolaire des Chênes
P.O. Box 846
457, rue des Écoles, Drummondville, QC J2B 6X1, Canada
Tél: 819-478-6700
commentaires@csdeschenes.qc.ca
www.csdeschenes.qc.ca
Number of Schools: 34 écoles primaires; 9 écoles secondaires; *Grades:* Pre - Sec; *Enrollment:* 13000; *Number of Employees:* 1 300
Christiane Desbiens, Directrice générale
christiane.desbiens@csdeschenes.qc.ca
Bernard Gauthier, Secrétaire générale
bernard.gauthier@csdeschenes.qc.ca
Carmen Lemire, Directrice, Service des ressources financières
carmen.lemire@csdeschenes.qc.ca
Daniel Dumaine, Directeur, Service des ressources humaines
daniel.dumaine@csdeschenes.qc.ca
Yves Gendron, Directeur, Service des ressources matérielles
yves.gendron@csdeschenes.qc.ca

East Angus: Commission scolaire des Hauts-Cantons
308, rue Palmer, East Angus, QC J0B 1R0, Canada
Tél: 819-832-4953; *Téléc:* 819-832-4863
info@cshc.qc.ca
www.cshc.qc.ca
Number of Schools: 30 écoles primaires; 3 écoles secondaires; *Grades:* Pre - Sec
Bernard Lacroix, Directeur général, 819-832-4953
Julie Morin, Directrice du service des ressources humaines, 819-583-2351, ext. 4200
Martial Gaudreau, Directeur du service de l'enseignement, 819-832-4953, ext. 4312
Véronique Fillion, Dir. des services des ressources financières et matérielles, 819-849-7051, ext. 4400
Gilbert Roy, Directeur des ressources informatiques, 819-832-4953, ext. 4337
Annie Garon, Secrétaire générale et responsable des communications, 819-832-4953, ext. 4319

Gaspé: Commission scolaire des Chic-Chocs
102, rue Jacques-Cartier, Gaspé, QC G4X 2S9, Canada
Tél: 418-368-3499; *Téléc:* 418-368-6531
informations@cschic-chocs.qc.ca
www.cschic-chocs.net
Number of Schools: 13 écoles primaires; 4 écoles secondaires; 3 écoles primaires et secondaires; *Grades:* Pre - Sec; *Enrollment:* 4430
Jean Letarte, Directeur général
Michel Morin, Directeur, Service du secrétariat général, 418-368-3499, ext. 5911
michel.morin@cschic-chocs.qc.ca
Daivd Smith, Coordonnateur des Services des ressources matérielles, 418-368-3499, ext. 5927
rm@cschic-chocs.net
Line Miville, Directrice des Services éducatifs, 418-368-3499, ext. 5941
marie.sylvestre@cschic-chocs.qc.ca

Gatineau: Commission scolaire au Coeur-des-Vallées
582, rue MacLaren est, Gatineau, QC J8L 2W2, Canada
Tél: 819-986-8511; *Téléc:* 819-986-9283
Ligne sans frais: 800-958-9966
info@cscv.qc.ca
www.cscv.qc.ca
Number of Schools: 17 écoles primaires; 5 écoles secondaires; *Grades:* Pre - Sec
Maurice Groulx, Directeur général

Gatineau: Commission scolaire des Draveurs
200, boul Maloney est, Gatineau, QC J8P 1K3, Canada
Tél: 819-663-9221; *Téléc:* 819-663-6176
reception@csdraveurs.qc.ca
www.csdraveurs.qc.ca
Number of Schools: 23 écoles primaires; 4 écoles secondaires; 2 entres d'éducation des adultes; *Grades:* Prim - Sec; *Enrollment:* 20000; *Number of Employees:* 3 500
Bernard Dufourd, Directeur général, 819-663-9221
dg@csdraveurs.qc.ca
Suzanne Côté, Directrice, Service des ressources éducatives jeunes & adults, 819-663-9221
sre@csdraveurs.qc.ca
Sara Duguay, Directrice, Service des ressources financières
srf@csdraveurs.qc.ca
Denis St-Onge, Directeur, Service des ressources humaines
srf@csdraveurs.qc.ca
Pascal Proulx, Directeur, Service des ressources informatique
srict@csdraveurs.qc.ca
Chantal Patrice, Directeur, Service des ressources matérielles
srm@csdraveurs.qc.ca
Yvon Landry, Secrétaire général
ssgc@csdraveurs.qc.ca

Gatineau: Commission scolaire des Portages-de-l'Outaouais
225, rue St-Rédempteur, Gatineau, QC J8X 2T3, Canada
Tél: 819-771-4548; *Téléc:* 819-771-6964
sgcspo@cspo.qc.ca
www.cspo.qc.ca
Number of Schools: 22 écoles primaires; 4 écoles secondaires; 2 centres de formation; 4 centres des adultes; *Grades:* Pre - Sec; éducation des adultes; *Enrollment:* 15599
Jean-Claude Bouchard, Directeur général
dgcspo@cspo.qc.ca
Pierre Ménard, Secrétaire général
Rémi Lupien, Directeur, Service des ressources financières
Luc Pelchat, Directeur, Service des ressources matérielles
Nadine Peterson, Directrice, Service des ressources éducatives

Granby: Commission scolaire du Val-des-Cerfs
P.O. Box 9000
55, rue Court, Granby, QC J2G 9H7, Canada
Tél: 450-372-0221; *Téléc:* 450-372-3150
descerfs@csvdc.qc.ca
www.csvdc.qc.ca
Number of Schools: 35 écoles primaires; 7 écoles secondaires; 2 centres d'éducation des adultes; *Grades:* Prim - Sec; éducatioin des adultes; *Enrollment:* 8800; *Number of Employees:* 1 650
André Messier, Directeur général
Chantale Cyr, Directrice du service des ressources humaines
chantale.cyr@csvdc.qc.ca
Ghislain Boutin, Directeur gén. adjoint, Ressources financières & matérielles
ghislain.boutin@csvdc.qc.ca
Katherine Plante, Secrétaire général
katherine.plante@csvdc.qc.ca

Havre-Saint-Pierre: Commission scolaire de la Moyenne-Côte-Nord
1235, rue de la Digue, Havre-Saint-Pierre, QC G0G 1P0, Canada
Tél: 418-538-3044; *Téléc:* 418-538-3268
www.csmcn.qc.ca
Number of Schools: 7 écoles primaires; 2 écoles secondaires; *Grades:* Pre - Sec
Marius Richard, Directeur général
Mario Cyr, Directeur des services éducatifs/Secrétaire général
Marius Richard, Directeur des ressources humaines (par intérim), 418-538-3044, ext. 3010
marius-richard@csmcn.qc.ca

Jonquière: Commission scolaire De La Jonquière
P.O. Box 1600
3644, rue St-Jules, Jonquière, QC G7X 7X4, Canada
Tél: 418-542-7551; *Téléc:* 418-542-1505
info@csjonquiere.qc.ca
www.csjonquiere.qc.ca
Number of Schools: 17 écoles primaires; 3 écoles secondaires; *Grades:* Prim - Sec; *Enrollment:* 10455; *Number of Employees:* 2 633
Aline Laforge, Directrice générale, 418-542-7551, ext. 4270
dgenerale@csjonquiere.qc.ca
Jacynthe Bond, Directrice, Services éducatifs jeunes et adultes, 418-542-7551, ext. 4218
jacynthe.bond@csjonquiere.qc.ca
Jean-François Leblanc, Directeur, Ressources financières, 418-542-7551, ext. 4234
jean-francois.leblanc@csjonquiere.qc.ca
Mario St-Pierre, Directeur, Ressources humaines, 418-542-7551, ext. 4276
rhumaines@csjonquiere.qc.ca
Christian St-Gelais, Directeur, Secrétariat général et communications, 418-542-7551, ext. 4302
sgeneral@csjonquiere.qc.ca

L'Étang-du-Nord: Commission scolaire des Iles
1419, ch de l'Étang-du-Nord, L'Étang-du-Nord, QC G4T 3B9, Canada
Tél: 418-986-5511; *Téléc:* 418-986-3552
secdgrh@csdesiles.qc.ca
www.csdesiles.qc.ca
Number of Schools: 5 écoles; 1 centre de formation professionnelle et de formation générale aux adultes; *Grades:* Pre - Sec; *Enrollment:* 1500; *Number of Employees:* 285
Brigitte Aucoin, Directrice générale, 418-986-5511, ext. 1101
Donald Chiasson, Directeur du service de secrétariat général, 418-986-5511, ext. 1201
Danielle Gallant, Directrice, Ressources financières, 418-986-5511, ext. 1301

La Malbaie: Commission scolaire de Charlevoix
575, boul de Comporté, La Malbaie, QC G5A 1T5, Canada
Tél: 418-665-3765; *Téléc:* 418-665-6805
www.cscharlevoix.qc.ca
Number of Schools: 15 écoles primaires; 3 écoles secondaires; *Grades:* Prim - Sec
Martine Vallée, Directrice générale, 418-665-3765, ext. 3000
dg@cscharlevoix.qc.ca
Julie Normandeau, Secrétaire générale, 418-665-3765, ext. 3006
julie.normandeau@cscharlevoix.qc.ca
Catherine Gélineau, Coordonnatrice, Services éducatifs, 418-435-2824, ext. 2007
catherine.gelineau@cscharlevoix.qc.ca
Kathleen Brassard, Bibliothécaire, 418-665-3765, ext. 3012
kathleen.brassard@cscharlevoix.qc.ca
France Chevrefils, Directrice, Services ressources humaines, 418-665-3765, ext. 3021
france.chevrefils@cscharlevoix.qc.ca
Stéphanie Marcotte, Directrice de service, Ressources financières, 418-435-2824, ext. 2006
stephanie.marcotte@cscharlevoix.qc.ca

La Prairie: Commission scolaire des Grandes-Seigneuries
50, boul Taschereau, La Prairie, QC J5R 4V3, Canada
Tél: 514-380-8899; *Téléc:* 514-380-8345
www.csdgs.qc.ca
www.facebook.com/csdgs.qc.ca
Number of Schools: 37 écoles primaires; 13 écoles secondaires; 2 centres de formation générale des adultes; *Grades:* Prim - Sec; *Enrollment:* 24400; *Number of Employees:* 3 355
Michelle Fournier, Directrice générale, 514-380-8899, ext. 3903
directiongenerale@csdgs.qc.ca
Nathalie Marceau, Directrice, Service du secrétariat général & de l'information, 514-380-8899, ext. 3917
secretariatgeneral@csdgs.qc.ca
André Guérard, Directeur, Services éducatifs, 514-380-8899, ext. 3957
se@csdgs.qc.ca
Michel Brochu, Directeur, Service des ressources humaines, 514-380-8899, ext. 3925
reshumaines@csdgs.qc.ca
Germen Brière, Directeur, Service des ressources financières, 514-380-8899, ext. 4971
resfinancieres@csdgs.qc.ca
Frédéric Grandioux, Directeur, Service des ressources matérielles, 514-380-8899, ext. 4947
resmaterielles@csdgs.qc.ca

La Sarre: Commission scolaire du Lac-Abitibi
500, rue Principale, La Sarre, QC J9Z 2A2, Canada
Tél: 819-333-5411; *Téléc:* 819-333-3044
SiteWeb@csdla.qc.ca
www.csdla.qc.ca
Number of Schools: 15 écoles primaires; 4 écoles secondaires
Huguette Théberge, Directrice générale, 819-333-5411, ext. 2224
Isabelle Godbout, Dir., Services des ressources humaines & Secrétariat général, 819-333-5411, ext. 2226
godbouti@csdla.qc.ca
Claudine Lachapelle, Directrice, Services éducatifs, 819-333-5411, ext. 2225
lachapellec@csdla.qc.ca
Isabelle Métivier, Directrice, Service des ressources financières, 819-333-5411, ext. 2222

Laval: Commission scolaire de Laval (CSDL)
955, boul Saint-Martin ouest, Laval, QC H7S 1M5, Canada
Tél: 450-662-7000
www2.cslaval.qc.ca
Number of Schools: 54 écoles primaires; 14 écoles secondaires; 8 centres formation professionnelle; *Grades:* Prim - Sec; éducation des adultes
Jean-Pierre Aubin, Directeur général, 450-662-7000, ext. 1001
Jean-Pierre Archambault, Secrétaire général, 450-662-7000, ext. 1201
secretariatgeneral@cslaval.qc.ca
Dominique Sylvain, Directrice, Service des ressources financières, 450-662-7000, ext. 1878
finances@cslaval.qc.ca
Élyse Des Roches, Directrice, Service des ressources humaines, 450-662-7000, ext. 1160
edesroches@cslaval.qc.ca

Longueuil: Commission scolaire Marie-Victorin
13, rue St-Laurent est, Longueuil, QC J4H 4B7, Canada
Tél: 450-670-0730
info@csmv.qc.ca
www.csmv.qc.ca
www.facebook.com/csmarievictorin
www.youtube.com/csmarievictorin
Number of Schools: 70 établissements; *Grades:* Pre - Sec; *Enrollment:* 33000; *Number of Employees:* 4 800
Raynald Thibeault, Directeur général
Anthony Bellini, Directeur général adjoint
Daniel Tremblay, Directeur général adjoint
Sylvie Caron, Directeur général adjoint

Magog: Commission scolaire des Sommets
449, rue Percy, Magog, QC J1X 1B5, Canada
Tél: 819-847-1610; *Téléc:* 819-847-2065
Ligne sans frais: 888-847-1610
info@csdessommets.qc.ca
www.csdessommets.qc.ca
Number of Schools: 27 écoles primaires; 4 écoles secondaires; *Grades:* Pre - Sec; *Enrollment:* 8550
Christian Provencher, Directeur général, 819 847-1610, ext. 18800
dgenerale@csdessommets.qc.ca
Lyne Beauchamp, Directrice, Secrétariat général, 819-847-1610, ext. 18853
Daniel Blais, Directeur, Service des ressources financières, 819-847-1610, ext. 18831
Chantal Larouche, Directrice, Ressources humaines, 819-847-1610, ext. 18825
Édith Pelletier, Directrice, Service des ressources éducatives, 819-847-1610, ext. 18825

Maniwaki: Commission scolaire des Hauts-Bois-de-l'Outaouais (CSHBO)
331, rue du Couvent, Maniwaki, QC J9E 1H5, Canada
Tél: 819-449-7866; *Téléc:* 819-449-2636
Ligne sans frais: 888-831-9606
info@cshbo.qc.ca
www.cshbo.qc.ca
Number of Schools: 11 écoles primaires; 3 écoles secondaires; 4 établissement des adultes; *Grades:* Prim-Sec; *Enrollment:* 3000; *Number of Employees:* 580
Harold Sylvain, Directeur général, 819-449-7866, ext. 237

Charles Millar
charles.millar@schbo.qc.ca
Richard Leblanc, Secrétaire général, 819-449-7866, ext. 217
Manon Riel, Directrice, Service des ressources financières, 819-449-7866, ext. 116
Stéphane Rondeau, Directeur, Service des ressources éducatives, 819-449-7866, ext. 225

Mont-Laurier: Commission scolaire Pierre-Neveu (CSPN)
525, rue de la Madone, Mont-Laurier, QC J9L 1S4, Canada
Tél: 819-623-4310; *Téléc:* 819-623-7979
Ligne sans frais: 866-334-4114
cspn@cspn.qc.ca
www.cspn.qc.ca
Number of Schools: 22 écoles primaires; 3 écoles secondaires; *Grades:* Prim - Sec
Normand Bélanger, Directeur général, 819-623-4114, ext. 5402
belanger.normand@cspn.qc.ca
Manon Plouffe, Directrice, Ressources Humaines, 819-623-4114, ext. 5432
plouffe.manon@cspn.qc.ca
Claudine Millaire, Directrice, Ressources éducatives, 819-623-4114, ext. 5462
millaire.claudine@cspn.qc.ca
Annie Lamoureux, Directrice, Ressources financiéres et taxation, 819-623-4114, ext. 5412
lamoureux.annie@cspn.qc.ca
Hugo Charbonneau, Directeur, Ressources matérielles, 819-623-4114, ext. 5442
charbonneau.hugo@cspn.qc.ca
Claude Boudrias, Secrétaire général, 819-623-4114, ext. 5452
boudrias.claude@cspn.qc.ca

Montmagny: Commission scolaire de la Côte-du-Sud
157, rue Saint-Louis, Montmagny, QC G5V 4N3, Canada
Tél: 418-248-1001; *Téléc:* 418-248-9797
info@cscotesud.qc.ca
www.cscotesud.qc.ca
www.facebook.com/commissionscolairecotedusud
Number of Schools: 39 écoles primaires; 9 écoles secondaires; *Grades:* Prim - Sec; *Enrollment:* 8100
André Chamard, Directeur général, 418-248-1001, ext. 8481
Pierre Côté, Directeur général adjoint/Secrétaire général, 418-248-1001, ext. 8483
Annie Ménard, Directrice, Ressources financières, 418-248-1001, ext. 8411
Louise Landry, Directrice, Ressources humaines, 418-248-1001, ext. 8471
Guy Bégin, Directeur, Ressources matérielles, 418-248-1001, ext. 8451

Montréal: Commission scolaire de la Pointe-de-l'Ile (CSPI)
550, 53e av, Montréal, QC H1A 2T7, Canada
Tél: 514-642-9520
www.cspi.qc.ca
Number of Schools: 41 écoles primaires; 7 écoles secondaires; 5 écoles spécialisées; 10 centres d'éducation des adultes; *Grades:* Prim - Sec; adultes; *Enrollment:* 35000; *Number of Employees:* 5 000
Pierre Boulay, Directeur général
Christiane St-Onge, Directrice, Services corporatifs et secrétariat général
Alain Bouchard, Directeur, Réseau - secteur des adultes
René Brodeur, Directeur, Ressources financières
Josée Dumouchel, Directrice, Ressources humaines
Normand Foucault, Directeur, Ressources matérielles
Sylvie Boudreault, Régisseure des services administratifs
sylvie-boudreault@cspi.qc.ca

Montréal: Commission scolaire de Montréal (CSDM)
3737, rue Sherbrooke est, Montréal, QC H1X 3B3, Canada
Tél: 514-596-6000
info@csdm.qc.ca
www.csdm.qc.ca
www.facebook.com/commission.scolaire.de.montreal
twitter.com/csdmqcca
Number of Schools: 200 établissements; *Grades:* Pre - Sec; *Enrollment:* 110000; *Number of Employees:* 8 000 enseignants
Gilles Petitclerc, Directeur général

Nicolet: Commission scolaire de la Riveraine
375, rue de Monseigneur-Brunault, Nicolet, QC J3T 1Y6, Canada
Tél: 819-293-5821; *Téléc:* 819-293-8691
information@csriveraine.qc.ca
www.csriveraine.qc.ca
Number of Schools: 25 écoles primaires; 3 écoles secondaires; 3 centres de formation professionnelle; 4 centres adultes; *Grades:* Prim - Sec; éducation des adultes; *Enrollment:* 9471
France Lefebvre, Directrice générale, 819-293-5821, ext. 4502
direction.generale@admin.csriveraine.qc.ca
Johane Croteau, Secrétaire générale, 819-293-5821, ext. 4506
Kathleen Haley, Directrice, Service des ressources financières, 819-293-5821, ext. 4511
service.rf@admin.csriveraine.qc.ca
Sophie Dubord, Directrice, Service des ressources humaines, 819-293-5821, ext. 4550
dubords@csriveraine.qc.ca
Michel Verreault, Coordonnateur, Service des ressources matérielles, 819-293-5821, ext. 4572
service.rm@admin.csriveraine.qc.ca

Québec: Commission scolaire de la Capitale
1900, rue Côté, Québec, QC G1N 3Y5, Canada
Tél: 418-686-4040; *Téléc:* 418-686-4032
adm2@cscapitale.qc.ca
www.cscapitale.qc.ca
Number of Schools: 65 établissements scolaires; *Grades:* K - 12; adultes; *Enrollment:* 26000; *Number of Employees:* 4 100
Pierre Lapointe, Directrice générale, 418-686-4040, ext. 2003
dgcapitale@cscapitale.qc.ca
Richard Vallée, Directeur général adjoint aux affaires administratives, 418-686-4040, ext. 2010
Johanne Chenard, Directrice générale adjointe aux affaires éducatives, 418-686-4040, ext. 2030
Érick Parent, Secrétaire général et directeur de l'information et des comm., 418-686-4040, ext. 2100
sg@cscapitale.qc.ca
Joanne Paradis, Directrice, Services éducatifs des jeunes, 418-686-4040, ext. 2200
sej@cscapitale.qc.ca
Maude Plourde, Directrice, Services de la formation professionnelle, 418-686-4040, ext. 2300
sfpea@cscapitale.qc.ca
Réjeanne Ducharme, Directrice, Services des ressources humaines, 418-686-4040, ext. 2400
srh@cscapitale.qc.ca
Marc Drolet, Directeur, Services des ressources financières, 418-686-4040, ext. 2600
srf@cscapitale.qc.ca
Éric Fortin, Directeur, Services des ressources matérielles, 418-686-4040, ext. 2500
srm@cscapitale.qc.ca

Québec: Commission scolaire des Découvreurs
#100, 945, av Wolfe, Québec, QC G1V 4E2, Canada
Tél: 418-652-2121; *Téléc:* 418-652-2146
www.csdecou.qc.ca
Number of Schools: 31; *Grades:* Prim - Sec; *Enrollment:* 10630; *Number of Employees:* 2 000
Reynald Deraspe, Directeur général, 418-652-2121
dirgen@csdecou.qc.ca
Jacky Tremblay, Secrétariat général, 418-652-2121, ext. 4241
secgen@csdecou.qc.ca
Christian Pleau, Directeur, Services éducatifs, 418-652-2121
seduc@csdecou.qc.ca
Brigitte Bouchard, Directeur, Ressources humaines, 418-652-2121, ext. 4111
srhum@csdecou.qc.ca
Julie Aubin, Directrice, Ressources matérielles, 418-652-2121, ext. 4197
srm@csdecou.qc.ca

Repentigny: Commission scolaire des Affluents (CSA)
80, rue Jean-Baptiste-Meilleur, Repentigny, QC J6A 6C5, Canada
Tél: 450-492-9400; *Téléc:* 450-492-3720
info@csaffluents.qc.ca
www.csaffluents.qc.ca
Number of Schools: 48 écoles primaires; 14 écoles secondaires; *Grades:* Prim - Sec; *Enrollment:* 34000; *Number of Employees:* 5000
Alain Vézina, Directeur général, 450-492-9400, ext. 2300
direction.generale@csaffluents.qc.ca
France-Lyne Masse, Directrice, Services éducatifs, 450-492-9400, ext. 1453
france-lyne.masse@re.csaffluents.qc.ca
Anne Turcotte, Directrice, Service des ressources financières, 450-492-9400
anne.turcotte@rf.csaffluents.qc.ca
Jacques Dufour, Secrétaire général et directeur des communications, 450-492-9400, ext. 1310
jacques.dufour@sg.csaffluents.qc.ca

Rimouski: Commission scolaire des Phares
435, av Rouleau, Rimouski, QC G5L 8V4, Canada
Tél: 418-723-5927; *Téléc:* 418-724-3350
webmestre@csphares.qc.ca
www.csphares.qc.ca
www.facebook.com/csphares
Number of Schools: 31 écoles primaires; 11 écoles secondaires; *Grades:* Prim - Sec; *Enrollment:* 8282; *Number of Employees:* 1 000
Jean-François Parent, Directeur général, 418-723-5927, ext. 1010
jf_parent@csphares.qc.ca
Mado Dugas, Directrice gén. adjointe et directrice des Services éducatifs, 418-723-5927, ext. 1120
mdugas@csphares.qc.ca
Cathy-Maude Croft, Dir. des Services du Secrétariat général et des communication, 418-723-5927, ext. 1020
cmcroft@csphares.qc.ca
Rock Bouffard, Directeur, Services des ressources humaines et de la paie, 418-723-5927, ext. 1040
rock_bouffard@csphares.qc.ca
Marc Girard, Dir. des Services des ressources financières & de la taxation, 418-723-5927, ext. 1060
mgirard@csphares.qc.ca
Carl Ruest, Dir. des Services des ressources matérielles et du transport, 418-723-5927, ext. 1080
cruest@csphares.qc.ca

Rivière-du-Loup: Commission scolaire de Kamouraska—Rivière-du-Loup
P.O. Box 910
464, rue Lafontaine, Rivière-du-Loup, QC G5R 3C2, Canada
Tél: 418-868-8201; *Téléc:* 418-862-0964
www.cskamloup.qc.ca
www.facebook.com/cskamloup.qc.ca
twitter.com/cskamloup
www.youtube.com/user/pavillondelavenir
Number of Schools: 15 écoles primaires; 2 écoles secondaires; *Grades:* Prim - Sec
Yvan Tardif, Directeur général

Roberval: Commission scolaire du Pays-des-Bleuets
828, boul Saint-Joseph, Roberval, QC G8H 2L5, Canada
Tél: 418-275-4136; *Téléc:* 418-275-6217
www.cspaysbleuets.qc.ca
www.facebook.com/309885304289
twitter.com/CSPaysBleuets
Number of Schools: 25 écoles primaires; 7 écoles secondaires; *Grades:* Prim - Sec; *Note:* Secteur Dolbeau-Mistassini: 1950, boul Sacré-Coeur, Dolbeau-Mistassini, 418-276-2012.
Serge Bergeron, Directeur général, 418-275-4136, ext. 1000
Guylaine Martel, Directeur, Service des ressources financières, 418-275-4136, ext. 4055
François Jeanrie, Directeur, Service des ressources humaines, 418-275-4136, ext. 1010
Stéphane Bilodeau, Directeur, Service des ressources informatiques, 418-275-4136, ext. 4023
Guylaine Martel, Directeur, Service des ressources matérielles, 418-275-4136, ext. 4055
Annie Tremblay, Service du secrétariat général et des communications, 418-275-4136, ext. 4006
Chantale Simard, Coordonnation des services de l'enseignement, 418-275-4136, ext. 1044
Jacqueline Lavertu, Coordonnation des services complémentaires, 418-275-4136, ext. 1042

Rouyn-Noranda: Commission scolaire de Rouyn-Noranda (CSRN)
P.O. Box 908
70, rue des Oblats est, Rouyn-Noranda, QC J9X 5C9, Canada
Tél: 819-762-8161; *Téléc:* 819-764-7170
webinfo@csrn.qc.ca
www.csrn.qc.ca
Number of Schools: 17 écoles primaires; 3 écoles secondaires; *Grades:* Prim - Sec
Yves Bédard, Directeur général, 819-762-8161, ext.1210
bedardy@csrn.qc.ca
Martial Drolet, Directeur, Ressources financières, 819-762-8161, ext. 1250
droletm@csrn.qc.ca
Paul-Ange Morin, Directeur, Ressources humaines, 819-762-8161, ext. 1240
morinpa@csrn.qc.ca
Patrick Fiset, Directeur, Ressources matérielles, 819-762-8161, ext. 1260
fisetp@csrn.qc.ca
Lyne Garneau, Secrétaire générale, 819-762-8161, ext. 1220
garneaul@csrn.qc.ca

***Saint-Eustache:* Commission scolaire de la Seigneurie-des-Mille-Iles**
430, boul Arthur-Sauvé, Saint-Eustache, QC J7R 6V6, Canada
Tél: 450-974-7000
info@cssmi.qc.ca
www.cssmi.qc.ca
www.facebook.com/150916731597957?ref=ts
www.twitter.com/cssmi
Number of Schools: 56 écoles primaires; 13 écoles secondaires; 2 centres de formation générale adulte; *Grades:* Prim-Sec; *Enrollment:* 40000; *Number of Employees:* 7 500
Jean-François Lachance, Directeur général, 450-974-7000, ext. 2001

***Saint-Félix-de-Valois:* Commission scolaire des Samares**
4671, rue Principale, Saint-Félix-de-Valois, QC J0K 2M0, Canada
Tél: 450-758-3500; *Téléc:* 450-889-8604
sg@cssamares.qc.ca
www.cssamares.qc.ca
Number of Schools: 67 écoles primaires; 12 écoles secondaires; *Grades:* K - 12
Sylvie Anctil, Directrice générale
dg@cssamares.qc.ca
Marie-Élène Laperrière, Directrice, Service du secrétariat général
sg@cssamares.qc.ca

***Saint-Hyacinthe:* Commission scolaire de Saint-Hyacinthe**
2255, av Sainte-Anne, Saint-Hyacinthe, QC J2S 5H7, Canada
Tél: 450-773-8401; *Téléc:* 450-773-6876
information@cssh.qc.ca
www.cssh.qc.ca
www.facebook.com/commissionscolairedesthyacinthe
Number of Schools: 30 écoles elementaires; 6 écoles secondaires; *Grades:* Prim - Sec
Caroline Dupré, Directrice générale, 450-773-8401, ext. 6559
caroline.dupre@cssh.qc.ca
Yvonne Scott, Secrétaire générale, 450-773-8401, ext. 6547
yvonne.scott@cssh.qc.ca
Karina St-Germain, Directrice, Services éducatifs, 450-773-8401, ext. 6247
karina.st-germain@cssh.qc.ca
Chantal Langelier, Directrice, Service des ressources humaines, 450-773-8401, ext. 6586
chantal.langelier@cssh.qc.ca
Sylvie Girard, Directrice, Service des ressources financières, 450-773-8401, ext. 6280
sylvie.girard@cssh.qc.ca
Jean-François Soumis, Directeur, Service des ressources matérielles et informatique, 450-773-8401, ext. 6585
jean-francois.soumis@cssh.qc.ca

***Saint-Jean-sur-Richelieu:* Commission scolaire des Hautes-Rivières**
210, rue Notre-Dame, Saint-Jean-sur-Richelieu, QC J3B 6N3, Canada
Tél: 450-359-6411; *Téléc:* 450-359-1569
Ligne sans frais: 877-359-6411
www.csdhr.qc.ca
www.facebook.com/CommissionScolaireDesHautesRivieres
Number of Schools: 49 écoles; *Grades:* Pre-Sec; adultes; *Enrollment:* 17361; *Number of Employees:* 2 500
Éric Blackburn, Directeur général, 450-359-6411, ext. 7240
cadg@csdhr.qc.ca
Silvie Mondat, Directrice, Ressources financières, 450-359-6411, ext. 7207
caressourcesfinancieres@csdhr.qc.ca
Katleen Loiselle, Directrice, Ressources humaines, 450-359-6411, ext. 7236
caressourceshumaines@csdhr.qc.ca
François Bergeron, Directeur, Ressources matérielles et du transport scolaire, 450-359-6411, ext. 7249
caressourcesmaterielles@csdhr.qc.ca
Mario Champagne, Directeur, Secrétariat général et communications, 450-359-6411, ext. 7510
secgen@csdhr.qc.ca

***Saint-Jérôme:* Commission scolaire de la Rivière-du-Nord (CSRDN)**
995, rue Labelle, Saint-Jérôme, QC J7Z 5N7, Canada
Tél: 450-438-3131
csrdn@csrdn.qc.ca
www.csrdn.qc.ca
www.facebook.com/431143150292431
twitter.com/CSRDN
Number of Schools: 39 écoles primaires; 7 écoles secondaires; *Grades:* Prim - Sec; *Enrollment:* 27000; *Number of Employees:* 3 600; *Note:* Centre administratif II: 795, rue Melançon, 450-438-3131.
Lise Allaire, Directrice générale

***Saint-Laurent:* Commission scolaire Marguerite-Bourgeoys (CSMB)**
1100, boul de la Côte-Vertu, Saint-Laurent, QC H4L 4V1, Canada
Tél: 514-855-4500; *Téléc:* 514-855-4749
www.csmb.qc.ca
www.facebook.com/csmbourgeoys
twitter.com//csmbourgeoys
www.linkedin.com/company/commission-scolaire-marguerite-bourgeoys
Number of Schools: 87 primaire; 12 secondaire; 6 FP; 6 FGA; *Enrollment:* 52000; *Number of Employees:* 8900
Yves Sylvain, Directeur général
Jean-Pierre Bédard, Directeur général adjoint
Richard Guillemette, Directeur général adjoint
Dominic Bertrand, Directeur général adjoint
Louise Gaudreault, Directeur général adjoint

***Saint-Romuald:* Commission scolaire des Navigateurs (CSDN)**
1860, 1ere rue, Saint-Romuald, QC G6W 5M6, Canada
Tél: 418-839-0500
dg@csnavigateurs.qc.ca
web.csdn.qc.ca
www.facebook.com/CSNavigateurs
twitter.com/csnavigateurs
Number of Schools: 35 primaires; 1 primaires-secondaires; 9 secondaires; 5 centres de formation professionnelle; *Grades:* Pre - Sec; *Enrollment:* 24000; *Number of Employees:* 3 500
Esther Lemieux, Directrice générale, 418-839-0500, ext. 51000
Claire Gagnon, Directrice, Services éducatifs - Jeunes, 418-839-0500, ext. 52000
Nicole Labrecque, Directrice adjointe, Enseignement général et bibliothèque, 418-839-0500
Denis Bourbeau, Directeur, Ressources humaines, 418-839-0500, ext. 56000
Bertin Fillion, Dir. général adjoint aux Services des ressources financières, 418-839-0500, ext. 57000
Richard Dion, Directeur, Ressources matérielles, 418-839-0500, ext. 58000

***Sainte-Agathe-des-Monts:* Commission scolaire des Laurentides (CSL)**
13, rue Saint-Antoine, Sainte-Agathe-des-Monts, QC J8C 2C3, Canada
Tél: 819-326-0333; *Téléc:* 819-326-2121
info@cslaurentides.qc.ca
www.cslaurentides.qc.ca
Number of Schools: 16 écoles primaires; 5 écoles secondaires; *Grades:* Prim - Sec; *Enrollment:* 8500; *Number of Employees:* 1 500
Claude Pouliot, Directeur général
direction.generale@cslaurentides.qc.ca
Antoine Déry, Directeur des services éducatifs, 819-326-0333, ext. 2008
ressources.educatives.direction@cslaurentides.qc.ca
Manon Bédard, Directrice adjointe, responsable des services complémentaires, 819-326-0333, ext. 2065
ressources.educatives.compl@cslaurentides.qc.ca
Denis Bertrand, Directeur formation professionnelle, 819-326-0333, ext. 2065
ressources.educatives.adultes@cslaurentides.qc.ca
Marie-Josée Lorion, Secrétaire générale et directrice des communications, 819-326-0333, ext. 2005
lorionm@cslaurentides.qc.ca
Réjean Cloutier, Directeur, Service des ressources financières, 819-326-0333, ext. 2015
ressources.financieres@cslaurentides.qc.ca
Josée Lapointe, Directrice, Service des ressources humaines, 819-326-0333, ext. 2013
ressources.humaines@cslaurentides.qc.ca
André Portugais, Directeur, Service des ressources matérielles, 819-326-0333, ext. 2017
ressources.materielles@cslaurentides.qc.ca

***Sept-Îles:* Commission scolaire du Fer**
30, rue Comeau, Sept-Îles, QC G4R 4N2, Canada
Tél: 418-968-9901; *Téléc:* 418-962-7760
www.csdufer.qc.ca
Number of Schools: 12 écoles primaires; 4 écoles secondaires; 4 centres de formation des adultes; *Grades:* Pre - Sec
Lucien Maltais, Directeur général, 418-964-2741
Solange Turgeon, Directrice des ressources humaines et secrétaire général, 418-964-2735
Richard Poirier, Directeur des services éducatifs, 418-964-2862
Anna Blais, Directrice des ressources financières et matérielles, 418-964-2727

***Sept-Îles:* Commission scolaire du Littoral**
789, rue Beaulieu, Sept-Îles, QC G4R 1P8, Canada
Tél: 418-962-5558; *Téléc:* 418-968-2942
Ligne sans frais: 877-745-7226
dglittoral@csdulittoral.qc.ca
www.csdulittoral.qc.ca
Number of Schools: 13; *Grades:* Pre - Sec; *Enrollment:* 530; *Number of Employees:* 190
Lucy de Mendonça, Administratrice, 418-962-5558, ext. 5560
dglittoral@csdulittoral.qc.ca
Marc-André Masse, Secrétaire général, Coordonnateur des ressources humaines, 418-962-5558, ext. 5520
rh@csdulittoral.qc.ca
Christian Denis, Directeur, Services des ressources financières, 418-962-5558, ext. 5564
cdenis@csdulittoral.qc.ca
Benoit Fequet, Coordonnateur des ressources matérielles, 418-962-5558, ext. 5205
bfequet@csdulittoral.qc.ca

***Shawinigan:* Commission scolaire de l'Énergie**
P.O. Box 580
2072, rue Gignac, Shawinigan, QC G9N 6V7, Canada
Tél: 819-539-6971; *Téléc:* 819-539-7797
Ligne sans frais: 1-888-711-0013
cse@csenergie.qc.ca
www.csenergie.qc.ca
Number of Schools: 36 écoles primaires; 7 écoles secondaires; 4 centres; *Grades:* Pre - Sec; *Enrollment:* 8683; *Number of Employees:* 2 200
Denis Lemaire, Directeur général, 819-539-6971, ext. 2223
dlemaire@csenergie.qc.ca
Serge Carpentier, Directeur général adjoint et secrétaire général, 819-539-6971, ext. 2227
scarpentier@csenergie.qc.ca
Renée Tremblay, Directeur général adjoint et des Services éducatifs jeunes, 819-539-6971, ext. 2258
rtremblay@csenergie.qc.ca
Serge Trudel, Directeur des Services des ressources financières, 819-539-6971, ext. 2241
setrudel@csenergie.qc.ca
Richard Boyer, Directeur des Services des ressources humaines, 819-539-6971, ext. 2233
rboyer@csenergie.qc.ca
Christian Lafrance, Directeur des Services des ressources matérielles, 819-539-6971, ext. 2305
clafrance@csenergie.qc.ca

***Sherbrooke:* Commission scolaire de la Région-de-Sherbrooke (CSRS)**
2955, boul de l'Université, Sherbrooke, QC J1K 2Y3, Canada
Tél: 819-822-5540; *Téléc:* 819-822-5530
www.csrs.qc.ca
www.facebook.com/CSsherbrooke
twitter.com/cssherbrooke
Number of Schools: 45 établissements; *Grades:* Prim - Sec; éducation des adultes; *Enrollment:* 22978; *Number of Employees:* 3 000
Michel Bernard, Directeur général
Gilles Millaire, Directeur, Service des ressources matérielles
RMTI@csrs.qc.ca
Daniel Samson, Directeur du Service des ressources humaines
711ressourceshumaines@csrs.qc.ca
Diane Blais, Directeur du Service des communications
Comm@csrs.qc.ca

***Sorel-Tracy:* Commission scolaire de Sorel-Tracy**
41, av de l'Hôtel-Dieu, Sorel-Tracy, QC J3P 1L1, Canada
Tél: 450-746-3990; *Téléc:* 450-746-4474
www.cs-soreltracy.qc.ca
Number of Schools: 15 écoles primaires; 3 écoles secondaires; 2 centres de formation professionnelle; *Grades:* Prim.-Sec.; *Enrollment:* 5442
Michel Lefebvre, Directeur général
Christine Marchand, Secrétariat général
Martine Cloutier, Directrice, Services éducatifs
Caroline Généreux, Directrice, Services des ressources humaines
Marie-Claude Larrivée, Directrice, Services des ressources financières
Élizabeth Mc Donough, Directrice, Services des ressources matérielles

***St-Bruno-de-Montarville:* Commission scolaire des Patriotes**
1740, rue Roberval, St-Bruno-de-Montarville, QC J3V 3R3, Canada
Tél: 450-441-2919; *Téléc:* 450-441-0838
courriel@csp.qc.ca
www.csp.qc.ca
www.facebook.com/Commissionscolairedespatriotes
twitter.com/cspatriotes

Number of Schools: 53 écoles primaires; 11 écoles secondaire; 2 centres de services spécialisés; *Grades:* Prim.-Sec.; *Enrollment:* 31077; *Number of Employees:* 4 825
Joseph Atalla, Directeur général

***St-Georges:* Commission scolaire de la Beauce-Etchemin**
1925, 118e rue, St-Georges, QC G5Y 7R7, Canada
Tél: 418-228-5541; *Téléc:* 418-228-5549
secretariat.general@csbe.qc.ca
www.csbe.qc.ca
www.facebook.com/csbeauceetchemin
Number of Schools: 55 écoles primaires; 10 écoles secondaires; 9 centres d'éducation des adultes; *Grades:* Prim - Sec; d'éducation des adultes; *Enrollment:* 16900
Normand Lessard, Directeur général, 418-228-5541, ext. 2503
direction.generale@csbe.qc.ca
Francis Isabel, Directeur du Secrétariat général et services corporatifs, 418-228-5541, ext. 2695
francis.isabel@csbe.qc.ca
Nataly Blondin, Directrice, Service de la formation professionnelle, 418-228-5541, ext. 2600
nataly.blondin@csbe.qc.ca
Patrick Beaudoin, Directeur, Service des finances, 418-228-5541, ext. 2520
patrick.beaudoin@csbe.qc.ca
Donald Busque, Directeur, Service des ressources humaines, 418-228-5541, ext. 2575
donald.busque@csbe.qc.ca
René Roy, Directeur, Service des ressources matérielles, 418-228-5541, ext. 2700
rene.roy@csbe.qc.ca

***Témiscouata-sur-le-Lac:* Commission scolaire du Fleuve-et-des-Lacs**
14, rue du Vieux-Chemin, Témiscouata-sur-le-Lac, QC G0L 1E0, Canada
Tél: 418-854-2370; *Téléc:* 418-854-2715
www.csfl.qc.ca
Number of Schools: 34 écoles primaires; 6 écoles secondaires; *Grades:* Pre - Sec
Bernard D'Amours, Directeur général, 418-854-2370, ext. 2114
dg@csfl.qc.ca
Daniel Beaulieu, Directeur général adjoint, 418-854-2370, ext. 2201
beaulieud@csfl.qc.ca
Stéphanie Dubé, Chef de secrétariat, 418-854-2370, ext. 2114
dubest@csfl.qc.ca
Catherine Boulay, Secrétaire générale, 418-854-2370, ext. 2104

***Thetford Mines:* Commission scolaire des Appalaches**
650, rue Lapierre, Thetford Mines, QC G6G 7P1, Canada
Tél: 418-338-7800; *Téléc:* 418-338-7845
ghebert@csappalaches.qc.ca
www.csappalaches.qc.ca
Number of Schools: 29 écoles primaires; 3 écoles secondaires; 2 centres de formation professionnelle; *Grades:* Prim - Sec; *Enrollment:* 6000; *Number of Employees:* 831
Camil Turmel, Directeur général
Alain Chabot, Directeur du Service des ressources financières
Martin Vallée, Directeur, Service des ressources humaines
André Dallaire, Directeur du Service des ressources matérielles

***Trois-Rivières:* Commission scolaire du Chemin-du-Roy**
1515, rue Ste-Marguerite, Trois-Rivières, QC G9A 5E7, Canada
Tél: 819-379-6565; *Téléc:* 819-379-2068
info@csduroy.qc.ca
www.csduroy.qc.ca
www.facebook.com/csduroy
www.youtube.com/user/csduroy
Number of Schools: 6 écoles primaires; 5 écoles secondaires; *Grades:* Pre - Sec; *Enrollment:* 18000
Hélène Corneau, Directrice générale, 819-379-5989, ext. 7272
dgduroy@csduroy.qc.ca
Chantal Morin, Directrice générale adjointe et Secrétariat général, 819-379-5989, ext. 7311
dga.cm@csduroy.qc.ca
Danielle Lemieux, Directrice générale adjointe, 819-379-5989, ext. 7311
dga.dl@csduroy.qc.ca
Yvan Beauregard, Directeur, Service des ressources humaines, 819-379-5989, ext. 7254
rh@csduroy.qc.ca
Marie-Claude Paillé, Directeur, Service des ressources financières, 819-379-5989, ext. 7371
rf.dir@csduroy.qc.ca

***Val-d'Or:* Commission scolaire de l'Or-et-des-Bois**
799, boul Forest, Val-d'Or, QC J9P 2L4, Canada
Tél: 819-825-4220; *Téléc:* 819-825-5305
info@csob.qc.ca
www.csob.qc.ca
www.facebook.com/profilcsob
Number of Schools: 15 écoles primaires; 4 écoles secondaires; *Grades:* Prim - Sec; *Enrollment:* 6138; *Number of Employees:* 1 100
Johanne Fournier, Directrice générale, 819-825-4220, ext. 3010
Nathalie Legault, Secrétaire générale, 819-825-4220, ext. 3011
Isabelle Bergeron, Directrice, Service des ressources humaines, 819-825-4220, ext. 3030
Louise Sylvestre, Directrice des ressources éducatives, 819-825-4220, ext. 3020
Alain Guillemette, Directeur, Service des ressources financières, 819-825-4220, ext. 3050
Rénald Dallaire, Directeur des ressources matérielles et informatiques, 819-825-4220, ext. 3040

***Vaudreuil-Dorion:* Commission scolaire des Trois-Lacs**
400, av St-Charles, Vaudreuil-Dorion, QC J7V 6B1, Canada
Tél: 514-477-7000; *Téléc:* 514-477-7022
www.cstrois-lacs.qc.ca
Number of Schools: 28 écoles primaires; 3 écoles secondaires; *Grades:* Prim - Sec; *Enrollment:* 15000
Sophie Proulx, Directrice générale, 514-477-7022
dgenerale@cstrois-lacs.qc.ca
Sandra Sheehy, Directrice, Service des ressources matérielles, 514-477-7000, ext. 1920
sandra.sheehy@cstrois-lacs.qc.ca
Chantal Beausoleil, Directrice, Service des ressources financières, 514-477-7000, ext. 1810
chantal.beausoleil@cstrois-lacs.qc.ca
Chantal Giasson, Directrice, Service des ressources humaines, 514-477-7000
chantal.giasson@cstrois-lacs.qc.ca
André Barrette, Secrétaire général, 514-477-7000, ext. 1210

***Victoriaville:* Commission scolaire des Bois-Francs**
P.O. Box 40
40, boul Bois-Francs nord, Victoriaville, QC G6P 6S5, Canada
Tél: 819-758-6453; *Téléc:* 819-758-5827
info@csbf.qc.ca
www.csbf.qc.ca
www.facebook.com/csboisfrancs
Number of Schools: 52 écoles et centres de formation; *Grades:* Prim - Sec; *Enrollment:* 13762; *Number of Employees:* 1 512
Daniel Sicotte, Directeur général
Jasmine Rochette, Directrice des Services éducatifs - jeunes
Michael Provencher, Secrétaire général
Brigitte Simoneau, Directrice du Service des ressources humaines
Josée Maheu, Directrice du Service des ressources financières
Frédéric Gagnon, Directeur, Service des ressources informatique & matérielles

***Ville-Marie:* Commission scolaire du Lac-Témiscamingue**
2, rue Maisonneuve, Ville-Marie, QC J9V 1V4, Canada
Tél: 819-629-2472; *Téléc:* 866-233-9122
courrier@cslactem.qc.ca
www.cslactem.qc.ca
Number of Schools: 14 écoles primaires; 4 écoles secondaires; 4 centres d'éducation des adultes; *Grades:* Prim.-Sec.
Éric Larivière, Directeur général, 819-629-2472, ext. 225
eric.lariviere@cslactem.qc.ca
Richard Provencher, Directeur, Services des ressources humaines et financières
Nicole Lavoie, Directrice, Services éducatifs du primaire et du secondaire
Joël Fleury, Directeur, Service des ressources matérielles
Martin Lefebvre, Secrétariat général et Service des communications

First Nations

***Mistissini:* Commission scolaire Crie Cree School Board**
203, rue Principale, Mistissini, QC G0W 1C0, Canada
Tel: 418-923-2764; *Toll-Free:* 1-866-999-2764
www.cscree.qc.ca
www.facebook.com/332475280170649
Number of Schools: 11
Abraham Jolly, Directeur général, 418-923-2764, ext. 201
ajolly@cscree.qc.ca
Bella Mianscum, Secretary General Director, 418-923-2764, ext. 218
bmianscum@cscree.qc.ca
Matthew Rabbitskin, Director, Financial Services, 418-923-2764, ext. 228
mrabbitskin@cscree.qc.ca
Moussa Habak, Director, Material Resources, 418-923-2764, ext. 208
mhabak@cscree.qc.ca
Natalie Petawabano, Director, Human Resources, 418-923-2764, ext. 211
npetawabano@cscree.qc.ca

***Saint-Laurent:* Commission scolaire Kativik Kativik School Board**
#400, 9800, boul Cavendish, Saint-Laurent, QC H4M 2V9, Canada
Tel: 514-482-8220; *Fax:* 514-482-8496
www.kativik.qc.ca
Number of Schools: 14; *Grades:* Prim - Sec
Annie Popert, Directrice générale, 514-482-8220, ext. 300
Harriet Keleutak, Secretary General, 514-482-8220, ext. 368
Diane Doucet, Director, Finance and Technical Services, 514-482-8220, ext. 321
Michèle Bertol, Director, Material Resources, 514-482-1585

Schools: Cégep

***Alma:* Collège d'Alma**
675, boul Auger ouest, Alma, QC G8B 2B7, Canada
Tél: 418-668-2387; *Téléc:* 418-668-7336
college@calma.qc.ca
www.collegealma.ca
www.facebook.com/CollegedAlma
twitter.com/collegealma
www.youtube.com/user/CollegeAlma
Grades: Préuniv., Techniques, Form. cont.
Jean Paradis, Directeur général

***Baie-Comeau:* Cégep de Baie-Comeau**
537, boul Blanche, Baie-Comeau, QC G5C 2B2, Canada
Tél: 418-589-5707; *Téléc:* 418-589-9842
Ligne sans frais: 1-800-463-2030
fraduval@cegep-baie-comeau.qc.ca
www.cegep-baie-comeau.qc.ca
www.facebook.com/cegepbaiecomeau
twitter.com0cegepbaiecomeau
Grades: Préuniv., Techniques, Form. cont.
Claude Montigny, Directeur général

***Chicoutimi:* Cégep de Chicoutimi**
534, rue Jacques-Cartier est, Chicoutimi, QC G7H 1Z6, Canada
Tél: 418-549-9520; *Téléc:* 418-549-1315
dirgene@cegep-chicoutimi.qc.ca
www.cegep-chicoutimi.qc.ca
www.facebook.com/CegepChicoutimi
Grades: Préuniv., Techniques, Form. cont.
Line Corneau, Présidente

***Drummondville:* Cégep de Drummondville**
960, rue St-Georges, Drummondville, QC J2C 6A2, Canada
Tél: 819-478-4671; *Téléc:* 819-474-6859
communications@cdrummond.qc.ca
www.cdrummond.qc.ca
Grades: Préuniv., Techniques; *Enrollment:* 1900
Hugo Houle, Président

***Gaspé:* Cégep de la Gaspésie et des Iles**
96, rue Jacques-Cartier, Gaspé, QC G4X 2S8, Canada
Tél: 418-368-2201; *Téléc:* 418-368-7003
Ligne sans frais: 1-888-368-2201
servicesauxclienteles@cegepgim.ca
www.cegepgim.ca
www.facebook.com/cegep.gaspesie.iles
twitter.com/cegepgim
www.youtube.com/user/cegepgim
Grades: Préuniv., Techniques, Form. cont.; *Enrollment:* 1140
Yves Galipeau, Directeur général

Campuses

Campus de Carleton-sur-Mer
776, boul Perron, Carleton-sur-Mer, QC G0C 1J0, Canada
Tél: 418-364-3341; *Téléc:* 418-364-7938
Ligne sans frais: 1-866-424-3341
www.cegepgim.ca

Campus des Iles-de-la-Madeleine
15, ch de la Piscine, L'Étang-du-Nord, QC G4T 3X4, Canada
Tél: 418-986-5187; *Téléc:* 418-986-6788
www.cegepgim.ca

École des pêches et de l'aquaculture du Québec
P.O. Box 220
167, La Frande-Allée est, Grande-Rivière, QC G0C 1V0, Canada
Tél: 418-385-2241; *Téléc:* 418-385-2888

***Gatineau:* Cégep Heritage College**
325, boul de la Cité des Jeunes, Gatineau, QC J8Y 6T3, Canada
Tel: 819-778-2270; *Fax:* 819-778-7364
www.cegep-heritage.qc.ca
www.youtube.com/user/heritagecollegevideo
Enrollment: 1387; *Note:* Career Programs (Nursing; Early Childhood Ed.; New Media & Publication Design; Electronics; Computer Science); Pre-University Programs: Liberal Arts, Sciences, Commerce, Social Sciences, Visual Arts; Continuing Ed.: French as a Second Language; Distance Education; Corporate Training.
Michael Randall, Director General
dg@cegep-heritage.qc.ca

***Gatineau, secteur Hull:* Cégep de l'Outaouais**
Campus Gabrielle-Roy
333, boul de la Cité-des-Jeunes, Gatineau, secteur Hull, QC J8Y 6M4, Canada
Tél: 819-770-4012; *Téléc:* 819-770-8167
Ligne sans frais: 866-770-4012
www.cegepoutaouais.qc.ca
www.facebook.com/148639948497211
twitter.com/CegepOutaouais
www.youtube.com/CegepOutaouais
Enrollment: 4418
Diana Dumitru, Directrice générale, 819-600-7665
diana.dumitru@videotron.ca

Campuses
Campus Félix-Leclerc
820, bou. de la Gappe, Gatineau, QC J8T 7T7, Canada
Tél: 819-770-4012; *Téléc:* 819- 24-3900

Campus Louis-Reboul
125, boul Sacré-Coeur, Gatineau, QC J8X 1C5, Canada
Tél: 819-770-4012; *Téléc:* 819-777-7594

***Granby:* Cégep de Granby Haute-Yamaska**
P.O. Box 7000
235, rue St-Jacques, Granby, QC J2G 9H7, Canada
Tél: 450-372-6614; *Téléc:* 450-372-6565
lfalvarez@cegepgranby.qc.ca
www.cegepgranby.qc.ca
www.facebook.com/CegepGranby
twitter.com/CegepGranby
www.youtube.com/CegepdeGranby
Yvan O'Connor, Directeur général

***Jonquière:* Cégep de Jonquière**
2505, rue St-Hubert, Jonquière, QC G7X 7W2, Canada
Tél: 418-547-2191; *Téléc:* 418-547-3359
cegep@cjonquiere.qc.ca
www.cjonquiere.qc.ca
www.facebook.com/cegepjonq
www.youtube.com/user/cegepdejonquiere
Jasmine Gauthier, Directrice des études
jasmine.gauthier@cjonquiere.qc.ca

***La Pocatière:* Cégep de La Pocatière**
140, 4e av, La Pocatière, QC G0R 1Z0, Canada
Tél: 418-856-1525; *Téléc:* 418-856-4589
information@cegeplapocatiere.qc.ca
www.cegeplapocatiere.qc.ca
www.facebook.com/cegeplapocatiere
twitter.com/cegeplapoc
Enrollment: 900
Marie-Claude Deschênes, Directrice générale intérimaire

***Lasalle:* Cégep André-Laurendeau**
1111, rue Lapierre, Lasalle, QC H8N 2J4, Canada
Tél: 514-364-3320; *Téléc:* 514-364-7130
www.claurendeau.qc.ca
www.facebook.com/165865462316
twitter.com/claurendeau
www.youtube.com/user/Claurendeau2008
Grades: Préuniv., Tech., Form. continue; *Enrollment:* 5000
Claude Roy, Directeur général

***Laval:* Collège Montmorency**
475, boul de l'Avenir, Laval, QC H7N 5H9, Canada
Tél: 450-975-6100; *Téléc:* 450-975-6116
communication@cmontmorency.qc.ca
www.cmontmorency.qc.ca
www.facebook.com/cmontmo
twitter.com/CMontmo
www.linkedin.com/company/c-gep-montmorency
Denyse Blanchet, Directrice générale

***Lévis:* Cégep de Lévis-Lauzon**
205, rte Mgr-Bourget, Lévis, QC G6V 6Z9, Canada
Tél: 418-833-5110; *Téléc:* 418-833-7323
cll.qc.ca
www.facebook.com/cegeplevislauzon
twitter.com/ComLevisLauzon
www.youtube.com/user/larouchm
Enrollment: 2885
Isabelle Fortier, Directrice générale

***Longueuil:* Collège Édouard-Montpetit**
945, ch de Chambly, Longueuil, QC J4H 3M6, Canada
Tél: 450-679-2631; *Téléc:* 450-679-5570
communications@cegepmontpetit.ca
www.college-em.qc.ca
www.facebook.com/CollegeEdouardM
twitter.com/collegeedouardm
www.youtube.com/collegeemontpetit
Number of Employees: 1000
Serge Brasset, Président

***Matane:* Cégep de Matane**
616, av St-Rédempteur, Matane, QC G4W 1L1, Canada
Tél: 418-562-1240; *Téléc:* 418-566-2115
Ligne sans frais: 1-800-463-4299
information@cegep-matane.qc.ca
www.cegep-matane.qc.ca
www.facebook.com/cegepdematane
twitter.com/cegepmatane
www.youtube.com/cegepdematane
Pierre Bédard, Directeur général

***Saint-Jérôme:* Cégep de Saint-Jérôme**
455, rue Fournier, Saint-Jérôme, QC J7Z 4V2, Canada
Tél: 450-436-1580; *Téléc:* 450-436-1756
Ligne sans frais: 877-450-2785
info@cstj.qc.ca
cstj.qc.ca
www.facebook.com/cstj1
Enrollment: 3300
Yves-André Bergeron, Directeur Général

***Mont-Tremblant:* Centre Collégial de Mont-Tremblant**
619, boul du Dr Gervais, Mont-Tremblant, QC J8E 2T3, Canada
Tél: 819-429-6155; *Téléc:* 819-429-5939
Ligne sans frais: 877-450-2785
ccmt.cstj.qc.ca

***Mont-Laurier:* Centre Collégial de Mont-Laurier**
700, rue Parent, Mont-Laurier, QC J9L 2K1, Canada
Tél: 819-623-1525; *Téléc:* 819-923-4749
Ligne sans frais: 877-450-2785
ccml.cstj.qc.ca

***Montréal:* Cégep de Saint-Laurent**
625, av Ste-Croix, Montréal, QC H4L 3X7, Canada
Tél: 514-747-6521; *Téléc:* 514-748-1249
info@cegepsl.qu.ca
www.cegepsl.qu.ca
www.facebook.com/137132236299536
twitter.com/webcsl
Enrollment: 2500
Mathieu Cormier, Directeur général

***Montréal:* Cégep du Vieux Montréal**
255, rue Ontario est, Montréal, QC H2X 1X6, Canada
Tél: 514-982-3437; *Téléc:* 514-982-3400
gestionnairew3@cvm.qc.ca
www.cvm.qc.ca
www.facebook.com/cegepduvieuxmontreal
twitter.com/cegepduvieuxmtl
Enrollment: 6000
Mylène Boisclair, Directrice générale
mboisclair@cvm.qc.ca

***Montréal:* Cégep Gérald-Godin**
15615, boul Gouin ouest, Montréal, QC H9H 5K8, Canada
Tél: 514-626-2666; *Téléc:* 514-626-6866
information@cgodin.qc.ca
www.cgodin.qc.ca
www.facebook.com/cegepgeraldgodin
twitter.com/geraldgodin
Enrollment: 1200
Christian Roy, Directeur général, 514-626-2666, ext. 5251
dg@cgodin.qc.ca

***Montréal:* Cégep Marie-Victorin**
7000, rue Marie-Victorin, Montréal, QC H1G 2J6, Canada
Tél: 514-325-0150; *Téléc:* 514-328-3830
promotion@collegemv.qc.ca
www.collegemv.qc.ca
www.facebook.com/cegepmarievictorin
twitter.com/cegepmarievic
www.linkedin.com/company/c-gep-marie-victorin
youtube.com/cegepmarievictorin
Enrollment: 3082
Nicole Rouillier, Directrice générale

***Montréal:* Collège Ahuntsic**
9155, rue St-Hubert, Montréal, QC H2M 1Y8, Canada
Tél: 514-389-5921; *Ligne sans frais:* 1-866-389-5921
webmestre@collegeahuntsic.qc.ca
www.collegeahuntsic.qc.ca
www.facebook.com/collegeahuntsic
twitter.com/CollegeAhuntsic
www.youtube.com/CollegeAhuntsic
Enrollment: 10100
Nathalie Valleé, Directrice générale

***Montréal:* Collège Dawson**
3040, rue Sherbrooke ouest, Montréal, QC H3Z 1A4, Canada
Tél: 514-931-8731; *Téléc:* 514-931-5181
www.dawsoncollege.qc.ca
www.facebook.com/dawsoncollege
twitter.com/mydawsoncollege
Enrollment: 10000
Richard Filion, Director General
rfilion@dawsoncollege.qc.ca
Robert Kavanagh, Academic Dean

***Montréal:* Collège de Bois-de-Boulogne**
10555, av de Bois-de-Boulogne, Montréal, QC H4N 1L4, Canada
Tél: 514-332-3000; *Téléc:* 514-332-5857
info@bdeb.qc.ca
www.bdeb.qc.ca
www.facebook.com/college.de.bois.de.boulogne
twitter.com/CollegeBdeB
www.linkedin.com/company/coll-ge-de-bois-de-boulogne
Grades: Préuniv., Techniques, Form. cont.
Maurice Piché, Directeur général
maurice.piche@bdeb.qc.ca

***Montréal:* Collège de Rosemont**
6400, 16e av, Montréal, QC H1X 2S9, Canada
Tél: 514-376-1620
www.crosemont.qc.ca
Patricia Hanigan, Directrice générale

***Québec:* Cégep de Sainte-Foy**
2410, ch Sainte-Foy, Québec, QC G1V 1T3, Canada
Tél: 418-659-6600; *Téléc:* 418-659-4563
info@cegep-ste-foy.qc.ca
www.cegep-ste-foy.qc.ca
www.facebook.com/cegepsaintefoy
www.twitter.com/cegepsaintefoy
ca.linkedin.com/pub/cégep-de-sainte-foy/45/90b/bb8
www.youtube.com/user/cegepdesaintefoy
Grades: Préuniv., Techniques, Form. cont.; *Enrollment:* 8000
Carole Lavoie, Directrice générale
carole.lavoie@cegep-ste-foy.qc.ca

***Québec:* Cégep François-Xavier-Garneau**
1660, boul de l'Entente, Québec, QC G1S 4S3, Canada
Tél: 418-688-8310; *Téléc:* 418-688-1539
communications@cegepgarneau.ca
www.cegepgarneau.ca
www.facebook.com/CegepGarneau
twitter.com/cegepgarneau
www.youtube.com/CollegeGarneau
Grades: Préuniv., Bacc. int'l, Tech.; *Enrollment:* 9000
Denise Trudeau, Directrice générale

***Québec:* Cégep Limoilou**
1300, 8e av, Québec, QC G1J 5L5, Canada
Tél: 418-647-6600; *Téléc:* 418-647-6798
info@climoilou.qc.ca
www.climoilou.qc.ca
www.facebook.com/CegepLimoilou
twitter.com/cegeplimoilou
www.linkedin.com/company/cegeplimoilou
www.youtube.com/webcegeplimoilou
Enrollment: 4470
Louis Grou, Directeur général, 418-647-6600, ext. 6602

Campuses
Campus de Charlesbourg
7600, av 3e est, Québec, QC G1H 7L4, Canada
Tél: 418-647-6600; *Téléc:* 418-647-5798

***Repentigny:* Cégep régional de Lanaudière**
781, rue Notre-Dame, Repentigny, QC J5Y 1B4, Canada
Tél: 450-470-0911; *Téléc:* 450-581-1567
infocom@collanaud.qc.ca
www.collanaud.qc.ca
twitter.com/cegeplanaudiere
www.linkedin.com/groups?home=&gid=2996990&trk=anet_ug_hm
www.youtube.com/user/Collanaud
Marcel Côté, Directeur général

Campuses
L'Assomption
180, rue Dorval, L'Assomption, QC J5W 6C1, Canada
Tel: 450-470-0922
www.cegep-lanaudiere.qc.ca/lassomption

Joliette
20, rue St-Charles sud, Joliette, QC J6E 4T1, Canada
Tel: 450-759-1661
www.cegep-lanaudiere.qc.ca/joliette
www.facebook.com/cegepjoliette
Enrollment: 2500

Terrebonne
2505, boul des Entreprises, Terrebonne, QC J6X 5S5, Canada
Tel: 450-470-0977
www.cegep-lanaudiere.qc.ca/terrebonne
Enrollment: 1700

***Rimouski:* Cégep de Rimouski**
60, rue de l'Évêché ouest, Rimouski, QC G5L 4H6, Canada
Tél: 418-723-1880; *Téléc:* 418-724-4961
Ligne sans frais: 1-800-463-0617
infoscol@cegep-rimouski.qc.ca
www4.cegep-rimouski.qc.ca
www.facebook.com/216198528401766
twitter.com/cegeprimouski
www.youtube.com/user/cegeprimouski
Enrollment: 2600; *Note:* Le Cégep emploie plus de 400 personnes et accueille annuellement 2600 étudiantes et étudiants inscrits dans 28 programmes à l'enseignement régulier. Quant à la Formation continue, 500 personnes y suivent des formations créditées ou non.
Dany April, Directeur des Services éducatifs

***Rivière-du-Loup:* Cégep de Rivière-du-Loup**
80, rue Frontenac, Rivière-du-Loup, QC G5R 1R1, Canada
Tél: 418-862-6903; *Téléc:* 418-862-4959
communications@cegep-rdl.qu.ca
www.cegep-rdl.qc.ca
www.facebook.com/cegeprdl
twitter.com/cegeprdl
www.youtube.com/user/cgrdl
Grades: Préuniv., Techniques, Form. cont.; *Enrollment:* 2200
René Gingras, Directeur général

***Rouyn-Noranda:* Cégep de l'Abitibi-Témiscamingue**
425, boul du Collège, Rouyn-Noranda, QC J9X 5E5, Canada
Tél: 819-762-0931; *Téléc:* 819-762-2071
Ligne sans frais: 1-866-234-3728
cegepat.qc.ca
www.facebook.com/CegepAbitibiTemiscamingue
twitter.com/cegepat
Grades: Préuniv., Techniques, Form. cont.; *Enrollment:* 2400
Sylvain Blais, Directeur général
sylvain.blais@cegepat.qc.ca

***Saint-Hyacinthe:* Cégep de Saint-Hyacinthe**
3000, av Boullé, Saint-Hyacinthe, QC J2S 1H9, Canada
Tél: 450-773-6800; *Téléc:* 450-773-9971
info@cegepsth.qc.ca
www.cegepsth.qc.ca
www.facebook.com/cegepsaintefoy
twitter.com/cegepsaintefoy
www.youtube.com/user/cegepdesaintefoy
Grades: Préuniv., Techniques, Form. cont.; *Enrollment:* 3200
Roger Sylvestre, Directeur général, 450-773-6800, ext. 2240
dirgenerale@cegepsth.qc.ca

***Saint-Jean-sur-Richelieu:* Cégep Saint-Jean-sur-Richelieu**
P.O. Box 1018
30, boul du Séminaire, Saint-Jean-sur-Richelieu, QC J3B 7B1, Canada
Tél: 450-347-5301; *Téléc:* 450-347-5259
communications@cstjean.qu.ca
www.cstjean.qc.ca
www.facebook.com/278415881842
Grades: Préuniv., Techniques, Form. cont.; *Enrollment:* 3600
Chantal Denis, Directrice générale, 450-347-5301, ext. 2277
chantal.denis@cstjean.qu.ca

***Sainte-Anne-de-Bellevue:* Cégep John Abbott College**
#21 - 257 Lakeshore Rd., Sainte-Anne-de-Bellevue, QC H9X 3L9, Canada
Tel: 514-457-6610; *Fax:* 514-457-4730
admissions@johnabbott.qc.ca
www.johnabbott.qc.ca
twitter.com/JACNews
Enrollment: 7600
John Halpin, Director General
john.halpin@johnabbott.qc.ca

***Sainte-Thérèse:* Collège Lionel-Groulx**
100, rue Duquet, Sainte-Thérèse, QC J7E 3G6, Canada
Tél: 450-430-3120; *Téléc:* 450-971-7883
info@clg.qc.ca
www.clg.qc.ca
www.facebook.com/collegelionelgroulx
twitter.com/clionelgroulx
Grades: Préuniv., Techniques, Form. cont.; *Enrollment:* 4109
Monique Laurin, Directrice générale

***Salaberry-de-Valleyfield:* Collège de Valleyfield**
169, rue Champlain, Salaberry-de-Valleyfield, QC J6T 1X6, Canada
Tél: 450-373-9441; *Téléc:* 450-373-7719
www.colval.qc.ca
Enrollment: 1200
Suzie Grondin, Directrice générale
dgvalleyfield@colval.qu.ca

***Sept-Iles:* Cégep de Sept-Iles**
175, rue De La Vérendrye, Sept-Iles, QC G4R 5B7, Canada
Tél: 418-962-9848
communications@cegep-sept-iles.qc.ca
www.cegep-sept-iles.qc.ca
www.facebook.com/cegepdeseptiles
twitter.com/Cegep_7iles
www.youtube.com/watch?v=KAaoUV_QSSQ
Donald Bhérer, Directeur général
donald.bherer@cegepsi.ca

***Shawinigan:* Collège Shawinigan**
P.O. Box 610
2263, av du Collège, Shawinigan, QC G9N 6V8, Canada
Tél: 819-539-6401; *Téléc:* 819-539-8819
information@collegeshawinigan.qc.ca
www.collegeshawinigan.qc.ca
www.facebook.com/collegeshawinigan?ref=profile
twitter.com/CShawinigan
Enrollment: 1500
Guy Dumais, Directeur général

***Sherbrooke:* Cégep de Sherbrooke**
475, rue du Cégep, Sherbrooke, QC J1E 4K1, Canada
Tél: 819-564-6350; *Téléc:* 819-564-1579
communications@cegepsherbrooke.qc.ca
www.cegepsherbrooke.qc.ca
www.facebook.com/cegepsherbrooke
twitter.com/cegepsherbrooke
Grades: Préuniv., Techniques, Form. cont.; *Enrollment:* 6000
Marie-France Bélanger, Directrice général

***Sherbrooke:* Champlain Regional College**
P.O. Box 5000
1301 Portland blvd., Sherbrooke, QC J1J 1S2, Canada
Tel: 819-564-3600; *Fax:* 819-564-2639
www.crc-sher.qc.ca
ca.linkedin.com/company/champlain-college_2?trk=ppro_cprof
Kenneth Robertson, Director General, 819-564-3600, ext. 613
krobertson@crcmail.net

Campuses
Champlain Lennoxville
P.O. Box 5003
2580 College St., Lennoxville, QC J1M 0C8, Canada
Tel: 819-564-3666; *Fax:* 819-564-5171
admissions@crc-lennox.qc.ca
www.crc-lennox.qc.ca
www.facebook.com/353253828656

Champlain St. Lambert
900 Riverside Dr., Saint-Lambert, QC J4P 3P2, Canada
Tel: 450-672-7360; *Fax:* 450-672-9299
InfoCenter@champlaincollege.qc.ca
www.champlainonline.com
www.facebook.com/Champlain.College.Saint.Lambert

Champlain St. Lawrence
790 Nérée-Tremblay Ave., Sainte-Foy, QC G1V 4K2, Canada
Tel: 418-656-6921; *Fax:* 418-656-6925
slccegep@slc.qc.ca
www.slc.qc.ca

***Sorel-Tracy:* Cégep de Sorel-Tracy**
3000, boul Tracy, Sorel-Tracy, QC J3R 5B9, Canada
Tél: 450-742-6651; *Téléc:* 450-742-1136
info@cegep-sorel-tracy.qc.ca
www.cegep-sorel-tracy.qc.ca
www.facebook.com/group.php?gid=2511302018
twitter.com/cegepsoreltracy
www.youtube.com/user/cegepsoreltracy
Grades: Préuniv., Techniques, Form. cont.
Fabienne Desroches, Directrice générale, 450-742-6651, ext. 2102
fabienne.desroches@cegepst.qc.ca

***Thetford Mines:* Cégep de Thetford**
671, boul Frontenac ouest, Thetford Mines, QC G6G 1N1, Canada
Tél: 418-338-8591; *Téléc:* 418-338-3498
www.cegepthetford.ca/
Enrollment: 1000
Christine Demers, Directrice Générale

***St-Agapit:* Campus Collégial de Lotbinière**
1080, av Bergeron, St-Agapit, QC G0S 1Z0, Canada
Tél: 418-338-8591; *Téléc:* 418-338-3498
www.cegepthetford.ca/
Enrollment: 1000

***St-Félicien:* Cégep de St-Félicien**
P.O. Box 7300
1105, boul Hamel, St-Félicien, QC G8K 2R8, Canada
Tél: 418-679-5412; *Téléc:* 418-679-0238
info@cegepstfe.ca
www.cstfelicien.qc.ca
www.facebook.com/cegepstfe
twitter.com/cstfelicien
www.youtube.com/user/cegepstfe
Grades: Préuniv., Techniques; *Enrollment:* 1000
M. Gilles Lapointe, Directeur général
glapointe@cegepstfe.ca

***St-Georges:* Cégep Beauce-Appalaches**
1055, 116e rue, St-Georges, QC G5Y 3G1, Canada
Tél: 418-228-8896; *Téléc:* 418-228-0562
Ligne sans frais: 1-800-893-5111
info@cegepba.qc.ca
www.cegepba.qc.ca
Enrollment: 1424
Mario Landry, Directeur général
cgarneau@cegepbceapp.qc.ca

***Trois-Rivières:* Cégep de Trois-Rivières**
P.O. Box 97
3500, rue De Courval, Trois-Rivières, QC G9A 5E6, Canada
Tél: 819-376-1721; *Téléc:* 819-693-8023
infoprog@cegeptr.qc.ca
www.cegeptr.qc.ca
www.facebook.com/cegeptr
twitter.com/cegeptr
www.linkedin.com/company/c-gep-de-trois-rivi-res
www.youtube.com/user/cegeptroisrivieres
Grades: Préuniv., Techniques, Form. cont.; *Enrollment:* 9475
Louis Gendron, Directeur général, 819-376-1721, ext. 2010
louis.gendron@cegeptr.qu.ca

***Victoriaville:* Cégep de Victoriaville**
475, rue Notre-Dame est, Victoriaville, QC G6P 4B3, Canada
Tél: 819-758-6401; *Téléc:* 819-758-6026
Ligne sans frais: 1-888-284-9476
information@cgpvicto.qc.ca
www.cgpvicto.qc.ca
www.facebook.com/CGPVICTO
www.linkedin.com/company/cegep-de-victoriaville
www.youtube.com/user/melissagosselin1
Number of Schools: 3
Paul Thériault, Directeur général, 819-758-6401, ext. 2400
dg@cegepvictor.ca

Schools: Specialized

First Nations

***Betsiamites:* École Nussim du conseil de bande de Betsiamites**
P.O. Box 70
4, rue Pulis, Betsiamites, QC G0H 1B0, Canada
Tél: 418-567-2215; *Téléc:* 418-567-8010
Grades: K-8

***Côte-Nord-du-Golfe-du-Saint-Lau:* École Olamen du Conseil des Montagnais (La Romaine)**
P.O. Box 222
Côte-Nord-du-Golfe-du-Saint-Lau, QC G0G 1M0, Canada
Tél: 418-229-2450
webmestre@olamen.qc.ca
Grades: K-12

***Kawawachikamach:* École Jimmy Sandy Memorial**
P.O. Box 5152
Kawawachikamach, QC G0G 2Z0, Canada
Tél: 418-585-3811; *Téléc:* 418-585-3347
Grades: K-4

***Malioténam:* École Tshishteshinu du conseil des Montagnais de Sept-Iles et Maliotenam**
P.O. Box 430 Moise
Maliotenam, QC G0G 2B0, Canada
Tél: 418-927-2956; *Téléc:* 418-927-3127
Grades: K-8

***Manawan:* École Otapi**
470, rue Otapi, Manawan, QC J0K 1M0, Canada
Tél: 819-971-1379
www.otapi.ca
Grades: 9-12

***Manawan:* École Simon P. Ottawa**
150, rue Wapoc, Manawan, QC J0K 1M0, Canada
Tél: 819-971-8817; *Téléc:* 819-871-8872
Grades: K-12

***Mashteuiatsh:* École Amishk**
225, rue Uapileu, Mashteuiatsh, QC G0W 2H0, Canada
Tél: 418-275-2473; *Téléc:* 418-275-0002
ecole.amishk@mashteuiatsh.ca
Grades: K-8; *Enrollment:* 300

***Mashteuiatsh:* École secondaire Kassinu Mamu**
507, rue Uapileu, Mashteuiatsh, QC G0W 2H0, Canada
Tél: 418-275-2473
kassinu.mamu@mashteuiatsh.ca
www.monecole-myschool.com/kassinumamu/
Grades: Sec.

***Natashquan:* École Uauitshitun Natashquan**
132, rue Tettaut RR1, Natashquan, QC G0G 2E0, Canada
Tél: 418-726-3368
uauitshitun@monecole-myschool.com
www.monecole-myschool.com/uauitshitun
Grades: K-12

***Obedjiwan:* École Mikisiw**
92, rue Tcikatnaw, Obedjiwan, QC G0W 3B0, Canada
Tél: 819-974-1221
Grades: 9-12

***Obedjiwan:* École Niska**
70, rue Niska Obedjiwan, Obedjiwan, QC G0W 3B0, Canada
Tél: 819-974-8842
Grades: K-8
Francine Gagnon Awashish, Directrice

***Pessamit:* École secondaire Uashkaikan du conseil de bande de Betsiamites**
63, rue Messek, Pessamit, QC G0H 1B0, Canada
Tél: 418-567-2271
Grades: 9-12

***Pikogan:* École Mikwan**
P.O. Box 36
RR#4, Pikogan, QC J9T 3A3, Canada
Tél: 819-732-5213
Grades: K-8

***Sept-Iles:* École Johnny-Pilot du conseil des Montagnais de Sept-Iles et Maliotenam**
P.O. Box 8000
100, rue Pashin, Sept-Iles, QC G4R 5V2, Canada
Tél: 418-962-5777; *Téléc:* 418-961-2666
ecolejonnypilot@globetrotter.net
Grades: K-8

***Sept-Iles:* École Manikanetish du conseil des Montagnais de Sept-Iles et Maliotenam**
P.O. Box 8000
1, rue Ukuias, Sept-Iles, QC G4R 2N5, Canada
Tél: 418-968-1550; *Téléc:* 418-962-6509
Grades: 9-12

***St-Augustin:* École Pakuashipi**
P.O. Box 68
52, rue Pakua, St-Augustin, QC G0G 2R0, Canada
Tél: 418-947-2729; *Téléc:* 418-947-2209
pakuashipi@yahoo.ca
www.monecole-myschool.com/pakuashipi/home.html
Grades: K-12

***Wemotaci:* École primaire Seskitin**
P.O. Box 214
41, rue Kenosi, Wemotaci, QC G0X 3R0, Canada
Tél: 819-666-2226
ericniquay@hotmail.com
www.monecole-myschool.com/seskitin
Grades: Elem.
Viviane Chilton, Directrice

***Wemotaci:* École secondaire Nikanik**
P.O. Box 222 B
20, rue Waratinak, Wemotaci, QC G0X 3R0, Canada
Tél: 819-666-2232
waratinak@monecole-myschool.com
www.monecole-myschool.com/waratinak
Nicole Potvin, Directrice

Hearing Impaired

***Montréal:* Mackay Centre School**
3500, boul Decarie, Montréal, QC H4A 3J5
Tel: 514-482-0001; *Fax:* 514-485-7254
www.emsb.qc.ca/mackay
Grades: 4-12 yrs; *Enrollment:* 147; *Number of Employees:* 32 teachers (4 for the deaf, 28 for the physically disabled); *Note:* School for the deaf/hearing impaired and children with disabilities.
Patricia Ciccarelli, Principal, 514-482-0001, ext. 1600
pciccarelli@emsb.qc.ca

Special Education

***Westmount:* École orale de Montréal pour le sourds Montreal Oral School for the Deaf**
4670, Ste. Catherine St. ouest, Westmount, QC H3Z 1S5
Tel: 514-488-4946; *Fax:* 514-488-0802
info@montrealoralschool.com
www.montrealoralschool.com
TTY: 514-488-4946
Note: School for the deaf with programs in both French and English.

Schools: Independent & Private

Faith-Based

***Dollard-des-Ormeaux:* Emmanuel Christian School École chrétienne Emmanuel**
4698 St-Jean Blvd., Dollard-des-Ormeaux, QC H9H 4S5, Canada
Tel: 514-696-6430; *Fax:* 514-696-3687
ladirection@emmanuelchristianschool.qc.ca
www.emmanuelchristianschool.qc.ca
Grades: JK - 12; Eng./Fr.; *Note:* A Christian education, with instruction in English & French.
George Van Kampen, Principal
gvankampen@emmanuelchristianschool.qc.ca

Catholic

***Anjou:* Le Collège d'Anjou**
11 000, Renaude Lapointe, Anjou, QC H1J 2V7, Canada
Tél: 514-322-8111; *Téléc:* 514-322-8112
info@collegedanjou.qc.ca
www.collegedanjou.qc.ca
www.facebook.com/132529583479406
Grades: Sec.
Luc Plante, Directeur général
Denis de Villers, Directeur des services pédagogiques

***Ayer's Cliff:* Collège Servite**
470, rue Main, Ayer's Cliff, QC J0B 1C0, Canada
Tél: 819-838-4221; *Téléc:* 819-838-4222
courrier@collegeservite.ca
www.collegeservite.ca
Grades: Sec.; Pens. & Ext.; *Note:* Confessionnelle catholique.
Carl Morissette, Directeur général
cmorissette@cnds.qc.ca
François Leblanc, Directeur du service aux élèves
fleblanc@cnds.qc.ca

***Baie-Comeau:* École secondaire Jean-Paul II**
20, av de Ramezay, Baie-Comeau, QC G4Z 1B2, Canada
Tél: 418-296-6212; *Téléc:* 418-296-3654
administration@jpii.ca
www.jpii.ca
Grades: Sec.
Dorsay Talaï, Directrice générale

***Coaticook:* Collège Rivier**
343, rue St-Jacques nord, Coaticook, QC J1A 2R2, Canada
Tél: 819-849-4833; *Téléc:* 819-849-3621
crivier@crivier.qc.ca
www.crivier.qc.ca
www.facebook.com/126425834079872
Grades: Sec.; Pens. & Ext.; *Note:* École catholique, privée et mixte.
Benoit Hélie, Directeur général
dgrivier@crivier.qc.ca

***Dolbeau-Mistassini:* Juvénat Saint-Jean**
200, boul Wallberg, Dolbeau-Mistassini, QC G8L 6A5, Canada
Tél: 418-276-3340; *Téléc:* 418-276-1757
juvenatstjean@hotmail.com
www.juvenatstjean.ca
Grades: Sec.; Pens. & Ext.
Marc Tremblay, Directeur général

***Grenville-sur-la-Rouge:* Séminaire du Sacré-Coeur**
2738, rte 148, Grenville-sur-la-Rouge, QC J0V 1B0, Canada
Tél: 819-242-0957; *Téléc:* 819-242-4089
administration@seminairedusacrecoeur.qc.ca
www.seminairedusacrecoeur.qc.ca
Grades: Sec.; Pens. & Ext.
Benoit Deschamps, Directeur général

***Lan-Saint-Jean:* Séminaire Marie-Reine-du-Clergé**
1569, rte 169 Métabetchouan-Lac-à-la-Croix, Lan-Saint-Jean, QC G8G 1A8, Canada
Tél: 418-349-2816; *Téléc:* 418-349-8055
direction@smrc.qc.ca
www.smrc.qc.ca
www.facebook.com/119850818032310
Grades: Sec.; Pens. & Ext.
Patrick Desmeules, Directeur général

***Lévis:* École Sainte-Famille (Fraternité St-Pie X) inc.**
10425, boul de la Rive-Sud, Lévis, QC G6V 7M5, Canada
Tél: 418-837-3028; *Téléc:* 418-837-7070
www.sspx.ca/fr/Quebec/L-Ecolle_Sainte_Famille
Grades: Prim./Sec.
Vincent d'André, Directeur

***Montréal:* Collège de Montréal**
1931, rue Sherbrooke ouest, Montréal, QC H3H 1E3, Canada
Tél: 514-933-7397; *Téléc:* 514-933-3225
cdm@college-montreal.qc.ca
www.college-montreal.qc.ca
Grades: Sec.; *Note:* École catholique privée.
Patricia Steben, Directrice générale

***Montréal:* École Augustin Roscelli inc.**
11960, boul de l'Acadie, Montréal, QC H3M 2T7, Canada
Tél: 514-334-0057; *Téléc:* 514-334-4060
info@ecoleaugustinroscelli.com
www.ecoleaugustinroscelli.com
Grades: Mat./Prim.; *Note:* École Catholique, privée, mixte.

***Montréal:* École Marie-Clarac**
École Marie-Clarac secondaire
3541, boul Gouin est, Montréal, QC H1H 5L8, Canada
Tél: 514-322-1161; *Téléc:* 514-322-6664
info@marie-clarac.qc.ca
ecolemarie-clarac.qc.ca
Grades: Mat./Prim./Sec.; mixte; filles; *Note:* Garderie et préscolaire/primaire (mixte); secondaire (filles); dirigée par les Soeurs de Charité de Sainte-Marie.
Sr. Martine Côté, Directrice générale

***Montréal:* École Saint-Joseph (1985) inc.**
4080, av De Lorimier, Montréal, QC H2K 3X7, Canada
Tél: 514-526-8288; *Téléc:* 514-526-5498
secretariat@stjoseph.qc.ca
www.stjoseph.qc.ca
Grades: Mat./Prim.
Frédéric Brazeau, Directeur général
fbrazeau@stjoseph.qc.ca

***Montréal:* Externat Mont-Jésus-Marie**
2755, ch de la Côte-Ste-Catherine, Montréal, QC H3T 1B5, Canada
Tél: 514-272-1035
www.montjesusmarie.com
Grades: Mat./Prim.

Sylvie Gagné, Directrice générale
Sylvie Judy Quinn, Directrice de la pédagogie

Montréal: **Pensionnat du Saint-Nom-de-Marie**
628, ch de la Côte Ste-Catherine, Montréal, QC H2V 2C5, Canada
Tél: 514-735-5261; *Téléc:* 514-735-5266
admission@psnm.qc.ca
www.psnm.qc.ca
Grades: Sec.; filles; Pens. & Ext.
Yves Petit, Directeur général

Montréal: **The Sacred Heart School of Montreal**
3635 Atwater Ave., Montréal, QC H3H 1Y4, Canada
Tel: 514-937-2845; *Fax:* 514-937-8214
info@sacredheart.qc.ca
www.sacredheart.qc.ca
www.facebook.com/SacredHeartMontreal
twitter.com/TheSHSM
Grades: Sec.; Girls; Eng.; Res & Day; *Note:* One of Canada's oldest, independent Catholic schools for girls.
Shawn O'Donnell, Head of School
sodonnell@sacredheart.qc.ca

Québec: **Collège Jésus-Marie de Sillery (CJMDS)**
2047, ch St-Louis, Québec, QC G1T 1P3, Canada
Tél: 418-687-9250; *Téléc:* 418-687-9847
admission@cjmds.qc.ca
collegejesusmarie.com
www.facebook.com/cjmds
twitter.com/cjmds
Grades: Mat - Sec.; filles; Pens. & Ext.; *Note:* Dirigé par la Congrégation des Religieuses de Jésus-Marie; programme enrichi au primaire, programme d'éducation internationale au secondaire.
Sylvie Gagné, Directrice générale

Québec: **Collège Saint-Charles-Garnier**
1150, boul René-Lévesque ouest, Québec, QC G1S 1V7, Canada
Tél: 418-681-0107; *Téléc:* 418-681-9631
cscg@collegegarnier.qc.ca
www.collegegarnier.qc.ca
www.facebook.com/collegesaintcharles
Grades: Sec.; *Note:* Propriétaire du Collège des Jésuites.
Mario Gagnon, Directeur général
mgagnon@collegegarnier.qc.ca

Québec: **Externat Saint-Coeur de Marie**
30, av des Cascades, Québec, QC G1E 2J8, Canada
Tél: 418-663-0605; *Téléc:* 418-663-9484
www.externat-scm.ca
Grades: Prim.; Pens. & Ext.
Richard Morin, Directeur général
richard.morin@externat-scm.ca

Rosemère: **Externat Sacré-Coeur**
535, rue Lefrançois, Rosemère, QC J7A 4R5, Canada
Tél: 450-621-6720; *Téléc:* 450-621-1525
courrier@externat.qc.ca
www.externat.qc.ca
Grades: Sec.; *Enrollment:* 1000
Denyse Hébert, Directrice générale

Saint-Augustin-de-Desmaures: **Séminaire Saint-François**
4900, rue Saint-Félix, Saint-Augustin-de-Desmaures, QC G3A 1X3, Canada
Tél: 418-872-0611; *Téléc:* 418-872-5845
www.ss-f.com
Grades: Sec.; Pens. & Ext.
Simon Robitaille, Directeur général
jmb@ss-f.com

Saint-Hyacinthe: **École secondaire Saint-Joseph de Saint-Hyacinthe**
2875, av Bourdages nord, Saint-Hyacinthe, QC J2S 5S3, Canada
Tél: 450-774-3775; *Téléc:* 450-774-6340
www.essj.qc.ca
Grades: Sec.; Pens. & Ext.
Simone Leblanc, Directrice général

Saint-Laurent: **École bilingue Notre-Dame de Sion**
1775, boul Décarie, Saint-Laurent, QC H4L 3N5, Canada
Tél: 514-747-3895; *Téléc:* 514-747-5492
cnicolet@ebnds.ca
www.ebnds.ca
Grades: Mat./Prim.; Fr./Angl.
Gisèle Séguin, Acting Principal
gseguin@ebnds.ca

Saint-Michel-de-Bellechasse: **Collège Dina-Bélanger**
P.O. Box 897
1, rue St-Georges, Saint-Michel-de-Bellechasse, QC G0R 3S0, Canada
Tél: 418-884-2360
secretariat@collegedina-belanger.qc.ca
collegedina-belanger.qc.ca
www.facebook.com/166864646784494
Grades: Sec.; Pens. & Ext.; *Enrollment:* 300; *Note:* Dirigé par les Religieuses de Jésus-Marie.
Sr Yvette Rioux, Directrice générale

Sherbrooke: **Collège du Sacré-Coeur**
155, rue Belvédère nord, Sherbrooke, QC J1H 4A7, Canada
Tél: 819-569-9457; *Téléc:* 819-820-0636
info@cscoeur.ca
www.cscoeur.ca
www.facebook.com/CSCoeur
www.youtube.com/user/CSCSherbrooke
Grades: Sec.; filles
Daniel Léveillé, Directeur général
dleveille@cscoeur.ca

St-Bruno-de-Montarville: **Collège Trinité**
1475, ch des Vingt, St-Bruno-de-Montarville, QC J3V 4P6, Canada
Tél: 450-653-2409; *Téléc:* 450-441-4786
secretariat@ctrinite.ca
www.collegetrinite.ca
www.facebook.com/188046491376814
www.youtube.com/channel/UC9EL_qg4jXfbUJVJbAIT4sg
Grades: Sec.
Christine Khoury, Directrice générale

Trois-Rivières: **Séminaire Saint-Joseph**
858, rue Laviolette, Trois-Rivières, QC G9A 5S3, Canada
Tél: 819-376-4459; *Téléc:* 819-378-0607
info@ssj.qc.ca
www.ssj.qc.ca
www.facebook.com/SeminaireSaintJoseph
www.youtube.com/SeminaireSaintJoseph
Grades: Sec.; garçons; Pens. & Ext.
Pierre Normand, Directeur général

Hearing Impaired

Montréal: **École orale de Montréal pour les sourds inc.**
Montreal Oral School for the Deaf Inc.
4670, rue Sainte-Catherine ouest, Montréal, QC H3Z 1S5, Canada
Tél: 514-488-4946; *Téléc:* 514-488-0802
info@montrealoralschool.com
www.montrealoralschool.com
Grades: Mat./Prim.; Éd. spéc.; *Note:* Mission: enseigner aux enfants sourds à parler & à communiquer verbalement. Programmes d'études et programmes d'intégration; services cliniques; counseling.
Martha Pérusse, Directrice

Special Education

Montréal: **L'École à Pas de Géant (Montréal)**
Giant Steps School (Montréal)
5460, av Connaught, Montréal, QC H4V 1X7, Canada
Tél: 514-935-1911; *Téléc:* 514-935-9768
info@giantstepsmontreal.com
giantstepsmontreal.com
www.facebook.com/185516821567574
Grades: Mat./Prim./Sec; Éd. spéc.; *Note:* Favoriser l'éducation et l'insertion scolaire et sociale des jeunes autistes.
Nick Katalifos, Président, Conseil d'administration

Montréal: **École Peter Hall inc.**
Peter Hall School
Campus Côte-Vertu & Centre administratif
840, boul de la Côte-Vertu, Montréal, QC H4L 1Y4, Canada
Tél: 514-748-6727; *Téléc:* 514-748-5122
info.ecole@peterhall.qc.ca
www.peterhall.qc.ca
Grades: Mat./Prim./Sec.; Fr./Angl.;Éd.Spec.; *Note:* Services éducatifs pour des élèves de 4 à 21 ans présentant une déficience intellectuelle.
Jean Laliberté, Directeur général
Maryvonne Robert, Principal

Campuses
École Peter Hall Ouimet
1455, rue Rochon, Québec, QC H4L 1W1, Canada
Tél: 514-748-1050; *Téléc:* 514-748-7544
ouimet@peterhall.qc.ca
www.peterhall.qc.ca
Grades: Mat./Prim./Sec.; Fr./Angl.;Éd.Spec.

Saint-Laurent: **Summit School**
École le Sommet
1750, rue Deguire, Saint-Laurent, QC H4L 1M7, Canada
Tel: 514-744-2867; *Fax:* 514-744-6410
admin@summit-school.com
www.summit-school.com
Grades: Pre./Elem./Sec.; Spec. Ed.; Eng.; *Enrollment:* 520; *Note:* Educational services for special needs students, from ages 4 to 21, with developmental disabilities such as autism, behavioral disturbances and other associated problems.
Herman Erdogmus, Director General

Independent & Private Schools

Baie-d'Urfé: **École internationale allemande Alexander von Humboldt inc. (AvH)**
Alexander von Humboldt German International School Inc.
216, rue Victoria, Baie-d'Urfé, QC H9X 2H9, Canada
Tél: 514-457-2886; *Téléc:* 514-457-2885
avh@avh.montreal.qc.ca
www.avh.montreal.qc.ca
www.facebook.com/avh.school
Grades: Mat./Prim./Sec.; Deutsche/Fr./Eng.; *Note:* Environnement multilingue: allemand, anglais, français; sciences naturelles & sociales; arts; Dipl. d'études sec. du Québec & bacc. allemand international; Deutsches Sprachdiplom der Kultusministerkonferenz.
Thomas Linse, Principal, 514-457-2886
linse@avh.montreal.qc.ca
Gitta Roes, Business Manager, 514-457-2886, ext. 223
roes@avh.montreal.qc.ca

Beauceville: **École Jésus-Marie de Beauceville**
670, 9e av, Beauceville, QC G5X 3P6, Canada
Tél: 418-774-3709; *Téléc:* 418-774-5749
secretariat@ejm.qc.ca
www.ejm.qc.com
www.facebook.com/ecolejesusmarie
www.flickr.com/photos/ejm_photos_web
Grades: Sec.; Pens. & Ext.

Boisbriand: **L'Académie des jeunes filles Beth Tziril**
251, av Beth Halevy, Boisbriand, QC J7E 4H4, Canada
Tél: 450-419-8881
cpetash@yahoo.com
Grades: Mat./Prim./Sec.

Boucherville: **École Les Trois Saisons**
570, boul de Mortagne, Boucherville, QC J4B 5E4, Canada
Tél: 450-641-2000; *Téléc:* 450-641-0927
Grades: Prim.
Katia Surprenant, Directrice générale

Brossard: **Académie Marie-Laurier**
Marie-Laurier Academy
1555, av Stravinski, Brossard, QC J4X 2H5, Canada
Tél: 450-923-2787; *Téléc:* 450-923-2291
academie@marielaurier.com
www.marielaurier.com
Grades: Mat./Prim./Sec.; Fr./Angl.; *Note:* Enseignement bilingue.

Châteauguay: **Collège Héritage de Châteauguay inc.**
P.O. Box 80036
270, boul d'Youville, Châteauguay, QC J6J 5X2, Canada
Tél: 450-692-5578
www.collegeheritage.ca
Grades: Prim./Sec.; *Enrollment:* 570
Jean-Guy Brais, Directeur

Chicoutimi: **École Apostolique de Chicoutimi (2A3)**
927, rue Jacques-Cartier est, Chicoutimi, QC G7H 2A3, Canada
Tél: 418-549-1055
accueil@soeursantoniennes.org
www.soeursantoniennes.org
Grades: Prim.
France Croussette, Supérieure générale

Chicoutimi: **Le Lycée du Saguenay**
658, rue Racine est, Chicoutimi, QC G7H 1V1, Canada
Tél: 418-543-4448
Grades: Sec.

Chicoutimi: **Séminaire de Chicoutimi**
679, rue Chabanel, Chicoutimi, QC G7H 1Z7, Canada
Tél: 418-549-0190; *Téléc:* 418-549-1524
seminaire@sdec.qc.ca
www.sdec.qc.ca
www.facebook.com/sdec.qc.ca
Grades: Sec.
Grant Bergeron, Directeur général
grant.baergen@sdec.qc.ca

***Compton:* École primaire Des Arbrisseaux**
6288, rte Louis-S.-St-Laurent, Compton, QC J0B 1L0, Canada
Tél: 819-835-9503
info@arbrisseaux.qc.ca
Grades: Prim.; Pens. & Ext.
Brigitte Raymond, Directrice

***Côte Saint-Luc:* L'Académie Hébraïque Inc. Hebrew Academy**
5700, av Kellert, Côte Saint-Luc, QC H4W 1T4, Canada
Tél: 514-489-5321; *Téléc:* 514-489-8607
www.ha-mtl.org
Grades: Mat. - 12é années; Angl./Fr.
Linda Lehrer, Directrice Exécutive
director@ha-montreal.org

***Dollard-des-Ormeaux:* Collège de l'Ouest de l'Ile West Island College**
851, rue Tecumseh, Dollard-des-Ormeaux, QC H9B 2L2, Canada
Tél: 514-683-4660; *Téléc:* 514-683-1702
office@westislandcollege.qc.ca
www.westislandcollege.qc.ca
www.youtube.com/user/westislandcollege
Grades: Sec.; Fr./Angl.
Robert Reid, Directeur des études
rreid@westislandcollege.qc.ca
Michel Lafrance, Directeur général
mlafrance@westislandcollege.qc.ca

***Dollard-des-Ormeaux:* Hebrew Foundation School École de formation hébraïque**
2, rue Hope, Dollard-des-Ormeaux, QC H9A 2V5, Canada
Tel: 514-684-6270; *Fax:* 514-684-1998
hebrewfoundation@gmail.com
206.132.176.122/BJEC_HebrewFoundation/index.php
Grades: Pre./Elem.; Eng./Fr.; *Note:* Programmes include M.E.L.S. French Immersion, traditional Jewish subjects, as well as the standard curriculum, dance & visual arts; instruction in English, French & Hebrew.
Rabbi Achiya Delouya, Head of School

***Dollard-des-Ormeaux:* The Learning Tree L'Arbre de Connaissance**
16, rue Séville, Dollard-des-Ormeaux, QC H9B 2V5
Tel: 514-683-8426
info@thelearningtree.ca
www.thelearningtree.ca
Grades: Preschool & Pre-Kindergarten; *Enrollment:* 160; *Number of Employees:* 25
Linda McPherson, Director

***Dorval:* Queen of Angels Academy**
100, boul Bouchard, Dorval, QC H9S 1A7, Canada
Tel: 514-636-0900; *Fax:* 514-633-8969
www.qaa.qc.ca
Other Information: Admissions: 514-636-0900 x 268
Grades: Sec.; Girls; Eng.
Mary Reynolds, Principal
reynolds.m@qaa.qc.ca

***Drummondville:* Collège Saint-Bernard**
25, av des Frères, Drummondville, QC J2B 6A2, Canada
Tél: 819-478-3330; *Téléc:* 819-478-2582
csb@csb.qc.ca
www.csb.qc.ca
www.facebook.com/lecollege
Grades: Mat - Sec.; Pens. & Ext.
Alexandre Cusson, Directeur général

***Gatineau:* Collège Saint-Alexandre**
2425, rue Saint-Louis, Gatineau, QC J8V 1E7, Canada
Tél: 819-561-3812; *Téléc:* 819-561-5205
www.college-stalexandre.qc.ca
www.facebook.com/amicalecsa
twitter.com/collstalexandre
www.youtube.com/channel/UCsPx8BuUnSPOARPqcXi3C5Q
Grades: Sec.; *Enrollment:* 970; *Number of Employees:* 90
Mario Vachon, Directeur général
mario.vachon@i-alex.qc.ca

***Gatineau:* Collège Saint-Joseph de Hull**
174, rue Notre-Dame-de-l'Ile, Gatineau, QC J8X 3T4, Canada
Tél: 819-776-3123; *Téléc:* 819-776-0992
direction@collegestjoseph.ca
www.collegestjoseph.ca
Grades: Sec.; filles
Georges Najm, Directeur général

***Gatineau:* École Montessori de l'Outaouais inc.**
161, rue Principale, Gatineau, QC J9H 7H4, Canada
Tél: 819-682-3299; *Téléc:* 819-682-7484
info.montessori@videotron.ca
www.montessori-outaouais.qc.ca
Grades: Mat./Prim.
Michèle Cusson, Directrice générale
directionmontessori@videotron.ca

***Granby:* Collège Mont-Sacré-Coeur**
210, rue Denison est, Granby, QC J2G 8E3, Canada
Tél: 450-372-6882; *Téléc:* 450-372-9219
info@college-msc.qc.ca
www.college-msc.qc.ca
www.facebook.com/134318786713143
www.youtube.com/channel/UC79hW8vx3txH26mRBuP3G_A
Grades: Sec.; *Note:* Programme Exploration; Programme sports instensifs; Programme anglais intensif.
Claude Lacroix, Directeur général

***Granby:* École secondaire du Verbe Divin**
P.O. Box 786
1021, rue Cowie, Granby, QC J2G 8W8, Canada
Tél: 450-378-1074; *Téléc:* 450-378-4566
pedagogie@verbedivin.com
www.verbedivin.com
Grades: Sec.; *Note:* Programmes - Immersion anglaise; Sports-Élite; Arts-Élite; Voyages; Programme Découverte.

***Joliette:* Académie Antoine Manseau**
P.O. Box 410
20, rue St-Charles-Borromée sud, Joliette, QC J6E 3Z9, Canada
Tél: 450-753-4271; *Téléc:* 450-753-3661
courrier@amanseau.qc.ca
www.amanseau.qc.ca
www.youtube.com/watch?v=A_XF9g_7CCM
Grades: Sec.
Christian Paul Carrière, Directeur général

***Joliette:* École les Mélèzes**
393, rue de Lanaudière, Joliette, QC J6E 3L9, Canada
Tél: 450-752-4433; *Téléc:* 450-752-4337
info@lesmelezes.qc.ca
www.lesmelezes.qc.ca
Grades: Mat./Prim.; Pens. & Ext.
Renée Champagne, Directrice générale
renee.champagne@lesmelezes.qc.ca

***Kirkland:* Académie Marie-Claire**
18190, boul Elkas, Kirkland, QC H9J 3Y4, Canada
Tél: 514-697-9995; *Téléc:* 514-697-5575
www.academiemarie-claire.qc.ca
Grades: Mat./Prim.; *Note:* 1ère année à 6ème année. Enseignement bilingue.
Marie-Claire Martin, Directrice
mmartin@amcca.ca

***Kirkland:* Kuper Academy**
High School
2975, rue Edmond, Kirkland, QC H9H 5K5, Canada
Tel: 514-426-3007; *Fax:* 514-426-0377
admissions@kuperacademy.ca
www.kuperacademy.ca
www.flickr.com/photos/69326354@N04
Grades: K.- 12; Eng.; *Note:* Liberal arts, mathematics, sciences, social sciences, & creative & performing arts.
Joan Salette, Head of School

***L'Assomption:* Collège de l'Assomption**
270, boul de l'Ange-Gardien, L'Assomption, QC J5W 1R7, Canada
Tél: 450-589-5621; *Téléc:* 450-589-2910
dirgen@classomption.qc.ca
www.classomption.qc.ca
Grades: Sec.
Danielle Lacroix, Directrice générale

***La Pocatière:* Collège de Sainte-Anne-de-la-Pocatière**
100, 4e av, La Pocatière, QC G0R 1Z0, Canada
Tél: 418-856-3012; *Téléc:* 418-856-5611
Ligne sans frais: 1-877-783-2663
info@leadercsa.com
www.leadercsa.com
Grades: Sec.; Pens. & Ext.; *Note:* Le programme Leader est offert.
Martine Dubé, Directrice générale

***La Prairie:* Collège Jean de la Mennais**
870, ch de St-Jean, La Prairie, QC J5R 2L5, Canada
Tél: 450-659-7657; *Téléc:* 450-659-3717
administration@jeandelamennais.qc.ca
www.jeandelamennais.qc.ca

Grades: Prim./Sec.
Richard Myre, Directeur général

***Laval:* Académie Lavalloise**
5290, boul des Laurentides Auteuil, Laval, QC H7K 2J8, Canada
Tél: 450-628-1430; *Téléc:* 866-550-2066
info@academielavalloise.com
academielavalloise.com
Grades: Mat./Prim.; *Enrollment:* 300
Tessa Zakaïb, Directrice
tessa.zakaib@academielavalloise.com

***Laval:* Collège Laurier**
1000, bloul. de l'Avenir, Laval, QC H7N 6J6, Canada
Tél: 514-287-1944
info@collegelaurier.ca
collegelaurier.ca
Grades: Sec.; *Enrollment:* 250
Myriam Stephens, Directrice générale

***Laval:* Collège Laval**
1275, av du Collège, Laval, QC H7C 1W8, Canada
Tél: 450-661-7714; *Téléc:* 450-661-7146
secretariat@collegelaval.ca
www.collegelaval.ca
www.facebook.com/collegelaval
Grades: Sec.; *Note:* Centre sportif, salle de théâtre, laboratoires informatiques, bibliothèque.
Michel Baillargeon, Directeur général
baillam@collegelaval.ca
Amélie Lapierre, Directrice des communications
lapiera@collegelaval.ca

***Laval:* Collège Letendre**
1000, boul de l'Avenir, Laval, QC H7N 6J6, Canada
Tél: 450-688-9933; *Téléc:* 450-688-3591
www.collegeletendre.com
Grades: Sec.
Yves Legault, Directeur
yves.legault@collegeletendre.qc.ca

***Laval:* École Charles-Perrault (Laval)**
1750, boul de la Concorde est, Laval, QC H7G 2E7, Canada
Tél: 450-975-2233
direction@charles-perrault-laval.com
www.ecolecharlesperrault.com/laval
Grades: Mat./Prim./Sec.; *Enrollment:* 380

***Laval:* École Démosthène**
1565, boul Saint-Martin ouest, Laval, QC H7S 1N1, Canada
Tél: 450-972-1800
demosthene@hcgm.org
socdem.org
Grades: Mat./Prim.; *Enrollment:* 218; *Note:* École privée de la communauté greque orthodoxe de Laval; formation générale; langues d'enseignement: française, greque.

***Laval:* École Notre-Dame de Nareg**
555, 67e Av, Laval, QC H7V 2M3, Canada
Tél: 450-680-1168
Grades: Mat./Prim.

***Lévis:* Juvénat Notre-Dame du Saint-Laurent**
30, rue du Juvénat, Lévis, QC G6V 6P5, Canada
Tél: 418-839-9592; *Téléc:* 418-839-5605
juvenat@jnd.qc.ca
www.jnd.qc.ca
www.facebook.com/juvenat222
www.youtube.com/user/jndsaintlaurent/videos
Grades: Sec.
Claude Gélinas, Directeur général, 418-839-9592, ext. 222
cgelinas@jnd.qc.ca

***Longueuil:* Collège Charles-Lemoyne inc. Administration générale/Campus Longueuil**
901, ch Tiffin, Longueuil, QC J4P 3G6, Canada
Tél: 514-875-0505; *Téléc:* 450-463-4494
college@cclemoyne.edu
www.cclemoyne.edu
www.facebook.com/collegecharleslemoyne
twitter.com/charleslemoyne
www.youtube.com/cclemoynetv
Grades: Sec.; *Note:* Campus Longueuil II: 2301, boul Fernand-Lafontaine; Campus Ville de Sainte-Catherine: 125, place Charles-Lemoyne.
David Bowles, Directeur général

***Longueuil:* Collège Français - Primaire Longueuil**
1391, rue Beauregard, Longueuil, QC J4K 2M3, Canada
Tél: 514-495-2581; *Téléc:* 514-279-5131
info@collegefrancais.ca
www.collegefrancais.ca
Grades: Mat./Prim.

Lélia Farout, Directrice
lfarout@collegefrancais.ca

Longueuil: Collège Notre-Dame-de-Lourdes
845, ch Tiffin, Longueuil, QC J4P 3G5, Canada
Tél: 450-670-4740; Téléc: 450-670-2800
collegendl@ndl.qc.ca
www.ndl.qc.ca
Grades: Sec.
Isabelle Marcotte, Directrice générale

Mont-Saint-Hilaire: Collège Saint-Hilaire inc.
800, rue Rouillard, Mont-Saint-Hilaire, QC J3G 4S6, Canada
Tél: 450-467-7001; Téléc: 450-467-9040
info@csh.qc.ca
www.csh.qc.ca
Grades: Sec.; Enrollment: 600
Diane Lavoie, Directrice générale

Montéal: École Alex Manoogian
755, rue Manoogian, Montéal, QC H4N 1Z5, Canada
Tél: 514-744-5636; Téléc: 514-744-2785
info@alexmanoogian.qc.ca
www.alexmanoogian.qc.ca
www.facebook.com/207468475974986
twitter.com/ecolealexman
www.linkedin.com/company/-cole-alex-manoogian-de-l-u-g-a-b
www.youtube.com/user/ecolealexmanoogian
Grades: Mat./Prim./Sec.; Fr./Eng./Armenian; Note: La première école arménienne au Canada; école privée.
Sébastien Stasse, Directeur

Montréal: Académie Beth Rivkah
5001, rue Vézina, Montréal, QC H3W 1C2, Canada
Tél: 514-731-3681
info@bethrivkah.com
www.bethrivkah.com
Grades: Mat./Prim./Sec.; filles; Enrollment: 500; Note: Une école pour filles juives, fondée en 1956 par le Rebbe Menachem Schneerson de Loubavitch.
Rabbi Yosef Minkowitz, Principal

Montréal: Académie Kells
Kells Academy
6865, boul de Maisonneuve ouest, Montréal, QC H4B 1T1, Canada
Tél: 514-485-8565; Téléc: 514-485-8505
kadmin@kells.ca
www.kells.ca
www.facebook.com/KellsAcademy
twitter.com/KellsAcademy
www.youtube.com/user/KellsAcademy1978
Grades: Prim./Sec.; Fr./Angl.; Éd. spéc.; Note: École mixte. Enseignement bilingue.
Irene Woods, Directrice
irenewoods@kells.ca

Montréal: Académie Louis-Pasteur
7220, rue Marie-Victorin, Montréal, QC H1G 2J5, Canada
Tél: 514-322-6123; Téléc: 514-322-6787
info@academielouispasteur.com
www.academielouispasteur.com
Grades: Mat./Prim.; Note: École primaire privée qui accueille des enfants de la maternelle à la 6e année.
Mark Passaretti, Directeur général
mpassaretti@academielouispasteur.com

Montréal: Académie Michèle-Provost inc.
1517, av des Pins ouest, Montréal, QC H3G 1B3, Canada
Tél: 514-934-0596; Téléc: 514-934-2390
info@academiemicheleprovost.qc.ca
www.academiemicheleprovost.qc.ca
www.facebook.com/AcademieMicheleProvost
Grades: Prim./Sec.; Pens. & Ext.
Michèle Provost, Présidente et Directrice générale

Montréal: Académie Saint-Louis de France
5320, rue d'Amos, Montréal, QC H1G 2Y1, Canada
Tél: 514-725-0340
www.academiesldf.com
Grades: Mat./Prim.; Enrollment: 150
Pascal Foucault, Directeur
pascal.foucault@academiesldf.ca

Montréal: The Akiva School
450 Kensington Ave., Montréal, QC H3Y 3A2, Canada
Tel: 514-939-2430; Fax: 514-939-2432
www.akivaschool.com
www.facebook.com/akivaschool
twitter.com/akivaschool
Grades: JK - 6; Eng./Fr./Hebrew; Note: Jewish community school; programmes include English Language Arts, Français, Judaic Studies, Music, Mathematics, Art, Media & Technology, Physical Education, & Ethics & Religious Cultures.
Jennifer Fraenkel, Head of School
jennifer@akivaschool.com

Montréal: Centennial Academy
L'Académie Centennale
3641, av Prud'homme, Montréal, QC H4A 3H6, Canada
Tel: 514-486-5533; Fax: 514-486-1401
aburgos@centennial.qc.ca
www.centennial.qc.ca
Grades: Sec.; Eng.
Angéla Burgos, Directrice

Montréal: Centre d'intégration scolaire inc.
6361, 6e av, Montréal, QC H1Y 2R7, Canada
Tél: 514-374-8490; Téléc: 514-374-3978
www.cisi.qc.ca
Grades: Prim./Sec.; Éd. spéc.
Patrice Allard, Directeur général, 514-374-8490, ext. 222
pallard@cisi.qc.ca

Montréal: Centre François-Michelle
10095, rue Meunier, Montréal, QC H3L 2Z1, Canada
Tel: 514-381-4418; Fax: 514-381-2895
dsormany@francois-michelle.qc.ca
www.francois-michelle.qc.ca
Grades: Mat./Prim./Sec.; Éd. spéc.
Marie-Claude Bénard, Directrice générale, 514-381-4418
mcbenard@francois-michelle.qc.ca

Montréal: Collège Beaubois
4901, rue du Collège Beaubois, Montréal, QC H8Y 3T4, Canada
Tél: 514-684-7642
info@collegebeaubois.qc.ca
www.collegebeaubois.qc.ca
www.facebook.com/271757196171526
twitter.com/collegebeaubois
www.linkedin.com/company/coll-ge-beaubois
www.youtube.com/user/Beaubois1967
Grades: Mat./Prim./Sec.
Daniel Trottier, Directeur général
dtrottier@collegebeaubois.qc.ca

Montréal: Collège Charlemagne inc.
5000, rue Pilon, Montréal, QC H9K 1G4, Canada
Tél: 514-626-7060; Téléc: 514-626-1654
admin@collegecharlemagne.com
www.collegecharlemagne.com
Grades: Mat./Prim./Sec.
Julie Beaudet, Directrice générale
jbeaudet@collegecharlemagne.com

Montréal: Collège Français - Secondaire Montréal
185, av Fairmount ouest, Montréal, QC H2T 2M6, Canada
Tél: 514-495-2581; Téléc: 514-271-2823
info@collegefrancais.ca
www.collegefrancais.ca
Grades: Sec.; Pens. & Ext.
J.L. Portal, Directeur
jlportal@collegefrancais.ca

Montréal: Collège international Marie de France
4635, ch Queen Mary, Montréal, QC H3W 1W3, Canada
Tél: 514-737-1177; Téléc: 514-737-0789
college@mariedefrance.qc.ca
www.mariedefrance.qc.ca
www.facebook.com/123134007735961?ref=ts&fref=ts
www.youtube.com/user/videocimf
Grades: Mat./Prim./Sec.; Enrollment: 1800
Brigitte Peytier, Directrice générale

Montréal: Collège Jean-Eudes
3535, boul Rosemont, Montréal, QC H1X 1K7, Canada
Tél: 514-376-5740
info@jeaneudes.qc.ca
www.jeaneudes.qc.ca
www.facebook.com/collegejeaneudes
Grades: Sec.; Enrollment: 1700
Nancy Desbiens, Directrice générale
ndesbiens@cje.qc.ca

Montréal: College Jeanne-Normandin
690, boul Crémazie est, Montréal, QC H2P 1E9, Canada
Tél: 514-381-3945; Téléc: 514-381-1695
info@jeanne-normandin.qc.ca
www.jeanne-normandin.qc.ca
www.facebook.com/143937785728317?fref=ts
Grades: Sec.; filles
Marie Robert, Directrice générale

Montréal: Collège Mont-Royal
2165, rue Baldwin, Montréal, QC H1L 5A7, Canada
Tél: 514-351-7851; Téléc: 514-351-3124
mradm@collegemont-royal.qc.ca
www.collegemont-royal.qc.ca
Grades: Sec.
Anne-Marie Blais, Directrice générale

Montréal: Collège Mont-Saint-Louis
1700, boul Henri-Bourassa est, Montréal, QC H2C 1J3, Canada
Tél: 514-382-1560; Téléc: 514-382-5886
info@msl.qc.ca
www.msl.qc.ca
Grades: Sec.
Sylvie Drolet, Directrice générale

Montréal: Collège Notre-Dame
3791, ch Queen Mary, Montréal, QC H3V 1A8, Canada
Tél: 514-739-3371
info@collegenotre-dame.qc.ca
www.collegenotre-dame.qc.ca
www.facebook.com/173636396052712
twitter.com/College_N_dame
Grades: Sec.
Lotfi Tazi, Directeur général

Montréal: College Prep International
7475, rue Sherbrooke ouest, Montréal, QC H4B 1S3, Canada
Tel: 514-489-7287; Fax: 514-489-7280
info@prepinternational.com
www.prepinternational.com
www.facebook.com/CollegePrepInternational
twitter.com/prepmontreal
Grades: Elem./Sec.; Eng.; Note: A private, non-sectarian & co-educational school.
Ursulene T. Mora, CEO

Montréal: Collège rabbinique du Canada
6405, av Westbury, Montréal, QC H3W 2X5, Canada
Tél: 514-735-2201; Téléc: 514-345-0275
Grades: Mat./Prim./Sec.; garçons; Note: École juive orthodoxe.

Montréal: Collège Regina Assumpta
1750, rue Sauriol est, Montréal, QC H2C 1X4, Canada
Tél: 514-382-4121; Téléc: 514-387-7825
info@reginaassumpta.qc.ca
www.reginaassumpta.qc.ca
www.facebook.com/CRAofficielle
Grades: Sec.; Note: Programme de musique; danse; centre culturel & sportif; chapelle.
Pierre Carle, Directeur général

Montréal: Collège Reine-Marie
9300, boul Saint-Michel, Montréal, QC H1Z 3H1, Canada
Tél: 514-382-0484; Téléc: 514-858-1401
info@reine-marie.qc.ca
www.reine-marie.qc.ca
www.facebook.com/college.reinemarie
www.youtube.com/user/CollegeReineMarie
Grades: Sec.; Enrollment: 500
Marc Tremblay, Directeur général

Montréal: Collège Sainte-Anne de Lachine
1250, boul St-Joseph, Montréal, QC H8S 2M8, Canada
Tél: 514-637-3571; Téléc: 514-637-8906
www.college-sainte-anne.qc.ca
www.facebook.com/csadl.ca
twitter.com/SainteAnne1861
www.linkedin.com/company/coll-ge-sainte-anne-de-lachine
www.youtube.com/user/collegeintsainteanne
Grades: Sec.
Ugo Cavenaghi, M.Éd., M.B.A., Directeur général
cavenaghiu@csadl.ca

Montréal: Collège Sainte-Marcelline
9155, boul Gouin ouest, Montréal, QC H4K 1C3, Canada
Tél: 514-334-9651; Téléc: 514-334-0210
college.marcelline.qc.ca
www.facebook.com/188810277886895
Grades: Mat./Prim/Sec.; Note: Enseignement préscolaire et primaire pour garçons et filles; et l'enseignement secondaire pour filles.
Sr. Teresa Belgiojoso, Directrice générale

Montréal: Collège St-Jean-Vianney
12630, boul Gouin est, Montréal, QC H1C 1B9, Canada
Tél: 514-648-3821; Téléc: 514-648-8401
college@st-jean-vianney.qc.ca
www.st-jean-vianney.qc.ca
www.facebook.com/collegestjeanvianney
twitter.com/collgestjeanvia
www.youtube.com/user/csjv2011
Grades: Sec.

Éric Deguire, Directeur général par intérim

***Montréal:* Collège Ville-Marie**
2850, rue Sherbrooke est, Montréal, QC H2K 1H3, Canada
Tél: 514-525-2516; *Téléc:* 514-525-7675
college@cvmarie.qc.ca
www.cvmarie.qc.ca
www.facebook.com/collegevillemarie
Grades: Sec.; *Note:* Programme d'Éducation internationale.
Hélène Sirois, Directrice générale

***Montréal:* L'école Ali Ibn Abi Talib**
1610, rue de Beauharnois ouest, Montréal, QC H4N 1J5, Canada
Tél: 514-744-0801; *Téléc:* 514-387-3457
info@ecoleali.com
www.ecoleali.com
Grades: Mat./Prim./Sec.
Bilal Jundi, Directeur

***Montréal:* L'École arménienne Sourp Hagop**
3400, rue Nadon, Montréal, QC H4J 1P5, Canada
Tél: 514-332-1373; *Téléc:* 514-332-8303
secretariat@ecolesourphagop.com
www.sourphagop.com
Grades: Mat./Prim./Sec.; *Enrollment:* 700
Léna Kadian, Directrice générale

***Montréal:* École au Jardin Bleu inc.**
1690, rue Sauvé est, Montréal, QC H2C 2A8, Canada
Tél: 514-388-4949
ecole@ecoleaujardinbleu.ca
www.ecoleaujardinbleu.ca
Grades: Mat./Prim.; *Note:* École privée française d'allégeance catholique.

***Montréal:* École Charles-Perrault (Pierrefonds)**
106, rue Cartier, Montréal, QC H8Y 1G8, Canada
Tél: 514-684-5043; *Téléc:* 514-684-5048
info@ecolecharles-perrault.ca
www.ecolecharles-perrault.ca
Grades: Mat./Prim.
Martine Azzouz, Directrice
direction@ecolecharles-perrault.ca

***Montréal:* L'École des Premières Lettres**
5210, rue Waverly, Montréal, QC H2T 2X7, Canada
Tél: 514-272-2229; *Téléc:* 514-272-3330
secretariat@premiereslettres.com
www.premiereslettres.com
Grades: Mat./Prim.
Anne Deguilhem, Directrice générale
adeguilhem@premiereslettres.com

***Montréal:* École Maïmonide**
Campus Jacob Safra
1900, rue Bourdon, Montréal, QC H4M 2X7, Canada
Tél: 514-744-5300; *Téléc:* 514-744-4838
admin@maimonide.ca
www.maimonide.ca
Grades: Mat./Prim./Sec.; *Note:* École de la communauté Sépharade de Montréal. Campus Parkhaven: 5615, rue Parkhaven, Côte Saint-Luc, 514-488-9224 (Michelle Serano, Directrice).
Lucienne Azoulay, Directrice générale

***Montréal:* École Michelet**
10550, av Pelletier, Montréal, QC H1H 3R5, Canada
Tél: 514-321-9551; *Téléc:* 514-321-9111
michelet@qc.aira.com
www.ecolemichelet.com
Grades: Prim.
Lucienne Mortier, Directrice générale

***Montréal:* École Montessori de Montréal**
1505, rue Serre, Montréal, QC H8N 1N3
Tél: 514-363-6603; *Téléc:* 514-363-0942
www.ecolemontessorimontreal.com
Grades: Pre.-6; *Enrollment:* 265
Anne Mansour, Directrice
annemansour@bellnet.ca

***Montréal:* École Montessori International**
10025, boul. de l'Acadie, Montréal, QC H4N 2S1
Tél: 514-331-1244
montessori_international@qc.aira.com
www.montessoriinternational.ca
Grades: Pre.-6; *Enrollment:* 250
Jeanette Kechichian, Directrice

Campuses
Pavillon Blainville
325, ch du Bas-de-Ste-Thérèse, Blainville, QC H4N 2S1
Tel: 450-965-7878
jgaron@emiblainville.com

***Montréal:* École Montessori Ville-Marie inc.**
760, rue Saint-Germain, Montréal, QC H4L 3R5, Canada
Tél: 514-335-6688; *Téléc:* 514-333-8988
ecolemontessorivillemarie.org
Grades: Mat./Prim.; *Note:* Campus Saint-Laurent: 760, rue St-Germain; Campus Laval-Duvernay: 755, rue Roland-Forget. Enseignement bilingue.
Claudette Debbané, Directrice

***Montréal:* École Pasteur**
12345, av de la Miséricorde, Montréal, QC H4J 2E8, Canada
Tél: 514-331-0850; *Téléc:* 514-331-2312
www.ecolepasteur.qc.ca
Grades: Mat./Prim./Sec.
Volta Ramirez, Directeur général

***Montréal:* École première Mesifta du Canada**
2355, av Ekers, Montréal, QC H3S 1C6, Canada
Tél: 514-738-1738
Grades: Mat./Prim./Sec.; *Note:* École juive.

***Montréal:* École primaire Socrates**
Socrates School
5757, av Wilderton, Montréal, QC H3S 2K8, Canada
Tél: 514-738-2421
socrates2@hcgm.org
socdem.org
Grades: Mat./Prim.; *Note:* Langues d'enseignement: française, greque et anglaise.
Chris Adamopoulos, Directeur général
cadamopoulos@hcgm.org

***Montréal:* École Rudolf Steiner de Montréal**
4855, av Kensington, Montréal, QC H3X 3S6, Canada
Tél: 514-481-5686; *Téléc:* 514-221-3677
info@ersm.org
www.ersm.org
Grades: Mat./Prim./Sec.; *Note:* Pédagogie Waldorf.

***Montréal:* École secondaire Duval**
260, boul Henri-Bourassa est, Montréal, QC H3L 1B8, Canada
Tél: 514-382-6070; *Téléc:* 514-382-7207
info@ecoleduval.com
www.ecoleduval.com
Grades: Sec.; *Note:* École sec. pour élèves qui ont abandonné leurs études régulières mais désirent obtenir leur diplôme dans les plus brefs délais, ou qui désirent satisfaire aux préalables d'un programme ou suivre un cours pour l'admission au collégial; cours individualisés ou cours de groupe.
Karl Duval, Directeur
karl.duval@ecoleduval.com

***Montréal:* Écoles musulmanes de Montréal**
Campus Secondaire
2255, boul Cavendish, Montréal, QC H4B 2L7, Canada
Tél: 514-484-5084
info@emms.ca
www.emms.ca
Grades: Prim./Sec.; *Note:* Campus Primaire: 7445, av Chester, (514) 484-8845 (Radjouh Idriss, directeur).

***Montréal:* Greaves Adventist Academy**
2330 West Hill Ave., Montréal, QC H4B 2S3, Canada
Tel: 514-486-5092; *Fax:* 514-486-0515
www.greavesadventistacademy.com
Grades: K - 11; *Note:* Greaves Adventist Academy is a private, non-subsidized English institution.
T. Z. Cousins, Principal

***Montréal:* Jewish People's Schools & Peretz Schools Inc.**
Les Écoles juives populaires et Les Écoles Peretz inc.
***Also known as:* JPPS-Bialik**
Head Office
6502, ch Kildare, Montréal, QC H4W 3B8, Canada
Tel: 514-731-3841
feedback@jppsbialik.ca
jppsbialik.ca
www.facebook.com/JPPSBialikSchool
twitter.com/JPPS_Bialik
Grades: Pre./Elem./Sec.; Eng./Fr.; *Note:* One educational system retaining the names of both founding schools, united in 1971. JPPS-Bialik is a Jewish day school system in Montréal, comprising: Bialik High School, 6500, ch Kildare, 514-481-2736; JPPS Elementary School, 5170, av Van Horne, 514-731-6456; and JPPS Children's Centre, 7950 ch Wavell, 514-488-1232. Instruction in English, French & Hebrew, with language programmes in French, Hebrew, Yiddish; mathematics, sciences & technology, Judaic Studies, Social Sciences, Arts; athletics; library.

***Montréal:* Lower Canada College**
4090, av Royale, Montréal, QC H4A 2M5, Canada
Tel: 514-482-9916; *Fax:* 514-482-0195
admin@lcc.ca
www.lcc.ca
Grades: K-11; Eng./Fr.
Christopher J. Shannon, Headmaster

***Montréal:* Loyola High School**
7272, rue Sherbrooke ouest, Montréal, QC H4B 1R2, Canada
Tel: 514-486-1101; *Fax:* 514-486-7266
admin@loyola.ca
www.loyola.ca
Grades: Sec.; Boys; Eng.
Éric McLean, Directeur

***Montréal:* Orchard House**
Maison Orchard
5565, ch Côte-Saint-Antoine, Montréal, QC H4A 1R3
Tel: 514-483-6556
admin@orchard-house.ca
www.orchard-house.ca
www.facebook.com/Orchard.House.Preschools
www.youtube.com/user/OrchardHouseMontreal
Yasmine Ghandour, Founder

Campuses
Pointe-Claire Campus
159, Place Frontenac, Montréal, QC H9R 4Z7
Tel: 514-630-3993
Stefanie Havas, Director

***Montréal:* Pensionnat Notre-Dame-des-Anges**
5680, boul Rosemont, Montréal, QC H1T 2H2, Canada
Tél: 514-254-6447; *Téléc:* 514-254-6261
pnda@pnda.qc.ca
ww.pnda.qc.ca
Grades: Prim.
France Mailloux, Directrice générale et pédagogique

***Montréal:* The Priory School inc.**
3120 The Boulevard, Montréal, QC H3Y 1R9, Canada
Tel: 514-935-5966; *Fax:* 514-935-1428
info@priory.qc.ca
www.priory.qc.ca
Grades: Pre./Elem.; Eng.
John Marinelli, Directeur

***Montréal:* St. George's School of Montreal**
École St-Georges de Montréal
3100 The Boulevard, Montréal, QC H3Y 1R9, Canada
Tel: 514-937-9289; *Fax:* 514-933-3621
info@stgeorges.qc.ca
stgeorges.qc.ca
www.facebook.com/stgeorgesschoolofmontreal
twitter.com/StGeorgesMtl
www.youtube.com/user/StGeorgesSchoolMtl
Grades: K - 11; Eng.; *Note:* A co-educational, non-denominational school.
James A. Officer, Head of School
james.officer@stgeorges.qc.ca

***Montréal:* Solomon Schechter Academy**
Académie Solomon Schechter
5555, ch de la Côte-St-Luc, Montréal, QC H3X 2C9, Canada
Tel: 514-485-0866; *Fax:* 514-485-2267
www.solomonschechter.ca
Grades: Pre.-6; Eng.,Fr. & Hebrew; *Enrollment:* 651; *Number of Employees:* 60 teachers; 75 assistants; 5 administrators; 5 librarians; 3 health professionals; *Note:* Committed to the values of Conservative Judaism; affiliated with the Shaare Zion Synagogue. Pre-Kindergarten to Gr. 6. Instruction in English, French & Hebrew.
Dr. Shimshon Hamerman, B.A., M.Sc., Ph.D., Head of School

***Montréal:* Talmud Torahs Unis de Montréal**
United Talmud Torahs of Montréal
4840, av Saint-Kevin, Montréal, QC H3W 1P2, Canada
Tél: 514-739-2291; *Téléc:* 514-739-3579
advancement@utt.qc.ca
www.herzliahsnowdon.qc.ca
www.facebook.com/457109797660792
Grades: Pre./Elem./Sec.; Eng./Fr.; *Note:* Instruction in Hebrew, French & English; college preparatory programme; Judaic Studies; athletics; arts; library.
Michelle Toledano, Principal

Montréal: **Trafalgar School for Girls**
3495, rue Simpson, Montréal, QC H3G 2J7, Canada
Tel: 514-935-2644; *Fax:* 513-935-2359
admissions@trafalgar.qc.ca
www.trafalgar.qc.ca
www.facebook.com/pages/Trafalgar-School-for-Girls/23292234724
Grades: Sec.; Girls; Eng.; *Enrollment:* 175; *Number of Employees:* 40
Geoffrey Dowd, Principal
gd@trafalgar.qc.ca

Montréal: **Villa Maria**
4245 Décarie Blvd., Montréal, QC H4A 3K4, Canada
Tel: 514-484-4950; *Fax:* 514-484-4492
info@villamaria.qc.ca
www.villamaria.qc.ca
www.facebook.com/VillaMariaMTL
www.youtube.com/user/EcoleSecondaireVilla
Grades: Sec.; Girls; Eng./Fr.; *Note:* Committed to students' proficiency in French & English; programmes include languages; arts (visual arts, drama, music); mathematics & sciences; technology; social sciences; ethics & religious culture; physical education & health.
Marie Anna Bacchi, Director General

Montréal: **Villa Sainte-Marcelline**
815, av Upper Belmont, Montréal, QC H3Y 1K5, Canada
Tel: 514-488-2528
info@villa.marcelline.qc.ca
villa.marcelline.qc.ca
Grades: Mat./Prim./Sec.; filles
Monique Pierre-Louis, Présidente

Montréal: **Yeshiva Gedola Merkaz Hatorah Section anglaise**
6155, ch Deacon, Montréal, QC H3S 2P4, Canada
Tel: 514-735-6611; *Fax:* 513-343-0083
mainoffice@yeshivagedola.org
www.yeshivagedola.com
Grades: Pre./Elem./Sec.; Eng./Fr.
Rabbi Moshe Glustein, Directeur

Montréal-Nord: **Centre Académique Fournier**
10339, av du Parc-Georges, Montréal-Nord, QC H1H 4Y4, Canada
Tél: 514-321-2642; *Téléc:* 514-321-0278
www.academiefournier.qc.ca
Grades: Prim./Sec.; Éd. spéc.
Paola Gravino, Directrice générale
paola.gravino@academiefournier.qc.ca

Nicolet: **Collège Notre-Dame-de-l'Assomption**
225, rue St-Jean-Baptiste, Nicolet, QC J3T 0A2, Canada
Tél: 819-293-4500; *Téléc:* 819-293-2099
info@cnda.qc.ca
www.cnda.qc.ca
www.facebook.com/CNDA.page.officielle
Grades: Sec.; Pens. & Ext.; *Note:* École privée mixte.
Mylène Proulx, Directrice générale

Outremont: **Belz Community School École communautaire Belz**
Also known as: Belz Girls School
1495, av Ducharme, Outremont, QC H2V 1E8, Canada
Tel: 514-271-0611; *Fax:* 514-271-9329
belz@belzschool.org
Grades: Pre./Elem./Sec.; Fr./Eng.; girls; *Enrollment:* 382; *Note:* Belz Boys School: 6508, Durocher, Outremont, (514) 270-5086.
Helen Liberman, Principal

Outremont: **Beth Jacob School Inc. École Beth Jacob inc.**
1750, av Glendale, Outremont, QC H2V 1B3, Canada
Tel: 514-739-3614
bjdrh@hotmail.com
Grades: Pre./Elem./Sec.; Eng./Fr.; Girls

Outremont: **Collège Stanislas - Montréal**
780, boul Dollard, Outremont, QC H2V 3G5, Canada
Tél: 514-273-9521; *Téléc:* 514-273-3409
direction@stanislas.qc.ca
www.stanislas.qc.ca
www.facebook.com/collegestanislasmontreal
twitter.com/stanmontreal
www.youtube.com/stanislasMontreal
Grades: Mat./Prim./Sec./Coll.; *Enrollment:* 2150
Philippe Warin, Proviseur/Directeur général

Campuses
Collège Stanislas - Québec
1605, ch Sainte-Foy, Québec, QC G1S 2P1, Canada
Tél: 418-527-9998; *Téléc:* 418-527-0399
quebec@stanislas.qc.ca
www.stanislas.qc.ca
www.facebook.com/334956659892267
twitter.com/stanquebec
www.youtube.com/StanislasQuebec
Grades: Mat./Prim./Sec./Coll.

Outremont: **École Buissonnière, centre de formation artistique inc.**
215, av de l'Épée, Outremont, QC H2V 3T3, Canada
Tél: 514-272-4739; *Téléc:* 514-907-5094
info@ecolebuissonniere.ca
www.ecolebuissonniere.ca
Grades: Mat./Prim.; *Note:* Intégration des arts aux programmes du Min. de l'Éducation; arts plastiques, musique, danse, art dramatique.
Hélène Bourduas, Directrice générale
Martine Duff, Directrice financière

Québec: **Académie Saint-Louis - préscolaire et primaire**
2200, de la Rive Boisée Nord, Québec, QC G2C 0J1, Canada
Tél: 416-787-2200; *Téléc:* 418-767-2211
www.aslouis.qc.ca
Grades: Prim.; *Note:* Programme d'éducation internationale.

Québec: **Académie Saint-Louis (Québec)**
1500, rue de La Rive-Boisée sud, Québec, QC G2C 2B3, Canada
Tél: 418-845-5121; *Téléc:* 418-845-5244
www.academielouispasteur.com
Grades: Sec.; *Note:* Programmes: Concentration Langues; Études-Sports: Hockey, Golf, Natation, Football, Cheerleading, et Soccer féminin.
Jocelyn Lee, Directeur général

Québec: **Centre Psycho-Pédagogique de Québec inc. (École Saint-François)**
1000, rue du Joli-Bois, Québec, QC G1V 3Z6, Canada
Tél: 418-650-1171; *Téléc:* 418-650-1145
adm@cppq.qc.ca
www.cppq.qc.ca
Grades: Prim./Sec./; Éd. spéc.; *Enrollment:* 200; *Note:* Favoriser l'intégration sociale de filles et garçons présentant des difficultés d'adaptation scolaire.
Jean-Marie Guay, Directeur

Québec: **Collège de Champigny**
1400, rte de l'Aéroport, Québec, QC G2G 1G6, Canada
Tél: 418-872-0508; *Téléc:* 418-872-1002
www.collegedechampigny.com
www.facebook.com/collegedechampigny
twitter.com/ColldeChampigny
Grades: Sec.
Guy Bouchard, Directeur général
guy.bouchard@collegedechampigny.com

Québec: **L'École des Ursulines de Québec et de Loretteville**
4, rue du Parloir, Québec, QC G1R 4S7, Canada
Tél: 418-692-2612; *Téléc:* 418-692-1240
secrectariat_euq@ursulinesquebec.com
ursulinesdequebec.laclefdelareussite.com
www.facebook.com/ursulinesquebec
twitter.com/ursulinesquebec
Grades: Prim./Sec.; filles; Pens. & Ext.; *Note:* Loretteville: 63, rue Racine, (418) 842-2949.
Jacques Ménard, Directeur
menardj@ursulinesquebec.com

Québec: **École Montessori de Québec inc.**
1265, av Du Buisson, Québec, QC G1T 2C4, Canada
Tél: 418-688-7646; *Téléc:* 418-687-5282
info@montessori-qc.net
www.montessori-qc.net
www.facebook.com/EcoleMontessoriDeQuebec
Grades: Mat./Prim.

Québec: **École secondaire François-Bourrin**
50, av des Cascades, Québec, QC G1E 2J7, Canada
Tél: 418-661-6978
efb@fbourrin.qc.ca
www.fbourrin.qc.ca
Grades: Sec.
M. Magella Beaulieu, Directeur général

Québec: **Externat Saint-Jean-Eudes**
650, av du Bourg-Royal, Québec, QC G2L 1M8, Canada
Tél: 418-627-1550; *Téléc:* 418-627-0770
info@sje.qc.ca
www.sje.qc.ca
Grades: Sec.; *Enrollment:* 1000
Édouard Malenfant, Directeur général

Québec: **Externat St-Jean-Berchmans**
2303, ch Saint-Louis, Québec, QC G1T 1R5, Canada
Tél: 418-687-5871; *Téléc:* 418-687-5886
sec@externatsjb.com
www.externatsjb.com
www.facebook.com/externatsjb
twitter.com/ExternatSJB
Grades: Mat./Prim.
Alain Roy, Directeur général

Québec: **Institut St-Joseph**
Pavillon Saint-Vallier
900, av. Joffre, Québec, QC G1S 4Z3, Canada
Tél: 418-688-0736; *Téléc:* 418-688-0737
www.st-joseph.qc.ca
www.facebook.com/institutstjoseph
Grades: Mat./Prim.
Jean-Guy Lussier, Directeur général

Québec: **Le Petit Séminaire de Québec**
6, rue de la Vielle-Université, Québec, QC G1R 5X8, Canada
Tél: 418-694-1020; *Téléc:* 418-694-1072
admission@collegefdl.ca
www.psq.qc.ca
www.facebook.com/collegefdl
Grades: Sec.
Marc Dallaire, Directeur général

Québec: **Réseau VISION**
Également connu sous le nom de: Écoles VISION Schools
Siège social
#300, 1995, rue Frank-Carrel, Québec, QC G1N 4H9, Canada
Tél: 418-653-3547; *Téléc:* 418-653-6435
Ligne sans frais: 866-553-3547
info@visionschools.com
www.visionschools.com
Number of Schools: 21; *Grades:* Mat./Prim./Sec.; *Enrollment:* 3000
Richard Dumais, Président

Québec: **Séminaire des Pères Maristes**
2315, ch Saint-Louis, Québec, QC G1T 1R5, Canada
Tél: 418-651-4944; *Téléc:* 418-651-6841
spmecole@spmaristes.qc.ca
www.spmaristes.qc.ca
Grades: Sec.
Jean-François Bussières, Directeur général
jfbussieres@spmaristes.qc.ca

Rawdon: **Collège Champagneur**
3713, rue Queen, Rawdon, QC J0K 1S0, Canada
Tél: 450-834-5401; *Téléc:* 450-834-6500
secretariat@champagneur.qc.ca
www.champagneur.qc.ca
Grades: Secondaire; *Note:* Privée mixte.
Johanne Lamy, Directrice générale

Rawdon: **École et Pensionnat Marie-Anne**
4567, rue du Mont-Pontbriand, Rawdon, QC J0K 1S0, Canada
Tél: 450-834-4668; *Téléc:* 855-266-4257
info@ecolemarieanne.org
www.ecolemarieanne.qc.ca
Grades: Mat./Prim.
Anne-Marie Breault, Directrice générale

Repentigny: **Académie François-Labelle**
1227, rue Notre-Dame, Repentigny, QC J5Y 3H2, Canada
Tél: 450-582-2020; *Téléc:* 450-582-9732
afl@academiefrancoislabelle.qc.ca
www.academiefrancoislabelle.qc.ca
www.facebook.com/173472472741596?fref=ts
Grades: Mat./Prim.
Michèle Beaudry, Directrice générale

Repentigny: **Centre Académique de Lanaudière**
930, boul L'Assomption, Repentigny, QC J6A 5H5, Canada
Tél: 450-654-5026
www.lecadl.com
Grades: Mat./Prim.
Roger Normandin, Directeur général

Rigaud: Collège Bourget
65, rue St-Pierre, Rigaud, QC J0P 1P0, Canada
Tél: 450-451-0815; *Téléc:* 450-451-4171
dg@collegebourget.qc.ca
www.collegebourget.qc.ca
Grades: Mat - 12è années
Jean-Marc St-Jacques, c.s.v., Directeur général

Rivière-du-Loup: Collège Notre-Dame
P.O. Box 786
56, rue Saint-Henri, Rivière-du-Loup, QC G5R 3Z5, Canada
Tél: 418-862-8257; *Téléc:* 418-862-8495
collegenotredame.ca
www.facebook.com/CollegeNotreDameRdLPageofficielle
Grades: Sec.; *Enrollment:* 500
Guy April, Directeur général
dg@collegenotredame.ca

Saint-Augustin-de-Desmaures: Collège Saint-Augustin
4950, rue Lionel-Groulx, Saint-Augustin-de-Desmaures, QC G3A 1V2, Canada
Tél: 418-872-0954
Grades: Sec.; Pens. & Ext.

Saint-Bruno-de-Montarville: Académie des Sacrés-Coeurs
1575, ch des Vingt, Saint-Bruno-de-Montarville, QC J3V 4P6, Canada
Tél: 450-653-3681; *Téléc:* 450-653-0816
info@academiedsc.ca
www.academiedessacrescoeurs.ca
Grades: Mat./Prim.; Pens. & Ext.
Christine Khoury, Directrice générale

Saint-Gabriel-de-Valcartier: École secondaire Mont-Saint-Sacrement
200, boul St-Sacrement, Saint-Gabriel-de-Valcartier, QC G0A 4S0, Canada
Tél: 418-844-3771; *Téléc:* 418-844-2926
secretariat@mss.qc.ca
www.mss.qc.ca
Grades: Sec.; *Note:* Programme Baccalauréat international; Programme Magellan.
Jean-Claude Grodin, Directeur général

Saint-Guillaume: Juvénat Saint-Louis-Marie
96, rue Saint-Jean-Baptiste, Saint-Guillaume, QC J0C 1L0, Canada
Tél: 819-396-2076
info@juvenat.ca
www.juvenat.ca
www.facebook.com/juvenat.stlouismarie
Grades: Sec.; Pens. & Ext.
Martin Girard, Directeur
juvenatmartin@hotmail.com
Luc Georgeff, Directeur
juvenatluc@hotmail.com

Saint-Hyacinthe: Collège Antoine-Girouard
700, rue Girouard est, Saint-Hyacinthe, QC J2S 2Y2, Canada
Tél: 514-773-4334
info@antoinegirouard.com
www.antoine-girouard.qc.ca
www.facebook.com/antoinegirouardcollege
Grades: Sec.

Saint-Hyacinthe: Collège Saint-Maurice
630, rue Girouard ouest, Saint-Hyacinthe, QC J2S 2Y3, Canada
Tél: 450-773-7478; *Téléc:* 450-773-1413
info.college@csm.qc.ca
www.csm.qc.ca
Grades: Sec.; filles; Pens. & Ext.; *Note:* École secondaire pour filles; Programme d'éducation internationale.
Jean-Pierre Jeannotte, Directeur général

Saint-Hyacinthe: La Petite Académie
1090, av Pratte, Saint-Hyacinthe, QC J2S 4B6, Canada
Tél: 450-771-0644; *Téléc:* 450-771-7242
info@lapetiteacademie.qc.ca
lapetiteacademie.qc.ca
Grades: Mat./Prim.
Lise Thiboutot, Directrice générale

Saint-Jacques: Collège Esther-Blondin
101, rue Ste-Anne, Saint-Jacques, QC J0K 2R0, Canada
Tél: 450-839-3672; *Téléc:* 450-839-3951
admin@collegeblondin.qc.ca
www.collegeblondin.qc.ca
Grades: Sec.; Pens. & Ext.; *Note:* Membre, Soc. des établissements du bacc. international du Québec, et Org. du bacc. international; le collège est reconnu École Verte Brundtland.
Stéphane Mayer, Directeur général

Saint-Jean-sur-Richelieu: École secondaire Marcellin-Champagnat
14, ch des Patriotes est, Saint-Jean-sur-Richelieu, QC J2X 5P9, Canada
Tél: 450-347-5343; *Téléc:* 450-347-2423
webmestre@esmc.qc.ca
www.esmc.qc.ca
Grades: Sec.
Richard Custeau, Directeur général
richard.custeau@i-esmc.qc.ca

Saint-Jérôme: Académie Lafontaine
2171, boul Maurice, Saint-Jérôme, QC J7Y 4M7, Canada
Tél: 450-431-3733; *Téléc:* 450-431-7390
info@academielafontaine.qc.ca
www.academielafontaine.qc.ca
Grades: Mat. - Sec.; *Note:* Camps du jour; piscine; cantine.
Claude Potvin, Directeur général

Saint-Lambert: Collège Durocher Saint-Lambert
Pavillon Durocher
857, rue Riverside, Saint-Lambert, QC J4P 1C2, Canada
Tél: 450-465-7213; *Téléc:* 450-465-0860
info@cdsl.qc.ca
www.cdsl.qc.ca
www.facebook.com/86410504648
Grades: Sec.; *Note:* Pavillon Saint-Lambert: 375, rue Riverside, 450-671-5585.
Isabelle Gélinas, Directrice générale

Saint-Laurent: École Jeunes musulmans canadiens
Également connu sous le nom de: École JMC
5919, boul Henri-Bourassa ouest, Saint-Laurent, QC H4R 1B7
Tél: 514-956-9559
admin@ecolejmc.ca
www.ecolejmc.ca
www.facebook.com/pages/%C3%89cole-JMC/20217550648227 4
Grades: Prim. - Sec.; *Enrollment:* 450
Layla Sawaf, Directrice générale

Saint-Laurent: École Vanguard Québec ltée (École primaire interculturelle)
Vanguard Québec School
5935, ch de la Côte-de-Liesse, Saint-Laurent, QC H4T 1C3, Canada
Tél: 514-747-5500; *Téléc:* 514-747-2831
cccaputo@vanguardquebec.qc.ca
www.vanguardquebec.qc.ca
www.facebook.com/pages/École-Vanguard-School/2508130817 26346
Grades: Prim./Sec.; Fr./Angl.; Éd. spéc.; *Note:* Services adaptés à des élèves présentant des difficultés graves d'apprentissage. École Vanguard Primaire Interculturelle: 1150, rue Deguire, (514) 747-3711 (Denise Bédard, directrice). École Vanguard Secondaire Francophone: 83, boul des Prairies, Laval, (450) 972-6268 (François Papineau, directeur). École Vanguard Secondaire Interculturelle: 175, rue Metcalfe, (514) 932-9770 (Maryse Bessette, directrice).
Carolyn Coffin-Caputo, Directrice générale, 514-747-5500

Saint-Laurent: Education Plus
1275, rue Hodge, Saint-Laurent, QC H4N 2B1, Canada
Tel: 514-733-9600; *Fax:* 514-733-3060
edplus@runbox.com
www.edplus.ca
Grades: 10 - 11; *Enrollment:* 40; *Note:* Relationship-based education, flexible structure, informal environment; Life Skills courses; drama; arts; English & French language skills.
James Watts, Director
j.watts@sympatico.ca

Sainte-Thérèse: Académie Ste-Thérèse
Campus Jacques-About
425, rue Blainville est, Sainte-Thérèse, QC J7E 1N7, Canada
Tél: 450-434-1130; *Téléc:* 450-434-0010
infostetherese@academie.ste-therese.com
www.academie.ste-therese.com
Grades: Mat./Prim./Sec.; Pens. & Ext.; *Note:* Campus Rosemère: 1, ch des Écoliers, Rosemère, 450-434-1130.
Rose De Angelis, Directrice générale
rdeangelis@academie.ste-therese.com

Sept-Îles: Institut d'enseignement de Sept-Iles inc.
737, av Gamache, Sept-Îles, QC G4R 2J8, Canada
Tél: 418-968-9104; *Téléc:* 418-962-8561
Grades: Sec.; *Enrollment:* 236
Jean-Sébastien Roy, Directeur général
jean-sebastien.roy@iesi.in

Shawinigan: Séminaire Sainte-Marie
5655, boul des Hêtres, Shawinigan, QC G9N 4V9, Canada
Tél: 819-539-5493
www.seminairestemarie.com
www.facebook.com/seminairesaintemarie
twitter.com/SemSteMarie
www.youtube.com/ssmpact
Grades: Prim./Sec.
Richard Gaudreault, Directeur général

Sherbrooke: Bishop's College School, Inc. (BCS)
P.O. Box 5001 Lennoxville
80, ch Moulton Hill, Sherbrooke, QC J1M 1Z8, Canada
Tel: 819-566-0238; *Fax:* 819-566-8182
Toll-Free: 1-877-570-7542
admissions@bishopscollegeschool.com
www.bishopscollegeschool.com
www.facebook.com/bishopscollegeschool
twitter.com/BCS_Today
www.youtube.com/BCStoday
Grades: 7-12; *Enrollment:* 216; *Number of Employees:* 30 teachers; *Note:* Bishop's College School is a bilingual boarding & day school.
William Mitchell, Head of School, 819-566-0227, ext. 201
wmitchell@bishopscollegeschool.com
Charles de Sainte Marie, Director, Development, 819-566-0227, ext. 203
John Haffenden, Executive Director, Finance & Operations, 819-566-0227, ext. 205
jhaffenden@bishopscollegeschool.com
Greg McConnell, Director, Admissions, 819-566-0227, ext. 296
gmcconnell@bishopscollegeschool.com

Sherbrooke: Collège du Mont-Sainte-Anne
2100, ch Ste-Catherine, Sherbrooke, QC J1N 3V5, Canada
Tél: 819-823-3003; *Téléc:* 819-569-9636
Ligne sans frais: 877-823-3003
secretariat@collegemsa.net
www.college-mont-sainte-anne.qc.ca
Grades: Sec.; garçons; Pens. & Ext.
André Ricard, Directeur général

Sherbrooke: Collège Mont Notre-Dame de Sherbrooke inc.
114, rue de la Cathédrale, Sherbrooke, QC J1H 4M1, Canada
Tél: 819-563-4104; *Téléc:* 819-563-8689
www.mont-notre-dame.qc.ca
www.facebook.com/423552584428886
www.youtube.com/user/CollegeMontNotreDame
Grades: Mat./Prim./Sec; filles; *Enrollment:* 500; *Note:* Programme d'éducation international; école de musique; école de danse; Espagnol; sports.
Éric Faucher, Directeur général
efaucher@mont-notre-dame.qc.ca

Sherbrooke: École Plein Soleil (Association coopérative)
300-458, rue de Montréal, Sherbrooke, QC J1H 1E5, Canada
Tél: 819-569-8359; *Téléc:* 819-569-3979
info@pleinsoleil.qc.ca
www.pleinsoleil.qc.ca
Grades: Mat./Prim.; *Note:* Programme d'éducation internationale.
Marie-Josée Mayrand, Directrice générale
mjmayrand@pleinsoleil.qc.ca

Sherbrooke: École secondaire de Bromptonville
125, rue du Frère-Théode, Sherbrooke, QC J1C 0S3, Canada
Tél: 819-846-2738; *Téléc:* 819-846-4808
esb@esb-fsc.ca
www.esb.bromptonville.qc.ca
Grades: Sec.; Pens. & Ext.
Simon Croteau, Directeur général
Simon.Croteau@esb-fsc.ca

Sherbrooke: Séminaire de Sherbrooke
195, rue Marquette, Sherbrooke, QC J1H 1L6, Canada
Tél: 819-563-2050; *Téléc:* 819-562-8261
courrier@seminaire-sherbrooke.qc.ca
www.seminaire-sherbrooke.qc.ca
Grades: Sec.; *Note:* Secondaire et collégial; formation continue.
Pierre Thériault, Recteur-Directeur général

Sherbrooke: Séminaire Salésien
135, rue Don Bosco nord, Sherbrooke, QC J1L 1E5, Canada
Tél: 819-566-2222; *Téléc:* 819-566-6969
lesalesien.com
www.facebook.com/lesalesien
twitter.com/salesien
www.youtube.com/leseminairesalesien

Grades: Sec.
Raymond Lepage, Directeur général

***Stanstead:* Stanstead College**
450 Dufferin St., Stanstead, QC J0B 3E0, Canada
Tel: 819-876-7891; *Fax:* 819-876-5891
admissions@stansteadcollege.com
www.stansteadcollege.com
www.facebook.com/78975058390
twitter.com/stansteadcolleg
www.youtube.com/user/StansteadSpartans
Grades: 7 - 12; *Enrollment:* 195; *Note:* Co-educational; curriculum/instruction in English, with programmes in French, arts, music, drama; athletics.
Michael T. Wolfe, Headmaster, 819-876-7891, ext. 230
michael.wolfe@stansteadcollege.com

***Terrebonne:* Collège Saint-Sacrement**
901, rue St-Louis, Terrebonne, QC J6W 1K1, Canada
Tél: 450-471-6615; *Téléc:* 450-471-5904
www.collegesaintsacrement.qc.ca
Grades: Sec.
Pierre Cofsky, Directeur général

***Trois-Rivières:* Collège Marie-de-l'Incarnation**
725, rue Hart, Trois-Rivières, QC G9A 5S3, Canada
Tél: 819-379-3223; *Téléc:* 819-379-3226
reception@cmitr.com
www.cmitr.qc.ca
www.facebook.com/cmitr
Grades: Mat./Prim./Sec.; Pens. & Ext.; *Note:* École pour filles; école de musique.
Réjean Lemay, Directeur général
Martine Talbot, Directrice pédagogique

***Trois-Rivières:* Institut secondaire Keranna (1992) inc.**
6205, boul des Chenaux, Trois-Rivières, QC G9A 5S3, Canada
Tél: 819-378-4833; *Téléc:* 819-378-2417
keranna@keranna.qc.ca
keranna.qc.ca
Grades: Sec.
Julie L'Heureux, Directrice générale
julie.lheureux@keranna.qc.ca

***Trois-Rivières:* Val Marie**
88, ch du Passage, Trois-Rivières, QC G8T 2M3, Canada
Tél: 819-379-8040; *Téléc:* 819-378-8559
secretariat@ecolevalmarie.qc.ca
www.ecolevalmarie.qc.ca
Grades: Mat./Prim.; Pens. & Ext.
France Vadeboncoeur, Directrice générale

***Val-Morin:* Académie Laurentienne**
1200, 14e av, Val-Morin, QC J0T 2R0, Canada
Tél: 819-322-2913; *Téléc:* 819-322-7086
info@al.qc.ca
www.academielaurentienne.ca
Grades: Prim./Sec.; Pens. & Ext.; *Note:* Programmes académiques et sportifs; installations sportives: piscines, palestre, gymnase double; terrains de jeux, de tennis; centre équestre.
Guy Richard, Directeur général
richard.guy@al.qc.ca

***Varennes:* Centre Éducatif Chante Plume**
104, boul de la Marine, Varennes, QC J3X 1Z5, Canada
Tél: 450-652-6869; *Téléc:* 450-652-5773
varennes@visionschools.com
varennes.visionschools.com
Grades: Mat./Prim.
Colette Cardin, Directrice propriétaire

***Varennes:* Collège Saint-Paul**
235, rue Sainte-Anne, Varennes, QC J3X 1P9, Canada
Tél: 450-652-2941; *Téléc:* 450-652-4461
reception@college-st-paul.qc.ca
www.college-st-paul.qc.ca
www.facebook.com/college.stpaul
Grades: Sec.; *Note:* Programme de formation générale; Programme d'éducation internationale.
Cathie Bouchard, Directrice générale
cbouchard@college-st-paul.qc.ca

***Vaudreuil-Dorion:* Éco-lita Trilingue**
1255, boul André-Chartrand, Vaudreuil-Dorion, QC J7V 0B7
Tél: 450-510-5454; *Téléc:* 450-510-0927
info@ecolita.ca
www.ecolita.ca
Grades: Pre.-6; *Enrollment:* 100
Michelle Vaudrin, Direction, fondatrice et directrice pédagogique

***Victoriaville:* Collège Clarétain**
663, rue Gamache, Victoriaville, QC G6R 0W3, Canada
Tél: 819-752-4571
administration@collegeclaretain.com
www.collegeclaretain.com
Grades: Sec.; Pens. & Ext.; *Note:* École privée mixte.
Christian Trudel, Directeur général

***Waterville:* Collège François-Delaplace**
365, rue Compton est, Waterville, QC J0B 3H0, Canada
Tél: 819-837-2882; *Téléc:* 819-837-0625
secretariat@moncfd.com
www.college-francois-delaplace.qc.ca
www.facebook.com/148860918474652
www.youtube.com/user/moncfd
Grades: Sec.; filles; *Note:* École Verte Brundtland; école secondaire privée pour filles (pensionnaires & externes).
Josée Hamel, Directrice générale
jhamel@college-francois-delaplace.qc.ca

***Westmount:* Miss Edgar's & Miss Cramp's School (ECS)**
525 Mount Pleasant Ave., Westmount, QC H3Y 3H6, Canada
Tel: 514-935-6357; *Fax:* 514-935-1099
info@ecs.qc.ca
www.ecs.qc.ca
www.facebook.com/207534389310982
twitter.com/EdgarCramp
Grades: K - 11; Girls; Eng. & Fr.; *Enrollment:* 344; *Note:* University-preparatory programme, to Gr. 11; French Immersion junior school; arts, athletics, math, sciences, languages, citizenship education; extended day programme; library.
Katherine Nikidis, B.Ed., MHSc, Head of School
nikidisk@ecs.qc.ca

***Westmount:* Selwyn House**
École Selwyn House
95 Côte-St-Antoine Rd., Westmount, QC H3Y 2H8, Canada
Tel: 514-931-9481; *Fax:* 514-931-6118
admission@selwyn.ca
www.selwyn.ca
Grades: Pre./Elem./Sec.; Eng.; Boys
Hal Hannford, Headmaster
hhannaford@selwyn.ca

***Westmount:* The Study**
3233, The Boulevard, Westmount, QC H3Y 1S4, Canada
Tel: 514-935-9352; *Fax:* 514-935-1721
info@thestudy.qc.ca
www.thestudy.qc.ca
www.facebook.com/pages/SOGA-Network/157775784348963
twitter.com/thestudyschool
www.youtube.com/thestudyschool
Grades: Pre./Elem./Sec.; Eng.; Girls; *Note:* Committed to best practices in education, with a focus on proficiency in both English & French, academics & athletics. The school is the first in Québec to introduce a Mandarin language program at the primary level.
Nancy Sweer, Head of School, 514-935-9352, ext. 226
nsweer@thestudy.qc.ca

Universities & Colleges

Universities

***Gatineau:* Université du Québec en Outaouais**
Pavillion Alexandre-Taché
283, boul Alexandre-Taché, Gatineau, QC J9A 1L8, Canada
Tél: 819-595-3900; *Téléc:* 819-595-3924
Ligne sans frais: 1-800-567-1283
questions@uqo.ca
www.uqo.ca
www.facebook.com/Universite.Quebec.Outaouais
twitter.com/uqo
www.linkedin.com/groups?home=&gid=3000070
www.youtube.com/uqovideo
Full Time Equivalency: 5200
Zacharie Bossinotte-Gosselin, Président

Campuses
Campus Saint-Jérôme
5, rue Saint-Joseph, Saint-Jérôme, QC J7Z 0B7, Canada
Tél: 450-530-7616; *Ligne sans frais:* 800-567-1283
uqo.ca/saint-jerome

***Montréal:* Concordia University**
Université Concordia
Sir George Williams Campus
1455, boul de Maisonneuve ouest, Montréal, QC H3G 1M8, Canada
Tel: 514-848-2424
www.concordia.ca
www.facebook.com/ConcordiaUniversity
twitter.com/Concordia
www.linkedin.com/company/concordia-university
www.youtube.com/ConcordiaUni
Full Time Equivalency: 35210
Alan Shepard, President & Vice-Chancellor
Graham Carr, Interim Provost & Vice-President, Academic Affairs
Bram Freedman, Vice-President, Advancement and External Relations
Leisha LeCouvie, Senior Director, Alumni Relations & Events
Denis Cossette, CFO
Graham Carr, Vice-President, Research and Graduate Studies
Roger Côté, Vice-President, Services
Philippe Beauregard, CCO

Faculties
Arts & Science
artsandscience.concordia.ca
Dr. David Graham, Dean
Engineering & Computer Science
encs.concordia.ca
Nabil Esmail, Dean
Fine Arts
finearts.concordia.ca
Catherine Wild, Dean
Graduate Studies & Research
Elizabeth Saccà, Dean
John Molson School of Business (JMSB)
Fax: 514-848-2816
gradprograms.jmsb@concordia.ca
johnmolson.concordia.ca
Other Information: Main Office: 514-848-2424, ext. 2727
Enrollment: 9222; *Note:* Civic address: 1450 Guy Street, Suite MB 6.201, Montreal, QC
Stéphane Brutus, Dean

Campuses
Loyola Campus
7141, rue Sherbrooke ouest, Montréal, QC H4B 1R6, Canada

***Montréal:* École de technologie supérieure**
1100, rue Notre-Dame ouest, Montréal, QC H3C 1K3, Canada
Tél: 514-396-8800; *Téléc:* 514-396-8950
Ligne sans frais: 1-888-394-7888
admission@etsmtl.ca
www.etsmtl.ca
www.facebook.com/etsmtl
twitter.com/etsmtl
www.youtube.com/user/etsmtl
Full Time Equivalency: 4800
Pierre Dumouchel, Directeur général

***Montréal:* HEC Montréal**
***Également connu sous le nom de:* École des Hautes Études Commerciales**
Université de Montréal
3000, ch de la Côte-Sainte-Catherine, Montréal, QC H3T 2A7, Canada
Tél: 514-340-6000; *Téléc:* 514-340-6411
webmestre@hec.ca
www.hec.ca
www.facebook.com/hecmontreal
twitter.com/HEC_Montreal
www.linkedin.com/company/hec-montreal
www.youtube.com/HECMontreal
Full Time Equivalency: 12000; *Note:* HEC Montréal est la première école de gestion au Canada. Affaires internationales; finance; gestion des opérations/logistique; gestion des ressources humaines; management; marketing; méthodes quantitatives de gestion; sciences comptables; technologies de l'information; économie appliquée. Édifice Decelles: 5255, av Decelles. Campus Laval: 2572, boul Daniel-Johnson, (450) 973-7741. Campus Longueuil: 101, place Charles-Lemoyne, (450) 651-5458. Bureau international à Paris: 15, rue du Louvre, 75001 Paris, 33(0)1 42 33 43 40.
Michel Patry, Directeur

***Montréal:* McGill University**
845 Sherbrooke St. West, Montréal, QC H3A 0G4
Tel: 514-398-4455
info.publicaffairs@mcgill.ca
www.mcgill.ca
www.facebook.com/McGillUniversity
twitter.com/mcgillu
www.linkedin.com/company/mcgill-university
plus.google.com/+mcgilluniversity/posts
Full Time Equivalency: 37170
Micheal Meighen, Chancellor
Stuart Cobbett, Chair of Board
Suzanne Fortier, Principal & Vice-Chancellor
Anthony C. Masi, Provost
Rose Goldstein, Vice-Principal, Research & International Relations
Michael Di Grappa, Vice-Principal, Administration & Finance
Stephen Strople, Secretary General
Marc Weinstein, Vice-Principal, Development & Alumni Relations
Olivier Marcil, Vice Principal, Communications & External Relations
Sarah Stroud, Associate Vice Principal, Research & International Relations

Faculties

Agricultural & Environmental Sciences
21111 Lakeshore Rd., Sainte-Anne-de-Bellevue, QC H9X 3V9
Tel: 514-398-7773
info.macdonald@mcgill.ca
www.mcgill.ca/macdonald
www.facebook.com/150355221657931
twitter.com/McGillMacCampus
www.linkedin.com/groups?gid=4331295
www.youtube.com/mcgilluniversity
Chandra A. Madramootoo, B.Sc., M.Sc., Ph.D., Dean

Faculty of Arts
Dawson Hall
#110, 853 Sherbrooke St. West, , QC H3A 2T6
Tel: 514-398-4212; *Fax:* 514-398-8102
www.mcgill.ca/arts
Christopher Manfredi, Dean
christopher.manfredi@mcgill.ca

Centre for Continuing Education
#1199, 688 Sherbrooke St. West, Montréal, QC H3A 3R1
Tel: 514-398-6200; *Fax:* 514-398-2650
info.conted@mcgill.ca
www.mcgill.ca/continuingstudies
Judith Potter, Dean

Faculty of Dentistry
#500, 2001 McGill College Ave., Montréal, QC H3A 1G1
Tel: 514-398-7203; *Fax:* 514-398-8900
undergrad.dentistry@mcgill.ca
www.mcgill.ca/dentistry
Paul Allison, Dean

Faculty of Education
3700 McTavish St., Montréal, QC H3A 1Y2
Tel: 514-398-7042; *Fax:* 514-398-4679
info@education.mcgill.ca
www.mcgill.ca/education
Dilson Rassier, Dean

Faculty of Engineering
Macdonald Engineering Bldg.
#378, 817 Sherbrooke St. West, Montréal, QC H3A 0C3
www.mcgill.ca/engineering
Jim A. Nicell, Dean

Graduate & Post-Doctoral Studies
3415 McTavish St., #MS13, Montréal, QC H3A 0C8
Tel: 514-398-7878
www.mcgill.ca/gps
www.facebook.com/mcgillgradschool
twitter.com/mcgillgradstudy
Martin Kreiswirth, Chair, Council of Graduate and Postdoctoral Studies

Faculty of Law
Old Chancellor Day Hall
3644 Peel St., Montréal, QC H3A 1W9
Tel: 514-398-6666
info.law@mcgill.ca
www.mcgill.ca/law
www.facebook.com/LawMcGill
twitter.com/LawMcGill
www.linkedin.com/groups?gid=126787
plus.google.com/101411088730700351673
Daniel Jutras, Dean
dean.law@mcgill.ca

Desautles Faculty of Management
Samuel Bronfman Building
1001 Sherbrooke St. West, Montréal, QC H3A 1G5
Tel: 514-398-4000; *Fax:* 514-398-3876
www.mcgill.ca/desautels
www.facebook.com/desautelsmcgill
twitter.com/desautelsmcgill
www.linkedin.com/groups?home=&gid=37970
instagram.com/desautelsmcgill
Morty Yalovsky, Interim Dean

Faculty of Medicine
McIntyre Building
3655 Promenade Sir William Osler, Montréal, QC H3G 1Y6
Tel: 514-398-1768; *Fax:* 514-398-3595
recep.med@mcgill.ca
www.mcgill.ca/medicine
Andrew Holmes, B.Sc., M.D., C.M., Dean

Schulich School of Music
Strathoona Music Bldg.
555 Sherbrooke St. West, Montréal, QC H3A 1E3
Tel: 514-398-4535; *Fax:* 514-398-1540
www.mcgill.ca/music
www.facebook.com/SchulichMusic
Sean Ferguson, Dean

Faculty of Religious Studies
Birks Bldg.
3520 University St., Montreal, QC H3A 2A7
Tel: 514-398-4121; *Fax:* 514-398-6665
web.relgstud@mcgill.ca
www.mcgill.ca/religiousstudies
www.facebook.com/328129725272
www.youtube.com/user/McGillFRS
Ian H. Henderson, Acting Dean

Faculty of Science
Dawson Hall
853 Sherbrooke St. West, Montréal, QC H3A 0G5
Tel: 514-398-4215
www.mcgill.ca/science
Martin Grant, Dean

Schools

Architecture
Macdonald-Harrington Building
815 Sherbrooke St. West, Montréal, QC H3A 0C2
Tel: 514-398-6700; *Fax:* 514-398-7372
www.mcgill.ca/architecture
Annmarie Adams, Director

Communication Sciences & Disorders
2001 McGill College Ave., 8th Fl., Montréal, QC H3A 1G1
Tel: 514-398-4137; *Fax:* 514-398-8123
scsd@mcgill.ca
www.mcgill.ca/scsd
www.facebook.com/50YearsSchoolOfCommunicationSciencesAndDisorders
Dr. Marc D. Pell, Associate Dean & Director

Faculty of Computer Science
McConnell Engineering Bldg.
#318, 3480 University St., Montréal, QC H3A 0E9
Tel: 514-398-7071; *Fax:* 514-398-3883
www.cs.mcgill.ca
Gregory Dudek, Director

School of Dietetics & Human Nutrition
Macdonald-Stewart Building
21111 Lakeshore Rd., Ste-Anne-de-Bellevu, QC H9X 3V9
Tel: 514-398-7773
www.mcgill.ca/dietetics
Dr. Kristine G. Koski, Director

Executive Institute
1001 rue Sherbrooke ouest, Montreal, QC H3A 1G5
Tel: 514-398-3970; *Fax:* 514-398-7443
Toll-Free: 888-419-0707
executive@mcgill.ca
executive.mcgill.ca
Peter Todd, Director

School of Physical & Occupational Therapy (SPOT)
3654 Promenade Sir William Osler, Montreal, QC H3G 1Y5
Tel: 514-398-4500; *Fax:* 514-398-6360
www.mcgill.ca/spot
www.facebook.com/McgillSchoolofPhysicalandOccupationalTherapy
instagram.com/mcgill_spot
Dr. Annette Majnemer, Director

Social Work
#300, 3508 rue University, Montreal, QC H3A 2A7
Tel: 514-398-7070; *Fax:* 514-397-4760
www.mcgill.ca/socialwork
Dr. Wendy Thomson, Director

School of Urban Planning
Tel: 514-398-4075; *Fax:* 514-398-8376
admissions.planning@mcgill.ca
www.mcgill.ca/urbanplanning
David Brown, Director

Affiliations

Macdonald Campus
21111, ch Bord-du-Lac, Sainte-Anne-de-Bellevue, QC H9X 3V9, Canada
Tel: 514-398-7707; *Fax:* 514-398-7766
info.macdonald@mcgill.ca
www.mcgill.ca/macdonald/
www.facebook.com/150355221657931?sk=wall
twitter.com/McGillMacCampus
www.linkedin.com/groups?gid=4331295&trk=hb_side_g
www.youtube.com/mcgilluniversity
Note: The Macdonald Campus of McGill University is the home of the University's Faculty of Agricultural & Environmental Sciences, the McGill School of Environment, & the School of Dietetics & Human Nutrition. Programmes leading to the degree of B.Sc.(Agr.), as well as graduate programs in agriculture, food, natural sciences, applied economics, environment, & engineering are offered.
Chandra A. Madramootoo, Dean, 514-398-7707
chandra.madramootoo@mcgill.ca

The Montreal Diocesan Theological College
3475, rue University, Montréal, QC H3A 2A8, Canada
Tel: 514-849-3004; *Fax:* 514-849-4113
info@dio-mdtc.ca
www.dio-mdtc.ca
facebook.com/dio.mdtc
Note: An Anglican theological college founded in 1873. Affiliated with McGill Univ. & l'Univ. de Montréal. Degree courses: B.Th., Dip.Min, M.Div. Advanced degrees, offered through McGill: S.T.M, M.A., Ph.D. Distance education courses leading to the Cert. in Theology, or Licentiate in Theology also available.
The Rev. Canon John Simons, Principal
Rev. Karen Egan, Director of Pastoral Studies
Rev. Tim Smart, Director of Lay Education
Rev. Dr. Elizabeth Rowlinson, Chaplain

The Presbyterian College, Montréal
Collège Presbytérien, Montréal
3495, rue University, Montréal, QC H3A 2A8
Tél: 514-288-5256; *Téléc:* 514-288-8072
www.presbyteriancollege.ca
www.facebook.com/PCleadershipcentre
Note: Founded in 1867 & affiliated with McGill Univ.
Dale Woods, Principal

Royal Victoria College
3425 University St., Montréal, QC H3A 2A8
Tel: 514-398-6378; *Fax:* 514-398-3159
www.mcgill.ca/accommodations/summer/rvc
Note: Royal Victoria College is McGill's only all women's residence.

The United Theological College
Le Séminaire Uni
3521 University St., Montréal, QC H3A 2A9
Tel: 514-849-2042; *Fax:* 514-849-8634
Toll-Free: 888-849-2042
admin@utc.ca
www.utc.ca
Note: A college of the United Church of Canada, committed to the training of persons, regardless of race, economic status, sexual orientation & gender identity, for various Christian ministries. Instruction in English & French is offered.
Philip L. Joudrey, Principal
pjoudrey@utc.ca
Angelika Piché, Director of French Leadership Development
apiche@utc.ca
Alyson Huntly, Director, Studies
ahuntly@utc.ca

Centres/Institutes

Business & Management Research Centre (B&MRC)
Bronfman Building
1001 Sherbrooke St. West, Montréal, QC H3A 1G5
Tel: 514-398-4000; *Fax:* 514-398-3876
www.mcgill.ca/desautels/research/centres/bmrc

Desmarais Global Finance Research Centre
1001 Sherbrooke St. West, Montréal, QC H3A 1G5
Tel: 514-398-8144; *Fax:* 514-398-3876
www.mcgill.ca/desautels/research/centres/dgfc
Vihang Errunza, Director
vihang.errunza@mcgill.ca

Marcel Desautels Institute for Integrated Management (MDIIM)
Bronfman Building
#104, 1001 Sherbrooke St. West, Montréal, QC H3A 1G5
Tel: 514-398-6061; *Fax:* 514-398-3876
mdiim.mgmt@mcgill.ca
www.mcgill.ca/desautels/integrated-management
Steve Maguire, Director

McGill Centre for the Convergence of Health & Economics (MCCHE)
Bronfman Building
1001 Sherbrooke St. West, Montréal, QC H3A 1G5
Tel: 514-398-3299; *Fax:* 514-398-8963
www.mcgill.ca/desautels/mcche
twitter.com/Desautels_MCCHE
Roba Al Ghoul, Project Administrator
roba.alghoul@mcgill.ca

Center for Strategy Studies in Organizations
Bronfman Building
1001 Sherbrooke St. West, Montréal, QC H3A 1G5
Tel: 514-398-4000
www.mcgill.ca/desautels/research/centres/csso
Robert David, Director
robert.david@mcgill.ca

Dobson Centre for Entrepreneurship
Bronfman Building
#649, 1001 Sherbrooke St. West, Montréal, QC H3A 1G5
Tel: 514-398-4000
www.mcgill.ca/desautels/research/centres/dces
Gregory Vit, Director
greg.vit@mcgill.ca

Management Science Research Centre
Bronfman Building
1001 Sherbrooke St. West, Montréal, QC H3A 1G5
Tel: 514-398-4000; *Fax:* 514-398-3876
www.mcgill.ca/desautels/research/centres/msrc
Shanling Li, Director

McGill Institute of Marketing (MIM)
Bronfman Building
1001 Sherbrooke St. West, Montréal, QC H3A 1G5
Tel: 514-398-4662; *Fax:* 514-398-3876
www.mcgill.ca/desautels/research/centres/marketing
Emine Sarigollu, Contact
emine.sarigollu@mcgill.ca

Research Institute of the McGill University Health Centre
Also known as: Research Institute of the MUHC
#500, 2155 Guy St., Montréal, QC H3H 2R9
Tel: 514-394-1934
ri.it@muhc.mcgill.ca
www.rimuhc.ca/web/research-institute-muhc
Vassilios Papadopoulos, Executive Director

Montréal: The United Theological College Le Séminaire Uni

3521, rue University, Montréal, QC H3A 2A9, Canada
Tel: 514-849-2042; *Fax:* 514-849-8634
Toll-Free: 888-849-2042
admin@utc.ca
www.utc.ca

Montréal: Université de Montréal

Pavillon J.-A.-DeSève
P.O. Box 6205
2332, boul Édouard-Montpetit, Montréal, QC H3C 3T5, Canada
Tél: 514-343-7076; *Téléc:* 514-343-5788
www.umontreal.ca
www.facebook.com/umontreal
twitter.com/UMontreal
www.youtube.com/udemvideo
Full Time Equivalency: 60000; *Note:* Facultés: Aménagement; Arts/Sciences; Droit; Éducation permanente; Études supérieures/postdoctorales; Médecine; Médecine dentaire; Médecine vétérinaire; Musique; Pharmacie; Sciences de l'éducation; Sciences infirmières; Théologie; Kinésiologie; Optometrie; Santé publique. Campus régionaux: Terrebonne; Ville de Laval; Longueuil; Québec.
Guy Breton, Recteur, 514-343-6991
guy.breton@umontreal.ca
Alexandre Chabot, Secrétaire général, 514-343-6111, ext. 6800
Raymond Lalande, Vice-recteur aux affaires académiques
Louise Béliveau, Vice-recteur aux affaires étudiantes et aux études
Marie-Josée Hébert, Vice recteur à la recherche, la création et l'innovation, 514-343-6662
marie-josee.herbert@umontreal.ca
Guy Lefebvre, Vice-recteur, relations internationales, à la Francophonie
Jean Charest, Vice-recteur aux ressources humaines et à la planification
Éric Filteau, Vice-recteur, des Finances et de l'Infrastructure

Affiliations
École Polytechnique de Montréal
Également connu sous le nom de: Polytechnique Montréal
P.O. Box 6079 Centre-ville
Montréal, QC H3C 3A7, Canada
Tél: 514-340-4711
www.polymtl.ca
www.facebook.com/polymtl
twitter.com/polymtl/
www.youtube.com/user/polymtlvideos/
Full Time Equivalency: 6900; *Number of Employees:* 248 professeurs; *Note:* Fondée en 1873, Le Polytechnique est une école d'ingénierie de classe internationale; programmes au baccalauréat, cycles supérieurs, formation continue; recherche; l'École se trouve à 2900, boul Édouard-Montpetit, Campus de l'Univ. de Montréal, 2500 ch de Polytechnique.
Christophe Guy, Directeur général
Steven Chamberland, Directeur, affaires académiques et la vie étudiante
Gilles Savard, Directeur, recherche, l'innovation & affaires internationales
Richard Hurteau, Directeur, l'administration
Philippe Duby, Directeur des ressources informationnelles

HEC Montréal
Également connu sous le nom de: École des Hautes Études Commerciales
3000, ch de la Côte-Sainte-Catherine, Montréal, QC H3T 2A7, Canada
Tél: 514-340-6000; *Téléc:* 514-340-6411
www.hec.ca
www.facebook.com/hecmontreal
twitter.com/HEC_Montreal
www.linkedin.com/company/hec-montreal
www.flickr.com/photos/hecmontreal

Centres/Institutes
Centre de recherche en éthique
P.O. Box 6128 Centre-ville
Montréal, QC H3C 3J7
Tél: 514-343-6111
www.lecre.umontreal.ca
www.facebook.com/208384185896720
Christine Tappolet, Directrice

Montréal: Université du Québec à Montréal (UQAM)

P.O. Box 8888 Centre-Ville
405, Rue Ste-Catherine Est, Montréal, QC H2L 2C4, Canada
Tél: 514-987-3000
general@uqam.ca
www.uqam.ca
www.facebook.com/uqam1
twitter.com/uqam
www.youtube.com/UQAMtv
Full Time Equivalency: 43140
Robert Proulx, Recteur, 514-987-3080
proulx.robert@uqam.ca

Campuses
Campus de Lanaudière
Pavillon D
#D106, 2700, boul des Entreprises, Terrebonne, QC J6X 4J8, Canada
Tél: 514-987-7002; *Téléc:* 450-477-8712
Ligne sans frais: 1-800-361-4567
lanaudiere@uqam.ca
www.etudier.uqam.ca/campus/lanaudiere
Amar Belhal, Coordonnateur, 450 662-1340
belhal.amar@uqam.ca

Campus de Laval
P.O. Box 4 ou 5
#A1950, 475, boul de l'Avenir, Laval, QC H7N 5H9, Canada
Tél: 450-662-1300; *Téléc:* 450-662-1244
laval@uqam.ca
www.etudier.uqam.ca/campus/laval

Campus de l'Ouest-de-l'île
#A-215, 3501, boul Saint-Charles, Kirkland, QC H9H 4S3, Canada
Tél: 514-428-1181
ouestdel'ile@uqam.ca
www.etudier.uqam.ca/campus/ouestdelile
Chantal Boucher, Coordonnatrice, 514 987-3000, ext. 2176
boucher.chantal@uqam.ca

Campus de Longueuil
#2050, 150, Place Charles-Le Moyne, Longueuil, QC J4K 0A8, Canada
Tél: 514-987-3063; *Téléc:* 514-987-4648
Ligne sans frais: 1-800-363-9290
longueuil@uqam.ca
www.etudier.uqam.ca/campus/longueuil

Québec: Université du Québec

475, rue Parvis, Québec, QC G1K 9H7
Tél: 418-657-3551; *Téléc:* 418-657-2132
information@uquebec.ca
www.uquebec.ca
fr-ca.facebook.com/pages/Université-du-Québec/141232909277771
twitter.com/ReseauUQ
www.linkedin.com/company/universit-du-qu-bec
www.youtube.com/user/reseauuq
André Roy, Secrétaire général
Isabelle Boucher, Vice-présidente à l'administration

Affiliations
Université du Québec en Abitibi-Témiscamingue (UQAT)
445, boul de l'Université, Rouyn-Noranda, QC J9X 5E4
Tél: 819-762-0971; *Téléc:* 819-797-4727
Ligne sans frais: 877-870-8728
information@uqat.ca
www.uqat.ca
www.facebook.com/uqat.ca
twitter.com/UQAT
www.youtube.com/user/uqatinformation
Full Time Equivalency: 3290

Université du Québec à Chicoutimi (UQAC)
555, boul de l'Université, Chicoutimi, QC G7H 2B1
Tél: 418-545-5011; *Téléc:* 418-545-5012
Ligne sans frais: 800-463-9880
www.uqac.ca
www.facebook.com/uqac.ca
twitter.com/UQAC
Full Time Equivalency: 6750
Martin Gauthier, Recteur

Université du Québec en Outaouais (UQO)
P.O. Box 1250 Hull
Gatineau, QC J8X 3X7
Tél: 819-595-3900; *Ligne sans frais:* 800-567-1283
dcr@uqo.ca
www.uqo.ca
www.facebook.com/Universite.Quebec.Outaouais
twitter.com/uqo
www.linkedin.com/groups?home=&gid=3000070
www.youtube.com/uqovideo
Full Time Equivalency: 6820

Université du Québec à Montréal (UQAM)
P.O. Box 8888 Centre-Ville
Montréal, QC H3C 3P8
Tél: 514-987-3000
general@uqam.ca
www.uqam.ca
Other Information: Urgence: 514-987-3131
www.facebook.com/uqam1
twitter.com/uqam
www.youtube.com/UQAMtv
Full Time Equivalency: 42040

Université du Québec à Rimouski
P.O. Box 3300 A
Rimouski, QC G5L 3A1
Tél: 418-723-1986; *Téléc:* 418-724-1525
Ligne sans frais: 800-511-3382
uqar@uqar.qc.ca
www.uqar.ca
www.facebook.com/accueil.uqar
twitter.com/UQAR
Full Time Equivalency: 7240

Université du Québec à Trois-Rivières (UQTR)
P.O. Box 500
Trois-Rivières, QC G9A 5H7
Tél: 819-376-5011; *Téléc:* 819-376-5210
Ligne sans frais: 800-365-0922
info@uqtr.ca
www.uqtr.ca
www.facebook.com/uqtr.ca
twitter.com/InformationUQTR
www.youtube.com/user/camerauqtr
Full Time Equivalency: 13710

École nationale d'administration publique (ENAP)
555, boul Charest est, Québec, QC G1K 9E5, Canada
Tél: 418-641-3000; *Téléc:* 418-641-3060
communication@enap.ca
www.enap.ca
www.facebook.com/ENAP.CA
twitter.com/info_enap
www.youtube.com/user/ENAPtv

École de technologie supérieure
1100, rue Notre-Dame ouest, Montréal, QC H3C 1K3
Tél: 514-396-8800; *Téléc:* 514-396-8950
communicationsETS@etsmtl.ca
www.etsmtl.ca
www.facebook.com/etsmtl
twitter.com/etsmtl
www.youtube.com/user/etsmtl

INRS-Institut Armand-Frappier
531, boul des Prairies, Laval, QC H7V 1B7
Tél: 450-687-5010; *Téléc:* 450-686-5566
info@iaf.inrs.ca
www.iaf.inrs.ca

Institut national de la recherche scientifique (INRS)
490, rue de la Couronne, Québec, QC G1K 9A9
Tél: 418-654-4677; *Téléc:* 418-654-3876
Ligne sans frais: 877-326-5762
communications@adm.inrs.ca
www.inrs.ca
www.facebook.com/UniversiteINRS
twitter.com/U_INRS
www.youtube.com/user/MyINRS
Full Time Equivalency: 600

Télé-université (TÉLUQ)
455, rue du Parvis, Québec, QC G1K 9H5
Tél: 418-657-2747; *Téléc:* 418-652-0176
Ligne sans frais: 888-843-4333
info@teluq.ca
www.teluq.uquebec.ca
www.facebook.com/universiteaujourdhui
twitter.com/teluq
www.linkedin.com/groups/TÉLUQ-2261708
www.youtube.com/channel/UCXA_KH9CeTMcioNX5nirn_A
Ginette Legault, Directrice générale

Télé-Université (Montréal)
#1105, 5800, rue Saint-Denis, Montréal, QC H2S 3L5
Tél: 514-843-2015

Québec: Université Laval
2325, rue de l'Université, Québec, QC G1V 0A6, Canada
Tél: 418-656-2131; *Ligne sans frais:* 1-877-785-2825
renseignements@ulaval.ca
www.ulaval.ca
www.facebook.com/ulaval.ca
twitter.com/universitelaval
www.linkedin.com/company/universite-laval
www.youtube.com/ulavaltv
Full Time Equivalency: 45400; *Note:* Première université francophone d'Amerique, ouverte sur le monde et animée d'une culture de l'exigence, l'Université Laval contribue au développement de la société par la formation de personnes compétentes, responsables et promotrice de changement, par l'avancement et le partage des connaissances, dans un environnement dynamique de recherche et de création
Denis Brière, Recteur

Campuses
Direction des Communications
Tel: 418-658-7266; *Fax:* 418-656-2809
info@adul.ulaval.ca
www.dc.ulaval.ca
Richard Fournier, Directeur

Centres/Institutes
Centre de recherche de l'Institut universitaire en santé mentale de Québec
2601, ch de la Canardière, Québec, QC G1J 2G3
Tél: 418-663-5741; *Téléc:* 418-663-9540
info@crulrg.ulaval.ca
www.crulrg.ulaval.ca/crulrg
Réjean Cantin, Président

Centre de recherche sur le cancer (CRC)
9, rue McMahon, Québec, QC G1R 3S3
Tél: 418-525-4444; *Téléc:* 418-691-5439
secretariat@crhdq.ulaval.ca
www.crc.ulaval.ca

Centre de recherche du CHU de Québec
2705, boul Laurier, Québec, QC G1V 4G2
Tél: 418-654-2296; *Téléc:* 418-654-2735
sec.drs@crchuq.ulaval.ca
www.crchudequebec.ulaval.ca

Serge Rivest, Directeur

Rimouski: Université du Québec à Rimouski
P.O. Box 3300 A
300, allée des Ursulines, Rimouski, QC G5L 3A1, Canada
Tél: 418-723-1986; *Téléc:* 418-724-1525
Ligne sans frais: 1-800-511-3382
uqar@uqar.qc.ca
www.uqar.ca
www.facebook.com/accueil.uqar
www.twitter.com/UQAR
Full Time Equivalency: 5400
Jean-Pierre Ouellet, Recteur
jean-pierre_ouellet@uqar.ca

Campuses
Campus de Lévis
1595, boul Alphonse-Desjardins, Lévis, QC G6V 0A6, Canada
Tél: 418-833-8800; *Téléc:* 418-833-1113
Ligne sans frais: 1-800-463-4712
campus_levis@uqar.ca

Rouyn-Noranda: Université du Québec en Abitibi-Témiscamingue (UQAT)
445, boul de l'Université, Rouyn-Noranda, QC J9X 5E4, Canada
Tél: 819-762-0971; *Téléc:* 819-797-4727
information@uqat.ca
www.uqat.ca
www.facebook.com/uqat.ca
twitter.com/UQAT
www.linkedin.com/company/uqat
www.youtube.com/uqatinformation
Johanne Jean, Rectrice, 819-762-0971, ext. 2246
Johanne.Jean@uqat.ca
Martine Rioux, Secrétaire générale, 819-762-0971, ext. 2245
Martine.Rioux@uqat.ca

Sherbrooke: Bishop's University
2600 College St., Sherbrooke, QC J1M 1Z7
Tel: 819-822-9600; *Fax:* 819-822-9661
businessoffice@ubishops.ca
www.ubishops.ca
www.facebook.com/bishops
twitter.com/ubishops
www.youtube.com/user/bishopsuniversity
Full Time Equivalency: 2850
Michael Goldbloom, Principal/Vice-Chancellor
principal@ubishops.ca
Victoria Meilkle, Secretary General & Vice-President, Government Relations

Sherbrooke: Université Bishop's
P.O. Box 5000
2600 College St., Sherbrooke, QC J1M 1Z7, Canada
Tél: 819-822-9600; *Téléc:* 819-822-9661
Ligne sans frais: 1-800-567-279
admissions@ubishops.ca
www.ubishops.ca
www.facebook.com/bishops
twitter.com/ubishops
www.linkedin.com/company/bishop%27s-university
www.youtube.com/user/bishopsuniversity
Full Time Equivalency: 2400
Brian Levitt, Chancellor
Yves Jodoin, Registrar & Secretary General
Joan Stadelman, Vice-President of Corporation
Sam Elkas, Chair
Michael Goldbloom, Principal & Vice-Chancellor
principal@ubishops.ca
Dr. Miles Turnbull, Vice-Principal, Academic, 819-822-9600, ext. 2227
miles.turnbull@ubishops.ca
Tony Addona, Director
Cathy Beauchamp, Director
Hans Rouleau, Liaison Coordinator
Damien Roy, Director
Suzanne Meeson, Continuing Education Coordinator
Pam McPhail, Director
Matt McBrine, Alumni Relations Coordinator
Patricia MacAulay, Manager
Jonathan Rittenhouse, Vice-Principal

Faculties
Williams School of Business
bucs@ubishops.ca
www.facebook.com/143674495704774
twitter.com/Williams_School
Dr. Francine Turmel, Dean, 819-822-9600, ext. 2622
francine.turmel@ubishops.ca

Mathematics Department
Dr. Trevoer Jones, Department Chairperson

Sociology Department
Dr. Steven J. Cole, Department Chairperson
scole@ubishops.ca

Sherbrooke: Université de Sherbrooke
2500, boul de l'Université, Sherbrooke, QC J1K 2R1, Canada
Tél: 819-821-7686
information@usherbrooke.ca
www.usherbrooke.ca
www.facebook.com/USherbrooke
twitter.com/usherbrooke
www.youtube.com/USherbrookeTV
Full Time Equivalency: 22140
Professeur Luce Samoisette, Rectrice de l'Université
Professeur Jacques Beauvais, Vice-recteur à la recherche, à l'innovation
Professeur Martin Buteau, Recteur adjoint et Vice-recteur aux ressources humaines
Professeur Jocelyne Faucher, Secrétaire générale et Vice-recteur à la vie étudiante
Professeur Lucie Laflamme, Vice-recteur aux études
Professeur Alain Webster, Vice-recteur au développement durable

Centres/Institutes
Centre d'imagerie moléculaire de Sherbrooke (CIMS)
3001, 12e av Nord, aile 8, 1er étage, Sherbrooke, QC J1H 5N4
Tél: 819-346-1110; *Téléc:* 819-829-3238
www.cims.med.usherbrooke.ca
Martin Lepage, Chaire, recherche du Canada en Imagerie par rés. magnétique
Johannes van Lier, Chaire, recherche Jeanne et Jean-Lous Lévesque en Radiobio.
David Fortin, Chaire, recherche en Neuro-oncologie de la Banque Nat. du CAN

Centre d'analyse et de traitement informatique du français québécois (CARIFQ)
2500, boul de l'Université, Sherbrooke, QC J1K 2R1
www.usherbrooke.ca/catifq
Professeur M. Wim Remysen, Directeur, 819-821-8000, ext. 65520
Wim.Remysen@USherbrooke.ca

Centre de recherche sur l'enseignement et l'apprentissage des sciences (CREAS)
Faculté d'éducation
2500, boul de l'Université, Sherbrooke, QC J1K 2R1
Tél: 819-821-8000; *Téléc:* 819-821-7009
www.creas.ca
Abdelkrim Hasni, Directeur, 819-821-8000, ext. 1049
a.hasni@usherbrooke.ca

Centre d'applications et de recherches en télédétection (CARTEL)
Faculté des lettres et sciences humaines
2500, boul de l'Université, Sherbrooke, QC J1K 2R1
Tél: 819-821-7180; *Téléc:* 819-821-7944
Cartel@USherbrooke.ca
www.usherbrooke.ca/cartel
Professeur Kalifa Goita, Directeur, 819-821-8000, ext. 62212
Kalifa.Goita@USherbrooke.ca

Centre de recherche en amélioration végétale
Également connu sous le nom de: Centre SEVE
Faculté des sciences, Département de biologie
2500, boul de l'Université, Sherbrooke, QC J1K 2R1
Tél: 819-821-8000; *Téléc:* 819-821-8049
www.centreseve.org
Anne-Marie Simao-Beaunoir, Responsable administrative, 819-821-8000, ext. 62001
Anne-Marie.Simao@USherbrooke.ca

Trois-Rivières: Université du Québec à Trois-Rivières
P.O. Box 500
3351, boul des Forges, Trois-Rivières, QC G9A 5H7, Canada
Tél: 819-376-5011; *Téléc:* 819-376-5210
Ligne sans frais: 1-800-365-0922
communications@uqtr.ca
www.uqtr.ca
www.facebook.com/uqtr.ca
twitter.com/InformationUQTR
www.flickr.com/photos/comuqtr
Full Time Equivalency: 11000
Patrick Lahaie, Directeur

Colleges

La Pocatière: Institut de technologie agroalimentaire
Campus de La Pocatière
401, rue Poiré, La Pocatière, QC G0R 1Z0, Canada
Tél: 418-856-1110; *Téléc:* 418-856-1719
scitalp@mapaq.gouv.qc.ca
www.ita.qc.ca
www.facebook.com/Institut.technologie.agroalimentaire.ITA
www.youtube.com/user/itamedias
Full Time Equivalency: 1000; *Note:* Spécialisé en agroalimentaire; Campus de Saint-Hyacinthe: 3230, rue Sicotte, (450) 778-6504; Collège Macdonald, Univ. McGill.
Rosaire Ouellet, Directeur général

Campuses
Campus de Saint-Hyacinthe
P.O. Box 70
3230, rue Sicotte, Saint-Hyacinthe, QC J2S 7B3, Canada
Tel: 450-778-6504; *Fax:* 450-778-6536
ita.st.hyacinthe@mapaq.gouv.qc.ca
www.ita.qc.ca

Montréal: École Polytechnique de Montréal
Également connu sous le nom de: Polytechnique de Montréal
Université de Montréal
2900, boul Édouard-Montpetit, Montréal, QC H3T 1J4, Canada
Tél: 514-340-4711
www.polymtl.ca
www.facebook.com/polymtl
twitter.com/polymtl
www.youtube.com/user/polymtlvideos
Full Time Equivalency: 6940; *Note:* Fondée en 1873, le Polytechnique est une école d'ingénierie de classes internationale; programmes au baccalauréat, cycles supérieures, formation continue; recherche. Adresse postale: CP 6079, succ. Centre-ville, Montréal, QC H3C 3A7.

Montréal: Institut de tourisme et d'hôtellerie du Québec
3535, rue Saint-Denis, Montréal, QC H2X 3P1
Tél: 514-282-5111; *Ligne sans frais:* 800-361-5111
info@ithq.qc.ca
www.ithq.qc.ca
www.facebook.com/ecoleITHQ
twitter.com/ITHQ
www.linkedin.com/company/ithq-montreal---canada
www.youtube.com/user/ITHQofficiel
Lucille Daoust, Directrice générale

Montréal: The Montreal Diocesan Theological College
3475, rue University, Montréal, QC H3A 2A8, Canada
Tel: 514-849-3004; *Fax:* 514-849-4113
info@dio-mdtc.ca
www.dio-mdtc.ca
facebook.com/dio.mdtc

Québec: Direction générale du Conservatoire de musique et d'art dramatique du Québec
225, Grande Allée est, Bloc C, 3e étage, Québec, QC G1R 5G5
Tél: 418-380-2327; *Téléc:* 418-380-2328
info@conservatoire.gouv.qc.ca
www.conservatoire.gouv.qc.ca
twitter.com/ConservatoireQc
www.youtube.com/my_videos?feature=mhee
Nicolas Desjardins, Directeur général

Campuses
Conservatoire de musique de Saguenay
202, rue Jacques-Cartier est, Chicoutimi, QC G7H 6R8, Canada
Tel: 418-698-3505; *Fax:* 418-698-3521
CMS@conservatoire.gouv.qc.ca
Régis Rousseau, Directeur

Conservatoire de musique de Gatineau
430, boul Alexandre-Taché, Gatineau, QC J9A 1M7, Canada
Tel: 819-772-3283; *Fax:* 819-772-3346
CMG@conservatoire.gouv.qc.ca
Marc Landry, Directeur

Conservatoire de musique de Montréal
4750, av Henri-Julien, 1e étage, Montréal, QC H2T 2C8, Canada
Tel: 514-873-4031; *Fax:* 514-873-4601
CMM@conservatoire.gouv.qc.ca
Manon Lafrance, Directrice
manon.lafrance@conservatoire.gouv.qc.ca

Conservatoire de musique de Québec
270, rue St-Amable, Québec, QC G1R 5G1, Canada
Tel: 418-643-2190; *Fax:* 418-644-9658
CMQ@conservatoire.gouv.qc.ca
Louis Dallaire, Directeur
louis.dallaire@conservatoire.gouv.qc.ca

Conservatoire de musique de Rimouski
22, rue Sainte-Marie, Rimouski, QC G5L 4E2, Canada
Tel: 418-727-3706; *Fax:* 418-727-3818
CMR@conservatoire.gouv.qc.ca
Benoît Plourde, Directeur
benoit.plourde@conservatoire.gouv.qc.ca

Conservatoire de musique de Trois-Rivières
587, rue Radisson, Trois-Rivières, QC G9A 2C8, Canada
Tel: 819-371-6748; *Fax:* 819-371-6955
CMT@conservatoire.gouv.qc.ca
Johanne Pothier, Directrice
johanne.pothier@conservatoire.gouv.qc.ca

Conservatoire de musique de Val-d'Or
88, rue Allard, Val-d'Or, QC J9P 2Y1, Canada
Tel: 819-354-4585; *Fax:* 819-354-4297
CMV@conservatoire.gouv.qc.ca
Jean Saint-Jules, Directeur
jean.st-jules@conservatoire.gouv.qc.ca

Conservatoire d'art dramatique de Montréal
4750, av Henri-Julien, 1e étage, Montréal, SK H2T 2C8, Canada
Tel: 514-873-4283; *Fax:* 514-864-2771
CADM@conservatoire.gouv.qc.ca
Benoit Dagenais, Directeur
benoit.dagenais@conservatoire.gouv.qc.ca

Conservatoire d'art dramatique de Québec
31, rue Mont-Carmel, Québec, QC G1R 4A6, Canada
Tel: 418-643-2139; *Fax:* 418-646-9255
CADQ@conservatoire.gouv.qc.ca
André Jean, Directeur
andre.jean@conservatoire.gouv.qc.ca

Cégep

Lévis: Collège de Lévis
9, rue Monseigneur Gosselin, Lévis, QC G6V 5K1, Canada
Tél: 418-833-1249; *Téléc:* 418-833-1974
info@collegedelevis.qc.ca
www.collegedelevis.qc.ca
www.facebook.com/collegedelevis
Grades: Sec.
David Lehoux, Directeur général
dlehoux@collegedelevis.qc.ca
Mélanie Lanouette, Directrice des services éducatifs
mlanouette@collegedelevis.qc.ca
Michelle Soucy, Directeur 1er cycle (1re et 2e secondaire)
msoucy@collegedelevis.qc.ca
Mélanie Champagne, Directrice de 2e cycle (3e, 4e et 5e secondaire)
mchampagne@collegedelevis.qc.ca

Montréal: Collège de Maisonneuve
3800, rue Sherbrooke Est, Montréal, QC H1X 2A2
Tél: 514-254-7131
communic@cmaisonneuve.qc.ca
www.cmaisonneuve.qc.ca
fr.facebook.ca/CollegeMaisonneuve
www.youtube.com/communicmaisonneuve
Grades: Préuniv., Techniques
Thomas Gulian, Directeur

Montréal: Collège Jean-de-Brébeuf inc.
3200, ch Côte Ste-Catherine, Montréal, QC H3T 1C1, Canada
Tél: 514-342-9342; *Téléc:* 514-342-6607
diradm@brebeuf.qc.ca
www.brebeuf.qc.ca
www.facebook.com/372651986136536
twitter.com/CollegeBrebeuf
www.linkedin.com/groups/Coll%C3%A8ge-JeandeBr%C3%A9beuf-1855359
www.youtube.com/user/collbrebeuf
Grades: Sec., Collégial
Michel April, Directeur générale

Saint-Laurent: Vanier College
821, av Ste-Croix, Saint-Laurent, QC H4L 3X9, Canada
Tel: 514-744-7500; *Fax:* 514-744-7505
info@vaniercollege.qc.ca
www.vaniercollege.qc.ca
www.facebook.com/pages/Vanier-College/164180234895
www.twitter.com/vaniercollege
www.linkedin.com/groups?mostPopular=&gid=3295473
www.youtube.com/user/vaniercollege
Full Time Equivalency: 6700; *Note:* An English Cégep.
Normand W. Bernier, Director General
dg@vaniercollege.qc.ca
Danielle Lafille, Academic Dean
academicdean@vaniercollege.qc.ca

Faculties
Faculty of Careers & Technical Programs
Michael Sendbuehler, Dean
sendbuem@vaniercollege.qc.ca

Faculty of Science & General Studies
Eric Lozowy, Dean
lozowye@vaniercollege.qc.ca

Faculty of Social Sciences, Commerce, Arts & Letters
Odette Côté, Dean
coteo@vaniercollege.qc.ca

Post Secondary/Technical

Brossard: Academy of Arts & Design
Académie des arts et de design
7305, Marie-Victorin, 2e étage, Brossard, QC J4W 1A6, Canada
Tel: 514-875-9777; *Toll-Free:* 800-268-9777
www.aadmtl.com
Note: Fashion Design, Fashion Merchandising, Interior Design, Advertising & Web Design, Animation Design. Instruction in French & English.
Serge Landry, Directeur général

Drummondville: Collège Ellis
Campus de Drummondville
235, rue Moisan, Drummondville, QC J2C 1W9, Canada
Tél: 819-477-3113; *Téléc:* 819-477-4556
www.ellis.qc.ca
www.facebook.com/160029390703893
twitter.com/CollegeEllis_
www.youtube.com/user/collegeellis
Alain Scalzo, Directeur général

Campuses
Campus de Longueuil
#2060, 150, place Charles-Le Moyne, Longueuil, QC J2C 1W9, Canada
Tél: 450-463-1500; *Téléc:* 450-670-3971
www.ellis.qc.ca

Campus de Trois-Rivières
90, rue Dorval, Trois-Rivières, QC G8T 5X7, Canada
Tél: 819-691-2600; *Téléc:* 819-691-3407
Ligne sans frais: 877-691-9800
www.ellis.qc.ca

Montréal: Collège André-Gasset
1001 Crémazie est, Montréal, QC H2M 1M3, Canada
Tél: 514-381-4293; *Téléc:* 514-381-7421
inform@grasset.qc.ca
www.grasset.qc.ca
www.facebook.com/CollegeAndreGrasset
Number of Employees: 75 professeurs; 40 l'enseignement technique; 60 personnel professionnel et administratif
Régent-Yves Desjardins, Président

Montréal: Collège d'enseignement en immobilier
#104 - 405, av Ogilvy, Montréal, QC H3M 1M3, Canada
Tél: 514-905-1551; *Téléc:* 514-904-1453
Ligne sans frais: 866-905-1551
info@collegecei.com
www.enseignementimmobilier.com
www.facebook.com/CollegeCEI
Shirley Soulard, Directeur général

Montréal: Collège D'Informatique Marsan
#400, boul de Pie-IX, Montréal, QC H1V 2C8, Canada
Tél: 514-525-3030; *Téléc:* 514-525-3314
info@collegemarsan.qc.ca
www.collegemarsan.qc.ca
www.facebook.com/pages/College-MARSAN/110908012260197
Carlos Richer, Directeur général

Montréal: Collège de photographie Marsan
#400 - 2030, boul Pie-IX, 4e étage, Montréal, QC H1V 2C8, Canada
Tél: 514-525-3030; *Téléc:* 514-525-3314
Ligne sans frais: 800-338-8643
info@collegemarsan.qc.ca
www.collegemarsan.qc.ca
Carlos Richer, Président & Directeur général, 514-525-3030, ext. 222

Montréal: College Inter Dec
#8000, 2000, rue Sainte-Catherine ouest, Montréal, QC H3H 2T2
Tel: 514-939-4444; *Toll-Free:* 1-877-341-4445
interdec@collegeinterdec.com
www.collegeinterdec.com
Note: Founded in 1983, Inter-Dec College is associated with LaSalle International. Fields of study include beauty, interior design, & digital arts.

Montréal: Collège Jean-de-Brébeuf
3200, ch de la côte Ste-Catherine, Montréal, QC H3T 1C1
Tél: 514-342-9342
www.brebeuf.qc.ca
Michel April, Directeur général
dirgen@brebeuf.qc.ca
France Lavoie, Directrice des ressources financières
Jacques Lemaire, Directeur des études au collégial

Montréal: Collège LaSalle
Lasalle College
2000, rue Sainte-Catherine ouest, Montréal, QC H3H 2T2, Canada
Tél: 514-939-2006; *Téléc:* 514-939-2015
Ligne sans frais: 800-363-3541
admission@clasalle.com
www.lasallecollege.com
www.facebook.com/collegelasalle
twitter.com/LaSalleCollege
www.youtube.com/lasallecollege
Jacques Marchand, Directeur général

Montréal: Collège Salette
418, rue Sherbrooke est, 3e étage, Montréal, QC H2L 1J6
Tél: 514-388-5725; *Téléc:* 514-388-5957
info@collegesalette.qc.ca
www.collegesalette.qc.ca
Note: Established in 1942, Collège Salette is a design school that offers programs in graphic design, web design & interactive media, & illustration advertising.

Montréal: École de Danse Contemporaine de Montréal
#211, 372, rue Ste-Catherine ouest, Montréal, QC H3B 1A2, Canada
Tél: 514-866-9814; *Téléc:* 514-866-5887
info@edcmtl.com
www.ladmmi.com
www.facebook.com/EcoleDeDanseContemporaineDeMontreal
twitter.com/edcmtl
Yves Rocray, Directeur général

Montréal: L'École du Show-Business (ESB)
7093. av du Parc, Montréal, QC H3N 1X7
Tél: 514-271-2244; *Ligne sans frais:* 1-877-271-2244
info@ecoledushowbusiness.com
www.ecoledushowbusiness.com
twitter.com/EcoleShowBizz
www.youtube.com/user/EcoleShowBizz#p/u
Note: Since 1999, the school has taught theatre trades. Programs include writing techniques, the production of advertising, scenography & set design, production of stage costumes, organizing an event, production techniques for cultural & corporate events, management of film & stage sets, web design techniques, & marketing & export of a product or service.

Montréal: École nationale de cirque
National Circus School
8181, 2e av, Montréal, QC H1Z 4N9, Canada
Tél: 514-982-0859; *Téléc:* 514-982-6025
Ligne sans frais: 800-267-0859
info@enc.qc.ca
www.enc.qc.ca
Marc Lalonde, Directeur général

Montréal: École nationale de l'humour
2120, rue Sherbrooke est, 7e étage, Montréal, QC H2K 1C3, Canada
Tél: 514-849-7876; *Téléc:* 514-849-3307
humour@enh.qc.ca
www.enh.qc.ca
Note: Formation professionnelle aux humoristes & aux auteurs. Reconnue par le Min. de l'Éducation, du Loisir & du Sport du Québec.
Louise Richer, Directrice générale

Montréal: L'École supérieure de ballet du Québec
4816, rue Rivard, Montréal, QC H2J 2N6
Tél: 514-849-4929; *Téléc:* 514-849-6107
info@esbq.ca
www.esbq.ca
www.facebook.com/ecolesuperieuredeballetduquebec
twitter.com/ecole_sup
Alix Laurent, Directeur général, 514-849-4929, ext. 224
Anik Bissonnette, Directrice artistique, 514-849-4929, ext. 221
Beverley Aitchison, Directrice associée aux programmes de formation, 514-849-4929, ext. 223
Claudine Balaux, Registraire et responsable, vie étudiante, 514-849-4929, ext. 225
Lili Marin, Responsable, communications et marketinge, 514-849-4929, ext. 249

Montréal: Institut supérieur d'informatique (ISI)
#100, 255, boul Crémazie est, Montréal, QC H2M 1M2
Tél: 514-842-2426; *Téléc:* 514-842-2084
info@isi-mtl.com
www.isi-mtl.com
www.facebook.com/isimtl
twitter.com/isimtl
www.youtube.com/user/isimtl
Note: Training is offered in networks & telecommunications, programming & internet technologies, integration of information systems, integration of websites, & IP telphony.

Montréal: Institut Teccart
3030, rue Hochelaga, Montréal, QC H1W 1G2
Tel: 514-526-2501; *Fax:* 514-526-9192
Toll-Free: 1-866-832-2278
www.teccart.qc.ca
Note: Programs are offered inthe areas of arts, design, & technology.

Montréal: The International College of Spiritual & Psychic Sciences
P.O. Box 1387 H
1974, boul de Maisonneuve ouest, Montréal, QC H3G 2N3, Canada
Tél: 514-937-8359; *Téléc:* 514-937-5380
info@iiihs.org
www.iiihs.org
Dr. Marilyn Zwaig Rossner, Ph.D., Dean
mrossner@iiihs.org

Montréal: International Florist Academy and School
École et Académie Internationale de Fleuristes
#111, 5491, av Victoria, Montréal, QC H3W 2P9
Tel: 514-739-7152; *Fax:* 514-419-5313
info@interfloristschool.com
www.interfloristschool.com

Montréal: National Theatre School of Canada (NTS)
École nationale de théâtre du Canada
5030, rue St-Denis, Montréal, QC H2J 2L8, Canada
Tel: 514-842-7954; *Fax:* 514-842-5661
Toll-Free: 866-547-7328
info@ent-nts.ca
www.ent-nts.qc.ca
www.facebook.com/entnts.montreal
www.youtube.com/user/ENTNTSMontreal
Enrollment: 160; *Number of Employees:* 25; *Note:* Offers training in acting, playwriting, directing, set & costume design & technical production in both English & French.
Gideon Arthurs, CEO
Michel Rafie, Director, Communications & Marketing
irenam@ent-nts.ca

Montréal: Trebas Institute
Institut Trebas
#600 - 550, rue Sherbrooke ouest, Montréal, QC H3A 1B9, Canada
Tel: 514-845-4141; *Fax:* 514-845-2581
Toll-Free: 866-587-3227
infomtl@trebas.com
www.trebas.com
Enrollment: 300
David P. Leonard, Président
Sat Balraj, Directeur les études

Campuses
Toronto
2340 Dundas St. West, 2nd Fl., Toronto, ON M6P 4A9, Canada
Tel: 416-966-3066; *Fax:* 416-966-0030
info@trebas.com
www.trebas.com
Enrollment: 300; *Note:* Audio Engineering & Production/DJ Arts, Entertainment Management, Film/Television Production
Peter Di Santo, Director

Outremont: École de Musique Vincent d'Indy
628, ch Côte-Sainte-Catherine, Outremont, QC H2V 2C5, Canada
Tél: 514-735-5261; *Téléc:* 514-735-5266
info@isdm-mode.com
www.emvi.qc.ca
Yves Petit, Directeur général

Québec: Collège Mérici
755, Grande Allée ouest, Québec, QC G1S 1C1, Canada
Tél: 418-683-1591; *Téléc:* 418-682-8938
Ligne sans frais: 800-208-1463
information@college-merici.qc.ca
merici.ca
www.facebook.com/collegemerici
twitter.com/CollegeMerici
Enrollment: 1200; *Note:* Le Collège Mérici est un établissement d'enseignement collégial privé accueillant environ 1200 étudiants.
Nicole Blodeau, Directeur général

Québec: Collège Radio Télévision de Québec Inc.
751, côte d'Abraham, Québec, QC G1R 1A2, Canada
Tél: 418-647-2095; *Téléc:* 418-522-5456
info@crtq.net
www.crtq.net
www.facebook.com/CRTQ-115152496860/
Christian Lavoie, Directeur

Québec: L'École de danse de Québec
Centre de production artistique et culturelle Aly
#214, 310, boul Langelier, Québec, QC G1K 5N3
Tél: 418-649-4715; *Téléc:* 418-649-4702
reception@ledq.qc.ca
www.ledq.qc.ca
Steve Huot, Directeur général, 418-649-4715
shuot@ledq.qc.ca
Lyne Binette, Directrice de la formation professionnelle, 418-649-4715, ext. 225
lbinette@ledq.qc.ca
Joëlle Turcotte, Directrice de l'école loisir, 418-649-4715, ext. 230
jturcotte@ledq.qc.ca
Natalie Lavallée, Responsable des communications, 418-649-4715, ext. 222
nlavallee@ledq.qc.ca
Jean-Pierre Parent, Responsable des services financiers, 418-649-4715, ext. 224
jpparent@ledq.qc.ca

Saint-Hubert: Académie de l'Entrepreneurship
4660, Montée St-Hubert, Saint-Hubert, QC J3Y 1V1, Canada
Tél: 450-676-5826; *Téléc:* 450-676-2261
Ligne sans frais: 888-676-5826
info@academie-ent.com
www.academie-ent.com
Johanne Bouchard, Directrice générale

Trois-Rivières: Collège Laflèche
1687, boul du Carmel, Trois-Rivières, QC G8Z 3R8, Canada
Tél: 819-375-7346; *Téléc:* 819-375-7347
college@clafleche.qc.ca
www.clafleche.qc.ca
Note: Le seul établissement collégial privé en Mauricie et au Centre-du-Québec à offrir à la fois des programmes préuniversitaires et techniques.
Julie Anne Trottier, Directeur général

Verdun: Collège de l'immobilier du Québec
600, ch du Golf, Verdun, QC H3E 1A8, Canada
Tél: 514-762-1862; *Téléc:* 514-762-4975
francine.forget@cigm.qc.ca
www.collegeimmobilier.com
Francine Forget, Directrice générale

Ville Mont-Royal: Collège Techniques de Montréal
#150 - 8255 Mountain Sights, Ville Mont-Royal, QC H4P 2B5, Canada
Tél: 514-932-6444; *Téléc:* 514-932-6448
info@mtccollege.com
www.mtccollege.com

Westmount: International Career School Canada
ICS Canada
#610, 245 Victoria Ave., Westmount, QC H3Z 2M6, Canada
Tel: 514-482-6951; *Fax:* 514-482-6868
Toll-Free: 1-888-427-2400
info@icslearn.ca
www.icslearn.ca
Enrollment: 12875; *Note:* At-home training in 50 career fields.
Connie C. Dempsey, Chief Academic Officer

Westmount: **Marianopolis College**
4873, ave Westmount, Westmount, QC H3Y 1K9, Canada
Tel: 514-931-8792; *Fax:* 514-931-8790
admissions@marianopolis.edu
www.marianopolis.edu
Len Even, Director General
DGsOffice@marianopolis.edu

Saskatchewan

Government Agencies

Regina: **Saskatchewan Ministry of Advanced Education**
Legislative Building
#307, 2405 Legislative Drive, Regina, SK S4S 0B3, Canada
Tel: 306-787-0341; *Fax:* 306-798-0263
minister.ae@gov.sk.ca
ae.gov.sk.ca
Hon. Scott Moe, Minister of Advanced Education, 306-787-0341

Regina: **Saskatchewan Ministry of Education**
Communciations Branch
2220 College Ave., 5th Fl., Regina, SK S4P 4V9, Canada
Tel: 306-787-2471; *Fax:* 306-787-1300
linquir@gov.sk.ca
www.education.gov.sk.ca
Other Information: Deputy Minister Julie MacRae:
julie.macrae@gov.sk.ca
Hon. Don Morgan, Q.C., Minister of Education, 306-787-0613
minister.edu@gov.sk.ca

School Boards/Districts/Divisions

Public

Creighton: **Creighton School Division #111**
P.O. Box 158
325 Main St., Creighton, SK S0P 0A0, Canada
Tel: 306-688-5138; *Fax:* 306-688-5740
creightonschooldivision.com
Enrollment: 394
Bob Smith, Director

Ile-a-la-Crosse: **Ile a la Crosse School Division #112**
P.O. Box 89
Ile-a-la-Crosse, SK S0M 1C0, Canada
Tel: 306-833-2141; *Fax:* 306-833-2104
icsd112.ca
Number of Schools: 1 elementary school; 1 high school; *Grades:* Pre - 12; adult education
Ernie Cychmistruk, Director, Education
ernie.c@icsd.ca
Dennis Moniuk, Secretary Treasurer
dmoniuk@icsd.ca

La Ronge: **Northern Lights School Division #113**
La Ronge Central Office
Bag Service #6500, La Ronge, SK S0J 1L0, Canada
Tel: 306-425-3302; *Fax:* 306-425-3377
centraloffice@nlsd113.net
www.nlsd113.com
Other Information: Beauval Sub-Office: 306-288-2310;
suboffice@nlsd113.net
Number of Schools: 22; *Grades:* K-12
Johnh Ulsifer, Director, Education
johnulsifer@nlsd113.net
Tom Harrington, Secretary-Treasurer
tomharrington@nlsd113.net
Cheryl Herman, First Nations/Metis Education Consultant
cherylherman@nlsd113.net
Mark Williment, Superintendent of Education
markwilliment@nlsd113.net
Jason Young, Superintendent of Education
jasonyoung@nlsd113.net
Dawn Ewart, Superintendent of Human Resources
dawnewart@nlsd113.net
Brian McKeand, Superintendent of Facilities
brianmceand@nlsd113.net

Langian: **Horizon School Division #205**
P.O. Box 100
110 Main st., Langian, SK S0K 2M0, Canada
Tel: 306-365-4888; *Fax:* 306-365-2808
Toll-Free: 877-365-4888
horizon@hzsd.ca
www.hzsd.ca
Number of Schools: 41; *Grades:* K - 12; *Enrollment:* 6992
Marc Danylchuk, Director, Education, 306-365-4888
marc.danylchuk@hzsd.ca
Lionel Diederichs, Chief Financial Officer
lionel.diederichs@hzsd.ca
Mark Fedak, Superintendent of Operations
mark.fedak@hzsd.ca
Anne Sloboda, Superintendent of Student Learning
anne.sloboda@hzsd.ca
Sylvia Lee, Superintendent of Human Resources
sylvia.lee@hzsd.ca
Darrell Paproski, Superintendent of Schools
darrell.paproski@hzsd.ca
Todd Gjevre, Superintendent of Schools
todd.gjevre@hzsd.ca
Crandall Hrynkiw, Superintendent of Schools
crandall.hrynkiw@hzsd.ca

Melfort: **North East School Division #200**
P.O. Box 6000
402 Main St., Melfort, SK S0E 1A0, Canada
Tel: 306-752-5741; *Fax:* 306-752-1933
Toll-Free: 888-752-5741
www.nesd.ca
Number of Schools: 22; *Grades:* Pre-K.-12; *Enrollment:* 5317
Don Rempel, Director of Education
Rosie Ottenbreit, Superintendent of Business Administration, 306-752-1214
Dean Biesenthal, Superintendent of Human Resources, 306-752-1205
careers@nesd.ca

Moose Jaw: **Holy Trinity Roman Catholic Separate School Division #22**
P.O. Box 1087
502 - 6 Ave. NE, Moose Jaw, SK S6H 4P8, Canada
Tel: 306-694-5333; *Fax:* 306-692-2238
contact@htcsd.ca
www.htcsd.ca
twitter.com/HolyTrinitySD
Number of Schools: 10; *Grades:* JK - 12
Celeste York, Director, Education, 306-694-5300
celeste.york@htcsd.ca
Gerry Gieni, Chief Financial Officer, 306-694-5333, ext. 2024
gerry.gieni@htcsd.ca
Geri Hall, Superintendent, Curriculum, Instruction & Assessment, 306-694-5333, ext. 2038
geri.hall@htcsd.ca
Dave DePape, Superintendent of Human Resources, 306-694-5333, ext. 2045
dave.depape@htcsd.ca
Elaine Oak, Superintendent of Education, 306-694-5333, ext. 2027
elaine.oak@htcsd.ca
Bernadette Day, Religious Education Consultant, 306-694-5333, ext. 2034
bernadette.cey@htcsd.ca

Moose Jaw: **Prairie South School Division #210**
15 Thatcher Dr. East, Moose Jaw, SK S6J 1L8, Canada
Tel: 306-694-1200; *Fax:* 306-694-4955
Toll-Free: 877-434-1200
www.prairiesouth.ca
www.facebook.com/206184285098
twitter.com/PrairieSouth
Number of Schools: 40; *Enrollment:* 6700; *Number of Employees:* 1,400
Jeff Finell, Director, Education, 306-694-1200
Bernie Girardin, Superintendent of Business & Operations, 306-694-1200
Ryan Boughen, Superintendent of Human Resources, 306-694-7524
Lori Meyer, Superintendent of Learning, 306-693-4631
Carol Coghill, Purchasing Officer, 306-694-7544

North Battleford: **Light of Christ Catholic School Division #16**
9301 - 19 Ave., North Battleford, SK S9A 3N5, Canada
Tel: 306-445-6158; *Fax:* 306-445-3993
loccsd@loccsd.ca
www.loccsd.ca
www.facebook.com/176370549066107
twitter.com/lightofchristsd
Number of Schools: 7; *Grades:* Pre-K.-12; *Enrollment:* 2100;
Note: This school division is an amalgamation of 4 boards: North Battleford RCSSD#16, Wilkie St. George RCSSD#85, Unity RCSSD#88 and Spiritwood RCSSD#82.
Herb Sutton, Director, Education, 306-445-6158
h.sutton@loccsd.ca
Karen Hrabinsky, Superintendent, Learning, 306-445-6158
k.hrabinsky@loccsd.ca
Jordan Kist, Chief Financial Officer, 306-445-6158
j.kist@loccsd.ca
Caralynn Gidych, Supervisor of Student Services, 306-445-6158
c.gidych@loccsd.ca

North Battleford: **Living Sky School Division #202**
509 Pioneer Ave., North Battleford, SK S9A 4A5, Canada
Tel: 306-937-7702; *Fax:* 306-445-4332
office@lskysd.ca
www.lskysd.ca
www.facebook.com/lskysd
twitter.com/SD202
www.pinterest.com/lskysd
Number of Schools: 31; *Grades:* K-12; *Enrollment:* 5700;
Number of Employees: 900+
Randy Fox, Director of Education, 306-937-7930
randy.fox@lskysd.ca
Lonny Darroch, Chief Financial Officer, 306-937-7924
lonny.darroch@lskysd.ca
Cathy Herrick, Superintendent of Curriculum and Instruction, 306-937-7939
cathy.herrick@lskysd.ca
Brian Quinn, Superintendent of Schools, Curriculum and Instruction, 306-937-7925
brian.quinn@lskysd.ca
Jim Shevchuk, Superintendent of Curriculum and Instruction, 306-937-7961
jim.shevchuk@lskysd.ca
Brenda Vickers, Superintendent of Human Resources, 306-937-7920
brenda.vickers@lskysd.ca
Nancy Schultz, Superintendent of Student Services, 306-937-7923
nancy.schultz@lskysd.ca

Prince Albert: **Prince Albert Roman Catholic Separate School Division #6**
Catholic Education Centre
118 - 11 St. East, Prince Albert, SK S6V 1A1, Canada
Tel: 306-953-7500; *Fax:* 306-763-1723
info@pacsd.ca
pacsd.ca
twitter.com/PACatholicSD
Number of Schools: 9; *Grades:* Pre - 12
Lorel Trumier, Director, Education
Louise Phaneuf, Superintendent of Human Resources
Helene Prefontaine, Superintendent of Education
Tricia McEwen, Superintendent of Education
Cal Martin, Chief Financial Officer

Prince Albert: **Saskatchewan Rivers School Division #119**
545 - 11 St. East, Prince Albert, SK S6V 1B1, Canada
Tel: 306-764-1571; *Fax:* 306-763-4460
www.srsd119.ca
Number of Schools: 32; *Grades:* Pre - 12; *Enrollment:* 9000
Robert Bratvold, Director, Education

Regina: **Prairie Valley School Division #208**
P.O. Box 1937
3080 Albert St. North, Regina, SK S4P 3E1, Canada
Tel: 306-949-3366; *Fax:* 306-543-1771
reception@pvsd.ca
www.pvsd.ca
Number of Schools: 38; *Grades:* K - 12; *Enrollment:* 8050;
Number of Employees: 1,100
Ben J. Grebinski, Director
Naomi Mellor, Chief Financial Officer/Deputy Director
Gloria Antifaiff, Superintendent of Education
Rhae Ann Holoien, Superintendent of Education
Kim Kinnear, Superintendent of Student Services
Terry Kuz, Superintendent of Education
Greg McJannet, Superintendent of Education
Lyle Stecyk, Superintendent of Project Management

Regina: **Regina Roman Catholic Separate School Division #81**
2160 Cameron St., Regina, SK S4T 2V6, Canada
Tel: 306-791-7200; *Fax:* 306-347-7699
rcs@rcsd.ca
www.rcsd.ca
Number of Schools: 24 elementary schools; 4 secondary schools; 3 alternative school; *Grades:* K-12; *Enrollment:* 10500;
Number of Employees: 1,100
Rob Currie, Director, Education, 306-791-7200, ext. 207
r.currie@rcsd.ca
Sandra Baragar, Superintendent, Human Resource Services, 306-791-7200, ext. 209
s.baragar@rcsd.ca
Michele Braun, Superintendent, Education Services, 306-791-7200, ext. 284
m.braun@rcsd.ca
Janet Chabot, Superintendent, Education Services, 306-791-7200, ext. 338
j.chabot@rcsd.ca
Sean Chase, Superintendent, Education Services, 306-791-7200
s.chase@rcsd.ca

Cheryl Exner, Superintendent, Education Services, 306-791-7200, ext. 308
c.exner@rcsd.ca
Brian Lach, Superintendent, Education Services, 306-791-7200, ext. 222
b.lach@rcsd.ca

Regina: Regina School Division #4
1600 - 4 Ave., Regina, SK S4R 8C8, Canada
Tel: 306-523-3000; *Fax:* 306-532-3031
info@rbe.sk.ca
www.rbe.sk.ca
Number of Schools: 41 elemtary schools; 9 secondary schools; 3 faith-based associate schools; *Grades:* JK - 12; *Enrollment:* 20000
Julie MacRae, Director, Education, 306-523-3017
julie.macrae@rbe.sk.ca
Debra Burnett, Secretary-Treasurer, 306-523-3018
debra.burnett@rbe.sk.ca
Paula Hesselink, Superintendent, Human Resources and Workplace Diversity, 306-523-3059
paula.hesselink@rbe.sk.ca

Rosetown: Sun West School Division #207
P.O. Box 700
Rosetown, SK S0L 2V0, Canada
Tel: 306-882-2677; *Fax:* 306-882-3366
Toll-Free: 1-866-375-2677
info@sunwestsd.ca
www.sunwestsd.ca
www.facebook.com/406487076079009?hc_location=timeline
twitter.com/SunWestSD207
Number of Schools: 14 K - 12 schools; 15 Hutterite colony schools; 7 elem.; 3 sec.; 1 distance ed; *Grades:* K - 12; *Enrollment:* 4400; *Number of Employees:* 800
Guy G. Tétrault, Director, Education
guy.tetrault@sunwestsd.ca
Tony Baldwin, Superintendent, Education
Shari Martin, Superintendent, Education
Tracy Dollansky, Superintendent, Education
Shelley Hengen, Superintendent, Education
Ryan Smith, Superintendent, Business
Roxan Foursha, Officer, Communications
Janine Walker, Officer, Human Resources
Doug Klassen, Supervisor, Technology
Earl McKnight, Supervisor, Transportation
Rob Minion, Supervisor, Facilities
Rhonda Saathoff, Supervisor, Business

Saskatoon: Greater Saskatoon Catholic Schools
420 - 22nd St. East, Saskatoon, SK S7K 1X3, Canada
Tel: 306-659-7000; *Fax:* 306-659-2011
info@gscs.sk.ca
www.scs.sk.ca
Number of Schools: 37 elementary schools; 6 secondary schools; 2 associate schools; *Grades:* Pre-K - 12; French, Cree, & Ukraini; *Enrollment:* 15000; *Number of Employees:* 1900+
Diane Boyko, Board Chair, 306-382-2832
DLBoyko@gscs.sk.ca
Greg Chatlain, Director, Education, 306-659-7001
Darryl Bazylak, Superintendent, Education, 306-659-7040
Al Boutin, Superintendent, Human Resource Services, 306-659-7048
Diane Cote, Superintendent, Education, 306-659-7090
Joel Lloyd, Superintendent, Administrative Services, 306-659-7021
Gordon Martell, Superintendent, Education, 306-659-7056
John McAuliffe, Superintendent, Education, 306-659-7044
Joanne Weninger, Superintendent, Education, 306-659-7041
Laurier Langlois, Manager, Corporate Services, 306-659-7023
llanglois@gscs.sk.ca

Saskatoon: Saskatoon Public Schools
310 - 21st St. East, Saskatoon, SK S7K 1M7, Canada
Tel: 306-683-8200; *Fax:* 306-657-3900
spsdinfo@spsd.sk.ca
www.spsd.sk.ca
www.facebook.com/SaskatoonPublicSchools
twitter.com/StoonPubSchools
Number of Schools: 43 elementary schools; 10 secondary schools; 2 assosciate schools; *Grades:* JK - 12; adult education; *Enrollment:* 21300; *Number of Employees:* 2,300
Avon Whittles, Director, Education
Garry Benning, Chief Financial Officer
Stan Laba, Superintendent of Facilities
Jaime Valentine, Superintendent of Human Resources
Bruce Bradshaw, Superintendent of Education
Dave Derksen, Superintendent of Education
Lisa Fleming, Superintendent of Education
Brenda Green, Superintendent of Education
Withman Jaigobin, Superintendent of Education
Dean Newton, Superintendent of Education
Shane Skjerven, Superintendent of Education

Donnalee Weinmaster, Superintendent of Education

Swift Current: Chinook School Division No. 211
P.O. Box 1809
2100 Gladstone St. East, Swift Current, SK S9H 4J8, Canada
Tel: 306-778-9200; *Fax:* 306-773-8011
Toll-Free: 1-877-321-9200
info@chinooksd.ca
www.chinooksd.ca
www.facebook.com/chinookschooldiv
twitter.com/ChinookSD
Number of Schools: 60; *Enrollment:* 6200; *Number of Employees:* 1125 teachers and administrative staff
Randy Beler, Chair
Liam Choo-Foo, Director of Education, 306-778-9200, ext. 209
Rod Quintin, CFO, 306-778-9200, ext. 201
Lee Cummins, Superintendent of Special Education & Student Services, 306-778-9200, ext. 206
Jan Pogorzelec, Superintendent of Schools, 306-778-9200, ext. 207
Dan Kerslake, Superintendent of Schools, 306-778-9200, ext. 226
Mark Benesh, Superintendent of Schools, 306-778-9200, ext. 205
J.P. Claire, Superintendent of Schools, 306-778-9200, ext. 204
Bob Vavra, Superintendent of Curriculum Instruction & Assessment, 306-778-9200, ext. 229

Turtleford: Northwest School Division #203
P.O. Box 280
Turtleford, SK S0M 2Y0, Canada
Tel: 306-845-2150; *Fax:* 306-845-3392
www.nwsd.ca
www.facebook.com/pages/Northwest-School-Division/689553387724712
twitter.com/northwestsd203
Number of Schools: 24; *Grades:* K - 12; *Enrollment:* 4910
Duane Hauk, Director, Education
duane.hauk@nwsd.ca
Charlie McCloud, Chief Financial Officer
charlie.mccloud@nwsd.ca
Cory Rideout, Superintendent of Human Resources
cory.rideout@nwsd.ca
Jennifer Williamson, Superintendent of Student Services
jennifer.williamson@nwsd.ca
Aaron Oakes, Superintendent of Curriculum & Instruction
aaron.oakes@nwsd.ca
Darrell Newton, Superintendent of Curriculum & Instruction
darrell.newton@nwsd.ca
Terry Craig, Superintendent of Schools
terry.craig@nwsd.ca

Warman: Prairie Spirit School Division #206
P.O. Box 809
121 Klassen St. East, Warman, SK S0K 4S0, Canada
Tel: 306-683-2800; *Fax:* 306-934-8221
www.spiritsd.ca
Number of Schools: 44; *Grades:* K - 12; *Enrollment:* 9400
Evelyn Novak, Director, Education
Jim Shields, Superintendent

Weyburn: Holy Family Rmonan Catholic Separate School District #140
110 Souris Ave., 3rd Fl., Weyburn, SK S4H 2Z8, Canada
Tel: 306-842-7025; *Fax:* 306-842-7033
www.holyfamilyrcssd.ca
Number of Schools: 5; *Grades:* K - 12; *Enrollment:* 981
Gwen Keith, Director, Education, 306-842-7025
gwen.keith@holyfamilyrcssd.ca
Bruno Tuchscherer, Chair
Christine Arnett, Superintendent of Finance, 306-842-7025
christine.arnett@holyfamilyrcssd.ca
Michael Zummack, Assistant Superintendent of Capital Operations, 306-539-4660
michael.zummack@holyfamilyrcssd.ca
Terry Jordens, Assessment & Instruction Coordinator, 306-842-7565
terry.jordens@holyfamilyrcssd.ca
Lynn Colquhoun, Religion & Curriculum Coordinator, 306-842-7565
lynn.colquhoun@holyfamilyrcssd.ca

Weyburn: South East Cornerstone School Division #209 (SECPSD)
80A - 18 St. NE, Weyburn, SK S4H 2W4, Canada
Tel: 306-848-0080; *Fax:* 306-848-4747
Toll-Free: 888-938-0080
contactus@cornerstonesd.ca
www.cornerstonesd.ca
Number of Schools: 39; *Grades:* K - 12; *Enrollment:* 8200
Marc Casavant, Director, Education, 306-848-4771
Shelley Toth, Superintendent of Business Services/CFO, 306-848-4727
Kelly Hilkewich, Superintendent of Schools- West, 306-848-4765
Velda Weatherald, Superintendent of Schools- East, 306-848-4766
Keith Keating, Superintendent of Schools- South, 306-848-4783
Gord Husband, Superintendent of Human Resources, 306-848-4786
Lynn Little, Superintendent of Education, 306-848-4732

Yorkton: Christ the Teacher Roman Catholic Separate School Division No. 212
45A Palliser Way, Yorkton, SK S3N 4C5, Canada
Tel: 306-783-8787; *Fax:* 306-783-4992
www.christtheteacher.ca
Number of Schools: 9; *Grades:* Pre-K.-12; *Enrollment:* 1800; *Note:* This division is an amalgamation of St. Henry's RCSSD #5, Yorkton RCSSD #86, St. Theodore RCSSD #138, Melville Rural RCSSD #217 and Yorkton Rural RCSSD #216.
Angie Rogalski, Chair
Darrell Zaba, Director of Education
Delmar Zwirsky, Secretary Treasurer
Barb Mackesey, Superintendent of Education
Chad Holinaty, Superintendent of Education

Yorkton: Good Spirit School Division #204 (GSSD)
Fairview Education Centre
63 King St. East, Yorkton, SK S3N 0T7, Canada
Tel: 306-786-5500; *Fax:* 306-783-0355
Toll-Free: 1-866-390-0773
info@gssd.ca
www.gssd.ca
Other Information: GSSD Distance Learning Center, Toll-Free Phone: 1-877-988-1122
facebook.com/gssd204
twitter.com/gssd204
Number of Schools: 28; *Grades:* JK - 12; *Enrollment:* 6231; *Number of Employees:* 1000
Raymond Sass, Chair
Dwayne Reeve, Director, Education
Juanita Brown, Superintendent of Education
Susan Maserek, Superintendent of Education
Darran Teneycke, Superintendent of Education
Alan Sharp, Superintendent of Education
Sherry Todosichuk, Superintendent, Business Administration

Faith-Based

Englefeld: Englefeld Protestant Separate School Division #132
Englefeld School
P.O. Box 100
Englefeld, SK S0K 1N0, Canada
Tel: 306-287-3568; *Fax:* 306-287-3569
admin.epssd@englefeld.ca
www.englefeld.ca/School/HomeSchool.html
Marie Stockbrugger, Secretary

French

Regina: Conseil des écoles fransaskoises
#201, 1440, 9e av Nord, Regina, SK S4R 8B1, Canada
Tel: 306-757-7541; *Fax:* 306-757-2040
regina@cefsk.ca
www.cefsk.ca
www.facebook.com/216496861783051
twitter.com/cefsk
Number of Schools: 14; *Grades:* K - 12; *Enrollment:* 1095
Donald Michaud, Directeur de l'éducation par intérim, 306-757-7541
direduc@cefsk.ca
Lise Gareau, Sec.-Treas.
Siriki Diabagaté, Direction des services financiers, 306-719-7424
sdiabagate@cefsk.ca
Andrée Myette, Directrice des communications, 306-719-7455
amyette@cefsk.ca

Schools: Cégep

French

Gravelbourg: Collège Mathieu
P.O. Box 989
308, 1ère av est, Gravelbourg, SK S0H 1X0
Tél: 306-648-3491; *Téléc:* 306-648-2295
Ligne sans frais: 1-800-663-5463
www.collegemathieu.sk.ca
www.facebook.com/CollegeMathieu
Francis Kasongo, Directeur général, 306-648-3129
direction@collegemathieu.sk.ca

Campuses
Campus de Saskatoon
#202, 308, 4e av nord, Saskatoon, SK S7K 2L7
Tel: 306-384-2722; *Fax:* 306-384-2469
Toll-Free: 866-524-4404

Campus de Regina
#217, 1440, 9e av nord, Regina, SK S4R 8B1
Tel: 306-565-3525; *Fax:* 306-569-2609

Schools: Specialized

Special Education

***Pilot Butte:* Ranch Ehrio Society**
P.O. Box 570
Pilot Butte, SK S0G 3Z0, Canada
Tel: 306-781-1800; *Fax:* 306-757-0599
inquiries@ranchehrlo.ca
www.ehrlo.com
www.facebook.com/RanchEhrlo
twitter.com/RanchEhrlo
www.youtube.com/user/ranchehrlo1
Grades: K-12; *Enrollment:* 192; *Note:* The Ranch is a residental school for children, youth, and young adults, who are experiencing social, psychological, mental, psychiatric, and/or physical disabilities, through the provision of holistic, psycho-social therapies.
Marion MacIver, President

Campuses
Buckland Campus
P.O. Box 1892
Prince Albert, SK S6V 6J9, Canada
Tel: 306-764-4511; *Fax:* 306-764-0042

Corman Park Campus
P.O. Box 500
Martensville, SK S0K 2T0, Canada
Tel: 306-659-3100; *Fax:* 306-956-2570

***Regina:* Cornwall Alternative School**
40 Dixon Cres., Regina, SK S4N 1V4, Canada
Tel: 306-522-0044; *Fax:* 306-359-0720
admin.cas@sasktel.net
www.cornwallalternativeschool.com
Grades: 7-10; *Enrollment:* 39
Gil Will, Acting Principal & CEO
David Halvorsen, Board Chairperson

***Saskatoon:* Radius Community Centre for Education & Employment**
P.O. Box 1812
Bay 1 - 611, 1st Ave. North, Saskatoon, SK S7K 1X7, Canada
Tel: 306-665-0362; *Fax:* 306-665-5579
info@radiuscentre.com
www.radiuscentre.com
www.facebook.com/profile.php?id=100008583871058&fref=ts&ref=br_tf
www.twitter.com/RadCentre1970
Gail McKenzie-Wilcox, Principal

Schools: Independent & Private

Faith-Based

***Battleford:* Heritage Christian School**
P.O. Box 490
11 - 20th St. West, Battleford, SK S0M 0E0, Canada
Tel: 306-446-3188; *Fax:* 306-446-3187
heritage@lskysd.ca
www.heritagechristianschool.lskysd.ca
Grades: K.-12; Days only; *Enrollment:* 59
Jeremy Verity, Principal

***Moose Jaw:* Cornerstone Christian School (CCS)**
43 Iroquois St. East, Moose Jaw, SK S6H 4S9
Tel: 306-693-2937; *Fax:* 306-694-1880
office@ccsmj.ca
www.ccsmj.ca
www.facebook.com/CornerstoneChristianSchoolAlumni
Grades: Kindergarten - 12; *Note:* The school is recognized by the Government of Saskatchewan as an Associate School. It is responsible to the local public school, the Prairie South School Division #210.
Ashley Taylor, Board Chair

***Outlook:* Lutheran Collegiate Bible Institute**
P.O. Box 459
Outlook, SK S0L 2N0, Canada
Tel: 306-867-8971; *Fax:* 306-867-9947
office@lcbi.sk.ca
www.lcbi.sk.ca
www.facebook.com/pages/LCBI-High-School/10150089137100296
twitter.com/LCBINews
Grades: 10-12; Residential only
Philip Guebert, Principal

***Regina:* Harvest City Christian Academy**
Harvest City Church
2202 - 8th Ave. North, Regina, SK S4R 7T9, Canada
Tel: 306-569-1935; *Fax:* 306-359-9047
www.harvestcitychristianacademy.com
Grades: K.-12 (Non-Denom.); Day only
Todd Harrison, Principal
todd.harrison@hccmail.ca

***Regina:* Regina Christian School (RCS)**
2505 - 23rd Ave., Regina, SK S4S 7K7, Canada
Tel: 306-775-0919; *Fax:* 306-775-3070
rcs.office@myaccess.ca
www.reginachristianschool.org
Other Information: development@reginachristianschool.org (E-mail, Development)
Grades: Pre - 12; *Enrollment:* 343; *Note:* The interdenominational school's academic program is offered with an evangelical Christian view.
Darryl Brown, Board Chair
Rod Rilling, B.Ed., B.A. (Hons), Principal
principal@reginachristianschool.org
Krista Munson, B.Ed., B.A., Vice Principal
krista.munson@rbe.sk.ca
Doreen Brace, B.Ed., Learning Leader & Resource Teacher
doreen.brace@rbe.sk.ca

***Rosthern:* Rosthern Junior College**
410 - 6th Ave., Rosthern, SK S0K 3R0, Canada
Tel: 306-232-4222; *Fax:* 306-232-5250
office@rjc.sk.ca
www.rjc.sk.ca
www.facebook.com/rosthernjc
twitter.com/RosthernJC
www.youtube.com/RosthernJrCollege
Grades: 10 - 12; *Note:* The Christian secondary school operates within a Mennonite school community, for students of any faith. Completion of enriched courses leads to a Saskatchewan senior matriculation.
Jim Epp, Principal
Kristen Hamm, Dean, Women
Ashley Wiebe, Dean, Women
David Attema, Dean, Men
Rowan Bezeau, Dean, Men
Val White, Contact, Admissions & Alumni

***Saskatoon:* Christian Centre Academy (CCA)**
102 Pinehouse Dr., Saskatoon, SK S7K 5H7, Canada
Tel: 306-242-7141
academy@christiancentre.ca
christiancentre.ca/academy
Grades: Kindergarten - 12; *Note:* The Accelerated Christian Education curriculum is used from kindergarten to grade 9 at the Christian Centre Academy. From grade 10 to 12, Saskatchewan Association of Independent Church Schools materials are used.

***Saskatoon:* Saskatoon Christian School**
P.O. Box 8
Site 510, RR#5, Saskatoon, SK S7K 3J8, Canada
Tel: 306-343-1494; *Fax:* 306-343-0366
info@saskatoonchristianschool.ca
www.saskatoonchristianschool.ca
Grades: K.-12; Day only; *Enrollment:* 350
Doug Wiebe, Principal
wiebedo@spsd.sk.ca

Catholic

***Wilcox:* Athol Murray College of Notre Dame**
P.O. Box 100
49 Main St., Wilcox, SK S0G 5E0, Canada
Tel: 306-732-2080; *Fax:* 306-732-4409
info@notredame.ca
www.notredame.sk.ca
www.facebook.com/48128406910
twitter.com/NotreDameHounds
Grades: 9-12; *Enrollment:* 350; *Note:* Athol Murray College of Notre Dame is an international coeducational & residential college preparatory school. It is dedicated to Catholic Christian education.
Rob Palmarin, B.Ed., M.Th., President, 306-732-1230
Britt Leeking, Director, Admissions, 306-732-1221
Kate MacLean, B.Ed, B.Sc., Director, Academics, 306-732-1240

Independent & Private Schools

***Caronport:* Caronport High School (CHS)**
c/o Briercrest College & Seminary
510 College Dr., Caronport, SK S0H 0S0, Canada
Tel: 306-756-3303; *Fax:* 306-756-5597
chs@briercrest.ca
www.briercrest.ca/chs
Grades: 9 - 12; *Number of Employees:* 22
Deborah Ike, Principal
George Willatt, Vice Principal
gwillatt@briercrest.ca

***Prince Albert:* Rivier Academy**
1405 Bishop Pascal Pl., Prince Albert, SK S6V 5J1, Canada
Tel: 306-764-6289; *Fax:* 306-763-1442
cec.pacsd6.sk.ca/Our-Schools/Rivier-Academy.html
Grades: 7 - 12; *Note:* An associate school of the Prince Albert Roman Catholic School Division 6, Rivier Academy is an independent, Catholic high school for young women. It provides a full course, as prescribed by Saskatchewan Learning.
Sr. Mary Woodward, Principal

***Regina:* Luther College High School**
1500 Royal St., Regina, SK S4T 5A5, Canada
Tel: 306-791-9150
www.facebook.com/LCHSRegina
Grades: 9-12
Brian Hills, Principal
bryan.hillis@luthercollege.edu

***Regina:* Regina Huda School**
40 Sheppard St., Regina, SK S4R 3M6, Canada
Tel: 306-565-1988; *Fax:* 306-565-2187
www.hudaschool.regina.sk.ca
Grades: Preschool - 12; *Note:* Regina Huda School strives to preserve the Islamic identity, by offering Islamic & Arabic studies for the Muslim community.
Dr. Ayman Aboguddah, Board President
aboguddah@gmail.com
Carla Natrasany, Principal

Universities & Colleges

Universities

***Caronport:* Briercrest College & Seminary**
510 College Dr., Caronport, SK S0H 0S0, Canada
Tel: 306-756-3200; *Fax:* 306-756-5500
Toll-Free: 800-667-5199
info@briercrest.ca
www.briercrest.ca
www.facebook.com/Briercrest
www.twitter.com/briercrest
www.youtube.com/briercrestcollegesem
Full Time Equivalency: 640; *Note:* The institution also operates the Caronport High School.

***Regina:* First Nations University of Canada**
1 First Nations Way, Regina, SK S4S 7K2, Canada
Tel: 306-790-5950; *Fax:* 306-790-5999
Toll-Free: 800-267-6303
www.fnuniv.ca
www.facebook.com/FNUNIV
twitter.com/FNUNIVCAN
pinterest.com/fnunivlibrary/
Full Time Equivalency: 750

Campuses
Saskatoon Campus
226 - 20th St. East, Saskatoon, SK S7K 0A6, Canada
Tel: 306-931-1800; *Fax:* 306-931-1849
Toll-Free: 800-267-6303

Northern Campus
1301 Central Ave., Prince Albert, SK S6V 4W1, Canada
Tel: 306-765-3333; *Toll-Free:* 800-267-6303

***Regina:* University of Regina**
3737 Wascana Pkwy., Regina, SK S4S 0A2
Tel: 306-585-4111; *Fax:* 306-585-5203
registrar@uregina.ca
www.uregina.ca
www.facebook.com/UniversityofRegina
twitter.com/UofRegina
www.linkedin.com/company/university-of-regina
www.linkedin.com/company/university-of-regina
Full Time Equivalency: 13580; *Number of Employees:* 2800
Jim Tomkins, Chancellor
Dr. Vianne Timmins, B.A., B.Ed., M.Ed., Ph.D., President & Vice-Chancellor

Dr. Thomas Chase, Provost & Vice-President, Academic
Dave Malloy, Vice-President, Research
Annette Revet, B.Sc.(Hons.), MBA, University Secretary
Dave Button, B.A., B.Ed., Vice-President, Administration
James D'Arcy, Registrar
Dr. Dena McMartin, Assoc. Vice-President, Academic & Research
John D. Smith, Assoc. Vice-President, Student Affairs
Kelly Kummerfield, B.Admin., Assoc. Vice-President, Human Resources
Nelson Wagner, Assoc. Vice-President, Facilities Management
Dale Schoffer, Assoc. Vice-President, Finance

Faculties

Faculty of Arts
3737 Wascana Pkwy., #CL426, Regina, SK S4S 0A2
Tel: 306-585-5653
www.uregina.ca/arts
www.facebook.com/UofRArts
twitter.com/UofRArts
Richard Kleer, Dean

Faculty of Business Administration
3737 Wascana Pkwy., 5th Fl., Regina, SK S4S 0A2
Tel: 306-585-4724; *Fax:* 306-585-5361
www.uregina.ca/business
www.facebook.com/pjhbusiness
twitter.com/HillSchoolofBus
Andrew Gaudes, Ph.D, Dean

Faculty of Education
3737 Wascana Pkwy., Regina, SK S4S 0A2
Tel: 306-585-4537; *Fax:* 306-585-4880
education.counselling@uregina.ca
www.uregina.ca/education
www.facebook.com/uredspc
Dr. Jennifer Tupper, B.A., Ph.D., Acting Dean

Faculty of Engineering & Applied Science
3737 Wascana Pkwy., Regina, SK S4S 0A2
Tel: 306-585-4734
engg@uregina.ca
www.urengineering.ca
Dr. Esam Hussein, Dean
esam.hussein@uregina.ca

Faculty of Fine Arts
269 Riddel Centre, University of Regina
Regina, SK S4S 0A2
Tel: 306-585-5557; *Fax:* 306-585-5544
finearts@uregina.ca
www.uregina.ca/finearts
Rae Staseson, Dean
Finearts.Dean@uregina.ca

Graduate Studies & Research
3737 Wascana Pkwy., Regina, SK S4S 0A2
Tel: 306-585-4161; *Fax:* 306-337-2444
grad.studies@uregina.ca
www.uregina.ca/gradstudies
Dr. Armin Eberlein, Dean
Grad.Dean@uregina.ca

Faculty of Kinesiology & Health Studies
3737 Wascana Pkwy., Regina, SK S4S 0A2
Tel: 306-585-4360; *Fax:* 306-585-4854
kinesiology@uregina.ca
www.uregina.ca/kinesiology
Dr. Craig Chamberlin, B.P.E., M.P.E., Ph.D., Dean

Faculty of Science
3737 Wascana Pkwy., Regina, SK S4S 0A2
Tel: 306-585-4143
www.uregina.ca/science
Dr. Daniel Gagnon, Dean

Faculty of Social Work
3737 Wascana Pkwy., Regina, SK S4S 0A2
Tel: 306-585-4554; *Fax:* 306-585-4872
sw.studentservices@uregina.ca
www.uregina.ca/socialwork
www.facebook.com/URsocialwork
www.youtube.com/user/URSocialWork
Dr. Judy White, Acting Dean

Conservatory of Performing Arts
3737 Wascana Pkwy., Regina, SK S4S 0A2
Tel: 306-585-5748; *Fax:* 306-585-5788
www.uregina.ca/cce/conservatory
Other Information: 306-585-5831
www.facebook.com/uofrcce
Christa Eidsness, Program Coordinator

Kenneth Levene Graduate School of Business
3737 Wascana Pkwy., Regina, SK S4S 0A2
Tel: 305-474-6294; *Fax:* 306-585-5361
www.uregina.ca/business/levene

Johnson-Shoyama Graduate School of Public Policy
Innocation Place
#110, 2 Research Dr., Regina, SK S4S 7H1
Tel: 306-585-5460; *Fax:* 306-585-5461
jsgs@uregina.ca
www.schoolofpublicpolicy.sk.ca
www.facebook.com/JSGSPP
twitter.com/JSGSPP
www.youtube.com/user/jsgspp
Dr. Michael Atkinson, B.A., M.A., Ph.D., Executive Director

School of Journalism
3737 Wascana Pkwy, Regina, SK S4S 0A2
Tel: 306-585-4420; *Fax:* 306-585-4867
journalism@uregina.ca
www.uregina.ca/arts/journalism
www.facebook.com/URJSchool
twitter.com/URJschool
Mitch Diamantopoulos, B.A. Hons., M.A., Department Head

Affiliations

Campion College
c/o University of Regina
3737 Wascana Pkwy., Regina, SK S4S 0A2, Canada
Tel: 306-586-4242; *Fax:* 306-359-1200
Toll-Free: 1-800-667-7282
campion.college@uregina.ca
www.campioncollege.sk.ca
www.facebook.com/campioncollege
twitter.com/CampionUR
www.youtube.com/user/URCampion
Full Time Equivalency: 1000; *Number of Employees:* 22 full-time professors; 17 full-time staff members; 1 campus minister
Dr. John Meehan, President, 306-359-1212
John.Meehan@uregina.ca
James Gustafson, Executive Director, Administration & Finance, 306-359-1231
James.Gustafson@uregina.ca
Joanne Kozlowski, Director of Communications & Marketing, 306-359-1244
joanne.kozlowski@uregina.ca
Kenneth Yanko, Director, Facilities & Operations, 306-359-1249
ken.yanko@uregina.ca
Stephanie Molloy, Campus Minister & Director of Pastoral Studies, 306-359-1235
stephanie.molloy@uregina.ca
Frank Obrigewitsch, Dean, 306-359-1237
frank.obrigewitsch@uregina.ca
Deborah Morrison, Registrar, 306-359-1226
deborah.morrison@uregina.ca

First Nations University of Canada
#207, 2553 Grasswood Rd. East, Regina, SK S7T 1C8
Tel: 306-790-5950; *Fax:* 306-790-5999
Toll-Free: 1-800-267-6303
www.fnuniv.ca
www.facebook.com/FNUNIV
www.pinterest.com/fnunivlibrary
Full Time Equivalency: 750; *Note:* At the First Nations University of Canada, students have the opportunity to learn in an environment of First Nations languages, traditions, & values.

Gabriel Dumont Institute (GDI)
917 - 22nd St. West, Saskatoon, SK S7M 0R9
Tel: 306-242-6070; *Fax:* 306-242-0002
Toll-Free: 877-488-6888
general@gdi.gdins.org
www.gdins.org
www.facebook.com/gabrieldumontinstitute
twitter.com/gdins_org
www.youtube.com/user/gabrieldumontins
Note: The Institute is designated as the official education arm of the Métis Nation-Saskatchewan (MN-S).
Geordy McCaffrey, Executive Director

Luther College
c/o University of Regina
3737 Wascana Pkwy., Regina, SK S4S 0A2, Canada
Tel: 306-585-5333; *Fax:* 306-585-2949
Toll-Free: 800-588-4378
lutheru@luthercollege.edu
www.luthercollege.edu
www.facebook.com/LCUR1971
Bryan Hillis, President, 306-585-5024
bryan.hillis@luthercollege.edu
Mark Duke, Director of Finance, 306-585-5023
mark.duke@luthercollege.edu
Franz Volker Greifenhagen, Dean, 306-585-4859
Franzvolker.greifenhagen@luthercollege.edu

Centres/Institutes

Centre on Aging & Health
Regina, SK S4S 0A2
Tel: 306-337-8477; *Fax:* 306-337-3204
CAH@uregina.ca
uregina.ca/hadjistt/centre_index.htm
twitter.com/UofRAgingCentre
Scott Wilson, Administrator
scott.j.wilson@uregina.ca

Collaborative Centre for Justice & Safety
3737 Wascana Pkwy., Regina, SK S4S 0A2
Tel: 306-337-2570
www.justiceandsafety.ca
Steve Palmer, Executive Director
steve.palmer@uregina.ca

Indigenous Peoples' Health Research Centre (IPHRC)
3737 Wascana Pkwy., Regina, SK S4S 0A2
Tel: 306-337-2461; *Fax:* 306-585-5694
iphrc.ca
www.facebook.com/IPHRC
twitter.com/iphrcsask
Jo-Ann Episkenew, Director
jo-ann.episkenew@uregina.ca

Saskatoon: College of Emmanuel & St. Chad
Also known as: University of Emmanuel College
114 Seminary Cres., Saskatoon, SK S7N 0X3, Canada
Tel: 306-975-3753; *Fax:* 306-934-2683
emmanuel.stchad@usask.ca
www.usask.ca/stu/emmanuel

Saskatoon: Lutheran Theological Seminary
114 Seminary Cres., Saskatoon, SK S7N 0X3, Canada
Tel: 306-966-7850; *Fax:* 306-966-7852
lutheran.seminary@usask.ca
www.usask.ca/stu/luther
www.facebook.com/LTSSaskatoon
Full Time Equivalency: 142; *Note:* Theological college at the University of Saskatchewan affiliated with the Evangelical Lutheran Church in Canada

Saskatoon: University of Saskatchewan
Administration Bldg.
105 Administration Pl., Saskatoon, SK S7N 5A2
Tel: 306-966-4343
www.usask.ca
www.facebook.com/usask
twitter.com/usask
www.linkedin.com/company/university-of-saskatchewan
instagram.com/usask
Full Time Equivalency: 20080
Blaine C. Favel, Chancellor
Peter Stoicheff, President & Vice-Chancellor
Ernie Barber, Interim Provost & Vice-President
Greg Fowler, Vice-President, Finance & Resources
Elizabeth Williamson, University Secretary
Russell Isinger, Registrar
Jim Basinger, Assoc. Vice-President, Research
jim.basinger@usask.ca
Karen Chad, Ph.D., Vice-President, Research
Jeff Dumba, Assoc. Vice-President, Financial Services & Controller
Ivan Muzychka, Assoc. Vice-President, Communications
Patti McDougall, Vice-Provost, Teaching & Learning
Mark Roman, Assoc. Vice-President, Information & Communications Tech

Faculties

College of Agriculture & Bioresources
51 Campus Dr., Saskatoon, SK S7N 5A8
Tel: 306-966-4056; *Fax:* 306-966-8894
agbio.reception@usask.ca
agbio.usask.ca
Mary Buhr, Dean

College of Arts & Science
9 Campus Dr., Saskatoon, SK S7N 5A5
Tel: 306-966-4232; *Fax:* 306-966-8839
officeofthedean@artsandscience.usask.ca
artsandscience.usask.ca
www.facebook.com/Arts.Science.UofS
twitter.com/usaskArtSci
www.youtube.com/user/artsandscienceUofS
Vacant, Dean

Edwards School of Business
#185, 25 Campus Dr., Saskatoon, SK S7N 5A7
Tel: 306-966-4785; *Fax:* 306-966-5408
undergrad@edwards.usask.ca
www.edwards.usask.ca
www.facebook.com/edwardsschoolofbusiness?ref=ts
twitter.com/edwards_school
www.youtube.com/ESBUofS

Daphne Taras, Dean

College of Dentistry

Toll-Free: 877-363-7275
dentistry@usask.ca
www.usask.ca/dentistry

Gerry Uswak, Dean, 306-966-5122
gerry.uswak@usask.ca

College of Education
28 Campus Dr., Saskatoon, SK S7N 0X1
Tel: 306-966-7647
edo.inquiries@usask.ca
www.usask.ca/education

Michelle Prytula, Dean
michelle.prytula@usask.ca

College of Engineering
57 Campus Dr., Saskatoon, SK S7N 5A9
Tel: 306-966-5273; *Fax:* 306-966-5205
coe.inquiries@usask.ca
www.engr.usask.ca
www.facebook.com/usask.engr
twitter.com/usask_engr

Georges Kipouros, Dean
georges.kipouros@usask.ca

School of Environment & Sustainability
Kirk Hall
#323, 117 Science Pl., Saskatoon, SK S7N 5C8
Tel: 306-966-1985; *Fax:* 306-966-2298
sens.info@usask.ca
www.usask.ca/sens
ca.linkedin.com/pub/sens-university-of-saskatchewan/3a/552/a4
www.flickr.com/photos/usask/sets/

Toddi Steelman, Executive Director
toddi.steelman@usask.ca

Graduate Studies & Research
105 Administration Pl., Saskatoon, SK S7N 5A2
Tel: 306-966-5751; *Fax:* 306-966-5756
gradstudies@usask.ca
www.usask.ca/cgsr

Adam Baxter-Jones, Dean

College of Kinesiology
87 Campus Dr., Saskatoon, SK S7N 5B2
Tel: 306-966-1060; *Fax:* 306-966-6464
kinesiology.usask.ca

Carol Rodgers, Ph.D., B.P.E., M.H.K., Dean
carol.rodgers@usask.ca

College of Law
15 Campus Dr., Saskatoon, SK S7N 5A6
Tel: 306-966-5869; *Fax:* 306-966-5900
law.usask.ca
www.youtube.com/user/CollegeOfLawUsask

Sanjeev Anand, Dean

College of Medicine
Health Sciences Bldg.
107 Wiggins Rd., #5D40, Saskatoon, SK S7N 5E5
Tel: 306-966-2673; *Fax:* 306-966-6164
medicine.communications@usask.ca
www.medicine.usask.ca

Preston Smith, M.D., Ph.D., FRCPC, Dean

College of Nursing
104 Clinic Pl., Saskatoon, SK S7N 2Z4
Tel: 306-966-6221; *Fax:* 306-966-6621
www.usask.ca/nursing
www.facebook.com/usaskNursing
twitter.com/uofsnursing
www.youtube.com/user/usasknursing

Lorna Butler, B.S.N., M.N., Ph.D., Dean

College of Pharmacy & Nutrition
Thorvaldson Building
#116, 110 Science Pl., Saskatoon, SK S7N 5C9
Tel: 306-966-6328; *Fax:* 306-966-6377
www.usask.ca/pharmacy-nutrition
www.facebook.com/327519416639

Kishor Wasan, Dean

School of Physical Therapy
1121 College Dr., Saskatoon, SK S7N 0W3
Tel: 306-966-6579; *Fax:* 306-966-6575
pt.generaloffice@usask.ca
www.medicine.usask.ca/pt

Elizabeth Harrison, Assoc. Dean

Veterinary Medicine
52 Campus Dr., Saskatoon, SK S7N 5B4
Tel: 306-966-7447; *Fax:* 306-966-8747
www.usask.ca/wcvm

Douglas Freeman, Dean
douglas.freeman@usask.ca

Affiliations

Briercrest Bible College & Biblical Seminary
510 College Dr., Caronport, SK S0H 0S0
Tel: 306-756-3200; *Fax:* 306-756-5500
info@briercrest.ca
www.briercrest.ca
www.facebook.com/Briercrest
twitter.com/briercrest
www.youtube.com/briercrestcollegesem

Dr Michael B. Pawelke, President

College of Emmanuel & St. Chad
114 Seminary Cres., Saskatoon, SK S7N 0X3
Tel: 306-975-3753; *Fax:* 306-934-2683
emmanuel.stchad@usask.ca
www.usask.ca/stu/emmanuel

The Rev David Irving, Chancellor
Rev. James Njegovan, President

Gabriel Dumont College
McLean Hall
#7, 106 Wiggins Rd., Saskatoon, SK S7M 5E6
Tel: 306-975-7095; *Fax:* 306-975-1108
gdins.org

Geordy McCaffrey, Executive Director, Gabriel Dumont Institute

Lutheran Theological Seminary
114 Seminary Cres., Saskatoon, SK S7N 0X3
Tel: 306-966-7850; *Fax:* 306-966-7852
lutheran.seminary@usask.ca
www.usask.ca/stu/luther
www.facebook.com/LTSSaskatoon

Kevin Ogilvie, President, 306-966-7863
kevin.ogilvie@usask.ca
Marla Mulloy, Chair
Vincent Gaudet, Director of Finance, 306-966-7862
finance.lts@usask.ca

St. Andrew's College
1121 College Dr., Saskatoon, SK S7N 0W3
Tel: 306-966-8970; *Fax:* 306-966-8981
Toll-Free: 1-877-644-8970
standrews.college@usask.ca
www.usask.ca/stu/standrews
www.facebook.com/StAndrewsCollegeSaskatoon
www.youtube.com/user/StAndrewsSaskatoon

Note: The College is a theological school of The United Church of Canada.
Lorne Calvert, Principal

St. Peter's College
P.O. Box 40
Muenster, SK S0K 2Y0
Tel: 306-682-7888; *Fax:* 306-682-4402
spc@stpeters.sk.ca
www.stpeterscollege.ca

Note: Affiliated with the University of Saskatchewan, the College provides Arts & Science, Agriculture, & Commerce courses to first and second year students.
Robert Harasymchuk, President
Barbara Langhorst, Coordinator, Humanities

St. Thomas More College (STM)
1437 College Dr., Saskatoon, SK S7N 0W6
Tel: 306-966-8900; *Fax:* 306-966-8904
Toll-Free: 1-800-667-2019
www.stmcollege.ca
www.facebook.com/stmcollege
twitter.com/stm1936
www.youtube.com/stm1936

Note: St. Thomas More College is a Catholic, liberal arts college, federated with the University of Saskatchewan. The college has 31 full-time tenure track faculty, 3 full-time term faculty, & 42 sessional faculty.

Centres/Institutes

Canadian Centre for Health & Safety in Agriculture (CCHSA)
P.O. Box 23
Saskatoon, SK S7N 2Z4
Tel: 306-966-8286; *Fax:* 306-966-8799
canadian.centre@usask.ca
www.cchsa-ccssma.usask.ca

Centre for Continuing & Distance Education (CCDE)
221 Cumberland Ave. North, Saskatoon, SK S7N 1M3
Tel: 306-966-5539; *Fax:* 306-966-5590
ccde.reg@usask.ca
ccde.usask.ca
www.facebook.com/CCDEUniversityofSaskatchewan

Bob Cram, Executive Director
bob.cram@usask.ca

Centre for Forensic Behavioural Science & Justice Studies
#110B, 9 Campus Dr., Saskatoon, SK S7N 5A5
Tel: 306-966-6818
www.usask.ca/cfbsjs

Stephen Wormith, Director
s.wormith@usask.ca

International Centre for Northern Governance & Development (ICNGD)
Kirk Hall
#234, 117 Science Pl., Saskatoon, SK S7N 5C8
Tel: 306-966-1665; *Fax:* 306-966-7780
artsandscience.usask.ca/icngd

Ken Coates, Director
ken.coates@usask.ca

Univesity Learning Centre
Murray Building
#106, 3 Campus Dr., Saskatoon, SK S7N 5A4
Tel: 306-966-2886; *Fax:* 306-966-6329
ulc@usask.ca
www.usask.ca/ulc
www.facebook.com/usaskULC
twitter.com/ULC_WritingHelp

Frank Bulk, Acting Program Director
frank.bulk@usask.ca

Centre for Integrative Medicine
HSC E-Wing, College of Medicine
#3227, 107 Wiggins Rd., Saskatoon, SK S7N 5E5
Tel: 306-966-7935
integrative.medicine@usask.ca
www.medicine.usask.ca/integrativemedicine
twitter.com/usask

Michael Epstein, Managing Director

Colleges

***Regina:* Luther College**
c/o University of Regina
3737 Wascana Pkwy., Regina, SK S4S 0A2, Canada
Tel: 306-585-5333; *Fax:* 306-585-2949
Toll-Free: 800-588-4378
lutheru@luthercollege.edu
www.luthercollege.edu
www.facebook.com/LCUR1971

Bryan Hillis, President, 306-585-5024
bryan.hillis@luthercollege.edu
Mark Duke, Director of Finance, 306-585-5023
mark.duke@luthercollege.edu
Franz Volker Greifenhagen, Dean, 306-585-4859
Franzvolker.greifenhagen@luthercollege.edu

***Saskatoon:* Gabriel Dumont Institute**
917 - 22nd St. West, Saskatoon, SK S7M 0R9, Canada
Tel: 306-242-6070; *Fax:* 306-242-0002
Toll-Free: 877-488-6888
general@gdi.gdins.org
www.gdins.org
www.facebook.com/gabrieldumontinstitute
twitter.com/gdins_org
www.youtube.com/channel/UCynvuqUsjiqxgyQ6Lrh6TUg

Note: Has partnerships with University of Saskatchewan & University of Regina; Educational arm of the Métis Nation-Saskatchewan

***Saskatoon:* Horizon College & Seminary**
***Also known as:* Central Pentecostal College**
1303 Jackson Ave., Saskatoon, SK S7H 2M9
Tel: 306-374-6655; *Fax:* 306-373-6968
Toll-Free: 877-374-6655
info@horizon.edu
www.horizon.edu
www.facebook.com/pages/Horizon-College-Seminary/18225432 1813848
twitter.com/HorizonCollege
www.youtube.com/user/HorizonCollegeSK

Jeromey Martini, President

Post Secondary/Technical

***Air Ronge:* Northlands College**
P.O. Box 1000
Air Ronge, SK S0J 3G0, Canada
Tel: 306-425-4480; *Fax:* 306-425-3002
Toll-Free: 1-888-311-1185
www.northlandscollege.sk.ca
www.linkedin.com/pub/northlands-college/67/a59/b34

Note: Program Centers are located in La Ronge (306-425-4353), Buffalo Narrows (306-235-1765), & Creighton (306-688-8838).
Kelvin (Toby) Greschnern, CEO, 306-425-4273

Campuses

La Ronge Program Center
P.O. Box 509
La Ronge, SK S0J 1L0, Canada
Tel: 306-425-4353; *Fax:* 306-425-2696

Buffalo Narrows Program Center
P.O. Box 190
Buffalo Narrows, SK S0M 0J0, Canada
Tel: 306-235-1765; *Fax:* 306-235-4346

Humboldt: Carlton Trail Regional College
P.O. Box 720
623 - 7 St., Humboldt, SK S0K 2A0, Canada
Tel: 306-682-2623; *Fax:* 306-682-3101
Toll-Free: 1-800-667-2623
humboldt@ctrc.sk.ca
www.ctrc.sk.ca/ctrc/

Number of Schools: 4 campuses
Rob Barber, CEO

Melville: Parkland Regional College Administration Office
P.O. Box 790
200 Block 9th Ave. East, Melville, SK S0A 2P0, Canada
Tel: 306-728-4471; *Fax:* 306-728-2576
www.parklandcollege.sk.ca

Number of Schools: 5 main campuses; 2 training centres
Fay Myers, CEO

Melville: Western Trade Training Institute (WTTI)
P.O. Box 790
Melville, SK S0A 2P0
Tel: 306-863-2278; *Fax:* 306-863-2263
d.mcmunn@wttionline.ca
www.wttionline.ca

Note: Offers apprenticeship level training Crane Operation and related sub trades.

Moose Jaw: T & H Academies Career Training Centre
Also known as: The Academies
345 Main St. North, Moose Jaw, SK
Tel: 306-694-2133; *Fax:* 306-692-9321
Toll-Free: 800-363-7999
www.theacademies.ca

Note: The Academies is a multifaceted training centre for careers in the beauty and spa industries.

Nipawin: Cumberland College
P.O. Box 2225
503 - 2nd St. East, Nipawin, SK S0E 1E0, Canada
Tel: 306-862-9833; *Fax:* 306-862-4940
www.cumberlandcollege.sk.ca

Valerie Mushinski, CEO
vmushinski@cumberlandcollege.sk.ca
Corinne Lam Ma, Manager, Learner Services, 506-873-3844
clamma@cumberlandcollege.sk.ca

Campuses

Nipawin Campus
P.O. Box 2225
501 - 6th St. East, Nipawin, SK S0E 1E0, Canada
Tel: 306-862-9833; *Fax:* 306-862-4940
crc.nipawin@cumberlandcollege.sk.ca

Melfort Campus
P.O. Box 2320
400 Burns Ave. East, Melfort, SK S0E 1A0, Canada
Tel: 306-752-2786; *Fax:* 306-752-3484
crc.melfort@cumberlandcollege.sk.ca

Hudson Bay Campus
P.O. Box 207
501 Prince St., Hudson Bay, SK S0E 0Y0, Canada
Tel: 306-865-2175; *Fax:* 306-865-2314
crc.hudsonbay@cumberlandcollege.sk.ca

Tisdale Campus
800 - 101 St., Tisdale, SK S0E 1T0, Canada
Tel: 306-873-2525; *Fax:* 306-873-4450
tisdale@cumberlandcollege.sk.ca

North Battleford: North West Regional College
10702 Diefenbaker Dr., North Battleford, SK S9A 4A8, Canada
Tel: 306-937-5100; *Fax:* 306-445-1575
www.nwrc.sk.ca

Enrollment: 823
Leo Murphy, Principal & Chief Executive

Regina: Avant-Garde College
1033 - 8th Ave., Regina, SK S4R 1E1
Tel: 306-522-5900; *Fax:* 306-522-3232
avant.garde@sasktel.net
www.avant-gardecollege.ca
www.facebook.com/jointhefight.sk#!/group.php?gid=5677166029 5

Note: Avant-Garde College has operates as a full-service educational salon.

Regina: Globe Theatre Conservatory
1801 Scarth St., Regina, SK S4P 2G9
auditions@globetheatrelive.com
globetheatrelive.com
www.facebook.com/pages/Globe-Theatre/33881883223
twitter.com/GlobeRegina
www.youtube.com/user/GlobeTheatreRegina

Note: Actor Training Program.

Regina: INtouch Career Advancement Training
Office of the Registrar
633 Park St., Regina, SK S4N 5N1, Canada
Tel: 306-781-0360; *Fax:* 306-781-0369
info@intouchcareercollege.com
www.intouchcareercollege.com

Note: Academic upgrading, employment preparation, computer education & business programs
Donna Singer, Principal
dsinger@intouchcareercollege.com

Regina: INtouch Career College
#500, 4400 - 4th Ave., Regina, SK S4T 0H8
Tel: 306-781-0360; *Fax:* 306-781-0369
info@intouchcareercollege.com
www.intouchcareercollege.com

Donna Singer, Principal/Manager
dsinger@intouchcareercollege.com

Regina: Jane's College of Medi-Aesthetics and Hair Design
9 Coventry Rd., Regina, SK S4T 5Z4
Tel: 306-205-8388; *Fax:* 306-205-8355
janescollege@myaccess,ca
www.janescollege.com

Regina: Richards Beauty College
434 Broad St., Regina, SK S4R 1X3
Tel: 306-522-2077
info@rbcollege.net
www.rbcollege.net
www.facebook.com/group.php?gid=39749152136&v=wall&viewas=0

Regina: Royal Canadian Mounted Police Training Academy
P.O. Box 6500
11th Ave., Regina, SK S4P 3J7
Tel: 306-780-6229; *Fax:* 306-780-3473
www.rcmp-grc.gc.ca/depot

Note: All cadets of the RCMP undergo their initial Basic Training here. They also provide the National Law Enforcement Training Program (NLET).

Regina: Schaller College
1652 Albert St., Regina, SK S4P 2S6
Tel: 306-751-2736; *Fax:* 306-751-2920
applications@ranchehrlo.ca
www.ehrlo.com/schaller/college

Note: Schaller College prepares students for careers in the field of Information Technology (IT).

Regina: Western College of Remedial Massage Therapies
832 McCarthy Blvd., Regina, SK S4T 6S7
Tel: 306-757-2242
informationcwesterncollege.ca
www.westerncollege.ca

Regina: Zoom Zoom Groom's Academy of Pet Grooming
1180 Winnipeg St., Regina, SK S4R 1J6
Tel: 306-533-9155
zzgroom@sasktel.net
www.zoomzoomgroom.com
www.facebook.com/zoomzoomgroom
twitter.com/zoomzoomgroom

Ridgedale: Stars & Stripes Heavy Equipment Training
P.O. Box 70
Ridgedale, SK S0E 1L0
Tel: 306-863-2239
startsandstripes2009@hotmail.com
www.starsandstripestraining.com

Note: Stars & Stripes Heavy Equipment Training is a Category 1 Private Vocational School.

Saskatoon: Academy of Fashion Design
218-B Ave. B South, Saskatoon, SK S7M 1M4, Canada
Tel: 306-978-9088; *Fax:* 306-933-9362
Toll-Free: 1-877-978-9088
fashiondesign@sasktel.net
www.aofdesign.com

Heather J. Brigidear, Program Coordinator

Saskatoon: McKay Career Training Inc.
133 - 3rd Ave. North, Saskatoon, SK S7K 2H4, Canada
Tel: 306-955-2622; *Fax:* 306-955-1601
www.mckaycareertraining.ca

Note: Medical & veterinary office assistant, graphic art/electronic prepress, multi media, massage therapy.
Gordon McKay

Saskatoon: Practicum Training Institute Inc. (PTI)
P.O. Box 30029
1624 - 33rd St. West, Saskatoon, SK S7L 7M6
Tel: 306-955-0079; *Fax:* 306-955-0343
pti@sasktel.net
www.practicumtraininginstitute.ca

Note: Practicum Training Institute provide practical hands on training to those in or wanting to enter into the Heavy Equipment Operating Industry.

Saskatoon: Professional Institute of Massage Therapy
#114, 701 Cynthia St., Saskatoon, SK S7L 6B7
Tel: 306-955-5833; *Fax:* 306-955-5864
saskatoon@pimtmassage.com
www.pimtmassage.com
www.facebook.com/280297472075
www.twitter.com/PIMTSaskatoon
www.youtube.com/PIMTSaskatoon

Campuses

Professional Institute of Massage Therapy - Calgary
805 - 14th St. NW, Calgary, AB T2N 2A4
Tel: 403-247-4319
saskatoon@pimtmassage.com
www.pimtmassage.com
www.facebook.com/280297472075
twitter.com/pimtcalgary

Saskatoon: The Recording Arts Institute of Saskatoon (RAIS)
#107, 120 Sonnenschein Way, Saskatoon, SK S7M 0W2
Tel: 306-292-6744; *Fax:* 306-220-6944
info@rais.ca
www.rais.ca
www.facebook.com/174117142631333

Note: RAIS offers programs in Audio Engineering and Motion Picture Arts.

Saskatoon: Redhouse College of Animation
#1, 505 - 23rd St. East, Saskatoon, SK S7K 4K7, Canada
Tel: 306-668-0013
info@redhousecollege.com
redhouse.sasktelwebhosting.com

Note: Three year animation program which includes basic animation principles and the process of writing, directing, and animating ones own film.
Gord Groat, Principal & Manager

Saskatoon: Saskatchewan Indian Institute of Technologies
c/o Asimakaniseekan Askiy Reserve
#118, 335 Packham Ave., Saskatoon, SK S7N 4S1, Canada
Tel: 306-244-4444; *Fax:* 306-244-1391
Toll-Free: 800-667-9704
www.siit.sk.ca

Ray Ahenakew, Acting President
Paul Ledoux, Registrar
Darlene Arcand, Director, Admission

Saskatoon: Saskatchewan Polytechnic
Administrative Offices, S.J. Cohen Centre
#400, 119 4th Ave. South, Saskatoon, SK S7K 5X2, Canada
Tel: 306-933-7331; *Toll-Free:* 866-467-4278
askaquestion@saskpolytech.ca
saskpolytech.ca
www.facebook.com/saskpolytech
www.twitter.com/saskpolytech
www.youtube.com/user/saskpolytech

Campuses

Saskatchewan Polytechnic - Saskatoon Campus
P.O. Box 1520
1130 Idylwyld Dr., Saskatoon, SK S7K 3R5, Canada
Tel: 306-659-4300
Gerry Bonsal, Director

Saskatchewan Polytechnic - Moose Jaw Campus
P.O. Box 1420
600 Saskatchewan St., Moose Jaw, SK S6H 4R4, Canada
Tel: 306-691-8200
Don Shanner, Director

Saskatchewan Polytechnic - Regina Campus
P.O. Box 556
4500 Wascana Pkwy., Regina, SK S4P 3A3, Canada
Tel: 306-775-7300
Noel Selinger, Director

Saskatchewan Polytechnic - Prince Albert Campus
P.O. Box 3003
1100 - 15 St. East, Prince Albert, SK S6V 6G1, Canada
Tel: 306-765-1500
Larry Fladager, Director

***Saskatoon:* Saskatoon Business College**
221 - 3rd Ave. North, Saskatoon, SK S7K 2H7, Canada
Tel: 306-244-6333; *Fax:* 306-652-4888
Toll-Free: 1-800-679-7711
www.saskbusinesscollege.com
twitter.com/sbccollege
Note: Business, health care, computer courses

***Saskatoon:* Saskatoon School of Horticulture (SSH)**
1021 Saskatchewan Cres. West, Saskatoon, SK S7M 5J6
Tel: 306-931-4769; *Fax:* 306-955-4769
growyourfuture@gmail.com
saskhort.com
www.facebook.com/saskatoon.horticulture

***Saskatoon:* Saskatoon Spa Academy Ltd.**
511J - 33rd St. West, Saskatoon, SK S7L 0V7
Tel: 306-477-0187; *Fax:* 306-477-0189
inquiries@SpaAcademy.ca
www.SpaAcademy.ca

***Saskatoon:* Universal Career College**
1202A Quebec Ave., Saskatoon, SK S7K 1V2, Canada
Tel: 306-373-8700; *Fax:* 306-373-8708
www.uccsaskatoon.ca
Note: Office & business management, travel & tourism
Laurette McCaig, Manager

***Saskatoon:* Western Academy Broadcasting College**
1222 Alberta Ave., Saskatoon, SK S7K 4E5, Canada
Tel: 306-665-1771; *Fax:* 306-244-1219
wabc@shaw.ca
www.wabcwesternacademy.com
Don Scott, Manager

***Shaunavon:* Great Plains College**
23 - 4th Ave. West, Shaunavon, SK S0N 2M0
Toll-Free: 866-296-2472
info@greatplainscollege.ca
www.greatplainscollege.ca
www.facebook.com/greatplainscollege
twitter.com/GPCollege
www.linkedin.com/company/great-plains-college
www.youtube.com/user/greatplainscollege
David Keast, CEO/President

Campuses

Kindersley Campus
P.O. Box 488
514 Main St., Kindersley, SK S0L 1S0, Canada
Tel: 306-463-6431; *Fax:* 306-463-1161
kindersley.office@greatplainscollege.ca

Swift Current Campus
P.O. Box 5000
129 - 2 Ave. NE, Swift Current, SK S9H 4G3, Canada
Tel: 306-773-1531; *Fax:* 306-773-2384
swiftcurrent.office@greatplainscollege.ca

Warman Campus
P.O. Box 1001
201 Central St., Warman, SK S0K 4S0, Canada
Tel: 306-242-5377; *Fax:* 306-242-8662
warman.office@greatplainscollege.ca

Biggar Program Centre
P.O. Box 700
701 Dominion St., Biggar, SK S0K 0MO, Canada
Tel: 306-948-3363; *Fax:* 306-948-2094
biggar.office@greatplainscollege.ca

Gravelbourg Program Centre
P.O. Box 652
7 Arthabasca St., Gravelbourg, SK S0H 1X0, Canada
Tel: 306-648-3244; *Fax:* 306-648-2983
gravelbourg.office@greatplainscollege.ca

Maple Creek Program Centre
P.O. Box 1738
20 Pacific Ave., Maple Creek, SK SON 1N0, Canada
Tel: 306-662-3829; *Fax:* 306-662-3849
maplecreek.office@greatplainscollege.ca

Nekaneet Program Centre
P.O. Box 548
Maple Creek, SK SON 1N0, Canada
Tel: 306-662-3660; *Fax:* 306-662-4160

Outlook Program Centre
P.O. Box 1237
104 Saskatchewan Ave., Outlook, SK S0L 2N0, Canada
Tel: 306-867-8857; *Fax:* 306-867-8722
outlook.office@greatplainscollege.ca

Macklin Training Centre
#1, 4801 Herald St., Macklin, SK S0L 2C0, Canada
Tel: 306-753-2143

Shaunavon Training Centre
499 Centre St., Shaunavon, SK S0N 2M0, Canada
Tel: 306-297-3462

***Tugaske:* Timeless Instruments**
P.O. Box 51
Tugaske, SK S0H 4B0
Tel: 306-759-2042; *Toll-Free:* 888-884-2753
david@timelessinstruments.com
www.timelessinstruments.com
www.facebook.com/pages/Timeless-Instruments/115399595203630
Note: Timeless Instruments is designed to prepare students to enter the work force as a self employed luthier or as a skilled worker in a shop.

***Weyburn:* Southeast Regional College Administrative Offices**
P.O. Box 1565
Weyburn, SK S4H 0T1, Canada
Tel: 306-848-2500; *Fax:* 306-848-2524
www.southeastcollege.org
Number of Schools: 7 centres & campuses
Graham Mickleborough, President

Yukon Territory

Government Agencies

***Whitehorse:* Yukon Department of Education**
P.O. Box 2703
1000 Lewes Blvd., Whitehorse, YT Y1A 2C6, Canada
Tel: 867-667-5141; *Fax:* 867-393-6254
Toll-Free: 800-661-0408
contact.education@gov.yk.ca
www.education.gov.yk.ca
Hon. Doug Graham, Minister of Education
doug.graham@gov.yk.ca

School Boards/Districts/Divisions

French

***Whitehorse:* Commission scolaire francophone du Yukon (CSFY)**
#3, 478 rue Range, Whitehorse, YT Y1A 3A2, Canada
Tel: 867-667-8680; *Fax:* 867-393-6946
Toll-Free: 800-661-0408
info@csfy.ca
commissionscolaire.csfy.ca
Grades: Pre-K.-12; *Enrollment:* 165; *Note:* The board operates the Yukon's only French first language school, École Émilie-Tremblay.
Edmond Ruest, Directeur général
edmond.ruest@gov.yk.ca
Lorraine Taillefer, Directrice générale, présentement en prêt de service
lorraine.taillefer@gov.yk.ca
Julie Dessureault, Secrétaire-trésorière
julie.dessureault@gov.yk.ca

Schools: Independent & Private

Independent & Private Schools

***Whitehorse:* Yukon Montessori School**
1191 First Ave., Whitehorse, YT Y1A 0K5
Tel: 867-334-7482
montessoriyukon@gmail.com
yukonmontessori.com
www.facebook.com/YukonMontessoriSchool
Grades: 1 - 6
Dominic Bradford, Head Teacher

Universities & Colleges

Colleges

***Whitehorse:* Yukon College**
P.O. Box 2799
500 College Dr., Whitehorse, YT Y1A 5K4, Canada
Tel: 867-668-8800; *Toll-Free:* 800-661-0504
www.yukoncollege.yk.ca
www.facebook.com/yukoncollege
www.twitter.com/yukoncollege
Karen Barnes, President & Vice-Chancellor
Jennifer Moorlag, Registrar
jmoorlag@yukoncollege.yk.ca
Gayle Corry, Director, Finance & Administrative Services
Brian Bonia, Director, Human Resources, 867-668-8787
bbonia@yukoncollege.yk.ca

Post Secondary/Technical

***Whitehorse:* Mile 918 Driver Development**
P.O. Box 322
Whitehorse, YT Y1A 1Y3
Tel: 867-667-6837; *Fax:* 867-668-2293
www.mile918driverdevelopment.ca
Note: Offers Class 1 and Class 3 Truck Driver Training, Air Brake Endorsement Courses, and Upgrade Training.

***Whitehorse:* Whitehorse Air Service**
40 Lodestar Lane, Whitehorse, YT Y1A 6E6
Tel: 867-456-2828; *Fax:* 867-668-6373
Note: Flying school offering courses in Commercial Pilot, Instructor Rating, Night Rating, Private Pilot, Recreational Pilot and VFR Over-The-Top Rating as outlined by Transport Canada.

Overseas Schools/Programs

***Bangladesh:* Dhaka District, Dhaka: Canadian International School**
200 Gulshan Ave. North, Gulshan - 2, Dhaka District, Dhaka, Bangladesh
info@canadaeducationbd.com
www.canadaeducationbd.com
Other Information: Phone: (+88) 02-881-3132 / (+88) 02-988-1231
Grades: 9 - 12; *Enrollment:* 200; *Note:* Manitoba curriculum.

***Bangladesh:* Gulshan-2, Dhaka: Canadian Trillinium School (CTS)**
House # 7, Road # 62, Gulshan-2, Dhaka, Bangladesh
contact@cts.edu.bd
www.cts.edu.bd
Other Information: Tel.: (+88) 02- 882-3958 / Fax: (+88) 02-882-3153
Grades: K - 12; *Note:* New Brunswick curriculum.

***Bermuda:* Hamilton: Mount Saint Agnes Academy**
19 Dundonald St. West, Hamilton, Bermuda
msaoffice@msa.bm
www.msa.bm
Other Information: Tel.: (+441) 292-4134 / Fax: (+441) 295-7265
Grades: K - 12; *Enrollment:* 362; *Note:* Alberta curriculum.

***Brazil:* Boa Viagem, Recife, PE: Colégio Santa Maria**
Rua Pe. Bernadino, Pessoa, 512, Boa Viagem, Recife, PE, Brazil
Other Information: Tel.: (+55) 51-020-210
Grades: K - 12; *Enrollment:* 25; *Note:* New Brunswick curriculum.

***Cambodia:* Chamkarmorn, Phnom Penh: Canadian International School of Phnom Penh**
Bassac Garden City, Preah Norodom Blvd.(41), Chamkarmorn, Phnom Penh, Cambodia
info@cisp.edu.kh
www.cisp.edu.kh
Other Information: Tel.: (+855) 23 727 788, / Fax: (+855) 23 727 766
www.facebook.com/CanadianInternationalSchoolOfPhnomPenh
Grades: K; *Enrollment:* 120; *Note:* New Brunswick curriculum.

Canada: Maple: Canadian College Italy - The Renaissance School
Canadian Head Office
59 Macamo Crt., Maple, ON L6A 1G1, Canada
Tel: 905-508-7108; *Fax:* 905-508-5480
Toll-Free: 800-422-0548
cciren@rogers.com
www.canadiancollegeitaly.com
Other Information: Int'l Phone: 39-(0872)-71-49-69; Fax: 39-(0872)-450-28
www.facebook.com/110636132290645
www.youtube.com/user/TheRenaissanceSchool
Grades: 9 - 12; *Enrollment:* 115; *Note:* Ontario curriculum. It is located at Via Cavour 13, Lanciano (CH), Italy 66034.

Canada: Vancouver: Maple Leaf Educational Systems
Vancouver Office
#400, 601 West Broadway, Vancouver, BC V5Z 4C2, Canada
Tel: 604-675-6910; *Fax:* 604-675-6911
info@mapleleafschools.com
www.mapleleafschools.com
Other Information: China Phone: 86-411-8790-6822; Fax: 86-411-8790-6811
www.linkedin.com/company/396267
Number of Schools: 24; *Grades:* Pre.-12; *Enrollment:* 10500; *Note:* Maple Leaf Educational Systems was founded in 1995, with the goal of blending Eastern & Western educational practices. Maple Leaf schools offer Canadian & Chinese accreditation & diplomas. The Chinese Office can be contacted at: Jinshitan National Holiday Resort, No. 9 Central St., Dalian, China 116650.

China: Wuhu, Anhui: Anhui Concord College of Sino-Canada (ACCSC)
Wanchunzhonglu, Chengdongxinqu, Wuhu, Anhui, China
www.accsc.com.cn
Grades: K - 12; *Enrollment:* 1000; *Note:* The Anhui Concord College of Sino-Canada [ACCSC] is a joint Canadian-Chinese boarding senior-high school. New Brunswick curriculum.

China: Beijing: Beijing Concord College of Sino-Canada (BCCSC)
Tongzhou District
Conglin, Zhuangyuan, Beijing, China
admissions@beijingccsc.com
www.ccsc.com.cn/english
Other Information: TEl.: (+86) 10 8959 1234 / Fax: (+86) 10 8959 9055
Grades: 10 - 12; *Enrollment:* 900; *Note:* New Brunswick curriculum.

China: Beijing: Beijing No. 25 Middle School
Dongcheng District
55 Dengshikou Dajie, Beijing, China
Other Information: Tel.: (+86) 010 65592140 ext 8212 / Fax: (+86) 010 65236510
Grades: 10 - 12; *Enrollment:* 108; *Note:* Nova Scotia curriculum.

China: Guangzhou, Guangdong Province: Huamei-Bond International College
Huamei Rd., Tianhe District, Guangzhou, Guangdong Province, China
wasdurhamsecondary@hotmail.com
www.hm163.com/englishvesion
Other Information: Phone: 020-87210372; Alternate Phone: 020-87210083
Grades: 9 - 12; *Note:* Ontario curriculum.

China: Jiangmen City: Boren Sino - Canadian School
65 Shuanglong Ave., Jiangmen City, China
academics@borenschool.com
en.borenschool.com
Other Information: Tel: 86 750 321 7848 / Fax: 86-750-321-9003
Grades: 9 - 12; *Note:* Ontario curriculum.
William D. Walter, Principal

China: Changchun City, Jilin Province: Canada Changchun Shiyi Secondary School
2666 Jingyang Da Lu, Changchun City, Jilin Province, China
normanxu_83@hotmail.com
www.cc11.net/canada/shownew.asp?46.html
Other Information: Phone: 0431-87662985 13204309767 18655182062
Grades: 10 - 12; *Enrollment:* 52; *Note:* British Columbia curriculum.

China: Haikou, Hainan Province: Canada Hainan Secondary School
Hainan ISIP Experimental School
Xiuying National High Tech Zone, Haikou, Hainan Province, China
www.canadahainanss.com
Other Information: Phone: 86-898-68612170; Fax: 86-898-68631818
Grades: Secondary; *Note:* Canada Hainan Secondary School is certified by the British Columbia Ministry of Education.
Chris Davidson, Canadian Principal
canvan123@yahoo.com
Yao Yuqin, Chinese Principal
susanyyq@163.com
Wu Yongxing, Foreign Affairs & External Liaison
della020@163.com
Brian Roodnick, Offshore Representative
roodnick@shaw.ca

China: Hefei, Anhui Province: Canada Hefei No. 1 Secondary School
2356 Xizang Road, Hefei, Anhui Province, China
www.hfbh.gov.cn/system/2008/10/17/002122263.shtml
Grades: 10 - 11; *Enrollment:* 153; *Note:* British Columbia curriculum.

China: Kunming, Yunnan Province: Canada Kunming No. 10 Secondary School
247 Baita Lu, Kunming, Yunnan Province, China
Grades: 10 - 12; *Enrollment:* 104; *Note:* British Columbia curriculum.

China: Langfang, Hebei Province: Canada Langfang Secondary School
350 Jianguo Road, Langfang, Hebei Province, China
Grades: 10 - 11; *Enrollment:* 78; *Note:* British Columbia curriculum.
Corri Gallicano, Principal
Rodger Lindstrom, Offshore Representative

China: New Territories, Hong Kong SAR: Renaissance College Hong Kong (RCHK)
5 Hang Ming St., New Territories, Hong Kong SAR, China
admissions@rchk.edu.hk
www.renaissance.edu.hk
Other Information: Phone: 852-3556-3556; Fax: 852-3556-3446
Harry Brown, Principal

China: Qingdao, Shandong Province: Canada Qingdao Secondary School
2 Yangxin Road, Shibei District, Qingdao, Shandong Province, China
Tel: 778-893-8566
info@cess.ca
www.csee.ca/18201.html
Grades: 10 - 11; *Enrollment:* 130; *Note:* British Columbia curriculum.

China: Tai'an, Shandong Province: Canada Shandong Secondary School
52 Wenhua Road, Tai'an, Shandong Province, China
Tel: 778-893-8566
info@cess.ca
www.csee.ca/14422.html
Grades: 10 - 12; *Enrollment:* 99; *Note:* British Columbia curriculum.

China: Weifang, Shandong Province: Canada Weifang No. 1 Secondary School
High Tech Zone
East Baotong St., Weifang, Shandong Province, China
www.csee.ca/9273.html
Grades: 10 - 12; *Enrollment:* 211; *Note:* British Columbia curriculum.

China: Zibo, Shandong Province: Canada Zibo No. 11 Secondary School
119 Liuquan Rd., Zhangdian District, Zibo, Shandong Province, China
www.zb11.net
Grades: 10 - 12; *Enrollment:* 103; *Note:* British Columbia curriculum.

China: Nanjing: Canadian International Academy of China
32 QingDao Rd., Nanjing, China
www.njisedu.cn
Other Information: Tel: 011-86-25-8320-8201; Fax: 011-86-25-8323-3866
Grades: 9 - 12; *Note:* Ontario curriculum.

China: Aberdeen, Hong Kong SAR: Canadian International School (Hong Kong)
36 Nam Long Shan Rd., Aberdeen, Hong Kong SAR, China
schoolinfo@cdnis.edu.hk
www.cdnis.edu.hk
Other Information: Phone: 011-852-2525-7088; Fax: 011-852-2525-7579
Grades: 9 - 12; *Enrollment:* 1332; *Note:* Ontario curriculum.

China: Beijing: Canadian International School of Beijing
38 Liangmaqiao, Lu Chaoyang District, Beijing, China
www.cisb.com.cn
Other Information: Phone: (+86) 10 6465 7788 / Fax: (+86) 10 6465 7788
Grades: K - 12; *Enrollment:* 1000; *Note:* New Brunswick curriculum.

China: Zhejiang Province, Wenzhou: Canadian Secondary Wenzhou No. 22 School
East Xueyuan Road, Zhejiang Province, Wenzhou, China
business_services@sd40.bc.ca
www.2ceducation.ca/#!wenzhou-no.-22-school
Other Information: Tel.: (+86) 577-88133357
Grades: 10-12; *Enrollment:* 73; *Note:* British Columbia curriculum.

China: Changchun, Jilin Province: Changchun Experimental High School
Jingyue Development Zone
2002 Fuzhi Road, Changchun, Jilin Province, China
Other Information: Tel.: (+86) 431 86801086 / Fax: (+86) 431 86801559
Grades: 10 - 12; *Enrollment:* 64; *Note:* Nova Scotia curriculum.

China: Chengdu, Sichuan Province: Chengdu Foreign Language School
High-tech West Zone
Yangxi Xian, Chengdu, Sichuan Province, China
www.cfls.net.cn
Other Information: Tel.: (+86) 2887820291
Grades: 10 - 12; *Enrollment:* 80; *Note:* Nova Scotia curriculum.

China: Kowloon City, Hong Kong SAR: Christian Alliance P.C. Lau Memorial International School (CAIS)
2 Fu Ning St., Kowloon City, Hong Kong SAR, China
info@cais.edu.hk
www.cais.edu.hk
Other Information: Phone: 852-2713-3733; Fax: 852-2760-4324
www.facebook.com/CAIS.HK
Grades: 10 - 12; *Enrollment:* 112; *Note:* Alberta curriculum.

Campuses
Lai Yiu Campus
Lai Yiu Estate
Wah Yiu Rd., Lai King, New Territories
lyoffice@cais.edu.hk
Other Information: Phone: 852-2778-3370; Fax: 852-2778-3326
Grades: K.-3

China: Guangzhou, Guangdong Province: Clifford School
Also known as: Clifford Experimental School
Clifford Estates
8 Shiguang Road, Clifford Estates Panyu, Guangzhou, Guangdong Province, China
international@clifford-school.org.cn
www.clifford-school.cn
Other Information: Phones: 86-20-8471-1441, 86-20-3477-4263
Grades: 1 - 12; *Enrollment:* 510; *Note:* Manitoba curriculum.

China: Quarry Bay, Hong Kong SAR: Delia School of Canada
Tai Fung Rd., Taikoo Shing, Quarry Bay, Hong Kong SAR, China
e.office@delia.edu.hk
www.delia.edu.hk
Other Information: Tel.: 852 2884 4165 / Fax: 852 2885 7824
Grades: 9 - 12; *Note:* Ontario curriculum.

Campuses
Secondary Section
Tai Fung Rd., Taikoo Shing, Quarry Bay, Hong Kong
Tel: 365-803-38; *Fax:* 288-578-24
s.office@delia.edu.hk
Grades: 7-12
P. Farrell, Head Teacher, Secondary Section

China: Guangzhou, Guangzhou Province: English School attached Guangdong University of Foreign Studies
599, Guanghua One, Dalang, Baiyun District, Guangzhou, Guangzhou Province, China
www.gwdwx.com/html/english/200703/intr/intr.html
Other Information: Tel.: (+86) 20 36276450 / Fax: (+86) 20 86074697
Grades: 10 - 12; *Enrollment:* 172; *Note:* Nova Scotia curriculum.

China: Ganzhou, Jiangxi: Ganzhou No. 3 Middle School (China)
30 Youth Rd., Ganzhou, Jiangxi, China
Other Information: Tel.: 0797-8200020 / Fax: 0797-8238816
Note: Prince Edward Island curriculum.

China: Tongxiang, Zhejiang Province: Grand Canadian Academy (Jiaxing) (GCA)
c/o Maodun High School (Tongxiang)
288 Zhenxing Donglu, Tongxiang, Zhejiang Province, China
www.gcahighschool.ca/jiaxing
Other Information: Phone & Fax: 573-8810-7576; Alt. Phone: 573-8810-7658
Grades: 9 - 12; *Enrollment:* 139; *Note:* British Columbia curriculum.

China: Guiyang, Guizhou: Guiyang Concord College of Sino-Canada (GCCSC)
Jinzhu West Rd., New World Terrace, Guanshan lake D, Guiyang, Guizhou, China
zsb@ccsc.com.cn
www.giccsc.com/english/index.aspx
Other Information: Tel.: (+86) 851-221-8058 / Fax: (+86) 400-659-8882
Grades: 1 - 12; *Note:* New Brunswick curriculum.

China: Guiyang, Guizhou Province: Guiyang No. 1 High School
1 Xingzhu East Road, Jinyang New District, Guiyang, Guizhou Province, China
Other Information: Tel.: (+86) 851 798 6168 / Fax: (+86) 851 798 6565
Grades: 10 - 12; *Enrollment:* 94; *Note:* Nova Scotia curriculum.

China: Harbin, Heilongjiang: Harbin Shenghengji Concord College of Sino-Canada (HSCCSC)
1357 Longzing Rd., Songbei District, Harbin, Heilongjiang, China
Other Information: Tel.: (+86) 451-8588-8599
Grades: 1 - 2, 5; *Note:* New Brunswick curriculum.

China: Zhengzhou, Henan Province: Henan Experimental High School
60 Wenhua Rd., Zhengzhou, Henan Province, China
Other Information: Tel.: (+86) 371 63913063 / Fax: (+86) 0242-3784954
Grades: 10 - 12; *Enrollment:* 586; *Note:* Nova Scotia curriculum.

China: Changsha, Hunan: Hunan Concord College of Sino-Canada (HCCSC)
99 jingyuan Rd., Yeulu District, Changsha, Hunan, China
www.hccsc.com.cn/EN/about.asp
Other Information: Tel.: (+86) 731-8299-1111
Grades: K - 12; *Note:* New Brunswick curriculum.

China: Shenzhen, Guangdong: International School of Nanshan Shenzhen (ISNS)
166 Nanguang Rd., Nanshan District, Shenzhen, Guangdong, China
www.isnsz.com
Other Information: Tel.: (+86) 755 2666-1000 / Fax: (+86) (755) 2645-4090
Grades: K - 12; *Enrollment:* 300; *Note:* New Brunswick curriculum.

China: Jiaxing City, Zhejiang Province: Jiaxing Senior High School
365 Hongyin Rd., Jiaxing City, Zhejiang Province, China
Grades: 10 - 12; *Enrollment:* 53; *Note:* British Columbia curriculum.

China: Jilin City, Jilin Province: Jilin No. 1 High School
155 Song Jiang West Rd., Jilin City, Jilin Province, China
Other Information: Tel.: (+86) 432 64852111 / Fax: (+86) 043 24826017
Grades: 10 - 12; *Enrollment:* 91; *Note:* Nova Scotia curriculum.

China: Karamay, Xin Jiang: Karamay Senior High School
58 Zhun Ge Er St., Karamay, Xin Jiang, China
Other Information: Tel.: (+86) 990 6236538
Grades: 10 - 12; *Enrollment:* 72; *Note:* Nova Scotia curriculum.

China: Luoyang, Henan Province: Luoyang No. 1 High School (East Campus)
1 Shuanglang St., Chenhe District, Luoyang, Henan Province, China
Other Information: Tel.: (+86) 186 2375 8712
Grades: 10 - 12; *Enrollment:* 58; *Note:* Nova Scotia curriculum.

China: Shanghai, Huangpu District: Luwan Senior High School
885 Xietu Rd., Shanghai, Huangpu District, China
Grades: 10 - 12; *Enrollment:* 85; *Note:* British Columbia curriculum.

China: Dalian, Liaoning Province: Maple Leaf Foreign Nationals School - Dalian
30 Gaoyan St., Zhongshan District, Dalian, Liaoning Province, China
mapleleafschools.com/ML_Dalian_Foreign_Nationals
Other Information: Phone: (+86) 4080-6301
Grades: K-9; *Enrollment:* 153; *Note:* British Columbia curriculum.

China: Wuhan, Hubei Province: Maple Leaf Foreign Nationals School - Wuhan
East Lake Hi-Tech Development Zone
1018 Minzu Ave., Wuhan, Hubei Province, China
info@mapleleafschools.com
www.mapleleafschools.com/ML_Wuhan_Foreign_Nationals
Other Information: Phone: 86-027-8192-5705; Fax: 86-027-8192-5704
Grades: 1 - 9; *Enrollment:* 26; *Note:* British Columbia curriculum.
Darrell Goss, Principal
dgoss@mapleleaf.net.ca
George Watson, Superintendent, BC Program, 604-675-6910
georgewatson.mapleleaf@gmail.com

China: Zhenjiang, Jiangsu Province: Maple Leaf International High School - Zhenjiang
Dagang High School, South Campus
Zhaosheng Road, Dagang Count, Zhenjiang, Jiangsu Province, China
www.mapleleafschools.com/schools/zhenjiang/
Other Information: Tel.: (+86) 4080-6301
Grades: 10 - 11; *Enrollment:* 130; *Note:* British Columbia curriculum.

China: Chongqing, Jiangsu Province: Maple Leaf International School - Chongqing
#1 Maple Leaf Rd., Chongqing, Jiangsu Province, China
www.mapleleafschools.com/schools/chongqing/
Other Information: Phone: (+86) 4080-6301 / Fax: (+86) 411-8790-0569
Grades: 10 - 12; *Enrollment:* 376; *Note:* British Columbia curriculum.

China: Dongguan, Guangdong: Mensa Kindergarten of Dongguan, Hou Jie Town
13 New Hou Sha Road, Chong Kou Village, Hou Jie, Dongguan, Guangdong, China
Other Information: Tel.: (86-769) 81525999 / Fax: (86-769) 81525222
Grades: K; *Enrollment:* 250; *Note:* New Brunswick curriculum.

China: Shijiazhuang City, Hebei Province: Middle School attached to Hebei Normal University - Shijiazhuang
315 Zhongshan East Rd., Shijiazhuang City, Hebei Provin, China
Other Information: Tel. (+86) 311 86060090
Grades: 10 - 12; *Enrollment:* 75; *Note:* Nova Scotia curriculum.

China: Nanchang, Jiangxi Province: Nanchang No. 2 High School
Honggutan, New District, Nanchang, Jiangxi Province, China
Other Information: Tel.: (+86) 791 31155 / Fax: (+86) 0791 3839518
Grades: 10 - 12; *Note:* Nova Scotia curriculum.

China: Nanjing, Jiangsu Province: Nanjing Foreign Language School British Columbia Academy (NFLS BC)
30 East Beijing Rd., Nanjing, Jiangsu Province, China
Grades: 10 - 12; *Enrollment:* 301; *Note:* British Columbia curriculum.

China: Nanjing, Jiangsu Province: Nanjing-Bond International College
Nanjing No. 13 High School
#14, Xijia Datang, Xuanwu District, Nanjing, Jiangsu Province, China
bond13z@yahoo.com.cn
bond.nj13z.cn
Other Information: Phone: 011-86-25-8326-9911; Fax: 011-86-25-8326-9927
Grades: 9 - 12; *Note:* Ontario curriculum.

China: Shenzhen, Guangdong Province: Oxstand-Bond International College
2040 Buxin Rd., Luohu District, Shenzhen, Guangdong Province, China
enquiry@oxstand.com.cn
oxstand.com.cn/ciep/index.html
Other Information: Phone: 011-86-755-2581-4853; Fax: 011-86-755-2581-3921
Grades: 9 - 12; *Note:* Ontario curriculum.

China: Xuhui District, Shanghai: Shanghai Nanyang Model High School
453 Lingling Rd., Xuhui District, Shanghai, China
www.shqj.com.cn/english.php?app=index&mod=imgdetails&id=94
Other Information: Tel.: (+86) 21 628 25748 / Fax: (+86) 21 628 26734
Grades: 10 - 12; *Enrollment:* 274; *Note:* British Columbia curriculum.

China: Minhang District, Shanghai: Shanghai United International School (SUIS)
55 Wan Yuan Rd., Minhang District, Shanghai, China
www.suis.com.cn
Other Information: Tel.: (+974) 5531-7348
Grades: 10 - 12; *Enrollment:* 257; *Note:* British Columbia curriculum.

China: Shenyang, Liaoning Province: Shenyang No. 2 High School (North Campus)
198 Shenbei Rd., Shenbei New District, Shenyang, Liaoning Province, China
Other Information: Tel.: (+86) 24 88043982 / Fax: (+86) 24 88041208
Grades: 10 - 12; *Enrollment:* 263; *Note:* Nova Scotia curriculum.

China: Nanshan District, Shenzhen, Gua: Shenzhen (Nanshan) Concord College of Sino-Canada (SCCSC)
166 Nanguang Rd., Nanshan District, Shenzhen, Gua, China
www.ccsc.cn/english.htm
Other Information: Tel.: (+86) 755 2656 8887 / Fax: (+86) 755 2657 8890
Grades: 10 - 12; *Enrollment:* 900; *Note:* New Brunswick curriculum.

China: Kaifeng City, Henan Province: Sino Bright School - Kaifeng
18th, SBS, No. 5, Jianguomenbei St. DongCheng, Kaifeng City, Henan Province, China
www.schoolbj.com
Other Information: Phone: 10-65537171; 10-65538727
Grades: 11; *Enrollment:* 145; *Note:* British Columbia curriculum.

China: Dongcheng District, Beijing, Fe: Sino Bright School No. 8
#1803, No. 5 Jianguomen North St., Dongcheng District, Beijing, Fe, China
www.schoolbj.com
Other Information: Tel.: (+86) 10-6553-8727 / Fax: (+86) 10-6553-7171
Grades: 12; *Enrollment:* 159; *Note:* British Columbia curriculum.

China: Wujiang City, Suzhou, Jiangsu P: Sino-Canada High School
Economic Development Zone
#1 Liannan Road Fen Hu, Wujiang City, Suzhou, Jiangsu P, China
www.sinocanadahighschool.com
Other Information: Phone: (+86) 512-6326-2288 / Fax: (+86) 12-632-62255
Grades: 10-12; *Enrollment:* 712; *Note:* British Columbia curriculum.

China: Suzhou, Jiangsu Province: Soochow University High School - Canadian Program
Suzhou Industrial Park
29 Dongzhen Rd., Suzhou, Jiangsu Province, China
Other Information: Tel.: (+86) 512 62526572 / Fax: (+86) 512 6758-1981
Grades: 10 - 12; *Enrollment:* 131; *Note:* Nova Scotia curriculum.

***China:* Jiangsu: Suzhou Industrial Park Foreign Language School**
Suzhou Industrial Park
89 Zhongnan St., Jiangsu, China
english.sfls.com.cn/contactus.aspx?channelid=8
Other Information: Tel.: (+86) 182-4889-9470
Grades: 10 - 12; *Enrollment:* 138; *Note:* British Columbia curriculum.

***China:* Lubei District, Tangshan, Hebei: Tangshan No. 1 High School**
369 Xiangyun Rd., Lubei District, Tangshan, Hebei, China
Other Information: Tel.: (+86) 315-259-5008 / Fax: (+86) 315-259-5008
Grades: 10 - 12; *Enrollment:* 224; *Note:* Nova Scotia curriculum.

***China:* Tongchuan, Shaanxi Province: Tongchuan No. 1 High School**
Chaoyang Road 10 New District Tongchuan, Tongchuan, Shaanxi Province, China
Other Information: Tel.: (+86) 919 3198121 / Fax: (+86) 919 3589821
Grades: 10 - 12; *Enrollment:* 28; *Note:* Nova Scotia curriculum.

***China:* Shenzhen, Guangdong Province: Tsinghua Experimental School (Shenzhen)**
Taoyuanju Qianjin Road, Baoan District, Shenzhen, Guangdong Province, China
Other Information: Tel.: (+86) 755 27452062 / Fax: (+86) 755 27451436
Grades: 10 - 12; *Enrollment:* 82; *Note:* Nova Scotia curriculum.

***China:* Shanghai, Baoshan District: Wusong Shanghai BC High School (WSBC)**
99 Tai He Road, Shanghai, Baoshan District, China
Grades: 10; *Enrollment:* 61; *Note:* British Columbia curriculum.

***China:* Xingtai, Hebei Province: Xingtai No. 1 High School**
118 Zhonghua dajie, Qiaoxi District, Xingtai, Hebei Province, China
Other Information: Tel.: (+86) 319 2217529 / Fax: (+86) 319 2222356
Grades: 10 - 12; *Enrollment:* 57; *Note:* Nova Scotia curriculum.

***China:* Yizhuang, Beijing: Yang Guang Qing International School of Beijing**
Beijing Economic & Development Zone
2 Tian Bao North St., Yizhuang, Beijing, China
bjetownschool@gmail.com
www.bdaschool.com
Other Information: Phone: 010-67872277; Fax: 010-67871129
Grades: 10 - 12; *Enrollment:* 127; *Note:* Manitoba curriculum.

***China:* WuQing District, Tianjin: Yinghua-Bond International College**
Yong Yang West Rd., WuQing District, Tianjin, China
www.tjyh2003.com/english/index.asp
Other Information: Phone: 011-86-22-5961-1023; Fax: 011-86-22-5961-1166
Grades: 9 - 12; *Note:* Ontario curriculum.

***Colombia:* La Estrella, Antioquia: Colegio Canadiense**
Cra 51 #97 Sur 137, La Estrella, Antioquia, Colombia
www.colegiocanadiense.edu.co
Other Information: Tel.: (+57) 300 530 5309
Grades: K - 12; *Enrollment:* 64; *Note:* British Columbia curriculum.

***Egypt:* El Sherouk City, Cairo: British Columbia Canadian International School (BCCIS)**
P.O. Box 11519/98
5th Settlement Section, 34 Suez Rd. Entrance, El Sherouk City, Cairo, Egypt
www.bccis.net
Other Information: Tel.: 01002128112; Fax: (202) 26300445
Grades: K - 12; *Enrollment:* 450; *Note:* British Columbia curriculum.

***Egypt:* Zone 4, New Greater Cairo: Canadian International School of Egypt**
El Tagamosa El Khames, Zone 4, New Greater Cairo, Egypt
cise-egypt.com
Other Information: Phone: 011-202-010-4482; Fax: 011-202-617-4500
Grades: 9 - 12; *Note:* Ontario curriculum.
Melanie Seifert, Principal
mseifert@cise-eg.com

***Egypt:* 6th of October City, Giza: Heritage International School**
Al-Yasmine Greenland, Second Touristic Village
P.O. Box 38
6th of October City, Giza, Egypt
info@heritageinternationalschool.com
www.heritageinternationalschool.com
Other Information: Phone: 202-38377251/2/4; Fax: 202-38377253
www.facebook.com/218640688193402
twitter.com/heritageegypt
Grades: K-12; *Enrollment:* 468; *Note:* Manitoba curriculum.

***Ghana:* Accra: Canadian Independent College of Ghana (CIC)**
Airport Residential Area
#Z-26 Patrice Lumumba Rd., Accra, Ghana
ghana@cicbaden.ca
www.ghanacic.com
Other Information: Phone: 233-302-760-571
www.facebook.com/GhanaCIC
twitter.com/GhanaCIC
Grades: Pre.-Sec.; *Note:* Manitoba curriculum.
Dr. Heather Bohez, B.Sc., N.D., Director
Donna Everitt, Coordinator, International Education, 204-945-1126

***India:* Bangalore: Canadian International School**
4&20 Manchenahalli, Yelahanka, Bangalore, India
info@cisb.org.in
www.canadianinternationalschool.com
Other Information: Tel.: +91 80 4249 4444
www.facebook.com/283666374991307
twitter.com/cisbweb
www.youtube.com/user/cisbindia
Grades: K - 12; *Enrollment:* 212; *Note:* Provides a learning experience to mainly expatriate and Indian students, representing over 25 nationalities. The school is accredited by the International Baccalaureate Organization and Ontario Ministry of Education, and is a member of the Council of International Schools.
Brian Tinker, Principal

***Japan:* Tokyo: Canadian International School (Japan)**
5-8-20 Kitashinagawa, Shinagawa-ku, Tokyo, Japan
study@cisjapan.net
cisjapan.net
Other Information: Phone: 03-5793-1392; Fax: 03-5793-3559
Grades: K - 12; *Enrollment:* 273; *Note:* Prince Edward Island curriculum.

***Japan:* Saitama, Tokyo: Columbia International School of Japan**
153 Matsugo, Tokorozawa, Saitama, Tokyo, Japan
Tel: 042-946-1911; *Fax:* 042-946-1955
office@columbia-ca.co.jp
columbia-ca.co.jp
Grades: 9 - 12; *Enrollment:* 280; *Note:* Ontario curriculum.

***Japan:* Tosa City, Kochi Prefecture: Meitoku Gijuku School**
Ryu Campus
564 Ryu Usa Cho, Tosa City, Kochi Prefecture, Japan
info@meitoku-gijuku.ed.jp
www.meitoku-gijuku.ed.jp
Other Information: Phone: 088-828-6688; Fax: 088-856-3060
Grades: 11; *Enrollment:* 5; *Note:* Manitoba curriculum.

***Macao:* Taipa: The International School of Macao (TIS)**
Block K, Macau University of Science & Technology
Avenida Wai Long, Taipa, Macao
tis@tis.edu.mo
www.tis.edu.mo
Other Information: Phone: 853-2853-3700; Fax: 853-2853-3702
www.facebook.com/117917438263544
Grades: 7 - 12; *Enrollment:* 809; *Note:* Alberta curriculum.

***Malaysia:* Petaling Jaya, Selangor: Sunway College (Canadian International Matriculation Programme)**
#3 Jalan Universiti, Jalan Kolej, Bandar Sunway, Petaling Jaya, Selangor, Malaysia
infosis@sunway.edu.my
www.sis.sunway.edu.my
Other Information: Phone: 011-603-7491-8623, ext. 8124; Fax: 011-603-5635-8630
Grades: 9 - 12; *Note:* Ontario curriculum.

***Malaysia:* Selangor: Taylor's College International Canadian Pre-University**
No. 1, Jalan SS15/8, 47500 Subang Jaya, Selangor, Malaysia
admission@taylors.edu.my
www.taylors.edu.my/en/college/programmes/pre-u/cpu
Other Information: Phone: 603-5636-2641; Fax: 603-5634-5209
www.facebook.com/166519953397649
www.youtube.com/user/taylorspreu
Grades: 9 - 12; *Enrollment:* 490; *Note:* Ontario curriculum.

***Mexico:* Acueducto Providencia, Guadalaj: Canadian School Guadalajara**
Montevideo 3306, Acueducto Providencia, Guadalaj, Mexico
www.canadianschool.com.mx
Other Information: Phones: 3610-17-06; 3641-64-52
www.facebook.com/176388335730456
Grades: K - 2; *Enrollment:* 132; *Note:* Alberta curriculum.

***Netherlands:* Brunssum: AFNORTH International School in the Netherlands**
Ferdinand Bolstraat 1, Brunssum, Netherlands
directorate@afnorth-is.com
www.afnorth-is.com
Other Information: Tel.: 31 45 527 8200 / Fax: 31 45 527 8277
twitter.com/AFNORTH_IS
Grades: 9 - 12; *Enrollment:* 900; *Note:* Institution offers programs following the curriculum of Ontario.

***Netherlands Antilles:* St. Maarten: Caribbean International Academy (CIA)**
P.O. Box 5454
Cupecoy, Tigris Rd., #4, Simpson Bay, St. Maarten, Netherlands Antilles
admission@carib-international.net
www.carib-international.net
Other Information: Phone: 011-721-545-3871; Fax: 011-721-545-3872
Grades: 9 - 12; *Note:* Ontario curriculum.

***Qatar:* Doha, Muaither: Hayat Universal School Qatar (HUBS)**
Muaither Bldg. 55, Area 53
P.O. Box 6124
Muaither St. North, Doha, Muaither, Qatar
info.qa@hayatschool.com
www.hayatschool.com
Other Information: Phone: 4468-7171; Fax: 4469-3352
Grades: K - 6; *Enrollment:* 773; *Note:* British Columbia curriculum.

***Qatar:* Doha: Qatar Canadian School (QCS)**
P.O. Box 24359
Doha, Qatar
qcs@cna-qatar.edu.qa
www.qcs.edu.qa
Other Information: Phone: 974-4421-7553/4; Fax: 974-4421-7556
Grades: K - 12; *Enrollment:* 264; *Note:* Alberta curriculum.

***Saint Lucia:* Rodney Bay: International School of St. Lucia (ISSL)**
P.O. Box 2407
Rodney Bay, Saint Lucia
internationalschoolstlucia@gmail.com
www.intschoolstlucia.org
Other Information: Tel.: (+758) 458 0989
Grades: 10 - 12; *Enrollment:* 50; *Note:* New Brunswick curriculum.

***Singapore:* Singapore: Canadian International School (Singapore)**
7 Jurong West St. 41, Singapore, Singapore
www.cis.edu.sg
Other Information: Phone: 65-6467-1732; Fax: 65-6467-1729
www.facebook.com/CIS.edu.sg
twitter.com/cissingapore
Number of Schools: 2; *Grades:* 9 - 12; *Enrollment:* 2500; *Note:* Ontario curriculum.

Campuses
Tanjong Katong Campus
371 Tanjong Katong Rd., Singapore 437128, Singapore
Other Information: Phone: 65-6345-1573; Fax: 65-6345-4057

***South Korea:* Seoul, Seocho-Dong: BC Collegiate Canada**
1449-9 Seocho-gu, Seoul, Seocho-Dong, South Korea
www.bccanada.net
Other Information: Tel.: 02)2135-2011 / Fax: 214-81-57057
www.facebook.com/pages/BC-Collegiate-Canada/14913566182 1651
twitter.com/BCA_Canada

Grades: K - 8; *Enrollment:* 267; *Note:* British Columbia curriculum.

South Korea: Gyeonggi-do: BIS Canada
200 Gumgok-dong, Seongnam-Si, Gyeonggi-do, South Korea
info@biscanada.org
www.biscanada.org
Other Information: Phone: 031-8022-7114; Fax: 031-8022-7115
Grades: K - 10; *Enrollment:* 300; *Note:* British Columbia curriculum.

South Korea: Gangdong-gu, Seoul: Canada BC International School (CBIS)
440 - 1 and 440- 11 Amsa-dong, Gangdong-gu, Seoul, South Korea
admin@cbis.or.kr
www.cbis.or.kr
Other Information: Phone: 02-6925-5430-1
Grades: K - 9; *Enrollment:* 112; *Note:* British Columbia curriculum.

South Korea: Nam-Gu, Incheon: Canada Maple International School (CMIS)
400-1 Mun-hak Dong, Nam-Gu, Incheon, South Korea
Tel: 032-715-8000; *Fax:* 032-715-8080
info@cmis.kr
www.cmis.kr
Other Information: Phone: (+82) 032-715-8000 / Fax: (+82) 032-715-8080
www.facebook.com/271476482896372
cafe.naver.com/cmis.cafe
Grades: K - 12; *Enrollment:* 142; *Note:* Manitoba curriculum.

South Korea: Sokcho, Gangwondo Province: SIS Canada (CISS)
#802, 38 Gyodong, Sokcho, Gangwondo Province, South Korea
ciss.kr
Other Information: Phone: 82-33-637-8817; Fax: 82-33-637-8815
twitter.com/siscanada2
blog.naver.com/sis8817
Grades: 1 - 11; *Enrollment:* 69; *Note:* British Columbia curriculum.

South Korea: Gwacheon-Si, Kyunggi-Do: Westminster Canadian Academy
Dolmugaegil #50, Gwacheon-Si, Kyunggi-Do, South Korea
Grades: K - 8; *Enrollment:* 44; *Note:* British Columbia curriculum.

Switzerland: Neuchâtel: Neuchâtel Junior College
Crêt-Taconnet, 4, Neuchâtel, Switzerland
admissions@neuchatel.org
www.njc.ch/school
Other Information: Tel.: 41-32-722-1860 / Fax: 41-32-722-1869
www.facebook.com/neuchateljuniorcollege
twitter.com/njcsuisse
www.linkedin.com/company/neuch-tel-junior-college
www.youtube.com/user/NJCNeuchatel
Grades: 12 & AP; *Enrollment:* 90; *Note:* Ontario curriculum.

Affiliations
Canadian Head Office
#1310, 44 Victoria St., Toronto, ON M5C 1Y2
Tel: 416-368-8169; *Fax:* 416-368-0956
Toll-Free: 800-263-2923
Note: The Canadian Head Office is responsible for admissions, alumni publications, events & records, & fundraising.
Dale Leishman, Director, Canadian Operations
dleishman@neuchatel.org
Brenda Neil, Director, Admission
admissions@neuchatel.org
Barbara Sutton, Director, Advancement
advancement@neuchatel.org

Thailand: Phasicharoen, Bangkok: British Columbia International School, Bangkok (BCISB)
606 Kalaprapruek Rd., Bangwar, Phasicharoen, Bangkok, Thailand
www.bcisb.net
Other Information: Phone: 662-802-1188, 802-2550; Fax: 662-802-2551, 802-1055#0
www.facebook.com/169194296453823
twitter.com/bcisb
Grades: 10 - 12; *Enrollment:* 30; *Note:* British Columbia curriculum.

Thailand: Nongkhaem District, Bangkok: Lertlah Schools
45, Soi Phetkasem 77, Nongkangploo, Nongkhaem District, Bangkok, Thailand
information@lertlah.com
www.lertlah.com
Other Information: Phone: 02-809-9081-5; Fax: 02-809-9898
www.facebook.com/LertlahGrapeSEED
Number of Schools: 3; *Grades:* K - 9; *Enrollment:* 1038; *Number of Employees:* 300; *Note:* Manitoba curriculum.
Seri Parndejpong, School Director
seri@lertlah.com

Trinidad: Petit Valley: Maple Leaf International School - Trinidad & Tobago
Alyce Heights Dr., Alyce Glen, Petit Valley, Trinidad
Tel: 868-632-9578
mlis@mapleleaf-school.com
www.mapleleaf-school.com
Other Information: Alternate Phone: 868-633-3173
Grades: 9 - 12; *Enrollment:* 350; *Note:* Ontario curriculum.
William Hargreaves, Principal
Al Tatem, Ontario Agent
altat@rogers.com
Michele Riley, BA, BEd, MEd, Vice President
Amanda Shaw, Manager, Finance & Operations
Marie Schuler, Coordinator, Academic Services & Admissions
Michelle Charles, BA, BEd, MEd, MTS, Coordinator, Academic Services & Admissions

Trinidad & Tobago: Chaguanas: Trillium International School
Liberty Centre
Hakim Juman St., Chaguanas, Trinidad & Tobago
Tel: 868-665-2641
trillium@tstt.net.tt
www.trilliumtt.com
Grades: 9 - 12; *Note:* Ontario curriculum.

United Arab Emirates: Abu Dhabi: Abu Dhabi Grammar School (Canada)
Tourist Club Area
P.O. Box 27161
Abu Dhabi, United Arab Emirates
ami@staff.ednet.ns.ca
www.agsgrmmr.sch.ae
Other Information: Tel.: (+971) 2 644 4703 / Fax: (+971) 2 645 4703
Grades: K - 12; *Enrollment:* 925; *Note:* Institution offers programs following the curriculum of Nova Scotia.

United Arab Emirates: Abu Dhabi: Canadian International School (Abu Dhabi) (CIS)
P.O. Box 3976
Khalifa A City, Abu Dhabi, United Arab Emirates
admin@cisabudhabi.com
www.cisabudhabi.com
Other Information: Phone: 971-2-556-4206; Fax: 971-2-556-4207
Grades: K-12; *Enrollment:* 550; *Note:* Alberta curriculum.

SECTION 7
GOVERNMENT: FEDERAL & PROVINCIAL

Listings in this section are as current as possible at the time of publication. For appointments made and results of elections held after publication, please refer to Canada's Information Resource Centre (CIRC), if your library subscribes to this online database.

Government Quick Reference Guide

ABORIGINAL AFFAIRS

Canadian Heritage, 15 Eddy St., Gatineau, QC K1A 0M5
819-997-0055, 866-811-0055,
PCH.info-info.PCH@canada.ca

Canadian Northern Economic Development Agency, Ottawa, ON K1A 0H4
855-897-2667, InfoNorth@CanNor.gc.ca

First Nations Tax Commission, #321, 345 Chief Alex Thomas Way, Kamloops, BC V2H 1H1
250-828-9857, Fax: 250-828-9858, 855-682-3682,
mailkamloops@fntc.ca

Indigenous & Northern Affairs, Terrasses de la Chaudière, 10 Wellington St., North Tower, Gatineau, QC K1A 0H4
Fax: 866-817-3977, 800-567-9604,
infopubs@aadnc-aandc.gc.ca

National Aboriginal Initiative, #750, 175 Hargrave St., Winnipeg, MA RC3 3R8
204-983-2189, Fax: 204-983-6132, 866-772-4880

Office of Intergovernmental Affairs, c/o Privy Council Office, #1000, 85 Slater St., Ottawa, ON K1A 0A3
613-957-5153, Fax: 613-957-5043, info@pco-bcp.gc.ca

Specific Claims Tribunal Canada, #400, 427 Laurier Ave. West, 4th Fl., PO Box 31, Ottawa, ON K1R 7Y2
613-947-0751, Fax: 613-943-0586,
claims.revendications@sct-trp.ca

Alberta

Alberta Indigenous Relations, Commerce Place, 10155 - 102 St. NW, 19th Fl., Edmonton, AB T5J 4G8
780-427-8407, Fax: 780-427-4019, -310-000

British Columbia

British Columbia Ministry of Aboriginal Relations & Reconciliation, 2957 Jutland Rd., PO Box 9100 Prov Govt, Victoria, BC V8W 9B1
250-387-6121, 800-663-7867, abrinfo@gov.bc.ca

British Columbia Treaty Commission, #700, 1111 Melville St., Vancouver, BC V6E 3V6
604-482-9200, Fax: 604-482-9222, 855-482-9200,
info@bctreaty.net

Native Economic Development Advisory Board, PO Box 9100 Prov Govt, Victoria, BC V8W 9B1
250-387-2536

Manitoba

Aboriginal Affairs Secretariat, #200, 500 Portage Ave., Winnipeg, MB R3C 3X1
204-945-2510, Fax: 204-945-3689

Manitoba Indigenous & Municipal Relations, Legislative Bldg, #344, 450 Broadway, Winnipeg, MB R3C OV8
204-945-3719, Fax: 204-945-8374, anaweb@gov.mb.ca

New Brunswick

Aboriginal Affairs Secretariat, Kings Place, #237, 440 King St., PO Box 6000, Fredericton, NB E3B 5H8
506-462-5177, Fax: 506-444-5142,
aboriginalaffairssecretariat@gnb.ca

Newfoundland & Labrador

Labrador & Aboriginal Affairs Office, Labrador Affairs, 21 Broomfield St., PO Box 3014, Happy Valley - Goose Bay, NL A0P 1E0
709-896-1780, Fax: 709-896-0045, 888-435-8111,
laa@gov.nl.ca

Northwest Territories

Northwest Territories Department of Aboriginal Affairs & Intergovernmental Relations, 4910 - 52nd St., PO Box 1320, Yellowknife, NT X1A 2L9
867-767-9025, Fax: 867-873-0233

Northwest Territories Department of Lands, Gallery Bldg., 4923 - 52nd St., 1st & 2nd Fl., PO Box 1320, Yellowknife, NT X1A 2L9
867-767-9185, Fax: 867-669-0905, NWTLands@gov.nt.ca

Nova Scotia

Office of Aboriginal Affairs, 5251 Duke St., 5th Fl., PO Box 1617, Halifax, NS B3J 2Y3
902-424-7409, Fax: 902-424-4225, oaa@gov.ns.ca

Nunavut

Nunavut Territory Department of Culture & Heritage, PO Box 1000 800, Iqaluit, NU X0A 0H0
867-975-5500, Fax: 867-975-5504, 866-934-2035

Ontario

Ontario Ministry of Indigenous Relations & Reconciliation, 160 Bloor St. East, 4th Fl., Toronto, ON M7A 2E6
416-326-4740, Fax: 416-326-4017, 866-381-5337

Québec

Secrétariat aux affaires autochtones, 905, av Honoré-Mercier, 1er étage, Québec, QC G1R 5M6
418-643-3166, Fax: 418-646-4918

Saskatchewan

Office of the Provincial Interlocutor, #210, 1855 Victoria Ave., Regina, SK S4P 3T2
306-798-0183, Fax: 306-787-5832, interlocutor@gov.sk.ca

Saskatchewan Government Relations, 1855 Victoria Ave., Regina, SK S4P 3T2
306-787-8885

ACTS & REGULATIONS

Justice Canada, East Memorial Bldg., 284 Wellington St., Ottawa, ON K1A 0H8
613-957-4222, Fax: 613-954-0811, webadmin@justice.gc.ca

Office of the Administrator of the Ship-source Oil Pollution Fund, #830, 180 Kent St., Ottawa, ON K1A 0N5
613-991-1726, Fax: 613-990-5423, info@sopf-cidphn.gc.ca

Office of the Senate Ethics Officer, Thomas D'Arcy McGee Bldg., #526, 90 Sparks St., Ottawa, ON K1P 5B4
613-947-3566, Fax: 613-947-3577, 800-267-7362,
cse-seo@sen.parl.gc.ca

Policy Horizons Canada, 360 Albert St., 15th Fl., Ottawa, ON K1R 7X7
613-947-3800, Fax: 613-995-6006,
questions@horizons.gc.ca

Public Prosecution Service of Canada, 284 Wellington St., 2nd Fl., Ottawa, ON K1A 0H8
613-957-6489, 877-505-7772, info@ppsc.gc.ca

Alberta

Alberta Justice & Solicitor General, Communications, Bowker Building, 9833 - 109 St., 5th Fl., Edmonton, AB T5K 2E8
780-427-2745, -310-0000

British Columbia

British Columbia Ministry of Justice, PO Box 9044 Prov Govt, Victoria, BC V8W 9E2

Manitoba

Manitoba Justice & Attorney General, Administration & Finance, #1110, 405 Broadway Ave., Winnipeg, MB R3C 3L6
204-945-2878, minjus@gov.mb.ca

New Brunswick

New Brunswick Department of Justice & Public Safety, Argyle Place, PO Box 6000, Fredericton, NB E3B 5H1
506-453-3992, DPS-MSP.Information@gnb.ca

Newfoundland & Labrador

Newfoundland & Labrador Department of Justice & Public Safety, Confederation Bldg., East Block, 4th Fl., PO Box 8700, St. John's, NL A1B 4J6
709-729-2869, Fax: 709-729-0469, justice@gov.nl.ca

Newfoundland & Labrador Department of Transportation & Works, Confederation Bldg., Prince Philip Dr., PO Box 8700, St. John's, NL A1B 4J6
709-729-2300, tw@gov.nl.ca

Northwest Territories

Northwest Territories Department of Justice, 4903 - 49th St., PO Box 1320, Yellowknife, NT X1A 2L9
867-767-9256

Nova Scotia

Nova Scotia Department of Justice, 1690 Hollis St., PO Box 7, Halifax, NS B3J 2L6
902-424-4030, justweb@gov.ns.ca

Nunavut

Nunavut Territory Department of Justice, Sivummut, 1st Fl., PO Box 1000 500, Iqaluit, NU X0A 0H0
867-975-6170, Fax: 867-975-6195, justice@gov.nu.ca

Ontario

Ontario Ministry of the Attorney General, McMurtry-Scott Bldg., 720 Bay St., 11th Fl., Toronto, ON M7A 2S9
416-326-2220, Fax: 416-326-4007, 800-518-7901,
attorneygeneral@ontario.ca

Prince Edward Island

Prince Edward Island Department of Justice & Public Safety, Shaw Bldg. South, 95 Rochford St., 4th Fl., PO Box 2000, Charlottetown, PE C1A 7N8
902-368-6410, Fax: 902-368-6488

Québec

Les Publications du Québec, 1000 rte de l'Église, 5e étage, Québec, QC G1V 3V9
418-643-5150, Fax: 418-643-6177, 800-463-2100,
publicationsduQuébec@cspq.gouv.qc.ca

Ministère de la Justice, Édifice Louis-Philippe-Pigeon, 1200, rte de l'Église, Québec, QC G1V 4M1
418-643-5140, 866-536-5140,
informations@justice.gouv.qc.ca

Saskatchewan

Saskatchewan Justice & Attorney General, 1874 Scarth St., Regina, SK S4P 4B3
306-787-7872

Yukon Territory

Yukon French Language Services Directorate, 305 Jarvis St., 3rd Fl., PO Box 2703, Whitehorse, YT Y1A 2C6
867-667-8260, Fax: 867-393-6226

Yukon Justice, Andrew Philipsen Law Centre, 2134 Second Ave., PO Box 2703, Whitehorse, YT Y1A 2C6
867-667-3033, Fax: 867-393-5790, justice@gov.yk.ca

ADOPTION

See Also: Child Welfare

Nunavut

Nunavut Territory Department of Family Services, PO Box 1000 950, Iqaluit, NU X0A 0H0
867-975-6038, Fax: 867-975-6091

AGRICULTURE

See Also: Land Resources

Agriculture & Agri-Food Canada, 1341 Baseline Rd., Ottawa, ON K1A 0C5
613-773-1000, Fax: 613-773-1081, 855-773-0241,
info@agr.gc.ca

Canadian Grain Commission, #600, 303 Main St., Winnipeg, MB R3C 3G8
204-984-0506, Fax: 204-983-2751, 800-853-6705,
contact@grainscanada.gc.ca

Crops & Aquatic Growth Facilities, c/o National Research Council, 1200 Montreal Rd., Ottawa, ON K1A 0R6

Farm Products Council of Canada, Building 59, Central Experimental Farm, 960 Carling Ave., Ottawa, ON K1A 0C6
613-759-1555, Fax: 613-759-1566, 855-611-1165,
fpcc-cpac@agr.gc.ca

Alberta

Agricultural Products Marketing Council, JG O'Donoghue Bldg., #305, 7000 - 113 St., Edmonton, AB T6H 5T6
780-427-2164, Fax: 780-422-9690,
marketingcouncil@gov.ab.ca

Agriculture Financial Services Corporation, 5718 - 56 Ave., Lacombe, AB T4L 1B1
403-782-8200, info@afsc.ca

Alberta Agriculture & Forestry, JG O'Donoghue Bldg., #100A, 7000 - 113th St., Edmonton, AB T6H 5T6
780-427-2727, -310-3276, duke@gov.ab.ca

Farmers' Advocate Office, JG O'Donoghue Bldg., #305, 7000 - 113 St., Edmonton, AB T6H 5T6
Fax: 780-427-3913, -310-3276,
farmers.advocate@gov.ab.ca

Northern Alberta Development Council, Peace River Office, Provincial Building, #206, 9621 - 96 Ave., PO Box 900-14, Peace River, AB T8S 1T4
780-624-6274, Fax: 780-624-6184, -310-0000,
nadc.council@gov.ab.ca

British Columbia

British Columbia Farm Industry Review Board, 780 Blanshard St., PO Box 9129 Prov Govt, Victoria, BC V8W 9B5
250-356-8945, Fax: 250-356-5131, firb@gov.bc.ca

British Columbia Ministry of Agriculture, PO Box 9043 Prov Govt, Victoria, BC V8W 9E2
888-221-7141, agriservicebc@gov.bc.ca

Manitoba

Agricultural Societies, 1129 Queens Ave., Brandon, MB R7A 1L9
204-726-6195, Fax: 204-726-6260

Food Development Centre, 810 Phillips St., PO Box 1240, Portage La Prairie, MB R1N 3J9
204-239-3150, 800-870-1044

Manitoba Agriculture, Legislative Bldg., #165, 450 Broadway, Winnipeg, MB R3C 0V8
204-945-3722, Fax: 204-945-3470, minagr@leg.gov.mb.ca

New Brunswick

New Brunswick Agricultural Insurance Commission, c/o Department of Agriculture, Aquaculture & Fisheries, PO Box 6000, Fredericton, NB E3B 5H1
506-453-2666, Fax: 506-453-7406, DAAF-MAAP@gnb.ca

New Brunswick Department of Agriculture, Aquaculture & Fisheries, Agricultural Research Station (Experimental Farm), PO Box 6000, Fredericton, NB E3B 5H1
506-453-2666, Fax: 506-453-7170, 888-622-4742,
DAAF-MAAP@gnb.ca

New Brunswick Grain Commission, c/o Department of Agriculture, Aquaculture & Fisheries, PO Box 6000, Fredericton, NB E3B 5H1
506-859-3309, Fax: 506-856-2092, DAAF-MAAP@gnb.ca

Northwest Territories

Northwest Territories Department of Environment & Natural Resources, #600, 5102 - 50 Ave., Yellowknife, NT X1A 3S8
867-767-9231

Nova Scotia

Agricultural Marshland Conservation Commission, NS

Farm Practices Board, NS

Farm Registration Appeal Board, NS

Livestock Health Services Board, NS

Nova Scotia Crop & Livestock Insurance Commission, 60 Research Dr., #A, PO Box 1092, Truro, NS B2N 5G9
902-893-6370, 800-565-6371, nsclic@gov.ns.ca

Nova Scotia Department of Agriculture, 1800 Argyle St., 6th Fl., PO Box 2223, Halifax, NS B3J 3C4
902-424-4560, Fax: 902-424-4671

Nova Scotia Farm Loan Board, PO Box 890, Truro, NS B2N 5G6
902-893-6506, Fax: 902-895-7693, FLBNS@gov.ns.ca

Ontario

Ontario Ministry of Agriculture, Food & Rural Affairs, Ontario Government Bldg., 1 Stone Rd. West, Guelph, ON N1G 4Y2
519-826-3100, Fax: 519-826-4335, 888-466-2372, about.omafra@ontario.ca

Prince Edward Island

Prince Edward Island Department of Agriculture & Fisheries, Jones Bldg., 11 Kent St., 5th Fl., PO Box 2000, Charlottetown, PE C1A 7N8
902-368-4880, Fax: 902-368-4857

Québec

La financière agricole de Québec, 1400, boul Guillaume-Couture, Lévis, QC G6W 8K7
418-838-5602, Fax: 418-833-3871, 800-749-3646, financiereagricole@fadq.qc.ca

Ministère de l'Agriculture, des Pêcheries et de l'Alimentation, 200, ch Sainte-Foy, Québec, QC G1R 4X6
418-380-2110, 888-222-6272

Saskatchewan

Agricultural Implements Board, #315, 3085 Albert St., Regina, SK S4S 0B1
306-787-8861, Fax: 306-787-8599

Farm Stress Unit, 3085 Albert St., Regina, SK S4S 0B1
800-667-4442

Farmland Security Board, #315, 3988 Albert St., Regina, SK S4S 3R1
306-787-5047, Fax: 306-787-8599

Prairie Agricultural Machinery Institute, 2215 - 8th Ave., PO Box 1150, Humboldt, SK S0K 2A0
306-682-5033, Fax: 306-682-5080, 800-567-7264, humboldt@pami.ca

Saskatchewan Agriculture, Walter Scott Bldg., 3085 Albert St., Regina, SK S4S 0B1
866-457-2377

Saskatchewan Sheep Development Board, 2213C Hanselman Crt., Saskatoon, SK S7L 6A8
306-933-5200, Fax: 306-933-7182, sheepdb@sasktel.net

AGRICULTURE & FOOD

Agriculture & Agri-Food Canada, 1341 Baseline Rd., Ottawa, ON K1A 0C5
613-773-1000, Fax: 613-773-1081, 855-773-0241, info@agr.gc.ca

Market & Industry Services Branch, Tower 5, 1341 Baseline Rd., Ottawa, ON K1A 0C5
613-759-1000, Fax: 613-773-1711

Science & Technology Branch, Tower 5, 1341 Baseline Rd., Ottawa, ON K1A 0C5
Fax: 613-773-1711

Strategic Policy Branch, Tower 7, 1341 Baseline Rd., Ottawa, ON K1A 0C5
613-759-1000, Fax: 613-773-2121

Alberta

Agricultural Products Marketing Council, JG O'Donoghue Bldg., #305, 7000 - 113 St., Edmonton, AB T6H 5T6
780-422-2164, Fax: 780-422-9690, marketingcouncil@gov.ab.ca

Agriculture Financial Services Corporation, 5718 - 56 Ave., Lacombe, AB T4L 1B1
403-782-8200, info@afsc.ca

Alberta Agriculture & Forestry, JG O'Donoghue Bldg., #100A, 7000 - 113th St., Edmonton, AB T6H 5T6
780-427-2727, -310-3276, duke@gov.ab.ca

Alberta Grains Council, JG O'Donoghue Bldg., #305, 7000 - 113 St., Edmonton, AB T6H 5T6
780-427-7329, Fax: 780-422-9690

Alberta Livestock & Meat Agency, Ellwood Office Park South, #101, 1003 Ellwood Rd. SW, Edmonton, AB T6X 0B3
780-638-1699, Fax: 780-638-6495, info@almaltd.ca

Farmers' Advocate Office, JG O'Donoghue Bldg., #305, 7000 - 113 St., Edmonton, AB T6H 5T6
Fax: 780-427-3913, -310-3276, farmers.advocate@gov.ab.ca

Irrigation Council, Provincial Bldg., 200 - 5 Ave. South, 3rd Fl., Lethbridge, AB T1J 4L1
403-381-5176, Fax: 403-382-4406

British Columbia

Agricultural Land Commission, #133, 4940 Canada Way, Burnaby, BC V5G 4K6
604-660-7000, Fax: 604-660-7033, ALCBurnaby@Victoria1.gov.bc.ca

British Columbia Broiler Hatching Egg Commission, #180, 32160 South Fraser Way, Abbotsford, BC V2T 1W5
604-850-1854, Fax: 604-850-1683, info@bcbhec.com

British Columbia Chicken Marketing Board, #101, 32450 Simon Ave., Abbotsford, BC V2T 4J2
604-859-2868, Fax: 604-859-2811, info@bcchicken.ca

British Columbia Cranberry Marketing Commission, PO Box 162 A, Abbotsford, BC V2T 6Z5
604-897-9252, cranberries@telus.net

British Columbia Egg Marketing Board, #250, 32160 South Fraser Way, Abbotsford, BC V2T 1W5
604-556-3348, Fax: 604-556-3410, bcemb@bcegg.com

British Columbia Hog Marketing Commission, PO Box 8000-280, Abbotsford, BC V2S 6H1
604-287-4647, Fax: 604-820-6647, info@bcpork.ca

British Columbia Milk Marketing Board, #200, 32160 South Fraser Way, Abbotsford, BC V2T 1W5
604-556-3444, Fax: 604-556-7717, info@milk-bc.com

British Columbia Ministry of Agriculture, PO Box 9043 Prov Govt, Victoria, BC V8W 9E2
888-221-7141, agriservicebc@gov.bc.ca

British Columbia Turkey Marketing Board, #106, 19329 Enterprise Way, Surrey, BC V3S 6J8
604-534-5644, Fax: 604-534-3651, info@bcturkey.com

British Columbia Vegetable Marketing Commission, #207, 15252 - 32nd Ave., Surrey, BC V3S 0R7
604-542-9734, Fax: 604-542-9735, info@bcveg.com

Manitoba

Agricultural Societies, 1129 Queens Ave., Brandon, MB R7A 1L9
204-726-6195, Fax: 204-726-6260

Farm Lands Ownership Board, #812, Norquay Bldg., 401 York Ave., Winnipeg, MB R3C 0P8
204-945-3149, Fax: 204-945-1489, 800-282-8069

Farm Machinery & Equipment Board, #812, 401 York Ave., Winnipeg, MB R3C 0P8
204-945-3854, Fax: 204-945-1489

Manitoba Agricultural Services Corporation, #100, 1525 First St. South, Brandon, MB R7A 7A1
204-726-6850, Fax: 204-726-6849, mailbox@masc.mb.ca

Manitoba Agriculture, Legislative Bldg., #165, 450 Broadway, Winnipeg, MB R3C 0V8
204-945-3722, Fax: 204-945-3470, minagr@leg.gov.mb.ca

New Brunswick

New Brunswick Agricultural Insurance Commission, c/o Department of Agriculture, Aquaculture & Fisheries, PO Box 6000, Fredericton, NB E3B 5H1
506-453-2666, Fax: 506-453-7406, DAAF-MAAP@gnb.ca

New Brunswick Farm Products Commission, c/o Department of Agriculture, Aquaculture & Fisheries, PO Box 6000, Fredericton, NB E3B 5H1
506-453-3647, Fax: 506-444-5969, DAAF-MAAP@gnb.ca

New Brunswick Grain Commission, c/o Department of Agriculture, Aquaculture & Fisheries, PO Box 6000, Fredericton, NB E3B 5H1
506-859-3309, Fax: 506-856-2092, DAAF-MAAP@gnb.ca

Newfoundland & Labrador

Chicken Farmers of Newfoundland & Labrador, Agriculture Canada Bldg. 6, 308 Brookfield Rd., PO Box 8098, St. John's, NL A1B 3M9
709-747-1493, Fax: 709-747-0544

Farm Industry Review Board, Fortis Bldg., PO Box 2006, Corner Brook, NL A2H 6J8
709-637-0806, Fax: 709-637-2365

Newfoundland & Labrador Department of Natural Resources, Natural Resources Bldg., 50 Elizabeth Ave., 7th Fl., PO Box 8700, St. John's, NL A1B 4J6
709-729-2920, Fax: 709-729-0059

Nova Scotia

Natural Products Marketing Council, 179 College Rd., PO Box 890, Truro, NS B2N 5G6
902-893-6511, Fax: 902-893-6573

Nova Scotia Crop & Livestock Insurance Commission, 60 Research Dr., #A, PO Box 1092, Truro, NS B2N 5G9
902-893-6370, 800-565-6371, nsclic@gov.ns.ca

Nova Scotia Department of Agriculture, 1800 Argyle St., 6th Fl., PO Box 2223, Halifax, NS B3J 3C4
902-424-4560, Fax: 902-424-4671

Ontario

Agricorp, 1 Stone Rd. West, 3rd Fl., PO Box 3660 Central, Guelph, ON N1H 8M4
Fax: 519-826-4118, 888-247-4999, contact@agricorp.com

Agricultural Research Institute of Ontario, 1 Stone Rd. West, 2nd Fl., Guelph, ON N1G 4Y2
519-826-4554, 888-466-2372, research.omafra@ontario.ca

Agriculture, Food & Rural Affairs Tribunal & Board of Negotiation, 1 Stone Rd. West, 2nd Fl., Guelph, ON N1G 4Y2
519-826-3433, Fax: 519-826-4232, 888-466-2372, appeals.tribunal.omafra@ontario.ca

Ontario Ministry of Agriculture, Food & Rural Affairs, Ontario Government Bldg., 1 Stone Rd. West, Guelph, ON N1G 4Y2
519-826-3100, Fax: 519-826-4335, 888-466-2372, about.omafra@ontario.ca

Prince Edward Island

Agricultural Insurance Corporation, 29 Indigo Cres., PO Box 1600, Charlottetown, PE C1A 7N3
902-368-4842, Fax: 902-368-6677

Agriculture Policy & Regulatory, Jones Bldg., 11 Kent St., 5th Fl., Charlottetown, PE C1A 7N8

BIO|FOOD|TECH, 101 Belvedere Ave., PO Box 2000, Charlottetown, PE C1A 7N8
902-368-5548, Fax: 902-368-5549, 877-368-5548, biofoodtech@biofoodtech.ca

Prince Edward Island Department of Agriculture & Fisheries, Jones Bldg., 11 Kent St., 5th Fl., PO Box 2000, Charlottetown, PE C1A 7N8
902-368-4880, Fax: 902-368-4857

Québec

Commission de protection du territoire agricole du Québec, 200, ch Ste-Foy, 2e étage, Québec, QC G1R 4X6
418-643-3314, Fax: 418-643-2261, 800-667-5294, info@cptaq.gouv.qc.ca

Ministère de l'Agriculture, des Pêcheries et de l'Alimentation, 200, ch Sainte-Foy, Québec, QC G1R 4X6
418-380-2110, 888-222-6272

Régie des marchés agricoles et alimentaires du Québec, 201, boul Crémazie est, 5e étage, Montréal, QC H2M 1L3
514-873-4024, Fax: 514-873-3984, rmaaqc@rmaaq.gouv.qc.ca

Saskatchewan

Agri-Food Council, #302, 3085 Albert St., Regina, SK S4S 0B1
306-787-5978, Fax: 306-787-5134, corey.ruud@gov.sk.ca

Saskatchewan Agriculture, Walter Scott Bldg., 3085 Albert St., Regina, SK S4S 0B1
866-457-2377

Saskatchewan Crop Insurance Corporation, 484 Prince William Dr., PO Box 3000, Melville, SK S0A 2P0
306-728-7200, Fax: 306-728-7202, 888-935-0000, customer.service@scic.gov.sk.ca

Saskatchewan Egg Producers, 496 Hoffer Dr., Regina, SK S4N 7A1
306-924-1505, Fax: 306-924-1515

Saskatchewan Milk Marketing Board, 444 McLeod St., Regina, SK S4N 4Y1
306-949-6999, Fax: 306-949-2605, info@saskmilk.ca

Saskatchewan Turkey Producers' Marketing Board, 1438 Fletcher Rd., Saskatoon, SK S7M 5T2
306-931-1050, saskaturkey@sasktel.net

Yukon Territory

Yukon Environment, 10 Burns Rd., PO Box 2703 V-3A, Whitehorse, YT Y1A 2C6
867-667-5652, Fax: 867-393-7197, environment.yukon@gov.yk.ca

AIR POLLUTION

See Also: Environment

Environmental Stewardship Branch, 351, boul St-Joseph, Gatineau, QC K1A 0H3
819-953-1711, Fax: 819-953-9452

International Joint Commission, 234 Laurier Ave. West, 22nd Fl., Ottawa, ON K1P 6K6
613-995-2984, Fax: 613-993-5583, commission@ottawa.ijc.org

Meteorological Service of Canada, 351, boul Saint-Joseph, Gatineau, QC K1A 0H3
819-934-5395, Fax: 819-934-1255

Alberta

Alberta Environment & Parks, Information Centre, Great West Life Bldg., 9920 - 108 St., Main Fl., Edmonton, AB T5K 2M4
780-427-2700, Fax: 780-427-4407, -310-3773, ESRD.Info-Centre@gov.ab.ca

British Columbia

British Columbia Ministry of Environment, PO Box 9339 Prov Govt, Victoria, BC V8W 9M1
250-387-9870, Fax: 250-387-6003, env.mail@gov.bc.ca

Manitoba

Manitoba Sustainable Development, 200 Saulteaux Cres., PO Box 22, Winnipeg, MB R3J 3W3
204-945-6784, 800-214-6497, mgi@gov.mb.ca

New Brunswick

New Brunswick Department of Energy & Resource Development, Hugh John Flemming Forestry Centre, 1350 Regent St., Fredericton, NB E3C 2G6
506-453-3826, Fax: 506-444-4367, dnr_mrnweb@gnb.ca

New Brunswick Department of Environment & Local Government, Marysville Place, PO Box 6000, Fredericton, NB E3B 5H1
506-453-2690, Fax: 506-457-4994, elg/egl-info@gnb.ca

Newfoundland & Labrador
Newfoundland & Labrador Department of Environment & Conservation, Confederation Bldg., West Block, 4th Fl., PO Box 8700, St. John's, NL A1B 4J6
709-729-2664, Fax: 709-729-6639, 800-563-6181, envcinquires@gov.nl.ca

Northwest Territories
Northwest Territories Department of Environment & Natural Resources, #600, 5102 - 50 Ave., Yellowknife, NT X1A 3S8
867-767-9231

Nova Scotia
Nova Scotia Department of Environment, #1800, 1894 Barrington St., PO Box 442, Halifax, NS B3J 2P8
902-424-3600, Fax: 902-424-0501, 877-936-8476

Nunavut
Nunavut Territory Department of Environment, PO Box 1000 1300, Iqaluit, NU X0A 0H0
867-975-7700, Fax: 867-975-7742, environment@gov.nu.ca

Ontario
Integrated Environmental Policy Division, 77 Wellesley St. West, 11th Fl., Toronto, ON M7A 2T5
416-314-6338, Fax: 416-314-6346

Ontario Ministry of Environment & Climate Change, Public Information Centre, Macdonald Block, 900 Bay St., 2nd Fl., Toronto, ON M7A 1N3
416-325-4000, Fax: 416-314-6713, 800-565-4923

Québec
Ministère du Développement durable, de l'Environnement et de la Lutte contre les changements climatiques, Édifice Marie-Guyart, 675, boul René-Lévesque est, 29e étage, Québec, QC G1R 5V7
418-521-3830, Fax: 418-646-5974, 800-561-1616, info@mddefp.gouv.qc.ca

Saskatchewan
Saskatchewan Environment, 3211 Albert St., 2nd Fl., Regina, SK S4S 5W6
306-787-2584, Fax: 306-787-9544, 800-567-4224, Centre.Inquiry@gov.sk.ca

Yukon Territory
Yukon Environment, 10 Burns Rd., PO Box 2703 V-3A, Whitehorse, YT Y1A 2C6
867-667-5652, Fax: 867-393-7197, environment.yukon@gov.yk.ca

AIRPORTS & AVIATION

See Also: Transportation

Canadian Air Transport Security Authority, 99 Bank St., 13th Fl., Ottawa, ON K1P 6B9
Fax: 613-990-1295, 888-294-2202

Transport Canada, Place de Ville, 330 Sparks St., Tower C, Ottawa, ON K1A 0N5
613-990-2309, Fax: 613-954-4731, 866-995-9737

Transportation Appeal Tribunal of Canada, #1201, 333 Laurier Ave. West, 12th Fl., Ottawa, ON K1A 0N5
613-990-6906, Fax: 613-990-9153, info@tatc.gc.ca

Newfoundland & Labrador
Newfoundland & Labrador Department of Transportation & Works, Confederation Bldg., Prince Philip Dr., PO Box 8700, St. John's, NL A1B 4J6
709-729-2300, tw@gov.nl.ca

Northwest Territories
Northwest Territories Department of Transportation, New Government Bldg., 5015 - 49 St., 4th Fl., PO Box 1320, Yellowknife, NT X1A 2L9
867-767-9089, Fax: 867-873-0606

Nunavut
Nunavut Territory Department of Community & Government Services, W.G. Brown Bldg., 4th Fl., PO Box 1000 700, Iqaluit, NU X0A 0H0
867-975-5400, Fax: 867-975-5305

Ontario
Ontario Ministry of Transportation, Ferguson Block, 77 Wellesley St. West, 3rd Fl., Toronto, ON M7A 1Z8
416-327-9200, Fax: 416-327-9185, 800-268-4686

Saskatchewan
Saskatchewan Highways & Infrastructure, Victoria Tower, 1855 Victoria Ave., Regina, SK S4P 3T2
306-787-4800, communications@highways.gov.sk.ca

Yukon Territory
Yukon Highways & Public Works, PO Box 2703, Whitehorse, YT Y1A 2C6
867-393-7193, Fax: 867-393-6218, 800-661-0408, hpw-info@gov.yk.ca

APPRENTICESHIP PROGRAMS

Canadian Council of Directors of Apprenticeship, 140 Promenade du Portage, 5th Fl, Phase IV, Gatineau, QC K1A 0J9
Fax: 819-994-0202, 877-599-6933, redseal-sceaurouge@hrsdc-rhdcc.gc.ca

Alberta
Alberta Advanced Education, Legislature Bldg., #403, 10800 - 97 Ave., Edmonton, AB T5K 2B6
780-422-5400, -310-0000

Apprenticeship & Student Aid Division, Commerce Place, 10155 - 102 St., 6th Fl., Edmonton, AB T5J 4L5

New Brunswick
New Brunswick Department of Post-Secondary Education, Training & Labour, Chestnut Complex, PO Box 6000, Fredericton, NB E3B 5H1
506-453-2597, Fax: 506-453-3618, dpetlinfo@gnb.ca

Northwest Territories
Apprenticeship, Trade & Occupations Certification Board, PO Box 1320, Yellowknife, NT X1A 2L9
867-873-7357, Fax: 867-873-0200

Prince Edward Island
Prince Edward Island Department of Workforce & Advanced Learning, Shaw Bldg., 105 Rochford St., 5th Fl., PO Box 2000, Charlottetown, PE C1A 7N8
902-368-5956, Fax: 902-368-5277

SkillsPEI, Atlantic Technology Centre, #212, 176 Great George St., Charlottetown, PE C1A 4K9
902-368-6290, Fax: 902-368-6340, 877-491-4766

Québec
Conseil consultatif du travail et de la main d'oeuvre, #17.100, 500, boul René-Lévesque ouest, Montréal, QC H2Z 1W7
514-873-2880, Fax: 514-873-1129, cctm@cctm.gouv.qc.ca

Saskatchewan
Saskatchewan Advanced Education, #1120, 2010 - 12 Ave., Regina, SK S4P 0M3
306-787-9478, aeeinquiry@gov.sk.ca

Saskatchewan Apprenticeship & Trade Certification Commission, 2140 Hamilton St., Regina, SK S4P 2E3
306-787-2444, Fax: 306-787-5105, 877-363-0536, apprenticeship@gov.sk.ca

Yukon Territory
Yukon Education, PO Box 2703, Whitehorse, YT Y1A 2C6
867-667-5141, Fax: 867-393-6339, contact.education@gov.yk.ca

AQUACULTURE

See: Fisheries

Aquatic & Crop Resource Development Industry Partnership Facility, 550 University Ave., Charlottetown, PE C1A 4P3
902-566-7000

Centre for Aquaculture & Environmental Research, 4160 Marine Dr., West Vancouver, BC V7V 1N6
604-666-7453, Fax: 604-666-3497

ARCTIC & NORTHERN AFFAIRS

Indigenous & Northern Affairs, Terrasses de la Chaudière, 10 Wellington St., North Tower, Gatineau, QC K1A 0H4
Fax: 866-817-3977, 800-567-9604, infopubs@aadnc-aandc.gc.ca

Polar Knowledge Canada, 2464 Sheffield Rd., Ottawa, ON K1B 4E5
613-943-8605, info@polar.gc.ca

British Columbia
Northern Development Initiative Trust, #301, 1268 Fifth Ave., Prince George, BC V2L 3L2
250-561-2525, Fax: 250-561-2563, info@northerndevelopment.bc.ca

Manitoba
Manitoba Indigenous & Municipal Relations, Legislative Bldg, #344, 450 Broadway, Winnipeg, MB R3C 0V8
204-945-3719, Fax: 204-945-8374, anaweb@gov.mb.ca

Northwest Territories
Northwest Territories Department of Environment & Natural Resources, #600, 5102 - 50 Ave., Yellowknife, NT X1A 3S8
867-767-9231

Nunavut
Nunavut Territory Department of Executive & Intergovernmental Affairs, 1084 Aeroplex bldg., PO Box 1000 200, Iqaluit, NU X0A 0H0
867-975-6000, Fax: 867-975-6099

Ontario
Northern Development Division, Roberta Bondar Place, #200, 70 Foster Dr., Sault Ste. Marie, ON P6A 6V8
705-945-5900, Fax: 705-945-5931, 800-461-2287

Ontario Ministry of Northern Development & Mines, 159 Cedar St., Sudbury, ON P3E 6A5
705-670-5755, Fax: 705-670-5818, 888-415-9845, ndmminister@ontario.ca

Yukon Territory
Yukon Economic Development, #209, 212 Main St., F-1, Whitehorse, YT Y1A 2A9
867-393-7191, Fax: 867-393-6412, 800-661-0408, ecdev@gov.yk.ca

ARTS & CULTURE

Canada Council for the Arts, 150 Elgin St., 2nd Fl., PO Box 1047, Ottawa, ON K1P 5V8
613-566-4414, Fax: 613-566-4390, 800-263-5588, info@canadacouncil.ca

Canada Place Corporation, 100 The Pointe, 999 Canada Place, Vancouver, BC V6C 3T4
604-775-7063

Canada Science & Technology Museum Corporation, PO Box 9724 T,Ottawa, ON K1G 5A3
613-991-3044, Fax: 613-993-7923, cts@techno-science.ca

Canadian Broadcasting Corporation, 181 Queen St., PO Box 3220 C,Ottawa, ON K1Y 1E4
613-288-6000, liaison@cbc.ca

Canadian Heritage, 15 Eddy St., Gatineau, QC K1A 0M5
819-997-0055, 866-811-0055, PCH.info-info.PCH@canada.ca

Canadian Museum for Human Rights, 85 Israel Asper Way, Winnipeg, MB R3C 0L5
204-289-2000, Fax: 204-289-2001, 877-877-6037, info@humanrights.ca

Canadian Museum of History, 100 Laurier St., Gatineau, QC K1A 0M8
819-776-7000, 800-555-5621

Canadian Museum of Nature, 240 McLeod St., PO Box 3443 D,Ottawa, ON K1P 6P4
613-566-4700, Fax: 613-364-4021, 800-263-4433

Library of Parliament, Parliamentary Buildings, Ottawa, ON K1A 0A9
613-992-4793, 866-599-4999, info@parl.gc.ca

National Arts Centre, 53 Elgin St., PO Box 1534 B,Ottawa, ON K1P 5W1
613-947-7000, Fax: 613-947-7112, 866-850-2787

National Film Board of Canada, Operational Headquarters, Norman McLaren Building, 3155, ch de la Côte-de-Liesse, CP 1600 Centre-ville,Montréal, QC H3C 3H5
514-283-9000, 800-267-7710

National Gallery of Canada, 380 Sussex Dr., PO Box 427 A,Ottawa, ON K1N 9N4
613-990-1985, Fax: 613-993-4385, 800-319-2787, info@gallery.ca

Parks Canada, National Office, 30 Victoria St., Gatineau, QC J8X 0B3
819-420-9486, 888-773-8888, information@pc.gc.ca

Telefilm Canada, #500, 360, rue Saint-Jacques, Montréal, QC H2Y 1P5
514-283-6363, Fax: 514-283-8212, 800-567-0890, info@telefilm.gc.ca

Alberta
Alberta Culture & Tourism, Communications Branch, Standard Life Centre, 10405 Jasper Ave., 7th Fl., Edmonton, AB T5J 4R7
780-427-6530, 800-232-7215, culture.communications@gov.ab.ca

British Columbia
Arts, Culture, Gaming Grants & Sport, PO Box 9490 Prov Govt, Victoria, BC V8W 9N7
250-356-6914, Fax: 250-387-7973

BC Place, 777 Pacific Blvd., Vancouver, BC V6B 4Y8
604-669-2300, Fax: 604-661-3412, stadium@bcpavco.com

British Columbia Arts Council, 800 Johnson St., PO Box 9819 Prov Govt, Victoria, BC V8W 9W3
250-356-1718, Fax: 250-387-4099, BCArtsCouncil@gov.bc.ca

British Columbia Ministry of Social Development & Social Innovation, PO Box 9058 Prov Govt, Victoria, BC V8W 9E1
800-663-7867, EnquiryBC@gov.bc.ca

British Columbia Pavilion Corporation, #200, 999 Canada Place, Vancouver, BC V6C 3C1
604-482-2200, Fax: 604-681-9017, info@bcpavco.com

Creative BC, 2225 West Broadway, Vancouver, BC V6K 2E4
604-736-7997, Fax: 604-736-7290

Islands Trust, #200, 1627 Fort St., Victoria, BC V8R 1H8
250-405-5151, Fax: 250-405-5155

Manitoba
Communications Services Manitoba, 155 Carlton St., 10th Fl., Winnipeg, MB R3C 3H8
204-945-3765

Heritage Grants Advisory Council, c/o Heritage Grants Program, #330, 213 Notre Dame Ave., Winnipeg, MB R3B 1N3
204-945-2213, Fax: 204-948-2086

Le Centre Culturel franco-manitobain/Franco-Manitoban Cultural Centre, 340, boul Provencher, Winnipeg, MB R2H 0G7
204-233-8972, Fax: 204-233-3324, communication@ccfm.mb.ca

Manitoba Arts Council, #525, 93 Lombard Ave., Winnipeg, MB R3B 3B1
204-945-2237, Fax: 204-945-5925, 866-994-2787, info@artscouncil.mb.ca
Manitoba Centennial Centre Corporation, #1000, 555 Main St., Winnipeg, MB R3B 1C3
204-956-1360, Fax: 204-944-1390, inquiries@mbccc.ca
Manitoba Film Classification Board, #216, 301 Weston St., Winnipeg, MB R3E 3H4
204-945-8962, Fax: 204-945-0890, 866-612-2399, mfcb@gov.mb.ca
Manitoba Heritage Council, 213 Notre Dame Ave., Main Fl., Winnipeg, MB R3B 1N3
204-945-2118, Fax: 204-948-2384, hrb@gov.mb.ca
Manitoba Museum, 190 Rupert Ave., Winnipeg, MB R3B 0N2
204-956-2830, Fax: 204-942-3679, info@manitobamuseum.ca
Multiculturalism Secretariat, 213 Notre Dame Ave., 7th Fl., Winnipeg, MB R3B 1N3
204-945-5632, multisec@gov.mb.ca

New Brunswick

Kings Landing Historical Settlement, 5804 Rte 102, Prince William, NB E6K 0A5
506-363-4999, Fax: 506-363-4989, info.kingslanding@gnb.ca
New Brunswick Arts Board, 649 Queen St., 2nd Fl., Fredericton, NB E3B 1C3
506-444-4444, Fax: 506-444-5543, 866-460-2787
New Brunswick Department of Social Development, Sartain MacDonald Bldg., 551 King St., PO Box 6000, Fredericton, NB E3B 5H1
506-453-2001, Fax: 506-453-2164, sd-ds@gnb.ca

Newfoundland & Labrador

Newfoundland & Labrador Arts Council, The Newman Bldg., 1 Springdale St., PO Box 98, St. John's, NL A1C 5H5
709-726-2212, Fax: 709-726-0619, 866-726-2212, nlacmail@nlac.ca
Newfoundland & Labrador Department of Business, Tourism, Culture & Rural Development, Confederation Bldg., West Block, 2nd Fl., PO Box 8700, St. John's, NL A1B 4J6
709-729-7000, btcrd@gov.nl.ca
Provincial Information & Library Resources Board, 48 St. George's Ave., Stephenville, NL A2H 1K9
709-643-0900, Fax: 709-643-0925

Northwest Territories

Northwest Territories Arts Council, PO Box 1320 Main, Yellowknife, NT X1A 2L9
867-920-6370, Fax: 867-873-0205, nwtartscouncil@gmail.com
Northwest Territories Department of Education, Culture & Employment, PO Box 1320, Yellowknife, NT X1A 2L9
ecepublicaffairs@gov.nt.ca

Nova Scotia

Art Gallery of Nova Scotia, 1723 Hollis St., PO Box 2262, Halifax, NS B3J 3C8
902-424-5280, Fax: 902-424-7359, infodesk@gov.ns.ca
Nova Scotia Business Inc., World Trade & Convention Centre, #701, 1800 Argyle St., PO Box 2374, Halifax, NS B3J 3N8
902-424-6650, Fax: 902-424-5739, 800-260-6682, info@nsbi.ca
Nova Scotia Museum, 1747 Summer St., Halifax, NS B3H 3A6
Fax: 902-424-0560, museum@gov.ns.ca

Nunavut

Nunavut Territory Department of Culture & Heritage, PO Box 1000 800, Iqaluit, NU X0A 0H0
867-975-5500, Fax: 867-975-5504, 866-934-2035

Ontario

Art Gallery of Ontario, 317 Dundas St. West, Toronto, ON M5T 1G4
416-977-0414, Fax: 416-979-6669, 877-225-4246
Corporate Services Division, 54 Wellesley St., 4th Fl., Toronto, ON M7A 2E7
416-325-6866, Fax: 416-314-7014, 888-664-6008
Ontario Arts Council, 151 Bloor St. West, 5th Fl., Toronto, ON M5S 1T6
416-961-1660, Fax: 416-961-7796, 800-387-0058, info@arts.on.ca
Ontario Film Review Board, #101B, 4950 Yonge St., Toronto, ON M1N 6K1
416-314-3626, Fax: 416-314-3632, 800-268-6024
Ontario Heritage Trust, 10 Adelaide St. East, Toronto, ON M5C 1J3
416-325-5000, Fax: 416-325-5071
Ontario Library Service - North, 334 Regent St., Sudbury, ON P3C 4E2
705-675-6467, Fax: 705-675-2285, 800-461-6348
Ontario Media Development Corporation, South Tower, #501, 175 Bloor St. East, Toronto, ON M4W 3R8
416-314-6858, Fax: 416-314-6876, reception@omdc.on.ca
Ontario Ministry of Tourism, Culture & Sport, Hearst Block, 900 Bay St., 9th Fl., Toronto, ON M7A 2E1
416-326-9326, Fax: 416-314-7854, 888-997-9015
Ontario Place Corporation, 955 Lake Shore Blvd. West, Toronto, ON M6K 3B9
416-314-9900, Fax: 416-314-9989, 866-663-4386
Ottawa Convention Centre, 55 Colonel By Dr., Ottawa, ON K1N 9J2
613-563-1984, Fax: 613-563-7646, 800-450-0077, info@ottawaconventioncentre.com
Royal Ontario Museum, 100 Queen's Park Cres., Toronto, ON M5S 2C6
416-586-5549, Fax: 416-586-5685, info@rom.on.ca
Southern Ontario Library Service, #902, 111 Peter St., Toronto, ON M5V 2H1
416-961-1669, Fax: 416-961-5122, 800-387-5765

Prince Edward Island

Prince Edward Island Department of Family & Human Services, Jones Bldg., 11 Kent St., 2nd Fl., PO Box 2000, Charlottetown, PE C1A 7N8
902-620-3777, Fax: 902-894-0242, 866-594-3777

Québec

Bibliothèque et Archives nationales du Québec (BAnQ), 2275, rue Holt, Montréal, QC H2G 3H1
514-873-1100, Fax: 514-873-9312, 800-363-9028
Commission des biens culturels du Québec, Bloc A-RC, 225, Grande Allée est, Québec, QC G1R 5G5
418-643-8378, Fax: 418-643-8591, info@cbcq.gouv.qc.ca
Conseil des arts et des lettres du Québec, 79, boul René-Lévesque est, 3e étage, Québec, QC G1R 5N5
418-643-1707, Fax: 418-643-4558, 800-897-1707, info@calq.gouv.qc.ca
Curateur public du Québec, 600, boul René-Lévesque ouest, Montréal, QC H3B 4W9
514-873-4074, 800-363-9020
Ministère de la Culture et Communications, 225, Grande Allée est, Québec, QC G1R 5G5
888-380-8882
Musée d'art contemporain de Montréal, 185, rue Ste-Catherine ouest, Montréal, QC H2X 3X5
514-847-6226, Fax: 514-847-6292, info@macm.org
Musée de la civilisation, 85, rue Dalhousie, CP 155 B,Québec, QC G1K 8R2
418-643-2158, Fax: 418-646-9705, 866-710-8031, mcqweb@mcq.org
Musée national des beaux-arts du Québec, Parc des Champs-de-Bataille, 1, av Wolfe-Montcalm, Québec, QC G1R 5H3
418-643-2150, 866-220-2150, info@mnba.qc.ca
Régie du cinéma, #100, 390, rue Notre-Dame ouest, Montréal, QC H2Y 1T9
514-873-2371, Fax: 514-873-8874, 800-463-2463
Société de développement des entreprises culturelles, #800, 215, rue Saint-Jacques, Montréal, QC H2Y 1M6
514-841-2200, Fax: 514-841-8606, 800-363-0401, info@sodec.gouv.qc.ca
Société de la Place des Arts de Montréal, 260, boul de Maisonneuve ouest, Montréal, QC H2X 1Y9
514-285-4200, Fax: 514-285-1968, info@pda.qc.ca
Société de télédiffusion du Québec (Télé-Québec), 1000, rue Fullum, Montréal, QC H2K 3L7
514-521-2424, Fax: 514-864-1970, info@teleQuébec.tv
Société du Grand Théâtre de Québec, 269, boul René-Lévesque est, Québec, QC G1R 2B3
418-643-8111, gtq@grandtheatre.qc.ca

Saskatchewan

Conexus Arts Centre, 200A Lakeshore Dr., Regina, SK S4S 7L3
306-565-4500, Fax: 306-565-3274, 800-667-8497, reception@conexusartscentre.ca
Provincial Capital Commission, 4607 Dewdney Ave., Regina, SK S4T 1B7
306-787-9261
Royal Saskatchewan Museum, 2445 Albert St., Regina, SK S4P 4W7
306-787-2815, Fax: 306-787-2820, rsminfo@gov.sk.ca
Saskatchewan Archives Board, #401, 1870 Albert St., PO Box 1665, Regina, SK S4P 3C6
306-787-4068, Fax: 306-787-1197
Saskatchewan Arts Board, 1355 Broad St., Regina, SK S4R 7V1
306-787-4056, Fax: 306-787-4199, 800-667-7526, info@artsboard.sk.ca
Saskatchewan Film & Video Classification Board, #500, 1919 Saskatchewan Dr., Regina, SK S4P 4H2
306-787-5550, Fax: 306-787-9779, 888-374-4636

Yukon Territory

Yukon Tourism & Culture, 100 Hanson St., PO Box 2703, Whitehorse, YT Y1A 2C6
867-667-5036, Fax: 867-667-3546

ASTRONOMY

See Also: Space & Astronomy

Canada-France-Hawaii Telescope, CFHT Corporation, #65, 1238 Mamalahoa Hwy., Kamuela, HI
808-885-7944, Fax: 808-885-7288, info@cfht.hawaii.edu
Canadian Astronomy Data Centre, NRC Herzberg Astronomy & Astrophysics, 5071 West Saanich Rd., Victoria, BC V9E 2E7
250-363-0001, Fax: 250-363-0045, cadc@nrc.gc.ca
Dominion Astrophysical Observatory, NRC Herzberg Astronomy & Astrophysics, 5071 West Saanich Rd., Victoria, BC V9E 2E7
250-363-0001, NRC.NSIHerzbergAstroInfoISN.CNRC@nrc-cnrc.gc.ca
Dominion Radio Astrophysical Observatory, 717 White Lake Rd., PO Box 248, Penticton, BC V2A 6J9
250-497-2300, NRC.DRAO-OFR.CNRC@nrc-cnrc.gc.ca
Gemini Observatory, 670 N. A'ohoku Place, Hilo, HI
808-974-2500, Fax: 808-974-2589

ATTORNEYS-GENERAL

See: Justice Departments

Public Prosecution Service of Canada, 284 Wellington St., 2nd Fl., Ottawa, ON K1A 0H8
613-957-6489, 877-505-7772, info@ppsc.gc.ca

Manitoba

Manitoba Justice & Attorney General, Administration & Finance, #1110, 405 Broadway Ave., Winnipeg, MB R3C 3L6
204-945-2878, minjus@gov.mb.ca

New Brunswick

New Brunswick Department of Justice & Public Safety, Argyle Place, PO Box 6000, Fredericton, NB E3B 5H1
506-453-3992, DPS-MSP.Information@gnb.ca
Office of the Attorney General, Chancery Place, PO Box 6000, Fredericton, NB E3B 5H1
506-462-5100, Fax: 506-453-3651, justice.comments@gnb.ca

Ontario

Ontario Ministry of the Attorney General, McMurtry-Scott Bldg., 720 Bay St., 11th Fl., Toronto, ON M7A 2S9
416-326-2220, Fax: 416-326-4007, 800-518-7901, attorneygeneral@ontario.ca

Saskatchewan

Saskatchewan Justice & Attorney General, 1874 Scarth St., Regina, SK S4P 4B3
306-787-7872

AUDITORS-GENERAL

Auditor General of Canada, 240 Sparks St., Ottawa, ON K1A 0G6
613-952-0213, Fax: 613-957-0474, 888-761-5953, infomedia@oag-bvg.gc.ca

Alberta

Alberta Office of the Auditor General, 9925 - 109 St., 8th Fl., Edmonton, AB T5K 2J8
780-427-4222, Fax: 780-422-9555, info@oag.ab.ca

British Columbia

Office of the Auditor General, PO Box 9036 Prov Govt, Victoria, BC V8W 9A2
250-419-6100, Fax: 250-387-1230
Office of the Auditor General for Local Government, #201, 10470 - 152nd St., Surrey, BC V3R 0Y3
604-930-7100

Manitoba

Office of the Auditor General, #500, 330 Portage Ave., Winnipeg, MB R3C 0C4
204-945-3790, Fax: 204-945-2169, oag.contact@oag.mb.ca

New Brunswick

Office of the Auditor General, HSBC Place, 520 King St., Fredericton, NB E3B 6G3
506-453-2243, Fax: 506-453-3067

Newfoundland & Labrador

Office of the Auditor General, PO Box 8700, St. John's, NL A1B 4J6
709-729-2695, Fax: 709-729-5970, oagmail@oag.nl.ca

Nova Scotia

Office of the Auditor General, Royal Centre, #400, 5161 George St., Halifax, NS B3J 1M7
902-424-5907, Fax: 902-424-4350

Ontario

Office of the Auditor General, 20 Dundas St. West, 15th Fl., PO Box 105, Toronto, ON M5G 2C2
416-327-2381, Fax: 416-327-9862, comments@auditor.on.ca

Prince Edward Island

Office of the Auditor General, Shaw Bldg., 105 Rochford St. North, 2nd Fl., PO Box 2000, Charlottetown, PE C1A 7N8
902-368-4520, Fax: 902-368-4598

Québec

Vérificateur général du Québec, 750, boulevard Charest est, 3e étage, Québec, QC G1K 9J6
418-691-5900, Fax: 418-644-4460, verificateur.general@vgq.qc.ca

Saskatchewan
Provincial Auditor Saskatchewan, Chateau Tower, #1500, 1920 Broad St., Regina, SK S4P 3V2
306-787-6398, Fax: 306-787-6383, info@auditor.sk.ca

AUTOMOBILE INSURANCE

See Also: Insurance (Life, Fire Property)

Alberta
Alberta Automobile Insurance Rate Board, Canadian Western Bank Place, #2440, 10303 Jasper Ave., Edmonton, AB T5J 3N6
780-427-5428, Fax: 780-638-4254, -310-0000, airb@gov.ab.ca

British Columbia
Insurance Corporation of British Columbia, 151 West Esplanade, North Vancouver, BC V7M 3H9
604-661-2800, 800-663-3051

Manitoba
Manitoba Public Insurance Corporation, #B100, 234 Donald St., PO Box 6300, Winnipeg, MB R3C 4A4
204-985-7000, Fax: 204-985-3525, 800-665-2410

Northwest Territories
Northwest Territories Department of Finance, PO Box 1320, Yellowknife, NT X1A 2L9
867-873-7500

Ontario
Financial Services Commission of Ontario, New York City Ctr., 5160 Yonge St., 17th Fl., PO Box 85, Toronto, ON M2N 6L9
416-250-7250, Fax: 416-590-7070, 800-668-0128, contactcentre@fsco.gov.on.ca

Québec
Société de l'assurance automobile du Québec, 333, boul Jean-Lesage, CP 19600 Terminus, Québec, QC G1K 8J6
418-643-7620, Fax: 418-644-0339, 800-361-7620

Saskatchewan
Automobile Injury Appeal Commission, #504, 2400 College Ave., Regina, SK S4P 1C8
306-798-5545, Fax: 306-798-5540, 866-798-5544, aiac@gov.sk.ca
Saskatchewan Government Insurance, 2260 - 11th Ave., Regina, SK S4P 0J9
306-751-1200, Fax: 306-787-7477, 800-667-8015, sgiinquiries@sgi.sk.ca

Yukon Territory
Yukon Justice, Andrew Philipsen Law Centre, 2134 Second Ave., PO Box 2703, Whitehorse, YT Y1A 2C6
867-667-3033, Fax: 867-393-5790, justice@gov.yk.ca

BANKING & FINANCIAL INSTITUTIONS

Bank of Canada, 234 Laurier Ave. West, Ottawa, ON K1A 0G9
613-782-8111, Fax: 613-782-7713, 800-303-1282, info@bankofcanada.ca
Business Development Bank of Canada, #400, 5, Place Ville-Marie, Montréal, QC H3B 5E7
877-232-2269
Canada Deposit Insurance Corporation, 50 O'Connor St., 17th Floor, Ottawa, ON K1P 6L2
Fax: 613-996-6095, 800-461-2342, info@cdic.ca
Finance Canada, 90 Elgin St., 14th Fl., Ottawa, ON K1A 0G5
613-369-3710, Fax: 613-369-4065, fin.financepublic-financepublique.fin@canada.ca
Financial Consumer Agency of Canada, 427 Laurier Ave. West, 6th Fl., Ottawa, ON K1R 1B9
613-960-4666, Fax: 613-941-1436, info@fcac-acfc.gc.ca
Office of the Superintendent of Financial Institutions, Kent Square, 255 Albert St., Ottawa, ON K1A 0H2
613-990-7788, Fax: 613-990-5591, 800-385-8647, information@osfi-bsif.gc.ca

Alberta
Alberta Treasury Board & Finance, Oxbridge Place, 9820 - 106 St., 9th Fl., Edmonton, AB T5K 1E7
780-427-3035, Fax: 780-427-1147, -310-0000
ATB Financial, #2100, 10020 - 100 St. NW, Edmonton, AB T5J 0N3
403-245-8110, 800-332-8383
Credit Union Deposit Guarantee Corporation, #2000, 10104 - 103 St., Edmonton, AB T5J 0H8
780-428-6680, Fax: 780-428-7571, 800-661-0351, mail@cudgc.ab.ca
Treasury & Risk Management Division, Federal Bldg., 9820 - 107 St., 8th Fl., Edmonton, AB T5K 1E7

British Columbia
British Columbia Ministry of Finance, PO Box 9417 Prov Govt, Victoria, BC V8W 9V1
877-388-4440, CTBTaxQuestions@gov.bc.ca
Financial Institutions Commission, #2800, 555 West Hastings, Vancouver, BC V6B 4N6
604-660-3555, Fax: 604-660-3365, 866-206-3030, FICOM@ficombc.ca

Manitoba
Deposit Guarantee Corporation of Manitoba, #390, 200 Graham Ave., Winnipeg, MB R3C 4L5
204-942-8480, Fax: 204-947-1723, 800-697-4447, mail@depositguarantee.mb.ca
Manitoba Finance, #109, Legislative Bldg., Winnipeg, MB R3C 0V8
204-945-3754, minfin@leg.gov.mb.ca
Manitoba Financial Services Agency, c/o Financial Institutions Regulation Branch, #207, 400 St. Mary Ave., Winnipeg, MB R3C 4K5
204-945-2542, Fax: 204-948-2268, 800-282-8069, insurance@gov.mb.ca

New Brunswick
New Brunswick Department of Finance, Chancery Place, 675 King St., PO Box 6000, Fredericton, NB E3B 5H1
506-453-2451, Fax: 506-457-4989, wwwfin@gnb.ca

Newfoundland & Labrador
Credit Union Deposit Guarantee Corporation, PO Box 340, Marystown, NL A0E 2M0
709-279-0170, Fax: 709-279-0177, 877-279-0170
Newfoundland & Labrador Department of Finance, Confederation Bldg., PO Box 8700, St. John's, NL A1B 4J6
709-729-3166, Fax: 709-729-2232, finance@gov.nl.ca

Northwest Territories
Northwest Territories Department of Finance, PO Box 1320, Yellowknife, NT X1A 2L9
867-873-7500

Nunavut
Nunavut Business Credit Corporation, Parnaivak Bldg., #100, PO Box 2548, Iqaluit, NU X0A 0H0
867-975-7891, Fax: 867-975-7897, 800-758-0038, credit@nbcc.nu.ca
Nunavut Territory Department of Finance, Bldg. 1079, 1st Fl., PO Box 1000 430, Iqaluit, NU X0A 0H0
867-975-5800, Fax: 867-975-5805

Ontario
Deposit Insurance Corporation of Ontario, #700, 4711 Yonge St., Toronto, ON M2N 6K8
416-325-9444, Fax: 416-325-9722, 800-268-6653, info@dico.com
Financial Services Commission of Ontario, New York City Ctr., 5160 Yonge St., 17th Fl., PO Box 85, Toronto, ON M2N 6L9
416-250-7250, Fax: 416-590-7070, 800-668-0128, contactcentre@fsco.gov.on.ca
Ontario Ministry of Finance, Frost Bldg. South, 7 Queen's Park Cres., 7th Fl., Toronto, ON M7A 1Y7
Fax: 866-888-3850, 866-668-8297, financecommunications.fin@ontario.ca
Provincial-Local Finance Division, College Park, 777 Bay St., 10th Fl., Toronto, ON M5G 2C8
416-327-0264, Fax: 416-325-7644

Prince Edward Island
Prince Edward Island Department of Finance, Shaw Bldg., 95 Rochford St. South, 2nd Fl., PO Box 2000, Charlottetown, PE C1A 7N8
902-368-4000, Fax: 902-368-5544

Québec
Caisse de dépôt et placement du Québec, 1000, place Jean-Paul-Riopelle, Montréal, QC H2Z 2B3
514-842-3261, Fax: 514-842-4833, 866-330-3936
Ministère des Finances, 12, rue Saint-Louis, Québec, QC G1R 5L3
418-528-9323, Fax: 418-646-1631, info@finances.gouv.qc.ca

Saskatchewan
Financial & Consumer Affairs Authority, #601, 1919 Saskatchewan Dr., Regina, SK S4P 4H2
306-787-5645, Fax: 306-787-5899, 877-880-5550, consumerprotection@gov.sk.ca
Saskatchewan Finance, 2350 Albert St., Regina, SK S4P 4A6
306-787-6768, Fax: 306-787-0241, communications@finance.gov.sk.ca

Yukon Territory
Yukon Finance, PO Box 2703, Whitehorse, YT Y1A 2C6
867-667-5343, Fax: 867-393-6217, fininfo@gov.yk.ca

BILINGUALISM

Canadian Heritage, 15 Eddy St., Gatineau, QC K1A 0M5
819-997-0055, 866-811-0055, PCH.info-info.PCH@canada.ca
Office of the Commissioner of Official Languages, 30 Victoria St., 6th Fl., Gatineau, ON K1A 0T8
819-420-4877, Fax: 819-420-4873, 877-996-6368

Manitoba
Le Centre Culturel franco-manitobain/Franco-Manitoban Cultural Centre, 340, boul Provencher, Winnipeg, MB R2H 0G7
204-233-8972, Fax: 204-233-3324, communication@ccfm.mb.ca

Northwest Territories
Office of the Languages Commissioner, Capital Suites - Zheh Gwizu', PO Box 2096, Inuvik, NT X0E 0T0
867-678-2200, Fax: 867-678-2201, 800-661-0889

Nunavut
Nunavut Territory Department of Culture & Heritage, PO Box 1000 800, Iqaluit, NU X0A 0H0
867-975-5500, Fax: 867-975-5504, 866-934-2035

Ontario
Office of Francophone Affairs, #200, 700 Bay St., 2nd Fl., Toronto, ON M7A 0A2
416-325-4949, Fax: 416-325-4980, 800-268-7507, ofa@ontario.ca
Ontario French-Language Education Communications Authority, 21 College St., Toronto, ON MRY 2M5
416-968-3536, Fax: 416-968-8203

Québec
Ministère des Relations internationales et Francophonie, Édifice Hector-Fabre, 525, boul Réne-Lévesque est, Québec, QC G1R 5R9
418-649-2300, Fax: 418-649-2656

Yukon Territory
Yukon French Language Services Directorate, 305 Jarvis St., 3rd Fl., PO Box 2703, Whitehorse, YT Y1A 2C6
867-667-8260, Fax: 867-393-6226

BIOTECHNOLOGY

Industrial Partnership Facility: Montréal, c/o Montréal (av Royalmount) Research Facilities, 6100, av Royalmount, Montréal, QC H4P 2R2

Alberta
Alberta Innovates - Bio Solutions, Phipps McKinnon Bldg., 10020 - 101A Ave., 18th Fl., Edmonton, AB T5J 3G2
780-427-1956, Fax: 780-427-3252, 877-828-0444, bio@albertainnovates.ca

Prince Edward Island
BIO|FOOD|TECH, 101 Belvedere Ave., PO Box 2000, Charlottetown, PE C1A 7N8
902-368-5548, Fax: 902-368-5549, 877-368-5548, biofoodtech@biofoodtech.ca

BOARDS OF REVIEW

Canada Industrial Relations Board, 240 Sparks St., 4th Fl. West, Ottawa, ON K1A 0X8
Fax: 613-995-9493, 800-575-9696
Canadian International Trade Tribunal, Standard Life Centre, 333 Laurier Ave. West, 15th Floor, Ottawa, ON K1A 0G7
613-990-2452, Fax: 613-990-2439, 855-307-2488, citt-tcce@tribunal.gc.ca
Canadian Nuclear Safety Commission, 280 Slater St., PO Box 1046 B,Ottawa, ON K1P 5S9
613-995-5894, Fax: 613-995-5086, 800-668-5284, cnsc.information.ccsn@canada.ca
Commission for Public Complaints Against the Royal Canadian Mounted Police, National Intake Office, PO Box 88689, Surrey, BC V3W 0X1
Fax: 604-501-4095, 800-665-6878
Committee on the Status of Endangered Wildlife in Canada, c/o Canadian Wildlife Service, 351 St. Joseph Blvd, 4th Fl., Gatineau, QC K1A 0H3
819-953-3215, Fax: 819-994-3684, cosewic/cosepac@ec.gc.ca
Immigration & Refugee Board of Canada, Canada Bldg, 344 Slater St., 12th Fl., Ottawa, ON K1A 0K1
613-995-6486, Fax: 613-943-1550, contact@irb-cisr.gc.ca
Mackenzie Valley Environmental Impact Review Board, 200 Scotia Centre, #5102, 50th Ave., PO Box 938, Yellowknife, NT X1A 2N7
867-766-7050, Fax: 867-766-7074, 866-912-3472
National Energy Board, 517 - 10 Ave. SW, Calgary, AB T2R 0A8
403-292-4800, Fax: 403-292-5503, 800-899-1265
Nunavut Impact Review Board, 29 Mitik St., PO Box 1360, Cambridge Bay, NU X0B 0C0
867-983-4600, Fax: 867-983-2594, 866-233-3033, info@nirb.ca
Nunavut Water Board, PO Box 119, Gjoa Haven, NU X0B 1J0
867-360-6338, Fax: 867-360-6369
Patented Medicine Prices Review Board, Standard Life Centre, #1400, 333 Laurier Ave. West, PO Box L40, Ottawa, ON K1P 1C1
613-954-8299, Fax: 613-952-7626, 877-861-2350, pmprb@pmprb-cepmb.gc.ca
Porcupine Caribou Management Board, PO Box 31723, Whitehorse, YT Y1A 6L3
867-633-4780, Fax: 867-393-3904, pcmb@taiga.net
Public Service Staffing Tribunal, 240 Sparks St., 6th Fl., Ottawa, ON K1A 0A5
613-949-6516, Fax: 613-949-6551, 866-637-4491, info@psst-tdfp.gc.ca

Royal Canadian Mounted Police External Review Committee, PO Box 1159 B, Ottawa, ON K1P 5R2
613-998-2134, Fax: 613-990-8969, org@erc-cee.gc.ca

Security Intelligence Review Committee, PO Box 2430 D,Ottawa, ON K1P 5W5
613-990-8441, Fax: 613-990-5230, info@sirc-csars.gc.ca

Veterans Review & Appeal Board, Daniel J. MacDonald Bldg., 161 Grafton St., PO Box 9900, Charlottetown, PE C1A 8V7
902-566-8751, Fax: 902-566-7850, 800-450-8006, vrab_tacra@vac-acc.gc.ca

Alberta

Alberta Review Board, Oxford Tower, #1120, 10235 - 101 St., Edmonton, AB T5J 3E9
780-422-5994, Fax: 780-427-1762

British Columbia

British Columbia Review Board, #1020, 510 Burrard St., Vancouver, BC V6C 3A8
604-660-8789, Fax: 604-660-8809, 877-305-2277

Manitoba

Manitoba Criminal Code Review Board, #2, 408 York Ave., Winnipeg, MB R3C 0P9
204-945-4438

Northwest Territories

Legal Services Board of the Northwest Territories, 4915 - 48th St., PO Box 1320, Yellowknife, NT X1A 2L9
867-873-7450, Fax: 867-873-5320, lsb@gov.nt.ca

Territorial Board of Revision, #600, 5201 - 50th Ave., Yellowknife, NT X1A 3S9
867-873-7125, Fax: 867-873-0609

Ontario

Animal Care Review Board, #530, 20 Dundas St. West, Toronto, ON M5G 2C2
416-212-0334, Fax: 416-314-4270, 855-444-7454, acrb.registrar@ontario.ca

Medical Eligibility Committee, 370 Select Dr., PO Box 168, Kingston, ON K7M 8T4
613-536-3058

Ontario Municipal Board & Board of Negotiation, #1500, 655 Bay St., Toronto, ON M5G 1E5
416-212-6349, Fax: 416-326-5370, 866-448-2248, ontario.municipal.board@ontario.ca

Ontario Review Board, 151 Bloor St. West, 10th Fl., Toronto, ON M5S 2T5
416-327-8866, Fax: 416-327-8867, orb@ontario.ca

Safety, Licensing Appeals & Standards Tribunals Ontario, #5230, 20 Dundas St. West, Toronto, ON M5G 2C2
416-212-0334, Fax: 416-314-4270, 855-444-7454, slastoinfo@ontario.ca

Québec

Bureau d'audiences publiques sur l'environnement, Édifice Lomer-Gouin, #2.10, 575, rue Saint-Amable, Québec, QC G1R 6A6
418-643-7447, Fax: 418-643-9474, 800-463-4732, communication@bape.gouv.qc.ca

Saskatchewan

Public & Private Rights Board, #23, 3085 Albert St., Regina, SK S4S 0B1
306-787-4071, Fax: 306-787-0088

Saskatchewan Film & Video Classification Board, #500, 1919 Saskatchewan Dr., Regina, SK S4P 4H2
306-787-5550, Fax: 306-787-9779, 888-374-4636

Surface Rights Board of Arbitration, 113 - 2nd Ave. East, PO Box 1597, Kindersley, SK S0L 1S0
306-463-5447, Fax: 306-463-5449, surfacerightsboard@gov.sk.ca

BROADCASTING

Canadian Broadcasting Corporation, 181 Queen St., PO Box 3220 C,Ottawa, ON K1Y 1E4
613-288-6000, liaison@cbc.ca

Canadian Radio-Television & Telecommunications Commission, Central Building, 1, Promenade du Portage, Les Terrasses de la Chaudière, Gatineau, QC J8X 4B1
819-997-0313, Fax: 819-994-0218, 877-249-2782

Alberta

Public Affairs Bureau, Federal Bldg., 9820 - 107 St., 7th Fl., Edmonton, AB T5K 1E7

British Columbia

Knowledge Network Corporation, 4355 Mathissi Pl., Burnaby, BC V5G 4S8
604-431-3222, Fax: 604-431-3387, 877-456-6988, info@knowledge.ca

Nova Scotia

Communications Nova Scotia, 1723 Hollis St., 3rd Fl., PO Box 608, Halifax, NS B3J 2R7
902-424-7690, Fax: 902-424-0515

Québec

Société de télédiffusion du Québec (Télé-Québec), 1000, rue Fullum, Montréal, QC H2K 3L7
514-521-2424, Fax: 514-864-1970, info@teleQuébec.tv

BUDGET PLANNING

Finance Canada, 90 Elgin St., 14th Fl., Ottawa, ON K1A 0G5
613-369-3710, Fax: 613-369-4065, fin.financepublic-financepublique.fin@canada.ca

Alberta

Alberta Treasury Board & Finance, Oxbridge Place, 9820 - 106 St., 9th Fl., Edmonton, AB T5K 1E7
780-427-3035, Fax: 780-427-1147, -310-0000

British Columbia

British Columbia Ministry of Finance, PO Box 9417 Prov Govt, Victoria, BC V8W 9V1
877-388-4440, CTBTaxQuestions@gov.bc.ca

Provincial Treasury, PO Box 9414 Prov Govt, Victoria, BC V8V 9V1
250-387-4541, Fax: 250-356-3041

Manitoba

Manitoba Finance, #109, Legislative Bldg., Winnipeg, MB R3C 0V8
204-945-3754, minfin@leg.gov.mb.ca

Treasury Division, #350, 363 Broadway, Winnipeg, MB R3C 3N9
204-945-3702, Fax: 204-948-2233

New Brunswick

New Brunswick Department of Finance, Chancery Place, 675 King St., PO Box 6000, Fredericton, NB E3B 5H1
506-453-2451, Fax: 506-457-4989, wwwfin@gnb.ca

Newfoundland & Labrador

Newfoundland & Labrador Department of Finance, Confederation Bldg., PO Box 8700, St. John's, NL A1B 4J6
709-729-3166, Fax: 709-729-2232, finance@gov.nl.ca

Northwest Territories

Financial Management Board Secretariat, c/o Secretary of the FMB / Comptroller General, 5003 - 49 St., PO Box 1320, Yellowknife, NT X1A 2L9
Fax: 867-873-0414

Northwest Territories Department of Finance, PO Box 1320, Yellowknife, NT X1A 2L9
867-873-7500

Nova Scotia

Nova Scotia Department of Finance & Treasury Board, Provincial Bldg., 1723 Hollis St., 7th Fl., PO Box 187, Halifax, NS B3J 2N3
902-424-5554, Fax: 902-424-0635, FinanceWeb@novascotia.ca

Nunavut

Nunavut Territory Department of Finance, Bldg. 1079, 1st Fl., PO Box 1000 430, Iqaluit, NU X0A 0H0
867-975-5800, Fax: 867-975-5805

Ontario

Office of the Budget, Frost Bldg. South, 7 Queen's Park Cres., 7th Fl., Toronto, ON M7A 1Y7

Ontario Ministry of Finance, Frost Bldg. South, 7 Queen's Park Cres., 7th Fl., Toronto, ON M7A 1Y7
Fax: 866-888-3850, 866-668-8297, financecommunications.fin@ontario.ca

Prince Edward Island

Prince Edward Island Department of Finance, Shaw Bldg., 95 Rochford St. South, 2nd Fl., PO Box 2000, Charlottetown, PE C1A 7N8
902-368-4000, Fax: 902-368-5544

Québec

Ministère des Finances, 12, rue Saint-Louis, Québec, QC G1R 5L3
418-528-9323, Fax: 418-646-1631, info@finances.gouv.qc.ca

Saskatchewan

Saskatchewan Finance, 2350 Albert St., Regina, SK S4P 4A6
306-787-6768, Fax: 306-787-0241, communications@finance.gov.sk.ca

Yukon Territory

Yukon Finance, PO Box 2703, Whitehorse, YT Y1A 2C6
867-667-5343, Fax: 867-393-6217, fininfo@gov.yk.ca

BUSINESS & FINANCE

Atlantic Canada Opportunities Agency, Blue Cross Centre, 644 Main St., 3rd Fl., PO Box 6051, Moncton, NB E1C 9J8
506-851-2271, Fax: 506-851-7403, 800-561-7862

Auditor General of Canada, 240 Sparks St., Ottawa, ON K1A 0G6
613-952-0213, Fax: 613-957-0474, 888-761-5953, infomedia@oag-bvg.gc.ca

Bank of Canada, 234 Laurier Ave. West, Ottawa, ON K1A 0G9
613-782-8111, Fax: 613-782-7713, 800-303-1282, info@bankofcanada.ca

Business Development Bank of Canada, #400, 5, Place Ville-Marie, Montréal, QC H3B 5E7
877-232-2269

Calgary, #2403, 308-4th Ave. SW, Calgary, AB T2P 0H7
403-817-6700, Fax: 403-817-6701

Canada Business Network, 235 Queen St., Ottawa, ON K1A 0H5
343-291-1818, 888-576-4444

Canada Deposit Insurance Corporation, 50 O'Connor St., 17th Floor, Ottawa, ON K1P 6L2
Fax: 613-996-6095, 800-461-2342, info@cdic.ca

Canada Economic Development for Québec Regions, Édifice Dominion Square, #900, 1255, rue Peel, Montréal, QC H3B 2T9
514-283-6412, Fax: 514-283-3302, 866-385-6412

Canada Mortgage & Housing Corporation, 700 Montreal Rd., Ottawa, ON K1A 0P7
613-748-2000, Fax: 613-748-2098, 800-668-2642, chic@cmhc-schl.gc.ca

Canada Pension Plan Investment Board, #2500, 1 Queen St. East, Toronto, ON M5C 2W5
416-868-4075, Fax: 416-868-8689, 866-557-9510, contact@cppib.com

Canada Revenue Agency, 875 Heron Rd., Ottawa, ON K1A 1A2
800-267-6999

Canada Savings Bonds, #201, 50 O'Connor St., PO Box 2770 D, Ottawa, ON K1P 1J7
905-754-2012, Fax: 613-782-8096, 800-575-5151, csb@csb.gc.ca

Canadian Commercial Corporation, #700, 350 Albert St., Ottawa, ON K1A 0S6
613-996-0034, Fax: 613-995-2121, 800-748-8191, communications@ccc.ca

Competition Bureau Canada, Place du Portage, Phase I, 50 Victoria St., Ottawa, ON K1A 0C9
819-997-4282, Fax: 819-997-0324, 800-348-5358

Competition Tribunal, Thomas D'Arcy McGee Bldg., #600, 90 Sparks St., Ottawa, ON K1P 5B4
613-957-3172, Fax: 613-957-3170, tribunal@ct-tc.gc.ca

Export Development Canada, 150 Slater St., Ottawa, ON K1A 1K3
613-598-2500, Fax: 613-598-3811, 800-267-8510

Farm Credit Canada, 1800 Hamilton St., Regina, SK S4P 2B8
306-780-8100, Fax: 306-780-8919, 888-332-3301, csc@fcc-fac.ca

Finance Canada, 90 Elgin St., 14th Fl., Ottawa, ON K1A 0G5
613-369-3710, Fax: 613-369-4065, fin.financepublic-financepublique.fin@canada.ca

Financial Transactions & Reports Analysis Centre of Canada, 234 Laurier Ave. West, 24th Fl., Ottawa, ON K1P 1H7
Fax: 613-943-7931, 866-346-8722, guidelines-lignesdirectrices@fintrac-canafe.gc.ca

Freshwater Fish Marketing Corporation, 1199 Plessis Rd., Winnipeg, MB R2C 3L4
204-983-6601, Fax: 204-983-6497, sandic@freshwaterfish.com

Global Affairs Canada, Enquiries Service, 125 Sussex Dr., Ottawa, ON K1A 0G2
613-944-4000, Fax: 613-996-9709, 800-267-8376

Innovation, Science & Economic Development Canada, C.D. Howe Building, 235 Queen St., Ottawa, ON K1A 0H5
613-954-5031, Fax: 613-954-2340, 800-328-6189, info@ic.gc.ca

North American Free Trade Agreement (NAFTA) Secretariat, Canadian Section, 111 Sussex Dr., 5th Fl., Ottawa, ON K1N 1J1
343-203-4274, Fax: 613-992-9392, webmaster@nafta-alena.gc.ca

Office of the Superintendent of Financial Institutions, Kent Square, 255 Albert St., Ottawa, ON K1A 0H2
613-990-7788, Fax: 613-990-5591, 800-385-8647, information@osfi-bsif.gc.ca

PPP Canada, #630, 100 Queen St., Ottawa, ON K1P 1J9
613-947-9480, Fax: 613-947-2289, 877-947-9480, info@p3canada.ca

Public Sector Pension Investment Board, #200, 440 Laurier Ave. West, Ottawa, ON K1R 7X6
613-782-3095, Fax: 613-782-6864, info@investpsp.ca

Royal Canadian Mint, 320 Sussex Dr., Ottawa, ON K1A 0G8
613-954-2626, Fax: 613-998-4130, 800-267-1871

Statistics Canada, R.H. Coats Bldg., Tunney's Pasture, 150 Tunney's Pasture Driveway, Ottawa, ON K1A 0T6
514-283-8300, Fax: 514-283-9350, 800-263-1136, STATCAN.infostats-infostats.STATCAN@canada.ca

Treasury Board of Canada Secretariat, East Tower, 140 O'Connor St., 9th Fl., Ottawa, ON K1A 0R5
613-957-2400, Fax: 613-941-4000, 877-636-0656

Western Economic Diversification Canada, Canada Place, #1500, 9700 Jasper Ave. NW, Edmonton, AB T5J 4H7
780-495-4164, Fax: 780-495-4557, 888-338-9378

Alberta

Agricultural Products Marketing Council, JG O'Donoghue Bldg., #305, 7000 - 113 St., Edmonton, AB T6H 5T6
780-427-2164, Fax: 780-422-9690, marketingcouncil@gov.ab.ca

Alberta Automobile Insurance Rate Board, Canadian Western Bank Place, #2440, 10303 Jasper Ave., Edmonton, AB T5J 3N6
780-427-5428, Fax: 780-638-4254, -310-0000, airb@gov.ab.ca

Alberta Capital Finance Authority, Sun Life Place, #2160, 10123 - 99 St. NW, Edmonton, AB T5J 3H1
780-427-9711, Fax: 780-422-2175, webacfa@gov.ab.ca
Alberta Enterprise Corporation Board, Alberta Enterprise Corporation, #1100, 10830 Jasper Ave., Edmonton, AB T5J 2B3
780-392-3901, Fax: 780-392-3908, info@alberta-enterprise.ca
Alberta Investment Management Corporation, #1100, 10830 Jasper Ave., Edmonton, AB T5J 2B3
780-392-3600, inquiries@aimco.alberta.ca
Alberta Office of the Auditor General, 9925 - 109 St., 8th Fl., Edmonton, AB T5K 2J8
780-427-4222, Fax: 780-422-9555, info@oag.ab.ca
Alberta Securities Commission, #600, 250 - 5th St. SW, Calgary, AB T2P 0R4
403-297-6454, Fax: 403-297-6156, 877-355-0585, inquiries@asc.ca
Alberta Treasury Board & Finance, Oxbridge Place, 9820 - 106 St., 9th Fl., Edmonton, AB T5K 1E7
780-427-3035, Fax: 780-427-1147, -310-0000
ATB Financial, #2100, 10020 - 100 St. NW, Edmonton, AB T5J 0N3
403-245-8110, 800-332-8383
Consumer & Registry Services, ATB Place South, 10020 - 100 St., 29th Fl., Edmonton, AB T5J 0N3
Credit Union Deposit Guarantee Corporation, #2000, 10104 - 103 St., Edmonton, AB T5J 0H8
780-428-6680, Fax: 780-428-7571, 800-661-0351, mail@cudgc.ab.ca
Financial & Corporate Services Division, ATB Place, 10025 Jasper Ave., 16th Fl., Edmonton, AB T5J 1S6
Treasury & Risk Management Division, Federal Bldg., 9820 - 107 St., 8th Fl., Edmonton, AB T5K 1E7

British Columbia

Auditor Certification Board, PO Box 9431 Prov Govt, Victoria, BC V8W 9V3
250-356-8658, Fax: 250-356-9422, Marda.Forbes@gov.bc.ca
BC Immigrant Investment Fund Ltd., #301, 865 Hornby St., Vancouver, BC V6Z 2G3
Fax: 250-952-0371
BC Renaissance Capital Fund Ltd., PO Box 9800 Prov Govt, BC V8W 9W1
Fax: 250-952-0371
British Columbia Innovation Council, 1188 West Georgia St., 9th Fl., Vancouver, BC V6E 4A2
604-683-2724, Fax: 604-683-6567, 800-665-7222, info@bcic.ca
British Columbia Lottery Corporation, 74 West Seymour St., Kamloops, BC V2C 1E2
250-828-5500, Fax: 250-828-5631, 866-815-0222
British Columbia Ministry of Finance, PO Box 9417 Prov Govt, Victoria, BC V8W 9V1
877-388-4440, CTBTaxQuestions@gov.bc.ca
British Columbia Ministry of International Trade (& Minister Responsible for Asia Pacific Strategy & Multiculturalism), PO Box 9063 Prov Gov,Victoria, BC V8W 9E2
250-953-0910, Fax: 250-953-0928
British Columbia Ministry of Social Development & Social Innovation, PO Box 9058 Prov Govt, Victoria, BC V8W 9E1
800-663-7867, EnquiryBC@gov.bc.ca
British Columbia Pension Corporation, 2995 Jutland Rd., PO Box 9460, Victoria, BC V8W 9V8
250-387-1014, Fax: 250-953-0429, 800-663-8823, PensionCorp@pensionsbc.ca
British Columbia Securities Commission, Pacific Centre, 701 West Georgia St., 12th Fl., PO Box 10142, Vancouver, BC V7Y 1L2
604-899-6500, Fax: 604-899-6506, 800-373-6393, inquiries@bcsc.bc.ca
Crown Agencies Resource Office, #344, 617 Government St., PO Box 9416 Prov Govt, Victoria, BC V8W 9V1
250-387-8499, Fax: 250-356-2001, caro@gov.bc.ca
Financial Institutions Commission, #2800, 555 West Hastings, Vancouver, BC V6B 4N6
604-660-3555, Fax: 604-660-3365, 866-206-3030, FICOM@ficombc.ca
Insurance Corporation of British Columbia, 151 West Esplanade, North Vancouver, BC V7M 3H9
604-661-2800, 800-663-3051
Insurance Council of British Columbia, #300, 1040 West Georgia St., PO Box 7, Vancouver, BC V6E 4H1
604-688-0321, Fax: 604-662-7767, 877-688-0321, info@insurancecouncilofbc.com
Office of the Auditor General, PO Box 9036 Prov Govt, Victoria, BC V8W 9A2
250-419-6100, Fax: 250-387-1230
Office of the Auditor General for Local Government, #201, 10470 - 152nd St., Surrey, BC V3R 0Y3
604-930-7100
Public Sector Employers' Council Secretariat, #210, 880 Douglas St., PO Box 9400 Prov Govt, Victoria, BC V8V 9V1
250-387-0842, Fax: 250-387-6258
Timber Export Advisory Committee, PO Box 9514 Prov Govt, Victoria, BC V8W 9C2
250-387-8916, Fax: 250-387-5050

Manitoba

Claimant Adviser Office, #200, 330 Portage Ave., Winnipeg, MB R3C 0C4
204-945-7413, Fax: 204-948-3157, cao@gov.mb.ca
Communities Economic Development Fund, 15 Moak Cres., Thompson, MB R8N 2B8
204-778-4138, Fax: 204-778-4313, 800-561-4315
Convention Centre Corporation Board of Directors, 375 York Ave., Winnipeg, MB R3C 3J3
204-956-1720, Fax: 204-943-0310, 800-565-7776, audra@wcc.mb.ca
Crown Corporations Council, #1130, 444 St. Mary Ave., Winnipeg, MB R3C 3T1
204-949-5270, Fax: 204-949-5283, info@crowncc.mb.ca
Deposit Guarantee Corporation of Manitoba, #390, 200 Graham Ave., Winnipeg, MB R3C 4L5
204-942-8480, Fax: 204-947-1723, 800-697-4447, mail@depositguarantee.mb.ca
Fiscal Research Division, #910, 386 Broadway, Winnipeg, MB R3C 3R6
204-945-3757, Fax: 204-945-5051
Heritage Grants Advisory Council, c/o Heritage Grants Program, #330, 213 Notre Dame Ave., Winnipeg, MB R3B 1N3
204-945-2213, Fax: 204-948-2086
Manitoba Agricultural Services Corporation, #100, 1525 First St. South, Brandon, MB R7A 7A1
204-726-6850, Fax: 204-726-6849, mailbox@masc.mb.ca
Manitoba Bureau of Statistics, #824, 155 Carlton St., Winnipeg, MB R3C 3H9
204-945-2406
Manitoba Finance, #109, Legislative Bldg., Winnipeg, MB R3C 0V8
204-945-3754, minfin@leg.gov.mb.ca
Manitoba Growth, Enterprise & Trade, The Paris Building, 259 Portage Ave., 9th Fl., Winnipeg, MB R3B 3P4
204-945-1995, Fax: 204-945-2964
Manitoba Municipal Government, #301, 450 Broadway Ave., Winnipeg, MB R3C 0V8
204-945-3744, 866-626-4862, mgi@gov.mb.ca
Manitoba Public Insurance Corporation, #B100, 234 Donald St., PO Box 6300, Winnipeg, MB R3C 4A4
204-985-7000, Fax: 204-985-3525, 800-665-2410
Manitoba Securities Commission, #500, 400 St. Mary Ave., Winnipeg, MB R3C 4K5
204-945-2548, Fax: 204-945-0330, 800-655-5244, securities@gov.mb.ca
Manitoba Trade & Investment Corporation, #1100, 259 Portage Ave., Winnipeg, MB R3B 3P4
204-945-2466, Fax: 204-957-1793, 800-529-9981, mbtrade@gov.mb.ca
Office of the Auditor General, #500, 330 Portage Ave., Winnipeg, MB R3C 0C4
204-945-3790, Fax: 204-945-2169, oag.contact@oag.mb.ca
Pension Commission of Manitoba, #1004, 401 York Ave., Winnipeg, MB R3C 0P8
204-945-2740, Fax: 204-948-2375, pensions@gov.mb.ca
Treasury Board Secretariat, #200, 386 Broadway, Winnipeg, MB R3C 3R6
204-945-4150, Fax: 204-948-4878

New Brunswick

Atlantic Lottery Corporation, 922 Main St., PO Box 5500, Moncton, NB E1C 8W6
800-561-3942, info@alc.ca
Financial & Consumer Services Commission, #300, 85 Charlotte St., Saint John, NB E2L 2J2
506-658-3060, Fax: 506-658-3059, 866-933-2222, info@fcnb.ca
New Brunswick Department of Finance, Chancery Place, 675 King St., PO Box 6000, Fredericton, NB E3B 5H1
506-453-2451, Fax: 506-457-4989, wwwfin@gnb.ca
New Brunswick Farm Products Commission, c/o Department of Agriculture, Aquaculture & Fisheries, PO Box 6000, Fredericton, NB E3B 5H1
506-453-3647, Fax: 506-444-5969, DAAF-MAAP@gnb.ca
New Brunswick Investment Management Corporation, York Tower, #581, 440 King St., Fredericton, NB E3B 5H8
506-444-5800, Fax: 506-444-5025, comments@nbimc.com
New Brunswick Jobs Board, Chancery Place, PO Box 6000, Fredericton, NB E3B 5H1
New Brunswick Lotteries & Gaming Corporation, Chancery Place, 4th Fl., PO Box 6000, Fredericton, NB E3B 5H1
506-453-2451, Fax: 506-453-2053
Office of the Auditor General, HSBC Place, 520 King St., Fredericton, NB E3B 6G3
506-453-2243, Fax: 506-453-3067
Office of the Comptroller, Chancery Place, 3rd Fl., PO Box 6000, Fredericton, NB E3B 5H1
506-453-2451, Fax: 506-457-6878, wwwooc@gnb.ca
Regional Development Corporation, Chancery Place, PO Box 6000, Fredericton, NB E3B 5H1
506-453-2277, Fax: 506-453-7988

Newfoundland & Labrador

Credit Union Deposit Guarantee Corporation, PO Box 340, Marystown, NL A0E 2M0
709-279-0170, Fax: 709-279-0177, 877-279-0170
Newfoundland & Labrador Department of Business, Tourism, Culture & Rural Development, Confederation Bldg., West Block, 2nd Fl., PO Box 8700, St. John's, NL A1B 4J6
709-729-7000, btcrd@gov.nl.ca
Newfoundland & Labrador Department of Finance, Confederation Bldg., PO Box 8700, St. John's, NL A1B 4J6
709-729-3166, Fax: 709-729-2232, finance@gov.nl.ca
Newfoundland & Labrador Municipal Financing Corporation, Confederation Bldg., PO Box 8700, St. John's, NL A1B 4J6
709-729-6686, Fax: 709-729-2095
Office of the Auditor General, PO Box 8700, St. John's, NL A1B 4J6
709-729-2695, Fax: 709-729-5970, oagmail@oag.nl.ca

Northwest Territories

Financial Management Board Secretariat, c/o Secretary of the FMB / Comptroller General, 5003 - 49 St., PO Box 1320, Yellowknife, NT X1A 2L9
Fax: 867-873-0414
Northwest Territories Department of Finance, PO Box 1320, Yellowknife, NT X1A 2L9
867-873-7500
Northwest Territories Department of Public Works & Services, Stuart M. Hodgson Bldg., 5009 - 49th St., PO Box 1320, Yellowknife, NT X1A 2L9

Nova Scotia

Nova Scotia Business Inc., World Trade & Convention Centre, #701, 1800 Argyle St., PO Box 2374, Halifax, NS B3J 3N8
902-424-6650, Fax: 902-424-5739, 800-260-6682, info@nsbi.ca
Nova Scotia Department of Business, Centennial Building, #600, 1660 Hollis St., PO Box 2311, Halifax, NS B3J 3C8
902-424-0377, Fax: 902-424-0500, business@novascotia.ca
Nova Scotia Department of Finance & Treasury Board, Provincial Bldg., 1723 Hollis St., 7th Fl., PO Box 187, Halifax, NS B3J 2N3
902-424-5554, Fax: 902-424-0635, FinanceWeb@novascotia.ca
Nova Scotia Provincial Lotteries & Casino Corporation, Summit Place, 1601 Lower Water St., 5th Fl., PO Box 1501, Halifax, NS B3J 2Y3
902-424-2203, Fax: 902-424-0724
Nova Scotia Securities Commission, Duke Tower, #400, 5251 Duke St., PO Box 458, Halifax, NS B3J 2P8
902-424-7768, Fax: 902-424-4625, 855-424-2499, NSSCinquiries@novascotia.ca
Office of the Auditor General, Royal Centre, #400, 5161 George St., Halifax, NS B3J 1M7
902-424-5907, Fax: 902-424-4350

Nunavut

Legal Registries, PO Box 1000 570, Iqaluit, NU X0A 0H0
867-975-6590, Fax: 867-975-6594, Legal.Registries@gov.nu.ca
Nunavut Territory Department of Finance, Bldg. 1079, 1st Fl., PO Box 1000 430, Iqaluit, NU X0A 0H0
867-975-5800, Fax: 867-975-5805

Ontario

Advertising Review Board, Macdonald Block, #M2-56, 900 Bay St., 2nd Fl., Toronto, ON M7A 1N3
416-327-2183, Fax: 416-327-2179
Agriculture, Food & Rural Affairs Tribunal & Board of Negotiation, 1 Stone Rd. West, 2nd Fl., Guelph, ON N1G 4Y2
519-826-3433, Fax: 519-826-4232, 888-466-2372, appeals.tribunal.omafra@ontario.ca
Deposit Insurance Corporation of Ontario, #700, 4711 Yonge St., Toronto, ON M2N 6K8
416-325-9444, Fax: 416-325-9722, 800-268-6653, info@dico.com
Financial Services Commission of Ontario, New York City Ctr., 5160 Yonge St., 17th Fl., PO Box 85, Toronto, ON M2N 6L9
416-250-7250, Fax: 416-590-7070, 800-668-0128, contactcentre@fsco.gov.on.ca
Grain Financial Protection Board, 1 Stone Rd. West, 1st Fl. Northeast, PO Box 3660 Central, Guelph, ON N1H 8M4
519-826-3949, Fax: 519-826-3367
Licence Appeal Tribunal, #530, 20 Dundas St. West, Toronto, ON M5G 2C2
416-314-4260, Fax: 416-314-4270, 800-255-2214

Liquor Control Board of Ontario, 55 Lake Shore Blvd. East, Toronto, ON M5E 1A4
416-365-5900, Fax: 416-864-2476, 800-668-5226, infoline@lcbo.com
Livestock Financial Protection Board, 1 Stone Rd. West, 5th Fl. Northwest, Guelph, ON N1G 4Y2
519-826-3886, Fax: 519-826-4375, 888-466-2372
Metro Toronto Convention Centre Corporation, 255 Front St. West, Toronto, ON M5V 2W6
416-585-8120, Fax: 416-585-8198, info@mtccc.com
Normal Farm Practices Protection Board, 1 Stone Rd. West, 3rd Fl., Guelph, ON N1G 4Y2
519-826-4047, Fax: 519-826-3259, 877-424-1300, ag.info.omafra@ontario.ca
Office of the Auditor General, 20 Dundas St. West, 15th Fl., PO Box 105, Toronto, ON M5G 2C2
416-327-2381, Fax: 416-327-9862, comments@auditor.on.ca
Ontario Electricity Financial Corporation, #1400, 1 Dundas St. West, Toronto, ON M7A 1Y7
416-325-8000, Fax: 416-325-8005
Ontario Farm Products Marketing Commission, 1 Stone Rd. West, 5th Fl. Southwest, Guelph, ON N1G 4Y2
519-826-4220, Fax: 519-826-3400, ontariofarm.productsmarketing.omafra@ontario.ca
Ontario Financing Authority, #1400, 1 Dundas St. West, Toronto, ON M7A 1Y7
416-325-8000, Fax: 416-204-3391, investor@ofina.on.ca
Ontario Food Terminal Board, 165 The Queensway, Toronto, ON M8Y 1H8
416-259-5479, Fax: 416-259-4303, oftboard@interlog.com
Ontario Lottery & Gaming Corporation, Roberta Bondar Pl., #800, 70 Foster Dr., Sault Ste. Marie, ON P6A 6V2
705-946-6464, Fax: 416-224-7000, 800-387-0098
Ontario Ministry of Economic Development & Growth, Hearst Block, 900 Bay St., 8th Fl., Toronto, ON M7A 2E1
416-325-6666, 800-268-7095
Ontario Ministry of Finance, Frost Bldg. South, 7 Queen's Park Cres., 7th Fl., Toronto, ON M7A 1Y7
Fax: 866-888-3850, 866-668-8297, financecommunications.fin@ontario.ca
Ontario Ministry of Government & Consumer Services, Mowat Block, 900 Bay St., 6th Fl., Toronto, ON M7A 1L2
416-212-2665, 844-286-8404
Ontario Place Corporation, 955 Lake Shore Blvd. West, Toronto, ON M6K 3B9
416-314-9900, Fax: 416-314-9989, 866-663-4386
Ontario Racing Commission, #400, 10 Carlson Crt., Toronto, ON M9W 6L2
416-213-0520, Fax: 416-213-7827, inquiry@ontarioracingcommission.ca
Ontario Securities Commission, #1903, 20 Queen St. West, Toronto, ON M5H 3S8
416-593-8314, Fax: 416-593-8122, 877-785-1555, inquiries@osc.gov.on.ca
Ottawa Convention Centre, 55 Colonel By Dr., Ottawa, ON K1N 9J2
613-563-1984, Fax: 613-563-7646, 800-450-0077, info@ottawaconventioncentre.com
Pay Equity Commission, #300, 180 Dundas St. West, Toronto, ON M7A 2S6
416-314-1896, Fax: 416-314-8741, 800-387-8813
Rural Economic Development (RED) Panel, 1 Stone Rd. West, 4th Fl., Guelph, ON N1G 4Y2
Fax: 519-826-4336, 888-588-4111, red.omafra@ontario.ca

Prince Edward Island

Agricultural Insurance Corporation, 29 Indigo Cres., PO Box 1600, Charlottetown, PE C1A 7N3
902-368-4842, Fax: 902-368-6677
Charlottetown Area Development Corporation, 4 Pownal St., PO Box 786, Charlottetown, PE C1A 7L9
902-892-5341, Fax: 902-368-1935
Office of the Auditor General, Shaw Bldg., 105 Rochford St. North, 2nd Fl., PO Box 2000, Charlottetown, PE C1A 7N8
902-368-4520, Fax: 902-368-4598
Prince Edward Island Department of Finance, Shaw Bldg., 95 Rochford St. South, 2nd Fl., PO Box 2000, Charlottetown, PE C1A 7N8
902-368-4000, Fax: 902-368-5544
Prince Edward Island Lending Agency, Homburg Financial Tower, 98 Fitzroy St., 2nd Fl., Charlottetown, PE C1A 1R7
902-368-6200, Fax: 902-368-6201
Risk Management & Insurance, Shaw Bldg., 95 Rochford St., PO Box 2000, Charlottetown, PE C1A 7N8
902-368-6170, Fax: 902-368-6243

Québec

Autorité des marchés financiers, Tour de la Bourse, 800, Square Victoria, 22e étage, Montréal, QC H4Z 1G3
514-395-0337, Fax: 514-873-3090, 877-525-0337, information@lautorite.qc.ca
Bureau de décision et de révision, #16.40, 500, boul René-Lévesque ouest, Montréal, QC H2Z 1W7
514-873-2211, Fax: 514-873-2162, 877-873-2211, secretariatBDR@bdr.gouv.qc.ca
Caisse de dépôt et placement du Québec, 1000, place Jean-Paul-Riopelle, Montréal, QC H2Z 2B3
514-842-3261, Fax: 514-842-4833, 866-330-3936
Centre du services partagés du Québec, 875, Grande Allée est, 4e étage, section 4.751, Québec, QC G1R 5W5
418-644-2777, Fax: 418-644-0462, 855-644-2777, cspq@cspq.gouv.qc.ca
Financement-Québec, 12, rue Saint-Louis, 3e étage, Québec, QC G1R 5L3
418-691-2203, Fax: 418-644-6214, financement.regroupe@finances.gouv.qc.ca
Fonds de la recherche en santé du Québec, #800, 500, rue Sherbrooke ouest, Montréal, QC H3A 3C6
514-873-2114, Fax: 514-873-8768
Le Protecteur du Citoyen, #1.25, 525, boul René-Lévesque est, Québec, QC G1R 5Y4
418-643-2688, Fax: 418-643-8759, 800-463-5070, protecteur@protecteurducitoyen.qc.ca
Ministère de l'Économie, de la Science et de l'Innovation, 710, place D'Youville, 3e étage, Québec, QC G1R 4Y4
418-691-5950, Fax: 418-644-0118, 866-680-1884
Ministère des Finances, 12, rue Saint-Louis, Québec, QC G1R 5L3
418-528-9323, Fax: 418-646-1631, info@finances.gouv.qc.ca
Ministère des Relations internationales et Francophonie, Édifice Hector-Fabre, 525, boul Réne-Lévesque est, Québec, QC G1R 5R9
418-649-2300, Fax: 418-649-2656
Revenu Québec, Direction des relations publiques/Communications, 3800, rue de Marly, Québec, QC G1X 4A5
418-652-6831, Fax: 418-646-0167, cabinet@revenuQuébec.ca
Régie des rentes du Québec, CP 5200, Sainte-Foy, QC G1K 7S9
418-643-5185, 800-463-5185
Secrétariat du Conseil du trésor, 875, Grande Allée est, 5e étage, secteur 500, Québec, QC G1R 5R8
418-643-1529, Fax: 418-643-9226, 866-552-5158, communication@sct.gouv.qc.ca
Société de financement des infrastructures locales, 12, rue Saint-Louis, Québec, QC G1R 5L3
Société du Centre des congrès de Québec, 900, boul René-Lévesque est, 2e étage, Québec, QC G1R 2B5
418-644-4000, Fax: 418-644-6455, 888-679-4000
Société du Palais des congrès de Montréal, 159, rue Saint-Antoine ouest, 9é étage, Montréal, QC H2Z 1H2
514-871-8122, Fax: 514-871-9389, 800-268-8122, info@congresmtl.com
Vérificateur général du Québec, 750, boulevard Charest est, 3e étage, Québec, QC G1K 9J6
418-691-5900, Fax: 418-644-4460, verificateur.general@vgq.qc.ca

Saskatchewan

Board of Revenue Commissioners, #480, 2151 Scarth St., Regina, SK S4P 2H8
306-787-6221, Fax: 306-787-1610
Crown Investments Corporation of Saskatchewan, #400, 2400 College Ave., Regina, SK S4P 1C8
306-787-6851, Fax: 306-787-8125
Energy & Resources, 2101 Scarth St., Regina, SK S4P SH9
306-787-2528
Financial & Consumer Affairs Authority, #601, 1919 Saskatchewan Dr., Regina, SK S4P 4H2
306-787-5645, Fax: 306-787-5899, 877-880-5550, consumerprotection@gov.sk.ca
Municipal Financing Corporation of Saskatchewan, 2350 Albert St., 6th Fl., Regina, SK S4P 4A6
306-787-8150, Fax: 306-787-8493
Provincial Auditor Saskatchewan, Chateau Tower, #1500, 1920 Broad St., Regina, SK S4P 3V2
306-787-6398, Fax: 306-787-6383, info@auditor.sk.ca
Saskatchewan Crop Insurance Corporation, 484 Prince William Dr., PO Box 3000, Melville, SK S0A 2P0
306-728-7200, Fax: 306-728-7202, 888-935-0000, customer.service@scic.gov.sk.ca
Saskatchewan Finance, 2350 Albert St., Regina, SK S4P 4A6
306-787-6768, Fax: 306-787-0241, communications@finance.gov.sk.ca
Saskatchewan Government Insurance, 2260 - 11th Ave., Regina, SK S4P 0J9
306-751-1200, Fax: 306-787-7477, 800-667-8015, sgiinquiries@sgi.sk.ca

Yukon Territory

Yukon Finance, PO Box 2703, Whitehorse, YT Y1A 2C6
867-667-5343, Fax: 867-393-6217, fininfo@gov.yk.ca
Yukon Lottery Commission/Lotteries Yukon, #101, 205 Hawkins St., Whitehorse, YT Y1A 1X3
867-633-7890, Fax: 867-668-7561, 800-661-0555, lotteriesyukon@gov.yk.ca

BUSINESS ASSISTANCE PROGRAMS

Canada Business Network, 235 Queen St., Ottawa, ON K1A 0H5
343-291-1818, 888-576-4444

BUSINESS DEVELOPMENT

See Also: Industry; Science & Technology

Atlantic Canada Opportunities Agency, Blue Cross Centre, 644 Main St., 3rd Fl., PO Box 6051, Moncton, NB E1C 9J8
506-851-2271, Fax: 506-851-7403, 800-561-7862
Business Development Bank of Canada, #400, 5, Place Ville-Marie, Montréal, QC H3B 5E7
877-232-2269
Canada Business Network, 235 Queen St., Ottawa, ON K1A 0H5
343-291-1818, 888-576-4444
Canada Economic Development for Québec Regions, Édifice Dominion Square, #900, 1255, rue Peel, Montréal, QC H3B 2T9
514-283-6412, Fax: 514-283-3302, 866-385-6412
Canadian Northern Economic Development Agency, Ottawa, ON K1A 0H4
855-897-2667, InfoNorth@CanNor.gc.ca
Export Development Canada, 150 Slater St., Ottawa, ON K1A 1K3
613-598-2500, Fax: 613-598-3811, 800-267-8510
Federal Economic Development Agency for Southern Ontario, #101, 139 Northfield Dr. West, Waterloo, ON N2L 5A6
Fax: 519-725-4976, 866-593-5505
FedNor (Federal Economic Development Initiative in Northern Ontario), C.D. Howe Bldg., 235 Queen St., 8th Fl., Ottawa, ON K1A 0H5
Fax: 613-941-4553, 877-333-6673
Innovation, Science & Economic Development Canada, C.D. Howe Building, 235 Queen St., Ottawa, ON K1A 0H5
613-954-5031, Fax: 613-954-2340, 800-328-6189, info@ic.gc.ca
Market & Industry Services Branch, Tower 5, 1341 Baseline Rd., Ottawa, ON K1A 0C5
613-759-1000, Fax: 613-773-1711
Western Economic Diversification Canada, Canada Place, #1500, 9700 Jasper Ave. NW, Edmonton, AB T5J 4H7
780-495-4164, Fax: 780-495-4557, 888-338-9378

Alberta

Alberta Enterprise Corporation Board, Alberta Enterprise Corporation, #1100, 10830 Jasper Ave., Edmonton, AB T5J 2B3
780-392-3901, Fax: 780-392-3908, info@alberta-enterprise.ca
Alberta Innovates - Technology Futures, 250 Karl Clark Rd., Edmonton, AB T6N 1E4
780-450-5111, Fax: 780-450-5333, referral@albertainnovates.ca
Northern Alberta Development Council, Peace River Office, Provincial Building, #206, 9621 - 96 Ave., PO Box 900-14, Peace River, AB T8S 1T4
780-624-6274, Fax: 780-624-6184, -310-0000, nadc.council@gov.ab.ca

British Columbia

British Columbia Innovation Council, 1188 West Georgia St., 9th Fl., Vancouver, BC V6E 4A2
604-683-2724, Fax: 604-683-6567, 800-665-7222, info@bcic.ca
British Columbia Ministry of International Trade (& Minister Responsible for Asia Pacific Strategy & Multiculturalism), PO Box 9063 Prov Gov,Victoria, BC V8W 9E2
250-953-0910, Fax: 250-953-0928
British Columbia Ministry of Jobs, Tourism, & Skills Training (& Responsible for Labour), PO Box 9846 Prov Govt, Victoria, BC V8W 9T2
EnquiryBC@gov.bc.ca
British Columbia Ministry of Social Development & Social Innovation, PO Box 9058 Prov Govt, Victoria, BC V8W 9E1
800-663-7867, EnquiryBC@gov.bc.ca
Economic Development Division, PO Box 9846 Prov Gov,Victoria, BC V8W 9T2
Northern Development Initiative Trust, #301, 1268 Fifth Ave., Prince George, BC V2L 3L2
250-561-2525, Fax: 250-561-2563, info@northerndevelopment.bc.ca

Manitoba

Manitoba Growth, Enterprise & Trade, The Paris Building, 259 Portage Ave., 9th Fl., Winnipeg, MB R3B 3P4
204-945-1995, Fax: 204-945-2964

Manitoba Mineral Resources, The Paris Building, 259 Portage Ave., 9th Fl., Winnipeg, MB R3B 3P4
204-945-6569, 800-223-5215, minesinfo@gov.mb.ca

Manitoba Trade & Investment Corporation, #1100, 259 Portage Ave., Winnipeg, MB R3B 3P4
204-945-2466, Fax: 204-957-1793, 800-529-9981, mbtrade@gov.mb.ca

New Brunswick

New Brunswick Jobs Board, Chancery Place, PO Box 6000, Fredericton, NB E3B 5H1

Opportunities New Brunswick, Place 2000, PO Box 6000, Fredericton, NB E3B 5H1
506-453-5471, Fax: 506-444-5277, 855-746-4662, info@onbcanada.ca

Regional Development Corporation, Chancery Place, PO Box 6000, Fredericton, NB E3B 5H1
506-453-2277, Fax: 506-453-7988

Newfoundland & Labrador

Newfoundland & Labrador Department of Business, Tourism, Culture & Rural Development, Confederation Bldg., West Block, 2nd Fl., PO Box 8700, St. John's, NL A1B 4J6
709-729-7000, btcrd@gov.nl.ca

Northwest Territories

Northwest Territories Department of Industry, Tourism & Investment, PO Box 1320, Yellowknife, NT X1A 2L9
867-767-9002

Nova Scotia

Innovacorp, #1400, 1801 Hollis St., Halifax, NS B3J 3N4
902-424-8670, Fax: 902-424-4679, 800-565-7051, info@innovacorp.ca

Nova Scotia Business Inc., World Trade & Convention Centre, #701, 1800 Argyle St., PO Box 2374, Halifax, NS B3J 3N8
902-424-6650, Fax: 902-424-5739, 800-260-6682, info@nsbi.ca

Nova Scotia Department of Business, Centennial Building, #600, 1660 Hollis St., PO Box 2311, Halifax, NS B3J 3C8
902-424-0377, Fax: 902-424-0500, business@novascotia.ca

Trade Centre Limited, 1800 Argyle St., PO Box 955, Halifax, NS B3J 2V9
902-421-8686, Fax: 902-422-2922

Nunavut

Nunavut Territory Department of Economic Development & Transportation, Inuksugait Plaza, Bldg. 1104A, PO Box 1000 1500, Iqaluit, NU X0A 0H0
867-975-7800, Fax: 867-975-7870, 888-975-5999, edt@gov.nu.ca

Ontario

Northern Development Division, Roberta Bondar Place, #200, 70 Foster Dr., Sault Ste. Marie, ON P6A 6V8
705-945-5900, Fax: 705-945-5931, 800-461-2287

Ontario Ministry of Economic Development & Growth, Hearst Block, 900 Bay St., 8th Fl., Toronto, ON M7A 2E1
416-325-6666, 800-268-7095

Ontario Ministry of Government & Consumer Services, Mowat Block, 900 Bay St., 6th Fl., Toronto, ON M7A 1L2
416-212-2665, 844-286-8404

Prince Edward Island

Charlottetown Area Development Corporation, 4 Pownal St., PO Box 786, Charlottetown, PE C1A 7L9
902-892-5341, Fax: 902-368-1935

Innovation PEI, 94 Euston St., PO Box 910, Charlottetown, PE C1A 7L9
902-368-6300, Fax: 902-368-6301, 800-563-3734, innovation@gov.pe.ca

Prince Edward Island Lending Agency, Homburg Financial Tower, 98 Fitzroy St., 2nd Fl., Charlottetown, PE C1A 1R7
902-368-6200, Fax: 902-368-6201

Québec

Commission de la capitale nationale du Québec, Edifice Hector-Fabre, 525 boul René-Lévesque Est, RC, Québec, QC G1R 5S9
418-528-0773, Fax: 418-528-0833, 800-442-0773, commission@capitale.gouv.qc.ca

Ministère des Finances, 12, rue Saint-Louis, Québec, QC G1R 5L3
418-528-9323, Fax: 418-646-1631, info@finances.gouv.qc.ca

Saskatchewan

Energy & Resources, 2101 Scarth St., Regina, SK S4P 5H9
306-787-2528

Yukon Territory

Yukon Development Corporation, PO Box 2703 D-1, Whitehorse, YT Y1A 2C6
867-456-3837, Fax: 867-393-7167

Yukon Economic Development, #209, 212 Main St., F-1, Whitehorse, YT Y1A 2A9
867-393-7191, Fax: 867-393-6412, 800-661-0408, ecdev@gov.yk.ca

BUSINESS REGULATIONS

Canada Revenue Agency, 875 Heron Rd., Ottawa, ON K1A 1A2
800-267-6999

Innovation, Science & Economic Development Canada, C.D. Howe Building, 235 Queen St., Ottawa, ON K1A 0H5
613-954-5031, Fax: 613-954-2340, 800-328-6189, info@ic.gc.ca

British Columbia

Corporate Services Division, PO Box 9415 Prov Govt, Victoria, BC V8W 9V1

Nova Scotia

Nova Scotia Business Inc., World Trade & Convention Centre, #701, 1800 Argyle St., PO Box 2374, Halifax, NS B3J 3N8
902-424-6650, Fax: 902-424-5739, 800-260-6682, info@nsbi.ca

Service Nova Scotia, c/o Public Enquiries - Service Nova Scotia, PO Box 2734, Halifax, NS B3J 3K5
902-424-5200, Fax: 902-424-0720, 800-670-4357

Nunavut

Nunavut Territory Department of Finance, Bldg. 1079, 1st Fl., PO Box 1000 430, Iqaluit, NU X0A 0H0
867-975-5800, Fax: 867-975-5805

Ontario

Office of the Fairness Commissioner, #1201, 595 Bay St., Toronto, ON M7A 2B4
416-325-9380, Fax: 416-326-6081, 877-727-5365, ofc@ontario.ca

ServiceOntario, College Park, 777 Bay St., 15th fl., Toronto, ON M7A 2J3
Fax: 416-326-1313, 800-267-8097

CABINETS & EXECUTIVE COUNCILS

See Also: Government (General Information); Parliament

The Canadian Ministry, Information Service, Parliament of Canada, Ottawa, ON K1A 0A9
613-992-4793, 866-599-4999, info@parl.gc.ca

Alberta

Executive Council, Legislature Building, 10800 - 97 Ave., Edmonton, AB T5K 2B6
780-427-2711, -310-0000

British Columbia

Executive Council of the Government of British Columbia, Cabinet Operations, 617 Government St., 1st Fl., PO Box 9487 Prov Govt, Victoria, BC V8W 9W6

Manitoba

Executive Council, Legislative Building, 450 Broadway Ave., Winnipeg, MB R3C 0V8

New Brunswick

Executive Council, Centennial Building, PO Box 6000, Fredericton, NB E3B 5H1
506-444-4417, Fax: 506-453-2266, Executivecouncilloffice@gnb.ca

Newfoundland & Labrador

Executive Council, c/o Communications Branch, East Block, Confederation Building, 10th Fl., St. John's, NL A1B 4J6
info@gov.nl.ca

Northwest Territories

Executive Council, PO Box 1320, Yellowknife, NT X1A 2L9
executive_communications@gov.nt.ca

Nova Scotia

Executive Council Office, One Government Place, 1700 Granville St., 5th Fl., PO Box 2125, Halifax, NS B3J 3B7
902-424-5970, Fax: 902-424-0667, execounc@gov.ns.ca

Nunavut

Executive Council, PO Box 2410, Iqaluit, NU X0A 0H0

Ontario

Cabinet of Ontario, Legislative Building, Queen's Park, Toronto, ON M7A 1A1

Prince Edward Island

Executive Council, Shaw Bldg., 5th Fl., PO Box 2000, Charlottetown, PE C1A 7N8
902-368-4502, Fax: 902-368-6118

Québec

Ministère du Conseil exécutif, 875, Grande Allée est, Québec, QC G1R 4Y8
418-643-2001, Fax: 418-528-9242

Saskatchewan

Executive Council, Communications Services, Executive Council, #130, 3085 Albert St., Regina, SK S4S 0B1
306-787-6276, Fax: 306-787-6123

Yukon Territory

Executive Council, 2071 Second Ave., PO Box 2703, Whitehorse, YT Y1A 2C6
867-667-5393, Fax: 867-393-6214, eco@gov.yk.ca

CANADIANS & SOCIETY

Beverly & Qamanirjuaq Caribou Management Board, Secretariat, PO Box 629, Stonewall, MB R0C 2Z0
204-467-2438, caribounews@arctic-caribou.com

Canada Council for the Arts, 150 Elgin St., 2nd Fl., PO Box 1047, Ottawa, ON K1P 5V8
613-566-4414, Fax: 613-566-4390, 800-263-5588, info@canadacouncil.ca

Canada Lands Company Ltd., #1200, 1 University Ave., Toronto, ON M5J 2P1
416-952-6112

Canadian Heritage, 15 Eddy St., Gatineau, QC K1A 0M5
819-997-0055, 866-811-0055, PCH.info-info.PCH@canada.ca

Canadian Human Rights Commission, 344 Slater St., 8th Fl., Ottawa, ON K1A 1E1
Fax: 613-996-9661, 888-214-1090, info.com@chrc-ccdp.gc.ca

Canadian Human Rights Tribunal, 160 Elgin St., 11th Fl., Ottawa, ON K1A 1J4
613-995-1707, Fax: 613-995-3484, registrar@chrt-tcdp.gc.ca

Canadian Race Relations Foundation, #225, 6 Garamond Ct., Toronto, ON M3C 1Z5
416-441-1900, Fax: 416-441-2752, 888-240-4936, info@crrf-fcrr.ca

Employment & Social Development Canada, 140 Promenade du Portage, Gatineau, QC K1A 0J9

First Nations Tax Commission, #321, 345 Chief Alex Thomas Way, Kamloops, BC V2H 1H1
250-828-9857, Fax: 250-828-9858, 855-682-3682, mailkamloops@fntc.ca

Global Affairs Canada, Enquiries Service, 125 Sussex Dr., Ottawa, ON K1A 0G2
613-944-4000, Fax: 613-996-9709, 800-267-8376

Government of Canada, c/o Canada Enquiry Centre, Service Canada, Ottawa, ON K1A 0J9
800-622-6232

Historic Sites & Monuments Board of Canada, 30 Victoria St., 3rd Fl., Gatineau, QC J8X 0B3
Fax: 819-420-9260, 855-283-8730, hsmbc-clmhc@pc.gc.ca

Immigration & Refugee Board of Canada, Canada Bldg, 344 Slater St., 12th Fl., Ottawa, ON K1A 0K1
613-995-6486, Fax: 613-943-1550, contact@irb-cisr.gc.ca

Immigration, Refugees & Citizenship, Jean Edmonds, South Tower, 365 Laurier Ave. West, Ottawa, ON K1A 1L1
888-242-2100

Indigenous & Northern Affairs, Terrasses de la Chaudière, 10 Wellington St., North Tower, Gatineau, QC K1A 0H4
Fax: 866-817-3977, 800-567-9604, infopubs@aadnc-aandc.gc.ca

Mental Health Commission of Canada, #600, 100 Sparks St., Ottawa, ON K1P 5B7
613-683-3755, Fax: 613-798-2989, info@mentalhealthcommission.ca

National Battlefields Commission, 390, av de Bernières, Québec, QC G1R 2L7
418-648-3506, Fax: 418-648-3638, information@ccbn-nbc.gc.ca

National Capital Commission, #202, 40 Elgin St., Ottawa, ON K1P 1C7
613-239-5000, Fax: 613-239-5063, 800-465-1867, info@ncc-ccn.ca

National Seniors Council, Phase IV, 8th Floor, Mail Stop 802, 140 Promenade du Portage, Gatineau, QC K1A 0J9
Fax: 819-953-9298, 800-622-6232

Networks of Centres of Excellence of Canada, 350 Albert Street, 16th Fl., Ottawa, ON K1A 1H5
613-995-6010, Fax: 613-992-7356, info@nce-rce.gc.ca

Nunavut Impact Review Board, 29 Mitik St., PO Box 1360, Cambridge Bay, NU X0B 0C0
867-983-4600, Fax: 867-983-2594, 866-233-3033, info@nirb.ca

Nunavut Planning Commission, PO Box 2101, Cambridge Bay, NU X0B 0C0
867-983-4625, Fax: 867-983-4626

Nunavut Water Board, PO Box 119, Gjoa Haven, NU X0B 1J0
867-360-6338, Fax: 867-360-6369

Office of the Commissioner of Official Languages, 30 Victoria St., 6th Fl., Gatineau, ON K1A 0T8
819-420-4877, Fax: 819-420-4873, 877-996-6368

Office of the Prime Minister, Liberal Party of Canada / Liberal Research Bureau, Langevin Block, 80 Wellington St., Ottawa, ON K1A 0A2
613-992-4211, Fax: 613-941-6900

Office of the Public Sector Integrity Commissioner of Canada, 60 Queen St., 7th Fl., Ottawa, ON K1P 5Y7
613-941-6400, Fax: 613-941-6535, 866-941-6400

Passport Canada, Passport Canada Program, Gatineau, QC K1A 0G3
800-567-6868

Porcupine Caribou Management Board, PO Box 31723, Whitehorse, YT Y1A 6L3
867-633-4780, Fax: 867-393-3904, pcmb@taiga.net

Public Health Agency of Canada, 130 Colonnade Rd., Ottawa, ON K1A 0K9

Social Sciences & Humanities Research Council of Canada, Constitution Sq., 350 Albert St., PO Box 1610 B,Ottawa, ON K1P 6G4
613-992-0691

Specific Claims Tribunal Canada, #400, 427 Laurier Ave. West, 4th Fl., PO Box 31, Ottawa, ON K1R 7Y2
613-947-0751, Fax: 613-943-0586, claims.revendications@sct-trp.ca

Status of Women Canada, PO Box 8097 T CSC,Ottawa, ON K1G 3H6
613-995-7835, Fax: 819-420-6906, 855-969-9922, communications@swc-cfc.gc.ca

Veterans Affairs Canada, 161 Grafton St., PO Box 7700, Charlottetown, PE C1A 8M9
866-522-2122, information@vac-acc.gc.ca

Veterans Review & Appeal Board, Daniel J. MacDonald Bldg., 161 Grafton St., PO Box 9900, Charlottetown, PE C1A 8V7
902-566-8751, Fax: 902-566-7850, 800-450-8006, vrab_tacra@vac-acc.gc.ca

Alberta

Alberta Health, PO Box 1360 Main,Edmonton, AB T5J 2N3
780-427-7164, -310-0000

Appeals Secretariat, Centre West Bldg., 10035 - 108 St., 6th Fl., Calgary, AB T5J 3E1
780-427-2709, Fax: 780-422-1088, appeals@gov.ab.ca

Labour Relations Board, Labour Building, #501, 10808 - 99 Ave., Edmonton, AB T5K 0G5
780-427-8547, Fax: 780-422-0970, 800-463-2572, alrbinfo@gov.ab.ca

Premier's Council on the Status of Persons with Disabilities, HSBC Building, #1110, 10055 - 106 St., Edmonton, AB T5J 1G3
780-422-1095, Fax: 780-415-0097, 800-272-8841, hs.pcspd@gov.ab.ca

Seniors Advisory Council for Alberta, Standard Life Centre, #600, 10405 Jasper Ave., 6th Fl., Edmonton, AB T5J 4R7
780-422-2321, Fax: 780-422-8762, -310-0000, saca@gov.ab.ca

Status of Women, Office of the Minister, Legislature Bldg., #208, 10800 - 97 Ave., Edmonton, AB T5K 2B6

British Columbia

British Columbia Ministry of Children & Family Development, PO Box 9770 Prov Govt, Victoria, BC V8W 9S5
250-387-7027, Fax: 250-356-3007, 877-387-7027, MCF.CorrespondenceManagement@gov.bc.ca

British Columbia Ministry of Community, Sport, & Cultural Development & Responsible for TransLink, PO Box 9490 Prov Govt, Victoria, BC V8W 9N7

British Columbia Treaty Commission, #700, 1111 Melville St., Vancouver, BC V6E 3V6
604-482-9200, Fax: 604-482-9222, 855-482-9200, info@bctreaty.net

Local Government, PO Box 9490 Prov Govt, Victoria, BC V8W 9N7
250-356-6575, Fax: 250-387-7973

Native Economic Development Advisory Board, PO Box 9100 Prov Govt, Victoria, BC V8W 9B1
250-387-2536

Manitoba

Aboriginal Affairs Secretariat, #200, 500 Portage Ave., Winnipeg, MB R3C 3X1
204-945-2510, Fax: 204-945-3689

Communications Services Manitoba, 155 Carlton St., 10th Fl., Winnipeg, MB R3C 3H8
204-945-3765

Communities Economic Development Fund, 15 Moak Cres., Thompson, MB R8N 2B8
204-778-4138, Fax: 204-778-4313, 800-561-4315

Healthy Living & Seniors, c/o Seniors & Healthy Aging Secretariat, #1610, 155 Carlton St., Winnipeg, MB R3C 3H8
204-945-6565, Fax: 204-948-2514, 800-665-6565, seniors@gov.mb.ca

Heritage Grants Advisory Council, c/o Heritage Grants Program, #330, 213 Notre Dame Ave., Winnipeg, MB R3B 1N3
204-945-2213, Fax: 204-948-2086

Le Centre Culturel franco-manitobain/Franco-Manitoban Cultural Centre, 340, boul Provencher, Winnipeg, MB R2H 0G7
204-233-8972, Fax: 204-233-3324, communication@ccfm.mb.ca

Manitoba Centennial Centre Corporation, #1000, 555 Main St., Winnipeg, MB R3B 1C3
204-956-1360, Fax: 204-944-1390, inquiries@mbccc.ca

Manitoba Education & Training, #168, Legislative Bldg., 450 Broadway, Winnipeg, MB R3C 0V8
204-945-3720, Fax: 204-945-1291, minedu@leg.gov.mb.ca

Manitoba Families, Legislative Building, #357, 450 Broadway, Winnipeg, MB R3C 0V8
204-945-3744, 866-626-4862

Manitoba Film Classification Board, #216, 301 Weston St., Winnipeg, MB R3E 3H4
204-945-8962, Fax: 204-945-0890, 866-612-2399, mfcb@gov.mb.ca

Manitoba Heritage Council, 213 Notre Dame Ave., Main Fl., Winnipeg, MB R3B 1N3
204-945-2118, Fax: 204-948-2384, hrb@gov.mb.ca

Manitoba Housing & Community Development, 352 Donald St., Winnipeg, MB R3B 2H8
204-945-4663, Fax: 204-948-2013, 800-661-4663, housing@gov.mb.ca

Manitoba Human Rights Commission, #700, 175 Hargrave St., Winnipeg, MB R3C 3R8
204-945-3007, Fax: 204-945-1292, 888-884-8681, hrc@gov.mb.ca

Manitoba Indigenous & Municipal Relations, Legislative Bldg, #344, 450 Broadway, Winnipeg, MB R3C 0V8
204-945-3719, Fax: 204-945-8374, anaweb@gov.mb.ca

Multiculturalism Secretariat, 213 Notre Dame Ave., 7th Fl., Winnipeg, MB R3B 1N3
204-945-5632, multisec@gov.mb.ca

Public Health & Primary Health Care, 300 Carlton St., 4th Floor, Winnipeg, MB R3B 3M9
204-788-6666

Status of Women, #409, 401 York Ave., Winnipeg, MB R3C 0P8
204-945-6281, Fax: 204-945-6511, 800-263-0234, msw@gov.mb.ca

New Brunswick

Intergovernmental Affairs Division, Chancery Place, 675 King St., 5th Fl., Fredericton, NB E3B 1E9
506-444-4948, Fax: 506-453-2995, iga@gnb.ca

New Brunswick Department of Health, HSBC Place, PO Box 5100, Fredericton, NB E3B 5G8
506-457-4800, Fax: 506-453-5243, Health.Sante@gnb.ca

New Brunswick Department of Social Development, Sartain MacDonald Bldg., 551 King St., PO Box 6000, Fredericton, NB E3B 5H1
506-453-2001, Fax: 506-453-2164, sd-ds@gnb.ca

New Brunswick Human Rights Commission, Barry House, PO Box 6000, Fredericton, NB E3B 5H1
506-453-2301, Fax: 506-453-2653, 888-471-2233, hrc.cdp@gnb.ca

Premier's Council on the Status of Disabled Persons, #648, 440 King St., Fredericton, NB E3B 5H8
506-444-3000, Fax: 506-444-3001, 800-442-4412, pcsdp@gnb.ca

Regional Development Corporation, Chancery Place, PO Box 6000, Fredericton, NB E3B 5H1
506-453-2277, Fax: 506-453-7988

Newfoundland & Labrador

C.A. Pippy Park Commission, Mount Scio House, 15 Mount Scio Rd., St. John's, NL A1B 3T2
709-737-3655, info@pippypark.com

Newfoundland & Labrador Department of Advanced Education & Skills, Confederation Building, West Block, 3rd Fl., PO Box 8700, St. John's, NL A1B 4J6
709-729-2480, aesweb@gov.nl.ca

Newfoundland & Labrador Department of Business, Tourism, Culture & Rural Development, Confederation Bldg., West Block, 2nd Fl., PO Box 8700, St. John's, NL A1B 4J6
709-729-7000, btcrd@gov.nl.ca

Newfoundland & Labrador Human Rights Commission, The Beothuk Bldg., 21 Crosbie Pl., PO Box 8700, St. John's, NL A1B 4J6
709-729-2709, Fax: 709-729-0790, 800-563-5808, humanrights@gov.nl.ca

Provincial Advisory Council on the Status of Women, #103, 15 Hallett Cres., St. John's, NL A1B 4C4
709-753-7270, Fax: 709-753-2606, 877-753-7270, info@pacsw.ca

Northwest Territories

Northwest Territories Department of Aboriginal Affairs & Intergovernmental Relations, 4910 - 52nd St., PO Box 1320, Yellowknife, NT X1A 2L9
867-767-9025, Fax: 867-873-0233

Northwest Territories Department of Municipal & Community Affairs, PO Box 1320, Yellowknife, NT X1A 2L9
867-767-9160, Fax: 867-873-0309

Office of the Languages Commissioner, Capital Suites - Zheh Gwizu', PO Box 2096, Inuvik, NT X0E 0T0
867-678-2200, Fax: 867-678-2201, 800-661-0889

Status of Women Council of the Northwest Territories, Northwest Tower, 4th Fl., PO Box 1320, Yellowknife, NT X1A 2L9
867-920-6177, Fax: 867-873-0285, 888-234-4485, council@statusofwomen.nt.ca

Nova Scotia

Nova Scotia Advisory Commission on AIDS, Barrington Tower, 1894 Barrington St., PO Box 31, Halifax, NS B3J 2L4
902-424-5730, aids@gov.ns.ca

Nova Scotia Advisory Council on the Status of Women, Quinpool Centre, #202, 6169 Quinpool Rd., PO Box 745, Halifax, NS B3J 2T3
902-424-8662, Fax: 902-424-0573, 800-565-8662, women@gov.ns.ca

Nova Scotia Department of Community Services, Nelson Place, 5675 Spring Garden Rd., 8th Fl., PO Box 696, Halifax, NS B3J 2T7
877-424-1177

Nova Scotia Department of Seniors, Barrington Tower, 1894 Barrington St., 15th Fl., Halifax, NS B3J 2R8
902-424-0770, Fax: 902-424-0561, 844-277-0770, seniors@NovaScotia.ca

Nova Scotia Disabled Persons Commission, Dartmouth Professional Center, #104, 277 Pleasant St., Dartmouth, NS B2Y 4B7
902-424-8280, 800-565-8280

Nova Scotia Human Rights Commission, Park Lane Terraces, #305, 5657 Spring Garden Rd., PO Box 2221, Halifax, NS B3J 3C4
902-424-4111, Fax: 902-424-0596, 877-269-7699, hrcinquiries@novascotia.ca

Pay Equity Commission, 5151 Terminal Rd., 6th Fl., PO Box 697, Halifax, NS B3J 2T8
902-424-8466, Fax: 902-424-0575

Service Nova Scotia, c/o Public Enquiries - Service Nova Scotia, PO Box 2734, Halifax, NS B3J 3K5
902-424-5200, Fax: 902-424-0720, 800-670-4357

Nunavut

Nunavut Territory Department of Family Services, PO Box 1000 950, Iqaluit, NU X0A 0H0
867-975-6038, Fax: 867-975-6091

Ontario

Anti-Racism Directorate, Ferguson Block, Queen's Park, 77 Wellesley St. West, 13th Fl., Toronto, ON M7A 1N3

Citizenship & Immigration Division, 400 University Ave., 3rd Fl., Toronto, ON M7A 2R9
416-314-7541, Fax: 416-314-7599

Office of Francophone Affairs, #200, 700 Bay St., 2nd Fl., Toronto, ON M7A 0A2
416-325-4949, Fax: 416-325-4980, 800-268-7507, ofa@ontario.ca

Ontario Heritage Trust, 10 Adelaide St. East, Toronto, ON M5C 1J3
416-325-5000, Fax: 416-325-5071

Ontario Human Rights Commission, #900, 180 Dundas St. West, Toronto, ON M7A 2R9
416-326-9511, Fax: 416-314-4494, 800-387-9080, info@ohrc.on.ca

Ontario Ministry of Citizenship & Immigration, 400 University Ave., 6th Fl., Toronto, ON M7A 2R9
416-327-2422, Fax: 416-327-1061, 800-267-7329, info.mci@ontario.ca

Ontario Ministry of Community & Social Services, Hepburn Block, 80 Grosvenor St., 6th Fl., Toronto, ON M7A 1E9
416-325-5666, Fax: 416-325-3347, 888-789-4199

Ontario Ministry of Government & Consumer Services, Mowat Block, 900 Bay St., 6th Fl., Toronto, ON M7A 1L2
416-212-2665, 844-286-8404

Ontario Ministry of Indigenous Relations & Reconciliation, 160 Bloor St. East, 4th Fl., Toronto, ON M7A 2E6
416-326-4740, Fax: 416-326-4017, 866-381-5337

Ontario Women's Directorate, College Park, 777 Bay St., 6th Fl., Toronto, ON M7A 2J4
416-314-0300, Fax: 416-314-0247, 866-510-5902, owd@ontario.ca

Royal Ontario Museum, 100 Queen's Park Cres., Toronto, ON M5S 2C6
416-586-5549, Fax: 416-586-5685, info@rom.on.ca

Prince Edward Island

Prince Edward Island Department of Family & Human Services, Jones Bldg., 11 Kent St., 2nd Fl., PO Box 2000, Charlottetown, PE C1A 7N8
902-620-3777, Fax: 902-894-0242, 866-594-3777

Prince Edward Island Human Rights Commission, 53 Water St., PO Box 2000, Charlottetown, PE C1A 7N8
902-368-4180, Fax: 902-368-4236, 800-237-5031, contact@peihumanrights.ca

Québec

Commission administrative des régimes de retraite et d'assurances (Québec), 475, rue Saint-Amable, Québec, QC G1R 5X3
418-643-4881, Fax: 418-644-3839, 800-463-5533

Commission des biens culturels du Québec, Bloc A-RC, 225, Grande Allée est, Québec, QC G1R 5G5
418-643-8378, Fax: 418-643-8591, info@cbcq.gouv.qc.ca

Conseil des arts et des lettres du Québec, 79, boul René-Lévesque est, 3e étage, Québec, QC G1R 5N5
418-643-1707, Fax: 418-643-4558, 800-897-1707, info@calq.gouv.qc.ca

Conseil du statut de la femme, #300, 800, place D'Youville, 3e étage, Québec, QC G1R 6E2
418-643-4326, Fax: 418-643-8926, 800-463-2851, csf@csf.gouv.qc.ca

Curateur public du Québec, 600, boul René-Lévesque ouest, Montréal, QC H3B 4W9
514-873-4074, 800-363-9020

Fonds québécois de la recherche sur la société et la culture, #470, 140, Grande Allée est, Québec, QC G1R 5M8
418-643-7582, Fax: 418-644-5248, frq.sc@frq.gouv.qc.ca

Ministère de l'Immigration, de la Diversité et de l'Inclusion, Édifice Gérald-Godin, 360, rue McGill, Montréal, QC H2Y 2E9
514-864-9191, Fax: 514-864-2899, 877-864-9191

Ministère de la Culture et Communications, 225, Grande Allée est, Québec, QC G1R 5G5
888-380-8882

Ministère de la Santé et des Services sociaux, Direction des communications, 1075, ch Sainte-Foy, 16e étage, Québec, QC G1S 2M1
418-643-9395, Fax: 418-643-4768, regisseur.web@msss.gouv.qc.ca

Ministère des Relations internationales et Francophonie, Édifice Hector-Fabre, 525, boul Réne-Lévesque est, Québec, QC G1R 5R9
418-649-2300, Fax: 418-649-2656

Ministère du Travail, de l'Emploi et de la Solidarité sociale, 200, ch Sainte-Foy, 5e étage, Québec, QC G1R 5S1
418-644-4545, Fax: 418-528-0559, 877-644-4545

Office des personnes handicapées du Québec, 309, rue Brock, Drummondville, QC J2B 1C5
Fax: 819-475-8753, 800-567-1465, aide@ophq.gouv.qc.ca

Secrétariat aux affaires autochtones, 905, av Honoré-Mercier, 1er étage, Québec, QC G1R 5M6
418-643-3166, Fax: 418-646-4918

Secrétariat aux affaires intergouvernementales canadiennes, 875, Grande Allée est, 3e étage, Québec, QC G1R 4Y8
418-643-4011, Fax: 418-528-0052

Société de développement des entreprises culturelles, #800, 215, rue Saint-Jacques, Montréal, QC H2Y 1M6
514-841-2200, Fax: 514-841-8606, 800-363-0401, info@sodec.gouv.qc.ca

Tribunal administratif du Québec, 575, rue Saint-Amable, Québec, QC G1R 5R4
418-643-3418, Fax: 418-643-5335, 800-567-0278, tribunal.administratif@taq.gouv.qc.ca

Saskatchewan

Saskatchewan Heritage Foundation, 3211 Albert St., 1st Fl., Regina, SK S4S 5W6
306-787-8600, Fax: 306-787-0069

Saskatchewan Human Rights Commission, Saskatoon Office, Sturdy Stone Bdg., #816, 122 - 3 Ave. North, 8th Fl., Saskatoon, SK S7K 2H6
306-933-5952, Fax: 306-933-7863, 800-667-9249, shrc@gov.sk.ca

Saskatchewan Social Services, 1920 Broad St., Regina, SK S4P 3V6
306-787-3700, 866-221-5200, socialservicesinquiry@gov.sk.ca

Yukon Territory

Yukon Community Services, PO Box 2703, Whitehorse, YT Y1A 2C6
867-667-5811, Fax: 867-393-6295, 800-661-0408, inquiry@gov.yk.ca

Yukon Health & Social Services, PO Box 2703, Whitehorse, YT Y1A 2C6
867-667-3673, Fax: 867-667-3096, 800-661-0408, hss@gov.yk.ca

Yukon Human Rights Commission, #101, 9010 Quartz St., Whitehorse, YT Y1A 2Z5
867-667-6226, Fax: 867-667-2662, 800-661-0535, humanrights@yhrc.yk.ca

Yukon Women's Directorate, #1, 404 Hason St., PO Box 2703, Whitehorse, YT Y1A 2C6
867-667-3030, Fax: 867-393-6270

CAREER PLANNING

Alberta

Alberta Labour, Legislature Bldg., #404, 10800 - 97 Ave., Edmonton, AB T5K 2B6
780-427-3731, 877-427-3731

British Columbia

British Columbia Ministry of Jobs, Tourism, & Skills Training (& Responsible for Labour), PO Box 9846 Prov Govt, Victoria, BC V8W 9T2
EnquiryBC@gov.bc.ca

Manitoba

Aboriginal Education Directorate, Murdo Scribe Centre, 510 Selkirk Ave., Winnipeg, MB R2W 2M7
204-945-7886, Fax: 204-948-2010, aedinfo@gov.mb.ca

New Brunswick

New Brunswick Department of Post-Secondary Education, Training & Labour, Chestnut Complex, PO Box 6000, Fredericton, NB E3B 5H1
506-453-2597, Fax: 506-453-3618, dpetlinfo@gnb.ca

Nova Scotia

Nova Scotia Department of Labour & Advanced Education, 5151 Terminal Rd., 6th Fl., PO Box 697, Halifax, NS B3J 2T8
902-424-5301, Fax: 902-424-2203

Ontario

Ontario Ministry of Advanced Education & Skills Development, Mowat Block, 900 Bay St., 14th Fl., Toronto, ON M7A 1L2
416-326-1600, Fax: 416-325-6348, 800-387-5514, information.met@ontario.ca

Ontario Ministry of Labour, 400 University Ave., 14th Fl., Toronto, ON M7A 1T7
416-326-7160, 800-531-5551

Saskatchewan

Saskatchewan Education, 2220 College Ave., Regina, SK S4P 4V9
linquiry@gov.sk.ca

Saskatchewan Labour Relations & Workplace Safety, #300, 1870 Albert St., Regina, SK S4P 4W1
306-787-7404, webmaster@lab.gov.sk.ca

CENSORSHIP (MEDIA)

Canadian Broadcasting Corporation, 181 Queen St., PO Box 3220 C,Ottawa, ON K1Y 1E4
613-288-6000, liaison@cbc.ca

Canadian Radio-Television & Telecommunications Commission, Central Building, 1, Promenade du Portage, Les Terrasses de la Chaudière, Gatineau, QC J8X 4B1
819-997-0313, Fax: 819-994-0218, 877-249-2782

Manitoba

Manitoba Film Classification Board, #216, 301 Weston St., Winnipeg, MB R3E 3H4
204-945-8962, Fax: 204-945-0890, 866-612-2399, mfcb@gov.mb.ca

Nunavut

Nunavut Territory Department of Community & Government Services, W.G. Brown Bldg., 4th Fl., PO Box 1000 700, Iqaluit, NU X0A 0H0
867-975-5400, Fax: 867-975-5305

Ontario

Ontario Film Review Board, #101B, 4950 Yonge St., Toronto, ON M1N 6K1
416-314-3626, Fax: 416-314-3632, 800-268-6024

Québec

Régie du cinéma, #100, 390, rue Notre-Dame ouest, Montréal, QC H2Y 1T9
514-873-2371, Fax: 514-873-8874, 800-463-2463

Saskatchewan

Saskatchewan Film & Video Classification Board, #500, 1919 Saskatchewan Dr., Regina, SK S4P 4H2
306-787-5550, Fax: 306-787-9779, 888-374-4636

CHILD WELFARE

See Also: Day Care Services

Alberta

Alberta Office of the Child & Youth Advocate, #600, 9925 - 109 St. NW, Edmonton, AB T5K 2J8
780-422-6056, Fax: 780-422-3675, 800-661-3446, ca.information@ocya.alberta.ca

British Columbia

Office of the Representative for Children & Youth, #400, 1019 Wharf St., Victoria, BC V8W 2Y9
250-356-6710, Fax: 250-356-0837, 800-476-3933, rcy@rcybc.ca

Manitoba

Manitoba Education & Training, #168, Legislative Bldg., 450 Broadway, Winnipeg, MB R3C 0V8
204-945-3720, Fax: 204-945-1291, minedu@leg.gov.mb.ca

Manitoba Healthy Child Office, 332 Bannatyne Ave., 3rd Fl., Winnipeg, MB R3A 0E2
204-945-2266, 888-848-0140, healthychild@gov.mb.ca

Newfoundland & Labrador

Newfoundland & Labrador Department of Child, Youth & Family Services, PO Box 8700, St. John's, NL A1B 4J6
709-729-0760

Newfoundland & Labrador Department of Education & Early Childhood Development, West Block, Confederation Bldg., 100 Prince Philip Dr., 3rd Fl., PO Box 8700, St. John's, NL A1B 4J6
709-729-5097, Fax: 709-729-5896, education@gov.nl.ca

Northwest Territories

Northwest Territories Department of Health & Social Services, 5015 - 49th St., PO Box 1320, Yellowknife, NT X1A 2L9
Fax: 867-873-0306

Nova Scotia

Nova Scotia Department of Education & Early Childhood Development, Trade Mart Bldg., 2021 Brunswick St., PO Box 578, Halifax, NS B3J 2S9
902-424-5168, Fax: 902-424-0511, 888-825-7770

Nunavut

Nunavut Territory Department of Family Services, PO Box 1000 950, Iqaluit, NU X0A 0H0
867-975-6038, Fax: 867-975-6091

Nunavut Territory Department of Health, PO Box 1000 1000, Iqaluit, NU X0A 0H0
867-975-5700, Fax: 867-975-5705, 800-661-0833

Ontario

Office of the Children's Lawyer, 393 University Ave., 14th Fl., Toronto, ON M5G 1W9
416-314-8000, Fax: 416-314-8050

Office of the Provincial Advocate for Children & Youth, #2200, 401 Bay St., Toronto, ON M7A 0A6
416-325-5669, Fax: 416-325-5681, 800-263-2841, advocacy@provincialadvocate.on.ca

Ontario Ministry of Children & Youth Services, Macdonald Block, #M-1B114, 900 Bay St., Toronto, ON M7A 1N3
Fax: 416-212-1977, 866-821-7770, mcsinfo@mcys.gov.on.ca

Prince Edward Island

Child & Family Services, Jones Bldg., 11 Kent St., 2nd Fl., PO Box 2000, Charlottetown, PE C1A 7N8
902-368-5294

Prince Edward Island Department of Education, Early Learning & Culture, Holman Centre, #101, 250 Water St., Summerside, PE C1N 1B6
902-438-4130, Fax: 902-438-4062

CITIZENSHIP

Immigration & Refugee Board of Canada, Canada Bldg, 344 Slater St., 12th Fl., Ottawa, ON K1A 0K1
613-995-6486, Fax: 613-943-1550, contact@irb-cisr.gc.ca

Manitoba

Manitoba Education & Training, #168, Legislative Bldg., 450 Broadway, Winnipeg, MB R3C 0V8
204-945-3720, Fax: 204-945-1291, minedu@leg.gov.mb.ca

Nova Scotia

Office of Immigration, #110A, 1741 Brunswick St., PO Box 1535, Halifax, NS B3J 2Y3
902-424-5230, Fax: 902-424-7936, 877-292-9597, nsnp@novascotia.ca

Ontario

Ontario Ministry of Citizenship & Immigration, 400 University Ave., 6th Fl., Toronto, ON M7A 2R9
416-327-2422, Fax: 416-327-1061, 800-267-7329, info.mci@ontario.ca

Québec

Ministère de l'Immigration, de la Diversité et de l'Inclusion, Édifice Gérald-Godin, 360, rue McGill, Montréal, QC H2Y 2E9
514-864-9191, Fax: 514-864-2899, 877-864-9191

CLIMATE & WEATHER

Atmospheric Science & Technology, 4905 Dufferin St., Toronto, ON M3H 5T4

Canadian Space Agency, John H. Chapman Space Centre, 6767, rte de l'Aéroport, Saint-Hubert, QC J3Y 8Y9
450-926-4800, Fax: 450-926-4352, asc.info.csa@canada.ca

Climatic Testing Facility, Ottawa Uplands Research Facilities, 2320 Lester Rd., Ottawa, ON K1V 1S2
613-998-9639

Environment & Climate Change Canada, 10 Wellington St., Gatineau, QC K1A 0H3
819-997-2800, Fax: 819-994-1412, 800-668-6767, enviroinfo@ec.gc.ca

Meteorological Service of Canada, 351, boul Saint-Joseph, Gatineau, QC K1A 0H3
819-934-5395, Fax: 819-934-1255

CLIMATE CHANGE

Alberta

Safety, Policy & Engineering Division, Twin Atria Building, 4999 - 98 Ave., Main Fl., Edmonton, AB T6B 2X3
780-427-8901, Fax: 780-415-0782, 800-666-5036

Newfoundland & Labrador

Office of Climate Change & Energy Efficiency, PO Box 8700, St. John's, NL A1B 4J6
709-729-1210, Fax: 709-729-1119, climatechange@gov.nl.ca

Québec

Ministère du Développement durable, de l'Environnement et de la Lutte contre les changements climatiques, Édifice Marie-Guyart, 675, boul René-Lévesque est, 29e étage, Québec, QC G1R 5V7
418-521-3830, Fax: 418-646-5974, 800-561-1616, info@mddefp.gouv.qc.ca

COAL

See Also: Energy

Alberta
Alberta Energy Regulator, #1000, 250 - 5 St. SW, Calgary, AB T2P 0R4
403-297-8311, Fax: 403-297-7336, 855-297-8311, inquiries@aer.ca
Ontario
Ontario Power Generation, 700 University Ave., Toronto, ON M5G 1X6
416-592-2555, 877-592-2555, webmaster@opg.com
Saskatchewan
Saskatchewan Power Corporation (SaskPower), 2025 Victoria Ave., Regina, SK S4P 0S1
306-566-2121, 888-757-6937

COMMUNICATIONS

See: Telecommunications
Canada Post Corporation, Corporate Secretariat, 2701 Riverside Dr., Ottawa, ON K1A 0B1
416-979-3033, 866-607-6301
Canadian Broadcasting Corporation, 181 Queen St., PO Box 3220 C,Ottawa, ON K1Y 1E4
613-288-6000, liaison@cbc.ca
Canadian Radio-Television & Telecommunications Commission, Central Building, 1, Promenade du Portage, Les Terrasses de la Chaudière, Gatineau, QC J8X 4B1
819-997-0313, Fax: 819-994-0218, 877-249-2782
Communications Research Centre Canada, 3701 Carling Ave., PO Box 11490 H, Ottawa, ON K2H 8S2
613-991-3313, Fax: 613-998-5355, info@crc.gc.ca
Spectrum, Information Technologies & Telecommunications, Journal Tower North, 300 Slater St., 20th Fl., Ottawa, ON K1A 0C8
613-998-0368, Fax: 613-952-1203
Alberta
Public Affairs Bureau, Federal Bldg., 9820 - 107 St., 7th Fl., Edmonton, AB T5K 1E7
Manitoba
Communications Services Manitoba, 155 Carlton St., 10th Fl., Winnipeg, MB R3C 3H8
204-945-3765
Ontario
Ontario Library Service - North, 334 Regent St., Sudbury, ON P3C 4E2
705-675-6467, Fax: 705-675-2285, 800-461-6348
Québec
Ministère de la Culture et Communications, 225, Grande Allée est, Québec, QC G1R 5G5
888-380-8882
Saskatchewan
Saskatchewan Telecommunications (SaskTel), 2121 Saskatchewan Dr., Regina, SK S4P 3Y2
306-777-3737, 800-727-5835, corporate.comments@sasktel.sk.ca

COMMUNITY & MUNICIPAL DEVELOPMENT

Atlantic Canada Opportunities Agency, Blue Cross Centre, 644 Main St., 3rd Fl., PO Box 6051, Moncton, NB E1C 9J8
506-851-2271, Fax: 506-851-7403, 800-561-7862
Canada Economic Development for Québec Regions, Édifice Dominion Square, #900, 1255, rue Peel, Montréal, QC H3B 2T9
514-283-6412, Fax: 514-283-3302, 866-385-6412
Canadian Northern Economic Development Agency, Ottawa, ON K1A 0H4
855-897-2667, InfoNorth@CanNor.gc.ca
Destination Canada, #800, 1045 Howe St., Vancouver, BC V6Z 2A9
604-638-8300
Federal Economic Development Agency for Southern Ontario, #101, 139 Northfield Dr. West, Waterloo, ON N2L 5A6
Fax: 519-725-4976, 866-593-5505
FedNor (Federal Economic Development Initiative in Northern Ontario), C.D. Howe Bldg., 235 Queen St., 8th Fl., Ottawa, ON K1A 0H5
Fax: 613-941-4553, 877-333-6673
Western Economic Diversification Canada, Canada Place, #1500, 9700 Jasper Ave. NW, Edmonton, AB T5J 4H7
780-495-4164, Fax: 780-495-4557, 888-338-9378
British Columbia
Local Government, PO Box 9490 Prov Govt, Victoria, BC V8W 9N7
250-356-6575, Fax: 250-387-7973
Manitoba
Manitoba Housing & Community Development, 352 Donald St., Winnipeg, MB R3B 2H8
204-945-4663, Fax: 204-948-2013, 800-661-4663, housing@gov.mb.ca
Manitoba Indigenous & Municipal Relations, Legislative Bldg, #344, 450 Broadway, Winnipeg, MB R3C 0V8
204-945-3719, Fax: 204-945-8374, anaweb@gov.mb.ca
New Brunswick
Regional Development Corporation, Chancery Place, PO Box 6000, Fredericton, NB E3B 5H1
506-453-2277, Fax: 506-453-7988
Newfoundland & Labrador
Newfoundland & Labrador Department of Health & Community Services, West Block, Confederation Bldg., PO Box 8700, St. John's, NL A1B 4J6
709-729-4984, healthinfo@gov.nl.ca
Northwest Territories
Northwest Territories Department of Municipal & Community Affairs, PO Box 1320, Yellowknife, NT X1A 2L9
867-767-9160, Fax: 867-873-0309
Nova Scotia
Nova Scotia Department of Municipal Affairs, Maritime Centre, 14 North, 1505 Barrington St., PO Box 216, Halifax, NS B3J 3K5
902-424-6642, 800-670-4357
Office of Aboriginal Affairs, 5251 Duke St., 5th Fl., PO Box 1617, Halifax, NS B3J 2Y3
902-424-7409, Fax: 902-424-4225, oaa@gov.ns.ca
Nunavut
Nunavut Territory Department of Community & Government Services, W.G. Brown Bldg., 4th Fl., PO Box 1000 700, Iqaluit, NU X0A 0H0
867-975-5400, Fax: 867-975-5305
Ontario
Ontario Ministry of Municipal Affairs, College Park, 777 Bay St., 17th Fl., Toronto, ON M5G 2E5
416-585-7000, Fax: 416-585-6470, mininfo@ontario.ca
Prince Edward Island
SkillsPEI, Atlantic Technology Centre, #212, 176 Great George St., Charlottetown, PE C1A 4K9
902-368-6290, Fax: 902-368-6340, 877-491-4766
Québec
Ministère des Affaires municipales et Occupation du territoire, Aile Chaveau, 10, rue Pierre-Olivier-Chauveau, Québec, QC G1R 4J3
418-691-2015, Fax: 418-643-7385, communications@mamrot.gouv.qc.ca
Ministère des Finances, 12, rue Saint-Louis, Québec, QC G1R 5L3
418-528-9323, Fax: 418-646-1631, info@finances.gouv.qc.ca
Saskatchewan
Saskatchewan Government Relations, 1855 Victoria Ave., Regina, SK S4P 3T2
306-787-8885

COMMUNITY FINANCING

Atlantic Canada Opportunities Agency, Blue Cross Centre, 644 Main St., 3rd Fl., PO Box 6051, Moncton, NB E1C 9J8
506-851-2271, Fax: 506-851-7403, 800-561-7862
Business Development Bank of Canada, #400, 5, Place Ville-Marie, Montréal, QC H3B 5E7
877-232-2269
Canada Economic Development for Québec Regions, Édifice Dominion Square, #900, 1255, rue Peel, Montréal, QC H3B 2T9
514-283-6412, Fax: 514-283-3302, 866-385-6412
Canada Savings Bonds, #201, 50 O'Connor St., PO Box 2770 D, Ottawa, ON K1P 1J7
905-754-2012, Fax: 613-782-8096, 800-575-5151, csb@csb.gc.ca
Finance Canada, 90 Elgin St., 14th Fl., Ottawa, ON K1A 0G5
613-369-3710, Fax: 613-369-4065, fin.financepublic-financepublique.fin@canada.ca
Western Economic Diversification Canada, Canada Place, #1500, 9700 Jasper Ave. NW, Edmonton, AB T5J 4H7
780-495-4164, Fax: 780-495-4557, 888-338-9378
Alberta
Alberta Capital Finance Authority, Sun Life Place, #2160, 10123 - 99 St. NW, Edmonton, AB T5J 3H1
780-427-9711, Fax: 780-422-2175, webacfa@gov.ab.ca
Manitoba
Communities Economic Development Fund, 15 Moak Cres., Thompson, MB R8N 2B8
204-778-4138, Fax: 204-778-4313, 800-561-4315
Newfoundland & Labrador
Newfoundland & Labrador Municipal Financing Corporation, Confederation Bldg., PO Box 8700, St. John's, NL A1B 4J6
709-729-6686, Fax: 709-729-2095
Nova Scotia
Nova Scotia Municipal Finance Corporation, Maritime Centre, 1505 Barrington St., 10th Fl. South, PO Box 850 M, Halifax, NS B3J 2V2
902-424-4590, Fax: 902-424-0525, gharding@gov.ns.ca
Ontario
Provincial-Local Finance Division, College Park, 777 Bay St., 10th Fl., Toronto, ON M5G 2C8
416-327-0264, Fax: 416-325-7644
Prince Edward Island
SkillsPEI, Atlantic Technology Centre, #212, 176 Great George St., Charlottetown, PE C1A 4K9
902-368-6290, Fax: 902-368-6340, 877-491-4766
Québec
Ministère des Affaires municipales et Occupation du territoire, Aile Chaveau, 10, rue Pierre-Olivier-Chauveau, Québec, QC G1R 4J3
418-691-2015, Fax: 418-643-7385, communications@mamrot.gouv.qc.ca
Yukon Territory
Yukon Economic Development, #209, 212 Main St., F-1, Whitehorse, YT Y1A 2A9
867-393-7191, Fax: 867-393-6412, 800-661-0408, ecdev@gov.yk.ca

COMMUNITY HEALTH

See: Health Services; Public Safety
New Brunswick
Wellness, Sartain MacDonald Bldg., PO Box 6000, Fredericton, NB E3B 5H1
506-453-4217, Fax: 506-444-5722, mieux-etre.wellness@gnb.ca

COMMUNITY SERVICES

British Columbia
British Columbia Ministry of Community, Sport, & Cultural Development & Responsible for TransLink, PO Box 9490 Prov Govt, Victoria, BC V8W 9N7
Manitoba
Local Government Development Division, 59 Elizabeth Dr., PO Box 33, Thompson, MB R8N 1X4
204-677-6794, Fax: 204-677-6525
New Brunswick
New Brunswick Department of Social Development, Sartain MacDonald Bldg., 551 King St., PO Box 6000, Fredericton, NB E3B 5H1
506-453-2001, Fax: 506-453-2164, sd-ds@gnb.ca
Newfoundland & Labrador
Newfoundland & Labrador Department of Health & Community Services, West Block, Confederation Bldg., PO Box 8700, St. John's, NL A1B 4J6
709-729-4984, healthinfo@gov.nl.ca
Northwest Territories
Northwest Territories Department of Municipal & Community Affairs, PO Box 1320, Yellowknife, NT X1A 2L9
867-767-9160, Fax: 867-873-0309
Nova Scotia
Community Sector Council of Nova Scotia, 1697 Brunswick St., Halifax, NS B3J 2G3
902-424-4585, information@csc-ns.ca
Nova Scotia Department of Community Services, Nelson Place, 5675 Spring Garden Rd., 8th Fl., PO Box 696, Halifax, NS B3J 2T7
877-424-1177
Nunavut
Nunavut Territory Department of Community & Government Services, W.G. Brown Bldg., 4th Fl., PO Box 1000 700, Iqaluit, NU X0A 0H0
867-975-5400, Fax: 867-975-5305
Ontario
Ontario Ministry of Community & Social Services, Hepburn Block, 80 Grosvenor St., 6th Fl., Toronto, ON M7A 1E9
416-325-5666, Fax: 416-325-3347, 888-789-4199
Prince Edward Island
Prince Edward Island Department of Family & Human Services, Jones Bldg., 11 Kent St., 2nd Fl., PO Box 2000, Charlottetown, PE C1A 7N8
902-620-3777, Fax: 902-894-0242, 866-594-3777
Saskatchewan
Saskatchewan Social Services, 1920 Broad St., Regina, SK S4P 3V6
306-787-3700, 866-221-5200, socialservicesinquiry@gov.sk.ca
Yukon Territory
Yukon Community Services, PO Box 2703, Whitehorse, YT Y1A 2C6
867-667-5811, Fax: 867-393-6295, 800-661-0408, inquiry@gov.yk.ca

CONFLICT OF INTEREST

Office of the Conflict of Interest & Ethics Commissioner, Commissioner's Office, 66 Slater St., 22nd Fl., PO Box 16, Ottawa, ON K1A 0A6
613-995-0721, Fax: 613-995-7308, ciec-ccie@parl.gc.ca
Office of the Senate Ethics Officer, Thomas D'Arcy McGee Bldg., #526, 90 Sparks St., Ottawa, ON K1P 5B4
613-947-3566, Fax: 613-947-3577, 800-267-7362, cse-seo@sen.parl.gc.ca

Alberta
Alberta Office of the Ethics Commissioner, #1250, 9925 - 109 St. NW, Edmonton, AB T5K 2J8
780-422-2273, Fax: 780-422-2261, generalinfo@ethicscommissioner.ab.ca

British Columbia
Office of the Conflict of Interest Commissioner, 421 Menzies St., 1st Fl., Victoria, BC V8V 1X4
250-356-0750, Fax: 250-356-6580, conflictofinterest@coibc.ca

Ontario
Conflict of Interest Commissioner, #1802, 2 Bloor St. East, Toronto, ON M4W 3J5
416-325-1571, Fax: 416-325-4330, 866-956-1191, coicommissioner@ontario.ca
Office of the Integrity Commissioner, #2100, 2 Bloor St. East, Toronto, ON M4W 3E2
416-314-8983, Fax: 416-314-8987, integrity.mail@oico.on.ca

Prince Edward Island
Office of the Conflict of Interest Commissioner, 197 Richmond St., 1st Fl., PO Box 2000, Charlottetown, PE C1A 7N8
902-368-5970, Fax: 902-368-5175

CONSERVATION & ECOLOGY

See Also: Heritage Resources; Natural Resources
Canadian Heritage, 15 Eddy St., Gatineau, QC K1A 0M5
819-997-0055, 866-811-0055, PCH.info-info.PCH@canada.ca
Commission for Environmental Cooperation, Secretariat, #200, 393, rue St-Jacques ouest, Montréal, QC H2Y 1N9
514-350-4300, Fax: 514-350-4314, info@cec.org
Environment & Climate Change Canada, 10 Wellington St., Gatineau, QC K1A 0H3
819-997-2800, Fax: 819-994-1412, 800-668-6767, enviroinfo@ec.gc.ca
Natural Resources Canada, 580 Booth St., Ottawa, ON K1A 0E4
343-292-6096, Fax: 613-992-7211
North American Bird Conservation Initiative, Canadian Wildlife Service, 351, boul St-Joseph, 3e étage, Gatineau, QC K1A 0H3
819-994-0512, Fax: 819-994-4445, nabci@ec.gc.ca
North American Waterfowl Management Plan, NAWCC (Canada) Secretariat, Place Vincent Massey, 351 St. Joseph Blvd., 7th Fl., Gatineau, QC K1A 0H3
819-934-6034, Fax: 819-934-6017, nawmp@ec.gc.ca
Parks Canada, National Office, 30 Victoria St., Gatineau, QC J8X 0B3
819-420-9486, 888-773-8888, information@pc.gc.ca
Polar Knowledge Canada, 2464 Sheffield Rd., Ottawa, ON K1B 4E5
613-943-8605, info@polar.gc.ca

Alberta
Alberta Environment & Parks, Information Centre, Great West Life Bldg., 9920 - 108 St., Main Fl., Edmonton, AB T5K 2M4
780-427-2700, Fax: 780-427-4407, -310-3773, ESRD.Info-Centre@gov.ab.ca
Alberta Environmental Appeals Board, Peace Hills Trust Tower, #306, 10011 - 109 St., Edmonton, AB T5J 3S8
780-427-6207, Fax: 780-427-4693
Alberta Used Oil Management Association, Empire Building, #1008, 10080 Jasper Ave., Edmonton, AB T5J 1V9
780-414-1510, Fax: 780-414-1519, 866-414-1510, auoma@usedoilrecycling.ca
Beverage Container Management Board, #100, 8616 - 51 Ave., Edmonton, AB T6E 6E6
780-424-3193, Fax: 780-428-4620, 888-424-7671, info@bcmb.ab.ca
Forestry Division, Petroleum Plaza ST, 9915 - 108 St. 10th Fl., Edmonton, AB T5K 2G8
Land Use Secretariat, Centre West Building, 10035 - 108 St., Edmonton, AB T5J 3E1
780-644-7972, Fax: 780-644-1034, luf@gov.ab.ca
Natural Resources Conservation Board, Sterling Place, 9940 - 106 St., 4th Fl., Edmonton, AB T5K 2N2
780-422-1977, Fax: 780-427-0607, 866-383-6722, info@nrcb.ca
Special Areas Board, Special Areas Board Administration, 212 - 2nd Ave. West, PO Box 820, Hanna, AB T0J 1P0
403-854-5600, Fax: 403-854-5527

British Columbia
British Columbia Assessment Authority, #400, 3450 Uptown Blvd., Victoria, BC V8Z 0B9
604-739-8588, Fax: 855-995-6209, 866-825-8322
British Columbia Ministry of Environment, PO Box 9339 Prov Govt, Victoria, BC V8W 9M1
250-387-9870, Fax: 250-387-6003, env.mail@gov.bc.ca
Environmental Appeal Board, 747 Fort St., 4th Fl., PO Box 9425 Prov Govt, Victoria, BC V8W 3E9
250-387-3464, Fax: 250-356-9923, eabinfo@gov.bc.ca
Forest Appeals Commission, 747 Fort St., 4th Fl., PO Box 9425 Prov Govt, Victoria, BC V8W 9V1
250-387-3464, Fax: 250-356-9923, facinfo@gov.bc.ca
Forest Practices Board, PO Box 9905 Prov Govt, Victoria, BC V8W 9R1
250-213-4700, Fax: 250-213-4725, 800-994-5899, fpboard@gov.bc.ca
North Area, 1011 - 4 Ave., 5th Fl., Prince George, BC V2L 3H9
250-565-6100

Manitoba
Clean Environment Commission, #305, 155 Carlton St., Winnipeg, MB R3C 3H8
204-945-0594, Fax: 204-945-0090, 800-597-3556, cec@gov.mb.ca
Ecological Reserves Advisory Committee, c/o Manitoba Conservation, Parks & Natural Areas Branch, 200 Saulteaux Cres., PO Box 53, Winnipeg, MB R3J 3W3
204-945-4148, Fax: 204-945-0012
Manitoba Sustainable Development, 200 Saulteaux Cres., PO Box 22, Winnipeg, MB R3J 3W3
204-945-6784, 800-214-6497, mgi@gov.mb.ca

New Brunswick
New Brunswick Department of Environment & Local Government, Marysville Place, PO Box 6000, Fredericton, NB E3B 5H1
506-453-2690, Fax: 506-457-4994, elg/egl-info@gnb.ca

Newfoundland & Labrador
Newfoundland & Labrador Department of Environment & Conservation, Confederation Bldg., West Block, 4th Fl., PO Box 8700, St. John's, NL A1B 4J6
709-729-2664, Fax: 709-729-6639, 800-563-6181, envcinquires@gov.nl.ca

Northwest Territories
Northwest Territories Department of Environment & Natural Resources, #600, 5102 - 50 Ave., Yellowknife, NT X1A 3S8
867-767-9231

Nova Scotia
Nova Scotia Department of Natural Resources, Founder's Square, 1701 Hollis St., 3rd Fl., PO Box 698, Halifax, NS B3J 2T9
902-424-5935, Fax: 902-424-7735, 800-565-2224

Ontario
Integrated Environmental Policy Division, 77 Wellesley St. West, 11th Fl., Toronto, ON M7A 2T5
416-314-6338, Fax: 416-314-6346
Niagara Escarpment Commission, 232 Guelph St., Georgetown, ON L7G 4B1
905-877-5191, Fax: 905-873-7452
Ontario Ministry of Environment & Climate Change, Public Information Centre, Macdonald Block, 900 Bay St., 2nd Fl., Toronto, ON M7A 1N3
416-325-4000, Fax: 416-314-6713, 800-565-4923
Ontario Ministry of Natural Resources & Forestry, 300 Water St., PO Box 7000, Peterborough, ON K9J 8M5
800-667-1940

Prince Edward Island
Prince Edward Island Department of Economic Development & Tourism, PO Box 2000, Charlottetown, PE C1A 7N8
902-368-5540, Fax: 902-368-5277, tpswitch@gov.pe.ca
Prince Edward Island Department of Justice & Public Safety, Shaw Bldg. South, 95 Rochford St., 4th Fl., PO Box 2000, Charlottetown, PE C1A 7N8
902-368-6410, Fax: 902-368-6488

Québec
Comité consultatif de l'environnement Kativik, CP 930, Kuujjuaq, QC J0M 1C0
819-964-2961, Fax: 819-964-0694, keac-ccek@krg.ca
Fondation de la faune du Québec, Place Iberville II, #420, 1175, av Lavigerie, Québec, QC G1V 4P1
418-644-7926, Fax: 418-643-7655, 877-639-0742, ffq@fondationdelafaune.qc.ca
Ministère du Développement durable, de l'Environnement et de la Lutte contre les changements climatiques, Édifice Marie-Guyart, 675, boul René-Lévesque est, 29e étage, Québec, QC G1R 5V7
418-521-3830, Fax: 418-646-5974, 800-561-1616, info@mddefp.gouv.qc.ca
Société de développement de la Baie James, #10, 462, 3e rue, Chibougamau, QC G8P 1N7
418-748-7777, Fax: 418-748-6868, chi@sdbj.gouv.qc.ca
Société québécoise de récupération et de recyclage, #411, 300, rue Saint-Paul, Québec, QC G1K 7R1
418-643-0394, Fax: 418-643-6507, 866-523-8290, info@recyc-Québec.gouv.qc.ca

Saskatchewan
Saskatchewan Assessment Management Agency, #200, 2201 - 11th Ave., Regina, SK S4P 0J8
306-924-8000, Fax: 306-924-8070, 800-667-7262, info.request@sama.sk.ca
Saskatchewan Conservation Data Centre, Fish & Wildlife Branch, Ministry of Environment, 3211 Albert St., Regina, SK S4S 5W6
306-787-7196, Fax: 306-787-9544
Saskatchewan Environment, 3211 Albert St., 2nd Fl., Regina, SK S4S 5W6
306-787-2584, Fax: 306-787-9544, 800-567-4224, Centre.Inquiry@gov.sk.ca
Saskatchewan Water Security Agency, #400, 111 Fairford St. East, Moose Jaw, SK S6H 7X9
306-694-3900, Fax: 306-694-3105, comm@wsask.ca
Wascana Centre Authority, 2900 Wascana Dr., PO Box 7111, Regina, SK S4P 3S7
306-522-3661, Fax: 306-565-2742, wca@wascana.ca

Yukon Territory
Alsek Renewable Resource Council, 180 Alaska Hwy., PO Box 2077, Haines Junction, YT Y0B 1L0
867-634-2524, Fax: 867-634-2527, admin@alsekrrc.ca
Carmacks Renewable Resource Council, PO Box 122, Carmacks, YT Y0B 1C0
867-863-6838, Fax: 867-863-6429, carmacksrrc@northwestel.net
Dawson District Renewable Resource Council, PO Box 1380, Dawson City, YT Y0B 1G0
867-993-6976, Fax: 867-993-6093, dawsonrrc@northwestel.net
Mayo District Renewable Resources Council, PO Box 249, Mayo, YT Y0B 1M0
867-996-2942, Fax: 867-996-2948, mayorrc@northwestel.net
North Yukon Renewable Resources Council, PO Box 80, Old Crow, YT Y0B 1N0
867-966-3034, Fax: 867-966-3036, nyrrc@northwestel.net
Selkirk Renewable Resources Council, PO Box 32, Pelly Crossing, YT Y0B 1P0
867-537-3937, Fax: 867-537-3939, selkirkrrc@northwestel.net
Teslin Renewable Resource Council, PO Box 186, Teslin, YT Y0A 1B0
867-390-2323, Fax: 867-390-2919, teslinrrc@northwestel.net
Yukon Environment, 10 Burns Rd., PO Box 2703 V-3A, Whitehorse, YT Y1A 2C6
867-667-5652, Fax: 867-393-7197, environment.yukon@gov.yk.ca
Yukon Land Use Planning Council, #201, 307 Jarvis St., Whitehorse, YT Y1A 2H3
867-667-7397, Fax: 867-667-4624, ylupc@planyukon.ca

CONSTRUCTION

Canada Mortgage & Housing Corporation, 700 Montreal Rd., Ottawa, ON K1A 0P7
613-748-2000, Fax: 613-748-2098, 800-668-2642, chic@cmhc-schl.gc.ca
Defence Construction Canada, Constitution Square, 350 Albert St., 19th Fl., Ottawa, ON K1A 0K3
613-998-9548, Fax: 613-998-1061, 800-514-3555, info@dcc-cdc.gc.ca
Hygrothermal Performance of Buildings Research Facilities, c/o National Research Council, 1200 Montreal Rd., Ottawa, ON K1A 0R6
613-993-9101
Infrastructure Canada, #1100, 180 Kent St., Ottawa, ON K1P 0B6
613-948-1148, 877-250-7154, info@infc.gc.ca

Alberta
Alberta Infrastructure, Infrastructure Building, 6950 - 113 St., Edmonton, AB T6H 5V7
780-415-0507, Fax: 780-427-2187, -310-0000, Infra.Contact.Us.m@gov.ab.ca
Alberta Transportation, Communications Branch, Twin Atria Building, 4999 - 98 Jasper Ave., 2nd Fl., Edmonton, AB T6B 2X3
780-427-2731, Fax: 780-466-3166, -310-0000, Trans.Contact.Us.m@gov.ab.ca
Corporate Strategies & Services Division, Infrastructure Bldg., 6950 - 113 St., 2nd Fl., Edmonton, AB T6H 5V7

British Columbia
British Columbia Ministry of Transportation & Infrastructure, PO Box 9850 Prov Govt, Victoria, BC V8W 9T5
250-387-3198, Fax: 250-356-7706, tran.webmaster@gov.bc.ca
Building Code Appeal Board, c/o Building & Safety Standards Branch, PO Box 9844 Prov Govt, Victoria, BC V8W 1A4
250-387-3133, Fax: 250-387-8164, Building.Safety@gov.bc.ca
Homeowner Protection Office, c/o BC Housing, #650, 4789 Kingway, Burnaby, BC V5H 0A3
604-646-7050, Fax: 604-646-7051, 800-407-7757, hpo@hpo.bc.ca

Partnerships BC, #2320, 1111 West Georgia St., PO Box 9478 Prov Govt, Vancouver, BC V8W 9W6
604-681-2443, Fax: 604-806-4190, partnershipsbc@partnershipsbc.ca

Manitoba
Manitoba Infrastructure, Legislative Building, #203, 450 Broadway Ave., Winnipeg, MB R3C 0V8
204-945-3723, Fax: 204-945-7610

New Brunswick
New Brunswick Department of Transportation & Infrastructure, Kings Place, PO Box 6000, Fredericton, NB E3B 5H1
506-453-3939, Fax: 506-453-7987, Transportation.Web@gnb.ca

Newfoundland & Labrador
Newfoundland & Labrador Department of Transportation & Works, Confederation Bldg., Prince Philip Dr., PO Box 8700, St. John's, NL A1B 4J6
709-729-2300, tw@gov.nl.ca

Nova Scotia
Nova Scotia Department of Transportation & Infrastructure Renewal, Johnston Bldg., 1672 Granville St., 2nd Fl., PO Box 186, Halifax, NS B3J 2N2
902-424-2297, Fax: 902-424-0532, 888-432-3233, tpwpaff@novascotia.ca

Nunavut
Nunavut Territory Department of Community & Government Services, W.G. Brown Bldg., 4th Fl., PO Box 1000 700, Iqaluit, NU X0A 0H0
867-975-5400, Fax: 867-975-5305

Ontario
Building Code Commission, 777 Bay St., 2nd Fl., Toronto, ON M5G 2E5
416-585-6666, Fax: 416-585-7531, codeinfo@ontario.ca
Building Materials Evaluation Commission, 777 Bay St., 2nd Fl., Toronto, ON M5G 2E5
416-585-4234, Fax: 416-585-7531
Infrastructure Ontario, College Park, 777 Bay St., 6th Fl., Toronto, ON M5G 2C8
416-212-7289, Fax: 416-325-4646, info@infrastructureontario.ca
Ontario Ministry of Economic Development & Growth, Hearst Block, 900 Bay St., 8th Fl., Toronto, ON M7A 2E1
416-325-6666, 800-268-7095
Ontario Ministry of Infrastructure, Hearst Block, 900 Bay St., 8th Fl., Toronto, ON M7A 2E1
416-325-6666, 800-268-7095
Waterfront Toronto, #1310, 20 Bay St., Toronto, ON M5J 2N8
416-241-1344, Fax: 416-214-4591, info@waterfrontoronto.ca

Prince Edward Island
Prince Edward Island Department of Transportation, Infrastructure & Energy, Jones Bldg., 11 Kent St., 3rd Fl., PO Box 2000, Charlottetown, PE C1A 7N8
902-368-5100, Fax: 902-368-5395

Québec
Commission de la capitale nationale du Québec, Edifice Hector-Fabre, 525 boul René-Lévesque Est, RC, Québec, QC G1R 5S9
418-528-0773, Fax: 418-528-0833, 800-442-0773, commission@capitale.gouv.qc.ca
Commission de la construction du Québec, 8485, av Christophe-Colomb, Montréal, QC H2M 0A7
514-341-7740, 888-842-8282
Modernisation des centres hospitaliers universitaires de Montréal, CHUM, CUSM, CHU Sainte-Justine, #10.049, 2021, rue Union, Montréal, QC H3A 2S9
514-864-9883, Fax: 514-873-7362, info.construction3chu@msss.gouv.qc.ca
Régie du bâtiment du Québec, 545, boul Crémazie est, 4e étage, Montréal, QC H2M 2V2
514-873-0976, Fax: 866-315-0106, 800-361-0761, crc@rbq.gouv.qc.ca
Société québécoise des infrastructures, Édifice Marie-Fitzbach, 1075, rue de l'Amérique-Française, 1er étage, Québec, QC G1R 5P8
418-646-1766, Fax: 418-646-6911, courrier@sqi.gouv.qc.ca

Saskatchewan
Saskatchewan Highways & Infrastructure, Victoria Tower, 1855 Victoria Ave., Regina, SK S4P 3T2
306-787-4800, communications@highways.gov.sk.ca
SaskBuilds, #720, 1855 Victoria Ave., Regina, SK S4P 3T2
306-798-8014, Fax: 306-798-0626, saskbuilds@gov.sk.ca

CONSUMER PROTECTION

See Also: Public Safety

Financial Consumer Agency of Canada, 427 Laurier Ave. West, 6th Fl., Ottawa, ON K1R 1B9
613-960-4666, Fax: 613-941-1436, info@fcac-acfc.gc.ca

Alberta
Consumer & Registry Services, ATB Place South, 10020 - 100 St., 29th Fl., Edmonton, AB T5J 0N3

British Columbia
Consumer Protection B.C., #307, 3450 Uptown Blvd., PO Box 9244, Victoria, BC V8W 0B9
Fax: 250-920-7181, 888-564-9963, info@consumerprotectionbc.ca

Manitoba
Healthy Living & Seniors, c/o Seniors & Healthy Aging Secretariat, #1610, 155 Carlton St., Winnipeg, MB R3C 3H8
204-945-6565, Fax: 204-948-2514, 800-665-6565, seniors@gov.mb.ca

Newfoundland & Labrador
Consumer Advocate, NL

Nunavut
Nunavut Territory Department of Community & Government Services, W.G. Brown Bldg., 4th Fl., PO Box 1000 700, Iqaluit, NU X0A 0H0
867-975-5400, Fax: 867-975-5305

Ontario
Ontario Ministry of Government & Consumer Services, Mowat Block, 900 Bay St., 6th Fl., Toronto, ON M7A 1L2
416-212-2665, 844-286-8404

Québec
Office de la protection du consommateur, #450, 400, boul Jean-Lesage, Québec, QC G1K 8W4
418-643-1484, Fax: 418-528-0979, 888-672-2556

Yukon Territory
Corporate Policy & Consumer Affairs Division, Berska Bldg., 307 Black St., 2nd Fl., Whitehorse, YT Y1A 2N1
Fax: 867-393-6943

CONVENTION FACILITIES

See: Tourism & Tourist Information

British Columbia
British Columbia Pavilion Corporation, #200, 999 Canada Place, Vancouver, BC V6C 3C1
604-482-2200, Fax: 604-681-9017, info@bcpavco.com
Vancouver Convention Centre, 1055 Canada Pl., Vancouver, BC V6C 0C3
604-689-8232, Fax: 604-647-7232, info@vancouverconventioncentre.com

COPYRIGHT

See: Patents & Copyright

Canadian Intellectual Property Office, Place du Portage I, #C-229, 50 Victoria St., Gatineau, QC K1A 0C9
819-997-1936, Fax: 819-953-2476, 866-997-1936, cipo.contact@ic.gc.ca

CORONERS

British Columbia
BC Coroners Service, Chief Coroner's Office, Metrotower II, #800, 4720 Kingsway, Burnaby, BC V5H 4N2
604-660-7745, Fax: 604-660-7766, CoronerRequest@gov.bc.ca

Manitoba
Office of the Chief Medical Examiner, #210, 1 Wesley Ave., Winnipeg, MB R3C 4C6
204-945-2088, 800-282-8069

Nova Scotia
Office of the Chief Medical Examiner, Dr. William D. Finn Centre for Forensic Medicine, 51 Garland Ave., Dartmouth, NS B3B 0J2
902-424-2722, Fax: 902-424-0607, 888-424-4336

Nunavut
Office of the Chief Coroner, c/o Court Services Division, PO Box 297, Iqaluit, NU X0A 0H0
867-975-6100, Fax: 867-975-6168, theofficeofthechiefcoroner@gov.nu.ca

Ontario
Office of the Chief Coroner & Ontario Forensic Pathology Service, 25 Morton Shulman Ave., Toronto, ON M3M 0B1
416-314-4000, Fax: 416-314-4030, 877-991-9959

Québec
Bureau du coroner, Édifice le Delta 2, #390, 2875, boul Laurier, Québec, QC G1V 5B1
418-643-1845, Fax: 418-643-6174, 866-312-7051, clientele.coroner@msp.gouv.qc.ca

Saskatchewan
Office of the Chief Coroner, #920, 1801 Hamilton St., Regina, SK S4P 4B4
306-787-5541, Fax: 306-787-5503, 866-592-7845, ocoroner@gov.sk.ca

CORRECTIONAL SERVICES

Correctional Service Canada, 340 Laurier Ave. West, Ottawa, ON K1A 0P9
613-992-5891, Fax: 613-943-1630
Office of the Correctional Investigator, PO Box 3421 D,Ottawa, ON K1P 6L4
Fax: 613-990-9091, 877-885-8848, org@oci-bec.gc.ca

British Columbia
Corrections Branch, PO Box 9278 Prov Govt, Victoria, BC V8W 9J7
250-387-6366, 888-952-7968

Manitoba
Corrections Division, #810, 405 Broadway Ave., Winnipeg, MB R3C 3L6
204-945-7804

Nunavut
Baffin Correctional Centre, PO Box 1000, Iqaluit, NU X0A 0H0
867-979-8100, Fax: 867-979-4646
Community Justice, PO Box 1000 500, Iqaluit, NU X0A 0H0
867-975-6363, Fax: 867-975-6160, communityjustice@gov.nu.ca

Saskatchewan
Office of the Minister of Corrections & Policing, Legislative Bldg., #345, 2405 Legislative Dr., Regina, SK S4S 0B3
306-787-4983, Fax: 306-787-5331

CRIMES COMPENSATION

Alberta
Criminal Injuries Review Board, #1502, 10025 - 102A Ave., Edmonton, AB T5J 2Z2
780-427-7330, Fax: 780-427-7347

Manitoba
Compensation for Victims of Crime, #1410, 405 Broadway, Winnipeg, MB R3C 3L6
204-945-0899, Fax: 204-948-3071, 800-262-9344

Northwest Territories
Victims Assistance Committee, c/o Community Justice & Community Policing Division, PO Box 1320, Yellowknife, NT X1A 2L9
867-920-6911, Fax: 867-873-0199

Ontario
Criminal Injuries Compensation Board, 439 University Ave., 4th Fl., Toronto, ON M5G 1Y8
416-326-2900, Fax: 416-326-2883, 800-372-7463, info.cicb@ontario.ca
Office for Victims of Crime, 700 Bay St., 3rd Fl., Toronto, ON M5G 1Z6
416-326-1682, Fax: 416-326-4497, 887-435-7661, ovc@ontario.ca

CROP MANAGEMENT

Aquatic & Crop Resource Development Industry Partnership Facility, 550 University Ave., Charlottetown, PE C1A 4P3
902-566-7000
Crops & Aquatic Growth Facilities, c/o National Research Council, 1200 Montreal Rd., Ottawa, ON K1A 0R6

CULTURE & HERITAGE

See: Arts & Culture

Canadian Heritage, 15 Eddy St., Gatineau, QC K1A 0M5
819-997-0055, 866-811-0055, PCH.info-info.PCH@canada.ca
Historic Sites & Monuments Board of Canada, 30 Victoria St., 3rd Fl., Gatineau, QC J8X 0B3
Fax: 819-420-9260, 855-283-8730, hsmbc-clmhc@pc.gc.ca
Indigenous & Northern Affairs, Terrasses de la Chaudière, 10 Wellington St., North Tower, Gatineau, QC K1A 0H4
Fax: 866-817-3977, 800-567-9604, infopubs@aadnc-aandc.gc.ca

Alberta
Intergovernmental Relations, Commerce Place, 10155 - 102 St., 12th Fl., Edmonton, AB T5J 4G8

British Columbia
British Columbia Ministry of Community, Sport, & Cultural Development & Responsible for TransLink, PO Box 9490 Prov Govt, Victoria, BC V8W 9N7

Manitoba
Manitoba Heritage Council, 213 Notre Dame Ave., Main Fl., Winnipeg, MB R3B 1N3
204-945-2118, Fax: 204-948-2384, hrb@gov.mb.ca

New Brunswick
New Brunswick Department of Tourism, Heritage & Culture, Centennial Building, PO Box 6000, Fredericton, NB E3B 5H1
506-453-3115, Fax: 506-457-4984, thctpcinfo@gnb.ca

Newfoundland & Labrador
Newfoundland & Labrador Department of Business, Tourism, Culture & Rural Development, Confederation Bldg., West Block, 2nd Fl., PO Box 8700, St. John's, NL A1B 4J6
709-729-7000, btcrd@gov.nl.ca

Northwest Territories
Northwest Territories Department of Aboriginal Affairs & Intergovernmental Relations, 4910 - 52nd St., PO Box 1320, Yellowknife, NT X1A 2L9
867-767-9025, Fax: 867-873-0233
Northwest Territories Department of Education, Culture & Employment, PO Box 1320, Yellowknife, NT X1A 2L9
ecepublicaffairs@gov.nt.ca

Nova Scotia
Office of African Nova Scotian Affairs, 1741 Brunswick St., 3rd Fl., PO Box 456 Central,Halifax, NS B3J 2R5
902-424-5555, Fax: 902-424-7189, 866-580-2672, ansa_newsletter@novascotia.ca
Office of Gaelic Affairs, 1741 Brunswick St., 3rd Fl., PO Box 456 Central,Halifax, NS B3J 2R5
902-424-4298, Fax: 902-424-0171, 888-842-3542, gaelicinfo@gov.ns.ca

Ontario
Anti-Racism Directorate, Ferguson Block, Queen's Park, 77 Wellesley St. West, 13th Fl., Toronto, ON M7A 1N3
Ontario Ministry of Tourism, Culture & Sport, Hearst Block, 900 Bay St., 9th Fl., Toronto, ON M7A 2E1
416-326-9326, Fax: 416-314-7854, 888-997-9015

Prince Edward Island
Housing Services, Jones Bldg., 11 Kent St., 2nd Fl., PO Box 2000, Charlottetown, PE C1A 7N8
902-620-3777, Fax: 902-894-0242

Québec
Commission de la capitale nationale du Québec, Edifice Hector-Fabre, 525 boul René-Lévesque Est, RC, Québec, QC G1R 5S9
418-528-0773, Fax: 418-528-0833, 800-442-0773, commission@capitale.gouv.qc.ca
Fonds québécois de la recherche sur la société et la culture, #470, 140, Grande Allée est, Québec, QC G1R 5M8
418-643-7582, Fax: 418-644-5248, frq.sc@frq.gouv.qc.ca
Secrétariat à la Capitale-Nationale, 700, boul René-Lévesque est, 31e étage, Québec, QC G1R 5H1
418-528-8549, Fax: 418-528-8558

Saskatchewan
Provincial Capital Commission, 4607 Dewdney Ave., Regina, SK S4T 1B7
306-787-9261
Saskatchewan Parks, Culture & Sport, 3211 Albert St., 1st Fl., Regina, SK S4S 5W6
306-787-5729, Fax: 306-798-0033, 800-205-7070, info@tpcs.gov.sk.ca
Wascana Centre Authority, 2900 Wascana Dr., PO Box 7111, Regina, SK S4P 3S7
306-522-3661, Fax: 306-565-2742, wca@wascana.ca

CURRENCY

Bank of Canada, 234 Laurier Ave. West, Ottawa, ON K1A 0G9
613-782-8111, Fax: 613-782-7713, 800-303-1282, info@bankofcanada.ca
Royal Canadian Mint, 320 Sussex Dr., Ottawa, ON K1A 0G8
613-954-2626, Fax: 613-998-4130, 800-267-1871

CUSTOMS

Canada Border Services Agency, Headquarters, 191 Laurier Ave. West, Ottawa, ON K1A 0L8
800-461-9999, contact@cbsa.gc.ca

DAIRY INDUSTRY

Agriculture & Agri-Food Canada, 1341 Baseline Rd., Ottawa, ON K1A 0C5
613-773-1000, Fax: 613-773-1081, 855-773-0241, info@agr.gc.ca
Canadian Dairy Commission, Central Experimental Farm, NCC Driveway, Bldg. 55, 960 Carling Ave., Ottawa, ON K1A 0Z2
613-792-2000, Fax: 613-792-2009, cdc-ccl@cdc-ccl.gc.ca

Alberta
Alberta Agriculture & Forestry, JG O'Donoghue Bldg., #100A, 7000 - 113th St., Edmonton, AB T6H 5T6
780-427-2727, -310-3276, duke@gov.ab.ca

British Columbia
British Columbia Milk Marketing Board, #200, 32160 South Fraser Way, Abbotsford, BC V2T 1W5
604-556-3444, Fax: 604-556-7717, info@milk-bc.com
British Columbia Ministry of Agriculture, PO Box 9043 Prov Govt, Victoria, BC V8W 9E2
888-221-7141, agriservicebc@gov.bc.ca

Manitoba
Manitoba Agriculture, Legislative Bldg., #165, 450 Broadway, Winnipeg, MB R3C 0V8
204-945-3722, Fax: 204-945-3470, minagr@leg.gov.mb.ca
Manitoba Milk Prices Review Commission, #812, 401 York Ave., Winnipeg, MB R3C 0P8
204-945-3854, Fax: 204-945-1489

New Brunswick
New Brunswick Department of Agriculture, Aquaculture & Fisheries, Agricultural Research Station (Experimental Farm), PO Box 6000, Fredericton, NB E3B 5H1
506-453-2666, Fax: 506-453-7170, 888-622-4742, DAAF-MAAP@gnb.ca

Nova Scotia
Nova Scotia Department of Agriculture, 1800 Argyle St., 6th Fl., PO Box 2223, Halifax, NS B3J 3C4
902-424-4560, Fax: 902-424-4671

Ontario
Ontario Ministry of Agriculture, Food & Rural Affairs, Ontario Government Bldg., 1 Stone Rd. West, Guelph, ON N1G 4Y2
519-826-3100, Fax: 519-826-4335, 888-466-2372, about.omafra@ontario.ca

Prince Edward Island
Prince Edward Island Department of Agriculture & Fisheries, Jones Bldg., 11 Kent St., 5th Fl., PO Box 2000, Charlottetown, PE C1A 7N8
902-368-4880, Fax: 902-368-4857

Québec
Ministère de l'Agriculture, des Pêcheries et de l'Alimentation, 200, ch Sainte-Foy, Québec, QC G1R 4X6
418-380-2110, 888-222-6272

Saskatchewan
Saskatchewan Agriculture, Walter Scott Bldg., 3085 Albert St., Regina, SK S4S 0B1
866-457-2377

DANGEROUS GOODS & HAZARDOUS MATERIALS

See Also: Occupational Safety; Waste Management

British Columbia
British Columbia Ministry of Transportation & Infrastructure, PO Box 9850 Prov Govt, Victoria, BC V8W 9T5
250-387-3198, Fax: 250-356-7706, tran.webmaster@gov.bc.ca

Northwest Territories
Northwest Territories Department of Transportation, New Government Bldg., 5015 - 49 St., 4th Fl., PO Box 1320, Yellowknife, NT X1A 2L9
867-767-9089, Fax: 867-873-0606

Nova Scotia
Nova Scotia Department of Transportation & Infrastructure Renewal, Johnston Bldg., 1672 Granville St., 2nd Fl., PO Box 186, Halifax, NS B3J 2N2
902-424-2297, Fax: 902-424-0532, 888-432-3233, tpwpaff@novascotia.ca

Ontario
Ontario Ministry of Transportation, Ferguson Block, 77 Wellesley St. West, 3rd Fl., Toronto, ON M7A 1Z8
416-327-9200, Fax: 416-327-9185, 800-268-4686

Prince Edward Island
Prince Edward Island Department of Transportation, Infrastructure & Energy, Jones Bldg., 11 Kent St., 3rd Fl., PO Box 2000, Charlottetown, PE C1A 7N8
902-368-5100, Fax: 902-368-5395

Québec
Ministère du Développement durable, de l'Environnement et de la Lutte contre les changements climatiques, Édifice Marie-Guyart, 675, boul René-Lévesque est, 29e étage, Québec, QC G1R 5V7
418-521-3830, Fax: 418-646-5974, 800-561-1616, info@mddefp.gouv.qc.ca

Saskatchewan
Saskatchewan Highways & Infrastructure, Victoria Tower, 1855 Victoria Ave., Regina, SK S4P 3T2
306-787-4800, communications@highways.gov.sk.ca

Yukon Territory
Yukon Highways & Public Works, PO Box 2703, Whitehorse, YT Y1A 2C6
867-393-7193, Fax: 867-393-6218, 800-661-0408, hpw-info@gov.yk.ca

DEBT MANAGEMENT

Finance Canada, 90 Elgin St., 14th Fl., Ottawa, ON K1A 0G5
613-369-3710, Fax: 613-369-4065, fin.financepublic-financepublique.fin@canada.ca

Manitoba
Treasury Division, #350, 363 Broadway, Winnipeg, MB R3C 3N9
204-945-3702, Fax: 204-948-2233

Prince Edward Island
Debt, Investment & Pension Management, Shaw Bldg. South, 95 Rochford St., 3rd Fl., PO Box 2000, Charlottetown, PE C1A 7N8
Fax: 902-368-4077

Saskatchewan
Provincial Mediation Board, #120, 2151 Scarth St., Regina, SK S4P 2H8
306-787-5408, Fax: 306-787-5574, 877-787-5408, pmb@gov.sk.ca
Saskatchewan Finance, 2350 Albert St., Regina, SK S4P 4A6
306-787-6768, Fax: 306-787-0241, communications@finance.gov.sk.ca

DEFENCE

See Also: Emergency Response; Public Safety
Canadian Joint Operations Command, National Defence Headquarters, MGen George R. Pearkes Bldg., 101 Colonel By Dr., Ottawa, ON K1A 0K2
866-377-0811
Canadian Special Operations Forces Command, CANSOFCOM Public Affairs, 101 Colonel By Dr., Ottawa, ON K1A 0K2
866-377-0811
Defence Construction Canada, Constitution Square, 350 Albert St., 19th Fl., Ottawa, ON K1A 0K3
613-998-9548, Fax: 613-998-1061, 800-514-3555, info@dcc-cdc.gc.ca
Defence Research & Development Canada, 101 Colonel By Dr., Ottawa, ON K1A 0K2
613-995-2534, 888-995-2534, information@forces.gc.ca
Department of National Defence & the Canadian Armed Forces, National Defence HQ, Major-General George R. Pearkes Bldg., 101 Colonel By Dr., Ottawa, ON K1A 0K2
613-995-2534, Fax: 613-992-4739, 888-995-2534, information@forces.gc.ca
Military Grievances External Review Committee, 60 Queen St., 10th Fl., Ottawa, ON K1P 5Y7
613-996-8529, Fax: 613-996-6491, 877-276-4193, mgerc-ceegm@mgerc-ceegm.gc.ca
Military Police Complaints Commission, 270 Albert St., 10th Fl., Ottawa, ON K1P 5G8
613-947-5625, Fax: 613-947-5713, 800-632-0566, commission@mpcc-cppm.gc.ca
Royal Canadian Air Force, MGen George R. Pearkes Building, 101 Colonel By Dr., Ottawa, ON K1A 0K2
Royal Canadian Navy, National Defence HQ, MGen George R. Pearkes Building, 101 Colonel By Dr., Ottawa, ON K1A 0K2
information@forces.gc.ca

DISABLED PERSONS SERVICES

Canadian Human Rights Commission, 344 Slater St., 8th Fl., Ottawa, ON K1A 1E1
Fax: 613-996-9661, 888-214-1090, info.com@chrc-ccdp.gc.ca

Alberta
Alberta Health, PO Box 1360 Main,Edmonton, AB T5J 2N3
780-427-7164, -310-0000
Alberta Human Services, Office of the Minister, Legislature Building, #224, 10800 - 97 Ave., Edmonton, AB T5K 2B6
780-644-5135, 866-644-5135
Appeals Secretariat, Centre West Bldg., 10035 - 108 St., 6th Fl., Calgary, AB T5J 3E1
780-427-2709, Fax: 780-422-1088, appeals@gov.ab.ca
Persons with Developmental Disabilities Community Boards, Centre West Bldg., 10035 - 108 St., 6th Fl., Edmonton, AB T5J 3E1
780-422-2775, -310-0000
Premier's Council on the Status of Persons with Disabilities, HSBC Building, #1110, 10055 - 106 St., Edmonton, AB T5J 1G3
780-422-1095, Fax: 780-415-0097, 800-272-8841, hs.pcspd@gov.ab.ca

British Columbia
Services to Adults with Developmental Disabilities, PO Box 9875 Prov Govt, Victoria, BC V8W 9R1
855-356-5609

Manitoba
Disability Programs & Early Learning & Child Care, c/o Disabilities Issues Office, #630, 240 Graham Ave., Winnipeg, MB R3C 0J7
204-945-7613, Fax: 204-948-2896, dio@gov.mb.ca

New Brunswick
Premier's Council on the Status of Disabled Persons, #648, 440 King St., Fredericton, NB E3B 5H8
506-444-3000, Fax: 506-444-3001, 800-442-4412, pcsdp@gnb.ca

Newfoundland & Labrador
Newfoundland & Labrador Department of Seniors, Wellness & Social Development, PO Box 8700, St. John's, NL A1B 4J6
709-729-0862, Fax: 709-729-0870, SWSDInfo@gov.nl.ca
Provincial Advisory Council for the Inclusion of Persons with Disabilities, c/o Department of Seniors, Wellness & Social Development, PO Box 8700, St. John's, NL A1B 4J6

Nova Scotia
Nova Scotia Disabled Persons Commission, Dartmouth Professional Center, #104, 277 Pleasant St., Dartmouth, NS B2Y 4B7
902-424-8280, 800-565-8280

Nunavut
Nunavut Territory Department of Culture & Heritage, PO Box 1000 800, Iqaluit, NU X0A 0H0
867-975-5500, Fax: 867-975-5504, 866-934-2035

Ontario
Health System Strategy & Policy Division, Hepburn Block, 80 Grosvenor St., 8th Fl., Toronto, ON M7A 1R3
416-327-8295, Fax: 416-327-5109

Québec
Office des personnes handicapées du Québec, 309, rue Brock, Drummondville, QC J2B 1C5
Fax: 819-475-8753, 800-567-1465, aide@ophq.gouv.qc.ca

DISCRIMINATION & EMPLOYMENT EQUITY

Canadian Human Rights Commission, 344 Slater St., 8th Fl., Ottawa, ON K1A 1E1
Fax: 613-996-9661, 888-214-1090, info.com@chrc-ccdp.gc.ca

Canadian Human Rights Tribunal, 160 Elgin St., 11th Fl., Ottawa, ON K1A 1J4
613-995-1707, Fax: 613-995-3484, registrar@chrt-tcdp.gc.ca

Office of the Public Sector Integrity Commissioner of Canada, 60 Queen St., 7th Fl., Ottawa, ON K1P 5Y7
613-941-6400, Fax: 613-941-6535, 866-941-6400

Alberta
Labour Relations Board, Labour Building, #501, 10808 - 99 Ave., Edmonton, AB T5K 0G5
780-427-8547, Fax: 780-422-0970, 800-463-2572, alrbinfo@gov.ab.ca

British Columbia
British Columbia Human Rights Tribunal, #1170, 605 Robson St., Vancouver, BC V6B 5J3
604-775-2000, Fax: 604-775-2020, 888-440-8844, BCHumanRightsTribunal@gov.bc.ca

Manitoba
Manitoba Human Rights Commission, #700, 175 Hargrave St., Winnipeg, MB R3C 3R8
204-945-3007, Fax: 204-945-1292, 888-884-8681, hrc@gov.mb.ca

New Brunswick
New Brunswick Human Rights Commission, Barry House, PO Box 6000, Fredericton, NB E3B 5H1
506-453-2301, Fax: 506-453-2653, 888-471-2233, hrc.cdp@gnb.ca

Newfoundland & Labrador
Newfoundland & Labrador Human Rights Commission, The Beothuk Bldg., 21 Crosbie Pl., PO Box 8700, St. John's, NL A1B 4J6
709-729-2709, Fax: 709-729-0790, 800-563-5808, humanrights@gov.nl.ca

Nova Scotia
Nova Scotia Human Rights Commission, Park Lane Terraces, #305, 5657 Spring Garden Rd., PO Box 2221, Halifax, NS B3J 3C4
902-424-4111, Fax: 902-424-0596, 877-269-7699, hrcinquiries@novascotia.ca

Ontario
Ontario Human Rights Commission, #900, 180 Dundas St. West, Toronto, ON M7A 2R9
416-326-9511, Fax: 416-314-4494, 800-387-9080, info@ohrc.on.ca

Prince Edward Island
Prince Edward Island Human Rights Commission, 53 Water St., PO Box 2000, Charlottetown, PE C1A 7N8
902-368-4180, Fax: 902-368-4236, 800-237-5031, contact@peihumanrights.ca

Québec
Commission de l'équité salariale, 200, ch Ste-Foy, 4e étage, Québec, QC G1R 6A1
418-528-8765, Fax: 418-528-6999, 888-528-8765, equite.salariale@ces.gouv.qc.ca

Saskatchewan
Saskatchewan Human Rights Commission, Saskatoon Office, Sturdy Stone Bdg., #816, 122 - 3 Ave. North, 8th Fl., Saskatoon, SK S7K 2H6
306-933-5952, Fax: 306-933-7863, 800-667-9249, shrc@gov.sk.ca

Yukon Territory
Yukon Human Rights Commission, #101, 9010 Quartz St., Whitehorse, YT Y1A 2Z5
867-667-6226, Fax: 867-667-2662, 800-661-0535, humanrights@yhrc.yk.ca

DIVORCE

Justice Canada, East Memorial Bldg., 284 Wellington St., Ottawa, ON K1A 0H8
613-957-4222, Fax: 613-954-0811, webadmin@justice.gc.ca

DRIVERS' LICENCES

Alberta
Alberta Transportation, Communications Branch, Twin Atria Building, 4999 - 98 Jasper Ave., 2nd Fl., Edmonton, AB T6B 2X3
780-427-2731, Fax: 780-466-3166, -310-0000, Trans.Contact.Us.m@gov.ab.ca

British Columbia
British Columbia Ministry of Transportation & Infrastructure, PO Box 9850 Prov Govt, Victoria, BC V8W 9T5
250-387-3198, Fax: 250-356-7706, tran.webmaster@gov.bc.ca

Manitoba
Manitoba Infrastructure, Legislative Building, #203, 450 Broadway Ave., Winnipeg, MB R3C 0V8
204-945-3723, Fax: 204-945-7610

Nova Scotia
Service Nova Scotia, c/o Public Enquiries - Service Nova Scotia, PO Box 2734, Halifax, NS B3J 3K5
902-424-5200, Fax: 902-424-0720, 800-670-4357

Ontario
Licence Appeal Tribunal, #530, 20 Dundas St. West, Toronto, ON M5G 2C2
416-314-4260, Fax: 416-314-4270, 800-255-2214

Ontario Ministry of Transportation, Ferguson Block, 77 Wellesley St. West, 3rd Fl., Toronto, ON M7A 1Z8
416-327-9200, Fax: 416-327-9185, 800-268-4686

Prince Edward Island
Prince Edward Island Department of Transportation, Infrastructure & Energy, Jones Bldg., 11 Kent St., 3rd Fl., PO Box 2000, Charlottetown, PE C1A 7N8
902-368-5100, Fax: 902-368-5395

Québec
Société de l'assurance automobile du Québec, 333, boul Jean-Lesage, CP 19600 Terminus, Québec, QC G1K 8J6
418-643-7620, Fax: 418-644-0339, 800-361-7620

Saskatchewan
Saskatchewan Government Insurance, 2260 - 11th Ave., Regina, SK S4P 0J9
306-751-1200, Fax: 306-787-7477, 800-667-8015, sgiinquiries@sgi.sk.ca

Yukon Territory
Driver Control Board, #102, 211 Hawkins St., PO Box 2703, Whitehorse, YT Y1A 2C6
867-667-5623, Fax: 867-667-5799, dcb@gov.yk.ca

DRUGS & ALCOHOL

See Also: Liquor Control

Canadian Centre on Substance Abuse, #500, 75 Albert St., Ottawa, ON K1P 5E7
613-235-4048, Fax: 613-235-8101, info@ccsa.ca

Alberta
Alberta Health Services, Corporate Office, North Tower, Seventh Street Plaza, 10030 - 107th St. NW, 14th Fl., Edmonton, AB T5J 3E4
780-342-2000, Fax: 780-342-2060, 888-342-2471, ahs.corp@albertahealthservices.ca

British Columbia
British Columbia Ministry of Health, 1515 Blanshard St., PO Box 9639 Prov Govt, Victoria, BC V8W 9P1
604-660-2421, 800-663-7100, hlth.health@gov.bc.ca

Québec
Ministère de la Santé et des Services sociaux, Direction des communications, 1075, ch Sainte-Foy, 16e étage, Québec, QC G1S 2M1
418-643-9395, Fax: 418-643-4768, regisseur.web@msss.gouv.qc.ca

Modernisation des centres hospitaliers universitaires de Montréal, CHUM, CUSM, CHU Sainte-Justine, #10.049, 2021, rue Union, Montréal, QC H3A 2S9
514-864-9883, Fax: 514-873-7362, info.construction3chu@msss.gouv.qc.ca

ECONOMIC DEVELOPMENT

See: Business Development

Canada Economic Development for Québec Regions, Édifice Dominion Square, #900, 1255, rue Peel, Montréal, QC H3B 2T9
514-283-6412, Fax: 514-283-3302, 866-385-6412

Canadian Northern Economic Development Agency, Ottawa, ON K1A 0H4
855-897-2667, InfoNorth@CanNor.gc.ca

Federal Economic Development Agency for Southern Ontario, #101, 139 Northfield Dr. West, Waterloo, ON N2L 5A6
Fax: 519-725-4976, 866-593-5505

FedNor (Federal Economic Development Initiative in Northern Ontario), C.D. Howe Bldg., 235 Queen St., 8th Fl., Ottawa, ON K1A 0H5
Fax: 613-941-4553, 877-333-6673

Alberta
Alberta Economic Development & Trade, Commerce Place, 10155 - 102 St., 12th Fl., Edmonton, AB T5J 4G8

British Columbia
Economic Development Division, PO Box 9846 Prov Gov,Victoria, BC V8W 9T2

Native Economic Development Advisory Board, PO Box 9100 Prov Govt, Victoria, BC V8W 9B1
250-387-2536

New Brunswick
Economic & Social Inclusion Corporation, Kings Place, PO Box 6000, Fredericton, NB E3B 5H1
506-444-2977, Fax: 506-444-2978, 888-295-4545, esic-sies@gnb.ca

New Brunswick Jobs Board, Chancery Place, PO Box 6000, Fredericton, NB E3B 5H1

Opportunities New Brunswick, Place 2000, PO Box 6000, Fredericton, NB E3B 5H1
506-453-5471, Fax: 506-444-5277, 855-746-4662, info@onbcanada.ca

Nunavut
Nunavut Territory Department of Economic Development & Transportation, Inuksugait Plaza, Bldg. 1104A, PO Box 1000 1500, Iqaluit, NU X0A 0H0
867-975-7800, Fax: 867-975-7870, 888-975-5999, edt@gov.nu.ca

Ontario
Ontario Ministry of Agriculture, Food & Rural Affairs, Ontario Government Bldg., 1 Stone Rd. West, Guelph, ON N1G 4Y2
519-826-3100, Fax: 519-826-4335, 888-466-2372, about.omafra@ontario.ca

Ontario Ministry of Economic Development & Growth, Hearst Block, 900 Bay St., 8th Fl., Toronto, ON M7A 2E1
416-325-6666, 800-268-7095

Ontario Ministry of Research, Innovation & Science, Hearst Block, 900 Bay St., 8th Fl., Toronto, ON M7A 2E1
416-325-6666, Fax: 416-325-6688, 866-668-4249

Rural Economic Development (RED) Panel, 1 Stone Rd. West, 4th Fl., Guelph, ON N1G 4Y2
Fax: 519-826-4336, 888-588-4111, red.omafra@ontario.ca

Prince Edward Island
Innovation PEI, 94 Euston St., PO Box 910, Charlottetown, PE C1A 7L9
902-368-6300, Fax: 902-368-6301, 800-563-3734, innovation@gov.pe.ca

Québec
Investissement Québec, #500, 1200, rte de l'Église, Québec, QC G1V 5A3
418-643-5172, Fax: 418-528-2063, 866-870-0437

Ministère de l'Économie, de la Science et de l'Innovation, 710, place D'Youville, 3e étage, Québec, QC G1R 4Y4
418-691-5950, Fax: 418-644-0118, 866-680-1884

Secrétariat à la Capitale-Nationale, 700, boul René-Lévesque est, 31e étage, Québec, QC G1R 5H1
418-528-8549, Fax: 418-528-8558

Saskatchewan
Municipal Financing Corporation of Saskatchewan, 2350 Albert St., 6th Fl., Regina, SK S4P 4A6
306-787-8150, Fax: 306-787-8493

Saskatchewan Economy, #300, 2103 - 11th Ave., Regina, SK S4P 3Z8
webmasterECON@gov.sk.ca

Yukon Territory
Yukon Economic Development, #209, 212 Main St., F-1, Whitehorse, YT Y1A 2A9
867-393-7191, Fax: 867-393-6412, 800-661-0408, ecdev@gov.yk.ca

EDUCATION

Canada School of Public Service, 373 Sussex Dr., Ottawa, ON K1N 6Z2
819-953-5400, Fax: 866-944-0454, 866-703-9598, info@csps-efpc.gc.ca

Canadian Council of Directors of Apprenticeship, 140 Promenade du Portage, 5th Fl, Phase IV, Gatineau, QC K1A 0J9
Fax: 819-994-0202, 877-599-6933, redseal-sceaurouge@hrsdc-rhdcc.gc.ca

Canadian Police College, PO Box 8900, Ottawa, ON K1G 3J2
613-993-9500, Fax: 613-990-9738, cpc-ccp@rcmp-grc.gc.ca

RCMP Training Academy, 6101 Dewdney Ave., PO Box 2500, Regina, SK S4P 3K7
306-780-5560, Fax: 306-780-5541

Alberta
Alberta Advanced Education, Legislature Bldg., #403, 10800 - 97 Ave., Edmonton, AB T5K 2B6
780-422-5400, -310-0000
Alberta Apprenticeship & Industry Training Board, Commerce Place, 10155 - 102 St., 10th Fl., Edmonton, AB T5J 4L5
780-427-8765, Fax: 780-422-7376, -310-0000
Alberta Council on Admissions & Transfer, Commerce Place, 10155 - 102 St., 11th Fl., Edmonton, AB T5J 4L5
780-422-9021, Fax: 780-422-3688, -310-0000, acat@gov.ab.ca
Alberta Education, Commerce Place, 10155 - 102 St., 7th Fl., Edmonton, AB T5J 4L5
780-427-7219, Fax: 780-427-0591, -310-0000
Alberta Teachers' Retirement Fund, Barnett House, #600, 11010 - 142 St. NW, Edmonton, AB T5N 2R1
780-451-4166, Fax: 780-452-3547, 800-661-9582, info@atrf.com
Apprenticeship & Student Aid Division, Commerce Place, 10155 - 102 St., 6th Fl., Edmonton, AB T5J 4L5
Campus Alberta Quality Council, Commerce Place, 10155 - 102 St., 8th Fl., Edmonton, AB T5J 4L5
780-427-8921, Fax: 780-641-9783
Council on Alberta Teaching Standards, Teaching & Leadership Excellence, Capital Boulevard Bldg., #44, 10044 - 108 St., 2nd Fl., Edmonton, AB T5J 5E6
780-427-2045, Fax: 780-422-4199, Teacher.Certification@gov.ab.ca

British Columbia
Auditor Certification Board, PO Box 9431 Prov Govt, Victoria, BC V8W 9V3
250-356-8658, Fax: 250-356-9422, Marda.Forbes@gov.bc.ca
British Columbia Council on Admissions & Transfer, #709, 555 Seymour St., Vancouver, BC V6B 3H6
604-412-7700, Fax: 604-683-0576, info@bccat.ca
British Columbia Ministry of Advanced Education, PO Box 9080 Prov Govt, Victoria, BC V8W 9E2
250-356-5170, AVED.GeneralInquiries@gov.bc.ca
British Columbia Ministry of Education, PO Box 9161 Prov Govt, Victoria, BC V8W 9H3
888-879-1166, EDUC.Correspondence@gov.bc.ca
Degree Quality Assessment Board, Degree Quality Assessment Board Secretariat, PO Box 9177 Prov Govt, Victoria, BC V8W 9H8
250-356-5406
Education Advisory Council, c/o Mike Roberts, Superintendent, Liaison, #1550, 555 West Hastings, PO Box 121110, Vancouver, BC V6B 4N6
604-660-1483, Fax: 604-660-2124
Justice Education Society, #260, 800 Hornby St., Vancouver, BC V6Z 2C3
604-660-9870, Fax: 604-775-3476, info@justiceeducation.ca
Leading Edge Endowment Fund Board, 1188 West Georgia St., 9th Fl., Vancouver, BC V6E 4A2
604-438-3220, contact@leefbc.ca
Premier's Technology Council, #1600, 800 Robson St., Vancouver, BC V6Z 3E7
604-827-4629, premiers.technologycouncil@gov.bc.ca
Private Career Training Institutions Agency, #203, 1155 West Pender St., Vancouver, BC V6E 2P4
604-569-0033, Fax: 778-945-0606, 800-661-7441, info@pctia.bc.ca
Teacher Regulation Branch, #400, 2025 West Broadway, Vancouver, BC V6J 1Z6
604-660-6060, Fax: 604-775-4859, 800-555-3684

Manitoba
Adult Learning & Literacy, #350, 800 Portage Ave., Winnipeg, MB R3G 0N4
204-945-8247, Fax: 204-948-1008, all@gov.mb.ca
Division du Bureau de l'éducation française, #509, 1181 av Portage, Winnipeg, MB R3C 0T3
204-945-6916, Fax: 204-948-2997
Manitoba Education & Training, #168, Legislative Bldg., 450 Broadway, Winnipeg, MB R3C 0V8
204-945-3720, Fax: 204-945-1291, minedu@leg.gov.mb.ca
Manitoba Education, Research & Learning Information Networks, University of Manitoba, #100, 135 Innovation Dr., Winnipeg, MB R3T 6A8
204-474-7800, Fax: 204-474-7830, 800-430-6404
Public Schools Finance Board, #506, 1181 Portage Ave., Winnipeg, MB R3G 0T3
204-945-6628, Fax: 204-948-2001
School Programs Division, #307, 1181 Portage Ave., Winnipeg, MB R3G 0T3
204-945-7934, Fax: 204-945-8303

New Brunswick
New Brunswick Department of Education & Early Childhood Development, Place 2000, PO Box 6000, Fredericton, NB E3B 5H1
506-453-3678, Fax: 506-453-4810, edcommunication@gnb.ca
New Brunswick Department of Post-Secondary Education, Training & Labour, Chestnut Complex, PO Box 6000, Fredericton, NB E3B 5H1
506-453-2597, Fax: 506-453-3618, dpetlinfo@gnb.ca

Newfoundland & Labrador
Newfoundland & Labrador Department of Advanced Education & Skills, Confederation Building, West Block, 3rd Fl., PO Box 8700, St. John's, NL A1B 4J6
709-729-2480, aesweb@gov.nl.ca
Newfoundland & Labrador Department of Education & Early Childhood Development, West Block, Confederation Bldg., 100 Prince Philip Dr., 3rd Fl., PO Box 8700, St. John's, NL A1B 4J6
709-729-5097, Fax: 709-729-5896, education@gov.nl.ca

Northwest Territories
Aurora Research Institute, 191 MacKenzie Rd., PO Box 1450, Inuvik, NT X0E 0T0
867-777-3298, Fax: 867-777-4264
Northwest Territories Department of Education, Culture & Employment, PO Box 1320, Yellowknife, NT X1A 2L9
ecepublicaffairs@gov.nt.ca

Nova Scotia
Council of Atlantic Ministers of Education & Training, PO Box 2044, Halifax, NS B3J 2Z1
902-424-5352, Fax: 902-424-8976, camet-camef@cap-cpma.ca
Nova Scotia Apprenticeship Agency, 2021 Brunswick St., PO Box 578, Halifax, NS B3J 2S9
902-424-5651, Fax: 902-424-0717, apprenticeship@gov.ns.ca
Nova Scotia Apprenticeship Board, 2021 Brunswick St., PO Box 578, Halifax, NS B3J 2S9
902-424-0872, Fax: 902-424-0717, 800-494-5651
Nova Scotia Department of Education & Early Childhood Development, Trade Mart Bldg., 2021 Brunswick St., PO Box 578, Halifax, NS B3J 2S9
902-424-5168, Fax: 902-424-0511, 888-825-7770
Nova Scotia Department of Labour & Advanced Education, 5151 Terminal Rd., 6th Fl., PO Box 697, Halifax, NS B3J 2T8
902-424-5301, Fax: 902-424-2203

Nunavut
Nunavut Territory Department of Education, Bldg. 1107, 2nd Fl., PO Box 1000 900, Iqaluit, NU X0A 0H0
867-975-5600, Fax: 867-975-5605, info.edu@gov.nu.ca

Ontario
Academic & Experience Requirements Committee of the Association of Ontario Land Surveyors, 1043 McNicoll Ave., Toronto, ON M1W 3W6
416-491-9020, Fax: 416-491-2576
College of Trades Appointments Council, Mowat Block, 900 Bay St., 23rd Fl., Toronto, ON M7A 1L2
416-326-5629, Fax: 416-326-5653, appointments.council@ontario.ca
College of Veterinarians of Ontario, 2106 Gordon St., Guelph, ON N1L 1G6
519-824-5600, Fax: 519-824-6497, 800-424-2856, inquiries@cvo.org
Financial Policy & Business Division, Mowat Block, 900 Bay St., 20th fl., Toronto, ON M7A 1L2
416-325-6127, Fax: 416-325-9560
Higher Education Quality Council of Ontario, #2402, 1 Yonge St., Toronto, ON M5E 1E5
416-212-3893, Fax: 416-212-3899, info@heqco.ca
Learning & Curriculum Division, Mowat Block, 900 Bay St., 22nd fl., Toronto, ON M7A 1L2
416-325-2135, Fax: 416-327-1182
Ontario French-Language Education Communications Authority, 21 College St., Toronto, ON MRY 2M5
416-968-3536, Fax: 416-968-8203
Ontario Graduate Scholarship Program Selection Board, 189 Red River Rd., 4th Fl., PO Box 4500, Thunder Bay, ON P7B 6G9
807-343-7257, Fax: 807-343-7278, 800-465-3957
Ontario Ministry of Advanced Education & Skills Development, Mowat Block, 900 Bay St., 14th Fl., Toronto, ON M7A 1L2
416-326-1600, Fax: 416-325-6348, 800-387-5514, information.met@ontario.ca
Ontario Ministry of Education, Mowat Block, 900 Bay St., 22nd Fl., Toronto, ON M7A 1L2
416-325-2929, Fax: 416-325-6348, 800-387-5514, information.met@ontario.ca
Ontario Student Assistance Program Financial Eligibility Advisory Committee, 77 Wellesley St. West, PO Box 276, Toronto, ON M7A 1N3
416-314-0714, Fax: 416-325-3096
Post-secondary Education Division, Mowat Block, 900 Bay St., 7th Fl., Toronto, ON M7A 1L2
416-325-2199, Fax: 416-326-3256
Post-secondary Education Quality Assessment Board, Mowat Block, 900 Bay St., 23rd Fl., Toronto, ON M7A 1L2
416-212-1230, Fax: 416-212-6620, peqab@ontario.ca
Training Completion Assurance Fund Advisory Board, Mowat Block, 900 Bay St., 9th Fl., Toronto, ON M7A 1L2
416-314-0500, Fax: 416-314-0499

Prince Edward Island
Prince Edward Island Department of Education, Early Learning & Culture, Holman Centre, #101, 250 Water St., Summerside, PE C1N 1B6
902-438-4130, Fax: 902-438-4062
Prince Edward Island Department of Workforce & Advanced Learning, Shaw Bldg., 105 Rochford St., 5th Fl., PO Box 2000, Charlottetown, PE C1A 7N8
902-368-5956, Fax: 902-368-5277
Prince Edward Island School Athletic Association, #101, 250 Water St., Summerside, PE C1N 1B6
902-438-4846, Fax: 902-438-4884

Québec
Comité-conseil sur les programmes d'études, 1035, de la Chevrotière, 17e étage, Québec, QC G1R 5A5
418-646-0133, Fax: 418-643-0056, ccpe@mels.gouv.qc.ca
Commission consultative de l'enseignement privé, 1035, rue de la Chevrotière, 14e étage, Québec, QC G1R 5A5
418-646-1249, Fax: 418-643-7752, commission.consultative@mels.gouv.qc.ca
Commission d'évaluation de l'enseignement collégial, 800, place d'Youville, 18e étage, Québec, QC G1R 5P4
418-643-9938, Fax: 418-643-9019, info@ceec.gouv.qc.ca
Commission de l'éducation en langue anglaise, 600, rue Fullum, 11e étage, Montréal, QC H2K 4L1
514-873-5656, Fax: 514-864-4181, cela-abee@mels.gouv.qc.ca
Conseil supérieur de l'éducation, #180, 1175, av Lavigerie, Québec, QC G1V 5B2
418-643-3850, Fax: 418-644-2530, panorama@cse.gouv.qc.ca
Ministère de l'Éducation et de l'Enseignement supérieur, 1035, rue De La Chevrotière, 28e étage, Québec, QC G1R 5A5
418-643-7095, Fax: 418-646-6561, 866-747-6626

Saskatchewan
Saskatchewan Advanced Education, #1120, 2010 - 12 Ave., Regina, SK S4P 0M3
306-787-9478, aeeinquiry@gov.sk.ca
Saskatchewan Education, 2220 College Ave., Regina, SK S4P 4V9
linquiry@gov.sk.ca
Saskatchewan Research Council, #125, 15 Innovation Blvd., Saskatoon, SK S7N 2X8
306-933-5400, Fax: 306-933-7446, info@src.sk.ca
Teachers' Superannuation Commission, #129, 3085 Albert St., Regina, SK S4S 0B1
306-787-6440, Fax: 306-787-1939, 877-364-8202, mail@stsc.gov.sk.ca

Yukon Territory
Yukon Education, PO Box 2703, Whitehorse, YT Y1A 2C6
867-667-5141, Fax: 867-393-6339, contact.education@gov.yk.ca

EDUCATION & TRAINING

Employment & Social Development Canada, 140 Promenade du Portage, Gatineau, QC K1A 0J9

Alberta
Alberta Human Services, Office of the Minister, Legislature Building, #224, 10800 - 97 Ave., Edmonton, AB T5K 2B6
780-644-5135, 866-644-5135
Alberta Labour, Legislature Bldg., #404, 10800 - 97 Ave., Edmonton, AB T5K 2B6
780-427-3731, 877-427-3731
Northern Alberta Development Council, Peace River Office, Provincial Building, #206, 9621 - 96 Ave., PO Box 900-14, Peace River, AB T8S 1T4
780-624-6274, Fax: 780-624-6184, -310-0000, nadc.council@gov.ab.ca

British Columbia
British Columbia Ministry of Technology, Innovation & Citizens' Services, PO Box 9068 Prov Govt, Victoria, BC V8W 9E2
250-952-7623, Fax: 250-952-7628, 800-663-7867, EnquiryBC@gov.bc.ca
Private Career Training Institutions Agency, #203, 1155 West Pender St., Vancouver, BC V6E 2P4
604-569-0033, Fax: 778-945-0606, 800-661-7441, info@pctia.bc.ca
Teacher Regulation Branch, #400, 2025 West Broadway, Vancouver, BC V6J 1Z6
604-660-6060, Fax: 604-775-4859, 800-555-3684

New Brunswick
New Brunswick Department of Post-Secondary Education, Training & Labour, Chestnut Complex, PO Box 6000, Fredericton, NB E3B 5H1
506-453-2597, Fax: 506-453-3618, dpetlinfo@gnb.ca

Northwest Territories
Northwest Territories Department of Education, Culture & Employment, PO Box 1320, Yellowknife, NT X1A 2L9
ecepublicaffairs@gov.nt.ca

Nova Scotia
Nova Scotia Department of Labour & Advanced Education, 5151 Terminal Rd., 6th Fl., PO Box 697, Halifax, NS B3J 2T8
902-424-5301, Fax: 902-424-2203

Ontario
Ontario Fire College, 1495 Muskoka Rd. North, Gravenhurst, ON P1P 1R8
705-687-2294, Fax: 705-687-7911, 800-565-0613
Ontario Ministry of Labour, 400 University Ave., 14th Fl., Toronto, ON M7A 1T7
416-326-7160, 800-531-5551
Training Completion Assurance Fund Advisory Board, Mowat Block, 900 Bay St., 9th Fl., Toronto, ON M7A 1L2
416-314-0500, Fax: 416-314-0499

Prince Edward Island
Prince Edward Island Department of Workforce & Advanced Learning, Shaw Bldg., 105 Rochford St., 5th Fl., PO Box 2000, Charlottetown, PE C1A 7N8
902-368-5956, Fax: 902-368-5277

Saskatchewan
Saskatchewan Advanced Education, #1120, 2010 - 12 Ave., Regina, SK S4P 0M3
306-787-9478, aeeinquiry@gov.sk.ca
Saskatchewan Police College, College West Bldg., University of Regina, #217, 3737 Wascana Pkwy., Regina, SK S4S 0A2
306-787-9292

ELECTED OFFICIALS & CONSTITUENCIES

Forty-second Parliament - Canada, House of Commons, Parliament Buildings, Ottawa, AB K1A 0A6

Alberta
Twenty-ninth Legislature - Alberta, Legislature Bldg., 10800 - 97 Ave., Edmonton, AB T5K 2B6
780-427-2826, laocommunications@assembly.ab.ca

British Columbia
Fourtieth Legislature - British Columbia, Parliament Buildings, Victoria, BC V8V 1X4
250-387-3785, Fax: 250-387-0942, ClerkHouse@leg.bc.ca

Manitoba
Forty-first Legislature - Manitoba, Legislative Building, 450 Broadway Ave., Winnipeg, MB R3C 0V8
204-945-3636, Fax: 204-948-2507, clerkla@leg.gov.mb.ca

New Brunswick
Fifty-eighth Legislative Assembly - New Brunswick, Centre Block, Legislative Building, 706 Queen St., PO Box 6000, Fredericton, NB E3B 5H1
506-453-2506, Fax: 506-453-7154, wwwleg@gnb.ca

Newfoundland & Labrador
Forty-Eighth House of Assembly - Newfoundland & Labrador, Confederation Building, PO Box 8700, St. John's, NL A1B 4J6
709-729-3405, ClerkHOA@gov.nl.ca

Northwest Territories
Eighteenth Legislative Assembly - Northwest Territories, 4570 - 48 St., PO Box 1320, Yellowknife, NT X1A 2L9
867-669-2200, Fax: 867-920-4735, 800-661-0784

Nova Scotia
Sixty-second General Assembly - Nova Scotia, Province House, 1726 Hollis St., Halifax, NS B3J 2Y3
902-424-4661, Fax: 902-424-0574

Nunavut
Fourth Legislative Assembly - Nunavut, PO Box 1200, Iqaluit, NU X0A 0H0

Ontario
Forty-first Provincial Parliament - Ontario, Clerk's Office, #104, Legislative Building, Queen's Park, Toronto, ON M7A 1A2
416-325-7500, Fax: 416-325-7489, web@ola.org

Prince Edward Island
Sixty-fifth General Assembly - Prince Edward Island, Province House, 165 Richmond St., 1st Fl., PO Box 2000, Charlottetown, PE C1A 7N8
902-368-5970, Fax: 902-368-5175, 877-315-5518

Québec
Quarante-et-unième assemblée nationale, Hôtel du Parlement, 1045, rue des Parlementaires, Québec, QC G1A 1A4
418-643-7239, Fax: 418-646-4271, 866-337-8837

Saskatchewan
Twenty-eighth Legislature - Saskatchewan, 2405 Legislative Dr., Regina, SK S4S 0B3

Yukon Territory
Thirty-third Legislative Assembly - Yukon Territory, Yukon Legislative Assembly Office, 2071 Second Ave., PO Box 2703, Whitehorse, YT Y1A 2C6
867-667-5498

ELECTIONS

Elections Canada, 30 Victoria St., Gatineau, ON K1A 0M6
613-993-2975, Fax: 613-954-8584, 800-463-6868
Office of the Commissioner of Canada Elections, 30 Victoria St., Gatineau, ON K1A 0M6
Fax: 819-939-1801, 855-759-6740, info@cef-cce.gc.ca

Alberta
Alberta Office of the Chief Electoral Officer / Elections Alberta, #100, 11510 Kingsway Ave., Edmonton, AB T5G 2Y5
780-427-7191, Fax: 780-422-2900, info@elections.ab.ca

British Columbia
Elections British Columbia, PO Box 9275 Prov Govt, Victoria, BC V8W 9J6
250-387-5305, Fax: 250-387-3578, 800-661-8683, electionsbc@elections.bc.ca

Manitoba
Elections Manitoba, #120, 200 Vaughan St., Winnipeg, MB R3C 1T5
204-945-3225, Fax: 204-945-6011, 866-628-6837, election@elections.mb.ca

New Brunswick
Office of the Chief Electoral Officer, #102, Sartain MacDonald Building, PO Box 6000, Fredericton, NB E3B 5H1
506-453-2218, Fax: 506-457-4926, 800-308-2922, info@electionsnb.ca

Newfoundland & Labrador
Office of the Chief Electoral Officer, 39 Hallett Cr., St. John's, NL A1B 4C4
709-729-0712, Fax: 709-729-0679, 877-729-7987, enl@gov.nl.ca

Northwest Territories
Elections NWT/Plebiscite Office, YK Centre East, #7, 4915-48th St., 3rd Fl., Yellowknife, NT X1A 3S4
867-767-9100, Fax: 867-920-9100, 844-767-9100, electionsnwt@gov.nt.ca

Nova Scotia
Elections Nova Scotia, #6, 7037 Mumford Rd., PO Box 2246, Halifax, NS B3J 3C8
902-424-8584, Fax: 902-424-6622, 800-565-1504

Nunavut
Nunavut Legislative Assembly, 926 Federal Rd., PO Box 1200, Iqaluit, NU X0A 0H0
867-975-5000, Fax: 867-975-5190, 877-334-7266, leginfo@assembly.nu.ca

Ontario
Elections Ontario, 51 Rolark Dr., Toronto, ON M1R 3B1
416-326-6300, Fax: 416-326-6200, 888-668-8683, info@elections.on.ca

Prince Edward Island
Elections Prince Edward Island, Atlantic Technology Centre, #160, 176 Great George St., Charlottetown, PE C1A 4K3
902-368-5895, Fax: 902-368-6500, 888-234-8783

Québec
Directeur général des Élections du Québec, Édifice René-Lévesque, 3460, rue de La Pérade, Québec, QC G1X 3Y5
418-528-0422, Fax: 418-643-7291, 888-353-2846, info@electionsQuébec.qc.ca

Saskatchewan
Elections Saskatchewan, 1702 Park St., Regina, SK S4N 6B2
306-787-4000, Fax: 306-787-4052, 877-958-8683, info@elections.sk.ca

EMERGENCY MEASURES

Emergency Management & Programs Branch, 340 Laurier Ave. West, Ottawa, ON K1A 0P8
Environment & Climate Change Canada, 10 Wellington St., Gatineau, QC K1A 0H3
819-997-2800, Fax: 819-994-1412, 800-668-6767, enviroinfo@ec.gc.ca
National Search & Rescue Secretariat, 269 Laurier Ave. West, 10th Fl., Ottawa, ON K1A 0P8
Fax: 613-996-3746, 800-727-9414, questions@nss-snrs.gc.ca
Public Safety Canada, 269 Laurier Ave. West, Ottawa, ON K1A 0P8
613-944-4875, Fax: 613-954-5186, 800-830-3118

Alberta
Alberta Emergency Management Agency, 2810 - 10303 Jasper Ave., Edmonton, AB T5J 3N6
780-422-9000, Fax: 780-644-1044, -310-0000, aema@gov.ab.ca
Alberta Environment & Parks, Information Centre, Great West Life Bldg., 9920 - 108 St., Main Fl., Edmonton, AB T5K 2M4
780-427-2700, Fax: 780-427-4407, -310-3773, ESRD.Info-Centre@gov.ab.ca

British Columbia
Emergency Management BC, PO Box 9201 Prov Govt, Victoria, BC V8W 9J1
250-952-4913, Fax: 250-952-4871
Provincial Emergency Program, PO Box 9201 Prov Govt, Victoria, BC V8W 9J1
250-952-4913, Fax: 250-952-4888, 800-663-3456

Manitoba
Emergency Measures Organization, #1525, 405 Broadway Ave., Winnipeg, MB R3C 3L6
204-945-4772, Fax: 204-945-4929, 888-267-8298, emo@gov.mb.ca

Newfoundland & Labrador
Fire & Emergency Services - Newfoundland & Labrador, 25 Hallett Cres., PO Box 8700, St. John's, NL A1B 4J6
709-729-1608, Fax: 709-729-2524
NL 911 Bureau Inc., c/o Fire & Emergency Services - NL, 25 Hallett Cres., PO Box 8700, St. John's, NL A1B 4J6

Nova Scotia
Emergency Management Office, PO Box 2581, Halifax, NS B3J 3N5
902-424-5620, Fax: 902-424-5376, 866-424-5620, emo@gov.ns.ca

Nunavut
Nunavut Emergency Management, PO Box 1000 700, Iqaluit, NU X0A 0H0
867-975-5403, Fax: 867-979-4221, 800-693-1666

Ontario
Emergency Management Ontario, 77 Wellesley St. West, PO Box 222, Toronto, ON M7A 1N3
416-314-3723, Fax: 416-314-3758, 877-314-3723
Office of the Fire Marshal & Emergency Management, Place Nouveau, 5775 Yonge St., 7th Fl., Toronto, ON M2M 4J1
416-325-3100, Fax: 416-325-3119

Saskatchewan
Emergency Management & Fire Safety, 1855 Victoria Ave., 5th Fl., Regina, SK S4P 3T2
306-787-3774, Fax: 306-787-7107, 866-757-5911

Yukon Territory
Emergency Measures Organization, Whitehorse Airport, Combined Services Bldg., 2nd Fl., 60 Norseman Rd., Whitehorse, YT Y1A 2C6
867-667-5220, Fax: 867-393-6266, 800-661-0408, emo.yukon@gov.yk.ca
Emergency Medical Services, Yukon Electrical Bldg., #200, 1100 First Ave., Whitehorse, YT Y1A 6K6

EMPLOYMENT

Public Service Commission, 22 Eddy St., Gatineau, QC K1A 0M7
613-992-9562, Fax: 613-992-9352, CFP.INFOCOM.PSC@cfp-psc.gc.ca

Alberta
Alberta Human Services, Office of the Minister, Legislature Building, #224, 10800 - 97 Ave., Edmonton, AB T5K 2B6
780-644-5135, 866-644-5135
Alberta Labour, Legislature Bldg., #404, 10800 - 97 Ave., Edmonton, AB T5K 2B6
780-427-3731, 877-427-3731
Corporate Human Resources, Peace Hills Trust Tower, 10011 - 109 St., 7th Fl., Edmonton, AB T5J 3S8
780-408-8400

British Columbia
British Columbia Public Service Agency, PO Box 9404 Prov Govt, Victoria, BC V8W 9V1
250-387-0518, Fax: 250-356-7074
Employment & Assistance Appeal Tribunal, PO Box 9994 Prov Govt, Victoria, BC V8W 9R7
250-356-6374, Fax: 250-356-9687, 866-557-0035, eaat@gov.bc.ca
Office of the Merit Commissioner, #502, 947 Fort St., PO Box 9037 Prov Govt, Victoria, BC V8W 9A3
250-953-4208, Fax: 250-953-4160, merit@meritcomm.bc.ca

Manitoba
Manitoba Civil Service Commission, #935, 155 Carlton St., Winnipeg, MB R3C 3H8
204-945-2332, Fax: 204-945-1486, 800-282-8069, csc@gov.mb.ca

New Brunswick
New Brunswick Department of Human Resources, Chancery Place, 675 King St., Fredericton, NB E3B 1E9
506-453-2264, Fax: 506-453-7195, Ohr-brh@gnb.ca
New Brunswick Jobs Board, Chancery Place, PO Box 6000, Fredericton, NB E3B 5H1

Newfoundland & Labrador
Labour Relations Agency, Beothuck Bldg., 20 Crosbie Pl., 3rd Fl., PO Box 8700, St. John's, NL A1B 4J6
709-729-2715, Fax: 709-729-1759, 877-563-1063, labour@gov.nl.ca

Newfoundland & Labrador Department of Advanced Education & Skills, Confederation Building, West Block, 3rd Fl., PO Box 8700, St. John's, NL A1B 4J6
709-729-2480, aesweb@gov.nl.ca

Newfoundland & Labrador Public Service Commission, 50 Mundy Pond Rd., PO Box 8700, St. John's, NL A1B 4J6
709-729-5810, Fax: 709-729-6234, 855-330-5810, contactpsc@gov.nl.ca

Northwest Territories

Northwest Territories Department of Human Resources, PO Box 1320, Yellowknife, NT X1A 2L9
867-678-6625, Fax: 867-873-0282, 866-475-8162, jobsyk@gov.nt.ca

Nova Scotia

Nova Scotia Public Service Commission, 1800 Argyle St., 5th Fl., PO Box 943, Halifax, NS B3J 2V9
902-424-7660

Ontario

Public Service Commission, Whitney Block, 99 Wellesley St. West, 5th Fl., Toronto, ON M7A 1W4
416-325-1750

Prince Edward Island

Prince Edward Island Department of Workforce & Advanced Learning, Shaw Bldg., 105 Rochford St., 5th Fl., PO Box 2000, Charlottetown, PE C1A 7N8
902-368-5956, Fax: 902-368-5277

Public Service Commission, Shaw Bldg. North, 105 Rochford St., 1st Fl., PO Box 2000, Charlottetown, PE C1A 7N8
902-368-4080, Fax: 902-368-4383

Québec

Commission de la fonction publique, 800, place D'Youville, 7e étage, Québec, QC G1R 3P4
418-643-1425, Fax: 418-643-7264, 800-432-0432, cfp@cfp.gouv.qc.ca

Emploi-Québec, Direction du Centre de communication avec la clientèle, 150, rue Monseigneur-Ross, 5e étage, Gaspé, QC G4X 2S7
514-873-4000, 877-767-8773

Ministère du Travail, de l'Emploi et de la Solidarité sociale, 200, ch Sainte-Foy, 5e étage, Québec, QC G1R 5S1
418-644-4545, Fax: 418-528-0559, 877-644-4545

Saskatchewan

Physician Recruitment Agency of Saskatchewan (SaskDocs), 309 - 4th Ave. North, Saskatoon, SK S7K 2L8
306-933-5000, Fax: 306-933-5115, 888-415-3627, info@saskdocs.ca

Public Service Commission, 2350 Albert St., Regina, SK S4P 4A6
306-787-7853, 866-319-5999, csinquiry@gov.sk.ca

Saskatchewan Advanced Education, #1120, 2010 - 12 Ave., Regina, SK S4P 0M3
306-787-9478, aeeinquiry@gov.sk.ca

Yukon Territory

Yukon Public Service Commission, Yukon Government Administration Bldg., 2071 Second Ave., PO Box 2703, Whitehorse, YT Y1A 2C6
867-667-5653, Fax: 867-667-5755, PSCWebsite@gov.yk.ca

EMPLOYMENT EQUITY

See: Discrimination & Employment Equity

Office of the Public Sector Integrity Commissioner of Canada, 60 Queen St., 7th Fl., Ottawa, ON K1P 5Y7
613-941-6400, Fax: 613-941-6535, 866-941-6400

British Columbia

Office of the Merit Commissioner, #502, 947 Fort St., PO Box 9037 Prov Govt, Victoria, BC V8W 9A3
250-953-4208, Fax: 250-953-4160, merit@meritcomm.bc.ca

Newfoundland & Labrador

Labour Relations Agency, Beothuck Bldg., 20 Crosbie Pl., 3rd Fl., PO Box 8700, St. John's, NL A1B 4J6
709-729-2715, Fax: 709-729-1759, 877-563-1063, labour@gov.nl.ca

EMPLOYMENT INSURANCE

Canada Employment Insurance Commission, 140, Promenade du Portage, Phase IV, Gatineau, QC K1A 0J9
800-206-7218

Service Canada, 140, Promenade du Portage, Gatineau, QC K1A 0J9
Fax: 613-941-1827, 800-622-6232

Saskatchewan

Saskatchewan Labour Relations & Workplace Safety, #300, 1870 Albert St., Regina, SK S4P 4W1
306-787-7404, webmaster@lab.gov.sk.ca

ENERGY

See Also: Natural Resources

Canadian Nuclear Safety Commission, 280 Slater St., PO Box 1046 B,Ottawa, ON K1P 5S9
613-995-5894, Fax: 613-995-5086, 800-668-5284, cnsc.information.ccsn@canada.ca

Indian Oil & Gas Canada, #100, 9911 Chiila Blvd., Tsuu T'ina (Sarcee), AB T2W 6H6
403-292-5625, Fax: 403-292-5618, ContactIOGC@inac-ainc.gc.ca

National Energy Board, 517 - 10 Ave. SW, Calgary, AB T2R 0A8
403-292-4800, Fax: 403-292-5503, 800-899-1265

Office of Energy Efficiency, CEF, Building 3, Observatory Cres., 930 Carling Ave., Ottawa, ON K1A 0Y3

Waste Biotreatability Facility, c/o Montréal (av Royalmount) Research Facilities, 6100, av Royalmount, Montréal, QC H4P 2R2

Alberta

Alberta Energy, North Petroleum Plaza, 9945 - 108 St., Edmonton, AB T5K 2G6
780-427-8050, Fax: 780-422-9522, -310-0000

Alberta Energy Regulator, #1000, 250 - 5 St. SW, Calgary, AB T2P 0R4
403-297-8311, Fax: 403-297-7336, 855-297-8311, inquiries@aer.ca

Alberta Innovates - Energy & Environmental Solutions, AMEC Place, #2540, 801 - 6th Ave. SW, Calgary, AB T2P 3W2
403-297-7089, Fax: 403-297-3638, ees@albertainnovates.ca

Alberta Utilities Commission, Fifth Avenue Place, 425 - 1st St. SW, 4th Fl., Calgary, AB T2P 3L8
403-592-8845, Fax: 403-592-4406, -310-0000, info@auc.ab.ca

Surface Rights Board, 1229 - 91 St. SW, Edmonton, AB T6X 1E9
780-427-2444, Fax: 780-427-5798, -310-0000, srb.lcb@gov.ab.ca

British Columbia

British Columbia Hydro, 6911 Southpoint Dr., Burnaby, BC V3N 4X8
604-224-9376, 800-224-9376

British Columbia Ministry of Energy & Mines (& Responsible for Core Review), PO Box 9060 Prov Govt, Victoria, BC V8W 9E3

British Columbia Utilities Commission, 900 Howe St., 6th Fl., PO Box 250, Vancouver, BC V6Z 2N3
604-660-4700, Fax: 604-660-1102, 800-663-1385, commission.secretary@bcuc.com

Columbia Power Corporation, #200, 445 - 13th Ave., Castlegar, BC V1N 1G1
250-304-6060, Fax: 250-304-6083, cpc.info@columbiapower.org

Oil & Gas Commission, #100, 10003 - 110 Ave., Fort St. John, BC V1J 6M7
250-794-5200, Fax: 250-794-5375

Powerex Corp., #1300, 666 Burrard St., Vancouver, BC V6C 2X8
604-891-5000, Fax: 604-891-6060, 800-220-4907

Powertech Labs Inc., 12388 - 88 Ave., Surrey, BC V8W 7R7
604-590-7500, Fax: 604-590-6611

Manitoba

Manitoba Hydro, 360 Portage Ave., PO Box 815 Main,Winnipeg, MB R3C 2P4
204-480-5900, Fax: 204-360-6155, 888-624-9376, publicaffairs@hydro.mb.ca

Manitoba Mineral Resources, The Paris Building, 259 Portage Ave., 9th Fl., Winnipeg, MB R3B 3P4
204-945-6569, 800-223-5215, minesinfo@gov.mb.ca

Power Engineers Advisory Board, Norquay Bldg., #500, 401 York Ave., Winnipeg, MB R3C 0P8
204-945-3373, Fax: 204-948-2309

New Brunswick

New Brunswick Department of Energy & Resource Development, Hugh John Flemming Forestry Centre, 1350 Regent St., Fredericton, NB E3C 2G6
506-453-3826, Fax: 506-444-4367, dnr_mrnweb@gnb.ca

Newfoundland & Labrador

Canada-Newfoundland & Labrador Offshore Petroleum Board, TD Place, 140 Water St., 5th Fl., St. John's, NL A1C 6H6
709-778-1400, Fax: 709-778-1473, information@cnlopb.ca

Churchill Falls (Labrador) Corporation Limited, Hydro Place, 500 Columbus Dr., PO Box 12500, St. John's, NL A1B 4K7
709-737-1859, Fax: 709-737-1816

Nalcor Energy, 500 Columbus Dr., St. John's, NL A1E 2B2
709-737-1400, Fax: 709-737-1800, info@nalcorenergy.com

Newfoundland & Labrador Board of Commissioners of Public Utilities, Prince Charles Bldg., #E-210, 120 Torbay Rd., PO Box 21040, St. John's, NL A1A 5B2
709-726-8600, Fax: 709-726-9604, 866-782-0006, ito@pub.nf.ca

Newfoundland & Labrador Hydro, Hydro Place, 500 Columbus Dr., PO Box 12400, St. John's, NL A1B 4K7
709-737-1400, Fax: 709-737-1800, 888-737-1296, hydro@nlh.nl.ca

Office of Climate Change & Energy Efficiency, PO Box 8700, St. John's, NL A1B 4J6
709-729-1210, Fax: 709-729-1119, climatechange@gov.nl.ca

Twin Falls Power Corporation, PO Box 12500, St. John's, NL A1B 3T5

Northwest Territories

Northwest Territories Department of Environment & Natural Resources, #600, 5102 - 50 Ave., Yellowknife, NT X1A 3S8
867-767-9231

Northwest Territories Power Corporation, 4 Capital Dr., Hay River, NT X0E 1G2
867-874-5200, info@ntpc.com

Nova Scotia

Canada-Nova Scotia Offshore Pétroleum Board, TD Centre, 1791 Barrington St., 8th Fl., Halifax, NS B3J 3K9
902-422-5588, Fax: 902-422-1799, info@cnsopb.ns.ca

Nova Scotia Department of Energy, Joseph Howe Bldg., 1690 Hollis St., PO Box 2664, Halifax, NS B3J 3J9
902-424-4575, Fax: 902-424-0528, enerinfo@novascotia.ca

Nova Scotia Utility & Review Board, Summit Place, 1601 Lower Water St., 3rd Fl., PO Box 1692 M,Halifax, NS B3J 3S3
902-424-4448, Fax: 902-424-3919, 855-442-4448, board@novascotia.ca

Ontario

Hydro One Inc., North Tower, 483 Bay St., 15th Fl., Toronto, ON M5G 2P5
416-345-5000, Fax: 905-944-3251, 877-955-1155, customercommunications@hydroone.com

Independent Electricity System Operator, #1600, 120 Adelaide St. West, Toronto, ON M5H 1T1
905-403-6900, Fax: 905-403-6921, 888-448-7777, customer.relations@ieso.ca

Ontario Energy Board, #2700, 2300 Yonge St., PO Box 2319, Toronto, ON M4P 1E4
416-481-1967, Fax: 416-440-7656, 888-632-6273

Ontario Ministry of Energy, Hearst Block, 900 Bay St., 4th Fl., Toronto, ON M7A 2E1
Fax: 416-325-8440, 888-668-4636

Ontario Ministry of Environment & Climate Change, Public Information Centre, Macdonald Block, 900 Bay St., 2nd Fl., Toronto, ON M7A 1N3
416-325-4000, Fax: 416-314-6713, 800-565-4923

Ontario Power Generation, 700 University Ave., Toronto, ON M5G 1X6
416-592-2555, 877-592-2555, webmaster@opg.com

Prince Edward Island

Prince Edward Island Department of Justice & Public Safety, Shaw Bldg. South, 95 Rochford St., 4th Fl., PO Box 2000, Charlottetown, PE C1A 7N8
902-368-6410, Fax: 902-368-6488

Prince Edward Island Energy Corporation, Sullivan Bldg., 16 Fitzroy St., PO Box 2000, Charlottetown, PE C1A 7N8

Québec

Agence de l'efficacité énergétique, #B406, 5700, 4e av ouest, Québec, QC G1H 6R1
418-627-6379, Fax: 418-643-5828, 877-727-6655, efficaciteenergetique@mern.gouv.qc.ca

Coopérative régionale d'électricité de Saint-Jean-Baptiste-de-Rouville, 3113, rue Principale, Saint-Jean-Baptiste, QC J0L 1B0
450-467-5583, Fax: 450-467-0092, 800-267-5583, info@coopsjb.com

Hydro-Québec, 75, boul René-Lévesque ouest, 19e étage, Montréal, QC H2Z 1A4
514-289-2211

Régie de l'énergie, Tour de la Bourse, #2.55, 800, Place Victoria, Montréal, QC H4Z 1A2
514-873-2452, Fax: 514-873-2070, 888-873-2452, secretariat@regie-energie.qc.ca

Société d'énergie de la Baie-James, #1200, 800, de Maisonneuve est, Montréal, QC H2L 4L8
514-286-2020

Saskatchewan

Energy & Resources, 2101 Scarth St., Regina, SK S4P SH9
306-787-2528

NorthPoint Energy Solutions Inc., 2025 Victoria Ave., Regina, SK S4P 0S1
306-566-2103, Fax: 306-566-3364, info@northpointenergy.com

Saskatchewan Power Corporation (SaskPower), 2025 Victoria Ave., Regina, SK S4P 0S1
306-566-2121, 888-757-6937

SaskEnergy Incorporated, 1777 Victoria Ave., Regina, SK S4P 4K5
306-777-9225, 800-567-8899

Yukon Territory

Yukon Energy, Mines & Resources, PO Box 2703, Whitehorse, YT Y1A 2C6
867-667-3130, Fax: 867-456-3965, 800-661-0408, emr@gov.yk.ca

ENGINEERING & CONSULTING

Canadian Environmental Assessment Agency, Place Bell Canada, 160 Elgin St., 22nd Fl., Ottawa, ON K1A 0H3
613-957-0700, Fax: 613-957-0862, 866-582-1884, info@ceaa-acee.gc.ca

Defence Construction Canada, Constitution Square, 350 Albert St., 19th Fl., Ottawa, ON K1A 0K3
613-998-9548, Fax: 613-998-1061, 800-514-3555, info@dcc-cdc.gc.ca

Infrastructure Canada, #1100, 180 Kent St., Ottawa, ON K1P 0B6
613-948-1148, 877-250-7154, info@infc.gc.ca

Natural Sciences & Engineering Research Council of Canada, Constitution Square, Tower II, 350 Albert St., Ottawa, ON K1A 1H5
613-995-4273, Fax: 613-992-5337, 855-275-2861

Alberta

Alberta Infrastructure, Infrastructure Building, 6950 - 113 St., Edmonton, AB T6H 5V7
780-415-0507, Fax: 780-427-2187, -310-0000, Infra.Contact.Us.m@gov.ab.ca

Safety, Policy & Engineering Division, Twin Atria Building, 4999 - 98 Ave., Main Fl., Edmonton, AB T6B 2X3
780-427-8901, Fax: 780-415-0782, 800-666-5036

British Columbia

British Columbia Ministry of Transportation & Infrastructure, PO Box 9850 Prov Govt, Victoria, BC V8W 9T5
250-387-3198, Fax: 250-356-7706, tran.webmaster@gov.bc.ca

Partnerships BC, #2320, 1111 West Georgia St., PO Box 9478 Prov Govt, Vancouver, BC V8W 9W6
604-681-2443, Fax: 604-806-4190, partnershipsbc@partnershipsbc.ca

Transportation Policy & Programs Department, PO Box 9850 Prov Govt, Victoria, BC V8W 9T5
250-387-5062, Fax: 250-387-6431

Manitoba

Manitoba Infrastructure, Legislative Building, #203, 450 Broadway Ave., Winnipeg, MB R3C 0V8
204-945-3723, Fax: 204-945-7610

Power Engineers Advisory Board, Norquay Bldg., #500, 401 York Ave., Winnipeg, MB R3C 0P8
204-945-3373, Fax: 204-948-2309

New Brunswick

New Brunswick Department of Transportation & Infrastructure, Kings Place, PO Box 6000, Fredericton, NB E3B 5H1
506-453-3939, Fax: 506-453-7987, Transportation.Web@gnb.ca

Nova Scotia

Nova Scotia Department of Transportation & Infrastructure Renewal, Johnston Bldg., 1672 Granville St., 2nd Fl., PO Box 186, Halifax, NS B3J 2N2
902-424-2297, Fax: 902-424-0532, 888-432-3233, tpwpaff@novascotia.ca

Ontario

Infrastructure Ontario, College Park, 777 Bay St., 6th Fl., Toronto, ON M5G 2C8
416-212-7289, Fax: 416-325-4646, info@infrastructureontario.ca

Ontario Ministry of Economic Development & Growth, Hearst Block, 900 Bay St., 8th Fl., Toronto, ON M7A 2E1
416-325-6666, 800-268-7095

Ontario Ministry of Infrastructure, Hearst Block, 900 Bay St., 8th Fl., Toronto, ON M7A 2E1
416-325-6666, 800-268-7095

Waterfront Toronto, #1310, 20 Bay St., Toronto, ON M5J 2N8
416-241-1344, Fax: 416-214-4591, info@waterfronttoronto.ca

Prince Edward Island

Prince Edward Island Department of Transportation, Infrastructure & Energy, Jones Bldg., 11 Kent St., 3rd Fl., PO Box 2000, Charlottetown, PE C1A 7N8
902-368-5100, Fax: 902-368-5395

Saskatchewan

Saskatchewan Highways & Infrastructure, Victoria Tower, 1855 Victoria Ave., Regina, SK S4P 3T2
306-787-4800, communications@highways.gov.sk.ca

SaskBuilds, #720, 1855 Victoria Ave., Regina, SK S4P 3T2
306-798-8014, Fax: 306-798-0626, saskbuilds@gov.sk.ca

ENVIRONMENT

Commissioner of the Environment & Sustainable Development, 240 Sparks St., Ottawa, ON K1A 0G6
613-952-0213, Fax: 613-941-8286

Environment & Climate Change Canada, 10 Wellington St., Gatineau, QC K1A 0H3
819-997-2800, Fax: 819-994-1412, 800-668-6767, enviroinfo@ec.gc.ca

Environmental Protection Review Canada, 240 Sparks St., 4th Fl. West, Ottawa, ON K1A 0X8
Fax: 613-907-1337, eprc-rpec@eprc-rpec.gc.ca

Alberta

Alberta Environment & Parks, Information Centre, Great West Life Bldg., 9920 - 108 St., Main Fl., Edmonton, AB T5K 2M4
780-427-2700, Fax: 780-427-4407, -310-3773, ESRD.Info-Centre@gov.ab.ca

Alberta Innovates - Energy & Environmental Solutions, AMEC Place, #2540, 801 - 6th Ave. SW, Calgary, AB T2P 3W2
403-297-7089, Fax: 403-297-3638, ees@albertainnovates.ca

British Columbia

British Columbia Ministry of Environment, PO Box 9339 Prov Govt, Victoria, BC V8W 9M1
250-387-9870, Fax: 250-387-6003, env.mail@gov.bc.ca

Manitoba

Manitoba Round Table for Sustainable Development, #160, 123 Main St., PO Box 70, Winnipeg, MB R3C 1A5
204-945-4391, Fax: 204-948-4730, mrtsd@gov.mb.ca

Manitoba Sustainable Development, 200 Saulteaux Cres., PO Box 22, Winnipeg, MB R3J 3W3
204-945-6784, 800-214-6497, mgi@gov.mb.ca

New Brunswick

New Brunswick Department of Environment & Local Government, Marysville Place, PO Box 6000, Fredericton, NB E3B 5H1
506-453-2690, Fax: 506-457-4994, elg/egl-info@gnb.ca

Newfoundland & Labrador

Newfoundland & Labrador Department of Environment & Conservation, Confederation Bldg., West Block, 4th Fl., PO Box 8700, St. John's, NL A1B 4J6
709-729-2664, Fax: 709-729-6639, 800-563-6181, envcinquires@gov.nl.ca

Northwest Territories

Northwest Territories Department of Environment & Natural Resources, #600, 5102 - 50 Ave., Yellowknife, NT X1A 3S8
867-767-9231

Nova Scotia

Agricultural Marshland Conservation Commission, NS

Nova Scotia Department of Environment, #1800, 1894 Barrington St., PO Box 442, Halifax, NS B3J 2P8
902-424-3600, Fax: 902-424-0501, 877-936-8476

Nova Scotia Lands Inc., Harbourside Pl., 45 Wabana Ct., PO Box 430 A,Sydney, NS B1P 6H2
Fax: 902-564-7903

Resource Recovery Fund Board Inc., #400, 35 Commercial St., Truro, NS B2N 3H9
902-895-7732, Fax: 902-897-3256, 877-313-7732, info@rrfb.com

Sydney Tar Ponds Agency, 1 Inglis St., PO Box 1028 A, Sydney, NS B1P 6J7
902-567-1035, Fax: 902-567-1037

Nunavut

Nunavut Territory Department of Environment, PO Box 1000 1300, Iqaluit, NU X0A 0H0
867-975-7700, Fax: 867-975-7742, environment@gov.nu.ca

Ontario

Environmental Commissioner of Ontario, #605, 1075 Bay St., Toronto, ON M5S 2B1
416-325-3377, Fax: 416-325-3370, 800-701-6454, commissioner@eco.on.ca

Ontario Ministry of Environment & Climate Change, Public Information Centre, Macdonald Block, 900 Bay St., 2nd Fl., Toronto, ON M7A 1N3
416-325-4000, Fax: 416-314-6713, 800-565-4923

Prince Edward Island

Environment, Jones Bldg., 11 Kent St., 4th Fl., PO Box 2000, Charlottetown, PE C1A 7N8
902-368-5028, Fax: 902-368-5830, 866-368-5044

Prince Edward Island Department of Justice & Public Safety, Shaw Bldg. South, 95 Rochford St., 4th Fl., PO Box 2000, Charlottetown, PE C1A 7N8
902-368-6410, Fax: 902-368-6488

Québec

Bureau d'audiences publiques sur l'environnement, Édifice Lomer-Gouin, #2.10, 575, rue Saint-Amable, Québec, QC G1R 6A6
418-643-7447, Fax: 418-643-9474, 800-463-4732, communication@bape.gouv.qc.ca

Ministère du Développement durable, de l'Environnement et de la Lutte contre les changements climatiques, Édifice Marie-Guyart, 675, boul René-Lévesque est, 29e étage, Québec, QC G1R 5V7
418-521-3830, Fax: 418-646-5974, 800-561-1616, info@mddefp.gouv.qc.ca

Saskatchewan

Saskatchewan Environment, 3211 Albert St., 2nd Fl., Regina, SK S4S 5W6
306-787-2584, Fax: 306-787-9544, 800-567-4224, Centre.Inquiry@gov.sk.ca

ENVIRONMENT DEPARTMENTS/MINISTRIES

Environment & Climate Change Canada, 10 Wellington St., Gatineau, QC K1A 0H3
819-997-2800, Fax: 819-994-1412, 800-668-6767, enviroinfo@ec.gc.ca

Alberta

Alberta Environment & Parks, Information Centre, Great West Life Bldg., 9920 - 108 St., Main Fl., Edmonton, AB T5K 2M4
780-427-2700, Fax: 780-427-4407, -310-3773, ESRD.Info-Centre@gov.ab.ca

British Columbia

British Columbia Ministry of Environment, PO Box 9339 Prov Govt, Victoria, BC V8W 9M1
250-387-9870, Fax: 250-387-6003, env.mail@gov.bc.ca

Manitoba

Manitoba Sustainable Development, 200 Saulteaux Cres., PO Box 22, Winnipeg, MB R3J 3W3
204-945-6784, 800-214-6497, mgi@gov.mb.ca

New Brunswick

New Brunswick Department of Environment & Local Government, Marysville Place, PO Box 6000, Fredericton, NB E3B 5H1
506-453-2690, Fax: 506-457-4994, elg/egl-info@gnb.ca

Newfoundland & Labrador

Newfoundland & Labrador Department of Environment & Conservation, Confederation Bldg., West Block, 4th Fl., PO Box 8700, St. John's, NL A1B 4J6
709-729-2664, Fax: 709-729-6639, 800-563-6181, envcinquires@gov.nl.ca

Northwest Territories

Northwest Territories Department of Environment & Natural Resources, #600, 5102 - 50 Ave., Yellowknife, NT X1A 3S8
867-767-9231

Nova Scotia

Nova Scotia Department of Environment, #1800, 1894 Barrington St., PO Box 442, Halifax, NS B3J 2P8
902-424-3600, Fax: 902-424-0501, 877-936-8476

Nunavut

Nunavut Territory Department of Environment, PO Box 1000 1300, Iqaluit, NU X0A 0H0
867-975-7700, Fax: 867-975-7742, environment@gov.nu.ca

Ontario

Ontario Ministry of Environment & Climate Change, Public Information Centre, Macdonald Block, 900 Bay St., 2nd Fl., Toronto, ON M7A 1N3
416-325-4000, Fax: 416-314-6713, 800-565-4923

Prince Edward Island

Prince Edward Island Department of Justice & Public Safety, Shaw Bldg. South, 95 Rochford St., 4th Fl., PO Box 2000, Charlottetown, PE C1A 7N8
902-368-6410, Fax: 902-368-6488

Québec

Ministère du Développement durable, de l'Environnement et de la Lutte contre les changements climatiques, Édifice Marie-Guyart, 675, boul René-Lévesque est, 29e étage, Québec, QC G1R 5V7
418-521-3830, Fax: 418-646-5974, 800-561-1616, info@mddefp.gouv.qc.ca

Saskatchewan

Saskatchewan Environment, 3211 Albert St., 2nd Fl., Regina, SK S4S 5W6
306-787-2584, Fax: 306-787-9544, 800-567-4224, Centre.Inquiry@gov.sk.ca

Yukon Territory

Yukon Environment, 10 Burns Rd., PO Box 2703 V-3A, Whitehorse, YT Y1A 2C6
867-667-5652, Fax: 867-393-7197, environment.yukon@gov.yk.ca

ENVIRONMENTAL ASSESSMENT

Canadian Environmental Assessment Agency, Place Bell Canada, 160 Elgin St., 22nd Fl., Ottawa, ON K1A 0H3
613-957-0700, Fax: 613-957-0862, 866-582-1884, info@ceaa-acee.gc.ca

Prince Edward Island

Environment, Jones Bldg., 11 Kent St., 4th Fl., PO Box 2000, Charlottetown, PE C1A 7N8
902-368-5028, Fax: 902-368-5830, 866-368-5044

Land & Environment, Jones Bldg., 11 Kent St., 3rd Fl., PO Box 2000, Charlottetown, PE C1A 7N8
902-368-5221, Fax: 902-368-5395

ENVIRONMENTAL HEALTH

Centre for Aquaculture & Environmental Research, 4160 Marine Dr., West Vancouver, BC V7V 1N6
604-666-7453, Fax: 604-666-3497

Environmental Protection Review Canada, 240 Sparks St., 4th Fl. West, Ottawa, ON K1A 0X8
Fax: 613-907-1337, eprc-rpec@eprc-rpec.gc.ca

Nova Scotia
Agricultural Marshland Conservation Commission, NS
Sydney Tar Ponds Agency, 1 Inglis St., PO Box 1028 A, Sydney, NS B1P 6J7
902-567-1035, Fax: 902-567-1037

Prince Edward Island
Environment, Jones Bldg., 11 Kent St., 4th Fl., PO Box 2000, Charlottetown, PE C1A 7N8
902-368-5028, Fax: 902-368-5830, 866-368-5044

EROSION CONTROL

Science & Technology Branch, Tower 5, 1341 Baseline Rd., Ottawa, ON K1A 0C5
Fax: 613-773-1711

Prince Edward Island
Agriculture Policy & Regulatory, Jones Bldg., 11 Kent St., 5th Fl., Charlottetown, PE C1A 7N8

Québec
Commission de protection du territoire agricole du Québec, 200, ch Ste-Foy, 2e étage, Québec, QC G1R 4X6
418-643-3314, Fax: 418-643-2261, 800-667-5294, info@cptaq.gouv.qc.ca

Saskatchewan
Saskatchewan Agriculture, Walter Scott Bldg., 3085 Albert St., Regina, SK S4S 0B1
866-457-2377

EXPORT DEVELOPMENT

Business Development Bank of Canada, #400, 5, Place Ville-Marie, Montréal, QC H3B 5E7
877-232-2269

Canadian Trade Commissioner Service, c/o Foreign Affairs & International Trade, 125 Sussex Dr., Ottawa, ON K1A 0G2
613-944-9991, Fax: 613-996-9709, 888-306-9991, enqserv@international.gc.ca

Export Development Canada, 150 Slater St., Ottawa, ON K1A 1K3
613-598-2500, Fax: 613-598-3811, 800-267-8510

Innovation, Science & Economic Development Canada, C.D. Howe Building, 235 Queen St., Ottawa, ON K1A 0H5
613-954-5031, Fax: 613-954-2340, 800-328-6189, info@ic.gc.ca

Western Economic Diversification Canada, Canada Place, #1500, 9700 Jasper Ave. NW, Edmonton, AB T5J 4H7
780-495-4164, Fax: 780-495-4557, 888-338-9378

Ontario
Ontario Ministry of Economic Development & Growth, Hearst Block, 900 Bay St., 8th Fl., Toronto, ON M7A 2E1
416-325-6666, 800-268-7095

Ontario Ministry of International Trade, College Park, #1836, 777 Bay St., Toronto, ON M5G 2E5

Québec
Ministère de l'Économie, de la Science et de l'Innovation, 710, place D'Youville, 3e étage, Québec, QC G1R 4Y4
418-691-5950, Fax: 418-644-0118, 866-680-1884

Saskatchewan
Energy & Resources, 2101 Scarth St., Regina, SK S4P SH9
306-787-2528

EXPROPRIATION

Canada Lands Company Ltd., #1200, 1 University Ave., Toronto, ON M5J 2P1
416-952-6112

Department of National Defence & the Canadian Armed Forces, National Defence HQ, Major-General George R. Pearkes Bldg., 101 Colonel By Dr., Ottawa, ON K1A 0K2
613-995-2534, Fax: 613-992-4739, 888-995-2534, information@forces.gc.ca

Justice Canada, East Memorial Bldg., 284 Wellington St., Ottawa, ON K1A 0H8
613-957-4222, Fax: 613-954-0811, webadmin@justice.gc.ca

Alberta
Land Compensation Board, 1229 - 91 St. SW, Edmonton, AB T6X 1E9
780-427-2444, Fax: 780-427-5798, -310-000, srb.lcb@gov.ab.ca

Manitoba
Manitoba Land Value Appraisal Commission, #1144, 363 Broadway, Winnipeg, MB R3C 3N9
204-945-5455, Fax: 204-948-2235

Québec
Ministère des Transports, de la Mobilité durable et de l'Électrification des transports, 700, boul René-Lévesque est, 29e étage, Québec, QC G1R 5H1
418-643-6980, Fax: 418-643-2033, 888-355-0511, communications@mtq.gouv.qc.ca

Saskatchewan
Public & Private Rights Board, #23, 3085 Albert St., Regina, SK S4S 0B1
306-787-4071, Fax: 306-787-0088

FAMILY BENEFITS

See Also: Income Security; Social Services

British Columbia
British Columbia Ministry of Children & Family Development, PO Box 9770 Prov Govt, Victoria, BC V8W 9S5
250-387-7027, Fax: 250-356-3007, 877-387-7027, MCF.CorrespondenceManagement@gov.bc.ca

Manitoba
Manitoba Families, Legislative Building, #357, 450 Broadway, Winnipeg, MB R3C 0V8
204-945-3744, 866-626-4862

New Brunswick
New Brunswick Department of Social Development, Sartain MacDonald Bldg., 551 King St., PO Box 6000, Fredericton, NB E3B 5H1
506-453-2001, Fax: 506-453-2164, sd-ds@gnb.ca

Newfoundland & Labrador
Newfoundland & Labrador Department of Advanced Education & Skills, Confederation Building, West Block, 3rd Fl., PO Box 8700, St. John's, NL A1B 4J6
709-729-2480, aesweb@gov.nl.ca

Newfoundland & Labrador Department of Child, Youth & Family Services, PO Box 8700, St. John's, NL A1B 4J6
709-729-0760

Northwest Territories
Northwest Territories Department of Education, Culture & Employment, PO Box 1320, Yellowknife, NT X1A 2L9
ecepublicaffairs@gov.nt.ca

Nunavut
Nunavut Territory Department of Family Services, PO Box 1000 950, Iqaluit, NU X0A 0H0
867-975-6038, Fax: 867-975-6091

Prince Edward Island
Child & Family Services, Jones Bldg., 11 Kent St., 2nd Fl., PO Box 2000, Charlottetown, PE C1A 7N8
902-368-5294

Québec
Conseil de gestion de l'assurance parentale, #104, 1122, Grande Allée ouest, Québec, QC G1S 1E5
418-643-1009, Fax: 418-643-6738, 888-610-7727

Ministère de la Famille, 425, rue Saint-Amable, 1er étage, Québec, QC G1R 4Z1
877-216-6202

Ministère du Travail, de l'Emploi et de la Solidarité sociale, 200, ch Sainte-Foy, 5e étage, Québec, QC G1R 5S1
418-644-4545, Fax: 418-528-0559, 877-644-4545

FEDERAL-PROVINCIAL AFFAIRS

Canadian Intergovernmental Conference Secretariat, 222 Queen St., 10th Fl., PO Box 488 A,Ottawa, ON K1N 8V5
613-995-2341, Fax: 613-996-6091, info@scics.gc.ca

Office of Intergovernmental Affairs, c/o Privy Council Office, #1000, 85 Slater St., Ottawa, ON K1A 0A3
613-957-5153, Fax: 613-957-5043, info@pco-bcp.gc.ca

Alberta
Intergovernmental Relations, Commerce Place, 10155 - 102 St., 12th Fl., Edmonton, AB T5J 4G8

British Columbia
Intergovernmental Relations Secretariat, PO Box 9433 Prov Govt, Victoria, BC V8W 9V3
250-387-0752, Fax: 250-387-1920, igrs@gov.bc.ca

New Brunswick
Intergovernmental Affairs Division, Chancery Place, 675 King St., 5th Fl., Fredericton, NB E3B 1E9
506-444-4948, Fax: 506-453-2995, iga@gnb.ca

Newfoundland & Labrador
Newfoundland & Labrador Department of Municipal & Intergovernmental Affairs, West Block, Main Fl., Confederation Bldg., PO Box 8700, St. John's, NL A1B 4J6
709-729-3046, Fax: 709-729-0943, mainfo@gov.nl.ca

Northwest Territories
Northwest Territories Department of Aboriginal Affairs & Intergovernmental Relations, 4910 - 52nd St., PO Box 1320, Yellowknife, NT X1A 2L9
867-767-9025, Fax: 867-873-0233

Nova Scotia
Nova Scotia Department of Intergovernmental Affairs, Duke Tower, 5251 Duke St., 5th Fl., PO Box 1617, Halifax, NS B3J 2Y3
902-424-5153, Fax: 902-424-0728

Nunavut
Nunavut Territory Department of Executive & Intergovernmental Affairs, 1084 Aeroplex bldg., PO Box 1000 200, Iqaluit, NU X0A 0H0
867-975-6000, Fax: 867-975-6099

Ontario
Ontario Ministry of Intergovernmental Affairs, Ferguson Block, 77 Wellesley St. West, 12th Fl., Toronto, ON M7A 1N3
416-326-1234

Québec
Secrétariat aux affaires intergouvernementales canadiennes, 875, Grande Allée est, 3e étage, Québec, QC G1R 4Y8
418-643-4011, Fax: 418-528-0052

FILM PRODUCTION & COLLECTIONS

Canadian Broadcasting Corporation, 181 Queen St., PO Box 3220 C,Ottawa, ON K1Y 1E4
613-288-6000, liaison@cbc.ca

National Film Board of Canada, Operational Headquarters, Norman McLaren Building, 3155, ch de la Côte-de-Liesse, CP 1600 Centre-ville,Montréal, QC H3C 3H5
514-283-9000, 800-267-7710

Telefilm Canada, #500, 360, rue Saint-Jacques, Montréal, QC H2Y 1P5
514-283-6363, Fax: 514-283-8212, 800-567-0890, info@telefilm.gc.ca

Alberta
Alberta Film, Whitemud Crossing, #140, 4211 - 106 St., Edmonton, AB T6J 6L7
888-813-1738

British Columbia
Creative BC, 2225 West Broadway, Vancouver, BC V6K 2E4
604-736-7997, Fax: 604-736-7290

Manitoba
Manitoba Film & Music, #410, 93 Lombard Ave., Winnipeg, MB R3B 3B1
204-947-2040, Fax: 204-956-5261, info@mbfilmmusic.ca

Newfoundland & Labrador
Newfoundland & Labrador Film Development Corporation, 12 King's Bridge Rd., St. John's, NL A1C 3K3
709-738-3456, Fax: 709-739-1680, 877-738-3456, info@nlfdc.ca

Nova Scotia
Nova Scotia Business Inc., World Trade & Convention Centre, #701, 1800 Argyle St., PO Box 2374, Halifax, NS B3J 3N8
902-424-6650, Fax: 902-424-5739, 800-260-6682, info@nsbi.ca

Ontario
Ontario Media Development Corporation, South Tower, #501, 175 Bloor St. East, Toronto, ON M4W 3R8
416-314-6858, Fax: 416-314-6876, reception@omdc.on.ca

FINANCE

See Also: Banking & Financial Institutions

Finance Canada, 90 Elgin St., 14th Fl., Ottawa, ON K1A 0G5
613-369-3710, Fax: 613-369-4065, fin.financepublic-financepublique.fin@canada.ca

Alberta
Alberta Securities Commission, #600, 250 - 5th St. SW, Calgary, AB T2P 0R4
403-297-6454, Fax: 403-297-6156, 877-355-0585, inquiries@asc.ca

Alberta Treasury Board & Finance, Oxbridge Place, 9820 - 106 St., 9th Fl., Edmonton, AB T5K 1E7
780-427-3035, Fax: 780-427-1147, -310-0000

British Columbia
British Columbia Ministry of Finance, PO Box 9417 Prov Govt, Victoria, BC V8W 9V1
877-388-4440, CTBTaxQuestions@gov.bc.ca

British Columbia Securities Commission, Pacific Centre, 701 West Georgia St., 12th Fl., PO Box 10142, Vancouver, BC V7Y 1L2
604-899-6500, Fax: 604-899-6506, 800-373-6393, inquiries@bcsc.bc.ca

Manitoba
Manitoba Finance, #109, Legislative Bldg., Winnipeg, MB R3C 0V8
204-945-3754, minfin@leg.gov.mb.ca

Manitoba Securities Commission, #500, 400 St. Mary Ave., Winnipeg, MB R3C 4K5
204-945-2548, Fax: 204-945-0330, 800-655-5244, securities@gov.mb.ca

New Brunswick
Financial & Consumer Services Commission, #300, 85 Charlotte St., Saint John, NB E2L 2J2
506-658-3060, Fax: 506-658-3059, 866-933-2222, info@fcnb.ca

New Brunswick Department of Finance, Chancery Place, 675 King St., PO Box 6000, Fredericton, NB E3B 5H1
506-453-2451, Fax: 506-457-4989, wwwfin@gnb.ca

Newfoundland & Labrador
Newfoundland & Labrador Department of Finance, Confederation Bldg., PO Box 8700, St. John's, NL A1B 4J6
709-729-3166, Fax: 709-729-2232, finance@gov.nl.ca

Northwest Territories
Northwest Territories Department of Finance, PO Box 1320, Yellowknife, NT X1A 2L9
867-873-7500

Nova Scotia
Nova Scotia Department of Finance & Treasury Board, Provincial Bldg., 1723 Hollis St., 7th Fl., PO Box 187, Halifax, NS B3J 2N3
902-424-5554, Fax: 902-424-0635, FinanceWeb@novascotia.ca

Nova Scotia Securities Commission, Duke Tower, #400, 5251 Duke St., PO Box 458, Halifax, NS B3J 2P8
902-424-7768, Fax: 902-424-4625, 855-424-2499, NSSCinquiries@novascotia.ca

Nunavut
Nunavut Territory Department of Finance, Bldg. 1079, 1st Fl., PO Box 1000 430, Iqaluit, NU X0A 0H0
867-975-5800, Fax: 867-975-5805

Ontario
Ontario Ministry of Finance, Frost Bldg. South, 7 Queen's Park Cres., 7th Fl., Toronto, ON M7A 1Y7
Fax: 866-888-3850, 866-668-8297, financecommunications.fin@ontario.ca

Ontario Securities Commission, #1903, 20 Queen St. West, Toronto, ON M5H 3S8
416-593-8314, Fax: 416-593-8122, 877-785-1555, inquiries@osc.gov.on.ca

Prince Edward Island
Prince Edward Island Department of Finance, Shaw Bldg., 95 Rochford St. South, 2nd Fl., PO Box 2000, Charlottetown, PE C1A 7N8
902-368-4000, Fax: 902-368-5544

Prince Edward Island Department of Workforce & Advanced Learning, Shaw Bldg., 105 Rochford St., 5th Fl., PO Box 2000, Charlottetown, PE C1A 7N8
902-368-5956, Fax: 902-368-5277

Québec
Bureau de décision et de révision, #16.40, 500, boul René-Lévesque ouest, Montréal, QC H2Z 1W7
514-873-2211, Fax: 514-873-2162, 877-873-2211, secretariatBDR@bdr.gouv.qc.ca

Ministère des Finances, 12, rue Saint-Louis, Québec, QC G1R 5L3
418-528-9323, Fax: 418-646-1631, info@finances.gouv.qc.ca

Saskatchewan
Saskatchewan Economy, #300, 2103 - 11th Ave., Regina, SK S4P 3Z8
webmasterECON@gov.sk.ca

Saskatchewan Finance, 2350 Albert St., Regina, SK S4P 4A6
306-787-6768, Fax: 306-787-0241, communications@finance.gov.sk.ca

Yukon Territory
Yukon Finance, PO Box 2703, Whitehorse, YT Y1A 2C6
867-667-5343, Fax: 867-393-6217, fininfo@gov.yk.ca

FINANCING & LOANS

See Also: Investment

Business Development Bank of Canada, #400, 5, Place Ville-Marie, Montréal, QC H3B 5E7
877-232-2269

Canada Mortgage & Housing Corporation, 700 Montreal Rd., Ottawa, ON K1A 0P7
613-748-2000, Fax: 613-748-2098, 800-668-2642, chic@cmhc-schl.gc.ca

Farm Credit Canada, 1800 Hamilton St., Regina, SK S4P 2B8
306-780-8100, Fax: 306-780-8919, 888-332-3301, csc@fcc-fac.ca

PPP Canada, #630, 100 Queen St., Ottawa, ON K1P 1J9
613-947-9480, Fax: 613-947-2289, 877-947-9480, info@p3canada.ca

Alberta
Alberta Capital Finance Authority, Sun Life Place, #2160, 10123 - 99 St. NW, Edmonton, AB T5J 3H1
780-427-9711, Fax: 780-422-2175, webacfa@gov.ab.ca

Alberta Enterprise Corporation Board, Alberta Enterprise Corporation, #1100, 10830 Jasper Ave., Edmonton, AB T5J 2B3
780-392-3901, Fax: 780-392-3908, info@alberta-enterprise.ca

ATB Financial, #2100, 10020 - 100 St. NW, Edmonton, AB T5J 0N3
403-245-8110, 800-332-8383

British Columbia
Provincial Treasury, PO Box 9414 Prov Govt, Victoria, BC V8V 9V1
250-387-4541, Fax: 250-356-3041

Manitoba
Business Services Division, #250, 240 Graham Ave., Winnipeg, MB R3C 0J7
204-945-8200, EMBinfo@gov.mb.ca

Manitoba Agricultural Services Corporation, #100, 1525 First St. South, Brandon, MB R7A 7A1
204-726-6850, Fax: 204-726-6849, mailbox@masc.mb.ca

Newfoundland & Labrador
Newfoundland & Labrador Department of Finance, Confederation Bldg., PO Box 8700, St. John's, NL A1B 4J6
709-729-3166, Fax: 709-729-2232, finance@gov.nl.ca

Northwest Territories
Northwest Territories Department of Industry, Tourism & Investment, PO Box 1320, Yellowknife, NT X1A 2L9
867-767-9002

Nova Scotia
Nova Scotia Farm Loan Board, PO Box 890, Truro, NS B2N 5G6
902-893-6506, Fax: 902-895-7693, FLBNS@gov.ns.ca

Nunavut
Nunavut Business Credit Corporation, Parnaivak Bldg., #100, PO Box 2548, Iqaluit, NU X0A 0H0
867-975-7891, Fax: 867-975-7897, 800-758-0038, credit@nbcc.nu.ca

Ontario
Ontario Electricity Financial Corporation, #1400, 1 Dundas St. West, Toronto, ON M7A 1Y7
416-325-8000, Fax: 416-325-8005

Ontario Financing Authority, #1400, 1 Dundas St. West, Toronto, ON M7A 1Y7
416-325-8000, Fax: 416-204-3391, investor@ofina.on.ca

Ontario Ministry of Agriculture, Food & Rural Affairs, Ontario Government Bldg., 1 Stone Rd. West, Guelph, ON N1G 4Y2
519-826-3100, Fax: 519-826-4335, 888-466-2372, about.omafra@ontario.ca

Prince Edward Island
Prince Edward Island Lending Agency, Homburg Financial Tower, 98 Fitzroy St., 2nd Fl., Charlottetown, PE C1A 1R7
902-368-6200, Fax: 902-368-6201

Québec
Caisse de dépôt et placement du Québec, 1000, place Jean-Paul-Riopelle, Montréal, QC H2Z 2B3
514-842-3261, Fax: 514-842-4833, 866-330-3936

Financement-Québec, 12, rue Saint-Louis, 3e étage, Québec, QC G1R 5L3
418-691-2203, Fax: 418-644-6214, financement.regroupe@finances.gouv.qc.ca

La financière agricole de Québec, 1400, boul Guillaume-Couture, Lévis, QC G6W 8K7
418-838-5602, Fax: 418-833-3871, 800-749-3646, financiereagricole@fadq.qc.ca

Yukon Territory
Yukon Economic Development, #209, 212 Main St., F-1, Whitehorse, YT Y1A 2A9
867-393-7191, Fax: 867-393-6412, 800-661-0408, ecdev@gov.yk.ca

FIRE PREVENTION

Fire Safety Testing Facility, National Fire Laboratory, Bldg. U-96, Concession 8, Mississippi Mills, ON K0A 1A0
613-993-9101

Alberta
Alberta Emergency Management Agency, 2810 - 10303 Jasper Ave., Edmonton, AB T5J 3N6
780-422-9000, Fax: 780-644-1044, -310-0000, aema@gov.ab.ca

British Columbia
Office of the Fire Commissioner, PO Box 9201 Prov Govt, Victoria, BC V8W 9J1
250-952-4913, Fax: 250-952-4888, 888-988-9488, OFC@gov.bc.ca

Newfoundland & Labrador
Eastern Waste Management Commission, #3, 255 Majors Path, St. John's, NL A1A 0L5
709-579-7960, Fax: 709-579-5392, info@easternwaste.ca

Fire & Emergency Services - Newfoundland & Labrador, 25 Hallett Cres., PO Box 8700, St. John's, NL A1B 4J6
709-729-1608, Fax: 709-729-2524

Northwest Territories
Northwest Territories Department of Municipal & Community Affairs, PO Box 1320, Yellowknife, NT X1A 2L9
867-767-9160, Fax: 867-873-0309

Nova Scotia
Emergency Management Office, PO Box 2581, Halifax, NS B3J 3N5
902-424-5620, Fax: 902-424-5376, 866-424-5620, emo@gov.ns.ca

Nunavut
Nunavut Emergency Management, PO Box 1000 700, Iqaluit, NU X0A 0H0
867-975-5403, Fax: 867-979-4221, 800-693-1666

Ontario
Emergency Management Ontario, 77 Wellesley St. West, PO Box 222, Toronto, ON M7A 1N3
416-314-3723, Fax: 416-314-3758, 877-314-3723

Fire Marshal's Public Fire Safety Council, Place Nouveau Bldg., 5775 Yonge St., 7th Fl., Toronto, ON M2M 4J1
416-325-3152, Fax: 416-325-3162, info@firesafetycouncil.com

Fire Safety Commission, Place Nouveau Bldg., 5775 Yonge St., 7th Fl., Toronto, ON M2M 4J1
416-325-3100, Fax: 416-314-1217

Office of the Fire Marshal & Emergency Management, Place Nouveau, 5775 Yonge St., 7th Fl., Toronto, ON M2M 4J1
416-325-3100, Fax: 416-325-3119

Ontario Fire College, 1495 Muskoka Rd. North, Gravenhurst, ON P1P 1R8
705-687-2294, Fax: 705-687-7911, 800-565-0613

Safety, Licensing Appeals & Standards Tribunals Ontario, #5230, 20 Dundas St. West, Toronto, ON M5G 2C2
416-212-0334, Fax: 416-314-4270, 855-444-7454, slastoinfo@ontario.ca

Québec
Commissariat des incendies, 455, rue Dupont, Québec, QC G1K 6N2
418-529-5706, Fax: 418-529-9922

Saskatchewan
Emergency Management & Fire Safety, 1855 Victoria Ave., 5th Fl., Regina, SK S4P 3T2
306-787-3774, Fax: 306-787-7107, 866-757-5911

Yukon Territory
Fire & Life Safety/Fire Marshal's Office, 91790 Alaska Hwy., PO Box 2703 C-20, Whitehorse, YT Y1A 2C6
Fax: 867-667-3165, 800-661-0408, inquiry@gov.yk.ca

FISH & GAME REGULATIONS

Newfoundland & Labrador
Fish Processing Licensing Board, c/o Fish Processing Licensing Board Secretariat, 30 Strawberry Marsh Rd., St. John's, NL A1B 4J6
fplbsecretariat@gov.nl.ca

FISHERIES

Fisheries & Oceans Canada, 200 Kent St., Ottawa, ON K1A 0E6
613-993-0999, Fax: 613-990-1866, info@dfo-mpo.gc.ca

Freshwater Fish Marketing Corporation, 1199 Plessis Rd., Winnipeg, MB R2C 3L4
204-983-6601, Fax: 204-983-6497, sandic@freshwaterfish.com

Gulf Fisheries Centre, 343, av Université, 5th Fl., CP 5030, Moncton, NB E1C 9B6
506-851-6227, Fax: 506-851-2435, info@dfo-mpo.gc.ca

British Columbia
British Columbia Ministry of Agriculture, PO Box 9043 Prov Govt, Victoria, BC V8W 9E2
888-221-7141, agriservicebc@gov.bc.ca

New Brunswick
Fisheries Resource Management, Hédard Robichaud Bldg., 22 St-Pierre Blvd. East, Caraquet, NB E1W 1B6
506-726-2400, Fax: 506-726-2419

New Brunswick Department of Agriculture, Aquaculture & Fisheries, Agricultural Research Station (Experimental Farm), PO Box 6000, Fredericton, NB E3B 5H1
506-453-2666, Fax: 506-453-7170, 888-622-4742, DAAF-MAAP@gnb.ca

Newfoundland & Labrador
Newfoundland & Labrador Department of Fisheries & Aquaculture, Petten Bldg., 30 Strawberry Marsh Rd., PO Box 8700, St. John's, NL A1B 4J6
709-729-3723, Fax: 709-729-6082, fisheries@gov.nl.ca

Northwest Territories
Northwest Territories Department of Environment & Natural Resources, #600, 5102 - 50 Ave., Yellowknife, NT X1A 3S8
867-767-9231

Nova Scotia
Fisheries & Aquaculture Loan Board, MacRae Library, PO Box 890, Truro, NS B2N 2P2
902-896-4800, Fax: 902-896-4812

Nova Scotia Department of Fisheries & Aquaculture, 1800 Argyle St., 6th fl., Halifax, NS B3J 2R5
902-424-4560, Fax: 902-424-4671, aquaculture@novascotia.ca

Ontario
Ontario Fish & Wildlife Heritage Commission, Robinson Pl., 300 Water St., PO Box 7000, Peterborough, ON K9J 8M5
705-755-1905, Fax: 705-755-1900

Prince Edward Island
Prince Edward Island Department of Agriculture & Fisheries, Jones Bldg., 11 Kent St., 5th Fl., PO Box 2000, Charlottetown, PE C1A 7N8
902-368-4880, Fax: 902-368-4857

FISHERIES & WILDLIFE

Beverly & Qamanirjuaq Caribou Management Board, Secretariat, PO Box 629, Stonewall, MB R0C 2Z0
204-467-2438, caribounews@arctic-caribou.com
Committee on the Status of Endangered Wildlife in Canada, c/o Canadian Wildlife Service, 351 St. Joseph Blvd, 4th Fl., Gatineau, QC K1A 0H3
819-953-3215, Fax: 819-994-3684, cosewic/cosepac@ec.gc.ca
Fisheries & Oceans Canada, 200 Kent St., Ottawa, ON K1A 0E6
613-993-0999, Fax: 613-990-1866, info@dfo-mpo.gc.ca
Natural Resources Canada, 580 Booth St., Ottawa, ON K1A 0E4
343-292-6096, Fax: 613-992-7211
North American Bird Conservation Initiative, Canadian Wildlife Service, 351, boul St-Joseph, 3e étage, Gatineau, QC K1A 0H3
819-994-0512, Fax: 819-994-4445, nabci@ec.gc.ca
North American Waterfowl Management Plan, NAWCC (Canada) Secretariat, Place Vincent Massey, 351 St. Joseph Blvd., 7th Fl., Gatineau, QC K1A 0H3
819-934-6034, Fax: 819-934-6017, nawmp@ec.gc.ca
Porcupine Caribou Management Board, PO Box 31723, Whitehorse, YT Y1A 6L3
867-633-4780, Fax: 867-393-3904, pcmb@taiga.net

Alberta
Alberta Environment & Parks, Information Centre, Great West Life Bldg., 9920 - 108 St., Main Fl., Edmonton, AB T5K 2M4
780-427-2700, Fax: 780-427-4407, -310-3773, ESRD.Info-Centre@gov.ab.ca

British Columbia
British Columbia Ministry of Environment, PO Box 9339 Prov Govt, Victoria, BC V8W 9M1
250-387-9870, Fax: 250-387-6003, env.mail@gov.bc.ca

Manitoba
Endangered Species Advisory Committee, 200 Saulteaux Cres., PO Box 24, Winnipeg, MB R3J 3W3
204-945-7775, Fax: 204-945-3077
Manitoba Habitat Heritage Corporation, #200, 1555 St. James St., Winnipeg, MB R3H 1B5
204-784-4350, Fax: 204-784-7359

New Brunswick
New Brunswick Department of Agriculture, Aquaculture & Fisheries, Agricultural Research Station (Experimental Farm), PO Box 6000, Fredericton, NB E3B 5H1
506-453-2666, Fax: 506-453-7170, 888-622-4742, DAAF-MAAP@gnb.ca

Newfoundland & Labrador
Newfoundland & Labrador Department of Fisheries & Aquaculture, Petten Bldg., 30 Strawberry Marsh Rd., PO Box 8700, St. John's, NL A1B 4J6
709-729-3723, Fax: 709-729-6082, fisheries@gov.nl.ca

Northwest Territories
Northwest Territories Department of Environment & Natural Resources, #600, 5102 - 50 Ave., Yellowknife, NT X1A 3S8
867-767-9231

Nova Scotia
Nova Scotia Department of Natural Resources, Founder's Square, 1701 Hollis St., 3rd Fl., PO Box 698, Halifax, NS B3J 2T9
902-424-5935, Fax: 902-424-7735, 800-565-2224

Ontario
Ontario Ministry of Natural Resources & Forestry, 300 Water St., PO Box 7000, Peterborough, ON K9J 8M5
800-667-1940

Prince Edward Island
Prince Edward Island Department of Justice & Public Safety, Shaw Bldg. South, 95 Rochford St., 4th Fl., PO Box 2000, Charlottetown, PE C1A 7N8
902-368-6410, Fax: 902-368-6488

Québec
Ministère de l'Agriculture, des Pêcheries et de l'Alimentation, 200, ch Sainte-Foy, Québec, QC G1R 4X6
418-380-2110, 888-222-6272
Ministère des Forêts, de la Faune et des Parcs, Service à la clientèle, #A409, 5700, 4e av ouest, Québec, QC G1H 6R1
Fax: 418-644-6513, 844-523-6738, services.clientele@mrnf.gouv.qc.ca

Yukon Territory
Yukon Environment, 10 Burns Rd., PO Box 2703 V-3A, Whitehorse, YT Y1A 2C6
867-667-5652, Fax: 867-393-7197, environment.yukon@gov.yk.ca
Yukon Fish & Wildlife Management Board, 106 Main St., 2nd Fl., PO Box 31104, Whitehorse, YT Y1A 5P7
867-667-3754, Fax: 867-393-6947, officemanager@yfwmb.ca

FOREST RESOURCES

Natural Resources Canada, 580 Booth St., Ottawa, ON K1A 0E4
343-292-6096, Fax: 613-992-7211

Alberta
Alberta Agriculture & Forestry, JG O'Donoghue Bldg., #100A, 7000 - 113th St., Edmonton, AB T6H 5T6
780-427-2727, -310-3276, duke@gov.ab.ca
Alberta Innovates - Bio Solutions, Phipps McKinnon Bldg., 10020 - 101A Ave., 18th Fl., Edmonton, AB T5J 3G2
780-427-1956, Fax: 780-427-3252, 877-828-0444, bio@albertainnovates.ca
Forestry Division, Petroleum Plaza ST, 9915 - 108 St. 10th Fl., Edmonton, AB T5K 2G8

British Columbia
British Columbia Ministry of Forests, Lands & Natural Resource Operations, PO Box 9049 Prov Govt, Victoria, BC V8W 9E2
800-663-7867, FLNRO.MediaRequests@gov.bc.ca
Forestry Innovation Investment Ltd., #1200, 1130 West Pender St., Vancouver, BC V6E 4A4
604-685-7507, Fax: 604-685-5373, info@bcfii.ca

New Brunswick
New Brunswick Forest Products Commission, Hugh John Flemming Forestry Centre, PO Box 6000, Fredericton, NB E3B 5H1
506-453-2196, Fax: 506-457-4966, dnr_mrnweb@gnb.ca

Nova Scotia
Nova Scotia Primary Forest Products Marketing Board, #202, 1256 Barrington St., Halifax, NS B3J 1Y6
902-424-7598, Fax: 902-424-6965, nspfpmb@gov.ns.ca

Nunavut
Nunavut Territory Department of Environment, PO Box 1000 1300, Iqaluit, NU X0A 0H0
867-975-7700, Fax: 867-975-7742, environment@gov.nu.ca

Ontario
Algonquin Forestry Authority - Huntsville, 222 Main St. West, Huntsville, ON P1H 1Y1
705-789-9647, Fax: 705-789-3353, info@algonquinforestry.on.ca
Algonquin Forestry Authority - Pembroke, Victoria Centre, 84 Isabella St., 2nd Fl., Pembroke, ON K8A 5S5
613-735-0173, Fax: 613-735-4192, info@algonquinforestry.on.ca
Policy Division, Whitney Block, #6540, 99 Wellesley St. West, Toronto, ON M7A 1W3
Fax: 416-314-1994, 800-667-1940

Québec
Ministère des Forêts, de la Faune et des Parcs, Service à la clientèle, #A409, 5700, 4e av ouest, Québec, QC G1H 6R1
Fax: 418-644-6513, 844-523-6738, services.clientele@mrnf.gouv.qc.ca

Yukon Territory
Yukon Energy, Mines & Resources, PO Box 2703, Whitehorse, YT Y1A 2C6
867-667-3130, Fax: 867-456-3965, 800-661-0408, emr@gov.yk.ca
Yukon Environment, 10 Burns Rd., PO Box 2703 V-3A, Whitehorse, YT Y1A 2C6
867-667-5652, Fax: 867-393-7197, environment.yukon@gov.yk.ca

FORESTRY & PAPER

Natural Resources Canada, 580 Booth St., Ottawa, ON K1A 0E4
343-292-6096, Fax: 613-992-7211

Alberta
Alberta Innovates - Bio Solutions, Phipps McKinnon Bldg., 10020 - 101A Ave., 18th Fl., Edmonton, AB T5J 3G2
780-427-1956, Fax: 780-427-3252, 877-828-0444, bio@albertainnovates.ca
Forestry Division, Petroleum Plaza ST, 9915 - 108 St. 10th Fl., Edmonton, AB T5K 2G8

British Columbia
British Columbia Ministry of Forests, Lands & Natural Resource Operations, PO Box 9049 Prov Govt, Victoria, BC V8W 9E2
800-663-7867, FLNRO.MediaRequests@gov.bc.ca
Forest Practices Board, PO Box 9905 Prov Govt, Victoria, BC V8W 9R1
250-213-4700, Fax: 250-213-4725, 800-994-5899, fpboard@gov.bc.ca
Timber Export Advisory Committee, PO Box 9514 Prov Govt, Victoria, BC V8W 9C2
250-387-8916, Fax: 250-387-5050

Newfoundland & Labrador
Newfoundland & Labrador Department of Natural Resources, Natural Resources Bldg., 50 Elizabeth Ave., 7th Fl., PO Box 8700, St. John's, NL A1B 4J6
709-729-2920, Fax: 709-729-0059

Nova Scotia
Nova Scotia Department of Natural Resources, Founder's Square, 1701 Hollis St., 3rd Fl., PO Box 698, Halifax, NS B3J 2T9
902-424-5935, Fax: 902-424-7735, 800-565-2224

Ontario
Algonquin Forestry Authority - Huntsville, 222 Main St. West, Huntsville, ON P1H 1Y1
705-789-9647, Fax: 705-789-3353, info@algonquinforestry.on.ca
Algonquin Forestry Authority - Pembroke, Victoria Centre, 84 Isabella St., 2nd Fl., Pembroke, ON K8A 5S5
613-735-0173, Fax: 613-735-4192, info@algonquinforestry.on.ca
Ontario Ministry of Natural Resources & Forestry, 300 Water St., PO Box 7000, Peterborough, ON K9J 8M5
800-667-1940

Québec
Ministère du Développement durable, de l'Environnement et de la Lutte contre les changements climatiques, Édifice Marie-Guyart, 675, boul René-Lévesque est, 29e étage, Québec, QC G1R 5V7
418-521-3830, Fax: 418-646-5974, 800-561-1616, info@mddefp.gouv.qc.ca

Saskatchewan
Saskatchewan Environment, 3211 Albert St., 2nd Fl., Regina, SK S4S 5W6
306-787-2584, Fax: 306-787-9544, 800-567-4224, Centre.Inquiry@gov.sk.ca

Yukon Territory
Yukon Environment, 10 Burns Rd., PO Box 2703 V-3A, Whitehorse, YT Y1A 2C6
867-667-5652, Fax: 867-393-7197, environment.yukon@gov.yk.ca

GAS

See: Oil & Natural Gas Resources
Gas Turbine Research Facility, c/o National Research Council, 1200 Montreal Rd., Ottawa, ON K1A 0R6
613-993-9101

GEOLOGICAL SERVICES

Earth Sciences Sector, 588 Booth St., Ottawa, ON K1A 0Y7
Geological Survey of Canada, 601 Booth St., Ottawa, ON K1A 0E8
Surveyor General Branch - Geomatics Canada, #605, 9700 Jasper Ave., Edmonton, AB T5J 4C3
780-495-2519, Fax: 780-495-4052

Alberta
Alberta Energy Regulator, #1000, 250 - 5 St. SW, Calgary, AB T2P 0R4
403-297-8311, Fax: 403-297-7336, 855-297-8311, inquiries@aer.ca

British Columbia
British Columbia Ministry of Energy & Mines (& Responsible for Core Review), PO Box 9060 Prov Govt, Victoria, BC V8W 9E3

Northwest Territories
Northwest Territories Geological Survey, 4601B - 52 Ave., PO Box 1320, Yellowknife, NT X1A 2L9
867-767-9211, Fax: 867-873-2652, ntgs@gov.nt.ca

Nova Scotia
Geomatics Centre, 160 Willow St., Amherst, NS B4H 3W5
902-667-7231, Fax: 902-667-6008, geoinfo@novascotia.ca

Ontario
Ontario Geological Survey, Willet Green Miller Centre, 933 Ramsey Lake Rd., Level B6, Sudbury, ON P3E 6B5
705-670-5758, Fax: 705-670-5818, 888-415-9845

Yukon Territory
Yukon Geological Survey, Elijah Smith Building, #102 & 230, 300 Main St., Whitehorse, YT Y1A 2B5
867-455-2800, geology@gov.yk.ca

GOVERNMENT

Auditor General of Canada, 240 Sparks St., Ottawa, ON K1A 0G6
613-952-0213, Fax: 613-957-0474, 888-761-5953, infomedia@oag-bvg.gc.ca
Bank of Canada, 234 Laurier Ave. West, Ottawa, ON K1A 0G9
613-782-8111, Fax: 613-782-7713, 800-303-1282, info@bankofcanada.ca
Business Development Bank of Canada, #400, 5, Place Ville-Marie, Montréal, QC H3B 5E7
877-232-2269
Canada Economic Development for Québec Regions, Édifice Dominion Square, #900, 1255, rue Peel, Montréal, QC H3B 2T9
514-283-6412, Fax: 514-283-3302, 866-385-6412

Canada Lands Company Ltd., #1200, 1 University Ave., Toronto, ON M5J 2P1
416-952-6112
Canada Revenue Agency, 875 Heron Rd., Ottawa, ON K1A 1A2
800-267-6999
Canadian Intergovernmental Conference Secretariat, 222 Queen St., 10th Fl., PO Box 488 A,Ottawa, ON K1N 8V5
613-995-2341, Fax: 613-996-6091, info@scics.gc.ca
Canadian Nuclear Safety Commission, 280 Slater St., PO Box 1046 B,Ottawa, ON K1P 5S9
613-995-5894, Fax: 613-995-5086, 800-668-5284, cnsc.information.ccsn@canada.ca
Committees of the House of Commons, Committees Directorate, House of Commons, 131 Queen St., 6th Fl., Ottawa, ON K1A 0A6
613-992-3150, Fax: 613-947-3089, cmteweb@parl.gc.ca
Defence Construction Canada, Constitution Square, 350 Albert St., 19th Fl., Ottawa, ON K1A 0K3
613-998-9548, Fax: 613-998-1061, 800-514-3555, info@dcc-cdc.gc.ca
Department of National Defence & the Canadian Armed Forces, National Defence HQ, Major-General George R. Pearkes Bldg., 101 Colonel By Dr., Ottawa, ON K1A 0K2
613-995-2534, Fax: 613-992-4739, 888-995-2534, information@forces.gc.ca
Elections Canada, 30 Victoria St., Gatineau, ON K1A 0M6
613-993-2975, Fax: 613-954-8584, 800-463-6868
Finance Canada, 90 Elgin St., 14th Fl., Ottawa, ON K1A 0G5
613-369-3710, Fax: 613-369-4065, fin.financepublic-financepublique.fin@canada.ca
First Nations Tax Commission, #321, 345 Chief Alex Thomas Way, Kamloops, BC V2H 1H1
250-828-9857, Fax: 250-828-9858, 855-682-3682, mailkamloops@fntc.ca
Forty-second Parliament - Canada, House of Commons, Parliament Buildings, Ottawa, AB K1A 0A6
Global Affairs Canada, Enquiries Service, 125 Sussex Dr., Ottawa, ON K1A 0G2
613-944-4000, Fax: 613-996-9709, 800-267-8376
Government of Canada, c/o Canada Enquiry Centre, Service Canada, Ottawa, ON K1A 0J9
800-622-6232
Governor General & Commander-in-Chief of Canada, Rideau Hall, 1 Sussex Dr., Ottawa, ON K1A 0A1
613-993-8200, Fax: 613-998-8760, 800-465-6890
House of Commons, Canada, House of Commons, Centre Block, Parliament Buildings, 111 Wellington St., Ottawa, ON K1A 0A6
613-992-4793, 866-599-4999, info@parl.gc.ca
Indigenous & Northern Affairs, Terrasses de la Chaudière, 10 Wellington St., North Tower, Gatineau, QC K1A 0H4
Fax: 866-817-3977, 800-567-9604, infopubs@aadnc-aandc.gc.ca
Innovation, Science & Economic Development Canada, C.D. Howe Building, 235 Queen St., Ottawa, ON K1A 0H5
613-954-5031, Fax: 613-954-2340, 800-328-6189, info@ic.gc.ca
International Development Research Centre, 150 Kent St., PO Box 8500, Ottawa, ON K1G 3H9
613-236-6163, Fax: 613-238-7230, info@idrc.ca
Justice Canada, East Memorial Bldg., 284 Wellington St., Ottawa, ON K1A 0H8
613-957-4222, Fax: 613-954-0811, webadmin@justice.gc.ca
North American Free Trade Agreement (NAFTA) Secretariat, Canadian Section, 111 Sussex Dr., 5th Fl., Ottawa, ON K1N 1J1
343-203-4274, Fax: 613-992-9392, webmaster@nafta-alena.gc.ca
Nunavut Impact Review Board, 29 Mitik St., PO Box 1360, Cambridge Bay, NU X0B 0C0
867-983-4600, Fax: 867-983-2594, 866-233-3033, info@nirb.ca
Nunavut Planning Commission, PO Box 2101, Cambridge Bay, NU X0B 0C0
867-983-4625, Fax: 867-983-4626
Office of Intergovernmental Affairs, c/o Privy Council Office, #1000, 85 Slater St., Ottawa, ON K1A 0A3
613-957-5153, Fax: 613-957-5043, info@pco-bcp.gc.ca
Office of the Commissioner of Official Languages, 30 Victoria St., 6th Fl., Gatineau, ON K1A 0T8
819-420-4877, Fax: 819-420-4873, 877-996-6368
Office of the Conflict of Interest & Ethics Commissioner, Commissioner's Office, 66 Slater St., 22nd Fl., PO Box 16, Ottawa, ON K1A 0A6
613-995-0721, Fax: 613-995-7308, ciec-ccie@parl.gc.ca
Office of the Leader, Bloc Québécois, Centre Block, 111 Wellington St., Ottawa, ON K1A 0A6
Office of the Leader, Green Party of Canada, Confederation Building, 244 Wellington St., Ottawa, ON K1A 0A6
613-996-1119, Fax: 613-996-0850, 866-868-3447, leader@greenparty.ca
Office of the Leader, Official Opposition, Conservative Party of Canada / Conservative Party Research Bureau, Centre Block, 111 Wellington St., Ottawa, ON K1A 0A6
613-995-1333, Fax: 613-995-1337
Office of the Ombudsman, PO Box 90026, Ottawa, ON K1V 1J8
Fax: 800-204-4193, 800-204-4198
Office of the Prime Minister, Liberal Party of Canada / Liberal Research Bureau, Langevin Block, 80 Wellington St., Ottawa, ON K1A 0A2
613-992-4211, Fax: 613-941-6900
Office of the Senate Ethics Officer, Thomas D'Arcy McGee Bldg., #526, 90 Sparks St., Ottawa, ON K1P 5B4
613-947-3566, Fax: 613-947-3577, 800-267-7362, cse-seo@sen.parl.gc.ca
Office of the Taxpayers' Ombudsman, #600, 150 Slater St., Ottawa, ON K1A 1K3
613-946-2310, Fax: 613-941-6319, 866-586-3839
Policy Horizons Canada, 360 Albert St., 15th Fl., Ottawa, ON K1R 7X7
613-947-3800, Fax: 613-995-6006, questions@horizons.gc.ca
Privy Council Office, #1000, 85 Sparks St., Ottawa, ON K1A 0A3
613-957-5153, Fax: 613-997-5043, info@pco-bcp.gc.ca
Public Service Commission, 22 Eddy St., Gatineau, QC K1A 0M7
613-992-9562, Fax: 613-992-9352, CFP.INFOCOM.PSC@cfp-psc.gc.ca
Public Service Staffing Tribunal, 240 Sparks St., 6th Fl., Ottawa, ON K1A 0A5
613-949-6516, Fax: 613-949-6551, 866-637-4491, info@psst-tdfp.gc.ca
Public Services & Procurement, Place du Portage, Phase III, 11, rue Laurier, Ottawa, ON K1A 0S5
questions@tpsgc-pwgsc.gc.ca
Royal Canadian Mint, 320 Sussex Dr., Ottawa, ON K1A 0G8
613-954-2626, Fax: 613-998-4130, 800-267-1871
Senate of Canada, Ottawa, QC K1A 0A4
sencom@sen.parl.gc.ca
Statistics Canada, R.H. Coats Bldg., Tunney's Pasture, 150 Tunney's Pasture Driveway, Ottawa, ON K1A 0T6
514-283-8300, Fax: 514-283-9350, 800-263-1136, STATCAN.infostats-infostats.STATCAN@canada.ca
The Canadian Ministry, Information Service, Parliament of Canada, Ottawa, ON K1A 0A9
613-992-4793, 866-599-4999, info@parl.gc.ca
Treasury Board of Canada Secretariat, East Tower, 140 O'Connor St., 9th Fl., Ottawa, ON K1A 0R5
613-957-2400, Fax: 613-941-4000, 877-636-0656

Alberta

Alberta Apprenticeship & Industry Training Board, Commerce Place, 10155 - 102 St., 10th Fl., Edmonton, AB T5J 4L5
780-427-8765, Fax: 780-422-7376, -310-0000
Alberta Infrastructure, Infrastructure Building, 6950 - 113 St., Edmonton, AB T6H 5V7
780-415-0507, Fax: 780-427-2187, -310-0000, Infra.Contact.Us.m@gov.ab.ca
Alberta Municipal Affairs, Communications Branch, Commerce Place, 10155 - 102 St., 18th Fl., Edmonton, AB T5J 4L4
780-427-2732, Fax: 780-422-1419, -310-0000
Alberta Office of the Auditor General, 9925 - 109 St., 8th Fl., Edmonton, AB T5K 2J8
780-427-4222, Fax: 780-422-9555, info@oag.ab.ca
Alberta Office of the Chief Electoral Officer / Elections Alberta, #100, 11510 Kingsway Ave., Edmonton, AB T5G 2Y5
780-427-7191, Fax: 780-422-2900, info@elections.ab.ca
Alberta Office of the Ethics Commissioner, #1250, 9925 - 109 St. NW, Edmonton, AB T5K 2J8
780-422-2273, Fax: 780-422-2261, generalinfo@ethicscommissioner.ab.ca
Alberta Office of the Ombudsman, Canadian Western Bank Building, #2800, 10303 Jasper Ave. NW, Edmonton, AB T5J 5C3
780-427-2756, Fax: 780-427-2759, 888-455-2756, info@ombudsman.ab.ca
Alberta Pensions Services Corporation, 5103 Windermere Blvd. SW, Edmonton, AB T6W 0S9
780-427-2782, 800-661-8198, memberservices@apsc.ca
Alberta Review Board, Oxford Tower, #1120, 10235 - 101 St., Edmonton, AB T5J 3E9
780-422-5994, Fax: 780-427-1762
Alberta Treasury Board & Finance, Oxbridge Place, 9820 - 106 St., 9th Fl., Edmonton, AB T5K 1E7
780-427-3035, Fax: 780-427-1147, -310-0000
Corporate Human Resources, Peace Hills Trust Tower, 10011 - 109 St., 7th Fl., Edmonton, AB T5J 3S8
780-408-8400
Executive Council, Legislature Building, 10800 - 97 Ave., Edmonton, AB T5K 2B6
780-427-2711, -310-0000
Government of Alberta, PO Box 1333, Edmonton, AB T5J 2N2
780-427-2711, Fax: 780-422-2852, -310-0000
Intergovernmental Relations, Commerce Place, 10155 - 102 St., 12th Fl., Edmonton, AB T5J 4G8
Legislative Assembly of Alberta, Legislature Annex, 9718 - 107 St., Edmonton, AB T5K 1E4
780-427-2826, Fax: 780-427-1623, laocommunications@assembly.ab.ca
Office of the Lieutenant Governor, Office of the Lieutenant Governor of AB, Legislature Bldg., 10800 - 97 Ave., 3rd Fl., Edmonton, AB T5K 2B6
780-427-7243, Fax: 780-422-5134, ltgov@gov.ab.ca
Office of the Premier, Office of the Premier, Legislature Building, #307, 10800 - 97 Ave., Edmonton, AB T5K 2B6
780-427-2251, Fax: 780-427-1349, -310-0000
Public Affairs Bureau, Federal Bldg., 9820 - 107 St., 7th Fl., Edmonton, AB T5K 1E7
Special Areas Board, Special Areas Board Administration, 212 - 2nd Ave. West, PO Box 820, Hanna, AB T0J 1P0
403-854-5600, Fax: 403-854-5527
Twenty-ninth Legislature - Alberta, Legislature Bldg., 10800 - 97 Ave., Edmonton, AB T5K 2B6
780-427-2826, laocommunications@assembly.ab.ca

British Columbia

Agricultural Land Commission, #133, 4940 Canada Way, Burnaby, BC V5G 4K6
604-660-7000, Fax: 604-660-7033, ALCBurnaby@Victoria1.gov.bc.ca
BC Legislative Assembly & Independent Offices, Clerk's Office, Parliament Bldgs., Victoria, BC V8V 1X4
250-387-3785, Fax: 250-387-0942, ClerkHouse@leg.bc.ca
British Columbia Assessment Authority, #400, 3450 Uptown Blvd., Victoria, BC V8Z 0B9
604-739-8588, Fax: 855-995-6209, 866-825-8322
British Columbia Pavilion Corporation, #200, 999 Canada Place, Vancouver, BC V6C 3C1
604-482-2200, Fax: 604-681-9017, info@bcpavco.com
British Columbia Public Service Agency, PO Box 9404 Prov Govt, Victoria, BC V8W 9V1
250-387-0518, Fax: 250-356-7074
British Columbia Treaty Commission, #700, 1111 Melville St., Vancouver, BC V6E 3V6
604-482-9200, Fax: 604-482-9222, 855-482-9200, info@bctreaty.net
British Columbia Utilities Commission, 900 Howe St., 6th Fl., PO Box 250, Vancouver, BC V6Z 2N3
604-660-4700, Fax: 604-660-1102, 800-663-1385, commission.secretary@bcuc.com
Court Services Branch, PO Box 9249 Prov Govt, Victoria, BC V8W 9J2
250-356-1550, Fax: 250-356-8152
Crown Agencies Resource Office, #344, 617 Government St., PO Box 9416 Prov Govt, Victoria, BC V8W 9V1
250-387-8499, Fax: 250-356-2001, caro@gov.bc.ca
Elections British Columbia, PO Box 9275 Prov Govt, Victoria, BC V8W 9J6
250-387-5305, Fax: 250-387-3578, 800-661-8683, electionsbc@elections.bc.ca
Executive Council of the Government of British Columbia, Cabinet Operations, 617 Government St., 1st Fl., PO Box 9487 Prov Govt, Victoria, BC V8W 9W6
Fourtieth Legislature - British Columbia, Parliament Buildings, Victoria, BC V8V 1X4
250-387-3785, Fax: 250-387-0942, ClerkHouse@leg.bc.ca
Government of British Columbia, Parliament Bldgs., Victoria, BC V8V 1X4
250-387-6121, 800-663-7867
Office of the Auditor General, PO Box 9036 Prov Govt, Victoria, BC V8W 9A2
250-419-6100, Fax: 250-387-1230
Office of the Auditor General for Local Government, #201, 10470 - 152nd St., Surrey, BC V3R 0Y3
604-930-7100
Office of the Conflict of Interest Commissioner, 421 Menzies St., 1st Fl., Victoria, BC V8V 1X4
250-356-0750, Fax: 250-356-6580, conflictofinterest@coibc.ca
Office of the Lieutenant Governor, Government House, 1401 Rockland Ave., Victoria, BC V8S 1V9
250-387-2080, Fax: 250-387-2078, ghinfo@gov.bc.ca
Office of the Ombudsperson, 947 Fort St., 2nd Fl., PO Box 9039 Prov Govt, Victoria, BC V8W 9A5
250-387-5855, Fax: 250-387-0198, 800-567-3247
Office of the Premier & Cabinet Office, West Annex, Parliament Bldgs., PO Box 9041 Prov Govt, Victoria, BC V8W 9E1
250-387-1715, Fax: 250-387-0087, premier@gov.bc.ca

Manitoba

Aboriginal Affairs Secretariat, #200, 500 Portage Ave., Winnipeg, MB R3C 3X1
204-945-2510, Fax: 204-945-3689
Board of Electrical Examiners, #500, 401 York Ave, Winnipeg, MB R3C 0P8
204-945-3373, Fax: 204-948-2309

Civil Service Commission Board, #935, 155 Carlton St., Winnipeg, MB R3C 3H8
204-945-1435, Fax: 204-945-1486
Crown Corporations Council, #1130, 444 St. Mary Ave., Winnipeg, MB R3C 3T1
204-949-5270, Fax: 204-949-5283, info@crowncc.mb.ca
Elections Manitoba, #120, 200 Vaughan St., Winnipeg, MB R3C 1T5
204-945-3225, Fax: 204-945-6011, 866-628-6837, election@elections.mb.ca
Executive Council, Legislative Building, 450 Broadway Ave., Winnipeg, MB R3C 0V8
Fiscal Research Division, #910, 386 Broadway, Winnipeg, MB R3C 3R6
204-945-3757, Fax: 204-945-5051
Forty-first Legislature - Manitoba, Legislative Building, 450 Broadway Ave., Winnipeg, MB R3C 0V8
204-945-3636, Fax: 204-948-2507, clerkla@leg.gov.mb.ca
Government of Manitoba, Legislative Building, Rm. 237, Winnipeg, MB R3C 0V8
204-945-3636, Fax: 204-948-2507, clerkla@leg.gov.mb.ca
Local Government Development Division, 59 Elizabeth Dr., PO Box 33, Thompson, MB R8N 1X4
204-677-6794, Fax: 204-677-6525
Manitoba Civil Service Commission, #935, 155 Carlton St., Winnipeg, MB R3C 3H8
204-945-2332, Fax: 204-945-1486, 800-282-8069, csc@gov.mb.ca
Manitoba Land Value Appraisal Commission, #1144, 363 Broadway, Winnipeg, MB R3C 3N9
204-945-5455, Fax: 204-948-2235
Manitoba Legislative Assembly, c/o Clerk's Office, Legislative Bldg., #237, 450 Broadway, Winnipeg, MB R3C 0V8
204-945-3636, Fax: 204-948-2507, clerkla@leg.gov.mb.ca
Manitoba Municipal Board, #1144, 363 Broadway, Winnipeg, MB R3C 3N9
204-945-2941, Fax: 204-948-2235
Manitoba Municipal Government, #301, 450 Broadway Ave., Winnipeg, MB R3C 0V8
204-945-3744, 866-626-4862, mgi@gov.mb.ca
Manitoba Office of the Ombudsman, Colony Square, #750, 500 Portage Ave., Winnipeg, MB R3C 3X1
204-982-9130, Fax: 204-942-7803, 800-665-0531, ombudsman@ombudsman.mb.ca
Office of the Auditor General, #500, 330 Portage Ave., Winnipeg, MB R3C 0C4
204-945-3790, Fax: 204-945-2169, oag.contact@oag.mb.ca
Office of the Lieutenant Governor, Legislative Building, #235, 450 Broadway Ave., Winnipeg, MB R3C 0V8
204-945-2753, Fax: 204-945-4329, ltgov@leg.gov.mb.ca
Office of the Premier, Legislative Building, #204, 450 Broadway Ave., Winnipeg, MB R3C 0V8
204-945-3714, Fax: 204-949-1484, premier@leg.gov.mb.ca
Treasury Board Secretariat, #200, 386 Broadway, Winnipeg, MB R3C 3R6
204-945-4150, Fax: 204-948-4878

New Brunswick

Executive Council, Centennial Building, PO Box 6000, Fredericton, NB E3B 5H1
506-444-4417, Fax: 506-453-2266, Executivecounciloffice@gnb.ca
Fifty-eighth Legislative Assembly - New Brunswick, Centre Block, Legislative Building, 706 Queen St., PO Box 6000, Fredericton, NB E3B 5H1
506-453-2506, Fax: 506-453-7154, wwwleg@gnb.ca
Government of New Brunswick, PO Box 6000, Fredericton, NB E3B 5H1
Intergovernmental Affairs Division, Chancery Place, 675 King St., 5th Fl., Fredericton, NB E3B 1E9
506-444-4948, Fax: 506-453-2995, iga@gnb.ca
Legislative Assembly of New Brunswick, Legislative Bldg., Centre Block, PO Box 6000, Fredericton, NB E3B 5H1
506-453-2506, Fax: 506-453-7154, wwwleg@gnb.ca
Office of the Auditor General, HSBC Place, 520 King St., Fredericton, NB E3B 6G3
506-453-2243, Fax: 506-453-3067
Office of the Chief Electoral Officer, #102, Sartain MacDonald Building, PO Box 6000, Fredericton, NB E3B 5H1
506-453-2218, Fax: 506-457-4926, 800-308-2922, info@electionsnb.ca
Office of the Comptroller, Chancery Place, 3rd Fl., PO Box 6000, Fredericton, NB E3B 5H1
506-453-2451, Fax: 506-457-6878, wwwooc@gnb.ca
Office of the Lieutenant-Governor, Government House, PO Box 6000, Fredericton, NB E3B 5H1
506-453-2505, Fax: 506-444-5280, LTgov@gnb.ca
Office of the Ombudsman, PO Box 6000, Fredericton, NB E3B 5H1
506-453-2789, Fax: 506-453-5599, 888-465-1100, nbombud@gnb.ca
Office of the Premier, Centennial Bldg., PO Box 6000, Fredericton, NB E3B 5H1
506-453-2144, Fax: 506-453-7407, premier@gnb.ca

Newfoundland & Labrador

Executive Council, c/o Communications Branch, East Block, Confederation Building, 10th Fl., St. John's, NL A1B 4J6
info@gov.nl.ca
Forty-Eighth House of Assembly - Newfoundland & Labrador, Confederation Building, PO Box 8700, St. John's, NL A1B 4J6
709-729-3405, ClerkHOA@gov.nl.ca
Government of Newfoundland & Labrador, Confederation Bldg., St. John's, NL A1B 4J6
info@gov.nl.ca
House of Assembly, c/o Clerk's Office, Confederation Bldg., PO Box 8700, St. John's, NL A1B 4J6
709-729-3405
Newfoundland & Labrador Department of Municipal & Intergovernmental Affairs, West Block, Main Fl., Confederation Bldg., PO Box 8700, St. John's, NL A1B 4J6
709-729-3046, Fax: 709-729-0943, mainfo@gov.nl.ca
Newfoundland & Labrador Department of Service NL, PO Box 8700, St. John's, NL A1B 4J6
709-729-4834, servicenlinfo@gov.nl.ca
Newfoundland & Labrador Municipal Financing Corporation, Confederation Bldg., PO Box 8700, St. John's, NL A1B 4J6
709-729-6686, Fax: 709-729-2095
Newfoundland & Labrador Public Service Commission, 50 Mundy Pond Rd., PO Box 8700, St. John's, NL A1B 4J6
709-729-5810, Fax: 709-729-6234, 855-330-5810, contactpsc@gov.nl.ca
Office of the Auditor General, PO Box 8700, St. John's, NL A1B 4J6
709-729-2695, Fax: 709-729-5970, oagmail@oag.nl.ca
Office of the Chief Electoral Officer, 39 Hallett Cr., St. John's, NL A1B 4C4
709-729-0712, Fax: 709-729-0679, 877-729-7987, enl@gov.nl.ca
Office of the Lieutenant Governor, Government House, 50 Military Rd., PO Box 5517, St. John's, NL A1C 5W4
709-729-4494, Fax: 709-729-2234, governmenthouse@gov.nl.ca
Office of the Premier, East Block, Confederation Bldg., PO Box 8700, St. John's, NL A1B 4J6
709-729-3570, Fax: 709-729-5875, premier@gov.nl.ca
Women's Policy Office, Confederation Bldg., 4th Fl., West Block, PO Box 8700, St. John's, NL A1B 4J6
709-729-5009, Fax: 709-729-1418

Northwest Territories

Eighteenth Legislative Assembly - Northwest Territories, 4570 - 48 St., PO Box 1320, Yellowknife, NT X1A 2L9
867-669-2200, Fax: 867-920-4735, 800-661-0784
Executive Council, PO Box 1320, Yellowknife, NT X1A 2L9
executive_communications@gov.nt.ca
Financial Management Board Secretariat, c/o Secretary of the FMB / Comptroller General, 5003 - 49 St., PO Box 1320, Yellowknife, NT X1A 2L9
Fax: 867-873-0414
Government of the Northwest Territories, PO Box 1320, Yellowknife, NT X1A 2L9
867-873-7500
Northwest Territories Department of Aboriginal Affairs & Intergovernmental Relations, 4910 - 52nd St., PO Box 1320, Yellowknife, NT X1A 2L9
867-767-9025, Fax: 867-873-0233
Northwest Territories Department of Public Works & Services, Stuart M. Hodgson Bldg., 5009 - 49th St., PO Box 1320, Yellowknife, NT X1A 2L9
NWT Legislative Assembly, 4570 - 48 St., PO Box 1320, Yellowknife, NT X1A 2L9
867-669-2200, 800-661-0784
Office of the Commissioner, 803 Northwest Tower, PO Box 1320, Yellowknife, NT X1A 2L9
867-873-7400, Fax: 867-873-0223, 888-270-3318, commissioner@gov.nt.ca
Office of the Premier, Legislative Assembly Bldg., PO Box 1320, Yellowknife, NT X1A 2L9
867-669-2311, Fax: 867-873-0385

Nova Scotia

Council of Atlantic Premiers, Council Secretariat, #1006, 5161 George St., PO Box 2044, Halifax, NS B3J 2Z1
902-424-7590, Fax: 902-424-8976, info@cap-cpma.ca
Crown Land Information Management Centre, Founders Square, 1701 Hollis St., PO Box 698, Halifax, NS B3J 2T9
902-424-7068, Fax: 902-424-3171, crownland@gov.ns.ca
Elections Nova Scotia, #6, 7037 Mumford Rd., PO Box 2246, Halifax, NS B3J 3C8
902-424-8584, Fax: 902-424-6622, 800-565-1504
Executive Council Office, One Government Place, 1700 Granville St., 5th Fl., PO Box 2125, Halifax, NS B3J 3B7
902-424-5970, Fax: 902-424-0667, execounc@gov.ns.ca
Government of Nova Scotia, Province House, 1726 Hollis St., Halifax, NS B3J 2Y3
800-670-4357
Legislative House of Assembly, c/o Clerk's Office, Province House, 1st Fl., PO Box 1617, Halifax, NS B3J 2Y3
902-424-5978, Fax: 902-424-0632
Nova Scotia Department of Internal Services, World Trade & Convention Centre, 1800 Argyle St., 5th Fl., PO Box 943, Halifax, NS B3J 2V9
902-424-5465, Fax: 902-424-0555
Nova Scotia Department of Municipal Affairs, Maritime Centre, 14 North, 1505 Barrington St., PO Box 216, Halifax, NS B3J 3K5
902-424-6642, 800-670-4357
Nova Scotia Public Service Commission, 1800 Argyle St., 5th Fl., PO Box 943, Halifax, NS B3J 2V9
902-424-7660
Nova Scotia Utility & Review Board, Summit Place, 1601 Lower Water St., 3rd Fl., PO Box 1692 M,Halifax, NS B3J 3S3
902-424-4448, Fax: 902-424-3919, 855-442-4448, board@novascotia.ca
Office of Acadian Affairs, Dennis Building, 1741 Brunswick St., PO Box 682, Halifax, NS B3J 2T3
902-424-0497, Fax: 902-428-0124, 866-382-5811, bonjour@novascotia.ca
Office of the Auditor General, Royal Centre, #400, 5161 George St., Halifax, NS B3J 1M7
902-424-5907, Fax: 902-424-4350
Office of the Lieutenant Governor, Government House, 1451 Barrington St., Halifax, NS B3J 1Z2
902-424-7001, Fax: 902-424-1790, lgoffice@novascotia.ca
Office of the Ombudsman, #700, 5670 Spring Garden Rd., PO Box 2152, Halifax, NS B3J 3B7
902-424-6780, Fax: 902-424-6675, 800-670-1111, ombudsman@gov.ns.ca
Office of the Premier, One Government Place, 1700 Granville St., 7th Fl., PO Box 726, Halifax, NS B3J 2T3
902-424-6600, Fax: 902-424-7648, 800-267-1993, premier@novascotia.ca
Service Nova Scotia, c/o Public Enquiries - Service Nova Scotia, PO Box 2734, Halifax, NS B3J 3K5
902-424-5200, Fax: 902-424-0720, 800-670-4357
Sixty-second General Assembly - Nova Scotia, Province House, 1726 Hollis St., Halifax, NS B3J 2Y3
902-424-4661, Fax: 902-424-0574

Nunavut

Executive Council, PO Box 2410, Iqaluit, NU X0A 0H0
Fourth Legislative Assembly - Nunavut, PO Box 1200, Iqaluit, NU X0A 0H0
Government of Nunavut, PO Box 1000 200, Iqaluit, NU X0A 0H0
867-975-6000, Fax: 867-975-6099, 877-212-6438, info@gov.nu.ca
Nunavut Legislative Assembly, 926 Federal Rd., PO Box 1200, Iqaluit, NU X0A 0H0
867-975-5000, Fax: 867-975-5190, 877-334-7266, leginfo@assembly.nu.ca
Nunavut Territory Department of Community & Government Services, W.G. Brown Bldg., 4th Fl., PO Box 1000 700, Iqaluit, NU X0A 0H0
867-975-5400, Fax: 867-975-5305
Nunavut Territory Department of Culture & Heritage, PO Box 1000 800, Iqaluit, NU X0A 0H0
867-975-5500, Fax: 867-975-5504, 866-934-2035
Nunavut Territory Department of Education, Bldg. 1107, 2nd Fl., PO Box 1000 900, Iqaluit, NU X0A 0H0
867-975-5600, Fax: 867-975-5605, info.edu@gov.nu.ca
Nunavut Territory Department of Environment, PO Box 1000 1300, Iqaluit, NU X0A 0H0
867-975-7700, Fax: 867-975-7742, environment@gov.nu.ca
Nunavut Territory Department of Executive & Intergovernmental Affairs, 1084 Aeroplex bldg., PO Box 1000 200, Iqaluit, NU X0A 0H0
867-975-6000, Fax: 867-975-6099
Nunavut Territory Department of Finance, Bldg. 1079, 1st Fl., PO Box 1000 430, Iqaluit, NU X0A 0H0
867-975-5800, Fax: 867-975-5805
Nunavut Territory Department of Health, PO Box 1000 1000, Iqaluit, NU X0A 0H0
867-975-5700, Fax: 867-975-5705, 800-661-0833
Office of the Commissioner, PO Box 2379, Iqaluit, NU X0A 0H0
867-975-5120, Fax: 867-975-5123, commissionerofnunavut@gov.nu.ca
Office of the Premier, PO Box 2410, Iqaluit, NU X0A 0H0
867-975-5050, Fax: 867-975-5051

Ontario

Cabinet of Ontario, Legislative Building, Queen's Park, Toronto, ON M7A 1A1
Cancer Care Ontario, 620 University Ave., 15th Fl., Toronto, ON M5G 2L7
416-971-9800, Fax: 416-971-6888

Elections Ontario, 51 Rolark Dr., Toronto, ON M1R 3B1
416-326-6300, Fax: 416-326-6200, 888-668-8683, info@elections.on.ca
Forty-first Provincial Parliament - Ontario, Clerk's Office, #104, Legislative Building, Queen's Park, Toronto, ON M7A 1A2
416-325-7500, Fax: 416-325-7489, web@ola.org
Government of Ontario, Queen's Park, Toronto, ON M7A 1A2
416-326-1234, 800-267-8097
Municipal Services Division, 777 Bay St., 16th Fl., Toronto, ON M5G 2E5
Fax: 416-585-6445
Office of the Auditor General, 20 Dundas St. West, 15th Fl., PO Box 105, Toronto, ON M5G 2C2
416-327-2381, Fax: 416-327-9862, comments@auditor.on.ca
Office of the Integrity Commissioner, #2100, 2 Bloor St. East, Toronto, ON M4W 3E2
416-314-8983, Fax: 416-314-8987, integrity.mail@oico.on.ca
Office of the Lieutenant Governor, Legislative Bldg., Queen's Park, Toronto, ON M7A 1A1
416-325-7780, Fax: 416-325-7787, lt.gov@ontario.ca
Office of the Ombudsman, Bell Trinity Sq., South Tower, 483 Bay St., 10th Fl., Toronto, ON M5G 2C9
416-586-3300, Fax: 416-586-3485, 800-263-1830, info@ombudsman.on.ca
Office of the Premier, Legislative Building, Queen's Park, Toronto, ON M7A 1A1
416-325-1941, Fax: 416-325-3745
Ontario Legislative Assembly, c/o Clerk of the Legislative Assembly, #104, Legislative Bldg., Queen's Park, Toronto, ON M7A 1A2
416-325-7500, Fax: 416-325-7489, web@ola.org
Ontario Mental Health Foundation, 180 Bloor St. West, #UC 101, Toronto, ON M5S 2V6
416-920-7721, Fax: 416-920-0026, grants@omhf.on.ca
Ontario Ministry of Infrastructure, Hearst Block, 900 Bay St., 8th Fl., Toronto, ON M7A 2E1
416-325-6666, 800-268-7095
Ontario Ministry of Intergovernmental Affairs, Ferguson Block, 77 Wellesley St. West, 12th Fl., Toronto, ON M7A 1N3
416-326-1234
Ontario Ministry of Municipal Affairs, College Park, 777 Bay St., 17th Fl., Toronto, ON M5G 2E5
416-585-7000, Fax: 416-585-6470, mininfo@ontario.ca
Ontario Pension Board, Sun Life Bldg., #2200, 200 King St. West, Toronto, ON M5H 3X6
416-364-8558, Fax: 416-364-7578, 800-668-6203, clientservice@opb.ca
Public Service Commission, Whitney Block, 99 Wellesley St. West, 5th Fl., Toronto, ON M7A 1W4
416-325-1750
Public Service Grievance Board, #600, 180 Dundas St. West, Toronto, ON M5G 1Z8
416-326-1388, Fax: 416-326-1396, psgb.psgb@ontario.ca
Treasury Board Secretariat, Ferguson Block, 77 Wellesley St. West, 8th Fl., Toronto, ON M7A 1N3
416-326-8525, Fax: 416-327-3790, 800-268-1142

Prince Edward Island

Elections Prince Edward Island, Atlantic Technology Centre, #160, 176 Great George St., Charlottetown, PE C1A 4K3
902-368-5895, Fax: 902-368-6500, 888-234-8783
Executive Council, Shaw Bldg., 5th Fl., PO Box 2000, Charlottetown, PE C1A 7N8
902-368-4502, Fax: 902-368-6118
Government of Prince Edward Island, Island Information Service, PO Box 2000, Charlottetown, PE C1A 7N8
902-368-4000, island@gov.pe.ca
Office of the Conflict of Interest Commissioner, 197 Richmond St., 1st Fl., PO Box 2000, Charlottetown, PE C1A 7N8
902-368-5970, Fax: 902-368-5175
Office of the Premier, Shaw Bldg., 95 Rochford St. South, 5th Fl., PO Box 2000, Charlottetown, PE C1A 7N8
902-368-4400, Fax: 902-368-4416, premier@gov.pe.ca
Prince Edward Island Legislative Assembly, 197 Richmond St., PO Box 2000, Charlottetown, PE C1A 7N8
902-368-5970, Fax: 902-368-5175, 877-315-5518, legislativelibrary@assembly.pe.ca
Public Service Commission, Shaw Bldg. North, 105 Rochford St., 1st Fl., PO Box 2000, Charlottetown, PE C1A 7N8
902-368-4080, Fax: 902-368-4383
Sixty-fifth General Assembly - Prince Edward Island, Province House, 165 Richmond St., 1st Fl., PO Box 2000, Charlottetown, PE C1A 7N8
902-368-5970, Fax: 902-368-5175, 877-315-5518

Québec

Bureau du coroner, Édifice le Delta 2, #390, 2875, boul Laurier, Québec, QC G1V 5B1
418-643-1845, Fax: 418-643-6174, 866-312-7051, clientele.coroner@msp.gouv.qc.ca
Cabinet du Lieutenant-gouverneur, Édifice André-Laurendeau, 1050, rue des Parlementaires R.C., Québec, QC G1A 1A1
418-643-5385, Fax: 418-644-4677, 866-791-0766
Cabinet du premier ministre, Édifice Honoré-Mercier, 835, boul René-Lévesque est, 3e étage, Québec, QC G1A 1B4
418-643-5321, Fax: 418-643-3924
Centre de recherche industrielle du Québec, 333, rue Franquet, Québec, QC G1P 4C7
418-659-1550, Fax: 418-652-2251, 800-667-2386, infocriq@criq.qc.ca
Centre du services partagés du Québec, 875, Grande Allée est, 4e étage, section 4.751, Québec, QC G1R 5W5
418-644-2777, Fax: 418-644-0462, 855-644-2777, cspq@cspq.gouv.qc.ca
Comité de déontologie policière, Tour du Saint-Laurent, #A-200, 2525, boul Laurier, 2e étage, Québec, QC G1V 4Z6
418-646-1936, Fax: 418-528-0987, comite.deontologie@msp.gouv.qc.ca
Commissaire à la déontologie policière, #1-40, 1200, rte de l'Église, Québec, QC G1V 4Y9
418-643-7897, Fax: 418-528-9473, 877-237-7897, deontologie-policiere.Québec@msp.gouv.qc.ca
Commissariat des incendies, 455, rue Dupont, Québec, QC G1K 6N2
418-529-5706, Fax: 418-529-9922
Commission de la fonction publique, 800, place D'Youville, 7e étage, Québec, QC G1R 3P4
418-643-1425, Fax: 418-643-7264, 800-432-0432, cfp@cfp.gouv.qc.ca
Commission de la fonction publique (Québec), 800, Place d'Youville, 7e étage, Québec, QC G1R 3P4
418-643-1425, Fax: 418-643-7264, 800-432-0432, cfp@cfp.gouv.qc.ca
Commission des droits de la personne et des droits de la jeunesse, 360, rue Saint-Jacques, 2e étage, Montréal, QC H2Y 1P5
514-873-5146, Fax: 514-873-6032, 800-361-6477, accueil@cdpdj.qc.ca
Commission québecoise des libérations conditionnelles, #1.32A, 300, boul Jean-Lesage, Québec, QC G1K 8K6
418-646-8300, Fax: 418-643-7217, cqlc@cqlc.gouv.qc.ca
Directeur général des Élections du Québec, Édifice René-Lévesque, 3460, rue de La Pérade, Québec, QC G1X 3Y5
418-528-0422, Fax: 418-643-7291, 888-353-2846, info@electionsQuébec.qc.ca
Financement-Québec, 12, rue Saint-Louis, 3e étage, Québec, QC G1R 5L3
418-691-2203, Fax: 418-644-6214, financement.regroupe@finances.gouv.qc.ca
Gouvernement du Québec, Hôtel du Parlement, 1045, rue des Parlementaires, Québec, QC G1A 1A3
418-644-4545, 877-644-4545
Institut de la statistique du Québec, 200, ch Ste-Foy, 1er étage, Québec, QC G1R 5T4
418-691-2401, Fax: 418-643-4129, 800-463-4090
L'Assemblée nationale, Hôtel du Parlement, 1045, rue des Parlementaires, Québec, QC G1A 1A3
418-643-7239, Fax: 418-646-4271, 866-337-8837, responsable.contenu@assnat.qc.ca
Ministère de l'Immigration, de la Diversité et de l'Inclusion, Édifice Gérald-Godin, 360, rue McGill, Montréal, QC H2Y 2E9
514-864-9191, Fax: 514-864-2899, 877-864-9191
Ministère des Affaires municipales et Occupation du territoire, Aile Chaveau, 10, rue Pierre-Olivier-Chauveau, Québec, QC G1R 4J3
418-691-2015, Fax: 418-643-7385, communications@mamrot.gouv.qc.ca
Ministère des Finances, 12, rue Saint-Louis, Québec, QC G1R 5L3
418-528-9323, Fax: 418-646-1631, info@finances.gouv.qc.ca
Ministère des Relations internationales et Francophonie, Édifice Hector-Fabre, 525, boul Réne-Lévesque est, Québec, QC G1R 5R9
418-649-2300, Fax: 418-649-2656
Ministère des Énergie et des Ressources naturelles, Service à la clientèle, #A409, 5700, 4e av ouest, Québec, QC G1H 6R1
Fax: 418-644-6513, 866-248-6936, services.clientele@mern.gouv.qc.ca
Ministère du Conseil exécutif, 875, Grande Allée est, Québec, QC G1R 4Y8
418-643-2001, Fax: 418-528-9242
Quarante-et-unième assemblée nationale, Hôtel du Parlement, 1045, rue des Parlementaires, Québec, QC G1A 1A4
418-643-7239, Fax: 418-646-4271, 866-337-8837
Régie des alcools, des courses et des jeux, 560, boul Charest est, Québec, QC G1K 3J3
418-643-7667, Fax: 418-643-5971, 800-363-0320
Secrétariat aux affaires intergouvernementales canadiennes, 875, Grande Allée est, 3e étage, Québec, QC G1R 4Y8
418-643-4011, Fax: 418-528-0052
Société des alcools du Québec, 905, av De Lorimier, Montréal, QC H2K 3V9
514-254-2020, 866-873-2020, info@saq.com
École nationale de police du Québec, 350, rue Marguerite-d'Youville, Nicolet, QC J3T 1X4
819-293-8631, Fax: 819-293-8630, courriel@enpq.qc.ca

Saskatchewan

Board of Revenue Commissioners, #480, 2151 Scarth St., Regina, SK S4P 2H8
306-787-6221, Fax: 306-787-1610
Elections Saskatchewan, 1702 Park St., Regina, SK S4N 6B2
306-787-4000, Fax: 306-787-4052, 877-958-8683, info@elections.sk.ca
Executive Council, Communications Services, Executive Council, #130, 3085 Albert St., Regina, SK S4S 0B1
306-787-6276, Fax: 306-787-6123
Government of Saskatchewan, 2405 Legislative Dr., Regina, SK S4S 0B3
Legislative Assembly of Saskatchewan, Office of the Clerk, Legislative Building, #239, 2405 Legislative Dr., Regina, SK S4S 0B3
info@legassembly.sk.ca
Office of the Lieutenant Governor, Government House, 4607 Dewdney Ave., Regina, SK S4T 1B7
306-787-4070, Fax: 306-787-7716, lgo@ltgov.sk.ca
Office of the Premier, Legislative Building, #226, 2405 Legislative Dr., Regina, SK S4S 0B3
306-787-9433, Fax: 306-787-0885
Ombudsman Saskatchewan, #150, 2401 Saskatchewan Dr., Regina, SK S4P 4H8
306-787-6211, Fax: 306-787-9090, 800-667-7180, ombreg@ombudsman.sk.ca
Provincial Auditor Saskatchewan, Chateau Tower, #1500, 1920 Broad St., Regina, SK S4P 3V2
306-787-6398, Fax: 306-787-6383, info@auditor.sk.ca
Public Service Commission, 2350 Albert St., Regina, SK S4P 4A6
306-787-7853, 866-319-5999, csinquiry@gov.sk.ca
Saskatchewan Central Services, 1920 Rose St., Regina, SK S4P 0A9
306-787-6911, Fax: 306-787-1061, GSReception@gs.gov.sk.ca
Twenty-eighth Legislature - Saskatchewan, 2405 Legislative Dr., Regina, SK S4S 0B3

Yukon Territory

Executive Council, 2071 Second Ave., PO Box 2703, Whitehorse, YT Y1A 2C6
867-667-5393, Fax: 867-393-6214, eco@gov.yk.ca
Government of the Yukon Territory, PO Box 2703, Whitehorse, YT Y1A 2C6
867-667-5811, 800-661-0408
Office of the Commissioner of Yukon, Taylor House, 412 Main St., Whitehorse, YT Y1A 2B7
867-667-5121, Fax: 867-393-6201, commissioner@gov.yk.ca
Office of the Premier, 2071 - 2nd Ave., PO Box 2703, Whitehorse, YT Y1A 2C6
867-667-8660, Fax: 867-393-6252, premier@gov.yk.ca
Thirty-third Legislative Assembly - Yukon Territory, Yukon Legislative Assembly Office, 2071 Second Ave., PO Box 2703, Whitehorse, YT Y1A 2C6
867-667-5498
Yukon Legislative Assembly, 2071 - 2nd Ave., PO Box 2703, Whitehorse, YT Y1A 2C6
867-667-5498, yla@gov.yk.ca
Yukon Public Service Commission, Yukon Government Administration Bldg., 2071 Second Ave., PO Box 2703, Whitehorse, YT Y1A 2C6
867-667-5653, Fax: 867-667-5755, PSCWebsite@gov.yk.ca

GOVERNMENT (GENERAL INFORMATION)

Auditor General of Canada, 240 Sparks St., Ottawa, ON K1A 0G6
613-952-0213, Fax: 613-957-0474, 888-761-5953, infomedia@oag-bvg.gc.ca
Correctional Service Canada, 340 Laurier Ave. West, Ottawa, ON K1A 0P9
613-992-5891, Fax: 613-943-1630
Department of National Defence & the Canadian Armed Forces, National Defence HQ, Major-General George R. Pearkes Bldg., 101 Colonel By Dr., Ottawa, ON K1A 0K2
613-995-2534, Fax: 613-992-4739, 888-995-2534, information@forces.gc.ca
Employment & Social Development Canada, 140 Promenade du Portage, Gatineau, QC K1A 0J9
Environment & Climate Change Canada, 10 Wellington St., Gatineau, QC K1A 0H3
819-997-2800, Fax: 819-994-1412, 800-668-6767, enviroinfo@ec.gc.ca
Fisheries & Oceans Canada, 200 Kent St., Ottawa, ON K1A 0E6
613-993-0999, Fax: 613-990-1866, info@dfo-mpo.gc.ca
Global Affairs Canada, Enquiries Service, 125 Sussex Dr., Ottawa, ON K1A 0G2
613-944-4000, Fax: 613-996-9709, 800-267-8376

Health Canada, Tunney's Pasture, Ottawa, ON K1A 0K9
613-957-2991, Fax: 613-941-5366, 866-225-0709, info@hc-sc.gc.ca

House of Commons, Canada, House of Commons, Centre Block, Parliament Buildings, 111 Wellington St., Ottawa, ON K1A 0A6
613-992-4793, 866-599-4999, info@parl.gc.ca

Immigration, Refugees & Citizenship, Jean Edmonds, South Tower, 365 Laurier Ave. West, Ottawa, ON K1A 1L1
888-242-2100

Indigenous & Northern Affairs, Terrasses de la Chaudière, 10 Wellington St., North Tower, Gatineau, QC K1A 0H4
Fax: 866-817-3977, 800-567-9604, infopubs@aadnc-aandc.gc.ca

Innovation, Science & Economic Development Canada, C.D. Howe Building, 235 Queen St., Ottawa, ON K1A 0H5
613-954-5031, Fax: 613-954-2340, 800-328-6189, info@ic.gc.ca

Office of the Prime Minister, Liberal Party of Canada / Liberal Research Bureau, Langevin Block, 80 Wellington St., Ottawa, ON K1A 0A2
613-992-4211, Fax: 613-941-6900

Public Affairs Branch, Tower 7, 1341 Baseline Rd., Ottawa, ON K1A 0C7
613-759-1000, Fax: 613-773-2772

Service Canada, 140, Promenade du Portage, Gatineau, QC K1A 0J9
Fax: 613-941-1827, 800-622-6232

Statistics Canada, R.H. Coats Bldg., Tunney's Pasture, 150 Tunney's Pasture Driveway, Ottawa, ON K1A 0T6
514-283-8300, Fax: 514-283-9350, 800-263-1136, STATCAN.infostats-infostats.STATCAN@canada.ca

Transport Canada, Place de Ville, 330 Sparks St., Tower C, Ottawa, ON K1A 0N5
613-990-2309, Fax: 613-954-4731, 866-995-9737

Treasury Board of Canada Secretariat, East Tower, 140 O'Connor St., 9th Fl., Ottawa, ON K1A 0R5
613-957-2400, Fax: 613-941-4000, 877-636-0656

Veterans Affairs Canada, 161 Grafton St., PO Box 7700, Charlottetown, PE C1A 8M9
866-522-2122, information@vac-acc.gc.ca

Alberta

Public Affairs Bureau, Federal Bldg., 9820 - 107 St., 7th Fl., Edmonton, AB T5K 1E7

Service Alberta, Government of Alberta, PO Box 1333, Edmonton, AB T5J 2N2
780-427-4088, -310-0000, service.alberta@gov.ab.ca

British Columbia

Service BC, PO Box 9804 Prov Govt, Victoria, BC V8W 9W1
250-387-6121, Fax: 250-387-5633, 800-663-7867

New Brunswick

Service New Brunswick, Westmorland Pl., PO Box 1998, Fredericton, NB E3B 5G4
506-457-3581, Fax: 506-444-2850, snb@snb.ca

Newfoundland & Labrador

Newfoundland & Labrador Department of Service NL, PO Box 8700, St. John's, NL A1B 4J6
709-729-4834, servicenlinfo@gov.nl.ca

Nova Scotia

Nova Scotia Department of Municipal Affairs, Maritime Centre, 14 North, 1505 Barrington St., PO Box 216, Halifax, NS B3J 3K5
902-424-6642, 800-670-4357

Service Nova Scotia, c/o Public Enquiries - Service Nova Scotia, PO Box 2734, Halifax, NS B3J 3K5
902-424-5200, Fax: 902-424-0720, 800-670-4357

Nunavut

Nunavut Territory Department of Executive & Intergovernmental Affairs, 1084 Aeroplex bldg., PO Box 1000 200, Iqaluit, NU X0A 0H0
867-975-6000, Fax: 867-975-6099

Ontario

ServiceOntario, College Park, 777 Bay St., 15th fl., Toronto, ON M7A 2J3
Fax: 416-326-1313, 800-267-8097

Québec

Services Québec, Bureau de la qualité, 800, place D'Youville, 20e étage, Québec, QC G1R 3P4

Yukon Territory

Government Inquiry Office, Government of Yukon Administration Bldg., 2071 - 2nd Ave., PO Box 2703, Whitehorse, YT Y1A 2C6
867-667-5811, 800-661-0408, inquiry.desk@gov.yk.ca

GOVERNMENT PURCHASING

See: Purchasing

Public Services & Procurement, Place du Portage, Phase III, 11, rue Laurier, Ottawa, ON K1A 0S5
questions@tpsgc-pwgsc.gc.ca

Saskatchewan

Saskatchewan Central Services, 1920 Rose St., Regina, SK S4P 0A9
306-787-6911, Fax: 306-787-1061, GSReception@gs.gov.sk.ca

GRANTS & SUBSIDIES

See Also: Student Aid

Atlantic Canada Opportunities Agency, Blue Cross Centre, 644 Main St., 3rd Fl., PO Box 6051, Moncton, NB E1C 9J8
506-851-2271, Fax: 506-851-7403, 800-561-7862

Business Development Bank of Canada, #400, 5, Place Ville-Marie, Montréal, QC H3B 5E7
877-232-2269

Canada Council for the Arts, 150 Elgin St., 2nd Fl., PO Box 1047, Ottawa, ON K1P 5V8
613-566-4414, Fax: 613-566-4390, 800-263-5588, info@canadacouncil.ca

Canada Economic Development for Québec Regions, Édifice Dominion Square, #900, 1255, rue Peel, Montréal, QC H3B 2T9
514-283-6412, Fax: 514-283-3302, 866-385-6412

Canada Mortgage & Housing Corporation, 700 Montreal Rd., Ottawa, ON K1A 0P7
613-748-2000, Fax: 613-748-2098, 800-668-2642, chic@cmhc-schl.gc.ca

Canadian Institutes of Health Research, 160 Elgin St., 9th Fl., Ottawa, ON K1A 0W9
613-941-2672, Fax: 613-954-1800, 888-603-4178, support@cihr-irsc.gc.ca

International Development Research Centre, 150 Kent St., PO Box 8500, Ottawa, ON K1G 3H9
613-236-6163, Fax: 613-238-7230, info@idrc.ca

National Film Board of Canada, Operational Headquarters, Norman McLaren Building, 3155, ch de la Côte-de-Liesse, CP 1600 Centre-ville,Montréal, QC H3C 3H5
514-283-9000, 800-267-7710

Natural Sciences & Engineering Research Council of Canada, Constitution Square, Tower II, 350 Albert St., Ottawa, ON K1A 1H5
613-995-4273, Fax: 613-992-5337, 855-275-2861

Networks of Centres of Excellence of Canada, 350 Albert Street, 16th Fl., Ottawa, ON K1A 1H5
613-995-6010, Fax: 613-992-7356, info@nce-rce.gc.ca

Western Economic Diversification Canada, Canada Place, #1500, 9700 Jasper Ave. NW, Edmonton, AB T5J 4H7
780-495-4164, Fax: 780-495-4557, 888-338-9378

Alberta

Municipal Assessment & Grants Division, Commerce Place, 10155 - 102 St., 15th Fl., Edmonton, AB T5J 4L4

Newfoundland & Labrador

Newfoundland & Labrador Municipal Financing Corporation, Confederation Bldg., PO Box 8700, St. John's, NL A1B 4J6
709-729-6686, Fax: 709-729-2095

Nova Scotia

Nova Scotia Department of Finance & Treasury Board, Provincial Bldg., 1723 Hollis St., 7th Fl., PO Box 187, Halifax, NS B3J 2N3
902-424-5554, Fax: 902-424-0635, FinanceWeb@novascotia.ca

Ontario

Ontario Trillium Foundation, 800 Bay St., 5th Fl., Toronto, ON M5S 3A9
416-963-4927, Fax: 416-963-8781, 800-263-2887, otf@otf.ca

Saskatchewan

Energy & Resources, 2101 Scarth St., Regina, SK S4P SH9
306-787-2528

HAZARDOUS MATERIALS

Atomic Energy of Canada Limited, Head Office, Chalk River Laboratories, 286 Plant Rd., Chalk River, ON K0J 1J0
888-220-2465, communications@aecl.ca

Canadian Nuclear Laboratories, Head Office, Chalk River Laboratories, 286 Plant Rd., Chalk River, ON K0J 1J0
866-513-2325, communications@cnl.ca

Health Canada, Tunney's Pasture, Ottawa, ON K1A 0K9
613-957-2991, Fax: 613-941-5366, 866-225-0709, info@hc-sc.gc.ca

Low-Level Radioactive Waste Management Office, 196 Toronto St., Port Hope, ON L1A 3V5
905-885-9488, Fax: 905-885-0273, 866-255-2755, info@llrwmo.org

Manitoba

Emergency Measures Organization, #1525, 405 Broadway Ave., Winnipeg, MB R3C 3L6
204-945-4772, Fax: 204-945-4929, 888-267-8298, emo@gov.mb.ca

Ontario

Ontario Ministry of Environment & Climate Change, Public Information Centre, Macdonald Block, 900 Bay St., 2nd Fl., Toronto, ON M7A 1N3
416-325-4000, Fax: 416-314-6713, 800-565-4923

Pesticides Advisory Committee, 135 St. Clair Ave. West, 15th Fl., Toronto, ON M4V 1P5
416-314-9230, Fax: 416-314-9237

HEALTH

Canadian Centre for Occupational Health & Safety, 135 Hunter St. East, Hamilton, ON L8N 1M5
905-572-2981, Fax: 905-572-4500, 800-668-4284

Canadian Centre on Substance Abuse, #500, 75 Albert St., Ottawa, ON K1P 5E7
613-235-4048, Fax: 613-235-8101, info@ccsa.ca

Canadian Food Inspection Agency, 1400 Merivale Rd., Ottawa, ON K1A 0Y9
613-225-2342, 800-442-2342

Health Canada, Tunney's Pasture, Ottawa, ON K1A 0K9
613-957-2991, Fax: 613-941-5366, 866-225-0709, info@hc-sc.gc.ca

Medical Device Facilities, Boucherville Research Facilities, 75, boul de Mortagne, Boucherville, QC J4B 6Y4
450-641-5100

National Seniors Council, Phase IV, 8th Floor, Mail Stop 802, 140 Promenade du Portage, Gatineau, QC K1A 0J9
Fax: 819-953-9298, 800-622-6232

Patented Medicine Prices Review Board, Standard Life Centre, #1400, 333 Laurier Ave. West, PO Box L40, Ottawa, ON K1P 1C1
613-954-8299, Fax: 613-952-7626, 877-861-2350, pmprb@pmprb-cepmb.gc.ca

Public Health Agency of Canada, 130 Colonnade Rd., Ottawa, ON K1A 0K9

Ste-Anne's Hospital, 305 boul des Anciens-Combattants, Sainte-Anne-de-Bellevue, QC H9X 1Y9
514-457-3440, 800-361-9287, steanne@vac-acc.gc.ca

Veterans Affairs Canada, 161 Grafton St., PO Box 7700, Charlottetown, PE C1A 8M9
866-522-2122, information@vac-acc.gc.ca

Zebrafish Screening Facility, 1411 Oxford St., Halifax, NS B3H 3Z1
902-426-8332

Alberta

Alberta Health, PO Box 1360 Main,Edmonton, AB T5J 2N3
780-427-7164, -310-0000

Alberta Health Advocates, Centre West Bldg., 10035 - 108 St., 12th Fl., Edmonton, AB T5J 3E1
780-422-1812, Fax: 780-422-0695, -310-0000, healthadvocates@gov.ab.ca

Alberta Health Services, Corporate Office, North Tower, Seventh Street Plaza, 10030 - 107th St. NW, 14th Fl., Edmonton, AB T5J 3E4
780-342-2000, Fax: 780-342-2060, 888-342-2471, ahs.corp@albertahealthservices.ca

Alberta Innovates - Health Solutions, #1500, 10104 - 103 Ave., Edmonton, AB T5J 4A7
780-423-5727, Fax: 780-429-3509, 877-423-5727, health@albertainnovates.ca

Alberta Seniors & Housing, PO Box 3100, Edmonton, AB T5J 4W3
780-644-9992, Fax: 780-422-5954, 877-644-9992

Financial & Corporate Services Division, ATB Place, 10025 Jasper Ave., 16th Fl., Edmonton, AB T5J 1S6

Health Quality Council of Alberta, #210, 811 - 14 St. NW, Calgary, AB T2N 2A4
403-297-8162, Fax: 403-297-8258, info@hqca.ca

Occupational Health & Safety Council, Standard Life Centre, 10405 Jasper Ave., Edmonton, AB T5J 3N4
780-412-8742, Fax: 780-412-8701

Office of the Chief Medical Officer of Health, ATB Place, 10025 Jasper Ave., 24th Fl., Edmonton, AB T5J 1S6
780-427-5263

Premier's Council on the Status of Persons with Disabilities, HSBC Building, #1110, 10055 - 106 St., Edmonton, AB T5J 1G3
780-422-1095, Fax: 780-415-0097, 800-272-8841, hs.pcspd@gov.ab.ca

Seniors Advisory Council for Alberta, Standard Life Centre, #600, 10405 Jasper Ave., 6th Fl., Edmonton, AB T5J 4R7
780-422-2321, Fax: 780-422-8762, -310-0000, saca@gov.ab.ca

British Columbia

British Columbia Centre for Disease Control, 655 West 12th Ave., Vancouver, BC V5Z 4R4
604-707-2400, Fax: 604-707-2401, admininfo@bccdc.ca

British Columbia Ministry of Health, 1515 Blanshard St., PO Box 9639 Prov Govt, Victoria, BC V8W 9P1
604-660-2421, 800-663-7100, hlth.health@gov.bc.ca

Manitoba

Addictions Foundation of Manitoba, 1031 Portage Ave., Winnipeg, MB R3G 0R8
204-944-6236, Fax: 204-944-7082, 866-638-2561, execoff@afm.mb.ca

Manitoba Council on Aging, #1610, 155 Carlton St., Winnipeg, MB R3C 3H8
204-945-6565, 800-665-6565, seniors@gov.mb.ca

Manitoba Drug Standards & Therapeutics Committee, #1014, 300 Carlton St., Winnipeg, MB R3B 3M9
204-786-7233

Manitoba Health, Seniors & Active Living, #100, 300 Carlton St., Winnipeg, MB R3B 3M9
204-945-3744, 866-626-4862, mgi@gov.mb.ca

Office of the Chief Medical Examiner, #210, 1 Wesley Ave., Winnipeg, MB R3C 4C6
204-945-2088, 800-282-8069

Public Health & Primary Health Care, 300 Carlton St., 4th Floor, Winnipeg, MB R3B 3M9
204-788-6666

New Brunswick

New Brunswick Department of Health, HSBC Place, PO Box 5100, Fredericton, NB E3B 5G8
506-457-4800, Fax: 506-453-5243, Health.Sante@gnb.ca

New Brunswick Department of Tourism, Heritage & Culture, Centennial Building, PO Box 6000, Fredericton, NB E3B 5H1
506-453-3115, Fax: 506-457-4984, thctpcinfo@gnb.ca

Premier's Council on the Status of Disabled Persons, #648, 440 King St., Fredericton, NB E3B 5H8
506-444-3000, Fax: 506-444-3001, 800-442-4412, pcsdp@gnb.ca

Senior & Healthy Aging Secretariat, Sartain MacDonald Bldg., 4th Fl., PO Box 6000, Fredericton, NB E3B 5H1
506-453-2001, Fax: 506-453-2164, seniors@gnb.ca

WorkSafeNB, 1 Portland St., PO Box 160, Saint John, NB E2L 3X9
506-632-2200, Fax: 506-632-4999, 800-222-9775, communications@ws-ts.nb.ca

Newfoundland & Labrador

Central Regional Health Authority, 21 Carmelite Rd., Grand Falls-Windsor, NL A2A 1Y4
888-799-2272, client.relations@centralhealth.nl.ca

Eastern Regional Health Authority, Health Sciences Centre, #1345, Prince Philip Dr., Level 1, St. John's, NL A1B 3V6
709-777-6500, Fax: 709-364-6460, 877-444-1399, client.relations@easternhealth.ca

Health Research Ethics Authority, #200, 95 Bonaventure Ave., 2nd Fl., St. John's, NL A1B 2X5
709-777-6974, Fax: 709-777-8776, info@hrea.ca

Labrador-Grenfell Regional Health Authority, Administration Bldg., PO Box 7000 C, Happy Valley-Goose Bay, NL A0P 1C0
709-897-2267, Fax: 709-896-4032

Newfoundland & Labrador Centre for Health Information, 70 O'Leary Ave., St. John's, NL A1B 2C7
709-752-6000, Fax: 709-752-6011, 877-752-6006, communications@nlchi.nl.ca

Newfoundland & Labrador Department of Health & Community Services, West Block, Confederation Bldg., PO Box 8700, St. John's, NL A1B 4J6
709-729-4984, healthinfo@gov.nl.ca

Newfoundland & Labrador Department of Seniors, Wellness & Social Development, PO Box 8700, St. John's, NL A1B 4J6
709-729-0862, Fax: 709-729-0870, SWSDInfo@gov.nl.ca

Newfoundland & Labrador Health Boards Association, Beothuck Bldg., 20 Crosbie Pl., 2nd Fl., St. John's, NL A1B 3Y8
709-364-7701, Fax: 709-364-6460

Western Regional Health Authority, Corporate Office, 1 Brookfield Ave., Corner Brook, NL A2H 6J7
709-637-5000

Northwest Territories

Northwest Territories Department of Health & Social Services, 5015 - 49th St., PO Box 1320, Yellowknife, NT X1A 2L9
Fax: 867-873-0306

Nova Scotia

Nova Scotia Advisory Commission on AIDS, Barrington Tower, 1894 Barrington St., PO Box 31, Halifax, NS B3J 2L4
902-424-5730, aids@gov.ns.ca

Nova Scotia Department of Health & Wellness, Barrington Tower., 1894 Barrington St., PO Box 488, Halifax, NS B3J 2R8
902-424-5818, 800-387-6665

Office of the Chief Medical Examiner, Dr. William D. Finn Centre for Forensic Medicine, 51 Garland Ave., Dartmouth, NS B3B 0J2
902-424-2722, Fax: 902-424-0607, 888-424-4336

Nunavut

Nunavut Territory Department of Culture & Heritage, PO Box 1000 800, Iqaluit, NU X0A 0H0
867-975-5500, Fax: 867-975-5504, 866-934-2035

Nunavut Territory Department of Health, PO Box 1000 1000, Iqaluit, NU X0A 0H0
867-975-5700, Fax: 867-975-5705, 800-661-0833

Office of the Chief Coroner, c/o Court Services Division, PO Box 297, Iqaluit, NU X0A 0H0
867-975-6100, Fax: 867-975-6168, theofficeofthechiefcoroner@gov.nu.ca

Ontario

Cancer Care Ontario, 620 University Ave., 15th Fl., Toronto, ON M5G 2L7
416-971-9800, Fax: 416-971-6888

Consent & Capacity Board, 151 Bloor St. West, 10th Fl., Toronto, ON M5S 2T5
416-327-4142, Fax: 416-924-8873, 866-777-7391, ccb@ontario.ca

Health Boards Secretariat, 151 Bloor St. West, 9th Fl., Toronto, ON M5S 2T5
416-327-8512, Fax: 416-327-8524, 866-282-2179

Health Services Information & Information Technology Cluster, 56 Wellesley St. West, 10th Fl., Toronto, ON M5S 2S3
416-314-0234, Fax: 416-314-4182

Health System Strategy & Policy Division, Hepburn Block, 80 Grosvenor St., 8th Fl., Toronto, ON M7A 1R3
416-327-8295, Fax: 416-327-5109

Medical Eligibility Committee, 370 Select Dr., PO Box 168, Kingston, ON K7M 8T4
613-536-3058

Ontario Mental Health Foundation, 180 Bloor St. West, #UC 101, Toronto, ON M5S 2V6
416-920-7721, Fax: 416-920-0026, grants@omhf.on.ca

Ontario Ministry of Health & Long-Term Care, Hepburn Block, 80 Grosvenor St., 10th Fl, Toronto, ON M7A 2C4
416-327-4327, 800-268-1153

Ontario Review Board, 151 Bloor St. West, 10th Fl., Toronto, ON M5S 2T5
416-327-8866, Fax: 416-327-8867, orb@ontario.ca

Pesticides Advisory Committee, 135 St. Clair Ave. West, 15th Fl., Toronto, ON M4V 1P5
416-314-9230, Fax: 416-314-9237

Trillium Gift of Life Network, #900, 522 University Ave., Toronto, ON M5G 1W7
416-363-4001, Fax: 416-363-4002, 800-263-2833

Prince Edward Island

BIO|FOOD|TECH, 101 Belvedere Ave., PO Box 2000, Charlottetown, PE C1A 7N8
902-368-5548, Fax: 902-368-5549, 877-368-5548, biofoodtech@biofoodtech.ca

Health PEI, 16 Garfield St., PO Box 2000, Charlottetown, PE C1A 7N8
902-368-6130, Fax: 902-368-6136, healthinput@gov.pe.ca

Prince Edward Island Department of Health & Wellness, 105 Rochford St. North, 4th Fl., PO Box 2000, Charlottetown, PE C1A 7N8
902-368-6414, Fax: 902-368-4121

Québec

Bureau du coroner, Édifice le Delta 2, #390, 2875, boul Laurier, Québec, QC G1V 5B1
418-643-1845, Fax: 418-643-6174, 866-312-7051, clientele.coroner@msp.gouv.qc.ca

Commission de la santé et de la sécurité du travail du Québec, 524, rue Bourdages, CP 1200 Terminus,Québec, QC G1K 7E2
Fax: 418-266-4015, 866-302-2778

Fonds de la recherche en santé du Québec, #800, 500, rue Sherbrooke ouest, Montréal, QC H3A 3C6
514-873-2114, Fax: 514-873-8768

Institut national d'excellence en santé et en services sociaux, 2535, boul Laurier, 5e étage, Québec, QC G1V 4M3
418-643-1339, Fax: 418-646-8349, inesss@inesss.qc.ca

Institut national de santé publique du Québec, 945, av Wolfe, Québec, QC G1V 5B3
418-650-5115, Fax: 418-646-9328, info@inspq.qc.ca

Ministère de la Santé et des Services sociaux, Direction des communications, 1075, ch Sainte-Foy, 16e étage, Québec, QC G1S 2M1
418-643-9395, Fax: 418-643-4768, regisseur.web@msss.gouv.qc.ca

Modernisation des centres hospitaliers universitaires de Montréal, CHUM, CUSM, CHU Sainte-Justine, #10.049, 2021, rue Union, Montréal, QC H3A 2S9
514-864-9883, Fax: 514-873-7362, info.construction3chu@msss.gouv.qc.ca

Régie de l'assurance maladie du Québec, 1125, Grande Allée ouest, Québec, QC G1S 1E7
418-646-4636, 800-561-9749

Secrétariat à l'accès aux services en langue anglaise et aux communautés ethnoculturelles, #840, 2021, av Union, Montréal, QC H3A 2S9
514-873-5163, Fax: 514-873-9876

Urgences-santé Québec, 3232, rue Bélanger, Montréal, QC H1Y 3H5
514-723-5600, info@urgences-sante.qc.ca

Saskatchewan

eHealth Saskatchewan, 2130 - 11th Ave., Regina, SK S4P 0J5
306-337-0600, 855-347-5465

Health Quality Council, Atrium Bldg., Innovation Place, 241, 111 Research Dr., Saskatoon, SK S7N 3R2
306-668-8810, Fax: 306-668-8820, info@hqc.sk.ca

Physician Recruitment Agency of Saskatchewan (SaskDocs), 309 - 4th Ave. North, Saskatoon, SK S7K 2L8
306-933-5000, Fax: 306-933-5115, 888-415-3627, info@saskdocs.ca

Saskatchewan Health, T.C. Douglas Bldg., 3475 Albert St., Regina, SK S4S 6X6
306-787-0146, 800-667-7766, info@health.gov.sk.ca

Saskatchewan Health Research Foundation, Atrium Bldg., Innovation Place, #253, 111 Research Dr., Saskatoon, SK S7N 3R2
306-975-1680, Fax: 306-975-1688, 800-975-1699

Yukon Territory

Yukon Health & Social Services, PO Box 2703, Whitehorse, YT Y1A 2C6
867-667-3673, Fax: 867-667-3096, 800-661-0408, hss@gov.yk.ca

HEALTH & SAFETY

Canadian Centre for Occupational Health & Safety, 135 Hunter St. East, Hamilton, ON L8N 1M5
905-572-2981, Fax: 905-572-4500, 800-668-4284

Canadian Coast Guard, Centennial Towers, #6S018, 200 Kent St., Ottawa, ON K1A 0E6
613-993-0999, Fax: 613-990-1866, info@dfo-mpo.gc.ca

Canadian Environmental Assessment Agency, Place Bell Canada, 160 Elgin St., 22nd Fl., Ottawa, ON K1A 0H3
613-957-0700, Fax: 613-957-0862, 866-582-1884, info@ceaa-acee.gc.ca

Canadian Food Inspection Agency, 1400 Merivale Rd., Ottawa, ON K1A 0Y9
613-225-2342, 800-442-2342

Department of National Defence & the Canadian Armed Forces, National Defence HQ, Major-General George R. Pearkes Bldg., 101 Colonel By Dr., Ottawa, ON K1A 0K2
613-995-2534, Fax: 613-992-4739, 888-995-2534, information@forces.gc.ca

Employment & Social Development Canada, 140 Promenade du Portage, Gatineau, QC K1A 0J9

Health Canada, Tunney's Pasture, Ottawa, ON K1A 0K9
613-957-2991, Fax: 613-941-5366, 866-225-0709, info@hc-sc.gc.ca

Public Health Agency of Canada, 130 Colonnade Rd., Ottawa, ON K1A 0K9

Public Safety Canada, 269 Laurier Ave. West, Ottawa, ON K1A 0P8
613-944-4875, Fax: 613-954-5186, 800-830-3118

Transportation Safety Board of Canada, 200, Promenade du Portage, 4th Fl., Gatineau, QC K1A 1K8
819-994-3741, Fax: 819-997-2239, 800-387-3557, communications@bst-tsb.gc.ca

Alberta

Alberta Emergency Management Agency, 2810 - 10303 Jasper Ave., Edmonton, AB T5J 3N6
780-422-9000, Fax: 780-644-1044, -310-0000, aema@gov.ab.ca

Alberta Health, PO Box 1360 Main,Edmonton, AB T5J 2N3
780-427-7164, -310-0000

Alberta Human Services, Office of the Minister, Legislature Building, #224, 10800 - 97 Ave., Edmonton, AB T5K 2B6
780-644-5135, 866-644-5135

Corporate Strategies & Services Division, Infrastructure Bldg., 6950 - 113 St., 2nd Fl., Edmonton, AB T6H 5V7

Occupational Health & Safety Council, Standard Life Centre, 10405 Jasper Ave., Edmonton, AB T5J 3N4
780-412-8742, Fax: 780-412-8701

Transportation Safety Board, North Office, Twin Atria Building, 4999 - 98 Ave., Main Fl., Edmonton, AB T6B 2X3
780-427-7178, Fax: 780-422-9739, -310-0000

Workers' Compensation Board, 9912 - 107 St., PO Box 2415, Edmonton, AB T5J 2S5
780-498-3999, Fax: 780-427-5863, 866-922-9221

British Columbia

British Columbia Centre for Disease Control, 655 West 12th Ave., Vancouver, BC V5Z 4R4
604-707-2400, Fax: 604-707-2401, admininfo@bccdc.ca

British Columbia Ministry of Health, 1515 Blanshard St., PO Box 9639 Prov Govt, Victoria, BC V8W 9P1
604-660-2421, 800-663-7100, hlth.health@gov.bc.ca

British Columbia Ministry of Technology, Innovation & Citizens' Services, PO Box 9068 Prov Govt, Victoria, BC V8W 9E2
250-952-7623, Fax: 250-952-7628, 800-663-7867, EnquiryBC@gov.bc.ca

Emergency Management BC, PO Box 9201 Prov Govt, Victoria, BC V8W 9J1
250-952-4913, Fax: 250-952-4871

Workers' Compensation Board of British Columbia, PO Box 5350 Terminal,Vancouver, BC V6B 5L5
604-276-3100, Fax: 604-276-3247, 888-621-7233

Manitoba

Advisory Council on Workplace Safety & Health, 401 York Ave., 2nd Fl., Winnipeg, MB R3C 0P8
204-945-3446, Fax: 204-948-2209, 866-888-8186, wshcompl@gov.mb.ca

Emergency Measures Organization, #1525, 405 Broadway Ave., Winnipeg, MB R3C 3L6
204-945-4772, Fax: 204-945-4929, 888-267-8298, emo@gov.mb.ca

Manitoba Health, Seniors & Active Living, #100, 300 Carlton St., Winnipeg, MB R3B 3M9
204-945-3744, 866-626-4862, mgi@gov.mb.ca

New Brunswick

New Brunswick Department of Health, HSBC Place, PO Box 5100, Fredericton, NB E3B 5G8
506-457-4800, Fax: 506-453-5243, Health.Sante@gnb.ca

New Brunswick Department of Post-Secondary Education, Training & Labour, Chestnut Complex, PO Box 6000, Fredericton, NB E3B 5H1
506-453-2597, Fax: 506-453-3618, dpetlinfo@gnb.ca

WorkSafeNB, 1 Portland St., PO Box 160, Saint John, NB E2L 3X9
506-632-2200, Fax: 506-632-4999, 800-222-9775, communications@ws-ts.nb.ca

Newfoundland & Labrador

Newfoundland & Labrador Department of Environment & Conservation, Confederation Bldg., West Block, 4th Fl., PO Box 8700, St. John's, NL A1B 4J6
709-729-2664, Fax: 709-729-6639, 800-563-6181, envcinquires@gov.nl.ca

Newfoundland & Labrador Department of Health & Community Services, West Block, Confederation Bldg., PO Box 8700, St. John's, NL A1B 4J6
709-729-4984, healthinfo@gov.nl.ca

Newfoundland & Labrador Workplace Health, Safety & Compensation Commission (WorkplaceNL), 146 - 148 Forest Rd., PO Box 9000, St. John's, NL A1A 3B8
709-778-1000, Fax: 709-738-1714, 800-563-9000, general.inquiries@whscc.nl.ca

Northwest Territories

Northwest Territories & Nunavut Workers' Safety & Compensation Commission, Centre Square Tower, 5022 - 49th St., 5th Fl., PO Box 8888, Yellowknife, NT X1A 2R3
867-920-3888, Fax: 867-873-4596, 800-661-0792

Northwest Territories Department of Health & Social Services, 5015 - 49th St., PO Box 1320, Yellowknife, NT X1A 2L9
Fax: 867-873-0306

Nova Scotia

Emergency Management Office, PO Box 2581, Halifax, NS B3J 3N5
902-424-5620, Fax: 902-424-5376, 866-424-5620, emo@gov.ns.ca

Nova Scotia Department of Health & Wellness, Barrington Tower., 1894 Barrington St., PO Box 488, Halifax, NS B3J 2R8
902-424-5818, 800-387-6665

Nova Scotia Department of Labour & Advanced Education, 5151 Terminal Rd., 6th Fl., PO Box 697, Halifax, NS B3J 2T8
902-424-5301, Fax: 902-424-2203

Nunavut

Nunavut Emergency Management, PO Box 1000 700, Iqaluit, NU X0A 0H0
867-975-5403, Fax: 867-979-4221, 800-693-1666

Ontario

Emergency Management Ontario, 77 Wellesley St. West, PO Box 222, Toronto, ON M7A 1N3
416-314-3723, Fax: 416-314-3758, 877-314-3723

Ontario Ministry of Government & Consumer Services, Mowat Block, 900 Bay St., 6th Fl., Toronto, ON M7A 1L2
416-212-2665, 844-286-8404

Ontario Ministry of Health & Long-Term Care, Hepburn Block, 80 Grosvenor St., 10th Fl, Toronto, ON M7A 2C4
416-327-4327, 800-268-1153

Ontario Ministry of Labour, 400 University Ave., 14th Fl., Toronto, ON M7A 1T7
416-326-7160, 800-531-5551

Road User Safety Division, Bldg A, #191, 1201 Wilson Ave., Downsview, ON M3M 1J8
416-235-2999, Fax: 416-235-4153

Prince Edward Island

Prince Edward Island Department of Health & Wellness, 105 Rochford St. North, 4th Fl., PO Box 2000, Charlottetown, PE C1A 7N8
902-368-6414, Fax: 902-368-4121

Prince Edward Island Workers Compensation Board, 14 Weymouth St., PO Box 757, Charlottetown, PE C1A 7L7
902-368-5680, Fax: 902-368-5696, 800-237-5049

Québec

Commission de la santé et de la sécurité du travail du Québec, 524, rue Bourdages, CP 1200 Terminus,Québec, QC G1K 7E2
Fax: 418-266-4015, 866-302-2778

Ministère de la Santé et des Services sociaux, Direction des communications, 1075, ch Sainte-Foy, 16e étage, Québec, QC G1S 2M1
418-643-9395, Fax: 418-643-4768, regisseur.web@msss.gouv.qc.ca

Ministère de la Sécurité publique, Tour des Laurentides, 2525, boul Laurier, 5e étage, Québec, QC G1V 2L2
418-646-6777, Fax: 418-643-0275, 866-644-6826

Ministère du Travail, de l'Emploi et de la Solidarité sociale, 200, ch Sainte-Foy, 5e étage, Québec, QC G1R 5S1
418-644-4545, Fax: 418-528-0559, 877-644-4545

Saskatchewan

Emergency Management & Fire Safety, 1855 Victoria Ave., 5th Fl., Regina, SK S4P 3T2
306-787-3774, Fax: 306-787-7107, 866-757-5911

Saskatchewan Health, T.C. Douglas Bldg., 3475 Albert St., Regina, SK S4S 6X6
306-787-0146, 800-667-7766, info@health.gov.sk.ca

Saskatchewan Labour Relations & Workplace Safety, #300, 1870 Albert St., Regina, SK S4P 4W1
306-787-7404, webmaster@lab.gov.sk.ca

Yukon Territory

Emergency Measures Organization, Whitehorse Airport, Combined Services Bldg., 2nd Fl., 60 Norseman Rd., Whitehorse, YT Y1A 2C6
867-667-5220, Fax: 867-393-6266, 800-661-0408, emo.yukon@gov.yk.ca

Emergency Medical Services, Yukon Electrical Bldg., #200, 1100 First Ave., Whitehorse, YT Y1A 6K6

Yukon Health & Social Services, PO Box 2703, Whitehorse, YT Y1A 2C6
867-667-3673, Fax: 867-667-3096, 800-661-0408, hss@gov.yk.ca

Yukon Workers' Compensation Health & Safety Board, 401 Strickland St., Whitehorse, YT Y1A 5N8
867-667-5645, Fax: 867-393-6279, 800-661-0443, worksafe@gov.yk.ca

HEALTH CARE INSURANCE

Health Canada, Tunney's Pasture, Ottawa, ON K1A 0K9
613-957-2991, Fax: 613-941-5366, 866-225-0709, info@hc-sc.gc.ca

British Columbia

Medical Services Commission, PO Box 9652 Prov Govt, Victoria, BC V8W 9P4
250-952-3073, Fax: 250-952-3133

Newfoundland & Labrador

Newfoundland & Labrador Department of Health & Community Services, West Block, Confederation Bldg., PO Box 8700, St. John's, NL A1B 4J6
709-729-4984, healthinfo@gov.nl.ca

Northwest Territories

Northwest Territories Department of Health & Social Services, 5015 - 49th St., PO Box 1320, Yellowknife, NT X1A 2L9
Fax: 867-873-0306

Nunavut

Nunavut Territory Department of Health, PO Box 1000 1000, Iqaluit, NU X0A 0H0
867-975-5700, Fax: 867-975-5705, 800-661-0833

Ontario

Health Services Information & Information Technology Cluster, 56 Wellesley St. West, 10th Fl., Toronto, ON M5S 2S3
416-314-0234, Fax: 416-314-4182

Prince Edward Island

Prince Edward Island Department of Health & Wellness, 105 Rochford St. North, 4th Fl., PO Box 2000, Charlottetown, PE C1A 7N8
902-368-6414, Fax: 902-368-4121

Québec

Régie de l'assurance maladie du Québec, 1125, Grande Allée ouest, Québec, QC G1S 1E7
418-646-4636, 800-561-9749

HEALTH SERVICES

See Also: Health Care Insurance; Occupational Safety

Canadian Centre for Occupational Health & Safety, 135 Hunter St. East, Hamilton, ON L8N 1M5
905-572-2981, Fax: 905-572-4500, 800-668-4284

Canadian Institutes of Health Research, 160 Elgin St., 9th Fl., Ottawa, ON K1A 0W9
613-941-2672, Fax: 613-954-1800, 888-603-4178, support@cihr-irsc.gc.ca

Health Canada, Tunney's Pasture, Ottawa, ON K1A 0K9
613-957-2991, Fax: 613-941-5366, 866-225-0709, info@hc-sc.gc.ca

Networks of Centres of Excellence of Canada, 350 Albert Street, 16th Fl., Ottawa, ON K1A 1H5
613-995-6010, Fax: 613-992-7356, info@nce-rce.gc.ca

Public Health Agency of Canada, 130 Colonnade Rd., Ottawa, ON K1A 0K9

Ste-Anne's Hospital, 305 boul des Anciens-Combattants, Sainte-Anne-de-Bellevue, QC H9X 1Y9
514-457-3440, 800-361-9287, steanne@vac-acc.gc.ca

Veterans Affairs Canada, 161 Grafton St., PO Box 7700, Charlottetown, PE C1A 8M9
866-522-2122, information@vac-acc.gc.ca

Alberta

Alberta Health, PO Box 1360 Main,Edmonton, AB T5J 2N3
780-427-7164, -310-0000

Alberta Health Advocates, Centre West Bldg., 10035 - 108 St., 12th Fl., Edmonton, AB T5J 3E1
780-422-1812, Fax: 780-422-0695, -310-0000, healthadvocates@gov.ab.ca

Alberta Seniors & Housing, PO Box 3100, Edmonton, AB T5J 4W3
780-644-9992, Fax: 780-422-5954, 877-644-9992

British Columbia

British Columbia Centre for Disease Control, 655 West 12th Ave., Vancouver, BC V5Z 4R4
604-707-2400, Fax: 604-707-2401, admininfo@bccdc.ca

British Columbia Ministry of Health, 1515 Blanshard St., PO Box 9639 Prov Govt, Victoria, BC V8W 9P1
604-660-2421, 800-663-7100, hlth.health@gov.bc.ca

Medical Services Commission, PO Box 9652 Prov Govt, Victoria, BC V8W 9P4
250-952-3073, Fax: 250-952-3133

Manitoba

Manitoba Health Appeal Board, #102, 500 Portage Ave., Winnipeg, MB R3C 3X1
204-945-5408, Fax: 204-948-2024, 866-744-3257, appeals@gov.mb.ca

Manitoba Health, Seniors & Active Living, #100, 300 Carlton St., Winnipeg, MB R3B 3M9
204-945-3744, 866-626-4862, mgi@gov.mb.ca

Manitoba Healthy Child Office, 332 Bannatyne Ave., 3rd Fl., Winnipeg, MB R3A 0E2
204-945-2266, 888-848-0140, healthychild@gov.mb.ca

New Brunswick

New Brunswick Department of Health, HSBC Place, PO Box 5100, Fredericton, NB E3B 5G8
506-457-4800, Fax: 506-453-5243, Health.Sante@gnb.ca

Senior & Healthy Aging Secretariat, Sartain MacDonald Bldg., 4th Fl., PO Box 6000, Fredericton, NB E3B 5H1
506-453-2001, Fax: 506-453-2164, seniors@gnb.ca

Newfoundland & Labrador

Central Regional Health Authority, 21 Carmelite Rd., Grand Falls-Windsor, NL A2A 1Y4
888-799-2272, client.relations@centralhealth.nl.ca

Eastern Regional Health Authority, Health Sciences Centre, #1345, Prince Philip Dr., Level 1, St. John's, NL A1B 3V6
709-777-6500, Fax: 709-364-6460, 877-444-1399, client.relations@easternhealth.ca

Health Research Ethics Authority, #200, 95 Bonaventure Ave., 2nd Fl., St. John's, NL A1B 2X5
709-777-6974, Fax: 709-777-8776, info@hrea.ca

Labrador-Grenfell Regional Health Authority, Administration Bldg., PO Box 7000 C, Happy Valley-Goose Bay, NL A0P 1C0
709-897-2267, Fax: 709-896-4032

Newfoundland & Labrador Centre for Health Information, 70 O'Leary Ave., St. John's, NL A1B 2C7
709-752-6000, Fax: 709-752-6011, 877-752-6006, communications@nlchi.nl.ca

Newfoundland & Labrador Department of Health & Community Services, West Block, Confederation Bldg., PO Box 8700, St. John's, NL A1B 4J6
709-729-4984, healthinfo@gov.nl.ca

Newfoundland & Labrador Department of Seniors, Wellness & Social Development, PO Box 8700, St. John's, NL A1B 4J6
709-729-0862, Fax: 709-729-0870, SWSDInfo@gov.nl.ca

Newfoundland & Labrador Health Boards Association, Beothuck Bldg., 20 Crosbie Pl., 2nd Fl., St. John's, NL A1B 3Y8
709-364-7701, Fax: 709-364-6460

Western Regional Health Authority, Corporate Office, 1 Brookfield Ave., Corner Brook, NL A2H 6J7
709-637-5000

Northwest Territories

Northwest Territories Department of Health & Social Services, 5015 - 49th St., PO Box 1320, Yellowknife, NT X1A 2L9
Fax: 867-873-0306

Nova Scotia

Nova Scotia Department of Health & Wellness, Barrington Tower., 1894 Barrington St., PO Box 488, Halifax, NS B3J 2R8
902-424-5818, 800-387-6665

Nunavut
Nunavut Territory Department of Health, PO Box 1000 1000, Iqaluit, NU X0A 0H0
867-975-5700, Fax: 867-975-5705, 800-661-0833
Ontario
Health Services Information & Information Technology Cluster, 56 Wellesley St. West, 10th Fl., Toronto, ON M5S 2S3
416-314-0234, Fax: 416-314-4182
Prince Edward Island
Health PEI, 16 Garfield St., PO Box 2000, Charlottetown, PE C1A 7N8
902-368-6130, Fax: 902-368-6136, healthinput@gov.pe.ca
Prince Edward Island Department of Health & Wellness, 105 Rochford St. North, 4th Fl., PO Box 2000, Charlottetown, PE C1A 7N8
902-368-6414, Fax: 902-368-4121
Québec
Institut national de santé publique du Québec, 945, av Wolfe, Québec, QC G1V 5B3
418-650-5115, Fax: 418-646-9328, info@inspq.qc.ca
Ministère de la Santé et des Services sociaux, Direction des communications, 1075, ch Sainte-Foy, 16e étage, Québec, QC G1S 2M1
418-643-9395, Fax: 418-643-4768, regisseur.web@msss.gouv.qc.ca
Saskatchewan
eHealth Saskatchewan, 2130 - 11th Ave., Regina, SK S4P 0J5
306-337-0600, 855-347-5465
Physician Recruitment Agency of Saskatchewan (SaskDocs), 309 - 4th Ave. North, Saskatoon, SK S7K 2L8
306-933-5000, Fax: 306-933-5115, 888-415-3627, info@saskdocs.ca
Saskatchewan Health, T.C. Douglas Bldg., 3475 Albert St., Regina, SK S4S 6X6
306-787-0146, 800-667-7766, info@health.gov.sk.ca
Saskatchewan Health Research Foundation, Atrium Bldg., Innovation Place, #253, 111 Research Dr., Saskatoon, SK S7N 3R2
306-975-1680, Fax: 306-975-1688, 800-975-1699

HERITAGE RESOURCES

See Also: Land Resources; Parks
Canadian Heritage, 15 Eddy St., Gatineau, QC K1A 0M5
819-997-0055, 866-811-0055, PCH.info-info.PCH@canada.ca
Parks Canada, National Office, 30 Victoria St., Gatineau, QC J8X 0B3
819-420-9486, 888-773-8888, information@pc.gc.ca
Alberta
Government House Foundation, 12845 - 102 Ave. NW, Edmonton, AB T5N 0M6
780-427-2281, Fax: 780-422-6508
Manitoba
Heritage Grants Advisory Council, c/o Heritage Grants Program, #330, 213 Notre Dame Ave., Winnipeg, MB R3B 1N3
204-945-2213, Fax: 204-948-2086
Manitoba Heritage Council, 213 Notre Dame Ave., Main Fl., Winnipeg, MB R3B 1N3
204-945-2118, Fax: 204-948-2384, hrb@gov.mb.ca
Newfoundland & Labrador
Heritage Foundation of Newfoundland & Labrador, The Newman Bldg., 1 Springdale St., PO Box 5171, St. John's, NL A1C 5V5
709-739-1892, Fax: 709-739-5413, 888-739-1892, info@heritagefoundation.ca
Nunavut
Nunavut Territory Department of Culture & Heritage, PO Box 1000 800, Iqaluit, NU X0A 0H0
867-975-5500, Fax: 867-975-5504, 866-934-2035
Ontario
Ontario Heritage Trust, 10 Adelaide St. East, Toronto, ON M5C 1J3
416-325-5000, Fax: 416-325-5071
Ontario Ministry of Tourism, Culture & Sport, Hearst Block, 900 Bay St., 9th Fl., Toronto, ON M7A 2E1
416-326-9326, Fax: 416-314-7854, 888-997-9015
Québec
Commission des biens culturels du Québec, Bloc A-RC, 225, Grande Allée est, Québec, QC G1R 5G5
418-643-8378, Fax: 418-643-8591, info@cbcq.gouv.qc.ca
Saskatchewan
Provincial Capital Commission, 4607 Dewdney Ave., Regina, SK S4T 1B7
306-787-9261
Saskatchewan Archives Board, #401, 1870 Albert St., PO Box 1665, Regina, SK S4P 3C6
306-787-4068, Fax: 306-787-1197
Saskatchewan Heritage Foundation, 3211 Albert St., 1st Fl., Regina, SK S4S 5W6
306-787-8600, Fax: 306-787-0069
Wanuskewin Heritage Park, RR#4 Penner Rd., Saskatoon, SK S7K 3J7
306-931-6767, Fax: 306-931-4522
Yukon Territory
Yukon Tourism & Culture, 100 Hanson St., PO Box 2703, Whitehorse, YT Y1A 2C6
867-667-5036, Fax: 867-667-3546

HISTORY & ARCHIVES

Canada Council for the Arts, 150 Elgin St., 2nd Fl., PO Box 1047, Ottawa, ON K1P 5V8
613-566-4414, Fax: 613-566-4390, 800-263-5588, info@canadacouncil.ca
Library & Archives Canada, 395 Wellington St., Ottawa, ON K1A 0N4
613-996-5115, Fax: 613-995-6274, 866-578-7777
Library of Parliament, Parliamentary Buildings, Ottawa, ON K1A 0A9
613-992-4793, 866-599-4999, info@parl.gc.ca
New Brunswick
Kings Landing Historical Settlement, 5804 Rte 102, Prince William, NB E6K 0A5
506-363-4999, Fax: 506-363-4989, info.kingslanding@gnb.ca
Ontario
Information, Privacy & Archives Division, 134 Ian Macdonald Blvd., Toronto, ON M7A 2C5
416-327-1600, Fax: 416-327-1999, 800-668-9933
Québec
Bibliothèque et Archives nationales du Québec (BAnQ), 2275, rue Holt, Montréal, QC H2G 3H1
514-873-1100, Fax: 514-873-9312, 800-363-9028
Saskatchewan
Saskatchewan Archives Board, #401, 1870 Albert St., PO Box 1665, Regina, SK S4P 3C6
306-787-4068, Fax: 306-787-1197

HOSPITALS

See Also: Health Care Insurance
Ste-Anne's Hospital, 305 boul des Anciens-Combattants, Sainte-Anne-de-Bellevue, QC H9X 1Y9
514-457-3440, 800-361-9287, steanne@vac-acc.gc.ca
Alberta
Alberta Health, PO Box 1360 Main,Edmonton, AB T5J 2N3
780-427-7164, -310-0000
British Columbia
British Columbia Ministry of Health, 1515 Blanshard St., PO Box 9639 Prov Govt, Victoria, BC V8W 9P1
604-660-2421, 800-663-7100, hlth.health@gov.bc.ca
Hospital Appeal Board, 747 Fort St., 4th Fl., PO Box 9425 Prov Govt, Victoria, BC V8W 9V1
250-387-3464, Fax: 250-356-9923, hab@gov.bc.ca
Northwest Territories
Northwest Territories Department of Health & Social Services, 5015 - 49th St., PO Box 1320, Yellowknife, NT X1A 2L9
Fax: 867-873-0306
Nunavut
Nunavut Territory Department of Health, PO Box 1000 1000, Iqaluit, NU X0A 0H0
867-975-5700, Fax: 867-975-5705, 800-661-0833
Prince Edward Island
Prince Edward Island Department of Health & Wellness, 105 Rochford St. North, 4th Fl., PO Box 2000, Charlottetown, PE C1A 7N8
902-368-6414, Fax: 902-368-4121
Québec
Ministère de la Santé et des Services sociaux, Direction des communications, 1075, ch Sainte-Foy, 16e étage, Québec, QC G1S 2M1
418-643-9395, Fax: 418-643-4768, regisseur.web@msss.gouv.qc.ca

HOUSING

Canada Mortgage & Housing Corporation, 700 Montreal Rd., Ottawa, ON K1A 0P7
613-748-2000, Fax: 613-748-2098, 800-668-2642, chic@cmhc-schl.gc.ca
Canadian Centre for Housing Technology, c/o National Research Council Canada, Building M-20, 1200 Montreal Rd., Ottawa, ON K1A 0R6
British Columbia
British Columbia Housing Management Commission (BC Housing), #1701, 4555 Kingsway, Burnaby, BC V5H 4V8
604-433-1711, Fax: 604-439-4722, webeditor@bchousing.org
British Columbia Ministry of Natural Gas Development (& Responsible for Housing), PO Box 9052 Prov Govt, Victoria, BC V8W 9E2
250-953-0900, Fax: 250-953-0927
Building Code Appeal Board, c/o Building & Safety Standards Branch, PO Box 9844 Prov Govt, Victoria, BC V8W 1A4
250-387-3133, Fax: 250-387-8164, Building.Safety@gov.bc.ca
Homeowner Protection Office, c/o BC Housing, #650, 4789 Kingway, Burnaby, BC V5H 0A3
604-646-7050, Fax: 604-646-7051, 800-407-7757, hpo@hpo.bc.ca
Local Government, PO Box 9490 Prov Govt, Victoria, BC V8W 9N7
250-356-6575, Fax: 250-387-7973
Safety Standards Appeal Board, 614 Humboldt St., 4th Fl., PO Box 9844 Prov Govt, Victoria, BC V8W 9T2
250-387-4021, Fax: 250-356-6645
Manitoba
Manitoba Housing & Community Development, 352 Donald St., Winnipeg, MB R3B 2H8
204-945-4663, Fax: 204-948-2013, 800-661-4663, housing@gov.mb.ca
New Brunswick
New Brunswick Department of Social Development, Sartain MacDonald Bldg., 551 King St., PO Box 6000, Fredericton, NB E3B 5H1
506-453-2001, Fax: 506-453-2164, sd-ds@gnb.ca
Newfoundland & Labrador
Newfoundland & Labrador Housing Corporation, Sir Brian Dunfield Bldg., 2 Canada Dr., PO Box 220, St. John's, NL A1C 5J2
709-724-3000, Fax: 709-724-3250
Northwest Territories
Northwest Territories Housing Corporation, Scotia Centre, 5102 - 50th Ave., PO Box 2100, Yellowknife, NT X1A 2P6
867-767-9080, Fax: 867-873-9426, 844-698-4663
Nova Scotia
Cape Breton Island Housing Authority, 18 Dolbin St., PO Box 1372, Sydney, NS B1P 6K3
902-539-8520, Fax: 902-539-0330, 800-565-3135
Cobequid Housing Authority, 114 Victoria East, PO Box 753, Amherst, NS B4H 4B9
902-667-8757, Fax: 902-667-1686, 800-934-2445
Eastern Mainland Housing Authority, 161 Terra Cotta Dr., New Glasgow, NS B2H 6B6
902-752-1225, Fax: 902-752-1315, 800-933-2101
Housing Nova Scotia, #3, 3770 Kempt Rd., Halifax, NS B3K 4X8
902-424-8445
Nova Scotia Department of Municipal Affairs, Maritime Centre, 14 North, 1505 Barrington St., PO Box 216, Halifax, NS B3J 3K5
902-424-6642, 800-670-4357
Nunavut
Nunavut Housing Corporation, PO Box 480, Arviat, NU X0C 0E0
867-857-3000, Fax: 867-857-3040
Nunavut Territory Department of Community & Government Services, W.G. Brown Bldg., 4th Fl., PO Box 1000 700, Iqaluit, NU X0A 0H0
867-975-5400, Fax: 867-975-5305
Ontario
Housing Division, College Park, 777 Bay St., 16th Fl., Toronto, ON M5G 2E5
416-585-6738, Fax: 416-585-6800
Ontario Ministry of Housing, College Park, 777 Bay St., 17th Fl., Toronto, ON M5G 2E5
416-585-6500, Fax: 416-585-4035, mininfo@ontario.ca
Québec
Société d'habitation du Québec, Aile St-Amable, 1054, rue Louis-Alexandre-Taschereau, 3e étage, Québec, QC G1R 5E7
Fax: 418-643-2533, 800-463-4315
Yukon Territory
Yukon Housing Corporation, 410G Jarvis St., PO Box 2703, Whitehorse, YT Y1A 2H5
867-667-5759, Fax: 867-667-3664, 800-661-0408, ykhouse@housing.yk.ca

HUMAN RIGHTS

See Also: Boards of Review
Canadian Human Rights Commission, 344 Slater St., 8th Fl., Ottawa, ON K1A 1E1
Fax: 613-996-9661, 888-214-1090, info.com@chrc-ccdp.gc.ca
Canadian Human Rights Tribunal, 160 Elgin St., 11th Fl., Ottawa, ON K1A 1J4
613-995-1707, Fax: 613-995-3484, registrar@chrt-tcdp.gc.ca
Canadian Museum for Human Rights, 85 Israel Asper Way, Winnipeg, MB R3C 0L5
204-289-2000, Fax: 204-289-2001, 877-877-6037, info@humanrights.ca
National Aboriginal Initiative, #750, 175 Hargrave St., Winnipeg, MA RC3 3R8
204-983-2189, Fax: 204-983-6132, 866-772-4880

Alberta
Alberta Human Rights Commission, Northern Regional Office, Standard Life Centre, #800, 10405 Jasper Ave., Edmonton, AB T5J 4R7
780-427-7661, Fax: 780-427-6013, 800-232-7215, humanrights@gov.ab.ca

British Columbia
British Columbia Human Rights Tribunal, #1170, 605 Robson St., Vancouver, BC V6B 5J3
604-775-2000, Fax: 604-775-2020, 888-440-8844, BCHumanRightsTribunal@gov.bc.ca

Manitoba
Manitoba Human Rights Commission, #700, 175 Hargrave St., Winnipeg, MB R3C 3R8
204-945-3007, Fax: 204-945-1292, 888-884-8681, hrc@gov.mb.ca

New Brunswick
New Brunswick Human Rights Commission, Barry House, PO Box 6000, Fredericton, NB E3B 5H1
506-453-2301, Fax: 506-453-2653, 888-471-2233, hrc.cdp@gnb.ca

Newfoundland & Labrador
Newfoundland & Labrador Human Rights Commission, The Beothuk Bldg., 21 Crosbie Pl., PO Box 8700, St. John's, NL A1B 4J6
709-729-2709, Fax: 709-729-0790, 800-563-5808, humanrights@gov.nl.ca

Nova Scotia
Nova Scotia Human Rights Commission, Park Lane Terraces, #305, 5657 Spring Garden Rd., PO Box 2221, Halifax, NS B3J 3C4
902-424-4111, Fax: 902-424-0596, 877-269-7699, hrcinquiries@novascotia.ca

Ontario
Ontario Human Rights Commission, #900, 180 Dundas St. West, Toronto, ON M7A 2R9
416-326-9511, Fax: 416-314-4494, 800-387-9080, info@ohrc.on.ca

Prince Edward Island
Prince Edward Island Human Rights Commission, 53 Water St., PO Box 2000, Charlottetown, PE C1A 7N8
902-368-4180, Fax: 902-368-4236, 800-237-5031, contact@peihumanrights.ca

Québec
Commission des droits de la personne et des droits de la jeunesse, 360, rue Saint-Jacques, 2e étage, Montréal, QC H2Y 1P5
514-873-5146, Fax: 514-873-6032, 800-361-6477, accueil@cdpdj.qc.ca

Saskatchewan
Saskatchewan Human Rights Commission, Saskatoon Office, Sturdy Stone Bdg., #816, 122 - 3 Ave. North, 8th Fl., Saskatoon, SK S7K 2H6
306-933-5952, Fax: 306-933-7863, 800-667-9249, shrc@gov.sk.ca

Yukon Territory
Yukon Human Rights Commission, #101, 9010 Quartz St., Whitehorse, YT Y1A 2Z5
867-667-6226, Fax: 867-667-2662, 800-661-0535, humanrights@yhrc.yk.ca

HYDRO, ELECTRIC POWER

National Energy Board, 517 - 10 Ave. SW, Calgary, AB T2R 0A8
403-292-4800, Fax: 403-292-5503, 800-899-1265

Alberta
Alberta Energy Regulator, #1000, 250 - 5 St. SW, Calgary, AB T2P 0R4
403-297-8311, Fax: 403-297-7336, 855-297-8311, inquiries@aer.ca
Alberta Utilities Commission, Fifth Avenue Place, 425 - 1st St. SW, 4th Fl., Calgary, AB T2P 3L8
403-592-8845, Fax: 403-592-4406, -310-0000, info@auc.ab.ca

British Columbia
British Columbia Hydro, 6911 Southpoint Dr., Burnaby, BC V3N 4X8
604-224-9376, 800-224-9376
Columbia Power Corporation, #200, 445 - 13th Ave., Castlegar, BC V1N 1G1
250-304-6060, Fax: 250-304-6083, cpc.info@columbiapower.org
Powertech Labs Inc., 12388 - 88 Ave., Surrey, BC V8W 7R7
604-590-7500, Fax: 604-590-6611

Manitoba
Manitoba Hydro, 360 Portage Ave., PO Box 815 Main,Winnipeg, MB R3C 2P4
204-480-5900, Fax: 204-360-6155, 888-624-9376, publicaffairs@hydro.mb.ca

Newfoundland & Labrador
Churchill Falls (Labrador) Corporation Limited, Hydro Place, 500 Columbus Dr., PO Box 12500, St. John's, NL A1B 4K7
709-737-1859, Fax: 709-737-1816
Nalcor Energy, 500 Columbus Dr., St. John's, NL A1E 2B2
709-737-1400, Fax: 709-737-1800, info@nalcorenergy.com
Newfoundland & Labrador Hydro, Hydro Place, 500 Columbus Dr., PO Box 12400, St. John's, NL A1B 4K7
709-737-1400, Fax: 709-737-1800, 888-737-1296, hydro@nlh.nl.ca
Twin Falls Power Corporation, PO Box 12500, St. John's, NL A1B 3T5

Northwest Territories
Northwest Territories Power Corporation, 4 Capital Dr., Hay River, NT X0E 1G2
867-874-5200, info@ntpc.com

Nova Scotia
Nova Scotia Utility & Review Board, Summit Place, 1601 Lower Water St., 3rd Fl., PO Box 1692 M,Halifax, NS B3J 3S3
902-424-4448, Fax: 902-424-3919, 855-442-4448, board@novascotia.ca

Ontario
Hydro One Inc., North Tower, 483 Bay St., 15th Fl., Toronto, ON M5G 2P5
416-345-5000, Fax: 905-944-3251, 877-955-1155, customercommunications@hydroone.com
Independent Electricity System Operator, #1600, 120 Adelaide St. West, Toronto, ON M5H 1T1
905-403-6900, Fax: 905-403-6921, 888-448-7777, customer.relations@ieso.ca
Ontario Power Generation, 700 University Ave., Toronto, ON M5G 1X6
416-592-2555, 877-592-2555, webmaster@opg.com

Québec
Coopérative régionale d'électricité de Saint-Jean-Baptiste-de-Rouville, 3113, rue Principale, Saint-Jean-Baptiste, QC J0L 1B0
450-467-5583, Fax: 450-467-0092, 800-267-5583, info@coopsjb.com
Hydro-Québec, 75, boul René-Lévesque ouest, 19e étage, Montréal, QC H2Z 1A4
514-289-2211
Société d'énergie de la Baie-James, #1200, 800, de Maisonneuve est, Montréal, QC H2L 4L8
514-286-2020

Saskatchewan
Saskatchewan Power Corporation (SaskPower), 2025 Victoria Ave., Regina, SK S4P 0S1
306-566-2121, 888-757-6937

IMMIGRATION

See Also: Citizenship
Immigration & Refugee Board of Canada, Canada Bldg, 344 Slater St., 12th Fl., Ottawa, ON K1A 0K1
613-995-6486, Fax: 613-943-1550, contact@irb-cisr.gc.ca
Immigration, Refugees & Citizenship, Jean Edmonds, South Tower, 365 Laurier Ave. West, Ottawa, ON K1A 1L1
888-242-2100
Passport Canada, Passport Canada Program, Gatineau, QC K1A 0G3
800-567-6868

Alberta
Alberta Labour, Legislature Bldg., #404, 10800 - 97 Ave., Edmonton, AB T5K 2B6
780-427-3731, 877-427-3731

British Columbia
BC Immigrant Investment Fund Ltd., #301, 865 Hornby St., Vancouver, BC V6Z 2G3
Fax: 250-952-0371

Manitoba
Manitoba Education & Training, #168, Legislative Bldg., 450 Broadway, Winnipeg, MB R3C 0V8
204-945-3720, Fax: 204-945-1291, minedu@leg.gov.mb.ca

Newfoundland & Labrador
Office of Immigration & Multiculturalism, c/o Department of Advanced Education & Skills, 100 Prince Phillip Dr., PO Box 8700, St. John's, NL A1B 4J6
709-729-6607, Fax: 709-729-7381, 888-632-4555, immigration@gov.nl.ca

Nova Scotia
Office of Immigration, #110A, 1741 Brunswick St., PO Box 1535, Halifax, NS B3J 2Y3
902-424-5230, Fax: 902-424-7936, 877-292-9597, nsnp@novascotia.ca

Prince Edward Island
Island Investment Development Inc., 94 Euston St., 2nd Fl., PO Box 1176, Charlottetown, PE C1A 7M8
902-620-3628, Fax: 902-368-5886, opportunitiespei@gov.pe.ca

Québec
Ministère de l'Immigration, de la Diversité et de l'Inclusion, Édifice Gérald-Godin, 360, rue McGill, Montréal, QC H2Y 2E9
514-864-9191, Fax: 514-864-2899, 877-864-9191

IMPORTS

See Also: Trade
Canada Border Services Agency, Headquarters, 191 Laurier Ave. West, Ottawa, ON K1A 0L8
800-461-9999, contact@cbsa.gc.ca
Canadian International Trade Tribunal, Standard Life Centre, 333 Laurier Ave. West, 15th Floor, Ottawa, ON K1A 0G7
613-990-2452, Fax: 613-990-2439, 855-307-2488, citt-tcce@tribunal.gc.ca
North American Free Trade Agreement (NAFTA) Secretariat, Canadian Section, 111 Sussex Dr., 5th Fl., Ottawa, ON K1N 1J1
343-203-4274, Fax: 613-992-9392, webmaster@nafta-alena.gc.ca

Québec
Revenu Québec, Direction des relations publiques/Communications, 3800, rue de Marly, Québec, QC G1X 4A5
418-652-6831, Fax: 418-646-0167, cabinet@revenuQuébec.ca

INCOME SECURITY

See Also: Social Services

Ontario
Ontario Ministry of Community & Social Services, Hepburn Block, 80 Grosvenor St., 6th Fl., Toronto, ON M7A 1E9
416-325-5666, Fax: 416-325-3347, 888-789-4199

Yukon Territory
Yukon Health & Social Services, PO Box 2703, Whitehorse, YT Y1A 2C6
867-667-3673, Fax: 867-667-3096, 800-661-0408, hss@gov.yk.ca

INCORPORATION OF COMPANIES & ASSOCIATIONS

Northwest Territories
Northwest Territories Department of Justice, 4903 - 49th St., PO Box 1320, Yellowknife, NT X1A 2L9
867-767-9256

Nova Scotia
Nova Scotia Department of Business, Centennial Building, #600, 1660 Hollis St., PO Box 2311, Halifax, NS B3J 3C8
902-424-0377, Fax: 902-424-0500, business@novascotia.ca
Registry of Joint Stock Companies, Maritime Centre, 1505 Barrington St., 9th Fl., PO Box 1529, Halifax, NS B3J 2Y4
902-424-7770, Fax: 902-424-4633, 800-225-8227, joint-stocks@gov.ns.ca

Nunavut
Legal Registries, PO Box 1000 570, Iqaluit, NU X0A 0H0
867-975-6590, Fax: 867-975-6594, Legal.Registries@gov.nu.ca

Ontario
ServiceOntario, College Park, 777 Bay St., 15th fl., Toronto, ON M7A 2J3
Fax: 416-326-1313, 800-267-8097

Saskatchewan
Courts & Tribunals Division, #1010, 1874 Scarth St., Regina, SK S4P 4B3
306-787-5359, Fax: 306-787-8737

Yukon Territory
Yukon Community Services, PO Box 2703, Whitehorse, YT Y1A 2C6
867-667-5811, Fax: 867-393-6295, 800-661-0408, inquiry@gov.yk.ca

INDUSTRIAL RELATIONS

See: Labour
Canada Industrial Relations Board, 240 Sparks St., 4th Fl. West, Ottawa, ON K1A 0X8
Fax: 613-995-9493, 800-575-9696

INDUSTRY

See Also: Business Development
Agriculture & Agri-Food Canada, 1341 Baseline Rd., Ottawa, ON K1A 0C5
613-773-1000, Fax: 613-773-1081, 855-773-0241, info@agr.gc.ca
Atlantic Canada Opportunities Agency, Blue Cross Centre, 644 Main St., 3rd Fl., PO Box 6051, Moncton, NB E1C 9J8
506-851-2271, Fax: 506-851-7403, 800-561-7862
Canada Mortgage & Housing Corporation, 700 Montreal Rd., Ottawa, ON K1A 0P7
613-748-2000, Fax: 613-748-2098, 800-668-2642, chic@cmhc-schl.gc.ca

Canadian Dairy Commission, Central Experimental Farm, NCC Driveway, Bldg. 55, 960 Carling Ave., Ottawa, ON K1A 0Z2
613-792-2000, Fax: 613-792-2009, cdc-ccl@cdc-ccl.gc.ca
Canadian Food Inspection Agency, 1400 Merivale Rd., Ottawa, ON K1A 0Y9
613-225-2342, 800-442-2342
Canadian Grain Commission, #600, 303 Main St., Winnipeg, MB R3C 3G8
204-984-0506, Fax: 204-983-2751, 800-853-6705, contact@grainscanada.gc.ca
Canadian International Trade Tribunal, Standard Life Centre, 333 Laurier Ave. West, 15th Floor, Ottawa, ON K1A 0G7
613-990-2452, Fax: 613-990-2439, 855-307-2488, citt-tcce@tribunal.gc.ca
Canadian Nuclear Safety Commission, 280 Slater St., PO Box 1046 B,Ottawa, ON K1P 5S9
613-995-5894, Fax: 613-995-5086, 800-668-5284, cnsc.information.ccsn@canada.ca
Canadian Radio-Television & Telecommunications Commission, Central Building, 1, Promenade du Portage, Les Terrasses de la Chaudière, Gatineau, QC J8X 4B1
819-997-0313, Fax: 819-994-0218, 877-249-2782
Canadian Space Agency, John H. Chapman Space Centre, 6767, rte de l'Aéroport, Saint-Hubert, QC J3Y 8Y9
450-926-4800, Fax: 450-926-4352, asc.info.csa@canada.ca
Communications Research Centre Canada, 3701 Carling Ave., PO Box 11490 H, Ottawa, ON K2H 8S2
613-991-3313, Fax: 613-998-5355, info@crc.gc.ca
Competition Bureau Canada, Place du Portage, Phase I, 50 Victoria St., Ottawa, ON K1A 0C9
819-997-4282, Fax: 819-997-0324, 800-348-5358
Competition Tribunal, Thomas D'Arcy McGee Bldg., #600, 90 Sparks St., Ottawa, ON K1P 5B4
613-957-3172, Fax: 613-957-3170, tribunal@ct-tc.gc.ca
Defence Construction Canada, Constitution Square, 350 Albert St., 19th Fl., Ottawa, ON K1A 0K3
613-998-9548, Fax: 613-998-1061, 800-514-3555, info@dcc-cdc.gc.ca
Earth Sciences Sector, 588 Booth St., Ottawa, ON K1A 0Y7
Export Development Canada, 150 Slater St., Ottawa, ON K1A 1K3
613-598-2500, Fax: 613-598-3811, 800-267-8510
Farm Credit Canada, 1800 Hamilton St., Regina, SK S4P 2B8
306-780-8100, Fax: 306-780-8919, 888-332-3301, csc@fcc-fac.ca
Farm Products Council of Canada, Building 59, Central Experimental Farm, 960 Carling Ave., Ottawa, ON K1A 0C6
613-759-1555, Fax: 613-759-1566, 855-611-1165, fpcc-cpac@agr.gc.ca
Fisheries & Oceans Canada, 200 Kent St., Ottawa, ON K1A 0E6
613-993-0999, Fax: 613-990-1866, info@dfo-mpo.gc.ca
Freshwater Fish Marketing Corporation, 1199 Plessis Rd., Winnipeg, MB R2C 3L4
204-983-6601, Fax: 204-983-6497, sandic@freshwaterfish.com
Global Affairs Canada, Enquiries Service, 125 Sussex Dr., Ottawa, ON K1A 0G2
613-944-4000, Fax: 613-996-9709, 800-267-8376
Indian Oil & Gas Canada, #100, 9911 Chiila Blvd., Tsuu T'ina (Sarcee), AB T2W 6H6
403-292-5625, Fax: 403-292-5618, ContactIOGC@inac-ainc.gc.ca
Innovation, Science & Economic Development Canada, C.D. Howe Building, 235 Queen St., Ottawa, ON K1A 0H5
613-954-5031, Fax: 613-954-2340, 800-328-6189, info@ic.gc.ca
National Energy Board, 517 - 10 Ave. SW, Calgary, AB T2R 0A8
403-292-4800, Fax: 403-292-5503, 800-899-1265
National Film Board of Canada, Operational Headquarters, Norman McLaren Building, 3155, ch de la Côte-de-Liesse, CP 1600 Centre-ville,Montréal, QC H3C 3H5
514-283-9000, 800-267-7710
National Research Council Canada, Building M-58, 1200 Montreal Rd., Ottawa, ON K1A 0R6
613-993-9101, Fax: 613-952-9907, 877-672-2672, info@nrc-cnrc.ca
Natural Resources Canada, 580 Booth St., Ottawa, ON K1A 0E4
343-292-6096, Fax: 613-992-7211
Natural Sciences & Engineering Research Council of Canada, Constitution Square, Tower II, 350 Albert St., Ottawa, ON K1A 1H5
613-995-4273, Fax: 613-992-5337, 855-275-2861
North American Free Trade Agreement (NAFTA) Secretariat, Canadian Section, 111 Sussex Dr., 5th Fl., Ottawa, ON K1N 1J1
343-203-4274, Fax: 613-992-9392, webmaster@nafta-alena.gc.ca
Office of the Superintendent of Financial Institutions, Kent Square, 255 Albert St., Ottawa, ON K1A 0H2
613-990-7788, Fax: 613-990-5591, 800-385-8647, information@osfi-bsif.gc.ca
Patented Medicine Prices Review Board, Standard Life Centre, #1400, 333 Laurier Ave. West, PO Box L40, Ottawa, ON K1P 1C1
613-954-8299, Fax: 613-952-7626, 877-861-2350, pmprb@pmprb-cepmb.gc.ca
PPP Canada, #630, 100 Queen St., Ottawa, ON K1P 1J9
613-947-9480, Fax: 613-947-2289, 877-947-9480, info@p3canada.ca
Spectrum, Information Technologies & Telecommunications, Journal Tower North, 300 Slater St., 20th Fl., Ottawa, ON K1A 0C8
613-998-0368, Fax: 613-952-1203
Standards Council of Canada, #600, 55 Metcalfe St., Ottawa, ON K1P 6L5
613-238-3222, Fax: 613-569-7808, info@scc.ca
Telefilm Canada, #500, 360, rue Saint-Jacques, Montréal, QC H2Y 1P5
514-283-6363, Fax: 514-283-8212, 800-567-0890, info@telefilm.gc.ca
Western Economic Diversification Canada, Canada Place, #1500, 9700 Jasper Ave. NW, Edmonton, AB T5J 4H7
780-495-4164, Fax: 780-495-4557, 888-338-9378

Alberta

Alberta Agriculture & Forestry, JG O'Donoghue Bldg., #100A, 7000 - 113th St., Edmonton, AB T6H 5T6
780-427-2727, -310-3276, duke@gov.ab.ca
Alberta Energy, North Petroleum Plaza, 9945 - 108 St., Edmonton, AB T5K 2G6
780-427-8050, Fax: 780-422-9522, -310-0000
Alberta Energy Regulator, #1000, 250 - 5 St. SW, Calgary, AB T2P 0R4
403-297-8311, Fax: 403-297-7336, 855-297-8311, inquiries@aer.ca
Alberta Grains Council, JG O'Donoghue Bldg., #305, 7000 - 113 St., Edmonton, AB T6H 5T6
780-427-7329, Fax: 780-422-9690
Alberta Innovates - Energy & Environmental Solutions, AMEC Place, #2540, 801 - 6th Ave. SW, Calgary, AB T2P 3W2
403-297-7089, Fax: 403-297-3638, ees@albertainnovates.ca
Alberta Livestock & Meat Agency, Ellwood Office Park South, #101, 1003 Ellwood Rd. SW, Edmonton, AB T6X 0B3
780-638-1699, Fax: 780-638-6495, info@almaltd.ca
Apprenticeship & Student Aid Division, Commerce Place, 10155 - 102 St., 6th Fl., Edmonton, AB T5J 4L5
Land Compensation Board, 1229 - 91 St. SW, Edmonton, AB T6X 1E9
780-427-2444, Fax: 780-427-5798, -310-000, srb.lcb@gov.ab.ca

British Columbia

Agricultural Land Commission, #133, 4940 Canada Way, Burnaby, BC V5G 4K6
604-660-7000, Fax: 604-660-7033, ALCBurnaby@Victoria1.gov.bc.ca
British Columbia Farm Industry Review Board, 780 Blanshard St., PO Box 9129 Prov Govt, Victoria, BC V8W 9B5
250-356-8945, Fax: 250-356-5131, firb@gov.bc.ca
British Columbia Hydro, 6911 Southpoint Dr., Burnaby, BC V3N 4X8
604-224-9376, 800-224-9376
British Columbia Ministry of Agriculture, PO Box 9043 Prov Govt, Victoria, BC V8W 9E2
888-221-7141, agriservicebc@gov.bc.ca
British Columbia Ministry of Energy & Mines (& Responsible for Core Review), PO Box 9060 Prov Govt, Victoria, BC V8W 9E3
British Columbia Ministry of Forests, Lands & Natural Resource Operations, PO Box 9049 Prov Govt, Victoria, BC V8W 9E2
800-663-7867, FLNRO.MediaRequests@gov.bc.ca
British Columbia Ministry of Jobs, Tourism, & Skills Training (& Responsible for Labour), PO Box 9846 Prov Govt, Victoria, BC V8W 9T2
EnquiryBC@gov.bc.ca
British Columbia Ministry of Technology, Innovation & Citizens' Services, PO Box 9068 Prov Govt, Victoria, BC V8W 9E2
250-952-7623, Fax: 250-952-7628, 800-663-7867, EnquiryBC@gov.bc.ca
British Columbia Utilities Commission, 900 Howe St., 6th Fl., PO Box 250, Vancouver, BC V6Z 2N3
604-660-4700, Fax: 604-660-1102, 800-663-1385, commission.secretary@bcuc.com
Columbia Power Corporation, #200, 445 - 13th Ave., Castlegar, BC V1N 1G1
250-304-6060, Fax: 250-304-6083, cpc.info@columbiapower.org
Financial Institutions Commission, #2800, 555 West Hastings, Vancouver, BC V6B 4N6
604-660-3555, Fax: 604-660-3365, 866-206-3030, FICOM@ficombc.ca
Forest Practices Board, PO Box 9905 Prov Govt, Victoria, BC V8W 9R1
250-213-4700, Fax: 250-213-4725, 800-994-5899, fpboard@gov.bc.ca
Insurance Council of British Columbia, #300, 1040 West Georgia St., PO Box 7, Vancouver, BC V6E 4H1
604-688-0321, Fax: 604-662-7767, 877-688-0321, info@insurancecouncilofbc.com
Oil & Gas Commission, #100, 10003 - 110 Ave., Fort St. John, BC V1J 6M7
250-794-5200, Fax: 250-794-5375
Real Estate Council of British Columbia, #900, 750 West Pender St., Vancouver, BC V6C 2T8
604-683-9664, Fax: 604-683-9017, 877-683-9664, info@recbc.ca

Manitoba

Advisory Council on Workplace Safety & Health, 401 York Ave., 2nd Fl., Winnipeg, MB R3C 0P8
204-945-3446, Fax: 204-948-2209, 866-888-8186, wshcompl@gov.mb.ca
Agricultural Societies, 1129 Queens Ave., Brandon, MB R7A 1L9
204-726-6195, Fax: 204-726-6260
Crown Corporations Council, #1130, 444 St. Mary Ave., Winnipeg, MB R3C 3T1
204-949-5270, Fax: 204-949-5283, info@crowncc.mb.ca
Farm Lands Ownership Board, #812, Norquay Bldg., 401 York Ave., Winnipeg, MB R3C 0P8
204-945-3149, Fax: 204-945-1489, 800-282-8069
Farm Machinery & Equipment Board, #812, 401 York Ave., Winnipeg, MB R3C 0P8
204-945-3854, Fax: 204-945-1489
Manitoba Agricultural Services Corporation, #100, 1525 First St. South, Brandon, MB R7A 7A1
204-726-6850, Fax: 204-726-6849, mailbox@masc.mb.ca
Manitoba Agriculture, Legislative Bldg., #165, 450 Broadway, Winnipeg, MB R3C 0V8
204-945-3722, Fax: 204-945-3470, minagr@leg.gov.mb.ca
Manitoba Bureau of Statistics, #824, 155 Carlton St., Winnipeg, MB R3C 3H9
204-945-2406
Manitoba Education & Training, #168, Legislative Bldg., 450 Broadway, Winnipeg, MB R3C 0V8
204-945-3720, Fax: 204-945-1291, minedu@leg.gov.mb.ca
Manitoba Growth, Enterprise & Trade, The Paris Building, 259 Portage Ave., 9th Fl., Winnipeg, MB R3B 3P4
204-945-1995, Fax: 204-945-2964
Manitoba Habitat Heritage Corporation, #200, 1555 St. James St., Winnipeg, MB R3H 1B5
204-784-4350, Fax: 204-784-7359
Manitoba Hydro, 360 Portage Ave., PO Box 815 Main,Winnipeg, MB R3C 2P4
204-480-5900, Fax: 204-360-6155, 888-624-9376, publicaffairs@hydro.mb.ca
Manitoba Indigenous & Municipal Relations, Legislative Bldg, #344, 450 Broadway, Winnipeg, MB R3C OV8
204-945-3719, Fax: 204-945-8374, anaweb@gov.mb.ca
Manitoba Minimum Wage Board, 614 - 401 York Ave., Winnipeg, MB R3C 0P8
204-945-8190, Fax: 204-948-2085, lmsd@gov.mb.ca
Manitoba Trade & Investment Corporation, #1100, 259 Portage Ave., Winnipeg, MB R3B 3P4
204-945-2466, Fax: 204-957-1793, 800-529-9981, mbtrade@gov.mb.ca
Taxicab Board, #200, 301 Weston St., Winnipeg, MB R3E 3H4
204-945-8919, Fax: 204-948-2315, taxicabboardoffice@gov.mb.ca
Tourism Secretariat, 213 Notre Dame Ave., 6th Fl., Winnipeg, MB R3B 1N3
204-945-0216
Workers Compensation Board of Manitoba, 333 Broadway Ave., Winnipeg, MB R3C 4W3
204-954-4321, Fax: 204-954-4999, 800-362-3340, wcb@wcb.mb.ca

New Brunswick

New Brunswick Department of Agriculture, Aquaculture & Fisheries, Agricultural Research Station (Experimental Farm), PO Box 6000, Fredericton, NB E3B 5H1
506-453-2666, Fax: 506-453-7170, 888-622-4742, DAAF-MAAP@gnb.ca
New Brunswick Department of Energy & Resource Development, Hugh John Flemming Forestry Centre, 1350 Regent St., Fredericton, NB E3C 2G6
506-453-3826, Fax: 506-444-4367, dnr_mrnweb@gnb.ca
New Brunswick Department of Environment & Local Government, Marysville Place, PO Box 6000, Fredericton, NB E3B 5H1
506-453-2690, Fax: 506-457-4994, elg/egl-info@gnb.ca
New Brunswick Department of Social Development, Sartain MacDonald Bldg., 551 King St., PO Box 6000, Fredericton, NB E3B 5H1
506-453-2001, Fax: 506-453-2164, sd-ds@gnb.ca
New Brunswick Farm Products Commission, c/o Department of Agriculture, Aquaculture & Fisheries, PO Box 6000, Fredericton, NB E3B 5H1
506-453-3647, Fax: 506-444-5969, DAAF-MAAP@gnb.ca

New Brunswick Liquor Corporation, 170 Wilsey Rd., PO Box 20787, Fredericton, NB E3B 5B8
506-452-6826, Fax: 506-462-2024, Receptionist@anbl.com
New Brunswick Research & Productivity Council, 921 College Hill Rd., Fredericton, NB E3B 6Z9
506-452-1212, Fax: 506-452-1395, 800-563-0844, info@rpc.ca
Regional Development Corporation, Chancery Place, PO Box 6000, Fredericton, NB E3B 5H1
506-453-2277, Fax: 506-453-7988
WorkSafeNB, 1 Portland St., PO Box 160, Saint John, NB E2L 3X9
506-632-2200, Fax: 506-632-4999, 800-222-9775, communications@ws-ts.nb.ca

Newfoundland & Labrador

Labour Relations Board, Beothuck Bldg., 20 Crosbie Pl., 5th Fl., PO Box 8700, St. John's, NL A1B 4J6
709-729-2707, Fax: 709-729-5738, lrb@gov.nl.ca
Nalcor Energy, 500 Columbus Dr., St. John's, NL A1E 2B2
709-737-1400, Fax: 709-737-1800, info@nalcorenergy.com
Newfoundland & Labrador Board of Commissioners of Public Utilities, Prince Charles Bldg., #E-210, 120 Torbay Rd., PO Box 21040, St. John's, NL A1A 5B2
709-726-8600, Fax: 709-726-9604, 866-782-0006, ito@pub.nf.ca
Newfoundland & Labrador Department of Fisheries & Aquaculture, Petten Bldg., 30 Strawberry Marsh Rd., PO Box 8700, St. John's, NL A1B 4J6
709-729-3723, Fax: 709-729-6082, fisheries@gov.nl.ca
Newfoundland & Labrador Department of Natural Resources, Natural Resources Bldg., 50 Elizabeth Ave., 7th Fl., PO Box 8700, St. John's, NL A1B 4J6
709-729-2920, Fax: 709-729-0059
Newfoundland & Labrador Housing Corporation, Sir Brian Dunfield Bldg., 2 Canada Dr., PO Box 220, St. John's, NL A1C 5J2
709-724-3000, Fax: 709-724-3250
Newfoundland & Labrador Hydro, Hydro Place, 500 Columbus Dr., PO Box 12400, St. John's, NL A1B 4K7
709-737-1400, Fax: 709-737-1800, 888-737-1296, hydro@nlh.nl.ca
Newfoundland & Labrador Liquor Corporation, 90 Kenmount Rd., PO Box 8750 A, St. John's, NL A1B 3V1
709-724-1100, Fax: 709-754-0321, info@nfliquor.com
Newfoundland & Labrador Municipal Financing Corporation, Confederation Bldg., PO Box 8700, St. John's, NL A1B 4J6
709-729-6686, Fax: 709-729-2095
Professional Fish Harvesters Certification Board, 368 Hamilton Ave., PO Box 8541, St. John's, NL A1B 3P2
709-722-8170, Fax: 709-722-8201, pfh@pfhcb.com

Northwest Territories

Northwest Territories Department of Environment & Natural Resources, #600, 5102 - 50 Ave., Yellowknife, NT X1A 3S8
867-767-9231
Northwest Territories Department of Industry, Tourism & Investment, PO Box 1320, Yellowknife, NT X1A 2L9
867-767-9002
Northwest Territories Housing Corporation, Scotia Centre, 5102 - 50th Ave., PO Box 2100, Yellowknife, NT X1A 2P6
867-767-9080, Fax: 867-873-9426, 844-698-4663
Northwest Territories Liquor Commission, #201, 31 Capital Dr., Hay River, NT X0E 1G2
867-874-8700, Fax: 867-874-8720
Northwest Territories Liquor Licensing Board, #204, 31 Capital Dr., Hay River, NT X0E 1G2
867-874-8715, Fax: 867-874-8722, 800-351-7770
Northwest Territories Power Corporation, 4 Capital Dr., Hay River, NT X0E 1G2
867-874-5200, info@ntpc.com

Nova Scotia

Crane Operators Appeal Board, 5151 Terminal Rd., 7th Fl., PO Box 697, Halifax, NS B3J 2T8
902-424-8595, Fax: 902-424-0217, fernanfs@gov.ns.ca
Elevators & Lifts Appeal Board, 5151 Terminal Rd., 7th Fl., PO Box 697, Halifax, NS B3J 2T8
902-424-8595, Fax: 902-424-0217
Innovacorp, #1400, 1801 Hollis St., Halifax, NS B3J 3N4
902-424-8670, Fax: 902-424-4679, 800-565-7051, info@innovacorp.ca
Nova Scotia Business Inc., World Trade & Convention Centre, #701, 1800 Argyle St., PO Box 2374, Halifax, NS B3J 3N8
902-424-6650, Fax: 902-424-5739, 800-260-6682, info@nsbi.ca
Nova Scotia Department of Agriculture, 1800 Argyle St., 6th Fl., PO Box 2223, Halifax, NS B3J 3C4
902-424-4560, Fax: 902-424-4671
Nova Scotia Department of Business, Centennial Building, #600, 1660 Hollis St., PO Box 2311, Halifax, NS B3J 3C8
902-424-0377, Fax: 902-424-0500, business@novascotia.ca
Nova Scotia Department of Natural Resources, Founder's Square, 1701 Hollis St., 3rd Fl., PO Box 698, Halifax, NS B3J 2T9
902-424-5935, Fax: 902-424-7735, 800-565-2224
Nova Scotia Farm Loan Board, PO Box 890, Truro, NS B2N 5G6
902-893-6506, Fax: 902-895-7693, FLBNS@gov.ns.ca
Nova Scotia Liquor Corporation, Bayers Lake Business Park, 93 Chain Lake Dr., Halifax, NS B3S 1A3
902-450-5874, 800-567-5874
Nova Scotia Utility & Review Board, Summit Place, 1601 Lower Water St., 3rd Fl., PO Box 1692 M,Halifax, NS B3J 3S3
902-424-4448, Fax: 902-424-3919, 855-442-4448, board@novascotia.ca
Power Engineers & Operators Appeal Committee, 5151 Terminal Rd., 7th Fl., PO Box 697, Halifax, NS B3J 2T8
902-424-8595, Fax: 902-424-0217
Trade Centre Limited, 1800 Argyle St., PO Box 955, Halifax, NS B3J 2V9
902-421-8686, Fax: 902-422-2922
Waterfront Development Corporation Ltd., The Cable Wharf, 1751 Lower Water St., 2nd Fl., Halifax, NS B3J 1S5
902-422-6591, Fax: 902-422-7582, info@wdcl.ca

Nunavut

Liquor Licensing Board, PO Box 1269, Iqaluit, NU X0A 0H0
867-975-6533, Fax: 867-975-6511, nllb@gov.nu.ca
Nunavut Territory Department of Economic Development & Transportation, Inuksugait Plaza, Bldg. 1104A, PO Box 1000 1500, Iqaluit, NU X0A 0H0
867-975-7800, Fax: 867-975-7870, 888-975-5999, edt@gov.nu.ca

Ontario

Agricorp, 1 Stone Rd. West, 3rd Fl., PO Box 3660 Central, Guelph, ON N1H 8M4
Fax: 519-826-4118, 888-247-4999, contact@agricorp.com
Agricultural Research Institute of Ontario, 1 Stone Rd. West, 2nd Fl., Guelph, ON N1G 4Y2
519-826-4554, 888-466-2372, research.omafra@ontario.ca
Building Code Commission, 777 Bay St., 2nd Fl., Toronto, ON M5G 2E5
416-585-6666, Fax: 416-585-7531, codeinfo@ontario.ca
Building Materials Evaluation Commission, 777 Bay St., 2nd Fl., Toronto, ON M5G 2E5
416-585-4234, Fax: 416-585-7531
Corporate Services Division, 56 Wellesley St., 4th Fl., Toronto, ON M7A 2E7
416-325-6866, Fax: 416-314-7014
Environmental Commissioner of Ontario, #605, 1075 Bay St., Toronto, ON M5S 2B1
416-325-3377, Fax: 416-325-3370, 800-701-6454, commissioner@eco.on.ca
Environmental Sciences & Standards Division, 135 St. Clair Ave. West, 14th Fl., Toronto, ON M4V 1P5
Fax: 416-314-6358
Health System Strategy & Policy Division, Hepburn Block, 80 Grosvenor St., 8th Fl., Toronto, ON M7A 1R3
416-327-8295, Fax: 416-327-5109
Hydro One Inc., North Tower, 483 Bay St., 15th Fl., Toronto, ON M5G 2P5
416-345-5000, Fax: 905-944-3251, 877-955-1155, customercommunications@hydroone.com
Independent Electricity System Operator, #1600, 120 Adelaide St. West, Toronto, ON M5H 1T1
905-403-6900, Fax: 905-403-6921, 888-448-7777, customer.relations@ieso.ca
Office of the Employer Advisor, #704, 151 Bloor St. West., Toronto, ON M5S 1S4
416-327-0020, Fax: 416-327-0726, 800-387-0774
Office of the Fairness Commissioner, #1201, 595 Bay St., Toronto, ON M7A 2B4
416-325-9380, Fax: 416-326-6081, 877-727-5365, ofc@ontario.ca
Ontario Media Development Corporation, South Tower, #501, 175 Bloor St. East, Toronto, ON M4W 3R8
416-314-6858, Fax: 416-314-6876, reception@omdc.on.ca
Ontario Ministry of Agriculture, Food & Rural Affairs, Ontario Government Bldg., 1 Stone Rd. West, Guelph, ON N1G 4Y2
519-826-3100, Fax: 519-826-4335, 888-466-2372, about.omafra@ontario.ca
Ontario Ministry of Economic Development & Growth, Hearst Block, 900 Bay St., 8th Fl., Toronto, ON M7A 2E1
416-325-6666, 800-268-7095
Ontario Ministry of Environment & Climate Change, Public Information Centre, Macdonald Block, 900 Bay St., 2nd Fl., Toronto, ON M7A 1N3
416-325-4000, Fax: 416-314-6713, 800-565-4923
Ontario Ministry of Government & Consumer Services, Mowat Block, 900 Bay St., 6th Fl., Toronto, ON M7A 1L2
416-212-2665, 844-286-8404
Ontario Ministry of Labour, 400 University Ave., 14th Fl., Toronto, ON M7A 1T7
416-326-7160, 800-531-5551
Ontario Ministry of Municipal Affairs, College Park, 777 Bay St., 17th Fl., Toronto, ON M5G 2E5
416-585-7000, Fax: 416-585-6470, mininfo@ontario.ca
Ontario Ministry of Natural Resources & Forestry, 300 Water St., PO Box 7000, Peterborough, ON K9J 8M5
800-667-1940
Ontario Ministry of Northern Development & Mines, 159 Cedar St., Sudbury, ON P3E 6A5
705-670-5755, Fax: 705-670-5818, 888-415-9845, ndmminister@ontario.ca
Ontario Ministry of Tourism, Culture & Sport, Hearst Block, 900 Bay St., 9th Fl., Toronto, ON M7A 2E1
416-326-9326, Fax: 416-314-7854, 888-997-9015
Ontario Power Generation, 700 University Ave., Toronto, ON M5G 1X6
416-592-2555, 877-592-2555, webmaster@opg.com
ServiceOntario, College Park, 777 Bay St., 15th fl., Toronto, ON M7A 2J3
Fax: 416-326-1313, 800-267-8097
Workplace Safety & Insurance Board, 200 Front St. West, Ground Fl., Toronto, ON M5V 3J1
416-344-1000, Fax: 416-344-4684, 800-387-0750

Prince Edward Island

Advisory Council on the Status of Women, Sherwood Business Centre, 161 St. Peter's Rd., Main Level, PO Box 2000, Charlottetown, PE C1A 7N8
902-368-4510, Fax: 902-368-3269, info@peistatusofwomen.ca
Agricultural Insurance Corporation, 29 Indigo Cres., PO Box 1600, Charlottetown, PE C1A 7N3
902-368-4842, Fax: 902-368-6677
Anne of Green Gables Licensing Authority Inc., 94 Euston St., PO Box 910, Charlottetown, PE C1A 7L9
902-368-5961
BIO|FOOD|TECH, 101 Belvedere Ave., PO Box 2000, Charlottetown, PE C1A 7N8
902-368-5548, Fax: 902-368-5549, 877-368-5548, biofoodtech@biofoodtech.ca
Charlottetown Area Development Corporation, 4 Pownal St., PO Box 786, Charlottetown, PE C1A 7L9
902-892-5341, Fax: 902-368-1935
Grain Elevators Corporation, 7 Gerald McCarville Dr., PO Box 250, Kensington, PE C0B 1M0
902-836-8935, Fax: 902-836-8926
Housing Services, Jones Bldg., 11 Kent St., 2nd Fl., PO Box 2000, Charlottetown, PE C1A 7N8
902-620-3777, Fax: 902-894-0242
Innovation PEI, 94 Euston St., PO Box 910, Charlottetown, PE C1A 7L9
902-368-6300, Fax: 902-368-6301, 800-563-3734, innovation@gov.pe.ca
Prince Edward Island Department of Agriculture & Fisheries, Jones Bldg., 11 Kent St., 5th Fl., PO Box 2000, Charlottetown, PE C1A 7N8
902-368-4880, Fax: 902-368-4857
Prince Edward Island Department of Economic Development & Tourism, PO Box 2000, Charlottetown, PE C1A 7N8
902-368-5540, Fax: 902-368-5277, tpswitch@gov.pe.ca
Prince Edward Island Department of Transportation, Infrastructure & Energy, Jones Bldg., 11 Kent St., 3rd Fl., PO Box 2000, Charlottetown, PE C1A 7N8
902-368-5100, Fax: 902-368-5395
Prince Edward Island Liquor Control Commission, 3 Garfield St., PO Box 967, Charlottetown, PE C1A 7M4
902-368-5710, Fax: 902-368-5735
Prince Edward Island Workers Compensation Board, 14 Weymouth St., PO Box 757, Charlottetown, PE C1A 7L7
902-368-5680, Fax: 902-368-5696, 800-237-5049
SkillsPEI, Atlantic Technology Centre, #212, 176 Great George St., Charlottetown, PE C1A 4K9
902-368-6290, Fax: 902-368-6340, 877-491-4766

Québec

Agence de l'efficacité énergétique, #B406, 5700, 4e av ouest, Québec, QC G1H 6R1
418-627-6379, Fax: 418-643-5828, 877-727-6655, efficaciteenergetique@mern.gouv.qc.ca
Centre de recherche industrielle du Québec, 333, rue Franquet, Québec, QC G1P 4C7
418-659-1550, Fax: 418-652-2251, 800-667-2386, infocriq@criq.qc.ca
Comité conjoint de chasse, de pêche et de piégeage, #C220, 383 rue Saint-Jacques, Montréal, QC H2Y 1N9
514-284-2151, Fax: 514-284-0039, cccppinfo@cccpp-hftcc.com
Commission de protection du territoire agricole du Québec, 200, ch Ste-Foy, 2e étage, Québec, QC G1R 4X6
418-643-3314, Fax: 418-643-2261, 800-667-5294, info@cptaq.gouv.qc.ca
Conseil consultatif du travail et de la main d'oeuvre, #17.100, 500, boul René-Lévesque ouest, Montréal, QC H2Z 1W7
514-873-2880, Fax: 514-873-1129, cctm@cctm.gouv.qc.ca

Financement-Québec, 12, rue Saint-Louis, 3e étage, Québec, QC G1R 5L3
418-691-2203, Fax: 418-644-6214, financement.regroupe@finances.gouv.qc.ca

Hydro-Québec, 75, boul René-Lévesque ouest, 19e étage, Montréal, QC H2Z 1A4
514-289-2211

La financière agricole de Québec, 1400, boul Guillaume-Couture, Lévis, QC G6W 8K7
418-838-5602, Fax: 418-833-3871, 800-749-3646, financiereagricole@fadq.qc.ca

Ministère de l'Agriculture, des Pêcheries et de l'Alimentation, 200, ch Sainte-Foy, Québec, QC G1R 4X6
418-380-2110, 888-222-6272

Ministère de la Culture et Communications, 225, Grande Allée est, Québec, QC G1R 5G5
888-380-8882

Ministère des Finances, 12, rue Saint-Louis, Québec, QC G1R 5L3
418-528-9323, Fax: 418-646-1631, info@finances.gouv.qc.ca

Ministère du Développement durable, de l'Environnement et de la Lutte contre les changements climatiques, Édifice Marie-Guyart, 675, boul René-Lévesque est, 29e étage, Québec, QC G1R 5V7
418-521-3830, Fax: 418-646-5974, 800-561-1616, info@mddefp.gouv.qc.ca

Ministère du Tourisme, #400, 900, boul René-Lévesque est, Québec, QC G1R 2B5
418-643-5959, Fax: 418-646-8723, 800-482-2433

Office de la sécurité du revenu des chasseurs et piègeurs cris, Édifice Champlain, #1100, 2700, boul Laurier, Québec, QC G1V 4K5
418-643-7300, Fax: 418-643-6803, 800-363-1560, courrier@osrcpc.ca

Régie des marchés agricoles et alimentaires du Québec, 201, boul Crémazie est, 5e étage, Montréal, QC H2M 1L3
514-873-4024, Fax: 514-873-3984, rmaaqc@rmaaq.gouv.qc.ca

Régie du bâtiment du Québec, 545, boul Crémazie est, 4e étage, Montréal, QC H2M 2V2
514-873-0976, Fax: 866-315-0106, 800-361-0761, crc@rbq.gouv.qc.ca

Société d'habitation du Québec, Aile St-Amable, 1054, rue Louis-Alexandre-Taschereau, 3e étage, Québec, QC G1R 5E7
Fax: 418-643-2533, 800-463-4315

Société de développement des entreprises culturelles, #800, 215, rue Saint-Jacques, Montréal, QC H2Y 1M6
514-841-2200, Fax: 514-841-8606, 800-363-0401, info@sodec.gouv.qc.ca

Société des alcools du Québec, 905, av De Lorimier, Montréal, QC H2K 3V9
514-254-2020, 866-873-2020, info@saq.com

Société du parc industriel et portuaire de Bécancour, 1000, boul Arthur-Sicard, Bécancour, QC G9H 2Z8
819-294-6656, Fax: 819-294-9020, spipb@spipb.com

Société québécoise de récupération et de recyclage, #411, 300, rue Saint-Paul, Québec, QC G1K 7R1
418-643-0394, Fax: 418-643-6507, 866-523-8290, info@recyc-Québec.gouv.qc.ca

Saskatchewan

Agri-Food Council, #302, 3085 Albert St., Regina, SK S4S 0B1
306-787-5978, Fax: 306-787-5134, corey.ruud@gov.sk.ca

Crown Investments Corporation of Saskatchewan, #400, 2400 College Ave., Regina, SK S4P 1C8
306-787-6851, Fax: 306-787-8125

Energy & Resources, 2101 Scarth St., Regina, SK S4P SH9
306-787-2528

Farm Stress Unit, 3085 Albert St., Regina, SK S4S 0B1
800-667-4442

Farmland Security Board, #315, 3988 Albert St., Regina, SK S4S 3R1
306-787-5047, Fax: 306-787-8599

Labour Relations Board, #1600, 1920 Broad St., Regina, SK S4P 3V2
306-787-2406, Fax: 306-787-2664

Prairie Agricultural Machinery Institute, 2215 - 8th Ave., PO Box 1150, Humboldt, SK S0K 2A0
306-682-5033, Fax: 306-682-5080, 800-567-7264, humboldt@pami.ca

Saskatchewan Agriculture, Walter Scott Bldg., 3085 Albert St., Regina, SK S4S 0B1
866-457-2377

Saskatchewan Crop Insurance Corporation, 484 Prince William Dr., PO Box 3000, Melville, SK S0A 2P0
306-728-7200, Fax: 306-728-7202, 888-935-0000, customer.service@scic.gov.sk.ca

Saskatchewan Environment, 3211 Albert St., 2nd Fl., Regina, SK S4S 5W6
306-787-2584, Fax: 306-787-9544, 800-567-4224, Centre.Inquiry@gov.sk.ca

Saskatchewan Lands Appeal Board, #315, 3085 Albert St., Regina, SK S4S 0B1
306-787-8861

Saskatchewan Liquor & Gaming Authority, 2500 Victoria Ave., PO Box 5054, Regina, SK S4P 3M3
306-787-5563, 800-667-7565, inquiry@slga.gov.sk.ca

Saskatchewan Power Corporation (SaskPower), 2025 Victoria Ave., Regina, SK S4P 0S1
306-566-2121, 888-757-6937

Saskatchewan Water Corporation (SaskWater), #200, 111 Fairford St. East, Moose Jaw, SK S6H 1C8
Fax: 306-694-3207, 888-230-1111, comm@saskwater.com

Saskatchewan Workers' Compensation Board, #200, 1881 Scarth St., Regina, SK S4P 4L1
306-787-4370, Fax: 306-787-4311, 800-667-7590, webmaster@wcbsask.com

SaskEnergy Incorporated, 1777 Victoria Ave., Regina, SK S4P 4K5
306-777-9225, 800-567-8899

Yukon Territory

Yukon Development Corporation, PO Box 2703 D-1, Whitehorse, YT Y1A 2C6
867-456-3837, Fax: 867-393-7167

Yukon Economic Development, #209, 212 Main St., F-1, Whitehorse, YT Y1A 2A9
867-393-7191, Fax: 867-393-6412, 800-661-0408, ecdev@gov.yk.ca

Yukon Environment, 10 Burns Rd., PO Box 2703 V-3A, Whitehorse, YT Y1A 2C6
867-667-5652, Fax: 867-393-7197, environment.yukon@gov.yk.ca

Yukon Housing Corporation, 410G Jarvis St., PO Box 2703, Whitehorse, YT Y1A 2H5
867-667-5759, Fax: 867-667-3664, 800-661-0408, ykhouse@housing.yk.ca

Yukon Liquor Corporation, 9031 Quartz Rd., Whitehorse, YT Y1A 4P9
867-667-5245, Fax: 867-393-6306, yukon.liquor@gov.yk.ca

Yukon Tourism & Culture, 100 Hanson St., PO Box 2703, Whitehorse, YT Y1A 2C6
867-667-5036, Fax: 867-667-3546

INDUSTRY & TRADE

Atlantic Canada Opportunities Agency, Blue Cross Centre, 644 Main St., 3rd Fl., PO Box 6051, Moncton, NB E1C 9J8
506-851-2271, Fax: 506-851-7403, 800-561-7862

Business Development Bank of Canada, #400, 5, Place Ville-Marie, Montréal, QC H3B 5E7
877-232-2269

Defence Construction Canada, Constitution Square, 350 Albert St., 19th Fl., Ottawa, ON K1A 0K3
613-998-9548, Fax: 613-998-1061, 800-514-3555, info@dcc-cdc.gc.ca

Export Development Canada, 150 Slater St., Ottawa, ON K1A 1K3
613-598-2500, Fax: 613-598-3811, 800-267-8510

Global Affairs Canada, Enquiries Service, 125 Sussex Dr., Ottawa, ON K1A 0G2
613-944-4000, Fax: 613-996-9709, 800-267-8376

Innovation, Science & Economic Development Canada, C.D. Howe Building, 235 Queen St., Ottawa, ON K1A 0H5
613-954-5031, Fax: 613-954-2340, 800-328-6189, info@ic.gc.ca

Market & Industry Services Branch, Tower 5, 1341 Baseline Rd., Ottawa, ON K1A 0C5
613-759-1000, Fax: 613-773-1711

Standards Council of Canada, #600, 55 Metcalfe St., Ottawa, ON K1P 6L5
613-238-3222, Fax: 613-569-7808, info@scc.ca

Western Economic Diversification Canada, Canada Place, #1500, 9700 Jasper Ave. NW, Edmonton, AB T5J 4H7
780-495-4164, Fax: 780-495-4557, 888-338-9378

British Columbia

British Columbia Ministry of International Trade (& Minister Responsible for Asia Pacific Strategy & Multiculturalism), PO Box 9063 Prov Gov,Victoria, BC V8W 9E2
250-953-0910, Fax: 250-953-0928

Timber Export Advisory Committee, PO Box 9514 Prov Govt, Victoria, BC V8W 9C2
250-387-8916, Fax: 250-387-5050

Manitoba

Manitoba Growth, Enterprise & Trade, The Paris Building, 259 Portage Ave., 9th Fl., Winnipeg, MB R3B 3P4
204-945-1995, Fax: 204-945-2964

New Brunswick

Regional Development Corporation, Chancery Place, PO Box 6000, Fredericton, NB E3B 5H1
506-453-2277, Fax: 506-453-7988

Northwest Territories

Northwest Territories Department of Environment & Natural Resources, #600, 5102 - 50 Ave., Yellowknife, NT X1A 3S8
867-767-9231

Nova Scotia

Nova Scotia Department of Agriculture, 1800 Argyle St., 6th Fl., PO Box 2223, Halifax, NS B3J 3C4
902-424-4560, Fax: 902-424-4671

Nova Scotia Department of Business, Centennial Building, #600, 1660 Hollis St., PO Box 2311, Halifax, NS B3J 3C8
902-424-0377, Fax: 902-424-0500, business@novascotia.ca

Pay Equity Commission, 5151 Terminal Rd., 6th Fl., PO Box 697, Halifax, NS B3J 2T8
902-424-8466, Fax: 902-424-0575

Workers' Compensation Board of Nova Scotia, 5668 South St., PO Box 1150, Halifax, NS B3J 2Y2
902-491-8999, 800-870-3331, info@wcb.gov.ns.ca

Ontario

Ontario Ministry of Economic Development & Growth, Hearst Block, 900 Bay St., 8th Fl., Toronto, ON M7A 2E1
416-325-6666, 800-268-7095

Ontario Ministry of Northern Development & Mines, 159 Cedar St., Sudbury, ON P3E 6A5
705-670-5755, Fax: 705-670-5818, 888-415-9845, ndmminister@ontario.ca

Prince Edward Island

Corporate Services, PO Box 2000, Charlottetown, PE C1A 7N8

Québec

Commission des lésions professionnelles, #700, 900, Place d'Youville, Québec, QC G1R 3P7
418-644-7777, Fax: 418-644-6443, 800-463-1591

Saskatchewan

Energy & Resources, 2101 Scarth St., Regina, SK S4P SH9
306-787-2528

Yukon Territory

Yukon Development Corporation, PO Box 2703 D-1, Whitehorse, YT Y1A 2C6
867-456-3837, Fax: 867-393-7167

INFORMATION & PRIVACY COMMISSIONER

Office of the Information Commissioner of Canada, 30 Victoria St., Gatineau, QC K1A 1H3
Fax: 819-994-1768, 800-267-0441, general@oic-ci.gc.ca

Privacy Commissioner of Canada, 30 Victoria St., Gatineau, QC K1A 1H3
819-994-5444, Fax: 819-994-5424, 800-282-1376

Alberta

Alberta Office of the Information & Privacy Commissioner, Office of the Information & Privacy Commissioner (Edmonton), #410, 9925 - 109 St., Edmonton, AB T5K 2J8
780-422-6860, Fax: 780-422-5682, 888-878-4044, generalinfo@oipc.ab.ca

British Columbia

Office of the Information & Privacy Commissioner for British Columbia, 947 Fort St., 4th Fl., PO Box 9038 Prov Govt, Victoria, BC V8W 9A4
250-387-5629, Fax: 250-387-1696, 800-663-7867, info@oipc.bc.ca

Nova Scotia

Office of the Information & Privacy Commissioner, Centennial Bldg., #1002, 1660 Hollis St., PO Box 181, Halifax, NS B3J 2M4
902-424-4684, Fax: 902-424-8303, 866-243-1564, oipcns@novascotia.ca

Ontario

Information & Privacy Commissioner of Ontario, #1400, 2 Bloor St. East, Toronto, ON M4W 1A8
416-326-3333, Fax: 416-325-9195, 800-387-0073, info@ipc.on.ca

Prince Edward Island

Office of the Information & Privacy Commissioner, J. Angus MacLean Bldg., 180 Richmond St., 2nd Fl., PO Box 2000, Charlottetown, PE C1A 7N8
902-368-4099, Fax: 902-368-5947

Saskatchewan

Information & Privacy Commissioner of Saskatchewan, #503, 1801 Hamilton St., Regina, SK S4P 4B4
306-787-8350, Fax: 306-798-1603, 877-748-2298, webmaster@oipc.sk.ca

Yukon Territory

Yukon Ombudsman & Privacy Commissioner, #201, 211 Hawkins St., Whitehorse, YT Y1A 2C6
867-667-8468, Fax: 867-667-8469, info@ombudsman.yk.ca

INFORMATION RESOURCES

Innovation, Science & Economic Development Canada, C.D. Howe Building, 235 Queen St., Ottawa, ON K1A 0H5
613-954-5031, Fax: 613-954-2340, 800-328-6189, info@ic.gc.ca

National Research Council Canada - National Science Library, 1200 Montreal Rd., Ottawa, ON K1A 0R6
613-998-8544, Fax: 613-998-2399, 800-668-1222, NRC.KMHelpdesk-BureaudaideGS.CNRC@nrc-cnrc.gc.ca
Public Services & Procurement, Place du Portage, Phase III, 11, rue Laurier, Ottawa, ON K1A 0S5
questions@tpsgc-pwgsc.gc.ca
Shared Services Canada, 434 Queen St., PO Box 9808 T CSC,Ottawa, ON K1G 4A8
613-947-6296, 855-215-3656, information@ssc-spc.gc.ca
Statistics Canada, R.H. Coats Bldg., Tunney's Pasture, 150 Tunney's Pasture Driveway, Ottawa, ON K1A 0T6
514-283-8300, Fax: 514-283-9350, 800-263-1136, STATCAN.infostats-infostats.STATCAN@canada.ca
Surveyor General Branch - Geomatics Canada, #605, 9700 Jasper Ave., Edmonton, AB T5J 4C3
780-495-2519, Fax: 780-495-4052

Newfoundland & Labrador
Office of the Chief Information Officer, 40 Higgins Line, PO Box 8700, St. John's, NL A1B 4J6
709-729-4000, Fax: 709-729-6767, ocio@gov.nl.ca

Nova Scotia
Geomatics Centre, 160 Willow St., Amherst, NS B4H 3W5
902-667-7231, Fax: 902-667-6008, geoinfo@novascotia.ca
Nova Scotia Department of Internal Services, World Trade & Convention Centre, 1800 Argyle St., 5th Fl., PO Box 943, Halifax, NS B3J 2V9
902-424-5465, Fax: 902-424-0555

Ontario
Ontario Geographic Names Board, Robinson Place, 300 Water St., 2nd Fl., PO Box 7000, Peterborough, ON K9J 8M5
705-755-2132
Science & Research Branch, Roberta Bondar Pl., 300 Water St., 4th Fl., Peterborough, ON K9J 8M5
705-755-2809, Fax: 705-755-2802

Saskatchewan
Saskatchewan Conservation Data Centre, Fish & Wildlife Branch, Ministry of Environment, 3211 Albert St., Regina, SK S4S 5W6
306-787-7196, Fax: 306-787-9544

INSURANCE

Alberta
Agriculture Financial Services Corporation, 5718 - 56 Ave., Lacombe, AB T4L 1B1
403-782-8200, info@afsc.ca

New Brunswick
New Brunswick Agricultural Insurance Commission, c/o Department of Agriculture, Aquaculture & Fisheries, PO Box 6000, Fredericton, NB E3B 5H1
506-453-2666, Fax: 506-453-7406, DAAF-MAAP@gnb.ca

INSURANCE (LIFE, FIRE, PROPERTY)

See Also: Automobile Insurance; Health Care Insurance
Canada Deposit Insurance Corporation, 50 O'Connor St., 17th Floor, Ottawa, ON K1P 6L2
Fax: 613-996-6095, 800-461-2342, info@cdic.ca
Office of the Superintendent of Financial Institutions, Kent Square, 255 Albert St., Ottawa, ON K1A 0H2
613-990-7788, Fax: 613-990-5591, 800-385-8647, information@osfi-bsif.gc.ca

Alberta
Economics & Fiscal Policy Division, Federal Bldg., 9820 - 107 St., 8th Fl., Edmonton, AB T5K 1E7

British Columbia
Insurance Council of British Columbia, #300, 1040 West Georgia St., PO Box 7, Vancouver, BC V6E 4H1
604-688-0321, Fax: 604-662-7767, 877-688-0321, info@insurancecouncilofbc.com

Manitoba
Manitoba Agricultural Services Corporation, #100, 1525 First St. South, Brandon, MB R7A 7A1
204-726-6850, Fax: 204-726-6849, mailbox@masc.mb.ca
Manitoba Financial Services Agency, c/o Financial Institutions Regulation Branch, #207, 400 St. Mary Ave., Winnipeg, MB R3C 4K5
204-945-2542, Fax: 204-948-2268, 800-282-8069, insurance@gov.mb.ca
Manitoba Public Insurance Corporation, #B100, 234 Donald St., PO Box 6300, Winnipeg, MB R3C 4A4
204-985-7000, Fax: 204-985-3525, 800-665-2410

Northwest Territories
Northwest Territories Department of Finance, PO Box 1320, Yellowknife, NT X1A 2L9
867-873-7500

Nova Scotia
Nova Scotia Crop & Livestock Insurance Commission, 60 Research Dr., #A, PO Box 1092, Truro, NS B2N 5G9
902-893-6370, 800-565-6371, nsclic@gov.ns.ca

Ontario
Deposit Insurance Corporation of Ontario, #700, 4711 Yonge St., Toronto, ON M2N 6K8
416-325-9444, Fax: 416-325-9722, 800-268-6653, info@dico.com
Financial Services Commission of Ontario, New York City Ctr., 5160 Yonge St., 17th Fl., PO Box 85, Toronto, ON M2N 6L9
416-250-7250, Fax: 416-590-7070, 800-668-0128, contactcentre@fsco.gov.on.ca
Workplace Safety & Insurance Board, 200 Front St. West, Ground Fl., Toronto, ON M5V 3J1
416-344-1000, Fax: 416-344-4684, 800-387-0750

Prince Edward Island
Agricultural Insurance Corporation, 29 Indigo Cres., PO Box 1600, Charlottetown, PE C1A 7N3
902-368-4842, Fax: 902-368-6677

Québec
Commission administrative des régimes de retraite et d'assurances (Québec), 475, rue Saint-Amable, Québec, QC G1R 5X3
418-643-4881, Fax: 418-644-3839, 800-463-5533

Saskatchewan
Financial & Consumer Affairs Authority, #601, 1919 Saskatchewan Dr., Regina, SK S4P 4H2
306-787-5645, Fax: 306-787-5899, 877-880-5550, consumerprotection@gov.sk.ca
Saskatchewan Crop Insurance Corporation, 484 Prince William Dr., PO Box 3000, Melville, SK S0A 2P0
306-728-7200, Fax: 306-728-7202, 888-935-0000, customer.service@scic.gov.sk.ca
Saskatchewan Government Insurance, 2260 - 11th Ave., Regina, SK S4P 0J9
306-751-1200, Fax: 306-787-7477, 800-667-8015, sgiinquiries@sgi.sk.ca

INTERGOVERNMENTAL AFFAIRS

See: Federal-Provincial Affairs; International Affairs
Canadian Intergovernmental Conference Secretariat, 222 Queen St., 10th Fl., PO Box 488 A,Ottawa, ON K1N 8V5
613-995-2341, Fax: 613-996-6091, info@scics.gc.ca
Destination Canada, #800, 1045 Howe St., Vancouver, BC V6Z 2A9
604-638-8300
Office of Intergovernmental Affairs, c/o Privy Council Office, #1000, 85 Slater St., Ottawa, ON K1A 0A3
613-957-5153, Fax: 613-957-5043, info@pco-bcp.gc.ca

Alberta
Intergovernmental Relations, Commerce Place, 10155 - 102 St., 12th Fl., Edmonton, AB T5J 4G8

British Columbia
Intergovernmental Relations Secretariat, PO Box 9433 Prov Govt, Victoria, BC V8W 9V3
250-387-0752, Fax: 250-387-1920, igrs@gov.bc.ca

Manitoba
Fiscal Research Division, #910, 386 Broadway, Winnipeg, MB R3C 3R6
204-945-3757, Fax: 204-945-5051

New Brunswick
Intergovernmental Affairs Division, Chancery Place, 675 King St., 5th Fl., Fredericton, NB E3B 1E9
506-444-4948, Fax: 506-453-2995, iga@gnb.ca

Newfoundland & Labrador
Labrador & Aboriginal Affairs Office, Labrador Affairs, 21 Broomfield St., PO Box 3014, Happy Valley - Goose Bay, NL A0P 1E0
709-896-1780, Fax: 709-896-0045, 888-435-8111, laa@gov.nl.ca
Newfoundland & Labrador Department of Municipal & Intergovernmental Affairs, West Block, Main Fl., Confederation Bldg., PO Box 8700, St. John's, NL A1B 4J6
709-729-3046, Fax: 709-729-0943, mainfo@gov.nl.ca

Northwest Territories
Northwest Territories Department of Aboriginal Affairs & Intergovernmental Relations, 4910 - 52nd St., PO Box 1320, Yellowknife, NT X1A 2L9
867-767-9025, Fax: 867-873-0233

Nova Scotia
Nova Scotia Department of Intergovernmental Affairs, Duke Tower, 5251 Duke St., 5th Fl., PO Box 1617, Halifax, NS B3J 2Y3
902-424-5153, Fax: 902-424-0728
Office of Acadian Affairs, Dennis Building, 1741 Brunswick St., PO Box 682, Halifax, NS B3J 2T3
902-424-0497, Fax: 902-428-0124, 866-382-5811, bonjour@novascotia.ca

Nunavut
Nunavut Territory Department of Executive & Intergovernmental Affairs, 1084 Aeroplex bldg., PO Box 1000 200, Iqaluit, NU X0A 0H0
867-975-6000, Fax: 867-975-6099

Ontario
Ontario Ministry of Intergovernmental Affairs, Ferguson Block, 77 Wellesley St. West, 12th Fl., Toronto, ON M7A 1N3
416-326-1234

Saskatchewan
Intergovernmental Affairs, #303, 3085 Albert St., Regina, SK S4S 0B1
306-787-8003

INTERNATIONAL AFFAIRS

See Also: Trade
Canadian International Trade Tribunal, Standard Life Centre, 333 Laurier Ave. West, 15th Floor, Ottawa, ON K1A 0G7
613-990-2452, Fax: 613-990-2439, 855-307-2488, citt-tcce@tribunal.gc.ca
Department of National Defence & the Canadian Armed Forces, National Defence HQ, Major-General George R. Pearkes Bldg., 101 Colonel By Dr., Ottawa, ON K1A 0K2
613-995-2534, Fax: 613-992-4739, 888-995-2534, information@forces.gc.ca
Destination Canada, #800, 1045 Howe St., Vancouver, BC V6Z 2A9
604-638-8300
Global Affairs Canada, Enquiries Service, 125 Sussex Dr., Ottawa, ON K1A 0G2
613-944-4000, Fax: 613-996-9709, 800-267-8376
International Development Research Centre, 150 Kent St., PO Box 8500, Ottawa, ON K1G 3H9
613-236-6163, Fax: 613-238-7230, info@idrc.ca

British Columbia
Intergovernmental Relations Secretariat, PO Box 9433 Prov Govt, Victoria, BC V8W 9V3
250-387-0752, Fax: 250-387-1920, igrs@gov.bc.ca

New Brunswick
Intergovernmental Affairs Division, Chancery Place, 675 King St., 5th Fl., Fredericton, NB E3B 1E9
506-444-4948, Fax: 506-453-2995, iga@gnb.ca

Ontario
Ontario Ministry of Intergovernmental Affairs, Ferguson Block, 77 Wellesley St. West, 12th Fl., Toronto, ON M7A 1N3
416-326-1234

Québec
Ministère des Relations internationales et Francophonie, Édifice Hector-Fabre, 525, boul René-Lévesque est, Québec, QC G1R 5R9
418-649-2300, Fax: 418-649-2656

INTERNATIONAL AID

Global Affairs Canada, Enquiries Service, 125 Sussex Dr., Ottawa, ON K1A 0G2
613-944-4000, Fax: 613-996-9709, 800-267-8376
International Development Research Centre, 150 Kent St., PO Box 8500, Ottawa, ON K1G 3H9
613-236-6163, Fax: 613-238-7230, info@idrc.ca

INTERNATIONAL TRADE

See: Trade
Canadian International Trade Tribunal, Standard Life Centre, 333 Laurier Ave. West, 15th Floor, Ottawa, ON K1A 0G7
613-990-2452, Fax: 613-990-2439, 855-307-2488, citt-tcce@tribunal.gc.ca
Global Affairs Canada, Enquiries Service, 125 Sussex Dr., Ottawa, ON K1A 0G2
613-944-4000, Fax: 613-996-9709, 800-267-8376

British Columbia
British Columbia Ministry of International Trade (& Minister Responsible for Asia Pacific Strategy & Multiculturalism), PO Box 9063 Prov Gov,Victoria, BC V8W 9E2
250-953-0910, Fax: 250-953-0928

Ontario
Ontario Ministry of Citizenship & Immigration, 400 University Ave., 6th Fl., Toronto, ON M7A 2R9
416-327-2422, Fax: 416-327-1061, 800-267-7329, info.mci@ontario.ca

INUIT

See: Aboriginal Affairs
Canadian Northern Economic Development Agency, Ottawa, ON K1A 0H4
855-897-2667, InfoNorth@CanNor.gc.ca

INVESTMENT

See Also: Business Development; Industry
Canada Economic Development for Québec Regions, Édifice Dominion Square, #900, 1255, rue Peel, Montréal, QC H3B 2T9
514-283-6412, Fax: 514-283-3302, 866-385-6412

Canada Pension Plan Investment Board, #2500, 1 Queen St. East, Toronto, ON M5C 2W5
416-868-4075, Fax: 416-868-8689, 866-557-9510, contact@cppib.com

Canada Savings Bonds, #201, 50 O'Connor St., PO Box 2770 D, Ottawa, ON K1P 1J7
905-754-2012, Fax: 613-782-8096, 800-575-5151, csb@csb.gc.ca

Canadian Northern Economic Development Agency, Ottawa, ON K1A 0H4
855-897-2667, InfoNorth@CanNor.gc.ca

Federal Economic Development Agency for Southern Ontario, #101, 139 Northfield Dr. West, Waterloo, ON N2L 5A6
Fax: 519-725-4976, 866-593-5505

FedNor (Federal Economic Development Initiative in Northern Ontario), C.D. Howe Bldg., 235 Queen St., 8th Fl., Ottawa, ON K1A 0H5
Fax: 613-941-4553, 877-333-6673

Finance Canada, 90 Elgin St., 14th Fl., Ottawa, ON K1A 0G5
613-369-3710, Fax: 613-369-4065, fin.financepublic-financepublique.fin@canada.ca

Innovation, Science & Economic Development Canada, C.D. Howe Building, 235 Queen St., Ottawa, ON K1A 0H5
613-954-5031, Fax: 613-954-2340, 800-328-6189, info@ic.gc.ca

Public Sector Pension Investment Board, #200, 440 Laurier Ave. West, Ottawa, ON K1R 7X6
613-782-3095, Fax: 613-782-6864, info@investpsp.ca

Alberta

Alberta Investment Management Corporation, #1100, 10830 Jasper Ave., Edmonton, AB T5J 2B3
780-392-3600, inquiries@aimco.alberta.ca

Alberta Securities Commission, #600, 250 - 5th St. SW, Calgary, AB T2P 0R4
403-297-6454, Fax: 403-297-6156, 877-355-0585, inquiries@asc.ca

Tax & Revenue Administration Division, Sir Frederick W. Haultain Building, 9811 - 109 St., 2nd Fl., Edmonton, AB T5K 2L5
780-427-3044, Fax: 780-427-0348, tra.revenue@gov.ab.ca

British Columbia

BC Immigrant Investment Fund Ltd., #301, 865 Hornby St., Vancouver, BC V6Z 2G3
Fax: 250-952-0371

BC Renaissance Capital Fund Ltd., PO Box 9800 Prov Govt, BC V8W 9W1
Fax: 250-952-0371

British Columbia Ministry of International Trade (& Minister Responsible for Asia Pacific Strategy & Multiculturalism), PO Box 9063 Prov Gov,Victoria, BC V8W 9E2
250-953-0910, Fax: 250-953-0928

British Columbia Securities Commission, Pacific Centre, 701 West Georgia St., 12th Fl., PO Box 10142, Vancouver, BC V7Y 1L2
604-899-6500, Fax: 604-899-6506, 800-373-6393, inquiries@bcsc.bc.ca

Forestry Innovation Investment Ltd., #1200, 1130 West Pender St., Vancouver, BC V6E 4A4
604-685-7507, Fax: 604-685-5373, info@bcfii.ca

Labour Market & Immigration Division, PO Box 9189 Prov Govt, Vancouver, BC V8W 9E6
250-953-3585, Fax: 250-387-6152

Manitoba

Manitoba Securities Commission, #500, 400 St. Mary Ave., Winnipeg, MB R3C 4K5
204-945-2548, Fax: 204-945-0330, 800-655-5244, securities@gov.mb.ca

Treasury Division, #350, 363 Broadway, Winnipeg, MB R3C 3N9
204-945-3702, Fax: 204-948-2233

New Brunswick

Financial & Consumer Services Commission, #300, 85 Charlotte St., Saint John, NB E2L 2J2
506-658-3060, Fax: 506-658-3059, 866-933-2222, info@fcnb.ca

New Brunswick Investment Management Corporation, York Tower, #581, 440 King St., Fredericton, NB E3B 5H8
506-444-5800, Fax: 506-444-5025, comments@nbimc.com

Opportunities New Brunswick, Place 2000, PO Box 6000, Fredericton, NB E3B 5H1
506-453-5471, Fax: 506-444-5277, 855-746-4662, info@onbcanada.ca

Northwest Territories

Northwest Territories Department of Industry, Tourism & Investment, PO Box 1320, Yellowknife, NT X1A 2L9
867-767-9002

Nova Scotia

Innovacorp, #1400, 1801 Hollis St., Halifax, NS B3J 3N4
902-424-8670, Fax: 902-424-4679, 800-565-7051, info@innovacorp.ca

Nova Scotia Securities Commission, Duke Tower, #400, 5251 Duke St., PO Box 458, Halifax, NS B3J 2P8
902-424-7768, Fax: 902-424-4625, 855-424-2499, NSSCinquiries@novascotia.ca

Ontario

Ontario Securities Commission, #1903, 20 Queen St. West, Toronto, ON M5H 3S8
416-593-8314, Fax: 416-593-8122, 877-785-1555, inquiries@osc.gov.on.ca

Prince Edward Island

Charlottetown Area Development Corporation, 4 Pownal St., PO Box 786, Charlottetown, PE C1A 7L9
902-892-5341, Fax: 902-368-1935

Debt, Investment & Pension Management, Shaw Bldg. South, 95 Rochford St., 3rd Fl., PO Box 2000, Charlottetown, PE C1A 7N8
Fax: 902-368-4077

Prince Edward Island Lending Agency, Homburg Financial Tower, 98 Fitzroy St., 2nd Fl., Charlottetown, PE C1A 1R7
902-368-6200, Fax: 902-368-6201

Québec

Financement-Québec, 12, rue Saint-Louis, 3e étage, Québec, QC G1R 5L3
418-691-2203, Fax: 418-644-6214, financement.regroupe@finances.gouv.qc.ca

Investissement Québec, #500, 1200, rte de l'Église, Québec, QC G1V 5A3
418-643-5172, Fax: 418-528-2063, 866-870-0437

JUSTICE

Justice Canada, East Memorial Bldg., 284 Wellington St., Ottawa, ON K1A 0H8
613-957-4222, Fax: 613-954-0811, webadmin@justice.gc.ca

Public Prosecution Service of Canada, 284 Wellington St., 2nd Fl., Ottawa, ON K1A 0H8
613-957-6489, 877-505-7772, info@ppsc.gc.ca

Alberta

Alberta Justice & Solicitor General, Communications, Bowker Building, 9833 - 109 St., 5th Fl., Edmonton, AB T5K 2E8
780-427-2745, -310-0000

Alberta Office of the Public Interest Commissioner, #2800, 10303 Jasper Ave. NW, Edmonton, AB T5J 5C3
780-641-8659, Fax: 780-427-2759, 855-641-8659, info@pic.alberta.ca

Justice Services Division, Bowker Building, 9833 - 109 St., 2nd Fl., Edmonton, AB T5K 2E8

British Columbia

British Columbia Ministry of Justice, PO Box 9044 Prov Govt, Victoria, BC V8W 9E2

British Columbia Ministry of Public Safety & Solicitor General, PO Box 9290 Prov Govt, Victoria, BC V8W 9J7
250-356-0149, Fax: 250-387-6224, 800-663-7867, EnquiryBC@gov.bc.ca

Justice Education Society, #260, 800 Hornby St., Vancouver, BC V6Z 2C3
604-660-9870, Fax: 604-775-3476, info@justiceeducation.ca

Manitoba

Manitoba Justice & Attorney General, Administration & Finance, #1110, 405 Broadway Ave., Winnipeg, MB R3C 3L6
204-945-2878, minjus@gov.mb.ca

New Brunswick

New Brunswick Department of Justice & Public Safety, Argyle Place, PO Box 6000, Fredericton, NB E3B 5H1
506-453-3992, DPS-MSP.Information@gnb.ca

Nova Scotia

Nova Scotia Department of Justice, 1690 Hollis St., PO Box 7, Halifax, NS B3J 2L6
902-424-4030, justweb@gov.ns.ca

Office of the Police Complaints Commissioner, #720, 1550 Bedford Hwy., PO Box 1573, Halifax, NS B3J 2Y3
902-424-3246, Fax: 902-424-1777, polcom@gov.ns.ca

Nunavut

Nunavut Territory Department of Justice, Sivummut, 1st Fl., PO Box 1000 500, Iqaluit, NU X0A 0H0
867-975-6170, Fax: 867-975-6195, justice@gov.nu.ca

Ontario

Ontario Ministry of the Attorney General, McMurtry-Scott Bldg., 720 Bay St., 11th Fl., Toronto, ON M7A 2S9
416-326-2220, Fax: 416-326-4007, 800-518-7901, attorneygeneral@ontario.ca

Special Investigations Unit, 5090 Commerce Blvd., Mississauga, ON L4W 5M4
416-622-0748, Fax: 416-622-2455, 800-787-8529

Québec

Ministère de la Justice, Édifice Louis-Philippe-Pigeon, 1200, rte de l'Église, Québec, QC G1V 4M1
418-643-5140, 866-536-5140, informations@justice.gouv.qc.ca

Saskatchewan

Saskatchewan Justice & Attorney General, 1874 Scarth St., Regina, SK S4P 4B3
306-787-7872

Yukon Territory

Yukon Justice, Andrew Philipsen Law Centre, 2134 Second Ave., PO Box 2703, Whitehorse, YT Y1A 2C6
867-667-3033, Fax: 867-393-5790, justice@gov.yk.ca

JUSTICE DEPARTMENTS

Justice Canada, East Memorial Bldg., 284 Wellington St., Ottawa, ON K1A 0H8
613-957-4222, Fax: 613-954-0811, webadmin@justice.gc.ca

Alberta

Alberta Justice & Solicitor General, Communications, Bowker Building, 9833 - 109 St., 5th Fl., Edmonton, AB T5K 2E8
780-427-2745, -310-0000

British Columbia

British Columbia Ministry of Justice, PO Box 9044 Prov Govt, Victoria, BC V8W 9E2

British Columbia Ministry of Public Safety & Solicitor General, PO Box 9290 Prov Govt, Victoria, BC V8W 9J7
250-356-0149, Fax: 250-387-6224, 800-663-7867, EnquiryBC@gov.bc.ca

Manitoba

Manitoba Justice & Attorney General, Administration & Finance, #1110, 405 Broadway Ave., Winnipeg, MB R3C 3L6
204-945-2878, minjus@gov.mb.ca

New Brunswick

New Brunswick Department of Justice & Public Safety, Argyle Place, PO Box 6000, Fredericton, NB E3B 5H1
506-453-3992, DPS-MSP.Information@gnb.ca

Newfoundland & Labrador

Newfoundland & Labrador Department of Justice & Public Safety, Confederation Bldg., East Block, 4th Fl., PO Box 8700, St. John's, NL A1B 4J6
709-729-2869, Fax: 709-729-0469, justice@gov.nl.ca

Northwest Territories

Northwest Territories Department of Justice, 4903 - 49th St., PO Box 1320, Yellowknife, NT X1A 2L9
867-767-9256

Nova Scotia

Nova Scotia Department of Justice, 1690 Hollis St., PO Box 7, Halifax, NS B3J 2L6
902-424-4030, justweb@gov.ns.ca

Nunavut

Nunavut Territory Department of Justice, Sivummut, 1st Fl., PO Box 1000 500, Iqaluit, NU X0A 0H0
867-975-6170, Fax: 867-975-6195, justice@gov.nu.ca

Ontario

Ontario Ministry of the Attorney General, McMurtry-Scott Bldg., 720 Bay St., 11th Fl., Toronto, ON M7A 2S9
416-326-2220, Fax: 416-326-4007, 800-518-7901, attorneygeneral@ontario.ca

Prince Edward Island

Prince Edward Island Department of Justice & Public Safety, Shaw Bldg. South, 95 Rochford St., 4th Fl., PO Box 2000, Charlottetown, PE C1A 7N8
902-368-6410, Fax: 902-368-6488

Québec

Ministère de la Justice, Édifice Louis-Philippe-Pigeon, 1200, rte de l'Église, Québec, QC G1V 4M1
418-643-5140, 866-536-5140, informations@justice.gouv.qc.ca

Saskatchewan

Saskatchewan Justice & Attorney General, 1874 Scarth St., Regina, SK S4P 4B3
306-787-7872

Yukon Territory

Yukon Justice, Andrew Philipsen Law Centre, 2134 Second Ave., PO Box 2703, Whitehorse, YT Y1A 2C6
867-667-3033, Fax: 867-393-5790, justice@gov.yk.ca

LABOUR

Canada Industrial Relations Board, 240 Sparks St., 4th Fl. West, Ottawa, ON K1A 0X8
Fax: 613-995-9493, 800-575-9696

Canadian Council of Directors of Apprenticeship, 140 Promenade du Portage, 5th Fl, Phase IV, Gatineau, QC K1A 0J9
Fax: 819-994-0202, 877-599-6933, redseal-sceaurouge@hrsdc-rhdcc.gc.ca

Employment & Social Development Canada, 140 Promenade du Portage, Gatineau, QC K1A 0J9

National Joint Council, C.D. Howe Building, 240 Sparks St. West, 7th Fl., PO Box 1525 B,Ottawa, ON K1P 5V2
613-990-1805, Fax: 613-990-7071, email.courrier@njc-cnm.gc.ca

Public Service Commission, 22 Eddy St., Gatineau, QC K1A 0M7
613-992-9562, Fax: 613-992-9352, CFP.INFOCOM.PSC@cfp-psc.gc.ca

Public Service Labour Relations Board, CD Howe Building, 240 Sparks St., 6th Fl., PO Box 1525 B, Ottawa, ON K1P 5V2
613-990-1800, Fax: 613-990-1849, 866-931-3454, mail.courrier@pslrb-crtfp.gc.ca

Public Service Staffing Tribunal, 240 Sparks St., 6th Fl., Ottawa, ON K1A 0A5
613-949-6516, Fax: 613-949-6551, 866-637-4491, info@psst-tdfp.gc.ca

Alberta

Alberta Apprenticeship & Industry Training Board, Commerce Place, 10155 - 102 St., 10th Fl., Edmonton, AB T5J 4L5
780-427-8765, Fax: 780-422-7376, -310-0000

Alberta Human Services, Office of the Minister, Legislature Building, #224, 10800 - 97 Ave., Edmonton, AB T5K 2B6
780-644-5135, 866-644-5135

Alberta Labour, Legislature Bldg., #404, 10800 - 97 Ave., Edmonton, AB T5K 2B6
780-427-3731, 877-427-3731

Apprenticeship & Student Aid Division, Commerce Place, 10155 - 102 St., 6th Fl., Edmonton, AB T5J 4L5

Corporate Human Resources, Peace Hills Trust Tower, 10011 - 109 St., 7th Fl., Edmonton, AB T5J 3S8
780-408-8400

Health Quality Council of Alberta, #210, 811 - 14 St. NW, Calgary, AB T2N 2A4
403-297-8162, Fax: 403-297-8258, info@hqca.ca

Labour Relations Board, Labour Building, #501, 10808 - 99 Ave., Edmonton, AB T5K 0G5
780-427-8547, Fax: 780-422-0970, 800-463-2572, alrbinfo@gov.ab.ca

Occupational Health & Safety Council, Standard Life Centre, 10405 Jasper Ave., Edmonton, AB T5J 3N4
780-412-8742, Fax: 780-412-8701

British Columbia

British Columbia Labour Relations Board, Oceanic Plaza, #600, 1066 West Hastings St., Vancouver, BC V6E 3X1
604-660-1300, Fax: 604-660-1892, information@lrb.bc.ca

British Columbia Ministry of Jobs, Tourism, & Skills Training (& Responsible for Labour), PO Box 9846 Prov Govt, Victoria, BC V8W 9T2
EnquiryBC@gov.bc.ca

British Columbia Ministry of Technology, Innovation & Citizens' Services, PO Box 9068 Prov Govt, Victoria, BC V8W 9E2
250-952-7623, Fax: 250-952-7628, 800-663-7867, EnquiryBC@gov.bc.ca

British Columbia Public Service Agency, PO Box 9404 Prov Govt, Victoria, BC V8W 9V1
250-387-0518, Fax: 250-356-7074

Employment Standards Tribunal, Oceanic Plaza, #650, 1066 West Hastings St., Vancouver, BC V6E 3X1
604-775-3512, Fax: 604-775-3372, registrar@bcest.bc.ca

Workers' Compensation Appeal Tribunal, #150, 4600 Jacombs Rd., Richmond, BC V6V 3B1
604-664-7800, Fax: 604-664-7898, 800-663-2782

Workers' Compensation Board of British Columbia, PO Box 5350 Terminal,Vancouver, BC V6B 5L5
604-276-3100, Fax: 604-276-3247, 888-621-7233

Manitoba

Advisory Council on Workplace Safety & Health, 401 York Ave., 2nd Fl., Winnipeg, MB R3C 0P8
204-945-3446, Fax: 204-948-2209, 866-888-8186, wshcompl@gov.mb.ca

Board of Electrical Examiners, #500, 401 York Ave, Winnipeg, MB R3C 0P8
204-945-3373, Fax: 204-948-2309

Civil Service Commission Board, #935, 155 Carlton St., Winnipeg, MB R3C 3H8
204-945-1435, Fax: 204-945-1486

Manitoba Civil Service Commission, #935, 155 Carlton St., Winnipeg, MB R3C 3H8
204-945-2332, Fax: 204-945-1486, 800-282-8069, csc@gov.mb.ca

Manitoba Education & Training, #168, Legislative Bldg., 450 Broadway, Winnipeg, MB R3C 0V8
204-945-3720, Fax: 204-945-1291, minedu@leg.gov.mb.ca

Manitoba Families, Legislative Building, #357, 450 Broadway, Winnipeg, MB R3C 0V8
204-945-3744, 866-626-4862

Manitoba Minimum Wage Board, 614 - 401 York Ave., Winnipeg, MB R3C 0P8
204-945-8190, Fax: 204-948-2085, lmsd@gov.mb.ca

Pension Commission of Manitoba, #1004, 401 York Ave., Winnipeg, MB R3C 0P8
204-945-2740, Fax: 204-948-2375, pensions@gov.mb.ca

Workers Compensation Board of Manitoba, 333 Broadway Ave., Winnipeg, MB R3C 4W3
204-954-4321, Fax: 204-954-4999, 800-362-3340, wcb@wcb.mb.ca

New Brunswick

New Brunswick Department of Human Resources, Chancery Place, 675 King St., Fredericton, NB E3B 1E9
506-453-2264, Fax: 506-453-7195, Ohr-brh@gnb.ca

New Brunswick Department of Post-Secondary Education, Training & Labour, Chestnut Complex, PO Box 6000, Fredericton, NB E3B 5H1
506-453-2597, Fax: 506-453-3618, dpetlinfo@gnb.ca

WorkSafeNB, 1 Portland St., PO Box 160, Saint John, NB E2L 3X9
506-632-2200, Fax: 506-632-4999, 800-222-9775, communications@ws-ts.nb.ca

Newfoundland & Labrador

Labour Relations Agency, Beothuck Bldg., 20 Crosbie Pl., 3rd Fl., PO Box 8700, St. John's, NL A1B 4J6
709-729-2715, Fax: 709-729-1759, 877-563-1063, labour@gov.nl.ca

Labour Relations Board, Beothuck Bldg., 20 Crosbie Pl., 5th Fl., PO Box 8700, St. John's, NL A1B 4J6
709-729-2707, Fax: 709-729-5738, lrb@gov.nl.ca

Newfoundland & Labrador Department of Advanced Education & Skills, Confederation Building, West Block, 3rd Fl., PO Box 8700, St. John's, NL A1B 4J6
709-729-2480, aesweb@gov.nl.ca

Newfoundland & Labrador Public Service Commission, 50 Mundy Pond Rd., PO Box 8700, St. John's, NL A1B 4J6
709-729-5810, Fax: 709-729-6234, 855-330-5810, contactpsc@gov.nl.ca

Newfoundland & Labrador Workplace Health, Safety & Compensation Commission (WorkplaceNL), 146 - 148 Forest Rd., PO Box 9000, St. John's, NL A1A 3B8
709-778-1000, Fax: 709-738-1714, 800-563-9000, general.inquiries@whscc.nl.ca

Northwest Territories

Apprenticeship, Trade & Occupations Certification Board, PO Box 1320, Yellowknife, NT X1A 2L9
867-873-7357, Fax: 867-873-0200

Northwest Territories & Nunavut Workers' Safety & Compensation Commission, Centre Square Tower, 5022 - 49th St., 5th Fl., PO Box 8888, Yellowknife, NT X1A 2R3
867-920-3888, Fax: 867-873-4596, 800-661-0792

Northwest Territories Department of Education, Culture & Employment, PO Box 1320, Yellowknife, NT X1A 2L9
ecepublicaffairs@gov.nt.ca

Nova Scotia

Labour Board of Nova Scotia, 5151 Terminal Rd., 7th Fl., PO Box 697, Halifax, NS B3J 2T8
902-424-6730, Fax: 902-424-1744, 877-424-6730, labourboard@gov.ns.ca

Nova Scotia Department of Labour & Advanced Education, 5151 Terminal Rd., 6th Fl., PO Box 697, Halifax, NS B3J 2T8
902-424-5301, Fax: 902-424-2203

Nova Scotia Public Service Commission, 1800 Argyle St., 5th Fl., PO Box 943, Halifax, NS B3J 2V9
902-424-7660

Pay Equity Commission, 5151 Terminal Rd., 6th Fl., PO Box 697, Halifax, NS B3J 2T8
902-424-8466, Fax: 902-424-0575

Workers' Advisers Program, #502, 5670 Spring Garden Rd., PO Box 1063, Halifax, NS B3J 2X1
Fax: 902-424-0530, 800-774-4712

Workers' Compensation Appeals Tribunal, #1002, 5670 Spring Garden Rd., Halifax, NS B3J 1H6
902-424-2250, Fax: 902-424-2321, 800-274-8281

Workers' Compensation Board of Nova Scotia, 5668 South St., PO Box 1150, Halifax, NS B3J 2Y2
902-491-8999, 800-870-3331, info@wcb.gov.ns.ca

Ontario

Grievance Settlement Board, Dundas/Edward Ctr., #600, 180 Dundas St. West, Toronto, ON M5G 1Z8
416-326-1388, Fax: 416-326-1396, gsb.gsb@ontario.ca

Office of the Employer Advisor, #704, 151 Bloor St. West., Toronto, ON M5S 1S4
416-327-0020, Fax: 416-327-0726, 800-387-0774

Office of the Worker Advisor, #1300, 123 Edward St., Toronto, ON M5G 1E2
416-325-8570, Fax: 416-325-4830, 800-660-6769, owaweb@ontario.ca

Ontario Labour Relations Board, 505 University Ave., 2nd Fl., Toronto, ON M5G 2P1
416-326-7500, Fax: 416-326-7531, 877-339-3335

Ontario Ministry of Advanced Education & Skills Development, Mowat Block, 900 Bay St., 14th Fl., Toronto, ON M7A 1L2
416-326-1600, Fax: 416-325-6348, 800-387-5514, information.met@ontario.ca

Ontario Ministry of Education, Mowat Block, 900 Bay St., 22nd Fl., Toronto, ON M7A 1L2
416-325-2929, Fax: 416-325-6348, 800-387-5514, information.met@ontario.ca

Ontario Ministry of Labour, 400 University Ave., 14th Fl., Toronto, ON M7A 1T7
416-326-7160, 800-531-5551

Pay Equity Commission, #300, 180 Dundas St. West, Toronto, ON M7A 2S6
416-314-1896, Fax: 416-314-8741, 800-387-8813

Public Service Commission, Whitney Block, 99 Wellesley St. West, 5th Fl., Toronto, ON M7A 1W4
416-325-1750

Treasury Board Secretariat, Ferguson Block, 77 Wellesley St. West, 8th Fl., Toronto, ON M7A 1N3
416-326-8525, Fax: 416-327-3790, 800-268-1142

Workplace Safety & Insurance Board, 200 Front St. West, Ground Fl., Toronto, ON M5V 3J1
416-344-1000, Fax: 416-344-4684, 800-387-0750

Prince Edward Island

Advisory Council on the Status of Women, Sherwood Business Centre, 161 St. Peter's Rd., Main Level, PO Box 2000, Charlottetown, PE C1A 7N8
902-368-4510, Fax: 902-368-3269, info@peistatusofwomen.ca

Prince Edward Island Department of Justice & Public Safety, Shaw Bldg. South, 95 Rochford St., 4th Fl., PO Box 2000, Charlottetown, PE C1A 7N8
902-368-6410, Fax: 902-368-6488

Prince Edward Island Workers Compensation Board, 14 Weymouth St., PO Box 757, Charlottetown, PE C1A 7L7
902-368-5680, Fax: 902-368-5696, 800-237-5049

Public Service Commission, Shaw Bldg. North, 105 Rochford St., 1st Fl., PO Box 2000, Charlottetown, PE C1A 7N8
902-368-4080, Fax: 902-368-4383

Workers Compensation Appeal Tribunal, 161 St. Peters Rd., 1st Fl., PO Box 2000, Charlottetown, PE C1A 7N8
902-894-0278, Fax: 902-620-3477

Québec

Commission de l'équité salariale, 200, ch Ste-Foy, 4e étage, Québec, QC G1R 6A1
418-528-8765, Fax: 418-528-6999, 888-528-8765, equite.salariale@ces.gouv.qc.ca

Commission de la construction du Québec, 8485, av Christophe-Colomb, Montréal, QC H2M 0A7
514-341-7740, 888-842-8282

Commission de la fonction publique, 800, place D'Youville, 7e étage, Québec, QC G1R 3P4
418-643-1425, Fax: 418-643-7264, 800-432-0432, cfp@cfp.gouv.qc.ca

Commission de la santé et de la sécurité du travail du Québec, 524, rue Bourdages, CP 1200 Terminus,Québec, QC G1K 7E2
Fax: 418-266-4015, 866-302-2778

Commission des lésions professionnelles, #700, 900, Place d'Youville, Québec, QC G1R 3P7
418-644-7777, Fax: 418-644-6443, 800-463-1591

Commission des normes du travail, Hall Est, 400, boul Jean-Lesage, 7e étage, Québec, QC G1K 8W1
514-873-7061, Fax: 418-646-3678, 800-265-1414

Commission des partenaires du marché du travail, Tour de la Place-Victoria, 800, rue du Square-Victoria, 28e étage, CP 100, Montréal, QC H4Z 1B7
514-873-5252, 800-334-6728, partenaires@mess.gouv.qc.ca

Commission des relations du travail, Hall est, 900, boul René-Lévesque est, 5e étage, Québec, QC G1R 6C9
418-643-3208, Fax: 418-643-8946, 866-864-3646, crtq@crt.gouv.qc.ca

Conseil consultatif du travail et de la main d'oeuvre, #17.100, 500, boul René-Lévesque ouest, Montréal, QC H2Z 1W7
514-873-2880, Fax: 514-873-1129, cctm@cctm.gouv.qc.ca

Ministère du Travail, de l'Emploi et de la Solidarité sociale, 200, ch Sainte-Foy, 5e étage, Québec, QC G1R 5S1
418-644-4545, Fax: 418-528-0559, 877-644-4545

Office des professions du Québec, 800, place D'Youville, 10e étage, Québec, QC G1R 5Z3
418-643-6912, Fax: 418-643-0973, 800-643-6912, courrier@opq.gouv.qc.ca

Régie du bâtiment du Québec, 545, boul Crémazie est, 4e étage, Montréal, QC H2M 2V2
514-873-0976, Fax: 866-315-0106, 800-361-0761, crc@rbq.gouv.qc.ca

Saskatchewan

Labour Relations Board, #1600, 1920 Broad St., Regina, SK S4P 3V2
306-787-2406, Fax: 306-787-2664

Minimum Wage Board, #400, 1870 Albert St., Regina, SK S4P 4W1

Office of the Worker's Advocate, #300, 1870 Albert St., Regina, SK S4P 4W1
306-787-2456, Fax: 306-787-0249, 877-787-2456

Public Service Commission, 2350 Albert St., Regina, SK S4P 4A6
306-787-7853, 866-319-5999, csinquiry@gov.sk.ca

Saskatchewan Education, 2220 College Ave., Regina, SK S4P 4V9
linquiry@gov.sk.ca
Saskatchewan Labour Relations & Workplace Safety, #300, 1870 Albert St., Regina, SK S4P 4W1
306-787-7404, webmaster@lab.gov.sk.ca
Saskatchewan Workers' Compensation Board, #200, 1881 Scarth St., Regina, SK S4P 4L1
306-787-4370, Fax: 306-787-4311, 800-667-7590, webmaster@wcbsask.com

Yukon Territory
Yukon Public Service Commission, Yukon Government Administration Bldg., 2071 Second Ave., PO Box 2703, Whitehorse, YT Y1A 2C6
867-667-5653, Fax: 867-667-5755, PSCWebsite@gov.yk.ca
Yukon Workers' Compensation Health & Safety Board, 401 Strickland St., Whitehorse, YT Y1A 5N8
867-667-5645, Fax: 867-393-6279, 800-661-0443, worksafe@gov.yk.ca

LAND RESOURCES

See Also: Agriculture; Forest Resources; Parks
Canada Lands Company Ltd., #1200, 1 University Ave., Toronto, ON M5J 2P1
416-952-6112
Natural Resources Canada, 580 Booth St., Ottawa, ON K1A 0E4
343-292-6096, Fax: 613-992-7211
Parks Canada, National Office, 30 Victoria St., Gatineau, QC J8X 0B3
819-420-9486, 888-773-8888, information@pc.gc.ca

Alberta
Land Use Secretariat, Centre West Building, 10035 - 108 St., Edmonton, AB T5J 3E1
780-644-7972, Fax: 780-644-1034, luf@gov.ab.ca
Special Areas Board, Special Areas Board Administration, 212 - 2nd Ave. West, PO Box 820, Hanna, AB T0J 1P0
403-854-5600, Fax: 403-854-5527

British Columbia
Surface Rights Board of British Columbia, #10, 10551 Shellbridge Way, Richmond, BC V6X 2W9
604-775-1740, Fax: 604-775-1742, 888-775-1740, office@surfacerightsboard.bc.ca

Manitoba
Farm Lands Ownership Board, #812, Norquay Bldg., 401 York Ave., Winnipeg, MB R3C 0P8
204-945-3149, Fax: 204-945-1489, 800-282-8069
Manitoba Land Value Appraisal Commission, #1144, 363 Broadway, Winnipeg, MB R3C 3N9
204-945-5455, Fax: 204-948-2235

Northwest Territories
Northwest Territories Department of Environment & Natural Resources, #600, 5102 - 50 Ave., Yellowknife, NT X1A 3S8
867-767-9231
Northwest Territories Department of Lands, Gallery Bldg., 4923 - 52nd St., 1st & 2nd Fl., PO Box 1320, Yellowknife, NT X1A 2L9
867-767-9185, Fax: 867-669-0905, NWTLands@gov.nt.ca
Northwest Territories Department of Municipal & Community Affairs, PO Box 1320, Yellowknife, NT X1A 2L9
867-767-9160, Fax: 867-873-0309

Nova Scotia
Nova Scotia Lands Inc., Harbourside Pl., 45 Wabana Ct., PO Box 430 A,Sydney, NS B1P 6H2
Fax: 902-564-7903

Nunavut
Nunavut Territory Department of Environment, PO Box 1000 1300, Iqaluit, NU X0A 0H0
867-975-7700, Fax: 867-975-7742, environment@gov.nu.ca

Prince Edward Island
Prince Edward Island Department of Justice & Public Safety, Shaw Bldg. South, 95 Rochford St., 4th Fl., PO Box 2000, Charlottetown, PE C1A 7N8
902-368-6410, Fax: 902-368-6488

Québec
Commission de protection du territoire agricole du Québec, 200, ch Ste-Foy, 2e étage, Québec, QC G1R 4X6
418-643-3314, Fax: 418-643-2261, 800-667-5294, info@cptaq.gouv.qc.ca
Territoire, #A313, 5700, 4e av ouest, Québec, QC G1H 6R1
418-627-6256, Fax: 418-528-2075

Saskatchewan
Saskatchewan Lands Appeal Board, #315, 3085 Albert St., Regina, SK S4S 0B1
306-787-8861

Yukon Territory
Yukon Land Use Planning Council, #201, 307 Jarvis St., Whitehorse, YT Y1A 2H3
867-667-7397, Fax: 867-667-4624, ylupc@planyukon.ca

LAND TITLES

See Also: Real Estate
Canada Lands Company Ltd., #1200, 1 University Ave., Toronto, ON M5J 2P1
416-952-6112

British Columbia
British Columbia Assessment Authority, #400, 3450 Uptown Blvd., Victoria, BC V8Z 0B9
604-739-8588, Fax: 855-995-6209, 866-825-8322

New Brunswick
Service New Brunswick, Westmorland Pl., PO Box 1998, Fredericton, NB E3B 5G4
506-457-3581, Fax: 506-444-2850, snb@snb.ca

Nunavut
Legal Registries, PO Box 1000 570, Iqaluit, NU X0A 0H0
867-975-6590, Fax: 867-975-6594, Legal.Registries@gov.nu.ca

Saskatchewan
Courts & Tribunals Division, #1010, 1874 Scarth St., Regina, SK S4P 4B3
306-787-5359, Fax: 306-787-8737

LANDLORD & TENANT REGULATIONS

Alberta
Alberta Justice & Solicitor General, Communications, Bowker Building, 9833 - 109 St., 5th Fl., Edmonton, AB T5K 2E8
780-427-2745, -310-0000

British Columbia
British Columbia Ministry of Natural Gas Development (& Responsible for Housing), PO Box 9052 Prov Govt, Victoria, BC V8W 9E2
250-953-0900, Fax: 250-953-0927
Surface Rights Board of British Columbia, #10, 10551 Shellbridge Way, Richmond, BC V6X 2W9
604-775-1740, Fax: 604-775-1742, 888-775-1740, office@surfacerightsboard.bc.ca

Northwest Territories
Northwest Territories Housing Corporation, Scotia Centre, 5102 - 50th Ave., PO Box 2100, Yellowknife, NT X1A 2P6
867-767-9080, Fax: 867-873-9426, 844-698-4663

Nunavut
Nunavut Housing Corporation, PO Box 480, Arviat, NU X0C 0E0
867-857-3000, Fax: 867-857-3040

Prince Edward Island
Prince Edward Island Regulatory & Appeals Commission, National Bank Tower, #501, 134 Kent St., PO Box 577, Charlottetown, PE C1A 7L1
902-892-3501, Fax: 902-566-4076, 800-501-6268, info@irac.pe.ca

Québec
Régie du logement du Québec, Village Olympique, #2360, 5199, rue Sherbrooke est, Montréal, QC H1T 3X1
514-873-2245, Fax: 514-864-8077, 800-683-2245

Saskatchewan
Office of Residential Tenancies, #304, 1855 Victoria Ave., Regina, SK S4P 3T2
306-787-2699, Fax: 306-787-5574, 888-215-2222, ort@gov.sk.ca
Provincial Mediation Board, #120, 2151 Scarth St., Regina, SK S4P 2H8
306-787-5408, Fax: 306-787-5574, 877-787-5408, pmb@gov.sk.ca

LANDS & SOILS

Agriculture & Agri-Food Canada, 1341 Baseline Rd., Ottawa, ON K1A 0C5
613-773-1000, Fax: 613-773-1081, 855-773-0241, info@agr.gc.ca
Canada Centre for Mapping & Earth Observation, #212, 50 Place de la Cité, PO Box 162, Sherbrooke, QC J1H 4G9
Earth Sciences Sector, 588 Booth St., Ottawa, ON K1A 0Y7
Indigenous & Northern Affairs, Terrasses de la Chaudière, 10 Wellington St., North Tower, Gatineau, QC K1A 0H4
Fax: 866-817-3977, 800-567-9604, infopubs@aadnc-aandc.gc.ca
Natural Resources Canada, 580 Booth St., Ottawa, ON K1A 0E4
343-292-6096, Fax: 613-992-7211

Alberta
Irrigation Council, Provincial Bldg., 200 - 5 Ave. South, 3rd Fl., Lethbridge, AB T1J 4L1
403-381-5176, Fax: 403-382-4406
Land Compensation Board, 1229 - 91 St. SW, Edmonton, AB T6X 1E9
780-427-2444, Fax: 780-427-5798, -310-000, srb.lcb@gov.ab.ca

British Columbia
British Columbia Ministry of Environment, PO Box 9339 Prov Govt, Victoria, BC V8W 9M1
250-387-9870, Fax: 250-387-6003, env.mail@gov.bc.ca
Forest Practices Board, PO Box 9905 Prov Govt, Victoria, BC V8W 9R1
250-213-4700, Fax: 250-213-4725, 800-994-5899, fpboard@gov.bc.ca
Timber Export Advisory Committee, PO Box 9514 Prov Govt, Victoria, BC V8W 9C2
250-387-8916, Fax: 250-387-5050

New Brunswick
New Brunswick Department of Energy & Resource Development, Hugh John Flemming Forestry Centre, 1350 Regent St., Fredericton, NB E3C 2G6
506-453-3826, Fax: 506-444-4367, dnr_mrnweb@gnb.ca
New Brunswick Department of Environment & Local Government, Marysville Place, PO Box 6000, Fredericton, NB E3B 5H1
506-453-2690, Fax: 506-457-4994, elg/egl-info@gnb.ca

Newfoundland & Labrador
Newfoundland & Labrador Department of Service NL, PO Box 8700, St. John's, NL A1B 4J6
709-729-4834, servicenlinfo@gov.nl.ca

Northwest Territories
Northwest Territories Department of Environment & Natural Resources, #600, 5102 - 50 Ave., Yellowknife, NT X1A 3S8
867-767-9231
Northwest Territories Department of Lands, Gallery Bldg., 4923 - 52nd St., 1st & 2nd Fl., PO Box 1320, Yellowknife, NT X1A 2L9
867-767-9185, Fax: 867-669-0905, NWTLands@gov.nt.ca

Nova Scotia
Nova Scotia Department of Natural Resources, Founder's Square, 1701 Hollis St., 3rd Fl., PO Box 698, Halifax, NS B3J 2T9
902-424-5935, Fax: 902-424-7735, 800-565-2224
Nova Scotia Lands Inc., Harbourside Pl., 45 Wabana Ct., PO Box 430 A,Sydney, NS B1P 6H2
Fax: 902-564-7903

Québec
Ministère du Développement durable, de l'Environnement et de la Lutte contre les changements climatiques, Édifice Marie-Guyart, 675, boul René-Lévesque est, 29e étage, Québec, QC G1R 5V7
418-521-3830, Fax: 418-646-5974, 800-561-1616, info@mddefp.gouv.qc.ca
Territoire, #A313, 5700, 4e av ouest, Québec, QC G1H 6R1
418-627-6256, Fax: 418-528-2075

Saskatchewan
Saskatchewan Assessment Management Agency, #200, 2201 - 11th Ave., Regina, SK S4P 0J8
306-924-8000, Fax: 306-924-8070, 800-667-7262, info.request@sama.sk.ca

Yukon Territory
Carmacks Renewable Resource Council, PO Box 122, Carmacks, YT Y0B 1C0
867-863-6838, Fax: 867-863-6429, carmacksrrc@northwestel.net
Selkirk Renewable Resources Council, PO Box 32, Pelly Crossing, YT Y0B 1P0
867-537-3937, Fax: 867-537-3939, selkirkrrc@northwestel.net
Yukon Environment, 10 Burns Rd., PO Box 2703 V-3A, Whitehorse, YT Y1A 2C6
867-667-5652, Fax: 867-393-7197, environment.yukon@gov.yk.ca
Yukon Land Use Planning Council, #201, 307 Jarvis St., Whitehorse, YT Y1A 2H3
867-667-7397, Fax: 867-667-4624, ylupc@planyukon.ca

LAW & JUSTICE

Auditor General of Canada, 240 Sparks St., Ottawa, ON K1A 0G6
613-952-0213, Fax: 613-957-0474, 888-761-5953, infomedia@oag-bvg.gc.ca
Canadian Human Rights Commission, 344 Slater St., 8th Fl., Ottawa, ON K1A 1E1
Fax: 613-996-9661, 888-214-1090, info.com@chrc-ccdp.gc.ca
Canadian Human Rights Tribunal, 160 Elgin St., 11th Fl., Ottawa, ON K1A 1J4
613-995-1707, Fax: 613-995-3484, registrar@chrt-tcdp.gc.ca
Canadian International Trade Tribunal, Standard Life Centre, 333 Laurier Ave. West, 15th Floor, Ottawa, ON K1A 0G7
613-990-2452, Fax: 613-990-2439, 855-307-2488, citt-tcce@tribunal.gc.ca
Canadian Judicial Council, Ottawa, ON K1A 0W8
613-288-1566, Fax: 613-288-1575
Canadian Police College, PO Box 8900, Ottawa, ON K1G 3J2
613-993-9500, Fax: 613-990-9738, cpc-ccp@rcmp-grc.gc.ca
Canadian Radio-Television & Telecommunications Commission, Central Building, 1, Promenade du Portage, Les Terrasses de la Chaudière, Gatineau, QC J8X 4B1
819-997-0313, Fax: 819-994-0218, 877-249-2782

Canadian Security Intelligence Service, PO Box 9732 T,Ottawa, ON K1G 4G4
613-993-9620, Fax: 613-231-0612
Commission for Public Complaints Against the Royal Canadian Mounted Police, National Intake Office, PO Box 88689, Surrey, BC V3W 0X1
Fax: 604-501-4095, 800-665-6878
Copyright Board of Canada, #800, 56 Sparks St., Ottawa, ON K1A 0C9
613-952-8621, Fax: 613-952-8630, secretariat@cb-cda.gc.ca
Correctional Service Canada, 340 Laurier Ave. West, Ottawa, ON K1A 0P9
613-992-5891, Fax: 613-943-1630
Defence Research & Development Canada, 101 Colonel By Dr., Ottawa, ON K1A 0K2
613-995-2534, 888-995-2534, information@forces.gc.ca
Financial Transactions & Reports Analysis Centre of Canada, 234 Laurier Ave. West, 24th Fl., Ottawa, ON K1P 1H7
Fax: 613-943-7931, 866-346-8722, guidelines-lignesdirectrices@fintrac-canafe.gc.ca
Immigration & Refugee Board of Canada, Canada Bldg, 344 Slater St., 12th Fl., Ottawa, ON K1A 0K1
613-995-6486, Fax: 613-943-1550, contact@irb-cisr.gc.ca
International Joint Commission, 234 Laurier Ave. West, 22nd Fl., Ottawa, ON K1P 6K6
613-995-2984, Fax: 613-993-5583, commission@ottawa.ijc.org
Justice Canada, East Memorial Bldg., 284 Wellington St., Ottawa, ON K1A 0H8
613-957-4222, Fax: 613-954-0811, webadmin@justice.gc.ca
Military Grievances External Review Committee, 60 Queen St., 10th Fl., Ottawa, ON K1P 5Y7
613-996-8529, Fax: 613-996-6491, 877-276-4193, mgerc-ceegm@mgerc-ceegm.gc.ca
Military Police Complaints Commission, 270 Albert St., 10th Fl., Ottawa, ON K1P 5G8
613-947-5625, Fax: 613-947-5713, 800-632-0566, commission@mpcc-cppm.gc.ca
Office of the Commissioner for Federal Judicial Affairs, 99 Metcalfe St., 8th Fl., Ottawa, ON K1A 1E3
613-995-5140, Fax: 613-995-5615, 877-583-4266
Office of the Conflict of Interest & Ethics Commissioner, Commissioner's Office, 66 Slater St., 22nd Fl., PO Box 16, Ottawa, ON K1A 0A6
613-995-0721, Fax: 613-995-7308, ciec-ccie@parl.gc.ca
Office of the Correctional Investigator, PO Box 3421 D,Ottawa, ON K1P 6L4
Fax: 613-990-9091, 877-885-8848, org@oci-bec.gc.ca
Office of the Ombudsman, PO Box 90026, Ottawa, ON K1V 1J8
Fax: 800-204-4193, 800-204-4198
Parole Board of Canada, Communications Division, National Office, 410 Laurier Ave. West, Ottawa, ON K1A 0R1
613-954-7474, Fax: 613-941-4981, info@pbc-clcc.gc.ca
Passport Canada, Passport Canada Program, Gatineau, QC K1A 0G3
800-567-6868
Public Prosecution Service of Canada, 284 Wellington St., 2nd Fl., Ottawa, ON K1A 0H8
613-957-6489, 877-505-7772, info@ppsc.gc.ca
RCMP Training Academy, 6101 Dewdney Ave., PO Box 2500, Regina, SK S4P 3K7
306-780-5560, Fax: 306-780-5541
Royal Canadian Mounted Police, 73 Leikin Dr., Ottawa, ON K1A 0R2
613-993-7267, Fax: 613-993-0260
Royal Canadian Mounted Police External Review Committee, PO Box 1159 B, Ottawa, ON K1P 5R2
613-998-2134, Fax: 613-990-8969, org@erc-cee.gc.ca
Security Intelligence Review Committee, PO Box 2430 D,Ottawa, ON K1P 5W5
613-990-8441, Fax: 613-990-5230, info@sirc-csars.gc.ca
Transportation Appeal Tribunal of Canada, #1201, 333 Laurier Ave. West, 12th Fl., Ottawa, ON K1A 0N5
613-990-6906, Fax: 613-990-9153, info@tatc.gc.ca
Transportation Safety Board of Canada, 200, Promenade du Portage, 4th Fl., Gatineau, QC K1A 1K8
819-994-3741, Fax: 819-997-2239, 800-387-3557, communications@bst-tsb.gc.ca
Veterans Review & Appeal Board, Daniel J. MacDonald Bldg., 161 Grafton St., PO Box 9900, Charlottetown, PE C1A 8V7
902-566-8751, Fax: 902-566-7850, 800-450-8006, vrab_tacra@vac-acc.gc.ca

Alberta

Alberta Justice & Solicitor General, Communications, Bowker Building, 9833 - 109 St., 5th Fl., Edmonton, AB T5K 2E8
780-427-2745, -310-0000
Alberta Office of the Ethics Commissioner, #1250, 9925 - 109 St. NW, Edmonton, AB T5K 2J8
780-422-2273, Fax: 780-422-2261, generalinfo@ethicscommissioner.ab.ca
Alberta Office of the Ombudsman, Canadian Western Bank Building, #2800, 10303 Jasper Ave. NW, Edmonton, AB T5J 5C3
780-427-2756, Fax: 780-427-2759, 888-455-2756, info@ombudsman.ab.ca
Alberta Review Board, Oxford Tower, #1120, 10235 - 101 St., Edmonton, AB T5J 3E9
780-422-5994, Fax: 780-427-1762
Criminal Injuries Review Board, #1502, 10025 - 102A Ave., Edmonton, AB T5J 2Z2
780-427-7330, Fax: 780-427-7347
Fatality Review Board, 4070 Bowness Rd. NW, Calgary, AB T3B 3R7
403-297-8123, Fax: 403-297-3429
Justice Services Division, Bowker Building, 9833 - 109 St., 2nd Fl., Edmonton, AB T5K 2E8
Land Compensation Board, 1229 - 91 St. SW, Edmonton, AB T6X 1E9
780-427-2444, Fax: 780-427-5798, -310-000, srb.lcb@gov.ab.ca
Law Enforcement Review Board, City Centre Place, #1502, 10025 - 102A Ave., Edmonton, AB T5J 2Z2
780-422-9376, Fax: 780-422-4782, lerb@gov.ab.ca
Legal Services Division, Bowker Building, 9833 - 109 St., 2nd Fl., Edmonton, AB T5K 2E8
780-422-0500
Public Security Division, John E. Brownlee Building, 10365 - 97 St., 10th Fl., Edmonton, AB T5J 3W7

British Columbia

British Columbia Law Institute, University of British Columbia, 1822 East Mall, Vancouver, BC V6T 1Z1
604-822-0142, Fax: 604-822-0144, bcli@bcli.org
British Columbia Ministry of Justice, PO Box 9044 Prov Govt, Victoria, BC V8W 9E2
British Columbia Ministry of Public Safety & Solicitor General, PO Box 9290 Prov Govt, Victoria, BC V8W 9J7
250-356-0149, Fax: 250-387-6224, 800-663-7867, EnquiryBC@gov.bc.ca
British Columbia Office of the Police Complaint Commissioner, #501, 947 Fort St., PO Box 9895 Prov Govt, Victoria, BC V8W 9T8
250-356-7458, Fax: 250-356-6503, 877-999-8707, info@opcc.bc.ca
British Columbia Review Board, #1020, 510 Burrard St., Vancouver, BC V6C 3A8
604-660-8789, Fax: 604-660-8809, 877-305-2277
Court Services Branch, PO Box 9249 Prov Govt, Victoria, BC V8W 9J2
250-356-1550, Fax: 250-356-8152
Judicial Council of British Columbia, Office of the Chief Judge, #337, 800 Hornby St., Vancouver, BC V6Z 2C5
604-660-2864, Fax: 604-660-1108, info@provincialcourt.bc.ca
Legal Services Society, #400, 510 Burrard St., Vancouver, BC V6C 3A8
604-601-6000
Office of the Conflict of Interest Commissioner, 421 Menzies St., 1st Fl., Victoria, BC V8V 1X4
250-356-0750, Fax: 250-356-6580, conflictofinterest@coibc.ca
Office of the Ombudsperson, 947 Fort St., 2nd Fl., PO Box 9039 Prov Govt, Victoria, BC V8W 9A5
250-387-5855, Fax: 250-387-0198, 800-567-3247
Office of the Representative for Children & Youth, #400, 1019 Wharf St., Victoria, BC V8W 2Y9
250-356-6710, Fax: 250-356-0837, 800-476-3933, rcy@rcybc.ca
Public Guardian & Trustee of British Columbia, #700, 808 West Hastings St., Vancouver, BC V6C 3L3
604-660-4444, Fax: 604-660-0374, 800-663-7867, clientservice@trustee.bc.ca

Manitoba

Advisory Council on Workplace Safety & Health, 401 York Ave., 2nd Fl., Winnipeg, MB R3C 0P8
204-945-3446, Fax: 204-948-2209, 866-888-8186, wshcompl@gov.mb.ca
Compensation for Victims of Crime, #1410, 405 Broadway, Winnipeg, MB R3C 3L6
204-945-0899, Fax: 204-948-3071, 800-262-9344
Health Information Privacy Committee, #4043, 300 Carlton St., Winnipeg, MB R3B 3M9
Highway Traffic Board/Motor Transport Board, #200, 301 Weston St., Winnipeg, MB R3E 3H4
204-945-8912, Fax: 204-783-6529
Law Enforcement Review Agency, #420, 155 Carlton St., Winnipeg, MB R3C 3H8
204-945-8667, Fax: 204-948-1014, 800-282-8069, lera@gov.mb.ca
Legal Aid Manitoba, 287 Broadway, 4th Fl., Winnipeg, MB R3C 0R9
204-985-8500, Fax: 204-944-8582, 800-261-2960, info@legalaid.mb.ca
License Suspension Appeal Board/Medical Review Committee, #200, 301 Weston St., Winnipeg, MB R3E 3H4
204-945-7350, Fax: 204-948-2682
Manitoba Criminal Code Review Board, #2, 408 York Ave., Winnipeg, MB R3C 0P9
204-945-4438
Manitoba Film Classification Board, #216, 301 Weston St., Winnipeg, MB R3E 3H4
204-945-8962, Fax: 204-945-0890, 866-612-2399, mfcb@gov.mb.ca
Manitoba Human Rights Commission, #700, 175 Hargrave St., Winnipeg, MB R3C 3R8
204-945-3007, Fax: 204-945-1292, 888-884-8681, hrc@gov.mb.ca
Manitoba Justice & Attorney General, Administration & Finance, #1110, 405 Broadway Ave., Winnipeg, MB R3C 3L6
204-945-2878, minjus@gov.mb.ca
Manitoba Land Value Appraisal Commission, #1144, 363 Broadway, Winnipeg, MB R3C 3N9
204-945-5455, Fax: 204-948-2235
Manitoba Law Reform Commission, #432, 405 Broadway, Winnipeg, MB R3C 3L6
204-945-2896, Fax: 204-948-2184, mail@manitobalawreform.ca
Manitoba Liquor & Lotteries, 830 Empress St., Winnipeg, MB R3G 3H3
204-957-2500, Fax: 204-284-3500, 800-265-3912
Manitoba Minimum Wage Board, 614 - 401 York Ave., Winnipeg, MB R3C 0P8
204-945-8190, Fax: 204-948-2085, lmsd@gov.mb.ca
Manitoba Office of the Ombudsman, Colony Square, #750, 500 Portage Ave., Winnipeg, MB R3C 3X1
204-982-9130, Fax: 204-942-7803, 800-665-0531, ombudsman@ombudsman.mb.ca
Office of the Auditor General, #500, 330 Portage Ave., Winnipeg, MB R3C 0C4
204-945-3790, Fax: 204-945-2169, oag.contact@oag.mb.ca
Office of the Chief Medical Examiner, #210, 1 Wesley Ave., Winnipeg, MB R3C 4C6
204-945-2088, 800-282-8069
Office of the Public Trustee, #500, 155 Carlton St., Winnipeg, MB R3C 5R9
204-945-2700, Fax: 204-948-2251, PGT@gov.mb.ca
Workers Compensation Board of Manitoba, 333 Broadway Ave., Winnipeg, MB R3C 4W3
204-954-4321, Fax: 204-954-4999, 800-362-3340, wcb@wcb.mb.ca

New Brunswick

New Brunswick Department of Justice & Public Safety, Argyle Place, PO Box 6000, Fredericton, NB E3B 5H1
506-453-3992, DPS-MSP.Information@gnb.ca
New Brunswick Human Rights Commission, Barry House, PO Box 6000, Fredericton, NB E3B 5H1
506-453-2301, Fax: 506-453-2653, 888-471-2233, hrc.cdp@gnb.ca
New Brunswick Liquor Corporation, 170 Wilsey Rd., PO Box 20787, Fredericton, NB E3B 5B8
506-452-6826, Fax: 506-462-2024, Receptionist@anbl.com
New Brunswick Police Commission, Fredericton City Centre, #202, 435 King St., Fredericton, NB E3B 1E5
506-453-2069, Fax: 506-457-3542, 888-389-1777, nbpc@gnb.ca
Office of the Attorney General, Chancery Place, PO Box 6000, Fredericton, NB E3B 5H1
506-462-5100, Fax: 506-453-3651, justice.comments@gnb.ca
Office of the Ombudsman, PO Box 6000, Fredericton, NB E3B 5H1
506-453-2789, Fax: 506-453-5599, 888-465-1100, nbombud@gnb.ca
WorkSafeNB, 1 Portland St., PO Box 160, Saint John, NB E2L 3X9
506-632-2200, Fax: 506-632-4999, 800-222-9775, communications@ws-ts.nb.ca

Newfoundland & Labrador

Newfoundland & Labrador Department of Justice & Public Safety, Confederation Bldg., East Block, 4th Fl., PO Box 8700, St. John's, NL A1B 4J6
709-729-2869, Fax: 709-729-0469, justice@gov.nl.ca
Newfoundland & Labrador Human Rights Commission, The Beothuk Bldg., 21 Crosbie Pl., PO Box 8700, St. John's, NL A1B 4J6
709-729-2709, Fax: 709-729-0790, 800-563-5808, humanrights@gov.nl.ca
Newfoundland & Labrador Legal Aid Commission, #300, 251 Empire Ave., St. John's, NL A1C 5J9
709-753-7860, Fax: 709-753-7851, 800-563-9911, nlac@legalaid.nl.ca

Royal Newfoundland Constabulary Public Complaints Commission, 689 Topsail Rd., PO Box 8700, St. John's, NL A1B 4J6
709-729-0950, Fax: 709-729-1302, rnccomplaintscommission@gov.nl.ca

Northwest Territories

Assessment Appeal Tribunal, #600, 5201 - 50th Ave., PO Box 1320, Yellowknife, NT X1A 3S9
867-873-7125, Fax: 867-873-0609

Legal Services Board of the Northwest Territories, 4915 - 48th St., PO Box 1320, Yellowknife, NT X1A 2L9
867-873-7450, Fax: 867-873-5320, lsb@gov.nt.ca

Northwest Territories & Nunavut Workers' Safety & Compensation Commission, Centre Square Tower, 5022 - 49th St., 5th Fl., PO Box 8888, Yellowknife, NT X1A 2R3
867-920-3888, Fax: 867-873-4596, 800-661-0792

Northwest Territories Department of Justice, 4903 - 49th St., PO Box 1320, Yellowknife, NT X1A 2L9
867-767-9256

Northwest Territories Liquor Commission, #201, 31 Capital Dr., Hay River, NT X0E 1G2
867-874-8700, Fax: 867-874-8720

Northwest Territories Liquor Licensing Board, #204, 31 Capital Dr., Hay River, NT X0E 1G2
867-874-8715, Fax: 867-874-8722, 800-351-7770

Territorial Board of Revision, #600, 5201 - 50th Ave., Yellowknife, NT X1A 3S9
867-873-7125, Fax: 867-873-0609

Victims Assistance Committee, c/o Community Justice & Community Policing Division, PO Box 1320, Yellowknife, NT X1A 2L9
867-920-6911, Fax: 867-873-0199

Nova Scotia

Nova Scotia Department of Justice, 1690 Hollis St., PO Box 7, Halifax, NS B3J 2L6
902-424-4030, justweb@gov.ns.ca

Nova Scotia Human Rights Commission, Park Lane Terraces, #305, 5657 Spring Garden Rd., PO Box 2221, Halifax, NS B3J 3C4
902-424-4111, Fax: 902-424-0596, 877-269-7699, hrcinquiries@novascotia.ca

Nova Scotia Legal Aid Commission, Office of the Executive Director, #920, 1701 Hollis St., Halifax, NS B3J 3M8
902-420-6578, 877-420-6578

Office of the Chief Medical Examiner, Dr. William D. Finn Centre for Forensic Medicine, 51 Garland Ave., Dartmouth, NS B3B 0J2
902-424-2722, Fax: 902-424-0607, 888-424-4336

Office of the Ombudsman, #700, 5670 Spring Garden Rd., PO Box 2152, Halifax, NS B3J 3B7
902-424-6780, Fax: 902-424-6675, 800-670-1111, ombudsman@gov.ns.ca

Pay Equity Commission, 5151 Terminal Rd., 6th Fl., PO Box 697, Halifax, NS B3J 2T8
902-424-8466, Fax: 902-424-0575

Workers' Compensation Appeals Tribunal, #1002, 5670 Spring Garden Rd., Halifax, NS B3J 1H6
902-424-2250, Fax: 902-424-2321, 800-274-8281

Workers' Compensation Board of Nova Scotia, 5668 South St., PO Box 1150, Halifax, NS B3J 2Y2
902-491-8999, 800-870-3331, info@wcb.gov.ns.ca

Nunavut

Baffin Correctional Centre, PO Box 1000, Iqaluit, NU X0A 0H0
867-979-8100, Fax: 867-979-4646

Legal Registries, PO Box 1000 570, Iqaluit, NU X0A 0H0
867-975-6590, Fax: 867-975-6594, Legal.Registries@gov.nu.ca

Legal Services Board of Nunavut, 1104-B Inuksugait Plaza, PO Box 29, Iqaluit, NU X0A 0H0
867-975-6395

Liquor Licensing Board, PO Box 1269, Iqaluit, NU X0A 0H0
867-975-6533, Fax: 867-975-6511, nllb@gov.nu.ca

Nunavut Territory Department of Justice, Sivummut, 1st Fl., PO Box 1000 500, Iqaluit, NU X0A 0H0
867-975-6170, Fax: 867-975-6195, justice@gov.nu.ca

Office of the Chief Coroner, c/o Court Services Division, PO Box 297, Iqaluit, NU X0A 0H0
867-975-6100, Fax: 867-975-6168, theofficeofthechiefcoroner@gov.nu.ca

Young Offenders Facility, 1548 Federal Rd., PO Box 1439, Iqaluit, NU X0A 0H0
867-979-4452, Fax: 867-979-5506

Ontario

Alcohol & Gaming Commission of Ontario, 90 Sheppard Ave. East, Toronto, ON M2N 0A4
416-326-8700, Fax: 416-326-5555, 800-522-2876, customer.service@agco.ca

Assessment Review Board, #1500, 655 Bay St., Toronto, ON M5G 1E5
416-212-6349, Fax: 416-314-3717, 866-448-2248, assessment.review.board@ontario.ca

Association of Ontario Land Surveyors, 1043 McNicoll Ave., Toronto, ON M1W 3W6
416-491-9020, Fax: 416-491-2576, 800-268-0718

Chief Inquiry Officer - Expropriations Act, McMurtry-Scott Bldg., 720 Bay St., 8th Fl., Toronto, ON M7A 2S9
416-314-2226

Commissioner for Community Safety, George Drew Bldg., North Side, 25 Grosvenor St., 11th fl., Toronto, ON M7A 1Y6
416-212-7656, Fax: 416-327-0469

Criminal Injuries Compensation Board, 439 University Ave., 4th Fl., Toronto, ON M5G 1Y8
416-326-2900, Fax: 416-326-2883, 800-372-7463, info.cicb@ontario.ca

Environmental Sciences & Standards Division, 135 St. Clair Ave. West, 14th Fl., Toronto, ON M4V 1P5
Fax: 416-314-6358

Judicial Appointments Advisory Committee, c/o Ministry of Government Services Mail Delivery, 77 Wellesley St. West, #M2B-88, Toronto, ON M7A 1N3
416-326-4060, Fax: 416-212-7316

Legal Aid Ontario, Atrium on Bay, #200, 40 Dundas St. West, Toronto, ON M5G 2H1
416-979-1446, Fax: 416-979-8669, 800-668-8258, info@lao.on.ca

Licence Appeal Tribunal, #530, 20 Dundas St. West, Toronto, ON M5G 2C2
416-314-4260, Fax: 416-314-4270, 800-255-2214

Liquor Control Board of Ontario, 55 Lake Shore Blvd. East, Toronto, ON M5E 1A4
416-365-5900, Fax: 416-864-2476, 800-668-5226, infoline@lcbo.com

Office for Victims of Crime, 700 Bay St., 3rd Fl., Toronto, ON M5G 1Z6
416-326-1682, Fax: 416-326-4497, 887-435-7661, ovc@ontario.ca

Office of the Children's Lawyer, 393 University Ave., 14th Fl., Toronto, ON M5G 1W9
416-314-8000, Fax: 416-314-8050

Office of the Integrity Commissioner, #2100, 2 Bloor St. East, Toronto, ON M4W 3E2
416-314-8983, Fax: 416-314-8987, integrity.mail@oico.on.ca

Office of the Ombudsman, Bell Trinity Sq., South Tower, 483 Bay St., 10th Fl., Toronto, ON M5G 2C9
416-586-3300, Fax: 416-586-3485, 800-263-1830, info@ombudsman.on.ca

Ontario Civilian Police Commission, #605, 250 Dundas St. West, Toronto, ON M7A 2T3
416-314-3004, Fax: 416-314-0198, 888-515-5005

Ontario Human Rights Commission, #900, 180 Dundas St. West, Toronto, ON M7A 2R9
416-326-9511, Fax: 416-314-4494, 800-387-9080, info@ohrc.on.ca

Ontario Labour Relations Board, 505 University Ave., 2nd Fl., Toronto, ON M5G 2P1
416-326-7500, Fax: 416-326-7531, 877-339-3335

Ontario Ministry of Community Safety & Correctional Services, George Drew Bldg., 25 Grosvenor St., 18th Fl., Toronto, ON M7A 1Y6
416-326-5000, Fax: 416-326-0498, 866-517-0571, mcscs.feedback@ontario.ca

Ontario Ministry of the Attorney General, McMurtry-Scott Bldg., 720 Bay St., 11th Fl., Toronto, ON M7A 2S9
416-326-2220, Fax: 416-326-4007, 800-518-7901, attorneygeneral@ontario.ca

Ontario Municipal Board & Board of Negotiation, #1500, 655 Bay St., Toronto, ON M5G 1E5
416-212-6349, Fax: 416-326-5370, 866-448-2248, ontario.municipal.board@ontario.ca

Ontario Parole Board, #1803, 415 Yonge St., Toronto, ON M5B 2E7
416-325-4480, Fax: 416-325-4485, 888-579-2888

Ontario Police Arbitration Commission, George Drew Bldg., 25 Grosvenor St., 1st Fl., Toronto, ON M7A 1Y6
416-314-3520, Fax: 416-314-3522, 866-517-0571

Ontario Review Board, 151 Bloor St. West, 10th Fl., Toronto, ON M5S 2T5
416-327-8866, Fax: 416-327-8867, orb@ontario.ca

OPSEU Pension Trust, #1200, 1 Adelaide St. East, Toronto, ON M5C 3A7
416-681-6161, Fax: 416-681-6175, 800-637-0024

Road User Safety Division, Bldg A, #191, 1201 Wilson Ave., Downsview, ON M3M 1J8
416-235-2999, Fax: 416-235-4153

Safety, Licensing Appeals & Standards Tribunals Ontario, #5230, 20 Dundas St. West, Toronto, ON M5G 2C2
416-212-0334, Fax: 416-314-4270, 855-444-7454, slastoinfo@ontario.ca

ServiceOntario, College Park, 777 Bay St., 15th fl., Toronto, ON M7A 2J3
Fax: 416-326-1313, 800-267-8097

Workplace Safety & Insurance Board, 200 Front St. West, Ground Fl., Toronto, ON M5V 3J1
416-344-1000, Fax: 416-344-4684, 800-387-0750

Prince Edward Island

Advisory Council on the Status of Women, Sherwood Business Centre, 161 St. Peter's Rd., Main Level, PO Box 2000, Charlottetown, PE C1A 7N8
902-368-4510, Fax: 902-368-3269, info@peistatusofwomen.ca

Housing Services, Jones Bldg., 11 Kent St., 2nd Fl., PO Box 2000, Charlottetown, PE C1A 7N8
902-620-3777, Fax: 902-894-0242

Office of the Auditor General, Shaw Bldg., 105 Rochford St. North, 2nd Fl., PO Box 2000, Charlottetown, PE C1A 7N8
902-368-4520, Fax: 902-368-4598

Office of the Conflict of Interest Commissioner, 197 Richmond St., 1st Fl., PO Box 2000, Charlottetown, PE C1A 7N8
902-368-5970, Fax: 902-368-5175

Prince Edward Island Human Rights Commission, 53 Water St., PO Box 2000, Charlottetown, PE C1A 7N8
902-368-4180, Fax: 902-368-4236, 800-237-5031, contact@peihumanrights.ca

Prince Edward Island Liquor Control Commission, 3 Garfield St., PO Box 967, Charlottetown, PE C1A 7M4
902-368-5710, Fax: 902-368-5735

Prince Edward Island Regulatory & Appeals Commission, National Bank Tower, #501, 134 Kent St., PO Box 577, Charlottetown, PE C1A 7L1
902-892-3501, Fax: 902-566-4076, 800-501-6268, info@irac.pe.ca

Prince Edward Island Workers Compensation Board, 14 Weymouth St., PO Box 757, Charlottetown, PE C1A 7L7
902-368-5680, Fax: 902-368-5696, 800-237-5049

Workers Compensation Appeal Tribunal, 161 St. Peters Rd., 1st Fl., PO Box 2000, Charlottetown, PE C1A 7N8
902-894-0278, Fax: 902-620-3477

Québec

Bureau du coroner, Édifice le Delta 2, #390, 2875, boul Laurier, Québec, QC G1V 5B1
418-643-1845, Fax: 418-643-6174, 866-312-7051, clientele.coroner@msp.gouv.qc.ca

Comité de déontologie policière, Tour du Saint-Laurent, #A-200, 2525, boul Laurier, 2e étage, Québec, QC G1V 4Z6
418-646-1936, Fax: 418-528-0987, comite.deontologie@msp.gouv.qc.ca

Commissaire à la déontologie policière, #1-40, 1200, rte de l'Église, Québec, QC G1V 4Y9
418-643-7897, Fax: 418-528-9473, 877-237-7897, deontologie-policiere.Québec@msp.gouv.qc.ca

Commissaire à la lutte contre la corruption (Unité permanente anticorruption), #UA8010, 600, rue Fullum, Montréal, QC H2K 3L6
514-228-3098, Fax: 514-873-0177, 855-567-8722

Commissariat des incendies, 455, rue Dupont, Québec, QC G1K 6N2
418-529-5706, Fax: 418-529-9922

Commission des droits de la personne et des droits de la jeunesse, 360, rue Saint-Jacques, 2e étage, Montréal, QC H2Y 1P5
514-873-5146, Fax: 514-873-6032, 800-361-6477, accueil@cdpdj.qc.ca

Commission des lésions professionnelles, #700, 900, Place d'Youville, Québec, QC G1R 3P7
418-644-7777, Fax: 418-644-6443, 800-463-1591

Commission des services juridiques, Tour de l'Est, #1404, 2, Complexe Desjardins, CP 123, Montréal, QC H5B 1B3
514-873-3562, Fax: 514-864-2351, info@csj.qc.ca

Commission québecoise des libérations conditionnelles, #1.32A, 300, boul Jean-Lesage, Québec, QC G1K 8K6
418-646-8300, Fax: 418-643-7217, cqlc@cqlc.gouv.qc.ca

Conseil de la justice administrative, #RC-01, 575, rue Saint-Amable, Québec, QC G1R 2G4
418-644-6279, Fax: 418-528-8471, 888-848-2581, president@cja.gouv.qc.ca

Conseil de la magistrature, #RC.01, 300, boul Jean-Lesage, Québec, QC G1K 8K6
418-644-2196, Fax: 418-528-1581, information@cm.gouv.qc.ca

Directeur des poursuites criminelles et pénales, Tour 1, #500, 2828, boul Laurier, Québec, QC G1V 0B9
418-643-4085, Fax: 418-643-7462, info@dpcp.gouv.qc.ca

Fonds d'aide aux recours collectifs, #10.30, 1, rue Notre-Dame est, Montréal, QC H2Y 1B6
514-393-2087

Le Protecteur du Citoyen, #1.25, 525, boul René-Lévesque est, Québec, QC G1R 5Y4
418-643-2688, Fax: 418-643-8759, 800-463-5070, protecteur@protecteurducitoyen.qc.ca

Ministère de la Justice, Édifice Louis-Philippe-Pigeon, 1200, rte de l'Église, Québec, QC G1V 4M1
418-643-5140, 866-536-5140, informations@justice.gouv.qc.ca

Ministère de la Sécurité publique, Tour des Laurentides, 2525, boul Laurier, 5e étage, Québec, QC G1V 2L2
418-646-6777, Fax: 418-643-0275, 866-644-6826
Régie des alcools, des courses et des jeux, 560, boul Charest est, Québec, QC G1K 3J3
418-643-7667, Fax: 418-643-5971, 800-363-0320
Société des alcools du Québec, 905, av De Lorimier, Montréal, QC H2K 3V9
514-254-2020, 866-873-2020, info@saq.com
Société québécoise d'information juridique, #600, 715, carré Victoria, Montréal, QC H2Y 2H7
514-842-8741, Fax: 514-844-8984
Sûreté du Québec, 1701, rue Parthenais, Montréal, QC H2K 3S7
514-598-4141, Fax: 514-598-4242
Tribunal administratif du Québec, 575, rue Saint-Amable, Québec, QC G1R 5R4
418-643-3418, Fax: 418-643-5335, 800-567-0278, tribunal.administratif@taq.gouv.qc.ca
Vérificateur général du Québec, 750, boulevard Charest est, 3e étage, Québec, QC G1K 9J6
418-691-5900, Fax: 418-644-4460, verificateur.general@vgq.qc.ca
École nationale de police du Québec, 350, rue Marguerite-d'Youville, Nicolet, QC J3T 1X4
819-293-8631, Fax: 819-293-8630, courriel@enpq.qc.ca

Saskatchewan

Financial & Consumer Affairs Authority, #601, 1919 Saskatchewan Dr., Regina, SK S4P 4H2
306-787-5645, Fax: 306-787-5899, 877-880-5550, consumerprotection@gov.sk.ca
Law Reform Commission of Saskatchewan, c/o University of Saskatchewan, College of Law, #185, 15 Campus Dr., Saskatoon, SK S7N 5A6
306-966-1625, Fax: 306-966-5900
Legal Aid Saskatchewan, #502, 201 - 21 St. East, Saskatoon, SK S7K 0B8
306-933-5300, Fax: 306-933-6764, 800-667-3764
Ombudsman Saskatchewan, #150, 2401 Saskatchewan Dr., Regina, SK S4P 4H8
306-787-6211, Fax: 306-787-9090, 800-667-7180, ombreg@ombudsman.sk.ca
Public & Private Rights Board, #23, 3085 Albert St., Regina, SK S4S 0B1
306-787-4071, Fax: 306-787-0088
Saskatchewan Film & Video Classification Board, #500, 1919 Saskatchewan Dr., Regina, SK S4P 4H2
306-787-5550, Fax: 306-787-9779, 888-374-4636
Saskatchewan Human Rights Commission, Saskatoon Office, Sturdy Stone Bdg., #816, 122 - 3 Ave. North, 8th Fl., Saskatoon, SK S7K 2H6
306-933-5952, Fax: 306-933-7863, 800-667-9249, shrc@gov.sk.ca
Saskatchewan Justice & Attorney General, 1874 Scarth St., Regina, SK S4P 4B3
306-787-7872
Saskatchewan Liquor & Gaming Authority, 2500 Victoria Ave., PO Box 5054, Regina, SK S4P 3M3
306-787-5563, 800-667-7565, inquiry@slga.gov.sk.ca
Saskatchewan Public Complaints Commission, #300, 1919 Saskatchewan Dr., Regina, SK S4P 4H2
306-787-6519, Fax: 306-787-6528, 866-256-6194
Saskatchewan Review Board, 188 - 11th St. West, Prince Albert, SK S6V 6G1
306-953-2812, Fax: 306-953-3342, lbutton-rowe@skprovcourt.ca
Saskatchewan Workers' Compensation Board, #200, 1881 Scarth St., Regina, SK S4P 4L1
306-787-4370, Fax: 306-787-4311, 800-667-7590, webmaster@wcbsask.com
Surface Rights Board of Arbitration, 113 - 2nd Ave. East, PO Box 1597, Kindersley, SK S0L 1S0
306-463-5447, Fax: 306-463-5449, surfacerightsboard@gov.sk.ca

Yukon Territory

Driver Control Board, #102, 211 Hawkins St., PO Box 2703, Whitehorse, YT Y1A 2C6
867-667-5623, Fax: 867-667-5799, dcb@gov.yk.ca
Law Society of Yukon - Discipline Committee, #202, 302 Steele St., Whitehorse, YT Y1A 3W8
867-668-4231, Fax: 867-667-7556
Law Society of Yukon - Executive, #202, 302 Steele St., Whitehorse, YT Y1A 2C5
867-668-4231, Fax: 867-667-7556
Yukon Human Rights Commission, #101, 9010 Quartz St., Whitehorse, YT Y1A 2Z5
867-667-6226, Fax: 867-667-2662, 800-661-0535, humanrights@yhrc.yk.ca
Yukon Judicial Council, PO Box 31222, Whitehorse, YT Y1A 5P7
867-667-5438, Fax: 867-393-6400, courtservices@gov.yk.ca
Yukon Justice, Andrew Philipsen Law Centre, 2134 Second Ave., PO Box 2703, Whitehorse, YT Y1A 2C6
867-667-3033, Fax: 867-393-5790, justice@gov.yk.ca
Yukon Law Foundation, PO Box 31789, Whitehorse, YT Y1A 6L3
867-667-7500, Fax: 867-393-3904
Yukon Legal Services Society/Legal Aid, #203, 2131 - 2nd Ave., Whitehorse, YT Y1A 1C3
867-667-5210, Fax: 867-667-8649, administration@legalaid.yk.ca
Yukon Liquor Corporation, 9031 Quartz Rd., Whitehorse, YT Y1A 4P9
867-667-5245, Fax: 867-393-6306, yukon.liquor@gov.yk.ca
Yukon Workers' Compensation Health & Safety Board, 401 Strickland St., Whitehorse, YT Y1A 5N8
867-667-5645, Fax: 867-393-6279, 800-661-0443, worksafe@gov.yk.ca

LEGAL & REGULATORY

Canadian Coast Guard, Centennial Towers, #6S018, 200 Kent St., Ottawa, ON K1A 0E6
613-993-0999, Fax: 613-990-1866, info@dfo-mpo.gc.ca
Commission for Environmental Cooperation, Secretariat, #200, 393, rue St-Jacques ouest, Montréal, QC H2Y 1N9
514-350-4300, Fax: 514-350-4314, info@cec.org
Office of the Public Sector Integrity Commissioner of Canada, 60 Queen St., 7th Fl., Ottawa, ON K1P 5Y7
613-941-6400, Fax: 613-941-6535, 866-941-6400
Public Servants Disclosure Protection Tribunal, #512, 90 Sparks St., Ottawa, ON K1P 5B4
613-943-8310, Fax: 613-943-8325, tribunal@psdpt-tpfd.gc.ca
Standards Council of Canada, #600, 55 Metcalfe St., Ottawa, ON K1P 6L5
613-238-3222, Fax: 613-569-7808, info@scc.ca
Standards Council of Canada, #200, 270 Albert Street, Ottawa, ON K1P 6N7
613-238-3222, Fax: 613-569-7808, info@scc.ca

Northwest Territories

Assessment Appeal Tribunal, #600, 5201 - 50th Ave., PO Box 1320, Yellowknife, NT X1A 3S9
867-873-7125, Fax: 867-873-0609

Nova Scotia

Crane Operators Appeal Board, 5151 Terminal Rd., 7th Fl., PO Box 697, Halifax, NS B3J 2T8
902-424-8595, Fax: 902-424-0217, fernanfs@gov.ns.ca
Elevators & Lifts Appeal Board, 5151 Terminal Rd., 7th Fl., PO Box 697, Halifax, NS B3J 2T8
902-424-8595, Fax: 902-424-0217
Pay Equity Commission, 5151 Terminal Rd., 6th Fl., PO Box 697, Halifax, NS B3J 2T8
902-424-8466, Fax: 902-424-0575
Power Engineers & Operators Appeal Committee, 5151 Terminal Rd., 7th Fl., PO Box 697, Halifax, NS B3J 2T8
902-424-8595, Fax: 902-424-0217
Workers' Advisers Program, #502, 5670 Spring Garden Rd., PO Box 1063, Halifax, NS B3J 2X1
Fax: 902-424-0530, 800-774-4712
Workers' Compensation Board of Nova Scotia, 5668 South St., PO Box 1150, Halifax, NS B3J 2Y2
902-491-8999, 800-870-3331, info@wcb.gov.ns.ca

Ontario

Environmental Commissioner of Ontario, #605, 1075 Bay St., Toronto, ON M5S 2B1
416-325-3377, Fax: 416-325-3370, 800-701-6454, commissioner@eco.on.ca
Ontario Ministry of Community Safety & Correctional Services, George Drew Bldg., 25 Grosvenor St., 18th Fl., Toronto, ON M7A 1Y6
416-326-5000, Fax: 416-326-0498, 866-517-0571, mcscs.feedback@ontario.ca
Road User Safety Division, Bldg A, #191, 1201 Wilson Ave., Downsview, ON M3M 1J8
416-235-2999, Fax: 416-235-4153

Prince Edward Island

Prince Edward Island Regulatory & Appeals Commission, National Bank Tower, #501, 134 Kent St., PO Box 577, Charlottetown, PE C1A 7L1
902-892-3501, Fax: 902-566-4076, 800-501-6268, info@irac.pe.ca

LEGAL AID SERVICES

British Columbia

Legal Services Society, #400, 510 Burrard St., Vancouver, BC V6C 3A8
604-601-6000

Manitoba

Legal Aid Manitoba, 287 Broadway, 4th Fl., Winnipeg, MB R3C 0R9
204-985-8500, Fax: 204-944-8582, 800-261-2960, info@legalaid.mb.ca

New Brunswick

New Brunswick Legal Aid Services Commission, #501, 500 Beaverbrook Ct., Fredericton, NB E3B 5X4
506-444-2776, Fax: 506-444-2290, info@legalaid.nb.ca

Newfoundland & Labrador

Newfoundland & Labrador Legal Aid Commission, #300, 251 Empire Ave., St. John's, NL A1C 5J9
709-753-7860, Fax: 709-753-7851, 800-563-9911, nlac@legalaid.nl.ca

Northwest Territories

Legal Services Board of the Northwest Territories, 4915 - 48th St., PO Box 1320, Yellowknife, NT X1A 2L9
867-873-7450, Fax: 867-873-5320, lsb@gov.nt.ca

Nova Scotia

Nova Scotia Legal Aid Commission, Office of the Executive Director, #920, 1701 Hollis St., Halifax, NS B3J 3M8
902-420-6578, 877-420-6578

Ontario

Legal Aid Ontario, Atrium on Bay, #200, 40 Dundas St. West, Toronto, ON M5G 2H1
416-979-1446, Fax: 416-979-8669, 800-668-8258, info@lao.on.ca

Prince Edward Island

Legal Aid, 40 Great George St., PO Box 2000, Charlottetown, PE C1A 7N8

Québec

Fonds d'aide aux recours collectifs, #10.30, 1, rue Notre-Dame est, Montréal, QC H2Y 1B6
514-393-2087

Saskatchewan

Legal Aid Saskatchewan, #502, 201 - 21 St. East, Saskatoon, SK S7K 0B8
306-933-5300, Fax: 306-933-6764, 800-667-3764

Yukon Territory

Yukon Legal Services Society/Legal Aid, #203, 2131 - 2nd Ave., Whitehorse, YT Y1A 1C3
867-667-5210, Fax: 867-667-8649, administration@legalaid.yk.ca

LEGISLATIVE ASSEMBLIES/NATIONAL ASSEMBLIES/HOUSES

House of Commons, Canada, House of Commons, Centre Block, Parliament Buildings, 111 Wellington St., Ottawa, ON K1A 0A6
613-992-4793, 866-599-4999, info@parl.gc.ca

Alberta

Legislative Assembly of Alberta, Legislature Annex, 9718 - 107 St., Edmonton, AB T5K 1E4
780-427-2826, Fax: 780-427-1623, laocommunications@assembly.ab.ca

British Columbia

BC Legislative Assembly & Independent Offices, Clerk's Office, Parliament Bldgs., Victoria, BC V8V 1X4
250-387-3785, Fax: 250-387-0942, ClerkHouse@leg.bc.ca

Manitoba

Manitoba Legislative Assembly, c/o Clerk's Office, Legislative Bldg., #237, 450 Broadway, Winnipeg, MB R3C 0V8
204-945-3636, Fax: 204-948-2507, clerkla@leg.gov.mb.ca

New Brunswick

Legislative Assembly of New Brunswick, Legislative Bldg., Centre Block, PO Box 6000, Fredericton, NB E3B 5H1
506-453-2506, Fax: 506-453-7154, wwwleg@gnb.ca

Newfoundland & Labrador

House of Assembly, c/o Clerk's Office, Confederation Bldg., PO Box 8700, St. John's, NL A1B 4J6
709-729-3405

Northwest Territories

NWT Legislative Assembly, 4570 - 48 St., PO Box 1320, Yellowknife, NT X1A 2L9
867-669-2200, 800-661-0784

Nova Scotia

Legislative House of Assembly, c/o Clerk's Office, Province House, 1st Fl., PO Box 1617, Halifax, NS B3J 2Y3
902-424-5978, Fax: 902-424-0632

Nunavut

Nunavut Legislative Assembly, 926 Federal Rd., PO Box 1200, Iqaluit, NU X0A 0H0
867-975-5000, Fax: 867-975-5190, 877-334-7266, leginfo@assembly.nu.ca

Ontario

Ontario Legislative Assembly, c/o Clerk of the Legislative Assembly, #104, Legislative Bldg., Queen's Park, Toronto, ON M7A 1A2
416-325-7500, Fax: 416-325-7489, web@ola.org

Prince Edward Island

Prince Edward Island Legislative Assembly, 197 Richmond St., PO Box 2000, Charlottetown, PE C1A 7N8
902-368-5970, Fax: 902-368-5175, 877-315-5518, legislativelibrary@assembly.pe.ca

Québec
L'Assemblée nationale, Hôtel du Parlement, 1045, rue des Parlementaires, Québec, QC G1A 1A3
418-643-7239, Fax: 418-646-4271, 866-337-8837, responsable.contenu@assnat.qc.ca

Saskatchewan
Legislative Assembly of Saskatchewan, Office of the Clerk, Legislative Building, #239, 2405 Legislative Dr., Regina, SK S4S 0B3
info@legassembly.sk.ca

Yukon Territory
Yukon Legislative Assembly, 2071 - 2nd Ave., PO Box 2703, Whitehorse, YT Y1A 2C6
867-667-5498, yla@gov.yk.ca

LEISURE CRAFT & VEHICLE REGULATIONS

Nova Scotia
Nova Scotia Department of Transportation & Infrastructure Renewal, Johnston Bldg., 1672 Granville St., 2nd Fl., PO Box 186, Halifax, NS B3J 2N2
902-424-2297, Fax: 902-424-0532, 888-432-3233, tpwpaff@novascotia.ca
Service Nova Scotia, c/o Public Enquiries - Service Nova Scotia, PO Box 2734, Halifax, NS B3J 3K5
902-424-5200, Fax: 902-424-0720, 800-670-4357

Ontario
Ontario Ministry of Transportation, Ferguson Block, 77 Wellesley St. West, 3rd Fl., Toronto, ON M7A 1Z8
416-327-9200, Fax: 416-327-9185, 800-268-4686

Québec
Ministère des Transports, de la Mobilité durable et de l'Électrification des transports, 700, boul René-Lévesque est, 29e étage, Québec, QC G1R 5H1
418-643-6980, Fax: 418-643-2033, 888-355-0511, communications@mtq.gouv.qc.ca

Saskatchewan
Saskatchewan Government Insurance, 2260 - 11th Ave., Regina, SK S4P 0J9
306-751-1200, Fax: 306-787-7477, 800-667-8015, sgiinquiries@sgi.sk.ca

LIBRARIES

Library & Archives Canada, 395 Wellington St., Ottawa, ON K1A 0N4
613-996-5115, Fax: 613-995-6274, 866-578-7777
Library of Parliament, Parliamentary Buildings, Ottawa, ON K1A 0A9
613-992-4793, 866-599-4999, info@parl.gc.ca
National Research Council Canada - National Science Library, 1200 Montreal Rd., Ottawa, ON K1A 0R6
613-998-8544, Fax: 613-998-2399, 800-668-1222, NRC.KMHelpdesk-BureaudaideGS.CNRC@nrc-cnrc.gc.ca

New Brunswick
Legislative Assembly of New Brunswick, Legislative Bldg., Centre Block, PO Box 6000, Fredericton, NB E3B 5H1
506-453-2506, Fax: 506-453-7154, wwwleg@gnb.ca

Newfoundland & Labrador
Provincial Information & Library Resources Board, 48 St. George's Ave., Stephenville, NL A2H 1K9
709-643-0900, Fax: 709-643-0925

Nova Scotia
Legislative House of Assembly, c/o Clerk's Office, Province House, 1st Fl., PO Box 1617, Halifax, NS B3J 2Y3
902-424-5978, Fax: 902-424-0632

Nunavut
Nunavut Territory Department of Culture & Heritage, PO Box 1000 800, Iqaluit, NU X0A 0H0
867-975-5500, Fax: 867-975-5504, 866-934-2035

Ontario
Ontario Library Service - North, 334 Regent St., Sudbury, ON P3C 4E2
705-675-6467, Fax: 705-675-2285, 800-461-6348
Southern Ontario Library Service, #902, 111 Peter St., Toronto, ON M5V 2H1
416-961-1669, Fax: 416-961-5122, 800-387-5765

Québec
Bibliothèque et Archives nationales du Québec (BAnQ), 2275, rue Holt, Montréal, QC H2G 3H1
514-873-1100, Fax: 514-873-9312, 800-363-9028

LIQUOR CONTROL

See Also: Drugs & Alcohol

British Columbia
Liquor Control & Licensing Branch, PO Box 9292 Prov Govt, Victoria, BC V8W 9J8
250-952-5787, Fax: 250-952-7066
Liquor Distribution Branch, 2625 Rupert St., Vancouver, BC V5M 3T5
604-252-3000, Fax: 604-252-3026, communications@bcliquorstores.com

Manitoba
Liquor & Gaming Authority of Manitoba, #800, 215 Garry St., Winnipeg, MB R3C 3P3
204-945-9400, Fax: 204-945-9450, 800-782-0363, gaminglicence@LGAmanitoba.ca
Manitoba Liquor & Lotteries, 830 Empress St., Winnipeg, MB R3G 3H3
204-957-2500, Fax: 204-284-3500, 800-265-3912

New Brunswick
New Brunswick Liquor Corporation, 170 Wilsey Rd., PO Box 20787, Fredericton, NB E3B 5B8
506-452-6826, Fax: 506-462-2024, Receptionist@anbl.com

Newfoundland & Labrador
Newfoundland & Labrador Liquor Corporation, 90 Kenmount Rd., PO Box 8750 A, St. John's, NL A1B 3V1
709-724-1100, Fax: 709-754-0321, info@nfliquor.com

Northwest Territories
Northwest Territories Liquor Commission, #201, 31 Capital Dr., Hay River, NT X0E 1G2
867-874-8700, Fax: 867-874-8720
Northwest Territories Liquor Licensing Board, #204, 31 Capital Dr., Hay River, NT X0E 1G2
867-874-8715, Fax: 867-874-8722, 800-351-7770

Nova Scotia
Nova Scotia Liquor Corporation, Bayers Lake Business Park, 93 Chain Lake Dr., Halifax, NS B3S 1A3
902-450-5874, 800-567-5874

Nunavut
Liquor Licensing Board, PO Box 1269, Iqaluit, NU X0A 0H0
867-975-6533, Fax: 867-975-6511, nllb@gov.nu.ca

Ontario
Alcohol & Gaming Commission of Ontario, 90 Sheppard Ave. East, Toronto, ON M2N 0A4
416-326-8700, Fax: 416-326-5555, 800-522-2876, customer.service@agco.ca
Liquor Control Board of Ontario, 55 Lake Shore Blvd. East, Toronto, ON M5E 1A4
416-365-5900, Fax: 416-864-2476, 800-668-5226, infoline@lcbo.com

Prince Edward Island
Prince Edward Island Liquor Control Commission, 3 Garfield St., PO Box 967, Charlottetown, PE C1A 7M4
902-368-5710, Fax: 902-368-5735

Québec
Régie des alcools, des courses et des jeux, 560, boul Charest est, Québec, QC G1K 3J3
418-643-7667, Fax: 418-643-5971, 800-363-0320
Société des alcools du Québec, 905, av De Lorimier, Montréal, QC H2K 3V9
514-254-2020, 866-873-2020, info@saq.com

Saskatchewan
Saskatchewan Liquor & Gaming Authority, 2500 Victoria Ave., PO Box 5054, Regina, SK S4P 3M3
306-787-5563, 800-667-7565, inquiry@slga.gov.sk.ca

Yukon Territory
Yukon Liquor Corporation, 9031 Quartz Rd., Whitehorse, YT Y1A 4P9
867-667-5245, Fax: 867-393-6306, yukon.liquor@gov.yk.ca

LOTTERIES & GAMING

British Columbia
Arts, Culture, Gaming Grants & Sport, PO Box 9490 Prov Govt, Victoria, BC V8W 9N7
250-356-6914, Fax: 250-387-7973
British Columbia Lottery Corporation, 74 West Seymour St., Kamloops, BC V2C 1E2
250-828-5500, Fax: 250-828-5631, 866-815-0222
Gaming Policy & Enforcement, PO Box 9311 Prov Govt, Victoria, BC V8W 9N1
250-387-1301, Fax: 250-387-1818, Gaming.branch@gov.bc.ca

Manitoba
Liquor & Gaming Authority of Manitoba, #800, 215 Garry St., Winnipeg, MB R3C 3P3
204-945-9400, Fax: 204-945-9450, 800-782-0363, gaminglicence@LGAmanitoba.ca
Manitoba Liquor & Lotteries, 830 Empress St., Winnipeg, MB R3G 3H3
204-957-2500, Fax: 204-284-3500, 800-265-3912

New Brunswick
Atlantic Lottery Corporation, 922 Main St., PO Box 5500, Moncton, NB E1C 8W6
800-561-3942, info@alc.ca
New Brunswick Lotteries & Gaming Corporation, Chancery Place, 4th Fl., PO Box 6000, Fredericton, NB E3B 5H1
506-453-2451, Fax: 506-453-2053

Newfoundland & Labrador
Newfoundland & Labrador Department of Service NL, PO Box 8700, St. John's, NL A1B 4J6
709-729-4834, servicenlinfo@gov.nl.ca

Nova Scotia
Nova Scotia Provincial Lotteries & Casino Corporation, Summit Place, 1601 Lower Water St., 5th Fl., PO Box 1501, Halifax, NS B3J 2Y3
902-424-2203, Fax: 902-424-0724

Nunavut
Nunavut Territory Department of Community & Government Services, W.G. Brown Bldg., 4th Fl., PO Box 1000 700, Iqaluit, NU X0A 0H0
867-975-5400, Fax: 867-975-5305

Ontario
Alcohol & Gaming Commission of Ontario, 90 Sheppard Ave. East, Toronto, ON M2N 0A4
416-326-8700, Fax: 416-326-5555, 800-522-2876, customer.service@agco.ca
Ontario Lottery & Gaming Corporation, Roberta Bondar Pl., #800, 70 Foster Dr., Sault Ste. Marie, ON P6A 6V2
705-946-6464, Fax: 416-224-7000, 800-387-0098

Québec
Régie des alcools, des courses et des jeux, 560, boul Charest est, Québec, QC G1K 3J3
418-643-7667, Fax: 418-643-5971, 800-363-0320
Société de financement des infrastructures locales, 12, rue Saint-Louis, Québec, QC G1R 5L3
Société des loteries du Québec, 500, rue Sherbrooke ouest, Montréal, QC H3A 3G6
514-282-8000, Fax: 514-873-8999

Saskatchewan
Saskatchewan Gaming Corporation (SaskGaming), 1880 Saskatchewan Dr., 3rd Fl., Regina, SK S4P 0B2
306-787-1590, 800-555-3189, contact@casinoregina.com
Saskatchewan Liquor & Gaming Authority, 2500 Victoria Ave., PO Box 5054, Regina, SK S4P 3M3
306-787-5563, 800-667-7565, inquiry@slga.gov.sk.ca

Yukon Territory
Yukon Lottery Commission/Lotteries Yukon, #101, 205 Hawkins St., Whitehorse, YT Y1A 1X3
867-633-7890, Fax: 867-668-7561, 800-661-0555, lotteriesyukon@gov.yk.ca

MAPS, CHARTS & AERIAL PHOTOGRAPHS

Canada Centre for Mapping & Earth Observation, #212, 50 Place de la Cité, PO Box 162, Sherbrooke, QC J1H 4G9
Surveyor General Branch - Geomatics Canada, #605, 9700 Jasper Ave., Edmonton, AB T5J 4C3
780-495-2519, Fax: 780-495-4052

Nova Scotia
Geomatics Centre, 160 Willow St., Amherst, NS B4H 3W5
902-667-7231, Fax: 902-667-6008, geoinfo@novascotia.ca

Ontario
Association of Ontario Land Surveyors, 1043 McNicoll Ave., Toronto, ON M1W 3W6
416-491-9020, Fax: 416-491-2576, 800-268-0718

MARINE NAVIGATION

Atlantic Pilotage Authority, Cogswell Tower, #910, 2000 Barrington St., Halifax, NS B3J 3K1
902-426-2550, Fax: 902-426-4004, 877-272-3477, dispatch@atlanticpilotage.com
Great Lakes Pilotage Authority, 202 Pitt St., 2nd fl., PO Box 95, Cornwall, ON K6H 5R9
613-933-2991, Fax: 613-932-3793
Pacific Pilotage Authority Canada, #1000, 1130 West Pender St., Vancouver, BC V6E 4A4
604-666-6771, Fax: 604-666-1647, info@ppa.gc.ca
St. Lawrence Seaway Management Corporation, 202 Pitt St., Cornwall, ON K6J 3P7
613-932-5170, Fax: 613-932-7286, marketing@seaway.ca

MARINE SCIENCES

Marine Performance Evaluation & Testing Facilities, c/o National Research Council, 1200 Montreal Rd., Ottawa, ON K1A 0R6

MEDICAL EXAMINERS

See: Coroners

Alberta
Justice Services Division, Bowker Building, 9833 - 109 St., 2nd Fl., Edmonton, AB T5K 2E8

MENTAL HEALTH

See: Health Services

Mental Health Commission of Canada, #600, 100 Sparks St., Ottawa, ON K1P 5B7
613-683-3755, Fax: 613-798-2989, info@mentalhealthcommission.ca

Alberta

Alberta Health, PO Box 1360 Main,Edmonton, AB T5J 2N3
780-427-7164, -310-0000

Alberta Health Advocates, Centre West Bldg., 10035 - 108 St., 12th Fl., Edmonton, AB T5J 3E1
780-422-1812, Fax: 780-422-0695, -310-0000, healthadvocates@gov.ab.ca

British Columbia

British Columbia Review Board, #1020, 510 Burrard St., Vancouver, BC V6C 3A8
604-660-8789, Fax: 604-660-8809, 877-305-2277

Mental Health Review Board, #302, 960 Quayside Dr., New Westminster, BC V3M 6G2
604-660-2325, Fax: 604-660-2403

New Brunswick

Psychiatric Patient Advocate Services Review Board, c/o Dept. of Health, Psychiatric Patient Advocate Services, #505, 860 Main St., Moncton, NB E1C 1G2
506-869-6818, Fax: 506-869-6101, 888-350-4133

Psychiatric Patient Advocate Services Tribunal, c/o Dept. of Health, Psychiatric Patient Advocate Services, #505, 860 Main St., Moncton, NB E1C 1G2
506-869-6818, Fax: 506-869-6101, 888-350-4133

Ontario

Ontario Mental Health Foundation, 180 Bloor St. West, #UC 101, Toronto, ON M5S 2V6
416-920-7721, Fax: 416-920-0026, grants@omhf.on.ca

Ontario Ministry of Community & Social Services, Hepburn Block, 80 Grosvenor St., 6th Fl., Toronto, ON M7A 1E9
416-325-5666, Fax: 416-325-3347, 888-789-4199

Ontario Ministry of Health & Long-Term Care, Hepburn Block, 80 Grosvenor St., 10th Fl, Toronto, ON M7A 2C4
416-327-4327, 800-268-1153

Saskatchewan

Saskatchewan Review Board, 188 - 11th St. West, Prince Albert, SK S6V 6G1
306-953-2812, Fax: 306-953-3342, lbutton-rowe@skprovcourt.ca

MINERALS, MINES & MINING

CanmetMATERIALS, 183 Longwood Rd. South, Hamilton, ON L8P 0A5

CanmetMINING, 555 Booth St., Ottawa, ON K1A 0G1
Fax: 613-947-6606

Earth Sciences Sector, 588 Booth St., Ottawa, ON K1A 0Y7

Alberta

Resource Development Policy Division, Petroleum Plaza NT, 9945 - 108 St. 8th Fl., Edmonton, AB T5K 2G6

British Columbia

British Columbia Ministry of Energy & Mines (& Responsible for Core Review), PO Box 9060 Prov Govt, Victoria, BC V8W 9E3

Mines & Mineral Resources Division, PO Box 9320 Prov Govt, Victoria, BC V8W 9N3
250-952-0470, Fax: 250-952-0491

Manitoba

Manitoba Mineral Resources, The Paris Building, 259 Portage Ave., 9th Fl., Winnipeg, MB R3B 3P4
204-945-6569, 800-223-5215, minesinfo@gov.mb.ca

Mining Board, #360, 1395 Ellice Ave., Winnipeg, MB R3G 3P2
Fax: 204-945-8427, 800-223-5215

New Brunswick

New Brunswick Department of Energy & Resource Development, Hugh John Flemming Forestry Centre, 1350 Regent St., Fredericton, NB E3C 2G6
506-453-3826, Fax: 506-444-4367, dnr_mrnweb@gnb.ca

Northwest Territories

Northwest Territories Department of Environment & Natural Resources, #600, 5102 - 50 Ave., Yellowknife, NT X1A 3S8
867-767-9231

Northwest Territories Department of Industry, Tourism & Investment, PO Box 1320, Yellowknife, NT X1A 2L9
867-767-9002

Nova Scotia

Nova Scotia Department of Energy, Joseph Howe Bldg., 1690 Hollis St., PO Box 2664, Halifax, NS B3J 3J9
902-424-4575, Fax: 902-424-0528, enerinfo@novascotia.ca

Nunavut

Nunavut Territory Department of Environment, PO Box 1000 1300, Iqaluit, NU X0A 0H0
867-975-7700, Fax: 867-975-7742, environment@gov.nu.ca

Ontario

Mines & Minerals Division, Willet Green Miller Centre, 933 Ramsey Lake Rd., Level B6, Sudbury, ON P3E 6B5
705-670-5755, Fax: 705-670-5818, 888-415-9845

Ontario Ministry of Northern Development & Mines, 159 Cedar St., Sudbury, ON P3E 6A5
705-670-5755, Fax: 705-670-5818, 888-415-9845, ndmminister@ontario.ca

Québec

Mines, Centre de service des Mines, #100, 1300, rue du Blizzard, Québec, QC G2K 0G9
418-627-6278, Fax: 418-644-8960, 800-363-7233, service.mines@mern.gouv.qc.ca

Énergie, #A407, 5700, 4e av ouest, Québec, QC G1H 6R1
418-627-6377, Fax: 418-643-0701

Saskatchewan

Energy & Resources, 2101 Scarth St., Regina, SK S4P 5H9
306-787-2528

Yukon Territory

Yukon Energy, Mines & Resources, PO Box 2703, Whitehorse, YT Y1A 2C6
867-667-3130, Fax: 867-456-3965, 800-661-0408, emr@gov.yk.ca

MINIMUM WAGES

See Also: Labour

British Columbia

British Columbia Ministry of Technology, Innovation & Citizens' Services, PO Box 9068 Prov Govt, Victoria, BC V8W 9E2
250-952-7623, Fax: 250-952-7628, 800-663-7867, EnquiryBC@gov.bc.ca

Québec

Commission des normes du travail, Hall Est, 400, boul Jean-Lesage, 7e étage, Québec, QC G1K 8W1
514-873-7061, Fax: 418-646-3678, 800-265-1414

Saskatchewan

Minimum Wage Board, #400, 1870 Albert St., Regina, SK S4P 4W1

MOTOR VEHICLES

See: Drivers' Licences

British Columbia

Office of the Superintendent of Motor Vehicles, PO Box 9254 Prov Govt, Victoria, BC V8W 9J2
250-387-7747, Fax: 250-356-5577, 855-387-7747, osmv.mailbox@gov.bc.ca

Vehicle Sales Authority of British Columbia, #208, 5455 - 152 St., Surrey, BC V3S 5A5
604-574-5050, Fax: 604-574-5883, consumer.services@mvsabc.com

Nova Scotia

Motor Vehicle Appeal Board, Maritime Centre, 1505 Barrington St., 9th Fl. North, Halifax, NS B3J 3K5
902-424-4256, 855-424-4256

MULTICULTURALISM

Canadian Race Relations Foundation, #225, 6 Garamond Ct., Toronto, ON M3C 1Z5
416-441-1900, Fax: 416-441-2752, 888-240-4936, info@crrf-fcrr.ca

Immigration & Refugee Board of Canada, Canada Bldg, 344 Slater St., 12th Fl., Ottawa, ON K1A 0K1
613-995-6486, Fax: 613-943-1550, contact@irb-cisr.gc.ca

Immigration, Refugees & Citizenship, Jean Edmonds, South Tower, 365 Laurier Ave. West, Ottawa, ON K1A 1L1
888-242-2100

British Columbia

British Columbia Ministry of Advanced Education, PO Box 9080 Prov Govt, Victoria, BC V8W 9E2
250-356-5170, AVED.GeneralInquiries@gov.bc.ca

British Columbia Ministry of International Trade (& Minister Responsible for Asia Pacific Strategy & Multiculturalism), PO Box 9063 Prov Gov,Victoria, BC V8W 9E2
250-953-0910, Fax: 250-953-0928

Industry Training Authority, 8100 Granville Ave., 8th Fl., Richmond, BC V6Y 3T6
778-328-8700, Fax: 778-328-8701, 866-660-6011, customerservice@itabc.ca

Manitoba

Adult Learning & Literacy, #350, 800 Portage Ave., Winnipeg, MB R3G 0N4
204-945-8247, Fax: 204-948-1008, all@gov.mb.ca

Manitoba Education & Training, #168, Legislative Bldg., 450 Broadway, Winnipeg, MB R3C 0V8
204-945-3720, Fax: 204-945-1291, minedu@leg.gov.mb.ca

Manitoba Ethnocultural Advisory & Advocacy Council, 215 Notre Dame Ave. 9th Fl., Winnipeg, MB R3B 1N3
204-945-2339, meaac@gov.mb.ca

Multiculturalism Secretariat, 213 Notre Dame Ave., 7th Fl., Winnipeg, MB R3B 1N3
204-945-5632, multisec@gov.mb.ca

Newfoundland & Labrador

Office of Immigration & Multiculturalism, c/o Department of Advanced Education & Skills, 100 Prince Phillip Dr., PO Box 8700, St. John's, NL A1B 4J6
709-729-6607, Fax: 709-729-7381, 888-632-4555, immigration@gov.nl.ca

Northwest Territories

Northwest Territories Department of Education, Culture & Employment, PO Box 1320, Yellowknife, NT X1A 2L9
ecepublicaffairs@gov.nt.ca

Nova Scotia

Nova Scotia Department of Communities, Culture & Heritage, 1741 Brunswick St., 3rd Fl., PO Box 456 Central,Halifax, NS B3J 2R5
902-424-2170, cch@novascotia.ca

Office of Immigration, #110A, 1741 Brunswick St., PO Box 1535, Halifax, NS B3J 2Y3
902-424-5230, Fax: 902-424-7936, 877-292-9597, nsnp@novascotia.ca

Prince Edward Island

Prince Edward Island Department of Education, Early Learning & Culture, Holman Centre, #101, 250 Water St., Summerside, PE C1N 1B6
902-438-4130, Fax: 902-438-4062

Québec

Ministère de l'Immigration, de la Diversité et de l'Inclusion, Édifice Gérald-Godin, 360, rue McGill, Montréal, QC H2Y 2E9
514-864-9191, Fax: 514-864-2899, 877-864-9191

Ministère de la Culture et Communications, 225, Grande Allée est, Québec, QC G1R 5G5
888-380-8882

MUNICIPAL & RURAL AFFAIRS

Canada Economic Development for Québec Regions, Édifice Dominion Square, #900, 1255, rue Peel, Montréal, QC H3B 2T9
514-283-6412, Fax: 514-283-3302, 866-385-6412

Canada Mortgage & Housing Corporation, 700 Montreal Rd., Ottawa, ON K1A 0P7
613-748-2000, Fax: 613-748-2098, 800-668-2642, chic@cmhc-schl.gc.ca

Indigenous & Northern Affairs, Terrasses de la Chaudière, 10 Wellington St., North Tower, Gatineau, QC K1A 0H4
Fax: 866-817-3977, 800-567-9604, infopubs@aadnc-aandc.gc.ca

Mackenzie Valley Environmental Impact Review Board, 200 Scotia Centre, #5102, 50th Ave., PO Box 938, Yellowknife, NT X1A 2N7
867-766-7050, Fax: 867-766-7074, 866-912-3472

Nunavut Impact Review Board, 29 Mitik St., PO Box 1360, Cambridge Bay, NU X0B 0C0
867-983-4600, Fax: 867-983-2594, 866-233-3033, info@nirb.ca

Nunavut Planning Commission, PO Box 2101, Cambridge Bay, NU X0B 0C0
867-983-4625, Fax: 867-983-4626

Alberta

Alberta Agriculture & Forestry, JG O'Donoghue Bldg., #100A, 7000 - 113th St., Edmonton, AB T6H 5T6
780-427-2727, -310-3276, duke@gov.ab.ca

Alberta Municipal Affairs, Communications Branch, Commerce Place, 10155 - 102 St., 18th Fl., Edmonton, AB T5J 4L4
780-427-2732, Fax: 780-422-1419, -310-0000

Municipal Government Board, Commerce Place, 10155 - 102 St., 15th Fl., Edmonton, AB T5J 4L4
780-427-4864, Fax: 780-427-0986, -310-0000, mgbmail@gov.ab.ca

British Columbia

Local Government, PO Box 9490 Prov Govt, Victoria, BC V8W 9N7
250-356-6575, Fax: 250-387-7973

Manitoba

Manitoba Indigenous & Municipal Relations, Legislative Bldg, #344, 450 Broadway, Winnipeg, MB R3C 0V8
204-945-3719, Fax: 204-945-8374, anaweb@gov.mb.ca

Manitoba Municipal Board, #1144, 363 Broadway, Winnipeg, MB R3C 3N9
204-945-2941, Fax: 204-948-2235

Manitoba Municipal Government, #301, 450 Broadway Ave., Winnipeg, MB R3C 0V8
204-945-3744, 866-626-4862, mgi@gov.mb.ca

New Brunswick

New Brunswick Department of Health, HSBC Place, PO Box 5100, Fredericton, NB E3B 5G8
506-457-4800, Fax: 506-453-5243, Health.Sante@gnb.ca

Regional Development Corporation, Chancery Place, PO Box 6000, Fredericton, NB E3B 5H1
506-453-2277, Fax: 506-453-7988

Newfoundland & Labrador

Municipal Assessment Agency Inc., 75 O'Leary Ave., St. John's, NL A1B 2C9
709-724-1532, 877-777-2807, info@maa.ca

Newfoundland & Labrador Department of Health & Community Services, West Block, Confederation Bldg., PO Box 8700, St. John's, NL A1B 4J6
709-729-4984, healthinfo@gov.nl.ca

Newfoundland & Labrador Department of Municipal & Intergovernmental Affairs, West Block, Main Fl., Confederation Bldg., PO Box 8700, St. John's, NL A1B 4J6
709-729-3046, Fax: 709-729-0943, mainfo@gov.nl.ca

Northwest Territories

Northwest Territories Department of Municipal & Community Affairs, PO Box 1320, Yellowknife, NT X1A 2L9
867-767-9160, Fax: 867-873-0309

Nova Scotia

Nova Scotia Department of Municipal Affairs, Maritime Centre, 14 North, 1505 Barrington St., PO Box 216, Halifax, NS B3J 3K5
902-424-6642, 800-670-4357

Nova Scotia Department of Transportation & Infrastructure Renewal, Johnston Bldg., 1672 Granville St., 2nd Fl., PO Box 186, Halifax, NS B3J 2N2
902-424-2297, Fax: 902-424-0532, 888-432-3233, tpwpaff@novascotia.ca

Ontario

Northern Development Division, Roberta Bondar Place, #200, 70 Foster Dr., Sault Ste. Marie, ON P6A 6V8
705-945-5900, Fax: 705-945-5931, 800-461-2287

Ontario Ministry of Agriculture, Food & Rural Affairs, Ontario Government Bldg., 1 Stone Rd. West, Guelph, ON N1G 4Y2
519-826-3100, Fax: 519-826-4335, 888-466-2372, about.omafra@ontario.ca

Ontario Ministry of Municipal Affairs, College Park, 777 Bay St., 17th Fl., Toronto, ON M5G 2E5
416-585-7000, Fax: 416-585-6470, mininfo@ontario.ca

Ontario Ministry of Northern Development & Mines, 159 Cedar St., Sudbury, ON P3E 6A5
705-670-5755, Fax: 705-670-5818, 888-415-9845, ndmminister@ontario.ca

Prince Edward Island

Prince Edward Island Department of Transportation, Infrastructure & Energy, Jones Bldg., 11 Kent St., 3rd Fl., PO Box 2000, Charlottetown, PE C1A 7N8
902-368-5100, Fax: 902-368-5395

Québec

Comité consultatif de l'environnement Kativik, CP 930, Kuujjuaq, QC J0M 1C0
819-964-2961, Fax: 819-964-0694, keac-ccek@krg.ca

Commission municipale du Québec, Mezzanine, aile Chauveau, 10, rue Pierre-Olivier-Chauveau, Québec, QC G1R 4J3
418-691-2014, Fax: 418-644-4676, 866-353-6767

Ministère des Affaires municipales et Occupation du territoire, Aile Chaveau, 10, rue Pierre-Olivier-Chauveau, Québec, QC G1R 4J3
418-691-2015, Fax: 418-643-7385, communications@mamrot.gouv.qc.ca

Ministère des Finances, 12, rue Saint-Louis, Québec, QC G1R 5L3
418-528-9323, Fax: 418-646-1631, info@finances.gouv.qc.ca

Saskatchewan

Municipal Financing Corporation of Saskatchewan, 2350 Albert St., 6th Fl., Regina, SK S4P 4A6
306-787-8150, Fax: 306-787-8493

Saskatchewan Government Relations, 1855 Victoria Ave., Regina, SK S4P 3T2
306-787-8885

Saskatchewan Municipal Board, #480, 2151 Scarth St., Regina, SK S4P 2H8
306-787-6221, Fax: 306-787-1610, info@smb.gov.sk.ca

Yukon Territory

Yukon Community Services, PO Box 2703, Whitehorse, YT Y1A 2C6
867-667-5811, Fax: 867-393-6295, 800-661-0408, inquiry@gov.yk.ca

MUNICIPAL AFFAIRS

Alberta

Alberta Municipal Affairs, Communications Branch, Commerce Place, 10155 - 102 St., 18th Fl., Edmonton, AB T5J 4L4
780-427-2732, Fax: 780-422-1419, -310-0000

British Columbia

Local Government, PO Box 9490 Prov Govt, Victoria, BC V8W 9N7
250-356-6575, Fax: 250-387-7973

Office of the Auditor General for Local Government, #201, 10470 - 152nd St., Surrey, BC V3R 0Y3
604-930-7100

Manitoba

Local Government Development Division, 59 Elizabeth Dr., PO Box 33, Thompson, MB R8N 1X4
204-677-6794, Fax: 204-677-6525

Manitoba Indigenous & Municipal Relations, Legislative Bldg, #344, 450 Broadway, Winnipeg, MB R3C OV8
204-945-3719, Fax: 204-945-8374, anaweb@gov.mb.ca

Manitoba Municipal Board, #1144, 363 Broadway, Winnipeg, MB R3C 3N9
204-945-2941, Fax: 204-948-2235

Manitoba Municipal Government, #301, 450 Broadway Ave., Winnipeg, MB R3C 0V8
204-945-3744, 866-626-4862, mgi@gov.mb.ca

New Brunswick

New Brunswick Department of Environment & Local Government, Marysville Place, PO Box 6000, Fredericton, NB E3B 5H1
506-453-2690, Fax: 506-457-4994, elg/egl-info@gnb.ca

Regional Development Corporation, Chancery Place, PO Box 6000, Fredericton, NB E3B 5H1
506-453-2277, Fax: 506-453-7988

Newfoundland & Labrador

Municipal Assessment Agency Inc., 75 O'Leary Ave., St. John's, NL A1B 2C9
709-724-1532, 877-777-2807, info@maa.ca

Newfoundland & Labrador Department of Municipal & Intergovernmental Affairs, West Block, Main Fl., Confederation Bldg., PO Box 8700, St. John's, NL A1B 4J6
709-729-3046, Fax: 709-729-0943, mainfo@gov.nl.ca

Newfoundland & Labrador Municipal Financing Corporation, Confederation Bldg., PO Box 8700, St. John's, NL A1B 4J6
709-729-6686, Fax: 709-729-2095

Northwest Territories

Northwest Territories Department of Municipal & Community Affairs, PO Box 1320, Yellowknife, NT X1A 2L9
867-767-9160, Fax: 867-873-0309

Nova Scotia

Nova Scotia Department of Municipal Affairs, Maritime Centre, 14 North, 1505 Barrington St., PO Box 216, Halifax, NS B3J 3K5
902-424-6642, 800-670-4357

Nova Scotia Municipal Finance Corporation, Maritime Centre, 1505 Barrington St., 10th Fl. South, PO Box 850 M, Halifax, NS B3J 2V2
902-424-4590, Fax: 902-424-0525, gharding@gov.ns.ca

Nunavut

Nunavut Territory Department of Community & Government Services, W.G. Brown Bldg., 4th Fl., PO Box 1000 700, Iqaluit, NU X0A 0H0
867-975-5400, Fax: 867-975-5305

Ontario

Ontario Ministry of Municipal Affairs, College Park, 777 Bay St., 17th Fl., Toronto, ON M5G 2E5
416-585-7000, Fax: 416-585-6470, mininfo@ontario.ca

Prince Edward Island

Prince Edward Island Department of Family & Human Services, Jones Bldg., 11 Kent St., 2nd Fl., PO Box 2000, Charlottetown, PE C1A 7N8
902-620-3777, Fax: 902-894-0242, 866-594-3777

Québec

Ministère des Affaires municipales et Occupation du territoire, Aile Chaveau, 10, rue Pierre-Olivier-Chauveau, Québec, QC G1R 4J3
418-691-2015, Fax: 418-643-7385, communications@mamrot.gouv.qc.ca

Saskatchewan

Municipal Financing Corporation of Saskatchewan, 2350 Albert St., 6th Fl., Regina, SK S4P 4A6
306-787-8150, Fax: 306-787-8493

Saskatchewan Municipal Board, #480, 2151 Scarth St., Regina, SK S4P 2H8
306-787-6221, Fax: 306-787-1610, info@smb.gov.sk.ca

MUSEUMS

Canada Science & Technology Museum Corporation, PO Box 9724 T,Ottawa, ON K1G 5A3
613-991-3044, Fax: 613-993-7923, cts@techno-science.ca

Canadian Heritage, 15 Eddy St., Gatineau, QC K1A 0M5
819-997-0055, 866-811-0055, PCH.info-info.PCH@canada.ca

Canadian Museum for Human Rights, 85 Israel Asper Way, Winnipeg, MB R3C 0L5
204-289-2000, Fax: 204-289-2001, 877-877-6037, info@humanrights.ca

Canadian Museum of History, 100 Laurier St., Gatineau, QC K1A 0M8
819-776-7000, 800-555-5621

Canadian Museum of Nature, 240 McLeod St., PO Box 3443 D,Ottawa, ON K1P 6P4
613-566-4700, Fax: 613-364-4021, 800-263-4433

Canadian War Museum, 1 Vimy Pl., Ottawa, ON K1A 0M8
819-776-7000, 800-555-5621

National Gallery of Canada, 380 Sussex Dr., PO Box 427 A,Ottawa, ON K1N 9N4
613-990-1985, Fax: 613-993-4385, 800-319-2787, info@gallery.ca

British Columbia

Royal BC Museum Corporation, 675 Belleville St., Victoria, BC V8W 9W2
250-356-7226, 888-447-7977, reception@royalbcmuseum.bc.ca

Manitoba

Manitoba Museum, 190 Rupert Ave., Winnipeg, MB R3B 0N2
204-956-2830, Fax: 204-942-3679, info@manitobamuseum.ca

New Brunswick

New Brunswick Museum, Exhibition Centre, Market Square, Saint John, NB E2L 4Z6
506-643-2300, Fax: 506-643-6081, 888-268-9595, nbmuseum@nbm-mnb.ca

Newfoundland & Labrador

The Rooms Corporation, 9 Bonaventure Ave., PO Box 1800 C, St. John's, NL A1C 5P9
709-757-8000, Fax: 709-757-8017, information@therooms.ca

Nova Scotia

Art Gallery of Nova Scotia, 1723 Hollis St., PO Box 2262, Halifax, NS B3J 3C8
902-424-5280, Fax: 902-424-7359, infodesk@gov.ns.ca

Nova Scotia Museum, 1747 Summer St., Halifax, NS B3H 3A6
Fax: 902-424-0560, museum@gov.ns.ca

Ontario

Corporate Services Division, 54 Wellesley St., 4th Fl., Toronto, ON M7A 2E7
416-325-6866, Fax: 416-314-7014, 888-664-6008

Royal Ontario Museum, 100 Queen's Park Cres., Toronto, ON M5S 2C6
416-586-5549, Fax: 416-586-5685, info@rom.on.ca

Québec

Ministère de la Culture et Communications, 225, Grande Allée est, Québec, QC G1R 5G5
888-380-8882

Musée d'art contemporain de Montréal, 185, rue Ste-Catherine ouest, Montréal, QC H2X 3X5
514-847-6226, Fax: 514-847-6292, info@macm.org

Musée de la civilisation, 85, rue Dalhousie, CP 155 B,Québec, QC G1K 8R2
418-643-2158, Fax: 418-646-9705, 866-710-8031, mcqweb@mcq.org

Musée national des beaux-arts du Québec, Parc des Champs-de-Bataille, 1, av Wolfe-Montcalm, Québec, QC G1R 5H3
418-643-2150, 866-220-2150, info@mnba.qc.ca

Saskatchewan

Royal Saskatchewan Museum, 2445 Albert St., Regina, SK S4P 4W7
306-787-2815, Fax: 306-787-2820, rsminfo@gov.sk.ca

Western Development Museum, Curatorial Centre, 2935 Lorne Ave., Saskatoon, SK S7J 0S5
306-934-1400, Fax: 306-934-4467, 800-363-6345, info@wdm.ca

Yukon Territory

Yukon Tourism & Culture, 100 Hanson St., PO Box 2703, Whitehorse, YT Y1A 2C6
867-667-5036, Fax: 867-667-3546

NATIVE AFFAIRS

See: Aboriginal Affairs

Canadian Northern Economic Development Agency, Ottawa, ON K1A 0H4
855-897-2667, InfoNorth@CanNor.gc.ca

Indigenous & Northern Affairs, Terrasses de la Chaudière, 10 Wellington St., North Tower, Gatineau, QC K1A 0H4
Fax: 866-817-3977, 800-567-9604, infopubs@aadnc-aandc.gc.ca

Alberta

Alberta Indigenous Relations, Commerce Place, 10155 - 102 St. NW, 19th Fl., Edmonton, AB T5J 4G8
780-427-8407, Fax: 780-427-4019, -310-000

British Columbia

British Columbia Ministry of Aboriginal Relations & Reconciliation, 2957 Jutland Rd., PO Box 9100 Prov Govt, Victoria, BC V8W 9B1
250-387-6121, 800-663-7867, abrinfo@gov.bc.ca

Manitoba

Manitoba Indigenous & Municipal Relations, Legislative Bldg, #344, 450 Broadway, Winnipeg, MB R3C OV8
204-945-3719, Fax: 204-945-8374, anaweb@gov.mb.ca

Northwest Territories

Northwest Territories Department of Aboriginal Affairs & Intergovernmental Relations, 4910 - 52nd St., PO Box 1320, Yellowknife, NT X1A 2L9
867-767-9025, Fax: 867-873-0233

Nova Scotia

Office of Aboriginal Affairs, 5251 Duke St., 5th Fl., PO Box 1617, Halifax, NS B3J 2Y3
902-424-7409, Fax: 902-424-4225, oaa@gov.ns.ca

Ontario
Ontario Ministry of Indigenous Relations & Reconciliation, 160 Bloor St. East, 4th Fl., Toronto, ON M7A 2E6
416-326-4740, Fax: 416-326-4017, 866-381-5337

Saskatchewan
Office of the Provincial Interlocutor, #210, 1855 Victoria Ave., Regina, SK S4P 3T2
306-798-0183, Fax: 306-787-5832, interlocutor@gov.sk.ca

NATIVE PEOPLES & NORTHERN AFFAIRS

Canadian Northern Economic Development Agency, Ottawa, ON K1A 0H4
855-897-2667, InfoNorth@CanNor.gc.ca
Indigenous & Northern Affairs, Terrasses de la Chaudière, 10 Wellington St., North Tower, Gatineau, QC K1A 0H4
Fax: 866-817-3977, 800-567-9604, infopubs@aadnc-aandc.gc.ca

Alberta
Alberta Indigenous Relations, Commerce Place, 10155 - 102 St. NW, 19th Fl., Edmonton, AB T5J 4G8
780-427-8407, Fax: 780-427-4019, -310-000

British Columbia
British Columbia Ministry of Aboriginal Relations & Reconciliation, 2957 Jutland Rd., PO Box 9100 Prov Govt, Victoria, BC V8W 9B1
250-387-6121, 800-663-7867, abrinfo@gov.bc.ca
North Area, 1011 - 4 Ave., 5th Fl., Prince George, BC V2L 3H9
250-565-6100

Manitoba
Manitoba Indigenous & Municipal Relations, Legislative Bldg, #344, 450 Broadway, Winnipeg, MB R3C OV8
204-945-3719, Fax: 204-945-8374, anaweb@gov.mb.ca

New Brunswick
Aboriginal Affairs Secretariat, Kings Place, #237, 440 King St., PO Box 6000, Fredericton, NB E3B 5H8
506-462-5177, Fax: 506-444-5142, aboriginalaffairssecretariat@gnb.ca

Northwest Territories
Northwest Territories Department of Aboriginal Affairs & Intergovernmental Relations, 4910 - 52nd St., PO Box 1320, Yellowknife, NT X1A 2L9
867-767-9025, Fax: 867-873-0233

Nova Scotia
Office of Aboriginal Affairs, 5251 Duke St., 5th Fl., PO Box 1617, Halifax, NS B3J 2Y3
902-424-7409, Fax: 902-424-4225, oaa@gov.ns.ca

Ontario
Ontario Ministry of Indigenous Relations & Reconciliation, 160 Bloor St. East, 4th Fl., Toronto, ON M7A 2E6
416-326-4740, Fax: 416-326-4017, 866-381-5337

Yukon Territory
Yukon Development Corporation, PO Box 2703 D-1, Whitehorse, YT Y1A 2C6
867-456-3837, Fax: 867-393-7167
Yukon Land Use Planning Council, #201, 307 Jarvis St., Whitehorse, YT Y1A 2H3
867-667-7397, Fax: 867-667-4624, ylupc@planyukon.ca

NATURAL GAS

See: Oil & Natural Gas Resources

Alberta
Alberta Utilities Commission, Fifth Avenue Place, 425 - 1st St. SW, 4th Fl., Calgary, AB T2P 3L8
403-592-8845, Fax: 403-592-4406, -310-0000, info@auc.ab.ca
Surface Rights Board, 1229 - 91 St. SW, Edmonton, AB T6X 1E9
780-427-2444, Fax: 780-427-5798, -310-0000, srb.lcb@gov.ab.ca

NATURAL RESOURCES

Canadian Museum of Nature, 240 McLeod St., PO Box 3443 D,Ottawa, ON K1P 6P4
613-566-4700, Fax: 613-364-4021, 800-263-4433
Natural Resources Canada, 580 Booth St., Ottawa, ON K1A 0E4
343-292-6096, Fax: 613-992-7211

Alberta
Natural Resources Conservation Board, Sterling Place, 9940 - 106 St., 4th Fl., Edmonton, AB T5K 2N2
780-422-1977, Fax: 780-427-0607, 866-383-6722, info@nrcb.ca

British Columbia
British Columbia Ministry of Environment, PO Box 9339 Prov Govt, Victoria, BC V8W 9M1
250-387-9870, Fax: 250-387-6003, env.mail@gov.bc.ca
British Columbia Ministry of Forests, Lands & Natural Resource Operations, PO Box 9049 Prov Govt, Victoria, BC V8W 9E2
800-663-7867, FLNRO.MediaRequests@gov.bc.ca
British Columbia Ministry of Natural Gas Development (& Responsible for Housing), PO Box 9052 Prov Govt, Victoria, BC V8W 9E2
250-953-0900, Fax: 250-953-0927

Manitoba
Manitoba Sustainable Development, 200 Saulteaux Cres., PO Box 22, Winnipeg, MB R3J 3W3
204-945-6784, 800-214-6497, mgi@gov.mb.ca

New Brunswick
New Brunswick Department of Energy & Resource Development, Hugh John Flemming Forestry Centre, 1350 Regent St., Fredericton, NB E3C 2G6
506-453-3826, Fax: 506-444-4367, dnr_mrnweb@gnb.ca

Newfoundland & Labrador
Newfoundland & Labrador Department of Natural Resources, Natural Resources Bldg., 50 Elizabeth Ave., 7th Fl., PO Box 8700, St. John's, NL A1B 4J6
709-729-2920, Fax: 709-729-0059

Northwest Territories
Northwest Territories Department of Environment & Natural Resources, #600, 5102 - 50 Ave., Yellowknife, NT X1A 3S8
867-767-9231

Nova Scotia
Nova Scotia Department of Natural Resources, Founder's Square, 1701 Hollis St., 3rd Fl., PO Box 698, Halifax, NS B3J 2T9
902-424-5935, Fax: 902-424-7735, 800-565-2224

Nunavut
Nunavut Territory Department of Environment, PO Box 1000 1300, Iqaluit, NU X0A 0H0
867-975-7700, Fax: 867-975-7742, environment@gov.nu.ca

Ontario
Ontario Ministry of Natural Resources & Forestry, 300 Water St., PO Box 7000, Peterborough, ON K9J 8M5
800-667-1940
Ontario Ministry of Northern Development & Mines, 159 Cedar St., Sudbury, ON P3E 6A5
705-670-5755, Fax: 705-670-5818, 888-415-9845, ndmminister@ontario.ca

Prince Edward Island
Prince Edward Island Department of Agriculture & Fisheries, Jones Bldg., 11 Kent St., 5th Fl., PO Box 2000, Charlottetown, PE C1A 7N8
902-368-4880, Fax: 902-368-4857
Prince Edward Island Department of Justice & Public Safety, Shaw Bldg. South, 95 Rochford St., 4th Fl., PO Box 2000, Charlottetown, PE C1A 7N8
902-368-6410, Fax: 902-368-6488

Québec
Ministère des Énergie et des Ressources naturelles, Service à la clientèle, #A409, 5700, 4e av ouest, Québec, QC G1H 6R1
Fax: 418-644-6513, 866-248-6936, services.clientele@mern.gouv.qc.ca
Ministère du Développement durable, de l'Environnement et de la Lutte contre les changements climatiques, Édifice Marie-Guyart, 675, boul René-Lévesque est, 29e étage, Québec, QC G1R 5V7
418-521-3830, Fax: 418-646-5974, 800-561-1616, info@mddefp.gouv.qc.ca

Saskatchewan
Energy & Resources, 2101 Scarth St., Regina, SK S4P SH9
306-787-2528
Saskatchewan Environment, 3211 Albert St., 2nd Fl., Regina, SK S4S 5W6
306-787-2584, Fax: 306-787-9544, 800-567-4224, Centre.Inquiry@gov.sk.ca
Wascana Centre Authority, 2900 Wascana Dr., PO Box 7111, Regina, SK S4P 3S7
306-522-3661, Fax: 306-565-2742, wca@wascana.ca

Yukon Territory
Yukon Energy, Mines & Resources, PO Box 2703, Whitehorse, YT Y1A 2C6
867-667-3130, Fax: 867-456-3965, 800-661-0408, emr@gov.yk.ca
Yukon Environment, 10 Burns Rd., PO Box 2703 V-3A, Whitehorse, YT Y1A 2C6
867-667-5652, Fax: 867-393-7197, environment.yukon@gov.yk.ca

NUCLEAR ENERGY

Atomic Energy of Canada Limited, Head Office, Chalk River Laboratories, 286 Plant Rd., Chalk River, ON K0J 1J0
888-220-2465, communications@aecl.ca
Canadian Nuclear Laboratories, Head Office, Chalk River Laboratories, 286 Plant Rd., Chalk River, ON K0J 1J0
866-513-2325, communications@cnl.ca
Canadian Nuclear Safety Commission, 280 Slater St., PO Box 1046 B,Ottawa, ON K1P 5S9
613-995-5894, Fax: 613-995-5086, 800-668-5284, cnsc.information.ccsn@canada.ca
Nuclear Legacy Liabilities Program, c/o AECL, Corporate Communications, #B700A, Chalk River Laboratories, Chalk River, ON K0J 1J0
613-584-8206, 800-364-6989, info@nuclearlegacyprogram.ca

Alberta
Alberta Energy, North Petroleum Plaza, 9945 - 108 St., Edmonton, AB T5K 2G6
780-427-8050, Fax: 780-422-9522, -310-0000

Ontario
Ontario Power Generation, 700 University Ave., Toronto, ON M5G 1X6
416-592-2555, 877-592-2555, webmaster@opg.com

Québec
Hydro-Québec, 75, boul René-Lévesque ouest, 19e étage, Montréal, QC H2Z 1A4
514-289-2211

NUTRITION

Science & Technology Branch, Tower 5, 1341 Baseline Rd., Ottawa, ON K1A 0C5
Fax: 613-773-1711

Manitoba
Manitoba Healthy Child Office, 332 Bannatyne Ave., 3rd Fl., Winnipeg, MB R3A 0E2
204-945-2266, 888-848-0140, healthychild@gov.mb.ca
Public Health & Primary Health Care, 300 Carlton St., 4th Floor, Winnipeg, MB R3B 3M9
204-788-6666

Newfoundland & Labrador
Newfoundland & Labrador Department of Health & Community Services, West Block, Confederation Bldg., PO Box 8700, St. John's, NL A1B 4J6
709-729-4984, healthinfo@gov.nl.ca

Northwest Territories
Northwest Territories Department of Health & Social Services, 5015 - 49th St., PO Box 1320, Yellowknife, NT X1A 2L9
Fax: 867-873-0306

Nunavut
Nunavut Territory Department of Health, PO Box 1000 1000, Iqaluit, NU X0A 0H0
867-975-5700, Fax: 867-975-5705, 800-661-0833

Ontario
Ontario Ministry of Health & Long-Term Care, Hepburn Block, 80 Grosvenor St., 10th Fl, Toronto, ON M7A 2C4
416-327-4327, 800-268-1153

Prince Edward Island
Prince Edward Island Department of Health & Wellness, 105 Rochford St. North, 4th Fl., PO Box 2000, Charlottetown, PE C1A 7N8
902-368-6414, Fax: 902-368-4121

Québec
Ministère de la Santé et des Services sociaux, Direction des communications, 1075, ch Sainte-Foy, 16e étage, Québec, QC G1S 2M1
418-643-9395, Fax: 418-643-4768, regisseur.web@msss.gouv.qc.ca

Saskatchewan
Saskatchewan Health, T.C. Douglas Bldg., 3475 Albert St., Regina, SK S4S 6X6
306-787-0146, 800-667-7766, info@health.gov.sk.ca

OCCUPATIONAL SAFETY

See Also: Dangerous Goods & Hazardous Materials
Canadian Centre for Occupational Health & Safety, 135 Hunter St. East, Hamilton, ON L8N 1M5
905-572-2981, Fax: 905-572-4500, 800-668-4284

Alberta
Alberta Labour, Legislature Bldg., #404, 10800 - 97 Ave., Edmonton, AB T5K 2B6
780-427-3731, 877-427-3731
Occupational Health & Safety Council, Standard Life Centre, 10405 Jasper Ave., Edmonton, AB T5J 3N4
780-412-8742, Fax: 780-412-8701

British Columbia
British Columbia Ministry of Technology, Innovation & Citizens' Services, PO Box 9068 Prov Govt, Victoria, BC V8W 9E2
250-952-7623, Fax: 250-952-7628, 800-663-7867, EnquiryBC@gov.bc.ca
Workers' Compensation Board of British Columbia, PO Box 5350 Terminal,Vancouver, BC V6B 5L5
604-276-3100, Fax: 604-276-3247, 888-621-7233

Manitoba
Advisory Council on Workplace Safety & Health, 401 York Ave., 2nd Fl., Winnipeg, MB R3C 0P8
204-945-3446, Fax: 204-948-2209, 866-888-8186, wshcompl@gov.mb.ca

New Brunswick
WorkSafeNB, 1 Portland St., PO Box 160, Saint John, NB E2L 3X9
506-632-2200, Fax: 506-632-4999, 800-222-9775, communications@ws-ts.nb.ca

Newfoundland & Labrador
Newfoundland & Labrador Workplace Health, Safety & Compensation Commission (WorkplaceNL), 146 - 148 Forest Rd., PO Box 9000, St. John's, NL A1A 3B8
709-778-1000, Fax: 709-738-1714, 800-563-9000, general.inquiries@whscc.nl.ca

Northwest Territories
Northwest Territories & Nunavut Workers' Safety & Compensation Commission, Centre Square Tower, 5022 - 49th St., 5th Fl., PO Box 8888, Yellowknife, NT X1A 2R3
867-920-3888, Fax: 867-873-4596, 800-661-0792

Nova Scotia
Occupational Health & Safety Advisory Council, PO Box 697, Halifax, NS B3J 2T8
902-424-2484, Fax: 902-424-5640
Workers' Compensation Board of Nova Scotia, 5668 South St., PO Box 1150, Halifax, NS B3J 2Y2
902-491-8999, 800-870-3331, info@wcb.gov.ns.ca

Ontario
Workplace Safety & Insurance Board, 200 Front St. West, Ground Fl., Toronto, ON M5V 3J1
416-344-1000, Fax: 416-344-4684, 800-387-0750

Prince Edward Island
Prince Edward Island Workers Compensation Board, 14 Weymouth St., PO Box 757, Charlottetown, PE C1A 7L7
902-368-5680, Fax: 902-368-5696, 800-237-5049

Québec
Commission de la santé et de la sécurité du travail du Québec, 524, rue Bourdages, CP 1200 Terminus,Québec, QC G1K 7E2
Fax: 418-266-4015, 866-302-2778
Commission des lésions professionnelles, #700, 900, Place d'Youville, Québec, QC G1R 3P7
418-644-7777, Fax: 418-644-6443, 800-463-1591

Saskatchewan
Office of the Worker's Advocate, #300, 1870 Albert St., Regina, SK S4P 4W1
306-787-2456, Fax: 306-787-0249, 877-787-2456
Saskatchewan Workers' Compensation Board, #200, 1881 Scarth St., Regina, SK S4P 4L1
306-787-4370, Fax: 306-787-4311, 800-667-7590, webmaster@wcbsask.com

Yukon Territory
Yukon Workers' Compensation Health & Safety Board, 401 Strickland St., Whitehorse, YT Y1A 5N8
867-667-5645, Fax: 867-393-6279, 800-661-0443, worksafe@gov.yk.ca

OCCUPATIONAL TRAINING

Canada School of Public Service, 373 Sussex Dr., Ottawa, ON K1N 6Z2
819-953-5400, Fax: 866-944-0454, 866-703-9598, info@csps-efpc.gc.ca

Alberta
Alberta Labour, Legislature Bldg., #404, 10800 - 97 Ave., Edmonton, AB T5K 2B6
780-427-3731, 877-427-3731
Apprenticeship & Student Aid Division, Commerce Place, 10155 - 102 St., 6th Fl., Edmonton, AB T5J 4L5

British Columbia
British Columbia Ministry of Technology, Innovation & Citizens' Services, PO Box 9068 Prov Govt, Victoria, BC V8W 9E2
250-952-7623, Fax: 250-952-7628, 800-663-7867, EnquiryBC@gov.bc.ca

Manitoba
Aboriginal Education Directorate, Murdo Scribe Centre, 510 Selkirk Ave., Winnipeg, MB R2W 2M7
204-945-7886, Fax: 204-948-2010, aedinfo@gov.mb.ca

New Brunswick
New Brunswick Department of Human Resources, Chancery Place, 675 King St., Fredericton, NB E3B 1E9
506-453-2264, Fax: 506-453-7195, Ohr-brh@gnb.ca
New Brunswick Department of Post-Secondary Education, Training & Labour, Chestnut Complex, PO Box 6000, Fredericton, NB E3B 5H1
506-453-2597, Fax: 506-453-3618, dpetlinfo@gnb.ca

Ontario
Ontario Ministry of Advanced Education & Skills Development, Mowat Block, 900 Bay St., 14th Fl., Toronto, ON M7A 1L2
416-326-1600, Fax: 416-325-6348, 800-387-5514, information.met@ontario.ca

Québec
École nationale de police du Québec, 350, rue Marguerite-d'Youville, Nicolet, QC J3T 1X4
819-293-8631, Fax: 819-293-8630, courriel@enpq.qc.ca
École nationale des pompiers du Québec, Palais de justice de Laval, #3.08, 2800, boul Saint-Martin ouest, Laval, QC H7T 2S9
450-680-6800, Fax: 450-680-6818, 866-680-3677, enpq@enpq.gouv.qc.ca

OCEANOGRAPHY

Bayfield Institute, Canada Centre for Inland Waters, 867 Lakeshore Rd., PO Box 5050, Burlington, ON L7R 4A6
905-336-6240
Bedford Institute of Oceanography, 1 Challenger Dr., PO Box 1006, Dartmouth, NS B2Y 4A2
Fax: 902-426-8484, WebmasterBIO-IOB@dfo-mpo.gc.ca
Fisheries & Oceans Canada, 200 Kent St., Ottawa, ON K1A 0E6
613-993-0999, Fax: 613-990-1866, info@dfo-mpo.gc.ca
Institut Maurice-Lamontagne, 850, rte de le Mer, CP 1000, Mont-Joli, QC G5H 3Z4
418-775-0500, Fax: 418-775-0730
Institute of Ocean Sciences, 9860 West Saanich Rd., PO Box 6000, Sidney, BC V8L 4B2
250-363-6517, Fax: 250-363-6390
Ocean Technology Enterprise Centre, PO Box 12093, St. John's, NL A1B 3T5
709-772-2469

OIL & NATURAL GAS RESOURCES

See Also: Energy; Natural Resources
Indian Oil & Gas Canada, #100, 9911 Chiila Blvd., Tsuu T'ina (Sarcee), AB T2W 6H6
403-292-5625, Fax: 403-292-5618, ContactIOGC@inac-ainc.gc.ca
National Energy Board, 517 - 10 Ave. SW, Calgary, AB T2R 0A8
403-292-4800, Fax: 403-292-5503, 800-899-1265
Northern Pipeline Agency Canada, #470, 588 Booth St., Ottawa, ON K1A 0Y7
613-995-1150, info@npa.gc.ca

Alberta
Alberta Energy, North Petroleum Plaza, 9945 - 108 St., Edmonton, AB T5K 2G6
780-427-8050, Fax: 780-422-9522, -310-0000
Alberta Energy Regulator, #1000, 250 - 5 St. SW, Calgary, AB T2P 0R4
403-297-8311, Fax: 403-297-7336, 855-297-8311, inquiries@aer.ca
Surface Rights Board, 1229 - 91 St. SW, Edmonton, AB T6X 1E9
780-427-2444, Fax: 780-427-5798, -310-0000, srb.lcb@gov.ab.ca

British Columbia
British Columbia Ministry of Natural Gas Development (& Responsible for Housing), PO Box 9052 Prov Govt, Victoria, BC V8W 9E2
250-953-0900, Fax: 250-953-0927
British Columbia Utilities Commission, 900 Howe St., 6th Fl., PO Box 250, Vancouver, BC V6Z 2N3
604-660-4700, Fax: 604-660-1102, 800-663-1385, commission.secretary@bcuc.com
Oil & Gas Commission, #100, 10003 - 110 Ave., Fort St. John, BC V1J 6M7
250-794-5200, Fax: 250-794-5375
Surface Rights Board of British Columbia, #10, 10551 Shellbridge Way, Richmond, BC V6X 2W9
604-775-1740, Fax: 604-775-1742, 888-775-1740, office@surfacerightsboard.bc.ca

Manitoba
Surface Rights Board, #360, 1395 Ellice Ave., Winnipeg, MB R3G 3P2
204-945-0731, Fax: 204-948-2578, 800-282-8069

New Brunswick
New Brunswick Department of Energy & Resource Development, Hugh John Flemming Forestry Centre, 1350 Regent St., Fredericton, NB E3C 2G6
506-453-3826, Fax: 506-444-4367, dnr_mrnweb@gnb.ca

Newfoundland & Labrador
Canada-Newfoundland & Labrador Offshore Petroleum Board, TD Place, 140 Water St., 5th Fl., St. John's, NL A1C 6H6
709-778-1400, Fax: 709-778-1473, information@cnlopb.ca

Nova Scotia
Canada-Nova Scotia Offshore Petroleum Board, TD Centre, 1791 Barrington St., 8th Fl., Halifax, NS B3J 3K9
902-422-5588, Fax: 902-422-1799, info@cnsopb.ns.ca
Nova Scotia Utility & Review Board, Summit Place, 1601 Lower Water St., 3rd Fl., PO Box 1692 M,Halifax, NS B3J 3S3
902-424-4448, Fax: 902-424-3919, 855-442-4448, board@novascotia.ca

Nunavut
Nunavut Territory Department of Environment, PO Box 1000 1300, Iqaluit, NU X0A 0H0
867-975-7700, Fax: 867-975-7742, environment@gov.nu.ca

Ontario
Ontario Ministry of Natural Resources & Forestry, 300 Water St., PO Box 7000, Peterborough, ON K9J 8M5
800-667-1940

Saskatchewan
NorthPoint Energy Solutions Inc., 2025 Victoria Ave., Regina, SK S4P 0S1
306-566-2103, Fax: 306-566-3364, info@northpointenergy.com
SaskEnergy Incorporated, 1777 Victoria Ave., Regina, SK S4P 4K5
306-777-9225, 800-567-8899

Yukon Territory
Oil & Gas Mineral Resources Division, PO Box 2703, Whitehorse, YT Y1A 2C6
867-667-5087, Fax: 867-393-6262, oilandgas@gov.yk.ca

OIL SPILLS

Canadian Coast Guard, Centennial Towers, #6S018, 200 Kent St., Ottawa, ON K1A 0E6
613-993-0999, Fax: 613-990-1866, info@dfo-mpo.gc.ca
Office of the Administrator of the Ship-source Oil Pollution Fund, #830, 180 Kent St., Ottawa, ON K1A 0N5
613-991-1726, Fax: 613-990-5423, info@sopf-cidphn.gc.ca

Newfoundland & Labrador
Canada-Newfoundland & Labrador Offshore Petroleum Board, TD Place, 140 Water St., 5th Fl., St. John's, NL A1C 6H6
709-778-1400, Fax: 709-778-1473, information@cnlopb.ca

OMBUDSMEN

Office of the Commissioner of Official Languages, 30 Victoria St., 6th Fl., Gatineau, ON K1A 0T8
819-420-4877, Fax: 819-420-4873, 877-996-6368
Office of the Correctional Investigator, PO Box 3421 D,Ottawa, ON K1P 6L4
Fax: 613-990-9091, 877-885-8848, org@oci-bec.gc.ca
Office of the Ombudsman, PO Box 90026, Ottawa, ON K1V 1J8
Fax: 800-204-4193, 800-204-4198
Office of the Procurement Ombudsman, Constitution Square Bldg., #1150, 340 Albert St., 11th Fl., PO Box 151, Ottawa, ON K1R 7Y6
Fax: 613-947-9800, 866-734-5169, boa-opo@boa-opo.gc.ca
Office of the Taxpayers' Ombudsman, #600, 150 Slater St., Ottawa, ON K1A 1K3
613-946-2310, Fax: 613-941-6319, 866-586-3839
Veterans Ombudsman (Charlottetown), 134 Kent St., PO Box 66, Charlottetown, PE C1A 7K2
902-626-2919, Fax: 888-566-7582, 877-330-4343, VAC.OVOInfo-InfoBOV.ACC@ombudsman-veterans.gc.ca
Veterans Ombudsman (Ottawa), #1560, 360 Albert St., Ottawa, ON K1R 7X7
Fax: 888-566-7582, 877-330-4343

Alberta
Alberta Office of the Ombudsman, Canadian Western Bank Building, #2800, 10303 Jasper Ave. NW, Edmonton, AB T5J 5C3
780-427-2756, Fax: 780-427-2759, 888-455-2756, info@ombudsman.ab.ca

British Columbia
Office of the Ombudsperson, 947 Fort St., 2nd Fl., PO Box 9039 Prov Govt, Victoria, BC V8W 9A5
250-387-5855, Fax: 250-387-0198, 800-567-3247

Manitoba
Manitoba Office of the Ombudsman, Colony Square, #750, 500 Portage Ave., Winnipeg, MB R3C 3X1
204-982-9130, Fax: 204-942-7803, 800-665-0531, ombudsman@ombudsman.mb.ca

New Brunswick
Office of the Ombudsman, PO Box 6000, Fredericton, NB E3B 5H1
506-453-2789, Fax: 506-453-5599, 888-465-1100, nbombud@gnb.ca

Nova Scotia
Office of the Ombudsman, #700, 5670 Spring Garden Rd., PO Box 2152, Halifax, NS B3J 3B7
902-424-6780, Fax: 902-424-6675, 800-670-1111, ombudsman@gov.ns.ca

Ontario
Office of the Ombudsman, Bell Trinity Sq., South Tower, 483 Bay St., 10th Fl., Toronto, ON M5G 2C9
416-586-3300, Fax: 416-586-3485, 800-263-1830, info@ombudsman.on.ca

Québec
Le Protecteur du Citoyen, #1.25, 525, boul René-Lévesque est, Québec, QC G1R 5Y4
418-643-2688, Fax: 418-643-8759, 800-463-5070, protecteur@protecteurducitoyen.qc.ca

Saskatchewan
Ombudsman Saskatchewan, #150, 2401 Saskatchewan Dr., Regina, SK S4P 4H8
306-787-6211, Fax: 306-787-9090, 800-667-7180, ombreg@ombudsman.sk.ca

PARKS

See Also: Land Resources

Alberta
Alberta Environment & Parks, Information Centre, Great West Life Bldg., 9920 - 108 St., Main Fl., Edmonton, AB T5K 2M4
780-427-2700, Fax: 780-427-4407, -310-3773, ESRD.Info-Centre@gov.ab.ca

Québec
Ministère des Forêts, de la Faune et des Parcs, Service à la clientèle, #A409, 5700, 4e av ouest, Québec, QC G1H 6R1
Fax: 418-644-6513, 844-523-6738, services.clientele@mrnf.gouv.qc.ca

PARKS & RECREATION

Canadian Heritage, 15 Eddy St., Gatineau, QC K1A 0M5
819-997-0055, 866-811-0055, PCH.info-info.PCH@canada.ca

Historic Sites & Monuments Board of Canada, 30 Victoria St., 3rd Fl., Gatineau, QC J8X 0B3
Fax: 819-420-9260, 855-283-8730, hsmbc-clmhc@pc.gc.ca

Parc Downsview Park Inc., 70 Canuck Ave., Toronto, ON M3K 2C5
416-954-0544, downsviewevents@clc.ca

Parks Canada, National Office, 30 Victoria St., Gatineau, QC J8X 0B3
819-420-9486, 888-773-8888, information@pc.gc.ca

Alberta
Parks Division, Oxbridge Place, 9820 - 106 St., 2nd Fl., Edmonton, AB T5K 2J6
780-427-3582, Fax: 780-427-5980, 866-427-3582

Special Areas Board, Special Areas Board Administration, 212 - 2nd Ave. West, PO Box 820, Hanna, AB T0J 1P0
403-854-5600, Fax: 403-854-5527

British Columbia
British Columbia Ministry of Environment, PO Box 9339 Prov Govt, Victoria, BC V8W 9M1
250-387-9870, Fax: 250-387-6003, env.mail@gov.bc.ca

Manitoba
Ecological Reserves Advisory Committee, c/o Manitoba Conservation, Parks & Natural Areas Branch, 200 Saulteaux Cres., PO Box 53, Winnipeg, MB R3J 3W3
204-945-4148, Fax: 204-945-0012

New Brunswick
New Brunswick Department of Tourism, Heritage & Culture, Centennial Building, PO Box 6000, Fredericton, NB E3B 5H1
506-453-3115, Fax: 506-457-4984, thctpcinfo@gnb.ca

Newfoundland & Labrador
Newfoundland & Labrador Department of Business, Tourism, Culture & Rural Development, Confederation Bldg., West Block, 2nd Fl., PO Box 8700, St. John's, NL A1B 4J6
709-729-7000, btcrd@gov.nl.ca

Northwest Territories
Northwest Territories Department of Environment & Natural Resources, #600, 5102 - 50 Ave., Yellowknife, NT X1A 3S8
867-767-9231

Nunavut
Nunavut Territory Department of Environment, PO Box 1000 1300, Iqaluit, NU X0A 0H0
867-975-7700, Fax: 867-975-7742, environment@gov.nu.ca

Ontario
Ontario Ministry of Economic Development & Growth, Hearst Block, 900 Bay St., 8th Fl., Toronto, ON M7A 2E1
416-325-6666, 800-268-7095

Prince Edward Island
Corporate Services, PO Box 2000, Charlottetown, PE C1A 7N8

Prince Edward Island Department of Economic Development & Tourism, PO Box 2000, Charlottetown, PE C1A 7N8
902-368-5540, Fax: 902-368-5277, tpswitch@gov.pe.ca

Québec
Ministère du Développement durable, de l'Environnement et de la Lutte contre les changements climatiques, Édifice Marie-Guyart, 675, boul René-Lévesque est, 29e étage, Québec, QC G1R 5V7
418-521-3830, Fax: 418-646-5974, 800-561-1616, info@mddefp.gouv.qc.ca

Société des établissements en plein air du Québec, Place de la Cité, Tour Cominar, #250, 2640, boul Laurier, 2e étage, Québec, QC G1V 5C2
418-686-4875, Fax: 418-643-8177, 800-665-6527, inforeservation@sepaq.com

Saskatchewan
Saskatchewan Parks, Culture & Sport, 3211 Albert St., 1st Fl., Regina, SK S4S 5W6
306-787-5729, Fax: 306-798-0033, 800-205-7070, info@tpcs.gov.sk.ca

Yukon Territory
Yukon Tourism & Culture, 100 Hanson St., PO Box 2703, Whitehorse, YT Y1A 2C6
867-667-5036, Fax: 867-667-3546

PARLIAMENT

See Also: Government (General Information; Protocol (State)

Forty-second Parliament - Canada, House of Commons, Parliament Buildings, Ottawa, AB K1A 0A6

Library of Parliament, Parliamentary Buildings, Ottawa, ON K1A 0A9
613-992-4793, 866-599-4999, info@parl.gc.ca

Office of the Leader, Bloc Québécois, Centre Block, 111 Wellington St., Ottawa, ON K1A 0A6

Office of the Leader, Green Party of Canada, Confederation Building, 244 Wellington St., Ottawa, ON K1A 0A6
613-996-1119, Fax: 613-996-0850, 866-868-3447, leader@greenparty.ca

Office of the Leader, Official Opposition, Conservative Party of Canada / Conservative Party Research Bureau, Centre Block, 111 Wellington St., Ottawa, ON K1A 0A6
613-995-1333, Fax: 613-995-1337

Office of the Prime Minister, Liberal Party of Canada / Liberal Research Bureau, Langevin Block, 80 Wellington St., Ottawa, ON K1A 0A2
613-992-4211, Fax: 613-941-6900

Privy Council Office, #1000, 85 Sparks St., Ottawa, ON K1A 0A3
613-957-5153, Fax: 613-997-5043, info@pco-bcp.gc.ca

The Canadian Ministry, Information Service, Parliament of Canada, Ottawa, ON K1A 0A9
613-992-4793, 866-599-4999, info@parl.gc.ca

Alberta
Legislative Assembly of Alberta, Legislature Annex, 9718 - 107 St., Edmonton, AB T5K 1E4
780-427-2826, Fax: 780-427-1623, laocommunications@assembly.ab.ca

British Columbia
BC Legislative Assembly & Independent Offices, Clerk's Office, Parliament Bldgs., Victoria, BC V8V 1X4
250-387-3785, Fax: 250-387-0942, ClerkHouse@leg.bc.ca

Manitoba
Manitoba Legislative Assembly, c/o Clerk's Office, Legislative Bldg., #237, 450 Broadway, Winnipeg, MB R3C 0V8
204-945-3636, Fax: 204-948-2507, clerkla@leg.gov.mb.ca

New Brunswick
Legislative Assembly of New Brunswick, Legislative Bldg., Centre Block, PO Box 6000, Fredericton, NB E3B 5H1
506-453-2506, Fax: 506-453-7154, wwwleg@gnb.ca

Northwest Territories
NWT Legislative Assembly, 4570 - 48 St., PO Box 1320, Yellowknife, NT X1A 2L9
867-669-2200, 800-661-0784

Nova Scotia
Legislative House of Assembly, c/o Clerk's Office, Province House, 1st Fl., PO Box 1617, Halifax, NS B3J 2Y3
902-424-5978, Fax: 902-424-0632

Nunavut
Nunavut Legislative Assembly, 926 Federal Rd., PO Box 1200, Iqaluit, NU X0A 0H0
867-975-5000, Fax: 867-975-5190, 877-334-7266, leginfo@assembly.nu.ca

Ontario
Ontario Legislative Assembly, c/o Clerk of the Legislative Assembly, #104, Legislative Bldg., Queen's Park, Toronto, ON M7A 1A2
416-325-7500, Fax: 416-325-7489, web@ola.org

Prince Edward Island
Prince Edward Island Legislative Assembly, 197 Richmond St., PO Box 2000, Charlottetown, PE C1A 7N8
902-368-5970, Fax: 902-368-5175, 877-315-5518, legislativelibrary@assembly.pe.ca

Québec
L'Assemblée nationale, Hôtel du Parlement, 1045, rue des Parlementaires, Québec, QC G1A 1A3
418-643-7239, Fax: 418-646-4271, 866-337-8837, responsable.contenu@assnat.qc.ca

Saskatchewan
Legislative Assembly of Saskatchewan, Office of the Clerk, Legislative Building, #239, 2405 Legislative Dr., Regina, SK S4S 0B3
info@legassembly.sk.ca

Yukon Territory
Yukon Legislative Assembly, 2071 - 2nd Ave., PO Box 2703, Whitehorse, YT Y1A 2C6
867-667-5498, yla@gov.yk.ca

PAROLE BOARDS

See Also: Correctional Services

Parole Board of Canada, Communications Division, National Office, 410 Laurier Ave. West, Ottawa, ON K1A 0R1
613-954-7474, Fax: 613-941-4981, info@pbc-clcc.gc.ca

Alberta
Crown Prosecution Service Division, Bowker Building, 9833 - 109 St., 2nd Fl., Edmonton, AB T5K 2E8

Manitoba
Corrections Division, #810, 405 Broadway Ave., Winnipeg, MB R3C 3L6
204-945-7804

New Brunswick
New Brunswick Department of Justice & Public Safety, Argyle Place, PO Box 6000, Fredericton, NB E3B 5H1
506-453-3992, DPS-MSP.Information@gnb.ca

Nunavut
Community Justice, PO Box 1000 500, Iqaluit, NU X0A 0H0
867-975-6363, Fax: 867-975-6160, communityjustice@gov.nu.ca

Ontario
Ontario Parole Board, #1803, 415 Yonge St., Toronto, ON M5B 2E7
416-325-4480, Fax: 416-325-4485, 888-579-2888

Safety, Licensing Appeals & Standards Tribunals Ontario, #5230, 20 Dundas St. West, Toronto, ON M5G 2C2
416-212-0334, Fax: 416-314-4270, 855-444-7454, slastoinfo@ontario.ca

Québec
Commission québecoise des libérations conditionnelles, #1.32A, 300, boul Jean-Lesage, Québec, QC G1K 8K6
418-646-8300, Fax: 418-643-7217, cqlc@cqlc.gouv.qc.ca

Saskatchewan
Community Justice Division, #610, 1874 Scarth St., Regina, SK S4P 4B3
306-787-5096, Fax: 306-787-0078

PASSPORT INFORMATION

See Also: Citizenship; Immigration

Passport Canada, Passport Canada Program, Gatineau, QC K1A 0G3
800-567-6868

PATENTS & COPYRIGHT

Canadian Intellectual Property Office, Place du Portage I, #C-229, 50 Victoria St., Gatineau, QC K1A 0C9
819-997-1936, Fax: 819-953-2476, 866-997-1936, cipo.contact@ic.gc.ca

Copyright Board of Canada, #800, 56 Sparks St., Ottawa, ON K1A 0C9
613-952-8621, Fax: 613-952-8630, secretariat@cb-cda.gc.ca

PAY EQUITY

Employment & Social Development Canada, 140 Promenade du Portage, Gatineau, QC K1A 0J9

British Columbia
British Columbia Ministry of Technology, Innovation & Citizens' Services, PO Box 9068 Prov Govt, Victoria, BC V8W 9E2
250-952-7623, Fax: 250-952-7628, 800-663-7867, EnquiryBC@gov.bc.ca

Employment Standards Tribunal, Oceanic Plaza, #650, 1066 West Hastings St., Vancouver, BC V6E 3X1
604-775-3512, Fax: 604-775-3372, registrar@bcest.bc.ca

New Brunswick
New Brunswick Department of Human Resources, Chancery Place, 675 King St., Fredericton, NB E3B 1E9
506-453-2264, Fax: 506-453-7195, Ohr-brh@gnb.ca

Nova Scotia
Pay Equity Commission, 5151 Terminal Rd., 6th Fl., PO Box 697, Halifax, NS B3J 2T8
902-424-8466, Fax: 902-424-0575

Ontario
Pay Equity Commission, #300, 180 Dundas St. West, Toronto, ON M7A 2S6
416-314-1896, Fax: 416-314-8741, 800-387-8813

Prince Edward Island
Workers Compensation Appeal Tribunal, 161 St. Peters Rd., 1st Fl., PO Box 2000, Charlottetown, PE C1A 7N8
902-894-0278, Fax: 902-620-3477

Québec
Commission de l'équité salariale, 200, ch Ste-Foy, 4e étage, Québec, QC G1R 6A1
418-528-8765, Fax: 418-528-6999, 888-528-8765, equite.salariale@ces.gouv.qc.ca

PENSIONS

Canada Pension Plan Investment Board, #2500, 1 Queen St. East, Toronto, ON M5C 2W5
416-868-4075, Fax: 416-868-8689, 866-557-9510, contact@cppib.com
Finance Canada, 90 Elgin St., 14th Fl., Ottawa, ON K1A 0G5
613-369-3710, Fax: 613-369-4065, fin.financepublic-financepublique.fin@canada.ca
Office of the Superintendent of Financial Institutions, Kent Square, 255 Albert St., Ottawa, ON K1A 0H2
613-990-7788, Fax: 613-990-5591, 800-385-8647, information@osfi-bsif.gc.ca
Public Sector Pension Investment Board, #200, 440 Laurier Ave. West, Ottawa, ON K1R 7X6
613-782-3095, Fax: 613-782-6864, info@investpsp.ca
Service Canada, 140, Promenade du Portage, Gatineau, QC K1A 0J9
Fax: 613-941-1827, 800-622-6232
Social Security Tribunal, PO Box 9812 T, Ottawa, ON K1G 6S3
613-952-8805, 877-227-8577, info.sst-tss@canada.gc.ca
Veterans Affairs Canada, 161 Grafton St., PO Box 7700, Charlottetown, PE C1A 8M9
866-522-2122, information@vac-acc.gc.ca
Veterans Review & Appeal Board, Daniel J. MacDonald Bldg., 161 Grafton St., PO Box 9900, Charlottetown, PE C1A 8V7
902-566-8751, Fax: 902-566-7850, 800-450-8006, vrab_tacra@vac-acc.gc.ca

Alberta

Alberta Pensions Services Corporation, 5103 Windermere Blvd. SW, Edmonton, AB T6W 0S9
780-427-2782, 800-661-8198, memberservices@apsc.ca
Alberta Teachers' Retirement Fund, Barnett House, #600, 11010 - 142 St. NW, Edmonton, AB T5N 2R1
780-451-4166, Fax: 780-452-3547, 800-661-9582, info@atrf.com

British Columbia

British Columbia Pension Corporation, 2995 Jutland Rd., PO Box 9460, Victoria, BC V8W 9V8
250-387-1014, Fax: 250-953-0429, 800-663-8823, PensionCorp@pensionsbc.ca

Manitoba

Pension Commission of Manitoba, #1004, 401 York Ave., Winnipeg, MB R3C 0P8
204-945-2740, Fax: 204-948-2375, pensions@gov.mb.ca
Teachers' Retirement Allowances Fund Board, #330 Johnston Terminal, 35 Forks Market Rd., Winnipeg, MB R3C 4S8
204-949-0048, Fax: 204-944-0361, 800-782-0714, info@traf.mb.ca

New Brunswick

New Brunswick Department of Human Resources, Chancery Place, 675 King St., Fredericton, NB E3B 1E9
506-453-2264, Fax: 506-453-7195, Ohr-brh@gnb.ca

Newfoundland & Labrador

Newfoundland & Labrador Government Money Purchase Pension Plan Committee, Confederation Bldg., PO Box 8700, St. John's, NL A1B 4J6
Pension Investment Committee, Confederation Bldg., PO Box 8700, St. John's, NL A1B 4J6

Nova Scotia

Nova Scotia Pension Agency, Purdy's Landing, #400, 1949 Upper Water St., PO Box 371, Halifax, NS B3J 2P8
902-424-5070, Fax: 902-424-0662, 800-774-5070, pensionsinfo@gov.ns.ca

Ontario

Financial Services Commission of Ontario, New York City Ctr., 5160 Yonge St., 17th Fl., PO Box 85, Toronto, ON M2N 6L9
416-250-7250, Fax: 416-590-7070, 800-668-0128, contactcentre@fsco.gov.on.ca
Ontario Pension Board, Sun Life Bldg., #2200, 200 King St. West, Toronto, ON M5H 3X6
416-364-8558, Fax: 416-364-7578, 800-668-6203, clientservice@opb.ca
Ontario Retirement Pension Plan Administration Corporation, 375 University Ave., Toronto, ON M5G 2J5
OPSEU Pension Trust, #1200, 1 Adelaide St. East, Toronto, ON M5C 3A7
416-681-6161, Fax: 416-681-6175, 800-637-0024
Provincial Judges Pension Board, c/o Ontario Pension Board, #2200, 200 King St. West, Toronto, ON M5H 3X6
416-601-3923, Fax: 416-364-9094
Provincial Judges Remuneration Commission, Ferguson Block, 77 Wellesley St. West, 13th Fl., Toronto, ON M7A 1N3
416-325-4141, Fax: 416-327-8402
Revenue Agencies Oversight Division, Frost Bldg. South, 7 Queen's Park Cres., 2nd Fl., Toronto, ON M7A 1Y7
416-325-0400

Prince Edward Island

Debt, Investment & Pension Management, Shaw Bldg. South, 95 Rochford St., 3rd Fl., PO Box 2000, Charlottetown, PE C1A 7N8
Fax: 902-368-4077

Québec

Commission administrative des régimes de retraite et d'assurances (Québec), 475, rue Saint-Amable, Québec, QC G1R 5X3
418-643-4881, Fax: 418-644-3839, 800-463-5533
Régie des rentes du Québec, CP 5200, Sainte-Foy, QC G1K 7S9
418-643-5185, 800-463-5185

Saskatchewan

Crown Investments Corporation of Saskatchewan, #400, 2400 College Ave., Regina, SK S4P 1C8
306-787-6851, Fax: 306-787-8125
Financial & Consumer Affairs Authority, #601, 1919 Saskatchewan Dr., Regina, SK S4P 4H2
306-787-5645, Fax: 306-787-5899, 877-880-5550, consumerprotection@gov.sk.ca
Municipal Employees' Pension Commission, #1000, 1801 Hamilton St., Regina, SK S4P 4W3
Fax: 306-787-8822
Saskatchewan Pension Plan, 608 Main St., PO Box 5555, Kindersley, SK S0L 1S0
306-463-5410, Fax: 306-463-3500, 800-667-7153, info@saskpension.com

PESTICIDES, HERBICIDES

Pest Management Regulatory Agency, 2720 Riverside Dr., Ottawa, ON K1A 0K9
613-736-3799, Fax: 613-736-3798, 800-267-6315, pmra.infoserv@hc-sc.gc.ca

Ontario

Pesticides Advisory Committee, 135 St. Clair Ave. West, 15th Fl., Toronto, ON M4V 1P5
416-314-9230, Fax: 416-314-9237

PIPELINES

National Energy Board, 517 - 10 Ave. SW, Calgary, AB T2R 0A8
403-292-4800, Fax: 403-292-5503, 800-899-1265
Northern Pipeline Agency Canada, #470, 588 Booth St., Ottawa, ON K1A 0Y7
613-995-1150, info@npa.gc.ca

Alberta

Alberta Energy, North Petroleum Plaza, 9945 - 108 St., Edmonton, AB T5K 2G6
780-427-8050, Fax: 780-422-9522, -310-0000
Alberta Energy Regulator, #1000, 250 - 5 St. SW, Calgary, AB T2P 0R4
403-297-8311, Fax: 403-297-7336, 855-297-8311, inquiries@aer.ca
Surface Rights Board, 1229 - 91 St. SW, Edmonton, AB T6X 1E9
780-427-2444, Fax: 780-427-5798, -310-0000, srb.lcb@gov.ab.ca

British Columbia

British Columbia Hydro, 6911 Southpoint Dr., Burnaby, BC V3N 4X8
604-224-9376, 800-224-9376

Northwest Territories

Northwest Territories Department of Environment & Natural Resources, #600, 5102 - 50 Ave., Yellowknife, NT X1A 3S8
867-767-9231

Nova Scotia

Nova Scotia Department of Energy, Joseph Howe Bldg., 1690 Hollis St., PO Box 2664, Halifax, NS B3J 3J9
902-424-4575, Fax: 902-424-0528, enerinfo@novascotia.ca
Nova Scotia Utility & Review Board, Summit Place, 1601 Lower Water St., 3rd Fl., PO Box 1692 M,Halifax, NS B3J 3S3
902-424-4448, Fax: 902-424-3919, 855-442-4448, board@novascotia.ca

Saskatchewan

SaskEnergy Incorporated, 1777 Victoria Ave., Regina, SK S4P 4K5
306-777-9225, 800-567-8899

POLICING SERVICES

Royal Canadian Mounted Police, 73 Leikin Dr., Ottawa, ON K1A 0R2
613-993-7267, Fax: 613-993-0260

Alberta

Alberta Justice & Solicitor General, Communications, Bowker Building, 9833 - 109 St., 5th Fl., Edmonton, AB T5K 2E8
780-427-2745, -310-0000
Public Security Division, John E. Brownlee Building, 10365 - 97 St., 10th Fl., Edmonton, AB T5J 3W7

British Columbia

British Columbia Ministry of Justice, PO Box 9044 Prov Govt, Victoria, BC V8W 9E2
British Columbia Ministry of Public Safety & Solicitor General, PO Box 9290 Prov Govt, Victoria, BC V8W 9J7
250-356-0149, Fax: 250-387-6224, 800-663-7867, EnquiryBC@gov.bc.ca

Manitoba

Health Information Privacy Committee, #4043, 300 Carlton St., Winnipeg, MB R3B 3M9
Law Enforcement Review Agency, #420, 155 Carlton St., Winnipeg, MB R3C 3H8
204-945-8667, Fax: 204-948-1014, 800-282-8069, lera@gov.mb.ca
Manitoba Justice & Attorney General, Administration & Finance, #1110, 405 Broadway Ave., Winnipeg, MB R3C 3L6
204-945-2878, minjus@gov.mb.ca

New Brunswick

New Brunswick Department of Justice & Public Safety, Argyle Place, PO Box 6000, Fredericton, NB E3B 5H1
506-453-3992, DPS-MSP.Information@gnb.ca
New Brunswick Police Commission, Fredericton City Centre, #202, 435 King St., Fredericton, NB E3B 1E5
506-453-2069, Fax: 506-457-3542, 888-389-1777, nbpc@gnb.ca

Newfoundland & Labrador

Newfoundland & Labrador Department of Justice & Public Safety, Confederation Bldg., East Block, 4th Fl., PO Box 8700, St. John's, NL A1B 4J6
709-729-2869, Fax: 709-729-0469, justice@gov.nl.ca
Royal Newfoundland Constabulary Public Complaints Commission, 689 Topsail Rd., PO Box 8700, St. John's, NL A1B 4J6
709-729-0950, Fax: 709-729-1302, rnccomplaintscommission@gov.nl.ca

Northwest Territories

Northwest Territories Department of Justice, 4903 - 49th St., PO Box 1320, Yellowknife, NT X1A 2L9
867-767-9256

Nova Scotia

Nova Scotia Department of Justice, 1690 Hollis St., PO Box 7, Halifax, NS B3J 2L6
902-424-4030, justweb@gov.ns.ca
Office of the Police Complaints Commissioner, #720, 1550 Bedford Hwy., PO Box 1573, Halifax, NS B3J 2Y3
902-424-3246, Fax: 902-424-1777, polcom@gov.ns.ca
Serious Incident Response Team, #203, 1256 Barrington St., Halifax, NS B3J 1Y6
902-424-2010, 855-450-2010, sirt@gov.ns.ca

Nunavut

Nunavut Territory Department of Justice, Sivummut, 1st Fl., PO Box 1000 500, Iqaluit, NU X0A 0H0
867-975-6170, Fax: 867-975-6195, justice@gov.nu.ca

Ontario

Ontario Ministry of the Attorney General, McMurtry-Scott Bldg., 720 Bay St., 11th Fl., Toronto, ON M7A 2S9
416-326-2220, Fax: 416-326-4007, 800-518-7901, attorneygeneral@ontario.ca
Ontario Provincial Police, Lincoln M. Alexander Bldg., 777 Memorial Ave., 3rd Fl., Orillia, ON L3V 7V3
705-329-6111, 888-310-1122
Special Investigations Unit, 5090 Commerce Blvd., Mississauga, ON L4W 5M4
416-622-0748, Fax: 416-622-2455, 800-787-8529

Québec

Ministère de la Justice, Édifice Louis-Philippe-Pigeon, 1200, rte de l'Église, Québec, QC G1V 4M1
418-643-5140, 866-536-5140, informations@justice.gouv.qc.ca
Sûreté du Québec, 1701, rue Parthenais, Montréal, QC H2K 3S7
514-598-4141, Fax: 514-598-4242

Saskatchewan

Saskatchewan Justice & Attorney General, 1874 Scarth St., Regina, SK S4P 4B3
306-787-7872
Saskatchewan Police College, College West Bldg., University of Regina, #217, 3737 Wascana Pkwy., Regina, SK S4S 0A2
306-787-9292
Saskatchewan Police Commission, #1850, 1881 Scarth St., Regina, SK S4P 4K9
306-787-9292, Fax: 306-798-4908
Saskatchewan Public Complaints Commission, #300, 1919 Saskatchewan Dr., Regina, SK S4P 4H2
306-787-6519, Fax: 306-787-6528, 866-256-6194

Yukon Territory

Yukon Justice, Andrew Philipsen Law Centre, 2134 Second Ave., PO Box 2703, Whitehorse, YT Y1A 2C6
867-667-3033, Fax: 867-393-5790, justice@gov.yk.ca

POLITICS & SOCIETY

Auditor General of Canada, 240 Sparks St., Ottawa, ON K1A 0G6
613-952-0213, Fax: 613-957-0474, 888-761-5953, infomedia@oag-bvg.gc.ca

Commission for Environmental Cooperation, Secretariat, #200, 393, rue St-Jacques ouest, Montréal, QC H2Y 1N9
514-350-4300, Fax: 514-350-4314, info@cec.org

Department of National Defence & the Canadian Armed Forces, National Defence HQ, Major-General George R. Pearkes Bldg., 101 Colonel By Dr., Ottawa, ON K1A 0K2
613-995-2534, Fax: 613-992-4739, 888-995-2534, information@forces.gc.ca

Finance Canada, 90 Elgin St., 14th Fl., Ottawa, ON K1A 0G5
613-369-3710, Fax: 613-369-4065, fin.financepublic-financepublique.fin@canada.ca

Global Affairs Canada, Enquiries Service, 125 Sussex Dr., Ottawa, ON K1A 0G2
613-944-4000, Fax: 613-996-9709, 800-267-8376

International Development Research Centre, 150 Kent St., PO Box 8500, Ottawa, ON K1G 3H9
613-236-6163, Fax: 613-238-7230, info@idrc.ca

International Joint Commission, 234 Laurier Ave. West, 22nd Fl., Ottawa, ON K1P 6K6
613-995-2984, Fax: 613-993-5583, commission@ottawa.ijc.org

National Capital Commission, #202, 40 Elgin St., Ottawa, ON K1P 1C7
613-239-5000, Fax: 613-239-5063, 800-465-1867, info@ncc-ccn.ca

Policy Horizons Canada, 360 Albert St., 15th Fl., Ottawa, ON K1R 7X7
613-947-3800, Fax: 613-995-6006, questions@horizons.gc.ca

Public Safety Canada, 269 Laurier Ave. West, Ottawa, ON K1A 0P8
613-944-4875, Fax: 613-954-5186, 800-830-3118

Public Services & Procurement, Place du Portage, Phase III, 11, rue Laurier, Ottawa, ON K1A 0S5
questions@tpsgc-pwgsc.gc.ca

Strategic Policy Branch, Tower 7, 1341 Baseline Rd., Ottawa, ON K1A 0C5
613-759-1000, Fax: 613-773-2121

Alberta

Intergovernmental Relations, Commerce Place, 10155 - 102 St., 12th Fl., Edmonton, AB T5J 4G8

Public Affairs Bureau, Federal Bldg., 9820 - 107 St., 7th Fl., Edmonton, AB T5K 1E7

British Columbia

British Columbia Ministry of Community, Sport, & Cultural Development & Responsible for TransLink, PO Box 9490 Prov Govt, Victoria, BC V8W 9N7

Newfoundland & Labrador

Newfoundland & Labrador Department of Service NL, PO Box 8700, St. John's, NL A1B 4J6
709-729-4834, servicenlinfo@gov.nl.ca

Newfoundland & Labrador Department of Transportation & Works, Confederation Bldg., Prince Philip Dr., PO Box 8700, St. John's, NL A1B 4J6
709-729-2300, tw@gov.nl.ca

Northwest Territories

Northwest Territories Department of Aboriginal Affairs & Intergovernmental Relations, 4910 - 52nd St., PO Box 1320, Yellowknife, NT X1A 2L9
867-767-9025, Fax: 867-873-0233

Northwest Territories Department of Public Works & Services, Stuart M. Hodgson Bldg., 5009 - 49th St., PO Box 1320, Yellowknife, NT X1A 2L9

Ontario

Environmental Commissioner of Ontario, #605, 1075 Bay St., Toronto, ON M5S 2B1
416-325-3377, Fax: 416-325-3370, 800-701-6454, commissioner@eco.on.ca

Prince Edward Island

Prince Edward Island Department of Health & Wellness, 105 Rochford St. North, 4th Fl., PO Box 2000, Charlottetown, PE C1A 7N8
902-368-6414, Fax: 902-368-4121

Yukon Territory

Emergency Measures Organization, Whitehorse Airport, Combined Services Bldg., 2nd Fl., 60 Norseman Rd., Whitehorse, YT Y1A 2C6
867-667-5220, Fax: 867-393-6266, 800-661-0408, emo.yukon@gov.yk.ca

POPULATION

See Also: Statistics

Statistics Canada, R.H. Coats Bldg., Tunney's Pasture, 150 Tunney's Pasture Driveway, Ottawa, ON K1A 0T6
514-283-8300, Fax: 514-283-9350, 800-263-1136, STATCAN.infostats-infostats.STATCAN@canada.ca

Manitoba

Manitoba Bureau of Statistics, #824, 155 Carlton St., Winnipeg, MB R3C 3H9
204-945-2406

Nunavut

Nunavut Territory Department of Executive & Intergovernmental Affairs, 1084 Aeroplex bldg., PO Box 1000 200, Iqaluit, NU X0A 0H0
867-975-6000, Fax: 867-975-6099

Québec

Institut de la statistique du Québec, 200, ch Ste-Foy, 1er étage, Québec, QC G1R 5T4
418-691-2401, Fax: 418-643-4129, 800-463-4090

POSTAL SERVICE

Canada Post Corporation, Corporate Secretariat, 2701 Riverside Dr., Ottawa, ON K1A 0B1
416-979-3033, 866-607-6301

PREMIERS & LEADERS

See Also: Cabinets & Executive Councils; Government (General Info)

Office of the Prime Minister, Liberal Party of Canada / Liberal Research Bureau, Langevin Block, 80 Wellington St., Ottawa, ON K1A 0A2
613-992-4211, Fax: 613-941-6900

Alberta

Office of the Premier, Office of the Premier, Legislature Building, #307, 10800 - 97 Ave., Edmonton, AB T5K 2B6
780-427-2251, Fax: 780-427-1349, -310-0000

British Columbia

Office of the Premier & Cabinet Office, West Annex, Parliament Bldgs., PO Box 9041 Prov Govt, Victoria, BC V8W 9E1
250-387-1715, Fax: 250-387-0087, premier@gov.bc.ca

Manitoba

Office of the Premier, Legislative Building, #204, 450 Broadway Ave., Winnipeg, MB R3C 0V8
204-945-3714, Fax: 204-949-1484, premier@leg.gov.mb.ca

New Brunswick

Office of the Premier, Centennial Bldg., PO Box 6000, Fredericton, NB E3B 5H1
506-453-2144, Fax: 506-453-7407, premier@gnb.ca

Newfoundland & Labrador

Office of the Premier, East Block, Confederation Bldg., PO Box 8700, St. John's, NL A1B 4J6
709-729-3570, Fax: 709-729-5875, premier@gov.nl.ca

Northwest Territories

Office of the Premier, Legislative Assembly Bldg., PO Box 1320, Yellowknife, NT X1A 2L9
867-669-2311, Fax: 867-873-0385

Nova Scotia

Council of Atlantic Premiers, Council Secretariat, #1006, 5161 George St., PO Box 2044, Halifax, NS B3J 2Z1
902-424-7590, Fax: 902-424-8976, info@cap-cpma.ca

Office of the Premier, One Government Place, 1700 Granville St., 7th Fl., PO Box 726, Halifax, NS B3J 2T3
902-424-6600, Fax: 902-424-7648, 800-267-1993, premier@novascotia.ca

Nunavut

Office of the Premier, PO Box 2410, Iqaluit, NU X0A 0H0
867-975-5050, Fax: 867-975-5051

Ontario

Office of the Premier, Legislative Building, Queen's Park, Toronto, ON M7A 1A1
416-325-1941, Fax: 416-325-3745

Prince Edward Island

Office of the Premier, Shaw Bldg., 95 Rochford St. South, 5th Fl., PO Box 2000, Charlottetown, PE C1A 7N8
902-368-4400, Fax: 902-368-4416, premier@gov.pe.ca

Québec

Cabinet du premier ministre, Édifice Honoré-Mercier, 835, boul René-Lévesque est, 3e étage, Québec, QC G1A 1B4
418-643-5321, Fax: 418-643-3924

Saskatchewan

Office of the Premier, Legislative Building, #226, 2405 Legislative Dr., Regina, SK S4S 0B3
306-787-9433, Fax: 306-787-0885

Yukon Territory

Office of the Premier, 2071 - 2nd Ave., PO Box 2703, Whitehorse, YT Y1A 2C6
867-667-8660, Fax: 867-393-6252, premier@gov.yk.ca

PROCUREMENT, GOODS & SERVICES

See: Purchasing

Public Services & Procurement, Place du Portage, Phase III, 11, rue Laurier, Ottawa, ON K1A 0S5
questions@tpsgc-pwgsc.gc.ca

Nova Scotia

Nova Scotia Department of Internal Services, World Trade & Convention Centre, 1800 Argyle St., 5th Fl., PO Box 943, Halifax, NS B3J 2V9
902-424-5465, Fax: 902-424-0555

Ontario

Supply Chain Ontario, 222 Jarvis St., 8th Fl., Toronto, ON M7A 0B6
Fax: 416-327-3573

Saskatchewan

Saskatchewan Central Services, 1920 Rose St., Regina, SK S4P 0A9
306-787-6911, Fax: 306-787-1061, GSReception@gs.gov.sk.ca

PROPERTY

See: Real Estate

New Brunswick

Service New Brunswick, Westmorland Pl., PO Box 1998, Fredericton, NB E3B 5G4
506-457-3581, Fax: 506-444-2850, snb@snb.ca

PROPERTY ASSESSMENT

British Columbia

British Columbia Assessment Authority, #400, 3450 Uptown Blvd., Victoria, BC V8Z 0B9
604-739-8588, Fax: 855-995-6209, 866-825-8322

New Brunswick

Assessment & Planning Appeal Board, City Centre, 435 King St., PO Box 6000, Fredericton, NB E3B 5H1
506-453-2126, Fax: 506-444-4881, lg/gl-info@gnb.ca

Newfoundland & Labrador

Municipal Assessment Agency Inc., 75 O'Leary Ave., St. John's, NL A1B 2C9
709-724-1532, 877-777-2807, info@maa.ca

Newfoundland & Labrador Department of Municipal & Intergovernmental Affairs, West Block, Main Fl., Confederation Bldg., PO Box 8700, St. John's, NL A1B 4J6
709-729-3046, Fax: 709-729-0943, mainfo@gov.nl.ca

Northwest Territories

Assessment Appeal Tribunal, #600, 5201 - 50th Ave., PO Box 1320, Yellowknife, NT X1A 3S9
867-873-7125, Fax: 867-873-0609

Prince Edward Island

Prince Edward Island Regulatory & Appeals Commission, National Bank Tower, #501, 134 Kent St., PO Box 577, Charlottetown, PE C1A 7L1
902-892-3501, Fax: 902-566-4076, 800-501-6268, info@irac.pe.ca

Saskatchewan

Saskatchewan Assessment Management Agency, #200, 2201 - 11th Ave., Regina, SK S4P 0J8
306-924-8000, Fax: 306-924-8070, 800-667-7262, info.request@sama.sk.ca

PROTOCOL (STATE)

See Also: Parliament

Governor General & Commander-in-Chief of Canada, Rideau Hall, 1 Sussex Dr., Ottawa, ON K1A 0A1
613-993-8200, Fax: 613-998-8760, 800-465-6890

PUBLIC SAFETY

See Also: Occupational Safety

Canadian Coast Guard, Centennial Towers, #6S018, 200 Kent St., Ottawa, ON K1A 0E6
613-993-0999, Fax: 613-990-1866, info@dfo-mpo.gc.ca

Canadian Security Intelligence Service, PO Box 9732 T,Ottawa, ON K1G 4G4
613-993-9620, Fax: 613-231-0612

Canadian Transportation Agency, Les Terrasses de la Chaudière, 15 Eddy St., Gatineau, QC J8X 4B3
Fax: 819-997-6727, 888-222-2592, info@otc-cta.gc.ca

Communications Security Establishment Canada, 1500 Bronson Ave., PO Box 9703 Terminal, Ottawa, ON K1A 0K2
613-991-7600, Fax: 613-991-8514

Department of National Defence & the Canadian Armed Forces, National Defence HQ, Major-General George R. Pearkes Bldg., 101 Colonel By Dr., Ottawa, ON K1A 0K2
613-995-2534, Fax: 613-992-4739, 888-995-2534, information@forces.gc.ca

Justice Canada, East Memorial Bldg., 284 Wellington St., Ottawa, ON K1A 0H8
613-957-4222, Fax: 613-954-0811, webadmin@justice.gc.ca

Office of the Communications Security Establishment Commissioner, PO Box 1984 B, Ottawa, ON K1P 5R5
613-992-3044

Public Safety Canada, 269 Laurier Ave. West, Ottawa, ON K1A 0P8
613-944-4875, Fax: 613-954-5186, 800-830-3118
Royal Canadian Mounted Police, 73 Leikin Dr., Ottawa, ON K1A 0R2
613-993-7267, Fax: 613-993-0260

Alberta
Alberta Justice & Solicitor General, Communications, Bowker Building, 9833 - 109 St., 5th Fl., Edmonton, AB T5K 2E8
780-427-2745, -310-0000
Public Security Division, John E. Brownlee Building, 10365 - 97 St., 10th Fl., Edmonton, AB T5J 3W7

British Columbia
British Columbia Ministry of Justice, PO Box 9044 Prov Govt, Victoria, BC V8W 9E2
British Columbia Ministry of Public Safety & Solicitor General, PO Box 9290 Prov Govt, Victoria, BC V8W 9J7
250-356-0149, Fax: 250-387-6224, 800-663-7867, EnquiryBC@gov.bc.ca
British Columbia Safety Authority, #200, 505 - 6th St., New Westminster, BC V3L 0E1
866-566-7233, info@safetyauthority.ca
Safety Standards Appeal Board, 614 Humboldt St., 4th Fl., PO Box 9844 Prov Govt, Victoria, BC V8W 9T2
250-387-4021, Fax: 250-356-6645

Manitoba
Manitoba Justice & Attorney General, Administration & Finance, #1110, 405 Broadway Ave., Winnipeg, MB R3C 3L6
204-945-2878, minjus@gov.mb.ca

New Brunswick
New Brunswick Department of Justice & Public Safety, Argyle Place, PO Box 6000, Fredericton, NB E3B 5H1
506-453-3992, DPS-MSP.Information@gnb.ca

Newfoundland & Labrador
Newfoundland & Labrador Department of Justice & Public Safety, Confederation Bldg., East Block, 4th Fl., PO Box 8700, St. John's, NL A1B 4J6
709-729-2869, Fax: 709-729-0469, justice@gov.nl.ca

Northwest Territories
Northwest Territories Department of Justice, 4903 - 49th St., PO Box 1320, Yellowknife, NT X1A 2L9
867-767-9256

Nova Scotia
Nova Scotia Department of Justice, 1690 Hollis St., PO Box 7, Halifax, NS B3J 2L6
902-424-4030, justweb@gov.ns.ca

Nunavut
Nunavut Territory Department of Justice, Sivummut, 1st Fl., PO Box 1000 500, Iqaluit, NU X0A 0H0
867-975-6170, Fax: 867-975-6195, justice@gov.nu.ca

Québec
Ministère de la Justice, Édifice Louis-Philippe-Pigeon, 1200, rte de l'Église, Québec, QC G1V 4M1
418-643-5140, 866-536-5140, informations@justice.gouv.qc.ca
Ministère de la Sécurité publique, Tour des Laurentides, 2525, boul Laurier, 5e étage, Québec, QC G1V 2L2
418-646-6777, Fax: 418-643-0275, 866-644-6826

Saskatchewan
Office of the Minister of Corrections & Policing, Legislative Bldg., #345, 2405 Legislative Dr., Regina, SK S4S 0B3
306-787-4983, Fax: 306-787-5331

Yukon Territory
Yukon Justice, Andrew Philipsen Law Centre, 2134 Second Ave., PO Box 2703, Whitehorse, YT Y1A 2C6
867-667-3033, Fax: 867-393-5790, justice@gov.yk.ca

PUBLIC SERVICES

Canada Deposit Insurance Corporation, 50 O'Connor St., 17th Floor, Ottawa, ON K1P 6L2
Fax: 613-996-6095, 800-461-2342, info@cdic.ca
Canada Post Corporation, Corporate Secretariat, 2701 Riverside Dr., Ottawa, ON K1A 0B1
416-979-3033, 866-607-6301
Canadian Broadcasting Corporation, 181 Queen St., PO Box 3220 C,Ottawa, ON K1Y 1E4
613-288-6000, liaison@cbc.ca
Canadian Centre for Occupational Health & Safety, 135 Hunter St. East, Hamilton, ON L8N 1M5
905-572-2981, Fax: 905-572-4500, 800-668-4284
Canadian Coast Guard, Centennial Towers, #6S018, 200 Kent St., Ottawa, ON K1A 0E6
613-993-0999, Fax: 613-990-1866, info@dfo-mpo.gc.ca
Canadian Security Intelligence Service, PO Box 9732 T,Ottawa, ON K1G 4G4
613-993-9620, Fax: 613-231-0612
Commission for Public Complaints Against the Royal Canadian Mounted Police, National Intake Office, PO Box 88689, Surrey, BC V3W 0X1
Fax: 604-501-4095, 800-665-6878
Correctional Service Canada, 340 Laurier Ave. West, Ottawa, ON K1A 0P9
613-992-5891, Fax: 613-943-1630
Department of National Defence & the Canadian Armed Forces, National Defence HQ, Major-General George R. Pearkes Bldg., 101 Colonel By Dr., Ottawa, ON K1A 0K2
613-995-2534, Fax: 613-992-4739, 888-995-2534, information@forces.gc.ca
Employment & Social Development Canada, 140 Promenade du Portage, Gatineau, QC K1A 0J9
Immigration & Refugee Board of Canada, Canada Bldg, 344 Slater St., 12th Fl., Ottawa, ON K1A 0K1
613-995-6486, Fax: 613-943-1550, contact@irb-cisr.gc.ca
Immigration, Refugees & Citizenship, Jean Edmonds, South Tower, 365 Laurier Ave. West, Ottawa, ON K1A 1L1
888-242-2100
MERX, Phase II, #103, 6 Antares Dr., Ottawa, ON K2E 8A9
613-727-4900, Fax: 888-235-5800, 800-964-6379, merx@merx.com
Military Police Complaints Commission, 270 Albert St., 10th Fl., Ottawa, ON K1P 5G8
613-947-5625, Fax: 613-947-5713, 800-632-0566, commission@mpcc-cppm.gc.ca
National Capital Commission, #202, 40 Elgin St., Ottawa, ON K1P 1C7
613-239-5000, Fax: 613-239-5063, 800-465-1867, info@ncc-ccn.ca
National Search & Rescue Secretariat, 269 Laurier Ave. West, 10th Fl., Ottawa, ON K1A 0P8
Fax: 613-996-3746, 800-727-9414, questions@nss-snrs.gc.ca
Parole Board of Canada, Communications Division, National Office, 410 Laurier Ave. West, Ottawa, ON K1A 0R1
613-954-7474, Fax: 613-941-4981, info@pbc-clcc.gc.ca
Public Service Commission, 22 Eddy St., Gatineau, QC K1A 0M7
613-992-9562, Fax: 613-992-9352, CFP.INFOCOM.PSC@cfp-psc.gc.ca
Public Service Staffing Tribunal, 240 Sparks St., 6th Fl., Ottawa, ON K1A 0A5
613-949-6516, Fax: 613-949-6551, 866-637-4491, info@psst-tdfp.gc.ca
Public Services & Procurement, Place du Portage, Phase III, 11, rue Laurier, Ottawa, ON K1A 0S5
questions@tpsgc-pwgsc.gc.ca
Royal Canadian Mounted Police, 73 Leikin Dr., Ottawa, ON K1A 0R2
613-993-7267, Fax: 613-993-0260
Royal Canadian Mounted Police External Review Committee, PO Box 1159 B, Ottawa, ON K1P 5R2
613-998-2134, Fax: 613-990-8969, org@erc-cee.gc.ca
Security Intelligence Review Committee, PO Box 2430 D,Ottawa, ON K1P 5W5
613-990-8441, Fax: 613-990-5230, info@sirc-csars.gc.ca
Service Canada, 140, Promenade du Portage, Gatineau, QC K1A 0J9
Fax: 613-941-1827, 800-622-6232
Veterans Affairs Canada, 161 Grafton St., PO Box 7700, Charlottetown, PE C1A 8M9
866-522-2122, information@vac-acc.gc.ca
Veterans Review & Appeal Board, Daniel J. MacDonald Bldg., 161 Grafton St., PO Box 9900, Charlottetown, PE C1A 8V7
902-566-8751, Fax: 902-566-7850, 800-450-8006, vrab_tacra@vac-acc.gc.ca

Alberta
Alberta Capital Finance Authority, Sun Life Place, #2160, 10123 - 99 St. NW, Edmonton, AB T5J 3H1
780-427-9711, Fax: 780-422-2175, webacfa@gov.ab.ca
Alberta Emergency Management Agency, 2810 - 10303 Jasper Ave., Edmonton, AB T5J 3N6
780-422-9000, Fax: 780-644-1044, -310-0000, aema@gov.ab.ca
Alberta Energy Regulator, #1000, 250 - 5 St. SW, Calgary, AB T2P 0R4
403-297-8311, Fax: 403-297-7336, 855-297-8311, inquiries@aer.ca
Alberta Health Services, Corporate Office, North Tower, Seventh Street Plaza, 10030 - 107th St. NW, 14th Fl., Edmonton, AB T5J 3E4
780-342-2000, Fax: 780-342-2060, 888-342-2471, ahs.corp@albertahealthservices.ca
Alberta Infrastructure, Infrastructure Building, 6950 - 113 St., Edmonton, AB T6H 5V7
780-415-0507, Fax: 780-427-2187, -310-0000, Infra.Contact.Us.m@gov.ab.ca
Alberta Justice & Solicitor General, Communications, Bowker Building, 9833 - 109 St., 5th Fl., Edmonton, AB T5K 2E8
780-427-2745, -310-0000
Alberta Municipal Affairs, Communications Branch, Commerce Place, 10155 - 102 St., 18th Fl., Edmonton, AB T5J 4L4
780-427-2732, Fax: 780-422-1419, -310-0000
Alberta Office of the Public Interest Commissioner, #2800, 10303 Jasper Ave. NW, Edmonton, AB T5J 5C3
780-641-8659, Fax: 780-427-2759, 855-641-8659, info@pic.alberta.ca
Alberta Pensions Services Corporation, 5103 Windermere Blvd. SW, Edmonton, AB T6W 0S9
780-427-2782, 800-661-8198, memberservices@apsc.ca
Corporate Human Resources, Peace Hills Trust Tower, 10011 - 109 St., 7th Fl., Edmonton, AB T5J 3S8
780-408-8400
Labour Relations Board, Labour Building, #501, 10808 - 99 Ave., Edmonton, AB T5K 0G5
780-427-8547, Fax: 780-422-0970, 800-463-2572, alrbinfo@gov.ab.ca
Legal Services Division, Bowker Building, 9833 - 109 St., 2nd Fl., Edmonton, AB T5K 2E8
780-422-0500
Municipal Government Board, Commerce Place, 10155 - 102 St., 15th Fl., Edmonton, AB T5J 4L4
780-427-4864, Fax: 780-427-0986, -310-0000, mgbmail@gov.ab.ca
Public Security Division, John E. Brownlee Building, 10365 - 97 St., 10th Fl., Edmonton, AB T5J 3W7

British Columbia
British Columbia Assessment Authority, #400, 3450 Uptown Blvd., Victoria, BC V8Z 0B9
604-739-8588, Fax: 855-995-6209, 866-825-8322
British Columbia Ferry Services Inc., c/o BC Ferry Authority, #500, 1321 Blanshard St., Victoria, BC V8W 0B7
250-381-1401, 888-223-3779, customerservice@bcferries.com
British Columbia Housing Management Commission (BC Housing), #1701, 4555 Kingsway, Burnaby, BC V5H 4V8
604-433-1711, Fax: 604-439-4722, webeditor@bchousing.org
British Columbia Ministry of Children & Family Development, PO Box 9770 Prov Govt, Victoria, BC V8W 9S5
250-387-7027, Fax: 250-356-3007, 877-387-7027, MCF.CorrespondenceManagement@gov.bc.ca
British Columbia Ministry of Justice, PO Box 9044 Prov Govt, Victoria, BC V8W 9E2
British Columbia Ministry of Public Safety & Solicitor General, PO Box 9290 Prov Govt, Victoria, BC V8W 9J7
250-356-0149, Fax: 250-387-6224, 800-663-7867, EnquiryBC@gov.bc.ca
British Columbia Public Service Agency, PO Box 9404 Prov Govt, Victoria, BC V8W 9V1
250-387-0518, Fax: 250-356-7074
British Columbia Transit, 520 Gorge Rd. East, Victoria, BC V8W 2P3
250-385-2551
Columbia Power Corporation, #200, 445 - 13th Ave., Castlegar, BC V1N 1G1
250-304-6060, Fax: 250-304-6083, cpc.info@columbiapower.org
Emergency Management BC, PO Box 9201 Prov Govt, Victoria, BC V8W 9J1
250-952-4913, Fax: 250-952-4871
Local Government, PO Box 9490 Prov Govt, Victoria, BC V8W 9N7
250-356-6575, Fax: 250-387-7973
Office of the Representative for Children & Youth, #400, 1019 Wharf St., Victoria, BC V8W 2Y9
250-356-6710, Fax: 250-356-0837, 800-476-3933, rcy@rcybc.ca

Manitoba
Advisory Council on Workplace Safety & Health, 401 York Ave., 2nd Fl., Winnipeg, MB R3C 0P8
204-945-3446, Fax: 204-948-2209, 866-888-8186, wshcompl@gov.mb.ca
Civil Service Commission Board, #935, 155 Carlton St., Winnipeg, MB R3C 3H8
204-945-1435, Fax: 204-945-1486
Deposit Guarantee Corporation of Manitoba, #390, 200 Graham Ave., Winnipeg, MB R3C 4L5
204-942-8480, Fax: 204-947-1723, 800-697-4447, mail@depositguarantee.mb.ca
Emergency Measures Organization, #1525, 405 Broadway Ave., Winnipeg, MB R3C 3L6
204-945-4772, Fax: 204-945-4929, 888-267-8298, emo@gov.mb.ca
Health Information Privacy Committee, #4043, 300 Carlton St., Winnipeg, MB R3B 3M9
Healthy Living & Seniors, c/o Seniors & Healthy Aging Secretariat, #1610, 155 Carlton St., Winnipeg, MB R3C 3H8
204-945-6565, Fax: 204-948-2514, 800-665-6565, seniors@gov.mb.ca
Local Government Development Division, 59 Elizabeth Dr., PO Box 33, Thompson, MB R8N 1X4
204-677-6794, Fax: 204-677-6525
Manitoba Bureau of Statistics, #824, 155 Carlton St., Winnipeg, MB R3C 3H9
204-945-2406

Manitoba Civil Service Commission, #935, 155 Carlton St., Winnipeg, MB R3C 3H8
204-945-2332, Fax: 204-945-1486, 800-282-8069, csc@gov.mb.ca

Manitoba Families, Legislative Building, #357, 450 Broadway, Winnipeg, MB R3C 0V8
204-945-3744, 866-626-4862

Manitoba Film Classification Board, #216, 301 Weston St., Winnipeg, MB R3E 3H4
204-945-8962, Fax: 204-945-0890, 866-612-2399, mfcb@gov.mb.ca

Manitoba Health, Seniors & Active Living, #100, 300 Carlton St., Winnipeg, MB R3B 3M9
204-945-3744, 866-626-4862, mgi@gov.mb.ca

Manitoba Human Rights Commission, #700, 175 Hargrave St., Winnipeg, MB R3C 3R8
204-945-3007, Fax: 204-945-1292, 888-884-8681, hrc@gov.mb.ca

Manitoba Hydro, 360 Portage Ave., PO Box 815 Main,Winnipeg, MB R3C 2P4
204-480-5900, Fax: 204-360-6155, 888-624-9376, publicaffairs@hydro.mb.ca

Manitoba Infrastructure, Legislative Building, #203, 450 Broadway Ave., Winnipeg, MB R3C 0V8
204-945-3723, Fax: 204-945-7610

Manitoba Justice & Attorney General, Administration & Finance, #1110, 405 Broadway Ave., Winnipeg, MB R3C 3L6
204-945-2878, minjus@gov.mb.ca

Manitoba Land Value Appraisal Commission, #1144, 363 Broadway, Winnipeg, MB R3C 3N9
204-945-5455, Fax: 204-948-2235

Manitoba Minimum Wage Board, 614 - 401 York Ave., Winnipeg, MB R3C 0P8
204-945-8190, Fax: 204-948-2085, lmsd@gov.mb.ca

Manitoba Public Insurance Corporation, #B100, 234 Donald St., PO Box 6300, Winnipeg, MB R3C 4A4
204-985-7000, Fax: 204-985-3525, 800-665-2410

Office of the Auditor General, #500, 330 Portage Ave., Winnipeg, MB R3C 0C4
204-945-3790, Fax: 204-945-2169, oag.contact@oag.mb.ca

Public Health & Primary Health Care, 300 Carlton St., 4th Floor, Winnipeg, MB R3B 3M9
204-788-6666

Workers Compensation Board of Manitoba, 333 Broadway Ave., Winnipeg, MB R3C 4W3
204-954-4321, Fax: 204-954-4999, 800-362-3340, wcb@wcb.mb.ca

New Brunswick

New Brunswick Department of Health, HSBC Place, PO Box 5100, Fredericton, NB E3B 5G8
506-457-4800, Fax: 506-453-5243, Health.Sante@gnb.ca

New Brunswick Department of Justice & Public Safety, Argyle Place, PO Box 6000, Fredericton, NB E3B 5H1
506-453-3992, DPS-MSP.Information@gnb.ca

New Brunswick Department of Post-Secondary Education, Training & Labour, Chestnut Complex, PO Box 6000, Fredericton, NB E3B 5H1
506-453-2597, Fax: 506-453-3618, dpetlinfo@gnb.ca

New Brunswick Department of Social Development, Sartain MacDonald Bldg., 551 King St., PO Box 6000, Fredericton, NB E3B 5H1
506-453-2001, Fax: 506-453-2164, sd-ds@gnb.ca

New Brunswick Human Rights Commission, Barry House, PO Box 6000, Fredericton, NB E3B 5H1
506-453-2301, Fax: 506-453-2653, 888-471-2233, hrc.cdp@gnb.ca

Office of the Ombudsman, PO Box 6000, Fredericton, NB E3B 5H1
506-453-2789, Fax: 506-453-5599, 888-465-1100, nbombud@gnb.ca

Premier's Council on the Status of Disabled Persons, #648, 440 King St., Fredericton, NB E3B 5H8
506-444-3000, Fax: 506-444-3001, 800-442-4412, pcsdp@gnb.ca

Service New Brunswick, Westmorland Pl., PO Box 1998, Fredericton, NB E3B 5G4
506-457-3581, Fax: 506-444-2850, snb@snb.ca

Newfoundland & Labrador

C.A. Pippy Park Commission, Mount Scio House, 15 Mount Scio Rd., St. John's, NL A1B 3T2
709-737-3655, info@pippypark.com

Eastern Waste Management Commission, #3, 255 Majors Path, St. John's, NL A1A 0L5
709-579-7960, Fax: 709-579-5392, info@easternwaste.ca

Income & Employment Support Appeal Board, Confederation Bldg., PO Box 8700, St. John's, NL A1B 4J6
709-729-2479, Fax: 709-729-5139

Newfoundland & Labrador Department of Advanced Education & Skills, Confederation Building, West Block, 3rd Fl., PO Box 8700, St. John's, NL A1B 4J6
709-729-2480, aesweb@gov.nl.ca

Newfoundland & Labrador Department of Justice & Public Safety, Confederation Bldg., East Block, 4th Fl., PO Box 8700, St. John's, NL A1B 4J6
709-729-2869, Fax: 709-729-0469, justice@gov.nl.ca

Newfoundland & Labrador Department of Municipal & Intergovernmental Affairs, West Block, Main Fl., Confederation Bldg., PO Box 8700, St. John's, NL A1B 4J6
709-729-3046, Fax: 709-729-0943, mainfo@gov.nl.ca

Newfoundland & Labrador Department of Service NL, PO Box 8700, St. John's, NL A1B 4J6
709-729-4834, servicenlinfo@gov.nl.ca

Newfoundland & Labrador Department of Transportation & Works, Confederation Bldg., Prince Philip Dr., PO Box 8700, St. John's, NL A1B 4J6
709-729-2300, tw@gov.nl.ca

Newfoundland & Labrador Legal Aid Commission, #300, 251 Empire Ave., St. John's, NL A1C 5J9
709-753-7860, Fax: 709-753-7851, 800-563-9911, nlac@legalaid.nl.ca

Newfoundland & Labrador Liquor Corporation, 90 Kenmount Rd., PO Box 8750 A, St. John's, NL A1B 3V1
709-724-1100, Fax: 709-754-0321, info@nfliquor.com

Newfoundland & Labrador Public Service Commission, 50 Mundy Pond Rd., PO Box 8700, St. John's, NL A1B 4J6
709-729-5810, Fax: 709-729-6234, 855-330-5810, contactpsc@gov.nl.ca

Royal Newfoundland Constabulary Public Complaints Commission, 689 Topsail Rd., PO Box 8700, St. John's, NL A1B 4J6
709-729-0950, Fax: 709-729-1302, rnccomplaintscommission@gov.nl.ca

Northwest Territories

Inuvialuit Water Board, Professional Bldg., #302, 125 Mackenzie Rd., PO Box 2531, Yellowknife, NT X0E 0T0
867-678-2942, Fax: 867-678-2943, info@inuvwb.ca

Northwest Territories Department of Health & Social Services, 5015 - 49th St., PO Box 1320, Yellowknife, NT X1A 2L9
Fax: 867-873-0306

Northwest Territories Department of Justice, 4903 - 49th St., PO Box 1320, Yellowknife, NT X1A 2L9
867-767-9256

Northwest Territories Department of Municipal & Community Affairs, PO Box 1320, Yellowknife, NT X1A 2L9
867-767-9160, Fax: 867-873-0309

Northwest Territories Department of Public Works & Services, Stuart M. Hodgson Bldg., 5009 - 49th St., PO Box 1320, Yellowknife, NT X1A 2L9

Northwest Territories Housing Corporation, Scotia Centre, 5102 - 50th Ave., PO Box 2100, Yellowknife, NT X1A 2P6
867-767-9080, Fax: 867-873-9426, 844-698-4663

Northwest Territories Power Corporation, 4 Capital Dr., Hay River, NT X0E 1G2
867-874-5200, info@ntpc.com

Victims Assistance Committee, c/o Community Justice & Community Policing Division, PO Box 1320, Yellowknife, NT X1A 2L9
867-920-6911, Fax: 867-873-0199

Nova Scotia

Emergency Management Office, PO Box 2581, Halifax, NS B3J 3N5
902-424-5620, Fax: 902-424-5376, 866-424-5620, emo@gov.ns.ca

Nova Scotia Department of Community Services, Nelson Place, 5675 Spring Garden Rd., 8th Fl., PO Box 696, Halifax, NS B3J 2T7
877-424-1177

Nova Scotia Department of Health & Wellness, Barrington Tower., 1894 Barrington St., PO Box 488, Halifax, NS B3J 2R8
902-424-5818, 800-387-6665

Nova Scotia Department of Justice, 1690 Hollis St., PO Box 7, Halifax, NS B3J 2L6
902-424-4030, justweb@gov.ns.ca

Nova Scotia Department of Transportation & Infrastructure Renewal, Johnston Bldg., 1672 Granville St., 2nd Fl., PO Box 186, Halifax, NS B3J 2N2
902-424-2297, Fax: 902-424-0532, 888-432-3233, tpwpaff@novascotia.ca

Nova Scotia Disabled Persons Commission, Dartmouth Professional Center, #104, 277 Pleasant St., Dartmouth, NS B2Y 4B7
902-424-8280, 800-565-8280

Nova Scotia Legal Aid Commission, Office of the Executive Director, #920, 1701 Hollis St., Halifax, NS B3J 3M8
902-420-6578, 877-420-6578

Nova Scotia Public Service Commission, 1800 Argyle St., 5th Fl., PO Box 943, Halifax, NS B3J 2V9
902-424-7660

Service Nova Scotia, c/o Public Enquiries - Service Nova Scotia, PO Box 2734, Halifax, NS B3J 3K5
902-424-5200, Fax: 902-424-0720, 800-670-4357

Workers' Advisers Program, #502, 5670 Spring Garden Rd., PO Box 1063, Halifax, NS B3J 2X1
Fax: 902-424-0530, 800-774-4712

Nunavut

Nunavut Emergency Management, PO Box 1000 700, Iqaluit, NU X0A 0H0
867-975-5403, Fax: 867-979-4221, 800-693-1666

Nunavut Territory Department of Community & Government Services, W.G. Brown Bldg., 4th Fl., PO Box 1000 700, Iqaluit, NU X0A 0H0
867-975-5400, Fax: 867-975-5305

Nunavut Territory Department of Family Services, PO Box 1000 950, Iqaluit, NU X0A 0H0
867-975-6038, Fax: 867-975-6091

Nunavut Territory Department of Finance, Bldg. 1079, 1st Fl., PO Box 1000 430, Iqaluit, NU X0A 0H0
867-975-5800, Fax: 867-975-5805

Nunavut Territory Department of Health, PO Box 1000 1000, Iqaluit, NU X0A 0H0
867-975-5700, Fax: 867-975-5705, 800-661-0833

Nunavut Territory Department of Justice, Sivummut, 1st Fl., PO Box 1000 500, Iqaluit, NU X0A 0H0
867-975-6170, Fax: 867-975-6195, justice@gov.nu.ca

Ontario

Advertising Review Board, Macdonald Block, #M2-56, 900 Bay St., 2nd Fl., Toronto, ON M7A 1N3
416-327-2183, Fax: 416-327-2179

Deposit Insurance Corporation of Ontario, #700, 4711 Yonge St., Toronto, ON M2N 6K8
416-325-9444, Fax: 416-325-9722, 800-268-6653, info@dico.com

Emergency Management Ontario, 77 Wellesley St. West, PO Box 222, Toronto, ON M7A 1N3
416-314-3723, Fax: 416-314-3758, 877-314-3723

Fire Safety Commission, Place Nouveau Bldg., 5775 Yonge St., 7th Fl., Toronto, ON M2M 4J1
416-325-3100, Fax: 416-314-1217

Health Services Information & Information Technology Cluster, 56 Wellesley St. West, 10th Fl., Toronto, ON M5S 2S3
416-314-0234, Fax: 416-314-4182

Human Rights Tribunal of Ontario, 655 Bay St., 14th Fl., Toronto, ON M7A 2A3
416-326-1312, Fax: 416-326-2199, 866-598-0322, hrto.tdpo@ontario.ca

Hydro One Inc., North Tower, 483 Bay St., 15th Fl., Toronto, ON M5G 2P5
416-345-5000, Fax: 905-944-3251, 877-955-1155, customercommunications@hydroone.com

Independent Electricity System Operator, #1600, 120 Adelaide St. West, Toronto, ON M5H 1T1
905-403-6900, Fax: 905-403-6921, 888-448-7777, customer.relations@ieso.ca

Office of the Employer Advisor, #704, 151 Bloor St. West., Toronto, ON M5S 1S4
416-327-0020, Fax: 416-327-0726, 800-387-0774

Office of the Worker Advisor, #1300, 123 Edward St., Toronto, ON M5G 1E2
416-325-8570, Fax: 416-325-4830, 800-660-6769, owaweb@ontario.ca

Ontario Ministry of Community & Social Services, Hepburn Block, 80 Grosvenor St., 6th Fl., Toronto, ON M7A 1E9
416-325-5666, Fax: 416-325-3347, 888-789-4199

Ontario Ministry of Community Safety & Correctional Services, George Drew Bldg., 25 Grosvenor St., 18th Fl., Toronto, ON M7A 1Y6
416-326-5000, Fax: 416-326-0498, 866-517-0571, mcscs.feedback@ontario.ca

Ontario Ministry of Infrastructure, Hearst Block, 900 Bay St., 8th Fl., Toronto, ON M7A 2E1
416-325-6666, 800-268-7095

Ontario Ministry of Municipal Affairs, College Park, 777 Bay St., 17th Fl., Toronto, ON M5G 2E5
416-585-7000, Fax: 416-585-6470, mininfo@ontario.ca

Ontario Ministry of the Attorney General, McMurtry-Scott Bldg., 720 Bay St., 11th Fl., Toronto, ON M7A 2S9
416-326-2220, Fax: 416-326-4007, 800-518-7901, attorneygeneral@ontario.ca

Ontario Ministry of Transportation, Ferguson Block, 77 Wellesley St. West, 3rd Fl., Toronto, ON M7A 1Z8
416-327-9200, Fax: 416-327-9185, 800-268-4686

Ontario Pension Board, Sun Life Bldg., #2200, 200 King St. West, Toronto, ON M5H 3X6
416-364-8558, Fax: 416-364-7578, 800-668-6203, clientservice@opb.ca

Ontario Power Generation, 700 University Ave., Toronto, ON M5G 1X6
416-592-2555, 877-592-2555, webmaster@opg.com

Public Service Commission, Whitney Block, 99 Wellesley St. West, 5th Fl., Toronto, ON M7A 1W4
416-325-1750

Public Service Grievance Board, #600, 180 Dundas St. West, Toronto, ON M5G 1Z8
416-326-1388, Fax: 416-326-1396, psgb.psgb@ontario.ca
Safety, Licensing Appeals & Standards Tribunals Ontario, #5230, 20 Dundas St. West, Toronto, ON M5G 2C2
416-212-0334, Fax: 416-314-4270, 855-444-7454, slastinfo@ontario.ca
Southern Ontario Library Service, #902, 111 Peter St., Toronto, ON M5V 2H1
416-961-1669, Fax: 416-961-5122, 800-387-5765

Prince Edward Island

Housing Services, Jones Bldg., 11 Kent St., 2nd Fl., PO Box 2000, Charlottetown, PE C1A 7N8
902-620-3777, Fax: 902-894-0242
Island Waste Management Corporation, 110 Watts Ave., Charlottetown, PE C1E 2C1
902-894-0330, Fax: 902-894-0331, 888-280-8111, info@iwmc.pe.ca
Prince Edward Island Department of Family & Human Services, Jones Bldg., 11 Kent St., 2nd Fl., PO Box 2000, Charlottetown, PE C1A 7N8
902-620-3777, Fax: 902-894-0242, 866-594-3777
Prince Edward Island Department of Health & Wellness, 105 Rochford St. North, 4th Fl., PO Box 2000, Charlottetown, PE C1A 7N8
902-368-6414, Fax: 902-368-4121
Public Service Commission, Shaw Bldg. North, 105 Rochford St., 1st Fl., PO Box 2000, Charlottetown, PE C1A 7N8
902-368-4080, Fax: 902-368-4383
SkillsPEI, Atlantic Technology Centre, #212, 176 Great George St., Charlottetown, PE C1A 4K9
902-368-6290, Fax: 902-368-6340, 877-491-4766

Québec

Centre du services partagés du Québec, 875, Grande Allée est, 4e étage, section 4.751, Québec, QC G1R 5W5
418-644-2777, Fax: 418-644-0462, 855-644-2777, cspq@cspq.gouv.qc.ca
Commissariat des incendies, 455, rue Dupont, Québec, QC G1K 6N2
418-529-5706, Fax: 418-529-9922
Commission administrative des régimes de retraite et d'assurances (Québec), 475, rue Saint-Amable, Québec, QC G1R 5X3
418-643-4881, Fax: 418-644-3839, 800-463-5533
Commission de la fonction publique, 800, place D'Youville, 7e étage, Québec, QC G1R 3P4
418-643-1425, Fax: 418-643-7264, 800-432-0432, cfp@cfp.gouv.qc.ca
Commission de la fonction publique (Québec), 800, Place d'Youville, 7e étage, Québec, QC G1R 3P4
418-643-1425, Fax: 418-643-7264, 800-432-0432, cfp@cfp.gouv.qc.ca
Commission municipale du Québec, Mezzanine, aile Chauveau, 10, rue Pierre-Olivier-Chauveau, Québec, QC G1R 4J3
418-691-2014, Fax: 418-644-4676, 866-353-6767
Hydro-Québec, 75, boul René-Lévesque ouest, 19e étage, Montréal, QC H2Z 1A4
514-289-2211
Institut de la statistique du Québec, 200, ch Ste-Foy, 1er étage, Québec, QC G1R 5T4
418-691-2401, Fax: 418-643-4129, 800-463-4090
Ministère de la Justice, Édifice Louis-Philippe-Pigeon, 1200, rte de l'Église, Québec, QC G1V 4M1
418-643-5140, 866-536-5140, informations@justice.gouv.qc.ca
Ministère de la Santé et des Services sociaux, Direction des communications, 1075, ch Sainte-Foy, 16e étage, Québec, QC G1S 2M1
418-643-9395, Fax: 418-643-4768, regisseur.web@msss.gouv.qc.ca
Ministère de la Sécurité publique, Tour des Laurentides, 2525, boul Laurier, 5e étage, Québec, QC G1V 2L2
418-646-6777, Fax: 418-643-0275, 866-644-6826
Ministère des Affaires municipales et Occupation du territoire, Aile Chaveau, 10, rue Pierre-Olivier-Chauveau, Québec, QC G1R 4J3
418-691-2015, Fax: 418-643-7385, communications@mamrot.gouv.qc.ca
Ministère du Travail, de l'Emploi et de la Solidarité sociale, 200, ch Sainte-Foy, 5e étage, Québec, QC G1R 5S1
418-644-4545, Fax: 418-528-0559, 877-644-4545
Modernisation des centres hospitaliers universitaires de Montréal, CHUM, CUSM, CHU Sainte-Justine, #10.049, 2021, rue Union, Montréal, QC H3A 2S9
514-864-9883, Fax: 514-873-7362, info.construction3chu@msss.gouv.qc.ca
Office des personnes handicapées du Québec, 309, rue Brock, Drummondville, QC J2B 1C5
Fax: 819-475-8753, 800-567-1465, aide@ophq.gouv.qc.ca
Régie de l'assurance maladie du Québec, 1125, Grande Allée ouest, Québec, QC G1S 1E7
418-646-4636, 800-561-9749
Régie du logement du Québec, Village Olympique, #2360, 5199, rue Sherbrooke est, Montréal, QC H1T 3X1
514-873-2245, Fax: 514-864-8077, 800-683-2245
Société d'habitation du Québec, Aile St-Amable, 1054, rue Louis-Alexandre-Taschereau, 3e étage, Québec, QC G1R 5E7
Fax: 418-643-2533, 800-463-4315
Société de l'assurance automobile du Québec, 333, boul Jean-Lesage, CP 19600 Terminus, Québec, QC G1K 8J6
418-643-7620, Fax: 418-644-0339, 800-361-7620
Urgences-santé Québec, 3232, rue Bélanger, Montréal, QC H1Y 3H5
514-723-5600, info@urgences-sante.qc.ca
Vérificateur général du Québec, 750, boulevard Charest est, 3e étage, Québec, QC G1K 9J6
418-691-5900, Fax: 418-644-4460, verificateur.general@vgq.qc.ca
École nationale des pompiers du Québec, Palais de justice de Laval, #3.08, 2800, boul Saint-Martin ouest, Laval, QC H7T 2S9
450-680-6800, Fax: 450-680-6818, 866-680-3677, enpq@enpq.gouv.qc.ca

Saskatchewan

Crown Investments Corporation of Saskatchewan, #400, 2400 College Ave., Regina, SK S4P 1C8
306-787-6851, Fax: 306-787-8125
Emergency Management & Fire Safety, 1855 Victoria Ave., 5th Fl., Regina, SK S4P 3T2
306-787-3774, Fax: 306-787-7107, 866-757-5911
Legal Aid Saskatchewan, #502, 201 - 21 St. East, Saskatoon, SK S7K 0B8
306-933-5300, Fax: 306-933-6764, 800-667-3764
Provincial Auditor Saskatchewan, Chateau Tower, #1500, 1920 Broad St., Regina, SK S4P 3V2
306-787-6398, Fax: 306-787-6383, info@auditor.sk.ca
Public Service Commission, 2350 Albert St., Regina, SK S4P 4A6
306-787-7853, 866-319-5999, csinquiry@gov.sk.ca
Saskatchewan Assessment Management Agency, #200, 2201 - 11th Ave., Regina, SK S4P 0J8
306-924-8000, Fax: 306-924-8070, 800-667-7262, info.request@sama.sk.ca
Saskatchewan Government Insurance, 2260 - 11th Ave., Regina, SK S4P 0J9
306-751-1200, Fax: 306-787-7477, 800-667-8015, sgiinquiries@sgi.sk.ca
Saskatchewan Justice & Attorney General, 1874 Scarth St., Regina, SK S4P 4B3
306-787-7872
Saskatchewan Power Corporation (SaskPower), 2025 Victoria Ave., Regina, SK S4P 0S1
306-566-2121, 888-757-6937
Saskatchewan Social Services, 1920 Broad St., Regina, SK S4P 3V6
306-787-3700, 866-221-5200, socialservicesinquiry@gov.sk.ca
Saskatchewan Transportation Company, 1717 Saskatchewan Dr., Regina, SK S4P 2E2
306-787-3347, Fax: 306-787-1633, info@stcbus.com
Saskatchewan Water Corporation (SaskWater), #200, 111 Fairford St. East, Moose Jaw, SK S6H 1C8
Fax: 306-694-3207, 888-230-1111, comm@saskwater.com
SaskEnergy Incorporated, 1777 Victoria Ave., Regina, SK S4P 4K5
306-777-9225, 800-567-8899

Yukon Territory

Emergency Measures Organization, Whitehorse Airport, Combined Services Bldg., 2nd Fl., 60 Norseman Rd., Whitehorse, YT Y1A 2C6
867-667-5220, Fax: 867-393-6266, 800-661-0408, emo.yukon@gov.yk.ca
Yukon Community Services, PO Box 2703, Whitehorse, YT Y1A 2C6
867-667-5811, Fax: 867-393-6295, 800-661-0408, inquiry@gov.yk.ca
Yukon Health & Social Services, PO Box 2703, Whitehorse, YT Y1A 2C6
867-667-3673, Fax: 867-667-3096, 800-661-0408, hss@gov.yk.ca
Yukon Housing Corporation, 410G Jarvis St., PO Box 2703, Whitehorse, YT Y1A 2H5
867-667-5759, Fax: 867-667-3664, 800-661-0408, ykhouse@housing.yk.ca
Yukon Justice, Andrew Philipsen Law Centre, 2134 Second Ave., PO Box 2703, Whitehorse, YT Y1A 2C6
867-667-3033, Fax: 867-393-5790, justice@gov.yk.ca
Yukon Public Service Commission, Yukon Government Administration Bldg., 2071 Second Ave., PO Box 2703, Whitehorse, YT Y1A 2C6
867-667-5653, Fax: 867-667-5755, PSCWebsite@gov.yk.ca
Yukon Utilities Board, #19, 1114 - 1st Ave., PO Box 31728, Whitehorse, YT Y1A 6L3
867-667-5058, Fax: 867-667-5059, yub@utilitiesboard.yk.ca

PUBLIC TRUSTEE

British Columbia

Public Guardian & Trustee of British Columbia, #700, 808 West Hastings St., Vancouver, BC V6C 3L3
604-660-4444, Fax: 604-660-0374, 800-663-7867, clientservice@trustee.bc.ca

Manitoba

Office of the Public Trustee, #500, 155 Carlton St., Winnipeg, MB R3C 5R9
204-945-2700, Fax: 204-948-2251, PGT@gov.mb.ca

Newfoundland & Labrador

Newfoundland & Labrador Department of Justice & Public Safety, Confederation Bldg., East Block, 4th Fl., PO Box 8700, St. John's, NL A1B 4J6
709-729-2869, Fax: 709-729-0469, justice@gov.nl.ca
Office of the Public Trustee, The Viking Bldg., #401, 136 Crosbie Rd., St. John's, NL A1B 3K3
709-729-0850, Fax: 709-729-3063

Nova Scotia

Public Trustee Office, #405, 5670 Spring Garden Rd., PO Box 685, Halifax, NS B3J 2T3
902-424-7760, Fax: 902-424-0616, publictrustee@gov.ns.ca

Ontario

Office of the Public Guardian & Trustee, Atrium on Bay, #800, 595 Bay St., 8th Fl., Toronto, ON M5G 2M6
416-314-2800, Fax: 416-326-1366, 800-366-0335

Québec

Curateur public du Québec, 600, boul René-Lévesque ouest, Montréal, QC H3B 4W9
514-873-4074, 800-363-9020

PUBLIC UTILITIES

Alberta

Alberta Energy Regulator, #1000, 250 - 5 St. SW, Calgary, AB T2P 0R4
403-297-8311, Fax: 403-297-7336, 855-297-8311, inquiries@aer.ca
Alberta Utilities Commission, Fifth Avenue Place, 425 - 1st St. SW, 4th Fl., Calgary, AB T2P 3L8
403-592-8845, Fax: 403-592-4406, -310-0000, info@auc.ab.ca

British Columbia

British Columbia Hydro, 6911 Southpoint Dr., Burnaby, BC V3N 4X8
604-224-9376, 800-224-9376
British Columbia Utilities Commission, 900 Howe St., 6th Fl., PO Box 250, Vancouver, BC V6Z 2N3
604-660-4700, Fax: 604-660-1102, 800-663-1385, commission.secretary@bcuc.com
Columbia Power Corporation, #200, 445 - 13th Ave., Castlegar, BC V1N 1G1
250-304-6060, Fax: 250-304-6083, cpc.info@columbiapower.org

Manitoba

Manitoba Hydro, 360 Portage Ave., PO Box 815 Main,Winnipeg, MB R3C 2P4
204-480-5900, Fax: 204-360-6155, 888-624-9376, publicaffairs@hydro.mb.ca

Newfoundland & Labrador

Churchill Falls (Labrador) Corporation Limited, Hydro Place, 500 Columbus Dr., PO Box 12500, St. John's, NL A1B 4K7
709-737-1859, Fax: 709-737-1816
Nalcor Energy, 500 Columbus Dr., St. John's, NL A1E 2B2
709-737-1400, Fax: 709-737-1800, info@nalcorenergy.com
Newfoundland & Labrador Board of Commissioners of Public Utilities, Prince Charles Bldg., #E-210, 120 Torbay Rd., PO Box 21040, St. John's, NL A1A 5B2
709-726-8600, Fax: 709-726-9604, 866-782-0006, ito@pub.nf.ca
Newfoundland & Labrador Hydro, Hydro Place, 500 Columbus Dr., PO Box 12400, St. John's, NL A1B 4K7
709-737-1400, Fax: 709-737-1800, 888-737-1296, hydro@nlh.nl.ca

Northwest Territories

Inuvialuit Water Board, Professional Bldg., #302, 125 Mackenzie Rd., PO Box 2531, Yellowknife, NT X0E 0T0
867-678-2942, Fax: 867-678-2943, info@inuvwb.ca
Northwest Territories Power Corporation, 4 Capital Dr., Hay River, NT X0E 1G2
867-874-5200, info@ntpc.com

Nova Scotia

Nova Scotia Utility & Review Board, Summit Place, 1601 Lower Water St., 3rd Fl., PO Box 1692 M,Halifax, NS B3J 3S3
902-424-4448, Fax: 902-424-3919, 855-442-4448, board@novascotia.ca

Ontario
Hydro One Inc., North Tower, 483 Bay St., 15th Fl., Toronto, ON M5G 2P5
416-345-5000, Fax: 905-944-3251, 877-955-1155, customercommunications@hydroone.com
Independent Electricity System Operator, #1600, 120 Adelaide St. West, Toronto, ON M5H 1T1
905-403-6900, Fax: 905-403-6921, 888-448-7777, customer.relations@ieso.ca
Ontario Power Generation, 700 University Ave., Toronto, ON M5G 1X6
416-592-2555, 877-592-2555, webmaster@opg.com

Prince Edward Island
Prince Edward Island Regulatory & Appeals Commission, National Bank Tower, #501, 134 Kent St., PO Box 577, Charlottetown, PE C1A 7L1
902-892-3501, Fax: 902-566-4076, 800-501-6268, info@irac.pe.ca

Québec
Coopérative régionale d'électricité de Saint-Jean-Baptiste-de-Rouville, 3113, rue Principale, Saint-Jean-Baptiste, QC J0L 1B0
450-467-5583, Fax: 450-467-0092, 800-267-5583, info@coopsjb.com
Hydro-Québec, 75, boul René-Lévesque ouest, 19e étage, Montréal, QC H2Z 1A4
514-289-2211
Régie de l'énergie, Tour de la Bourse, #2.55, 800, Place Victoria, Montréal, QC H4Z 1A2
514-873-2452, Fax: 514-873-2070, 888-873-2452, secretariat@regie-energie.qc.ca

Saskatchewan
Saskatchewan Power Corporation (SaskPower), 2025 Victoria Ave., Regina, SK S4P 0S1
306-566-2121, 888-757-6937
Saskatchewan Water Corporation (SaskWater), #200, 111 Fairford St. East, Moose Jaw, SK S6H 1C8
Fax: 306-694-3207, 888-230-1111, comm@saskwater.com
SaskEnergy Incorporated, 1777 Victoria Ave., Regina, SK S4P 4K5
306-777-9225, 800-567-8899

Yukon Territory
Yukon Utilities Board, #19, 1114 - 1st Ave., PO Box 31728, Whitehorse, YT Y1A 6L3
867-667-5058, Fax: 867-667-5059, yub@utilitiesboard.yk.ca

PUBLIC WORKS

Infrastructure Canada, #1100, 180 Kent St., Ottawa, ON K1P 0B6
613-948-1148, 877-250-7154, info@infc.gc.ca
Public Services & Procurement, Place du Portage, Phase III, 11, rue Laurier, Ottawa, ON K1A 0S5
questions@tpsgc-pwgsc.gc.ca

Alberta
Alberta Infrastructure, Infrastructure Building, 6950 - 113 St., Edmonton, AB T6H 5V7
780-415-0507, Fax: 780-427-2187, -310-0000, Infra.Contact.Us.m@gov.ab.ca
Alberta Transportation, Communications Branch, Twin Atria Building, 4999 - 98 Jasper Ave., 2nd Fl., Edmonton, AB T6B 2X3
780-427-2731, Fax: 780-466-3166, -310-0000, Trans.Contact.Us.m@gov.ab.ca

British Columbia
British Columbia Ministry of Technology, Innovation & Citizens' Services, PO Box 9068 Prov Govt, Victoria, BC V8W 9E2
250-952-7623, Fax: 250-952-7628, 800-663-7867, EnquiryBC@gov.bc.ca
British Columbia Ministry of Transportation & Infrastructure, PO Box 9850 Prov Govt, Victoria, BC V8W 9T5
250-387-3198, Fax: 250-356-7706, tran.webmaster@gov.bc.ca
Partnerships BC, #2320, 1111 West Georgia St., PO Box 9478 Prov Govt, Vancouver, BC V8W 9W6
604-681-2443, Fax: 604-806-4190, partnershipsbc@partnershipsbc.ca

Manitoba
Manitoba Infrastructure, Legislative Building, #203, 450 Broadway Ave., Winnipeg, MB R3C 0V8
204-945-3723, Fax: 204-945-7610

New Brunswick
New Brunswick Department of Transportation & Infrastructure, Kings Place, PO Box 6000, Fredericton, NB E3B 5H1
506-453-3939, Fax: 506-453-7987, Transportation.Web@gnb.ca

Newfoundland & Labrador
Newfoundland & Labrador Department of Transportation & Works, Confederation Bldg., Prince Philip Dr., PO Box 8700, St. John's, NL A1B 4J6
709-729-2300, tw@gov.nl.ca

Northwest Territories
Northwest Territories Department of Public Works & Services, Stuart M. Hodgson Bldg., 5009 - 49th St., PO Box 1320, Yellowknife, NT X1A 2L9

Nova Scotia
Nova Scotia Department of Internal Services, World Trade & Convention Centre, 1800 Argyle St., 5th Fl., PO Box 943, Halifax, NS B3J 2V9
902-424-5465, Fax: 902-424-0555
Nova Scotia Department of Transportation & Infrastructure Renewal, Johnston Bldg., 1672 Granville St., 2nd Fl., PO Box 186, Halifax, NS B3J 2N2
902-424-2297, Fax: 902-424-0532, 888-432-3233, tpwpaff@novascotia.ca

Nunavut
Nunavut Territory Department of Community & Government Services, W.G. Brown Bldg., 4th Fl., PO Box 1000 700, Iqaluit, NU X0A 0H0
867-975-5400, Fax: 867-975-5305

Ontario
Infrastructure Ontario, College Park, 777 Bay St., 6th Fl., Toronto, ON M5G 2C8
416-212-7289, Fax: 416-325-4646, info@infrastructureontario.ca
Ontario Ministry of Economic Development & Growth, Hearst Block, 900 Bay St., 8th Fl., Toronto, ON M7A 2E1
416-325-6666, 800-268-7095
Ontario Ministry of Infrastructure, Hearst Block, 900 Bay St., 8th Fl., Toronto, ON M7A 2E1
416-325-6666, 800-268-7095

Prince Edward Island
Prince Edward Island Department of Transportation, Infrastructure & Energy, Jones Bldg., 11 Kent St., 3rd Fl., PO Box 2000, Charlottetown, PE C1A 7N8
902-368-5100, Fax: 902-368-5395

Saskatchewan
Saskatchewan Highways & Infrastructure, Victoria Tower, 1855 Victoria Ave., Regina, SK S4P 3T2
306-787-4800, communications@highways.gov.sk.ca
SaskBuilds, #720, 1855 Victoria Ave., Regina, SK S4P 3T2
306-798-8014, Fax: 306-798-0626, saskbuilds@gov.sk.ca

Yukon Territory
Yukon Highways & Public Works, PO Box 2703, Whitehorse, YT Y1A 2C6
867-393-7193, Fax: 867-393-6218, 800-661-0408, hpw-info@gov.yk.ca

PUBLICATIONS

Public Services & Procurement, Place du Portage, Phase III, 11, rue Laurier, Ottawa, ON K1A 0S5
questions@tpsgc-pwgsc.gc.ca

Nova Scotia
Communications Nova Scotia, 1723 Hollis St., 3rd Fl., PO Box 608, Halifax, NS B3J 2R7
902-424-7690, Fax: 902-424-0515

Nunavut
Nunavut Legislative Assembly, 926 Federal Rd., PO Box 1200, Iqaluit, NU X0A 0H0
867-975-5000, Fax: 867-975-5190, 877-334-7266, leginfo@assembly.nu.ca

Québec
Ministère de la Culture et Communications, 225, Grande Allée est, Québec, QC G1R 5G5
888-380-8882

Yukon Territory
Yukon Highways & Public Works, PO Box 2703, Whitehorse, YT Y1A 2C6
867-393-7193, Fax: 867-393-6218, 800-661-0408, hpw-info@gov.yk.ca

PURCHASING

MERX, Phase II, #103, 6 Antares Dr., Ottawa, ON K2E 8A9
613-727-4900, Fax: 888-235-5800, 800-964-6379, merx@merx.com

Alberta
Alberta Infrastructure, Infrastructure Building, 6950 - 113 St., Edmonton, AB T6H 5V7
780-415-0507, Fax: 780-427-2187, -310-0000, Infra.Contact.Us.m@gov.ab.ca

British Columbia
British Columbia Ministry of Technology, Innovation & Citizens' Services, PO Box 9068 Prov Govt, Victoria, BC V8W 9E2
250-952-7623, Fax: 250-952-7628, 800-663-7867, EnquiryBC@gov.bc.ca
Procurement, PO Box 9476 Prov Govt, Victoria, BC V8W 9W6
250-387-7300, Fax: 250-387-7309, purchasing@gov.bc.ca

Newfoundland & Labrador
Government Purchasing Agency, 30 Strawberry Marsh Rd., St. John's, NL A1B 4R4
709-729-3348, Fax: 709-729-5817, tenders@gov.nl.ca
Newfoundland & Labrador Department of Service NL, PO Box 8700, St. John's, NL A1B 4J6
709-729-4834, servicenlinfo@gov.nl.ca

Northwest Territories
Northwest Territories Department of Public Works & Services, Stuart M. Hodgson Bldg., 5009 - 49th St., PO Box 1320, Yellowknife, NT X1A 2L9

Nunavut
Nunavut Territory Department of Community & Government Services, W.G. Brown Bldg., 4th Fl., PO Box 1000 700, Iqaluit, NU X0A 0H0
867-975-5400, Fax: 867-975-5305

Ontario
Ontario Ministry of Infrastructure, Hearst Block, 900 Bay St., 8th Fl., Toronto, ON M7A 2E1
416-325-6666, 800-268-7095
Supply Chain Ontario, 222 Jarvis St., 8th Fl., Toronto, ON M7A 0B6
Fax: 416-327-3573

Prince Edward Island
Prince Edward Island Department of Transportation, Infrastructure & Energy, Jones Bldg., 11 Kent St., 3rd Fl., PO Box 2000, Charlottetown, PE C1A 7N8
902-368-5100, Fax: 902-368-5395

RAIL TRANSPORTATION

See Also: Transportation
Transportation Safety Board of Canada, 200, Promenade du Portage, 4th Fl., Gatineau, QC K1A 1K8
819-994-3741, Fax: 819-997-2239, 800-387-3557, communications@bst-tsb.gc.ca
VIA Rail Canada Inc., CP 8116 A,Montréal, QC H3C 3N3
514-871-6000, Fax: 514-871-6104, 888-842-7245, customer_relations@viarail.ca

Alberta
Alberta Transportation, Communications Branch, Twin Atria Building, 4999 - 98 Jasper Ave., 2nd Fl., Edmonton, AB T6B 2X3
780-427-2731, Fax: 780-466-3166, -310-0000, Trans.Contact.Us.m@gov.ab.ca

Manitoba
Manitoba Infrastructure, Legislative Building, #203, 450 Broadway Ave., Winnipeg, MB R3C 0V8
204-945-3723, Fax: 204-945-7610

New Brunswick
New Brunswick Department of Transportation & Infrastructure, Kings Place, PO Box 6000, Fredericton, NB E3B 5H1
506-453-3939, Fax: 506-453-7987, Transportation.Web@gnb.ca

Newfoundland & Labrador
Newfoundland & Labrador Department of Transportation & Works, Confederation Bldg., Prince Philip Dr., PO Box 8700, St. John's, NL A1B 4J6
709-729-2300, tw@gov.nl.ca

Nova Scotia
Nova Scotia Department of Transportation & Infrastructure Renewal, Johnston Bldg., 1672 Granville St., 2nd Fl., PO Box 186, Halifax, NS B3J 2N2
902-424-2297, Fax: 902-424-0532, 888-432-3233, tpwpaff@novascotia.ca

Ontario
Metrolinx, 97 Front St. West, Toronto, ON M5J 1E6
416-874-5900, Fax: 416-869-1755
Ontario Northland Transportation Commission, 555 Oak St. East, North Bay, ON P1B 8L3
705-472-4500, Fax: 705-476-5598, 800-363-7512, info@ontarionorthland.ca

Québec
Société du port ferroviaire Baie-Comeau-Haute-Rive, 18, rte Maritime, Baie-Comeau, QC G4Z 2L6
418-296-6785, Fax: 418-296-2377, societeduport@globetrotter.net

Saskatchewan
Saskatchewan Grain Car Corporation, #1210, 1855 Victoria Ave., Regina, SK S4P 3T2
306-787-1137, Fax: 306-798-0931
Saskatchewan Highways & Infrastructure, Victoria Tower, 1855 Victoria Ave., Regina, SK S4P 3T2
306-787-4800, communications@highways.gov.sk.ca

REAL ESTATE

See Also: Land Titles
Canada Mortgage & Housing Corporation, 700 Montreal Rd., Ottawa, ON K1A 0P7
613-748-2000, Fax: 613-748-2098, 800-668-2642, chic@cmhc-schl.gc.ca

British Columbia
Real Estate Council of British Columbia, #900, 750 West Pender St., Vancouver, BC V6C 2T8
604-683-9664, Fax: 604-683-9017, 877-683-9664, info@recbc.ca
Nova Scotia
Nova Scotia Department of Municipal Affairs, Maritime Centre, 14 North, 1505 Barrington St., PO Box 216, Halifax, NS B3J 3K5
902-424-6642, 800-670-4357
Service Nova Scotia, c/o Public Enquiries - Service Nova Scotia, PO Box 2734, Halifax, NS B3J 3K5
902-424-5200, Fax: 902-424-0720, 800-670-4357
Nunavut
Legal Registries, PO Box 1000 570, Iqaluit, NU X0A 0H0
867-975-6590, Fax: 867-975-6594, Legal.Registries@gov.nu.ca

RECREATION

See Also: Tourism & Tourist Information
Canada Place Corporation, 100 The Pointe, 999 Canada Place, Vancouver, BC V6C 3T4
604-775-7063
Canadian Heritage, 15 Eddy St., Gatineau, QC K1A 0M5
819-997-0055, 866-811-0055, PCH.info-info.PCH@canada.ca
National Battlefields Commission, 390, av de Bernières, Québec, QC G1R 2L7
418-648-3506, Fax: 418-648-3638, information@ccbn-nbc.gc.ca
Parks Canada, National Office, 30 Victoria St., Gatineau, QC J8X 0B3
819-420-9486, 888-773-8888, information@pc.gc.ca
British Columbia
British Columbia Lottery Corporation, 74 West Seymour St., Kamloops, BC V2C 1E2
250-828-5500, Fax: 250-828-5631, 866-815-0222
British Columbia Ministry of Social Development & Social Innovation, PO Box 9058 Prov Govt, Victoria, BC V8W 9E1
800-663-7867, EnquiryBC@gov.bc.ca
Manitoba
Convention Centre Corporation Board of Directors, 375 York Ave., Winnipeg, MB R3C 3J3
204-956-1720, Fax: 204-943-0310, 800-565-7776, audra@wcc.mb.ca
Manitoba Horse Racing Commission, #812, 401 York Ave., PO Box 46086 Westdale, Winnipeg, MB R3R 3S3
204-885-7770, Fax: 204-831-0942
Tourism Secretariat, 213 Notre Dame Ave., 6th Fl., Winnipeg, MB R3B 1N3
204-945-0216
New Brunswick
Atlantic Lottery Corporation, 922 Main St., PO Box 5500, Moncton, NB E1C 8W6
800-561-3942, info@alc.ca
New Brunswick Department of Tourism, Heritage & Culture, Centennial Building, PO Box 6000, Fredericton, NB E3B 5H1
506-453-3115, Fax: 506-457-4984, thctpcinfo@gnb.ca
New Brunswick Lotteries & Gaming Corporation, Chancery Place, 4th Fl., PO Box 6000, Fredericton, NB E3B 5H1
506-453-2451, Fax: 506-453-2053
Newfoundland & Labrador
C.A. Pippy Park Commission, Mount Scio House, 15 Mount Scio Rd., St. John's, NL A1B 3T2
709-737-3655, info@pippypark.com
Newfoundland & Labrador Department of Business, Tourism, Culture & Rural Development, Confederation Bldg., West Block, 2nd Fl., PO Box 8700, St. John's, NL A1B 4J6
709-729-7000, btcrd@gov.nl.ca
Nova Scotia
Nova Scotia Provincial Lotteries & Casino Corporation, Summit Place, 1601 Lower Water St., 5th Fl., PO Box 1501, Halifax, NS B3J 2Y3
902-424-2203, Fax: 902-424-0724
Ontario
Alcohol & Gaming Commission of Ontario, 90 Sheppard Ave. East, Toronto, ON M2N 0A4
416-326-8700, Fax: 416-326-5555, 800-522-2876, customer.service@agco.ca
Metro Toronto Convention Centre Corporation, 255 Front St. West, Toronto, ON M5V 2W6
416-585-8120, Fax: 416-585-8198, info@mtccc.com
Niagara Parks Commission, Oak Hall Administration Bldg., 7400 Portage Rd. South, PO Box 150, Niagara Falls, ON L2E 6T2
905-356-2241, Fax: 905-354-6041, 877-642-7275
Ontario Lottery & Gaming Corporation, Roberta Bondar Pl., #800, 70 Foster Dr., Sault Ste. Marie, ON P6A 6V2
705-946-6464, Fax: 416-224-7000, 800-387-0098
Ontario Ministry of Tourism, Culture & Sport, Hearst Block, 900 Bay St., 9th Fl., Toronto, ON M7A 2E1
416-326-9326, Fax: 416-314-7854, 888-997-9015
Ontario Place Corporation, 955 Lake Shore Blvd. West, Toronto, ON M6K 3B9
416-314-9900, Fax: 416-314-9989, 866-663-4386
Ontario Racing Commission, #400, 10 Carlson Crt., Toronto, ON M9W 6L2
416-213-0520, Fax: 416-213-7827, inquiry@ontarioracingcommission.ca
Ottawa Convention Centre, 55 Colonel By Dr., Ottawa, ON K1N 9J2
613-563-1984, Fax: 613-563-7646, 800-450-0077, info@ottawaconventioncentre.com
St. Lawrence Parks Commission, 13740 County Rd. 2, Morrisburg, ON K0C 1X0
613-543-3704, Fax: 613-543-2847, 800-437-2233, getaway@parks.on.ca
Prince Edward Island
Maritime Provinces Harness Racing Commission, 5 Gerald McCarville Dr., PO Box 128, Kensington, PE C0B 1M0
902-836-5500, Fax: 902-836-5320
Prince Edward Island Department of Economic Development & Tourism, PO Box 2000, Charlottetown, PE C1A 7N8
902-368-5540, Fax: 902-368-5277, tpswitch@gov.pe.ca
Prince Edward Island Department of Family & Human Services, Jones Bldg., 11 Kent St., 2nd Fl., PO Box 2000, Charlottetown, PE C1A 7N8
902-620-3777, Fax: 902-894-0242, 866-594-3777
Québec
Comité conjoint de chasse, de pêche et de piégeage, #C220, 383 rue Saint-Jacques, Montréal, QC H2Y 1N9
514-284-2151, Fax: 514-284-0039, cccppinfo@cccpp-hftcc.com
Régie des alcools, des courses et des jeux, 560, boul Charest est, Québec, QC G1K 3J3
418-643-7667, Fax: 418-643-5971, 800-363-0320
Société de financement des infrastructures locales, 12, rue Saint-Louis, Québec, QC G1R 5L3
Société des établissements en plein air du Québec, Place de la Cité, Tour Cominar, #250, 2640, boul Laurier, 2e étage, Québec, QC G1V 5C2
418-686-4875, Fax: 418-643-8177, 800-665-6527, inforeservation@sepaq.com
Saskatchewan
Saskatchewan Liquor & Gaming Authority, 2500 Victoria Ave., PO Box 5054, Regina, SK S4P 3M3
306-787-5563, 800-667-7565, inquiry@slga.gov.sk.ca
Wascana Centre Authority, 2900 Wascana Dr., PO Box 7111, Regina, SK S4P 3S7
306-522-3661, Fax: 306-565-2742, wca@wascana.ca
Yukon Territory
Yukon Lottery Commission/Lotteries Yukon, #101, 205 Hawkins St., Whitehorse, YT Y1A 1X3
867-633-7890, Fax: 867-668-7561, 800-661-0555, lotteriesyukon@gov.yk.ca
Yukon Tourism & Culture, 100 Hanson St., PO Box 2703, Whitehorse, YT Y1A 2C6
867-667-5036, Fax: 867-667-3546

RECYCLING

Alberta
Alberta Recycling Management Authority, Scotia Tower 1, #1800, 10060 Jasper Ave., PO Box 189, Edmonton, AB T5J 2J1
780-990-1111, Fax: 780-990-1122, 888-999-8762, info@albertarecycling.ca
Newfoundland & Labrador
Multi-Materials Stewardship Board, PO Box 8131 A, St. John's, NL A1B 3M9
709-753-0948, Fax: 709-753-0974, 800-901-6672, inquiries@mmsb.nl.ca
Nova Scotia
Resource Recovery Fund Board Inc., #400, 35 Commercial St., Truro, NS B2N 3H9
902-895-7732, Fax: 902-897-3256, 877-313-7732, info@rrfb.com

RESEARCH

Canada Foundation for Innovation, #450, 230 Queen St., Ottawa, ON K1P 5E4
613-947-6496, Fax: 613-943-0923, feedback@innovation.ca
Policy Horizons Canada, 360 Albert St., 15th Fl., Ottawa, ON K1R 7X7
613-947-3800, Fax: 613-995-6006, questions@horizons.gc.ca
Alberta
Alberta Advanced Education, Legislature Bldg., #403, 10800 - 97 Ave., Edmonton, AB T5K 2B6
780-422-5400, -310-0000
Alberta Innovates - Health Solutions, #1500, 10104 - 103 Ave., Edmonton, AB T5J 4A7
780-423-5727, Fax: 780-429-3509, 877-423-5727, health@albertainnovates.ca
British Columbia
British Columbia Law Institute, University of British Columbia, 1822 East Mall, Vancouver, BC V6T 1Z1
604-822-0142, Fax: 604-822-0144, bcli@bcli.org
Ontario
Ontario Ministry of Research, Innovation & Science, Hearst Block, 900 Bay St., 8th Fl., Toronto, ON M7A 2E1
416-325-6666, Fax: 416-325-6688, 866-668-4249
Québec
Fonds de recherche du Québec, #800, 500, rue Sherbrooke Ouest, Montréal, QC H3A 3C6
514-873-2114

RESEARCH & DEVELOPMENT

Aerospace Manufacturing Technologies Centre, Campus Université de Montréal, 5145, av Decelles, Montréal, QC H3T 2B2
Aquatic & Crop Resource Development Industry Partnership Facility, 550 University Ave., Charlottetown, PE C1A 4P3
902-566-7000
Atomic Energy of Canada Limited, Head Office, Chalk River Laboratories, 286 Plant Rd., Chalk River, ON K0J 1J0
888-220-2465, communications@aecl.ca
Automotive & Surface Transportation Facilities, Ottawa Uplands Research Facilities, 2320 Lester Rd., Ottawa, ON K1V 1S2
613-998-9639
Bayfield Institute, Canada Centre for Inland Waters, 867 Lakeshore Rd., PO Box 5050, Burlington, ON L7R 4A6
905-336-6240
Bedford Institute of Oceanography, 1 Challenger Dr., PO Box 1006, Dartmouth, NS B2Y 4A2
Fax: 902-426-8484, WebmasterBIO-IOB@dfo-mpo.gc.ca
Canada Centre for Mapping & Earth Observation, #212, 50 Place de la Cité, PO Box 162, Sherbrooke, QC J1H 4G9
Canada Foundation for Innovation, #450, 230 Queen St., Ottawa, ON K1P 5E4
613-947-6496, Fax: 613-943-0923, feedback@innovation.ca
Canada-France-Hawaii Telescope, CFHT Corporation, #65, 1238 Mamalahoa Hwy., Kamuela, HI
808-885-7944, Fax: 808-885-7288, info@cfht.hawaii.edu
Canadian Astronomy Data Centre, NRC Herzberg Astronomy & Astrophysics, 5071 West Saanich Rd., Victoria, BC V9E 2E7
250-363-0001, Fax: 250-363-0045, cadc@nrc.gc.ca
Canadian Centre for Housing Technology, c/o National Research Council Canada, Building M-20, 1200 Montreal Rd., Ottawa, ON K1A 0R6
Canadian Hydrographic Services & Oceanographic Services, 615 Booth St., Ottawa, ON K1A 0E6
chsinfo@dfo-mpo.gc.ca
Canadian Nuclear Laboratories, Head Office, Chalk River Laboratories, 286 Plant Rd., Chalk River, ON K0J 1J0
866-513-2325, communications@cnl.ca
Canadian Photonics Fabrication Centre, c/o National Research Council Canada, Building M-50, 1200 Montreal Rd., Ottawa, ON K1A 0R6
613-993-9101
Canadian Space Agency, John H. Chapman Space Centre, 6767, rte de l'Aéroport, Saint-Hubert, QC J3Y 8Y9
450-926-4800, Fax: 450-926-4352, asc.info.csa@canada.ca
Cell Culture Pilot Plant, c/o Montréal (av Royalmount) Research Facilities, 6100, av Royalmount, Montréal, QC H4P 2R2
514-496-6100
Centre for Aquaculture & Environmental Research, 4160 Marine Dr., West Vancouver, BC V7V 1N6
604-666-7453, Fax: 604-666-3497
Civil Infrastructure & Related Structures Testing Facilities, c/o National Research Council, 1200 Montreal Rd., Ottawa, ON K1A 0R6
613-993-9101
Climatic Testing Facility, Ottawa Uplands Research Facilities, 2320 Lester Rd., Ottawa, ON K1V 1S2
613-998-9639
Cultus Lake Salmon Research Lab, 4222 Columbia Valley Hwy., Cultus Lakw, BC V2R 5B6
Dominion Astrophysical Observatory, NRC Herzberg Astronomy & Astrophysics, 5071 West Saanich Rd., Victoria, BC V9E 2E7
250-363-0001, NRC.NSIHerzbergAstroInfoISN.CNRC@nrc-cnrc.gc.ca
Dominion Radio Astrophysical Observatory, 717 White Lake Rd., PO Box 248, Penticton, BC V2A 6J9
250-497-2300, NRC.DRAO-OFR.CNRC@nrc-cnrc.gc.ca
Fire Safety Testing Facility, National Fire Laboratory, Bldg. U-96, Concession 8, Mississippi Mills, ON K0A 1A0
613-993-9101

Freshwater Institute Science Laboratory, 501 University Cres., Winnipeg, MB R3T 2N6
204-983-5000, Fax: 204-983-6285

Gas Turbine Research Facility, c/o National Research Council, 1200 Montreal Rd., Ottawa, ON K1A 0R6
613-993-9101

Gemini Observatory, 670 N. A'ohoku Place, Hilo, HI
808-974-2500, Fax: 808-974-2589

Hydraulics Laboratories, c/o National Research Council, 1200 Montreal Rd., Ottawa, ON K1A 0R6

Hygrothermal Performance of Buildings Research Facilities, c/o National Research Council, 1200 Montreal Rd., Ottawa, ON K1A 0R6
613-993-9101

Indoor Environment Testing Facilities, c/o National Research Council, 1200 Montreal Rd., Ottawa, ON K1A 0R6
613-993-9101

Industrial Partnership Facility: Montréal, c/o Montréal (av Royalmount) Research Facilities, 6100, av Royalmount, Montréal, QC H4P 2R2

Institut Maurice-Lamontagne, 850, rte de le Mer, CP 1000, Mont-Joli, QC G5H 3Z4
418-775-0500, Fax: 418-775-0730

Institute of Ocean Sciences, 9860 West Saanich Rd., PO Box 6000, Sidney, BC V8L 4B2
250-363-6517, Fax: 250-363-6390

Marine Performance Evaluation & Testing Facilities, c/o National Research Council, 1200 Montreal Rd., Ottawa, ON K1A 0R6

Material Emissions Testing Facilities, c/o National Research Council, 1200 Montreal Rd., Ottawa, ON K1A 0R6

Medical Device Facilities, Boucherville Research Facilities, 75, boul de Mortagne, Boucherville, QC J4B 6Y4
450-641-5100

Microbial Fermentation Pilot Plant, c/o Montréal (av Royalmount) Research Facilities, 6100, av Royalmount, Montréal, QC H4P 2R2
514-496-6100

National Research Council Canada, Building M-58, 1200 Montreal Rd., Ottawa, ON K1A 0R6
613-993-9101, Fax: 613-952-9907, 877-672-2672, info@nrc-cnrc.ca

National Research Council Canada - Industrial Research Assistance Program, 1200 Montreal Rd., Ottawa, ON K1A 0R6
Fax: 613-952-1086, 877-994-4727, publicinquiries.irap-pari@nrc-cnrc.gc.ca

Natural Sciences & Engineering Research Council of Canada, Constitution Square, Tower II, 350 Albert St., Ottawa, ON K1A 1H5
613-995-4273, Fax: 613-992-5337, 855-275-2861

Networks of Centres of Excellence of Canada, 350 Albert Street, 16th Fl., Ottawa, ON K1A 1H5
613-995-6010, Fax: 613-992-7356, info@nce-rce.gc.ca

Ocean Technology Enterprise Centre, PO Box 12093, St. John's, NL A1B 3T5
709-772-2469

Pacific Biological Station, 3190 Hammond Bay Rd., Nanaimo, BC V9T 6N7
250-756-7000, Fax: 250-756-7053

Printable Electronics Labs, c/o National Research Council, 1200 Montreal Rd., Ottawa, ON K1A 0R6

Science & Technology Branch, Tower 5, 1341 Baseline Rd., Ottawa, ON K1A 0C5
Fax: 613-773-1711

Sea Lamprey Control Centre, 1219 Queen St. East, Sault Ste Marie, ON P6A 2E5

St. Andrews Biological Station, 531 Brandy Cove Rd., St Andrews, NB E5B 2L9
506-529-8854, Fax: 506-529-5862, XMARSABS@mar.dfo-mpo.gc.ca

Waste Biotreatability Facility, c/o Montréal (av Royalmount) Research Facilities, 6100, av Royalmount, Montréal, QC H4P 2R2

Wind Tunnel Testing Facilities, c/o National Research Council, 1200 Montreal Rd., Ottawa, ON K1A 0R6

Zebrafish Screening Facility, 1411 Oxford St., Halifax, NS B3H 3Z1
902-426-8332

Alberta

Alberta Advanced Education, Legislature Bldg., #403, 10800 - 97 Ave., Edmonton, AB T5K 2B6
780-422-5400, -310-0000

Alberta Economic Development & Trade, Commerce Place, 10155 - 102 St., 12th Fl., Edmonton, AB T5J 4G8

Alberta Innovates - Bio Solutions, Phipps McKinnon Bldg., 10020 - 101A Ave., 18th Fl., Edmonton, AB T5J 3G2
780-427-1956, Fax: 780-427-3252, 877-828-0444, bio@albertainnovates.ca

Alberta Innovates - Energy & Environmental Solutions, AMEC Place, #2540, 801 - 6th Ave. SW, Calgary, AB T2P 3W2
403-297-7089, Fax: 403-297-3638, ees@albertainnovates.ca

Alberta Research & Innvoation Authority, John J. Bowlen Bldg., #620 - 7 Ave. SW, 9th Fl., Calgary, AB T2P 0Y8
403-297-3022, Fax: 403-297-6435, aria@albertainnovates.ca

British Columbia

Powertech Labs Inc., 12388 - 88 Ave., Surrey, BC V8W 7R7
604-590-7500, Fax: 604-590-6611

New Brunswick

New Brunswick Research & Productivity Council, 921 College Hill Rd., Fredericton, NB E3B 6Z9
506-452-1212, Fax: 506-452-1395, 800-563-0844, info@rpc.ca

Newfoundland & Labrador

Newfoundland & Labrador Research & Development Corporation, 68 Portugal Cove Rd., St. John's, NL A1B 2L9
709-758-0913, Fax: 709-758-0927, info@rdc.org

Northwest Territories

Aurora Research Institute, 191 MacKenzie Rd., PO Box 1450, Inuvik, NT X0E 0T0
867-777-3298, Fax: 867-777-4264

Ontario

Ontario Ministry of Research, Innovation & Science, Hearst Block, 900 Bay St., 8th Fl., Toronto, ON M7A 2E1
416-325-6666, Fax: 416-325-6688, 866-668-4249

Science & Research Branch, Roberta Bondar Pl., 300 Water St., 4th Fl., Peterborough, ON K9J 8M5
705-755-2809, Fax: 705-755-2802

Prince Edward Island

Agricultural Insurance Corporation, 29 Indigo Cres., PO Box 1600, Charlottetown, PE C1A 7N3
902-368-4842, Fax: 902-368-6677

BIO|FOOD|TECH, 101 Belvedere Ave., PO Box 2000, Charlottetown, PE C1A 7N8
902-368-5548, Fax: 902-368-5549, 877-368-5548, biofoodtech@biofoodtech.ca

Québec

Centre de recherche industrielle du Québec, 333, rue Franquet, Québec, QC G1P 4C7
418-659-1550, Fax: 418-652-2251, 800-667-2386, infocriq@criq.qc.ca

Fonds de la recherche en santé du Québec, #800, 500, rue Sherbrooke ouest, Montréal, QC H3A 3C6
514-873-2114, Fax: 514-873-8768

Fonds de recherche du Québec, #800, 500, rue Sherbrooke Ouest, Montréal, QC H3A 3C6
514-873-2114

Fonds québécois de la recherche sur la nature et les technologies, #450, 140, Grande Allée est, Québec, QC G1R 5M8
418-643-8560, Fax: 418-643-1451, info.nt@frq.gouv.qc.ca

Fonds québécois de la recherche sur la société et la culture, #470, 140, Grande Allée est, Québec, QC G1R 5M8
418-643-7582, Fax: 418-644-5248, frq.sc@frq.gouv.qc.ca

Ministère de l'Économie, de la Science et de l'Innovation, 710, place D'Youville, 3e étage, Québec, QC G1R 4Y4
418-691-5950, Fax: 418-644-0118, 866-680-1884

Saskatchewan

Prairie Agricultural Machinery Institute, 2215 - 8th Ave., PO Box 1150, Humboldt, SK S0K 2A0
306-682-5033, Fax: 306-682-5080, 800-567-7264, humboldt@pami.ca

Saskatchewan Health Research Foundation, Atrium Bldg., Innovation Place, #253, 111 Research Dr., Saskatoon, SK S7N 3R2
306-975-1680, Fax: 306-975-1688, 800-975-1699

Saskatchewan Opportunities Corporation, Innovation Place, #114, 14 Innovation Blvd., Saskatoon, SK S7N 2X8
306-933-6295, Fax: 306-933-8215, saskatoon@innovationplace.com

Saskatchewan Power Corporation (SaskPower), 2025 Victoria Ave., Regina, SK S4P 0S1
306-566-2121, 888-757-6937

Saskatchewan Research Council, #125, 15 Innovation Blvd., Saskatoon, SK S7N 2X8
306-933-5400, Fax: 306-933-7446, info@src.sk.ca

ROUND TABLES

Manitoba

Manitoba Round Table for Sustainable Development, #160, 123 Main St., PO Box 70, Winnipeg, MB R3C 1A5
204-945-4391, Fax: 204-948-4730, mrtsd@gov.mb.ca

SALES TAX

Alberta

Financial Sector Regulation & Policy Division, Terrace Building, 9515 - 107 St., 4th Fl., Edmonton, AB T5K 2C3
780-427-8322

British Columbia

Employment & Labour Market Services Division, PO Box 9762 Prov Govt, Victoria, BC V8W 1A4
250-953-3921, Fax: 250-953-3928

Manitoba

Taxation Division, #101, 401 York Ave., Winnipeg, MB R3C 0P8
204-945-5603, Fax: 204-945-0896, 800-782-0318

Northwest Territories

Northwest Territories Department of Finance, PO Box 1320, Yellowknife, NT X1A 2L9
867-873-7500

Nova Scotia

Provincial Tax Commission, Maritime Centre, 1505 Barrington St., 9th Fl., PO Box 1003, Halifax, NS B3J 2X1
902-424-6300, Fax: 902-424-7434, 800-565-2336, taxcommission@gov.ns.ca

Service Nova Scotia, c/o Public Enquiries - Service Nova Scotia, PO Box 2734, Halifax, NS B3J 3K5
902-424-5200, Fax: 902-424-0720, 800-670-4357

Nunavut

Nunavut Territory Department of Finance, Bldg. 1079, 1st Fl., PO Box 1000 430, Iqaluit, NU X0A 0H0
867-975-5800, Fax: 867-975-5805

Saskatchewan

Revenue Division, 2350 Albert St., 5th Fl., PO Box 200, Regina, SK S4P 2Z6
306-787-6645, Fax: 306-787-0776, 800-667-6102

SCHOOL BOARDS

See: Education

Nova Scotia

Annapolis Valley Regional School Board, 121 Orchard St., PO Box 340, Berwick, NS B0P 1E0
902-538-4600, Fax: 902-538-4630, 800-850-3887

Cape Breton-Victoria Regional School Board, 275 George St., Sydney, NS BIP IJ7
902-564-8293, Fax: 902-564-0123

Chignecto-Central Regional School Board, 60 Lorne St., Truro, NS B2N 3K3
800-770-0008

Conseil scolaire acadien provincial, CP 88, Saulnierville, NS B0W 2Z0
902-769-5458, Fax: 902-769-5459, 888-533-2727

Halifax Regional School Board, 33 Spectacle Lake Dr., Dartmouth, NS B3B 1X7
902-464-2000

South Shore Regional School Board, 69 Wentzell Dr., Bridgewater, NS B4V 0A2
902-543-2468, Fax: 902-541-3051, 888-252-2217, receptionist@ssrsb.ca

Strait Regional School Board, 16 Cemetery Rd., Port Hastings, NS B9A 1K6
902-625-2191, Fax: 902-625-2281, 800-650-4448, srsb@srsb.ca

Tri-County Regional School Board, 79 Water St., Yarmouth, NS B5A 1L4
902-749-5696, Fax: 902-749-5697, 800-915-0113

Prince Edward Island

French Language School Board, 1596, rte 124, Abram-Village, PE C0B 2E0
902-854-2975, Fax: 902-854-2981, cslf@edu.pe.ca

SCIENCE & NATURE

Agriculture & Agri-Food Canada, 1341 Baseline Rd., Ottawa, ON K1A 0C5
613-773-1000, Fax: 613-773-1081, 855-773-0241, info@agr.gc.ca

Beverly & Qamanirjuaq Caribou Management Board, Secretariat, PO Box 629, Stonewall, MB R0C 2Z0
204-467-2438, caribounews@arctic-caribou.com

Canada Centre for Mapping & Earth Observation, #212, 50 Place de la Cité, PO Box 162, Sherbrooke, QC J1H 4G9

Canadian Institutes of Health Research, 160 Elgin St., 9th Fl., Ottawa, ON K1A 0W9
613-941-2672, Fax: 613-954-1800, 888-603-4178, support@cihr-irsc.gc.ca

Canadian Nuclear Safety Commission, 280 Slater St., PO Box 1046 B,Ottawa, ON K1P 5S9
613-995-5894, Fax: 613-995-5086, 800-668-5284, cnsc.information.ccsn@canada.ca

Canadian Space Agency, John H. Chapman Space Centre, 6767, rte de l'Aéroport, Saint-Hubert, QC J3Y 8Y9
450-926-4800, Fax: 450-926-4352, asc.info.csa@canada.ca

CanmetMINING, 555 Booth St., Ottawa, ON K1A 0G1
Fax: 613-947-6606

Cell Culture Pilot Plant, c/o Montréal (av Royalmount) Research Facilities, 6100, av Royalmount, Montréal, QC H4P 2R2
514-496-6100

Commission for Environmental Cooperation, Secretariat, #200, 393, rue St-Jacques ouest, Montréal, QC H2Y 1N9
514-350-4300, Fax: 514-350-4314, info@cec.org

Committee on the Status of Endangered Wildlife in Canada, c/o Canadian Wildlife Service, 351 St. Joseph Blvd, 4th Fl., Gatineau, QC K1A 0H3
819-953-3215, Fax: 819-994-3684, cosewic/cosepac@ec.gc.ca
Crops & Aquatic Growth Facilities, c/o National Research Council, 1200 Montreal Rd., Ottawa, ON K1A 0R6
Cultus Lake Salmon Research Lab, 4222 Columbia Valley Hwy., Cultus Lakw, BC V2R 5B6
Earth Sciences Sector, 588 Booth St., Ottawa, ON K1A 0Y7
Ecosystems & Fisheries Management, 200 Kent St., Ottawa, ON K1A 0E6
Environment and Climate Change Canada, 10 Wellington St., Gatineau, QC K1A 0H3
819-997-2800, Fax: 819-994-1412, 800-668-6767, enviroinfo@ec.gc.ca
Fisheries & Oceans Canada, 200 Kent St., Ottawa, ON K1A 0E6
613-993-0999, Fax: 613-990-1866, info@dfo-mpo.gc.ca
Geological Survey of Canada, 601 Booth St., Ottawa, ON K1A 0E8
Indian Oil & Gas Canada, #100, 9911 Chiila Blvd., Tsuu T'ina (Sarcee), AB T2W 6H6
403-292-5625, Fax: 403-292-5618, ContactIOGC@inac-ainc.gc.ca
International Development Research Centre, 150 Kent St., PO Box 8500, Ottawa, ON K1G 3H9
613-236-6163, Fax: 613-238-7230, info@idrc.ca
Mackenzie Valley Environmental Impact Review Board, 200 Scotia Centre, #5102, 50th Ave., PO Box 938, Yellowknife, NT X1A 2N7
867-766-7050, Fax: 867-766-7074, 866-912-3472
National Energy Board, 517 - 10 Ave. SW, Calgary, AB T2R 0A8
403-292-4800, Fax: 403-292-5503, 800-899-1265
National Research Council Canada, Building M-58, 1200 Montreal Rd., Ottawa, ON K1A 0R6
613-993-9101, Fax: 613-952-9907, 877-672-2672, info@nrc-cnrc.ca
Natural Resources Canada, 580 Booth St., Ottawa, ON K1A 0E4
343-292-6096, Fax: 613-992-7211
Natural Sciences & Engineering Research Council of Canada, Constitution Square, Tower II, 350 Albert St., Ottawa, ON K1A 1H5
613-995-4273, Fax: 613-992-5337, 855-275-2861
Networks of Centres of Excellence of Canada, 350 Albert Street, 16th Fl., Ottawa, ON K1A 1H5
613-995-6010, Fax: 613-992-7356, info@nce-rce.gc.ca
North American Bird Conservation Initiative, Canadian Wildlife Service, 351, boul St-Joseph, 3e étage, Gatineau, QC K1A 0H3
819-994-0512, Fax: 819-994-4445, nabci@ec.gc.ca
North American Waterfowl Management Plan, NAWCC (Canada) Secretariat, Place Vincent Massey, 351 St. Joseph Blvd., 7th Fl., Gatineau, QC K1A 0H3
819-934-6034, Fax: 819-934-6017, nawmp@ec.gc.ca
Nunavut Impact Review Board, 29 Mitik St., PO Box 1360, Cambridge Bay, NU X0B 0C0
867-983-4600, Fax: 867-983-2594, 866-233-3033, info@nirb.ca
Nunavut Water Board, PO Box 119, Gjoa Haven, NU X0B 1J0
867-360-6338, Fax: 867-360-6369
Pest Management Regulatory Agency, 2720 Riverside Dr., Ottawa, ON K1A 0K9
613-736-3799, Fax: 613-736-3798, 800-267-6315, pmra.infoserv@hc-sc.gc.ca
Polar Knowledge Canada, 2464 Sheffield Rd., Ottawa, ON K1B 4E5
613-943-8605, info@polar.gc.ca
Porcupine Caribou Management Board, PO Box 31723, Whitehorse, YT Y1A 6L3
867-633-4780, Fax: 867-393-3904, pcmb@taiga.net
Sea Lamprey Control Centre, 1219 Queen St. East, Sault Ste Marie, ON P6A 2E5
Social Sciences & Humanities Research Council of Canada, Constitution Sq., 350 Albert St., PO Box 1610 B,Ottawa, ON K1P 6G4
613-992-0691
Strategic Policy, 200 Kent St., Ottawa, ON K1A 0E6

Alberta

Alberta Agriculture & Forestry, JG O'Donoghue Bldg., #100A, 7000 - 113th St., Edmonton, AB T6H 5T6
780-427-2727, -310-3276, duke@gov.ab.ca
Alberta Energy, North Petroleum Plaza, 9945 - 108 St., Edmonton, AB T5K 2G6
780-427-8050, Fax: 780-422-9522, -310-0000
Alberta Environmental Appeals Board, Peace Hills Trust Tower, #306, 10011 - 109 St., Edmonton, AB T5J 3S8
780-427-6207, Fax: 780-427-4693
Alberta Innovates - Energy & Environmental Solutions, AMEC Place, #2540, 801 - 6th Ave. SW, Calgary, AB T2P 3W2
403-297-7089, Fax: 403-297-3638, ees@albertainnovates.ca
Alberta Innovates - Health Solutions, #1500, 10104 - 103 Ave., Edmonton, AB T5J 4A7
780-423-5727, Fax: 780-429-3509, 877-423-5727, health@albertainnovates.ca
Alberta Livestock & Meat Agency, Ellwood Office Park South, #101, 1003 Ellwood Rd. SW, Edmonton, AB T6X 0B3
780-638-1699, Fax: 780-638-6495, info@almaltd.ca
Alberta Recycling Management Authority, Scotia Tower 1, #1800, 10060 Jasper Ave., PO Box 189, Edmonton, AB T5J 2J1
780-990-1111, Fax: 780-990-1122, 888-999-8762, info@albertarecycling.ca
Alberta Research & Innvoation Authority, John J. Bowlen Bldg., #620 - 7 Ave. SW, 9th Fl., Calgary, AB T2P 0Y8
403-297-3022, Fax: 403-297-6435, aria@albertainnovates.ca
Alberta Used Oil Management Association, Empire Building, #1008, 10080 Jasper Ave., Edmonton, AB T5J 1V9
780-414-1510, Fax: 780-414-1519, 866-414-1510, auoma@usedoilrecycling.ca
Beverage Container Management Board, #100, 8616 - 51 Ave., Edmonton, AB T6E 6E6
780-424-3193, Fax: 780-428-4620, 888-424-7671, info@bcmb.ab.ca
Irrigation Council, Provincial Bldg., 200 - 5 Ave. South, 3rd Fl., Lethbridge, AB T1J 4L1
403-381-5176, Fax: 403-382-4406
Land Compensation Board, 1229 - 91 St. SW, Edmonton, AB T6X 1E9
780-427-2444, Fax: 780-427-5798, -310-000, srb.lcb@gov.ab.ca
Natural Resources Conservation Board, Sterling Place, 9940 - 106 St., 4th Fl., Edmonton, AB T5K 2N2
780-422-1977, Fax: 780-427-0607, 866-383-6722, info@nrcb.ca
Special Areas Board, Special Areas Board Administration, 212 - 2nd Ave. West, PO Box 820, Hanna, AB T0J 1P0
403-854-5600, Fax: 403-854-5527

British Columbia

Agricultural Land Commission, #133, 4940 Canada Way, Burnaby, BC V5G 4K6
604-660-7000, Fax: 604-660-7033, ALCBurnaby@Victoria1.gov.bc.ca
British Columbia Farm Industry Review Board, 780 Blanshard St., PO Box 9129 Prov Govt, Victoria, BC V8W 9B5
250-356-8945, Fax: 250-356-5131, firb@gov.bc.ca
British Columbia Ministry of Agriculture, PO Box 9043 Prov Govt, Victoria, BC V8W 9E2
888-221-7141, agriservicebc@gov.bc.ca
British Columbia Ministry of Energy & Mines (& Responsible for Core Review), PO Box 9060 Prov Govt, Victoria, BC V8W 9E3
British Columbia Ministry of Environment, PO Box 9339 Prov Govt, Victoria, BC V8W 9M1
250-387-9870, Fax: 250-387-6003, env.mail@gov.bc.ca
British Columbia Ministry of Forests, Lands & Natural Resource Operations, PO Box 9049 Prov Govt, Victoria, BC V8W 9E2
800-663-7867, FLNRO.MediaRequests@gov.bc.ca
Environmental Appeal Board, 747 Fort St., 4th Fl., PO Box 9425 Prov Govt, Victoria, BC V8W 3E9
250-387-3464, Fax: 250-356-9923, eabinfo@gov.bc.ca
Environmental Protection Division, PO Box 9339, Victoria, BC V8W 9M1
250-387-1288, Fax: 250-387-5669
Forest Appeals Commission, 747 Fort St., 4th Fl., PO Box 9425 Prov Govt, Victoria, BC V8W 9V1
250-387-3464, Fax: 250-356-9923, facinfo@gov.bc.ca
Forest Practices Board, PO Box 9905 Prov Govt, Victoria, BC V8W 9R1
250-213-4700, Fax: 250-213-4725, 800-994-5899, fpboard@gov.bc.ca
Forestry Innovation Investment Ltd., #1200, 1130 West Pender St., Vancouver, BC V6E 4A4
604-685-7507, Fax: 604-685-5373, info@bcfii.ca
Islands Trust, #200, 1627 Fort St., Victoria, BC V8R 1H8
250-405-5151, Fax: 250-405-5155
Oil & Gas Commission, #100, 10003 - 110 Ave., Fort St. John, BC V1J 6M7
250-794-5200, Fax: 250-794-5375
Timber Export Advisory Committee, PO Box 9514 Prov Govt, Victoria, BC V8W 9C2
250-387-8916, Fax: 250-387-5050

Manitoba

Aboriginal Affairs Secretariat, #200, 500 Portage Ave., Winnipeg, MB R3C 3X1
204-945-2510, Fax: 204-945-3689
Agricultural Societies, 1129 Queens Ave., Brandon, MB R7A 1L9
204-726-6195, Fax: 204-726-6260
Clean Environment Commission, #305, 155 Carlton St., Winnipeg, MB R3C 3H8
204-945-0594, Fax: 204-945-0090, 800-597-3556, cec@gov.mb.ca
Ecological Reserves Advisory Committee, c/o Manitoba Conservation, Parks & Natural Areas Branch, 200 Saulteaux Cres., PO Box 53, Winnipeg, MB R3J 3W3
204-945-4148, Fax: 204-945-0012
Endangered Species Advisory Committee, 200 Saulteaux Cres., PO Box 24, Winnipeg, MB R3J 3W3
204-945-7775, Fax: 204-945-3077
Farm Lands Ownership Board, #812, Norquay Bldg., 401 York Ave., Winnipeg, MB R3C 0P8
204-945-3149, Fax: 204-945-1489, 800-282-8069
Farm Machinery & Equipment Board, #812, 401 York Ave., Winnipeg, MB R3C 0P8
204-945-3854, Fax: 204-945-1489
Local Government Development Division, 59 Elizabeth Dr., PO Box 33, Thompson, MB R8N 1X4
204-677-6794, Fax: 204-677-6525
Manitoba Agriculture, Legislative Bldg., #165, 450 Broadway, Winnipeg, MB R3C 0V8
204-945-3722, Fax: 204-945-3470, minagr@leg.gov.mb.ca
Manitoba Habitat Heritage Corporation, #200, 1555 St. James St., Winnipeg, MB R3H 1B5
204-784-4350, Fax: 204-784-7359
Manitoba Hydro, 360 Portage Ave., PO Box 815 Main,Winnipeg, MB R3C 2P4
204-480-5900, Fax: 204-360-6155, 888-624-9376, publicaffairs@hydro.mb.ca
Manitoba Indigenous & Municipal Relations, Legislative Bldg, #344, 450 Broadway, Winnipeg, MB R3C OV8
204-945-3719, Fax: 204-945-8374, anaweb@gov.mb.ca
Manitoba Mineral Resources, The Paris Building, 259 Portage Ave., 9th Fl., Winnipeg, MB R3B 3P4
204-945-6569, 800-223-5215, minesinfo@gov.mb.ca
Manitoba Sustainable Development, 200 Saulteaux Cres., PO Box 22, Winnipeg, MB R3J 3W3
204-945-6784, 800-214-6497, mgi@gov.mb.ca

New Brunswick

New Brunswick Department of Agriculture, Aquaculture & Fisheries, Agricultural Research Station (Experimental Farm), PO Box 6000, Fredericton, NB E3B 5H1
506-453-2666, Fax: 506-453-7170, 888-622-4742, DAAF-MAAP@gnb.ca
New Brunswick Department of Energy & Resource Development, Hugh John Flemming Forestry Centre, 1350 Regent St., Fredericton, NB E3C 2G6
506-453-3826, Fax: 506-444-4367, dnr_mrnweb@gnb.ca
New Brunswick Department of Environment & Local Government, Marysville Place, PO Box 6000, Fredericton, NB E3B 5H1
506-453-2690, Fax: 506-457-4994, elg/egl-info@gnb.ca
New Brunswick Farm Products Commission, c/o Department of Agriculture, Aquaculture & Fisheries, PO Box 6000, Fredericton, NB E3B 5H1
506-453-3647, Fax: 506-444-5969, DAAF-MAAP@gnb.ca
New Brunswick Research & Productivity Council, 921 College Hill Rd., Fredericton, NB E3B 6Z9
506-452-1212, Fax: 506-452-1395, 800-563-0844, info@rpc.ca

Newfoundland & Labrador

C.A. Pippy Park Commission, Mount Scio House, 15 Mount Scio Rd., St. John's, NL A1B 3T2
709-737-3655, info@pippypark.com
Newfoundland & Labrador Department of Environment & Conservation, Confederation Bldg., West Block, 4th Fl., PO Box 8700, St. John's, NL A1B 4J6
709-729-2664, Fax: 709-729-6639, 800-563-6181, envcinquires@gov.nl.ca
Newfoundland & Labrador Department of Fisheries & Aquaculture, Petten Bldg., 30 Strawberry Marsh Rd., PO Box 8700, St. John's, NL A1B 4J6
709-729-3723, Fax: 709-729-6082, fisheries@gov.nl.ca
Newfoundland & Labrador Department of Natural Resources, Natural Resources Bldg., 50 Elizabeth Ave., 7th Fl., PO Box 8700, St. John's, NL A1B 4J6
709-729-2920, Fax: 709-729-0059
Professional Fish Harvesters Certification Board, 368 Hamilton Ave., PO Box 8541, St. John's, NL A1B 3P2
709-722-8170, Fax: 709-722-8201, pfh@pfhcb.com

Northwest Territories

Aurora Research Institute, 191 MacKenzie Rd., PO Box 1450, Inuvik, NT X0E 0T0
867-777-3298, Fax: 867-777-4264
Northwest Territories Department of Environment & Natural Resources, #600, 5102 - 50 Ave., Yellowknife, NT X1A 3S8
867-767-9231

Nova Scotia

Crown Land Information Management Centre, Founders Square, 1701 Hollis St., PO Box 698, Halifax, NS B3J 2T9
902-424-7068, Fax: 902-424-3171, crownland@gov.ns.ca
Geomatics Centre, 160 Willow St., Amherst, NS B4H 3W5
902-667-7231, Fax: 902-667-6008, geoinfo@novascotia.ca

Natural Products Marketing Council, 179 College Rd., PO Box 890, Truro, NS B2N 5G6
902-893-6511, Fax: 902-893-6573

Nova Scotia Department of Agriculture, 1800 Argyle St., 6th Fl., PO Box 2223, Halifax, NS B3J 3C4
902-424-4560, Fax: 902-424-4671

Nova Scotia Department of Natural Resources, Founder's Square, 1701 Hollis St., 3rd Fl., PO Box 698, Halifax, NS B3J 2T9
902-424-5935, Fax: 902-424-7735, 800-565-2224

Nova Scotia Farm Loan Board, PO Box 890, Truro, NS B2N 5G6
902-893-6506, Fax: 902-895-7693, FLBNS@gov.ns.ca

Nunavut

Nunavut Territory Department of Environment, PO Box 1000 1300, Iqaluit, NU X0A 0H0
867-975-7700, Fax: 867-975-7742, environment@gov.nu.ca

Ontario

Algonquin Forestry Authority - Huntsville, 222 Main St. West, Huntsville, ON P1H 1Y1
705-789-9647, Fax: 705-789-3353, info@algonquinforestry.on.ca

Algonquin Forestry Authority - Pembroke, Victoria Centre, 84 Isabella St., 2nd Fl., Pembroke, ON K8A 5S5
613-735-0173, Fax: 613-735-4192, info@algonquinforestry.on.ca

Animal Care Review Board, #530, 20 Dundas St. West, Toronto, ON M5G 2C2
416-212-0334, Fax: 416-314-4270, 855-444-7454, acrb.registrar@ontario.ca

Association of Ontario Land Surveyors, 1043 McNicoll Ave., Toronto, ON M1W 3W6
416-491-9020, Fax: 416-491-2576, 800-268-0718

Cancer Care Ontario, 620 University Ave., 15th Fl., Toronto, ON M5G 2L7
416-971-9800, Fax: 416-971-6888

Environmental Commissioner of Ontario, #605, 1075 Bay St., Toronto, ON M5S 2B1
416-325-3377, Fax: 416-325-3370, 800-701-6454, commissioner@eco.on.ca

Environmental Sciences & Standards Division, 135 St. Clair Ave. West, 14th Fl., Toronto, ON M4V 1P5
Fax: 416-314-6358

Huronia Historical Parks, 16164 Hwy. 12, PO Box 160, Midland, ON L4R 4K8
705-526-7838, Fax: 705-526-9193

Lake of the Woods Control Board, c/o Executive Engineer, 373 Sussex Dr., Block E1, Ottawa, ON K1A 0H3
Fax: 888-702-9632, 800-661-5922, secretariat@lwcb.ca

Livestock Medicines Advisory Committee, 1 Stone Rd. West, 3rd Fl. Northeast, Guelph, ON N1G 4Y2
519-826-4110, Fax: 519-826-3254, ag.info.omafra@ontario.ca

Mines & Minerals Division, Willet Green Miller Centre, 933 Ramsey Lake Rd., Level B6, Sudbury, ON P3E 6B5
705-670-5755, Fax: 705-670-5818, 888-415-9845

Niagara Parks Commission, Oak Hall Administration Bldg., 7400 Portage Rd. South, PO Box 150, Niagara Falls, ON L2E 6T2
905-356-2241, Fax: 905-354-6041, 877-642-7275

Ontario Clean Water Agency, 1 Yonge St., 17th Fl., Toronto, ON M5E 1E5
416-314-5600, 800-667-6292, ocwa@ocwa.com

Ontario Drinking Water Advisory Council, 40 St. Clair Ave. West, 3rd Fl., Toronto, ON M4V 1M2
416-212-7779, Fax: 416-212-7595

Ontario Fish & Wildlife Heritage Commission, Robinson Pl., 300 Water St., PO Box 7000, Peterborough, ON K9J 8M5
705-755-1905, Fax: 705-755-1900

Ontario Geographic Names Board, Robinson Place, 300 Water St., 2nd Fl., PO Box 7000, Peterborough, ON K9J 8M5
705-755-2132

Ontario Ministry of Agriculture, Food & Rural Affairs, Ontario Government Bldg., 1 Stone Rd. West, Guelph, ON N1G 4Y2
519-826-3100, Fax: 519-826-4335, 888-466-2372, about.omafra@ontario.ca

Ontario Ministry of Environment & Climate Change, Public Information Centre, Macdonald Block, 900 Bay St., 2nd Fl., Toronto, ON M7A 1N3
416-325-4000, Fax: 416-314-6713, 800-565-4923

Ontario Ministry of Natural Resources & Forestry, 300 Water St., PO Box 7000, Peterborough, ON K9J 8M5
800-667-1940

Ontario Ministry of Northern Development & Mines, 159 Cedar St., Sudbury, ON P3E 6A5
705-670-5755, Fax: 705-670-5818, 888-415-9845, ndmminister@ontario.ca

Ontario Moose & Bear Allocation Advisory Committee, PO Box 964, Sioux Lookout, ON P8T 1B3
807-737-2615, Fax: 807-737-4173

Ontario Science Centre, 770 Don Mills Rd., Toronto, ON M3C 1T3
416-696-1000, Fax: 416-696-3166, 888-696-1110

Ottawa River Regulation Planning Board, c/o Ottawa River Regulation Secretariat, Block E1, 373 Sussex Dr., Ottawa, ON K1A 0H3
613-995-3443, 800-778-1246, secretariat@ottawariver.ca

Pesticides Advisory Committee, 135 St. Clair Ave. West, 15th Fl., Toronto, ON M4V 1P5
416-314-9230, Fax: 416-314-9237

Provincial Services Division, #6540, 99 Wellesley St. West, Toronto, ON M7A 1W3
416-326-9504

Rabies Advisory Committee, DNA Bldg, Trent University, 2140 East Bank Dr., PO Box 4840, Peterborough, ON K9J 7B8
705-755-2270

Royal Botanical Gardens, 680 Plains Rd. West, Burlington, ON L7T 4H4
905-527-1158, Fax: 905-577-0375, 800-694-4769, info@rbg.ca

Safety, Licensing Appeals & Standards Tribunals Ontario, #5230, 20 Dundas St. West, Toronto, ON M5G 2C2
416-212-0334, Fax: 416-314-4270, 855-444-7454, slastoinfo@ontario.ca

Science & Research Branch, Roberta Bondar Pl., 300 Water St., 4th Fl., Peterborough, ON K9J 8M5
705-755-2809, Fax: 705-755-2802

Science North, 100 Ramsey Lake Rd., Sudbury, ON P3E 5S9
705-522-3701, Fax: 705-522-4954, 800-461-4898, contactus@sciencenorth.ca

Shibogama Interim Planning Board, PO Box 105, Wunnumin, ON P0V 2Z0
807-442-2559, Fax: 807-442-2627

St. Lawrence Parks Commission, 13740 County Rd. 2, Morrisburg, ON K0C 1X0
613-543-3704, Fax: 613-543-2847, 800-437-2233, getaway@parks.on.ca

Windigo Interim Planning Board, PO Box 299, Sioux Lookout, ON P8T 1A3
807-737-1585, Fax: 807-737-3133

Prince Edward Island

Agricultural Insurance Corporation, 29 Indigo Cres., PO Box 1600, Charlottetown, PE C1A 7N3
902-368-4842, Fax: 902-368-6677

Grain Elevators Corporation, 7 Gerald McCarville Dr., PO Box 250, Kensington, PE C0B 1M0
902-836-8935, Fax: 902-836-8926

Prince Edward Island Department of Agriculture & Fisheries, Jones Bldg., 11 Kent St., 5th Fl., PO Box 2000, Charlottetown, PE C1A 7N8
902-368-4880, Fax: 902-368-4857

Prince Edward Island Energy Corporation, Sullivan Bldg., 16 Fitzroy St., PO Box 2000, Charlottetown, PE C1A 7N8

Québec

Bureau d'audiences publiques sur l'environnement, Édifice Lomer-Gouin, #2.10, 575, rue Saint-Amable, Québec, QC G1R 6A6
418-643-7447, Fax: 418-643-9474, 800-463-4732, communication@bape.gouv.qc.ca

Comité consultatif de l'environnement Kativik, CP 930, Kuujjuaq, QC J0M 1C0
819-964-2961, Fax: 819-964-0694, keac-ccek@krg.ca

Fondation de la faune du Québec, Place Iberville II, #420, 1175, av Lavigerie, Québec, QC G1V 4P1
418-644-7926, Fax: 418-643-7655, 877-639-0742, ffq@fondationdelafaune.qc.ca

Fonds québécois de la recherche sur la nature et les technologies, #450, 140, Grande Allée est, Québec, QC G1R 5M8
418-643-8560, Fax: 418-643-1451, info.nt@frq.gouv.qc.ca

Ministère de l'Agriculture, des Pêcheries et de l'Alimentation, 200, ch Sainte-Foy, Québec, QC G1R 4X6
418-380-2110, 888-222-6272

Ministère des Énergie et des Ressources naturelles, Service à la clientèle, #A409, 5700, 4e av ouest, Québec, QC G1H 6R1
Fax: 418-644-6513, 866-248-6936, services.clientele@mern.gouv.qc.ca

Régie de l'énergie, Tour de la Bourse, #2.55, 800, Place Victoria, Montréal, QC H4Z 1A2
514-873-2452, Fax: 514-873-2070, 888-873-2452, secretariat@regie-energie.qc.ca

Société de développement de la Baie James, #10, 462, 3e rue, Chibougamau, QC G8P 1N7
418-748-7777, Fax: 418-748-6868, chi@sdbj.gouv.qc.ca

Saskatchewan

Agri-Food Council, #302, 3085 Albert St., Regina, SK S4S 0B1
306-787-5978, Fax: 306-787-5134, corey.ruud@gov.sk.ca

Agricultural Implements Board, #315, 3085 Albert St., Regina, SK S4S 0B1
306-787-8861, Fax: 306-787-8599

Farm Stress Unit, 3085 Albert St., Regina, SK S4S 0B1
800-667-4442

Health Quality Council, Atrium Bldg., Innovation Place, 241, 111 Research Dr., Saskatoon, SK S7N 3R2
306-668-8810, Fax: 306-668-8820, info@hqc.sk.ca

Prairie Agricultural Machinery Institute, 2215 - 8th Ave., PO Box 1150, Humboldt, SK S0K 2A0
306-682-5033, Fax: 306-682-5080, 800-567-7264, humboldt@pami.ca

Saskatchewan Agriculture, Walter Scott Bldg., 3085 Albert St., Regina, SK S4S 0B1
866-457-2377

Saskatchewan Conservation Data Centre, Fish & Wildlife Branch, Ministry of Environment, 3211 Albert St., Regina, SK S4S 5W6
306-787-7196, Fax: 306-787-9544

Saskatchewan Crop Insurance Corporation, 484 Prince William Dr., PO Box 3000, Melville, SK S0A 2P0
306-728-7200, Fax: 306-728-7202, 888-935-0000, customer.service@scic.gov.sk.ca

Saskatchewan Environment, 3211 Albert St., 2nd Fl., Regina, SK S4S 5W6
306-787-2584, Fax: 306-787-9544, 800-567-4224, Centre.Inquiry@gov.sk.ca

Saskatchewan Lands Appeal Board, #315, 3085 Albert St., Regina, SK S4S 0B1
306-787-8861

Saskatchewan Research Council, #125, 15 Innovation Blvd., Saskatoon, SK S7N 2X8
306-933-5400, Fax: 306-933-7446, info@src.sk.ca

Saskatchewan Science Centre, 2903 Powerhouse Dr., Regina, SK S4N 0A1
306-522-4629, 800-667-6300, info@sasksciencecentre.com

Saskatchewan Sheep Development Board, 2213C Hanselman Crt., Saskatoon, SK S7L 6A8
306-933-5200, Fax: 306-933-7182, sheepdb@sasktel.net

Saskatchewan Turkey Producers' Marketing Board, 1438 Fletcher Rd., Saskatoon, SK S7M 5T2
306-931-1050, saskaturkey@sasktel.net

Surface Rights Board of Arbitration, 113 - 2nd Ave. East, PO Box 1597, Kindersley, SK S0L 1S0
306-463-5447, Fax: 306-463-5449, surfacerightsboard@gov.sk.ca

Yukon Territory

Alsek Renewable Resource Council, 180 Alaska Hwy., PO Box 2077, Haines Junction, YT Y0B 1L0
867-634-2524, Fax: 867-634-2527, admin@alsekrrc.ca

Carmacks Renewable Resource Council, PO Box 122, Carmacks, YT Y0B 1C0
867-863-6838, Fax: 867-863-6429, carmacksrrc@northwestel.net

Dawson District Renewable Resource Council, PO Box 1380, Dawson City, YT Y0B 1G0
867-993-6976, Fax: 867-993-6093, dawsonrrc@northwestel.net

Mayo District Renewable Resources Council, PO Box 249, Mayo, YT Y0B 1M0
867-996-2942, Fax: 867-996-2948, mayorrc@northwestel.net

North Yukon Renewable Resources Council, PO Box 80, Old Crow, YT Y0B 1N0
867-966-3034, Fax: 867-966-3036, nyrrc@northwestel.net

Selkirk Renewable Resources Council, PO Box 32, Pelly Crossing, YT Y0B 1P0
867-537-3937, Fax: 867-537-3939, selkirkrrc@northwestel.net

Teslin Renewable Resource Council, PO Box 186, Teslin, YT Y0A 1B0
867-390-2323, Fax: 867-390-2919, teslinrrc@northwestel.net

Yukon Development Corporation, PO Box 2703 D-1, Whitehorse, YT Y1A 2C6
867-456-3837, Fax: 867-393-7167

Yukon Environment, 10 Burns Rd., PO Box 2703 V-3A, Whitehorse, YT Y1A 2C6
867-667-5652, Fax: 867-393-7197, environment.yukon@gov.yk.ca

Yukon Fish & Wildlife Management Board, 106 Main St., 2nd Fl., PO Box 31104, Whitehorse, YT Y1A 5P7
867-667-3754, Fax: 867-393-6947, officemanager@yfwmb.ca

Yukon Land Use Planning Council, #201, 307 Jarvis St., Whitehorse, YT Y1A 2H3
867-667-7397, Fax: 867-667-4624, ylupc@planyukon.ca

SCIENCE & TECHNOLOGY

See Also: Business Development

Aerospace Manufacturing Technologies Centre, Campus Université de Montréal, 5145, av Decelles, Montréal, QC H3T 2B2

Atomic Energy of Canada Limited, Head Office, Chalk River Laboratories, 286 Plant Rd., Chalk River, ON K0J 1J0
888-220-2465, communications@aecl.ca

Bedford Institute of Oceanography, 1 Challenger Dr., PO Box 1006, Dartmouth, NS B2Y 4A2
Fax: 902-426-8484, WebmasterBIO-IOB@dfo-mpo.gc.ca

Canada Centre for Mapping & Earth Observation, #212, 50 Place de la Cité, PO Box 162, Sherbrooke, QC J1H 4G9

Canada Foundation for Innovation, #450, 230 Queen St., Ottawa, ON K1P 5E4
613-947-6496, Fax: 613-943-0923, feedback@innovation.ca
Canada Science & Technology Museum Corporation, PO Box 9724 T,Ottawa, ON K1G 5A3
613-991-3044, Fax: 613-993-7923, cts@techno-science.ca
Canadian Centre for Housing Technology, c/o National Research Council Canada, Building M-20, 1200 Montreal Rd., Ottawa, ON K1A 0R6
Canadian Food Inspection Agency, 1400 Merivale Rd., Ottawa, ON K1A 0Y9
613-225-2342, 800-442-2342
Canadian Institutes of Health Research, 160 Elgin St., 9th Fl., Ottawa, ON K1A 0W9
613-941-2672, Fax: 613-954-1800, 888-603-4178, support@cihr-irsc.gc.ca
Canadian Nuclear Laboratories, Head Office, Chalk River Laboratories, 286 Plant Rd., Chalk River, ON K0J 1J0
866-513-2325, communications@cnl.ca
Canadian Photonics Fabrication Centre, c/o National Research Council Canada, Building M-50, 1200 Montreal Rd., Ottawa, ON K1A 0R6
613-993-9101
Canadian Space Agency, John H. Chapman Space Centre, 6767, rte de l'Aéroport, Saint-Hubert, QC J3Y 8Y9
450-926-4800, Fax: 450-926-4352, asc.info.csa@canada.ca
CanmetMINING, 555 Booth St., Ottawa, ON K1A 0G1
Fax: 613-947-6606
Cultus Lake Salmon Research Lab, 4222 Columbia Valley Hwy., Cultus Lakw, BC V2R 5B6
Freshwater Institute Science Laboratory, 501 University Cres., Winnipeg, MB R3T 2N6
204-983-5000, Fax: 204-983-6285
Hydraulics Laboratories, c/o National Research Council, 1200 Montreal Rd., Ottawa, ON K1A 0R6
Institut Maurice-Lamontagne, 850, rte de la Mer, CP 1000, Mont-Joli, QC G5H 3Z4
418-775-0500, Fax: 418-775-0730
Institute of Ocean Sciences, 9860 West Saanich Rd., PO Box 6000, Sidney, BC V8L 4B2
250-363-6517, Fax: 250-363-6390
International Development Research Centre, 150 Kent St., PO Box 8500, Ottawa, ON K1G 3H9
613-236-6163, Fax: 613-238-7230, info@idrc.ca
National Research Council Canada, Building M-58, 1200 Montreal Rd., Ottawa, ON K1A 0R6
613-993-9101, Fax: 613-952-9907, 877-672-2672, info@nrc-cnrc.gc.ca
National Research Council Canada - National Science Library, 1200 Montreal Rd., Ottawa, ON K1A 0R6
613-998-8544, Fax: 613-998-2399, 800-668-1222, NRC.KMHelpdesk-BureaudaideGS.CNRC@nrc-cnrc.gc.ca
Natural Sciences & Engineering Research Council of Canada, Constitution Square, Tower II, 350 Albert St., Ottawa, ON K1A 1H5
613-995-4273, Fax: 613-992-5337, 855-275-2861
Networks of Centres of Excellence of Canada, 350 Albert Street, 16th Fl., Ottawa, ON K1A 1H5
613-995-6010, Fax: 613-992-7356, info@nce-rce.gc.ca
Pacific Biological Station, 3190 Hammond Bay Rd., Nanaimo, BC V9T 6N7
250-756-7000, Fax: 250-756-7053
Science, Technology & Innovation Council, 235 Queen St., 9th Fl., Ottawa, ON K1A 0H5
343-291-2362, Fax: 613-952-0459, info@stic-csti.ca
Sea Lamprey Control Centre, 1219 Queen St. East, Sault Ste Marie, ON P6A 2E5
Spectrum, Information Technologies & Telecommunications, Journal Tower North, 300 Slater St., 20th Fl., Ottawa, ON K1A 0C8
613-998-0368, Fax: 613-952-1203
St. Andrews Biological Station, 531 Brandy Cove Rd., St Andrews, NB E5B 2L9
506-529-8854, Fax: 506-529-5862, XMARSABS@mar.dfo-mpo.gc.ca
Strategic Policy, 200 Kent St., Ottawa, ON K1A 0E6

Alberta

Alberta Innovates - Energy & Environmental Solutions, AMEC Place, #2540, 801 - 6th Ave. SW, Calgary, AB T2P 3W2
403-297-7089, Fax: 403-297-3638, ees@albertainnovates.ca

British Columbia

BC Renaissance Capital Fund Ltd., PO Box 9800 Prov Govt, BC V8W 9W1
Fax: 250-952-0371
British Columbia Innovation Council, 1188 West Georgia St., 9th Fl., Vancouver, BC V6E 4A2
604-683-2724, Fax: 604-683-6567, 800-665-7222, info@bcic.ca
Leading Edge Endowment Fund Board, 1188 West Georgia St., 9th Fl., Vancouver, BC V6E 4A2
604-438-3220, contact@leefbc.ca
Powertech Labs Inc., 12388 - 88 Ave., Surrey, BC V8W 7R7
604-590-7500, Fax: 604-590-6611
Premier's Technology Council, #1600, 800 Robson St., Vancouver, BC V6Z 3E7
604-827-4629, premiers.technologycouncil@gov.bc.ca

Manitoba

Industrial Technology Centre, #200, 78 Innovation Dr., Winnipeg, MB R3T 6C2
204-480-3333, Fax: 204-480-0345, 800-728-7933, tech@itc.mb.ca
Manitoba Education, Research & Learning Information Networks, University of Manitoba, #100, 135 Innovation Dr., Winnipeg, MB R3T 6A8
204-474-7800, Fax: 204-474-7830, 800-430-6404
Manitoba Mineral Resources, The Paris Building, 259 Portage Ave., 9th Fl., Winnipeg, MB R3B 3P4
204-945-6569, 800-223-5215, minesinfo@gov.mb.ca

New Brunswick

New Brunswick Research & Productivity Council, 921 College Hill Rd., Fredericton, NB E3B 6Z9
506-452-1212, Fax: 506-452-1395, 800-563-0844, info@rpc.ca

Northwest Territories

Aurora Research Institute, 191 MacKenzie Rd., PO Box 1450, Inuvik, NT X0E 0T0
867-777-3298, Fax: 867-777-4264

Nova Scotia

Innovacorp, #1400, 1801 Hollis St., Halifax, NS B3J 3N4
902-424-8670, Fax: 902-424-4679, 800-565-7051, info@innovacorp.ca

Ontario

Environmental Sciences & Standards Division, 135 St. Clair Ave. West, 14th Fl., Toronto, ON M4V 1P5
Fax: 416-314-6358
Ontario Science Centre, 770 Don Mills Rd., Toronto, ON M3C 1T3
416-696-1000, Fax: 416-696-3166, 888-696-1110
Science North, 100 Ramsey Lake Rd., Sudbury, ON P3E 5S9
705-522-3701, Fax: 705-522-4954, 800-461-4898, contactus@sciencenorth.ca

Québec

Centre de recherche industrielle du Québec, 333, rue Franquet, Québec, QC G1P 4C7
418-659-1550, Fax: 418-652-2251, 800-667-2386, infocriq@criq.qc.ca
Commission de l'éthique en science et en technologie, 1150, Grande Allée ouest, 1er étage, Québec, QC G1S 4Y9
418-691-5989, Fax: 418-646-0920, ethique@ethique.gouv.qc.ca
Fonds québécois de la recherche sur la nature et les technologies, #450, 140, Grande Allée est, Québec, QC G1R 5M8
418-643-8560, Fax: 418-643-1451, info.nt@frq.gouv.qc.ca
Ministère de l'Économie, de la Science et de l'Innovation, 710, place D'Youville, 3e étage, Québec, QC G1R 4Y4
418-691-5950, Fax: 418-644-0118, 866-680-1884

Saskatchewan

Prairie Agricultural Machinery Institute, 2215 - 8th Ave., PO Box 1150, Humboldt, SK S0K 2A0
306-682-5033, Fax: 306-682-5080, 800-567-7264, humboldt@pami.ca
Saskatchewan Opportunities Corporation, Innovation Place, #114, 14 Innovation Blvd., Saskatoon, SK S7N 2X8
306-933-6295, Fax: 306-933-8215, saskatoon@innovationplace.com
Saskatchewan Research Council, #125, 15 Innovation Blvd., Saskatoon, SK S7N 2X8
306-933-5400, Fax: 306-933-7446, info@src.sk.ca
Saskatchewan Science Centre, 2903 Powerhouse Dr., Regina, SK S4N 0A1
306-522-4629, 800-667-6300, info@sasksciencecentre.com

Yukon Territory

Yukon Energy, Mines & Resources, PO Box 2703, Whitehorse, YT Y1A 2C6
867-667-3130, Fax: 867-456-3965, 800-661-0408, emr@gov.yk.ca

SECURITIES ADMINISTRATION

See Also: Finance

Alberta

Alberta Securities Commission, #600, 250 - 5th St. SW, Calgary, AB T2P 0R4
403-297-6454, Fax: 403-297-6156, 877-355-0585, inquiries@asc.ca

British Columbia

British Columbia Securities Commission, Pacific Centre, 701 West Georgia St., 12th Fl., PO Box 10142, Vancouver, BC V7Y 1L2
604-899-6500, Fax: 604-899-6506, 800-373-6393, inquiries@bcsc.bc.ca

Manitoba

Manitoba Securities Commission, #500, 400 St. Mary Ave., Winnipeg, MB R3C 4K5
204-945-2548, Fax: 204-945-0330, 800-655-5244, securities@gov.mb.ca

New Brunswick

Financial & Consumer Services Commission, #300, 85 Charlotte St., Saint John, NB E2L 2J2
506-658-3060, Fax: 506-658-3059, 866-933-2222, info@fcnb.ca

Northwest Territories

Northwest Territories Department of Justice, 4903 - 49th St., PO Box 1320, Yellowknife, NT X1A 2L9
867-767-9256

Nova Scotia

Nova Scotia Securities Commission, Duke Tower, #400, 5251 Duke St., PO Box 458, Halifax, NS B3J 2P8
902-424-7768, Fax: 902-424-4625, 855-424-2499, NSSCinquiries@novascotia.ca

Ontario

Ontario Securities Commission, #1903, 20 Queen St. West, Toronto, ON M5H 3S8
416-593-8314, Fax: 416-593-8122, 877-785-1555, inquiries@osc.gov.on.ca

Québec

Autorité des marchés financiers, Tour de la Bourse, 800, Square Victoria, 22e étage, Montréal, QC H4Z 1G3
514-395-0337, Fax: 514-873-3090, 877-525-0337, information@lautorite.qc.ca

Saskatchewan

Financial & Consumer Affairs Authority, #601, 1919 Saskatchewan Dr., Regina, SK S4P 4H2
306-787-5645, Fax: 306-787-5899, 877-880-5550, consumerprotection@gov.sk.ca

SENIOR CITIZENS SERVICES

National Seniors Council, Phase IV, 8th Floor, Mail Stop 802, 140 Promenade du Portage, Gatineau, QC K1A 0J9
Fax: 819-953-9298, 800-622-6232
Social Security Tribunal, PO Box 9812 T, Ottawa, ON K1G 6S3
613-952-8805, 877-227-8577, info.sst-tss@canada.gc.ca
Veterans Affairs Canada, 161 Grafton St., PO Box 7700, Charlottetown, PE C1A 8M9
866-522-2122, information@vac-acc.gc.ca

Alberta

Alberta Health, PO Box 1360 Main,Edmonton, AB T5J 2N3
780-427-7164, -310-0000
Alberta Health Advocates, Centre West Bldg., 10035 - 108 St., 12th Fl., Edmonton, AB T5J 3E1
780-422-1812, Fax: 780-422-0695, -310-0000, healthadvocates@gov.ab.ca
Alberta Seniors & Housing, PO Box 3100, Edmonton, AB T5J 4W3
780-644-9992, Fax: 780-422-5954, 877-644-9992
Seniors Advisory Council for Alberta, Standard Life Centre, #600, 10405 Jasper Ave., 6th Fl., Edmonton, AB T5J 4R7
780-422-2321, Fax: 780-422-8762, -310-0000, saca@gov.ab.ca

British Columbia

Office of the Seniors Advocate, PO Box 9561 Prov Govt, Victoria, BC V8W 9P4
250-952-3034, 877-952-3181, info@seniorsadvocatebc.ca

Manitoba

Healthy Living & Seniors, c/o Seniors & Healthy Aging Secretariat, #1610, 155 Carlton St., Winnipeg, MB R3C 3H8
204-945-6565, Fax: 204-948-2514, 800-665-6565, seniors@gov.mb.ca
Manitoba Health, Seniors & Active Living, #100, 300 Carlton St., Winnipeg, MB R3B 3M9
204-945-3744, 866-626-4862, mgi@gov.mb.ca

New Brunswick

Senior & Healthy Aging Secretariat, Sartain MacDonald Bldg., 4th Fl., PO Box 6000, Fredericton, NB E3B 5H1
506-453-2001, Fax: 506-453-2164, seniors@gnb.ca

Newfoundland & Labrador

Ministerial Council on Aging & Seniors, c/o Department of Seniors, Wellness & Social Development, PO Box 8700, St. John's, NL A1B 4J6
Newfoundland & Labrador Department of Seniors, Wellness & Social Development, PO Box 8700, St. John's, NL A1B 4J6
709-729-0862, Fax: 709-729-0870, SWSDInfo@gov.nl.ca

Nova Scotia

Nova Scotia Department of Seniors, Barrington Tower, 1894 Barrington St., 15th Fl., Halifax, NS B3J 2R8
902-424-0770, Fax: 902-424-0561, 844-277-0770, seniors@NovaScotia.ca

Nunavut

Nunavut Territory Department of Culture & Heritage, PO Box 1000 800, Iqaluit, NU X0A 0H0
867-975-5500, Fax: 867-975-5504, 866-934-2035

Ontario
Ontario Seniors' Secretariat, #601C, 777 Bay St., 6th Fl., Toronto, ON M7A 2J4
416-326-7076, Fax: 416-326-7078, infoseniors@ontario.ca
Québec
Comité national d'éthique sur le vieillissement et les changements démographiques, #700, 875, Grande Allée est, 5e étage, Québec, QC G1R 5W5
418-643-0098, Fax: 418-643-0082
Ministère de la Famille, 425, rue Saint-Amable, 1er étage, Québec, QC G1R 4Z1
877-216-6202
Ministère de la Santé et des Services sociaux, Direction des communications, 1075, ch Sainte-Foy, 16e étage, Québec, QC G1S 2M1
418-643-9395, Fax: 418-643-4768, regisseur.web@msss.gouv.qc.ca
Secrétariat aux aînés, #4.09, 930, ch Sainte-Foy, 4e étage, Québec, QC G1S 2L4
Yukon Territory
Yukon Health & Social Services, PO Box 2703, Whitehorse, YT Y1A 2C6
867-667-3673, Fax: 867-667-3096, 800-661-0408, hss@gov.yk.ca

SOCIAL AFFAIRS

Alberta
Social Care Facilities Review Committee, Sterling Place, 9940 - 106 St., 3rd Fl., Edmonton, AB T5K 2N2

SOCIAL SERVICES

See Also: Community Services
Service Canada, 140, Promenade du Portage, Gatineau, QC K1A 0J9
Fax: 613-941-1827, 800-622-6232
Alberta
Appeals Secretariat, Centre West Bldg., 10035 - 108 St., 6th Fl., Calgary, AB T5J 3E1
780-427-2709, Fax: 780-422-1088, appeals@gov.ab.ca
Social Care Facilities Review Committee, Sterling Place, 9940 - 106 St., 3rd Fl., Edmonton, AB T5K 2N2
British Columbia
British Columbia College of Social Workers, #1430, 1200 West 73 Ave., Vancouver, BC V6P 6G5
604-737-4916, Fax: 604-737-6809, 877-576-6740, info@bccsw.ca
British Columbia Ministry of Community, Sport, & Cultural Development & Responsible for TransLink, PO Box 9490 Prov Govt, Victoria, BC V8W 9N7
Manitoba
Social Services Appeal Board, 175 Hargrave St., 7th Fl., Winnipeg, MB R3C 3R8
204-945-3003, Fax: 204-945-1736, 800-282-8069
New Brunswick
Economic & Social Inclusion Corporation, Kings Place, PO Box 6000, Fredericton, NB E3B 5H1
506-444-2977, Fax: 506-444-2978, 888-295-4545, esic-sies@gnb.ca
New Brunswick Department of Social Development, Sartain MacDonald Bldg., 551 King St., PO Box 6000, Fredericton, NB E3B 5H1
506-453-2001, Fax: 506-453-2164, sd-ds@gnb.ca
Newfoundland & Labrador
Newfoundland & Labrador Department of Advanced Education & Skills, Confederation Building, West Block, 3rd Fl., PO Box 8700, St. John's, NL A1B 4J6
709-729-2480, aesweb@gov.nl.ca
Northwest Territories
Northwest Territories Department of Health & Social Services, 5015 - 49th St., PO Box 1320, Yellowknife, NT X1A 2L9
Fax: 867-873-0306
Nova Scotia
Housing Nova Scotia, #3, 3770 Kempt Rd., Halifax, NS B3K 4X8
902-424-8445
Nunavut
Nunavut Territory Department of Family Services, PO Box 1000 950, Iqaluit, NU X0A 0H0
867-975-6038, Fax: 867-975-6091
Nunavut Territory Department of Health, PO Box 1000 1000, Iqaluit, NU X0A 0H0
867-975-5700, Fax: 867-975-5705, 800-661-0833
Ontario
Ontario Ministry of Community & Social Services, Hepburn Block, 80 Grosvenor St., 6th Fl., Toronto, ON M7A 1E9
416-325-5666, Fax: 416-325-3347, 888-789-4199
Ontario Ministry of Housing, College Park, 777 Bay St., 17th Fl., Toronto, ON M5G 2E5
416-585-6500, Fax: 416-585-4035, mininfo@ontario.ca
Québec
Comité consultatif de lutte contre la pauvreté et l'exclusion sociale, 425, rue Saint-Amable, RC 145, Québec, QC G1R 4Z1
418-528-9866, Fax: 418-643-6623, infocclp@mess.gouv.qc.ca
Conseil de gestion de l'assurance parentale, #104, 1122, Grande Allée ouest, Québec, QC G1S 1E5
418-643-1009, Fax: 418-643-6738, 888-610-7727
Ministère de la Santé et des Services sociaux, Direction des communications, 1075, ch Sainte-Foy, 16e étage, Québec, QC G1S 2M1
418-643-9395, Fax: 418-643-4768, regisseur.web@msss.gouv.qc.ca
Saskatchewan
Saskatchewan Social Services, 1920 Broad St., Regina, SK S4P 3V6
306-787-3700, 866-221-5200, socialservicesinquiry@gov.sk.ca

SOIL RESOURCES

Soils & Crops Research & Development Centre, 2560, boul Hochelaga, Québec, QC G1V 2J3
418-657-7980, Fax: 418-648-2402
Nova Scotia
Nova Scotia Department of Agriculture, 1800 Argyle St., 6th Fl., PO Box 2223, Halifax, NS B3J 3C4
902-424-4560, Fax: 902-424-4671
Québec
Commission de protection du territoire agricole du Québec, 200, ch Ste-Foy, 2e étage, Québec, QC G1R 4X6
418-643-3314, Fax: 418-643-2261, 800-667-5294, info@cptaq.gouv.qc.ca

SOLICITORS GENERAL

Alberta
Alberta Justice & Solicitor General, Communications, Bowker Building, 9833 - 109 St., 5th Fl., Edmonton, AB T5K 2E8
780-427-2745, -310-0000
Newfoundland & Labrador
Newfoundland & Labrador Department of Justice & Public Safety, Confederation Bldg., East Block, 4th Fl., PO Box 8700, St. John's, NL A1B 4J6
709-729-2869, Fax: 709-729-0469, justice@gov.nl.ca
Nova Scotia
Nova Scotia Department of Justice, 1690 Hollis St., PO Box 7, Halifax, NS B3J 2L6
902-424-4030, justweb@gov.ns.ca
Ontario
Ontario Ministry of Community Safety & Correctional Services, George Drew Bldg., 25 Grosvenor St., 18th Fl., Toronto, ON M7A 1Y6
416-326-5000, Fax: 416-326-0498, 866-517-0571, mcscs.feedback@ontario.ca
Québec
Ministère de la Sécurité publique, Tour des Laurentides, 2525, boul Laurier, 5e étage, Québec, QC G1V 2L2
418-646-6777, Fax: 418-643-0275, 866-644-6826
Yukon Territory
Yukon Justice, Andrew Philipsen Law Centre, 2134 Second Ave., PO Box 2703, Whitehorse, YT Y1A 2C6
867-667-3033, Fax: 867-393-5790, justice@gov.yk.ca

SPACE & ASTRONOMY

Canada Science & Technology Museum Corporation, PO Box 9724 T,Ottawa, ON K1G 5A3
613-991-3044, Fax: 613-993-7923, cts@techno-science.ca
Canadian Space Agency, John H. Chapman Space Centre, 6767, rte de l'Aéroport, Saint-Hubert, QC J3Y 8Y9
450-926-4800, Fax: 450-926-4352, asc.info.csa@canada.ca

SPORTS

See: Recreation
Alberta
Alberta Sport Connection, HSBC Bldg., #500, 10055 - 106 St., Edmonton, AB T5J 1G3
780-415-1167, Fax: 780-415-0308, -310-0000
British Columbia
Arts, Culture, Gaming Grants & Sport, PO Box 9490 Prov Govt, Victoria, BC V8W 9N7
250-356-6914, Fax: 250-387-7973
British Columbia Ministry of Community, Sport, & Cultural Development & Responsible for TransLink, PO Box 9490 Prov Govt, Victoria, BC V8W 9N7
New Brunswick
New Brunswick Department of Tourism, Heritage & Culture, Centennial Building, PO Box 6000, Fredericton, NB E3B 5H1
506-453-3115, Fax: 506-457-4984, thctpcinfo@gnb.ca
Newfoundland & Labrador
Marble Mountain Development Corporation, PO Box 947, Corner Brook, NL A2H 6J2
709-637-7601, Fax: 709-634-1702, 888-462-7253
Newfoundland & Labrador Department of Seniors, Wellness & Social Development, PO Box 8700, St. John's, NL A1B 4J6
709-729-0862, Fax: 709-729-0870, SWSDInfo@gov.nl.ca
Ontario
Ontario Ministry of Tourism, Culture & Sport, Hearst Block, 900 Bay St., 9th Fl., Toronto, ON M7A 2E1
416-326-9326, Fax: 416-314-7854, 888-997-9015
Prince Edward Island
Prince Edward Island School Athletic Association, #101, 250 Water St., Summerside, PE C1N 1B6
902-438-4846, Fax: 902-438-4884
Sport & Recreation, Sullivan Bldg., 16 Fitzroy St., 3rd Fl., PO Box 2000, Charlottetown, PE C1A 7N8
902-368-4789, Fax: 902-368-4224
Québec
Ministère de l'Éducation et de l'Enseignement supérieur, 1035, rue De La Chevrotière, 28e étage, Québec, QC G1R 5A5
418-643-7095, Fax: 418-646-6561, 866-747-6626
Régie des installations olympiques/Parc olympique Québec, 4141, av Pierre-De Coubertin, Montréal, QC H1V 3N7
514-252-4141, Fax: 514-252-0372, 877-997-0919, rio@rio.gouv.qc.ca
Saskatchewan
Saskatchewan Parks, Culture & Sport, 3211 Albert St., 1st Fl., Regina, SK S4S 5W6
306-787-5729, Fax: 306-798-0033, 800-205-7070, info@tpcs.gov.sk.ca

STANDARDS

Standards Council of Canada, #600, 55 Metcalfe St., Ottawa, ON K1P 6L5
613-238-3222, Fax: 613-569-7808, info@scc.ca

STATISTICS

See Also: Vital Statistics
Statistics Canada, R.H. Coats Bldg., Tunney's Pasture, 150 Tunney's Pasture Driveway, Ottawa, ON K1A 0T6
514-283-8300, Fax: 514-283-9350, 800-263-1136, STATCAN.infostats-infostats.STATCAN@canada.ca
Manitoba
Manitoba Bureau of Statistics, #824, 155 Carlton St., Winnipeg, MB R3C 3H9
204-945-2406
Nunavut
Nunavut Territory Department of Executive & Intergovernmental Affairs, 1084 Aeroplex bldg., PO Box 1000 200, Iqaluit, NU X0A 0H0
867-975-6000, Fax: 867-975-6099
Prince Edward Island
Prince Edward Island Department of Health & Wellness, 105 Rochford St. North, 4th Fl., PO Box 2000, Charlottetown, PE C1A 7N8
902-368-6414, Fax: 902-368-4121
Québec
Institut de la statistique du Québec, 200, ch Ste-Foy, 1er étage, Québec, QC G1R 5T4
418-691-2401, Fax: 418-643-4129, 800-463-4090

STATISTICS (ENVIRONMENTAL)

Statistics Canada, R.H. Coats Bldg., Tunney's Pasture, 150 Tunney's Pasture Driveway, Ottawa, ON K1A 0T6
514-283-8300, Fax: 514-283-9350, 800-263-1136, STATCAN.infostats-infostats.STATCAN@canada.ca

STUDENT AID

Nunavut
Nunavut Territory Department of Education, Bldg. 1107, 2nd Fl., PO Box 1000 900, Iqaluit, NU X0A 0H0
867-975-5600, Fax: 867-975-5605, info.edu@gov.nu.ca
Ontario
Post-secondary Education Division, Mowat Block, 900 Bay St., 7th Fl., Toronto, ON M7A 1L2
416-325-2199, Fax: 416-326-3256
Saskatchewan
Saskatchewan Education, 2220 College Ave., Regina, SK S4P 4V9
linquiry@gov.sk.ca
Yukon Territory
Advanced Education, PO Box 2703, Whitehorse, YT Y1A 2C6
867-667-5131, Fax: 867-667-8555, contact.education@gov.yk.ca

SUSTAINABLE DEVELOPMENT

Commissioner of the Environment & Sustainable Development, 240 Sparks St., Ottawa, ON K1A 0G6
613-952-0213, Fax: 613-941-8286

Alberta

Alberta Energy, North Petroleum Plaza, 9945 - 108 St., Edmonton, AB T5K 2G6
780-427-8050, Fax: 780-422-9522, -310-0000

Manitoba

Manitoba Round Table for Sustainable Development, #160, 123 Main St., PO Box 70, Winnipeg, MB R3C 1A5
204-945-4391, Fax: 204-948-4730, mrtsd@gov.mb.ca

Newfoundland & Labrador

Newfoundland & Labrador Department of Environment & Conservation, Confederation Bldg., West Block, 4th Fl., PO Box 8700, St. John's, NL A1B 4J6
709-729-2664, Fax: 709-729-6639, 800-563-6181, envcinquires@gov.nl.ca

Québec

Ministère du Développement durable, de l'Environnement et de la Lutte contre les changements climatiques, Édifice Marie-Guyart, 675, boul René-Lévesque est, 29e étage, Québec, QC G1R 5V7
418-521-3830, Fax: 418-646-5974, 800-561-1616, info@mddefp.gouv.qc.ca

Yukon Territory

Yukon Energy, Mines & Resources, PO Box 2703, Whitehorse, YT Y1A 2C6
867-667-3130, Fax: 867-456-3965, 800-661-0408, emr@gov.yk.ca

TAXATION

See Also: Sales Tax

Canada Revenue Agency, 875 Heron Rd., Ottawa, ON K1A 1A2
800-267-6999

First Nations Tax Commission, #321, 345 Chief Alex Thomas Way, Kamloops, BC V2H 1H1
250-828-9857, Fax: 250-828-9858, 855-682-3682, mailkamloops@fntc.ca

Office of the Taxpayers' Ombudsman, #600, 150 Slater St., Ottawa, ON K1A 1K3
613-946-2310, Fax: 613-941-6319, 866-586-3839

Alberta

Financial Sector Regulation & Policy Division, Terrace Building, 9515 - 107 St., 4th Fl., Edmonton, AB T5K 2C3
780-427-8322

Manitoba

Taxation Division, #101, 401 York Ave., Winnipeg, MB R3C 0P8
204-945-5603, Fax: 204-945-0896, 800-782-0318

Nova Scotia

Provincial Tax Commission, Maritime Centre, 1505 Barrington St., 9th Fl., PO Box 1003, Halifax, NS B3J 2X1
902-424-6300, Fax: 902-424-7434, 800-565-2336, taxcommission@gov.ns.ca

Service Nova Scotia, c/o Public Enquiries - Service Nova Scotia, PO Box 2734, Halifax, NS B3J 3K5
902-424-5200, Fax: 902-424-0720, 800-670-4357

Saskatchewan

Board of Revenue Commissioners, #480, 2151 Scarth St., Regina, SK S4P 2H8
306-787-6221, Fax: 306-787-1610

Revenue Division, 2350 Albert St., 5th Fl., PO Box 200, Regina, SK S4P 2Z6
306-787-6645, Fax: 306-787-0776, 800-667-6102

TELECOMMUNICATIONS

See Also: Broadcasting

Canadian Broadcasting Corporation, 181 Queen St., PO Box 3220 C,Ottawa, ON K1Y 1E4
613-288-6000, liaison@cbc.ca

Canadian Radio-Television & Telecommunications Commission, Central Building, 1, Promenade du Portage, Les Terrasses de la Chaudière, Gatineau, QC J8X 4B1
819-997-0313, Fax: 819-994-0218, 877-249-2782

Communications Research Centre Canada, 3701 Carling Ave., PO Box 11490 H, Ottawa, ON K2H 8S2
613-991-3313, Fax: 613-998-5355, info@crc.gc.ca

Shared Services Canada, 434 Queen St., PO Box 9808 T CSC,Ottawa, ON K1G 4A8
613-947-6296, 855-215-3656, information@ssc-spc.gc.ca

Spectrum, Information Technologies & Telecommunications, Journal Tower North, 300 Slater St., 20th Fl., Ottawa, ON K1A 0C8
613-998-0368, Fax: 613-952-1203

Québec

Ministère de la Culture et Communications, 225, Grande Allée est, Québec, QC G1R 5G5
888-380-8882

Société de télédiffusion du Québec (Télé-Québec), 1000, rue Fullum, Montréal, QC H2K 3L7
514-521-2424, Fax: 514-864-1970, info@teleQuébec.tv

Saskatchewan

Saskatchewan Telecommunications (SaskTel), 2121 Saskatchewan Dr., Regina, SK S4P 3Y2
306-777-3737, 800-727-5835, corporate.comments@sasktel.sk.ca

TOURISM & TOURIST INFORMATION

Destination Canada, #800, 1045 Howe St., Vancouver, BC V6Z 2A9
604-638-8300

Old Port of Montréal Corporation Inc., 333, rue de la Commune ouest, Montréal, QC H2Y 2E2
514-283-5256, 800-971-7678

Parks Canada, National Office, 30 Victoria St., Gatineau, QC J8X 0B3
819-420-9486, 888-773-8888, information@pc.gc.ca

Alberta

Alberta Culture & Tourism, Communications Branch, Standard Life Centre, 10405 Jasper Ave., 7th Fl., Edmonton, AB T5J 4R7
780-427-6530, 800-232-7215, culture.communications@gov.ab.ca

Northern Alberta Development Council, Peace River Office, Provincial Building, #206, 9621 - 96 Ave., PO Box 900-14, Peace River, AB T8S 1T4
780-624-6274, Fax: 780-624-6184, -310-0000, nadc.council@gov.ab.ca

Travel Alberta, #400, 1601 - 9 Ave. SE, Calgary, AB T2G 0H4
403-648-1000, Fax: 403-648-1111, 800-252-3782, info@travelalberta.com

British Columbia

British Columbia Ministry of Jobs, Tourism, & Skills Training (& Responsible for Labour), PO Box 9846 Prov Govt, Victoria, BC V8W 9T2
EnquiryBC@gov.bc.ca

British Columbia Pavilion Corporation, #200, 999 Canada Place, Vancouver, BC V6C 3C1
604-482-2200, Fax: 604-681-9017, info@bcpavco.com

Tourism British Columbia, #300, 1803 Douglas St., Victoria, BC V8W 9W5
604-660-2861, Fax: 604-660-3383, ContactTourism@DestinationBC.ca

Manitoba

Tourism Secretariat, 213 Notre Dame Ave., 6th Fl., Winnipeg, MB R3B 1N3
204-945-0216

Travel Manitoba, 21 Forks Market Rd., Winnipeg, MB R3C RT7
204-927-7838, 800-665-0040, contactus@travelmanitoba.com

New Brunswick

New Brunswick Department of Tourism, Heritage & Culture, Centennial Building, PO Box 6000, Fredericton, NB E3B 5H1
506-453-3115, Fax: 506-457-4984, thctpcinfo@gnb.ca

Newfoundland & Labrador

Newfoundland & Labrador Department of Business, Tourism, Culture & Rural Development, Confederation Bldg., West Block, 2nd Fl., PO Box 8700, St. John's, NL A1B 4J6
709-729-7000, btcrd@gov.nl.ca

Northwest Territories

Northwest Territories Department of Industry, Tourism & Investment, PO Box 1320, Yellowknife, NT X1A 2L9
867-767-9002

Nova Scotia

Tourism Nova Scotia, 8 Water St., PO Box 667, Windsor, NS B0N 2T0
902-798-6700, Fax: 902-798-6610, 800-565-0000, TNS@gov.ns.ca

Ontario

Huronia Historical Parks, 16164 Hwy. 12, PO Box 160, Midland, ON L4R 4K8
705-526-7838, Fax: 705-526-9193

Ontario Ministry of Tourism, Culture & Sport, Hearst Block, 900 Bay St., 9th Fl., Toronto, ON M7A 2E1
416-326-9326, Fax: 416-314-7854, 888-997-9015

Ontario Tourism Marketing Partnership Corporation, #900, 10 Dundas St. East, Toronto, ON M7A 2A1
416-212-0757, Fax: 416-325-6004, 800-668-2746

Tourism Policy & Development Division, Hearst Block, 900 Bay St., 10th Fl., Toronto, ON M7A 2E1
416-326-9326, Fax: 416-325-6985

Prince Edward Island

Eastlink Centre Charlottetown, 46 Kensington Rd., Charlottetown, PE C1A 5H7
902-629-6600, Fax: 902-629-6650

Prince Edward Island Department of Economic Development & Tourism, PO Box 2000, Charlottetown, PE C1A 7N8
902-368-5540, Fax: 902-368-5277, tpswitch@gov.pe.ca

Québec

Commission de la capitale nationale du Québec, Edifice Hector-Fabre, 525 boul René-Lévesque Est, RC, Québec, QC G1R 5S9
418-528-0773, Fax: 418-528-0833, 800-442-0773, commission@capitale.gouv.qc.ca

Ministère du Tourisme, #400, 900, boul René-Lévesque est, Québec, QC G1R 2B5
418-643-5959, Fax: 418-646-8723, 800-482-2433

Régie des installations olympiques/Parc olympique Québec, 4141, av Pierre-De Coubertin, Montréal, QC H1V 3N7
514-252-4141, Fax: 514-252-0372, 877-997-0919, rio@rio.gouv.qc.ca

Secrétariat à la Capitale-Nationale, 700, boul René-Lévesque est, 31e étage, Québec, QC G1R 5H1
418-528-8549, Fax: 418-528-8558

Société des établissements en plein air du Québec, Place de la Cité, Tour Cominar, #250, 2640, boul Laurier, 2e étage, Québec, QC G1V 5C2
418-686-4875, Fax: 418-643-8177, 800-665-6527, inforeservation@sepaq.com

Société du Centre des congrès de Québec, 900, boul René-Lévesque est, 2e étage, Québec, QC G1R 2B5
418-644-4000, Fax: 418-644-6455, 888-679-4000

Société du Palais des congrès de Montréal, 159, rue Saint-Antoine ouest, 9é étage, Montréal, QC H2Z 1H2
514-871-8122, Fax: 514-871-9389, 800-268-8122, info@congresmtl.com

Saskatchewan

Tourism Saskatchewan, #189, 1621 Albert St., Regina, SK S4P 2S5
306-787-9600, Fax: 306-787-2866, 877-237-2273, travel.info@sasktourism.com

Yukon Territory

Yukon Tourism & Culture, 100 Hanson St., PO Box 2703, Whitehorse, YT Y1A 2C6
867-667-5036, Fax: 867-667-3546

TRADE

See Also: Business Development; Imports

Business Development Bank of Canada, #400, 5, Place Ville-Marie, Montréal, QC H3B 5E7
877-232-2269

Canadian Commercial Corporation, #700, 350 Albert St., Ottawa, ON K1A 0S6
613-996-0034, Fax: 613-995-2121, 800-748-8191, communications@ccc.ca

Canadian International Trade Tribunal, Standard Life Centre, 333 Laurier Ave. West, 15th Floor, Ottawa, ON K1A 0G7
613-990-2452, Fax: 613-990-2439, 855-307-2488, citt-tcce@tribunal.gc.ca

Canadian Trade Commissioner Service, c/o Foreign Affairs & International Trade, 125 Sussex Dr., Ottawa, ON K1A 0G2
613-944-9991, Fax: 613-996-9709, 888-306-9991, enqserv@international.gc.ca

Commission for Environmental Cooperation, Secretariat, #200, 393, rue St-Jacques ouest, Montréal, QC H2Y 1N9
514-350-4300, Fax: 514-350-4314, info@cec.org

Export Development Canada, 150 Slater St., Ottawa, ON K1A 1K3
613-598-2500, Fax: 613-598-3811, 800-267-8510

Market & Industry Services Branch, Tower 5, 1341 Baseline Rd., Ottawa, ON K1A 0C5
613-759-1000, Fax: 613-773-1711

North American Free Trade Agreement (NAFTA) Secretariat, Canadian Section, 111 Sussex Dr., 5th Fl., Ottawa, ON K1N 1J1
343-203-4274, Fax: 613-992-9392, webmaster@nafta-alena.gc.ca

Alberta

Alberta Economic Development & Trade, Commerce Place, 10155 - 102 St., 12th Fl., Edmonton, AB T5J 4G8

British Columbia

British Columbia Ministry of Social Development & Social Innovation, PO Box 9058 Prov Govt, Victoria, BC V8W 9E1
800-663-7867, EnquiryBC@gov.bc.ca

Economic Development Division, PO Box 9846 Prov Gov,Victoria, BC V8W 9T2

Labour Market & Immigration Division, PO Box 9189 Prov Govt, Vancouver, BC V8W 9E6
250-953-3585, Fax: 250-387-6152

Manitoba

Manitoba Growth, Enterprise & Trade, The Paris Building, 259 Portage Ave., 9th Fl., Winnipeg, MB R3B 3P4
204-945-1995, Fax: 204-945-2964

Nova Scotia

Nova Scotia Department of Business, Centennial Building, #600, 1660 Hollis St., PO Box 2311, Halifax, NS B3J 3C8
902-424-0377, Fax: 902-424-0500, business@novascotia.ca

Nova Scotia Department of Intergovernmental Affairs, Duke Tower, 5251 Duke St., 5th Fl., PO Box 1617, Halifax, NS B3J 2Y3
902-424-5153, Fax: 902-424-0728

Ontario

Ontario Ministry of International Trade, College Park, #1836, 777 Bay St., Toronto, ON M5G 2E5

Québec

Ministère des Finances, 12, rue Saint-Louis, Québec, QC G1R 5L3
418-528-9323, Fax: 418-646-1631, info@finances.gouv.qc.ca

Ministère des Relations internationales et Francophonie, Édifice Hector-Fabre, 525, boul Réne-Lévesque est, Québec, QC G1R 5R9
418-649-2300, Fax: 418-649-2656

Yukon Territory

Yukon Economic Development, #209, 212 Main St., F-1, Whitehorse, YT Y1A 2A9
867-393-7191, Fax: 867-393-6412, 800-661-0408, ecdev@gov.yk.ca

TRADE-MARKS

See: Patents & Copyright

Canadian Intellectual Property Office, Place du Portage I, #C-229, 50 Victoria St., Gatineau, QC K1A 0C9
819-997-1936, Fax: 819-953-2476, 866-997-1936, cipo.contact@ic.gc.ca

Prince Edward Island

Anne of Green Gables Licensing Authority Inc., 94 Euston St., PO Box 910, Charlottetown, PE C1A 7L9
902-368-5961

TRAINING

See: Apprenticeship Programs; Occupational Training

Alberta

Alberta Advanced Education, Legislature Bldg., #403, 10800 - 97 Ave., Edmonton, AB T5K 2B6
780-422-5400, -310-0000

TRANSPORTATION

Atlantic Pilotage Authority, Cogswell Tower, #910, 2000 Barrington St., Halifax, NS B3J 3K1
902-426-2550, Fax: 902-426-4004, 877-272-3477, dispatch@atlanticpilotage.com

Automotive & Surface Transportation Facilities, Ottawa Uplands Research Facilities, 2320 Lester Rd., Ottawa, ON K1V 1S2
613-998-9639

Canadian Air Transport Security Authority, 99 Bank St., 13th Fl., Ottawa, ON K1P 6B9
Fax: 613-990-1295, 888-294-2202

Canadian Coast Guard, Centennial Towers, #6S018, 200 Kent St., Ottawa, ON K1A 0E6
613-993-0999, Fax: 613-990-1866, info@dfo-mpo.gc.ca

Canadian Transportation Agency, Les Terrasses de la Chaudière, 15 Eddy St., Gatineau, QC J8X 4B3
Fax: 819-997-6727, 888-222-2592, info@otc-cta.gc.ca

Federal Bridge Corporation Limited, #1210, 55 Metcalfe St., Ottawa, ON K1P 6L5
613-998-8427, Fax: 613-993-6945, info@federalbridge.ca

Great Lakes Pilotage Authority, 202 Pitt St., 2nd fl., PO Box 95, Cornwall, ON K6H 5R9
613-933-2991, Fax: 613-932-3793

Laurentian Pilotage Authority, Head Office, #1401, 999, boul Maisonneuve ouest, Montréal, QC H3A 3L4
514-283-6320, Fax: 514-496-2409, administration@apl.gc.ca

Marine Atlantic Inc., Corporate Office, Baine Johnston Centre, #302, 10 Fort William Pl., St. John's, NL A1C 1K4
800-897-2797, customer_relations@marine-atlantic.ca

Old Port of Montréal Corporation Inc., 333, rue de la Commune ouest, Montréal, QC H2Y 2E2
514-283-5256, 800-971-7678

Pacific Pilotage Authority Canada, #1000, 1130 West Pender St., Vancouver, BC V6E 4A4
604-666-6771, Fax: 604-666-1647, info@ppa.gc.ca

St. Lawrence Seaway Management Corporation, 202 Pitt St., Cornwall, ON K6J 3P7
613-932-5170, Fax: 613-932-7286, marketing@seaway.ca

Transport Canada, Place de Ville, 330 Sparks St., Tower C, Ottawa, ON K1A 0N5
613-990-2309, Fax: 613-954-4731, 866-995-9737

Transportation Appeal Tribunal of Canada, #1201, 333 Laurier Ave. West, 12th Fl., Ottawa, ON K1A 0N5
613-990-6906, Fax: 613-990-9153, info@tatc.gc.ca

Transportation Safety Board of Canada, 200, Promenade du Portage, 4th Fl., Gatineau, QC K1A 1K8
819-994-3741, Fax: 819-997-2239, 800-387-3557, communications@bst-tsb.gc.ca

VIA Rail Canada Inc., CP 8116 A,Montréal, QC H3C 3N3
514-871-6000, Fax: 514-871-6104, 888-842-7245, customer_relations@viarail.ca

Alberta

Alberta Automobile Insurance Rate Board, Canadian Western Bank Place, #2440, 10303 Jasper Ave., Edmonton, AB T5J 3N6
780-427-5428, Fax: 780-638-4254, -310-0000, airb@gov.ab.ca

Alberta Infrastructure, Infrastructure Building, 6950 - 113 St., Edmonton, AB T6H 5V7
780-415-0507, Fax: 780-427-2187, -310-0000, Infra.Contact.Us.m@gov.ab.ca

Alberta Transportation, Communications Branch, Twin Atria Building, 4999 - 98 Jasper Ave., 2nd Fl., Edmonton, AB T6B 2X3
780-427-2731, Fax: 780-466-3166, -310-0000, Trans.Contact.Us.m@gov.ab.ca

Corporate Strategies & Services Division, Infrastructure Bldg., 6950 - 113 St., 2nd Fl., Edmonton, AB T6H 5V7

Safety, Policy & Engineering Division, Twin Atria Building, 4999 - 98 Ave., Main Fl., Edmonton, AB T6B 2X3
780-427-8901, Fax: 780-415-0782, 800-666-5036

Transportation Safety Board, North Office, Twin Atria Building, 4999 - 98 Ave., Main Fl., Edmonton, AB T6B 2X3
780-427-7178, Fax: 780-422-9739, -310-0000

British Columbia

British Columbia Ferry Commission, PO Box 9279 Prov Govt, Victoria, BC V8W 9J7
250-952-0112, info@bcferrycommission.com

British Columbia Ferry Services Inc., c/o BC Ferry Authority, #500, 1321 Blanshard St., Victoria, BC V8W 0B7
250-381-1401, 888-223-3779, customerservice@bcferries.com

British Columbia Ministry of Transportation & Infrastructure, PO Box 9850 Prov Govt, Victoria, BC V8W 9T5
250-387-3198, Fax: 250-356-7706, tran.webmaster@gov.bc.ca

British Columbia Transit, 520 Gorge Rd. East, Victoria, BC V8W 2P3
250-385-2551

Passenger Transportation Board, #202, 940 Blanshard St., PO Box 9850 Prov Govt, Victoria, BC V8W 9T5
250-953-3777, Fax: 250-953-3788, ptboard@gov.bc.ca

Transportation Policy & Programs Department, PO Box 9850 Prov Govt, Victoria, BC V8W 9T5
250-387-5062, Fax: 250-387-6431

Manitoba

Highway Traffic Board/Motor Transport Board, #200, 301 Weston St., Winnipeg, MB R3E 3H4
204-945-8912, Fax: 204-783-6529

License Suspension Appeal Board/Medical Review Committee, #200, 301 Weston St., Winnipeg, MB R3E 3H4
204-945-7350, Fax: 204-948-2682

Manitoba Infrastructure, Legislative Building, #203, 450 Broadway Ave., Winnipeg, MB R3C 0V8
204-945-3723, Fax: 204-945-7610

Taxicab Board, #200, 301 Weston St., Winnipeg, MB R3E 3H4
204-945-8919, Fax: 204-948-2315, taxicabboardoffice@gov.mb.ca

New Brunswick

New Brunswick Department of Transportation & Infrastructure, Kings Place, PO Box 6000, Fredericton, NB E3B 5H1
506-453-3939, Fax: 506-453-7987, Transportation.Web@gnb.ca

Vehicle Management Agency, Vehicle Management Centre, PO Box 6000, Fredericton, NB E3B 5H1
506-453-3939, Fax: 506-453-3628, Transportation.Web@gnb.ca

Newfoundland & Labrador

Newfoundland & Labrador Department of Transportation & Works, Confederation Bldg., Prince Philip Dr., PO Box 8700, St. John's, NL A1B 4J6
709-729-2300, tw@gov.nl.ca

Northwest Territories

Northwest Territories Department of Transportation, New Government Bldg., 5015 - 49 St., 4th Fl., PO Box 1320, Yellowknife, NT X1A 2L9
867-767-9089, Fax: 867-873-0606

Nova Scotia

Nova Scotia Department of Transportation & Infrastructure Renewal, Johnston Bldg., 1672 Granville St., 2nd Fl., PO Box 186, Halifax, NS B3J 2N2
902-424-2297, Fax: 902-424-0532, 888-432-3233, tpwpaff@novascotia.ca

Nunavut

Nunavut Territory Department of Community & Government Services, W.G. Brown Bldg., 4th Fl., PO Box 1000 700, Iqaluit, NU X0A 0H0
867-975-5400, Fax: 867-975-5305

Nunavut Territory Department of Economic Development & Transportation, Inuksugait Plaza, Bldg. 1104A, PO Box 1000 1500, Iqaluit, NU X0A 0H0
867-975-7800, Fax: 867-975-7870, 888-975-5999, edt@gov.nu.ca

Ontario

Licence Appeal Tribunal, #530, 20 Dundas St. West, Toronto, ON M5G 2C2
416-314-4260, Fax: 416-314-4270, 800-255-2214

Metrolinx, 97 Front St. West, Toronto, ON M5J 1E6
416-874-5900, Fax: 416-869-1755

Ontario Highway Transport Board, 151 Bloor St. West, 10th Fl., Toronto, ON M5S 2T5
416-326-6732, Fax: 416-326-6738, ohtb@mto.gov.on.ca

Ontario Ministry of Infrastructure, Hearst Block, 900 Bay St., 8th Fl., Toronto, ON M7A 2E1
416-325-6666, 800-268-7095

Ontario Ministry of Transportation, Ferguson Block, 77 Wellesley St. West, 3rd Fl., Toronto, ON M7A 1Z8
416-327-9200, Fax: 416-327-9185, 800-268-4686

Ontario Northland Transportation Commission, 555 Oak St. East, North Bay, ON P1B 8L3
705-472-4500, Fax: 705-476-5598, 800-363-7512, info@ontarionorthland.ca

Owen Sound Transportation Company Ltd., 717875, Hwy. 6, Owen Sound, ON N4K 5N7
519-376-8740, 800-265-3163

Road User Safety Division, Bldg A, #191, 1201 Wilson Ave., Downsview, ON M3M 1J8
416-235-2999, Fax: 416-235-4153

Prince Edward Island

Prince Edward Island Department of Transportation, Infrastructure & Energy, Jones Bldg., 11 Kent St., 3rd Fl., PO Box 2000, Charlottetown, PE C1A 7N8
902-368-5100, Fax: 902-368-5395

Québec

Agence métropolitaine de transport, 700, rue de la Gauchetière ouest, 26e étage, Montréal, QC H3B 5M2
514-287-2464

Commission des transports du Québec, 200, ch Sainte-Foy, 7e étage, Québec, QC G1R 5V5
514-873-6424, Fax: 418-644-8034, 888-461-2433, courier@ctq.gouv.qc.ca

Ministère des Transports, de la Mobilité durable et de l'Électrification des transports, 700, boul René-Lévesque est, 29e étage, Québec, QC G1R 5H1
418-643-6980, Fax: 418-643-2033, 888-355-0511, communications@mtq.gouv.qc.ca

Société de l'assurance automobile du Québec, 333, boul Jean-Lesage, CP 19600 Terminus, Québec, QC G1K 8J6
418-643-7620, Fax: 418-644-0339, 800-361-7620

Société des traversiers du Québec, 250, rue Saint-Paul, Québec, QC G1K 9K9
418-643-2019, Fax: 418-643-7308, 877-787-7483, stq@traversiers.gouv.qc.ca

Société du parc industriel et portuaire de Bécancour, 1000, boul Arthur-Sicard, Bécancour, QC G9H 2Z8
819-294-6656, Fax: 819-294-9020, spipb@spipb.com

Société du port ferroviaire Baie-Comeau-Haute-Rive, 18, rte Maritime, Baie-Comeau, QC G4Z 2L6
418-296-6785, Fax: 418-296-2377, societeduport@globetrotter.net

Saskatchewan

Global Transportation Hub Authority, #350, 1777 Victoria Ave., Regina, SK S4P 4K5
306-787-4842, Fax: 306-798-4600

Highway Traffic Board, 1621A mcDonald St., Regina, SK S4N 5R2
306-775-8336, Fax: 306-775-6618, contactus@highwaytrafficboard.sk.ca

Saskatchewan Highways & Infrastructure, Victoria Tower, 1855 Victoria Ave., Regina, SK S4P 3T2
306-787-4800, communications@highways.gov.sk.ca

Saskatchewan Transportation Company, 1717 Saskatchewan Dr., Regina, SK S4P 2E2
306-787-3347, Fax: 306-787-1633, info@stcbus.com

Yukon Territory

Driver Control Board, #102, 211 Hawkins St., PO Box 2703, Whitehorse, YT Y1A 2C6
867-667-5623, Fax: 867-667-5799, dcb@gov.yk.ca

Yukon Community Services, PO Box 2703, Whitehorse, YT Y1A 2C6
867-667-5811, Fax: 867-393-6295, 800-661-0408, inquiry@gov.yk.ca

Yukon Highways & Public Works, PO Box 2703, Whitehorse, YT Y1A 2C6
867-393-7193, Fax: 867-393-6218, 800-661-0408, hpw-info@gov.yk.ca

TRANSPORTATION OF DANGEROUS GOODS

Nova Scotia
Nova Scotia Department of Transportation & Infrastructure Renewal, Johnston Bldg., 1672 Granville St., 2nd Fl., PO Box 186, Halifax, NS B3J 2N2
902-424-2297, Fax: 902-424-0532, 888-432-3233, tpwpaff@novascotia.ca

Ontario
Road User Safety Division, Bldg A, #191, 1201 Wilson Ave., Downsview, ON M3M 1J8
416-235-2999, Fax: 416-235-4153

Prince Edward Island
Prince Edward Island Department of Transportation, Infrastructure & Energy, Jones Bldg., 11 Kent St., 3rd Fl., PO Box 2000, Charlottetown, PE C1A 7N8
902-368-5100, Fax: 902-368-5395

Saskatchewan
Saskatchewan Highways & Infrastructure, Victoria Tower, 1855 Victoria Ave., Regina, SK S4P 3T2
306-787-4800, communications@highways.gov.sk.ca

TRAPPING & FUR INDUSTRY

Ontario
Ontario Moose & Bear Allocation Advisory Committee, PO Box 964, Sioux Lookout, ON P8T 1B3
807-737-2615, Fax: 807-737-4173

Québec
Comité conjoint de chasse, de pêche et de piégeage, #C220, 383 rue Saint-Jacques, Montréal, QC H2Y 1N9
514-284-2151, Fax: 514-284-0039, cccppinfo@cccpp-hftcc.com

Office de la sécurité du revenu des chasseurs et piègeurs cris, Édifice Champlain, #1100, 2700, boul Laurier, Québec, QC G1V 4K5
418-643-7300, Fax: 418-643-6803, 800-363-1560, courrier@osrcpc.ca

Saskatchewan
Saskatchewan Environment, 3211 Albert St., 2nd Fl., Regina, SK S4S 5W6
306-787-2584, Fax: 306-787-9544, 800-567-4224, Centre.Inquiry@gov.sk.ca

TREASURY SERVICES

See Also: Finance

Treasury Board of Canada Secretariat, East Tower, 140 O'Connor St., 9th Fl., Ottawa, ON K1A 0R5
613-957-2400, Fax: 613-941-4000, 877-636-0656

Alberta
Alberta Treasury Board & Finance, Oxbridge Place, 9820 - 106 St., 9th Fl., Edmonton, AB T5K 1E7
780-427-3035, Fax: 780-427-1147, -310-0000

Treasury & Risk Management Division, Federal Bldg., 9820 - 107 St., 8th Fl., Edmonton, AB T5K 1E7

British Columbia
Provincial Treasury, PO Box 9414 Prov Govt, Victoria, BC V8V 9V1
250-387-4541, Fax: 250-356-3041

Manitoba
Treasury Board Secretariat, #200, 386 Broadway, Winnipeg, MB R3C 3R6
204-945-4150, Fax: 204-948-4878

Treasury Division, #350, 363 Broadway, Winnipeg, MB R3C 3N9
204-945-3702, Fax: 204-948-2233

Nova Scotia
Nova Scotia Department of Finance & Treasury Board, Provincial Bldg., 1723 Hollis St., 7th Fl., PO Box 187, Halifax, NS B3J 2N3
902-424-5554, Fax: 902-424-0635, FinanceWeb@novascotia.ca

Nunavut
Nunavut Territory Department of Finance, Bldg. 1079, 1st Fl., PO Box 1000 430, Iqaluit, NU X0A 0H0
867-975-5800, Fax: 867-975-5805

Ontario
Treasury Board Secretariat, Ferguson Block, 77 Wellesley St. West, 8th Fl., Toronto, ON M7A 1N3
416-326-8525, Fax: 416-327-3790, 800-268-1142

Prince Edward Island
Treasury Board, Shaw Bldg., 95 Rochford St. South, 3rd Fl., PO Box 2000, Charlottetown, PE C1A 7N8

Québec
Secrétariat du Conseil du trésor, 875, Grande Allée est, 5e étage, secteur 500, Québec, QC G1R 5R8
418-643-1529, Fax: 418-643-9226, 866-552-5158, communication@sct.gouv.qc.ca

URBAN RENEWAL & DESIGN

See Also: Municipal Affairs

Newfoundland & Labrador
Newfoundland & Labrador Housing Corporation, Sir Brian Dunfield Bldg., 2 Canada Dr., PO Box 220, St. John's, NL A1C 5J2
709-724-3000, Fax: 709-724-3250

Northwest Territories
Northwest Territories Department of Municipal & Community Affairs, PO Box 1320, Yellowknife, NT X1A 2L9
867-767-9160, Fax: 867-873-0309

Ontario
Ontario Ministry of Municipal Affairs, College Park, 777 Bay St., 17th Fl., Toronto, ON M5G 2E5
416-585-7000, Fax: 416-585-6470, mininfo@ontario.ca

Prince Edward Island
SkillsPEI, Atlantic Technology Centre, #212, 176 Great George St., Charlottetown, PE C1A 4K9
902-368-6290, Fax: 902-368-6340, 877-491-4766

Québec
Société d'habitation du Québec, Aile St-Amable, 1054, rue Louis-Alexandre-Taschereau, 3e étage, Québec, QC G1R 5E7
Fax: 418-643-2533, 800-463-4315

VETERANS AFFAIRS

Veterans Affairs Canada, 161 Grafton St., PO Box 7700, Charlottetown, PE C1A 8M9
866-522-2122, information@vac-acc.gc.ca

VICE-REGAL REPRESENTATIVES

Canadian Secretary to The Queen, 427 Laurier St., Ottawa, ON K1A 0M5

Governor General & Commander-in-Chief of Canada, Rideau Hall, 1 Sussex Dr., Ottawa, ON K1A 0A1
613-993-8200, Fax: 613-998-8760, 800-465-6890

Alberta
Office of the Lieutenant Governor, Office of the Lieutenant Governor of AB, Legislature Bldg., 10800 - 97 Ave., 3rd Fl., Edmonton, AB T5K 2B6
780-427-7243, Fax: 780-422-5134, ltgov@gov.ab.ca

British Columbia
Office of the Lieutenant Governor, Government House, 1401 Rockland Ave., Victoria, BC V8S 1V9
250-387-2080, Fax: 250-387-2078, ghinfo@gov.bc.ca

Manitoba
Office of the Lieutenant Governor, Legislative Building, #235, 450 Broadway Ave., Winnipeg, MB R3C 0V8
204-945-2753, Fax: 204-945-4329, ltgov@leg.gov.mb.ca

New Brunswick
Office of the Lieutenant-Governor, Government House, PO Box 6000, Fredericton, NB E3B 5H1
506-453-2505, Fax: 506-444-5280, LTgov@gnb.ca

Newfoundland & Labrador
Office of the Lieutenant Governor, Government House, 50 Military Rd., PO Box 5517, St. John's, NL A1C 5W4
709-729-4494, Fax: 709-729-2234, governmenthouse@gov.nl.ca

Northwest Territories
Office of the Commissioner, 803 Northwest Tower, PO Box 1320, Yellowknife, NT X1A 2L9
867-873-7400, Fax: 867-873-0223, 888-270-3318, commissioner@gov.nt.ca

Nova Scotia
Office of the Lieutenant Governor, Government House, 1451 Barrington St., Halifax, NS B3J 1Z2
902-424-7001, Fax: 902-424-1790, lgoffice@novascotia.ca

Nunavut
Office of the Commissioner, PO Box 2379, Iqaluit, NU X0A 0H0
867-975-5120, Fax: 867-975-5123, commissionerofnunavut@gov.nu.ca

Ontario
Office of the Lieutenant Governor, Legislative Bldg., Queen's Park, Toronto, ON M7A 1A1
416-325-7780, Fax: 416-325-7787, lt.gov@ontario.ca

Prince Edward Island
Office of the Lieutenant Governor, Government House, PO Box 846, Charlottetown, PE C1A 7L9
902-368-5480, Fax: 902-368-5481

Québec
Cabinet du Lieutenant-gouverneur, Édifice André-Laurendeau, 1050, rue des Parlementaires R.C., Québec, QC G1A 1A1
418-643-5385, Fax: 418-644-4677, 866-791-0766

Saskatchewan
Office of the Lieutenant Governor, Government House, 4607 Dewdney Ave., Regina, SK S4T 1B7
306-787-4070, Fax: 306-787-7716, lgo@ltgov.sk.ca

Yukon Territory
Office of the Commissioner of Yukon, Taylor House, 412 Main St., Whitehorse, YT Y1A 2B7
867-667-5121, Fax: 867-393-6201, commissioner@gov.yk.ca

VIOLENCE

See Also: Policing Services

New Brunswick
New Brunswick Department of Social Development, Sartain MacDonald Bldg., 551 King St., PO Box 6000, Fredericton, NB E3B 5H1
506-453-2001, Fax: 506-453-2164, sd-ds@gnb.ca

Nova Scotia
Nova Scotia Department of Community Services, Nelson Place, 5675 Spring Garden Rd., 8th Fl., PO Box 696, Halifax, NS B3J 2T7
877-424-1177

Nunavut
Nunavut Territory Department of Family Services, PO Box 1000 950, Iqaluit, NU X0A 0H0
867-975-6038, Fax: 867-975-6091

VITAL STATISTICS

Alberta
Open Government, Telus House at ATB Place, 10020 - 100 St., 29th Fl., Edmonton, AB T5J 0N3

British Columbia
British Columbia Vital Statistics Agency, PO Box 9657 Prov Govt, Victoria, BC V8W 9P3
250-952-2681, Fax: 250-952-9097, VSOFFCEO@gov.bc.ca

Nova Scotia
Service Nova Scotia, c/o Public Enquiries - Service Nova Scotia, PO Box 2734, Halifax, NS B3J 3K5
902-424-5200, Fax: 902-424-0720, 800-670-4357

Vital Statistics, 300 Horseshoe Lake Dr., PO Box 157, Halifax, NS B3J 2M9
902-424-4381, Fax: 902-450-7311, 877-848-2578, vstat@gov.ns.ca

Prince Edward Island
Prince Edward Island Department of Health & Wellness, 105 Rochford St. North, 4th Fl., PO Box 2000, Charlottetown, PE C1A 7N8
902-368-6414, Fax: 902-368-4121

Québec
Directeur de l'état civil, 2535, boul Laurier, Québec, QC G1V 5C5
418-644-4545, 877-644-4545, etatcivil@dec.gouv.qc.ca

Saskatchewan
eHealth Saskatchewan, 2130 - 11th Ave., Regina, SK S4P 0J5
306-337-0600, 855-347-5465

WASTE & GARBAGE

Atomic Energy of Canada Limited, Head Office, Chalk River Laboratories, 286 Plant Rd., Chalk River, ON K0J 1J0
888-220-2465, communications@aecl.ca

Canadian Nuclear Laboratories, Head Office, Chalk River Laboratories, 286 Plant Rd., Chalk River, ON K0J 1J0
866-513-2325, communications@cnl.ca

Low-Level Radioactive Waste Management Office, 196 Toronto St., Port Hope, ON L1A 3V5
905-885-9488, Fax: 905-885-0273, 866-255-2755, info@llrwmo.org

Newfoundland & Labrador
Newfoundland & Labrador Department of Municipal & Intergovernmental Affairs, West Block, Main Fl., Confederation Bldg., PO Box 8700, St. John's, NL A1B 4J6
709-729-3046, Fax: 709-729-0943, mainfo@gov.nl.ca

Newfoundland & Labrador Department of Service NL, PO Box 8700, St. John's, NL A1B 4J6
709-729-4834, servicenlinfo@gov.nl.ca

Nova Scotia
Resource Recovery Fund Board Inc., #400, 35 Commercial St., Truro, NS B2N 3H9
902-895-7732, Fax: 902-897-3256, 877-313-7732, info@rrfb.com

Ontario
Ontario Ministry of Environment & Climate Change, Public Information Centre, Macdonald Block, 900 Bay St., 2nd Fl., Toronto, ON M7A 1N3
416-325-4000, Fax: 416-314-6713, 800-565-4923

Québec
Bureau d'audiences publiques sur l'environnement, Édifice Lomer-Gouin, #2.10, 575, rue Saint-Amable, Québec, QC G1R 6A6
418-643-7447, Fax: 418-643-9474, 800-463-4732, communication@bape.gouv.qc.ca

Société québécoise de récupération et de recyclage, #411, 300, rue Saint-Paul, Québec, QC G1K 7R1
418-643-0394, Fax: 418-643-6507, 866-523-8290, info@recyc-Québec.gouv.qc.ca

WASTE MANAGEMENT

See Also: Dangerous Goods & Hazardous Materials

Atomic Energy of Canada Limited, Head Office, Chalk River Laboratories, 286 Plant Rd., Chalk River, ON K0J 1J0
888-220-2465, communications@aecl.ca

Canadian Nuclear Laboratories, Head Office, Chalk River Laboratories, 286 Plant Rd., Chalk River, ON K0J 1J0
866-513-2325, communications@cnl.ca

Nuclear Legacy Liabilities Program, c/o AECL, Corporate Communications, #B700A, Chalk River Laboratories, Chalk River, ON K0J 1J0
613-584-8206, 800-364-6989, info@nuclearlegacyprogram.ca

Waste Biotreatability Facility, c/o Montréal (av Royalmount) Research Facilities, 6100, av Royalmount, Montréal, QC H4P 2R2

Alberta

Alberta Environment & Parks, Information Centre, Great West Life Bldg., 9920 - 108 St., Main Fl., Edmonton, AB T5K 2M4
780-427-2700, Fax: 780-427-4407, -310-3773, ESRD.Info-Centre@gov.ab.ca

Alberta Recycling Management Authority, Scotia Tower 1, #1800, 10060 Jasper Ave., PO Box 189, Edmonton, AB T5J 2J1
780-990-1111, Fax: 780-990-1122, 888-999-8762, info@albertarecycling.ca

Alberta Used Oil Management Association, Empire Building, #1008, 10080 Jasper Ave., Edmonton, AB T5J 1V9
780-414-1510, Fax: 780-414-1519, 866-414-1510, auoma@usedoilrecycling.ca

Beverage Container Management Board, #100, 8616 - 51 Ave., Edmonton, AB T6E 6E6
780-424-3193, Fax: 780-428-4620, 888-424-7671, info@bcmb.ab.ca

Newfoundland & Labrador

Multi-Materials Stewardship Board, PO Box 8131 A, St. John's, NL A1B 3M9
709-753-0948, Fax: 709-753-0974, 800-901-6672, inquiries@mmsb.nl.ca

Northwest Territories

Northwest Territories Department of Municipal & Community Affairs, PO Box 1320, Yellowknife, NT X1A 2L9
867-767-9160, Fax: 867-873-0309

Ontario

Integrated Environmental Policy Division, 77 Wellesley St. West, 11th Fl., Toronto, ON M7A 2T5
416-314-6338, Fax: 416-314-6346

Prince Edward Island

Island Waste Management Corporation, 110 Watts Ave., Charlottetown, PE C1E 2C1
902-894-0330, Fax: 902-894-0331, 888-280-8111, info@iwmc.pe.ca

Québec

Société québécoise de récupération et de recyclage, #411, 300, rue Saint-Paul, Québec, QC G1K 7R1
418-643-0394, Fax: 418-643-6507, 866-523-8290, info@recyc-Québec.gouv.qc.ca

Saskatchewan

Saskatchewan Environment, 3211 Albert St., 2nd Fl., Regina, SK S4S 5W6
306-787-2584, Fax: 306-787-9544, 800-567-4224, Centre.Inquiry@gov.sk.ca

Yukon Territory

Yukon Environment, 10 Burns Rd., PO Box 2703 V-3A, Whitehorse, YT Y1A 2C6
867-667-5652, Fax: 867-393-7197, environment.yukon@gov.yk.ca

WATER & WASTEWATER

Bedford Institute of Oceanography, 1 Challenger Dr., PO Box 1006, Dartmouth, NS B2Y 4A2
Fax: 902-426-8484, WebmasterBIO-IOB@dfo-mpo.gc.ca

Canadian Hydrographic Services & Oceanographic Services, 615 Booth St., Ottawa, ON K1A 0E6
chsinfo@dfo-mpo.gc.ca

Civil Infrastructure & Related Structures Testing Facilities, c/o National Research Council, 1200 Montreal Rd., Ottawa, ON K1A 0R6
613-993-9101

Environment & Climate Change Canada, 10 Wellington St., Gatineau, QC K1A 0H3
819-997-2800, Fax: 819-994-1412, 800-668-6767, enviroinfo@ec.gc.ca

Fisheries & Oceans Canada, 200 Kent St., Ottawa, ON K1A 0E6
613-993-0999, Fax: 613-990-1866, info@dfo-mpo.gc.ca

Freshwater Institute Science Laboratory, 501 University Cres., Winnipeg, MB R3T 2N6
204-983-5000, Fax: 204-983-6285

Institut Maurice-Lamontagne, 850, rte de le Mer, CP 1000, Mont-Joli, QC G5H 3Z4
418-775-0500, Fax: 418-775-0730

Institute of Ocean Sciences, 9860 West Saanich Rd., PO Box 6000, Sidney, BC V8L 4B2
250-363-6517, Fax: 250-363-6390

Nunavut Water Board, PO Box 119, Gjoa Haven, NU X0B 1J0
867-360-6338, Fax: 867-360-6369

Alberta

Alberta Environment & Parks, Information Centre, Great West Life Bldg., 9920 - 108 St., Main Fl., Edmonton, AB T5K 2M4
780-427-2700, Fax: 780-427-4407, -310-3773, ESRD.Info-Centre@gov.ab.ca

Alberta Transportation, Communications Branch, Twin Atria Building, 4999 - 98 Jasper Ave., 2nd Fl., Edmonton, AB T6B 2X3
780-427-2731, Fax: 780-466-3166, -310-0000, Trans.Contact.Us.m@gov.ab.ca

Alberta Utilities Commission, Fifth Avenue Place, 425 - 1st St. SW, 4th Fl., Calgary, AB T2P 3L8
403-592-8845, Fax: 403-592-4406, -310-0000, info@auc.ab.ca

Irrigation Council, Provincial Bldg., 200 - 5 Ave. South, 3rd Fl., Lethbridge, AB T1J 4L1
403-381-5176, Fax: 403-382-4406

British Columbia

British Columbia Ministry of Environment, PO Box 9339 Prov Govt, Victoria, BC V8W 9M1
250-387-9870, Fax: 250-387-6003, env.mail@gov.bc.ca

British Columbia Utilities Commission, 900 Howe St., 6th Fl., PO Box 250, Vancouver, BC V6Z 2N3
604-660-4700, Fax: 604-660-1102, 800-663-1385, commission.secretary@bcuc.com

Manitoba

Manitoba Sustainable Development, 200 Saulteaux Cres., PO Box 22, Winnipeg, MB R3J 3W3
204-945-6784, 800-214-6497, mgi@gov.mb.ca

Manitoba Water Council, 200 Saulteaux Cres., PO Box 38, Winnipeg, MB R3J 3W3
info@manitobawatercouncil.ca

New Brunswick

New Brunswick Department of Energy & Resource Development, Hugh John Flemming Forestry Centre, 1350 Regent St., Fredericton, NB E3C 2G6
506-453-3826, Fax: 506-444-4367, dnr_mrnweb@gnb.ca

New Brunswick Department of Environment & Local Government, Marysville Place, PO Box 6000, Fredericton, NB E3B 5H1
506-453-2690, Fax: 506-457-4994, elg/egl-info@gnb.ca

Newfoundland & Labrador

Newfoundland & Labrador Board of Commissioners of Public Utilities, Prince Charles Bldg., #E-210, 120 Torbay Rd., PO Box 21040, St. John's, NL A1A 5B2
709-726-8600, Fax: 709-726-9604, 866-782-0006, ito@pub.nf.ca

Newfoundland & Labrador Department of Environment & Conservation, Confederation Bldg., West Block, 4th Fl., PO Box 8700, St. John's, NL A1B 4J6
709-729-2664, Fax: 709-729-6639, 800-563-6181, envcinquires@gov.nl.ca

Northwest Territories

Inuvialuit Water Board, Professional Bldg., #302, 125 Mackenzie Rd., PO Box 2531, Yellowknife, NT X0E 0T0
867-678-2942, Fax: 867-678-2943, info@inuvwb.ca

Northwest Territories Department of Environment & Natural Resources, #600, 5102 - 50 Ave., Yellowknife, NT X1A 3S8
867-767-9231

Nova Scotia

Nova Scotia Department of Natural Resources, Founder's Square, 1701 Hollis St., 3rd Fl., PO Box 698, Halifax, NS B3J 2T9
902-424-5935, Fax: 902-424-7735, 800-565-2224

Nova Scotia Utility & Review Board, Summit Place, 1601 Lower Water St., 3rd Fl., PO Box 1692 M,Halifax, NS B3J 3S3
902-424-4448, Fax: 902-424-3919, 855-442-4448, board@novascotia.ca

Waterfront Development Corporation Ltd., The Cable Wharf, 1751 Lower Water St., 2nd Fl., Halifax, NS B3J 1S5
902-422-6591, Fax: 902-422-7582, info@wdcl.ca

Ontario

Lake of the Woods Control Board, c/o Executive Engineer, 373 Sussex Dr., Block E1, Ottawa, ON K1A 0H3
Fax: 888-702-9632, 800-661-5922, secretariat@lwcb.ca

Ontario Clean Water Agency, 1 Yonge St., 17th Fl., Toronto, ON M5E 1E5
416-314-5600, 800-667-6292, ocwa@ocwa.com

Ontario Ministry of Environment & Climate Change, Public Information Centre, Macdonald Block, 900 Bay St., 2nd Fl., Toronto, ON M7A 1N3
416-325-4000, Fax: 416-314-6713, 800-565-4923

Ontario Ministry of Natural Resources & Forestry, 300 Water St., PO Box 7000, Peterborough, ON K9J 8M5
800-667-1940

Walkerton Clean Water Centre, 20 Ontario Rd., PO Box 160, Walkerton, ON N0G 2V0
519-881-2003, Fax: 519-881-4947, 866-515-0550, inquiry@wcwc.ca

Prince Edward Island

Prince Edward Island Department of Justice & Public Safety, Shaw Bldg. South, 95 Rochford St., 4th Fl., PO Box 2000, Charlottetown, PE C1A 7N8
902-368-6410, Fax: 902-368-6488

Québec

Ministère du Développement durable, de l'Environnement et de la Lutte contre les changements climatiques, Édifice Marie-Guyart, 675, boul René-Lévesque est, 29e étage, Québec, QC G1R 5V7
418-521-3830, Fax: 418-646-5974, 800-561-1616, info@mddefp.gouv.qc.ca

Saskatchewan

Saskatchewan Environment, 3211 Albert St., 2nd Fl., Regina, SK S4S 5W6
306-787-2584, Fax: 306-787-9544, 800-567-4224, Centre.Inquiry@gov.sk.ca

Saskatchewan Water Corporation (SaskWater), #200, 111 Fairford St. East, Moose Jaw, SK S6H 1C8
Fax: 306-694-3207, 888-230-1111, comm@saskwater.com

Saskatchewan Water Security Agency, #400, 111 Fairford St. East, Moose Jaw, SK S6H 7X9
306-694-3900, Fax: 306-694-3105, comm@wsask.ca

Water Appeal Board, #217, 3085 Albert St., Regina, SK S4S 0B1
306-798-7462, Fax: 306-787-8558

Yukon Territory

Yukon Environment, 10 Burns Rd., PO Box 2703 V-3A, Whitehorse, YT Y1A 2C6
867-667-5652, Fax: 867-393-7197, environment.yukon@gov.yk.ca

WATER POLLUTION

See: Environment; Water Resources

Office of the Administrator of the Ship-source Oil Pollution Fund, #830, 180 Kent St., Ottawa, ON K1A 0N5
613-991-1726, Fax: 613-990-5423, info@sopf-cidphn.gc.ca

Saskatchewan

Water Appeal Board, #217, 3085 Albert St., Regina, SK S4S 0B1
306-798-7462, Fax: 306-787-8558

WATER RESOURCES

See Also: Oceanography

Environmental Stewardship Branch, 351, boul St-Joseph, Gatineau, QC K1A 0H3
819-953-1711, Fax: 819-953-9452

Freshwater Institute Science Laboratory, 501 University Cres., Winnipeg, MB R3T 2N6
204-983-5000, Fax: 204-983-6285

International Joint Commission, 234 Laurier Ave. West, 22nd Fl., Ottawa, ON K1P 6K6
613-995-2984, Fax: 613-993-5583, commission@ottawa.ijc.org

Nunavut Water Board, PO Box 119, Gjoa Haven, NU X0B 1J0
867-360-6338, Fax: 867-360-6369

Water Science & Technology, 200, boul Sacré-Coeur, Gatineau, QC K1A 0H3
819-994-4533

Alberta

Alberta Environment & Parks, Information Centre, Great West Life Bldg., 9920 - 108 St., Main Fl., Edmonton, AB T5K 2M4
780-427-2700, Fax: 780-427-4407, -310-3773, ESRD.Info-Centre@gov.ab.ca

British Columbia

Environmental Protection Division, PO Box 9339, Victoria, BC V8W 9M1
250-387-1288, Fax: 250-387-5669

Manitoba

Manitoba Water Council, 200 Saulteaux Cres., PO Box 38, Winnipeg, MB R3J 3W3
info@manitobawatercouncil.ca

New Brunswick

New Brunswick Department of Environment & Local Government, Marysville Place, PO Box 6000, Fredericton, NB E3B 5H1
506-453-2690, Fax: 506-457-4994, elg/egl-info@gnb.ca

Northwest Territories

Inuvialuit Water Board, Professional Bldg., #302, 125 Mackenzie Rd., PO Box 2531, Yellowknife, NT X0E 0T0
867-678-2942, Fax: 867-678-2943, info@inuvwb.ca

Nova Scotia

Nova Scotia Department of Agriculture, 1800 Argyle St., 6th Fl., PO Box 2223, Halifax, NS B3J 3C4
902-424-4560, Fax: 902-424-4671

Nunavut
Nunavut Territory Department of Health, PO Box 1000 1000, Iqaluit, NU X0A 0H0
867-975-5700, Fax: 867-975-5705, 800-661-0833
Ontario
Drinking Water Management Division, 135 St. Clair Ave. West, 14th Fl., Toronto, ON M4V 1P5
416-314-4475, Fax: 416-314-6935
Integrated Environmental Policy Division, 77 Wellesley St. West, 11th Fl., Toronto, ON M7A 2T5
416-314-6338, Fax: 416-314-6346
Ontario Clean Water Agency, 1 Yonge St., 17th Fl., Toronto, ON M5E 1E5
416-314-5600, 800-667-6292, ocwa@ocwa.com
Ontario Drinking Water Advisory Council, 40 St. Clair Ave. West, 3rd Fl., Toronto, ON M4V 1M2
416-212-7779, Fax: 416-212-7595
Walkerton Clean Water Centre, 20 Ontario Rd., PO Box 160, Walkerton, ON N0G 2V0
519-881-2003, Fax: 519-881-4947, 866-515-0550, inquiry@wcwc.ca
Prince Edward Island
Energy & Minerals, Jones Bldg., 4th Fl., PO Box 2000, Charlottetown, PE C1A 7N8
902-894-0288, Fax: 902-894-0290
Québec
Ministère du Développement durable, de l'Environnement et de la Lutte contre les changements climatiques, Édifice Marie-Guyart, 675, boul René-Lévesque est, 29e étage, Québec, QC G1R 5V7
418-521-3830, Fax: 418-646-5974, 800-561-1616, info@mddefp.gouv.qc.ca
Saskatchewan
Environmental Protection & Audit Division, 3211 Albert St., 5th Fl., Regina, SK S4S 5W6
Fax: 306-787-2947
Saskatchewan Environment, 3211 Albert St., 2nd Fl., Regina, SK S4S 5W6
306-787-2584, Fax: 306-787-9544, 800-567-4224, Centre.Inquiry@gov.sk.ca
Saskatchewan Water Corporation (SaskWater), #200, 111 Fairford St. East, Moose Jaw, SK S6H 1C8
Fax: 306-694-3207, 888-230-1111, comm@saskwater.com
Saskatchewan Water Security Agency, #400, 111 Fairford St. East, Moose Jaw, SK S6H 7X9
306-694-3900, Fax: 306-694-3105, comm@wsask.ca
Water Appeal Board, #217, 3085 Albert St., Regina, SK S4S 0B1
306-798-7462, Fax: 306-787-8558
Yukon Territory
Yukon Environment, 10 Burns Rd., PO Box 2703 V-3A, Whitehorse, YT Y1A 2C6
867-667-5652, Fax: 867-393-7197, environment.yukon@gov.yk.ca

WEATHER

Environment & Climate Change Canada, 10 Wellington St., Gatineau, QC K1A 0H3
819-997-2800, Fax: 819-994-1412, 800-668-6767, enviroinfo@ec.gc.ca
Wind Tunnel Testing Facilities, c/o National Research Council, 1200 Montreal Rd., Ottawa, ON K1A 0R6

WEIGHTS & MEASURES

Standards Council of Canada, #600, 55 Metcalfe St., Ottawa, ON K1P 6L5
613-238-3222, Fax: 613-569-7808, info@scc.ca

WILDLIFE RESOURCES

Committee on the Status of Endangered Wildlife in Canada, c/o Canadian Wildlife Service, 351 St. Joseph Blvd, 4th Fl., Gatineau, QC K1A 0H3
819-953-3215, Fax: 819-994-3684, cosewic/cosepac@ec.gc.ca
North American Bird Conservation Initiative, Canadian Wildlife Service, 351, boul St-Joseph, 3e étage, Gatineau, QC K1A 0H3
819-994-0512, Fax: 819-994-4445, nabci@ec.gc.ca
North American Waterfowl Management Plan, NAWCC (Canada) Secretariat, Place Vincent Massey, 351 St. Joseph Blvd., 7th Fl., Gatineau, QC K1A 0H3
819-934-6034, Fax: 819-934-6017, nawmp@ec.gc.ca
Manitoba
Endangered Species Advisory Committee, 200 Saulteaux Cres., PO Box 24, Winnipeg, MB R3J 3W3
204-945-7775, Fax: 204-945-3077
Nunavut
Nunavut Territory Department of Environment, PO Box 1000 1300, Iqaluit, NU X0A 0H0
867-975-7700, Fax: 867-975-7742, environment@gov.nu.ca
Ontario
Ontario Fish & Wildlife Heritage Commission, Robinson Pl., 300 Water St., PO Box 7000, Peterborough, ON K9J 8M5
705-755-1905, Fax: 705-755-1900
Ontario Ministry of Environment & Climate Change, Public Information Centre, Macdonald Block, 900 Bay St., 2nd Fl., Toronto, ON M7A 1N3
416-325-4000, Fax: 416-314-6713, 800-565-4923
Québec
Fondation de la faune du Québec, Place Iberville II, #420, 1175, av Lavigerie, Québec, QC G1V 4P1
418-644-7926, Fax: 418-643-7655, 877-639-0742, ffq@fondationdelafaune.qc.ca
Ministère des Forêts, de la Faune et des Parcs, Service à la clientèle, #A409, 5700, 4e av ouest, Québec, QC G1H 6R1
Fax: 418-644-6513, 844-523-6738, services.clientele@mrnf.gouv.qc.ca
Ministère des Énergie et des Ressources naturelles, Service à la clientèle, #A409, 5700, 4e av ouest, Québec, QC G1H 6R1
Fax: 418-644-6513, 866-248-6936, services.clientele@mern.gouv.qc.ca

WOMEN'S ISSUES

See Also: Pay Equity
Status of Women Canada, PO Box 8097 T CSC,Ottawa, ON K1G 3H6
613-995-7835, Fax: 819-420-6906, 855-969-9922, communications@swc-cfc.gc.ca
Alberta
Status of Women, Office of the Minister, Legislature Bldg., #208, 10800 - 97 Ave., Edmonton, AB T5K 2B6
Manitoba
Manitoba Women's Advisory Council, #409, 401 York Ave., Winnipeg, MB R3C 0P8
204-945-6281, Fax: 204-945-6511, 800-263-0234, msw@gov.mb.ca
Status of Women, #409, 401 York Ave., Winnipeg, MB R3C 0P8
204-945-6281, Fax: 204-945-6511, 800-263-0234, msw@gov.mb.ca
New Brunswick
New Brunswick Department of Social Development, Sartain MacDonald Bldg., 551 King St., PO Box 6000, Fredericton, NB E3B 5H1
506-453-2001, Fax: 506-453-2164, sd-ds@gnb.ca
Women's Equality Branch, Sartain MacDonald Bldg., PO Box 6000, Fredericton, NB E3B 5H1
506-453-8126, Fax: 506-453-7977, WEB-EDF@gnb.ca
Newfoundland & Labrador
Provincial Advisory Council on the Status of Women, #103, 15 Hallett Cres., St. John's, NL A1B 4C4
709-753-7270, Fax: 709-753-2606, 877-753-7270, info@pacsw.ca
Women's Policy Office, Confederation Bldg., 4th Fl., West Block, PO Box 8700, St. John's, NL A1B 4J6
709-729-5009, Fax: 709-729-1418
Northwest Territories
Status of Women Council of the Northwest Territories, Northwest Tower, 4th Fl., PO Box 1320, Yellowknife, NT X1A 2L9
867-920-6177, Fax: 867-873-0285, 888-234-4485, council@statusofwomen.nt.ca
Nova Scotia
Nova Scotia Advisory Council on the Status of Women, Quinpool Centre, #202, 6169 Quinpool Rd., PO Box 745, Halifax, NS B3J 2T3
902-424-8662, Fax: 902-424-0573, 800-565-8662, women@gov.ns.ca
Nunavut
Nunavut Territory Department of Culture & Heritage, PO Box 1000 800, Iqaluit, NU X0A 0H0
867-975-5500, Fax: 867-975-5504, 866-934-2035
Ontario
Ontario Women's Directorate, College Park, 777 Bay St., 6th Fl., Toronto, ON M7A 2J4
416-314-0300, Fax: 416-314-0247, 866-510-5902, owd@ontario.ca
Québec
Conseil du statut de la femme, #300, 800, place D'Youville, 3e étage, Québec, QC G1R 6E2
418-643-4326, Fax: 418-643-8926, 800-463-2851, csf@csf.gouv.qc.ca
Ministère de la Famille, 425, rue Saint-Amable, 1er étage, Québec, QC G1R 4Z1
877-216-6202
Secrétariat à la condition féminine, 905, avenue Honoré-Mercier, 3e étage, Québec, QC G1R 5M6
418-643-9052, Fax: 418-643-4991
Yukon Territory
Yukon Women's Directorate, #1, 404 Hason St., PO Box 2703, Whitehorse, YT Y1A 2C6
867-667-3030, Fax: 867-393-6270

WORKERS' COMPENSATION

Alberta
Appeals Commission for Alberta Workers' Compensation, #2300, 801 - 6th Ave. SW, Calgary, AB T2P 3W2
780-412-8700, Fax: 780-412-8701, -310-0000, AC.AcesAdmin@gov.ab.ca
Workers' Compensation Board, 9912 - 107 St., PO Box 2415, Edmonton, AB T5J 2S5
780-498-3999, Fax: 780-427-5863, 866-922-9221
British Columbia
Workers' Compensation Appeal Tribunal, #150, 4600 Jacombs Rd., Richmond, BC V6V 3B1
604-664-7800, Fax: 604-664-7898, 800-663-2782
Workers' Compensation Board of British Columbia, PO Box 5350 Terminal,Vancouver, BC V6B 5L5
604-276-3100, Fax: 604-276-3247, 888-621-7233
Manitoba
Workers Compensation Board of Manitoba, 333 Broadway Ave., Winnipeg, MB R3C 4W3
204-954-4321, Fax: 204-954-4999, 800-362-3340, wcb@wcb.mb.ca
New Brunswick
WorkSafeNB, 1 Portland St., PO Box 160, Saint John, NB E2L 3X9
506-632-2200, Fax: 506-632-4999, 800-222-9775, communications@ws-ts.nb.ca
Newfoundland & Labrador
Newfoundland & Labrador Workplace Health, Safety & Compensation Commission (WorkplaceNL), 146 - 148 Forest Rd., PO Box 9000, St. John's, NL A1A 3B8
709-778-1000, Fax: 709-738-1714, 800-563-9000, general.inquiries@whscc.nl.ca
Northwest Territories
Northwest Territories & Nunavut Workers' Safety & Compensation Commission, Centre Square Tower, 5022 - 49th St., 5th Fl., PO Box 8888, Yellowknife, NT X1A 2R3
867-920-3888, Fax: 867-873-4596, 800-661-0792
Nova Scotia
Workers' Compensation Board of Nova Scotia, 5668 South St., PO Box 1150, Halifax, NS B3J 2Y2
902-491-8999, 800-870-3331, info@wcb.gov.ns.ca
Ontario
Workplace Safety & Insurance Board, 200 Front St. West, Ground Fl., Toronto, ON M5V 3J1
416-344-1000, Fax: 416-344-4684, 800-387-0750
Prince Edward Island
Prince Edward Island Workers Compensation Board, 14 Weymouth St., PO Box 757, Charlottetown, PE C1A 7L7
902-368-5680, Fax: 902-368-5696, 800-237-5049
Québec
Commission de la santé et de la sécurité du travail du Québec, 524, rue Bourdages, CP 1200 Terminus,Québec, QC G1K 7E2
Fax: 418-266-4015, 866-302-2778
Commission des lésions professionnelles, #700, 900, Place d'Youville, Québec, QC G1R 3P7
418-644-7777, Fax: 418-644-6443, 800-463-1591
Saskatchewan
Saskatchewan Workers' Compensation Board, #200, 1881 Scarth St., Regina, SK S4P 4L1
306-787-4370, Fax: 306-787-4311, 800-667-7590, webmaster@wcbsask.com
Yukon Territory
Yukon Workers' Compensation Health & Safety Board, 401 Strickland St., Whitehorse, YT Y1A 5N8
867-667-5645, Fax: 867-393-6279, 800-661-0443, worksafe@gov.yk.ca

YOUNG OFFENDERS

Justice Canada, East Memorial Bldg., 284 Wellington St., Ottawa, ON K1A 0H8
613-957-4222, Fax: 613-954-0811, webadmin@justice.gc.ca
Alberta
Alberta Justice & Solicitor General, Communications, Bowker Building, 9833 - 109 St., 5th Fl., Edmonton, AB T5K 2E8
780-427-2745
British Columbia
British Columbia Ministry of Justice, PO Box 9044 Prov Govt, Victoria, BC V8W 9E2
Office of the Representative for Children & Youth, #400, 1019 Wharf St., Victoria, BC V8W 2Y9
250-356-6710, Fax: 250-356-0837, 800-476-3933, rcy@rcybc.ca
Northwest Territories
Northwest Territories Department of Justice, 4903 - 49th St., PO Box 1320, Yellowknife, NT X1A 2L9
867-767-9256

Nova Scotia
Nova Scotia Department of Justice, 1690 Hollis St., PO Box 7, Halifax, NS B3J 2L6
902-424-4030, justweb@gov.ns.ca

Nunavut
Young Offenders Facility, 1548 Federal Rd., PO Box 1439, Iqaluit, NU X0A 0H0
867-979-4452, Fax: 867-979-5506

YOUTH SERVICES

Federal Economic Development Agency for Southern Ontario, #101, 139 Northfield Dr. West, Waterloo, ON N2L 5A6
Fax: 519-725-4976, 866-593-5505

Alberta
Alberta Office of the Child & Youth Advocate, #600, 9925 - 109 St. NW, Edmonton, AB T5K 2J8
780-422-6056, Fax: 780-422-3675, 800-661-3446, ca.information@ocya.alberta.ca

British Columbia
Provincial Services, PO Box 9717 Prov Govt, Victoria, BC V8W 9S1
250-387-0978, Fax: 250-356-2079

Newfoundland & Labrador
Newfoundland & Labrador Department of Child, Youth & Family Services, PO Box 8700, St. John's, NL A1B 4J6
709-729-0760

Nunavut
Nunavut Territory Department of Culture & Heritage, PO Box 1000 800, Iqaluit, NU X0A 0H0
867-975-5500, Fax: 867-975-5504, 866-934-2035

Ontario
Office of the Provincial Advocate for Children & Youth, #2200, 401 Bay St., Toronto, ON M7A 0A6
416-325-5669, Fax: 416-325-5681, 800-263-2841, advocacy@provincialadvocate.on.ca

Ontario Ministry of Children & Youth Services, Macdonald Block, #M-1B114, 900 Bay St., Toronto, ON M7A 1N3
Fax: 416-212-1977, 866-821-7770, mcsinfo@mcys.gov.on.ca

Québec
Commission des droits de la personne et des droits de la jeunesse, 360, rue Saint-Jacques, 2e étage, Montréal, QC H2Y 1P5
514-873-5146, Fax: 514-873-6032, 800-361-6477, accueil@cdpdj.qc.ca

Ministère de la Santé et des Services sociaux, Direction des communications, 1075, ch Sainte-Foy, 16e étage, Québec, QC G1S 2M1
418-643-9395, Fax: 418-643-4768, regisseur.web@msss.gouv.qc.ca

ZONING

British Columbia
British Columbia Ministry of Community, Sport, & Cultural Development & Responsible for TransLink, PO Box 9490 Prov Govt, Victoria, BC V8W 9N7

Manitoba
Manitoba Municipal Board, #1144, 363 Broadway, Winnipeg, MB R3C 3N9
204-945-2941, Fax: 204-948-2235

Québec
Commission municipale du Québec, Mezzanine, aile Chauveau, 10, rue Pierre-Olivier-Chauveau, Québec, QC G1R 4J3
418-691-2014, Fax: 418-644-4676, 866-353-6767

Government of Canada

c/o Canada Enquiry Centre, Service Canada, Ottawa, ON K1A 0J9
Toll-Free: 800-622-6232
TTY: 800-926-9105
www.canada.ca
twitter.com/canada

All political authority in Canada is divided between the federal & provincial governments, according to the provisions of the Constitution Act, 1867. Local municipalities are a concern of the provinces, & derive their authority from Acts of provincial legislation. The Parliament of Canada consists of Her Majesty Queen Elizabeth II (represented in Canada by the Governor General, His Excellency the Right Honourable David Johnston), an Upper House called the Senate, & an elected House of Commons.

Governor General & Commander-in-Chief of Canada / Gouverneur général et Commandant en chef du Canada

Rideau Hall, 1 Sussex Dr., Ottawa, ON K1A 0A1
Tel: 613-993-8200; *Fax:* 613-998-8760
Toll-Free: 800-465-6890
www.gg.ca

Canada is a constitutional monarchy. Under the terms of its Constitution, Her Majesty Queen Elizabeth II is the Head of State. The duties of the Head of State in Canada are undertaken by the Governor General as the Crown's representative. He is also Commander-in-Chief of the Canadian Forces, Chancellor & Principal Companion of the Order of Canada, Chancellor & Commander of the Order of Military Merit, & Head of the Canadian Heraldic Authority. The Office of the Governor General encompasses a number of responsibilities, both constitutional & traditional in nature. The Governor General of Canada exercises powers & responsibilities belonging to the Sovereign, with the advice of members of the Privy Council. He is involved in the promotion of Canadian sovereignty at home & represents Canada abroad. Canadian values, diversity, inclusion, culture, & heritage are promoted by the Governor General. National honours, decorations, & awards to recognize people who have demonstrated excellence, valour, bravery, or exceptional dedication to service are presented by the Governor General.

Governor General & Commander-in-Chief of Canada, Right Hon. David Johnston, CC, CMM, COM, CD, FRSC(hon), FRCPSC(hon)
Tel: 613-993-8200; *Fax:* 613-993-1967

Secretary to the Governor General, Stephen Wallace
Tel: 613-993-0259; *Fax:* 613-993-1967

Superintendent, Associated Services - Security, Sylvian Côté
Tel: 613-993-9332; *Fax:* 613-993-8641

The Chancellery of Honours / Chancellerie

1 Sussex Dr., Ottawa, ON K1A 0A1
Tel: 613-998-8732; *Fax:* 613-991-1681

Deputy Secretary & Deputy Herald Chancellor, Office of the Secretary to the Governor General, The Chancellery of Honours, Emmanuelle Sajous
Tel: 613-998-8731; *Fax:* 613-991-1681

Director, Honours, Orders, Darcy De Marsico
Tel: 613-993-3524; *Fax:* 613-991-1681

Director, Honours, Decorations & Medals, Denis Poirier
Tel: 613-991-5845; *Fax:* 613-991-1681

Chief Herald of Canada & Director, The Canadian Heraldic Authority, Claire Boudreau
Tel: 613-991-2227; *Fax:* 613-990-5818

Deputy Chief Herald of Canada & Assistant Director, The Canadian Heraldic Authority, Bruce Patterson
Tel: 613-991-2229; *Fax:* 613-990-5818

Corporate Services Branch / Direction générale des Services ministériels

1 Sussex Dr., Ottawa, ON K1A 0A1

Director General, Fady Abdul-Nour
Tel: 613-991-9091; *Fax:* 613-998-8762

Policy, Program & Protocol Branch / Politique, programme et protocole

1 Sussex Dr., Ottawa, ON K1A 0A1

Deputy Secretary, Patricia Jaton
Tel: 613-990-9006; *Fax:* 613-993-4728

Executive Director, Events, Household & Visitor Services, Christine MacIntyre
Tel: 613-993-1901; *Fax:* 613-991-5113

Privy Council Office (PCO) / Bureau du Conseil privé (BCP)

#1000, 85 Sparks St., Ottawa, ON K1A 0A3
Tel: 613-957-5153; *Fax:* 613-997-5043
TTY: 613-957-5741
info@pco-bcp.gc.ca
www.pco-bcp.gc.ca
Other Communication: Media Phone: 613-957-5420

The Privy Council Office provides non-partisan advice & information from across the Public Service to the Prime Minister, the Cabinet, & its decision-making structures. The key roles of the Privy Council are as follows: advising the Prime Minister & supporting the Cabinet; managing the Cabinet's decision-making system & facilitating its efficient & effective functioning on a daily basis; & providing public service leadership, including the management of the appointments process for Crown corporations & agencies, & senior positions in federal departments. The Privy Council is led by the Clerk of the Privy Council. A member of the Privy Council is awarded the title, "Honourable," for life. The Governor General, the Prime Minister, & the Chief Justice of Canada are accorded the title, "The Right Honourable," for life.

President, Queen's Privy Council for Canada; Minister, Democratic Institutions; Minister Responsible, Elections Canada, Hon. Maryam Monsef, P.C.
Tel: 613-995-6411; *Fax:* 613-996-9800
Maryam.Monsef@parl.gc.ca

Leader of the Government in the House of Commons, Hon. Bardish Chagger, P.C.
Tel: 613-996-5928; *Fax:* 613-992-6251
Bardish.Chagger@parl.gc.ca

Chief Government Whip, Andrew Leslie
Tel: 613-995-1800; *Fax:* 613-995-6298
Andrew.Leslie@parl.gc.ca

Clerk of the Privy Council & Secretary to the Cabinet, Michael Wernick
Tel: 613-957-5400
www.clerk.gc.ca
Social Media: twitter.com/Clerk_GC
Note: Michael Wernick was appointed Clerk of the Privy Council & Secretary to the Cabinet on January 22, 2016.

National Security Advisor to the Prime Minister, Daniel Jean
Tel: 613-957-5056

Deputy National Security Advisor to the Prime Minister, David McGovern
Tel: 613-957-5015

Special Advisor, Human Smuggling & Illegal Migration, Ward P.D. Elcock
Tel: 613-996-3713

Deputy Clerk of the Privy Council & Associate Secretary to the Cabinet, Serge Dupont
Tel: 613-957-5466

Deputy Secretary to the Cabinet, Operations, Les Linklater
Tel: 613-957-5417

Deputy Secretary to the Cabinet, Plans & Consultations & Intergovernmental Affairs, Stephen Lucas
Tel: 613-957-5462

Deputy Secretary to the Cabinet, Legislation & House Planning / Machinery of Government, & Counsel to the Clerk of the Privy Council, Ian McCowan, Q.C.
Tel: 613-957-5792

Deputy Secretary to the Cabinet, Results & Delivery, Matthew Mendelsohn
Tel: 613-952-7544

Deputy Secretary to the Cabinet, Senior Personnel, Business Transformation & Renewal, Janine Sherman
Tel: 613-957-5465

Chief of Staff, Office of the Clerk of the Privy Council & Secretary to the Cabinet, Barbara Henry
Tel: 613-957-5063

Director General, Legislation & House Planning, Randall Koops
Tel: 613-947-3639

Director General, Operations, Laurent Marcoux
Tel: 613-957-5456

Executive Director, Security Operations, Security & Intelligence, Louise Lacelle
Tel: 613-957-5387

Director, Corporate & Media Affairs, Raymond Rivet
Tel: 613-957-5233

Privy Council Members & Date When Sworn In

Hon. Paul Theodore Hellyer, Apr. 26, 1957
H.R.H. Prince Phillip, The Duke of Edinburg, Oct. 14, 1957
Hon. Allan Joseph MacEachen, Apr. 22, 1963
Hon. Yvon Dupuis, Feb. 3, 1964
Right Hon. John Napier Turner, Dec. 18, 1965
Right Hon. Joseph Jacques Jean Chrétien, Apr. 4, 1967
Hon. Alexander Bradshaw Campbell, Jul. 5, 1967
Hon. Donald Stovel Macdonald, Apr. 20, 1968
Hon. Jean-Eudes Dubé, Jul. 6, 1968
Hon. Otto Emil Lang, Jul. 6, 1968
Hon. Robert D. George Stanbury, Oct. 20, 1969
Hon. Alastair William Gillespie, Aug. 12, 1971
Hon. William Warren Allmand, Nov. 27, 1972
Hon. James Hugh Faulkner, Nov. 27, 1972
Hon. André Ouellet, Nov. 27, 1972
Hon. Marc Lalonde, Nov. 27, 1972
Hon. J. Judd Buchanan, Aug. 8, 1974
Hon. Marcel Lessard, Sep. 26, 1975
Hon. Leonard Stephen Marchand, Sep. 15, 1976
Hon. Monique Bégin, Sep. 15, 1976
Hon. Jean-Jacques Blais, Sep. 15, 1976
Hon. Francis Fox, Sep. 15, 1976
Hon. Anthony Chisholm Abbott, Sep. 15, 1976
Hon. Iona Campagnolo, Sep. 15, 1976
Hon. Norman A. Cafik, Sep. 16, 1977
Hon. J. Gilles Lamontagne, Jan. 19, 1978
Hon. John M. Reid, Nov. 24, 1978
Hon. Pierre De Bané, Nov. 24, 1978
Right Hon. Charles Joseph Clark, Jun. 4, 1979
Hon. James Aloysius McGrath, Jun. 4, 1979
Hon. John Carnell Crosbie, Jun. 4, 1979
Hon. David Samuel Horne MacDonald, Jun. 4, 1979
Right Hon. Donald Frank Mazankowski, Jun. 4, 1979
Hon. Elmer MacIntosh MacKay, Jun. 4, 1979
Hon. Arthur Jacob Epp, Jun. 4, 1979
Hon. John Allen Fraser, Jun. 4, 1979
Hon. Sinclair McKnight Stevens, Jun. 4, 1979
Hon. Ronald George Atkey, Jun. 4, 1979
Hon. David Edward Crombie, Jun. 4, 1979
Hon. Henry Perrin Beatty, Jun. 4, 1979
Hon. J. Robert Howie, Jun. 4, 1979
Hon. Michael Holcombe Wilson, Jun. 4, 1979
Hon. Gerald Augustine Regan, Mar. 3, 1980
Hon. James Sydney Clark Fleming, Mar. 3, 1980
Hon. William H. Rompkey, Mar. 3, 1980
Hon. Pierre Bussières, Mar. 3, 1980
Hon. Charles Lapointe, Mar. 3, 1980
Hon. Edward C. Lumley, Mar. 3, 1980
Hon. Yvon Pinard, Mar. 3, 1980
Hon. Donald James Johnston, Mar. 3, 1980
Hon. Lloyd Axworthy, Mar. 3, 1980
Hon. Paul James Cosgrove, Mar. 3, 1980
Hon. Judith A. Erola, Mar. 3, 1980
Hon. Jacob Austin, Sep. 22, 1981
Hon. Serge Joyal, Sep. 22, 1981
Hon. John Edward Broadbent, Apr. 17, 1982
Hon. William Grenville Davis, Apr. 17, 1982
Hon. John MacLennan Buchanan, Apr. 17, 1982
Hon. Alfred Brian Peckford, Apr. 17, 1982
Hon. James Matthew Lee, Apr. 17, 1982
Hon. David Michael Collenette, Aug. 12, 1983
Hon. Céline Hervieux-Payette, Aug. 12, 1983
Hon. Roger Simmons, Aug. 12, 1983
Hon. David Paul Smith, Aug. 12, 1983
Hon. Roy MacLaren, Aug. 17, 1983
Hon. Peter Michael Pitfield, Apr. 19, 1984
Right Hon. Martin Brian Mulroney, May 7, 1984
Right Hon. Edward Richard Schreyer, Jun. 3, 1984
Hon. Herb Breau, Jun. 30, 1984
Hon. Joseph Roger Rémi Bujold, Jun. 30, 1984
Hon. Ralph Ferguson, Jun. 30, 1984
Hon. Jack Burnett Murta, Sep. 17, 1984
Hon. Otto John Jelinek, Sep. 17, 1984
Hon. Thomas Edward Siddon, Sep. 17, 1984
Hon. Charles James Mayer, Sep. 17, 1984
Hon. William Hunter McKnight, Sep. 17, 1984
Hon. Rev. Walter Franklin McLean, Sep. 17, 1984
Hon. Thomas Michael McMillan, Sep. 17, 1984
Hon. Patricia Carney, Sep. 17, 1984
Hon. André Bissonnette, Sep. 17, 1984
Hon. Suzanne Blais-Grenier, Sep. 17, 1984
Hon. Benoît Bouchard, Sep. 17, 1984
Hon. Andrée Champagne, Sep. 17, 1984
Hon. Michel Côté, Sep. 17, 1984
Hon. Barbara Jean McDougall, Sep. 17, 1984
Hon. Monique Vézina, Sep. 17, 1984
Hon. Saul Mark Cherniack, Nov. 30, 1984
Hon. Paule Gauthier, Nov. 30, 1984
Hon. Stewart Donald McInnes, Aug. 20, 1985
Hon. Frank Oberle, Nov. 20, 1985
Hon. Gordon F. Joseph Osbaldeston, Feb. 13, 1986
Hon. Lowell Murray, Jun. 30, 1986
Hon. Paul Wyatt Dick, Jun. 30, 1986
Hon. Pierre H. Cadieux, Jun. 30, 1986
Hon. Jean J. Charest, Jun. 30, 1986
Hon. Thomas Hockin, Jun. 30, 1986
Hon. Monique Landry, Jun. 30, 1986
Hon. Bernard Valcourt, Jun. 30, 1986

Hon. Gerry Weiner, Jun. 30, 1986
Hon. John William Bosley, Jun. 30, 1987
Hon. Douglas Grinslade Lewis, Aug. 27, 1987
Hon. Pierre Blais, Aug. 27, 1987
Hon. Gerry St. Germain, Mar. 31, 1988
Hon. Lucien Bouchard, Mar. 31, 1988
Hon. John Horton McDermid, Sep. 15, 1988
Hon. Shirley Martin, Sep. 15, 1988
Hon. Mary Collins, Jan. 30, 1989
Hon. Alan Redway, Jan. 30, 1989
Hon. William Charles Winegard, Jan. 30, 1989
Right Hon. A. Kim Campbell, Jan. 30, 1989
Hon. Gilles Loiselle, Jan. 30, 1989
Hon. Marcel Danis, Feb. 23, 1990
Hon. Audrey McLaughlin, Jan. 10, 1991
Hon. Pauline Browes, Apr. 21, 1991
Hon. J.J. Michel Robert, Dec. 5, 1991
Hon. Marcel Prud'homme, Jul. 1, 1992
Hon. Lorne Edmund Nystrom, Jul. 1, 1992
Hon. John Charles Polanyi, Jul. 1, 1992
Hon. Maurice F. Strong, Jul. 1, 1992
Hon. Antonine Maillet, Jul. 1, 1992
Hon. Richard Cashin, Jul. 1, 1992
Hon. Paul M. Tellier, Jul. 1, 1992
Hon. David Robert Peterson, Jul. 1, 1992
Hon. Charles Rosner Bronfman, Oct. 21, 1992
Hon. Pierre H. Vincent, Jan. 4, 1993
Hon. James Stewart Edwards, Jun. 25, 1993
Hon. Robert Douglas Nicholson, Jun. 25, 1993
Hon. Barbara Jane Sparrow, Jun. 25, 1993
Hon. Peter L. McCreath, Jun. 25, 1993
Hon. Ian Angus Ross Reid, Jun. 25, 1993
Hon. Larry Schneider, Jun. 25, 1993
Hon. Garth Turner, Jun. 25, 1993
Hon. David Anderson, Nov. 4, 1993
Hon. Ralph Edward Goodale, Nov. 4, 1993
Hon. David Charles Dingwall, Nov. 4, 1993
Hon. Ron Irwin, Nov. 4, 1993
Hon. Brian Tobin, Nov. 4, 1993
Hon. Joyce Fairbairn, Nov. 4, 1993
Hon. Sheila Maureen Copps, Nov. 4, 1993
Hon. Sergio Marchi, Nov. 4, 1993
Hon. John Manley, Nov. 4, 1993
Right Hon. Paul Martin, Nov. 4, 1993
Hon. Douglas Young, Nov. 4, 1993
Hon. Michel Dupuy, Nov. 4, 1993
Hon. Arthur C. Eggleton, Nov. 4, 1993
Hon. Marcel Massé, Nov. 4, 1993
Hon. Anne McLellan, Nov. 4, 1993
Hon. Allan Rock, Nov. 4, 1993
Hon. Fernand Robichaud, Nov. 4, 1993
Hon. Ethel Blondin-Andrew, Nov. 4, 1993
Hon. Lawrence MacAulay, Nov. 4, 1993
Hon. Raymond Chan, Nov. 4, 1993
Hon. Jon Gerrard, Nov. 4, 1993
Hon. Douglas Peters, Nov. 4, 1993
Hon. Alfonso Gagliano, Sep. 15, 1994
Hon. Lucienne Robillard, Feb. 22, 1995
Hon. Jane Stewart, Jan. 25, 1996
Hon. Stéphane Dion, Jan. 25, 1996
Hon. Pierre Pettigrew, Jan. 25, 1996
Hon. Martin Cauchon, Jan. 25, 1996
Hon. Hedy Fry, Jan. 25, 1996
Hon. James Andrew Grant, Sep. 30, 1996
Hon. Don Boudria, Oct. 4, 1996
Hon. Lyle Vanclief, Jun. 11, 1997
Hon. Herb Dhaliwal, Jun. 11, 1997
Hon. David Kilgour, Jun. 11, 1997
Hon. James Scott Peterson, Jun. 11, 1997
Hon. Andrew Mitchell, Jun. 11, 1997
Hon. Gilbert Normand, Jun. 18, 1997
Hon. Robert (Bob) Keith Rae, Apr. 30, 1998
Hon. Claudette Bradshaw, Nov. 23, 1998
Hon. Jocelyne Bourgon, Dec. 14, 1998
Hon. Raymond A. Speaker, Jun. 9, 1999
Hon. Frank Joseph McKenna, Jun. 9, 1999
Hon. George Baker, Aug. 3, 1999
Hon. Robert Daniel Nault, Aug. 3, 1999
Hon. Maria Minna, Aug. 3, 1999
Hon. Elinor Caplan, Aug. 3, 1999
Hon. Denis Coderre, Aug. 3, 1999
Hon. J. Bernard Boudreau, Oct. 4, 1999
Right Hon. Beverley M. McLachlin, Jan. 12, 2000
Hon. Sharon Carstairs, Jan. 9, 2001
Hon. Robert G. Thibault, Jan. 9, 2001
Hon. Rey Pagtakhan, Jan. 9, 2001
Hon. Gary Albert Filmon, Oct. 4, 2001
Hon. Susan Whelan, Jan. 15, 2002
Hon. Maurizio Bevilacqua, Jan. 15, 2002
Hon. Paul DeVillers, Jan. 15, 2002
Hon. Gar Knutson, Jan. 15, 2002
Hon. Denis Paradis, Jan. 15, 2002
Hon. Claude Drouin, Jan. 15, 2002
Hon. John McCallum, Jan. 15, 2002
Hon. Stephen Owen, Jan. 15, 2002
Hon. William Graham, Jan. 16, 2002
Hon. Gerry Byrne, Jan. 16, 2002
Hon. Jean Augustine, May 26, 2002
Hon. Arnold Wayne Easter, Oct. 22, 2002
Hon. Baljit Singh Chadha, Feb. 20, 2003
Hon. Steven W. Mahoney, Apr. 11, 2003
Hon. Roy J. Romanow, Nov. 13, 2003
Hon. Albina Guarnieri, Dec. 12, 2003
Hon. Stan Kazmierczak Keyes, Dec. 12, 2003
Hon. Robert Speller, Dec. 12, 2003
Hon. Geoff Regan, Dec. 12, 2003
Hon. Tony Valeri, Dec. 12, 2003
Hon. David Pratt, Dec. 12, 2003
Hon. Irwin Cotler, Dec. 12, 2003
Hon. Judy Sgro, Dec. 12, 2003
Hon. Hélène Chalifour Scherrer, Dec. 12, 2003
Hon. Ruben John Efford, Dec. 12, 2003
Hon. Liza Frulla, Dec. 12, 2003
Hon. Joseph Robert Comuzzi, Dec. 12, 2003
Hon. Giuseppe (Joseph) Volpe, Dec. 12, 2003
Hon. Joseph McGuire, Dec. 12, 2003
Hon. Dr. Carolyn Bennett, Dec. 12, 2003
Hon. Jacques Saada, Dec. 12, 2003
Hon. M. Aileen Carroll, Dec. 12, 2003
Hon. André Harvey, Dec. 12, 2003
Hon. Susan Barnes, Dec. 12, 2003
Hon. David Price, Dec. 12, 2003
Hon. Jim Karygiannis, Dec. 12, 2003
Hon. Shawn Murphy, Dec. 12, 2003
Hon. Joseph Louis Jordan, Dec. 12, 2003
Hon. Roger Gallaway, Dec. 12, 2003
Hon. Paul Bonwick, Dec. 12, 2003
Hon. Eleni Bakopanos, Dec. 12, 2003
Hon. Georges Farrah, Dec. 12, 2003
Hon. Mark Eyking, Dec. 12, 2003
Hon. Dan McTeague, Dec. 12, 2003
Hon. Walt Lastewka, Dec. 12, 2003
Hon. Brenda Kay Chamberlain, Dec. 12, 2003
Hon. Larry Bagnell, Dec. 12, 2003
Hon. Gurbax Singh Malhi, Dec. 12, 2003
Hon. Yvon Charbonneau, Dec. 12, 2003
Hon. Joseph Frank Fontana, Dec. 12, 2003
Hon. Jerry Pickard, Dec. 12, 2003
Hon. John McKay, Dec. 12, 2003
Hon. Scott Brison, Dec. 12, 2003
Hon. John Ferguson Godfrey, Dec. 12, 2003
Hon. Andrew Telegdi, Jan. 30, 2004
Hon. Rev. William Alexander Blaikie, Feb. 19, 2004
Hon. Grant Hill, Feb. 19, 2004
Right Hon. Stephen Joseph Harper, May 4, 2004
Hon. Joseph Mario Jacques Olivier, May 5, 2004
Hon. Ujjal Dosanjh, Jul. 20, 2004
Hon. Ken Dryden, Jul. 20, 2004
Hon. David Emerson, Jul. 20, 2004
Hon. Tony Ianno, Jul. 20, 2004
Hon. Peter Adams, Jul. 20, 2004
Hon. Sarmite Bulte, Jul. 20, 2004
Hon. Roy Cullen, Jul. 20, 2004
Hon. Marlene Jennings, Jul. 20, 2004
Hon. Dominic Leblanc, Jul. 20, 2004
Hon. Judi Longfield, Jul. 20, 2004
Hon. Paul Macklin, Jul. 20, 2004
Hon. Keith P. Martin, Jul. 20, 2004
Hon. Karen Redman, Jul. 20, 2004
Hon. Raymond Simard, Jul. 20, 2004
Hon. Patricia Ann Torsney, Jul. 20, 2004
Hon. Bryon Wilfert, Jul. 20, 2004
Hon. Belinda Stronach, May 17, 2005
Hon. Aldéa Landry, Q.C., Jun. 24, 2005
Right Hon. Adrienne Clarkson, Oct. 3, 2005
Hon. Navdeep Bains, Oct. 7, 2005
Hon. Anita Neville, Oct. 7, 2005
Hon. Charles Hubbard, Oct. 7, 2005
Hon. Jean-Pierre Blackburn, Feb. 6, 2006
Hon. Gregory Francis Thompson, Feb. 6, 2006
Hon. Marjory LeBreton, Feb. 6, 2006
Hon. Monte Solberg, Feb. 6, 2006
Hon. Charles (Chuck) Strahl, Feb. 6, 2006
Hon. Gary Lunn, Feb. 6, 2006
Hon. Peter Gordon MacKay, Feb. 6, 2006
Hon. Loyola Hearn, Feb. 6, 2006
Hon. Stockwell Burt Day, Feb. 6, 2006
Hon. Carol Skelton, Feb. 6, 2006
Hon. Vic Toews, Feb. 6, 2006
Hon. Rona Ambrose, Feb. 6, 2006
Hon. Michael D. Chong, Feb. 6, 2006
Hon. Diane Finley, Feb. 6, 2006
Hon. Gordon O'Connor, Feb. 6, 2006
Hon. Beverley J. (Bev) Oda, Feb. 6, 2006
Hon. Jim Prentice, Feb. 6, 2006
Hon. John Baird, Feb. 6, 2006
Hon. Maxime Bernier, Feb. 6, 2006
Hon. Lawrence Cannon, Feb. 6, 2006
Hon. Tony Clement, Feb. 6, 2006
Hon. Josée Verner, Feb. 6, 2006
Hon. Michael Fortier, Feb. 6, 2006
Hon. John Reynolds, Feb. 6, 2006
Hon. Jay D. Hill, Feb. 16, 2006
Hon. Peter Van Loan, Nov. 27, 2006
Hon. Jason Kenney, Jan. 4, 2007
Hon. Gerry Ritz, Jan. 4, 2007
Hon. Helena Guergis, Jan. 4, 2007
Hon. Christian Paradis, Jan. 4, 2007
Hon. Daniel Philip Hays, Jan. 22, 2007
Hon. James Abbott, Oct. 15, 2007
Hon. Diane Ablonczy, Aug. 14, 2007
Hon. James Moore, Jun. 25, 2008
Hon. Denis Losier, Sep. 3, 2008
Hon. Arthur Thomas Porter, Sep. 3, 2008
Hon. Leona Aglukkaq, Oct. 30, 2008
Hon. Keith Ashfield, Oct. 30, 2008
Hon. Steven John Fletcher, Oct. 30, 2008
Hon. Dr. Gary Goodyear, Oct. 30, 2008
Hon. Peter Kent, Oct. 30, 2008
Hon. Denis Lebel, Oct. 30, 2008
Hon. Rob Merrifield, Oct. 30, 2008
Hon. Lisa Raitt, Oct. 30, 2008
Hon. Gail Shea, Oct. 30, 2008
Hon. Lynne Yelich, Oct. 30, 2008
Hon. Leonard Joseph Gustafson, Jan. 8, 2009
Hon. Frances Lankin, Jan. 22, 2009
Hon. Kevin Lynch, May 11, 2009
Hon. Rob Moore, Jan. 19, 2010
Hon. Michael Grant Ignatieff, May 7, 2010
Hon. Philippe Couillard, Jun. 21, 2010
Hon. John Duncan, Aug. 6, 2010
Hon. Rick Casson, Oct. 1, 2010
Hon. Laurie Hawn, Oct. 1, 2010
Hon. Julian Fantino, Jan. 4, 2011
Hon. Ted Menzies, Jan. 4, 2011
Hon. Steven Blaney, May 18, 2011
Hon. Edward Fast, May 18, 2011
Hon. Joe Oliver, May 18, 2011
Hon. Peter Penashue, May 18, 2011
Hon. Tim Uppal, May 18, 2011
Hon. Alice Wong, May 18, 2011
Hon. Bal Gosal, May 18, 2011
Hon. Peter Andrew Stewart Milliken, May 8, 2012
Hon. Ronald Cannan, Sep. 13, 2012
Hon. Mike Lake, Sep. 13, 2012
Hon. Thomas J. Mulcair, Sep. 14, 2012
Right Hon. Michaëlle Jean, Sep. 26, 2012
Hon. Kerry-Lynne D. Findlay, Feb. 22, 2013
Hon. Ernest Preston Manning, Mar. 6, 2013
Hon. Deborah Grey, Apr. 22, 2013
Hon. Shelly Glover, Jul. 15, 2013
Hon. Chris Alexander, Jul. 15, 2013
Hon. Kellie Leitch, Jul. 15, 2013
Hon. Kevin Sorenson, Jul. 15, 2013
Hon. Pierre Poilievre, Jul. 15, 2013
Hon. Candice Bergen, Jul. 15, 2013
Hon. Greg Rickford, Jul. 15, 2013
Hon. Michelle Rempel, Jul. 15, 2013
Hon. L. Yves Fortier, Aug. 8, 2013
Hon. Claude Carignan, Sep. 3, 2013
Hon. Gerald J. Comeau, Sep. 19, 2013
Hon. Deepak Obhrai, Sep. 19, 2013
Hon. Cyril Eugene McLean, Mar. 6, 2014
Hon. Ed Holder, Mar. 19, 2014
H.R.H. Prince of Wales Charles Philip Arthur George, May 18, 2014
Hon. Wayne G. Wouters, Dec. 10, 2014
Hon. Erin O'Toole, Jan. 5, 2015
Hon. Ian Carl Holloway, Q.C., Jan. 30, 2015
Hon. Noël A. Kinsella, Feb. 23, 2015
Hon. Marie-Lucie Morin, Apr. 20, 2015
Right Hon. Justin Pierre James Trudeau, Nov. 4, 2015
Hon. William Francis Morneau, Nov. 4, 2015
Hon. Jody Wilson-Raybould, Nov. 4, 2015

Hon. Judy M. Foote, Nov. 4, 2015
Hon. Chrystia Freeland, Nov. 4, 2015
Hon. Jane Philpott, Nov. 4, 2015
Hon. Jean-Yves Duclos, Nov. 4, 2015
Hon. Marc Garneau, Nov. 4, 2015
Hon. Marie-Claude Bibeau, Nov. 4, 2015
Hon. James Gordon Carr, Nov. 4, 2015
Hon. Mélanie Joly, Nov. 4, 2015
Hon. Diane Lebouthillier, Nov. 4, 2015
Hon. Kent Hehr, Nov. 4, 2015
Hon. Catherine McKenna, Nov. 4, 2015
Hon. Harjit Singh Sajjan, Nov. 4, 2015
Hon. MaryAnn Mihychuk, Nov. 4, 2015
Hon. Amarjeet Sohi, Nov. 4, 2015
Hon. Maryam Monsef, Nov. 4, 2015
Hon. Carla Qualtrough, Nov. 4, 2015
Hon. Hunter Tootoo, Nov. 4, 2015
Hon. Kirsty Duncan, Nov. 4, 2015
Hon. Patricia A. Hajdu, Nov. 4, 2015
Hon. Bardish Chagger, Nov. 4, 2015
Hon. Andrew Brooke Leslie, Feb. 15, 2016
Hon. Ginette C. Petitpas Taylor, Feb. 15, 2016
Hon. V. Peter Harder, Apr. 6, 2016

Corporate Services / Services ministériels
Tel: 613-957-5151; *Fax:* 613-957-5138

Assistant Deputy Minister, Michelle Doucet
Tel: 613-957-5151
Chief Information Officer; Executive Director, IMST, Jennaeya McTavish
Tel: 613-957-5709
Executive Director, Finance & Corporate Planning Division, Karen Cahill
Tel: 613-957-5180
Executive Director, Human Resources Division, Renée de Bellefeuille
Tel: 613-952-4802

Office of Intergovernmental Affairs (IGA) / Affaires intergouvernementales

c/o Privy Council Office, #1000, 85 Slater St., Ottawa, ON K1A 0A3
Tel: 613-957-5153; *Fax:* 613-957-5043
TTY: 613-957-5741
info@pco-bcp.gc.ca
www.pco-bcp.gc.ca/aia

The federal government office is responsible for the management of federal-provincial-territorial relations (FPTR). The office supports & advises the Prime Minister & the Minister of Intergovernmental Affairs about issues related to federal-provincial-territorial relations, such as communications, policies, & parliamentary affairs. Fiscal federalism, the evolution of the federation, & Canadian unity are key areas for the IGA.

Prime Minister; Minister, Intergovernmental Affairs, Right Hon. Justin Pierre James Trudeau, P.C., B.A., B.Ed.
Tel: 613-995-0253; *Fax:* 613-947-0310
justin.trudeau@parl.gc.ca
Deputy Secretary to the Cabinet, Stephen Lucas
Tel: 613-957-5462
Acting Assistant Secretary to the Cabinet, Patrick Tanguy
Tel: 613-944-5432
Director, Operations, Provincial & Territorial Analysis, Catherine Demers
Tel: 613-947-4069
Acting Director, First Ministers' Meetings (FMM) & Multilateral Relations, Jonathan DeWolfe
Tel: 613-944-4780

Senate of Canada / Sénat du Canada

Ottawa, QC K1A 0A4
sencom@sen.parl.gc.ca
www.sen.parl.gc.ca
twitter.com/SenateCA

Senators are appointed by the Governor General, upon the recommendation of the Prime Minister of Canada. Senators hold their positions only until they attain the age of 75 years.
To be eligible for appointment, a senatorial candidate must be a Canadian citizen, & be at least 30 years of age. The person must own $4,000 of equity in land in his or her province or territory, & have a personal net worth of at least $4,000. A senator must also be a resident of the province or territory for which he or she is appointed.
The main tasks of the Senate are as follows: to examine bills; to approve, reject, or amend legislation; to investigate policy matters & to present recommendations; & to examine the government's spending proposals. No bill may become law unless it is passed by the Senate.
The main thrust of the Senate's work is carried out in committees, where bills are interpreted & reviewed clause by clause, & evidence is heard from groups & individuals who may be affected by the particular bill under review. Senators' committees, or study groups, investigate key issues, such as poverty, terrorism, literacy, children's rights, Aboriginal peoples, constitutional affairs, & foreign affairs. The Senate reports produced from these legislations have proved to be valuable, & have often led to changes in government policy or legislation.
The Senate, as originally constituted at Confederation, consisted of 72 members. Through the addition of new provinces & territories, & the general growth of Canada, the Senate now has 105 regular members. On January 29, 2014, Liberal Leader Justin Trudeau removed all 32 Liberal senators from the national Liberal caucus, but they still technically sit as Liberals.
Following the 2015 general election, Prime Minister Trudeau announced the creation of an independent advisory body to recommend Senate nominees through a merit-based system.
By provinces & territories, representation in the Senate of Canada is as follows (Sept. 2016):
Alberta 6;
British Columbia 5;
Manitoba 4;
New Brunswick 8;
Newfoundland & Labrador 6;
Northwest Territories 1;
Nova Scotia 8;
Nunavut 1;
Ontario 18:
Prince Edward Island 3;
Québec 18;
Saskatchewan 6;
Yukon 1.
By party affiliation, representation is as follows (Sept. 2016):
Conservative 41;
Liberal 21;
Non-affiliated 23;
Vacant 20;
Total 105.

Political Officers
Speaker of the Senate, Hon. George Furey, Non-affiliated
Tel: 613-992-4416
Toll-free: 800-267-7362; *Fax:* 613-992-9772
Speaker-President@sen.parl.gc.ca
Speaker pro tempore, Hon. Nicole Eaton, Conservative Party
Tel: 613-947-4047
Toll-free: 800-267-7362; *Fax:* 613-947-4044
nicole.eaton@sen.parl.gc.ca
Government Representative in the Senate; Leader of the Government in the Senate, Hon. Peter Harder, Non-affiliated
Tel: 613-995-0222
Toll-free: 800-267-7362; *Fax:* 613-995-0207
peter.harder@sen.parl.gc.ca
Legislative Deputy to the Government Representative in the Senate; Deputy Leader of the Government in the Senate, Hon. Diane Bellemare, Non-affiliated
Tel: 613-943-1555
Toll-free: 800-267-7362; *Fax:* 613-943-1565
diane.bellemare@sen.parl.gc.ca
Senate Liberal Leader, Hon. James S. Cowan, Liberal
Tel: 613-995-4268
Toll-free: 800-267-7362; *Fax:* 613-995-4287
jim.cowan@sen.parl.gc.ca
Leader of the Opposition in the Senate, Hon. Claude Carignan, Conservative Party
Tel: 613-992-0240
Toll-free: 800-267-7362; *Fax:* 613-992-0246
claude.carignan@sen.parl.gc.ca
Deputy Leader of the Senate Liberals, Hon. Joan Fraser, Liberal
Tel: 613-943-9556
Toll-free: 800-267-7362; *Fax:* 613-943-9558
joan.fraser@sen.parl.gc.ca
Deputy Leader of the Opposition in the Senate, Hon. Yonah Martin, Conservative Party
Tel: 613-943-4078
Toll-free: 800-267-7362; *Fax:* 613-943-4082
martin@sen.parl.gc.ca
Government Liaison; Government Whip in the Senate, Hon. Grant Mitchell, Non-affiliated
Tel: 613-995-4254
Toll-free: 800-267-7362; *Fax:* 613-995-4265
grant.mitchell@sen.parl.gc.ca
Senate Liberal Whip, Hon. Jim Munson, Liberal
Tel: 613-947-2504
Toll-free: 800-267-7362; *Fax:* 613-947-2506
jim.munson@sen.parl.gc.ca
Opposition Whip in the Senate, Hon. Donald Neil Plett, Conservative Party
Tel: 613-992-0180
Toll-free: 800-267-7362; *Fax:* 613-992-0186
don.plett@sen.parl.gc.ca
Deputy Opposition Whip in the Senate, Hon. Stephen Greene, Conservative Party
Tel: 613-947-4210
Toll-free: 800-267-7362; *Fax:* 613-947-4224
stephen.greene@sen.parl.gc.ca
Chair, Senate Liberal Caucus, Hon. Percy E. Downe, Liberal
Tel: 613-943-8107
Toll-free: 800-267-7362; *Fax:* 613-943-8109
percy.downe@sen.parl.gc.ca

Senators, with appointment year & political affiliation
Hon. Raynell Andreychuk, 1993, Conservative Party
Tel: 613-947-2239
Toll-free: 800-267-7362; *Fax:* 613-947-2241
raynell.andreychuk@sen.parl.gc.ca
raynellandreychuk.sencanada.ca
Hon. Salma Ataullahjan, 2010, Conservative Party
Tel: 613-947-5906
Toll-free: 800-267-7362; *Fax:* 613-947-5908
salma.ataullahjan@sen.parl.gc.ca
senatorsalma.sencanada.ca
Hon. George S. Baker, P.C., 2002, Liberal
Tel: 613-947-2517
Toll-free: 800-267-7362; *Fax:* 613-947-1525
george.baker@sen.parl.gc.ca
Hon. Denise Batters, 2013, Conservative Party
Tel: 613-996-8922
Toll-free: 800-267-7362; *Fax:* 613-996-8964
denise.batters@sen.parl.gc.ca
denisebatters.ca
Hon. Diane Bellemare, 2012, Non-affiliated
Tel: 613-943-1555
Toll-free: 800-267-7362; *Fax:* 613-943-1565
diane.bellemare@sen.parl.gc.ca
dianebellemaresen.ca
Hon. Lynn Beyak, 2013, Conservative Party
Tel: 613-996-8680
Toll-free: 800-267-7362; *Fax:* 613-996-8673
lynn.beyak@sen.parl.gc.ca
lynnbeyak.sencanada.ca
Hon. Douglas Black, 2013, Non-affiliated
Tel: 613-996-8757
Toll-free: 800-267-7362; *Fax:* 613-996-8862
doug.black@sen.parl.gc.ca
dougblack.ca
Hon. Pierre-Hugues Boisvenu, 2010, Non-affiliated
Tel: 613-943-4030
Toll-free: 800-267-7362; *Fax:* 613-943-4029
boisvp@sen.parl.gc.ca
www.boisvenu.ca
Note: Senator Boisvenu left the Conservative caucus on June 4, 2015, amid the growing Senate expense scandal.
Hon. Patrick Brazeau, 2008, Non-affiliated
Hon. Larry W. Campbell, 2005, Non-affiliated
Tel: 613-995-4050
Toll-free: 800-267-7362; *Fax:* 613-995-4056
larry.campbell@sen.parl.gc.ca
www.larrycampbell.ca
Hon. Claude Carignan, 2009, Conservative Party
Tel: 613-992-0240
Toll-free: 800-267-7362; *Fax:* 613-992-0246
claude.carignan@sen.parl.gc.ca
www.claudecarignan.ca
Hon. Anne C. Cools, 1984, Non-affiliated
Tel: 613-992-2808
Toll-free: 800-267-7362; *Fax:* 613-992-8513
anne.cools@sen.parl.gc.ca
senatorcools.sencanada.ca
Hon. Jane Marie Cordy, 2000, Liberal
Tel: 613-995-8409
Toll-free: 800-267-7362; *Fax:* 613-995-8432
jane.cordy@sen.parl.gc.ca
sen.parl.gc.ca/jcordy
Hon. James S. Cowan, 2005, Liberal
Tel: 613-995-4268
Toll-free: 800-267-7362; *Fax:* 613-995-4287
jim.cowan@sen.parl.gc.ca
Hon. Jean-Guy Dagenais, 2012, Conservative Party
Tel: 613-996-7644
Toll-free: 800-267-7362; *Fax:* 613-996-7649
jean-guy.dagenais@sen.parl.gc.ca
senateurdagenais.ca
Hon. Dennis Dawson, 2005, Liberal
Tel: 613-995-3978
Toll-free: 800-267-7362; *Fax:* 613-995-3998
dennis.dawson@sen.parl.gc.ca
Hon. Joseph A. Day, 2001, Liberal
Tel: 613-992-0833
Toll-free: 800-267-7362; *Fax:* 613-992-1175
joseph.day@sen.parl.gc.ca
jday.sencanada.ca
Hon. Jacques Demers, 2009, Non-affiliated
Tel: 613-992-0151
Toll-free: 800-267-7362; *Fax:* 613-992-0128
line.tessier@sen.parl.gc.ca
jacquesdemers.sencanada.ca
Hon. Percy E. Downe, 2003, Liberal
Tel: 613-943-8107
Toll-free: 800-267-7362; *Fax:* 613-943-8109

Percy.Downe@sen.parl.gc.ca
sen.parl.gc.ca/pdowne
Hon. Norman E. Doyle, 2012, Conservative Party
Tel: 613-996-7483
Toll-free: 800-267-7362; *Fax:* 613-996-7466
norman.doyle@sen.parl.gc.ca
normanedoyle.sencanada.ca
Hon. Michael Duffy, 2009, Non-affiliated
Tel: 613-947-4163
Toll-free: 800-267-7362; *Fax:* 613-947-4157
Michael.Duffy@sen.parl.gc.ca
www.mikeduffy.ca
Hon. Lillian Eva Dyck, 2005, Liberal
Tel: 613-995-4318
Toll-free: 800-267-7362; *Fax:* 613-995-4331
lillian.dyck@sen.parl.gc.ca
sen.parl.gc.ca/ldyck
Hon. Nicole Eaton, 2009, Conservative Party
Tel: 613-947-4047
Toll-free: 800-267-7362; *Fax:* 613-947-4044
nicole.eaton@sen.parl.gc.ca
nicoleeaton.sencanada.ca
Hon. Art Eggleton, P.C., 2005, Liberal
Tel: 613-995-4230
Toll-free: 800-267-7362; *Fax:* 613-995-4237
art.eggleton@sen.parl.gc.ca
www.senatorarteggleton.ca
Hon. Tobias C. Enverga Jr., 2012, Conservative Party
Tel: 613-943-1945
Toll-free: 800-267-7362; *Fax:* 613-943-1938
tobias.enverga@sen.parl.gc.ca
senatorenverga.com
Hon. Joan Fraser, 1998, Liberal
Tel: 613-943-9556
Toll-free: 800-267-7362; *Fax:* 613-943-9558
joan.fraser@sen.parl.gc.ca
sen.parl.gc.ca/jfraser
Hon. Linda Frum, 2009, Conservative Party
Tel: 613-992-0310
Toll-free: 800-267-7362; *Fax:* 613-992-0316
linda.frum@sen.parl.gc.ca
www.lindafrum.ca
Hon. George Furey, 1999, Non-affiliated
Tel: 613-992-4416
Toll-free: 800-267-7362; *Fax:* 613-943-1792
george.furey@sen.parl.gc.ca
sen.parl.gc.ca/gfurey
Hon. Raymonde Gagné, 2016, Non-affiliated
Tel: 613-943-4323
Toll-free: 800-267-7362; *Fax:* 613-943-4327
Raymonde.Gagne@sen.parl.gc.ca
Hon. Stephen Greene, 2009, Conservative Party
Tel: 613-947-4210
Toll-free: 800-267-7362; *Fax:* 613-947-4224
stephen.greene@sen.parl.gc.ca
stephengreene.sencanada.ca
Hon. Peter Harder, 2016, Non-affiliated
Tel: 613-995-0222
Toll-free: 800-267-7362; *Fax:* 613-995-0207
peter.harder@sen.parl.gc.ca
Hon. Leo Housakos, 2009, Conservative Party
Tel: 613-947-4237
Toll-free: 800-267-7362; *Fax:* 613-947-4239
Leo.Housakos@sen.parl.gc.ca
sen.parl.gc.ca/leohousakos
Hon. Elizabeth Hubley, 2001, Liberal
Tel: 613-992-1177
Toll-free: 800-267-7362; *Fax:* 613-992-1516
elizabeth.hubley@sen.parl.gc.ca
sen.parl.gc.ca/ehubley
Hon. Mobina S.B. Jaffer, 2001, Liberal
Tel: 613-992-0189
Toll-free: 800-267-7362; *Fax:* 613-992-0673
mobina.jaffer@sen.parl.gc.ca
mobinajaffer.ca
Hon. Janis G. Johnson, 1990, Conservative Party
Tel: 613-943-1430
Toll-free: 800-267-7362; *Fax:* 613-992-5029
janis.johnson@sen.parl.gc.ca
janisjohnson.ca
Hon. Serge Joyal, P.C., 1997, Liberal
Tel: 613-943-0434
Toll-free: 800-267-7362; *Fax:* 613-943-0441
serge.joyal@sen.parl.gc.ca
sergejoyal.sencanada.ca
Hon. Colin Kenny, 1984, Liberal
Tel: 613-996-2877
Toll-free: 800-267-7362; *Fax:* 613-996-3737
colin.kenny@sen.parl.gc.ca
www.colinkenny.ca
Hon. Daniel Lang, 2009, Conservative Party
Tel: 613-947-4050
Toll-free: 800-267-7362; *Fax:* 613-947-4049
daniel.lang@sen.parl.gc.ca
www.danlang.ca
Hon. Frances Lankin, 2016, Non-affiliated
Tel: 613-995-2795
Toll-free: 800-267-7362; *Fax:* 613-995-2789
Frances.Lankin@sen.parl.gc.ca
Hon. Sandra M. Lovelace Nicholas, 2005, Liberal
Tel: 613-943-3635
Toll-free: 800-267-7362; *Fax:* 613-943-3637
carole.smith@sen.parl.gc.ca
Hon. Michael L. MacDonald, 2009, Conservative Party
Tel: 613-995-1866
Toll-free: 800-267-7362; *Fax:* 613-995-1853
michael.macdonald@sen.parl.gc.ca
www.capebretonsenator.ca
Hon. Ghislain Maltais, 2012, Conservative Party
Tel: 613-996-7377
Toll-free: 800-267-7362; *Fax:* 613-996-7260
ghislain.maltais@sen.parl.gc.ca
ghislainmaltais.sencanada.ca
Hon. Fabian Manning, 2011, Conservative Party
Tel: 613-947-4203
Toll-free: 800-267-7362; *Fax:* 613-947-4170
fabian.manning@sen.parl.gc.ca
www.fabianmanning.ca
Hon. Elizabeth (Beth) Marshall, 2010, Conservative Party
Tel: 613-943-4011
Toll-free: 800-267-7362
elizabeth.marshall@sen.parl.gc.ca
elizabethmarshall.ca
Hon. Yonah Martin, 2009, Conservative Party
Tel: 613-943-4078
Toll-free: 800-267-7362; *Fax:* 613-943-4082
martin@sen.parl.gc.ca
yonahmartin.sencanada.ca
Hon. Paul J. Massicotte, 2003, Liberal
Tel: 613-943-8110
Toll-free: 800-267-7362; *Fax:* 613-943-8129
paul.massicotte@sen.parl.gc.ca
pauljmassicotte.sencanada.ca
Hon. Elaine McCoy, 2005, Non-affiliated
Tel: 613-995-4293
Toll-free: 800-267-7362; *Fax:* 613-995-4304
elaine.mccoy@sen.parl.gc.ca
www.albertasenator.ca
Note: Elaine McCoy sits as a Non-affiliated Progressive Conservative.
Hon. Thomas Johnson McInnis, 2012, Conservative Party
Tel: 613-943-1662
Toll-free: 800-267-7362; *Fax:* 613-943-1683
thomasjohnson.mcinnis@sen.parl.gc.ca
senatormcinnis.sencanada.ca
Hon. Paul E. McIntyre, Q.C., 2012, Conservative Party
Tel: 613-943-1756
Toll-free: 800-267-7362; *Fax:* 613-943-1751
paul.mcintyre@sen.parl.gc.ca
paulmcintyre.sencanada.ca
Hon. Terry M. Mercer, 2003, Liberal
Tel: 613-996-2657
Toll-free: 800-267-7362; *Fax:* 613-947-2345
terry.mercer@sen.parl.gc.ca
Hon. Pana Merchant, 2002, Liberal
Tel: 613-944-7777
Toll-free: 800-267-7362; *Fax:* 613-944-7778
pana.merchant@sen.parl.gc.ca
Hon. Don Meredith, 2010, Non-affiliated
Tel: 613-996-8572
Toll-free: 800-267-7362; *Fax:* 613-996-8570
don.meredith@sen.parl.gc.ca
donmeredith.sencanada.ca
Hon. Grant Mitchell, 2005, Non-affiliated
Tel: 613-995-4254
Toll-free: 800-267-7362; *Fax:* 613-995-4265
grant.mitchell@sen.parl.gc.ca
senatorgrantmitchell.ca
Hon. Percy Mockler, 2009, Conservative Party
Tel: 613-947-4225
Toll-free: 800-267-7362; *Fax:* 613-947-4227
percy.mockler@sen.parl.gc.ca
percymockler.sencanada.ca
Hon. Wilfred P. Moore, 1996, Liberal
Tel: 613-947-1921
Toll-free: 800-267-7362; *Fax:* 613-943-1995
wp.moore@sen.parl.gc.ca
Hon. Jim Munson, 2003, Liberal
Tel: 613-947-2504
Toll-free: 800-267-7362; *Fax:* 613-947-2506
jim.munson@sen.parl.gc.ca
senatormunson.ca
Hon. Richard Neufeld, 2009, Conservative Party
Tel: 613-947-4055
Toll-free: 800-267-7362; *Fax:* 613-947-4065
richard.neufeld@sen.parl.gc.ca
senatorrichardneufeld.com
Hon. Thanh Hai Ngo, 2012, Conservative Party
Tel: 613-943-1599
Toll-free: 800-267-7362; *Fax:* 613-943-1592
thanhhai.ngo@sen.parl.gc.ca
www.senatorngo.com
Hon. Kelvin Kenneth Ogilvie, 2009, Conservative Party
Tel: 613-992-0331
Toll-free: 800-267-7362; *Fax:* 613-992-0334
kelvin.ogilvie@sen.parl.gc.ca
senatorkelvinogilvie.sencanada.ca
Hon. Victor Oh, 2013, Conservative Party
Tel: 613-943-1880
Toll-free: 800-267-7362; *Fax:* 613-943-1882
senator.oh@sen.parl.gc.ca
victoroh.ca
Hon. Ratna Omidvar, 2016, Non-affiliated
Tel: 613-943-4330
Toll-free: 800-267-7362; *Fax:* 613-943-4328
Ratna.Omidvar@sen.parl.gc.ca
victoroh.ca
Hon. Dennis Glen Patterson, 2009, Conservative Party
Tel: 613-992-0480
Toll-free: 800-267-7362; *Fax:* 613-992-0495
dennis.patterson@sen.parl.gc.ca
www.dennispatterson.ca
Hon. Chantal Petitclerc, 2016, Non-affiliated
Tel: 613-995-0298
Toll-free: 800-267-7362; *Fax:* 613-995-0276
Chantal.Petitclerc@sen.parl.gc.ca
Hon. Donald Neil Plett, 2009, Conservative Party
Tel: 613-992-0180
Toll-free: 800-267-7362; *Fax:* 613-992-0186
don.plett@sen.parl.gc.ca
www.donplett.ca
Hon. Rose-May Poirier, 2010, Conservative Party
Tel: 613-943-4027
Toll-free: 800-267-7362; *Fax:* 613-943-4026
rosemay.poirier@sen.parl.gc.ca
rosemaypoirier.sencanada.ca
Hon. André Pratte, 2016, Non-affiliated
Tel: 613-995-0300
Toll-free: 800-267-7362; *Fax:* 613-995-0318
Andre.Pratte@sen.parl.gc.ca
Hon. Nancy Greene Raine, 2009, Conservative Party
Tel: 613-947-4052
Toll-free: 800-267-7362; *Fax:* 613-947-4054
nancy.raine@sen.parl.gc.ca
sen.parl.gc.ca/nraine
Hon. Pierrette Ringuette, 2002, Non-affiliated
Tel: 613-943-2248
Toll-free: 800-267-7362; *Fax:* 613-943-2245
pierrette.ringuette@sen.parl.gc.ca
pringuette.sencanada.ca
Hon. Bob Runciman, 2010, Conservative Party
Tel: 613-943-4020
Toll-free: 800-267-7362; *Fax:* 613-943-4022
bob.runciman@sen.parl.gc.ca
www.bobrunciman.com
Hon. Nancy Ruth, 2005, Conservative Party
Tel: 613-995-4174
Toll-free: 800-267-7362; *Fax:* 613-995-4188
nancy.ruth@sen.parl.gc.ca
www.nancyruth.ca
Hon. Judith Seidman, 2009, Conservative Party
Tel: 613-992-0110
Toll-free: 800-267-7362; *Fax:* 613-992-0118
judith.seidman@sen.parl.gc.ca
www.judithseidman.ca
Hon. Nick G. Sibbeston, 1999, Non-affiliated
Tel: 613-943-7790
Toll-free: 800-267-7362; *Fax:* 613-943-7792
sibnic@sen.parl.gc.ca
sen.parl.gc.ca/nsibbeston
Hon. Murray Sinclair, 2016, Non-affiliated
Tel: 613-995-0234
Toll-free: 800-267-7362; *Fax:* 613-995-0273
Murray.Sinclair@sen.parl.gc.ca
Hon. Larry W. Smith, 2011, Conservative Party
Tel: 613-996-8555
Toll-free: 800-267-7362; *Fax:* 613-996-8565
larry.smith@sen.parl.gc.ca
larrysmith.sencanada.ca
Hon. Carolyn Stewart Olsen, 2009, Conservative Party
Tel: 613-992-0121
Toll-free: 800-267-7362; *Fax:* 613-992-0124
carolyn.stewartolsen@sen.parl.gc.ca
carolynstewartolsen.sencanada.ca
Hon. Scott Tannas, 2013, Conservative Party
Tel: 613-943-2240
Toll-free: 800-267-7362; *Fax:* 613-943-2280

scott.tannas@sen.parl.gc.ca
scotttannas.com
Hon. Claudette Tardif, 2005, Liberal
Tel: 613-947-3589
Toll-free: 800-267-7362; *Fax:* 613-947-3609
claudette.tardif@sen.parl.gc.ca
claudettetardif.ca
Hon. David Tkachuk, 1993, Conservative Party
Tel: 613-947-3196
Toll-free: 800-267-7362; *Fax:* 613-947-3198
david.tkachuk@sen.parl.gc.ca
senatortkachuk.com
Hon. Betty E. Unger, 2012, Conservative Party
Tel: 613-996-7420
Toll-free: 800-267-7362; *Fax:* 613-996-7407
betty.unger@sen.parl.gc.ca
www.bettyunger.ca
Hon. Josée Verner, P.C., 2011, Conservative Party
Tel: 613-996-6999
Toll-free: 800-267-7362; *Fax:* 613-996-7004
josee.verner@sen.parl.gc.ca
joseeverner.sencanada.ca
Hon. John D. Wallace, 2009, Non-affiliated
Tel: 613-947-4240
Toll-free: 800-267-7362; *Fax:* 613-947-4252
john.wallace@sen.parl.gc.ca
johnwallace.sencanada.ca
Hon. Pamela Wallin, O.C., S.O.M., 2009, Non-affiliated
Tel: 613-996-2794
Toll-free: 800-267-7362
pamela.wallin@sen.parl.gc.ca
www.pamelawallin.com
Hon. Charlie Watt, 1984, Liberal
Tel: 613-992-2981
Toll-free: 800-267-7362; *Fax:* 613-990-5453
charlie.watt@sen.parl.gc.ca
Hon. David M. Wells, 2013, Conservative Party
Tel: 613-943-1788
Toll-free: 800-267-7362; *Fax:* 613-943-1926
claudine.courtois@sen.parl.gc.ca
www.davidwells.ca
Hon. Vernon White, 2012, Conservative Party
Tel: 613-996-7602
Toll-free: 800-267-7362; *Fax:* 613-996-7654
senatorwhite@sen.parl.gc.ca
sen.parl.gc.ca/vwhite

Clerk of the Senate & Clerk of the Parliaments
Parliament Hill, Centre Block, #185-S, Ottawa, ON K1A 0A4
Clerk of the Senate & Clerk of the Parliaments, Charles Robert
Tel: 613-992-2493
Law Clerk, Michel Patrice
Director, Communications Directorate, Mélisa Leclerc
Tel: 613-996-2751; *Fax:* 613-995-4998
Principal Clerk, Committees Directorate, Blair Armitage
Tel: 613-996-5588
Principal Clerk, Chamber & Procedure Office, Heather Lank
Tel: 613-996-0397
Usher of the Black Rod, J. Greg Peters
Tel: 613-992-8483
Director General & Clerk Assistant, International & Interparliamentary Affairs, Eric Janse
Tel: 613-992-6637; *Fax:* 613-992-3674
Director, Information Services Directorate, Hélène Bouchard
Tel: 613-993-5299
Director, Legislative Systems & Broadcasting Directorate, Diane Boucher
Tel: 613-992-1222
Clerk Assistant & Director General, International & Interparliamentary Affairs, Eric Janse
Tel: 613-992-6637; *Fax:* 613-992-3674
Chief Financial Officer, Finance & Procurement Directorate, Pascale Legault
Tel: 613-943-0197; *Fax:* 613-643-4030
Acting Director, Human Resources Directorate, Angela Vanikiotis
Tel: 613-996-1096; *Fax:* 613-992-1995

Parliamentary Precinct Services
Chambers Bldg., 40 Elgin St., 13th Fl., Ottawa, ON K1A 0A4
Director General, Gilles Duguay
Tel: 613-992-4787

House of Commons, Canada / Chambre des communes

House of Commons, Centre Block, Parliament Buildings, 111 Wellington St., Ottawa, ON K1A 0A6
Tel: 613-992-4793
Toll-Free: 866-599-4999
TTY: 613-995-2266
info@parl.gc.ca
www.parl.gc.ca
Information Service, Parliament of Canada
Ottawa, ON K1A 0A9

The House of Commons is the major law-making unit in Canada. The 338 members of the House represent each constituency, or riding, across Canada.
Members are elected in general elections, held at least once every five years. During general elections, one candidate per riding is elected, based on the largest number of votes, even if his or her vote is less than half the total. When a member resigns or dies between general elections, a by-election is held. The party that wins the largest number of seats in the general election usually forms the government. The party with the second largest number of votes becomes the Official Opposition. A minority government is created when one particular party holds no clear majority of seats in the House. In this case, the government is usually led by the party with the most seats in Parliament, providing it can sustain the support from other minor parties that enable it to pass legislation.
Any bills within federal jurisdiction must be passed by a majority of House members to become law. Members usually vote on proposed legislation according to party affiliation. They may vote against their party. They may also leave their elected party to sit as an independent within the House.
The Speaker of the House of Commons is a Member of Parliament, who is selected by fellow Members of Parliament through a secret ballot process. The Speaker's roles are to ensure that all procedures & rules are followed in the House, & to oversee administration in the House.

Officers & Officials of the House of Commons
Speaker of the House of Commons, Hon. Geoff Regan, P.C., B.A., LL.B.
Tel: 613-996-3085; *Fax:* 613-996-6988
geoff.regan@parl.gc.ca
Deputy Speaker; Chair, Committees of the Whole, Bruce Stanton
Tel: 613-992-6582; *Fax:* 613-996-3128
bruce.stanton@parl.gc.ca
Leader of the Government in the House of Commons, Hon. Bardish Chagger, P.C.
Tel: 613-996-5928; *Fax:* 613-992-6251
Bardish.Chagger@parl.gc.ca
Note: Web Site: www.houseleader.gc.ca
House Leader, Official Opposition; House Leader, Conservative Party, Hon. Candice Bergen
Tel: 613-995-9511; *Fax:* 613-947-0313
candice.bergen@parl.gc.ca
House Leader, New Democratic Party, Peter Julian, B.A.
Tel: 613-992-4214; *Fax:* 613-947-9500
peter.julian@parl.gc.ca
Chief Government Whip; Whip, Liberal Party, Andrew Leslie
Tel: 613-995-1800; *Fax:* 613-995-6298
Andrew.Leslie@parl.gc.ca
Chief Opposition Whip; Whip, Conservative Party, Gordon Brown, B.A. (Hons)
Tel: 613-992-8756; *Fax:* 613-996-9171
gord.brown@parl.gc.ca
Whip, New Democratic Party, Marjolaine Boutin-Sweet
Tel: 613-947-4576; *Fax:* 613-947-4579
marjolaine.boutin-sweet@parl.gc.ca
Caucus Chair, Liberal Party, Francis Scarpaleggia, B.A., M.A., M.B.A.
Tel: 613-995-8281; *Fax:* 613-996-0828
francis.scarpaleggia@parl.gc.ca
Caucus Chair, Conservative Party, David Sweet
Tel: 613-996-4984; *Fax:* 613-996-4986
David.Sweet@parl.gc.ca
Responsible, Liberal Party Research Office, Right Hon. Justin Pierre James Trudeau, P.C., B.A., B.Ed., Liberal
Tel: 613-995-0253; *Fax:* 613-947-0310
justin.trudeau@parl.gc.ca
www.pm.gc.ca
Responsible, Conservative Party Research Office (Interim), Hon. Rona Ambrose, P.C., B.A., M.A.
Tel: 613-996-9778; *Fax:* 613-996-0785
rona.ambrose@parl.gc.ca
Responsible, New Democratic Party Research Office, Hon. Thomas J. Mulcair, P.C., B.C.L. (Civil Law). LL.B (Common Law), New Democratic Party
Tel: 613-947-0867; *Fax:* 613-947-0868
thomas.mulcair@parl.gc.ca
www.ndp.ca/tom
Social Media: twitter.com/ThomasMulcair, www.facebook.com/ThomasMulcair
Clerk, House of Commons, Audrey Elizabeth O'Brien
Tel: 613-992-2986; *Fax:* 613-995-6668
audrey.obrien@parl.gc.ca
Deputy Clerk, House of Commons; Acting Clerk, House of Commons, Marc Bosc
Tel: 613-992-2986; *Fax:* 613-995-6668
marc.bosc@parl.gc.ca
Acting Sergeant-at-Arms; Deputy Sergeant-at-Arms, Pat McDonell
Tel: 613-995-7020
patrick.mcdonell@parl.gc.ca
Office of the Sergeant-at-Arms, House of Commons
111 Wellington St.
Ottawa, ON K1A 0A6
Parliamentary Secretary to the Leader of the Government in the House of Commons, Kevin Lamoureux
Tel: 613-996-6417; *Fax:* 613-996-9713
kevin.lamoureux@parl.gc.ca

Committees of the House of Commons / Comités de la chambre des communes
Committees Directorate, House of Commons, 131 Queen St., 6th Fl., Ottawa, ON K1A 0A6
Tel: 613-992-3150; *Fax:* 613-947-3089
cmteweb@parl.gc.ca
www.parl.gc.ca/committeebusiness

A committee consists of parliamentarians from the House of Commons, the Senate, or both. Committee members are selected for study & consideration of matters, including bills. Items for consideration by committees are referred by the House of Commons or the Senate.
Types of committees include the following: Committees of the Whole; Joint Committees; Legislative Committees; Liaison Committee; Standing Committees; & Special Committees.
The following were the House of Commons Committees as of Sept. 2016:
Access to Information, Privacy, & Ethics;
Agriculture & Agri-Food;
Canadian Heritage;
Citizenship & Immigration;
Electoral Reform;
Environment & Sustainable Development;
Finance;
Fisheries & Oceans;
Foreign Affairs & International Development;
Government Operations & Estimates;
Health;
Human Resources, Skills & Social Development, & the Status of Persons with Disabilities;
Indigenous & Northern Affairs;
Industry, Science, & Technology;
International Trade;
Justice & Human Rights;
Liaison;
National Defence;
Natural Resources;
Official Languages;
Pay Equity (Special Committee);
Procedure & House Affairs;
Public Accounts;
Public Safety & National Security;
Status of Women;
Transport, Infrastructure, & Communities;
& Veterans Affairs.
Principal Clerk, Committees, Jeffrey LeBlanc
Tel: 613-995-0516; *Fax:* 613-947-3089
jeffrey.leblanc@parl.gc.ca
Principal Clerk, Committees, Ian McDonald
Tel: 613-943-9484; *Fax:* 613-947-0309
ian.mcdonald@parl.gc.ca
Clerk, Access to Information, Privacy, & Ethics Committee, Michel Marcotte
Tel: 613-992-1240; *Fax:* 613-947-3089
ethi@parl.gc.ca
parl.gc.ca/ETHI-e
Clerk, Agriculture & Agri-Food Committee, David Chandonnet
Tel: 613-947-6732; *Fax:* 613-947-3089
agri@parl.gc.ca
parl.gc.ca/AGRI-e
Clerk, Canadian Heritage Committee, Jean-François Lafleur
Tel: 613-947-6729; *Fax:* 613-947-3089
chpc@parl.gc.ca
parl.gc.ca/CHPC-e
Clerk, Citizenship & Immigration Committee, Erica Pereira
Tel: 613-995-8525; *Fax:* 613-947-3089
cimm@parl.gc.ca
parl.gc.ca/CIMM-e
Clerk, Environment & Sustainable Development Committee, Cynara Corbin
Tel: 613-992-5023; *Fax:* 613-947-3089
envi@parl.gc.ca
parl.gc.ca/ENVI-e

Clerk, Finance Committee, Suzie Cadieux
Tel: 613-992-9753; *Fax:* 613-947-3089
fina@parl.gc.ca
parl.gc.ca/FINA-e

Clerk, Fisheries & Oceans Committee, David Chandonnet
Tel: 613-996-3105; *Fax:* 613-947-3089
fopo@parl.gc.ca
parl.gc.ca/FOPO-e

Clerk, Foreign Affairs & International Development Committee, Angela Crandall
Tel: 613-996-1540; *Fax:* 613-947-3089
faae@parl.gc.ca
parl.gc.ca/FAAE-e

Clerk, Government Operations & Estimates Committee, Leif-Erik Aune
Tel: 613-995-9469; *Fax:* 613-947-3089
oggo@parl.gc.ca
parl.gc.ca/OGGO-e

Clerk, Health Committee, David Gagnon
Tel: 613-995-4108; *Fax:* 613-947-3089
hesa@parl.gc.ca
parl.gc.ca/HESA-e

Clerk, Human Resources, Skills, & Social Development & the Status of Persons with Disabilities Committee, Julie Geoffrion
Tel: 613-996-1542; *Fax:* 613-947-3089
huma@parl.gc.ca
parl.gc.ca/HUMA-e

Clerk, Indigenous & Northern Affairs Committee, Michelle Legault
Tel: 613-996-1173; *Fax:* 613-947-3089
inan@parl.gc.ca
parl.gc.ca/INAN-e

Clerk, Industry, Science, & Technology Committee, Roger Préfontaine
Tel: 613-947-1971; *Fax:* 613-947-3089
indu@parl.gc.ca
parl.gc.ca/INDU-e

Clerk, International Trade Committee, Rémi Bourgault
Tel: 613-944-4364; *Fax:* 613-947-3089
ciit@parl.gc.ca
parl.gc.ca/CIIT-e

Clerk, Justice & Human Rights Committee, Michael MacPherson
Tel: 613-996-1553; *Fax:* 613-947-3089
just@parl.gc.ca
parl.gc.ca/JUST-e

Clerk, Liaison Committee, Ian McDonald
Tel: 613-943-9484; *Fax:* 613-947-3089
liai@parl.gc.ca
parl.gc.ca/LIAI-e

Clerk, National Defence Committee, Philippe Grenier-Michaud
Tel: 613-995-9461; *Fax:* 613-947-3089
nddn@parl.gc.ca
parl.gc.ca/NDDN-e

Clerk, Natural Resources Committee, Michel Marcotte
Tel: 613-995-0047; *Fax:* 613-947-3089
rnnr@parl.gc.ca
parl.gc.ca/RNNR-e

Clerk, Official Languages Committee, Georges Etoka
Tel: 613-947-8891; *Fax:* 613-947-3089
lang@parl.gc.ca
parl.gc.ca/LANG-e

Clerk, Pay Equity Special Committee, Julie Lalande Prud'homme
Tel: 613-995-2622; *Fax:* 613-947-3089
espe@parl.gc.ca
parl.gc.ca/ESPE-e

Clerk, Procedure & House Affairs Committee, Joann Garbig
Tel: 613-996-0506; *Fax:* 613-947-3089
proc@parl.gc.ca
parl.gc.ca/PROC-e

Clerk, Public Accounts Committee, Caroline Massicotte
Tel: 613-996-1664; *Fax:* 613-947-3089
pacp@parl.gc.ca
parl.gc.ca/PACP-e

Clerk, Public Safety & National Security Committee, Jean-Marie David
Tel: 613-944-5635; *Fax:* 613-947-3089
secu@parl.gc.ca
parl.gc.ca/SECU-e

Clerk, Status of Women Committee, Danielle Widmer
Tel: 613-995-6119; *Fax:* 613-947-3089
fewo@parl.gc.ca
parl.gc.ca/FEWO-e

Clerk, Transport, Infrastructure, & Communities Committee, Andrew Bartholomew Chaplin
Tel: 613-996-4663; *Fax:* 613-947-3089
tran@parl.gc.ca
parl.gc.ca/TRAN-e

Clerk, Veterans Affairs Committee, Hughes La Rue
Tel: 613-944-9354; *Fax:* 613-947-3089
acva@parl.gc.ca
parl.gc.ca/ACVA-e

Finance Services / Services des Finances

Chief Financial Officer, Daniel Paquette
Tel: 613-996-0485; *Fax:* 613-995-4970
daniel.g.paquette@parl.gc.ca

Senior Director, Corporate Accounting, Systems & Internal Control, José Fernandez
Tel: 613-947-2570
jose.fernandez@parl.gc.ca

Acting Senior Director, Financial Planning, Resource Management & Corporate Policies, Sanjiv Sandhu
Tel: 613-992-6169; *Fax:* 613-947-3571
sanjiv.sandhu@parl.gc.ca

Human Resources Services / Services en ressources humaines

Chief Human Resources Officer, Pierre Parent
Tel: 613-992-0100; *Fax:* 613-947-0001
pierre.parent@parl.gc.ca

Senior Director, Corporate Preparedness & Planning, Jill Anne Joseph
Tel: 613-944-9390
jillanne.joseph@parl.gc.ca

Information Services / Services de l'information

Chief Information Officer, Stéphan Aubé
Tel: 613-995-8884; *Fax:* 613-947-3547
stephan.aube@parl.gc.ca

Chief Technology Officer, Soufiane Ben Moussa
Tel: 613-947-5599; *Fax:* 613-947-3547
soufiane.benmoussa@parl.gc.ca

Senior Director, IT Operations & Services, Louis Lefebvre
Tel: 613-944-5272; *Fax:* 613-947-6292
louis.lefebvre@parl.gc.ca

Law Clerk & Parliamentary Counsel / Légiste et Conseiller parlementaire

Law Clerk & Parliamentary Counsel, Philippe Dufresne
Tel: 613-996-1057
philippe.dufresne@parl.gc.ca

Deputy Law Clerk & Parliamentary Counsel, Richard Denis
Tel: 613-943-2601; *Fax:* 613-947-5556
richard.denis@parl.gc.ca

Chief, Administrative Services, Suzanne Dupuis
Tel: 613-947-1997; *Fax:* 613-947-5556
suzanne.c.dupuis@parl.gc.ca

Office of the Clerk & Secretariat / Bureau de la greffière et secrétariat

Clerk of the House of Commons, Audrey O'Brien
Tel: 613-992-2986; *Fax:* 613-995-6668
audrey.obrien@parl.gc.ca

Deputy Clerk of the House of Commons; Acting Clerk of the House of Commons, Marc Bosc
Tel: 613-992-2986; *Fax:* 613-995-6668
marc.bosc@parl.gc.ca

Chief Audit Executive, Internal Audit, Jennifer Wall
Tel: 613-944-4080
jennifer.wall@parl.gc.ca

Acting Head, Corporate Communications, Nathalie Hannah
Tel: 613-947-4876; *Fax:* 613-995-3052
nathalie.hannah@parl.gc.ca

Parliamentary Precinct Operations / Opérations de la Cité parlementaire

Tel: 613-995-7521; *Fax:* 613-995-1650

Director General, Parliamentary Precinct Operations, Benoit Giroux
Tel: 613-995-1990; *Fax:* 613-995-1650
benoit.giroux@parl.gc.ca

Procedural Services / Services de la procédure

Acting Deputy Clerk of the House of Commons, André Gagnon
Tel: 613-947-5623; *Fax:* 613-995-1449
andre.gagnon@parl.gc.ca

Principal Clerk, Committees, Jeffrey LeBlanc
Tel: 613-995-0516; *Fax:* 613-947-3089
jeffrey.leblanc@parl.gc.ca

Acting Principal Clerk, Chamber Business & Parliamentary Publications, Jeremy LeBlanc
Tel: 613-996-1086; *Fax:* 613-995-3331
jeremy.leblanc@parl.gc.ca

Principal Clerk, Committees & Legislative Services Directorate, Ian McDonald
Tel: 613-943-9484; *Fax:* 613-947-0309
ian.mcdonald@parl.gc.ca

Principal Clerk, Information Management, Pierre Rodrigue
Tel: 613-944-5652; *Fax:* 613-995-2997
pierre.rodrigue@parl.gc.ca

Office of the Prime Minister, Liberal Party of Canada / Liberal Research Bureau

Langevin Block, 80 Wellington St., Ottawa, ON K1A 0A2
Tel: 613-992-4211; *Fax:* 613-941-6900
TTY: 613-957-5741
www.pm.gc.ca

The Prime Minister is the Head of Government in Canada & usually the leader of the party in power in the House of Commons.
The Prime Minister recommends the appointment of the Governor General to the monarchy, & is responsible for selecting a team of ministers, who are then appointed by the Governor General to the Queen's Privy Council. In addition, he or she also controls the appointment of senators, judges, & parliamentary secretaries. It is customary that the Prime Minister is also appointed to the Imperial Privy Council & is thus titled, "The Right Honourable". The Prime Minister has the right to dissolve parliament & can therefore control the timing of general elections.
The Prime Minister's Office is a central agency that features the executive staff of the Prime Minister, such as partisan political advisors & administrators, who provide support to the Prime Minister exclusively.
The Right Hon. Justin Trudeau was sworn in as Canada's 23rd Prime Minister at a ceremony held Nov. 4, 2015, at Rideau Hall.

Prime Minister; Responsible, Liberal Party Research Office, Right Hon. Justin Pierre James Trudeau, P.C., B.A., B.Ed.
Tel: 613-995-0253; *Fax:* 613-947-0310
justin.trudeau@parl.gc.ca

Leader of the Government in the House of Commons; Liberal Party House Leader, Hon. Bardish Chagger, P.C.
Tel: 613-996-5928; *Fax:* 613-992-6251
Bardish.Chagger@parl.gc.ca

Caucus Chair, Liberal Party, Francis Scarpaleggia, B.A., M.A., M.B.A.
Tel: 613-995-8281; *Fax:* 613-996-0828
francis.scarpaleggia@parl.gc.ca

Chief Government Whip, Hon. Andrew Leslie, C.M.M., M.Sc., M.S.M., C.D., P.C.
Tel: 613-995-1800; *Fax:* 613-995-6298
Andrew.Leslie@parl.gc.ca

Deputy Government Whip, Hon. Ginette Petitpas Taylor, P.C.
Tel: 613-992-8072; *Fax:* 613-992-8083
Ginette.PetitpasTaylor@parl.gc.ca

Parliamentary Secretary to the Prime Minister, Celina Caesar-Chavannes
Tel: 613-992-6344; *Fax:* 613-992-8320
Celina.Caesar-Chavannes@parl.gc.ca

Parliamentary Secretary to the Prime Minister (Intergovernmental Affairs), Adam Vaughan
Tel: 613-992-2352; *Fax:* 613-992-6301
Adam.Vaughan@parl.gc.ca

Parliamentary Secretary to the Prime Minister (Youth), Peter Schiefke
Tel: 613-957-3744; *Fax:* 613-952-0874
Peter.Schiefke@parl.gc.ca

Chief of Staff, Katie Telford

Principal Secretary, Gerald Butts

Office of the Leader, Official Opposition, Conservative Party of Canada / Conservative Party Research Bureau

Centre Block, 111 Wellington St., Ottawa, ON K1A 0A6
Tel: 613-995-1333; *Fax:* 613-995-1337
www.conservative.ca
twitter.com/cpc_hq
www.facebook.com/cpcpcc

The Conservative Party of Canada became the Official Opposition after losing to the Liberals in the 2015 general election. Former Prime Minister Stephen Harper resigned as Leader following the party's defeat. Rona Ambrose was chosen as the party's new Interim Leader at a meeting held Nov. 5, 2015.

Interim Leader, Official Opposition; Interim Party Leader, Conservative Party of Canada; Responsible, Conservative Party Research Office, Hon. Rona Ambrose, P.C., B.A., M.A.
Tel: 613-996-9778; *Fax:* 613-996-0785
rona.ambrose@parl.gc.ca

Deputy Leader, Conservative Party of Canada, Hon. Denis Lebel, P.C.
Tel: 613-996-6236; *Fax:* 613-996-6252
denis.lebel@parl.gc.ca

House Leader, Official Opposition, Hon. Candice Bergen
Tel: 613-995-9511; *Fax:* 613-947-0313
candice.bergen@parl.gc.ca

Caucus Chair, Conservative Party of Canada, David Sweet
Tel: 613-996-4984; *Fax:* 613-996-4986
David.Sweet@parl.gc.ca

Chief Opposition Whip, Gordon Brown, B.A. (Hons)
Tel: 613-992-8756; *Fax:* 613-996-9171
gord.brown@parl.gc.ca
Deputy Opposition Whip, Dave MacKenzie
Tel: 613-995-4432; *Fax:* 613-995-4433
dave.mackenzie@parl.gc.ca
Director, Caucus Services, Policy & Research, Conservative Research Bureau, Martin Bélanger
Tel: 613-996-5084; *Fax:* 613-943-8727
martin.belanger@parl.gc.ca
Interim Executive Director, Conservative Party of Canada, Simon Thompson

Office of the Leader, New Democratic Party / New Democratic Party Research Bureau

Centre Block, 111 Wellington St., Ottawa, ON K1A 0A6
Tel: 613-995-7224; *Fax:* 613-995-4565
www.npd.ca
www.facebook.com/NDP.NPD
www.youtube.com/user/NDPCanada

Thomas Mulcair was elected leader of the Official Opposition & Leader of the New Democratic Party of Canada on March 24, 2011. Mulcair's election followed the August 2011 death of Jack Layton, Former Leader of the Official Opposition & Leader of the New Democratic Party. From July 28, 2011 to March 23, 2012, Nycole Turmel was the interim leader. After the 2015 general election, the NDP fell to Third Party status; Thomas Mulcair stayed on as Leader.

Party Leader, New Democratic Party, Hon. Thomas J. Mulcair, P.C., B.C.L. (Civil Law), LL.B (Common Law)
Tel: 613-947-0867; *Fax:* 613-947-0868
thomas.mulcair@parl.gc.ca
Social Media: twitter.com/ThomasMulcair,
www.facebook.com/ThomasMulcair
House Leader, New Democratic Party, Peter Julian, B.A.
Tel: 613-992-4214; *Fax:* 613-947-9500
peter.julian@parl.gc.ca
Deputy House Leader, New Democratic Party, Matthew Dubé, B.A.
Tel: 613-992-6035; *Fax:* 613-995-6223
Matthew.Dube@parl.gc.ca
Caucus Chair, New Democratic Party, Charlie Angus
Tel: 613-992-2919; *Fax:* 613-995-0747
charlie.angus@parl.gc.ca
Whip, New Democratic Party Caucus, Marjolaine Boutin-Sweet
Tel: 613-947-4576; *Fax:* 613-947-4579
marjolaine.boutin-sweet@parl.gc.ca
Deputy Whip, New Democratic Party, Irene Mathyssen, B.A.(Hons), B.Ed.
Tel: 613-995-2901; *Fax:* 613-943-8717
irene.mathyssen@parl.gc.ca
President, New Democratic Party of Canada, Marit Stiles
Social Media: twitter.com/maritstiles,
www.facebook.com/maritstilesNDP,
ca.linkedin.com/in/marit-stiles-a197874
National Director, New Democratic Party of Canada, Karl Bélanger
Social Media: twitter.com/karlbelanger

Office of the Leader, Bloc Québécois / Bureau du chef, Bloc Québécois

Centre Block, 111 Wellington St., Ottawa, ON K1A 0A6
www.blocquebecois.org
twitter.com/blocquebecois
www.facebook.com/blocquebecois
www.youtube.com/user/blocquebecois

Following the May 2011 general election, Gilles Duceppe resigned as Leader of the Bloc Québécois party. On December 11, 2011, Daniel Paillé became the Leader & President of the Bloc Québécois. Paillé resigned on December 16, 2013, for health-related reasons. Mario Beaulieu was chosen to be the Bloc's new Leader on June 14, 2014. Former Leader Gilles Duceppe returned to the position on June 10, 2015, with Beaulieu staying on as Party President. Following the 2015 general election, Duceppe resigned again, & Rhéal Fortin took over as Interim Leader.

Interim Party Leader, Bloc Québécois, Rhéal Fortin
Rheal.Fortin@parl.gc.ca
House Leader, Bloc Québécois, Luc Thériault, B.A., M.A., D.E.S.S.
Tel: 613-992-0164; *Fax:* 613-992-5341
Luc.Theriault@parl.gc.ca
Caucus Chair, Bloc Québécois, Louis Plamondon, B.A.Ped., B.A.An
Tel: 613-995-9241; *Fax:* 613-995-6784
louis.plamondon@parl.gc.ca
Whip, Bloc Québécois, Monique Pauzé
Tel: 613-992-5257; *Fax:* 613-996-4338
Monique.Pauze@parl.gc.ca
Party President, Bloc Québécois, Mario Beaulieu

Office of the Leader, Green Party of Canada

Confederation Building, 244 Wellington St., Ottawa, ON K1A 0A6
Tel: 613-996-1119; *Fax:* 613-996-0850
Toll-Free: 866-868-3447
leader@greenparty.ca
www.greenparty.ca
Other Communication: General Information, E-mail: info@greenparty.ca; Media Requests, E-mail: media@greenparty.ca
twitter.com/canadiangreens
www.facebook.com/GreenPartyofCanada
www.youtube.com/user/canadiangreenparty

Elizabeth May was elected the Leader of the Green Party of Canada in 2006. In the May 2011 election, May became the first Green Party candidate to be elected to the House of Commons. She was re-elected in the 2015 general election.

Leader, Green Party of Canada, Elizabeth May, O.C., LL.B.
Tel: 613-996-1119; *Fax:* 613-996-0850
elizabeth.may@parl.gc.ca
Social Media: twitter.com/elizabethmay,
www.facebook.com/ElizabethMayGreenLeader,
www.linkedin.com/pub/elizabeth-may/3/a91/69
Deputy Leader, Green Party of Canada, Daniel Green
Deputy Leader, Green Party of Canada, Bruce Hyer
brucehyer.ca
Social Media: twitter.com/brucehyer,
www.facebook.com/brucehyer

The Canadian Ministry / The Cabinet

Information Service, Parliament of Canada, Ottawa, ON K1A 0A9
Tel: 613-992-4793
Toll-Free: 866-599-4999
TTY: 613-995-2266
info@parl.gc.ca
www.parl.gc.ca

The Canadian Ministry, or Cabinet, is the most significant of all federal government committees or councils. Cabinet members are selected & led by the Prime Minister. They must also be or become members of the Queen's Privy Council.
Cabinet ministers determine specific policies & are responsible for them in the House of Commons. The Cabinet is responsible for initiating all public bills in the House of Commons, & in some instances can create regulations that have the strength of law, termed decisions of the Governor-in-Council.
Cabinet meetings are usually closed to the public, allowing members to discuss their opinions on particular policy in secret. Once decided, members usually support all policy uniformly. If a minister is unable to support the Ministry, he or she is obligated to resign. Ministers are responsible to Parliament for their actions & the actions of their department.
The mailing address for all Cabinet members on Parliament Hill in Ottawa is as follows: House of Commons, Parliament Buildings, Ottawa, Ontario, K1A 0A6.
Members of the The Canadian Ministry are presented in order of precedence:

Members of The Canadian Ministry (Cabinet)

Prime Minister; Minister, Intergovernmental Affairs; Minister, Youth, Right Hon. Justin Pierre James Trudeau, P.C., B.A., B.Ed.
Tel: 613-995-0253; *Fax:* 613-947-0310
justin.trudeau@parl.gc.ca
Social Media: twitter.com/JustinTrudeau,
www.facebook.com/JustinPJTrudeau,
ca.linkedin.com/in/justintrudeau
Note: Web Sites: www.justin.ca (Personal); www.pm.gc.ca (Prime Minister of Canada); www.liberal.ca (Party)
Right Hon. Justin Pierre James Trudeau, Prime Minister, Office of the Prime Minister, Langevin Block
80 Wellington St.
Ottawa, ON K1A 0A2
Minister, Public Safety & Emergency Preparedness, Hon. Ralph Goodale, P.C., B.A., LL.B.
Tel: 613-947-1153; *Fax:* 613-996-9790
ralph.goodale@parl.gc.ca
Social Media: twitter.com/RalphGoodale,
www.facebook.com/ralphgoodale
Note: Web Sites: ralphgoodale.liberal.ca (Personal); www.publicsafety.gc.ca/cnt/bt/mnstr-eng.aspx (Public Safety Canada)
Minister, Agriculture & Agri-Food, Hon. Lawrence MacAulay, P.C.
Tel: 613-995-9325; *Fax:* 613-995-2754
lawrence.macaulay@parl.gc.ca
Social Media: www.facebook.com/lawrence.macaulay
Note: Web Sites: lawrencemacaulay.liberal.ca (Personal); www.agr.gc.ca/eng/about-us/minister/?id=1369864009036 (Agriculture & Agri-Food Canada)
Minister, Foreign Affairs, Hon. Stéphane Dion, P.C., B.A., M.A., Ph.D.
Tel: 613-996-5789; *Fax:* 613-996-6562
stephane.dion@parl.gc.ca
Social Media: twitter.com/HonStephaneDion,
www.facebook.com/stephanedionmp
Note: Web Sites: stephanedion.liberal.ca (Personal); www.international.gc.ca/dfatd-maecd/dion.aspx?lang=eng (Foreign Affairs)
Minister, Immigration, Refugees & Citizenship, Hon. John McCallum, P.C., B.A., Ph.D.
Tel: 613-996-3374; *Fax:* 613-992-3921
john.mccallum@parl.gc.ca
Social Media: twitter.com/honjohnmccallum,
www.facebook.com/McCallumj1
Note: Web Sites: johnmccallum.ca (Personal); www.cic.gc.ca/english/department/minister/mccallum.asp (Immigration, Citizenship & Refugees)
Minister, Indigenous & Northern Affairs, Hon. Dr. Carolyn Bennett, P.C., M.D.
Tel: 613-995-9666; *Fax:* 613-947-4622
carolyn.bennett@parl.gc.ca
Social Media: twitter.com/Carolyn_Bennett,
www.facebook.com/carolyn.bennett.stpauls,
www.linkedin.com/pub/carolyn-bennett/13/a3/811
Note: Web Sites: carolynbennett.liberal.ca (Personal); www.aadnc-aandc.gc.ca (Indigenous & Northern Affairs)
President, Treasury Board, Hon. Scott Brison, P.C., B.Comm.
Tel: 613-995-8231; *Fax:* 613-996-9349
scott.brison@parl.gc.ca
Social Media: twitter.com/scottbrison,
www.facebook.com/scott.a.brison,
www.linkedin.com/pub/scott-brison/9/a43/1a6
Note: Web Sites: www.brison.ca (Personal); www.tbs-sct.gc.ca (Treasury Board of Canada)
Minister, Fisheries, Oceans & the Canadian Coast Guard, Hon. Dominic Leblanc, P.C., B.A., LL.B., LL.M.
Tel: 613-992-1020; *Fax:* 613-992-3053
dominic.leblanc@parl.gc.ca
Social Media: www.facebook.com/19671249720
Note: Web Sites: www.dominicleblanc.ca (Personal); www.houseleader.gc.ca (Leader of the Government in the House of Commons); www.dfo-mpo.gc.ca (Fisheries & Oceans Canada)
Minister, Innovation, Science & Economic Development, Hon. Navdeep Bains, P.C., B.A., M.B.A., C.M.A.
Tel: 613-995-7784; *Fax:* 613-996-9817
Navdeep.Bains@parl.gc.ca
Social Media: twitter.com/navdeepsbains,
www.facebook.com/NavdeepSinghBains,
ca.linkedin.com/pub/navdeep-bains/37/269/48
Note: Web Sites: navdeepbains.liberal.ca (Personal); www.ic.gc.ca/eic/site/icgc.nsf/eng/h_07539.html (Innovation, Science & Economic Development)
Minister, Finance, Hon. Bill Morneau, P.C.
Tel: 613-992-1377; *Fax:* 613-992-1383
Bill.Morneau@parl.gc.ca
Social Media: twitter.com/Bill_Morneau,
www.facebook.com/morneau.bill
Note: Web Sites: billmorneau.liberal.ca (Personal); www.fin.gc.ca/comment/minfin-eng.asp (Finance)
Minister, Justice & Attorney General of Canada, Hon. Jody Wilson-Raybould, P.C.
Tel: 613-992-1416; *Fax:* 613-992-1460
Jody.Wilson-Raybould@parl.gc.ca
Social Media: twitter.com/Puglaas,
www.facebook.com/JodyWRLiberal
Note: Web Sites: jody.liberal.ca (Personal); www.justice.gc.ca (Department of Justice)
Minister, Public Services & Procurement, Hon. Judy Foote, P.C., B.A., B.Ed
Tel: 613-992-8655; *Fax:* 613-992-5324
Judy.Foote@parl.gc.ca
Note: Web Site: judyfoote.liberal.ca (Personal); www.tpsgc-pwgsc.gc.ca (Public Services & Procurement)
Minister, International Trade, Hon. Chrystia Freeland, P.C.
Tel: 613-992-5234; *Fax:* 613-996-9607
chrystia.freeland@parl.gc.ca
Social Media: twitter.com/cafreeland,
www.facebook.com/freelandchrystia
Note: Web Sites: chrystiafreeland.liberal.ca (Personal); www.international.gc.ca/dfatd-maecd/freeland.aspx?lang=eng (International Trade)
Minister, Health, Hon. Jane Philpott, P.C.
Tel: 613-992-3640; *Fax:* 613-992-3642
Jane.Philpott@parl.gc.ca
Social Media: twitter.com/janephilpott,
www.facebook.com/janepaulinephilpott
Note: Web Sites: janephilpott.liberal.ca (Personal); www.healthycanadians.gc.ca/minister-ministre/jane-philpott-eng.php (Health)
Minister, Families, Children & Social Development, Hon. Jean-Yves Duclos, P.C.
Jean-Yves.Duclos@parl.gc.ca
Social Media: twitter.com/jyduclos,

www.facebook.com/jyduclosliberal
Note: Web Sites: jeanyvesduclos.liberal.ca (Personal); www.esdc.gc.ca (Employment & Social Development)

Minister, Transport, Hon. Marc Garneau, P.C., C.C., C.D., B.Sc., Ph.D., F.C.A.S.I.
Tel: 613-996-7267; *Fax:* 613-995-8632
marc.garneau@parl.gc.ca
Social Media: twitter.com/MarcGarneau, www.facebook.com/marcgarneaump
Note: Web Sites: marcgarneau.liberal.ca (Personal); www.tc.gc.ca/eng/minister-menu.htm (Transport Canada)

Minister, International Development & La Francophonie, Hon. Marie-Claude Bibeau, P.C.
Tel: 613-995-2024; *Fax:* 613-992-1696
Marie-Claude.Bibeau@parl.gc.ca
Social Media: twitter.com/mclaudebibeau, www.facebook.com/mclaudebibeau, www.linkedin.com/in/marie-claude-bibeau-b0b72518
Note: Web Sites: marieclaudebibeau.liberal.ca (Personal); www.international.gc.ca/dfatd-maecd/bibeau.aspx (International Development); www.international.gc.ca/franco/index.aspx (La Francophonie)

Minister, Natural Resources, Hon. James Carr, O.M., P.C., B.A.
Tel: 613-992-9475; *Fax:* 613-992-9586
Jim.Carr@parl.gc.ca
Social Media: twitter.com/jimcarr_wpg, www.facebook.com/jim.carr.lib
Note: Web Sites: www.jimcarrmp.ca (Personal); www.nrcan.gc.ca/media-room/minister/1905 (Natural Resources)

Minister, Canadian Heritage, Hon. Mélanie Joly, P.C.
Tel: 613-992-0983; *Fax:* 613-992-1932
Melanie.Joly@parl.gc.ca
Social Media: twitter.com/melaniejoly, www.facebook.com/melanie.joly.965
Note: Web Sites: melaniejoly.liberal.ca (Personal); www.pch.gc.ca (Canadian Heritage)

Minister, National Revenue, Hon. Diane Lebouthillier, P.C.
Tel: 613-992-6188; *Fax:* 613-992-6194
Diane.Lebouthillier@parl.gc.ca
Social Media: twitter.com/dilebouthillier, www.facebook.com/lebouthillierd
Note: Web Sites: dianelebouthillier.liberal.ca (Personal); www.cra-arc.gc.ca/gncy/mnstr/menu-eng.html (Canada Revenue Agency)

Minister, Veterans Affairs; Associate Minister, National Defence, Hon. Kent Hehr, P.C.
Tel: 613-995-1561; *Fax:* 613-995-1862
Kent.Hehr@parl.gc.ca
Social Media: twitter.com/KentHehr, www.facebook.com/KentHehrj, ca.linkedin.com/in/kenthehr
Note: Web Sites: kenthehr.liberal.ca (Personal); www.veterans.gc.ca/eng/about-us/department-officials/minister (Veterans Affairs); www.forces.gc.ca (National Defence)

Minister, Environment & Climate Change, Hon. Catherine Mary McKenna, P.C.
Tel: 613-996-5322; *Fax:* 613-996-5323
Catherine.McKenna@parl.gc.ca
Social Media: twitter.com/cathmckenna, www.facebook.com/McKenna.Ottawa, ca.linkedin.com/in/catherine-mckenna-a0333025
Note: Web Sites: catherinemckennamp.ca (Personal); www.ec.gc.ca (Environment Canada)

Minister, National Defence, Hon. Harjit S. Sajjan, P.C.
Tel: 613-995-7052; *Fax:* 613-995-2962
HarjitS.Sajjan@parl.gc.ca
Social Media: twitter.com/HarjitSajjan, www.facebook.com/harjit.sajjan.7
Note: Web Sites: harjitsajjan.liberal.ca (Personal); www.forces.gc.ca (National Defence)

Minister, Employment, Workforce Development & Labour, Hon. MaryAnn Mihychuk, P.C., B.Sc., M.Sc., P.Geo.
Tel: 613-992-7148; *Fax:* 613-996-9125
MaryAnn.Mihychuk@parl.gc.ca
Social Media: twitter.com/mpmihychuk, www.facebook.com/MaryAnn.Mihychuk.KSP, ca.linkedin.com/in/maryann-mihychuk-m-sc-p-geo-50253516
Note: Web Sites: maryannmihychuk.liberal.ca (Personal); www.labour.gc.ca (Employment, Workforce Development & Labour)

Minister, Infrastructure & Communities, Hon. Amarjeet Sohi, P.C.
Tel: 613-992-1013; *Fax:* 613-992-1026
Amarjeet.Sohi@parl.gc.ca
Social Media: twitter.com/SohiAmarjeet
Note: Web Sites: amarjeetsohi.liberal.ca (Personal); www.infrastructure.gc.ca (Infrastructure)

Minister, Democratic Institutions; Minister Responsible, Elections Canada; President, Queen's Privy Council for Canada, Hon. Maryam Monsef, P.C.
Tel: 613-995-6411; *Fax:* 613-996-9800
Maryam.Monsef@parl.gc.ca
Other Communications: ca.linkedin.com/in/maryam-monsef-44733655
Social Media: twitter.com/MaryamMonsef
Note: Web Sites: maryammonsef.liberal.ca (Personal); www.elections.ca (Elections Canada); www.democraticreform.gc.ca (Democratic Reform)

Minister, Sport & Persons with Disabilities, Hon. Carla Qualtrough, P.C.
Tel: 613-992-2957; *Fax:* 613-992-3192
Carla.Qualtrough@parl.gc.ca
Social Media: twitter.com/CQualtro, www.facebook.com/CarlaQ2015, ca.linkedin.com/in/carla-qualtrough-0b229ab3
Note: Web Sites: carlaqualtrough.liberal.ca (Personal); www.pch.gc.ca (Canadian Heritage); www.esdc.gc.ca (Employment & Social Development)

Minister, Science, Hon. Kirsty Duncan, P.C., B.A., PhD
Tel: 613-995-4702; *Fax:* 613-995-8359
kirsty.duncan@parl.gc.ca
Social Media: twitter.com/kirstyduncanmp, www.facebook.com/KirstyDuncanMP
Note: Web Sites: kirstyduncan.liberal.ca (Personal); www.science.gc.ca (Science)

Minister, Status of Women, Hon. Patricia Hajdu, P.C.
Tel: 613-996-4792; *Fax:* 613-996-9785
Patty.Hajdu@parl.gc.ca
Social Media: twitter.com/PattyHajdu, ca.linkedin.com/in/patty-hajdu-825326a
Note: Web Sites: pattyhajdu.liberal.ca (Personal); www.swc-cfc.gc.ca (Status of Women)

Leader of the Government in the House of Commons; Minister, Small Business & Tourism, Hon. Bardish Chagger, P.C.
Tel: 613-996-5928; *Fax:* 613-992-6251
Bardish.Chagger@parl.gc.ca
Social Media: twitter.com/BardishKW, www.facebook.com/bardish.chagger
Note: Web Sites: bardishchagger.liberal.ca (Personal); www.ic.gc.ca/eic/site/icgc.nsf/eng/h_07540.html (Small Business & Tourism)

Forty-second Parliament - Canada

House of Commons, Parliament Buildings, Ottawa, AB K1A 0A6

www.parl.gc.ca

Members of the House of Commons are elected by the people. The Speaker is elected by the House.
Last General Election: Oct. 19, 2015.
Political Party Leaders (May 2016):
Liberal Party of Canada - The Right Hon. Justin Trudeau;
Conservative Party of Canada - Hon. Rona Ambrose (Interim);
New Democratic Party - Thomas J. Mulcair;
Green Party of Canada - Elizabeth May;
Bloc Québécois - Rhéal Fortin (Interim);
Representation in the House of Commons by province is as follows (Sept. 2016):
Alberta - Conservative Party of Canada 26, Liberal Party of Canada 4, New Democratic Party 1, Vacant 2, Total 34;
British Columbia - Liberal Party of Canada 17, New Democratic Party 14, Conservative Party of Canada 10, Green Party of Canada 1, Total 42;
Manitoba - Liberal Party of Canada 7, Conservative Party of Canada 5, New Democratic Party 2, Total 14;
New Brunswick - Liberal Party of Canada 10, Total 10;
Newfoundland & Labrador - Liberal Party of Canada 7, Total 7;
Northwest Territories - Liberal Party of Canada 1, Total 1;
Nova Scotia - Liberal Party of Canada 11, Total 11;
Nunavut - Independent 1, Total 1;
Ontario - Liberal Party of Canada 79, Conservative Party of Canada 33, New Democratic Party 8, Vacant 1, Total 121;
Prince Edward Island - Liberal Party of Canada 4, Total 4;
Québec - Liberal Party of Canada 40, New Democratic Party 16, Conservative Party of Canada 12, Bloc Québécois 10, Total 78;
Saskatchewan - Conservative Party of Canada 9, New Democratic Party 3, Liberal Party of Canada 1, Total 13;
Yukon - Liberal Party of Canada 1, Total 1.
Representation in the House of Commons by party affiliation is as follows (Sept. 2016):
Liberal Party of Canada 182;
Conservative Party of Canada 95;
New Democratic Party 44;
Bloc Québécois 10;
Green Party of Canada 1;
Independent 1;
Vacant 5;
Total 338.
Indemnities, Salaries, & Allowances (2014):
The basic sessional indemnity for each member of the House of Commons is $163,700. In addition to the indemnity, members who occupy certain positions in the House of Commons receive additional remuneration.
Prime Minister: $163,700, plus a car allowance of $2,000;
Minister $78,300, plus a car allowance of $2,000;
Minister of State: $58,700;
Secretary of State: $58,700;
Parliamentary Secretary: $16,300;
Speaker of the House of Commons: $78,300, plus a car allowance of $1,000;
Deputy Speaker of the House of Commons: $40,600;
Leader of the Opposition in the House of Commons: $78,300, plus a car allowance of $2,000;
Leaders of Other Parties: $55,600;
Opposition House Leader: $40,600;
House Leader of Other Parties: $16,300;
Deputy House Leaders of Government & Official Opposition: $16,300;
Deputy House Leaders of Other Parties: $5,800;
Chief Government Whip: $29,400;
Chief Opposition Whip: $29,400;
Whip of Other Parties: $11,500;
Chief Government Whip's Assistant: $11,500;
Deputy Whip of the Official Opposition: $11,500;
Deputy Whip of Other Parties: $5,800;
Caucus Chair of the Government & the Official Opposition: $11,500;
Caucus Chair of Other Parties: $5,800;
Deputy Chair, Committees of the Whole: $16,300;
Assistant Deputy Chair, Committees of the Whole: $16,300;
Chair of Standing & Standing Joint Committee (excluding the Liaison Committee & the Standing Joint Committee on the Library of Parliament): $11,500;
Vice-Chair of Standing & Standing Joint Committee (excluding the Liaison Committee & the Standing Joint Committee on the Library of Parliament): $0.
Mail may be sent postage-free to any Member of Parliament at the following address: House of Commons, Parliament Buildings, Ottawa, Ontario, K1A 0A6.
The following is a list of Members of Parliament, as of May 2016, with their constituency, number of electors on lists for the 2015 election, party affiliation, & contact information:

Members of the Parliament of Canada

Ziad Aboultaif
Constituency: Edmonton — Manning, Alberta *No. of Constituents:* 80,111, Conservative Party
Tel: 613-992-0946; *Fax:* 613-992-0973
Ziad.Aboultaif@parl.gc.ca
ziadaboultaif.conservative.ca
Social Media: www.facebook.com/ziad4manning
Constituency Office
#204A, 8119 - 160 Ave.
Edmonton, AB T5Z 0G3

Dan Albas
Constituency: Central Okanagan — Similkameen — Nicola, British Columbia *No. of Constituents:* 86,093, Conservative Party
Tel: 613-995-1702
Toll-free: 800-665-8711; *Fax:* 613-995-1154
dan.albas@parl.gc.ca
www.danalbas.com
Other Communications: Constituency Fax: 250-707-2153
Social Media: twitter.com/DanAlbas
Constituency Office
#10, 2483 Main St.
West Kelowna, BC V4T 2E8

Harold Albrecht, D.D.S.
Constituency: Kitchener — Conestoga, Ontario *No. of Constituents:* 68,623, Conservative Party
Tel: 613-992-4633; *Fax:* 613-992-9932
harold.albrecht@parl.gc.ca
haroldalbrechtmp.ca
Other Communications: Constituency Phone: 519-578-3777; Fax: 519-578-0138
Social Media: twitter.com/Albrecht4KitCon, www.facebook.com/Harold.Albrecht.MP
Constituency Office
#624, 1187 Fischer-Hallman Rd.
Kitchener, ON N2E 4H9

John Aldag
Constituency: Cloverdale — Langley City *No. of Constituents:* 77,044, Liberal
Tel: 613-992-0884; *Fax:* 613-992-0898
John.Aldag@parl.gc.ca
johnaldag.ca
Other Communications: Constituency Phone: 604-514-2500; Fax: 604-215-2504
Social Media: twitter.com/jwaldag, www.facebook.com/JohnAldagLPC
Constituency Office
#5, 19211 Fraser Hwy.
Surrey, BC V3S 7C9

Omar Alghabra, P. Eng, M.B.A.
Constituency: Mississauga Centre, Ontario *No. of Constituents:* 82,443, Liberal
Tel: 613-992-1301; *Fax:* 613-992-1321
Omar.Alghabra@parl.gc.ca
omaralghabra.liberal.ca
Other Communications: Constituency Phone: 905-848-8595; Fax: 905-848-2712
Social Media: twitter.com/OmarAlghabra,

www.facebook.com/oalghabra,
ca.linkedin.com/in/omaralghabra
Constituency Office
#400, 151 City Centre Dr.
Mississauga, ON L5B 1M7

Leona Alleslev
Constituency: Aurora — Oak Ridges — Richmond Hill, Ontario *No. of Constituents:* 78,848, Liberal
Tel: 613-992-0700; *Fax:* 613-992-0716
Leona.Alleslev@parl.gc.ca
leonaalleslev.liberal.ca
Other Communications: Constituency Phone: 905-773-8358; Fax: 905-773-8374
Social Media: twitter.com/LeonaAlleslev, www.facebook.com/leonaalleslev
Constituency Office
#202, 12820 Yonge St.
Richmond Hill, ON L4E 4H1

Dean Allison, B.A.
Constituency: Niagara West, Ontario *No. of Constituents:* 68,937, Conservative Party
Tel: 613-995-2772; *Fax:* 613-992-2727
dean.allison@parl.gc.ca
www.deanallison.ca
Other Communications: Constituency Phone: 905-563-7900; Fax: 905-563-7500
Social Media: twitter.com/DeanAllisonMP
Constituency Office
4994 King St.
Beamsville, ON L0R 1B0

Interim Official Opposition Leader; Interim Leader, Conservative Party of Canada, Hon. Rona Ambrose, P.C., B.A., M.A.
Constituency: Sturgeon River — Parkland, Alberta *No. of Constituents:* 84,952, Conservative Party
Tel: 613-996-9778; *Fax:* 613-996-0785
rona.ambrose@parl.gc.ca
www.ronaambrose.com
Other Communications: Constituency Phone: 780-823-2050; Fax: 780-823-2055
Social Media: twitter.com/ronaambrose, www.facebook.com/ronaambrose
Constituency Office
#102, 4807 - 44 Ave.
Stony Plain, AB T7Z 1V5

William Amos
Circonscription électorale: Pontiac, Quebec *Nombre de constituants:* 87,365, Liberal
Tél: 613-995-3950; *Téléc:* 613-992-6802
William.Amos@parl.gc.ca
williamamos.liberal.ca
Autres numéros: Chelsea: 819-827-5161; Gracefield: 819-463-0112
Les réseaux sociaux: twitter.com/WillAAmos, www.facebook.com/willamoscanada
Constituency Office
164, ch Old Chelsea
Chelsea, QC J9B 1J4

Gary Anandasangaree
Constituency: Scarborough — Rouge Park, Ontario *No. of Constituents:* 71,950, Liberal
Tel: 613-992-1351; *Fax:* 613-992-1373
Gary.Anandasangaree@parl.gc.ca
garyanandasangaree.liberal.ca
Other Communications: Constituency Phone: 416-283-1414; Fax: 416-283-5012
Social Media: twitter.com/gary_srp, www.facebook.com/garyforsrp
Constituency Office
#3, 3600 Ellesmere Rd.
Toronto, ON M1C 4Y8

David Anderson, B.A., M.Div
Constituency: Cypress Hills — Grasslands, Saskatchewan *No. of Constituents:* 50,426, Conservative Party
Tel: 613-992-0657; *Fax:* 613-992-5508
david.anderson@parl.gc.ca
www.davidanderson.ca
Other Communications: Constituency Phone: 306-778-4480; Fax: 306-778-6981
Social Media: twitter.com/DavidAndersonSK, www.facebook.com/DavidAndersonSK, www.linkedin.com/pub/dave-anderson-mp/13/582/b9a
Constituency Office
#2, 240 Central Ave. North
Swift Current, SK S9H 0L2

Caucus Chair, New Democratic Party, Charlie Angus
Constituency: Timmins — James Bay, Ontario *No. of Constituents:* 60,692, New Democratic Party
Tel: 613-992-2919; *Fax:* 613-995-0747
charlie.angus@parl.gc.ca
www.charlieangus.ndp.ca
Social Media: twitter.com/CharlieAngusNDP, www.facebook.com/charlie.angus.58

Mel Arnold
Constituency: North Okanagan — Shuswap, British Columbia *No. of Constituents:* 96,243, Conservative Party
Tel: 613-995-9095; *Fax:* 613-992-3195
Mel.Arnold@parl.gc.ca
www.melarnold.ca
Other Communications: Constituency Phone: 250-260-5020; Fax: 250-260-5025
Social Media: twitter.com/melarnoldmp, www.facebook.com/mel.arnold.754, ca.linkedin.com/in/mel-arnold-11372561
Constituency Office
3105 - 29th St.
Vernon, BC V1T 5A8

René Arseneault
Constituency: Madawaska — Restigouche, New Brunswick *No. of Constituents:* 50,871, Liberal
Tel: 613-995-0581; *Fax:* 613-996-9736
Rene.Arseneault@parl.gc.ca
renearseneault.liberal.ca
Other Communications: Campbellton: 506-789-4593; Edmunston: 506-739-0285
Constituency Office
#204, 19 Aberdeen St.
Campbellton, NB E3N 3G4

Chandra Arya
Constituency: Nepean, Ontario *No. of Constituents:* 82,976, Liberal
Tel: 613-992-1325; *Fax:* 613-992-1336
Chandra.Arya@parl.gc.ca
chandraarya.liberal.ca
Other Communications: Constituency Phone: 613-825-5505; Fax: 613-825-2055
Social Media: twitter.com/ChandraNepean, www.facebook.com/ElectChandra
Constituency Office
#201A, 240 Kennevale Dr.
Nepean, ON K2J 6B6

Niki Ashton, B.A., M.A.
Constituency: Churchill — Keewatinook Aski, Manitoba *No. of Constituents:* 49,036, New Democratic Party
Tel: 613-992-3018; *Fax:* 613-996-5817
niki.ashton@parl.gc.ca
nikiashton.ndp.ca
Other Communications: Thompson: 204-677-1333; The Pas: 204-627-8716
Social Media: twitter.com/nikiashton, www.facebook.com/niki.ashton
Constituency Office
83 Churchill Dr.
Thompson, MB R8N 0L6

Robert Aubin, B.A.
Circonscription électorale: Trois-Rivières, Québec *Nombre de constituants:* 90,900, New Democratic Party
Tél: 613-992-2349; *Téléc:* 613-995-9498
robert.aubin@parl.gc.ca
robertaubin.ndp.ca
Autres numéros: Constituency Phone: 819-371-5901; Fax: 819-371-5912
Les réseaux sociaux: twitter.com/RobertAubinNPD, www.facebook.com/robertaubin.npd
Constituency Office
214, rue Bonaventure
Trois-Rivières, QC G9A 2B1

Ramez Ayoub
Circonscription électorale: Thérèse — De Blainville, Quebec *Nombre de constituants:* 79,347, Liberal
Tél: 613-992-2617; *Téléc:* 613-992-6069
Ramez.Ayoub@parl.gc.ca
ramezayoub.liberal.ca
Autres numéros: Constituency Phone: 450-965-1188; Fax: 450-965-3221
Les réseaux sociaux: twitter.com/ramezayoub, www.facebook.com/ramez.ayoub, ca.linkedin.com/in/ramez-ayoub-0a71654
Constituency Office
#401, 201, boul Curé-Labelle
Sainte-Thérèse, QC J7E 2X6

Vance Badawey
Constituency: Niagara Centre, Ontario *No. of Constituents:* 82,305, Liberal
Tel: 613-995-0988; *Fax:* 613-995-5245
Vance.Badawey@parl.gc.ca
vancebadawey.liberal.ca
Other Communications: Constituency Phone: 905-788-2204; Fax: 905-788-0071
Social Media: twitter.com/VBadawey, www.facebook.com/vancebadaweyliberal, ca.linkedin.com/in/vance-badawey-78a66619
Constituency Office
#103, 136 East Main St.
Welland, ON L3B 3W6

Hon. Larry Bagnell, P.C., B.A., B.Sc.
Constituency: Yukon, Yukon *No. of Constituents:* 26,283, Liberal
Tel: 613-995-9368; *Fax:* 613-995-0945
Larry.Bagnell@parl.gc.ca
larrybagnell.liberal.ca
Other Communications: Constituency Phone: 867-668-6565; Fax: 867-668-6570
Social Media: twitter.com/LarryBagnell, www.facebook.com/pages/Larry-Bagnell/6750956837, www.linkedin.com/pub/larry-bagnell/3b/32/967
Constituency Office
#204, 204 Black St.
Whitehorse, YT Y1A 2M9

Minister, Innovation, Science & Economic Development, Hon. Navdeep Bains, P.C., B.A., M.B.A., C.M.A.
Constituency: Mississauga — Malton, Ontario *No. of Constituents:* 74,448, Liberal
Tel: 613-995-7784; *Fax:* 613-996-9817
Navdeep.Bains@parl.gc.ca
navdeepbains.liberal.ca
Other Communications: Constituency Phone: 905-564-0228; Fax: 905-564-1147
Social Media: twitter.com/navdeepsbains, www.facebook.com/NavdeepSinghBains, ca.linkedin.com/pub/navdeep-bains/37/269/48
Constituency Office
#210, 6660 Kennedy Rd.
Mississauga, ON L5T 2M9

John Barlow
Constituency: Foothills, Alberta *No. of Constituents:* 82,380, Conservative Party
Tel: 613-995-8471; *Fax:* 613-996-9770
John.Barlow@parl.gc.ca
johnbarlow.conservative.ca
Other Communications: Constituency Phone: 403-603-3665; Fax: 403-603-3669
Social Media: twitter.com/johnbarlowmp, www.facebook.com/johnbarlowmp, ca.linkedin.com/in/john-barlow-14003743
Constituency Office
109 - 4th Ave. SW
High River, AB T1V 1M5

Xavier Barsalou-Duval
Circonscription électorale: Pierre-Boucher — Les Patriotes — Verchères, Québec *Nombre de constituants:* 78,738, Bloc Québécois
Tél: 613-996-2998; *Téléc:* 613-995-1062
Xavier.Barsalou-Duval@parl.gc.ca
www.blocquebecois.org/depute-xavier-barsalou-duval
Autres numéros: Constituency Phone: 450-652-4442; Fax: 450-652-4447
Les réseaux sociaux: twitter.com/XavierBarsalouD, www.facebook.com/xavierbarsalouduval, www.linkedin.com/in/xavierbarsalouduval
Constituency Office
#202, 1625, boul Lionel-Boulet
Varennes, QC J3X 1P7

Frank Baylis
Circonscription électorale: Pierrefonds—Dollard, Québec *Nombre de constituants:* 85,216, Liberal
Tél: 613-992-2689; *Téléc:* 613-996-8478
Frank.Baylis@parl.gc.ca
frankbaylis.liberal.ca
Autres numéros: Constituency Phone: 514-624-5725; Fax: 514-624-5728
Les réseaux sociaux: twitter.com/frankbaylis, www.facebook.com/frankbaylisliberal, www.linkedin.com/in/frankbaylis
Constituency Office
#501, 3883, boul St-Jean
Dollard-des-Ormeaux, QC H9G 3B9

Mario Beaulieu
Circonscription électorale: La Pointe-de-l'Île, Québec *Nombre de constituants:* 84,507, Bloc Québécois
Tél: 613-995-6327; *Téléc:* 613-996-5173
Mario.Beaulieu@parl.gc.ca
www.blocquebecois.org/depute-mario-beaulieu
Autres numéros: Constituency Phone: 514-645-0101; Fax: 514-645-0032
Les réseaux sociaux: twitter.com/mario_beaulieu, www.facebook.com/mariobeaulieu101
Constituency Office
#100, 12500, boul Industriel
Montréal, QC H1B 5P5

Terry Beech
Constituency: Burnaby North — Seymour, British Columbia *No. of Constituents:* 74,071, Liberal
Tel: 613-992-0802; *Fax:* 613-992-0824
Terry.Beech@parl.gc.ca
terrybeech-parl.ca
Other Communications: Constituency Phone: 604-718-8870; Fax: 604-718-8874
Social Media: twitter.com/terrybeech, www.facebook.com/terryjamesbeech, www.linkedin.com/in/terrybeech
Constituency Office

3906 Hastings St.
Burnaby, BC V5C 6C1
Minister, Indigenous & Northern Affairs, Hon. Dr. Carolyn Bennett, P.C., M.D.
Constituency: St. Paul's, Ontario *No. of Constituents:* 77,433, Liberal
Tel: 613-995-9666; *Fax:* 613-947-4622
carolyn.bennett@parl.gc.ca
carolynbennett.liberal.ca
Other Communications: Constituency Phone: 416-952-3990; Fax: 416-952-3995
Social Media: twitter.com/Carolyn_Bennett, www.facebook.com/carolyn.bennett.stpauls, www.linkedin.com/pub/carolyn-bennett/13/a3/811
Constituency Office
#103, 1650 Yonge St.
Toronto, ON M4T 2A2

Sheri Benson
Constituency: Saskatoon West, Saskatchewan *No. of Constituents:* 55,886, New Democratic Party
Tel: 613-992-1899; *Fax:* 613-992-3085
Sheri.Benson@parl.gc.ca
sheribenson.ndp.ca
Other Communications: Constituency Phone: 306-975-6555; Fax: 306-975-5786
Social Media: twitter.com/SheriRBenson, www.facebook.com/sheribensonndp, www.linkedin.com/in/sheribenson
Constituency Office
904E - 22nd St. West
Saskatoon, SK S7M 0S1

House Leader, Official Opposition; House Leader, Conservative Party of Canada, Hon. Candice Bergen, P.C.
Constituency: Portage — Lisgar, Manitoba *No. of Constituents:* 62,153, Conservative Party
Tel: 613-995-9511; *Fax:* 613-947-0313
candice.bergen@parl.gc.ca
www.candicebergen.ca
Social Media: twitter.com/CandiceBergenMP, www.facebook.com/CandiceBergenMp

Hon. Maxime Bernier, P.C., B.Comm., LL.B.
Circonscription électorale: Beauce, Québec *Nombre de constituants:* 85,547, Conservative Party
Tél: 613-992-8053; *Téléc:* 613-995-0687
maxime.bernier@parl.gc.ca
www.maximebernier.com
Les réseaux sociaux: twitter.com/maximebernier, www.facebook.com/hon.maximebernier, ca.linkedin.com/in/maximebernier

Luc Berthold
Circonscription électorale: Mégantic — L'Érable, Québec *Nombre de constituants:* 71,469, Conservative Party
Tél: 613-995-1377; *Téléc:* 613-943-1562
Luc.Berthold@parl.gc.ca
Autres numéros: Constituency Phone: 418-338-2903; Fax: 418-338-3631
Les réseaux sociaux: twitter.com/LucBerthold, www.facebook.com/lucbertholdmeganticlerable, www.linkedin.com/in/lucberthold
Constituency Office
105A, rue Notre-Dame est
Thetford Mines, QC G6G 2J9

James Bezan
Constituency: Selkirk — Interlake —Eastman, Manitoba *No. of Constituents:* 71,331, Conservative Party
Tel: 613-992-2032; *Fax:* 613-992-6224
james.bezan@parl.gc.ca
www.jamesbezan.com
Other Communications: Constituency Phone: 204-785-6151; Fax: 204-785-6153
Social Media: twitter.com/jamesbezan, www.facebook.com/jamesbezan
Constituency Office
374 Main St.
Selkirk, MB R1A 1T7

Minister, International Development & La Francophonie, Hon. Marie-Claude Bibeau, P.C.
Circonscription électorale: Compton — Stanstead, Québec *Nombre de constituants:* 81,867, Liberal
Tél: 613-995-2024; *Téléc:* 613-992-1696
Marie-Claude.Bibeau@parl.gc.ca
mclaudebibeau.liberal.ca
Autres numéros: Constituency Phone: 819-347-2598; Fax: 819-347-3583
Les réseaux sociaux: twitter.com/mclaudebibeau, www.facebook.com/mclaudebibeau, www.linkedin.com/in/marie-claude-bibeau-b0b72518
Constituency Office
#204, 175 Queen St.
Sherbrooke, QC J1M 1K1

Chris Bittle
Constituency: St. Catharines, Ontario *No. of Constituents:* 84,474, Liberal
Tel: 613-992-3352; *Fax:* 613-947-4402
Chris.Bittle@parl.gc.ca
chrisbittle.liberal.ca
Other Communications: Constituency Phone: 905-934-6767; Fax: 905-934-1577
Social Media: twitter.com/Chris_Bittle, www.facebook.com/ChrisBittleMP, ca.linkedin.com/in/chris-bittle-6085989
Constituency Office
#1, 61 Geneva St.
St Catharines, ON L2M 4M6

Daniel Blaikie
Constituency: Elmwood — Transcona, Manitoba *No. of Constituents:* 65,207, New Democratic Party
Tel: 613-995-6339; *Fax:* 613-995-6688
Daniel.Blaikie@parl.gc.ca
danielblaikie.ndp.ca
Other Communications: Constituency Phone: 204-984-2499; Fax: 204-984-2502
Social Media: twitter.com/daniel_blaikie, www.facebook.com/daniel.blaikie.5
Constituency Office
#210, 1100 Concordia Ave.
Winnipeg, MB R2K 4B8

Bill Blair
Constituency: Scarborough Southwest, Ontario *No. of Constituents:* 72,164, Liberal
Tel: 613-995-0284; *Fax:* 613-996-6309
Bill.Blair@parl.gc.ca
billblair.liberal.ca
Other Communications: Constituency Phone: 416-261-8613; Fax: 416-261-5268
Social Media: twitter.com/BillBlair, www.facebook.com/williamsterlingblair
Constituency Office
2263 Kingston Rd.
Scarborough, ON M1N 1T8

Rachel Blaney
Constituency: North Island — Powell River, British Columbia *No. of Constituents:* 80,730, New Democratic Party
Tel: 613-992-2503; *Fax:* 613-996-3306
Rachel.Blaney@parl.gc.ca
rachelblaney.ndp.ca
Other Communications: Constituency Phone: 250-287-9388; Fax: 250-287-9361
Social Media: twitter.com/RABlaney, www.facebook.com/Rachel.a.blaney, ca.linkedin.com/in/rachelablaney
Constituency Office
908 Island Hwy.
Campbell River, BC V9W 4B2

Hon. Steven Blaney, P.C., M.B.A.
Circonscription électorale: Bellechasse — Les Etchemins — Lévis, Québec *Nombre de constituants:* 92,420, Conservative Party
Tél: 613-992-7434; *Téléc:* 613-995-6856
steven.blaney@parl.gc.ca
stevenblaney.ca
Les réseaux sociaux: twitter.com/stevenblaneypcc, www.facebook.com/HonStevenBlaney, ca.linkedin.com/in/steven-blaney-41801143

Kelly Block
Constituency: Carlton Trail — Eagle Creek, Saskatchewan *No. of Constituents:* 55,048, Conservative Party
Tel: 613-995-1551; *Fax:* 613-943-2010
kelly.block@parl.gc.ca
kellyblockmp.ca
Other Communications: Martensville: 306-975-4004; Humboldt: 306-682-1611
Social Media: twitter.com/kellyblockmp, www.facebook.com/kellyblockmp
Constituency Office
#2-B, 725 Centennial Dr. South
Martensville, SK S0K 2T0

Randy Boissonnault
Constituency: Edmonton Centre, Alberta *No. of Constituents:* 78,131, Liberal
Tel: 613-992-4524; *Fax:* 613-943-0044
Randy.Boissonnault@parl.gc.ca
randyboissonnault.liberal.ca
Other Communications: Constituency Phone: 780-442-1888; Fax: 780-442-1891
Social Media: twitter.com/randyb4yeg, www.facebook.com/R.Boissonnault, ca.linkedin.com/in/randyb123
Constituency Office
#103, 10235 - 124 St.
Edmonton, AB T5N 1P9

Mike Bossio
Constituency: Hastings — Lennox & Addington, Ontario *No. of Constituents:* 72,641, Liberal
Tel: 613-992-5321; *Fax:* 613-996-8652
Mike.Bossio@parl.gc.ca
mikebossio.ca
Other Communications: Constituency Phone: 613-354-0909; Fax: 613-354-0913
Social Media: twitter.com/MikeBossio, www.facebook.com/mike.bossio.liberal, ca.linkedin.com/in/mikebossio
Constituency Office
20-B Richmond Blvd.
Napanee, ON K7R 4A4

Sylvie Boucher
Circonscription électorale: Beauport — Côte-de-Beaupré — Ile d'Orléans — Chlevoix, Québec *Nombre de constituants:* 76,452, Conservative Party
Tél: 613-995-9732; *Téléc:* 613-996-2656
Sylvie.Boucher@parl.gc.ca
Autres numéros: Constituency Phone: 418-827-6776; Fax: 418-827-7077
Les réseaux sociaux: twitter.com/sboucherm, www.facebook.com/sylvie.boucher.9235, www.linkedin.com/in/sylvie-boucher-81b45736
Constituency Office
9749, boul Sainte-Anne
Ste-Anne-de-Beaupre, QC G0A 3C0

Michel Boudrias
Circonscription électorale: Terrebonne, Québec *Nombre de constituants:* 84,298, Bloc Québécois
Tél: 613-947-4788; *Téléc:* 613-947-4879
Michel.Boudrias@parl.gc.ca
www.blocquebecois.org/depute-michel-boudrias
Autres numéros: Constituency Phone: 450-964-9417; Fax: 450-964-1234
Les réseaux sociaux: www.facebook.com/michelboudrias101
Constituency Office
730-732, rue St. Louis
Terrebonne, QC J6W 1J6

Alexandre Boulerice, B.A.
Circonscription électorale: Rosemont — La Petite-Patrie, Québec *Nombre de constituants:* 84,403, New Democratic Party
Tél: 613-992-0423; *Téléc:* 613-992-0878
Alexandre.Boulerice@parl.gc.ca
www.boulerice.org
Autres numéros: Constituency Phone: 514-729-5342; Fax: 514-729-5875
Les réseaux sociaux: twitter.com/alexboulerice, www.facebook.com/alexandreboulerice
Constituency Office
#208, 1453, rue Beaubien est
Montréal, QC H2G 3C6

Whip, New Democratic Party, Marjolaine Boutin-Sweet
Circonscription électorale: Hochelaga, Québec *Nombre de constituants:* 82,783, New Democratic Party
Tél: 613-947-4576; *Téléc:* 613-947-4579
marjolaine.boutin-sweet@parl.gc.ca
marjolaineboutinsweet.ndp.ca
Autres numéros: Constituency Phone: 514-283-2655; Fax: 514-283-6485
Les réseaux sociaux: twitter.com/marjboutinsweet, www.facebook.com/marjolaineboutinsweet
Constituency Office
#225, 2030, boul Pie-IX
Montréal, QC H1V 2C8

John Brassard
Constituency: Barrie — Innisfil, Ontario *No. of Constituents:* 76,831, Conservative Party
Tel: 613-992-3394; *Fax:* 613-996-7923
John.Brassard@parl.gc.ca
johnbrassard.com
Other Communications: Constituency Phone: 705-726-5959; Fax: 705-726-3340
Social Media: twitter.com/johnbrassardcpc, www.facebook.com/BarrieInnisfil, www.linkedin.com/in/johnbrassard
Constituency Office
#204-B, 480 Huronia Rd.
Barrie, ON L4N 6M2

Bob Bratina
Constituency: Hamilton East — Stoney Creek, Ontario *No. of Constituents:* 80,042, Liberal
Tel: 613-992-6535; *Fax:* 613-992-7764
Bob.Bratina@parl.gc.ca
bbratina.liberal.ca
Other Communications: Constituency Phone: 905-662-4763; Fax: 905-662-2285
Social Media: twitter.com/bratinabobhesc, www.facebook.com/BratinaHESC
Constituency Office
#2, 40 Centennial Pkwy. North
Hamilton, ON L8E 1H6

Pierre Breton
Circonscription électorale: Shefford, Québec *Nombre de constituants:* 88,355, Liberal
Tél: 613-992-5279; *Téléc:* 613-992-7871
Pierre.Breton@parl.gc.ca
pierrebreton.liberal.ca
Autres numéros: Constituency Phone: 450-378-3221; Fax:

450-378-3380
Les réseaux sociaux: twitter.com/pierrebretonplc, www.facebook.com/PierreBretonPLC, www.linkedin.com/in/pierre-breton-69101721
Constituency Office
#101, 400, rue Principale
Granby, QC J2G 2W6

President, Treasury Board, Hon. Scott Brison, P.C., B.Comm.
Constituency: Kings — Hants, Nova Scotia *No. of Constituents:* 66,454, Liberal
Tel: 613-995-8231; *Fax:* 613-996-9349
scott.brison@parl.gc.ca
www.brison.ca
Other Communications: Constituency Phone: 902-542-4010; Fax: 902-542-4184
Social Media: twitter.com/scottbrison, www.facebook.com/scott.a.brison, www.linkedin.com/pub/scott-brison/9/a43/1a6
Constituency Office
#101A, 24 Harbourside Dr.
Wolfville, NS B4P 2C1

Ruth Ellen Brosseau
Circonscription électorale: Berthier — Maskinongé, Québec *Nombre de constituants:* 82,803, New Democratic Party
Tél: 613-992-5681; *Téléc:* 613-992-7276
RuthEllen.Brosseau@parl.gc.ca
ruthellenbrosseau.ndp.ca
Autres numéros: Constituency Phone: 819-228-1210; Fax: 819-228-1181
Les réseaux sociaux: twitter.com/RE_Brosseau, www.facebook.com/RuthEllenBrosseau, ca.linkedin.com/in/ruth-ellen-brosseau-ab99b155
Constituency Office
343, av St-Laurent
Louiseville, QC J5V 1K2

Chief Opposition Whip; Whip, Conservative Party, Gordon Brown, B.A. (Hons)
Constituency: Leeds — Grenville — Thousand Islands & Rideau Lakes, Ontario *No. of Constituents:* 79,195, Conservative Party
Tel: 613-992-8756; *Fax:* 613-996-9171
gord.brown@parl.gc.ca
www.gordbrownmp.ca
Other Communications: Constituency Phone: 613-498-3096; Fax: 613-498-3100
Social Media: www.facebook.com/MP-Gord-Brown-370174663083749
Constituency Office
#120, 2399 Parkedale Ave.
Brockville, ON K6V 3G9

Celina Caesar-Chavannes
Constituency: Whitby, Ontario *No. of Constituents:* 91,891, Liberal
Tel: 613-992-6344; *Fax:* 613-992-8320
Celina.Caesar-Chavannes@parl.gc.ca
celina.liberal.ca
Other Communications: Constituency Phone: 905-665-8182; Fax: 905-665-8124
Social Media: twitter.com/celinachavannes, www.facebook.com/CelinaCaesarChavannes, ca.linkedin.com/in/celina-r-caesar-chavannes-7bb85b7
Constituency Office
#206, 701 Rossland Rd. East
Whitby, ON L1N 8Y9

Blaine Calkins, B.Sc.
Constituency: Red Deer — Lacombe, Alberta *No. of Constituents:* 86,609, Conservative Party
Tel: 613-995-8886; *Fax:* 613-996-9860
blaine.calkins@parl.gc.ca
www.blainecalkinsmp.ca
Other Communications: Constituency Phone: 403-783-5530; Fax: 403-783-5532
Social Media: twitter.com/blainecalkinsmp, www.facebook.com/208129505866377
Constituency Office
#6A, 4612 - 50th St.
Ponoka, AB T4J 1S7

Richard Cannings
Constituency: South Okanagan — West Kootenay, British Columbia *No. of Constituents:* 90,694, New Democratic Party
Tel: 613-996-8036; *Fax:* 613-943-0922
Richard.Cannings@parl.gc.ca
richardcannings.ndp.ca
Other Communications: Penticton: 250-770-4480; Castlegar: 250-365-2792
Social Media: twitter.com/CanningsNDP, www.facebook.com/richardjcannings, ca.linkedin.com/in/richard-cannings-0160a536
Constituency Office
#202, 301 Main St.
Penticton, BC V2A 5B7

Guy Caron, B.A., M.A.
Circonscription électorale: Rimouski-Neigette — Témiscouata — Les Basques, Québec *Nombre de constituants:* 70,079, New Democratic Party
Tél: 613-992-5302; *Téléc:* 613-996-8298
Guy.Caron@parl.gc.ca
guycaron.ndp.ca
Autres numéros: Constituency Phone: 418-725-2562; Fax: 418-725-3993
Les réseaux sociaux: twitter.com/GuyCaronNPD, www.facebook.com/GuyCaronNPD
Constituency Office
#109, 140, rue Saint-Germain
Rimouski, QC G5L 4B5

Minister, Natural Resources, Hon. James Carr, O.M., P.C., B.A.
Constituency: Winnipeg South Centre, Manitoba *No. of Constituents:* 69,799, Liberal
Tel: 613-992-9475; *Fax:* 613-992-9586
Jim.Carr@parl.gc.ca
www.jimcarrmp.ca
Other Communications: Constituency Phone: 204-983-1355; Fax: 204-984-3979
Social Media: twitter.com/jimcarr_wpg, www.facebook.com/jim.carr.lib
Constituency Office
#12, 611 Corydon Ave.
Winnipeg, MB R3L 0P3

Colin Carrie, B.Sc. (Hons.), D.C.
Constituency: Oshawa, Ontario *No. of Constituents:* 95,561, Conservative Party
Tel: 613-996-4756; *Fax:* 613-992-1357
colin.carrie@parl.gc.ca
www.colincarriemp.ca
Other Communications: Constituency Phone: 905-440-4868; Fax: 905-440-4872
Social Media: twitter.com/ColinCarrie, www.facebook.com/colin.carrie.1
Constituency Office
#2B, 57 Simcoe St. South
Oshawa, ON L1H 4G4

Bill Casey, B.Sc.Eng.
Constituency: Cumberland — Colchester, Nova Scotia *No. of Constituents:* 64,923, Liberal
Tel: 613-992-3366; *Fax:* 613-992-7220
Bill.Casey@parl.gc.ca
billcasey.liberal.ca
Other Communications: Amherst: 902-667-8679; Truro: 902-667-0742
Social Media: twitter.com/billcaseyns, www.facebook.com/BillCaseyNS
Constituency Office
35 Church St.
Amherst, NS B4H 3A7

Sean Casey, Q.C., B.B.A., LL.B.
Constituency: Charlottetown, Prince Edward Island *No. of Constituents:* 27,891, Liberal
Tel: 613-996-4714; *Fax:* 613-995-7685
sean.casey@parl.gc.ca
seancasey.ca
Other Communications: Constituency Phone: 902-566-7770; Fax: 902-566-7780
Social Media: twitter.com/seancaseylpc, www.facebook.com/SeanCaseyCharlottetown, www.linkedin.com/in/seancaseycharlottetown
Constituency Office
#201, 75 Fitzroy Rd.
Charlottetown, PE C1A 1R6

Leader of the Government in the House of Commons; Minister, Small Business & Tourism, Hon. Bardish Chagger, P.C.
Constituency: Waterloo, Ontario *No. of Constituents:* 78,527, Liberal
Tel: 613-996-5928; *Fax:* 613-992-6251
Bardish.Chagger@parl.gc.ca
bardishchagger.liberal.ca
Other Communications: Constituency Phone: 519-746-1573; Fax: 519-746-6436
Social Media: twitter.com/BardishKW, www.facebook.com/bardish.chagger
Constituency Office
#360, 100 Regina St. South
Waterloo, ON N2J 4A8

François-Philippe Champagne
Circonscription électorale: Saint-Maurice — Champlain, Québec *Nombre de constituants:* 92,086, Liberal
Tél: 613-995-4895; *Téléc:* 613-996-6883
Francois-Philippe.Champagne@parl.gc.ca
francoisphilippechampagne.liberal.ca
Autres numéros: Shawinigan: 819-538-5291; La Tuque: 819-523-2696
Les réseaux sociaux: twitter.com/FP_Champagne, facebook.com/FrancoisPhilippeChampagne.ca, www.linkedin.com/in/francoisphilippechampagne
Constituency Office
#01, 632 - 6th av
Shawinigan, QC G9T 2H5

Arnold Chan
Constituency: Scarborough — Agincourt, Ontario *No. of Constituents:* 69,888, Liberal
Tel: 613-992-4501; *Fax:* 613-995-1612
arnold.chan@parl.gc.ca
arnoldchan.liberal.ca
Other Communications: Constituency Phone: 416-321-5454; Fax: 416-321-5456
Social Media: twitter.com/arnoldchanlib, www.facebook.com/ArnoldChan.Agincourt, ca.linkedin.com/pub/arnold-chan/10/7a0/974
Constituency Office
#110, 2190 McNicoll Ave.
Toronto, ON M1V 0B3

Shaun Chen
Constituency: Scarborough North, Ontario *No. of Constituents:* 64,827, Liberal
Tel: 613-996-9681; *Fax:* 613-996-6643
Shaun.Chen@parl.gc.ca
shaunchen.liberal.ca
Other Communications: Constituency Phone: 416-321-2436; Fax: 416-298-6035
Social Media: twitter.com/shaun_chen, www.facebook.com/ShaunChenLiberal
Constituency Office
4386 Sheppard Ave. East, #C
Toronto, ON M1S 1T8

Hon. Michael D. Chong, P.C.
Constituency: Wellington — Halton Hills, Ontario *No. of Constituents:* 89,653, Conservative Party
Tel: 613-992-4179; *Fax:* 613-996-4907
michael.chong@parl.gc.ca
www.michaelchong.ca
Social Media: twitter.com/michaelchongmp, www.facebook.com/M.P.MichaelChong, www.linkedin.com/pub/michael-chong/15/632/353

François Choquette, B.Ed., M.Lit.
Circonscription électorale: Drummond, Québec *Nombre de constituants:* 81,303, New Democratic Party
Tél: 613-947-4550; *Téléc:* 613-947-4551
francois.choquette@parl.gc.ca
francoischoquette.ndp.ca
Autres numéros: Constituency Phone: 819-477-3611; Fax: 819-477-7116
Les réseaux sociaux: twitter.com/F_Choquette, www.facebook.com/François-Choquette-401582226692843
Constituency Office
#100, 150 Marchand St.
Drummondville, QC J2S 4N1

David Christopherson
Constituency: Hamilton Centre, Ontario *No. of Constituents:* 68,087, New Democratic Party
Tel: 613-995-1757; *Fax:* 613-992-8356
david.christopherson@parl.gc.ca
davidchristopherson.ndp.ca
Other Communications: Constituency Phone: 905-526-0770; Fax: 905-526-9943
Social Media: twitter.com/davechrismp, www.facebook.com/DavidChristophersonNDP, ca.linkedin.com/in/david-christopherson-1b357678
Constituency Office
22 Tisdale St. South
Hamilton, ON L8N 2V9

Alupa Clarke
Circonscription électorale: Beauport — Limoilou, Québec *Nombre de constituants:* 78,530, Conservative Party
Tél: 613-992-4406; *Téléc:* 613-992-4544
Alupa.Clarke@parl.gc.ca
Autres numéros: Constituency Phone: 418-663-2113; Fax: 418-663-2989
Les réseaux sociaux: twitter.com/Alupa_Clarke, www.facebook.com/AlupaClarke
Constituency Office
#101, 2000, av Sanfaçon
Québec, QC G1E 3R7

Hon. Tony Clement, P.C., B.A., LL.B.
Constituency: Parry Sound — Muskoka, Ontario *No. of Constituents:* 75,642, Conservative Party
Tel: 613-944-7740; *Fax:* 613-992-5092
tony.clement@parl.gc.ca
www.tonyclement.ca
Social Media: twitter.com/TonyclementCPC, www.facebook.com/tonyclementpsm

Michael Cooper
Constituency: St. Albert — Edmonton, Albert *No. of Constituents:* 83,841, Conservative Party
Tel: 613-996-4722; *Fax:* 613-995-8880
Michael.Cooper@parl.gc.ca
michaelcoopermp.ca
Other Communications: Constituency Phone: 780-459-0809; Fax: 780-460-1246
Social Media: twitter.com/Cooper4SAE, facebook.com/michaelcooper4stalbertedmonton
Constituency Office
#220, 20 Perron St.
St. Albert, AB T8N 1E4

Serge Cormier
Constituency: Acadie — Bathurst, New Brunswick *No. of Constituents:* 66,594, Liberal
Tel: 613-992-2165; *Fax:* 613-992-4558
Serge.Cormier@parl.gc.ca
sergecormier.liberal.ca
Other Communications: Constituency Phone: 506-726-5398; Fax: 506-726-5394
Social Media: twitter.com/sergecormierlib, www.facebook.com/sergecormierliberal
Constituency Office
#314, 220 St-Pierre Blvd. West
Caraquet, NB E1W 1B5

Nathan Cullen, B.A.
Constituency: Skeena — Bulkley Valley, British Columbia *No. of Constituents:* 63,459, New Democratic Party
Tel: 613-993-6654; *Fax:* 613-993-9007
nathan.cullen@parl.gc.ca
www.nathancullen.com
Other Communications: Smithers: 250-877-4140; Terrace: 250-615-5339
Social Media: twitter.com/nathancullen, www.facebook.com/nathan.cullen1, www.linkedin.com/pub/nathan-cullen/21/24a/a36
Constituency Office
#100, 3891 - 1st Ave.
Smithers, BC V0J 2N0

Rodger Cuzner, B.A.
Constituency: Cape Breton — Canso, Nova Scotia *No. of Constituents:* 60,666, Liberal
Tel: 613-992-6756; *Fax:* 613-992-4053
rodger.cuzner@parl.gc.ca
rodgercuzner.liberal.ca
Other Communications: Constituency Phone: 902-842-9763; Fax: 902-842-9025
Social Media: twitter.com/RodgerCuzner, www.facebook.com/rodger.cuzner, ca.linkedin.com/in/rodger-cuzner-68a127b8
Constituency Office
78 Commercial St., #G & E
Dominion, NS B1G 1B4

Julie Dabrusin
Constituency: Toronto — Danforth, Ontario *No. of Constituents:* 77,158, Liberal
Tel: 613-992-9381; *Fax:* 613-992-9389
Julie.Dabrusin@parl.gc.ca
juliedabrusin.liberal.ca
Other Communications: Constituency Phone: 416-405-8914; Fax: 416-405-8915
Social Media: twitter.com/juliedabrusin, www.facebook.com/TorDanLibs, ca.linkedin.com/in/julie-dabrusin-412938a3
Constituency Office
1180 Danforth Ave.
Toronto, ON M4J 1M3

Pam Damoff
Constituency: Oakville North — Burlington, Ontario *No. of Constituents:* 85,462, Liberal
Tel: 613-992-1338; *Fax:* 613-992-1344
Pam.Damoff@parl.gc.ca
pamdamoff.liberal.ca
Other Communications: Constituency Phone: 905-847-4043; Fax: 905-847-3037
Social Media: twitter.com/PamDamoff, www.facebook.com/PamDamoff, ca.linkedin.com/in/pam-damoff-32038b47
Constituency Office
#590, 2525 Old Brunte Rd.
Oakville, ON L6M 4J2

Don Davies, B.A., LL.B.
Constituency: Vancouver Kingsway, British Columbia *No. of Constituents:* 71,206, New Democratic Party
Tel: 613-943-0267; *Fax:* 613-943-0219
don.davies@parl.gc.ca
dondavies.ca
Other Communications: Constituency Phone: 604-775-6263; Fax: 604-775-6284
Social Media: twitter.com/dondavies, www.facebook.com/DonDaviesNDP, www.linkedin.com/pub/don-davies/30/3ab/934
Constituency Office
2951 Kingsway
Vancouver, BC V5R 5J4

Matt DeCourcey
Constituency: Fredericton, New Brunswick *No. of Constituents:* 60,587, Liberal
Tel: 613-992-1067; *Fax:* 613-996-9955
Matt.DeCourcey@parl.gc.ca
mattdecourcey.liberal.ca
Other Communications: Constituency Phone: 506-452-4110; Fax: 506-452-4076
Social Media: twitter.com/MattDeCourcey, www.facebook.com/mattdecourceyforfredericton, www.linkedin.com/in/mattdecourcey
Constituency Office
#300, 494 Queen St.
Fredericton, NB E3B 1B6

Gérard Deltell
Circonscription électorale: Louis-Saint-Laurent, Québec *Nombre de constituants:* 92,119, Conservative Party
Tél: 613-996-4151; *Téléc:* 613-954-2269
Gerard.Deltell@parl.gc.ca
Autres numéros: Constituency Phone: 418-842-5552; Fax: 418-842-7333
Les réseaux sociaux: twitter.com/gerarddeltell, www.facebook.com/deltell.gerard
Constituency Office
#200, 9195, boul L'Ormière
Québec, QC G2B 3K2

Sukh Dhaliwal, P.Eng.
Constituency: Surrey — Newton, British Columbia *No. of Constituents:* 64,798, Liberal
Tel: 613-992-0666; *Fax:* 613-992-1965
Sukh.Dhaliwal@parl.gc.ca
sukhdhaliwal.liberal.ca
Other Communications: Constituency Phone: 604-598-2200; Fax: 604-598-2212
Social Media: twitter.com/sukhdhaliwal, www.facebook.com/sukhsinghdhaliwal
Constituency Office
#202, 12992 - 76th Ave.
Surrey, BC V2W 2V6

Anju Dhillon
Circonscription électorale: Dorval — Lachine — LaSalle, Québec *Nombre de constituants:* 85,587, Liberal
Tél: 613-995-2251; *Téléc:* 613-996-1481
Anju.Dhillon@parl.gc.ca
www.anjudhillon.ca
Autres numéros: Constituency Phone: 514-639-4497; Fax: 514-639-7407
Les réseaux sociaux: twitter.com/adhillonmp, www.facebook.com/anjudhillonliberals
Constituency Office
735, rue Notre-Dame
Lachine, QC H8S 2B5

Nicola Di Iorio
Circonscription électorale: Saint-Léonard — Saint-Michel, Québec *Nombre de constituants:* 76,531, Liberal
Tél: 613-995-9414; *Téléc:* 613-992-8523
Nicola.DiIorio@parl.gc.ca
nicoladiiorio.liberal.ca
Autres numéros: Constituency Phone: 514-256-4548; Fax: 514-256-8828
Les réseaux sociaux: twitter.com/DiIorioLiberal, www.facebook.com/nicoladiiorio2015, www.linkedin.com/in/nicoladiiorio
Constituency Office
8370, boul Lacordaire
Saint-Léonard, QC H1R 3Y6

Minister, Foreign Affairs, Hon. Stéphane Dion, P.C., B.A., M.A., Ph.D.
Circonscription électorale: Saint-Laurent, Québec *Nombre de constituants:* 69,078, Liberal
Tél: 613-996-5789; *Téléc:* 613-996-6562
stephane.dion@parl.gc.ca
stephanedion.liberal.ca
Autres numéros: Constituency Phone: 514-335-6655; Fax: 514-335-2712
Les réseaux sociaux: twitter.com/HonStephaneDion, www.facebook.com/stephanedionmp
Constituency Office
#440, 750, boul Marcel Laurin
Saint-Laurent, QC H4M 2M4

Kerry Diotte
Constituency: Edmonton Griesbach, Alberta *No. of Constituents:* 79,980, Conservative Party
Tel: 613-992-3821; *Fax:* 613-992-6898
Kerry.Diotte@parl.gc.ca
www.kerrydiotte.com
Other Communications: Constituency Phone: 780-495-3261; Fax: 780-495-5142
Social Media: twitter.com/KerryDiotte, facebook.com/KerryDiotteEdmontonGriesbach, ca.linkedin.com/in/kerry-diotte-a439344
Constituency Office
#102, 10212 - 127th Ave. NW
Edmonton, AB T5E 0B8

Todd Doherty
Constituency: Cariboo — Prince George, British Columbia *No. of Constituents:* 78,356, Conservative Party
Tel: 613-995-6704; *Fax:* 613-996-9850
Todd.Doherty@parl.gc.ca
todddoherty.conservative.ca
Other Communications: Constituency Phone: 250-564-7771; Fax: 250-564-6224
Social Media: twitter.com/ToddDohertyMP, www.facebook.com/ToddDohertyMP, www.linkedin.com/in/todddohertyformp
Constituency Office
1520 - 3rd Ave.
Prince George, BC V2L 3G4

Fin Donnelly, B.A.
Constituency: Port Moody — Coquitlam, British Columbia *No. of Constituents:* 78,693, New Democratic Party
Tel: 613-947-4455; *Fax:* 613-947-4458
fin.donnelly@parl.gc.ca
findonnelly.ndp.ca
Other Communications: Constituency Phone: 604-664-9229; Fax: 604-664-9231
Social Media: twitter.com/FinDonnelly, www.facebook.com/fin.donnelly, www.linkedin.com/pub/fin-donnelly/4/968/919
Constituency Office
1116 Austin Ave.
Coquitlam, BC V3K 3P5

Earl Dreeshen, B.Ed.
Constituency: Red Deer — Mountainview, Alberta *No. of Constituents:* 86,737, Conservative Party
Tel: 613-995-0590; *Fax:* 613-995-6831
earl.dreeshen@parl.gc.ca
www.earldreeshen.ca
Social Media: twitter.com/earl_dreeshen, www.facebook.com/10400775935, ca.linkedin.com/in/earl-dreeshen-a7aa878a

Francis Drouin
Constituency: Glengarry — Prescott — Russell *No. of Constituents:* 85,388, Liberal
Tel: 613-992-0490; *Fax:* 613-996-9123
Francis.Drouin@parl.gc.ca
francisdrouin.liberal.ca
Other Communications: Constituency Phone: 613-446-6310; Fax: 613-446-5666
Social Media: twitter.com/Francis_Drouin, www.facebook.com/FrancisDrouinGPR, ca.linkedin.com/in/francis-drouin-16825413
Constituency Office
#201, 1468 Laurier St.
Rockland, ON K4K 1C8

Deputy House Leader, New Democratic Party, Matthew Dubé, B.A.
Circonscription électorale: Beloeil — Chambly, Québec *Nombre de constituants:* 91,068, New Democratic Party
Tél: 613-992-6035; *Téléc:* 613-995-6223
Matthew.Dube@parl.gc.ca
matthewdube.ndp.ca
Autres numéros: Constituency Phone: 450-658-0088; Fax: 450-658-0885
Les réseaux sociaux: twitter.com/MattDube, www.facebook.com/matthew.dube
Constituency Office
#105, 1991, boul De Périgny
Chambly, QC J3L 4C3

Emmanuel Dubourg, C.P.A., M.B.A.
Circonscription électorale: Bourassa, Québec *Nombre de constituants:* 70,815, Liberal
Tél: 613-995-6108; *Téléc:* 613-995-9755
Emmanuel.Dubourg@parl.gc.ca
emmanueldubourg.liberal.ca
Autres numéros: Constituency Phone: 514-323-1212; Fax: 514-323-2875
Les réseaux sociaux: twitter.com/EmmanuelDubourg, www.facebook.com/dubourgemmanuel
Constituency Office
#203, 5835, boul Léger
Montréal-Nord, QC H1G 6E1

Minister, Families, Children & Social Development, Hon. Jean-Yves Duclos, P.C.
Circonscription électorale: Québec, Québec *Nombre de constituants:* 79,157, Liberal
Tél: 613-992-8865; *Téléc:* 613-995-2805
Jean-Yves.Duclos@parl.gc.ca
jeanyvesduclos.liberal.ca
Autres numéros: Constituency Phone: 418-523-6666; Fax: 418-523-6672
Les réseaux sociaux: twitter.com/jyduclos, www.facebook.com/jyduclosliberal, ca.linkedin.com/in/jean-yves-duclos-6405a344
Constituency Office
275, boul Charest est
Québec, QC G1K 3G8

Terry Duguid
Constituency: Winnipeg South, Manitoba *No. of Constituents:* 63,798, Liberal
Tel: 613-995-7517; *Fax:* 613-943-1466
Terry.Duguid@parl.gc.ca
terryduguid.liberal.ca
Other Communications: Constituency Phone: 204-984-6787; Fax: 204-984-6792
Social Media: twitter.com/TerryDuguid, www.facebook.com/terryduguidmp
Constituency Office

#103, 2800 Pembina Hwy.
Winnipeg, MB R3T 5P3

Minister, Science, Hon. Kirsty Duncan, P.C., B.A., Ph.D.
Constituency: Etobicoke North, Ontario *No. of Constituents:* 68,063, Liberal
Tel: 613-995-4702; *Fax:* 613-995-8359
kirsty.duncan@parl.gc.ca
kirstyduncan.liberal.ca
Other Communications: Constituency Phone: 416-747-6003; Fax: 416-747-8295
Social Media: twitter.com/kirstyduncanmp, www.facebook.com/KirstyDuncanMP
Constituency Office
815 Albion Rd.
Toronto, ON M9V 1A3

Linda Francis Duncan, B.A., LL.B., LL.M.
Constituency: Edmonton — Strathcona, Alberta *No. of Constituents:* 76,160, New Democratic Party
Tel: 613-995-7325; *Fax:* 613-995-5342
linda.duncan@parl.gc.ca
lindaduncan.ndp.ca
Other Communications: Constituency Phone: 780-495-8404; Fax: 780-495-8403
Social Media: twitter.com/LindaDuncanMP, www.facebook.com/LindaDuncanMP
Constituency Office
10049 - 81st Ave.
Edmonton, AB T6E 1W7

Pierre-Luc Dusseault
Circonscription électorale: Sherbrooke, Québec *Nombre de constituants:* 87,299, New Democratic Party
Tél: 613-943-7896; *Téléc:* 613-943-7902
pierre-luc.dusseault@parl.gc.ca
pierrelucdusseault.ndp.ca
Autres numéros: Constituency Phone: 819-564-4200; Fax: 819-564-3745
Les réseaux sociaux: twitter.com/PLDusseault, www.facebook.com/PLDusseault
Constituency Office
#130, 100, rue Belvédère sud
Sherbrooke, QC J1H 4B5

Scott Duvall
Constituency: Hamilton Mountain, Ontario *No. of Constituents:* 76,886, New Democratic Party
Tel: 613-995-9389; *Fax:* 613-992-7802
Scott.Duvall@parl.gc.ca
scottduvall.ndp.ca
Other Communications: Constituency Phone: 905-574-3331; Fax: 905-574-4980
Social Media: twitter.com/sduvall07, www.facebook.com/scott.r.duvall
Constituency Office
#2, 555 Concession St, Level 2
Hamilton, ON L8V 1A8

Julie Dzerowicz
Constituency: Davenport, Ontario *No. of Constituents:* 72,082, Liberal
Tel: 613-992-2576; *Fax:* 613-995-8202
Julie.Dzerowicz@parl.gc.ca
juliedzerowicz.liberal.ca
Other Communications: Constituency Phone: 416-654-8048; Fax: 416-654-5083
Social Media: twitter.com/JulieDzerowicz, www.facebook.com/voteforjuliedzerowicz, www.linkedin.com/pub/julie-dzerowicz/a/33a/593
Constituency Office
1202 Bloor St. West
Toronto, ON M6H 1N2

Hon. Arnold Wayne Easter, P.C., Dipl.T., LL.D.(Hon.)
Constituency: Malpeque, Prince Edward Island *No. of Constituents:* 28,556, Liberal
Tel: 613-992-2406
Toll-free: 800-442-4050; *Fax:* 613-995-7408
wayne.easter@parl.gc.ca
wayneeaster.parl.liberal.ca
Other Communications: Constituency Fax: 902-964-3242
Social Media: twitter.com/WayneEaster, www.facebook.com/wayne.easterMP, ca.linkedin.com/in/wayne-easter-91a62339
Constituency Office
#1, 4283 Rte. 13
Hunter River, PE C0A 1N0

Jim Eglinski
Constituency: Yellowhead, Alberta *No. of Constituents:* 73,996, Conservative Party
Tel: 613-992-1653; *Fax:* 613-992-3459
Jim.Eglinski@parl.gc.ca
jimeglinski.ca
Social Media: twitter.com/jimeglinski, www.facebook.com/425390920918995, ca.linkedin.com/in/jim-eglinski-13b050114

Ali Ehsassi
Constituency: Willowdale, Ontario *No. of Constituents:* 75,172, Liberal
Tel: 613-992-4964; *Fax:* 613-992-1158
Ali.Ehsassi@parl.gc.ca
aliehsassi.liberal.ca
Other Communications: Constituency Phone: 416-223-2858; Fax: 416-223-9715
Social Media: twitter.com/AliEhsassi, www.facebook.com/ali.ehsassi
Constituency Office
115 Sheppard Ave. West
Toronto, ON M2N 1M7

Fayçal El-Khoury, B.Eng.
Circonscription électorale: Laval — Les Iles, Québec *Nombre de constituants:* 82,297, Liberal
Tél: 613-992-2659; *Téléc:* 613-992-9469
Faycal.El-Khoury@parl.gc.ca
faycalelkhoury.liberal.ca
Autres numéros: Constituency Phone: 450-689-4594; Fax: 450-689-5092
Les réseaux sociaux: twitter.com/F_ElKhoury, www.facebook.com/elkhoury2015
Constituency Office
#200, 674, Place Publique
Laval, QC H7X 1G1

Neil Ellis
Constituency: Bay of Quinte, Ontario *No. of Constituents:* 83,954, Liberal
Tel: 613-992-0752; *Fax:* 613-992-0759
Neil.Ellis@parl.gc.ca
neilellis.liberal.ca
Other Communications: Constituency Phone: 613-969-3300; Fax: 613-969-3313
Social Media: twitter.com/NeilREllis, www.facebook.com/neilrellis
Constituency Office
100 Station St.
Belleville, ON K8N 2S5

Nathaniel Erskine-Smith
Constituency: Beaches — East York, Ontario *No. of Constituents:* 76,173, Liberal
Tel: 613-992-2115; *Fax:* 613-996-7942
Nathaniel.Erskine-Smith@parl.gc.ca
nathanielerskinesmith.liberal.ca
Other Communications: Constituency Phone: 416-467-0860; Fax: 416-467-0905
Social Media: twitter.com/beynate, www.facebook.com/beynatemp, ca.linkedin.com/in/nerskinesmith
Constituency Office
1902 Danforth Ave.
Toronto, ON M4C 1J4

Hon. Mark Eyking, P.C.
Constituency: Sydney — Victoria, Nova Scotia *No. of Constituents:* 59,761, Liberal
Tel: 613-995-6459; *Fax:* 613-995-2963
mark.eyking@parl.gc.ca
markeyking.liberal.ca
Other Communications: Constituency Phone: 902-567-6275; Fax: 902-564-2479
Social Media: twitter.com/MarkEyking_MP, www.facebook.com/MarkEykingMP, ca.linkedin.com/in/mark-eyking-57217557
Constituency Office
500 Kings Rd.
Sydney, NS B1S 1B2

Doug Eyolfson
Constituency: Charleswood — St. James — Assiniboia — Headingley, Manitoba *No. of Constituents:* 63,466, Liberal
Tel: 613-995-5609; *Fax:* 613-992-3199
Doug.Eyolfson@parl.gc.ca
dougeyolfson.liberal.ca
Other Communications: Constituency Phone: 204-984-6432; Fax: 204-984-6451
Social Media: twitter.com/DougEyolfson, www.facebook.com/DougEyolfson
Constituency Office
3092 Portage Ave., #D
Winnipeg, MB R3K 0Y2

Ted Falk
Constituency: Provencher, Manitoba *No. of Constituents:* 64,598, Conservative Party
Tel: 613-992-3128; *Fax:* 613-995-1049
ted.falk@parl.gc.ca
tedfalk.ca
Other Communications: Constituency Phone: 204-326-9889; Fax: 204-346-9874
Social Media: twitter.com/mptedfalk, www.facebook.com/ted.falk.14, ca.linkedin.com/in/ted-falk-7508b53a
Constituency Office
76 Provincial Trunk Hwy. 12 North
Steinbach, MB T5G 1T4

Hon. Edward Fast, P.C., LL.B.
Constituency: Abbotsford, British Columbia *No. of Constituents:* 68,154, Conservative Party
Tel: 613-995-0183; *Fax:* 613-996-9795
ed.fast@parl.gc.ca
www.edfast.ca
Other Communications: Constituency Phone: 604-557-7888; Fax: 604-557-9918
Social Media: twitter.com/HonEdFast, www.facebook.com/EdFastMP
Constituency Office
#205, 2825 Clearbrook Rd.
Abbotsford, BC V2T 6S3

Greg Fergus
Circonscription électorale: Hull — Aylmer, Québec *Nombre de constituants:* 78,773, Liberal
Tél: 613-992-7550; *Téléc:* 613-992-7599
Greg.Fergus@parl.gc.ca
gregfergus.liberal.ca
Autres numéros: Constituency Phone: 819-994-8844; Fax: 819-994-8557
Les réseaux sociaux: twitter.com/GregFergus, www.facebook.com/GregFergusLiberal
Constituency Office
179, promenade Du Portage
Gatineau, QC J8X 2K5

Andy Fillmore
Constituency: Halifax, Nova Scotia *No. of Constituents:* 71,363, Liberal
Tel: 613-995-7614; *Fax:* 613-992-8569
Andy.Fillmore@parl.gc.ca
andyfillmore.liberal.ca
Other Communications: Constituency Phone: 902-426-8691; Fax: 902-426-8693
Social Media: twitter.com/AndyFillmoreHFX, www.facebook.com/AndyFillmoreHFX, ca.linkedin.com/pub/andy-fillmore/22/a82/4ab
Constituency Office
#808, 1888 Brunswick St.
Halifax, NS B3J 3J8

Hon. Diane Finley, P.C., B.A., M.B.A.
Constituency: Haldimand — Norfolk, Ontario *No. of Constituents:* 82,621, Conservative Party
Tel: 613-996-4974; *Fax:* 613-996-9749
diane.finley@parl.gc.ca
www.dianefinley.ca
Other Communications: Constituency Phone: 519-426-3400; Fax: 519-426-0003
Social Media: twitter.com/dianefinleymp
Constituency Office
76 Kent St. South
Simcoe, ON N3Y 2Y1

Pat Finnigan
Constituency: Miramichi — Grand Lake, New Brunswick *No. of Constituents:* 48,158, Liberal
Tel: 613-992-5335; *Fax:* 613-996-8418
Pat.Finnigan@parl.gc.ca
patfinnigan.liberal.ca
Other Communications: Constituency Phone: 506-778-8448; Fax: 506-778-8150
Social Media: twitter.com/patricefinnigan, www.facebook.com/patfinniganliberal
Constituency Office
514 Water St.
Miramichi, NB E1V 2G5

Darren Fisher
Constituency: Dartmouth — Cole Harbour, Nova Scotia *No. of Constituents:* 73,066, Liberal
Tel: 613-995-9378; *Fax:* 613-995-9379
Darren.Fisher@parl.gc.ca
darrenfisher.liberal.ca
Other Communications: Constituency Phone: 902-462-6453; Fax: 902-462-6493
Social Media: twitter.com/DarrenFisherNS, www.facebook.com/DarrenFisherNS
Constituency Office
#200, 82 Tacoma Dr.
Darmouth, NS B2W 3E5

Peter Fonseca, B.A., B.Ed.
Constituency: Mississauga East — Cooksville, Ontario *No. of Constituents:* 81,736, Liberal
Tel: 613-996-0420; *Fax:* 613-996-0279
Peter.Fonseca@parl.gc.ca
peterfonseca.liberal.ca
Other Communications: Constituency Phone: 905-566-0009; Fax: 905-566-0017
Social Media: twitter.com/VoteFonseca, www.facebook.com/PeterFonsecaMP
Constituency Office
#303, 918 Dundas St. East
Mississauga, ON L4Y 4H9

Minister, Public Services & Procurement, Hon. Judy Foote, P.C., B.A., B.Ed
Constituency: Bonavista — Burin — Trinity, Newfoundland & Labrador *No. of Constituents:* 61,475, Liberal
Tel: 613-992-8655; *Fax:* 613-992-5324
Judy.Foote@parl.gc.ca

judyfoote.liberal.ca
Other Communications: Constituency Phone: 709-832-1383; Fax: 709-832-1380
Social Media: twitter.com/judyfootemp, www.facebook.com/judy.foote.146
Constituency Office
3 Church St.
PO Box 370
Grand Bank, NL A0E 1W0

Interim Party Leader, Bloc Québécois, Rhéal Fortin
Circonscription électorale: Rivière-du-Nord, Québec *Nombre de constituants:* 89,381, Bloc Québécois
Tél: 613-992-3257; *Téléc:* 613-992-2156
Rheal.Fortin@parl.gc.ca
www.blocquebecois.org/depute-rheal-fortin
Autres numéros: Constituency Phone: 450-565-0061; Fax: 450-565-0118
Les réseaux sociaux: twitter.com/rhealfortin, www.facebook.com/566791310126350
Constituency Office
#305 161, rue de la Gare
Saint-Jérôme, QC J7Z 2B9

Peter Fragiskatos
Constituency: London North Centre, Ontario *No. of Constituents:* 88,819, Liberal
Tel: 613-992-0805; *Fax:* 613-992-9613
Peter.Fragiskatos@parl.gc.ca
peterfragiskatos.liberal.ca
Other Communications: Constituency Phone: 519-663-9777; Fax: 519-663-2238
Social Media: twitter.com/pfragiskatos, www.facebook.com/pfragiskatos
Constituency Office
885 Adelaide St. North
London, ON N5Y 2M2

Colin Fraser
Constituency: West Nova, Nova Scotia *No. of Constituents:* 66,796, Liberal
Tel: 613-995-5711; *Fax:* 613-996-9857
Colin.Fraser@parl.gc.ca
colinfraser.liberal.ca
Other Communications: Yarmouth: 902-742-6808; Middleton: 902-825-3327
Social Media: twitter.com/colinjmfraser, www.facebook.com/colinjmfraser
Constituency Office
#200, 396 Main St.
Yarmouth, NS B5A 1E9

Sean Fraser
Constituency: West Nova, Nova Scotia *No. of Constituents:* 59,585, Liberal
Tel: 613-992-6022
Toll-free: 844-641-5886; *Fax:* 613-992-2337
Sean.Fraser@parl.gc.ca
seanfraser.liberal.ca
Other Communications: Antigonish Phone: 902-867-2919
Social Media: twitter.com/seanfrasermp, www.facebook.com/SeanFraserMP, ca.linkedin.com/pub/sean-fraser/54/90/795
Constituency Office
#2A, 115 MacLean St.
New Glasgow, NS B2H 4M5

Minister, International Trade, Hon. Chrystia Freeland, P.C.
Constituency: University — Rosedale, Ontario *No. of Constituents:* 73,963, Liberal
Tel: 613-992-5234; *Fax:* 613-996-9607
chrystia.freeland@parl.gc.ca
chrystiafreeland.liberal.ca
Other Communications: Constituency Phone: 416-928-1451; Fax: 416-928-2377
Social Media: twitter.com/cafreeland, www.facebook.com/freelandchrystia
Constituency Office
#510, 344 Bloor St. West
Toronto, ON M5S 3A7

Hon. Hedy Fry, P.C., M.D., L.R.C.P.S.I., L.M.
Constituency: Vancouver Centre, British Columbia *No. of Constituents:* 86,663, Liberal
Tel: 613-992-3213; *Fax:* 613-995-0056
hedy.fry@parl.gc.ca
www.hedyfry.com
Other Communications: Constituency Phone: 604-666-0135; Fax: 604-666-0114
Social Media: twitter.com/hedyfry, www.facebook.com/drhedyfry, ca.linkedin.com/in/hon-hedy-fry-6710b868
Constituency Office
#106, 1030 Denman St.
Vancouver, BC V6G 2M6

Stephen Fuhr
Constituency: Kelowna — Lake Country, British Columbia *No. of Constituents:* 89,033, Liberal
Tel: 613-992-7006; *Fax:* 613-992-7636
Stephen.Fuhr@parl.gc.ca
stephenfuhr.liberal.ca
Other Communications: Constituency Phone: 250-470-5075; Fax: 250-470-5077
Social Media: twitter.com/fuhr2015, www.facebook.com/fuhr2015
Constituency Office
#102, 1420 St. Paul St.
Kelowna, BC V1Y 2E6

Cheryl Gallant, B.Sc.
Constituency: Renfrew — Nipissing — Pembroke, Ontario *No. of Constituents:* 78,080, Conservative Party
Tel: 613-992-7712; *Fax:* 613-995-2561
cheryl.gallant@parl.gc.ca
www.cherylgallant.com
Other Communications: Constituency Phone: 613-732-4404; Fax: 613-732-4697
Social Media: twitter.com/cherylgallant, www.facebook.com/CherylGallant, www.linkedin.com/pub/cheryl-gallant/36/336/366
Constituency Office
84 Isabella St., 1st Fl.
Pembroke, ON K8A 5S5

Minister, Transport, Hon. Marc Garneau, P.C., C.C., C.D., B.Sc., Ph.D., F.C.A.S.I.
Circonscription électorale: Notre-Dame-de-Grâce — Westmount, Québec *Nombre de constituants:* 79,597, Liberal
Tél: 613-996-7267; *Téléc:* 613-995-8632
marc.garneau@parl.gc.ca
marcgarneau.liberal.ca
Autres numéros: Constituency Phone: 514-283-2013; Fax: 514-283-9790
Les réseaux sociaux: twitter.com/MarcGarneau, www.facebook.com/marcgarneaump
Constituency Office
#340, 4060, rue Sainte-Catherine ouest
Westmount, QC H3Z 2Z3

Randall Garrison, M.A.
Constituency: Esquimalt — Saanich — Sooke, British Columbia *No. of Constituents:* 89,523, New Democratic Party
Tel: 613-996-2625; *Fax:* 613-996-9779
randall.garrison@parl.gc.ca
www.randallgarrison.ca
Other Communications: Constituency Phone: 250-405-6550; Fax: 250-405-6554
Social Media: twitter.com/r_garrison, www.facebook.com/RandallGarrisonPage
Constituency Office
2904 Tillicum Rd.
Victoria, BC V9A 2A5

Bernard Généreux
Circonscription électorale: Montmagny — L'Islet — Kamouraska — Rivière-du-Loup, Québec *Nombre de constituants:* 78,489, Conservative Party
Tél: 613-995-0265; *Téléc:* 613-943-1229
Bernard.Genereux@parl.gc.ca
bernardgenereux.conservateur.ca
Autres numéros: Montmagny: 418-248-1211 Riviere-du-Loup: 418-868-1280
Les réseaux sociaux: twitter.com/genereuxbernard, www.facebook.com/bernardgenereuxpc
Constituency Office
#101, 6, rue St-Jean Baptiste est
Montmagny, QC G5V 1J7

Garnett Genuis
Constituency: Sherwood Park — Fort Saskatchewan, Alberta *No. of Constituents:* 88,876, Conservative Party
Tel: 613-995-3611; *Fax:* 613-995-3612
Garnett.Genuis@parl.gc.ca
www.garnettgenuis.ca
Other Communications: Constituency Phone: 780-467-4944; Fax: 780-449-1471
Social Media: twitter.com/GarnettGenuis, www.facebook.com/173928532656310
Constituency Office
#214, 2018 Sherwood Dr.
Sherwood Park, AB T8A 5V3

Mark Gerretsen
Constituency: Kingston and the Islands, Ontario *No. of Constituents:* 89,990, Liberal
Tel: 613-996-1955; *Fax:* 613-996-1958
Mark.Gerretsen@parl.gc.ca
markgerretsen.liberal.ca
Other Communications: Constituency Phone: 613-542-3243; Fax: 613-542-5461
Social Media: twitter.com/MarkGerretsen, www.facebook.com/markgerretsen, ca.linkedin.com/in/markgerretsen
Constituency Office
841 Princess St.
Kingston, ON K7L 1G7

Marilène Gill
Circonscription électorale: Manicouagan, Québec *Nombre de constituants:* 75,030, Bloc Québécois
Tél: 613-992-2363; *Téléc:* 613-996-7954
Marilene.Gill@parl.gc.ca
blocquebecois.org/depute-marilene
Autres numéros: Baie-Comeau: 418-589-0573; Sept-Iles: 418-960-1411
Les réseaux sociaux: twitter.com/gillmarilene, www.facebook.com/marilenegill.blocquebecois
Constituency Office
955, rue de Parfondeval
Baie-Comeau, QC G5C 2W8

Marilyn Gladu
Constituency: Sarnia — Lambton, Ontario *No. of Constituents:* 80,565, Conservative Party
Tel: 613-957-2649; *Fax:* 613-957-2655
Marilyn.Gladu@parl.gc.ca
marilyngladu.com
Other Communications: Constituency Phone: 519-383-6600; Fax: 519-383-0609
Social Media: www.facebook.com/Gladu2015, ca.linkedin.com/pub/marilyn-gladu/13/747/55
Constituency Office
#2, 1000 Finch Dr.
Sarnia, ON N7S 6G5

Joël Godin
Circonscription électorale: Portneuf — Jacques-Cartier, Québec *Nombre de constituants:* 87,782, Conservative Party
Tél: 613-992-2798; *Téléc:* 613-995-1637
Joel.Godin@parl.gc.ca
Autres numéros: Constituency Phone: 418-870-1571; Fax: 418-870-1577
Les réseaux sociaux: twitter.com/pcc_hq, www.facebook.com/JoelGodinPJC, ca.linkedin.com/in/joël-godin-16511749
Constituency Office
#230, 334 Rd. 138
Saint-Augustin-de-Desmaures, QC G3A 1G8

Pam Goldsmith-Jones
Constituency: West Vancouver — Sunshine Coast — Sea to Sky Country, British Columbia *No. of Constituents:* 89,459, Liberal
Tel: 613-947-4617; *Fax:* 613-947-4620
Pam.Goldsmith-Jones@parl.gc.ca
pamgoldsmithjones.liberal.ca
Other Communications: Constituency Phone: 604-913-2660; Fax: 604-913-2664
Social Media: twitter.com/pgoldsmithjones, www.facebook.com/PamelaGoldsmithJones, ca.linkedin.com/in/pam-goldsmith-jones-2467b247
Constituency Office
6367 Bruce St. West
West Vancouver, BC V7W 2B8

Minister, Public Safety & Emergency Preparedness, Hon. Ralph Goodale, P.C., B.A., LL.B.
Constituency: Regina — Wascana, Saskatchewan *No. of Constituents:* 56,656, Liberal
Tel: 613-947-1153; *Fax:* 613-996-9790
ralph.goodale@parl.gc.ca
ralphgoodale.liberal.ca
Other Communications: Constituency Phone: 306-585-2202; Fax: 306-585-2280
Social Media: twitter.com/RalphGoodale, www.facebook.com/ralphgoodale
Constituency Office
310 University Park Dr.
Regina, SK S4V 0Y8

Karina Gould
Constituency: Burlington, Ontario *No. of Constituents:* 95,624, Liberal
Tel: 613-995-0881; *Fax:* 613-995-1091
Karina.Gould@parl.gc.ca
karinagould.liberal.ca
Other Communications: Constituency Phone: 905-639-5757; Fax: 905-639-6031
Social Media: twitter.com/karinagould, www.facebook.com/karina.gould, ca.linkedin.com/in/karinagould
Constituency Office
#209, 777 Guelph Line
Burlington, ON L7R 3N2

Jacques Gourde
Circonscription électorale: Lévis — Lotbinière, Québec *Nombre de constituants:* 87,103, Conservative Party
Tél: 613-992-2639; *Téléc:* 613-992-1018
jacques.gourde@parl.gc.ca
jacquesgourde.conservateur.ca
Autres numéros: Constituency Phone: 418-836-0970; Fax: 418-836-6177
Les réseaux sociaux: twitter.com/JacquesGourde, www.facebook.com/jacquesgourde2025
Constituency Office
2677, rue Lagueux
Lévis, QC G6J 1B7

David de Burgh Graham
Circonscription électorale: Laurentides — Labelle, Québec *Nombre de constituants:* 96,737, Liberal

Tél: 613-992-2289; *Téléc:* 613-992-6864
David.Graham@parl.gc.ca
davidgraham.ca
Autres numéros: Constituency Phones: 819-326-4724; 819-440-3091
Les réseaux sociaux: twitter.com/daviddbgraham, www.facebook.com/daviddebgraham
Constituency Office
80A, boul Norbert-Morin
Sainte-Agathe-des-Monts, QC J8C 2V8

Raj Grewal
Constituency: Brampton East, Ontario *No. of Constituents:* 67,721, Liberal
Tel: 613-992-0769; *Fax:* 613-992-0777
Raj.Grewal@parl.gc.ca
rajgrewal.liberal.ca
Other Communications: Constituency Phone: 905-458-1474; Fax: 905-458-8615
Social Media: twitter.com/rajliberal, www.facebook.com/RajLiberal
Constituency Office
#204, 1 Gateway Blvd.
Brampton, ON L6T 0G3

Minister, Status of Women, Hon. Patricia Hajdu, P.C.
Constituency: Thunder Bay — Superior North, Ontario *No. of Constituents:* 63,995, Liberal
Tel: 613-996-4792; *Fax:* 613-996-9785
Patty.Hajdu@parl.gc.ca
pattyhajdu.liberal.ca
Other Communications: Constituency Phone: 807-766-2090; Fax: 807-766-2094
Social Media: twitter.com/PattyHajdu, ca.linkedin.com/in/patty-hajdu-825326a
Constituency Office
#3, 705 Red River Rd.
Thunder Bay, ON P7B 1J3

Cheryl Hardcastle
Constituency: Windsor — Tecumseh, Ontario *No. of Constituents:* 86,864, New Democratic Party
Tel: 613-947-3445; *Fax:* 613-947-3448
Cheryl.Hardcastle@parl.gc.ca
cherylhardcastle.ndp.ca
Other Communications: Constituency Phone: 519-979-2707; Fax: 519-979-7747
Social Media: twitter.com/CHardcastleNDP, www.facebook.com/CherylHardcastleNDP
Constituency Office
#2, 9733 Tecumseh Rd. East
Windsor, ON N8R 1A5

Rachael Harder
Constituency: Lethbridge, Ontario *No. of Constituents:* 82,225, Conservative Party
Tel: 613-992-4516; *Fax:* 613-992-6181
Rachael.Harder@parl.gc.ca
rachaelharder.ca
Other Communications: Constituency Phone: 403-320-0070; Fax: 403-380-4026
Social Media: twitter.com/rachaelhardermp, www.facebook.com/RachaelHarderMP
Constituency Office
255 - 8th St. South
Lethbridge, AB T1J 4Y1

Ken Hardie
Constituency: Fleetwood — Port Kells, British Columbia *No. of Constituents:* 74,286, Liberal
Tel: 613-996-2205; *Fax:* 613-995-7139
Ken.Hardie@parl.gc.ca
kenhardie.liberal.ca
Other Communications: Constituency Phone: 604-501-5900; Fax: 604-501-5901
Social Media: twitter.com/KenHardie, www.facebook.com/KenHardieLiberal, www.linkedin.com/pub/ken-hardie/11/26b/b7
Constituency Office
#301, 16088 - 84th Ave.
Surrey, BC V4N 0V9

T.J. Harvey
Constituency: Tobique — Mactaquac, New Brunswick *No. of Constituents:* 53,870, Liberal
Tel: 613-947-4431; *Fax:* 613-947-4434
TJ.Harvey@parl.gc.ca
tjharvey.liberal.ca
Other Communications: Constituency Phone: 506-392-5807; Fax: 506-392-5826
Social Media: twitter.com/TJHarveyLib, www.facebook.com/TJHarveyLib, ca.linkedin.com/pub/dir/T.j./Harvey/ca-0-Canada
Constituency Office
9160 Main St.
Florenceville, NB E7L 2A6

Minister, Veterans Affairs; Associate Minister, National Defence, Hon. Kent Hehr, P.C.
Constituency: Calgary Centre, Alberta *No. of Constituents:* 84,960, Liberal
Tel: 613-995-1561; *Fax:* 613-995-1862
Kent.Hehr@parl.gc.ca
kenthehr.liberal.ca
Other Communications: Constituency Phone: 403-244-1880; Fax: 403-245-3468
Social Media: twitter.com/KentHehr, www.facebook.com/KentHehrj, ca.linkedin.com/in/kenthehr
Constituency Office
950 - 6th Ave. SW
Calgary, AB T2P 1E4

Randy Hoback
Constituency: Prince Albert, Saskatchewan *No. of Constituents:* 56,563, Conservative Party
Tel: 613-995-3295; *Fax:* 613-995-6819
randy.hoback@parl.gc.ca
www.mprandyhoback.ca
Social Media: twitter.com/MPRandyHoback, www.facebook.com/MPRandyHoback, ca.linkedin.com/in/mprandyhoback

Mark Holland, B.A.
Constituency: Ajax, Ontario *No. of Constituents:* 84,584, Liberal
Tel: 613-995-8042; *Fax:* 613-996-1289
Mark.Holland@parl.gc.ca
markholland.liberal.ca
Other Communications: Constituency Phone: 905-426-6808; Fax: 905-426-9564
Social Media: twitter.com/markhollandlib, www.facebook.com/mark.hollandlib, ca.linkedin.com/in/mark-holland-70966135
Constituency Office
#1, 100 Old Kingston Rd.
Ajax, ON L1T 2Z9

Anthony Housefather
Circonscription électorale: Mont-Royal, Québec *Nombre de constituants:* 74,374, Liberal
Tél: 613-995-0121; *Téléc:* 613-992-6762
Anthony.Housefather@parl.gc.ca
anthonyhousefather.liberal.ca
Autres numéros: Constituency Phone: 514-283-0171; Fax: 514-283-2407
Les réseaux sociaux: twitter.com/AHousefather, www.facebook.com/anthonyhousefather, www.linkedin.com/in/anthony-housefather-5984791
Constituency Office
#316, 4770, av Kent
Montréal, QC H3W 1H2

Carol Hughes
Constituency: Algoma — Manitoulin — Kapuskasing, Ontario *No. of Constituents:* 62,625, New Democratic Party
Tel: 613-996-5376; *Fax:* 613-995-6661
carol.hughes@parl.gc.ca
carolhughes.ndp.ca
Social Media: twitter.com/CarolHughesMP, www.facebook.com/38326584416

Ahmed Hussen
Constituency: York South — Weston, Ontario *No. of Constituents:* 70,361, Liberal
Tel: 613-995-0777; *Fax:* 613-992-2949
Ahmed.Hussen@parl.gc.ca
ahmedhussen.liberal.ca
Other Communications: Constituency Phone: 416-656-2526; Fax: 416-656-9908
Social Media: twitter.com/ahmedhussenlib, www.facebook.com/AhmedHussenLib, ca.linkedin.com/in/ahmed-hussen-0282726
Constituency Office
99D Ingram Dr.
Toronto, ON M6M 2L7

Gudie Hutchings
Constituency: Long Range Mountains, Newfoundland & Labrador *No. of Constituents:* 71,037, Liberal
Tel: 613-996-5511; *Fax:* 613-996-9632
Gudie.Hutchings@parl.gc.ca
gudiehutchings.liberal.ca
Other Communications: Constituency Phone: 709-637-4540; Fax: 709-637-4537
Social Media: twitter.com/Gudie, www.facebook.com/gudiehutchings, ca.linkedin.com/pub/gudrid-hutchings/6/74/77b
Constituency Office
#49, 51 Park St.
Corner Brook, NL A2H 2X1

Angelo Iacono
Circonscription électorale: Alfred-Pellan, Québec *Nombre de constituants:* 78,288, Liberal
Tél: 613-992-0611; *Téléc:* 613-992-8556
Angelo.Iacono@parl.gc.ca
angeloiacono.liberal.ca
Autres numéros: Constituency Phone: 450-661-4117; Fax: 450-661-5623
Les réseaux sociaux: twitter.com/AngeloIacono, www.facebook.com/iaconoplc, ca.linkedin.com/in/angelo-iacono-86690427
Constituency Office
#300, 3131, de la Concorde est
Laval, QC H7E 4W4

Matt Jeneroux, B.A.
Constituency: Edmonton Riverbend, Alberta *No. of Constituents:* 80,938, Conservative Party
Tel: 613-992-3594; *Fax:* 613-992-3616
Matt.Jeneroux@parl.gc.ca
mattjeneroux.ca
Other Communications: Constituency Phone: 780-495-4351; Fax: 780-495-4485
Social Media: twitter.com/jeneroux, www.facebook.com/mattjeneroux, ca.linkedin.com/pub/matt-jeneroux/13/787/49a
Constituency Office
#204, 596 Riverbend Sq.
Edmonton, AB T6R 2E3

Gord Johns
Constituency: Courtenay — Alberni, British Columbia *No. of Constituents:* 90,998, New Democratic Party
Tel: 613-992-0903; *Fax:* 613-992-0913
Gord.Johns@parl.gc.ca
gordjohns.ndp.ca
Other Communications: Constituency Phone: 250-947-2140; Fax: 250-947-2144
Social Media: twitter.com/GordJohns
Constituency Office
#12A, 1209 East Island
Parksville, BC V9P 1R5

Georgina Jolibois
Constituency: Desnethé — Missinippi — Churchill River, Saskatchewan *No. of Constituents:* 44,320, New Democratic Party
Tel: 613-995-8321; *Fax:* 613-995-7697
Georgina.Jolibois@parl.gc.ca
georginajolibois.ndp.ca
Other Communications: La Loche: 306-822-2289; La Ronge: 306-425-2643
Social Media: twitter.com/GeorginaNDP, www.facebook.com/GeorginaJoliboisNDP
Constituency Office
#117, 23 La Loche Ave.
La Loche, SK S0M 1G0

Minister, Canadian Heritage, Hon. Mélanie Joly, P.C.
Circonscription électorale: Ahuntsic-Cartierville, Québec *Nombre de constituants:* 82,948, Liberal
Tél: 613-992-0983; *Téléc:* 613-992-1932
Melanie.Joly@parl.gc.ca
melaniejoly.liberal.ca
Autres numéros: Constituency Phone: 514-383-3709; Fax: 514-383-3589
Les réseaux sociaux: twitter.com/melaniejoly, www.facebook.com/melanie.joly.965, ca.linkedin.com/in/mjoly
Constituency Office
#1109, 225, Chabanel ouest
Montréal, QC H2N 2C9

Yvonne Jones
Constituency: Labrador, Newfoundland & Labrador *No. of Constituents:* 19,917, Liberal
Tel: 613-996-4630; *Fax:* 613-996-7132
yvonne.jones@parl.gc.ca
yvonnejones.liberal.ca
Other Communications: Constituency Phones: 709-896-2483; 709-927-5210
Social Media: twitter.com/YvonneJJones, www.facebook.com/yvonnejonesliberal
Constituency Office
217 Hamilton River Rd., #B
PO Box 119
Happy Valley-Goose Bay, NL A0P 1E0

Bernadette Jordan
Constituency: South Shore, Nova Scotia *No. of Constituents:* 75,904, Liberal
Tel: 613-996-0877; *Fax:* 613-996-0878
Bernadette.Jordan@parl.gc.ca
bernadettejordan.liberal.ca
Other Communications: Constituency Phone: 902-527-5655; Fax: 902-527-5656
Social Media: twitter.com/bernjordanmp, www.facebook.com/bernadettesouthshore
Constituency Office
#106, 129 Aberdeen Rd.
Bridgewater, NS B4V 2S7

Majid Jowhari
Constituency: Richmond Hill, Ontario *No. of Constituents:* 80,402, Liberal
Tel: 613-992-3802; *Fax:* 613-996-1954
Majid.Jowhari@parl.gc.ca
majidjowhari.liberal.ca
Other Communications: Constituency Phone: 905-707-9701; Fax: 905-707-9705
Social Media: twitter.com/MajidJowhari, www.facebook.com/Majid.Jowhari.Liberal.RichmondHill, ca.linkedin.com/in/majidjowhari

Constituency Office
#407, 9140 Leslie St.
Richmond Hill, ON L4B 0A9

House Leader, New Democratic Party, Peter Julian, B.A.
Constituency: New Westminster — Burnaby, British Columbia *No. of Constituents:* 79,176, New Democratic Party
Tel: 613-992-4214; *Fax:* 613-947-9500
peter.julian@parl.gc.ca
peterjulian.ndp.ca
Other Communications: Constituency Phone: 604-775-5707; Fax: 604-775-5743
Social Media: twitter.com/MPJulian, www.facebook.com/MPPeterJulian
Constituency Office
7615 - 6th St.
Burnaby, BC V3N 3M6

Darshan Singh Kang
Constituency: Calgary Skyview, Alberta *No. of Constituents:* 73,643, Liberal
Tel: 613-947-4487; *Fax:* 613-947-4490
DarshanSingh.Kang@parl.gc.ca
www.electkang.ca
Other Communications: Constituency Phone: 403-291-0018; Fax: 403-291-9516
Social Media: twitter.com/darshankang, www.facebook.com/CalgarySkyviewLPCA
Constituency Office
#140, 2635 - 37th Ave. NE
Calgary, AB T1Y 5Z6

Pat Kelly
Constituency: Calgary Rocky Ridge, Alberta *No. of Constituents:* 87,323, Conservative Party
Tel: 613-992-0826; *Fax:* 613-992-0845
Pat.Kelly@parl.gc.ca
patkelly.conservative.ca
Other Communications: Constituency Phone: 403-282-7980; Fax: 403-282-3587
Social Media: twitter.com/patkelly_mp, www.facebook.com/239513849576273, ca.linkedin.com/in/pat-kelly-15605742
Constituency Office
#202, 400 Crowfoot Cres.
Calgary, AB T3G 5H6

Hon. Peter Kent, P.C.
Constituency: Thornhill, Ontario *No. of Constituents:* 81,106, Conservative Party
Tel: 613-992-0253; *Fax:* 613-992-0887
peter.kent@parl.gc.ca
www.peterkent.ca
Other Communications: Constituency Phone: 905-886-9911; Fax: 905-886-5267
Social Media: twitter.com/KentThornhillMP, www.facebook.com/PeterKentMP, www.linkedin.com/pub/peter-kent/2a/aaa/888
Constituency Office
#41B, 7378 Yonge St.
Thornhill, ON L4J 8J1

Iqra Khalid
Constituency: Mississauga — Erin Mills, Ontario *No. of Constituents:* 82,348, Liberal
Tel: 613-995-7321; *Fax:* 613-992-6708
Iqra.Khalid@parl.gc.ca
iqrakhalid.liberal.ca
Other Communications: Constituency Phone: 905-820-8814; Fax: 905-820-4068
Social Media: twitter.com/iamIqraKhalid, www.facebook.com/iqrakhalidliberal
Constituency Office
#35, 3100 Ridgeway Dr.
Mississauga, ON L5L 5M5

Kamal Khera
Constituency: Brampton West, Ontario *No. of Constituents:* 70,734, Liberal
Tel: 613-992-0778; *Fax:* 613-992-0800
Kamal.Khera@parl.gc.ca
kamalkhera.ca
Other Communications: Constituency Phone: 905-454-4758; Fax: 905-454-3192
Social Media: twitter.com/KamalKheraLib, www.facebook.com/Kamal.Khera.Lib
Constituency Office
#10/10A, 35 Van Kirk Dr.
Brampton, ON L7A 1A5

Robert Gordon Kitchen
Constituency: Souris — Moose Mountain, Saskatchewan *No. of Constituents:* 52,093, Conservative Party
Tel: 613-992-7685; *Fax:* 613-995-8908
Robert.Kitchen@parl.gc.ca
sourismoosemountain.conservative.ca
Other Communications: Constituency Phone: 306-634-3000; Fax: 306-634-4835
Social Media: twitter.com/cpc_hq
Constituency Office
#308, 1133 - 4th St.
Estevan, SK S4A 0W6

Tom Kmiec, B.A., M.A.
Constituency: Calgary Shepard, Alberta *No. of Constituents:* 96,769, Conservative Party
Tel: 613-992-0846
Toll-free: 855-852-5710; *Fax:* 613-992-0883
Tom.Kmiec@parl.gc.ca
www.tomkmiec.ca
Social Media: twitter.com/tomkmiec, ca.linkedin.com/in/tomkmiec
Constituency Office
#1220, 2784 Glenmore Trail SE
Calgary, AB T2C 2E6

Jenny Kwan, B.A.
Constituency: Vancouver East, British Columbia *No. of Constituents:* 87,657, New Democratic Party
Tel: 613-992-6030; *Fax:* 613-995-7412
Jenny.Kwan@parl.gc.ca
jennykwan.ndp.ca
Social Media: twitter.com/JennyKwanBC, www.facebook.com/JennyKwanVanEast

Hon. Mike Lake, P.C., B.Comm.
Constituency: Edmonton — Wetaskiwin, Alberta *No. of Constituents:* 98,502, Conservative Party
Tel: 613-995-8695; *Fax:* 613-995-6465
mike.lake@parl.gc.ca
www.mikelake.ca
Other Communications: Constituency Phone: 780-495-2149; Fax: 780-495-2147
Social Media: twitter.com/MikeLakeMP, www.facebook.com/MikeLakeMP
Constituency Office
1230 - 91 St. SW
Edmonton, AB T6X 0P2

David Lametti, B.A., LL.B., B.C.L., LL.M., D.Phil.
Circonscription électorale: LaSalle — Émard — Verdun, Québec *Nombre de constituants:* 83,824, Liberal
Tél: 613-943-6636; *Téléc:* 613-943-6637
David.Lametti@parl.gc.ca
davidlametti.liberal.ca
Autres numéros: Constituency Phone: 514-363-0954; Fax: 514-367-5533
Les réseaux sociaux: twitter.com/DavidLametti, www.facebook.com/DLamettiLasalleVerdun
Constituency Office
6415, boul Monk
Montréal, QC H4E 3H8

Kevin Lamoureux
Constituency: Winnipeg North, Manitoba *No. of Constituents:* 57,627, Liberal
Tel: 613-996-6417; *Fax:* 613-996-9713
kevin.lamoureux@parl.gc.ca
kevinlamoureux.liberal.ca
Other Communications: Constituency Phone: 204-984-1767; Fax: 204-984-1766
Social Media: twitter.com/kevin_lamoureux, www.facebook.com/mpkevin.ca, ca.linkedin.com/in/kevin-lamoureux-16541a5a
Constituency Office
98 Mandalay Dr.
Winnipeg, MB R2P 1V8

Linda Lapointe
Circonscription électorale: Rivière-des-Mille-Iles, Québec *Nombre de constituants:* 81,429, Liberal
Tél: 613-992-7330; *Téléc:* 613-992-2602
Linda.Lapointe@parl.gc.ca
lindalapointe.liberal.ca
Autres numéros: Constituency Phone: 450-420-5525; Fax: 450-420-2575
Les réseaux sociaux: twitter.com/LapointeLinda, www.facebook.com/1605859372964304, ca.linkedin.com/in/linda-lapointe-ba430112
Constituency Office
61, rue de la Grande-Côte
Boisbriand, QC J7G 1C8

Guy Lauzon
Constituency: Stormont — Dundas — South Glengarry, Ontario *No. of Constituents:* 78,706, Conservative Party
Tel: 613-992-2521; *Fax:* 613-996-2119
guy.lauzon@parl.gc.ca
www.guylauzon.ca
Other Communications: Constituency Phone: 613-937-3331; Fax: 613-937-3251
Social Media: twitter.com/GuyLauzonMP, www.facebook.com/lauzonguy
Constituency Office
621 Pitt St.
Cornwall, ON K6J 3R8

Stéphane Lauzon
Circonscription électorale: Argenteuil — La Petite-Nation, Québec *Nombre de constituants:* 78,626, Liberal
Tél: 613-992-0902; *Téléc:* 613-992-2935
Stephane.Lauzon@parl.gc.ca
stephanelauzon.liberal.ca
Autres numéros: Lachute: 450-562-0737; Gatineau: 819-281-2626
Les réseaux sociaux: twitter.com/stephanelauzon5, www.facebook.com/stephane.lauzon.988
Constituency Office
#204, 505, av Bethany
Lachute, QC J8H 4A6

Hélène Laverdière, Ph.D.
Circonscription électorale: Laurier — Sainte-Marie, Québec *Nombre de constituants:* 84,142, New Democratic Party
Tél: 613-992-6779; *Téléc:* 613-995-8461
Helene.Laverdiere@parl.gc.ca
helenelaverdiere.ndp.ca
Autres numéros: Constituency Phone: 514-522-1339; Fax: 514-522-9899
Les réseaux sociaux: twitter.com/HLaverdiereNPD, www.facebook.com/Helene.Laverdiere.deputee
Constituency Office
#507, 101, boul Maisonneuve est
Montréal, QC H2L 4P9

Deputy Leader, Conservative Party of Canada, Hon. Denis Lebel, P.C.
Circonscription électorale: Lac-Saint-Jean, Québec *Nombre de constituants:* 85,337, Conservative Party
Tél: 613-996-6236; *Téléc:* 613-996-6252
denis.lebel@parl.gc.ca
www.denislebel.com
Autres numéros: Roberval: 418-275-2768; Alma: 418-275-2768
Les réseaux sociaux: twitter.com/denislebelpcc, www.facebook.com/DenisLebelPCC
Constituency Office
#102, 797, boul Saint-Joseph
Roberval, QC G8H 2L4

Minister, Fisheries, Oceans & the Canadian Coast Guard, Hon. Dominic Leblanc, P.C., B.A., LL.B., LL.M.
Constituency: Beauséjour, New Brunswick *No. of Constituents:* 66,170, Liberal
Tel: 613-992-1020; *Fax:* 613-992-3053
dominic.leblanc@parl.gc.ca
www.dominicleblanc.ca
Other Communications: Constituency Phone: 506-533-5700; Fax: 506-533-5888
Social Media: www.facebook.com/leblancdominic
Constituency Office
328 Main St., #I
Shediac, NB E4P 2E3

Minister, National Revenue, Hon. Diane Lebouthillier, P.C.
Circonscription électorale: Gaspésie — Les Iles-de-la-Madeleine, Québec *Nombre de constituants:* 65,623, Liberal
Tél: 613-992-6188; *Téléc:* 613-992-6194
Diane.Lebouthillier@parl.gc.ca
dianelebouthillier.liberal.ca
Autres numéros: Constituency Phones: 418-385-4264; 418-986-1489
Les réseaux sociaux: twitter.com/dilebouthillier, www.facebook.com/lebouthillierd
Constituency Office
#104, 153, La Grande Allée est
Grande-Rivière, QC G0C 1V0

Paul Lefebvre
Constituency: Sudbury, Ontario *No. of Constituents:* 71,594, Liberal
Tel: 613-996-8962; *Fax:* 613-995-2569
Paul.Lefebvre@parl.gc.ca
paullefebvre.liberal.ca
Other Communications: Constituency Phone: 705-673-7107; Fax: 705-673-0944
Social Media: twitter.com/lefebvrepaul, www.facebook.com/paullefebvre.sudbury, ca.linkedin.com/pub/paul-lefebvre/58/885/a1a
Cosntituency Office
152 Durham St.
Sudbury, ON P3E 3M7

Hon. Dr. Kellie Leitch, P.C., O.Ont., M.D., M.B.A., F.R.C.S.(C)
Constituency: Simcoe — Grey, Ontario *No. of Constituents:* 97,145, Conservative Party
Tel: 613-992-4224; *Fax:* 613-992-2164
kellie.leitch@parl.gc.ca
www.kellieleitch.ca
Social Media: twitter.com/KellieLeitch, www.facebook.com/KellieLeitchMP, www.linkedin.com/pub/dr-k-kellie-leitch/17/584/96

Denis Lemieux
Circonscription électorale: Chicoutimi — Le Fjord, Québec *Nombre de constituants:* 66,639, Liberal
Tél: 613-992-7207; *Téléc:* 613-992-0431
Denis.Lemieux@parl.gc.ca
denislemieux.liberal.ca
Autres numéros: Constituency Phone: 418-698-5648; Fax: 418-698-5611
Les réseaux sociaux: twitter.com/DenisLemieuxLib,

www.facebook.com/denislemieuxlib,
ca.linkedin.com/in/denis-lemieux-7b9332a7
Constituency Office
#70, 345, rue des Saguenéens
Chicoutimi, QC G7H 6K9

Chief Government Whip; Whip, Liberal Party, Hon. Andrew Leslie, C.M.M., M.Sc., M.S.M., C.D., P.C.
Constituency: Orléans, Ontario *No. of Constituents:* 96,174, Liberal
Tel: 613-995-1800; *Fax:* 613-995-6298
Andrew.Leslie@parl.gc.ca
andrewleslie.liberal.ca
Other Communications: Constituency Phone: 613-834-1800; Fax: 613-590-1201
Social Media: twitter.com/andrewlesliemp, www.facebook.com/andrewleslieorleans
Constituency Office
255 Centrum Blvd.
Orléans, ON K1E 3W3

Michael Levitt
Constituency: York Centre, Ontario *No. of Constituents:* 64,297, Liberal
Tel: 613-941-6339; *Fax:* 613-941-2421
Michael.Levitt@parl.gc.ca
michaellevitt.liberal.ca
Other Communications: Constituency Phone: 416-638-3700; Fax: 416-638-1407
Social Media: twitter.com/LevittMichael, www.facebook.com/LevittYorkCentre
Constituency Office
660 Wilson Ave.
Toronto, ON M3K 1E1

Ron Liepert
Constituency: Calgary Signal Hill, Alberta *No. of Constituents:* 84,765, Conservative Party
Tel: 613-992-3066; *Fax:* 613-992-3256
Ron.Liepert@parl.gc.ca
ronliepert.ca
Other Communications: Constituency Phone: 403-292-6666; Fax: 403-292-6670
Social Media: twitter.com/ronliepert, www.facebook.com/ronliepert, ca.linkedin.com/in/ron-liepert-6a32a128
Constituency Office
#2216, 8561 - 8A Ave. SW
Calgary, AB T3H 0V5

Joël Lightbound
Circonscription électorale: Louis-Hébert, Québec *Nombre de constituants:* 81,109, Liberal
Tél: 613-995-4995; *Téléc:* 613-996-8292
Joel.Lightbound@parl.gc.ca
joellightbound.liberal.ca
Autres numéros: Constituency Phone: 418-648-3244; Fax: 418-648-3260
Les réseaux sociaux: twitter.com/JoelLightbound, www.facebook.com/joellightbound
Constituency Office
#110, 3700, rue du Campanile
Québec, QC G1X 4G6

Ben Lobb, B.Sc. Admin.
Constituency: Huron — Bruce, Ontario *No. of Constituents:* 80,355, Conservative Party
Tel: 613-992-8234; *Fax:* 613-995-6350
ben.lobb@parl.gc.ca
www.benlobb.com
Social Media: twitter.com/benlobbmp, www.facebook.com/LobbBen, ca.linkedin.com/in/ben-lobb-188083b1

Alaina Lockhart
Constituency: Fundy Royal, New Brunswick *No. of Constituents:* 62,713, Liberal
Tel: 613-996-2332; *Fax:* 613-995-4286
Alaina.Lockhart@parl.gc.ca
alainalockhart.liberal.ca
Other Communications: Constituency Phone: 506-832-4200; Fax: 506-832-4235
Social Media: twitter.com/AlainaLockhart, www.facebook.com/AlainaFundyRoyal
Constituency Office
#104, 599 Main St.
Hampton, NB E5N 6C2

Wayne Long
Constituency: Saint John — Rothesay, New Brunswick *No. of Constituents:* 61,236, Liberal
Tel: 613-947-2700; *Fax:* 613-947-4574
Wayne.Long@parl.gc.ca
waynelong.liberal.ca
Other Communications: Constituency Phone: 506-657-2500; Fax: 506-657-2504
Social Media: twitter.com/WayneLongSJ, www.facebook.com/WayneLongSJ, ca.linkedin.com/pub/wayne-long/82/399/748
Constituency Office
1 Market Sq., #N306
Saint John, NB E2L 4Z6

Lloyd Longfield
Constituency: Guelph, Ontario *No. of Constituents:* 95,761, Liberal
Tel: 613-996-4758; *Fax:* 613-996-9922
Lloyd.Longfield@parl.gc.ca
www.lloydlongfield.ca
Other Communications: Constituency Phone: 519-837-8276; Fax: 519-837-8443
Social Media: twitter.com/lloydlongfield, www.facebook.com/lloyd4guelph, ca.linkedin.com/in/lloyd-longfield-544a1b7
Constituency Office
40 Cork St. East
Guelph, ON N1H 2W8

Karen Ludwig, M.A., M.Ed., CITP
Constituency: New Brunswick Southwest, New Brunswick *No. of Constituents:* 51,376, Liberal
Tel: 613-995-5550; *Fax:* 613-995-5226
Karen.Ludwig@parl.gc.ca
karenludwig.liberal.ca
Other Communications: Constituency Phones: 506-466-3928; 506-738-3634
Social Media: twitter.com/karenludwigmp, www.facebook.com/karenludwigNB, ca.linkedin.com/pub/karen-ludwig/19/568/4b3
Constituency Office
49 King St.
St. Stephen, NB E3L 2C1

Tom Lukiwski
Constituency: Moose Jaw — Lake Centre — Lanigan, Saskatchewan *No. of Constituents:* 57,471, Conservative Party
Tel: 613-992-4573; *Fax:* 613-996-6885
tom.lukiwski@parl.gc.ca
www.tomlukiwski.com
Other Communications: Constituency Phone: 306-691-3577; Fax: 306-391-3579
Social Media: twitter.com/TomLukiwski, www.facebook.com/TomLukiwski, ca.linkedin.com/in/tom-lukiwski-3b0b187a
Constituency Office
#1, 54 Stadacona St. West
Moose Jaw, SK S6H 1Z1

Minister, Agriculture & Agri-Food, Hon. Lawrence MacAulay, P.C.
Constituency: Cardigan, Prince Edward Island *No. of Constituents:* 28,777, Liberal
Tel: 613-995-9325; *Fax:* 613-995-2754
lawrence.macaulay@parl.gc.ca
lawrencemacaulay.liberal.ca
Other Communications: Constituency Phone: 902-838-4139; Fax: 902-838-3790
Social Media: www.facebook.com/lawrence.macaulay
Constituency Office
551 Main St.
PO Box 1150
Montague, PE C0A 1R0

Alistair MacGregor
Constituency: Cowichan — Malahat — Langford, British Columbia *No. of Constituents:* 80,298, New Democratic Party
Tel: 613-943-2180; *Fax:* 613-993-5577
Alistair.MacGregor@parl.gc.ca
alistairmacgregor.ndp.ca
Other Communications: Constituency Phone: 250-746-4896; Fax: 250-746-2354
Social Media: twitter.com/AMacGregor4CML, www.facebook.com/alistair4ndp, www.linkedin.com/in/alistair-macgregor-239552
Constituency Office
#101, 126 Ingram St.
Duncan, BC V9L 1P1

Deputy Opposition Whip, Dave MacKenzie
Constituency: Oxford, Ontario *No. of Constituents:* 83,431, Conservative Party
Tel: 613-995-4432; *Fax:* 613-995-4433
dave.mackenzie@parl.gc.ca
www.davemackenzie.ca
Social Media: twitter.com/davemackenziemp, www.facebook.com/DaveMacKenzieMP

Steven MacKinnon
Circonscription électorale: Gatineau, Québec *Nombre de constituants:* 84,097, Liberal
Tél: 613-992-4351; *Téléc:* 613-992-1037
Steven.MacKinnon@parl.gc.ca
stevemackinnon.liberal.ca
Autres numéros: Constituency Phone: 819-561-5555; Fax: 819-561-0005
Les réseaux sociaux: twitter.com/stevenmackinnon, ca.linkedin.com/in/mackinnonsteven
Constituency Office
#204, 160, boul de l'Hôpital
Gatineau, QC J8T 8J1

Larry Maguire
Constituency: Brandon — Souris, Manitoba *No. of Constituents:* 60,427, Conservative Party
Tel: 613-995-9372; *Fax:* 613-992-1265
Larry.Maguire@parl.gc.ca
larrymaguire.ca
Other Communications: Constituency Phone: 204-726-7600; Fax: 204-726-7699
Social Media: twitter.com/larrymaguiremp, www.facebook.com/larrymaguiremp
Constituency Office
#8, 223 - 18th St. North
Brandon, MB R7A 2V8

Sheila Malcolmson
Constituency: Nanaimo — Ladysmith, British Columbia *No. of Constituents:* 93,578, New Democratic Party
Tel: 613-992-5243; *Fax:* 613-992-9112
Sheila.Malcolmson@parl.gc.ca
sheilamalcolmson.ndp.ca
Other Communications: Constituency Phone: 250-734-6400; Fax: 250-734-6404
Social Media: twitter.com/S_Malcolmson, www.facebook.com/SheilaMalcolmsonNDP
Constituency Office
#103, 495 Dunsmuir St.
Nanaimo, BC V9R 6B9

James Maloney
Constituency: Etobicoke — Lakeshore, Ontario *No. of Constituents:* 92,100, Liberal
Tel: 613-995-9364; *Fax:* 613-992-5880
James.Maloney@parl.gc.ca
jamesmaloney.liberal.ca
Other Communications: Constituency Phone: 416-251-5510; Fax: 416-251-2845
Social Media: twitter.com/j_maloney, www.facebook.com/jamesmaloney.etobicoke
Constituency Office
#203, 1092 Islington Ave.
Toronto, ON M8Z 4R9

Simon Marcil
Circonscription électorale: Mirabel, Québec *Nombre de constituants:* 87,622, Bloc Québécois
Tél: 613-992-1227; *Téléc:* 613-992-1245
Simon.Marcil@parl.gc.ca
www.blocquebecois.org/depute-simon-marcil
Autres numéros: Constituency Phone: 450-430-5535; Fax: 450-430-5155
Les réseaux sociaux: www.facebook.com/simon.marcil
Constituency Office
#102, 13479, boul Curé-Labelle
Mirabel, QC J7J 1H1

Brian Masse, B.A. (Hons.)
Constituency: Windsor West, Ontario *No. of Constituents:* 84,699, New Democratic Party
Tel: 613-996-1541; *Fax:* 613-992-5397
brian.masse@parl.gc.ca
brianmasse.ndp.ca
Other Communications: Constituency Phone: 519-255-1631; Fax: 519-255-7913
Social Media: twitter.com/BrianMasseMP, www.facebook.com/brianmassemp
Constituency Office
#2, 1398 Ouellette Ave.
Windsor, ON N8X 1J8

Rémi Massé
Circonscription électorale: Avignon — La Mitis — Matane — Matapédia, Québec *Nombre de constituants:* 60,801, Liberal
Tél: 613-995-1013; *Téléc:* 613-995-5184
Remi.Masse@parl.gc.ca
remimasse.liberal.ca
Autres numéros: Matane: 418-562-0343; Carleton-sur-Mer: 418-364-6254
Les réseaux sociaux: twitter.com/remi_masse1, www.facebook.com/remi.masse.federal, ca.linkedin.com/in/remimasse
Constituency Office
290, av Saint-Jérôme
Matane, QC G4W 3A9

Deputy Whip, New Democratic Party, Irene Mathyssen, B.A.(Hons), B.Ed.
Constituency: London — Fanshawe, Ontario *No. of Constituents:* 85,788, New Democratic Party
Tel: 613-995-2901; *Fax:* 613-943-8717
irene.mathyssen@parl.gc.ca
www.irenemathyssen.ca
Other Communications: Constituency Phone: 519-685-4745; Fax: 519-685-1462
Social Media: twitter.com/irenemathyssen, www.facebook.com/MP.Mathyssen, ca.linkedin.com/in/irene-mathyssen-8aa01672
Constituency Office
1700 Dundas St., #D
London, ON N5W 3C9

Bryan May
Constituency: Cambridge, Ontario *No. of Constituents:* 82,916, Liberal
Tel: 613-996-1307; *Fax:* 613-996-8340
Bryan.May@parl.gc.ca
bryanmay.liberal.ca
Other Communications: Constituency Phone: 519-624-7440; Fax: 519-624-3517
Social Media: twitter.com/_BryanMay, www.facebook.com/bryanmaycambridge
Constituency Office
534 Hespeler Rd., #A4
Cambridge, ON N1R 6J7

Leader, Green Party of Canada, Elizabeth May, O.C., LL.B.
Constituency: Saanich — Gulf Islands, British Columbia *No. of Constituents:* 85,839, Green Party of Canada
Tel: 613-996-1119; *Fax:* 613-996-0850
elizabeth.may@parl.gc.ca
www.elizabethmaymp.ca
Other Communications: Constituency Phone: 250-657-2000; Fax: 250-657-2004
Social Media: twitter.com/elizabethmay, www.facebook.com/ElizabethMayGreenLeader, www.linkedin.com/pub/elizabeth-may/3/a91/69
Constituency Office
9711 Fourth St., #1
Sidney, BC V8L WY8

Minister, Immigration, Refugees & Citizenship, Hon. John McCallum, P.C., B.A., Ph.D.
Constituency: Markham — Unionville, Ontario *No. of Constituents:* 82,534, Liberal
Tel: 613-996-3374; *Fax:* 613-992-3921
john.mccallum@parl.gc.ca
johnmccallum.ca
Other Communications: Constituency Phone: 905-479-8100; Fax: 905-479-3440
Social Media: twitter.com/honjohnmccallum, www.facebook.com/McCallumj1
Constituency Office
#21-22, 7750 Birchmount Rd.
Markham, ON L3R 0B4

Kelly McCauley
Constituency: Edmonton West, Alberta *No. of Constituents:* 79,446, Conservative Party
Tel: 780-392-2515; *Fax:* 780-392-2519
Kelly.McCauley@parl.gc.ca
kellymccauley.ca
Other Communications: Constituency Phone: 780-392-2515; Fax: 780-392-2519
Social Media: twitter.com/KellyMcCauleyMP, www.facebook.com/KellyMcCauleyforEdmontonWest, ca.linkedin.com/in/kjmccauley
Constituency Office
5613 - 199th St.
Edmonton, AB T6M 0M8

Phil McColeman, B.A.
Constituency: Brantford — Brant, Ontario *No. of Constituents:* 96,290, Conservative Party
Tel: 613-992-3118; *Fax:* 613-992-6382
phil.mccoleman@parl.gc.ca
www.philmccolemanmp.ca
Other Communications: Constituency Phone: 519-754-4300
Social Media: twitter.com/Phil4Brant, www.facebook.com/phil.mccoleman, ca.linkedin.com/in/phil-mccoleman-53660386
Constituency Office
#3, 108 St. George St.
Brantford, ON N3R 1V6

Karen McCrimmon
Constituency: Kanata — Carleton, Ontario *No. of Constituents:* 79,831, Liberal
Tel: 613-992-1119; *Fax:* 613-992-1043
Karen.McCrimmon@parl.gc.ca
karenmccrimmon.liberal.ca
Other Communications: Constituency Phone: 613-592-3469; Fax: 613-592-4756
Social Media: twitter.com/karenmccrimmon, www.facebook.com/karen.mccrimmon.ca, ca.linkedin.com/in/karen-mccrimmon-ba2a5429
Constituency Office
#121, 555 Legget Dr.
Kanata, ON K2K 2X3

Ken McDonald
Constituency: Avalon, Newfoundland & Labrador *No. of Constituents:* 67,781, Liberal
Tel: 613-992-4133; *Fax:* 613-992-7277
Ken.McDonald@parl.gc.ca
kenmcdonald.liberal.ca
Other Communications: Constituency Phone: 709-834-3424; Fax: 709-834-3628
Social Media: twitter.com/avalonmpken, www.facebook.com/1636440659937941
Constituency Office
#105, 120 Conception Bay Hwy.
Conception Bay South, NL A1W 3A6

David J. McGuinty, Dip. Agr., B.A., LL.B, LL.M.
Constituency: Ottawa South, Ontario *No. of Constituents:* 86,708, Liberal
Tel: 613-992-3269; *Fax:* 613-995-1534
david.mcguinty@parl.gc.ca
davidmcguinty.liberal.ca
Other Communications: Constituency Phone: 613-990-8640; Fax: 613-990-2592
Social Media: twitter.com/DavidMcGuinty, www.facebook.com/davidmcguinty, ca.linkedin.com/in/davidmcguinty
Constituency Office
1883 Bank St., #A
Ottawa, ON K1V 7Z9

Hon. John McKay, P.C., B.A., LL.B.
Constituency: Scarborough — Guildwood, Ontario *No. of Constituents:* 63,885, Liberal
Tel: 613-992-1447; *Fax:* 613-992-8968
john.mckay@parl.gc.ca
www.johnmckaymp.on.ca
Other Communications: Constituency Phone: 416-283-1226; Fax: 416-283-7935
Social Media: twitter.com/JohnMcKayLib
Constituency Office
#10, 3785 Kingston Rd.
Toronto, ON M1J 3H4

Minister, Environment & Climate Change, Hon. Catherine Mary McKenna, P.C.
Constituency: Ottawa Centre, Ontario *No. of Constituents:* 91,625, Liberal
Tel: 613-996-5322; *Fax:* 613-996-5323
Catherine.McKenna@parl.gc.ca
catherinemckennamp.ca
Other Communications: Constituency Phone: 613-946-8682; Fax: 613-946-8680
Social Media: twitter.com/cathmckenna, www.facebook.com/McKenna.Ottawa, ca.linkedin.com/in/catherine-mckenna-a0333025
Constituency Office
107 Catherine St.
Ottawa, ON K2P 0P4

Ron McKinnon
Constituency: Coquitlam — Port Coquitlam, British Columbia *No. of Constituents:* 84,120, Liberal
Tel: 613-992-9650; *Fax:* 613-992-9868
Ron.McKinnon@parl.gc.ca
ronmckinnon.liberal.ca
Other Communications: Constituency Phone: 604-927-1080; Fax: 604-927-1084
Social Media: twitter.com/RonMcKinnonLib, www.facebook.com/25722340150, ca.linkedin.com/in/ron-mckinnon-92b1a93
Constituency Office
#101, 3278 Westwood St.
Port Coquitlam, BC V3C 3L8

Cathy McLeod, B.Sc., M.Sc.
Constituency: Kamloops — Thompson — Cariboo, British Columbia *No. of Constituents:* 93,877, Conservative Party
Tel: 613-995-6931; *Fax:* 613-995-9897
cathy.mcleod@parl.gc.ca
cathymcleod.ca
Other Communications: Constituency Phone: 250-851-4991; Fax: 250-851-4994
Social Media: twitter.com/Cathy_McLeod, www.facebook.com/cathymcleodMP
Constituency Office
#6, 275 Seymour St.
Kamloops, BC V2C 2E7

Michael McLeod
Constituency: Northwest Territories, Northwest Territories *No. of Constituents:* 29,432, Liberal
Tel: 613-992-4587; *Fax:* 613-992-1586
Michael.McLeod@parl.gc.ca
michaelmcleod.liberal.ca
Other Communications: Constituency Phone: 867-873-6995; Fax: 867-920-4233
Social Media: twitter.com/MMcLeodNWT, www.facebook.com/1599103463663052
Constituency Office
#114, 5109 - 48th St.
Yellowknife, NT X1A 1N5

Alexandra Mendes
Circonscription électorale: Brossard — Saint-Lambert, Québec *Nombre de constituants:* 83,587, Liberal
Tél: 613-995-9301; *Téléc:* 613-992-7273
Alexandra.Mendes@parl.gc.ca
alexandramendes.liberal.ca
Autres numéros: Constituency Phone: 450-466-6872; Fax: 450-466-9822
Les réseaux sociaux: twitter.com/AlexandraBrStL, www.facebook.com/AlexandraMendesLiberal2015, ca.linkedin.com/in/amendes
Constituency Office
#225, 6955, boul Taschereau
Brossard, QC J4Z 1A7

Marco Mendicino, B.A., LL.B.
Constituency: Eglinton — Lawrence, Ontario *No. of Constituents:* 77,463, Liberal
Tel: 613-992-6361; *Fax:* 613-992-9791
Marco.Mendicino@parl.gc.ca
marcomendicinomp.ca
Other Communications: Constituency Phone: 416-781-5583; Fax: 416-781-5586
Social Media: twitter.com/marcomendicino, www.facebook.com/marcoelmendicino
Constituency Office
511 Lawrence Ave. West
Toronto, ON M6A 1A3

Minister, Employment, Workforce Development & Labour, Hon. MaryAnn Mihychuk, P.C., B.Sc., M.Sc., P.Geo.
Constituency: Kildonan — St. Paul, Manitoba *No. of Constituents:* 61,604, Liberal
Tel: 613-992-7148; *Fax:* 613-996-9125
MaryAnn.Mihychuk@parl.gc.ca
maryannmihychuk.liberal.ca
Other Communications: Constituency Phone: 204-984-6322; Fax: 204-984-6415
Social Media: twitter.com/mpmihychuk, www.facebook.com/MaryAnn.Mihychuk.KSP, ca.linkedin.com/in/maryann-mihychuk-m-sc-p-geo-50253516
Constituency Office
1575 Main St.
Winnipeg, MB R2W 3W5

Larry Miller
Constituency: Bruce — Grey — Owen Sound, Ontario *No. of Constituents:* 82,056, Conservative Party
Tel: 613-996-5191; *Fax:* 613-952-0979
larry.miller@parl.gc.ca
www.larrymiller.ca
Other Communications: Constituency Phone: 519-371-1059; Fax: 519-371-1752
Social Media: twitter.com/LarryMillerMP, www.facebook.com/LarryMillerMP, ca.linkedin.com/in/larry-miller-computer-3b44296a
Constituency Office
#208, 1131 - 2nd Ave. East
Owen Sound, ON N4K 2J1

Marc Miller
Circonscription électorale: Ville-Marie — Le Sud-Ouest — Ile-des-Soeurs, Québec *Nombre de constituants:* 84,387, Liberal
Tél: 613-995-6403; *Téléc:* 613-995-6404
Marc.Miller@parl.gc.ca
marcmiller.liberal.ca
Autres numéros: Constituency Phone: 514-496-4885; Fax: 514-496-8097
Les réseaux sociaux: twitter.com/MarcMillerVM, www.facebook.com/MarcMillerVilleMarie
Constituency Office
3175, rue Saint-Jacques
Montréal, QC H4C 1G7

Minister, Democratic Institutions; Minister Responsible, Elections Canada; President, Queen's Privy Council for Canada, Hon. Maryam Monsef, P.C.
Constituency: Peterborough — Kawartha, Ontario *No. of Constituents:* 91,180, Liberal
Tel: 613-995-6411; *Fax:* 613-996-9800
Maryam.Monsef@parl.gc.ca
maryammonsef.liberal.ca
Other Communications: Constituency Phone: 705-745-2108; Fax: 705-741-4123
Social Media: twitter.com/MaryamMonsef, ca.linkedin.com/in/maryam-monsef-44733655
Constituency Office
#4, 417 Bethune St.
Peterborough, ON K9H 3Z1

Christine Moore, B.A.
Circonscription électorale: Abitibi — Témiscamingue, Quebec *Nombre de constituants:* 82,839, New Democratic Party
Tél: 613-996-3250; *Téléc:* 613-992-3672
christine.moore@parl.gc.ca
christinemoore.ndp.ca
Autres numéros: Rouyn-Noranda: 819-762-3733 Ville-Marie: 819-629-2726
Les réseaux sociaux: twitter.com/moorenpd, www.facebook.com/ChristineMooreNPD, www.linkedin.com/in/christine-moore-493b8285
Constituency Office
33-A, rue Gamble ouest, RC15
Rouyn-Noranda, QC J9X 2R3

Minister, Finance, Hon. Bill Morneau, P.C.
Constituency: Toronto Centre, Ontario *No. of Constituents:* 70,578, Liberal
Tel: 613-992-1377; *Fax:* 613-992-1383
Bill.Morneau@parl.gc.ca
billmorneau.liberal.ca

Other Communications: Constituency Phone: 416-972-9749; Fax: 416-972-9891
Social Media: twitter.com/Bill_Morneau, www.facebook.com/morneau.bill
Constituency Office
430 Parliament St.
Toronto, ON M5A 3A2

Robert J. Morrissey
Constituency: Egmont, Prince Edward Island *No. of Constituents:* 27,751, Liberal
Tel: 613-992-9223
Toll-free: 800-224-0018; *Fax:* 613-992-1974
Robert.Morrissey@parl.gc.ca
robertmorrissey.liberal.ca
Other Communications: Constituency Fax: 902-432-6853
Social Media: twitter.com/MorrisseyEgmont, www.facebook.com/MorrisseyEgmont
Constituency Office
263 Heather Moyse Dr.
Summerside, PE C1N 5P1

Party Leader, New Democratic Party of Canada; Responsible, New Democratic Party Research Office, Hon. Thomas J. Mulcair, P.C., B.C.L. (Civil Law), LL.B (Common Law)
Circonscription électorale: Outremont, Québec *Nombre de constituants:* 70,559, New Democratic Party
Tél: 613-947-0867; *Téléc:* 613-947-0868
thomas.mulcair@parl.gc.ca
www.ndp.ca/tom
Autres numéros: Constituency Phone: 514-736-2727; Fax: 514-736-2726
Les réseaux sociaux: twitter.com/ThomasMulcair, www.facebook.com/ThomasMulcair
Constituency Office
#302, 154, av Laurier ouest
Montréal, QC H2T 2N7

Joyce Murray, M.B.A.
Constituency: Vancouver Quadra, British Columbia *No. of Constituents:* 74,633, Liberal
Tel: 613-992-2430; *Fax:* 613-995-0770
joyce.murray@parl.gc.ca
joycemurray.liberal.ca
Other Communications: Constituency Phone: 604-664-9220; Fax: 604-664-9221
Social Media: twitter.com/joycemurray, www.facebook.com/mpjoycemurray, www.linkedin.com/pub/joyce-murray/31/144/b64
Constituency Office
#206, 2112 West Broadway
Vancouver, BC V6K 2C8

Pierre Nantel
Circonscription électorale: Longueuil — Saint-Hubert, Québec *Nombre de constituants:* 85,766, New Democratic Party
Tél: 613-992-8514; *Téléc:* 613-992-2744
pierre.nantel@parl.gc.ca
pierrenantel.ndp.ca
Autres numéros: Constituency Phone: 450-928-4288; Fax: 450-928-4293
Les réseaux sociaux: twitter.com/pierrenantel, www.facebook.com/pierrenantel
Constituency Office
#200, 192, rue Saint-Jean
Longueuil, QC J4H 2X5

Eva Nassif
Circonscription électorale: Vimy, Québec *Nombre de constituants:* 85,889, Liberal
Tél: 613-995-7398; *Téléc:* 613-996-1195
Eva.Nassif@parl.gc.ca
evanassif.liberal.ca
Autres numéros: Constituency Phone: 450-967-3641; Fax: 450-967-3645
Les réseaux sociaux: twitter.com/EvaNassifVimy, www.facebook.com/EvaNassif.LiberalLaval, ca.linkedin.com/in/evanassif
Constituency Office
#415, 1695, boul Laval
Laval, QC H7S 2M2

John Nater
Constituency: Perth — Wellington, Ontario *No. of Constituents:* 76,097, Conservative Party
Tel: 613-992-6124; *Fax:* 613-998-7902
John.Nater@parl.gc.ca
johnnater.ca
Other Communications: Stratford: 519-273-1400; Harriston: 519-338-3589
Social Media: twitter.com/jlnater, www.facebook.com/jlnater2014, www.linkedin.com/in/jlnater
Constituency Office
59 Lorne Ave. East, #A
Stratford, ON N5A 6S4

Hon. Robert Nault, P.C.
Constituency: Kenora, Ontario *No. of Constituents:* 42,548, Liberal
Tel: 613-996-1161; *Fax:* 613-996-1759
Bob.Nault@parl.gc.ca
bobnault.liberal.ca
Other Communications: Kenora: 807-468-2170; Sioux Lookout: 807-737-4934
Social Media: twitter.com/VoteBobNault, www.facebook.com/votebobnault
Constituency Office
#202, 301 First Ave. South
Kenora, ON P9N 1W2

Hon. Robert Douglas Nicholson, P.C., Q.C., B.A., LL.B.
Constituency: Niagara Falls, Ontario *No. of Constituents:* 102,602, Conservative Party
Tel: 613-995-1547; *Fax:* 613-992-7910
rob.nicholson@parl.gc.ca
www.robnicholson.ca
Social Media: twitter.com/honrobnicholson

Alex Nuttall
Circonscription électorale: Barrie — Springwater — Oro-Medonte, Ontario *Nombre de constituants:* 75,207, Conservative Party
Tél: 613-992-0718; *Téléc:* 613-992-0745
Alex.Nuttall@parl.gc.ca
www.alexnuttallmp.ca
Les réseaux sociaux: twitter.com/AlexNuttallMP, www.facebook.com/MPNuttallBSOM, ca.linkedin.com/in/votealexnuttall

Hon. Deepak Obhrai, P.C.
Constituency: Calgary Forest Lawn, Alberta *No. of Constituents:* 74,620, Conservative Party
Tel: 613-947-4566; *Fax:* 613-947-4569
deepak.obhrai@parl.gc.ca
www.deepakobhrai.com
Other Communications: Constituency Phone: 403-207-3030; Fax: 403-207-3035
Social Media: twitter.com/deepakobhrai, www.facebook.com/DeepakObhrai
Constituency Office
#225, 525 - 28th St. SE
Calgary, AB T2A 6W9

Jennifer O'Connell, B.A.
Constituency: Pickering — Uxbridge, Ontario *No. of Constituents:* 85,794, Liberal
Tel: 613-995-8082; *Fax:* 613-993-6587
Jennifer.OConnell@parl.gc.ca
jenniferoconnell.liberal.ca
Other Communications: Constituency Phone: 905-839-2878; Fax: 905-839-2423
Social Media: twitter.com/jenoconnell_, www.facebook.com/423193734535043
Constituency Office
#4, 1154 Kingston Rd.
Pickering, ON L1V 1B4

Rev. Dr. Robert Oliphant, B. Comm., M. Div., D. Min.
Circonscription électorale: Don Valley West, Ontario *Nombre de constituants:* 70,524, Liberal
Tél: 613-992-2855; *Téléc:* 613-995-1635
Rob.Oliphant@parl.gc.ca
roboliphant.liberal.ca
Autres numéros: Constituency Phone: 416-467-7275; Fax: 416-467-8550
Les réseaux sociaux: twitter.com/Rob_Oliphant, www.facebook.com/roboliphantdvw, www.linkedin.com/in/robert-oliphant-1598989
Constituency Office
#310, 1670 Bayview Ave.
Toronto, ON M4G 3C2

John Oliver
Constituency: Oakville, Ontario *No. of Constituents:* 88,179, Liberal
Tel: 613-995-4014; *Fax:* 613-992-0520
John.Oliver@parl.gc.ca
johnoliver.mp
Other Communications: Constituency Phone: 905-338-2008; Fax: 905-338-5432
Social Media: twitter.com/johnolivermp, www.facebook.com/JohnOliverMP
Constituency Office
301 Robinson St.
Oakville, ON L6J 1G7

Seamus O'Regan
Constituency: St. John's South—Mount Pearl, Newfoundland & Labrador *No. of Constituents:* 66,936, Liberal
Tel: 613-992-0927; *Fax:* 613-995-7858
Seamus.ORegan@parl.gc.ca
seamusoregan.liberal.ca
Other Communications: Constituency Phone: 709-772-4608; Fax: 709-772-4776
Social Media: twitter.com/SeamusORegan, www.facebook.com/VoteSeamus, ca.linkedin.com/in/seamus-o-regan-5b8b4b83
Constituency Office
689 Topsail Rd., 2nd Fl.
St. John's, NL A1E 2E3

Hon. Erin O'Toole, P.C., C.D., B.A., LL.B.
Constituency: Durham, Ontario *No. of Constituents:* 93,455, Conservative Party
Tel: 613-992-2792; *Fax:* 613-992-2794
Erin.OToole@parl.gc.ca
erinotoole.ca
Other Communications: Constituency Phone: 905-697-1699; Fax: 905-697-1678
Social Media: twitter.com/erinotoolemp, www.facebook.com/erinotoolecpc, ca.linkedin.com/in/erin-o-toole-67307416
Constituency Office
#103, 54 King St. East
Bowmanville, ON L1C 1N3

Robert-Falcon Ouellette
Constituency: Winnipeg Centre, Manitoba *No. of Constituents:* 55,633, Liberal
Tel: 613-992-5308; *Fax:* 613-992-2890
Robert-Falcon.Ouellette@parl.gc.ca
robertfalconouellette.liberal.ca
Other Communications: Constituency Phone: 204-984-1675; Fax: 204-984-1676
Social Media: twitter.com/DrRobbieO, www.facebook.com/RFalconOuellette, ca.linkedin.com/in/robert-falcon-ouellette-7b123040
Constituency Office
594 Ellice Ave.
Winnipeg, MB R3G 0A3

Hon. Denis Paradis, P.C., B.Comm., LL.L.
Circonscription électorale: Brome — Missisquoi, Québec *Nombre de constituants:* 85,051, Liberal
Tél: 613-947-8185; *Téléc:* 613-947-8188
Denis.Paradis@parl.gc.ca
denisparadis.liberal.ca
Autres numéros: Magog: 819-868-1305; Cowansville: 450-263-0025
Les réseaux sociaux: www.facebook.com/denisparadisbromemissisquoi
Constituency Office
353, rue Principale ouest
Magog, QC J1X 2B1

Pierre Paul-Hus
Circonscription électorale: Charlesbourg — Haute-Saint-Charles, Québec *Nombre de constituants:* 84,596, Conservative Party
Tél: 613-995-8857; *Téléc:* 613-995-1625
Pierre.Paul-Hus@parl.gc.ca
www.pierrepaul-hus.ca
Autres numéros: Constituency Phone: 418-624-0022; Fax: 418-624-1095
Les réseaux sociaux: twitter.com/pierrepaulhus, www.facebook.com/pierrepaulhus2015, ca.linkedin.com/in/pierre-paul-hus-0abb6035
Constituency Office
#204, 8400, boul Henri-Bourassa
Québec, QC G1G 4E2

Whip, Bloc Québécois, Monique Pauzé
Circonscription électorale: Repentigny, Québec *Nombre de constituants:* 91,986, Bloc Québécois
Tél: 613-992-5257; *Téléc:* 613-996-4338
Monique.Pauze@parl.gc.ca
www.blocquebecois.org/depute-monique-pauze
Autres numéros: Constituency Phone: 450-581-3896; Fax: 450-581-9958
Les réseaux sociaux: twitter.com/m_pauze, www.facebook.com/monique.pauze1
Constituency Office
#201, 184, rue Notre-Dame
Repentigny, QC J6A 2P9

Joe Peschisolido, B.A., LL.B.
Constituency: Steveston — Richmond East, British Columbia *No. of Constituents:* 71,526, Liberal
Tel: 613-992-1385; *Fax:* 613-992-1410
Joe.Peschisolido@parl.gc.ca
joepeschisolido.ca
Other Communications: Constituency Phone: 604-257-2900; Fax: 604-257-2904
Social Media: twitter.com/jpeschisolido, www.facebook.com/Peschisolido, ca.linkedin.com/in/joepeschisolido
Constituency Office
#120, 11080 No. 5 Rd.
Richmond, BC V7A 4E7

Kyle Peterson, B.A., M.A., J.D., M.B.A.
Constituency: Newmarket — Aurora, Ontario *No. of Constituents:* 83,108, Liberal
Tel: 613-992-9310; *Fax:* 613-992-9407
Kyle.Peterson@parl.gc.ca
kylepeterson.liberal.ca
Other Communications: Constituency Phone: 905-953-7515; Fax: 905-953-7527
Social Media: twitter.com/kylejpeterson, www.facebook.com/kyle.peterson.newmarketaurora
Constituency Office
#202, 16600 Bayview Ave.
Newmarket, ON L3X 1Z9

Deputy Government Whip, Hon. Ginette Petitpas Taylor, P.C.
Constituency: Moncton — Riverview — Dieppe, New Brunswick *No. of Constituents:* 71,350, Liberal
Tel: 613-992-8072; *Fax:* 613-992-8083
Ginette.PetitpasTaylor@parl.gc.ca
ginettepetitpastaylor.liberal.ca
Other Communications: Constituency Phone: 506-851-3310; Fax: 506-851-3273
Social Media: twitter.com/gptaylormrd, www.facebook.com/ginetteptaylor, ca.linkedin.com/in/ginette-petitpas-taylor-041390b0
Constituency Office
#110, 272 St-George St.
Moncton, NB E1C 1W6

Minister, Health, Hon. Jane Philpott, P.C.
Circonscription électorale: Markham—Stouffville, Ontario *Nombre de constituants:* 87,460, Liberal
Tél: 613-992-3640; *Téléc:* 613-992-3642
Jane.Philpott@parl.gc.ca
janephilpott.liberal.ca
Autres numéros: Constituency Phone: 905-640-1125; Fax: 905-640-1184
Les réseaux sociaux: twitter.com/janephilpott, www.facebook.com/janepaulinephilpott, ca.linkedin.com/in/janephilpott
Constituency Office
6060 Main St.
Stouffville, ON L4A 1B8

Michel Picard
Circonscription électorale: Montarville, Québec *Nombre de constituants:* 75,521, Liberal
Tél: 613-996-2416; *Téléc:* 613-995-6973
Michel.Picard@parl.gc.ca
michelpicard.liberal.ca
Autres numéros: Constituency Phone: 450-653-8383; Fax: 450-653-0550
Les réseaux sociaux: twitter.com/MPicardLiberal, www.facebook.com/michelpicardplc
Constituency Office
#203, 1428, rue Montarville
Saint-Bruno-de-Montarville, QC J3V 3T5

Caucus Chair, Bloc Québécois, Louis Plamondon, B.A.Ped., B.A.An
Circonscription électorale: Bécancour — Nicolet — Saurel, Québec *Nombre de constituants:* 78,607, Bloc Québécois
Tél: 613-995-9241; *Téléc:* 613-995-6784
louis.plamondon@parl.gc.ca
www.louisplamondon.com
Les réseaux sociaux: www.facebook.com/LouisPlamondonBQ, www.linkedin.com/pub/louis-plamondon/36/b11/771

Hon. Pierre Poilievre, P.C., B.A.
Constituency: Carleton, Ontario *No. of Constituents:* 73,418, Conservative Party
Tel: 613-992-2772; *Fax:* 613-992-1209
pierre.poilievre@parl.gc.ca
pierremp.ca
Other Communications: Constituency Phone: 613-692-3331; Fax: 613-692-3303
Social Media: twitter.com/PierrePoilievre, www.facebook.com/pierre.poilievre
Constituency Office
1139 Mill St.
Manotick, ON K4M 1A5

Jean-Claude Poissant
Circonscription électorale: La Prairie, Québec *Nombre de constituants:* 82,318, Liberal
Tél: 613-992-1084; *Téléc:* 613-992-1116
Jean-Claude.Poissant@parl.gc.ca
jeanclaudepoissant.liberal.ca
Autres numéros: Constituency Phone: 450-632-3383; Fax: 450-632-2033
Les réseaux sociaux: twitter.com/PLCLaPrairieJCP, www.facebook.com/jeanclaudepoissantlaprairie
Constituency Office
#200, 66, rte. 132
Delson, QC J5B 0A1

Anne Minh-Thu Quach, B.A.
Circonscription électorale: Salaberry — Suroît, Québec *Nombre de constituants:* 92,280, New Democratic Party
Tél: 613-995-2532; *Téléc:* 613-941-3300
anneminh-thu.quach@parl.gc.ca
anneminhthuquach.ndp.ca
Autres numéros: Constituency Phone: 450-371-0644; Fax: 450-371-3330
Les réseaux sociaux: twitter.com/AnneMTQuach, www.facebook.com/188474554625330
Constituency Office
#230, 30, av du Centenaire
Salaberry-de-Valleyfield, QC J6S 5X4

Minister, Sport & Persons with Disabilities, Hon. Carla Qualtrough, P.C.
Constituency: Delta, British Columbia *No. of Constituents:* 74,267, Liberal
Tel: 613-992-2957; *Fax:* 613-992-3192
Carla.Qualtrough@parl.gc.ca
carlaqualtrough.liberal.ca
Other Communications: Constituency Phone: 778-591-0549; Fax: 778-593-8549
Social Media: twitter.com/CQualtro, www.facebook.com/CarlaQ2015, ca.linkedin.com/in/carla-qualtrough-0b229ab3
Constituency Office
#110, 8295 - 120th St.
Delta, BC V4C 0R1

Hon. Lisa Raitt, P.C., B.Sc., M.Sc., LL.B.
Constituency: Milton, Ontario *No. of Constituents:* 71,754, Conservative Party
Tel: 613-996-7046; *Fax:* 613-992-0851
lisa.raitt@parl.gc.ca
www.lisaraittmp.ca
Other Communications: Constituency Phone: 905-693-0166; Fax: 905-693-0704
Social Media: twitter.com/lraitt, www.facebook.com/lisaraitt
Constituency Office
86 Main St. East
Milton, ON L9T 1N3

Tracey Ramsey
Constituency: Essex, Ontario *No. of Constituents:* 91,816, New Democratic Party
Tel: 613-992-1812; *Fax:* 613-995-0033
Tracey.Ramsey@parl.gc.ca
traceyramsey.ndp.ca
Other Communications: Constituency Phone: 519-776-4700; Fax: 519-776-1383
Social Media: twitter.com/TraceyRam, www.facebook.com/TraceyRamseyNDP
Constituency Office
316 Talbot St. North
Essex, ON N8M 2E1

Murray Rankin, Q.C., LL.B
Constituency: Victoria, British Columbia *No. of Constituents:* 92,574, New Democratic Party
Tel: 613-996-2358; *Fax:* 613-952-1458
Murray.Rankin@parl.gc.ca
murrayrankin.ndp.ca
Other Communications: Constituency Phone: 250-363-3600; Fax: 250-363-8422
Social Media: twitter.com/MurrayRankin, www.facebook.com/MurrayRankinMP
Constituency Office
1057 Fort St.
Victoria, BC V8V 3K5

Yasmin Ratansi, C.G.A.
Constituency: Don Valley East, Ontario *No. of Constituents:* 62,682, Liberal
Tel: 613-992-0919; *Fax:* 613-992-0945
Yasmin.Ratansi@parl.gc.ca
yasminratansi.liberal.ca
Other Communications: Constituency Phone: 416-443-0343; Fax: 416-443-1393
Social Media: twitter.com/Yasmin_Ratansi, www.facebook.com/yasmin.ratansi, ca.linkedin.com/in/yasminratansi
Constituency Office
#309, 220 Duncan Mill Rd.
Toronto, ON M3B 3J5

Alain Rayes
Circonscription électorale: Richmond — Arthabaska, Québec *Nombre de constituants:* 85,652, Conservative Party
Tél: 613-995-1554; *Téléc:* 613-995-2026
Alain.Rayes@parl.gc.ca
www.alainrayes.ca
Autres numéros: Constituency Phone: 819-751-1375; Fax: 819-751-5517
Les réseaux sociaux: twitter.com/AlainRayes, www.facebook.com/alainrayes
Constituency Office
3, rue de la Gare
Victoriaville, QC G6P 6S4

Speaker of the House of Commons, Hon. Geoff Regan, P.C., B.A., LL.B.
Constituency: Halifax West, Nova Scotia *No. of Constituents:* 70,089, Liberal
Tel: 613-996-3085; *Fax:* 613-996-6988
geoff.regan@parl.gc.ca
www.geoffregan.ca
Other Communications: Constituency Phone: 902-426-2217; Fax: 902-426-8339
Social Media: twitter.com/geoffregan, www.facebook.com/geoffreganNS
Constituency Office
#222, 1496 Bedford Hwy.
Bedford, NS B4A 1E5

Scott Reid, B.A., M.A.
Constituency: Lanark — Frontenac — Kingston, Ontario *No. of Constituents:* 78,826, Conservative Party
Tel: 613-947-2277; *Fax:* 613-947-2278
scott.reid@parl.gc.ca
www.scottreid.ca
Social Media: twitter.com/ScottReidCPC, www.facebook.com/scott.reid.73594

Hon. Michelle Rempel, P.C., B.A.
Constituency: Calgary Nose Hill, Alberta *No. of Constituents:* 81,582, Conservative Party
Tel: 613-992-4275; *Fax:* 613-947-9475
michelle.rempel@parl.gc.ca
www.michellerempel.ca
Social Media: twitter.com/MichelleRempel, www.facebook.com/126806667378661, ca.linkedin.com/in/hon-michelle-rempel-pc-mp-75665aab

Blake Richards, B.A.
Constituency: Banff — Airdrie, Alberta *No. of Constituents:* 91,222, Conservative Party
Tel: 613-996-5152; *Fax:* 613-947-4601
blake.richards@parl.gc.ca
www.blakerichards.ca
Other Communications: Constituency Phone: 403-948-5103; Fax: 403-948-0879
Social Media: twitter.com/BlakeRichardsMP
Constituency Office
#16, 620 - 1st Ave. NW
Airdrie, AB T4B 2R3

Jean R. Rioux
Circonscription électorale: Saint-Jean, Québec *Nombre de constituants:* 88,414, Liberal
Tél: 613-992-5296; *Téléc:* 613-992-9849
Jean.Rioux@parl.gc.ca
jeanrioux.liberal.ca
Autres numéros: Constituency Phone: 450-357-9100; Fax: 450-357-9109
Les réseaux sociaux: twitter.com/jeanriouxplc, www.facebook.com/jeanriouxsaintjean, ca.linkedin.com/in/jean-r-rioux-ba5271a0
Constituency Office
#1, 211, Mayrand
Saint-Jean-sur-Richelieu, QC J3B 3L1

Hon. Gerry Ritz, P.C.
Constituency: Battlefords — Lloydminster, Saskatchewan *No. of Constituents:* 49,763, Conservative Party
Tel: 613-995-7080; *Fax:* 613-996-8472
gerry.ritz@parl.gc.ca
www.gerryritz.ca
Other Communications: Constituency Phone: 306-445-2004; Fax: 306-445-0207
Social Media: twitter.com/gerryritzmp, www.facebook.com/gerryritzmp
Constituency Office
1322 - 100th St.
North Battleford, SK S9A 0V8

Yves Robillard
Circonscription électorale: Marc-Aurèle-Fortin, Québec *Nombre de constituants:* 76,162, Liberal
Tél: 613-992-1120; *Téléc:* 613-992-1163
Yves.Robillard@parl.gc.ca
yvesrobillard.liberal.ca
Autres numéros: Constituency Phone: 450-622-2992; Fax: 450-622-3003
Les réseaux sociaux: twitter.com/yrobillardplc, www.facebook.com/YvesRobillardPLC, ca.linkedin.com/in/yves-robillard-4a59307a
Constituency Office
#101, 2968, boul Dagenais ouest
Laval, QC H7P 1T1

Pablo Rodriguez, B.A.A
Circonscription électorale: Honoré-Mercier, Québec *Nombre de constituants:* 78,744, Liberal
Tél: 613-995-0580; *Téléc:* 613-992-1710
Pablo.Rodriguez@parl.gc.ca
pablorodriguez.liberal.ca
Autres numéros: Constituency Phone: 514-353-5044; Fax: 514-353-3050
Les réseaux sociaux: twitter.com/Rodriguez_Pab, www.facebook.com/liberalpablo, www.linkedin.com/in/pabrodriguez
Constituency Office
#208, 8595, boul Maurice-Duplessis
Montréal, QC H1E 4H7

Sherry Romanado
Circonscription électorale: Longueuil — Charles-LeMoyne, Québec *Nombre de constituants:* 83,719, Liberal
Tél: 613-998-5961; *Téléc:* 613-954-0707
Sherry.Romanado@parl.gc.ca
sherryromanado.liberal.ca
Autres numéros: Constituency Phone: 450-671-1222; Fax: 450-671-8884
Les réseaux sociaux: twitter.com/SherryRomanado, www.facebook.com/sherryromanado, ca.linkedin.com/in/sherryromanado
Constituency Office
#150, 2120, Victoria Ave.
Greenfield Park, QC J4V 1M9

Anthony Rota, B.A., M.B.A.
Circonscription électorale: Nipissing — Timiskaming, Ontario *Nombre de constituants:* 70,820, Liberal
Tél: 613-995-6255; *Téléc:* 613-996-7993
Anthony.Rota@parl.gc.ca
www.anthonyrota.ca
Autres numéros: Constituency Phones: 705-474-3700; 705-647-6262
Les réseaux sociaux: twitter.com/AnthonyRota, www.facebook.com/anthony.rota.148, www.linkedin.com/in/anthony-rota-9353a723
Constituency Office
375 Main St. West
North Bay, ON P1B 2T9

Kim Rudd
Constituency: Northumberland — Peterborough South, Ontario *No. of Constituents:* 89,128, Liberal
Tel: 613-992-8585; *Fax:* 613-995-7536
Kim.Rudd@parl.gc.ca
kimrudd.ca
Other Communications: Constituency Phone: 905-372-8757; Fax: 905-372-1500
Social Media: twitter.com/ruddkim
Constituency Office
#4, 12 Elgin St. East
Cobourg, ON K9A 0C5

Dan Ruimy
Circonscription électorale: Pitt Meadows — Maple Ridge, British Columbia *Nombre de constituants:* 71,682, Liberal
Tél: 613-947-4613; *Téléc:* 613-947-4615
Dan.Ruimy@parl.gc.ca
danruimy.liberal.ca
Autres numéros: Constituency Phone: 604-466-2761; Fax: 604-466-7593
Les réseaux sociaux: twitter.com/danruimymp, www.facebook.com/danruimy2015, www.linkedin.com/in/dan-ruimy-1855561
Constituency Office
22369 Lougheed Hwy.
Maple Ridge, BC V2X 2T3

Don Rusnak
Constituency: Thunder Bay — Rainy River, Ontario *No. of Constituents:* 62,773, Liberal
Tel: 613-992-3061; *Fax:* 613-995-3515
Don.Rusnak@parl.gc.ca
donrusnak.liberal.ca
Other Communications: Constituency Phone: 807-625-1160; Fax: 807-623-6001
Social Media: twitter.com/donrusnakmp, www.facebook.com/rusnak2015
Constituency Office
#1, 905 East Victoria Ave.
Thunder Bay, ON P7C 1B3

Romeo Saganash, LL.B.
Circonscription électorale: Abitibi — Baie-James — Nunavik — Eeyou, Quebec *Nombre de constituants:* 63,226, New Democratic Party
Tél: 613-992-3030; *Téléc:* 613-996-0828
romeo.saganash@parl.gc.ca
romeosaganash.ndp.ca
Autres numéros: Val-d'Or: 819-824-2942; Chibougamau: 418-748-7870
Les réseaux sociaux: twitter.com/RomeoSaganash, www.facebook.com/RomeoSaganash
Constituency Office
#204, 888 - 3rd Ave.
Val'd-Or, QC J9P 5E6

Ruby Sahota
Constituency: Brampton North, Ontario *No. of Constituents:* 73,321, Liberal
Tel: 613-995-4843; *Fax:* 613-995-7003
Ruby.Sahota@parl.gc.ca
rubysahota.liberal.ca
Other Communications: Constituency Phone: 905-840-0505; Fax: 905-840-1778
Social Media: twitter.com/mprubysahota, www.facebook.com/MPRubySahota
Constituency Office
#307, 50 Sunny Meadow Blvd.
Brampton, ON L6R 0Y7

Raj Saini
Constituency: Kitchener Centre, Ontario *No. of Constituents:* 76,797, Liberal
Tel: 613-995-8913; *Fax:* 613-996-7329
Raj.Saini@parl.gc.ca
rajsaini.liberal.ca
Other Communications: Constituency Phone: 519-741-2001; Fax: 519-579-2404
Social Media: twitter.com/rajsainimp, www.facebook.com/RajSainiMP
Constituency Office
#202, 209 Frederick St.
Kitchener, ON N2H 2M7

Minister, National Defence, Hon. Harjit S. Sajjan, P.C.
Constituency: Vancouver South, British Columbia *No. of Constituents:* 86,663, Liberal
Tel: 613-995-7052; *Fax:* 613-995-2962
HarjitS.Sajjan@parl.gc.ca
harjitsajjan.liberal.ca
Other Communications: Constituency Phone: 604-775-5323; Fax: 604-775-5420
Social Media: twitter.com/HarjitSajjan, www.facebook.com/harjit.sajjan.7
Constituency Office
6406 Victoria Dr.
Vancouver, BC V5P 3X7

Darrell Samson
Constituency: Sackville — Preston — Chezzetcook, Nova Scotia *No. of Constituents:* 67,401, Liberal
Tel: 613-995-5822; *Fax:* 613-996-9655
Darrell.Samson@parl.gc.ca
darrellsamson.liberal.ca
Other Communications: Constituency Phone: 902-861-2311; Fax: 902-861-4620
Social Media: twitter.com/darrellsamson, www.facebook.com/darrellsamsonliberal
Constituency Office
2900 Hwy. 2, 2nd Fl.
Fall River, NS B2T 1W4

Ramesh Sangha
Constituency: Brampton Centre, Ontario *No. of Constituents:* 64,640, Liberal
Tel: 613-992-9105; *Fax:* 613-947-0443
Ramesh.Sangha@parl.gc.ca
rameshsangha.ca
Social Media: twitter.com/sangharamesh, www.facebook.com/liberalsangha

Brigitte Sansoucy
Circonscription électorale: Saint-Hyacinthe — Bagot, Québec *Nombre de constituants:* 80,787, New Democratic Party
Tél: 613-996-4585; *Téléc:* 613-992-1815
Brigitte.Sansoucy@parl.gc.ca
brigittesansoucy.npd.ca
Autres numéros: Constituency Phone: 450-771-0505; Fax: 450-771-0767
Les réseaux sociaux: twitter.com/bsansoucynpd, www.facebook.com/brigitte.sansoucy.npd
Constituency Office
2193, av Sainte-Anne
Saint-Hyacinthe, QC J2S 5H5

Randeep Sarai
Constituency: Surrey Centre, British Columbia *No. of Constituents:* 70,493, Liberal
Tel: 613-992-2922; *Fax:* 613-992-0252
Randeep.Sarai@parl.gc.ca
randeepsarai.liberal.ca
Other Communications: Constituency Phone: 604-589-2441; Fax: 604-589-2445
Social Media: twitter.com/randeepssarai, www.facebook.com/profile.php?id=891695511
Constituency Office
#170, 10362 King George Blvd.
Surrey, BC V3T 2W5

Bob Saroya
Constituency: Markham — Unionville, Ontario *No. of Constituents:* 82,534, Conservative Party
Tel: 613-992-1178; *Fax:* 613-992-1206
Bob.Saroya@parl.gc.ca
bobsaroya.conservative.ca
Other Communications: Constituency Phone: 905-470-2024; Fax: 905-470-1366
Social Media: twitter.com/bobsaroya, www.facebook.com/bobsaroya
Constituency Office
#201, 8300 Woodbine Ave.
Markham, ON L3R 9Y7

Caucus Chair, Liberal Party, Francis Scarpaleggia, B.A., M.A., M.B.A.
Circonscription électorale: Lac-Saint-Louis, Québec *Nombre de constituants:* 85,727, Liberal
Tél: 613-995-8281; *Téléc:* 613-996-0828
francis.scarpaleggia@parl.gc.ca
www.scarpaleggia.ca
Autres numéros: Constituency Phone: 514-695-6661; Fax: 514-695-3708
Les réseaux sociaux: twitter.com/scarpaleggialsl, www.facebook.com/Fscarpaleggia, ca.linkedin.com/in/francis-scarpaleggia-b9a59755
Constituency Office, Tour est
#635, 1, av Holiday
Pointe-Claire, QC H9R 5N3

Peter Schiefke
Circonscription électorale: Vaudreuil — Soulanges, Québec *Nombre de constituants:* 90,607, Liberal
Tél: 613-957-3744; *Téléc:* 613-952-0874
Peter.Schiefke@parl.gc.ca
peterschiefke.liberal.ca
Autres numéros: Constituency Phone: 450-510-2305; Fax: 450-510-2383
Les réseaux sociaux: twitter.com/peterschiefke, www.facebook.com/PeterSchiefkeLiberal, ca.linkedin.com/in/peter-schiefke-62b63a37
Constituency Office
223, av St. Charles
Vaudreuil-Dorion, QC J7V 2L6

Jamie Schmale
Constituency: Haliburton — Kawartha Lakes — Brock, Ontario *No. of Constituents:* 91,208, Conservative Party
Tel: 613-992-2474; *Fax:* 613-996-9656
Jamie.Schmale@parl.gc.ca
jamieschmale.ca
Other Communications: Constituency Phone: 705-324-2400; Fax: 705-324-0880
Social Media: twitter.com/jamie_schmale, www.facebook.com/216582391864869, ca.linkedin.com/pub/jamie-schmale/6/43/1a2
Constituency Office
68 McLaughlin Rd.
Lindsay, ON K9V 6B5

Deb Schulte
Constituency: King — Vaughan, Ontario *No. of Constituents:* 84,925, Liberal
Tel: 613-992-1461; *Fax:* 613-992-1470
Deb.Schulte@parl.gc.ca
debschulte.ca
Other Communications: Constituency Phone: 905-303-5000; Fax: 905-303-5002
Social Media: twitter.com/_DebSchulte, www.facebook.com/DebSchulte82
Constituency Office
#115, 9401 Jane St.
Vaughan, ON L6A 4H7

Marc Serré
Constituency: Nickel Belt, Ontario *No. of Constituents:* 72,828, Liberal
Tel: 613-995-9107; *Fax:* 613-995-9109
Marc.Serre@parl.gc.ca
marcserre.liberal.ca
Other Communications: Val Caron: 705-897-2222; Sturgeon Falls: 705-580-2584
Social Media: twitter.com/marcserremp, www.facebook.com/marcserreMP, ca.linkedin.com/in/marcgserre
Constituency Office
#203, 2945 Hwy. 69 North
Val Caron, ON P3N 1N3

Hon. Judy Sgro, P.C.
Constituency: Humber River — Black Creek, Ontario *No. of Constituents:* 60,994, Liberal
Tel: 613-992-7774; *Fax:* 613-947-8319
judy.sgro@parl.gc.ca
www.judysgro.com
Other Communications: Constituency Phone: 416-744-1882; Fax: 416-952-1696
Social Media: twitter.com/judysgromp, www.facebook.com/GoWithSgro, www.linkedin.com/in/judysgro
Constituency Office
#25, 2201 Finch Ave. West
Toronto, ON M9M 2Y9

Brenda Shanahan, B.A., B.S.W., M.B.A.
Circonscription électorale: Châteauguay — Lacolle, Québec *Nombre de constituants:* 75,924, Liberal
Tél: 613-996-7265; *Téléc:* 613-996-9287
Brenda.Shanahan@parl.gc.ca
brendashanahan.liberal.ca
Autres numéros: Constituency Phone: 450-691-7044; Fax: 450-691-3114
Les réseaux sociaux: twitter.com/BShanahanLib, www.facebook.com/BrendaShanahan2015
Constituency Office
253, boul D'anjou
Châteauguay, QC J6J 2R4

Terry Sheehan
Constituency: Sault Ste. Marie, Ontario *No. of Constituents:* 63,555, Liberal
Tel: 613-992-9723; *Fax:* 613-992-1954
Terry.Sheehan@parl.gc.ca
terrysheehan.liberal.ca
Other Communications: Constituency Phone: 705-941-2900; Fax: 705-941-2903
Social Media: twitter.com/terrysheehanmp, www.facebook.com/terrysheehanmp
Constituency Office
#102, 369 Queen St. East
Sault Ste. Marie, ON P6A 1Z4

Martin Shields
Constituency: Bow River, Alberta *No. of Constituents:* 75,146, Conservative Party
Tel: 613-992-0761
Toll-free: 844-241-0020; *Fax:* 613-992-0768

Martin.Shields@parl.gc.ca
martinshieldsbowriver.ca
Other Communications: Constituency Fax: 403-793-6778
Social Media: twitter.com/MartinBowRiver,
www.facebook.com/MartininBowRiver
Constituency Office
#2, 403 - 2nd Ave. West
Brooks, AB T1R 0S3

Bev Shipley
Constituency: Lambton — Kent — Middlesex, Ontario *No. of Constituents:* 80,666, Conservative Party
Tel: 613-947-4581
Toll-free: 800-586-4614; *Fax:* 613-947-4584
bev.shipley@parl.gc.ca
www.bevshipley.ca
Other Communications: Constituency Faxes: 519-245-6736; 519-627-4635
Social Media: twitter.com/BevShipleyMP,
www.facebook.com/BevShipleyMP,
www.linkedin.com/pub/bev-shipley/40/511/0
Constituency Office
380 Albert St.
Strathroy, ON N7G 1W7

Jati Sidhu
Constituency: Mission — Matsqui — Fraser Canyon, British Columbia *No. of Constituents:* 62,486, Liberal
Tel: 613-992-1248; *Fax:* 613-992-1298
Jati.Sidhu@parl.gc.ca
jatisidhu.liberal.ca
Other Communications: Constituency Phone: 604-814-5710; Fax: 604-814-5714
Social Media: twitter.com/VoteJatiSidhu,
www.facebook.com/jatisidhuMP
Constituency Office
32081 Lougheed Hwy., #B3
Mission, BC V2V 1A3

Sonia Sidhu
Constituency: Brampton South, Ontario *No. of Constituents:* 72,111, Liberal
Tel: 613-995-5381; *Fax:* 613-995-6796
Sonia.Sidhu@parl.gc.ca
soniasidhu.liberal.ca
Other Communications: Constituency Phone: 905-846-0076; Fax: 905-846-3901
Social Media: twitter.com/SoniaLiberal,
www.facebook.com/soniasidhuliberal,
ca.linkedin.com/in/sonia-sidhu-13a4622a
Constituency Office
#600, 24 Queen St. East
Brampton, ON L6V 1A3

Gagan Sikand
Constituency: Mississauga — Streetsville, Ontario *No. of Constituents:* 83,122, Liberal
Tel: 613-943-1762; *Fax:* 613-943-1768
Gagan.Sikand@parl.gc.ca
gagansikand.liberal.ca
Other Communications: Constituency Phone: 905-812-1811; Fax: 905-812-8464
Social Media: twitter.com/gagansikand,
www.facebook.com/gagansikandliberal
Constituency Office
#8G, 6990 Financial Dr.
Mississauga, ON L5N 8J4

Scott Simms, B.Comm.
Constituency: Coast of Bays — Central — Notre Dame, Newfoundland & Labrador *No. of Constituents:* 63,891, Liberal
Tel: 613-996-3935; *Fax:* 613-996-7622
scott.simms@parl.gc.ca
www.scottsimms.com
Social Media: twitter.com/Scott_Simms,
www.facebook.com/ScottSimmsCanada

Minister, Infrastructure & Communities, Hon. Amarjeet Sohi, P.C.
Constituency: Edmonton Mill Woods, Alberta *No. of Constituents:* 73,323, Liberal
Tel: 613-992-1013; *Fax:* 613-992-1026
Amarjeet.Sohi@parl.gc.ca
asohi.liberal.ca
Other Communications: Constituency Phone: 780-497-3524; Fax: 780-497-3511
Social Media: twitter.com/SohiAmarjeet
Constituency Office
9225 - 28th Ave.
Edmonton, AB T6N 1N1

Robert Sopuck, B.Sc., M.Sc.
Constituency: Dauphin — Swan River — Marquette, Manitoba *No. of Constituents:* 63,187, Conservative Party
Tel: 613-992-3176; *Fax:* 613-992-0930
robert.sopuck@parl.gc.ca
www.robertsopuck.ca
Social Media: twitter.com/robertsopuck,
www.facebook.com/RobertSopuckMP

Francesco Sorbara
Constituency: Vaughan — Woodbridge, Ontario *No. of Constituents:* 73,924, Liberal
Tel: 613-996-4971; *Fax:* 613-996-4973
Francesco.Sorbara@parl.gc.ca
francescosorbara.liberal.ca
Other Communications: Constituency Phone: 905-264-6446; Fax: 905-264-8637
Social Media: twitter.com/Votesorbara,
www.facebook.com/FrancescoSorbaraMP,
ca.linkedin.com/in/francesco-sorbara-7a33265
Constituency Office
#6A, 8633 Weston Rd.
Woodbridge, ON L4L 9R6

Hon. Kevin Sorenson, P.C.
Constituency: Battle River — Crowfoot, Alberta *No. of Constituents:* 80,698, Conservative Party
Tel: 613-947-4608; *Fax:* 613-947-4611
kevin.sorenson@parl.gc.ca
www.kevinsorenson.ca
Other Communications: Constituency Phone: 780-608-4600; Fax: 780-608-4603
Social Media: twitter.com/kevinasorenson,
www.facebook.com/SorensonKevinA
Constituency Office
4945 - 50th St.
Camrose, AB T4V 1P9

Sven Spengemann, B.Sc., LL.B., LL.M., S.J.D.
Constituency: Mississauga — Lakeshore, Ontario *No. of Constituents:* 86,308, Liberal
Tel: 613-992-4848; *Fax:* 613-996-3267
Sven.Spengemann@parl.gc.ca
svenspengemann.liberal.ca
Other Communications: Constituency Phone: 905-273-8033; Fax: 905-273-5040
Social Media: twitter.com/SvenTrueNorth,
www.facebook.com/votesven,
ca.linkedin.com/pub/sven-spengemann/53/63a/508
Constituency Office
#30, 1077 North Service Rd.
Mississauga, ON L4Y 1A6

Bruce Stanton
Constituency: Simcoe North, Ontario *No. of Constituents:* 86,208, Conservative Party
Tel: 613-992-6582; *Fax:* 613-996-3128
bruce.stanton@parl.gc.ca
www.brucestanton.ca
Social Media: twitter.com/bruce_stanton,
www.facebook.com/6236822310,
www.linkedin.com/pub/bruce-stanton/28/19/95

Gabriel Ste-Marie
Circonscription électorale: Joliette, Québec *Nombre de constituants:* 85,981, Bloc Québécois
Tél: 613-996-6910; *Téléc:* 613-995-2818
Gabriel.Ste-Marie@parl.gc.ca
www.blocquebecois.org/depute-gabriel-ste-marie
Autres numéros: Constituency Phone: 450-752-1940; Fax: 450-752-1719
Les réseaux sociaux: twitter.com/gabriel_smarie,
www.facebook.com/gabrielstemarieblocquebecois,
ca.linkedin.com/in/gabrielstemarie
Constituency Office
436, St-Viateur
Joliette, QC J6E 3B2

Wayne Stetski
Constituency: Kootenay—Columbia, British Columbia *No. of Constituents:* 85,653, New Democratic Party
Tel: 613-995-7246; *Fax:* 613-996-9923
Wayne.Stetski@parl.gc.ca
waynestetski.ndp.ca
Other Communications: Constituency Phone: 250-417-2250; Fax: 250-417-2253
Social Media: twitter.com/WayneStetski,
www.facebook.com/StetskiNDP,
ca.linkedin.com/in/wayne-stetski-b0771417
Constituency Office
111 - 7th Ave. South
Cranbrook, BC V1C 2J3

Kennedy Stewart, B.A., M.A., Ph.D.
Constituency: Burnaby South, British Columbia *No. of Constituents:* 75,263, New Democratic Party
Tel: 613-996-5597; *Fax:* 613-992-5501
kennedy.stewart@parl.gc.ca
www.kennedystewart.ca
Other Communications: Constituency Phone: 604-291-8863; Fax: 604-666-0727
Social Media: twitter.com/kennedystewart,
www.facebook.com/kennedy.stewart,
www.linkedin.com/pub/kennedy-stewart/14/817/540
Constituency Office
4940 Kingsway
Burnaby, BC V5H 2E2

Mark Strahl
Constituency: Chilliwack — Hope, British Columbia *No. of Constituents:* 71,703, Conservative Party
Tel: 613-992-2940; *Fax:* 613-944-9376
mark.strahl@parl.gc.ca
www.markstrahl.com
Other Communications: Constituency Phone: 604-847-9711; Fax: 604-847-9744
Social Media: twitter.com/markstrahl,
www.facebook.com/MPmarkstrahl
Constituency Office
#102, 7388 Vedder Rd.
Chilliwack, BC V2R 4E4

Shannon Stubbs
Constituency: Lakeland, Alberta *No. of Constituents:* 79,334, Conservative Party
Tel: 613-992-4171; *Fax:* 613-996-9011
Shannon.Stubbs@parl.gc.ca
Other Communications: Constituency Phone: 780-657-7075; Fax: 780-657-7079
Social Media: twitter.com/shannonstubbsmp,
www.facebook.com/ShannonLakeland,
ca.linkedin.com/in/shannonlstubbs
Constituency Office
5009 - 40th St.
Two Hills, AB T0B 4K0

Caucus Chair, Conservative Party, David Sweet
Constituency: Flamborough — Glanbrook, Ontario *No. of Constituents:* 78,865, Conservative Party
Tel: 613-996-4984; *Fax:* 613-996-4986
David.Sweet@parl.gc.ca
www.davidsweet.ca
Other Communications: Constituency Phone: 905-574-0474
Social Media: twitter.com/DavidSweetMP,
ca.linkedin.com/in/david-sweet-71373160
Constituency Office
#4, 1760 Upper James St.
Hamilton, ON L9B 1K9

Marwan Tabbara
Constituency: Kitchener South — Hespeler, Ontario *No. of Constituents:* 72,359, Liberal
Tel: 613-992-1063; *Fax:* 613-992-1082
Marwan.Tabbara@parl.gc.ca
marwantabbara.liberal.ca
Other Communications: Constituency Phone: 519-571-5509; Fax: 519-571-5515
Social Media: twitter.com/marwantabbaramp,
www.facebook.com/marwantabbaramp,
ca.linkedin.com/in/marwan-tabbara-b3aaa986
Constituency Office
#2A, 153 Country Hill Dr.
Kitchener, ON N2E 2G7

Geng Tan
Constituency: Don Valley North, Ontario *No. of Constituents:* 71,812, Liberal
Tel: 613-995-4988; *Fax:* 613-995-1686
Geng.Tan@parl.gc.ca
gengtan.liberal.ca
Other Communications: Constituency Phone: 416-443-0623; Fax: 416-443-9819
Social Media: twitter.com/gengtanmp,
www.facebook.com/votegengtan
Constituency Office
422 McNicoll Ave.
Toronto, ON M2H 2E1

Filomena Tassi
Constituency: Hamilton West — Ancaster — Dundas, Ontario *No. of Constituents:* 84,350, Liberal
Tel: 613-992-1034; *Fax:* 613-992-1050
Filomena.Tassi@parl.gc.ca
filomenatassi.liberal.ca
Other Communications: Constituency Phone: 905-529-5435; Fax: 905-529-4123
Social Media: twitter.com/votetassi,
www.facebook.com/votetassi
Constituency Office
1686 Main St. West
Hamilton, ON L8S 0A2

House Leader, Bloc Québécois, Luc Thériault, B.A., M.A., D.E.S.S.
Circonscription électorale: Montcalm, Québec *Nombre de constituants:* 83,532, Bloc Québécois
Tél: 613-992-0164
Ligne sans frais: 800-263-5726; *Téléc:* 613-992-5341
Luc.Theriault@parl.gc.ca
www.blocquebecois.org/depute-luc-theriault
Autres numéros: Constituency Fax: 450-474-1585
Les réseaux sociaux:
www.facebook.com/Luc-Thériault-396754053854614
Constituency Office
1095, Montée Masson
Mascouche, QC J7K 2M1

David Allan Tilson, Q.C., B.A., LL.B.
Constituency: Dufferin — Caledon, Ontario *No. of Constituents:* 92,461, Conservative Party
Tel: 613-995-7813; *Fax:* 613-992-9789

david.tilson@parl.gc.ca
www.davidtilson.ca
Other Communications: Orangeville: 519-941-1832; Bolton: 905-857-6080
Social Media: twitter.com/davidtilson, www.facebook.com/profile.php?id=100000267832446
Constituency Office
#2, 229 Broadway
Orangeville, ON L9W 1K4

Hon. Hunter Tootoo, P.C.
Constituency: Nunavut, Nunavut *No. of Constituents:* 19,223, Independent
Tel: 613-992-2848; *Fax:* 613-996-9764
Hunter.Tootoo@parl.gc.ca
Other Communications: Constituency Phone: 867-979-4193; Fax: 867-979-4196
Social Media: twitter.com/huntertootoo, www.facebook.com/hunter.tootoo.1
Constituency Office
#101, 922 Niagunngusiaq Rd.
Iqaluit, NU X0A 0H0

Brad Trost, B.A., B.Sc.
Constituency: Saskatoon — University, Saskatchewan *No. of Constituents:* 57,274, Conservative Party
Tel: 613-992-8052; *Fax:* 613-996-9899
brad.trost@parl.gc.ca
www.bradtrost.ca
Other Communications: Constituency Phone: 306-975-6133; Fax: 306-975-6670
Social Media: twitter.com/BradTrostCPC, www.facebook.com/183289298385094
Constituency Office
505-B Nelson Rd.
Saskatoon, SK S7S 1P4

Prime Minister; Minister, Intergovernmental Affairs; Minister, Youth, Right Hon. Justin Pierre James Trudeau, P.C., B.A., B.Ed.
Circonscription électorale: Papineau, Québec *Nombre de constituants:* 78,649, Liberal
Tél: 613-995-0253; *Téléc:* 613-947-0310
justin.trudeau@parl.gc.ca
www.justin.ca
Autres numéros: Constituency Phone: 514-277-6020; Fax: 514-277-3454
Les réseaux sociaux: twitter.com/JustinTrudeau, www.facebook.com/JustinPJTrudeau, ca.linkedin.com/in/justintrudeau
Constituency Office
#302, 529, rue Jarry est
Montréal, QC H2P 1V4

Karine Trudel
Circonscription électorale: Jonquière, Québec *Nombre de constituants:* 72,802, New Democratic Party
Tél: 613-995-8425; *Téléc:* 613-947-2748
Karine.Trudel@parl.gc.ca
karinetrudel.npd.ca
Autres numéros: Constituency Phone: 418-695-4477; Fax: 418-695-4467
Les réseaux sociaux: twitter.com/trudel_karine
Constituency Office
1930 Davis St.
Jonquiere, QC G7S 3B6

Dave Van Kesteren
Constituency: Chatham-Kent — Leamington, Ontario *No. of Constituents:* 79,160, Conservative Party
Tel: 613-992-2612; *Fax:* 613-992-1852
dave.vankesteren@parl.gc.ca
www.davevankesteren.ca
Social Media: twitter.com/dvk_ckl, www.facebook.com/davevankesteren

Hon. Peter Van Loan, P.C., B.A., LL.B., M.A., M.Sc.Pl.
Constituency: York — Simcoe, Ontario *No. of Constituents:* 75,570, Conservative Party
Tel: 613-996-7752; *Fax:* 613-992-8351
peter.vanloan@parl.gc.ca
www.petervanloan.com
Other Communications: Constituency Phone: 905-898-1600; Fax: 905-898-4600
Social Media: twitter.com/petervanloan, ca.linkedin.com/in/peter-van-loan-53503110a
Constituency Office
#10, 45 Grist Mill Rd.
Holland Landing, ON L9N 1M7

Dan Vandal
Constituency: Saint Boniface — Saint Vital, Manitoba *No. of Constituents:* 65,626, Liberal
Tel: 613-995-0579; *Fax:* 613-996-7571
Dan.Vandal@parl.gc.ca
danvandal.liberal.ca
Other Communications: Constituency Phone: 204-983-3183; Fax: 204-983-4274
Social Media: twitter.com/stbstvdan, www.facebook.com/danvandalforstboniface
Constituency Office
#4, 213 St. Mary's Rd.
Winnipeg, MB R2H 1J2

Anita Vandenbeld
Constituency: Ottawa West — Nepean, Ontario *No. of Constituents:* 83,195, Liberal
Tel: 613-996-0984; *Fax:* 613-996-9880
Anita.Vandenbeld@parl.gc.ca
www.electanita.ca
Other Communications: Constituency Phone: 613-990-7720; Fax: 613-993-6501
Social Media: twitter.com/Vote_Anita, ca.linkedin.com/pub/anita-vandenbeld/6/499/2a0
Constituency Office
1315 Richmond Rd.
Ottawa, ON K2B 7Y4

Adam Vaughan
Constituency: Spadina — Fort York, Ontario *No. of Constituents:* 74,958, Liberal
Tel: 613-992-2352; *Fax:* 613-992-6301
Adam.Vaughan@parl.gc.ca
adamvaughan.liberal.ca
Other Communications: Constituency Phone: 416-533-2710; Fax: 416-533-2236
Social Media: twitter.com/TOAdamVaughan, www.facebook.com/adamvaughan.toronto
Constituency Office
215 Spadina Ave., 4th Fl.
Toronto, ON M5T 2C7

Karen Louise Vecchio
Constituency: Elgin — Middlesex — London, Ontario *No. of Constituents:* 82,892, Conservative Party
Tel: 613-990-7769; *Fax:* 613-996-0194
Karen.Vecchio@parl.gc.ca
karenvecchio.ca
Other Communications: Constituency Phone: 519-637-2255; Fax: 519-637-3358
Social Media: twitter.com/karen_vecchio, www.facebook.com/karen.vecchio.33, ca.linkedin.com/in/karen-vecchio-510a9a24
Constituency Office
#203, 750 Talbot St.
St. Thomas, ON N5P 1E2

Arnold Viersen
Constituency: Peace River — Westlock, Alberta *No. of Constituents:* 75,362, Conservative Party
Tel: 613-996-1783
Toll-free: 800-667-8450; *Fax:* 613-995-1415
Arnold.Viersen@parl.gc.ca
www.arnoldviersen.ca
Other Communications: Constituency Fax: 780-305-0343
Social Media: twitter.com/arnoldviersen, www.facebook.com/arnold.viersen
Constituency Office
5124 - 50th St.
PO Box 4458
Barrhead, AB T7N 1A3

Arif Virani, B.A., LL.B.
Constituency: Parkdale — High Park, Ontario *No. of Constituents:* 78,241, Liberal
Tel: 613-992-2936; *Fax:* 613-995-1629
Arif.Virani@parl.gc.ca
arifvirani.liberal.ca
Other Communications: Constituency Phone: 416-769-5072; Fax: 416-769-8343
Social Media: twitter.com/viraniarif, www.facebook.com/ArifViraniMP, ca.linkedin.com/in/arifvirani
Constituency Office
1596 Bloor St. West
Toronto, ON M6P 1A7

Cathay Wagantall
Constituency: Yorkton — Melville, Saskatoon *No. of Constituents:* 53,694, Conservative Party
Tel: 613-992-4394; *Fax:* 613-992-8676
Cathay.Wagantall@parl.gc.ca
www.cathaywagantall.ca
Other Communications: Constituency Phone: 306-782-3309; Fax: 306-786-7207
Social Media: twitter.com/cathayw, www.facebook.com/CathayWagantallForMP, ca.linkedin.com/in/cathay-wagantall-06a11116
Constituency Office
43 Betts Ave.
Yorkton, SK S3N 1M1

Mark Warawa
Constituency: Langley — Aldergrove, British Columbia *No. of Constituents:* 81,812, Conservative Party
Tel: 613-992-1157; *Fax:* 613-943-1823
mark.warawa@parl.gc.ca
www.markwarawa.com
Other Communications: Constituency Phone: 604-534-5955; Fax: 604-534-5970
Social Media: twitter.com/MPmarkwarawa, www.facebook.com/markwarawa
Constituency Office
#104, 4769 - 222nd St.
Langley, BC V2Z 3C1

Chris Warkentin
Constituency: Grande Prairie — Mackenzie, Alberta *No. of Constituents:* 80,511, Conservative Party
Tel: 613-992-5685; *Fax:* 613-947-4782
chris.warkentin@parl.gc.ca
www.chriswarkentin.ca
Other Communications: Constituency Phone: 780-538-1677; Fax: 780-538-9257
Social Media: twitter.com/chriswarkentin, www.facebook.com/chriswarkentin
Constituency Office
#201, 10625 West Side Dr.
Grande Prairie, AB T8V 8E6

Dianne L. Watts
Constituency: South Surrey — White Rock, British Columbia *No. of Constituents:* 76,078, Conservative Party
Tel: 613-947-4497; *Fax:* 613-947-4500
Dianne.Watts@parl.gc.ca
diannewattsmp.ca
Social Media: twitter.com/diannelwatts, www.facebook.com/DianneLWatts1, ca.linkedin.com/pub/dianne-watts/63/575/915

Kevin Waugh
Constituency: Saskatoon — Grasswood, Saskatchewan *No. of Constituents:* 58,810, Conservative Party
Tel: 613-995-5653; *Fax:* 613-995-0126
Kevin.Waugh@parl.gc.ca
kevinwaugh.ca
Other Communications: Constituency Phone: 306-975-6472; Fax: 306-975-6492
Social Media: twitter.com/kevinwaugh_cpc, www.facebook.com/kevinwaughmp, ca.linkedin.com/in/kevin-waugh-97383340
Constituency Office
#5, 2720 - 8th St. East
Saskatoon, SK S7H 0V8

Len Webber
Constituency: Calgary Confederation, Alberta *No. of Constituents:* 88,854, Conservative Party
Tel: 613-996-2756; *Fax:* 613-992-2537
Len.Webber@parl.gc.ca
www.lenwebber.ca
Social Media: twitter.com/Webber4Confed, www.facebook.com/lenwebberyyc, ca.linkedin.com/in/lenwebber

Erin Weir
Constituency: Regina — Lewvan, Saskatoon *No. of Constituents:* 63,894, New Democratic Party
Tel: 613-992-9115; *Fax:* 613-992-0131
Erin.Weir@parl.gc.ca
www.erinweir.ca
Social Media: twitter.com/TeamWeir, www.facebook.com/ErinWeirNDP

Nick Whalen, LL.B., B.Sc., M.Sc.
Constituency: St. John's East, Newfoundland & Labrador *No. of Constituents:* 65,499, Liberal
Tel: 613-996-7269; *Fax:* 613-992-2178
Nick.Whalen@parl.gc.ca
nickwhalen.liberal.ca
Other Communications: Constituency Phone: 709-772-7171; Fax: 709-772-7175
Social Media: twitter.com/nickwhalenmp
Constituency Office
120 Torbay Rd., #E130
St. John's, NL A1A 2G8

Jonathan Wilkinson
Constituency: North Vancouver, British Columbia *No. of Constituents:* 84,093, Liberal
Tel: 613-995-1225; *Fax:* 613-992-7319
Jonathan.Wilkinson@parl.gc.ca
jonathanwilkinson.liberal.ca
Other Communications: Constituency Phone: 604-775-6333; Fax: 604-775-6332
Social Media: twitter.com/JonathanWNV, www.facebook.com/JonathanWilkinsonNorthVancouver
Constituency Office
102 - 3rd St. West
North Vancouver, BC V7M 1E8

Attorney General; Minister, Justice, Hon. Jody Wilson-Raybould, P.C.
Constituency: Vancouver Granville, British Columbia *No. of Constituents:* 79,154, Liberal
Tel: 613-992-1416; *Fax:* 613-992-1460
Jody.Wilson-Raybould@parl.gc.ca
jwilson-raybould.liberal.ca
Other Communications: Constituency Phone: 604-717-1140; Fax: 604-717-1144
Social Media: twitter.com/Puglaas, www.facebook.com/JodyWRLiberal
Constituency Office
#104, 1245 West Broadway
Vancouver, BC V6H 1G7

Hon. Alice Wong, P.C., Ph.D.
Constituency: Richmond Centre, British Columbia *No. of Constituents:* 68,991, Conservative Party
Tel: 613-995-2021; *Fax:* 613-995-2174
alice.wong@parl.gc.ca
alicewong.ca
Other Communications: Constituency Phone: 604-775-5790; Fax: 604-775-6291
Social Media: twitter.com/AliceWongCanada
Constituency Office
#360, 5951 Number 3 Rd.
Richmond, BC V6X 2E3

Borys Wrzesnewskyj, B.Comm.
Constituency: Etobicoke Centre, Ontario *No. of Constituents:* 87,440, Liberal
Tel: 613-947-5000; *Fax:* 613-947-4276
Borys.Wrzesnewskyj@parl.gc.ca
boryswrzesnewskyj.liberal.ca
Other Communications: Constituency Phone: 416-249-7322; Fax: 416-249-6117
Social Media: twitter.com/boryswrz, www.facebook.com/VoteBorys
Constituency Office
#2, 577 Burnhamthorpe Rd.
Etobicoke, ON M9C 2Y3

Kate Young
Constituency: London West, Ontario *No. of Constituents:* 92,326, Liberal
Tel: 613-996-6674; *Fax:* 613-996-6772
Kate.Young@parl.gc.ca
kateyoung.liberal.ca
Other Communications: Constituency Phone: 519-473-5955; Fax: 519-473-7333
Social Media: twitter.com/kateyoungmp, www.facebook.com/kateyoungmp, ca.linkedin.com/in/kate-young-20414014
Constituency Office
#200, 390 Commissioners Rd. West
London, ON N6J 1Y3

David Yurdiga
Constituency: Fort McMurray — Cold Lake, Alberta *No. of Constituents:* 76,190, Conservative Party
Tel: 613-992-1154; *Fax:* 613-992-4603
David.Yurdiga@parl.gc.ca
fortmcmurraycoldlake.conservative.ca
Other Communications: Constituency Phone: 780-743-2201; Fax: 780-743-2287
Social Media: twitter.com/DavidYurdiga, www.facebook.com/david.yurdiga
Constituency Office
#112, 10021 Biggs Ave.
Fort McMurray, AB T9H 1S4

Salma Zahid
Constituency: Scarborough Centre, Ontario *No. of Constituents:* 70,594, Liberal
Tel: 613-992-6823; *Fax:* 613-943-1045
Salma.Zahid@parl.gc.ca
salmazahid.liberal.ca
Other Communications: Constituency Phone: 416-752-2358; Fax: 416-752-4624
Social Media: twitter.com/SalmaZahid15, www.facebook.com/salmazahid15
Constituency Office
#5, 2155 Lawrence Ave. East
Toronto, ON M1R 5G9

Bob Zimmer, B.A.
Constituency: Prince George — Peace River — Northern Rockies, British Columbia *No. of Constituents:* 76,312, Conservative Party
Tel: 613-947-4524
Toll-free: 855-767-4567; *Fax:* 613-947-4527
Bob.Zimmer@parl.gc.ca
www.bobzimmer.ca
Other Communications: Constituency Phones: 250-787-1192; 250-719-684
Social Media: twitter.com/bobzimmermp, www.facebook.com/bobzimmercpc
Constituency Office
9916 - 100th Ave.
Fort St. John, BC V1J 1Y5

Vacant
Constituency: Calgary Heritage, Alberta
Note: Former Prime Minister Stephen Harper resigned his seat in Aug. 2016.

Vacant
Constituency: Medicine Hat — Cardston — Warner, Alberta
Note: Conservative MP Jim Hillyer died on March 23, 2016, at age 41.

Vacant
Constituency: Ottawa — Vanier, Ontario
Note: The Hon. Mauril Bélanger died on Aug. 16, 2016, at age 61, after a battle with ALS.

Vacant
Constituency: Regina — Qu'Appelle, Saskatchewan *No. of Constituents:* 53,204
Note: Conservative MP Andrew Scheer resigned his seat September 13, 2016.

Vacant
Constituency: Calgary Midnapore, Alberta *No. of Constituents:* 87,158
Note: Conservative MP Jason Kenney resigned his seat in September 2016 in order to run for leader of the Alberta PC party.

Federal Government Departments & Agencies / Agences et départements du gouvernement fédéral

Editor's Note: The entries listed below are entered alphabetically, using applied titles as registered by the Federal Identity Program. Cross references are used to help you to locate the entry quickly. The two departments that incorporate Department of as part of their applied titles (Department of Finance Canada; Department of Justice Canada) are nevertheless listed alphabetically under Finance & Justice.

Office of the Administrator of the Ship-source Oil Pollution Fund (SOPF) / Administrateur de la caisse d'indemnisation des dommages dus à la pollution par les hydrocarbures causée par les navires

#830, 180 Kent St., Ottawa, ON K1A 0N5
Tel: 613-991-1726; *Fax:* 613-990-5423
info@sopf-cidphn.gc.ca
www.ssopfund.ca

The Administrator oversees the Ship-source Oil Pollution Fund, which provides compensation for oil spills from ships, & handles all claims filed against it.

Administrator, Alfred H. Popp, Q.C.
Tel: 613-991-1726
Director, Corporate Services, Monique Pronovost
Tel: 613-993-5439; *Fax:* 613-990-5423
Payroll & Finance Officer, Dianne Richer
Tel: 613-990-6852

Agriculture & Agri-Food Canada / Agriculture et agro-alimentaire Canada

1341 Baseline Rd., Ottawa, ON K1A 0C5
Tel: 613-773-1000; *Fax:* 613-773-1081
Toll-Free: 855-773-0241
TTY: 613-773-2600
info@agr.gc.ca
www.agr.gc.ca
Other Communication: Toll-Free Phone: AgriInvest & AgriStability, 1-866-367-8506; Agricultural Innovation Program, 1-877-246-4682; Prairie Shelterbelt Program, 1-866-766-2284

Agriculture & Agri-Food Canada is responsible for all matters related to agriculture. Examples of services provided by Agriculture & Agri-Food Canada include the following: research, development, & technology; policies & programs; the inspection & regulation of animals & plant-life forms; the coordination of rural development; the support of agricultural productivity & trade; the stabilization of farm incomes; & the provision of information. The goals of Agriculture & Agri-Food Canada are as follows: to achieve security of the food system; to ensure health of the environment; & to provide innovation for growth. Agriculture & Agri-Food Canada reports to Parliament & Canadians through the Minister of Agriculture & Agri-Food. The department was responsible for the Canadian Wheat Board prior to its privatization. On April 15, 2015, the sale of the Canadian Wheat Board to the G3 Global Grain Group was announced, creating G3 Canada Limited. The G3 Global Grain Group owns 50.1%, while the rest is kept in trust for farmers delivering grain to the company.

Minister, Agriculture & Agri-Food, Hon. Lawrence MacAulay, P.C.
Tel: 613-995-9325; *Fax:* 613-995-2754
lawrence.macaulay@parl.gc.ca
Social Media: www.facebook.com/lawrence.macaulay
Parliamentary Secretary, Jean-Claude Poissant
Tel: 613-992-1084; *Fax:* 613-992-1116
Jean-Claude.Poissant@parl.gc.ca
Chief of Staff, Mary Jean McFall
Tel: 613-773-1059; *Fax:* 613-773-1081
maryjean.mcfall@canada.ca
Director, Communications, Guy Gallant
Tel: 613-773-1018; *Fax:* 613-773-1081
guy.gallant@canada.ca
Director, Policy, Maxime Dea
Tel: 613-773-1059; *Fax:* 613-773-1081
maxime.dea@canada.ca
Communications Advisor, Oliver Anderson
Tel: 613-773-1059; *Fax:* 613-773-1081
oliver.anderson@canada.ca

Associated Agencies, Boards & Commissions:

•Canada Agricultural Review Tribunal (CART) / Commission de révision agricole du Canada (CRAC)
Bldg. 60
Birch Dr.
Ottawa, ON K1A 0C6
Tel: 613-792-2087; *Fax:* 613-792-2088
infotribunal@cart-crac.gc.ca
www.cart-crac.gc.ca
The Tribunal provides independent oversight of the use of Administrative Monetary Penalties by federal agencies, with regards to agriculture & agri-food.

•Canadian Dairy Commission (CDC) / Commission canadienne du lait
See Entry Name Index for detailed listing.

•Canadian Food Inspection Agency (CFIA) / Agence canadienne d'inspection des aliments
See Entry Name Index for detailed listing.

•Canadian Grain Commission (CGC) / Commission canadienne des grains
See Entry Name Index for detailed listing.

•Canadian International Grains Institute / Institut international du Canada pour le grain
#1000, 303 Main St.
Winnipeg, MB R3C 3G7
Tel: 204-983-5344; *Fax:* 204-983-2642
cigi@cigi.ca
cigi.ca

•Canadian Pari-Mutuel Agency (CPMA) / Agence canadienne du pari mutuel (ACPM)
PO Box 5904 Merivale
Ottawa, ON K2C 3X7
Tel: 613-949-0735; *Fax:* 613-949-0750
Toll-free: 800-268-8835
cpmawebacpm@agr.gc.ca
www4.agr.gc.ca/AAFC-AAC/display-afficher.do?id=1204043533186&lang
Other Communication: Equine Drug Control Program, Phone: 613-949-0745; Fax: 613-949-1538

•Farm Credit Canada (FCC) / Financement agricole Canada
See Entry Name Index for detailed listing.

•Farm Products Council of Canada (FPCC) / Conseil des produits agricoles du Canada (CPAC)
Canada Bldg.
344 Slater St., 10th Fl.
Ottawa, ON K1R 7Y3
Tel: 613-995-6752; *Fax:* 613-995-2097
TTY: 613-943-3707
fpcc-cpac@agr.gc.ca
www.fpcc-cpac.gc.ca

Agriculture & Food Inspection Legal Services / Services juridiques - Agriculture et inspection des aliments

Tower 7, 1341 Baseline Rd., Ottawa, ON K1A 0C5
Tel: 613-759-1000; *Fax:* 613-773-2929

General Counsel & Deputy Executive Director, Louise Sénéchal
Tel: 613-773-2901; *Fax:* 613-773-2929
louise.senechal@agr.gc.ca
Business Manager, Aysha Johnson
Tel: 613-773-2915; *Fax:* 613-773-2929
aysha.johnson@agr.gc.ca
Executive Director & Senior General Counsel, Shalene Curtis-Micallef
Tel: 613-773-5772; *Fax:* 613-773-2929
Senior Counsel, Jane Dudley
Tel: 613-773-6015; *Fax:* 613-773-6093

Corporate Management Branch

Tower 7, 1341 Baseline Rd., Ottawa, ON K1A 0C5
Tel: 613-759-1000; *Fax:* 613-773-0911

Assistant Deputy Minister, Pierre Corriveau
Tel: 613-773-1330; *Fax:* 613-773-1233
pierre.corriveau@agr.gc.ca
Director General, Asset Management & Capital Planning, Lynden Hillier
Tel: 613-773-0923; *Fax:* 613-773-0966
lynden.hillier@agr.gc.ca
Acting Director General, Finance & Resource Management Services, Angela Murphy
Tel: 613-773-0776; *Fax:* 613-773-2199
angela.murphy@agr.gc.ca
Director General, Strategic Management, Vacant
Executive Director, Canadian Pari-Mutuel Agency, Steve Suttie
Tel: 613-759-6448; *Fax:* 613-759-6230
steve.suttie@agr.gc.ca
#100, 1130 Morrison Dr., Room 121
PO Box 5904
Ottawa, ON K2C 3X7

Human Resources / Ressources humaines

Tower 4, 1341 Baseline Rd., Ottawa, ON K1A 0C5
Tel: 613-759-1000; *Fax:* 613-773-1211

Director General, Human Resources Directorate, Matthew Shea
Tel: 613-773-1329; *Fax:* 613-773-2727
matthew.shea@agr.gc.ca
Director General, Workplace Relations, Roxanne Savage
Tel: 613-773-1293; *Fax:* 613-773-2193
Roxanne.Savage@agr.gc.ca
Director, Human Resources Planning, Measurement & Systems, Scott Aughey
Tel: 613-773-2380; *Fax:* 613-773-3637
scott.aughey@agr.gc.ca
Director, Leadership, Learning & Talent Management, Laurie Hunter
Tel: 613-773-3493; *Fax:* 613-773-1222
laurie.hunter@agr.gc.ca
Executive Director, Human Resources, Maureen Power
Tel: 613-773-3444; *Fax:* 613-773-0966
maureen.power@agr.gc.ca

Deputy Minister's Office / Bureau du sous-ministre
Tower 7, 1341 Baseline Rd., Ottawa, ON K1A 0C5
Tel: 613-759-1011; *Fax:* 613-759-1040

The Deputy Minister's Office oversees the following organizations: Corporate Secretariat; Food Safety Review Secretariat; & Portfolio Coordination Secretariat.
Deputy Minister, Agriculture & Agri-Food Canada, Andrea Lyon
Tel: 613-773-1011; *Fax:* 613-773-1040
andrea.lyon@agr.gc.ca
Associate Deputy Minister, Agriculture & Agri-Food Canada, Chris Forbes
Tel: 613-773-1011; *Fax:* 613-773-1040
chris.forbes@agr.gc.ca
Director, Parliamentary Relations Office & Portfolio Coordination Secretariat, Kristen Bassett
Tel: 613-773-1019; *Fax:* 613-773-2299
kristen.bassett@agr.gc.ca
Manager, Finance & Administration, Corporate Secretariat, Jeanne Johnson
Tel: 613-773-1057; *Fax:* 613-773-1061
jeanne.johnson@agr.gc.ca

Information Systems Branch / Direction générale des systèmes d'information
Tower 4, 1341 Baseline Rd., Ottawa, ON K1A 0C5
Tel: 613-759-1000; *Fax:* 613-773-0666

The Information Systems Branch of Agriculture & Agri-Food Canada is reponsible for the following organizations: Applications Development Directorate; Information Management Services; IT Operations; & the Strategic Management Directorate.
Chief Information Officer, Michel Lessard
Tel: 613-773-1395; *Fax:* 613-773-0666
michel.lessard@agr.gc.ca
Director General, Applications Development Directorate, Angus Howieson
Tel: 613-759-7735; *Fax:* 613-759-6045
angus.howieson@agr.gc.ca
Director General, Transformation & Modernization Services, Jeff Lamirande
Tel: 613-773-0304; *Fax:* 613-773-0666
jeff.lamirande@agr.gc.ca
Acting Director General, Strategic Management, Robert Jackson
Tel: 613-773-0348; *Fax:* 613-773-0666
robert.jackson@agr.gc.ca
Director, Corporate & Collaborative Solutions, Cameron MacDonald
Tel: 613-759-6940; *Fax:* 613-773-2600
cameron.macdonald@agr.gc.ca
Manager, Information Services, Ingrit Monasterios
Tel: 613-773-1448; *Fax:* 613-773-1499
ingrit.monasterios@agr.gc.ca

Market & Industry Services Branch (MISB) / Direction générale des services à l'industrie et aux marchés
Tower 5, 1341 Baseline Rd., Ottawa, ON K1A 0C5
Tel: 613-759-1000; *Fax:* 613-773-1711

The Market & Industry Services Branch of Agriculture & Agri-Food Canada oversees the following organizations: Bilateral Relations & Technical Trade Policy Directorate; Food Value Chain Bureau; International Markets Bureau; Market Access Secretariat; Negotiations & Multilateral Trade Policy Directorate; & the Operations Directorate. The Operations Directorate operates regional offices throughout Canada, which provide access to market & trade programs & services. Marketing & trade officers offer the following information: statistics by country & product; market access advice; investment opportunities; regulatory issues; export counselling; & news about promotional events.
Assistant Deputy Minister, Fred Gorrell
Tel: 613-773-1790; *Fax:* 613-773-1711
fred.gorrell@agr.gc.ca
Director General, Market Access Secretariat, Kris Panday
Tel: 613-773-1512; *Fax:* 613-773-1616
kris.panday@agr.gc.ca
Director General, Sector Development & Analysis Directorate, Andrea Johnston
Tel: 613-773-2323; *Fax:* 613-773-0300
andrea.johnston@agr.gc.ca
Director General, Trade Agreements & Negotiations, Frédéric Seppey
Tel: 613-773-0985; *Fax:* 613-773-1755
frederic.seppey@agr.gc.ca
Director General, Regional Operations Directorate, Sandra Gagné
Tel: 514-315-6170; *Fax:* 514-496-3966
sandra.gagne@agr.gc.ca

Market & Industry Services Branch Regional Offices

Alberta & Territories Regional Office
#720, 9700 Jasper Ave., Edmonton, AB T5J 4G5
Tel: 780-495-4144; *Fax:* 780-495-3324
Regional Director, Rodney Dlugos
Tel: 780-495-5525; *Fax:* 780-495-3324
rodney.dlugos@agr.gc.ca
Acting Deputy Director, Cheryl McClellan-Moody
Tel: 780-495-4948; *Fax:* 780-495-3324
cheryl.mcclellan-moody@agr.gc.ca

Atlantic Regional Office
#405, 1791 Barrington St., PO Box 248 Halifax, NS B3J 2N7
Tel: 902-426-3198; *Fax:* 902-426-3439
The Atlantic Regional Office in Halifax, Nova Scotia, is the headquarters for the following operations: New Brunswick Operations (Phone: 506-452-3706, Fax: 506-452-3509); Newfoundland & Labrador Operations (Phone: 709-772-4063, Fax: 709-772-4803); Nova Scotia Operations (Phone: 902-896-0332, Fax: 902-896-0100); & Prince Edward Island Operations (Phone: 902-566-7300, Fax: 902-566-7316).
Regional Director, Janet Steele
Tel: 902-426-7171; *Fax:* 902-426-3439
janet.steele@agr.gc.ca
Deputy Director, Prince Edward Island Operations, Heath Coles
Tel: 902-370-1507; *Fax:* 902-370-1511
heath.coles@agr.gc.ca
Deputy Director, Nova Scotia Operations, Shelley Manning
Tel: 902-896-0098; *Fax:* 902-896-0100
shelley.manning@agr.gc.ca

British Columbia Regional Office
#420, 4321 Stillcreek Dr., Burnaby, BC V5C 6S7
Fax: 604-292-5891
Deputy Director, Michelle Soucie
Tel: 604-292-5869; *Fax:* 604-292-5891
michelle.soucie@agr.gc.ca

Ontario Regional Office
174 Stone Rd. West, Guelph, ON N1G 4S9
Tel: 519-837-9400; *Fax:* 226-217-8187
Deputy Director, Fred Brandenburg
Tel: 226-217-8048; *Fax:* 226-217-8187
fred.brandenburg@agr.gc.ca
Deputy Director, Michael Metson
Tel: 226-217-8061; *Fax:* 226-217-8187
michael.metson@agr.gc.ca

Québec Regional Office
2001, boul Robert-Bourassa, 7e étage, Montréal, QC H3A 3N2
Tel: 514-283-8888; *Fax:* 514-496-3966
Regional Director, Sandra Gagné
Tel: 514-315-6170; *Fax:* 514-496-3966
sandra.gagne@agr.gc.ca
Acting Deputy Director, Simon Glance
Tel: 613-773-1876; *Fax:* 613-773-1500
simon.glance@agr.gc.ca

Saskatchewan Regional Office
2010 - 12th Ave., Regina, SK S4P 0M3
Tel: 306-780-5545; *Fax:* 306-780-7360
Acting Deputy Director, Deb Niekamp
Tel: 306-523-6529; *Fax:* 306-523-6558
Deborah.Niekamp@agr.gc.ca
Acting Market & Trade Officer, Catherine Duczek
Tel: 306-523-6531; *Fax:* 306-780-7360
catherine.duczek@agr.gc.ca
Regional Director, Bob Nawolsky
Tel: 204-259-4068; *Fax:* 204-259-4088
bob.nawolsky@agr.gc.ca

Office of Audit & Evaluation
Tower 4, 1341 Baseline Rd., Ottawa, ON K1A 0C5
Tel: 613-759-1000; *Fax:* 613-773-2727

Agriculture & Agri-Food Canada's Office of Audit & Evaluation is responsible for the following services: evaluation; governance & review; & internal audit & assurance.
Director General, Nancy Hamzawi
Tel: 613-773-3551; *Fax:* 613-773-0666
Nancy.Hamzawi@agr.gc.ca
Director, Internal Audit, Lyne Castonguay
Tel: 613-773-0669; *Fax:* 613-773-0666
lyne.castonguay@agr.gc.ca
Director, Evaluation Services, Christine Torrie
Tel: 613-773-2315; *Fax:* 613-773-0666
christine.torrie@agr.gc.ca

Programs Branch / Direction générale des programmes
Tower 7, 1341 Baseline Rd., Ottawa, ON K1A 0C5
Tel: 613-759-1000; *Fax:* 613-773-2121

The Programs Branch of Agriculture & Agri-Food Canada oversees the following organizations: Agriculture Transformation Programs Directorate; Business Risk Management Program Development; Centre of Program Excellence (COPE); Farm Income Programs Directorate; Finance & Renewal Programs Directorate; & Service Policy & Transformation Directorate.
Assistant Deputy Minister, Tina Namiesniowski
Tel: 613-773-2815; *Fax:* 613-773-2121
tina.namiesniowski@agr.gc.ca
Director General, Farm Income Programs Directorate, Jocelyn Beaudette
Tel: 204-259-5800; *Fax:* 204-259-5888
jocelyn.beaudette@agr.gc.ca
Grain Exchange Bldg.
167 Lombard Ave., 10th Fl.
PO Box 6100
Winnipeg, MB R3C 4N3
Director General, Service & Program Excellence Directorate, Ray Edwards
Tel: 613-773-0612; *Fax:* 613-773-1911
ray.edwards@agr.gc.ca
Grain Exchange Bldg.
167 Lombard Ave., 10th Fl.
PO Box 6100
Winnipeg, MB R3C 4N3
Director General, Business Risk Management Programs Directorate, Rosser Lloyd
Tel: 613-773-2116; *Fax:* 613-773-2198
rosser.lloyd@agr.gc.ca
Director General, Business Development & Competitiveness Directorate, Lynn Renaud
Tel: 613-773-0213; *Fax:* 613-773-2121
Lynn.Renaud@agr.gc.ca
Director General, Community Pastures Program, Alan Parkinson
Tel: 306-523-6838; *Fax:* 306-780-5018
alan.parkinson@agr.gc.ca
#408, 1800 Hamilton St.
Regina, SK S4P 4L2
Director General, Innovation Programs Directorate, John Fox
Tel: 613-773-3017; *Fax:* 613-773-1922
john.fox@agr.gc.ca

Public Affairs Branch
Tower 7, 1341 Baseline Rd., Ottawa, ON K1A 0C7
Tel: 613-759-1000; *Fax:* 613-773-2772
Assistant Deputy Minister, Jane Taylor
Tel: 613-773-2922; *Fax:* 613-773-2772
jane.taylor@agr.gc.ca
Director General, Strategic Planning, Advice & Coordination, Steven Jurgutis
Tel: 613-773-2760; *Fax:* 613-773-2772
steven.jurgutis@agr.gc.ca
Director General, Communications Services, Pierre Leduc
Tel: 613-773-2840; *Fax:* 613-773-2772
Pierre.Leduc@agr.gc.ca

Science & Technology Branch / Direction générale des sciences et de la technologie
Tower 5, 1341 Baseline Rd., Ottawa, ON K1A 0C5
Fax: 613-773-1711

Agriculture & Agri-Food Canada's Research Branch consists of the following organizations: Innovation Directorate; International Scientific Cooperation Bureau; Land Resources; Science Centres Directorate, Science Partnerships Directorate; & Science Policy & Planning. Scientists from Agriculture & Agri-Food Canada work on projects to benefit the agricultural & agri-food sector at research centres located across Canada.
Assistant Deputy Minister, Brian T. Gray
Tel: 613-773-1860; *Fax:* 613-773-1717
brian.gray@agr.gc.ca
Associate Assistant Deputy Minister, Gilles Saindon, Ph.D.
Tel: 613-773-1840; *Fax:* 613-773-1844
gilles.saindon@agr.gc.ca
Director General, Cross-Sectoral Strategic Direction, Michael Whittaker
Tel: 613-773-2308; *Fax:* 613-773-1855
michael.j.whittaker@agr.gc.ca
Director General, Coastal Ecozone, Christiane Deslauriers, Ph.D.
Tel: 902-365-8514; *Fax:* 902-365-8455
christiane.deslauriers@agr.gc.ca
Acting Director General, Prairie/Boreal Plain Ecozone, Gabriel Piette

Tel: 450-768-7902; *Fax:* 450-768-7851
gabriel.piette@agr.gc.ca

Research Centres

Agroforestry Development Centre
PO Box 940 Indian Head, SK S0G 2K0
Fax: 306-956-7248

Coordinating Biologist, Agroforestry Development Centre, Henry C. de Gooijer
Tel: 306-695-5102; *Fax:* 306-695-2568
henry.degooijer@agr.gc.ca

Research Manager, Bill R. Schroeder
Tel: 306-695-5126; *Fax:* 306-695-2568
bill.schroeder@agr.gc.ca

Atlantic Cool Climate Crop Research Centre
308 Brookfield Rd., PO Box 39088 St. John's, NL A1E 5Y7
Tel: 709-772-4619; *Fax:* 709-772-6064

Associate Director, Research, Development & Technology, Sandy Todd, PAg
Tel: 709-772-4606; *Fax:* 709-772-3820
sandy.todd@agr.gc.ca

Atlantic Food & Horticulture Research Centre
32 Main St., Kentville, NS B4N 1J5
Tel: 902-679-5333; *Fax:* 902-365-8477

Associate Director, Research Development & Technology, Dr. Mark Hodges, Ph.D.
Tel: 902-365-8500; *Fax:* 902-365-8455
mark.hodges@agr.gc.ca

Manager, Farm, Innovation & Renewal, David L. Bowlby
Tel: 902-368-8587; *Fax:* 902-365-8588
david.bowlby@agr.gc.ca

Brandon Research Centre
2701 Grand Valley Rd., PO Box 1000A Brandon, MB R7A 5Y3
Tel: 204-726-7650; *Fax:* 204-728-3858

Associate Director, Research, Development & Technology, Byron Irvine, Ph.D.
Tel: 204-578-6539; *Fax:* 204-578-6528
byron.irvine@agr.gc.ca

Research Assistant, Clayton J. Jackson, P.Ag.
Tel: 204-578-6615; *Fax:* 204-578-6524
clayton.jackson@agr.gc.ca

Canada-Manitoba Crop Diversification Centre
PO Box 309 Carberry, MB R0K 0H0
Tel: 204-834-6000; *Fax:* 204-834-3777

Canada-Saskatchewan Irrigation Diversification Centre
901 McKenzie St. South, PO Box 700 Outlook, SK S0L 2N0
Tel: 306-867-5400; *Fax:* 306-867-9656
csidc@agr.gc.ca

Cereal Research Centre
#100, 101 Rte. 100, Morden, MB R6M 1Y5
Tel: 204-822-7506; *Fax:* 204-822-7507

Associate Director, Research, Development & Technology, Dr. David Wall
Tel: 204-822-7535; *Fax:* 204-822-7507
david.wall@agr.gc.ca

Crops & Livestock Research Centre
440 University Ave., Charlottetown, PE C1A 4N6
Tel: 902-370-1400; *Fax:* 902-370-1444

The Crops & Livestock Research Centre (CLRC) in Charlottetown, Prince Edward Island is one of Agriculture and Agri-Food Canada's network of 19 research centres. The Centre's mandate is to develop scientific knowledge & new technologies in agriculture with the prime focus on Prince Edward Island & Atlantic Canada.

Director, Research, Development & Technology, Eric van Bochove
Tel: 902-370-1399
eric.vanBochove@agr.gc.ca

Associate Director, Research, Development & Technology, Dr. Maria Rodriguez
Tel: 902-370-1420; *Fax:* 902-370-1444
maria.rodriguez@agr.gc.ca

Dairy & Swine Research & Development Centre
2000, rue College, Succ Lennoxville, Sherbrooke, QC J1M 0C8
Tél: 819-565-9171

The Dairy & Swine Research & Development Centre oversees the operations of the Beef Research Farm in Kapuskasing, Ontario, as well as the Office of Intellectual Property & Commercialization in Sherbrooke, Québec.

Director, Research & Development, Jacques Surprenant, PhD, MPA
Tel: 819-780-7101
jacques.surprenant@agr.gc.ca

Associate Director, Research, Development & Technology, Dr. Alain Giguère
Tel: 819-780-7103
alain.giguere@agr.gc.ca

Acting Associate Director, Research, Development & Technology, Jean-Pierre Charuest
Tel: 819-780-7105; *Fax:* 819-564-5507
jeanpierre.charuest@agr.gc.ca

Eastern Cereal & Oilseed Research Centre
960 Carling Ave., Ottawa, ON K1A 0C6
Tel: 613-759-1858; *Fax:* 613-759-1970

Director, Research & Development, Michèle Marcotte, Ph.D., Eng.
Tel: 613-759-1525; *Fax:* 613-759-1970
michele.marcotte@agr.gc.ca

Associate Director, Research, Development & Technology, Dr. Marc Savard
Tel: 613-759-1683; *Fax:* 613-759-1970
marc.savard@agr.gc.ca

Manager, Research Support, Pierre Descent
Tel: 613-759-1544; *Fax:* 613-759-6566
Pierre.Descent@agr.gc.ca

Food Research & Development Centre
3600, boul Casavant ouest, Saint-Hyacinthe, QC J2S 8E3
Tel: 450-768-7999; *Fax:* 450-768-7851

Acting Director, Research, Development & Technology, Alain Houde
Tel: 450-768-7899; *Fax:* 450-768-7851
alain.houde@agr.gc.ca

Greenhouse & Processing Crops Research Centre
2585 Country Rd. 20, Harrow, ON N0R 1G0
Tel: 519-738-2251; *Fax:* 519-738-2929

Director, Research, Development & Technology, Della Johnston
Tel: 519-738-1218
della.johnston@agr.gc.ca

Associate Director, Research, Development & Technology, Karl Volkmar
Tel: 519-953-6688
karl.volkmar@agr.gc.ca

Manager, Greenhouse, Saeed Akhtar
Tel: 519-738-1212; *Fax:* 519-738-2929
saeed.akhtar@agr.gc.ca

Guelph Food Research Centre
93 Stone Rd. West, Guelph, ON N1G 5C9
Tel: 519-829-2400; *Fax:* 519-829-2602

Director, Research & Development, Gabriel Piette
Tel: 450-768-3304
gabriel.pietter@agr.gc.ca

Associate Director, Research, Development & Technology, Dr. Punidadas Piyasena
Tel: 226-217-8109
puni.piyasena@agr.gc.ca

Horticulture Research & Development Centre
430, boul Gouin, Saint-Jean-sur-Richelieu, QC J3B 3E6
Tel: 450-346-4494; *Fax:* 450-346-7740

Director, Research, Development & Technology, Gabriel Piette
Tel: 450-768-3304
gabriel.piette@agr.gc.ca

Associate Director, Research, Development & Technology, Roger Chagnon
Tel: 450-515-2002
roger.chagnon@agr.gc.ca

Lacombe Research Centre
6000 C & E Trail, Lacombe, AB T4L 1W1
Tel: 403-782-8100; *Fax:* 403-782-4308

The Lacombe Research Centre is responsible for the operations of research farms in Beaverlodge & Fort Vermilion in Alberta.

Acting Director, Research, Development & Technology, François Eudes
Tel: 403-317-2208
francois.eudes@agr.gc.ca

Associate Director, Research, Development & Technology, Mueen Aslam
Tel: 403-782-8110
mueen.aslam@agr.gc.ca

Lethbridge Research Centre
5403 - 1st Ave. South, Lethbridge, AB T1J 4B1
Tel: 403-327-4561; *Fax:* 403-382-3156

The Lethbridge Research Centre oversees the operations of the Onefour Research Substation, the Stavely Research Substation, & the Vauxhall Research Substation in Alberta.

Acting Director, Research, Development & Technology, François Eudes
Tel: 403-317-2208
francois.eudes@agr.gc.ca

Associate Director, Research, Development & Technology, Yves Plante
Tel: 403-317-3445
yves.plante@agr.gc.ca

Pacific Agri-Food Research Centre (PARC)
4200 Hwy. 97, Summerland, BC V0H 1Z0
Tel: 250-494-7711; *Fax:* 250-494-0755

The Pacific Agri-Food Research Centre oversees the following organizations: the Agassiz Site, the Kamloops Range Research Unit, & the Summerland Site.

Acting Director, Research, Development & Technology, Kenna MacKenzie
Tel: 250-494-6358
kenna.mackenzie@agr.gc.ca

Associate Director, Research, Development & Technology, Dr. Sankaran KrishnaRaj
Tel: 604-796-6122; *Fax:* 604-796-6133
sankaran.krishnaraj@agr.gc.ca

Potato Research Centre
850 Lincoln Rd., PO Box 20280 Fredericton, NB E3B 4Z7
Tel: 506-460-4300

The Potato Research Centre is also responsible for the Senator Hervé J. Michaud Research Farm, located in Bouctouche, New Brunswick.

Associate Director, Research, Development & Technology, Edward Hurley
Tel: 506-460-4340
j.edward.hurley@agr.gc.ca

Acting Director, Research, Development & Technology, Joyce Boye
Tel: 450-768-3232
joyce.boye@agr.gc.ca

Manager, Farm, Larry McMillan
Tel: 506-460-4510; *Fax:* 506-460-4377
larry.mcmillan@agr.gc.ca

Saskatoon Research Centre
107 Science Pl., Saskatoon, SK S7N 0X2
Tel: 306-385-9301; *Fax:* 306-385-9482

Acting Director, Research, Development & Technology, Bruce McArthur
Tel: 306-778-7270
bruce.mcarthur@agr.gc.ca

Associate Director, Research, Development & Technology, Ranjana Sharma
Tel: 306-385-9310
ranjana.sharma@agr.gc.ca

Semiarid Prairie Agricultural Research Centre
PO Box 1030 Swift Current, SK S9H 3X2
Tel: 306-770-4400

The Semiarid Prairie Agricultural Research Centre is responsible for the operations of research farms in Indian Head & Regina, Saskatchewan.

Director, Research, Development & Technology, Bruce McArthur
Tel: 306-770-4420
bruce.mcarthur@agr.gc.ca

Associate Director, Research, Development & Technology, Alain Giguère
Tel: 306-385-9320
alain.giguere@agr.gc.ca

Supervisor, Indian Head Research Farm, Darren Pollock
Tel: 306-695-5264; *Fax:* 306-695-3445
darren.pollock@agr.gc.ca

Soils & Crops Research & Development Centre
2560, boul Hochelaga, Québec, QC G1V 2J3
Tel: 418-657-7980; *Fax:* 418-648-2402

The Soils & Crops Research & Development Centre is also responsible for a research farm in Normandin, Québec.

Director, Research, Development & Technology, Jacques Surprenant
Tel: 819-780-7101
jacques.surprenant@agr.gc.ca

Associate Director, Research, Development & Technology, Geneviève Levasseur
Tel: 418-210-5002
genevieve.levasseur@agr.gc.ca

Southern Crop Protection & Food Research Centre
1391 Sandford St., London, ON N5V 4T3
Tel: 519-457-1470; *Fax:* 519-457-3997

The Southern Crop Protection & Food Research Centre oversees the operations of research farms in Delhi & Vineland, Ontario, as well as an Office of Intellectual Property & Commercialization in London, Ontario.

Director, Research, Development & Technology, Della Johnston
Tel: 519-738-1218
della.johnston@agr.gc.ca

Associate Director, Research, Development & Technology, Dr. Karl Volkmar
Tel: 519-457-1470 ext: 206
karl.volkmar@agr.gc.ca

Research Scientist, Vineland Research Farm, Antonet Svircev
Tel: 905-562-2018; *Fax:* 905-562-4335
antonet.svircev@agr.gc.ca

Strategic Policy Branch / Direction générale des politiques stratégiques

Tower 7, 1341 Baseline Rd., Ottawa, ON K1A 0C5

Tel: 613-759-1000; *Fax:* 613-773-2121

The Strategic Policy Branch of Agriculture & Agri-Food Canada includes the following organizations: Policy Development & Analysis Directorate; Policy, Planning, & Integration Directorate; & the Research & Analysis Directorate.

Assistant Deputy Minister, Greg Meredith
Tel: 613-773-2930; *Fax:* 613-773-2121
greg.meredith@agr.gc.ca

Director General, Policy, Planning & Integration Directorate, Andrew Goldstein
Tel: 613-773-0259; *Fax:* 613-773-2333
andrew.goldstein@agr.gc.ca

Director General, Research & Analysis Directorate, Greg Stain
Tel: 613-773-1207; *Fax:* 613-773-2444
greg.strain@agr.gc.ca

Policy Advisor, Gemma Boag
Tel: 613-773-2082
gemma.boag@agr.gc.ca

Atlantic Canada Opportunities Agency (ACOA) / Agence de promotion économique du Canada atlantique (APECA)

Blue Cross Centre, 644 Main St., 3rd Fl., PO Box 6051 Moncton, NB E1C 9J8

Tel: 506-851-2271; *Fax:* 506-851-7403
Toll-Free: 800-561-7862
TTY: 877-456-6500
www.acoa-apeca.gc.ca
twitter.com/acoacanada

The role of the Atlantic Canada Opportunities Agency is the development of opportunities for economic growth in Atlantic Canada. The agency achieves its mission in the following ways: assisting businesses to become more innovative, productive, & competitive; promoting the strengths of Atlantic Canada; & helping communities to develop more diversified local economies. In March 2014, the ACOA assumed responsibility for economic development in Cape Breton, after the closing of Enterprise Cape Breton Corporation.

Minister Responsible; Minister, Innovation, Science & Economic Development, Hon. Navdeep Bains, P.C., B.A., M.B.A., C.M.A.
Tel: 613-995-7784; *Fax:* 613-996-9817
Navdeep.Bains@parl.gc.ca

President, Paul J. LeBlanc
Tel: 506-851-6128

Chief, Financial Planning & Analysis, Mariline Belliveau
Tel: 506-851-3769

Director General, Human Resources, Charlene Sullivan
Tel: 506-851-2141; *Fax:* 506-851-7403

Executive Director & General Counsel, Legal Services, Mark Belliveau
Tel: 506-851-7593; *Fax:* 506-851-3304

Director, Public Affairs, Deborah Corey
Tel: 506-851-2133; *Fax:* 506-851-7403

Director, General Communications, Kevin Dubé
Tel: 613-948-3986; *Fax:* 613-946-2858

Director, Energy, Environment Policy, & Coordination, Daniel McCarthy
Tel: 613-952-8216; *Fax:* 613-995-1719

Finance & Corporate Services / Finances et services corporatifs

Vice-President, Denise Frenette
Tel: 506-851-6438; *Fax:* 506-851-7403

Director General, Chief Information Officer Directorate, Marc Gagnon
Tel: 506-851-6511; *Fax:* 506-851-7403

Acting Director General, Finance & Administration, Stephane Legace
Tel: 506-851-2359

Director & Coordinator, ATIP, Diane Cormier
Tel: 506-381-4270; *Fax:* 506-851-7403

Deputy Chief, Ministerial Liaison Office, Carolee Sandell
Tel: 613-948-1498

Director, Branch Coordination & Management Services, Nancy Menchions
Tel: 506-227-8278; *Fax:* 506-851-7403

Policy & Programs / Politiques et programmes

Vice-President, Daryell Nowlan
Tel: 506-851-3805; *Fax:* 506-851-7403

Director General, Policy, Wade Aucoin
Tel: 506-381-0324; *Fax:* 506-851-7403

Director General, Advocacy & Industrial Benefits, Madonna Kent
Tel: 613-952-7494; *Fax:* 613-995-1719

Acting Director, Strategic Policy Development, Diana Zandberg
Tel: 506-871-2067; *Fax:* 506-851-7403

Director, Innovation & Entrepreneurship, Lyne Lirette-LeBlanc
Tel: 506-851-7954; *Fax:* 506-851-7403

Acting Director General, Community Development, William Grandy
Tel: 506-851-6496

Director General, Community Development, Gilbert Philion
Tel: 506-851-3818

Regional Offices

New Brunswick Regional Office

570 Queen St., 3rd Fl., PO Box 578 Fredericton, NB E3B 5A6

Tel: 506-452-3184; *Fax:* 506-452-3285
Toll-Free: 800-561-4030
TTY: 877-456-6500

The New Brunswick Regional Office oversees operations at the following offices: Campbellton (Phone: 506-789-4735); Edmundston (Phone: 506-735-4236); Fundy Region (Phone: 506-636-4485); Miramichi (506-625-1443); Northeast (Phone: 506-548-7420); Northwest (Phone: 506-473-5556); Southeast (Phone: 506-851-6432); & Tracadie-Sheila (506-395-1024).

Vice-President, New Brunswick, Kent Estabrooks
Tel: 506-452-3342; *Fax:* 506-452-3261

Director General, Regional Operations, André Charron
Tel: 506-452-2413

Director, Finance & Corporate Services, Barbara Gagnon-Thériault
Tel: 506-444-6164

Director General, Policy, Advocacy & Coordination, Kalie Hatt-Kilburn
Tel: 506-444-6144

Director, Policy, Advocacy, & Coordination, Monique LeBlanc
Tel: 506-452-2451

Manager, Strategic Initiatives, New Brunswick Federal Council, Paulianne Howe
Tel: 506-444-6133

Newfoundland & Labrador Regional Office

John Cabot Building, 10 Barter's Hill, 11th Fl., PO Box 1060 Stn. C, St. John's, NL A1C 5M5

Tel: 709-772-2751; *Fax:* 709-772-2712
Toll-Free: 800-668-1010
TTY: 877-456-6500

The Newfoundland & Labrador Regional Office oversees the following offices throughout the province: Clarenville (Phone: 709-466-5980); Corner Brook (Phone: 709-637-4477); Gander (Phone: 709-651-4457); Grand Falls-Windsor (Phone: 709-489-6600); Labrador (709-896-2741); & Marystown (709-279-5608).

Vice-President, Newfoundland & Labrador, Paul Mills
Tel: 709-772-4150

Director General, Policy, Advocacy, & Coordination, Susan Drodge
Tel: 709-772-2334

Director, Communications, Julie Afonso
Tel: 709-772-2984

Director, Communications, Douglas Burgess
Tel: 709-772-2935

Director, Community Development, John Kennedy
Tel: 709-772-2741

Director, Finance & Management Services, Geoffrey Hudson
Tel: 709-772-3367

Director General Regional Operations, Kenneth Martin
Tel: 709-772-0212

Director, Community Development, Karen Skinner
Tel: 709-772-2753

Regional Coordinator, Newfoundland & Labrador Federal Council, Mary Thorne-Gosse
Tel: 709-772-2781

Nova Scotia Regional Office

#700, 1801 Hollis St., PO Box 2284 Stn. C, Halifax, NS B3J 3C8

Tel: 902-426-8361; *Fax:* 902-426-2054
Toll-Free: 800-565-1228
TTY: 877-456-6500

The Nova Scotia Regional Office of the Atlantic Canada Opportunities Agency oversees the following offices throughout Nova Scotia: Antigonish (Phone: 902-867-6075); Bridgewater (Phone: 902-541-5543); Church Point (Phone: 902-260-3590); Sydney (902-564-3600); Shelburne/Queens (902-875-7324); Truro (902-895-2743); Windsor (902-472-3607); & Yarmouth (Phone: 902-742-0809).

Vice-President, Nova Scotia, Peter Hogan
Tel: 902-426-8364

Director General, Policy, Advocacy & Coordination, Laurie Cameron
Tel: 902-426-4260

Director General, Commercial Development, Joe Cashin
Tel: 902-564-7356; *Fax:* 902-564-3825

Director General, Regional Operations, Charles (Chuck) Maillet
Tel: 902-426-5790

Director General, Corporate Services, Lori Marenick
Tel: 902-564-3825; *Fax:* 902-564-3825

Director General, Community Development, Tom Plumridge
Tel: 902-564-3846; *Fax:* 902-564-3825

Executive Director, Nova Scotia Federal Council, Lisa Muton
Tel: 902-426-8622

Director, Corporate Services, Jeff Pottie
Tel: 902-802-4271

Director, Communications, Alexander Smith
Tel: 902-426-9417; *Fax:* 902-426-5843

Ottawa Office

60 Queen St., 4th Fl., PO Box 1667 Stn. B, Ottawa, ON K1P 5R5

Tel: 613-954-2422; *Fax:* 613-954-0429

Prince Edward Island Regional Office

Royal Bank Building, 100 Sydney St., 3rd Floor, PO Box 40 Charlottetown, PE C1A 7K2

Tel: 902-566-7492; *Fax:* 902-566-7098
Toll-Free: 800-871-2596
TTY: 877-456-6500

Vice-President, Prince Edward Island & Tourism, Patrick Dorsey
Tel: 902-368-0760

Director General, Atlantic Tourism, Robert McCloskey
Tel: 902-626-2479; *Fax:* 902-566-7098

Director, Corporate Programs & Services, Lynne Beairsto
Tel: 902-566-7499

Director, Enterprise Development, Michael Dillon
Tel: 902-368-0737; *Fax:* 902-566-7098

Director, Trade & Investment & Canada Business, Patti-Sue Lee
Tel: 902-626-2481

Director, Community Economic Development & Infrastructure, Marilyn Murphy
Tel: 902-368-0987

Acting Director, Communicatons, Christopher Brooks
Tel: 902-566-7569; *Fax:* 902-566-7098

Account Manager, Infrastructure Programs, Kandace McEntee
Tel: 902-218-0414; *Fax:* 902-566-7098

Atlantic Pilotage Authority (APA) / Administration de pilotage de l'Atlantique

Cogswell Tower, #910, 2000 Barrington St., Halifax, NS B3J 3K1

Tel: 902-426-2550; *Fax:* 902-426-4004
Toll-Free: 877-272-3477
dispatch@atlanticpilotage.com
www.atlanticpilotage.com
Other Communication: Toll-Free Fax: 1-877-745-3477; Fax to Email Direct: 1-866-774-2477

The Federal Crown Corporation is responsible for the safe & efficient operation, maintenance & administration of marine pilotage service to Atlantic Canada.

Chief Executive Officer, Sean Griffiths
Tel: 902-426-2553

Chief Financial Officer, Peter L. MacArthur
Tel: 902-426-8657

Atomic Energy of Canada Limited (AECL) / Énergie atomique du Canada Ltée (EACL)

Head Office, Chalk River Laboratories, 286 Plant Rd., Chalk River, ON K0J 1J0

Toll-Free: 888-220-2465
communications@aecl.ca
www.aecl.ca

Atomic Energy of Canada develops peaceful applications from nuclear technology. Services include research, design, engineering, waste management, & decommissioning.
It was announced on February 28, 2013, that the Government of Canada is seeking to shift management & operation of AECL's Nuclear Laboratories to a Government-owned, Contractor-operated (GoCo) model, similar to models in the US & UK. Canadian Nuclear Laboratories was created in 2014 in the first phase of this shift. In June 2015 it was announced that the Canadian National Energy Alliance won the contract to operate Canadian Nuclear Laboratories, leaving AECL as a small Crown corporation dedicated to managing the contract.

Acting Transition Officer & Vice-President, Decommissioning & Waste Management Oversight, Richard Sexton

Vice-President; General Counsel; Corporate Secretary, Grant Gardiner

Vice-President, Site Operations & Infrastructure Oversight, Frank Gibbs

Vice-President, Business Operations & Chief Financial Officer, David Smith

Canadian Nuclear Laboratories (CNL) / Laboratoires Nucléaires Canadiens (LNC)
Head Office, Chalk River Laboratories, 286 Plant Rd., Chalk River, ON K0J 1J0
Toll-Free: 866-513-2325
communications@cnl.ca
www.cnl.ca
Other Communication: Community Enquiries: 1-800-364-6989; Media Enquiries: 1-866-886-2325; Library Requests: 613-584-3311, ext. 43900
twitter.com/CNL_LNC
www.linkedin.com/company/9191967
www.youtube.com/c/CNLCanada

Canadian Nuclear Laboratories was created as a subsidiary of Atomic Energy of Canada during the organization's restructuring. As of November 2014, CNL is responsible for all day-to-day operations of AECL sites.
The following offices & laboratories are part of Atomic Energy of Canada/Canadian Nuclear Laboratories: Whiteshell Laboratories in Pinawa, Manitoba (204-753-2311); Low-Level Radioactive Waste Management in Ottawa, Ontario (613-998-9442); AECL Ottawa (613-237-3270); Port Hope Office & Laboratory in Port Hope, Ontario (905-885-9488); Port Hope Area Initiative (905-885-0291); Centre for Nuclear Energy Research at the University of New Brunswick in Fredericton (506-453-5111); & Wrap Up Office in Oakville, Ontario (905-829-3333).

Chair, Mark Morant
President & CEO, Mark Lesinski
Vice-President, Human Resources, Esther Zdolec
Vice-President, Finance & Chief Financial Officer, Barry Casselman
Vice-President, Research & Development, Thomas Blejwas
Vice-President, Operations & Chief Nuclear Officer, William Pilkington
Vice-President, Business Development & Commercial Ventures, Bill Mangan
Vice-President, Legal, Mark Richards
Vice-President, Decommissioning & Waste Management, Kurt Kehler
Vice-President, Health, Safety, Security, Environment & Quality, Kevin Daniels

Low-Level Radioactive Waste Management Office (LLRWMO) / Bureau de gestion des déchets radioactifs de faible activité (BGDRFA)
196 Toronto St., Port Hope, ON L1A 3V5
Tel: 905-885-9488; *Fax:* 905-885-0273
Toll-Free: 866-255-2755
info@llrwmo.org
www.llrwmo.org

Carries out the responsibilities of the federal government for low-level radioactive waste (LLRW) management in Canada.

Nuclear Legacy Liabilities Program (NLLP) / Programme des responsabilités nucléaires héritées (PRNH)
c/o AECL, Corporate Communications, #B700A, Chalk River Laboratories, Stn. 700A, Chalk River, ON K0J 1J0
Tel: 613-584-8206
Toll-Free: 800-364-6989
info@nuclearlegacyprogram.ca
www.nuclearlegacyprogram.ca

Established in 2006 to manage Canada's nuclear legacy liabilities at Canadian Nuclear Laboratories (CNL) sites. Natural Resources Canada oversees the program, while CNL is responsible for implementation.

Auditor General of Canada / Vérificateur général du Canada

240 Sparks St., Ottawa, ON K1A 0G6
Tel: 613-952-0213; *Fax:* 613-957-0474
Toll-Free: 888-761-5953
TTY: 613-954-8042
infomedia@oag-bvg.gc.ca
www.oag-bvg.gc.ca
Other Communication: Media Relations Phone: 1-888-761-5953; Work Opportunities, E-mail: emplo@oag-bvg.gc.ca
twitter.com/OAG_BVG

The Office of the Auditor General of Canada was established in 1878. Today, the head office in Ottawa & regional offices in Halifax, Montréal, Edmonton, & Vancouver employ approximately 575 employees. The Office of the Auditor General of Canada provides objective, fact-based information required by Parliament to hold the federal government accountable for its stewardship of public funds. An Officer of Parliament, the Auditor General of Canada is responsible for auditing the following organizations: federal government departments; federal government agencies; most Crown corporations; many federal organizations; the government of the Yukon; the government of the Northwest Territories; & the government of Nunavut. The Auditor General, Michael Ferguson, reports publicly to the House of Commons about matters he believes should be brought to the attention of the House of Commons. The report can include chapters on audits & studies, sustainable development strategies, & environmental petitions.

Auditor General, Michael Ferguson, FCA
Assistant Auditor General, Professional Practices, Stuart Barr
Tel: 613-952-0213 ext: 545
Assistant Auditor General, National Defence, Veterans Affairs Canada, Jerome Berthelette
Tel: 613-952-0213 ext: 450
Assistant Auditor General, IC, Aboriginal Issues, HRMA, Nunavut, Industry, & NRC, Vacant
Assistant Auditor General, Crown Corporations Group, Nancy Cheng
Tel: 613-952-0213 ext: 626; *Fax:* 613-941-8284
Assistant Auditor General, Yukon & the Northwest Territories, Terrance DeJong
Tel: 613-952-0213 ext: 248
Assistant Auditor General, CBC, CRTC, CC, Maurice Laplante
Tel: 613-952-0213 ext: 547
Assistant Auditor General, CBSA, CIDA, CSIS, CIC, CSC, IRB, Justice, Public Safety, & RCMP, Vacant
Assistant Auditor General, CDIC, CMHC, OP, FI, EDC, FCC, IDRC, & PSPIB, Clyde MacLellan
Tel: 613-952-0213 ext: 522
Assistant Auditor General, CRA, AA, SO, Income Tax, GST, FS, ILO, Marian McMahon
Tel: 613-952-0213 ext: 221
Assistant Auditor General, Corporate Services, Sylvain Ricard
Tel: 613-952-0213 ext: 535
Assistant Auditor General, Corporate Services, Sylvain Ricard
Tel: 613-952-0213 ext: 535
Principal, Canadian Heritage, Martin Dompierre
Tel: 613-952-0213 ext: 429
Director, Parliamentary Liaison, Marie-Josée Gougeon
Tel: 613-952-0213 ext: 636

Commissioner of the Environment & Sustainable Development / Commissaire à l'environnement et au développement durable
240 Sparks St., Ottawa, ON K1A 0G6
Tel: 613-952-0213; *Fax:* 613-941-8286
oag-bvg.gc.ca/internet/English/cesd_fs_e_921.html
Commissioner, Environment & Sustainable Development, Julie Gelfand
Tel: 613-952-0213 ext: 640
Principal, Sustainable Development Strategies, Audits, & Studies, Sharon Clark
Tel: 613-952-0213 ext: 642
Principal, Sustainable Development Strategies, Audits, & Studies, Kimberly Leach
Tel: 613-952-0213 ext: 624

Regional Offices

Edmonton
Canada Place, #1635, 9700 Jasper Ave., Edmonton, AB T5J 4C3
Tel: 780-495-2028; *Fax:* 780-495-2031
Principal, Guy LeGras
Tel: 780-495-2029

Halifax/Dartmouth
Maritime Centre, #1140, 1505 Barrington St., Halifax, NS B3J 3K5
Tel: 902-426-9241; *Fax:* 902-426-8591
Principal, Heather McManaman
Tel: 902-426-7728

Montréal
#545, 1255, rue Peel, Montréal, QC H3B 2T9
Tél: 514-283-6086; *Téléc:* 514-283-1715
Principal, René Béliveau
Tel: 514-283-8324

Vancouver
#805, 1550 Alberni St., Vancouver, BC V6G 1A5
Tel: 604-666-3596; *Fax:* 604-666-6162
Principal, Lana Dar
Tel: 604-666-7613

Bank of Canada / Banque du Canada

234 Laurier Ave. West, Ottawa, ON K1A 0G9
Tel: 613-782-8111; *Fax:* 613-782-7713
Toll-Free: 800-303-1282
TTY: 888-418-1461
info@bankofcanada.ca
www.bankofcanada.ca
Other Communication: Access to information & privacy issues, E-mail: ATIP-AIPRP@bankofcanada.ca; Media, E-mail: communications@bankofcanada.ca
twitter.com/bankofcanada
www.linkedin.com/company/12682
www.youtube.com/user/bankofcanadaofficial

Founded in 1934, the Bank of Canada was orignially a privately owned corporation. It became a Crown corporation, belonging to the federal government, in 1938. As Canada's central bank, the role of the Bank of Canada is the promotion of the economic & financial welfare of the nation. The following are the main responsibilities of the Bank of Canada: Canada's financial system; monetary policy; funds management; & bank notes. The Governor & Senior Deputy of the Bank of Canada are appointed by the Bank's Board of Directors, with the approval of the Cabinet. Regional offices of the Bank of Canada are located in the following cities: Halifax; Montréal; Toronto; Calgary; Vancouver; & New York. Head office staff have been relocated to 234 Laurier Ave. West due to major renovations occurring at the original 234 Wellington St. address. The change will be in effect from 2013 to 2016.

Governor, Stephen S. Poloz
Senior Deputy Governor, Carolyn Wilkins
Deputy Governor, Timothy Lane
Deputy Governor, Sylvain Leduc
Deputy Governor, Lynn Patterson
Deputy Governor, Lawrence Schembri
Chief Operating Officer, Filipe Dinis

Audit / Vérification
Chief Internal Auditor, Julie Champagne

Canadian Economic Analysis / Analyses de l'économie canadienne
Chief, Eric Santor

Communications / Services de communications
Chief, Jill Vardy

Corporate Services / Services de gestion
Chief, Dinah Maclean

Currency / Monnaie
Chief, Richard Wall

Executive & Legal Services / Services à la Haute Direction et Services juridiques
General Counsel & Corporate Secretary, Jeremy S.T. Farr

Financial Markets / Marchés financiers
Chief, Toni Gravelle

Financial Services / Services financiers
Chief Financial Officer, Carmen Vierula

Financial Stability / Stabilité financière
Chief, Ron Morrow

Funds Management & Banking / Gestion financière et bancaire
Chief, Grahame Johnson

Human Resources / Services des ressources humaines
Chief, Alexis Corbett

Information Technology Services / Services des technologies de l'information
Chief, Sylvian Chalut

International Economic Analysis / Analyses de l'économie internationale
Chief, Césaire Meh

Business Development Bank of Canada (BDC) / Banque de développement du Canada (BDC)

#400, 5, Place Ville-Marie, Montréal, QC H3B 5E7
Toll-Free: 877-232-2269
www.bdc.ca
Other Communication: Toll-Free Fax 1-877-329-9232
twitter.com/BDC_News
www.facebook.com/bdc.ca
www.linkedin.com/companies/bdc
www.youtube.com/BDCBanx

The Business Development Bank of Canada is a financial institution which is wholly owned by the Government of Canada. It was created by an Act of Parliament in 1944. The Bank is governed by an independent Board of Directors, & reports to the

Minister of Industry. The mission of the Business Development Bank of Canada is to assist in the establishment & development of Canadian businesses in all industries. The Bank focuses its efforts on small & medium-sized enterprises. The following services are carried out by the Business Development Bank of Canada: consulting services; flexible financing, such as long term business financing & subordinate financing; & venture capital. Branches of the Business Development Bank of Canada are located throughout Canada. Smaller communities are served by satellite branches, consultants & travelling account managers.

Chair, Samuel L. Duboc
President & Chief Executive Officer, Michael Denham
Executive Vice-President & Chief Financial & Risk Officer, Paul Buron
Executive Vice-President, Financing, Pierre Dubreuil
Executive Vice-President, BDC Capital, Jérôme Nycz
Senior Vice President & Chief Information & Innovation Officer, Chantal Belzile
Senior Vice President, Marketing & Public Affairs, Michel Bergeron
Senior Vice President, Human Resources, Mary Karamanos
Senior Vice President, Legal Affairs; Corporate Secretary, Louise Paradis

Alberta Branches

Calgary Area Branch
Barclay Centre, #110, 444 - 7 Ave. SW, Calgary, AB T2P 0X8
Fax: 403-292-6616
Toll-Free: 888-463-6232

Calgary North Branch
#100, 1935 - 32 Ave. NE, Calgary, AB T2E 7C8
Fax: 403-292-6651
Toll-Free: 888-463-6232

Calgary South Branch
#200, 6700 MacLeod Trail SE, Calgary, AB T2H 0L3
Fax: 403-292-4345
Toll-Free: 888-463-6232

Edmonton Branch
#200, 10665 Jasper Ave., Edmonton, AB T5J 3S9
Fax: 780-495-6616
Toll-Free: 888-463-6232

Edmonton South Branch
#201, 4628 Calgary Trail NW, Edmonton, AB T6H 6A1
Fax: 780-495-7198
Toll-Free: 888-463-6232

Edmonton West Branch
236 Mayfield Common, Edmonton, AB T5P 4B3
Fax: 780-495-3102
Toll-Free: 888-463-6232

Grande Prairie Branch
#203, 10625 West Side Dr., Grande Prairie, AB T8V 8E6
Fax: 780-539-5130
Toll-Free: 888-463-6232

Lethbridge Branch
#701, 400 - 4th Ave. South, Lethbridge, AB T1J 4E1
Fax: 403-382-3162
Toll-Free: 888-463-6232

Medicine Hat Branch
#112, 640 - 3rd St. SE, PO Box 18 Medicine Hat, AB T1A 0H5
Fax: 403-528-6899
Toll-Free: 888-463-6232

Office by appointment.

Red Deer Branch
#200, 4900 - 50th Ave., Red Deer, AB T4N 1X7
Fax: 403-340-4243
Toll-Free: 888-463-6232

British Columbia Branches

Cranbrook Branch
205B Cranbrook St. North, Cranbrook, BC V1C 3R1
Fax: 250-417-2213
Toll-Free: 888-463-6232

Fort St. John Branch
#7, 10230 - 100th St., Fort St. John, BC V1J 3Y9
Fax: 250-787-9423
Toll-Free: 888-463-6232

Fraser Valley Branch
#301, 5577 - 153A St., Surrey, BC V3S 5K7
Fax: 604-586-2430
Toll-Free: 888-463-6232

Kamloops Branch
205 Victoria St., Kamloops, BC V2C 2A1
Fax: 250-851-4925
Toll-Free: 888-463-6232

Kelowna Branch
313 Bernard Ave., Kelowna, BC V1Y 6N6
Fax: 250-470-4832
Toll-Free: 888-463-6232

Nanaimo Branch
#500, 6581 Aulds Rd., Nanaimo, BC V9T 6J6
Fax: 250-390-5753
Toll-Free: 888-463-6232

Nelson Branch
#1, 619B Front St., Nelson, BC V1L 4B6
Fax: 250-352-3809
Toll-Free: 888-463-6232

North Vancouver Branch
#3, 221 West Esplanade, North Vancouver, BC V7M 3J3
Fax: 604-666-1957
Toll-Free: 888-463-6232

Prince George Branch
#150, 177 Victoria St., Prince George, BC V2L 5R8
Fax: 250-561-5512
Toll-Free: 888-463-6232

Terrace Branch
3233 Emerson St., Terrace, BC V8G 5L2
Fax: 250-615-5320
Toll-Free: 888-463-6232

Tri-Cities Branch
#370, 2755 Lougheed Highway, Port Coquitlam, BC V3B 5Y9
Fax: 604-927-1415
Toll-Free: 888-463-6232

Vancouver Branch
One Bentall Centre, #2100, 505 Burrard St., PO Box 6 Vancouver, BC V7X 1M6
Fax: 604-666-1068
Toll-Free: 888-463-6232

Victoria Branch
990 Fort St., Victoria, BC V8V 3K2
Fax: 250-363-8029
Toll-Free: 888-463-6232

Manitoba Branches

Brandon Branch
#10, 940 Princess Ave., Brandon, MB R7A 0P6
Fax: 204-726-7555
Toll-Free: 888-463-6232

Winnipeg Branch
#1100, 155 Carlton St., Winnipeg, MB R3C 3H8
Fax: 204-983-0870
Toll-Free: 888-463-6232

Winnipeg West Branch
130 Commerce Dr., Winnipeg, MB R3P 0Z6
Fax: 204-983-6531
Toll-Free: 888-463-6232

New Brunswick Branches

Bathurst Branch
#205, 275 Main St., Bathurst, NB E2A 1A9
Fax: 506-548-7381
Toll-Free: 888-463-6232

Edmundston Branch
#407, 121, rue de l'Église, Edmundston, NB E3V 1J9
Télec: 506-735-0019
Ligne sans frais: 888-463-6232

Office by appointment.

Fredericton Branch
#504, 570 Queen St., PO Box 754 Fredericton, NB E3B 5B4
Fax: 506-452-2416
Toll-Free: 888-463-6232

Moncton Branch
766 Main St., Moncton, NB E1C 1E6
Fax: 506-851-6033
Toll-Free: 888-463-6232

Saint John Branch
#100, 53 King St., Saint John, NB E2L 1G5
Fax: 506-636-3892
Toll-Free: 888-463-6232

Newfoundland & Labrador Branches

Corner Brook Branch
4 Herald Ave., 1st Fl., Corner Brook, NL A2H 4B4
Fax: 709-637-4522
Toll-Free: 888-463-6232

Grand Falls-Windsor Branch
42 High St., PO Box 744 Grand Falls-Windsor, NL A2A 2M4
Fax: 709-489-6569
Toll-Free: 888-463-6232

St. John's Branch
215 Water St., PO Box 520 St. John's, NL A1C 5K4
Fax: 709-772-2516
Toll-Free: 888-463-6232

Northwest Territories & Nunavut Branches

Yellowknife & Nunavut Branch
4912 - 49th St., Yellowknife, NT X1A 1P3
Fax: 867-873-3501
Toll-Free: 888-463-6232

Nova Scotia Branches

Halifax Branch
#1400, 2000 Barrington St., Halifax, NS B3J 2Z7
Fax: 902-426-6783
Toll-Free: 888-463-6232

Sydney Branch
#117, 275 Charlotte St., Sydney, NS B1P 1C6
Fax: 902-564-3975
Toll-Free: 888-463-6232

Truro Branch
#2, 733 Prince St., PO Box 1378 Truro, NS B2N 1G7
Fax: 902-893-7957
Toll-Free: 888-463-6232

Yarmouth Branch
103 Water St., PO Box 98 Yarmouth, NS B5A 4B1
Fax: 902-742-8180
Toll-Free: 888-463-6232

Ontario Branches

Barrie Branch
#201, 126 Wellington St. West, Barrie, ON L4N 1K9
Fax: 705-739-0467
Toll-Free: 888-463-6232

Belleville Branch
284B Wallbridge-Loyalist Rd., Belleville, ON K8N 5B3
Fax: 613-969-4018
Toll-Free: 888-463-6232

Office by appointment.

Brampton Branch
#100, 24 Queen St. East, Brampton, ON L6V 1A3
Fax: 905-450-7514
Toll-Free: 888-463-6232

Burlington / Halton Branch
#401, 4145 North Service Rd., Burlington, ON L7L 6A3
Fax: 905-315-9243
Toll-Free: 888-463-6232

Durham (Whitby) Branch
400 Dundas St. West, Whitby, ON L1N 2M7
Fax: 905-666-1059
Toll-Free: 888-463-6232

Etobicoke Branch
#1001, 1243 Islington Ave., Toronto, ON M8X 1Y9
Fax: 416-954-2631
Toll-Free: 888-463-6232

Guelph Branch
#100, 120 Research Lane, Guelph, ON N1G 0B5
Fax: 519-826-2662
Toll-Free: 888-463-6232

Hamilton Branch
#1900, 25 Main St. West, Hamilton, ON L8P 1H1
Fax: 905-572-4282
Toll-Free: 888-463-6232

Kenora Branch
227 - 2nd St. South, Kenora, ON P9N 1G1
Fax: 807-467-3533
Toll-Free: 888-463-6232

Kingston Branch
#201, 1000 Gardiners Rd., Kingston, ON K7P 3C4
Fax: 613-389-2543
Toll-Free: 888-463-6232

Kitchener-Waterloo Branch
#110, 50 Queen St. North, Kitchener, ON N2H 6P4
Fax: 519-571-6685
Toll-Free: 888-463-6232

London Branch
#1000, 148 Fullarton St., London, ON N6A 5P3
Fax: 519-645-5450
Toll-Free: 888-463-6232

Markham Branch
#201, 3985 Hwy. 7 East, Markham, ON L3R 2A2
Fax: 905-305-1969
Toll-Free: 888-463-6232

Mississauga Branch
#100, 4310 Sherwoodtowne Blvd., Mississauga, ON L4Z 4C4
Fax: 905-566-6425
Toll-Free: 888-463-6232

North Bay Branch
#203, 1145 Cassells St., North Bay, ON P1B 4B4
Fax: 705-495-5707
Toll-Free: 888-463-6232

North York Branch
#502, 1120 Finch Ave. West, North York, ON M3J 3H7
Fax: 416-736-3425
Toll-Free: 888-463-6232

Ottawa Branch
55 Metcalfe St., Ground Fl., Ottawa, ON K1P 6L5
Fax: 613-995-9045
Toll-Free: 888-463-6232

Ottawa West Branch
#100, 700 Silver Seven Rd., Kanata, ON K2V 1C3
Fax: 613-592-5053
Toll-Free: 888-463-6232

Peterborough Branch
Peterborough Square Tower, 340 George St. North, 4th Fl., PO Box 1419 Peterborough, ON K9J 7H6
Fax: 705-750-4808
Toll-Free: 888-463-6232

Sarnia Branch
#101, 1086 Modeland Rd., Sarnia, ON N7S 6L2
Fax: 519-383-1849
Toll-Free: 888-463-6232
Office by appointment.

Sault Ste. Marie Branch
153 Great Northern Rd., Sault Ste. Marie, ON P6B 4Y9
Fax: 705-941-3040
Toll-Free: 888-463-6232

Scarborough Branch
#112, 305 Milner Ave., Toronto, ON M1B 3V4
Fax: 416-954-0716
Toll-Free: 888-463-6232

St Catharines Branch
#202, 25 Corporate Park Dr., St Catharines, ON L2S 3W2
Fax: 905-988-2890
Toll-Free: 888-463-6232

Stratford Branch
516 Huron St., Stratford, ON N5A 5T7
Fax: 519-271-8472
Toll-Free: 888-463-6232

Sudbury Branch
#10, 233 Brady St., Sudbury, ON P3B 4H5
Fax: 705-670-5333
Toll-Free: 888-463-6232

Thunder Bay Branch
#102, 1136 Alloy Dr., Thunder Bay, ON P7B 6M9
Tel: 807-346-1780
Toll-Free: 888-463-6232

Timmins Branch
#202, 85 Pine St. South, Timmins, ON P4N 2K1
Fax: 705-268-5437
Toll-Free: 888-463-6232
Office by appointment.

Toronto Branch
#1200, 121 King St. West, Toronto, ON M5H 3T9
Fax: 416-954-5009
Toll-Free: 888-463-6232
The King Street West branch offers corporate financing for the Greater Toronto Area.

Vaughan Branch
#600, 3901 Hwy. 7 West, Vaughan, ON L4L 8L5
Fax: 905-264-2122
Toll-Free: 888-463-6232

Windsor Branch
#200, 2485 Ouellette Ave., Windsor, ON N8X 1L5
Fax: 519-257-6811
Toll-Free: 888-463-6232

Prince Edward Island Branches

Charlottetown Branch
#230, 119 Kent St., PO Box 488 Charlottetown, PE C1A 7L1
Fax: 902-566-7459
Toll-Free: 888-463-6232

Québec Branches

Alma Branch
#101, 65, rue Saint-Joseph Sud, Alma, QC G8B 6V4
Téléc: 418-698-5678
Ligne sans frais: 888-463-6232

Boucherville Branch
#300, 1570, rue Ampère, Boucherville, QC J4B 7L4
Téléc: 450-645-2055
Ligne sans frais: 888-463-6232

Brossard Branch
#200, 4255, boul Lapinière, Brossard, QC J4Z 0C7
Téléc: 450-926-7221
Ligne sans frais: 888-463-6232

Chaudière - Appalaches (Saint-Romuald) Regional Branch
#100, 1175, boul Guillaume-Couture, Lévis, QC G6W 5M6
Téléc: 418-834-1855
Ligne sans frais: 888-463-6232

Des Moulins/L'Assomption & Lanaudière North Branch
2785, av Claude Léveillée, Terrebonne, QC J6X 4J9
Téléc: 450-964-8773
Ligne sans frais: 888-463-6232

Drummondville Branch
1010, boul René-Lévesque, Drummondville, QC J2C 5W4
Téléc: 819-478-5864
Ligne sans frais: 888-463-6232

Eastern Montréal Branch
6347, rue Jean-Talon Est, Saint-Léonard, QC H1S 3E7
Téléc: 514-251-2758
Ligne sans frais: 888-463-6232

Granby Branch
#102, 90, rue Robinson Sud, Granby, QC J2G 7L4
Téléc: 450-372-2423
Ligne sans frais: 888-463-6232

Laval Branch
#100, 2525, Daniel-Johnson, Laval, QC H7T 1S9
Téléc: 450-973-6860
Ligne sans frais: 888-463-6232

Montréal Branch
#12525, 5, Place Ville-Marie, Montréal, QC H3B 5E7
Téléc: 514-496-7974
Ligne sans frais: 888-463-6232

Pointe-Claire Branch
#210, 6500, rte Trans-Canada, Pointe-Claire, QC H9R 0A5
Téléc: 514-697-3160
Ligne sans frais: 888-463-6232

Québec Branch
#300, 1035, av Wilfrid Pelletier, Québec, QC G1W 0C5
Téléc: 418-648-5525
Ligne sans frais: 888-463-6232

Québec North West Branch
#310, 1165, boul Lebourgneuf, Québec, QC G2K 2C9
Téléc: 418-648-4745
Ligne sans frais: 888-463-6232

Rimouski Branch
#004, 180, rue des Gouverneurs, Rimouski, QC G5L 8G1
Téléc: 418-722-3362
Ligne sans frais: 888-463-6232

Rouyn-Noranda Branch
#301, 139, boul Québec, Rouyn-Noranda, QC J9X 6M8
Téléc: 819-764-5472
Ligne sans frais: 888-463-6232

Saguenay / Lac St-Jean Branch
#300, 315, rue Hôtel-de-ville, Saguenay, QC G7H 4W8
Téléc: 418-698-5678
Ligne sans frais: 888-463-6232

Saint-Jérôme Branch
#102, 55, rue Castonguay, Saint-Jérôme, QC J7Y 2H9
Téléc: 450-432-8366
Ligne sans frais: 888-463-6232

Saint-Laurent Branch
#210, 8250, boul Décarie, Saint-Laurent, QC H4P 2P5
Téléc: 514-496-7510
Ligne sans frais: 888-463-6232

Sherbrooke Branch
#200, 1802, rue King Ouest, Sherbrooke, QC J1J 0A2
Téléc: 819-564-4276
Ligne sans frais: 888-463-6232

Thérèse-de-Blainville (Boisbriand) Regional Branch
3000, rue Cours le Corbusier, Boisbriand, QC J7G 3E8
Téléc: 450-420-4904
Ligne sans frais: 888-463-6232

Trois-Rivières Branch
#150, 1500, rue Royale, Trois-Rivières, QC G9A 6E6
Téléc: 819-371-5220
Ligne sans frais: 888-463-6232

Vaudreuil-Soulanges
#206, 11, boul de la Cité des Jeunes, Vaudreuil-Dorion, QC J7V 0N3
Téléc: 450-455-8126
Ligne sans frais: 888-463-6232

Saskatchewan Branches

Prince Albert Branch
75 South Industrial Dr., #A, Prince Albert, SK S6V 7L7
Fax: 306-953-1343
Toll-Free: 888-463-6232
Office by appointment.

Regina
#320, 2220 - 12th Ave., Regina, SK S4P 0M8
Fax: 306-780-7516
Toll-Free: 888-463-6232

Saskatoon
135 - 21st St. East, Main Fl., Saskatoon, SK S7K 0B4
Fax: 306-975-5955
Toll-Free: 888-463-6232

Yukon Branches

Whitehorse
#210, 2237 - 2 Ave., Whitehorse, YT Y1A 0K7
Fax: 867-667-4058
Toll-Free: 888-463-6232

Canada Border Services Agency (CBSA) / Agence des services frontaliers du Canada (ASFC)

Headquarters, 191 Laurier Ave. West, Ottawa, ON K1A 0L8
Toll-Free: 800-461-9999
TTY: 866-335-3237
contact@cbsa.gc.ca
www.cbsa-asfc.gc.ca
Other Communication: Border Information Service, Service in French, Toll-Free Phone: 1-800-959-2036; Public Safety Canada, Phone: 613-944-4875, Toll-Free: 1-800-830-3118
twitter.com/CanBorder
www.facebook.com/CanBorder
www.youtube.com/CanBorder

Established in 2003, as a response to the need for increased border services, the Canada Border Services Agency ensures the security & prosperity of Canada. The agency is responsible for managing the access of people & goods to & from Canada. To carry out its mission, Canada Border Services Agency administers more than ninety pieces of legislation. Some of the agencies duties include the following: managing over 100 border crossings; offering services at points throughout Canada & internationally; operating detention centres across the nation; conducting marine operations at the ports of Prince Rupert, Vancouver, Montréal, & Halifax; managing postal services at major mail centres in Montréal, Toronto, & Vancouver; & forming part of more than twenty Integrated Border Enforcement Teams across Canada.

Minister, Public Safety & Emergency Preparedness, Hon. Ralph Goodale, P.C., B.A., LL.B.
Tel: 613-947-1153; *Fax:* 613-996-9790
ralph.goodale@parl.gc.ca

President, Linda Lizotte-MacPherson
Tel: 613-952-3200; *Fax:* 613-948-3177

Executive Vice-President, Nada Semaan
Tel: 613-952-3200; *Fax:* 613-952-1851

Regional Director General, Southern Ontario, Rick Comerford
Tel: 905-354-5353

Acting Regional Executive General, Southern Ontario, Dan Badour
Tel: 519-967-4010

Executive Director, Québec, Benoît Chiquette
Tel: 514-283-6201

Regional Director General, Atlantic, Calvin Christiansen
Tel: 902-426-2914

Regional Director General, Northern Ontario, Lisa Janes
Tel: 613-991-0566

Regional Director General, Pacific Region, Roslyn MacVicar
Tel: 604-666-0760

Regional Director General, Greater Toronto Area, Goran Vragrovic
Tel: 905-803-5595

Director, Atlantic Region, Southern New Brunswick & Prince Edward Island District, Don Collins
Tel: 506-636-4506
Other Communications: Administrative Assistant, Phone: 506-426-4501

Director, Atlantic Region, Northwestern New Brunswick District, John Dolimount
Tel: 506-328-9211
Other Communications: Administrative Assistant, Phone: 506-324-8660

District Director, Metro Vancouver, John Dyck
Tel: 604-775-6790; *Fax:* 604-775-6792

District Director, Northern Ontario Region, Northwest District, Tuula Schuler
Tel: 705-941-3052
District Director, Pacific Region, Vancouver Airport District, Sari Hellsten
Tel: 604-666-1800; *Fax:* 604-666-1812
Other Communications: Executive Assistant, Phone: 604-666-9337
Director, Prairie Region, Southern Alberta & Southern Saskatchewan District, Kevin Hewson
Tel: 403-344-2061
Director, Québec Region, Montérégie District, Chantal Laurin
Tel: 450-246-2272
Director, Pacific Region, Okanagan & Kootenay District, Glyn Lee
Tel: 250-770-4512; *Fax:* 250-482-5983
District Director, Northern Ontario Region, St. Lawrence District, Lance Markell
Tel: 613-382-8495
Director, Atlantic Region, Newfoundland & Labrador, & Nova Scotia, Rick Patterson
Tel: 902-426-7184
Director, Pacific Region, West Coast & Yukon District, Ivan Peterson
Tel: 250-363-3365; *Fax:* 250-363-8261
Director, Québec Region, St-Lawrence District, Éric Lapierre
Tel: 514-350-6100; *Fax:* 514-283-8591
Other Communications: Executive Assistant, Phone: 514-350-6100
Director, Québec Region, Airports District, Pierre Provost
Tel: 514-633-7702
District Director, Pacific Region, Pacific Highway District, Kim Scoville
Tel: 778-538-3602; *Fax:* 604-541-5968
Other Communications: Executive Assistant, Phone: 778-545-5559
Director, Central Manitoba, Central Saskatchewan & NT District, Mike Shoobert
Tel: 306-780-7356; *Fax:* 306-780-8222
District Director, Northern Ontario Region, Ottawa District, Steve MacNaughton
Tel: 613-949-1900

Corporate Affairs Branch
191 Laurier Ave. West, 6th Fl., Ottawa, ON K1A 0L8
Vice-President, Caroline Webber
Tel: 613-960-6596; *Fax:* 613-960-6599
Director General, Recourse Directorate, Tammy Branch
Tel: 343-291-7187
Director General, Communications Directorate, Joanne John
Tel: 613-946-4875
Director General, Corporate Planning & Reporting Directorate, Melanie Larocque
Tel: 613-948-9863
Director General, Corporate Secretariat Directorate, Robert Mundie
Tel: 613-954-1909
Director General, Internal Audit & Program Evaluation Directorate, Dena Palamedes
Tel: 613-941-7216
Executive Director, Cabinet, Parliamentary & Regulatory Affairs Division, Colin Boyd
Tel: 613-948-7882
Executive Director, Communications Directorate, Marc Raider
Tel: 613-948-9048

Comptrollership Branch
219 Laurier Ave. West, 9th Fl., Ottawa, ON K1A 0L8
Vice-President, Christine Walker
Tel: 613-948-8604
Chief Financial Officer, Operations Branch, Eva Jacobs
Tel: 613-948-9296
Chief Financial Officer, Comptrollership Branch, Caroline Sanders
Tel: 613-948-7849
Comptroller, Operations Branch, Nathalie Fleurent
Tel: 613-948-9333
Director General, Infrastructure & Environmental Operations Directorate, Sylvain Cyr
Tel: 343-291-5803
Director General, Security & Professional Standards Directorate, Pierre Giguère
Tel: 343-291-7726
Director General, Agency Comptroller Directorate, Jen O'Donoghue
Tel: 343-291-5684
Director General, Resource Management Directorate, John Pinsent
Tel: 613-941-6388
Director General, Transformation & Oversight Directorate, Scott Taymun
Tel: 613-960-1625

Human Resources Branch
99 Metcalfe St., 3rd Fl., Ottawa, ON K1A 0L8
Vice-President, Jean-Stéphen Piché
Tel: 613-948-3180; *Fax:* 613-952-1783
Director General, Training & Development Directorate, Jacqueline Rigg
Tel: 613-948-3328
Director General, Labour Relations & Compensation Directorate, Marc Thibodeau
Tel: 613-948-9861; *Fax:* 613-948-9838
Director General, HR Programs Directorate, Philippe Thompson
Tel: 613-948-1164
Executive Director, Executive Group Services, Leadership & Talent Management Division, France Guèvremont
Tel: 613-948-9828
Executive Director, Ethics & Employee Support Directorate, Steven Levecque
Tel: 613-948-9115
Executive Director, Learning Design Solutions Division, Jennifer Richens
Tel: 434-291-6691
Executive Director, Client Services Division, Jean-Philippe Lapointe
Tel: 343-291-6033

Information, Science & Technology Branch
191 Laurier Ave. West, 7th Fl., Ottawa, ON K1A 0L8
Vice-President, Maurice Chénier
Tel: 613-946-4884
Associate Vice-President, Louis-Paul Normand
Tel: 613-948-9694
Director General, Travellers Project Portfolio Directorate, Victor Abele
Tel: 343-291-6859
Acting Director General, CBSA Assessment & Revenue Management Directorate, Sylvie Cloutier
Tel: 343-291-5235
Director General, Business Application Services Directorate, Minh Doan
Tel: 343-291-6018
Director General, Science & Engineering Directorate, Diane Keller
Tel: 613-954-2200
Director General, Enterprise Architecture & Information Management Directorate, Gino Lechasseur
Tel: 343-291-7415
Director General, Business, Corporate Projects & Portfolio Management Directorate, Lucie Loignon
Tel: 343-291-5020
Director General, Enterprise Services Directorate, Brendan Dunne
Tel: 343-391-6655
Director General, Commercial Project Portfolio Directorate, Bruna Rados
Tel: 343-291-6176

Operations Branch
191 Laurier Ave. West, 18th Fl., Ottawa, ON K1A 0L8
Vice-President, Martin Bolduc
Tel: 613-948-4445
Associate Vice-President, Caroline Xavier
Tel: 613-952-5269; *Fax:* 613-948-7130
Director General, National Border Operations Centre, Calvin Christiansen
Tel: 613-991-1773; *Fax:* 613-991-1407
Acting Director General, Enforcement & Intelligence Operations Directorate, Andrew LeFrank
Tel: 613-948-0423
Director General, International Region Directorate, Jacques Cloutier
Tel: 613-948-1846
Director General, Border Operations Directorate, Denis R. Vinette
Tel: 613-954-6990; *Fax:* 613-957-9723
Executive Director, Border Operations Directorate, Raymond Bédard
Tel: 613-941-4565

Programs Branch
191 Laurier Ave. West, 15th Fl., Ottawa, ON K1A 0L8
Vice-President, Richard Wex
Tel: 613-954-7220; *Fax:* 613-952-2622
Associate Vice-President, Peter Hill
Tel: 613-952-2531; *Fax:* 613-952-2622
Director General, Global Border Management & Data Analytics Directorate, Charles Slowey
Tel: 613-946-3183
Director General, Enforcement & Intelligence Programs Directorate, Monik Beauregard
Tel: 613-948-9041
Director General, Commercial Program Directorate, Megan Imrie
Tel: 613-954-6431
Director General, Trade & Anti-dumping Programs Directorate, Brent McRoberts
Tel: 613-954-7338
Director General, Traveller Program Directorate, Arianne Reza
Tel: 613-952-3266
Director General, Beyond the Border Governance & Coordination Directorate, Kristine Stolarik
Tel: 613-954-7282
Executive Director, Commercial Program Directorate, Beverly Boyd
Tel: 343-291-5522
Executive Director, Global Border Management & Data Analytics Directorate, Kym Martin
Tel: 613-957-1286
Executive Director, Enforcement & Intelligence Programs Directorate, Lesley Soper
Tel: 613-957-6044

Canada Business Network / Réseau Entreprises Canada

235 Queen St., Ottawa, ON K1A 0H5
Tel: 343-291-1818
Toll-Free: 888-576-4444
TTY: 800-457-8466
www.canadabusiness.ca
twitter.com/CanadaBusiness
www.facebook.com/244892072221776
www.youtube.com/CanadaBusinessCBN

Canada Business provides a wide range of information on government services, programs & regulations to Canadian business people. The base framework is an organized network of centres across Canada, one in each province & territory. The network of Canada Business is expanding to include regional access partners in many other communities across Canada. The centres offer various products & services aimed at helping clients obtain quick, accurate & comprehensive business information. Each centre exists as a result of cooperative arrangements between federal & provincial governments, & the private sector in some cases. Administration & management of the CBSC varies depending on location between the following federal agencies: Innovation, Science & Economic Development; Atlantic Canada Opportunities Agency; Canada Economic Development for Quebec Regions; Canadian Northern Economic Development Agency; Federal Economic Development Agency for Southern Ontario; & Western Economic Diversification Canada.

Acting Senior Manager, Canada Business Network Operations, Sophie Nowak
Tel: 613-462-9315; *Fax:* 613-954-5463
Program Officer, Canada Business Network Operations, Louise Cardinal
Tel: 343-291-1743; *Fax:* 613-954-5463

Regional Offices

Business InfoCentre at the World Trade Centre Winnipeg (BIC)
219 Provencher Blvd., 3rd Fl., Winnipeg, MB R2H 0G4
Tel: 204-984-2272; *Fax:* 204-983-3852
Toll-Free: 800-665-2019
TTY: 800-457-8466
cbn@wtcwinnipeg.com
www.wtcwinnipeg.com/bic
twitter.com/WTCWinnipeg
www.facebook.com/WorldTradeCentreWinnipeg
www.youtube.com/channel/UC4iM28J39PfY7qS6g1_xc4g

Business Link - Alberta's Business Information Service
10160 - 103th St. NW, Edmonton, AB T5J 1B1
Tel: 780-422-7722; *Fax:* 780-422-0055
Toll-Free: 888-576-4444
TTY: 800-457-8466
askus@businesslink.ca
businesslink.ca
Other Communication: Research Services Phone: 780-422-7780; Aboriginal Business Development Services: 1-800-272-9675
twitter.com/BusinessLinkAB
www.facebook.com/BusinessLinkAB
linkedin.com/company/the-business-link-business-service-centre

Canada Business Nova Scotia
#700, 1801 Hollis St., Halifax, NS B3J 3C8
Toll-Free: 888-576-4444
TTY: 800-457-8466

Canada Business NWT (CBNWT) / Entreprises Canada TNO
#701, 5201 - 50 Ave., Yellowknife, NT X1A 3S9
Tel: 876-873-7958
Toll-Free: 888-576-4444
TTY: 800-457-8466

Canada Business Ontario
151 Yonge St., 4th Fl., Toronto, ON M5C 2W7
Tel: 416-775-3456
Toll-Free: 888-576-4444
TTY: 800-457-8466
www.cbo-eco.ca

Canada Business Prince Edward Island
PO Box 40 Charlottetown, PE C1A 7K2
Toll-Free: 888-576-4444
TTY: 800-457-8466

Canada Business Yukon
#101, 307 Jarvis St., Whitehorse, YT Y1A 2H3
Tel: 867-667-2000; *Fax:* 867-667-2001
Toll-Free: 888-576-4444
TTY: 800-457-8466

Info entrepreneurs
#W204, 380, rue St-Antoine ouest, local 6000, Montréal, QC H2Y 3X7
Tél: 514-496-4636; *Téléc:* 514-496-5934
Ligne sans frais: 888-576-4444
TTY: 800-457-8466
www.infoentrepreneurs.org
Autres nombres: Toll-Free Fax: 1-888-417-0442; Québec, Phone: 418-649-6116; Fax: 418-682-1144
twitter.com/chambremontreal
www.facebook.com/chambremontreal

New Brunswick Business Service Centre
PO Box 5002 Campbellton, NB E3N 3L3
Fax: 506-789-4737
Toll-Free: 888-576-4444
TTY: 800-457-8466

Newfoundland & Labrador Business Service Centre
John Cabot Bldg., 10 Barter's Hill, 11th Fl., St. John's, NL A1C 5M5
Tel: 709-772-6022; *Fax:* 709-772-2712
Toll-Free: 888-576-4444
TTY: 800-457-8466

Nunavut Service Centre
Inuksugait Plaza, PO Box 1480 Iqaluit, NU X0A 0H0
Tel: 867-975-7860; *Fax:* 867-975-7885
Toll-Free: 888-576-4444
TTY: 800-457-8466
Other Communication: Rankin Inlet, Phone: 867-645-8450, Fax: 867-645-8455; Cambridge Bay, Phone: 867-983-7383, Fax: 967-983-7380

Small Business BC
82 - 601 West Cordova St., Vancouver, BC V6B 1G1
Tel: 604-775-5525; *Fax:* 604-775-5520
Toll-Free: 800-667-2272
TTY: 800-457-8466
askus@smallbusinessbc.ca
www.smallbusinessbc.ca
Other Communication: Feedback E-mail: feedback@smallbusinessbc.ca
twitter.com/smallbusinessbc
www.facebook.com/smallbusinessbc
www.linkedin.com/groups/Small-Business-BC-2397794

Square One: Saskatchewan's Business Resource Centre
250 - 3rd Ave. South, Saskatoon, SK S7K 1L9
Tel: 306-242-4101; *Fax:* 306-242-4136
Toll-Free: 888-576-4444
TTY: 800-457-8466
info@squareonesask.ca
squareonesask.ca
twitter.com/squareonesask
www.facebook.com/SquareOneSask
www.linkedin.com/company/squareonesask

Canada Council for the Arts / Conseil des Arts du Canada

150 Elgin St., 2nd Fl., PO Box 1047 Ottawa, ON K1P 5V8
Tel: 613-566-4414; *Fax:* 613-566-4390
Toll-Free: 800-263-5588
TTY: 866-585-5559
info@canadacouncil.ca
www.canadacouncil.ca
twitter.com/canadacouncil
www.facebook.com/canadacouncil
www.youtube.com/canadacouncil

The Canada Council for the Arts is a national arm's-length agency created by an Act of Parliament in 1957. According to the Canada Council Act, the role of the Council is to foster & promote the study & enjoyment of, & the production of works in the arts. To fulfill this mandate, the Council offers a broad range of grants & services to professional Canadian artists & arts organizations in dance, interdisciplinary work & performance art, media arts, music, interdisciplinary work, theatre, visual arts, & writing & publishing. The Council awards more than 100 prizes every year. It administers the Killam Program of scholarly awards, the Governor General's Literary Awards & the Governor General's Awards in Visual & Media Arts. The Canadian Commission for UNESCO & the Public Lending Right Commission operate under its aegis.

Chair, Pierre Lassonde, C.M., O.Q.
Vice-Chair, Nathalie Bondil
Director & CEO, Simon Brault
Tel: 613-566-4414 ext: 420
director@canadacouncil.ca
Chief Financial Officer & Director General, Corporate Services Division, Linda Drainville
Tel: 613-566-4414 ext: 510
Linda.Drainville@canadacouncil.ca
Director, Marketing Communications, Geneviève Vallerand
Tel: 613-566-4414 ext: 514
genevieve.vallerand@canadacouncil.ca

Canada Deposit Insurance Corporation (CDIC) / Société d'assurance-dépôts du Canada (SADC)

50 O'Connor St., 17th Floor, Ottawa, ON K1P 6L2
Fax: 613-996-6095
Toll-Free: 800-461-2342
info@cdic.ca
www.cdic.ca
Other Communication: Toll Free: 1-800-461-7232 (French); E-mail (French): info@sadc.ca; URL (French): www.sadc.ca
twitter.com/CDIC_SADC
linkedin.com/company/canada-deposit-insurance-corporation
www.youtube.com/user/cdicchannel

CDIC, a Crown corporation established in 1967, ensures eligible deposits in member institutions (banks, trust companies, loan companies & cooperative credit associations) in case a member becomes insolvent. Funding is provided by its member institutions through premiums paid on insured deposits. Reports to government through the Minister of Finance. CDIC responsibilities include: providing deposit insurance in case of member failure; contributing to the stability of the Canadian financial system.

Chair, Bryan P. Davies
President & Chief Executive Officer, Michèle Bourque
Senior Vice-President, Insurance & Risk Assessment, Dean A. Cosman
Senior Vice-President, Complex Resolution Division, Michael Mercer
Vice-President, Finance & Administration & Chief Financial Officer, Anthony Carty
Vice-President, Corporate Affairs & General Counsel, Chantal Richer

Canada Economic Development for Québec Regions / Développement économique Canada pour les régions du Québec

Édifice Dominion Square, #900, 1255, rue Peel, Montréal, QC H3B 2T9
Tel: 514-283-6412; *Fax:* 514-283-3302
Toll-Free: 866-385-6412
TTY: 844-805-8727
www.dec-ced.gc.ca
Secondary Address: 165, rue Hôtel de Ville Place du Portage, Phase IIPO Box 1110 B Sta. Gatineau, QC J8X 3X5
Alt. Fax: 819-997-3340

Defines federal objectives relating to development opportunities & delivers business assistance programs for small- & medium-sized businesses in Québec for innovation, entrepreneurial & market development purposes. Supports a series of programs for appropriate environmental initiatives in various regions of Québec. The agency fosters alliances among the various environmental industry stakeholders including small- & medium-sized enterprises & industrial associations. Goals include a strengthening of existing & new partnerships, & an improvement of access to government programs. The agency also provides a significant amount of support for research & development in areas of environmental technology, demonstration, marketing & transfer projects. Supports initiatives that contribute to making Montréal an industrial centre of excellence in the environment. Aids small- & medium-sized firms in gaining access to federal procurement process, & encourages training & education focusing on business management. Helps business develop export markets through cooperative efforts with Innovation, Science & Economic Development & Foreign Affairs & International Trade Canada

Minister Responsible; Minister, Innovation, Science & Economic Development, Hon. Navdeep Bains, P.C., B.A., M.B.A., C.M.A.
Tel: 613-995-7784; *Fax:* 613-996-9817
Navdeep.Bains@parl.gc.ca
Acting Deputy Minister & President, Pierre-Marc Mongeau
Tel: 514-283-4843; *Fax:* 514-283-7778
Chief of Staff & Departmental Advisor, Marie-Eve Harvey
Tel: 514-283-8119; *Fax:* 514-283-7778
Officer, Ministerial Correspondence, Sophie Lavoie
Tel: 514-283-7459; *Fax:* 514-283-7778

Corporate Services Sector / Secteur Services Corporatifs

Tel: 514-283-4651; *Fax:* 514-283-1549
Executive Director, Marc Lemieux
Tel: 514-283-4565; *Fax:* 514-296-5449
Chief of Staff, Brigitte Flamand
Tel: 514-283-0161; *Fax:* 514-496-5449

Legal Services

Tel: 514-283-2997; *Fax:* 514-283-1549
Executive Director & General Counsel, Christine Calvé
Tel: 514-283-2997; *Fax:* 514-283-1549

Operations / Opérations

Tel: 514-283-3510; *Fax:* 514-283-4547
Vice-President, Pierre-Marc Mongeau
Tel: 514-283-3510; *Fax:* 514-283-4547

Branch & Regional Operations

Director General, Branch, Regional Operations - Group A, Gilles Pelletier
Tel: 514-283-0703; *Fax:* 514-283-3637
Director General, Regional Operations - Group B, Georges Arseneau
Tel: 514-283-4188; *Fax:* 514-283-4547

Policy & Communications

Tel: 514-283-1294; *Fax:* 514-283-5940
Vice-President, Marie-Chantal Girard
Tel: 514-283-1294
Acting Chief of Staff, Nathalie Jutras
Tel: 514-496-2941; *Fax:* 514-283-5940
Director, Government Affairs Branch, France Pitre
Tel: 819-997-7716; *Fax:* 819-997-8519
Director General, Policy, Research & Programs Branch, Sonia LeBris
Tel: 514-283-2664; *Fax:* 514-283-8429
Director, Communications Branch, Nadine Blackburn
Tel: 514-283-8817

Regional Offices

Abitibi-Témiscamingue
906, 5e av, Val-d'Or, QC J9P 1B9
Fax: 819-825-3245
Toll-Free: 800-567-6451
Regional Director, Sandra Lafleur
Tel: 819-825-5260; *Fax:* 819-825-3245

Bas St-Laurent
Édifice Trust général du Canada, #310, 2, rue Saint-Germain Est, Rimouski, QC G5L 8T7
Tel: 418-722-3282; *Fax:* 418-722-3285
Regional Director, Pierre Roberge
Tel: 418-722-3255; *Fax:* 418-722-3285

Centre-du-Québec
#105, 1100 boul René-Lévesque, Drummondville, QC J2C 5W4
Tel: 819-478-4664; *Fax:* 819-478-4666

Côte-Nord
#202B, 701, boul Laure, PO Box 698 Sept-Îles, QC G4R 4K9
Fax: 418-968-0806
Toll-Free: 800-463-1707
Regional Director, Stéphane Lacroix
Tel: 418-968-3285

Estrie
Place Andrew Paton, #100, 202, rue Wellington nord, Sherbrooke, QC J1H 5C6
Tel: 819-564-5904; *Fax:* 819-564-5912
Regional Director, Mariette Larochelle
Tel: 819-564-5904; *Fax:* 819-564-5912

Gaspésie—Iles-de-la-Madeleine
Place Jacques-Cartier, 120, rue de la Reine, 3e étage, Gaspé, QC G4X 2S1
Fax: 418-368-6256
Toll-Free: 866-368-0044
Senior Advisor, Érick St-Laurent
Tel: 418-368-5879

Greater Montréal
Édifice Dominion Square, #900, 1255, rue Peel, Montréal, QC H3B 2T9
Tel: 514-283-3628; *Fax:* 514-283-7491
Regional Director, Jean-Philippe Brassard
Tel: 514-496-5341

Mauricie
#350, 125, rue des Forges, Trois-Rivières, QC G9A 2G7
Tel: 819-371-5182; *Fax:* 819-371-5186
Toll-Free: 800-567-8637

Regional Director, Pierre Lacoursière
Tel: 819-371-5182; *Fax:* 819-371-5186

Outaouais
#202, 259 boul Saint-Joseph, Gatineau, QC J8Y 6T1
Fax: 819-994-7846
Toll-Free: 800-561-4353

Regional Director, Marc Boily
Tel: 819-994-7442; *Fax:* 819-994-7846

Québec - Chaudière - Appalaches
Place Iberville IV, #030, 2954, boul Laurier, Québec, QC G1V 4T2
Tel: 418-648-4451; *Fax:* 418-648-7291

Regional Director, Christian Audet
Tel: 418-648-4451; *Fax:* 418-648-7291

Saguenay - Lac-Saint-Jean
#203, 100, rue Saint-Joseph sud, Alma, QC G8B 7A6
Fax: 418-668-7584
Toll-Free: 800-463-9808

Regional Director, Charles Lambert
Tel: 418-668-3084; *Fax:* 418-688-7584

Canada Foundation for Innovation (CFI) / Fondation canadienne pour l'innovation (FCI)

#450, 230 Queen St., Ottawa, ON K1P 5E4
Tel: 613-947-6496; *Fax:* 613-943-0923
feedback@innovation.ca
www.innovation.ca
twitter.com/innovationca
www.facebook.com/innovationincanada
www.youtube.com/user/InnovationCanada

Established by the Canadian government in 1997, the Foundation's mission is to strengthen the nation's ability to undertake research & technological initiatives. The CFI helps fund research facilities in universities, colleges, hospitals, & non-profit institutions across the country.

Chair, Kevin P.D. Smith
President & CEO, Gilles G. Patry
Tel: 613-947-7260
gilles.patry@innovation.ca

External Relations & Communications

Vice-President, Pierre Normand
Tel: 613-943-0211
pierre.normand@innovation.ca
Director, Communications, Elizabeth Shilts
Tel: 613-996-4421
elizabeth.shilts@innovation.ca

Finance & Corporate Services

Vice-President, Manon Harvey
Tel: 613-947-6497
manon.harvey@innovation.ca
Director, Corporate Services, John Fryer
Tel: 613-947-3208
john.fryer@innovation.ca

Programs & Planning

Vice-President, Guy Levesque
Tel: 613-996-3109
guy.levesque@innovation.ca
Director, Programs, Mohamed Nasser-Eddine
Tel: 613-996-3110
mohamad.nasser-eddine@innovation.ca

Canada Industrial Relations Board (CIRB) / Conseil canadien des relations industrielles (CCRI)

240 Sparks St., 4th Fl. West, Ottawa, ON K1A 0X8
Fax: 613-995-9493
Toll-Free: 800-575-9696
TTY: 800-855-0511
www.cirb-ccri.gc.ca

The Board is an independent, administrative, quasi-judicial tribunal which administers Part I & certain provisions of Part II of the Canada Labour Code. Its responsibilities include the granting or revoking of collective bargaining rights, the mediation & adjudication of unfair labour practice complaints, the determination of unlawful strikes & lockouts & other matters. As of April 2013, the Board is responsible for the duties formerly carried out by the Canadian Artists & Producers Professional Relations Tribunal.

Chair, Ginette Brazeau
Tel: 613-995-7046; *Fax:* 613-947-3894
Vice-Chair, Annie Berthiaume
Toll-free: 800-575-9696
Vice-Chair, Graham Clarke
Toll-free: 800-575-9696; *Fax:* 613-947-5407
Vice-Chair, Louise Fecteau
Toll-free: 800-575-9696; *Fax:* 514-283-3590
Vice-Chair, Judith F. MacPherson
Toll-free: 800-575-9696; *Fax:* 613-947-5407
Vice-Chair, Allison Smith
Toll-free: 800-575-9696
Vice-Chair, Claude Roy
Toll-free: 800-575-9696; *Fax:* 514-283-3590
Executive Director, Sylvie Guilbert
Tel: 613-947-5429

Case Management Secretariat Directorate

Director, Communications Case Management Services, Justine Abel
Tel: 613-947-5432
Manager, Operational Policy & Procedures, Christine Brûlé-Charron
Tel: 613-947-5421

Legal Services

Senior Counsel, Susan Nicholas
Tel: 613-947-5456; *Fax:* 613-947-5460

Regional Offices

Canada Lands Company Ltd. (CLCL) / Société immobilière du Canada limitée (SICL)

#1200, 1 University Ave., Toronto, ON M5J 2P1
Tel: 416-952-6112
clc.ca

CLCL is a Crown corporation with a mandate to enhance the quality of life of the communities in which it conducts business, to generate best value for the taxpayer through the orderly disposal of strategic real estate properties no longer required by the federal government, as well as the management of certain other select properties. The agency reports to government through the Minister of Transport, Infrastructure & Communities.

Chair, Grant B. Walsh
gwalsh@walshdeltagroup.com
President & CEO, John McBain
Chief Operating Officer, CN Tower, Jack Robinson
Chief Financial Officer & Executive Vice-President, Corporate Services, Jurgen H. Dirks
Vice-President, Real Estate, Western Region, Doug Cassidy
Director, Corporate Communications, Manon Lapensée
mlapensee@clc.ca

Old Port of Montréal Corporation Inc. / Société du Vieux port de Montréal

333, rue de la Commune ouest, Montréal, QC H2Y 2E2
Tél: 514-283-5256
Ligne sans frais: 800-971-7678
www.oldportcorporation.com

Parc Downsview Park Inc.

70 Canuck Ave., Toronto, ON M3K 2C5
Tel: 416-954-0544
downsviewevents@clc.ca
www.downsviewpark.ca
Other Communication: Media Phone: 416-952-6112
twitter.com/downsviewpark
www.facebook.com/DownsviewParkOfficialPage
www.youtube.com/user/DownsviewPark

Canada Mortgage & Housing Corporation (CMHC) / Société canadienne d'hypothèques et de logement (SCHL)

700 Montreal Rd., Ottawa, ON K1A 0P7
Tel: 613-748-2000; *Fax:* 613-748-2098
Toll-Free: 800-668-2642
TTY: 613-748-2447
chic@cmhc-schl.gc.ca
www.cmhc-schl.gc.ca
Other Communication: Canadian Housing Information Centre: 613-748-2367
twitter.com/CMHC_ca
www.facebook.com/cmhc.schl
www.linkedin.com/company/canada-mortgage-and-housing-corporation
www.youtube.com/CMHCca

CMHC works closely with a network of professional associations, groups & institutions concerned with regional planning & the residential sector. It prepares various research projects for the examination of relationships between urban areas, housing & sustainable development issues. Involved in numerous technical research projects addressing interrelationships between housing, energy & resource use. Through its research & information transfer function, CMHC will undertake initiatives such as identifying approaches & solutions that lead to more sustainable & healthy communities, examining barriers to potential development of brownfield sites. CMHC will focus on ways to reduce residential energy consumption in multiple-unit housing, educate consumers on energy-saving changes to homes. The Net Zero Healthy Healthy Housing Initiative combines passive solar, energy-efficient design, construction & appliances, integrated with renewable energy systems, to achieve net zero energy consumption on an annual basis, significantly reducing environmental impacts & GHG emissions. Twenty demonstration projects across Canada are underway.

Chair, Robert Kelly
President & Chief Executive Officer; Board Member, Evan Siddall
Tel: 613-748-2186
Senior Vice-President, Corporate Development, Policy & Research, Debra Darke
Tel: 613-748-2994
Senior Vice-President, General Counsel & Corporate Secretary, Sebastien Gignac
Tel: 613-748-2892
Senior Vice-President, Regional Operations & Assisted Housing, Charles MacArthur
Tel: 613-748-2251
Senior Vice-President, Insurance, Steven Mennill
Tel: 613-748-2772
Chief Financial Officer, Brian Naish
Tel: 613-748-2958
Chief Risk Officer, Remy Bowers
Tel: 613-748-2818
Senior Vice-President, Human Resources, Marie-Claude Tremblay
Tel: 613-748-2082
Senior Vice-President, Capital Markets, Wojciech (Wojo) Zielonka
Tel: 613-748-2012
Vice President, Afforadable Housing, Carla Staresina
Vice President, Insurance Operations, Glen Trevisani
Tel: 613-748-4049
Vice-President, Audit, Nadine Leblanc

Regional Business Centres

Atlantic Region
Barrington Tower, 9th Fl., 1894 Barrington St., Halifax, NS B3J 2A8
Tel: 902-426-3530; *Fax:* 902-426-9991
TTY: 800-309-3388

General Manager, Audrey Moritz
Tel: 902-426-1813
Principal, Marketing, Info & Communications, Caroline Arsenault
Tel: 902-426-8127

British Columbia
#2000, 1111 West Georgia St., Vancouver, BC V6E 4M3
Tel: 604-731-5733; *Fax:* 604-737-4139
TTY: 800-309-3388

Regional Vice-President, Caroline Sanfaçon

Ontario
#300, 100 Sheppard Ave. East, Toronto, ON M2N 6Z1
Tel: 416-221-2642; *Fax:* 416-218-3310
Toll-Free: 866-389-1742
TTY: 800-309-3388

Regional Vice-President, Christina Haddad
Tel: 416-218-3300

Prairie & Territories Region
#200, 1000 - 7 Ave. SW, Calgary, AB T2P 5L5
Tel: 403-515-3000; *Fax:* 403-515-2930
Toll-Free: 877-499-7245
TTY: 800-309-3388

Regional Vice-President, Prairie & Territories Business Centre, Fatima Barros

Québec
1100, boul René-Levesque ouest, 1er étage, Montréal, QC H3B 5J7
Tél: 514-283-2222
Ligne sans frais: 888-772-0772
TTY: 800-309-3388

General Manager, Isabelle Bougie
Tel: 514-283-3023

Canada Pension Plan Investment Board / Office d'investissement du Régime de pensions du Canada

#2500, 1 Queen St. East, Toronto, ON M5C 2W5
Tel: 416-868-4075; *Fax:* 416-868-8689
Toll-Free: 866-557-9510
contact@cppib.com
www.cppib.ca
twitter.com/cppib
www.linkedin.com/company/23230
www.youtube.com/user/CPPIB

The CPP Investment Board is a Crown corporation created as part of 1997 reforms designed to ensure the soundness & sustainability of the CPP. The Board operates under similar investment rules as other pension plans in Canada, which require the prudent management of pension plan assets in the interests of plan contributors & beneficiaries.

Chair, Board of Directors, Heather Munroe-Blum

President & CEO, Mark Machin
Senior Managing Director & Head of International; President, CPPIB Asia Inc., Vacant
Senior Managing Director & Global Head, Private Investments, Mark Jenkins
Senior Managing Director, General Counsel & Corporate Secretary, Patrice Walch-Watson
Senior Managing Director & Global Head, Real Estate Investments, Graeme Eadie
Senior Managing Director & Global Head, Investment Partnerships & Chief Talent Officer, Pierre Lavallée
Senior Managing Director & Global Head, Public Affairs & Communications, Michel Leduc
Senior Managing Director & Chief Investment Strategist, Edwin D. Cass
Senior Managing Director & Chief Financial Officer, Benita M. Warmbold
Senior Managing Director & Global Head, Public Market Investments, Eric M. Wetlaufer
Senior Managing Director & Chief Operations Officer, Nicholas Zelenczuk

Canada Place Corporation / Corporation Place du Canada

100 The Pointe, 999 Canada Place, Vancouver, BC V6C 3T4
Tel: 604-775-7063
www.canadaplace.ca
Other Communication: Media Phone: 604-665-9267
twitter.com/canadaplace
www.facebook.com/CanadaPlace
www.youtube.com/user/CanadaPlaceCorp

The Corporation, which merged with Port Metro Vancouver, is the landlord & in charge of property management at Canada Place in Vancouver, which includes a cruise ship facility, a trade & convention centre, a hotel, an IMAX theatre, & a parking structure

Canada Post Corporation / Société canadienne des postes

Corporate Secretariat, 2701 Riverside Dr., Ottawa, ON K1A 0B1
Tel: 416-979-3033
Toll-Free: 866-607-6301
TTY: 800-267-2797
www.canadapost.ca
Other Communication: Postal Security, Phone: 1-800-267-1177

Federal commercial Crown corporation responsible for Canada's postal system. Reports to government through the Minister of Transportation. For postal rates, codes, abbreviations & other general information; see Postal Information in the main Index.

Minister Reponsible; Minister, Public Services & Procurement, Hon. Judy Foote, P.C., B.A., B.Ed
Tel: 613-992-8655; *Fax:* 613-992-5324
Judy.Foote@parl.gc.ca
Chair, Siân M. Matthews
President & Chief Executive Officer, Deepak Chopra
Group President, Physical Delivery Network, Jacques Côté
Chief Financial Officer, Wayne Cheeseman
Senior Vice-President, Parcels, René Desmarais
Senior Vice-President, Strategy & Corporate Marketing, Leonard Diplock
Senior Vice-President, Delivery & Customer Experience, Douglas Jones
Chief Human Resources Officer, Scott G. McDonald
Chief Operating Officer, Mary Traversy
Chief Information Technology Officer, André Turgeon
Vice-President, Engineering, Bill Davidson
Vice-President, Operations Integration, Manon Fortin
Vice-President, Pension Fund & Chief Investment Officer, Douglas Greaves
Vice-President, Marketing & Commercial Products, Bill Gunton
Vice-President, Human Resources, Ann Therese MacEachern
Vice-President, Finance & Comptroller, Barbara MacKenzie
Vice-President, Government Relations & Policy, Susan Margles
Vice-President, Sales, Serge Pitre
Vice-President, Communications & Public Affairs, Jo-Anne Polak
Vice-President, Operations, Brian Wilson

ePost / Postel

#1300, 393 University Ave., Toronto, ON M5G 2P7
Toll-Free: 877-376-1212
epoinfo@canadapost.ca

Office of the Ombudsman / Bureau de l'ombudsman

PO Box 90026 Ottawa, ON K1V 1J8
Fax: 800-204-4193
Toll-Free: 800-204-4198
www.ombudsman.postescanadapost.ca

Ombudsman, Nabil R. Allaf

Canada Post Communications Offices

Atlantic Division
6175 Almon St., Halifax, NS B3K 5N2
Tel: 902-494-4711

Greater Toronto Area & Regions
4567 Dixie Rd., Mississauga, ON L4W 1S2
Tel: 905-214-9595; *Fax:* 905-214-9244

Huron Division
951 Highbury Ave., London, ON N5Y 1B0
Tel: 519-457-5362; *Fax:* 519-457-5346

Pacific Division
349 West Georgia St., PO Box 2110 Stn. STN Terminal, Vancouver, BC V6B 4Z3
Tel: 604-662-1606

Prairie Division
#1300, 10020 - 101A Ave., Edmonton, AB T5J 4J4
Tel: 780-944-3137; *Fax:* 780-944-3140
Secondary Address: #409, 266 Graham Ave.
Winnipeg Office:
Winnipeg, MB R3C 0K0
Alt. Fax: 204-987-5110

Québec Division
#503, 300, rue St-Paul, Québec, QC G1K 3W0
Tel: 418-694-3161; *Fax:* 418-694-6993
Secondary Address: #1506, 555, rue McArthur
Montréal Office:
Saint-Laurent, QC H4T 1T4
Alt. Fax: 514-345-4307

Canada Revenue Agency (CRA) / Agence du revenu du Canada

875 Heron Rd., Ottawa, ON K1A 1A2
Toll-Free: 800-267-6999
TTY: 800-665-0354
www.cra-arc.gc.ca
Other Communication: Individual Income Tax Enquiries: 1-800-959-8281; Telerefund: 1-800-959-1956; Business & Self-Employed Individuals: 1-800-959-5525; GST/HST Credit: 1-800-959-1953
twitter.com/canrevagency
www.youtube.com/canrevagency

The Canada Revenue Agency administers tax laws for the Canadian federal government & for most provincial & territorial governments. The Agency is also responsible for various social & economic benefit & incentive programs, which are delivered through the tax system.

Minister, National Revenue, Hon. Diane Lebouthillier, P.C.
Tel: 613-992-6188; *Fax:* 613-992-6194
Diane.Lebouthillier@parl.gc.ca
Parliamentary Secretary, Emmanuel Dubourg
Tel: 613-995-6108; *Fax:* 613-995-9755
Emmanuel.Dubourg@parl.gc.ca
Commissioner & Chief Executive Officer, Andrew Treusch
Tel: 613-957-3688; *Fax:* 613-952-1547
Chief of Staff to the Minister, Josée Guilmette
Tel: 613-995-2960; *Fax:* 613-952-6608
Chief of Staff to the Commissioner, Sheriff Abdou
Tel: 613-957-3688; *Fax:* 613-952-1547

Appeals Branch / Direction générale des appels

Assistant Commissioner, Anne-Marie Lévesque
Tel: 613-960-2388; *Fax:* 613-952-5965
Director General, Program Management & Analysis Directorate, Lynn Atkinson
Tel: 613-960-2374; *Fax:* 613-952-4281
Director General, Tax & Charities Appeals Directorate, Catherine Letellier de St-Just
Tel: 613-960-2308; *Fax:* 613-941-8088
Director General, Taxpayer Relief & Service Complaints Directorate, Joanne Pellerin-Dunbar
Tel: 613-960-2232; *Fax:* 613-952-5825

Assessment & Benefit Services Branch / Direction générale des services de cotisation et de prestations

Assistant Commissioner, Frank Vermaeten
Tel: 613-941-5007; *Fax:* 613-954-4434
Deputy Assistant Commissioner, Cynthia Leblanc
Tel: 613-954-6614
Director General, Individual Returns Directorate, Clément Bouchard
Tel: 613-957-7497; *Fax:* 613-941-2090
Director General, Benefit Programs Directorate, Nathalie Dumais
Tel: 613-957-9338; *Fax:* 613-946-6719
Director General, Business Returns Directorate, Josée Dussault
Tel: 613-954-7979; *Fax:* 613-941-8539
Director General, Horizontal Integration Directorate, Michael Honcoop
Tel: 613-954-5755; *Fax:* 613-957-3365

Audit, Evaluation & Risk Branch / Direction générale de la vérification, de l'évaluation et des risques

Assistant Commissioner & Chief Audit Executive, Brian Philbin
Tel: 613-670-9375; *Fax:* 613-952-0512

Collections & Verifications Branch / Direction Générale des Recouvrements et de la Vérification

Assistant Commissioner, Michael Snaauw
Tel: 613-954-1269; *Fax:* 613-952-6395
Deputy Assistant Commissioner, Mireille Laroche
Tel: 613-957-8174; *Fax:* 613-952-6395
Director General, Technology & Business Intelligence Directorate, Enikö Vermes
Tel: 613-957-1863; *Fax:* 613-960-0340
Director General, Branch Management Services Directorate, Vacant
Director General, Collections Directorate, Vacant
Director General, Debt Management Compliance Directorate, Kevin McKenzie
Tel: 613-954-1284; *Fax:* 613-954-2243

Compliance Programs Branch / Programmes d'observation de la législation

Fax: 613-952-6772

Assistant Commissioner, Terrance I. McAuley
Tel: 613-957-3709; *Fax:* 613-952-6772
Acting Assistant Commissioner, Richard Montroy
Tel: 613-957-3709; *Fax:* 613-952-6772
Assistant Commissioner, Ted Gallivan
Tel: 613-946-9684; *Fax:* 613-952-6772
Director General, International & Large Business Directorate, Lisa Anawati
Tel: 613-952-7425; *Fax:* 613-941-9673
Director General, Small & Medium Enterprises Directorate, Susan Betts
Tel: 613-946-3447; *Fax:* 613-957-3623
Acting Director General, Small & Medium Enterprises Directorate, Marianne Fitzgerald
Tel: 613-941-6756; *Fax:* 613-957-3623
Director General, Business Intelligence & Corporate Management Directorate, Martin Leigh
Tel: 613-941-5126; *Fax:* 613-960-0328
Other Communications: Alternate Telephone: 613-791-6880
Director General, Business Intelligence & Corporate Management Directorate, Maria Pagliarello
Tel: 613-941-5126; *Fax:* 613-960-0328
Senior Advisor/Director General, Internal & Large Business Directorate, Jeff Sadrian
Tel: 613-941-0410
Director General, GST/HST Directorate, Girish Shah
Tel: 613-948-4581; *Fax:* 613-957-3622
Director General, Criminal Investigations Directorate, Johanne Charbonneau
Tel: 613-957-3648; *Fax:* 613-941-9609

Finance & Administration Branch / Direction générale des finances et de l'administration

Assistant Commissioner & Chief Financial Officer, Roch Huppé
Tel: 613-946-1763; *Fax:* 613-948-5776
Assistant Commissioner & Agency Comptroller, Johanne Bernard
Tel: 613-948-5240; *Fax:* 613-948-5776
Director General, Security & Internal Affairs Directorate, Dana-Lynne Hills
Tel: 613-948-2449; *Fax:* 613-952-2019
Director General, Financial Administration Directorate, Annie Boudreau
Tel: 613-957-7343; *Fax:* 613-952-3087
Director General, Resource Management Directorate, Janique Caron
Tel: 613-957-7339; *Fax:* 613-954-4199
Director General, Administration Directorate, Roger Houde
Tel: 613-947-3262; *Fax:* 613-941-2264
Acting Director General, Real Property & Service Integration Directorate, Lisa Lafosse
Tel: 613-670-8889; *Fax:* 613-998-6414
Director General, Strategic Management & Program Support Directorate, Michael K. Walker
Tel: 613-957-7502; *Fax:* 613-957-7613

Human Resources Branch / Direction générale des ressources humaines

Fax: 613-957-2306

Assistant Commissioner, Diane Lorenzato
Tel: 613-954-8200

Deputy Assistant Commissioner, Dan Couture
Tel: 613-946-4527; *Fax:* 613-952-8557

Employment Programs Directorate / Direction des programmes d'emploi
Director General, Roxanne Descoteaux
Tel: 613-954-1623; *Fax:* 613-954-4194

Executive Personnel Programs Directorate / Direction des programmes pour les cadres de direction

Human Resources Operations Directorate / Direction des opérations des ressources humaines
Director General, Geneviève Béland
Tel: 613-670-9260; *Fax:* 613-946-4513

Strategic Business Integration Directorate / Direction de l'intégration stratégique d'affaire
Director General, Nathalie Kachulis
Tel: 613-954-8166

Training & Learning Directorate / Direction de la formation et de l'apprentissage
Director General, Karen Butcher
Tel: 613-670-9164

Workplace Relations & Compensation Directorate / Direction des relations en milieu de travail et de la rémunération
Director General, Claude P. Tremblay
Tel: 613-954-8150

Information Technology Branch / Direction générale de l'informatique
Fax: 613-957-9058
Assistant Commissioner & Chief Information Officer, Annette Butikofer
Tel: 613-946-6494; *Fax:* 613-960-5683
Deputy Assistant Commissioner, Solutions, Keith Barrass
Tel: 613-941-4250; *Fax:* 613-946-6103
Deputy Assistant Commissioner, Corporate Systems & Support, Vacant
Acting Director General, Branch Business Management Directorate, Denis Lafrenière
Tel: 613-946-9473; *Fax:* 613-946-4992
Director General, Data & Business Intelligence Directorate, Marc Butler
Tel: 613-948-0396
Director General, Solutions Architecture & Integration Directorate, François Dicaire
Tel: 613-946-9405; *Fax:* 613-954-9222
Director General, Compliance & Debt Management Directorate, Brett Hodges
Tel: 613-952-6742; *Fax:* 613-952-8141
Director General, Individual Returns & Benefits Directorate, Guy Mathieu
Tel: 613-941-1250; *Fax:* 613-941-2626
Director General, Branch Business Management Directorate, Denis Lafrenière
Tel: 613-946-9473; *Fax:* 613-946-4992
Director General, Business & Enterprise Solutions Directorate, France Bilodeau
Tel: 613-952-2658; *Fax:* 613-948-4315
Director General, Systems Integrity Directorate, Santo Scarfo
Tel: 613-948-0814; *Fax:* 613-948-1000
Director General, Corporate Enterprise Solutions Directorate, Lyne Sincennes
Tel: 613-954-9039
Director General, Revenue & Accounting Systems Directorate, Robert Stanzel
Tel: 613-952-2658

Legal Services Branch / Direction générale des services juridiques
Fax: 613-954-6282
Senior General Counsel, Richard Gobeil
Tel: 613-957-2358; *Fax:* 613-957-2371

Legislative Policy & Regulatory Affairs / Politiques législatives et affaires réglementaires
Assistant Commissioner, Geoff Trueman
Tel: 613-957-3708; *Fax:* 613-957-2067
Director General, Legislative Policy Directorate, Costa Dimitrakopoulos
Tel: 613-670-9560; *Fax:* 613-954-0896
Director General, Registered Plans Directorate, Michael Godwin
Tel: 613-954-0933; *Fax:* 613-952-1343
Director General, Charities Directorate, Cathy Hawara
Tel: 613-670-9570; *Fax:* 613-954-2586
Director General, Excise & GST/HST Rulings Directorate, Danielle Laflèche
Tel: 613-948-4398; *Fax:* 613-941-4451
Acting Director General, Income Tax Rulings Directorate, Randy Hewlett
Tel: 613-670-9058; *Fax:* 613-957-2088

Public Affairs Branch / Direction générale des affaires publiques
Assistant Commissioner, PAB & Chief Privacy Officer, Susan Gardner-Barclay
Tel: 613-957-3508; *Fax:* 613-954-7955
Director General, Ministerial Services & Operations Directorate, Louise Dorval
Tel: 613-957-8438; *Fax:* 613-941-0914
Director General, Communications Directorate, Jane Hazel
Tel: 613-948-4847

Strategy & Integration Branch / Direction generale de la stratégie et de l'intégration
Assistant Commissioner, Yves Giroux
Tel: 613-952-3660; *Fax:* 613-941-3438
Director General, Agency Strategy & Reporting Directorate, Ann Marie Hume
Tel: 613-954-6082; *Fax:* 613-952-0061
Director General, Agency Change & Innovation Directorate, Mireille Éthier
Tel: 613-957-7623; *Fax:* 613-954-5885
Director General, Information & Relationship Management Directorate, Wayne Lepine
Tel: 613-941-9964; *Fax:* 613-941-0181
Director General, Intelligence, Statistics & Data Directorate, Patricia Whitridge
Tel: 613-957-8706; *Fax:* 613-952-6715

Tax Services Offices
Toll-Free: 800-959-8281
TTY: 800-665-0354
Other Communication: For Business or Self-Employed, Toll-Free: 1-800-959-5525

Atlantic Region
Bathurst
201 George St., PO Box 8888 Bathurst, NB E2A 4L8
Fax: 506-548-7176
Toll-Free: 800-959-8281

Charlottetown
161 St. Peters Rd., PO Box 8500 Charlottetown, PE C1A 8L3
Fax: 902-566-7197

Halifax (Nova Scotia)
Ralston Bldg., 1557 Hollis St., PO Box 638 Halifax, NS B3J 2T5
Fax: 902-426-7170

Moncton
Assumption Place, #217, 770 Main St., PO Box 1070 Moncton, NB E1C 8P2
Fax: 506-851-7018

St. John's (Newfoundland & Labrador)
Sir Humphrey Gilbert Building, 165 Duckworth St., PO Box 12075 St. John's, NL A1B 4R5
Fax: 709-754-5928

Saint John
126 Prince William St., Saint John, NB E2L 4H9
Fax: 506-636-5200

Sydney
47 Dorchester St., PO Box 1300 Sydney, NS B1P 6K3
Fax: 902-564-3095

Pacific Region
Burnaby-Fraser
9755 King George Blvd., Surrey, BC V3T 5E1
Fax: 604-587-2010

Kelowna (Southern Interior)
#100, 1620 Dickson Ave., Kelowna, BC V1Y 9Y2
Fax: 250-492-8346

Prince George (Northern BC & Yukon)
280 Victoria St., Prince George, BC V2L 4X3
Fax: 250-561-7869

Penticton (Southern Interior)
277 Winnipeg St., Penticton, BC V2A 1N6
Fax: 250-492-8346

Vancouver
1166 West Pender St., Vancouver, BC V6E 3H8
Fax: 604-689-7536

Victoria (Vancouver Island)
1415 Vancouver St., Victoria, BC V8V 3W4
Fax: 250-363-8188

Prairie Region
Brandon
#210, 153 - 11th St., Brandon, MB R7A 7K6
Fax: 204-726-7868

Calgary
220 - 4 Ave. SE, Calgary, AB T2G 0L1
Fax: 403-264-5843

Edmonton
#10, 9700 Jasper Ave., Edmonton, AB T5J 4C8
Fax: 780-495-3533

Lethbridge
#200, 419 - 7 St. South, PO Box 3009 Stn. Main, Lethbridge, AB T1J 4A9
Fax: 403-382-4765

Red Deer
4996 - 49 Ave., Red Deer, AB T4N 6X2
Fax: 403-341-7053

Regina
#260, 1783 Hamilton St., PO Box 557 Regina, SK S4P 3A3
Fax: 306-757-1412

Saskatoon
340 - 3rd Ave. North, Saskatoon, SK S7K 0A8
Fax: 306-652-3211

Winnipeg
325 Broadway, Winnipeg, MB R3C 4T4
Fax: 204-984-5164

Ontario Region
Barrie
81 Mulcaster St., Barrie, ON L4M 6T7
Fax: 705-721-0056

Belleville (East Central Ontario)
11 Station St., Belleville, ON K8N 2S3
Fax: 613-969-7845

Hamilton (Hamilton Niagara)
55 Bay St., PO Box 2220 Hamilton, ON L8N 3E1
Fax: 905-546-1615

Kingston (East Central Ontario)
31 Hyperion Ct., PO Box 2600 Kingston, ON K7L 5P3
Fax: 613-545-3272

Kitchener-Waterloo
166 Frederick St., Kitchener, ON N2H 0A9
Fax: 519-579-4532

London
451 Talbot St., London, ON N6A 5E5
Fax: 519-645-4029

Ottawa & Nunavut
333 Laurier Ave. West, Ottawa, ON K1A 0L9
Fax: 613-238-7125

Ottawa Technology Centre
875 Heron Rd., Ottawa, ON K1A 1A2
Fax: 613-739-1147

Peterborough (East Central Ontario)
1161 Crawford Dr., Peterborough, ON K9J 6X6

St Catharines (Hamilton Niagara)
32 Church St., St Catharines, ON L2R 3B9
Fax: 905-688-5996

Sudbury
1050 Notre Dame Ave., Sudbury, ON P3A 5C1
Fax: 705-671-3994

Thunder Bay
130 South Syndicate Ave., Thunder Bay, ON P7E 1C7
Fax: 807-622-8512

Toronto Centre
1 Front St. West, Toronto, ON M5J 2X6
Fax: 416-360-8908
Other Communication: Non-Resident Tax/Regulation, Fax: 416-954-8528

Toronto East
200 Town Centre Ct., Toronto, ON M1P 4Y3
Fax: 416-973-5126

Toronto North
5001 Yonge St., Toronto, ON M2N 6R9
Fax: 416-512-2558
Other Communication: Non-Resident Tax/Regulation, Fax: 416-954-8528

Toronto West
5800 Hurontario St., Mississauga, ON L5R 4B4
Fax: 905-566-6182

Windsor
185 Ouellette Ave., Windsor, ON N9A 5S8
Fax: 519-257-6558

Québec Region
Brossard (Montérégie-Rive-Sud)
3250, boul Lapinière, Brossard, QC J4Z 3T8
Téléc: 450-926-7100

Chicoutimi (Est-du-Québec)
CP 1600 Succ Bureau-chef, Jonquière, QC G7S 4L3
Téléc: 418-698-6387
Autres nombres: Adresse du bureau: 100, rue La Fontaine, Chicoutimi, QC G7H 6X2

Gatineau (Outaouais et Rouyn-Noranda)
85, ch de La Savane, Gatineau, QC K1A 1L4
Téléc: 819-994-1103

Laval
3400, av Jean-Béraud, Laval, QC H7T 2Z2
Téléc: 514-496-1309

Montréal
305, boul René-Lévesque ouest, Montréal, QC H2Z 1A6
Téléc: 514-496-1309

Québec
165, rue de la Pointe-aux-Lièvres sud, Québec, QC G1K 5Y8
Téléc: 418-649-6478

Rimouski
#101, 180, av de la Cathédrale, Rimouski, QC G5L 5H9
Téléc: 418-722-3027

Rouyn-Noranda (Outaouais et Rouyn-Noranda)
44, av du Lac, Rouyn-Noranda, QC J9X 6Z9
Téléc: 819-797-8366

Sherbrooke
50, Place de la Cité, CP 1300 Sherbrooke, QC J1H 5L8
Téléc: 819-821-8582

Trois-Rivières
2250, rue St-Olivier, Trois-Rivières, QC G9A 4E9
Téléc: 819-371-2744

Canada School of Public Service (CCMD) / École de la fonction publique du Canada (EEPC)

373 Sussex Dr., Ottawa, ON K1N 6Z2
Tel: 819-953-5400; *Fax:* 866-944-0454
Toll-Free: 866-703-9598
info@csps-efpc.gc.ca
www.csps-efpc.gc.ca
Other Communication: Media, Phone: 613-996-2744; E-mail: media@csps-efpc.gc.ca
twitter.com/School_GC
www.linkedin.com/company/canada-school-of-public-service

Learning provider for the Public Service of Canada. The School brings together three well-established federal public service learning organizations: the Canadian Centre for Management Development, & from the Public Service Commission, Training & Development Canada & Language Training Canada. Contributes to building & maintaining a modern, high-quality, professional public service that is at the leading-edge of knowledge in modern public administration & public sector management. Through up-to-date adult learning techniques, it provides public servants across the country with access to the common learning opportunities they require to effectively serve Canada & Canadians

Minister Responsible; President, Treasury Board, Hon. Scott Brison, P.C., B.Comm.
Tel: 613-995-8231; *Fax:* 613-996-9349
scott.brison@parl.gc.ca
Deputy Minister & President, Wilma Vreeswijk
Tel: 613-992-8165; *Fax:* 613-943-1038
President Emeritus, Jocelyne Bourgon
Tel: 613-943-4311; *Fax:* 613-947-3130
Vice-President, Learning Programs, Jean-François Fleury
Tel: 613-992-8346; *Fax:* 613-992-3663
Vice-President, Strategic Directions & Service Excellence, Catherine MacQuarrie
Tel: 613-943-0321; *Fax:* 613-947-3706
Other Communications: Executive Assistant, Phone: 613-943-4296
Vice-President & Chief Financial Officer, Corporate Services, Danielle May-Cuconato
Tel: 613-943-8917
Director General, Registrar & Service Excellence, René Bouchard
Tel: 613-996-5489; *Fax:* 613-947-3706
Director General, Leadership & Professional Development, David Henley
Tel: 613-943-5607; *Fax:* 613-947-3130
Administrative & Financial Control Officer, Human Resources & Workplace Management, Denis Galarneau
Tel: 613-797-9022; *Fax:* 613-995-0331
Director General, Functional Communities, Authority Delegation & Orientation, Joanne Lalonde
Tel: 819-934-7692
Other Communications: Executive Assistant, Phone: 613-295-7355
Acting Senior Director, Regional Operations, Language Training & Business Development, Marta Anderson
Tel: 613-943-0153; *Fax:* 613-992-3663
Senior Director, Executive Leadership & Transformation, Annie Champagne
Tel: 819-956-7945; *Fax:* 819-953-7298
Senior Director, Regional Operations, Language Training & Business Development, John Prentice
Tel: 819-994-4970
Senior Director, Marketing, Communications & Parliamentary Affairs, Marc Sanderson
Tel: 613-943-4304; *Fax:* 613-943-5651

Canada Science & Technology Museum Corporation (CSTM) / Musée des sciences et de la technologie du Canada (MSTC)

PO Box 9724 Stn. T, Ottawa, ON K1G 5A3
Tel: 613-991-3044; *Fax:* 613-993-7923
cts@techno-science.ca
techno-science.ca

The Corporation is the only comprehensive science & technology collecting institution in Canada, & focuses on the following major subject areas: aviation, communications, manufacturing, natural resources, renewable resources including agriculture, scientific instrumentation, & transportation. The Corporation operates three Museums: the Canada Agriculture Museum, the Canada Aviation Museum & the Canada Science & Technology Museum.

President & Chief Operating Officer, Alex Benay
Vice-President, Collection, Research & Corporate Governance, Monique Horth
Tel: 613-991-9508

Canadian Broadcasting Corporation (CBC) / Société Radio-Canada (SRC)

181 Queen St., PO Box 3220 Stn. C, Ottawa, ON K1Y 1E4
Tel: 613-288-6000
TTY: 613-288-6455
liaison@cbc.ca
www.cbc.radio-canada.ca
Other Communication: Toll Free: 1-866-306-4636
twitter.com/CBCRadioCanada
www.facebook.com/CBCRadioCanada

The Canadian Broadcasting Corporation (CBC) is a Crown corporation governed by the 1991 Broadcasting Act & subject to regulations of the Canadian Radio-television & Telecommunications Commission (CRTC). The CBC operates four national radio networks, CBC Radio One & CBC Radio Two in English, & ICI Radio-Canada Première & Espace musique in French, featuring information & general interest programs as well as classical music & cultural programs; two self-supporting specialty cable television services, CBC News Network in English & Ici RDI in French, which feature news & information programs 24 hours a day, seven days a week; & radio & television services for Canada's North in English, French & eight aboriginal languages. CBC also provides, on behalf of the Government of Canada, an online multilingual service called Radio Canada International (formerly a shortwave radio service), which publishes content in five languages.

Chair, Board of Directors, Rémi Racine
President & Chief Executive Officer, Hubert T. Lacroix
Executive Vice-President, English Services, Heather Conway
Executive Vice-President, French Services, Louis Lalonde
Vice-President, Legal Services, General Counsel & Corporate Secretary, Sylvie Gadoury
Vice-President, People & Culture, Josée Girard
Executive Vice-President, Media Technology & Infrastructure Services, Steven Guiton
Vice-President, Strategy & Public Affairs, Alex Johnston
Executive Vice-President & CFO, Judith Purves

CBC/Radio-Canada - English Services

PO Box 500 Stn. A, Toronto, ON M5W 1E6
Toll-Free: 866-306-4636
TTY: 866-220-6045
www.cbc.radio-canada.ca

CBC/Radio-Canada - French Services / ICI Radio-Canada

1400, boul René-Lévesque Est, CP 6000 Succ Centre-ville, Montréal, QC H3C 3A8
Tél: 514-597-6000
Ligne sans frais: 866-306-4636
TTY: 514-597-6013
www.radio-canada.ca
twitter.com/CBCRadioCanada
www.facebook.com/CBCRadioCanada
www.linkedin.com/grp/home?gid=2280703
instagram.com/cbcradiocanada

CBC/Radio-Canada - Ombudsmen

www.ombudsman.cbc.radio-canada.ca

Ombudsman, CBC, English Services, Esther Enkin
Tel: 416-205-2978; *Fax:* 416-205-2825
ombudsman@cbc.ca
Social Media: twitter.com/CBCOmbudsman
PO Box 500 A Sta.
Toronto, ON M5W 1E6

Ombudsman, Radio-Canada, French Services, Guy Gendron
Tél: 514-597-4757
Ligne sans frais: 877-846-4737; *Téléc:* 514-597-5253
ombudsman@radio-canada.ca
Les réseaux sociaux: twitter.com/ombudsmanrc
PO Box 6000
Montreal, QC H3C 3A8

Radio Canada International

1400, boul René-Lévesque est, CP 6000 Montréal, QC H2L 2M2
Tél: 514-597-7461
info@rcinet.ca
www.rcinet.ca
twitter.com/RCInet
www.facebook.com/rcinet

Radio Canada International was transitioned to an online-only service in 2012. It now produces online content in five languages: English, French, Spanish, Arabic & Chinese. The aim of RCInet.ca is to produce programs for people who know little or nothing about Canada, & to accomplish this the service publishes a variety of interviews, feature reports, columns, news, a current affairs blog & a multimedia section.

CBC Regional Offices

Alberta (English & French)
123 Edmonton City Centre, 10062 - 102nd Ave., PO Box 555 Edmonton, AB T5J 2P4
Tel: 780-468-7500
www.cbc.ca/edmonton/contact

Atlantic Provinces (French Services) / Radio-Canada Acadie
#15, 165, rue Main, Moncton, NB E1C 1B8
Tel: 506-853-6666
www.cbc.ca/nb/contact

British Columbia (English & French)
700 Hamilton St., PO Box 4600 Vancouver, BC V6B 4A2
Tel: 604-662-6000
Toll-Free: 866-306-4636
www.cbc.ca/bc/contact

CBC North
PO Box 160 Yellowknife, NT X1A 2N2
Tel: 867-920-5400
www.cbc.ca/north/contact

CBC North also operates offices in the Yukon (867-668-8400), Nunavut (867-979-6100), & Québec (1-877-597-4369).

Canadian Broadcasting Centre
PO Box 500 Stn. A, Toronto, ON M5W 1E6
Tel: 416-205-3311
www.cbc.ca/toronto/contact

Manitoba (English & French)
541 Portage Ave., Winnipeg, MB R3B 2G1
Tel: 204-788-3222
TTY: 866-220-6045
www.cbc.ca/manitoba/contact

Maritimes (English)
PO Box 3000 Halifax, NS B3J 3E9
Tel: 902-420-8311
www.cbc.ca/ns/contact

Newfoundland (English)
PO Box 12010 Stn. A, St. John's, NL A1B 3T8
Tel: 709-576-5000
www.cbc.ca/nl/contact

Ottawa Production Centre
181 Queen St., PO Box 3220 Stn. C, Ottawa, ON K1Y 1E4
Tel: 613-288-6000
www.cbc.ca/ottawa/contact

Prince Edward Island (English & French)
430 University Ave., PO Box 2230 Charlottetown, PE C1A 8B9
Tel: 902-629-6400
www.cbc.ca/pei/contact

Québec (English) / Maison de Radio-Canada
CP 6000 Montréal, QC H3C 3A8
Tél: 514-597-6000
www.cbc.ca/montreal/contact

Québec (French) / Société Radio-Canada
CP 18800 Québec, QC G1K 9L4

Saskatchewan (English & French)
2440 Broad St., Regina, SK S4P 4A1
Tel: 306-347-9540
www.cbc.ca/sask/contact

Canadian Centre for Occupational Health & Safety (CCOHS) / Centre canadien d'hygiène et de sécurité au travail (CCHST)

135 Hunter St. East, Hamilton, ON L8N 1M5
Tel: 905-572-2981; *Fax:* 905-572-4500
Toll-Free: 800-668-4284
www.ccohs.ca
twitter.com/ccohs
www.facebook.com/CCOHS
www.youtube.com/ccohs

Provides occupational health & safety & environmental information in the form of publications, responses to inquiries & a computerized information service available in various formats. Topics include: environmental acts & regulations; occupational & environmental health data; toxic effects of chemical substances; transport of dangerous goods; chemical evaluation; hazardous substances; & domestic substances listed under the Canadian Environmental Protection Act; biological hazards; ergonomics

Acting Chair, Council of Governors, Leslie Galway
Acting President & CEO; Vice-President, Operations, Gareth Jones
Tel: 905-572-2981 ext: 453
Chief Financial Officer; Vice-President, Finance, Frank Leduc
Tel: 905-572-2981 ext: 440
Director, Marketing Communications, Lynda Brown
Tel: 905-572-2981 ext: 447

Canadian Centre on Substance Abuse (CCSA) / Centre canadien de lutte contre l'alcoolisme et les toxicomanies (CCLAT)

#500, 75 Albert St., Ottawa, ON K1P 5E7
Tel: 613-235-4048; *Fax:* 613-235-8101
info@ccsa.ca
www.ccsa.ca
Other Communication: Publications, Email: publications@ccsa.ca
twitter.com/CCSAcanada
linkedin.com/company/canadian-centre-on-substance-abusse-ccsa-
www.youtube.com/user/CCSACCLAT

CCSA is a non-profit organization working to minimize the harm associated with the use of alcohol, tobacco, & other drugs.

Interim Chair, Paula Tyler
Tel: 613-235-4048 ext: 232
Chief Executive Officer, Rita Notarandrea
Tel: 613-235-4048 ext: 227
Deputy Chief Executive Officer, Rhowena Martin
Tel: 613-235-4048 ext: 239
Interim Director, Public Affairs & Communications, Wendy Cumming
Tel: 613-235-4048 ext: 276
Director, Strategic Partnerships & Knowledge Mobilization, Robert Eves
Tel: 613-235-4048 ext: 260
Interim Director, Finance, Darwin Ewert
Tel: 613-235-4048 ext: 231
Director, Information Systems & Performance Measurement, Rebecca Jesseman
Tel: 613-235-4048 ext: 228
Director, Human Resources, Darlene Pinto
Tel: 613-235-4048 ext: 254
Director, Research & Policy, Amy Porath-Waller
Tel: 613-235-4048 ext: 252

Canadian Commercial Corporation (CCC) / Corporation commerciale canadienne

#700, 350 Albert St., Ottawa, ON K1A 0S6
Tel: 613-996-0034; *Fax:* 613-995-2121
Toll-Free: 800-748-8191
communications@ccc.ca
www.ccc.ca

A Crown Corporation mandated to facilitate international trade, particularly in government markets. CCC specializes in international procurement markets for Canadian companies & provides services to help them win, negotiate & manage export contracts. As prime contractor, CCC offers a government-to-government agreement that simplifies customer access to Canadian technology & expertise. CCC contracts have a government guarantee for performance.

Interim Chair, Stephen Sorocky
President & Chief Executive Officer, Martin Zablocki
Tel: 613-996-0042; *Fax:* 613-992-2134
Other Communications: Alternate Phone: 613-996-0043
Vice-President, Business Development & Sales, Cameron McKenzie
Tel: 613-943-3719; *Fax:* 613-995-2121
Chief Financial Officer & Vice-President, Corporate Services, Ernie Briard
Tel: 613-995-4658; *Fax:* 613-995-2121
Vice-President, Defence & Contract Management, Jacques Greffe
Tel: 613-996-0161; *Fax:* 613-995-2121
Vice-President, General Counsel & Corporate Secretary, Legal Services, Tamara Parschin-Rybkin, Q.C.
Tel: 613-992-4419; *Fax:* 613-947-3903

Canadian Dairy Commission (CDC) / Commission canadienne du lait (CCL)

Central Experimental Farm, NCC Driveway, Bldg. 55, 960 Carling Ave., Ottawa, ON K1A 0Z2
Tel: 613-792-2000; *Fax:* 613-792-2009
TTY: 613-792-2082
cdc-ccl@cdc-ccl.gc.ca
www.cdc-ccl.gc.ca/CDC/index-eng.php
Other Communication: Special Milk Class Permits, Phone: 613-792-2057; Dairy Imports & Exports, Phone: 613-792-2010

The federal Crown corporation serves the interests of all dairy stakeholders, including producers, processors, further processors, exporters, consumers & governments. The following are the key objectives of the CDC: providing efficient milk & cream producers with the opportunity to obtain a fair return for their labour & investment; & ensuring an adequate supply of high quality dairy products for consumers.

Chair, Alistair Johnston
Chief Executive Officer, Jacques Laforge
Tel: 613-792-2060; *Fax:* 613-792-2064
jlaforge@cdc-ccl.gc.ca
Commissioner, Henricus Bos
Tel: 613-792-2063; *Fax:* 613-792-2064
henricus.bos@cdc-ccl.gc.ca
Director, Audit & Evaluation, Hossein Behzadi
Tel: 613-222-2468; *Fax:* 613-792-2009
hossein.behzadi@cdc-ccl.gc.ca
Director, Finance & Administration, Chantal Laframbois
Tel: 613-792-2056; *Fax:* 613-792-2009
chantal.laframboise@cdc-ccl.gc.ca

Canadian Environmental Assessment Agency (CEAA) / Agence canadienne d'évaluation environnementale (ACEE)

Place Bell Canada, 160 Elgin St., 22nd Fl., Ottawa, ON K1A 0H3
Tel: 613-957-0700; *Fax:* 613-957-0862
Toll-Free: 866-582-1884
info@ceaa-acee.gc.ca
www.ceaa-acee.gc.ca

The Canadian Environmental Assessment Agency (CEAA) was established to administer the Canadian Environmental Assessment Act (the Act). The environmental assessment process identifies the environmental effects of proposed projects & measures to address those effects, in support of sustainable development. CEAA promotes environmental assessment as a tool to protect & sustain a healthy environment in harmony with a growing economy. The CEAA advocates high-quality environmental assessments by assisting federal departments & agencies with training & guidance & by investing in the research & development of best practices. CEAA provides administrative support to mediators & review panels & ensures that the public has opportunities to participate effectively in the environmental assessment process. Public participation strengthens the quality & credibility of environmental assessments by providing local & traditional knowledge, & insight into possible environmental effects. A publicly accessible master index of environmental assessments carried out by federal departments is available in the Canadian Environmental Assessment Registry (projects beginning before November 2003 are available in the Federal Environmental Assessment Index) located on the CEAA we b site. In addition, CEAA's participant funding program provides limited funds to ensure that interested individuals & groups have the opportunity to participate in mediations & panel reviews. Accountable to the Minister of the Environment.

President, Ron Hallman
Tel: 613-948-2671
Ron.Hallman@ceaa-acee.gc.ca
Vice-President, Policy Development, Christine Loth-Bown
Tel: 613-948-2662; *Fax:* 613-957-0897
Vice-President, Operations, Heather Smith
Tel: 613-948-2665; *Fax:* 613-957-0935
heather.smith@ceaa-acee.gc.ca
Director General, Regional Operations Sector, Sylvain Ouellet
Tel: 613-948-2663; *Fax:* 613-957-0935
sylvain.ouellet@ceaa-acee.gc.ca
Vice-President, Corporate Services, Juliet Woodfield
Tel: 613-960-0897
juliet.woodfield@ceaa-acee.gc.ca
Director, National Programs Division, Steve Chapman
Tel: 613-957-0294
steve.chapman@ceaa-acee.gc.ca
Director, Operational Support, Andrée Chevrier
Tel: 613-957-0641; *Fax:* 613-948-1354
andree.chevrier@ceaa-acee.gc.ca
Director, Communications, Kirstan Gagnon
Tel: 613-957-0712
Kirstan.Gagnon@ceaa-acee.gc.ca

Regional Offices

Alberta, Prairie & Northwest Territories
#425, 10115 - 100A St., Edmonton, AB T5J 2W2
Tel: 780-495-2037; *Fax:* 780-495-2876

Atlantic Region
#200, 1801 Hollis St., Halifax, NS B3J 3N4
Tel: 902-426-0564; *Fax:* 902-426-6550

Ontario
#907, 55 St. Clair Ave. East, Toronto, ON M4T 1M2
Tel: 416-952-1576; *Fax:* 416-952-1573

Pacific & Yukon
#410, 701 Georgia St. West, Vancouver, BC V7Y 1K8
Tel: 604-666-2431; *Fax:* 604-666-6990

Québec
#901, 1550, av d'Estimauville, Québec, QC G1J 0C1
Tél: 418-649-6444; *Téléc:* 418-649-6443

Canadian Food Inspection Agency (CFIA) / Agence canadienne d'inspection des aliments (ACIA)

1400 Merivale Rd., Ottawa, ON K1A 0Y9
Tel: 613-225-2342
Toll-Free: 800-442-2342
TTY: 800-465-7735
www.inspection.gc.ca
Other Communication: Atlantic Area, Phone: 506-777-3939; Ontario Area: 226-217-8555; Québec Area: 514-283-8888; Western Area: 587-230-2200
twitter.com/CFIA_food
www.facebook.com/CFIACanada
www.linkedin.com/company/canadian-food-inspection-agency

The agency is responsible for all inspection services related to food safety, economic fraud, trade-related requirements, & animal & plant health programs.

Minister Responsible; Minister, Health, Hon. Jane Philpott, P.C.
Tel: 613-992-3640; *Fax:* 613-992-3642
Jane.Philpott@parl.gc.ca
President, Bruce Archibald
Tel: 613-773-6000
Bruce.Archibald@inspection.gc.ca
Executive Vice-President, Carolina Giliberti
Tel: 613-773-6500; *Fax:* 613-773-6060
Carolina.Giliberti@inspection.gc.ca
Acting Chief of Staff, Merril Bawden
Tel: 613-773-5359
Merril.Bawden@inspection.gc.ca
Chief Food Safety Officer & Vice-President, Science, Dr. Martine Dubuc
Tel: 613-773-5722; *Fax:* 613-773-5797
martine.dubuc@inspection.gc.ca
Director, Strategic Initiatives Division, Plant & Animal Programs, Gregory Wolff
Tel: 613-773-7060
greg.wolff@inspection.gc.ca
Chief Redress Officer of Integrity & Redress Secretariat, Susan Shaw
Tel: 613-773-5400; *Fax:* 613-773-5694
Susan.Shaw@inspection.gc.ca
Chief Financial Officer & Vice-President, Corporate Management, Yves Bacon
Tel: 613-773-5759; *Fax:* 613-773-5792
Yves.Bacon@inspection.gc.ca
Vice-President, Operations, Gérard Étienne
Tel: 613-773-5725; *Fax:* 613-773-5795
Gerard.Etienne@inspection.gc.ca
Vice-President, Communications & Public Affairs, Geneviève Desjardins
Tel: 613-773-5776; *Fax:* 613-773-5559
Genevieve.Desjardins@inspection.gc.ca
Vice-President, Human Resources, Colleen Barnes
Tel: 613-773-5310; *Fax:* 613-773-5795
Colleen.Barnes@inspection.gc.ca
Vice-President, Information Management & Information Technology, Michel Lessard
Tel: 613-773-1395; *Fax:* 613-773-0666
Michel.Lessard@canada.ca

Vice-President, Policy & Programs, Paul Mayers
Tel: 613-773-5747; *Fax:* 613-773-5969
Paul.Mayers@inspection.gc.ca

Associate Vice-President, Policy & Programs, Barbara A. Jordan
Tel: 613-773-5745
Barbara.Jordan@inspection.gc.ca

Acting Executive Director & Senior General Counsel, Legal Services, Louise Sénéchal
Tel: 613-773-5772; *Fax:* 613-773-5670
Louise.Senechal@agr.gc.ca

Executive Director, Audit & Evaluation, Theresa Iuliano
Tel: 613-773-7194
Theresa.Iuliano@inspection.gc.ca

Canadian Grain Commission (CGC) / Commission canadienne des grains (CCG)

#600, 303 Main St., Winnipeg, MB R3C 3G8
Tel: 204-984-0506; *Fax:* 204-983-2751
Toll-Free: 800-853-6705
TTY: 866-317-4289
contact@grainscanada.gc.ca
www.grainscanada.gc.ca
Other Communication: Grain Sanitation & Infestation Control Industry Services, Fax: 204-984-7550; Licensing & Security Unit, Fax: 204-983-4654; Statistics Unit, Phone: 204-983-2739
twitter.com/Grain_Canada
www.youtube.com/user/GrainCommission

The CGC is Canada's official grain quality assurance agency. The CGC offers a wide range of programs & services. It regulates grain handling in Canada & establishes & maintains quality standards for Canadian grains. Responsibilities are as follows: officially inspecting & grading grain; weighing grain at terminal & transfer elevators; licensing grain elevators & dealers; conducting & publishing statistical & economic studies; & performing basic & applied research on Canadian grain.

Acting Chief Commissioner, Jim Smolik
Tel: 204-983-2730; *Fax:* 204-983-2751

Commissioner, Murdoch MacKay
Tel: 204-983-2732; *Fax:* 204-983-2751

Chief Financial Officer, Cheryl Blahey
Tel: 204-984-7042; *Fax:* 204-984-7213

Chief Informatics Officer, Karl Daher
Tel: 204-984-6948; *Fax:* 204-983-0248

Chief Operating Officer, Gordon Miles
Tel: 204-983-2731; *Fax:* 204-983-2751

Director, Human Resources, Michelle Dedieu
Tel: 204-984-7486; *Fax:* 204-983-5382

Director, Industry Services, Nathan Gerelus
Tel: 204-291-3960; *Fax:* 204-983-7550

Director, Grain Research Laboratory, Stefan Wagener
Tel: 204-983-2764; *Fax:* 204-983-0724

Coordinator, Communications, Louise Worster
Tel: 204-983-2748

Canadian Heritage / Patrimoine canadien

15 Eddy St., Gatineau, QC K1A 0M5
Tel: 819-997-0055
Toll-Free: 866-811-0055
TTY: 888-997-3123
PCH.info-info.PCH@canada.ca
www.pch.gc.ca
twitter.com/CdnHeritage
www.facebook.com/CdnHeritage
www.youtube.com/CdnHeritage

Canadian Heritage works to achieve a more cohesive & creative nation. Goals of the department are for Canadians to express & share their cultural experiences with others in their own country & globally & for Canadians to live in an inclusive society with intercultural understanding & citizen participation.
Responsibilities are carried out by the following sectors: Citizenship & Heritage; Cultural Affairs; Sport, Major Events & Regions; & Strategic Policy, Planning & Corporate Affairs.

Minister, Canadian Heritage, Hon. Mélanie Joly, P.C.
Tel: 613-992-0983; *Fax:* 613-992-1932
Melanie.Joly@parl.gc.ca

Minister, Status of Women, Hon. Patricia Hajdu, P.C.
Tel: 613-996-4792; *Fax:* 613-996-9785
Patty.Hajdu@parl.gc.ca

Minister, Sport & Persons with Disabilities, Hon. Carla Qualtrough, P.C.
Tel: 613-992-2957; *Fax:* 613-992-3192
Carla.Qualtrough@parl.gc.ca

Deputy Minister, Graham Flack
Tel: 819-994-1132; *Fax:* 819-997-0979
Graham.Flack@pch.gc.ca

Parliamentary Secretary to the Minister of Canadian Heritage, Randy Boissonnault
Tel: 613-992-4524; *Fax:* 613-943-0044
Randy.Boissonnault@parl.gc.ca

Parliamentary Secretary to the Minister of Status of Women, Anju Dhillon
Tel: 613-995-2251; *Fax:* 613-996-1481
Anju.Dhillon@parl.gc.ca

Parliamentary Secretary to the Minister of Sport & Persons with Disabilities, Stéphane Lauzon
Tel: 613-992-0902; *Fax:* 613-992-2935
Stephane.Lauzon@parl.gc.ca

Director General, Communications, Veronique Deriger
Tel: 819-997-0231; *Fax:* 819-953-5382
veronique.deriger@canada.ca

Associated Agencies, Boards & Commissions:

•Canada Council for the Arts / Conseil des Arts du Canada
See Entry Name Index for detailed listing.

•Canada Science & Technology Museum Corporation / Musée des sciences et de la technologie du Canada
See Entry Name Index for detailed listing.

•Canadian Broadcasting Corporation (CBC) / Société Radio-Canada (SRC)
See Entry Name Index for detailed listing.

•Canadian Museum of History / Musée canadien de l'histoire
See Entry Name Index for detailed listing.

•Canadian Museum of Nature (CMN) / Musée canadien de la nature (MCN)
See Entry Name Index for detailed listing.

•Canadian Radio-television & Telecommunications Commission (CRTC) / Conseil de la radiodiffusion et des télécommunications canadiennes
See Entry Name Index for detailed listing.

•Library & Archives Canada
See Entry Name Index for detailed listing.

•National Arts Centre (NAC) / Centre national des Arts (CNA)
See Entry Name Index for detailed listing.

•National Battlefields Commission / Commission des champs de bataille nationaux
See Entry Name Index for detailed listing.

•National Film Board of Canada / Office national du film du Canada
See Entry Name Index for detailed listing.

•National Gallery of Canada / Musée des Beaux-Arts du Canada
See Entry Name Index for detailed listing.

•Public Service Commission of Canada / Commission de la fonction publique du Canada
See Entry Name Index for detailed listing.

•Status of Women Canada / Condition féminine Canada
See Entry Name Index for detailed listing.

•Telefilm Canada / Téléfilm Canada
See Entry Name Index for detailed listing.

Canadian Secretary to The Queen / Secrétaire canadien de la Reine

427 Laurier St., Ottawa, ON K1A 0M5

The Canadian Secretary to The Queen acts as the primary means of communication between the monarch & the Canadian Government, provincial governments, & the governments of other Commonwealth realms. The Canadian Secretary also drafts speeches the Queen will deliver, chairs (ex-officio) the Advisory Committee on Vice-Regal Appointments, & is responsible for tours of Canada conducted by members of the Royal Family.

Canadian Secretary to The Queen, Kevin MacLeod, CVO, CD
Tel: 613-947-7035

Citizenship & Heritage Sector / Citoyenneté et patrimoine

Assistant Deputy Minister, Hubert Lussier
Tel: 819-997-2832; *Fax:* 819-994-5032
Hubert.Lussier@pch.gc.ca

Director General, Citizen Participation, William Fizet
Tel: 819-953-5999; *Fax:* 819-953-3515
William.Fizet@pch.gc.ca

Director General, Canadian Conservation Institute, Patricia Kell
Tel: 613-998-3721 ext: 115; *Fax:* 613-952-1431
Patricia.Kell@pch.gc.ca

Director, Policy, Research Planning & Regional Affairs, Paul Turcotte
Tel: 819-934-6260
paul.turcotte@canada.ca

Director General, Citizen Participation, Michel Lemay
Tel: 819-953-5999; *Fax:* 819-953-3515
Michel.Lemay@pch.gc.ca

Director, Canadian Heritage Information Network (CHIN), Charlie Costain
Tel: 613-998-3721 ext: 162; *Fax:* 613-998-4721
charlie.costain@canada.ca

Senior Director, Policy & Research, Yvan M. Déry
Tel: 819-994-2224; *Fax:* 819-994-3697
yvan.dery@pch.gc.ca

Regional Offices

Atlantic
#106, 1045 Main St., Moncton, NB E1C 1H1
Tel: 506-851-7066; *Fax:* 506-851-7079
Toll-Free: 866-811-0055
TTY: 888-997-3123
pch-atlan@pch.gc.ca

Regional Executive Director, Paul Landry
Tel: 506-851-7069; *Fax:* 506-851-7079
Paul.Landry@pch.gc.ca

Ontario
#400, 150 John St., Toronto, ON M5V 3T6
Tel: 416-954-0395; *Fax:* 416-954-2909
Toll-Free: 866-811-0055
TTY: 888-997-3123
pch-ontario@pch.gc.ca

Executive Director, Marie Moliner
Tel: 416-954-0396; *Fax:* 416-954-2909
marie.moliner@pch.gc.ca

Prairies & Northern Region
#510, 240 Graham Ave., PO Box 2160 Winnipeg, MB R3C 3R5
Tel: 204-983-3601; *Fax:* 204-984-6996
Toll-Free: 866-811-0055
TTY: 888-997-3123
pnr-rpn@pch.gc.ca

Regional Executive Director, Louis Chagnon
Tel: 204-983-0261; *Fax:* 204-984-2303
Louis.Chagnon@pch.gc.ca

Québec
Complexe Guy-Favreau, Tour Ouest, 200, boul René-Lévesque ouest, 6e étage, Montréal, QC H2Z 1X4
Tel: 514-283-5191
Toll-Free: 866-811-0055
TTY: 888-997-3123
pch-qc@pch.gc.ca

Regional Executive Director, Michel Saint Denis
Tel: 514-283-5797; *Fax:* 514-283-8762
Michel.SaintDenis@pch.gc.ca

Western
#205, 351 Abbott St., Vancouver, BC V6B 6C6
Tel: 604-666-0176; *Fax:* 604-666-3508
Toll-Free: 866-811-0055
TTY: 888-997-3123
wr-ro@pch.gc.ca
Other Communication: LAN Fax: 604-666-8801

Regional Executive Director, Patrick Tobin
Patrick.Tobin@pch.gc.ca

Canadian Human Rights Commission / Commission canadienne des droits de la personne

344 Slater St., 8th Fl., Ottawa, ON K1A 1E1
Fax: 613-996-9661
Toll-Free: 888-214-1090
TTY: 888-643-3304
info.com@chrc-ccdp.gc.ca
www.chrc-ccdp.gc.ca
Other Communication: Library, E-mail: library@chrc-ccdp.ca; Media Relations, E-mail: communications@chrc-ccdp.gc.ca
twitter.com/cdnhumanrights
www.facebook.com/CanadianHumanRightsCommission

The Commission administers the Canadian Human Rights Act, which applies to federal government departments & agencies, & businesses under federal jurisdiction. The Commission accepts complaints of discrimination based on race, national or ethnic origin, colour, religion, age, sex, marital & family status, pardoned offence, disability & sexual orientation. It also administers the Employment Equity Act to remove barriers for four designated groups: women, Aboriginal peoples, persons with disabilities & members of visible minorities. Collect calls accepted throughout Canada.

Chief Commissioner, Marie-Claude Landry, Ad.E.

Deputy Chief Commissioner, David Langtry
Tel: 613-943-9148

Commissioner, Tara Erskine

Commissioner, Judy C. Mintz

Acting Director General, Human Rights Promotion Branch, Piero Narducci
Tel: 613-943-9028

Director General, Corporate Management Branch & CFO, Heather Throop
Tel: 613-943-9033; *Fax:* 613-941-6808

Executive Director, Ian Fine
Tel: 613-943-9090

Director, Resolution Services Division, Suzanne Best
Tel: 613-943-0191

Director, Policy & International Relations Division, Natalie Dagenais
Tel: 613-943-9133

Director, Employment Equity Compliance Division, Marie-Claude Girard
Tel: 613-943-9064
Director, Communications, Outreach & Communications Branch, Natalie Babin-Dufresne
Tel: 613-943-9138
Acting Director & Senior Counsel, Litigation Services Division, Fiona Keith
Tel: 613-943-9520
Acting Director, Prevention Initiatives & Liaison Division, Marie-Anne St-Amour
Tel: 613-295-4660
Director, Financial & Administrative Services Division, Luc Bélanger
Tel: 613-943-9002
Director, Legal Advisory Services & Senior Counsel, Sheila Osborne-Brown
Tel: 613-943-9107
Acting Director, Human Resources Division, Mélanie Godin
Tel: 613-943-9024

National Aboriginal Initiative (NAI) / Initiative Nationale Autochtone
#750, 175 Hargrave St., Winnipeg, MA RC3 3R8
Tel: 204-983-2189; *Fax:* 204-983-6132
Toll-Free: 866-772-4880
TTY: 866-772-4840
www.doyouknowyourrights.ca
twitter.com/cdnhumanrights
www.facebook.com/CanadianHumanRightsCommission
The National Aboriginal Initiative offers human rights expertise to First Nations governments & other Aboriginal organizations.
Director, Sherri Helgason
Tel: 204-983-4648

Regional Offices
Eastern Region
#903, 425, boul de Maisonneuve ouest, Montréal, QC H3A 3G5
Fax: 514-283-5084
Toll-Free: 800-999-6899
Regional Manager, Élisabeth Gauthier
Tel: 514-496-2932; *Fax:* 514-283-5084
Western Region
Canada Place, #1645, 9700 Jasper Ave., Edmonton, AB T5J 4C3
Fax: 780-495-4044
Toll-Free: 800-999-6899
Regional Manager, Hilda Andresen
Tel: 780-232-3579

Canadian Human Rights Tribunal (CHRT) / Tribunal canadien des droits de la personne (TCDP)

160 Elgin St., 11th Fl., Ottawa, ON K1A 1J4
Tel: 613-995-1707; *Fax:* 613-995-3484
TTY: 613-947-1070
registrar@chrt-tcdp.gc.ca
www.chrt-tcdp.gc.ca
Quasi-judicial body that adjudicates complaints of discrimination referred to it by the Canadian Human Rights Commission & determines whether the activities violate the Canadian Human Rights Act.
Chair, David Thomas
Vice-Chair, Susheel Gupta
Acting Executive Director & Registrar; Director, Corporate & Internal Services, Amal Picard
Tel: 613-947-1038

Canadian Institutes of Health Research (CIHR) / Instituts de recherche en santé du Canada (IRSC)

160 Elgin St., 9th Fl., Ottawa, ON K1A 0W9
Tel: 613-941-2672; *Fax:* 613-954-1800
Toll-Free: 888-603-4178
support@cihr-irsc.gc.ca
www.cihr-irsc.gc.ca
Promotes health research excellence in Canada through training & funding programs in basic, clinical, health systems & services, & population health research. Research is carried out in universities, in the health sciences faculties, affiliated hospitals & institutions & other faculties where research projects are highly relevant to human health. University-Industry programs create the opportunity for collaboration between Canadian companies & researchers conducting research in Canadian universities or affiliated institutions. Also manages the health-related Networks of Centres of Excellence & operates 13 "virtual" institutes, which link & support researchers pursuing common goals in specific areas of focus.
President, Alain Beaudet
Tel: 613-954-1808
Executive Vice-President, Chief Scientific Officer & Vice-President, Research & Knowledge Translation, Dr. Jane E. Aubin
Tel: 613-954-1805
VPResearch@cihr-irsc.gc.ca
Chief Financial Officer & Vice-President, Resource Planning & Management, Thérèse Roy, CPA, CA
Tel: 613-954-1946
therese.roy@cihr-irsc.gc.ca
Vice-President, External Affairs and Business Development, Michel Perron
Tel: 613-957-6134
Director General, Information Management, Technology & Security, Martin Bernier
Tel: 613-957-6140
Executive Director, Secretariat on Responsible Conduct of Research, Susan Zimmerman
Tel: 613-947-7148
Director, Institute Affairs, Vacant
Director, Human Resources, Daryl Gauthier
Tel: 613-957-8762
Director General, Finance & Administration, Anick Ouellette
Tel: 613-957-6127
Director General, Communications & Public Outreach, Christina Cefaloni
Tel: 613-954-1812

Canadian Intergovernmental Conference Secretariat (CICS) / Secrétariat des conférences intergouvernementales canadiennes

222 Queen St., 10th Fl., PO Box 488 Stn. A, Ottawa, ON K1N 8V5
Tel: 613-995-2341; *Fax:* 613-996-6091
info@scics.gc.ca
www.scics.gc.ca
twitter.com/cics_info
CICS is a conference support body which provides the administrative services required for the planning & the conduct of federal-provincial-territorial & provincial-territorial conferences at the First Ministers, ministers & deputy ministers level. The agency is at the disposal of individual federal, provincial & territorial government departments which may be called upon to organize & chair such meetings.
Secretary, André M. McArdle
Tel: 613-995-2345
Director, Corporate Services, Laurent Bissonnette
Tel: 613-995-9943
Director, Information Services, Bernard Latulippe
Tel: 613-995-4203
Director, Conference Services, Rodrigue Hurtubise
Tel: 613-995-4328
Rodrigue.Hurtubise@scics.gc.ca

Canadian International Trade Tribunal (CITT) / Tribunal canadien du commerce extérieur (TCCE)

Standard Life Centre, 333 Laurier Ave. West, 15th Floor, Ottawa, ON K1A 0G7
Tel: 613-990-2452; *Fax:* 613-990-2439
Toll-Free: 855-307-2488
citt-tcce@tribunal.gc.ca
www.citt-tcce.gc.ca
Other Communication: Media, Phone: 613-949-2309
The Tribunal is an independent, quasi-judicial body, which carries out both judicial & advisory functions relating to trade remedies for the North American Free Trade Agreement. In this capacity, the Tribunal succeeds the Procurement Review Board of Canada. Reports to government through the Minister of Finance.
Acting Chair, Jean Bédard, LL.L., LL.M., M.B.A.
Executive Director & General Counsel, Nick Covelli
Tel: 613-990-2420
Acting Director, Trade Remedies Investigations, Gayatri Shankarraman
Tel: 613-998-8512
Senior Counsel & Director, Legal Services, Eric Wildhaber
Tel: 613-998-8623

Canadian Judicial Council / Conseil canadien de la magistrature

Ottawa, ON K1A 0W8
Tel: 613-288-1566; *Fax:* 613-288-1575
www.cjc-ccm.gc.ca
The members of the Council include the Chief Justice of Canada (who acts as Chair), the Chief Justices & Associate Chief Justices of each Superior Court or Branch or Division thereof, the senior judges of the Supreme Court of the Yukon Territory, the Supreme Court of the Northwest Territories & the Nunavut Court of Justice, the Chief Judge & Associate Chief Judge of the Tax Court of Canada, & the Chief Justice of the Court Martial Court of Canada.
Executive Director & General Counsel, Norman Sabourin
Tel: 613-288-1566 ext: 301
Senior Administrative Officer, Odette Dagenais
Tel: 613-288-1566 ext: 302
Director, Committees Management, Josée Desjardins
Tel: 613-288-1566 ext: 309
Director, Communications & Strategic Issues, Johanna Laporte
Tel: 613-288-1566

Canadian Museum for Human Rights (CMHR) / Musée canadien des droits de la personne (MCDP)

85 Israel Asper Way, Winnipeg, MB R3C 0L5
Tel: 204-289-2000; *Fax:* 204-289-2001
Toll-Free: 877-877-6037
TTY: 204-289-2050
info@humanrights.ca
humanrights.ca
twitter.com/cmhr_news
www.facebook.com/canadianmuseumforhumanrights
www.youtube.com/user/HumanRightsMuseum
The Canadian Museum for Human Rights was established in 2008 to explore the topic of human rights with particular attention to Canada, to encourage reflection & discussion & promote respect for others. The museum officially opened in September 2014.
Chair, Board of Trustees, Eric Hughes, CA
Vice-Chair, Board of Trustees, J. Pauline Rafferty
President & CEO, John Young
john.young@humanrights.ca
Chief Operating Officer, Gail Stephens
gail.stephens@humanrights.ca
Chief Financial Officer, Susanne Robertson
susanne.robertson@humanrights.ca
Vice-President, Visitor Experience & Engagement, Jacques Lavergne
jacques.lavergne@humanrights.ca
Vice-President, Exhibitions, Research & Design, Corey Timpson
corey.timpson@humanrights.ca
Vice-President, Public Affairs & Programs, Angela Cassie
angela.cassie@humanrights.ca
Director, Learning & Programming, June Creelman
june.creelman@humanrights.ca
Director, Information Technology, Christopher Rivers
chris.rivers@humanrights.ca
Director, Human Resources, Catherine Schinkel
catherine.schinkel@humanrights.ca

Canadian Museum of History (CMH) / Musée canadien de l'histoire

100 Laurier St., Gatineau, QC K1A 0M8
Tel: 819-776-7000
Toll-Free: 800-555-5621
TTY: 819-776-7003
www.civilization.ca
twitter.com/civilization
www.facebook.com/museumofcivilization
www.youtube.com/user/CanMusCiv
The Canadian Museum of History (formerly the Museum of Civilization Corporation) was established by the Museums Act. The Crown corporation manages the Canadian Museum of History, the Canadian War Museum & the Virtual Museum of New France in its efforts to promote increased awareness & understanding of Canadian history, culture & identity.
President & Chief Executive Officer, Mark O'Neill
Tel: 819-776-7116
Chief Financial Officer, Melissa MacKenzie
Tel: 819-776-8363
Chief Operating Officer & Senior Vice-President, David Loye
Tel: 819-776-8258
Director General & Vice-President, Jean-Marc Blais
Tel: 819-776-8302
Vice-President, Development, Yves Gadler
Tel: 819-776-8468
Vice-President, Human Resources, Manon Rochon
Tel: 819-776-8268
manon.rochon@historymuseum.ca
Vice-President, Corporate Affairs & Publishing, Chantal Schryer
Tel: 819-776-8499
chantal.schryer@historymuseum.ca
Director, Business Partnerships & Information Management, Nicolas Gauvin
Tel: 819-776-8407
Director, Collections Management & Conservation, Wanda McWilliams
Tel: 819-776-8434

Director, Research, Dean Oliver, Ph.D.
Tel: 819-776-7172
Director, Visitor Services & Corporate Security, Heather Paszkowski
Tel: 819-776-8288

Canadian War Museum (CWM) / Musée canadien de la guerre
1 Vimy Pl., Ottawa, ON K1A 0M8
Tel: 819-776-7000
Toll-Free: 800-555-5621
TTY: 819-776-7003
www.warmuseum.ca
twitter.com/CanWarMuseum
www.facebook.com/warmuseum
www.youtube.com/user/CanWarMus

The Canadian War Museum presents Canada's military heritage from earliest times to the present.

Director General, Canadian War Museum; Vice-President, Canadian History Museum, Stephen Quick
Tel: 819-776-8523
stephen.quick@warmuseum.ca
Director, Collections, James Whitham
Tel: 819-776-8646
james.whitham@warmuseum.ca
Acting Director, Research, Tony Glen
Tel: 819-776-8619
tony.glen@warmuseum.ca
Director, Public Affairs, Yasmine Mingay
Tel: 819-776-8606
yasmine.mingay@warmuseum.ca
Librarian, Lara Andrews
Tel: 819-776-8680
lara.andrews@warmuseum.ca

Canadian Museum of Nature (CMN) / Musée Canadien de la Nature (MCN)

240 McLeod St., PO Box 3443 Stn. D, Ottawa, ON K1P 6P4
Tel: 613-566-4700; *Fax:* 613-364-4021
Toll-Free: 800-263-4433
TTY: 613-566-4770
www.nature.ca
Other Communication: Toll-Free TTY: 1-866-600-8801
twitter.com/MuseumofNature
www.facebook.com/canadianmuseumofnature
www.youtube.com/user/canadanaturemuseum

A diverse natural history collection encompassing some 10 million specimens, & thousands of species. Provides access to specimens & data for research & access to knowledge on biodiversity, biosystematics & the environment. Carries out research on management & care of collections & employs a staff of researchers working on national & international projects. Through public programs, CMN communicates knowledge & promotes understanding of science & nature to diverseaudiences. It includes permanent, special & travelling exhibits, curriculum-based & interpretive programs, & print, electronic, audiovisual & multimedia publications.

President & Chief Executive Officer, Meg Beckel
Tel: 613-566-4733; *Fax:* 613-364-4020
Interim Vice-President, Corporate Services, Charles Bloom
Tel: 613-566-4732; *Fax:* 613-364-4020
Vice-President, Experience & Engagement, Ailsa Barry
Tel: 613-566-4744; *Fax:* 613-566-4759
Other Communications: Alt. Phone: 613-566-4286
Vice-President, Research & Collections, Mark Graham
Tel: 613-566-4743
Corporate Secretary, Irene Byrne
Tel: 613-566-4738

Canadian Northern Economic Development Agency (CanNor) / Agence canadienne de développement économique du Nord

Ottawa, ON K1A 0H4
Toll-Free: 855-897-2667
InfoNorth@CanNor.gc.ca
www.cannor.gc.ca
Other Communication: NU Phone: 867-975-3746, E-mail: ecdevnunavut@cannor.gc.ca; NT Phone: 855-897-2667, E-mail: ecdevnwt@cannor.gc.ca; YT Phone: 867-667-3263, E-mail ytinfo@cannor.gc.ca
Inuksugait Plaza IIPO Box 40 Sta. Iqaluit, NU X0A 0H0

CanNor was established in 2009 to promote growth & development in Northern Canada through economic development programs & collaboration between northern & southern partnerships. The agency also coordinates the activities of other federal departments in relation to northern project development through the Northern Projects Management Office (NPMO). Programs offered by the agency include: Strategic Investments in Northern Economic Development (SINED); Aboriginal Economic Development (AED); Northern Adult Basic Education Program (NABEP); Community Infrastructure Improvement Fund (CIIF); & promotion of official language minority communities.

Minister Responsible; Minister, Innovation, Science & Economic Development, Hon. Navdeep Bains, P.C., B.A., M.B.A., C.M.A.
Tel: 613-995-7784; *Fax:* 613-996-9817
Navdeep.Bains@parl.gc.ca
President, Janet King
Tel: 613-947-0221; *Fax:* 613-947-0242

Northern Projects Management Office (NPMO) / Bureau de gestion des projets nordiques
Nova Plaza, 5019 - 52nd St., 3rd Fl., PO Box 1500 Yellowknife, NT X1A 2R3
Tel: 867-920-6766

The NMPO provides the following services: issues management & advice for industry & communities; coordinating the participation of federal departments in the regulatory review process; providing transparency through publicly tracking the progress of projects.

Director General, Matthew Spence
Tel: 867-669-2593; *Fax:* 867-766-8401

Regional Offices

Iqaluit
Allavvik Bldg., 1106 Inuksugait Plaza, PO Box 40 Iqaluit, NU X0A 0H0
Acting Director General, Operations, Peter Rinaldi
Tel: 867-975-3721; *Fax:* 867-975-3724
Executive Director, Nunavut Federal Council, Hagar Idlout-Sudlovenick
Tel: 867-975-4771; *Fax:* 867-975-4773
Regional Director, Sylvie Renaud
Tel: 867-975-3737; *Fax:* 867-975-3740

Ottawa
400 Cooper St., 5th Fl., Ottawa, ON K1A 0H4
Chief Financial Officer & Director, Corporate Services, Yves Robineau
Tel: 613-992-5072; *Fax:* 613-995-9495
Vice-President, Policy, Planning, Communications & NPMO, Mitch Bloom
Tel: 613-995-9432; *Fax:* 613-995-9472

Whitehorse
#215, 305 Main St., Whitehorse, YT V1A 2B3
Regional Director, Michael Bloor
Tel: 867-667-3310; *Fax:* 867-667-3801

Yellowknife
Nova Plaza, 5019 - 52nd St., 3rd Fl., PO Box 1500 Yellowknife, NT X1A 2R3
Executive Director, Northwest Territories Federal Council, Trevor Sinclair
Tel: 867-766-8451
Regional Director, Kevin Lewis
Tel: 867-766-8405; *Fax:* 867-766-8401

Canadian Nuclear Safety Commission (CNSC) / Commission canadienne de sûreté nucléaire (CCSN)

280 Slater St., PO Box 1046 Stn. B, Ottawa, ON K1P 5S9
Tel: 613-995-5894; *Fax:* 613-995-5086
Toll-Free: 800-668-5284
cnsc.information.ccsn@canada.ca
www.nuclearsafety.gc.ca
Other Communication: Alt. E-mails: cnsc.interventions.ccsn@cnsc-ccsn.gc.ca (Hearings & Meetings); cnsc.pfp.ccsn@cnsc-ccsn.gc.ca (Participant Funding Program)
www.facebook.com/CanadianNuclearSafetyCommission
www.youtube.com/user/cnscccsn

Federal agency which regulates activities involving nuclear energy & prescribed substances in the interests of health & safety for workers & the public. Areas covered under the AECB's licensing process include the nuclear fuel cycle (from mining to waste disposal), heavy water plants, research reactors & accelerators, & radioisotopes. Operations ensure that the use of nuclear energy in Canada does not pose undue risk to health, safety, security & the environment. The Research & Support Program (RSP) augments & extends the AECB's regulatory program beyond the capability of in-house resources. It produces pertinent & independent information that will assist the Board & its staff in making sound, timely & credible decisions on regulating nuclear facilities & materials. The nine sectors of the program include: safety of nuclear facilities; radioactive waste management; health physics; physical security; development of regulatory processes; & social services

President, Michael Binder
Tel: 613-992-8828
Executive Vice-President & Chief Regulatory Operations Officer, Ramzi Jammal
Tel: 613-947-8899
Other Communications: Executive Assistant, Phone: 613-947-8896
Chief Financial Officer & Vice-President, Corporate Services Branch, Stéphane Cyr
Tel: 613-995-0104
Vice-President, Regulatory Affairs & Chief Communications Officer, Jason K. Cameron
Tel: 613-947-3773
Vice-President, Technical Support Branch, Terry Jamieson
Tel: 613-947-8931
Other Communications: Executive Assistant, Phone: 613-996-0260
Director General, Security & Safeguards, Raoul R. Awad
Tel: 613-992-2943
Director General, Nuclear Cycle & Facilities Regulation, David Newland
Tel: 613-943-8948
Director General, Assessment & Analysis, Gerry Frappier
Tel: 613-995-2031
Director General, Safety Management, Kathleen Heppell-Masys
Tel: 613-991-3220
Director General, Information Management & Technology Directorate, Hugh Robertson
Tel: 613-949-9498
Director General, Strategic Communications Directorate, Sunni Locatelli
Tel: 613-995-2903
Director General, Nuclear Substance Regulation, Colin Moses
Tel: 613-993-7699; *Fax:* 613-995-5086
colin.moses@canada.ca
Director General, Power Reactor Regulation, Barclay Howden
Tel: 613-995-2655; *Fax:* 613-995-5086
barclay.howden@canada.ca
Director General, Strategic Planning Directorate, Liane Sauer
Tel: 613-943-7662; *Fax:* 613-995-5086
liane.sauer@canada.ca
Director General, Finance & Administration Directorate, Daniel Schnob
Tel: 613-995-8273; *Fax:* 613-995-5086
Director General, Regulatory Improvement & Major Projects Management, Haidy Tadros
Tel: 613-943-0179; *Fax:* 613-995-5086
Director General, Environmental & Radiation Protection & Assessment, Patsy Thompson
Tel: 613-943-9650; *Fax:* 613-995-5086
patsy.thompson@canada.ca
Director General, Regulatory Policy Directorate, Brian Torrie
Tel: 613-947-3728
Director General, Human Resources Directorate, Louise Youdale
Tel: 613-995-7464

Canadian Race Relations Foundation (CRRF) / Fondation canadienne des relations raciales (TCRR)

#225, 6 Garamond Ct., Toronto, ON M3C 1Z5
Tel: 416-441-1900; *Fax:* 416-441-2752
Toll-Free: 888-240-4936
info@crrf-fcrr.ca
www.crr.ca
Other Communication: Toll-Free Fax: 1-888-399-0333
twitter.com/CRRF
www.facebook.com/133251670048639

Crown corporation operating at arms length from the federal government from which it receives no funding. The Foundation is committed to building a national framework for the fight against racism in Canadian society.

Minister Responsible; Minister, Canadian Heritage, Hon. Mélanie Joly, P.C.
Tel: 613-992-0983; *Fax:* 613-992-1932
Melanie.Joly@parl.gc.ca
Chair, Albert C. Lo
Executive Director, Anita Bromberg
Tel: 416-441-2714
Director, Finance & Administration, Arsalan Tavassoli
Tel: 416-952-5063
atavassoli@crrf-fcrr.ca

Canadian Radio-Television & Telecommunications Commission (CRTC) / Conseil de la radiodiffusion et des télécommunications Canadiennes

Central Building, 1, Promenade du Portage, Les Terrasses de la Chaudière, Gatineau, QC J8X 4B1
Tel: 819-997-0313; *Fax:* 819-994-0218
Toll-Free: 877-249-2782
TTY: 819-994-0423
www.crtc.gc.ca
Other Communication: Toll-Free TTY: 1-877-909-2782
Mailing Address: CRTC
Ottawa, ON K1A 0N2
twitter.com/CRTCeng
www.youtube.com/user/CRTCgcca

The CRTC is vested with the authority to regulate & supervise all aspects of the Canadian broadcasting system, as well as to regulate telecommunications common carriers & service providers that fall under federal jurisdiction. Reports to Parliament through the Minister of Canadian Heritage.

Chair & Chief Executive Officer, Jean-Pierre Blais
Tel: 819-997-3430; *Fax:* 819-953-1555
Vice-Chair, Telecommunications, Peter Menzies
Tel: 819-997-4645; *Fax:* 819-994-0218
Vice-Chair, Broadcasting, Vacant
Tel: 819-997-8766; *Fax:* 819-997-4923
Commissioner, Quebec, Yves Dupras
Tel: 514-244-5071
Commissioner, Atlantic/Nunavut Regions, Christopher MacDonald
Tel: 902-426-2644
Commissioner, Manitoba/Saskatchewan Regions, Candice J. Molnar
Tel: 306-780-3422
Commissioner, Ontario Region, Raj Shoan
Tel: 416-954-6269
Commissioner, British Columbia/Yukon Regions, Stephen B. Simpson
Tel: 604-666-2914
Commissioner, Alberta/Northwest Territories Regions, Linda Vennard
Tel: 403-292-6663; *Fax:* 403-292-6686
Secretary General, Danielle May-Cuconato
Tel: 819-953-5889
Senior General Counsel & Executive Director, Christianne Laizner
Tel: 819-953-3990
Executive Director, Communications & External Relations, Claude Doucet
Tel: 819-997-9372
Executive Director, Broadcasting, Scott Hutton
Tel: 819-997-4573; *Fax:* 819-994-0218
Executive Director, Telecommunications, Chris Seidl
Tel: 819-956-4480; *Fax:* 819-997-4550
Chief Compliance & Enforcement Officer, Manon Bombardier
Tel: 819-997-3749; *Fax:* 819-994-5610
Chief Consumer Officer, Barbara Motzney
Tel: 819-997-4534

Regional Offices

Alberta
#574, 220 - 4th Ave. SW., Calgary, AB T2G 4X3
Tel: 403-292-6660; *Fax:* 403-292-6686

British Columbia
#290, 858 Beatty St., Vancouver, BC V6B 1C1
Tel: 604-666-2111; *Fax:* 604-666-8322

Manitoba
#970, 360 Main St., Winnipeg, MB R3C 3Z3
Tel: 204-983-6306; *Fax:* 204-983-6317

Nova Scotia
Metropolitan Place, #1410, 99 Wyse Rd., Dartmouth, NS B3A 4S5
Tel: 902-426-7997; *Fax:* 902-426-2721

Ontario
#624, 55 St. Clair Ave. East, Toronto, ON M4T 1M2
Tel: 416-954-6271

Québec
#205, 505, boul de Maisonneuve ouest, Montréal, QC H3A 3C2
Tel: 514-283-6607

Saskatchewan
#403, 1975 Scarth St., Regina, SK S4P 2H1
Tel: 306-780-3422

Canadian Security Intelligence Service (CSIS) / Service canadien du renseignement de sécurité

PO Box 9732 Stn. T, Ottawa, ON K1G 4G4
Tel: 613-993-9620; *Fax:* 613-231-0612
TTY: 613-991-9228
www.csis.gc.ca
twitter.com/csiscanada

CSIS is part of Canada's national security establishment. It investigates threats, analyzes information & produces intelligence in order to advise the government on protecting the country & its citizens.

Director, Michael Coulombe
Tel: 613-993-9620

Canadian Space Agency (CSA) / Agence spatiale canadienne (ASC)

John H. Chapman Space Centre, 6767, rte de l'Aéroport, Saint-Hubert, QC J3Y 8Y9
Tel: 450-926-4800; *Fax:* 450-926-4352
asc.info.csa@canada.ca
www.asc-csa.gc.ca
twitter.com/csa_asc
www.facebook.com/CanadianSpaceAgency
www.youtube.com/user/Canadianspaceagency

Established in 1989, & responsible for coordinating all civil, space-related policies & programs on behalf of the Government of Canada. Scientific research & industrial development in earth observation, space science & exploration, satellite communications, & space awareness & learning. RADARSAT International (RSI) develops products & services demanded by world markets. RADARSAT-1, the first Canadian commercial Earth Observation (EO) satellite, is uniquely capable of responding to disasters around the world. The system can support the operational mapping & monitoring of natural disasters in four critical ways: prevention, preparedness, emergency response & recovery. Moreover, the development of the high performance RADARSAT-2, launched in 2007, further enhances Canada's competitive position. RADARSAT-2 offers improved quality of data images to meet the growing world demand of Earth observation information. The SCISAT satellite is used in ozone depletion research. The RADARSAT Constellation is currently in development, with a proposed launch date of 2018, & will provide total coverage of Canada's land & oceans via a three-satellite configuration.

Minister, Innovation, Science & Economic Development, Hon. Navdeep Bains, P.C., B.A., M.B.A., C.M.A.
Tel: 613-995-7784; *Fax:* 613-996-9817
Navdeep.Bains@parl.gc.ca
President & CEO, Sylvain Laporte
Tel: 450-926-4301
Vice-President, Luc Brûlé
Tel: 450-926-4750; *Fax:* 450-926-4315
Chief Financial Officer, Marie-Claude Guérard
Tel: 450-926-4407; *Fax:* 450-926-4424
Chief Scientist, Life Sciences, Nicole Buckley
Tel: 450-926-4744
Chief Medical Officer, Operational Space Medicine, Raffi Kuyumjian
Tel: 450-926-5785; *Fax:* 450-926-4707
Chief Medical Officer, Operational Space Medicine, Jean-Marc Comtois
Tel: 450-926-4755
Director General, Programs & Integrated Planning, Colleen Merchant
Tel: 613-993-4783
Director General, Space Utilization, Éric Laliberté
Tel: 450-926-4461; *Fax:* 450-926-6521
Director General, Space Exploration, Gilles Leclerc
Tel: 450-926-4606; *Fax:* 450-926-4323
Director General, Space Science & Technology, Jean Claude Piedboeuf
Tel: 450-926-4770; *Fax:* 450-926-4766
Executive Director, Corporate Services & Human Resources, Yves Saulnier
Tel: 450-926-4667; *Fax:* 450-926-4612

Canadian Transportation Agency (CTA) / Office des transports du Canada (OTC)

Les Terrasses de la Chaudière, 15 Eddy St., Gatineau, QC J8X 4B3
Fax: 819-997-6727
Toll-Free: 888-222-2592
TTY: 800-669-5575
info@otc-cta.gc.ca
www.cta-otc.gc.ca
twitter.com/CTA_gc

Responsible for the economic regulation of transportation in Canada. The agency requires that all applications for new railway lines, modifications to existing railway lines, disputed railway crossings at grade, grade separation, utility crossings & private crossings be accompanied by an environment impact assessment

Chair & Chief Executive Officer, Scott Streiner
Tel: 819-953-7600; *Fax:* 819-953-9979
Vice-Chair, Sam Barone
Tel: 819-953-8915; *Fax:* 819-953-9979
sam.barone@otc-cta.gc.ca
Director General, Ghislain Blanchard
Tel: 613-301-9261; *Fax:* 819-953-5564
ghislain.blanchard@otc-cta.gc.ca
Chief Dispute Resolution Officer, Douglas Smith
Tel: 819-953-5074; *Fax:* 819-953-5562
Douglas.Smith@otc-cta.gc.ca
Acting Director, Workplace & Workforce, Hannya Rizk
Tel: 819-997-6764; *Fax:* 819-953-9842
Hannya.Rizk@otc-cta.gc.ca
Senior Director, Air Determinations, Carole Girard
Tel: 819-997-8761; *Fax:* 819-953-8957
carole.girard@otc-cta.gc.ca
Chief Corporate Officer, Internal Services Branch, Jacqueline Bannister
Tel: 819-953-7666; *Fax:* 819-953-8353
jacqueline.bannister@otc-cta.gc.ca
Director, Communications, Alexandre Robertson
Tel: 819-953-8926; *Fax:* 819-953-8353
Alexandre.Robertson@otc-cta.gc.ca
Chief Strategy Officer, Analysis & Outreach Branch, Randall Meades
Tel: 819-953-0327; *Fax:* 819-953-9979
Randall.Meades@otc-cta.gc.ca

Regional Enforcement Officers

Atlantic
#109, 1045 Main St., Moncton, NB E1C 1H1
Tel: 506-851-6950; *Fax:* 506-851-2518
conformite-compliance@otc-cta.gc.ca

Central
#702, 269 Main St., PO Box 27007 Stn. Winnipeg Square, Winnipeg, MB R3C 4T3
Tel: 204-984-6092; *Fax:* 204-984-6093
conformite-compliance@otc-cta.gc.ca

Ontario
#300, 4900 Yonge St., Toronto, ON M2N 6A5
Tel: 416-952-7895; *Fax:* 416-952-7897
conformite-compliance@otc-cta.gc.ca

Pacific
#219, 800 Burrard St., Vancouver, BC V6Z 2V8
Tel: 604-666-0620; *Fax:* 604-666-1267
conformite-compliance@otc-cta.gc.ca

Québec
#1C, 700, place Leigh-Capreol, Dorval, QC H4Y 1G7
Tel: 514-420-5999; *Fax:* 514-450-5182
conformite-compliance@otc-cta.gc.ca

Western
#1135, 9700 Jasper Ave. NW, Edmonton, AB T5J 4C3
Tel: 780-495-6618; *Fax:* 780-495-5639
conformite-compliance@otc-cta.gc.ca

Office of the Conflict of Interest & Ethics Commissioner / Commissariat aux conflits d'intérêts et à l'éthique

Commissioner's Office, 66 Slater St., 22nd Fl., PO Box 16 Ottawa, ON K1A 0A6
Tel: 613-995-0721; *Fax:* 613-995-7308
ciec-ccie@parl.gc.ca
www.ciec-ccie.gc.ca
twitter.com/CIEC_CCIE

The Conflict of Interest & Ethics Commissioner is an independent Officer of Parliament. Responsibilities include assisting elected & appointed officials to avoid conflicts between their private interests & public duties.

Conflict of Interest & Ethics Commissioner, Mary E. Dawson
Tel: 613-995-0721; *Fax:* 613-995-7308
Director, Advisory & Compliance, Lyne Robinson-Dalpé
Tel: 613-996-6020; *Fax:* 613-995-7308
General Counsel, Legal Services, Matine Richard
Tel: 613-996-6028; *Fax:* 613-995-7308

Copyright Board of Canada / Commission du droit d'auteur du Canada

#800, 56 Sparks St., Ottawa, ON K1A 0C9
Tel: 613-952-8621; *Fax:* 613-952-8630
secretariat@cb-cda.gc.ca
www.cb-cda.gc.ca

The Board is an economic regulatory body empowered to establish, either mandatorily or at the request of an interested party, the royalties to be paid for the use of copyrighted works, when the administration of such copyright is entrusted to a collective-administration society. The Board also has the right to supervise agreements between users & licensing bodies & issues licences when the copyright owner cannot be located.

Chair, Robert A. Blair

Vice-Chair & Chief Executive Officer, Claude Majeau
Tel: 613-952-8621

Secretary General, Gilles McDougall
Tel: 613-952-8624
gilles.mcdougall@cb-cda.gc.ca

Senior Legal Counsel, Sylvain Audet
Tel: 613-960-8356
sylvain.audet@cb-cda.gc.ca

Director, Research & Analysis, Raphael Solomon
Tel: 613-946-4456
raphael.solomon@cb-cda.gc.ca

Office of the Correctional Investigator / L'Enquêteur correctionnel Canada

PO Box 3421 Stn. D, Ottawa, ON K1P 6L4
Fax: 613-990-9091
Toll-Free: 877-885-8848
org@oci-bec.gc.ca
www.oci-bec.gc.ca

Investigates complaints from inmates in Canadian institutions. Reports on problems inmates have that fall within the responsibility of the Department of Public Safety & Emergency Preparedness & meet certain conditions.

Correctional Investigator, Howard Sapers
Tel: 613-990-2689

Executive Director & General Counsel, Ivan Zinger
Tel: 613-990-2690; *Fax:* 613-990-9091

Director, Policy & Research, David Hooey
Tel: 613-990-2693; *Fax:* 613-990-0563

Director of Investigations, Marie-France Kingsley
Tel: 613-998-6960; *Fax:* 613-990-9091

Director, Corporate Services & Planning, Manuel Marques
Tel: 613-991-9002; *Fax:* 613-990-0563

Director, Investigations, Paul McKenzie
Tel: 613-990-2691; *Fax:* 613-990-9091

Correctional Service Canada (CSC) / Service correctionnel Canada

340 Laurier Ave. West, Ottawa, ON K1A 0P9
Tel: 613-992-5891; *Fax:* 613-943-1630
www.csc-scc.gc.ca
twitter.com/csc_scc_en
www.youtube.com/user/CSCsccEN

An agency within Public Safety & Emergency Preparedness Canada responsible for the administration of sentences with respect to convicted offenders sentenced to two or more years as decided by the federal courts, & certain provincial inmates who have been transferred to a federal institution. CSC is also responsible for the supervision of inmates who have been granted conditional release by the authority of the National Parole Board.

Minister, Public Safety & Emergency Preparedness, Hon. Ralph Goodale, P.C., B.A., LL.B.
Tel: 613-947-1153; *Fax:* 613-996-9790
ralph.goodale@parl.gc.ca

Commissioner, Don Head
Tel: 613-995-5781; *Fax:* 613-943-1630

Senior Deputy Commissioner, Anne Kelly
Tel: 613-947-0643; *Fax:* 613-943-1630

Associate Assistant Commissioner, Public Affairs Directorate, Amy Jarrette
Tel: 613-996-5476; *Fax:* 613-947-1184

Director General, Aboriginal Initiatives Directorate, Lisa Allgaier
Tel: 613-995-5465; *Fax:* 613-943-0493

Director General & Chief Information Officer, Information Management Services, Dung-Chi Tran
Tel: 613-995-3912; *Fax:* 613-995-7647

Chief Audit Executive, Internal Audit, Sylvie Soucy
Tel: 613-943-0330; *Fax:* 613-995-0026

Executive Director & General Counsel, Legal Services, Barbara Massey
Tel: 613-992-9009; *Fax:* 613-995-9971

Communications & Engagement / Communications et Engagement

Assistant Commissioner, Scott Harris
Tel: 613-995-6867

Corporate Services / Services corporatifs

Assistant Commissioner, Corporate Services & Chief Financial Officer, Liette Dumas-Sluyter
Tel: 613-996-4242; *Fax:* 613-992-8443

Director General & Deputy Chief Financial Officer, Resource Management Branch, Denis Bombardier
Tel: 613-992-8432

Director General, Technical Services, Ghislain Sauvé
Tel: 613-943-0976; *Fax:* 613-996-9421

Senior Director, Facilities, Philippe Poirier
Tel: 613-995-2015; *Fax:* 613-996-9421

Correctional Operations & Programs / Opérations et programmes correctionnels

Assistant Commissioner, Fraser Macaulay
Tel: 613-943-0499; *Fax:* 613-996-6174

Associate Assistant Commissioner, Vacant

Chief Executive Officer, CORCAN, Lynn Garrow
Tel: 613-996-4530; *Fax:* 613-996-9864
www.csc-scc.gc.ca/corcan

Director General, Offender Programs & Reintegration, Michael Bettmann
Tel: 613-995-6547; *Fax:* 613-996-0428

Associate Director General, Chaplaincy, Bill Rasmus
Tel: 613-943-3145; *Fax:* 613-952-8464

Director General, Community Reintegration Branch, Carmen Long
Tel: 613-943-9256

Director General, Correctional Operations & Programs, Nick Fabiano
Tel: 613-943-1135

Health Services / Services de santé

Assistant Commissioner, Michele Brenning
Tel: 613-995-8023; *Fax:* 613-943-4546

Director General, Clinical Services, Henry de Souza
Tel: 613-947-1013; *Fax:* 613-995-6277

Director General, Public Health, Kate Jackson
Tel: 613-992-8792; *Fax:* 613-943-9600

Director General, Mental Health, Vacant

Human Resource Management / Gestion des ressources humaines

Assistant Commissioner, Kathryn Howard
Tel: 613-995-8899; *Fax:* 613-992-9208

Director General, Learning & Development, Bev Arseneault
Tel: 613-996-8124

Director General, Classification, Recruitment & Staffing Programs, Bobbi Grant
Tel: 613-947-2755; *Fax:* 613-947-1356

Policy / Politiques

Assistant Commissioner, Larry Motiuk
Tel: 613-996-2180; *Fax:* 613-995-3606

Director General, Rights, Redress & Resolution, Julie Keravel
Tel: 613-992-9281; *Fax:* 613-943-4391

Acting Director General, Values, Integrity & Conflict Management, Jacques Vanasse
Tel: 613-943-0511; *Fax:* 613-996-8397

Director, Evaluation, Brigitte de Blois
Tel: 613-943-2827; *Fax:* 613-996-3287

Senior Director, Research NHQ, Kelly Taylor
Tel: 613-900-0000; *Fax:* 613-941-8477

Women Offender Sector / Secteur des délinquantes

Deputy Commissioner for Women, Jennifer Wheatley
Tel: 613-992-6067; *Fax:* 613-992-4692

Director General, Interventions, Kelly Hartle
Tel: 613-947-0238; *Fax:* 613-992-4692

Regional Headquarters

Atlantic
1045 Main St., 2nd Fl., Moncton, NB E1C 1H1
Tel: 506-851-6313; *Fax:* 506-851-6316

Deputy Commissioner, Thérèse Leblanc
Tel: 506-851-6377; *Fax:* 506-851-2418

Ontario
443 Union St., PO Box 1174 Kingston, ON K7L 4Y8
Tel: 613-536-4527; *Fax:* 613-545-8684

Regional Director, Fiona Jordan
Tel: 613-634-3304

Pacific
#100, 33991 Gladys Ave., PO Box 4500 Abbotsford, BC V2S 2E8
Tel: 604-870-2501; *Fax:* 604-870-2430

Acting Director, Sundeep Cheema
Tel: 604-870-2413

Prairies
2313 Hanselman Pl., PO Box 9223 Saskatoon, SK S7K 3X5
Tel: 306-975-4850; *Fax:* 306-975-5186

Québec
#200, 3, pl Laval, Laval, QC H7N 1A2
Tel: 450-967-3333; *Fax:* 450-967-3326

Regional Director, Youssef Mani
Tel: 450-664-6640 ext: 391; *Fax:* 450-664-6641

District Offices

Central Ontario
#215, 180 Dundas St. West, Toronto, ON M5G 1Z8
Tel: 416-973-2393; *Fax:* 416-973-1779

East & West Québec
#202, 212, boul. Curé-Labelle, Sainte-Thérèse, QC J7E 2X7
Tel: 450-435-3932; *Fax:* 450-420-7600

Fraser Valley
#100, 32544 George Ferguson Way, Abbotsford, BC V2T 4Y1
Tel: 604-870-2730; *Fax:* 604-870-2731

Hamilton & Niagara
55 Bay St. North, 2nd Fl., Hamilton, ON L8R 3P7
Tel: 905-572-2695; *Fax:* 905-572-2072

Manitoba/Sask/Northwestern Ontario
#102, 123 Main St., Winnipeg, MB R3C 1A3
Tel: 204-983-4306; *Fax:* 204-983-5869

Montréal-Métropolitan
#917, Tour Ouest, 200, boul René-Lévesque ouest, Montréal, QC H2Z 1X4
Tél: 514-283-1776; *Téléc:* 514-283-1783

New Brunswick & PEI
1 Factory Lane, 1st Fl., Moncton, NB E1C 9M3
Tel: 506-851-3038; *Fax:* 506-851-2057

Newfoundland & Labrador
531 Charter Ave., St. John's, NL A1A 1P7
Tel: 709-772-5359; *Fax:* 709-772-6415

Northeast Ontario
249 Slater St., Ottawa, ON K1P 5H9
Tel: 613-996-7011; *Fax:* 613-954-1687

Northern Alberta, NWT
9530 - 101 Ave., 2nd Fl., Edmonton, AB T5H 0B3
Tel: 780-495-4900; *Fax:* 780-495-4975

Northern/Interior Area
1863 Bredin Rd., Kelowna, BC V1Y 7S9
Tel: 250-470-5166; *Fax:* 250-470-5173

Nova Scotia
#102, 2131 Gottingen St., Halifax, NS B3K 5Z7
Tel: 902-426-3408; *Fax:* 902-426-6579

Nunavut
1043 Woodhouse St., Iqaluit, NU X0A 0H0
Tel: 867-979-8892; *Fax:* 867-979-7441

Saskatchewan
#603, 230 - 22 St. East, Saskatoon, SK S7K 0E9
Tel: 306-975-4070; *Fax:* 306-975-4532

Southern Alberta
#140, 1925 - 18 Ave. NE, Calgary, AB T2E 7T8
Tel: 403-292-5522; *Fax:* 403-292-5510

Vancouver Area
#401, 877 Expo Blvd., Vancouver, BC V6B 1K9
Tel: 604-666-8004; *Fax:* 604-666-2000

Vancouver Island
#200, 256 Wallace St., Nanaimo, BC V9R 5B3
Tel: 250-754-0264; *Fax:* 250-754-0266

District Director, Dave Keating

Western Ontario
#117, 255 Woodlawn Rd. West, Guelph, ON N1H 8J1
Tel: 519-826-2139; *Fax:* 519-826-2143

Defence Construction Canada (DCC) / Construction de Défense Canada (CDC)

Constitution Square, 350 Albert St., 19th Fl., Ottawa, ON K1A 0K3
Tel: 613-998-9548; *Fax:* 613-998-1061
Toll-Free: 800-514-3555
info@dcc-cdc.gc.ca
www.dcc-cdc.gc.ca
twitter.com/dcc_cdc
www.facebook.com/dcc.cdc
www.linkedin.com/company/693781
www.youtube.com/user/DCCCommunications

Federal government crown corporation responsible for the contracting & supervising of major military construction & maintenance projects required by National Defence. Services include construction, project management, environmental services & operational support services. DCC provides environmental science & environmental engineering services to help fulfill the Department of National Defence's sustainable development strategy, including: environmental impact & site assessment; environmental site remediation; environmental support for project & program management; sustainable development strategy support services; policy, compliance & advisory services; site decommissioning services; facility deconstruction & demolition; firing range decommissioning;

waste management auditing & planning; waste reduction planning; landfill inventories & investigations; hazardous waste management; UST removals; training & education; ISO 14000 environmental management systems; environmental CIS applications; environmental checklists for property transactions & decommissioning; environmental monitoring & compliance auditing; designated substances inventories; environmental disclosures reporting; treatment & disposal facilities conceptual designs; environmental contrac ting & contract management; energy conservation. Projects include: the DEW (Distant Early Warning) Line cleanup; Hanger 1 at 8 Wing Trenton; P3 development of the new Communications Security Establishment Canada facility; creation of the Building Information Modelling tool; removal of unexploded ordinance; overhaul of the Fleet Maintenance Facility (FMF) Cape Breton Shop at CFB Esquimalt; & Goose Bay Remediation Project.

President & Chief Executive Officer, James S. Paul
Tel: 613-998-9541; *Fax:* 613-998-1218
Vice-President, Operations, Daniel Benjamin, P.Eng., ing
Tel: 613-949-7721; *Fax:* 613-998-1218
Vice-President, Operations, Mélinda Nycholat
Tel: 613-991-9313; *Fax:* 613-991-9953
Vice-President, Operations, Ross Welsman
Tel: 613-990-2869; *Fax:* 613-998-9547
Corporate Secretary, Alison Lawford
Tel: 613-990-2867; *Fax:* 613-998-1218
Director, Ontario Region, John Graham, P.Eng., PMP
Tel: 613-384-1256 ext: 230; *Fax:* 613-384-7747
Howard Maitland Building
#205, 780 Midpark Dr.
Kingston, ON K7M 7P6
Director, Western Region, Stephen G. Karpyshin, P.Eng.
Tel: 780-495-5442; *Fax:* 780-495-5959
#210, 13220 St. Albert Trail
Edmonton, AB T5L 4W1
Director, Québec Region, Grant Sayers, C.E.T.
Tel: 514-496-2729; *Fax:* 514-283-8347
#224, 2030, boul Pie-IX
Montréal, QC H1V 2C8
Director, Atlantic Region, George Theoharopoulos, P.Eng.
Tel: 902-426-4040; *Fax:* 902-426-9655
#202, 1597 Bedford Hwy.
Bedford, NS B4A 1E7
Regional Director, National Capital Region, Elizabeth Mah
Tel: 613-949-7718; *Fax:* 613-998-9547
#202, 1597 Bedford Hwy.
Bedford, NS B4A 1E7

Defence Research & Development Canada / Recherche et développement pour la défense Canada

101 Colonel By Dr., Ottawa, ON K1A 0K2
Tel: 613-995-2534
Toll-Free: 888-995-2534
TTY: 800-467-9877
information@forces.gc.ca
www.drdc-rddc.gc.ca
Other Communication: mlo-blm@forces.gc.ca

Provides research & development both nationally & internationally by providing the Canadian Forces with relevant & timely technologies, while at the same time offering attractive collaborative opportunities to other government departments, the private sector, academia & international allies.

Chief Executive Officer & Assistant Deputy Minister, Science & Technology, Dr. Marc Fortin
Tel: 613-996-2020
Director General, Science & Technology Centre Operations, Jocelyn Tremblay
Tel: 613-992-0737
Director General, Corporate Services, Mylène Ouellet
Tel: 613-992-6105
Director General, Military Personnel Research & Analysis, Susan Truscott
Tel: 613-992-6162

Destination Canada (DC)

#800, 1045 Howe St., Vancouver, BC V6Z 2A9
Tel: 604-638-8300
en.destinationcanada.com
twitter.com/DestinationCAN
www.facebook.com/ExploreCanada
www.linkedin.com/company/destination-canada
www.youtube.com/user/CTCNewsNouvellesCCT

Formerly known as the Canadian Tourism Commission, Destination Canada is a unique partnership between tourism business & associations, provincial & territorial governments, & the Government of Canada. Destination Canada's mission is to sustain a vibrant & profitable Canadian tourism industry. The agency maintains offices in the following countries: Australia, Brazil, China, France, Germany, India, Japan, Mexico, South Korean, the United Kingdom & the United States.

Chair, Olga Ilich
President & Chief Executive Officer, David Goldstein
Chief Financial Officer & Vice-President, Finance & Operations, André Joannette
Chief Marketing Officer & Senior Vice-President, Marketing Strategy, Jon Mamela
Vice-President, International, Emmanuelle Legault
Vice-President, Strategy & Corporate Communications, Gilles Verret
General Counsel & Corporate Secretary, Sarah Sidhu

Elections Canada / Élections Canada

30 Victoria St., Gatineau, ON K1A 0M6
Tel: 613-993-2975; *Fax:* 613-954-8584
Toll-Free: 800-463-6868
TTY: 800-361-8935
www.elections.ca
Other Communication: Toll-Free Fax: 1-888-524-1444; Toll-Free Phone (Mexico): 001-800-514-6868
twitter.com/ElectionsCan_E
www.facebook.com/ElectionsCanE
youtube.com/c/ElectionsCanadaE

The Chief Electoral Officer of Canada is responsible for the conduct of federal elections & referendums in Canada & for ensuring that all provisions of the Canada Elections Act are complied with & enforced. Major activities include the maintenance of the National Register of Electors, the production of lists of electors, the training of returning officers, the revisions of polling division boundaries & the acquisition of election materials & supplies. Elections Canada is also responsible for the compilation & publishing of statutory & statistical reports, & the provision of advice & assistance to Parliament, as required. The agency also implements public education & information programs. As well, its mandate includes the registration of political parties & third parties engaged in election advertising, & the certification of statutory payments to be made to auditors, political parties, & candidates under the election expenses provisions of the Act. Following each decennial census, the Chief Electoral Officer must calculate the number of electoral districts to be assigned to each province according to rules contained in s. 51 of the Constitution Act, prepare population distribution maps for use by the ten electoral boundaires commissions (one per province) that are directly responsible for readjusting federal electoral boundaries & publishing their reports.

Minister Responsible; Minister, Democratic Institutions, Hon. Maryam Monsef, P.C.
Tel: 613-995-6411; *Fax:* 613-996-9800
Maryam.Monsef@parl.gc.ca
Parliamentary Secretary to the Minister of Democratic Institutions, Mark Holland
Tel: 613-995-8042; *Fax:* 613-996-1289
Mark.Holland@parl.gc.ca
Chief Electoral Officer, Marc Mayrand
Tel: 613-993-2975; *Fax:* 613-954-8584
Chief of Staff, Office of the CEO, Vivian Cousineau
Tel: 819-939-2012; *Fax:* 819-939-1811

Chief Information Officer Sector / Secteur du dirigeant principal de l'information

Fax: 819-939-1204

Chief Information Officer, Jacques Mailloux
Tel: 819-939-1230; *Fax:* 819-939-1204
Director, IT Infrastructure Operations, Robert Chassé
Tel: 819-939-1240; *Fax:* 819-939-1204
Acting Director, Business Solutions Development & Maintenance, Tarek Houssari
Tel: 819-939-1300; *Fax:* 819-939-1204
Director, Information Management, Suzanne Lépinay
Tel: 819-939-1294; *Fax:* 819-939-1810

Electoral Events / Scrutins

Fax: 613-954-2874

Deputy Chief Electoral Officer, Michel Roussel
Tel: 819-939-1755; *Fax:* 819-939-1757
Senior Director, Electoral Data Management & Readiness, Maurice Bastarache
Tel: 819-939-1731; *Fax:* 819-939-1675
Senior Director, Field Readiness & Event Management, Dani Srour
Tel: 819-939-2208; *Fax:* 819-939-1757
Senior Director, Electoral Data Management & Readiness, Duncan Toswell
Tel: 819-939-1456; *Fax:* 819-939-1750
Director, Field Programs & Services, Denis Bazinet
Tel: 819-939-1400; *Fax:* 819-939-1204
Director, Field Personnel Readiness, Nathalie Chalifoux
Tel: 819-939-1794
Director, National Register of Electors, Céline Desbiens
Tel: 819-939-1686
Director, Electoral Geography, Pierre Desjardins
Tel: 819-939-1734; *Fax:* 819-939-1675
Director, Analysis & Quantity, Daniel Larrivée
Tel: 819-939-1729; *Fax:* 819-939-1732
Director, Alternative Voting Methods, Paul Legault
Tel: 613-949-0101
Director, Field Personnel Readiness, Larry Li
Tel: 819-939-1751; *Fax:* 613-990-7583
Director, Special Projects, Nan Smith
Tel: 819-939-1730; *Fax:* 613-939-1750

Integrated Services, Policy & Public Affairs / Services intégrés, Politique et Affaires publiques

Fax: 819-939-1920

Deputy Chief Electoral Officer, Belaineh Deguefé
Tel: 819-939-1890
Senior Director, Public Affairs, Susan Torosian
Tel: 819-939-1856; *Fax:* 613-939-1920
Director, Outreach, Lisa Drouillard
Tel: 819-939-2296; *Fax:* 819-939-1925
Director, Corporate Strategy Office, Bill Duncan
Tel: 819-939-1516; *Fax:* 613-939-1589
Director, External Relations, Jane Dunlop
Tel: 819-939-1898
Director, Advertising & Publication Services, Marc Lamontagne
Tel: 819-939-1910; *Fax:* 819-939-1925
Acting Director, Outreach, Mario Lavoie
Tel: 819-939-1855; *Fax:* 819-939-1920
Acting Director, Policy & Research, Alain Pelletier
Tel: 819-939-1912; *Fax:* 819-939-1920

Office of the Chief Financial & Planning Officer / Bureau du dirigeant principal des finances et de la planification

Chief Financial & Planning Officer, Hughes St-Pierre
Tel: 819-939-1461; *Fax:* 819-939-1529
Controller & Deputy Chief Financial Officer, France Labine
Tel: 819-939-1466; *Fax:* 819-939-1532
Director, Resource Management, Michel Leblanc
Tel: 819-939-1465

Political Financing / Financement politique

Tel: 819-939-1945; *Fax:* 819-939-1997

Deputy Chief Electoral Officer, Sylvian Dubois
Tel: 819-939-1944; *Fax:* 819-939-1997

Regulatory Affairs / Affaires régulatoires

Deputy Chief Electoral Officer, Stéphane Perrault
Tel: 819-939-2082
General Counsel & Senior Director, Anne Lawson
Tel: 819-939-2088
Senior Director, Electoral Integrity Office, Lyne H. Morin
Tel: 819-939-1742
Director, Political Financing & Audit, François LeBlanc
Tel: 819-939-1943; *Fax:* 819-939-1803
Director, Regulatory Instruments & Systems, Jeff Merrett
Tel: 819-939-2044; *Fax:* 819-939-1803

Employment & Social Development Canada / Emploi et Développement social Canada

140 Promenade du Portage, Gatineau, QC K1A 0J9
www.esdc.gc.ca
Other Communication: Media enquiries: 819-994-5559
twitter.com/SocDevSoc
www.youtube.com/hrsdcanada

In Nov. 2015, Prime Minister Trudeau created two new portfolios to fall under Employment & Social Development Canada: Families, Children & Social Development, & Employment, Workforce Development & Labour.

The department works to build a competitive country & to support Canadians in making choices to live productively. The following are key responsibilities of the federal department: developing policies to assist Canadians to use their talents, skills & resources to participate in learning, work, & their community; creating programs to support initiative to help citizens in life transitions; improving outcomes for people through services offered by Service Canada & other partners; & establishing a healthy work environment.

Minister, Families, Children & Social Development, Hon. Jean-Yves Duclos, P.C.
Jean-Yves.Duclos@parl.gc.ca
Minister, Employment, Workforce Development & Labour, Hon. MaryAnn Mihychuk, P.C., B.Sc., M.Sc., P.Geo.
Tel: 613-992-7148; *Fax:* 613-996-9125
MaryAnn.Mihychuk@parl.gc.ca
Minister, Sport & Persons with Disabilities, Hon. Carla Qualtrough, P.C.
Tel: 613-992-2957; *Fax:* 613-992-3192
Carla.Qualtrough@parl.gc.ca
Deputy Minister, Louise Levonian
Tel: 819-654-7047; *Fax:* 819-953-5603
Parliamentary Secretary to the Minister of Employment, Workforce Development & Labour, Rodger Cuzner, B.A.
Tel: 613-992-6756; *Fax:* 613-992-4053
rodger.cuzner@parl.gc.ca

Parliamentary Secretary to the Minister of Families, Children & Social Development, Terry Duguid
Tel: 613-995-7517; *Fax:* 613-943-1466
Terry.Duguid@parl.gc.ca
Associate Deputy Minister, Benoit Robidoux
Tel: 819-934-6330; *Fax:* 819-953-5603
benoit.robidoux@hrsdc-rhdcc.gc.ca
Senior General Counsel, Mark McCombs
Tel: 819-654-1965; *Fax:* 819-953-7317
mark.mccombs@hrsdc-rhdcc.gc.ca
Director General, Legal Services, Caroline Cyr
Tel: 819-654-3872; *Fax:* 819-956-8998
caroline.cyr@hrsdc-rhdcc.gc.ca
Director General, Legal Services, Zahra Pourjafar-Ziaei
Tel: 819-654-3874; *Fax:* 819-994-2291
zahra.pourjafarziaei@hrsdc-rhdcc.gc.ca
Director, Regional Affairs, Marie Tremblay
Tel: 418-648-2430; *Fax:* 418-648-7984
marie.qc.tremblay@hrsdc-rhdcc.gc.ca
Director, Paliamentary Affairs, Daniel Boudria
Tel: 819-654-5546
Director, Communications, Mathieu Filion
Tel: 819-654-5546; *Fax:* 819-994-5222
Director, Operations & Quebec Desk, Michel Archambault
Tel: 819-654-5611
Director, Policy, Mathieu Laberge
Tel: 819-654-5546

Associated Agencies, Boards & Commissions:

•Canada Employment Insurance Commission (CEIC) / Commission de l'assurance-emploi du Canada (CAEC)
140, Promenade du Portage, Phase IV
Gatineau, QC K1A 0J9
Toll-free: 800-206-7218
www.esdc.gc.ca/en/ei/commission.page
Manages the Employment Insurance Program.

•Canada Industrial Relations Board / Conseil canadien des relations industrielles
See Entry Name Index for detailed listing.

•Canadian Centre for Occupational Health & Safety / Centre canadien d'hygiène et de sécurité au travail
See Entry Name Index for detailed listing.

•Canadian Council of Directors of Apprenticeship (CCDA) / Conseil canadien des directeurs de l'apprentissage
140 Promenade du Portage, 5th Fl, Phase IV
Gatineau, QC K1A 0J9
Fax: 819-994-0202
Toll-free: 877-599-6933
TTY: 800-926-9105
redseal-sceaurouge@hrsdc-rhdcc.gc.ca
www.red-seal.ca
A national body responsible for the certification of skilled workers, in the regulated trade, under the Interprovincial Standards (Red Seal) Program. This program is designed to facilitate the mobility of workers employed in the apprenticeable occupations in Canada through the establishment of common standards for certification. The apprenticeship program is generally administered by provincial & territorial departments responsible for education, labour & training (under the direction of the provincial & territorial Director of Apprenticeship) with authority delegated from the legislation in each province & territory. Through the program, apprentices who have completed their training & certified journeymen are able to obtain a Red Seal endorsement on their Certificate of Qualification by successfully completing an Interprovincial Standards Examination. The program encourages standardization of provincial & territorial apprenticeship training & certification programs. The Red Seal allows qualified trade persons to practice the trade in any province or territory in Canada where the trade is designated without having to write further examinations.

•Social Security Tribunal (SST) / Tribunal de la sécurité sociale (TSS)
PO Box 9812 T
Ottawa, ON K1G 6S3
Tel: 613-952-8805
Toll-free: 877-227-8577
TTY: 800-465-7735
info.sst-tss@canada.gc.ca
www.canada.gc.ca/sst-tss
Other Communication: Toll-Free Fax: 1-855-814-4117
The Social Security Tribunal was created April 1, 2013 to function as an independent administrative tribunal & provide appeal processes for Employment Insurance (EI), Canada Pension Plan (CPP) & Old Age Security (OAS) decisions.

Office of the Minister of Employment, Workforce Development & Labour / Cabinet de la ministre de l'Emploi, du Développement de la main-d'ouvre et du Travail
The new Ministry of Employment, Workforce Development and Labour was created Nov. 2015 by Prime Minister Trudeau.
Minister, Employment, Workforce Development & Labour, Hon. MaryAnn Mihychuk, P.C., B.Sc., M.Sc., P.Geo.
Tel: 819-654-5611
MaryAnn.Mihychuk@parl.gc.ca
Director, Policy, David Foster
Tel: 819-953-5646; *Fax:* 819-994-5168
david.foster@labour-travail.gc.ca
Director, Communications, John O'Leary
Tel: 819-654-5611

Office of the Minister Family, Children & Social Development / Cabinet de Ministre de la Famille, de l'Enfance et du Développement social
The new Ministry of Family, Children and Social Development was created Nov. 2015 by Prime Minister Trudeau.
Minister Families, Children & Social Development, Hon. Jean-Yves Duclos
Tel: 819-654-5546; *Fax:* 819-994-0448
jeanyves.duclos@hrsdc-rhdcc.gc.ca
Chief of Staff, Josée Duplessis
Tel: 819-654-5546; *Fax:* 819-953-0357
Director, Communications, Mathieu Filion
Tel: 819-654-5546; *Fax:* 819-994-5222
Director, Policy, Mathieu Laberge
Tel: 819-654-5546
Director, Issues Management, Marianne Goodwin
Tel: 819-654-5546
Director, Regional Affairs, Marie Tremblay
Tel: 418-648-2430; *Fax:* 418-648-7984
marie.qc.tremblay@hrsdc-rhdcc.gc.ca
Director General, Social Development, Labour & Service Canada Communications, Krista Wilcox
Tel: 819-654-5577
krista.wilcox@hrsdc-rhdcc.gc.ca

Corporate Secretariat / Secrétariat du Ministère
Corporate Secretary, Cheryl Fischer
Tel: 819-994-1122
cheryl.fischer@hrsdc-rhdcc.gc.ca

Chief Financial Officer's Office / Bureau de l'agent principal des finances
Chief Financial Officer, Alain P. Séguin
Tel: 819-654-6634; *Fax:* 819-997-0699
alain.p.seguin@hrsdc-rhdcc.gc.ca
Senior Director General, Corporate Accounting & Reporting, Patrick Amyot
Tel: 819-654-6437; *Fax:* 819-997-6149
patrick.amyot@hrsdc-rhdcc.gc.ca
Senior Director General, Investment, Asset & Procurement Management, Alain R. Gélinas
Tel: 819-654-5847; *Fax:* 819-994-1114
alain.r.gelinas@hrsdc-rhdcc.gc.ca
Senior Director, Financial Management Services, Ken Baker
Tel: 819-654-6562
ken.baker@hrsdc-rhdcc.gc.ca
Acting Senior Director, Corporate Accounting, Julie N. Charbonneau
Tel: 819-654-6437; *Fax:* 819-953-0831
julie.n.charbonneau@hrsdc-rhdcc.gc.ca
Senior Director, Enabling Services, Sara Lantz
Tel: 819-654-6546
sara.lantz@hrsdc-rhdcc.gc.ca
Senior Director General, Corporate Accounting & Reporting, Annie Péladeau
Tel: 819-654-6434; *Fax:* 819-997-6149
annie.peladeau@hrsdc-rhdcc.gc.ca
Senior Director, Planning & Expenditure Management, Michel Racine
Tel: 819-654-6561; *Fax:* 819-994-6411
michel.racine@hrsdc-rhdcc.gc.ca
Senior Director, Strategic Financial Analysis & Costing, Frédéric Souligny
Tel: 819-654-6531
frederic.souligny@hrsdc-rhdcc.gc.ca
Director, SAP ISSO, Antoine Thibodeau
Tel: 819-654-6325; *Fax:* 819-953-8637
antoine.thibodeau@hrsdc-rhdcc.gc.ca

Internal Audit Services Branch / Direction générale des services de vérification interne
Chief Audit Executive, Vincent DaLuz
Tel: 819-654-5767; *Fax:* 819-953-0177
vincent.daluz@hrsdc-rhdcc.gc.ca
Senior Director, Audit Operations, Brigitte Marois
Tel: 819-654-5779; *Fax:* 819-953-0177
brigitte.marois@hrsdc-rhdcc.gc.ca

Human Resources Services Branch / Direction générale des services des ressources humaines
Human Resources Services provides human resource services & technical expertise to the ministry, including succession planning, career development, orientation & training; compensation & benefits; classification & staffing; organizational renewal design & development; labour relations; occupational health & safety; & employment equity & official languages.
Assistant Deputy Minister, Peter Larose
Tel: 819-654-6909; *Fax:* 819-934-6620
peter.larose@hrsdc-rhdcc.gc.ca
Executive Director, National Human Resources Service Centre, Johanne Brault
Tel: 438-892-0101; *Fax:* 514-496-2001
johanne.brault@hrsdc-rhdcc.gc.ca
Director General, Strategic Directions, Marie-Claude Pelletier
Tel: 819-654-6920
marieclaude.pelletier@hrsdc-rhdcc.gc.ca
Director General, Branch Management Services, Sylvain Patenaude
Tel: 819-654-6892; *Fax:* 819-954-6097
sylvain.patenaude@hrsdc-rhdcc.gc.ca
Director General, Centre of Expertise, Sandra Webber
Tel: 819-654-4936; *Fax:* 819-953-1100
sandra.webber@hrsdc-rhdcc.gc.ca

Income Security & Social Development Branch / Direction générale de la sécurité du revenu et du développement social
Income Security & Social Development is the focal point for social policy & programs designed to ensure that children, families, seniors, people with disabilities, the homeless & those at risk of homelessness, communities & others who are facing social challenges have the support, knowledge, & information they need to maintain their well-being & facilitate their participation in society.
Senior Assistant Deputy Minister, Kathryn McDade
Tel: 819-654-2099; *Fax:* 819-934-5331
kathryn.mcdade@hrsdc-rhdcc.gc.ca
Senior Director, Program Information, Management & Analysis, Jackie Holden
Tel: 819-654-6972
jackie.holden@hrsdc-rhdcc.gc.ca
Director General, Office for Disability Issues, Nancy Milroy-Swainson
Tel: 819-624-7687; *Fax:* 819-994-8634
nancy.milroyswainson@hrsdc-rhdcc.gc.ca
Other Communications: Secure Phone: 819-624-7688
Director, Federal, Provincial & Territorial & Stakeholder Relations, Lisa Legault
Tel: 819-654-2267; *Fax:* 819-654-2695
lisa.legault@hrsdc-rhdcc.gc.ca

Innovation, Information & Technology Branch / Direction générale d'innovation, information et technologie
Innovation, Information & Technology provides information & technology services to the ministry, including business applications that support & streamline work processes, access data, & process millions of benefit-related transactions to address Canadians' needs. It is also responsible for the provision & management of telephony & data networks, applications & data stores, & new processes & technologies.
Chief Information Officer, Charles Nixon
Tel: 819-654-1400; *Fax:* 819-654-1306
charles.nixon@hrsdc-rhdcc.gc.ca
Director General, Client Service Operations & Solutions Development, Mario Bégin
Tel: 819-654-1050; *Fax:* 819-654-1008
mario.begin@hrsdc-rhdcc.gc.ca
Executive Director, Enterprise Services, Barbara Cretzman
Tel: 819-654-0468
barbara.cretzman@hrsdc-rhdcc.gc.ca
Director General, Transformation, Charles McColgan
Tel: 819-654-1147
charles.mccolgan@hrsdc-rhdcc.gc.ca
Director General, Strategy, Planning, Architecture & Management, Lorne Sundby
Tel: 587-756-0700; *Fax:* 780-495-6431
lorne.sundby@hrsdc-rhdcc.gc.ca
Acting Executive Director, Client Service Operations & Solutions Development, Nathalie Beaulieu
Tel: 819-654-0163
nathalie.beaulieu@hrsdc-rhdcc.gc.ca
Director General, Business Relationship Management, Linda Stutchbury
Tel: 587-756-0688
linda.stutchbury@hrsdc-rhdcc.gc.ca
Director General, Enterprise Services, Vidya Shankarnarayan
Tel: 819-654-1205
vidya.shankarnarayan@hrsdc-rhdcc.gc.ca

Labour Program / Programme du travail
The Labour Program promotes safe, healthy, cooperative & productive workplaces. They develop, administer & enforce workplace legislation & regulations, such as the Canada Labour Code, which covers industrial relations, health & safety & employment standards, & the Employment Equity Act, which promotes workplace equality by removing the barriers faced by women, Aboriginal peoples, persons with disabilities & visible

minorities while on the job. These laws cover federally regulated workers & employers.

Assistant Deputy Minister, Compliance, Operations & Program Development, Gary Robertson
Tel: 819-654-4558
gary.robertson@labour-travail.gc.ca

Assistant Deputy Minister, Policy, Dispute Resolution & International Affairs, Anthony Giles
Tel: 819-654-6776; *Fax:* 819-934-8679
anthony.giles@labour-travail.gc.ca

Executive Director & Senior Counsel, Occupational Health & Safety Tribunal Canada, Marie-Claude Turgeon
Tel: 613-957-4105; *Fax:* 613-954-6404
marieclaude.turgeon@ohstc-tsstc.gc.ca

Director General, Federal Mediation & Conciliation Service, Guy Baron
Tel: 819-654-4080; *Fax:* 819-997-1693
guy.baron@labour-travail.gc.ca
Other Communications: Secure Phone: 819-654-4079

Director General, Workplace Directorate, Brenda Baxter
Tel: 819-654-4410; *Fax:* 819-953-8883
brenda.baxter@labour-travail.gc.ca

Director General, Federal Programs, Maggie Trudel-Maggiore
Tel: 819-654-4529
maggie.trudelmaggiore@labour-travail.gc.ca

Acting Director General, Strategic Integration, Planning & Coordination, Carole A. Norton
Tel: 819-654-4484; *Fax:* 819-934-8679
carole.norton@labour-travail.gc.ca

Director General, Regional Operations & Compliance Directorate, Annik Wilson
Tel: 819-654-4370
annik.wilson@labour-travail.gc.ca

Director General, International & Intergovernmental Labour Affairs, Patry Rakesh
Tel: 819-654-1689
rakesh.patry@labour-travail.gc.ca

Learning Branch / Apprentissage

The Learning branch helps Canadians attend college, university & trade schools by providing advice, loans, assistance, grants to students, by encouraging individuals & organizations to save for a child's post-secondary education, & by assisting children from low-income families through grants. It is responsible for programs & services related to learning, including student financial assistance, savings incentives for post-secondary education, & literacy.

Assistant Deputy Minister, Gail Johnson
Tel: 819-654-8707; *Fax:* 819-654-8714
gail.e.johnson@hrsdc-rhdcc.gc.ca

Director General, Program Policy Planning, Danièle Besner
Tel: 819-654-8739; *Fax:* 819-994-1868
daniele.besner@hrsdc-rhdcc.gc.ca

Director, Program Delivery, Canada Student Loans Directorate, Colette Cibula
Tel: 819-654-8511; *Fax:* 819-654-8588
colette.cibula@hrsdc-rhdcc.gc.ca

Director, Program Integrity & Accountability, Canada Student Loans Directorate, Jonathan Wallace
Tel: 819-654-8446; *Fax:* 819-654-8357
jonathan.wallace@hrsdc-rhdcc.gc.ca

Director General, Canada Education Savings Program, David Swol
Tel: 819-654-8605; *Fax:* 819-654-8703
david.swol@hrsdc-rhdcc.gc.ca

Office of the Deputy Minister of Labour / Cabinet de Sous-ministre du travail

Deputy Minister of Labour, Lori Sterling
Tel: 819-934-3320; *Fax:* 819-934-7066
lori.sterling@labour-travail.gc.ca

Director General, Catherine A. Drew
Tel: 819-997-8850; *Fax:* 819-934-7066
catherine.a.drew@labour-travail.gc.ca

Senior Advisor to the Deputy Minister of Labour, Christian Beaulieu
Tel: 819-994-5633; *Fax:* 819-934-7066
christian.beaulieu@labour-travail.gc.ca

Program Operations / Opérations des programmes

Program Operations handles the operation & coordination of the Grant & Contributions programs across the Department.

Assistant Deputy Minister, Joanne Lamothe
Tel: 819-654-2447; *Fax:* 819-934-7614
joanne.lamothe@hrsdc-rhdcc.gc.ca

Director General, Centre of Expertise (Gs &Cs Delivery), Shelley Dooher
Tel: 819-654-2641
shelley.dooher@hrsdc-rhdcc.gc.ca

Director General, Program & Services Oversight, Robert Smith
Tel: 819-654-2476
robert.smith@servicecanada.gc.ca

Director General, Strategic Directions, Nancy Gardiner
Tel: 819-654-2558; *Fax:* 819-953-9898
nancy.gardiner@hrsdc-rhdcc.gc.ca

Public Affairs & Stakeholder Relations / Affaires publiques et Relations avec les intervenants

Public Affairs & Stakeholder Relations informs Canadians about HRSDC's mandate, policies & programs. It also supports departmental activities in engaging & communicating with stakeholders & citizens.

Assistant Deputy Minister, James Gilbert
Tel: 819-654-1741; *Fax:* 819-934-5751
james.gilbert@hrsdc-rhdcc.gc.ca

Director General, Labour, Seniors & Social Development Communications Directorate, Barry Frewer
Tel: 819-654-1883
barry.frewer@hrsdc-rhdcc.gc.ca

Director General, Strategic Communications & Stakeholders Relations, Benoit Trottier
Tel: 819-654-1744
benoit.trottier@hrsdc-rhdcc.gc.ca

Director, Jobs & Training Communications, Brian Laghi
Tel: 819-654-1914
brian.laghi@hrsdc-rhdcc.gc.ca

Director, Branch Management Services, Aline Michaud
Tel: 819-654-1729
aline.michaud@hrsdc-rhdcc.gc.ca

Service Canada

140, Promenade du Portage, Gatineau, QC K1A 0J9
Fax: 613-941-1827
Toll-Free: 800-622-6232
TTY: 800-926-9105
www.servicecanada.gc.ca
Other Communication: Media enquiries: 819-994-5559; Twitter (French): twitter.com/ServiceCanada_F; YouTube (French): www.youtube.com/user/ServiceCanadaF
twitter.com/ServiceCanada_E
www.youtube.com/user/ServiceCanadaE

Service Canada provides convenient access to a great range of Government of Canada programs & services. Service Canada Centres, as well as scheduled outreach sites, are located throughout Canada. The Service Canada web site & call centres are also available to assist Canadian citizens.
The following contact information is for frequently used programs:
Apprenticeship Grants: Toll-Free Phone 1-866-742-3644, TTY 1-800-255-4786;
Canada Pension Plan (CPP): Toll-Free Phone 1-800-277-9914, TTY 1-800-255-4786;
Employer Contact Centre: Toll-Free Phone 1-800-367-5693, TTY 1-855-881-9874;
Employment Insurance (EI): Toll-Free Phone 1-800-206-7218, TTY 1-800-529-3742;
Old Age Security (OAS): Toll-Free Phone 1-800-277-9914, TTY 1-800-255-4786;
Passports: Toll-Free Phone: 1-800-567-6868, TTY 1-866-255-7655;
Social Insurance Number (SIN): Toll-Free Phone: 1-800-206-7218;
Wage Earner Protection Program (WEPP): Toll-Free Phone 1-866-683-6516, TTY 1-800-926-9105.

Senior Associate Deputy Minister; Chief Operating Officer, Service Canada, Louise Levonian
Tel: 819-654-5754; *Fax:* 819-934-5770
louise.levonian@hrsdc-rhdcc.gc.ca

Assistant Deputy Minister, Integrity Services, Louis Beauséjour
Tel: 819-654-4826; *Fax:* 819-934-9312
louis.beausejour@hrsdc-rhdcc.gc.ca

Assistant Deputy Minister, Citizen Services, Peter Simeoni
Tel: 819-654-5079; *Fax:* 819-997-5433
peter.simeoni@servicecanada.gc.ca

Senior Assistant Deputy Minister, Processing & Payment Services, Benoit Long
Tel: 819-654-6949
benoit.long@hrsdc-rhdcc.gc.ca

Senior Executive Director, Office Payments Services - Quebec, Rui Costa
Tel: 438-892-1270; *Fax:* 514-496-6794
rui.costa@servicecanada.gc.ca

Senior Executive Director, Citizen Services & Program Delivery - Ontario, Geoff Anderton
Tel: 647-790-9513
geoff.anderton@servicecanada.gc.ca

Senior Executive Director, Payments & Processing - Atlantic, Doug Johnson
Tel: 709-772-6261; *Fax:* 709-772-5703
doug.johnson@servicecanada.gc.ca
Other Communications: Secure Phone: 709-979-0302

Senior Executive Director, Citizen Services & Program Delivery - Quebec, Esther Lessard
Tel: 438-892-1353; *Fax:* 514-282-7271
esther.lessard@servicecanada.gc.ca

Executive Director, EI Modernization, Fred Begley
Tel: 819-654-7566; *Fax:* 613-954-6105
fred.begley@hrsdc-rhdcc.gc.ca

Executive Director, Processing & Payment Services Branch, Carol Sabourin
Tel: 819-654-7709
carol.sabourin@servicecanada.gc.ca

Executive Director, Ontario Federal Council, Vacant

Executive Director, OAS & CPP Business Operations, Michael A. Kidd
Tel: 819-654-7784
michael.a.kidd@servicecanada.gc.ca

Director General, Strategic Services - Atlantic, Trevor Kraus
Tel: 902-536-4614
trevor.kraus@servicecanada.gc.ca

Acting Senior Director, EI Operations, Sonja Adcock
Tel: 819-654-7572
sonja.adcock@servicecanada.gc.ca

Senior Executive Director, Citizen Services Maritime, Jeff E. Tapely
Tel: 506-247-0588; *Fax:* 506-452-3213
jeff.tapley@servicecanada.gc.ca

Executive Director, Phone Ops & ICM, Daniel Tremblay
Tel: 819-654-6865
daniel.tremblay@servicecanada.gc.ca

Director General, Strategic Directions Directorate, Jason Choueiri
Tel: 819-654-6662
jason.choueiri@servicecanada.gc.ca

Senior Director General, Service Policy, Partnerships & Performance, Cheryl Fisher
Tel: 819-654-6139
cheryl.fisher@servicecanada.gc.ca

Director General, Identity Policy & Programs Directorate, Anik Dupont
Tel: 819-654-4751
anik.dupont@servicecanada.gc.ca

Director General, Integrity Operations, Marc LeBrun
Tel: 819-654-4728; *Fax:* 819-953-2633
marc.l.lebrun@servicecanada.gc.ca

Senior Executive Director, Stephanie A. Hébert
Tel: 438-892-1812; *Fax:* 514-283-1691
stephanie.a.hebert@servicecanada.gc.ca

Director General, Strategic Projects Office, Peter Boyd
Tel: 819-654-5132
peter.boyd@servicecanada.gc.ca

Director General, Service Canada - Marketing, Christine M. Burton
Tel: 819-654-5023
christine.burton@servicecanada.gc.ca

Director General, Strategic Directions, Roger C. Butt
Tel: 819-654-5119; *Fax:* 819-997-5433
roger.c.butt@servicecanada.gc.ca

Director General & Departmental Security Officer, Internal Integrity & Security & DSO, Daniel J. Comeau
Tel: 819-654-4669; *Fax:* 819-994-9616
daniel.j.comeau@servicecanada.gc.ca

Director General, CPP & OAS Renewal, Cliff G. Groen
Tel: 819-654-6944
cliff.groen@servicecanada.gc.ca

Senior Executive Director, Citizen Services & Program Delivery Branch, Cathy M. Hennessey
Tel: 647-790-9076
cathy.hennessey@servicecanada.gc.ca

Director General, Partnerships & Service Offerings, Julie Lalonde-Goldenberg
Tel: 819-654-5099; *Fax:* 819-934-2148
julie.lalondegoldenberg@servicecanada.gc.ca

Director General, Digital Service Directorate, Lucie Kempffer
Tel: 819-654-6854
lucie.kempffer@hrsdc-rhdcc.gc.ca

Director General, Call Centre Directorate, Vacant

Director General, Benefits Processing, Ron Meighan
Tel: 819-654-7573
ron.meighan@servicecanada.gc.ca

Director General, Identity Policy & Programs Directorate, Joanne Roy-Aubrey
Tel: 819-654-4765; *Fax:* 819-953-4144
joanne.royaubrey@servicecanada.gc.ca

Alberta Service Canada Centres

Brooks
Cassils Plaza, 608 - 2 St. West, Brooks, AB T1R 1A8

Calgary - 4th Ave. SE
Calgary Centre Service Canada Centre, Harry Hays Building, #270, 220 - 4 Ave. SE, Calgary, AB T2G 4X3

Calgary - Crowchild Trail NW
Calgary North Service Canada Centre, One Executive Place, 1816 Crowchild Trail NW, Main Fl., Calgary, AB T2M 3Y7

Calgary - Fisher St. SE
Calgary South Service Canada Centre, Fisher Park Place II, #100, 6712 Fisher St. SE, Calgary, AB T2H 2A7

Calgary - Marlborough Way NE
Calgary East Service Canada Centre, #1502, 515 Marlborough Way NE, Calgary, AB T2A 7E7

Camrose
Federal Building, 4901 - 50 Ave., 2nd Fl., Camrose, AB T4V 0S2

Canmore
Building C, #113, 802 Bow Valley Trail, Canmore, AB T1W 1N6

Edmonton - 87th Ave. NW
Edmonton Meadowlark Service Canada, Meadowlark Shopping Ctr, #120, 15710 - 87th Ave. NW, Edmonton, AB T5R 5W9

Edmonton - 137th Ave. NW
Edmonton North Service Canada Centre, Northgate Centre, #2000, 9499 - 137th Ave. NW, Edmonton, AB T5E 5R8
Tel: 780-495-3904
Toll-Free: 800-622-6232

Edmonton - Jasper Ave.
Edmonton Canada Place Service Canada Centre, Canada Place, 9700 Jasper Ave., Main Fl., Edmonton, AB T5J 4C3

Edmonton - Millbourne Shopping Centre NW
Edmonton Millbourne Service Canada Centre, #148, Millbourne Shopping Centre NW, Edmonton, AB T6K 3L6

Edson
4905 - 4 Ave., Edson, AB T7E 1T5

Fort McMurray
#107, 8530 Manning Ave., Main Fl., Fort McMurray, AB T9H 5G2

Grande Prairie
Towne Centre Mall, #100, 9845 - 99 Ave., Grande Prairie, AB T8V 0R3

Lethbridge
Crowsnest Trail Plaza, 101, 920 - 2A Ave. North, Lethbridge, AB T1H 0E3

Lloydminster
4114 - 70th Ave., Lloydminster, AB T9V 2X3

Medicine Hat
Northside Centre, 78 - 8 St. NW, Medicine Hat, AB T1A 6P1

Red Deer
#101, 4901 - 46th St., Red Deer, AB T4N 1N2

St Paul
4807 - 50 Ave., St Paul, AB T0A 3A0

Slave Lake
Sawridge Plaza, 100 Main St. South, Slave Lake, AB T0G 2A3

Service Canada Outreach Sites - Alberta
Toll-Free: 800-622-6232
TTY: 800-926-9105

The following places in Alberta are scheduled outreach sites for Service Canada:
Athabasca (Duniece Centre, 4810 - 50th St., 3rd Fl.);
Barrhead (6203 - 49 St.);
Blairmore (Provincial Building, 12501 - 20th Ave.);
Cold Lake (Cold Lake Public Library, 5513B - 48th Ave.);
Drayton Valley (5136 - 1 Ave., 2nd Fl.);
Drumheller (90 - 3rd Ave., 4th Fl.);
Falher (308 Main St.);
Grande Cache (4500 Pine Plaza);
High Level (Provincial Building, 10106 - 100 Ave.);
High Prairie (5226 - 53 Ave., 2nd Fl.);
Hinton (568 Carmichael Lane);
Hobbema (Maskwacis Health Centre);
Jasper (Château Jasper, 96 Geikie St.);
Lac La Biche (Provincial Building, 503 Beaver Hill Rd.);
Peace River (Valley Chrysler Building, 9603 - 90 Ave.);
Rocky Mountain House (4919 - 51st St.);
Stettler (4835 - 50 St.);
Taber (5324 - 48th Ave.);
Vegreville (5121 - 49 St.);
Wabasca-Desmarais (891 Mistassiniy Rd.);
Westlock (11304 - 99 St.);
Whitecourt (Midtown Mall, 5115 - 49th St.).

British Columbia Service Canada Centres

Abbotsford
100, 32525 Simon Ave., Abbotsford, BC V2T 6T6

Burnaby
#100, 3480 Gilmore Way, Burnaby, BC V5G 4Y1

Campbell River
#101, 950 Alder St., Campbell River, BC V9W 2P8

Chilliwack
#100, 9345 Main St., Chilliwack, BC V2P 4M3

Coquitlam
#100, 2963 Glen Dr., Coquitlam, BC V3B 2P7

Courtenay
Comox Valley Service Canada Centre, 130 - 19 St., Courtenay, BC V9N 8S1

Cranbrook
1113 Baker St., Cranbrook, BC V1C 1A7

Dawson Creek
#103, 1508 - 102 Ave., Dawson Creek, BC V1G 2E2

Duncan
Cowichan Service Canada Centre, 211 Jubilee St., Duncan, BC V9L 1W8

Kamloops
317 Seymour St., 1st Fl., Kamloops, BC V2C 2E8

Kelowna
#106, 471 Queensway, Kelowna, BC V1Y 6S5

Langley
#102, 8747 - 204 St., Langley, BC V1M 2Y5

Maple Ridge
Ridge Meadows Service Canada Centre, 22325 Lougheed Hwy., Maple Ridge, BC V2X 2T3

Nanaimo
#201, 60 Front St., Nanaimo, BC V9R 5H7

Nelson
Chahko Mika Mall, 1125 Lakeside Dr., Main Fl., Nelson, BC V1L 5Z3

New Westminster
#201, 620 Royal Ave., New Westminster, BC V3M 1J2

North Vancouver
North Shore Service Canada Centre, #100, 221 West Esplanade, North Vancouver, BC V7M 3N7

Penticton
#101, 386 Ellis St., Penticton, BC V2A 8C9

Port Alberni
4805 Mar St., #A, Port Alberni, BC V9Y 8J5

Powell River
7061 Duncan St., #A, Powell River, BC V8A 1W1

Prince George
1363 - 4 Ave., Prince George, BC V2L 3J6

Prince Rupert
#100, 215 - 3 St., Prince Rupert, BC V8J 3J9

Quesnel
283 Reid St. East, Quesnel, BC V2J 2M1

Richmond
#350, 5611 Cooney Rd., Richmond, BC V6X 3J6

Salmon Arm
191 Shuswap St. NW, 1st Fl., Salmon Arm, BC V1E 4P6

Smithers
1020 Murray St., Smithers, BC V0J 2N0

Squamish
1440 Winnipeg St., Squamish, BC V8B 0C3

Surrey - 104th Ave.
Surrey North Service Canada Centre, 13889 - 104 Ave., Surrey, BC V3T 1W8

Surrey - Hwy. 10
Surrey South Service Canada Centre, #103, 15295 Hwy. 10, Surrey, BC V3S 0X9

Terrace
4630 Lazelle Ave., Terrace, BC V8G 1S6

Trail
#101, 1101 Dewdney Ave., Trail, BC V1R 4T1

Vancouver - Broadway
Vancouver (West Broadway) Service Centre, 1263 West Broadway, Vancouver, BC V6H 1G7

Vancouver - Hastings St. West
Sinclair Centre Service Canada Centre, #125, 757 Hastings St. West, Vancouver, BC V6C 1A1

Vancouver - Kingsway
Vancouver East Service Canada Centre, 1420 Kingsway, Vancouver, BC V5N 2R5

Vanderhoof
189 Stewart St. East, RR#2, Vanderhoof, BC V0J 3A2

Vernon
3202 - 31st St., Vernon, BC V1T 2H3

Victoria - Douglas St.
1401 Douglas St., Victoria, BC V8W 2G2

Victoria - Jacklin Rd.
Victoria West Shore Service Canada Centre, 3179 Jacklin Rd., Victoria, BC V9B 3Y7

Williams Lake
79 - Fourth Ave. South, Williams Lake, BC V2G 1J6

Service Canada Outreach Sites - British Columbia
Toll-Free: 800-622-6232
TTY: 800-926-9105

The following places in British Columbia are scheduled outreach sites for Service Canada:
Alert Bay (Namgis Health Centre, 48 School Rd.);
Bella Bella (Heiltsuk Social Development Office);
Cache Creek (Village of Cache Creek Offices, 1389 Quartz Rd.);
Clearwater (Community Resource Centre for the North Thompson, 751 Clearwater Village Rd.);
Fort St John (10600 - 100th St.);
Hope (895 - 3rd Ave.);
Lytton (Village of Lytton Office, 380 Main St.);
Mackenzie (64 Centennial Dr.);
Masset (1666 Orr St.);
Merritt (Rail Yard Mall, 2194 Coutlee Ave.);
Port Hardy (8785 Gray St.);
Richmond - Multi-Language Extension Services in Cantonese & Mandarin (Immigrant Services Society, #150, 8400 Alexandra Rd.);
Sechelt (#102, 5710 Teredo St.);
Surrey - Multi-Language Extension Services in Punjabi (#205, 12725 - 80th Ave.);
Surrey - Multi-Language Extension Services in Punjabi (DiverseCity, #1107, 7330 - 137th St.);
Vancouver - Multi-Language Extension Services in Cantonese & Mandarin (MOSAIC, 1720 Grant St., Fl. 2);
Vancouver - Multi-Language Extension Services in Cantonese & Mandarin (SUCCESS, 28 West Pender St.);
Vancouver - Multi-Language Extension Services in Punjabi (Progressive Intercultural Community Services Society, 8153 Main St.);
Whistler (Whistler Chamber of Commerce, #201, 4230 Gateway Dr.).

Manitoba Service Canada Centres

Brandon
Government of Canada Building, #100, 1039 Princess Ave., Brandon, MB R7A 4J5

Churchill
1 Mantayo Seepee Meskanow, Churchill, MB R0B 0E0

Dauphin
181 - 1st Ave. NE, Dauphin, MB R7N 1A6
Tel: 800-622-6232; *Fax:* 204-622-4045

Flin Flon
Government of Canada Building, 111 Main St., Flin Flon, MB R8A 1J9

Morden
Government of Canada Building, 158 Stephen St., Morden, MB R6M 1T3

Notre Dame de Lourdes
51 Rodgers St., Notre Dame de Lourdes, MB R0G 1M0

Portage la Prairie
Government of Canada Building, 1016 Saskatchewan Ave. East, Portage La Prairie, MB R1N 3V2

Saint Pierre Jolys
427 Sabourin St., Saint Pierre Jolys, MB R0A 1V0

Selkirk
51 Main St., Selkirk, MB R1A 1P9
Fax: 204-785-6222

Steinbach
Steinbach Place, 321 Main St., Main Fl., Steinbach, MB R5G 1Z2

Swan River
#1, 355 Kelsey Trail, Swan River, MB R0L 1Z0

The Pas
Uptown Mall, 333 Edwards Ave., PO Box 660 The Pas, MB R9A 1K7

Thompson
60 Moak Cres., Thompson, MB R8N 2B7

Winnipeg - Henderson Hwy.
Winnipeg NE Service Canada Ctr., Kildonan Village Mall, 1122 Henderson Hwy., Winnipeg, MB R2G 1L1

Winnipeg - Portage Ave.
Winnipeg South-West Service Canada Centre, Westwood Centre, 3338 Portage Ave., Winnipeg, MB R3K 0Z1

Winnipeg - St. Mary's Rd.
Winnipeg St-Vital Service Canada Centre, 1001 St. Mary's Rd., Winnipeg, MB R2M 3S4

Winnipeg - York Ave.
Winnipeg Centre Service Canada Ctr., Stanley Knowles Bldg., 391 York Ave., Winnipeg, MB R3C 0P4
Service Canada Outreach Sites - Manitoba
Toll-Free: 800-622-6232
TTY: 800-926-9105
The following places in Manitoba are scheduled outreach sites for Service Canada:
Arborg (317 River Rd.);
Ashern (Fieldstone Ventures Education & Training Centre, 61 Main St.);
Beausejour (20 - 1st St. South);
Carberry (112 Main St.);
Carman (15 - 1st Ave. SW);
Deloraine (220 South Railway Ave. West);
Fisher Branch (23 Main St.);
Gillam (323 Railway Ave.);
Gimli (62 - 2nd Ave., 2nd Fl.);
Gladstone (MAFRI Gladstone GO Centre, 37 Morris Ave. North);
Killarney (318 Williams Ave.);
Lac du Bonnet (4 Park Ave.);
McCreary (436 - 2nd Ave.);
Minnedosa (Yellowhead Regional Employment Skills & Services, 133 Main St. South);
Morris (220 Main St. North);
Neepawa (290 Davidson St.);
Russell (IGA Mall, Main St. & Lawrence Ave.);
Saint-Georges (Allard Library, 104086 Hwy. #11);
Saint Laurent (Saint Laurent Recreation Cente, Lot 825, Hwy. #6);
Shoal Lake (438 Station St.);
Snow Lake (Snow Lake Family Resource Centre, 131 Balsam St.);
Sprague (East Borderland Primary Health Care Centre, Hwy. #12 & Rd. 308);
Stonewall (South Interlake Regional Library, 419 Main St.);
Teulon (19 Beach Rd.);
Virden (227 Wellington St. West);
Winnipeg (#100, 614 des Meurons St.);
Winnipegosis (Village of Winnipegosis Office, 130 - 2 nd St.)

New Brunswick Service Canada Centres

Bathurst
Nicolas Denys Building, 120 Harbourview Blvd., 1st Fl., Bathurst, NB E2A 7R2
Campbellton
Campbellton City Center Mall, #111, 157 Water St., Campbellton, NB E3N 3L4
Caraquet
Bellevue Place, 20E St. Pierre Blvd. West, Caraquet, NB E1W 1B6
Dalhousie
Darlington Mall, 110 Plaza Blvd., Dalhousie, NB E8C 2E2
Edmundston
Federal Building, 22 Emmerson St., Edmundston, NB E3V 1R8
Fredericton
Federal Building, 633 Queen St., Fredericton, NB E3B 1C3
Grand Falls / Grand-Sault
#100, 441 Madawaska Rd., Grand Falls, NB E3Y 1C6
Miramichi
Roach Building, 150 Pleasant St., Miramichi, NB E1V 1Y1
Moncton
Heritage Court, #310, 95 Foundry St., Moncton, NB E1C 5H7
Richibucto
Cartier Place, 25 Cartier Blvd., Richibucto, NB E4W 3W7
Sackville
East Main Plaza, 170 Main St., Sackville, NB E4L 4B4
Saint John
1 Agar Pl., 1st Fl., Saint John, NB E2L 5G4
Saint Quentin
193 Canada St., Saint-Quentin, NB E8A 1J8
St. Stephen
Post Office Building, 93 Milltown Blvd., St. Stephen, NB E3L 1G5
Shediac
Centre-Ville Mall, 342 Main St., Shediac, NB E4P 2E7
Shippagan
196A J.D. Gauthier Blvd., 1st Fl., Shippagan, NB E8S 1P2
Sussex
Mapleton Place, 10 Gateway St., Sussex, NB E4E 1T1
Tracadie-Sheila
Le Rond Point Shopping Center, #17, 3409 Principale St., Tracadie-Sheila, NB E1X 1C7
Woodstock
Post Office Building, 680 Main St., Woodstock, NB E7M 5Z9
Service Canada Outreach Sites - New Brunswick
Toll-Free: 800-622-6232
TTY: 800-926-9105
The following places in New Brunswick are scheduled outreach sites for Service Canada:
Baie-Sainte-Anne (5383 Rte. 117);
Doaktown (328 Main St.);
Florenceville-Bristol (#1, 8768 Main St.);
Grand Manan (North Head Grand Manan Business Center, 130 Rte. 776);
Minto (420 Pleasant Dr.);
Neguac (430 Principale St.);
Perth-Andover (588E East Riverside Dr.);
Rogersville (11117 Main St.);
Fredericton (Kchikhusis Complex, 150 Cliffe St., Fl. 3);
Tobique Narrows (Tobique Employment & Training Centre, 278 Main St.).

Newfoundland & Labrador Service Canada Centres

Channel-Port-aux-Basques
#4, 10 High St., Channel-Port-aux-Basques, NL A0M 1C0
Clarenville
Park Place, 50 Manitoba Dr., Clarenville, NL A5A 1K5
Corner Brook
Joseph R. Smallwood Building, 1 Regent Sq., Corner Brook, NL A2H 7K6
Gander
McCurdy Complex, 1 Markham Place, 3rd Fl., Gander, NL A1V 0A8
Grand Falls-Windsor
Bayley Building, #100, 4A Bayley St., Grand Falls, NL A2A 2T5
Happy Valley-Goose Bay
23 Broomfield St., Happy Valley-Goose Bay, NL A0P 1E0
Harbour Grace
Babb Building, 33-35 Harvey St., Harbour Grace, NL A0A 2M0
Labrador City
Labrador Mall, 500 Vanier Ave., Labrador City, NL A2V 2W7
Marystown
Jerrett Building, #130, 140 Ville Marie Dr., Marystown, NL A0E 2M0
Placentia
Dalfens Mall, 61 Blockhouse Rd., Placentia, NL A0B 2Y0
Rocky Harbour
Budgeon Building, 118 Pond Rd., Rocky Harbour, NL A0K 4N0
St. Anthony
Viking Mall, 1 Goose Cove Rd., St. Anthony, NL A0K 4S0
St. John's
Building 223, Pleasantville, 223 Churchill Ave., St. John's, NL A1A 1N3
Springdale
Wells Building, 130 Main St., RR#2, Springdale, NL A0J 1T0
Stephenville
133 Carolina Ave., Stephenville, NL A2N 2S5
Service Canada Outreach Sites - Newfoundland & Labrador
Toll-Free: 800-622-6232
TTY: 800-926-9105
The following places in Newfoundland & Labrador are scheduled outreach sites for Service Canada:
Baie Verte (Barker Building, 325 Hwy. #410);
Bonavista (Bonavista Campus, College of the North Atlantic, #A118, 301 Confederation Dr.);
Burgeo (142 Reach Rd.);
Forteau (32 Main St.);
Harbour Breton (Halfyard Building, #30, 42 Canada Dr.);
Mainland (School & Community Centre of Sainte-Anne, Rte. 463);
Newville (Development Association Building, Rte. 340);
Old Perlican (John Hoskins Community Centre, 575A Main St.);
Pollards Point (Main St.);
Port Saunders (Dobbin Building, 90 Main St.);
Ramea (21 Main St.);
Saint Alban's (St. Alban's Resource Centre, 3 Cormier Ave.);
Sheshatshiu (Innu Nation Building, Main Fl.);
Trepassey (Opportunities Complex, Main Hwy.);
Wesleyville (Employment Assistance Office, Cape Freels Development Association, 344 Main St.)

Northwest Territories Service Canada Centres

Fort Simpson
Federal Building, 9606 - 100th St., Fort Simpson, NT X0E 0N0
Fort Smith
Federal Building, 149 McDougal Rd., Fort Smith, NT X0E 0P0
Hay River
Federal Building, #204, 41 Capital Dr., Hay River, NT X0E 1G2
Inuvik
85 Kingmingya Rd., Inuvik, NT X0E 0T0
Yellowknife
Greenstone Building, 5101 - 50 Ave., Main Fl., Yellowknife, NT X1A 3Z4
Service Canada Outreach Sites - Northwest Territories
Toll-Free: 800-622-6232
TTY: 800-926-9105
The following places in the Northwest Territories are scheduled outreach sites for Service Canada:
Behchoko (Tli Cho Government Building);
Deline (Deline Charter Community Office);
Fort Liard (Deh Cho Health & Social Services);
Fort Providence (Zhati Koe Friendship Centre);
Fort Resolution (Deninu Ku'e First Nation Office);
Tuktoyaktuk (Tuktoyaktuk Community Corporation Office).

Nova Scotia Service Canada Centres

Amherst
#202, 26-28 Prince Arthur St., Amherst, NS B4H 1V6
Antigonish
Federal Building, 325 Main St., 2nd Fl., Antigonish, NS B2G 2C3
Bedford
Royal Bank Building, 1597 Bedford Hwy., 2nd Fl., Bedford, NS B4A 1E7
Bridgewater
Dawson B. Dauphinee Building, 77 Dufferin St., Bridgewater, NS B4V 9A2
Dartmouth
Belmont House, 33 Alderney Dr., 3rd Fl., Dartmouth, NS B2Y 2N4
Digby
98 Sydney St., Digby, NS B0V 1A0
Glace Bay
Senator's Place, #101, 633 Main St., Glace Bay, NS B1A 6J3
Guysborough
Chedabucto Centre, 9996 Hwy. #16, Guysborough, NS B0H 1N0
Halifax
Tower 2, Mumford Towers, 7001 Mumford Rd., Halifax, NS B3L 4R3
Inverness
15926 Central Ave., Inverness, NS B0E 1N0
Kentville
Federal Building, 495 Main St., 2nd Fl., Kentville, NS B4N 3W5
New Glasgow
340 East River Rd., New Glasgow, NS B2H 3P7
North Sydney
105 King St., Main Fl., North Sydney, NS B2A 3S1
Port Hawkesbury
Shediac Shopping Centre, #8, 811 Reeves St., Port Hawkesbury, NS B9A 2S4
Shelburne
Loyalist Plaza, 218 Water St., Shelburne, NS B0T 1W0
Sydney
Commerce Tower, 15 Dorchester St., 1st Fl., Sydney, NS B1P 5Y9
Truro
181 Willow St., Truro, NS B2N 4Z9
Windsor
80 Water St., Windsor, NS B0N 2T0
Yarmouth
Canada Post Office Building, 13 Willow St., 2nd Fl., Yarmouth, NS B5A 1T8
Service Canada Outreach Sites - Nova Scotia
Toll-Free: 800-622-6232
TTY: 800-926-910
The following places in Nova Scotia are scheduled outreach sites for Service Canada:
Church Point (Sainte-Anne University Campus, 1649 Rte. 1);
Sheet Harbour (Bluewater Building, 22756 Hwy. 7, 2nd Fl.).

Nunavut Service Canada Centres

Cambridge Bay
16 Mitik St., 1st Fl., PO Box 2010 Cambridge Bay, NU X0B 0C0

Iqaluit
#306, Iqaluit House, Building 622, Main Fl., Queen Elizabeth Way, PO Box 639 Iqaluit, NU X0A 0H0
Tel: 867-975-4700

Rankin Inlet
Rockland Building, PO Box 97 Rankin Inlet, NU X0C 0G0

Ontario Service Canada Centres

Ajax
#200, 274 Mackenzie Ave., Ajax, ON L1S 2E9

Arnprior
Heritage Square, #1 & 2, 75 Elgin St. West, Arnprior, ON K7S 3T9

Bancroft
Fairway Plaza, 5 Fairway Blvd., Bancroft, ON K0L 1C0

Barrie
48 Owen St., 1st Fl., Barrie, ON L4M 3H1

Belleville
Business Building, 1 North Front St., 2nd Fl., Belleville, ON K8P 5G9

Bracebridge
Federal Bldg., 98 Manitoba St., 2nd Fl., Bracebridge, ON P1L 2B5

Brampton
Human Resources Development Canada, 18 Corporation Dr., Brampton, ON L6S 6B2

Brantford
58 Dalhousie St., 2nd Fl., Brantford, ON N3T 2J2

Brockville
Thomas Fuller Building, 14 Court House Ave., 1st Fl., Brockville, ON K6V 4T1

Burlington
#108E, 676 Appleby Line, Burlington, ON L7L 5Y1

Cambridge
#2C, 350 Conestoga Blvd., Cambridge, ON N1R 7L7

Carleton Place
46 Lansdowne Ave., Carleton Place, ON K7C 2T8

Chatham
Chatham-Kent Service Canada Centre, Federal Building, 120 Wellington St. West, Chatham, ON N7M 3P3

Cobourg
1005 Elgin St. West, Cobourg, ON K9A 5J4

Collingwood
44 Hurontario St., Collingwood, ON L9Y 2L6

Cornwall
#100, 111 Water St. East, Cornwall, ON K6H 6S2

Dryden
119 King St., Dryden, ON P8N 1C1

East Gwillimbury
Newmarket Service Canada Centre, #1, 18183 Yonge St. East, East Gwillimbury, ON L9N 0H9

Elliot Lake
Ministry, Training, Colleges & Universities, Employment Ctr, 50 Hillside Dr. North, Elliot Lake, ON P5A 1X4

Espanola
#2, 721 Centre St., Espanola, ON P5E 1T3

Fort Frances
301 Scott St., Fort Frances, ON P9A 1H1

Gananoque
5 Charles St. South, Gananoque, ON K7G 1V9

Georgetown
232 Guelph St., 1st Fl., Georgetown, ON L7G 4B1

Geraldton
208 Beamish Ave. West, Geraldton, ON P0T 1M0

Goderich
52 East St., Goderich, ON N7A 1N3

Guelph
259 Woodlawn Rd. West, #C, Guelph, ON N1H 8J1

Hamilton - Barton St. East
Hamilton East Service Canada Centre, Red Hill Creek Centre, 2255 Barton St. East, Hamilton, ON L8H 7T4

Hamilton - Upper James St.
Hamilton Main Service Canada Centre, 1550 Upper James St., 1st Fl., Hamilton, ON L9B 2L6

Hawkesbury
521 Main St. East, Hawkesbury, ON K6A 1B3

Kapuskasing
8 Queen St., Kapuskasing, ON P5N 1G7

Kenora
Kenora Market Square, #201, 308 - 2nd St. South, Kenora, ON P9N 1G4

Kingston
Frontenac Mall, 1300 Bath Rd., 1st Fl., Kingston, ON K7M 4X4

Kirkland Lake
Ontario Northlands Telecommunications Building, 10 Government Rd. East, Kirkland Lake, ON P2N 1A2

Kitchener
409 Weber St. West, Kitchener, ON N2H 4B1

Leamington
Leamington Mall, 215 Talbot St. East, Leamington, ON N8H 3X5

Lindsay
65 Kent St. West, Lindsay, ON K9V 2Y3

Listowel
210 Main St. East, Listowel, ON N4W 2B7

London
Dominion Public Building, 457 Richmond St., London, ON N6A 3E3

Malton
#5, 6877 Goreway Dr., Malton, ON L4V 1L9

Marathon
#105, 52 Peninsula Rd., Marathon, ON P0T 2E0

Markham
#14, 5051 Hwy. #7 East, Markham, ON L3R 1N3

Midland
Huronia Mall, 9225 Hwy. #93, RR#2, Midland, ON L4R 4K4

Milton
Trafalgar Square, 310 Main St. East, Milton, ON L9T 1P4

Mississauga - Dixie Rd.
Mississauga East Service Canada Centre, 2525 Dixie Rd., Mississauga, ON L4Y 2A1

Mississauga - Glen Erin Dr.
Mississauga West Service Canada Centre, 3085A Glen Erin Dr., Mississauga, ON L5L 1J3

Napanee
Murphy's Plaza, 2 Dairy Ave., Napanee, ON K7R 3T1

New Liskeard
280 Armstrong St. North, RR#3, New Liskeard, ON P0J 1P0

Niagara Falls
Customs Building, 5853 Peer St., Niagara Falls, ON L2G 1X4

North Bay
Canada Place, #102, 107 Shirreff Ave., North Bay, ON P1B 7K8

Oakville
#5B, 117 Cross Ave., Oakville, ON L6J 2W7

Orangeville
#102, 210 Broadway Ave., Orangeville, ON L9W 5G4

Orillia
#101, 50 Andrew St. South, Orillia, ON L3V 7T5

Oshawa
Midtown Mall, #6C, 200 John St. West, Oshawa, ON L1J 2B4

Ottawa - Carling Ave.
Ottawa West Service Canada Centre, Lincoln Fields Galleria, 2525 Carling Ave., 1st Fl., Ottawa, ON K2B 7Z2

Ottawa - Laurier Ave. West
Ottawa Government Service Centre, 110 Laurier Ave. West, Ottawa, ON K1P 1J1

Ottawa - Laurier Ave. West
Ottawa Centre Service Canada Centre, L'Esplanade Laurier, 300 Laurier Ave. West, 2nd Fl., Ottawa, ON K1A 0R3

Ottawa - Ogilvie Rd.
Ottawa East Service Canada Centre, Beacon Hill Shopping Ctr, 2339 Ogilvie Rd., Ottawa, ON K1J 8M6

Owen Sound
Heritage Place Shopping Centre, 1350 - 16 St. East, Owen Sound, ON N4K 6N7

Parry Sound
74 James St., 2nd Fl., Parry Sound, ON P2A 1T8

Pembroke
141 Lake St., Pembroke, ON K8A 5L8

Perth
The Factory, 40 Sunset Blvd., Perth, ON K7H 2Y4

Peterborough
219 George St. North, Peterborough, ON K9J 3G7

Picton
229 Main St., Picton, ON K0K 2T0

Prescott
292 Centre St., Prescott, ON K0E 1T0
Tel: 613-925-2808; *Fax:* 613-925-3846
ontario.inquiry@hrsdc-rhdcc.gc.ca

Renfrew
350 Raglan St. South, Renfrew, ON K7V 1R7

Richmond Hill
35 Beresford Dr., Richmond Hill, ON L4B 4M3

St Catherines
Henley Square Plaza, 395 Ontario St., #E & F, St Catharines, ON L2N 7N6

St Thomas
#34, 1010 Talbot St., St Thomas, ON N5P 4N2

Sarnia
529 Exmouth St., Sarnia, ON N7T 5P6

Sault Ste. Marie
22 Bay St., 1st Fl., Sault Ste. Marie, ON P6A 5S2

Simcoe
5 Queensway East, Simcoe, ON N3Y 5K2

Smiths Falls
#115, 91 Cornelia St. West, Smiths Falls, ON K7A 5L3

Stratford
#2, 61 Lorne Ave. East, Ground Fl., Stratford, ON N5A 6S4

Sudbury
Federal Building, 19 Lisgar St., Main Fl., Sudbury, ON P3E 3L4

Thunder Bay
975 Alloy Dr., Thunder Bay, ON P7B 5Z8

Tillsonburg
Livingston Centre, 96 Tillson Ave., Tillsonburg, ON N4G 3A1

Timmins
120 Cedar St. South, 1st Fl., Timmins, ON P4N 2G8

Toronto - Chesswood Dr.
Toronto North Service Canada Centre, 3737 Chesswood Dr., Toronto, ON M3J 2P6

Toronto - College St.
#100, 559 College St., Toronto, ON M6G 1A9

Toronto - Dundas St. West
Toronto Etobicoke Service Canada Centre, 5343 Dundas St. West, Toronto, ON M9B 6K6

Toronto - Gerrard St. East
Gerrard Square Mall, 1000 Gerrard St. East, #DD10/11, 2nd Fl., Toronto, ON M4M 1Z3

Toronto - Lawrence Ave. West
Lawrence Square, #103-105, 700 Lawrence Ave. West, Toronto, ON M6A 3B3

Toronto - Queen St. West
Toronto City Hall Service Canada Centre, City Hall, 100 Queen St. West, 1st Fl., Toronto, ON M5H 2N2

Toronto - St. Clair Ave. East
Toronto Centre Service Canada Ctr., Arthur Meighen Building, 25 St. Clair Ave. East, 1st Fl., Toronto, ON M4T 3A4

Toronto - Tapscott Rd.
Toronto Malvern Service Canada Ctr., Malvern Town Ctr. Mall, 31 Tapscott Rd., Toronto, ON M1B 4Y7

Toronto - Town Centre Ct.
Toronto Scarborough Service Canada Centre, Canada Centre, 200 Town Centre Ct., 1st Fl., Toronto, ON M1P 4X9

Toronto - Yonge St.
Toronto Willowdale Service Canada Ctr., Joseph Shepard Bldg, 4900 Yonge St., 1st Fl., Toronto, ON M2N 6B1

Trenton
50 Dundas St. West, Trenton, ON K8V 6R5

Walkerton
200 McNab St., Walkerton, ON N0G 2V0

Wallaceburg
Municipal Service Centre, 786 Dufferin Ave., 2nd Fl., Wallaceburg, ON N8A 2V3

Welland
250 Thorold Rd. West, Welland, ON L3C 3W2
Tel: 905-988-2700; *Fax:* 905-735-7036

Windsor
#103, 400 City Hall Sq. East, Windsor, ON N9A 7K6

Woodstock
#101, 959 Dundas St., Woodstock, ON N4S 1H2

Service Canada Outreach Sites - Ontario
Toll-Free: 800-622-6232
TTY: 800-926-9105

The following places in Ontario are scheduled outreach sites for Service Canada:
Alliston (49 Wellington St. West);
Amherstburg (179 Victoria St. South);
Ancaster (Ancaster Square, 300 Wilson St. East);
Atikokan (Atikokan Employment Centre, #206, 214 Main St. West);
Attawapiskat (Attawapiskat Development Corporation, 1001 Riverside Rd. West);
Aylmer (Aylmer Community Services, 25 Centre St.);
Bearskin Lake (Bearskin Lake Band Office);
Belle River (499 Notre Dame St.);
Big Trout Lake (Big Trout Lake Band Council Office);
Blind River (62 Queen Ave.);
Bolton (Caledon Community Services, 18 King St. East, Upper Fl.);
Bowmanville (132 Church St.);
Brampton (Community Door, 7700 Hurontario St.);
Cat Lake (Cat Lake First Nation Band Office;
Chapleau (Sudbury Manitoulin District Social Services Administration Board Office, 12 Birch St.);
Cochrane (143 Fourth Ave.);
Cornwall Island (CIA 111 Building);
Deer Lake (Deer Lake First Nation Band Office);
Dundas (Old Town Hall, 60 Main St., Main Fl.);
Dunnville (Dunnville Employment Centre, St. Leonard's Community Services, 208 Broad St. East);
Embrun (La Cité Collégiale, 993 Notre Dame St.);
Exeter (349 Main St. South);
Fenelon Falls (Fenelon Falls Branch, Kawartha Lakes Public Library, 19 Market St.);
Fergus (552 Wellington County Rd. 18 West);
Flamborough (#117, 7 Innovation Dr.);
Flinton (3641 Flinton Rd.);
Forest (6247 Indian Lane, RR#2);
Fort Albany (Peetabeck Health Services);
Fort Erie (469 Central Ave.);
Fort Hope (Fort Hope Band Council Office);
Fort Severn (Fort Severn Band Council Office);
Gore Bay (35 Merideth St.);
Grimsby (63 Main St. West);
Haliburton (49 Maple Ave.);
Hamilton (71 Main St. West, 1st Fl.);
Havelock (13 Quebec St.);
Hearst (523 Hwy. 11 East);
Hudson (Lac Seul First Nation Band Office);
Huntsville (207 Main St. West);
Iroquois Falls (33 Ambridge Dr.);
Kasabonika (Kasabonika First Nations Band Council);
Kashechewan (13B Riverside Rd. West);
Keewaydin (Keewaywin First Nation Band Office);
Kemptville (#3 & 4, 125 Prescott St.);
Kenora (Dalles First Nation Band Office);
Keswick (90 Wexford Dr.);
Kincardine (727 Queen St.);
Kingfisher Lake (Kingfisher Lake Band Council Office);
Lansdowne House (Lansdowne House First Nation Band Office);
Madoc (20 Davidson St.);
Mindemoya (6020 Hwy. #542);
Monetville (Dokis Reserve Rd.);
Moose Factory (22 Jonathan Cheechoo Dr.);
Moosonee (34 Revillion Rd. North);
Muncey (300 East River Rd.);
Muskrat Dam (Muskrat Dam Band Council Office);
New Osnaburgh (Mishkeegogamang First Nation Band Office);
Nipigon (5 Wadsworth Dr., 1st Fl.);
North Spirit Lake (North Spirit Lake First Nation Band Office);
Petrolia (4200 Petrolia Line);
Pikangikum (Pikangikum Band Council Office);
Poplar Hill (Poplar Hill Band Council Office);
Port Colborne (92 Charlotte St.);
Port Perry (#3, 119 Perry St.);
Red Lake (227 Howey St.);
Sachigo Lake (Sachigo Band Council Office);
Sandy Lake (Sandy Lake Band Council Office);
Seaforth (138 Main St. South);
Shelburne (167 Centre St.);
Shoal Lake (Shoal Lake First Nation Band Office);
Sioux Lookout (80 Front St.);
Sioux Narrows (Northwest Angle First Nation Band Office);
Slate Falls (48 Lakeview Dr.);
Southwold (Oneida First Nation Administrative Building;
Strathroy (34 Frank St.);
Sturgeon Falls (109 Third St.)
Summer Beaver (Summer Beaver First Nation Band Office);
Terrace Bay (Hwy, #17 & Selkirk Ave.);
Tilbury (20 Queen St. North);
Thessalon (214 Main St.);
Toronto (220 Attwell Dr.);
Toronto (58 Cecil St.);
Toronto (55 John St.);
Toronto (779 The Queensway);
Toronto (605 Rogers Rd.);
Toronto (29 St. Dennis Dr.);
Toronto (2900 Warden Ave.);
Uxbridge (#201, 2 Campbell Dr.);
Vaughan (9100 Jane St.);
Wasaga Beach (30 Lewis St.);
Wawa (48 Mission Rd.);
Webequie (Webequie First Nation Band Council);
West Lorne (160 Main St.);
Wiarton (542 Berford St.);
Wikwemikong (19A Complex Dr.);
Wingham (152 Josephine St.);
Woodbridge (8401 Weston Rd.);
Wunnumin Lake (Wunnumin Lake First Nation Band Council Office)

Prince Edward Island Service Canada Centres

Charlottetown
Jean Canfield Government of Canada Building, 191 University Ave., 1st Fl., Charlottetown, PE C1A 4L2

Montague
491 Main St., Montague, PE C0A 1R0

O'Leary
371 Main St., O'Leary, PE C0B 1V0

Souris
Save Easy Mall, 173 Main St., 2nd Fl., Souris, PE C0A 2B0

Summerside
Government of Canada Building, 294 Church St., Summerside, PE C1N 0C1

Service Canada Outreach Sites - Prince Edward Island
Toll-Free: 800-622-6232
TTY: 800-926-9105

The following place in Prince Edward Island is a scheduled outreach site for Service Canada: 48 Mill Rd., Wellington, PE, C0B 2E0.

Québec Service Canada Centres

Alma
Complexe Jacques-Gagnon, #105, 100, rue St-Joseph sud, Alma, QC G8B 7A6

Amos
502, 4e rue est, Amos, QC J9T 2R9

Asbestos
#204, 309, rue Chassé, Asbestos, QC J1T 2B4

Baie-Comeau
Centre d'achats Laflèche, #204, 625, boul Laflèche ouest, Baie-Comeau, QC G5C 1C4

Bécancour
#200, 1580, boul de Port-Royal, 1e étage, Bécancour, QC G9H 1X6

Brossard
Centre de ressources humaines Canada, 2501, boul Lapinière, 1e étage, Brossard, QC J4Z 3P1

Campbell's Bay
2, rue John, Campbell's Bay, QC J0X 1K0

Cap-aux-Meules
Centre de ressources humaines Canada, #200, 380, ch Principal, Cap-aux-Meules, QC G4T 1S2

Causapscal
8, rue Saint-Jacques nord, Causapscal, QC G0J 1J0

Chandler
#201, 75, boul René-Lévesque est, Chandler, QC G0C 1K0

Châteauguay
#101, 245, boul St-Jean Baptiste, Châteauguay, QC J6K 3C3

Chibougamau
623, 3e rue, Chibougamau, QC G8P 3A2

Chicoutimi
98, rue Racine est, Chicoutimi, QC G7H 1R1

Chisasibi
453, rue Wolverine, Chisasibi, QC J0M 1E0

Coaticook
#300, 14, rue Adams, Coaticook, QC J1A 1K3

Cote Saint-Luc
Côte-des-Neiges Service Canada Centre, Carré Décarie, #3015, 6900, boul Décarie, 3e étage, Cote-St-Luc, QC H3X 2T8

Cowansville
224, rue du Sud, 2e étage, Cowansville, QC J2K 2X4

Dolbeau -Mistassini
1400, rue des Érables, Dolbeau-Mistassini, QC G8L 2W7

Donnacona
#110, 100, rte 138, Donnacona, QC G3M 1B5

Drummondville
Édifice Surprenant, 1525, boul Saint-Joseph, Drummondville, QC J2C 2E9

Forestville
Centre Forestville, #800, 25, rte 138 est, Forestville, QC G0T 1E0

Gaspé
Édifice Frédérica-Giroux, 98, rue de la Reine, 1e étage, Gaspé, QC G4X 2V4

Gatineau - Bellehumeur
L'Atrium, #150, 85, rue Bellehumeur, Gatineau, QC J8T 8B7

Gatineau - MacLaren est
Buckingham (Gatineau) Service Canada Center, 101, rue MacLaren est, 2e étage, Gatineau, QC J8L 1J9

Gatineau - Saint-Joseph
Hull-Aylmer (Gatineau) Service Canada Centre, 920, boul Saint-Joseph, Gatineau, QC J8Z 1S9

Granby
82, rue Robinson sud, Granby, QC J2G 7L4

Joliette
Comlexe Joliette, #100, 46, rue Gauthier sud, Joliette, QC J6E 4J4

Jonquière
#102, 3750, boul du Royaume, Jonquière, QC G7X 0A4

Kuujjuaq
Nunavik Service Canada Center, 5207, ch de l'Aéroport, Kuujjuaq, QC J0M 1C0

La Malbaie
541, rue St-Étienne, La Malbaie, QC G5A 1J3

La Pocatière
Les Cours Painchaud, #103, 708, 4e av, La Pocatière, QC G0R 1Z0

La Sarre
Carrefour La Sarre Marketplace, #30, 255, 3e rue est, La Sarre, QC J9Z 3N7

La Tuque
Carrefour La Tuque Inc., 290, rue Saint-Joseph, La Tuque, QC G9X 3Z8

Lac Mégantic
#201, 5200, rue Frontenac, 2e étage, Lac-Mégantic, QC G6B 1H3

Laval
1041, boul des Laurentides, Laval, QC H7G 2W2

Lévis
Place Lévis, #175, 50, rte du Président-Kennedy, Lévis, QC G6V 6W8

Longueuil
#100, 1195, ch du Tremblay, Longueuil, QC J4N 1R4

Louiseville
507, rue Marcel, Louiseville, QC J5V 1N1

Magog
#100A, 1700, rue Sherbrooke, Magog, QC J1X 5B4

Maniwaki
Galeries Maniwaki, #220, 100, rue Principale sud, Maniwaki, QC J9E 3L4

Matane
Les Galeries du Vieux-Port, #220, 750, av du Phare ouest, Matane, QC G4W 3W8

Mont-Laurier
431, rue de la Madone, 1e étage, Mont-Laurier, QC J9L 1S1

Montmagny
37, av Sainte-Brigitte sud, Montmagny, QC G5V 2Y3

Montréal - Chauveau
Mercier (Montréal) Service Canada Centre, 5455, rue Chauveau, 1e étage, Montréal, QC H1N 1G8
Téléc: 514-255-0624

Montréal - Jarry est
Villeray (Montréal) Service Canada Centre, #300, 1415, rue Jarry est, 3e étage, Montréal, QC H2E 3B2

Montréal - Jean-Talon est
Saint-Léonard (Montréal) Service Canada Centre, #500, 6020, rue Jean-Talon est, Montréal, QC H1S 3B1

Montréal - Newman
Lasalle (Montréal) Service Canada Centre, 7655, boul Newman, Montréal, QC H8N 1X7

Montréal - René-Lévesque ouest
Montréal Downtown Service Canada Centre, Place Guy-Favreau, #034, 200, boul René-Lévesque ouest, Montréal, QC H2Z 1X4
Montréal - Sherbrooke est
Pointe-aux-Trembles (Montréal) Service Canada Centre, 13313, rue Sherbrooke est, Montréal, QC H1A 1C2
Montréal - Transcanadienne
Pointe-Claire (Montréal) Service Canada Centre, #100, 6500, aut Transcanadienne, 1e étage, Montréal, QC H9R 0A5
Montréal - Wellington
Verdun Service Canada Centre, 4110, rue Wellington, 2e étage, Montréal, QC H4G 1V7
New Richmond
Carrefour Baie-des-Chaleurs, 122, boul Perron ouest, 2e étage, New Richmond, QC G0C 2B0
Québec - Gare-du-Palais
Québec (Centre-Ville) Service Canada Centre, 330, rue de la Gare-du-Palais, Québec, QC G1K 3X2
Québec - Montmorency
La Cité-Limoilou Service Canada Centre, #101, 2500, boul Montmorency, Québec, QC G1J 5C7
Québec - Quatre-Bourgeois
Sainte-Foy (Québec) Service Canada Centre, #200, 3229, ch des Quatre-Bourgeois, 3e étage, Québec, QC G1W 0C1
Repentigny
Place Repentigny, #54, 155, rue Notre-Dame, Repentigny, QC J6A 7G5
Rimouski
Édifice Boisé Langevin, #102, 287, rue Pierre-Saindon, Rimouski, QC G5L 9A7
Rivière-du-Loup
298, boul Armand-Thériault, 2e étage, Rivière-du-Loup, QC G5R 4C2
Roberval
Plaza Roberval, #202, 755, boul Saint-Joseph, Roberval, QC G8H 2L4
Rouyn-Noranda
Édifice Réal-Caouette, #300, 151, av du Lac, Rouyn-Noranda, QC J9X 6C3
Saint-Eustache
250, boul Arthur-Sauvé, Saint-Eustache, QC J7R 2H9
Saint-Georges
Centre de ressources humaines Canada, 11400 - 1re av est, 2e étage, Saint-Georges, QC G5Y 7H2
Saint-Hyacinthe
Galeries St-Hyacinthe Shopping Mall, #2500, 3225, av Cusson, 2e étage, Saint-Hyacinthe, QC J2S 0H7
Saint-Jean-sur-Richelieu
#106, 320, boul du Séminaire nord, Saint-Jean-sur-Richelieu, QC J3B 5K9
Saint-Jérôme
#100, 339, boul Jean-Paul-Hogue, Saint-Jérôme, QC J7Z 7A5
Sainte-Agathe-des-Monts
118, rue Principale est, 2e étage, Sainte-Agathe-des-Monts, QC J8C 1L8
Sainte-Anne-des-Monts
230, 1ére av ouest, Sainte-Anne-des-Monts, QC G4V 1E2
Sainte-Thérèse
#110, 100, boul Ducharme, Sainte-Thérèse, QC J7E 1X2
Salaberry-de-Valleyfield
Valleyfield Service Canada Centre, #100, 73, rue Maden, Salaberry-de-Valleyfield, QC J6S 3V4
Senneterre
761 - 10e av, Senneterre, QC J0Y 2M0
Sept-Îles
701, boul Laure, 3e étage, Sept-Îles, QC G4R 1X8
Shawinigan
444 - 5e rue, Shawinigan, QC G9N 1E6
Sherbrooke
124, rue Wellington nord, Sherbrooke, QC J1H 5X8
Sorel-Tracy
101, rue Augusta, Sorel-Tracy, QC J3P 1A8
Terrebonne
835, montée Masson, Terrebonne, QC J6W 2C7
Thetford Mines
#500, 350, boul Frontenac ouest, Thetford Mines, QC G6G 6N7
Trois-Rivières
#100, 1660, rue Royale, Trois-Rivières, QC G9A 4K3
Val-d'Or
400, av Centrale, Val-d'Or, QC J9P 1P3
Vaudreuil-Dorion
2555, rue Dutrisac, Vaudreuil-Dorion, QC J7V 7E6
Victoriaville
84, boul Labbé sud, Victoriaville, QC G6S 1K4
Ville-Marie
69B, rue Sainte-Anne, Ville-Marie, QC J9V 2B6

Service Canada Outreach Sites - Québec
Ligne sans frais: 800-622-6232
TTY: 800-926-9105
The following places in Québec are scheduled outreach sites for Service Canada:
L'Anse-Saint-Jean (La Petite École Community Centre, 239, rue St-Jean-Baptiste);
Baie-Saint-Paul (René-Richard Library, 9, rue Forget);
Belleterre (Saint-Andre School, 255, 3e av);
Cadillac (2, rue Dumont est);
Chapeau (120, rue King);
Chénéville (90A, rue Albert Ferland);
Dégelis (663, 6e rue ouest);
Fortierville (Fortierville Municipal Library, 198A, rue de la Fabrique);
Grande-Entrée (Auberge La Salicorne, 355, rte 199);
Grande-Vallée (1, rue du Vieux Pont);
Lac-Sainte-Marie (Lac-Ste-Marie City Hall, 106, ch Lac-Ste-Marie);
Lachute (Maison populaire d'Argenteuil, 335, rue Principale);
Lamarche (100, rue Principale);
Lebel-sur-Quévillon (107, rue Principal sud);
Les Escoumins (459, rte 138);
Lyster (2375, rue Bécancour);
Matagami (180, place du Commerce);
Matapédia (City Hall, 1, rue de l'Hôtel-de-ville);
Mont-Joli (1572, boul Jacque Cartier);
Mont-Louis (40, 7e rue est);
New Carisle (208, rue Gerard D. Levesque);
Normandin (Town Hall, 1048, rue Saint-Cyrille);
Notre-Dame-de-Montauban (421, rue Principal);
Notre-Dame-du-Laus (Municipal Library, 4, rue de l'Église);
Pohénégamook (1309, rue Principale);
Potton (The Re illy House, 302, rue Principale);
Port-Cartier (4C, boul des îles);
Rivière-Rouge (Municipal Library, 230, rue de L'Annonciation sud);
Sacré-Coeur (88, rue Principale nord);
Saint-Fabien-de-Panet (195, rue Bilodeau);
Saint-Michel-des-Saints (521, rue Brassard);
Saint-Pamphile (164, rue de l'Église ouest);
Taschereau (52, rue Morin);
Témiscaming (Le Centre, 20, rue Humphrey);
Weedon (Weedon Community Centre, #314, 209 rue des Érables).

Saskatchewan Service Canada Centres

Estevan
#10, 419 Kensington Ave., Estevan, SK S4A 2A1
La Ronge
1016 La Ronge Ave., La Ronge, SK S0J 1L0
Melfort
McKendry Plaza, 104 McKendry Ave. West, Melfort, SK S0E 1A0
Moose Jaw
Victoria Place, #501, 111 Fairford St. East, Moose Jaw, SK S6H 7X5
North Battleford
Territorial Place, #15, 9800 Territorial Dr., North Battleford, SK S9A 3N6
Prince Albert
1288 Central Ave., Prince Albert, SK S6V 4V8
Regina
Alvin Hamilton Building, 1783 Hamilton St., Regina, SK S4P 2B6
Saskatoon
Federal Building, 101 - 22 St. East, Saskatoon, SK S7K 0E1
Swift Current
Chinook Building, 250 Central Ave. North, Swift Current, SK S9H 0L2
Weyburn
City Centre Mall, 110 Souris Ave., Main Fl., Weyburn, SK S4H 2Z8
Yorkton
Imperial Plaza, 214 Smith St. East, Yorkton, SK S3N 3S6

Service Canada Outreach Sites - Saskatchewan
Toll-Free: 800-622-6232
TTY: 800-926-9105
The following places in Saskatchewan are scheduled outreach sites for Service Canada:
Assiniboia (313 Centre St.);
Beauval (Lavoie St.);
Black Lake (Black Lake First Nation Band Office);
Buffalo Narrows (#4, 1491 Pederson Ave.);
Carlyle (100 Main St.);
Clearwater River (Clearwater Dene Nation Band Office);
Davidson (204 Washington St.);
Debden (204 - 2nd Ave. East);
Domremy (Domremy Fransaskois Community Centre, 109 - 1st St. North);
Fond-du-Lac (Fond-du-Lac First Nation Band Office;
Gravelbourg (133 - 5th Ave. East);
Hudson Bay (501 Prince St.);
Humboldt (623 - 7th St.);
Ile-à-la-Crosse (Lajeunesse Ave.);
Kindersley (207 Main St.);
La Loche (La Loche Recreation Centre (Montgrand St.);
Maple Creek (114 Jasper St.);
Meadow Lake (Meadow Lake Tribal Council Main Office, 8155 Flying Dust First Nation);
Nipawin (233 Centre St.);
North Battleford (1371 - 103rd St.);
Ponteix (Royer Cultural Centre, 110 Railway Ave.);
Preeceville (27 Main St. North);
Regina (3115 - 5th Ave.);
St. Isidore-de-Bellevue (Bellevue Cultural Association, 716 Hwy. #225);
Shaunavon (23 - 4th Ave. West);
Stony Rapids (Transwest Air Terminal, 2nd Fl.);
Uranium City (Northern Settlement of Uranium City Office, 205 Fredette Rd.);
Wollaston Lake (Economic Development Office);
Wynyard (400A Ave. D West);
Zenon Park (Zenon Park Fransaskoise Association, 755 Main St.).

Yukon Service Canada Centres

Whitehorse
Elijah Smith Building, #125, 300 Main St., Whitehorse, YT Y1A 2B5

Service Canada Outreach Sites - Yukon
The following places in the Yukon are scheduled outreach sites for Service Canada:
Dawson City (Oak Hall, 1017 - 2nd Ave.);
Watson Lake (Yukon College Campus, Robert Campbell Hwy.).

Skills & Employment Branch / Direction générale des compétences et de l'emploi

Skills & Employment provides programs & initiatives that promote skills development, labour market participation & inclusiveness, as well as ensuring labour market efficiency. Specifically, these programs seek to address the employment & skills needs of those facing employment barriers, & contribute to life long learning & building a skilled inclusive labour force. Other programs that support an efficient labour market include the labour market integration of recent immigrants, the entry of temporary foreign workers, the mobility of workers across Canada & the dissemination of labour market information. This branch is also responsible for programs that provide temporary income support to eligible unemployed workers.

Senior Assistant Deputy Minister, Paul Thompson
Tel: 819-654-2795
paul.thompson@hrsdc-rhdcc.gc.ca
Executive Director, EI Part II, Benefits & Measures, Monika Bertrand
Tel: 819-654-3345; *Fax:* 819-934-7107
monika.bertrand@hrsdc-rhdcc.gc.ca
Executive Director, Federal/Provincial/Territorial Partnerships, Catherine Demers
Tel: 819-654-3367; *Fax:* 819-934-7818
catherine.demers@hrsdc-rhdcc.gc.ca
Director General, Employment Programs & Parnerships Directorate, John Atherton
Tel: 819-654-3289; *Fax:* 819-934-7107
john.atherton@hrsdc-rhdcc.gc.ca
Other Communications: Secure Phone: 819-654-3294
Director General, Horizontal Management & Integration Directorate, Michel C. Caron
Tel: 819-654-2814; *Fax:* 819-934-5333
michel.caron@hrsdc-rhdcc.gc.ca
Director General, Temporary Foreign Workers, Alexis Jonathan Conrad
Tel: 819-654-3203; *Fax:* 819-997-5979
alexis.conrad@hrsdc-rhdcc.gc.ca
Director General, Employment Insurance Policy, Annette Ryan
Tel: 819-654-3056; *Fax:* 819-934-6631
annette.ryan@hrsdc-rhdcc.gc.ca
Director General, Labour Market Integration, Catherine Scott
Tel: 819-654-2892; *Fax:* 819-994-0202
catherine.scott@hrsdc-rhdcc.gc.ca

Director General, Aboriginal Affairs Directorate, James Sutherland
Tel: 819-654-3109; *Fax:* 819-994-3297
james.sutherland@hrsdc-rhdcc.gc.ca
Director General, Workplace Partnerships Directorate, Stephen Johnson
Tel: 819-654-3801; *Fax:* 819-934-2425
stephen.johnson@hrsdc-rhdcc.gc.ca

Strategic Policy & Research Branch / Direction générale de la politique stratégique et de la recherche

Strategic Policy & Research leads on integrating human resources & social development issues in strategic policy, evaluation, & knowledge & research dissemination. It also leads on emerging & long-term policy development, corporate planning, & central agency, intergovernmental & international relations.

Senior Assistant Deputy Minister, Jacques Paquette
Tel: 819-654-6101; *Fax:* 819-934-1505
jacques.paquette@hrsdc-rhdcc.gc.ca
Senior Director, Data Management, Alan D. Bulley
Tel: 819-654-1655
alan.bulley@hrsdc-rhdcc.gc.ca
Director General, Evaluation Directorate, Yves Gingras
Tel: 819-654-3450; *Fax:* 819-953-7887
yves.gingras@hrsdc-rhdcc.gc.ca
Other Communications: Secure Phone: 613-784-0976
Director General, Social Policy, Siobhan Harty
Tel: 819-654-3660; *Fax:* 819-953-9119
siobhan.harty@hrsdc-rhdcc.gc.ca
Director General, Economic Policy Directorate, Jonathan R. Will
Tel: 819-654-3763; *Fax:* 819-997-7329
jonathan.r.will@hrsdc-rhdcc.gc.ca
Director, Resource Management Directorate, Lissa Dornan
Tel: 819-654-3820; *Fax:* 819-994-9677
lissa.dornan@hrsdc-rhdcc.gc.ca
Director General, Strategy & Intergovernmental Relations, John S. McDowell
Tel: 819-654-3512; *Fax:* 819-953-4701
john.mcdowell@hrsdc-rhdcc.gc.ca
Director General, Policy Research Directorate, François Weldon
Tel: 819-654-3576; *Fax:* 819-953-8868
francois.weldon@hrsdc-rhdcc.gc.ca
Other Communications: Secure Phone: 819-654-3577
Senior Director, Labour Market Analysis, Philippe Massé
Tel: 819-654-3771; *Fax:* 819-953-0519
philippe.masse@hrsdc-rhdcc.gc.ca
Senior Director, Social Development Policy, Doug Murphy
Tel: 819-654-3685; *Fax:* 819-953-9119
doug.murphy@hrsdc-rhdcc.gc.ca

Environment & Climate Change Canada / Environnement et du Changement climatique

10 Wellington St., Gatineau, QC K1A 0H3
Tel: 819-997-2800; *Fax:* 819-994-1412
Toll-Free: 800-668-6767
TTY: 819-994-0736
enviroinfo@ec.gc.ca
www.ec.gc.ca
Other Communication: Environmental Emergencies (24-hour): 819-997-3742; TTY: 819-994-0736
twitter.com/environmentca
www.facebook.com/environmentcan
www.youtube.com/user/environmentcan

Environment became Environment & Climate Change in Nov. 2015, under Prime Minister Trudeau. The department fosters a national capacity for sustainable development in cooperation with other governments, departments of government & the private sector that will result in a safe & healthy environment & a sound & prosperous economy by: undertaking & promoting programs to augment understanding of the environment; supporting environmentally responsible public & private decision-making; warning Canadians of risks to & from the environment; engaging Canadians as partners in measurably beneficial action to conserve, protect & restore the integrity of Canada's environment for the benefit of present & future generations.

Minister, Environment & Climate Change, Hon. Catherine Mary McKenna, P.C.
Tel: 613-996-5322; *Fax:* 613-996-5323
Catherine.McKenna@parl.gc.ca
Deputy Minister, Michael Martin
Tel: 819-938-9047; *Fax:* 819-953-6897
Parliamentary Secretary, Jonathan Wilkinson
Tel: 613-995-1225; *Fax:* 613-992-7319
Jonathan.Wilkinson@parl.gc.ca
Director General, Audit & Evaluation, Robert D'Aoust
Tel: 819-938-5017; *Fax:* 819-938-5453
robert.daoust@canada.ca

Associated Agencies, Boards & Commissions:

•Committee on the Status of Endangered Wildlife in Canada (COSEWIC) / Comité sur la situation des espèces en péril au Canada
c/o Canadian Wildlife Service
351 St. Joseph Blvd, 4th Fl.
Gatineau, QC K1A 0H3
Tel: 819-953-3215; *Fax:* 819-994-3684
cosewic/cosepac@ec.gc.ca
www.cosewic.gc.ca
Other Communication: Species at Risk Act Public Registry: www.sararegistry.gc.ca

Committee of experts that assesses & designates which wild species are in some danger of disappearing from Canada. COSEWIC determines the national status of wild Canadian species, subspecies & separate populations suspected of being at risk. COSEWIC bases its decisions on the best up-to-date scientific information & Aboriginal traditional knowledge available. All native mammals, birds, reptiles, amphibians, fish, mollusks, lepidopterans (butterflies & moths), vascular plants, mosses & lichens are included in its current mandate. In its 2010 Annual report, COSEWIC's assessment results indicate there are 602 species in the risk category (extirpated, endangered, threatened or of special concern) & 13 species found to be extinct.

•North American Waterfowl Management Plan (NAWMP) / Le plan nord-américain de gestion de la sauvagine
NAWCC (Canada) Secretariat, Place Vincent Massey
351 St. Joseph Blvd., 7th Fl.
Gatineau, QC K1A 0H3
Tel: 819-934-6034; *Fax:* 819-934-6017
nawmp@ec.gc.ca
www.nawmp.ca

The North American Waterfowl Management Plan is an international action plan to conserve migratory birds throughout the continent. The Plan's goal is to return waterfowl populations to their 1970's levels by conserving wetland & upland habitat. Canada & the United States signed the Plan in 1986 in reaction to critically low numbers of waterfowl. Mexico joined in 1994 making it a truly continental effort. The Plan is a partnership of federal, provincial/state & municipal governments, non-governmental organizations, private companies & many individuals, all working towards achieving better wetland habitat for the benefit of migratory birds, other wetland-associated species & people. The Plan's unique combination of biology, landscape conservation & partnerships comprise its exemplary conservation legacy. Plan projects are international in scope, but implemented at regional levels. These projects contribute to the protection of habitat & wildlife species across the North American landscape.

•North American Bird Conservation Initiative (NABCI)
Canadian Wildlife Service
351, boul St-Joseph, 3e étage
Gatineau, QC K1A 0H3
Tel: 819-994-0512; *Fax:* 819-994-4445
nabci@ec.gc.ca
www.nabci.net

The NABCI is a coordinated effort among Canada, the United States & Mexico to maintain the diversity & abundance of all North American birds. National coordination of this effort in Canada occurs through the NABCI Canada Council, chaired by the Asst. Deputy Minister of Environment Canada's Environmental Conservation Service. Council members include representatives from provincial governments, non-government organizations, four bird plans (waterfowl, landbirds, shorebirds, waterbirds), & habitat joint ventures. In Canada, there are four habitat joint ventures (Pacific Birds Habitat, Canadian Intermountain, Prairie Habitat, Eastern Habitat) & three species (Arctic Goose, Black Duck, Sea Duck).

Enforcement Branch / Direction générale de l'application de la loi

401 Burrard St., Vancouver, BC V6C 3S5
Tel: 604-666-6496; *Fax:* 604-666-0048

The Branch is built around the principle of ensuring that companies & individuals comply with the pollution prevention & conservation goals of environmental & wildlife protection acts & regulations. Enforcement is delivered through the work of in-the-field enforcement officers across Canada working through the Environmental Enforcement Directorate & The Wildlife Enforcement Directorate. Their work is carried out in cooperation with other federal, provincial & territorial governments & with international organizations involved in enforcement such as the United States Fish & Wildlife Service, the United States Environmental Protection Agency & Interpol.

Chief Enforcement Officer, Gordon T. Owen
Tel: 819-938-5281; *Fax:* 819-997-0086
National Director, Enforcement Services, Kim Hibbeln
Tel: 819-938-5315; *Fax:* 819-938-5386
Director General, Wildlife Enforcement, Sheldon Jordan
Tel: 819-938-5381; *Fax:* 819-938-3617
sheldon.jordan@canada.ca
Director General, Environmental Enforcement Directorate, Margaret Meroni
Tel: 819-938-5281
Executive Director, Wildlife Enforcement Directorate, Kathy A. Graham
Tel: 819-938-5374; *Fax:* 819-994-5836
kathy.graham@canada.ca

Environmental Stewardship Branch / Direction générale de l'intendance environnementale

351, boul St-Joseph, Gatineau, QC K1A 0H3
Tel: 819-953-1711; *Fax:* 819-953-9452

Assessment & management of risk associated with domestic & international sources of pollution. The range of activity is broad, assessment of substances & practices that pose a risk to the environment, development & implementation of environmental protection measures including pollution prevention, regulations, permits & technology advancement & ensuring compliance with federal pollution & wildlife laws. These activities lead to improvements in environmental quality which helps to support the health of Canadians & their economic security.

Assistant Deputy Minister, Mike Beale
Tel: 819-420-7871
mike.beale@canada.ca
Director General, Environmental Protection Operations, Marc D'Iorio
Tel: 819-420-7600; *Fax:* 819-934-6531
marc.diorio@canada.ca
Other Communications: Alternate Phone: 613-355-2010
Director General, Energy & Transportation, Helen Ryan
Tel: 819-420-8055
helen.ryan@canada.ca
Director General, Industrial Sectors Directorate, Vacant
Director General, Legislative & Regulatory Affairs, John Moffet
Tel: 819-420-7907; *Fax:* 819-420-7391
john.moffet@canada.ca
Director General, Industrial sectors, Chemicals & Waste Directorate, Virginia Poter
Tel: 819-938-4291; *Fax:* 819-938-4293
virginia.poter@canada.ca
Executive Director, Mining & Processing, Carolyne Blain
Tel: 819-420-7680; *Fax:* 819-420-7381
carolyne.blain@canada.ca
Executive Director, Oil, Gas & Alternative Energy, Mark Cauchi
Tel: 819-420-8028
mark.cauchi@canada.ca
Executive Director, Environmental Assessment & Marine Programs, Mary J. Taylor
Tel: 819-938-4021
mary.taylor@canada.ca
Executive Director, Legislative Governance, Laura Farquharson
Tel: 819-420-7876; *Fax:* 819-997-9806
laura.farquharson@canada.ca
Executive Director, Chemicals Management, Vacant

Finance Branch / Direction générale des finances
Tel: 819-953-4736; *Fax:* 819-953-4064

Assistant Deputy Minister, Carol Najm
Tel: 819-938-9149
Director General & Deputy Chief Financial Officer, Finance Directorate, Yves Bacon
Tel: 819-938-9156; *Fax:* 819-953-2459
Director General, Corporate Management, Karen Turcotte
Tel: 819-953-5842; *Fax:* 819-953-3388

Human Resources Branch / Direction générale des ressources humaines

Assistant Deputy Minister, Lynette Cox
Tel: 819-938-4744; *Fax:* 819-938-4685
Director General, Human Resources Business Transformation Directorate, Jocelyne Kharyati
Tel: 819-938-4583
jocelyne.kharyati@canada.ca
Director General, Integrated Classification & Staffing Solutions, Dominique Boily
Tel: 819-938-4690
dominique.boily@canada.ca
Director General, Workforce Development & Wellness Services, Michelle Laframboise
Tel: 819-938-4670; *Fax:* 819-938-4674
michelle.laframboise@canada.ca
Other Communications: Alternate Phone: 819-210-1988

International Affairs / Direction générale des affaires internationales

200, boul Sacré-Coeur, Gatineau, QC K1A 0H3
Tel: 819-934-6020; *Fax:* 819-953-9412

Assistant Deputy Minister & Chief Negotiator for Climate Change, Louise Métivier
Tel: 819-938-3722; *Fax:* 819-938-3725
louise.metivier@ec.gc.ca

Director General, Climate Change International, France Jacovella
Tel: 819-938-3749; *Fax:* 819-938-3769
Director General, Multilateral & Bilateral Affairs, Daniel Wolfish
Tel: 819-937-3676
daniel.wolfish@canada.ca
Director General, Americas, Catherine Stewart
Tel: 819-938-3784
catherine.stewart2@canada.ca

Legal Services / Services juridiques
351, boul Saint-Joseph, Gatineau, QC K1A 0H3
Senior General Counsel & Executive Director, Legal Services, Jane Allain
Tel: 819-938-4938; *Fax:* 819-938-4952
jane.allain@canada.ca

Meteorological Service of Canada (MSC) / Le service météorologique du Canada (SMC)
351, boul Saint-Joseph, Gatineau, QC K1A 0H3
Tel: 819-934-5395; *Fax:* 819-934-1255
The Meteorological Service of Canada monitors water quantities, provides information & conducts research on climate, atmospheric science, air quality, ice & other environmental issues.
Assistant Deputy Minister, David Grimes
Tel: 819-938-4385; *Fax:* 819-934-1255
Director General, Monitoring & Data Services Directorate, Geneviève Béchard
Tel: 819-938-4564
genevieve.bechard@canada.ca
Director General, Prediction Services Directorate, Diane E. Campbell
Tel: 819-938-4440
diane.campbell@canada.ca
Director General, Canadian Centre for Meteorological & Environmental Prediction, Michel Jean
Tel: 514-421-4601; *Fax:* 514-421-7250
michel.jean2@canada.ca
Director General, Policy, Planning & Partnerships Directorate, Danielle Lacasse
Tel: 819-938-4373; *Fax:* 819-938-5349
danielle.lacasse@canada.ca
Executive Director, Policy & Partnerships Division, Michael Crowe
Tel: 819-938-4379
michael.crowe@canada.ca
Executive Director, National Programs & Business Development, Ken Macdonald
Tel: 819-938-4446
ken.macdonald2@canada.ca
Other Communications: Alternate Phone: 613-762-8394

Science & Technology Branch / Direction générale des sciences et de la technologie
351, boul Saint-Joseph, Gatineau, QC K1A 0H3
Tel: 819-994-4751; *Fax:* 819-997-1541
Assistant Deputy Minister, Karen L. Dodds
Tel: 819-938-3435; *Fax:* 819-938-3497
karen.dodds@canada.ca

Atmospheric Science & Technology / Sciences et technologie atmosphériques
4905 Dufferin St., Toronto, ON M3H 5T4
Director General, Charles A. Lin
Tel: 416-739-4995; *Fax:* 416-739-4265
charles.lin@canada.ca
Executive Director, Air Quality Research Division, Catharine Banic
Tel: 416-739-4613; *Fax:* 416-739-4224
cathy.banic@canada.ca
Other Communications: Alternate Phone: 416-912-1294

Science & Risk Assessment Directorate / Direction générale de Science et évaluation des risques
351, boul St-Joseph, Gatineau, QC K1A 0H3
Tel: 819-953-3091; *Fax:* 819-953-5371
Director General, David Morin
Tel: 819-938-5200; *Fax:* 819-938-5212
david.morin@canada.ca

Science & Technology Strategies / Science et technologies, statégies
200, boul Sacré-Coeur, 11e étage, Gatineau, QC K1A 0H3
Tel: 905-336-4503
Director General, Eric Gagné
Tel: 819-938-3466
eric.gagne@canada.ca

Water Science & Technology / Science et technologie de l'eau
200, boul Sacré-Coeur, Gatineau, QC K1A 0H3
Tel: 819-994-4533
Director General, David Boerner
Tel: 819-938-3523
david.boerner@canada.ca

Wildlife & Landscape Science / Sciences de la faune et du paysage
1125 Colonel By Dr., Ottawa, ON K1A 0H3
Tel: 613-998-0313; *Fax:* 613-998-0315
Director General, Kevin J. Cash
Tel: 613-998-0329; *Fax:* 613-998-0458
kevin.cash@canada.ca

Strategic Policy / Direction générale de la politique stratégique
Assistant Deputy Minister, Dan E. McDougall
Tel: 819-938-3782; *Fax:* 819-938-3323
Dan.McDougall@ec.gc.ca
Director General, Economic Analysis Directorate, Derek Hermanutz
Tel: 873-469-1471; *Fax:* 819-938-3374
derek.hermanutz@canada.ca
Director General, Strategic Policy Directorate, Matt Parry
Tel: 873-469-1505; *Fax:* 819-938-3639
matt.parry@canada.ca
Director General, Intergovernmental & Stakeholder Relations Directorate, Roger Roberge
Tel: 819-938-3716; *Fax:* 819-994-6787
roger.roberge@canada.ca
Other Communications: Alternate Phone: 613-302-0803
Director General, Sustainability Directorate, Tony Young
Tel: 873-469-1400
tony.young@canada.ca
Acting Director, Intergovernmental Affairs, Angela Gillis
Tel: 819-938-3711
angela.gillis@canada.ca

Environment Canada Regional Offices
Atlantic & Québec Regions
1550, av d'Estimauville, Québec, QC G1J 0C3
Toll-Free: 800-668-6767
enviroinfo@ec.gc.ca
Regional Director General, Atlantic & Quebec Regions, Philippe Morel
Tel: 418-648-4077; *Fax:* 418-649-6213
Other Communications: Secure Fax: 418-649-6668
Associate Regional Director General, Atlantic & Quebec Regions, Geoff Mercer
Tel: 902-426-4824; *Fax:* 902-426-5168
Other Communications: Alternate Phone: 902-802-1701
45 Alderney Dr.
Dartmouth, NS B2Y 2N6

British Columbia & Yukon (Pacific & Yukon Region)
401 Burrard St., Vancouver, BC V6C 3S5
Tel: 604-664-9100; *Fax:* 604-713-9517
enviroinfo@ec.gc.ca
Regional Director General, Paul Kluckner
Tel: 604-664-9145; *Fax:* 604-664-9190
Associate Regional Director General, Cheryl Baraniecki
Tel: 780-951-8687; *Fax:* 780-495-3086
Other Communications: Alternate Phone: 587-336-3211
9250 - 49th St. NW
Edmonton, AB T6B 1K5

Ontario
4905 Dufferin St., Toronto, ON M3H 5T4
Tel: 416-739-4826; *Fax:* 416-739-4776
enviroinfo.ontario@ec.gc.ca
Regional Director General, Michael Goffin
Tel: 416-739-4936; *Fax:* 416-739-4691
Associate Regional Director General, Susan V. Humphrey
Tel: 416-739-5882; *Fax:* 416-739-4691

Joint Venture Coordinators
www.ec.gc.ca/pch-hjv

Commission for Environmental Cooperation (CEC) / Commission coopération environnementale

Secretariat, #200, 393, rue St-Jacques ouest, Montréal, QC H2Y 1N9
Tel: 514-350-4300; *Fax:* 514-350-4314
info@cec.org
www.cec.org
twitter.com/CECweb
www.facebook.com/CECconnect
www.youtube.com/CECweb
The Commission for Environmental Cooperation (CEC) is an international organization created by Canada, Mexico & the United States under the North American Agreement on Environmental Cooperation (NAAEC). The CEC was established to address regional environmental concerns, help prevent potential trade & environmental conflicts & to promote the effective enforcement of environmental law. The Agreement complements the environmental provisions of the North American Free Trade Agreement (NAFTA).
Executive Director, César Rafael Chávez
Tel: 514-350-4317
crchavez@cec.org
Director, Administration & Finances, Riccardo Embriaco
Tel: 514-350-4356
rembriaco@cec.org
Director, Submissions on Enforcement Matters Unit, Robert Moyer
Tel: 514-350-4340
rmoyer@cec.org
Director, Programs, Karen Richardson
Tel: 514-350-4326
krichardson@cec.org
Council Liaison & Organizational Performance Officer, Nathalie Daoust
Tel: 514-350-4310
ndaoust@cec.org

Environmental Protection Review Canada / Révision de la protection de l'environnement Canada

240 Sparks St., 4th Fl. West, Ottawa, ON K1A 0X8
Fax: 613-907-1337
eprc-rpec@eprc-rpec.gc.ca
www.eprc-rpec.gc.ca
Environmental Protection Review Canada is a group of expert adjudicators, entirely separate from Environment & Climate Change, that conducts reviews of Environmental Protection Compliance Orders (EPCOs). Under the Canadian Environmental Protection Act, 1999 (CEPA, 1999), enforcement officers have the power to issue EPCOs to prevent a violation, to stop an on-going violation or to require that violations be corrected. Any person who has been issued an EPCO may ask for an independent review conducted by a Review Officer. Review Officers have the authority to confirm or cancel an EPCO. They may also amend, suspend, add or delete a term or condition of the Order. The decisions of Review Officers may be appealed to the Federal Court, Trial Division.
Chief Review Officer, Allan Pope
Tel: 613-997-4060; *Fax:* 613-992-4918

Export Development Canada (EDC) / Exportation et développement Canada (SEE)

150 Slater St., Ottawa, ON K1A 1K3
Tel: 613-598-2500; *Fax:* 613-598-3811
Toll-Free: 800-267-8510
TTY: 866-574-0451
www.edc.ca
twitter.com/ExportDevCanada
www.facebook.com/ExportDevCanada
www.linkedin.com/company/export-development-canada
www.youtube.com/ExportDevCanada
A financial services corporation assisting Canadian business to succeed in foreign markets. EDC provides a wide range of financial solutions to exporters across Canada & their customers around the world. The corporation's risk management services include: export-credit insurance protecting exporters against losses due to non-payment relating to commercial & political risks; & flexible medium- or long-term financing & guarantees. As a financially self-sustaining Crown corporation, EDC operates on commercial principles, charging fees & premiums for its products & interest on its loans. EDC is governed by a board of directors composed of representatives from both the private & public sectors, & reports to Parliament through the minister for international trade. An Environmental Review Directive is used to assess the environmental impacts of projects EDC is asked to support. EDC pursues an international multilateral consensus on environmental review practices so that all exporters are subject to the same rules. EDC has adopted & implemented the OECD Recommendation on Common Approaches on Environment & Officially Supported Export Credits. EDC has signed the UNEP Statement of Financial Institutions. Through the EnviroExport initiative, EDC helps Canadia n environmental exporters succeed internationally through financing products. Where EDC is considering providing financing support, political risk insurance or equity to the sponsor of a Category A project under the Environmental Review Directive, EDC will seek consent to inform the public on its website that it is considering support to such a project.
President & CEO, Benoit Daignault
Senior Vice-President & Global Head, Financing & Investments, Carl Burlock
Senior Vice-President, Human Resources, Stephanie Butt Thibodeau
Senior Vice-President, Corporate Affairs, Catherine Decarie
Senior Vice-President & Chief Risk Officer, Enterprise Risk Management, Al Hamdani
Chief Financial Officer & Senior Vice-President, Finance & Technology, Ken Kember
Senior Vice-President, Strategy & Innovation, Derek Layne

Senior Vice-President, Business Development, Mairead Lavery
Senior Vice-President & Chief Corporate Advisor, Jim McArdle
Senior Vice-President, Insurance, Clive Witter
Chief Compliance & Ethics Officer, Scott Driscoll

EDC Regional Offices

Calgary
#2403, 308-4th Ave. SW, Calgary, AB T2P 0H7
Tel: 403-817-6700; *Fax:* 403-817-6701
Vice-President, Western Region, Linda Morris
LMorris@edc.ca

Edmonton
#3400, 10810 - 101 St., Edmonton, AB T5J 3S4
Tel: 780-801-5402; *Fax:* 780-801-5333

Halifax
Tower 2, #1605, 1969 Upper Water St., Halifax, NS B3J 3R7
Tel: 902-450-7600; *Fax:* 902-450-7601
Toll-Free: 888-332-3343
Vice-President, Atlantic Region, David Surrette
Tel: 902-450-7610
DSurrette@edc.ca

London
#1512, 148 Fullarton St., London, ON N6A 5P3
Tel: 519-963-5400; *Fax:* 519-963-5407

Moncton
#400, 735 Main St., Moncton, NB E1C 1E5
Tel: 506-851-6066; *Fax:* 506-851-6406

Montréal
Tour de la Bourse, #4520, 800, Place Victoria, CP 124 Montréal, QC H4Z 1C3
Tél: 514-908-9200; *Téléc:* 514-878-9891
Vice-présidente, Région du Québec, Julie Potter
JPottier@edc.ca

Québec
D-3, #600, 2875, boul Laurier, Québec, QC G1V 2M2
Tel: 418-577-7408; *Fax:* 418-577-7419

St. John's
510 Topsail Rd., St. John's, NL A1E 2C2
Tel: 709-772-8808; *Fax:* 709-772-8693

Toronto
#3120, 155 Wellington St. West, Toronto, ON M5V 3L3
Tel: 416-349-6515; *Fax:* 416-349-6516

Vancouver
Bentall Four, #400, 1055 Dunsmuir St., PO Box 49086 Vancouver, BC V7X 1G4
Tel: 604-678-2240; *Fax:* 604-678-2241
Toll-Free: 866-838-0031

Winnipeg
Commodity Exchange Tower, #2075, 360 Main St., Winnipeg, MB R3C 3Z3
Tel: 204-975-5090; *Fax:* 204-975-5094

Farm Credit Canada / Financement agricole Canada

1800 Hamilton St., Regina, SK S4P 2B8
Tel: 306-780-8100; *Fax:* 306-780-8919
Toll-Free: 888-332-3301
TTY: 306-780-6974
csc@fcc-fac.ca
www.fcc-fac.com
twitter.com/FCCagriculture
www.facebook.com/fccagriculture
www.linkedin.com/company/farm-credit-canada
www.youtube.com/fcctvonline

Federal Crown corporation reporting to Parliament through the Minister of Agriculture & Agri-Food. Under the Farm Credit Canada Act FCC offers financing to primary producers & agribusiness through 100 offices in rural communities across Canada.

President & Chief Executive Officer, Michael Hoffort, P.Ag.
Executive Vice-President & Chief Financial Officer, Rick Hoffman, CMA, MBA
Executive Vice-President & Chief Risk Officer, Corinna Mitchell-Beaudin
Executive Vice-President & Chief Operating Officer, Sophie Perreault
Executive Vice-President & Chief Information Officer, Travis Asmundson
Executive Vice-President & Chief Marketing Officer, Todd Klink
Executive Vice-President & Chief Human Resource Officer, Greg Honey
Senior Vice-President, Law & Corporate Secretary, Greg Willner, B.Admin., LL.B.

Farm Products Council of Canada (FPCC) / Conseil des produits agricoles du Canada (CPAC)

Building 59, Central Experimental Farm, 960 Carling Ave., Ottawa, ON K1A 0C6
Tel: 613-759-1555; *Fax:* 613-759-1566
Toll-Free: 855-611-1165
TTY: 613-759-1737
fpcc-cpac@agr.gc.ca
www.fpcc-cpac.gc.ca

In 1972, the Nationanl Farm Products Council was established by Parliament. The National Farm Products Council became known as the Farm Products Council of Canada in 2009.
The mission of the council is as follows: to oversee the national supply management agencies for poultry & eggs & the national promotion research agencies; to liaise with provincial governments interested in the work of the national agencies; to review operations of the national agencies to ensure they act in accordance with the *Farm Products Agencies Act*; to investigate complaints in relation to national agency decisions & to hold public hearings if necessary; to administer the *Agricultural Products Marketing Act* & to encourage effective marketing of farm products; & to advise the Minister on matters related to the national agencies.
The Council consists of at least three members & up to seven. Members of the Council are appointed by Cabinet.

Chair, Laurent Pellerin
Tel: 613-759-1265; *Fax:* 613-759-1566
laurent.pellerin@agr.gc.ca
Vice-Chair, Mike Pickard
Director, Council Operations & Communications, Nathalie Vanasse
Tel: 613-759-1562; *Fax:* 613-759-1505
Director, Corporate & Regulatory Affairs, Marc Chamaillard
Tel: 613-759-1706; *Fax:* 613-759-1566
marc.chamaillard@agr.gc.ca
Manager, Policy Analysis, Hélène Devost
Tel: 613-759-1589; *Fax:* 613-759-1505
helene.devost@agr.gc.ca
Officer, Web & Publications, Chantal Lafontaine
Tel: 613-759-1742; *Fax:* 613-759-1505

Federal Economic Development Agency for Southern Ontario (FedDev Ontario) / Agence fédérale de développement économique pour le Sud de l'Ontario

#101, 139 Northfield Dr. West, Waterloo, ON N2L 5A6
Fax: 519-725-4976
Toll-Free: 866-593-5505
www.feddevontario.gc.ca
twitter.com/FedDevOntario

FedDev Ontario was launched in 2009, & has the mandate to strengthen the economy in Southern Ontario. It accomplishes this through investment, job creation & programs. Examples of programs & initiatives are as follows: Applied Research & Commercialization Initiative; Building Canada Fund-Communities Component; Canada-Ontario Infrastructure Program; Canada-Ontario Municipal Rural Infrastructure Fund; Canada Strategic Infrastructure Fund; Community Adjustment Fund; Community Infrastructure Improvement Fund; Community Futures Program; Eastern Ontario Development Program; Economic Development Initiative; Graduate Enterprise Internship; Investing in Business Innovation; Municipal Rural Infrastructure Fund Top-Up; Ontario Potable Water Program; Prosperity Initiative; Recreational Infrastructure Canada Program in Ontario; Scientists & Engineers in Business; Southern Ontario Development Program; Technology Development Program; & Youth STEM.

Minister Responsible; Minister, Innovation, Science & Economic Development, Hon. Navdeep Bains, P.C., B.A., M.B.A., C.M.A.
Tel: 613-995-7784; *Fax:* 613-996-9817
Navdeep.Bains@parl.gc.ca
President, Nancy Horsman
Tel: 519-883-2560; *Fax:* 519-725-4976
Chief Financial Officer, Susan Anzolin
Tel: 519-883-2590
Director General, Human Resources, Colleen Robinson
Tel: 519-883-2570; *Fax:* 519-725-9663
Director General, Communications, Peter Yendall
Tel: 613-960-6154

Business, Innovation & Community Development / Innovation, commerciale et développement communautaire

Vice-President, Alain Beaudoin
Tel: 519-883-2553; *Fax:* 613-960-7742
Director General, Innovation & Community Development, Patrick Tobin
Tel: 416-952-4083
Acting Director General, Infrastructure & Business Development, Alexia Touralias
Tel: 416-775-3440

Policy, Partnerships & Performance Management / Politiques, partenariats et gestion de rendement

Director General, Partnerships & External Relations Directorate, Annie Cuerrier
Tel: 416-973-5958
Acting Director General, Strategic Policy, David McNabb
Tel: 613-960-7757; *Fax:* 613-791-1557

Regional Offices

Ottawa
155 Queen St., 14th Fl., Ottawa, ON K1P 6L1
Fax: 613-952-9026
Toll-Free: 866-593-5505

Toronto
151 Yonge St., 3rd Fl., Toronto, ON M5C 2W7
Fax: 416-954-6654
Toll-Free: 866-593-5505

Peterborough
143 Simcoe St., Peterborough, ON K9H 0A3
Fax: 705-750-4827
Toll-Free: 866-593-5505

Office of the Commissioner for Federal Judicial Affairs / Commissariat à la magistrature fédérale Canada

99 Metcalfe St., 8th Fl., Ottawa, ON K1A 1E3
Tel: 613-995-5140; *Fax:* 613-995-5615
Toll-Free: 877-583-4266
www.fja-cmf.gc.ca

Established in 1978, the Office of the Commissioner for Federal Judicial Affairs is responsible for the administration of Part I of the Judges Act. Federally appointed judges are provided with administrative services independent of the Department of Justice. Approximately 1,100 active judges & 800 retired judges are served by the Commissioners' Office.
The Office is also engaged in the following duties: management of the Judicial Appointments Secretariat & the Federal Courts Reports Section; coordination of initiatives related to the judiciary's role in international cooperation; preparation of a budget; administration of a judical intranet & a virtual library; & the provision of language training to judges.

Commissioner for Federal Judicial Affairs Canada, William A. Brooks
Tel: 613-947-1793; *Fax:* 613-995-5192
Deputy Commissioner, Marc A. Giroux
Tel: 613-947-1875; *Fax:* 613-995-5615
Executive Director, Judicial Appointments; Senior Legal Counsel, Véronique Joly
Tel: 613-992-9400; *Fax:* 613-941-0607
Executive Editor, Federal Courts Reports, François Boivin
Tel: 613-947-8491; *Fax:* 613-995-5615
Director, Compensation, Pension, Benefits, & Human Resources, Nikki Clemenhagen
Tel: 613-947-9899; *Fax:* 613-995-5615
Director, Finance & Administration, Errolyn Humphreys
Tel: 613-947-8492; *Fax:* 613-995-5615
Director, Judges' Language Training, Dominique Allard
Tel: 613-992-2950; *Fax:* 613-947-8503
Director, International Programs, Oleg Shakov
Tel: 613-992-2990; *Fax:* 613-995-5615

Finance Canada / Finances Canada

90 Elgin St., 14th Fl., Ottawa, ON K1A 0G5
Tel: 613-369-3710; *Fax:* 613-369-4065
TTY: 613-369-3230
fin.financepublic-financepublique.fin@canada.ca
www.fin.gc.ca
Other Communication: Media: 613-369-4000
twitter.com/financecanada
www.youtube.com/user/financecanada

The Department of Finance Canada is responsible for providing the federal government with analysis & advice on financial & economic issues. It also monitors & researches the performance of the Canadian economy's major factors (output, growth, employment, income, price stability, monetary policy, & long-term change). Interacting with various other federal departments & agencies, the Department encourages coordination in all federal initiatives with an impact on the economy. Emphasis is placed on consulting with the public regarding policy directions & options.

Minister, Finance, Hon. Bill Morneau, P.C.
Tel: 613-992-1377; *Fax:* 613-992-1383
Bill.Morneau@parl.gc.ca
Deputy Minister, Paul Rochon
Tel: 613-369-4434
Parliamentary Secretary, François-Philippe Champagne
Tel: 613-995-4895; *Fax:* 613-996-6883
Francois-Philippe.Champagne@parl.gc.ca
Associate Deputy Minister, Marta Morgan
Tel: 613-369-4431

Associate Deputy Minister & G7/G20 & FSB Deputy for Canada, Timothy Sargent
Tel: 613-369-4219

Associated Agencies, Boards & Commissions:

•Auditor General of Canada / Vérificateur Général du Canada
See Entry Name Index for detailed listing.

•Bank of Canada / Banque du Canada
See Entry Name Index for detailed listing.

•Canada Deposit Insurance Corporation / Société d'assurance-dépôts du Canada
See Entry Name Index for detailed listing.

•Canada Savings Bonds (CSB) / Obligations d'épargne du Canada (OEC)
#201, 50 O'Connor St.
PO Box 2770 D
Ottawa, ON K1P 1J7
Tel: 905-754-2012; *Fax:* 613-782-8096
Toll-free: 800-575-5151
TTY: 800-354-2222
csb@csb.gc.ca
www.csb.gc.ca
Other Communication: Payroll Savings, Employees: 1-877-899-3599; Employers: 1-888-467-5999; Buying Bonds: 1-888-773-9999; Financial Institutions & Investment Dealers: 1-888-646-2626

•Canada Revenue Agency / Agence du revenu du Canada
See Entry Name Index for detailed listing.

•Financial Consumer Agency of Canada / Agence de la consommation en matière financière du Canada
See Entry Name Index for detailed listing.

•Financial Transactions & Reports Analysis Centre of Canada (FINTRAC) / Centre d'analyse des opérations et déclarations financières du Canada (CANAFE)
234 Laurier Ave. West, 24th Fl.
Ottawa, ON K1P 1H7
Fax: 613-943-7931
Toll-free: 866-346-8722
guidelines-lignesdirectrices@fintrac-canafe.gc.ca
www.fintrac.gc.ca
Other Communication: Electronic Reporting: F2R@fintrac-canafe.gc.ca; Law Enforcement & Partner Agencies: partner-partenaire@fintrac-canafe.gc.ca

Created in 2000, FINTRAC is Canada's financial intelligence unit, a specialized agency created to collect, analyze & disclose financial information & intelligence on suspected money laundering & terrorist activities financing.

•Office of the Superintendent of Financial Institutions / Bureau du surintendant des institutions financières Canada
See Entry Name Index for detailed listing.

Consultations & Communications Branch / Direction des consultations et des communications
Assistant Deputy Minister, Pamela Aung-Thin
Tel: 613-369-3212

Corporate Services Branch / Direction des services ministériels
Provides joint services for the federal Treasury Board Secretariat & Finance Canada.
Assistant Deputy Minister, Randy Larkin
Tel: 613-369-3490
Executive Director & Chief Information Officer, Information Management & Technology, Philippe Lajeunesse
Tel: 613-369-3509
Deputy Chief Financial Officer & Executive Director, Financial Management, Christopher Meyers
Tel: 613-369-3473
Executive Director, Human Resources Division, Edward Poznanski
Tel: 613-369-3595
Senior Director, Corporate Planning, Rosie Dénot
Tel: 613-369-3493
Senior Director, Client Services Delivery, Marc Robillard
Tel: 613-369-3431

Economic & Fiscal Policy Branch / Direction de la politique économique et fiscale
Assistant Deputy Minister, Jean-François Perrault
Tel: 613-369-4018

Economic Development & Corporate Finance / Développement économique et finances intégrées
Assistant Deputy Minister, Richard Botham
Tel: 613-369-3623
General Director, Ailish Campbell
Tel: 613-369-9248

Federal-Provincial Relations & Social Policy Branch / Direction des relations fédérales-provinciales et de la politique sociale
Assistant Deputy Minister, Diane Lafleur
Tel: 613-369-4129
General Director, Catherine A. Adam
Tel: 613-369-4186

Financial Sector Policy Branch / Direction de la politique du secteur financier
Assistant Deputy Minister, Rob Stewart
Tel: 613-369-3878
General Director, Leah Anderson
Tel: 613-369-3620

International Trade & Finance / Finances et échanges internationaux
Assistant Deputy Minister, Stewart Rick
Tel: 613-369-5691
General Director, Paul Samson
Tel: 613-369-3603

Law Branch / Direction juridique
Assistant Deputy Minister & Counsel, Sandra Hassan
Tel: 613-369-3305
Deputy Assistant Deputy Minister, Justice Canada, Michel LeFrançois
Tel: 613-369-3300
General Counsel & Executive Director, General Legal Services Division, Cindy Shipton-Mitchell
Tel: 613-369-3316
General Counsel & Director, Tax Counsel Division, Robert Wong
Tel: 613-369-3335

Tax Policy Branch / Direction de la politique de l'impôt
Senior Assistant Deputy Minister, Andrew Marsland
Tel: 613-369-3739
General Director, Tax Policy, Brian Ernewein
Tel: 613-369-3743
General Director, Analysis, Miodrag Jovanovic
Tel: 613-369-3738
Director, Intergovernmental Tax Policy, Evaluation & Research Division, Maude Lavoie
Tel: 613-369-3805
Director, Tax Legislation, Alexandra MacLean
Tel: 613-369-3669

Financial Consumer Agency of Canada (FCAC) / Agence de la consommation en matière financière du Canada (ACFC)

427 Laurier Ave. West, 6th Fl., Ottawa, ON K1R 1B9
Tel: 613-960-4666; *Fax:* 613-941-1436
TTY: 866-914-6097
info@fcac-acfc.gc.ca
www.fcac-acfc.gc.ca
Other Communication: Toll-Free: 1-866-461-FCAC (3222) for services in English; 1-866-461-ACFC (2232) for services in French
twitter.com/fcacan
www.facebook.com/FCACan
linkedin.com/company/financial-consumer-agency-of-canada
www.youtube.com/fcacan

Created by Parliament in 2001, the Financial Consumer Agency of Canada (FCAC) exists to protect Canada's financial consumers; to make them aware of their rights & responsibilities; & to inform Canadians about the financial products & services available to them. The FCAC ensures that the nearly 500 federally regulated financial institutions respect the consumer provisions in the laws that govern them & monitors the voluntary codes of conduct financial institutions have adopted. As well as informing people about their rights as financial consumers, the FCAC provides information & tools to help consumers shop around for the best financial product/service for their situation. As of July 2010, the FCAC oversees payment card network operators & their commerical practices.

Commissioner, Lucie Tedesco
Tel: 613-941-4335
Deputy Commissioner, Brigitte Goulard
Tel: 613-641-4300; *Fax:* 613-941-1436
Financial Literacy Leader, Jane Rooney
Tel: 613-941-1528
Senior Counsel, Legal Services, Ekaterina Ohandjanian
Tel: 613-941-1425
Director, Marketing & Communications Branch, André-Marc Allain
Tel: 613-941-4770
Acting Director, Education, Research & Policy, Teresa Frick
Tel: 613-960-4657
Director, Corporate Services Branch, Martin Pachéco
Tel: 613-941-4239
Director, Compliance & Enforcement Branch, John Rossi
Tel: 613-941-3929

Director, Information Management/Information Technology, André Gilbert
Tel: 613-960-4622

Office of the Superintendent of Financial Institutions (OSFI) / Bureau du surintendant des institutions financières Canada (BSIF)

Kent Square, 255 Albert St., Ottawa, ON K1A 0H2
Tel: 613-990-7788; *Fax:* 613-990-5591
Toll-Free: 800-385-8647
TTY: 613-943-3980
information@osfi-bsif.gc.ca
www.osfi-bsif.gc.ca
Other Communication: Information (Ottawa-Gatineau), Phone: 613-943-3950

Responsible for regulating & supervising financial institutions & pension plans under federal jurisdiction. Included under federal jurisdiction are: banks, some insurance companies, trust companies, loan companies, cooperative credit associations, & fraternal benefit societies. OSFI monitors & examines these institutions & pension plans for solvency, liquidity, & compliance with legislation, regulations & Office guidelines. Provides actuarial services & advice to the Government of Canada. Reports to government through the Minister of Finance.

Superintendent, Jeremy Rudin
Tel: 613-990-3667; *Fax:* 613-993-6782
jeremy.rudin@osfi-bsif.gc.ca
Capital Consultant, Robert J. Hanna
Tel: 613-990-7278; *Fax:* 613-993-6525
bob.hanna@osfi-bsif.gc.ca
Director, Security & Administrative Services & DSO, Raymond Bullard
Tel: 613-990-7781; *Fax:* 613-990-0081
raymond.bullard@osfi-bsif.gc.ca
Director, Communications, Margaret Pearcy
Tel: 613-993-0577; *Fax:* 613-660-5591
margaret.pearcy@osfi-bsif.gc.ca

Corporate Services Sector / Secteur des services intégrés
Fax: 613-949-3968
Other Communication: Toronto Fax: 613-993-6782
Assistant Superintendent, Gary Walker
Tel: 613-990-8761; *Fax:* 613-990-6328
gary.walker@osfi-bsif.gc.ca
Chief Information Officer, Janet Harris-Campbell
Tel: 613-991-0469; *Fax:* 613-991-0195
Janet.Harris-Campbell@osfi-bsif.gc.ca

Office of the Chief Actuary / Bureau de l'actuaire en chef
Fax: 613-990-9900
Chief Actuary, Jean-Claude Ménard
Tel: 613-990-7577; *Fax:* 613-990-9900
jean-claude.menard@osfi-bsif.gc.c
Managing Director, OCA & Chief Actuary, EI Premium, Canada Student Loans & Employment Insurance Section, Michel Millette
Tel: 613-990-4589; *Fax:* 613-990-9900
michel.millette@osfi-bsif.gc.ca

Regulation Sector / Secteur de la réglementation
Fax: 613-993-6525
Deputy Superintendent, Mark Zelmer
Tel: 613-949-7643; *Fax:* 613-990-0081
mark.zelmer@osfi-bsif.gc.ca
Senior Director, Research Division, Walter Engert
Tel: 613-991-0427; *Fax:* 613-990-0081
walter.engert@osfi-bsif.gc.ca
Senior Director, Legislation, Approvals & Strategic Policy, Patricia A. Evanoff
Tel: 613-990-9004; *Fax:* 613-990-0081
patty.evanoff@osfi-bsif.gc.ca
Executive Director & General Counsel, Legal Services Division, Gino Richer
Tel: 613-949-8933; *Fax:* 613-990-0081
gino.richer@osfi-bsif.gc.ca
Senior Director, Accounting, Karen F. Stothers
Tel: 416-973-0744; *Fax:* 416-952-1662
karen.stothers@osfi-bsif.gc.ca
Senior Director, Actuarial Division, Stuart Wason
Tel: 416-973-2056; *Fax:* 416-952-0664
Stuart.Wason@osfi-bsif.gc.ca
Managing Director, Modeling & Mortgage Insurance, Capital Division, Michael Bean
Tel: 416-954-0503; *Fax:* 416-952-1662
Michael.Bean@osfi-bsif.gc.ca
Managing Director, Approvals & Precedents, Judy Cameron
Tel: 613-990-7337; *Fax:* 613-990-7394
judy.cameron@osfi-bsif.gc.ca
Managing Director, Private Pension Plans Division, Tamara DeMos
Tel: 613-990-7857; *Fax:* 613-990-7394
tamara.demos@osfi-bsif.gc.ca

Managing Director, Insurance Capital, Capital Insurance, Bernard Dupont
Tel: 613-990-7797; *Fax:* 613-990-0081
bernard.dupont@osfi-bsif.gc.ca
Senior Director, Bank Capital, Capital Banking, Richard F. Gresser
Tel: 613-990-7336; *Fax:* 613-990-0081
richard.gresser@osfi-bsif.gc.ca
Managing Director, Legislation & Policy Initiatives, Philipe A. Sarrazin
Tel: 613-998-4190; *Fax:* 613-990-0081
philipe.sarrazin@osfi-bsif.gc.ca
Senior Director, Actuarial Division, Chris Townsend
Tel: 416-952-4129; *Fax:* 416-952-0664
chris.townsend@osfi-bsif.gc.ca

Supervision Support Group / Groupe de soutien de la surveillance
Senior Director, Philippe Sarfati
Tel: 416-973-8145; *Fax:* 416-954-3170
philippe.sarfati@osfi-bsif.gc.ca
Managing Director, Capital Markets Risk Assessment Services, Mate Glavota
Tel: 416-973-3950; *Fax:* 416-954-3170
mate.glavota@osfi-bsif.gc.ca
Senior Director, Property & Casualty Insurance Group, Penny M. Lee
Tel: 416-952-0557; *Fax:* 416-954-6478
penny.lee@osfi-bsif.gc.ca
Managing Director, Credit Risk Division, Marc Desautels
Tel: 416-973-9041; *Fax:* 416-954-3167
marc.desautels@osfi-bsif.gc.ca
Senior Director, Supervision Support Group, Paul Marchand
Tel: 416-952-7274; *Fax:* 416-954-3170
paul.marchand@osfi-bsif.gc.ca
Senior Director, Supervisory Practices Division, Bruce J. Rutherford
Tel: 416-973-4378; *Fax:* 416-952-1663
bruce.rutherford@osfi-bsif.gc.ca
Managing Director, Operational Risk Division, Bob Hassan
Tel: 416-952-3246; *Fax:* 416-954-3170
bob.hassan@osfi-bsif.gc.ca
Director, Supervision, Calvin Johansson
Tel: 416-973-7017; *Fax:* 416-952-1663
calvin.johansson@osfi-bsif.gc.ca
Managing Director, Risk Measurement & Analytics Assessment Services (RMAAS), Ka Ying (Timothy) Fong
Tel: 416-952-0690; *Fax:* 416-952-1663
timothy.fong@osfi-bsif.gc.ca
Director, Supervision, Adri van Hilten
Tel: 416-973-0716; *Fax:* 416-973-1168
adri.vanhilten@osfi-bsif.gc.ca
Managing Director, Corporate Governance, Maria Moutafis
Tel: 416-973-3699; *Fax:* 416-973-8994
maria.moutafis@osfi-bsif.gc.ca
Managing Director, Credit Risk Division, Richard Mark Newman
Tel: 416-952-6497; *Fax:* 416-973-8966
mark.newman@osfi-bsif.gc.ca
Managing Director, Property & Casualty Insurance Group, Wayne Proctor
Tel: 416-973-6761; *Fax:* 416-954-6478
wayne.proctor@osfi-bsif.gc.ca
Managing Director, Risks, Surveillance & Analytics Division, Stephen Wright
Tel: 416-954-6486; *Fax:* 416-973-1171
stephen.wright@osfi-bsif.gc.ca

Fisheries & Oceans Canada (DFO) / Pêches et Océans Canada (MPO)

200 Kent St., Ottawa, ON K1A 0E6
Tel: 613-993-0999; *Fax:* 613-990-1866
TTY: 800-465-7735
info@dfo-mpo.gc.ca
www.dfo-mpo.gc.ca
twitter.com/DFO_MPO
www.youtube.com/user/fisheriescanada

The Department of Fisheries & Oceans (DFO), on behalf of the Government of Canada, is responsible for policies & programs in support of Canada's economic, ecological & scientific interests in the oceans & freshwater fish habitat; for the conservation & sustainable utilization of Canada's fisheries resources in marine & inland waters; & for safe, effective & environmentally sound marine services responsive to the needs of Canadians in a global economy. The Department's mandate is extremely broad & covers management & protection of the marine & fisheries resources inside the 200-mile exclusive economic zone; management & protection of freshwater fisheries resources; marine safety along the world's longest coastline; facilitation of marine transportation; protection of the marine environment; support to other federal government institutions & objectives, as the government's civilian marine service; & research to support government priorities such as climate change & biodiversity. Because of its broad mandate, DFO does not operate alone. Federal & provincial governments share jurisdiction in a number of areas related to the Department's mandate.

Minister, Fisheries, Oceans & the Canadian Coast Guard, Hon. Dominic LeBlanc, P.C., B.A., LL.B., LL.M.
Tel: 613-992-1020; *Fax:* 613-992-3053
dominic.leblanc@parl.gc.ca
Deputy Minister, Catherine Blewett
Parliamentary Secretary, Serge Cormier
Tel: 613-992-2165; *Fax:* 613-992-4558
Serge.Cormier@parl.gc.ca
Associate Deputy Minister, Leslie MacLean
Tel: 613-998-1464; *Fax:* 613-993-2194
Acting Director General, Communications, Rhonda Walker-Sisttie
Tel: 613-990-0219; *Fax:* 613-993-8277
Deputy Head & General Counsel, Legal Services Unit, Rose-Gabrielle Birba
Tel: 613-993-5692

Associated Agencies, Boards & Commissions:

·Freshwater Fish Marketing Corporation / Office de commercialisation du poisson d'eau douce
See Entry Name Index for detailed listing.

Canadian Coast Guard (CCG) / Garde côtière canadienne
Centennial Towers, #6S018, 200 Kent St., Ottawa, ON K1A 0E6
Tel: 613-993-0999; *Fax:* 613-990-1866
TTY: 800-465-7735
info@dfo-mpo.gc.ca
www.ccg-gcc.gc.ca
Other Communication: Coast Guard College, Toll-Free: 1-888-582-9090; E-mail: CCGCregistrar@dfo-mpo.gc.ca
twitter.com/CCG_GCC
www.youtube.com/user/CCGrecruitmentGCC

The Canadian Coast Guard provides the following maritime programs & services: search & rescue; marine communications & traffic services, including radio communications & radio navigational aids services; marine navigation services, a program which establishes & maintains navigational aids to assist vessels in safe navigation; enrvironmental response program, which works to minimize impacts of marine pollution incidents & to provide humanitarian aid in disasters; aids to navigation, such as the Differential Global Positioning System (DGPS) & Notices to Mariners (NOTMAR); icebreaking services; & client relations & international affairs.

Commissioner, Jody Thomas
Tel: 613-990-5813; *Fax:* 613-990-2780
Assistant Commissioner, Canadian Coast Guard, Roger Girouard
Tel: 250-480-2766
Director General, Integrated Business Management Services, Bill Kroll
Tel: 613-998-1440; *Fax:* 613-990-3480
Assistant Commissioner, Central & Arctic Region, Julie Gascon
Tel: 514-283-0050
Deputy Commissioner, Operations, Mario Pelletier
Tel: 613-998-1575; *Fax:* 613-990-2780
Director General, Integrated Technical Services, Sam Ryan
Tel: 613-998-1638; *Fax:* 613-993-5333
Director General, National Strategies, Chris Henderson
Tel: 613-991-3007; *Fax:* 613-991-4982
Director General, Operations, Wade Spurrell
Tel: 709-772-5150; *Fax:* 613-995-4700
Deputy Commissioner, Vessel Procurement, Michel G. Vermette
Tel: 613-994-9220
Director, Horizontal CCG Priorities, Maritime Services, Tanya Alvaro
Tel: 613-998-1411; *Fax:* 613-998-8428
Director, Engagement Strategies, Bruno Bond
Tel: 613-990-9541
Acting Director, Fleet Operational Business, Gary A. Walsh
Tel: 613-991-0262; *Fax:* 613-993-3421

Business Modernization / Modernisation des operations
200 Kent St., Ottawa, ON K1A 0E6
Senior Assistant Deputy Minister, David Balfour
Tel: 613-998-1488; *Fax:* 613-993-9547
Director General, Jaime Caceres
Tel: 613-993-9291; *Fax:* 613-991-0061

Ecosystems & Fisheries Management / Gestion des écosystèmes et des pêches
200 Kent St., Ottawa, ON K1A 0E6
Responsible for the management & development of all federal fisheries & habitat in Canada. The division conserves, protects, develops & enhances fishery resources & habitats, encompassing the Atlantic & Pacific sectors, adjacent provinces, & the 200-mile offshore zone. Also manages Canadian parts of trans-boundary rivers.
Senior Assistant Deputy Minister, Kevin Stringer
Tel: 613-990-9864; *Fax:* 613-990-9557
Assistant Deputy Minister, EFM Operations, Philippe Morel
Tel: 613-993-1914; *Fax:* 613-990-9557
Director General, Ecosystems Management, Sharon Ashley
Tel: 613-990-0007
Director General, Ecosystem Program Policy, Vacant
Director General, Aquaculture Management, Eric Gilbert
Tel: 613-993-1884; *Fax:* 613-993-8607
Acting Director General, Licensing & Planning, Sylvie Lapointe
Tel: 613-993-6853; *Fax:* 613-990-7051
Director General, Small Craft Harbours, Micheline Leduc
Tel: 613-990-8989
Director General, Oceans & Fisheries Policy, Jeff MacDonald
Tel: 613-990-7556
Director General, Conservation & Protection, Allan D. MacLean
Tel: 613-993-1414; *Fax:* 613-941-2718
Director General, Aboriginal Affairs, David Millette
Tel: 613-990-7201; *Fax:* 613-993-7651
Director General, Licensing & Planning, Jean-François LaRue
Tel: 613-949-4922
Director General, Conservation & Protection, Paul Steele
Tel: 613-998-9537
Executive Director, Fisheries Protection Program, Christine Stoneman
Tel: 613-991-6355; *Fax:* 613-993-7493

Ecosystems & Oceans Science / Océans et science
200 Kent St., Ottawa, ON K1A 0E6
www2.mar.dfo-mpo.gc.ca/science/ocean/sci/sci-e.html
Services include: oceans sciences (ocean's physical properties, behaviour of organic & inorganic materials & their impact on fish & ecosystems, pollutants); regulation, enforcement & management of fisheries resources & habitat that are exploited for aboriginal, commercial & recreational purposes. The Marine Protected Areas Policy & the National Framework for Establishing & Managing Marine Protected Areas represents DFO's approach to establishing & maintaining MPOs in Canada.
Assistant Deputy Minister, Trevor Swerdfager
Tel: 613-949-4919
Director General, Ecosystem Science Directorate, Arran McPherson
Tel: 613-990-0271
Director General, Strategic & Regulatory Science, Wayne Moore
Tel: 613-990-0001; *Fax:* 613-990-0313

Canadian Hydrographic Services & Oceanographic Services (CHS) / Service hydrographique et services océanographiques du Canada
615 Booth St., Ottawa, ON K1A 0E6
chsinfo@dfo-mpo.gc.ca
www.chs-shc.gc.ca
Federal program which offers the following: conducts field studies & gathers hydrographic information on tides, water levels & currents; compiles & publishes navigational charts & manuals for Canadian & adjacent international waters; works with Natural Resources Canada to cooperatively map boundary waters.
Director General, Denis Hains
Tel: 613-990-6234
Executive Director, Canada Meteorological & Oceanographic Society, Vacant
Executive Director Emeritus, Canada Meteorological & Oceanographic Society, Uri Schwarz
Tel: 613-991-0151

Human Resources & Corporate Services / Services généraux
200 Kent St., Ottawa, ON K1A 0E6
Assistant Deputy Minister, Diane Orange
Tel: 613-993-8726; *Fax:* 613-993-3246
Chief Information Officer & Director General, Information Management & Technology Services, Hachem Ben Essalah
Tel: 613-993-2051
Director General, Human Resources, Tom Balfour
Tel: 613-990-0013
Acting Director General, Real Property & Environmental Management, Bill Varvaris
Tel: 613-993-9291; *Fax:* 613-991-0061
Senior Director, Infrastructure & Operations, Abdelaziz Essoltani
Tel: 613-998-0235
Senior Director, Real Property Transformation, Kathleen White
Tel: 613-993-9248; *Fax:* 613-993-3246

Strategic Policy / Politiques stratégiques
200 Kent St., Ottawa, ON K1A 0E6
Provides leadership in recommending, developing & monitoring policy frameworks that advance DFO's initiatives, support DFO programs, & are responsive to the changing needs of DFO clients. Provides strategic advice on departmental programs, develops long-term planning priorities for the department & coordinates cross-sectoral activities in support of government goals & departmental objectives.
Senior Assistant Deputy Minister, Tom Rosser
Tel: 613-993-1808; *Fax:* 613-993-6958

Director General, Economic Analysis & Statistics, Robert Elliott
Tel: 613-993-8597; *Fax:* 613-991-3254
Director General, Strategic Policy Directorate, Beth MacNeil
Tel: 613-990-0287; *Fax:* 613-993-5085
Other Communications: Alt. Phone: 613-852-7243
Acting Director General, Executive Secretariat, Caroline Douglas
Tel: 613-998-5012
Acting Director, International Fisheries Management/Bilateral Relations, Élise Lavigne
Tel: 613-990-5374; *Fax:* 613-993-5995
Senior Director, Policy & Integration, David Creasey
Tel: 613-991-4842

Regional Directors

Central & Arctic
520 Exmouth St., Sarnia, ON N7T 8B1
Tel: 519-383-1813; *Fax:* 519-464-5128
Toll-Free: 866-290-3731
www.dfo-mpo.gc.ca/regions/central/index-eng.htm
Regional Director General, David Burden
Tel: 519-383-1810; *Fax:* 519-464-5128

Gulf
Gulf Fisheries Centre, 343, av Université, PO Box 5030 Moncton, NB E1C 9B6
Tel: 506-851-7747; *Fax:* 506-851-2435
www.glf.dfo-mpo.gc.ca
twitter.com/DFO_GULF
Associate Regional Director General, Jackey Richard
Tel: 506-851-7754; *Fax:* 506-851-2428

Maritimes
Marine House, 176 Portland St., PO Box 1035 Halifax, NS B2Y 4T3
Tel: 902-426-3550; *Fax:* 902-426-5995
www.inter.dfo-mpo.gc.ca/Maritimes/Home
twitter.com/DFO_MAR
Regional Director General, Morley B. Knight
Tel: 902-426-2581
Regional Director General, Faith G. Scattolon
Tel: 902-426-7315; *Fax:* 902-426-2706

Newfoundland & Labrador
Northwest Atlantic Fisheries Centre, 80 East White Hills, PO Box 5667 St. John's, NL A1C 5X1
Tel: 709-772-4423; *Fax:* 709-772-4880
www.nfl.dfo-mpo.gc.ca
twitter.com/DFO_NL
Acting Regional Director General, Lily K. Abbass
Tel: 709-772-4417; *Fax:* 709-772-2387
Regional Director General, Michael J. Alexander
Tel: 709-772-4417

Pacific
#200, 401 Burrard St., Vancouver, BC V6C 3S4
Tel: 604-666-0384; *Fax:* 604-666-1847
www.pac.dfo-mpo.gc.ca
twitter.com/DFO_Pacific
Regional Director General, Susan Farlinger
Tel: 604-666-6098

Québec
104, rue Dalhousie, Québec, QC G1K 7Y7
Tél: 418-648-2239; *Téléc:* 418-648-4758
www.qc.dfo-mpo.gc.ca
twitter.com/DFO_CCG_Quebec
Regional Director General, Richard Nadeau
Tel: 418-648-4158; *Fax:* 418-648-4758

Research Facilities
www.dfo-mpo.gc.ca/science/regions/index-eng.htm

Bayfield Institute
Canada Centre for Inland Waters, 867 Lakeshore Rd., PO Box 5050 Burlington, ON L7R 4A6
Tel: 905-336-6240
Comprises fisheries research, habitat management, hydrographic surveys & chart production & ships support. Together with the Freshwater Institute in Winnipeg, it provides the federal Fisheries & Oceans science programs for the Central & Arctic Region. Multiple partnerships with a variety of external stakeholders allow the Institute to be recognized internationally as a site of leading research in freshwater science.
Regional Director, Science, Michelle Wheatley
Tel: 204-983-2420; *Fax:* 204-984-2401

Bedford Institute of Oceanography (BIO) / L'institut océanographique de Bedford
1 Challenger Dr., PO Box 1006 Dartmouth, NS B2Y 4A2
Fax: 902-426-8484
WebmasterBIO-IOB@dfo-mpo.gc.ca
www.bio.gc.ca
Administered by Fisheries & Oceans, Bedford Institute of Oceanography (BIO) is Canada's largest centre for ocean research. Scientists, engineers & technicians primarily from Fisheries & Oceans, & Natural Resources Canada, (smaller components are from National Defense & Environment & Climate Change) perform targeted research & provide advice on Atlantic marine environments. Programs include: fisheries research, ocean sciences & management, habitat ecology, marine chemistry, Canadian Hydrographic Service (producing navigation charts for the Atlantic & Arctic areas), marine environmental regional & resources geoscience, & seabird research & management. BIO based staff also conduct joint projects, such as sea floor mapping & exploration, & provide scientific response to marine environmental emergencies. Also located at Bedford is the Canadian Shark Research Laboratory & the Otolith Research Laboratory.
Regional Director, Science, Alain Vézina
Tel: 902-426-3492; *Fax:* 902-426-8484
Director, Natural Resources Canada - Geological Survey of Canada (Atlantic), Stephen Locke
Tel: 902-426-2730; *Fax:* 902-426-1466

Centre for Aquaculture & Environmental Research / Centre de recherche sur l'aquaculture et l'environnement
4160 Marine Dr., West Vancouver, BC V7V 1N6
Tel: 604-666-7453; *Fax:* 604-666-3497
The Center for Aquaculture & Environmental Research (CAER) is a specialized centre for aquaculture & coastal research co-founded by Fisheries & Oceans Canada & the University of British Columbia.
Facility Manager, Leo van Kalsbeek
Tel: 250-363-6320; *Fax:* 250-363-6787
Head, Environmental & Aquaculture Research, Steve MacDonald
Tel: 604-666-6286

Cultus Lake Salmon Research Lab / Laboratoire de recherche sur le saumon du lac Cultus
4222 Columbia Valley Hwy., Cultus Lakw, BC V2R 5B6
The facility houses several laboratories, including an inorganic chemistry laboratory & a radioisotope laboratory. Artificial streams, ponds & an experimental hatchery are located on-site.

Freshwater Institute Science Laboratory / Laboratoire scientifique de l'Institut des eaux douces
501 University Cres., Winnipeg, MB R3T 2N6
Tel: 204-983-5000; *Fax:* 204-983-6285
www.dfo-mpo.gc.ca/regions/central/pub/fresh-douces/index-eng.htm
Main areas of research are: fish habitats; limnology emphasizing mechanisms & processes of biological production & decomposition in lakes; studies related to energy development use, acidification, radionuclide & heavy metal pollution. Arctic research emphasizes commercially important fish & marine mammals & associated ecosystems, & the effects of hydroelectric developments & toxic chemical pollution on aquatic ecosystems. The Institute supports a major field camp at the Experimental Lakes Area. Activities include freshwater & arctic science, science oceans initiative, fish habitat management, fisheries management, small craft harbours, corporate services, communications & regional senior management. The federal fish inspection program, recently transferred to the new Canadian Food Inspection Agency (CFIA), continues to operate out of the FWI.
Regional Director, Science, Michelle Wheatley
Tel: 204-983-2420; *Fax:* 204-984-2401

Gulf Fisheries Centre (GFC) / Centre de poissonerie du gulfe
343, av Université, 5th Fl., CP 5030 Moncton, NB E1C 9B6
Tél: 506-851-6227; *Téléc:* 506-851-2435
info@dfo-mpo.gc.ca
www.glf.dfo-mpo.gc.ca/Gulf/Who-We-Are/Gulf-Fisheries-Centre
The Gulf Fisheries Centre is home to one of two laboratories in Canada that specialize in shellfish health. Also contains the Mère Juliette Library, which is open to the general public. The library's collection contains 20,000 books & reports, 100 scientific journals, 10,000 microfiches & over a hundred videos.
Regional Director, Fisheries & Aquaculture Management Branch, Andrew Maw
Tel: 506-851-6667; *Fax:* 506-851-7732

Institut Maurice-Lamontagne (IML) / Maurice Lamontagne Institute (MLI)
850, rte de le Mer, CP 1000 Mont-Joli, QC G5H 3Z4
Tél: 418-775-0500; *Téléc:* 418-775-0730
www.qc.dfo-mpo.gc.ca/iml-mli/institut-institute/index-eng.asp
Provides extensive research on: fisheries, fish habitat, oceanography, hydrography; development of marine renewable resources in the fields of fisheries, ocean industry development, commercial shipping & recreational boating. Main area of focus centres on the Gulf of St. Lawrence & estuary, Saguenay Fjord, Canadian Arctic, & the James, Hudson & Ungava Bays. Also performs the following research: environmental chemistry research on the distribution, transport & fate of contaminants in sediments, water & the food chain; ecotoxicology research & field assessments for biomarkers, fish pathology & embryotoxicity; molecular toxicology research for biomarkers, fish reproduction & steroid hormones; bioremediation study on the microbial degradation of petroleum oil hydrocarbons & microbial bioassays. Projects include the temporal & spatial monitoring of organic & inorganic contaminants in fish, shellfish & sediments of the St. Lawrence gulf & estuary. Also studying the effects of pulp & paper effluents & mercury & municipal effluents on the reproduction of fish.
Regional Director, Regional Science Branch, Yves de Lafontaine
Tel: 418-775-0555; *Fax:* 418-775-0730

Institute of Ocean Sciences (IOS) / Institut des sciences de la mer (ISM)
9860 West Saanich Rd., PO Box 6000 Sidney, BC V8L 4B2
Tel: 250-363-6517; *Fax:* 250-363-6390
Science divisions at IOS include: Canadian Hydrographic Service, Marine Environment & Habitat Science, Ocean Science & Productivity. Other departments & organizations at the IOS facility include: GSC Pacific - Sidney Pacific Geoscience Centre, Canadian Wildlife Service, Canadian Coast Guard, North Pacific Marine Science Organization (PICES).
Manager, Ocean Sciences Directorate, Robin Brown
Tel: 250-363-6378; *Fax:* 250-363-6690

Pacific Biological Station (PBS) / La station de biologie du Pacifique
3190 Hammond Bay Rd., Nanaimo, BC V9T 6N7
Tel: 250-756-7000; *Fax:* 250-756-7053
Research at PBS responds to stock assessment, aquaculture, marine environment & habitat science, & ocean science & productivity priorities.
Regional Director, Science Branch, Carmel Lowe
Tel: 250-756-7177; *Fax:* 250-729-8360
Other Communications: Alt. Phone: 250-363-6335

Resolute Bay Laboratories / Laboratoires de Resolute Bay
Resolute Bay, NT
The Eastern Arctic field camp at Resolute Bay has been inactive for several years due to deteriorating conditions. However, with increasing interest in how global warming is affecting arctic marine conditions, the site, which includes a laboratory, warehouse & living quarters may be re-opened in the future.

St. Andrews Biological Station (SABS) / La Station biologique de St. Andrews
531 Brandy Cove Rd., St Andrews, NB E5B 2L9
Tel: 506-529-8854; *Fax:* 506-529-5862
XMARSABS@mar.dfo-mpo.gc.ca
www.mar.dfo-mpo.gc.ca/sabs
Chemical & ecological studies on the interaction between oceanography & fisheries/aquaculture & the aquatic environment. Stock assessments & associated research on commercially important groundfish, pelagic finfish, invertebrate species in the Bay of Fundy & other areas of Atlantic Canada. Research in support of the existing salmon aquaculture industry & research on other species with potential for aquaculture in Atlantic Canada. Major environmental research projects include: risk assessment of organic chemicals to fisheries; biochemical indicators of health of aquatic animals; aquatic toxicity of marine phytotoxins; molluscan toxins, techniques & improvements; phytotoxin research; aquaculture ecology research; effectiveness of acid rain control programs; effects of aquaculture in the coastal environment.

Sea Lamprey Control Centre / Centre de contôle de la lamproie de mer
1219 Queen St. East, Sault Ste Marie, ON P6A 2E5
The Centre is a combined office, lab, warehouse, aquarium, & maintenance & chemical storage facility that houses Canada's Sea Lamprey Control program & the research lab of the Great Lakes Laboratory for Fisheries & Aquatic Sciences (GLLFAS). It is located on the grounds of the Sault Ste. Marie Canal National Historic Site.
Division Manager, Paul Sullivan
Tel: 705-941-3010; *Fax:* 705-941-3025

Freshwater Fish Marketing Corporation / Office de commercialisation du poisson d'eau douce

1199 Plessis Rd., Winnipeg, MB R2C 3L4
Tel: 204-983-6601; *Fax:* 204-983-6497
sandic@freshwaterfish.com
www.freshwaterfish.com
The Corporation is a buyer, processor & marketer of freshwater fish, harvested from over 400 lakes in Manitoba, Saskatchewan, Alberta, the Northwest Territories & Northwestern Ontario. Reports to the government through the Minister of Fisheries & Oceans.
President & Chief Executive Officer, Donald Salkeld
Chief Financial Officer, Stan Lazar
Vice-President, Sales & Marketing, Paul Cater
Vice-President, Operations, Jon Goertzen
Vice-President, Human Resources & Government Services, Wendy Matheson

Global Affairs Canada (GAC) / Affaires mondiales Canada (AMC)

Enquiries Service, 125 Sussex Dr., Ottawa, ON K1A 0G2
Tel: 613-944-4000; *Fax:* 613-996-9709
Toll-Free: 800-267-8376
TTY: 613-944-1310
www.international.gc.ca
Other Communication: Emergencies, Phone: 613-996-8885; Jules Léger Library: 613-992-6150; Canadian Foreign Service Institute: 819-994-6932; Media Relations Office: 343-203-7700
twitter.com/CanadaTrade
www.facebook.com/CanadaAndTheWorld
www.linkedin.com/groups?gid=1808582
www.youtube.com/channel/UCIVMBvs03h74NSdQMH31jKA

In 1909, the Canada Department of External Affairs was established. Prior to the 2015 general election, the department was known as Foreign Affairs, Trade & Development Canada. After the election, Prime Minister Trudeau renamed the department Global Affairs Canada.

The department's mandate includes the following responsibilities: to manage the nation's diplomatic & consular relations; to ensure that foreign policy advances national interests; to promote international trade; to strengthen trading arrangements; to increase free & fair market access at bilateral, regional, & global levels; & to work with partners to attain improved economic opportunity & enhanced security for Canadians at home & abroad.

The department funds the following programs in Canada & throughout the world: Anti-Crime Capacity Building Program; Canada in La Francophonie; Canadian International Arctic Fund; Counter-Terrorism Capacity Building Program; Global Commerce Support Program (Invest Canada-Community Initiatives, Going Global Innovation, & Global Opportunities for Associations); Global Partnership Program; Global Peace and Security Fund (Global Peace & Security Program, Global Peace Operations Program, & Glyn Berry Program); International Education & Youth; International Science & Technology Partnerships Program; Investment Cooperation Program; Permanent Secretariat of the UN Convention on Biological Diversity; United Nations Trust Fund on Indigenous Issues; & United Nations Voluntary Fund for Victims of Torture.

The department also offers travel reports & warnings, such as information about security, entry requirements, health conditions, & local customs & laws (travel.gc.ca/travelling/advisories).

In March 2013, the Canadian International Development Agency (CIDA) merged with the former Department of Foreign Affairs & International Trade (DFAIT).

Minister, Foreign Affairs, Hon. Stéphane Dion, P.C., B.A., M.A., Ph.D.
Tel: 613-996-5789; *Fax:* 613-996-6562
stephane.dion@parl.gc.ca
Minister, International Trade, Hon. Chrystia Freeland, P.C.
Tel: 613-992-5234; *Fax:* 613-996-9607
chrystia.freeland@parl.gc.ca
Minister, International Development & La Francophonie, Hon. Marie-Claude Bibeau, P.C.
Tel: 613-995-2024; *Fax:* 613-992-1696
Marie-Claude.Bibeau@parl.gc.ca
Ambassador of Religious Freedom, Andrew P.W. Bennett
Senior General Counsel & Executive Director, Legal Services, Isabelle Jacques
Tel: 343-203-2274

Associated Agencies, Boards & Commissions:

•Canadian Commercial Corporation
See Entry Name Index for detailed listing.
•Export Development Canada
See Entry Name Index for detailed listing.
•International Development Research Centre
See Entry Name Index for detailed listing.
•International Joint Commission
See Entry Name Index for detailed listing.
•National Capital Commission
See Entry Name Index for detailed listing.
•North American Free Trade Agreement (NAFTA) Canadian Secretariat
See Entry Name Index for detailed listing.

Office of the Minister, Foreign Affairs

The Minister of Foreign Affairs is responsible for Canada's foreign policy & issues related to external affairs. The Minister oversees the International Centre for Human Rights & Democratic Development, the International Development Research Centre, the International Joint Commission, & the National Capital Commission.

Minister, Foreign Affairs, Hon. Stéphane Dion, P.C., B.A., M.A., Ph.D.
Tel: 613-996-5789; *Fax:* 613-996-6562
stephane.dion@parl.gc.ca
Parliamentary Secretary (Consular Affairs), Omar Alghabra
Tel: 613-992-1301; *Fax:* 613-992-1321
Parliamentary Secretary, Pamela Goldsmith-Jones
Tel: 613-947-4617; *Fax:* 613-947-4620
Pam.Goldsmith-Jones@parl.gc.ca
Chief of Staff, Julian Ovens
Tel: 343-203-1851
Director, Parliamentary Affairs, Jamie Innes
Tel: 343-203-1851
Director, Communications, Joseph Pickerill
Tel: 343-203-1851
Director, Policy, Christopher Berzins
Tel: 343-203-1851

Office of the Minister, International Development & Minister for La Francophonie

www.international.gc.ca/development-developpement/index.aspx
twitter.com/dfatd_dev
www.facebook.com/DFATDDevelopment

The Minister of International Development is responsible for Canada's international development & humanitarian objectives through managing support & resources, & engaging in policy development in Canada & internationally.

Minister, International Development & La Francophonie, Hon. Marie-Claude Bibeau, P.C.
Tel: 613-995-2024; *Fax:* 613-992-1696
Marie-Claude.Bibeau@parl.gc.ca
Parliamentary Secretary, Karina Gould
Tel: 613-995-0881; *Fax:* 613-995-1091
Karina.Gould@parl.gc.ca
Chief of Staff, Geoffroi Montpetit
Tel: 343-203-6238
Director, Parliamentary Affairs, Russell Milon
Tel: 343-203-5975
Senior Departmental Advisor, Carlos Rojas-Arbulú
Tel: 343-203-4781
Press Secretary, Bernard Boutin
Tel: 343-203-6238

Office of the Minister, International Trade

Responsibilities of the Minister of Foreign Affairs include international trade & commerce. The Minister oversee the Canadian Commercial Corporation, Export Development Canada, & NAFTA - Canadian Secretariat.

Minister, International Trade, Hon. Chrystia Freeland, P.C.
Tel: 613-992-5234; *Fax:* 613-996-9607
chrystia.freeland@parl.gc.ca
Parliamentary Secretary, David Lametti, B.A., LL.B., B.C.L., LL.M., D.Phil.
Tel: 613-943-6636; *Fax:* 613-943-6637
David.Lametti@parl.gc.ca
Chief of Staff, Brian Clow
Tel: 343-203-7332
Director, Parliamentary Affairs, Vincent Garneau
Tel: 343-203-7332

Office of the Minister of State (Foreign Affairs & Consular)

Responsibilities of foreign affairs personnel include diplomatic & consular relations & the the administration of the Foreign Service & Canada's missions abroad.

Office of the Deputy Minister, Foreign Affairs

Deputy Minister, Foreign Affairs, Ian Shugart
Tel: 343-203-4911
Senior Director, USS, Vera Alexander
Tel: 343-203-5986
Deputy Director, Office of the Deputy Minister, Foreign Affairs, David Hutchison
Tel: 343-203-5988

Office of the Senior Associate Deputy Minister, Foreign Affairs

Director, Office of the Senior Associate Deputy Minister, Emi Furuya
Tel: 343-203-5983

Office of the Deputy Minister, International Development

Deputy Minister, International Development, Peter Boehm
Tel: 343-203-2771
Executive Advisor, Nicole Martel
Tel: 343-203-6622

Office of the Deputy Minister, International Trade

Deputy Minister, International Trade, Christine Hogan
Tel: 343-203-5000
Executive Director, Owen Teo
Tel: 343-203-5961

Americas / Amériques

Assistant Deputy Minister, David Morrison
Tel: 343-203-3555
Director General, North America Strategy Bureau, Martin Benjamin
Tel: 343-203-3547
Director General, Americas Programming Bureau, Isabelle Bérard
Tel: 343-203-4591
Director General, Mission Support & Geo Coordination, Antoine Chevrier
Tel: 343-203-3645
Director General, North America Advocacy & Operations Bureau, Jim Nickel
Tel: 343-203-3585
Director General, Latin America & Caribbean Bureau, André Frenette
Tel: 343-203-2707
Director, Mission Support, Evelyne Coulombe
Tel: 343-203-3647
Director, North America Policy & Relations Division, Sylvian Fabi
Tel: 343-203-3548
Director, Central America & Caribbean, Johanne Forest
Tel: 343-203-3275
Director, Strategic Operations & Planning, Carla Hogan Rufelds
Tel: 343-203-4590
Director, Latin America & Caribbean - South America, Sylvia Cesaratto
Tel: 343-203-3277
Director, Programming, Marie Legault
Tel: 343-203-4574
Director, North America Advocacy, Mark McLaughlin
Tel: 343-203-3586; *Fax:* 613-943-8174
Director, Hemispheric Affairs, Andrew Shore
Tel: 343-203-2709
Director, North America Commercial Programs, Lynda Watson
Tel: 343-203-3560
Director, U.S. Transboundary Affairs Division, Christopher Wilkie
Tel: 343-203-3533; *Fax:* 343-943-8808

Asia Pacific / Asie-Pacifique

Assistant Deputy Minister, Susan Gregson
Tel: 343-203-2197
Susan.Gregson@international.gc.ca
Director General, South, Southeast Asia & Oceania, Peter MacArthur
Tel: 343-203-3406
Director General, Programming, Jeff Nankivell
Tel: 343-203-4510
Director General, Trade & Diplomacy North Asia, Graham Shantz
Tel: 343-203-3463; *Fax:* 613-944-2535
Executive Director, Greater China, David B. Hartman
Tel: 343-203-3460
Senior Director, Sri Lanka, Pakistan & Afghanistan Division, Louis Verret
Tel: 343-203-4505
Director, South Asia Division, Julia Bentley
Tel: 343-203-3407
Director, Northeast Asia Division, Christopher Burton
Tel: 343-203-3366; *Fax:* 343-943-1068
Executive Director, South, Southeast Asia & Oceania Commercial Relations, Rosaline Kwan
Tel: 343-203-1880
Director, Southeast Asia & Oceania Relations, Evelyn Puxley
Tel: 343-203-3395
Other Communications: Secure Phone: 613-992-6807
Director, Strategic Planning Operations, Andrew (Drew) Smith
Tel: 343-203-4509
Director, Burma/Mongolia/Philippines, Susan Steffan
Tel: 343-203-4666

Canadian Trade Commissioner Service (TCS) / Service des délégués commerciaux du Canada (SDC)

c/o Foreign Affairs & International Trade, 125 Sussex Dr., Ottawa, ON K1A 0G2
Tel: 613-944-9991; *Fax:* 613-996-9709
Toll-Free: 888-306-9991
enqserv@international.gc.ca
www.tradecommissioner.gc.ca
Other Communication: Alternate Twitter:
twitter.com/invest_canada; twitter.com/Canada_Trade
twitter.com/tcs_sdc
www.facebook.com/CanadaTrade
www.linkedin.com/groups?mostPopular=&gid=1808582
www.youtube.com/user/investincanada

The Canadian Trade Commissioner Service was founded in 1894, & now has offices across Canada & in 160 countries worldwide. With a mandate to help Canadian businesses succeed in the global marketplace, the TCS offers intelligence, qualified contacts, partnership opportunities & practical advice on foreign markets. Note that the Virtual Trade Commissioner has closed, & information on trade commissioners' coordinates, market information & events by region, sector & country can be found on the TCS website.

Director General, Trade Commissioner Service Operations, Duane McMullen
Tel: 343-203-1879
Director, Investment Cooperation Program, Martin Jensen
Tel: 343-203-4034; *Fax:* 613-943-3919

Trade Offices in Canada
www.tradecommissioner.gc.ca/eng/offices-in-canada.jsp
Atlantic Region - Halifax Regional Office
#415, 1791 Barrington St., Halifax, NS B3J 3L1
Fax: 902-426-5218
Toll-Free: 888-306-9991
roatl-atlantic@international.gc.ca
www.tradecommisioner.gc.ca/ns
Senior Trade Commissioner & Director, Kathryn Aleong
Tel: 902-426-6360
kathryn.aleong@international.gc.ca
Ontario Region - Toronto Regional Office
Yonge-Richmond Centre, 151 Yonge St., 4th Fl., Toronto, ON M5C 2W7
Fax: 416-973-8161
Toll-Free: 888-306-9991
Ontario.TCS-SDC@international.gc.ca
www.tradecommisioner.gc.ca/ont
Director & Senior Trade Commissioner, Jim Fein
Tel: 416-954-6326
Pacific Region - Vancouver Regional Office
#2000, 300 West Georgia St., Vancouver, BC V6B 6E1
Fax: 604-666-0954
Toll-Free: 888-306-9991
pacific-pacifique.tcs-sdc@international.gc.ca
www.tradecommissioner.gc.ca/bc
Senior Trade Commissioner, Christian Hansen
Tel: 604-666-8888
Prairies & Northwest Territories Region - Calgary Regional Office
#300, 639 - 5 Ave. SW, Calgary, AB T2P 0M9
Fax: 403-292-4578
Toll-Free: 888-306-9991
Prairies.TCS-SDC@international.gc.ca
www.tradecommissioner.gc.ca/alta
Secondary Address: #300, 639 - 5 Ave. SW
Physical Address:
Calgary, AB
Senior Trade Commissioner & Director, Patricia Elliott
Tel: 403-292-6409
Quebec Region & Nunavut - Montréal Regional Office
Place Bonaventure, Portail Sud-Ouest, #8750, 800, rue de la Gauchetiere ouest, Montréal, QC H5A 1K6
Fax: 514-283-8794
Toll-Free: 888-306-9991
quebec.tcs-sdc@international.gc.ca
www.tradecommissioner.gc.ca/que
Acting Director, Michel Lamarre
Tel: 514-283-3531

Chief Audit Executive / Dirigeant principal de la vérification
Chief Audit Executive, Brahim Achtoutal
Tel: 343-203-5354
Director, Anne Weldon-Lacroix
Tel: 343-203-5353
Internal Auditor, Ion-Mircea Ghinda
Tel: 343-203-5302
Acting Manager, Practice Management, Sophie Frenette
Tel: 613-203-5319
Acting Audit Manager, Daniel Steeves
Tel: 343-203-5305

Consular, Security, & Legal (Legal Adviser) / Services consulaires, sécurité, affaires juridiques (Jurisconsulte)
Deputy Legal Adviser & Director General, Legal Affairs, Hugh Adsett
Tel: 343-203-2556
Deputy Legal Adviser & Director General, Trade Law, Robert Brookfield
Tel: 343-203-2499
Director General, Security & Emergency Management (Departmental Security Officer), Robert Derouin
Tel: 343-203-1733
Director General, Consular Policy, Beatrice Maille
Tel: 343-203-2758
Director General, Consular Operations Bureau, Donica Pottie
Tel: 343-203-2756
Director, Emergency Operations & Planning, Francois Lafond
Tel: 343-203-2656
Director, Ocean & Environmental Law, Catherine Boucher
Tel: 343-203-9001
Director, Case Management, Victoria Fuller
Tel: 343-203-2749
Director, Business Management Office, Jean-Jules Renaud
Tel: 343-203-2876
Director, Market Access & Trade Remedies Law, Dominic Gingras
Tel: 343-203-2500; *Fax:* 613-944-0027
Director, Criminal, Security & Diplomatic Law, Roland Legault
Tel: 343-203-2534
Director, Consular Policy & Programs, Tristan Landry
Tel: 343-203-1829; *Fax:* 613-943-2158
Director, Treaty Law, Gary Luton
Tel: 343-203-2465; *Fax:* 613-947-0342
Director, Task Force on Security Funding, Jamie Bell
Tel: 343-203-4878
Director, Consular Corporate Management & Innovation, Bill Milner
Tel: 343-203-2248
Director, United Nations, Human Rights & Economic Law, Carolyn Knobel
Tel: 343-203-2450
Director, Policy, Governance & Partnerships, Ken England
Tel: 343-203-2648; *Fax:* 613-996-4381
Director, Continental Shelf, Stephen P. Randall
Tel: 343-203-2202
Director, Training, Exercises & Resilience, Valerie Sorel
Tel: 343-203-2691
Director, Corporate Security Division & MCO Renewal, Derrick Stewart
Tel: 343-203-3075
Director, Investment & Services Law, Sylvie T. Tabet
Tel: 343-203-2224; *Fax:* 613-944-5857

Corporate Planning, Finance & Information Technology / Planification ministérielle, finance et technologie de l'information
Assistant Deputy Minister & Chief Financial Officer, Arun Thangaraj
Tel: 343-203-1433
Acting Chief of Staff to the ADM & CFO, Louise Chevrier
Tel: 343-203-1228
Chief Information Officer & Director General, Information Management & Technology, Martin Loken
Tel: 343-203-1196
Acting Director General, Corporate Accounting, Sophie Bainbridge
Tel: 343-203-8088
Acting Director General, Financial Planning & Management, Jeffrey Johnson
Tel: 343-203-1462
Director, Financial Planning & Management, Clinton Lawrence-Whyte
Tel: 343-203-1603
Director General, Corporate Planning, Performance & Risk, Bob L. Lawson
Tel: 343-203-6363
Director General, Grants & Contributions Management, Mark Lusignan
Tel: 343-203-5583
mark.lusignan@international.gc.ca
Executive Director, Information Management & Business Management, Yann Blais
Tel: 343-203-5829
Deputy CIO & Executive Director, Client Relations & Information Technology Governance, Allison Young
Tel: 343-203-1218
Executive Director, Information Technology Client Support, Alain Lefebvre
Tel: 343-203-1197; *Fax:* 819-934-0632
Executive Director, Information Management & Business Management, Yann Blais
Tel: 343-203-5829
Executive Director & Deputy CIO, Client Relations & Information Technology Governance, Allison Young
Tel: 343-203-1218
Chief Librarian, Library Services (Jules Léger Library), Jo-Anne H. Valentine
Tel: 343-203-2640
www.international.gc.ca/library-bibliotheque/index.aspx

Corporate Secretary / Secrétaire des services intégrés
Corporate Secretary & Director General, Alison LeClaire
Tel: 343-203-3506; *Fax:* 613-943-6584

Europe, Middle East, & Maghreb / Europe, Moyen-Orient et Maghreb
Assistant Deputy Minister, Alex Bugailiskis
Tel: 343-203-3445
Director General, Middle East-Maghreb, Masud Husain
Tel: 343-203-3304
Director General, Europe & Eurasia, Matthew Levin
Tel: 343-203-3662; *Fax:* 613-995-1277
Other Communications: Secure Phone: 613-992-8333
Director General, Europe-Middle East Programming, Dave Metcalfe
Tel: 343-203-4513
Director, AMMAN MENA Developement, Sean Boyd
Tel: 343-203-4571
Director, Maghreb & Regional Commercial Relations, Sebastien Carriere
Tel: 343-203-3291
Director, EU-EFTA Commercial Relations, Edith St-Hilaire
Tel: 343-203-3704
Director, Business Management Office for Europe, Middle East, Maghreb & Africa, Margaret Felisiak
Tel: 343-203-3630
Director, Eastern Europe & Eurasia Relations, Kevin Hamilton
Tel: 343-203-3603; *Fax:* 613-995-1277
Executive Director, Middle East Relations, Sebastien Beaulieu
Tel: 343-203-3296
Director, Gulf State Relations, Emmanuelle Lamoureux
Tel: 343-203-3293
Director, EU-EFTA Relations, Olivier Nicoloff
Tel: 343-203-3691; *Fax:* 613-995-5772
Other Communications: Secure Fax: 613-944-2158
Director, Planning & Operations, Rory O'Connor
Tel: 343-203-4511
Rory.Oconnor@international.gc.ca
Director, Maghreb & Regional Commercial Relations, Simon Pomel
Tel: 343-203-3431
Trade Commissioner, EU-EFTA Commercial Relations, Marilou Denis
Tel: 343-203-3706
Deputy Director, Trade, Maghreb & Regional Commercial Relations, Peter E. Stulken
Tel: 343-203-3312

Global Issues & Development / Enjeux mondiaux et du développement
Assistant Deputy Minister, Diane Jacovella
Tel: 343-203-6089
Director General, Health & Nutrition, Amy Baker
Tel: 343-203-6241
Acting Director General, Social Development, Julie Shouldice
Tel: 343-203-5071
Director General, International Organizations, Sarah A. Fountain Smith
Tel: 343-203-2437
Director General, Food Security & Environment, Caroline Leclerc
Tel: 343-203-4725; *Fax:* 819-953-6356
caroline.leclerc@international.gc.ca
Director General, International Humanitarian Assistance, Heather Jeffrey
Tel: 343-203-6098
Director General, Economic Development, Patricia Pena
Tel: 343-203-4782
Director, Global Health, Gloria Wiseman
Tel: 343-203-6242
Director, Natural Resources & Governance, Sharon Peake
Tel: 343-203-4779
Director, Humanitarian Organizations & Food Assistance, Christina Buchan
Tel: 343-203-6088
christina.buchan@international.gc.ca
Director, Food Security, Vacant
Director, United Nations, Rebecca Netley
Tel: 343-203-2438
Director, Economic Growth & IFIs, Andrew Clark
Tel: 343-203-6099
Director, Commonwealth & Francophonie Affairs, Virginie Saint-Louis
Tel: 343-203-2425
Director, International Humanitarian Assistance Operations, Stephen Salewicz
Tel: 343-203-6094
stephen.salewicz@international.gc.ca
Acting Director General, Social Development, Julie Shouldice
Tel: 343-203-5071
Director General, International Organizations, Sarah Fountain Smith
Tel: 343-203-2437

Human Resources / Ressources humaines
Assistant Deputy Minister, Francis Trudel
Tel: 343-203-2009; *Fax:* 613-944-2411
Director General, Assignments & Executive Management, Chris Cooter
Tel: 343-203-2008
Director General, Canadian Foreign Service Institute, Lillian Thomsen
Tel: 343-203-8155; *Fax:* 613-994-9525
Executive Director, Assignment & Pool Management, Mark Fletcher
Tel: 343-203-2054
Executive Director, Executive Services & Talent Management, Colin Gascon
Tel: 343-203-1943

Inspector General / Inspecteur général
Inspector General, Barbara Richardson
Tel: 343-203-1507
Executive Director, Mission Inspection, Benoit Prefontaine
Tel: 343-203-1506

Director, Special Investigations Division, Jérôme Bernier
Tel: 343-203-1538
Director, Values & Ethics & Workplace Well-being, Barbara Carswell
Tel: 343-203-1505
Director, Evaluation, Stephen Kester
Tel: 343-203-1509; *Fax:* 343-203-1511

International Business Development, Investment & Innovation / Développement du commerce international, investissement et innovation

Assistant Deputy Minister, International Business, Susan Bincoletto
Tel: 343-203-1875
Director General, Trade Sectors, Cameron MacKay
Tel: 343-203-3828; *Fax:* 613-944-3214
Director General, Regional Trade Operations & Intergovernmental Relations, Michael Danagher
Tel: 343-203-2112
Director General, Investment & Innovation, Louis Marcotte
Tel: 343-203-4113; *Fax:* 613-944-3178
Director General, Trade Portfolio Strategy & Coordination, Randle Wilson
Tel: 343-203-1877
Director, Investor Services, Tracy Reynolds
Tel: 343-203-4140
Director, Science, Technology & Innovation, Jennifer Daubeny
Tel: 343-203-4047
Director, Investor Outreach, Caroline Chrétien
Tel: 343-203-6558; *Fax:* 613-944-3178
Director, Sustainable Technologies Sector Practice, Hilary Esmonde-White
Tel: 343-203-3815
Director, Missions Consultations & Outreach, John Gartke
Tel: 343-203-2769
Director, Systems & Analysis Division, Alain Gendron
Tel: 343-203-4033
Director, Regional Network & Intergovernmental Relations, Luc Santerre
Tel: 343-203-2111; *Fax:* 613-995-6576
Executive Director, Multi-Sectors Practices, Wayne Robson
Tel: 343-203-3726; *Fax:* 613-996-2635
Director, Trade Strategy & Analysis, Stéphane Lambert
Tel: 343-203-1882
Director, Trade Planning & Coordination, Catherine Nagy
Tel: 343-203-3095
Director, International Trade Portfolio, Francine Noftle
Tel: 343-203-2336
Director, Aerospace, Automotive, Defence & ICT Practices, Kyle M. Nunas
Tel: 343-203-3862
Director, Strategy & Analysis Division, Stanley Psutka
Tel: 343-203-4121
Acting Director, Trade & Economic Analysis, Aaron Sydor
Tel: 343-203-2403; *Fax:* 613-992-4695
Director, Trade Commissioner Support, Alan Minz
Tel: 343-203-6880
Director, International Education, Andreas Weichert
Tel: 343-203-1766; *Fax:* 613-944-1448

International Platform / Plateforme internationale

Assistant Deputy Minister, Dan Danagher
Tel: 343-203-1484
Acting Director General, IPB Corporate Services Bureau, Dominique Bélanger
Tel: 343-203-1487
Director, Mission Procurement Operations, Josephine Dahan
Tel: 343-203-1339
Director General, Client Relations & Missions Operations, Marie-José Lacroix
Tel: 343-203-1927
Director General, Foreign Service Directives, Leslie Scanlon
Tel: 343-203-1354
Director General, Physical Resources, David McKinnon
Tel: 343-203-8355
Director General, Locally Engaged Staff, Andrew Stirling
Tel: 343-203-3902; *Fax:* 819-994-5950
Executive Director, Strategic Policy & Planning, Todd Sandrock
Tel: 343-203-8348; *Fax:* 343-957-0530

International Security / Sécurité internationale

Director General, Freedom & Human Rights, Richard Arbeiter
Tel: 343-203-3615
Director General, Security & Intelligence Bureau, David Drake
Tel: 343-203-3176
Director General, Stabilization & Reconstruction Task Force, Tamara Guttman
Tel: 343-203-2825
Director General, Non-Proliferation & Security Threat Reduction, Heidi Hulan
Tel: 343-203-3935; *Fax:* 613-944-1130
Director, Democracy, Tara Denham
Tel: 343-203-2322
Executive Director, Human Rights, Mark Allen
Tel: 343-203-2907
Director, International Crime & Terrorism Division, Mark Berman
Tel: 613-203-3236; *Fax:* 343-944-3105
Director, Global Partnership Program, Manon S. Dumas
Tel: 343-203-3932
Acting Director, Humanitarian Affairs & Disasters Response, Craig Weichel
Tel: 343-203-2800
Director, Non-Proliferation & Disarmament, Martin Larose
Tel: 343-203-3166
Director & Deputy Head of START, Stabilization & Reconstruction Programs, Pamela O'Donnell
Tel: 343-203-2848
Director, Deployment & Coordination Division, Caroline Delany
Tel: 343-203-2786
Executive Director, Defence & Security Relations, Rouben Khatchadourian
Tel: 343-203-3196
Director, Conflict Policy & Security Coherence Secretariat, Shannon Smith
Tel: 343-203-2827
Director, Business Management Office IFM-BMO, Melissa Shepard Legault
Tel: 343-203-3142; *Fax:* 613-944-2104
Director, Democracy, Eric Laporte
Tel: 613-404-4423
Director, Capacity Building Programs, Nell Stewart
Tel: 343-203-3215

Office of Protocol / Bureau du Protocole

Chief of Protocol, Angela Bogdan
Tel: 343-203-3005
Director, Diplomatic Corps Services, Lisette Ramcharan
Tel: 343-203-3015
Deputy Chief of Protocol & Director, Official Visits, Geoffrey J. Dean
Tel: 343-203-2990
Director, Summits, Official Events & Management Services, Daniel Desfossés
Tel: 343-203-0803
Director, Hospitality (Westin Contractor), Official Events, Alexandre Lincourt
Tel: 613-944-7283
Coordinator, Official Events, Daniel Grenier
Tel: 343-203-2977; *Fax:* 343-944-0020

Partnerships for Development Innovation / Partenariats pour l'innovation dans le développement

Assistant Deputy Minister, Elissa A. Golberg
Tel: 343-203-6494; *Fax:* 819-953-6357
Director General, Social Development Partnerships, Lilian Chatterjee
Tel: 343-203-6508
lilian.chatterjee@international.gc.ca
Director General, Engaging Canadians, Ariel Delouya
Tel: 343-203-6485; *Fax:* 819-953-6357
Director General, Sustainable Economic Growth Partnerships, Francois F. Montour
Tel: 343-203-6507; *Fax:* 819-994-3834
Director, Health & Food Security, Diane Harper
Tel: 343-203-6516
Director, Food Security Partnerships, Marie Nyiramana
Tel: 343-203-6489; *Fax:* 613-996-9276
marie.nyiramana@international.gc.ca
Director General, Engaging Canadians, Ariel Delouya
Tel: 343-203-6485; *Fax:* 613-995-0667

Public Affairs / Affaires publiques

Assistant Deputy Minister, Ken J. MacKillop
Tel: 343-203-1650
Director, Foreign Affairs & Consular, Gregory Galligan
Tel: 343-203-1685
Director General, Strategic Communications, Charles Mojsej
Tel: 343-203-1711
Executive Director, Corporate Communications, Fiona Nelson
Tel: 343-203-6181; *Fax:* 819-997-7397
Executive Director, Digital Media, Mark Stokes
Tel: 343-203-1656
Director, Media Relations Office, Adam Barratt
Tel: 343-203-1695
Director, Trade, Strategic Communications, Latifa Belmahdi
Tel: 343-203-1660
Director, Social Media, Charles Brisebois
Tel: 343-203-1718; *Fax:* 613-992-2432
Director, Business Management Office for Public Affairs & Special Bureaux, Linda Young
Tel: 343-203-6817
Director, E-Communications & Communications Products, Yan Michaud
Tel: 343-203-1729
Director, Development, Strategic Communications, Jacqueline Théoret
Tel: 343-203-6182
Director, Development, Strategic Communications, Alexandra Young
Tel: 343-203-6182

Strategic Policy / Politique stratégique

Assistant Deputy Minister, Vincent Rigby
Tel: 343-203-6680
vincent.rigby@international.gc.ca
Director General, International Assistance Envelope Management, Nicole Giles
Tel: 343-203-4731
Director General, Development Policy Planning, Deirdre Kent
Tel: 343-203-4729
Director General, Office of the Senior Arctic Official, Susan Harper
Tel: 343-203-2320
Director General, International Economic Policy, Marc-Yves Bertin
Tel: 343-203-5147
Executive Director, Circumpolar Affairs, Chris Shapardanov
Tel: 343-203-2865
Director, Prosperity & Development, Tom Bui
Tel: 343-203-4784
Director, Development Relations, Janet Durno
Tel: 343-203-4726; *Fax:* 613-992-3492
Director, IAE Priorities & Allocation, Susan Greene
Tel: 343-203-4727
Director, Development Evaluation, David Heath
Tel: 343-203-5285
Director, Development Research, Lilly Nicholls
Tel: 343-203-6307
Director, Program Coherence & Effectiveness, Vaughn Lantz
Tel: 343-203-5148
Director, Foreign Policy Planning, Michael Walma
Tel: 343-203-2100
Acting Director, Foreign Policy Research, Neil Brennan
Tel: 343-203-2086

Sub-Saharan Africa / Afrique subsaharienne

Assistant Deputy Minister, Lise Filiatrault
Tel: 343-203-4945
Director General, Southern & Eastern Africa Bureau, Norton Leslie
Tel: 343-203-4928
Director General, Pan-Africa Bureau, Lisa Stadelbauer
Tel: 343-203-3339
Director General, West & Central Africa Bureau, Kenneth Neufeld
Tel: 343-203-5029
Senior Director, Pan-Africa & Regional Development Division, Edmond Wega
Tel: 343-203-4929
Director, Pan-Africa Affairs Division, Nadia Ahmad
Tel: 343-203-3420
Director, Pan-Africa Affairs Division, Nadia Ahmad
Tel: 343-203-3420
Director, South Sudan Program, Southern & Eastern Africa, Chantal Labelle
Tel: 343-203-4974
Director General, Southern & Eastern Africa Bureau, Leslie Norton
Tel: 343-203-4928
Director, Democratic Republic of Congo & Nigeria, Benin, Burkina Faso, DRC & Nigeria Development Division, James Parsons
Tel: 343-203-5024
Director, Operations, Planning & Strategic Coordination Division, Renata E. Wielgosz
Tel: 343-203-3319

Trade Agreements & Negotiations Branch / Accords commerciaux et négociations

Acting Assistant Deputy Minister, Kirsten Hillman
Tel: 343-203-4120
Associate Assistant Deputy Minister, Vacant
Chief Trade Negotiator, Canada-India Comprehensive Economic Partnership Agreement, Don Stephenson
Tel: 343-203-4082
Chief Trade Negotiator, Canada-European Union, Steve Verheul
Tel: 343-203-4455
Chief Air Negotiator/Director General, Intellectual Property & Services Trade, Bruce Christie
Tel: 343-203-4453
Director General, Trade & Export Controls, Wendy Gilmour
Tel: 343-203-4337
Director General, Market Access, Marvin Hildebrand
Tel: 343-203-4414
Director General, Trade Negotiations, David Usher
Tel: 343-203-4229

Director General, North America & Investment, Martin Moen
Tel: 343-203-4190
Secretary & Executive Director, Trade Agreements & NAFTA Secretariat, Deborah Gowling
Tel: 343-203-4268; *Fax:* 613-992-9392

Great Lakes Pilotage Authority (GLPA) / Administration de pilotage des Grands Lacs (APGL)

202 Pitt St., 2nd fl., PO Box 95 Cornwall, ON K6H 5R9
Tel: 613-933-2991; *Fax:* 613-932-3793
www.glpa-apgl.com

The Authority provides pilotage services in the waters of the St. Lawrence River commencing at the northern entrance of St. Lambert Lock, the Great Lakes area & the Port of Churchill, Manitoba. Reports to government through the Minister of Transport.

Chief Executive Officer, Robert Lemire, C.A.
rlemire@glpa-apgl.com
Chief Financial Officer, Stéphane Bissonnette
sbissonnette@glpa-apgl.com
Director, Operations, Diane Couture
dcouture@glpa-apgl.com

Regional Offices

Head Office & Cornwall Dispatch
202 Pitt St., 2nd Fl., Cornwall, ON K6H 5R79
Tel: 613-933-2991; *Fax:* 613-932-3793

Thorold Office
Lock 7, Welland Canal, Thorold, ON
Tel: 905-688-3399; *Fax:* 905-688-5599

Health Canada / Santé Canada

Tunney's Pasture, Ottawa, ON K1A 0K9
Tel: 613-957-2991; *Fax:* 613-941-5366
Toll-Free: 866-225-0709
info@hc-sc.gc.ca
www.hc-sc.gc.ca
twitter.com/healthcanada
www.facebook.com/HealthyCdns
www.youtube.com/user/healthcanada

In partnership with provincial & territorial governments, Health Canada (HC) develops health policy, enforces health regulations, promotes disease prevention, & enhances healthy living for all Canadians. HC ensures that health services are available & accessible to First Nations & Inuit communities. It works closely with other federal departments, agencies & health stakeholders to reduce health & safety risks to Canadians. Through its Health Intelligence Network, HC works with other levels of government & the health care system in the surveillance, prevention, control & research of disease outbreaks across Canada & around the world. It also monitors health & safety risks related to the sale & use of drugs, food, chemicals, pesticides, medical devices & certain consumer products. HC negotiates agreements regarding hazardous materials in the workplace, performs medical assessments for pilots & air traffic controllers, & conducts environmental health assessments. As of April 1, 2013, Health Canada assumed the responsibilities & functions under the Hazardous Materials Information Review Act, formerly carried out by the Hazardous Materials Information Review Commission.

Minister, Health, Hon. Jane Philpott, P.C.
Tel: 613-992-3640; *Fax:* 613-992-3642
Jane.Philpott@parl.gc.ca
Parliamentary Secretary, Kamal Khera
Tel: 613-992-0778; *Fax:* 613-992-0800
Kamal.Khera@parl.gc.ca
Director, Parliamentary Affairs, Peter Cleary
Tel: 613-957-0200
Director, Communications, David Clements
Tel: 613-957-0200
Director, Policy, Caroline Pitfield

Associated Agencies, Boards & Commissions:

•Canadian Institutes of Health Research / Instituts de recherche en santé du Canada
See Entry Name Index for detailed listing.

•Mental Health Commission of Canada (MHCC) / Commission de la santé mentale du Canada
#600, 100 Sparks St.
Ottawa, ON K1P 5B7
Tel: 613-683-3755; *Fax:* 613-798-2989
info@mentalhealthcommission.ca
The Mental Health Commission of Canada is mandated to improve the mental health system & help change Canadians' attitudes & behaviours around mental health issues.

•Pest Management Regulatory Agency (PMRA) / Agence de réglementation de la lutte antiparasitaire (ARLA)
See Entry Name Index for detailed listing.

•Public Health Agency of Canada / Agence de santé publique du Canada
130 Colonnade Rd.
Ottawa, ON K1A 0K9
www.phac-aspc.gc.ca
Other Communication: Alberta/NWT: 780-495-2754; Atlantic: 902-426-2700; BC/Yukon: 604-666-2083; Manitoba/Saskatchewan: 204-789-2000; Ontario/Nunavut: 416-973-0003; Quebec: 514-283-2858
Promotes & protects the health & safety of all Canadians. Its activities focus on preventing chronic diseases, including cancer & heart disease, preventing injuries, & responding to public health emergencies & infectious disease outbreaks.

Health Canada Regulations Section / Section de la réglementation
General Counsel & Director, Claude Lesage
Tel: 613-952-9645

Legal Services / Services juridiques
www.hc-sc.gc.ca/ahc-asc/branch-dirgen/ls-sj/index-eng.php
Senior General Counsel & Head, Legal Services, Irit Weiser
Tel: 613-957-3766; *Fax:* 613-954-9485
Senior Administrative Officer, Ginette Morin
Tel: 613-941-5343

Chief Financial Officer Branch (CFOB) / Direction générale du contrôleur ministériel (DGCM)
hc-sc.gc.ca/ahc-asc/branch-dirgen/cfob-dgcm/index-eng.php
Other Communication: Management Accountability Division, E-mail: mcs-sfcm@hc-sc.gc.ca
The CFOB is the departmental focal point of accountability to ensure rigorous stewardship of resources & managing for results. The CFO provides the Minister, Deputy Minister, Associate Deputy Minister & the Departmental Executive with strategic advice on efficiency of expenditures & value-for-money, as well as anticipating & promoting future trends. The CFO reports directly to the Deputy Minister & is a key member of Health Canada's Senior Management Board. The CFO is also the lead executive with Central Agencies for overall financial management, with a functional reporting relationship to the Comptroller General of Canada.
Assistant Deputy Minister & Chief Financial Officer, Jamie Tibbetts
Tel: 613-952-3985

Financial Operations Directorate
Director General, Todd Mitton
Tel: 613-957-7762

Planning & Corporate Management Practices Directorate
Director General, Marc Desjardins
Tel: 613-948-6357

Resource Management Directorate
Director General, Edward de Sousa
Tel: 613-946-6358
Executive Director, Financial Management Office, Nadia Dellavalle
Tel: 613-957-1048

Communications & Public Affairs Branch / Direction générale des affaires publiques et des communications
The Communications & Public Affairs Branch integrates national & regional perspectives into all of its policies & strategies, communications & consultation functions. The Branch plays a key role in delivering Health Canada's commitment to transparency. Through the branch, Health Canada aims to continue improving communications & the flow of information to & from stakeholders, clients, partners, media & the Canadian public.
Assistant Deputy Minister, Michelle Kovacevic
Tel: 613-960-2176
Acting Director General, Public Health Strategic & Communications Directorate, Erika-Kirsten Easton
Tel: 613-952-8155
Acting Director General, Public Affairs Directorate, Renee Couturier
Tel: 613-957-0215; *Fax:* b13-948-8092
Director General, Ministerial Services & Integrated Communications Directorate, Marian Hubley
Tel: 613-960-6040
Director General, Health Strategic Communications Directorate, Vacant

Corporate Services Branch (CSB) / Direction générale aux services de gestion
The CSB provides corporate support & services across the Department in the following areas: human resources management; official languages; real property & facilities management; occupational health, safety emergency & security management; information technology & information management; executive correspondence; & access to information & privacy requests/issues.
Assistant Deputy Minister, Debbie Beresford-Green
Tel: 613-946-3200
Chief Information Officer, Information Management, Kirk Shaw
Tel: 613-595-1307
Director General, Human Resources, Robert Ianiro
Tel: 613-957-3236
Director General, Real Property & Security Directorate, Martin Tomkin
Tel: 613-952-6190
Executive Director, Learning, Development & Talent Management, Vacant
Executive Director, National Real Property Management Division, Paul Bortolotti
Tel: 613-952-0936
Executive Director, Strategic Human Resources Management & Executive Group Services Division, Peter Hooey
Tel: 613-668-7893
Executive Director & DSO, Security Management Division, Louis Lahaie
Tel: 613-952-9550
Executive Director, Workplace Relations & Organizational Wellbeing, Delroy Lawrence
Tel: 613-954-2248
Executive Director, Regional Operations Division, Caroline Legare
Tel: 613-941-4214
Executive Director, Strategic Human Resources Management & Executive Group Services Division, Joanne Lirette
Tel: 613-957-3253
Executive Director, Solutions Centre, Tracey Sampson
Tel: 613-595-1371
Executive Director, Client Services Division, Cathy Peters
Tel: 613-957-3253
Executive Director, IT Service Delivery Division, Vacant
Executive Director, Regional Real Property Division, Ian Skinner
Tel: 613-941-1791
Director, Facilities & Operations Division, Carole Proulx
Tel: 613-447-6025
Executive Director, Service Management Division, Karl Ghiara
Tel: 613-595-1287

Deputy Minister's Office / Bureau de la Sous-Ministre
Deputy Minister, Simon Kennedy
Tel: 613-957-0212
Associate Deputy Minister, Paul Glover
Tel: 613-954-5904
Executive Director, Inspection Review, Todd Cain
Tel: 613-948-6420
Executive Director, Deputy Minister's Office, Lara Boulanger-Stewart
Tel: 613-957-9515
Ombudsman Services Officer, Organizational Ombudsman, Lorrain C. Kelly
Tel: 613-954-2238

First Nations & Inuit Health Branch (FNIHB) / Direction générale de la santé des Premières nations et des Inuits (DGSPNI)
Assists First Nations & Inuit communities & people to address health inequalities & diseases threats through health surveillance & population health interventions. Ensures the availability of, or access to, health services for First Nations & Inuit people. Devolves control & management of community-based health services to First Nations & Inuit communities & organizations. The Environmental Health Division addresses conditions in the environment that could affect the health of community members, such as drinking water quality, mould, food safety, facilities inspections, transportation of dangerous goods. The Environmental Research Division conducts, coordinates & funds contaminants-related research, coordinates the replacement or upgrading of diesel-fuel tanks & remediation of fuel oil-contaminated sites, lab services for testing of PCBs & mercury, drinking water-related research & testing.
Senior Assistant Deputy Minister, Sony Perron
Tel: 613-957-7701
Acting Assistant Deputy Minister, Regional Operations, Keith Conn
Tel: 613-946-1722
Executive Director, Internal Client Services & Transition, Susan Russell
Tel: 613-952-3151
Director General, British Columbia Tripartite Initiative, Vacant
Director General, Non-Insured Health Benefits Directorate, Sandra Bruce
Tel: 613-954-8825
Executive Director, Capacity, Infrastructure, Accountability, Paula Hadden-Jokiel
Tel: 613-941-3757
Director General, Strategic Policy, Planning & Information, Mary-Luisa Kapelus
Tel: 613-954-2445

Acting Director, Population Health & Wellness Division, Andrea Challis
Tel: 613-612-1329
Executive Director, Primary Health Care, Robin Buckland
Tel: 613-957-6359
Executive Director, Policy & Partnerships, Jon Rogers
Tel: 613-960-6595
Executive Director, Capacity, Infrastructure & Accountability, Catherine Jones
Tel: 613-941-3757; *Fax:* 613-960-3788
Chief Medical Officer of Health & Executive Director, Population & Public Health, Tom Wong
Tel: 613-952-9616
Director, Environmental Public Health Division, Ivy Chan
Tel: 613-948-7773
Director, Home and Preventative Care Division, Marlene Nose
Tel: 613-948-5445
Director, Primary Health Care Systems, Leila Gillis
Tel: 613-952-7492
Director, Communicable Disease Control, Erin E. Henry
Tel: 613-957-1151
Director, Population Health & Wellness, Halina Cyr
Tel: 613-948-6412

Health Products & Food Branch (HPFB) / Direction générale des produits de santé et des aliments (DGPSA)

HPFB's mandate is to take an integrated approach to the management of risks & benefits related to health products & food by minimizing health factors to Canadians while maximizing the safety provided by the regulatory system for health products & food; & to promote conditions that enable Canadians to make healthy choices & provide information so that they can make informed decisions about their health. The Environmental Impact Initiative develops strategy & policy in response to the Canadian Environmental Protection Act requirement that all new substances for use in Canada must be assessed for direct & indirect impact on human health & the environment.

Associate Assistant Deputy Minister, Anne Lamar
Tel: 613-957-6817; *Fax:* 613-957-3954
Acting Chief Finance & Administration Officer, Bureau of Business Systems & Operations, Denise Berthiaume
Tel: 613-957-0365; *Fax:* 613-957-1784
Director General, Veterinary Drugs Directorate, Daniel Chaput
Tel: 613-954-1873; *Fax:* 613-954-5694
Director General, HPFB Inspectorate - Ottawa, Robin Chiponski
Tel: 613-957-6836
Director General, Biologics & Genetic Therapies Directorate, Cathy Parker
Tel: 613-946-0099
Acting Director General, Resource Management & Operations Directorate, Deryck Trehearne
Tel: 613-957-6690
Senior Medical Officer, Centre for Evaluation of Radiopharmaceuticals & Biotherapeutics, Jerieta Waltin-James
Tel: 613-790-4541
Director General, Food Directorate, Karen McIntyre
Tel: 613-957-1821
Director General, Office of Nutrition Policy & Promotion, Dr. Hasan Hutchinson
Tel: 613-957-8330
Director General, Therapeutic Products Directorate, Marion Law
Tel: 613-957-6466
Interim Director General, Marketed Health Products Directorate, John Patrick Stewart
Tel: 613-941-8889
Director General, Policy, Planning & International Affairs Directorate, Edward Morgan
Tel: 613-952-8149
Executive Director, Licensing & Inspection, Etienne Ouimette
Tel: 613-954-2996
Executive Director, Risk Management, Steven Schwendt
Tel: 613-952-5804
Director, Centre for Biologics Evaluation, Lindsay Elmgren
Tel: 613-957-1061
Director, Centre for Evaluation of Radiopharmaceuticals & Biotherapeutics, Agnes V. Klein
Tel: 613-954-5706
Acting Director, Business Integration & Risk Management, Marianne Tang
Tel: 613-957-6468
Acting Director, Policy & International Collaboration, Liz Anne Gillham-Eisen
Tel: 613-960-5315
Director, Office of Regulatory Affairs, Georgette Roy
Tel: 613-957-1488; *Fax:* 613-952-7756
Director, Bureau of Chemical Safety, Barbara Lee
Tel: 613-957-0973; *Fax:* 613-952-7756
Director, Bureau of Food Surveillance & Science Integration, Danielle Bruie
Tel: 613-957-1923
Acting Director, Bureau of Microbial Hazards, Martin Duplessis
Tel: 613-957-0880
Director, Bureau of Nutritional Sciences, William Yan
Tel: 613-948-8478
Acting Director, Bureau of Policy, Intergovernmental & International Affairs, Denise MacGillivray
Tel: 613-957-8417
Director, Policy & Strategic Planning, Kim Dayman-Rutkus
Tel: 613-954-6785
Director, Bureau of Strategic Initiatives & Planning, Melinda Piecki
Tel: 613-957-6660
Director, Marketed Biologics, Biotechnology & Natural Health Products, Duc Vu
Tel: 613-954-0731
Acting Director, Marketed Health Products Safety & Effectiveness Information, Mary Raphael
Tel: 613-960-6685
Director, Marketed Pharmaceuticals & Medical Devices, Kimby Barton
Tel: 613-952-6239
Director, Therapeutic Effectiveness & Policy Bureau, Lisa Lange
Tel: 613-946-6509
Director, Planning & Evaluation, Kim LaForce
Tel: 613-948-6319
Director, Environmental Impact Initiative, Gordon Stringer
Tel: 613-960-3747
Director, International Affairs, Louise Dery
Tel: 613-948-7787
Director, Office of Legislative & Regulatory Modernization, David K. Lee
Tel: 613-946-6586
Acting Director, Bureau of Cardiology, Allergy & Neurological Sciences, Sophie Sommerer
Tel: 613-954-6498
Director, Bureau of Gastroenterolgy, Infection & Viral Diseases, Ceila Lourenco
Tel: 613-941-2588
Director, Bureau of Metabolism, Oncology & Reproductive Sciences, Kelly Robinson
Tel: 613-941-1154
Director, Bureau of Pharmaceutical Sciences, Karen Reynolds
Tel: 613-948-4273
Director, Bureau of Policy, Science & International Programs, Patrice Lemyre
Tel: 613-957-6451; *Fax:* 613-941-1812
Interim Director, Planning, Performance & Review Services, Carey Agnew
Tel: 613-941-1248
Director, Office of Clinical Trials, Carole Legare
Tel: 613-954-6494; *Fax:* 613-954-4474
Director, Office of Planning, Performance & Review Services, Therapeutic Products, Vacant
Director, Office of Submissions & Intellectual Property, Therapeutic Products, Anne Bowes
Tel: 613-941-0842; *Fax:* 613-946-5610

Healthy Environments & Consumer Safety (HECSB) / Direction générale, santé environnementale et sécurité des consommateurs (DGSESC)

The HECSB mission is to help Canadians to maintain & improve their health by promoting healthy & safe living, working & recreational environments & by reducing the harm caused by tobacco, alcohol, controlled substances, environmental contaminants, & unsafe consumer & industrial products.

Assistant Deputy Minister, Hilary Geller
Tel: 613-946-6701
Director General, Environmental & Radiation Health Sciences, Andrew Adams
Tel: 613-954-3859
Director General, Consumer Product Safety Directorate, Tina Green
Tel: 613-957-1422
Acting Director General, Environmental and Radiation Health Sciences, Tim Singer
Tel: 613-954-3859

Safe Environments Programme (SEP) / Programme de la sécurité des milieux (PSM)

Other Communication: URL: www.hc-sc.gc.ca/ahc-asc/branch-dirgen/hecs-dgsesc/sep-psm/index-eng.php

Investigates, monitors & assesses health risks in the work, home & natural environments. Areas investigated & regulated include: medical devices, chemicals & biotechnology products in the environment, drinking water, air quality, tobacco, hazardous products & toxic waste, as well as anything that emits radiation from natural & human sources. Aims to protect Canadians from health hazards associated with natural & man-made environments through assessment & investigation of the health effects of environmental pollutants & health hazards associated with radiation sources & hazardous products.

Director General, Safe Environments Directorate, Amanda Jane Preece
Tel: 613-954-0291

Workplace Hazardous Materials Information System (WHMIS) / Système d'information sur les matières dangereuses utilisées au travail (SIMDUT)

Fax: 613-952-1994
www.hc-sc.gc.ca/ewh-semt/occup-travail/whmis-simdut/index_e.html

A nationwide hazard communication system providing information on hazardous materials used in the workplace. Key elements of the system are cautionary labelling on containers of hazardous materials, material safety data sheets (MSDSs) that contain more detailed information, & worker training. Suppliers must ensure that products are appropriately labelled & that MSDSs are provided to purchasers. Employers are required to make MSDSs available to their employees & provide workers with training on WHMIS & the safe use of hazardous materials. WHMIS supports the workers' right to know the hazards of the materials they use. WHMIS requirements are administered through federal & provincial coordinators.

Director General, Workplace Hazardous Materials Directorate, Daniel Wolfish
Tel: 613-952-7585

Pest Management Regulatory Agency (PMRA) / Agence de réglementation de la lutte antiparasitaire (ARLA)

2720 Riverside Dr., Ottawa, ON K1A 0K9

Tel: 613-736-3799; *Fax:* 613-736-3798
Toll-Free: 800-267-6315
TTY: 800-465-7735
pmra.infoserv@hc-sc.gc.ca
www.hc-sc.gc.ca/cps-spc/pest/index-eng.php
Other Communication: Agency URL: www.hc-sc.gc.ca/ahc-asc/branch-dirgen/pmra-arla/index-eng.php

Created in 1995, The PMRA determines if proposed pesticides can be used safely when label directions are followed & will be effective for their intended use. If there is reasonable certainty from scientific evaluation that no harm to human health, future generations or the environment will result from exposure to or use of a pesticide, its registration for use in Canada will be approved. Once the pesticides are on the market, the PMRA monitors their use through a series of education, compliance & enforcement programs. Pesticides are also reviewed every fifteen years or sooner as new information is discovered & as science evolves. Companies are also required to report any incident they receive about their products,just as the public is encouraged to report any incidents to these companies or through the Incident Reporting Program. The PMRA administers the Pest Control Products Act on behalf of the Minister of Health.

Executive Director, Richard Aucoin
Tel: 613-736-3701; *Fax:* 613-736-3707
Director General, Health Evaluation Directorate, Peter Chan, PhD
Tel: 613-736-3510
Director General, Value Assessment & Re-evaluation Management Directorate, Margherita Conti
Tel: 613-736-3485
Director General, Compliance, Lab Services & Regional Operations Directorate, Diana Dowthwaite
Tel: 613-736-3484
Director, Policy, Communications & Regulatory Affairs, Jason Flint
Tel: 613-736-3914
Acting Director General, Environmental Assessment Directorate, Scott Kirby
Tel: 613-736-3715

Regions & Programs Branch / Direction générale des régions et des programmes

Acting Senior Director General, Peter Brander
Tel: 613-954-0690
Executive Director, DAS National & Laboratory Coordination, Guy Aucoin
Tel: 450-928-4100
Acting Executive Director, Specialized Health Services Directorate, Ken Moore
Tel: 613-957-7669

Regional Offices

Alberta

Canada Place, #710, 9700 Jasper Ave., Edmonton, AB T5J 4C3

Tel: 780-495-6815; *Fax:* 780-495-5551
TTY: 800-465-7735

Atlantic

#1525, 1505 Barrington St., Halifax, NS B3J 3Y6

Tel: 902-426-2038; *Fax:* 902-426-3768
TTY: 800-465-7735

Regional Director General, Krista Locke
Tel: 902-407-7810; *Fax:* 902-426-6659

British Columbia
Winch Bldg., Sinclair Centre, #410, 757 West Hastings St., Vancouver, BC V6C 1A1
Tel: 604-666-2083; *Fax:* 604-666-2258
TTY: 800-465-7735
Regional Director General, Bruce Cuddihey
Tel: 604-775-7003; *Fax:* 604-775-8716
Manitoba
#300, 391 York Ave., Winnipeg, MB R3C 4W1
Tel: 204-983-4199; *Fax:* 204-983-6018
TTY: 800-465-7735
Ontario
180 Queen St. West, Toronto, ON M5V 3L7
Tel: 416-973-4389; *Fax:* 416-973-1423
Toll-Free: 866-999-7612
TTY: 800-465-7735
Regional Director General, Lucy Butts
Tel: 416-954-3592; *Fax:* 416-954-3599
lucy.butts@hc-sc.gc.ca
Québec
Guy-Favreau Complexe, Tour Est, 200, boul René-Lévesque ouest, 2e étage, Montréal, QC H2Z 1X4
Tél: 450-646-1353; *Téléc:* 514-283-6739
Ligne sans frais: 800-561-3350
TTY: 800-465-7735
Regional Director General, Marie-France Bérard
Tel: 514-283-2856; *Fax:* 514-283-0910
Saskatchewan
2045 Broad St., 1st Fl., Regina, SK S4P 3T7
Tél: 306-780-5449; *Téléc:* 306-780-3129
TTY: 800-465-7735
Autres nombres: Alternate phone: 306-780-5038
Regional Director General, Ward Chickoski
Tel: 780-495-3857

Strategic Policy Branch (SPB) / Direction générale de la politique stratégique (DGPS)
The SPB plays a lead role in health policy, communications & consultations. The SPB's objective is to promote national coordination & development of a strong, shared knowledge base to address health & health care priorities for all Canadians. They also aim to facilitate successful health system adaptation to changes in technology, society, industry & the environment, such that Canadians will continue to be protected from health risks, have access to quality health care, & gain positive health benefits from information & innovation.
Assistant Deputy Minister, Abby Hoffman
Tel: 613-946-1791
Director General, Policy Coordination & Planning Directorate, Cheryl Grant
Tel: 613-957-1940
Director General, Health Care Programs & Policy Directorate, Helen McElroy
Tel: 613-954-0834
Director General, Applied Research & Analysis Directorate, Vacant
Director General, Health Care Strategies Directorate, Marcel Saulnier
Tel: 613-960-9712
Director, Office of Pharmaceuticals Management Strategies, Frances Hall
Tel: 613-952-6451
Executive Director, Official Language Community Development Bureau, Roger Farley
Tel: 613-954-7467
Executive Director, Health Programs & Strategic Initiatives, Cindy Moriarty
Tel: 613-946-9375
Executive Director, Office of Pharmaceuticals Management Strategies, Jean Pruneau
Tel: 613-957-1692
Executive Director, Science Policy, Laird Roe
Tel: 613-941-3003; *Fax:* 613-941-9093
Director, Health Care System Division, Gavin Brown
Tel: 613-957-8994; *Fax:* 613-648-4663

Immigration & Refugee Board of Canada (IRB) / Commission de l'immigration et du statut de réfugié du Canada (CISR)

Canada Bldg, 344 Slater St., 12th Fl., Ottawa, ON K1A 0K1
Tel: 613-995-6486; *Fax:* 613-943-1550
contact@irb-cisr.gc.ca
www.irb-cisr.gc.ca
The IRB is an independent administrative tribunal that reports to Parliament through the Minister of Immigration, Refugees & Citizenship. The Board's mission, on behalf of Canadians, is to make well-reasoned decisions on immigration & refugee matters efficiently, fairly, & in accordance with the law. As Canada's largest federal tribunal, the IRB consists of three divisions. The Refugee Protection Division decides claims for refugee protection made by persons in Canada. The Immigration Division conducts detention reviews & immigration inquiries for certain categories of people believed to be inadmissable, or removable from, Canada. The Immigration Appeal Division hears appeals of sponsorship applications refused by officials of Immigration, Refugees & Citizenship; appeals from certain removal orders made against permanent residents, refugees & other protected persons, & holders of permanent resident visas; appeals by permanent residents who have been found outside Canada not to have fulfilled their residency obligation; & appeals by Immigration, Refugees & Citizenship from decisions of the Immigration Division at admissability hearings.
Chair, Mario Dion
Executive Director, Ross Pattee
Tel: 613-670-6857
Deputy Chair, Immigration Appeal Division, Paul Aterman
Tel: 613-670-6900
Deputy Chair, Immigration Division, Susan Bibeau
Tel: 514-963-9278
Deputy Chair, Refugee Protection Division, Sylvia Cox-Duquette
Tel: 613-670-6993; *Fax:* 613-947-4860
Deputy Chair, Refugee Appeal Division, Ken Sandhu
Tel: 613-670-6909
Director General, Policy, Planning & Research Branch, Greg Kipling
Tel: 613-996-0942
Director General, Registry & Regional Support Services, Rebecca McTaggart
Tel: 416-954-1224; *Fax:* 416-952-7517
Acting Director General, Strategic Communication & Partnerships Branch, Aarin Masson
Tel: 613-670-6886
Director General, Human Resources & Professional Development Branch, Barbara Wyant
Tel: 613-670-6985

Immigration, Refugees & Citizenship / Immigration, des Réfugiés et de la Citoyenneté

Jean Edmonds, South Tower, 365 Laurier Ave. West, Ottawa, ON K1A 1L1
Toll-Free: 888-242-2100
TTY: 888-576-8502
www.cic.gc.ca
twitter.com/CitImmCanada
www.facebook.com/CitCanada
www.youtube.com/CitImmCanada
The Department of Immigration, Refugees & Citizenship (formerly Citizenship & Immigration (CIC), renamed Nov. 2015 by Prime Minister Trudeau) administers Canada's citizenship & immigration policies, procedures & service. The department is responsible for the following: examining immigrants, visitors & people claiming refugee status at land borders, seaports & airports; processing applications for permanent residence, extensions of visitor status requests & sponsorships for relatives & refugees overseas; admitting students, temporary workers & qualified business immigrants; investigating & removing people who are in Canada illegally; working with & helping fund a network of settlement agencies & services to help immigrants adapt to & participate in day-to-day Canadian life; promoting the acceptance of immigrants by Canadians; cooperating with various levels of government on enforcement, program development & the delivery of services; accepting applications & verifying the eligibility & documentation of applicants; granting citizenship & administration of the Oath of numerous community facilities across Canada; confirming Canadian citizenship status &; issuing proofs of citizenship to Canadians. The Immigration & Refugee Board reports to Parliament through the minister.
Minister, Immigration, Refugees & Citizenship, Hon. John McCallum, P.C., B.A., Ph.D.
Tel: 613-996-3374; *Fax:* 613-992-3921
john.mccallum@parl.gc.ca
Parliamentary Secretary, Arif Virani, B.A., LL.B.
Tel: 613-992-2936; *Fax:* 613-995-1629
Arif.Virani@parl.gc.ca
Chief of Staff to the Minister, Mathieu Belanger
Tel: 613-954-1064
Director, Issues Management, Bernie Derible
Tel: 613-954-1064
Policy Advisor, Kyle Nicholson
Tel: 613-954-1064

Canada Immigration Centres & Citizenship Offices / Centres d'immigration et de citoyenneté
Immigration visa offices are located in most Canadian Embassies & Consulates abroad. Immigration centres are located at most ports of entry in Canada, & citizenship & immigration offices in major cities throughout the country. For specific addresses & other information contact 1-888-242-2100.

Office of the Deputy Minister / Cabinet du sous-ministre
Fax: 613-954-3509
Other Communication: Secure Fax: 613-954-5448
Deputy Minister, Anita Biguzs
Tel: 613-954-3501
Associate Deputy Minister, Richard Wex
Tel: 613-954-5117
Executive Director & Senior General Counsel, Legal Services, Marie Bourry
Tel: 613-437-6745; *Fax:* 613-952-4777
Deputy Executive Director & General Counsel, Legal Services, Kristine Allen
Tel: 613-437-6722

Communications Branch / Direction générale des communications
Tel: 613-954-9019; *Fax:* 613-941-7099
Director General, David Hickey
Tel: 613-437-7634; *Fax:* 613-941-7099

Office of Internal Audit & Accountability / Bureau de vérification interne et responsabilisation
Fax: 613-952-6556
Director General, Raymond Kunze
Tel: 613-437-7226

Office of the Assistant Deputy Minister, Chief Financial Officer / Bureau de la sous-ministre adjointe, administrateur principal des finances
Fax: 613-957-2772
Assistant Deputy Minister/Chief Financial Officer, Tony Matson
Tel: 613-437-9182; *Fax:* 613-946-6048
Director General, Financial Management, Daniel Mills
Tel: 613-437-6396; *Fax:* 613-952-9772
Acting Director General, Financial Operations, Benoit St-Jean
Tel: 819-934-2135; *Fax:* 819-934-3884

Office of the Assistant Deputy Minister, Corporate Services / Bureau de la sous-ministre adjointe, Services ministériels
Fax: 613-954-7360
Assistant Deputy Minister, Stefanie Beck
Tel: 613-437-9190
Chief Information Officer/Director General, Soyoung Park
Tel: 613-437-6881; *Fax:* 613-954-6209
Director General, Administration, Security & Accommodation, Bob Lanouette
Tel: 613-437-9206; *Fax:* 613-954-3754
Acting Director General, Human Resources, Holly Flowers Code
Tel: 613-437-7776
Director General, Corporate Affairs, Michael Olsen
Tel: 613-437-7103; *Fax:* 613-957-5946
Executive Director, Application Management Services, Marie-Andrée Roy
Tel: 873-408-0051

Office of the Assistant Deputy Minister, Operations / Bureau de la sous-ministre adjointe, Opérations
Fax: 613-957-8887
Assistant Deputy Minister, Robert Orr
Tel: 613-437-9166; *Fax:* 613-957-8887
Associate Assistant Deputy Minister, Dawn Edlund
Tel: 613-952-1770; *Fax:* 613-957-8887

Biometrics Project Office / Bureau de projet de la biométrie
Fax: 613-960-5877
Director General, Vacant

Case Management Branch / Règlement des cas
Other Communication: Secure Fax: 613-941-6970
Director General, Heather Primeau
Tel: 613-437-6563

Centralized Processing Region / Région des processus centralisés
Fax: 613-941-7020
Director General, Paul Armstrong
Tel: 613-437-5581

Citizenship & Passport Program Operational Coordination / La Coordination opérationnelle des programmes de citoyenneté et de passeport
Fax: 613-957-8887
Director General, Passport Operational Coordination, Caitlin Imrie
Tel: 613-437-9766
Executive Director, Business Strategy & Innovation, Jean-Pierre Lamarche
Tel: 613-437-9722
Director, Service Management, Rouba Dabboussy
Tel: 613-437-9740
Director, Citizenship Program Delivery, Mary-Ann Hubers
Tel: 613-437-7581
Director, Integration, Coordination, & Advancement, Donna Price
Tel: 819-639-9053

Director, Integration, Coordination, & Advancement, Doug Temple
Tel: 613-437-9762

Integration Program Management Branch / Bureau de la gestion du programme d'intégration
Fax: 613-998-1534
Director General, Heather Primeau
Tel: 613-991-2215; *Fax:* 613-998-1534

International Region / Région internationale
Fax: 613-957-5802
Director General, Angela Gawel
Tel: 613-437-7266; *Fax:* 613-957-5802

Migration Health Branch / Direction générale migration et santé
Fax: 613-941-2179
Director General, André Valotaire
Tel: 613-437-7303; *Fax:* 613-941-2179

Operational Management & Coordination / Gestion opérationnelle et coordination
Fax: 613-952-5382
Director General, Mike MacDonald
Tel: 613-437-7132

Operations Performance Management Branch / Gestion des opérations de performance
Director General, Stephanie Kirkland
Tel: 613-437-5813; *Fax:* 613-960-5877

Strategic Projects Office / Bureau de projets stratégiques
Fax: 613-960-7659
Director General, Caroline Melis
Tel: 613-437-9391
Executive Director, Bruce Grundison
Tel: 613-437-9386; *Fax:* 613-952-7094

Office of the Assistant Deputy Minister, Strategic & Program Policy / Cabinet du sous-ministre adjoint, Politiques stratégiques et de programmes
Fax: 613-946-6048
Assistant Deputy Minister, Catrina Tapley
Tel: 613-437-9160; *Fax:* 613-946-6048
Acting Associate Assistant Deputy Minister, David Manicom
Tel: 613-437-9152; *Fax:* 613-946-6048

Admissibility Branch / Direction générale de l'admissibilité
Fax: 613-952-9187
Director General, Larisa Galadza
Tel: 613-437-5937

Immigration Branch / Direction générale de l'immigration
Fax: 613-941-9323
Director General, Maia Welbourne
Tel: 613-437-7534; *Fax:* 613-954-5896

Integration / FCRO Branch / Intégration / BORTCÉ
Tel: 613-957-4483; *Fax:* 613-954-9144
Director General, Corinne Prince St-Amand
Tel: 613-437-6249
Senior Director, Horizontal Policy & Program, Brenna MacNeil
Tel: 613-437-6285; *Fax:* 613-952-7416

International & Intergovernmental Relations / Relations internationales et intergouvernementales
Fax: 613-954-4322
Director General, Mark Davidson
Tel: 613-437-7492; *Fax:* 613-954-4322

Refugee Affairs / Affaires des réfugiés
Fax: 613-957-5869
Director General, Sarita Bhatla
Tel: 613-437-7433; *Fax:* 613-957-5869

Research & Evaluation Branch / Recherche et évaluation
Fax: 613-957-5936
Director General, Ümit Kiziltan
Tel: 613-437-6106; *Fax:* 613-957-5936

Strategic Policy & Planning / Politiques stratégiques et planification
Fax: 613-954-5896
Director General, Fraser Valentine
Tel: 613-437-9196

Passport Canada / Passeport Canada
Passport Canada Program, Gatineau, QC K1A 0G3
Toll-Free: 800-567-6868
TTY: 866-255-7655
www.ppt.gc.ca
Other Communication: Phone from outside Canada or USA: 819-997-8338
Secondary Address: 22, rue de Varennes
Passport Canada Program
Gatineau, QC J8T 8R1
twitter.com/passportcan
www.facebook.com/passportcan
www.youtube.com/passportcan

Passport Canada issues six types of Canadian passports, as well as two types of travel documents for refugees & stateless persons who live in Canada. Passports include regular passports, diplomatic passports, special passports, emergency travel documents, & temporary passports. Examples of Canadian travel documents are refugee travel documents & certificates of identity.
Passport Canada service locations include Passport Canada regional offices, selected Canada Post counters, Service Canada Centres, & Government of Canada offices abroad. Only these locations are authorized to collect passport processing fees.
Non-Canadians may use Passport Canada's central office in Gatineau, Québec. It is responsible for certificates of identity & travel documents.
Persons who are sixteen years of age or older must apply for a passport using general adult application forms, which are available free of charge. An application must include the completed application form, proof of Canadian citizenship, two photographs, a document to support identity, plus the required fee.
Child applications must be complete for all Canadians who are under sixteen years of age. As of October 1, 2012, all applications for a child's passport require a detailed proof of parentag e document to demonstrate a child & parent relationship.
Since 2009, everyone who travels to the United States by land, sea, or air, including Canadian & U.S. citizens, must present a valid passport or another secure document.
Passport Canada always make final decisions about passport entitlement.
As of July 1, 2013, all new Canadian passports are issued as ePassports, which contain enhanced security features & embedded electronic chips.
On July 2, 2013, responsibility for the passport program was assumed by Citizenship & Immigration. Service Canada now oversees passport operations including the network of passport offices.

Director, Business Solutions, Josee Bessette
Tel: 819-953-3461
Director, Investigation Division, Peter Bulatovic
Tel: 819-934-8525; *Fax:* 819-953-8737
Director, Planning & Foreign Operations Division, René Côté
Tel: 819-994-1963
Director, Intelligence Divison, Malcolm Eales
Tel: 819-934-3143
Director, Strategic Management Division, Hubert Laferrière
Tel: 819-934-3841

Passport Canada Offices
Persons who plan to travel within the next twenty business days should apply in person at a Passport Canada office.
Passport Canada offices are also able to deal with complex cases, such as lost, stolen, damaged, or inaccessible passports, absence of a guarantor, & applications for children when only one parent is participating.

Brampton
#401, 40 Gillingham Dr., Brampton, ON L6X 4X7
Urgent service is unavailable at the Brampton office. Clients who require express or pick-up service may use the Mississauga Passport Canada office.

Calgary - 4th Ave.
Harry Hays Building, #150, 220 - 4th Ave. SE, Calgary, AB T2G 4X3

Calgary - Macleod Trail SW
14331 Macleod Trail SW, Calgary, AB T2Y 1M7
Urgent service is unavailable at this office. Persons who need express or pick-up service are encouraged to apply at the 4th Avenue South East office in Calgary.

Chicoutimi
98, rue Racine est, Chicoutimi, QC G7H 1R1

Edmonton
Canada Place Building NW, #126, 9700 Jasper Ave., Edmonton, AB T5J 4C3

Fredericton
Frederick Square, #430, 77 Westmorland St., Fredericton, NB E3B 6Z3

Gatineau
Place du Centre, 200, Promenade du Portage, Commercial Level 2, Gatineau, QC K1A 0G4

Halifax
Maritime Centre, #1508, 1505 Barrington St.. 15th Fl., Halifax, NS B3J 3K5

Hamilton
Standard Life Building, 120 King St. West, Plaza Level, Hamilton, ON L8P 4V2

Kelowna
Capri Centre, #110, 1835 Gordon Dr., Kelowna, BC V1Y 3H4
In-person service & express service are available. Urgent service is unavailable at the Kelowna office.

Kitchener
40 Weber St. East, Mezzanine Level, Kitchener, ON N2H 6R3

Laval
Place Laval, #500, 3, place Laval, Laval, QC H7N 1A2

London
Cherryhill Village Mall, #76, 301 Oxford St. West, London, ON N6H 1S6

Mississauga
Central Parkway Mall, #116, 377 Burnhamthorpe Rd. East, 2nd Fl., Mississauga, ON L5A 3Y1

Montréal - Marcel-Laurin
#100, 2089, boul Marcel-Laurin, Montréal, QC H4R 1K4

Montréal - René-Levesque ouest
Tour Ouest, Complexe Guy Favreau, #103, 200, boul René-Lévesque ouest, Montréal, QC H2Z 1X4

Montréal - Transcanadienne
Le Centre Commercial Fairview Pointe-Claire, #C-022A, 6815, aut Transcanadienne, Montréal, QC H9R 1C4

Ottawa
#115, 885 Meadowlands Dr. East, Ottawa, ON K2C 3N2
Secondary Address: 1430 Prince of Wales Dr.
Ottawa, ON K2C 1N6

Québec
Tour Cominar, Place de la Cité, #200, 2640, boul Laurier, 2e étage, Québec, QC G1V 5C2

Regina
#500, 1870 Albert St., Regina, SK S4P 4B7

Richmond
#310, 5611 Cooney Rd., Richmond, BC V6X 3J6
Urgent service is not available at the Richmond location. In-person & express service are available, however. Passports must be picked up at the the Vancouver Passport Canada office.

St. Catharines
Pen Centre Shopping Plaza, #604, 221 Glendale Ave., St Catharines, ON L2T 2K9

St. John's
TD Place, #802, 140 Water St., St. John's, NL A1C 6H6

Saskatoon
Federal Building, #405, 101 - 22 St. East, Saskatoon, SK S7K 0E1

Surrey
Central City Shopping Centre, #1109, 10153 King George Blvd., Surrey, BC V3T 2W1

Thunder Bay
979 Alloy Dr., 2nd Fl., Thunder Bay, ON P7B 5Z8

Toronto - Town Centre Crt.
#210, 200 Town Centre Crt., Toronto, ON M1P 4Y7

Toronto - Victoria St.
#300, 74 Victoria St., Toronto, ON M5C 2A5

Toronto - Yonge St.
Joseph Sheppard Building, #380, 4900 Yonge St., Toronto, ON M2N 6A4

Vancouver
Sinclair Centre, #200, 757 Hastings St. West, Vancouver, BC V6C 1A1

Victoria
Bay Centre, 1150 Douglas St., Level 4, Victoria, BC V8W 3M9

Whitby
Whitby Mall, #6, 1615 Dundas St. East, Whitby, ON L1N 2L1
Urgent service is not available at the Whitby location. In-person & express service are available, however. Passports must be picked up at the the Scarborough Passport Canada office.

Windsor
CIBC Building, #503, 100 Ouellette Ave., Windsor, ON N9A 6T3

Winnipeg
#400, 433 Main St., Winnipeg, MB R3B 1B3

Canada Post Receiving Agents
To facilitate access to passport services throughout Canada, Canada Post acts as a passport receiving agent on behalf of Passport Canada.
General passport applications for adults & children & simplified renewal passport applications are collected, along with citizenship documents & application fees. Application packages are sent to Passport Canada to be processed.
A $20 non-refundable convenience fee, plus applicable taxes, is payable to Canada Post for each general adult & child's passport application.

Acton
Acton Stn. Main, 53 Bower St., Acton, ON L7J 1E0
Toll-Free: 800-267-1177

Ancaster
Meadowlands Post Office, 27 Legend Crt., Ancaster, ON L9K 1J0
Toll-Free: 800-267-1177

Belleville
Belleville Stn. Main, 21 College St. West, #D, Belleville, ON K8N 3B0
Toll-Free: 800-267-1177

Boucherville
BP Boucherville, 131, rue Jacques-Ménard, Boucherville, QC J4B 5B0
Toll-Free: 800-267-1177

Bracebridge
Bracebridge Stn. Main, 98 Manitoba St., Bracebridge, ON P1L 1A0
Toll-Free: 800-267-1177

Brantford
Brantford Stn. Main, 58 Dalhousie St., PO Box 1962 Brantford, ON N3T 2J0
Toll-Free: 800-267-1177

Brossard
BP Brossard, 10, de la Place-du-Commerce, Brossard, QC J4W 4T0
Toll-Free: 800-267-1177

Cambridge
Cambridge CSC, 33 Water St. North, Cambridge, ON N1R 3B0
Toll-Free: 800-267-1177

Charlottetown
Charlottetown Stn. Central, 101 Kent St., Charlottetown, PE C1A 1M0
Toll-Free: 800-267-1177

Chatham
Chatham Post Office, 120 Wellington St. West, Chatham, ON N7M 4V0
Toll-Free: 800-267-1177

Guelph
Guelph Stn. Main, 88 Wyndham St. North, Guelph, ON N1H 4E0
Toll-Free: 800-267-1177

Kingston
Kingston Post Office, 120 Clarence St., Kingston, ON K7L 1X0
Toll-Free: 800-267-1177

Lévis
Succ. Lévis, 4870, boul de la Rive sud, Lévis, QC G6V 3P0
Toll-Free: 800-267-1177

Midland
Midland Post Office, 525 Dominion Ave., Midland, ON L4R 1P0
Toll-Free: 800-267-1177

Moncton
Moncton Main Post Office, 281 St. George St., Moncton, NB E1C 1H0
Toll-Free: 800-267-1177

Montréal - Donegani
BP Pointe-Claire, 15 av Donegani, Montréal, QC H9R 2V0
Toll-Free: 800-267-1177

Montréal - Joseph-Renaud
Succ. Anjou, 7200, boul Joseph-Renaud, Montréal, QC H1K 3X0
Toll-Free: 800-267-1177

Newmarket
Newmarket Stn. Main, 190 Mulock Dr., Newmarket, ON L3Y 3N0
Toll-Free: 800-267-1177

North Bay
North Bay Main Post Office, 101 Worthington St. East, North Bay, ON P1B 1H0
Toll-Free: 800-267-1177

Oakville
146 Lakeshore West, Oakville, ON L6K 1E0
Toll-Free: 800-267-1177

Orillia
Orillia Stn. Main, 25 Peter St. North, Orillia, ON L3V 4Y0
Toll-Free: 800-267-1177

Ottawa - Riverside Dr.
Canada Post Place Post Office, 2701 Riverside Dr., Ottawa, ON K1A 0B1
Toll-Free: 800-267-1177

Ottawa - Sandford Fleming Ave.
Ottawa Post Office, 1424 Sanford Fleming Ave., Ottawa, ON K1A 0C1
Toll-Free: 800-267-1177

Owen Sound
Owen Sound Stn. Main, 901 - 3rd Ave. East, Owen Sound, ON N4K 2K0
Toll-Free: 800-267-1177

Peterborough
Peterborough Post Office, 150 King St., Peterborough, ON K9J 2R0
Toll-Free: 800-267-1177

Pickering
Pickering Main Post Office, 1740 Kingston Rd., Pickering, ON L1V 1C0
Toll-Free: 800-267-1177

Prince George
Prince George Stn. A, 1323 - 5th Ave., Prince George, BC V2L 3L0
Toll-Free: 800-267-1177

Québec - Bouvier
Succ. Québec Centre, #145, 710, rue Bouvier, Québec, QC G2J 1C0
Toll-Free: 800-267-1177

Québec - Chaudière
Succ. Cap-Rouge, #122, 1100, boul de la Chaudière, Québec, QC G1Y 1C0
Toll-Free: 800-267-1177

Québec - Fort
BP Québec Haute-Ville, 5, rue du Fort, Québec, QC G1R 2J0
Toll-Free: 800-267-1177

Rimouski
Rimouski Succ. A, 136, rue St-Germain ouest, Rimouski, QC G5L 4B0
Toll-Free: 800-267-1177

Saint Bruno
Saint-Bruno Succ. Bureau-Chef, 50, rue de la Rabastalière ouest, Saint-Bruno, QC J3V 1Y0
Toll-Free: 800-267-1177

Saint John
Saint John Area Stn. Main, 125 Rothesay Ave., Saint John, NB E2L 2B0
Toll-Free: 800-267-1177

Sarnia
Sarnia Stn. Main, 105 Christina St. South, Sarnia, ON N7T 2M0
Toll-Free: 800-267-1177

Sault Ste Marie
Sault Ste Marie Main Post Office, 451 Queen St. East, Sault Ste Marie, ON P6A 1Z0
Toll-Free: 800-267-1177

Stratford
Stratford Stn. Main, 75 Waterloo St. South, Stratford, ON N5A 4A0
Toll-Free: 800-267-1177

Sudbury - Lasalle Blvd.
Sudbury Stn. A, 1776 Lasalle Blvd., Sudbury, ON P3A 2A0
Toll-Free: 800-267-1177

Sudbury - Lisgar St.
Sudbury Stn. B, 1 Lisgar St., Sudbury, ON P3E 3L0
Toll-Free: 800-267-1177

Summerside
Summerside Main Post Office, 454 Granville St., Summerside, PE C1N 3K0
Toll-Free: 800-267-1177

Sydney
Sydney Stn. A, 269 Charlotte St., Sydney, NS B1P 1T0
Toll-Free: 800-267-1177

Toronto
Toronto Stn. K, 2384 Yonge St., Toronto, ON M4P 2E0
Toll-Free: 800-267-1177

Trois-Rivières
BP Trois-Rivières, 1285, rue Notre-Dame, Trois-Rivières, QC G9A 4X0
Toll-Free: 800-267-1177

Uxbridge
Uxbridge Stn. Main, 67 Brock St. West, Uxbridge, ON L9P 1A0
Toll-Free: 800-267-1177

Woodstock
Woodstock Stn. Main, 433 Norwich Ave., Woodstock, ON N4S 3W0
Toll-Free: 800-267-1177

Yarmouth
Yarmouth Main Post Office, 15 Willow St., Yarmouth, NS B5A 1T0
Toll-Free: 800-267-1177

Service Canada Receiving Agents

As a receiving agent, a Service Canada Centre accepts general passport applications for both adults & children, as well as simplified renewal passport applications. Application packages are then sent to Passport Canada for processing. When Passport Canada has approved & issued passports, they are delivered to the mailing addresses on the applications. The service provided by Service Canada is free of charge.

Abbotsford
#100, 32525 Simon Ave., Abbotsford, BC V2T 6T6

Ajax
#200, 274 Mackenzie Ave., Ajax, ON L1S 2E9

Amherst
#202, 26-28 Prince Arthur St., Amherst, NS B4H 1V6

Asbestos
#204, 309, rue Chassé, Asbestos, QC J1T 2B4

Baie Comeau
Centre d'achats Laflèche, #204, 625, boul Laflèche ouest, Baie-Comeau, QC G5C 1C4

Barrie
48 Owen St., 1st Fl., Barrie, ON L4M 3H1

Bedford
Royal Bank Building, 1597 Bedford Hwy., 2nd Fl., Bedford, NS B4A 1E7

Bracebridge
Federal Building, 98 Manitoba St., 2nd Fl., Bracebridge, ON P1L 2B5

Brandon
Government of Canada Building, #100, 1039 Princess Ave., Brandon, MB R7A 4J5

Bridgewater
Dawson B. Dauphinee Building, 77 Dufferin St., Bridgewater, NS B4V 9A2

Brockville
The Fuller Building, 14 Court House Ave., 1st Fl., Brockville, ON K6V 4T1

Brooks
Cassils Shopping Plaza, 608 - 2 St. West, Brooks, AB T1R 1A8

Brossard
2501, boul Lapiniere, 1e étage, Brossard, QC J4Z 3P1

Burnaby
#100, 3480 Gilmore Way, Burnaby, BC V5G 4Y1

Calgary - Crowchild Trail NW
Calgary North Service Canada Centre, One Executive Place, 1816 Crowchild Trail NW, Main Fl., Calgary, AB T2M 3Y7

Calgary - Fisher St. SE
Calgary South Service Canada Centre, Fisher Park Place II, #100, 6712 Fisher St. SE, Calgary, AB T2H 2A7

Calgary - Marlborough Way NE
Calgary East Service Canada Centre, Marlborough Mall, #1502, 515 Marlborough Way NE, Calgary, AB T2A 7E7

Campbellton
Campbellton City Center Mall, #111, 157 Water St., Campbellton, NB E3N 3L4

Cambridge Bay
16 Mitik St., 1st Fl., PO Box 2010 Cambridge Bay, NU X0B 0C0

Canmore
Building C, Canmore Gateway Shops, #113, 802 Bow Valley Trail, Canmore, AB T1W 1N6

Charlottetown
Jean Canfield Government of Canada Building, 191 University Ave., 1st Fl., Charlottetown, PE C1A 4L2

Chibougamau
623, 3e rue, Chibougamau, QC G8P 3A2

Chilliwack
#100, 9345 Main St., Chilliwack, BC V2P 4M3

Coaticook
289, rue Baldwin, Coaticook, QC J1A 2A2
Collingwood
44 Hurontario St., Collingwood, ON L9Y 2L6
Coquitlam
#100, 2963 Glen Dr., Coquitlam, BC V3B 2P7
Corner Brook
Joseph R. Smallwood Building, 1 Regent Sq., Corner Brook, NL A2H 7K6
Cornwall
#100, 111 Water St. East, Cornwall, ON K6H 6S2
Courtenay
Comox Valley Service Canada Centre, 130 - 19th St., Courtenay, BC V9N 8S1
Cowansville
224, rue du Sud, 2e étage, Cowansville, QC J2K 2X4
Cranbrook
1113 Baker St., Cranbrook, BC V1C 1A7
Drummondville
Édifice Surprenant, 1525, boul Saint-Joseph, Drummondville, QC J2C 2E9
East Gwillimbury
Newmarket Service Canada Centre, #1, 18183 Yonge St., East Gwillimbury, ON L9N 0H9
Edmonton - 87th Ave. NW
Edmonton Meadowlark Service Canada, Meadowlark Shopping Ctr, #120, 15710 - 87th Ave. NW, Edmonton, AB T5R 5W9
Edmonton - 50th St. NW
Hermitage Square, 12735 - 50th St. NW, Edmonton, AB T5A 4L8
Edmonton - Millbourne Market Mall
Edmonton Millbourne Service Canada Centre, #148, Millbourne Market Mall, Edmonton, AB T6K 3L6
Edmundston
Federal Building, 22 Emmerson St., Edmundston, NB E3V 1R8
Edson
4905 - 4th Ave., Edson, AB T7E 1C6
Elliot Lake
White Mountain Academy Of The Arts, #2, 99 Spine Rd., Elliot Lake, ON P5A 3S9
Espanola
#2, 721 Centre St., Espanola, ON P5E 1T3
Estevan
#10, 419 Kensington Ave., Estevan, SK S4A 2A1
Flin Flon
Government of Canada Building, 111 Main St., Flin Flon, MB R8A 1J9
Fort Frances
301 Scott St., Fort Frances, ON P9A 1H1
Fort McMurray
#107, 8530 Manning Ave., Main Fl., Fort McMurray, AB T9H 5G2
Fort Simpson
Federal Building, 9606 - 100th St., Fort Simpson, NT X0E 0N0
Fort Smith
Federal Building, 136 McDougal Rd., Fort Smith, NT X0E 0P0
Gander
McCurdy Complex, 1 Markham Pl., 3rd Fl., Gander, NL A1V 0A8
Gaspé
Édifice Frederica-Giroux, 98, rue de la Reine, 1e étage, Gaspé, QC G4X 2V4
Georgetown
232 Guelph St., 1st Fl., Georgetown, ON L7G 4B1
Glace Bay
Senator's Place, #101, 633 Main St., Glace Bay, NS B1A 6J3
Grand Falls / Grand-Sault
#100, 441 Madawaska Rd., Grand Falls, NB E3Y 1C6
Grande Prairie
Towne Centre Mall, #100, 9845 - 99th Ave., Grande Prairie, AB T8V 0R3
Happy Valley-Goose Bay
23 Broomfield St., Happy Valley-Goose Bay, NL A0P 1E0
Hawkesbury
521 Main St. East, Hawkesbury, ON K6A 1B3
Hay River
Federal Building, #204, 41 Capital Dr., Hay River, NT X0E 1G2
Inuvik
85 Kingmingya Rd., Inuvik, NT X0E 0T0
Iqaluit
#306, 933 Mivvik St., Iqaluit, NU X0A 0H0
Kamloops
520 Seymour St., 1st Fl., Kamloops, BC V2C 2G9
Kapuskasing
8 Queen St., Kapuskasing, ON P5N 1G7
Kelowna
#106, 471 Queensway, Kelowna, BC V1Y 6S5
Kenora
Kenora Market Square, #201, 308 - 2nd St., Kenora, ON P9N 1G4
Kentville
Federal Building, 495 Main St., 2nd Fl., Kentville, NS B4N 3W5
La Tuque
Carrefour La Tuque Inc., #14, 290, rue St-Joseph, La Tuque, QC G9X 3Z8
Labrador City
Labrador Mall, 500 Vanier Ave., Labrador City, NL A2V 2W7
Langley
#202, 8747 - 204th St., Langley, BC V1M 2Y5
Lethbridge
Crowsnest Trail Plaza, #101, 920 - 2A Ave. North, Lethbridge, AB T1H 0E3
Lévis
Place Lévis, #175, 50, rte du Président-Kennedy, Lévis, QC G6V 6W8
Lloydminster
4114 - 70th Ave., Lloydminster, AB T9V 2X3
Longueuil
#100, 1195, ch du Tremblay, Longueuil, QC J4N 1R4
Magog
#100A, 1700, rue Sherbrooke, Magog, QC J1X 5B4
Maple Ridge
Ridge Meadows Service Canada Centre, 22325 Lougheed Hwy., Maple Ridge, BC V2X 2T3
Marystown
Jerrett Building, #130, 140 Ville-Marie Dr., Marystown, NL A0E 2M0
Medicine Hat
Northside Centre, 78 - 8th St. NW, Medicine Hat, AB T1A 6P1
Melfort
McKendry Plaza, 104 McKendry Ave. West, Melfort, SK S0E 1A0
Miramichi
139 Douglastown Blvd., Miramichi, NB E1V 0A4
Moncton
Heritage Court, #110, 95 Foundry St., Moncton, NB E1C 5H7
Montague
491 Main St., Montague, PE C0A 1R0
Montréal - Newman
Lasalle (Montréal) Service Canada Centre, 7655, boul Newman, Montréal, QC H8N 1X7
Montréal - Wellington
Verdun Service Canada Centre, 4110, rue Wellington St., 2e étage, Montréal, QC H4G 1V7
Moose Jaw
Victoria Place, #501, 111 Fairford St. East, Moose Jaw, SK S6H 7X5
Morden
Government of Canada Building, 158 Stephen St., Morden, MB R6M 1T3
Nanaimo
#201, 60 Front St., Nanaimo, BC V9R 5H7
Nelson
Chahko Mika Mall, 1125 Lakeside Dr., Main Fl., Nelson, BC V1L 5Z3
New Glasgow
340 East River Rd., New Glasgow, NS B2H 3P7
New Liskeard
280 Armstrong St. North, New Liskeard, ON P0J 1P0
New Westminster
#201, 620 Royal Ave., New Westminster, BC V3M 1J2
North Battleford
1401 - 101st St., North Battleford, SK S9A 1A1
North Bay
Canada Place, #102, 107 Shirreff Ave., North Bay, ON P1B 7K8
North Vancouver
North Shore Service Canada Centre, #100, 221 West Esplanade, North Vancouver, BC V7M 3N7
Notre Dame de Lourdes
51 Rodgers St., Notre Dame de Lourdes, MB R0G 1M0
O'Leary
371 Main St., O'Leary, PE C0B 1V0
Oakville
#5B, 117 Cross Ave., Oakville, ON L6J 2W7
Orangeville
#102, 210 Broadway Ave., Orangeville, ON L9W 5G4
Oshawa
Midtown Mall, #6C, 200 John St. West, Oshawa, ON L1J 2B4
Ottawa - Carling Ave.
Ottawa West Service Canada Centre, Lincoln Fields Galleria, 2525 Carling Ave., 1st Fl., Ottawa, ON K2B 7Z2
Ottawa - Ogilvie Rd.
Ottawa East Service Canada Centre, Beacon Hill Shopping Ctr, 2339 Ogilvie Rd., Ottawa, ON K1J 8M6
Owen Sound
Heritage Place Shopping Centre, 1350 - 16th St. East, Owen Sound, ON N4K 6N7
Parry Sound
74 James St., 2nd Fl., Parry Sound, ON P2A 1T8
Pembroke
141 Lake St., Pembroke, ON K8A 5L8
Penticton
#101, 386 Ellis St., Penticton, BC V2A 8C9
Peterborough
219 George St. North, Peterborough, ON K9J 3G7
Placentia
Dalfens Mall, 61 Blockhouse Rd., Placentia, NL A0B 2Y0
Powell River
7061 Duncan St., #A, Powell River, BC V8A 1W1
Prince Albert
South Hill Mall, 2995 - 2nd Ave. West, Prince Albert, SK S6V 5V5
Prince George
1363 - 4th Ave., Prince George, BC V2L 3J6
Rankin Inlet
#164, 1 Mivvik Ave., PO Box 97 Rankin Inlet, NU X0C 0G0
Red Deer
#101, 4901 - 46th St., Red Deer, AB T4N 1N2
Regina
Alvin Hamilton Building, 1783 Hamilton St., Regina, SK S4P 2B6
Repentigny
#200, 667, rue Notre-Dame, Repentigny, QC J6A 2W5
Richmond Hill
35 Beresford Dr., Richmond Hill, ON L4B 4M3
Rouyn-Noranda
Édifice Réal Caouette, #300, 151, av du Lac, Rouyn-Noranda, QC J9X 6C3
St. Anthony
Viking Mall, 1 Goose Cove Rd., St. Anthony, NL A0K 4S0
Saint-Hyacinthe
Galeries St-Hyacinthe Shopping Mall, #2550, 3225, av Cusson, 2e étage, Saint-Hyacinthe, QC J2S 0H7
Saint John
1 Agar Pl., 1st Fl., Saint John, NB E2L 5G4
Saint-Quentin
193 Canada St., Saint-Quentin, NB E8A 1J8
St Stephen
Canada Post Building, 93 Milltown Blvd., St Stephen, NB E3L 1G5
Salaberry-de-Valleyfield
Valleyfield Service Canada Centre, #100, 73, rue Maden, Salaberry-de-Valleyfield, QC J6S 3V4
Salmon Arm
191 Shuswap St. NW, 1st Fl., Salmon Arm, BC V1E 4P6
Sault Ste. Marie
22 Bay St., 1st Fl., Sault Ste. Marie, ON P6A 5S2

Sept-îles
701, boul Laure, 3e étage, Sept-îles, QC G4R 1X8
Shediac
Centre-Ville Mall, 342 Main St., Shediac, NB E4P 2E7
Sherbrooke
124, rue Wellington nord, Sherbrooke, QC J1H 5X8
Souris
IGA Mall, 173 Main St., 2nd Fl., Souris, PE C0A 2B0
Steinbach
Steinbach Place, 321 Main St., Main Fl., Steinbach, MB R5G 1Z2
Summerside
Government of Canada Building, 294 Church St., Summerside, PE C1N 0C1
Terrace
4630 Lazelle Ave., Terrace, BC V8G 1S6
The Pas
Uptown Mall, 333 Edwards Ave., The Pas, MB R9A 1K7
Thetford Mines
#500, 350, boul Frontenac ouest, Thetford Mines, QC G6G 6N7
Thompson
40-B Moak Cres., Thompson, MB R8N 2B7
Timmins
120 Cedar St. South, 1st Fl., Timmins, ON P4N 2G8
Toronto - College St.
#100, 559 College St., Toronto, ON M6G 1A9
Toronto - Lawrence Ave. West
Lawrence Square, #103-105, 700 Lawrence Ave. West, Toronto, ON M6A 3B3
Toronto - St. Clair Ave. East
Toronto Centre Service Canada Ctr., Arthur Meighen Building, 25 St. Clair Ave. East, 1st Fl., Toronto, ON M4T 3A4
Trois-Rivières
#100, 1660, rue Royale, Trois-Rivières, QC G9A 4K3
Val d'Or
400, av Centrale, Val-d'Or, QC J9P 1P3
Vancouver
1263 West Broadway, Vancouver, BC V6H 1G7
Victoria
Victoria West Shore Service Canada Centre, 3179 Jacklin Rd., Victoria, BC V9B 3Y7
Weyburn
City Centre Mall, 110 Souris Ave., Main Fl., Weyburn, SK S4H 2Z8
Whitehorse
Elijah Smith Building, #125, 300 Main St., Whitehorse, YT Y1A 2B5
Woodstock
Canada Post Building, 680 Main St., Woodstock, NB E7M 5Z9
Yellowknife
Greenstone Building, 5101 - 50th Ave., Main Fl., Yellowknife, NT X1A 3Z4
Yorkton
Imperial Plaza, 214 Smith St. East, Yorkton, SK S3N 3S6

Indigenous & Northern Affairs / Affaires autochtones et du Nord

Terrasses de la Chaudière, 10 Wellington St., North Tower, Gatineau, QC K1A 0H4
Fax: 866-817-3977
Toll-Free: 800-567-9604
TTY: 866-553-0554
infopubs@aadnc-aandc.gc.ca
www.aadnc-aandc.gc.ca
twitter.com/AANDCanada
www.facebook.com/AANDCanada
www.youtube.com/AANDCanada; www.flickr.com/aandcanada

The Department of Indigenous & Northern Affairs (formerly Aboriginal Affairs & Northern Development Canada, renamed in Nov. 2015 by Prime Minister Trudeau) supports First Nations, Inuit & Métis people in their effort to develop healthy, sustainable communities & achieve their economic & social aspirations. This mandate is derived largely from the Department of Indian & Northern Development Act, the Indian Act, territorial acts & legal obligations arising from section 91(24) of the Constitution Act, 1867. The department administers over 50 statutes. On March 25, 2014, the Northwest Territories Devolution Act gained royal assent, transferring power over land & resources to the government of the Northwest Territories as of April 1, 2014.

Minister, Indigenous & Northern Affairs, Hon. Dr. Carolyn Bennett, P.C., M.D.
Tel: 613-995-9666; *Fax:* 613-947-4622
carolyn.bennett@parl.gc.ca
Deputy Minister, Hélène Laurendeau
Tel: 819-997-0133; *Fax:* 819-953-2251
Parliamentary Secretary, Yvonne Jones
Tel: 613-996-4630; *Fax:* 613-996-7132
yvonne.jones@parl.gc.ca
Acting Director General, Communications, Shirley Anne Off
Tel: 819-997-9595; *Fax:* 819-934-3555
Director General, Human Resources & Workplace Services, Maryse Pesant
Tel: 819-997-9646; *Fax:* 819-953-1311
Executive Director, Indian Residential School Adjudication Secretariat, Shelley Trevethan
Tel: 819-934-0318; *Fax:* 819-934-0802

Associated Agencies, Boards & Commissions:

•Beverly & Qamanirjuaq Caribou Management Board
Secretariat
PO Box 629
Stonewall, MB R0C 2Z0
Tel: 204-467-2438
caribounews@arctic-caribou.com
www.arctic-caribou.com
Group of hunters, biologists & wildlife managers working together to conserve Canada's vast Beverly & Qamanirjuaq caribou herds for the welfare of traditional caribou-using communities in northern Manitoba, Saskatchewan, Northwest Territories & Nunavut.

•First Nations Tax Commission (FNTC) / Commission de la fiscalité des premières nations (CFPN)
#321, 345 Chief Alex Thomas Way
Kamloops, BC V2H 1H1
Tel: 250-828-9857; *Fax:* 250-828-9858
Toll-free: 855-682-3682
mailkamloops@fntc.ca
www.fntc.ca
Other Communication: National Capital Region Email: mail@fntc.ca
The FNTC operates in the larger context of First Nation issues which goes beyond property tax. The FNTC is concerned with reducing the barriers to economic development on First Nation lands, increasing investor certainty, and enabling First Nations to be part of their regional economies. The FNTC is working to fill the institutional vacuum that has prevented First Nations from participating in the market economy and creating a national regulatory framework for First Nation tax systems that meets or beats the standards of provinces.

•Indian Oil & Gas Canada (IOGC) / Pétrole et gaz des Indiens du Canada
#100, 9911 Chiila Blvd.
Tsuu T'ina (Sarcee), AB T2W 6H6
Tel: 403-292-5625; *Fax:* 403-292-5618
ContactIOGC@inac-ainc.gc.ca
www.pgic-iogc.gc.ca
Indian Oil & Gas Canada (IOGC) is an organization committed to managing and regulating oil and gas resources on First Nation reserve lands. It is a special operating agency within Indigenous & Northern Affairs.

•Mackenzie Valley Environmental Impact Review Board
200 Scotia Centre
#5102, 50th Ave.
PO Box 938
Yellowknife, NT X1A 2N7
Tel: 867-766-7050; *Fax:* 867-766-7074
Toll-free: 866-912-3472
www.reviewboard.ca
In 1998, the Mackenzie Valley Environmental Impact Review Board was established under the Mackenzie Valley Resources Management Act. The co-management Review Board is made up of members nominated by First Nations & federal & territorial governments. Board members represent the interests of all residents of the Mackenzie Valley.

•Nunavut Impact Review Board
29 Mitik St.
PO Box 1360
Cambridge Bay, NU X0B 0C0
Tel: 867-983-4600; *Fax:* 867-983-2594
Toll-free: 866-233-3033
info@nirb.ca
www.nirb.ca
An institution of the government established under the Nunavut Land Claims Agreement to conduct environmental & socio-economic assessments. The NIRB process involves participation by members of the community, Inuit organizations, the Government of Nunavut & the Government of Canada through the entire environmental assessment. Under the Canadian Environmental Assessment Act, the federal departments with specific responsibilities for the project must ensure that the requirements of the Act are met throughout the assessment process. This open process facilitates sound environmental stewardship & promotes economic & sustainable development.

•Nunavut Planning Commission
PO Box 2101
Cambridge Bay, NU X0B 0C0
Tel: 867-983-4625; *Fax:* 867-983-4626
www.nunavut.ca
Responsible for land use planning & environmental reporting & management in Nunavut.

•Nunavut Water Board
PO Box 119
Gjoa Haven, NU X0B 1J0
Tel: 867-360-6338; *Fax:* 867-360-6369
www.nunavutwaterboard.org
Responsible for the regulation, use & management of water in the Nunavut Settlement Area.

•Polar Knowledge Canada (POLAR) / Savoir polaire Canada (POLAIRE)
See Entry Name Index for detailed listing.

•Porcupine Caribou Management Board
PO Box 31723
Whitehorse, YT Y1A 6L3
Tel: 867-633-4780; *Fax:* 867-393-3904
pcmb@taiga.net
taiga.net/pcmb
Works to manage the Porcupine Caribou herd, one of the largest herds of migratory caribou in North America, & to protect & maintain its habitat.

•Truth & Reconciliation Commission of Canada
c/o National Centre for Truth & Reconciliation
Chancellor's Hall, 177 Dysart Rd.
Winnipeg, MB R3T 2N2
Tel: 204-474-6069
Toll-free: 855-415-4534
NCTR@umanitoba.ca
nctr.ca
The Commission was established as part of the Indian Residential Schools Settlement Agreement, to learn the truth about what happened in Canada's residential schools & report those findings to the Canadian public.
As of December 18, 2015, the Commission completed its mandate, & its work transferred to the National Centre for Truth & Reconciliation at the University of Manitoba.

Chief Financial Officer Sector / Secteur du dirigeant principal des finances

Tel: 819-953-1201; *Fax:* 819-953-4094
Chief Financial Officer, Paul Thoppil
Tel: 819-956-8188; *Fax:* 819-956-8193
Chief Information Officer, Information Management Branch, Tim Eryou
Tel: 819-994-3334; *Fax:* 819-956-8739
Senior Director, Corporate Information Management Directorate, Monica Fuijkschot
Tel: 819-953-7062; *Fax:* 819-953-3265
Director, Enterprise IM/IT Strategic Services, Philippe Jourdeuil
Tel: 819-934-0408; *Fax:* 819-956-8739

Education & Social Development Programs & Partnerships / Secteur des programmes et des partenariats en matière d'éducation et de développement social

Fax: 819-953-3624
Assistant Deputy Minister, Paula Isaak
Tel: 819-997-0020; *Fax:* 819-953-4094
Director General, Social Policy & Programs Branch, Margaret Buist
Tel: 819-953-0978; *Fax:* 819-934-4094
Director General, Education Branch, Chris Rainer
Tel: 819-934-3971; *Fax:* 819-934-1478

Lands & Economic Development / Terres et Développement économique

Fax: 819-953-0248
Manages land-related statutory duties under the Indian Act & duties related to transferring land management services to First Nations. The Environment Directorate maintains an Inventory of Contaminated Sites on reserve land & coordinates remediation planning; responsible for the design & implementation of the Indian & Inuit Affairs Program Environmental Stewardship Strategy Action Plan; development of First Nations capacity, tools & enabling legislation in order that First Nations undertake their own environmental protection initiatives; supports First Nation, Métis & Inuit communities in efforts to promote environmental stewardship in a manner that is consistent with the principles of sustainable development.
Assistant Deputy Minister, Sheilagh Murphy
Tel: 819-997-0114; *Fax:* 819-934-1983

Director General, Economic Research & Policy Development Branch, Allan Clarke
Tel: 819-953-3004; *Fax:* 819-934-1983
Director General, Economic & Business Opportunities, Vacant
Tel: 819-953-0517; *Fax:* 819-953-0649
Director General, Lands & Environmental Management Branch, Susan Waters
Tel: 819-997-8883; *Fax:* 819-953-3201

Northern Affairs / Affaires du Nord

Fax: 819-953-6121

Supports northern political & economic development through the management of federal interests; promotes sustainable development of the North's natural resources & northern communities. Works toward the devolution of all province-like responsibilities to northern governments Nunavut & the Yukon. Develops & coordinates policies & programs related to northern environment & conservation, like the federal Northern Affairs Program Sustainable Development Strategy, the cleanup of northern hazardous waste sites, climate change & interdepartmental liaison with key policy departments like Environment & Climate Change. Northern Contaminants Program is managed by Indigenous & Northern Affairs in partnership with the federal departments of Health, Environment & Fisheries & Oceans, the territorial governments, Aboriginal organizations & university researchers, & its aim is to work toward reducing & eliminating, where possible, contaminants in traditionally harvested foods. The Northern Information Network is designed to link users to information about the Yukon, the Northwest Territories & Nunavut for more effective decision-making in areas such as resource management & economic development. NIN supports various research initiatives about the North, including project impact assessments, sustainable development strategies, wildlife management planning, land use planning & emergency preparedness. NIN has a directory of geo-referenced databases, provides a forum for discussion & has information & research documents pertaining to the North.

Assistant Deputy Minister, Stephen Van Dine
Tel: 819-953-3760; *Fax:* 819-953-6121
Director General, Natural Resources & Environment Branch, Mark Hopkins
Tel: 819-997-9381; *Fax:* 819-953-8766
Director General, Northern Governance Branch, Nancy Kearnan
Tel: 819-997-0223; *Fax:* 819-953-9323
Executive Director, Northern Contaminated Sites Program Branch, Joanna Ankersmit
Tel: 819-997-7247; *Fax:* 819-934-9229
Senior Director, Environment & Renewable Resources Directorate, Catherine Conrad
Tel: 819-997-2728; *Fax:* 819-953-2590
Director, Circumpolar Affairs Directorate, Sarah Cox
Tel: 819-997-8318; *Fax:* 819-953-0546

Policy & Strategic Direction / Politique et direction stratégique

Fax: 819-953-5082

Senior Assistant Deputy Minister, Françoise Ducros
Tel: 819-994-7555; *Fax:* 819-953-5082
Acting Director General, Litigation Management & Resolution Branch, Michelle Adkins
Tel: 819-953-4968; *Fax:* 819-997-1679
Director General, Planning, Research & Statistics Branch, Gonzague Guéranger
Tel: 819-994-7213; *Fax:* 819-953-6010
Director General, Strategic Policy, Cabinet & Parliamentary Affairs Branch, Nicole Kennedy
Tel: 819-997-8359; *Fax:* 819-953-3320
Director General, Aboriginal & External Relations, Francois Weldon
Tel: 819-934-9361; *Fax:* 819-934-6461
Director General, Strategic Policy, Cabinet & Parliamentary Affairs Branch, Nicole Kennedy
Tel: 819-997-8359; *Fax:* 819-953-3320
Senior Director, Legislative, Parliamentary & Regulatory Affairs Branch, Lynne Newman
Tel: 819-953-6167; *Fax:* 819-953-4250

Regional Operations / Opérations régionales

Fax: 819-953-9406

Senior Assistant Deputy Minister, Lynda Clairmont
Tel: 819-953-5577; *Fax:* 819-953-9406
Director General, Sector Operations Branch, Serge Beaudoin
Tel: 819-934-1828; *Fax:* 819-934-1034
Director General, Community Infrastructure Branch, Daniel Leclair
Tel: 819-953-4636; *Fax:* 819-953-3321

Resolution & Individual Affairs / Résolution et affaires individuelles

Fax: 613-996-2811

Assistant Deputy Minister, Joëlle Montminy
Tel: 819-934-3217; *Fax:* 819-997-9167
Director General, Individual Affairs Branch, Claudia Ferland
Tel: 819-953-6764; *Fax:* 819-953-3371
Acting Director General, Settlement Agreement Operations, Tara Shannon
Tel: 819-934-3216; *Fax:* 613-996-3053
Executive Director, Indian Registration & Integrated Program Management, Nathalie Nepton
Toll-free: 800-567-9604; *Fax:* 819-997-6296

Treaties & Aboriginal Government / Traités et gouvernement autochtone

Fax: 819-953-3246

Senior Assistant Deputy Minister, Joe Wild
Tel: 819-953-3180; *Fax:* 819-953-3246
Director General, Policy Development & Coordination Branch, Perry Billingsley
Tel: 819-953-4315; *Fax:* 819-953-3855
Director General, Negotiations - West, Anita Boscariol
Tel: 604-775-7234; *Fax:* 604-775-7149
Director General, Specific Claims Branch, Stephen Gagnon
Tel: 819-994-2323; *Fax:* 819-994-4123
Director General, Implementation Branch, Allan MacDonald
Tel: 819-994-3434; *Fax:* 819-953-6430
Director General, Negotiations - Central, David Millette
Tel: 819-953-4365; *Fax:* 819-956-7011
Director General, Negotiations - East, Sylvain Ouellet
Tel: 819-994-7521; *Fax:* 819-953-6768
Senior Director, Negotiations - South, Jim Barkwell
Tel: 604-775-7105; *Fax:* 604-775-7149
Senior Director, NWT Directorate, Vacant
Senior Director, Negotiation, Blake McLaughlin
Tel: 819-994-1210; *Fax:* 819-994-1831

Treaty Negotiation Office

Vancouver
#600, 1138 Melville St., Vancouver, BC V6E 4S3
Tel: 604-775-7114; *Fax:* 604-775-7149
Other Communication: Alternate Phone: 604-775-5100

Regional Offices

Alberta
Canada Place, #630, 9700 Jasper Ave., Edmonton, AB T5J 4G2
Tel: 780-495-2773; *Fax:* 780-495-4088
Regional Director General, Jim Sisson
Tel: 780-495-2835

Atlantic
40 Havelock St., PO Box 160 Amherst, NS B4H 3Z3
Tel: 902-661-6200; *Fax:* 902-661-6237
Toll-Free: 800-567-9604
Regional Director General, Christopher McDonell
Tel: 902-661-6262

British Columbia
#600, 1138 Melville St., Vancouver, BC V6E 4S3
Tel: 604-775-5100; *Fax:* 604-775-7149
Toll-Free: 866-553-0554
Other Communication: Alternate Phone: 604-775-5100
Regional Director General, Eric Magnuson
Tel: 604-666-5201; *Fax:* 604-775-7149

Manitoba
#200, 365 Hargrave St., Winnipeg, MB R3B 3A3
Fax: 204-983-2936
Toll-Free: 800-567-9604
Regional Director General, John de Francesco
Tel: 204-983-2474

Northwest Territories
PO Box 1500 Yellowknife, NT X1A 2R3
Tel: 867-669-2500; *Fax:* 867-669-2709
Regional Director General, Mohan Denetto
Tel: 867-669-2501; *Fax:* 867-669-2703

Nunavut
PO Box 2200 Iqaluit, NU X0A 0H0
Tel: 867-975-4500; *Fax:* 867-975-4560
Acting Regional Director General, Stephen Traynor
Tel: 867-975-4501

Ontario
25 St. Clair Ave. East, 8th Fl., Toronto, ON M4T 1M2
Tel: 416-973-6234; *Fax:* 416-954-6329
Regional Director General, Mauricette Howlett
Tel: 416-973-6201; *Fax:* 416-954-4326

Québec
Complexe Jacques-Cartier, #400, 320, rue St-Joseph est, Québec, QC G1K 9J2
Téléc: 418-648-2266
Ligne sans frais: 800-567-9604
Autres nombres: Alternate Toll-Free Phone: 1-800-263-5592
Regional Director General, Luc Dumont
Tel: 418-648-3270

Saskatchewan
1827 Albert St., Regina, SK S4P 2S9
Tel: 306-780-5392; *Fax:* 306-780-7305
Regional Director General, Anna Fontaine
Tel: 306-780-6486

Yukon
#415C, 300 Main St., Whitehorse, YT Y1A 2B5
Tel: 867-667-3888; *Fax:* 867-667-3801
Regional Director General, Dionne Savill
Tel: 867-667-3300

Office of the Information Commissioner of Canada / Commissariat à l'information du Canada

30 Victoria St., Gatineau, QC K1A 1H3

Fax: 819-994-1768
Toll-Free: 800-267-0441
general@oic-ci.gc.ca
www.oic-ci.gc.ca
twitter.com/OIC_CI_Canada
www.facebook.com/OICCANADA

The Office of the Information Commissioner of Canada was established in 1983. It investigates complaints from people & organizations who believe they have been denied rights under the Access of Information Act, Canada's freedom of information legislation.
An independent ombudsperson appointed by Parliament, the Information Commissioner has strong investigative powers. The Information Commissioner mediates between government institutions & dissatisfied applicants, & may refer cases to the Federal Court for resolution.

Information Commissioner, Suzanne Legault
Tel: 819-994-0002; *Fax:* 819-994-1768
Assistant Commissioner, Complaints Resolution & Compliance, Emily McCarthy
Tel: 819-994-0003; *Fax:* 819-994-1768
Director General, Corporate Services Branch, Layla Michaud
Tel: 819-994-0004; *Fax:* 819-994-1768

Infrastructure Canada

#1100, 180 Kent St., Ottawa, ON K1P 0B6

Tel: 613-948-1148
Toll-Free: 877-250-7154
TTY: 800-465-7735
info@infc.gc.ca
www.infrastructure.gc.ca
Other Communication: Media Relations, Phone: 613-960-9251, E-mail: media@infc.gc.ca
twitter.com/INFC_eng

Infrastructure Canada is engaged in the following tasks to ensure modern public infrastructure for the benefit of Canadians: developing policies; establishing partnerships; fostering knowledge; making investments; & delivering programs.
To address local, regional, & national priorities, Infrastructure Canada works with municipalities, provinces & territories, other federal departments & agencies, as well as private companies & the non-profit sector to build & revitalize the infrastructure required by Canadians.

Minister, Infrastructure & Communities, Hon. Amarjeet Sohi, P.C.
Tel: 613-992-1013; *Fax:* 613-992-1026
Amarjeet.Sohi@parl.gc.ca
Deputy Minister, Jean-François Tremblay
Tel: 613-948-2845
jean-francois.tremblay@canada.ca
Parliamentary Secretary, Pablo Rodriguez
Tel: 613-995-0580; *Fax:* 613-992-1710
Pablo.Rodriguez@parl.gc.ca
Associate Deputy Minister, Yazmine Laroche
Tel: 613-948-8157; *Fax:* 613-948-2963
yazmine.laroche@infc.gc.ca

Audit & Evaluation Branch

Independent audits are conducted to ensure proper processes of Infrastructure Canada. Evaluation programs are also carried out to assess the value of the department's programs & initiatives. The work of the Audit & Evaluation Branch supports decision making within Infrastructure Canada.

Chief Audit & Evaluation Executive, Isabelle Trépanier
Tel: 613-954-4879; *Fax:* 613-941-5050
isabelle.trepanier@infc.gc.ca
Director, Audit, Christopher MacDonald
Tel: 613-946-8751; *Fax:* 613-941-5050
christopher.macdonald@infc.gc.ca

Corporate Services Branch

The Corporate Services Branch supports corporate functions & provides information management & technology services. Specific duties include administration, human resources services, procurement, financial services, & maintenance of the Shared Information Management System for Infrastructure.

Assistant Deputy Minister, Darlene Boileau
Tel: 613-948-9161; *Fax:* 613-960-6348
darlene.boileau@infc.gc.ca
Chief Information Officer & Director General, Angus Howieson
Tel: 613-946-0509; *Fax:* 613-948-2963
angus.howieson@infc.gc.ca
Director General, Corporate Services, Finance & Contracting, Cynthia Cantile
Tel: 613-948-4424; *Fax:* 613-960-6348
cynthia.cantlie@infc.gc.ca
Director General, Human Resources, Security, & Administration, Nancy Martel
Tel: 613-948-3773; *Fax:* 613-948-3772
nancy.martel@infc.gc.ca
Director General, Planning, Reporting & Coordination, Jocelyne St. Jean
Tel: 613-948-3996; *Fax:* 613-960-9428
jocelyne.stjean@canada.ca
Director, Operational Support & Web Services, Patrick Boulé
Tel: 613-948-8002; *Fax:* 613-960-9648
pat.boule@canada.ca
Director, Application Services, Sherry Shaaked
Tel: 613-948-9719; *Fax:* 613-941-5050
sherry.shaaked@canada.ca

Policy & Communications Branch

The following responsibilities are handled by the Policy & Communications Branch: identifying infrastructure priorities; conducting research that contributes to policy development; assessing investments; providing correspondence services; & coordinating communications on infrastructure & sharing knowledge.

Assistant Deputy Minister, Jeff Moore
Tel: 613-946-5188; *Fax:* 613-960-9648
jeff.moore@infc.gc.ca
Director General, Policy & Priority Initiatives Directorate, Alain Desruisseaux
Tel: 613-954-7786; *Fax:* 613-960-9648
alain.desruisseaux@canada.ca
Director General, Communications, Peter Wallace
Tel: 613-948-2940; *Fax:* 613-960-9649
peter.wallace@info.gc.ca
Director, Public Affairs, Tim Hillier
Tel: 613-946-0517; *Fax:* 613-960-9649
tim.hillier@canada.ca
Director, Strategic Communications, Vacant
Director, Strategic Policy & Priority Initiatives, Environmental Initiatives, Sonya Read
Tel: 613-948-9160; *Fax:* 613-948-6062
sonya.read@canada.ca
Director, Economic & Community Initiatives, Michael Rutherford
Tel: 613-960-5656; *Fax:* 613-960-6948
michael.rutherford@infc.gc.ca
Director, Policy, Stephanie Tanton
Tel: 613-946-9922; *Fax:* 613-960-6948
stephanie.tanton@infc.gc.ca

Program Operations Branch

The Program Operations Branch is responsible for the following activities: implementing programs; administering funding agreements; managing the federal Gas Tax transfer to Canadian municipalities to support environmentally sustainable infrastructure; & conducting environment assessments & program evaluations.

Assistant Deputy Minister, Marc Fortin
Tel: 613-948-8003; *Fax:* 613-960-9423
marc.fortin@canada.ca
Director General, Program Integration, Laura Di Paolo
Tel: 613-948-9392; *Fax:* 613-960-9428
laura.dipaolo@canada.ca
Director General, Québec / West, Éric Landry
Tel: 613-960-9500; *Fax:* 613-960-9428
eric.landry@canada.ca
Director General, North / Atlantic / Ontario, John Hnatyshyn
Tel: 613-960-6774; *Fax:* 613-960-9423
john.hnatyshyn@canada.ca
Director, West, Québec / West, Maxine Bilodeau
Tel: 613-941-7922; *Fax:* 613-960-9428
maxine.bilodeau@canada.ca
Director, Atlantic, North / Atlantic / Ontario, Johanne Lafleur
Tel: 613-960-6802; *Fax:* 613-960-9423
johanne.lafleur@canada.ca
Director, Québec, Québec / West, Nathalie Lechasseur
Tel: 613-960-6140; *Fax:* 613-948-2965
nathalie.lechasseur@canada.ca
Director, Program Integration, Bogdan Makuc
Tel: 613-960-9247; *Fax:* 613-960-9428
bogdan.makuc@canada.ca
Director, Ontario, North / Atlantic / Ontario, Chad Westmacott
Tel: 613-960-9422; *Fax:* 613-960-9423
chad.westmacott@canada.ca

Innovation, Science & Economic Development Canada / Innovation, des science et du développement économique

C.D. Howe Building, 235 Queen St., Ottawa, ON K1A 0H5
Tel: 613-954-5031; *Fax:* 613-954-2340
Toll-Free: 800-328-6189
TTY: 866-694-8389
info@ic.gc.ca
www.ic.gc.ca
www.linkedin.com/company/industry-canada
www.youtube.com/user/IndustryCanadaGC

The mission of Innovation, Science & Economic Development (formerly Industry Canada, renamed by Prime Minister Trudeau after the 2015 general election) is to help make Canadians more productive & competitive in a global, knowledge-based economy. The department's policies, programs & services assist in the creation of an economy that provides more & better-paying jobs for Canadians; supports stronger business growth through sustained improvements in productivity; & gives consumers, businesses & investors confidence that the marketplace is fair, efficient & competitive. To reach its clients, the department collaborates extensively with partners at all levels of government & the private sector.

Minister, Innovation, Science & Economic Development, Hon. Navdeep Bains, P.C., B.A., M.B.A., C.M.A.
Tel: 613-995-7784; *Fax:* 613-996-9817
Navdeep.Bains@parl.gc.ca
Minister, Small Business & Tourism, Hon. Bardish Chagger, P.C.
Tel: 613-996-5928; *Fax:* 613-992-6251
Bardish.Chagger@parl.gc.ca
Minister, Science, Hon. Kirsty Duncan, P.C., B.A., PhD
Tel: 613-995-4702; *Fax:* 613-995-8359
kirsty.duncan@parl.gc.ca
Deputy Minister, John Knubley
Tel: 343-291-2804; *Fax:* 613-954-3272
Parliamentary Secretary to the Minister of Science, Terry Beech
Tel: 613-992-0802; *Fax:* 613-992-0824
Terry.Beech@parl.gc.ca
Parliamentary Secretary to the Minister of Innovation, Science & Economic Development, Greg Fergus
Tel: 613-992-7550; *Fax:* 613-992-7599
Greg.Fergus@parl.gc.ca
Parliamentary Secretary to the Minister of Small Business & Tourism, Gudie Hutchings
Tel: 613-996-5511; *Fax:* 613-996-9632
Gudie.Hutchings@parl.gc.ca
Associate Deputy Minister, Kelly Gillis
Tel: 343-291-2870; *Fax:* 343-291-2508

Associated Agencies, Boards & Commissions:

•Communications Research Centre Canada (CRC) / Centre de recherches sur les communications
3701 Carling Ave.
PO Box 11490 H
Ottawa, ON K2H 8S2
Tel: 613-991-3313; *Fax:* 613-998-5355
info@crc.gc.ca
www.crc.gc.ca
Dedicated to advanced communications research & development for over 50 years. Key research areas include radio science, terrestrial wireless systems, satellite communications broadcasting & broadband network technologies. CRC has a long history of technology transfer. CRC operates an Innovation Centre, a technology incubator for small & medium-sized high-tech start-ups, which provides increased access to CRC's technologies, research expertise & unique laboratories & facilities.

•Competition Tribunal (CT) / Tribunal de la concurrence (TC)
Thomas D'Arcy McGee Bldg.
#600, 90 Sparks St.
Ottawa, ON K1P 5B4
Tel: 613-957-3172; *Fax:* 613-957-3170
tribunal@ct-tc.gc.ca
www.ct-tc.gc.ca
Hears & decides all applications made under Parts V11.1 & VIII of the Competition Act.

•Destination Canada (DC)
See Entry Name Index for detailed listing.

•Patent Appeal Board (PAB) / Commission d'appel des brevets (CAB)
The Patent Appeal Board reviews rejected applications, chairs re-examination boards, reviews rejections of re-issue applications & provides other functions.

•Science, Technology & Innovation Council (STIC) / Conseil des sciences, de la technologie et de l'innovation (CSTI)
235 Queen St., 9th Fl.
Ottawa, ON K1A 0H5
Tel: 343-291-2362; *Fax:* 613-952-0459
info@stic-csti.ca
www.stic-csti.ca
Provides the Minister of Industry with policy advice on science & technology & measures Canada's science & technology performance against international standards.

•Standards Council of Canada (SCC) / Conseil canadien des normes (CCN)
#200, 270 Albert Street
Ottawa, ON K1P 6N7
Tel: 613-238-3222; *Fax:* 613-569-7808
info@scc.ca
www.scc.ca
The Standards Council of Canada (SCC) works to promote the development & use of national & international standards & reports to Parliament through the Minister of Industry. It consists of 13 members & a staff of 90.

Audit & Evaluation Branch / Direction générale de la vérification et de l'évaluation
Tel: 343-291-2356; *Fax:* 343-291-2485
Chief Audit Executive & Director General, Audit & Evaluation, Brian Gear, CAE
Tel: 343-291-2355; *Fax:* 343-291-2485

Canadian Intellectual Property Office (CIPO) / Office de la propriété intellectuelle du Canada (OPIC)
Place du Portage I, #C-229, 50 Victoria St., Gatineau, QC K1A 0C9
Tel: 819-997-1936; *Fax:* 819-953-2476
Toll-Free: 866-997-1936
TTY: 866-442-2476
cipo.contact@ic.gc.ca
www.cipo.ic.gc.ca
Other Communication: International Calls: 819-934-0544; OPIC Fax: 819-953-6742
twitter.com/CIPO_Canada
www.linkedin.com/company/canadian-intellectual-property-office
Chief Executive Officer; Commissioner of Patents, Registrar of Trade-marks, Johanne Bélisle
Tel: 819-997-1057; *Fax:* 819-997-1890
Assistant Commissioner, Patent Branch, Agnes L. Lajoie
Tel: 819-997-2949; *Fax:* 819-994-1989
Director General, Programs branch, Martin Cloutier
Tel: 819-934-9133; *Fax:* 819-953-5059
Executive Director, Corporate Strategies & Services, Vacant
Senior Director, Information Branch, Louise Baird
Tel: 819-953-3293; *Fax:* 819-953-6004
Senior Director, Information Branch, Michèle Langlois
Tel: 819-635-5731; *Fax:* 819-953-6004
Senior Director, Policy, Planning, International Affairs & Research Office, Konstantinos Georgaras
Tel: 819-994-2757; *Fax:* 819-953-8638

Chief Information Office Sector / Secteur du bureau principal de l'information
Tel: 613-954-3570; *Fax:* 613-941-1938
Chief Information Officer, Rick Rinholm
Tel: 343-291-1444; *Fax:* 613-941-1938
Director General, Strategy & Information Services Branch, Kelly Acton
Tel: 343-291-1573; *Fax:* 343-291-1606
Director General, Enterprise & Corporate Services Branch, Daniel Boulet
Tel: 343-291-1576; *Fax:* 343-291-1607
Director General, Workplace Technology Services Branch, Pierre Gravel
Tel: 343-291-1404
Director General, Business Services Branch, Patti Pomeroy
Tel: 343-291-1292
Acting Director, CIO Business Management Directorate, Julie Correia
Tel: 343-291-1407; *Fax:* 343-291-1604

Communications & Marketing Branch / Direction générale des communications et du marketing
Director, Aparna Kurl
Tel: 343-291-1686; *Fax:* 343-291-2466

Competition Bureau Canada / Bureau de la concurrence Canada
Place du Portage, Phase I, 50 Victoria St., Ottawa, ON K1A 0C9
Tel: 819-997-4282; *Fax:* 819-997-0324
Toll-Free: 800-348-5358
TTY: 800-642-3844
www.competitionbureau.gc.ca
twitter.com/CompBureau
www.facebook.com/competitionbureaucanada
www.youtube.com/user/competitionbureau

The Competition Bureau is the organization responsible for the enforcement of the Competition Act, the Consumer Packaging & Labelling Act except as it relates to food, the Precious Metals Marking Act & the Textile Labelling Act. The Competition Bureau ensures compliance by the business community with legislation administered by the Bureau, & oversees the development of policy & dissemination of information aimed at ensuring optimal compliance levels.

Commissioner of Competition, John Pecman
Tel: 819-997-3304
Executive Director & Senior General Counsel, Legal Services, Jonathan Chaplan
Tel: 819-994-7714

Corporate Management Sector / Secteur de la gestion intégrée
Tel: 613-941-9578; *Fax:* 613-998-6950
Chief Financial Officer, David Enns
Tel: 343-291-2970; *Fax:* 613-998-6950
Director General, Resource Planning & Investments Branch, Michelle Baron
Tel: 343-291-2715; *Fax:* 343-291-3296
Director General, Corporate Finance, Systems & Procurement Branch, Simon Brault
Tel: 343-291-2967; *Fax:* 613-941-0319
Director General, Corporate Planning & Governance, Barbara Gibbon
Tel: 613-960-8800; *Fax:* 613-957-4788
Director General, Human Resources Branch, Caroline Dunn
Tel: 343-291-3251; *Fax:* 613-952-0239
Director General, Corporate Facilities & Security Branch, Garima Dwivedi
Tel: 613-954-5074

Industry Sector / Secteur de l'industrie
Tel: 613-954-3395; *Fax:* 613-941-1134

Industry Sector (IS) assists Canadian industry & businesses compete, expand & create jobs in the knowledge-based economy. IS contributes to Innovation, Science & Economic Development's strategic objectives, trade, investment, innovation, connectedness & marketplace. It facilitates delivery of industrial, related policy analyses & strategies to promote global competitiveness of Canadian industry. IS provides a broad range of services, information resources, sector policies & strategies to support business growth. IS provides Canadian businesses with timely information products, business tools, research, strategic analyses, data & information resources.

Assistant Deputy Minister, Philip Jennings
Tel: 343-291-2116; *Fax:* 613-941-1134

Aerospace, Defence & Marine Branch / Aérospatiale, defense et la marine
Tel: 343-291-2105; *Fax:* 613-998-6703
Director General, Mary Gregory
Tel: 343-291-2128; *Fax:* 613-998-6703
Deputy Director, Space & Marine Directorate, Guillaume Cote
Tel: 613-618-2117; *Fax:* 866-694-8389
Senior Director, Aerospace, André Bernier
Tel: 343-291-2097; *Fax:* 613-952-5822

Automotive & Transportation Industries Branch / Direction générale des industries de l'automobile et des transports
Tel: 613-952-0441; *Fax:* 613-952-8088
Director General, Colette Downie
Tel: 343-291-2114; *Fax:* 613-952-8088

Manufacturing & Life Sciences Branch / Industries de la fabrication et des sciences de la vie
Tel: 613-954-2892; *Fax:* 613-954-3107
Director General, Gerard Peets
Tel: 343-291-2129; *Fax:* 343-291-2480

Investment Review Branch / Direction générale de l'examen des investissements
Tel: 343-291-1887; *Fax:* 343-291-2469
Director General, Patricia Brady
Tel: 343-291-2706; *Fax:* 343-291-2469
Corporate Secretary, Shelley Dooher
Tel: 343-291-2811; *Fax:* 343-291-2506

Science & Innovation Sector / Secteur science et innovation
Tel: 613-995-9605; *Fax:* 613-995-2233
Assistant Deputy Minister, Lawrence Hanson
Tel: 343-291-2366; *Fax:* 613-995-2233
Director General, Policy Branch, Shannon Glenn
Tel: 343-291-2376; *Fax:* 613-996-7887
Director General, Program Coordination Branch, Alison McDermott
Tel: 343-291-2428; *Fax:* 613-996-7887
Executive Director, Science, Technology & Innovation Council Secretariat, Dianne Caldbick
Tel: 343-291-2365; *Fax:* 613-952-0459
Executive Director, Industrial Technologies Office, Lisa Setlakwe
Tel: 343-291-2294; *Fax:* 613-954-5649
Senior Director, Strategic Planning & Management Services, Michel Galipeau
Tel: 343-291-2290; *Fax:* 613-954-5649
Senior Director, S&T Policy Advice Directorate, Marie-Hélène Légaré
Tel: 343-291-2384; *Fax:* 613-996-7887

Small Business, Tourism & Marketplace Services / Services axés sur le marché, le tourisme et la petite entreprise
Tel: 613-995-9605; *Fax:* 613-948-9088
Assistant Deputy Minister, Shereen Benzvy Miller
Tel: 343-291-1800; *Fax:* 613-948-9088
Director General, Services for Business, Christian Laverdure
Tel: 343-291-1809

Corporations Canada
365 Laurier Ave. West, Ottawa, ON K1A 0C8
Tel: 613-941-4550; *Fax:* 613-941-0601
corporationscanada.ic.gc.ca
Director General, Corporations Canada, Virginie Éthier
Tel: 343-291-3420; *Fax:* 343-291-3407

Measurement Canada / Mesures Canada
151 Tunney's Pasture Driveway, Ottawa, ON K1A 0C9
Tel: 613-952-0652; *Fax:* 613-957-1265
mc.ic.gc.ca
President, Alan Johnston
Tel: 613-952-0655; *Fax:* 613-957-1265
Vice-President, Engineering & Laboratory Services, Jean Lafortune
Tel: 613-952-0635; *Fax:* 613-952-1754
Vice-President, Innovative Services Directorate, Sonia Roussy
Tel: 613-952-4285; *Fax:* 613-952-1736
Vice-President, Program Development Directorate, Carl Cotton
Tel: 613-941-8918; *Fax:* 613-952-1736
Director, Ontario Region, John McCarty
Tel: 905-943-8729; *Fax:* 905-943-8738
232 Yorktech Dr.
Markham, ON L6G 1A6
Director, Prairie & Northern Region, John Pheifer
Tel: 204-983-8919; *Fax:* 204-983-5511
232 Yorktech Dr.
Markham, ON L6G 1A6
Director, Eastern Region, Jeffrey Watters
Tel: 514-496-7511; *Fax:* 514-283-7230
232 Yorktech Dr.
Markham, ON L6G 1A6

Office of the Superintendent of Bankruptcy / Bureau du surintendant des faillites
155 Queen St., Ottawa, ON K1A 0H5
Tel: 613-941-1000; *Fax:* 613-941-2862
osb-bsf.ic.gc.ca
Superintendent of Bankruptcy, Bill James
Tel: 613-941-2691; *Fax:* 613-946-9205
Deputy Superintendent, Roula Eatrides
Tel: 613-946-2157; *Fax:* 613-948-6367
Chief of Staff, Program Policy & Regulatory Affairs, Elisabeth Lang
Tel: 819-997-5222; *Fax:* 819-953-5013
Director General, Outreach Services, Harvey Wong
Tel: 613-941-2854; *Fax:* 613-941-2862
Director, Eastern Region, Samra Rabie
Tel: 514-283-3422; *Fax:* 514-283-5130
1155, rue Metcalfe
Montréal, QC H3B 2V6
Director, Central Region, Jack Steinman
Tel: 416-954-6310; *Fax:* 416-973-6964
25 St. Clair Ave. East
Toronto, ON M4T 1M2

Small Business Branch / Direction générale de la petite entreprise
Tel: 343-291-1790; *Fax:* 343-291-2474
Acting Director General, Christopher Johnstone
Tel: 343-291-2637; *Fax:* 343-291-2638

Tourism Branch / Direction générale du tourisme
Tel: 613-948-8009; *Fax:* 613-952-0290
Director General, Ilona Rehberg
Tel: 343-291-1779; *Fax:* 613-960-5770

Spectrum, Information Technologies & Telecommunications / Spectre, technologies de l'information et télécommunications
Journal Tower North, 300 Slater St., 20th Fl., Ottawa, ON K1A 0C8
Tel: 613-998-0368; *Fax:* 613-952-1203
www.ic.gc.ca/eic/site/020.nsf/eng/h_00593.html

Contributes to the Innovation, Science & Economic Development mandate by fostering the early development & use of information & communications technologies, infrastructures & services. The sector uses its policy & regulatory rule-making powers, & marketplace & industry sectoral development services to ensure Canada has a world-class telecommunications & information infrastructure; promote the international competitiveness of Canadian information technologies by all sectors of the Canadian economy; & ensure effective & efficient use of the radio frequency spectrum.

Senior Assistant Deputy Minister, Corinne Charette
Tel: 343-291-3939; *Fax:* 613-952-1203
Assistant Deputy Minister, Éric Dagenais
Tel: 343-291-3940; *Fax:* 343-291-3874
Director General, Information & Communications Technologies Branch, Krista Campbell
Tel: 613-954-5598; *Fax:* 613-957-4076
Acting Director General, Engineering, Planning & Standards Branch, Martin Proulx
Tel: 343-291-1500; *Fax:* 343-291-1906
Director General, Spectrum Licensing Policy Branch, Fiona Gilfillan
Tel: 343-291-1270; *Fax:* 343-291-1269
Director General, Governance, Policy Coordination & Planning, Shirley Anne Scharf
Tel: 343-291-3827
Director General, Connecting Canadians Branch, Susan Hart
Tel: 343-291-3803
Director General, Spectrum Management Operations Branch, Peter Hill
Tel: 343-291-3462; *Fax:* 343-291-3526
Director General, Digital Policy Branch, Krista Campbell
Tel: 613-954-5598; *Fax:* 613-957-4076
Senior Director, Spectrum Management Operations, Lynne Fancy
Tel: 343-291-3488; *Fax:* 343-291-3526
Director, Spectrum - Central and Western Ontario District, Lou Battiston
Tel: 905-639-6508; *Fax:* 905-639-6551
Director, Spectrum - Western Region Spectrum Operations, Morris Bodnar
Tel: 250-470-5040; *Fax:* 250-470-5045

Digital Policy Branch / Direction générale des politiques numériques
Tel: 613-991-1177; *Fax:* 613-957-1201

Formerly known as the Electronic Commerce Branch. Coordinates the development & implementation of a national electronic commerce strategy. It is responsible for both domestic & international aspects of electronic commerce. The Canadian Electronic Commerce Strategy was announced in September 1998. The Strategy, which was developed in collaboration with provincial & territorial governments, industry & consumer groups, among others, establishes a framework, goals, timetable, & implementation plan for electronic commerce domestically. The Strategy involves coordinating strategic elements that fall within the federal government's responsibilities, including the policy development areas of encryption & privacy. The branch develops policies, legislation & regulations that promote business innovation, competition, & growth in the online marketplace.

Director General, Krista Campbell
Tel: 613-954-5598; *Fax:* 613-957-4076

Strategic Policy Sector / Secteur de la politique stratégique
Tel: 613-943-7152; *Fax:* 613-947-2959
Assistant Deputy Minister, Mitch Davies
Tel: 343-291-2643; *Fax:* 343-291-2493
Director General, Telecommunications Policy Branch, Pamela Miller
Tel: 343-291-2634; *Fax:* 613-998-1256
Acting Director General, Office of Consumers Affairs, Anne-Marie Monteith
Tel: 343-291-3057; *Fax:* 343-291-1880
Director General, Economic Research & Policy Analysis Branch, Joy Senack
Tel: 343-291-2614; *Fax:* 343-952-1936
Deputy Director General, Productivity & Competitiveness Analysis, Larry Shute
Tel: 343-291-2617; *Fax:* 613-952-1936
Director General, Strategic Policy Branch, Nipun Vats
Tel: 343-291-2649; *Fax:* 613-952-8761
151 Yonge St.
Toronto, ON M5C 2W7
Executive Director, Strategic Policy Sector - Atlantic Region, Patricia Hearn
Tel: 709-772-4866; *Fax:* 709-772-3306

10 Barters Hill
PO Box 8950
St. John's, NL A1B 3R9
Executive Director, Strategic Policy Sector - Quebec Region, Julie Insley
Tel: 514-283-2058; *Fax:* 514-283-2269
10 Barters Hill
PO Box 8950
St. John's, NL A1B 3R9
Executive Director, Strategic Policy Sector - Pacific Region, Doug Kinsey
Tel: 604-666-1400; *Fax:* 604-666-8330
300 West Georgia St.
Vancouver, BC V6B 6E1
Executive Director, Strategic Policy Sector - Prairie & Northern Region, David Migadel
Tel: 780-495-2951; *Fax:* 780-495-4582
9700 Jasper Ave.
Edmonton, AB T5J 4C3
Director, Strategic Policy Branch, Paul Sandhar-Cruz
Tel: 343-291-3721

FedNor (Federal Economic Development Initiative in Northern Ontario) / FedNor (Initiative fédérale du développement économique dans le Nord de l'Ontario)
C.D. Howe Bldg., 235 Queen St., 8th Fl., Ottawa, ON K1A 0H5
Fax: 613-941-4553
Toll-Free: 877-333-6673
TTY: 866-694-8389
fednor.gc.ca
twitter.com/FedNor

FedNor is the responsibility of the Minister of Innovation, Science & Economic Development.
Director General, Aime Dimatteo
Tel: 705-671-0723; *Fax:* 705-670-6103
Director, Communcations, Linda Menard
Tel: 705-671-0696; *Fax:* 705-670-5331

International Development Research Centre (IDRC) / Centre de recherches pour le développement international (CRDI)

150 Kent St., PO Box 8500 Ottawa, ON K1G 3H9
Tel: 613-236-6163; *Fax:* 613-238-7230
info@idrc.ca
www.idrc.ca
Other Communication: Library Reference Desk: library@idrc.ca; Careers: careers@idrc.ca; Fellowships & Awards: awards@idrc.ca
twitter.com/Idrc_crdi
www.facebook.com/IDRC.CRDI
www.youtube.com/idrccrdi

Helps scientists in developing countries identify long-term, practical solutions to pressing development problems. Support is given directly to scientists working in universities, private enterprise, government & non-profit-making organizations. Priority is given to research aimed at achieving equitable & sustainable development. One of the three program areas of focus is Environmental & Natural Resource Management. Initiatives in this area include a rural poverty & environment program initiative, an urban poverty & environment program, ecosystem approaches to human health, an international model forest network, biodiversity & regional water demand initiative. Reports to Parliament through the Minister of Foreign Affairs.

Chair, Margaret Biggs
President, Jean Lebel
Tel: 613-236-6163 ext: 253; *Fax:* 613-238-7230
jlebel@idrc.ca
Vice-President, Resources Branch & Chief Financial Officer, Sylvain Dufour
Tel: 613-236-6163 ext: 237; *Fax:* 613-236-6074
sdufour@idrc.ca
Acting Vice-President, Program & Partnership Branch, Stephen McGurk
Tel: 613-236-6163 ext: 203; *Fax:* 613-567-7748
smcgurk@idrc.ca
Vice-President, Corporate Strategy & Communications, Joanne Charette
Tel: 613-236-6163 ext: 232; *Fax:* 613-565-8212
jcharette@idrc.ca
Director, Grants Administration Division, Geneviève Leguerrier
Tel: 613-236-6163 ext: 243; *Fax:* 613-238-7230
gleguerrier@idrc.ca
Acting Director, Agriculture & Environment, Dominique Charron
Tel: 613-236-6163 ext: 207; *Fax:* 613-567-7748
dcharron@idrc.ca
Director, Finance & Administration Division, Rana Auditto
Tel: 613-236-6163 ext: 253; *Fax:* 613-238-7230
rauditto@idrc.ca
Director, Human Resources Division, Véronique Duvieusart
Tel: 613-236-6163 ext: 251; *Fax:* 613-236-5594
vduvieusart@idrc.ca
Director, Corporate Communications, Christel Binnie
Tel: 613-236-6163 ext: 205; *Fax:* 613-563-2476
cbinnie@idrc.ca
Director, Information Management & Technology Division, Gilles Dupuis
Tel: 613-236-6163 ext: 260; *Fax:* 613-563-1139
gdupuis@idrc.ca

Regional Offices

Asia
IDRC, 208 Jor Bagh, New Delhi, 110003 India
aro@idrc.ca
www.idrc.ca/aro
Other Communication: Tel: 91-11-2461-9411; Fax: 91-11-2462-2707

Latin America & the Caribbean
Avenida Brasil 2655, Montevideo, 11300 Uruguay
lacro@idrc.ca
www.idrc.ca/lacro
Other Communication: Tel: 598-2-709-0042; Fax: 598-2-708-6776

Middle East & North Africa
8 Ahmed Nessim St., 8th fl., PO Box 14 Giza, Cairo
mero@idrc.ca
www.idrc.ca/mero
Other Communication: Tel: 20-2-336-7051; Fax: 20-2-336-7056

Sub-Saharan Africa
IDRC, Liasion House, 2nd Floor, State House Avenue, Nairobi, 62084 00200 Kenya
rossa@idrc.ca
www.idrc.ca/rossa
Other Communication: Tel: 254-20-2713160; Fax: 254-20-2711063

International Joint Commission (IJC) / Commission mixte internationale (CMI)

234 Laurier Ave. West, 22nd Fl., Ottawa, ON K1P 6K6
Tel: 613-995-2984; *Fax:* 613-993-5583
commission@ottawa.ijc.org
www.ijc.org
twitter.com/IJCsharedwaters
www.facebook.com/internationaljointcommission
www.flickr.com/photos/internationaljointcommission

Established by the Boundary Waters Treaty of 1909 & is responsible for approving (by Order of Approval) certain works in boundary waters which affect levels & flows on both sides of the Canada-US border. The commission provides recommendations on matters along the common boundary which have been referred to the Commission by the governments. Also monitors & assesses the Great Lakes Water Quality Agreement (GLWQA) & is responsible for reviewing & commenting on Remedial Action Plans (RAPs) in coordination with eight US states & the province of Ontario.

Acting Canadian Chair, Gordon Walker
Commissioner, Hon. Benoit Bouchard
Commissioner, Richard Morgan
Director, Sciences & Engineering, Pierre Yves Caux
Tel: 613-992-5727
cauxpy@ottawa.ijc.org

Great Lakes Regional Office / Bureau régional des Grands Lacs
100 Ouellette Ave., 8th fl., Windsor, ON N9A 6T3
Tel: 519-257-6700; *Fax:* 519-257-6740
Director, Great Lakes Regional Office, Trish Morris

United States Section / Section des États-Unis
#615, 2000 L St., NW, Washington, DC 20440 USA
Tel: 202-736-9009; *Fax:* 202-632-2006
commission@washington.ijc.org
Chair & Commissioner, Lana Pollack
Tel: 202-632-2007
Commissioner, Dereth Glance
Commissioner, Rich Moy
Secretary, Charles A. Lawson
Tel: 202-736-9008
lawsonc@washington.ijc.org
Public Information Officer, Frank Bevacqua
Tel: 202-736-9024
bevacquaf@washington.ijc.org

Justice Canada

East Memorial Bldg., 284 Wellington St., Ottawa, ON K1A 0H8
Tel: 613-957-4222; *Fax:* 613-954-0811
TTY: 613-992-4556
webadmin@justice.gc.ca
www.justice.gc.ca
Other Communication: Media Relations Phone: 613-957-4207; Access to Information and Privacy Phone: 613-952-8361
twitter.com/JusticeCanadaEN
www.facebook.com/JusticeCanadaEn
www.youtube.com/user/JusticeCanadaEn

The Department ensures that the Canadian justice system is fair, accessible & efficient. Responsibilities are as follows: provision of policy & program advice & direction by the development of the legal content of bills, regulations, & guidelines; prosecution of federal offences throughout Canada; litigation of civil cases by or on behalf of the federal Crown; & provision of legal advice to federal law enforcement agencies & other government departments.

Minister, Justice & Attorney General of Canada, Hon. Jody Wilson-Raybould, P.C.
Tel: 613-992-1416; *Fax:* 613-992-1460
Jody.Wilson-Raybould@parl.gc.ca
Deputy Minister & Deputy Attorney General, William F. Pentney
Tel: 613-957-4998
Parliamentary Secretary, Bill Blair
Tel: 613-995-0284; *Fax:* 613-996-6309
Bill.Blair@parl.gc.ca
Parliamentary Secretary, Sean Casey, Q.C., B.B.A., LL.B.
Tel: 613-996-4714; *Fax:* 613-995-7685
sean.casey@parl.gc.ca
Associate Deputy Minister, Pierre Legault
Tel: 613-941-4073; *Fax:* 613-941-4074
Director, Political Operations, Lea MacKenzie
Tel: 613-992-4621; *Fax:* 613-990-7255
Chief Audit Executive, Inanc Yazar
Tel: 613-670-6434; *Fax:* 613-948-7411
Federal Ombudsman for Victims of Crime, Sue O'Sullivan
Tel: 613-957-6554; *Fax:* 613-941-3498
www.victimsfirst.gc.ca
Social Media: twitter.com/OFOVC_BOFVAC
Assistant Deputy Minister, Change Management Office, France Pégeot
Tel: 613-952-3816

Aboriginal Affairs Portfolio / Portfeuille des affaires autochtones
Fax: 613-954-4737
Assistant Deputy Minister, Pamela McCurry
Tel: 613-907-3648; *Fax:* 613-954-4737
Acting Deputy Assistant Deputy Minister, Paul Shenher
Tel: 780-495-2978; *Fax:* 780-495-8491
Other Communications: Alt. Phone: 613-907-3672
Senior General Counsel & Senior Advisor to the ADAG, Ronald S. Stevenson
Tel: 613-907-3621; *Fax:* 613-954-4737
Acting Director General & Senior General Counsel, Aboriginal Law Centre, Caroline Clark
Tel: 613-907-3630; *Fax:* 613-954-4737
Acting Chief, Executive & Legal Support Services, Wendy Hickey
Tel: 613-907-3606; *Fax:* 613-957-4737
Senior General Counsel; Head, Legal Services Unit, Indigenous & Northern Development Canada-Legal Services, Alain Lafontaine
Tel: 819-994-4141; *Fax:* 819-953-4225

Business & Regulatory Law Portfolio / Portefeuille du droit des affaires et du droit réglementaire
Fax: 613-946-9988
Acting Assistant Deputy Minister, Lynn Lovett
Tel: 613-957-4944; *Fax:* 613-946-9988
Acting Deputy Assistant Deputy Minister, Francisco Couto
Tel: 613-957-4638
Director General, Employment & Social Development Canada, Caroline Cyr
Tel: 819-654-3872; *Fax:* 819-956-8998
Director General, Employment & Social Development Canada, Zahra Pourjafar-Ziaei
Tel: 819-654-3874; *Fax:* 819-956-8998

Central Agencies Portfolio / Groupes centraux
Fax: 613-995-7223
Assistant Deputy Minister, Sandra Hassan
Tel: 613-369-3305
Deputy Assistant Deputy Minister, Michel Lefrançois
Tel: 613-369-3300
Executive Director & Senior General Counsel, Treasury Board Secretariat - Legal Services, Dora Benbaruk
Tel: 613-952-3379; *Fax:* 613-954-5806

Executive Director & General Counsel, PSC Legal Services, Jean-Daniel Bélanger
Tel: 819-420-6658
Executive Director & General Counsel, Office of the Superintendent of Financial Institutions, Gino Richer
Tel: 613-949-8933; *Fax:* 613-990-0081

Communications Branch
284 Wellington St., Ottawa, ON K1A 0H8
Fax: 613-941-2329
Director General, Tracie Noftle
Tel: 613-957-9596; *Fax:* 613-954-0811
Deputy Director General, Strategic Communications Division, Joe de Mora
Tel: 613-954-6327

Legislative Services Branch / Division des services législatifs
275 Sparks St., Ottawa, ON K1A 0H8
Chief Legislative Counsel, Philippe Hallée
Tel: 613-941-4178; *Fax:* 613-941-1193
Deputy Chief Legislative Counsel (Regulations), Peter Beaman
Tel: 613-957-0077; *Fax:* 613-941-1193
Deputy Chief Legislative Counsel (Legislation), Jean-Charles Bélanger
Tel: 613-957-0031; *Fax:* 613-957-7866

Litigation Branch / Direction du contentieux
50 O'Connor St., Ottawa, ON K1A 0H8
Assistant Deputy Attorney General, Geoffrey M. Bickert
Tel: 613-670-6357; *Fax:* 613-941-1972
Director General & Senior General Counsel, International Assistance Group, Janet Henchey
Tel: 613-948-3003; *Fax:* 613-957-8412
Director General & Senior General Counsel, Civil Litigation Section, Alain Préfontaine
Tel: 613-670-6257; *Fax:* 613-954-1920
Deputy Director General & General Counsel, Civil Litigation Section, Catherine Lawrence
Tel: 613-670-6258; *Fax:* 613-954-1920

Management & CFO Sector / Secteur de la gestion et de la DPF
Fax: 613-952-2178
Assistant Deputy Minister & Chief Financial Officer, Marie-Josée Thivierge
Tel: 613-907-3724; *Fax:* 613-957-6377
Corporate Counsel, Deborah MacNair
Tel: 613-952-1578; *Fax:* 613-946-2216
Chief Information Officer, Marj Akerley
Tel: 613-941-3444
Director General, Human Resources Branch, Michel Brazeau
Tel: 613-941-1867; *Fax:* 613-954-5740
Director General, Business Practice & Intelligence Branch, Vacant
Director General, Corporate Services Branch, Ivan Sicard
Tel: 613-907-3709; *Fax:* 613-941-0220
Director General, Workplace Branch, Bruno Thériault
Tel: 613-941-2818; *Fax:* 613-952-3932
Director General & Deputy Chief Financial Officer, Finance & Planning Branch, Eric Trépanier
Tel: 613-948-5117; *Fax:* 613-946-1389
Acting Senior Director, Business Practices Division, Yves Marion
Tel: 613-957-4959; *Fax:* 613-946-3411

Policy Sector / Secteur des politiques
Fax: 613-957-9949
Senior Assistant Deputy Minister, Donald K. Piragoff
Tel: 613-957-4730; *Fax:* 613-957-9949
Director General & General Counsel, International Legal Programs Section, Deborah Friedman
Tel: 613-946-9283; *Fax:* 613-948-8910
Director General, Programs Branch, Elizabeth Hendy
Tel: 613-957-4344; *Fax:* 613-954-4893
Director General, Policy Integration & Coordination Section, Stan E. Lipinski
Tel: 613-941-2267; *Fax:* 613-957-4019
Director General & General Counsel, Youth Justice & Strategic Initiatives Section, Danièle Ménard
Tel: 613-954-2730; *Fax:* 613-954-3275
Director & General Counsel, Criminal Law Policy Section, Phaedra Glushek
Tel: 613-957-4690; *Fax:* 613-941-9310
Director General & Senior General Counsel, Criminal Law Policy Section, Carole Morency
Tel: 613-941-4044; *Fax:* 613-941-9310
Senior Director, Policy Implementation Directorate, Sean Malone
Tel: 613-941-1085; *Fax:* 613-941-5446
Senior General Counsel, Family, Children & Youth Section, Elissa Lieff
Tel: 613-957-1200; *Fax:* 613-952-5740

Public Law & Legislative Services Sector / Secteur du droit public et des services législatifs
Fax: 613-952-4137
Assistant Deputy Minister, Laurie Wright
Tel: 613-941-7890; *Fax:* 613-957-1403
Director General & Senior General Counsel, Constitutional, Administrative & International Law Section, Edward Livingstone
Tel: 613-941-2317; *Fax:* 613-941-1937
Director General & Senior General Counsel, Human Rights Law Section, Nancy Othmer
Tel: 613-960-3420; *Fax:* 613-952-4137

Public Safety, Defence & Immigration Portfolio / Sécurité Publique, défense & immigration
Assistant Deputy Minister, Elisabeth Eid
Tel: 613-952-4774; *Fax:* 613-952-7370
Executive Director & Senior General Counsel, Immigration, Refugees & Citizenship Canada, Marie Bourry
Tel: 613-437-6745; *Fax:* 613-952-4777
Executive Director & General Counsel, Carole Johnson
Tel: 613-954-1248; *Fax:* 613-957-7840
Executive Director & Senior General Counsel, Canada Border Services Agency, Tom Saunders
Tel: 613-946-2506; *Fax:* 613-946-2570
Executive Director & Senior General Counsel, Office of the Deputy Assistant Deputy Minister, Paul Shuttle
Tel: 613-948-1463; *Fax:* 613-957-7840
Senior General Counsel, National Security Litigation & Advisory Group, Mylène Bouzigon
Tel: 613-842-1197; *Fax:* 613-842-1345
Other Communications: Secure Fax: 613-744-9631
Senior General Counsel, Office of the Assistant Deputy Minister, Michael W. Duffy
Tel: 613-960-0880; *Fax:* 613-957-7840
Other Communications: Secure Fax: 613-948-9808
Senior General Counsel, Royal Canadian Mounted Police, Liliana Longo
Tel: 613-843-4451; *Fax:* 613-825-1241
DND/CF Legal Advisor & Senior General Counsel, National Defence & Canadian Forces, Legal Services, Leigh Taylor
Tel: 613-995-0828; *Fax:* 613-995-0943

Tax Law Services Portfolio / Services du droit fiscal
99 Bank St., Ottawa, ON K1A 0H8
Fax: 613-941-1221
Assistant Deputy Attorney General, Micheline Van-Erum
Tel: 613-670-6416; *Fax:* 613-941-1221
Associate Assistant Deputy Attorney General, Anick Pelletier
Tel: 613-670-6409; *Fax:* 613-941-1221
Senior General Counsel, Tax Law Services, Gordon Bourgard
Tel: 613-670-6439; *Fax:* 613-941-2293
Senior General Counsel, Canada Revenue Agency, Richard Gobeil
Tel: 613-957-2358; *Fax:* 613-957-2371

Laurentian Pilotage Authority (LPA) / Administration de pilotage des Laurentides (APL)

Head Office, #1401, 999, boul Maisonneuve ouest, Montréal, QC H3A 3L4
Tél: 514-283-6320; *Téléc:* 514-496-2409
administration@apl.gc.ca
www.pilotagestlaurent.gc.ca
Autres nombres: Dispatch Center, Toll-Free Phone: 800-361-0747; E-mail: pilote-mtl@apl.gc.ca; Billing Department, Phone: 514-283-6320; E-mail: facturation-billing@apl.gc.ca

In 1972, the Laurentian Pilotage Authority was created under the Pilotage Act.
The Crown corporation has the following objectives: to operate a pilotage service in Canadian waters in & around the province of Québec, except the waters of Cap d'Espoir & Chaleur Bay; to maintain a service in the interest of navigational safety; & to charge pilotage tariffs in order to finance operations.

Chief Executive Officer, Fulvio Fracassi
Tel: 514-283-6320 ext: 204
Director, Administrative Services, Claude Lambert
Tel: 514-283-6320 ext: 212
Director, Dispatch Services, Steve Lapointe
Tel: 514-283-6320 ext: 300
Senior Director, Operations, Sylvia Masson
Tel: 514-283-6320
Advisor, Human Resources, Isabelle Roy
Tel: 514-283-6320 ext: 213
Secretary; Legal Advisor, Mario St-Pierre
Tel: 514-283-6320 ext: 209

Library & Archives Canada (LAC) / Bibliothèque et archives Canada

395 Wellington St., Ottawa, ON K1A 0N4
Tel: 613-996-5115; *Fax:* 613-995-6274
Toll-Free: 866-578-7777
TTY: 866-299-1699
www.bac-lac.gc.ca
Other Communication: Media Relations, Phone: 613-293-4298; Interlibrary Loans: 819-996-7527; Theses Canada: 819-994-6882; Copyright Bureau: 613-992-2567
twitter.com/@LibraryArchives
www.facebook.com/LibraryArchives
www.youtube.com/user/LibraryArchiveCanada

The mission of Library & Archives Canada is to collect & preserve the documentary heritage of Canada. Library & Archives Canada ensures that publications, archival records, photographs, sound & audio-visual materials, & electronic documents are accessible to all Canadians. The organization also works to facilitate cooperation among communities involved in the acquisition, preservation, & diffusion of knowledge. Library & Archives Canada provides services the the public, government, plus libraries, archives, & publishers.

Librarian & Archivist of Canada, Guy Berthiaume
Tel: 819-934-5800; *Fax:* 819-934-5888
guy.berthiaume@canada.ca
Chief of Staff, Sébastien Goupil
Tel: 819-934-5799; *Fax:* 819-934-5888
sebastien.goupil@canada.ca
Director General, Communications, Renee Harden
Tel: 819-994-6766; *Fax:* 819-934-5839
renee.harden@canada.ca
Executive Director, Friends of Library & Archives Canada, Georgia Ellis
Tel: 613-943-1544; *Fax:* 613-943-2343
georgia.ellis@canada.ca

Corporate Services / Services Corporatifs
Assistant Deputy Minister & Chief Financial Officer, Hervé Déry
Tel: 819-934-4618; *Fax:* 819-934-5264
herve.dery@canada.ca
Senior Director General & Chief Financial Officer, Mark C. Melanson
Tel: 819-934-4627; *Fax:* 819-934-4428
mark.melanson@canada.ca
Senior Director General & Chief Information Officer, Paul Wagner
Tel: 819-997-4111; *Fax:* 819-994-6835
paul.wagner@canada.ca
Director General, Strategic Planning & Infrastructure Management, Serge Corbeil
Tel: 819-934-5876; *Fax:* 819-934-5267
serge.corbeil@canada.ca
Director General, Innovation & Digital Transformation, Michael Corbett
Tel: 613-818-7471
michael.corbett@canada.ca

Corporate Secretary / Secrétaire général
Corporate Secretary, Fabien Lengellé
Tel: 819-994-6982; *Fax:* 819-934-4422
fabien.lengelle@canada.ca

Operations Sector / Secteur des opérations
Chief Operating Officer, Normand Charbonneau
Tel: 819-934-5790
normand.charbonneau@canada.ca
Director General, Evaluation & Acquisitions Branch, Chantal Marin-Comeau
Tel: 819-934-5860; *Fax:* 819-934-7534
chantal.marin-comeau@canada.ca
Director General, Government Records Branch, Robert McIntosh
Tel: 613-762-9354; *Fax:* 819-934-5393
robert.mcintosh@canada.ca
Director General, Public Services Branch, Johanna Smith
Tel: 613-897-4742
johanna.smith@canada.ca

Library of Parliament / Bibliothèque du Parlement

Parliamentary Buildings, Ottawa, ON K1A 0A9
Tel: 613-992-4793
Toll-Free: 866-599-4999
TTY: 613-995-2266
info@parl.gc.ca
www.lop.parl.gc.ca/About/Library/VirtualLibrary/index-e.asp
Other Communication: Visitor Information, Phone: 613-996-0896
twitter.com/LoPResearch
twitter.com/LoPInformation

The Library of Parliament provides services to parliamentarians & the public.
The Library of Parliament's Parliamentary Budget Officer offers analysis to Parliament about the country's finances & trends in

the Canadian economy. Information is also available about proposed legislation, plus legislative summaries & research publications.
Services to the public include information about Parliament, classroom resources, & guided tours of the Parliament buildings.

Parliamentary Librarian, Sonia L'Heureux
Tel: 613-992-3122
Parliamentary Budget Officer, Jean-Denis Fréchette
Tel: 613-992-8026
Director General, Economic & Fiscal Analysis, Mostafa Askari Rankouhi
Tel: 613-992-8045
Director General, Information & Document Resource Service, Lynn Brodie
Tel: 613-996-8558
Director General, Corporate Services, Lynn Potter
Tel: 613-992-6826
Senior Director, Legal & Social Affairs, Kristen Douglas
Tel: 613-995-3476
Senior Director, Reference & Strategic Analysis, Joseph Jackson
Tel: 613-995-6363
Senior Director, Econ. & Fiscal Analysis & Forec., Chris Matier
Tel: 613-992-8004
Senior Director, Public Education Programs, Benoit Morin
Tel: 613-943-6401
Senior Director, Economics, Resources & International Affairs, Marcus Pistor
Tel: 613-947-6330
Senior Director, Costing & Program Analysis, Peter Weltman
Tel: 613-992-8044

Marine Atlantic Inc. / Marine Atlantique

Corporate Office, Baine Johnston Centre, #302, 10 Fort William Pl., St. John's, NL A1C 1K4
Toll-Free: 800-897-2797
customer_relations@marine-atlantic.ca
www.marine-atlantic.ca
twitter.com/MAferries
www.youtube.com/user/maferries

Marine Atlantic is a Crown corporation that strives to provide safe & environmentally responsible ferry service between the island of Newfoundland & the province of Nova Scotia.
Two routes are available. A year round service is provided between Port aux Basques, Newfoundland & Labrador & North Sydney, Nova Scotia. The second route is available between mid-June & late September between Argentia, Newfoundland & Labrador & North Sydney, Nova Scotia.

Acting Chair, President & CEO, Paul John Griffin
Chief Information Officer, Colin Tibbo
Vice-President, Customer Experience, Donald Barnes
Vice-President, Finance, Shawn Leamon
Director, Passenger Services, Neil Paterson
Manager, Marketing, Vicki Rose

Military Grievances External Review Committee / Comité externe d'examen des griefs militaires

60 Queen St., 10th Fl., Ottawa, ON K1P 5Y7
Tel: 613-996-8529; *Fax:* 613-996-6491
Toll-Free: 877-276-4193
TTY: 877-986-1666
mgerc-ceegm@mgerc-ceegm.gc.ca
mgerc-ceegm.gc.ca
Other Communication: Toll-Free Fax: 1-866-716-6601

Formerly known as the Canadian Forces Grievance Board, the Committee is an administrative tribunal with quasi-judicial powers, independent from the Department of National Defence (DND) & the Canadian Forces (CF). The former Board was created on March 1, 2000, in accordance with legislation enacted in December 1998 that contained amendments to the National Defence Act. The Committee was renamed on June 19, 2013, with the enactment of Bill C-15.
The Committee conducts objective & transparent reviews of grievances with due respect to fairness & equity for each individual member of the CF, regardless of rank or position. It plays a unique role within the military grievance review process because it ensures that the rights of CF personnel are considered fairly & impartially in the best interests of both parties concerned, thus balancing the rights of the grievor against the legal & operational requirements of the CF.

Chair, Bruno Hamel
Tel: 613-996-6453; *Fax:* 613-995-8129
Other Communications: Executive Assistant, Phone: 613-996-8621
Vice-Chair, Sonia Gaal
Tel: 613-996-8628
Executive Director, Corporate Services, Christine Guérette
Tel: 613-996-7027
Director, Operations/General Counsel, Caroline Maynard
Tel: 613-995-5552; *Fax:* 613-996-6491
Other Communications: Executive Assistant, Phone: 613-995-5127
Registrar, Stéphanie King
Tel: 613-995-5126
Senior Legal Counsel, Operations Directorate, Ann Boivin
Tel: 613-995-5599; *Fax:* 613-996-6491

National Arts Centre (NAC) / Centre national des Arts (CNA)

53 Elgin St., PO Box 1534 Stn. B, Ottawa, ON K1P 5W1
Tel: 613-947-7000; *Fax:* 613-947-7112
Toll-Free: 866-850-2787
www.nac-cna.ca
twitter.com/canadasnac
www.facebook.com/CanadasNAC
www.youtube.com/user/NACvideosCNA

The National Arts Centre is a multidisciplinary, bilingual performing arts centre that was created by an Act of the Parliament of Canada & opened to the public in 1969. It is home to the National Arts Centre Orchestra. The National Arts Centre works to develop performing arts in the National Capital Region & to help the Canada Council develop performing arts throughout Canada.
The Centre raises approximately half of its revenues from ticket, food, & parking sales, & well as hall rental fees & fundraising through the National Arts Centre Foundation. Other revenues are derived from the federal government.

Chair, National Arts Centre Board of Trustees, Adrian Burns
President & CEO, Peter Herrndorf
Tel: 613-947-7000 ext: 200; *Fax:* 613-238-4556
Peter.Herrndorf@nac-cna.ca
Chief Executive Officer, National Arts Centre Foundation, Jayne Watson
Tel: 613-947-7000 ext: 331; *Fax:* 613-947-8786
Jayne.Watson@nac-cna.ca
Chief Financial Officer & Director, Finance, Daniel Senyk
Tel: 613-947-7000 ext: 585; *Fax:* 613-943-1399
Daniel.Senyk@nac-cna.ca
Managing Director, NAC Orchestra, Christopher Deacon
Tel: 613-947-7000 ext: 363; *Fax:* 613-943-1400
Christopher.Deacon@nac-cna.ca
Managing Director, English Theatre, Nathan Medd
Tel: 613-947-7000 ext: 319; *Fax:* 613-943-1401
Nathan.Medd@nac-cna.ca
Director, Music Education & Community Engagement, Geneviève Cimon
Tel: 613-947-7000 ext: 374; *Fax:* 613-992-5225
Genevieve.Cimon@nac-cna.ca
Director, Human Resources, Debbie Collins
Tel: 613-947-7000 ext: 518; *Fax:* 613-943-1402
Debbie.Collins@nac-cna.ca
Director, Production Operations, Mike Damato
Tel: 613-947-7000 ext: 288; *Fax:* 613-943-8692
production@nac-cna.ca
Director, Administrative Services & Information Technology, Doug Eide
Tel: 613-947-7000 ext: 403; *Fax:* 613-952-7682
Douglas.Eide@nac-cna.ca
Artistic Director, French Theatre, Brigitte Haentjens
Tel: 613-947-7000 ext: 312; *Fax:* 613-943-1401
Brigitte.Haentjens@nac-cna.ca
Director, Marketing, Diane Landry
Tel: 613-947-7000 ext: 328; *Fax:* 613-996-2828
Diane.Landry@nac-cna.ca
Director, Operations, David McCuaig
Tel: 613-947-7000 ext: 650; *Fax:* 613-947-4512
David.McCuaig@nac-cna.ca
Director, Communications & Public Affairs, Rosemary Thompson
Tel: 613-947-7000 ext: 260; *Fax:* 613-996-9578
Rosemary.Thompson@nac-cna.ca
Director, Patron Services & New Media, Maurizio Ortolani
Tel: 613-947-7000 ext: 275; *Fax:* 613-947-7112
Maurizio.Ortolani@nac-cna.ca

National Battlefields Commission (NBC) / Commission des champs de bataille nationaux

390, av de Bernières, Québec, QC G1R 2L7
Tel: 418-648-3506; *Fax:* 418-648-3638
information@ccbn-nbc.gc.ca
www.ccbn-nbc.gc.ca
Other Communication: Communications, Phone: 418-649-6251; Customer Service: 418-649-6159; Archives: 418-648-2589; Finances: 418-648-4666; Activities: 418-648-4071
www.facebook.com/plainsofabraham

In 1908, an Act was passed to create the National Battlefields Commission. The purpose of the Commission is to acquire & preserve historical battlefields & to create national parks from these battlefields for the benefit of the public. The federal government agency, with its nine-member board of directors, operates under the portfolio of the Minister of Canadian Heritage.
The Commission has a sustainable development policy for the conservation of the Plains of Abraham park.

Secretary - Director General, André Beaudet
Tel: 418-648-3553; *Fax:* 418-648-3638
Director, Institutional Affairs, Anne Chouinard
Tel: 418-648-2540; *Fax:* 418-648-3638
Director, Communications & Cultural & Heritage Production, Joanne Laurin
Tel: 418-649-6251; *Fax:* 418-648-3809
Director, Administration, Paule Veilleux
Tel: 418-648-4666; *Fax:* 418-649-6345

National Capital Commission (NCC) / Commission de la capitale nationale (CCN)

#202, 40 Elgin St., Ottawa, ON K1P 1C7
Tel: 613-239-5000; *Fax:* 613-239-5063
Toll-Free: 800-465-1867
TTY: 866-661-3530
info@ncc-ccn.ca
www.ncc-ccn.gc.ca
Other Communication: Emergency Service, Phone: 613-239-5353; Gatineau Park Visitor Centre: 819-827-2020; Volunteer Centre: 613-239-5373; Skateway: 613-239-5234; Sponsorship: 613-239-5625
www.youtube.com/user/nccvidccn

The National Capital Commission is a Crown corporation. It was established by Parliament in 1959 to act as a steward for federal buildings & lands in Canada's National Capital Region.
The Commission works to ensure that the region is a place of national significance & pride. It consists of the following corporate, advisory, & special committees: Executive; Audit; Governance; Advisory Committee on Planning, Design, & Realty; Advisory Committee on Communications, Marketing, & Programming; Advisory Committee on the Official Residences of Canada; & Canadiana Fund.
In accordance with the *National Capital Act*the Commission's board of directors is appointed by the Minister of Foreign Affairs, with the approval of the Governor-in-Council. The National Capital Commission is accountable to Parliament & reports through the Minister of Foreign Affairs.

Minister Responsible; Minister, Canadian Heritage, Hon. Mélanie Joly, P.C.
Tel: 613-992-0983; *Fax:* 613-992-1932
Melanie.Joly@parl.gc.ca
Chair, Russell Andrew Mills
Chief Executive Officer, Mark Kristmanson
Tel: 613-239-5678 ext: 526; *Fax:* 613-239-5039
Chief Financial Officer & Senior Vice-President, Finance & Information Technology Services, Pierre Désautels
Tel: 613-239-5678 ext: 508; *Fax:* 613-239-5007
Vice-President, Capital Lands & Parks Branch, Steve Blight
Tel: 613-239-5678 ext: 558; *Fax:* 613-239-5336
Acting Vice-President, Capital Planning & Environmental Management, Fred Gaspar
Tel: 613-239-5678 ext: 577; *Fax:* 613-239-5302
Vice-President, Public Affairs, Communications & Marketing, Natalie Page
Tel: 613-239-5678 ext: 518
Vice-President, Real Estate Management, Design & Construction, Claude Robert
Tel: 613-239-5678 ext: 565; *Fax:* 613-239-5302
Vice-President, Human Resources, Manon Rochon
Tel: 613-239-5678 ext: 557; *Fax:* 613-239-5552
Director, Audit, Research, Evaluation & Ethics; Chief Audit Executive, Jayne Hinchliff-Milne
Tel: 613-239-5678 ext: 562; *Fax:* 613-239-5695

Department of National Defence & the Canadian Armed Forces / Le Ministère de la Défense nationale et les Forces armées canadiennes

National Defence HQ, Major-General George R. Pearkes Bldg., 101 Colonel By Dr., Ottawa, ON K1A 0K2
Tel: 613-995-2534; *Fax:* 613-992-4739
Toll-Free: 888-995-2534
TTY: 800-467-9877
information@forces.gc.ca
www.forces.gc.ca
Other Communication: CF Recruiting, Phone: 1-800-856-8488; Access to Information, Phone: 613-992-0996; Media Inquiries, Phone: 613-996-2353 or 1-866-377-0811
twitter.com/CanadianForces
www.facebook.com/CanadianForces
www.linkedin.com/company/1564
www.youtube.com/user/CanadianForcesVideos

The Department of National Defence, the Canadian Armed Forces, & related organizations provide services to defend Canada & Canadian interests.
The Defence Portfolio comprises the following organizations,

which are the responsibility of the Minister of National Defence: The Office of the Legal Advisor to the Department of National Defence & the Canadian Forces; National Search & Rescue Secretariat; Defence Research & Development Canada; Communications Security Establishment; Cadets & Junior Canadian Rangers; Canadian Forces Housing Agency; Judge Advocate General; Military Police Complaints Commission; Canadian Forces Grievance Board; Office of the Chief Military Judge; The Office of the National Defence & Canadian Forces Ombudsman; & the Canadian Forces Personnel Support Agency.
Some of the Canadian Forces' current operations include: Operation Impact, against the Islamic State of Iraq & the Levant (ISIL), also known as Daesh, in the Republic of Iraq; Operation Caribbe in the Caribbean Sea; Operation Artemis at sea; Operation Calumet in the Sinai Peninsula; & Operation Nunalivut in Nunavut.

Governor General; Commander-in-Chief of Canada, Right Hon. David Johnston, CC, CMM, COM, CD, FRSC(hon), FRCPSC(hon)
Tel: 613-993-8200; *Fax:* 613-998-8760
TTY: 800-465-6890
Social Media: twitter.com/GGDavidJohnston, www.facebook.com/GGDavidJohnston
Rideau Hall
1 Sussex Dr.
Ottawa, ON K1A 0A1

Minister, National Defence, Hon. Harjit S. Sajjan, P.C.
Tel: 613-995-7052; *Fax:* 613-995-2962
HarjitS.Sajjan@parl.gc.ca
Note: Web Site: www.forces.gc.ca/en/about-org-structure/minister-national-defence.page

Associate Minister, National Defence, Hon. Kent Hehr, P.C.
Tel: 613-995-1561; *Fax:* 613-995-1862
Kent.Hehr@parl.gc.ca

Parliamentary Secretary, Hon. John McKay, P.C., B.A., LL.B.
Tel: 613-992-1447; *Fax:* 613-992-8968
john.mckay@parl.gc.ca

Chief of Defence Staff for the Canadian Forces, Gen Jonathan Vance
Tel: 613-992-7405

Vice-Chief of Defence Staff, VAdm Mark Norman

Chair, Defence Science Advisory Board, Wayne Williams
Tel: 613-992-4070; *Fax:* 613-996-9168

Ombudsman, Gary Walbourne
Tel: 613-996-2089; *Fax:* 613-996-3280
Other Communications: Secure Fax: 613-996-9562

Chief of Staff to the Minister, Brian Bohunicky
Tel: 613-996-3100

Chief of Staff to the Associate Minister, Vacant

Director, Parliamentary Affairs, Louis Landry
Tel: 613-996-3100

Director, General Operations, Robyn Hynes
Tel: 613-992-0787; *Fax:* 613-992-3167

Director, Strategic Planning & Research, Mary Kirby
Tel: 613-992-0787; *Fax:* 613-992-3167

Director, Communications, Renée Filiatrault
Tel: 613-996-3100

Associated Agencies, Boards & Commissions:

•Communications Security Establishment Canada / Centre de la sécurité des telecommunications Canada
1500 Bronson Ave.
PO Box 9703 Terminal
Ottawa, ON K1A OK2
Tel: 613-991-7600; *Fax:* 613-991-8514
www.cse-cst.gc.ca
The Communications Security Establishment is Canada's national cryptologic agency, providing the Government of Canada with two key services: foreign signals intelligence in support of defence & foreign policy, & the protection of electronic information & communication.

•Office of the Communications Security Establishment Commissioner / Bureau du Commissaire du Centre de la sécurité des télécommunications
PO Box 1984 B
Ottawa, ON K1P 5R5
Tel: 613-992-3044
www.ocsec-bccst.gc.ca
The Commissioner reviews the activities of the Communications Security Establishment for compliance with the law; advises the Minister of National Defence & the Attorney General of Canada of any CSE activity not in compliance with the law; receives complaints about CSE activities; carries out specific duties under the public interest provisions of the Security of Information Act.

•Military Police Complaints Commission / Commission d'examen des plaintes concernant la police militaire
270 Albert St., 10th Fl.
Ottawa, ON K1P 5G8
Tel: 613-947-5625; *Fax:* 613-947-5713
Toll-free: 800-632-0566
commission@mpcc-cppm.gc.ca
www.mpcc-cppm.gc.ca
Other Communication: Toll Free Fax: 1-877-947-5713
Quasi-judicial, independent civilian agency examines complaints arising from either the conduct of military police members in the exercise of policing duties or functions or from interference in or obstruction of their police investigations.

Deputy Minister of National Defence / Sous-ministre de la Défense nationale

The following positions report to the Deputy Minister of National Defence: Associate Deputy Minister of National Defence; Assistant Deputy Minister, Finance & Corporate Services; Assistant Deputy Minister, Human Resources - Civilian; Assistant Deputy Minister, Infrastructure & Environment; Assistant Deputy Minister, Policy; & Assistant Deputy Minister, Materiel.
The following positions report to both the Deputy Minister of National Defence & the Chief of the Defence Staff: Vice Chief of the Defence Staff; Assistant Deputy Minister, Information Management; Assistant Deputy Minister, Public Affairs; Assistant Deputy Minister, Science & Technology; Chief Review, Services; & the Department of National Defence & Canadian Forces Legal Advisor.
The Judge Advocate General is responsible to the Minister of National Defence & accountable for legal advice given to the Deputy Minister of National Defence & the Chief of the Defence Staff.

Deputy Minister, National Defence, John Forster
Tel: 613-992-4258; *Fax:* 613-995-2028
Senior Associate Deputy Minister, National Defence, W. (Bill) Davern Jones
Tel: 613-992-0275; *Fax:* 613-995-2028
Assistant Deputy Minister, Review Services, Amipal Manchanda
Tel: 613-992-7975; *Fax:* 613-947-5843
Corporate Secretary, Larry Surtees
Tel: 613-996-6402; *Fax:* 613-992-0313
Director General, Audit, Jean-Francois Riel
Tel: 613-992-4936; *Fax:* 613-992-0528
Executive Director, Evaluation Operations, Vacant
Tel: 613-992-0345; *Fax:* 613-992-0528

Chief Military Personnel (CMP) / Chef - Personnel militaire (CPM)

www.cmp-cpm.forces.gc.ca
Other Communication: Media Liaison Office, Phone: 1-866-377-0811; CF Member Assistance Program: 1-800-268-7708; CF Pension Program: 1-800-267-0325; Honours & Recognition: 1-877-741-8332
The Chief Military Personnel has the following responsibilities: providing guidance to the Canadian Forces about military personnel management issues; establishing policies & programs to maintain the profession of arms; monitoring compliance with Canadian Forces personnel management policies; & overseeing the management of the Canadian Forces Personnel System.
The Chief Military Personnel manages programs & services such as compensation & benefits, careers & training, work environment, human resources intiatives, & health services.

Chief of Military Personnel, LGen C.T. Whitecross, CMM, MSM, CD
Surgeon General / Commander, Canadian Forces Health Services Group, BGen H.C. MacKay, OMM, CD, QHP
Director General, Military Personnel Research & Analysis, Susan Truscott
Tel: 613-992-6162; *Fax:* 613-995-5785

Finance & Corporate Services / Finances et serices du ministère

Assistant Deputy Minister, Claude C.R. Rochette
Tel: 613-992-5669; *Fax:* 613-992-9693
Director General, Financial Management, Werner Liedtke
Tel: 613-992-6907; *Fax:* 613-992-4639
Director General, Financial Operations, Dale MacMillan
Tel: 613-971-6506; *Fax:* 613-971-6507
Director General, Strategic Finance & Financial Arrangements, Ian Poulter
Tel: 613-943-5279; *Fax:* 613-992-8712

Human Resources - Civilian / Ressources humaines - Civils

Assistant Deputy Minister, Kin Choi
Tel: 613-971-0245; *Fax:* 613-971-0247
Director General, Workforce Development, Joe Dragon, PhD
Tel: 613-971-0332; *Fax:* 613-971-0320
Director General, Workplace Management, Susan Harrison
Tel: 613-971-0202; *Fax:* 613-971-0103
Director General, Human Resources Strategic Directions, Vacant
Tel: 613-971-0248; *Fax:* 613-971-0236
Director General, Civilian Human Resources Management Operations, Vacant
Tel: 613-971-0524; *Fax:* 613-971-0103

Information Management / Gestion de l'information

Assistant Deputy Minister, Len Bastien
Tel: 613-995-2017; *Fax:* 613-995-2189
Chief of Staff, MGen Gregory Loos
Tel: 613-992-5420; *Fax:* 613-995-2189
Director General, Information Management Technology & Strategic Planning, Guy Charron
Tel: 613-992-1674; *Fax:* 613-992-4223
Director General, Information Management Project Delivery, Tony Hoe
Tel: 613-992-9119
Director General, Enterprise Application Services, Claude Lareau
Tel: 613-960-9915; *Fax:* 613-960-9920

Infrastructure & Environment / Infrastructure et environnement

Assistant Deputy Minister, Jaime Pitfield
Tel: 613-947-4061
Chief of Staff, Vacant
Chief Executive Officer, Canadian Forces Housing Agency, Dominique Francoeur
Tel: 613-998-5904; *Fax:* 613-991-1988
Director General, Portfolio Requirements, Susan Chambers
Tel: 613-995-0923; *Fax:* 613-995-1031
Director General, Environment, Rose Kattackal
Tel: 613-995-5586; *Fax:* 613-995-1031

Judge Advocate General's Office / Juge-avocat général
101 Colonel By Dr., Ottawa, ON K1A 0K2
Tel: 613-992-5678; *Fax:* 613-992-1211

Judge Advocate General, MGen Blaise Cathcart
Tel: 613-992-3019; *Fax:* 613-992-5678
Acting Deputy Judge Advocate General, Operations, Cdr. Geneviève Bernachez
Tel: 613-996-6456; *Fax:* 613-945-0242
Deputy Judge Advocate General, Regional Services - Ottawa, Vacant
Tel: 613-996-6456
Deputy Judge Advocate General, Military Justice & Administrative Law, Vacant

Materiel / Matériels

Assistant Deputy Minister, Patrick Finn
Tel: 613-992-6622; *Fax:* 613-945-0949
Chief of Staff, André Fillion
Tel: 613-992-6622; *Fax:* 613-995-0028
Director General, Major Project Services (Air), Troy Crosby
Tel: 819-997-6306; *Fax:* 819-997-9699
Director, Major Project Services, Vacant
Tel: 819-997-6134; *Fax:* 819-997-6072
Director, Major Project Delivery (Land & Sea), Ian Mack
Tel: 819-939-6963; *Fax:* 819-997-7252

Aerospace Equipment Program Management / Gestion du programme d'équipement aérospatial

Director General, Vacant
Tel: 613-939-3354; *Fax:* 613-990-5236

International & Industry Programs / Programmes Internationaux et industriels

Director General, Vacant
Tel: 613-992-3730; *Fax:* 613-995-0028

Land Equipment Program Management / Gestion du programme d'équipement terrestre

Director General, Vacant
Tel: 819-997-9474; *Fax:* 819-994-3143

Maritime Equipment Program Management / Gestion du programme d'équipement maritime

Director General, Vacant
Tel: 819-939-3500; *Fax:* 819-992-7058

Materiel Systems & Supply Chain / Systèmes de matériel et chaîne d'approvisionnement

Director General, Vacant
Tel: 819-994-9461; *Fax:* 819-994-1627

Procurement Services / Services d'acquisition

Director General, Vacant
Tel: 613-997-3356; *Fax:* 613-997-3211

Policy / Politiques

Assistant Deputy Minister, Gordon Venner
Tel: 613-992-3458; *Fax:* 613-995-6631
Director General, International Security Policy, Vacant
Tel: 613-992-2769; *Fax:* 613-992-3990
Director General, Policy Planning, Vacant
Tel: 613-992-0799; *Fax:* 613-995-0446
Director General, Policy Coordination, Nada Vrany
Tel: 613-995-8332; *Fax:* 613-995-2876

Public Affairs / Affaires publiques

Assistant Deputy Minister, Edison Stewart
Tel: 613-996-0562; *Fax:* 613-995-2610
Chief of Staff & Director, Vacant
Tel: 613-995-1497
Director General, Marketing, Janice Keenan
Tel: 819-997-1846; *Fax:* 819-997-1880
Director General, Public Affairs Strategic Planning, Sophie Galarneau
Tel: 613-943-5353; *Fax:* 613-995-2610

Science & Technology / Science et technologie

Assistant Deputy Minister, Dr. Marc Fortin
Tel: 613-996-2020; *Fax:* 613-995-3402
Chief of Staff, Camille Boulet
Tel: 613-996-7215; *Fax:* 613-995-3402
Director General, Defence Research & Development Canada - Centre for Security Science, Mark Williamson
Tel: 613-944-8195; *Fax:* 613-995-0002
Director General, Research & Development Corporate Services, Mylène Ouellet
Tel: 613-992-6105; *Fax:* 613-996-0038

Office of the Chief of the Defence Staff / Chef d'état-major de la défense

The following organizations report to the Chief of the Defence Staff: Canadian Army; Royal Canadian Air Force; Royal Canadian Navy; Canadian Joint Operations Command; Canadian Special Operations Forces Command; & Chief of Military Personnel.
The following positions report to both the Chief of the Defence Staff & the Deputy Minister of National Defence: Vice Chief of the Defence Staff; Chief, Review Services; Department of National Defence & Canadian Forces Legal Advisor; Assistant Deputy Minister, Information Management; Assistant Deputy Minister, Public Affairs; & Assistant Deputy Minister, Science & Technology.
Chief of Defence Staff for the Canadian Forces, Gen Jonathan Vance
Tel: 613-992-7405
Vice-Chief of Defence Staff, VAdm Mark Norman

Canadian Army / Armée canadienne
National Defence HQ, MGen George R. Pearkes Building, 110 Colonel By Dr., Ottawa, K1A 0K2

Tel: 613-995-2534
Toll-Free: 888-995-2534
TTY: 800-467-9877
information@forces.gc.ca
www.army.forces.gc.ca
twitter.com/canadianarmy
www.facebook.com/CANArny
www.youtube.com/CanadianArmyNews

The land component of the combined Canadian Forces is the Canadian Army. To provide trained, combat-ready troops in order to meet the nation's defense objectives around the globe is the mission of the Canadian Army. The Army has more than 400 regular & reserve units located throughout Canada, with over 41,000 soldiers.
The following are the types of units that make up the Canadian Army: infantry, armour, artillery, engineers, signals, & combat support.
In addition to several training facilities, the Army operates the following major support bases: Gagetown, New Brunswick; Valcartier, Québec; Montréal, Québec; Petawawa, Ontario; Kingston, Ontario; Shilo, Manitoba; & Edmonton, Alberta.
Commander, Canadian Army, LGen Paul Wynnyk, CMM, MSM, CD
Social Media: twitter.com/Army_Comd
Deputy Commander, Canadian Army, MGen J.C.G. Juneau, OMM, MSM, CD
Army Sergeant Major, CWO A. Guimond, MMM, CD
Chief of Staff, Army Strategy, BGen S.M. Cadden, CD
Chief of Staff, Army Operations, BGen J.P.H.H. Gosselin, OMM, MSM, CD
Chief of Staff, Army Reserve, BGen R.R.E. MacKenzie, OMM, CD
Commander, Canadian Army Doctrine & Training Centre Headquarters, MGen J.M. Lanthier, OMM, MSC, MSM, CD

Land Force Doctrine & Training System (LFDTS) / Système de la doctrine et de l'instruction de la Force terrestre (SDIFT)
Canadian Forces Base Kingston, PO Box 17000 Stn. Forces, Kingston, ON K7K 7B4

www.army-armee.forces.gc.ca/en/doctrine-training/index.page
Other Communication: Public Affairs, Phone: 613-541-5010, ext. 4538, Fax: 613-540-8028

The Land Force Doctrine & Training System is responsible for leading land warfare intellectual development & land operations training for the Canadian Army. Land Force training & doctrine development includes simulation & digitization.
The following are units of the Land Force Doctrine & Training System: Headquarters; Canadian Land Force Command & Staff College; Peace Support Training Centre; 2 Electronic Warfare Squadron; Combat Training Centre, located at CFB Gagetown, New Brunswick & 8 Wing Trenton, Ontario; & the Canadian Manoeuvre Training Centre in Wainwright, Alberta.
Commander, Land Force Doctrine & Training System, MGen J.M. Lanthier, OMM, MSC, MSM, CD
Chief Warrant Officer, CWO D.C. Tofts

2nd Canadian Division / 2e Division du Canada
Pierre Le Moyne d'Iberville Building, CP 600 Succ K, Montréal, QC H1N 3R2

Tél: 514-252-2777
www.army-armee.forces.gc.ca/en/quebec/index.page
Autres nombres: Media, Phone: 514-252-2777, ext. 4211, Fax: 514-252-2029
www.facebook.com/2DivCA

Established in 1992, the 2nd Canadian Division (formerly Land Force Québec Area) comprises Regular & Reserve Land Force units in the province of Québec. The mission of the 2nd Canadian Division is the provision of combat-ready, versatile land forces.
Commander, 2nd Canadian Division & Joint Task Force East, BGen Stéphane Lafaut, OMM, MSC, CD

3rd Canadian Division / 3e Division du Canada
700 Vimy Ave., PO Box 10500 Stn. Forces, Edmonton, AB T5J 4J5

Tel: 780-973-4011
Toll-Free: 877-973-1944
www.army-armee.forces.gc.ca/en/western/index.page
Other Communication: Public Affairs, Phone: 780-973-1942, Fax: 780-973-1939
twitter.com/3CdnDiv
www.facebook.com/3CdnDiv
www.youtube.com/c/ThirdCanadianDivision

The 3rd Canadian Division (formerly Land Force Western Area) was established in 1991. The role of the 3rd Canadian Division is to oversee all regular & reserve army units from Thunder Bay, Ontario to Vancouver Island, British Columbia.
The following organizations are part of Land Force Western Area: One Regular Mechanized Brigade Group, One Area Support Group, three Reserve Brigade Groups, & the Western Area Training Centre.
Commander, 3rd Canadian Division & Joint Task Force West, BGen W.D. Eyre, MSC, CD

4th Canadian Division / 4e Division du Canada
The LCol George Taylor Denison III Armoury, 1 Yukon Lane, Toronto, ON M3K 0A1

Tel: 416-633-6200
www.army-armee.forces.gc.ca/en/central/index.page
Other Communication: Media, Phone: 416-633-6200, ext. 5500
twitter.com/4CdnDiv4DivCA
www.facebook.com/4CdnDiv4DivCA
www.flickr.com/photos/lfca_multimedia

The 4th Canadian Division (formerly Land Force Central Area) is the Canadian Army in Ontario. The mandate of Land Force Central Area is the generation & maintenance of combat capable, multi-purpose land forces to handle the defence objectives of the nation. The 4th Canadian Division consists of over 21,000 personnel in 35 communities throughout Ontario. The Area's largest regular force units are Canadian Forces Base Kingston & Canadian Forces Base Petawawa.
Commander, 4th Canadian Division & Joint Task Force Central, BGen Lowell Thomas, OMM, CD
Sergeant Major, CWO Stuart Hartnell, MMM, MSM, CD

5th Canadian Division / 5e Division du Canada
PO Box 99000 Stn. Forces, Halifax, NS B3K 5X5

Tel: 902-427-7576
www.army-armee.forces.gc.ca/en/atlantic/index.page
twitter.com/5CdnDiv
www.facebook.com/CANArmyAtlantic
www.youtube.com/user/CANArmyAtlantic

All Army Regular & Reserve Force elements in New Brunswick, Nova Scotia, Prince Edward Island, & Newfoundland & Labrador are the responsibility of the 5th Canadian Division (formerly Land Force Atlantic Area). Exceptions are the 2nd Battalion, The Royal Canadian Regiment & the Combat Training Centre in Gagetown, New Brunswick. The Area comprises approximately 7,000 personnel.
The Land Force Atlantic Areas is involved in recruiting, training, & forging units ready for peacekeeping, peace support, & peace enforcement operations throughout the world.
Commander, BGen Carl Turenne, OMM, MSC, CD
Division Chief Warrant Officer, CWO S.E. Croucher, MMM, CD

Canadian Forces Base Edmonton (CFB Edmonton) / Base des Forces canadiennes Edmonton (BFC Edmonton)
PO Box 10500 Stn. Forces, Edmonton, AB T5J 4J5

www.army-armee.forces.gc.ca/en/cfb-edmonton/index.page

CFB Edmonton provides infrastructure & support to units located in & near Edmonton as well as to elements situated in the Northwest Territories & Yukon.
Commander, Col S.M. Lacroix
Sergeant Major, CWO J.M. Doppler
Officer, Public Affairs, Capt Donna Riguidel
Tel: 780-973-4011 ext: 802
donna.riguidel@forces.gc.ca

Canadian Forces Base Gagetown (CFB Gagetown) / Base des Forces canadiennes Gagetown (BFC Gagetown)
PO Box 17000 Stn. Forces, Oromocto, NB E2V 4J5

Tel: 506-422-2000
www.army-armee.forces.gc.ca/en/5-cdsb-gagetown/index.page
www.facebook.com/CanadianForcesBaseGagetown

Opened in 1958, CFB Gagetown is the largest military facility in eastern Canada.
Operational units situated at CFB Gagetown include the 2nd Battalion of the Royal Canadian Regiment, 4 Engineer Support Regiment, 4 Air Defence Regiment, 403 Operational (Helicopter) Training Squadron, & C Squadron of the Royal Canadian Dragoons. The base also features the Joint Meteorological Centre, the Land Force Atlantic Area Training Centre, the Land Force Trials & Evaluation Unit, & the Argonaut Army Cadet Summer Training Centre.
Commanding Officer, CFB Gagetown, Col D.A. MacIsaac

Canadian Forces Base Kingston (CFB Kingston) / Base des Forces canadiennes Kingston (BFC Kingston)
PO Box 17000 Stn. Forces, Kingston, ON K7K 7B4

Tel: 613-541-5010
www.army-armee.forces.gc.ca/en/cfb-kingston/index.page
Other Communication: Base Duty Centre: 613-541-5330; Military Police: 613-541-5648

The following units are located at CFB Kingston: 1st Canadian Division; Canadian Forces Recruiting Centre Detachment Kingston; CF Joint Signal Regiment; 2 Area Support Group Signal Squadron Detachment Kingston; CF Joint Support Group; 21 Electronic Warfare Regiment; 1 Wing Kingston; Canadian Forces National Counter-Intelligence Unit Detachment Kingston; 2 MP Regiment Detachment Kingston; Kingston Garrison Learning & Career Centre; Canadian Forces School of Military Intelligence; Canadian Forces National Counter-Intelligence Unit Detachment Kingston; Canadian Forces Crypto Maintenance Unit; Land Force Doctrine & Training System; Canadian Forces School of Communications & Electronics; Canadian Defence Academy; 1 Dental Unit - Detachment Kingston; 33 CF Health Services Centre; Civilian Human Resources Office; Dispute Resolution Centre; Canadian Forces Housing Unit; MPO 305 Vimy Post Office, & the Military Communications & Electronics Museum. The base also serves base & cadet units.
Commander, Col S.R. Kelsey, CD
Sergeant Major, CWO Terry Garand, MMM, CD

Canadian Forces Base Montréal (CFB Montréal) / Base des Forces canadiennes Montréal (BFC Montréal)
Richelain, QC J0J 1R0

www.army-armee.forces.gc.ca/en/cfb-montreal/index.page

The Montréal base supports lodger & integral units in the area as well as reserves & cadets
Commander, Col Sébastien Bouchard
Sergeant Major, CWO Mario Tremblay

Canadian Forces Base Petawawa (CFB Petawawa) / Base des Forces candiennes Petawawa (BFC Petawawa)
CFB/ASU Petawawa Base HQ, Building S-111, 101 Menin Rd., PO Box 9999 Stn. Main, Petawawa, ON K8H 2X3

Tel: 613-687-5511
petawawapublicaffairs@forces.gc.ca
www.army-armee.forces.gc.ca/en/cfb-petawawa/index.page
twitter.com/GarrisonPet
www.facebook.com/100533039582

Garrison support services are provided for 2 Canadian Mechanized Brigade Group & lodger units at CFB Petawawa. There are approximately 5,400 military members at the base.
Commander, Col J.R.M. Gagné, MSM, CD
Sergeant Major, CWO W.A. Richards, MMM, MSM, CD

Canadian Forces Base Shilo (CFB Shilo) / Base des Forces canadiennes Shilo (BFC Shilo)
CFB Shilo, PO Box 5000 Stn. Main, Shilo, MB R0K 2A0

Tel: 204-765-3000
www.army-armee.forces.gc.ca/en/cfb-shilo/index.page

Canadian Forces Base / Area Support Unit Shilo, located in southwestern Manitoba, is home to the Second Battalion Princess Patricia's Canadian Light Infantry & the First Regiment Royal Canadian Horse Artillery, which are both part of 1 Canadian Mechanized Brigade Group. The base also features part of the Western Area Training Centre, 11 CF Health Services Centre, 742 Signals Squadron Detachment Shilo, & RCA Brandon's Reserve Unit.
Commander, LCol John Cochrane

Canadian Forces Base Suffield (CFB Suffield) / Base des Forces canadiennes Suffield (BFC Suffield)
CFB Suffield Headquarters, Building 393, Falaise St., PO Box 6000 Stn. Main, Medicine Hat, AB T1A 8K8

Tel: 403-544-4405
www.army-armee.forces.gc.ca/en/cfb-suffield/index.page

Under the Canadian Army command of the Land Forces Western Area, CFB Suffield hosts the largest military training area in Canada. The range & training area is used by organizations such as Defence Research & Development Canada - Suffield & the British Army Training Unit Suffield.

Commander, LCol John C. Scott

Base Regimental Sergeant Major, CWO Richard Stacey, MMM, SMV, CD

Canadian Forces Base Valcartier (CFB Valcartier) / Base des forces canadiennes Valcartier (BFC Valcartier)
CP 100 Succ Forces, Courcelette, QC G0A 4Z0

www.army-armee.forces.gc.ca/en/cfb-valcartier/index.page

CFB Valcartier is home to the 5th Canadian Mechanized Brigade Group.

Commander, Col Sébastien Bouchard

Sergeant Major, CWO Mario Tremblay

Canadian Forces Base Wainwright (CFB Wainwright) / Base des forces canadiennes Wainwright (BFC Wainwright)
Wainwright Garrison, General Delivery, Stn. Main, Denwood, AB T0B 1B0

www.army-armee.forces.gc.ca/en/cfb-wainwright/index.page

CFB Wainwright features the Canadian Manoeuvre Training Centre.

Public Affairs Officer, Capt. Denny Brown
Tel: 780-842-1363 ext: 120
denny.brown@forces.gc.ca

Royal Canadian Air Force (RCAF) / Aviation royale canadienne (ARC)
MGen George R. Pearkes Building, 101 Colonel By Dr., Ottawa, ON K1A 0K2

www.rcaf-arc.forces.gc.ca
Other Communication: Media Liaison: 613-996-2353; 1-866-377-0811
twitter.com/RCAF_ARC
www.facebook.com/rcaf1924
www.youtube.com/user/RCAFIMAGERY

The Commander of Air Command & Chief of the Air Forces Staff is responsible for training, generating, & maintaining multi-purpose, combat capable air forces to serve the nation. The Commander of 1 Canadian Air Division oversees operational & tactical control of the air force. There are wings in the following locations throughout Canada: Bagotville, Québec; Borden, Ontario; Cold Lake, Alberta; Comox, British Columbia; Gander, Newfoundland & Labrador; Goose Bay, Newfoundland & Labrador; Greenwood, Nova Scotia; Kingston, Ontario; Moose Jaw, Saskatchewan; North Bay, Ontario; Shearwater, Nova Scotia; Trenton, Ontario; & Winnipeg, Manitoba.
Operations include missions in areas of conflict, support operations for troops, & support for humanitarian aid & diplomatic missions. Locations of recent operations include Haiti, Libya, Afghanistan & Mali.

Commander of the Royal Canadian Air Force, L.Gen M.J. Hood, CMM, CD

Commander, 1 Canadian Air Division, MGen D.L.R. Wheeler

Chief Warrant Officer of the Royal Canadian Air Force, CWO Gérard Poitras

Canadian Forces Station Alert (CFS Alert)
c/o 8 Wing / CFB Trenton, PO Box 1000 Stn. Forces, Astra, ON K0K 3W0

Tel: 613-392-2811
www.rcaf-arc.forces.gc.ca/en/8-wing/alert.page

The Air Force commands CFS Alert. The station is a unit of 8 Wing Trenton, Ontario.

Canadian Forces Base Bagotville: 3 Wing (CFB Bagotville) / Base des Forces canadiennes Bagotville: 3e escadre (BFC Bagotville)
CP 5000 Succ Bureau-chef, Alouette, QC G0V 1A0

3escbagotville@forces.gc.ca
www.rcaf-arc.forces.gc.ca/en/3-wing/index.page
Autres nombres: Public Affairs, Fax: 418-677-4073

The following are 3 Wing Squadrons: 414 Electronic Warfare Squadron; 425 Tactical Fighter Squadron; 439 Combat Support Squadron; 3 Air Maintenance Squadron; & 12 Radar Squadron.

Wing Commander, Col Darcy Molstad, CD

Canadian Forces Base Borden: 16 Wing (CFB Borden) / Base des Forces canadiennes Borden: 16 escadre (BFC Borden)
16 Wing Headquarters, PO Box 1000 Stn. Main, Borden, ON L0M 1C0

Tel: 705-424-1200
www.rcaf-arc.forces.gc.ca/en/16-wing/index.page
Other Communication: Public Affairs, Phone: 705-424-1200, ext. 3162
www.facebook.com/CanadianForcesBaseBorden

The following schools at Borden provide air force technical training & professional development: Air Command Academy; Canadian Forces School of Aerospace Technology & Engineering; & Canadian Forces School of Aerospace Control Operations.

Wing Commander, Col Yve Thomson, CD

Canadian Forces Base Cold Lake: 4 Wing (CFB Cold Lake) / Base des Forces canadiennes Cold Lake: 4 escadre (BFC Cold Lake)
PO Box 6550 Stn. Forces, Cold Lake, AB T9M 2C6

4wingcoldlake@forces.gc.ca
www.rcaf-arc.forces.gc.ca/en/4-wing/index.page
Other Communication: Public Affairs, Phone: 780-840-8000, ext 8121, Fax: 780-840-7300

Fighter pilot training for the Canadian Forces takes place at Cold Lake. The base deploys & supports fighter aircraft to meet the domestic & international commitments of the Royal Canadian Air Force.
4 Wing is home to the following squadrons: 409 Tactical Fighter Squadron; 410 Tactical Fighter Squadron; 417 Combat Support Squadron; 419 Tactical Fighter Training Squadron; 1 Air Maintenance Squadron; CF-18 Weapon System Manager Detachment Cold Lake; 42 Radar Squadron; 10 Field Technical Training Squadron; & 4 Airfield Defence Detachment.

Wing Commander, Col E.J. Kenny, MSM, CD

Canadian Forces Base Comox: 19 Wing (CFB Comox) / Base des Forces canadiennes Commox: 19e escadre (BFC Comox)
PO Box 1000 Stn. Main, Lazo, BC V0R 2K0

Tel: 250-339-8211
19WingPublicAffairs@forces.gc.ca
www.rcaf-arc.forces.gc.ca/en/19-wing/index.page
Other Communication: Public Affairs, Phone; 250-339-8201; Fax: 250-339-8120; Joint Rescue Coordination Ctr., Phone: 250-413-8937; Wing Operations (Noise Complaints), Phone: 250-339-8231

Based on Vancouver Island, British Columbia, 19 Wing is known for its CP-140 Aurora Long Range Patrol Aircraft crews that embark on surveillance missions over the Pacific Ocean. Search & rescue teams, which are part of the 442 Transport & Rescue Squadron based at 19 Wing, fly the CC-115 Buffalo Search & Rescue Aircraft & CH-149 Cormorant Helicopters on operations from the Arctic to the border between British Columbia & Washington, & from the Pacific Ocean to the Rocky Mountains. The Wing is also home to the Canadian Forces School of Search & Rescue & the Regional Cadet Gliding School (Pacific).

Wing Commander, Col Tom Dunne, CD

Canadian Forces Base Gander: 9 Wing (CFB Gander) / Base des Forces canadiennes Gander: 9e escadre (BFC Gander)
PO Box 6000 Gander, NL A1V 1X1

Tel: 709-256-1703; *Fax:* 709-256-1735
www.rcaf-arc.forces.gc.ca/en/9-wing/index.page
Other Communication: Public Affairs, Phone: 709-256-1703, ext. 1126

The Gander base is a major military establishment in Newfoundland & Labrador. It supports the Canadian Forces Recruiting Centre Detachment Corner Brook, plus several Cadet Corps. Armouries are maintained in Corner Brook, Stepheville, & Grand Falls-Windsor.
9 Wing Gander is responsible for search & rescue services in Newfoundland & Labrador & northeastern Québec.
The base is also home to CFS Lietrim Detachment Gander. Its role is the operation & maintenance of signals intelligence.
The Wing also features Canadian Coastal Radar, which it operates & maintains on behalf of Fighter Group Canadian NORAD Region Headquarters.

Wing Commander, LCol Pierre Haché

Canadian Forces Base Goose Bay: 5 Wing (CFB Goose Bay) / Base des Forces canadiennes Goose Bay: 5e escadre (BFC Goose Bay)
PO Box 7002 Stn. A, Happy Valley-Goose Bay, NL A0P 1S0

www.rcaf-arc.forces.gc.ca/en/5-wing/index.page
Other Communication: Public Affairs, Phone: 709-896-6928, Fax: 709-896-6997; SERCO Customer Service Help Desk: 709-896-6900, ext. 6946, csc.bmx@serco-na.com

5 Wing Goose Bay supports Canadian Forces, North American Aerospace Defense Command (NORAD), & Allied training & operations.

Wing Commander, LCol Luc Sabourin

Canadian Forces Base Greenwood: 14 Wing (CFB Greenwood) / Base des Forces canadiennes Greenwood: 14e escadre (BFC Greenwood)
PO Box 5000 Stn. Main, Greenwood, NS B0P 1N0

Tel: 902-765-1494
www.rcaf-arc.forces.gc.ca/en/14-wing/index.page
Other Communication: Public Affairs, Phone: 902-765-1494, ext. 5101, Fax: 902-765-1757

The roles of 14 Wing Greenwood include sovereignty & surveillance missions over the Atlantic Ocean by CP-140 Aurora Long Range Patrol Aircraft crews, as well as search & rescue services throughout Atlantic Canada & eastern Québec. 413 Transport & Rescue Squadron members use CC-130 Hercules Aircraft & CH-149 Cormorant Helicopters during their operations.

Wing Commander, Col Patrick Thauberger, CD

Canadian Forces Base Kingston: 1 Wing (CFB Kingston) / Base des Forces canadiennes Kingston: 1re escadre (BFC Kingston)
Sergeant KS Smith CD Building, PO Box 17000 Stn. Forces, Kingston, ON K7K 7B4

Tel: 613-541-5010
1wingpublicaffairs@forces.gc.ca
www.rcaf-arc.forces.gc.ca/en/1-wing/index.page
Other Communication: Public Affairs, Phone: 613-541-5010, ext. 8251

Equipped with a fleet of CH-146 Griffons, 1 Wing supports the Canadian Army by airlifting troops & equipment around the world. The headquarters for 1 Wing is situated in Kingston, with seven tactical helicopter & training squadrons throughout Canada.
The following squadrons are part of 1 Wing: 403 Helicopter Operational Training Squadron at Gagetown, New Brunswick; 430 Escadron tactique d'helicoptères at Valcartier, Québec; 438 Escadron tactique d'helicoptères at St-Hubert, Québec; 427 Special Operations Aviation Squadron & 450 Tactical Helicopter Squadron at Petawawa, Ontario; 400 Tactical Helicopter Squadron; & 408 Tactical Helicopter Squadron at Edmonton, Alberta.

Wing Commander, Col Scott Clancy, OMM, MSM, CD

Canadian Forces Base Moose Jaw: 15 Wing (CFB Moose Jaw) / Base des Forces canadiennes Moose Jaw: 15e escadre (BFC Moose Jaw)
PO Box 5000 Moose Jaw, SK S6H 7Z8

15wingpao@forces.gc.ca
www.rcaf-arc.forces.gc.ca/en/15-wing/index.page
Other Communication: Public Affairs, Phone: 306-694-2823, Fax: 306-694-2880

The Moose Jaw Saskatchewan base is home to the military air demonstration team, the Canadian Forces Snowbirds, 2 Canadian Forces Flying Training School, 3 Canadian Forces Flying Training School, & the North Atlantic Treaty Organization (NATO) Flying Training in Canada program.

Wing Commander, Col A.R. Day

Canadian Forces Base North Bay: 22 Wing (CFB North Bay) / Base des Forces canadiennes North Bay: 22e escadre (BFC North Bay)
General Delivery, Hornell Heights, ON POH 1PO

Tel: 705-494-2011; *Fax:* 705-494-6261
22WgPublicAffairsOff@forces.gc.ca
www.rcaf-arc.forces.gc.ca/en/22-wing/index.page

The role of 22 Wing North Bay is the provision of surveillance, identification, control, & warning for the aerospace defence of Canada & North Americ. Radar information is received via satellite from the North Warning System across the Canadian Arctic, coastal radars on the east & west coasts of Canada, & Airborne Warning & Control System Aircraft. Members of 21 Aerospace Control & Warning Squadron are on guard every hour of every day. 51 Aerospace Control & Warning Operational Training Squadron is also located at North Bay.

Wing Commander, Col Henrik N. Smith, CD

Canadian Forces Base Shearwater: 12 Wing (CFB Shearwater) / Base des Forces canadiennes Shearwater: 12e escadre (BFC Shearwater)
PO Box 5000 Stn. Main, Shearwater, NS B0J 3A0

www.rcaf-arc.forces.gc.ca/en/12-wing/index.page
Other Communication: Public Affairs, Phone: 902-720-1996

12 Wing Shearwater supports the Navy with helicopter air detachments for both domestic & international operations. Helicopter air detachments deploy with Navy ships. Operations in recent years have included Operation LAMA to help Newfoundland communities affected by Hurricane Igor, Operation HESTIA to assist persons affected by the earthquake in Haiti, & Operation SAIPH to counter piracy activity off the Horn of Africa.

Wing Commander, Col P.C. Allan, CD

Canadian Forces Base Trenton: 8 Wing (CFB Trenton) / Base des Forces canadiennes Trenton: 8e escadre (BFC Trenton)
PO Box 1000 Stn. Forces, Astra, ON K0K 3W0

Tel: 613-392-2811
www.rcaf-arc.forces.gc.ca/en/8-wing/index.page
Other Communication: Public Affairs, Phone: 613-392-2811, ext. 4565

8 Wing at CFB Trenton conducts search & rescue operations for a region under the jurisdiction of the Joint Rescue Coordination Centre Trenton. The Wing is also engaged in airlifting troops, equipment, supplies, & humanitarian aid throughout the world. CFB Trenton also hosts the parachute demonstration team known as the Skyhawks.

Wing Commander, Col C. Keiver, MSM, CD

Canadian Forces Base Winnipeg: 17 Wing (CFB Winnnipeg) / Base des Forces canadiennes Winnipeg: 17e escadre (BFC Winnipeg)
PO Box 17000 Stn. Forces, Winnipeg, MB R3J 3Y5
PubAffairs@forces.gc.ca
www.rcaf-arc.forces.gc.ca/en/17-wing/index.page
Other Communication: Public Affairs, Phone: 204-833-2500, ext. 6499, Fax: 204-833-2594
17 Wing Winnipeg supports units from the border between Alberta & Saskatchewan to Thunder Bay Ontario, & from the high Arctic to the 49th Parallel.
Command elements include 1 Canadian Air Division / Canadian North American Aerospace Defense Command (NORAD) Region Headquarters, 2 Canadian Air Division / Air Force Training & Doctrine, & 38 Canadian Brigade Group Headquarters.
The Wing also comprises the following training schools: 1 Canadian Forces Flying Training School; The Canadian Forces School of Aerospace Studies; THe Canadian Forces School of Meteorology; & The Canadian Forces School of Survival & Aeromedical Training.
Wing Commander, Col Andy Cook

Royal Canadian Navy (RCN) / Marine royale canadienne (MRC)
National Defence HQ, MGen George R. Pearkes Building, 101 Colonel By Dr., Ottawa, ON K1A 0K2
information@forces.gc.ca
www.navy-marine.forces.gc.ca
Other Communication: Public Affairs, Phone: 613-995-2534, Toll free: 1-888-995-2534
twitter.com/rcn_mrc
www.youtube.com/user/RoyalCanadianNavy
The Royal Canadian Navy carries out the following mission: to provide a multipurpose, combat-capable force; to exercise sovereignty over Canadian waters; to monitor & safeguard Canada's maritime approaches; to protect offshore natural resources; & to contribute to global security.
The following are some of the Royal Canadian Navy's recent operations: participation in counter-narcotic operations in the Caribbean Basin; joint North Atlantic Treaty Organization training exercises in the Black Sea; & participation in Operation Artimis, counterterrorism & maritime security operations in the Red Sea, the Gulf of Aden, the Gulf of Oman & the Indian Ocean.
Commander of the Royal Canadian Navy, VAdm M.A.G. Norman, CMM, CD
Chief Petty Officer of the Navy, CPO1 Tom Riefesel, CD

Maritime Forces Atlantic (MARLANT) / Forces maritimes de l'Atlantique (FMARA)
Maritime Forces Atlantic Headquarters, PO Box 99000 Stn. Forces, Halifax, NS B3K 5X5
www.navy-marine.forces.gc.ca/en/about/structure-marlant-home.page
Other Communication: Public Affairs, Fax: 902-452-5280; Media Inquiries, Phone: 902-427-3766
Maritime Forces Atlantic consists of the Her Majesty's Canadian (HMC) Dockyard, CFB Stadacona, the CF Station at St. John's, & the Atlantic Fleet of ships.
The Commander of Maritime Forces Atlantic carries out the following responsibitlities: generation of ships & sailors that can respond to events that affect Canadian interests; command of the Royal Canadian Navy's Atlantic Fleet & the Halifax Search & Rescue Region; support to government departments & agencies in areas such as fisheries protection & environmental monitoring; & support for members of the sea, air, & army cadets in the Atlantic provinces.
Commander, Maritime Forces Atlantic; Commander, Joint Task Force Atlantic, RAdm John Newton, OMM, MSM, CD
Formation Chief Petty Officer, CPO1 Pierre Auger

Maritime Forces Pacific (MARPAC) / Forces maritimes du Pacifique (FMARP)
Maritime Forces Pacific Headquarters, PO Box 17000 Stn. Forces, Victoria, BC V9A 7N2
www.navy-marine.forces.gc.ca/en/about/structure-marpac-home.page
Other Communication: Public Affairs, Phone: 250-363-5789, Fax: 250-363-5202
twitter.com/marpac
www.facebook.com/maritime.forces.pacific
www.youtube.com/navywebmaster
Maritime Forces Pacific consists of the following organizations: Joint Task Force (Pacific); 443 Maritime Helicopter Squadron; Joint Rescue Co-ordination Centre Victoria; Regional Joint Operations Centre (Pacific); VENTURE, The Naval Officers Training Centre; Canadian Forces Fleet School Equimalt; Regional Cadet Support Unit (Pacific); RAVEN Aboriginal Youth Initiative; Canadian Forces Ammunition Depot Rocky Point; & the Victoria In-Service Support Contract On-Site Management Team, in support of Canadian Submarine Extended Docking Work Periods.
Commander, Maritime Forces Pacific, RAdm Gilles Couturier, OMM, CD
Maritime Forces Pacific Chief Petty Officer, CPO1 M. Feltham, MMM, CD

The Naval Reserve / La Réserve navale
Naval Reserve Headquarters, PO Box 1000 Stn. Forces, Courcelette, QC G0A 4Z0
www.navy-marine.forces.gc.ca/en/about/structure-navres-home.page
Other Communication: Public Affairs, Phone: 418-694-5560, ext. 5303, Fax: 418-694-5377
Naval Reservists serve on a part time basis to augment the Regular Force. They do not have to participate in missions overseas. Roles for The Naval Reserve include the operation of Maritime Coastal Defence Vessels, port security, diving, & public relations.
Commander, Naval Reserve, Cmdre M.B. Mulkins, OMM, CD
Formation Chief, CPO1 David R. Arsenault, MMM, CD

Canadian Forces Base Esquimalt (CFB Equimalt) / Base des Forces canadiennes Esquimalt (BFC Esquimalt)
PO Box 17000 Stn. Forces, Victoria, BC V9A 7N2
cfbesquimalt@outlook.com
Other Communication: Public Affairs, Phone: 250-363-4006, Fax: 250-363-5527
CFB Esquimalt is home to the Canadian Pacific Naval Fleet. The base provides support services to ships & personnel of the Martime Forces Pacific & the Joint Task Force Pacific. CFB Esquimalt also features organizations such as the the Naval Officers Training Centre, the Canadian Forces Fleet School, the Port Operations & Emergency Services Branch, & Canadian Forces Health Services Centre (Pacific).

Canadian Forces Base Halifax (CFB Halifax) / Base des Forces canadiennes Halifax (BFC Halifax)
PO Box 99000 Stn. Forces, Halifax, NS B3K 5X5
Other Communication: Public Affairs, Fax: 902-427-2218; Media Request Line: 902-427-3766
CFB Halifax is the home port of the Atlantic Fleet. The base provides harbour support, emergency response services, logistics, environmental management, & construction engineering to Maritime Forces Atlantic.

Canadian Forces Station St. John's (CFS St. John's) / Station des Forces canadiennes St. John's (SFC St. John's)
115 The Boulevard, St. John's, NL A1A 0P5
Tel: 709-773-3900
www.cg.cfpsa.ca
Canadian Forces Station St. John's supports Royal Canadian Navy personnel as they work to protect Canada's Atlantic waters. The station also hosts training for sea, air & army cadets.

Canadian Joint Operations Command (CJOC) / Commandement des opérations interarmées du Canada (COIC)
National Defence Headquarters, MGen George R. Pearkes Bldg., 101 Colonel By Dr., Ottawa, ON K1A 0K2
Toll-Free: 866-377-0811
www.forces.gc.ca/en/operations.page
Other Communication: Public Affairs, Phone: 613-996-2353, Fax: 613-996-8330
twitter.com/CFOperations
www.flickr.com/photos/cfoperations
Canadian Joint Operations Command of the Canadian Forces uses an integrated command structure to develop, generate, & integrate joint force capabilities in order to conduct operations in North America & throughout the world.
Canadian Joint Operations Command consists of the following: headquarters in Ottawa, Ontario; regional Joint Task Force headquarters throughout Canada; units that make up the Canadian Forces Joint Operational Support Group across Canada; task forces deployed on continental operations in Canada & North America; & task forces deployed on expeditionary operations throughout the world.
Commander, Canadian Joint Operations Command, LGen Stephen Bowes

Canadian Special Operations Forces Command (CANSOFCOM) / Commandement des Forces d'opérations spéciales du Canada (COMFOSCAN)
CANSOFCOM Public Affairs, 101 Colonel By Dr., Ottawa, ON K1A 0K2
Toll-Free: 866-377-0811
www.forces.gc.ca/en/operations-special-forces/index.page
Other Communication: Public Affairs, Phone: 613-996-2353, Fax: 613-996-8330
Canadian Special Operations Forces Command is engaged in the following strategic tasks: generating deployable Special Operations Forces; developing the capabilities of Special Operation Forces; commanding Special Operations Forces; giving advice on special operations to the Chief of the Defence Staff & other Canadian Forces commanders; & maintaining relationships with allied special operations forces & security partners.
Canadian Special Operations Forces Command is comprised of the following organizations: Joint Task Force 2; 427 Special Operations Aviation Squadron; Canadian Joint Incident Response Unit; & Canadian Special Operations Regiment.
Examples of operational tasks performed by personnel of the Canadian Special Operations Forces Command include the following: maritime counter-terrorism; hostage rescue; support for non-combatant evacuation operations; & protection of Government of Canada personnel.
Commander, Canadian Special Operations Forces, Command Headquarters, Maj-Gen Mike Rouleau, OMM, MSC, CD

National Energy Board (NEB) / Office national de l'énergie (ONE)

517 - 10 Ave. SW, Calgary, AB T2R 0A8
Tel: 403-292-4800; *Fax:* 403-292-5503
Toll-Free: 800-899-1265
TTY: 800-632-1663
www.neb-one.gc.ca
Other Communication: Toll-free Fax: 1-877-288-8803
twitter.com/nebcanada
www.youtube.com/user/NationalEnergyBoard
Federal regulatory tribunal whose powers include: authorizing oil, natural gas & electricity exploration; certifying interprovincial & international pipelines & designated power lines; & setting tolls & tariffs for oil & gas pipelines under federal jurisdiction. The NEB reviews Canadian supply of all major commodities, with emphasis on electricity, oil, natural gas, & oil & natural gas by-products. It also reviews the demand for Canadian energy in Canada & in export markets. In addition to its regulatory role, the NEB is responsible for advising the government on the development & use of energy resources. Its responsibilities include regulating exploration, development & production of oil & gas on frontier lands in a manner that promotes worker safety, environmental protection & resource conservation. The NEB is responsible for environmental matters relating to the construction & operation of facilities & programs within its jurisdiction. Its environmental activities are carried out in three phases: The first phase involves evaluating the potential environmental effects of proposed projects. In the second phase, the environment is protected through monitoring & enforcement of terms & conditions attached to project approval. The third phase include s ongoing monitoring of operations to ensure that cleanup, restoration & maintenance of sites & rights of way are conducted to acceptable standards. The Board also verifies that emergency response plans are in place & that it or the operator can respond immediately to any incidents.
Chair & Chief Executive Officer, Peter Watson

National Film Board of Canada (NFB) / Office national du film du Canada (ONF)

Operational Headquarters, Norman McLaren Building, 3155, ch de la Côte-de-Liesse, CP 1600 Succ Centre-ville, Montréal, QC H3C 3H5
Tél: 514-283-9000
Ligne sans frais: 800-267-7710
www.onf-nfb.gc.ca
Autres nombres: Alt. URL: www.nfb.ca
twitter.com/thenfb
www.facebook.com/nfb.ca
www.youtube.com/nfb
Created by an act of Parliament in 1939, the National Film Board is Canada's public producer & distributor of audiovisual works that feature distinctive & innovative Canadian content. The federal cultural agency works to achieve its mandate to produce, distribute, & promote Canadian films, in accordance with the *National Film Act*. The National Film Board specializes in documentaries about social issues, animated films, & alternative drama that offer a unique Canadian perpective for Canadians & other countries.
Canadians can access National Film Board productions in both English & French in each region of the country through public libraries that hold collections of National Film Board films & an online "Screening Room". Works can also be viewed on television, in theatres, & on mobile devices.
The National Film Board carries out its mission within the Department of Canadian Heritage.

Government Film Commissioner; Chair, National Film Board of Canada, Claude Joli-Coeur
Tel: 514-283-9245

Director General, Creation & Innovation, André Picard
Tel: 514-242-0376

Director General, Finance, Operations, & Technology, Luisa Frate
Tel: 514-283-9051

Director General, French Program, Michèle Bélanger
Tel: 514-283-9285

Director General, Legal & Human Resources Services, François Tremblay
Tel: 438-938-3670

Director General, English Program, Michelle van Beusekom
Tel: 514-242-0376

National Film Board of Canada Studios
Edmonton - North West Centre (English)
#100, 10815 - 104 Ave., Edmonton, AB T5J 4N6
Tel: 780-495-3013; *Fax:* 780-495-6412
northwest@nfb.ca
Executive Producer, David Christensen
Tel: 780-495-3015
Halifax - Atlantic Centre (English)
Cornwallis House, #201, 5475 Spring Garden Rd., Halifax, NS B3J 3T2
Tel: 902-426-6000; *Fax:* 902-426-8901
atlantic@nfb.ca
Executive Producer, Kent Martin
Tel: 902-426-7351
Moncton - Canadian Francophonie Studio - Acadie (French)
Heritage Court, #100, 95 Foundry St., Moncton, NB E1C 5H7
Tel: 506-851-6104; *Fax:* 506-851-2246
Toll-Free: 866-663-8331
infofrancophonieacadie@nfb.ca
Executive Producer, Jacques Turgeon
Tel: 506-851-6105
Montréal - Digital Studio (French)
3155, ch de la Côte-de-Liesse, Montréal, QC H4N 2N4
Tel: 514-283-0733; *Fax:* 514-283-6403
Executive Producer, Hugues Sweeney
h.sweeney@onf.ca
Montréal - English Animation Studio
3155, ch de la Côte-de-Liesse, Montréal, QC H4N 2N4
Tel: 514-261-1650; *Fax:* 514-283-3211
animation@nfb.ca
Executive Producer, Michael Fukushima
Montréal - French Animation & Youth Studio (French)
3155, ch de la Côte-de-Liesse, Montréal, QC H4N 2N4
Tel: 514-283-9332; *Fax:* 514-283-4443
animation@nfb.ca
Executive Producer & Producer, Julie Roy
Montréal - Québec Centre (English)
3155, ch de la Côte-de-Liesse, Montréal, QC H4N 2N4
Tel: 514-827-5048
quebeccentre@nfb.ca
Montréal - Québec Studio (French)
3155, ch de la Côte-de-Liesse, Montréal, QC H4N 2N4
Tel: 514-496-1171; *Fax:* 514-283-7914
studioquebec@onf.ca
Executive Producer & Producer, Colette Loumède
St. John's - Atlantic Centre (English)
#102, 28 Cochrane St., St. John's, NL A1C 3L3
Tel: 709-763-0425
atlantic@nfb.ca
Executive Producer, Annette Clarke
Toronto - Canadian Francophonie Studio (French)
150 John St., 3rd Fl., Toronto, ON M5V 3C3
Tel: 416-973-5382; *Fax:* 416-973-2594
Toll-Free: 866-663-7668
infofrancophonie@nfb.ca
Executive Producer, Dominic Desjardins
Toronto - Ontario Centre (English)
150 John St., 3rd Fl., Toronto, ON M5V 3C3
Tel: 416-973-6856; *Fax:* 416-973-9640
ontarioinfo@nfb.ca
Executive Producer, Anita Lee
Vancouver - Digital Studio (English)
#250, 351 Abbott St., Vancouver, BC V6B 0G6
Tel: 604-666-3838
interactiveproposals@nfb.ca
Executive Producer, Loc Dao
Vancouver - Pacific & Yukon Centre (English)
#250, 351 Abbott St., Vancouver, BC V6B 0G6
Executive Producer, Shirley Vercruysse
s.vercruysse@nfb.ca
Winnipeg - North West Centre (English)
145 McDermot Ave., Winnipeg, MB R3B 0R9
Tel: 204-983-5852; *Fax:* 204-983-0742
northwest@nfb.ca

National Gallery of Canada (NGC) / Musée des Beaux-Arts du Canada (MBAC)

380 Sussex Dr., PO Box 427 Stn. A, Ottawa, ON K1N 9N4
Tel: 613-990-1985; *Fax:* 613-993-4385
Toll-Free: 800-319-2787
TTY: 613-990-0777
info@gallery.ca
www.gallery.ca
Other Communication: Box Office, Phone: 1-888-541-8888; Group Tours, Phone: 613-990-4888; Library, Phone: 613-998-8949, E-mail: erefel@gallery.ca; Archives, Phone: 613-990-0597
twitter.com/gallerydotca
www.facebook.com/nationalgallerycanada
www.youtube.com/user/ngcmedia

The National Gallery of Canada contains the most comprehensive collection of contemporary & historic Canadian art. The collection is accessible to the public for appreciation, advancement of knowledge, & research.
The Board of Trustees of the National Gallery of Canada serves as the gallery's governing body & acts in accordance with the *Museums Act*. The Board, which consists of eleven members, is assisted by the following committees: the Executive Committee; the Acquisitions Committee; the Audit & Finance Committee; the Governance & Nominating Committee; the Human Resources Committee; & the Porgrammes & Advancement Committee. The Board of Trustees reports to Parliament through the Minister of Canadian Heritage & Official Languages.

Chair, Michael J. Tims
Vice-Chair, Harriet E. Walker
Chief Executive Officer & Director, Marc Mayer
Chief Curator; Deputy Director, Collections, Research & Education, Paul Lang
Chief Financial Officer & Deputy Director, Administration, Julie Peckham
Deputy Director, Advancement & Public Engagement, Jean-François Bilodeau
Director, Conservation & Technical Research, Stephen Gritt
Tel: 613-990-1941
Director, Human Resources, Sylvie Sarault
Director, Facilities Planning Management, Edmond Richard
Tel: 613-993-9355
Chief, Bookstore, Patrick Aubin
Tel: 613-990-8566
Chief, Technical Services, Jean-François Castonguay
Tel: 613-990-4998
Chief, Finance, M.J. Lacombe
Chief, Design Services, Gordon Filewych
Tel: 613-990-8908
Chief, Information Technology Systems, Nigel Holmes
Tel: 613-990-2453
Chief, Restoration & Conservation, John McElhone
Tel: 613-991-0011
Chief, Publications & Copyright, Ivan Parisien
Tel: 613-990-0532
Chief, Education & Public Programs, Megan Richardson
Tel: 613-990-0574
Chief, Protection Services, Gary Rousseau
Tel: 613-990-6432
Chief, Collections Management & Outreach, Stacey Wakeford
Chief, Strategic Management, Christine Sadler
Tel: 613-990-7549
Chief, Strategic Planning & Risk Management, Margaret Skulskau
Tel: 613-990-3483
Chief, Visitor Services, Léo Tousignant
Tel: 613-990-5572
Chief, Membership & Annual Giving, Taylor van Blokland
Curator, Contemporary Art, Josée Drouin-Brisebois
Tel: 613-990-7645
Curator, Canadian Art, Katerina Atanassova
Curator, Indigenous Art, Greg Hill
Tel: 613-949-0327
Curator, Photographs Collection, Ann Thomas
Tel: 613-990-1961

National Joint Council (NJC) / Conseil national mixte (CNM)

C.D. Howe Building, 240 Sparks St. West, 7th Fl., PO Box 1525 Stn. B, Ottawa, ON K1P 5V2
Tel: 613-990-1805; *Fax:* 613-990-7071
email.courrier@njc-cnm.gc.ca
www.njc-cnm.gc.ca

The National Joint Council was established in 1944. As part of the Public Service of Canada, the Council provides a forum for consultation on workplace policies & information sharing between public service bargaining agents & the government as employer.
The parties work together to resolve workplace problems & to establish terms of employment. The National Joint Council's working committees consist of representatives from both sides of the Council. The following committees address labour relations issues: Executive; Foreign Service Directives; Government Travel; Isolated Posts & Government Housing; Joint Employment Equity; Occupational Health & Safety; Official Languages; Relocation; Service-Wide Committee on Occupational Health & Safety; Union Management Relations; & Work Force Adjustment.

General Secretary, Deborah Cooper
Deborah.Cooper@njc-cnm.gc.ca
Committee Advisor, Joint Employment Equity Committtee, Government Travel Committee, & Foreign Service Directives Committee, Jennifer Purdy
Jennifer.Purdy@njc-cnm.gc.ca
Secretary to the NJC & Manager, NJC Operations, Roxanne Lépine
Tel: 613-990-1806; *Fax:* 613-990-7071
Roxanne.Lepine@njc-cnm.gc.ca
Committee Advisor, Occupational Health & Safety Committee, Service-Wide Committee on Occupational Health & Safety, Relocation Committee, Official Languages Committee & Work Force Adjustment Committee, Virginie Martel
Virginie.Martel@njc-cnm.gc.ca
Committee Advisor, Isolated Posts & Government Housing Committee, Dental Care Board of Management, & Disability Insurance Board of Management, Catherine Molina
Catherine.Molina@njc-cnm.gc.ca

National Research Council Canada (NRC) / Conseil national de recherches Canada (CNRC)

Building M-58, 1200 Montreal Rd., Ottawa, ON K1A 0R6
Tel: 613-993-9101; *Fax:* 613-952-9907
Toll-Free: 877-672-2672
TTY: 613-949-3042
info@nrc-cnrc.gc.ca
www.nrc-cnrc.gc.ca
Other Communication: Media Relations, Toll-free Phone: 1-855-282-1637; E-mail: media@nrc-cnrc.gc.ca
twitter.com/nrc_cnrc
www.linkedin.com/company/8417
www.youtube.com/researchcouncilcan

The National Research Council is the Government of Canada's agency for research & development. Reporting to Parliament is through the Minister of Industry. The Council works with partners & clients to meet industrial & societal needs, in accordance with the *National Research Council Act*.
Technical & advisory services are available to assist enterprises solve technical problems. The following are some examples of the specialized services available: analytical chemistry services, calibration services, cold regions techologies & services, molecular biology services, environmental hydraulics services, marine performance & evaluation services, flight test & evaluation services, surface transportation services, medical diagnostics, nuclear magnetic resonance services, & protein purification services.
The National Research Council encourages & engages in research & business partnerships. Licensing opportunities are available for research & development solutions.

Chair, Paul Thomas Jenkins
President, John R. McDougall
Tel: 613-993-2024
Acting Executive Vice-President, Pam Bjornson
Tel: 613-998-3664; *Fax:* 613-998-3839
Vice-President, Industrial Research Assistance Program, Bogdan Ciobanu
Tel: 613-993-0695; *Fax:* 613-954-0501
Vice-President, Human Resources, Isabelle Gingras
Tel: 613-993-9136; *Fax:* 613-952-6078
Isabelle.Gingras@canada.ca
Vice-President, Corporate Management; Chief Financial Officer, Michel A. Piché
Tel: 613-991-5457; *Fax:* 613-952-1628
Vice-President, Engineering, Ian Potter
Tel: 613-949-5955; *Fax:* 613-949-5987
Vice-President, Life Sciences, Roman Szumski
Tel: 613-993-9244; *Fax:* 613-954-2066
Vice-President, Emerging Technologies, Danial D. Wayner
Tel: 613-998-5404; *Fax:* 613-949-1314
Secretary General, Dick Bourgeois-Doyle
Tel: 613-993-1906; *Fax:* 613-991-0398
Chief Audit & Evaluation Executive, Alexandra Dagger
Tel: 613-993-9962; *Fax:* 613-941-0986
Acting Director General, Information Technology Services, Marc Dabros
Tel: 613-991-3199; *Fax:* 613-954-2561
Director General, Planning & Reporting Services, Gary Fudge
Tel: 613-949-0542; *Fax:* 613-949-7539

Director General, Administrative Services & Property Management, Frank Jefferies
Tel: 613-993-6835; *Fax:* 613-957-9828
Director General, Finance, Gail McLellan
Tel: 613-993-5673; *Fax:* 613-954-5884
Director General, Communications Branch, Andrew Norgaard
Tel: 613-990-7438; *Fax:* 613-952-9907
Acting Director General, Knowledge Management, Kathleen O'Connell
Tel: 613-993-2341; *Fax:* 613-952-9112
Director General, Government & International Relations, Judith Young
Tel: 613-993-4758; *Fax:* 613-941-0986
Acting Director General, Design & Fabrication Services, Pierre Mayette
Tel: 613-993-7460
pierre.mayette@canada.ca
General Manager, Information & Communications Technologies, François Cordeau
Tel: 613-993-4444; *Fax:* 613-949-1325
Acting General Manager, Human Health Therapeutics, Bernard Massie
Tel: 514-496-6131
bernard.massie@canada.ca
General Manager, Automotive & Surface Transportation, Michel Dumoulin
Tel: 450-641-5181; *Fax:* 450-641-5101
General Manager, NRC Herzberg Astronomy & Astrophysics, Gregory Fahlman
Tel: 250-363-0040; *Fax:* 250-363-8483
General Manager, Aerospace, Jerzy Komorowski
Tel: 613-993-0141; *Fax:* 613-952-7214
General Manager, Aquatic & Crop Resource Development, Denise LeBlanc
Tel: 902-426-2496; *Fax:* 902-426-8514
General Manager, Ocean, Coastal & River Engineering, Terry Lindstrom
Tel: 613-993-2417; *Fax:* 613-952-7679
General Manager, Energy, Mining & Environment, Andrew Reynolds
Tel: 604-221-3024; *Fax:* 604-221-3002
General Manager, Measurement Science & Standards, Alan Steele
Tel: 613-993-9384; *Fax:* 613-952-8154
General Manager, Security & Disruptive Technologies, Duncan Stewart
Tel: 613-990-0915
General Manager, Construction, Richard Tremblay
richard.tremblay5@canada.ca
Acting General Manager, Medical Devices, Tristan Booth
Tel: 514-496-6251
tristan.booth@canada.ca

National Research Council Canada - National Science Library / Bibliothèque scientifique nationale
1200 Montreal Rd., Ottawa, ON K1A 0R6
Tel: 613-998-8544; *Fax:* 613-998-2399
Toll-Free: 800-668-1222
NRC.KMHelpdesk-BureaudaideGS.CNRC@nrc-cnrc.gc.ca
nsl-bsn.nrc-cnrc.gc.ca
www.facebook.com/cisti.icist
Formerly known as the Canada Institute for Scientific & Technical Information (l'Institut canadien de l'information scientifique et technique), the National Science Library was founded in 1924. Under the *National Research Council Act*the NRC is mandated to operate & maintain a national library. The Library supports Canada's research, innovation, & health communities by supplying resources & services to aid in discoveries & commercialization.
The main library, located in Ottawa, is open to the public (all branch libraries across Canada were closed by the end of 2012). Library users have online access to the NRC-CISTI Public Catalogue in order to search for & order print & electronic holdings in the areas of science, technology, engineering, & medicine. Interlibrary Loan services are handled by Infotrieve. The Library features the following online services: DataCite Canada; DOCLINE in Canada; PubMed Central Canada; & the NRC Archives. The Archives service offers information about the development of scientific research at the Council & the history of science in Canada.
The National Science Library is governed by a Director General & an Advisory Board that comprises national & international stakeholders from the library, publishing, academic, & business sectors. Board members are appointed by the Council of the National Research Council Canada.
Director General, Knowledge Management, Kathleen M. O'Connell
Tel: 613-993-2341
kathleen.oconnell@canada.ca

National Research Council Canada - Industrial Research Assistance Program (NRC-IRAP) / Programme d'aide à la recherche industrielle (PARI)
1200 Montreal Rd., Ottawa, ON K1A 0R6
Fax: 613-952-1086
Toll-Free: 877-994-4727
publicinquiries.irap-pari@nrc-cnrc.gc.ca
www.nrc-cnrc.gc.ca/eng/irap/index.html
The Industrial Research Assistance Program offers advisory & funding services to help businesses with their research & development projects. Firms are assisted in both the development & commercialization of technologies.
For information about the Industrial Research Assistance Program or to consult an Industrial Technology Advisor, contact one of the regional offices located across Canada. Industrial Technology Advisors are available to support clients through each stage of their projects, by connecting firms with national & international industry experts & possible business partners.
Vice-President, Bogdan Ciobanu
Tel: 613-993-0695; *Fax:* 613-954-0501
Executive Director, National Office, Jason Charron
Tel: 613-998-2626
jason.charron@canada.ca
Director, Program Expertise, Alain Brizard
Tel: 613-990-9475; *Fax:* 613-952-1079
Director, Concierge Service, Christopher Labrador
Tel: 519-497-5121
Manager, Advisory Services, Kathy Keast
Tel: 705-671-4472; *Fax:* 705-671-4564
Manager, Program Development Office, Brian C. Wilson
Tel: 613-993-4089; *Fax:* 613-952-1086

IRAP Regional Offices

Boucherville - Québec Region
#111P, 75, boul de Mortagne, Boucherville, QC J4B 6Y4
Tel: 450-641-5300; *Fax:* 450-641-5301
In Québec, Industrial Technology Advisors have expertise in important industrial sectors located in the province, such as manufacturing, construction, software, & the environment.
Executive Director, Claude Attendu
Tel: 450-641-5305; *Fax:* 450-641-5301
Director, Québec East-West, Patrice Audet-Lapointe
Tel: 450-641-5324; *Fax:* 450-641-5301
Director, Québec Periphery, Yves Lamarche
Tel: 450-641-5804; *Fax:* 450-641-5301
Director, Québec Montréal, Richard O'Shaughnessey
Tel: 450-641-5314; *Fax:* 450-641-5301

Calgary - West Region
3608 - 33rd St. NW, Calgary, AB T2L 2A6
Tel: 403-292-6450; *Fax:* 403-292-6452
Toll-Free: 877-994-4727
Serves Alberta & the Northwest Territories. Specialists are available for the following key industrial sectors in the western region: energy, environmental technologies, agricultural & food sciences, construction, transportation, telecommunications, advanced chemisty & manufacturing, & health care & pharmaceuticals.
Executive Director, Drew McNaughton
Tel: 403-292-6460
Director, Robert Faulder
Tel: 403-292-6466; *Fax:* 403-292-6452

Charlottetown - Atlantic & Nunavut Region
550 University Ave., Charlottetown, PE C1A 4P3
Toll-Free: 877-994-4727
Director, Michelle C. Lazaratos
Tel: 902-566-7636; *Fax:* 902-566-7641

Edmonton - West Region
#208, 9650 - 20 Ave, Edmonton, AB T6N 1G1
Tel: 780-495-6509; *Fax:* 780-495-6510
Toll-Free: 877-994-4727
Serves Alberta & the Northwest Territories.
Director, Kashmir Gill
Tel: 780-495-2136; *Fax:* 780-495-6510

Halifax - Atlantic & Nunavut Region
1411 Oxford St., Halifax, NS B3H 3Z1
Fax: 902-426-1624
Toll-Free: 877-994-4727
The expertise of Industrial Technology Advisors in the Atlantic & Nunavut area covers both established & developing industrial sectors. Examples of areas where assistance is available include aquaculture, agriculture, wood products, manufacturing, telecommunications, & biotechnology.
Executive Director, Bradley C. Goodyear
Tel: 902-426-1055; *Fax:* 902-426-1624

Markham - Ontario Region
7271 Warden Ave., Markham, ON L3R 5X5
Director, Angelo Del Duca
Tel: 905-479-9034; *Fax:* 416-973-3253

Oakville - Ontario Region
#302, 690 Dorval Dr., Oakville, ON L6K 3W7

Ottawa - Ontario Region
Shirley's Bay, 3701 Carling Ave., Ottawa, ON K2H 8S2
Director, L.M. Plante
Tel: 613-998-6947; *Fax:* 613-949-0071

St. John's - Atlantic & Nunavut Region
Memorial University Campus, Arctic Ave., PO Box 12093 St. John's, NL A1B 3T5
Fax: 709-772-5067
Toll-Free: 877-994-4727
The St. John's office serves Newfoundland & Labrador & Nunavut.
Director, Kristi McBride
Tel: 709-743-7988; *Fax:* 709-772-5067

Toronto - Ontario Region
#903, 55 St. Clair Ave. East, Toronto, ON M4T 1M2
Fax: 416-973-4303
Toll-Free: 877-994-4727
Industrial Technology Advisors are located at offices throughout Ontario. They offer a full range of expertise in areas such as manufacturing, construction, software, electronics, manufacturing, medical devices, life sciences, & aerospace.
Executive Director, David Lisk
Tel: 416-973-4483; *Fax:* 416-973-4303
Director, Ontario St. Clair, Manfred Hubert
Tel: 416-952-4459; *Fax:* 416-973-4303

Winnipeg - West Region
435 Ellice Ave., Winnipeg, MB R3B 1Y6
Tel: 204-983-0092; *Fax:* 204-983-8835
Saskatoon - Saskatchewan Region: #4460, 110 Gymnasium Place, Saskatoon, SK S7N 0W9; Tel: 306-975-4748; Toll-Free: 1-877-994-4727; Fax: 306-975-4717
Director, Saskatoon, Brendan Reding
Tel: 306-975-4730; *Fax:* 306-975-4717
Director, Winnipeg, Vivian Sullivan
Tel: 204-984-6477; *Fax:* 204-983-8835

Vancouver - Pacific Region
#650, 1185 West Georgia St., Vancouver, BC V6E 4E6
Tel: 604-666-6062; *Fax:* 604-666-7204
British Columbia & the Yukon are served by Pacific region personnel. Expertise reflects the industrial activity in the area, such as mining, forestry, construction, industrial engineering, electronics, & information technologies.
Executive Director, Pacific Region, Christopher Ryan
Tel: 604-221-3163; *Fax:* 604-221-3101
Director, Pacific Kelowna, Byron D. De Kergommeaux
Tel: 250-712-4301; *Fax:* 250-712-4306
Director, Pacific Vancouver, Neil Bailey
Tel: 604-666-6365; *Fax:* 604-666-7204
Director, Pacific Vancouver, Olga Kargina
Tel: 604-666-7304; *Fax:* 604-666-7204
Director, Pacific Vancouver, James Wilkin
Tel: 604-666-6646; *Fax:* 604-666-7204

Waterloo - Ontario Region
Waterloo Research & Technology Park, 29 Hagey Blvd., Waterloo, ON N2L 6R5
Director, Tomas Matulis
Tel: 519-763-8046; *Fax:* 519-763-2112

National Research Council Canada - Research Facilities
nrc-cnrc.gc.ca/eng/solutions/facilities/index.html
The National Research Council provides Canadian businesses access to research facilities & research experts. The research infrastructure enables businesses to pursue research & development opportunities & to accelerate product development.

Advanced, Non-Linear Optical Imaging & Microscopy Facility (CARSLab) / Imagerie et microscopie optiques non linéaires de pointe (CARSLab)
100 Sussex Dr., Ottawa, ON K1N 5A2
CARSLab stands for Coherent Anti-Stokes Raman Scattering Laboratory. Clients are offered state-of-the-art multimodal imaging capability. Workshops & hands on training is available for person to learn more about the CARS technique. The CARSLab facility can be available to Centres of Research Excellence & other research groupings.
Contact, Aaron Rodericks
Tel: 613-998-5663
Aaron.Rodericks@nrc-cnrc.gc.ca

Aerospace Manufacturing Technologies Centre (AMTC) / Le centre de technologies de fabrication en aérospatiale
Campus Université de Montréal, 5145, av Decelles, Montréal, QC H3T 2B2
www.nrc-cnrc.gc.ca/eng/solutions/facilities/amtc_index.html
Industries are assisted in the implementation of advanced manufacturing methods for aerospace. Examples of technologies investigated include automation & robotics, metal

forming & joining, fabrication of composite structures, & material removal.
Contact, Matthew Tobin
Tel: 613-990-0765
Matthew.Tobin@nrc-cnrc.gc.ca

Cell Culture Pilot Plant / Usine pilote, culture cellulaire
c/o Montréal (av Royalmount) Research Facilities, 6100, av Royalmount, Montréal, QC H4P 2R2
Tél: 514-496-6100
The pilot plant offers expertise in viral infection processes, virus recovery & purification, cell culture in bioreactors, & HPLC assays.
Team Leader, Cell Culture Scale-Up, Sven Ansorge
Tel: 514-283-3915
Sven.Ansorge@cnrc-nrc.gc.ca

Aquatic & Crop Resource Development Industry Partnership Facility / Installation de partenariat de développment des cultures et des ressources aquatiques
550 University Ave., Charlottetown, PE C1A 4P3
Tel: 902-566-7000
The Industry Partnership Facility in Charlottetown serves scientists from industries with commercial potential for products connected to aquatic & crop resource development.
Contact, Paul Neima
Tel: 902-566-7444
Paul.Neima@nrc-cnrc.gc.ca
#232, 550 University Ave.
Charlottetown, PE C1A 4P3

Atacama Large Millimetre/submillimetre Array (ALMA) / Observatoire ALMA (Atacama Large Millimetre/submillimetre Array)
Santiago Central Office, Alonso de Córdova 3107, Vitacura - Santiago
www.almaobservatory.org
Other Communication: International Phone: 56-2-2467-6100
Secondary Address: Kilómetro 121, Carretera CH 23
Operations Support Facility
San Pedro de Atacama, Chile
twitter.com/ALMAObs
www.facebook.com/ALMA.Radiotelescope
www.youtube.com/user/almaobservatory
Located in Chile, the ALMA Observatory studies the millimetre & sub-millimetre universe at high angular resolution & with great sensitivity. It is funded & operated by an international partnership involving North America, Europe & East Asia. The NRC is partnered with the US National Radio Astronomy Observatory as part of the North American component of the project.
Contact, Gerald Schieven
Tel: 250-363-6919
gerald.schieven@nrc-cnrc.gc.ca

Automotive & Surface Transportation Facilities / Installations d'Automobile et transport de surface
Ottawa Uplands Research Facilities, 2320 Lester Rd., Ottawa, ON K1V 1S2
Tel: 613-998-9639
The Ottawa location of the National Research Council's Surface Transportation research facilities feature areas to test road, military, & rail vehicles & components. Examples of facilities include environmental chambers, the compression & tension facility, the heavy vehicle tilt facility, the rail vehicle impact facility, vibration testing facilities, as well as the railway, wheel, bearing, & brake facility.
Portfolio Business Advisor, Craig A. Ceppetelli, BSc., MBA
Tel: 613-998-9388
Craig.Ceppetelli@nrc-cnrc.gc.ca
Contact, Aluminium Technology Centre, Stéphan Simard
Tel: 418-545-5544
Stephan.Simard@cnrc-nrc.gc.ca
501, boul Université est
Saguenay, QC G7H 8C3
Contact, Wind Tunnel Testing Facilities, Matthew Tobin
Tel: 613-990-0765
Matthew.Tobin@nrc-cnrc.gc.ca
1200 Monteal Rd.
Ottawa, ON K1A 0R6

Canada-France-Hawaii Telescope (CFHT) / Télescope Canada-France-Hawaï (TCFH)
CFHT Corporation, #65, 1238 Mamalahoa Hwy., Kamuela, HI 96743 USA
Tel: 808-885-7944; *Fax:* 808-885-7288
info@cfht.hawaii.edu
www.cfht.hawaii.edu
twitter.com/CFHTelescope
www.facebook.com/cfhtelescope
Located in Hawaii, the CFHT is a joint facility of the NRC, the Centre National de la Recherche Scientifique, France, & the University of Hawaii.

Contact, J.J. Kavelaars
Tel: 250-363-8694
JJ.Kavelaars@nrc-cnrc.gc.ca

Canadian Astronomy Data Centre (CADC) / Centre canadien de données astronomiques (CCDA)
NRC Herzberg Astronomy & Astrophysics, 5071 West Saanich Rd., Victoria, BC V9E 2E7
Tel: 250-363-0001; *Fax:* 250-363-0045
cadc@nrc.gc.ca
www.cadc-ccda.hia-iha.nrc-cnrc.gc.ca
Established in 1986 by the NRC, through a grant from the Canadian Space Agency (CSA). Operates as one of three world-wide distribution centres for astronomical data obtained with the Hubble Space Telescope (HST).
General Manager, NRC Herzberg, Gregory Fahlman
Tel: 250-363-0040; *Fax:* 250-363-8483

Canadian Centre for Housing Technology (CCHT) / Centre canadien des technologies résidentielles
c/o National Research Council Canada, Building M-20, 1200 Montreal Rd., Ottawa, ON K1A 0R6
www.ccht-cctr.gc.ca
Operated jointly by the National Research Council, Natural Resources Canada, & the Canada Mortgage & Housing Corporation, the Canadian Centre for Housing Technology offers research & demonstrations related to innovative technology in housing. The present focus is upon energy efficiency & energy conversion systems.
Facilities on the six acre site include two research houses, the InfoCentre, & four serviced lots to develop & build new concepts. The testing facilities are available to the construction industry on a fee-for-service basis.
Contact, General & Project Inquiries, Mike Swinton
Tel: 613-993-9708
Mike.Swinton@nrc-cnrc.gc.ca

Canadian Photonics Fabrication Centre (CPFC) / Centre canadien de fabrication de dispositifs photoniques
c/o National Research Council Canada, Building M-50, 1200 Montreal Rd., Ottawa, ON K1A 0R6
Tel: 613-993-9101
The Canadian Photonics Fabrication Centre has test & measurement capabilities for experts to assist companies in the diagnosis of material & fabrication related problems.
Contact, George Ross
Tel: 613-949-3717
George.Ross@nrc-cnrc.gc.ca

Civil Infrastructure & Related Structures Testing Facilities / Installation d'essai des infrastructures civiles et des structures annexes
c/o National Research Council, 1200 Montreal Rd., Ottawa, ON K1A 0R6
Tel: 613-993-9101
Testing facilities are available to evaluate the design, performance, rehabilitation, & management of concrete structures & buried utilities.
Contact, Dino Zuppa
Tel: 613-949-0073
Dino.Zuppa@nrc-cnrc.gc.ca

Climatic Testing Facility / Installation d'essais climatiques
Ottawa Uplands Research Facilities, 2320 Lester Rd., Ottawa, ON K1V 1S2
Tel: 613-998-9639
Evaluates the performance of commercial & military equipment, vehicles, & components under severe climatic conditions.
Portfolio Business Advisor, Craig A. Ceppetelli, BSc., MBA
Tel: 613-998-9388
Craig.Ceppetelli@nrc-cnrc.gc.ca

Crops & Aquatic Growth Facilities / Installations pour la croissance des plantes et des algues
c/o National Research Council, 1200 Montreal Rd., Ottawa, ON K1A 0R6
Repeatable cultivation & growing conditions for plants & algae are provided to companies & collaborators. Facilities include sunrooms, a transgenic plant center, a crop greenhouse, conviron environmental growth chambers, wet labs, a chemostat laboratory, & aquatic greenhouses.
Contact, Paul Neima
Tel: 902-566-7444
Paul.Neima@nrc-cnrc.gc.ca

Dominion Astrophysical Observatory (DAO) / Observatoire fédéral d'astrophysique
NRC Herzberg Astronomy & Astrophysics, 5071 West Saanich Rd., Victoria, BC V9E 2E7
Tel: 250-363-0001
NRC.NSIHerzbergAstroInfoISN.CNRC@nrc-cnrc.gc.ca
Operating since 1916, the DAO operates the 1.8-metre Plaskett Telescope & the 1.2-metre telescope, featuring the high-resolution McKellar spectrograph.

General Manager, NRC Herzberg, Gregory Fahlman
Tel: 250-363-0040; *Fax:* 250-363-8483

Dominion Radio Astrophysical Observatory (DRAO) / Observatoire fédéral de radioastrophysique
717 White Lake Rd., PO Box 248 Penticton, BC V2A 6J9
Tel: 250-497-2300
NRC.DRAO-OFR.CNRC@nrc-cnrc.gc.ca
The DRAO operates three telescopes: a 26-metre fully steerable dish, a seven-antenna aperture synthesis array & a solar radio flux monitor.

Fire Safety Testing Facility / Installations d'essais en sécurité incendie
National Fire Laboratory, Bldg. U-96, Concession 8, Mississippi Mills, ON K0A 1A0
Tel: 613-993-9101
Secondary Address: 1200 Montreal Rd.
c/o National Research Council
Ottawa, ON K1A 0R6
The Mississippi Mills location offers a Burn Hall & 10-storey Smoke Tower complex with full-sized stair, elevator & service shafts.
The Ottawa location offers column, floor & wall test furnaces & an intermediate-scale furnace.
Contact, Dino Zuppa
Tel: 613-949-0073
Dino.Zuppa@nrc-cnrc.gc.ca

Gas Turbine Research Facility / Installation de recherche sur les turbines à gaz
c/o National Research Council, 1200 Montreal Rd., Ottawa, ON K1A 0R6
Tel: 613-993-9101
The National Research Council helps industries develop & evaluate gas turbine engines & components to meet operational, safety, & environmental requirements.
Contact, Matthew Tobin
Tel: 613-990-0765
Matthew.Tobin@nrc-cnrc.gc.ca

Gemini Observatory / Observatoire Gemini
670 N. A'ohoku Place, Hilo, HI 96720 USA
Tel: 808-974-2500; *Fax:* 808-974-2589
Secondary Address: Casilla 603
c/o AURA
La Serena, Chile
www.facebook.com/GeminiObservatory
Twin 8.1-metre diameter optical/infrared telescopes located in Hawaii & Chile, operated by a partnership of five countries: Canada, the US, Australia, Brazil & Argentina.
Contact, Dr. Stéphanie Côté
Stephanie.Cote@nrc-cnrc.gc.ca

Hydraulics Laboratories / Laboratoires hydrauliques
c/o National Research Council, 1200 Montreal Rd., Ottawa, ON K1A 0R6
The National Research Council operates hydraulics laboratories for applied research & commercial studies. Studies focus upon civil engineering hydraulics, port & harbour developments, coastal science & engineering, & offshore energy projects.

Hygrothermal Performance of Buildings Research Facilities / Les installations de recherche en performance hygrothermique
c/o National Research Council, 1200 Montreal Rd., Ottawa, ON K1A 0R6
Tel: 613-993-9101
The Envelope Environmental Exposure Facility has an automated environmental chamber, so that interior & exterior climatic conditions can be simulated. This testing can lead to improved design, construction, & operation of energy-efficient building systems.
The Guarded Hot Box Environmental Test Facility helps builders of wall systems & manufacturers of insulation determine the thermal resistance of products.
The Dynamic Roofing Facility is used to evaluate the dynamic wind uplift performance of roofing assemblies. The facility is important to manufacturers that want to sell their products in areas that experience high wind conditions, such as the southern & eastern coasts of North America.
Contact, Dino Zuppa
Tel: 613-949-0073
Dino.Zuppa@nrc-cnrc.gc.ca

Indoor Environment Testing Facilities / Installations d'essai sur l'environnement intérieur
c/o National Research Council, 1200 Montreal Rd., Ottawa, ON K1A 0R6
Tel: 613-993-9101
The National Research Council's indoor envrionment testing facilities include an indoor air testing facility, an indoor environment facility, a floor sound transmission testing facility, & a wall sound transmission testing facility. Through testing,

industries can develop technologies for the design & operation of energy-efficient, cost-effective, & healthy indoor environments.
Contact, Dino Zuppa
Tel: 613-949-0073
Dino.Zuppa@nrc-cnrc.gc.ca

Industrial Partnership Facility: Montréal (IPF) / Installation de partenariat industriel à Montréal
c/o Montréal (av Royalmount) Research Facilities, 6100, av Royalmount, Montréal, QC H4P 2R2
The scientific complex offers services to companies engaged in biotechnology research & development. Both large & small businesses have access to these advanced facilities & experts to create & test new technologies.
Property Officer, Québec, Leasing & Property, Louise Demers-Thorne
Tel: 514-496-1733
Louise.Demers-Thorne@cnrc-nrc.gc.ca

Marine Performance Evaluation & Testing Facilities / Installation d'essais et évaluation en performance marine
c/o National Research Council, 1200 Montreal Rd., Ottawa, ON K1A 0R6
St. John's Research FacilitiesPO Box 12093 Sta. St. John's, NL A1B 3T5
Marine performance evaluation & testing facilities in Ottawa, Ontario include the following: an ice tank, a large scale wave flume, a large area basin, a coastal wave basin, & a multidirectional wave basin.
The following facilities are located in St. John's Newfoundland & Labrador: cold room laboratories, a towing tank, an ice tank, & an offshore energy basin.
Research is conducted into problems involving marine environments, vessels, & structures.
Contact, Ottawa, Enzo Gardin
Tel: 613-991-2987
Enzo.Gardin@nrc-cnrc.gc.ca
Contact, St. John's, Mark Murphy
Tel: 709-772-2105
Mark.Murphy@nrc-cnrc.gc.ca

Material Emissions Testing Facilities / Laboratoire des émissions émanant des matériaux
c/o National Research Council, 1200 Montreal Rd., Ottawa, ON K1A 0R6
The materiel emissions testing facilities are able to measure the emission of volatile organic compounds from building materials & consumer products. Equipment is also capable of determining the efficiency of air cleaning devices.
Contact, Dino Zuppa
Tel: 613-949-0073
Dino.Zuppa@nrc-cnrc.gc.ca

Medical Device Facilities / Installations de dispositifs médicaux
Boucherville Research Facilities, 75, boul de Mortagne, Boucherville, QC J4B 6Y4
Tel: 450-641-5100
Secondary Address: 435 Ellice Ave.
Winnipeg Research Facilities
Winnipeg, MB R3B 1Y6
The National Research Council's medical device facilities offer assistance to healthcare organizations with research & development needs. Facilities are located in Boucherville Québec, Winnipeg Manitoba, & Halifax Nova Scotia.
The Boucherville site provides expertise in functional nanomaterials & virtual reality surgical planning for surgical oncology.
The Winnipeg facility's areas of interest include early stage disease diagnoses that are minially invasive & techology that reduces or eliminates hospital stays.
The Halifax locations focus upon translational neuroscience. Halifax's Neuroimaging Research Laboratory is situated at the QEII's Health Sciences Centre's Halifax Infirmary (#3900, 1796 Summer St, Halifax, NS B3H 3A7). The city's Clinicial Laboratory for Magnetoencephalography / Biomedical MRI Research is located at the IWK Health Centre (Goldbloom Pavillion, 5850 University Ave, Halifax, NS B3K 6R8).
Contact, Eileen Raymond
Tel: 514-496-6349
Eileen.Raymond@nrc-cnrc.gc.ca

Microbial Fermentation Pilot Plant / Usine pilote spécialisée en fermentation microbienne
c/o Montréal (av Royalmount) Research Facilities, 6100, av Royalmount, Montréal, QC H4P 2R2
Tel: 514-496-6100
Secondary Address: 100 Sussex Dr.
Sussex Drive Research Facilities
Ottawa, ON K1N 5A2
The following are some of the services in the areas of molecular biology, microbial physiology, & microbial fermentation technology offered by the pilot plant: training & scientific & technical guidance; testing new control & monitoring equipment; screening activities; analytical services to support bioprocessing operations; product purification; handling methanol-oxidizing microorganisms; & selection of recombinant strains such as E.coli.
Team Leader, Microbial Fermentation, Luke Masson
Tel: 514-496-3123
Luke.Masson@cnrc-nrc.gc.ca

Ocean Technology Enterprise Centre (OTEC) / Centre des entreprises de technologies océaniques
PO Box 12093 St. John's, NL A1B 3T5
Tel: 709-772-2469
Opened in 2003, the Ocean Technology Enterprise Centre conducts ocean engineering research to benefit the Canadian marine industry. The Centre, which is housed within the National Research Council's Industry Partnership Facility on the campus of Memorial University, provides facilities & expertise to assist ocean technology companies in the development of technologies.
Contact, Noel Murphy
Tel: 709-772-4939
Noel.Murphy@nrc-cnrc.gc.ca

Printable Electronics Labs / Le laboratoire du programme-phare Électronique imprimable
c/o National Research Council, 1200 Montreal Rd., Ottawa, ON K1A 0R6
Secondary Address: 75, boul de Mortagne
Boucherville Research Facilities
Boucherville, QC J4B 6Y4
Focuses on applications of state-of-the-art, multi-functional printing tools.
The Ottawa facility provides the following: large-scale inkjet printing; sheet-to-sheet gravure; flexographic & screen printing; organic & inorganic solution processing.
The Boucherville facility offers automated nano imprinting & nano embossing.
Contact, Michael Davison
Tel: 613-998-9414
Michael.Davison@nrc-cnrc.gc.ca

Waste Biotreatability Facility / Services d'évaluation de la biotraitabilité
c/o Montréal (av Royalmount) Research Facilities, 6100, av Royalmount, Montréal, QC H4P 2R2
The Waste Biotreatability Facility is engaged in the evaluation of organic waste for its biotreatability & its potential to produce energy such as hydrogen & methane. The facility is part of the Industrial Partnership Facility: Montréal.
Property Officer, Québec, Leasing & Property, Louise Demers-Thorne
Tel: 514-496-1733
Louise.Demers-Thorne@cnrc-nrc.gc.ca

Wind Tunnel Testing Facilities / Installations d'essais en souffleries
c/o National Research Council, 1200 Montreal Rd., Ottawa, ON K1A 0R6
To support the research of government, industries, & universities, the National Research Council provides six wind tunnels, plus experties in aerodynamic noise measurement, pressure sensitive paint technology, & flow mapping. Part of the Automotive & Surface Transportation Facilities.
Contact, Matthew Tobin
Tel: 613-990-0765
Matthew.Tobin@nrc-cnrc.gc.ca

Zebrafish Screening Facility
1411 Oxford St., Halifax, NS B3H 3Z1
Tel: 902-426-8332
Testing services are available for pharmacological & toxicology activity. The National Research Council's Zebrafish Screening Facility can be accessed by companies & research organizations by entering into a technical service agreement or research collaboration.
Contact, James De Pater
Tel: 613-614-9547
James.DePater@nrc-cnrc.gc.ca

National Search & Rescue Secretariat / Secrétariat national de recherches et sauvetage

269 Laurier Ave. West, 10th Fl., Ottawa, ON K1A 0P8
Fax: 613-996-3746
Toll-Free: 800-727-9414
questions@nss-snrs.gc.ca
www.nss.gc.ca
Provides a central managerial role in the overall coordination of search & rescue. It addresses program & policy issues related to the National Search & Rescue Program, & advises the Lead Minister for search & rescue.
Director, Dominik Breton
Tel: 613-996-2581
Senior Finance Officer/Comptroller, Finance & Administration, Paul Langelier
Tel: 613-989-9708; *Fax:* 613-996-3746
Chief, Non-Federal Programs, Policy & Programs, Vacant
Toll-free: 800-727-9414; *Fax:* 613-996-3746
Chief, Communications & Outreach, Manon Langlois
Tel: 613-996-6411; *Fax:* 613-996-3746

National Seniors Council (NSC) / Conseil national des aînés (CNA)

Phase IV, 8th Floor, Mail Stop 802, 140 Promenade du Portage, Gatineau, QC K1A 0J9
Fax: 819-953-9298
Toll-Free: 800-622-6232
TTY: 800-926-9105
www.seniorscouncil.gc.ca
The Council, formerly known as the National Advisory Council on Aging, advises the Minister of Employment & Social Development, the Minister of Health, & the Minister of State (Seniors) on issues related to the aging of the Canadian population & the quality of life of seniors. It reviews the needs & problems of seniors & recommends remedial action, liaises with other groups interested in aging, encourages public discussion & publishes & disseminates information on aging.
Chair, Andrew Wister

Natural Resources Canada (NRCan) / Ressources naturelles Canada (RNCan)

580 Booth St., Ottawa, ON K1A 0E4
Tel: 343-292-6096; *Fax:* 613-992-7211
TTY: 613-996-4397
www.nrcan.gc.ca
Other Communication: Media, Phone: 343-292-6100; E-mail: NRCan.media_relations-media_relations.RNCan@canada.ca
twitter.com/NRCan
www.youtube.com/user/NaturalResourcesCa
Advances development of Canada's economy by contributing to the development & use of Canada's mineral & energy resources in a manner consistent with federal environmental & social objectives; advances knowledge of the Canadian landmass through scientific & science-related activities.
Minister, Natural Resources, Hon. James Carr, O.M., P.C., B.A.
Tel: 613-992-9475; *Fax:* 613-992-9586
Jim.Carr@parl.gc.ca
Deputy Minister, Bob Hamilton
Tel: 343-292-6799; *Fax:* 613-992-3828
bob.hamilton@canada.ca
Parliamentary Secretary, Kim Rudd
Tel: 613-992-8585; *Fax:* 613-995-7536
Kim.Rudd@parl.gc.ca
Associate Deputy Minister, Michael Keenan
Tel: 343-292-6799; *Fax:* 613-992-3828
michael.keenan@canada.ca
Chief of Staff, Janet Annesley
Tel: 343-292-6837
janet.annesley@canada.ca
Chief Audit Executive, Christian Asselin
Tel: 343-292-8752; *Fax:* 613-992-8799
Christian.Asselin@NRCan-RNCan.gc.ca
Executive Director, Task Force on Energy Security, Prosperity & Sustainability, Gregory Jack
Tel: 613-943-5764; *Fax:* 613-992-1392
Gregory.Jack@NRCan-RNCan.gc.ca
#244, 155 Queen St., 2nd Fl.
Ottawa, ON K1A 0E4
Acting Director, Office of the Chief Scientist, Dr. Nabil Bouzoubaâ
Tel: 343-292-8727
nabil.bouzoubaa@canada.ca
Director, Operations, Northern Pipeline Agency, Vacant
Director, Communications, Laurel Munroe
Tel: 343-292-6837
laurel.munroe@canada.ca

Associated Agencies, Boards & Commissions:
•**National Energy Board**
See Entry Name Index for detailed listing.

Canadian Forest Service (CFS) / Service canadien des forêts
Tel: 613-995-0947; *Fax:* 613-947-7395
TTY: 613-996-4397
www.nrcan.gc.ca/forests
Promotes the sustainable development of Canada's forests & competitiveness of the Canadian forest sector for the well-being of present & future generations of Canadians. It focuses on forest science & technology, & related national policy coordination. The CFS maintains five research centres across the country that share responsibility for research in the areas of biodiversity; biotechnology; climate change; ecology &

ecosytems; entomology; forest conditions, monitoring & reporting; forest fires; forest & landscape management; pathology; silviculture & regeneration; & socioeconomics.

Assistant Deputy Minister, Glenn Mason
Tel: 343-292-8555; *Fax:* 613-947-7395
glenn.mason@canada.ca

Planning, Operations & Information Branch / Direction de la planification, des opérations et de l'information

Director General, Joanne Frappier
Tel: 343-292-8558; *Fax:* 613-947-9100
joanne.frappier@canada.ca

Policy, Economics & Industry Branch / Direction de la politique, de l'économie et de l'industrie

Acting Director General, Darcy Booth
Tel: 613-947-9051; *Fax:* 613-947-9020
Darcie.Booth@NRCan-RNCan.gc.ca

Science & Programs Branch / Direction des sciences et des programmes

Acting Director General, Mike Fullerton
Tel: 343-292-8588; *Fax:* 613-947-9035
mike.fullerton@canada.ca

CFS Regional Offices

Atlantic Forestry Centre (AFC) / Centre de foresterie de l'Atlantique (CFA)

1350 Regent St. South, PO Box 4000 Fredericton, NB E3B 5P7

Tel: 506-452-3500; *Fax:* 506-452-3525
www.nrcan.gc.ca/forests/research-centres/afc/13447

Responsible for the overall Canadian Forest Service operations & programs in the Atlantic region. Liaises & negotiates with provincial government, industry officials, & other sector-related senior management on behalf of the CFS in the region.

Regional Director General, Derek MacFarlane
Tel: 506-452-3508
Derek.MacFarlane@NRCan-RNCan.gc.ca

Canadian Wood Fibre Centre (CWFC) / Centre canadien sur la fibre de bois (CCFB)

580 Booth St., 7th Floor, Ottawa, ON K1A 0E4

Tel: 613-947-9001; *Fax:* 613-947-9033
www.nrcan.gc.ca/forests/research-centres/cwfc/13457

The Canadian Wood Fibre Centre (CWFC) brings together forest sector researchers to develop solutions for the Canadian forest sector's wood fibre related industries in an environmentally responsible manner. Its mission is to create innovative knowledge to expand the economic opportunities for the forest sector to benefit from Canadian wood fibre.

Executive Director, George Alexande Bruemmer
Tel: 613-947-7331; *Fax:* 613-947-8863
GeorgeAlexande.Bruemmer@NRCan-RNCan.gc.ca

Great Lakes Forestry Centre (GLFC) / Centre de foresterie des Grands Lacs (CFGL)

1219 Queen St. East, PO Box 490 Sault Ste Marie, ON P6A 2E5

Tel: 705-949-9461; *Fax:* 705-541-5700
www.nrcan.gc.ca/forests/research-centres/glfc/13459

Responsibilities include: forest research & regional forestry activities in Ontario; provides the primary federal focus for forestry in Ontario; emphasis on boreal mixed wood forest management & environmental impacts of pollutants & forestry practices; efforts also directed at the reduction of losses from insects, disease & fire; ecosystem dynamics & classification; nutrient problems & impacts from forestry practices; acid rain impacts (carbon dioxide/nitrogen oxide interactions).

Director General, David Nanang
Tel: 705-541-5555
David.Nanang@NRCan-RNCan.gc.ca

Laurentian Forestry Centre (LFC) / Centre de foresterie des Laurentides (CFL)

1055, rue du PEPS, CP 10380 Succ Sainte-Foy, Québec, QC G1V 4C7

www.nrcan.gc.ca/forests/research-centres/lfc/13473

Responsibilities include: increasing scientific & technical knowledge in the area of forest biology which includes biodiversity, tree biotechnology & advanced genetics, pest management methods, & in the area of forest ecosystem which cover forest ecosystem processes, effects of forestry practices, landscape management & climate change.

Director General, Jacinthe Leclerc
Tel: 418-648-5847
Jacinthe.Leclerc@RNCan-NRCan.gc.ca

Northern Forestry Centre (NFC) / Centre de foresterie du Nord (CFN)

5320 - 122 St., Edmonton, AB T6H 3S5

Tel: 780-435-7210; *Fax:* 780-435-7359
www.nrcan.gc.ca/forests/research-centres/nofc/13485

Responsibilities include: socio-economics & forest sociology; fire ecology, environment, & advanced fire management & prediction systems; climate change & forest interactions; carbon budget modeling; forest health, insect, & disease monitoring & management systems; remote sensing applications & landscape level classification systems; ecosystems productivity; biodiversity. Regional coordination of national programs relating to Model Forests & First Nation Forestry. Responsible for the direction of forestry programs in the provinces of Alberta, Saskatchewan, Manitoba & the NWT, including R&D, & four federal-provincial partnership agreements in forestry.

Director General, Michael Norton
Tel: 780-435-7202; *Fax:* 780-435-7396
michael.norton@canada.ca

Pacific Forestry Centre (PFC) / Centre de foresterie du Pacifique (CFP)

506 West Burnside Rd., Victoria, BC V8Z 1M5

Tel: 250-363-0600; *Fax:* 250-363-6004
www.nrcan.gc.ca/forests/research-centres/pfc/13489

Responsibilities include: forest management of federal lands; first nations programs; first nations land claims resource analysis; economic analysis of the regional forest sector (value-added, labour costs, & industrial sustainability); national strategic planning for the forestry practices & landscape management networks; science & technology programs in both forest biology (ecosystems processes, climate change, pest management, & tree biotechnology). Advises the CFS ADM on all forestry matters relating to the Pacific & Yukon region. The Mountain Pine Beetle Action Plan 2005-2010 set out strategies for confronting the infestation.

Director General, Judi Beck
Tel: 250-298-2300
judi.beck@nrcan-rncan.gc.ca

Corporate Management & Services Sector / Secteur de la gestion et des services intégrés

Fax: 613-922-8922

Assistant Deputy Minister, CMSS & Chief Financial Officer, Kami Ramcharan
Tel: 343-292-8168; *Fax:* 613-992-8922
kami.ramcharan@canada.ca

Director General, Finance & Procurement Branch, Marc Bélisle
Tel: 613-943-8763; *Fax:* 613-996-2151
Marc.Belisle@NRCan-RNCan.gc.ca

Director General & Chief Human Resources Officer, Cheri Crosby
Tel: 613-995-1261; *Fax:* 613-995-4289
Cheri.Crosby@NRCan-RNCan.gc.ca

Director General & Chief Information Officer, Chief Information Office & Security Branch, Pierre Ferland
Tel: 613-943-0469
Pierre.Ferland@NRCan-RNCan.gc.ca

Executive Director, Planning & Operations Branch, Kelly Morrison
Tel: 613-947-2758; *Fax:* 613-992-8922
Kelly.Morrison@NRCan-RNCan.gc.ca

Senior Director, Executive Services & Talent Management Division, Michel Brazeau
Tel: 613-947-8243; *Fax:* 613-947-2034
Michel.Brazeau@NRCan-RNCan.gc.ca

Senior Director, Workplace Services, Tambrae Knapp
Tel: 613-947-2039; *Fax:* 613-995-3800
Tambrae.Knapp@NRCan-RNCan.gc.ca

Earth Sciences Sector / Secteur des sciences de la Terre
588 Booth St., Ottawa, ON K1A 0Y7

ww.nrcan.gc.ca/earth-sciences

Provides Canadians with timely & reliable geomatics & geoscience knowledge, products & services of the highest standards & in the most cost-effective manner possible. The Earth Sciences Sector is a predominantly science- & technology-based sector & includes the Geological Survey of Canada, Geomatics Canada, & the Polar Continental Shelf Project. These groups are major contributors to the comprehensive geoscience knowledge base of Canada & provide surveying, mapping, remote sensing, & digital information services describing the Canadian landmass.

Chief Scientist & Assistant Deputy Minister, Judith Bossé
Tel: 343-292-6605; *Fax:* 613-995-1509
judith.bosse@canada.ca

Canada Centre for Mapping & Earth Observation / Centre canadien de cartographie et d'observation de la Terre
#212, 50 Place de la Cité, PO Box 162 Sherbrooke, QC J1H 4G9

Remote sensing data for Canada; development of remote sensing technology & applications in conjunction with the private sector, & in support of environmental monitoring; development of the Canadian geospatial data infrastructure for distribution of remote sensing & other geographical databases, in partnership with other departments; development of GIS applications.

Director General, Prashant Shukle
Tel: 613-759-1196; *Fax:* 613-759-1204
prashant.shukle@canada.ca

Geological Survey of Canada (GSC) / Commission géologique du Canada
601 Booth St., Ottawa, ON K1A 0E8

www.nrcan.gc.ca/earth-sciences

Geoscientific information & research, geoscience surveys, sustainable development of Canada's resources, environmental protection, technology innovation.

Director General, Central & Northern Canada Branch, Vacant

Director General, Atlantic & Western Canada Branch, Daniel Lebel
Tel: 613-992-1400; *Fax:* 613-995-6575
daniel.lebel@canada.ca

Science-Business Programs Advisor, Dan Richardson
Tel: 613-996-9151; *Fax:* 613-996-6575
dan.richardson@canada.ca

Surveyor General Branch - Geomatics Canada (SGB) / Direction de l'arpenteur général - Géomatique Canada (DAG)
#605, 9700 Jasper Ave., Edmonton, AB T5J 4C3

Tel: 780-495-2519; *Fax:* 780-495-4052
nrcan.gc.ca/earth-sciences/geomatics/canada-lands-surveys/10780

Surveys Canadian lands & waters; prepares & distributes topographic, geographic, electoral & aeronautical maps & digital products, surveys federal-provincial boundaries; manages a national program for acquiring & using remote sensing data. Associated offices include the Canada Map Office, Geogrpahical Names Board of Canada & National Air Photo Library.

Surveyor General/International Boundary Commissioner, Peter Sullivan
Tel: 780-495-7347; *Fax:* 780-495-4052
Peter.Sullivan@NRCan-RNCan.gc.ca

Strategic Policy & Operations Branch / Direction de la politique stratégique et des opérations
588 Booth St., Ottawa, ON K1A 0Y7

Director General, Mary Preville
Tel: 343-292-6515; *Fax:* 613-996-9670
mary.preville@canada.ca

Energy Sector / Secteur de la politique énergétique

Fax: 613-992-1405
www.nrcan.gc.ca/energy

Develops & promotes economic, regulatory & voluntary approaches to encourage sustainable development of energy resources to meet domestic needs & export markets. Advises the government on federal energy policies, strategies, emergency plans & activities; promotes efficient energy use.

Assistant Deputy Minister, Jay Khosla
Tel: 343-292-6265; *Fax:* 613-992-1405
jay.khosla@canada.ca

Electricity Resources Branch / Direction des ressources en électricité

Legislative, policy & regulatory responsibilities for renewable energies, electricity, oil & gas, frontier lands activities. Provides leadership on policy on nuclear energy, uranium, radioactive waste & related environmental issues.

Director General, Niall O'Dea
Tel: 343-292-6200; *Fax:* 613-947-4205
niall.odea@canada.ca

Energy Policy Branch / Direction de la politique énergétique

Developing, planning & coordinating policy matters relating to the energy sector, including management of petroleum exploration & development, electricity markets & alternative energy, & the design or delivery of specific energy efficiency programs & services.

Director General, Drew Leyburne
Tel: 343-292-6448; *Fax:* 613-996-5943
drew.leyburne@canada.ca

Energy Safety & Security / Sûreté énergétique et sécurité

Director General, Jeff Labonté
Tel: 343-292-6258; *Fax:* 613-992-8738
jeff.labonte@canada.ca

Office of Energy Efficiency (OEE) / Office de l'efficacité énergétique
CEF, Building 3, Observatory Cres., 930 Carling Ave., Ottawa, ON K1A 0Y3

www.nrcan.gc.ca/energy/offices-labs/office-energy-efficiency

Policy & programs in support of efficient use of energy, use of alternative energy & transportation fuels. Grants & incentives, workshops, statistics & analysis & free publications are offered.

Director General, Patricia Fuller
Tel: 343-292-6310
patricia.fuller@canada.ca

Petroleum Resources Branch / Direction des ressources pétrolières

Legislative, policy & regulatory responsibilities for all sources of energy supplies, such as renewable energies, electricity, oil & gas, frontier lands activities.

Director General, Terence Hubbard
Tel: 343-292-6165; *Fax:* 613-992-8738
terence.hubbard@canada.ca

Innovation & Energy Technology Sector / Secteur de l'innovation et de la technologie énergétique

Assistant Deputy Minister, Frank Des Rosiers
Tel: 343-292-8817; *Fax:* 613-944-4747
frank.desrosiers@canada.ca

CanmetENERGY Research Centres

Office of Energy Research & Development (OERD) / Bureau de recherche et développement énergétique (BRDE)

Fax: 613-995-6146

Coordinates the following federal funding programs: Clean Energy Fund; ecoENERGY Innovation Initiative; ecoENERGY Technology Initiative; & Energy Research & Development (PERD). PERD is intended for research & development in energy efficiency & climate change, transportation & renewable energy. The OERD coordinates & represents Canada in international collaboration energy R&D through international mechanisms such as the International Energy Agency & the MOU with US DOE International Energy Agency.

Director General, Yiota Kokkinos
Tel: 343-292-8951
yiota.kokkinos@canada.ca

Major Projects Management Office / Bureau de gestion des grands projets
580 Booth St., Ottawa, ON K1A 0E4

Assistant Deputy Minister, Erin O'Gorman
Tel: 343-292-8830; *Fax:* 613-995-7555
erin.ogorman@canada.ca

Director General, Jim Clarke
Tel: 343-292-8825; *Fax:* 613-995-7555
jim.clarke@canada.ca

Director General, Policies, Mollie Johnson
Tel: 343-292-8824
mollie.johnson2@canada.ca

Director General, Strategic Projects Secretariat, Timothy Gardiner
Tel: 343-292-8805
timothy.gardiner@canada.ca

Minerals & Metals Sector / Secteur des minéraux et des métaux

www.nrcan.gc.ca/mining-materials/mining

MMS is the federal government's primary source of scientific & technological knowledge, & policy advice, on Canada's mineral & metal resources & on explosives regulation & technology. In addition to housing three scientific research institutions, MMS has the government lead in promoting sustainable development & responsible use of Canada's mineral & metal resources. The Sector is a leader in the generation & dissemination of knowledge on the Canadian minerals & metals industry, & collaborates with & provides research services to governmental, institutional & industrial clients for the development of new technology with economic, environmental & social benefits to Canadians.

Assistant Deputy Minister, Marian Campbell Jarvis
Tel: 343-292-8722; *Fax:* 613-996-7425
marian.campbelljarvis@canada.ca

CanmetMATERIALS / CanmetMATÉRIAUX
183 Longwood Rd. South, Hamilton, ON L8P 0A5

CanmetMATERIALS focuses on the fabrication, processing & evaluation of metals & materials. It operates facilities in Hamilton & Calgary, & is the largest research centre of its kind in Canada.

Director General, Philippe Dauphin
Tel: 905-645-0698; *Fax:* 905-645-0831
philippe.dauphin@canada.ca

CanmetMINING / CanmetMINES
555 Booth St., Ottawa, ON K1A 0G1

Fax: 613-947-6606

CanmetMINING leads & participates in mining & innovative national collaborations to develop green mining science & technologies.

Director General, Magdi Habib
Tel: 613-995-4776; *Fax:* 613-992-8928
magdi.habib@canada.ca

Explosives Safety & Security Branch / Direction de la sécurité et de ls sûreté des explosifs

Director General, Patrick O'Neill
Tel: 343-292-8748; *Fax:* 613-948-5195
patrick.oneill@canada.ca

Industry & Economic Analysis Branch / Direction de l'analyse industrielle et économique

Acting Director General, David McNabb
Tel: 343-292-6083
david.mcnabb@canada.ca

Minerals, Metals & Materials Policy Branch / Direction de la politique des minéraux, métaux et matériaux

Director General, Stefania Trombetti
Tel: 343-292-8704; *Fax:* 613-952-7501
stefania.trombetti@canada.ca

Public Affairs & Portfolio Management Sector / Secteur de la gestion des affaires publiques et du portefeuille

Assistant Deputy Minister, Jean-Michel Catta
Tel: 343-292-8922
jean-michel.catta@canada.ca

Director General, Communications Services, Jennifer Hollington
Tel: 343-292-6483; *Fax:* 613-947-1426
jennifer.hollington@canada.ca

Director General, Portfolio Management & Corporate Secretariat Branch, Lorraine McKenzie Presley
Tel: 343-292-8844; *Fax:* 613-947-9033
lorraine.mckenziepresley@canada.ca

Associate Director General, Public Affairs Branch, Vacant

Natural Sciences & Engineering Research Council of Canada (NSERC) / Conseil des recherches en sciences naturelles et en génie du Canada (CRSNG)

Constitution Square, Tower II, 350 Albert St., Ottawa, ON K1A 1H5

Tel: 613-995-4273; *Fax:* 613-992-5337
Toll-Free: 855-275-2861
www.nserc-crsng.gc.ca
twitter.com/nserc_crsng
www.facebook.com/EurekaCanadaEnglish
www.youtube.com/user/NSERCTube

Science & Engineering Research Canada (NSERC) is a federal agency whose role is to make investments in people, discovery & innovation for the benefit of all Canadians. With an annual budget of more than $860 million, it supports more than 20,000 university students & postdoctoral fellows in their advanced studies. NSERC promotes discovery by funding more than 10,000 university professors every year & helps make innovation happen by encouraging more than 500 Canadian companies to participate & invest in university research projects.

President, Mario Pinto
Tel: 613-995-5840
pres@nserc-crsng.gc.ca

Vice-President & Chair, Daniel F. Muzyka

Chief Financial Officer & Vice-President, Common Administrative Services, Patricia Sauvé-McCuan
Tel: 613-995-3914; *Fax:* 613-944-1760
Patricia.Sauve-McCuan@nserc-crsng.gc.ca

Vice-President, Research Grants & Scholarships Directorate, Pierre Charest
Tel: 613-995-5833
Pierre.Charest@nserc-crsng.gc.ca

Vice-President, Communications, Corporate & International Affairs Directorate, Alfred LeBlanc
Tel: 613-943-5317
Alfred.Leblanc@nserc-crsng.gc.ca

Vice-President, Research Partnerships Programs, Bettina Hamelin
Tel: 613-992-1585
Bettina.Hamelin@nserc-crsng.gc.ca

Acting Associate Vice-President, NCE, Jean Saint-Vil
Tel: 613-995-6010
Jean.Saint-Vil@nserc-crsng.gc.ca

Executive Director, Corporate Planning & Policy Division, Kevin Fitzgibbons
Tel: 613-995-6449
Kevin.Fitzgibbons@nserc-crsng.gc.ca

Director General & Chief Information Officer, Information & Innovation Solutions, Christina Cavazzoni
Tel: 613-996-8820
Christiana.Cavazzoni@nserc-crsng.gc.ca

Director General, Human Resources, Jennifer Gualtieri
Tel: 613-944-9264
Jennifer.Gualtieri@nserc-crsng.gc.ca

Director General & Deputy Chief Financial Officer, Finance & Awards Administration Division, Nathalie Manseau
Tel: 613-996-8269
Nathalie.Manseau@nserc-crsng.gc.ca

Networks of Centres of Excellence of Canada (NCE) / Réseaux de centres d'excellence (RCE)

350 Albert Street, 16th Fl., Ottawa, ON K1A 1H5

Tel: 613-995-6010; *Fax:* 613-992-7356
info@nce-rce.gc.ca
www.nce-rce.gc.ca
twitter.com/nce_rce
www.facebook.com/networksofcentresofexcellence
www.linkedin.com/company/networks-of-centres-of-excellence

The Networks of Centres of Excellence (NCE) is mandated to persue discoveries in the fields of natural sciences, engineering, social sciences & health sciences, in order to transform them into products, services & processes that improve the lives of Canadians. In partnership with Innovation, Science & Economic Development & Health Canada, NCE is jointly administered by The Canadian Institutes of Health Research (CIHR), the Natural Sciences & Engineering Research Council (NSERC) & the Social Sciences & Humanities Research Council (SSHRC).

Acting Chair, Management Committee, Kevin Fitzgibbons

Program Deputy Director, Réginald Thériault
Tel: 613-947-8894
Reginald.Theriault@nce-rce.gc.ca

North American Free Trade Agreement (NAFTA) Secretariat / Secrétariat de l'ALÉNA

Canadian Section, 111 Sussex Dr., 5th Fl., Ottawa, ON K1N 1J1

Tel: 343-203-4274; *Fax:* 613-992-9392
webmaster@nafta-alena.gc.ca
www.nafta-alena.gc.ca

The NAFTA Secretariat, comprised of a Canadian Section, a United States Section & a Mexican Section, is responsible for the administration of the dispute settlement provisions of the North American Free Trade Agreement. The Canadian Section also carries responsibility for similar provisions under the Canada-Chile, Canada-Israel & Canada-Costa Rica free trade agreements.

Canadian Secretary & Executive Director, Deborah Gowling
Tel: 343-203-4268; *Fax:* 613-992-9392
Deborah.Gowling@international.gc.ca

Registrar, Feleke Bogale
Tel: 343-203-4277; *Fax:* 613-992-9392

Northern Pipeline Agency Canada (NPAC) / Administration du pipe-line du Nord Canada (APNC)

#470, 588 Booth St., Ottawa, ON K1A 0Y7

Tel: 613-995-1150
info@npa.gc.ca
npa.gc.ca
Secondary Address: 444 - 7th Ave. SW
Calgary, AB T2P 0X8

Established to carry out federal responsibilities in relation to the planning & construction of the Canadian portion of the Alaska Natural Gas Transportation System.

Commissioner, Bob Hamilton
Tel: 343-292-6799; *Fax:* 613-992-3828
bob.hamilton@canada.ca

Office of the Commissioner of Official Languages / Commissariat aux langues officielles

30 Victoria St., 6th Fl., Gatineau, ON K1A 0T8

Tel: 819-420-4877; *Fax:* 819-420-4873
Toll-Free: 877-996-6368
TTY: 800-880-1990
www.ocol-clo.gc.ca
twitter.com/OCOLCanada
www.facebook.com/officiallanguages

Responsible for ensuring the equality of English & French in Parliament, within the Government of Canada, the federal administration, & the institutions subject to the Official Languages Act; the preservation & development of official language communities in Canada; & the equality of English & French in Canadian society.

Commissioner of Official Languages, Graham Fraser
Tel: 819-420-4875; *Fax:* 819-420-4839
Other Communications: Executive Assistant, Phone: 819-420-4810

Assistant Commissioner, Policy & Communications Branch, Mary Donaghy
Tel: 819-420-4832; *Fax:* 819-420-4828

Assistant Commissioner, Corporate Management Branch, Eric Trépanier
Tel: 819-420-4850; *Fax:* 819-420-4873

Assistant Commissioner, Compliance Assurance Branch, Ghislaine Saikaley
Tel: 819-420-4853; *Fax:* 819-420-4854

Pacific Pilotage Authority Canada / Administration de pilotage du Pacifique Canada

#1000, 1130 West Pender St., Vancouver, BC V6E 4A4

Tel: 604-666-6771; *Fax:* 604-666-1647
info@ppa.gc.ca
www.ppa.gc.ca
Other Communication: Vancouver Dispatch: 604-666-6776, Fax: 604-666-6093; Victoria Dispatch: 250-363-3878, Fax: 250-363-3293

Operates pilotage services in Canadian waters in & around British Columbia. Reports to government through the Minister of Transportation.

Chief Executive Officer, Kevin Obermeyer

Chair, Lorraine Cunningham
Director, Finance, Stefan Woloszyn
Director, Marine Operations, Capt. Brian Young

Parks Canada / Parcs Canada

National Office, 30 Victoria St., Gatineau, QC J8X 0B3
Tel: 819-420-9486
Toll-Free: 888-773-8888
TTY: 866-787-6221
information@pc.gc.ca
www.pc.gc.ca
twitter.com/ParksCanada
www.facebook.com/ParksCanada
www.youtube.com/user/ParksCanadaAgency

Responsible for the protection, management, operation & maintenance of national parks, historic sites, canals & other significant examples of Canada's natural & cultural heritage, for the benefit, understanding & enjoyment of Canadians. Administers one of the largest park systems in the world. There are 46 national parks & national park reserves in total. In addition to the national parks, national historic sites & national marine conservation areas, Parks Canada coordinates other heritage programs, including federal heritage buildings, heritage railway stations, grave sites of Canadian Prime Ministers, heritage rivers, archaeology programs, international programs.

Minister, Environment & Climate Change; Minister Responsible, Parks Canada, Hon. Catherine Mary McKenna, P.C.
Tel: 613-996-5322; *Fax:* 613-996-5323
Catherine.McKenna@parl.gc.ca

Chief Executive Officer, Daniel L. Watson
Tel: 819-420-5146

Chief Audit & Evaluation Executive, Office of Internal Audit & Evaluation, Brian Evans
Tel: 819-420-5132; *Fax:* 819-420-5133
Other Communications: Alt. Phone: 613-889-1675

Ombudsman & Director, Centre for Values & Ethics, Maryse Lavigne
Tel: 819-420-5033; *Fax:* 819-420-5036

Chief of Staff & Corporate Secretary, Jesse Fleming
Tel: 819-420-5145; *Fax:* 819-420-5144

Associated Agencies, Boards & Commissions:

•Historic Sites & Monuments Board of Canada / Commission des lieux et monuments historiques du Canada
30 Victoria St., 3rd Fl.
Gatineau, QC J8X 0B3
Fax: 819-420-9260
Toll-free: 855-283-8730
hsmbc-clmhc@pc.gc.ca
www.pc.gc.ca/eng/clmhc-hsmbc/index.aspx

A seventeen-member advisory board which reports to the Minister of Environment & recommends whether persons, places or events are of national historic &/or architectural significance, & therefore warrant commemoration. The board also makes recommendations concerning the designation of heritage railway stations.

Chief Financial Officer Directorate / Dirigeante principale des finances

Chief Financial Officer, Sylvain Michaud
Tel: 819-420-9518

External Relations & Visitor Experience Directorate / Direction générale des relations externes et expériences des visiteurs

Vice-President, External Relations & Visitor Experience, Michael Nadler
Tel: 819-420-9409

Human Resources Directorate / Direction générale des ressources humaines

Chief Human Resources Officer, Pierre Richer de La Flèche
Tel: 819-420-9133; *Fax:* 819-420-9135

Indigenous Affairs, Heritage Conservation & Commemoration Directorate / Direction générale des affaires authochtones, de la conservation et de la commémoration du patrimoine

Vice-President, George Green
Tel: 819-420-9256

Director, Cultural Heritage Policies, Genevieve Charrois
Tel: 819-420-9255; *Fax:* 819-953-4909

Protected Areas Establishment & Conservation Directorate / Direction générale de l'Établissement et conservation des aires protégées

Vice-President, Rob Prosper
Tel: 819-420-9267; *Fax:* 819-420-9273
Other Communications: Alternate Phone: 613-889-6900

Chief Ecosystem Scientist, Gilles Seutin
Tel: 819-420-9269; *Fax:* 819-420-9273
Other Communications: Alternate Phone: 613-277-8447

Executive Director, World Conservation Congress Lead, Natural Resource Conservation Branch, Mike P. Wong
Tel: 819-420-9271; *Fax:* 819-420-9273

Executive Director, Natural Resource Conservation Branch, Nadine Crookes
Tel: 250-726-7165; *Fax:* 250-726-3520

Strategic Policy & Investment Directorate / Direction générale des Politiques stratégiques et investissement

Vice-President, Strategic Policy & Investment, Jane Pearse
Tel: 819-420-9114
Other Communications: Alternate Phone: 613-614-0644

Chief Information Officer, Greg Thompson
Tel: 403-762-1528; *Fax:* 403-762-1555

Canal Offices

Carillon
230, rue du Barrage, Saint-André-d'Argenteuil, QC J0V 1X0
Tel: 450-537-3534; *Fax:* 450-658-2428
info.canal@pc.gc.ca
www.pc.gc.ca/canalcarillon
twitter.com/quebeccanals

Chambly
1899, boul Périgny, Chambly, QC J3L 4C3
Tel: 450-658-4381; *Fax:* 450-658-2428
info.canal@pc.gc.ca
www.pc.gc.ca/canalchambly
Other Communication: Lock #9 (Saint-Jean), Phone: 450-348-3392
twitter.com/quebeccanals

Lachine
105, rue McGill, 6e étage, Montréal, QC H2Y 2E7
Tel: 514-283-6054; *Fax:* 514-496-1263
info.canal@pc.gc.ca
www.pc.gc.ca/canallachine
twitter.com/lachinecanal

Rideau
34 Beckwith St. South, Smiths Falls, ON K7A 2A8
Tel: 613-283-5170; *Fax:* 613-283-0677
RideauCanal-info@pc.gc.ca
www.pc.gc.ca/canalrideau
twitter.com/RideauCanalNHS
www.facebook.com/RideauCanalNHS

Sainte-Anne-de-Bellevue
170, rue Sainte-Anne, Sainte-Anne, QC H9X 1N1
Tel: 514-457-5546; *Fax:* 450-658-2428
info.canal@pc.gc.ca
www.pc.gc.ca/canalsteanne
twitter.com/quebeccanals

Saint-Ours
2930, ch des Patriotes, Saint-Ours, QC J0G 1P0
Tél: 450-785-2212; *Téléc:* 450-658-2428
info.canal@pc.gc.ca
www.pc.gc.ca/canalstours
twitter.com/quebeccanals

St. Peters
160 Toulouse St., PO Box 8 St Peters, NS B0E 3B0
Tel: 902-295-2069; *Fax:* 902-295-3496
information@pc.gc.ca
www.pc.gc.ca/stpeterscanal
Other Communication: Summer Phone: 902-535-2118
twitter.com/ParksCanada_NS
www.facebook.com/StPetersCanal

Sault Ste Marie
1 Canal Dr., Sault Ste Marie, ON P6A 6W4
Tel: 705-941-6262; *Fax:* 705-941-6206
info-saultcanal@pc.gc.ca
www.pc.gc.ca/eng/lhn-nhs/on/ssmarie/index.aspx
twitter.com/SaultCanalNHS
www.facebook.com/SaultCanalNHS

Trent-Severn Waterway
PO Box 567 Peterborough, ON K9J 6Z6
Tel: 705-750-4900; *Fax:* 705-742-9644
TTY: 705-750-4949
Ont.Trentsevern@pc.gc.ca
www.pc.gc.ca/trentsevern
twitter.com/TrentSevernNHS
www.facebook.com/TrentSevernNHS

Atlantic National Parks/National Historic Sites

Alexander Graham Bell Historic Site of Canada
PO Box 159 Baddeck, NS B0E 1B0
Tel: 902-295-2069; *Fax:* 902-295-3496
information@pc.gc.ca
www.pc.gc.ca/eng/lhn-nhs/ns/grahambell/index.aspx
twitter.com/ParksCanada_NS
www.facebook.com/AGBNHS

Ardgowan National Historic Site of Canada
2 Palmer's Lane, Charlottetown, PE C1A 5V8
Tel: 902-566-7050; *Fax:* 902-566-7226
www.pc.gc.ca/eng/lhn-nhs/pe/ardgowan/index.aspx
twitter.com/ParksCanadaPEI

Bank Fishery National Heritage Exhibit
PO Box 9080 Stn. A, Halifax, NS B3K 5M7
Tel: 902-426-5080; *Fax:* 902-426-4228
information@pc.gc.ca
www.pc.gc.ca/lhn-nhs/ns/bank/index.aspx
twitter.com/ParksCanada_NS

Boishébert & Beaubears Shipbuilding National Historic Sites of Canada
186, route 117, Kouchibouguac National Park, NB E4X 2P1
Tel: 506-876-2443; *Fax:* 506-876-4802
TTY: 506-876-4205
kouch.info@pc.gc.ca
www.pc.gc.ca/lhn-nhs/nb/boishebert/index.aspx
twitter.com/nhsnb

Canso Islands National Historic Site of Canada
1465 Union St., PO Box 159 Baddeck, NS B0E 1B0
Tel: 902-295-2069; *Fax:* 902-295-3496
information@pc.gc.ca
www.pc.gc.ca/lhn-nhs/ns/canso/index.aspx
Other Communication: Summer Phone: 902-366-3136
twitter.com/ParksCanada_NS
www.facebook.com/cansoislands

Cape Breton Highlands National Park of Canada
Ingonish Beach, NS B0C 1L0
Tel: 902-224-2306; *Fax:* 902-285-2866
cbhnp.info@pc.gc.ca
www.pc.gc.ca/pn-np/ns/cbreton/index.aspx
twitter.com/ParksCanada_NS
www.facebook.com/CBHNP

Cape Spear National Historic Site of Canada
PO Box 1268 St. John's, NL A1C 5M9
Tel: 709-772-5367; *Fax:* 709-772-6302
cape.spear@pc.gc.ca
www.pc.gc.ca/lhn-nhs/nl/spear/index.aspx
twitter.com/ParksCanadaNL

Carleton Martello Tower National Historic Site of Canada
454 Whipple St., Saint John, NB E2M 2R3
Tel: 506-636-4011; *Fax:* 506-636-4574
TTY: 506-887-6015
info.martello@pc.gc.ca
www.pc.gc.ca/lhn-nhs/nb/carleton/index.aspx

Castle Hill National Historic Site of Canada
PO Box 10 Stn. Jerseyside, Placentia Bay, NL A0B 2G0
Tel: 709-227-2401; *Fax:* 709-227-2452
castle.hill@pc.gc.ca
www.pc.gc.ca/lhn-nhs/nl/castlehill/index.aspx
Other Communication: Off-season: 709-772-6709, Fax: 709-772-6388
Off-season AddressPO Box 1268 Sta. St. John's, NL A1C 5M9
twitter.com/ParksCanadaNL

Fort Amherst/Port-La-Joye National Historic Site of Canada
2 Palmers Lane, Charlottetown, PE C1A 5V8
Tel: 902-566-7050; *Fax:* 902-566-7226
pljfa.info@pc.gc.ca
www.pc.gc.ca/lhn-nhs/pe/amherst/index.aspx
twitter.com/ParksCanadaPEI

Fort Anne National Historic Site of Canada
PO Box 9 Annapolis Royal, NS B0S 1A0
Tel: 902-532-2397; *Fax:* 902-532-2232
information@pc.gc.ca
www.pc.gc.ca/lhn-nhs/ns/fortanne/index.aspx
Other Communication: Off-season: 902-532-2321
twitter.com/ParksCanada_NS

Fort Beauséjour National Historic Site of Canada
111 Fort Beauséjour Rd., Aulac, NB E4L 2W5
Tel: 506-364-5080; *Fax:* 506-536-4399
fort.beausejour@pc.gc.ca
www.pc.gc.ca/lhn-nhs/nb/beausejour/index.aspx

Fort Edward National Historic Site of Canada
PO Box 9 Annapolis Royal, NS B0S 1A0
Tel: 902-532-2321; *Fax:* 902-532-2232
information@pc.gc.ca
www.pc.gc.ca/lhn-nhs/ns/edward/index.aspx
Other Communication: June - Sept.: 902-798-2639; West Hants Historical Society: 902-798-4706
twitter.com/ParksCanada_NS

Fort McNab National Historic Site of Canada
c/o Halifax Citadel National Historic Site, PO Box 9080 Stn. A, Halifax, NS B3K 5M7
Tel: 902-426-5080; *Fax:* 902-426-4228
halifax.citadel@pc.gc.ca
www.pc.gc.ca/lhn-nhs/ns/mcnab/index.aspx
twitter.com/ParksCanada_NS

Fortress of Louisbourg National Historic Site
259 Park Service Rd., Louisbourg, NS B1C 2L2
Tel: 902-733-3552; *Fax:* 902-733-2362
louisbourg.info@pc.gc.ca
www.pc.gc.ca/lhn-nhs/ns/louisbourg/index.aspx
twitter.com/ParksCanada_NS
www.facebook.com/FortressOfLouisbourgNHS

Fundy National Park of Canada
PO Box 1001 Alma, NB E4H 1B4
Tel: 506-887-6000; *Fax:* 506-887-6008
TTY: 506-887-6015
fundy.info@pc.gc.ca
www.pc.gc.ca/pn-np/nb/fundy/index.aspx

Grand Pré National Historic Site of Canada
PO Box 150 Grand Pré, NS B0P 1M0
Tel: 902-542-3631; *Fax:* 902-542-1691
Toll-Free: 866-542-3631
grandpre.info@pc.gc.ca
www.pc.gc.ca/lhn-nhs/ns/grandpre/index.aspx
twitter.com/ParksCanada_NS
www.facebook.com/GrandPreNHS

Georges Island National Historic Site of Canada
c/o Halifax Citadel National Historic Site of Canada, PO Box 9080 Stn. A, Halifax, NS B3K 5M7
Tel: 902-426-5080; *Fax:* 902-426-4228
halifax.citadel@pc.gc.ca
www.pc.gc.ca/lhn-nhs/ns/georges/index.aspx
twitter.com/ParksCanada_NS

Green Gables Heritage Place
2 Palmer's Lane, Charlottetown, PE C1A 5V6
Tel: 902-963-7874; *Fax:* 902-963-7869
greengables.info@pc.gc.ca
www.pc.gc.ca/lhn-nhs/pe/greengables/index.aspx
twitter.com/ParksCanadaPEI

Gros Morne National Park of Canada
PO Box 130 Rocky Harbour, NL A0K 4N0
Tel: 709-458-2417; *Fax:* 709-458-2059
TTY: 709-772-4564
grosmorne.info@pc.gc.ca
www.pc.gc.ca/pn-np/nl/grosmorne/index.aspx
Other Communication: Emergency: 1-877-852-3100
twitter.com/ParksCanadaNL

Halifax Citadel National Historic Site of Canada
PO Box 9080 Stn. A, Halifax, NS B3K 5M7
Tel: 902-426-5080; *Fax:* 902-426-4228
halifax.citadel@pc.gc.ca
www.pc.gc.ca/lhn-nhs/ns/halifax/index.aspx
twitter.com/ParksCanada_NS

Hawthorne Cottage National Historic Site of Canada
PO Box 5542 St. John's, NL A1C 5W4
Tel: 709-753-9262; *Fax:* 709-753-0879
info@historicsites.ca
www.pc.gc.ca/lhn-nhs/nl/hawthorne/index.aspx
Other Communication: Off-season: 709-528-4004
twitter.com/ParksCanadaNL

Kejimkujik National Park of Canada
PO Box 236 Maitland Bridge, NS B0T 1B0
Tel: 902-682-2772
Toll-Free: 888-773-8888
kejimkujik.info@pc.gc.ca
www.pc.gc.ca/pn-np/ns/kejimkujik/index_e.asp
twitter.com/ParksCanada_NS
www.facebook.com/Kejimkujik

Kouchibouguac National Park of Canada
186, Route 117, Kouchibouguac National Park, NB E4X 2P1
Tel: 506-876-2443; *Fax:* 506-876-4802
Toll-Free: 888-773-8888
TTY: 506-876-4205
kouch.info@pc.gc.ca
www.pc.gc.ca/pn-np/nb/kouchibouguac/index.aspx

L'Anse aux Meadows National Historic Site of Canada
PO Box 70 St-Lunaire-Griquet, NL A0K 2X0
Tel: 709-623-2608; *Fax:* 709-623-2028
viking.lam@pc.gc.ca
www.pc.gc.ca/lhn-nhs/nl/meadows/index.aspx
twitter.com/ParksCanadaNL

Marconi National Historic Site of Canada
PO Box 159 Baddeck, NS B0E 1B0
Tel: 902-295-2069; *Fax:* 902-295-3496
information@pc.gc.ca
www.pc.gc.ca/lhn-nhs/ns/marconi/index.aspx
Other Communication: Summer Phone: 902-842-2530
twitter.com/ParksCanada_NS
www.facebook.com/MarconiNHS

Monument Lefebvre National Historic Site of Canada
480 Centrale Rd., Memramcook, NB E4K 3S6
Tel: 506-758-9808; *Fax:* 506-758-9813
monument@nbnet.nb.ca
www.pc.gc.ca/lhn-nhs/nb/lefebvre/index.aspx

Port-au-Choix National Historic Site of Canada
PO Box 140 Port au Choix, NL A0K 4C0
Tel: 709-458-2417; *Fax:* 709-861-3827
pac-historic-site@pc.gc.ca
www.pc.gc.ca/lhn-nhs/nl/portauchoix/index.aspx
Other Communication: Seasonal: 709-861-3522
twitter.com/ParksCanadaNL

Port Royal National Historic Site of Canada
PO Box 9 Annapolis Royal, NS B0S 1A0
Tel: 902-532-2898; *Fax:* 902-532-2232
information@pc.gc.ca
www.pc.gc.ca/lhn-nhs/ns/portroyal/index.aspx
Other Communication: Off-season: 902-532-2321
twitter.com/ParksCanada_NS

Prince Edward Island National Park of Canada
2 Palmers Lane, Charlottetown, PE C1A 5V8
Tel: 902-672-6350; *Fax:* 902-672-6370
pnipe.peinp@pc.gc.ca
www.pc.gc.ca/pn-np/pe/pei-ipe/index.aspx
twitter.com/ParksCanadaPEI
www.facebook.com/PEInationalpark

Prince of Wales Tower National Historic Site
c/o Halifax Citadel National Historic Site, PO Box 9080 Stn. A, Halifax, NS B3K 5M7
Tel: 902-426-5080; *Fax:* 902-426-4228
halifax.citadel@pc.gc.ca
www.pc.gc.ca/lhn-nhs/ns/prince/index.aspx
twitter.com/ParksCanada_NS

Province House National Historic Site of Canada
2 Palmer's Lane, Charlottetown, PE C1A 5V8
Tel: 902-566-7050; *Fax:* 902-566-7226
www.pc.gc.ca/lhn-nhs/pe/provincehouse/index.aspx
twitter.com/ParksCanadaPEI

Red Bay National Historic Site of Canada
PO Box 103 Red Bay, NL A0K 4K0
Tel: 709-920-2142; *Fax:* 709-458-2144
redbay.info@pc.gc.ca
www.pc.gc.ca/lhn-nhs/nl/redbay/index.aspx
Other Communication: Summer: 709-458-2417; Fax: 709-458-2059
twitter.com/ParksCanadaNL

Ryan Premises National Historic Site
PO Box 1451 Bonavista, NL A0C 1B0
Tel: 709-468-1600; *Fax:* 709-468-1604
ryan.premises@pc.gc.ca
www.pc.gc.ca/lhn-nhs/nl/ryan/index.aspx
twitter.com/ParksCanadaNL

Sable Island National Park Reserve
c/o Halifax Citadel National Historic Site, PO Box 9080 Stn. A, Halifax, NS B3K 5M7
Tel: 902-426-1993; *Fax:* 902-426-4228
sable@pc.gc.ca
www.pc.gc.ca/eng/pn-np/ns/sable/index.aspx
twitter.com/ParksCanada_NS

St. Andrews Blockhouse National Historic Site of Canada
454 Whipple St., Saint John, NB E2M 2R3
Tel: 506-636-4011; *Fax:* 506-636-4574
TTY: 506-887-6015
fundy.info@pc.gc.ca
www.pc.gc.ca/lhn-nhs/nb/standrews/index.aspx
Other Communication: Summer: 506-529-4270

St. Peters Canada National Historic Site of Canada
160 Toulouse St., PO Box 8 St Peter's, NS B0E 3B0
Tel: 902-295-2069; *Fax:* 902-295-3496
information@pc.gc.ca
www.pc.gc.ca/lhn-nhs/ns/stpeters/index.aspx
Other Communication: Summer Phone: 902-535-2118
twitter.com/ParksCanada_NS
www.facebook.com/StPetersCanal

Signal Hill National Historic Site of Canada
PO Box 1268 St. John's, NL A1C 5M9
Tel: 709-772-5367; *Fax:* 709-772-6302
signal.hill@pc.gc.ca
www.pc.gc.ca/lhn-nhs/nl/signalhill/index.aspx
twitter.com/ParksCanadaNL
www.facebook.com/SignalHillNHS

Terra Nova National Park of Canada
General Delivery, Glovertown, NL A0G 2L0
Tel: 709-533-2801; *Fax:* 709-533-2706
info.tnnp@pc.gc.ca
www.pc.gc.ca/pn-np/nl/terranova/index.aspx
twitter.com/ParksCanadaNL
www.facebook.com/TerraNovaNP

York Redoubt National Historic Site of Canada
c/o Halifax Citadel National Historic Site, PO Box 9080 Stn. A, Halifax, NS B3K 5M7
Tel: 902-426-5080; *Fax:* 902-426-4228
halifax.citadel@pc.gc.ca
www.pc.gc.ca/lhn-nhs/ns/york/index.aspx
twitter.com/ParksCanada_NS

Ontario National Parks/National Historic Sites

Battle of the Windmill National Historic Site of Canada
370 Vankoughnet St., PO Box 479 Prescott, ON K0E 1T0
Tel: 613-925-2896; *Fax:* 613-925-1536
ont.wellington@pc.gc.ca
www.pc.gc.ca/lhn-nhs/on/windmill/index.aspx

Bellevue House National Historic Site of Canada
35 Centre St., Kingston, ON K7L 4E5
Tel: 613-545-8666; *Fax:* 613-545-8721
bellevue.house@pc.gc.ca
www.pc.gc.ca/lhn-nhs/on/bellevue/index.aspx

Bethune Memorial House National Historic Site of Canada
235 John St. North, Gravenhurst, ON P1P 1G4
Tel: 705-687-4261; *Fax:* 705-687-4935
ont-bethune@pc.gc.ca
www.pc.gc.ca/lhn-nhs/on/bethune/index.aspx

Bois Blanc Island Lighthouse National Historic Site of Canada
c/o Fort Malden N.H.S., 100 Laird Ave., PO Box 38 Amherstburg, ON N9V 2Z2
Tel: 519-736-5416; *Fax:* 519-736-6603
ont.fort-malden@pc.gc.ca
www.pc.gc.ca/lhn-nhs/on/boisblanc/index.aspx
www.facebook.com/FortMaldenNHS

Bruce Peninsula National Park
PO Box 189 Tobermory, ON N0H 2R0
Tel: 519-596-2233; *Fax:* 519-596-2298
bruce-fathomfive@pc.gc.ca
www.pc.gc.ca/pn-np/on/bruce/index.aspx
twitter.com/BrucePNP
www.facebook.com/BrucePeninsulaNP

Butler's Barracks c/o Fort George National Historic Site
c/o Niagara National Historic Sites, 26 Queen St., PO Box 787 Niagara-on-the-Lake, ON L0S 1J0
Tel: 905-468-6614; *Fax:* 905-468-8523
ont-niagara@pc.gc.ca
www.pc.gc.ca/lhn-nhs/on/fortgeorge/index.aspx
twitter.com/FortGeorgeNHS
www.facebook.com/FortGeorgeNHS

Fort George National Historic Site of Canada
c/o Niagara National Historic Sites, 26 Queen St., PO Box 787 Niagara-on-the-Lake, QC L0S 1J0
Tel: 905-468-6614; *Fax:* 905-468-8523
ont-niagara@pc.gc.ca
www.pc.gc.ca/lhn-nhs/on/fortgeorge/index.aspx
twitter.com/FortGeorgeNHS
www.facebook.com/FortGeorgeNHS

Fathom Five National Marine Park of Canada
PO Box 189 Tobermory, ON N0H 2R0
Tel: 519-596-2233; *Fax:* 519-596-2298
bruce-fathomfive@pc.gc.ca
www.pc.gc.ca/eng/amnc-nmca/on/fathomfive/index.aspx
twitter.com/BrucePNP
www.facebook.com/BrucePeninsulaNP

Fort Malden National Historic Site
100 Laird Ave., PO Box 38 Amherstburg, ON N9V 2Z2
Tel: 519-736-5416; *Fax:* 519-736-6603
ont.fort-malden@pc.gc.ca
www.pc.gc.ca/eng/lhn-nhs/on/malden/index.aspx
www.facebook.com/FortMaldenNHS

Fort Mississauga c/o Fort George National Historic Site
c/o Niagara National Historic Sites, 26 Queen St., PO Box 787 Niagara on the Lake, ON L0S 1J0
Tel: 905-468-6614; *Fax:* 905-468-8523
ont-niagara@pc.gc.ca
www.pc.gc.ca/lhn-nhs/on/fortgeorge/natcul/natcul2b.aspx

Fort St. Joseph National Historic Site of Canada
PO Box 220 Richards Landing, ON P0R 1J0
Tel: 705-246-2664; *Fax:* 705-246-1796
fortstjoseph-info@pc.gc.ca
www.pc.gc.ca/lhn-nhs/on/stjoseph.aspx
twitter.com/FortStJosephNHS
www.facebook.com/FortStJosephNHS

Fort Wellington National Historic Site of Canada
PO Box 479 Prescott, ON K0E 1T0
Tel: 613-925-2896; *Fax:* 613-925-1536
TTY: 613-925-2896
ont-wellington@pc.gc.ca
www.pc.gc.ca/lhn-nhs/on/wellington.aspx

Georgian Bay Islands National Park of Canada
901 Wye Valley Rd., PO Box 9 Midland, ON L4R 4K6
Tel: 705-527-7200; *Fax:* 705-526-5939
info.gbi@pc.gc.ca
www.pc.gc.ca/eng/pn-np/on/georg/index.aspx
twitter.com/GBINP

Inverarden House National Historic Site of Canada
370 Vankoughnet St., PO Box 479 Prescott, ON K0E 1T0
Tel: 613-925-2896; *Fax:* 613-925-1536
ont-wellington@pc.gc.ca
www.pc.gc.ca/lhn-nhs/on/inverarden/index.aspx

Kingston Martello Towers
c/o Bellevue House N.H.S., 35 Centre St., Kingston, ON K7L 4E5
Tel: 613-545-8666; *Fax:* 613-545-8721
Bellevue.House@pc.gc.ca
www.pc.gc.ca/lhn-nhs/on/bellevue/index.aspx

Laurier House National Historic Site of Canada
335 Laurier Ave. East, Ottawa, ON K1A 6R4
Tel: 613-992-8142; *Fax:* 613-947-4851
laurier-house@pc.gc.ca
www.pc.gc.ca/lhn-nhs/on/laurier.aspx

Point Clark Lighthouse National Historic Site of Canada
c/o Georgian Bay Islands National Park of Canada, 901 Wye Valley Rd., PO Box 9 Midland, ON L4R 4K6
Tel: 705-526-9804; *Fax:* 705-526-5939
www.pc.gc.ca/lhn-nhs/on/clark.aspx

Point Pelee National Park of Canada
407 Monarch Lane, RR#1, Leamington, ON N8H 3V4
Tel: 519-322-2365; *Fax:* 519-322-1277
Toll-Free: 888-773-8888
TTY: 866-787-6221
pelee.info@pc.gc.ca
www.pc.gc.ca/fra/pn-np/on/pelee.aspx
twitter.com/PointPeleeNP
www.facebook.com/PointPeleeNP

Pukaskwa National Park of Canada
PO Box 212 Heron Bay, ON P0T 1R0
Tel: 807-229-0801; *Fax:* 807-229-2097
ont-pukaskwa@pc.gc.ca
www.pc.gc.ca/pn-np/on/pukaskwa.aspx
twitter.com/PukaskwaNP
www.facebook.com/PukaskwaNP

Queenston Heights & Brock's Monument
14184 Niagara River Pky., Niagara-on-the-Lake, ON L0S 1J0
Tel: 905-262-4759
ont-niagara@pc.gc.ca
www.pc.gc.ca/lhn-nhs/on/queenston/index.aspx
twitter.com/FortGeorgeNHS
www.facebook.com/FortGeorgeNHS

St. Lawrence Islands National Park of Canada
2 County Rd. 5, RR#3, Mallorytown, ON K0E 1R0
Tel: 613-923-5261; *Fax:* 613-923-1021
ont-sli@pc.gc.ca
www.pc.gc.ca/pn-np/on/lawren/index.aspx
twitter.com/TINationalPark
www.facebook.com/TINationalPark

Sir John Johnson National Historic Site of Canada
c/o Fort Wellington National Historic Site, 370 Vanhoughnet St., PO Box 479 Prescott, ON K0E 1T0
Tel: 613-925-2896; *Fax:* 613-925-1536
ont.wellington@pc.gc.ca
www.pc.gc.ca/lhn-nhs/on/johnjohnson/index.aspx
Other Communication: Sir John Johnson Manor House Committee, Phone: 613-347-2356; E-mail: sirjohnjohnson@sympatico.ca

Woodside National Historic Site of Canada
528 Wellington St. North, Kitchener, ON N2H 5L5
Tel: 519-571-5684; *Fax:* 519-571-5686
Toll-Free: 888-773-8888
ont-woodside@pc.gc.ca
www.pc.gc.ca/lhn-nhs/on/woodside/index.aspx
twitter.com/ParksCanada
www.facebook.com/WoodsideNHS

Québec National Parks/National Historic Sites

Artillery Park c/o Fortifications of Québec National Historic Site of Canada
2, rue d'Auteuil, Québec, QC G1R 5C2
Tél: 418-648-7016
Ligne sans frais: 888-773-8888
TTY: 866-787-6221
information@pc.gc.ca
www.pc.gc.ca/lhn-nhs/qc/fortifications/index.aspx

Battle of the Châteauguay National Historic Site of Canada
2371 Rivière Châteauguay Rd., Howick, QC J0S 1G0
Tél: 450-829-2003; *Téléc:* 450-829-3325
bataille.chateauguay@pc.gc.ca
www.pc.gc.ca/lhn-nhs/qc/chateauguay/index.aspx
Autres nombres: Hors saison: 819-423-6965

Battle of the Restigouche National Historic Site of Canada
Route 132, CP 359 Pointe-à-la-Croix, QC G0C 1L0
Tél: 418-788-5676; *Téléc:* 418-788-5895
Ligne sans frais: 888-773-8888
TTY: 866-787-6221
information@pc.gc.ca
www.pc.gc.ca/lhn-nhs/qc/ristigouche.aspx

Carillon Barracks National Historic Site of Canada
308A, ch du Fleuve, Coteau-du-Lac, QC J0P 1B0
Tél: 450-763-5631; *Téléc:* 450-763-1654
Ligne sans frais: 888-773-8888
TTY: 866-787-6221
information@pc.gc.ca
www.pc.gc.ca/lhn-nhs/qc/carillon/index.aspx
Autres nombres: Hors saison: 819-423-6965

Cartier-Brébeuf National Historic Site of Canada
2, rue D'Auteuil, Québec, QC G1R 5C2
Tél: 418-648-7016
Ligne sans frais: 888-773-8888
TTY: 866-787-6221
information@pc.gc.ca
www.pc.gc.ca/lhn-nhs/qc/cartierbrebeuf.aspx

Coteau-du-Lac National Historic Site of Canada
308A, ch du Fleuve, Coteau-du-Lac, QC J0P 1B0
Tél: 450-763-5631
Ligne sans frais: 888-773-8888
TTY: 866-787-6221
reservations.coteau@pc.gc.ca
www.pc.gc.ca/lhn-nhs/qc/coteaudulac.aspx

Forges du Saint-Maurice National Historic Site of Canada
10000, boul des Forges, Trois-Rivières, QC G9C 1B1
Tél: 819-378-5116
Ligne sans frais: 888-773-8888
information@pc.gc.ca
www.pc.gc.ca/lhn-nhs/qc/saintmaurice.aspx
Autres nombres: Hors saison: 514-283-2282

Forillon National Park of Canada
122, boul Gaspé, Gaspé, QC G4X 1A9
Tél: 418-368-5505; *Téléc:* 418-368-6837
Ligne sans frais: 888-773-8888
TTY: 866-787-6221
information@pc.gc.ca
www.pc.gc.ca/pn-np/qc/forillon.aspx
twitter.com/ForillonNP
www.facebook.com/ForillonNP

Fort Chambly National Historic Site of Canada
2, rue de Richelieu, Chambly, QC J3L 2B9
Tél: 450-658-1585; *Téléc:* 450-658-7216
Ligne sans frais: 888-773-8888
TTY: 866-787-6221
information@pc.gc.ca
www.pc.gc.ca/lhn-nhs/qc/fortchambly/index.aspx

Fort Lennox National Historic Site of Canada
1, 61e av, St-Paul-de-l'Ile-aux-Noix, QC J0J 1G0
Tél: 450-291-5700; *Téléc:* 450-291-4389
information@pc.gc.ca
www.pc.gc.ca/lhn-nhs/qc/lennox.aspx
Autres nombres: Hors saison: 450-658-1585

Fort Témiscamingue National Historic Site of Canada
834, ch du Vieux-Fort, Duhamel ouest, QC J9V 1N7
Tél: 819-629-3222; *Téléc:* 819-629-2977
Ligne sans frais: 888-773-8888
TTY: 866-787-6221
information@pc.gc.ca
www.pc.gc.ca/fra/lhn-nhs/qc/temiscamingue.aspx
Autres nombres: Hors saison: 514-283-2282

Fortifications of Québec National Historic Site of Canada
2, rue d'Auteuil, Québec, QC G1R 5C2
Tél: 418-648-7016
Ligne sans frais: 888-773-8888
TTY: 866-787-6221
information@pc.gc.ca
www.pc.gc.ca/lhn-nhs/qc/fortifications/index.aspx

Grosse Ile & the Irish Memorial National Historic Site of Canada
2, rue D'Auteuil, Québec, QC G1R 5C2
Tél: 418-234-8841; *Téléc:* 866-790-8991
Ligne sans frais: 888-773-8888
TTY: 866-787-6221
information@pc.gc.ca
www.pc.gc.ca/lhn-nhs/qc/grosseile/index.aspx

La Mauricie National Park of Canada
702, 5e rue, Shawinigan, QC G9N 1E9
Tél: 819-538-3232; *Téléc:* 819-536-3661
Ligne sans frais: 888-773-8888
information@pc.gc.ca
www.pc.gc.ca/fra/pn-np/qc/mauricie.aspx
www.facebook.com/MauricieNP

Lévis Forts National Historic Site of Canada
41, ch du Gouvernement, Québec, QC G1R 5C2
Tél: 418-835-5182; *Téléc:* 418-948-9119
information@pc.gc.ca
www.pc.gc.ca/lhn-nhs/qc/levis/index.aspx

Louis S. St-Laurent National Historic Site of Canada
6790, rte Louis-St-Laurent, Compton, QC J0B 1L0
Tél: 819-835-5448; *Téléc:* 819-835-9101
Ligne sans frais: 888-773-8888
TTY: 866-787-6221
information@pc.gc.ca
www.pc.gc.ca/fra/lhn-nhs/qc/stlaurent.aspx
Autres nombres: Hors saison: 450-658-1585

Manoir Papineau National Historic Site of Canada
500, rue Notre-Dame, Montebello, QC J0V 1L0
Tél: 819-423-6965; *Téléc:* 819-423-6455
Ligne sans frais: 888-773-8888
TTY: 866-787-6221
manoir.papineau@pc.gc.ca
www.pc.gc.ca/fra/lhn-nhs/qc/manoirpapineau/index.aspx

Mingan Archipelago National Park Reserve of Canada
1340, rue de la Digue, Havre-Saint-Pierre, QC G0G 1P0
Tél: 418-538-3331; *Téléc:* 418-538-3595
information@pc.gc.ca
www.pc.gc.ca/pn-np/qc/mingan.aspx
Autres nombres: Information et / ou réservations: 418-538-3285; 418-949-2126
twitter.com/MinganNPR
www.facebook.com/MinganNPR

Pointe-au-Père Lighthouse National Historic Site of Canada
1034, rue du Phare, Pointe-au-Père, QC G5M 1L8
Tél: 418-368-5505
Ligne sans frais: 888-773-8888
TTY: 866-787-6221
information@pc.gc.ca
www.pc.gc.ca/lhn-nhs/qc/pointaupere/index.aspx

Saguenay St. Lawrence Marine Park of Canada
182, rte de l'Église, Tadoussac, QC G0T 2A0
Tél: 418-235-4703; *Téléc:* 418-235-4686
info.marinepark@pc.gc.ca
www.pc.gc.ca/amnc-nmca/qc/saguenay/default.aspx

Sir George-Étienne Cartier National Historic Site of Canada
458, rue Notre-Dame est, Montréal, QC H2Y 1C8
Tél: 514-283-2282; *Téléc:* 514-283-5560
Ligne sans frais: 888-773-8888
TTY: 866-558-2950
information@pc.gc.ca
www.pc.gc.ca/lhn-nhs/qc/etiennecartier.aspx

Sir Wilfrid Laurier National Historic Site of Canada
945, 12e av, St-Lin-Laurentides, QC J5M 2W4
Tél: 450-439-3702; *Téléc:* 450-439-5721
Ligne sans frais: 888-773-8888
TTY: 866-787-6221
reservations.wilfridlaurier@pc.gc.ca
www.pc.gc.ca/fra/lhn-nhs/qc/wilfridlaurier.aspx
Autres nombres: Hors saison: 819-423-6965

The Fur Trade at Lachine National Historic Site of Canada
1255, boul Saint-Joseph, Lachine, QC H8S 2M2
Tél: 514-637-7433; *Téléc:* 514-637-5325
information@pc.gc.ca
www.pc.gc.ca/lhn-nhs/qc/lachine/index.aspx
Autres nombres: Hors saison: 514-283-2282

Western & Northern Canada National Parks/National Historic Sites

Aulavik National Park of Canada
PO Box 29 Sachs Harbour, NT X0E 0Z0
Tel: 867-777-8800; *Fax:* 867-777-8820
www.pc.gc.ca/pn-np/nt/aulavik/index_e.asp

Auyuittuq National Park of Canada
PO Box 353 Pangnirtung, NU X0A 0R0
Tel: 867-473-2500; *Fax:* 867-473-8612
nunavut.info@pc.gc.ca
www.pc.gc.ca/pn-np/nu/auyuittuq/index_e.asp
twitter.com/ParksCanNunavut
www.facebook.com/ParksCanadaNunavut

Banff National Park of Canada
PO Box 900 Banff, AB T1L 1K2
Tel: 403-762-1550; *Fax:* 403-762-1551
banff.vrc@pc.gc.ca
www.pc.gc.ca/pn-np/ab/banff/index_e.asp
twitter.com/banffnp
www.facebook.com/BanffNP
www.youtube.com/view_play_list?p=7ABD4B2249F753EB

Banff Park Museum National Historic Site of Canada
PO Box 900 Banff, AB T1L 1K2
Tel: 403-762-1558; *Fax:* 403-762-1565
banff.vrc@pc.gc.ca
www.pc.gc.ca/eng/lhn-nhs/ab/banff/index.aspx

Bar U Ranch National Historic Site of Canada
PO Box 168 Longview, AB T0L 1H0
Tel: 403-395-2212; *Fax:* 403-395-2331
BarU.Info@pc.gc.ca
www.pc.gc.ca/lhn-nhs/ab/baru/index_e.asp

Batoche National Historic Site of Canada
RR#1 Box 1040, Wakaw, SK S0K 4P0
Tel: 306-423-6227; *Fax:* 306-423-5400
TTY: 306-423-5540
batoche.info@pc.gc.ca
www.pc.gc.ca/eng/lhn-nhs/sk/batoche/index.aspx
twitter.com/parkscanada_sk
www.facebook.com/saskNHS

Cave & Basin National Historic Site of Canada
PO Box 900 Banff, AB T1L 1K2
Tel: 403-762-1566; *Fax:* 403-762-1565
caveandbasin@pc.gc.ca
pc.gc.ca/eng/lhn-nhs/ab/caveandbasin/index.aspx

Chilkoot Trail National Historic Site of Canada
#205, 300 Main St., Whitehorse, YT Y1A 2B5
Tel: 867-667-3910; *Fax:* 867-393-6701
Toll-Free: 800-661-0486
whitehorse.info@pc.gc.ca
www.pc.gc.ca/lhn-nhs/yt/chilkoot/index_e.asp
twitter.com/ParksCanYukon
www.facebook.com/ParksCanadaYukon

Dawson Historical Complex National Historic Site of Canada
PO Box 390 Dawson City, YT Y0B 1G0
Tel: 867-993-7200; *Fax:* 867-993-7203
dawson.info@pc.gc.ca
www.pc.gc.ca/lhn-nhs/yt/klondike.aspx
twitter.com/ParksCanYukon
www.facebook.com/ParksCanadaYukon

Dredge No. 4 National Historic Site of Canada
PO Box 390 Dawson City, YT Y0B 1G0
Tel: 867-993-7200; *Fax:* 867-993-7203
dawson.info@pc.gc.ca
www.pc.gc.ca/lhn-nhs/yt/klondike.aspx
twitter.com/ParksCanYukon
www.facebook.com/ParksCanadaYukon

Elk Island National Park of Canada
#1, 54401 Range Road 203, Fort Saskatchewan, AB T8L 0V3
Tel: 780-992-5790; *Fax:* 780-992-2951
elk.island@pc.gc.ca
www.pc.gc.ca/pn-np/ab/elkisland/index_e.asp
twitter.com/ElkIslandNP
www.facebook.com/ParksCanada

Fisgard Lighthouse National Historic Site of Canada
603 Fort Rodd Hill Rd., Victoria, BC V9C 2W8
Tel: 250-478-5849; *Fax:* 250-478-2816
fort.rodd@pc.gc.ca
www.pc.gc.ca/lhn-nhs/bc/fisgard/index_e.asp
twitter.com/FortRoddFisgard
www.facebook.com/FortRoddFisgardNHS

Fort Battleford National Historic Site of Canada
PO Box 70 Battleford, SK S0M 0E0
Tel: 306-937-2621; *Fax:* 306-937-3370
TTY: 306-937-3199
battleford.info@pc.gc.ca
www.pc.gc.ca/lhn-nhs/sk/battleford/index_e.asp
twitter.com/parkscanada_sk
www.facebook.com/saskNHS

Fort Langley National Historic Site of Canada
23433 Mavis Ave., PO Box 129 Fort Langley, BC V1M 2R5
Tel: 604-513-4777; *Fax:* 604-513-4798
fort.langley@pc.gc.ca
www.pc.gc.ca/lhn-nhs/bc/langley/index_e.asp
twitter.com/FortLangleyNHS
www.facebook.com/FortLangleyNHS

Fort Rodd Hill National Historic Site of Canada
603 Fort Rodd Hill Rd., Victoria, BC V9C 2W8
Tel: 250-478-5849; *Fax:* 250-478-2816
fort.rodd@pc.gc.ca
www.pc.gc.ca/lhn-nhs/bc/fortroddhill/index_e.asp
twitter.com/FortRoddFisgard
www.facebook.com/FortRoddFisgardNHS

Fort St. James National Historic Site of Canada
PO Box 1148 Fort St James, BC V0J 1P0
Tel: 250-996-7191; *Fax:* 250-996-8566
stjames@pc.gc.ca
www.pc.gc.ca/lhn-nhs/bc/stjames/index_e.asp

Fort Walsh National Historic Site of Canada
PO Box 278 Maple Creek, SK S0N 1N0
Tel: 306-662-3590; *Fax:* 306-662-2711
TTY: 306-662-3124
fort.walsh@pc.gc.ca
www.pc.gc.ca/eng/lhn-nhs/sk/walsh/index.aspx
Other Communication: Administration: 306-662-2645
twitter.com/parkscanada_sk
www.facebook.com/saskNHS

Gitwangak Battle Hill National Historic Site of Canada
PO Box 37 Queen Charlotte, BC V0T 1S0
Tel: 250-559-8818; *Fax:* 250-559-8366
TTY: 250-559-8139
gwaii.haanas@pc.gc.ca
www.pc.gc.ca/lhn-nhs/bc/kitwanga/index_E.asp

Glacier National Park of Canada
PO Box 350 Revelstoke, BC V0E 2S0
Tel: 250-837-7500; *Fax:* 250-837-7536
TTY: 866-787-6221
www.pc.gc.ca/pn-np/bc/glacier/index_e.asp
www.facebook.com/MRGnationalparks

Grasslands National Park of Canada
PO Box 150 Val Marie, SK S0N 2T0
Tel: 306-476-2018; *Fax:* 306-298-2042
Toll-Free: 877-345-2257
grasslands.info@pc.gc.ca
www.pc.gc.ca/eng/pn-np/sk/grasslands/index.aspx
twitter.com/parkscanada_sk
www.facebook.com/grasslandsNP

Gulf Islands National Park Reserve of Canada
2220 Harbour Rd., Sidney, BC V8L 2P6
Tel: 250-654-4000; *Fax:* 250-654-4014
Toll-Free: 866-944-1744
gulf.islands@pc.gc.ca
www.pc.gc.ca/pn-np/bc/gulf/index_E.asp
twitter.com/GulfIslandsNPR
www.facebook.com/GulfIslandsNPR

Gulf of Georgia Cannery National Historic Site of Canada
12138 - 4 Ave., Richmond, BC V7E 3J1
Tel: 604-664-9009; *Fax:* 604-664-9008
gog.info@pc.gc.ca
www.pc.gc.ca/lhn-nhs/bc/georgia/index_e.asp

Gwaii Haanas National Park Reserve & Haida Heritage Site of Canada
Haida Heritage Centre, 60 Second Beach Rd., PO Box 37 Queen Charlotte, BC V0T 1S0
Tel: 250-559-8818; *Fax:* 250-559-8366
Toll-Free: 877-559-8818
gwaii.haanas@pc.gc.ca
www.pc.gc.ca/gwaiihaanas
www.facebook.com/GwaiiHaanas

Ivvavik National Park of Canada
PO Box 1840 Inuvik, NT X0E 0T0
Tel: 867-777-8800; *Fax:* 867-777-8820
inuvik.info@pc.gc.ca
www.pc.gc.ca/pn-np/yt/ivvavik/index_e.asp

Jasper National Park of Canada
PO Box 10 Jasper, AB T0E 1E0
Tel: 780-852-6176; *Fax:* 780-852-1865
pnj.jnp@pc.gc.ca
www.pc.gc.ca/pn-np/ab/jasper/index_e.asp
twitter.com/JasperNP
www.facebook.com/JasperNP

Kluane National Park & Reserve of Canada
PO Box 5495 Haines Junction, YT Y0B 1L0
Tel: 867-634-7207; *Fax:* 867-634-7208
kluane.info@pc.gc.ca
www.pc.gc.ca/pn-np/yt/kluane/index_e.asp
twitter.com/ParksCanYukon
www.facebook.com/ParksCanadaYukon

Kootenay National Park of Canada
PO Box 220 Radium Hot Springs, BC V0A 1M0
Tel: 250-347-9505
Toll-Free: 888-773-8888
kootenay.info@pc.gc.ca
www.pc.gc.ca/pn-np/bc/kootenay/index_e.asp
twitter.com/KootenayNP
www.facebook.com/KootenayNP

Lower Fort Garry National Historic Site of Canada
5925 Highway 9, St. Andrews, MB R1A 4A8
Tel: 204-785-6050; *Fax:* 204-482-5887
Toll-Free: 888-773-8888
TTY: 866-787-6221
lfg.info@pc.gc.ca
www.pc.gc.ca/lhn-nhs/mb/fortgarry/index_e.asp
twitter.com/ParksCanadaWPG
www.facebook.com/ParksCanadaWPG

Motherwell Homestead National Historic Site of Canada
PO Box 70 Abernethy, SK S0A 0A0
Tel: 306-333-2116; *Fax:* 306-333-2210
Motherwell.Homestead@pc.gc.ca
www.pc.gc.ca/eng/lhn-nhs/sk/motherwell/index.aspx
twitter.com/parkscanada_sk
www.facebook.com/saskNHS

Mount Revelstoke National Park of Canada
PO Box 350 Revelstoke, BC V0E 2S0
Tel: 250-837-7500; *Fax:* 250-837-7536
TTY: 866-787-6221
www.pc.gc.ca/pn-np/bc/revelstoke/index_e.asp
www.facebook.com/MRGnationalparks

Nahanni National Park Reserve of Canada
10002 - 100 St., PO Box 348 Fort Simpson, NT X0E 0N0
Tel: 867-695-7750; *Fax:* 867-695-2446
nahanni.info@pc.gc.ca
www.pc.gc.ca/pn-np/nt/nahanni/index_e.asp

Pacific Rim National Park Reserve of Canada
2040 Pacific Rim Hwy., PO Box 280 Ucluelet, BC V0R 3A0
Tel: 250-726-3500; *Fax:* 250-726-3520
pacrim.info@pc.gc.ca
www.pc.gc.ca/pn-np/bc/pacificrim/index_e.asp
twitter.com/pacificrimNPR
www.facebook.com/PacificRimNPR

Prince Albert National Park of Canada
PO Box 100 Waskesiu Lake, SK S0J 2Y0
Tel: 306-663-4522
panp.info@pc.gc.ca
www.pc.gc.ca/eng/pn-np/sk/princealbert/index.aspx
twitter.com/parkscanada_sk

Prince of Wales Fort National Historic Site of Canada
PO Box 127 Churchill, MB R0B 0E0
Tel: 204-675-8863; *Fax:* 204-675-2026
TTY: 866-787-6221
mannorth.nhs@pc.gc.ca
www.pc.gc.ca/lhn-nhs/mb/prince/index_e.asp

Qausuittuq National Park of Canada
nunavut.info@pc.gc.ca
twitter.com/ParksCanNunavut
www.facebook.com/ParksCanadaNunavut

Quttinirpaaq National Park of Canada
PO Box 278 Iqaluit, NU X0A 0H0
Tel: 867-975-4673; *Fax:* 867-975-4674
nunavut.info@pc.gc.ca
www.pc.gc.ca/pn-np/nu/quttinirpaaq/index_e.asp
twitter.com/ParksCanNunavut
www.facebook.com/ParksCanadaNunavut

Riding Mountain National Park of Canada
PO Box 299 Onanole, MB R0J 2H0
Tel: 204-848-7275; *Fax:* 204-848-2596
rmnp.info@pc.gc.ca
www.pc.gc.ca/pn-np/mb/riding/index_e.asp
twitter.com/@RidingNP
www.facebook.com/RidingNP

Riel House National Historic Site of Canada
330 River Rd. (St. Vidal), Winnipeg, MB R1A 3Y3
Tel: 204-983-6757; *Fax:* 204-984-0679
TTY: 866-787-6221
riel.info@pc.gc.ca
www.pc.gc.ca/lhn-nhs/mb/riel/index_E.asp
twitter.com/ParksCanadaWPG
www.facebook.com/ParksCanadaWPG

Rocky Mountain House National Historic Site of Canada
Site 127, Comp 6, RR#4, Rocky Mountain House, AB T4T 2A4
Tel: 403-845-2412; *Fax:* 403-845-5320
rocky.info@pc.gc.ca
www.pc.gc.ca/lhn-nhs/ab/rockymountain/index_E.asp

Sirmilik National Park of Canada
PO Box 300 Pond Inlet, NU X0A 0S0
Tel: 867-899-8092; *Fax:* 867-899-8104
sirmilik.info@pc.gc.ca
www.pc.gc.ca/pn-np/nu/sirmilik/index_E.asp
twitter.com/ParksCanNunavut
www.facebook.com/ParksCanadaNunavut

SS Keno National Historic Site of Canada
PO Box 390 Dawson City, YT Y0B 1G0
Tel: 867-993-7200; *Fax:* 867-993-7203
dawson.info@pc.gc.ca
www.pc.gc.ca/lhn-nhs/yt/sskeno/index_e.asp
twitter.com/ParksCanYukon
www.facebook.com/ParksCanadaYukon

SS Klondike National Historic Site of Canada
#205, 300 Main St., Whitehorse, YT Y1A 2B5
Tel: 867-667-3910; *Fax:* 867-393-6701
Toll-Free: 800-661-0486
whitehorse.info@pc.gc.ca
www.pc.gc.ca/lhn-nhs/yt/ssklondike/index_E.asp
Other Communication: Summer: 867-667-4511
twitter.com/ParksCanYukon
www.facebook.com/ParksCanadaYukon

St. Andrews Rectory National Historic Site of Canada
374, chemin River, St. Andrews, MB R1A 2Y1
Tel: 204-785-6050; *Fax:* 204-482-5887
Toll-Free: 888-773-8888
TTY: 866-787-6221
lfg.info@pc.gc.ca
www.pc.gc.ca/lhn-nhs/mb/standrews/contact_e.asp

The Forks National Historic Site of Canada
Manitoba Field Unit, 145 McDermot Ave., Winnipeg, MB R3B 0R9
Tel: 204-983-6757; *Fax:* 204-984-0679
Toll-Free: 888-773-8888
TTY: 866-787-6221
forks.fourche@pc.gc.ca
www.pc.gc.ca/lhn-nhs/mb/forks/index_e.asp
twitter.com/ParksCanadaWPG
www.facebook.com/ParksCanadaWPG

Tuktut Nogait National Park of Canada
PO Box 91 Paulatuk, NT X0E 1N0
Tel: 867-580-3233; *Fax:* 867-580-3234
inuvik.info@pc.gc.ca
www.pc.gc.ca/pn-np/nt/tuktutnogait/index_e.asp

Ukkusiksalik National Park of Canada
PO Box 220 Repulse Bay, NU X0C 0H0
Tel: 867-462-4500; *Fax:* 867-462-4095
ukkusiksalik.info@pc.gc.ca
www.pc.gc.ca/pn-np/nu/ukkusiksalik/index_E.asp
twitter.com/ParksCanNunavut
www.facebook.com/ParksCanadaNunavut

Vuntut National Park of Canada
PO Box 19 Old Crow, YT Y0B 1N0
Tel: 867-667-3910; *Fax:* 867-393-6701
vuntut.info@pc.gc.ca
www.pc.gc.ca/pn-np/yt/vuntut/index_E.asp
twitter.com/ParksCanYukon
www.facebook.com/ParksCanadaYukon

Wapusk National Park of Canada
Churchill Office, PO Box 127 Churchill, MB R0B 0E0
Tel: 204-675-8863; *Fax:* 204-675-2026
Toll-Free: 888-773-8888
TTY: 866-787-6221
wapusk.np@pc.gc.ca
www.pc.gc.ca/pn-np/mb/wapusk/index_e.asp

Waterton Lakes National Park of Canada
PO Box 200 Waterton Park, AB T0K 2M0
Tel: 403-859-5133; *Fax:* 403-859-5152
waterton.info@pc.gc.ca
www.pc.gc.ca/pn-np/ab/waterton/index_E.asp
twitter.com/watertonlakesnp
www.facebook.com/WatertonLakesNP

Wood Buffalo National Park of Canada
PO Box 750 Fort Smith, NT X0E 0P0
Tel: 867-872-7900; *Fax:* 867-872-3910
TTY: 867-872-7961
wbnp.info@pc.gc.ca
www.pc.gc.ca/pn-np/nt/woodbuffalo/index_e.asp
Other Communication: 24 Hour Hotline: 867-872-7962

Yoho National Park of Canada
PO Box 99 Field, BC V0A 1G0
Tel: 250-343-6783
yoho.info@pc.gc.ca
www.pc.gc.ca/pn-np/bc/yoho/index_E.asp

York Factory National Historic Site of Canada
PO Box 127 Churchill, MB R0B 0E0
Tel: 204-675-8863; *Fax:* 204-675-2026
mannorth.nhs@pc.gc.ca
www.pc.gc.ca/lhn-nhs/mb/yorkfactory/index_E.asp

Parole Board of Canada (PBC) / Commission des libérations conditionnelles du Canada (CLCC)

Communications Division, National Office, 410 Laurier Ave. West, Ottawa, ON K1A 0R1
Tel: 613-954-7474; *Fax:* 613-941-4981
info@pbc-clcc.gc.ca
www.pbc-clcc.gc.ca
Other Communication: Record Suspension Information: 1-800-874-2652, suspension@pbc-clcc.gc.ca; Victim Information: 1-866-789-4636; Media Relations: 613-960-1856, media@pbc-clcc.gc.ca
www.youtube.com/user/PBCclcc

The Parole Board of Canada is an agency within the portfolio of Public Safety Canada. The chairperson of the Board reports to Parliament through Public Safety Canada.
The role of the Parole Division of Canada is to make independent, conditional release & record suspension decisions. The independent administrative tribunal is also responsible for making clemency recommendations. The Parole Board of Canada acts under the authority of the *Corrections & Conditional Release Act* & regulations, the *Criminal Code of Canada*the *Criminal Records Act* & regulations, the *Letters Patent*& the *Privacy & Access to Information* Acts.
The national office in Ottawa contains the Appeal Division of the Board. Regional offices are located throughout the country.

Chair, Harvey J. Cenaiko
Tel: 613-954-1154
Executive Director General, Talal Dakalbab
Tel: 613-954-1153
Chief Financial Officer, Cathy Gaudet
Tel: 613-957-2325
Director General, Policy & Operations Division, Suzanne Brisebois
Tel: 613-941-3380
Director, Public Affairs, Jennifer McNaughton
Tel: 613-954-6547
Acting Director, Record Suspension Program, Amélie Brisebois
Tel: 613-954-5973; *Fax:* 613-941-4981
Director, Clemency & Record Suspension, Denis Ladouceur
Tel: 613-954-5913; *Fax:* 613-941-4981
Director, Corporate Services, Eric McMullen
Tel: 613-954-7771; *Fax:* 613-957-7729
Director, Board Members Training & Development, Céline St-Onge
Tel: 613-954-5944; *Fax:* 613-941-6444
Other Communications: Alternate Phone: 613-608-7334

Regional Offices of the Parole Board of Canada

Abbotsford - Pacific Regional Office
1925 McCallum Rd., 2nd Fl., Abbotsford, BC V2S 3N2
Tel: 604-870-2468; *Fax:* 604-870-2498
Regional Director General, Harold Massey

Edmonton - Prairies Regional Office
Scotia 2, Scotia Place, #401, 10060 Jasper Ave. NW, 4th Fl., Edmonton, AB T5J 3R8
Tel: 780-495-3404; *Fax:* 780-495-3475
Acting Regional Director General, Talal Dakalbab
Tel: 780-442-6770

Kingston - Ontario & Nunavut Regional Office
516 O'Connor Dr., Kingston, ON K7P 1N3
Tel: 613-634-3857; *Fax:* 613-634-3862
Regional Director General, Denise Preston
Tel: 613-384-7621

Moncton - Atlantic Regional Office
#101, 1045 Main St., Moncton, NB E1C 1H1
Tel: 506-851-6345; *Fax:* 506-851-6926
Regional Director General, Gisèle Smith
Tel: 506-851-6492

Montréal - Québec Regional Office
Tour ouest, Place Guy-Favreau, #1001, 200, boul René-Lévesque ouest, Montréal, QC H2Z 1X4
Tel: 514-283-4584; *Fax:* 514-283-5484
Regional Director General, Martin J. van Ginhoven
Tel: 514-283-4584

Saskatoon - Prairies Regional Office
101 - 22 St. East, 6th Fl., Saskatoon, SK S7K 0E1
Tel: 306-975-4228; *Fax:* 306-975-5892
This office serves Saskatchewan & Manitoba.
Acting Regional Director General, Talal Dakalbab
Tel: 780-442-6770

Patented Medicine Prices Review Board / Conseil d'examen du prix des médicaments brevetés

Standard Life Centre, #1400, 333 Laurier Ave. West, PO Box L40 Ottawa, ON K1P 1C1
Tel: 613-954-8299; *Fax:* 613-952-7626
Toll-Free: 877-861-2350
TTY: 613-957-4373
pmprb@pmprb-cepmb.gc.ca
www.pmprb-cepmb.gc.ca
twitter.com/PMPRB_CEPMB

The Patented Medicine Prices Review Board (PMPRB) is an independent quasi-judicial body established by Parliament in 1987 under the Patent Act (Act). The PMPRB is responsible for regulating the prices that patentees charge, the "factory-gate" price, for prescription & non-prescription patented drugs sold in Canada, to wholesalers, hospitals or pharmacies, for human and veterinary use to ensure that they are not excessive. The PMPRB regulates the price of each patented drug product, including each strength of each dosage form of each patented medicine sold in Canada.

Chair, Mary Catherine Lindberg
Tel: 613-952-3300
Vice-Chair, Mitchell Levine
Tel: 613-960-4570; *Fax:* 613-952-7626
Executive Director, Douglas Clark
Tel: 613-957-3656; *Fax:* 613-952-7626
Director, Board Secretariat & Communications, Guillaume Couillard
Tel: 613-954-8299; *Fax:* 613-952-7626
Director, Corporate Services, Ramona Kenney
Tel: 613-952-3304; *Fax:* 613-952-7626
Director, Policy & Economic Analysis Branch, Tanya Potashnik
Tel: 613-952-9406; *Fax:* 613-952-7626
Director, Regulatory Affairs & Outreach, Ginette Tognet
Tel: 613-954-8297; *Fax:* 613-952-7626

Polar Knowledge Canada (POLAR) / Savoir polaire Canada (POLAIRE)

2464 Sheffield Rd., Ottawa, ON K1B 4E5
Tel: 613-943-8605
info@polar.gc.ca
www.canada.ca/en/polar-knowledge
Other Communication: Archived Canadian Polar Commission Web Site: www.polarcom.gc.ca
Secondary Address: 360 Albert St., 17th Fl. Science & Technology Program Interim Office Ottawa, ON K1R 1A4

Polar Knowledge Canada was created in 2015, merging the mandate of the Canadian Polar Commission with the Canadian High Arctic Research Station (CHARS) initiative at Indigenous & Northern Affairs. POLAR will be located at the Canadian High Arctic Research Station in Cambridge Bay, Nunavut, once it is

completed in 2017.
The former Canadian Polar Commission was mandated to enhance the public's awareness of polar regions & to foster both international & domestic liaison & cooperation in circumpolar research & technology development. One of the Commission's main objectives in the short term is focus on climate change & energy. Maintains the Canadian Polar Information System (CPIS) which, in addition to polar data & information, includes services such as the Polar Science Forum, Researcher's Directory, Researcher's Toolbox, & links to International Partners. Research funding initiatives include the Scientific Committee on Antarctic Research (SCAR) Fellowship, Northern Scientific Training Program, & Canadian Northern Studies Trust.

Minister Responsible; Minister, Indigenous & Northern Affairs, Hon. Dr. Carolyn Bennett, P.C., M.D.
Tel: 613-995-9666; *Fax:* 613-947-4622
carolyn.bennett@parl.gc.ca

President, David J. Scott, Ph.D
Tel: 613-943-8606

Policy Horizons Canada / Horizons de politiques Canada

360 Albert St., 15th Fl., Ottawa, ON K1R 7X7
Tel: 613-947-3800; *Fax:* 613-995-6006
questions@horizons.gc.ca
www.horizons.gc.ca

Formerly known as the Policy Research Initiative, Policy Horizons Canada serves the deputy minister & federal policy communities within the government by providing insight & research to help policymakers create new policies at a faster, more productive rate.

Director General, Paul De Civita
Tel: 613-943-2400; *Fax:* 613-947-3809
paul.decivita@horizons.gc.ca

Director, Samantha McDonald
Tel: 613-992-5193; *Fax:* 613-947-3809

Chief Futurist, Peter Padbury
Tel: 613-943-8412; *Fax:* 613-947-3809
peter.padbury@horizons.gc.ca

Director, John Giraldez
Tel: 613-992-3660; *Fax:* 613-947-3809
john.giraldez@horizons.gc.ca

PPP Canada

#630, 100 Queen St., Ottawa, ON K1P 1J9
Tel: 613-947-9480; *Fax:* 613-947-2289
Toll-Free: 877-947-9480
info@p3canada.ca
www.p3canada.ca
Other Communication: Media Inquiries, Phone: 613-947-9480; Toll-Free: 1-877-947-9480; E-mail: media@p3canada.ca
www.linkedin.com/company/p3-canada

PPP Canada is a Crown corporation whose mandate it is to assess public-private partnership opportunities & to provide funding for such projects through the P3 Canada Fund. The corporation reports to Parliament through the Minister of Finance.

Chair, Anthony Comper
Chief Executive Officer, John McBride
Chief Financial Officer & Vice-President, Finance, Risk & Administration, Greg Smith
Vice-President, Project Development, Carol Beaulieu
Vice-President, Investment, Michael Mills
Vice-President, Strategy & Organizational Development, Kim Butler

Privacy Commissioner of Canada / Commissariat à la protection de la vie privée du Canada

30 Victoria St., Gatineau, QC K1A 1H3
Tel: 819-994-5444; *Fax:* 819-994-5424
Toll-Free: 800-282-1376
TTY: 819-994-6591
www.priv.gc.ca
twitter.com/PrivacyPrivee

The Privacy Commissioner of Canada is an Officer of Parliament mandated to protect & promote privacy rights, working independently from Government, reporting directly to the House of Commons & the Senate. The Privacy Commissioner oversees two federal privacy laws: the Privacy Act, which covers the federal government, & the new Personal Information Protection & Electronic Documents (PIPEDA) Act, which covers the collection use & disclosure of personal information in the course of commercial activities, except in provinces which have not, by then, enacted legislation that is deemed to be substantially similar to the federal law. The Privacy Commissioner's powers include: investigating complaints & conducting audits under both federal privacy laws; publishing information about personal information handling practices in the public & private sectors; conducting research into privacy issues; & promoting awareness & understanding of privacy issues in Canada.

Privacy Commissioner, Daniel Therrien
Tel: 819-994-5841; *Fax:* 819-994-5424
Other Communications: Executive Assistant, Phone: 819-994-5835

Chief Financial Officer & Director General, Corporate Services Branch, Daniel Nadeau
Tel: 819-994-6503; *Fax:* 819-994-5424

Chief Privacy Officer & Director, Access to Information & Privacy, Johane Lessard
Tel: 819-994-5970; *Fax:* 819-994-5424

Director General, Communications Branch, Anne-Marie Hayden
Tel: 819-994-5581; *Fax:* 819-994-5424
Anne-Marie.Hayden@priv.gc.ca

Director General, PIPEDA Investigations Branch, Brent Homan
Tel: 819-994-6261; *Fax:* 819-994-5424

Director General & Senior General Counsel, Legal Services, Policy & Research, Patricia Kosseim
Tel: 819-994-6005; *Fax:* 819-994-5424

Director General, Audit & Review, Steven Morgan
Tel: 819-994-6046; *Fax:* 819-994-5424

Public Prosecution Service of Canada (PPSC) / Service des poursuites pénales du Canada (SPPC)

284 Wellington St., 2nd Fl., Ottawa, ON K1A 0H8
Tel: 613-957-6489
Toll-Free: 877-505-7772
info@ppsc.gc.ca
www.ppsc-sppc.gc.ca

The Public Prosecution Service of Canada prosecutes criminal offences under federal jurisdiction & seeks to strengthen the criminal justice system by fulfilling the responsibilities of the Attorney General of Canada. Types of cases handled by the PPSC include ones involving drugs, organized crime, terrorism, tax law, the proceeds of crime, crimes against humanity & war crimes, Criminal Code offences in the territories & federal regulatory offences.

Minister, Justice & Attorney General of Canada, Hon. Jody Wilson-Raybould, P.C.
Tel: 613-992-1416; *Fax:* 613-992-1460
Jody.Wilson-Raybould@parl.gc.ca

Director of Public Prosecutions, Brian J. Saunders
Tel: 613-957-4756; *Fax:* 613-954-2958

Deputy Director of Public Prosecutions, Drug, National Security & Northern Prosecutions Branch, George Dolhai
Tel: 613-941-2653; *Fax:* 613-941-8742

Chief Financial Officer, Finance & Acquisitions Directorate, Lucie Bourcier
Tel: 613-957-4842; *Fax:* 613-941-9398

Chief Information Officer, Information Management & Technology Directorate, Victor Gatt
Tel: 613-946-7989; *Fax:* 613-960-3434

Chief Audit Executive, Internal Audit, Julie Betts
Tel: 613-960-0884

Chief, Executive Secretariat, Robert Doyle
Tel: 613-952-0267; *Fax:* 613-954-2958

Director General, Human Resources Directorate, Denis Deshamais
Tel: 613-957-2310; *Fax:* 613-946-9982

Senior General Counsel & Director General, Corporate Counsel Office, Jef Richstone
Tel: 613-960-4852; *Fax:* 613-954-2958

Office of the Commissioner of Canada Elections / Bureau du Commissaire aux élections fédérales

30 Victoria St., Gatineau, ON K1A 0M6
Fax: 819-939-1801
Toll-Free: 855-759-6740
info@cef-cce.gc.ca
www.cef-cce.gc.ca
Other Communication: Media Relations, Toll-Free Phone: 1-855-759-6737

The Commissioner of Canada Elections was transferred from Elections Canada to the Public Prosecution Service of Canada on October 1, 2014.

Commissioner of Canada Elections, Yves Côté
Tel: 819-939-1800

Senior Director, Investigations, Eric Ferron
Tel: 819-939-2062

Director & Senior Counsel, Legal Services, Marc Chénier
Tel: 819-939-2253

Regulatory & Economic Prosecutions & Management Branch / Direction des poursuites réglementaires et économiques et de la gestion

Deputy Director of Public Prosecutions, Kathleen Roussel
Tel: 613-957-4762

Senior General Counsel & Director General, Law Practice Management & Regulatory & Economic Prosecutions, Jeff Richstone
Tel: 613-960-4852; *Fax:* 613-954-2958

Executive Director & Senior Counsel, Ministerial & External Relations, Cyril McIntyre
Tel: 613-952-1525; *Fax:* 613-946-9977

Senior General Counsel, Supreme Court Coordination, François Lacasse
Tel: 613-957-4770; *Fax:* 613-941-7865

Director, Communications, Daniel Brien
Tel: 613-946-3821

Director, Strategic Planning & Performance Management, Francine Chartrand
Tel: 613-946-7991; *Fax:* 613-946-9977

Director, Agent Affairs, Marius Nault
Tel: 613-952-0284; *Fax:* 613-957-8478

Director, Administration Services, Juan-Luis Vásquez
Tel: 613-946-8880; *Fax:* 613-946-9977
Other Communications: Alternate Phone: 613-791-3036

Regional Offices

Edmonton
EPCOR Tower, #700, 10423 - 101st St., Edmonton, AB T5H 0E7
Tel: 780-495-3553
Chief Federal Prosecutor, Wes Smart, Q.C.
Tel: 780-495-6608; *Fax:* 780-495-6940

Halifax
Duke Tower, #1400, 5251 Duke St., Halifax, NS B3J 1P3
Tel: 902-426-5535
Chief Federal Prosecutor, Peter Chisholm
Tel: 902-426-7142; *Fax:* 902-426-7274

Iqaluit
PO Box 1030 Iqaluit, NU X0A 0H9
Tel: 867-975-4600
Chief Federal Prosecutor, Barry Nordin
Tel: 867-975-4635; *Fax:* 867-979-0101

Montréal
Tour Est, Complexe Guy-Favreau, 200, boul René-Lévesque ouest, 9e étage, Montréal, QC H2Z 1X4
Tél: 514-283-2935
Procureur fédéral en chef, André A. Morin, Ad. E.
Tél: 514-283-9929

Ottawa - National Capital Region
#806, 160 Elgin St., Ottawa, ON K1A 0H8
Tel: 613-957-7000
Chief Federal Prosecutor, Tom Raganold
Tel: 613-957-7142

Saskatoon
123 Second Ave. South, 10th Floor, Saskatoon, SK S7K 7E6
Tel: 306-975-5477
Chief Federal Prosecutor, Christine Haynes
Tel: 306-975-4766; *Fax:* 306-975-4507

Toronto
Exchange Tower, #3400, 2 First Canadian Pl., PO Box 36 Toronto, ON M5X 1K6
Tel: 416-973-0960
Chief Federal Prosecutor, Morris Pistyner
Tel: 416-973-3150; *Fax:* 416-973-8253

Vancouver
Robson Ct., #900, 840 Howe St., Vancouver, BC V6Z 2S9
Tel: 604-666-5250
Chief Federal Prosecutor, Robert Prior
Tel: 604-775-7475; *Fax:* 604-666-1599

Whitehorse
Elijah Smith Bldg., #200, 300 Main St., Whitehorse, YT Y1A 2B5
Tel: 867-667-8100
Chief Federal Prosecutor, John Phelps
Tel: 867-393-6884; *Fax:* 867-667-3979

Winnipeg
#515, 234 Donald St., Winnipeg, MB R3C 1M8
Tel: 204-983-5738
Chief Federal Prosecutor, Ian Mahon
Tel: 204-983-2398; *Fax:* 204-984-1350

Yellowknife
Joe Tobie Bldg., 5020 - 48th St., 3rd Fl., PO Box 8 Yellowknife, NT X1A 2N1
Tel: 867-669-6900
Chief Federal Prosecutor, Sandra Aitken
Tel: 867-669-6900; *Fax:* 867-920-4022

Local Offices

Brampton
#600, 201 County Court Blvd., Brampton, ON L6W 4L2
Tel: 905-454-2424

Calgary
#510, 606 - 4th St. SW, Calgary, AB T2P 1T1
Tel: 403-299-3978

Kitchener
#202, 15 - 29 Duke St., Kitchener, ON N2H 1A0
Tel: 519-585-2970

Moncton
#400, 777 Main St., Moncton, NB E1C 1E9
Tel: 506-851-4391

St. John's
Atlantic Place, #812, 215 Water St., St. John's, NL A1C 6C9
Tel: 709-772-8046

Yellowknife - Nunavut Local Office
Joe Tobie Bldg., 5020 - 48th St., 2nd Fl., PO Box 8
Yellowknife, NT X1A 2N1
Tel: 867-669-6931

Public Safety Canada / Sécurité publique Canada

269 Laurier Ave. West, Ottawa, ON K1A 0P8
Tel: 613-944-4875; *Fax:* 613-954-5186
Toll-Free: 800-830-3118
TTY: 866-865-5667
www.publicsafety.gc.ca
Other Communication: National Crime Prevention Centre E-mail: ps.prevention-prevention.sp@canada.ca; National Office for Victims Toll-Free: 1-866-525-0554; Media Relations: 613-991-0657
twitter.com/safety_canada
www.youtube.com/user/SafetyinCanada

Public Safety Canada works to keep Canadians safe in cases of natural disasters, crime, & terrorism. Policies are developed, & programs & services are delivered in the following areas: emergency management, including information about emergency preparedness; national security, which features the administration of the Government Operations Centre to monitor potential threats to the national interest; law enforcement, including the contribution of funds for policing services in First Nations & Inuit communities; federal corrections effectiveness, efficiency & accountability, with the development of federal policy & legislation; & crime prevention, such as work with other governments, businesses, & volunteer groups to support projects to reduce offences.

Minister, Public Safety & Emergency Preparedness, Hon. Ralph Goodale, P.C., B.A., LL.B.
Tel: 613-947-1153; *Fax:* 613-996-9790
ralph.goodale@parl.gc.ca
Deputy Minister, Malcolm Brown
Tel: 613-991-2895; *Fax:* 613-990-8312
Parliamentary Secretary, Michel Picard
Tel: 613-996-2416; *Fax:* 613-995-6973
Michel.Picard@parl.gc.ca
Chief of Staff, Minister's Office, Vacant
Tel: 613-991-2924
Chief Audit & Evaluation Executive, Internal Audit & Evaluation Directorate, Denis Gorman
Tel: 613-990-2646
Director, Legal Services, Sophie Beecher
Tel: 613-949-3184

Associated Agencies, Boards & Commissions:

•Canada Border Services Agency (CBSA) / Agence des services frontaliers du Canada (ASFC)
See Entry Name Index for detailed listing.

•Canadian Security Intelligence Service (CSIS) / Service canadien du renseignement de sécurité (SCRS)
See Entry Name Index for detailed listing.

•Commission for Public Complaints Against the Royal Canadian Mounted Police / Commission des plaintes du public contre la Gendarmerie royale du Canada
National Intake Office
PO Box 88689
Surrey, BC V3W 0X1
Fax: 604-501-4095
Toll-free: 800-665-6878
TTY: 866-432-5837
www.crcc-ccetp.gc.ca
The Commission is responsible for the receipt of complaints from the public about the conduct of members of the RCMP. It is also responsible for the review of complaints when complainants are not satisfied with the disposition of their complaints by the RCMP. The Commission can inquire into complaints by means of public hearings & the chair of the Commission can investigate complaints. Annually, the chair reports to Parliament through the Minister of Public Safety Canada.

•Correctional Service of Canada (CSC) / Service correctionnel Canada (SCC)
See Entry Name Index for detailed listing.

•Parole Board of Canada (PBC) / Commission des libérations conditionnelles du Canada (CLCC)
See Entry Name Index for detailed listing.

•Royal Canadian Mounted Police (RCMP) / Gendarmerie royale du Canada (GRC)
See Entry Name Index for detailed listing.

•Royal Canadian Mounted Police External Review Committee / Comité externe d'examen de la Gendarmerie royale du Canada
PO Box 1159 B
Ottawa, ON K1P 5R2
Tel: 613-998-2134; *Fax:* 613-990-8969
org@erc-cee.gc.ca
www.erc-cee.gc.ca
The RCMP External Review Committee is an independent agency reporting to Parliament through the Minister of Public Safety Canada. It aims to independently and impartially promote fair and equitable labour relations within the RCMP, in accordance with applicable principles of law. To this end the Committee conducts an independent review of appeals in disciplinary and discharge and demotion matters, as well as certain categories of grievances that can be referred to it pursuant to s. 33 of the RCMP Act and s. 36 of the RCMP Regulations.

Communications Directorate / Direction générale des communications
Director General, Jamie Tomlinson
Tel: 613-990-2642
Manager, Communications, Communication Services Division, Athena MacKenzie
Tel: 613-949-4462

Community Safety & Countering Crime Branch / Secteur de la sécurité communautaire et de la réduction du crime
340 Laurier Ave. West, Ottawa, ON K1A 0P8
www.publicsafety.gc.ca/cnt/cntrng-crm
The Community Safety & Countering Crime Branch consists of the Aboriginal Policing Directorate, the Corrections & Criminal Justice Directorate, & the National Crime Prevention Centre.
Assistant Deputy Minister, Kathy Thompson
Tel: 613-990-2703

Aboriginal Policing Policy Directorate / Direction des politiques de police autochtones
Director, Micheline Lavoie
Tel: 613-990-8771

Corrections & Criminal Justice Directorate / Direction générale des affaires correctionnelles et de la ustice pénale
Director General, Angela Connidis
Tel: 613-991-2952

Corporate Management Branch / Secteur de la gestion ministérielle
340 Laurier Ave. West, Ottawa, ON K1A 0P8
Chief Financial Officer & Assistant Deputy Minister, Mark Perlman
Tel: 613-990-2615; *Fax:* 613-949-8441
Chief Information Officer, Christianne Poirier
Tel: 613-944-4878
Comptroller & Deputy Chief Financial Officer, Judy Cosby
Tel: 613-998-0053; *Fax:* 613-991-1227
Director General, Corporate Services, David Conabree
Tel: 613-949-0477
Director General, Human Resources, Philippe Thompson
Tel: 613-949-9925; *Fax:* 613-991-4534
Acting Senior Director, Financial Services & Systems & Resource Management, Douglas McConnachie
Tel: 613-991-2836

Emergency Management & Programs Branch / Secteur de la gestion des urgences et des programmes
340 Laurier Ave. West, Ottawa, ON K1A 0P8
The Emergency Management & National Security Branch consists of the following directorates & secretariat: Coordination Directorate; Emergency Management Policy Directorate; National Security Policy Directorate; Operations Directorate; Preparedness & Recovery Directorate; & the Cyber Security Strategy Secretariat.
Assistant Deputy Minister, Lori MacDonald
Tel: 613-993-4325
Senior Director, Emergency Management Programs, Michèle Kingsley
Tel: 613-990-3110
Director General, Emergency Management Policy & Outreach, Stéphanie Durand
Tel: 613-991-2799
Director General, Programs Directorate, Bobby Matheson
Tel: 613-957-9639; *Fax:* 613-946-9996
Director General, Government Operations Centre (GOC), Craig Oldham
Tel: 613-991-7728
Senior Director, Emergency Programs, Dave Neville
Tel: 613-990-3110
Director General, Programs, Bobby Matheson
Tel: 613-957-9639; *Fax:* 613-946-9996

Law Enforcement & Policing Branch / Secteur de la Police, et de l'application de la loi
340 Laurier Ave. West, Ottawa, ON K1A 0P8
Assistant Deputy Minister, Vacant
Director General, Law Enforcement & Border Strategies Directorate, Trevor Bhupsingh
Tel: 613-991-4281
Director General, Policing Policy, Mark Potter
Tel: 613-991-1632
Senior Director, RCMP Policy Division, Annie LeBlanc
Tel: 613-991-2842; *Fax:* 613-993-5252

National & Cyber Security Branch / Secteur de la sécurité et de la cyber-sécurité nationale
269 Laurier Ave. West, Ottawa, ON K1A 0P8
Tel: 613-990-4976
www.publicsafety.gc.ca/cyber
Other Communication: Get Cyber Safe URL: www.getcybersafe.gc.ca
twitter.com/getcybersafe
www.facebook.com/GetCyberSafe
www.youtube.com/channel/UCOY1X4VeHhjYe0V44hZowMQ
Senior Assistant Deputy Minister, Lynda Clairmont
Tel: 613-990-4976
Assistant Deputy Minister, Gary Robertson
Tel: 613-991-9633
Director General, National Cyber Security Directorate, Peter Hammerschmidt
Tel: 613-990-2661

Portfolio Affairs & Communications / Secteur des affaires du portefeuillet et des communications
340 Laurier Ave. West, Ottawa, ON K1A 0P8
Assistant Deputy Minister, Paul MacKinnon
Tel: 613-949-6435
Director General, Border Policy & Intergovernmental Affairs, Jill Wherrett
Tel: 613-949-7260

Office of the Public Sector Integrity Commissioner of Canada (PSIC) / Commissariat à l'intégrité du secteur public du Canada (ISPC)

60 Queen St., 7th Fl., Ottawa, ON K1P 5Y7
Tel: 613-941-6400; *Fax:* 613-941-6535
Toll-Free: 866-941-6400
www.psic-ispc.gc.ca
Other Communication: Secure Fax: 613-946-2151

A independent Agency of Parliament, established in 2007 under the Public Servants Disclosure Protection Act, that provides a means for public servants or members of the public to disclose possible wrongdoing in the federal public sector. The Commissioner reports directly to parliament.

Public Sector Integrity Commissioner of Canada, Joe Friday
Tel: 613-948-9178; *Fax:* 613-941-6535
Executive Director, France Duquette
Tel: 613-946-2142; *Fax:* 613-941-6535
Executive Services Manager, Monqie Halloran
Tel: 613-948-9178; *Fax:* 613-941-6535
Director, Operations, Raynald Lampron
Tel: 613-941-6304; *Fax:* 613-941-6535

Public Servants Disclosure Protection Tribunal (PSDPT) / Tribunal de la protection des fonctionnaires divulgateurs (TPFD)

#512, 90 Sparks St., Ottawa, ON K1P 5B4
Tel: 613-943-8310; *Fax:* 613-943-8325
tribunal@psdpt-tpfd.gc.ca
www.psdpt-tpfd.gc.ca

The Tribunal exists to hear reprisal complaints referred by the Public Sector Integrity Commissioner, & has the power to discipline persons who take reprisals while granting remedies to complainants.

Minister Responsible; Minister, Public Services & Procurement, Hon. Judy Foote, P.C., B.A., B.Ed
Tel: 613-992-8655; *Fax:* 613-992-5324
Judy.Foote@parl.gc.ca
Chair, Hon. Marie-Josée Bédard
Member, Hon. Peter B. Annis
Member, Hon. Martine St-Louis
Executive Director, Rachel Boyer
Tel: 613-947-0740

Public Service Commission (PSC) / Commission de la fonction publique (CFP)

22 Eddy St., Gatineau, QC K1A 0M7
Tel: 613-992-9562; *Fax:* 613-992-9352
TTY: 800-532-9397
CFP.INFOCOM.PSC@cfp-psc.gc.ca
www.psc-cfp.gc.ca
twitter.com/PSCofCanada

An independent agency that reports directly to Parliament. For administrative purposes, the Minister of Canadian Heritage speaks on its behalf in the House of Commons, but has no jurisdiction over it. The commission is also responsible for safeguarding the values of a professional Public Service: competence, non-partisanship & representatives.

Minister Responsible; Minister, Public Services & Procurement, Hon. Judy Foote, P.C., B.A., B.Ed
Tel: 613-992-8655; *Fax:* 613-992-5324
Judy.Foote@parl.gc.ca

President, Anne-Marie Robinson
Tel: 819-420-6559

Commissioner, Susan Cartwright
Tel: 819-420-6566

Commissioner, Daniel Tucker
Tel: 819-420-6567

Executive Director & General Counsel, Jean-Daniel Bélanger
Tel: 819-420-6658; *Fax:* 819-420-6660

Audit & Data Services / Vérification et des services de données

Vice-President, Jacqueline Bogden
Tel: 819-420-8808

Director General, Audit, Blair Haddock
Tel: 819-420-8866

Director General, Data Services & Analysis, Raman Srivastava
Tel: 819-420-8819

Corporate Management / Gestion ministérielle

Vice-President, Omer Boudreau
Tel: 819-420-8378

Director General & Chief Information Officer, Information Technology Services, Cindy Cripps-Prawak
Tel: 819-420-8433; *Fax:* 819-420-8408

Director General, Human Resources Management, Judith Flynn-Bédard
Tel: 819-420-6604

Director General, Communications & Parliamentary Affairs, Andrew McGillivary
Tel: 819-420-6543

Director General, Finance & Administration, Philip Morton
Tel: 819-420-8374

Investigations / Direction générale des enquêtes

Vice-President, Denis Bilodeau
Tel: 819-420-8916; *Fax:* 819-420-8855

Policy / Politiques

Senior Vice-President, Christine Donoghue
Tel: 819-420-8505; *Fax:* 819-420-8953

Acting Senior Vice-President, Gerry Thom
Tel: 819-420-8511

Director General, Policy Development, Jennifer Miles
Tel: 819-420-6501; *Fax:* 819-420-6460

Director General, Political Activities & Non-Partisanship, Kathy Nakamura
Tel: 819-420-6469

Acting Director General, Delegation & Accountability, Janelle Wright
Tel: 819-420-6432

Chief, Financial Planning & Reporting, Danièle Allaire
Tel: 819-420-8946; *Fax:* 819-420-8953

Regional Offices

Alberta, British Columbia, Northwest Territories & Yukon
Sinclair Centre, #210, 757 West Hastings St., Vancouver, BC V6C 3M2
Fax: 604-666-6808
Toll-Free: 800-645-5605
cfp.emplois-jobs.psc@cfp-psc.gc.ca

Atlantic
Maritime Centre Bldg., #1729, 1505 Barrington St., Halifax, NS B3J 3K5
Fax: 902-426-0507
Toll-Free: 800-645-5605
cfp.emplois-jobs.psc@cfp-psc.gc.ca

Ontario / Central Prairies & Nunavut
1 Front St. West, 6th Fl., Toronto, ON M5J 2X5
Tel: 416-973-3131; *Fax:* 416-973-1883
cfp.emplois-jobs.psc@cfp-psc.gc.ca

Québec
Complexe Guy-Favreau, Tour Est, 200, boul René-Lévesque ouest, 8e étage, Montréal, QC H2Z 1X4
Tel: 514-496-5069; *Fax:* 866-667-4936
cfp.emplois-jobs.psc@cfp-psc.gc.ca

Staffing & Assessment Services / Services de dotation et d'évaluation

Director General, Personnel Psychology Centre, Stan Lee
Tel: 819-420-8626; *Fax:* 819-420-8506

Public Service Staffing Tribunal (PSSRB) / Tribunal de la dotation de la fonction publique

240 Sparks St., 6th Fl., Ottawa, ON K1A 0A5
Tel: 613-949-6516; *Fax:* 613-949-6551
Toll-Free: 866-637-4491
TTY: 866-389-6901
info@psst-tdfp.gc.ca
www.psst-tdfp.gc.ca

Established under the Public Service Employment Act, the Tribunal deals with complaints related to internal appointments & lay offs in the federal public service. The Tribunal conducts hearings & provides mediation services in order to resolve complaints.

Chair & Chief Executive Officer, Guy Giguère
Tel: 613-949-5435; *Fax:* 613-949-5514

Director, Planning, Communications & Information Management, Brian Boudreau
Tel: 613-949-5513; *Fax:* 613-949-6551
brian.boudreau@psst-tdfp.gc.ca

Director, Registry, Operations & Policy, Louise Bourgeois
Tel: 613-949-6518; *Fax:* 613-949-6551
louise.bourgeois@psst-tdfp.gc.ca

Director, Human Resources & Corporate Services, Julie Brunet
Tel: 613-949-9753; *Fax:* 613-949-5514

Director, Dispute Resolution, Serge Roy
Tel: 613-949-6515; *Fax:* 613-949-6551
serge.roy@psst-tdfp.gc.ca

Public Services & Procurement / Services publics et de l'Approvisionnement

Place du Portage, Phase III, 11, rue Laurier, Ottawa, ON K1A 0S5
TTY: 800-926-9105
questions@tpsgc-pwgsc.gc.ca
www.tpsgc-pwgsc.gc.ca
Other Communication: Access to Government of Canada Tenders: buyandsell.gc.ca
twitter.com/PWGSC_TPSGC
www.linkedin.com/company/pwgsc
www.youtube.com/user/PWGSCanada

Public Works & Government Services Canada was renamed Public Services & Procurement by Prime Minister Trudeau in Nov. 2015. It is the primary department responsible for purchasing goods & services for the Government of Canada. The department purchases a variety of goods & services, construction, architectural, engineering & maintenance services & provides leasing services related to federal government works & facilities. It also maintains source lists of potential suppliers for some products, & ensures that the government's operational requirements are met in a cost-effective & timely manner, while taking into account the government's objectives including environmental considerations. As builders & caretakers of buildings, the department protects the environment by reducing solid waste, greening the construction & operation of buildings, conserving energy & water, improving fleet management, minimizing the effects of operations on climate change, & increasing environmental protection & conservation.

Minister, Public Services & Procurement, Hon. Judy Foote, P.C., B.A., B.Ed
Tel: 613-992-8655; *Fax:* 613-992-5324
Judy.Foote@parl.gc.ca

Deputy Minister & Deputy Receiver General for Canada, Marie Lemay
Tel: 819-956-1706
marie.lemay@tpsgc-pwgsc.gc.ca

Parliamentary Secretary, Leona Alleslev
Tel: 613-992-0700; *Fax:* 613-992-0716
Leona.Alleslev@parl.gc.ca

Associate Deputy Minister, Gavin Liddy
Tel: 819-956-4472
Gavin.Liddy@tpsgc-pwgsc.gc.ca

Chief of Staff, Office of the Minister, A. Gianluca Cairo
Tel: 819-997-5421
gianluca.cairo@canada.ca

Chief of Staff, Deputy Minister's Office, Emma Orawiec
Tel: 819-956-1710
Emma.Orawiec@tpsgc-pwgsc.gc.ca

Acting Chief of Staff, Associate Deputy Minister's Office, Madeleine Chabot
Tel: 819-956-1804
madeleine.chabot@tpsgc-pwgsc.gc.ca

Senior General Counsel & Executive Director, Legal Services Branch, Alain Vauclair
Tel: 819-420-2838; *Fax:* 819-953-3974
alain.vauclair@tpsgc-pwgsc.gc.ca

Director, Communications, Annie Trépanier
Tel: 819-997-5421; *Fax:* 819-956-8920
annie.trepanier@tpsgc-pwgsc.gc.ca

Director, Operations, Lucio Durante
Tel: 819-997-5421; *Fax:* 819-956-8920
lucio.durante@canada.ca

Press Secretary, Office of the Minister, Jessica Turner
Tel: 819-997-5421; *Fax:* 819-956-8920
jessica.turner2@canada.ca

Associated Agencies, Boards & Commissions:

•Defence Construction Canada / Construction de Défense Canada
See Entry Name Index for detailed listing.

•Public Service Labour Relations Board (PSLREB) / Commission des relations de travail et de l'emploi dans la fonction publique (CRTEFP)
CD Howe Building
240 Sparks St., 6th Fl.
PO Box 1525 B
Ottawa, ON K1P 5V2
Tel: 613-990-1800; *Fax:* 613-990-1849
Toll-free: 866-931-3454
TTY: 866-389-6901
mail.courrier@pslrb-crtfp.gc.ca
www.pslreb-crtefp.gc.ca
Other Communication: Jacob Finkelman Library: 613-990-1800; library-bibliotheque@pslrb-crtfp.gc.ca; Staffing Complaints: 613-949-6516; Fax: 613-949-6551; 1-866-637-4491

Independent, quasi-judicial statutory tribunal responsible for administering the collective bargaining & grievance adjudication systems in the federal Public & Parliamentary Service. Also provides mediation & conflict resolution services, compensation analysis & research services. The PSLREB was created with the merger of the Public Service Labour Relations Board (PSLRB) & the Public Service Staffing Tribunal (PSST) in November 2014.

Accounting, Banking & Compensation Branch / Direction générale de la comptabilité, gestion bancaire et rémunération

Responsible for managing the operations of the federal treasury, including issuing Receiver General payments for major government programs as well as maintaining the Accounts of Canada & producing the Government's financial statements. Responsible for providing government-wide accounting & reporting services. Directs the management & delivery of the administration of the public service pension & group insurance plans & maintains accounts for the various pension funds. Focuses in the financial management & control framework for the Department.

Assistant Deputy Minister, Accounting, Banking & Compensation, Brigitte Fortin
Tel: 819-420-5286; *Fax:* 819-934-0932
brigitte.fortin@tpsgc-pwgsc.gc.ca

Acting Director General, Central Accounting & Reporting Sector, Jean-René Drapeau
Tel: 819-420-5281; *Fax:* 819-956-8400
jean-rene.drapeau@tpsgc-pwgsc.gc.ca

Director General, Transformation of Pay Administration, Kristine Renic
Tel: 819-954-8394
kristine.renic@tpsgc-pwgsc.gc.ca

Acting Director General, Pension Modernization Project Directorate, Jeff Marcantonio
Tel: 613-948-6218; *Fax:* 613-952-7989
jeff.marcantonio@tpsgc-pwgsc.gc.ca

Director General, Compensation, Carrie Roussin
Tel: 819-956-0481; *Fax:* 819-956-3000
carrie.roussin@tpsgc-pwgsc.gc.ca

Director General, Government of Canada Pension Centre, David Stevens
Tel: 506-533-5555; *Fax:* 506-533-5607
david.stevens@pwgsc-tpsgc.gc.ca

Acquisitions Branch / Direction générale des approvisionnements

Provides departments & agencies with expert assistance at each stage of the supply cycle & offers tools that simplify & accelerate the acquisition of goods & services. It ensures that the government exercises due diligence & maintains the integrity of the procurement process. It is a primary service provider offering client departments a broad base of procurement solutions aimed at securing best value for their procurement dollar.

Assistant Deputy Minister, Lisa Campbell
Tel: 819-420-6168; *Fax:* 819-953-1058
Lisa.Campbell@tpsgc-pwgsc.gc.ca

Director General, Office of Small & Medium Enterprises & Strategic Engagement, Desmond Gray
Tel: 819-956-8416; *Fax:* 819-956-6859
desmond.gray@tpsgc-pwgsc.gc.ca
Director General, Traffic Management Directorate, Jacques Amyot
Tel: 819-956-7301; *Fax:* 819-956-4644
jacques.amyot@tpsgc-pwgsc.gc.ca
Director General, Business Management Sector, Robin Dubeau
Tel: 819-420-1518
robin.dubeau@tpsgc-pwgsc.gc.ca
Director General, Policy, Risk, Integrity & Strategic Management Sector, Gail Bradshaw
Tel: 819-956-0299; *Fax:* 819-956-0355
gail.bradshaw@tpsgc-pwgsc.gc.ca
Director General, Marine Sector, Scott Leslie
Tel: 613-943-3338; *Fax:* 613-944-7870
scott.leslie@tpsgc-pwgsc.gc.ca
Director General, Defence Procurement, Washington Region, Lorna Prosper
Tel: 202-682-7604; *Fax:* 202-682-7613
Lorna.Prosper@tpsgc-pwgsc.gc.ca
Director General, Services & Technology Acquisition Management Sector, Normand Masse
Tel: 819-956-3937; *Fax:* 819-956-2675
normand.masse@tpsgc-pwgsc.gc.ca
Director General, Defence & Major Projects Sector, Cathy A. Sabiston
Tel: 819-956-0010; *Fax:* 819-956-9110
cathy.sabiston@tpsgc-pwgsc.gc.ca
Senior Director, Risk, Quality & Integrity Management Directorate, Matthew Sreter
Tel: 819-956-0920; *Fax:* 819-956-0400
matthew.sreter@tpsgc-pwgsc.gc.ca
Director General, Land & Aerospace Equipment Procurement & Support Sector, Sylvain Cyr
Tel: 819-956-7113; *Fax:* 819-956-5650
sylvain.cyr@tpsgc-pwgsc.gc.ca

Chief Information Officer Branch / Direction générale du dirigeant principal de l'information

Acting Chief Information Officer, Luc Lafrance
Tel: 819-420-5991
Luc.Lafrance@tpsgc-pwgsc.gc.ca
Senior Director, Enterprise Case & Information Management Solutions, Shannon Archibald
Tel: 819-420-5841
shannon.archibald@tpsgc-pwgsc.gc.ca
Director, Support Services Competency Centre, Mark Armstrong
Tel: 819-956-3508
Mark.Armstrong@tpsgc-pwgsc.gc.ca
Director General, Chief Technology Officer, Rachel Porteous
Tel: 819-956-4745
rachel.porteous@tpsgc-pwgsc.gc.ca
Director, IT Project Portfolio Management, Michael Bennett
Tel: 819-420-5847
michael.bennett@tpsgc-pwgsc.gc.ca
Senior Director, Enterprise Architecture & Innovation, Mark Steski
Tel: 819-956-3101
Mark.Steski@tpsgc-pwgsc.gc.ca
Director, Strategic Planning & Management Services, Philip Quinlan
Tel: 819-934-5125
Philip.Quinlan@tpsgc-pwgsc.gc.ca
Director General, Solution Design, John MacKenzie
Tel: 819-420-5740; *Fax:* 819-956-2960
john.mackenzie@tpsgc-pwgsc.gc.ca
Director, Shared Case Management System, Justin Blanchette
Tel: 613-513-5996
justin.blanchette@tpsgc-pwgsc.gc.ca
Director General, In-Service Support, Robert Templeton
Tel: 819-420-0386
robert.templeton@tpsgc-pwgsc.gc.ca

Departmental Oversight Branch / Direction générale de la surveillance

Assistant Deputy Minister, Barbara Glover
Tel: 819-997-1094; *Fax:* 819-956-9949
barbara.glover@tpsgc-pwgsc.gc.ca
Chief Audit & Evaluation Executive, Linda Anglin
Tel: 819-420-5909; *Fax:* 819-956-9721
linda.anglin@tpsgc-pwgsc.gc.ca
Director General, Forensic Accounting Management Group, Micheline Nehmé
Tel: 819-956-3360; *Fax:* 819-956-7860
Director General, Operational Integrity Sector, Simona Wambera
Tel: 819-956-9978; *Fax:* 819-956-6402
simona.wambera@tpsgc-pwgsc.gc.ca
Director General, Industrial Security Sector, Jennifer E. Stewart
Tel: 613-948-1777; *Fax:* 613-948-4144
jennifer.stewart@pwgsc-tpsgc.gc.ca

Director, Continuous Audit & Advisory Services, Renaud Génier
Tel: 819-420-5853; *Fax:* 819-956-9721
renaud.genier@tpsgc-pwgsc.gc.ca
Senior Director, Canadian Industrial Security Directorate, Pascal Girard
Tel: 613-952-7907
pascal.girard@tpsgc-pwgsc.gc.ca

Finance & Administration Branch / Direction générale des finances et de l'administration

Acting Chief Financial Officer, Julie Charron
Tel: 819-420-5660; *Fax:* 819-956-0162
julie.charron@tpsgc-pwgsc.gc.ca
Director General, SIGMA, André-Guy Chéchippe
Tel: 819-934-1057; *Fax:* 819-934-6955
andre-guy.chechippe@tpsgc-pwgsc.gc.ca
Acting Head, Financial Operations, Monique Arnold
Tel: 873-469-4244
monique.arnold@tpsgc-pwgsc.gc.ca
Director General, Financial Management, Jacques Cormier
Tel: 819-420-6163; *Fax:* 819-956-7956
jacques.cormier@tpsgc-pwgsc.gc.ca
Director General, Corporate Accommodation & Materiel Management, Helen Bélanger
Tel: 819-420-2155
helen.belanger@tpsgc-pwgsc.gc.ca
Director, Financial Services for Finance & Administration Branch & ISB, Michel Brunette
Tel: 819-420-6164; *Fax:* 819-956-7956
michel.brunette@tpsgc-pwgsc.gc.ca
Senior Director, Budget Management, Mohammad Rahman
Tel: 819-420-5221; *Fax:* 819-956-0162
mohammad.rahman@tpsgc-pwgsc.gc.ca

Human Resources Branch / Direction générale des ressources humaines

Fax: 819-956-7724

Acting Assistant Deputy Minister, André Latreille
Tel: 819-420-1579; *Fax:* 819-934-2523
andre.v.latreille@tpsgc-pwgsc.gc.ca
Director General, Labour Relations & Ethics, OHS, Compensation & Well-being, Marielle Doyon
Tel: 819-420-1575
marielle.doyon@tpsgc-pwgsc.gc.ca
Director General, Corporate Human Resources Policies & Programs, Danielle Jean-Venne
Tel: 819-956-9716; *Fax:* 819-956-9955
danielle.jean-venne@tpsgc-pwgsc.gc.ca
Director General, Human Resources Operations, Karl Shepherd
Tel: 819-956-8365; *Fax:* 819-956-4760
Karl.shepherd@tpsgc-pwgsc.gc.ca

Integrated Services Branch / Direction generale des services intégrés

Assistant Deputy Minister, Sarah Paquet
Tel: 613-992-0679
sarah.paquet@tpsgc-pwgsc.gc.ca
Acting Director General, Business Planning & Management Services, Debbie Roberts
Tel: 613-943-6434
debbie.roberts@tpsgc-pwgsc.gc.ca
Director General, Service Integration Sector, Réa McKay
Tel: 613-992-2999 ext: 9
rea.mckay@tpsgc-pwgsc.gc.ca
Director General, Government Information Services Sector, Marc Saint-Pierre
Tel: 613-992-9218; *Fax:* 613-947-6949
marc.saint-pierre@tpsgc-pwgsc.gc.ca
Acting Director General, Shared Services Integration Sector, Stéphane J. Guèvremont
Tel: 613-282-4273; *Fax:* 613-943-6435
stephane.guevremont@tpsgc-pwgsc.gc.ca
Acting Director Director, Shared Services Integration Sector, Jacqueline Jodoin
Tel: 613-387-3414; *Fax:* 613-992-5980
jacqeline.jodoin@tpsgc-pwgsc.gc.ca
Director, GCDOCS Enterprise Program Management Office, Jennifer Woods
Tel: 613-513-9683
jennifer.woods@tpsgc-pwgsc.gc.ca

MERX

Phase II, #103, 6 Antares Dr., Ottawa, ON K2E 8A9

Tel: 613-727-4900; *Fax:* 888-235-5800
Toll-Free: 800-964-6379
merx@merx.com
www.merx.com
Other Communication: Agencies, Crown & Private Corporations, E-mail: priv@merx.com

The federal government's Government Electronic Tendering Service (GETS) contracts MERX to advertise government procurement opportunities online. Architectural & engineering consulting services, or services related to real property above $84,000 are advertised on MERX; below $84,000, they are handled through SELECT. Construction opportunities above $100,000 are advertised through MERX; below are handled through SELECT. MERX is used for printing services valued at $10,000 or above, & most goods & services valued at $25,000 or above. Below this level Public Services & Procurement uses a variety of bid solicitation methods: T-buys (purchasing by telephone when the product or service is required quickly & can easily be identified over the phone); RFQ (Request for Quotation); an Invitation to Tender (ITT) is used for straightforward requirements above $25,000 & where the lowest price will determine the awarding of the contract; RFP (Request for Proposal) for more complex requirements above $25,000; RFSO (Request for Standing Offer); RFSA (Request for Supply Arrangement); Sole-sourcing, subject to trade agreements & government contracting regulations. For products, individual departments have authority to buy up to $5,000 directly from suppliers; above $5,000, the department must go to Public Services & Procurement. Departments have authority to purchase nearly all their services; for program delivery services, departments may buy directly from suppliers up to $400,000 competitively or up to $100,000 without competition; they may also buy competitively up to $2 million when they advertise their requirements through MERX. Subscribers to MERX have access to an opportunity matching service, may view historical opportunities, review contract awards & international opportunities

Office of the Procurement Ombudsman / Bureau de l'ombudsman de l'approvisionnement

Constitution Square Bldg., #1150, 340 Albert St., 11th Fl., PO Box 151 Ottawa, ON K1R 7Y6

Fax: 613-947-9800
Toll-Free: 866-734-5169
TTY: 800-926-9105
boa-opo@boa-opo.gc.ca
opo-boa.gc.ca
twitter.com/OPO_Canada

The Procurement Ombudsman reviews complaints with respect to awarded contracts for the acquisition of goods below $25,000 & services below $100,000; reviews complaints with respect to the administration of contracts, no matter the value; reviews departmental practices for acquiring goods & services; & helps provide an alternative dispute resolution process if agreeable to both parties.

Acting Procurement Ombudsman, Lorenzo Ieraci
Director, Quality Assurance & Risk Management, Janet Barrington
Director, Procurement Inquiries & Reviews, Eimer Sim
Director, Communications & Corporate Management, David Rabinovitch

Parliamentary Precinct Branch / Direction générale de la cité parlementaire

Assistant Deputy Minister, Rob Wright
Tel: 819-775-7325; *Fax:* 819-775-7479
rob.wright@tpsgc-pwgsc.gc.ca
Acting General, Owner-Investor, Program, Portfolio & Client Relationship Management, William Harris
Tel: 819-775-7415; *Fax:* 819-775-7313
william.harris@tpsgc-pwgsc.gc.ca
Director General, LTVP Project Management & Delivery, Ezio DiMillo
Tel: 819-775-7412; *Fax:* 819-775-7321
ezio.dimillo@tpsgc-pwgsc.gc.ca
Senior Director, Wellington & Senate Accommodations, Thierry Montpetit
Tel: 819-775-5731; *Fax:* 819-775-7179
thierry.montpetit@tpsgc-pwgsc.gc.ca

Policy, Planning & Communications Branch / Direction générale des politiques, de la planification et des communications

Assistant Deputy Minister, Alfred MacLeod
Tel: 819-420-5341; *Fax:* 819-956-5145
alfred.macleod@tpsgc-pwgsc.gc.ca
Director General, Ministerial Services & Access to Information, Anne-Marie Pelletier
Tel: 819-956-5132; *Fax:* 819-956-9538
anne-marie.pelletier@tpsgc-pwgsc.gc.ca
Director General, Office of Greening Government Operation, Vacant
Tel: 613-948-2430

Real Property Branch / Biens immobiliers

Fax: 613-736-2789

Manages office space & other general-purpose property; acts as custodian for $7.6 billion of real property holdings; administers 2,000 lease contracts; provides working space for 241,000 public servants in 1,810 locations across Canada; provides professional & technical services to government departments & agencies. Government buildings are 34 per cent more energy efficient & 24 per cent more greenhouse gas efficient than in 1990. Green Leases address key environmental standards such as proper management of wastewater, indoor air quality, recycling, energy efficient lighting fixtures, greenhouse gas reduction. Works with other departments on the remediation of contaminated sites & is the federal lead in the cleanup of the Sydney Tar Ponds in Nova Scotia.

Assistant Deputy Minister, Kevin Radford
Tel: 819-956-3189
Kevin.Radford@tpsgc-pwgsc.gc.ca

Director General, AFD Sector, Mark Campbell
Tel: 819-775-7217; *Fax:* 819-775-7279
mark.campbell@tpsgc-pwgsc.gc.ca

Director General, Accommodation, Portfolio Management & Real Estate Services, Terry Homma
Tel: 819-420-2640; *Fax:* 819-956-1600
terry.homma@tpsgc-pwgsc.gc.ca

Director General, Special Initiatives Sector, Ralph Collins
Tel: 613-736-3298; *Fax:* 613-947-9300
ralph.collins@tpsgc-pwgsc.gc.ca

Director General, Professional & Technical Service Management, Veronica Silva
Tel: 873-469-3571; *Fax:* 819-956-2021
veronica.silva@tpsgc-pwgsc.gc.ca

Director, Program Management Sector, Suzanne Bastien
Tel: 613-816-1575
suzanne.bastien@tpsgc-pwgsc.gc.ca

Director, Project Management Directorate, Carole Beauchamp
Tel: 819-775-7216
carole.beauchamp@tpsgc-pwgsc.gc.ca

Director General, Client Consultancy & Real Property Solutions, Toby Greenbaum
Tel: 613-960-6713; *Fax:* 613-960-6399
toby.greenbaum@tpsgc-pwgsc.gc.ca

Director General, Engineering Assets Strategy, Marilea Pirie
Tel: 604-666-5191; *Fax:* 604-775-6806
marilea.pirie@pwgsc-tpsgc.gc.ca

Acting Director General, CRA Portfolio, Lisa Lafosse
Tel: 613-670-8889
lisa.lafosse@tpsgc-pwgsc.gc.ca

Senior Director, Real Property Branch Transformation, Guylaine Boucher
Tel: 613-944-5403
Guylaine.Boucher@tpsgc-pwgsc.gc.ca

Director General, Program Management Sector, Stephen Twiss
Tel: 819-420-2693; *Fax:* 819-934-0980
stephen.twiss@tpsgc-pwgsc.gc.ca

Director General, Major Crown Projects, Jean Vézina
Tel: 819-956-4935; *Fax:* 819-956-7384
jean.vezina@tpsgc-pwgsc.gc.ca

Director, Energy Services Acquisition Program, Tomasz Smetny-Sowa
Tel: 613-736-2644
tomasz.smetny-sowa@tpsgc-pwgsc.gc.ca

Director, Special Initiatives Sector, John Paul Lamberti
Tel: 613-808-4279
johnpaul.lamberti@tpsgc-pwgsc.gc.ca

Translation Bureau / Bureau de traduction
Cremazie Bldg., 70 Cremazie St., Gatineau, QC K1A 0S5
Fax: 819-997-9227

Chief Executive Officer, Donna Achimov
Tel: 819-997-8825; *Fax:* 819-934-1008
donna.achimov@tpsgc-pwgsc.gc.ca
Other Communications: Alternate Phone: 613-240-2552

Vice-President, Corporate Services, Lucie Séguin
Tel: 819-994-5221
Lucie.Seguin@tpsgc-pwgsc.gc.ca

Vice-President, Linguistic Services, Adam Gibson
Tel: 819-994-1391; *Fax:* 819-953-3827
adam.gibson@tpsgc-pwgsc.gc.ca

Acting Vice-President, Service Strategies & Partnership, Nancy Gauthier
Tel: 819-997-7620; *Fax:* 819-997-8197
Nancy.Gauthier@tpsgc-pwgsc.gc.ca

Royal Canadian Mint / Monnaie royale canadienne

320 Sussex Dr., Ottawa, ON K1A 0G8
Tel: 613-954-2626; *Fax:* 613-998-4130
Toll-Free: 800-267-1871
TTY: 613-949-7731
www.mint.ca
twitter.com/CanadianMint
www.facebook.com/RoyalCanadianMint
www.youtube.com/user/canadianmint

The RCM has two plants located in Ottawa & Winnipeg. Foreign & domestic circulating coinage is manufactured in Winnipeg. The Ottawa facility is responsible for the production of foreign & domestic numismatic products, precious metals & the refining of gold. The RCM also operates boutiques in Ottawa, Winnipeg & Vancouver. Reports to government through Public Services & Procurement.

Chair, Carman Joynt, FCPA, FCA, ICD.D
President & CEO, Sanda L. Hanington, ICD.D
Tel: 613-993-1716

Vice-President, Corporate & Legal Affairs & Corporate Secretary, Simon Kamel
Tel: 613-993-1732; *Fax:* 613-990-4465

Chief Financial Officer & Vice-President, Finance & Administration, Jennifer Camelon
Tel: 613-998-9835

Royal Canadian Mounted Police (RCMP) / Gendarmerie royale du Canada (GRC)

73 Leikin Dr., Ottawa, ON K1A 0R2
Tel: 613-993-7267; *Fax:* 613-993-0260
TTY: 613-825-1391
www.rcmp-grc.gc.ca
twitter.com/rcmpgrcpolice
www.facebook.com/rcmpgrc
www.youtube.com/rcmpgrcpolice

In 1873 the North West Mounted Police was constituted to provide Police protection in the unsettled portions of the North West. In 1904 the title Royal was given to the Force. In 1920 The Dominion Police was amalgamated with this Force & the name changed to Royal Canadian Mounted Police. The headquarters was moved from Regina to Ottawa & the Force may be called upon to perform duties in any portion of the Dominion. In 1928 the RCMP absorbed the Saskatchewan Provincial Police & in 1932 the Provincial Police Forces of Alberta, Manitoba, New Brunswick, Nova Scotia & PEI were absorbed in like manner.

Commissioner, Bob Paulson
Tel: 613-843-6400

Director General, Occupational Health & Safety, Sylvie Châteauvert
Tel: 613-843-5319

Deputy Commissioner, Specialized Policing Services, Peter Henschel
Tel: 613-843-4631

Chief Financial & Administrative Officer, Corporate Management & Comptrollership, Alain Duplantie
Tel: 613-843-4629

Director General, Canadian Criminal Real Time Identification Services, Guylaine Dansereau
Tel: 613-998-6140

Director General, Criminal Intelligence Directorate, Robert Fahlman
Tel: 613-993-4256

Director General, International Policing, Barbara A.S. Fleury
Tel: 613-993-5168; *Fax:* 613-991-4876

Director General, Real Property Management, Sheila Jamieson
Tel: 613-843-3808

Director General, Assets Management & Programs Branch, Milton Jardine
Tel: 613-843-3769; *Fax:* 613-825-7518

Director General, Intelligence Analysis & Communications, Criminal Analysis Branch, Agnes Jelking
Tel: 613-993-6466

Director General, National Security Program, Dan Killam
Tel: 613-993-0297

Director General, Criminal Intelligence, Robert Fahlman
Tel: 613-998-4256

Director General, Procurement & Contracting Branch, Heather MacDonald
Tel: 613-843-6942

Director General, Financial Management, Denise Nesrallah
Tel: 613-843-6907

Director General, Internal Policing, Barbara Fleury
Tel: 613-993-5168

Director General, National Communication Services, Christine Pappas
Tel: 613-825-7267

Director, Business Operations, Barbara Oattes
Tel: 613-998-0869

Director General, Intelligence Analysis & Communications, Agnes Jelking
Tel: 613-993-6466

Director General, Corporate Management Systems, Alain Séguin
Tel: 613-843-5054

Director General, Financial Crime, Stephen White
Tel: 613-990-1670

Director, Organized Crime Branch, Michel Aubin
Tel: 613-991-4673

RCMP Divisions & Commanding Officers

A Division
155 McArthur Ave., Ottawa, ON K1A 0R4
Tel: 613-993-8860; *Fax:* 613-993-5870

Acting Commanding Officer, Allen Nause
Tel: 613-993-8860; *Fax:* 613-993-5870

B Division
PO Box 9700 Stn. B, St. John's, NL A1A 3T5
Tel: 709-772-5465

C Division
4225, boul Dorchester ouest, Westmount, QC H3Z 1V5
Tél: 514-939-8300; *Téléc:* 514-283-2169
Ligne sans frais: 800-771-5401

D Division
1091 Portage Ave., PO Box 5650 Winnipeg, MB R3C 3K2
Tel: 204-983-5420

E Division
657 - 37th Ave. West, Vancouver, BC V5Z 1K6
Tel: 604-264-3111

Commanding Officer, Craig Callens

F Division
6101 Dewdney Ave., PO Box 2500 Regina, SK S4P 3K7
Tel: 306-780-5560; *Fax:* 306-780-5541

Acting Commanding Officer, Harper Boucher

G Division
PO Box 5000 Yellowknife, NT X1A 2R3
Tel: 867-669-5200; *Fax:* 867-669-5175
gdiv_yellowknife_detachment@rcmp-grc.gc.ca

Commanding Officer & Chief Superintendent, E.W. Summerfield
Tel: 403-669-5101

H Division
3139 Oxford St., PO Box 2286 Halifax, NS B3J 3E1
Tel: 902-426-3940; *Fax:* 902-426-2481

Acting Commanding Officer, D.L. Bishop
Tel: 902-426-3940

J Division
1445 Regent St., PO Box 3900 Fredericton, NB E3B 4Z8
Tel: 506-452-3400

K Division
11140 - 109 St., Edmonton, AB T5G 2T4
Tel: 780-945-5444; *Fax:* 780-945-5601

Commanding Officer, Dale McGowan

L Division
450 University Ave., PO Box 1360 Charlottetown, PE C1A 7N1
Tel: 902-566-7112

M Division
4100 - 4th Ave., Whitehorse, YT Y1A 1H5
Tel: 867-667-5551; *Fax:* 867-393-6791

Commanding Officer & Chief Superintendent, A.B. Harvie
Tel: 867-633-8611

O Division
130 Dufferin Ave., 5th Fl., PO Box 3240 Stn. B, London, ON N6A 4K3
Tel: 519-640-7267
Toll-Free: 800-387-0020

V Division
PO Box 500 Stn. B, Iqaluit, NU X0A 0H0
Tel: 867-975-4409; *Fax:* 867-975-4434

Training Facilities

Canadian Police College / École de police canadienne
PO Box 8900 Ottawa, ON K1G 3J2
Tel: 613-993-9500; *Fax:* 613-990-9738
cpc-ccp@rcmp-grc.gc.ca
www.cpc.gc.ca
twitter.com/cpc1976ccp
www.facebook.com/262605970429119
www.youtube.com/user/CanPoliceCollege

Chair, Advisory Board, Kim Armstrong
Director General, Cal Corley
Tel: 613-998-0883
cal.corley@rcmp-grc.gc.ca

RCMP Training Academy / Académie d'entrainement
6101 Dewdney Ave., PO Box 2500 Regina, SK S4P 3K7
Tel: 306-780-5560; *Fax:* 306-780-5541
www.rcmp-grc.gc.ca/depot/about-ausujet/index-eng.htm

Known as the "Depot" Division, the RCMP Academy has been training cadets since 1885. The Academy also trains national & international law enforcement agencies through the National Law Enforcement Training Program (NLET), & is the home of the the Police Dog Training Centre & the RCMP Heritage Centre.

St. Lawrence Seaway Management Corporation (SLSMC) / Corporation de Gestion de la Voie Maritime du Saint-Laurent (CGVMSL)

202 Pitt St., Cornwall, ON K6J 3P7
Tel: 613-932-5170; *Fax:* 613-932-7286
marketing@seaway.ca
www.greatlakes-seaway.com
Other Communication: Statistics/Research: billing@seaway.ca; Publications: publications@seaway.ca

A not-for-profit corporation responsible for the safe & efficient movement of marine traffic through Canadian Seaway facilities. It shares operations with its American counterpart, the Saint Lawrence Seaway Development Corporation, in operating & maintaining 15 locks between Montréal & Lake Erie.

Chair, Tim Dool
President & CEO, Terence F. Bowles
Chief Financial Officer, Karen Dumoulin
Corporate Environment Officer & Vice-President, External Relations, Jean Aubry-Morin

Regional Offices

Maisonneuve
151, rue Écluse, Saint-Lambert, QC J4R 2V6
Tel: 450-672-4110; *Fax:* 450-672-7098
Other Communication: Vessel Location, Phone: 450-672-4115

Niagara
508 Glendale Ave., St Catharines, ON L2R 6V8
Tel: 905-641-1932; *Fax:* 905-682-4525
Other Communication: Vessel Location, Phone: 905-688-6462

Security Intelligence Review Committee (SIRC) / Comité de Surveillance des activités de renseignement de sécurité (CSARS)

PO Box 2430 Stn. D, Ottawa, ON K1P 5W5
Tel: 613-990-8441; *Fax:* 613-990-5230
info@sirc-csars.gc.ca
www.sirc-csars.gc.ca
Other Communication: Media Liaison, Phone: 613-990-8441

Has as its mandate, under the Canadian Security Intelligence Service Act, to carry out the independent & external review of the Canadian Security Intelligence Service (CSIS) & to investigate complaints about CSIS activities. It is also required to investigate complaints from individuals who have had their employment prospects affected by the denial of a security clearance, & complaints referred to it by the Human Rights Commission. It is required to investigate reports made to it by the Minister of Immigration, Refugees & Citizenship, & the Solicitor General of Canada, which relate to national security or to an individual's involvement in organized crime. The Committee is required to report annually to Parliament through the Minister of Public Safety & Emergency Preparedness on these matters.

Chair, Hon. Pierre Blais
Tel: 613-991-9111; *Fax:* 613-990-5230
Executive Director, Michael Doucet, MBA
Tel: 613-991-9111; *Fax:* 613-990-5230
Director, Research Division, Sacha Richard
Tel: 613-949-4120; *Fax:* 613-990-5230

Office of the Senate Ethics Officer (SEO) / Bureau du conseiller sénatorial en éthique (CSE)

Thomas D'Arcy McGee Bldg., #526, 90 Sparks St., Ottawa, ON K1P 5B4
Tel: 613-947-3566; *Fax:* 613-947-3577
Toll-Free: 800-267-7362
cse-seo@sen.parl.gc.ca
sen.parl.gc.ca/seo-cse

The Senate Ethics Officer is responsible for administering, interpreting & applying the Conflict of Interest Code for Senators, which seeks to enhance public trust in senators & the Senate, provide guidance to senators on conflict of interest matters & to establish standards & a transparent system for proper conduct.

Senate Ethics Officer, Lyse Ricard
lyse.ricard@sen.parl.gc.ca
Assistant Senate Ethics Officer & General Counsel, Deborah Palumbo
deborah.palumbo@sen.parl.gc.ca
Chief Advisor, Jacques Lalonde
jacques.lalonde@sen.parl.gc.ca
Special Advisor, Willard Dionne
willard.dionne@sen.parl.gc.ca
Administrator & Ethics Advisor, Louise Dalphy
louise.dalphy@sen.parl.gc.ca

Shared Services Canada (SSC) / Services Partagés Canada (SPC)

434 Queen St., PO Box 9808 Stn. T CSC, Ottawa, ON K1G 4A8
Tel: 613-947-6296
Toll-Free: 855-215-3656
information@ssc-spc.gc.ca
www.ssc-spc.gc.ca
Other Communication: Media, Phone: 613-947-6276; E-mail: media@ssc-spc.gc.ca; ATIP, Phone: 613-996-0756; E-mail: ATIP-AIPRP@ssc-spc.gc.ca
twitter.com/ssc_ca
www.flickr.com/photos/ssc_spc

Created in 2011, Shared Services Canada is responsible for delivering email, data centre & telecommunication services to 43 federal departments & agencies (known as Partner Organizations). It reports to Parliament through the Minister of Public Services & Procurement.

Minister Responsible; Minister, Public Services & Procurement, Hon. Judy Foote, P.C., B.A., B.Ed
Tel: 613-992-8655; *Fax:* 613-992-5324
Judy.Foote@parl.gc.ca
President, Liseanne Forand
Tel: 613-992-3850; *Fax:* 613-992-5851
liseanne.forand@ssc-spc.gc.ca
Chief Operating Officer, John A. Glowacki Jr.
Tel: 613-943-7558
john.glowacki@ssc-spc.gc.ca
Chief of Staff, James van Raalte
Tel: 613-992-5547
James.vanRaalte@ssc-spc.gc.ca
Chief Audit & Evaluation Executive, Yves Genest
Tel: 613-941-1576; *Fax:* 613-941-1611
yves.genest@canada.ca
Director General, Strategic Policy Integration, Graham Barr
Tel: 613-943-7559
graham.barr@ssc-spc.gc.ca

Chief Financial Officer's Office & Corporate Services / Bureau du Chef des services financiers et services ministériels

Acting Senior Assistant Deputy Minister, Elizabeth Tromp
Tel: 613-995-5622; *Fax:* 613-995-0930
Elizabeth.Tromp@ssc-spc.gc.ca
Associate Assistant Deputy Minister, Corporate Services, Camille Therriault-Power
Tel: 613-996-0024
Camille.Therriault-Power@ssc-spc.gc.ca
Senior Director General, Organizational Effectiveness, Frances McRae
Tel: 613-996-0627
Frances.McRae@ssc-spc.gc.ca
Director General, Procurement & Vendor Relationships, Pat Breton
Tel: 613-960-7028; *Fax:* 613-292-5029
pat.breton@canada.ca
Director General, Finance & DCFO Services, Manon N. Fillion
Tel: 613-608-3507; *Fax:* 613-608-3507
manon.fillion@canada.ca
Director General, Human Resources & Workplace, Rose Kattackal
rose.kattackal@canada.ca
Director General, Corporate Secretariat's Office, Violaine Sauvé
violaine.sauve@canada.ca
Director General, Chief Information & Security Office, Pankaj Sehgal
Tel: 613-996-0195
pankaj.sehgal@canada.ca
Director General, Communications, Organizational Effectiveness, Michelle Shipman
Tel: 613-410-3890
michelle.shipman@canada.ca

Operations / Opérations

Senior Assistant Deputy Minister, Kevin Radford
Tel: 613-996-0002
kevin.radford@ssc-spc.gc.ca
Director General, EDC Delivery Management, Nasser Alsukayri
Tel: 613-818-1799
nasser.alsukayri@canada.ca
Director General, Cyber Protection & IT Security Operations, Eric Belzile
Tel: 613-290-8682
Eric.Belzile@ssc-spc.gc.ca
Director General, Resource Planning & Change Readiness, Sylvie Bussière
Tel: 613-943-8322; *Fax:* 613-996-0930
sylvie.bussiere@canada.ca
Acting Director General, Finance Portfolio, Ken Canam
Tel: 613-948-0976
Ken.Canam@ssc-spc.gc.ca
Director General, Data Centre Horizontal, Guy Charron
Tel: 613-954-9562
guy.charron@ssc-spc.gc.ca
Director General, Economic & International Portfolio Lead (ATD), Jocelyn Côté
Tel: 343-203-1174; *Fax:* 613-944-0044
Jocelyn.Cote@ssc-spc.gc.ca
Director General, Enterprise IT Service Management, Brendan Dunne
Tel: 613-748-2646
brendan.dunne@canada.ca
Director General, National Security Portfolio, José Gendron
Tel: 613-960-4360; *Fax:* 613-301-4485
jose.gendron@canada.ca
Director General, Science Portfolio, Surinder S. Komal
Tel: 613-952-1210; *Fax:* 613-993-8930
surinder.komal@canada.ca
Director General, Enterprise Network & Telecom Services, Patrice Nadeau
Tel: 613-952-1202
patrice.nadeau@canada.ca
Director General, Enterprise Data Centres, Patrice Rondeau
patrice.rondeau@canada.ca

Projects & Client Relationships / Projets et Relations clients

Senior Assistant Deputy Minister, Peter Bruce
Tel: 613-996-0970
Peter.Bruce@ssc-spc.gc.ca
Director General, Telecom & Cyber Security Projects, Afif Chaaban
Tel: 613-952-3687
afif.chaaban@canada.ca
Director General, Client Relations & Business Intake, Jean-François Lymburner
Tel: 613-868-5049
jean-francois.lymburner@canada.ca
Acting Director General, Enterprise Data Centre Projects, Ken MacDonald
Tel: 613-222-6018
ken.macdonald@canada.ca
Director General, Project Management Centre of Excellence, Rama Rai
Tel: 819-997-8909
rama.rai@canada.ca

Transformation, Service Strategy & Design / Transformation, stratégie de services et conception

Director General, Transformation Program Office, Gilles Dufour
Tel: 613-302-6514
gilles.dufour@canada.ca
Director General, Distributed Computing Transformation Program, Gail Eagen
Tel: 613-952-1399; *Fax:* 613-941-2784
gail.eagen@canada.ca
Other Communications: Alt. Phone: 613-286-7563
Director General, Telecommunications Transformation Program, Michel Fortin
Tel: 613-948-7670
michel.fortin@canada.ca
Director General, Enterprise Architecture, Shirley Ivan
Tel: 613-793-9143
shirley.ivan@canada.ca
Acting Director General, Cyber & IT Security Transformation Program, Simon Levesque
Tel: 613-668-0060
simon.levesque@canada.ca
Director General, Data Centre Consolidation, Peter Littlefield
Tel: 613-954-0255
peter.littlefield@canada.ca
Director General, Cyber & IT Security Transformation Program, Raj Thuppal
Tel: 613-960-3600
Raj.thuppal@ssc-spc.gc.ca
Manager, Executive Office, Sylvie Labelle
Tel: 613-995-5715

Social Sciences & Humanities Research Council of Canada (SSHRC) / Conseil de recherches en sciences humaines du Canada (CRSH)

Constitution Sq., 350 Albert St., PO Box 1610 Stn. B, Ottawa, ON K1P 6G4
Tel: 613-992-0691
www.sshrc-crsh.gc.ca
twitter.com/SSHRC_CRSH
www.facebook.com/108668929196739
www.youtube.com/user/SSHRC1

The key national research agency investing in the knowledge & skills Canada needs to build the quality of its social, cultural & economic life. SSHRC supports university-based research & training in the human sciences. It funds basic, applied & collaborative research, student training, research partnerships, knowledge transfer & the communication of research findings in all disciplines of the social sciences & humanities. Grants & fellowships are awarded through national competitions adjudicated by eminent researchers & scholars.

President, Ted Hewitt
Tel: 613-995-5488
ted.hewitt@sshrc-crsh.gc.ca
Vice-President & Chair, Jack Mintz
Executive Vice-President, Brent Herbert-Copley
Tel: 613-995-5457
Brent.Herbert-Copley@sshrc-crsh.gc.ca
Vice-President, Research Programs, Dominique Bérubé
Tel: 613-995-5495
Dominique.Berube@sshrc-crsh.gc.ca
CFO & Vice-President, Common Administrative Services, Alfred Tsang
Tel: 613-995-3914; *Fax:* 613-944-1760
Alfred.Tsang@sshrc-crsh.gc.ca

Specific Claims Tribunal Canada (SCT) / Tribunal des revendications particulières Canada (TRP)

#400, 427 Laurier Ave. West, 4th Fl., PO Box 31 Ottawa, ON K1R 7Y2
Tel: 613-947-0751; *Fax:* 613-943-0586
claims.revendications@sct-trp.ca
www.sct-trp.ca

Created in 2008 as part of the federal government's Justice at Last policy. The Tribunal is an independent group of six federal judges who can make binding rulings on monetary damage claims filed by First Nations groups against the Crown.

Chair, Hon. Harry Slade
Executive Director, Rachel Boyer
Tel: 613-947-0740

Standards Council of Canada (SCC) / Conseil canadien des normes (CCN)

#600, 55 Metcalfe St., Ottawa, ON K1P 6L5
Tel: 613-238-3222; *Fax:* 613-569-7808
info@scc.ca
www.scc.ca
twitter.com/StandardsCanada
www.facebook.com/635631173146666
www.linkedin.com/company/standards-council-of-canada
www.youtube.com/user/StandardsCanada

Federal Crown corporation with the mandate to promote efficient & effective standardization. The organization reports to Parliament through the Minister of Industry & oversees Canada's National Standards System. The National Standards System comprises organizations & individuals involved in voluntary standards development, promotion & implementation. In addition, more than 400 organizations have been accredited by the Standards Council, including environmental management systems (EMS) registration organizations that perform registrations to ISO 14000 series standards. The Council offers accreditation to registration bodies for specialized environmental management systems in industry-specific areas, including sustainable forestry management (CAN/CSZ809-02). Manages the Program for the Accreditation of Laboratories - Canada (PALCAN) which seeks to identify & accredit competent testing laboratories. Initial assessment is made & regular follow-up audits are performed; accredited organizations are included in the Standards Council directory of accredited testing organizations. Users of testing services can eliminate or reduce their need to establish the competence of a prospective lab. In cooperation with the Canadian Association of Environmental Analy tical Laboratories (CAEAL), SCC operates an accreditation program for environmental analytical laboratories. SCC's website provides free access to a wide variety of standards information, including searchable databases containing information on Canadian, foreign & international standards, regulations & SCC-accredited organizations. More speacialized information is available through SCC's information & Research Service. Other accreditation programs include ones for registrars of ISO 14000 environmental management systems; environmental auditor certifiers & auditor training course providers.

Chair, Kathy Milsom
Chief Executive Officer, John Walter
Tel: 613-238-3222 ext: 400
Chief Financial Officer & Vice-President, Corporate Services, Ernie Briard
Tel: 613-238-3222 ext: 467
Vice-President, Strategy, Michel Girard
Tel: 613-238-3222 ext: 499
Vice-President, Accreditation Services, Chantal Guay
Tel: 613-238-3222 ext: 432
Vice-President, Standards Solutions, Sylvie C. Lafontaine, CA
Tel: 613-238-3222 ext: 410
Corporate Secretary & Vice-President, Communications & Corporate Planning, Sandra E. Watson
Tel: 613-238-3222 ext: 403

Statistics Canada / Statistique Canada

R.H. Coats Bldg., Tunney's Pasture, 150 Tunney's Pasture Driveway, Ottawa, ON K1A 0T6
Tel: 514-283-8300; *Fax:* 514-283-9350
Toll-Free: 800-263-1136
TTY: 800-363-7629
STATCAN.infostats-infostats.STATCAN@canada.ca
www.statcan.ca
twitter.com/statcan_eng
www.facebook.com/statisticscanada
www.youtube.com/statisticscanada

Agency of the federal government, headed by the Chief Statistician of Canada which reports to Parliament through the Minister of Industry. As Canada's central statistical agency, it has a mandate to collect, compile, analyse, abstract & publish statistical information relating to the commercial, industrial, financial, social, economic & general activities & condition of the people of Canada; coordinates activities with its federal & provincial partners in the national statistical system to avoid duplication of effort & to ensure the consistency & usefulness of statistics. The agency profiles & measures both social & economic changes in Canada. It presents a comprehensive picture of the national economy through statistics on manufacturing, agriculture, retail sales, services, prices, productivity changes, trade, transportation, employment & unemployment, & aggregate measures such as gross domestic product. It also presents a comprehensive picture of social conditions through statistics on demography, health, areas. In Nov. 2015, Prime Minister Trudeau reintroduced the long-form census, which had been replaced by the Conservatives in 2010 with the National Household Survey.

Chief Statistician of Canada, Anil Arora
Tel: 613-951-9757; *Fax:* 613-951-3883
Chief Audit Executive, Internal Audit & Evaluation Services, Patrice Prud'homme
Tel: 613-951-1062; *Fax:* 613-952-9099
patrice.prudhomme@canada.ca
Other Communications: Alternate Phone: 613-818-2262
Departmental Secretary, Preston Poon
Tel: 613-951-4245; *Fax:* 613-951-1134
preston.poon@canada.ca

Analysis & Development & Health Statistics

Director General, Analysis & Development Branch, Garnett Picot
Tel: 613-951-8214; *Fax:* 613-951-5403
garnett.picot@statcan.gc.ca
Director, Family & Labour Studies, Vacant

Analytical Studies, Methodology & Statistical Infrastructure

Assistant Chief Statistician, Sylvie Michaud
Tel: 613-951-9482; *Fax:* 613-951-0556
Sylvie.Michaud@statcan.gc.ca
Director General, Analytical Studies Branch, Isabelle Amano
Tel: 613-951-3807
Isabelle.Amano@statcan.gc.ca
Director General, Statistical Infrastructure, Claude Graziadei
Tel: 613-951-6128; *Fax:* 613-951-0411
Claude.Graziadei@statcan.gc.ca
Director General, Methodology, Claude Julien
Tel: 613-951-6937; *Fax:* 613-951-1462
claude.julien@canada.ca
Other Communications: Alternate Phone: 613-850-6246

Census, Operations & Communications

Assistant Chief Statistician, Connie Graziadei
Tel: 613-951-7081; *Fax:* 613-951-1394
Connie.Graziadei@statcan.gc.ca
Other Communications: Alternate Phone: 613-290-0794
Director General, Communications Division, Gabrielle Beaudoin
Tel: 613-951-2808; *Fax:* 613-951-2827
Gabrielle.Beaudoin@statcan.gc.ca
Other Communications: Alternate Phone: 613-218-0854
Director General, Census Management Office, Marc Hamel
Tel: 613-951-2495; *Fax:* 613-951-9300
Marc.Hamel@statcan.gc.ca
Director General, Operations, Yves Béland
Tel: 613-951-1494
yves.beland@canada.ca
Other Communications: Alternate Phone: 613-293-3048
Director General, Collection & Regional Services, Geoff Bowlby
Tel: 613-951-5077; *Fax:* 613-951-2105
geoff.bowlby@canada.ca
Other Communications: Alternate Phone: 613-724-0270

Corporate Services

Assistant Chief Statistician & Chief Financial Officer, Stéphane Dufour
Tel: 613-951-9866; *Fax:* 613-951-5290
Stephane.Dufour@statcan.gc.ca
Other Communications: Alternate Phone: 613-371-1491
Director General & Chief Information Officer, Informatics Branch, Lise Duquet
Tel: 613-951-7114; *Fax:* 613-951-4674
Lise.Duquet@statcan.gc.ca
Director General, Human Resources, Deirdre Keane
Tel: 613-951-9955; *Fax:* 613-951-0967
Deirdre.Keane@statcan.gc.ca
Director General, Finance Branch, Monia Lahaie
Tel: 613-951-1376
Monia.Lahaie@statcan.gc.ca
Section Chief, Information Technology Systems, Janique Godin
Tel: 613-301-6239
Janique.Godin@statcan.gc.ca

Economic Statistics

Assistant Chief Statistician, André Loranger
Tel: 613-951-3674; *Fax:* 613-951-0556
Andre.Loranger@statcan.gc.ca
Director General, Industry Statistics, Daniela Ravindra
Tel: 613-951-3514; *Fax:* 613-951-0411
daniela.ravindra@canada.ca
Other Communications: Alternate Phone: 613-851-4745
Director General, Economy-wide Statistics, Craig Kuntz
Tel: 613-951-7092; *Fax:* 613-951-0411
Craig.Kuntz@statcan.gc.ca
Other Communications: Alternate Phone: 613-795-1909
Director General, Agriculture, Technology & Transportation Statistics, Jean-Pierre Simard
Tel: 613-951-0741; *Fax:* 613-951-0411
Jean-Pierre.Simard@statcan.gc.ca
Other Communications: Alternate Phone: 613-447-0049
Director General, Macroeconomic Accounts Branch, James Tebrake
Tel: 613-951-0538; *Fax:* 613-951-9031
James.Tebrake@statcan.gc.ca

Social, Health & Labour Statistics

Assistant Chief Statistician, Peter Morrison
Tel: 613-951-4692; *Fax:* 613-951-3231
Peter.Morrison@statcan.gc.ca
Director General, Census Subject Matter, Social & Demographic Statistics, Johanne Denis
Tel: 613-951-0402; *Fax:* 613-951-7178
johanne.denis@canada.ca
Director General, Health, Justice & Special Surveys, Lynn Barr-Telford
Tel: 613-951-1518; *Fax:* 613-951-7333
Lynn.Barr-Telford@statcan.gc.ca
Assistant Chief Statistician, Education, Labour & Income Statistics, Jane Badets
Tel: 613-951-2561; *Fax:* 613-951-2869
jane.badets@canada.ca

Statistics Canada Regional Reference Centres/Centres de Référence Régionaux

Calgary
First Street Plaza, #401, 138 - 4 Ave. SE, Calgary, AB T2G 4Z6
Tel: 403-292-6717; *Fax:* 403-292-4958
Toll-Free: 800-263-1136

Edmonton
Park Square, 10001 Bellamy Hill, 9th Fl., Edmonton, AB T5J 3B6
Tel: 403-495-3027; *Fax:* 403-495-5318
Toll-Free: 800-263-1136

Halifax
1770 Market St., 3rd Fl., Halifax, NS B3J 3M3

Montréal
Tour Est, Complexe Guy-Favreau, 200, boul René-Lévesque ouest, 4e étage, Montréal, QC H2Z 1X4

Ottawa
R.H. Coats Bldg., Lobby, Holland Ave., Ottawa, ON K1A 0T6

Regina
Avord Tower, 2002 Victoria Ave., 9th Fl., Regina, SK S4P 0R7
Tel: 306-780-5405; *Fax:* 306-780-5403
Toll-Free: 800-263-1136
statcan@sk.sympatico.ca

Toronto
Arthur Meighen Bldg., 25 St. Clair Ave. East, 10th Fl., Toronto, ON M4T 1M4

Vancouver
Library Square Tower, #1600, 300 West Georgia St., Vancouver, BC V6B 6C9
Tel: 606-666-5946; *Fax:* 604-666-3043
Toll-Free: 866-787-7472

Winnipeg
Via Rail Bldg., #200, 123 Main St., Winnipeg, MB R3C 4V9

Status of Women Canada (SWC) / Condition féminine Canada (CFC)

PO Box 8097 Stn. T CSC, Ottawa, ON K1G 3H6
Tel: 613-995-7835; *Fax:* 819-420-6906
Toll-Free: 855-969-9922
TTY: 819-420-6905
communications@swc-cfc.gc.ca
www.swc-cfc.gc.ca
Secondary Address: 22 Eddy St., 10th Fl.
Gatineau, QC J8X 2V6
twitter.com/Canada_swc
www.youtube.com/user/CanadaSWC

The federal government agency promotes gender equality, & the participation of women in the economic, social, cultural, & political life in Canada. Status of Women Canada focuses its work in the following areas: improvement of women's economic autonomy & well-being; elimination of systemic violence against women & children; & the advancement of women's human rights. To achieve results, SWC works with & supports research organizations, equality-seeking organizations, the non-governmental, voluntary & private sectors, & international organizations.

Minister, Status of Women, Hon. Patricia Hajdu, P.C.
Tel: 613-996-4792; *Fax:* 613-996-9785
Patty.Hajdu@parl.gc.ca

Coordinator/Head of Agency, Meena Ballantyne
Tel: 819-420-6801; *Fax:* 819-420-6805
meena.ballantyne@cfc-swc.gc.ca

Senior Director General, Women's Program & Regional Operations Directorate, Linda Savoie
Tel: 819-420-6850; *Fax:* 819-420-6907
linda.savoie@cfc-swc.gc.ca

Director General, Policy & External Relations, Justine Akman
Tel: 819-420-6871; *Fax:* 819-420-6908
justine.akman@cfc-swc.gc.ca

Director General, Communications & Public Affairs, Nanci-Jean Waugh
Tel: 819-420-6810; *Fax:* 819-420-6906
nanci-jean.waugh@cfc-swc.gc.ca

Office of the Taxpayers' Ombudsman (OTO) / Bureau de l'ombudsman des contribuables (BOC)

#600, 150 Slater St., Ottawa, ON K1A 1K3
Tel: 613-946-2310; *Fax:* 613-941-6319
Toll-Free: 866-586-3839
www.oto-boc.gc.ca
Other Communication: Toll-Free Fax: 1-866-586-3855
twitter.com/OTO_Canada

The Office of the Taxpayers' Ombudsman seeks to hold the Canada Revenue Agency accountable to taxpayers & benefit recipients. The Office is organized into five operating units: Intake, Complaint Investigation, Systemic Investigation, Communications & Corporate Services.

Taxpayers' Ombudsman, Sherra Profit

Director, Josée M. Labelle
Tel: 613-946-2975

Manager, Intake & Complaint Investigations, Joan Alain
Tel: 613-946-2520

Manager, Systemic Examinations, Lorna Riopelle
Tel: 613-941-6225

Telefilm Canada / Téléfilm Canada

#500, 360, rue Saint-Jacques, Montréal, QC H2Y 1P5
Tél: 514-283-6363; *Téléc:* 514-283-8212
Ligne sans frais: 800-567-0890
info@telefilm.gc.ca
www.telefilm.ca
www.facebook.com/telefilmcanada

Telefilm Canada is a Crown corporation reporting to Parliament through the Department of Canadian Heritage. Headquartered in Montréal, Telefilm provides services to the Canadian audiovisual industry by means of four regional offices located in Vancouver, Toronto, Montréal & Halifax. Dedicated to the development & promotion of the Canadian audiovisual industry.

Chair, Michel Roy
Executive Director, Carolle Brabant, C.P.A., C.A., MBA
Director, International Promotion, Sheila de La Varende
Director, National Promotion & Communications, Francesca Accinelli
Director, Business Affairs & Coproduction, Roxanne Girard
Director, Public & Government Affairs, Jean-Claude Mahé
Director, Marketing & Communications, Évelyne Morrisseau
Director, Legal Services & Access to Information; Corporate Secretary, Stéphane Odesse
Director, Administration & Corporate Services, Denis Pion
Director, Projects Financing, Michel Pradier

Regional Offices

Atlantic Region
1717 Barrington St., 4th Fl., Halifax, NS B3J 2A4
Tel: 902-426-8425; *Fax:* 902-426-4445
Toll-Free: 800-565-1773
info@telefilm.ca

Ontario & Nunavut
#100, 474 Bathurst St., Toronto, ON M5T 2S6
Tel: 416-973-6436; *Fax:* 416-973-8606
Toll-Free: 800-463-4607
info@telefilm.ca

Western Region
210 West Georgia St., Vancouver, BC V6B 0L9
Tel: 604-666-1566; *Fax:* 604-666-7754
Toll-Free: 800-663-7771
info@telefilm.ca

Transport Canada (TC) / Transports Canada

Place de Ville, 330 Sparks St., Tower C, Ottawa, ON K1A 0N5
Tel: 613-990-2309; *Fax:* 613-954-4731
Toll-Free: 866-995-9737
TTY: 888-675-6863
www.tc.gc.ca
twitter.com/transport_gc
www.facebook.com/401846167974
www.youtube.com/TransportCanada

Using EMS 14000 standards, Transport Canada incorporates environmental considerations in all decision-making to fulfill the department's sustainable development strategy. Working with airports & airlines to minimize environmental effects of de-icing fluids; working with Environment & Climate Change & industry to more effectively manage road salt; participating with ICAO's Committee on Aviation Environmental Protection (CAEP) concerning aircraft emissions, noise & land use planning. Ongoing contaminated sites management program. The Moving on Sustainable Transportation (MOST) Program supports projects that educate, raise awareness & provide tools to understand, promote & encourage sustainable transportation, such as neighbourhood transit passes, idle-free workplaces, school walking routes. Development of strategies to reduce greenhouse gas emissions from freight transportation; information on fuel consumption. Urban Transportation Showcase Program aims to reduce greenhouse gas emissions through showcasing demonstrations in communities across Canada (www.tc.gc.ca/pdtu).

Minister, Transport, Hon. Marc Garneau, P.C., C.C., C.D., B.Sc., Ph.D., F.C.A.S.I.
Tel: 613-996-7267; *Fax:* 613-995-8632
marc.garneau@parl.gc.ca

Deputy Minister, Michael Keenan
Tel: 613-990-4509; *Fax:* 613-991-0851
michael.keenan@tc.gc.ca

Parliamentary Secretary, Kate Young
Tel: 613-996-6674; *Fax:* 613-996-6772
Kate.Young@parl.gc.ca

Associate Deputy Minister, Helena Borges
Tel: 613-949-2960; *Fax:* 613-991-0851
helena.borges@tc.gc.ca

Chief of Staff, Jean-Philippe Arseneau
Tel: 613-991-0700; *Fax:* 613-995-0327
jean-philippe.arseneau@tc.gc.ca

Chief, Audit & Evaluation Executive & Integrity Officer, Martin Rubenstein
Tel: 613-990-5462; *Fax:* 613-990-6455
martin.rubenstein@tc.gc.ca

Director General, Corporate Secretariat, Simon Dubé
Tel: 613-952-4315; *Fax:* 613-990-1878
simon.dube@tc.gc.ca

Executive Director to the Deputy Minister, Ana Renart
Tel: 613-990-9002; *Fax:* 613-991-0851
ana.renart@tc.gc.ca

Executive Director, Legal Services, Henry K. Schultz
Tel: 613-990-5768; *Fax:* 613-990-5777
henry.schultz@tc.gc.ca

Associated Agencies, Boards & Commissions:

•Atlantic Pilotage Authority Canada / Administration de pilotage de l'Atlantique Canada
See Entry Name Index for detailed listing.

•Canada Lands Company / Société Immobilière du Canada
See Entry Name Index for detailed listing.

•Canada Mortgage & Housing Corporation / Société canadienne d'hypothèques et de logement
See Entry Name Index for detailed listing.

•Canada Post Corporation / Société canadienne des postes
See Entry Name Index for detailed listing.

•Canadian Air Transport Security Authority (CATSA) / Administration canadienne de la sûreté du transport aérien (ACSTA)
99 Bank St., 13th Fl.
Ottawa, ON K1P 6B9
Fax: 613-990-1295
Toll-free: 888-294-2202
TTY: 613-949-5534
www.catsa-acsta.gc.ca
CATSA secures critical elements of the air transportation system - from passenger screening to baggage screening - & encourages Canadians to Pack Smart for the benefit of all air travellers.

•Canadian Transportation Agency / Office des transports du Canada
See Entry Name Index for detailed listing.

•Federal Bridge Corporation Limited (FBCL) / Société des ponts fédéraux Limitée
#1210, 55 Metcalfe St.
Ottawa, ON K1P 6L5
Tel: 613-998-8427; *Fax:* 613-993-6945
info@federalbridge.ca
www.federalbridge.ca
Other Communication: Cornwall Phone: 613-932-3629; Sault Ste. Marie Phone: 705-256-8208
The FBCL was incorporated in 1998 to assume the non-navigational management responsibilities of the St. Lawrence Seaway Authority, including the Jacques Cartier & Champlain Bridges Incorporated, & in a joint venture with its U.S. partner, the Seaway International Bridge Corporation, Ltd. At the same time, the FBCL assumed responsibility for the management of the Canadian portion of the Thousand Islands International Bridge. In 2000, the FBCL acquired the Canadian half of the Sault Ste. Marie International Bridge.

•Great Lakes Pilotage Authority / Administration de pilotage des Grands Lacs
See Entry Name Index for detailed listing.

•Laurentian Pilotage Authority / Administration de pilotage des Laurentides Canada
See Entry Name Index for detailed listing.

•Marine Atlantic Inc. / Marine Atlantique
See Entry Name Index for detailed listing.

•Pacific Pilotage Authority / Administration de Pilotage du Pacifique Canada
See Entry Name Index for detailed listing.

•Royal Canadian Mint / Monnaie royale canadienne
See Entry Name Index for detailed listing.

•Transportation Appeal Tribunal of Canada / Anciennement le Tribunal de l'aviation civile
#1201, 333 Laurier Ave. West, 12th Fl.
Ottawa, ON K1A 0N5
Tel: 613-990-6906; *Fax:* 613-990-9153
info@tatc.gc.ca
www.tatc.gc.ca
The Tribunal provides an independent review process for anyone who has been given notice of an administrative or enforcement action taken by the Minister of Transport, railway safety inspectors or the Canadian Transportation Agency under various federal transportation Acts.

•Transportation Safety Board of Canada / Bureau de la sécurité des transports du Canada
See Entry Name Index for detailed listing.

•VIA Rail Canada Inc.
See Entry Name Index for detailed listing.

Communications Group / Groupe Communications
Tel: 613-993-0055; *Fax:* 613-991-6719

Director General, Dan Dugas
Tel: 613-990-6138; *Fax:* 613-991-6719
dan.dugas@tc.gc.ca

Executive Director, Marie-Claude Petit
Tel: 613-993-7649
marie-claude.petit@tc.gc.ca

Acting Director, Web, Outreach & Creative Services, Anick Rainville
Tel: 613-949-6588; *Fax:* 613-990-0680
anick.rainville@tc.gc.ca

Corporate Services / Services généraux
Tel: 613-991-6567; *Fax:* 613-991-0426
Corporate Services is part of the Department's administration business line & is responsible for providing services & functional expertise in the areas of finance & administration, technology & information management, human resources & access to information, Crown corporation portfolio coordination, internal audit & evaluation services.
Assistant Deputy Minister & Chief Financial Officer, Corporate Services, André Lapointe
Tel: 613-991-6565; *Fax:* 613-991-0426
andre.lapointe@tc.gc.ca
Director General, Financial Planning & Resource Management, Claude Corbin
Tel: 613-990-3800; *Fax:* 613-998-1337
claude.corbin@tc.gc.ca
Executive Director, Corporate Planning & Reporting, Isabelle Trépanier
Tel: 613-993-5769; *Fax:* 613-991-0426
isabelle.trepanier@tc.gc.ca

Finance & Administration / Finances et administration
Director General, Deloranda Munro
Tel: 613-993-4307; *Fax:* 613-991-4410
deloranda.munro@tc.gc.ca

Human Resources Directorate / Direction générale des ressources humaines
Director General, Linda Brouillette
Tel: 613-991-6317
linda.brouillette@tc.gc.ca
Executive Director, Executive Resourcing & Classification, Michèle Ouellette
Tel: 613-991-5913; *Fax:* 613-949-4202
michele.ouellette@tc.gc.ca
Senior Director, Corporate, HR Policy, Programs, Planning & Systems, Robert Sincennes
Tel: 613-991-6485; *Fax:* 613-998-4065
robert.sincennes@tc.gc.ca
Chief, Resources, Projects & Issues Management Branch, Patrice Faria
Tel: 613-993-7900; *Fax:* 613-998-4614
patrice.faria@tc.gc.ca

Technology & Information Management Services Directorate / Direction générale des services de gestion de la technologie et de l'information
Chief Information Officer & Director General, Chris Molinski
Tel: 613-998-6465; *Fax:* 613-990-2469
chris.molinski@tc.gc.ca
Director, Application Services, Tracey Boicey
Tel: 613-998-0739; *Fax:* 613-954-4493
tracey.boicey@tc.gc.ca
Director, Production Operations & Service Management, Louise Séguin
Tel: 613-991-6599
louise.seguin@tc.gc.ca

Policy Group / Groupe de politiques
Responsible for setting policies relating to rail, marine, highways & borders, motor carrier, air, airports & accessible transportation, as well as setting departmental strategic policy & coordinating intergovernmental relations; assessing the performance of the overall transportation systems & its components, & developing supporting databases, forecasts & economic analysis; administering the management agreement with the St. Lawrence Seaway Management Corporation; & supporting rail passenger services through payments to VIA Rail & three regional railways, & ferry services through payments to Marine Atlantic & to provincial & private operators & border infrastructure improvements.
Assistant Deputy Minister, Shawn Tupper
Tel: 613-998-1880; *Fax:* 613-991-1440
shawn.tupper@tc.gc.ca

Air Policy / Politique du transport aérien
Fax: 613-991-6445
Director General, Sara Wiebe
Tel: 613-993-0054; *Fax:* 613-991-6445
sara.wiebe@tc.gc.ca
Executive Director, International Air Policy, Marc Rioux
Tel: 613-993-1718; *Fax:* 613-991-6445
marc.rioux@tc.gc.ca
Manager, Senior Policy Advisor, Keith Jones
Tel: 613-991-6446; *Fax:* 613-991-6445
keith.jones@tc.gc.ca

Crown Corporation Governance / Gouvernance de société d'État
Executive Director, Crown Corporations & Portfolio Governance, April Nakatsu
Tel: 613-991-2998; *Fax:* 613-991-4277
april.nakatsu@tc.gc.ca

Economic Analysis / Analyse économiques
Tel: 613-877-8066; *Fax:* 613-957-3280
Director General, Transportation & Economic Analysis & Chief Economist, Christian Dea
Tel: 613-949-7217
christian.dea@tc.gc.ca

Environmental Policy / Politiques environnementales
Director General, Ellen Burack
Tel: 613-949-2677; *Fax:* 613-949-9415
ellen.burack@tc.gc.ca

International & Intergovernmental Relations / Relations internationales et intergouvernementales
Director General, Sandra LaFortune
Tel: 613-991-6500; *Fax:* 613-990-6422
sandra.lafortune@tc.gc.ca

Marine Policy / Politique maritime
Fax: 613-998-1845
Director General, Vacant
Chief, International Marine Policy, Doug O'Keefe
Tel: 613-991-6526; *Fax:* 613-998-1845
doug.okeefe@tc.gc.ca

Strategic Policy & Innovation / Politiques stratégiques
Tel: 613-949-9596; *Fax:* 613-990-1719
Director General, Craig Hutton
Tel: 613-949-7277; *Fax:* 613-990-1719
craig.hutton@tc.gc.ca
Senior Director, Policy Integration & Research, Jacques Rochon
Tel: 613-991-2967; *Fax:* 613-990-1719
jacques.rochon@tc.gc.ca

Surface Transportation Policy / Politiques sur le transport terrestre des marchandises
Fax: 613-998-2686
Director General, Lenore Duff
Tel: 613-998-2689; *Fax:* 613-998-2686
lenore.duff@tc.gc.ca

Programs Group / Groupe des programmes
www.tc.gc.ca/eng/programs-menu.htm
Responsible for the transfer of ports, harbours & airports to communities & other interests; the oversight & lease management of divested facilities; the operation of facilities not yet divested; & real property management. Responsible for environmental programs & policies, including environmental management system, sustainable development strategies, environmental assessment & national environmental issues in transportation, such as climate change.
Assistant Deputy Minister, Programs, Natasha Rascanin
Tel: 613-990-3001; *Fax:* 613-990-1427
natasha.rascanin@tc.gc.ca
Senior Director, Detroit River International Crossing, Windsor Gateway Project, Marie-Hélène Lévesque
Tel: 613-991-4702; *Fax:* 613-990-9639
marie-helene.levesque@tc.gc.ca

Air & Marine Programs / Programmes aériens et maritimes
Tel: 613-949-4904; *Fax:* 613-990-8889
Director General, Vacant
Senior Director, New Bridge for the St. Lawrence Project Team, Vacant

Environmental Affairs / Affaires environnementales
Fax: 613-957-4260
Director General, Sustainable Transportation Stewardship, Jim Lothrop
Tel: 613-991-5995; *Fax:* 613-993-8674
jim.lothrop@tc.gc.ca
Acting Director, Multimodal Investment Strategies, Dominic Cliche
Tel: 613-990-5891; *Fax:* 613-993-8674
dominic.cliche@tc.gc.ca
Senior Director, Environmental Management, Alec Simpson
Tel: 613-990-0512
alec.simpson@tc.gc.ca

Transportation Infrasturcture Programs / Programmes d'infrastructure de transport
Fax: 613-990-9639
Director General, Jane Weldon
Tel: 613-998-8137
jane.weldon@tc.gc.ca

Safety & Security Group / Groupe de sécurité et sûreté
Tel: 613-990-9262; *Fax:* 613-990-2947
The ADM, Safety & Security, directs the development of transportation safety & security legislation, regulations & national standards; is responsible for the uniform implementation of monitoring, testing, inspection, research & development, & subsidy programs in the aviation, marine, rail & road modes of transport; oversees the delivery of aircraft services to government & other transportation bodies; & is responsible for development & enforcement of regulations & standards under federal jurisdiction, to protect public safety in the transportation of dangerous goods, & to prevent unlawful interference in the aviation, marine & railways modes of transport, as well as ensuring that the department is prepared to respond to transportation & transportation-related emergencies.
Associate Assistant Deputy Minister, Donald Roussel
Tel: 613-949-2394; *Fax:* 613-990-2791
donald.roussel@tc.gc.ca
Executive Director, Centre of Enforcement Expertise, Allan R. Bartley
Tel: 613-949-1442; *Fax:* 613-990-2848
allan.bartley@tc.gc.ca

Aircraft Services / Services des aéronefs
Tel: 613-998-7991; *Fax:* 613-991-0365
Director General, Aircraft Services & Multimodal Training, Gérald Toupin
Tel: 613-998-3316; *Fax:* 613-991-0365
gerald.toupin@tc.gc.ca

Civil Aviation / Aviation civile
Tel: 613-773-8383; *Fax:* 613-996-9178
Director General, Aaron McCrorie
Tel: 613-990-1322
aaron.mccrorie@tc.gc.ca

Marine Safety & Security / Sécurité et sûreté maritimes
www.tc.gc.ca/eng/marine-menu.htm
Responsible for the administration of national & international laws designed to ensure the safe operation, navigation, design & maintenance of ships, protection of life & property, & prevention of ship-source pollution. Transport Canada has assumed responsibility for environmental response from Fisheries & Oceans Canada. Strictly enforces pollution prevention regulations through the inspection of ships for compliance with pollution prevention regulations & through investigation of pollution incidents.
Acting Director, Marine Security Operations, Lucie Bergeron
Tel: 613-990-1450; *Fax:* 613-949-3906
lucie.bergeron@tc.gc.ca
Executive Director, Navigation Safety & Environmental Programs, Naim Nazha
Tel: 613-991-3131; *Fax:* 613-949-9444
naim.nazha@tc.gc.ca
Director, Strategic Planning & Technical Training Services, Ted Mackay
Tel: 613-998-9293
ted.mackay@tc.gc.ca

Rail Safety / Sécurité ferroviaire
www.tc.gc.ca/eng/rail-menu.htm
Administers the Railway Safety Act & associated regulations; provides funding for improvements to railway grade crossings; administers Part II of the Canada Labour Code, relating to the safety & health of employees; & ensures, for specific railway works, that environmental impacts are assessed in compliance with the Canadian Environmental Assessment Act.
Director General, Brigitte Diogo
Tel: 613-998-8697; *Fax:* 613-990-7767
brigitte.diogo@tc.gc.ca

Road Safety & Motor Vehicle Registration / Direction de la sécurité routière et de la réglementation automobile
Fax: 613-990-2914
Toll-Free: 800-333-0371
www.tc.gc.ca/eng/road-menu.htm
Administers the Motor Vehicle Safety Act by developing vehicle & motor vehicle equipment safety standards, emission standards & testing procedures; responds to public enquiries & complaints of alleged vehicle safety defects, emission defects & fuel consumption deficiencies; &, in conjunction with Natural Resources Canada, provides fuel consumption information through vehicle labels & the Fuel Consumption Guide. Also administers the Motor Vehicle Transport Act, which governs the safety fitness of extra-provincial trucks & buses. The enforcement of this act is largely delegated to the provinces.
Director General, Kim Benjamin
Tel: 613-998-7851; *Fax:* 613-993-8628
kim.benjamin@tc.gc.ca

Security Program Support / Soutien au programme de sûreté
Responsible for the development & enforcement of regulations & standards to prevent unlawful interference with air, rail & marine transportation; management of departmental security.
Executive Director, Emergency Preparedness, Julie L. Spallin
Tel: 613-947-5076
julie.spallin@tc.gc.ca

Transportation of Dangerous Goods / Transport des marchandises dangereuses
Regulatory development, information & guidance on dangerous goods transport for the public, industry & government. Represents Canada on international organizations responsible for establishing uniform international requirements, such as the United Nations Committee of Experts on the Transport of Dangerous Goods, Association of American Railroads (AAR) Tankcar Committee & International Civil Aviation Organization (ICAO) Dangerous Goods Panel. Branches are responsible for

regulatory affairs, research, evaluation, compliance & response, review of remedial measures, development of training programs.

Regional Offices

Atlantic

Heritage Court, 95 Foundry St., 6th Fl., PO Box 42 Moncton, NB E1C 8K6

Tel: 506-851-7314; *Fax:* 855-726-7495
Toll-Free: 800-305-2059
TTY: 888-675-6863
Questions@tc.gc.ca
www.tc.gc.ca/eng/atlantic/menu.htm

Regional Director General, Marc Fortin
Tel: 506-851-7315; *Fax:* 506-851-3099
marc.fortin@tc.gc.ca

Ontario

#300, 4900 Yonge St., Toronto, ON M2N 6A5

Tel: 416-952-0215; *Fax:* 416-952-0196
www.tc.gc.ca/eng/ontario/menu.htm

Regional Director General, Michael R. Stephenson
Tel: 416-952-2170; *Fax:* 416-952-2174
michael.stephenson@tc.gc.ca

Pacific

#620, 800 Burrard St., Vancouver, BC V6Z 2J8

Tel: 604-666-5575; *Fax:* 604-666-4839
pacific-pacifique@tc.gc.ca
www.tc.gc.ca/eng/pacific/menu.htm
Other Communication: Civil Aviation Services, E-mail: services@tc.gc.ca

Regional Director General, Michael A. Henderson
Tel: 604-666-5849
michael.henderson@tc.gc.ca

Prairie & Northern

344 Edmonton St., 1st Fl., PO Box 8550 Winnipeg, MB R3C 0P6

Tel: 204-983-4341; *Fax:* 204-984-2069
Toll-Free: 888-463-0521
pnrweb@tc.gc.ca
www.tc.gc.ca/eng/prairieandnorthern/menu.htm
Other Communication: Regional HQ, Direct Phone: 204-983-3152

Regional Director General, Michele Taylor
Tel: 204-984-8105; *Fax:* 204-984-8119
michele.taylor@tc.gc.ca

Québec

700, Leigh Capréol, 2e étage, Dorval, QC H4Y 1G7

Tel: 514-633-3580; *Fax:* 514-633-3585
www.tc.gc.ca/eng/quebec/menu.htm

Regional Director General, Albert Deschamps
Tel: 514-633-2717; *Fax:* 514-633-2720
albert.deschamps@tc.gc.ca

Transportation Safety Board of Canada (TSB) / Bureau de la sécurité des transports du Canada (BST)

200, Promenade du Portage, 4th Fl., Gatineau, QC K1A 1K8

Tel: 819-994-3741; *Fax:* 819-997-2239
Toll-Free: 800-387-3557
TTY: 819-953-7287
communications@bst-tsb.gc.ca
www.tsb.gc.ca
twitter.com/TSBCanada
www.youtube.com/tsbcanada

The Board is an independent agency reporting to Parliament through the President of the Queen's Privy Council. The formal name for the Board is the Canadian Transportation Accident Investigation & Safety Board. Its sole aim is the advancement of transportation safety in the marine, rail, pipeline & air modes of transport. The TSB conducts independent investigations into selected transportation occurences in order to make findings as to their causes & contributing factors; identifies safety deficiences, & makes recommendations designed to prevent further occurences. Because the Board is independent, its transportation accident investigations are completely separate from the regulatory agencies responsible for transportation. In making findings & recommendations it is not the function of the Board to assign fault or determine civil liability.

Chair, Kathy Fox
Tel: 819-994-8000; *Fax:* 819-994-9759
kathy.fox@bst-tsb.gc.ca

Chief Operating Officer, Jean L. Laporte
Tel: 819-994-8004; *Fax:* 819-994-9759
Jean.Laporte@bst-tsb.gc.ca

Director, Investigations, Air, Mark Clitsome
Tel: 819-994-3813; *Fax:* 819-953-9586
Mark.Clitsome@bst-tsb.gc.ca

Director, Investigations, Rail/Pipeline, Kirby Jang
Tel: 819-953-6470; *Fax:* 819-953-7876
Kirby.jang@bst-tsb.gc.ca
Other Communications: Administrative Assistant, Phone: 819-953-1646

Director, Investigations, Marine, Marc-André Poisson
Tel: 819-953-1398
Marc-Andre.Poisson@bst-tsb.gc.ca

Director, Communications, Jacqueline Roy
Tel: 819-994-8051; *Fax:* 819-953-1733
jacqueline.roy@bst-tsb.gc.ca

Corporate Services Directorate / Direction générale des services intégrés

Director General, Chantal Lemyre
Tel: 819-994-8003; *Fax:* 819-953-9648
chantal.lemyre@bst-tsb.gc.ca

Operations Services Branch / Services à l'appui des opérations

Director, Leo Donati
Tel: 819-994-4135; *Fax:* 819-953-2160
leo.donati@bst-tsb.gc.ca
Other Communications: Alternate Phone: 613-990-0999

Treasury Board of Canada Secretariat / Secrétariat du Conseil du Trésor du Canada

East Tower, 140 O'Connor St., 9th Fl., Ottawa, ON K1A 0R5

Tel: 613-957-2400; *Fax:* 613-941-4000
Toll-Free: 877-636-0656
TTY: 613-957-9090
www.tbs-sct.gc.ca
twitter.com/tbs_Canada
www.youtube.com/channel/UCV7uvs-FoatgAuyzjpJTS3g

The Treasury Board is a Cabinet Committee of government headed by the President of the Treasury Board. The committee constituting the Treasury Board includes, in addition to the President, the Minister of Finance & four other ministers appointed by the Governor-in-Council. The main role of the Treasury Board is the management of the government's financial, personnel & administrative responsibilities. The Treasury Board derives its authority primarily from the Financial Administration Act & is supported by the Treasury Board Secretariat.

President, Treasury Board, Hon. Scott Brison, P.C., B.Comm.
Tel: 613-995-8231; *Fax:* 613-996-9349
scott.brison@parl.gc.ca

Parliamentary Secretary, Joyce Murray
Tel: 613-992-2430; *Fax:* 613-995-0770
joyce.murray@parl.gc.ca

Secretary, Yaprak Baltacioglu
Tel: 613-369-3176

Associate Secretary, Iain Stewart
Tel: 613-369-3184

Chief of Staff, President's Office, Sabina Saini
Tel: 613-369-3170

Executive Director & Senior General Counsel, Treasury Board Secretariat Legal Services, Dora Benbaruk
Tel: 613-952-3379; *Fax:* 613-954-5806

Director General, Internal Audit & Evaluation Bureau, Mike Milito
Tel: 613-369-9674

Director, Parliamentary Affairs, President's Office, Edward Rawlinson
Tel: 613-369-3170

Director, Evaluation, Internal Audit & Evaluation Bureau, Elena Petrus
Tel: 613-404-9960

Director, Policy, President's Office, Tisha Ashton
Tel: 613-369-3170

Press Secretary, Jean-Luc Ferland
Tel: 613-369-3170

Associated Agencies, Boards & Commissions:

•Public Sector Pension Investment Board / Office d'investissement des régimes de pensions du secteur public
#200, 440 Laurier Ave. West
Ottawa, ON K1R 7X6
Tel: 613-782-3095; *Fax:* 613-782-6864
info@investpsp.ca
www.investpsp.ca

Crown corporation established by Parliament by the Public Sector Pension Investment Board Act (September 1999). The mandate of PSP Investments is to manage employer & employee contributions made after April 1, 2000 to the federal Public Service, the Canadian Forces & the Royal Canadian Mounted Police pension funds.

Chief Information Officer Branch / Direction du dirigeant principal de l'information

Chief Information Officer of the Government of Canada, John Messina
Tel: 613-369-9633

Deputy Chief Information Officer, Dave Adamson
Tel: 613-369-9637; *Fax:* 613-818-0431

Chief Technology Officer of the Government of Canada, Wade Daley
Tel: 613-369-9652; *Fax:* 613-946-4334

Executive Director, IT Project Review & Oversight, Leslie Crone
Tel: 613-369-9671

Executive Director, Information Management & Open Government, Stephen B. Walker
Tel: 613-369-9699

Executive Director, Security & Identity Management, Rita Whittle
Tel: 613-369-9683

Executive Director, Service Policy, Service & GC 2.0 Policy & Community Enablement Division, Nicholas Wise
Tel: 613-369-9655; *Fax:* 613-266-6204

Senior Director, IT Architecture, Information Technology, Serge Caron
Tel: 613-369-9650

Senior Director, Cyber Security, Security & Identity Management, Daniel Couillard
Tel: 613-369-9679; *Fax:* 613-790-2435

Senior Director, IT Policy Development & Oversight, Information Technology, Catherine Droessler
Tel: 613-369-9649

Senior Director, Corporate Engagement, Governance & Renewal, Web Standard Office, Michel Laviolette
Tel: 613-716-5816; *Fax:* 613-954-6811

Director, IT-Enabled Project Review, Claire Pereira
Tel: 613-946-5055; *Fax:* 613-946-4334

Corporate Services Sector / Secteur des services ministériels

Assistant Secretary, Corporate Services & CFO, Renée Lafontaine
Tel: 613-369-9440

Executive Director, Financial Management Directorate, Grace Chennette
Tel: 613-369-9441

Executive Director & Chief Information Officer, Paul Girard
Tel: 613-992-4306; *Fax:* 613-943-2077

Executive Director & Chief Information Officer, Marc Brouillard
Tel: 613-369-9599; *Fax:* 613-816-3365

Director, Corporate Administration & Security, Jodi C. Doyle
Tel: 613-369-3059; *Fax:* 613-898-6765

Economic Sector / Secteur des programmes économiques

Assistant Secretary, Taki Sarantakis
Tel: 613-369-9500

Executive Director, Industrial Division, Gibby Armstrong
Tel: 613-369-9497

Executive Director, Resource Division, Samantha Tattersall
Tel: 613-369-9503; *Fax:* 613-948-6062

Expenditure Management Sector / Secteur de la gestion des dépenses

Assistant Secretary, Brian Pagan
Tel: 613-369-9581

Deputy Assistant Secretary, Vacant

Executive Director, Program Performance & Evaluation Division, Kiran Hanspal
Tel: 613-369-9568

Executive Director, Expenditure Strategies & Estimates, Marcia Santiago
Tel: 613-369-9589

Executive Director, Expenditure Analysis & Compensation Planning, Richard Stuart
Tel: 613-369-9573

Director, Strategic Review, Spending Review Coordination, Erik De Vries
Tel: 613-369-9582

Senior Director, Spending Reviews & Expenditure Policy, Tom Roberts
Tel: 613-369-9495

Senior Director, Centre of Excellence for Evaluation, Anne Routhier
Tel: 613-369-9622

Senior Director, Expend Operations & Estimates, Strategies, Darryl Sprecher
Tel: 613-369-9590

Federal Contaminated Sites Inventory / Inventaire des sites contaminés fédéraux

www.tbs-sct.gc.ca/fcsi-rscf

Includes all known federal contaminated sites for which federal departments & agencies (excluding Crown corporations) are accountable. Also includes some non-federal sites for which the government has accepted some or all responsibility. Sites are classified at the time of assessment for contaminants, in a system developed by the Canadian Council of Ministers of Environment.

Government Operations Sector / Secteur des opérations gouvernementales

Assistant Secretary, Nancy Chahwan
Tel: 613-369-9538

Executive Director, Government Operations & Services Directorate, Alexis Conrad
Tel: 613-868-7004; *Fax:* 613-995-2873

Human Resources Division / Division des ressources humaines

Executive Director, Caroline Curran
Tel: 613-369-9468

International Affairs, Security & Justice Sector / Secteur des affaires internationales, de la sécurité et de la justice

Assistant Secretary, Michael Vandergrift
Tel: 613-369-9530
Executive Director, International Affairs, Immigration & Defense, Mieke Bos
Tel: 613-369-9527
Executive Director, Security & Justice Division, Rob Chambers
Tel: 613-369-9526
Executive Director, International Affairs & Development Division, Mélanie Robert
Tel: 613-369-9557

Office of the Comptroller General (OCG) / Bureau du contrôleur général (BCG)

www.tbs-sct.gc.ca/ocg-bcg

Comptroller General of Canada, Bill Matthews
Tel: 613-369-3081
Assistant Comptroller General, Internal Audit, Anthea English
Tel: 613-369-3093
Assistant Comptroller General, Financial Management, Patricia Sauvé-McCuan
Tel: 613-369-3126; *Fax:* 613-952-2399
Assistant Comptroller General, Acquired Services & Assets, Elisa Mayhew
Tel: 613-369-3148
Assistant Comptroller General, Acquired Services & Assets, Marc O'Sullivan
Tel: 613-369-3079
Assistant Comptroller General, Financial Management, Roger Ermuth
Tel: 613-369-3119; *Fax:* 613-952-9613
Executive Director, Policy & Liaison, Terry Hunt
Tel: 613-369-3095; *Fax:* 613-952-3698
Executive Director, Costing Centre of Expertise, Michael Lionais
Tel: 613-369-3118
Executive Director, Government Accounting Policy & Reporting, Diane Peressini
Tel: 613-369-3107
Senior Director, Corporate Financial Systems, Daniel Banville
Tel: 613-808-9947; *Fax:* 613-943-3166
Senior Director, Real Property & Materiel Policy Division, Kevin Colenutt
Tel: 613-369-3141
Senior Director, Cost Assessment Operations, Donna Dériger
Tel: 613-369-3116
Senior Executive Director, Strategic Planning & Information Management, Dorene Hartling
Tel: 613-218-2568; *Fax:* 613-369-3115
Executive Director, Audit Operations, Hugo Pagé
Tel: 613-369-3091
Manager, Procurement Policy, Danielle Aubin
Tel: 613-415-6014
Senior Director, Investment Planning & Project Management, Lisa Reynolds
Tel: 613-369-3142
Director, Financial Management Community Development, Sylvie Séguin
Tel: 613-369-3102
Senior Director, Public Accounts Policy & Reporting, Darlene Bess
Tel: 613-369-3105

Office of the Chief Human Resources Officer (OCHRO) / Bureau du dirigeant principal des ressources humaines (BDPRH)

www.tbs-sct.gc.ca/chro-dprh

Formerly known as Canada Public Service Agency, the Office of the Chief Human Resources Officer is responsible for matters relating to human resources, pensions & benefits, labour relations & compensation.

Chief Human Resources Officer, Anne Marie Smart
Tel: 613-952-1225
Chief of Staff, Christiane Allard
Tel: 613-960-6915
Assistant Deputy Minister, Compensation & Labour Relations Sector, Manon Brassard
Tel: 613-952-3000
Assistant Deputy Minister, Pensions & Benefits, Bayla Kolk
Tel: 613-957-6410; *Fax:* 613-946-6200
Visitng Assistant Deputy Minister, ADM Collective Management, Susan MacGowan
Tel: 613-992-9160; *Fax:* 613-992-5412
Assistant Deputy Minister, Governance, Planning & Policy Sector, Sally Thornton
Tel: 613-952-1173
Associate Assistant Deputy Minister, Compensation & Labour Relations Sector, Carl Trottier
Tel: 613-960-3845; *Fax:* 613-952-8100
Executive Director, Executive Policies, Luna Bengio
Tel: 613-943-7925
Executive Director, Labour Relations, Don Graham
Tel: 613-952-2962; *Fax:* 613-952-9421
Executive Director, Pension Policy & Program, Dominique Laporte
Tel: 613-952-3262
Executive Director, Business Intelligence & Modernization, Myriam Boudreault
Tel: 613-948-9476
Executive Director, Official Languages Centre of Excellence, Marc Tremblay
Tel: 613-948-2932
Executive Director, People Management & Community Engagement, Margaret Van Amelsvoort-Thoms
Tel: 613-957-9684; *Fax:* 613-941-9450
Executive Director, Strategic Compensation Management, Baxter Williams
Tel: 613-946-3069
Senior Director, Non-Core Public Administration, David Belovich
Tel: 613-952-2952; *Fax:* 613-952-3002
Senior Director, Workplace Wellness & Productivity Strategy, Ashique Biswas
Tel: 613-952-3261; *Fax:* 613-946-6200
Senior Director, Equitable Compensation, Renée Caron
Tel: 613-948-5097; *Fax:* 613-952-9421
Senior Director, Pension Policy & Stakeholder Relations, Kim Gowing
Tel: 613-952-3121; *Fax:* 613-954-0013
Executive Director, Labour Relations, Drew Heavens
Tel: 613-952-2962; *Fax:* 613-952-0701
Senior Director, Workforce Organization & Classification, Laurie Pratt-Tremblay
Tel: 613-952-3278
Senior Director, Strategic CPA Compensation Management, Kevin R. Marchand
Tel: 613-952-3295; *Fax:* 613-952-3295
Senior Director, ADM Collective Management, Elaine Coldwell
Tel: 613-943-3088
Executive Director, HR Project Management & Implementation, Debra Tattrie
Tel: 613-960-9441
Senior Director, Union Engagement & NJC Support, Claudia Zovatto
Tel: 613-957-9678; *Fax:* 613-952-3002

Office of the Commissioner of Lobbying (OCL) / Commissariat au lobbying du Canada (CAL)

255 Albert St., 10th Fl., Ottawa, ON K1A 0R5

Tel: 613-957-2760; *Fax:* 613-957-3078
questionslobbying@ocl-cal.gc.ca
www.ocl-cal.gc.ca

Commissioner of Lobbying, Karen E. Shepherd
Deputy Commissioner, René Leblanc

Priorities & Planning / Priorités et planification

Assistant Secretary, Roger Scott-Douglas
Tel: 613-369-9433
Executive Director, MAF & Risk Management Directorate, Paule Labbé
Tel: 613-369-9427; *Fax:* 613-952-1782
Executive Director, Strategic Policy, Kathleen Owens
Tel: 613-369-9423

Regulatory Affairs / Affaires réglementaires

Assistant Secretary, Francis Bilodeau
Tel: 613-369-9542
Executive Director, Regulatory Affairs Directorate, Doug Band
Tel: 613-369-9515

Social & Cultural Sector / Secteur des programmes sociaux et culturels

Assistant Secretary, Annette Gibbons
Tel: 613-369-9487
Executive Director, ESDC & Canadian Heritage, Jennifer Aitken
Tel: 613-369-9486
Executive Director, Heritage, Cultural & Veterans Affairs, Vacant
Executive Director, INAC, Health & Veterans, Isabella Chan
Tel: 613-369-9483

Strategic Communications & Ministerial Affairs / Communications stratégiques et affaires ministérielles

Assistant Secretary, Jayne Huntley
Tel: 613-369-9369
Executive Director, Strategic Communications & Parliamentary Relations, Louise Baird
Tel: 613-369-3199
Senior Director, Ministerial Services, Janice Young
Tel: 613-369-3195; *Fax:* 613-952-6596

Veterans Affairs Canada / Anciens combattants Canada

161 Grafton St., PO Box 7700 Charlottetown, PE C1A 8M9

Toll-Free: 866-522-2122
information@vac-acc.gc.ca
www.veterans.gc.ca
Other Communication: Toll-Free French: 1-866-522-2022; Media Relations: 613-992-7468
Secondary Address: 66 Slater St.
Ottawa, ON K1A 0P4
twitter.com/veteransENG_ca
www.facebook.com/VeteransAffairsCanada
www.youtube.com/user/VeteransAffairsCa

Provides pensions for disability or death, economic support in the form of allowances, & health care benefits & services to veterans & members of the Canadian Armed Forces, members & ex-members of the RCMP, & their dependents.

Minister, Veterans Affairs, Hon. Kent Hehr, P.C.
Tel: 613-995-1561; *Fax:* 613-995-1862
Kent.Hehr@parl.gc.ca
Parliamentary Secretary, Karen McCrimmon
Tel: 613-992-1119; *Fax:* 613-992-1043
Karen.McCrimmon@parl.gc.ca
Chief of Staff, Christine Tabbert
Tel: 613-996-4649
Director, Parliamentary Affairs, Jeff Valois
Tel: 613-996-4649
Director, Communications, Norbert Cyr
Tel: 613-996-4649; *Fax:* 613-954-1054
Director, Policy, Paul McCarthy
Tel: 613-996-4649

Associated Agencies, Boards & Commissions:

•Veterans Review & Appeal Board (VRAB) / Tribunal des anciens combattants (révision et appel) (TACRA)
Daniel J. MacDonald Bldg.
161 Grafton St.
PO Box 9900
Charlottetown, PE C1A 8V7
Tel: 902-566-8751; *Fax:* 902-566-7850
Toll-free: 800-450-8006
vrab_tacra@vac-acc.gc.ca
www.vrab-tacra.gc.ca
Other Communication: Ligne sans frais: 1-877-368-0859

The Board is an independent Board with full and exclusive jurisdiction to hear appeals from the decisions of the Minister of Veterans Affairs. The Board may affirm, vary or reverse the Minister's decisions, or refer decisions back to the Minister for reconsideration. The Board is completely independent from the Department of Veterans Affairs.

Deputy Minister's Office (Charlottetown)

Deputy Minister, Gen (Ret) Walter Natynczyk
Tel: 902-566-8666
Associate Deputy Minister, Karen Ellis
Tel: 902-370-4853; *Fax:* 902-566-7868
Executive Director & General Counsel, Legal Services, Laura Nicholson
Tel: 902-566-8798; *Fax:* 902-566-8793

Audit & Evaluation Division / Direction générale de la vérification et de l'évaluation

Director General, Sheri Ostridge
Tel: 902-566-8018; *Fax:* 902-566-8343

Bureau of Pensions Advocates (BPA) / Bureau de services juridiques des pensions (BSJP)

Toll-Free: 877-396-6761

Executive Director & Chief Pensions Advocate, Anthony Saez
Tel: 902-566-8916; *Fax:* 902-566-7804
Other Communications: Alt. Phone: 604-666-3627
Director, Appeals & Legal Issues, Charles Keliher
Tel: 902-566-8058; *Fax:* 902-566-7804
Director, Strategic Planning & Management Support Directorate, Sue Lemaistre
Tel: 902-566-6923; *Fax:* 902-368-0450

Human Resources & Corporate Services Branch / Secteur des ressources humaines et services Ministériels

Assistant Deputy Minister, Charlotte Stewart
Tel: 902-566-8047; *Fax:* 902-566-8521
Director General, Information Technology & Information Management Division, Mitch Freeman
Tel: 902-566-8236
Acting Director General, Human Resources Division (Charlottetown), Louise Wallis
Tel: 902-566-8408; *Fax:* 902-566-8425
Director General, Finance Division, Maureen Sinnott
Tel: 902-566-8320; *Fax:* 902-368-0411

Senior Director, Corporate Finance, Christina Hutchins
Tel: 902-566-8531; *Fax:* 902-368-0411

Policy, Communications & Commemoration / Politiques, communications et commémoration
Assistant Deputy Minister, Sue Foster
Tel: 902-566-8100; *Fax:* 902-566-8780
Associate Assistant Deputy Minister, Bernard Butler
Tel: 902-566-6890; *Fax:* 902-566-8780
Director General, European Operations Directorate, Greg Kenney
Other Communications: International Phone: 011-333-2150-6867
Vimy Memorial
Vimy, Nord-Pas-de-Calais, 62580 France
Director General, Commemoration Division (Charlottetown), André Levesque
Tel: 902-566-8026; *Fax:* 902-566-7056
Director General, Policy & Research Division, Faith McIntyre
Tel: 902-566-7438; *Fax:* 902-370-4533
faith.mcintyre@vac-acc.gc.ca
Director General, Communications Division (Charlottetown), Paul Thomson
Tel: 902-566-8321; *Fax:* 902-566-8508
Senior Director, Strategic Policy Integration, Janice Burke
Tel: 902-566-8977; *Fax:* 902-368-0441
Senior Director, Strategic Communications & Public Affairs, Jane Hicks
Tel: 613-992-4903; *Fax:* 613-996-9969
Senior Director, Communications Division (Charlottetown), Michael Zinck
Tel: 902-368-0136; *Fax:* 902-566-8508

Service Delivery Branch / Prestation des services
Assistant Deputy Minister, Michel Doiron
Tel: 902-626-2723; *Fax:* 902-566-8172
Director General, Field Operations, Charlotte Bastien
Tel: 514-496-6413; *Fax:* 514-496-7303
Director General & Office Manager, Service Delivery & Program Management Division, Sonia Gogoh
Tel: 902-368-0649; *Fax:* 902-566-8073
Director General, Business Re-engineering, Andrée Métivier
Tel: 902-995-8114
Acting Director General, Centralized Operations Division, Colleen Solterman
Tel: 902-566-8644; *Fax:* 902-566-8337
Senior Director, Strategic & Enabling Initiatives, Elizabeth Douglas
Tel: 902-368-0076; *Fax:* 902-370-4827

Ste-Anne's Hospital / Hôpital Sainte-Anne
305 boul des Anciens-Combattants, Sainte-Anne-de-Bellevue, QC H9X 1Y9
Tel: 514-457-3440
Toll-Free: 800-361-9287
steanne@vac-acc.gc.ca
www.veterans.gc.ca/eng/steannes-hospital

The Hospital provides Veterans with long-term or respite care in addition to offering support services, through its day centre, to clients who still reside in the community & to Veterans & other clients who require mental health services or short-term hospitalization, through the National Centre for Operational Stress Injuries (NCOSI).

Executive Director, Rachel Corneille-Gravel
Tel: 514-457-8400; *Fax:* 514-457-5741
Director, Commemoration & Communications, Maggie Michaudville
Tel: 514-457-8455; *Fax:* 514-457-5741

Deputy Minister's Office (Ottawa)
Deputy Minister, Gen (Ret) Walter Natynczyk
Tel: 613-996-6881; *Fax:* 613-952-7709
walter.natynczyk@vac-acc.gc.ca
Associate Deputy Minister, Karen Ellis
Tel: 613-944-1710

Veterans Ombudsman (Charlottetown) / Ombudsman des vétérans (Charlottetown)
134 Kent St., PO Box 66 Charlottetown, PE C1A 7K2
Tel: 902-626-2919; *Fax:* 888-566-7582
Toll-Free: 877-330-4343
VAC.OVOInfo-InfoBOV.ACC@ombudsman-veterans.gc.ca
www.ombudsman-veterans.gc.ca
twitter.com/VetsOmbudsman
www.facebook.com/VeteransOmbudsman
www.youtube.com/user/ovoview

Director, Corporate Services & Charlottetown Operations, Michel Guay
Tel: 902-626-2663; *Fax:* 902-566-7582
Communications Officer, Troy Fraser
Tel: 902-626-4941; *Fax:* 902-566-7582

Veterans Ombudsman (Ottawa) / Ombudsman des vétérans (Ottawa)
#1560, 360 Albert St., Ottawa, ON K1R 7X7
Fax: 888-566-7582
Toll-Free: 877-330-4343
www.ombudsman-veterans.gc.ca
twitter.com/VetsOmbudsman
www.facebook.com/VeteransOmbudsman
www.youtube.com/user/ovoview

Veterans Ombudsman, Guy Parent
Tel: 613-944-2944; *Fax:* 613-943-3088
Deputy Ombudsman & Executive Director, Operations, Sharon Squire
Tel: 613-944-2943; *Fax:* 613-944-2939
Director, Strategic Review & Analysis, Amanda Jane
Tel: 613-943-3057; *Fax:* 613-944-2939

Regional Offices
Atlantic Region
40 Alderney Dr., 3rd Fl., Dartmouth, NS B2Y 2N5
Tel: 902-426-0629; *Fax:* 902-426-7447
Ontario Region
8 Oakes Ave., Kirkland Lake, ON P2N 3R3
Tel: 705-567-9571; *Fax:* 705-568-2517
Associate Regional Director General, R.D. Singh
Tel: 905-755-8872
Québec Region
Place Bonaventure, #6505, 800, rue de la Gauchetière Ouest, Montréal, QC H5A 1L8
Regional Associate Director General, Michel Bento
Tel: 514-496-6416; *Fax:* 514-496-7303
Western Region (Vancouver)
#1000, 605 Robson St., Vancouver, BC V6B 5J3
Western Region (Winnipeg)
#610, 234 Donald St., PO Box 6050 Winnipeg, MB R3C 4G5

VIA Rail Canada Inc.

CP 8116 Succ A, Montréal, QC H3C 3N3
Tél: 514-871-6000; *Téléc:* 514-871-6104
Ligne sans frais: 888-842-7245
TTY: 800-268-9503
customer_relations@viarail.ca
www.viarail.ca
Autres nombres: Customer Relations, Toll-Free Phone: 1-800-681-2561
twitter.com/VIA_Rail
www.facebook.com/viarailcanada
www.youtube.com/user/VIARailCanadaInc

Established in 1977, VIA Rail Canada is a Crown corporation that manages the national passenger rail network. The corporation serves 450 communities throughout Canada. VIA works to offer safe, efficient, & environmentally responsible public transportation.
Environmental intiatives include a reduction in emissions & a reduce, re-use & recycle program. Under the capital investment plan, older locomotives & passenger cars are being rebuilt. The corporation also offers a Green Procurement Guide to promote the use of environmentally responsible products in all its activities.

President & CEO, Yves Desjardins-Siciliano
Chief Commercial Officer, Martin Landry
Chief Capital Asset Management Officer, Robert St-Jean
Chief Human Resources Officer, Laurent F. Caron
Chief Legal & Risk Officer; Corporate Secretary, Jean-François Legault
Chief Business Transformation Officer, Sonia Corriveau
Chief Financial Officer, Patricia Jasmin
Chief Transportation & Safety Officer, Marc Beaulieu

Western Economic Diversification Canada (WD) / Diversification de l'économie de l'Ouest Canada (DEO)

Canada Place, #1500, 9700 Jasper Ave. NW, Edmonton, AB T5J 4H7
Tel: 780-495-4164; *Fax:* 780-495-4557
Toll-Free: 888-338-9378
TTY: 877-303-3388
www.wd-deo.gc.ca
twitter.com/wd_canada

Responsible for promoting economic growth & diversification in the West. By investing in innovation, fostering entrepreneurship & using partnerships to enhance community sustainability, WD is helping to create a more prosperous future for western Canadians.Invests in R&D & commercialization in environmental technologies as a focus area for innovation strategies.

Minister Responsible; Minister, Innovation, Science & Economic Development, Hon. Navdeep Bains, P.C., B.A., M.B.A., C.M.A.
Tel: 613-995-7784; *Fax:* 613-996-9817
Navdeep.Bains@parl.gc.ca
Deputy Minister, Daphne Meredith
Tel: 780-495-5772; *Fax:* 780-495-6222
Other Communications: Ottawa: 613-952-9382
Chief of Staff to the Minister, Jerra Kosick
Tel: 613-952-7418; *Fax:* 613-957-1155
Director, Communications, Nicholas Insley
Tel: 613-954-8097; *Fax:* 613-957-1155

Headquarters / Administration centrale
Tel: 780-495-4164; *Fax:* 780-495-5808
Executive Director, Finance & Corporate Management, Cathy McLean
Tel: 780-495-4301; *Fax:* 780-495-7618
Director General, Finance & Management Accountability, Kathryn Mattern
Tel: 780-495-4407; *Fax:* 780-495-4434
Director, Information Management & Information Technology, Grant Gaudin
Tel: 780-495-6734; *Fax:* 780-495-5808
Director, Human Resources, Patrick Faulkner
Tel: 780-495-2992; *Fax:* 780-495-6874

Regional Offices
Alberta (Edmonton)
Canada Place, #1500, 9700 Jasper Ave. Northwest, Edmonton, AB T5J 4H7
Tel: 780-495-4164; *Fax:* 780-495-4557
Toll-Free: 888-338-9378
TTY: 877-303-3388
Assistant Deputy Minister, Doug Maley
Tel: 780-495-4168; *Fax:* 780-495-6222
Other Communications: Executive Assistant, Phone: 780-495-4960
Director General, Operations, Nadean Langlois
Tel: 780-495-4973; *Fax:* 780-495-4557
British Columbia (Vancouver)
Price Waterhouse Bldg., #700, 333 Seymour St., Vancouver, BC V6B 5G9
Tel: 604-666-6256; *Fax:* 604-666-2353
Toll-Free: 888-338-9378
TTY: 877-303-3388
Assistant Deputy Minister, Gerry Salembier
Tel: 604-666-6366; *Fax:* 604-666-1510
Director General, Operations, Naina Sloan
Tel: 604-666-7011; *Fax:* 604-666-2353
Manager, Consultations, Marketing & Communications, Jaime Burke
Tel: 604-666-1318; *Fax:* 604-666-2353
Manitoba (Winnipeg)
The Cargill Bldg., #620, 240 Graham Ave., Winnipeg, MB R3C 0J7
Tel: 204-983-4472; *Fax:* 204-983-4694
Toll-Free: 888-338-9378
TTY: 877-303-3388
Assistant Deputy Minister, Vacant
Tel: 204-983-5715; *Fax:* 204-983-0966
Other Communications: Executive Assistant, Phone: 204-983-4467
Executive Director, Manitoba Federal Council Secretariat, Glenn Armstrong
Tel: 204-984-6815
Director General, Operations, France Guimond
Tel: 204-984-2438; *Fax:* 204-983-1280
Policy & Strategic Direction (Ottawa)
#500, 141 Laurier Ave. West, Ottawa, ON K1P 5J3
Tel: 613-952-2768; *Fax:* 613-952-9384
TTY: 877-303-3388
Assistant Deputy Minister, James Meddings
Tel: 613-952-7096; *Fax:* 613-954-1044
Director General, Strategic Services & Advocacy, Francesco Del Bianco
Tel: 613-954-9640; *Fax:* 613-952-3434
Director General, Planning & Programs, Donald MacDonald
Tel: 780-495-8437; *Fax:* 780-495-6876
Director, Consultations, Marketing & Communications, Janet Chen
Tel: 613-952-7101; *Fax:* 613-952-6775
Saskatchewan (Saskatoon)
#601, 119 - 4 Ave. South, PO Box 2025 Saskatoon, SK S7K 3S7
Tel: 306-975-4373; *Fax:* 306-975-5484
Toll-Free: 888-338-9378
TTY: 877-303-3388
Assistant Deputy Minister, Brenda LePage
Tel: 306-975-5858; *Fax:* 306-975-5484
Executive Director, Saskatchewan Federal Council, Deanne Belisle
Tel: 306-975-6093; *Fax:* 306-975-5484

Director General, Operations, Doug Zolinsky
Tel: 306-975-6988; *Fax:* 306-975-5484

Government of Alberta

Seat of Government: PO Box 1333 Edmonton, AB T5J 2N2
Tel: 780-427-2711; *Fax:* 780-422-2852
Toll-Free: -310-0000
TTY: 800-232-7125
www.alberta.ca
Other Communication: TTY: 780-427-9999 (in Edmonton)
twitter.com/YourAlberta
www.facebook.com/youralberta.ca
www.youtube.com/user/YourAlberta

Alberta was proclaimed as a province on September 1, 1905. The province has an elected Legislative Assembly, consisting of 87 members. The Premier & the Cabinet exercise executive power. The representative of the Crown is the Lieutenant Governor, who is appointed by the Governor General. The population as of the 2011 StatsCan census was 3,645,257. Alberta has a land area of 640,081.87 sq km.

Office of the Lieutenant Governor

Office of the Lieutenant Governor of AB, Legislature Bldg., 10800 - 97 Ave., 3rd Fl., Edmonton, AB T5K 2B6
Tel: 780-427-7243; *Fax:* 780-422-5134
ltgov@gov.ab.ca
www.lieutenantgovernor.ab.ca
www.flickr.com/photos/lieutenantgovernorofalberta

The representative of the Crown in Alberta is the Lieutenant Governor, who is appointed by the Governor General, with the advice of the Prime Minister of Canada.

Lieutenant Governor, Hon. Lois Mitchell, CM, AOE, LLD
Private Secretary to the Lieutenant Governor, Brian Roach
Tel: 780-427-8308; *Fax:* 780-422-5134
brian.roach@gov.ab.ca
Communications Officer, Janet Resta
Tel: 780-427-9222; *Fax:* 780-422-5134
janet.resta@gov.ab.ca

Office of the Premier

Office of the Premier, Legislature Building, #307, 10800 - 97 Ave., Edmonton, AB T5K 2B6
Tel: 780-427-2251; *Fax:* 780-427-1349
Toll-Free: -310-0000
alberta.ca/premier.cfm

The head of government in Alberta is the Premier. The Premier of the province is the leader of the political party that has the most seats in the Legislative Assembly. The Premier is head of the Executive Council, which works to put government policy into practice.

NDP Leader Rachel Notley was elected as Alberta's seventeenth Premier in a general election held May 5, 2015. Her win marked the end of the PC Party's four-decade reign in the province.

The following services are provided by the Office of the Premier: the provision of support to the Premier; issues management; the provision of strategic advice; correspondence; & scheduling.

Premier; President, Executive Council, Hon. Rachel Notley
Tel: 780-427-2251; *Fax:* 780-427-1349
premier@gov.ab.ca
Social Media: twitter.com/RachelNotley,
www.facebook.com/rachelnotley
Chief of Staff, Brian Topp

Executive Council

Legislature Building, 10800 - 97 Ave., Edmonton, AB T5K 2B6
Tel: 780-427-2711
Toll-Free: -310-0000
www.alberta.ca/premier-cabinet.aspx

The Executive Council consists of the Premier & cabinet ministers. Cabinet ministers are selected by the Premier from elected members of the Premier's party.

The Cabinet carries out the following functions: approving Orders in Council; ratifying policy matters; & acting as the final authority on issues related to the operation of the government. The following is a list of members of the Executive Council, presented in order of precedence:

Premier; President, Executive Council, Hon. Rachel Notley
Tel: 780-427-2251; *Fax:* 780-427-1349
premier@gov.ab.ca
alberta.ca/premier.cfm
Social Media: twitter.com/RachelNotley,
www.facebook.com/rachelnotley
Legislature Building
#408, 10800 - 97 Ave.
Edmonton, AB T5K 2B6
Deputy Premier; Minister, Health, Hon. Sarah Hoffman
Tel: 780-427-3665; *Fax:* 780-415-0961
www.health.alberta.ca/about/minister-bio.html
Social Media: twitter.com/shoffmanab
Minister, Infrastructure; Minister, Transportation; Government House Leader, Hon. Brian Mason
Tel: 780-427-5041; *Fax:* 780-422-2722
transportation.minister@gov.ab.ca
www.transportation.alberta.ca
Social Media: twitter.com/bmasonNDP,
www.facebook.com/brianmasonNDP
Legislature Bldg.
#324, 10800 - 97 Ave.
Edmonton, AB T5K 2B6
Minister, Education, Hon. David Eggen
Tel: 780-427-5010; *Fax:* 780-427-5018
education.minister@gov.ab.ca
www.education.alberta.ca
Social Media: twitter.com/davideggenAB,
www.facebook.com/ElectDavidEggen
Minister, Economic Development & Trade; Deputy Government House Leader, Hon. Deron Bilous
Tel: 780-644-8554; *Fax:* 780-644-8572
Social Media: twitter.com/DeronBilous,
www.facebook.com/electderonbilous
Minister, Finance; President, Treasury Board, Hon. Joe Ceci
Tel: 780-415-4855; *Fax:* 780-415-4853
www.finance.alberta.ca/ministry/minister_finance.html
Social Media: twitter.com/joececiyyc,
www.facebook.com/joe.ceci.ndp
Legislature Bldg.
#323, 10800 - 97 Ave.
Edmonton, AB T5K 2B6
Minister, Justice & Solicitor General, Hon. Kathleen Ganley
Tel: 780-427-2339; *Fax:* 780-422-6621
justice.alberta.ca
Social Media: www.facebook.com/buffaloNDP
Minister, Environment & Parks; Minister Responsible, Climate Change Office, Hon. Shannon Phillips
Tel: 780-427-2391; *Fax:* 780-422-6259
aep.minister@gov.ab.ca
esrd.alberta.ca/about-esrd/ministers-office/default.aspx
Social Media: twitter.com/sphillipsab,
www.facebook.com/ShannonPhillipsLethbridge
Minister, Agriculture & Forestry; Deputy Government House Leader, Hon. Oneil Carlier
Tel: 780-427-2137; *Fax:* 780-422-6035
www.agric.gov.ab.ca
Social Media: twitter.com/oneilcarlier,
www.facebook.com/oneilcarliermla
Minister, Municipal Affairs, Hon. Danielle Larivee
Tel: 780-427-3744; *Fax:* 780-422-9550
minister.municipalaffairs@gov.ab.ca
www.municipalaffairs.alberta.ca
Minister, Energy, Hon. Margaret McCuaig-Boyd
Tel: 780-427-3740; *Fax:* 780-644-1222
minister.energy@gov.ab.ca
www.energy.alberta.ca/About_Us/991.asp
Social Media: www.facebook.com/1558169337770701
Minister, Human Services, Hon. Irfan Sabir
Tel: 780-643-6210; *Fax:* 780-643-6214
calgary.mccall@assembly.ab.ca
humanservices.alberta.ca
Minister, Seniors & Housing, Hon. Lori Sigurdson
Tel: 780-415-9550; *Fax:* 780-415-9411
www.iae.alberta.ca
Social Media: twitter.com/lorisigurdson,
www.facebook.com/lorisigurdson.ndp
Minister, Indigenous Relations, Hon. Richard Feehan
Tel: 780-422-4144; *Fax:* 780-638-4052
ir.ministeroffice@gov.ab.ca
www.municipalaffairs.alberta.ca
Minister, Labour; Minister Responsible, Democratic Renewal, Hon. Christina Gray
Tel: 780-638-9400; *Fax:* 780-638-9401
labour.minister@gov.ab.ca
www.municipalaffairs.alberta.ca
Minister, Service Alberta; Minister, Status of Women, Hon. Stephanie McLean
Tel: 780-422-6880; *Fax:* 780-422-2496
ministersa@gov.ab.ca
www.municipalaffairs.alberta.ca
Minister, Culture & Tourism, Hon. Ricardo Miranda
Tel: 780-422-3559; *Fax:* 780-427-5018
culturetourism.minister@gov.ab.ca
www.municipalaffairs.alberta.ca
Minister, Advanced Education, Hon. Marlin Schmidt
Tel: 780-427-5777; *Fax:* 780-422-8733
ae.minister@gov.ab.ca
www.municipalaffairs.alberta.ca
Associate Minister, Health, Hon. Brandy Payne
Tel: 780-427-3665; *Fax:* 780-415-0961
health.minister@gov.ab.ca
www.municipalaffairs.alberta.ca

Deputy Minister's Office

Executive Branch, Legislature Building, #305, 10800 - 97th Ave., Edmonton, AB T5K 2B6
alberta.ca/executive-council.cfm

The Executive Council Office is led by the Deputy Minister of the Executive Council.

Deputy Minister, Executive Council, Marcia Nelson
Deputy Secretary, Cabinet, Cabinet Coordination Office, Andre Tremblay
Tel: 780-415-0552
andre.tremblay@gov.ab.ca
Chief of Staff to the Deputy Minister, Evan Romanow
Tel: 780-644-1276
evan.romanow@gov.ab.ca

Cabinet Coordination Office

Legislature Bldg., #402, 10800 - 97 Ave., Edmonton, AB T5K 2B6
Deputy Clerk, Executive Council & Deputy Secretary to Cabinet, Andre Tremblay
Tel: 780-415-0552
andre.tremblay@gov.ab.ca
Executive Director, Brandy Cox
Tel: 780-415-9786
brandy.cox@gov.ab.ca

Corporate Services

Federal Bldg., 9820 - 107 St., 7th Fl., Edmonton, AB T5K 1E7
Executive Director, Finance & Administration, Jennifer Hibbert
Tel: 780-427-9233
jennifer.hibbert@gov.ab.ca
Executive Director, Human Resources, Kim McCrary
Tel: 780-427-9234
kim.mccrary@gov.ab.ca

Intergovernmental Relations

Commerce Place, 10155 - 102 St., 12th Fl., Edmonton, AB T5J 4G8
Associate Deputy Minister, Garry Pocock
Tel: 780-422-0453; *Fax:* 780-427-0939
garry.pocock@gov.ab.ca
Executive Director, Economics & Resources, Don Kwas
Tel: 780-422-0487
don.kwas@gov.ab.ca
Executive Director, Federal / Provincial Relations, Bruce Tait
Tel: 780-422-1127; *Fax:* 780-427-0939
bruce.tait@gov.ab.ca
Executive Director, Social Policy, Gordon Vincent
Tel: 780-415-6548; *Fax:* 780-427-0939
gordon.vincent@gov.ab.ca

Operations & Machinery of Government

Federal Bldg., 9820 - 107 St., 7th Fl., Edmonton, AB T5K 1E7
Executive Director, Kristin Stolarz
Tel: 780-644-8815

Policy Coordination Office

Federal Bldg., 9820 - 107 St., 7th Fl., Edmonton, AB T5K 1E7
Deputy Minister, John Heaney
Tel: 780-422-5353
john.heaney@gov.ab.ca
Assistant Deputy Minister, Community Policy & Regulations Coordination, Jessica Bowering
Tel: 780-644-8276
jessica.bowering@gov.ab.ca
Assistant Deputy Minister, Economic Policy, Doug Lammie
Tel: 780-422-5933
douglas.lammie@gov.ab.ca
Assistant Deputy Minister, Social Policy, Lisa Sadownik
Tel: 780-638-4141
andre.tremblay@gov.ab.ca

Protocol

Federal Bldg., 9820 - 107 St., 9th Fl., Edmonton, AB T5K 1E7
Chief, Protocol, Katherine Huising
Tel: 780-422-2236; *Fax:* 780-422-0786
katherine.huising@gov.ab.ca
Deputy Chief, Protocol, Norm Davies
Tel: 780-422-1845; *Fax:* 780-422-0786
norm.davies@gov.ab.ca

Public Affairs Bureau

Federal Bldg., 9820 - 107 St., 7th Fl., Edmonton, AB T5K 1E7
Communications are provided by the Public Affairs Bureau to support Alberta's government ministries. The Public Affairs Bureau provides information about government policies & programs to Albertans. The Bureau is also responsible for coordinating communications during public emergencies.

Managing Director, Mark Wells
Tel: 780-644-3024; *Fax:* 780-427-1010
mark.wells@gov.ab.ca
Assistant Deputy Minister, Strategic Communications & Marketing, Social Portfolio, Carol Chawrun

Tel: 780-427-9274
carol.chawrun@gov.ab.ca
Executive Director, Planning & Consultation, Vacant
Tel: 780-415-1541
Executive Director, Issues Management, Vacant
Assistant Deputy Minister, Strategic Communications & Engagement, Resources & Economics Portfolio, Christopher McPherson
Tel: 780-643-9341
christopher.mcpherson@gov.ab.ca

Cabinet Policy Committees
www.alberta.ca/government-committees.aspx
The following are Alberta's cabinet policy committees: Climate Leadership Policy; Economic Development Policy; Legislative Review; Municipal Governance; Social Policy; & Treasury Board
President, Treasury Board, Hon. Joe Ceci
Chair, Climate Leadership Policy Committee, Hon. Christina Gray
Chair, Economic Development Policy Committee, Hon. Deron Bilous
Chair, Legislative Review Committee, Hon. Kathleen Ganley
Chair, Municipal Governance Committee, Hon. Deron Bilous
Chair, Social Policy Committee, Hon. Shannon Phillips

Legislative Assembly of Alberta

Legislature Annex, 9718 - 107 St., Edmonton, AB T5K 1E4
Tel: 780-427-2826; *Fax:* 780-427-1623
laocommunications@assembly.ab.ca
www.assembly.ab.ca
Other Communication: Reference information: library.requests@assembly.ab.ca; Visitor Services Office: visitorinfo@assembly.ab.ca
twitter.com/LegAssemblyofAB
www.facebook.com/431884683512474
www.youtube.com/user/AlbertaLegislature
The Legislative Assembly of Alberta is elected by voters. It consists of government members & opposition members.
The Legislative Assembly Office carries out the following main responsibilities: supporting the Speaker of the Legislative Assembly; supporting members; recording proceedings & maintaining records of the Legislative Assembly; educating the public; & providing services to external clients.
The Legislative Assembly Office is organized by services such as the following: management & communication services; house & committee services; legal services; human resource services; financial management & administrative services; visitor, ceremonial, & security services; library services; public information & reporting services; & information technology services.
Clerk, Rob Reynolds
Tel: 780-427-1347
rob.reynolds@assembly.ab.ca
Note: The Clerk acts as the Chief Executive Officer of the Legislative Assembly Office. In the Chamber, the Clerk advises the Speaker about procedure. He also calls out the daily order of business.
Senior Parliamentary Counsel; Director, House Services; Law Clerk & Director, Interparliamentary Relations, Shannon Dean
Tel: 780-427-1345; *Fax:* 780-427-0744
shannon.dean@assembly.ab.ca
Note: Main duties of House Services include producing the Order Paper, Votes, & Proceedings, & the Journals, as well as maintaining the Assembly's current & historical records.
Senior Financial Officer; Director, Financial Management & Administrative Services, Scott Ellis
Tel: 780-427-1566; *Fax:* 780-415-1714
scott.ellis@assembly.ab.ca
Note: Financial Management & Administrative Services is responsible for financial processing, reporting, & control.
Sergeant-at-Arms; Director, Visitor, Ceremonial & Security Services, Brian Hodgson
Tel: 780-427-6048; *Fax:* 780-415-5829
brian.hodgson@assembly.ab.ca
Note: The following duties are performed: management of visitors' services for the Legislative Assembly; provision of security services; & the execution of ceremonial functions for the Legislative Assembly.
Director, Human Resources, Information Technology & Broadcast Services, Cheryl Scarlett
Tel: 780-427-1368; *Fax:* 780-427-6436
cheryl.scarlett@assembly.ab.ca
Note: Customized human resource management services are provided to support the operation of the Legislative Assembly of Alberta.
Legislature Librarian, Valerie Footz
Tel: 780-427-0202; *Fax:* 780-427-6016
val.footz@assembly.ab.ca
Note: The Legislature Library provides services to Members of the Legislative Assembly of Alberta, Members' staff, Legislative Assembly Office staff, & the general public.

Office of the Speaker
Legislative Branch, Legislature Building, #325, 10800 - 97th Ave., Edmonton, AB T5K 2B6
The Speaker of the Alberta Legislative Assembly maintains orderly debate in the Chamber. He cannot engage in debate in the Assembly. As head of the Legislative Assembly Office, the Speaker also plays a role in the maintenance of records of the Assembly & the provision of services to members.
Speaker, Hon. Robert Wanner
Constituency: Medicine Hat, New Democratic Party
Tel: 780-427-2464; *Fax:* 780-422-9553
medicine.hat@assembly.ab.ca
Deputy Speaker, Debbie Jabbour
Constituency: Peace River, New Democratic Party
Tel: 780-638-1423; *Fax:* 780-638-1431
peace.river@assembly.ab.ca

Government Members' Caucus Office
Federal Bldg., 9820 - 107 St., 6th Fl., Edmonton, AB T5K 1E7
Tel: 780-427-1800; *Fax:* 780-415-0701
nd@assembly.ab.ca
www.albertandp.ca
twitter.com/AlbertaNDP
www.facebook.com/AlbertaNDP
www.youtube.com/user/AlbertaNDP
Alberta's New Democratic Party hold the most seats in the Legislature & are the governing party in Alberta.
Government House Leader, Hon. Brian Mason
Tel: 780-427-5041; *Fax:* 780-422-2722
edmonton.highlandsnorwood@assembly.ab.ca
Deputy Government House Leader, Hon. Deron Bilous
Tel: 780-644-8554; *Fax:* 780-644-8572
edmonton.beverlyclareview@assembly.ab.ca
Deputy Government House Leader, Hon. Oneil Carlier
Tel: 780-427-2137; *Fax:* 780-422-6035
as.minister.m@gov.ab.ca
Executive Director, Government Caucus, Jim Gurnett
Tel: 780-644-6842; *Fax:* 780-415-0701
jim.gurnett@assembly.ab.ca

Wildrose Alliance Party of Alberta Office
Federal Bldg., 9820 - 107 St., 5th Fl., Edmonton, AB T5K 1E7
Tel: 780-638-3505; *Fax:* 780-638-3506
www.wildrose.ca
twitter.com/TeamWildrose
www.youtube.com/user/WildroseTV
The Wildrose Alliance Party of Alberta, led by Brian Jean, is the Official Opposition.
Leader, Alberta Wildrose Alliance, Brian Jean
Tel: 780-427-1031; *Fax:* 780-638-3506
fortmcmurray.conklin@assembly.ab.ca
Social Media: twitter.com/brianjeanwrp, www.facebook.com/brianjeanwrp
Chief of Staff, Kevin Thomas
Tel: 780-638-9576; *Fax:* 780-638-3506
kevin.thomas@assembly.ab.ca
Principal Secretary & Director, Caucus Operations, Matt Solberg
Tel: 780-643-9114; *Fax:* 780-638-3506
matt.solberg@assembly.ab.ca

Progressive Conservative Party Caucus Office
Federal Bldg., 9820 - 107 St., 4th Fl., Edmonton, AB T5K 1E7
Tel: 780-427-1879; *Fax:* 780-427-0968
www.pcalberta.org
twitter.com/PC_Alberta
www.facebook.com/pc.alberta
Interim Leader, Alberta Progressive Conservative Party, Ric McIver
Tel: 780-643-9091; *Fax:* 780-415-0968
calgary.hays@assembly.ab.ca
Social Media: twitter.com/RicMcIver, www.facebook.com/RicMcIver, www.linkedin.com/pub/ric-mciver/10/498/34a
Note: Former Premier & PC Leader Jim Prentice quit politics after his party's defeat in the May 5, 2015, general election. Ric McIver was appointed Interim Leader on May 11, 2015.
Chief of Staff, Kevin Weidlich
Tel: 780-427-1879; *Fax:* 780-427-0968
kevin.weidlich@assembly.ab.ca
Director, Policy & Research, Nicholas Burris
Tel: 780-427-1879; *Fax:* 780-427-0968
nicholas.burris@assembly.ab.ca
Director, Communications, Christine Way
Tel: 780-638-9514; *Fax:* 780-427-0968
christine.way@assembly.ab.ca

Liberal Caucus Office
Federal Bldg., 9820 - 107 St., 6th Fl., Edmonton, AB T5K 1E7
Tel: 780-427-2292; *Fax:* 780-427-3697
liberal.correspondence@assembly.ab.ca
www.albertaliberal.com
twitter.com/albertaliberals
www.facebook.com/ablib
www.youtube.com/user/AlbertaLiberalCaucus
Leader, Liberal Party of Alberta, Dr. David Swann
Tel: 780-422-1582; *Fax:* 780-427-3697
calgary.mountainview@assembly.ab.ca
Chief of Staff, Carmen Remenda
Tel: 780-644-7796; *Fax:* 780-427-3697
carmen.remenda@assembly.ab.ca
Director, Communications, Stephen Binder
Tel: 780-644-7719; *Fax:* 780-427-3697
stephen.binder@assembly.ab.ca

Alberta Party Caucus Office
Federal Bldg., 9820 - 107 St., 5th Fl., Edmonton, AB T5K 1E7
www.albertaparty.ca
twitter.com/AlbertaParty
www.facebook.com/albertaparty
www.youtube.com/user/TheAlbertaParty
Leader, Alberta Party, Greg Clark
Tel: 780-644-7033; *Fax:* 780-644-7004
calgary.elbow@assembly.ab.ca
Caucus & Legislative Affairs Coordinator, Barbara Currie
Tel: 780-644-7020; *Fax:* 780-644-7004
barbara.currie@assembly.ab.ca

Committees of the Legislative Assembly of Alberta
Legislative Branch, Legislature Annex, #801, 9718 - 107 St., Edmonton, AB T5K 1E4
Tel: 780-427-1350; *Fax:* 780-427-5688
committees@assembly.ab.ca
www.assembly.ab.ca/committees
Committees of the Legislative Assembly of Alberta include select special committees, special standing committees, legislative policy committees, & standing committees.
The current select special committee is the Ethics & Accountability Committee.
There is currently one special standing committee, Members' Services.
Legislative policy committees include the following: Alberta's Economic Future; Families & Communities; & Resource Stewardship.
Current standing committees are as follows: Alberta Heritage Savings Trust Fund; Legislative Offices; Private Bills; Privileges & Elections, Standing Orders & Printing; & Public Accounts.
Chair, Select Special Ethics & Accountability Committee, Jessica Littlewood
Constituency: Fort Saskatchewan-Vegreville, New Democratic Party
Tel: 780-644-5748; *Fax:* 780-415-0701
fortsaskatchewan.vegreville@assembly.ab.ca
Chair, Special Standing Committee on Members' Services, Hon. Robert Wanner
Constituency: Medicine Hat, New Democratic Party
Tel: 780-427-2464; *Fax:* 780-422-9553
medicine.hat@assembly.ab.ca
Chair, Standing Committee on Alberta's Economic Future, Graham D. Sucha
Constituency: Calgary-Shaw, New Democratic Party
Tel: 780-644-5779; *Fax:* 780-415-0701
calgary.shaw@assembly.ab.ca
Chair, Standing Committee on Families & Communities, Nicole Goehring
Constituency: Edmonton-Castle Downs, New Democratic Party
Tel: 780-644-5719; *Fax:* 780-415-0701
edmonton.castledowns@assembly.ab.ca
Chair, Standing Committee on Resource Stewardship, Rod Loyola
Constituency: Edmonton-Ellerslie, New Democratic Party
Tel: 780-644-5737; *Fax:* 780-415-0701
edmonton.ellerslie@assembly.ab.ca
Chair, Standing Committee on the Alberta Heritage Savings Trust Fund, Barb Miller
Constituency: Red Deer-South, New Democratic Party
Tel: 780-638-1403; *Fax:* 780-638-1431
reddeer.south@assembly.ab.ca
Chair, Standing Committee on Legislative Offices, David Shepherd
Constituency: Edmonton-Centre, New Democratic Party
Tel: 780-638-1424; *Fax:* 780-415-0701
edmonton.centre@assembly.ab.ca
Chair, Standing Committee on Private Bills, Karen M. McPherson
Constituency: Calgary-Mackay-Nose Hill, New Democratic Party
Tel: 780-638-1401; *Fax:* 780-638-1430
calgary.mackay.nosehill@assembly.ab.ca

Chair, Standing Committee on Privileges & Elections, Standing Orders & Printing, Maria Fitzpatrick
Constituency: Lethbridge-East, New Democratic Party
Tel: 780-638-1409; *Fax:* 780-638-1430
lethbridge.east@assembly.ab.ca
Chair, Standing Committee on Public Accounts, Derek Fildebrandt
Constituency: Strathmore-Brooks, Wildrose Alliance Party of Alberta
Tel: 780-427-4099; *Fax:* 780-638-3506
strathmore.brooks@assembly.ab.ca

Twenty-ninth Legislature - Alberta

Legislature Bldg., 10800 - 97 Ave., Edmonton, AB T5K 2B6
Tel: 780-427-2826
laocommunications@assembly.ab.ca
www.assembly.ab.ca
Other Communication: Reference Information, E-mail: library.requests@assembly.ab.ca
twitter.com/LegAssemblyofAB
www.facebook.com/431884683512474
www.youtube.com/user/AlbertaLegislature
Last General Election, May 5, 2015.
Party Leaders:
New Democratic Party: Rachel Notley.
Wildrose Alliance Party: Brian Jean.
Progressive Conservative Party: Ric McIver.
Liberal Party: David Swann.
Alberta Party: Greg Clark.
Party Standings (Sept. 2016):
New Democratic Party 54;
Wildrose Alliance Party 22;
Progressive Conservative Party 9;
Alberta Liberal 1;
Alberta Party 1;
Total 87.
Indemnities, Salaries, & Allowances:
MLA indemnity $134,000, with no MLA tax free allowance.
In addition to this are the following indemnities & allowances:
Premier $83,750;
Speaker $67,000;
Ministers with portfolio $67,000;
Ministers without portfolio $30,150;
Leader of the Official Opposition $67,000;
Deputy Speaker & Chair, Committees $33,500;
Deputy Chair of Committees $16,750;
Leader of a recognized opposition party $30,150.
The following are special members' allowances:
Official Opposition House Leader: $16,750;
Third Party House Leader (recognized opposition party): $13,400;
Chief Government Whip: $13,400;
Assistant Government Whip: $8,040;
Chief Opposition Whip: $10,050;
Assistant Opposition Whip: $8,040;
Third Party Whip: $8,040.
The following is a list of members, with their constituency, the number of electors in their electoral division, their party affiliation, & contact information:

Members of the Legislative Assembly of Alberta

Leela Sharon Aheer
Constituency: Chestermere-Rocky View *No. of Constituents:* 32,094, Wildrose Alliance Party of Alberta
Tel: 780-422-0315
Toll-free: 866-643-4314; *Fax:* 780-638-3506
chestermere.rockyview@assembly.ab.ca
Other Communications: Constituency Phone: 403-207-9889; Fax: 403-216-2225
Social Media: www.facebook.com/leela.aheer
Constituency Office
#215, 175 Chestermere Station Way
Chestermere, AB T1X 0G1
Shaye Anderson
Constituency: Leduc-Beaumont *No. of Constituents:* 35,566, New Democratic Party
Tel: 780-644-5739; *Fax:* 780-415-0701
leduc.beaumont@assembly.ab.ca
Other Communications: Constituency Phone: 780-929-3290; Fax: 780-929-7881
Constituency Office
#106, 6202 - 29 Ave.
Beaumont, AB T4X 0H5
Wayne Anderson
Constituency: Highwood *No. of Constituents:* 33,937, Wildrose Alliance Party of Alberta
Tel: 780-427-7855; *Fax:* 780-638-3506
highwood@assembly.ab.ca
Other Communications: Constituency Phone: 403-995-5488; Fax: 403-995-5490
Social Media: twitter.com/wildrosewayne
Constituency Office
#5, 49 Elizabeth St.
PO Box 568 Main Sta.
Okotoks, AB T1S 1A7
Erin Babcock
Constituency: Stony Plain *No. of Constituents:* 31,324, New Democratic Party
Tel: 780-638-1422; *Fax:* 780-415-0701
stony.plain@assembly.ab.ca
Other Communications: Constituency Phone: 780-963-1444; Fax: 780-963-1730
Social Media: www.facebook.com/erinndp
Constituency Office
5004 - 50 Ave.
Stony Plain, AB T7Z 1T2
Drew Barnes
Constituency: Cypress-Medicine Hat *No. of Constituents:* 30,324, Wildrose Alliance Party of Alberta
Tel: 780-427-6662
Toll-free: 866-339-2191; *Fax:* 780-638-3506
cypress.medicinehat@assembly.ab.ca
Other Communications: Constituency Phone: 403-528-2191; Fax: 403-528-2278
Social Media: twitter.com/drewbarnesmla, www.facebook.com/barneswildrose
Constituency Office, Trans Canada Place
#5, 1299 Trans Canada Way
Medicine Hat, AB T1B 1H9
Minister, Economic Development & Trade; Deputy Government House Leader, Hon. Deron Bilous
Constituency: Edmonton-Beverly-Clareview *No. of Constituents:* 34,963, New Democratic Party
Tel: 780-644-8554; *Fax:* 780-644-8572
edmonton.beverlyclareview@assembly.ab.ca
Other Communications: Constituency Phone: 780-476-6467; Fax: 780-476-6473
Social Media: twitter.com/DeronBilous, www.facebook.com/electderonbilous
Constituency Office, Hermitage Mall
#552, 40 St. & Hermitage Rd.
Edmonton, AB T5A 4N2
Minister, Agriculture & Forestry; Deputy Government House Leader, Hon. Oneil Carlier
Constituency: Whitecourt-Ste. Anne *No. of Constituents:* 26,502, New Democratic Party
Tel: 780-427-2137
Toll-free: 800-786-7136; *Fax:* 780-422-6035
as.minister.m@gov.ab.ca
Other Communications: Constituency Phone: 780-786-1997; Fax: 780-786-1995
Social Media: twitter.com/oneilcarlier, www.facebook.com/oneilcarliermla
Constituency Office
4811 Crockett St.
PO Box 3618
Mayerthorpe, AB T0E 1N0
Jon Carson
Constituency: Edmonton-Meadowlark *No. of Constituents:* 28,936, New Democratic Party
Tel: 780-638-1402; *Fax:* 780-638-1431
edmonton.meadowlark@assembly.ab.ca
Other Communications: Constituency Phone: 780-414-0711; Fax: 780-414-0713
Social Media: twitter.com/joncmla
Constituency Office
#220, 8944 - 182 St.
Edmonton, AB T5T 2E3
Minister, Finance; President, Treasury Board, Hon. Joe Ceci
Constituency: Calgary-Fort *No. of Constituents:* 29,623, New Democratic Party
Tel: 780-415-4855; *Fax:* 780-415-4853
calgary.fort@assembly.ab.ca
Other Communications: Constituency Phone: 403-216-5454; Fax: 403-216-5452
Social Media: twitter.com/joececiyyc, www.facebook.com/joe.ceci.ndp
Constituency Office
#151, 2710 - 17th Ave. SE
Calgary, AB T2A 0P6
Leader, Alberta Party, Greg Clark
Constituency: Calgary-Elbow *No. of Constituents:* 32,288, Alberta Party
Tel: 780-644-7033; *Fax:* 780-644-7004
calgary.elbow@assembly.ab.ca
Other Communications: Constituency Phone: 403-252-0346; Fax: 403-252-0520
Social Media: twitter.com/AlbertaParty, www.facebook.com/albertaparty
Note: Greg Clark made history in the May 5, 2015, general election by being the first member of the Alberta Party to win a seat in the legislature.
Constituency Office
#205, 5005 Elbow Dr. SW
Calgary, AB T2S 2T6
Michael Connolly
Constituency: Calgary-Hawkwood *No. of Constituents:* 33,523, New Democratic Party
Tel: 780-644-6922; *Fax:* 780-415-0701
calgary.hawkwood@assembly.ab.ca
Other Communications: Constituency Phone: 403-216-5444; Fax: 403-216-5442
Social Media: twitter.com/ndpmikec, www.facebook.com/MichaelConnollyNDP
Constituency Office
#29, 735 Ranchlands Blvd. NW
Calgary, AB T3G 3A9
Craig Coolahan
Constituency: Calgary-Klein *No. of Constituents:* 31,499, New Democratic Party
Tel: 780-638-1419; *Fax:* 780-415-0701
calgary.klein@assembly.ab.ca
Other Communications: Constituency Phone: 403-216-5430; Fax: 403-216-5432
Social Media: twitter.com/craigcoolahan, www.facebook.com/181313855292530
Constituency Office
#9, 2400 Centre St. NE
Calgary, AB T2E 2T9
Nathan M. Cooper
Constituency: Olds-Didsbury-Three Hills *No. of Constituents:* 31,043, Wildrose Alliance Party of Alberta
Tel: 780-427-5498; *Fax:* 780-638-3506
oldsdidsbury.threehills@assembly.ab.ca
Other Communications: Constituency Phone: 403-556-3132; Fax: 403-556-3120
Social Media: twitter.com/wildrosenathan, www.facebook.com/nathancooperODT
Constituency Office
4905 B - 50 Ave.
PO Box 3909
Olds, AB T4H 1P6
Estefania Cortes-Vargas
Constituency: Strathcona-Sherwood Park *No. of Constituents:* 30,188, New Democratic Party
Tel: 780-638-1417; *Fax:* 780-415-0701
strathcona.sherwoodpark@assembly.ab.ca
Other Communications: Constituency Phone: 780-416-2492; Fax: 780-416-7093
Constituency Office
#19, 99 Wye Rd.
Sherwood Park, AB T8B 1M1
Scott Cyr
Constituency: Bonnyville-Cold Lake *No. of Constituents:* 23,774, Wildrose Alliance Party of Alberta
Tel: 780-422-3690; *Fax:* 780-638-3506
bonnyville.coldlake@assembly.ab.ca
Other Communications: Constituency Phone: 780-826-5658; Fax: 780-826-2165
Social Media: twitter.com/scottjcyr, www.facebook.com/ScottJCyr
Constituency Office
#2, 4428 - 50 Ave.
PO Box 5160
Bonnyville, AB T9N 2G4
Lorne Dach
Constituency: Edmonton-McClung *No. of Constituents:* 28,287, New Democratic Party
Tel: 780-638-1427; *Fax:* 780-415-0701
edmonton.mcclung@assembly.ab.ca
Other Communications: Constituency Phone: 780-408-1860; Fax: 780-408-1864
Social Media: twitter.com/lornedach, www.facebook.com/dachndp
Constituency Office
#301, 6650 - 177 St.
Edmonton, A T5T 4J5
Thomas Dang
Constituency: Edmonton-South West *No. of Constituents:* 35,600, New Democratic Party
Tel: 780-638-1406; *Fax:* 780-638-1431
edmonton.southwest@assembly.ab.ca
Other Communications: Constituency Phone: 780-643-9153; Fax: 780-415-8693
Social Media: twitter.com/thomasdangab, www.facebook.com/ThomasDangAB
Constituency Office
5160 Currents Dr.
Edmonton, A T6W 0L9
Deborah Drever
Constituency: Calgary-Bow *No. of Constituents:* 29,711, New Democratic Party
Tel: 780-644-7467; *Fax:* 780-644-2406
calgary.bow@assembly.ab.ca
Other Communications: Constituency Phone: 403-216-5400; Fax: 403-216-5402
Constituency Office
6307 Bowness Rd. NW
Calgary, AB T3B 0E4
Wayne Drysdale
Constituency: Grande Prairie-Wapiti *No. of Constituents:*

33,349, Progressive Conservative
Tel: 780-415-0107; *Fax:* 780-415-0968
grandeprairie.wapiti@assembly.ab.ca
Other Communications: Constituency Phone: 780-538-1800; Fax: 780-538-1802
Social Media: twitter.com/MLA_W_Drysdale, www.facebook.com/waynedrysdalemla, www.linkedin.com/pub/wayne-drysdale/1a/159/473
Constituency Office
#207, 10605 West Side Dr.
Grande Prairie, AB T8V 8E6

Minister, Education, Hon. David Eggen
Constituency: Edmonton-Calder *No. of Constituents:* 33,326, New Democratic Party
Tel: 780-427-5010; *Fax:* 780-427-5018
education.minister@gov.ab.ca
Other Communications: Constituency Phone: 780-451-2345; Fax: 780-451-2344
Social Media: twitter.com/davideggenAB, www.facebook.com/ElectDavidEggen
Constituency Office
10212 - 127 Ave., #A
Edmonton, AB T5E 0B8

Mike Ellis
Constituency: Calgary-West *No. of Constituents:* 29,209, Progressive Conservative
Tel: 780-644-2395; *Fax:* 780-415-0968
calgary.west@assembly.ab.ca
Other Communications: Constituency Phone: 403-216-5439; Fax: 403-216-5441
Social Media: twitter.com/mikeellispc
Constituency Office
#234, 333 Aspen Glen Landing SW
Calgary, AB T3H 0N6

Minister, Indigenous Relations, Hon. Richard Feehan
Constituency: Edmonton-Rutherford *No. of Constituents:* 26,885, New Democratic Party
Tel: 780-422-4144; *Fax:* 780-638-4052
ir.ministeroffice@gov.ab.ca
Other Communications: Constituency Phone: 780-414-1311; Fax: 780-414-1314
Social Media: twitter.com/feehanrichard, www.facebook.com/Feehan4NDPRutherford
Constituency Office
308 Saddleback Rd.
Edmonton, AB T6J 4R7

Derek Gerhard Fildebrandt
Constituency: Strathmore-Brooks *No. of Constituents:* 33,215, Wildrose Alliance Party of Alberta
Tel: 780-427-4099; *Fax:* 780-638-3506
strathmore.brooks@assembly.ab.ca
Other Communications: Constituency Phone: 403-362-6973; Fax: 403-362-5923
Social Media: twitter.com/dfildebrandt, www.facebook.com/derekfildebrandtwildrose
Constituency Office
116 - 2nd Ave. West
PO Box 873
Brooks, AB T1R 1B7

Maria Fitzpatrick
Constituency: Lethbridge-East *No. of Constituents:* 32,483, New Democratic Party
Tel: 780-638-1409; *Fax:* 780-638-1430
lethbridge.east@assembly.ab.ca
Other Communications: Constituency Phone: 403-320-1011; Fax: 403-328-6613
Social Media: twitter.com/mfitzpatrickndp, www.facebook.com/MariaFitzpatrickNDP
Constituency Office
543 - 13 St. South
Lethbridge, AB T1J 2W1

Rick Fraser
Constituency: Calgary-South East *No. of Constituents:* 42,002, Progressive Conservative
Tel: 780-643-9188; *Fax:* 780-415-0968
calgary.southeast@assembly.ab.ca
Other Communications: Constituency Phone: 403-215-8930; Fax: 403-215-8932
Social Media: www.facebook.com/RickFraserYYCSE, ca.linkedin.com/pub/rick-fraser/30/192/55
Constituency Office
#202, 5126 - 126 Ave. SE
Calgary, AB T2Z 0H2

Minister, Justice & Solicitor General, Hon. Kathleen Ganley
Constituency: Calgary-Buffalo *No. of Constituents:* 28,411, New Democratic Party
Tel: 780-427-2339; *Fax:* 780-422-6621
ministryofjustice@gov.ab.ca
Other Communications: Constituency Phone: 403-244-7737; Fax: 403-541-9106
Social Media: www.facebook.com/buffaloNDP
Constituency Office
#130, 1177 - 11 Ave. SW
Calgary, AB T2R 1K9

Prab Gill
Constituency: Calgary-Greenway, Progressive Conservative
Tel: 780-427-2877; *Fax:* 780-415-0968
calgary.greenway@assembly.ab.ca
Other Communications: Constituency Phone: 403-248-4487; Fax: 403-273-2898
Note: Prab Gill was elected in a by-election held March 22, 2016. The by-election was held to fill the vacancy after PC member Manmeet Bhullar died in a car crash in November 2015.
Constituency Office
#754, 2220 - 68 St. NE
Calgary, A T1Y 6Y7

Nicole Goehring
Constituency: Edmonton-Castle Downs *No. of Constituents:* 35,641, New Democratic Party
Tel: 780-644-5719; *Fax:* 780-415-0701
edmonton.castledowns@assembly.ab.ca
Other Communications: Constituency Phone: 780-414-0705; Fax: 780-414-0707
Social Media: www.facebook.com/nicolegoehringndp
Constituency Office
12120 - 161 Ave.
Edmonton, AB T5X 5M8

Richard Gotfried
Constituency: Calgary-Fish Creek *No. of Constituents:* 29,254, Progressive Conservative
Tel: 780-643-6541; *Fax:* 780-415-0968
calgary.fishcreek@assembly.ab.ca
Other Communications: Constituency Phone: 403-278-4444; Fax: 403-278-7875
Social Media: www.facebook.com/RichardGotfried4FishCreek
Constituency Office
#7, 1215 Lake Sylvan Dr. SE
Calgary, AB T2J 3Z5

Minister, Labour; Minister Responsible, Democratic Renewal, Hon. Christina Gray
Constituency: Edmonton-Mill Woods *No. of Constituents:* 25,978, New Democratic Party
Tel: 780-638-9400; *Fax:* 780-638-9401
labour.minister@gov.ab.ca
Other Communications: Constituency Phone: 780-414-1000; Fax: 780-414-1278
Social Media: twitter.com/christinandp, www.facebook.com/ChristinaNDP
Constituency Office
#101, 9807 - 34 Ave.
Edmonton, AB T6E 5X9

David Hanson
Constituency: Lac La Biche-St. Paul-Two Hills *No. of Constituents:* 20,243, Wildrose Alliance Party of Alberta
Tel: 780-422-4902
Toll-free: 866-674-6999; *Fax:* 780-638-3506
laclabiche.stpaul.twohills@assembly.ab.ca
Other Communications: Constituency Phone: 780-645-6999; Fax: 780-645-5787
Constituency Office
4331 - 50 Ave.
St. Paul, AB T0A 3A3

Bruce Hinkley
Constituency: Wetaskiwin-Camrose *No. of Constituents:* 26,990, New Democratic Party
Tel: 780-638-1413; *Fax:* 780-638-1430
wetaskiwin.camrose@assembly.ab.ca
Other Communications: Constituency Phone: 780-672-0000; Fax: 780-672-6945
Social Media: twitter.com/brucehinkleyndp, www.facebook.com/BruceHinkleyNDP
Constituency Office
4870 - 51 St.
Camrose, AB T4V 1S1

Minister, Health; Deputy Premier, Hon. Sarah Hoffman
Constituency: Edmonton-Glenora *No. of Constituents:* 30,764, New Democratic Party
Tel: 780-427-3665; *Fax:* 780-415-0961
health.minister@gov.ab.ca
Other Communications: Constituency Phone: 780-455-7979; Fax: 780-455-2197
Social Media: twitter.com/shoffmanab
Constituency Office
10649 - 124 St.
Edmonton, AB T5N 1S5

Trevor Horne
Constituency: Spruce Grove-St. Albert *No. of Constituents:* 37,658, New Democratic Party
Tel: 780-638-1415; *Fax:* 780-638-1431
sprucegrove.stalbert@assembly.ab.ca
Other Communications: Constituency Phone: 780-962-6606; Fax: 780-962-1568
Social Media: twitter.com/trevor_horne, www.facebook.com/trevor.horne
Constituency Office
#60, 210 McLeod Ave.
Spruce Grove, AB T7X 2K5

Grant Hunter
Constituency: Cardston-Taber-Warner *No. of Constituents:* 23,918, Wildrose Alliance Party of Alberta
Tel: 780-422-1550
Toll-free: 888-600-6080; *Fax:* 780-638-3506
cardston.taberwarner@assembly.ab.ca
Other Communications: Constituency Phone: 403-223-0001; Fax: 403-223-0002
Social Media: www.facebook.com/673551522750547
Constituency Office
5224 - 48 Ave.
Taber, AB T1G 1S1

Debbie Jabbour
Constituency: Peace River *No. of Constituents:* 18,699, New Democratic Party
Tel: 780-638-1423; *Fax:* 780-638-1431
peace.river@assembly.ab.ca
Other Communications: Constituency Phone: 780-624-5400; Fax: 780-624-5464
Social Media: twitter.com/debjabbour, www.facebook.com/DebbieJabbourNDP
Constituency Office, Riverside Mall
#2, 10122 - 100 St.
PO Box 6299
Peace River, AB T8S 1S2

Sandra Jansen
Constituency: Calgary-North West *No. of Constituents:* 35,946, Progressive Conservative
Tel: 780-427-8156; *Fax:* 780-415-0968
calgary.northwest@assembly.ab.ca
Other Communications: Constituency Phone: 403-297-7104; Fax: 403-297-7121
Social Media: twitter.com/SANDRAYYCNW, www.linkedin.com/pub/sandra-jansen/25/148/288
Constituency Office
#7223, 8650 - 112th Ave. NW
Calgary, AB T3R 0R5

Leader, Wildrose Alliance Party of Alberta, Brian Jean
Constituency: Fort McMurray-Conklin *No. of Constituents:* 13,182, Wildrose Alliance Party of Alberta
Tel: 780-427-1031; *Fax:* 780-638-3506
fortmcmurray.conklin@assembly.ab.ca
Other Communications: Constituency Phone: 780-588-7979; Fax: 780-588-7970
Social Media: twitter.com/brianjeanwrp, www.facebook.com/brianjeanwrp
Constituency Office
#1, 9912 Franklin Ave.
Fort McMurray, AB T9H 4Z4

Anam Kazim
Constituency: Calgary-Glenmore *No. of Constituents:* 37,109, New Democratic Party
Tel: 780-638-1400; *Fax:* 780-638-1430
calgary.glenmore@assembly.ab.ca
Other Communications: Constituency Phone: 403-216-5421; Fax: 403-216-5423
Social Media: www.facebook.com/1378322999162086
Note: Anam Kazim won the riding of Calgary-Glenmore in a recount, after the initial vote led to a tie.
Constituency Office
#A208, 1600 - 90th Ave. SW
Calgary, AB T2V 5A8

Jamie Kleinsteuber
Constituency: Calgary-Northern Hills *No. of Constituents:* 36,248, New Democratic Party
Tel: 780-644-6939; *Fax:* 780-415-0701
calgary.northernhills@assembly.ab.ca
Other Communications: Constituency Phone: 403-274-1931; Fax: 403-275-8421
Social Media: www.facebook.com/andpcalgarynorthernhills
Constituency Office
#104, 200 Country Hills Landing NW
Calgary, AB T3K 5P3

Minister, Municipal Affairs, Hon. Danielle Larivee
Constituency: Lesser Slave Lake *No. of Constituents:* 19,051, New Democratic Party
Tel: 780-427-3744
Toll-free: 866-625-0648; *Fax:* 780-422-9550
lesser.slavelake@assembly.ab.ca
Other Communications: Constituency Phone: 780-849-3479; Fax: 780-843-0115
Social Media: twitter.com/daniellelarivee, www.facebook.com/DanielleLariveeNDP
Constituency Office
225 - 2nd Ave. NW
PO Box 416
Slave Lake, AB T0G 2A1

Jessica Littlewood
Constituency: Fort Saskatchewan-Vegreville *No. of Constituents:* 37,187, New Democratic Party
Tel: 780-644-5748; *Fax:* 780-415-0701
fortsaskatchewan.vegreville@assembly.ab.ca
Other Communications: Constituency Phone: 780-992-6560; Fax: 780-992-6562

Social Media: twitter.com/jlittlewoodndp, www.facebook.com/JLittlewoodNDP
Constituency Office
9925B - 104 St.
Fort Saskatchewan, AB T8L 2E7

Todd Loewen
Constituency: Grande Prairie-Smoky *No. of Constituents:* 28,752, Wildrose Alliance Party of Alberta
Tel: 780-427-5967; *Fax:* 780-638-3506
grandeprairie.smoky@assembly.ab.ca
Other Communications: Constituency Phone: 780-513-1233; Fax: 780-513-1247
Social Media: twitter.com/dtloewen
Constituency Office
#102, 9201 Lakeland Dr.
Grande Prairie, AB T8X 0K8

Rod Loyola
Constituency: Edmonton-Ellerslie *No. of Constituents:* 31,588, New Democratic Party
Tel: 780-644-5737; *Fax:* 780-415-0701
edmonton.ellerslie@assembly.ab.ca
Other Communications: Constituency Phone: 780-414-2000; Fax: 780-414-6383
Social Media: twitter.com/rod_loyola, www.facebook.com/rodloyola1
Constituency Office
5732 - 19A Ave.
Edmonton, AB T6L 1L8

Robyn Luff
Constituency: Calgary-East *No. of Constituents:* 32,739, New Democratic Party
Tel: 780-638-1412; *Fax:* 780-638-1430
calgary.east@assembly.ab.ca
Other Communications: Constituency Phone: 403-216-5450; Fax: 403-216-5452
Social Media: twitter.com/rluff, www.facebook.com/robynluffndp
Constituency Office
#550, 2710 - 17th Ave. SE
Calgary, A T2A 0P6

Don MacIntyre
Constituency: Innisfail-Sylvan Lake *No. of Constituents:* 27,529, Wildrose Alliance Party of Alberta
Tel: 780-427-7651; *Fax:* 780-638-3506
innisfail.sylvanlake@assembly.ab.ca
Other Communications: Constituency Phone: 403-887-9575; Fax: 403-887-6154
Social Media: twitter.com/wildrose_don, www.facebook.com/784610181631744
Constituency Office
Bay 2, 160 Hewlett Park Landing
Sylvan Lake, AB T4S 2J3

Brian Malkinson
Constituency: Calgary-Currie *No. of Constituents:* 33,747, New Democratic Party
Tel: 780-638-1420; *Fax:* 780-415-0701
calgary.currie@assembly.ab.ca
Other Communications: Constituency Phone: 403-246-4794; Fax: 403-686-1543
Social Media: twitter.com/brianmalkinson, www.facebook.com/brianmalkinsonndp
Constituency Office
2108B - 33 Ave. SW
Calgary, A T2T 1Z6

Minister, Infrastructure; Minister, Transportation; Government House Leader, Hon. Brian Mason
Constituency: Edmonton-Highlands-Norwood *No. of Constituents:* 30,985, New Democratic Party
Tel: 780-427-5041; *Fax:* 780-422-2722
edmonton.highlandsnorwood@assembly.ab.ca
Other Communications: Constituency Phone: 780-414-0682; Fax: 780-414-0684
Social Media: twitter.com/bmasonNDP, www.facebook.com/brianmasonNDP
Constituency Office
6519 - 112 Ave.
Edmonton, AB T5W 0P1

Minister, Energy, Hon. Margaret McCuaig-Boyd
Constituency: Dunvegan-Central Peace-Notley *No. of Constituents:* 14,905, New Democratic Party
Tel: 780-427-3740; *Fax:* 780-644-1222
dunvegan.centralpeace.notley@assembly.ab.ca
Other Communications: Constituency Phone: 780-835-7211; Fax: 780-835-7212
Social Media: www.facebook.com/1558169337770701
Constituency Office
10410 - 110 St.
PO Box 9
Fairview, AB T0H 1L0

Interim Leader, Alberta Progressive Conservative Party, Ric McIver
Constituency: Calgary-Hays *No. of Constituents:* 30,865, Progressive Conservative
Tel: 780-643-9091; *Fax:* 780-415-0968
calgary.hays@assembly.ab.ca
Other Communications: Constituency Phone: 403-215-4380; Fax: 403-215-4383
Social Media: twitter.com/RicMcIver, www.facebook.com/RicMcIver, www.linkedin.com/pub/ric-mciver/10/498/34a
Constituency Office
#255, 11488 - 24 St. SE
Calgary, AB T2Z 4C9

Annie McKitrick
Constituency: Sherwood Park *No. of Constituents:* 33,455, New Democratic Party
Tel: 780-644-5750; *Fax:* 780-415-0701
sherwood.park@assembly.ab.ca
Other Communications: Constituency Phone: 780-417-4747; Fax: 780-417-4748
Social Media: twitter.com/mckitrick_annie
Constituency Office
#116B, 937 Fir St.
Sherwood Park, AB T8A 4N6

Minister, Service Alberta; Minister, Status of Women, Hon. Stephanie McLean
Constituency: Calgary-Varsity *No. of Constituents:* 30,132, New Democratic Party
Tel: 780-422-6880; *Fax:* 780-422-2496
ministersa@gov.ab.ca
Other Communications: Constituency Phone: 403-216-5436; Fax: 403-216-5438
Social Media: twitter.com/ndpstephanie
Constituency Office
#101, 5403 Crowchild Trail NW
Calgary, AB T3B 4Z1

Karen M. McPherson
Constituency: Calgary-Mackay-Nose Hill *No. of Constituents:* 36,930, New Democratic Party
Tel: 780-638-1401; *Fax:* 780-638-1430
calgary.mackay.nosehill@assembly.ab.ca
Other Communications: Constituency Phone: 403-215-7710; Fax: 403-216-5410
Social Media: twitter.com/ndpkaren, www.facebook.com/935141689871831
Constituency Office
#16, 5440 - 4th St. NW
Calgary, AB T2K 1A8

Barb Miller
Constituency: Red Deer-South *No. of Constituents:* 35,912, New Democratic Party
Tel: 780-638-1403; *Fax:* 780-638-1431
reddeer.south@assembly.ab.ca
Other Communications: Constituency Phone: 403-340-3565; Fax: 403-346-9260
Constituency Office
#503, 4901 - 48 St.
Red Deer, AB T4N 6M4

Minister, Culture & Tourism, Hon. Ricardo Miranda
Constituency: Calgary-Cross *No. of Constituents:* 29,867, New Democratic Party
Tel: 780-422-3559; *Fax:* 780-427-0188
calgary.cross@assembly.ab.ca
Other Communications: Constituency Phone: 403-280-4022; Fax: 403-280-3877
Social Media: twitter.com/_ricardoyyc, www.facebook.com/Ricardo4CalgaryCross
Constituency Office
#215, 5401 Temple Dr. NE
Calgary, AB T1Y 3R7

Chris Nielsen
Constituency: Edmonton-Decore *No. of Constituents:* 30,940, New Democratic Party
Tel: 780-638-1405; *Fax:* 780-638-1431
edmonton.decore@assembly.ab.ca
Other Communications: Constituency Phone: 780-414-1328; Fax: 780-414-1330
Social Media: www.facebook.com/230106293857775
Constituency Office
#5, 9228 - 144 Ave.
Edmonton, AB T5E 6A3

Jason Nixon
Constituency: Rimbey-Rocky Mountain House-Sundre *No. of Constituents:* 31,993, Wildrose Alliance Party of Alberta
Tel: 780-643-9111
rimbey.rockymountainhouse.sundre@assembly.ab.ca
Other Communications: Constituency Phone: 403-638-5029; 403-638-0035
Social Media: www.facebook.com/jason.j.nixon
Constituency Office
Bay 4, 117 Centre St. South
PO Box 1547
Sundre, AB T0M 1X0

Premier; President, Executive Council; Leader, Alberta New Democratic Party, Hon. Rachel Notley
Constituency: Edmonton-Strathcona *No. of Constituents:* 28,283, New Democratic Party
Tel: 780-427-2251; *Fax:* 780-427-1349
edmonton.strathcona@assembly.ab.ca
Other Communications: Constituency Phone: 780-414-0702; Fax: 780-414-0703
Social Media: twitter.com/RachelNotley, www.facebook.com/rachelnotley
Constituency Office, Strathcona Professional Centre
#101, 10328 - 81 Ave.
Edmonton, AB T6E 1X2

Ronald Orr
Constituency: Lacombe-Ponoka *No. of Constituents:* 26,926, Wildrose Alliance Party of Alberta
Tel: 780-638-3275
Toll-free: 800-565-6432; *Fax:* 780-638-3506
lacombe.ponoka@assembly.ab.ca
Other Communications: Constituency Phone: 403-782-7725; 403-782-3307
Social Media: twitter.com/RonOrrMLA
Constituency Office
#101, 4892 - 46 St.
Lacombe, AB T4L 2B4

Prasad Panda
Constituency: Calgary-Foothills, Wildrose Alliance Party of Alberta
Tel: 780-644-8319; *Fax:* 780-638-3505
Other Communications: Constituency Phone: 403-288-4453
Note: Although former Premier Jim Prentice won the riding in the May 5, 2015, general election, he quit both the seat & as Leader of the PC Party following the party's overall defeat. Prasad Panda won the seat in a by-election held Sept. 3, 2015.

Associate Minister, Health, Hon. Brandy Payne
Constituency: Calgary-Acadia *No. of Constituents:* 27,830, New Democratic Party
Tel: 780-427-3665; *Fax:* 780-415-0961
health.minister@gov.ab.ca
Other Communications: Constituency Phone: 403-640-1363; Fax: 403-592-8171
Constituency Office
#10, 8318 Fairmount Dr. SE
Calgary, AB T2H 0Y8

Minister, Environment & Parks; Minister Responsible, Climate Change Office, Hon. Shannon Phillips
Constituency: Lethbridge-West *No. of Constituents:* 30,228, New Democratic Party
Tel: 780-427-2391; *Fax:* 780-422-6259
aep.minister@gov.ab.ca
Other Communications: Constituency Phone: 403-329-4644; Fax: 403-329-4289
Social Media: twitter.com/sphillipsab, www.facebook.com/ShannonPhillipsLethbridge
Constituency Office
402 - 8 St. South
Lethbridge, AB T1J 2J7

Colin Piquette
Constituency: Athabasca-Sturgeon-Redwater *No. of Constituents:* 25,826, New Democratic Party
Tel: 780-638-1425; *Fax:* 780-415-0701
athabasca.sturgeon.redwater@assembly.ab.ca
Other Communications: Constituency Phone: 780-675-3232; Fax: 780-675-2396
Social Media: twitter.com/colinpiquette, ca.linkedin.com/pub/colin-piquette/8/183/653
Constituency Office
B-4705 - 49 Ave.
Athabasca, AB T9S 0B5

Angela Pitt
Constituency: Airdrie *No. of Constituents:* 38,195, Wildrose Alliance Party of Alberta
Tel: 780-644-7121
Toll-free: 888-948-8741; *Fax:* 780-638-3506
airdrie@assembly.ab.ca
Other Communications: Constituency Phone: 403-948-8741; Fax: 403-948-8744
Social Media: twitter.com/AngelaPittMLA, www.facebook.com/AngelaPittAirdrie
Constituency Office
209 Bowers St.
Airdrie, AB T4B 0R6

Marie Renaud
Constituency: St. Albert *No. of Constituents:* 33,486, New Democratic Party
Tel: 780-644-6924; *Fax:* 780-415-0701
st.albert@assembly.ab.ca
Other Communications: Constituency Phone: 780-459-9113; Fax: 780-460-9815
Social Media: twitter.com/mariefrenaud, www.facebook.com/MarieRenaudMLA
Constituency Office
#109B, 50 St. Thomas St.
St. Albert, AB T8N 6Z8

Dave Rodney
Constituency: Calgary-Lougheed *No. of Constituents:* 30,847, Progressive Conservative
Tel: 780-415-1325; *Fax:* 780-415-0968

calgary.lougheed@assembly.ab.ca
Other Communications: Constituency Phone: 403-238-1212; Fax: 403-251-5453
Social Media: twitter.com/DaveRodneyMLA, www.facebook.com/daverodneypc
Constituency Office
#311A, 2525 Woodview Dr. SW
Calgary, AB T2W 4N4

Eric Rosendahl
Constituency: West Yellowhead *No. of Constituents:* 21,424, New Democratic Party
Tel: 780-638-1426
Toll-free: 800-661-6517; *Fax:* 780-415-0701
west.yellowhead@assembly.ab.ca
Other Communications: Constituency Phone: 780-865-9796; Fax: 780-865-9760
Constituency Office
#102, 1336 Switzer Dr.
Hinton, AB T7V 2C1

Minister, Human Services, Hon. Irfan Sabir
Constituency: Calgary-McCall *No. of Constituents:* 27,243, New Democratic Party
Tel: 780-643-6210; *Fax:* 780-643-6214
calgary.mccall@assembly.ab.ca
Other Communications: Constituency Phone: 403-216-5424; Fax: 403-216-5426
Constituency Office
#311, 7 Wetwinds Cres. NE
Calgary, AB T3J 5H2

Minister, Advanced Education, Hon. Marlin Schmidt
Constituency: Edmonton-Gold Bar *No. of Constituents:* 33,381, New Democratic Party
Tel: 780-427-5777; *Fax:* 780-422-8733
ae.minister@gov.ab.ca
Other Communications: Constituency Phone: 780-414-1015; Fax: 780-414-1017
Social Media: ca.linkedin.com/pub/marlin-schmidt/0/71a/2a0
Constituency Office
7510 - 82 Ave.
Edmonton, AB T6C 0X9

David A. Schneider
Constituency: Little Bow *No. of Constituents:* 23,769, Wildrose Alliance Party of Alberta
Tel: 780-644-7134
Toll-free: 800-563-0917; *Fax:* 780-638-3506
little.bow@assembly.ab.ca
Other Communications: Constituency Phone: 403-485-3160; Fax: 403-485-3166
Social Media: twitter.com/dschneiderdave, www.facebook.com/dschneiderwrp
Constituency Office
125 Centre St.
PO Box 231
Vulcan, AB T0L 2B0

Kim Schreiner
Constituency: Red Deer-North *No. of Constituents:* 32,082, New Democratic Party
Tel: 780-638-1407; *Fax:* 780-638-1430
reddeer.north@assembly.ab.ca
Other Communications: Constituency Phone: 403-342-2263; Fax: 403-340-3185
Social Media: www.facebook.com/779018965547018
Constituency Office
#200, 4814 Ross St.
Red Deer, AB T4N 1X4

David Shepherd
Constituency: Edmonton-Centre *No. of Constituents:* 29,240, New Democratic Party
Tel: 780-638-1424; *Fax:* 780-415-0701
edmonton.centre@assembly.ab.ca
Other Communications: Constituency Phone: 780-414-0743; Fax: 780-414-0772
Social Media: twitter.com/dshepyeg, www.facebook.com/dmshepYEG
Constituency Office
10208 - 112 St.
Edmonton, AB T5K 1M4

Minister, Seniors & Housing, Hon. Lori Sigurdson
Constituency: Edmonton-Riverview *No. of Constituents:* 28,566, New Democratic Party
Tel: 780-427-5777; *Fax:* 780-422-8733
edmonton.riverview@assembly.ab.ca
Other Communications: Constituency Phone: 780-414-0719; Fax: 780-414-0721
Social Media: twitter.com/lorisigurdson, www.facebook.com/lorisigurdson.ndp
Constituency Office
9202B - 149 St.
Edmonton, AB T5R 1C3

Mark Smith
Constituency: Drayton Valley-Devon *No. of Constituents:* 24,930, Wildrose Alliance Party of Alberta
Tel: 780-644-7146
Toll-free: 800-542-7307; *Fax:* 780-638-3506
draytonvalley.devon@assembly.ab.ca
Other Communications: Constituency Phone: 780-542-3355; Fax: 780-542-3331
Social Media: twitter.com/mwsmithab
Constituency Office
5136B - 52 Ave.
Drayton Valley, AB T7A 1S5

Richard Starke
Constituency: Vermilion-Lloydminster *No. of Constituents:* 24,079, Progressive Conservative
Tel: 780-638-1306
Toll-free: 800-567-7644; *Fax:* 780-415-0968
vermilion.lloydminster@assembly.ab.ca
Other Communications: Constituency Phone: 780-853-4202; Fax: 780-853-5770
Social Media: twitter.com/RichardStarke, www.linkedin.com/pub/richard-starke/3b/a3/903
Constituency Office
5036 - 49 Ave.
Vermilion, AB T9X 1B7

Pat Stier
Constituency: Livingstone-Macleod *No. of Constituents:* 29,454, Wildrose Alliance Party of Alberta
Tel: 780-427-1707
Toll-free: 800-565-0962; *Fax:* 780-638-3506
livingstone.macleod@assembly.ab.ca
Other Communications: Constituency Phone: 403-646-6256; Fax: 403-646-6250
Social Media: twitter.com/PatStier_WR, www.facebook.com/PatStierWildrose
Constituency Office
2019 - 20 Ave.
Nanton, AB T0L 1R0

Rick Strankman
Constituency: Drumheller-Stettler *No. of Constituents:* 24,897, Wildrose Alliance Party of Alberta
Tel: 780-427-7237; *Fax:* 780-638-3506
drumheller.stettler@assembly.ab.ca
Other Communications: Constituency Phone: 403-742-4284; Fax: 403-742-4295
Social Media: twitter.com/RickStrankman, www.facebook.com/wildroserick
Constituency Office
4820 - 50 St.
PO Box 2022
Stettler, AB T0C 2L2

Graham Sucha
Constituency: Calgary-Shaw *No. of Constituents:* 30,458, New Democratic Party
Tel: 780-644-5779; *Fax:* 780-415-0701
calgary.shaw@assembly.ab.ca
Other Communications: Constituency Phone: 403-256-8969; Fax: 403-256-8970
Social Media: twitter.com/grahamsucha, www.facebook.com/grahamndp
Constituency Office
#328, 22 Midlake Blvd. SE
Calgary, AB T2X 2X7

Leader, Liberal Party of Alberta, Dr. David Swann
Constituency: Calgary-Mountain View *No. of Constituents:* 32,484, Liberal
Tel: 780-422-1582; *Fax:* 780-427-3697
calgary.mountainview@assembly.ab.ca
www.albertaliberal.com
Other Communications: Constituency Phone: 403-216-5445; Fax: 403-216-5447
Social Media: twitter.com/davidswann, www.facebook.com/515014295
Constituency Office
#102, 723 - 14 St. NW
Calgary, AB T2N 2A4

Heather Sweet
Constituency: Edmonton-Manning *No. of Constituents:* 31,609, New Democratic Party
Tel: 780-644-5727; *Fax:* 780-415-0701
edmonton.manning@assembly.ab.ca
Other Communications: Constituency Phone: 780-414-0714; Fax: 780-414-0716
Social Media: twitter.com/heathersweetndp, www.facebook.com/heathersweetndp
Constituency Office
5523 - 137 Ave.
Edmonton, AB T5A 3L4

Wes Taylor
Constituency: Battle River-Wainwright *No. of Constituents:* 25,371, Wildrose Alliance Party of Alberta
Tel: 780-644-7151; *Fax:* 780-638-3506
battleriver.wainwright@assembly.ab.ca
Other Communications: Constituency Phone: 780-842-6177; Fax: 780-842-3171
Social Media: twitter.com/westaylorwrp, www.facebook.com/WesTaylorWRP
Constituency Office
#201, 1006 - 4 Ave.
Wainwright, AB T9W 2R3

Dr. Bob Turner
Constituency: Edmonton-Whitemud *No. of Constituents:* 34,825, New Democratic Party
Tel: 780-638-1410; *Fax:* 780-415-0701
edmonton.whitemud@assembly.ab.ca
Other Communications: Constituency Phone: 780-413-5970; Fax: 780-413-5971
Social Media: twitter.com/doctorcanbob
Constituency Office
#203, 596 Riverbend Square
Edmonton, AB T6R 2E3

Glenn Van Dijken
Constituency: Barrhead-Morinville-Westlock *No. of Constituents:* 28,176, Wildrose Alliance Party of Alberta
Tel: 780-644-7152; *Fax:* 780-638-3506
barrhead.morinville.westlock@assembly.ab.ca
Other Communications: Constituency Phone: 780-674-3225; Fax: 780-674-6183
Social Media: twitter.com/glennvandijken, www.facebook.com/glenn.van.dijken
Constituency Office
5106 - 50 St.
PO Box 4250
Barrhead, AB T7N 1A3

Speaker, Hon. Robert Wanner
Constituency: Medicine Hat *No. of Constituents:* 30,596, New Democratic Party
Tel: 780-427-2464; *Fax:* 780-422-9553
medicine.hat@assembly.ab.ca
Other Communications: Constituency Phone: 403-527-5622; Fax: 403-527-5112
Social Media: twitter.com/bobwanner
Constituency Office
537 - 4th St. SE
Medicine Hat, AB T1A 0K7

Cameron Westhead
Constituency: Banff-Cochrane *No. of Constituents:* 35,672, New Democratic Party
Tel: 780-638-1418
Toll-free: 866-760-8281; *Fax:* 780-415-0701
banff.cochrane@assembly.ab.ca
Other Communications: Constituency Phone: 403-609-4509; Fax: 403-609-4513
Constituency Office
#102, 721 Main St.
PO Box 8650
Canmore, AB T1W 0B9

Denise Woollard
Constituency: Edmonton-Mill Creek *No. of Constituents:* 32,437, New Democratic Party
Tel: 780-638-1404; *Fax:* 780-638-1431
edmonton.millcreek@assembly.ab.ca
Other Communications: Constituency Phone: 780-466-3737
Social Media: twitter.com/denisewoollard

Tany Yao
Constituency: Fort McMurray-Wood Buffalo *No. of Constituents:* 23,488, Wildrose Alliance Party of Alberta
Tel: 780-644-7129; *Fax:* 780-638-3506
fortmcmurray.woodbuffalo@assembly.ab.ca
Other Communications: Constituency Phone: 780-790-6014; Fax: 780-791-3683
Social Media: twitter.com/tanyyao, www.facebook.com/1625388114349662
Constituency Office
#102, 9912 Franklin Ave.
Fort McMurray, AB T9H 2K4

Alberta Government Departments & Agencies

Alberta Advanced Education

Legislature Bldg., #403, 10800 - 97 Ave., Edmonton, AB T5K 2B6

Tel: 780-422-5400
Toll-Free: -310-0000
www.iae.alberta.ca

On Oct. 22, 2015, Premier Notley created Alberta Economic Development & Trade, drawing from parts of Innovation & Advanced Education, and leaving Advanced Education as its own portfolio. The key responsibilities of Advanced Education include post-secondary matters, apprenticeship & industry training & adult learning.

The following are some specific activities: funding public post-secondary institutions in Alberta; developing program standards with industry; counselling apprentices & employers; certifying apprentices & occupational trainees; providing student financial assistance; funding education providers; & funding apprentices.

Minister, Advanced Education, Hon. Marlin Schmidt
Tel: 780-427-5777; *Fax:* 780-422-8733
ae.minister@gov.ab.ca

Deputy Minister, Rod Skura
Tel: 780-415-4744
rod.skura@gov.ab.ca
Executive Director, Human Resources, Gerry Jacubo
Tel: 780-422-5324; *Fax:* 780-427-3316
gerry.jacubo@gov.ab.ca
Director, Strategy & Planning, Jackie Hammond
Tel: 780-644-5278; *Fax:* 780-422-1801
jackie.hammond@gov.ab.ca
Director, Communications, John Muir
Tel: 780-422-1562; *Fax:* 780-427-0821
john.muir@gov.ab.ca

Associated Agencies, Boards & Commissions:

•Alberta Apprenticeship & Industry Training Board
Commerce Place
10155 - 102 St., 10th Fl.
Edmonton, AB T5J 4L5
Tel: 780-427-8765; *Fax:* 780-422-7376
Toll-free: -310-0000
TTY: 780-427-9999
tradesecrets.gov.ab.ca
Other Communication: TTY Toll-Free: 1-800-232-7215
Board members are appointed by the Lieutenant Governor in Council, upon recommendation of the Minister of Advanced Education. The mission of the board is to maintain high quality training & certification standards in the apprenticeship & industry training system. The board offers recommendations to the Minister about the needs of the labour market in Alberta & the training & certification of persons in designated trades & occupations.

•Alberta Council on Admissions & Transfer (ACAT)
Commerce Place
10155 - 102 St., 11th Fl.
Edmonton, AB T5J 4L5
Tel: 780-422-9021; *Fax:* 780-422-3688
Toll-free: -310-0000
TTY: 780-427-9999
acat@gov.ab.ca
www.acat.gov.ab.ca
Other Communication: TTY Toll-Free: 1-800-232-7215
Established in 1974, the independent body advocates for learners by working to ensure transferability of educational courses & programs to benefit students. The role of the council is to develop policies & procedures to facilitate transfer agreements among post-secondary institutions.

•Campus Alberta Quality Council (CAQC)
Commerce Place
10155 - 102 St., 8th Fl.
Edmonton, AB T5J 4L5
Tel: 780-427-8921; *Fax:* 780-641-9783
www.caqc.gov.ab.ca
The arms-length quality assurance agency makes recommendations to the Minister of Advanced Education & Technology on applications from post-secondary institutions that want to offer new degree programs. All degree programs, except for degrees in divinity, offered by resident institutions & non-resident institutions in Alberta must be approved by the Minister.

Advanced Learning & Community Partnerships Division
Commerce Place, 10155 - 102 St., 7th Fl., Edmonton, AB T5J 4L5
Assistant Deputy Minister, Peter Leclaire
Tel: 780-641-9349
peter.leclaire@gov.ab.ca
Executive Director, External Relations Sector, Erin Gregg
Tel: 780-644-1856
erin.gregg@gov.ab.ca
Executive Director, Operations, Gilbert Perras
Tel: 780-638-3588
gilbert.perras@gov.ab.ca
Executive Director, Campus Alberta Sector, David E. Williams
Tel: 780-415-9668
david.e.williams@gov.ab.ca

Apprenticeship & Student Aid Division
Commerce Place, 10155 - 102 St., 6th Fl., Edmonton, AB T5J 4L5
Assistant Deputy Minister, Andy Weiler
Tel: 780-644-7732
andy.weiler@gov.ab.ca
Executive Director, Policy & Standards, Carla Corbett
Tel: 780-422-1193
carla.corbett@gov.ab.ca
Executive Director, Student Aid, Maggie DesLauriers
Tel: 780-422-4498; *Fax:* 780-422-4517
maggie.deslauriers@gov.ab.ca
Acting Executive Director, Operations & Client Connections, John St. Arnaud
Tel: 780-427-5770; *Fax:* 780-422-7376
john.starnaud@gov.ab.ca

Strategic & Corporate Services Division
Phipps-McKinnon Bldg., 10020 - 101A Ave., 5th Fl., Edmonton, AB T5J 3G2
Assistant Deputy Minister, Dan Rizzoli
Tel: 780-415-2966
dan.rizzoli@gov.ab.ca
Executive Director & SFO, Corporate Services, Darrell Dancause
Tel: 780-427-1897
darrell.dancause@gov.ab.ca
Executive Director, Strategic Policy & Planning, Jennifer M. McGill
Tel: 780-643-1748
jennifer.m.mcgill@gov.ab.ca
Executive Director & CIO, Information & Technology Management, Leslie Sim
Tel: 780-415-0813
leslie.sim@gov.ab.ca
Senior Director, Governance Services, Susan Bocock
Tel: 780-415-8985
susan.bocock@gov.ab.ca
Senior Director, Strategic Policy, Sandra Duxbury
Tel: 780-427-4498
sandra.duxbury@gov.ab.ca
Senior Director, International & Intergovernmental Relations, Carolyn Fewkes
Tel: 780-422-4062
carolyn.fewkes@gov.ab.ca
Director, Legal & Legislative Services, Nancy Reid Jones
Tel: 780-427-4699
nancy.reid@gov.ab.ca

Alberta Agriculture & Forestry

JG O'Donoghue Bldg., #100A, 7000 - 113th St., Edmonton, AB T6H 5T6
Tel: 780-427-2727
Toll-Free: -310-3276
duke@gov.ab.ca
www.agric.gov.ab.ca
twitter.com/AlbertaAg
www.facebook.com/259215474123606
www.youtube.com/user/AlbertaAgriculture
The department changed from Agriculture & Rural Development to Agriculture & Forestry following the May 2015 general election, when it absorbed the Forestry Division from Environment & Sustainable Resource Development (renamed Environment & Parks after the election).
Minister, Agriculture & Forestry, Hon. Oneil Carlier
Tel: 780-427-2137; *Fax:* 780-422-6035
Deputy Minister, Bev Yee
Tel: 780-427-2145; *Fax:* 780-415-6002
bev.yee@gov.ab.ca
Executive Director, Extension & Communication Services Division, Katrina Bluetchen
Tel: 780-427-4532; *Fax:* 780-422-6317
katrina.bluetchen@gov.ab.ca
Executive Director/Senior Financial Officer, Financial Services Division, Anne Halldorson
Tel: 780-427-3216; *Fax:* 780-422-6529
anne.halldorson@gov.ab.ca

Associated Agencies, Boards & Commissions:

•Agriculture Financial Services Corporation (AFSC)
5718 - 56 Ave.
Lacombe, AB T4L 1B1
Tel: 403-782-8200
info@afsc.ca
www.afsc.ca
The Agriculture Financial Services Corporation provides loans, crop insurance & farm income disaster assistance to farmers, agricultural & small businesses. Although the AFSC is a provincial crown corporation, it has a public sector board of directors, & works closely with private sector companies through business alliances.

•Agricultural Products Marketing Council
JG O'Donoghue Bldg.
#305, 7000 - 113 St.
Edmonton, AB T6H 5T6
Tel: 780-427-2164; *Fax:* 780-422-9690
marketingcouncil@gov.ab.ca
www.agriculture.alberta.ca/marketingcouncil
The Alberta Agricultural Products Marketing Council supports legislation & regulations & offers policy advice to the Minister of Agriculture & Rural Development & industry organizations.

•Alberta Grains Council (AGC)
JG O'Donoghue Bldg.
#305, 7000 - 113 St.
Edmonton, AB T6H 5T6
Tel: 780-427-7329; *Fax:* 780-422-9690
www1.agric.gov.ab.ca/$department/deptdocs.nsf/all/agc2620
The Alberta Grains Council makes recommendations to the Minister of Agriculture & Rural Affairs about issues in the grain industry.

•Alberta Livestock & Meat Agency (ALMA)
Ellwood Office Park South
#101, 1003 Ellwood Rd. SW
Edmonton, AB T6X 0B3
Tel: 780-638-1699; *Fax:* 780-638-6495
info@almaltd.ca
www.alma.alberta.ca
The provincial government agency was established to advance the Alberta Livestock & Meat Strategy. The goal of the Alberta Livestock & Meat Agency is to develop a profitable & competitive Alberta livestock & meat industry, by offering information & investment opportunities to the industry & the Government of Alberta.

•Irrigation Council
Provincial Bldg.
200 - 5 Ave. South, 3rd Fl.
Lethbridge, AB T1J 4L1
Tel: 403-381-5176; *Fax:* 403-382-4406
www1.agric.gov.ab.ca/$department/deptdocs.nsf/all/irc9432
The Irrigation Council was established under Section 50 of the Irrigation Districts Act. The provincial agency reports to the Minister of Agriculture & Rural Development.

•Farmers' Advocate Office (FAO)
JG O'Donoghue Bldg.
#305, 7000 - 113 St.
Edmonton, AB T6H 5T6
Fax: 780-427-3913
Toll-free: -310-3276
farmers.advocate@gov.ab.ca
www.farmersadvocate.gov.ab.ca
The Farmers' Advocate Office offers rural consumer protection, rural opportunities, & fair process for rural Albertans. The Office supports programs to settle disputes or offer appeals privately.

Human Resource Services & Facilities Management Services
JG O'Donoghue Bldg., 7000 - 113 St., 3rd Fl., Edmonton, AB T6H 5T6
Executive Director, Heather K.M. Behman
Tel: 780-427-2430; *Fax:* 780-427-3398
heather.behman@gov.ab.ca

Food Safety & Technology Sector
3rd fl. JG O'Donoghue Bldg., 7000 - 113 St., Edmonton, AB T6H 5T6
Tel: 780-427-6159
Assistant Deputy Minister, Jamie Curran
Tel: 780-422-6166; *Fax:* 780-422-6317
jamie.curran@gov.ab.ca

Animal Health & Assurance Division
OS Longman Bldg., 6909 - 116 St., Edmonton, AB T6H 4P2
Executive Director & Chief Provincial Veterinarian, Dr. Gerald Hauer
Tel: 780-427-3448; *Fax:* 780-415-0810
gerald.hauer@gov.ab.ca
Assistant Chief Provincial Veterinarian, Dr. Krystil Jones
Tel: 780-638-2334
krystil.jones@gov.ab.ca

Corporate Innovation & Planning Division
JG O'Donoghue Bldg, 7000 - 113 St., 3rd Fl., Edmonton, AB T6H 5T6
Executive Director, Greg Rudolf
Tel: 780-644-3029; *Fax:* 780-422-3655
greg.rudolf@gov.ab.ca

Food Safety & Animal Welfare Division
JG O'Donoghue Bldg., 7000 - 113 St., 3rd Fl., Edmonton, AB T6H 5T6
Tel: 780-422-7197; *Fax:* 780-422-4513
Executive Director, Jeff Stewart
Tel: 780-641-9084
jeff.stewart@gov.ab.ca

Information Technology Division
JG O'Donoghue Bldg., 7000 - 113 St., 2nd Fl., Edmonton, AB T6H 5T6
Executive Director, Information Technology, Rob Pungor
Tel: 780-422-6660; *Fax:* 780-422-4004
rob.pungor@gov.ab.ca

Forestry Division
Petroleum Plaza ST, 9915 - 108 St. 10th Fl., Edmonton, AB T5K 2G8
Assistant Deputy Minister, Bruce Mayer
Tel: 780-427-3542; *Fax:* 780-427-0923
bruce.mayer@gov.ab.ca
Executive Director, Wildfire Management Branch, Wally Born
Tel: 780-638-3948
wally.born@gov.ab.ca

Executive Director, Forest Industry Development Branch, Daniel Lux
Tel: 780-644-2246; *Fax:* 780-644-5728
daniel.lux@gov.ab.ca
Executive Director, Forest Management Branch, Darren Tapp
Tel: 780-427-5324; *Fax:* 780-427-0085
darren.tapp@gov.ab.ca

Industry & Rural Development Sector
JG O'Donoghue Bldg., 7000 - 113 St., 3rd Fl., Edmonton, AB T6H 5T6
Assistant Deputy Minister, John Brown
Tel: 780-427-2439; *Fax:* 780-422-6317
john.brown@gov.ab.ca

Crop Research & Extension Division
5712 - 48 Ave., Camrose, AB T4V 0K1
Tel: 403-782-8029; *Fax:* 403-782-5514
Executive Director, Dr. James Calpas
Tel: 403-782-8614
james.calpas@gov.ab.ca

Food & Bio-Processing Division
Food Processing Development Centre, 6309 - 45 St., Leduc, AB T9E 7C5
Tel: 780-986-4793; *Fax:* 780-986-5138
Executive Director, Ken Gossen
Tel: 780-980-4860; *Fax:* 780-986-5138
ken.gossen@gov.ab.ca

Rural Development Division
Provincial Building, 4709 - 44 Ave., Stony Plain, AB T7Z 1N4
Tel: 780-968-3516; *Fax:* 780-963-4709
Executive Director, Rod Carlyon
Tel: 780-968-3512; *Fax:* 780-963-4709
rod.carlyon@gov.ab.ca

Policy & Environment Sector
JG O'Donoghue Bldg., 7000 - 113 St., 3rd Fl., Edmonton, AB T6H 5T6
Assistant Deputy Minister, Dave Burdek
Tel: 780-427-1957; *Fax:* 780-422-6317
dave.burdek@gov.ab.ca

Economics & Competitiveness Division
JG O'Donoghue Bldg., 7000 - 113 St., 3rd Fl., Edmonton, AB T6H 5T6
Tel: 780-422-3771; *Fax:* 780-427-5220
Executive Director, Don Brown
Tel: 780-644-5634; *Fax:* 780-427-5220
don.brown@gov.ab.ca

Environmental Stewardship Division
JG O'Donoghue Bldg., 7000 - 113 St., 3rd Fl., Edmonton, AB T6H 5T6
Executive Director, Sean Royer
Tel: 780-427-0674; *Fax:* 780-422-9745
sean.royer@gov.ab.ca

Irrigation & Farm Water Division
JG O'Donoghue Building, 7000 - 113 St., 2nd Fl., Edmonton, AB T6H 5T6
Executive Director, Jamie Wuite
Tel: 780-427-3747; *Fax:* 780-422-0474
jamie.wuite@gov.ab.ca

Policy, Strategy, & Intergovernmental Affairs Division
JG O'Donoghue Bldg., 7000 - 113 St., 2nd Fl., Edmonton, AB T6H 5T6
Tel: 780-422-9167; *Fax:* 780-427-5921
Executive Director, Darren Chase
Tel: 780-427-3338; *Fax:* 780-427-5921
darren.chase@gov.ab.ca

Alberta Office of the Auditor General

9925 - 109 St., 8th Fl., Edmonton, AB T5K 2J8
Tel: 780-427-4222; *Fax:* 780-422-9555
info@oag.ab.ca
www.oag.ab.ca
Secondary Address: #820, 600 - 6th Ave. SW
Calgary, AB T2P 0S5
Alt. Fax: 403-297-5195

The Auditor General of Alberta is the independent auditor of all Government of Alberta ministries, departments, regulated funds, & agencies. Audits identify areas where improvement is required for the use of public resources & provide recommendations to improve practices.

Auditor General, Merwan Noshir Saher, FCPA, FCA
Tel: 780-422-6195
Assistant Auditor General, Robert Driesen
Tel: 780-422-8445
rdriesen@oag.ab.ca
Assistant Auditor General, Brad Ireland
Tel: 780-422-6447
bireland@oag.ab.ca
Assistant Auditor General, Eric Leonty
Tel: 780-422-8448
eleonty@oag.ab.ca
Assistant Auditor General, Doug Wylie
Tel: 780-422-8372
dwylie@oag.ab.ca
Senior Financial Officer, Loulou Eng, CMA
Tel: 780-422-6355
leng@oag.ab.ca
General Counsel, Kerry Langford, LLB
Tel: 780-422-6359
klangford@oag.ab.ca
Chief Operating Officer, Corporate Services, Ruth McHugh
Tel: 780-422-6517
rmchugh@oag.ab.ca

Alberta Office of the Child & Youth Advocate

#600, 9925 - 109 St. NW, Edmonton, AB T5K 2J8
Tel: 780-422-6056; *Fax:* 780-422-3675
Toll-Free: 800-661-3446
ca.information@ocya.alberta.ca
www.ocya.alberta.ca
Other Communication: Southern Alberta Advocacy Services, Phone: 403-297-8435, Fax: 403-297-4456
Secondary Address: #406, 301 - 14 St. NW
Southern Alberta Advocacy Services, Professional Bldg.
Calgary, AB T2N 2A1
twitter.com/AlbertaCYA

As of April 1, 2012, the Child & Youth Advocate is an independent officer reporting to the Legislature under the Child & Youth Advocate Act.

Child & Youth Advocate, Del Graff
Tel: 780-422-6056; *Fax:* 780-422-3675
del.graff@ocya.alberta.ca
Executive Director, Child & Youth Advocacy, Jackie Stewart
Tel: 780-644-2363
jackie.stewart@ocya.alberta.ca

Alberta Culture & Tourism

Communications Branch, Standard Life Centre, 10405 Jasper Ave., 7th Fl., Edmonton, AB T5J 4R7
Tel: 780-427-6530
Toll-Free: 800-232-7215
TTY: 780-427-9999
culture.communications@gov.ab.ca
www.culture.alberta.ca
Other Communication: Toll-Free TTY: 1-800-232-7215; Privacy E-mail: ccs.communications@gov.ab.ca
twitter.com/AlbertaCulture
www.youtube.com/user/AlbertaCulture

Formerly known as Culture, Culture & Community Services, & before that Culture & Community Spirit, the ministry was merged with Tourism in 2014 under Premier Jim Prentice.
Alberta's Culture continues to support arts & cultural industries throughout Alberta. Financial assistance is provided to the non-profit sector, film, the arts, & heritage.
Alberta Tourism (formerly known as Tourism, Parks, & Recreation, established in 2008) works to develop the tourism industry in Alberta by facilitating the profitability & sustainability of both existing & new tourism operations, positioning land for tourism, creating a positive policy environment, assisting with regulatory processes, & promoting tourism investment.

Minister, Culture & Tourism, Hon. Ricardo Miranda
Tel: 780-422-3559; *Fax:* 780-427-5018
Deputy Minister, Darlene Bouwsema
Tel: 780-427-2921
darlene.bouwsema@gov.ab.ca
Executive Director, Human Resources, John Kelly
Tel: 780-422-5779; *Fax:* 780-422-3142
john.kelly@gov.ab.ca
Executive Director, Francophone Secretariat, Cindie LeBlanc
Tel: 780-415-3232; *Fax:* 780-422-7533
cindie.leblanc@gov.ab.ca
Other Communications: Main Secretariat Number: 780-415-3348
Executive Director, Policy & Legislative Services, David Middagh
Tel: 780-427-0617
david.middagh@gov.ab.ca

Associated Agencies, Boards & Commissions:

•Alberta Film
Whitemud Crossing
#140, 4211 - 106 St.
Edmonton, AB T6J 6L7
Toll-free: 888-813-1738
www.albertafilm.ca
Alberta Film is mandated to support the screen-based production industry in Alberta, through areas such as marketing, location scouting & industry development. The Alberta Production Grant provides funding for screen-based production.

•Alberta Foundation for the Arts (AFA)
10708 - 105 Ave.
Edmonton, AB T5H 0A1
Tel: 780-427-9968
Toll-free: -310-0000
www.affta.ab.ca
The Foundation supports the development of arts throughout Alberta. It works to maintain & expand the AFA art collection for Albertans.

•Alberta Historical Resources Foundation (AHRF)
Old St. Stephen's College
8820 - 112 St.
Edmonton, AB T6G 2P8
Tel: 780-431-2300
www.culture.alberta.ca/ahrf
Established through the Historical Resources Act, The Alberta Historical Resource Foundation raises awareness of Alberta's heritage.

•Alberta Sport Connection
HSBC Bldg.
#500, 10055 - 106 St.
Edmonton, AB T5J 1G3
Tel: 780-415-1167; *Fax:* 780-415-0308
Toll-free: -310-0000
www.albertasport.ca
Supported by the Alberta Lottery Fund, Alberta Sport Connection (the Alberta Sport, Recreation, Parks, & Wildlife Foundation) reports to the Minister of Alberta Culture & Tourism. The Foundation's objectives are provided in the Alberta, Sport, Recreation, Parks, & Wildlife Foundation Act.
Alberta Sport Connection's mandate changed to focus solely on sport in November 2013. Alberta Sport Connection develops partnerships with sport programs in order to encourage & enhance athletic excellence & active lifestyles. The Foundation funds Sport Associations & Sport Development Centres.

•Government House Foundation
12845 - 102 Ave. NW
Edmonton, AB T5N 0M6
Tel: 780-427-2281; *Fax:* 780-422-6508
history.alberta.ca/governmenthouse
Established in 1976, the Government House Foundation consists of a board of up to 12 directors. The Lieutenant Governor appoints the directors who are responsible to the Minister of Culture & Tourism.
The board of directors is engaged in the following activities: advising the Minister about the preservation of Government House, raising public awareness of the architectural development of Government House, & soliciting property for display in Government House.

•Travel Alberta
#400, 1601 - 9 Ave. SE
Calgary, AB T2G 0H4
Tel: 403-648-1000; *Fax:* 403-648-1111
Toll-free: 800-252-3782
info@travelalberta.com
www.travelalberta.com
Other Communication: Alt. E-mail: info@travelalberta.com
Travel Alberta is a marketing organization that is engaged in the following activities: promotion of Alberta as a tourist destination; administration of the Tourism Information System; management of the Travel Alberta Contact / Distribution Centre; & the operation of a network of Visitor Information Centres.

Creative & Community Development Division
Standard Life Centre, 9th Fl., 10405 Jasper Ave., 9th Fl., Edmonton, AB T5J 4R7
Assistant Deputy Minister, Lora Pillipow
Tel: 780-644-1515; *Fax:* 780-422-2891
lora.pillipow@gov.ab.ca
Executive Director, Cultural Industries Branch, Jeff Brinton
Tel: 780-422-8581
Toll-free: 888-813-1738; *Fax:* 780-422-8582
jeff.brinton@gov.ab.ca
#140, 4211 - 106 St.
Edmonton, AB T6J 6L7
Executive Director, Arts Branch, Jeffrey Anderson
Tel: 780-415-0283; *Fax:* 780-422-9132
jeffrey.anderson@gov.ab.ca
Executive Director, Community Engagement Branch, Carol Moerth
Tel: 780-415-4874; *Fax:* 780-427-4155
carol.moerth@gov.ab.ca

Heritage Division
Old St. Stephen's College, 8820 - 112 St., Edmonton, AB T6G 2P8
Assistant Deputy Minister, David Link
Tel: 780-431-2313; *Fax:* 780-427-5598
david.link@gov.ab.ca
Executive Director & Provincial Archivist, Provincial Archives of Alberta, Leslie Latta
Tel: 780-427-0058; *Fax:* 780-427-4646

leslie.latta@gov.ab.ca
Other Communications: Provincial Archives of Alberta, Phone: 780-427-1750
Provincial Archives of Alberta
8555 Roper Rd.
Edmonton, AB T6E 5W1
Executive Director, Royal Tyrrell Museum of Palaeontology, Andy Neuman
Tel: 403-820-6201; *Fax:* 403-823-7131
andrew.neuman@gov.ab.ca
PO Box 7500
Drumheller, AB T0J 0Y0
Executive Director, Royal Alberta Museum, Chris Robinson
Tel: 780-453-9168; *Fax:* 780-454-6629
chris.robinson@gov.ab.ca
12845 - 102 Ave.
Edmonton, AB T5N 0M6
Executive Director, Historic Resources Management Branch, Matthew Wangler
Tel: 780-438-8503
matthew.wangler@gov.ab.ca
Executive Director, Historic Sites & Museums, Catherine Whalley
Tel: 780-431-2306; *Fax:* 780-427-5598
catherine.whalley@gov.ab.ca

Policy & Strategic Corporate Services
Standard Life Centre, 10405 Jasper Ave., 7th Fl., Edmonton, AB T5J 4R7
Assistant Deputy Minister, Brian Fischer
Tel: 780-427-0437; *Fax:* 780-427-0255
brian.fischer@gov.ab.ca
Senior Financial Officer / Executive Director, Financial Services Branch, Pam Arnston
Tel: 780-427-0120; *Fax:* 780-427-0255
pam.arnston@gov.ab.ca
Executive Director & Chief Information Officer, Information Management & Technology Services, Howard Grossman
Tel: 780-644-3974; *Fax:* 780-644-1286
howard.grossman@gov.ab.ca
Executive Director, Policy & Legislative Services Branch, David Middagh
Tel: 780-427-0617; *Fax:* 780-427-0255
david.middagh@gov.ab.ca

Recreation & Physical Activity Division
Standard Life Centre, 10405 Jasper Ave., 9th Fl., Edmonton, AB T5J 4R7
Executive Director, Roger Kramers
Tel: 780-422-3305; *Fax:* 780-427-5140
roger.kramers@gov.ab.ca

Tourism Division
Commerce Place, 10155 - 102 St., 6th Fl., Edmonton, AB T5J 4L6
Assistant Deputy Minister, Chris Heseltine
Tel: 780-643-1997; *Fax:* 780-422-1759
chris.heseltine@gov.ab.ca
Executive Director, Destination Development & Visitor Services Branch, Yvette Ng
Tel: 780-643-1368
yvette.ng@gov.ab.ca

Alberta Economic Development & Trade

Commerce Place, 10155 - 102 St., 12th Fl., Edmonton, AB T5J 4G8
economic.alberta.ca
Created in 2015, Economic Development & Trade focuses on the following priorities: Economic Development & Small & Medium-Sized Enterprises; Science & Innovation (including the Alberta Innovated programs); & Trade & Investment Attraction (including Alberta's international offices).
The following international offices work to promote trade & to attract investment & other interests such as culture & education: Alberta China Office; Alberta Hong Kong Office; Alberta New Delhi Office; Alberta Japan Office; Alberta Korea Office; Alberta Guangzhou Office; Alberta Mexico Office; Alberta Shanghai Office; Alberta Singapore Office; Alberta Taiwan Office; Alberta United Kingdom Office; & Alberta Washington, D.C. Office.
Minister, Economic Development & Trade, Hon. Deron Bilous
Tel: 780-644-8554; *Fax:* 780-644-8572
Deputy Minister, Jason Krips
Tel: 780-415-0900; *Fax:* 780-415-6114
jason.krips@gov.ab.ca
Director, Communications, Jeannie Smith
Tel: 780-422-2524; *Fax:* 780-422-2635
jeannie.smith@gov.ab.ca

Associated Agencies, Boards & Commissions:

•Alberta Enterprise Corporation Board
Alberta Enterprise Corporation
#1100, 10830 Jasper Ave.
Edmonton, AB T5J 2B3
Tel: 780-392-3901; *Fax:* 780-392-3908
info@alberta-enterprise.ca
www.alberta-enterprise.ca
The Alberta Enterprise Corporation Board was established in 2008 through the Alberta Enterprise Corporation Act. The Alberta Enterprise Fund is the corporation's fund that targets technology venture capital funds.

•Alberta Innovates - Bio Solutions (AI Bio)
Phipps McKinnon Bldg.
10020 - 101A Ave., 18th Fl.
Edmonton, AB T5J 3G2
Tel: 780-427-1956; *Fax:* 780-427-3252
Toll-free: 877-828-0444
bio@albertainnovates.ca
bio.albertainnovates.ca
Alberta Innovates Bio Solutions was established in 2010 under the Alberta Research & Innovation Act. It is part of the Alberta Innovates system, which reports to the Minister of Alberta Advanced Education & Technology. Investments are made in research & innovation to benefit Alberta's forestry, agriculture, & food sectors.
In April 2016, the government of Alberta announced plans to consolidate Alberta Innovates into a single organization.

•Alberta Innovates - Energy & Environmental Solutions
AMEC Place
#2540, 801 - 6th Ave. SW
Calgary, AB T2P 3W2
Tel: 403-297-7089; *Fax:* 403-297-3638
ees@albertainnovates.ca
ai-ees.ca
The Alberta energy & environmental research organization works to develop innovative methods for the conversion of natural resources into environmentally responsible, market-ready energy.
In April 2016, the government of Alberta announced plans to consolidate Alberta Innovates into a single organization.

•Alberta Innovates - Health Solutions (AIHS)
#1500, 10104 - 103 Ave.
Edmonton, AB T5J 4A7
Tel: 780-423-5727; *Fax:* 780-429-3509
Toll-free: 877-423-5727
health@albertainnovates.ca
www.ahfmr.ab.ca
Alberta Innovates - Health Solutions supports research & innovation for the improvement of Albertans' health & well-being. The organization also works to create health related social & economic benefits.
In April 2016, the government of Alberta announced plans to consolidate Alberta Innovates into a single organization.

•Alberta Innovates - Technology Futures
250 Karl Clark Rd.
Edmonton, AB T6N 1E4
Tel: 780-450-5111; *Fax:* 780-450-5333
referral@albertainnovates.ca
www.albertatechfutures.ca
As part of the research & innovation system in Alberta, the organization works to build healthy, sustainable businesses. Technology Futures offers technical services, program funding, as well as regionally accessible commercialization support.
In April 2016, the government of Alberta announced plans to consolidate Alberta Innovates into a single organization.

•Alberta Research & Innvoation Authority (ARIA)
John J. Bowlen Bldg.
#620 - 7 Ave. SW, 9th Fl.
Calgary, AB T2P 0Y8
Tel: 403-297-3022; *Fax:* 403-297-6435
aria@albertainnovates.ca
aria.albertainnovates.ca
The advisory body offers recommendations to the Government of Alberta about research, emerging technologies & policy direction.

Economic Development & SMEs Division
Commerce Place, 10155 - 102 St., 5th Fl., Edmonton, AB T5J 4L6
Assistant Deputy Minister, Shannon Flint
Tel: 780-422-8463; *Fax:* 780-422-2091
shannon.flint@gov.ab.ca
Executive Director, Innovation System Engagement, Lisa Bowes
Tel: 780-422-3117; *Fax:* 780-422-2091
lisa.bowes@gov.ab.ca
Executive Director, Energy Value & Supply Chain, Luciano Dalla-Longa
Tel: 780-427-6987; *Fax:* 780-422-2091
luciano.dalla-longa@gov.ab.ca
Director, Economic Development Policy, Toby Schneider
Tel: 780-427-6617; *Fax:* 780-422-2091
toby.schneider@gov.ab.ca
Executive Director, Entrepreneurship & Regional Development, Tom Mansfield
Tel: 780-427-6483; *Fax:* 780-422-2091
tom.mansfield@gov.ab.ca
Senior Director, Strategic Initiatives, Vacant
Senior Director, Small Business & Entrepreneurship, Nicole Martel
Tel: 780-643-9467; *Fax:* 780-422-5804
nicole.martel@gov.ab.ca
Senior Director, Regional Economic Development Services, Tammy Powell
Tel: 780-865-8210
tammy.powell@gov.ab.ca

Science & Innovation Division
Phipps-McKinnon Bldg., 10020 - 101A Ave., 5th Fl., Edmonton, AB T5J 3G2
Assistant Deputy Minister, Justin Riemer
Tel: 780-427-6303
justin.riemer@gov.ab.ca
Executive Director, Technology Partnerships & Investments Branch, Brent Lakeman
Tel: 780-643-6511
brent.lakeman@gov.ab.ca
Senior Director, Emerging Technology Industries Unit, Mathew Anil
Tel: 780-415-8751
mathew.anil@gov.ab.ca
Senior Director, Science & Research - Special Initiatives, Daphne Cheel
Tel: 780-422-0054
daphne.cheel@gov.ab.ca
Senior Director, Integrated Science & Research Initiatives, Chris Van Tighem
Tel: 780-427-5229
chris.vantighem@gov.ab.ca
Senior Director, Life Sciences Industries Unit, Hubert Eng
Tel: 780-427-0649
hubert.eng@gov.ab.ca
Senior Director, ICT Industries Unit, Tim Olsen
Tel: 780-644-4970
tim.olsen@gov.ab.ca
Senior Director, Emerging Science & Technology Initiatives, Lori Querengesser
Tel: 780-427-6616
lori.querengesser@gov.ab.ca
Senior Director, Innovation Policy & Strategy, Alex Umnikov
Tel: 780-427-6620
alex.umnikov@gov.ab.ca

Strategic Policy & Corporate Services
Commerce Pl., 10155 - 102 St., 13th Fl., Edmonton, AB T5J 4G8
Tel: 780-427-6543
Assistant Deputy Minister, Lorne Harvey
Tel: 780-422-2429; *Fax:* 780-422-2635
lorne.harvey@gov.ab.ca
Executive Director, Human Resources, Pat Connolly
Tel: 780-422-1341; *Fax:* 780-422-1272
pat.connolly@gov.ab.ca
Executive Director, Finance & Administration, Howard Wong
Tel: 780-427-0793; *Fax:* 780-644-8141
howard.wong@gov.ab.ca

Trade & Investment Attraction Division
Commerce Place, 10155 - 102 St., 4th Fl., Edmonton, AB T5J 4L6
Tel: 780-427-6543; *Fax:* 780-427-0699
Assistant Deputy Minister, Matthew Machielse
Tel: 780-427-4442; *Fax:* 780-422-9127
matthew.machielse@gov.ab.ca
Executive Director, Trade Policy - International, Daryl Hanak
Tel: 780-422-1339
daryl.hanak@gov.ab.ca
Executive Director, Asia Pacific Branch, Nancy Wu
Tel: 780-643-1660; *Fax:* 780-427-0699
nancy.wu@gov.ab.ca
Executive Director, Emerging Markets, Greg Jardine
Tel: 780-427-6368
greg.jardine@gov.ab.ca
Executive Director, Europe, Beverlee Loat
Tel: 780-638-4392
beverlee.loat@gov.ab.ca
Standard Life Building
639 - 5 Ave. SW, 3rd Fl.
Calgary, AB T2P 0M9
Executive Director, United States, Tristan Sanregret
Tel: 780-427-4605
tristan.sanregret@gov.ab.ca

Alberta International Offices

The manadate for each Alberta international office is to meet the province's priorities in the region.

Alberta Japan Office Managing Director, David Anderson
Other Communications: Phone: 011-81-3-3475-1298; Fax: 011-81-3-3470-3939
Place Canada, 3rd Fl.
3-37 Akasaka 7 - chome Minato-ku
Tokyo, 107-0052 Japan

Alberta South Korea Office Managing Director, Gregory Baker
greg.baker@gov.ab.ca
Other Communications: Phone: 82-2-3783-6140; Fax: 82-2-3783-6147
c/o Embassy of Canada
21 Jeongdong-gil (Jeong-dong), Jung-gu
Seoul, 110-1202 South Korea

Alberta Washington DC Office Director, Alberta - USA Relations, Mary Ballantyne
Tel: 202-448-6474; *Fax:* 202-448-6477
mary.ballantyne@international.gc.ca
Canadian Embassy
501 Pennsylvania Ave. NW
Washington, DC 20001 USA

Alberta Mexico Office Managing Director, Klaus Buttner
klaus.buttner@international.gc.ca
Other Communications: Phone: 011-52-55-5387-9302; Fax: 011-52-55-5724-7913
Calle Schiller No 529, Colonia Polanco, Del Miguel Hidalgo
Mexico City, 11560 Mexico

Alberta Taiwan Office Representative, Li-an Chen
lian.chen@international.gc.ca
Other Communications: Phone: 011-886-2-8789-2006; Fax: 011-886-2-8789-1878
Canadian Trade Office
6F, No. 1, Song Zhi Rd., XinYi District
Taipei City, 11047 Taiwan

Alberta China Office Managing Director, Vacant
Other Communications: Phone: 011-86-10-5139-4272; Fax: 011-86-10-5139-4465
c/o Canadian Embassy
19 Dongzhimenwai Dajie, Chaoyang District
Beijing, 100600 China

Alberta's Senior Representative - Hong Kong Office, Ron Hoffmann
Other Communications: Phone: 011-852-2528-4729; Fax: 011-852-2529-8115
Tower Two, Admiralty Centre
#1004, 18 Harcourt Rd.
Hong Kong, China

Alberta Singapore Office Managing Director, Robert Simmons
robert.simmons@international.gc.ca
Other Communications: Phone: 011-65-6854-5872; Fax: 011-656-8545-5915
#11-01, One George St.

Alberta Shanghai Office Senior Commercial Officer, Yvonna Zou
yvonna.zou@internationa.gc.ca
Other Communications: Phone: 011-86-21-3279-2896; Fax: 011-86-21-3279-2801
1788 Nanjing Xi Lu
Shanghai, 200040 China

Alberta United Kingdom Office Managing Director, Vacant
Other Communications: Phone: 011-44-20-7004-6361
Canada House, Trafalgar Square
London, SW1Y 5BJ UK

Alberta Education

Commerce Place, 10155 - 102 St., 7th Fl., Edmonton, AB T5J 4L5

Tel: 780-427-7219; *Fax:* 780-427-0591
Toll-Free: -310-0000
TTY: 780-427-9999
www.education.alberta.ca
Other Communication: Media Inquiries, Phone: 780-422-4495
twitter.com/albertaed
www.facebook.com/AlbertaEducation
www.youtube.com/user/InspiringEducation

From Early Childhood Services (ECS) to Grade 12, Alberta Education provides support for students, parents, teachers & administrators. The Ministry is engaged in the following activities: developing & evaluating curriculum; setting standards; assessing outcomes; supporting the education of special needs, Aboriginal, & francophone students; developing & certifying teachers; funding & supporting school boards; overseeing educational policies & regulations; & managing the Alberta Initiative for School Improvement (AISI).

Minister, Education, Hon. David Eggen
Tel: 780-427-5010; *Fax:* 780-427-5018
education.minister@gov.ab.ca

Deputy Minister, Dr. Curtis Clarke
Tel: 780-427-3659; *Fax:* 780-427-7733
curtis.clarke@gov.ab.ca

Associated Agencies, Boards & Commissions:

•Council on Alberta Teaching Standards (COATS)
Teaching & Leadership Excellence, Capital Boulevard Bldg.
#44, 10044 - 108 St., 2nd Fl.
Edmonton, AB T5J 5E6
Tel: 780-427-2045; *Fax:* 780-422-4199
Teacher.Certification@gov.ab.ca
www.teachingquality.ab.ca

Established by a Ministerial Order in 1985, the Council on Alberta Teaching Standards offers recommendations related to teaching to the Minister. Advice is provided on matters such as teacher certification, teacher preparation, & practice review.

First Nations, Metis & Inuit (FNMI) Education Division

44 Capital Blvd., 10044 - 108 St. NW, 9th Fl., Edmonton, AB T5J 5E6

Assistant Deputy Minister, Jane Martin
Tel: 780-415-6192; *Fax:* 780-638-3871
jane.martin@gov.ab.ca

Executive Director, Division, Dan K. Smith
Tel: 780-638-9423
dan.k.smith@gov.ab.ca

Executive Director, FNMI & Inuit Education Sector, Eileen Marthiensen
Tel: 780-644-7956; *Fax:* 780-415-9306
eileen.marthiensen@gov.ab.ca

Program & System Support Division

Commerce Place, 10155 - 102 St., 7th Fl., Edmonton, AB T5J 4L5

Assistant Deputy Minister, Dean Lindquist
Tel: 780-427-2051; *Fax:* 780-415-8938
dean.lindquist@gov.ab.ca

Executive Director, Capital Planning Sector, Laura Cameron
Tel: 780-427-0289; *Fax:* 780-644-2284
laura.cameron@gov.ab.ca

Executive Director, Learning & Technology Resources, Bette Gray
Tel: 780-427-1509; *Fax:* 780-415-1091
bette.gray@gov.ab.ca

Executive Director, Information & Technology Management Sector, Aziza Jivraj
Tel: 780-427-3880; *Fax:* 780-422-0880
aziza.jivraj@gov.ab.ca

Executive Director, Field Services Sector, Mark Swanson
Tel: 780-427-6272; *Fax:* 780-422-9682
mark.swanson@gov.ab.ca

Executive Director, Education Supports Sector, David Woloshyn
Tel: 780-422-6554; *Fax:* 780-643-1188
david.woloshyn@gov.ab.ca

Strategic Services & Governance Division

Commerce Place, 10155 - 102 St., 7th Fl., Edmonton, AB T5J 4L5

Assistant Deputy Minister, Michael Walter
Tel: 780-427-3663; *Fax:* 780-422-0408
michael.walter@gov.ab.ca

Executive Director, Results-Based Budgeting Team, Vacant

Acting Executive Director, Policy & Planning, Jeff Willan
Tel: 780-427-9998; *Fax:* 780-422-5126
jeff.willan@gov.ab.ca

Executive Director, Strategic Financial Services Sector, Brad J. Smith
Tel: 780-422-0920; *Fax:* 780-422-6996
bsmith@gov.ab.ca

Student Learning Standards Division

44 Capital Blvd., 10044 - 108 St., 8th Fl., Edmonton, AB T5J 5E6

Tel: 780-427-7484; *Fax:* 780-422-1400

Assistant Deputy Minister, Ellen Hambrook
Tel: 780-427-7484; *Fax:* 780-422-1400
ellen.hambrook@gov.ab.ca

Executive Director, Programs of Study & Resources Sector, Merla Bolender
Tel: 780-644-2530; *Fax:* 780-422-3745
merla.bolender@gov.ab.ca
10044 - 108 St., 8th Fl.
Edmonton, AB T5J 5E6

Executive Director, Operations & Implementation Support Sector, Neil Fenske
Tel: 780-422-0629; *Fax:* 780-422-3745
neil.fenske@gov.ab.ca
10044 - 108 St., 8th Fl.
Edmonton, AB T5J 5E6

Acting Executive Director, French Education Services Sector, Gilbert Guimont
Tel: 780-422-7793; *Fax:* 780-422-1947
gilbert.guimont@gov.ab.ca
10044 - 108 St., 9th Fl.
Edmonton, AB T5J 5E6

Executive Director, Provincial Assessment Sector, Paul Lamoureux
Tel: 780-422-4848; *Fax:* 780-422-4200
paul.lamoureux@gov.ab.ca
10044 - 108 St., 9th Fl.
Edmonton, AB T5J 5E6

System Excellence Division

44 Capital Blvd., 10044 - 108 St., 2nd Fl., Edmonton, AB T5J 5E6

Assistant Deputy Minister, Gene Williams
Tel: 780-644-3578; *Fax:* 780-638-3272
gene.williams@gov.ab.ca

Executive Director, Research, System Assurance Engagement & Teacher Relations Sector, Doug Aitkenhead
Tel: 780-643-1277
doug.aitkenhead@gov.ab.ca

Executive Director & Registrar, Teaching & Leadership Excellence Sector, Paul Macleod
Tel: 780-422-6947; *Fax:* 780-422-4199
paul.macleod@gov.ab.ca

Executive Director, Human Resources Branch, Bernadette Welham
Tel: 780-644-7503; *Fax:* 780-422-5362
bernadette.welham@gov.ab.ca

Alberta Office of the Chief Electoral Officer / Elections Alberta (OOCEO)

#100, 11510 Kingsway Ave., Edmonton, AB T5G 2Y5

Tel: 780-427-7191; *Fax:* 780-422-2900
info@elections.ab.ca
www.elections.ab.ca
twitter.com/ElectionsAB
www.facebook.com/electionsalberta
ca.linkedin.com/pub/elections-alberta/15/286/4b5
plus.google.com/115240326572053097224

The Office of the Chief Electoral Officer is engaged in the following activities: administering impartial, open, & fair elections; offering necessary information to political participants & voters; providing a high standard of customer service; training election officials; & adopting best practices & new technologies.

Chief Electoral Officer, Glen L. Resler, CPA, CMA
Tel: 780-427-1035
glen.resler@elections.ab.ca

Deputy Chief Electoral Officer; Director, Election Operations & Communications, Drew Westwater
Tel: 780-427-6860
drew.westwater@elections.ab.ca

Senior Financial Compliance Officer, Matthew Dennis
Tel: 780-427-6698
matthew.dennis@elections.ab.ca

Alberta Energy

North Petroleum Plaza, 9945 - 108 St., Edmonton, AB T5K 2G6

Tel: 780-427-8050; *Fax:* 780-422-9522
Toll-Free: -310-0000
TTY: 780-427-9999
www.energy.gov.ab.ca
Other Communication: Calgary, Phone: 403-297-8955; TTY Toll-Free: 1-800-232-7215
twitter.com/Alberta_Energy

Alberta Energy is responsible for the development of Alberta's non-renewable resources & renewable energy. Non-renewable resources include natural gas, conventional oil & oil sands, coal, & minerals. Renewable resources include wind, solar, geothermal, & hydro.

Other responsibilities of Alberta Energy are as follows: establishing & administering fiscal & royalty systems; granting the right to explore & develop resources; promoting energy conservation; & encouraging investment to create economic prosperity.

Minister, Energy, Hon. Margaret McCuaig-Boyd
Tel: 780-427-3740; *Fax:* 780-644-1222
minister.energy@gov.ab.ca

Deputy Minister, Colleen Volk
Tel: 780-415-8434; *Fax:* 780-427-7737
coleen.volk@gov.ab.ca

Associated Agencies, Boards & Commissions:

•Alberta Utilities Commission (AUC)
Fifth Avenue Place
425 - 1st St. SW, 4th Fl.
Calgary, AB T2P 3L8
Tel: 403-592-8845; *Fax:* 403-592-4406
Toll-free: -310-0000
info@auc.ab.ca
www.auc.ab.ca
Other Communication: Edmonton Office, Phone: 780-427-4901; Edmonton Office, Fax: 780-427-6970

The Alberta Utilities Commission was established by the Government of Alberta as a quasi-judicial independent agency. It is responsible for regulating the utilities sector & the electricity & natural gas markets in Alberta to ensure that the delivery of utility service is responsible, fair, & in the public interest.

•Alberta Energy Regulator (AER)
#1000, 250 - 5 St. SW
Calgary, AB T2P 0R4
Tel: 403-297-8311; *Fax:* 403-297-7336
Toll-free: 855-297-8311
inquiries@aer.ca
www.aer.ca
As an independent, quasi-judicial agency of the Government of Alberta, the Alberta Energy Regulator is responsible for regulating the safe & responsible development of energy resources in Alberta, assuming all duties & responsibilities performed by the former Energy Resources Conservation Board, as of July 2013. The province's energy resources include coal, natural gas, oil, & oil sands.

Electricity & Sustainable Energy Division

North Petroleum Plaza, 9945 - 108 St., 8th Fl., Edmonton, AB T5K 2G6

Assistant Deputy Minister, James E. Allen
Tel: 780-644-7126; *Fax:* 780-427-7737
james.e.allen@gov.ab.ca
Executive Director, Generation, Transmission & Wholesale Branch, Andrew Buffin
Tel: 780-415-6414
andrew.buffin@gov.ab.ca
Executive Director, Strategy & Integration Branch, David James
Tel: 780-644-8135
david.james@gov.ab.ca
Executive Director, Retail & Distribution Branch, Kristin Stolarz
Tel: 780-644-1232
kristin.stolarz@gov.ab.ca

Ministry Services Division

Petroleum Plaza NT, 9945 - 108 St., 6th Fl., Edmonton, AB T5K 2G6

Assistant Deputy Minister, Douglas Borland
Tel: 780-427-6223; *Fax:* 780-427-7737
douglas.borland@gov.ab.ca
Executive Director, Energy Information & Analysis, Matthew Foss
Tel: 780-422-5059
matthew.foss@gov.ab.ca
Executive Director, Human Resources, Noelle Green
Tel: 780-427-6294
noelle.green@gov.ab.ca

Oil Sands Division

Petroleum Plaza NT, 9945 - 108 St., 8th Fl., Edmonton, AB T5K 2G6

Assistant Deputy Minister, Steve Tkalcic
Tel: 780-422-9121; *Fax:* 780-422-0692
steve.tkalcic@gov.ab.ca
Executive Director, Oil Sands Policy, Roger Ramcharita
Tel: 780-422-9212
roger.ramcharita@gov.ab.ca
Executive Director, Oil Sands Operations, Larry Ziegenhagel
Tel: 780-427-6384
larry.ziegenhagel@gov.ab.ca

Resource Development Policy Division

Petroleum Plaza NT, 9945 - 108 St. 8th Fl., Edmonton, AB T5K 2G6

Assistant Deputy Minister, Al Sanderson
Tel: 780-422-6656
al.sanderson@gov.ab.ca
Executive Director, Energy Technical Services, Christopher Holly
Tel: 780-422-9206
chris.holly@gov.ab.ca
Executive Director, Resource Land Access, Audrey Murray
Tel: 780-427-6383; *Fax:* 780-422-3044
audrey.murray@gov.ab.ca
Executive Director, Resource Policy Development, Sharla Rauschning
Tel: 780-427-6230; *Fax:* 780-644-3604
sharla.rauschning@gov.ab.ca

Resource Revenue & Operations Division

Petroleum Plaza NT, 9945 - 108 St., 8th Fl., Edmonton, AB T5K 2G6

Assistant Deputy Minister, Mike Ekelund
Tel: 780-422-9119; *Fax:* 780-427-7737
mike.ekelund@gov.ab.ca
Chief Executive Officer, PETRINEX (Edmonton / Calgary), Wally Goeres
Tel: 780-415-2079; *Fax:* 780-422-0229
wally.goeres@gov.ab.ca
Executive Director, Tenure, Brenda Allbright
Tel: 780-422-9393; *Fax:* 780-422-1123
brenda.allbright@gov.ab.ca
Acting Executive Director, Petroleum Marketing & Valuation, & Royalty-In-Kind Operations, Ann Blackmore
Tel: 403-297-5503
ann.blackmore@gov.ab.ca
Executive Director, Compliance & Assurance, Larry McGuinness
Tel: 403-297-6742; *Fax:* 403-297-5199
larry.mcguinness@gov.ab.ca
Executive Director, Royalty Operations, Salim Merali
Tel: 780-422-9124; *Fax:* 780-427-0865
salim.merali@gov.ab.ca
Branch Head, Coal & Mineral Development, Gary V. White
Tel: 780-415-0349; *Fax:* 780-422-5447
gary.v.white@gov.ab.ca

Strategic Initiatives Division

Petroleum Plaza NT, 9945 - 108 St., 8th Fl., Edmonton, AB T5K 2G6

Assistant Deputy Minister, Mike Ekelund
Tel: 780-422-9119
mike.ekelund@gov.ab.ca

Strategy & Market Access Division

Petroleum Plaza NT, 9945 - 108 St., 8th Fl., Edmonton, AB T5K 2G6

Assistant Deputy Minister, Cynthia Farmer
Tel: 780-644-1750; *Fax:* 780-415-9669
cynthia.farmer@gov.ab.ca
Executive Director, Market Diversification Branch, Mike Fernandez
Tel: 780-643-1668
mike.fernandez@gov.ab.ca
Executive Director, Strategic Energy Secretariat, Barbra Korol
Tel: 780-644-6838
barbra.korol@gov.ab.ca
Executive Director, International Energy Policy Branch, Alisa Neuman
Tel: 780-422-9149
alisa.neuman@gov.ab.ca

Alberta Environment & Parks

Information Centre, Great West Life Bldg., 9920 - 108 St., Main Fl., Edmonton, AB T5K 2M4

Tel: 780-427-2700; *Fax:* 780-427-4407
Toll-Free: -310-3773
ESRD.Info-Centre@gov.ab.ca
esrd.alberta.ca
Other Communication: Toll-Free Outside AB: 1-877-944-0313; 24-hour Environment Hotline (to report an environmental emergency or file a complaint): 1-800-222-6514
twitter.com/ABGovWildfire
www.facebook.com/AlbertaParks
www.flickr.com/photos/srdalberta
Environment & Sustainable Resource Development was changed to Environment & Parks after the May 2015 general election, with its Forestry Division being moved to the modified Agriculture & Forestry department (formerly Agriculture & Rural Development).

Minister, Environment & Parks, Hon. Shannon Phillips
Tel: 780-427-2391; *Fax:* 780-422-6259
ESRD.Minister@gov.ab.ca

Deputy Minister, Andre Corbould
Tel: 780-427-1799; *Fax:* 780-415-9669
andre.corbould@gov.ab.ca
Petroleum Plaza ST
9915 - 108 St., 10th Fl.
Edmonton, AB T5K 2G8

Executive Director, Human Resources Services, Mike Boyle
Tel: 780-644-1398; *Fax:* 780-427-2513
mike.boyle@gov.ab.ca

Manager, Correspondence & Client Support Unit, Wanda Gruenheidt
Tel: 780-644-2742
wanda.gruenheidt@gov.ab.ca

Associated Agencies, Boards & Commissions:

•Alberta Environmental Appeals Board
Peace Hills Trust Tower
#306, 10011 - 109 St.
Edmonton, AB T5J 3S8
Tel: 780-427-6207; *Fax:* 780-427-4693
www.eab.gov.ab.ca
The Environmental Appeals Board strives to offer fair, impartial, & efficient resolutions to matters in order to advance the protection & enhancement of the environment in Alberta.

•Alberta Recycling Management Authority (ARMA)
Scotia Tower 1
#1800, 10060 Jasper Ave.
PO Box 189
Edmonton, AB T5J 2J1
Tel: 780-990-1111; *Fax:* 780-990-1122
Toll-free: 888-999-8762
info@albertarecycling.ca
www.albertarecycling.ca
Other Communication: Toll-Free Fax: 1-866-990-1122; Electronics Recycling: electronics@albertarecycling.ca; Tire Recycling: tires@albertarecycling.ca; Paint: paint@albertarecycling.ca
Reporting to the Minister of Environment, the not-for-profit association manages tire, paint, & electronics recycling programs throughout Alberta.

•Alberta Used Oil Management Association (AUOMA)
Empire Building
#1008, 10080 Jasper Ave.
Edmonton, AB T5J 1V9
Tel: 780-414-1510; *Fax:* 780-414-1519
Toll-free: 866-414-1510
auoma@usedoilrecycling.ca
www.usedoilrecycling.com/en/ab
Other Communication: Info Line (for information about the nearest Alberta Eco Centre / Collection Facility): 1-888-922-2298
The not-for-profit association encourages Albertans to return used oil, filters, & containers to collection facilities so they can be disposed of properly. The program is funded by an Environmental Handling Charge, & a Return Incentive is paid to private sector collectors.

•Beverage Container Management Board (BCMB)
#100, 8616 - 51 Ave.
Edmonton, AB T6E 6E6
Tel: 780-424-3193; *Fax:* 780-428-4620
Toll-free: 888-424-7671
info@bcmb.ab.ca
www.bcmb.ab.ca
The Beverage Container Management Board is an alliance of the Alberta Government, municipalities, beverage manufacturers, environmental organizations, & the public. It was established in 1997 as a management board, under the Beverage Container Recycling Regulation pursuant to Section 175 of the Environmental Protection & Enhancement Act. The Beverage Container Management Board oversees the collection & recycling of beverage containers throughout Alberta. Its policy parameters are established by the Minister of Environment. Funding is through a levy based on the returns of beverage containers.

•Disabled Hunter Review Committee
c/o Fish & Wildlife Div, Sustainable Resource Development
9920 - 108 St.
Edmonton, AB T5K 2M4
Toll-free: -310-0000
The Disabled Hunter Review Committee is engaged in hearing appeals & reviewing applications by persons who received a negative decision when attempting to obtain a licences or permit for hunting. Depending upon the number of applications, the Committee holds hearings annually.

•Environmental Response Centre
Twin Atria Bldg.
4999 - 98 Ave., 1st Fl.
Edmonton, AB T6B 2X3
Tel: 780-427-2700
Other Communication: Environment Hotline (for reporting an environmental emergency or filing a complaint): 1-800-222-6514
Complaints about contraventions of the Environmental Protection & Enhancement Act are investigated.

•Land Compensation Board (LCB)
1229 - 91 St. SW
Edmonton, AB T6X 1E9
Tel: 780-427-2444; *Fax:* 780-427-5798
Toll-free: -310-000
srb.lcb@gov.ab.ca
www.landcompensation.gov.ab.ca
The Land Compensation Board listens to disputes & delivers a decision, within it legislated mandate, about the compensation for landowners or tenants when land is taken by an authority for public works projects. Applications to the Board can be made through forms found in the Expropriation Act Rules of Procedure & Practice.

•Natural Resources Conservation Board (NRCB)
Sterling Place
9940 - 106 St., 4th Fl.
Edmonton, AB T5K 2N2
Tel: 780-422-1977; *Fax:* 780-427-0607
Toll-free: 866-383-6722
info@nrcb.ca
www.nrcb.ca

Established in 1991 by the Government of Alberta, the Natural Resources Conservation Board carries out its responsibilities under the Natural Resources Conservation Board Act. The quasi-judicial agency, which is accountable to the Minister of Sustainable Resource Development, reviews non-energy natural resource projects. The Board considers environmental, economic, & social effects in deciding if a project is in the public interest.

In accordance with the Agricultural Operation Practices Act, the Natural Resources Conservation Board also has regulatory authority for confined feeding operations in Alberta. Its work in this area includes administering policies, fulfilling applications, & conducting board reviews.

•Surface Rights Board (SRB)
1229 - 91 St. SW
Edmonton, AB T6X 1E9
Tel: 780-427-2444; *Fax:* 780-427-5798
Toll-free: -310-0000
srb.lcb@gov.ab.ca
www.surfacerights.gov.ab.ca

The Surface Rights Board holds hearings on disputes related to energy activities & land access. The hearing usually involves a panel of three members of the Surface Rights Board. Members of the Board are appointed by an Order in Counsel, according to the Surface Rights Act. Affected parties may also participate in the hearings, which are open to the public.

The Board delivers decisions, within its legislated mandate, about compensation to landowners, surrounding issues such as oil & gas & power line activity. In determining compensation, the Board considers factors such as the value of the land, loss of use, inconvenience, nuisance, & noise, & adverse effects on remaining land.

•Wildfire Costs Assessment Committee
c/o Office of the Farmer's Advocate, JG O'Donoghue Building
7000 - 113 St., 3rd Fl.
Edmonton, AB T6H 5T6

The Wildfire Costs Assessment Committee is administered by the Farmers' Advocate Office. When a party is deemed responsible for starting a wildfire, the Committee evaluates that party's ability to pay the cost of fighting the fire.

•Wildlife Predator & Shot Livestock Compensation Committee
9920 - 108 St.
Edmonton, AB T5K 2M4

The reimbursement paid to a livestock producer, when an animal has been injured by a wildlife predator, or shot, is determined by the Predator & Shot Livestock Compensation Committee of Alberta. Compensation provided to the livestock owner is based upon a schedule for losses or injury to specified livestock.

Corporate Services Division

Petroleum Plaza ST, 9915 - 108 St., 10th Fl, Edmonton, AB T5K 2G8
Tel: 780-643-0890; *Fax:* 780-644-8469

Assistant Deputy Minister, Tom Davis
Tel: 780-644-3205; *Fax:* 780-427-0923
tom.davis@gov.ab.ca

Acting Chief Information Officer & Executive Director, Informatics Branch, Lee George
Tel: 780-415-2463
lee.george@gov.ab.ca
Oxbridge Place
9820 - 106 St.
Edmonton, AB T5K 2J6

Executive Director, Corporate Performance Branch, Marilea Pattison Perry
Tel: 780-644-1157
marilea.pattisonperry@gov.ab.ca

Executive Director & Senior Financial Officer, Finance Branch, Kevin Peterson
Tel: 780-427-9148; *Fax:* 780-427-0923
kevin.peterson@gov.ab.ca

Acting Chief Data Officer, Ray Keller
Tel: 780-427-0533
ray.keller@gov.ab.ca

Environmental Monitoring

Petroleum Plaza ST, 9915 - 108 St., 10th Fl., Edmonton, AB T5K 2G8
Tel: 780-427-6236; *Fax:* 780-427-0923

Executive Director, Information Systems, Roger Burns
Tel: 780-644-5065
roger.burns@gov.ab.ca

Operations Division

Petroleum Plaza ST, 9915 - 108 St., 10th Fl., Edmonton, AB T5K 2G8
Tel: 780-427-1335

Assistant Deputy Minister, Graham Statt
Tel: 780-644-4948; *Fax:* 780-422-5141
graham.statt@gov.ab.ca

Executive Director, Infrastructure Branch, David Ardell
Tel: 403-297-5892
dave.ardell@gov.ab.ca

Executive Director, Alberta Environmental Support & Emergency Response Team (ASERT), John Conrad
Tel: 780-422-7669; *Fax:* 780-427-2278
john.conrad@gov.ab.ca

Executive Director, Resilience & Mitigation Branch, Cathy Maniego
Tel: 780-638-3066
cathy.maniego@gov.ab.ca

Executive Regional Director, Red Deer - North Saskatchewan Region, Randall Barrett
Tel: 780-427-0689
randall.barrett@gov.ab.ca

Executive Regional Director, Peace Region, Darcy Beach
Tel: 780-624-6541
darcy.beach@gov.ab.ca

Executive Regional Director, Upper Athabasca Region, George Robertson
Tel: 780-778-7159
george.robertson@gov.ab.ca

Executive Regional Director, Lower Athabasca Region, Terry Zitnak
Tel: 780-623-5379
terry.zitnak@gov.ab.ca

Parks Division

Oxbridge Place, 9820 - 106 St., 2nd Fl., Edmonton, AB T5K 2J6
Tel: 780-427-3582; *Fax:* 780-427-5980
Toll-Free: 866-427-3582

Executive Director, Parks Program Coordination, Steve Donelon
Tel: 780-422-4407; *Fax:* 780-427-5980
steve.donelon@gov.ab.ca

Executive Director, Parks Regional Operations, Robert Hugill
Tel: 403-362-1203
rob.hugill@gov.ab.ca

Policy & Planning Division

Petroleum Plaza ST, 9915 - 108 St., 11th Fl., Edmonton, AB T5K 2G8
Tel: 780-427-1799; *Fax:* 780-415-9669

Assistant Deputy Minister, Shannon Flint
Tel: 780-422-8463; *Fax:* 780-427-0923
shannon.flint@gov.ab.ca

Executive Director, Wildlife Management Branch, Ron Bjorge
Tel: 780-427-9503
ron.bjorge@gov.ab.ca

Executive Director, Planning Branch, Scott Milligan
Tel: 780-422-0672
scott.milligan@gov.ab.ca

Air & Climate Change Policy Branch

Baker Centre, 10025 - 106 St., 12th Fl., Edmonton, AB T5J 1G4

Executive Director, Kate Rich
Tel: 780-644-5290; *Fax:* 780-415-1718
kathleen.rich@gov.ab.ca

Fish & Wildlife Policy Branch

Great West Life Bldg., 9920 - 108 St., 2nd Fl., Edmonton, AB T5K 2M4
Tel: 780-427-5185; *Fax:* 780-422-9559

Executive Director, Travis Ripley
Tel: 780-427-7763
travis.ripley@gov.ab.ca

Land & Forestry Policy Branch

Oxbridge Pl., 9820 - 106 St., 10th Fl., Edmonton, AB T5K 2J6

Executive Director, Kem Singh
Tel: 780-427-7012; *Fax:* 780-422-4192
kem.singh@gov.ab.ca

Policy Integration Branch

Oxbridge Pl., 9820 - 106 St., 10th Fl., Edmonton, AB T5K 2J6

Executive Director, Heather von Hauff
Tel: 780-643-9369; *Fax:* 780-422-4192
heather.vonhauff@gov.ab.ca

Water Policy Branch

Oxbridge Pl., 9820 - 106 St., 7th Fl., Edmonton, AB T5K 2J6
Tel: 780-644-4959; *Fax:* 780-644-4955

Executive Director, Andy Ridge
Tel: 780-638-4198
andy.ridge@gov.ab.ca

Policy Management Office

Petroleum Plaza ST, 9915 - 108 St., 8th Fl., Edmonton, AB T5K 2G6

Assistant Deputy Minister, Al Sanderson
Tel: 780-422-6656; *Fax:* 780-427-7737
al.sanderson@gov.ab.ca

Executive Director, Policy & Regulatory Alignment, Wade Clark
Tel: 780-427-7426
wade.clark@gov.ab.ca

Executive Director, Policy Systems & Engagement, Lori Enns
Tel: 780-427-3607
lori.enns@gov.ab.ca

Strategy Division

Petroleum Plaza ST, 9915 - 108 St., 11th Fl., Edmonton, AB T5K 2G8

Assistant Deputy Minister, Rick Blackwood
Tel: 780-427-1139; *Fax:* 780-415-9669
rick.blackwood@gov.ab.ca

Executive Director, Strategy Development & Foresight, Cam Lane
Tel: 780-427-9451
cam.lane@gov.ab.ca

Executive Director, Strategic Relationships & Engagement, Robert Stokes
Tel: 780-422-2690
robert.stokes@gov.ab.ca

Land Use Secretariat

Centre West Building, 10035 - 108 St., Edmonton, AB T5J 3E1
Tel: 780-644-7972; *Fax:* 780-644-1034
luf@gov.ab.ca
www.landuse.alberta.ca

The Land Use Secretariat is a leader in the implementation of Alberta's Land-use Framework. The Secretariat assists regional advisory councils in offering advice to government about developing regional plans.

Stewardship Commissioner, Rick Blackwood
Tel: 780-427-1139; *Fax:* 780-415-9669
rick.blackwood@gov.ab.ca

Executive Director, Crystal Damer
Tel: 780-644-5014; *Fax:* 780-644-1034
crystal.damer@gov.ab.ca

Alberta Office of the Ethics Commissioner

#1250, 9925 - 109 St. NW, Edmonton, AB T5K 2J8
Tel: 780-422-2273; *Fax:* 780-422-2261
generalinfo@ethicscommissioner.ab.ca
www.ethicscommissioner.ab.ca

Established in 1992, the Office of the Ethics Commissioner for the Province of Alberta is engaged in the promotion of public confidence in the ethics of each Member of the Legislative Assembly. The Hon. Marguerite Trussler, Q.C., is Alberta's fourth Ethics Commissioner & was officially sworn in on June 4, 2014.

Alberta Ethics Commissioner, Marguerite Trussler, Q.C.

Chief Administrative Officer, Kent Ziegler
Tel: 780-422-4974; *Fax:* 780-422-2261
kziegler@ethicscommissioner.ab.ca

Registrar, Lobbyists Act, & General Counsel, Lana Robins
Tel: 780-644-3879; *Fax:* 780-422-2261
lrobins@ethicscommissioner.ab.ca

Alberta Health

PO Box 1360 Stn. Main, Edmonton, AB T5J 2N3
Tel: 780-427-7164
Toll-Free: -310-0000
TTY: 800-232-7215
www.health.alberta.ca
twitter.com/goahealth
www.flickr.com/photos/albertahealth

Formerly Alberta Health & Wellness, Alberta Health is involved in the following activities: establishing legislation, policy, & standards; supporting the health system; allocating resources; & administering provincial programs.

In 2012, Alberta Health absorbed elements of the former Alberta Seniors. In 2014, Premier Jim Prentice made Seniors a separate department again.

Minister, Health, Hon. Sarah Hoffman
Tel: 780-427-3665; *Fax:* 780-415-0961
health.minister@gov.ab.ca

Associate Minister, Health, Hon. Brandy Payne
Tel: 780-427-3665; *Fax:* 780-415-0961

Deputy Minister, Carl Amrhein
Tel: 780-422-0747; *Fax:* 780-427-1016
carl.amrhein@gov.ab.ca

Chief Addiction & Mental Health Officer, Dr. Michael Trew
Tel: 780-641-8639

Chief Delivery Officer, Glenn Monteith
Tel: 780-415-2745
glenn.monteith@gov.ab.ca

Executive Director, Alberta Mental Health Review, Sandra Klashinsky
Tel: 780-427-7242
sandra.klashinsky@gov.ab.ca

Director, Executive Correspondence & Issues Management Unit, Monica Ulmer
Tel: 780-638-4562; *Fax:* 780-427-1851
monica.ulmer@gov.ab.ca

Senior Medical Advisor, Dr. Alan Casson
Tel: 780-644-1450; *Fax:* 780-638-3811
alan.casson@gov.ab.ca

Senior Nursing Advisor, Dr. Valerie Grdisa
Tel: 780-427-5488; *Fax:* 780-638-3811
valerie.grdisa@gov.ab.ca

Associated Agencies, Boards & Commissions:

•Alberta Health Advocates (AHA)
Centre West Bldg.
10035 - 108 St., 12th Fl.
Edmonton, AB T5J 3E1
Tel: 780-422-1812; *Fax:* 780-422-0695
Toll-free: -310-0000
healthadvocates@gov.ab.ca
www.albertahealthadvocates.ca
The Office of the Health Advocate opened April 1, 2014, & is divided into three divisions: Health, Mental Health (created in 1990) & Seniors.

•Alberta Health Services (AHS)
Corporate Office, North Tower, Seventh Street Plaza
10030 - 107th St. NW, 14th Fl.
Edmonton, AB T5J 3E4
Tel: 780-342-2000; *Fax:* 780-342-2060
Toll-free: 888-342-2471
ahs.corp@albertahealthservices.ca
www.albertahealthservices.ca
Other Communication: Board Office, Phone: 866-943-1120; Fax: 403-943-1124, E-mail: ahs.board@ahs.ca
Alberta Health Services was established in 2008, & became operational in 2009. The provincial health authority plans & delivers health services throughout Alberta. In December 2013, plans were finalized to privatize all diagnostic lab services in Edmonton.

•Health Quality Council of Alberta (HQCA)
#210, 811 - 14 St. NW
Calgary, AB T2N 2A4
Tel: 403-297-8162; *Fax:* 403-297-8258
info@hqca.ca
www.hqca.ca
Other Communication: Edmonton Office, Phone: 780-429-3008, Fax: 780-429-0985
The Health Quality Council of Alberta is legislated under the Regional Health Authorities Act. The Council's responsibilities are set forth in the Health Quality Council of Alberta Regulation. The independent organization strives to improve the health service quality, patient safety, & performance of the health system in Alberta.

Office of the Chief Medical Officer of Health (OCMOH)
ATB Place, 10025 Jasper Ave., 24th Fl., Edmonton, AB T5J 1S6
Tel: 780-427-5263
The Office of the Chief Medical Officer of Health offers guidelines to Alberta Health Services about public health policy. The Office also provides information to the public about communicable diseases & public health programs.
The Chief Medical Officer of Health works under the authority of the Public Health Act to promote & protect the health of the people of Alberta.
Chief Medical Officer of Health, Dr. Karen Grimsrud
Tel: 780-641-8638; *Fax:* 780-427-7683
Deputy Chief Medical Officer of Health, Dr. Martin Lavoie
Tel: 780-644-7557; *Fax:* 780-427-7683
martin.lavoie@gov.ab.ca

Financial & Corporate Services Division
ATB Place, 10025 Jasper Ave., 16th Fl., Edmonton, AB T5J 1S6
Assistant Deputy Minister, Martin Chamberlain, Q.C.
Tel: 780-422-1045; *Fax:* 780-422-3672
martin.chamberlain@gov.ab.ca
Executive Director, Corporate Services, Stephen Arthur
Tel: 780-415-0201; *Fax:* 780-427-1643
stephen.arthur@gov.ab.ca
Executive Director, Health Facilities Planning, Wayne Campbell
Tel: 780-638-3546; *Fax:* 780-422-3672
wayne.campbell@gov.ab.ca
Executive Director, Human Resources, Marina Christopherson
Tel: 780-641-9521; *Fax:* 780-422-1700
marina.christopherson@gov.ab.ca
Executive Director, Health Economics & Funding Branch, Dee-Jay King
Tel: 780-427-8596; *Fax:* 780-427-1577
dee-jay.king@gov.ab.ca
Acting Executive Director, Financial Planning Branch, Scott McIntyre
Tel: 780-427-6011; *Fax:* 780-422-3672
scott.mcintyre@gov.ab.ca

Health Information Technology & Systems Division
ATB Place, 10025 Jasper Ave., 21st Fl., Edmonton, AB T5J 1S6
Acting Assistant Deputy Minister & Chief Information Officer; Executive Director, Strategic IMT Services Branch, Kim Wieringa
Tel: 780-415-2492; *Fax:* 780-422-5176
kim.wieringa@gov.ab.ca
Executive Director, Information Management Branch, Sue Kessler
Tel: 780-415-2788; *Fax:* 780-422-6663
sue.kessler@gov.ab.ca
Executive Director, Information Technology & Operations, Blaine Steward
Tel: 780-415-1562; *Fax:* 780-644-3091
blaine.steward@gov.ab.ca

Health Services
ATB Place, 10025 Jasper Ave., 18th Fl., Edmonton, AB T5J 1S6
Assistant Deputy Minister, Ruby Brown
Tel: 780-644-7666; *Fax:* 780-415-0570
ruby.brown@gov.ab.ca
Executive Director, Primary Health Care Branch & Addiction & Mental Health Branch, Shannon Berg
Tel: 780-641-9067; *Fax:* 780-427-8055
shannon.berg@gov.ab.ca
Acting Executive Director, Acute Care Branch, Marie Lyle
Tel: 780-415-2780; *Fax:* 780-422-0134
marie.lyle@gov.ab.ca
Executive Director, Wellness Branch, Corinne Parker
Tel: 780-415-2759
corinne.parker@gov.ab.ca
Executive Director, Continuing Care Branch, Corinne Schalm
Tel: 780-644-3621; *Fax:* 780-422-1515
corinne.schalm@gov.ab.ca
Provincial MES Medical Director, Hal Canham
Tel: 780-422-2061
hal.canham@gov.ab.ca

Health System Accountability & Performance Division
ATB Place, 10025 Jasper Ave., 24th Fl., Edmonton, AB T5J 1S6
Assistant Deputy Minister, Linda Mattern
Tel: 780-422-2720; *Fax:* 780-422-3671
linda.mattern@gov.ab.ca
Executive Director, Health Protection, Dawn Friesen
Tel: 780-415-2818; *Fax:* 780-427-1470
dawn.friesen@gov.ab.ca
Executive Director, Health Analytics, Deb Kaweski
Tel: 780-415-0212
deb.kaweski@gov.ab.ca
Executive Director, Surveillance & Assessment, Kathy Ness
Tel: 780-422-2561; *Fax:* 780-427-1470
kathy.ness@gov.ab.ca
Executive Director, Health System Monitoring, John Quince
Tel: 780-415-1505; *Fax:* 780-422-3672
john.quince@gov.ab.ca
Executive Director, Compliance & Monitoring Branch, Cheryl Whitten
Tel: 780-415-2174; *Fax:* 780-415-0963
cheryl.whitten@gov.ab.ca

Professional Services & Health Benefits Division
ATB Place, 10025 Jasper Ave., 10th Fl., Edmonton, AB T5J 1S6
Assistant Deputy Minister, Miin Alikhan
Tel: 780-427-1572; *Fax:* 780-415-8455
miin.alikhan@gov.ab.ca
Executive Director, Workforce Strategy, Health Human Resources Planning & Strategy Branch, Bernard Anderson
Tel: 780-415-2749; *Fax:* 780-415-1094
bernard.anderson@gov.ab.ca
Executive Director, Pharmaceuticals & Supplementary Health Benefits Branch, Michele Evans
Tel: 780-427-8019; *Fax:* 780-422-3646
michele.evans@gov.ab.ca
Executive Director, Provider Compensation & Strategic Partnerships Branch, Maryna Korchagina
Tel: 780-644-8066
maryna.korchagina@gov.ab.ca
Executive Director, Health Insurance Programs Branch, Donna Manuel
Tel: 780-644-3149; *Fax:* 780-644-1445
donna.manuel@gov.ab.ca

Strategic Planning & Policy Development Division
ATB Place, 10025 Jasper Ave., 19th Fl., Edmonton, AB T5J 1S6
Assistant Deputy Minister, Denise Perret
Tel: 780-422-8989
denise.perret@gov.ab.ca
Executive Director, Research & Innovation Branch, Joseph Gebran
Tel: 780-415-0221
joseph.gebran@gov.ab.ca
Acting Executive Director, Strategic Policy Branch; Director, Intergovernmental & Aboriginal Relations, Lyn Bilida
Tel: 780-422-6589
lyn.bilida@gov.ab.ca

Alberta Human Services

Office of the Minister, Legislature Building, #224, 10800 - 97 Ave., Edmonton, AB T5K 2B6
Tel: 780-644-5135
Toll-Free: 866-644-5135
www.humanservices.alberta.ca
Other Communication: Alberta Supports Contact Centre, Toll-Free Phone: 1-877-644-9992; Family Violence Info Line: 310-1818; Bullying Help Line: 1-888-456-2323
twitter.com/ABHumanServices
The Ministry of Human Services was created in 2011, under Premier Redford. The ministry is responsible for programs & services in the following areas: children & youth; employment & immigration; homelessness support; & Alberta Supports.
Children & youth services include the following: adoption, child care & early childhood development, child intervention, family support for children with disabilities, & the prevention of family violence & bullying.
Employment & immigration services oversee Alberta Works, employment standards, labour market information, labour relations, occupational health & safety, & immigration.
Homelessness support is involved in the administration of Alberta's Plan to End Homelessness, the Alberta Secretariat for Action on Homelessness, the Gunn Centre, & emergency shelters.
Alberta Supports includes the Alberta Supports Contact Centre.
As of 2014, Human Services is also responsible for programs relating to persons with disabilities.

Minister, Human Services, Hon. Irfan Sabir
Tel: 780-643-6210; *Fax:* 780-643-6214

Deputy Minister, Human Services, David Morhart
Tel: 780-427-6448
david.morhart@gov.ab.ca

Chief Delivery Officer, Lori Cooper
Tel: 780-644-7520
lori.cooper@gov.ab.ca

Executive Director, Human Resources, Lynn Cook
Tel: 780-427-0441
lynn.cook@gov.ab.ca

Associated Agencies, Boards & Commissions:

•Appeals Secretariat
Centre West Bldg.
10035 - 108 St., 6th Fl.
Calgary, AB T5J 3E1
Tel: 780-427-2709; *Fax:* 780-422-1088
appeals@gov.ab.ca
humanservices.alberta.ca/department/appeals-secretariat.html
Other Communication: Child & Youth/Persons in Care, Phone: 780-644-2513; Persons & Children with Disabilities/Child Care Licensing, Phone: 780-422-2775
Provides appeal options for people in Alberta whose benefits through Assured Income for the Severely Handicapped Act (AISH) or Alberta Works Income Supports (IESA) have been denied, changed or cancelled.

•Persons with Developmental Disabilities Community Boards
Centre West Bldg.
10035 - 108 St., 6th Fl.
Edmonton, AB T5J 3E1
Tel: 780-422-2775
Toll-free: -310-0000
humanservices.alberta.ca/disability-services/pdd.html
Six Persons with Developmental Disabilities Community Boards were established by the Persons with Developmental Disabilities Community Governance Act. The boards deliver supports to adults with developmental disabilities. The following services are funded by the program: community living supports for persons in their home environment; employment supports to educate & train individuals; community access supports; & specialized community supports.

•Premier's Council on the Status of Persons with Disabilities
HSBC Building
#1110, 10055 - 106 St.
Edmonton, AB T5J 1G3
Tel: 780-422-1095; *Fax:* 780-415-0097
Toll-free: 800-272-8841
hs.pcspd@gov.ab.ca
humanservices.alberta.ca/department/premiers-council.html
Established in 1988, the mandate for the Premier's Council on the Status of Persons with Disabilities is outlined in the Premier's Council on the Status of Persons with Disabilities Act. The Premier's Council consists of up to fifteen volunteer members who communicate the concerns of Alberta's disability community to the provincial government.

•Social Care Facilities Review Committee
Sterling Place
9940 - 106 St., 3rd Fl.
Edmonton, AB T5K 2N2
humanservices.alberta.ca/department/15042.html
Other Communication: Complaint Line: 780-427-3010

Aboriginal Engagement & Strategy Division
Sterling Place, 9940 - 106 St., 5th Fl., Edmonton, AB T5K 2N2
Assistant Deputy Minister, Gloria Iatridis
Tel: 780-415-2209; *Fax:* 780-422-0562
gloria.iatridis@gov.ab.ca

Child & Family Services Division
Sterling Place, 9940 - 106 St., 10th Fl., Edmonton, AB T5K 2N2
Tel: 780-422-0305; *Fax:* 780-422-5415
Services for Alberta's families & children are delivered from ten Child & Family Services Authorities located in regions throughout the province.
Assistant Deputy Minister, Mark Hattori
Tel: 780-415-1548; *Fax:* 780-422-5415
mark.hattori@gov.ab.ca
Regional Director, Northeast Alberta, Ron Benson
Tel: 780-743-7462; *Fax:* 780-743-7474
ron.benson@gov.ab.ca
Other Communications: Main Phone: 780-743-7416
Children & Youth Services, Northeast Alberta Region, Provincial Building
9915 Franklin Ave., 4th Fl.
Fort McMurray, AB T9H 2K4
Regional Director, Northwest Alberta, Rick Flette
Tel: 780-538-5248; *Fax:* 780-538-5137
rick.flette@gov.ab.ca
Other Communications: Main Phone: 780-538-5122
Children & Youth Services, Northwest Alberta Region, Place South
#214, 10130 - 99th Ave., 4th Fl.
Grande Prairie, AB T8V 2V4
Acting Regional Director, Métis Settlements, Bryan Huygen
Tel: 780-415-0182; *Fax:* 780-415-0177
bryan.huygen@gov.ab.ca
Other Communications: Main Phone: 780-427-1033
Children & Youth Services, Métis Settlement Region, Centurion Plaza
#210, 10335 - 172 St.
Edmonton, AB T5S 1K9
Regional Director, Calgary & Area, Jon Reeves
Tel: 403-297-8076
jon.reeves@gov.ab.ca
Other Communications: Main Phone: 403-297-6100
Children & Youth Services, Calgary & Area Region
1240 Kensington Rd. NW, 2nd Fl.
Calgary, AB T2N 3P7
Regional Director, North Central Alberta, Dr. David Rideout
Tel: 780-305-2435; *Fax:* 780-305-2444
david.rideout@gov.ab.ca
Other Communications: Main Phone: 780-305-2440
Children & Youth Services, North Central Alberta Region, Administrative Building
5143 - 50th St., 2nd Fl.
Barrhead, AB T7N 1A6
Regional Director, Southeast Alberta, Lonnie Slezina
Tel: 403-529-3756; *Fax:* 403-528-5244
Other Communications: Main Phone: 403-529-3753
Children & Youth Services, Southeast Alberta Region, Provincial Building
346 - 3rd St. SE, 1st Fl.
Medicine Hat, A T1A 0G7
Regional Director, Southwest Alberta, Lonnie Slezina
Tel: 403-381-5570; *Fax:* 403-381-5791
lonnie.slezina@gov.ab.ca
www.southwestalbertacfsa.gov.ab.ca
Other Communications: Main Phone: 403-381-5543
Children & Youth Services, Southwest Alberta Region, Lethbridge Centre Tower
#709, 400 - 4th Ave. South
Lethbridge, AB T1J 4E1
Regional Director, Central Alberta, David Tunney
Tel: 403-341-8655; *Fax:* 403-755-6184
david.tunney@gov.ab.ca
www.centralalbertacfsa.gov.ab.ca
Other Communications: Main Phone: 403-341-8642
Children & Youth Services, Central Alberta Region, Bishop's Place
4826 Ross St., 3rd Fl.
Red Deer, AB T4N 1X4
Regional Director, Edmonton & Area, Vacant
Tel: 780-415-2291; *Fax:* 780-422-6864
www.edmontonandareacfsa.gov.ab.ca
Other Communications: Main Phone: 780-422-3355
Children & Youth Services, Edmonton & Area Region, Oxbridge Place
9820 - 106th St., 7th Fl.
Edmonton, AB T5K 2J6

Common Service Access Division
Standard Life Centre, 10405 Jasper Ave., 4th Fl., Edmonton, AB T5J 4R7
Assistant Deputy Minister, Stephen Gauk
Tel: 780-422-7960; *Fax:* 780-638-2821
stephen.gauk@gov.ab.ca
Executive Director, Common Service Transformation Office, Tricia Smith
Tel: 780-643-1308; *Fax:* 780-638-2821
tricia.smith@gov.ab.ca
Executive Director, Common Service Delivery, Chris Wells
Tel: 780-644-1911; *Fax:* 780-415-1667
chris.wells@gov.ab.ca

Corporate Services Division
Standard Life Centre, 10405 Jasper Ave., 2nd Fl., Edmonton, AB T5J 4R7
Tel: 780-638-3560; *Fax:* 780-644-2524
Assistant Deputy Minister, Carol Ann Kushlyk
Tel: 780-422-8550; *Fax:* 780-644-2524
carolann.kushlyk@gov.ab.ca
Acting Executive Director, Corporate Finance & Senior Financial Officer & Director, Financial Services & Accountability, Mahmud Dhala
Tel: 780-427-2190; *Fax:* 780-644-2524
mahmud.dhala@gov.ab.ca
Executive Director, Business Services, Kevin Molcak
Tel: 780-644-1125; *Fax:* 780-427-9376
kevin.molcak@gov.ab.ca

Disability Services Division
Standard Life Centre, 10405 Jasper Ave., 3rd Fl., Edmonton, AB T5J 4R7
Acting Assistant Deputy Minister, Brenda Lee Doyle
Tel: 780-644-2790; *Fax:* 780-427-1689
jillian.carson@gov.ab.ca
Public Trustee, Frances Barbara Martini
Tel: 780-422-3141; *Fax:* 780-422-9136
Public Guardian - Calgary, Graham Badry
Tel: 403-592-4099; *Fax:* 403-297-3427
graham.badry@gov.ab.ca
Public Guardian - Central Region, Betty Lou Bowles
Tel: 403-340-5502; *Fax:* 403-340-7131
bettylou.bowles@gov.ab.ca
Public Guardian - South, Connie MacDonald
Tel: 403-381-5653; *Fax:* 403-381-5774
connie.macdonald@gov.ab.ca
Public Guardian - North, Teresa Overgaard
Tel: 780-645-6252; *Fax:* 780-645-6260
teresa.overgaard@gov.ab.ca
Public Guardian - Edmonton, Shirley Peleshytyk
Tel: 780-427-9950; *Fax:* 780-422-9138
shirley.peleshytyk@gov.ab.ca
Executive Lead, One Disability Initiative, Sheryl Fricke
Tel: 780-415-2221; *Fax:* 780-427-1689
sheryl.fricke@gov.ab.ca

Early Childhood & Community Supports Division
Sterling Place, 9940 - 106 St., 10th Fl., Edmonton, AB T5K 2N2
Tel: 780-427-6428; *Fax:* 780-422-9045
Assistant Deputy Minister, Michele Kirchner
Tel: 780-427-5634; *Fax:* 780-422-9045
michele.kirchner@gov.ab.ca
Executive Director, Early Childhood Development, Suzanne Anselmo
Tel: 780-422-4538; *Fax:* 780-427-1258
suzanne.anselmo@gov.ab.ca
Executive Director, Family & Community Support Services, Ken Dropko
Tel: 780-644-2485; *Fax:* 780-644-2671
ken.dropko@gov.ab.ca
Executive Director, Alberta's Promise Secretariat, Judy Eng-Hum
Tel: 403-297-2599; *Fax:* 403-297-6664
judy.eng-hum@gov.ab.ca
Executive Director, Prevention & Early Intervention Supports, Silvia Vajushi
Tel: 780-638-1266; *Fax:* 780-644-2671
silvia.vajushi@gov.ab.ca

Employment & Financial Supports Division
Milner Bldg., 10040 - 104 St., 12th Fl., Edmonton, AB T5J 0Z2
Tel: 780-427-1245; *Fax:* 780-427-5148
Toll-Free: 866-477-8589
Acting Assistant Deputy Minister, Sherri Wilson
Tel: 780-644-4731; *Fax:* 780-427-5148
sherri.wilson@gov.ab.ca
Executive Director, Business Innovations, Brian Payne
Tel: 780-427-6678; *Fax:* 780-422-6768
brian.payne@gov.ab.ca
Executive Director, Program Policy, David Schneider
Tel: 780-415-9106; *Fax:* 780-422-0032
david.schneider@gov.ab.ca
Executive Director, Assured Income for the Severely Handicapped (AISH) Delivery Services, Vacant
Tel: 780-644-4731
Toll-free: 877-644-9992; *Fax:* 780-644-3299

Family Violence Prevention & Homeless Supports Division
Capital Boulevard, #44, 10044 - 108 St., 3rd Fl., Edmonton, AB T5J 5E6
Tel: 780-643-6648; *Fax:* 780-644-5796
Assistant Deputy Minister, Susan Taylor
Tel: 780-415-8907; *Fax:* 780-644-5796
susan.taylor@gov.ab.ca
Executive Director, Program Policy Integration, Brian Bechtel
Tel: 780-638-1135; *Fax:* 780-427-2039
brian.bechtel@gov.ab.ca
Executive Director, Housing & Homeless Supports, Jason Chance
Tel: 780-643-9477; *Fax:* 780-415-9345
jason.chance@gov.ab.ca
Executive Director, Family & Community Safety, Paulette Rodziewicz
Tel: 403-643-6651; *Fax:* 403-427-2039
paulette.rodziewicz@gov.ab.ca

Planning & Quality Assurance Division
Sterling Place, 9940 - 106 St., 12th Fl., Edmonton, AB T5K 2N2
Assistant Deputy Minister, Tracy Wyrstiuk
Tel: 780-422-9562
tracy.wyrstiuk@gov.ab.ca
Acting Executive Director, Child & Family Services Council for Quality Assurance, Robert Hopkins
Tel: 780-415-9610
robert.hopkins@gov.ab.ca
Other Communications: Council Main Phone: 780-415-0720
Acting Executive Director, Governance Services, Shafana Mitha
Tel: 780-644-2509; *Fax:* 780-644-6880
shafana.mitha@gov.ab.ca
Executive Director, Quality Assurance & Continuous Improvement, Dale Sobkovich
Tel: 780-415-4503; *Fax:* 780-415-5841
dale.sobkovich@gov.ab.ca

Policy & Community Engagement Division
Sterling Place, 9940 - 106 St., 12th Fl., Edmonton, AB T5K 2N2
Assistant Deputy Minister, Vacant
Tel: 780-415-2583
Executive Director, Strategic Policy Initiatives, John Thomson
Tel: 780-643-1157; *Fax:* 780-427-5971
john.thomson@gov.ab.ca

Strategic Technology & Data Integration Division
Standard Life Centre, 10405 Jasper Ave., 8th Fl., Edmonton, AB T5J 4R7
Assistant Deputy Minister, Chi Loo
Tel: 780-422-3179; *Fax:* 780-427-9376
chi.loo@gov.ab.ca
Chief Information Officer, Information & Technology Services, Vicki Ozaruk
Tel: 780-427-8398; *Fax:* 780-427-4310
vicki.ozaruk@gov.ab.ca

Alberta Indigenous Relations

Commerce Place, 10155 - 102 St. NW, 19th Fl., Edmonton, AB T5J 4G8
Tel: 780-427-8407; *Fax:* 780-427-4019
Toll-Free: -310-000
indigenous.alberta.ca
twitter.com/AboriginalRel
www.youtube.com/user/aralberta
Indigenous Relations works with Aboriginal communities & other partners to enhance social & economic opportunities for Alberta's Aboriginal people.
Minister, Indigenous Relations, Hon. Richard Feehan
Tel: 780-422-4144; *Fax:* 780-638-4052
ir.ministeroffice@gov.ab.ca
Deputy Minister, Donavon Young
Tel: 780-643-9081; *Fax:* 780-422-2745
donavon.young@gov.ab.ca
Director, Communications, Jessica L. Johnson
Tel: 780-427-4210; *Fax:* 780-415-9548
jessica.l.johnson@gov.ab.ca

Associated Agencies, Boards & Commissions:

•Métis Settlements Appeal Tribunal (MSAT)
#200, 10335 - 172 St.
Edmonton, AB T5S 1K9
Tel: 780-422-1541; *Fax:* 780-422-0019
Toll-free: 800-661-8864
www.msat.gov.ab.ca

•Northern Alberta Development Council (NADC)
Peace River Office, Provincial Building
#206, 9621 - 96 Ave.
PO Box 900-14
Peace River, AB T8S 1T4
Tel: 780-624-6274; *Fax:* 780-624-6184
Toll-free: -310-0000
nadc.council@gov.ab.ca
www.nadc.ca
Other Communication: Bursary Information, E-mail: nadc.bursary@gov.ab.ca
The Northern Alberta Development Council focuses on the advancement of the northern economy. The Council is engaged in projects involving tourism, transportation, educational initiatives, value-added agriculture, & inter-jurisdictional projects.

Consultation & Land Claims
Commerce Place, 10155 - 102 St., 20th Fl., Edmonton, AB T5J 4G8
Tel: 780-427-0417; *Fax:* 780-427-0401
Assistant Deputy Minister, Stan Rutwind, Q.C.
Tel: 780-643-1731; *Fax:* 780-427-0401
stan.rutwind@gov.ab.ca
Executive Director, Aboriginal Consultation, Lawrence Aimoe
Tel: 780-644-1036; *Fax:* 780-427-0401
lawrence.aimoe@gov.ab.ca
Acting Executive Director, Stewardship & Policy Integration, Carcey Hincz
Tel: 780-638-4375; *Fax:* 780-643-1948
carcey.hincz@gov.ab.ca
Director, Land Claims, Steven Andres
Tel: 780-427-6084; *Fax:* 780-427-0401
steven.andres@gov.ab.ca

First Nations & Metis Relations
Commerce Place, 10155 - 102 St., 19th Fl., Edmonton, AB T5J 4G8
Tel: 780-427-8407; *Fax:* 780-427-4019
Assistant Deputy Minister, Clay Buchanan
Tel: 780-422-5925; *Fax:* 780-427-4019
clay.buchanan@gov.ab.ca
Assistant Deputy Minister, Aboriginal Women's Initiatives & Research, Tracy Balash
Tel: 780-638-5656; *Fax:* 780-427-4019
tracy.balash@gov.ab.ca
Assistant Deputy Minister, Strategic Directions, John Donner
Tel: 780-643-3880
john.donner@gov.ab.ca
Executive Director, Métis Relations, Thomas Droege
Tel: 780-427-9431; *Fax:* 780-427-4019
thomas.droege@gov.ab.ca
Executive Director, First Nations Relations, Cynthia Dunnigan
Tel: 780-415-6141; *Fax:* 780-427-1760
cynthia.dunnigan@gov.ab.ca

Policy & Planning
Commerce Place, 10155 - 102 St., 20th Fl., Edmonton, AB T5J 4G8
Tel: 780-644-1119; *Fax:* 780-427-0401
Executive Director, Cameron Henry
Tel: 780-427-2008; *Fax:* 780-427-4019
cameron.henry@gov.ab.ca
Director, Economic Policy & Intergovernmental Relations, Erin McGregor
Tel: 780-644-7707; *Fax:* 780-427-4019
erin.mcgregor@gov.ab.ca
Director, Social Policy, Marnie Robb
Tel: 780-644-4668; *Fax:* 780-427-0401
marnie.robb@gov.ab.ca
Director, Corporate Planning & Research, Ellen Tian
Tel: 780-422-4061; *Fax:* 780-427-0401
ellen.tian@gov.ab.ca

Alberta Office of the Information & Privacy Commissioner

Office of the Information & Privacy Commissioner (Edmonton), #410, 9925 - 109 St., Edmonton, AB T5K 2J8
Tel: 780-422-6860; *Fax:* 780-422-5682
Toll-Free: 888-878-4044
generalinfo@oipc.ab.ca
www.oipc.ab.ca
Other Communication: Calgary Office, Phone: 403-297-2728, Fax: 403-297-2711
Secondary Address: #2460, 801 - 6th Ave. SW
Calgary, AB T2P 3W2
twitter.com/ABoipc
The Information & Privacy Commissioner has offices in Calgary & Edmonton. In Calgary, issues related to the Personal Information Protection Act are addressed. The Edmonton office handles issues under the Freedom of Information & Protection of Privacy Act & the Health Information Act.
Information & Privacy Commissioner, Jill Clayton
Tel: 780-422-6860; *Fax:* 780-422-5682
jclayton@oipc.ab.ca
Assistant Commissioner, LeRoy Brower
Tel: 780-422-7617; *Fax:* 780-422-5682
leroy.brower@gov.ab.ca

Alberta Infrastructure

Infrastructure Building, 6950 - 113 St., Edmonton, AB T6H 5V7
Tel: 780-415-0507; *Fax:* 780-427-2187
Toll-Free: -310-0000
Infra.Contact.Us.m@gov.ab.ca
www.infrastructure.alberta.ca
The Ministry supports the provision of well-designed, high-quality public infrastructure for the people of Alberta.
Minister, Infrastructure, Hon. Brian Mason
Tel: 780-427-5041; *Fax:* 780-422-2722
infrastructure.minister@gov.ab.ca
Deputy Minister, Vacant
Tel: 780-427-3835; *Fax:* 780-422-6565
Executive Director, Human Resources Branch, Susan Tanghe
Tel: 780-644-3579
susan.tanghe@gov.ab.ca
Executive Director, Strategic Partnerships Division, Neil Kjelland
Tel: 780-415-1028
neil.kjelland@gov.ab.ca

Corporate Strategies & Services Division
Infrastructure Bldg., 6950 - 113 St., 2nd Fl., Edmonton, AB T6H 5V7
Assistant Deputy Minister, David Breakwell
Tel: 780-415-1599; *Fax:* 780-643-0803
david.breakwell@gov.ab.ca
Executive Director, Strategic Services Branch, Cynthia Evans
Tel: 780-644-1833
cynthia.evans@gov.ab.ca
Executive Director & Senior Financial Officer, Finance Branch, Faye McCann
Tel: 780-644-8774; *Fax:* 780-643-0803
faye.mccann@gov.ab.ca

Health & Government Facilities Division
Infrastructure Building, 6950 - 113 St., 2nd Fl., Edmonton, AB T6H 5V7
Assistant Deputy Minister, Andrew Sharman
Tel: 780-641-9080
andrew.sharman@gov.ab.ca
Executive Director, Health Facilities Branch, Vince Farmer
Tel: 780-644-2739
vince.farmer@gov.ab.ca
Executive Director, Government Facilities, Neil McFarlane
Tel: 780-422-7554; *Fax:* 780-422-9749
neil.mcfarlane@gov.ab.ca
Executive Director, Technical Services Branch, Krista Berezowski
Tel: 780-641-9352; *Fax:* 780-422-7479
krista.berezowski@gov.ab.ca

Learning Facilities Division
Infrastructure Building, 6950 - 113 St., 2nd Fl., Edmonton, AB T6H 5V7
Assistant Deputy Minister, Brian Fedor
Tel: 780-422-0616
brian.fedor@gov.ab.ca
Executive Director, Learning Facilities Branch, Roy Roth
Tel: 780-643-1080
roy.roth@gov.ab.ca

Properties Division
Infrastructure Building, 6950 - 113 St., 3rd Fl., Edmonton, AB T6H 5V7
Tel: 780-427-3881
Assistant Deputy Minister, Dave Bentley
Tel: 780-422-7489
dave.bentley@gov.ab.ca
Executive Director, Reality Services Branch, Tracy Hayden
Tel: 780-641-9635
tracy.hayden@gov.ab.ca
Executive Director, Asset Management Branch, Jason Nault
Tel: 780-643-6737
jason.nault@gov.ab.ca
Executive Director, Property Management Branch, Leonid Oukrainski
Tel: 780-422-4606
leonid.oukrainski@gov.ab.ca
Director, Land Services, Richard Landry
Tel: 780-427-0695
richard.landry@gov.ab.ca

Alberta Justice & Solicitor General

Communications, Bowker Building, 9833 - 109 St., 5th Fl., Edmonton, AB T5K 2E8
Tel: 780-427-2745
Toll-Free: -310-0000
justice.alberta.ca
twitter.com/AlbertaJSG
www.facebook.com/AlbertaSafeCommunities
www.youtube.com/user/absolgen
In 2012, then-Premier Alison Redford announced the creation of the Ministry of Justice & Solicitor General, through the merger of Alberta Solicitor General & Public Security with Alberta Justice. The mission of Alberta Justice & Solicitor General is to provide a fiar & safe province. Its core businesses are as follows: promoting safe communities for the people of Alberta; facilitating access to justice; & providing legal & strategic services to government.
Minister, Justice; Solicitor General, Hon. Kathleen Ganley
Tel: 780-427-2339; *Fax:* 780-422-6621
Deputy Minister, Justice; Deputy Attorney General, Philip Bryden
Tel: 780-427-5032
philip.bryden@gov.ab.ca
Executive Director, Policy & Planning Services Branch, Matthew Barker
Tel: 780-643-6845
matthew.barker@gov.ab.ca
Executive Director, Human Resources, Vacant

Associated Agencies, Boards & Commissions:

•Alberta Human Rights Commission
Northern Regional Office, Standard Life Centre
#800, 10405 Jasper Ave.
Edmonton, AB T5J 4R7
Tel: 780-427-7661; *Fax:* 780-427-6013
Toll-free: 800-232-7215
humanrights@gov.ab.ca
www.albertahumanrights.ab.ca
Other Communication: Education & Community Services, Phone: 403-297-8407
The Alberta Human Rights Act established the Alberta Human Rights Commission. In accordance with the Alberta Human Rights Act, the Commission works to foster equality & to reduce discrimination.
The address of the Alberta Human Rights Commission's Southern Regional Office is as follows: J.J. Bowlen Building, #200, 620 - 7 Ave. SW, Calgary, AB T2P 0Y8. The confidential inquiry line for the Southern Regional Office is 403-297-6571. TTY service is also available for persons who are deaf or hard of hearing. The TTY number in Calgary is 403-297-5639. The fax number for the Southern Regional Office is 403-297-6567.

•Alberta Review Board
Oxford Tower
#1120, 10235 - 101 St.
Edmonton, AB T5J 3E9
Tel: 780-422-5994; *Fax:* 780-427-1762
The Alberta Review Board is composed of nine members who are appointed by the Lieutenant Governor in Council.
The Board is responsible for making or reviewing dispositions about any accused person for whom one of the following verdicts is rendered: unfit to stand trial, or not criminally responsible because of mental disorder. The Alberta Review Board also determines whether a person is subject to a detention order, a conditional discharge, or an absolute discharge.

•Criminal Injuries Review Board (CIRB)
#1502, 10025 - 102A Ave.
Edmonton, AB T5J 2Z2
Tel: 780-427-7330; *Fax:* 780-427-7347
Established in 1997, the Criminal Injuries Review Board operates as an autonomous body, in accordance with the Victims of Crime Act. Members of the Board are appointed by the Lieutenant Governor in Council, as recommended by the Minister. They review the decisions of the Director of Victims of Crime Financial Benefits Program, or his or her designate.

•Fatality Review Board
4070 Bowness Rd. NW
Calgary, AB T3B 3R7
Tel: 403-297-8123; *Fax:* 403-297-3429
The Lieutenant Governor in Council appoints the members of the Fatality Review Board. The board consists of the chief medical examiner, a physician, a lawyer, & a layperson.
The Fatality Review Board reviews deaths investigated by the Office of the Chief Medical Examiner & makes recommendations to the Minister of Justice & Solicitor General about whether or not a public fatality inquiry should take place in order to prevent similar deaths in the future.

•Law Enforcement Review Board (LERB)
City Centre Place
#1502, 10025 - 102A Ave.
Edmonton, AB T5J 2Z2
Tel: 780-422-9376; *Fax:* 780-422-4782
lerb@gov.ab.ca
Established under Alberta's Police Act, the Law Enforcement Review Board conducts its business as an independent, quasi-judicial organization. Members of the Board are appointed by the Lieutenant Governor in Council as recommended by the Minister. They are charged with the responsibility of reviewing public complaints about the conduct of police officers & appeals by police officers.

Corporate Services Division
Bowker Building, 9833 - 109 St., 2nd Fl., Edmonton, AB T5K 2E8
Assistant Deputy Minister, Gerald Lamoureux
Tel: 780-427-3301
gerald.lamoureux@gov.ab.ca
Executive Director, Alberta First Responders Radio Communication Sytstem (AFRRCS), Vacant
Executive Director, IMTS Service Delivery Branch, Ayaaz Janmohamed
Tel: 780-644-3171
ayaaz.janmohamed@gov.ab.ca
Executive Director, Business Services Branch, Michael Michalski
Tel: 780-427-7516
michael.michalski@gov.ab.ca
Executive Director, Project Support Office, Gail Thomsen
Tel: 780-644-8417
gail.thomsen@gov.ab.ca
Executive Director & Senior Financial Officer, Financial Management Branch, Brad Wells
Tel: 780-415-1946
brad.wells@gov.ab.ca

Correctional Services Division
John E. Brownlee Building, 10365 - 97 St., 10th Fl., Edmonton, AB T5J 3W7
The following branches make up the Correctional Services Division: adult centre operations; community corrections & release program; strategic services; & young offenders.
Assistant Deputy Minister, Kim Sanderson
Tel: 780-427-3440; *Fax:* 780-427-5905
kim.sanderson@gov.ab.ca
Executive Director, Young Offender Branch, Judith Barlow
Tel: 780-422-5019; *Fax:* 780-422-0732
judith.barlow@gov.ab.ca
Executive Director, Strategic Services Branch, Fiona Lavoy
Tel: 780-644-2092
fiona.lavoy@gov.ab.ca
Executive Director, Community Corrections & Release Programs, Joanne Panasiuk
Tel: 780-427-3154
joanne.panasiuk@gov.ab.ca
Executive Director, Adult Centre Operations Branch, Wayne Reddon
Tel: 780-427-3644
wayne.reddon@gov.ab.ca

Crown Prosecution Service Division
Bowker Building, 9833 - 109 St., 2nd Fl., Edmonton, AB T5K 2E8
Assistant Deputy Minister, Eric Tolppanen
Tel: 780-427-5046; *Fax:* 780-422-9639
eric.tolppanen@gov.ab.ca
Executive Director, Specialized Prosecutions (Edmonton), Sheila Brown, Q.C.
Tel: 780-422-0640; *Fax:* 780-422-1217
sheila.brown@gov.ab.ca
John E. Brownlee Building
10365 - 97 St., 5th Fl.
Edmonton, AB T5J 3W7
Executive Director, Strategic & Business Services, Peter Teasdale, Q.C.
Tel: 780-427-5050; *Fax:* 780-988-7639
peter.teasdale@gov.ab.ca
Executive Director, Appeals, Education, & Prosecution Policy Branch, Josh Hawkes, Q.C.
Tel: 403-297-6005; *Fax:* 403-297-3453
josh.hawkes@gov.ab.ca
Centrium Place
#300, 332 - 6th Ave. SW
Calgary, AB T2P 0B2
Assistant Executive Director, Specialized Prosecutions (Calgary), Brian Holtby, Q.C.
Tel: 403-297-8477; *Fax:* 403-355-4518
brian.holtby@gov.ab.ca
Centrium Place
#300, 332 - 6th Ave. SW
Calgary, AB T2P 0B2

Justice Services Division
Bowker Building, 9833 - 109 St., 2nd Fl., Edmonton, AB T5K 2E8
The Justice Services Division oversees claims & recoveries, the maintenance enforcement program, & the Medical Examiner's Office.
Assistant Deputy Minister, Rae-Ann Lajeunesse
Tel: 780-638-4618
rae-ann.lajeunesse@gov.ab.ca
Executive Director, Claims & Recoveries, Suzanne Harbottle
Tel: 780-427-8255
suzanne.harbottle@gov.ab.ca
Sun Life Building
10123 - 99 St., 6th Fl.
Edmonton, AB T5J 3H1
Executive Director, Specialized Programs & Divisional Strategy Branch, Leslie Noel
Tel: 780-415-1953
leslie.noel@gov.ab.ca
Sun Life Building
10123 - 99 St., 6th Fl.
Edmonton, AB T5J 3H1
Executive Director, Maintenance Enforcement Program, David Peace
Tel: 780-422-5555; *Fax:* 780-401-7575
david.peace@gov.ab.ca
www.justice.gov.ab.ca/mep
Other Communications: MEP E-mail: albertamep@gov.ab.ca
John E. Brownlee Building
10365 - 97 St., 7th Fl.
Edmonton, AB T5J 3W7
Chief Medical Examiner, Dr. Jeffery Gofton
Tel: 403-297-8213; *Fax:* 403-297-3429
jeffery.gofton@gov.ab.ca
4070 Bowness Rd. NW
Calgary, AB T3B 3R7
Chief Toxicologist, Graham Jones
Tel: 780-427-4987; *Fax:* 780-422-1265
graham.jones@gov.ab.ca
7007 - 116 St.
Edmonton, AB T6H 5R8
Property Rights Advocate, Lee Cutforth
Tel: 403-388-1781; *Fax:* 403-388-1788
lee.cutforth@gov.ab.ca
Provincial Bldg.
200 - 5th Ave. South
Lethbridge, AB T1J 4L1
Access & Privacy Officer, Dana R. Johnson
Tel: 780-427-4987; *Fax:* 780-422-4063
dana.r.johnson@gov.ab.ca
7007 - 116 St.
Edmonton, AB T6H 5R8

Legal Services Division
Bowker Building, 9833 - 109 St., 2nd Fl., Edmonton, AB T5K 2E8
Tel: 780-422-0500
The following branches are part of the Legal Services Division: divisional planning & management; government client services; & legal policy & ministerial services.
Assistant Deputy Minister, Frank Bosscha
Tel: 780-643-1352; *Fax:* 780-422-9639
frank.bosscha@gov.ab.ca
Executive Director, Corporate Legal Services, R. Neil Dunne, Q.C.
Tel: 780-422-8787; *Fax:* 780-425-0307
r.neil.dunne@gov.ab.ca
Executive Director, Departmental Legal Services Delivery, Government Client Services Branch, Barbara Mason
Tel: 780-427-9618; *Fax:* 780-425-0310
barb.mason@gov.ab.ca
Executive Director, Legal Services Coordination, Government Client Services Branch, Lorne Merryweather, Q.C.
Tel: 780-422-9501; *Fax:* 780-427-1230
lorne.merryweather@gov.ab.ca
Executive Director, Legal Policy & Ministerial Services Branch, Nolan Steed, Q.C.
Tel: 780-422-9653; *Fax:* 780-425-0307
nolan.steed@gov.ab.ca
Executive Director, Departmental Legal Services Delivery, Government Client Services Branch, Rita Sumka
Tel: 780-422-3715; *Fax:* 780-427-5914
rita.sumka@gov.ab.ca
Chief Legislative Counsel, Legislative Counsel Office, Peter Pagano, Q.C.
Tel: 780-427-0303; *Fax:* 780-422-7366
peter.pagano@gov.ab.ca

Public Security Division
John E. Brownlee Building, 10365 - 97 St., 10th Fl., Edmonton, AB T5J 3W7
The following branches are part of the Public Security Division: commercial vehicle enforcement; fish & wildlife enforcement; law enforcement & oversight; parks enforcement; policy & program development; & sheriffs branch. The division is also responsible for the Alberta Serious Incident Response Team.
Assistant Deputy Minister, Bill Sweeney
Tel: 780-427-3457; *Fax:* 780-427-1194
bill.sweeney@gov.ab.ca
Chief Fish & Wildlife Officer, Fish & Wildlife Enforcement Branch, Daniel Boyco
Tel: 780-427-2372; *Fax:* 780-422-9560
daniel.boyco@gov.ab.ca
Great West Life Building
9920 - 108 St., 3rd Fl.
Edmonton, AB T5K 2M4
Chief, Commercial Vehicle Enforcement Branch, Steve Callahan
Tel: 403-340-5225; *Fax:* 403-340-5074
steve.callahan@gov.ab.ca
Provincial Building
4920 - 51 St., 4th Fl.
Red Deer, AB T4N 6K8
Executive Director, Policy & Program Development Branch, Kathy Collins
Tel: 780-427-7051; *Fax:* 780-422-4213
kathy.collins@gov.ab.ca
Executive Director, Alberta Serious Incident Response Team (ASIRT), Susan Hughson
Tel: 780-644-1487; *Fax:* 780-644-1497
sue.hughson@gov.ab.ca
Petroleum Plaza
9915 - 108 St., 14th Fl.
Edmonton, AB T5K 2G8
Chief Sheriff / Executive Director, Sheriffs Branch, Lee Newton
Tel: 780-638-1190; *Fax:* 780-422-3365
lee.newton@gov.ab.ca
Oxford Tower
#702, 10025 - 102A Ave.
Edmonton, AB T5J 2Z2
Executive Director, Law Enforcement & Oversight Branch, Gloria Ohrt
Tel: 780-427-6887; *Fax:* 780-427-5916
gloria.ohrt@gov.ab.ca

Resolution & Court Administration Services Division (RCAS)
Brownlee Bldg., 10365 - 97 St., Edmonton, AB T5J 3W7
The Resolution & Court Administration Services Division oversees the Court of Appeal, the Court of Queen's Bench, the Provincial Court, Law Information Centres, & Alberta Law Libraries.
Assistant Deputy Minister, Lynn Varty
Tel: 780-427-9620; *Fax:* 780-422-9639
lynn.varty@gov.ab.ca
Registrar, Court of Appeal, Mary MacDonald
Tel: 780-422-7710; *Fax:* 780-422-7710
mary.macdonald@gov.ab.ca
Law Courts Building South
1A Sir Winston Churchill Sq., 5th Fl.
Edmonton, AB T5J 0R2
Acting Executive Director, Edmonton Law Courts Building, Brenda Haynes
Tel: 780-427-7869
brenda.haynes@gov.ab.ca
Law Courts Building South
1A Sir Winston Churchill Sq., Mezzanine Fl.
Edmonton, AB T5J 0R2
Executive Director, Court of Queen's Bench, Corinne Jamieson
Tel: 403-297-2877; *Fax:* 403-297-8625
corinne.jamieson@gov.ab.ca
Calgary Courts Centre
601 - 5th St. SW
Calgary, AB T2P 5P7
Executive Director, Provincial Court Administration, Sharon Lepetich
Tel: 403-297-2313; *Fax:* 403-297-7152
sharon.lepetich@gov.ab.ca
Calgary Courts Centre
601 - 5th St, SW
Calgary, AB T2P 5P7
Executive Director, Organizational Alignment, Gail Matheson
Tel: 780-644-7652
gail.matheson@gov.ab.ca
Executive Director, Programs & Services, Faye Morrison
Tel: 780-968-3463
faye.morrison@gov.ab.ca

Alberta Labour

Legislature Bldg., #404, 10800 - 97 Ave., Edmonton, AB T5K 2B6

Tel: 780-427-3731
Toll-Free: 877-427-3731
work.alberta.ca
Other Communication: Temporary Foreign Workers, Phone: 780-644-9955; Toll-Free Phone: 1-877-944-9955; Occupational Health & Safety, Phone: 780-415-8690; Toll-Free Phone: 1-866-415-8690
twitter.com/Work_Alberta

The Ministry of Labour is mandated to provide support to both employees & employers, with an emphasis on maintaining safe, fair & healthy workplaces.

Minister, Labour, Hon. Christina Gray
Tel: 780-638-9400; *Fax:* 780-638-9401
Deputy Minister, Jeff Parr
Tel: 780-643-1725; *Fax:* 780-641-9351
jeff.parr@gov.ab.ca
Assistant Deputy Minister, WCB Review Secretariat, Lenore Neudorf
Tel: 780-644-8498
lenore.neudorf@gov.ab.ca
Assistant Deputy Minister, Strategy & Policy Division, Leann Wagner
Tel: 780-643-1348
leann.wagner@gov.ab.ca
Executive Director, Human Resources Branch, Judi Carmichael
Tel: 780-427-2184
judi.carmichael@gov.ab.ca

Associated Agencies, Boards & Commissions:

•Appeals Commission for Alberta Workers' Compensation
#2300, 801 - 6th Ave. SW
Calgary, AB T2P 3W2
Tel: 780-412-8700; *Fax:* 780-412-8701
Toll-free: -310-0000
AC.AcesAdmin@gov.ab.ca
www.appealscommission.ab.ca
Other Communication: Toll-Free Phone Outside Alberta: 1-866-222-4109; Calgary, Phone: 403-508-8800; Fax: 780-508-8822
The Appeals Commission for Alberta Workers' Compensation strives to offer an independent, fair, & timely appeals process. The Commission works to operate consistently with legislation & policy.

•Labour Relations Board (ALRB)
Labour Building
#501, 10808 - 99 Ave.
Edmonton, AB T5K 0G5
Tel: 780-427-8547; *Fax:* 780-422-0970
Toll-free: 800-463-2572
alrbinfo@gov.ab.ca
www.alrb.gov.ab.ca
Other Communication: Calgary Phone: 403-297-4334; Fax: 403-297-5884
The independent & impartial tribunal is involved in the application & interpretation of labour lawa in Alberta. The Alberta Labour Relations Board administers the Labour Relations Code to handle disputes between trade unions & employers.

•Occupational Health & Safety Council (OHSC)
Standard Life Centre
10405 Jasper Ave.
Edmonton, AB T5J 3N4
Tel: 780-412-8742; *Fax:* 780-412-8701
work.alberta.ca/occupational-health-safety/6446.html
Under the Occupational Health & Safety Act, the Occupational Health & Safety Council advises the Minister about matters related to the health & safety of Alberta's workers. Nine members serve on the Council, including the chair & representatives from employers, employees, & the public.

•Workers' Compensation Board (WCB)
9912 - 107 St.
PO Box 2415
Edmonton, AB T5J 2S5
Tel: 780-498-3999; *Fax:* 780-427-5863
Toll-free: 866-922-9221
TTY: 780-498-7895
www.wcb.ab.ca
Other Communication: Calgary, Phone: 403-517-6000; Toll-Free Phone, outside Alberta: 1-800-661-9608; Claims, Toll-Free Fax: 1-800-661-1993
The independent organization manages workers' compensation insurance, based on legislation. The Alberta Workers' Compensation Board compensates injured workers for costs such as lost income & health care.

Corporate Services & Information

Labour Bldg., 10808 - 99 Ave., 9th Fl., Edmonton, AB T5K 0G5

Assistant Deputy Minister, Melissa Banks
Tel: 780-415-0632
melissa.banks@gov.ab.ca
Executive Director, Finance & Administration, Shelley Engstrom
Tel: 780-427-0034
shelley.engstrom@gov.ab.ca
Executive Director, Information Management & Information Technology, Stacey Shenfield
Tel: 780-641-9340
stacy.shenfield@gov.ab.ca

Safe, Fair & Healthy Workplaces Division

Labour Bldg., 10808 - 99 Ave., 10th Fl., Edmonton, AB T5K 0G5

Tel: 780-644-1500; *Fax:* 780-643-1392
Assistant Deputy Minister, Brent McEwan
Tel: 780-643-1391; *Fax:* 780-643-1392
brent.mcewan@gov.ab.ca
Executive Director, Employment Standards Program Delivery, Darren Caul
Tel: 780-422-5932; *Fax:* 780-644-5424
darren.caul@gov.ab.ca
Executive Director, Occupational Health & Safety Program Delivery, Rob Feagan
Tel: 780-415-0603; *Fax:* 780-644-1508
rob.feagan@gov.ab.ca
Executive Director, Mediation Services, Bertha Greenstein
Tel: 780-415-0530; *Fax:* 780-427-6327
bertha.greenstein@gov.ab.ca
Executive Director, Occupational Health & Safety Policy & Program Development, Ross Nairne
Tel: 780-644-8672; *Fax:* 780-422-0014
ross.nairne@gov.ab.ca
Executive Director, Workplace Policy, Legislation & Program Development, Tim Thompson
Tel: 780-415-0527; *Fax:* 780-422-0014
tim.thompson@gov.ab.ca

Workforce Strategies Division

Labour Bldg., 10808 - 99 Ave., 10th Fl., Edmonton, AB T5K 0G5

Tel: 780-638-3138; *Fax:* 780-422-2889
Assistant Deputy Minister, Maryann Everett
Tel: 780-422-9493; *Fax:* 780-422-2889
maryann.everett@gov.ab.ca
Executive Director, Labour Qualifications & Mobility, Gosia Cichy-Weclaw
Tel: 780-422-1851; *Fax:* 780-422-6400
gosia.cichy-weclaw@gov.ab.ca
Executive Director, Labour Attraction & Retention, Danielle Comeau
Tel: 780-427-0528; *Fax:* 780-422-0249
danielle.comeau@gov.ab.ca
Executive Director, Policy & Evaluation, Vacant
Executive Director, Workforce Initiatives, Sue Welke
Tel: 780-644-7431
sue.welke@gov.ab.ca
Director, Industry & Workforce Partnerships & Employment Programs, Geoff Perry
Tel: 780-644-8708; *Fax:* 780-638-1168
geoff.perry@gov.ab.ca

Alberta Municipal Affairs

Communications Branch, Commerce Place, 10155 - 102 St., 18th Fl., Edmonton, AB T5J 4L4

Tel: 780-427-2732; *Fax:* 780-422-1419
Toll-Free: -310-0000
www.municipalaffairs.alberta.ca
twitter.com/ABMuniAffairs

In 2011, under then-Premier Redford, the Ministry of Municipal Affairs took on the responsibilities of the former Ministry of Housing & Urban Affairs.
Alberta's Ministry of Municipal Affairs is engaged in the following activities: assisting Alberta's municipalities in the provision of well-managed, accountable local government; managing municipal & library system boards; administering a safety system for the construction & maintenance of equipment & buildings; ensuring safe, affordable, & sustainable housing for Albertans; & assisting urban communities.

Minister, Municipal Affairs, Hon. Danielle Larivee
Tel: 780-427-3744; *Fax:* 780-422-9550
lesser.slavelake@assembly.ab.ca
Deputy Minister, Brad Pickering
Tel: 780-427-4826; *Fax:* 780-422-9561
brad.pickering@gov.ab.ca
Executive Director, Human Resource Services, Rick Nisbet
Tel: 780-422-8681; *Fax:* 780-422-0214
rick.nisbet@gov.ab.ca

Associated Agencies, Boards & Commissions:

•Alberta Emergency Management Agency (AEMA)
2810 - 10303 Jasper Ave.
Edmonton, AB T5J 3N6
Tel: 780-422-9000; *Fax:* 780-644-1044
Toll-free: -310-0000
aema@gov.ab.ca
www.aema.alberta.ca
Other Communication: Alberta Emergency Management Agency Response Readiness Centre, Phone: 1-866-618-2362
The Alberta Emergency Management Agency coordinates organizations, such as government, municipalities, & first responders, which are involved in the prevention, preparedness, & response to emergencies.

•Capital Region Board
Bell Tower
#1100, 10104 - 103 Ave.
Edmonton, AB T5J 0H8
Tel: 780-638-6000; *Fax:* 780-638-6009
www.capitalregionboard.ab.ca
The Government of Alberta established the Capital Region Board in 2008. The Board consists of members from twenty-four participating municipalities. They serve on the following committees: land use; transit; Geographic Information Services; housing; & governance.
The following are the municipalities of the Capital Region Board: Town of Beaumont; Town of Bon Accord; Town of Bruderheim; Town of Calmar; Town of Devon; City of Edmonton; City of Fort Saskatchewan; Town of Gibbons; Lamont County; Town of Lamont; City of Leduc; Leduc County; Town of Legal; Town of Morinville; Parkland County; Town of Redwater; City of St. Albert; City of Spruce Grove; Town of Stony Plain; Strathcona County; Sturgeon County; Village of Thorsby; Village of Wabamun; & the Village of Warburg.

•McCullough Centre
PO Box 130
Gunn, AB T0E 1A0
Tel: 780-967-2221; *Fax:* 780-967-3494
Since 1941, the McCullough Centre (formerly the Gunn Centre) has offered services to disadvantaged men. The Centre provides temporary accommodation & support services to help men reestablish their lives.

•Municipal Government Board (MGB)
Commerce Place
10155 - 102 St., 15th Fl.
Edmonton, AB T5J 4L4
Tel: 780-427-4864; *Fax:* 780-427-0986
Toll-free: -310-0000
mgbmail@gov.ab.ca
www.municipalaffairs.alberta.ca
Operating as an independent & impartial body, the Municipal Government Board decides upon certain appeals & disputes from the Municipal Government Act. Examples of issues dealt with by the Municipal Government Board are as follows: disputes between municipalities; annexation matters; linear property assessment complaints; & appeals about equalized assessment & subdivisions.

•Safety Codes Council (SCC)
#1000, 10665 Jasper Ave. NW
Edmonton, AB T5J 3S9
Tel: 780-413-0099; *Fax:* 780-424-5134
Toll-free: 888-413-0099
sccinfo@safetycodes.ab.ca
www.safetycodes.ab.ca
The Safety Codes Council is a corporation that supports the Ministry of Municipal Affairs' administration of the Safety Codes Act. The Council has the following business units: Accreditation & Appeals; Administration; Certification & Policy; Electronic Business Solutions; & Training.

•Special Areas Board
Special Areas Board Administration
212 - 2nd Ave. West
PO Box 820
Hanna, AB T0J 1P0
Tel: 403-854-5600; *Fax:* 403-854-5527
www.specialareas.ab.ca
Other Communication: Hanna, Phone: 403-854-5625; Oyen, Phone: 403-664-3618, Fax: 403-664-3320; Consort, Phone: 403-577-3523, Fax: 403-577-2446; Youngstown, Phone: 403-779-3733
The Special Areas Board is responsible for the management of public land in Alberta's three Special Areas. The Board also provides municipal services to eastern Alberta's dryland region. The following are examples of programs & services offered by the Special Areas Board: protective & emergency services; construction & maintenance of local roads; provision of water services; management of public land; operation & maintenance of Special Areas recreational parks & community pastures; conservation programming; agricultural development; & economic development programs.

Corporate Strategic Services Division
Assistant Deputy Minister, Anthony Lemphers
Tel: 780-415-9099; *Fax:* 780-422-4923
anthony.lemphers@gov.ab.ca
Executive Director & Senior Financial Officer, Financial Services, Dan Balderston
Tel: 780-644-8098; *Fax:* 780-422-5840
dan.balderston@gov.ab.ca
Executive Director, Corporate Planning & Policy, Indira Breitkreuz
Tel: 780-422-7317; *Fax:* 780-422-4923
indira.breitkreuz@gov.ab.ca
Manager, Flood Recovery Unit, Jess Kevan
Tel: 780-644-1010
kevan.jess@gov.ab.ca
Director & Chief Information Officer, Information Technology, Heather Cox
Tel: 780-427-6097; *Fax:* 780-422-0776
heather.cox@gov.ab.ca

Municipal Assessment & Grants Division
Commerce Place, 10155 - 102 St., 15th Fl., Edmonton, AB T5J 4L4
Assistant Deputy Minister, Meryl Whittaker
Tel: 780-427-9660; *Fax:* 780-427-0453
meryl.whittaker@gov.ab.ca
Executive Director, Grants & Education Property Tax Branch, Janice Romanyshyn
Tel: 780-415-0833; *Fax:* 780-644-2114
janice.romanyshyn@gov.ab.ca
Executive Director, Assessment Services Branch, Steve White
Tel: 780-422-1377; *Fax:* 780-422-3110
steve.white@gov.ab.ca

Municipal Services & Legislation Division
Commerce Place, 10155 - 102 St., 17th Fl., Edmonton, AB T5J 4L4
Assistant Deputy Minister, Gary Sandberg
Tel: 780-422-8034; *Fax:* 780-420-1016
gary.sandberg@gov.ab.ca
Executive Director, Municipal Services Branch, Stephanie Clarke
Tel: 780-641-9245; *Fax:* 780-420-1016
stephanie.clarke@gov.ab.ca
Executive Director, Major Legislative Projects & Strategic Planning, Alex Nnamonu
Tel: 780-644-2905; *Fax:* 780-644-4941
alexander.nnamonu@gov.ab.ca

Public Safety Division
Commerce Place, 10155 - 102 St., 16th Fl., Edmonton, AB T5J 4L4
Assistant Deputy Minister, Bruce McDonald
Tel: 780-644-5624; *Fax:* 780-427-2538
bruce.mcdonald@gov.ab.ca
Executive Director, Safety Services Branch, Alex Morrison
Tel: 780-644-1010; *Fax:* 780-427-8686
safety.services@gov.ab.ca
Executive Director & Fire Commissioner, Trent West
Tel: 780-643-0842; *Fax:* 780-415-8663
trent.west@gov.ab.ca
Registrar, New Home Buyers Protection Act; Director, Operations, Monte Krueger
Tel: 780-427-6133; *Fax:* 780-427-2538
monte.krueger@gov.ab.ca

Alberta Office of the Ombudsman

Canadian Western Bank Building, #2800, 10303 Jasper Ave. NW, Edmonton, AB T5J 5C3
Tel: 780-427-2756; *Fax:* 780-427-2759
Toll-Free: 888-455-2756
info@ombudsman.ab.ca
www.ombudsman.ab.ca
Secondary Address: #2560, 801 - 6 Ave. SW
Calgary Regional Office
Calgary, AB T2P 3W2
Alt. Fax: 403-297-5121

As an Officer of the Legislative Assembly of Alberta, the Alberta Ombudsman reports directly to the Legislative Assembly. The Ombudsman carries out his role under the authority of Alberta's Ombudsman Act.
The Alberta Ombudsman operates independently from the Alberta government to investigate & respond to written complaints about unfair treatment from Alberta government authorities, designated professional organizations. The Ombudsman also handles the patient concerns resolution process of Alberta Health Services.
Ombudsman, Peter Hourihan
peter.hourihan@ombudsman.ab.ca
Deputy Ombudsman, Joe Loran
joe.loran@ombudsman.ab.ca
General Counsel, Sandy Hermiston
paul.michna@ombudsman.ab.ca

Alberta Office of the Public Interest Commissioner (PIC)

#2800, 10303 Jasper Ave. NW, Edmonton, AB T5J 5C3
Tel: 780-641-8659; *Fax:* 780-427-2759
Toll-Free: 855-641-8659
info@pic.alberta.ca
yourvoiceprotected.ca
Secondary Address: #2560, 801 - 6th Ave. West
Calgary, AB T2P 3W2
Alt. Fax: 403-297-5121

The Office of the Public Interest Commissioner investigates disclosures of wrongdoing & complaints of reprisals for employees of government ministries, agencies, boards & commissions, & other public entities.
Public Interest Commissioner & Alberta Ombudsman, Peter Hourihan
Tel: 780-641-8659
peter.hourihan@ombudsman.ab.ca
Note: Alberta Ombudsman Peter Hourihan was appointed as the province's first Public Interest Commissioner in April 2013.
Director, Ted Miles
Tel: 780-641-8659
ted.miles@pic.alberta.ca

Alberta Seniors & Housing

PO Box 3100 Edmonton, AB T5J 4W3
Tel: 780-644-9992; *Fax:* 780-422-5954
Toll-Free: 877-644-9992
TTY: 800-232-7215
www.seniors.alberta.ca

Alberta Seniors & Housing is responsible for programming for seniors, as well as housing & community services.
Minister, Hon. Lori Sigurdson
Tel: 780-415-9550; *Fax:* 780-415-9411
seniors.minister@gov.ab.ca
Deputy Minister, Shannon Marchand
Tel: 780-644-2023
shannon.marchand@gov.ab.ca
Executive Director, Human Resources, Liz Kennedy
Tel: 780-408-8443
liz.kennedy@gov.ab.ca

Associated Agencies, Boards & Commissions:

•Seniors Advisory Council for Alberta (SACA)
Standard Life Centre
#600, 10405 Jasper Ave., 6th Fl.
Edmonton, AB T5J 4R7
Tel: 780-422-2321; *Fax:* 780-422-8762
Toll-free: -310-0000
saca@gov.ab.ca
www.seniors.alberta.ca/seniors/SACA.html
The Seniors Advisory Council for Alberta consults with senior citizens & seniors' organizations in communities throughout Alberta. The Council then informs the Government of Alberta, through the Minister of Seniors & Community Supports, about the issues that affect Alberta's seniors.
The Seniors Advisory Council for Alberta is also engaged in planning the Seniors' Week celebration each years, supporting workshops for frontline workers & seniors, & participating in research projects.

Housing Division
44 Capital Blvd., 10044 - 108 St., 3rd Fl., Edmonton, AB T5J 5E6
Tel: 780-422-0122
Other Communication: Rural & Native Mortgage Portfolio, Phone: 780 427-6897
Assistant Deputy Minister, Mike Leathwood
Tel: 780-643-1020; *Fax:* 780-422-5124
mike.leathwood@gov.ab.ca
Executive Director, Housing Funding & Accountability, Robert Lee
Tel: 780-643-1324; *Fax:* 780-427-0418
robert.lee@gov.ab.ca
Executive Director, Stakeholder Relations & Housing Strategies, Dean Lussier
Tel: 780-427-1751; *Fax:* 780-422-5124
dean.lussier@gov.ab.ca
Executive Director, Housing Capital Initiatives, Don Squire
Tel: 780-427-5786; *Fax:* 780-644-7482
don.squire@gov.ab.ca

Seniors Services Division
Standard Life Centre, 10405 Jasper Ave., 6th Fl., Edmonton, AB T5J 4R7
Assistant Deputy Minister, John Cabral
Tel: 780-422-7270; *Fax:* 780-644-7602
john.cabral@gov.ab.ca
Executive Director, Seniors Strategic Planning Branch, Kindy Joseph
Tel: 780-644-8613; *Fax:* 780-422-8762
kindy.joseph@gov.ab.ca
Executive Director, Seniors Program Delivery Branch, Neil McDonald
Tel: 780-422-8522; *Fax:* 780-422-5954
neil.mcdonald@gov.ab.ca

Strategic Services Division
44 Capital Blvd., 10044 - 108 St., 3rd Fl., Edmonton, AB T5J 5E6
Assistant Deputy Minister, MaryAnne Wilkinson
Tel: 780-641-9865; *Fax:* 780-644-5586
maryanne.wilkinson@gov.ab.ca
Chief Information Officer, Chris Kearney
Tel: 780-415-2704; *Fax:* 780-644-5586
chris.kearney@gov.ab.ca
Executive Director, Policy, Planning & Legislative Services Branch, Bree Claude
Tel: 780-638-4115; *Fax:* 780-644-5586
bree.claude@gov.ab.ca
Senior Financial Officer, Financial Services Branch, Darren Baptista
Tel: 780-422-0927; *Fax:* 780-644-5586
darren.baptista@gov.ab.ca

Service Alberta

Government of Alberta, PO Box 1333 Edmonton, AB T5J 2N2
Tel: 780-427-4088
Toll-Free: -310-0000
service.alberta@gov.ab.ca
www.servicealberta.ca
Other Communication: Consumer Information, E-mail: cs@gov.ab.ca; Corporate Registry, E-mail: cr@gov.ab.ca; Land Titles, E-mail: lto@gov.ab.ca; Landlords & Tenants, E-mail: rta@gov.ab.ca
twitter.com/ServiceAlberta
www.facebook.com/youthconsumerchampions

The Ministry of Service Alberta offers information, services & products to Albertans. The following are examples of the ministry's services: delivery of shared services to ministries, such as printing documents & technical support; management of the government's vehicle fleet; administration of the Freedom of Information & Protection of Privacy legislation; provision of licensing & registry services; & enforcement of high standards of consumer protection.
Minister, Service Alberta, Hon. Stephanie McLean
Tel: 780-422-6880; *Fax:* 780-422-2496
Deputy Minister, Tim Grant
Tel: 780-427-1990
tim.grant@gov.ab.ca
Executive Director, Human Resource Services, Dana Thompson
Tel: 780-422-4623
dana.thompson@gov.ab.ca
Executive Director, Policy & Strategic Partnerships, Andrew Dore
Tel: 780-427-1466
andrew.dore@gov.ab.ca

Associated Agencies, Boards & Commissions:

•Alberta Funeral Services Regulatory Board (AFSRB)
11810 Kingsway Ave.
Edmonton, AB T5G 0X5
Tel: 780-452-6130; *Fax:* 780-452-6085
Toll-free: 800-563-4652
afsrb@telusplanet.net
www.afsrb.ab.ca
In 1992, the Alberta Funeral Services Regulatory Board was established under the Licensing of Trades & Businesses Act & the Funeral Services Business Licensing Regulation.
The Board provides the following services: establishing educational standards; licensing pre-need salespeople, funeral directors, embalmers, funeral businesses, & crematories; monitoring performance standards; & investigating consumer complaints.

•Alberta Motor Vehicle Industry Council (AMVIC)
#303, 9945 - 50 St.
Edmonton, AB T6A 0L4
Tel: 780-466-1140; *Fax:* 780-462-0633
www.amvic.org
The Alberta Motor Vehicle Industry Council is responsible for the administration & enforcement of automotive industry regulations, under Alberta's Fair Trading Act.

•Money Mentors
Quikcard Centre
#175, 17010 - 103rd Ave.
Edmonton, AB T5S 1K7
Fax: 780-423-2791
Toll-free: 888-294-0076
www.moneymentors.ca

Formerly known as Credit Counselling Services of Alberta, Money Mentors is a not-for-profit credit counselling & money coaching organization. It serves Albertans by educating them about personal money management & offering alternatives for those who encounter financial difficulties.

•Real Estate Council of Alberta (RECA)
#350, 4954 Richard Rd. SW
Calgary, AB T3E 6L1
Tel: 403-228-2954; *Fax:* 403-228-3065
Toll-free: 888-425-2754
info@reca.ca
www.reca.ca
Operating under the Real Estate Act of Alberta, the Real Estate Council of Alberta is responsible for the regulation of professionals in the real estate, real estate appraisal, & mortgage broker industries. The Council is made up of the following committees: Audit, Finance, Governance, Hearings, & the Education Ad Hoc Committee.

Consumer & Registry Services

ATB Place South, 10020 - 100 St., 29th Fl., Edmonton, AB T5J 0N3

The Consumers division administers & enforces consumer protection legislation, in support of a fair & effective marketplace for Albertans. The Office of the Utilities Consumer Advocate is also the responsibility of Consumer Services. It ensures that consumers have the information & protection required for the electricity & natural gas markets in Alberta.

Assistant Deputy Minister, Colin Lloyd
Tel: 780-427-2300; *Fax:* 780-422-0956
colin.lloyd@gov.ab.ca
Utilities Consumer Advocate, Chris Hunt
Tel: 403-592-2600
Toll-free: -10 -822; *Fax:* 403-592-2604
chris.hunt@gov.ab.ca
www.ucahelps.alberta.ca
Other Communications: General E-mail: ucahelps@gov.ab.ca
TD Tower
10088 - 102 Ave., 17th Fl.
Edmonton, AB T5J 2Z1
Executive Director, Consumer Services Programs, Rob Phillips
Tel: 780-422-8177; *Fax:* 780-427-3033
rob.phillips@gov.ab.ca
Executive Director, Motor Vehicles & Agent Support, Steve Burford
Tel: 780-415-2847; *Fax:* 780-644-1040
steve.burford@gov.ab.ca
Executive Director, Land Titles & Surveys, Les Speakman
Tel: 780-427-0108; *Fax:* 780-422-3105
les.speakman@gov.ab.ca

Open Government

Telus House at ATB Place, 10020 - 100 St., 29th Fl., Edmonton, AB T5J 0N3

Open Government supports government accountability & transparency initiatives.

Assistant Deputy Minister, Cathryn Landreth
Tel: 780-427-0057; *Fax:* 780-422-0956
cathryn.landreth@gov.ab.ca
Chief Advisor, Open Government Program, Mark Diner
Tel: 780-644-4389; *Fax:* 780-422-9694
mark.diner@gov.ab.ca
Executive Director, Information Management Branch, Laurel Frank
Tel: 780-422-0267; *Fax:* 780-422-0818
laurel.frank@gov.ab.ca
Executive Director, Information Access & Protection, Doug Morrison
Tel: 780-644-4964; *Fax:* 780-427-1120
doug.morrison@gov.ab.ca

Service Modernization

ATB Place South, 10020 - 100 St., 29th Fl., Edmonton, AB T5J 0N3

Service Modernization uses information & communication technology to modernize how the government interacts with Albertans.

Assistant Deputy Minister, Mark Brisson
Tel: 780-644-4529
mark.brisson@gov.ab.ca
Chief Information Officer & Executive Director, Business Solutions Services, Dennis Mudryk
Tel: 780-643-9332
dennis.mudryk@gov.ab.ca
Executive Director, Corporate Information Security Office, Martin Dinel
Tel: 780-427-2429; *Fax:* 780-427-0238
martin.dinel@gov.ab.ca
Executive Director, Client Relationship Management, Tim Dickinson
Tel: 780-643-1881; *Fax:* 780-638-5948
tim.dickinson@gov.ab.ca
Executive Director, Business Development, Architecture, Innovation & Technology Solutions, Rob Godin
Tel: 780-644-4541; *Fax:* 780-427-0238
rob.godin@gov.ab.ca
Executive Director, Infrastructure Operations, Dale Huhtala
Tel: 780-427-2295; *Fax:* 780-638-5949
dale.huhtala@gov.ab.ca

Shared Services

Telus House at ATB Place, 10020 - 100 St., 29th Fl., Edmonton, AB T5J 0N3

Assistant Deputy Minister, Laura Wood
Tel: 780-415-2272; *Fax:* 780-422-0956
laura.wood@gov.ab.ca
Executive Director, Service Delivery, Ray Keroack
Tel: 780-427-0254; *Fax:* 780-427-0254
ray.keroack@gov.ab.ca
Executive Director, Client Services Operations, Chris Mochulski
Tel: 780-644-8344
chris.mochulski@gov.ab.ca
Executive Director, Procurement Services, Bill Moulton
Tel: 780-427-4120; *Fax:* 780-422-9672
bill.moulton@gov.ab.ca
Executive Director, Service Development & Quality (SDQ), Sonya Johnston
Tel: 780-415-9260
sonya.johnston@gov.ab.ca

Strategic Planning & Financial Services

Commerce Place, 10155 - 102 St., 13th Fl., Edmonton, AB T5J 4G8

Executive Director & Senior Financial Officer, Strategic Planning & Financial Services, Althea Hutchinson
Tel: 780-415-8975; *Fax:* 780-427-0307
althea.hutchinson@gov.ab.ca

Status of Women

Office of the Minister, Legislature Bldg., #208, 10800 - 97 Ave., Edmonton, AB T5K 2B6

www.humanservices.alberta.ca/family-community/14870.html

Created in 2015, Status of Women seeks to improve gender equality in Alberta. Two programs were moved to the ministry upon its creation: Women's Equality & Advancement, & Women in Leadership.

Minister Responsible, Status of Women, Hon. Stephanie McLean
Tel: 780-422-6880; *Fax:* 780-422-2496
Deputy Minister, Kim Armstrong
Tel: 780-644-7559
kim.armstrong@gov.ab.ca
Chief of Staff, Amy Nugent
Tel: 780-422-6880
amy.nugent@gov.ab.ca

Alberta Transportation

Communications Branch, Twin Atria Building, 4999 - 98 Jasper Ave., 2nd Fl., Edmonton, AB T6B 2X3

Tel: 780-427-2731; *Fax:* 780-466-3166
Toll-Free: -310-0000
Trans.Contact.Us.m@gov.ab.ca
www.transportation.alberta.ca
www.facebook.com/EndDrunkDriving

Alberta's Ministry of Transportation consists of the Department of Transportation & the Transportation Safety Board. The Ministry strives to provide a safe & sustainable transportation system & water management infrastructure throughout the province.
Key activities of the Department are as follows: leading the planning, construction & preservation of highways across Alberta; offering information & education about transportation safety services & enforcement programs; designing, building, & maintaining the water management infrastructure in the province; managing grant programs to assist municipalities; & representing Alberta at all levels of government to ensure regulatory harmonization.

Associated Agencies, Boards & Commissions:

•Transportation Safety Board
North Office, Twin Atria Building
4999 - 98 Ave., Main Fl.
Edmonton, AB T6B 2X3
Tel: 780-427-7178; *Fax:* 780-422-9739
Toll-free: -310-0000
www.atsb.alberta.ca
The Alberta Transportation Safety Board reports to the Minister of Transportation, through the Chair. The Board's members are chosen through a public recruitment process.
The Board hears appeals about licence suspensions & vehicle seizures. Its decisions are made in accordance with the Traffic Safety Act & the Railway (Alberta) Act.

Corporate Services & Information Division

Twin Atria Building, 4999 - 98 Ave., 3rd Fl., Edmonton, AB T6B 2X3

Assistant Deputy Minister, Ranjit Tharmalingam
Tel: 780-422-7672; *Fax:* 780-644-7220
ranjit.tharmalingam@gov.ab.ca
Senior Financial Officer, Finance Branch, Michael Lundquist
Tel: 780-644-5114; *Fax:* 780-427-8327
michael.lundquist@gov.ab.ca

Delivery Services Division

Twin Atria Building, 4999 - 98 Ave., 2nd Fl., Edmonton, AB T6B 2X3

Assistant Deputy Minister, Manon Plante
Tel: 780-643-1682
manon.plante@gov.ab.ca
Executive Director, Regional Services Operations & Planning, Darrell Camplin
Tel: 780-638-9419
darrell.camplin@gov.ab.ca
Executive Director, Major Capital Projects Branch, Landon Reppert
Tel: 780-644-1199; *Fax:* 780-415-0475
landon.reppert@gov.ab.ca

Safety, Policy & Engineering Division

Twin Atria Building, 4999 - 98 Ave., Main Fl., Edmonton, AB T6B 2X3

Tel: 780-427-8901; *Fax:* 780-415-0782
Toll-Free: 800-666-5036

The division supports initiatives such as barrier-free transportation, climate change initiatives & border crossing issues, as well as leading reviews & changes to statutes & regulations.

Assistant Deputy Minister, Shaun Hammond
Tel: 780-415-1146; *Fax:* 780-415-0782
shaun.hammond@gov.ab.ca
Executive Director, Safety & Compliance Services, Denis Boissonnault
Tel: 780-422-3759; *Fax:* 780-422-9193
denis.boissonnault@gov.ab.ca
Executive Director, Strategy & Policy Branch, & Planning & Investment Strategies Branch, Ross Danyluk
Tel: 780-644-2663
ross.danyluk@gov.ab.ca
Executive Director, Office of Traffic Safety, Wendy Doyle
Tel: 780-427-6588; *Fax:* 780-422-3682
wendy.doyle@gov.ab.ca
Executive Director, Technical Standards Branch, Moh Lali
Tel: 780-415-1083; *Fax:* 780-422-2027
moh.lali@gov.ab.ca
Executive Director, Driver Programs, Terry Wallace
Tel: 780-427-7508; *Fax:* 780-422-6612
terry.wallace@gov.ab.ca

Alberta Treasury Board & Finance

Oxbridge Place, 9820 - 106 St., 9th Fl., Edmonton, AB T5K 1E7

Tel: 780-427-3035; *Fax:* 780-427-1147
Toll-Free: -310-0000
www.finance.alberta.ca
twitter.com/AB_TB_Finance

Alberta's Treasury Board manages government spending by carrying out the following responsibilities: leading the provincial government's capital planning process; providing advice & analysis on costs & capital spending; identifying alternatives for financing capital projects; & ensuring accounting standards & financial reporting. The ministry also oversees economic development & corporate human resources.
Alberta Finance offers financial, economic, & fiscal policy advice to government. The Ministry also provides tax & regulatory administration to support strong government finances & to ensure that Alberta has a productive & competitive economy.
The two ministries were combined in 2012 by then-Premier Redford.

Minister, Finance; President, Treasury Board, Hon. Joe Ceci
Tel: 780-415-4855; *Fax:* 780-415-4853
tbf.minister@gov.ab.ca
Legislature Building
#323, 10800 - 97 Ave.
Edmonton, AB T5K 2B6
Deputy Minister, Lorna Rosen
Tel: 780-415-4515; *Fax:* 780-427-6596
lorna.rosen@gov.ab.ca
Senior Assistant Deputy Minister, Mark Prefontaine
Tel: 780-638-5627
mark.prefontaine@gov.ab.ca
Executive Director, Human Resource Services, Dawn White
Tel: 780-415-8694; *Fax:* 780-422-0421
dawn.white@gov.ab.ca

Director, Strategic Priorities, Briegh Anne Albert
Tel: 780-643-1697
brieghanne.albert@gov.ab.ca
Director, Policy & Legislative Coordination, Jessica Ellison
Tel: 780-415-8396; *Fax:* 780-427-6596
jessica.ellison@gov.ab.ca

Associated Agencies, Boards & Commissions:

•Alberta Automobile Insurance Rate Board (AIRB)
Canadian Western Bank Place
#2440, 10303 Jasper Ave.
Edmonton, AB T5J 3N6
Tel: 780-427-5428; *Fax:* 780-638-4254
Toll-free: -310-0000
airb@gov.ab.ca
www.airb.alberta.ca
The Automobile Insurance Rate Board is engaged in the following activities: setting premiums for basic coverage; monitoring premiums for optional coverage; & reviewing & approving rating programs for new insurers.

•Alberta Capital Finance Authority (ACFA)
Sun Life Place
#2160, 10123 - 99 St. NW
Edmonton, AB T5J 3H1
Tel: 780-427-9711; *Fax:* 780-422-2175
webacfa@gov.ab.ca
www.acfa.gov.ab.ca
Other Communication: Rate Information Line: 780-422-2632
Established in 1956, the Alberta Capital Finance Authority is a non-profit corporation that acts under the authority of the Alberta Capital Finance Authority Act (Alberta). Flexible funding for capital projects is provided by the provincial authority to Alberta's municipalities, school boards, & other local entities, at interest rates based on the cost of its borrowings.

•Alberta Investment Management Corporation (AIMCo)
#1100, 10830 Jasper Ave.
Edmonton, AB T5J 2B3
Tel: 780-392-3600
inquiries@aimco.alberta.ca
www.aimco.alberta.ca
Other Communication: Toronto Office, Phone: 416-304-1160; Media Inquiries, Phone: 403-538-5645
Established as a Crown corporation in 2008, the Alberta Investment Management Corporation provides investment management services for a group of Alberta public sector funds.

•Alberta Pensions Services Corporation (APS)
5103 Windermere Blvd. SW
Edmonton, AB T6W 0S9
Tel: 780-427-2782
Toll-free: 800-661-8198
memberservices@apsc.ca
www.apsc.ca
Other Communication: Alternate E-mails: employerservices@apsc.ca; pay@apsc.ca; privacy@apsc.ca; mediacontact@apsc.ca
Alberta Pensions Services Corporation was incorporated in 1995, under the Business Corporations Act of Alberta. The Crown Corporation administers seven statutory pension plans & two supplementary retirement plans.

•Alberta Securities Commission (ASC)
#600, 250 - 5th St. SW
Calgary, AB T2P 0R4
Tel: 403-297-6454; *Fax:* 403-297-6156
Toll-free: 877-355-0585
inquiries@asc.ca
www.albertasecurities.com
Other Communication: Alt. E-mails: complaints@asc.ca; checkfirst@asc.ca; sedar.sedi@asc.ca; records.requests@asc.ca; registration@asc.ca; media@asc.ca; registrar@asc.ca; webmaster@asc.ca
The Alberta Securities Commission is a regulatory agency that is responsible for the administration of the Alberta Securities Act. The capital market in Alberta is regulated by the Alberta Securities Commission to protect investors.
The Alberta Securities Commission also works as a member of the Canadian Securities Administrators to coordinate & improve the regulation of Canada's capital markets.

•Alberta Teachers' Retirement Fund (ATRF)
Barnett House
#600, 11010 - 142 St. NW
Edmonton, AB T5N 2R1
Tel: 780-451-4166; *Fax:* 780-452-3547
Toll-free: 800-661-9582
info@atrf.com
www.atrf.com
Other Communication: Alt. E-mails: member@atrf.com (Member Plan Inquiries); retiredmember@atrf.com (Retired Members); helpdesk@atrf.com (Employer Inquiries)
Established under the Teachers' Pension Plans Act, the Alberta Teachers' Retirement Fund has administered a pension plan for teachers employed in Alberta's school jurisdictions & charter schools since 1939.
The independent corporation also administers the Private School Teachers' Pension Plan for teachers at Alberta's private schools that have joined the plan.

•ATB Financial
#2100, 10020 - 100 St. NW
Edmonton, AB T5J 0N3
Tel: 403-245-8110
Toll-free: 800-332-8383
www.atb.com
Other Communication: Privacy, Phone: 1-866-858-4175; Online Banking, Phone: 1-866-282-4932; Business Online Banking, Phone: 1-888-655-5152; MasterCard, Phone: 1-800-661-2266
Established in 1938, ATB Financial has been a provincial Crown corporation since 1997. As the largest Alberta-based financial institution, ATB Financial serves people across Alberta through 165 branches, 131 agencies, & a Customer Contact Centre.

•Credit Union Deposit Guarantee Corporation (CUDGC)
#2000, 10104 - 103 St.
Edmonton, AB T5J 0H8
Tel: 780-428-6680; *Fax:* 780-428-7571
Toll-free: 800-661-0351
mail@cudgc.ab.ca
www.cudgc.ab.ca
Established untder the Alberta Credit Union Act, the Credit Union Deposit Guarantee Corporation is a provincial corporation. The Corporation is administered by a Board of Directors, who are appointed by the Lieutenant Governor in Council of Alberta. The Credit Union Deposit Guarantee Corporation guarantees deposits held with Alberta's credit unions & works to ensure that credit unions employ sound business practices.

Public Sector Working Group
Canadian Western Bank Bldg., 10303 Jasper Ave., 28th Fl., Edmonton, AB T5J 5C3
Tel: 780-638-9550
Assistant Deputy Minister, Wendy Boje
Tel: 780-644-7942
wendy.boje@gov.ab.ca
Executive Director, Public Sector Labour Research & Analytics, Bernard Anderson
Tel: 780-638-9550
bernard.anderson@gov.ab.ca

Budget Development & Reporting Division
Federal Bldg., 9820 - 107 St., 9th Fl., Edmonton, AB T5K 1E7
The Budget Development & Reporting Division is responsible for preparing the annual Budget, as well as annual reports & consolidated financial statements.
Assistant Deputy Minister, Aaron Neumeyer
Tel: 780-644-8078; *Fax:* 780-644-3907
aaron.neumeyer@gov.ab.ca
Executive Director, Corporate Planning, Reporting & Evaluation, Tanya Bowerman
Tel: 780-415-9167; *Fax:* 780-422-2164
tanya.bowerman@gov.ab.ca
Executive Director, Budget Development & Reporting 2, Greg Findlay
Tel: 780-415-9258; *Fax:* 780-644-3907
greg.findlay@gov.ab.ca
Executive Director, Revenue & Reporting, James Forrest
Tel: 780-427-8752; *Fax:* 780-644-3907
james.forrest@gov.ab.ca
Executive Director, Budget Development & Reporting 4, Dale Fulford
Tel: 780-427-8736; *Fax:* 780-644-3907
dale.fulford@gov.ab.ca
Executive Director, Budget Development & Reporting 1, Ken Gray
Tel: 780-427-7635; *Fax:* 780-644-3907
ken.gray@gov.ab.ca
Executive Director, Budget Development & Reporting 3, Glen Savitsky
Tel: 780-427-8196; *Fax:* 780-644-3907
glen.savitsky@gov.ab.ca

Corporate Internal Audit Services
Terrace Bldg., 9515 - 107 St., 3rd Fl., Edmonton, AB T5K 2C3
Tel: 780-644-7185
Corporate Internal Audit Services works with Alberta's government ministries to identify areas for improvement. Following the performance of internal audits, recommendations are provided to better operations & fiscal management.
Chief Internal Auditor, Vacant
Executive Director, Enterprise Audits & Professional Practice, Kathleen Gora
Tel: 780-644-5271; *Fax:* 780-644-4761
kathleen.gora@gov.ab.ca
Executive Director, Internal Audit Operations, Michael Hocken
Tel: 780-644-7153; *Fax:* 780-644-4761
michael.hocken@gov.ab.ca

Corporate Human Resources (CHR)
Peace Hills Trust Tower, 10011 - 109 St., 7th Fl., Edmonton, AB T5J 3S8
Tel: 780-408-8400
www.chr.alberta.ca
Corporate Human Resources offers advice to the Alberta provincial government about human resource administration. The following are some of the tasks performed by Corporate Human Resources: providing a corporate executive search program; coordinating job postings; delivering information about benefits, workplace health, labour relations, & other issues; advancing employee engagement; & offering learning opportunities to provincial government employees.
Deputy Minister, Corporate Human Resources & Public Service Commissioner, Lana Lougheed
Tel: 780-408-8450
lana.lougheed@gov.ab.ca
Senior Assistant Deputy Minister, Leadership & Talent Development, Christine Couture
Tel: 780-643-9287
christine.couture@gov.ab.ca
Assistant Deputy Minister, Leadership & Talent Development, Margot Ross-Graham
Tel: 780-408-8462
margot.ross-graham@gov.ab.ca
Assistant Deputy Minister, Labour & Employment Practices, Dean Screpnek
Tel: 780-408-8477
dean.screpnek@gov.ab.ca
Assistant Deputy Minister, Strategic Services & Human Resources Transformation, Bryce Stewart
Tel: 780-408-8488
bryce.stewart@gov.ab.ca
Chief Information Officer, Judy Cui
Tel: 780-408-8496; *Fax:* 780-638-3064
judy.cui@gov.ab.ca
Senior Financial Officer, Strategic Services & Human Resources Transformation, Greg Kliparchuk
Tel: 780-638-3199; *Fax:* 780-638-3064
greg.kliparchuk@gov.ab.ca
Acting Executive Director, Learning & Development, Tracy Bell
Tel: 780-644-3899
tracy.bell@gov.ab.ca
Executive Director, Alberta Public Service Communications & Engagement, Kim Capstick
Tel: 780-422-4807
kim.capstick@gov.ab.ca
Executive Director, Talent Management, Michelle Dorval
Tel: 780-427-1294
michelle.dorval@gov.ab.ca
Executive Director, Strategic Policy, Bryan Karbonik
Tel: 780-644-2230
bryan.karbonik@gov.ab.ca
Executive Director, Labour Relations & Workplace Health, Myles Morris
Tel: 780-408-8417
myles.morris@gov.ab.ca
Executive Director, Human Resources Services, Dawn White
Tel: 780-415-8964
dawn.white@gov.ab.ca

Economics & Fiscal Policy Division
Federal Bldg., 9820 - 107 St., 8th Fl., Edmonton, AB T5K 1E7
Assistant Deputy Minister, Mark Parsons
Tel: 780-427-8790; *Fax:* 780-426-3951
mark.parsons@gov.ab.ca
Chief Economist & Executive Director, Economics & Revenue Forecasting, Catherine Rothrock
Tel: 780-427-2758; *Fax:* 780-426-3951
catherine.rothrock@gov.ab.ca
Executive Director, Tax Policy, Joffre Hotz
Tel: 780-427-8727
joffre.hotz@gov.ab.ca
Executive Director, Fiscal Planning & Analysis, Stephen Tkachyk
Tel: 780-427-8804; *Fax:* 780-427-1296
stephen.tkachyk@gov.ab.ca
Chief Statistician/Director, Office of Statistics & Information (OSI), Annik Foreman
Tel: 780-643-1074; *Fax:* 780-426-3951
annik.foreman2@gov.ab.ca

Financial Sector Regulation & Policy Division (FSRP)
Terrace Building, 9515 - 107 St., 4th Fl., Edmonton, AB T5K 2C3
Tel: 780-427-8322
Acting Assistant Deputy Minister; Acting Superintendent of Financial Institutions, Insurance & Pensions, Nilam Jetha
Tel: 780-427-9722; *Fax:* 780-427-1636
nilam.jetha@gov.ab.ca
Deputy Superintendent, Financial Institutions Regulation, Peter Baba
Tel: 780-415-2450; *Fax:* 780-420-0752
peter.baba@gov.ab.ca

Deputy Superintendent, Pensions, Paul Owens
Tel: 780-415-0516; *Fax:* 780-422-4283
paul.owens@gov.ab.ca
Deputy Superintendent, Insurance Regulations & Market Conduct, David Sorensen
Tel: 780-427-8896; *Fax:* 780-420-0752
david.sorensen@gov.ab.ca
Executive Director, Pension Policy, Dale Beesley
Tel: 780-415-0513; *Fax:* 780-644-7771
dale.beesley@gov.ab.ca

Office of the Controller

Terrace Bldg., 9515 - 107 St., 3rd Fl., Edmonton, AB T5K 2C3
Tel: 780-427-3076; *Fax:* 780-422-2164

The Office of the Controller handles the following responsibilities: overseeing financial management & control policies; ensuring government accounting standards; reporting financial information; & planning.

Acting Controller, Dan Stadlwieser
dan.stadlwieser@gov.ab.ca
Executive Director, Corporate Consolidations & Reporting, Richard Isaak
Tel: 780-415-9149
richard.isaak@gov.ab.ca
Executive Director, Financial Accounting & Standards, Vacant
Tel: 780-415-9253

Strategic & Business Services Division

Terrace Building, 9515 - 107 St., 4th Fl., Edmonton, AB T5K 2C3
Tel: 780-427-3052
Other Communication: Air Charter Services, Phone: 780-427-5251

Assistant Deputy Minister, Darren Hedley
Tel: 780-422-2730; *Fax:* 780-427-1296
darren.hedley@gov.ab.ca
Acting Chief Information Officer/Chief Technology Officer, Patrick Marshall
Tel: 780-644-4289; *Fax:* 780-644-5016
patrick.marshall@gov.ab.ca
Executive Director, Financial Services, Shakeeb Siddiqui
Tel: 780-644-8622; *Fax:* 780-422-2163
shakeeb.siddiqui@gov.ab.ca

Tax & Revenue Administration Division (TRA)

Sir Frederick W. Haultain Building, 9811 - 109 St., 2nd Fl., Edmonton, AB T5K 2L5
Tel: 780-427-3044; *Fax:* 780-427-0348
tra.revenue@gov.ab.ca
www.finance.alberta.ca/publications/tax_rebates

Assistant Deputy Minister, Ian Ayton
Tel: 780-427-9403; *Fax:* 780-422-0899
ian.ayton@gov.ab.ca
Executive Director, Revenue Operations, Kent Heine
Tel: 780-644-4257; *Fax:* 780-644-4921
kent.heine@gov.ab.ca
Executive Director, Tax Services, Angelina Leung
Tel: 780-644-4064; *Fax:* 780-427-5074
angelina.leung@gov.ab.ca
Acting Executive Director, Audit, Tracy Teng
Tel: 780-644-4248; *Fax:* 780-422-2090
tracy.teng@gov.ab.ca

Treasury & Risk Management Division

Federal Bldg., 9820 - 107 St., 8th Fl., Edmonton, AB T5K 1E7

Assistant Deputy Minister, Lowell Epp
Tel: 780-422-4052; *Fax:* 780-427-0780
lowell.epp@gov.ab.ca
Executive Director, Risk Management & Insurance, Mark Day
Tel: 780-644-4045; *Fax:* 780-422-5271
mark.day@gov.ab.ca
Executive Director, Financial Institutions Policy, James Flett
Tel: 780-415-9233; *Fax:* 780-644-7759
james.flett@gov.ab.ca
Executive Director, Capital Markets, Stephen J. Thompson
Tel: 780-644-5011
stephen.j.thompson@gov.ab.ca

Government of British Columbia

Seat of Government: Parliament Bldgs., Victoria, BC V8V 1X4
Tel: 250-387-6121
Toll-Free: 800-663-7867
TTY: 800-661-8773
www2.gov.bc.ca
Other Communication: Vancouver, Phone: 604-660-2421; Vancouver, TDD: 604-775-0303; Outside BC, Phone: 604-660-2421
twitter.com/BCGovNews
www.facebook.com/BCProvincialGovernment
www.youtube.com/user/ProvinceofBC

The Province of British Columbia entered Confederation on July 20, 1871. According to the 2011 StatsCan census, the population of the province is 4,400,057. British Columbia's land area is 922,509.29 sq km.

Office of the Lieutenant Governor

Government House, 1401 Rockland Ave., Victoria, BC V8S 1V9
Tel: 250-387-2080; *Fax:* 250-387-2078
ghinfo@gov.bc.ca
www.ltgov.bc.ca
www.facebook.com/BCGovernmentHouse

The Hon. Judith Guichon was sworn in as the 29th Lieutenant Governor of British Columbia on November 2, 2012.

Lieutenant Governor, Hon. Judith Guichon, OBC
Tel: 250-387-2080
Social Media: twitter.com/LGJudithGuichon, www.facebook.com/LGJudithGuichon
Private Secretary to the Lieutenant Governor & Executive Director, Government House, Jerymy Brownridge
Tel: 250-387-2083; *Fax:* 250-387-2078
Director, Programmes, Events & Outreach, Heidi Elliott
Tel: 250-356-0925
Director, Operations & Management Services, Thandi Williams
Tel: 250-387-2087

Office of the Premier & Cabinet Office

West Annex, Parliament Bldgs., PO Box 9041 Stn. Prov Govt, Victoria, BC V8W 9E1
Tel: 250-387-1715; *Fax:* 250-387-0087
premier@gov.bc.ca
www.gov.bc.ca/premier
Other Communication: Premier's Vancouver Office, Phone: 604-775-1600, Fax: 604-775-1688

Christy Clark won the leadership of the Liberal party in February 2011, following the resignation of former premier, Gordon Campbell. She was sworn in as the 35th Premier of British Columbia on March 14, 2011. She led the Liberal party to victory in the May 2013 provincial election, but lost her Vancouver-Point Grey seat to NDP candidate David Eby. She remained Premier, however, opting to run in a July by-election for the seat of Westside-Kelowna, which she won on July 10, 2013.

Premier; President, Executive Council, Hon. Christy Clark
Tel: 250-387-1715; *Fax:* 250-387-0087
premier@gov.bc.ca
Social Media: twitter.com/christyclarkbc, www.facebook.com/ChristyClarkForBC
Chief of Staff, Dan Doyle
Deputy Chief of Staff, Operations, Michele Cadario
Press Secretary, Stephen Smart
Executive Director, Communications & Issues Management, Ben Chin
Managing Director, Correspondence, Antoinette De Wit
Tel: 250-387-3570; *Fax:* 250-356-1385
Antoinette.DeWit@gov.bc.ca
Director, Communications, Katy Merrifield; *Fax:* 250-356-1385

Cabinet Operations

PO Box 9487 Stn. Prov Govt, Victoria, BC V8W 9W6
Fax: 250-387-7392

Cabinet Secretary; Deputy Minister to the Premier; Head of the Public Service, Kim Henderson
Deputy Cabinet Secretary, Elizabeth MacMillan
Tel: 250-387-6020; *Fax:* 250-387-7392
Executive Director, Cabinet Operations, Steve Anderson
Tel: 250-387-0782; *Fax:* 250-387-7392
steve.anderson@gov.bc.ca
Executive Director, Lynne Holt
Tel: 250-387-5541; *Fax:* 250-387-7392
Lynn.Holt@gov.bc.ca
Executive Director, Anne Preyde
Tel: 250-387-7380; *Fax:* 250-387-7392
Anne.Preyde@gov.bc.ca

Deputy Minister's Office

PO Box 9041 Stn. Prov Govt, Victoria, BC V8W 9E1
Tel: 250-387-2226; *Fax:* 250-356-7258

Deputy Minister to the Premier; Cabinet Secretary; Head of the Public Service, Kim Henderson
Deputy Minister, Corporate Policy & Intergovernmental Relations, Neil Sweeney
Tel: 250-387-5830; *Fax:* 250-356-7258
Associate Deputy Minister, Corporate Policy, Bobbi Plecas
Tel: 250-356-2206; *Fax:* 250-356-7258

Intergovernmental Relations Secretariat (IGRS)

PO Box 9433 Stn. Prov Govt, Victoria, BC V8W 9V3
Tel: 250-387-0752; *Fax:* 250-387-1920
igrs@gov.bc.ca
www.igrs.gov.bc.ca
Other Communication: Alternate E-mail: protocol@gov.bc.ca

The Intergovernmental Relations Secretariat consists of the following sections: Intergovernmental & International Relations; Office of Protocol; & the Francophone Affairs Program.
The mission of Intergovernmental & International Relations is to ensure that the province's relations with provincial & territorial governments, the federal government, the United States, the Asia-Pacific region, & other international governments advance British Columbia's interests. Advice is given to the Premier & cabinet ministers.
The Office of Protocol offers leadership in government protocol, ceremonial, & diplomatic events. Examples of these activities include the installation of cabinet members & the opening of the legislature.
Information on the Government of British Columbia's Francophone Affairs Program can be found here: www2.gov.bc.ca/gov/content/governments/organizational-structure/office-of-the-premier/intergovernmental-relations-secretariat/francophone.

Deputy Minister, Neil Sweeney
Tel: 250-387-2987; *Fax:* 250-387-1920
Associate Deputy Minister, Pierrette Maranda
Tel: 250-387-0752; *Fax:* 250-387-1920
Pierrette.Maranda@gov.bc.ca
Executive Director, Economic Policy & Asia Pacific Relations, Donald Haney
Tel: 250-387-5628; *Fax:* 250-387-1920
Donald.Haney@gov.bc.ca
Executive Director, US Relations & Partnerships, Jeremy Hewitt
Tel: 250-387-1134; *Fax:* 250-387-1920
Executive Director & Chief of Protocol, Lucy Lobmeier
Tel: 250-356-6177
Lucy.Lobmeier@gov.bc.ca
PO Box 9422 Prov Govt Sta.
Victoria, BC V8W 9N3
Executive Director, Strategic Policy & Planning, Sukumar Periwal
Tel: 250-387-0761; *Fax:* 250-387-1920
Sukumar.Periwal@gov.bc.ca
Executive Director, Federalism & Canadian Intergovernmental Policy, Grant H. Smith
Tel: 250-356-1042; *Fax:* 250-387-1920

Executive Council of the Government of British Columbia

Cabinet Operations, 617 Government St., 1st Fl., PO Box 9487 Stn. Prov Govt, Victoria, BC V8W 9W6
www.gov.bc.ca/premier/cabinet_ministers

Cabinet Ministers

Premier; President, Executive Council, Hon. Christy Clark
Tel: 250-387-1715; *Fax:* 250-387-0087
premier@gov.bc.ca
www.bcliberals.com/premier
Social Media: twitter.com/christyclarkbc, www.facebook.com/ChristyClarkForBC
PO Box 9041 Prov Govt Sta.
Victoria, BC V8W 9E1
Deputy Premier; Minister, Natural Gas Development; Minister Responsible, Housing, Hon. Rich Coleman
Tel: 250-953-0900; *Fax:* 250-950-0927
MNGH.minister@gov.bc.ca
www.gov.bc.ca/mngd
Social Media: twitter.com/colemancountry
PO Box 9052 Prov Govt Sta.
Victoria, BC V8W 9E2
Minister, Aboriginal Relations & Reconciliation, Hon. John Rustad
Tel: 250-953-4844; *Fax:* 250-953-4856
ABR.Minister@gov.bc.ca
www.gov.bc.ca/arr
Social Media: www.facebook.com/john.rustad
PO Box 9055 Prov Govt Sta.
Victoria, BC V8W 9E2
Minister, Advanced Education, Hon. Andrew Wilkinson
Tel: 250-356-0179; *Fax:* 250-952-0260
AVED.Minister@gov.bc.ca
www.gov.bc.ca/aved
Social Media: twitter.com/Wilkinson4BC
PO Box 9080 Prov Govt Sta.
Victoria, BC V8W 9E2
Minister, Agriculture, Hon. Norm Letnick
Tel: 250-387-1023; *Fax:* 250-387-1522
AGR.Minister@gov.bc.ca
www.gov.bc.ca/agri
Social Media: twitter.com/normletnick, www.facebook.com/normletnickmla, www.linkedin.com/pub/norm-letnick/15/8a0/589
PO Box 9043 Prov Govt Sta.
Victoria, BC V8W 9E2
Minister, Children & Family Development, Hon. Stephanie Cadieux
Tel: 250-387-9699; *Fax:* 250-387-9722
MCF.Minister@gov.bc.ca

www.gov.bc.ca/mcf
Social Media: twitter.com/mlacadieux,
www.facebook.com/stephaniecadieux
PO Box 9057 Prov Govt Sta.
Victoria, BC V8W 9E2

Minister, Community, Sport & Cultural Development; Minister Responsible for TransLink, Hon. Peter Fassbender
Tel: 250-387-2283; *Fax:* 250-387-4312
CSCD.Minister@gov.bc.ca
www.gov.bc.ca/cscd
Social Media: twitter.com/FassbenderMLA,
www.facebook.com/PeterFassbenderSurreyFleetwood

Minister, Education, Hon. Mike Bernier
Tel: 250-387-1977; *Fax:* 250-356-0948
educ.minister@gov.bc.ca
www.gov.bc.ca/bced
Social Media: twitter.com/mike_a_bernier,
www.facebook.com/mayormike.bernier
PO Box 9045 Prov Govt Sta.
Victoria, BC V8W 9E2

Minister, Energy & Mines; Minister Responsible for Core Review, Hon. Bill Bennett
Tel: 250-387-5896; *Fax:* 250-387-4312
MEM.Minister@gov.bc.ca
www.gov.bc.ca/ener
Social Media: twitter.com/KootenayBill,
www.facebook.com/kootenay.bill
PO Box 9069 Prov Govt Sta.
Victoria, BC V8W 9E2

Minister, Environment, Hon. Mary Polak
Tel: 250-387-1187; *Fax:* 250-387-1356
ENV.Minister@gov.bc.ca
www.gov.bc.ca/env
Social Media: www.facebook.com/maryforbc
PO Box 9047 Prov Govt Sta.
Victoria, BC V8W 9E2

Minister, Finance; Government House Leader, Hon. Michael de Jong, Q.C.
Tel: 250-387-3751; *Fax:* 250-387-5594
FIN.Minister@gov.bc.ca
www.gov.bc.ca/fin
Social Media: twitter.com/mike_de_jong,
www.facebook.com/michaeldejongbc
PO Box 9048 Prov Govt Sta.
Victoria, BC V8W 9E2

Minister, Forests, Lands & Natural Resource Operations, Hon. Steve Thomson
Tel: 250-387-6240; *Fax:* 250-387-1040
FLNR.Minister@gov.bc.ca
www.gov.bc.ca/for
Social Media: twitter.com/Steve4Kelowna,
www.facebook.com/Steve4Kelowna
PO Box 9049 Prov Govt Sta.
Victoria, BC V8W 9E2

Minister, Health, Hon. Terry Lake
Tel: 250-953-3547; *Fax:* 250-356-9587
hlth.minister@gov.bc.ca
www.gov.bc.ca/health
Social Media: twitter.com/TerryLakeMLA
PO Box 9050 Prov Govt Sta.
Victoria, BC V8W 9E2

Minister, International Trade; Minister Responsible for the Asia Pacific Strategy & Multiculturalism, Hon. Teresa Wat
Tel: 250-953-0910; *Fax:* 250-953-0928
MIT.Minister@gov.bc.ca
www.gov.bc.ca/mit
Social Media: twitter.com/Teresa_Wat,
www.facebook.com/TeresaWatBC
PO Box 9063 Prov Govt Sta.
Victoria, BC V8W 9E2

Minister, Jobs, Tourism & Skills Training; Minister Responsible for Labour, Hon. Shirley Bond
Tel: 250-356-2771; *Fax:* 250-356-3000
JTST.Minister@gov.bc.ca
www.gov.bc.ca/jtst
Social Media: twitter.com/shirleybond,
www.facebook.com/shirley.bond
PO Box 9071 Prov Govt Sta.
Victoria, BC V8W 9E2

Minister, Justice; Attorney General, Hon. Suzanne Anton
Tel: 250-387-1866; *Fax:* 250-387-6411
JAG.Minister@gov.bc.ca
www.gov.bc.ca/justice
Social Media: twitter.com/SuzanneAnton,
www.facebook.com/suzanne.anton
PO Box 9044 Prov Govt Sta.
Victoria, BC V8W 9E2

Minister, Public Safety & Solicitor General, Hon. Mike Morris
Tel: 250-356-2178; *Fax:* 250-356-2142
mike.morris.mla@leg.bc.ca
www.gov.bc.ca/justice
Social Media: twitter.com/MikeMorrisforBC,
www.facebook.com/MikeMorrisforBC
PO Box 9044 Prov Govt Sta.
Victoria, BC V8W 9E2

Minister, Small Business & Red-Tape Reduction; Minister Responsible for the Liquor Distribution Branch, Hon. Coralee Oakes
Tel: 250-356-8247; *Fax:* 250-356-8250
coralee.oakes.mla@leg.bc.ca
Social Media: twitter.com/CoraleeOakes,
www.facebook.com/teamcoralee

Minister, Social Development & Social Innovation; Caucus Chair, Hon. Michelle Stilwell
Tel: 250-356-7750; *Fax:* 250-356-7292
SDSI.minister@gov.bc.ca
www.gov.bc.ca/sdsi
Social Media: twitter.com/Stilwell2013,
www.facebook.com/MichelleStilwellMLA
PO Box 9058 Prov Govt Sta.
Victoria, BC V8W 9E2

Minister of State for Emergency Preparedness, Hon. Naomi Yamamoto
Tel: 250-356-8213; *Fax:* 250-356-8223
naomi.yamamoto.mla@leg.bc.ca
Social Media: twitter.com/naomiyamamoto,
www.facebook.com/naomiyamamoto.northvan

Minister, Technology, Innovation & Citizens' Services, Hon. Amrik Virk
Tel: 250-952-7623; *Fax:* 250-952-7628
TIACS.minister@gov.bc.ca
www.gov.bc.ca/citz
Social Media: twitter.com/amrikvirkbc,
www.facebook.com/amrikvirkbc
PO Box 9068 Prov Govt Sta.
Victoria, BC V8W 9E2

Minister, Transportation & Infrastructure; Deputy House Leader, Hon. Todd Stone
Tel: 250-387-1978; *Fax:* 250-356-2290
Minister.Transportation@gov.bc.ca
www.gov.bc.ca/tran
Social Media: twitter.com/toddstonebc
PO Box 9055 Prov Govt Sta.
Victoria, BC V8W 9E2

BC Legislative Assembly & Independent Offices

Clerk's Office, Parliament Bldgs., Victoria, BC V8V 1X4
Tel: 250-387-3785; *Fax:* 250-387-0942
ClerkHouse@leg.bc.ca
www.leg.bc.ca

Clerk of the House, Craig James
Tel: 250-387-3785
ClerkHouse@leg.bc.ca

Speaker, Legislative Assembly, Hon. Linda Reid
Tel: 250-387-3952; *Fax:* 250-387-2813
linda.reid.mla@leg.bc.ca
#207, Parliament Bldgs.
Victoria, BC V8V 1X4

Sergeant-at-Arms, Gary Lenz
Tel: 250-387-0953

Auditor General, Carol Bellringer, FCPA, FCA
Tel: 250-419-6100
bcauditor@bcauditor.com
www.bcauditor.com

Chief Electoral Officer, Elections British Columbia, Keith Archer
Tel: 250-387-5305; *Fax:* 250-387-3578
ElectionsBC@elections.bc.ca
www.elections.bc.ca

Conflict of Interest Commissioner, Paul D.K. Fraser, Q.C.
Tel: 250-356-0750; *Fax:* 250-356-6580
conflictofinterest@coibc.ca
www.coibc.ca

Acting Information & Privacy Commissioner, Drew McArthur
info@oipc.bc.ca
www.oipc.bc.ca
Note: On March 22, 2016, Elizabeth Denham announced she would be stepping down as Information & Privacy Commissioner once her term ended on July 6, 2016.

Merit Commissioner, Fiona Spencer
Tel: 250-953-4208; *Fax:* 250-953-4160
merit@meritcomm.bc.ca
www.meritcomm.bc.ca

Ombudsperson, Jay Chalke
Tel: 250-356-1559; *Fax:* 250-387-0198
outreach@bcombudsperson.ca
www.ombudsman.bc.ca

Police Complaint Commissioner, Stan T. Lowe
Tel: 250-356-7458; *Fax:* 250-356-6503
info@opcc.bc.ca
www.opcc.bc.ca

Representative for Children & Youth, Mary Ellen Turpel-Lafond
Tel: 250-356-6710; *Fax:* 250-356-0837
rcy@rcybc.ca
www.rcybc.ca

Director, Legislative Library Administration Office, Peter Gourlay
Tel: 250-387-6508
llbc.ref@leg.bc.ca
www.leg.bc.ca/learn-about-us/legislative-library
Other Communications: Library Phone: 250-387-6510; Fax: 250-356-1373

Director, Hansard Production, Rob Sutherland
Tel: 250-387-0944; *Fax:* 250-356-5681
robert.sutherland@leg.bc.ca
www.leg.bc.ca/learn-about-us/hansard-services
Other Communications: Hansard E-mail: HansardServices@leg.bc.ca

Government Caucus Office (Liberal)
East Annex, Parliament Buildings, Victoria, BC V8V 1X4
Tel: 250-356-6171; *Fax:* 250-356-6176
www.governmentcaucus.bc.ca
twitter.com/bcliberalcaucus
www.facebook.com/BCLiberalCaucus
www.youtube.com/user/BCGovCaucus

Premier; President, Executive Council; Leader, Liberal Party of British Columbia, Hon. Christy Clark, Liberal
Tel: 250-387-1715; *Fax:* 250-387-0087
premier@gov.bc.ca
Social Media: twitter.com/christyclarkbc,
www.facebook.com/ChristyClarkForBC

Government House Leader; Minister, Finance, Hon. Michael de Jong, Q.C., Liberal
Tel: 250-387-3751; *Fax:* 250-387-5594
FIN.Minister@gov.bc.ca
Social Media: twitter.com/mike_de_jong,
www.facebook.com/michaeldejongbc

Deputy House Leader; Minister, Transportation & Infrastructure, Hon. Todd Stone
Tel: 250-387-1978; *Fax:* 250-356-2290
todd.stone.mla@leg.bc.ca
Social Media: twitter.com/toddstonebc

Caucus Chair; Minister, Social Development & Social Innovation, Hon. Michelle Stilwell
Tel: 250-356-7750; *Fax:* 250-356-7292
michelle.stilwell.mla@leg.bc.ca

Government Whip, Eric Foster
Tel: 250-356-9574; *Fax:* 250-356-0596
eric.foster.mla@leg.bc.ca

Deputy Government Whip, Linda Larson
Tel: 250-952-6784; *Fax:* 250-356-0596
linda.larson.mla@leg.bc.ca

Executive Director, Government Caucus, Primrose Carson
Tel: 250-387-2950; *Fax:* 250-387-9066

Director, Communications, Ben James
Tel: 250-356-9131

Director, Research, Rosa Ellithorpe
Tel: 250-387-8943; *Fax:* 250-356-0329

Director, Outreach, Lorne Mayencourt
Tel: 250-952-7283; *Fax:* 250-387-9066

Office of the Opposition (New Democrat)
#201, Parliament Bldgs., Victoria, BC V8V 1X4
Tel: 250-387-3655; *Fax:* 250-387-4680
ndp@leg.bc.ca
bcndpcaucus.ca
twitter.com/bcndpcaucus
www.youtube.com/user/BCNDPCaucus

Leader, Official Opposition, John Horgan
Tel: 250-387-3655; *Fax:* 250-387-4680
john.horgan.mla@leg.bc.ca
Note: Adrian Dix announced his intention to resign as leader of the NDP on September 19, 2013. He was replaced by John Horgan on May 4, 2014.

Opposition House Leader, Mike Farnworth
Tel: 250-387-3655; *Fax:* 250-387-4680
mike.farnworth.mla@leg.bc.ca

Opposition Caucus Chair, Shane Simpson
Tel: 250-387-3655; *Fax:* 250-387-4680
shane.simpson.mla@leg.bc.ca

Opposition Caucus Whip, Maurine Karagianis
Tel: 250-387-3655; *Fax:* 250-387-4680
maurine.karagianis.mla@leg.bc.ca

Deputy Opposition House Leader, Michelle Mungall
Tel: 250-387-3655; *Fax:* 250-387-4680
michelle.mungall.mla@leg.bc.ca

Opposition Caucus Vice-Chair, Kathy Corrigan
Tel: 250-387-3655; *Fax:* 250-387-4680
kathy.corrigan.mla@leg.bc.ca

Deputy Opposition Whip, Scott Fraser
Tel: 250-387-3655; *Fax:* 250-387-4680
scott.fraser.mla@leg.bc.ca

Chief of Staff, Suzanne Christensen
Tel: 250-953-4707

Executive Director, Mike Lowe
Tel: 250-953-4645

Legislative Committees
#224, Parliament Bldgs., Victoria, BC V8V 1X4
Tel: 250-356-2933; *Fax:* 250-356-8172
www.leg.bc.ca/cmt
www.facebook.com/157086584375374

At the beginning of each session, Select Standing Committees are established by the Legislative Assembly in British Columbia. The following Select Standing Committees have been established: Aboriginal Affairs; Children & Youth; Crown Corporations; Education; Finance & Government Services; Health; Legislative Initiatives; Parliamentary Reform, Ethical Conduct, Standing Orders & Private Bills; & Public Accounts.

Deputy Clerk & Clerk of Committees, Kate Ryan-Lloyd
Tel: 250-356-2895; *Fax:* 250-356-8172
ClerkComm@leg.bc.ca

Fortieth Legislature - British Columbia

Parliament Buildings, Victoria, BC V8V 1X4
Tel: 250-387-3785; *Fax:* 250-387-0942
ClerkHouse@leg.bc.ca
www.leg.bc.ca
twitter.com/BCLegislature
www.facebook.com/157086584375374

Last General Election: May 14, 2013.
Next General Election: May 9, 2017.
Party Standings (Sept. 2016):
Liberal 48;
New Democratic Party 35;
Independent 2;
Total 85.
Salaries, Indemnities, & Allowances: (2009):
Annual Basic Compensation per Member $101,859.00.
Additional Salaries:
Premier $91,673.10;
Leader of the Official Opposition $50,929.50;
Leader of a recognized political party other than the government or the Official Opposition $25,464.75;
Member, Executive Council with portfolio $50,929.50;
Member, Executive Council without portfolio $35,650.65;
Speaker $50,929.50;
Deputy Speaker $35,650.65;
Assistant Deputy Speaker $35,650.65;
Government Whip $20,371.80;
Deputy Government Whip $15,278.85;
Official Opposition Whip $20,371.80;
Official Opposition Deputy Whip $15,278.85
Party Whip of a recognized political party other than the government or the Official Opposition $10,185.90;
House Leader $20,371.80;
House Leader of a recognized political party other than the government or the Official Opposition $10,185.90;
Deputy Chair, Committee of the Whole $20,371.80;
Parliamentary Secretary $15,278.85.
The following is a list of each Member of the Legislative Assembly of British Columbia, including the constituency, the total number of registered voters for the 2013 provincial general election, party affiliation, & contact information:

Members of the Legislative Assembly of British Columbia

Minister, Justice; Attorney General, Hon. Suzanne Anton
Constituency: Vancouver-Fraserview *No. of Constituents:* 39,849, Liberal
Tel: 250-387-1866; *Fax:* 250-387-6411
suzanne.anton.mla@leg.bc.ca
Other Communications: Constituency Phone: 604-660-2035; Fax: 604-660-2368
Social Media: twitter.com/SuzanneAnton, www.facebook.com/suzanne.anton
Note: Web Site: www.gov.bc.ca/justice (Ministry of Justice)
Constituency Office
#112, 2609 East 49th Ave.
Vancouver, BC V5S 1J9

Dan Ashton
Constituency: Penticton *No. of Constituents:* 43,483, Liberal
Tel: 250-356-1745
Toll-free: 866-487-4402; *Fax:* 250-952-7263
dan.ashton.mla@leg.bc.ca
danashtonmla.ca
Other Communications: Constituency Phone: 250-487-4400; Fax: 250-487-4405
Social Media: twitter.com/MLADanAshton, www.facebook.com/ElectDanAshton
Constituency Office
#210, 300 Riverside Dr.
Penticton, BC V2A 9C9

Robin Austin
Constituency: Skeena *No. of Constituents:* 21,164, New Democratic Party
Tel: 250-387-3655; *Fax:* 250-387-4680
robin.austin.mla@leg.bc.ca
bcndpcaucus.ca/mla/robin-austin
Other Communications: Terrace: 250-638-7906; Kitimat: 250-632-9886
Social Media: twitter.com/Robin4skeena, www.facebook.com/Robin4Skeena, www.linkedin.com/pub/robin-austin/30/89a/984
Constituency Office
#112, 4710 Lazelle Ave.
Terrace, BC V8G 1T2

Harry Bains
Constituency: Surrey-Newton *No. of Constituents:* 33,367, New Democratic Party
Tel: 250-387-3655; *Fax:* 250-387-4680
harry.bains.mla@leg.bc.ca
harrybains.ca
Other Communications: Constituency Phone: 604-597-8248; Fax: 604-597-8882
Social Media: twitter.com/HarryBainsSN, www.facebook.com/373406402773313
Constituency Office
#102, 7093 King George Blvd.
Surrey, BC V3W 5A5

Donna Barnett
Constituency: Cariboo-Chilcotin *No. of Constituents:* 21,585, Liberal
Tel: 250-387-3820; *Fax:* 250-387-9066
donna.barnett.mla@leg.bc.ca
donnabarnettmla.bc.ca
Other Communications: 100 Mile: 250-395-3916; Will. Lake: 250-305-3800
Constituency Office
#7, 530 Horse Lake Rd.
PO Box 95
100 Mile House, BC V0K 1E0

Minister, Energy & Mines; Minister Responsible for Core Review, Hon. Bill Bennett
Constituency: Kootenay East *No. of Constituents:* 30,733, Liberal
Tel: 250-387-5896
Toll-free: 866-417-6022; *Fax:* 250-387-4312
bill.bennett.mla@leg.bc.ca
www.bill-bennett.ca
Other Communications: Constituency Phone: 250-417-6022; Fax: 250-417-6026
Social Media: twitter.com/KootenayBill, www.facebook.com/kootenay.bill
Note: Web Site: www.gov.bc.ca/ener (Ministry of Energy & Mines)
Constituency Office
100C Cranbrook St. North
Cranbrook, BC V1C 3P9

Minister, Education, Hon. Mike Bernier
Constituency: Peace River South *No. of Constituents:* 26,142, Liberal
Tel: 250-387-1977
Toll-free: 855-582-3430; *Fax:* 250-356-0948
educ.minister@gov.bc.ca
www.mikebernierbc.ca
Other Communications: Constituency Phone: 250-782-3430; Fax: 250-782-6454
Social Media: twitter.com/Mike_A_Bernier, www.facebook.com/mayormike.bernier
Note: Web Site: www.gov.bc.ca/bced (Ministry of Education)
Constituency Office
#103B, 1100 Alaska Ave.
Dawson Creek, BC V1G 4V8

Doug Bing
Constituency: Maple Ridge-Pitt Meadows *No. of Constituents:* 40,050, Liberal
Tel: 250-953-0971; *Fax:* 250-387-9100
doug.bing.mla@leg.bc.ca
dougbingmla.ca
Other Communications: Constituency Phone: 604-465-9299; Fax: 604-465-9294
Social Media: twitter.com/douglasbing, www.facebook.com/dougbingmla
Constituency Office
#104, 20130 Lougheed Hwy.
Maple Ridge, BC V2X 2P7

Minister, Jobs, Tourism & Skills Training; Minister Responsible for Labour, Hon. Shirley Bond
Constituency: Prince George-Valemount *No. of Constituents:* 35,433, Liberal
Tel: 250-356-2771; *Fax:* 250-356-3000
shirley.bond.mla@leg.bc.ca
shirleybondmla.bc.ca
Other Communications: Constituency Phone: 250-612-4181; Fax: 250-612-4188
Social Media: twitter.com/shirleybond, www.facebook.com/shirley.bond
Note: Web Site: www.gov.bc.ca/jtst (Ministry of Jobs, Tourism & Skills Training)
Constituency Office
1350 - 5th Ave.
Prince George, BC V2L 3L4

Minister, Children & Family Development, Hon. Stephanie Cadieux
Constituency: Surrey-Cloverdale *No. of Constituents:* 52,817, Liberal
Tel: 250-387-9699; *Fax:* 250-387-9722
stephanie.cadieux.mla@leg.bc.ca
stephaniecadieuxmla.bc.ca
Other Communications: Constituency Phone: 604-576-3792; Fax: 604-576-2635
Social Media: twitter.com/MLACadieux, www.facebook.com/stephaniecadieux
Note: Web Site: www.gov.bc.ca/mcf (Ministry of Children & Family Development)
Constituency Office
#101, 5658 - 176th St.
Surrey, BC V3S 4C6

Spencer Chandra Herbert
Constituency: Vancouver-West End *No. of Constituents:* 37,609, New Democratic Party
Tel: 250-387-3655; *Fax:* 250-387-4680
s.chandraherbert.mla@leg.bc.ca
www.spencerchandraherbert.ca
Other Communications: Constituency Phone: 604-660-7307; Fax: 604-660-7300
Social Media: twitter.com/SChandraHerbert
Constituency Office
929 Denman St.
Vancouver, BC V6G 2L9

Raj Chouhan
Constituency: Burnaby-Edmonds *No. of Constituents:* 37,132, New Democratic Party
Tel: 250-387-3655; *Fax:* 250-387-4680
raj.chouhan.mla@leg.bc.ca
www.rajchouhan.ca
Other Communications: Constituency Phone: 604-660-7301; Fax: 604-660-7304
Social Media: twitter.com/rajchouhan, www.facebook.com/rajchouhan.ndp
Constituency Office
5234 Rumble St.
Burnaby, BC V5J 2B6

Premier; President, Executive Council, Hon. Christy Clark
Constituency: Westside-Kelowna *No. of Constituents:* 45,389, Liberal
Tel: 250-387-1715; *Fax:* 250-387-0087
premier@gov.bc.ca
www.bcliberals.com/premier
Other Communications: Constituency Phone: 250-768-8426; Fax: 250-768-8436
Social Media: twitter.com/christyclarkbc, www.facebook.com/ChristyClarkForBC
Constituency Office
#3, 2429 Dobbin Rd.
West Kelowna, BC V4T 2L4

Deputy Premier; Minister, Natural Gas Development; Minister Responsible, Housing, Hon. Rich Coleman
Constituency: Fort Langley-Aldergrove *No. of Constituents:* 48,163, Liberal
Tel: 250-953-0900; *Fax:* 250-953-0927
rich.coleman.mla@leg.bc.ca
richcolemanmla.bc.ca
Other Communications: Constituency Phone: 604-882-3151; Fax: 604-882-3154
Social Media: twitter.com/colemancountry
Note: Web Site: www.gov.bc.ca/mngd (Ministry of Natural Gas Development & Responsible for Housing)
Constituency Office
#130, 7888 - 200th St.
Langley, BC V2Y 3J4

Katrine Conroy
Constituency: Kootenay West *No. of Constituents:* 31,793, New Democratic Party
Tel: 250-387-3655
Toll-free: 888-755-0556; *Fax:* 250-387-4680
katrine.conroy.mla@leg.bc.ca
www.katrineconroy.ca
Other Communications: Constituency Phone: 250-304-2783; Fax: 250-304-2655
Social Media: twitter.com/KatrineConroy, www.facebook.com/7840309339
Constituency Office
#2, 1006 - 3rd St.
Castlegar, BC V1N 3X6

Opposition Caucus Vice-Chair, Kathy Corrigan
Constituency: Burnaby-Deer Lake *No. of Constituents:* 35,520, New Democratic Party
Tel: 250-387-3655; *Fax:* 250-387-4680
kathy.corrigan.mla@leg.bc.ca
www.kathycorrigan.ca
Other Communications: Constituency Phone: 604-775-2414; Fax: 604-775-2550
Social Media: twitter.com/kathycorrigan, www.facebook.com/58134129421
Constituency Office

#150, 5172 Kingsway
Burnaby, BC V5H 2E8

Marc Dalton
Constituency: Maple Ridge-Mission *No. of Constituents:* 45,230, Independent
Tel: 250-953-4769
Toll-free: 877-899-3215; *Fax:* 250-387-9100
marc.dalton.mla@leg.bc.ca
marcdaltonmla.bc.ca
Other Communications: Constituency phone: 604-476-4530; Fax: 604-476-4531
Social Media: twitter.com/MarcDalton, www.facebook.com/MarcDalton4MR.Mis
Constituency Office
#102, 23015 Dewdney Trunk Rd.
Maple Ridge, BC V2X 3K9

Judy Darcy
Constituency: New Westminster *No. of Constituents:* 46,875, New Democratic Party
Tel: 250-387-3655; *Fax:* 250-387-4680
judy.darcy.mla@leg.bc.ca
bcndpcaucus.ca/mla/judy-darcy
Other Communications: Constituency Phone: 604-775-2101; Fax: 604-775-2121
Social Media: twitter.com/DarcyJudy, www.facebook.com/JudyDarcyBC
Constituency Office
737 - 6th St.
New Westminster, BC V3L 3C6

Minister, Finance; Government House Leader, Hon. Michael de Jong, Q.C.
Constituency: Abbotsford West *No. of Constituents:* 31,910, Liberal
Tel: 250-387-3751; *Fax:* 250-387-5594
mike.dejong.mla@leg.bc.ca
www.mikedejong.com
Other Communications: Constituency Phone: 604-870-5486; Fax: 604-870-5444
Social Media: twitter.com/mike_de_jong, www.facebook.com/michaeldejongbc
Note: Web Site: www.gov.bc.ca/fin (Ministry of Finance)
Constituency Office
#103, 32660 George Ferguson Way
Abbotsford, BC V2T 4V6

Adrian Dix
Constituency: Vancouver-Kingsway *No. of Constituents:* 37,946, New Democratic Party
Tel: 250-387-3655; *Fax:* 250-387-4680
adrian.dix.mla@leg.bc.ca
adriandixmla.ca
Other Communications: Constituency Phone: 604-660-0314; Fax: 604-660-1131
Social Media: twitter.com/adriandix, www.facebook.com/adriandixbcndp
Note: Adrian Dix announced his intention to resign as leader of the NDP party on September 19, 2013. He was replaced by John Horgan on May 4, 2014. Dix stayed on as MLA of Vancouver-Kingsway.
Constituency Office
5022 Joyce St.
Vancouver, BC V5R 4G6

Doug Donaldson
Constituency: Stikine *No. of Constituents:* 13,845, New Democratic Party
Tel: 250-387-3655; *Fax:* 250-387-4680
doug.donaldson.mla@leg.bc.ca
dougdonaldson.ca
Other Communications: Hazelton: 250-842-6338; Smithers: 250-847-8841
Social Media: twitter.com/DonaldsonDoug, www.facebook.com/doug.donaldson.stikine
Constituency Office
4345 Field St.
PO Box 227
Hazelton, BC V0J 1Y0

David Eby
Constituency: Vancouver-Point Grey *No. of Constituents:* 41,091, New Democratic Party
Tel: 250-387-3655; *Fax:* 250-387-4680
david.eby.mla@leg.bc.ca
Other Communications: Constituency Phone: 604-660-1297; Fax: 604-660-0862
Social Media: twitter.com/Dave_Eby, www.facebook.com/dave.eby
Constituency Office
2909 West Broadway
Vancouver, B V6K 2G6

Mable Elmore
Constituency: Vancouver-Kensington *No. of Constituents:* 38,755, New Democratic Party
Tel: 250-387-3655; *Fax:* 250-387-4680
mable.elmore.mla@leg.bc.ca
mableelmore.ca
Other Communications: Constituency Phone: 604-775-1033; Fax: 604-775-1330
Social Media: twitter.com/mableelmore, www.facebook.com/VancouverKensingtonNDP
Constituency Office
6106 Fraser St.
Vancouver, BC V5W 3A1

Opposition House Leader, Mike Farnworth
Constituency: Port Coquitlam *No. of Constituents:* 37,056, New Democratic Party
Tel: 250-387-3655; *Fax:* 250-387-4680
mike.farnworth.mla@leg.bc.ca
bcndpcaucus.ca/mla/mike-farnworth
Other Communications: Constituency Phone: 604-927-2088; Fax: 604-927-2090
Social Media: twitter.com/mikefarnworthbc, www.facebook.com/MikeFarnworthPoco
Constituency Office
#107A, 2748 Lougheed Hwy.
Port Coquitlam, BC V3B 6P2

Minister, Community, Sport & Cultural Development; Minister Responsible for TransLink, Hon. Peter Fassbender
Constituency: Surrey-Fleetwood *No. of Constituents:* 35,692, Liberal
Tel: 250-387-2283; *Fax:* 250-387-4312
peter.fassbender.mla@leg.bc.ca
www.fassbender.ca
Other Communications: Constituency Phone: 604-501-3227; Fax: 604-501-3232
Social Media: twitter.com/FassbenderMLA, www.facebook.com/PeterFassbenderSurreyFleetwood
Note: Web Site: www.gov.bc.ca/cscd (Ministry of Community, Sport, Cultural Development)
Constituency Office
#301A, 15930 Fraser Hwy.
Surrey, BC V4N 0X8

Rob Fleming
Constituency: Victoria-Swan Lake *No. of Constituents:* 39,275, New Democratic Party
Tel: 250-387-3655; *Fax:* 250-387-4680
rob.fleming.mla@leg.bc.ca
www.robflemingmla.ca
Other Communications: Constituency Phone: 250-356-5013; Fax: 250-360-2027
Social Media: twitter.com/Rob_Fleming, www.facebook.com/RobFlemingVictoria
Constituency Office
1020 Hillside Ave.
Victoria, BC V8T 2A3

Government Whip, Eric Foster
Constituency: Vernon-Monashee *No. of Constituents:* 47,129, Liberal
Tel: 250-356-9574; *Fax:* 250-356-0596
eric.foster.mla@leg.bc.ca
ericfostermla.bc.ca
Other Communications: Constituency Phone: 250-503-3600; Fax: 250-503-3603
Constituency Office
3209 - 31st Ave.
Vernon, BC V1T 2H2

Deputy Opposition Whip, Scott Fraser
Constituency: Alberni-Pacific Rim *No. of Constituents:* 31,892, New Democratic Party
Tel: 250-387-3655
Toll-free: 866-870-4190; *Fax:* 250-387-4680
scott.fraser.mla@leg.bc.ca
Other Communications: Constituency Phone: 250-720-4515; Fax: 250-720-4511
Constituency Office
3945B Johnston Rd.
Port Alberni, BC V9Y 5N4

Simon Gibson
Constituency: Abbotsford-Mission *No. of Constituents:* 36,510, Liberal
Tel: 250-953-0974
Toll-free: 866-370-6203; *Fax:* 250-387-9100
simon.gibson.mla@leg.bc.ca
simongibsonmla.ca
Other Communications: Constituency Phone: 604-820-6203; Fax: 604-820-6211
Social Media: twitter.com/SimonGibsonMLA, www.facebook.com/SimonGibsonForMLA
Constituency Office
33058 First Ave.
Mission, BC V2V 1G3

Scott Hamilton
Constituency: Delta North *No. of Constituents:* 36,169, Liberal
Tel: 250-953-5144; *Fax:* 250-387-9100
scott.hamilton.mla@leg.bc.ca
mlascotthamilton.ca
Other Communications: Constituency Phone: 604-597-1488; Fax: 604-597-1466
Social Media: twitter.com/scott4delta, www.facebook.com/Scott4Delta
Constituency Office
8350 - 112th St.
Delta, BC V4C 7A2

Sue Hammell
Constituency: Surrey-Green Timbers *No. of Constituents:* 31,271, New Democratic Party
Tel: 250-387-3655; *Fax:* 250-387-4680
sue.hammell.mla@leg.bc.ca
www.suehammellmla.ca
Other Communications: Constituency Phone: 604-590-5868; Fax: 604-590-5873
Social Media: twitter.com/suehammell, www.facebook.com/SueHammellNDP
Constituency Office
#100, 9030 King George Blvd.
Victoria, BC V3V 7Y3

George Heyman
Constituency: Vancouver-Fairview *No. of Constituents:* 45,698, New Democratic Party
Tel: 250-387-3655; *Fax:* 250-387-4680
george.heyman.mla@leg.bc.ca
www.georgeheyman.ca
Other Communications: Constituency Phone: 604-775-2453; Fax: 604-660-6821
Social Media: twitter.com/georgeheyman, www.facebook.com/georgeheyman
Constituency Office
642 West Broadway
Vancouver, BC V5Z 1G1

Gordon Hogg
Constituency: Surrey-White Rock *No. of Constituents:* 40,254, Liberal
Tel: 250-952-7638; *Fax:* 250-387-9100
gordon.hogg.mla@leg.bc.ca
gordonhoggmla.bc.ca
Other Communications: Constituency Phone: 604-542-3930; Fax: 604-542-3933
Constituency Office
#130, 1959 - 152nd St.
Surrey, BC V4A 9E3

Gary Holman
Constituency: Saanich North & the Islands *No. of Constituents:* 45,800, New Democratic Party
Tel: 250-387-3655
Toll-free: 855-955-5711; *Fax:* 250-387-4680
gary.holman.mla@leg.bc.ca
www.garyholmanmla.ca
Other Communications: Constituency Phone: 250-655-5711
Social Media: twitter.com/HolmanGary, www.facebook.com/GaryHolmanMLA
Constituency Office
2393 beacon Ave.
Sidney, BC V8L 1W9

Leader, Official Opposition, John Horgan
Constituency: Juan de Fuca *No. of Constituents:* 40,002, New Democratic Party
Tel: 250-387-3655; *Fax:* 250-387-4680
john.horgan.mla@leg.bc.ca
www.johnhorgan.com
Other Communications: Constituency Phone: 250-391-2801; Fax: 250-391-2804
Social Media: twitter.com/jjhorgan, www.facebook.com/JuandeFucaNDP
Note: John Horgan was acclaimed Leader of the Official Opposition on May 4, 2014.
Constituency Office
#122, 2806 Jacklin Rd.
Victoria, BC V9B 5A4

Marvin Hunt
Constituency: Surrey-Panorama *No. of Constituents:* 45,415, Liberal
Tel: 250-952-7271; *Fax:* 250-387-9100
marvin.hunt.mla@leg.bc.ca
marvinhuntmla.ca
Other Communications: Constituency Phone: 604-574-5662; Fax: 604-574-5691
Social Media: twitter.com/marvinhunt4bc, www.facebook.com/37802741947, www.linkedin.com/pub/marvin-hunt/1a/10/9aa
Constituency Office
#120, 5455 - 152nd St.
Surrey, BC V3S 5A5

Vicki Huntington
Constituency: Delta South *No. of Constituents:* 34,989, Independent
Tel: 250-952-7594; *Fax:* 250-952-7598
vicki.huntington.mla@leg.bc.ca
vickihuntington.org
Other Communications: Constituency Phone: 604-940-7924; Fax: 604-940-7927
Social Media: twitter.com/vickihuntington, www.facebook.com/Vicki.J.Huntington
Constituency Office
4805 Delta St.
Delta, BC V4K 2T7

Carole James
Constituency: Victoria-Beacon Hill *No. of Constituents:* 44,550, New Democratic Party
Tel: 250-387-3655; *Fax:* 250-387-4680
carole.james.mla@leg.bc.ca
www.carolejamesmla.ca
Other Communications: Constituency Phone: 250-952-4211; Fax: 250-952-4586
Social Media: twitter.com/carolejames, www.facebook.com/carolejames
Constituency Office
1084 Fort St.
Victoria, BC V8V 3K4

Opposition Caucus Whip, Maurine Karagianis
Constituency: Esquimalt-Royal Roads *No. of Constituents:* 39,253, New Democratic Party
Tel: 250-387-3655; *Fax:* 250-387-4680
maurine.karagianis.mla@leg.bc.ca
www.maurinekaragianis.ca
Other Communications: Constituency Phone: 250-479-8326; Fax: 250-479-5003
Social Media: twitter.com/mkaragianis, www.facebook.com/7661314937
Constituency Office
#A5, 100 Aldersmith Pl.
Victoria, BC V9A 7M8

Leonard Krog
Constituency: Nanaimo *No. of Constituents:* 40,545, New Democratic Party
Tel: 250-387-3655; *Fax:* 250-387-4680
leonard.krog.mla@leg.bc.ca
leonardkrog-mla.ca
Other Communications: Constituency Phone: 250-714-0630; Fax: 250-714-0859
Social Media: twitter.com/LeonardKrogMla
Constituency Office
#4, 77 Victoria Cres.
Nanaimo, BC V9R 5B9

Greg Kyllo
Constituency: Shuswap *No. of Constituents:* 41,547, Liberal
Tel: 250-953-0965
Toll-free: 877-771-7557; *Fax:* 250-952-7263
greg.kyllo.mla@leg.bc.ca
gregkyllomla.ca
Other Communications: Constituency Phone: 250-833-7414; Fax: 250-833-7422
Social Media: twitter.com/KylloGreg, www.facebook.com/gregkylloshuswap
Constituency Office
#202A, 371 Alexander St. NE
Salmon Arm, BC V1E 4N7

Minister, Health, Hon. Terry Lake
Constituency: Kamloops-North Thompson *No. of Constituents:* 40,610, Liberal
Tel: 250-953-3547; *Fax:* 250-356-9587
terry.lake.mla@leg.bc.ca
terrylakemla.bc.ca
Other Communications: Constituency Phone: 250-554-5413; Fax: 250-554-5417
Social Media: twitter.com/TerryLakeMLA
Note: Web Site: www.gov.bc.ca/health (Ministry of Health)
Constituency Office
618-B Transquille Rd.
Kamloops, BC V2B 3H6

Deputy Government Whip, Linda Larson
Constituency: Boundary-Similkameen *No. of Constituents:* 29,682, Liberal
Tel: 250-952-6784
Toll-free: 855-498-5122; *Fax:* 250-356-0596
linda.larson.mla@leg.bc.ca
lindalarsonmla.ca
Other Communications: Constituency Phone: 250-498-5122; Fax: 250-498-5427
Constituency Office
6369 Main St.
PO Box 998
Oliver, BC V0H 1T0

Deputy Speaker, Richard T. Lee
Constituency: Burnaby North *No. of Constituents:* 41,227, Liberal
Tel: 250-356-3052; *Fax:* 250-387-9100
richard.lee.mla@leg.bc.ca
richardleemla.bc.ca
Other Communications: Constituency Phone: 604-775-0778; Fax: 604-775-0833
Social Media: twitter.com/Richard_T_Lee, www.linkedin.com/in/richardleemla
Constituency Office
1833 Willingdon Ave.
Burnaby, BC V5C 5R3

Minister, Agriculture, Hon. Norm Letnick
Constituency: Kelowna-Lake Country *No. of Constituents:* 45,028, Liberal
Tel: 250-387-1023
Toll-free: 866-765-8516; *Fax:* 250-387-1522
norm.letnick.mla@leg.bc.ca
normletnickmla.bc.ca
Other Communications: Constituency Phone: 250-765-8516; Fax: 250-765-7283
Social Media: twitter.com/normletnick, www.facebook.com/normletnickmla, www.linkedin.com/pub/norm-letnick/15/8a0/589
Note: Web Site: www.gov.bc.ca/agri (Ministry of Agriculture)
Constituency Office
#101, 330 Hwy. 33 West
Kelowna, BC V1X 1X9

Norm Macdonald
Constituency: Columbia River-Revelstoke *No. of Constituents:* 25,072, New Democratic Party
Tel: 250-387-3655
Toll-free: 866-870-4188; *Fax:* 350-387-4680
norm.macdonald.mla@leg.bc.ca
www.normmacdonald.ca
Other Communications: Constituency Phone: 250-344-4816; Fax: 350-344-4815
Constituency Office
#104, 806 - 9th St. North
Golden, BC V0A 1H0

Melanie Mark
Constituency: Vancouver-Mount Pleasant, New Democratic Party
Tel: 250-387-3655; *Fax:* 250-387-4680
melanie.mark.mla@leg.bc.ca
Social Media: twitter.com/melaniejmark, www.facebook.com/melaniemarkvmp, ca.linkedin.com/in/melanie-mark-95598b97
Note: Melanie Mark won the riding in a by-election held Feb. 2, 2016.

John Martin
Constituency: Chilliwack *No. of Constituents:* 37,784, Liberal
Tel: 250-953-4613
Toll-free: 866-424-8350; *Fax:* 250-387-9100
john.martin.mla@leg.bc.ca
johnmartinmla.ca
Other Communications: Constituency Phone: 604-702-5214; Fax: 604-702-5223
Social Media: twitter.com/JohnMartinMLA
Constituency Office
#1, 45953 Airport Rd.
Chilliwack, BC V2P 1A3

Don McRae
Constituency: Comox Valley *No. of Constituents:* 50,456, Liberal
Tel: 250-356-0963; *Fax:* 250-952-7263
don.mcrae.mla@leg.bc.ca
donmcraemla.bc.ca
Other Communications: Constituency Phone: 250-703-2422; Fax: 250-703-2425
Social Media: twitter.com/DonMcRaeMLA, www.facebook.com/donmcrae
Constituency Office
437 - 5th St.
Courtenay, BC V9N 1J7

Minister, Public Safety & Solicitor General, Hon. Mike Morris
Constituency: Prince George-Mackenzie *No. of Constituents:* 33,587, Liberal
Tel: 250-356-2178; *Fax:* 250-356-2142
mike.morris.mla@leg.bc.ca
mikemorrismla.ca
Other Communications: Constituency Phone: 250-612-4194; Fax: 250-612-4191
Social Media: twitter.com/MikeMorrisforBC, www.facebook.com/MikeMorrisforBC
Constituency Office
1621 Nicholson St. South
Prince George, BC V2N 1V7

Deputy Opposition House Leader, Michelle Mungall
Constituency: Nelson-Creston *No. of Constituents:* 28,262, New Democratic Party
Tel: 250-387-3655
Toll-free: 87- 38- 449; *Fax:* 250-387-4680
michelle.mungall.mla@leg.bc.ca
www.michellemungall.com
Other Communications: Constituency Phone: 250-354-5944; Fax: 250-354-5937
Social Media: twitter.com/michellemungall, www.facebook.com/michelle.mungall
Constituency Office
#204, 402 Baker St.
Nelson, BC V1L 4H8

Minister, Small Business & Red-Tape Reduction; Minister Responsible for the Liquor Distribution Branch, Hon. Coralee Oakes
Constituency: Cariboo North *No. of Constituents:* 23,838, Liberal
Tel: 250-356-8247; *Fax:* 250-356-8250
coralee.oakes.mla@leg.bc.ca
coraleeoakesmla.ca
Other Communications: Constituency Phone: 250-991-0296; Fax: 250-992-5629
Social Media: twitter.com/CoraleeOakes, www.facebook.com/teamcoralee
Constituency Office
644A Front St.
Quesnel, BC V2J 2K8

Pat Pimm
Constituency: Peace River North *No. of Constituents:* 26,142, Independent
Tel: 250-953-4892; *Fax:* 250-387-1522
pat.pimm.mla@leg.bc.ca
patpimmmla.bc.ca
Other Communications: Constituency Phone: 250-263-0101; Fax: 250-263-0104
Social Media: twitter.com/pat_pimm, www.facebook.com/430620263692782
Constituency Office
10104 - 100th St.
Fort St. John, BC V1J 3Y7

Darryl Plecas
Constituency: Abbotsford South *No. of Constituents:* 36,280, Liberal
Tel: 250-952-7275; *Fax:* 250-387-9100
darryl.plecas.mla@leg.bc.ca
darrylplecasmla.ca
Other Communications: Constituency Phone: 604-744-0700; Fax: 604-744-0701
Social Media: twitter.com/DarrylPlecas, www.facebook.com/DarrylPlecasforMLA
Constituency Office
33553 Marshall Rd.
Abbotsford, BC V2S 1K8

Minister, Environment, Hon. Mary Polak
Constituency: Langley *No. of Constituents:* 46,414, Liberal
Tel: 250-387-1187; *Fax:* 250-387-1356
mary.polak.mla@leg.bc.ca
marypolakmla.bc.ca
Other Communications: Constituency Phone: 604-514-8206; Fax: 604-514-0195
Social Media: www.facebook.com/maryforbc
Note: Web Site: www.gov.bc.ca/env (Ministry of Environment)
Constituency Office
#102, 20611 Fraser Hwy.
Langley, BC V3A 4G4

Lana Popham
Constituency: Saanich South *No. of Constituents:* 39,213, New Democratic Party
Tel: 250-387-3655; *Fax:* 250-387-4680
lana.popham.mla@leg.bc.ca
saanichsouth.blogspot.com
Other Communications: Constituency Phone: 250-479-4154; Fax: 250-479-4176
Social Media: twitter.com/lanapopham, www.facebook.com/LanaPophamSaanichSouth
Constituency Office
4085 Quadra St.
Victoria, BC V8X 1K5

Bruce Ralston
Constituency: Surrey-Whalley *No. of Constituents:* 37,138, New Democratic Party
Tel: 250-387-3655; *Fax:* 250-387-4680
bruce.ralston.mla@leg.bc.ca
www.bruceralstonmla.ca
Other Communications: Constituency Phone: 604-586-2740; Fax: 604-586-2800
Social Media: twitter.com/BruceRalston, www.facebook.com/bruceralstonsurrey
Constituency Office
10574 King George Blvd.
Surrey, BC V3T 2X3

Speaker, Hon. Linda Reid
Constituency: Richmond East *No. of Constituents:* 45,048, Liberal
Tel: 250-387-3952; *Fax:* 250-387-2813
linda.reid.mla@leg.bc.ca
lindareidmla.bc.ca
Other Communications: Constituency Phone: 604-775-0891; Fax: 604-775-0999
Social Media: twitter.com/MLAReid
Constituency Office
#130, 8040 Garden City Rd.
Richmond, BC V6Y 2N9

Linda Reimer
Constituency: Port Moody-Coquitlam *No. of Constituents:* 35,731, Liberal
Tel: 250-387-2203; *Fax:* 250-387-9100
linda.reimer.mla@leg.bc.ca
www.lindareimer.ca
Other Communications: Constituency Phone: 604-469-5430; Fax: 604-469-5435
Social Media: twitter.com/LindaReimerMLA, www.facebook.com/LindaReimerForMLA
Constituency Office

#203, 130 Brew St.
Port Moody, BC V3H 0E3
Jennifer Rice
Constituency: North Coast *No. of Constituents:* 15,500, New Democratic Party
Tel: 250-387-3655
Toll-free: 866-624-7734; *Fax:* 250-387-4680
jennifer.rice.mla@leg.bc.ca
bcndpcaucus.ca/mla/jennifer-rice
Other Communications: Constituency Phone: 250-624-7734; Fax: 250-624-7737
Social Media: twitter.com/JenniferRice6, www.facebook.com/NDPJenniferRice
Constituency Office
818 - 3rd Ave. West
Prince Rupert, BC V8J 1M6
Selina Robinson
Constituency: Coquitlam-Maillardville *No. of Constituents:* 38,623, New Democratic Party
Tel: 250-387-3655; *Fax:* 250-387-4680
selina.robinson.mla@leg.bc.ca
selinarobinson.wordpress.com
Other Communications: Constituency Phone: 604-933-2001; Fax: 604-933-2002
Social Media: twitter.com/selinarobinson, www.facebook.com/selina.d.robinson.7
Constituency Office
#102, 1108 Austin Ave.
Coquitlam, BC V3K 3P5
Bill Routley
Constituency: Cowichan Valley *No. of Constituents:* 43,183, New Democratic Party
Tel: 250-387-3655
Toll-free: 877-715-0127; *Fax:* 250-387-4680
bill.routley.mla@leg.bc.ca
billroutley.com
Other Communications: Constituency Phone: 250-715-0127; Fax: 250-715-0139
Social Media: twitter.com/brotherbillr, www.facebook.com/billroutleyndp
Constituency Office
273 Trunk Rd.
PO Box 599
Duncan, BC V9L 3X9
Doug Routley
Constituency: Nanaimo-North Cowichan *No. of Constituents:* 41,036, New Democratic Party
Tel: 250-387-3655; *Fax:* 250-387-4680
douglas.routley.mla@leg.bc.ca
www.dougroutley.ca
Other Communications: Ladysmith: 250-245-9375; Nanaimo: 250-716-5221
Social Media: twitter.com/DougRoutleyNDP, www.facebook.com/DougRoutleyNDP
Constituency Office
#1, 16 High St.
PO Box 269
Ladysmith, BC V9G 1A2
Minister, Aboriginal Relations & Reconciliation, Hon. John Rustad
Constituency: Nechako Lakes *No. of Constituents:* 17,002, Liberal
Tel: 250-953-4844
Toll-free: 877-964-5650; *Fax:* 250-953-4856
john.rustad.mla@leg.bc.ca
johnrustadmla.bc.ca
Other Communications: Constituency Phone: 250-567-6820; Fax: 250-567-6822
Social Media: www.facebook.com/john.rustad
Note: Web Site: www.gov.bc.ca/arr (Aboriginal Relations & Reconciliation)
Constituency Office
183 First St.
PO Box 421
Vanderhoof, BC V0J 3A0
Jane Jae Kyung Shin
Constituency: Burnaby-Lougheed *No. of Constituents:* 36,366, New Democratic Party
Tel: 250-387-3655; *Fax:* 250-387-4680
jane.shin.mla@leg.bc.ca
Other Communications: Constituency Phone: 604-660-5058
Social Media: www.facebook.com/janeshin.ndp
Constituency Office
#3, 8699 - 10th Ave.
Burnaby, BC V3N 2S9
Nicholas Simons
Constituency: Powell River-Sunshine Coast *No. of Constituents:* 37,727, New Democratic Party
Tel: 250-387-3655; *Fax:* 250-387-4680
nicholas.simons.mla@leg.bc.ca
bcndpcaucus.ca/mla/nicholas-simons
Other Communications: Powell River: 604-485-1249; Sechelt: 604-741-0792
Social Media: twitter.com/NicholasSimons, www.facebook.com/54770956910
Constituency Office
#109, 4675 Marine Ave.
Powell River, BC V8A 2L2
Opposition Caucus Chair, Shane Simpson
Constituency: Vancouver-Hastings *No. of Constituents:* 40,751, New Democratic Party
Tel: 250-387-3655; *Fax:* 250-387-4680
shane.simpson.mla@leg.bc.ca
www.shanesimpson.ca
Other Communications: Constituency Phone: 604-775-2277; Fax: 604-775-2352
Social Media: twitter.com/ShaneSimpsonMLA, www.facebook.com/shane.simpson.94
Constituency Office
2365 Hastings St. East
Vancouver, BC V5L 1V6
Minister, Social Development & Social Innovation; Caucus Chair, Hon. Michelle Stilwell
Constituency: Parksville-Qualicum *No. of Constituents:* 42,898, Liberal
Tel: 250-356-7750; *Fax:* 250-356-7292
michelle.stilwell.mla@leg.bc.ca
michellestilwellmla.ca
Other Communications: Constituency Phone: 250-248-2625; Fax: 250-248-2787
Social Media: twitter.com/Stilwell2013, www.facebook.com/MichelleStilwellMLA
Note: Web Site: www.gov.bc.ca/sdsi (Ministry of Social Development & Social Innovation)
Constituency Office
#2B, 1209 Island Hwy. East
Parksville, BC V9P 2E5
Moira Stilwell
Constituency: Vancouver-Langara *No. of Constituents:* 38,853, Liberal
Tel: 250-952-7653; *Fax:* 250-387-9066
moira.stilwell.mla@leg.bc.ca
moirastilwellmla.bc.ca
Other Communications: Constituency Phone: 604-660-8380; Fax: 604-660-8383
Social Media: twitter.com/DrMoiraStilwell
Constituency Office
7283 Cambie St.
Vancouver, BC V6P 3H2
Minister, Transportation & Infrastructure; Deputy House Leader, Hon. Todd Stone
Constituency: Kamloops-South Thompson *No. of Constituents:* 42,372, Liberal
Tel: 250-387-1978; *Fax:* 250-356-2290
todd.stone.mla@leg.bc.ca
toddstonemla.ca
Other Communications: Constituency Phone: 250-374-2880; Fax: 250-377-3448
Social Media: twitter.com/toddstonebc
Note: Web Site: www.gov.bc.ca/tran (Ministry of Transportation & Infrastructure)
Constituency Office
446 Victoria St.
Kamloops, BC V2C 2A7
Jordan Sturdy
Constituency: West Vancouver-Sea to Sky *No. of Constituents:* 38,053, Liberal
Tel: 250-356-1631; *Fax:* 250-387-9100
jordan.sturdy.mla@leg.bc.ca
www.jordansturdy.ca
Other Communications: Constituency Phone: 604-922-1153; Fax: 604-922-1167
Social Media: twitter.com/jordansturdy, www.facebook.com/JordanWestVanSeatoSky
Constituency Office
6392 Bay St.
West Vancouver, BC V7W 2G9
Sam Sullivan
Constituency: Vancouver-False Creek *No. of Constituents:* 43,157, Liberal
Tel: 250-953-0916; *Fax:* 250-387-9100
sam.sullivan.mla@leg.bc.ca
www.samsullivan.ca
Other Communications: Constituency Phone: 604-775-2601; Fax: 604-775-2607
Social Media: twitter.com/sam_sullivan, www.facebook.com/samsullivancampaign, www.linkedin.com/pub/sam-sullivan/61/426/a59
Constituency Office
#201, 1168 Hamilton St.
Vancouver, BC V6B 2S2
Ralph Sultan
Constituency: West Vancouver-Capilano *No. of Constituents:* 39,246, Liberal
Tel: 250-356-9495; *Fax:* 250-387-9066
ralph.sultan.mla@leg.bc.ca
www.ralphsultanmla.ca
Other Communications: Constituency Phone: 604-981-0050; Fax: 604-981-0055
Social Media: twitter.com/ralph_sultan, www.facebook.com/sultanralph
Constituency Office
#409, 545 Clyde Ave.
West Vancouver, BC V7T 1C5
Jackie Tegart
Constituency: Fraser-Nicola *No. of Constituents:* 22,187, Liberal
Tel: 250-952-7616
Toll-free: 877-378-4802; *Fax:* 250-387-9066
jackie.tegart.mla@leg.bc.ca
jackietegartmla.ca
Other Communications: Constituency Phone: 250-453-9726; Fax: 250-453-9765
Social Media: twitter.com/tegart_jackie, www.facebook.com/561577033860025
Constituency Office
405 Railway Ave.
PO Box 279
Ashcroft, BC V0K 1A0
Minister, Forests, Lands & Natural Resource Operations, Hon. Steve Thomson
Constituency: Kelowna-Mission *No. of Constituents:* 45,230, Liberal
Tel: 250-387-6240; *Fax:* 250-387-1040
steve.thomson.mla@leg.bc.ca
stevethomsonmla.bc.ca
Other Communications: Constituency Phone: 250-712-3620; Fax: 250-712-3626
Social Media: twitter.com/Steve4Kelowna, www.facebook.com/Steve4Kelowna
Note: Web Site: www.gov.bc.ca/for (Ministry of Forests, Lands & Natural Resource Operations)
Constituency Office
#102, 2121 Ethel St.
Kelowna, BC V1Y 2Z6
Jane Thornthwaite
Constituency: North Vancouver-Seymour *No. of Constituents:* 38,786, Liberal
Tel: 250-387-2796; *Fax:* 250-387-9066
jane.thornthwaite.mla@leg.bc.ca
janethornthwaitemla.bc.ca
Other Communications: Constituency Phone: 604-983-9852; Fax: 604-983-9978
Social Media: twitter.com/jthornthwaite, www.facebook.com/JThornthwaite
Constituency Office
#217, 1233 Lynn Valley Rd.
North Vancouver, BC V7J 0A1
Laurie Throness
Constituency: Chilliwack-Hope *No. of Constituents:* 35,848, Liberal
Tel: 250-952-7270; *Fax:* 250-387-9100
laurie.throness.mla@leg.bc.ca
www.lauriethroness.ca
Other Communications: Chilliwack: 604-858-5299; Hope: 604-860-2113
Social Media: twitter.com/LaurieThroness, www.facebook.com/lauriethroness
Constituency Office
#10, 7300 Vedder Rd.
Chilliwack, BC V2R 4G6
Claire Trevena
Constituency: North Island *No. of Constituents:* 41,222, New Democratic Party
Tel: 250-387-3655
Toll-free: 866-387-5100; *Fax:* 250-387-4680
claire.trevena.mla@leg.bc.ca
www.clairetrevena.ca
Other Communications: Campbell Riv.: 250-287-5100; Port Hardy: 250 949-9473
Social Media: twitter.com/clairetrevena, www.facebook.com/64295031941
Constituency Office
908 Island Hwy.
Campbell River, BC V9W 2C3
Minister, Technology, Innovation & Citizens' Services, Hon. Amrik Virk
Constituency: Surrey-Tynehead *No. of Constituents:* 36,881, Liberal
Tel: 250-952-7623; *Fax:* 250-952-7628
amrik.virk.MLA@leg.bc.ca
amrikvirkmla.ca
Other Communications: Constituency Phone: 604-586-3747; Fax: 604-584-4741
Social Media: twitter.com/amrikvirkbc, www.facebook.com/amrikvirkbc
Note: Web Site: www.gov.bc.ca/citz (Ministry of Technology, Innovation & Citizens' Services)
Constituency Office
#201, 15135 - 101 Ave.
Surrey, BC V3R 7Z1

Minister, International Trade; Minister Responsible for the Asia Pacific Strategy & Multiculturalism, Hon. Teresa Wat
Constituency: Richmond Centre *No. of Constituents:* 43,915, Liberal
Tel: 250-953-0910; *Fax:* 250-953-0928
teresa.wat.mla@leg.bc.ca
teresawatmla.ca
Other Communications: Constituency Phone: 604-775-0754; Fax: 604-775-0898
Social Media: twitter.com/Teresa_Wat, www.facebook.com/TeresaWatBC
Note: Web Site: www.gov.bc.ca/mit (Ministry of International Trade)
Constituency Office
#300, 8120 Granville Ave.
Richmond, BC V6Y 1P3

Andrew J. Weaver
Constituency: Oak Bay-Gordon Head *No. of Constituents:* 38,267, Green Party of Canada
Tel: 250-387-8347; *Fax:* 250-387-8338
andrew.weaver.mla@leg.bc.ca
www.andrewweavermla.ca
Other Communications: Constituency Phone: 250-472-8528; Fax: 250-472-6163
Social Media: twitter.com/AJWVictoriaBC, www.facebook.com/AndrewWeaverMLA
Note: Andrew J. Weaver was the first Green Party member ever to be elected in a Canadian provincial legislature.
Constituency Office
#219, 3930 Shelbourne St.
Victoria, BC V8P 5P6

Jodie Wickens
Constituency: Coquitlam-Burke Mountain, New Democratic Party
Tel: 250-387-3655; *Fax:* 250-387-4680
jodie.wickens.mla@leg.bc.ca
Other Communications: Constituency Phone: 604-942-5020; Fax: 604-942-5099
Social Media: twitter.com/jbtwickens, www.facebook.com/jodiewickensndp
Note: Jodie Wickens won the riding in a by-election held Feb. 2, 2016.
Constituency Office
#510, 2950 Glen Dr.
Coquitlam, BC V3B 0J1

Minister, Advanced Education, Hon. Andrew Wilkinson
Constituency: Vancouver-Quilchena *No. of Constituents:* 38,095, Liberal
Tel: 250-356-0179; *Fax:* 250-952-0260
andrew.wilkinson.mla@leg.bc.ca
andrewwilkinsonmla.ca
Other Communications: Constituency Phone: 604-664-0748; Fax: 604-664-0750
Social Media: twitter.com/Wilkinson4BC
Note: Web Site: www.gov.bc.ca/aved (Ministry of Advanced Education)
Constituency Office
5640 Dunbar St.
Vancouver, BC V6N 1W7

Minister of State for Emergency Preparedness, Hon. Naomi Yamamoto
Constituency: North Vancouver-Lonsdale *No. of Constituents:* 40,528, Liberal
Tel: 250-356-8213; *Fax:* 250-356-8223
naomi.yamamoto.mla@leg.bc.ca
naomiyamamotomla.bc.ca
Other Communications: Constituency Phone: 604-981-0033; Fax: 604-981-0044
Social Media: twitter.com/naomiyamamoto, www.facebook.com/naomiyamamoto.northvan
Constituency Office
#5, 221 West Esplanade
North Vancouver, BC V7M 3J3

John Yap
Constituency: Richmond-Steveston *No. of Constituents:* 42,581, Liberal
Tel: 250-953-0919; *Fax:* 250-387-9100
john.yap.mla@leg.bc.ca
johnyapmla.bc.ca
Other Communications: Constituency Phone: 604-241-8452; Fax: 604-241-8493
Social Media: twitter.com/John_Yap, www.facebook.com/JohnYapSteveston
Constituency Office
#115, 4011 Bayview St.
Richmond, BC V7E 0A4

British Columbia Government Departments & Agencies

British Columbia Ministry of Aboriginal Relations & Reconciliation

2957 Jutland Rd., PO Box 9100 Stn. Prov Govt, Victoria, BC V8W 9B1
Tel: 250-387-6121
Toll-Free: 800-663-7867
abrinfo@gov.bc.ca
www.gov.bc.ca/arr
Other Communication: Vancouver Phone: 604-660-2421; Information, Toll-Free Line: 1-800-880-1022

The Ministry of Aboriginal Relations & Reconciliation works to achieve the following goals: reconciliation with Aboriginal peoples; negotiation of lasting agreements; strengthening relationships with the Métis Nation; development of partnerships with Aboriginal people, organizations, & communities; support of capacity building in Aboriginal communities; provision of advice on policy related to Aboriginal people; & revitalization of Aboriginal language & culture.

Minister, Aboriginal Relations & Reconciliation, Hon. John Rustad
Tel: 250-953-4844; *Fax:* 250-953-4856
ABR.Minister@gov.bc.ca

Deputy Minister, Aboriginal Relations & Reconciliation, Doug Caul
Tel: 250-356-1394; *Fax:* 250-387-6073
PO Box 9100 Prov Govt Sta.
Victoria, BC V8W 9B1

Executive Director, Strategic Planning, Maria Wilkie
Tel: 250-356-1645; *Fax:* 250-387-6073
Maria.Wilkie@gov.bc.ca

Director, Executive Operations, Shawna French
Tel: 250-356-6330; *Fax:* 250-387-6073
Shawna.French@gov.bc.ca

Manager, Workforce Strategies Branch, Jeanne Zoschke
Tel: 250-812-7984; *Fax:* 250-356-9230
Jeanne.Zoschke@gov.bc.ca

Associated Agencies, Boards & Commissions:

•British Columbia Treaty Commission (BCTC)
#700, 1111 Melville St.
Vancouver, BC V6E 3V6
Tel: 604-482-9200; *Fax:* 604-482-9222
Toll-free: 855-482-9200
info@bctreaty.net
www.bctreaty.net
The independent & neutral body facilitates treaty negotiations among the governments of Canada, British Columbia, & First Nations in BC.

•Native Economic Development Advisory Board
PO Box 9100 Prov Govt
Victoria, BC V8W 9B1
Tel: 250-387-2536
Supporting sustainable Aboriginal economic development throughout British Columbia is the role of the Native Economic Development Advisory Board.

Fiscal Negotiations Team
Fax: 250-387-5213

Chief Negotiator, Rob Draeseke
Tel: 250-356-8768; *Fax:* 250-356-5213
Rob.Draeseke@gov.bc.ca

Acting Fiscal Negotiator, Mike Scharf
Tel: 250-387-0026
Mike.R.Scharf@gov.bc.ca

Director, Cost-sharing & Financial Mandates, Elisabeth Ellis
Tel: 250-356-9070; *Fax:* 250-356-6073
Elisabeth.Ellis@gov.bc.ca

Director, Fiscal Arrangements & Climate Change, Michael Matsubuchi
Tel: 250-387-6387; *Fax:* 250-356-5312
Michael.Matsubuchi@gov.bc.ca
Other Communications: Cell Phone: 250-744-7454

Negotiations & Regional Operations Division
Fax: 250-387-6073

Assistant Deputy Minister, Christian Kittleson
Tel: 250-356-1086

Chief Negotiator, Heinz Dyck
Tel: 250-356-8769; *Fax:* 250-356-6159
Heinz.Dyck@gov.bc.ca

Chief Negotiator, Mark Lofthouse
Tel: 250-387-0024; *Fax:* 250-387-0887
Mark.Lofthouse@gov.bc.ca
Other Communications: Cell Phone: 250-480-8899

Partnerships & Community Renewal Division
Fax: 250-387-6073

Chief Negotiator, Negotiations & Regional Operations Division, Roger Graham
Tel: 250-356-6599; *Fax:* 250-356-0366
Roger.Graham@gov.bc.ca
Other Communications: Cell Phone: 250-812-8244

Executive Director, Intergovernmental & Community Relations, Ken Armour
Tel: 250-387-2161; *Fax:* 250-356-9467
Ken.Armour@gov.bc.ca

Executive Director, David Stevenson
Tel: 250-387-5522; *Fax:* 250-356-9467
David.Stevenson@gov.bc.ca

Strategic Initiatives Division
Fax: 250-387-6073

Assistant Deputy Minister, Neilane Mayhew
Tel: 250-387-6838

Divisional Coordinator, Janice Franklin
Tel: 250-356-0213
Janice.Franklin@gov.bc.ca

Executive Director, Strategic Policy & Planning Branch, Jaclynn Hunter
Tel: 250-356-5267; *Fax:* 250-356-0366
Jaclynn.Hunter@gov.bc.ca

Executive Director, Cross Government Initiatives, Mary Sue Maloughney
Tel: 250-356-7214; *Fax:* 250-387-0887
MarySue.Maloughney@gov.bc.ca
Other Communications: Cell Phone: 250-589-0931

Executive Director, LNG & Major Projects, Giovanni Puggioni
Tel: 250-952-0530; *Fax:* 250-356-0366
Giovanni.Puggioni@gov.bc.ca

Executive Director, Lands & Resources Branch, John Pyper
Tel: 250-356-5267; *Fax:* 250-387-0887
John.Pyper@gov.bc.ca
Other Communications: Cell Phone: 250-889-4124

Executive Director, South East Coal, Peter Robb
Tel: 250-952-0927; *Fax:* 250-356-0366
Peter.Robb@gov.bc.ca

Executive Director, Implementation & Legislation, Lloyd Roberts
Tel: 250-356-2595
Lloyd.Roberts@gov.bc.ca

Director, Land Programs, Dugald Smith
Tel: 250-952-4960
Dugald.Smith@gov.bc.ca

British Columbia Ministry of Advanced Education

PO Box 9080 Stn. Prov Govt, Victoria, BC V8W 9E2
Tel: 250-356-5170
AVED.GeneralInquiries@gov.bc.ca
www.gov.bc.ca/aved

The Ministry of Advanced Education is responsible for the following: universities; colleges; post-secondary policy & accountability; post secondary financing; student financial assistance; research, innovation, & technology; & multiculturalism.

Minister, Advanced Education, Hon. Andrew Wilkinson
Tel: 250-356-0179; *Fax:* 250-952-0260
AVED.Minister@gov.bc.ca

Deputy Minister, Sandra Carroll
Tel: 250-356-5173; *Fax:* 250-356-5468
AVED.DeputyMinister@gov.bc.ca
PO Box 9884 Prov Govt Sta.
Victoria, BC V8W 9T6

Deputy Minister, Government Communications & Public Engagement, John Paul Fraser
Tel: 250-356-2277; *Fax:* 250-356-6942
JohnPaul.Fraser@gov.bc.ca
www.gov.bc.ca/gcpe

Chief of Staff, Jennifer Chalmers
Tel: 250-356-0179; *Fax:* 250-952-0260
Jennifer.Chalmers@gov.bc.ca

Director, Executive Operations & Strategic Support, Jennifer Meadows
Tel: 250-952-6842; *Fax:* 250-356-5468

Manager, Operations & Ministerial Correspondence & Research Unit, Judy Johnstone
Tel: 250-356-6284; *Fax:* 250-356-5468

Associated Agencies, Boards & Commissions:

•British Columbia Council on Admissions & Transfer (BCCAT)
#709, 555 Seymour St.
Vancouver, BC V6B 3H6
Tel: 604-412-7700; *Fax:* 604-683-0576
info@bccat.ca
www.bccat.ca

•Degree Quality Assessment Board (DQAB)
Degree Quality Assessment Board Secretariat
PO Box 9177 Prov Govt
Victoria, BC V8W 9H8
Tel: 250-356-5406
www.aved.gov.bc.ca/degree-authorization/board/welcome.htm

The Degree Quality Assessment Board reviews applications from British Columbia public post-secondary institutions, & private & out-of-province public post-secondary institutions. Applications concern new degree programs & exempt status, & the use of the word university. Recommendations are then made to the Minister of Advanced Education & Labour Market Development.

•Private Career Training Institutions Agency (PCTIA)
#203, 1155 West Pender St.
Vancouver, BC V6E 2P4
Tel: 604-569-0033; *Fax:* 778-945-0606
Toll-free: 800-661-7441
info@pctia.bc.ca
www.pctia.bc.ca
Other Communication: Board Inquiries, E-mail: board@pctia.bc.ca
The Private Career Training Institutions Agency is the regulatory agency for private training institutions in British Columbia. The Agency works in accordance with the Private Career Training Institutions Act, Regulations & Bylaws.

Board Resourcing & Development Office
Tel: 604-660-1170; *Fax:* 604-775-0158
abc@gov.bc.ca
www.gov.bc.ca/brdo
The Board Resourcing & Development Office has the following responsibilities: forming guidelines for appointments to agencies; ensuring an open & consistent appointment process; & confirming that appointees to agencies receive orientation & continuing professional development.
Director, Natalya Brodie
Tel: 604-775-1683; *Fax:* 604-775-0158
Natalya.Brodie@gov.bc.ca

Government Communications & Public Engagement
PO Box 9409 Stn. Prov Govt, Victoria, BC V8W 9V1
Tel: 250-387-1337; *Fax:* 250-387-3534
Deputy Minister, John Paul Fraser
Tel: 250-356-2277
JohnPaul.Fraser@gov.bc.ca

Corporate Priorities & Communications Operations
PO Box 9409 Stn. Prov Govt, Victoria, BC V8W 9V1
Assistant Deputy Minister, Matt Gordon
Tel: 250-356-7398
Matt.Gordon@gov.bc.ca
Corporate Director, Katherine Laurence
Tel: 604-775-1669
Katherine.Laurence@gov.bc.ca
Executive Director, Comminications Operations, Nick Koolsbergen
Tel: 250-361-6913
Nick.Koolsbergen@gov.bc.ca

Strategic Communications Services
PO Box 9409 Stn. Prov Govt, Victoria, BC V8W 9V1
Fax: 250-356-2872
Assistant Deputy Minister, Kelly Gleeson
Tel: 250-356-8608; *Fax:* 250-356-2872
Kelly.Gleeson@gov.bc.ca
Executive Director, Marketing & Communications Support Service, Mary Dila
Tel: 250-356-7823; *Fax:* 250-387-6070
Mary.Dila@gov.bc.ca
Director, Coporate Planning, Carleen Kerr
Tel: 250-387-5033; *Fax:* 250-387-6070
Carleen.Kerr@gov.bc.ca
Director, Graphic Design, Andrew Pratt
Tel: 250-356-8120; *Fax:* 250-387-6070
Andrew.Pratt@gov.bc.ca
Director, Advertising & Marketing Services, Kevin Watt
Tel: 250-882-4374; *Fax:* 250-387-1435
Kevin.Watt@gov.bc.ca

Strategic Initiatives Division
PO Box 9439 Stn. Prov Govt, Victoria, BC V8W 9V3
Fax: 250-387-7391
Assistant Deputy Minister, Denise Champion
Tel: 250-953-4685; *Fax:* 250-387-7971
Denise.Champion@gov.bc.ca
Executive Director, Corporate Online Services, Walter Moser
Tel: 250-217-6017
Walter.Moser@gov.bc.ca
Executive Director, Citizen Engagement, David Hume
Tel: 250-589-9043; *Fax:* 250-356-7391
David.Hume@gov.bc.ca
Director, Strategic Business Transformation, Irene Guglielmi
Tel: 250-216-7038; *Fax:* 250-387-2144
Irene.Guglielmi@gov.bc.ca
Director, Enterprise Data Services, Elaine Dawson
Tel: 250-952-7957; *Fax:* 250-387-2144
Elaine.Dawson@gov.bc.ca
Director, Financial Operations & Workplace Support Services, Jack Taekema
Tel: 778-698-2313; *Fax:* 250-387-6687
Jack.Taekema@gov.bc.ca
Director, Citizen Engagement, Tanya Twynstra
Tel: 250-507-2163; *Fax:* 250-387-0718
Tanya.Twynstra@gov.bc.ca
Executive Director, Citizen Engagement, David Hume
Tel: 250-589-9043; *Fax:* 250-356-7391
David.Hume@gov.bc.ca

Financial & Management Services Division
PO Box 9134 Stn. Prov Govt, Victoria, BC V8W 9B5
Tel: 250-356-2496; *Fax:* 250-356-5468
Assistant Deputy Minister & EFO, Kevin Brewster
Tel: 250-356-2496; *Fax:* 250-356-5468
Chief Financial Officer, Donna Porter
Tel: 250-356-6819; *Fax:* 250-356-8851
Donna.Porter@gov.bc.ca
Chief Information Officer & Executive Director, Technology & Business Transformation Branch, Trevor Hurst
Tel: 250-415-5899; *Fax:* 250-952-0739
Trevor.Hurst@gov.bc.ca
Executive Director, Sector Business Innovation, Jeanne Sedun
Tel: 250-952-7412
Jeanne.Sedun@gov.bc.ca
Executive Director, Post-Secondary Finance, Vacant
Tel: 250-387-8820
Manager, Capital Asset Management, Vacant
Director, Post-Secondary Finance, Donna Friedlander
Tel: 250-387-6142
Donna.Friedlander@gov.bc.ca
Director, Technology Solutions, Marijan Sajko
Tel: 250-514-8026; *Fax:* 250-952-0739
Executive Director, Sector Business Innovation, Jeanne Sedun
Tel: 250-952-7412; *Fax:* 250-356-5468
Jeanne.Sedun@gov.bc.ca
Director, Student Services Finance, Rosilyn Soo
Tel: 250-508-5039
AVED.PostSecondaryFinanceBranch@gov.bc.ca

Governance, Legislation & Strategic Policy
PO Box 9157 Stn. Prov Govt, Victoria, BC V8W 9H2
Tel: 250-356-0826; *Fax:* 250-356-5468
Assistant Deputy Minister, Claire Avison
Tel: 250-356-0826; *Fax:* 250-356-5468
Executive Director, Strategic Policy & Planning, Susan B. Brown
Tel: 250-387-6193
Susan.B.Brown@gov.bc.ca
Executive Director, Governance & Quality Assurance Branch, Mary Shaw
Tel: 250-356-5406
Executive Director, Post-Secondary Audit & Accountability Branch, Jacqui Stewart
Tel: 250-387-5029; *Fax:* 250-387-1377
Jacqui.Stewart@gov.bc.ca
Director, Stakeholder Relations, Debbie Azaransky
Tel: 250-387-6160
Director, Compliance & Investigation, Sharlane Callow
Tel: 250-356-7210; *Fax:* 250-387-1377
Sharlane.Callow@gov.bc.ca
Director, Strategic Policy & Planning, Kate Cotie
Tel: 250-387-6197
Kate.Cotie@gov.bc.ca
Director, Research & Analysis, Justin Jones
Tel: 250-387-1105; *Fax:* 250-356-5440
Justin.Jones@gov.bc.ca
Director, Quality Assurance, Dorothy Rogers
Tel: 250-387-6298
Director, Strategic Sector Engagement, Niya West
Tel: 250-387-8874
Niya.West@gov.bc.ca

Institutions & Programs Division
PO Box 9877 Stn. Prov Govt, Victoria, BC V8W 9T6
Tel: 250-952-0697; *Fax:* 250-356-5468
Acting Assistant Deputy Minister, Nicola Lemmer
Tel: 250-952-0697; *Fax:* 250-356-5468
Executive Director, Teaching Universities, Institutes & Aboriginal Programs Branch, Deborah Hull
Tel: 250-387-1446; *Fax:* 250-952-6110
Deborah.Hull@gov.bc.ca
Executive Director, Colleges & Skills Development Branch, Nicola Lemmer
Tel: 250-387-1950; *Fax:* 250-952-6110
Nicola.Lemmer@gov.bc.ca
Executive Director, Research Universities, International Education & Health Programs Branch, Tony Loughran
Tel: 250-387-8871; *Fax:* 250-387-2360
Director, Research Universities, Susan Burns
Tel: 250-356-6114; *Fax:* 250-387-2360
Director, Teaching Universities, Institutes & Aboriginal Programs Branch, Nell Hodges
Tel: 250-387-6182; *Fax:* 250-952-6110
AVED.TeachingUniversInstits&AboriginalProgsBr@gov.bc.ca
Acting Director, Health Programs, Kevin Perrault
Tel: 250-356-8257
Director, Adult Education, Bryan Dreilich
Tel: 250-387-3395; *Fax:* 250-952-6110
Bryan.Dreilich@gov.bc.ca
Director, Colleges, Melanie Nielsen
Tel: 250-387-6156; *Fax:* 250-952-6110
Melanie.Nielsen@gov.bc.ca
Director, Skills Development, Vincent Portal
Tel: 250-516-8439; *Fax:* 250-952-6110
Vincent.Portal@gov.bc.ca
Director, Aboriginal Programs, Vacant

British Columbia Ministry of Agriculture

PO Box 9043 Stn. Prov Govt, Victoria, BC V8W 9E2
Toll-Free: 888-221-7141
agriservicebc@gov.bc.ca
www.gov.bc.ca/agri
Other Communication: Agriculture Communications Office, Phone: 250-356-1674
The mission of the Ministry of Agriculture to stabilize & expand agrifoods production & incomes, to safeguard animal, plant, & human health, & to encourage environmental stewardship. Responsibilities include agriculture, acquacultures & food industry development, fish processing, meat processing policy, food safety & quality, & crop insurance.
Minister, Agriculture, Hon. Norm Letnick
Tel: 250-387-1023; *Fax:* 250-387-1522
AGR.Minister@gov.bc.ca
PO Box 9043 Prov Govt Sta.
Victoria, BC V8W 9E2
Deputy Minister, Agriculture, Derek Sturko
Tel: 250-356-1800; *Fax:* 250-356-8392
Chief of Staff, Karen Bill
Tel: 250-387-1023; *Fax:* 250-387-1522
Karen.Bill@gov.bc.ca
PO Box 9120 Prov Govt Sta.
Victoria, BC V8W 9B4
Manager, Executive Operations, Stefan Morales
Tel: 250-356-5126; *Fax:* 250-356-7279
Stefan.Morales@gov.bc.ca

Associated Agencies, Boards & Commissions:

•Agricultural Land Commission (ALC)
#133, 4940 Canada Way
Burnaby, BC V5G 4K6
Tel: 604-660-7000; *Fax:* 604-660-7033
ALCBurnaby@Victoria1.gov.bc.ca
www.alc.gov.bc.ca
The independent Crown agency strives to preserve agricultural land in British Columbia. The Provincial Agricultural Land Commission also works to encourage & enable farm businesses throughout the province. The Commission's chief responsibility is the administration of the Agricultural Land Commission Act.

•AgriStability
Tel: 877-343-2767; *Fax:* 877-605-8467
AgriStability@gov.bc.ca
www.agf.gov.bc.ca/agristability
Responsibility for AgriStability was transferred to the British Columbia Ministry of Agriculture from Agriculture & Agri-Food Canada in January 2010. AgriStability offices are as follows: 1767 Angus Campbell Rd., Abbotsford, BC V3G 2M3; #201, 583 Fairview Rd., Oliver, BC V0H 1T0; #200, 1500 Hardy St., Kelowna, BC V1Y 8H2; 10043 - 100th St., Fort St. John, BC V1J 3Y5.

•British Columbia Broiler Hatching Egg Commission (BCBHEC)
#180, 32160 South Fraser Way
Abbotsford, BC V2T 1W5
Tel: 604-850-1854; *Fax:* 604-850-1683
info@bcbhec.com
www.bcbhec.com
The British Columbia Broiler Hatching Egg Commission was formed in 1988 under the British Columbia Natural Products Marketing Act, & seeks to promote a better understanding of the broiler hatching egg industry.

•British Columbia Chicken Marketing Board (BCCMB)
#101, 32450 Simon Ave.
Abbotsford, BC V2T 4J2
Tel: 604-859-2868; *Fax:* 604-859-2811
info@bcchicken.ca
www.bcchicken.ca
The purpose of the BC Chicken Marketing Board is to monitor & regulate the production of chicken in British Columbia. The Board works closely with hatcheries, growers, truckers & processors, & carries out field inspections, to accomplish this.

•British Columbia Cranberry Marketing Commission (BCCMC)
PO Box 162 A
Abbotsford, BC V2T 6Z5
Tel: 604-897-9252
cranberries@telus.net
www.bccranberries.com
Since 1968 the BCCMC has administered the British Columbia Cranberry Marketing Scheme, established under the Natural Products Marketing (BC) Act. The Commission reports to the British Columbia Farm Industry Review Board.

•British Columbia Egg Marketing Board (BCEMB)
#250, 32160 South Fraser Way
Abbotsford, BC V2T 1W5
Tel: 604-556-3348; *Fax:* 604-556-3410
bcemb@bcegg.com
www.bcegg.com
The BCEMB was established in 1967 in order to better regulate the price of eggs.

•British Columbia Farm Industry Review Board (BCFIRB)
780 Blanshard St.
PO Box 9129 Prov Govt
Victoria, BC V8W 9B5
Tel: 250-356-8945; *Fax:* 250-356-5131
firb@gov.bc.ca
www.firb.gov.bc.ca
The British Columbia Farm Industry Review Board is a statutory appeal body. It is engaged in the general supervision of marketing boards & commodity boards which operate in the agricultural & aquaculture sectors.

•British Columbia Hog Marketing Commission (BCHMC)
PO Box 8000-280
Abbotsford, BC V2S 6H1
Tel: 604-287-4647; *Fax:* 604-820-6647
info@bcpork.ca
www.bcpork.ca
The Commission seeks to promote BC-grown pork through the use of its logo on all BC pork products.

•British Columbia Milk Marketing Board (BCMMB)
#200, 32160 South Fraser Way
Abbotsford, BC V2T 1W5
Tel: 604-556-3444; *Fax:* 604-556-7717
info@milk-bc.com
bcmilkmarketing.worldsecuresystems.com
The Board is reponsible for promoting, controlling & regulating the production, transportation, packing, storing & marketing of all BC milk products.

•British Columbia Turkey Marketing Board (BCTMB)
#106, 19329 Enterprise Way
Surrey, BC V3S 6J8
Tel: 604-534-5644; *Fax:* 604-534-3651
info@bcturkey.com
www.bcturkey.com
Established in 1966, the Board oversees the licensing of turkey farmers and processors; prices for live turkeys; maintaining of a quota system; & promoting turkey products, under the authority of the Natural Products Marketing (BC) Act.

•British Columbia Vegetable Marketing Commission (BCVMC)
#207, 15252 - 32nd Ave.
Surrey, BC V3S 0R7
Tel: 604-542-9734; *Fax:* 604-542-9735
info@bcveg.com
bcveg.com
The Commission is responsible for promoting controlled marketing for BC vegetable producers, under the authority of the Natural Products Marketing (BC) Act.

Agriculture Science & Policy
PO Box 9120 Stn. Prov Govt, Victoria, BC V8W 9B4
Tel: 250-356-1816; *Fax:* 250-356-7279
Assistant Deputy Minister, James Mack
Tel: 250-356-1821
Director, Plant & Animal Health Branch, Jane Pritchard
Tel: 604-556-3013; *Fax:* 604-556-3015
Jane.Pritchard@gov.bc.ca
Executive Director, Corporate Governance, Policy & Legislation Branch, Lorie Hrycuik
Tel: 250-356-8299; *Fax:* 250-387-0357
Lorie.Hrycuik@gov.bc.ca

Business Development Division
PO Box 9120 Stn. Prov Govt, Victoria, BC V8W 9B4
Tel: 250-356-1122; *Fax:* 250-356-7279
Assistant Deputy Minister, Arif Lalani
Tel: 250-356-1122
Director, Business Risk Management Branch, Gary Falk
Tel: 250-861-7206; *Fax:* 250-861-7490
Gary.Falk@gov.bc.ca
Director, Sector Development Branch, Ken Nickel
Tel: 604-556-3103; *Fax:* 604-556-3030
Ken.Nickel@gov.bc.ca
780 Blanshard St.
PO Box 9308 Prov Govt Sta.
Victoria, BC V8W 9N1

Office of the Auditor General

PO Box 9036 Stn. Prov Govt, Victoria, BC V8W 9A2
Tel: 250-419-6100; *Fax:* 250-387-1230
www.bcauditor.com
twitter.com/BCAuditorGen
www.facebook.com/OAGBC
ca.linkedin.com/company/office-of-the-auditor-general-of-bc
www.youtube.com/user/BCAuditorGeneral
The chief responsibility of the Office of the Auditor General is auditing most of the British Columbia provincial government, with its ministries, Crown corporations, & other organizations.
Auditor General, Carol Bellringer, FCPA, FCA
Tel: 250-419-6100
bcauditor@bcauditor.com
Deputy Auditor General, Russ Jones, FCPA, FCA
Tel: 250-419-6103
Executive Operations Manager, Elaine Hepburn
Tel: 250-419-6108
ehepburn@bcauditor.com

Corporate Services
Assistant Auditor General, Cornell Dover
Tel: 250-419-6139
Manager, Executive Operations, Elaine Hepburn
Tel: 250-419-6108
ehepburn@bcauditor.com
Manager, Communications, Colleen Rose
Tel: 250-419-6207
crose@bcauditor.com

Financial Audit
Assistant Auditor General, Bill Gilhooly, BEcon, CPA, CA
Tel: 250-419-6102
bgilhooly@bcauditor.com
Executive Director, Peter Bourne, CPA, CA, CIA
Tel: 250-419-6141
pbourne@bcauditor.com
Other Communications: Alternate Phone: 250-387-5600
Executive Director, Lisa Moore, CPA, CA
Tel: 250-419-6188
lmoore@bcauditor.com

IT Audit
Director, Ada Chiang
Tel: 250-419-6144
achiang@bcauditor.com
Director, David K. Lau
Tel: 250-419-6118
dlau@bcauditor.com
Director, IT Audit, Pam Hamilton
Tel: 250-419-6164
phamilton@bcauditor.com

Performance Audit
Assistant Auditor General, Sheila Dodds, CPA, CA, CIA
Tel: 250-419-6149
sdodds@bcauditor.com
Assistant Auditor General, Malcolm Gaston, CPA, CMA, CPFA
Tel: 250-419-6105
mgaston@bcauditor.com
Assistant Auditor General, Morris Sydor, MBA, CPA, CA
Tel: 250-419-6106
msydor@bcauditor.com
Executive Director, Laura Hatt
Tel: 250-419-6168
lhatt@bcauditor.com
Executive Director, Peter Nagati
Tel: 250-419-6176
pnagati@bcauditor.com
Director, Paul Nyquist
Tel: 250-419-6194
pnyquist@bcauditor.com

Office of the Auditor General for Local Government (AGLG)

#201, 10470 - 152nd St., Surrey, BC V3R 0Y3
Tel: 604-930-7100
www.aglg.ca
The Office was created through the Auditor General for Local Government Act in 2012, & is mandated to assist local governments in improving their operations.
Chair, Audit Council, Anthony Ariganello
Auditor General for Local Government, Gordon Ruth
Deputy Auditor General for Local Government, Terri Van Sleuwen
Tel: 604-930-7108
Terri.VanSleuwen@aglg.ca
Director, Finance & Corporate Services, Vicki Yeats
Tel: 604-930-7114
Vicki.Yeats@aglg.ca

British Columbia Centre for Disease Control (BCCDC)

655 West 12th Ave., Vancouver, BC V5Z 4R4
Tel: 604-707-2400; *Fax:* 604-707-2401
admininfo@bccdc.ca
www.bccdc.ca
Other Communication: Media/Communications, Phone: 604-707-2412
twitter.com/cdcofbc
The BCCDC is both a provincial & national leader in public health as it detects, treats, & prevents diseases in its patients. Not only does it offer direct services for people with diseases & health concerns, but it also provides analytical & policy support to health authorities at all levels of government.
Executive Medical Director & Deputy Provincial Health Officer, Dr. Mark Tyndall
Interm Medical Director, Communicable Disease Prevention & Control Service, Dr. Eleni Galanis

British Columbia Ministry of Children & Family Development (MCFD)

PO Box 9770 Stn. Prov Govt, Victoria, BC V8W 9S5
Tel: 250-387-7027; *Fax:* 250-356-3007
Toll-Free: 877-387-7027
TTY: 800-667-4770
MCF.CorrespondenceManagement@gov.bc.ca
www.gov.bc.ca/mcf
Other Communication: Helpline for Children: 310-1234; Emergencies outside office hours: 604-660-4927 (Vancouver); 604-660-8180 (Lower Mainland); 1-800-663-9122 (remainder of province)
The Ministry of Children & Family Development works to support healthy child development, to maximize the potential of children & youth, & to achieve meaningful outcomes for children, youth, & families. A client-centered approach is used to deliver services. The following services are available to families throughout British Columbia: adoption services; early childhood development & child care services; child safety, family support, & children in care services; services for children & youth with special needs; mental health services for children & youth; & youth justice services.
Minister, Children & Family Development, Hon. Stephanie Cadieux
Tel: 250-387-9699; *Fax:* 250-387-9722
MCF.Minister@gov.bc.ca
PO Box 9057 Prov Govt Sta.
Victoria, BC V8W 9E2
Deputy Minister, Mark Sieben
Tel: 250-387-1541; *Fax:* 250-356-2920
mcf.deputyministersoffice@gov.bc.ca
PO Box 9721 Prov Govt Sta.
Victoria, BC V8W 9S2
Chief of Staff, Debbie MacLean
Tel: 250-387-9699; *Fax:* 250-387-9722
PO Box 9767 Prov Govt Sta.
Victoria, BC V8W 9S5
Deputy Director, Child Welfare, Alex Scheiber
Tel: 250-387-7418
Regional Executive Director, Service, Office of the Provincial Director of Child Welfare, Nancy McComb
Tel: 250-354-6470; *Fax:* 250-354-6530
Executive Director, Executive Operations, Carolyn Kamper
Tel: 250-387-3717; *Fax:* 250-356-2920

Associated Agencies, Boards & Commissions:

•British Columbia College of Social Workers (BCCSW)
#1430, 1200 West 73 Ave.
Vancouver, BC V6P 6G5
Tel: 604-737-4916; *Fax:* 604-737-6809
Toll-free: 877-576-6740
info@bccsw.ca
www.bccollegeofsocialworkers.ca
The regulatory body for the practice of social work in British Columbia is the Board of Registration for Social Workers in BC. The Board's responsibility is establishing & supporting high standards for Registered Social Workers in the province.

Aboriginal Services
PO Box 9777 Stn. Prov Govt, Victoria, BC V8W 9S5
Tel: 250-387-5275; *Fax:* 250-387-1732
Executive Director, Denise Devenny
Tel: 250-387-0726
Director, Aboriginal Policy & Legislation Team; Jordan's Principle Implementation Team, Dena Carroll
Tel: 250-356-5581; *Fax:* 250-387-1732

Other Communications: Team Phone: 250-356-9791, Fax: 250-387-1732

Finance & Corporate Services
PO Box 9721 Stn. Prov Govt, Victoria, BC V8W 9S2
Tel: 250-387-5275; *Fax:* 250-356-6534

Assistant Deputy Minister, Reg Bawa
Tel: 250-356-0988; *Fax:* 250-356-0988
Chief Financial Officer, Anne Minnings
Tel: 250-356-2954; *Fax:* 250-356-2899
Anne.Minnings@gov.bc.ca
Chief Information Officer & Executive Director, Modelling, Analysis & Information Management Branch, Martin P. Wright
Tel: 250-387-7406; *Fax:* 250-387-7618
Executive Director, Legislation & Litigation, Michael Turanski
Tel: 250-387-6434; *Fax:* 250-356-8182
Executive Director, CYMH Policy, Sandy Wiens
Tel: 250-387-1551; *Fax:* 250-356-0580
Director, Accounting Operations, Financial Practice & Control, Financial Services, Katherine Jess
Tel: 250-387-7724; *Fax:* 250-387-1101
Director, Financial Planning & Reporting, Financial Services, Kathy Jones
Tel: 250-356-7817; *Fax:* 250-356-2899
Director, Financial & Corporate Support, Provincial Office, Financial Services, Sreeni Keshava
Tel: 250-356-2792; *Fax:* 250-356-2899
Director, Child & Youth Mental Health Policy, Integrated Policy & Legislation, Robert Lampard
Tel: 250-356-5201; *Fax:* 250-356-0580
Director, Children & Youth with Special Needs Policy, Aleksandra Stevanovic
Tel: 250-387-1828; *Fax:* 250-356-0399

Policy & Provincial Services
PO Box 9738 Stn. Prov Govt, Victoria, BC V8W 9S2
Tel: 250-387-5954; *Fax:* 250-387-2481

Assistant Deputy Minister, Christine Massey
Tel: 250-387-7090; *Fax:* 250-387-2481
Director, Aboriginal Policy, Dena Carroll
Tel: 250-356-5581; *Fax:* 250-356-2995
865 Hornby St., 9th Fl.
Vancouver, BC V6Z 9S2
Director, Applied Practice Research & Learning, Kim Shelford
Tel: 250-387-7089; *Fax:* 250-387-7421
PO Box 9766 Prov Govt Sta.
Victoria, BC V8W 9S1
Executive Director, CYMH Policy, Sandy Wiens
Tel: 250-387-1551; *Fax:* 250-356-0580
PO Box 9766 Prov Govt Sta.
Victoria, BC V8W 9S1

Provincial Services
PO Box 9717 Stn. Prov Govt, Victoria, BC V8W 9S1
Tel: 250-387-0978; *Fax:* 250-356-2079

Executive Director, Youth Custody Services, Lenora Angel
Tel: 604-356-1970; *Fax:* 604-356-2079
PO Box 9719 Prov Govt Sta.
Victoria, BC V8W 9S5
Assistant Executive Director, Youth Custody Services, Rick Faoro
Tel: 778-452-2065; *Fax:* 778-452-2076
Provincial Director, Youth Forensic Psychiatric Services, Andre Picard
Tel: 778-452-2202; *Fax:* 778-452-2201
Provincial Clinical Director, Youth Forensic Psychiatric Services, Dr. Kulwant Riar
Tel: 778-452-2205; *Fax:* 778-452-2201
Director, Youth Justice Policy & Program Support, Chris Zatylny
Tel: 250-387-1335; *Fax:* 250-356-2079

Strategic Human Resource & Sectoral Relations
PO Box 9757 Stn. Prov Govt, Victoria, BC V8W 9S3
Tel: 250-356-6883; *Fax:* 250-952-6880

Executive Director, Tim Orborne
Tel: 250-356-1621
Director, Workforce Reporting & Occupational Safety, Cheryl Howarth
Tel: 250-387-7659
Director, Strategic Workplace Initiatives, Michelle Perren
Tel: 250-387-2466
Director, Learning & Development, Anita Misri
Tel: 250-387-2192

Regional Offices

Fraser & Vancouver Coastal Regions
#601, 700 West Georgia St., Vancouver, BC V7Y 1B6
Tel: 604-660-2433; *Fax:* 604-660-1090
Assistant Deputy Minister, Beverly Dicks
Tel: 604-660-2433; *Fax:* 604-660-1090
Acting Assistant Deputy Minister, Coast Fraser Surrey Office, Barbara Walsh
Tel: 604-660-2433; *Fax:* 604-596-4153
Executive Director of Service, Vancouver Coastal Regional Office, Dennis Padmore
Tel: 604-660-2433; *Fax:* 604-660-1090
Executive Director, Practice, Coast Fraser Surrey Office, Bruce McNeill
Tel: 604-586-4109; *Fax:* 604-586-4153
Director, Support to Operations, Coast Fraser Surrey Office, Donna Mathiasen
Tel: 604-586-4148; *Fax:* 604-596-4151
Director, Practice, Coast Fraser Surrey Office, Susan Waldron
Tel: 604-775-2740; *Fax:* 604-586-4153
Director, Aboriginal Service Change, Coast Fraser Surrey Office, Virge Silveira
Tel: 604-586-4132; *Fax:* 604-586-4153
Director, Practice Fraser South, Coast Fraser Surrey Office, Amarjit Sahota
Tel: 604-586-2628; *Fax:* 604-586-4153
Executive Director of Service, Fraser East, Vancouver Coastal Regional Office, Holden Chu
Tel: 604-660-4121; *Fax:* 604-660-1090
Acting Director, Finance & Administration, Vancouver Coastal Regional Office, Phillip Dong
Tel: 604-999-8237; *Fax:* 604-660-1090
Executive Director of Service, North Fraser, Vancouver Coastal Regional Office, Sheila Robinson
Tel: 604-660-2433; *Fax:* 604-660-5072

Victoria South Island Office
PO Box 9727 Stn. Prov Govt, Victoria, BC V8W 9S5
Tel: 250-952-4707; *Fax:* 250-952-4282

North Region
Tel: 250-565-4367; *Fax:* 250-565-4427
Acting Assistant Deputy Minister, Robert Watts
Tel: 250-565-4367
Executive Director of Services, Northwest, Shirley Reimer
Tel: 250-565-4367
Director, Quality Assurance, Rob Rail
Tel: 250-565-4367
Director, Operations, Brenda Lewis
Tel: 250-387-7418

Vancouver Island
PO Box 9767 Stn. Prov Govt, Victoria, BC V8W 9S5
Tel: 250-387-7744; *Fax:* 250-387-7756
Director, Egagement, Partnerships & Strategic Initiatives, Sobhana Daniel
Tel: 250-387-1205
Project Manager, Michele Haddon
Tel: 250-387-7402

Columbia Power Corporation (CPC)

#200, 445 - 13th Ave., Castlegar, BC V1N 1G1
Tel: 250-304-6060; *Fax:* 250-304-6083
cpc.info@columbiapower.org
www.columbiapower.org
twitter.com/columbiapower
www.linkedin.com/company/4818136

Columbia Power Corporation was established under the Company Act in 1994. A Crown corporation, it is wholly owned & controlled by the Province of British Columbia. On a joint venture basis with the Columbia Basin Trust, Columbia Power Corporation undertakes power project investments as the agent of the Province of British Columbia. Some power projects include the following: Arrow Lakes Generating Station, Brilliant Expansion Project, & Waneta Expansion Project.

Chair, Lee Doney
Vice-Chair, Tim Stanley
President & Chief Executive Officer, Frank Wszelaki
Frank.Wszelaki@columbiapower.org
Vice-President, Capital Projects, Giulio Ambrosone
Giulio.Ambrosone@columbiapower.org
Vice-President, Operations, Sue Dyer
Sue.Dyer@columbiapower.org
Vice-President, Project Development, Karim Hirji
Karim.Hirji@columbiapower.org

British Columbia Ministry of Community, Sport, & Cultural Development & Responsible for TransLink

PO Box 9490 Stn. Prov Govt, Victoria, BC V8W 9N7
www.gov.bc.ca/cscd
Other Communication: Media Inquiries, Phone: 250-953-3677, Fax: 250-356-1070

Enabling local governments & citizens of British Columbia to build well-governed communities with opportunities to participate in the arts & sports is the goal of the Ministry of Community, Sport, & Cultural Development.
The following are examples of the ministry's responsibilities: providing policies & programs so that local governments can govern effectively; offering advice & funding for community economic growth; ensuring a fair & flexible property assessment system; & supporting the provincial sport system, cultural organizations, & artists.

Minister, Community, Sport & Cultural Development; Minister Responsible for TransLink, Hon. Peter Fassbender
Tel: 250-387-2283; *Fax:* 250-387-4312
CSCD.Minister@gov.bc.ca
Deputy Minister, Community, Sport, & Cultural Development & Responsible for Translink, Jacquie Dawes
Tel: 250-953-3677; *Fax:* 250-356-1070
Jacquie.Dawes@gov.bc.ca
Chief of Staff, Joan Dick
Tel: 250-387-2283; *Fax:* 250-387-4312
Administrative Coordinator, Lia Robbins
Tel: 250-387-2283; *Fax:* 250-387-4312
Director, Executive Operations, Vanessa Gedney
Tel: 250-356-7152; *Fax:* 250-387-7973
Vanessa.Gedney@gov.bc.ca

Associated Agencies, Boards & Commissions:

•British Columbia Arts Council (BCAC)
800 Johnson St.
PO Box 9819 Prov Govt
Victoria, BC V8W 9W3
Tel: 250-356-1718; *Fax:* 250-387-4099
BCArtsCouncil@gov.bc.ca
www.bcartscouncil.ca
The BC Arts Council supports arts & cultural activities across the province, including professional dance companies, art galleries, local museums & music festivals.

•British Columbia Assessment Authority (BCAA)
#400, 3450 Uptown Blvd.
Victoria, BC V8Z 0B9
Tel: 604-739-8588; *Fax:* 855-995-6209
Toll-free: 866-825-8322
www.bcassessment.ca
The British Columbia Assessment Authority is an independent, provincial Crown corporation. Governed by a Board of Directors, the role of BC Assessment is the production of annual property assessments for each property owner in British Columbia. Area offices are located across the province.

•British Columbia Games Society
#200, 990 Fort St.
Victoria, BC V8V 3K2
Tel: 250-387-1375; *Fax:* 250-387-4489
www.bcgames.org
The BC Games Society is incorporated under the Societies Act. With responsibility to British Columbia's Minister of Healthy Living & Sport, the Crown Agency works with its partners to provide event management leadership. The Society strives to create development opportunities for athletes, coaches, & officials, sport organizations, & host communities.

•Creative BC
2225 West Broadway
Vancouver, BC V6K 2E4
Tel: 604-736-7997; *Fax:* 604-736-7290
www.creativebc.com
Creative BC's mission is to ensure that film & television production thrives for Canadian & international clients. As one of the largest production centres in North America, the province offers film producers & production companies a great range of services.

•Islands Trust
#200, 1627 Fort St.
Victoria, BC V8R 1H8
Tel: 250-405-5151; *Fax:* 250-405-5155
www.islandstrust.bc.ca
Other Communication: Northern Office: 250-247-2063; Salt Spring Office: 250-537-9144
The Islands Trust area covers the following islands & waters between the British Columbia mainland & southern Vancouver Island: Bowen, Denman, Gabriola, Galiano, Gambier, Hornby, Lasqueti, Mayne, North Pender, Salt Spring, Saturna, South Pender, & Thetis. The Trust is a federation of independent local governments. The federation plans land use & regulates development to preserve & protect the area and its environment.

•Property Assessment Appeal Board (PAAB)
#10, 10551 Shellbridge Way
Richmond, BC V6X 2W9
Tel: 604-775-1740; *Fax:* 604-775-1742
Toll-free: 888-775-1740
office@paab.bc.ca
www.assessmentappeal.bc.ca
Other Communication: Toll-Free Fax: 1-888-775-1742
The Board assists with assessment appeals for all types of properties, dealing with issues such as market value, classification, and qualification for tax exemption.

•Royal BC Museum Corporation
675 Belleville St.
Victoria, BC V8W 9W2
Tel: 250-356-7226
Toll-free: 888-447-7977
reception@royalbcmuseum.bc.ca
www.royalbcmuseum.bc.ca
The Royal BC Museum Corporation was created through the proclamation of the Museum Act. It is British Columbia's provincial museum & archives.

•Tourism British Columbia
#300, 1803 Douglas St.
Victoria, BC V8W 9W5
Tel: 604-660-2861; *Fax:* 604-660-3383
ContactTourism@DestinationBC.ca
www.hellobc.com
Tourism British Columbia is a Crown corporation which provides information for industry & the media. Its goals are increases in revenue, economic benefits, & employment in British Columbia, through the promotion of development & growth in the tourism industry. The organization is accountable to the Minister of Tourism, Culture & The Arts.

Arts, Culture, Gaming Grants & Sport
PO Box 9490 Stn. Prov Govt, Victoria, BC V8W 9N7
Tel: 250-356-6914; *Fax:* 250-387-7973
In March 2014, this branch assumed responsibility for outreach programs, such as Capital for Kids, formerly administered by the BC Provincial Capital Commission.
Assistant Deputy Minister, Melanie Stewart
Tel: 250-356-7139; *Fax:* 250-387-8720
Executive Director, Arts, Culture & BC Arts Council, Gillian Wood
Tel: 250-356-1725; *Fax:* 250-387-4099
Gillian.Wood@gov.bc.ca
Executive Director, Sport Branch, Margo Ross
Tel: 250-356-7168; *Fax:* 250-356-2842
Margo.Ross@gov.bc.ca
Executive Director, Sport Branch, Margo Ross
Tel: 250-356-7168
Associate Director, BC Arts Council, Sarah Durno
Tel: 250-356-7013; *Fax:* 250-387-4099
Sarah.Durno@gov.bc.ca
Policy Analyst/Sport Consultant, Sport Branch, Sharon White
Tel: 250-387-5651; *Fax:* 250-356-2842
Sharon.D.White@gov.bc.ca

Integrated Policy, Legislation & Operations
PO Box 9847 Stn. Prov Govt, Victoria, BC V8W 9T2
Fax: 250-387-7973
Executive Lead, Heather Brazier
Tel: 250-387-3860
Heather.Brazier@gov.bc.ca
Senior Director, Integrated Policy, Trudy Rotgans
Tel: 250-356-7875
Trudy.Rotgans@gov.bc.ca
Director, Integrated Legislation, Meagan Gergley
Tel: 250-387-4052
Meagan.Gergley@gov.bc.ca
Director, Integrated Operations, Vacant
Tel: 250-356-9037

Local Government
PO Box 9490 Stn. Prov Govt, Victoria, BC V8W 9N7
Tel: 250-356-6575; *Fax:* 250-387-7973
www.cd.gov.bc.ca/lgd
Working with a great range of partners, the Local Government Department develops communities that can manage change & offer affordable services to residents of British Columbia. The Department's programs include the following: developing local government legislation; facilitating partnerships with local governments & First Nations; fostering positive inter-governmental relations to facilitate community & regional planning; offering financial support; & providing information & advice.
Assistant Deputy Minister, Tara Faganello
Tel: 250-356-6575; *Fax:* 250-387-7973
Executive Director, Local Government Infrastructure & Finance, Liam Edwards
Tel: 250-387-4067; *Fax:* 250-356-1873
800 Johnson St., 4th Fl.
PO Box 9838 Prov Govt Sta.
Victoria, BC V8W 9T1
Executive Director, Intergovernmental Relations & Planning, Vacant
Tel: 250-356-1128; *Fax:* 250-387-6212
800 Johnson St., 6th Fl.
PO Box 9841 Prov Govt Sta.
Victoria, BC V8W 9T2
Executive Director, Governance & Structure, Nicola Marotz
Tel: 250-356-6257; *Fax:* 250-387-6212
Nicola.Marotz@gov.bc.ca
800 Johnson St., 6th Fl.
PO Box 9847 Prov Govt Sta.
Victoria, BC V8W 9T2
Executive Director, Property Assessment Services, Rob Fraser
Tel: 250-356-7835; *Fax:* 250-356-6924
Rob.Fraser@gov.bc.ca
800 Johnson St., 4th Fl.
PO Box 9839 Prov Govt Sta.
Victoria, BC V8W 9T1
Director, Local Government Structure, Governance & Structure, Marijke Edmondson
Tel: 250-387-4058; *Fax:* 250-387-7972
Marijke.Edmondson@gov.bc.ca
800 Johnson St., 4th Fl.
PO Box 9839 Prov Govt Sta.
Victoria, BC V8W 9T1
Director, Advisory Services, Governance & Structure, Michelle Dann
Tel: 250-387-4059; *Fax:* 250-387-7972
Michelle.Dann@gov.bc.ca
800 Johnson St., 4th Fl.
PO Box 9839 Prov Govt Sta.
Victoria, BC V8W 9T1
Director, Community Relations, Governance & Structure, Vacant
Tel: 250-387-4057; *Fax:* 250-387-7972
800 Johnson St., 4th Fl.
PO Box 9839 Prov Govt Sta.
Victoria, BC V8W 9T1
Executive Director, Intergovernmental Relations, Intergovernmental Relations & Planning Division, Meggin Messenger
Tel: 250-387-4045; *Fax:* 250-387-6212
Meggin.Messenger@gov.bc.ca
800 Johnson St., 4th Fl.
PO Box 9839 Prov Govt Sta.
Victoria, BC V8W 9T1
Director, Intergovernmental Relations & Planning Division, Karen Rothe
Tel: 250-356-7064; *Fax:* 250-387-6212
Karen.Rothe@gov.bc.ca
800 Johnson St., 4th Fl.
PO Box 9839 Prov Govt Sta.
Victoria, BC V8W 9T1
Director, Infrastructure & Engineering, Local Government Infrastructure & Finance, Brian Bedford
Tel: 250-356-0700; *Fax:* 250-387-7972
Brian.Bedford@gov.bc.ca
800 Johnson St., 4th Fl.
PO Box 9839 Prov Govt Sta.
Victoria, BC V8W 9T1
Director, Local Government Finance, Local Government Infrastructure & Finance, Sean Grant
Tel: 250-387-4036; *Fax:* 250-387-7972
800 Johnson St., 4th Fl.
PO Box 9839 Prov Govt Sta.
Victoria, BC V8W 9T1

Management Services
PO Box 9842 Stn. Prov Govt, Victoria, BC V8W 9T2
Tel: 250-387-8705; *Fax:* 250-387-7973
Assistant Deputy Minister, David Curtis
Tel: 250-387-9180; *Fax:* 250-387-7973
George.Farkas@gov.bc.ca
Executive Director/Chief Information Officer, Information Systems, Bruce Klette
Tel: 250-356-0803; *Fax:* 250-387-1590
Bruce.Klette@gov.bc.ca
800 Johnson St., 3rd Fl.
PO Box 9802 Prov Govt Sta.
Victoria, BC V8W 9W1
Executive Director, Strategic Human Resources, Sarah Francis
Tel: 250-387-1478
800 Johnson St., 2nd Fl.
PO Box 9806 Prov Govt Sta.
Victoria, BC V8W 9W1
Director/Chief Financial Officer, Finance & Administrative Services, Jim MacAulay
Tel: 250-387-9179; *Fax:* 250-387-1590
Jim.MacAulay@gov.bc.ca
800 Johnson St., 3rd Fl.
PO Box 9843 Prov Govt Sta.
Victoria, BC V8W 9T2
Director, Internal Planning, Corporate Planning & Priorities, Shannon Mullen
Tel: 250-953-4334; *Fax:* 250-387-1407
Shannon.Mullen@gov.bc.ca
800 Johnson St., 3rd Fl.
PO Box 9843 Prov Govt Sta.
Victoria, BC V8W 9T2
Executive Director, Strategic Human Resources, Sarah Francis
Tel: 250-387-1478; *Fax:* 250-387-1407
800 Johnson St., 3rd Fl.
PO Box 9843 Prov Govt Sta.
Victoria, BC V8W 9T2

Office of the Conflict of Interest Commissioner

421 Menzies St., 1st Fl., Victoria, BC V8V 1X4
Tel: 250-356-0750; *Fax:* 250-356-6580
conflictofinterest@coibc.ca
www.coibc.ca
The Conflict of Interest Commissioner is an independent Officer of the Legislative Assembly. The following roles are carried out by the Commissioner: advising Members of the Legislative Assembly; meeting with Members of the Legislative Assembly for review of disclosure of Members' interests, & obligations imposed by the Members' Conflict of Interest Act; & undertaking investigations into alleged contraventions of the Act or the Constitution Act, section 25.
Commissioner, Paul D. K. Fraser, Q.C.
Tel: 250-356-9283
Executive Coordinator, Linda Pink
Tel: 250-356-0750

Destination BC Corp.

#12, 510 Burrard St., Victoria, BC V6C 3A8
Tel: 604-660-2861; *Fax:* 604-660-3383
Toll-Free: 800-822-7899
ContactTourism@DestinationBC.ca
www.destinationbc.ca
Other Communication: Tourism URL: www.hellobc.com; Tourism Business Customer Service, E-mail: ProductServices@gov.bc.ca
twitter.com/Destination_BC
www.facebook.com/HelloBC
www.youtube.com/user/TourismBC
Operating as Destination British Columbia, the corporation was founded in 2012 under the British Columbia Business Corporations Act, & operates as a crown corporation under the Destination BC Corp. Act. Its mandate is to work with tourism stakeholders across BC to market the province as a tourism destination at the international, national & provincial levels.
Chair, Andrea Shaw
President & CEO, Marsha Walden
Tel: 604-660-3676
Marsha.Walden@DestinationBC.ca
Chief Financial Officer & Executive Director, Corporate Services, Dean Skinner
Tel: 604-356-5648
Dean.Skinner@DestinationBC.ca
Vice-President, Global Marketing, Maya Lange
Tel: 604-660-2837
Maya.Lange@DestinationBC.ca
Vice-President, Destination & Industry Development, Grant Mackay
Tel: 604-660-6319
Grant.Mackay@DestinationBC.ca
Vice-President, Corporate Development, Richard Porges
Tel: 250-356-9936
Richard.Porges@DestinationBC.ca
Director, Overseas Marketing, Maria Greene
Tel: 604-660-3769
Maria.Greene@DestinationBC.ca
Director, Partnership Marketing, Peter Harrison
Tel: 250-387-8578
Peter.Harrison@DestinationBC.ca
Director, Sector Development & Consortium Co-op, Richard Lewis
Tel: 604-660-3701
Richard.Lewis@DestinationBC.ca
Manager, Brand, Mary Elliot
Tel: 604-660-6383
Mary.Elliott@DestinationBC.ca
Director, Visitor Experiences & Industry Development, Ninette Ollgaard
Tel: 250-356-0453
Ninette.Ollgaard@DestinationBC.ca
Director, Digital Strategy & Analytics, Daniel Vasquez
Tel: 604-775-0116
Daniel.Vasquez@DestinationBC.ca

British Columbia Ministry of Education

PO Box 9161 Stn. Prov Govt, Victoria, BC V8W 9H3
Toll-Free: 888-879-1166
TTY: 800-661-8773
EDUC.Correspondence@gov.bc.ca
www.gov.bc.ca/bced
Other Communication: Media Inquiries, Phone: 250-356-5963
The Ministry of Education works with stakeholders in all stages of the education system, from early learning programs & kindergarten to grade 12 to life-long literacy. Early learning programs include the ministry initiative, StrongStart. Life-long

literacy initiatives include programs at community learning centres & public libraries.

Minister, Education, Hon. Mike Bernier
Tel: 250-387-1977; *Fax:* 250-356-0948
educ.minister@gov.bc.ca

Deputy Minister, Education, Dave Byng
Tel: 250-356-1234; *Fax:* 250-356-6007
dm.education@gov.bc.ca

Parliamentary Secretary, Independent Schools, Simon Gibson
Tel: 250-953-0974; *Fax:* 250-387-9100
simon.gibson.mla@leg.bc.ca

Chief of Staff, Matt Holme
Tel: 250-387-1977

Associated Agencies, Boards & Commissions:

•Education Advisory Council
c/o Mike Roberts, Superintendent, Liaison
#1550, 555 West Hastings
PO Box 121110
Vancouver, BC V6B 4N6
Tel: 604-660-1483; *Fax:* 604-660-2124
The purpose of the Education Advisory Council is to advise the Minister of Education on all areas of the education system, including: curriculum & assessment; the teaching profession; system governance; & finance.

•Teacher Regulation Branch
#400, 2025 West Broadway
Vancouver, BC V6J 1Z6
Tel: 604-660-6060; *Fax:* 604-775-4859
Toll-free: 800-555-3684
www.bcteacherregulation.ca
The Teacher Regulation Branch ensures that standards for education at met and maintained by the teachers in the province.

Knowledge Management & Accountability Division
PO Box 9146 Stn. Prov Govt, Victoria, BC V8W 9H1
Tel: 250-356-6760; *Fax:* 250-953-3225
EDUC.GovernanceDepartment@gov.bc.ca

Assistant Deputy Minister, Ian Rongve
Tel: 250-356-6760
EDUC.KMA@gov.bc.ca

Executive Director, Governance & Accountability, Dave Duerksen
Tel: 250-387-8037; *Fax:* 250-953-3225
Dave.Duerksen@gov.bc.ca

Director, International Education, Brenda Neufeld
Tel: 250-216-7168; *Fax:* 250-953-4908
International.Education@gov.bc.ca

Executive Director, Knowledge Management, Darlene Therrien
Tel: 250-217-2818
Darlene.Therrien@gov.bc.ca

Director, Applied Research & Evaluation, Gerald Morton
Tel: 250-216-5774; *Fax:* 250-953-3225
Gerald.Morton@gov.bc.ca

Learning Division
PO Box 9887 Stn. Prov Govt, Victoria, BC V8W 9T6
Tel: 250-216-6038; *Fax:* 250-387-6315
EDUC.learningdivision@gov.bc.ca

Acting Assistant Deputy Minister, Jennifer McCrea
Tel: 250-896-3735; *Fax:* 250-387-6315
EDUC.learningdivision@gov.bc.ca

Liason Division
Tel: 604-660-1415; *Fax:* 604-660-2124
www.bced.gov.bc.ca/departments/liaison

Partner Relations Division
PO Box 9161 Stn. Prov Govt, Victoria, BC V8W 9H3
Tel: 250-356-0891
EDUCADMO@Victoria1.gov.bc.ca

Assistant Deputy Minister, Paige MacFarlane
Tel: 250-356-0891
EDUCADMO@Victoria1.gov.bc.ca

Executive Director, Teacher Regulation Branch, Wilma Clarke
Tel: 604-775-4817; *Fax:* 604-775-4860
Wilma.Clarke@gov.bc.ca

Director, Libraries, Mari Martin
Tel: 250-886-2584; *Fax:* 250-953-4985
llb@gov.bc.ca

Executive Director, Partner & Intergovernmental Relations, Kevena Bamford
Tel: 250-360-7336

Executive Director, People & Workplace Intiatives, Heather Beaton
Tel: 250-216-4244; *Fax:* 250-953-3225
PWI@gov.bc.ca

Resource Management Division
PO Box 9151 Stn. Prov Govt, Victoria, BC V8W 9H1
Tel: 250-356-2588; *Fax:* 250-953-4985
www.bced.gov.bc.ca/departments/resource_man/

Assistant Deputy Minister, Deborah Fayad
Tel: 250-356-2588

Director, School District Financial Reporting, Ian Aaron
Tel: 250-415-1073; *Fax:* 250-953-4985

Director, Funding & Allocation, Rebecca John
Tel: 778-676-4471

Executive Director, Chief Financial Officer, Financial Services Branch, Brian Fraser
Tel: 250-387-6282; *Fax:* 250-953-4985
Financial.Services@gov.bc.ca

Manager, Business Operations, Aleesa Paulson
Tel: 250-217-2478; *Fax:* 250-953-4985

Services & Technology Division
PO Box 9132 Stn. Prov Govt, Victoria, BC V8W 9B5
Tel: 250-356-8363

Assistant Deputy Minister, Jill Kot
Jill.Kot@gov.bc.ca

Executive Director, Service Delivery Branch, Kerry Pridmore
Tel: 250-507-1485
Kerry.Pridmore@gov.bc.ca

Elections British Columbia

PO Box 9275 Stn. Prov Govt, Victoria, BC V8W 9J6
Tel: 250-387-5305; *Fax:* 250-387-3578
Toll-Free: 800-661-8683
TTY: 888-456-5448
electionsbc@elections.bc.ca
www.elections.bc.ca
Other Communication: Toll-free Fax: 1-866-466-0665
twitter.com/ElectionsBC
www.facebook.com/67197771286
www.youtube.com/ElectionsBConline

Elections British Columbia is a non-partisan, independent Office of the Legislature. Its responsibility is the administration of the electoral process in the province, including provincial general elections, by-elections, provincial referendums, & recall & initiative petitions & votes.

Chief Electoral Officer, Keith Archer, Ph.D.

Deputy Chief Electoral Officer, Electoral Operations, Anton Boegman
Tel: 250-356-2713
Anton.Boegman@elections.bc.ca

Deputy Chief Electoral Officer, Funding & Disclosure, Nola Western
Tel: 250-387-4141
Nola.Western@elections.bc.ca

Director, Information Technology, Yvonne Koehn
Tel: 250-387-1945
Yvonne.Koehn@elections.bc.ca

Director, Corporate Planning & Event Leader, Jill Lawrance
Tel: 250-387-7258
Jill.Lawrance@elections.bc.ca

Director, Voter Registration & Boundaries, Tim Strocel
Tel: 250-356-7677
Tim.Strocel@elections.bc.ca

British Columbia Ministry of Energy & Mines (& Responsible for Core Review)

PO Box 9060 Stn. Prov Govt, Victoria, BC V8W 9E3
www.gov.bc.ca/ener

In September 2012, changes were made to the Ministry of Energy & Mines to reinforce natural gas, which is an economic development priority of the provincial government.
The development of sustainable & competitive energy & mineral resource sectors in British Columbia is the focus of the Ministry of Energy & Mines. To develop legislation & guidelines, the ministry consults with other ministries & levels of government, as well as communities, First Nations, the public, energy & mining companies, & environmental organizations.

Minister, Energy & Mines; Minister Responsible for Core Review, Hon. Bill Bennett
Tel: 250-387-5896; *Fax:* 250-387-4312
MEM.Minister@gov.bc.ca

Deputy Minister, Elaine McKnight
PO Box 9319 Prov Govt Sta.
Victoria, BC V8W 9N3

Chief of Staff, Eric Wallace-Deering
Tel: 250-387-5896

Director, Cabinet & Legislative Initiatives & Executive Operations, Rhonda De Champlain
Tel: 250-952-0253; *Fax:* 250-952-0269
Rhonda.DeChamplain@gov.bc.ca

Associated Agencies, Boards & Commissions:

•Surface Rights Board of British Columbia (SRB)
#10, 10551 Shellbridge Way
Richmond, BC V6X 2W9
Tel: 604-775-1740; *Fax:* 604-775-1742
Toll-free: 888-775-1740
office@surfacerightsboard.bc.ca
www.surfacerightsboard.bc.ca
Other Communication: Toll-Free Fax: 1-888-775-1742
The Board is mandated to help solve disputes between landowners & companies requiring access to private land for the purpose of exploring, developing or producing Crown-owned resources such as oil, gas, coal, minerals & geothermal.

Corporate Initiatives Branch
PO Box 9315 Stn. Prov Govt, Victoria, BC V8W 9N1
Fax: 250-952-0258

Executive Director, Fraser Marshall
Tel: 250-952-0274
Fraser.Marshall@gov.bc.ca

Director, Corporate Policy & External Relations, Guy Gensey
Tel: 250-356-0185
Guy.Gensey@gov.bc.ca

Director, Corporate Policy & Planning, Daymon Trachsel
Tel: 250-953-3730
Daymon.Trachsel@gov.bc.ca

Director, Corporate Initiatives, Gayle Cho
Tel: 250-952-0165
Gayle.Cho@gov.bc.ca

Electricity & Alternative Energy Division
PO Box 9314 Stn. Prov Govt, Victoria, BC V8W 9N1
Tel: 250-952-0673; *Fax:* 250-952-0258

Assistant Deputy Minister, Les MacLaren
Tel: 250-952-0204; *Fax:* 250-952-0926
Les.MacLaren@gov.bc.ca

Executive Director, Columbia River Treaty (CRT) Review Team, Kathy Eichenberger
Tel: 250-952-3368
Kathy.Eichenberger@gov.bc.ca

Executive Director, Innovative Clean Energy (ICE) Fund, Dan Green
Tel: 250-952-0279; *Fax:* 250-952-0351
Dan.Green@gov.bc.ca

Executive Director, Alternative Energy; Renewable Energy Development Branch, Paul Wieringa
Tel: 250-952-0651; *Fax:* 250-952-0657
Paul.Wieringa@gov.bc.ca

Director, Renewable & Low Carbon Fuels, Michael Rensing
Tel: 250-952-0265
Michael.Rensing@gov.bc.ca

Acting Director, Electricity Generation & Regulation Branch, Chris Trumpy
Tel: 250-952-6390
Chris.Trumpy@gov.bc.ca

Director, ICE Fund, Liz Wouters
Tel: 250-387-2883; *Fax:* 250-952-0351
Liz.Wouters@gov.bc.ca

Coordinator, Energy Efficiency Branch, Joy Beauchamp
Tel: 250-356-1168
Joy.Beauchamp@gov.bc.ca

Coordinator, Electricity Transmission/Inter-jurisdictional Branch, Michele West
Tel: 250-952-0286
Michele.West@gov.bc.ca

Mines & Mineral Resources Division
PO Box 9320 Stn. Prov Govt, Victoria, BC V8W 9N3
Tel: 250-952-0470; *Fax:* 250-952-0491

Assistant Deputy Minister, David Morel
Tel: 250-952-0473; *Fax:* 250-952-0491
David.Morel@gov.bc.ca

Chief Inspector/Executive Director, Health & Safety, Health & Safety & Permitting Branch, Al Hoffman
Tel: 250-952-0494; *Fax:* 250-952-0491
Al.Hoffman@gov.bc.ca

Chief Geologist & Executive Director, British Columbia Geological Survey, Stephen Rowins
Tel: 250-952-0454; *Fax:* 250-952-0381
Stephen.Rowins@gov.bc.ca

Chief Gold Commissioner & Executive Director, Mineral Titles, May Mah-Paulson
Tel: 250-952-0335
May.Mah-Paulson@gov.bc.ca

Deputy Chief Gold Commissioner & Director, Mineral Titles (Vancouver), Mark Messmer
Tel: 604-660-2814; *Fax:* 604-660-2653
Mark.Messmer@gov.bc.ca

Executive Director, Policy, Legislation & Issues Resolution Branch, Nathaniel Amann-Blake
Tel: 250-952-0868; *Fax:* 250-952-0271
Nathaniel.Amann-Blake@gov.bc.ca

Director, Coal Titles, Jennifer Anthony
Tel: 250-356-0185; *Fax:* 250-952-0541
Jennifer.Anthony@gov.bc.ca
Director, Cordilleran Geoscience, Adrian Hickin
Tel: 250-953-3801; *Fax:* 250-952-0381
Adrian.Hickin@gov.bc.ca
Director, Resource Information Section, Larry Jones
Tel: 250-952-0386; *Fax:* 250-952-0381
Larry.Jones@gov.bc.ca
Director, Mineral Development Office, Bruce Madu
Tel: 604-660-2094; *Fax:* 604-775-0313
Bruce.Madu@gov.bc.ca
Director, Policy & Regulatory Reform, Chris Smith
Tel: 250-952-0317; *Fax:* 250-952-0271
Chris.Smith@gov.bc.ca

British Columbia Ministry of Environment

PO Box 9339 Stn. Prov Govt, Victoria, BC V8W 9M1
Tel: 250-387-9870; *Fax:* 250-387-6003
env.mail@gov.bc.ca
www.gov.bc.ca/env
Other Communication: Environmental Emergencies: 1-800-663-3456; Report All Poachers & Polluters (RAPP): 1-877-952-7277; Media Enquiries, Phone: 250-387-9973

The following responsibilities are handled by the Ministry of the Environment: establishment of standards; administration of legislation; promotion of stewardship & sustainability, through environmental protection; development of partnerships, by engaging stakeholders, First Nations, & citizens in policy & program development; & conservation, maintenance, & enhancement of ecosystems & native species.

Minister, Environment, Hon. Mary Polak
Tel: 250-387-1187; *Fax:* 250-387-1356
ENV.Minister@gov.bc.ca
Deputy Minister, Environment, Wes Shoemaker
Tel: 250-387-5429
Deputy Minister, Climate Leadership, Fazil Mihlar
Fazil.Mihlar@gov.bc.ca
Parliamentary Secretary, Energy Literacy & the Environment, Jordan Sturdy
Tel: 250-356-1631; *Fax:* 250-387-9100
jordan.sturdy.mla@leg.bc.ca
Chief of Staff, Martina Kapac de Frias
Tel: 250-387-1187

Associated Agencies, Boards & Commissions:

•British Columbia Environmental Assessment Office
See Entry Name Index for detailed listing.

BC Parks & Conservation Officer Service

PO Box 9376 Stn. Prov Govt, Victoria, BC V8W 9M1
Tel: 250-356-9234; *Fax:* 250-356-9197
conservation.officer.service@gov.bc.ca
www.env.gov.bc.ca/cos/
Other Communication: Wildlife conflict: 1-877-952-7277

Assistant Deputy Minister, Lori Halls
Tel: 250-387-9997; *Fax:* 250-953-3414
Executive Director, Regional Operations, Robert C. Austad
Tel: 250-356-9247; *Fax:* 250-387-5757
Bob.Austad@gov.bc.ca
Executive Director, Visitor Services, Christine Houghton
Tel: 250-356-9241; *Fax:* 250-387-5757
Christine.Houghton@gov.bc.ca
Executive Director, Parks Planning & Management, Brian Bawtinheimer
Tel: 250-387-4355; *Fax:* 250-387-5757
Brian.Bawtinheimer@gov.bc.ca
Chief Conservation Officer, Enforcement Program/Conservation Officer Service, Kelly Larkin
Tel: 250-356-9100; *Fax:* 250-356-9197
Kelly.Larkin@gov.bc.ca
Chief Superintendent, Program Governance, Lance Sundquist
Tel: 250-751-3119; *Fax:* 250-751-7383
Lance.Sundquist@gov.bc.ca
Other Communications: Alternate Phone: 250-356-9121
Chief Superintendent, Provincial Operations, Barry Farynuk
Tel: 250-354-6336; *Fax:* 250-354-6277
Barry.Farynuk@gov.bc.ca

Climate Action Secretariat

PO Box 9486 Stn. Prov Govt, Victoria, BC V8W 9W6
Fax: 250-356-7286
climateactionsecretariat@gov.bc.ca
www.env.gov.bc.ca/cas//index.html

Head, James Mack
Tel: 250-387-9456; *Fax:* 250-356-7286
Chief Negotiator/Executive Director, Business Development, Tim Lesiuk
Tel: 250-387-9216; *Fax:* 250-356-7286
Other Communications: Cell Phone: 250-216-5893
Executive Director, Climate Policy, Liz Lilly
Tel: 250-356-7917; *Fax:* 250-356-7286
Liz.Lilly@gov.bc.ca
Executive Director, Carbon Neutral Government & Climate Action Outreach, Rob Abbott
Tel: 250-356-5826; *Fax:* 250-356-7286
Director, Business Development/Lead Negotiator, Jessica Verhagen
Tel: 604-836-1942; *Fax:* 250-356-7286
Jessica.Verhagen@gov.bc.ca
Manager, Business Partnerships, Diane Beattie
Tel: 250-953-4884; *Fax:* 250-356-7286
Diane.Beattie@gov.bc.ca

Correspondence Unit

PO Box 9339 Stn. Prov Govt, Victoria, BC V8W 9M1
Fax: 250-356-9836

Manager, Correspondence Projects, Sara Nicoll
Tel: 250-387-9874; *Fax:* 250-356-9836
Sara.Nicoll@gov.bc.ca
Coordinator, Correspondence, Greg Visco
Tel: 250-387-9885; *Fax:* 250-356-9836
Assistant Deputy Minister, Dave Nikolejsin
Tel: 250-356-7475; *Fax:* 250-356-6448
eaoinfo@gov.bc.ca

Environmental Protection Division

PO Box 9339 Victoria, BC V8W 9M1
Tel: 250-387-1288; *Fax:* 250-387-5669
www.env.gov.bc.ca/epd/

Assistant Deputy Minister, Jim Standen
Tel: 250-387-1288; *Fax:* 250-387-5669
Jim.Standen@gov.bc.ca
Executive Director, Environmental Management, Jim Hofweber
Tel: 250-387-9971; *Fax:* 250-387-8897
Jim.Hofweber@gov.bc.ca
Executive Director, Environmental Standards Branch, David Ranson
Tel: 250-387-9933; *Fax:* 250-356-7197
David.Ranson@gov.bc.ca
Director, Regional Operations, Jennifer McGuire
Tel: 250-356-6027; *Fax:* 250-356-5496
Assistant Director, Regional Operations, Christa Zacharias-Homer
Tel: 250-490-8227; *Fax:* 250-356-5496
Christa.ZachariasHomer@gov.bc.ca
Regional Manager, Thompson Regional Office, Cassandra Caunce
Tel: 250-371-6225; *Fax:* 250-828-4000
Cassandra.Caunce@gov.bc.ca
1259 Dalhousie Dr.
Kamloops, BC V2C 5Z5
Director, Environmental Protection Division, West Coast Region, Randy Alexander
Tel: 250-751-3176; *Fax:* 250-751-3103
Randy.Alexander@gov.bc.ca
2080A Labieux Rd.
Nanaimo, BC V9T 6J9
Regional Manager, Environmental Protection, Lower Mainland Regional Office, Jonn Braman
Tel: 604-582-5284; *Fax:* 604-584-9751
Jonn.Braman@gov.bc.ca
10470 - 152nd St., 2nd Fl.
Surrey, BC V3R 0Y3
Regional Director, Omineca Regional Office, Edward Hoffman
Tel: 250-565-6443; *Fax:* 250-565-6629
Edward.Hoffman@gov.bc.ca
1011 - 4th Ave., 3rd Fl.
Prince George, BC V2L 3H9
Regional Director, Kootenay & Okanagan Regional Office, Robyn Roome
Tel: 250-354-6362; *Fax:* 250-354-6332
Robyn.Roome@gov.bc.ca
#401, 333 Victoria St.
Nelson, BC V1L 4K3
Regional Manager, Environmental Protection, Skeena Regional Office, Ian Sharpe
Tel: 250-847-7251; *Fax:* 250-847-7591
Ian.Sharpe@gov.bc.ca
3726 Alfred Ave.
PO Box 5000
Smithers, BC V0J 2N0
Section Head, Cariboo Regional Office, Douglas Hill
Tel: 250-398-4542; *Fax:* 250-398-4214
Doug.Hill@gov.bc.ca
#400, 640 Borland St.
Williams Lake, BC V2G 4T1
Director, Land Remediation, Mike Macfarlane
Tel: 250-356-0557
Mike.Macfarlane@gov.bc.ca
#400, 640 Borland St.
Williams Lake, BC V2G 4T1

Environmental Sustainability & Strategic Policy Division

PO Box 9335 Stn. Prov Govt, Victoria, BC V8W 9M1
Tel: 250-387-9666; *Fax:* 250-387-8894

Assistant Deputy Minister, Mark Zacharias
Tel: 250-356-0121; *Fax:* 250-387-5669
Executive Director, Strategic Policy Branch, Anthony J. Danks
Tel: 250-387-8483; *Fax:* 250-387-8894
Anthony.Danks@gov.bc.ca
Acting Director, Ecosystems Branch, Alec Dale
Tel: 250-387-9731; *Fax:* 250-356-5104
Alec.Dale@gov.bc.ca
Director, Knowledge Management Branch, Fern Schultz
Tel: 250-387-6722; *Fax:* 250-356-1202
Fern.Schultz@gov.bc.ca
Director, Water Protection & Sustainability Branch, Lynn Kriwoken
Tel: 250-387-9446; *Fax:* 250-356-1202
Lynn.Kriwoken@gov.bc.ca

British Columbia Ferry Services Inc.

c/o BC Ferry Authority, #500, 1321 Blanshard St., Victoria, BC V8W 0B7
Tel: 250-381-1401
Toll-Free: 888-223-3779
customerservice@bcferries.com
www.bcferries.com
Other Communication: Outside North America Phone: 250-386-3431
twitter.com/BCFerries
www.facebook.com/119019564797374
plus.google.com/+bcferries; instagram.com/bcferries

BC Ferries operates as the primary provider of coastal ferry service in British Columbia. The fleet covers 25 routes. BC Ferry Authority holds the single issued voting share of BC Ferries.

Chair, BC Ferry Authority, Roderick D. Deward
President & Chief Executive Officer, Mike Corrigan
Executive Vice-President, Human Resources & Corporate Development, Glen N. Schwartz

British Columbia Ministry of Finance

PO Box 9417 Stn. Prov Govt, Victoria, BC V8W 9V1
Toll-Free: 877-388-4440
CTBTaxQuestions@gov.bc.ca
www.gov.bc.ca/fin
Other Communication: Media Inquiries, Phone: 250-356-9872, Fax: 250-356-2822

The Ministry of Finance establishes, implements, & reviews the government's financial management, fiscal, economic, & taxation policies. Responsibilities are as follows: economic planning, budgeting, & reporting; policy development for the financial, corporate, & real estate sectors; overseeing financial & administrative governance for the public service; banking & risk management services for government; tax & non-tax administration; loan administration & collection; administering a governance framework for Crown agencies; & regulating the financial services & real estate sectors.

Minister, Finance; Government House Leader, Hon. Michael de Jong, Q.C.
Tel: 250-387-3751; *Fax:* 250-387-5594
FIN.Minister@gov.bc.ca
PO Box 9048 Prov Govt Sta.
Victoria, BC V8W 9E2
Deputy Minister, Finance, Athana Mentzelopoulos
Athana.Mentzelopoulos@gov.bc.ca
PO Box 9417 Prov Govt Sta.
Victoria, BC V8W 9V1
Chief of Staff, Penelope Chandler
Tel: 250-387-3751; *Fax:* 250-387-5594
Chief of Staff, Brian Menzies
Tel: 250-387-3751; *Fax:* 250-387-5594
Associate Deputy Minister, Cheryl Wenezenki-Yolland
Tel: 250-387-8499; *Fax:* 250-387-1655
Assistant Deputy Minister, Strategic Initiatives, Doug Foster
Tel: 250-387-9022; *Fax:* 250-387-1655
Doug.Foster@gov.bc.ca
Manager, Ministry Correspondence Unit, Jessica Gillies
Tel: 250-387-3513; *Fax:* 250-387-1655
Jessica.Gillies@gov.bc.ca

Associated Agencies, Boards & Commissions:

•Auditor Certification Board
PO Box 9431 Prov Govt
Victoria, BC V8W 9V3
Tel: 250-356-8658; *Fax:* 250-356-9422
Marda.Forbes@gov.bc.ca

The Auditor Certification Board is authorized under the Business Corporations Act. The Board receives applications from individuals who apply to becertified as auditors. Persons with the necessary qualifications are then certified.

•British Columbia Securities Commission (BCSC)
Pacific Centre
701 West Georgia St., 12th Fl.
PO Box 10142
Vancouver, BC V7Y 1L2
Tel: 604-899-6500; *Fax:* 604-899-6506
Toll-free: 800-373-6393
inquiries@bcsc.bc.ca
www.bcsc.bc.ca
The British Columbia Securities Commission is an independent provincial government agency. Through administration of the Securities Act, the Commission regulates securities trading in British Columbia.

•British Columbia Lottery Corporation (BCLC)
74 West Seymour St.
Kamloops, BC V2C 1E2
Tel: 250-828-5500; *Fax:* 250-828-5631
Toll-free: 866-815-0222
www.bclc.com
Other Communication: Vancouver Phone: 604-215-0649

•Crown Agencies Resource Office (CARO)
#344, 617 Government St.
PO Box 9416 Prov Govt
Victoria, BC V8W 9V1
Tel: 250-387-8499; *Fax:* 250-356-2001
caro@gov.bc.ca
www.gov.bc.ca/caro
Implementation of the governance framework for British Columbia's Crown agencies is the role of the Crown Agencies Secretariat. The Secretariat advises Ministries & Crown agencies on the requirements of the Crown Agency Accountability System. It also maintains the Crown Agency Registry.

•Financial Institutions Commission (FICOM)
#2800, 555 West Hastings
Vancouver, BC V6B 4N6
Tel: 604-660-3555; *Fax:* 604-660-3365
Toll-free: 866-206-3030
FICOM@ficombc.ca
www.fic.gov.bc.ca
Other Communication: HR@ficombc.ca; CUandTrusts@ficombc.ca; DepositInsurance@ficombc.ca; Insurance@ficombc.ca; Pensions@ficombc.ca; RealEstate@ficombc.ca; MortgageBrokers@ficombc.ca
The Financial Institutions Commission is a regulatory agency of British Columbia's Ministry of Finance. The Commission's responsibility is the administration of statutes that regulate the financial services, pension, & real estate sectors in the province.

•Insurance Council of British Columbia
#300, 1040 West Georgia St.
PO Box 7
Vancouver, BC V6E 4H1
Tel: 604-688-0321; *Fax:* 604-662-7767
Toll-free: 877-688-0321
info@insurancecouncilofbc.com
www.insurancecouncilofbc.com
The Insurance Council of British Columbia reports to the province's Minister of Finance. The Council has the following responsibilities: Licensing insurance agents, salespersons, & adjusters; Regulating insurance licensees; & Investigating & disciplining licensees.

•Partnerships BC
#2320, 1111 West Georgia St.
PO Box 9478 Prov Govt
Vancouver, BC V8W 9W6
Tel: 604-681-2443; *Fax:* 604-806-4190
partnershipsbc@partnershipsbc.ca
www.partnershipsbc.ca
Partnerships BC is mandated to plan, deliver & provide oversight of major infrastructure projects in the province.

•Public Sector Employers' Council Secretariat (PSEC)
#210, 880 Douglas St.
PO Box 9400 Prov Govt
Victoria, BC V8V 9V1
Tel: 250-387-0842; *Fax:* 250-387-6258
www.fin.gov.bc.ca/psec
The coordination of the management of labour relations policies & practices in the public sector is the principal responsibility of the Public Sector Employers' Council. The Council consists of the following members: eight Ministers or Deputy Ministers; Commissioner of the BC Public Service Agency; & representatives from six public sector employers' associations. The Public Sector Employers' Council Secretariat carries out the work of the Council.

•Real Estate Council of British Columbia (RECBC)
#900, 750 West Pender St.
Vancouver, BC V6C 2T8
Tel: 604-683-9664; *Fax:* 604-683-9017
Toll-free: 877-683-9664
info@recbc.ca
www.recbc.ca
The Real Estate Council of British Columbia is a regulatory agency with the following responsibilities under the requirements of the Real Estate Services Act: Licensing individuals & brokerages involved in real estate sales, rental & strata property management; Enforcing licensing qualifications & licensee conduct; & Investigating complaints against licensees & imposing discipline.

Crown Agencies Resource Office
PO Box 9416 Stn. Prov Govt, Victoria, BC V8W 9V1
Tel: 250-387-8499; *Fax:* 250-356-2001
CARO@gov.bc.ca
www.gov.bc.ca/caro

Executive Director, Kate Fagan Taylor
Tel: 250-356-8291; *Fax:* 250-356-2001

Corporate Information & Records Management Office
PO Box 9417 Stn. Prov Govt, Victoria, BC V8W 9V1
Tel: 250-387-1655

Executive Director, Strategic Policy & Projects, Charmaine Lowe
Executive Director, Information Management Act Implementation, Shirley Mitrou
Executive Director, Privacy, Compliance & Training, Sharon Plater
Executive Director, Information Access Operations, Brad Williams
Tel: 250-387-9807; *Fax:* 250-387-9843
Acting Executive Director, Government Records Service, Alexander Wright

Corporate Services Division
PO Box 9415 Stn. Prov Govt, Victoria, BC V8W 9V1
Assistant Deputy Minister & Executive Financial Officer, Tara Richards
Tel: 250-387-8139
Tara.Richards@gov.bc.ca
Chief Financial Officer & Executive Director, Corporate Financial & Facilities Services, Steve Klak
Tel: 250-356-1387; *Fax:* 250-356-7326
Steve.Klak@gov.bc.ca
Chief Information Officer & Executive Director, Information Management, Michael Carpenter
Tel: 250-387-3485; *Fax:* 250-356-1494
Michael.Carpenter@gov.bc.ca
PO Box 9424 Prov Govt Sta.
Victoria, BC V8W 9V1
Executive Director, Strategic Human Resources, Elaine Jones
Tel: 250-387-2984; *Fax:* 250-356-7326
Elaine.F.Jones@gov.bc.ca
PO Box 9420 Prov Govt Sta.
Victoria, BC V8W 9V1
Executive Director, Performance Management & Corporate Priorities Branch, Kashi Tanaka
Tel: 250-387-4733; *Fax:* 250-356-7326
Kashi.Tanaka@gov.bc.ca

Deputy Secretary to Treasury Board
PO Box 9417 Stn. Prov Govt, Victoria, BC V8W 9V8
Tel: 250-387-8675; *Fax:* 250-356-9054
Assistant Deputy Minister/Deputy Secretary to Treasury Board, George Farkas
Tel: 250-387-8675; *Fax:* 250-387-9054
George.Farkas@gov.bc.ca
Chief Economist & Executive Director, Economic Forecasting & Policy Analysis, Sadaf Mirza
Tel: 250-387-9023
Sadaf.Mirza@gov.bc.ca
Executive Director, Economic Development, Alex Chandler
Tel: 250-387-3943; *Fax:* 250-387-9054
Alex.Chandler@gov.bc.ca
Executive Director, SUCH Ministries, Gord Enemark
Tel: 250-356-5032; *Fax:* 250-387-9054
Gord.Enemark@gov.bc.ca
Executive Director, Social Policy, Keith Godin
Tel: 250-356-5900
Keith.Godin@gov.bc.ca
Executive Director, Capital, Heather Hill
Tel: 250-387-9007
Jonathan.Dube@gov.bc.ca
Executive Director, Fiscal Planning, Dave Riley
Tel: 250-387-9030; *Fax:* 250-387-0300
Dave.Riley@gov.bc.ca

Gaming Policy & Enforcement
PO Box 9311 Stn. Prov Govt, Victoria, BC V8W 9N1
Tel: 250-387-1301; *Fax:* 250-387-1818
Gaming.branch@gov.bc.ca
www.gaming.gov.bc.ca

Assistant Deputy Minister, John Mazure
Tel: 250-953-4482; *Fax:* 250-387-1818
Gaming.branch@gov.bc.ca
Executive Director, Racing, Michael Brown
Tel: 604-660-7405; *Fax:* 604-660-7414
Michael.Brown@gov.bc.ca
Executive Director, Community Supports Division, David Horricks
Tel: 250-387-3211; *Fax:* 250-387-1818
David.Horricks@gov.bc.ca
Other Communications: Cell Phone: 250-516-4362
Executive Director, Strategic Policy & Projects, Michele Jaggi-Smith
Tel: 250-356-1109; *Fax:* 250-356-1910
Michele.JaggiSmith@gov.bc.ca
Executive Director, Compliance Division, Len Meilleur
Tel: 250-356-6320; *Fax:* 250-356-0794
Len.Meilleur@gov.bc.ca
Executive Director, Licensing, Registration & Certification Division, Angela Swan
Tel: 250-356-2980; *Fax:* 250-356-0782
Angela.Swan@gov.bc.ca

Internal Audit & Advisory Services
PO Box 9413 Stn. Prov Govt, Victoria, BC V8W 9V1
Tel: 250-387-6303; *Fax:* 250-356-2001
www.fin.gov.bc.ca/ocg/ias/ias.htm

Assistant Deputy Minister, Chris Brown
Tel: 250-387-8198
Chris.Brown@gov.bc.ca
Director, IM/IT Audit, Alexsandro Amaral
Tel: 250-387-9235
Director, Jane Bryant
Tel: 250-387-8177
Director, Stephen Ward
Tel: 250-387-0283

Office of the Comptroller General
PO Box 9413 Stn. Prov Govt, Victoria, BC V8W 9V1
Fax: 250-356-2001
Comptroller.General@gov.bc.ca
www.fin.gov.bc.ca/ocg.htm
Other Communication: Legal Encumbrance Inquiries, Phone: 250-387-3364
The Office of the Comptroller General oversees the quality & integrity of the government's financial management & control systems.
Comptroller General, Stuart Newton
Tel: 250-387-6692; *Fax:* 250-356-2001
Stuart.Newton@gov.bc.ca
Executive Director, Financial Reporting & Advisory Services, Carl Fischer
Tel: 250-356-9272; *Fax:* 250-356-8388
Carl.Fischer@gov.bc.ca
Executive Director, Corporate Compliance & Controls Monitoring, Greg Gudgeon
Tel: 250-356-7434; *Fax:* 250-356-0560
greg.gudgeon@gov.bc.ca
Executive Director, Financial Management Branch, Tamara McLeod
Tel: 250-216-6057; *Fax:* 250-356-6164
Tamara.McLeod@gov.bc.ca
Executive Director, Corporate Accounting Services, Steve Rossander
Tel: 250-415-7673; *Fax:* 250-356-6164
Steve.Rossander@gov.bc.ca

Policy & Legislation Division
Tel: 250-356-9911; *Fax:* 250-952-0137
Assistant Deputy Minister, Heather Wood
Tel: 250-356-9911; *Fax:* 250-952-0137
Executive Lead, Liquefied Natural Gas (LNG) Taxation, Pat Parkinson
Tel: 250-387-8990; *Fax:* 250-952-0137
Executive Director, Strategic Projects & Policy, Elizabeth Cole
Tel: 604-660-2971; *Fax:* 604-660-3365
Elizabeth.Cole@gov.bc.ca
Executive Director, Liquefied Natural Gas (LNG) Taxation, Christina Dawkins
Tel: 250-356-5068; *Fax:* 250-387-9061
Executive Director, Tax Policy Branch, Paul Flanagan
Tel: 250-387-9014; *Fax:* 250-387-9061
Paul.Flanagan@gov.bc.ca
Executive Director, Intergovernmental Fiscal Relations, Rory Molnar
Tel: 250-387-7511; *Fax:* 250-387-9061
Rory.Molnar@gov.bc.ca

Executive Director, Financial & Corporate Sector Policy Branch, Vacant
Tel: 250-387-7567; *Fax:* 250-387-9093
Senior Director, Income Tax, Richard Purnell
Tel: 250-387-9072; *Fax:* 250-387-9061
Richard.Purnell@gov.bc.ca

Provincial Treasury
PO Box 9414 Stn. Prov Govt, Victoria, BC V8V 9V1
Tel: 250-387-4541; *Fax:* 250-356-3041
www.fin.gov.bc.ca/pt.htm

Assistant Deputy Minister, Jim Hopkins
Tel: 250-387-5729; *Fax:* 250-356-3041
Jim.Hopkins@gov.bc.ca
Chief Security Officer, Risk Mitigation & Government Security, Shaun Fynes
Tel: 250-387-0522; *Fax:* 250-356-6222
Shaun.Fynes@gov.bc.ca
Executive Director, Banking & Cash Management, Kevin MacMillen
Tel: 250-387-7105
Executive Director, Risk Management, Linda Irvine
Tel: 250-387-0521; *Fax:* 250-356-6222
Acting Executive Director, Debt Management, David Latham
Tel: 250-387-8815; *Fax:* 250-387-3024

Revenue Division
Fax: 250-387-3000

Assistant Deputy Minister, Elan Symes
Tel: 250-387-0665; *Fax:* 250-387-3000
Elan.Symes@gov.bc.ca
Executive Director, Public Information & Corporate Services Branch, Ann Davies
Tel: 250-953-3672
Ann.Davies@gov.bc.ca
Executive Director, Property Taxation Branch, Steven B. Emery
Tel: 250-387-0532; *Fax:* 250-387-2210
Executive Director, Receivables Management Office, Dennis Forbes
Tel: 250-356-8031; *Fax:* 250-356-5604
Dennis.Forbes@gov.bc.ca
Executive Director, Consumer Taxation Programs Branch, Jordan Goss
Tel: 250-387-0611
Jordan.Goss@gov.bc.ca
Executive Director, Income Taxation Branch, Paula Harper
Tel: 250-387-3968; *Fax:* 250-356-9243
Executive Director, Mineral, Oil & Gas Revenue Branch, Andrew Ritonja
Tel: 250-387-1182; *Fax:* 250-952-0191
Andrew.Ritonja@gov.bc.ca
Executive Director, Revenue Solutions Branch, David Sherwood
Tel: 250-387-5785; *Fax:* 250-356-1706
David.Sherwood@gov.bc.ca
Executive Director, Tax Appeals & Litigation Branch, Hilary Vance
Tel: 250-387-0662; *Fax:* 250-387-5883
Hilary.Vance@gov.bc.ca

British Columbia Ministry of Forests, Lands & Natural Resource Operations

PO Box 9049 Stn. Prov Govt, Victoria, BC V8W 9E2
Toll-Free: 800-663-7867
TTY: 800-661-8773
FLNRO.MediaRequests@gov.bc.ca
www.gov.bc.ca/for
Other Communication: Media Phone: 250-356-5261

The Ministry of Forests, Lands & Natural Resource Operations establishes policies for access to & use of British Columbia's forests, land, & natural resources. Services provided enable stewardship & sustainable management of the province's resources. Responsibilities of the ministry include Aboriginal consultation; Crown land administration policy; resource roads & bridges policy; forest, range, & grazing stewardship policy; pest & disease management policy; water use planning; timber supply & sales; fish, wildlife, & habitat management; licensing for hunting, trapping, & angling; recreation sites & trails; & wildfire management.

Minister, Forests, Lands & Natural Resource Operations, Hon. Steve Thomson
Tel: 250-387-6240; *Fax:* 250-387-1040
FLNR.Minister@gov.bc.ca
Deputy Minister, Tim Sheldan
Tel: 250-952-6500; *Fax:* 250-387-3291
Tim.Sheldan@gov.bc.ca
Parliamentary Secretary to the Minister of Forests, Lands & Natural Resource Operations, John Martin
Tel: 250-953-4613; *Fax:* 250-387-9100
john.martin.MLA@leg.bc.ca
Chief of Staff, Bruce Strongitharm
Bruce.Strongitharm@gov.bc.ca
Associate Deputy Minister, Forest Sector, Jason Fisher

Associated Agencies, Boards & Commissions:

•Assayers Certification Board of Examiners (ACBE)
PO Box 9333 Prov Govt
Victoria, BC V8W 9N3
Tel: 250-952-0374
commons.bcit.ca/assayercert/exam.html
The Board of Examiners administers the Assayers Certification Program, invigilate the examinations, grade papers, and recommend candidates for qualification to the Responsible Minister. The Board operates under the Ministry of Energy & Mines Act.

•Forest Practices Board (FPB)
PO Box 9905 Prov Govt
Victoria, BC V8W 9R1
Tel: 250-213-4700; *Fax:* 250-213-4725
Toll-free: 800-994-5899
fpboard@gov.bc.ca
www.bcfpb.ca
British Columbia's Forest Practices Board is responsible for reporting to the government & public about compliance with the Forest & Range Practices Act. The Board engages in the following activities: Investigation of public complaints; Undertaking special investigations; Auditing forest practices of government, government enforcement of the Forest & Range Practices Act, & licence holders on public lands; Participation in appeals; & Provision of reports & recommendations.

•Muskwa-Kechika Advisory Board (M-KAB)
MKMASupport@shaw.ca
www.muskwa-kechika.com
The Board oversees the preservation of the Muskwa-Kechika Management Area, & ensures that activities carried out within the area meet the standards set by the Muskwa-Kechika Management Plan.

•Timber Export Advisory Committee
PO Box 9514 Prov Govt
Victoria, BC V8W 9C2
Tel: 250-387-8916; *Fax:* 250-387-5050

Corporate Initiatives
PO Box 9352 Stn. Prov Govt, Victoria, BC V8W 9M1
Executive Director, Rose Ellis
Tel: 250-387-9707
Rose.Ellis@gov.bc.ca
Director, Strategic Initiatives & Legislation, Katherine Rowe
Tel: 250-387-8606
Director, Major Projects, Brenda Hartley
Tel: 250-828-4443; *Fax:* 250-387-2335
Brenda.Hartley@gov.bc.ca

Corporate Services for the Natural Resouces Sector
Assistant Deputy Minister, CSNR & Executive Financial Officer, Forests, Lands & Natural Resource Operations, Trish Dohan
Tel: 250-953-4745
Trish.Dohan@gov.bc.ca
Assistant Deputy Minister & Executive Financial Officer, MARR, AGRI, ENV, MEM & NGD, Wes Boyd
Tel: 250-387-9878

Client Services Branch
Executive Director, Wendy Byrnes
Tel: 250-371-6232
Wendy.Byrnes@gov.bc.ca
Director, Provincial Client Operations, Tracey Edwards
Tel: 250-356-9221
Tracey.Edwards@gov.bc.ca
Provincial Manager, Fleet & Assets, Kevin Doran
Tel: 250-387-6804; *Fax:* 250-387-6609
Kevin.Doran@gov.bc.ca
Manager, Warehousing & Fleet, Kim Pilotte
Tel: 250-952-4428; *Fax:* 250-952-4925
Kim.Pilotte@gov.bc.ca

Financial Services Branch
Chief Financial Officer & Executive Director, Murray Jacobs
Tel: 250-387-4702
Murray.Jacobs@gov.bc.ca
Director, Financial Planning & Reporting, Mary Myers
Tel: 250-952-0229
Mary.Myers@gov.bc.ca
Director, Revenue, Nicole Wright
Tel: 778-676-1951
Nicole.Wright@gov.bc.ca
Manager, Financial Planning & Reporting, Michael McNally-Dawes
Tel: 250-387-5376
Michael.McNallyDawes@gov.bc.ca
Manager, Revenue Programs, Helen Li-Hennessey
Tel: 778-676-4648
Helen.LiHennessey@gov.bc.ca
Manager, Water Revenue, Marie Curtis
Tel: 250-387-6037
Marie.Curtis@gov.bc.ca

Information Management
PO Box 9364 Stn. Prov Govt, Victoria, BC V8W 9M3
Chief Information Officer & Executive Director, Denise Rossander
Tel: 250-952-0944
Director, Architecture, Fary Eriksson
Tel: 250-387-5277
Fary.Eriksson@gov.bc.ca
Director, Infrastructure Services, Fredo Vanlierop
Director, Technology Services, Dave Rejminiak
Tel: 250-387-6358
Dave.Rejminiak@gov.bc.ca
Director, Communication Services, Tina St. Hilaire
Tel: 250-588-5310
Tina.St.Hilaire@gov.bc.ca

Executive Operations
PO Box 9352 Stn. Prov Govt, Victoria, BC V8W 9M1
Fax: 250-387-3291

Chief of Staff, Cynthia Petrie
Tel: 250-387-4471
Cynthia.Petrie@gov.bc.ca
Manager, Correspondence Services, Vacant
Tel: 250-356-9638
FLNR.Correspondence@gov.bc.ca

Integrated Resource Operations Division
PO Box 9352 Stn. Prov Govt, Victoria, BC V8W 9M1
Tel: 250-356-1874; *Fax:* 250-387-3291
Assistant Deputy Minister, Robert Turner
Tel: 250-356-1874
Executive Director, GeoBC, Andrew Calarco
Tel: 250-952-6581
Andrew.Calarco@gov.bc.ca
Executive Director, Mountain Resorts, Norman Lee
Tel: 250-952-0478
Norman.K.Lee@gov.bc.ca
Director, Compliance & Enforcement, Kevin Edquist
Tel: 250-387-8372; *Fax:* 250-387-2569
Kevin.Edquist@gov.bc.ca
Director, Recreation Sites & Trails BC, John Hawkings
Tel: 604-898-2105
John.Hawkings@gov.bc.ca
Executive Director, BC Wildfire Services, Madeline Maley
Tel: 250-387-6368; *Fax:* 250-387-5685
Madeline.Maley@gov.bc.ca
Director, Archaeology Branch, Justine Batten
Tel: 250-953-3355; *Fax:* 250-953-3340
Justine.Batten@gov.bc.ca
Director, Heritage Branch, Richard Linzey
Tel: 250-356-1434; *Fax:* 250-356-2842
Richard.Linzey@gov.bc.ca
Manager, Resource Registry & Research, GeoBC, Janet Adams
Tel: 250-952-5309; *Fax:* 250-356-5797
Janet.Adams@gov.bc.ca

Regional Operations Offices
Coast
2100 Labieux Rd., Nanaimo, BC V9T 6E9
Tel: 250-751-7001; *Fax:* 250-751-7190
Forests.CoastRegionOffice@gov.bc.ca
www.for.gov.bc.ca/rco
Assistant Deputy Minister, Craig Sutherland
Tel: 250-387-9773; *Fax:* 250-356-2150
Regional Executive Director, West Coast, Sharon Hadway
Tel: 250-751-7161; *Fax:* 250-751-7196
Sharon.Hadway@gov.bc.ca
Regional Executive Director, South Coast, Heather MacKnight
Tel: 604-586-2892; *Fax:* 604-586-4434
Heather.MacKnight@gov.bc.ca
Director, Resource Management (West Coast), Larry Barr
Tel: 250-751-7105; *Fax:* 250-741-5686
Larry.Barr@gov.bc.ca
Director, Pricing/Tenures/Mines (West Coast), Denis Collins
Tel: 250-751-7121; *Fax:* 250-751-7196
Denis.Collins@gov.bc.ca
Director, Authorizations (West Coast), Myles Mana
Tel: 250-751-7308; *Fax:* 250-751-7081
Myles.Mana@gov.bc.ca
Director, Resource Management (South Coast), Julia Berardinucci
Tel: 604-586-4433; *Fax:* 604-586-4434
Julia.Berardinucci@gov.bc.ca
Director, Resource Authorization (South Coast), Alec Drysdale
Tel: 604-586-4420; *Fax:* 604-586-4419
Alec.Drysdale@gov.bc.ca
Director, Resource Initiatives Office (South Coast), Kevin Haberl
Tel: 604-898-2145; *Fax:* 604-586-4434
Kevin Haberl@gov.bc.ca
Manager, Strategic Initiatives, Chris Tunnoch
Tel: 604-924-2224; *Fax:* 250-356-9299
Chris.Tunnoch@gov.bc.ca

Manager, Permit & Authorization Service Bureau, Yvonne Foxall
Tel: 250-387-3787; *Fax:* 250-387-1814
Yvonne.Foxall@gov.bc.ca

North Area

1011 - 4 Ave., 5th Fl., Prince George, BC V2L 3H9
Tel: 250-565-6100
www.for.gov.bc.ca/mi

Assistant Deputy Minister, Kevin Kriese
Tel: 250-952-0596
Executive Director, Butch Morningstar
Tel: 250-387-0844
Butch.Morningstar@gov.bc.ca
Executive Director, Strategic Projects, Gary Reay
Tel: 250-751-7007
Executive Coordinator, Leona Frenette
Tel: 250-356-5304
Regional Executive Director, Northeast, Dale Morgan
Tel: 250-784-1200
Dale.Morgan@gov.bc.ca
Regional Executive Director, Skeena, Eamon O'Donoghue
Tel: 250-847-7495; *Fax:* 250-847-7347
Eamon.ODonoghue@gov.bc.ca
Regional Executive Director, Omineca, Bill Warner
Tel: 250-565-6102; *Fax:* 250-565-6671
Bill.Warner@gov.bc.ca
Director, Authorizations (Prince George), Greg Rawling
Tel: 250-565-6234; *Fax:* 250-565-6671
Greg.Rawling@gov.bc.ca
Director, Resource Management (Omenica), Normand Bilodeau
Tel: 250-565-4457
Director, Major Projects (Northeast), Todd Bondaroff
Tel: 250-784-1245; *Fax:* 250-787-3219
Todd.Bondaroff@gov.bc.ca
Regional Director, Pricing & Tenures (Omineca), Heather Cullen
Tel: 250-565-6102; *Fax:* 250-565-6671
Heather.Cullen@gov.bc.ca
Director, Resource Management (Skeena), Jane Lloyd-Smith
Tel: 250-847-7340; *Fax:* 250-847-7728
Jane.LloydSmith@gov.bc.ca
Acting Director, Authorizations (Skeena), Nick Thomas
Tel: 250-847-7517; *Fax:* 250-847-7347
Nicholas.Thomas@gov.bc.ca
Director, Resource Authorizations (Northeast), Karrilyn Vince
Tel: 250-787-3534; *Fax:* 250-787-3219
Karrilyn.Vince@gov.bc.ca
District Manager, Resource Operations (Vanderhoof/Fort St. James), Lynda Currie
Tel: 250-996-5241; *Fax:* 250-996-5290
Lynda.Currie@gov.bc.ca
District Manager, Resource Operations (Mackenzie), Dave Francis
Tel: 250-997-2203; *Fax:* 250-997-2203
Dave.Francis@gov.bc.ca
District Manager, Resource Operations (Dawson Creek), Robert Kopecky
Tel: 250-784-1205; *Fax:* 250-784-1203
District Manager, Resource Operations (Fort Nelson), Steve Lindsey
Tel: 250-774-5520; *Fax:* 250-774-3704
Steve.Lindsey@gov.bc.ca
District Manager, Coast Mountains Resource District, Barry Dobbin
Tel: 250-638-5100; *Fax:* 250-638-5176
Barry.Dobbin@gov.bc.ca
District Manager, Nadina, Josh Pressey
Tel: 250-692-2224; *Fax:* 250-692-7461
Josh.Pressey@gov.bc.ca

South

441 Columbia St., Kamloops, BC V2C 2T3
Tel: 250-828-4131; *Fax:* 250-828-4154
www.for.gov.bc.ca/rsi

Assistant Deputy Minister, Richard Manwaring
Tel: 250-828-4449
Acting Executive Director, Madeline Maley
Tel: 250-828-4114
Other Communications: Alternate Phone: 250-371-3747
Regional Executive Director, Southern Interior Region, Kevin Dickenson
Tel: 250-828-4445; *Fax:* 250-828-4442
Kevin.Dickenson@gov.bc.ca
Regional Executive Director, Cariboo, Gerry MacDougall
Gerry.MacDougall@gov.bc.ca
Regional Executive Director, Kootenay Boundary, Tony Wideski
Tel: 250-426-1741; *Fax:* 250-426-1767
Tony.Wideski@gov.bc.ca
Director, Resource Management (Kootenay), Paul Rasmussen
Tel: 250-354-6947
Paul.Rasmussen@gov.bc.ca
Director, Resource Authorizations (Kamloops), Peter Lishman
Tel: 250-828-4239; *Fax:* 250-828-4442
Peter.Lishman@gov.bc.ca
Director, Resource Management (Kamloops), Dan Peterson
Tel: 250-828-4124; *Fax:* 250-828-4154
Dan.Peterson@gov.bc.ca
Director, Pricing & Tenures (Kamloops), Jim Schafthuizen
Tel: 250-828-4625; *Fax:* 250-828-4154
Jim.Schafthuizen@gov.bc.ca
Director, Resource Management (Cariboo), Rodger Stewart
Tel: 250-398-4549; *Fax:* 250-398-4214
Rodger.Stewart@gov.bc.ca
Other Communications: Cell Phone: 250-305-8536
Director, Resource Authorizations (Cariboo), Ken Vanderburgh
Tel: 250-398-4225; *Fax:* 250-398-4836
Ken.Vanderburgh@gov.bc.ca
District Manager, Natural Resource Operations (100 Mile House), Patrick Byrne
Tel: 250-395-7804; *Fax:* 250-395-7810
Pat.Byrne@gov.bc.ca
District Manager, Natural Resource Operations (Quensel), Steve Dodge
Tel: 250-992-4465; *Fax:* 250-992-4403
Steve.Dodge@gov.bc.ca
District Manager, Natural Resource Operations (Kamloops), Rick Sommer
Tel: 250-371-6501
Rick.B.Sommer@gov.bc.ca
District Manager, Natural Resource Operations (Okanagan Shuswap), Dave Hails
Tel: 250-558-1729; *Fax:* 250-549-5485
Dave.Hails@gov.bc.ca
District Manager, Natural Resource Operations (Cascades), Charles van Hemmen
Tel: 250-378-8402; *Fax:* 250-378-8481
Charles.vanHemmen@gov.bc.ca
Other Communications: Cell Phone: 250-315-3773
District Manager, Resource Operations (Central Cariboo/Chilcotin), Mike Pedersen
Tel: 250-398-4355; *Fax:* 250-398-4790
Mike.Pedersen@gov.bc.ca
Other Communications: Alternate Phone: 250-398-4345

Resource Stewardship Division

PO Box 9352 Stn. Prov Govt, Victoria, BC V8W 9M1
Tel: 250-356-0972; *Fax:* 250-356-2150

Assistant Deputy Minister, Tom Ethier
Tel: 250-356-0972; *Fax:* 250-356-2150
Director, Resource Management Objectives, Allan Lidstone
Tel: 250-356-6255; *Fax:* 250-356-5341
Allan.Lidstone@gov.bc.ca
Director, Tree Improvement Branch, Brian Barber
Tel: 250-356-0888; *Fax:* 250-356-8124
Brian.Barber@gov.bc.ca
Other Communications: URL: www.for.gov.bc.ca/hti/
Director & Comptroller, Water Rights, Water Management, Glen Davidson, P.Eng
Tel: 250-387-6949; *Fax:* 250-356-0605
Glen.Davidson@gov.bc.ca
Director, Resource Management Objectives, Allan Lidstone
Tel: 250-356-6255; *Fax:* 250-387-2410
Allan.Lidstone@gov.bc.ca
Director, Forest Analysis & Inventory Branch, Albert Nussbaum
Tel: 250-356-5958; *Fax:* 250-387-5999
Forests.ForestAnalysisBranchOffice@gov.bc.ca
Director, Resource Practices Branch, Jennifer Davis
Tel: 250-387-0088; *Fax:* 250-387-1467
Jennifer.C.Davis@gov.bc.ca
Director, Operations, Keith Thomas
Tel: 250-387-4895; *Fax:* 250-356-2150
Keith.Thomas@gov.bc.ca
Director, Fish & Wildlife, Dan Peterson
Tel: 250-387-3637; *Fax:* 250-387-9568
Deputy Director, Fish, Wildlife & Habitat Management, Yvonne Foxall
Tel: 250-356-0874; *Fax:* 250-387-9568
Yvonne.Foxall@gov.bc.ca
Manager, Fish & Wildlife Policy, Jeff Morgan
Tel: 250-371-6347
Jeff.Morgan@gov.bc.ca

Tenures, Competitiveness & Innovation Division

PO Box 9352 Stn. Prov Govt, Victoria, BC V8W 9M1
Tel: 250-387-1057; *Fax:* 250-953-3603

Ensures that forestry laws are being followed in BC's public forests, & takes action where there is non-compliance. C&E staff enforce forest management laws & combat forest crimes such as theft, arson & mischief. Officials conduct more than 16,000 inspections a year to assess compliance with forest laws. Where there is evidence of a contravention, an investigation is conducted, which may lead to the issuance of a violation ticket, penalty or other enforcement action. The most serious forest crimes are prosecuted through the court system.

Assistant Deputy Minister, Dave Peterson
Tel: 250-387-1057; *Fax:* 250-356-6791
Director, LNG, Crown Land Opportunities & Restoration Branch, Myles Mana
Tel: 250-387-8787; *Fax:* 250-356-6791
Myles.Mana@gov.bc.ca
Director, Compensation & Business Analysis Branch, Sinclair Tedder
Tel: 250-387-8608; *Fax:* 250-356-7903
Sinclair.Tedder@gov.bc.ca
Director, Forest Tenures Branch, Doug Stewart
Tel: 250-387-8729; *Fax:* 250-356-7903
Doug.B.Stewart@gov.bc.ca
Director, Competitiveness & Innovation Branch, James Sandland
Tel: 250-953-3988; *Fax:* 250-356-7903
Paul.S.Knowles@gov.bc.ca
Director, Land Tenures, Michelle Porter
Tel: 250-387-1832
Michelle.Porter@gov.bc.ca

Timber Operations, Pricing & First Nations Division

PO Box 9352 Stn. Prov Govt, Victoria, BC V8W 9M1
Fax: 250-387-3291

Assistant Deputy Minister, Tom Jensen
Tel: 250-387-0902; *Fax:* 250-387-3291
Tom.Jensen@gov.bc.ca
Chief Engineer, Brian Chow
Tel: 250-953-4370; *Fax:* 250-953-3687
Brian.Chow@gov.bc.ca
Executive Director, Field Operations, Mike Falkiner
Tel: 250-387-8309; *Fax:* 250-953-3687
Mike.Falkiner@gov.bc.ca
Director, Timber Pricing, Steve Kozuki
Tel: 250-356-9807
Steve.Kozuki@gov.bc.ca
Director, Resource Worker Safety, Tom Jackson
Tel: 250-949-0888; *Fax:* 250-387-3291
Tom.Jackson@gov.bc.ca
Director, First Nation Relations Branch, Charles Hunter
Tel: 250-387-6719
Charles.Hunter@gov.bc.ca
Director, Engineering Branch, Peter Wyatt
Tel: 250-387-1295; *Fax:* 250-953-3687
Peter.Wyatt@gov.bc.ca

British Columbia Ministry of Health

1515 Blanshard St., PO Box 9639 Stn. Prov Govt, Victoria, BC V8W 9P1
Tel: 604-660-2421
Toll-Free: 800-663-7100
hlth.health@gov.bc.ca
www.gov.bc.ca/health
Other Communication: Media Inquiries, Phone: 250-952-1887, Fax: 250-952-1883

The Ministry of Health is responsible for ensuring quality, timely, & cost effective health services for all citizens of British Columbia. To guide & enhance British Columbia's health services, the ministry works with health authorities, agencies, care providers, & other groups.

Minister, Health, Hon. Terry Lake
Tel: 250-953-3547; *Fax:* 250-356-9587
hlth.minister@gov.bc.ca
Deputy Minister, Health, Stephen Brown
Tel: 250-952-1590; *Fax:* 250-952-1909
hlth.dmoffice@gov.bc.ca
Parliamentary Secretary to the Minister of Health for Seniors, Darryl Plecas
Tel: 250-952-7275; *Fax:* 250-387-9100
darryl.plecas.mla@leg.bc.ca
Chief of Staff, Martyn Lafrance
Tel: 250-953-3547
Executive Director, Strategic Management & Organizational Development, Debbie Godfrey
Tel: 250-952-1026; *Fax:* 250-952-1909

Associated Agencies, Boards & Commissions:

•British Columbia Ambulance Service (BCAS)
The BCAS operates under the Emergency Health Services Commission, legislated by the Emergency & Health Services Act.

•Hospital Appeal Board (HAB)
747 Fort St., 4th Fl.
PO Box 9425 Prov Govt
Victoria, BC V8W 9V1
Tel: 250-387-3464; *Fax:* 250-356-9923
hab@gov.bc.ca
www.hab.gov.bc.ca
The Hospital Appeal Board of British Columbia is an independent, quasi-judicial administrative appeal tribunal, which was created by the Hospital Act. The Board provides an appeal process for medical practitioners. The role of the Board is to review hospital board of management decisions concerning

hospital privileges. Board members are appointed by British Columbia's Minister of Health.

•Medical Services Commission (MSC)
PO Box 9652 Prov Govt
Victoria, BC V8W 9P4
Tel: 250-952-3073; *Fax:* 250-952-3133
The Medical Services Commission is a statutory body made up of nine members. In accordance with the Medicare Protection Act & Regulations, the Commission acts on behalf of the Government of British Columbia to manage the Medical Services Plan. The Commission works to ensure British Columbia residents have access to medical care, & to manage the provision & payment of medical services.

•Mental Health Review Board (MHRB)
#302, 960 Quayside Dr.
New Westminster, BC V3M 6G2
Tel: 604-660-2325; *Fax:* 604-660-2403
www.mentalhealthreviewboard.gov.bc.ca

Corporate Services
Fax: 250-952-1909
Associate Deputy Minister, Sabine Feulgen
Tel: 250-952-1764
Assistant Deputy Minister, Health Sector IM/IT, Lindsay Kislock
Tel: 250-952-2791
Assistant Deputy Minister, Health Sector Workforce Division, Ted Patterson
Tel: 250-952-3166
Ted.Patterson@gov.bc.ca
Assistant Deputy Minister, Finance & Corporate Services, Manjit Sidhu
Tel: 250-952-2066

Health Services
Tel: 250-952-2402; *Fax:* 250-952-1390
Associate Deputy Minister, Lynn Stevenson
Tel: 250-952-2402
Assistant Deputy Minister, Health Sector Planning & Innovation Division, Heather Davidson
Tel: 250-952-2569
Assistant Deputy Minister, Health Services Policy & Quality Assurance Division, Doug Hughes
Tel: 250-952-1049
Assistant Deputy Minister, Population & Public Health, Arlene Paton
Tel: 250-952-1731
Assistant Deputy Minister, Medical Beneficiary & Pharmaceutical Services, Barbara Walman
Tel: 250-952-1705
Executive Lead, Strategic Initiatives, Deborah Shera
Tel: 250-952-1343

HealthLink BC
PO Box 9600 Stn. Prov Govt, Victoria, BC V8W 9P1
Fax: 250-952-2970
healthlinkbc@gov.bc.ca
www.HealthLinkBC.ca
Other Communication: HealthLink BC hotline: 8-1-1; TTY: 7-1-1
HealthLink BC allows residents of British Columbia to access health care information by phone or online, and incorporates the following previously existing services: BC HealthGuide, BC HealthFiles, BC NurseLine & Pharmacist service, & Dial-a-Dietitian.
Executive Director, Clinical Services, Marie Root
Tel: 604-215-5118; *Fax:* 250-952-6509
Director, Dietitian Services, Barbara Leslie
Tel: 604-215-5138
Director, Nursing Services, Kim Schmidt
Tel: 604-215-5103

Office of the Provincial Health Officer
Tel: 250-952-1330; *Fax:* 250-952-1362
Provincial Health Officer, Dr. Perry Kendall
Perry.Kendall@gov.bc.ca
Deputy Provincial Health Officer, Dr. Bonnie Henry
Provincial Drinking Water Officer, Lynne Magee
Tel: 250-952-1572

Office of the Seniors Advocate
PO Box 9561 Stn. Prov Govt, Victoria, BC V8W 9P4
Tel: 250-952-3034
Toll-Free: 877-952-3181
info@seniorsadvocatebc.ca
www.seniorsadvocatebc.ca
Seniors Advocate, Isobel Mackenzie
Tel: 250-952-3033
Deputy Seniors Advocate, Mark Blandford
Tel: 250-952-2999
Executive Director, Bruce Ronayne
Tel: 250-952-2298
Director, Communications, Sara Darling
Tel: 250-952-3035

British Columbia Hydro

6911 Southpoint Dr., Burnaby, BC V3N 4X8
Tel: 604-224-9376
Toll-Free: 800-224-9376
www.bchydro.com
Secondary Address: 333 Dunsmuir St.
Corporate Address
Vancouver, BC V6B 5R3
twitter.com/bchydro
www.facebook.com/bchydro
www.youtube.com/bchydro
The Clean Energy Act consolidated BC Hydro & the BC Transmission Corporation in 2010. BC Hydro is a crown corporation that reports to the British Columbia Ministry of Energy, Mines, & Natural Gas. The mission of the corporation is the delivery of energy, in an envrionmentally & socially responsible manner, to meet the province's demand for electricity. Four million customers are provided with power via a network of over 77,000 km of transmission & distribution lines, 334,000 individual transformers, & over 290 substations.
Chair, W.J. Brad Bennett
President & Chief Executive Officer, Jessica McDonald
Deputy CEO & Capital Infrastructure Project Delivery, Chris O'Riley
Executive Vice-President, Transmission, Distribution & Customer Service, Greg Reimer
Executive Vice-President, Finance & Supply Chain & Chief Financial Officer, Cheryl Yaremko
Senior Vice-President, Corporate Services & General Counsel, Ray Aldeguer
Senior Vice-President, Energy, Regulatory & Business Planning, Janet Fraser
Senior Vice-President & Chief Human Resources Officer, Debbie Nagle
Senior Vice-President, Generation Operations, Janet Fraser

Associated Agencies, Boards & Commissions:

•Powerex Corp.
#1300, 666 Burrard St.
Vancouver, BC V6C 2X8
Tel: 604-891-5000; *Fax:* 604-891-6060
Toll-free: 800-220-4907
www2.powerex.com
A wholly-owned subsidiary of BC Hydro, Powerex Corp. markets wholesale energy products & services to utilities, power pools, industrials, & power marketers in North America, particularly western Canada, the western United States.

•Powertech Labs Inc.
12388 - 88 Ave.
Surrey, BC V8W 7R7
Tel: 604-590-7500; *Fax:* 604-590-6611
www.powertechlabs.com
A wholly owned subsidiary of BC Hydro, Powertech Labs offers environmental, mechanical, electrical, metallurgical, civil, chemical, gas technologies, & structural engineering to deal with technical problems with power equipment & systems.

Office of the Information & Privacy Commissioner for British Columbia (OIPC)

947 Fort St., 4th Fl., PO Box 9038 Stn. Prov Govt, Victoria, BC V8W 9A4
Tel: 250-387-5629; *Fax:* 250-387-1696
Toll-Free: 800-663-7867
info@oipc.bc.ca
www.oipc.bc.ca
Other Communication: Vancouver Phone: 604-660-2421
twitter.com/@BCInfoPrivacy
Operating independently from the government, the Office of the Information & Privacy Commissioner is responsible for monitoring & enforcing the following acts in British Columbia: Freedom of Information & Protection of Privacy Act; & Personal Information Protection Act.
Acting Commissioner, Drew McArthur
Note: On March 22, 2016, Elizabeth Denham announced she would be stepping down as Information & Privacy Commissioner once her term ended on July 6, 2016.
Deputy Commissioner, Michael McEvoy
Deputy Registrar & Assistant Commissioner, Investigation & Mediation, Jay Fedorak
Registrar of Inquiries, Cindy Hamilton
Tel: 250-387-2686
Director, Communications, Cara McGregor
Senior Investigator, Audit & Compliance, Tanya Allen
Senior Investigator, Patrick Egan
Coordinator, Lobbyist Registry, Carol Searle

Insurance Corporation of British Columbia (ICBC)

151 West Esplanade, North Vancouver, BC V7M 3H9
Tel: 604-661-2800
Toll-Free: 800-663-3051
www.icbc.com
Other Communication: New Claims, Lower Mainland Phone: 604-520-8222; Elsewhere in BC, Toll Free: 1-800-910-4222; TIPS Lower Mainland, Phone: 604-661-6844; TIPS BC Line: 1-800-661-6844
A provincial Crown corporation, The Insurance Corporation of British Columbia was established in 1973. The main responsibilities of the Insurance Corporation of British Columbia are as follows: Provision of universal auto insurance to motorists in British Columbia; Registration & licensing of vehicles; & Driver licensing.
Chair, Ron Olynyk
President/Chief Executive Officer, Mark Blucher
Chief Financial Officer, Geri Prior
Vice-President, Corporate & Stakeholder Governance, Steve Crombie
Vice-President, Claims, Brian Jarvis
Vice-President, Corporate Services, Barbara Meens Thistle
Vice-President, Insurance & Driver Licensing, Steve Yendall

British Columbia Ministry of International Trade (& Minister Responsible for Asia Pacific Strategy & Multiculturalism)

PO Box 9063 Stn. Prov Gov, Victoria, BC V8W 9E2
Tel: 250-953-0910; *Fax:* 250-953-0928
www.gov.bc.ca/mit
Other Communication: Trade & Invest BC: www.britishcolumbia.ca/invest
twitter.com/BCTradeInvest
www.linkedin.com/company/trade-&-invest-british-columbia
www.youtube.com/user/BCTradeInvest
The Ministry of International Trade & Minister Responsible for Asia Pacific Strategy & Multiculturalism seeks to increase British Columbia's exports, establish international partnerships, increase the province's competitiveness, work out trade deals & attract investments from foreign companies.
Minister, International Trade; Minister Responsible for the Asia Pacific Strategy & Multiculturalism, Hon. Teresa Wat
Tel: 250-953-0910; *Fax:* 250-953-0928
MIT.Minister@gov.bc.ca
Deputy Minister, Clark Roberts
Tel: 250-952-0242; *Fax:* 250-952-0137
Clark.Roberts@gov.bc.ca
Chief of Staff, Jay Denney
Tel: 250-953-0910; *Fax:* 250-953-0928
Director, Operations, Debbie Smollett
Tel: 250-952-0710
Debbie.Smollett@gov.bc.ca

Associated Agencies, Boards & Commissions:

•BC Immigrant Investment Fund Ltd. (BCIIF)
#301, 865 Hornby St.
Vancouver, BC V6Z 2G3
Fax: 250-952-0371
bciif.ca
BCIIF is wholly owned by the Province of British Columbia & was incorporated in 2000 under the Company Act of British Columbia. It utilizes funds provided under the federal Immigrant Investor Program (IIP) & has an investment portfolio structured into the following three asset classes: Money Market & Central Depository Investments; Infrastructure Investments; & Venture Capital Investments.

•BC Renaissance Capital Fund Ltd. (BCRCF)
PO Box 9800 Prov Govt
Fax: 250-952-0371
bciif.ca
The BC Renaissance Capital Fund Ltd. is a Crown corporation wholly owned by the BC Immigrant Investment Fund. Its purpose is to develop innovative technology companies in BC through the attraction of venture capital investment.

•Forestry Innovation Investment Ltd. (FII)
#1200, 1130 West Pender St.
Vancouver, BC V6E 4A4
Tel: 604-685-7507; *Fax:* 604-685-5373
info@bcfii.ca
www.bcfii.ca
British Columbia's Forestry Innovation Investment strives to support a prosperous & environmentally sustainable forest economy in the province. The role of the organization includes the following activities: Promotion of British Columbia's forest practices & wood products to international markets; Working in partnership with the forestry sector, the Government of British Columbia, & the Government of Canada; & Assisting the forestry sector with issues such as Mountain Pine Beetle outbreak.

•Multicultural Advisory Council of BC (MAC)
Multiculturalism & Inclusive Communities Office
605 Robson St., 5th Fl.
Vancouver, BC V6B 5J3
Tel: 604-775-0643; *Fax:* 604-775-0670
mac@gov.bc.ca
www.embracebc.ca/embracebc/multiculturalism
Other Communication: Alternate Phone: 604-660-5140
Members of the Multicultural Advisory Council advise the minister responsible for multiculturalism about issues related to multiculturalism & anti-racism. The Multiculturalism Act of British Columbia guides the council.

Corporate Initiatives & Multiculturalism Division
PO Box 9855 Stn. Prov Gov, Victoria, BC V8W 9T5
Executive Lead, Dean Sekyer
Tel: 250-952-0409; *Fax:* 250-952-0646
Dean.Sekyer@gov.bc.ca
Senior Director, Corporate Planning & Strategic Initiatives, Gail Greenwood
Tel: 250-952-0664; *Fax:* 250-952-0137
Gail.Greenwood@gov.bc.ca
Director, Corporate Initiatives, Tom Graham
Tel: 250-356-1705
Tom.Graham@gov.bc.ca
Director, Multiculturalism, Mark Seeley
Tel: 604-868-7768; *Fax:* 604-660-1320
Mark.Seeley@gov.bc.ca
Director, Community Engagement, Philip Yung
Tel: 604-660-5809; *Fax:* 604-660-1320
Philip.Yung@gov.bc.ca

International Business Development Division
Tel: 604-775-2100; *Fax:* 604-660-1320
Assistant Deputy Minister, Vacant
Tel: 604-775-0005; *Fax:* 604-660-1320
Executive Director, Technology & Innovation, Brian Krieger
Tel: 604-660-0220; *Fax:* 604-775-2197
Brian.Krieger@gov.bc.ca
Director, Technology & Innovation, Nina Cagic
Tel: 604-660-5883
Nina.Cagic@gov.bc.ca
Director, Technology & Innovation, David Collier
Tel: 604-218-9036
David.Collier@gov.bc.ca
Director, Transportation, Rob O'Brien
Rob.OBrien@gov.bc.ca
Director, International Missions & Corporate Events, Maureen Yelovatz
Tel: 250-952-6024
Maureen.Yelovatz@gov.bc.ca

International Markets
Fax: 604-775-2197
Executive Director, Henry Han
Tel: 604-660-5888
Henry.Han@gov.bc.ca

International Markets - East Asia
Fax: 604-775-2197
Executive Director, Paul Irwin
Tel: 604-660-5906
Paul.Irwin@gov.bc.ca

International Strategy & Competitiveness Division
Other Communication: Venture Capital Program Information, Toll-Free Phone: 1-800-665-6597
Executive Director, Trade Policy & Negotiations, Sohee Ahn
Tel: 250-952-0708
Sohee.Ahn@gov.bc.ca
Executive Director, Strategy, Business Intelligence & International Marketing, Hayden Lansdell
Tel: 250-387-7553; *Fax:* 250-952-0137
Executive Director, Investment Capital, Nathan Nankivell
Tel: 250-387-8131; *Fax:* 250-952-0371
Nathan.Nankivell@gov.bc.ca
Acting Executive Director, International Trade Policy, Janel Quiring
Tel: 250-356-5867; *Fax:* 250-952-0351
Janel.Quiring@gov.bc.ca
Executive Director, Investment Capital, Bindi Sawchuk
Tel: 250-952-0614; *Fax:* 250-952-0371
Bindi.Sawchuk@gov.bc.ca

Management Services Division
PO Box 9842 Stn. Prov Govt, Victoria, BC V8W 9T2
Tel: 250-387-8705; *Fax:* 250-387-7973
Acting Assistant Deputy Minister, Tracy Campbell
Tel: 250-387-9180; *Fax:* 250-387-7973
Tracy.Campbell@gov.bc.ca
Director, Operations, Financial Services, Mike Holt
Tel: 250-387-5440; *Fax:* 250-387-2815
Mike.Holt@gov.bc.ca
Chief Information Officer & Executive Director, Information Systems Branch, Bruce Klette
Tel: 250-356-0803; *Fax:* 250-387-1590
Bruce.Klette@gov.bc.ca
Executive Director, Strategic Initiatives, Shannon Baillie
Tel: 250-356-0364; *Fax:* 250-387-7973
Shannon.Baillie@gov.bc.ca
Executive Director, Corporate Planning & Priorities, Daniel Leduc
Tel: 250-356-1079; *Fax:* 250-387-8772
Danine.Leduc@gov.bc.ca
Executive Director, Karyn Scott
Tel: 250-356-7004; *Fax:* 250-356-1873
Karyn.Scott@gov.bc.ca

British Columbia Ministry of Jobs, Tourism, & Skills Training (& Responsible for Labour)

PO Box 9846 Stn. Prov Govt, Victoria, BC V8W 9T2
EnquiryBC@gov.bc.ca
www.gov.bc.ca/jti
Other Communication: Media Relations, Phone: 250-387-2799; Fax: 250-356-9829; E-mail: JTST.MediaRequests@gov.bc.ca
In September 2012, the Ministry of Jobs, Tourism, & Innovation was reorganized to become the Ministry of Jobs, Tourism, & Skills Training. The minister of the ministry is also responsible for Labour. The change was made to ensure citizens of British Columbia are equipped with useful skills to preserve a strong economy.
General responsibilities of the ministry are as follows: WorkSafeBC; export market development; trade initiatives; the Canada-BC Business Service Centre; the Community Business Loans Program; labour relations; employment standards; regional economic & rural development; Rural BC Secretariat; tourism strategies; Aboriginal tourism; industry training; & occupational health & safety.
Minister, Jobs, Tourism & Skills Training; Minister Responsible, Labour, Hon. Shirley Bond
Tel: 250-356-2771; *Fax:* 250-356-3000
JTST.Minister@gov.bc.ca
Deputy Minister, Jobs, Tourism, & Skills Training, Shannon Baskerville
Tel: 250-952-0103
Shannon.Baskerville@gov.bc.ca
Director, Executive Operations & Planning, Lianna Olson
Tel: 250-952-0104; *Fax:* 250-356-1195
Manager, Small Business Roundtable Secretariat, Sean Kincross
Tel: 250-387-9083; *Fax:* 250-952-0113
Sean.Kincross@gov.bc.ca

Associated Agencies, Boards & Commissions:

•British Columbia Labour Relations Board
Oceanic Plaza
#600, 1066 West Hastings St.
Vancouver, BC V6E 3X1
Tel: 604-660-1300; *Fax:* 604-660-1892
information@lrb.bc.ca
www.lrb.bc.ca
The British Columbia Labour Relations Board is an independent, administrative tribunal. The Board is responsible for mediating & adjudicating employment & labour relations matters related to unionized workplaces.

•Employment Standards Tribunal
Oceanic Plaza
#650, 1066 West Hastings St.
Vancouver, BC V6E 3X1
Tel: 604-775-3512; *Fax:* 604-775-3372
registrar@bcest.bc.ca
www.bcest.bc.ca
Established under the Employment Standards Act, the Employment Standards Tribunal operates as an administrative tribunal. The responsibility of the Tribunal is to provide an independent appeal of Determinations made by the Director of Employment Standards.

•Industry Training Authority (ITA)
8100 Granville Ave., 8th Fl.
Richmond, BC V6Y 3T6
Tel: 778-328-8700; *Fax:* 778-328-8701
Toll-free: 866-660-6011
customerservice@itabc.ca
www.itabc.ca
British Columbia's Industry Training Authority is a provincial government agency which oversees the province's training & apprenticeship system. The ITA works with industry, employers, training providers, trainees, & apprentices.

•Leading Edge Endowment Fund Board (LEEF)
1188 West Georgia St., 9th Fl.
Vancouver, BC V6E 4A2
Tel: 604-438-3220
contact@leefbc.ca
www.leefbc.ca
To encourage social & economic development in British Columbia, the provincial government established the Leading Edge Endowment Fund in 2002. The Fund establishes Leadership Research Chairs at the province's public, post-secondary institutions, & Regional Innovation Chairs through colleges, university-colleges, & institutes.

•Northern Development Initiative Trust
#301, 1268 Fifth Ave.
Prince George, BC V2L 3L2
Tel: 250-561-2525; *Fax:* 250-561-2563
info@northerndevelopment.bc.ca
northerndevelopment.bc.ca
The Northern Trust consists of a Board of Directors which makes funding decisions for programs of the Trust. According to provincial legislation, investments can be made in the following areas: agriculture, economic development, energy, forestry, mining, Olympic opportunities; pine beetle recovery, small business, tourism, & transportation.

•Southern Interior Development Initiative Trust
#103, 2802 - 30th St.
Vernon, BC V1T 8G7
Tel: 250-545-6829; *Fax:* 250-545-6896
admin@sidit-bc.ca
www.sidit-bc.ca
The government of British Columbia enacted legislation in 2006 to establish the Southern Interior Development Initiative Trust. The mission of the Trust is to grow & diversify the economy of the Southern Interior of British Columbia through investments in economic development projects that will benefit the area.

•Workers' Compensation Appeal Tribunal (WCAT)
#150, 4600 Jacombs Rd.
Richmond, BC V6V 3B1
Tel: 604-664-7800; *Fax:* 604-664-7898
Toll-free: 800-663-2782
www.wcat.bc.ca
The Workers' Compensation Appeal Tribunal of British Columbia is an independent appeal tribunal, which was established by the Workers Compensation Amendment Act (No. 2), 2002. The Tribunal decides appeals from workers & employers from decisions of the Workers' Compensation Board (WorkSafeBC).

Economic Development Division
PO Box 9846 Stn. Prov Gov, Victoria, BC V8W 9T2
Assistant Deputy Minister, Economic Development & Major Investments, Okenge Yuma Morisho
Tel: 250-952-0385
Executive Director, Cross Sector Initiatives, Chris Gilmore
Tel: 250-952-0139
Christopher.Gilmore@gov.bc.ca
Executive Director, Regional Economic Policy & Projects, Sarah Fraser
Tel: 250-952-0644; *Fax:* 250-952-0351
Sarah.Fraser@gov.bc.ca
Executive Director, Economic Policy & Strategic Initiatives, Angelo Cocco
Tel: 250-952-0612; *Fax:* 250-952-0646
Angelo.Cocco@gov.bc.ca
Director, Economic Policy & Strategic Initiatives, Jeff Rafuse
Tel: 250-952-0652; *Fax:* 250-952-0646
Jeff.Rafuse@gov.bc.ca
Director, Regional Economic Policy & Projects, Greg Goodwin
Tel: 250-356-0778; *Fax:* 250-952-0351

Major Investments
PO Box 9325 Stn. Prov Govt, Victoria, BC V8W 2G5
Fax: 250-356-7578
Senior Executive, Ron Bronstein
Tel: 250-356-7528
Ron.Bronstein@gov.bc.ca
Executive Director, Strategic Initiatives, Jane Burnes
Tel: 250-889-1054
Jane.Burnes@gov.bc.ca
Executive Project Director, Sean Darling
Tel: 250-356-7520
Sean.Darling@gov.bc.ca

Labour
Assistant Deputy Minister, Industrial Relations & Labour Programs, Trevor Hughes
Tel: 250-356-1346; *Fax:* 250-356-5186
Trevor.Hughes@gov.bc.ca
PO Box 9594 Prov Gov Sta.
Victoria, BC V8W 9K4
Executive Director, Labour Policy & Legislation, John Blakely
Tel: 250-356-9987; *Fax:* 250-356-5186
John.Blakely@gov.bc.ca
Other Communications: Alt. E-mail: SDL.Policy@gov.bc.ca
PO Box 9594 Prov Gov Sta.
Victoria, BC V8W 9K4
Executive Director, Employment Standards Branch, Chris M. Johnson
Tel: 250-387-3300; *Fax:* 250-356-1886

SDL.EmploymentStandards@gov.bc.ca
PO Box 9570 Prov Gov Sta.
Victoria, BC V8W 9K1

Workers' Advisers Office (WAO)
Tel: 604-713-0360; *Fax:* 604-713-0311
Toll-Free: 800-663-4261
wao@wao-bc.org
www.labour.gov.bc.ca/wab

The Workers' Advisers Office is independent of WorkSafeBC, & is to be consulted by workers & their dependants when disagreements with WorkSafeBC decisions arise.

Executive Director, Vacant
Tel: 604-713-0364
Regional Manager, Vacant
Tel: 604-713-0386
Program Manager, Alex Taylor
Tel: 604-741-5514

Labour Market & Immigration Division
PO Box 9189 Stn. Prov Govt, Vancouver, BC V8W 9E6
Tel: 250-953-3585; *Fax:* 250-387-6152

Assistant Deputy Minister, Scott MacDonald
Tel: 250-953-3585; *Fax:* 250-387-6152
D.Scott.MacDonald@gov.bc.ca
Manager, Operations, Sheila Purdy
Tel: 250-953-3707; *Fax:* 250-387-6152
Sheila.Purdy@gov.bc.ca
Executive Director, Trades Training, Strategic Planning & Engagement, David Muter
Tel: 250-217-5385
David.Muter@gov.bc.ca
Acting Executive Director, Labour Market Programs, Catherine Poole
Tel: 250-387-3661
Catherine.Poole@gov.bc.ca
Director, Employment Services & Supports Programs, Sunjit Mark
Tel: 250-952-0642
Director, Corporate Initiatives & Stakeholder Relations, Rishi Sharma
Tel: 250-387-6132; *Fax:* 250-387-0878
Rishi.Sharma@gov.bc.ca
Executive Director, Labour Market Information, Jeremy Higgs
Tel: 250-387-5631
Director, Finance & Performance, Julio Galleguillos
Tel: 250-952-7584
Julio.Galleguillos@gov.bc.ca
Director, Sector & Project Based Programs, Shannon Renault
Tel: 250-387-6661
Acting Director, Strategic Planning & Evaluation, Genevieve Casault
Tel: 250-415-5832
Genevieve.Casault@gov.bc.ca
Acting Director, Canada/BC Job Grant, Canada Job Grant & Performance Management, Laura Elliott
Tel: 250-387-7570
Laura.Elliott@gov.bc.ca
Director, Trades Training, Marc Black
Tel: 250-216-3513
Marc.Black@gov.bc.ca
Director, Program Management & Planning, Troy Machan
Tel: 604-660-0059; *Fax:* 604-660-4092
Director, Client Engagement, Products & Services, Renee Derksen
Tel: 250-387-3517; *Fax:* 250-356-0033
Renee.Derksen@gov.bc.ca

Tourism Policy
PO Box 9327 Stn. Prov Gov, Victoria, BC V8W 9N3
Fax: 250-952-0351

Executive Director, Tourism & Creative Sectors, Asha Bhat
Tel: 250-387-0130; *Fax:* 250-952-0351
Asha.Bhat@gov.bc.ca
Director, Strategic Issues, Vacant
Tel: 250-356-7861; *Fax:* 250-952-0351
Director, Governance & Legislation, Amber Crofts
Tel: 250-356-1489
Director, Policy & Investment Alignment, Amy Schneider
Tel: 250-356-5632
Amy.Schneider@gov.bc.ca
Director, Intergovernmental Relations, Andrew Little
Tel: 250-952-6022
Andrew.Little@gov.bc.ca

Management Services Division
PO Box 9842 Stn. Prov Govt, Victoria, BC V8W 9T2
Tel: 250-387-8705; *Fax:* 250-387-7973

British Columbia Ministry of Justice

PO Box 9044 Stn. Prov Govt, Victoria, BC V8W 9E2
www.gov.bc.ca/justice

The Ministry of Justice works to ensure safety for the people of British Columbia by seeing that public affairs are administered according to the law & by leading law reform.
The following are examples of general responsibilities of the ministry: legal services to government; consumer services; crime prevention programs; emergency social services; provincial emergency management; criminal justice; legal aid; court administration; police & correctional services; victim assistance; & the protection order registry.

Minister, Justice; Attorney General, Hon. Suzanne Anton
Tel: 250-387-1866; *Fax:* 250-387-6411
JAG.Minister@gov.bc.ca
Deputy Minister & Deputy Attorney General, Richard Fyfe, Q.C.
Tel: 250-356-0149; *Fax:* 250-387-6224
PO Box 9290 Prov Govt Sta.
Victoria, BC V8W 9J7
Chief of Staff, Josh Stewart
Tel: 250-387-1866; *Fax:* 250-387-6411
Director, Investigation & Standards Office, Sydney Swift
Tel: 250-387-5912; *Fax:* 250-356-9875
Sydney.Swift@gov.bc.ca

Associated Agencies, Boards & Commissions:

•British Columbia Ferry Commission
PO Box 9279 Prov Govt
Victoria, BC V8W 9J7
Tel: 250-952-0112
info@bcferrycommission.com
www.bcferrycommission.com

The British Columbia Ferry Commission was established under the Coastal Ferry Act, 2003. The fares & service levels of the province's ferry operator, British Columbia Ferry Services Inc., are regulated by the Commission. The Commission is a quasi-judicial regulatory agency independent of both the provincial government and of BC Ferries.

•British Columbia Human Rights Tribunal
#1170, 605 Robson St.
Vancouver, BC V6B 5J3
Tel: 604-775-2000; *Fax:* 604-775-2020
Toll-free: 888-440-8844
TTY: 604-775-2021
BCHumanRightsTribunal@gov.bc.ca
www.bchrt.bc.ca

The independent, quasi-judicial body was established by the British Columbia Human Rights Code. The British Columbia Human Rights Tribunal is engaged in accepting, screening, mediating, & adjudicating human rights complaints.

•British Columbia Law Institute (BCLI)
University of British Columbia
1822 East Mall
Vancouver, BC V6T 1Z1
Tel: 604-822-0142; *Fax:* 604-822-0144
bcli@bcli.org
www.bcli.org

The Institute was created in 1997 under the Provincial Society Act, & is tasked with promoting clarity in modern law; improvement in the administration of justice; & scholarly legal research. Formerly known as the British Columbia Law Reform Commission.

•British Columbia Office of the Police Complaint Commissioner
#501, 947 Fort St.
PO Box 9895 Prov Govt
Victoria, BC V8W 9T8
Tel: 250-356-7458; *Fax:* 250-356-6503
Toll-free: 877-999-8707
info@opcc.bc.ca
www.opcc.bc.ca

Provides impartial civilian oversight of complaints by the public involving municipal police.

•British Columbia Review Board
#1020, 510 Burrard St.
Vancouver, BC V6C 3A8
Tel: 604-660-8789; *Fax:* 604-660-8809
Toll-free: 877-305-2277
www.bcrb.bc.ca

The British Columbia Review Board was created in accordance with the Criminal Code of Canada. The Board is an independent tribunal, with responsibility for holding hearings to establish & review dispositions. The dispositions involve persons who have been charged with criminal offenses & received verdicts of not criminally responsible on account of mental disorder, or unfit to stand trial on account of mental disorder.

•Elections British Columbia
See Entry Name Index for detailed listing.

•Environmental Appeal Board (EAB)
747 Fort St., 4th Fl.
PO Box 9425 Prov Govt
Victoria, BC V8W 3E9
Tel: 250-387-3464; *Fax:* 250-356-9923
eabinfo@gov.bc.ca
www.eab.gov.bc.ca

Hears appeals from decisions made by government officials related to environmental issues, under the following acts: Environmental Management Act, Greenhouse Gas Industrial Reporting & Control Act, Greenhouse Gas Reduction (Renewable and Low Carbon Fuels) Act, Integrated Pest Management Act, Water Stewardship Act, Water Users' Communities Act, & Wildlife Act.

•Forest Appeals Commission (FAC)
747 Fort St., 4th Fl.
PO Box 9425 Prov Govt
Victoria, BC V8W 9V1
Tel: 250-387-3464; *Fax:* 250-356-9923
facinfo@gov.bc.ca
www.fac.gov.bc.ca

The independent agency hears appeals under the following statutes: Forest Practices Code of British Columbia Act; Forest & Range Practices Act; Private Managed Forest Land Act; Wildfire Act; Forest Act; Range Act.

•Judicial Council of British Columbia
Office of the Chief Judge
#337, 800 Hornby St.
Vancouver, BC V6Z 2C5
Tel: 604-660-2864; *Fax:* 604-660-1108
info@provincialcourt.bc.ca
www.provincialcourt.bc.ca/judicial-council

As designated by the Provincial Court Act, the Judicial Council of British Columbia consists of nine members. The process of the Judicial Council is governed by a Procedure Bylaw. The overall goal of the Council is the improvement of the quality of judicial service in the province.

•Justice Education Society (JES)
#260, 800 Hornby St.
Vancouver, BC V6Z 2C3
Tel: 604-660-9870; *Fax:* 604-775-3476
info@justiceeducation.ca
www.justiceeducation.ca

Formerly the Law Courts Education Society, renamed in 2009, the Justice Education Society seeks to promote the understanding of, and access to, Canada's justice system for all groups of people, but especially youth, Aboriginals, ethnic & immigrant communities, deaf people, those with learning disabilities, & other groups as required.

•Legal Services Society (LSS)
#400, 510 Burrard St.
Vancouver, BC V6C 3A8
Tel: 604-601-6000
www.lss.bc.ca
Other Communication: Call Centre: 1-866-577-2525; 604-408-2172 (Greater Vancouver)

The Legal Services Society was established by the Legal Services Society Act. The non-profit Society provides legal information, advice, & representation services to assist British Columbians in the resolution of their legal issues. Regional centres & local agents' offices are located throughout the province.

•Office of the Representative for Children & Youth (RCY)
#400, 1019 Wharf St.
Victoria, BC V8W 2Y9
Tel: 250-356-6710; *Fax:* 250-356-0837
Toll-free: 800-476-3933
rcy@rcybc.ca
www.rcybc.ca
Other Communication: Northern Office - Prince George: 250-561-4626; Lower Mainland Office - Burnaby: 604-775-3213

Acting in accordance with British Columbia's Representative for Children and Youth Act, the Representative for Children & Youth is responsible for advocacy, monitoring, & investigation.

•Public Guardian & Trustee of British Columbia (PGT)
#700, 808 West Hastings St.
Vancouver, BC V6C 3L3
Tel: 604-660-4444; *Fax:* 604-660-0374
Toll-free: 800-663-7867
clientservice@trustee.bc.ca
www.trustee.bc.ca
Other Communication: Communications & Media Relations: 604-660-4474; Child & Youth Svs.: 604-775-3480; Estate & Personal Trust Svs.: 604-660-4444; E-mail: estates@trustee.bc.ca

The Public Guardian & Trustee of British Columbia was established under the Public Guardian & Trustee Act. The corporation offers the following programs: Child & Youth

Services; Services to Adults; & Estate & Personal Trust Services.

Justice & Public Safety Secretariat
PO Box 9290 Stn. Prov Govt, Victoria, BC V8W 9J7
Tel: 250-356-1143

Executive Lead, Allan Castle
Tel: 250-356-0111
Allan.Castle@gov.bc.ca

Corporate Management Services Branch
Assistant Deputy Minister, Shauna Brouwer
Tel: 250-387-5258
Chief Financial Officer & Executive Director, Finance & Administration Division, David Hoadley
Tel: 250-356-5393; *Fax:* 250-356-3739
Executive Director, Facilities Services Division, Betty Chen-Mack
Tel: 250-356-7159; *Fax:* 250-356-9528
Betty.ChenMack@gov.bc.ca
Executive Director, Organizational Development Team Office, Julie Spiteri
Tel: 250-415-7580; *Fax:* 250-356-6323
Julie.Spiteri@gov.bc.ca

Court Services Branch
PO Box 9249 Stn. Prov Govt, Victoria, BC V8W 9J2
Tel: 250-356-1550; *Fax:* 250-356-8152
Assistant Deputy Minister, Court Services, Lynda Cavanaugh
Tel: 250-356-1527; *Fax:* 250-387-4743
Lynda.Cavanaugh@gov.bc.ca
Chief Sheriff & Executive Director, Sheriff Services Corporate Programs, Paul Corrado
Tel: 250-660-8089
Executive Director, Service Reform, Bernard Achampong
Tel: 250-387-7847; *Fax:* 250-356-8152
Bernard.Achampong@gov.bc.ca
Executive Director, Corporate Support, Brenda Miller
Tel: 250-356-1525; *Fax:* 250-387-4743
Brenda.L.Miller@gov.bc.ca
Director, Court Innovation, Kevin Conn
Tel: 604-660-0226
Kevin.Conn@gov.bc.ca

Criminal Justice Branch
PO Box 9276 Stn. Prov Govt, Victoria, BC V8W 9J7
Tel: 250-387-3840; *Fax:* 250-387-0090
www.ag.gov.bc.ca/prosecution-service
Assistant Deputy Attorney General, Joyce DeWitt-Van Oosten, Q.C.
Tel: 250-387-3840; *Fax:* 250-387-0090

Information Systems Branch
PO Box 9262 Stn. Prov Govt, Victoria, BC V8W 9J4
Tel: 250-356-8787; *Fax:* 250-356-7699
Chief Information Officer, Bobbi Sadler
Tel: 250-387-5910
Chief Application Architect, Business Services Division, Enterprise Architecture, Glenn Mahoney
Tel: 250-387-5191
Glenn.Mahoney@gov.bc.ca
Chief Security Architect, Technical Support Services, John Zimmerman
Tel: 250-356-7121
John.Zimmermann@gov.bc.ca

Justice Services Branch
agjuserv@gov.bc.ca
Acting Assistant Deputy Minister, James Deitch
Tel: 250-356-6582; *Fax:* 250-356-2721
James.Deitch@gov.bc.ca
Provincial Executive Director, Family Justice Services, Dan VanderSluis
Tel: 250-387-5903; *Fax:* 250-356-1279
www.ag.gov.bc.ca/family-justice
Executive Director, Maintenance Enforcement & Locate Services, Christopher Beresford
Tel: 604-660-2528; *Fax:* 604-660-1346
Chris.Beresford@gov.bc.ca
Executive Director, Civil Policy & Legislation Office, Nancy Carter
Tel: 250-356-6182; *Fax:* 250-387-4525
Nancy.Carter@gov.bc.ca
Acting Executive Director, Criminal Justice & Legal Access Policy Division, Kathleen Rawlinson
Tel: 250-356-8083; *Fax:* 250-356-6552
Kathleen.Rawlinson@gov.bc.ca
Executive Director, Dispute Resolution Office, David Merner
Tel: 250-387-6888; *Fax:* 250-387-1189
David.Merner@gov.bc.ca

Legal Services Branch
PO Box 9280 Stn. Prov Govt, Victoria, BC V8W 9J7
Tel: 250-356-9260; *Fax:* 250-356-5111
Assistant Deputy Attorney General, Kurt Sandstrom
Tel: 250-356-9260; *Fax:* 250-356-5111
Kurt.Sandstrom@gov.bc.ca
Chief Legislative Counsel, Corinne Swystun; *Fax:* 250-356-5758
Executive Director, Business Operations & Strategic Initiatives, Aaron Plater
Tel: 250-952-7550
Aaron.Plater@gov.bc.ca

Office of the Merit Commissioner

#502, 947 Fort St., PO Box 9037 Stn. Prov Govt, Victoria, BC V8W 9A3
Tel: 250-953-4208; *Fax:* 250-953-4160
merit@meritcomm.bc.ca
www.meritcomm.bc.ca

The Merit Commissioner is an independent officer reporting directly to the Legislative Assembly of British Columbia. The Commissioner is reponsible for upholding the principle of merit as outlined in The Public Service Act, which governs the hiring of public servants based on their qualifications, rather than their political beliefs.

Merit Commissioner, Fiona Spencer
Tel: 250-953-4208

British Columbia Ministry of Natural Gas Development (& Responsible for Housing)

PO Box 9052 Stn. Prov Govt, Victoria, BC V8W 9E2
Tel: 250-953-0900; *Fax:* 250-953-0927
www.gov.bc.ca/mngd

The Ministry of Natural Gas Development & Responsible for Housing is mandated to ensure that the province benefits economically from its natural gas resources, with a focus on the liquefied natural gas sector. The ministry also seeks to provide British Columbians with safe, affordable & appropriate housing.

Minister, Natural Gas Development; Minister Responsible, Housing; Deputy Premier, Hon. Rich Coleman
Tel: 250-953-0900; *Fax:* 250-953-0927
MNGH.minister@gov.bc.ca
Deputy Minister, Dave Nikolejsin
Tel: 250-952-0504; *Fax:* 250-952-0269
Dave.Nikolejsin@gov.bc.ca
PO Box 9319 Prov Govt Sta.
Victoria, BC V8W 9N3
Chief of Staff, Tobie Myers
Tel: 250-953-0900
MNGH.minister@gov.bc.ca
Director, Cabinet & Legislative Initiatives & Executive Operations, Rhonda De Champlain
Tel: 250-952-0253; *Fax:* 250-952-0269
Rhonda.DeChamplain@gov.bc.ca
Legal Counsel, Simon Coley
Tel: 250-952-0105; *Fax:* 250-952-0269
Simon.Coley@gov.bc.ca
Administrative Assistant, Luella Barneston
Tel: 250-953-0900
MNGH.minister@gov.bc.ca

Associated Agencies, Boards & Commissions:

•British Columbia Housing Management Commission (BC Housing)
#1701, 4555 Kingsway
Burnaby, BC V5H 4V8
Tel: 604-433-1711; *Fax:* 604-439-4722
webeditor@bchousing.org
bchousing.org
Other Communication: tenantinquiries@bchousing.org; media@bchousing.org; FOIPP@bchousing.org; purchasing@bchousing.org; imt@bchousing.org; hpo@hpo.bc.ca
BC Housing develops, manages & administers subsidized housing across British Columbia.

•British Columbia Safety Authority
#200, 505 - 6th St.
New Westminster, BC V3L 0E1
Toll-free: 866-566-7233
info@safetyauthority.ca
safetyauthority.ca
Other Communication: Toll-Free Fax: 1-888-660-3508; Media Contact, Phone: 778-396-2164; E-mail: media@safetyauthority.ca
Oversees the safe installation & operation of technical systems & equipment.

•Building Code Appeal Board (BCAB)
c/o Building & Safety Standards Branch
PO Box 9844 Prov Govt
Victoria, BC V8W 1A4
Tel: 250-387-3133; *Fax:* 250-387-8164
Building.Safety@gov.bc.ca
www.housing.gov.bc.ca/bcab

•Homeowner Protection Office (HPO)
c/o BC Housing
#650, 4789 Kingway
Burnaby, BC V5H 0A3
Tel: 604-646-7050; *Fax:* 604-646-7051
Toll-free: 800-407-7757
hpo@hpo.bc.ca
www.hpo.bc.ca
Other Communication: Toll-Free Fax: 1-877-476-6657
The Homeowner Protection Office seeks to protect buyers of new homes, to regulate the quality of residential construction, & to support residential construction research & education in British Columbia.

•Oil & Gas Commission (OGC)
#100, 10003 - 110 Ave.
Fort St. John, BC V1J 6M7
Tel: 250-794-5200; *Fax:* 250-794-5375
www.bcogc.ca
Other Communication: Incident Reporting: 1-800-663-3456; Victoria: 250-419-4400
The Oil & Gas Commission was enacted under the Oil & Gas Commission Act, The Commission regulates British Columbia's oil & gas activities & pipelines.

•Safety Standards Appeal Board
614 Humboldt St., 4th Fl.
PO Box 9844 Prov Govt
Victoria, BC V8W 9T2
Tel: 250-387-4021; *Fax:* 250-356-6645
www.housing.gov.bc.ca/SSAB
Resolves appeals from decisions made under the Safety Standards Act & the Homeowner Protection Act.

Corporate Initiatives Branch
PO Box 9315 Stn. Prov Govt, Victoria, BC V8W 9N1
Fax: 250-952-0637
Executive Director, Fraser Marshall
Tel: 250-952-0274
Fraser.Marshall@gov.bc.ca
Director, Corporate Initiatives, Gayle Cho
Tel: 250-952-0165; *Fax:* 250-356-5092
Gayle.Cho@gov.bc.ca
Director, Corporate Policy & External Relations, Guy Gensey
Tel: 250-952-0283
Guy.Gensey@gov.bc.ca
Director, Corporate Policy & Planning, Daymon Trachsel
Tel: 250-953-3730
Daymon.Trachsel@gov.bc.ca

LNG Initiatives
PO Box 9318 Stn. Prov Govt, Victoria, BC V8W 9N3
Fax: 250-952-0269
Assistant Deputy Minister/Lead Negotiator, Energy & LNG Initiatives, Brian Hansen
Tel: 250-952-0124
Brian.Hansen@gov.bc.ca
Executive Director, LNG Task Force, Suzanne Manahan
Tel: 250-952-0729
Suzanne.Manahan@gov.bc.ca
Director, Policy & Decision Support, Kursti Calder
Tel: 250-356-9825
Kursti.Calder@gov.bc.ca
Director, International Markets & Energy Outlook, Jennifer Wray
Tel: 250-952-0523
Jennifer.Wray@gov.bc.ca

Office of Housing & Construction Standards
PO Box 9844 Stn. Prov Govt, Victoria, BC V8W 9T2
Assistant Deputy Minister, Jeff Vasey
Tel: 250-387-2001; *Fax:* 250-387-8164
Jeff.Vasey@gov.bc.ca
Acting Executive Director, Building & Safety Standards Branch, Jarrett Hutchinson
Tel: 250-208-7277; *Fax:* 250-356-9377
Jarrett.Hutchinson@gov.bc.ca
Acting Executive Director, Housing Policy Branch, Roger Lam
Tel: 250-208-6695; *Fax:* 250-356-8182
Roger.Lam@gov.bc.ca
Director, Safety Policy & BC Safety Authority Liaison, Shannon Horner
Tel: 250-882-0017; *Fax:* 250-256-9377
building.safety@gov.bc.ca

Oil & Strategic Initiatives
Fax: 250-953-3770
Assistant Deputy Minister, Vacant
Executive Director, Linda Beltrano
Tel: 250-356-1183; *Fax:* 250-952-0255
Linda.Beltrano@gov.bc.ca
Director, Best Practices & Strategic Planning, Olga Klimko
Tel: 250-953-3766; *Fax:* 250-952-0255
Olga.Klimko@gov.bc.ca

Upstream Development Division

Fax: 250-952-0926

Assistant Deputy Minister, Ines Piccinino
Tel: 250-952-0115
Ines.Piccinino@gov.bc.ca
Executive Director, Tenure & Geoscience Branch, Garth Thoroughgood
Tel: 250-952-6382; *Fax:* 250-952-0331
Garth.Thoroughgood@gov.bc.ca
Executive Director, Policy & Royalty Branch, Richard Grieve
Tel: 250-387-1584; *Fax:* 250-953-3770
Director, Resource Development, Vacant
Director, Petroleum Geology, Fil Ferri
Tel: 250-952-0377; *Fax:* 250-952-0255
Fil.Ferri@gov.bc.ca
Director, Tenure & Revenue Management, Debbie Fischer
Tel: 250-952-0336; *Fax:* 250-952-0291
Debbie.Fischer@gov.bc.ca
Director, Pricing, Tenure & Royalty Policy, Geoff Turner
Tel: 250-952-0709; *Fax:* 250-953-3770
Geoff.Turner@gov.bc.ca
Director, Regulatory Policy, Michelle Schwabe
Tel: 250-387-1585; *Fax:* 250-953-3770
Michelle.Schwabe@gov.bc.ca
Executive Director, Resource Access & Strategic Engagement, Matt Austin
Tel: 250-952-0198; *Fax:* 250-952-0926
Matt.Austin@gov.bc.ca

Office of the Ombudsperson

947 Fort St., 2nd Fl., PO Box 9039 Stn. Prov Govt, Victoria, BC V8W 9A5
Tel: 250-387-5855; *Fax:* 250-387-0198
Toll-Free: 800-567-3247
www.ombudsman.bc.ca
www.youtube.com/user/bcombudsperson

Complaints about the services of public agencies are submitted to the Office of the Ombudsperson. The responsibility of the Office of the Ombudsperson is to investigate impartially these inquiries about the practices of public agencies within its jurisdiction. The Office determines if public agencies acted fairly in accordance with relevant legislation & policies.

Ombudsperson, Jay Chalke
Tel: 250-356-1559
Deputy Ombudsperson, David Paradiso
Tel: 250-387-0189
Executive Director, Corporate Services, Dave Van Swieten
Tel: 250-387-4896
Executive Director, Investigations, Bruce Clarke
Tel: 250-356-5723
Acting Director, Intake & Innovation, David Murray
Tel: 250-953-4143

British Columbia Pavilion Corporation (PavCo)

#200, 999 Canada Place, Vancouver, BC V6C 3C1
Tel: 604-482-2200; *Fax:* 604-681-9017
info@bcpavco.com
www.bcpavco.com

The BC Pavilion Corporation is a provincial crown corporation of British Columbia's Ministry of Transportation & Infrastructure. The corporation's divisions include Corporate Office, BC Place, & the Vancouver Convention Centre.

Chair, Stuart McLaughlin
Interim President & CEO, Ken Cretney
Chief Finance Officer, Rehana Din

BC Place
777 Pacific Blvd., Vancouver, BC V6B 4Y8
Tel: 604-669-2300; *Fax:* 604-661-3412
stadium@bcpavco.com
www.bcplacestadium.com
twitter.com/bcplace

Director, Sales & Marketing, Graham Ramsay

Vancouver Convention Centre
1055 Canada Pl., Vancouver, BC V6C 0C3
Tel: 604-689-8232; *Fax:* 604-647-7232
info@vancouverconventioncentre.com
www.vancouverconventioncentre.com

Assistant General Manager, Craig Lehto
Vice-President, Sales & Marketing, Claire Smith, CMP

British Columbia Pension Corporation

2995 Jutland Rd., PO Box 9460 Victoria, BC V8W 9V8
Tel: 250-387-1014; *Fax:* 250-953-0429
Toll-Free: 800-663-8823
PensionCorp@pensionsbc.ca
www.pensionsbc.ca
Other Communication: College Pension Plan: 250-953-4324; Municipal Pension Plan: 250-953-3000; Public Service Pension Plan: 250-953-3033; Teachers' Pension Plan: 250-953-3022

Established under the Public Sector Pension Plans Act, the Pension Corporation administers the College, Municipal, Public Service, Teachers' & WorkSafeBC pension plans.

Chair, Wayne Jefferson
Chief Executive Officer, Laura Nashman
Tel: 250-387-8203
Chief Financial Officer & Vice-President, Corporate Services, Trevor Fedyna
Vice-President, Transformation & Information Services, Dave Marecek
Vice-President, Member Experience, Kevin Olinek
Vice-President, Pension Operations, Lanny Smith
Vice-President, Board Services, Aaron Walker-Duncan

British Columbia Ministry of Public Safety & Solicitor General

PO Box 9290 Stn. Prov Govt, Victoria, BC V8W 9J7
Tel: 250-356-0149; *Fax:* 250-387-6224
Toll-Free: 800-663-7867
EnquiryBC@gov.bc.ca

The Ministry of Public Safety & Solicitor General was re-established by Premier Clark in December 2015, & works jointly with the Ministry of Justice to oversee the administration of justice, protection of rights & public safety in the province.

Minister, Public Safety & Solicitor General, Hon. Mike Morris
Tel: 250-356-2178; *Fax:* 250-356-2142
PSSG.Minister@gov.bc.ca
Deputy Minister & Deputy Solicitor General, Mark Sieben
Tel: 250-356-0149

Associated Agencies, Boards & Commissions:

•Consumer Protection B.C.
#307, 3450 Uptown Blvd.
PO Box 9244
Victoria, BC V8W 0B9
Fax: 250-920-7181
Toll-free: 888-564-9963
info@consumerprotectionbc.ca
www.consumerprotectionbc.ca

Established in 2004 under the Business Practices & Consumer Protection Authority Act, Consumer Protection B.C. administers the following consumer protection laws: Business Practices & Consumer Protection Act, the Cremation, Interment & Funeral Services Act, & the Motion Picture Act.

•Vehicle Sales Authority of British Columbia (VSA)
#208, 5455 - 152 St.
Surrey, BC V3S 5A5
Tel: 604-574-5050; *Fax:* 604-574-5883
consumer.services@mvsabc.com
mvsabc.com
Other Communication: Alt. Emails: licensing@mvsabc.com; compensationfund@mvsabc.com; training@mvsabc.com; communications@mvsabc.com

The VSA licenses motor vehicle dealerships & salespeople; certifies & provides continuing education for salespeople; assists consumers; investigates consumer complaints & provides dispute resolution; & carries out compliance action.

Corporate Policy & Planning Office
PO Box 9283 Stn. Prov Govt, Victoria, BC V8W 9J7
Tel: 250-387-0306

Executive Director, Toby Louie
Tel: 250-356-6389
Toby.Louie@gov.bc.ca

BC Coroners Service
Chief Coroner's Office, Metrotower II, #800, 4720 Kingsway, Burnaby, BC V5H 4N2
Tel: 604-660-7745; *Fax:* 604-660-7766
CoronerRequest@gov.bc.ca
www.pssg.gov.bc.ca/coroners

BC Coroners Service investigates all unexpected, unnatural, unexplained, & unattended deaths in the province. Improvements to public safety & recommendations to prevent similar deaths are made by the Coroners Service.

Chief Coroner, Lisa Lapointe
Deputy Chief Coroner, Operations, Pat Cullinane
Tel: 250-356-9362
Pat.Cullinane@gov.bc.ca
Deputy Chief Coroner, Vincent Stancato
Tel: 604-660-7745; *Fax:* 604-660-7766
Executive Director, Medical Unit, Kelly Barnard
Tel: 604-660-2597
Kelly.Barnard@gov.bc.ca

Community Safety & Crime Prevention Branch
Fax: 604-660-5340
VictimServicesandCrimePrevention@gov.bc.ca
www.pssg.gov.bc.ca/victimservices
Other Communication: Civil Forfeiture Office, E-mail: CivilFO@gov.bc.ca

Assistant Deputy Minister, Patricia Boyle
Tel: 604-660-5272; *Fax:* 604-660-5340
Executive Director, Victim Services & Crime Prevention Division, Taryn Walsh
Tel: 604-660-5199
VictimServices@gov.bc.ca

Corporate Management Services Branch
Assistant Deputy Minister, Shauna Brouwer
Tel: 250-387-5258; *Fax:* 250-387-0081
Chief Financial Officer & Executive Director, Finance & Administration Division, David Hoadley
Tel: 250-356-5393; *Fax:* 250-356-3739
Executive Director, Organizational Development Team Office, Julie Spiteri
Tel: 250-415-7580; *Fax:* 250-356-6323
Julie.Spiteri@gov.bc.ca

Corrections Branch
PO Box 9278 Stn. Prov Govt, Victoria, BC V8W 9J7
Tel: 250-387-6366
Toll-Free: 888-952-7968
www.pssg.gov.bc.ca/corrections
Other Communication: Adult Custody Phone: 250-387-5098; Community Corrections & Corporate Programs Phone: 250-356-7930

The Corrections Branch consists of the Adult Custody Division & the Community Corrections & Corporate Programs Division. The Adult Custody Division operates correctional centres for persons awaiting trial or serving a provincial custody sentence. The Community Corrections & Corporate Programs Division operates over fifty community corrections offices throughout British Columbia.

Assistant Deputy Minister, Corrections, Brent Merchant
Tel: 250-387-5363; *Fax:* 250-387-5698
Provincial Director, Strategic Operations, Elenore Clark
Tel: 250-387-5936; *Fax:* 250-387-5039
Elenore.Clark@gov.bc.ca
Provincial Director, Capital Team, Tedd Howard
Tel: 604-368-1844; *Fax:* 250-952-6883
Tedd.Howard@gov.bc.ca
Provincial Director, Adult Custody Division, Stephanie Macpherson
Tel: 250-387-5098; *Fax:* 250-952-6883
Provincial Director, Community Corrections & Corporate Programs Division, Bill Small
Tel: 250-356-7930; *Fax:* 250-952-6883
Bill.Small@gov.bc.ca

Information Systems
PO Box 9262 Stn. Prov Govt, Victoria, BC V8W 9J4
Tel: 250-356-8787; *Fax:* 250-356-7699

Assistant Deputy Minister & Chief Financial Officer, Bobbi Sadler
Tel: 250-387-5910
Chief Security Architect, Security Division, John Zimmerman
Tel: 250-356-7121; *Fax:* 250-356-7699
John.Zimmermann@gov.bc.ca
Executive Director, Business Services Division, Lois Fraser
Tel: 250-356-6061
Lois.Fraser@gov.bc.ca

Office of the Superintendent of Motor Vehicles (OSMV)
PO Box 9254 Stn. Prov Govt, Victoria, BC V8W 9J2
Tel: 250-387-7747; *Fax:* 250-356-5577
Toll-Free: 855-387-7747
osmv.mailbox@gov.bc.ca
www.pssg.gov.bc.ca/osmv
twitter.com/RoadSafetyBC

The Office of the Superintendent of Motor Vehicles is responsible for regulating drivers in British Columbia. The following services are provided: establishment & maintenance of standards for driving behaviour & medical fitness; provision of an independent method of appeal of certain Insurance Corporation of British Columbia decisions; scheduling & hearing evidence related to proposals by the Insurance Corporation of British Columbia concerning licences, driving training schools, & AirCare Certified repair facilities; & reviewing driving prohibitions & vehicle impoundments imposed by police.

Superintendent of Motor Vehicles, Sam MacLeod
Tel: 250-387-5692
Deputy Superintendent of Motor Vehicles, Steven Roberts
Tel: 250-953-3818; *Fax:* 250-356-5577
Steven.Roberts@gov.bc.ca

Policing & Security Programs Branch
PO Box 9285 Stn. Prov Govt, Victoria, BC V8W 9J7
Tel: 250-387-1100; *Fax:* 250-356-7747
sgpcsb@gov.bc.ca
Assistant Deputy Minister & Director, Police Services, Clayton J.D. Pecknold
Clayton.Pecknold@gov.bc.ca
Executive Director, Security Services, Sandra Sajko
Tel: 250-356-1504; *Fax:* 250-387-1911
sgspdsec@gov.bc.ca
Executive Director, Policing, Security & Law Enforcement Infrastructure & Finance, Alana Standish
Tel: 250-356-8146

British Columbia Public Service Agency

PO Box 9404 Stn. Prov Govt, Victoria, BC V8W 9V1
Tel: 250-387-0518; *Fax:* 250-356-7074
search.employment.gov.bc.ca

The provision of human resource management services is the responsibility of the British Columbia Service Agency. The services are provided to persons & organizations working in the provinces's public sector.

Deputy Minister, Lori Halls
Tel: 250-952-6296; *Fax:* 250-356-7074
Assistant Deputy Minister, Employee Relations, John Davison
Tel: 250-356-3090
Assistant Deputy Minister, Talent Management, Alison Paine
Tel: 250-952-0913
Assistant Deputy Minister, Service Operations, Debi Upton
Tel: 250-387-0758
Chief Financial Officer, Financial Management Office, Libby Oulton
Tel: 250-387-7437
Libby.Oulton@gov.bc.ca
Executive Director, Executive Account Management & Consulting, Alison Looysen
Tel: 250-508-0417
Executive Director, Business Performance Division, Bruce Richmond
Tel: 250-387-0222; *Fax:* 250-387-0593
Bruce.Richmond@gov.bc.ca
Executive Lead, Lean BC Office, Colleen Sparks
Tel: 250-507-9391
Colleen.Sparks@gov.bc.ca

British Columbia Ministry of Small Business & Red Tape Reduction

PO Box 9054 Stn. Prov Govt, Victoria, BC V8W 9E2
Tel: 250-387-2283

The ministry is responsible for liquor distribution as well as supporting small business.

Minister; Minister responsible for the Liquor Distribution Branch, Hon. Coralee Oakes
Tel: 250-356-8247; *Fax:* 250-356-8250
SBRt.Minister@gov.bc.ca
Deputy Minister, Tim McEwan
Tel: 604-660-3757
Tim.McEwan@gov.bc.ca
Parliamentary Secretary, Liquor Reform, John Yap
Tel: 250-953-0919; *Fax:* 250-387-9100
John.Yap.MLA@leg.bc.ca

Associated Agencies, Boards & Commissions:

•Liquor Distribution Branch (LDB)
2625 Rupert St.
Vancouver, BC V5M 3T5
Tel: 604-252-3000; *Fax:* 604-252-3026
communications@bcliquorstores.com
www.bcldb.com
Other Communication: Retail Stores: www.bcliquorstores.com; Direct Sales: ldbdatam@bcldb.com; Liquor Licensing: lclb.lclb@gov.bc.ca

The LDB is responsible for the beverage alcohol industry in British Columbia, with the sole right to purchase alcohol for sale & reuse. It operates a wholesale & retail beverage alcohol business with locations across the province.

Liquor Control & Licensing Branch (LCLB)
PO Box 9292 Stn. Prov Govt, Victoria, BC V8W 9J8
Tel: 250-952-5787; *Fax:* 250-952-7066
www.pssg.gov.bc.ca/lclb
Assistant Deputy Minister, Douglas Scott
Tel: 250-952-5777; *Fax:* 259-852-7066
Deputy General Manager, Licensing, Suzanne Bell
Tel: 250-952-7046; *Fax:* 250-952-7060
Suzanne.Bell@gov.bc.ca
Deputy General Manager, Compliance & Enforcement Division, Raymond Tetzel
Tel: 604-775-0137; *Fax:* 250-952-7059
Raymond.Tetzel@gov.bc.ca
Executive Director, Compliance & Enforcement Committee Secretariat, Wendy Taylor
Tel: 250-952-6161; *Fax:* 250-952-7059
Acting Director, Policy, Planning & Communications, Elaine Vale
Tel: 250-952-7037; *Fax:* 250-952-7066

Management Services Division
PO Box 9842 Stn. Prov Govt, Victoria, BC V8W 9T2
Tel: 250-387-8705; *Fax:* 250-387-7973
Acting Assistant Deputy Minister, Tracy Campbell
Tel: 250-387-9180
Tracy.Campbell@gov.bc.ca
Executive Director, Strategic Initiatives, Shannon Baillie
Tel: 250-356-0364
Shannon.Baillie@gov.bc.ca
Executive Director, Strategic Financial Initiatives, Karyn Scott
Tel: 250-387-4056
Karyn.Scott@gov.bc.ca
Chief Information Officer & Executive Director, Information Systems Branch, Bruce Klette
Tel: 250-356-0803
Bruce.Klette@gov.bc.ca
Executive Director, Corporate Planning & Priorities, Vacant
Tel: 250-356-2036
Director, Operations, Financial Services, Mike Holt
Tel: 250-387-5440
Mike.Holt@gov.bc.ca
Executive Director, Strategic Human Resources, Sarah Francis
Tel: 250-361-5714

Small Business & Regulatory Reform Division
PO Box 9854 Stn. Prov Govt, Victoria, BC V8W 9T5
Tel: 250-387-0661; *Fax:* 250-952-0113
Assistant Deputy Minister, Christine Little
Tel: 250-387-0661
Christine.Little@gov.bc.ca
Executive Director, Small Business, Jaclynn Hunter
Tel: 250-387-1548
Jaclynn.Hunter@gov.bc.ca
Manager, Small Business Roundtable Secretariat, Sean Kincross
Tel: 250-387-9083
Sean.Kincross@gov.bc.ca
Director, Small Business Programs, Patricia Summers
Tel: 250-952-0519
Patricia.Summers@gov.bc.ca
Director, Strategic Initiatives, Jordan Bennett
Tel: 250-356-8783
Jordan.Bennett@gov.bc.ca

British Columbia Ministry of Social Development & Social Innovation

PO Box 9058 Stn. Prov Govt, Victoria, BC V8W 9E1
Toll-Free: 800-663-7867
TTY: 800-661-8773
EnquiryBC@gov.bc.ca
www.gov.bc.ca/sdsi

The main responsibilities of the Ministry of Social Development & Social Innovation include supporting community living services that assist persons with developmental disabilities; providing employment programs & services to unemployed & underemploye persons; & delivering income assistance to persons in need.

Minister, Social Development & Social Innovation, Hon. Michelle Stilwell
Tel: 250-356-7750; *Fax:* 250-356-7292
SDSI.minister@gov.bc.ca
Deputy Minister, Sheila Taylor
Tel: 250-387-3471; *Fax:* 250-387-5775
PO Box 9934 Prov Govt Sta.
Victoria, BC V8W 9R2
Parliamentary Secretary, Accessibility, Linda Larson
Tel: 250-952-6784; *Fax:* 250-356-0596
linda.larson.MLA@leg.bc.ca
PO Box 9934 Prov Govt Sta.
Victoria, BC V8W 9R2
Advocate for Service Quality, Leanne Dospital
Executive Director, Corporate Planning & Strategic Initiatives, Mark S. Medgyesi
Tel: 250-387-2001
Manager, Executive Operations, Karen MacMillan
Tel: 250-387-2807; *Fax:* 250-387-5775
Acting Manager, Executive Correspondence Services, Adriana Di Castri
Tel: 250-387-7660; *Fax:* 250-387-5775

Associated Agencies, Boards & Commissions:

•Employment & Assistance Appeal Tribunal
PO Box 9994 Prov Govt
Victoria, BC V8W 9R7
Tel: 250-356-6374; *Fax:* 250-356-9687
Toll-free: 866-557-0035
eaat@gov.bc.ca
www.gov.bc.ca/eaat
Other Communication: Toll-Free Fax: 1-877-356-9687

Corporate Services Division
PO Box 9940 Stn. Prov Govt, Victoria, BC V8W 9R2
Tel: 250-387-3159; *Fax:* 250-387-2418
Assistant Deputy Minister & Executive Financial Officer, Len Dawes
Tel: 250-387-7035; *Fax:* 250-387-2418
Chief Financial Officer & Executive Director, Financial & Administrative Services Branch, Martha Thomas
Tel: 778-676-3739; *Fax:* 250-356-5994
Martha.Thomas@gov.bc.ca
Executive Director, People Strategies, Angela Scammell
Tel: 250-216-6596; *Fax:* 250-387-4264
Director, Budgets Planning & Analytics, Keith Parker
Tel: 250-217-1807
Keith.C.Parker@gov.bc.ca
Director, Communications & Engagement, Elaine Cross
Tel: 250-507-1380; *Fax:* 250-387-4264
Elaine.Cross@gov.bc.ca
Director, Financial Operations, Laurie Farquharson
Tel: 250-514-6315; *Fax:* 250-356-1051
Laurie.Farquharson@gov.bc.ca
Director, Facilities & Workplace Solutions, Joel Crocker
Tel: 250-217-4971; *Fax:* 250-356-5994

Employment & Labour Market Services Division
PO Box 9762 Stn. Prov Govt, Victoria, BC V8W 1A4
Tel: 250-953-3921; *Fax:* 250-953-3928
Assistant Deputy Minister, Nichola Manning
Tel: 250-953-3921; *Fax:* 250-953-3928
Executive Director, Program Management & Development, Sergei Bouslov
Tel: 250-387-6012; *Fax:* 250-387-2069
Manager, Contract & Policy, Jay Marchant
Tel: 250-387-6036; *Fax:* 250-387-2089
Jay.Marchant@gov.bc.ca
Executive Director, Service Delivery, Hovan Baghdassarian
Tel: 250-356-0050; *Fax:* 250-356-2734
Director, Operations, Engagement, Partnerships & Strategic Initiatives, Eugene Johnson
Tel: 250-387-3717; *Fax:* 250-387-8164
Director, Business Supports & Systems, ICM Branch, ELMSD, Dexter Ratcliff
Tel: 250-216-8721
Executive Director, Operations, Service Delivery, Hovan Baghdassarian
Tel: 250-356-0050; *Fax:* 250-356-2734
Hovan.Baghdassarian@gov.bc.ca
Executive Director, Finance, Planning & Reporting, Tiffany Ma
Tel: 250-217-9165; *Fax:* 250-387-2069
Tiffany.Ma@gov.bc.ca

Services to Adults with Developmental Disabilities
PO Box 9875 Stn. Prov Govt, Victoria, BC V8W 9R1
Toll-Free: 855-356-5609
Acting Executive Director, Paula Grant
Tel: 250-953-4538
Director, Integrated Services & Supports - Prince George/Kamloops, Rob Rail
Tel: 250-645-4011
Rob.Rail@gov.bc.ca
Director, Corporate/Vancouver Island, Lynn Forbes
Tel: 250-387-2098
Lynn.Forbes@gov.bc.ca
Director, Fraser Region/Provincial Practice Lead, Sonia Hall
Tel: 604-575-7586
Sonia.Hall@gov.bc.ca
Manager, Program Development & Performance, Lauren Nackman

Information Services Division
PO Box 9436 Stn. Prov Govt, Victoria, BC V8W 9W3
Tel: 250-356-6633
Acting Assistant Deputy Minister, Rob Byers
Tel: 250-387-9169
Acting Executive Director, Business Operations, Nancy Allen
Tel: 250-356-2688
Executive Director & Chief Technology Officer, Wency Lum
Tel: 250-387-5129
Executive Director, Strategic Planning & Initiatives, Erika Taylor
Tel: 250-387-9169

Research, Innovation & Policy Division
PO Box 9936 Stn. Prov Govt, Victoria, BC V8W 9R2
Tel: 250-356-5065; *Fax:* 250-387-5775

Assistant Deputy Minister, Molly Harrington
Tel: 250-356-5065; *Fax:* 250-387-2418
Executive Director, Research Branch, Robert Bruce
Tel: 250-356-6787; *Fax:* 250-387-8164
Robert.Bruce@gov.bc.ca
Executive Director, Strategic Policy, Ian Ross
Tel: 250-953-3923; *Fax:* 250-387-8164
Ian.Ross@gov.bc.ca
Executive Director, Social Innovation, Robin McLay
Tel: 250-356-1074; *Fax:* 250-387-5775
Executive Director, Accessibility Secretariat, Susan Mader
Tel: 250-356-0923
Susan.Mader@gov.bc.ca
Executive Director, Ministry of Social Development-Ministry of Children & Family Development Legislation, Litigation & Appeals Branch, Michael Turnaski
Tel: 250-387-6434; *Fax:* 250-356-8182
Michael.Turanski@gov.bc.ca
Director, Child & Family Development Legislation & Legal Support, Leah M. Bailey
Tel: 250-387-0372; *Fax:* 250-356-8182
Leah.Bailey@gov.bc.ca
Executive Director, Accessibility Secretariat, Susan Mader
Tel: 250-356-0923; *Fax:* 250-387-8164
Susan.Mader@gov.bc.ca
Director, Analytics & Forecasting, Research Branch, Linda DeBenedictis
Tel: 250-387-4622; *Fax:* 250-387-8164
Linda.DeBenedictis@gov.bc.ca
Director, Policy, Shannon Pendergast
Tel: 250-356-5002; *Fax:* 250-387-8164

Service Delivery Division
Assistant Deputy Minister, Debi Upton
Tel: 250-387-6905
Executive Director, Strategic Transformation Branch, Raymond Fieltsch
Tel: 250-356-2220
Raymond.Fieltsch@gov.bc.ca
Supervisor, Employment Plans & Eligibility Reviews, Roline Sims
Tel: 250-828-4712
Director, Engagement, Partnerships & Strategic Initiatives, Dana Jensen
Tel: 250-387-3865; *Fax:* 250-952-6450
Manager, Strategic Planning, Planning, Innovation, & Performance, Debra Choo
Tel: 250-387-9271; *Fax:* 250-952-6450

Prevention & Loss Management Services
Executive Director, Kim Saastad
Tel: 250-377-2648

British Columbia Ministry of Technology, Innovation & Citizens' Services

PO Box 9068 Stn. Prov Govt, Victoria, BC V8W 9E2
Tel: 250-952-7623; *Fax:* 250-952-7628
Toll-Free: 800-663-7867
EnquiryBC@gov.bc.ca
www.gov.bc.ca/citz
Other Communication: Victoria, Phone: 250-387-6121; Vancouver, Phone: 604-660-2421

The Ministry of Technology, Innovation & Citizens' Services & Open Government oversees the following: BC OnLine; BC Stats; Enquiry BC (Service BC Contact Centre); Service BC; Network BC; Shared Services BC; Hosting Solutions BC; Freedom of Information; & the Office of the Chief Information Officer. The Ministry seeks to further develop the technology industry in BC while improving accessible services & information for citizens.

Minister, Technology, Innovation & Citizens' Services, Hon. Amrik Virk
Tel: 250-952-7623; *Fax:* 250-952-7628
LCTZ.Minister@gov.bc.ca
PO Box 9068 Prov Govt Sta.
Victoria, BC V8W 9E2
Deputy Minister, Technology, Innovation & Citizens' Services (including Shared Services BC), John Jacobson
Tel: 250-387-8852; *Fax:* 250-387-8561
PO Box 9440 Prov Govt Sta.
Victoria, BC V8W 9V3
Chief of Staff, Nick Facey
Tel: 250-952-7623; *Fax:* 250-952-7628

Associated Agencies, Boards & Commissions:

•British Columbia Innovation Council (BCIC)
1188 West Georgia St., 9th Fl.
Vancouver, BC V6E 4A2
Tel: 604-683-2724; *Fax:* 604-683-6567
Toll-free: 800-665-7222
info@bcic.ca
www.bcic.ca
Other Communication: Program Inquiries, E-mail: programs@bcic.ca

The British Columbia Innovation Council strives to advance innovation & commercialization by focusing on the following strategies: developing, recruiting & retaining science & technology professionals; fostering innovation & entrepreneurship; & bringing innovation to commercial success by establishing partnerships.

•Knowledge Network Corporation
4355 Mathissi Pl.
Burnaby, BC V5G 4S8
Tel: 604-431-3222; *Fax:* 604-431-3387
Toll-free: 877-456-6988
info@knowledge.ca
www.knowledge.ca
Other Communication: E-mails: acquisitions@knowledge.ca (Acquisitions); hr@knowledge.ca (Employment); partners@knowledge.ca (Knowledge Partners); press@knowledge.ca (Press)

The Knowledge Network Corporation is a provincial Crown agency, operating under British Columbia's Ministry of Technology, Innovation & Citizens' Services. The corporation is British Columbia's public broadcaster, which is licensed by the Canadian Radio-television & Telecommunications Commission. Arts & culture & children's programs are featured through television & the Internet.
The network is commercial-free. Funds for the provision of educational broadcasting services are received the British Columbia provincial government, public supporters, & Knowledge Partners.

•Premier's Technology Council (PTC)
#1600, 800 Robson St.
Vancouver, BC V6Z 3E7
Tel: 604-827-4629
premiers.technologycouncil@gov.bc.ca
www.gov.bc.ca/premier/technology_council

The 23 member Premier's Technology Council advises the Premier on all technology related issues that affect British Columbia & its residents.

Office of the Associate Deputy Minister - Citizens' Services
PO Box 9440 Stn. Prov Govt, Victoria, BC V8W 9V3
Fax: 250-387-8561
Associate Deputy Minister, Sarf Ahmed
Tel: 250-387-0315; *Fax:* 250-387-8561
Sarf.Ahmed@gov.bc.ca

Corporate Services Division
Tel: 250-952-7635; *Fax:* 250-387-5693
Assistant Deputy Minister & Executive Financial Officer, Colin McEwan
Tel: 250-952-7635
Chief Financial Officer & Executive Director, Financial & Administrative Services Branch, Teri Lavine
Tel: 250-516-6812; *Fax:* 250-952-8286
Teri.Lavine@gov.bc.ca
Ministry Chief Information Officer & Executive Director, Information Management Branch, Corinne Timmermann
Tel: 250-952-9528
Corinne.Timmermann@gov.bc.ca
Executive Director, Planning, Performance & Communications, Vacant
Executive Director, Corporate Projects, Tracey Colins
Tel: 250-507-2284
Tracey.Colins@gov.bc.ca
Director, Strategic HR, Tina van der Lee
Tel: 250-514-0075; *Fax:* 250-387-9651
Tina.vanderLee@gov.bc.ca
Director, Facilities Management, Laurie Gowans
Tel: 250-213-1449
Laurie.Gowans@gov.bc.ca
Director, Financial Policy, Reporting & Operations, Sandra Hall
Tel: 250-356-1324
Sandra.Hall@gov.bc.ca
Director, Strategic Planning & Support Services, Daisy Jassar
Tel: 250-217-9270; *Fax:* 250-356-2643
Daisy.Jassar@gov.bc.ca
Director, Internal Communications, Anne McKinnon
Tel: 250-588-9241
Anne.McKinnon@gov.bc.ca
Director, Information Management Branch, Service Operations & Continual Improvement, Shelley Mendez
Tel: 250-952-8593; *Fax:* 250-356-2643
Shelley.Mendez@gov.bc.ca
Director, Applications Management, Craig Randle
Tel: 250-952-8586; *Fax:* 250-356-2643
Craig.Randle@gov.bc.ca
Director, Budgets & Corporate Reporting, Tony Dierick
Tel: 250-356-1322
Tony.Dierick@gov.bc.ca

Logistics & Business Services Division
Tel: 250-952-7983
Assistant Deputy Minister, Wes Boyd
Tel: 250-508-5791
Executive Director, Supply Services, Dawson Brenner
Tel: 250-356-0600; *Fax:* 250-387-0388
Dawson.Brenner@gov.bc.ca
Senior Director, Access & Open Information, Chad Hoskins
Tel: 250-356-7343; *Fax:* 250-387-9843
Chad.Hoskins@gov.bc.ca
Senior Director, Product Distribution Centre, Gary Heuer
Tel: 604-927-2296
Gary.Heuer@gov.bc.ca
Other Communications: Toll-Free Fax: 1-800-988-1155
Senior Manager, Financial Planning & Reporting, Kim Torrell
Tel: 778-678-2584; *Fax:* 250-356-6036
Kim.Torrell@gov.bc.ca
Executive Director, Business Development & Procurement Transformation, Brooke Hayes
Tel: 778-698-2243
Brooke.Hayes@gov.bc.ca
Director, Staff Administration, Elizabeth Vander Beesen
Tel: 250-387-1430; *Fax:* 250-387-9843
Elizabeth.vanderBeesen@gov.bc.ca
Director, Asset Investment Recovery & Distribution Centre Victoria, Leslie Walden
Tel: 250-952-4561; *Fax:* 250-952-4224
Leslie.Walden@gov.bc.ca
Director, Government Records Service, Alexander Wright
Tel: 250-588-4057; *Fax:* 250-387-9843
Alexander.Wright@gov.bc.ca

Procurement
PO Box 9476 Stn. Prov Govt, Victoria, BC V8W 9W6
Tel: 250-387-7300; *Fax:* 250-387-7309
purchasing@gov.bc.ca
www.pss.gov.bc.ca

Offers procurement & supply services, using internal & private sector resources.

Executive Director, Duncan McLelland
Tel: 250-387-7312; *Fax:* 250-387-7310
Duncan.McLelland@gov.bc.ca
Senior Manager, Commercial Services, Steve Bradbury
Tel: 778-698-2341; *Fax:* 250-387-7310
Steve.Bradbury@gov.bc.ca
Senior Director, IM/IT Procurement Services, Bedrija Hromic
Tel: 250-217-2481; *Fax:* 250-356-0303
Bedrija.Hromic@gov.bc.ca
Director, eProcurement & Sourcing Solutions, Adam McKinnon
Tel: 250-217-4377; *Fax:* 250-387-7309
Adam.McKinnon@gov.bc.ca

Queen's Printer
PO Box 9452 Stn. Prov Govt, Victoria, BC V8W 9V7
Tel: 250-387-3309; *Fax:* 250-356-6036
Toll-Free: 800-663-6105
www.pss.gov.bc.ca/printing/printing.html
Other Communication: BC Mail Plus, URL: www.pss.gov.bc.ca/bcmp; BC Gazette, E-mail: QPGazette@gov.bc.ca; QP LegalEze, E-mail: QPLegalEze@gov.bc.ca

British Columbia's Queen's Printer provides printing & specialized scanning services, plus multimedia duplication to the province's government ministries & the public sector.

Senior Director, Queen's Printer / BC Mail Plus, Don Swagar
Tel: 250-387-6691; *Fax:* 250-356-7380
Don.Swagar@gov.bc.ca
Director, Queen's Printer, Spencer Tickner
Tel: 250-589-0111; *Fax:* 250-387-1120
Spencer.Tickner@gov.bc.ca
Manager, Crown Publications, Wendy Pope
Tel: 250-356-5392; *Fax:* 250-387-1120
Wendy.Pope@gov.bc.ca

Real Property Division
4000 Seymour Pl., PO Box 9412 Victoria, BC V8W 9V1
Tel: 250-387-8280; *Fax:* 250-952-8289
Assistant Deputy Minister, Brian Fellows
Tel: 250-387-8280
Executive Director, Real Estate Release of Assets for Economic Generation, David Greer
Tel: 250-387-6337
David.Greer@gov.bc.ca
Executive Director, Accommodation Management, Lorne DeLarge
Tel: 250-952-5407; *Fax:* 250-952-8293
Lorne.DeLarge@gov.bc.ca
Executive Director, Asset Management Branch, Jon Burbee
Tel: 250-213-7439; *Fax:* 250-952-8289
Jon.Burbee@gov.bc.ca
Executive Director, Real Estate Business Services, Stephen Marquet
Tel: 250-889-7876; *Fax:* 250-952-8285
Stephen.Marguet@gov.bc.ca
Executive Director, Facilities Management Services, Patricia A. Marsh
Tel: 250-952-4130; *Fax:* 250-952-8407
Patricia.A.Marsh@gov.bc.ca

Executive Director, Workplace Development Services, Jim Thompson
Tel: 250-952-9527; *Fax:* 250-952-7403
Jim.Thompson@gov.bc.ca
Director, Corporate Sustainability, Bernie Gaudet
Tel: 250-920-8435; *Fax:* 250-952-8407
Bernie.Gaudet@gov.bc.ca
Director, Operations, Robb Gillis
Tel: 250-952-4830
Robert.Gillis@gov.bc.ca
Project Director, Contract Governance, Karen Liversedge
Tel: 250-952-8867
Karen.Liversedge@gov.bc.ca
Director, Leasing Services, John Marsh
Tel: 250-952-8412; *Fax:* 250-952-8288
John.Marsh@gov.bc.ca
Director, Workplace Strategies & Planning, Rob Macdonald
Tel: 250-952-8315; *Fax:* 250-952-8293
Robert.Macdonald@gov.bc.ca
Director, Real Estate Business, Lorraine McMillan
Tel: 250-952-8321; *Fax:* 250-952-8285
Lorraine.McMillan@gov.bc.ca
Acting Director, Governance & Performance Management, Kim Chow
Tel: 250-952-8770
Kim.Chow@gov.bc.ca
Director, Financial Planning & Reporting, May Yu
Tel: 250-356-7118
May.Yu@gov.bc.ca

Office of the Chief Information Officer (OCIO)
PO Box 9412 Stn. Prov Govt, Victoria, BC V8W 9V1
Tel: 250-356-7970; *Fax:* 250-387-1940
Toll-Free: 800-663-7867
LCTZ.ChiefInformationOfficer@gov.bc.ca
www.cio.gov.bc.ca
Other Communication: To report an information incident, such as a privacy breach, phone: 1-866-660-0811, option 3; BC Privacy Helpline, Phone: 250-356-1851; Fax: 250-953-0455

The Office of the Chief Information Officer guides & promotes the management of government information as an asset to business.
Examples of responsibilities include records management, legislation that governs the protection of privacy & personal information, freedom of information requests, & governance for corporate IM/IT policy, such as technology architecture & standards, data access, & information security.

Associate Deputy Minister & Government Chief Information Officer for the Province of British Columbia, Bette-Jo Hughes
Tel: 250-387-0401; *Fax:* 250-387-1940
BetteJo.Hughes@gov.bc.ca
Assistant Deputy Minister, Strategic Initiatives & and Partnerships, David Morel
Tel: 778-698-2332
Executive Director, Finance, Vacant
Tel: 250-356-8321
Executive Director, IM/IT Capital Investment, Philip Twyford
Tel: 250-516-0268; *Fax:* 250-953-3555
Philip.Twyford@gov.bc.ca

Privacy & Legislation Branch
PO Box 9493 Stn. Prov Govt, Victoria, BC V8W 9N7
Tel: 250-356-0361; *Fax:* 250-356-1182
Other Communication: Privacy Helpline: 250-356-1851; E-mail: CPIAADMIN@gov.bc.ca

Executive Director, Sharon Plater
Tel: 250-356-0322
Sharon.Plater@gov.bc.ca
Director, Legislation, Vacant
Tel: 250-356-7787
Director, Strategic Privacy Practices, Vacant
Tel: 250-356-0322
Director, Operations & Privacy Management, Sukhy Sidhu
Tel: 250-356-0378; *Fax:* 250-356-1182

Technology Solutions
PO Box 9412 Stn. Prov Govt, Victoria, BC V8W 9V1
Tel: 250-387-4779; *Fax:* 250-387-5693

Assistant Deputy Minister, Ian Bailey
Tel: 250-387-4779; *Fax:* 250-387-5693
Executive Director, Transformation & Architecture, Stephen Gordon
Tel: 250-634-8448
Stephen.Gordon@gov.bc.ca
Executive Director, Hosting, Niki Sedmak
Tel: 250-744-9193; *Fax:* 250-387-1940
Niki.Sedmak@gov.bc.ca
Director, Contracts, Device Services, Gary Armstrong
Tel: 250-514-1761; *Fax:* 250-387-9451
Gary.Armstrong@gov.bc.ca
Executive Director, Hosting Delivery, Ian Donaldson
Tel: 250-387-9462; *Fax:* 250-387-9451
Ian.Donaldson@gov.bc.ca
Director, Hosting Administrators Office, Michael P. Hayes
Tel: 250-217-9617; *Fax:* 250-387-1940
Michael.P.Hayes@gov.bc.ca
Director, Business Management, Leanne Howes
Tel: 250-952-6026; *Fax:* 250-387-1940
Leanne.Howes@gov.bc.ca
Director, Contract Management & Reporting, Pete Provan
Tel: 250-516-4115
Pete.Provan@gov.bc.ca
Director, Business Management, Device Services, Ralph Roberts
Tel: 250-415-6820; *Fax:* 250-387-9451
Ralph.Roberts@gov.bc.ca

Service BC
PO Box 9804 Stn. Prov Govt, Victoria, BC V8W 9W1
Tel: 250-387-6121; *Fax:* 250-387-5633
Toll-Free: 800-663-7867
TTY: 800-661-8773
www.servicebc.gov.bc.ca
Other Communication: Vancouver & outside B.C., Phone: 604-660-2421; Southeast Service BC Centre, Phone: 250-354-6109; Vancouver Island / South Coast Service BC Centre: 250-356-7302

Service BC provides frontline government services & information to businesses, residents, & visitors in British Columbia. Areas of service include education, training, employment & labour standards, doing business in the province, licensing & registration, taxation, health services, legal services, family support services, property, transportation, tourism, recreation, & publications. Service is available by phone, online, or in person at Service BC Centres throughout the province.

Assistant Deputy Minister, Beverly Dicks
Tel: 250-387-9170; *Fax:* 250-387-5633

BC OnLine
#E415, 4000 Seymour Pl., PO Box 9412 Stn. Prov Govt, Victoria, BC V8W 9V1
Fax: 250-952-6115
Toll-Free: 800-663-6102
bconline@apicanada.com
www.bconline.gov.bc.ca
Other Communication: Help Desk, Phone: 250-953-8200; E-mail: bcolhelp@apicanada.com (Support Issues)

BC OnLine serves government, legal, & business professionals by providing access to provincial government computer systems through the Internet. Examples of e-government services include Court Services Online, Land Title & Survey Authority Electronic Services, Personal Property Registry, Corporate Registry, Gas & Electrical Permits, & the Wills Registry.

Registries & Online Services
PO Box 9431 Stn. Prov Govt, Victoria, BC V8W 9V3
Tel: 250-387-7848; *Fax:* 250-356-9422
Toll-Free: 877-526-1526
BCRegistries@gov.bc.ca
www.bcregistryservices.gov.bc.ca
Other Communication: Societies & Cooperatives: 250-356-8609; Personal Property Registry: 250-952-7976

BC Registry Services support commerce by overseeing the Corporate Registry, the Personal Property Registry, the Manufactured Home Registry, & the OneStop Business Registry.

Executive Director, Carol Prest
Tel: 250-356-8658
Carol.Prest@gov.bc.ca
Deputy Registrar, Debbie Turner
Tel: 250-356-8669
Debbie.Turner@gov.bc.ca
Director, Business & Project Services, Ian Armstrong
Tel: 250-356-2024
Ian.Armstrong@gov.bc.ca
Manager, Registries Operations, Robyn Andrew
Tel: 250-953-4748
Robyn.Andrew@gov.bc.ca
Senior Registry Analyst, Barb Baker
Tel: 250-356-7716; *Fax:* 250-387-3055
Barb.Baker@gov.bc.ca
Manager, Administration, Rob Bowes
Tel: 250-356-9417; *Fax:* 250-356-9422
Rob.Bowes@gov.bc.ca
Team Lead, Corporations/Societies, Tammy Wiedeman
Tel: 250-356-8656; *Fax:* 250-356-8923
Tammy.Wiedeman@gov.bc.ca

BC Stats
553 Superior St., PO Box 9410 Stn. Prov Govt, Victoria, BC V8W 9V1
Fax: 250-387-0380
BC.Stats@gov.bc.ca
www.bcstats.gov.bc.ca

Operating under the direction of the British Columbia Statistics Act, R.S.B.C. 1996, C. 439, BC Stats is the central statistical agency of the Province of British Columbia. The organization serves government & voluntary clients through the dissemination of general statistical information.

Executive Director, Elizabeth Vickery
Tel: 250-217-5055
Elizabeth.Vickery@gov.bc.ca
Manager, Student Outcomes, Jim Martell
Tel: 778-676-3975
Jim.Martell@gov.bc.ca
Director, Demographic Analysis, Jackie Storen
Tel: 250-216-2291
Jackie.Storen@gov.bc.ca
Manager, Public Sector Research & Evaluation, Angela Matheson
Tel: 250-507-1148; *Fax:* 250-387-0380
Angela.Matheson@gov.bc.ca
Manager, Economic Account & Analysis, Lillian Hallin
Tel: 250-387-0366; *Fax:* 250-387-0380
Lillian.Hallin@gov.bc.ca
Manager, Performance Measurement & Reporting Program, Brooke Somers
Tel: 250-818-3143; *Fax:* 250-387-0380
Brooke.Somers@gov.bc.ca
Manager, Trade & Business Statistics, Dan Schrier
Tel: 250-812-0175; *Fax:* 250-387-0380
Dan.Schrier@gov.bc.ca

Service Delivery
PO Box 9804 Stn. Prov Govt, Victoria, BC V8W 9W1
Tel: 250-356-2038; *Fax:* 250-387-5633

Executive Director, Ron Hinshaw
Tel: 250-356-2031; *Fax:* 250-387-5633
Ron.Hinshaw@gov.bc.ca
Director, Contact Centre, Jeannette Eason
Tel: 778-698-2045; *Fax:* 250-387-5633
Jeannette.Eason@gov.bc.ca

Service BC Contact Centre
PO Box 9804 Stn. Prov Govt, Victoria, BC V8W 9W1
Fax: 250-387-5633
Toll-Free: 800-663-7867
TTY: 800-661-8773
EnquiryBC@gov.bc.ca
Other Communication: Vancouver, Phone: 604-660-2421

Inquiries are handled about services provided by provincial governmen ministries, Crown corporations, & public agencies. Formerly known as Enquiry BC.

Strategic Initiatives & Partnerships Division
PO Box 9412 Stn. Prov Govt, Victoria, BC V8W 9V1
Tel: 250-216-7511

Assistant Deputy Minister, David Morel
Tel: 778-698-2332
Executive Lead, Administrator's Office, Susan Stanford
Tel: 778-698-2349
Executive Director, Technology & Innovation, Kevin Butterworth
Tel: 250-356-1894
Kevin.Butterworth@gov.bc.ca
Executive Director, Network BC, Howard Randell
Tel: 250-953-3978
Executive Director, Negotiations Finance, Vitali Kozubenko
Tel: 250-415-9411; *Fax:* 250-387-3040
Vitali.Kozubenko@gov.bc.ca
Executive Director, Service Architecture & Planning/Regulatory Affairs, Roman Mateyko
Tel: 250-356-1789; *Fax:* 250-387-1940
Roman.Mateyko@gov.bc.ca
Executive Director, Contract Management, Malcolm Barrington
Tel: 250-387-9637; *Fax:* 250-953-3555
Executive Director, Relationship Management, Janice Larson
Tel: 250-807-9412
Janice.Larson@gov.bc.ca
Executive Director, Commercialization Initiatives, Government Initiatives, Peter Watkins
Tel: 250-514-2739; *Fax:* 250-387-4722
Peter.Watkins@gov.bc.ca
Executive Director, Strategic Partnership Office, Pelle Agerup
Tel: 250-882-0455
Pelle.Agerup@gov.bc.ca
Acting Director, Knowledge Transfer & Commercialization, Technology & Innovation, Christine Fast
Tel: 250-216-2713
Christine.Fast@gov.bc.ca
Director, Business Priorities, Strategic Partnership Office, Dan Cope
Tel: 250-508-7606; *Fax:* 250-387-7309
Dan.Cope@gov.bc.ca
Director, Strategy & Support, Geoff Haines
Tel: 250-953-6217
Geoff.Haines@gov.bc.ca
Director, Contract Management, Caroline Hergt
Tel: 778-679-5404; *Fax:* 250-953-3555
Caroline.Hergt@gov.bc.ca
Other Communications: Cell Phone: 778-679-5404

Director, Strategic Partnership Office, Mike Kishimoto
Tel: 604-398-3597
Mike.Kishimoto@gov.bc.ca
Director, Research & Knowledge Development, Technology & Innovation, Cecile Lacombe
Tel: 250-387-6157
Cecile.Lacombe@gov.bc.ca
Director, Portfolio Management, Scarlette Verjinschi
Tel: 250-356-5511; *Fax:* 250-387-3066
Scarlette.Verjinschi@gov.bc.ca
Director, Business Development, Strategic Partnership Office, Erik Wanless
Tel: 250-217-0185
Erik.Wanless@gov.bc.ca
Director, Planning & Operations, Jerri Wilkins
Tel: 250-812-3970; *Fax:* 250-387-1940
Jerri.Wilkins@gov.bc.ca

British Columbia Ministry of Transportation & Infrastructure

PO Box 9850 Stn. Prov Govt, Victoria, BC V8W 9T5
Tel: 250-387-3198; *Fax:* 250-356-7706
tran.webmaster@gov.bc.ca
www.th.gov.bc.ca
Other Communication: Media Enquiries, Phone: 250-387-7787, Fax: 250-356-2950

The mission of the Ministry of Transportation & Infrastructure is to plan tranportation networks, to establish policies, to provide transportation services & infrastructure, & to administer acts & regulations related to transportation & infrastructure.
Specific responsibilities include the following: working with partners to fund cost-effective public transit, ferry services, & cycling networks; managing funding for public infrastructure; maintaining highways; setting commercial vehicle operating standards & overseeing vehicle safety inspections; & licensing commercial passenger transporation.

Minister, Transportation & Infrastructure; Deputy House Leader, Hon. Todd Stone
Tel: 250-387-1978; *Fax:* 250-356-2290
Minister.Transportation@gov.bc.ca
Minister of State for Emergency Preparedness, Hon. Naomi Yamamoto
Tel: 250-356-8213; *Fax:* 250-356-8223
naomi.yamamoto.mla@leg.bc.ca
Deputy Minister, Grant Main
Tel: 250-387-3280; *Fax:* 250-387-6431
Grant.Main@gov.bc.ca
PO Box 9850 Prov Govt Sta.
Victoria, BC V8W 9T5
Deputy Minister, Emergency Preparedness, Becky Denlinger
Emergency.Management.Deputy.Minister@gov.bc.ca
Chief of Staff, Jordan Bell
Jordan.Bell@gov.bc.ca
Chief of Staff, Kit Sauder
Tel: 250-356-8213
Kit.Sauder@gov.bc.ca
Manager, Divisional Operations, Partnerships Division, Elizabeth Nicholls
Tel: 250-387-9753; *Fax:* 250-387-6431
Elizabeth.Nicholls@gov.bc.ca

Associated Agencies, Boards & Commissions:

•British Columbia Ferry Services Inc.
See Entry Name Index for detailed listing.

•British Columbia Pavilion Corporation (PavCo)
See Entry Name Index for detailed listing.

•British Columbia Railway Company
#600, 221 West Esplanade
North Vancouver, BC V7M 3J3
Tel: 604-678-4735; *Fax:* 604-678-4736
www.bcrco.com

•British Columbia Transit
520 Gorge Rd. East
Victoria, BC V8W 2P3
Tel: 250-385-2551
www.bctransit.com
Other Communication: Community transit information: transitinfo@bctransit.com
A provincial crown agency, BC Transit coordinates the delivery of public transportation in British Columbia, outside the Greater Vancouver Regional District. The corporation's specific role, in accordance with the BC Transit Act, is the planning, acquisition, construction, operation, & maintenance of public passenger transportation systems & rail systems.

•Passenger Transportation Board
#202, 940 Blanshard St.
PO Box 9850 Prov Govt
Victoria, BC V8W 9T5
Tel: 250-953-3777; *Fax:* 250-953-3788
ptboard@gov.bc.ca
www.ptboard.bc.ca
The Passenger Transportation Board carries out its responsibilities in accordance with the Passenger Transportation Act. The independent tribunal makes decisions regarding the operation of passenger directed vehicles and inter-city buses in British Columbia.

Emergency Management BC (EMBC)

PO Box 9201 Stn. Prov Govt, Victoria, BC V8W 9J1
Tel: 250-952-4913; *Fax:* 250-952-4871
www.embc.gov.bc.ca
Other Communication: Disaster & Emergency Reporting, Toll-Free Phone: 1-800-663-3456

Emergency Management BC oversees the Coroners Service of British Columbia, the Office of the Fire Commissioner, & the Provincial Emergency Program.
Assistant Deputy Minister, Patrick Quealey
Tel: 250-952-5013

Provincial Emergency Program

PO Box 9201 Stn. Prov Govt, Victoria, BC V8W 9J1
Tel: 250-952-4913; *Fax:* 250-952-4888
Toll-Free: 800-663-3456
embc.gov.bc.ca/em

The Provincial Emergency Program provides training & support to local governments.
Executive Director, Emergency Management, Chris Duffy
Tel: 250-952-4544; *Fax:* 250-952-4888
Chris.Duffy@gov.bc.ca
Director, Organizational Learning, Carol McClintock
Tel: 250-952-4811; *Fax:* 250-952-4888
Carol.McClintock@gov.bc.ca
Executive Director, Strategic Planning, Policy & Legislation, Cam Filmer
Tel: 250-952-4881; *Fax:* 250-952-4888
Cam.Filmer@gov.bc.ca

Finance & Management Services Department

PO Box 9850 Victoria, BC V8W 9T5
Tel: 250-387-3100; *Fax:* 250-387-6431

Assistant Deputy Minister, Finance & Management Services, Nancy Bain
Tel: 250-387-3100; *Fax:* 250-387-6431
Nancy.Bain@gov.bc.ca
Director, Financial Planning & Reporting, Sandra Jackson
Tel: 250-356-2267; *Fax:* 250-387-7645
Sandra.Jackman@gov.bc.ca
Executive Director, Crown Agencies, Carol Bishop
Tel: 250-387-1936; *Fax:* 250-356-7706
Carol.Bishop@gov.bc.ca
Other Communications: Cell Phone: 250-888-1251
Executive Director/Chief Information Officer, Information Management Branch, Debbie Fritz
Tel: 250-387-3580; *Fax:* 250-356-7184
Debbie.Fritz@gov.bc.ca
Director, Accounting & Operations, Ellen Slanina
Tel: 250-387-3104; *Fax:* 250-387-7645
Ellen.Slanina@gov.bc.ca
Director, Finance (British Columbia Transportation Finance Authority), Gary So
Tel: 250-387-7873; *Fax:* 250-387-7645
Gary.So@gov.bc.ca

Highways Department

PO Box 9850 Victoria, BC V8W 9T5
Tel: 250-387-3260; *Fax:* 250-387-6431

Assistant Deputy Minister, Kevin Richter
Tel: 250-387-7671; *Fax:* 250-387-6431
Kevin.Richter@gov.bc.ca
Chief Engineer, Dirk Nyland
Tel: 250-356-0723; *Fax:* 250-387-7735
Dirk.Nyland@gov.bc.ca
Other Communications: Cell Phone: 250-812-6645
Director, Provincial Field Services, Keith Callander
Tel: 250-828-4151; *Fax:* 250-828-4277
Keith.Callander@gov.bc.ca
Other Communications: Cell Phone: 604-880-2336
Director, Construction & Maintenance, Rodney Chapman
Tel: 250-387-7626; *Fax:* 250-356-8143
Rodney.Chapman@gov.bc.ca
Other Communications: Cell Phone: 250-213-7499
Director, Rehabilitation & Maintenance, Ian Pilkington
Tel: 250-387-7627; *Fax:* 250-356-7276
Ian.Pilkington@gov.bc.ca
Director, Social Media Branch, Russel Lolacher
Tel: 250-356-9682; *Fax:* 250-356-8767
Russel.Lolacher@gov.bc.ca
Other Communications: Cell Phone: 778-679-2482
Director, Commercial Vehicle Safety & Enforcement Branch, Brian Murray
Tel: 250-953-4024; *Fax:* 250-952-0578
Brian.Murray@gov.bc.ca
Other Communications: Cell Phone: 778-888-8436
Director, Business Management Services, Sandra Toth Nacey
Tel: 250-356-9768; *Fax:* 250-256-8767
Sandra.TothNacey@gov.bc.ca
Other Communications: Cell Phone: 778-679-2483
Director, Engineering Systems, Al Szczawinski
Tel: 250-387-7777; *Fax:* 250-387-8081
Al.Szczawinski@gov.bc.ca

Office of the Fire Commissioner

PO Box 9201 Stn. Prov Govt, Victoria, BC V8W 9J1
Tel: 250-952-4913; *Fax:* 250-952-4888
Toll-Free: 888-988-9488
OFC@gov.bc.ca
www.embc.gov.bc.ca/ofc

The Office of the Fire Commissioner administers & enforces fire safety legislation, trains local assistants to the fire commissioner, certifies fire fighters, provides public fire safety education, advises local governments, responds to major fires, & investigates fires.
Fire Commissioner, Gordon Anderson
Tel: 250-952-5048
Deputy Fire Commissioner, Vacant
Tel: 250-952-4913

Partnerships Division

PO Box 9850 Stn. Prov Govt, Victoria, BC V8W 9T5
Tel: 250-356-1403; *Fax:* 250-387-6431

Assistant Deputy Minister, Lindsay Kislock
Tel: 250-387-5062; *Fax:* 250-387-6431
Lindsay.Kislock@gov.bc.ca
Director, Properties & Land Management Branch, Svein Haugen
Tel: 250-356-7904; *Fax:* 250-356-6970
Svein.Haugen@gov.bc.ca
Administrator, Transit Branch, Sheila Smith
Tel: 250-387-3059; *Fax:* 250-387-5012
Sheila.M.Smith@gov.bc.ca
Director, Real Esate, Richard Myhill Jones
Tel: 604-678-4703; *Fax:* 604-678-4702
Richard.MyhillJones@gov.bc.ca
Director, Corporate Planning & Strategic Initiatives, Jesse Skulmoski
Tel: 250-356-7108; *Fax:* 250-356-0897
Jesse.Skulmoski@gov.bc.ca
Executive Director, Transit & Crown Agency Programs, Kevin Volk
Tel: 250-387-4851; *Fax:* 250-387-5012
Kevin.Volk@gov.bc.ca

Transportation Policy & Programs Department

PO Box 9850 Stn. Prov Govt, Victoria, BC V8W 9T5
Tel: 250-387-5062; *Fax:* 250-387-6431

Assistant Deputy Minister, Deborah Bowman
Tel: 250-356-6225
Deborah.Bowman@gov.bc.ca
Registrar/Director, Passenger Transportation Branch, Kristin Vanderkuip
Tel: 604-527-2201
Kristin.Vanderkuip@gov.bc.ca
Executive Director, Pacific Gateway Branch, Lisa Gow
Tel: 250-387-2672; *Fax:* 250-387-5812
Lisa.Gow@gov.bc.ca
Executive Director, Transportation Policy Branch, Greg Gilks
Tel: 250-387-0882; *Fax:* 250-356-0897
Greg.Gilks@gov.bc.ca
Director, Transportation Trade Network Strategies & Business Development, Danielle Prpich
Tel: 250-387-2175; *Fax:* 250-387-5812
Danielle.Prpich@gov.bc.ca

Infrastructure Department

PO Box 9850 Stn. Prov Govt, Victoria, BC V8W 9T5
Tel: 250-387-6742; *Fax:* 250-387-6431

Assistant Deputy Minister, Patrick Livolsi
Tel: 250-387-7671; *Fax:* 250-387-6431
Patrick.Livolsi@gov.bc.ca
Executive Director, Planning & Programming Branch, David Marr
Tel: 250-356-2100; *Fax:* 250-356-0897
David.Marr@gov.bc.ca
Senior Project Advisor, Jon Buckle
Tel: 604-927-4452; *Fax:* 604-927-4453
Jon.Buckle@gov.bc.ca
Director, Marine Branch, Krik Handrahan
Tel: 250-952-0678; *Fax:* 250-356-0897
Kirk.Handrahan@gov.bc.ca

British Columbia Utilities Commission

900 Howe St., 6th Fl., PO Box 250 Vancouver, BC V6Z 2N3
Tel: 604-660-4700; *Fax:* 604-660-1102
Toll-Free: 800-663-1385
commission.secretary@bcuc.com
www.bcuc.com
twitter.com/BCutilitiescom

The British Columbia Utilities Commission is an independent regulatory agency of the Provincial Government of British Columbia. The Commission's regulates the province's natural gas & electricity utilities. Other activities of the Utilities Commission include the regulation of universal compulsory automobile insurance & intra-provincial pipelines.

Chair & CEO, Len Kelsey
Tel: 604-660-4714
Commission Secretary, Erica Hamilton
Tel: 604-660-4727
Erica.Hamilton@bcuc.com
Director, Policy, Planning & Customer Relations, Alison Thorson
Tel: 604-660-4185; *Fax:* 604-660-1102
alison.thorson@bcuc.com
Director, Energy, Doug Chong
Tel: 604-660-4737
doug.chong@bcuc.com
Acting Director, Performance Monitoring, Conduct & Compliance, Ian W. Homer
Tel: 604-660-1728
ian.homer@bcuc.com
Director, Rates, Philip W. Nakoneshny
Tel: 604-660-4736
philip.nakoneshny@bcuc.com
Director, Infrastructure, J. Todd Smith
Tel: 604-660-4723
Director, Human Resources & Finance, Viki Vourlis
Tel: 604-660-4719
Viki.Vourlis@bcuc.com

British Columbia Vital Statistics Agency

PO Box 9657 Stn. Prov Govt, Victoria, BC V8W 9P3
Tel: 250-952-2681; *Fax:* 250-952-9097
VSOFFCEO@gov.bc.ca
www.vs.gov.bc.ca

The Vital Statistics Agency operates under the Ministry of Health, & offers the following services: Birth registration; marriage certificates; death certificates; wills; name changes; & geneaology.

Registrar General, Jack Shewchuk
Tel: 250-952-9039; *Fax:* 250-952-9097
Jack.Shewchuk@gov.bc.ca
Director, Information Technology Services, Suzanne Jennings
Tel: 250-952-9084
Suzanne.Jennings@gov.bc.ca

Workers' Compensation Board of British Columbia

PO Box 5350 Stn. Terminal, Vancouver, BC V6B 5L5
Tel: 604-276-3100; *Fax:* 604-276-3247
Toll-Free: 888-621-7233
www.worksafebc.com
Other Communication: Claims: 604-231-8888, Fax: 604-233-9777; Employer services/Assessments: 604-244-6181
Secondary Address: 6951 Westminster Hwy.
Head Office Street Address
Richmond, BC
twitter.com/WorkSafeBC
www.facebook.com/133870710003535
www.linkedin.com/company/worksafebc
www.youtube.com/user/WorkSafeBC

The Workers' Compensation Board of British Columbia, or WorkSafeBC, assists workers & employers in British Columbia by promoting health & safety in workplaces. WorkSafeBC's key responsiblities are as follows: consultation with & education of employers & workers; monitoring compliance with the Occupational Health & Safety Regulation; & provision of return-to-work compensation, rehabilitation, health care benefits, & other services for parties affected by work-related injuries or diseases.

Chair, George Morfitt
governance@worksafebc.com
President & CEO, Diana Miles
Chief Financial Officer & Senior Vice-President, Finance Division, Brian Erickson
Senior Vice-President, Operations, Worker & Employer Services Division, Trevor Alexander
Senior Vice-President, Human Resources & Corporate Affairs, Roberta Ellis
Vice-President, Prevention Services, Al Johnson
Vice-President, Business Analysis, Corporate Communications & Marketing, Kevin LaFreniere
Vice-President, Claims Services, Todd McDonald
Vice-President, Employer, Industry & Worker Services, Ian Munroe
General Counsel & Secretary, Ian Shaw

Government of Manitoba

Seat of Government: Legislative Building, Rm. 237, Winnipeg, MB R3C 0V8
Tel: 204-945-3636; *Fax:* 204-948-2507
clerkla@leg.gov.mb.ca
www.gov.mb.ca
twitter.com/MBGov
www.facebook.com/ManitobaGovernment
www.youtube.com/ManitobaGovernment

The Province of Manitoba entered Confederation July 15, 1870. It has a land area of 647,797 sq km, & the StatsCan census population in 2011 was 1,208,268.
The 41st general election of Manitoba was held April 19, 2016, in which the Progressive Conservative Party of Manitoba won a majority over the incumbent New Democratic Party of Manitoba. Certain post-election details, such as full changes to departmental structure, were not available at the time of publication. For these & other updates, please see subsequent editions of *Governments Canada*& Canada's Information Resource Centre (CIRC) online.

Office of the Lieutenant Governor

Legislative Building, #235, 450 Broadway Ave., Winnipeg, MB R3C 0V8
Tel: 204-945-2753; *Fax:* 204-945-4329
ltgov@leg.gov.mb.ca
www.manitobalg.ca

Lieutenant Governor, Hon. Janice Filmon, CM, OM
Chief of Staff/Private Secretary, Phyllis Fraser
Tel: 204-945-2752
Government House Event Coordinator, Lisa Vermette
Tel: 204-945-2753

Office of the Premier

Legislative Building, #204, 450 Broadway Ave., Winnipeg, MB R3C 0V8
Tel: 204-945-3714; *Fax:* 204-949-1484
premier@leg.gov.mb.ca
www.gov.mb.ca/minister/premier

Premier; President, Executive Council; Minister, Intergovernmental Affairs; Minister responsible, International Relations, Hon. Brian Pallister
Tel: 204-945-3714; *Fax:* 204-945-1484
premier@leg.gov.mb.ca
Deputy Premier; Keeper of the Great Seal; Minister, Justice & Attorney General, Hon. Heather Stefanson
Tel: 204-945-3728; *Fax:* 204-945-2517
minjus@leg.gov.mb.ca
Deputy Minister, Intergovernmental Affairs & International Relations, Fredrick (Rick) Mantey
Tel: 204-945-2213; *Fax:* 204-945-1717
Deputy Secretary to Cabinet, Outcomes & Results, Michael D. Richards
Tel: 204-945-2670
Chief of Staff to the Premier, Philip Houde
Tel: 204-945-2271
Principal Secretary, Jonathan Scarth
Tel: 204-945-0346

Executive Council

Legislative Building, 450 Broadway Ave., Winnipeg, MB R3C 0V8
www.gov.mb.ca/minister

The following is a list of Cabinet Ministers of the Government of Manitoba in order of precedence:

Premier; President, Executive Council; Minister, Intergovernmental Affairs; Minister responsible, International Relations, Hon. Brian Pallister
Tel: 204-945-3714; *Fax:* 204-945-1484
premier@leg.gov.mb.ca
Legislative Building
#204, 450 Broadway
Winnipeg, MB R3C 0V8
Deputy Premier; Keeper of the Great Seal; Minister, Justice & Attorney General, Hon. Heather Stefanson
Tel: 204-945-3728; *Fax:* 204-945-2517
minjus@leg.gov.mb.ca
Minister, Finance; Minister responsible, Civil Service Commission, Hon. Cameron Friesen
Tel: 204-945-3952; *Fax:* 204-948-6057
minfin@leg.gov.mb.ca
Minister, Health, Seniors & Active Living, Hon. Kelvin Goertzen
Tel: 204-945-3731; *Fax:* 204-945-0441
minhsal@leg.gov.mb.ca
Minister, Education & Training, Hon. Ian Wishart
Tel: 204-945-3720; *Fax:* 204-945-1291
minedu@leg.gov.mb.ca
Minister, Families, Hon. Scott Fielding
Tel: 204-945-4337; *Fax:* 204-945-5149
minfs@leg.gov.mb.ca
Minister, Infrastructure, Hon. Blaine Pedersen
Tel: 204-945-3723; *Fax:* 204-945-7610
minmi@leg.gov.mb.ca
Minister, Indigenous & Municipal Relations, Hon. Eileen Clarke
Tel: 204-945-3788; *Fax:* 204-945-1383
minim@leg.gov.mb.ca
Minister, Sustainable Development, Hon. Cathy Cox
Tel: 204-945-3730; *Fax:* 204-945-3586
minsdev@leg.gov.mb.ca
Minister, Growth, Enterprise & Trade, Hon. Cliff Cullen
Tel: 204-945-0067; *Fax:* 204-945-4882
minget@leg.gov.mb.ca
Minister, Agriculture, Hon. Ralph Eichler
Tel: 204-945-3722; *Fax:* 204-945-3470
minagr@leg.gov.mb.ca
Minister, Sport, Culture & Heritage; Minister responsible for Francophone Affairs & Status of Women, Hon. Rochelle Squires
Tel: 204-945-3729; *Fax:* 204-945-5223
minsch@leg.gov.mb.ca
Minister, Crown Services, Hon. Ron Schuler
Tel: 204-945-8020; *Fax:* 204-948-7700
mincrown@leg.gov.mb.ca

Manitoba Legislative Assembly

c/o Clerk's Office, Legislative Bldg., #237, 450 Broadway, Winnipeg, MB R3C 0V8
Tel: 204-945-3636; *Fax:* 204-948-2507
clerkla@leg.gov.mb.ca
www.gov.mb.ca/legislature

Clerk of the Legislative Assembly, Patricia Chaychuk
Tel: 204-945-3636
clerk@leg.gov.mb.ca
Deputy Clerk of the Legislative Assembly, Rick Yarish
Tel: 204-945-0245
Speaker of the House, Hon. Myrna Driedger
Tel: 204-945-3706; *Fax:* 204-945-1443
speaker@leg.gov.mb.ca
Chief Electoral Officer, Shipra Verma, CPA, CA
Tel: 204-945-3225
Toll-free: 866-628-6837; *Fax:* 204-945-6011
election@elections.mb.ca
www.electionsmanitoba.ca
Ombudsman, Charlene Paquin
Tel: 204-982-9130; *Fax:* 204-942-7803
ombudsman@ombudsman.mb.ca
www.ombudsman.mb.ca
Lobbyist Registrar & Conflict of Interest Commissioner, Jeffrey Schnoor, Q.C.
Tel: 204-948-1018
mbcoic@legassembly.mb.ca
www.mbcoic.ca/commissioner.html
Children's Advocate, Darlene MacDonald, MSW, RSW
Tel: 204-988-7440
Toll-free: 800-263-7146; *Fax:* 204-988-7472
info@childrensadvocate.mb.ca
www.childrensadvocate.mb.ca
Auditor General, Norman J. Ricard, CA
Tel: 204-945-3790
norman.ricard@oag.mb.ca
www.oag.mb.ca
Journals Clerk / Clerk Assistant, Claude Michaud
Tel: 204-945-6331
claude.michaud@leg.gov.mb.ca

Government Caucus Office (Progressive Conservative Party)
Legislative Building, #227, 450 Broadway Ave., Winnipeg, MB R3C 0V8
Tel: 204-945-3709; *Fax:* 204-945-1284
Toll-Free: 800-282-8069
pccaucus@leg.gov.mb.ca
www.pcmanitoba.com
twitter.com/Brian_Pallister
www.facebook.com/BrianPallister
www.youtube.com/PCManitobadotcom

Premier & Leader, Hon. Brian Pallister
Tel: 204-945-3714; *Fax:* 204-945-1484
premier@leg.gov.mb.ca
Caucus Chair, Wayne Ewasko
wayne.ewasko@leg.gov.mb.ca
Caucus Whip, Cliff Graydon
cliff.graydon@leg.gov.mb.ca

Government House Leader, Andrew Micklefield
andrew.micklefield@leg.gov.mb.ca
Director, Administration, Barb Craven
Tel: 204-945-3709

Official Opposition Office (New Democratic Party)
Legislative Bldg., #234, 450 Broadway Ave., Winnipeg, MB R3C 0V8
Tel: 204-945-3710; *Fax:* 204-948-2005
www.facebook.com/manitobandpcaucus
www.youtube.com/user/yourmanitoba

Interim Leader, Manitoba New Democratic Party, Flor Marcelino
Tel: 204-945-3710; *Fax:* 204-945-2005
flor.marcelino@leg.gov.mb.ca
Social Media: twitter.com/flormarcelino, www.facebook.com/flormarcelinoMB, www.linkedin.com/pub/flor-marcelino/37/245/b36
Interim Deputy Leader; Caucus Whip, Amanda Lathlin
Amanda.Lathlin@leg.gov.mb.ca
Caucus Chair, Rob Altemeyer
rob.altemeyer@leg.gov.mb.ca
Opposition House Leader, Jim Maloway
jim.maloway@leg.gov.mb.ca
Deputy House Leader; Deputy Whip, Ted Marcelino
ted.marcelino@leg.gov.mb.ca
Director, Policy & Communications, Christopher Sanderson
Tel: 204-945-8438

Office of the Liberal Party of Canada in Manitoba
635 Broadway Ave., Winnipeg, MB R3C 0X1
Tel: 204-988-9380; *Fax:* 204-284-1492
Toll-Free: 800-567-5746
Executive.Director@ManitobaLiberals.ca
www.manitobaliberals.ca
Other Communication: Media, E-mail: media@manitobaliberals.ca; Manitoba Young Liberals, Facebook: www.facebook.com/ManitobaYoungLiberals
www.facebook.com/manitobaliberals
www.youtube.com/user/manitobaliberals

Leader, Rana Bokhari
Social Media: twitter.com/rana4manitoba
Director, Communications & Research, Liz Gonsalves
Tel: 204-945-5194
Director, Administration, Mie Larsen
Tel: 204-945-5194

Legislative Committees
Committees Branch, Legislative Building, #251, 450 Broadway Ave., Winnipeg, MB R3C 0V8
Fax: 204-945-0038
gov.mb.ca/legislature/committees/index.html

At the beginning of the first session of each Legislature, a Special Committee consisting of seven members recommends a list of members to serve on the various committees. Once the Special Committee's report is adopted, the standing committees are created. The following standing committees have been established: Agriculture & Food; Crown Corporations; Human Resources; Intergovernmental Affairs; Justice; Legislative Affairs; Private Bills; Public Accounts; Rules of the House; Social & Economic Development; & Statutory Regulations & Orders.

Committee Clerk, Monique Grenier
Tel: 204-945-0796
monique.grenier@leg.gov.mb.ca
Committee Clerk, Andrea Signorelli
Tel: 204-945-4729
andrea.signorelli@leg.gov.mb.ca

Forty-first Legislature - Manitoba

Legislative Building, 450 Broadway Ave., Winnipeg, MB R3C 0V8
Tel: 204-945-3636; *Fax:* 204-948-2507
clerkla@leg.gov.mb.ca
www.gov.mb.ca/legislature

Last General Election: Apr. 19, 2016.
Next General Election: Apr. 2020.
Party Standings (Sept. 2016):
Progressive Conservative 40;
New Democratic Party 14;
Liberal 3;
Total - 57.
MLA Pay (effective April 1, 2014):
MLA basic annual salary $89,500;
Additional Annual Salaries:
Premier $55,944;
Cabinet Ministers $36,745;
Cabinet Ministers without portfolio $32,570;
Speaker $49,000;
Deputy Speaker $10,042;
Leader of the Official Opposition $49,000;
Deputy Chairperson of the Committee of the Whole $7,172;
Government House Leader $10,042;
Government Whip $7,172;
Official Opposition House Leader $7,172;
Official Opposition Whip $5,739;
Leader of Other Recognized Parties $41,300;
Other Opposition House Leader $5,739;
Other Opposition Whip $4,306;
Caucus Chair $6,182;
Permanent Chairperson, Standing or Special Committees $185.00 per meeting to an annual maximum of $4,306.
All members of the Legislative Assembly of Manitoba may be reached at the following address: 450 Broadway, Winnipeg, MB R3C 0V8.
The following is a list of Mmembers of the Legislative Assembly of Manitoba, with their constituency, number of registered voters in the constituency, party affiliation, & contact information:

Members of the Legislative Assembly of Manitoba

James Allum
Constituency: Fort Garry-Riverview, New Democratic Party
Tel: 204-945-3710; *Fax:* 204-945-2005
james.allum@leg.gov.mb.ca
jamesallum.ca
Other Communications: Constituency Phone: 204-475-2270; Fax: 204-475-2293
Social Media: twitter.com/jamesallummb, www.facebook.com/jamesallumMB
Constituency Office
565 1/2 Osborne St. South
Winnipeg, MB R3L 2B3

Rob Altemeyer
Constituency: Wolseley, New Democratic Party
Tel: 204-945-3710; *Fax:* 204-948-2005
rob.altemeyer@leg.gov.mb.ca
robaltemeyer.ca
Other Communications: Constituency Phone: 204-775-8575; Fax: 204-779-0326
Social Media: www.facebook.com/RobAltemeyerMLA
Constituency Office
#202, 222 Furby St.
Winnipeg, MB R3C 2A7

Kelly Bindle
Constituency: Thompson, Progressive Conservative
Tel: 204-945-3709; *Fax:* 204-945-1284
kelly.bindle@leg.gov.mb.ca
www.votekelly.ca
Social Media: www.facebook.com/Vote-Kelly-Bindle-531086180375656

Kevin Chief
Constituency: Point Douglas, New Democratic Party
Tel: 204-945-3710; *Fax:* 204-945-2005
kevin.chief@leg.gov.mb.ca
kevinchief.ca
Other Communications: Constituency Phone: 204-421-9126; Fax: 204-421-9127
Social Media: twitter.com/kevin_chief, www.facebook.com/kchiefer
Constituency Office
804 Selkirk Ave.
Winnipeg, MB R2W 2N6

Minister, Indigenous & Municipal Relations, Hon. Eileen Clarke
Constituency: Agassiz, Progressive Conservative
Tel: 204-945-3788; *Fax:* 204-945-1383
minim@leg.gov.mb.ca
www.eileenclarke.ca
Social Media: www.facebook.com/eileen.clarke.351

Minister, Sustainable Development, Hon. Cathy Cox
Constituency: River East, Progressive Conservative
Tel: 204-945-3730; *Fax:* 204-945-3586
minsdev@leg.gov.mb.ca
www.votecathycox.ca
Social Media: twitter.com/cathymcox

Minister, Growth, Enterprise & Trade, Hon. Cliff Cullen
Constituency: Spruce Woods, Progressive Conservative
Tel: 204-945-0067; *Fax:* 204-945-4882
minget@leg.gov.mb.ca
www.cliffcullen.ca
Other Communications: Constituency Phone: 204-827-3956; Fax: 204-827-3957
Constituency Office
101 Broadway St.
PO Box 129
Glenboro, MB R0K 0X0

Nic Curry
Constituency: Kildonan, Progressive Conservative
Tel: 204-945-3709; *Fax:* 204-945-1284
nic.curry@leg.gov.mb.ca
www.niccurry.ca
Social Media: twitter.com/nicjamescurry, www.facebook.com/Nic4Kildonan

Speaker of the House, Hon. Myrna Driedger
Constituency: Charleswood, Progressive Conservative
Tel: 204-945-3706; *Fax:* 204-945-1443
myrna.driedger@leg.gov.mb.ca
www.myrnadriedger.com
Other Communications: Constituency Phone: 204-885-0594; Fax: 204-885-5525
Social Media: twitter.com/MyrnaBDriedger
Constituency Office
5120-B Roblin Blvd.
Winnipeg, MB R3R 0G9

Minister, Agriculture, Hon. Ralph Eichler
Constituency: Lakeside, Progressive Conservative
Tel: 204-945-3722; *Fax:* 204-945-3470
minagr@leg.gov.mb.ca
www.ralpheichler.com
Other Communications: Constituency Phone: 204-467-9482; Fax: 204-467-7580
Social Media: twitter.com/rocklakeside
Constituency Office
319 Main St.
PO Box 1845
Stonewall, MB ROC 2Z0

Wayne Ewasko
Constituency: Lac du Bonnet, Progressive Conservative
Tel: 204-945-3709; *Fax:* 204-945-1284
wayne.ewasko@leg.gov.mb.ca
www.wayneewasko.com
Other Communications: Constituency Phone: 204-268-3282; Fax: 204-268-3976
Social Media: www.linkedin.com/pub/wayne-ewasko/74/a0/860
Constituency Office
638 Park Ave.
PO Box 1299
Beausejour, MB R0E 0C0

Minister, Families, Hon. Scott Fielding
Constituency: Kirkfield Park, Progressive Conservative
Tel: 204-945-4337; *Fax:* 204-945-5149
minfs@leg.gov.mb.ca
www.votescottfielding.ca
Social Media: twitter.com/scottfielding25, www.facebook.com/scott.fielding.1029

Hon. Steven Fletcher, P.C.
Constituency: Assiniboia, Progressive Conservative
Tel: 204-945-3709; *Fax:* 204-945-1284
steven.fletcher@leg.gov.mb.ca
www.pcmanitoba.com/steven_fletcher
Social Media: twitter.com/honsfletcher, www.facebook.com/StevenFletcherMP

Nahanni Fontaine
Constituency: St. Johns, New Democratic Party
Tel: 204-945-3710; *Fax:* 204-945-2005
nahanni.fontaine@leg.gov.mb.ca
todaysndp.ca/mla/nahanni-fontaine
Social Media: twitter.com/NahanniFontaine, www.facebook.com/NahanniFontaineMB, ca.linkedin.com/in/nahanni-fontaine-8359b085

Minister, Finance; Minister responsible, Civil Service Commission, Hon. Cameron Friesen
Constituency: Morden-Winkler, Progressive Conservative
Tel: 204-945-3952; *Fax:* 204-948-6057
minfin@leg.gov.mb.ca
www.cameronfriesen.ca
Other Communications: Constituency Phone: 204-822-1088; Fax: 204-822-1086
Social Media: twitter.com/mordenwinkler, www.facebook.com/CameronFriesen.MordenWinkler
Constituency Office
108A - 8th St.
Morden, MB R6M 1Y7

Hon. Jon Gerrard, P.C.
Constituency: River Heights, Liberal
Tel: 204-945-5194; *Fax:* 204-948-3220
jon.gerrard@leg.gov.mb.ca
jongerrard.manitobaliberals.ca
Social Media: twitter.com/drjongerrard, www.facebook.com/manitobaliberaljongerrard, ca.linkedin.com/in/jon-gerrard-0362b819
MLA Office, Legislative Building
#167, 450 Broadway
Winnipeg, MB R3C 0V8

Minister, Health, Seniors & Active Living, Hon. Kelvin Goertzen
Constituency: Steinbach, Progressive Conservative
Tel: 204-945-3731; *Fax:* 204-945-0441
minhsal@leg.gov.mb.ca
www.kelvingoertzen.com
Other Communications: Constituency Phone: 204-326-5763; Fax: 204-346-9913
Social Media: twitter.com/kelvin_goertzen, www.facebook.com/KelvingoertzenMLA
Constituency Office
227 Main St.
Steinbach, MB R5G 1Y7

Cliff Graydon
Constituency: Emerson, Progressive Conservative
Tel: 204-945-3709; *Fax:* 204-945-1284
cliff.graydon@leg.gov.mb.ca
www.cliffgraydon.ca
Other Communications: Constituency Phone: 204-324-9901; Fax: 204-324-9902

Social Media: twitter.com/cliffgraydonmla
Constituency Office
67 St. NE
PO Box 2099
Altona, MB R0G 0B0

Sarah Guillemard
Constituency: Fort Richmond, Progressive Conservative
Tel: 204-945-3709; *Fax:* 204-945-1284
sarah.guillemard@leg.gov.mb.ca
www.sarahguillemard.ca
Social Media: www.facebook.com/fortrichmondvoices

Reg Helwer
Constituency: Brandon West, Progressive Conservative
Tel: 204-945-3709; *Fax:* 204-945-1284
reg.helwer@leg.gov.mb.ca
www.pcmanitoba.com/reg_helwer
Other Communications: Constituency Phone: 204-728-2410; Fax: 204-726-4740
Social Media: twitter.com/reghelwer, www.facebook.com/Reg-Helwer-PC-145964902129507
Constituency Office
#2, 20 - 18th St.
Brandon, MB R7A 5A3

Len IsLeifson
Constituency: Brandon East, Progressive Conservative
Tel: 204-945-3709; *Fax:* 204-945-1284
len.isleifson@leg.gov.mb.ca
www.votelen.ca
Social Media: twitter.com/LenIsleifson, www.facebook.com/len.isleifson

Derek Johnson
Constituency: Interlake, Progressive Conservative
Tel: 204-945-3709; *Fax:* 204-945-1284
derek.johnson@leg.gov.mb.ca
www.derekjohnson.ca
Social Media: twitter.com/interlakepc

Scott Johnston
Constituency: St. James, Progressive Conservative
Tel: 204-945-3709; *Fax:* 204-945-1284
scott.johnston@leg.gov.mb.ca
www.votescottjohnston.ca

Wab Kinew
Constituency: Fort Rouge, New Democratic Party
Tel: 204-945-3710; *Fax:* 204-945-2005
wab.kinew@leg.gov.mb.ca
wabkinew.ca
Social Media: twitter.com/WabKinew, www.facebook.com/WabKinew

Judy Klassen
Constituency: Kewatinook, Liberal
Tel: 204-945-5427; *Fax:* 204-948-3220
judy.klassen@leg.gov.mb.ca
judyklassen.manitobaliberals.ca
Social Media: www.facebook.com/970363999696016

Bob Lagassé
Constituency: Dawson Trail, Progressive Conservative
Tel: 204-945-3709; *Fax:* 204-945-1284
bob.lagasse@leg.gov.mb.ca
www.boblagasse.ca
Social Media: twitter.com/baszel90

Alan Lagimodiere
Constituency: Selkirk, Progressive Conservative
Tel: 204-945-3709; *Fax:* 204-945-1284
alan.lagimodiere@leg.gov.mb.ca
www.alanlagimodiere.ca
Social Media: twitter.com/AlanLagimodiere

Cindy Lamoureux
Constituency: Burrows, Liberal
Tel: 204-945-5177; *Fax:* 204-948-3220
cindy.lamoureux@leg.gov.mb.ca
cindylamoureux.manitobaliberals.ca
Social Media: twitter.com/08cindylam, www.facebook.com/Cindy4Burrows

Amanda Lathlin
Constituency: The Pas, New Democratic Party
Tel: 204-945-3710; *Fax:* 204-948-2005
Amanda.Lathlin@leg.gov.mb.ca
todaysndp.ca/mla/amanda-lathlin-0
Other Communications: Constituency Phone: 204-623-2034; Fax: 204-623-2068
Social Media: www.facebook.com/AmandaLathlinMLA
Constituency Office
1416 Gordon Ave.
The Pas, MB R9A 1L8

Tom Lindsey
Constituency: Flin Flon, New Democratic Party
Tel: 204-945-3710; *Fax:* 204-945-2005
tom.lindsey@leg.gov.mb.ca
todaysndp.ca/candidate/tom-lindsey
Social Media: twitter.com/tomlindseyndp, www.facebook.com/TomLindseyForFlinFlon

Jim Maloway
Constituency: Elmwood, New Democratic Party
Tel: 204-945-3710; *Fax:* 204-948-2005
jim.maloway@leg.gov.mb.ca
todaysndp.ca/mla/jim-maloway
Other Communications: Constituency Phone: 204-415-1122; Fax: 204-414-9414
Social Media: www.facebook.com/JimMalowayMB
Constituency Office
46 Stadacona St.
Winnipeg, MB R2L 2C8

Interim Leader, Manitoba New Democratic Party, Flor Marcelino
Constituency: Logan, New Democratic Party
Tel: 204-945-3710; *Fax:* 204-945-2005
flor.marcelino@leg.gov.mb.ca
todaysndp.ca/flor-marcelino
Other Communications: Constituency Phone: 204-788-0800; Fax: 204-788-4444
Social Media: twitter.com/flormarcelino, www.facebook.com/flormarcelinoMB, www.linkedin.com/pub/flor-marcelino/37/245/b36
Constituency Office
849 Notre Dame Ave.
Winnipeg, MB R3E OM4

Ted Marcelino
Constituency: Tyndall Park, New Democratic Party
Tel: 204-945-3710; *Fax:* 204-948-2005
ted.marcelino@leg.gov.mb.ca
todaysndp.ca/mla/ted-marcelino-0
Other Communications: Constituency Phone: 204-421-9493; Fax: 204-421-9496
Constituency Office
#24, 360 Keewatin St.
Winnipeg, MB R2X 2Y3

Shannon Martin
Constituency: Morris, Progressive Conservative
Tel: 204-945-3709; *Fax:* 204-945-1284
shannon.martin@leg.gov.mb.ca
www.shannonmartin.ca
Other Communications: Constituency Phone: 204-736-3610; Fax: 204-736-3821
Social Media: twitter.com/MartinforMorris

Colleen Mayer
Constituency: St. Vital, Progressive Conservative
Tel: 204-945-3709; *Fax:* 204-945-1284
colleen.mayer@leg.gov.mb.ca
www.votecolleen.ca
Social Media: twitter.com/colleen_mayer, www.facebook.com/politiciancolleenmayer

Brad Michaleski
Constituency: Dauphin, Progressive Conservative
Tel: 204-945-3709; *Fax:* 204-945-1284
brad.michaleski@leg.gov.mb.ca
www.bradmichaleski.ca
Social Media: twitter.com/bradmichaleski, www.facebook.com/bradmichaleskipc

Government House Leader, Hon. Andrew Micklefield
Constituency: Rossmere, Progressive Conservative
Tel: 204-945-2709; *Fax:* 204-945-1284
andrew.micklefield@leg.gov.mb.ca
www.voteandrewmicklefield.ca
Social Media: twitter.com/a_micklefield, www.facebook.com/andrew.micklefield

Janice Morley-Lecomte
Constituency: Seine River, Progressive Conservative
Tel: 204-945-2709; *Fax:* 204-945-1284
janice.morley-lecomte@leg.gov.mb.ca
janicemorleylecomte.ca
Social Media: twitter.com/janicemlpcseine, www.facebook.com/Janice-Morley-Lecomte-993832983963008

Greg Nesbitt
Constituency: Riding Mountain, Progressive Conservative
Tel: 204-945-3709; *Fax:* 204-945-1284
greg.nesbitt@leg.gov.mb.ca
www.gregnesbitt.ca
Social Media: twitter.com/gregnesbittpc, www.facebook.com/greg.nesbitt.pcridingmountain, ca.linkedin.com/in/greg-nesbitt-a2731b33

Premier; President, Executive Council; Minister, Intergovernmental Affairs; Minister responsible, International Relations, Hon. Brian Pallister
Constituency: Fort Whyte, Progressive Conservative
Tel: 204-945-3714; *Fax:* 204-945-1484
premier@leg.gov.mb.ca
www.brianpallister.com
Other Communications: Constituency Phone: 204-489-0828
Social Media: twitter.com/Brian_Pallister, www.facebook.com/BrianPallister
Constituency Office
#143, 99 Scurfield Blvd.
Winnipeg, MB R3Y 1Y1

Minister, Infrastructure, Hon. Blaine Pedersen
Constituency: Midland, Progressive Conservative
Tel: 204-945-3723; *Fax:* 204-945-7610
minmi@leg.gov.mb.ca
www.blainepedersen.com
Other Communications: Constituency Phone: 204-745-2203; Fax: 204-745-2205
Social Media: twitter.com/BlainePedersen1
Constituency Office
148 Main St.
PO Box 1944
Carman, MB R0G OJO

Doyle Piwniuk
Constituency: Arthur-Virden, Progressive Conservative
Tel: 204-945-3709; *Fax:* 204-945-1284
doyle.piwniuk@leg.gov.mb.ca
doylepiwniuk.com
Other Communications: Constituency Phone: 204-748-6443; Fax: 204-748-6492
Social Media: twitter.com/doylepiwniuk, www.facebook.com/doyle.piwniuk.7, www.linkedin.com/pub/doyle-piwniuk/5a/934/0
Constituency Office
250 Nelson St. West
Virden, MB R0M 2C0

Jon Reyes
Constituency: St. Norbert, Progressive Conservative
Tel: 204-945-3709; *Fax:* 204-945-1284
jon.reyes@leg.gov.mb.ca
www.pcmanitoba.com/jon_reyes
Social Media: twitter.com/jonreyes204, www.facebook.com/jonreyesinthecommunity

Mohinder Saran
Constituency: The Maples, New Democratic Party
Tel: 204-945-3710; *Fax:* 204-945-2005
mohinder.saran@leg.gov.mb.ca
todaysndp.ca/mla/mohinder-saran-0
Other Communications: Constituency Phone: 204-632-7933; Fax: 204-697-2031
Social Media: www.linkedin.com/pub/mohinder-saran/66/508/6b
Constituency Office
80 Mandalay Dr.
Winnipeg, MB R2P 1V8

Minister, Crown Services, Hon. Ron Schuler
Constituency: St. Paul, Progressive Conservative
Tel: 204-945-8020; *Fax:* 204-948-7700
mincrown@leg.gov.mb.ca
www.ronschuler.com
Other Communications: Constituency Phone: 204-444-4371; Fax: 204-444-4372
Social Media: twitter.com/ronrschuler, www.facebook.com/ron.r.schuler
Constituency Office
#3, 777 Cedar Pl.
PO Box 150
Oakbank, MB R0E 1J0

Gregory Selinger
Constituency: St. Boniface *No. of Constituents:* 14,496, New Democratic Party
Tel: 204-945-3710; *Fax:* 204-945-2005
greg.selinger@leg.gov.mb.ca
www.gregselinger.ca
Other Communications: Constituency Phone: 204-237-9247; Fax: 204-237-9488
Social Media: twitter.com/gregselinger, www.facebook.com/TodaysNDP
Constituency Office
123 Enfield Cres.
Winnipeg, MB R2H 1A8

Andrew Smith
Constituency: Southdale, Progressive Conservative
Tel: 204-945-3709; *Fax:* 204-945-1284
andrew.smith@leg.gov.mb.ca
www.voteandrewsmith.ca
Social Media: www.facebook.com/www.smith4southdale.ca, ca.linkedin.com/in/andrew-smith-79563a42

Dennis Smook
Constituency: La Verendrye, Progressive Conservative
Tel: 204-945-3709; *Fax:* 204-945-1284
dennis.smook@leg.gov.mb.ca
www.dennissmook.ca
Other Communications: Constituency Phone: 204-424-5406; Fax: 204-424-5458
Social Media: twitter.com/DennisSmookMLA
Constituency Office
217B Fournier St.
La Broquerie, MB R0A 0W0

Minister, Sport, Culture & Heritage; Minister responsible for Francophone Affairs & Status of Women, Hon. Rochelle Squires
Constituency: Riel, Progressive Conservative
Tel: 204-945-3729; *Fax:* 204-945-5223
minsch@leg.gov.mb.ca
www.voterochelle.ca
Social Media: twitter.com/rochellesquires

Deputy Premier; Keeper of the Great Seal; Minister, Justice & Attorney General, Hon. Heather Stefanson

Constituency: Tuxedo, Progressive Conservative
Tel: 204-945-3728; *Fax:* 204-945-2517
minjus@leg.gov.mb.ca
www.heatherstefanson.com
Other Communications: Constituency Phone: 204-487-0013; Fax: 204-487-0078
Social Media: twitter.com/HeatherStef, www.linkedin.com/pub/heather-stefanson/50/503/1ab
Constituency Office
1840 Grant Ave.
Winnipeg, MB R3N 0N4

Andrew Swan
Constituency: Minto, New Democratic Party
Tel: 204-945-3710; *Fax:* 204-948-2005
andrew.swan@leg.gov.mb.ca
andrewswan.ca
Other Communications: Constituency Phone: 204-783-9860; Fax: 204-772-6129
Social Media: www.facebook.com/andrew.swan.777
Constituency Office
892 Sargent Ave.
Winnipeg, MB R3E 0C7

James Teitsma
Constituency: Radisson, Progressive Conservative
Tel: 204-945-3709; *Fax:* 204-945-1284
james.teitsma@leg.gov.mb.ca
jamesteitsma.ca
Social Media: twitter.com/JamesTeitsma

Jeff Wharton
Constituency: Gimli, Progressive Conservative
jeff.wharton@leg.gov.mb.ca
jeffwharton.ca
Social Media: twitter.com/jeffwharton2win, www.facebook.com/JeffWhartonGimli

Matt Wiebe
Constituency: Concordia, New Democratic Party
Tel: 204-945-3710; *Fax:* 204-948-2005
matt.wiebe@leg.gov.mb.ca
todaysndp.ca/mla/matt-wiebe-0
Other Communications: Constituency Phone: 204-654-1857; Fax: 204-663-1943
Social Media: twitter.com/mattwiebemb
Constituency Office
#106, 1111 Munroe Ave.
Winnipeg, MB R2K 3Z5

Minister, Education & Training, Hon. Ian Wishart
Constituency: Portage la Prairie, Progressive Conservative
Tel: 204-945-3720; *Fax:* 204-945-1291
minedu@leg.gov.mb.ca
www.ianwishart.ca
Other Communications: Constituency Phone: 204-857-9267; Fax: 204-857-9841
Social Media: twitter.com/wishartportage
Constituency Office
46 Saskatchewan Ave. East
Portage la Prairie, MB R1N 0L2

Rick Wowchuk
Constituency: Swan River, Progressive Conservative
rick.wowchuk@leg.gov.mb.ca
www.rickwowchuk.ca
Social Media: www.facebook.com/rick4swan

Blair Yakimoski
Constituency: Transcona, Progressive Conservative
blair.yakimoski@leg.gov.mb.ca
www.blairyakimoski.ca
Social Media: twitter.com/blairyak

Manitoba Government Departments & Agencies

Manitoba Agriculture

Legislative Bldg., #165, 450 Broadway, Winnipeg, MB R3C 0V8
Tel: 204-945-3722; *Fax:* 204-945-3470
minagr@leg.gov.mb.ca
www.gov.mb.ca/agriculture

Manitoba Agriculture, Food & Rural Development was renamed to Manitoba Agriculture following the 2016 general election.

Minister, Agriculture, Hon. Ralph Eichler
Tel: 204-945-3722; *Fax:* 204-945-3470
minagr@leg.gov.mb.ca

Deputy Minister, Dori Gingera-Beauchemin
Tel: 204-945-3734; *Fax:* 204-948-2095

Chief Veterinary Officer, Dr. Megan Bergman
Tel: 204-945-7684

Acting Director, Financial & Administrative Services, Diane Dempster
Tel: 204-945-7347

Associated Agencies, Boards & Commissions:

•Agricultural Societies
1129 Queens Ave.
Brandon, MB R7A 1L9
Tel: 204-726-6195; *Fax:* 204-726-6260
Promotes improvement in agriculture & development of Manitoba agricultural products. Provide organizational assistance to rural & urban people.

•Agri-Food Research & Development Initiative Program Council (ARDI)
c/o Manitoba Agriculture
810 Phillips St.
PO Box 1240
Portage la Prairie, MB R1N 3J9

•Animal Care Appeal Board

•Farm Lands Ownership Board
#812, Norquay Bldg.
401 York Ave.
Winnipeg, MB R3C 0P8
Tel: 204-945-3149; *Fax:* 204-945-1489
Toll-free: 800-282-8069
www.gov.mb.ca/agriculture/programs/aaa23s03.html

•Farm Machinery & Equipment Board
#812, 401 York Ave.
Winnipeg, MB R3C 0P8
Tel: 204-945-3854; *Fax:* 204-945-1489
www.gov.mb.ca/agriculture/programs/aaa14s01.html

•Farm Practices Protection Board
#812, 401 York Ave.
Winnipeg, MB R3C 0P8
Tel: 204-945-3854; *Fax:* 204-945-1489
www.gov.mb.ca/agriculture/programs/aaa25s03.html

•Farm Products Marketing Council
#812, 401 York Ave.
Winnipeg, MB R3C 0P8
Tel: 204-945-0630; *Fax:* 204-945-1489
www.gov.mb.ca/agriculture/programs/aaa31s02.html

•Food Development Centre
810 Phillips St.
PO Box 1240
Portage La Prairie, MB R1N 3J9
Tel: 204-239-3150
Toll-free: 800-870-1044
www.gov.mb.ca/agriculture/fdc
The Food Development Centre (FDC) is a Special Operating Agency of Manitoba Agriculture, Food & Rural Initiatives (MAFRI). Its mandate is to assist the agri-food industry in the development & commercialization of conventional & functional foods & natural health products.

•Manitoba Agricultural Services Corporation (MASC)
#100, 1525 First St. South
Brandon, MB R7A 7A1
Tel: 204-726-6850; *Fax:* 204-726-6849
mailbox@masc.mb.ca
www.masc.mb.ca
Formerly the Manitoba Agricultural Credit Corporation & the Manitoba Crop Insurance Corporation. Manitoba Agricultural Services Corporation (MASC) fully supports the province's producers & rural communities, through innovative & targeted risk management & financial programs. MASC is represented across Manitoba by 19 insurance offices & 16 lending offices, with corporate offices located in Portage la Prairie & Brandon.

•Manitoba Farm Mediation Board
#812, 401 York Ave.
Winnipeg, MB R3C 0P8
Tel: 204-945-0359; *Fax:* 204-945-1489
www.gov.mb.ca/agriculture/programs/aaa25s01.html
Mediates options to legal action by creditors when farmers cannot meet their obligations.

•Manitoba Horse Racing Commission
#812, 401 York Ave.
PO Box 46086 Westdale
Winnipeg, MB R3R 3S3
Tel: 204-885-7770; *Fax:* 204-831-0942
www.manitobahorsecomm.org
Governs, directs, controls, & regulates horse racing & the operation of all race tracks in Manitoba.

•Manitoba Milk Prices Review Commission
#812, 401 York Ave.
Winnipeg, MB R3C 0P8
Tel: 204-945-3854; *Fax:* 204-945-1489
www.gov.mb.ca/agriculture/programs/aaa22s08.html

•Veterinary Services Commission
c/o Livestock Knowledge Centre
#204, 545 University Cres.
Winnipeg, MB R3T 5S6
Tel: 204-945-6311; *Fax:* 204-945-4327
www.gov.mb.ca/agriculture/programs/aaa11s08.html

Agri-Food & Rural Development Division

Assistant Deputy Minister, Leloni Scott
Tel: 204-945-3735

Chief Operating Officer & General Manager, Food Development Centre, Lynda Lowry
Tel: 204-239-3624

Executive Director, Strategic Planning Directorate, Maurice Bouvier
Tel: 204-792-5406

Director, Value Added & Rural Economic Advancement Knowledge Centre, Mona Cornock
Tel: 204-726-6410

Director, GO Teams, Gerald Huebner
Tel: 204-797-4522

Director, Economic Development Initiatives, Leo Prince
Tel: 204-945-2427

Growing Opportunities (GO) Offices

Central Plains
Morris Ave., PO Box 532 Gladstone, MB R0J 0T0
Tel: 204-385-6633

Eastman
20 First St. South, PO Box 50 Beausejour, MB R0E 0C0
Tel: 204-268-6094
GO Team Manager, Shaunda Rossington
Tel: 204-268-6099

North Interlake
317 River Rd., PO Box 2000 Arborg, MB R0C 0A0
Tel: 204-376-3300

North Parkland
27 Second Ave. SW, Dauphin, MB R7N 3E5
Tel: 204-622-2007
GO Team Manager, Jana Schott
Tel: 204-648-3925

Northern

Pembina
279 Carlton St., PO Box 189 Somerset, MB R0G 2L0
Tel: 204-744-4050
GO Team Manager, Shane Dobson
Tel: 204-871-5800

Red River
67 - 2 St. NE, PO Box 969 Altona, MB R0G 0B0
Tel: 204-324-2804
GO Team Manager, Curtis Weeks
Tel: 204-304-0239

South Interlake
77 Main St., PO Box 70 Teulon, MB R0C 3B0
Tel: 204-886-2696
GO Team Manager, Wray Whitmore
Tel: 204-861-2298

South Parkland
221 Elm St., Hwy 21 North, PO Box 50 Hamiota, MB R0M 0T0
Tel: 204-764-3010

Southwest
247 Wellington St., PO Box 850 Virden, MB R0M 2C0
Tel: 204-748-4770

Urban
#13, 59 Scurfield Blvd., Winnipeg, MB R3Y 1V2
Tel: 204-945-4521

Valleys North
120 - 6th Ave. North, PO Box 370 Swan River, MB R0L 1Z0
Tel: 204-734-3417

Agri-Industry Development & Innovation Division

Acting Assistant Deputy Minister, Tracy Gilson
Tel: 204-945-3736

Chief Veterinary Officer, Food Safety Knowledge Centre, Wayne Lees
Tel: 204-945-7685

Director, Agri-Food Innovation & Adaptation, Daryl Domitruk
Tel: 204-823-1145

Director, Livestock Knowledge Centre, Melinda German
Tel: 204-573-1563

Director, Crops, Mike Kagan
Tel: 204-745-5653

Policy & Agri-Innovation Division

Acting Assistant Deputy Minister, Mike Lesiuk
Tel: 204-945-3910

Acting Director, Policy Analysis, Kim Beilby
Tel: 204-726-7023

Director, Knowledge Management, Margot Cathcart
Tel: 204-726-6207

Director, Boards, Commissions & Legislation, Debora Durnin-Richards
Tel: 204-945-0630

Director, Program Review & Evaluation, Marvin Richter
Tel: 204-797-8017

Office of the Auditor General

#500, 330 Portage Ave., Winnipeg, MB R3C 0C4
Tel: 204-945-3790; *Fax:* 204-945-2169
oag.contact@oag.mb.ca
www.oag.mb.ca
Other Communication: Reporting concerns, E-mail: citizens.concerns@oag.mb.ca

Established under The Auditor General Act, the Office of the Auditor General is an independent office of the Legislative Assembly. Through audit of management practices & accountability reports, the Office contributes to effective governance & public trust.

Auditor General, Norman J. Ricard, CA
Tel: 204-945-3790
Assistant Auditor General, VFM Audit Services, Sandra Cohen
Tel: 204-945-6896
Assistant Auditor General, Professional Practice, Greg MacBeth
Tel: 204-945-6883
Assistant Auditor General, Financial Statement Audits, Tyson D. Shtykalo
Tel: 204-945-1355
Assistant Auditor General, Investigations, Brian E. Wirth
Tel: 204-945-1620

Manitoba Civil Service Commission

#935, 155 Carlton St., Winnipeg, MB R3C 3H8
Tel: 204-945-2332; *Fax:* 204-945-1486
Toll-Free: 800-282-8069
TTY: 204-945-1437
csc@gov.mb.ca
www.gov.mb.ca/csc
Other Communication: Recruitment Support Services, Phone: 204-945-1334; Fax: 204-948-2193; E-mail: govjobs@gov.mb.ca

Minister Responsible; Minister, Finance, Hon. Cameron Friesen
Tel: 204-945-3952; *Fax:* 204-948-6057
minfin@leg.gov.mb.ca
Commissioner, Lynn Romeo
Assistant Deputy Minister, Corporate Services Division, Ilana Dadds
Tel: 204-945-1469

Associated Agencies, Boards & Commissions:

•Civil Service Commission Board
#935, 155 Carlton St.
Winnipeg, MB R3C 3H8
Tel: 204-945-1435; *Fax:* 204-945-1486

•Civil Service Superannuation Board
#1200, 444 St. Mary Ave.
Winnipeg, MB R3C 3T1
Tel: 204-946-3200
Toll-free: 800-432-5134
askus@cssb.mb.ca
www.cssb.mb.ca

Manitoba Education & Training

#168, Legislative Bldg., 450 Broadway, Winnipeg, MB R3C 0V8
Tel: 204-945-3720; *Fax:* 204-945-1291
minedu@leg.gov.mb.ca
www.edu.gov.mb.ca

Manitoba Education & Advanced Learning was renamed Education & Training after the 2016 general election.

Minister, Education & Training, Hon. Ian Wishart
Tel: 204-945-3720; *Fax:* 204-945-1291
minedu@leg.gov.mb.ca
Deputy Minister, Bramwell (Bram) Strain
Director, Private Vocational Institutions & Designation, Manitoba Student Aid, Riel Dion
Tel: 204-945-8502
Director, Schools' Finance Branch, Lynne Mavins
Tel: 204-945-4061
Program Director, Professional Certification & Student Records Unit, Allan Tataryn
Tel: 204-773-2998
Director, Education Administration Services, David Yeo
Tel: 204-945-8664

Associated Agencies, Boards & Commissions:

•Board of Reference

•Manitoba Ethnocultural Advisory & Advocacy Council (MEAAC)
215 Notre Dame Ave. 9th Fl.
Winnipeg, MB R3B 1N3
Tel: 204-945-2339
meaac@gov.mb.ca
www.gov.mb.ca/immigration/multiculturalism/meaac.html

•Multiculturalism Secretariat
213 Notre Dame Ave., 7th Fl.
Winnipeg, MB R3B 1N3
Tel: 204-945-5632
multisec@gov.mb.ca
www.gov.mb.ca/immigration/multiculturalism

•Public Schools Finance Board
#506, 1181 Portage Ave.
Winnipeg, MB R3G 0T3
Tel: 204-945-6628; *Fax:* 204-948-2001

•Teachers' Retirement Allowances Fund Board (TRAF)
#330 Johnston Terminal
35 Forks Market Rd.
Winnipeg, MB R3C 4S8
Tel: 204-949-0048; *Fax:* 204-944-0361
Toll-free: 800-782-0714
info@traf.mb.ca
www.traf.mb.ca

Administration & Finance

Acting Executive Director, Claude Fortier
Tel: 204-945-1117
Director, Innovative Technology Services, Calvin Hawley
Tel: 204-479-0873
Translator/French Language Coordinator, Translation Services, Rene Tondji-Simen
Tel: 204-945-6889

Adult Learning & Literacy

#350, 800 Portage Ave., Winnipeg, MB R3G 0N4
Tel: 204-945-8247; *Fax:* 204-948-1008
all@gov.mb.ca
www.gov.mb.ca/mal/all
Other Communication: Toll-Free Phone: 1-800-282-8069, ext. 8247

Executive Director, Nancy Buchanan
Tel: 204-945-4399
Director & Registrar, Programs, Monika Idzikowski
Tel: 204-945-6203

Division du Bureau de l'éducation française / French Language Education Office

#509, 1181 av Portage, Winnipeg, MB R3C 0T3
Tél: 204-945-6916; *Téléc:* 204-948-2997
www.edu.gov.mb.ca/m12/polapp/direction.html

Sous-ministre adjoint par interim, Marcel Berube
Tél: 204-945-6928
Directeur, Programmes de langues officielles et services administratifs, Kassy Assie
Tél: 204-945-6029
Directrice, La production de Bibliothèque et Matériaux, Lynette Chartier
Tél: 204-945-1342
Directrice par interim, Services de soutien en éducation, Sandy Drzystek
Tél: 204-945-6939
Directeur, Developpement et implantation des programmes, Gilbert Michaud
Tél: 204-945-6022

Immigration

#700, 213 Notre Dame Ave., Winnipeg, MB R3B 1N3
Tel: 204-945-2806
Toll-Free: 800-665-8332
immigratemanitoba@gov.mb.ca
www.immigratemanitoba.com
Other Communication: Immigrating to Manitoba, Phone: 204-945-6300

Assistant Deputy Minister, Immigration, Ben Rempel
Tel: 204-945-0077
Director, Provincial-Territorial Immigration Secretariat, Vanessa Arrojado
Tel: 204-945-1831
Director, Immigration & Employment Programs, Fanny Levy
Tel: 204-945-5935
Director, International Qualifications Recognition, Margot Morrish
Tel: 204-945-5906
Director, Settlement & Language Training, Liz Robinson
Tel: 204-945-5429
Director, Research, Legislation & Policy; FIPPA Access & Privacy Coordinator, Glenda Segal
Tel: 204-945-4889
Director, Business Immigration & Investment, Richard Zebinski
Tel: 204-945-8234
pnp-b@gov.mb.ca
www.manitoba.ca/businessimmigration

Manitoba Healthy Child Office

332 Bannatyne Ave., 3rd Fl., Winnipeg, MB R3A 0E2
Tel: 204-945-2266
Toll-Free: 888-848-0140
healthychild@gov.mb.ca
www.gov.mb.ca/healthychild

Office provides leadership & encourages actions that address health concerns & reduces the need for medical care for children. Following the 2016 general election, the Manitoba Healthy Child Office became part of Manitoba Education & Training.

Assistant Deputy Minister; Associate Secretary to Healthy Child Committee of Cabinet, Rob Santos
Tel: 204-945-8670
Executive Director, Programs & Administration, Susan Tessler
Tel: 204-945-1275
Director, Policy Development, Research & Evaluation, Leanne Boyd
Tel: 204-945-5447
Director, Parenting Initiatives, Steven Feldgaier
Tel: 204-945-3084

MB4Youth

Tel: 204-945-3556
www.gov.mb.ca/cyo/youth
Other Communication: Toll-Free Phone: 1-800-282-8069, ext. 3556

MB4Youth helps youth up to age 29 in Manitoba find employment through internships, grants, job referrals, mentorship & bursary opportunities & wage incentives, as well as striving to be the single source for all government youth programs & services. The organization works with youth, businesses, not-for-profit organizations, community groups, educational institutions, provincial departments & other levels of government to achieve these goals.

Director, Annette Willborn
Tel: 204-945-0371

School Programs Division

#307, 1181 Portage Ave., Winnipeg, MB R3G 0T3
Tel: 204-945-7934; *Fax:* 204-945-8303

Assistant Deputy Minister, Aileen Najduch
Tel: 204-945-7935
Chief Operating Officer, Manitoba Text Book Bureau, Brenda McKinny
Tel: 204-483-5035
Director, Program & Student Services, Allan Hawkins
Tel: 204-945-7911; *Fax:* 204-945-7914
Director, Instruction, Curriculum & Assessment, Daryl Gervais
Tel: 204-945-0294

Aboriginal Education Directorate

Murdo Scribe Centre, 510 Selkirk Ave., Winnipeg, MB R2W 2M7
Tel: 204-945-7886; *Fax:* 204-948-2010
aedinfo@gov.mb.ca
www.edu.gov.mb.ca/aed

The Aboriginal Education Directorate operates from within the following departments: Manitoba Education, Manitoba Advanced Education & Literacy & Manitoba Aboriginal & Northern Affairs.

Director, Helen Robinson-Settee
Tel: 204-945-4763
Assistant Director, Dino Altieri
Tel: 204-945-6181; *Fax:* 204-948-2010
dino.altieri@gov.mb.ca

Elections Manitoba

#120, 200 Vaughan St., Winnipeg, MB R3C 1T5
Tel: 204-945-3225; *Fax:* 204-945-6011
Toll-Free: 866-628-6837
election@elections.mb.ca
www.electionsmanitoba.ca
twitter.com/electionsMB
www.facebook.com/ElectionsManitoba

Independent from government, Elections Manitoba conducts fair elections. It ensures that political financing laws are followed, & increases public awareness of the electoral process

Chief Electoral Officer, Shipra Verma, CPA, CA
Tel: 204-945-3225
Commissioner of Elections, Bill Bowles
Tel: 204-944-9105; *Fax:* 204-947-1536
info@commissionerofelections.mb.ca
www.commissionerofelections.mb.ca
Note: The Commissioner of Elections is an independent officer, appointed by the Chief Electoral Officer; responsibility is to ensure compliance with & enforcement of The Elections Act & The Election Financing Act.
#5, 165 Kennedy St.
Winnipeg, MB R3C 1S6

Manitoba Families

Legislative Building, #357, 450 Broadway, Winnipeg, MB R3C 0V8
Tel: 204-945-3744
Toll-Free: 866-626-4862
TTY: 204-945-4796
www.gov.mb.ca/fs

Manitoba Family Services was renamed to Manitoba Families following the 2016 general election. The department supports citizens in need to achieve fuller participation in society & greater self-suffiency & independence. Helps keep children, families & communities safe & secure & promotes healthy citizen development & well-being. Mission is accomplished through: provision of financial support; provision of supports & services for adults & children with disabilities; provision of child protection & related services; assistance to people facing family violence or family disruption; provision of services & supports to promote the healthy development & well-being of children & families; assistance to Manitobans to access safe, appropriate & affordable housing; fostering community capacity & engaging the broader community to participate in & contribute to decision-making; & respectful & appropriate delivery of programs & services.

Minister, Families, Hon. Scott Fielding
Tel: 204-945-4337; *Fax:* 204-945-5149
minfs@leg.gov.mb.ca

Deputy Minister, Joy Cramer
Tel: 204-945-6704; *Fax:* 204-945-1896
dmfs@leg.gov.mb.ca

Legislative Assistant, Janice Morley-Lecomte
Tel: 204-945-2709; *Fax:* 204-945-1284
janice.morley-lecomte@leg.gov.mb.ca

Associated Agencies, Boards & Commissions:

•Advisory Council on Workplace Safety & Health
401 York Ave., 2nd Fl.
Winnipeg, MB R3C 0P8
Tel: 204-945-3446; *Fax:* 204-948-2209
Toll-free: 866-888-8186
wshcompl@gov.mb.ca
www.gov.mb.ca/labour/safety

•Board of Electrical Examiners
#500, 401 York Ave
Winnipeg, MB R3C 0P8
Tel: 204-945-3373; *Fax:* 204-948-2309

•Building Standards Board
Norquay Building
#508, 401 York Ave.
Winnipeg, MB R3C 0P8
Tel: 204-945-3322; *Fax:* 204-948-2089
Toll-free: 800-282-8069
firecomm@gov.mb.ca
www.firecomm.gov.mb.ca/codes_mbsb.html

•Construction Industry Wages Board
Norquay Building
#604, 401 York Ave.
Winnipeg, MB R3C 0P8
Tel: 204-945-3352; *Fax:* 204-948-3046
Toll-free: 800-821-4307

•Disabilities Issues Office
#630, 240 Graham Ave.
Winnipeg, MB R3C 0J7
Tel: 204-945-7613; *Fax:* 204-948-2896
TTY: 204-948-2901
dio@gov.mb.ca
www.gov.mb.ca/dio

•Elevator Board
Norquay Building
#500, 401 York Ave.
Winnipeg, MB R3C 0P8
Tel: 204-945-3373; *Fax:* 204-948-2309

•Propane Gas Advisory Board
Norquay Bldg.
#500, 401 York Ave.
Winnipeg, MB R3C 0P8
Tel: 204-945-3373; *Fax:* 204-948-2309

•Manitoba Labour Board
#500, 175 Hargrave St.
Winnipeg, MB R3C 3R8
Tel: 204-945-3783; *Fax:* 204-945-1296
mlb@gov.mb.ca
www.gov.mb.ca/labour/labbrd

•Manitoba Minimum Wage Board
614 - 401 York Ave.
Winnipeg, MB R3C 0P8
Tel: 204-945-8190; *Fax:* 204-948-2085
lmsd@gov.mb.ca
www.gov.mb.ca/labour/labmgt/wages/minwagbd.html

•Manitoba Women's Advisory Council
#409, 401 York Ave.
Winnipeg, MB R3C 0P8
Tel: 204-945-6281; *Fax:* 204-945-6511
Toll-free: 800-263-0234
msw@gov.mb.ca
www.gov.mb.ca/msw/mwac

•Pension Commission of Manitoba
#1004, 401 York Ave.
Winnipeg, MB R3C 0P8
Tel: 204-945-2740; *Fax:* 204-948-2375
TTY: 204-945-4796
pensions@gov.mb.ca
www.gov.mb.ca/labour/pension/index.html

•Power Engineers Advisory Board
Norquay Bldg.
#500, 401 York Ave.
Winnipeg, MB R3C 0P8
Tel: 204-945-3373; *Fax:* 204-948-2309

•Social Services Appeal Board
175 Hargrave St., 7th Fl.
Winnipeg, MB R3C 3R8
Tel: 204-945-3003; *Fax:* 204-945-1736
Toll-free: 800-282-8069
TTY: 204-948-2037
www.gov.mb.ca/fs/ssab

Administration & Finance
#500, 326 Broadway Ave., Winnipeg, MB R3C 0S5
Tel: 204-945-3242
fadmin@gov.mb.ca

Assistant Deputy Minister, Aurel Tess
Tel: 204-945-5943
Acting Director, Innovation, Information & Technology, Jody Black
Tel: 204-945-5494
Acting Director, Agency Accountability & Support Unit, Marilyn McEachern
Tel: 204-945-1109
Director, Innovation, Information & Technology, Brian Konopski
Tel: 204-945-4807
Director, Financial & Administrative Services, Wayne Pestun
Tel: 204-945-4005

Child & Family Services
#216, 114 Garry St., Winnipeg, MB R3C 4V4
Tel: 204-945-6656
cfsd@gov.mb.ca

Assistant Deputy Minister, Carolyn Loeppky
Tel: 204-945-3257
Acting Assistant Deputy Minister, Ben Van Haute
Tel: 204-945-3257
Acting Executive Director, Child Protection, Brian Ridd
Tel: 204-945-4575
Director, Community Support & Development, Tom Moody
Tel: 204-945-2345
Acting Director, Intersectoral Activities/Community Supports, Daphne Penrose
Tel: 204-945-5782
Chief Executive Officer, General Child & Family Services Authority, Debbie Besant

Community Service Delivery
#119, 114 Garry St., Winnipeg, MB R3C 4V4
Tel: 204-945-1634
csd@gov.mb.ca

Assistant Deputy Minister, Charlene Paquin
Tel: 204-945-2204
Executive Director, Rural & Northern Services, Debbie Besant
Tel: 204-945-4998
Executive Director, Winnipeg Services, Michelle Dubik
Tel: 204-945-2685
Executive Director, Child & Family Services of Central MB, Kathleen Wightman
Tel: 204-857-8751
Executive Director, Service Delivery Support, Tom Sidebottom
Tel: 204-945-1268
Director, Provincial Services, Kathy Brooks
Tel: 204-945-6854

Manitoba Developmental Centre
3rd St. NE, Portage la Prairie, MB R1N 3C6
Tel: 204-856-4200; *Fax:* 204-856-4258
Toll-Free: 800-473-4603
csd@gov.mb.ca
www.gov.mb.ca/fs/pwd/mdc

Chief Executive Officer, Cynthia Winram
Tel: 204-856-4237
Director, Administration & Operations, Alan Dell
Tel: 204-856-4247
Director, Speciality Programs, Brenda Solomon
Tel: 204-856-4206
Director, Habilitation/Specialty Program, Barb St. Goddard
Tel: 204-856-4223

Disability Programs & Early Learning & Child Care
c/o Disabilities Issues Office, #630, 240 Graham Ave., Winnipeg, MB R3C 0J7
Tel: 204-945-7613; *Fax:* 204-948-2896
TTY: 204-948-2901
dio@gov.mb.ca
www.gov.mb.ca/dio

Acting Assistant Deputy Minister, Denise Koss
Tel: 204-945-6374
Vulnerable Persons' Commissioner, JoAnne Reinsch
Tel: 204-945-0564
Acting Executive Director, Disability Programs, Carly Johnston
Tel: 204-945-3848
Director, Manitoba Early Learning & Child Care, Margaret Ferniuk
Tel: 204-945-2668

Manitoba Finance

#109, Legislative Bldg., Winnipeg, MB R3C 0V8
Tel: 204-945-3754
minfin@leg.gov.mb.ca
www.gov.mb.ca/finance

Established in 1969 under authority of the Financial Administration Act. Responsible for central accounting, payroll & financial reporting services for the government, consumer & corporate affairs & central financial control of cost-shared agreements. The ministry manages government borrowing programs & is responsible for federal-provincial relations.

Minister, Finance; Minister responsible, Civil Service Commission, Hon. Cameron Friesen
Tel: 204-945-3952; *Fax:* 204-948-6057
minfin@leg.gov.mb.ca

Deputy Minister, Finance; Deputy Minister, Crown Services, Jim Hrichishen
Tel: 204-945-5343; *Fax:* 204-945-1640
dmfin@leg.gov.mb.ca

Tax Appeals Commissioner, Dan Torbiak
Tel: 204-945-1002

Director, Insurance & Risk Management, Jim Swanson
Tel: 204-945-1919

Associated Agencies, Boards & Commissions:

•Crown Corporations Council / Conseil des corporations de la Couronne
#1130, 444 St. Mary Ave.
Winnipeg, MB R3C 3T1
Tel: 204-949-5270; *Fax:* 204-949-5283
info@crowncc.mb.ca
www.crowncc.mb.ca

•Deposit Guarantee Corporation of Manitoba
#390, 200 Graham Ave.
Winnipeg, MB R3C 4L5
Tel: 204-942-8480; *Fax:* 204-947-1723
Toll-free: 800-697-4447
mail@depositguarantee.mb.ca
depositguarantee.mb.ca

•Manitoba Securities Commission
#500, 400 St. Mary Ave.
Winnipeg, MB R3C 4K5
Tel: 204-945-2548; *Fax:* 204-945-0330
Toll-free: 800-655-5244
securities@gov.mb.ca
www.msc.gov.mb.ca

The Manitoba Securities Commission is an independent agency of the Government of Manitoba that protects investors & promotes fair & efficient capital markets throughout the province.

Comptroller Division
Provides central accounting, payroll & financial reporting services, & central financial control of cost-shared agreements for the government. The division develops government-wide financial systems, policies & procedures, & provides policy advice for financial & management systems. The division coordinates, develops & maintains departmental data processing systems, & provides direction to the government on the effective use of information systems technology

Provincial Comptroller, Betty-Anne Pratt
Tel: 204-945-4919
Director, Internal Audit & Consulting Services, Jane Holatko
Tel: 204-945-8110
Director, All Charities Campaign, Debra Laturnus
Tel: 204-945-5621
Director, Disbursements & Accounting, Terry Patrick
Tel: 204-945-1343

Corporate Services Division
Assistant Deputy Minister, Ilana Dadds
Tel: 204-945-1469

Executive Director, Information Communication Technology Shared Services Branch, Michael Antonio
Tel: 204-232-3560
Director, Information Support Services for CSC, Phong Duong
Tel: 204-391-1535
Acting Director, Corporate Policy Branch, Silvester Komlodi
Tel: 204-945-3960

Fiscal Research Division
#910, 386 Broadway, Winnipeg, MB R3C 3R6
Tel: 204-945-3757; *Fax:* 204-945-5051
www.gov.mb.ca/finance/fedprov

Provides research & analytical support for national/provincial fiscal & economic matters & inter-governmental financial relations. Also administers fiscal arrangements & tax collection agreements with the federal government & tax credit programs with federal & municipal governments

Assistant Deputy Minister, Richard Groen
Tel: 204-945-1476
Director, Economic & Fiscal Analysis, Narendra Budhia
Tel: 204-945-5078
Director, Federal Provinical Relations, Lezlee Dunn
Tel: 204-945-2947

Manitoba Financial Services Agency (MFSA)
c/o Financial Institutions Regulation Branch, #207, 400 St. Mary Ave., Winnipeg, MB R3C 4K5
Tel: 204-945-2542; *Fax:* 204-948-2268
Toll-Free: 800-282-8069
insurance@gov.mb.ca
www.mbfinancialinstitutions.ca

As part of the MFSA, the Financial Institutions Regulation Branch (FIRB) is responsible for administering The Insurance Act, The Credit Unions & Caisses Populaires Act, The Cooperatives Act & Part XXIV of The Corporations Act. The Manitoba Securities Commission is also part of the MFSA.

Chief Administrative Officer, Donald Murray
Tel: 204-945-2551
Superintendent, Financial Institutions, Jim Scalena
Tel: 204-945-3911
Deputy Superintendent, Insurance, Scott Moore
Tel: 204-945-1150

Priorities & Planning Secretariat
Executive Director, Planning, Jim August
Tel: 204-945-1116
Secretary / Executive Director, Policy, Tom Garrett
Tel: 204-945-0346
Director, Jamie Dumont
Tel: 204-945-5379
Director, Nammi Poorooshasb
Tel: 204-945-0460

Taxation Division
#101, 401 York Ave., Winnipeg, MB R3C 0P8
Tel: 204-945-5603; *Fax:* 204-945-0896
Toll-Free: 800-782-0318
www.gov.mb.ca/finance/taxation

Treasury Board Secretariat
#200, 386 Broadway, Winnipeg, MB R3C 3R6
Tel: 204-945-4150; *Fax:* 204-948-4878
www.gov.mb.ca/finance/tb

The Treasury Board Secretariat provides financial and analytical support and advice to the Minister of Finance and Treasury Board.

Secretary to the Treasury Board, Lynn Zapshala-Kelln
Tel: 204-945-1102
Assistant Deputy Minister, Analysis & Strategic Management, Chris Roed
Tel: 204-945-1524
Assistant Deputy Minister, Fiscal Management & Capital Planning, Giselle Martel
Tel: 204-945-1096

Treasury Division
#350, 363 Broadway, Winnipeg, MB R3C 3N9
Tel: 204-945-3702; *Fax:* 204-948-2233
www.gov.mb.ca/finance/treasury

Created as a separate entity in 1976, to address the need for placing greater emphasis on the management of substantial amounts of money, debt & investments. Currency & interest rate risk management programs have been developed due to the increase in volumes & dollar values. The division assists with the arrangement of financing for municipalities, schools & hospitals

Assistant Deputy Minister, Garry Steski
Tel: 204-945-6637
Director, Risk Management & Banking Branch, Lynne Peloquin
Tel: 204-945-0363
Director, Capital Markets, Don Delisle
Tel: 204-945-5404
Director, Treasury Operations, Scott Wiebe
Tel: 204-945-6677

Manitoba Growth, Enterprise & Trade

The Paris Building, 259 Portage Ave., 9th Fl., Winnipeg, MB R3B 3P4
Tel: 204-945-1995; *Fax:* 204-945-2964
www.gov.mb.ca/jec

Manitoba Jobs & the Economy was renamed Manitoba Growth, Enterprise & Trade after the 2016 general election. The department's mission is to support the growth of business in the province, to meet provincial labour demands, to increase training opportunities & to expand global trade relations.

Minister, Growth, Enterprise & Trade, Hon. Cliff Cullen
Tel: 204-945-0067; *Fax:* 204-945-4882
minget@leg.gov.mb.ca
Deputy Minister, James Wilson
Legislative Assistant, Kelly Bindle
Tel: 204-945-3709; *Fax:* 204-945-1284
kelly.bindle@leg.gov.mb.ca

Associated Agencies, Boards & Commissions:

•Apprenticeship & Certification Board
#100, 111 Lombard Ave.
Winnipeg, MB R3B OT4
Tel: 204-945-3337; *Fax:* 204-948-2539
www.gov.mb.ca/wdis/apprenticeship/boardpac
The Board is an advisory body which makes recommendations regarding the designation & regulation of trades & which approves apprenticeship training standards.

•Companies Office Advisory Board
#1010, 405 Broadway
Winnipeg, MB R3C 3L6
Tel: 204-945-2500; *Fax:* 204-945-1459
Toll-free: 888-246-8353
companies@gov.mb.ca
www.companiesoffice.gov.mb.ca

•Convention Centre Corporation Board of Directors
375 York Ave.
Winnipeg, MB R3C 3J3
Tel: 204-956-1720; *Fax:* 204-943-0310
Toll-free: 800-565-7776
audra@wcc.mb.ca
The Board manages & administers the affairs of the corporation.

•Industrial Technology Centre
#200, 78 Innovation Dr.
Winnipeg, MB R3T 6C2
Tel: 204-480-3333; *Fax:* 204-480-0345
Toll-free: 800-728-7933
tech@itc.mb.ca
www.itc.mb.ca

•Manitoba Education, Research & Learning Information Networks (MERLIN)
University of Manitoba
#100, 135 Innovation Dr.
Winnipeg, MB R3T 6A8
Tel: 204-474-7800; *Fax:* 204-474-7830
Toll-free: 800-430-6404
www.merlin.mb.ca

•Manitoba Opportunity Fund (MOF)
#600, 259 Portage Ave.
Winnipeg, MB R3B 2A9
Tel: 204-945-1872
MOF holds and invests the Provincial allocation of immigrants investments made through the Federal Department of Citizenship and Immigration Canada's Immigrant Investor Program.

•Manitoba Taking Charge! Inc.
276 Colony St.
Winnipeg, MB R3C 1W3
Tel: 204-945-1100; *Fax:* 204-925-1105
Taking Charge! Inc. is a non-profit organization under the leadership & direction of a Board of Directors that also oversees the employment programming & Taking Care, the licensed day care.

Administration & Finance Division
Assistant Deputy Minister, Corporate Services, Craig Halwachs
Tel: 204-945-3675
Acting Executive Director, Financial & Administrative Corporate Services, Melissa Ballantyne
Tel: 204-945-7281
Director, Information Technology, Wilma Wong
Tel: 204-945-4596

Manitoba Bureau of Statistics (MBS)
#824, 155 Carlton St., Winnipeg, MB R3C 3H9
Tel: 204-945-2406
www.gov.mb.ca/mbs

Chief Statistician, Wilf Falk
Tel: 204-945-2988
Labour Market & Survey Statistician, Melissa Luff
Tel: 204-945-2985
Demographics & Census Statistician, Tara Newton
Tel: 204-945-2406
tnewton@mbs.gov.mb.ca

Business Transformation & Technology
#1100, 215 Garry St., Winnipeg, MB R3C 3Z1
Tel: 204-945-2342; *Fax:* 204-948-3385
btt@gov.mb.ca
ww.gov.mb.ca/jec/busdev/btt/index.html

Assistant Deputy Minister, Vacant
Executive Director, ICT Service Delivery Infrastructure Services, Ric Coy
Tel: 204-945-2324
Executive Director, Business Operations, Marion Guinn
Tel: 204-945-7629
Acting Manager, Customer Service, Kathy Kupfer
Tel: 204-232-0652
Executive Director, Business Transformation, Shannon Roe
Tel: 204-945-6829

Entrepreneurship Manitoba
#1010, 405 Broadway, Winnipeg, MB R3C 3L6
Tel: 204-945-8200
Toll-Free: 855-836-7250
embinfo@gov.mb.ca
www.gov.mb.ca/ctt/emb
Other Communication: Business & Corporate Inquiries & Feedback, Phone: 204-945-2500; Fax: 204-945-1459; Toll-Free Phone: 1-888-246-8353

To encourage & facilitate entrepreneurial & employment opportunities within the Province through the establishment of new businesses or the expansion/retention of existing Manitoba businesses. The Branch promotes increased access to capital for industry by serving as a principal source of financial advice & assistance for businesses to expand or locate in Manitoba. The Branch develops & administers a number of third party delivered pools of risk capital.

Director, Companies Office, Myron Pawlowsky
Tel: 204-945-4206
Director, Small Business Development, Tony Romeo
Tel: 204-945-2019
Deputy Director, Legal, Companies Office, Stacey Belding
Tel: 204-945-4994
Senior Manager, Competitiveness Initiatives, Paul Pierlot
Tel: 204-945-5633
Chief Financial Officer, Companies Office, David Rudy
Tel: 204-945-2650

Business Services Division
#250, 240 Graham Ave., Winnipeg, MB R3C 0J7
Tel: 204-945-8200
TTY: 855-836-7250
EMBinfo@gov.mb.ca

Senior Executive Director, Financial Services, James Kilgour
Tel: 204-945-7626
Senior Manager, Industry Consulting & Marketing Support, David Sprange
Tel: 204-945-7938

Legislative Building Information Systems
Office Manager, Corazon Magnayon
Tel: 204-945-6219

Science, Innovation & Business Development
ww.gov.mb.ca/jec/busdev/sibd
Senior Executive Director, Douglas McCartney
Tel: 204-945-6298
Director, Research & Innovation Policy, Thomas Penner
Tel: 204-945-0152

Trade & International Relations
Executive Director, Manitoba Trade & Investment, Don Callis
Tel: 204-945-8695
Director, Canada-US & International Relations, Elliott Brown
Tel: 204-945-5346
Senior Manager, Asia Pacific, Charles Daniels
Tel: 204-945-7820
Senior Manager, Trade Operations, Sean Hogan
Tel: 204-945-1639

Workforce Development & Income Support
Assistant Deputy Minister, Jan Foster
Tel: 204-945-3990
Executive Director, Industry Services, Wayne Copet
Tel: 204-945-5452
Executive Director, Employment & Income Assistance Programs, Dave Fisher
Tel: 204-945-8730
Executive Director, Technology, Training & Information Services, Cheryl Lavallee
Tel: 204-945-7103
Executive Director, Apprenticeship Manitoba, Pierrette Buisson
Tel: 204-945-8501

Director, Employment & Training Services, Shelley Biblow
Tel: 204-945-1040
Director, Policy & Program Development, Catherine Gates
Tel: 204-945-0028
Director, Industry Services, Lynn Houghton
Tel: 204-945-0122
Director, Quality Assurance & Program Support, Darren Macdonald
Tel: 204-945-5660
Director, Technology Services, Ken Sanderson
Tel: 204-945-5708

Manitoba Health, Seniors & Active Living

#100, 300 Carlton St., Winnipeg, MB R3B 3M9
Tel: 204-945-3744
Toll-Free: 866-626-4862
mgi@gov.mb.ca
www.gov.mb.ca/health/index.html

Renamed Health, Seniors & Active Living after the 2016 general election, the department is responsible for the overall quality of the health system in the province, for maintaining the health system, & for ensuring that the health needs of Manitobans are met. Services are provided through regional delivery systems, hospitals & other health care facilities. The Department also makes insured benefits claims payments for residents of Manitoba related to the cost of medical, hospital, personal care, pharmacare & other health services. To lead the way to quality health care, built with creativity, compassion, confidence, trust & respect; empower Manitobans through knowledge, choices & access to the best possible health resources; & build partnerships & alliances for healthy & supportive communities. To foster innovation in the health care system. This is accomplished through: developing mechanisms to assess & monitor quality of care, utilization & cost effectiveness; fostering behaviours & environments which promote health; & promoting responsiveness & flexibility of delivery systems, & alternative & less expensive services.

Minister, Health, Seniors & Active Living, Hon. Kelvin Goertzen
Tel: 204-945-3731; *Fax:* 204-945-0441
minhsal@leg.gov.mb.ca
Deputy Minister, Karen Herd
Tel: 204-945-3771; *Fax:* 204-945-4564
dmhlt@leg.gov.mb.ca
Chief Provincial Public Health Officer, Dr. Michael Routledge, M.D., M.Sc., C.C.F.P., F.R.C.P.C.
Tel: 204-788-6636
Deputy Chief Provincial Public Health Officer, Dr. Elise Weiss, M.D., C.C.F.P., F.C.F.P., M.Sc.
Tel: 204-788-6636

Associated Agencies, Boards & Commissions:

•Addictions Foundation of Manitoba (AFM) / Fondation manitobaine de lutte contre les dépendances
1031 Portage Ave.
Winnipeg, MB R3G 0R8
Tel: 204-944-6236; *Fax:* 204-944-7082
Toll-free: 866-638-2561
execoff@afm.mb.ca
www.afm.mb.ca
Other Communication: General Inquiries, Phone: 204-944-6200; Library, E-mail: library@afm.mb.ca

•Appeal Panel for Home Care
c/o Manitoba Health Appeal Board
#102, 500 Portage Ave.
Winnipeg, MB R3C 3X1
Tel: 204-945-5408; *Fax:* 204-948-2024
Toll-free: 866-744-3257
appeals@gov.mb.ca
www.gov.mb.ca/health/appealboard/appeals.html

•Automobile Injury Compensation Appeal Commission
#301, 428 Portage Ave.
Winnipeg, MB R3C 0E2
Tel: 204-945-4155; *Fax:* 204-948-2402
Toll-free: 800-282-8069
autoinjury@gov.mb.ca
www.gov.mb.ca/cca/auto
Other Communication: Toll-Free Phone: 1-800-282-8069, ext. 4155

•CancerCare Manitoba (CCMB)
Tel: 204-787-2197
Toll-free: 866-561-1026
www.cancercare.mb.ca
Other Communication: Twitter: twitter.com/cancercaremb

•Claimant Adviser Office (CAO)
#200, 330 Portage Ave.
Winnipeg, MB R3C 0C4
Tel: 204-945-7413; *Fax:* 204-948-3157
TTY: 800-855-0511
cao@gov.mb.ca
www.gov.mb.ca/cca/claimant
Other Communication: Toll-Free Phone: 1-800-282-8069, ext. 7413

•Funeral Board of Manitoba
254 Portage Ave.
Winnipeg, MB R3C 0B6
Tel: 204-947-1098; *Fax:* 204-945-0424
funeralboard@gov.mb.ca
www.gov.mb.ca/funeraldirectorsboard

•Health Information Privacy Committee (HIPC)
#4043, 300 Carlton St.
Winnipeg, MB R3B 3M9
www.gov.mb.ca/health/hipc

•Hearing Aid Board
#302, 258 Portage Ave.
Winnipeg, MB R3C 0B6
Tel: 204-945-3800; *Fax:* 204-945-0728
Toll-free: 800-782-0067

•Manitoba Association of Architects Council
137 Bannatyne Ave., 2nd Fl.
Winnipeg, MB R3B 0R3
Tel: 204-925-4620; *Fax:* 204-925-4624
info@mbarchitects.org
www.mbarchitects.org/council.php

•Manitoba Council on Aging
#1610, 155 Carlton St.
Winnipeg, MB R3C 3H8
Tel: 204-945-6565
Toll-free: 800-665-6565
seniors@gov.mb.ca
www.gov.mb.ca/shas/manitobacouncil

•Manitoba Drug Standards & Therapeutics Committee (MDSTC)
#1014, 300 Carlton St.
Winnipeg, MB R3B 3M9
Tel: 204-786-7233
www.gov.mb.ca/health/mdbif/review.html
Other Communication: Toll-Free Phone: 1-800-297-8099, ext. 7233

•Manitoba Health Appeal Board
#102, 500 Portage Ave.
Winnipeg, MB R3C 3X1
Tel: 204-945-5408; *Fax:* 204-948-2024
Toll-free: 866-744-3257
appeals@gov.mb.ca
www.gov.mb.ca/health/appealboard
Quasi-judicial body responsible for making decisions on appeals under The Health Services Insurance Act, The Ambulance Services Act & The Mental Health Act.

•Manitoba Liquor Control Commission
See Entry Name Index for detailed listing.

•Residential Tenancies Commission
#1650, 155 Carlton St.
Winnipeg, MB R3C 3H8
Tel: 204-945-2028; *Fax:* 204-945-5453
Toll-free: 800-782-8403
rtc@gov.mb.ca
www.gov.mb.ca/cca/residtc

Administration & Finance

Acting Associate Deputy Minister & Chief Financial Officer, Nardia Maharaj
Tel: 204-788-2525
Controller, Tony Messner
Tel: 204-786-7135
Acting Executive Director, Finance, Rhonda Hogg
Tel: 204-788-7138
Executive Director, Health Information Management, Deborah Malazdrewicz
Tel: 204-786-7149
Executive Director, Management Services, Scott Murray
Tel: 204-786-7230
Acting Director, Regional Finance, Jason Perez
Tel: 204-788-6393
Acting Director, Management Services, Ron Oberlin
Tel: 204-786-7312

Health Workforce Secretariat

Assistant Deputy Minister, Bethy Beaupre
Tel: 204-786-6674
Executive Director, Medical Labour Relations, Lori Kroeker
Tel: 204-786-7277
Director, Health Human Resource Planning, Sean Brygidyr
Tel: 204-788-6767
Director, Fee for Service/Insured Benefits, Gayle Martens
Tel: 204-788-6623
Director, Contracts & Negotiations, Pearl Reimer
Tel: 204-788-6374

Healthy Living & Seniors

c/o Seniors & Healthy Aging Secretariat, #1610, 155 Carlton St., Winnipeg, MB R3C 3H8
Tel: 204-945-6565; *Fax:* 204-948-2514
Toll-Free: 800-665-6565
seniors@gov.mb.ca
www.gov.mb.ca/healthyliving

Assistant Deputy Minister, Marcia Thomson
Tel: 204-784-3908
Executive Director, Addictions Policy & Support Branch, Tina Leclair
Tel: 204-784-3913
Executive Director, Mental Health & Spiritual Health Care, Carly Johnston
Tel: 204-786-7281
Executive Director, Healthy Living & Healthy Populations, Debbie Nelson
Tel: 204-788-6654

Provincial Policy & Programs

Fax: 204-775-3712

Assistant Deputy Minister, Bernadette Preun
Tel: 204-788-6439
Executive Director, Capital Planning, Norman Blackie
Tel: 204-788-6691
Executive Director, Provincial Drug Programs, Robert Shaffer
Tel: 204-786-7333
Acting Director, Information Systems, Kevin Dack
Tel: 204-788-2518
Director, Corporate Services, Jeff Gunter
Tel: 204-788-6749
Acting Director, Drug Management Policy, Jeff Onyskiw
Tel: 204-788-6436
Acting Manager, Protection for Persons in Care, Chris Campbell
Tel: 204-786-7264
Coordinator, French Language Services, Richard Loiselle
Tel: 204-788-6698; *Fax:* 204-772-2943

Public Health & Primary Health Care

300 Carlton St., 4th Floor, Winnipeg, MB R3B 3M9
Tel: 204-788-6666
www.gov.mb.ca/health/publichealth
Other Communication: Primary Care, Phone: 204-788-6732; Fax: 204-943-5305; E-mail: phc@gov.mb.ca; URL: www.gov.mb.ca/health/primarycare

Mission is to encourage the prevention of illness & injury, coordinate access to health care, & strengthen existing primary health care services with new initiatives

Assistant Deputy Minister, Avis Gray
Tel: 204-788-6656
Medical Officer of Health, Immunization Strategy & STBBI, Denise Koh
Tel: 204-788-6794
Executive Director, First Nations, Metis & Inuit Health, Barry Mathers
Tel: 204-788-6647
Executive Director, Public Health Programs & Strategies, Anita Moore
Tel: 204-788-6781
Director, Primary Health Care, Kristin Anderson
Tel: 204-788-6746
Acting Director, Communicable Disease Control, Richard Baydack
Tel: 204-788-6715
Lead Epidemiologist & Director, Epidemiology & Surveillance, Patricia Caetano
Tel: 204-788-6700
Director, Northern Nursing Stations, Kim Hutcheson
Tel: 204-788-6642
Director, Northern Health, Jennifer White
Tel: 204-788-6429
Director, Environment Health & Emergency Preparedness, Peter Parys
Tel: 204-788-6745
Director, Maternal & Child Health, Val Steeves
Tel: 204-788-6364

Regional Policy & Programs

Assistant Deputy Minister, Jean Cox
Tel: 204-786-7301
Acting Chief Provincial Psychiatrist, Hugh Andrew
Tel: 204-788-6677
Chief Provincial Psychiatrist, Richard Zloty
Tel: 204-788-6677
Executive Director, Continuing Care, Lorraine Dacombe Dewar
Tel: 204-788-6649

Executive Director, Health Emergency Management, Gerry Delorme
Tel: 204-945-6382
Executive Director, Acute, Tertiary & Specialty Care, Brie DeMone
Tel: 204-788-6331
Executive Director, Provincial Cancer & Diagnostic Services Branch, Teresa Mrozek
Tel: 204-786-7358
Executive Director, Urban Regional Support Services, Vacant
Acting Director, Office of Disaster Management, Barbara Crumb
Tel: 204-945-4228
Director, Continuing Care, Hana Forbes
Tel: 204-786-7323
Acting Director, Emergency Medical Services, Brenda Gregory
Tel: 204-945-0711
Director, MTCC, John Jones
Tel: 204-571-8863
Director, Diagnostic Services, Provincial Cancer & Diagnostic Services Branch, Michele Mathae-Hunter
Tel: 204-788-6628
Director, Office of Provincial Renal, Transplant & Transfusion Services, Wendy Peppel
Tel: 204-786-7374
Director, Provincial Blood Programs, Carol Renner
Tel: 204-786-6353

Associated Agencies, Boards & Commissions:

•Interlake-Eastern Regional Health Authority
233A Main St.
Selkirk, MB R1A 1S1
Tel: 204-785-4700; *Fax:* 204-482-4300
Toll-free: 855-347-8500
info@ierha.ca
www.ierha.ca

•Northern Health Region
84 Church St.
Flin Flon, MB R8A 1L8
Tel: 204-687-1300; *Fax:* 204-687-6405
Toll-free: 888-340-6742

•Prairie Mountain Health
192 - 1st Ave. West
PO Box 579
Souris, MB R0K 2C0
Tel: 204-483-5000; *Fax:* 204-483-5005
Toll-free: 888-682-2253
pmh@pmh-mb.ca
pmh-mb.ca

•Southern Health / Santé Sud
94 Principale St.
PO Box 470
La Broquerie, MB R0A 0W0
Tel: 204-424-5880; *Fax:* 204-424-5888
Toll-free: 800-742-6509
info@southernhealth.ca
www.southernhealth.ca

•Winnipeg Regional Health Authority
650 Main St., 4th Fl.
Winnipeg, MB R3B 1E2
Tel: 204-926-7000; *Fax:* 204-926-7007
www.wrha.mb.ca

Manitoba Housing & Community Development

352 Donald St., Winnipeg, MB R3B 2H8
Tel: 204-945-4663; *Fax:* 204-948-2013
Toll-Free: 800-661-4663
housing@gov.mb.ca
www.gov.mb.ca/housing

Minister, Families, Hon. Scott Fielding
Tel: 204-945-4337; *Fax:* 204-945-5149
minfs@leg.gov.mb.ca
Deputy Minister, Families, Joy Cramer
Tel: 204-945-6704; *Fax:* 204-945-1896
dmfs@leg.gov.mb.ca

Associated Agencies, Boards & Commissions:

•ALL Aboard Committee
Tel: 204-945-3380
allaboard@gov.mb.ca
www.gov.mb.ca/allaboard

•Cooperative Loans & Loans Guarantee Board
#400, 352 Donald St.
Winnipeg, MB R3B 2H8
Tel: 204-945-3379; *Fax:* 204-948-1065
Toll-free: 866-479-6155
co-ops@gov.mb.ca
www.gov.mb.ca/housing/coop/coop_loanboard.html

•Cooperative Promotion Board
B18, 25 Tupper St.
Portage La Prairie, MB R1N 3K1
Tel: 204-239-3883; *Fax:* 204-239-3690
Toll-free: 866-479-6155
co-ops@gov.mb.ca
www.gov.mb.ca/housing/coop/coop_promoboard.html

•Manitoba Community Services Council, Inc. (MCSC)
#102, 90 Garry St.
Winnipeg, MB R3C 4H1
Tel: 204-940-4450; *Fax:* 204-453-2692
applications@mbcsc.ca
www.mbcsc.ca

Community Development & Strategic Initiatives
Assistant Deputy Minister, Community Development & Strategic Initiatives, Craig Marchinko
Tel: 204-945-6975
Executive Director, Integrated Community Initiatives Branch, Lissa Donner
Tel: 204-945-3312
Executive Director, Community & Cooperative Development, Joy Goertzen
Tel: 204-945-1147
Director, Community Relations Branch, Nadine Delisle
Tel: 204-945-4464
Director, Community Places, Mark Ranson
Tel: 204-945-1374

Corporate Services
Assistant Deputy Minister & Chief Financial Officer, Vacant
Executive Director, Corporate Management Services Branch, Sherry Zajac
Tel: 204-945-0032
Director, Financial Services, Brian Brown
Tel: 204-945-4699
Director, Legal Services & Corporate Secretary, Azim Jiwa
Tel: 204-945-7495

Manitoba Housing
www.gov.mb.ca/housing/about_mbhousing.html
Chief Executive Officer, Darrell Jones
Tel: 204-945-7647
Chief Operating Officer, Social Housing Management, Steven Spry
Tel: 204-945-5529
Executive Director, Asset Management, Brent Timmerman
Tel: 204-945-6887
Executive Director, Property Services, Gord Thomas
Tel: 204-945-7716
Director, Procurement, Gina Barnett
Tel: 204-945-2573
Director, Capital Planning & Project Management, David Besant
Tel: 204-945-5674
Director, Security, David Grayston
Tel: 204-945-5880
Director, Tenant Services, Lisa May
Tel: 204-945-8129
Acting Director, Portfolio Administration, Pat Moore
Tel: 204-945-8290
Director, Land Development, Dwayne Rewniak
Tel: 204-945-4703

Manitoba Human Rights Commission (MHRC)

#700, 175 Hargrave St., Winnipeg, MB R3C 3R8
Tel: 204-945-3007; *Fax:* 204-945-1292
Toll-Free: 888-884-8681
TTY: 888-897-2811
hrc@gov.mb.ca
www.manitobahumanrights.ca
www.facebook.com/ManitobaHumanRightsCommission

Chair, Yvonne Peters

Manitoba Hydro

360 Portage Ave., PO Box 815 Stn. Main, Winnipeg, MB R3C 2P4
Tel: 204-480-5900; *Fax:* 204-360-6155
Toll-Free: 888-624-9376
TTY: 855-287-6809
publicaffairs@hydro.mb.ca
www.hydro.mb.ca
twitter.com/manitobahydro
www.facebook.com/ManitobaHydro
www.linkedin.com/company/manitoba-hydro
www.youtube.com/user/ManitobaHydro

Manitoba Hydro (MH) is a major energy utility. One of the largest electricity & natural gas utilities in Canada, it serves 561,869 electric customers throughout Manitoba & 274,817 gas customers in various communities throughout southern Manitoba. Virtually all electricity generated by the provincial Crown Corporation is from self-renewing water power. MH is the major distributor of natural gas in the province. Developing & implementing an environmental management system consistent with ISO standards. Actively pursuing a vairety or projects & programs aimed at reducing GHG & vehicle emissions, recycling, conserving energy, digging out contaminated soils, partnering with NGOs.

Chair, H. Sanford Riley
President & CEO, Kelvin Shepherd
Vice-President, Corporate Relations, Ruth Kristjanson
Vice-President, Customer Care & Energy Conservation, Lloyd Kuczek
Vice-President, Human Resources & Corporate Services, Bryan Luce
Vice-President, Transmission, Shane Mailey
Vice-President, Finance & Regulatory, Darren Rainkie
Vice-President, Customer Service & Distribution, Brent Reed
Vice-President, General Counsel & Corporate Secretary, Ken Tennenhouse
Vice-President, Corporate Communications & Public Affairs, Siobhan Vinish

Manitoba Indigenous & Municipal Relations

Legislative Bldg, #344, 450 Broadway, Winnipeg, MB R3C 0V8
Tel: 204-945-3719; *Fax:* 204-945-8374
anaweb@gov.mb.ca
www.gov.mb.ca/ana

Aboriginal & Northern Affairs was renamed Indigenous & Municipal Relations following the 2016 general election. The department's goals are as follows: to improve the quality of life & opportunities for Aboriginal & Northern people; to facilitate better services, opportunities & results for Manitoba's Aboriginal & northern people; to support the mental, emotional, physical & spiritual health of northern communities & Aboriginal people; to resolve outstanding provincial obligations to Aboriginal/northern communities; to foster self-determination, accountability & sustainable growth; & to strengthen the participation of Aboriginal & northern people in Manitoba's economy.

Minister, Indigenous & Municipal Relations, Hon. Eileen Clarke
Tel: 204-945-3788; *Fax:* 204-945-1383
minim@leg.gov.mb.ca
Deputy Minister, Municipal Relations; Associate Clerk, Executive Council, Fred Meier
Deputy Minister, Indigenous Relations, Robert Wavey
Director, Finance & Administrative Services, Angel Anderson
Tel: 204-677-6609
Director, Sports Secretariat, Michael Benson
Tel: 204-945-8834

Associated Agencies, Boards & Commissions:

•Northern Affairs Capital Approval Board
PO Box 2532
The Pas, MB R9A 1M3

•Communities Economic Development Fund (CEDF)
15 Moak Cres.
Thompson, MB R8N 2B8
Tel: 204-778-4138; *Fax:* 204-778-4313
Toll-free: 800-561-4315
www.cedf.mb.ca

Aboriginal Affairs Secretariat
#200, 500 Portage Ave., Winnipeg, MB R3C 3X1
Tel: 204-945-2510; *Fax:* 204-945-3689
Director, Policy & Strategic Initiatives, Eleanor Brockington
Tel: 204-945-0572
Director, Agreements Management, David Hicks
Tel: 204-945-2506
Acting Director, Aboriginal Consultation Unit, Jason Fontaine
Tel: 204-945-5120; *Fax:* 204-945-2274

Local Government Development Division
59 Elizabeth Dr., PO Box 33 Thompson, MB R8N 1X4
Tel: 204-677-6794; *Fax:* 204-677-6525

The Local Government Development Division provides support to 50 northern & remote communities, including public works, environmental services, & infrastructure development. It promotes cooperative, community-driven sustainable development.

Executive Director, Vacant
Tel: 204-677-6795
Director, Program Planning & Development - Winnipeg, Paul Doolan
Tel: 204-945-2161; *Fax:* 204-948-2389

Regional Offices

Dauphin
Provincial Bldg., 27 - 2nd Ave. SW, PO Box 15 Dauphin, MB R7N 3E5
Tel: 204-622-2110; *Fax:* 204-622-2305

Regional Director, Karen Barker
Tel: 204-622-2152
kbarker@gov.mb.ca

Thompson
59 Elizabeth Dr., PO Box 27 Thompson, MB R8N 1X4
Tel: 204-677-6786; *Fax:* 204-677-6525
Regional Director, Armand Barbeau
Tel: 204-677-6737

Manitoba Infrastructure

Legislative Building, #203, 450 Broadway Ave., Winnipeg, MB R3C 0V8
Tel: 204-945-3723; *Fax:* 204-945-7610
www.gov.mb.ca/mit

Manitoba Infrastructure & Transportation was renamed Manitoba Infrastructure after the 2016 general election.

Minister, Infrastructure, Hon. Blaine Pedersen
Tel: 204-945-3723; *Fax:* 204-945-7610
minmi@leg.gov.mb.ca
Deputy Minister, Lance Vigfusson
Legislative Assistant, Derek Johnson
Tel: 204-945-3709; *Fax:* 204-945-1284
derek.johnson@leg.gov.mb.ca

Associated Agencies, Boards & Commissions:

•Disaster Assistance Appeal Board
#1144, 363 Broadway
Winnipeg, MB R3C 3N9
Tel: 204-945-8550; *Fax:* 204-948-2235
Toll-free: 888-267-8298
emo@gov.mb.ca
www.gov.mb.ca/emo/home/dfa/appeal.html

•Highway Traffic Board/Motor Transport Board
#200, 301 Weston St.
Winnipeg, MB R3E 3H4
Tel: 204-945-8912; *Fax:* 204-783-6529
www.gov.mb.ca/mit/boards/traffic.html

•Manitoba East Side Road Authority (ESRA)
#200, 155 Carlton St.
Winnipeg, MB R3C 3H8
Tel: 204-945-4900; *Fax:* 204-948-2462
Toll-free: 866-356-6355
floodway@gov.mb.ca
www.floodwayauthority.mb.ca
The Authority oversees the safety, reliability & improvement of transportation services between communities on the east side of Lake Winnipeg & the the rest of the province.

•Manitoba Floodway Authority (MFA)
#200, 155 Carlton St.
Winnipeg, MB R3C 3H8
Tel: 204-945-4900; *Fax:* 204-948-2462
Toll-free: 866-356-6355
floodway@gov.mb.ca
www.floodwayauthority.mb.ca
Separate, independent, publicly accountable provincial agency that will manage the expansion & maintenance of the Red River Floodway on behalf of Manitobans.

•License Suspension Appeal Board/Medical Review Committee
#200, 301 Weston St.
Winnipeg, MB R3E 3H4
Tel: 204-945-7350; *Fax:* 204-948-2682
www.gov.mb.ca/mit/boards/medical.html

•Manitoba Land Value Appraisal Commission
#1144, 363 Broadway
Winnipeg, MB R3C 3N9
Tel: 204-945-5455; *Fax:* 204-948-2235
www.gov.mb.ca/mit/boards/land.html

Accommodation Services Division

Tel: 204-945-7532; *Fax:* 204-945-5933
Assistant Deputy Minister, Chris Hauch
Tel: 204-945-7535
Director, Green Building Coordination Team, Cindy Choy
Tel: 204-945-8665
Director, Real Estate & Contract Services, Andrea Clarke
Tel: 204-945-7588
Acting Director, Project Services, Michael Erlanger
Tel: 204-794-6052
Director, Major Capital Projects, Patrick Kuzyk
Tel: 204-945-1094
Director, Operations, Susanne Parent
Tel: 204-945-7528

Administrative Services Division

Tel: 204-945-6831; *Fax:* 204-945-5115
Assistant Deputy Minister, Ian Hasanally
Tel: 204-945-2964
Director, Financial Services, Jennifer Hibber
Tel: 204-945-3883
Acting Director, Information Technology Services, Brian LaPointe
Tel: 204-797-3564
Acting Director, Occupational Safety, Health & Risk Management, Tim Lucko
Tel: 204-803-1582
Acting Director, Corporate Information Branch; Director, Transformation & Innovation Office, Randy Pitz
Tel: 204-771-5390

Emergency Measures Organization (EMO)

#1525, 405 Broadway Ave., Winnipeg, MB R3C 3L6
Tel: 204-945-4772; *Fax:* 204-945-4929
Toll-Free: 888-267-8298
emo@gov.mb.ca
www.gov.mb.ca/emo
Other Communication: Disaster Financial Assistance, Phone: 204) 945-3050; Fax: 204) 948-2278; E-mail: dfa@gov.mb.ca
Coordinates emergency response, municipal emergency planning & training, & disaster recovery programs
Acting Executive Director, Lee Spencer
Tel: 204-945-4772
Director, Operations, Michael Gagne
Tel: 204-945-4772
Acting Director, Recovery, Christa Jacobucci
Tel: 204-945-2780
Director, Planning, Don Mackinnon
Tel: 204-945-4772

Engineering & Operations Division

Assistant Deputy Minister, Ron Weatherburn
Tel: 204-945-3775
Executive Director, Highway Engineering, Walter T. Burdz
Tel: 204-945-3772
Executive Director, Construction & Maintenance, Larry Halayko
Tel: 204-945-7035
Executive Director, Highway Regional Operations, Don McKibbin
Tel: 204-726-6807

Motor Carrier Division

Tel: 204-945-3890; *Fax:* 204-948-2078
Assistant Deputy Minister, Esther Nagtegaal
Tel: 204-945-5199
Executive Director, Darren Christie
Tel: 204-945-7693
Director, Motor Carrier Permits & Development, Sheila Champagne
Tel: 204-945-8909
Director, Motor Carrier Safety Programs, Bruce McCormick
Tel: 204-945-6651
Director, Motor Carrier Strategic Initiatives Branch, Lawrence Mercer
Tel: 204-945-1894

Supply & Services Division

Tel: 204-945-6343; *Fax:* 204-948-2509
Assistant Deputy Minister, Tracey Danowski
Tel: 204-791-0516
Chief Operating Officer, Materials Distribution Agency, David Bishop
Tel: 204-945-6043; *Fax:* 204-948-5077
#7, 1715 St. James St.
Winnipeg, MB R3H 1H3
Chief Operating Officer, Crown Lands & Property Agency, Grace Delong
Tel: 204-239-3561
Toll-free: 866-210-9589; *Fax:* 204-239-3560
#308, 25 Tupper St. North
POrtage la Prairie, MB R1N 3K1
Chief Operating Officer, Vehicle & Equipment Management Agency, Al Franchuk
Tel: 204-945-0275; *Fax:* 204-948-1109
626 Henry Ave.
Winnipeg, MB R3A 1P7

Transportation Policy Division

Tel: 204-945-6701; *Fax:* 204-945-5539
Assistant Deputy Minister, Esther Nagtegaal
Tel: 204-945-5199
Director, Transportation Policy & Service Development, Richard Danis
Tel: 204-945-0800
Acting Director, Transportation Systems Planning & Development, & Senior Tranportation Systems Planning Engineer, David B. Duncan
Tel: 204-945-3646
Director, Legislative & Regulatory Services, Lucille McLaughlin
Tel: 204-945-7996

Water Management & Structures Division

Assistant Deputy Minister, Doug McMahon
Tel: 204-945-3113
Chief Design Engineer, Al Nelson
Tel: 204-771-1507
Executive Director, Hydrologic Forecasting & Water Management, Steven Topping
Tel: 204-945-7488

Manitoba Justice & Attorney General

Administration & Finance, #1110, 405 Broadway Ave., Winnipeg, MB R3C 3L6
Tel: 204-945-2878
minjus@gov.mb.ca
www.gov.mb.ca/justice

Promotes a safe, just & peaceful society supported by a justice system that is fair, effective, trusted & understood by: providing a fair & effective prosecution service; managing offenders in an environment that promotes public safety & rehabilitation; providing mechanisms for timely & peaceful resolution of civil & criminal matters; providing legal advice & services to government; providing programs which assist in protecting & enforcing individual & collective rights; providing support & assistance to victims of crime; & promoting effective policing & crime prevention initiatives. Manitoba Justice employees may be reached by contacting Manitoba Government Inquiry, Phone: 204-945-3744; Toll-Free Phone: 1-866-626-4862; TTY: 204-945-4796; E-mail: mgi@gov.mb.ca; URL: www.gov.mb.ca/contact.

Deputy Premier; Keeper of the Great Seal; Minister, Justice & Attorney General, Hon. Heather Stefanson
Tel: 204-945-3728; *Fax:* 204-945-2517
minjus@leg.gov.mb.ca
Deputy Minister & Deputy Attorney General, Julie Frederickson

Associated Agencies, Boards & Commissions:

•Compensation for Victims of Crime
#1410, 405 Broadway
Winnipeg, MB R3C 3L6
Tel: 204-945-0899; *Fax:* 204-948-3071
Toll-free: 800-262-9344
www.gov.mb.ca/justice/victims/services/compensation.html
The Compensation for Victims of Crime Program provides compensation for personal injury or death resulting from certain crimes occurring within Manitoba.

•Law Enforcement Review Agency (LERA)
#420, 155 Carlton St.
Winnipeg, MB R3C 3H8
Tel: 204-945-8667; *Fax:* 204-948-1014
Toll-free: 800-282-8069
lera@gov.mb.ca
www.gov.mb.ca/justice/lera
The mission of the Law Enforcement Review Agency (LERA) is to deliver a judicious, timely, impartial, client-oriented service to the public and to the police services and police officers within its jurisdiction.

•Legal Aid Manitoba
287 Broadway, 4th Fl.
Winnipeg, MB R3C 0R9
Tel: 204-985-8500; *Fax:* 204-944-8582
Toll-free: 800-261-2960
info@legalaid.mb.ca
www.legalaid.mb.ca
Legal Aid Manitoba works to ensure people with low incomes have the protections guaranteed in Canada by the The Charter of Rights & Freedoms, enacted as part of The Constitution Act in 1982.

•Manitoba Criminal Code Review Board
#2, 408 York Ave.
Winnipeg, MB R3C 0P9
Tel: 204-945-4438

•Manitoba Human Rights Commission
See Entry Name Index for detailed listing.

•Manitoba Law Reform Commission
#432, 405 Broadway
Winnipeg, MB R3C 3L6
Tel: 204-945-2896; *Fax:* 204-948-2184
mail@manitobalawreform.ca
www.manitobalawreform.ca
The Manitoba Law Reform Commission is an independent agency of the Government of Manitoba established by The Law Reform Commission Act, C.C.S.M. c. L95. The Commission's duties are to inquire into & consider any matter relating to law in Manitoba with a view to making recommendations for the improvement, modernization & reform of law.

•Office of the Chief Medical Examiner
#210, 1 Wesley Ave.
Winnipeg, MB R3C 4C6
Tel: 204-945-2088
Toll-free: 800-282-8069
www.gov.mb.ca/justice/family/chief.html
Other Communication: After-Hours, Phone: 204-945-2088

The Chief Medical Examiner's Office investigates deaths where the cause is not readily known or when the death is a result of violence.

•**Office of the Public Trustee**
#500, 155 Carlton St.
Winnipeg, MB R3C 5R9
Tel: 204-945-2700; *Fax:* 204-948-2251
PGT@gov.mb.ca
www.gov.mb.ca/publictrustee
The Public Trustee of Manitoba is a provincial government Special Operating Agency that manages & protects the affairs of Manitobans who are unable to do so themselves & have no one else willing or able to act. This includes mentally incompetent & vulnerable adults, deceased estates, & children.

Civil Legal Services
Director, C. Lynn Romeo
Director, Constitutional Law, Heather Leonoff
Tel: 204-945-0679; *Fax:* 204-945-0053
Director, Family Law, Joan A. MacPhail, Q.C.
Tel: 204-945-0268
www.gov.mb.ca/justice/family/law
Other Communications: Toll-Free Phone: 1-800-282-8069, ext. 0268

Corrections Division
#810, 405 Broadway Ave., Winnipeg, MB R3C 3L6
Tel: 204-945-7804
www.gov.mb.ca/justice/criminal/corrections
Other Communication: Adult Corrections, Phone: 204-945-7309
Associate Deputy Minister, Greg Graceffo
Tel: 204-945-7291
Executive Director, Adult Probation Services, Bob Dojack
Tel: 204-945-0882; *Fax:* 204-945-5537
Executive Director, Community & Youth Corrections, Louis Goulet
Tel: 204-945-6063; *Fax:* 204-945-5537
Executive Director, Adult Custody, Ronald (Ron) Leslie
Tel: 204-945-6041; *Fax:* 204-948-2166

Courts Division
www.gov.mb.ca/justice/court
Assistant Deputy Minister, Shauna Curtin
Tel: 204-945-3027
Executive Director, Judicial Services, Karen Fulham
Tel: 204-945-0413
Executive Director, Winnipeg & Regional Courts, Debbie Baker
Tel: 204-945-5883

Criminal Justice Division
www.gov.mb.ca/justice/criminal
Assistant Deputy Minister, Mike Horn
Tel: 204-945-2887
Executive Director, Victim Services, Suzanne Gervais
Tel: 204-945-4589
Toll-free: 866-484-2846
suzanne.gervais@gov.mb.ca
www.gov.mb.ca/justice/victims/services

Legislative Counsel Division
#410, 405 Broadway Ave., Winnipeg, MB R3C 3L6
Legislative Counsel & Assistant Deputy Minister, Jake Harms
Tel: 204-945-1737; *Fax:* 204-945-1940
jake.harms@gov.mb.ca
Director, Legal Translation, Michel Nantel
Tel: 204-945-4597; *Fax:* 204-945-1940
michelalbert.nantel@gov.mb.ca

Prosecutions Division
#510, 405 Broadway Ave., Winnipeg, MB R3C 3L6
Tel: 204-945-2852
Assistant Deputy Attorney General, Michael Mahon
Tel: 204-945-2852
Director, Winnipeg Prosecutions, Jacqueline St. Hill
Tel: 204-945-3228
Director, Policy Development & Analysis, Vacant

Liquor & Gaming Authority of Manitoba (LGA)

#800, 215 Garry St., Winnipeg, MB R3C 3P3
Tel: 204-945-9400; *Fax:* 204-945-9450
Toll-Free: 800-782-0363
gaminglicence@LGAmanitoba.ca
lgamanitoba.ca
Other Communication: Liquor Licensing, Phone: 204-474-5619; Toll-Free Phone: 1-888-898-6522; E-mail: liquorlicence@LGAmanitoba.ca; Liquor Permits, E-mail: permit@LGAmanitoba.ca
The Liquor & Gaming Authority of Manitoba was created in 2014 with the merger of the Manitoba Gaming Control Commission & the Regulatory Services Division of the Manitoba Liquor Control Commission. The new authority licenses liquor sales, service & manufacturing, & licenses gaming employees, products & operations.

Chair, Donna Roed
Vice-Chairperson, Vic Wonnacott
Executive Director, Rick Josephson

Manitoba Liquor & Lotteries (MBLL)

830 Empress St., Winnipeg, MB R3G 3H3
Tel: 204-957-2500; *Fax:* 204-284-3500
Toll-Free: 800-265-3912
www.mbll.ca
twitter.com/ImpactTeamMB
www.facebook.com/MBLLImpactTeam
www.linkedin.com/company/manitoba-lotteries
www.youtube.com/liquormarts
The Crown Corporation was formed with the merger of the Manitoba Liquor Control Commission & Manitoba Lotteries Corporation in 2014. This coincided with the creation of the Liquor & Gaming Authority of Manitoba.
Manitoba Liquor & Lotteries operates the following: Liquor Marts & Liquor Mart Express stores; Club Regent Casino; McPhillips Station Casino; Video Lotto & PlayNow.com; & distributes & sells Western Canada Lottery products through a network of lottery ticket retailers.
Chair, Polly Craik
Chief Executive Officer, John Stinson
Chief Financial Officer, John Stinson
Chief Corporate Services Officer, Peter Hak
Chief Community Relations & Marketing Officer, Larry Wandowich
Vice-President, Corporate Communications & Social Responsibility, Susan Olynik

Manitoba Mineral Resources

The Paris Building, 259 Portage Ave., 9th Fl., Winnipeg, MB R3B 3P4
Tel: 204-945-6569
Toll-Free: 800-223-5215
minesinfo@gov.mb.ca
www.manitoba.ca/iem
Minister, Growth, Enterprise & Trade, Hon. Cliff Cullen
Tel: 204-945-0067; *Fax:* 204-945-4882
minget@leg.gov.mb.ca
Deputy Minister, Growth, Enterprise & Trade, James Wilson

Associated Agencies, Boards & Commissions:

•**Manitoba Health Research Council**
#205, 445 Ellice Ave.
Winnipeg, MB R3B 3P5
Tel: 204-775-1096; *Fax:* 204-786-5401
info@mhrc.mb.ca
mhrc.mb.ca

•**Mining Board**
#360, 1395 Ellice Ave.
Winnipeg, MB R3G 3P2
Fax: 204-945-8427
Toll-free: 800-223-5215
www.manitoba.ca/iem/mrd/board/mboard.html
Arbitration of disputes between surface rights holders & mineral rights holders with respect to accessing of minerals other than oil & gas.

•**Surface Rights Board**
#360, 1395 Ellice Ave.
Winnipeg, MB R3G 3P2
Tel: 204-945-0731; *Fax:* 204-948-2578
Toll-free: 800-282-8069
www.manitoba.ca/iem/mrd/board/srboard.html
Other Communication: Toll-Free Phone: 1-800-282-8069, ext. 0731
Arbitrates disputes relating to right of entry or compensation for surface rights used by holders of oil & gas rights.

Administration & Finance
Assistant Deputy Minister, Corporate Services, Craig Halwachs
Tel: 204-945-3675
Executive Director, Finance & Accountability, Peter Moreira
Tel: 204-945-7281
Director, Comptrollership, Peter Szewczuk
Tel: 204-945-4789
Director, Information Technology, Wilma Wong
Tel: 204-945-4596

Mineral Resources Division
#360, 1395 Ellice Ave., Winnipeg, MB R3G 3P2
Assistant Deputy Minister, Tim Friesen
Tel: 204-945-4317
Acting Director, Manitoba Geological Survey, Christian Bohm
Tel: 204-945-6549
Chief Mining Engineer, Calvin Liske
Tel: 204-945-6517
Director, Petroleum Branch, Keith Lowdon
Tel: 204-945-6574

Manitoba Municipal Government

#301, 450 Broadway Ave., Winnipeg, MB R3C 0V8
Tel: 204-945-3744
Toll-Free: 866-626-4862
mgi@gov.mb.ca
www.gov.mb.ca/ia
Manitoba Municipal Government was folded into Indigenous & Municipal Relations following the 2016 general election. The department's mission is to improve the economic, social & environmental wellbeing of Manitoba communities & citizens. The Department serves individuals, local governments, community organizations & businesses; & establishes a legislative, financial, planning & policy framework that supports democratic, accountable, effective & financially efficient local government, & the sustainable development of our communities. Programs are aimed at meeting particular needs for training, on-going advice, technical analysis & funding related to community revitalization & development, infrastructure development, land management, business support & local governance. The Department functions as an advocate of community needs, a catalyst & co-ordinator of action, promotes & participates in partnerships with private sector & non-government organizations & intergovernmental alliances.
Minister, Indigenous & Municipal Relations, Hon. Eileen Clarke
Tel: 204-945-3788; *Fax:* 204-945-1383
minim@leg.gov.mb.ca
Deputy Minister, Municipal Relations; Associate Clerk of Executive Council, Fred Meier

Associated Agencies, Boards & Commissions:

•**Manitoba Municipal Board**
#1144, 363 Broadway
Winnipeg, MB R3C 3N9
Tel: 204-945-2941; *Fax:* 204-948-2235
www.gov.mb.ca/municipalboard

•**Manitoba Water Services Board (MWSB)**
2010 Currie Blvd.
PO Box 22080
Brandon, MB R7A 6Y9
Tel: 204-726-6076; *Fax:* 204-726-7196
mwsb@gov.mb.ca
www.gov.mb.ca/ia/mwsb
A Crown Corporation that develops safe, affordable & sustainable water & wastewater infrastructure for rural Manitobans.

•**Taxicab Board**
#200, 301 Weston St.
Winnipeg, MB R3E 3H4
Tel: 204-945-8919; *Fax:* 204-948-2315
taxicabboardoffice@gov.mb.ca
www.gov.mb.ca/ia/taxicab/taxicab.html

Canada-Manitoba Infrastructure Secretariat
#1140, 363 Broadway, Winnipeg, MB R3C 3N9
Tel: 204-945-4074; *Fax:* 204-945-2035
Toll-Free: 800-268-4883
infra@gov.mb.ca
www.infrastructure.mb.ca
Executive Director, Karlene Debance
Tel: 204-945-4431
Director, Infrastructure Programs, Barb Harrison
Tel: 204-945-7624
Director, Economic Development Programs, Tara Pratt
Tel: 204-945-8666

Community Planning & Development
Assistant Deputy Minister, Ramona Mattix
Tel: 204-945-6117
Director, Planning Policy & Programs, Jon Gunn
Tel: 204-945-3864
Director, Community & Regional Planning, David Neufeld
Tel: 204-945-2192

Energy Division
www.gov.mb.ca/iem/energy
Executive Director, Jim Crone
Tel: 204-945-1874
jim.crone@gov.mb.ca
Director, Industrial Research Consortium, John Murray
Tel: 204-945-7533
Director, Energy Strategic Initiatives, Doug Smith
Tel: 204-945-8379

Provincial-Municipal Support Services
Assistant Deputy Minister, Laurie Davidson
Tel: 204-945-2565; *Fax:* 204-948-2107
Provincial Municipal Assessor, Assessment Branch, Mark Boreskie
Tel: 204-945-2604; *Fax:* 204-945-1994
assessment@gov.mb.ca
www.gov.mb.ca/assessment

Director, Information Systems, Debbie Champagne
Tel: 204-945-2602; *Fax:* 204-945-1994
Director, Municipal Finance & Advisory Services, Matt Dryburgh
Tel: 204-945-1944; *Fax:* 204-948-2780
muniadvice@gov.mb.ca

Manitoba Office of the Ombudsman

Colony Square, #750, 500 Portage Ave., Winnipeg, MB R3C 3X1
Tel: 204-982-9130; *Fax:* 204-942-7803
Toll-Free: 800-665-0531
ombudsman@ombudsman.mb.ca
www.ombudsman.mb.ca
Secondary Address: #202, 1011 Rosser Ave.
Scotia Towers
Brandon, MB R7A 0L5
Alt. Fax: 204-571-5157
www.facebook.com/manitobaombudsman
www.youtube.com/user/manitobaombudsman

The Ombudsman, an independent & non-partisan Officer of the Legislative Assembly, investigates complaints from persons who feel they have been unfairly dealt with by government departments or agencies.

Manitoba Ombudsman, Charlene Paquin
Tel: 204-982-9130

Manitoba Public Insurance Corporation

#B100, 234 Donald St., PO Box 6300 Winnipeg, MB R3C 4A4
Tel: 204-985-7000; *Fax:* 204-985-3525
Toll-Free: 800-665-2410
TTY: 204-985-8832
www.mpi.mb.ca
Other Communication: Out-of-Province Claims, Toll-Free Phone: 1-800-661-6051

Administers Manitoba's Public Automobile Insurance Program & sells extension auto coverage on a competitive basis.

Chair, Brent VanKoughnet
President & CEO, Dan Guimond
Chief Information Officer & Vice-President, Information Technology & Business Transformation, Brad Bunko
Chief Product Officer & Vice-President, Business Development & Communications, Ward Keith
Chief Operating Officer & Vice-President, Customer Service, Christine Martin
Chief Financial Officer & Vice-President, Finance, Heather Reichert

Manitoba Sport, Culture & Heritage

www.gov.mb.ca/chc

Manitoba Tourism, Culture, Heritage, Sport & Consumer Protection was renamed to Sport, Culture & Heritage following the 2016 general election. The department is committed to the development & implementation of programs & services which promote & enhance the well-being, identity & creativity of Manitobans & which contribute to Manitoba's continued economic growth & steadily rising quality of life. Working with its partners in the community & with government, the department raises the national & international profile of the talents & abilities of Manitobans, encourages healthy active living, promotes pride of place, creates jobs & attracts & maintains investment in the province.

Minister, Sport, Culture & Heritage; Minister responsible for Francophone Affairs & Status of Women, Hon. Rochelle Squires
Tel: 204-945-3729; *Fax:* 204-945-5223
minsch@leg.gov.mb.ca
Deputy Minister, Mala Sachdeva
Legislative Assistant, Sarah Guillemard
Tel: 204-945-3709; *Fax:* 204-945-1284
sarah.guillemard@leg.gov.mb.ca
Director, Sport Secretariat, Michael Benson
Tel: 204-945-8834

Associated Agencies, Boards & Commissions:

•Le Centre Culturel franco-manitobain/Franco-Manitoban Cultural Centre (CCFM)
340, boul Provencher
Winnipeg, MB R2H 0G7
Tel: 204-233-8972; *Fax:* 204-233-3324
communication@ccfm.mb.ca
www.ccfm.mb.ca

•Heritage Grants Advisory Council
c/o Heritage Grants Program
#330, 213 Notre Dame Ave.
Winnipeg, MB R3B 1N3
Tel: 204-945-2213; *Fax:* 204-948-2086
www.gov.mb.ca/chc/grants/hgp.html

•Manitoba Arts Council (MAC)
#525, 93 Lombard Ave.
Winnipeg, MB R3B 3B1
Tel: 204-945-2237; *Fax:* 204-945-5925
Toll-free: 866-994-2787
info@artscouncil.mb.ca
www.artscouncil.mb.ca

An arms-length agency of the provincial government dedicated to artistic excellence. It offers a broad-based granting program for professional artists & arts organizations. It promotes, preserves, supports & advocates for the arts as essential to the quality of life of all the people of Manitoba.

•Manitoba Centennial Centre Corporation
#1000, 555 Main St.
Winnipeg, MB R3B 1C3
Tel: 204-956-1360; *Fax:* 204-944-1390
inquiries@mbccc.ca
www.mbccc.ca

•Manitoba Combative Sports Commission (MCSC)
#420, 213 Notre Dame Ave.
Winnipeg, MB R3B 1N3
Tel: 204-945-1788; *Fax:* 204-948-3649
www.mbcombativesports.com
Other Communication: Twitter: twitter.com/MBCombatSports

The Manitoba Combative Sports Commission regulates all professional contests or exhibitions of boxing, kick boxing & mixed martial arts, including the licensing & supervision of officials, athletes & promoters.

•Manitoba Film Classification Board
#216, 301 Weston St.
Winnipeg, MB R3E 3H4
Tel: 204-945-8962; *Fax:* 204-945-0890
Toll-free: 866-612-2399
mfcb@gov.mb.ca
www.gov.mb.ca/chc/mfcb

•Manitoba Heritage Council
213 Notre Dame Ave., Main Fl.
Winnipeg, MB R3B 1N3
Tel: 204-945-2118; *Fax:* 204-948-2384
hrb@gov.mb.ca
www.gov.mb.ca/chc/hrb

Protects, interprets & promotes the heritage resources of the province; offers advice & recommendations on places & events which should be protected by the department; protection of significant buildings & sites.

•Manitoba Museum / Musée du Manitoba
190 Rupert Ave.
Winnipeg, MB R3B 0N2
Tel: 204-956-2830; *Fax:* 204-942-3679
info@manitobamuseum.ca
www.manitobamuseum.ca

•Manitoba Film & Music (MFM)
#410, 93 Lombard Ave.
Winnipeg, MB R3B 3B1
Tel: 204-947-2040; *Fax:* 204-956-5261
info@mbfilmmusic.ca
mbfilmmusic.ca
Other Communication: Twitter: twitter.com/MBFilmMusic

Pomotes the province's film & sound recording artists & industries.

•Public Library Advisory Board
#300, 1011 Rosser Ave.
Brandon, MB R7A 0L5
Tel: 204-726-6590; *Fax:* 204-726-6868
Toll-free: 800-252-9998
pls@gov.mb.ca

•Public Utilities Board
#400, 330 Portage Ave.
Winnipeg, MB R3C 0C4
Tel: 204-945-2638; *Fax:* 204-945-2643
Toll-free: 866-854-3698
publicutilities@gov.mb.ca
www.pub.gov.mb.ca

•Sport Manitoba
145 Pacific Ave.
Winnipeg, MB R3B 2Z6
Tel: 204-925-5600; *Fax:* 204-925-5916
info@sportmanitoba.ca
www.sportmanitoba.ca

•Venture Manitoba Tours Ltd.
PO Box 1000
Riverton, MB R0C 2R0
Tel: 204-378-2769; *Fax:* 204-378-2734
vmt@mts.net

Administration & Finance Division

Executive Financial Officer, David Paton
Tel: 204-945-2233
IT Director, Information Systems, Lori Constant
Tel: 204-330-2895
Director, Financial Services, Helen Hasiuk
Tel: 204-945-3946

Communications Services Manitoba

155 Carlton St., 10th Fl., Winnipeg, MB R3C 3H8
Tel: 204-945-3765
Acting Assistant Deputy Minister, Debbie MacKenzie
Tel: 204-945-4271
Director, Production & Media Procurement, Heather A. Coleman
Tel: 204-945-7121
Acting Director, Public Affairs, Angela Jamieson
Tel: 204-945-4971
Director, Creative Services & Advertising & Program Promotion, Cam McCullough
Tel: 204-945-8830
Manager, Internet & New Media Services, Carol Bartmanovich
Tel: 204-945-0870

Consumer Protection

Tel: 204-945-3744
Toll-Free: 866-626-4862
www.gov.mb.ca/cca
Assistant Deputy Minister, Alexandra Morton, Q.C.
Tel: 204-945-3742
Director, Consumer Protection Office, Gail Anderson
Tel: 204-945-3696
Director, Research & Planning, Beatrice Dyce
Tel: 204-945-4259
Acting Director, Consumer Protection Office, Beatrice Dyce
Tel: 204-945-4259
Director, Residential Tenancies Branch, Laura Gowerluk
Tel: 204-945-0377
Director, Claimant Adviser Office, Bob Sample
Tel: 204-945-8171

Culture & Heritage Programs

Assistant Deputy Minister, Veronica Dyck
Tel: 204-945-4078
Director, Arts Branch, Sandy Baardman
Tel: 204-945-4579
Director, Public Library Services, Trevor Surgenor
Tel: 204-726-6864
#200, 1595 - 1 St.
Brandon, MB R7A 7A1

Historic Resources

213 Notre Dame, Winnipeg, MB R3B 1N3
Tel: 204-945-2118; *Fax:* 204-948-2384
hrb@gov.mb.ca
www.gov.mb.ca/chc/hrb
Director, Donna Dul
Tel: 204-945-4389

The Property Registry

276 Portage Ave., Winnipeg, MB R3C 0B6
Tel: 204-945-3123; *Fax:* 204-948-2492
ppr@gov.mb.ca
www.gov.mb.ca/tpr
Other Communication: Land Titles Office, E-mail: tpradmin@gov.mb.ca
Registrar-General & Chief Operating Officer, Barry C. Effler
Tel: 204-945-0446
Registrar, Personal Property Security, Donna Woroniak
Tel: 204-945-2661
Director, Information Technology, Cecilia Antonio
Tel: 204-945-2244
Acting Director, Finance, Grant Kernested
Tel: 204-945-1946

Provincial Services

#100, 200 Vaughan St., Winnipeg, MB R3C 1T5
Legislative Librarian, Tannis Gretzinger
Tel: 204-945-4245
Archivist of Manitoba, Scott Goodine
Tel: 204-945-6140
Director, Information & Privacy Policy Secretariat, Michael Baudic
Tel: 204-945-2523
Acting Director, Translation Services, Anne Dubouloz Gislason
Tel: 204-945-3096

Status of Women

#409, 401 York Ave., Winnipeg, MB R3C 0P8
Tel: 204-945-6281; *Fax:* 204-945-6511
Toll-Free: 800-263-0234
msw@gov.mb.ca
www.gov.mb.ca/msw
Executive Director, Beth Ulrich
Tel: 204-945-6281

Tourism Secretariat
213 Notre Dame Ave., 6th Fl., Winnipeg, MB R3B 1N3
Tel: 204-945-0216
www.gov.mb.ca/chc/tourism_sec/index.html
Executive Director, Tourism Manitoba, Michelle Wallace
Tel: 204-945-2449

Manitoba Sustainable Development

200 Saulteaux Cres., PO Box 22 Winnipeg, MB R3J 3W3
Tel: 204-945-6784
Toll-Free: 800-214-6497
mgi@gov.mb.ca
www.gov.mb.ca/conservation

Manitoba Conservation & Water Stewardship was renamed to Sustainable Development after the 2016 general election. The department protects, conserves, manages & sustains development of forest, fisheries, wildlife, water, energy & Crown & Park land resources. It also protects environmental integrity, & ensures a high level of environmental quality.
The department is the lead agency for providing outdoor recreational opportunities for Manitobans & visitors.
It is a contributor to the economic development & well-being of the province, through resource-based harvesting operations, & in cooperation with other departments responsible for agriculture & tourism. Protecting people & property from floods, wildfires, & adverse effects of other natural occurrences, are also major roles.
The department administers legislation & regulations protecting the environment & public health, participates in approval, licensing & appeals for industrial development activities, administers waste reduction & pollution prevention activities, & monitors environmental quality.

Minister, Sustainable Development, Hon. Cathy Cox
Tel: 204-945-3730; *Fax:* 204-945-3586
minsdev@leg.gov.mb.ca
Deputy Minister, Sustainable Development, Grant Doak
Tel: 204-945-3785; *Fax:* 204-948-2403
Legislative Assistant, Rick Wowchuk
rick.wowchuk@leg.gov.mb.ca
Executive Director, Corporate Crown Lands Policy, Marlene Zyluk
Tel: 204-945-7370

Associated Agencies, Boards & Commissions:

•Clean Environment Commission
#305, 155 Carlton St.
Winnipeg, MB R3C 3H8
Tel: 204-945-0594; *Fax:* 204-945-0090
Toll-free: 800-597-3556
cec@gov.mb.ca
www.cecmanitoba.ca
Arm's-length provincial agency that holds public hearings on the subject of the regulation of a broad range of private industry, municipal or provincial government operations. Investigates environmental matters or considers proposed abatement projects with public hearings. Reports to the Minister with advice & recommendations & acts as a mediator between two or more parties to an environmental dispute.

•Conservation Agreements Board
c/o Manitoba Habitat Heritage Corporation
#200, 1555 St James St.
Winnipeg, MB R3H 1B5
Tel: 204-784-4350
mhhc@mhhc.mb.ca
www.gov.mb.ca/conservation/wildlife/habcons/consagree.html

•Ecological Reserves Advisory Committee
c/o Manitoba Conservation, Parks & Natural Areas Branch
200 Saulteaux Cres.
PO Box 53
Winnipeg, MB R3J 3W3
Tel: 204-945-4148; *Fax:* 204-945-0012
www.gov.mb.ca/conservation/parks/ec_reserves/reserves.html

•Endangered Species Advisory Committee
200 Saulteaux Cres.
PO Box 24
Winnipeg, MB R3J 3W3
Tel: 204-945-7775; *Fax:* 204-945-3077

•Lake Winnipeg Stewardship Board (LWSB)
PO Box 305
Gimli, MB R0C 1B0
Tel: 204-642-4899
www.lakewinnipeg.org
Established in 2003 to assist the government of Manitoba to achieve the main commitments in the Lake Winnipeg Action Plan of reducing phosphorus & nitrogen in the lake to pre-1970 levels. The Lake Winnipeg Stewardship Board's Interim Report (Jan. 2005), contained 32 sets of recommendations & was followed by public discussions. The board's mandate finished in 2010, but former board members may still be contacted as follows:

•Lake of the Woods Control Board (LWCB)
c/o Executive Engineer
373 Sussex Dr., Block E1
Ottawa, ON K1A 0H3
Fax: 888-702-9632
Toll-free: 800-661-5922
secretariat@lwcb.ca
www.lwcb.ca

•Manitoba Habitat Heritage Corporation
#200, 1555 St. James St.
Winnipeg, MB R3H 1B5
Tel: 204-784-4350; *Fax:* 204-784-7359
www.mhhc.mb.ca

•Manitoba Hazardous Waste Management Corporation Board
1803 Hekla Ave.
Winnipeg, MB R2R 0K3

•Manitoba Round Table for Sustainable Development (MRT)
#160, 123 Main St.
PO Box 70
Winnipeg, MB R3C 1A5
Tel: 204-945-4391; *Fax:* 204-948-4730
mrtsd@gov.mb.ca
www.gov.mb.ca/conservation/susresmb/mrtsd
The Manitoba Round Table for Sustainable Development is an advisory body to the provincial government. It provides advice & support to decision makers toward making responsible resource, land use, environment, social, & economic development decisions for the province.

•Manitoba Water Council
200 Saulteaux Cres.
PO Box 38
Winnipeg, MB R3J 3W3
info@manitobawatercouncil.ca
www.manitobawatercouncil.ca
Assists rural residents outside Winnipeg in developing safe & sustainable water &/or sewerage facilities.

Administration & Finance Division
Assistant Deputy Minister, Bruce Gray
Tel: 204-945-3840
Director, Comptrollership, Grants & Contract Review, Rodney Dieleman
Tel: 204-945-4187
Director, Financial Services, Matthew Wiebe
Tel: 204-945-8266
Director, Business Transformation & Technology, Maria Villarba
Tel: 204-945-2929

Climate Change & Environmental Protection
Acting Assistant Deputy Minister, Jocelyn Baker
Tel: 204-945-6658
Divisional Administrative Officer, Sue Tacter
Tel: 204-945-0003
Assistant Divisional Administrator, Brenda Enns
Tel: 204-945-7055
Director, Environmental Approvals, Tracey Braun
Tel: 204-945-7071
Director, Climate Change, Neil Cunningham
Tel: 204-945-8793
Director, Don Labossiere
Tel: 204-945-7005
Director, Environmental Programs & Strategies, Laurie Streich
Tel: 204-945-7482

Conservation Programs Division
Manages Manitoba's natural resources, parks, lands, forests, fish, wildlife, & the environment. Implements the principles of sustainable development.
Assistant Deputy Minister, Serge Scrafield
Tel: 204-945-7008

Forestry
Tel: 204-945-7989
forestinfo@gov.mb.ca
www.gov.mb.ca/conservation/forestry
Director, John Dojack
Tel: 204-945-7998
Divisional Administrative Officer, Carol Legge
Tel: 204-945-7999

GeoManitoba
1007 Century St., Winnipeg, MB R3H OW4
Tel: 204-945-6666; *Fax:* 204-945-1365
Toll-Free: 877-627-7226
geomanitoba@gov.mb.ca
www.gov.mb.ca/conservation/geomanitoba
The division is responsible for: Geospatial Data Acquisition & Product Development; Geospatial Information, Distribution & Support; & Geospatial Technology Management.
Director, Greg Carlson
Tel: 204-945-7952
Director, Geospatial Data Acquisition & Product Development, Wayne Leeman
Tel: 204-945-0011

Green Manitoba
#1200, 155 Carlton St., Winnipeg, MB R3C 3H8
Tel: 204-945-3268; *Fax:* 204-943-0031
Toll-Free: 866-460-3118
greenmanitoba.ca
twitter.com/greenmanitoba
www.facebook.com/GreenManitoba
Chief Operating Officer, Christina McDonald, Ph.D.
Tel: 204-945-1819
Senior Manager, Waste Policy & Programs, Jim Ferguson
Tel: 204-945-7042

Lands
www.gov.mb.ca/conservation/lands_branch
Director, Lori Stevenson
Tel: 204-476-0053
lori.stevenson@gov.mb.ca
Senior Manager, Crown Land & Aboriginal Land Programs, Jamie Patrick
Tel: 204-945-6680
jaime.patrick@gov.mb.ca

Wildlife & Ecosystem Protection
Tel: 204-945-7775; *Fax:* 204-945-3077
www.gov.mb.ca/conservation/wildlife
Director, James Duncan
Tel: 204-945-7465

Corporate Policy
Executive Director, Jocelyn Baker
Tel: 204-945-6658
Director, Aboriginal Relations, Ron Missyabit
Tel: 204-945-7088
Director, Sustainable Resource & Policy Management, Charlotte Price
Tel: 204-945-6944

Regional Services & Parks
Tel: 204-945-6784
Toll-Free: 800-214-6497
www.gov.mb.ca/conservation/parks
Other Communication: Camping Information, Phone: 204-945-6784; Camping Reservations, Phone: 204-948-3333; Toll-Free Phone: 1-888-482-2267
Operates six regional offices in rural Manitoba & co-ordinated from Headquarters operations in Winnipeg. The Division co-ordinates the delivery of programs & services at the community level.
Assistant Deputy Minister, Bruce Bremner
Tel: 204-945-4842
Director, Parks & Natural Areas, Mike Gilbertson
Tel: 204-471-9338
Director, Regional Support Services, Blair McTavish
Tel: 204-945-6647
Divisional Administrative Officer, Regional Support Services, Dianne Arjoon
Tel: 204-945-6803

Regional Offices

Central
75 - 7th Ave., PO Box 6000 Gimli, MB R0C 1B0
Tel: 204-642-6070; *Fax:* 204-642-6108
Regional Director, Rob Nedotiafko
Tel: 204-642-6096

Eastern
Provincial Hwy. #502, CP 4000 Lac du Bonnet, MB R0E 1A0
Tél: 204-345-1431; *Téléc:* 204-345-1440
Supervisor, Regional Park Operations, Don Hallett
Tel: 204-345-1480

Northeastern
59 Elizabeth Dr., PO Box 28 Thompson, MB R8N 1X4
Tel: 204-677-6648; *Fax:* 204-677-6359
Regional Director, Pierce Roberts
Tel: 204-677-6893

Northwestern
3rd St. & Ross Ave., PO Box 2550 The Pas, MB R9A 1M4
Tel: 204-627-8215; *Fax:* 204-623-5733
Regional Director, Wayde Roberts
Tel: 204-627-8399

Western
1129 Queens Ave., PO Box 13 Brandon, MB R7A 1L9
Tel: 204-726-6441; *Fax:* 204-726-6301
Regional Director, Perry Stonehouse
Tel: 204-573-7411

Water Stewardship Division
Tel: 204-945-6784
Toll-Free: 800-214-6497
www.gov.mb.ca/waterstewardship

Divisional Administrative Officer, Sheila Gair
Tel: 204-945-5554
Director, Watersheds & Protected Areas, Planning & Coordination, Rhonda McDougal
Tel: 204-945-8271

Fisheries Branch
Tel: 204-945-6640
fish@gov.mb.ca
www.gov.mb.ca/waterstewardship/fish
Director, Brian Parker
Tel: 204-945-7814

Office of Drinking Water
1007 Century St., Winnipeg, MB R3H OW4
Tel: 204-945-5762; *Fax:* 204-945-1365
www.gov.mb.ca/waterstewardship/drinking_water
Director, Kim Philip
Tel: 204-945-7010

Regulatory Services
www.gov.mb.ca/waterstewardship/licensing
Manager, Water Use Licensing Section, Rob Matthews
Tel: 204-945-6118

Water Science & Management Branch
Tel: 204-945-6784
Toll-Free: 800-214-6497
www.gov.mb.ca/waterstewardship/water_quality/water_science.html
Director, Nicole Armstrong
Tel: 204-945-3991

Manitoba Trade & Investment Corporation

#1100, 259 Portage Ave., Winnipeg, MB R3B 3P4
Tel: 204-945-2466; *Fax:* 204-957-1793
Toll-Free: 800-529-9981
mbtrade@gov.mb.ca
www.gov.mb.ca/trade
Part of Manitoba Growth, Enterprise & Trade, the corporation provides financial services & manages financial instruments on behalf of the Province of Manitoba to assist with economic development initiatives.
In April 2014, the Manitoba Development Corporation Act amalgamated the Manitoba Development Corporation, Economic Innovation & Technology Council & Manitoba Trade & Investment Corporation.
Minister, Growth, Enterprise & Trade, Hon. Cliff Cullen
Tel: 204-945-0067; *Fax:* 204-945-4882
minget@leg.gov.mb.ca
Deputy Minister, Growth, Enterprise & Trade, James Wilson
Chief Executive Officer, Don Callis
Tel: 204-945-8695

Travel Manitoba

21 Forks Market Rd., Winnipeg, MB R3C RT7
Tel: 204-927-7838
Toll-Free: 800-665-0040
contactus@travelmanitoba.com
www.travelmanitoba.com
twitter.com/travelmanitoba
www.facebook.com/TravelManitoba
www.youtube.com/TravelManitoba
President & CEO, Colin Ferguson
Tel: 204-291-9355
coferguson@travelmanitoba.com
Senior Vice-President, Strategy & Market Development, Brigitte Sandron
Tel: 204-795-8698
bsandron@travelmanitoba.com
Vice-President, Marketing & Communications, Linda Whitfield
Tel: 204-927-7825
lwhitfield@travelmanitoba.com

Workers Compensation Board of Manitoba (WCB)

333 Broadway Ave., Winnipeg, MB R3C 4W3
Tel: 204-954-4321; *Fax:* 204-954-4999
Toll-Free: 800-362-3340
wcb@wcb.mb.ca
www.wcb.mb.ca
twitter.com/WCBManitoba
Chair, Michael Werier
President & CEO, Winston Maharaj
Chief Financial Officer, Finance & Administrative Services, Lorena Trann
Chief Operating Officer, SAFE Work Manitoba, Jamie Hall
Chief Information Officer, Stu Charles
General Counsel & Vice-President, Compliance & Corporate Services, Lori Ferguson Sain
Vice-President, Compensation Services, Darren Oryniak
Vice-President, Assessments, Innovation & Technology, Alice Sayant
Vice-President, Human Resources & Strategy Division, Dave Scott

Government of New Brunswick

Seat of Government: PO Box 6000 Fredericton, NB E3B 5H1
www.gnb.ca
twitter.com/Gov_NB
www.facebook.com/GovNB
www.youtube.com/user/gnbca
The Province of New Brunswick entered Confederation July 1, 1867. It has a land area of 71,355.12 sq km. The StatsCan census population in 2011 was 751,171.

Office of the Lieutenant-Governor

Government House, PO Box 6000 Fredericton, NB E3B 5H1
Tel: 506-453-2505; *Fax:* 506-444-5280
LTgov@gnb.ca
www.gnb.ca/lg
The Lieutenant-Governor represents The Queen of Canada, Her Majesty Queen Elizabeth II in New Brunswick. The Lieutenant-Governor is appointed by the Governor General-in-Council on the recommendation of the Prime Minister of Canada.
The following are some responsibilities of the Lieutenant-Governor: opening, proroguing, & dissolving the Legislative Assembly of New Brunswick; swearing in the Premier & cabinet ministers; delivering the Speech from the Throne; giving royal assents to bills passed by the legislature; presenting awards; lending patronage to non-for-profit organizations; & participating in dedications & investitures.
Lieutenant-Governor of New Brunswick / Lieutenant-gouverneur du Nouveau-Brunswick, Hon. Jocelyne Roy-Vienneau, ONB
jocelyne.roy-vienneau@gnb.ca
Principal Secretary, Tim Richardson
tim.richardson@gnb.ca

Office of the Premier / Cabinet du Premier ministre

Centennial Bldg., PO Box 6000 Fredericton, NB E3B 5H1
Tel: 506-453-2144; *Fax:* 506-453-7407
premier@gnb.ca
www.gnb.ca/premier
Premier; President, Executive Council; Minister Responsible, Education & New Economy Fund; Innovation, Women's Equality, Rural Affairs & Premier's Council on the Status of Disabled Persons, Hon. Brian Gallant
Tel: 506-453-2548; *Fax:* 506-453-2144
premier@gnb.ca
Principal Secretary, Greg Byrne
Tel: 506-453-2144
greg.byrne@gnb.ca
Chief of Staff, Jordan O'Brien
Tel: 506-453-2144
Jordan.OBrien@gnb.ca
Press Secretary, Julie Robichaud
Tel: 506-453-2144
julie.robichaud@gnb.ca
Director, Stakeholder Engagement, Grégoire Carrière
Tel: 506-453-2144
gregoire.carriere@gnb.ca
Director, Strategic Planning, Michael Pearson
Tel: 506-453-2144
michael.pearson@gnb.ca
Director, Communications, Tina Robichaud
Tel: 506-453-2144
tina.robichaud@gnb.ca

Executive Council / Conseil exécutif

Centennial Building, PO Box 6000 Fredericton, NB E3B 5H1
Tel: 506-444-4417; *Fax:* 506-453-2266
Executivecounciloffice@gnb.ca
www.gnb.ca/0012/index-e.asp
The following members of The Cabinet of the Government of New Brunswick are listed in the order their departments appear in the Executive Council Act:
Premier; President, Executive Council; Minister Responsible, Education & New Economy Fund, Innovation, Women's Equality, Rural Affairs & Premier's Council on the Status of Disabled Persons, Hon. Brian Gallant
Tel: 506-453-2548; *Fax:* 506-453-2144
premier@gnb.ca
Office of the Premier, Centennial Building
670 King St.
PO Box 6000
Fredericton, NB E3B 5H1
Deputy Premier; Minister, Familes & Children; Minister Responsible, Military Affairs, Hon. Stephen Horsman
Stephen.Horsman@gnb.ca
Minister, Justice & Public Safety, Hon. Denis Landry
denis.landry2@gnb.ca
Minister, Post-Secondary Education, Training & Labour; Minister responsible, Intergovernmental Affairs, Official Languages & Regional Development Corporation, Hon. Donald Arseneault
donald.arseneault@gnb.ca
Minister, Agriculture, Aquaculture & Fisheries; Minister, Energy & Resource Development; Government House Leader, Hon. Rick Doucet
rick.doucet@gnb.ca
Minister, Health; Deputy Government House Leader, Hon. Victor Éric Boudreau
victor.boudreau@gnb.ca
Minister, Service New Brunswick; Minister Responsible, Aboriginal Affairs, Poverty Reduction, & the Economic & Social Inclusion Corporation, Hon. Ed Doherty
Ed.Doherty@gnb.ca
Minister, Education & Early Childhood Development, Hon. Brian Kenny
brian.kenny@gnb.ca
Minister, Transportation & Infrastructure; Minister responsible, Northern & Miramichi funds, Hon. Bill Fraser
bill.fraser@gnb.ca
President, Treasury Board; Minister responsible, Trade Policy, Hon. Roger Melanson
Roger.L.Melanson@gnb.ca
Minister, Economic Development; Minister responsible, La Francophonie, Opportunities NB, Hon. Francine Landry
Francine.Landry@gnb.ca
Minister, Finance; Minister responsible, Literacy, Hon. Cathy Rogers
Cathy.Rogers@gnb.ca
Attorney General; Minister, Environment & Local Government, Hon. Serge Rousselle, Q.C.
Tel: 506-453-3678; *Fax:* 506-457-4810
Serge.Rousselle@gnb.ca
Minister, Tourism, Heritage & Culture, Hon. John Ames
John.Ames@gnb.ca
Minister, Seniors & Long-Term Care; Minister Responsible, Celtic Affairs, Hon. Lisa Harris
Lisa.Harris@gnb.ca

Executive Council Office / Bureau du Conseil exécutif

Chancery Place, 6th Fl., PO Box 6000 Fredericton, NB E3B 5H1
Tel: 506-444-4417; *Fax:* 506-453-2266
executivecounciloffice@gnb.ca
www.gnb.ca/0012/index-e.asp
The Executive Council Office is responsible for the provision of secretariat & administrative services to the following: the Executive Council; ministers with policy coordination responsibilities; & the Policy & Priorities Committee.
Premier; President, Executive Council, Hon. Brian Gallant
Tel: 506-453-2548; *Fax:* 506-453-2144
premier@gnb.ca
Clerk of the Executive Council; Secretary to Cabinet & Deputy Minister of the Executive Council Office, Judy Wagner
Tel: 506-444-4775
Judy.Wagner@gnb.ca
Assistant Secretary to the Policy & Priorities Committee of Cabinet, Patricia Mackenzie
Tel: 506-453-2314
patricia.mackenzie@gnb.ca
Acting Chief Information Officer, Cheryl Hansen
Tel: 506-457-6885
cheryl.hansen@gnb.ca
Chief Legal Advisor to the Premier; Government of New Brunswick's First Nations Representative, Judith Keating
Tel: 506-444-4417
Judith.Keating@gnb.ca
Chief of Strategy Management, Jane Washburn
Tel: 506-444-5734
jane.washburn@gnb.ca
Director, Communications, Bruce MacFarlane
Tel: 506-444-4583
bruce.macfarlane@gnb.ca
Director, Operations, Sabrina Noble
Tel: 506-444-4417
sabrina.noble@gnb.ca

Associated Agencies, Boards & Commissions:

·New Brunswick Jobs Board
Chancery Place
PO Box 6000
Fredericton, NB E3B 5H1
The NB Jobs Board was announced in February 2015, with a mandate to focus on job creation & economic growth.

Aboriginal Affairs Secretariat / Secrétariat des affaires autochtones
Kings Place, #237, 440 King St., PO Box 6000 Fredericton, NB E3B 5H8
Tel: 506-462-5177; *Fax:* 506-444-5142
aboriginalaffairssecretariat@gnb.ca
www.gnb.ca/aboriginal
The Aboriginal Affairs Secretariat strives to enhance the Government of New Brunswick's relationship with Mi'kmaq & Maliseet (or Wolastoqiyik) communities & Aboriginal organizations. The Secretariat acts as a gateway for contact between First Nations & the province. It works with all provincial departments to address issues such as health, housing, education, family & community services, economic development, & natural resource management.
Minister Responsible, Hon. Ed Doherty
Tel: 506-643-2001
Ed.Doherty@gnb.ca
Deputy Minister, Patrick Francis
Tel: 506-462-5177
Patrick.Francis@gnb.ca
Executive Director, John Smith
Tel: 506-462-5177
John.Smith6@gnb.ca
Director, Economic Development & Social, John Adam
Tel: 506-462-5177
john.adam@gnb.ca
Director, Aboriginal Relations & Consultation, Susanne Derrah
Tel: 506-462-5177
Susi.Derrah@gnb.ca

Intergovernmental Affairs Division
Chancery Place, 675 King St., 5th Fl., Fredericton, NB E3B 1E9
Tel: 506-444-4948; *Fax:* 506-453-2995
iga@gnb.ca
The Intergovernmental Affairs Division manages relations with other governments, communities, & organizations.
Minister Responsible, Hon. Donald Arseneault
Donald.Arseneault@gnb.ca
Assistant Deputy Minister, Eric Beaulieu
Tel: 506-444-4948
eric.beaulieu@gnb.ca
Chief of Protocol, Lana Tingley-Lacroix
Tel: 506-453-2671
lana.tingleylacroix@gnb.ca
Executive Director, Trade Policy Division, Elaine Campbell
Tel: 506-444-5788
elaine.campbell@gnb.ca
Director, Canadian Francophonie & Official Languages Branch, Line Pinet
Tel: 506-444-4948
line.pinet@gnb.ca
Director, Multilateral Francophonie Branch, James Thériault
Tel: 506-444-5364
james.theriault@gnb.ca

Women's Equality Branch
Sartain MacDonald Bldg., PO Box 6000 Fredericton, NB E3B 5H1
Tel: 506-453-8126; *Fax:* 506-453-7977
WEB-EDF@gnb.ca
www.gnb.ca/women
Women's Issues, a branch of the Executive Council Office, consists of the following units: Violence Prevention Initiatives; Wage Gap Reduction Initiatives; & Policy Assessment & Advice. The branch provides support on women's issues to the Minister Responsible for Women's Issues & to departments of the provincial government.
Premier; Minister Responsible, Hon. Brian Gallant
Tel: 506-453-2548; *Fax:* 506-453-2144
premier@gnb.ca
Assistant Deputy Minister, Jocelyne Mills
Tel: 506-444-5179
jocelyne.mills@gnb.ca
Director, Policy & Strategic Initiatives, Nicole McCarty
Tel: 506-453-8126
Nicole.McCarty@gnb.ca
Director, Violence Prevention & Community Partnerships, Martine Stewart
Tel: 506-453-8126
Martine.Stewart@gnb.ca

Legislative Assembly of New Brunswick / Assemblée législative

Legislative Bldg., Centre Block, PO Box 6000 Fredericton, NB E3B 5H1
Tel: 506-453-2506; *Fax:* 506-453-7154
wwwleg@gnb.ca
www.gnb.ca/legis/index-e.asp
The Office of the Legislative Assembly is responsible for the following services: assisting Members of the Legislative Assembly, their staff, & the public; recording the proceedings of the Legislative Assembly; maintaining the records of the Legislative Assembly; & providing information services on behalf of the Legislative Assembly.
Speaker of the Legislative Assembly, Hon. Chris Collins
Tel: 506-453-2907; *Fax:* 506-453-7154
Chris.Collins@gnb.ca
Note: Premier Gallant & the government caucus announced on Oct. 7, 2014, that they would support Chris Collins as Speaker. He was officially named on Oct. 24, 2014.
Deputy Speaker, Bernard LeBlanc
Tel: 506-453-2506; *Fax:* 506-453-7154
bernard.leblanc@gnb.ca
Clerk of the Legislative Assembly, Donald J. Forestell
Tel: 506-453-2506; *Fax:* 506-453-7154
don.forestell@gnb.ca
Sergeant-at-Arms, Daniel Bussières
Tel: 506-453-2527; *Fax:* 506-453-7154
dan.bussieres@gnb.ca
Commissioner, Office of the Conflict of Interest, Vacant
Tel: 506-457-7890; *Fax:* 506-444-5224
coi@gnb.ca
www.gnb.ca/legis/conflict
Edgecombe House
736 King St.
Fredericton, NB E3B 1G2
Official Reporter, Hansard Office, Linda Fahey
Tel: 506-453-8352; *Fax:* 506-453-3199
linda.fahey@gnb.ca
West Block
96 Saint John St.
PO Box 6000
Fredericton, NB E3B 5H1
Legislative Librarian, Kenda Clark-Gorey
Tel: 506-453-8346; *Fax:* 506-444-5889
kenda.clark.gorey@gnb.ca
Director, Finance & Human Resources, Katie Hill
Tel: 506-453-2506; *Fax:* 506-444-3331
Katie.Hill@gnb.ca

Government Members Office (Liberal Party)
West Block, Departmental Bldg., PO Box 6000 Fredericton, NB E3B 5H1
Tel: 506-453-2548; *Fax:* 506-453-3956
Leader of the Government (Premier); President, Executive Council; Minister Responsible, Education & New Economy Fund, Innovation, Women's Equality, Rural Affairs & Premier's Council on the Status of Disabled Persons, Hon. Brian Gallant
Tel: 506-453-2548; *Fax:* 506-453-2144
premier@gnb.ca
Office of the Premier, Centennial Building
670 King St.
PO Box 6000
Fredericton, NB E3B 5H1
Minister, Agriculture, Aquaculture &d Fisheries; Minister, Energy & Resource Development; Government House Leader, Rick Doucet
Rick.Doucet@gnb.ca
Chief Government Whip, Hédard Albert
Tel: 506-453-2548; *Fax:* 506-453-3956
hedard.albert@gnb.ca
Chair, Government Caucus, Monique LeBlanc
Tel: 506-453-2548; *Fax:* 506-453-3956
Monique.A.LeBlanc@gnb.ca

Office of the Official Opposition (Progressive Conservative Party) / Bureau de l'opposition officielle
East Block, Old Education Bldg., PO Box 6000 Fredericton, NB E3B 5H1
Tel: 506-453-7494; *Fax:* 506-453-3461
Interim Leader, Official Opposition, R. Bruce Fitch
Tel: 506-453-7494; *Fax:* 506-453-3461
bruce.fitch@gnb.ca
Note: Former Premier David Alward resigned as leader of the PC Party of New Brunswick after failing to win the 2014 General Election.
House Leader, Official Opposition, Madeleine Dubé
Tel: 506-453-7494; *Fax:* 506-453-3461
Madeleine.Dube@gnb.ca
Whip, Official Opposition, Carl Urquhart
Tel: 506-453-7494; *Fax:* 506-453-3461
carl.urquhart@gnb.ca
Caucus Chair, Official Opposition, Pam Lynch
Tel: 506-453-7494; *Fax:* 506-453-3461
Pam.Lynch@gnb.ca
Chief of Staff, Greg Lutes
Tel: 506-453-7494
Greg.Lutes@gnb.ca
Director, Communications, Robert Fowlie
Tel: 506-453-7494
bob.fowlie@gnb.ca
Director, Office of the Chief of Staff, Paul Robichaud
Tel: 506-453-7494
Paul.Robichaud@gnb.ca

Office of the Third Party (Green Party)
West Block, Departmental Bldg., PO Box 6000 Fredericton, NB E3B 5H1
Tel: 506-457-6842; *Fax:* 506-453-7154
www.greenpartynb.ca
twitter.com/greenpartynb
www.facebook.com/GPNB.PVNB
www.youtube.com/user/GPVNB
On October 3, 2014, Premier Gallant announced that the Green Party would be given official Third Party status in the legislature, a first in New Brunswick history.
Leader, Green Party, David Coon
Tel: 506-455-0936
David.Coon@gnb.ca
Social Media: twitter.com/DavidCCoon, www.facebook.com/david.coon.fredsouth, ca.linkedin.com/pub/david-coon/71/624/493
Chief of Staff, Meredith Brewer
Tel: 506-457-6842
Merredith.Brewer@gnb.ca

Standing Committees of the Legislative Assembly of New Brunswick
www1.gnb.ca/legis/committees/comm-index-e.asp
The following are the Standing Committees of the Legislative Assembly of New Brunswick: Crown Corporations; Economic Policy; Estimates & Fiscal Policy; Law Amendments; Legislative Administration; Private Bills; Procedure, Privileges & Legislative Officers; Public Accounts; & Social Policy.
Chair, Standing Committee on Crown Corporations, Bertrand LeBlanc
Constituency: Kent North, Liberal
Bertrand.LeBlanc@gnb.ca
Chair, Standing Committee on Economic Policy, Gilles LePage
Constituency: Restigouche West, Liberal
Gilles.LePage@gnb.ca
Chair, Standing Committee on Estimates & Fiscal Policy, Bernard LeBlanc
Constituency: Memramcook-Tantramar, Liberal
Bernard.LeBlanc@gnb.ca
Chair, Standing Committee on Law Amendments, Hon. Serge Rousselle, Q.C.
Constituency: Tracadie-Sheila, Liberal
Serge.Rousselle@gnb.ca
Chair, Legislative Administration Committee, Hon. Chris Collins
Constituency: Moncton Centre, Liberal
Chris.Collins@gnb.ca
Chair, Standing Committee on Private Bills, Wilfred Roussel
Constituency: Shippagan-Lamèque-Miscou, Liberal
Wilfred.Roussel@gnb.ca
Chair, Standing Committee on Procedure, Privileges & Legislative Officers, Hédard Albert
Constituency: Caraquet, Liberal
Hedard.Albert@gnb.ca
Chair, Standing Committee on Public Accounts, Trevor A. Holder
Constituency: Portland-Simonds, Progressive Conservative
Trevor.Holder@gnb.ca
Chair, Standing Committee on Social Policy, Monique LeBlanc
Constituency: Moncton East, Liberal
Monique.A.LeBlanc@gnb.ca

Select Committees of the Legislative Assembly of New Brunswick
The House may appoint a Select Committee to consider & report on a particular subject or to undertake a specific task or inquiry. As of Sept. 2016, the current Select Committee is the Select Committee on Climate Change.

Fifty-eighth Legislative Assembly - New Brunswick

Centre Block, Legislative Building, 706 Queen St., PO Box 6000 Fredericton, NB E3B 5H1
Tel: 506-453-2506; *Fax:* 506-453-7154
wwwleg@gnb.ca
www.gnb.ca/legis
Last General Election, September 22, 2014.
Next General Election: September 24, 2018.
Party Standings (Sept. 2016):
Liberal 26;
Progressive Conservative 22;

Green 1;
Total 49.
Members' Salaries, Indemnities, & Allowances (2010):
Members' annual indemnity $85,000.
Additional Members' Salaries, Indemnities, & Allowances:
Premier $79,000;
Cabinet Ministers $52,614;
Leader of the Opposition $55,300;
Leader of a Registered Political Party: $19,750;
Speaker $52,614;
Deputy Speaker $26,307;
Government Whip $26,307;
Official Opposition Whip $19,730;
Government House Leader $26,307;
Opposition House Leader $19,730.
Members of the Legislative Assembly may be reached at the following address: Members of the Legislative Assembly, Province of New Brunswick, PO Box 6000, Fredericton, NB E3B 5H1.
The following is a list of Members of the Legislative Assembly with preliminary information after the 2014 election, including their riding, the number of electors, party affiliation, & contact information:

Members of the Legislative Assembly of New Brunswick

Chief Government Whip, Hédard Albert
Constituency: Caraquet, Electoral District 6 *No. of Constituents:* 11,137, Liberal
Tel: 506-453-2548; *Fax:* 506-453-3956
hedard.albert@gnb.ca
nbliberal.ca/support/hedard-albert
Other Communications: Constituency Phone: 506-726-2929; Fax: 506-726-2966
Social Media: www.facebook.com/HedardAlbertLiberal
Constituency Office
#25, 7 St. Pierre Blvd. West
Caraquet, NB E1W 1B8

Minister, Tourism, Heritage & Culture, John B. Ames
Constituency: Charlotte-Campobello, Electoral District 36 *No. of Constituents:* 12,391, Liberal
John.Ames@gnb.ca
nbliberal.ca/support/john-b-ames
Social Media: twitter.com/JohnBAmes, www.facebook.com/JohnBAmes, www.linkedin.com/in/johnbames
Constituency Office
#5, 78 Milltown Blvd.
St Stephen, NB E3L 1G6

Minister, Post-Secondary Education, Training & Labour; Minister Responsible, Intergovernmental Affairs, Official Languages & the Regional Development Corporation, Hon. Donald Arseneault
Constituency: Campbellton-Dalhousie, Electoral District 2 *No. of Constituents:* 11,642, Liberal
donald.arseneault@gnb.ca
nbliberal.ca/support/donald-arseneault
Other Communications: Constituency Phone: 506-685-5252; Fax: 506-685-5255
Social Media: twitter.com/donarseneault, www.facebook.com/donald.arseneault.7, ca.linkedin.com/pub/donald-arseneault/3b/b71/732
Constituency Office
#2, 389 Adelaide St.
Dalhousie, NB E8C 1B5

Minister, Health; Deputy Government House Leader, Hon. Victor Éric Boudreau
Constituency: Shediac-Beaubassin-Cap-Pelé, Electoral District 15 *No. of Constituents:* 12,554, Liberal
Tel: 506-457-4800; *Fax:* 506-453-5442
victor.boudreau@gnb.ca
nbliberal.ca/support/victor-boudreau
Other Communications: Constituency Phone: 506-533-3450; Fax: 506-533-3452
Social Media: www.facebook.com/victor.boudreau.9
Constituency Office
328 Main St., #H
Shediac, NB E4P 2E3

Benoît Bourque
Constituency: Kent South, Electoral District 13 *No. of Constituents:* 12,424, Liberal
Tel: 506-743-0335
Benoit.Bourque@gnb.ca
nbliberal.ca/support/benoit-bourque
Social Media: www.facebook.com/benoitbourqueliberal
Constituency Office
#202, 291 Irving Blvd.
Bouctouche, NB E4S 3K6

Jeff Carr
Constituency: New Maryland-Sunbury, Electoral District 39 *No. of Constituents:* 12,380, Progressive Conservative
Tel: 506-453-7494; *Fax:* 506-453-3461
Jeff.Carr@gnb.ca
pcnb.ca/jeff-carr
Other Communications: Constituency Phone: 506-368-2938; Fax: 506-368-2939
Social Media: twitter.com/jeffcarr4nms, www.facebook.com/492631777502937
Constituency Office
189A Sunbury Dr.
Fredericton, NB E5L 1R5

Jody Carr
Constituency: Oromocto-Lincoln, Electoral District 37 *No. of Constituents:* 11,144, Progressive Conservative
Tel: 506-453-7494; *Fax:* 506-453-3461
jody.carr@gnb.ca
pcnb.ca/jody-carr
Other Communications: Constituency Phone: 506-357-4141; Fax: 506-357-4147
Social Media: twitter.com/jodycarr_mla, www.facebook.com/6189731133
Constituency Office
#102, 2398 Lincoln Rd.
Lincoln, NB E3B 7G1

Chuck Chiasson
Constituency: Victoria-La Vallée, Electoral District 47 *No. of Constituents:* 11,685, Liberal
Tel: 506-475-1124
Chuck.Chiasson@gnb.ca
nbliberal.ca/support/chuck-chiasson
Social Media: twitter.com/ChuckChiasson, www.facebook.com/chuck.chiasson, www.linkedin.com/profile/view?id=101415355
Constituency Office
#11, 385 Broadway Blvd.
Grand Falls, NB E3Y 2K5

Speaker, Hon. Chris Collins
Constituency: Moncton Centre, Electoral District 19 *No. of Constituents:* 10,841, Liberal
Tel: 506-453-2907; *Fax:* 506-453-7154
chris.collins@gnb.ca
nbliberal.ca/support/chris-collins-2
Other Communications: Constituency Phone: 506-453-2548; Fax: 506-453-3956
Social Media: twitter.com/ChrisCollinsMLA, www.facebook.com/chris.collins.77985741, ca.linkedin.com/pub/chris-collins/18/859/118
Note: Premier Gallant & the government caucus announced on Oct. 7, 2014, that they would support Chris Collins as Speaker. He was officially named on Oct. 24, 2014.
Constituency Office
118 Mountain Rd.
Moncton, NB E1C 2K7

Leader, Third Party (Green Party), David Coon
Constituency: Fredericton South, Electoral District 40 *No. of Constituents:* 10,417, Green Party of Canada
Tel: 506-455-0936
David.Coon@gnb.ca
www.greenpartynb.ca
Social Media: twitter.com/DavidCCoon, www.facebook.com/david.coon.fredsouth, ca.linkedin.com/pub/david-coon/71/624/493
Note: David Coon is the first Green Party member ever to be elected to the New Brunswick Legislative Assembly.
Constituency Office
#1, 133 King St.
Fredericton, NB E3B 1C8

Gary Crossman
Constituency: Hampton, Electoral District 27 *No. of Constituents:* 11,767, Progressive Conservative
Tel: 506-453-7494; *Fax:* 506-453-3461
Gary.Crossman@gnb.ca
pcnb.ca/gary-crossman
Other Communications: Constituency Phone: 506-832-5700; Fax: 506-832-5549
Social Media: twitter.com/GaryCrossman1, www.facebook.com/GaryCrossmanNB, www.linkedin.com/pub/gary-crossman/59/164/a90
Constituency Office
39 Railway Ave.
Hampton, NB E5N 5L2

Minister, Service New Brunswick; Minister Responsible, Aboriginal Affairs, Poverty Reduction, & Economic & Social Inclusion Corporation, Hon. Ed Doherty
Constituency: Saint John Harbour, Electoral District 32 *No. of Constituents:* 11,093, Liberal
Ed.Doherty@gnb.ca
nbliberal.ca/support/ed-doherty-2
Social Media: twitter.com/dohertyed, www.facebook.com/doherty4Harbour
Constituency Office
#124, 100 Prince Edward St.
Saint John, NB E2L 4M5

Minister, Agriculture, Aquaculture & Fisheries; Minister, Energy & Resource Development; Government House Leader, Hon. Rick Doucet
Constituency: Fundy-The Isles-Saint John West, Electoral District 35 *No. of Constituents:* 11,538, Liberal
rick.doucet@gnb.ca
nbliberal.ca/support/rick-doucet
Social Media: twitter.com/Rick_Doucet, ca.linkedin.com/pub/hon-rick-doucet/30/19a/171
Constituency Office
28 Mt. Pleasant St.
St George, NB E5C 3K4

House Leader, Official Opposition, Madeleine Dubé
Constituency: Edmundston-Madawaska Centre, Electoral District 48 *No. of Constituents:* 11,343, Progressive Conservative
Tel: 506-735-2528; *Fax:* 506-735-2583
madeleine.dube@gnb.ca
pcnb.ca/madeleine-mado-dube
Constituency Office
59 de l'Église St.
Edmundston, NB E3V 1J6

Stewart Fairgrieve
Constituency: Carleton, Electoral District 45
Note: On Oct. 5, 2015, PC candidate Stewart Fairgrieve won a by-election in the riding of Carleton, called after former Premier David Alward resigned his seat, in May 2015.

Interim Leader of the Official Opposition, R. Bruce Fitch
Constituency: Riverview, Electoral District 23 *No. of Constituents:* 11,547, Progressive Conservative
Tel: 506-453-7494; *Fax:* 506-453-3461
bruce.fitch@gnb.ca
brucefitch.ca
Other Communications: Constituency Phone: 506-869-6117; Fax: 506-869-6114
Social Media: twitter.com/brucefitchmla
Constituency Office
#18A, 567 Coverdale Rd.
Riverview, NB E1B 3K7

Hugh John (Ted) Flemming III, Q.C.
Constituency: Rothesay, Electoral District 29 *No. of Constituents:* 10,956, Progressive Conservative
Tel: 506-453-7494; *Fax:* 506-453-3461
hugh.flemming@gnb.ca
pcnb.ca/hugh-j-ted-flemming
Other Communications: Constituency Phone: 506-848-5440; Fax: 506-848-5442
Social Media: twitter.com/tedflemming, www.facebook.com/flemmingforrothesay
Constituency Office
70 Hampton Rd.
Rothesay, NB

Minister, Transportation & Infrastructure; Minister responsible, Northern & Miramichi funds, Hon. Bill Fraser
Constituency: Miramichi, Electoral District 10 *No. of Constituents:* 11,248, Liberal
bill.fraser@gnb.ca
nbliberal.ca/support/bill-fraser
Other Communications: Constituency Phone: 506-624-5516; Fax: 506-624-5517
Social Media: twitter.com/billfrasermla, www.facebook.com/billfrasermla
Constituency Office
1202 Water St., #B
Miramichi, NB E1N 1A2

Premier; President, Executive Council; Minister Responsible, Education & New Economy Fund, Innovation, Women's Equality, Rural Affairs & Premier's Council on the Status of Disabled Persons, Hon. Brian Gallant
Constituency: Shediac Bay-Dieppe, Electoral District 14 *No. of Constituents:* 12,643, Liberal
Tel: 506-453-2548; *Fax:* 506-453-2144
Brian.Gallant@gnb.ca
nbliberal.ca/meet-brian
Other Communications: Constituency Phone: 506-869-7000; Fax: 506-869-7007
Social Media: twitter.com/BrianGallantNB
Constituency Office
#203, 650 Champlain St.
Dieppe, NB E1A 1P5

Deputy Government Whip, Daniel Guitard
Constituency: Restigouche-Chaleur, Electoral District 3 *No. of Constituents:* 11,397, Liberal
Tel: 506-453-2548; *Fax:* 506-453-3956
Daniel.Guitard@gnb.ca
nbliberal.ca/support/daniel-guitard
Other Communications: Constituency Phone: 506-542-2424; Fax: 506-542-2425
Social Media: www.facebook.com/danielguitard.liberal
Constituency Office
691 Principale St.
Petit-Rocher, NB E8J 1G1

Minister, Seniors & Long-Term Care; Minister responsible, Celtic Affairs, Lisa Harris
Constituency: Miramichi Bay-Neguac, Electoral District 9 *No. of Constituents:* 11,888, Liberal
Tel: 506-453-2506; *Fax:* 506-453-7154
Lisa.Harris@gnb.ca
nbliberal.ca/support/lisa-harris
Other Communications: Constituency Phone: 506-778-8713; Fax: 506-836-1804

Constituency Office
1 Marina Dr.
Miramichi, NB E1V 6S8

Andrew Harvey
Constituency: Carleton-Victoria, Electoral District 46 *No. of Constituents:* 11,804, Liberal
Tel: 506-273-4598; *Fax:* 506-273-4772
Andrew.Harvey@gnb.ca
nbliberal.ca/support/andrew-harvey
Social Media: www.facebook.com/AndrewHarveyCarletonVictoria
Constituency Office
117 Fort Rd.
Perth-Andover, NB E7H 2B9

Blaine Higgs
Constituency: Quispamsis, Electoral District 28 *No. of Constituents:* 11,710, Progressive Conservative
Tel: 506-848-5422; *Fax:* 506-848-5429
blaine.higgs@gnb.ca
pcnb.ca/blaine-higgs
Other Communications: Constituency Phone: 506-848-5422; Fax: 506-848-5429
Social Media: twitter.com/BlaineHiggs, www.facebook.com/BlaineHiggsMLA
Constituency Office
25 William Ct.
Quispamsis, NB E2E 4B1

Trevor Holder
Constituency: Portland-Simonds, Electoral District 31 *No. of Constituents:* 11,093, Progressive Conservative
Tel: 506-453-7494; *Fax:* 506-453-3461
trevor.holder@gnb.ca
pcnb.ca/trevor-holder
Other Communications: Constituency Phone: 506-657-2335; Fax: 506-642-2588
Social Media: twitter.com/TrevorHolderPC, www.facebook.com/TrevorHolderSJ
Constituency Office
#2, 229 Churchill Blvd.
Saint John, NB E2K 3E2

Deputy Premier; Minister, Families & Children; Minister Responsible, Military Affairs, Hon. Stephen Horsman
Constituency: Fredericton North, Electoral District 41 *No. of Constituents:* 11,511, Liberal
Stephen.Horsman@gnb.ca
nbliberal.ca/support/stephen-horsman
Social Media: www.facebook.com/StephanHorsmanFrederictonNorth
Constituency Office
150 Cliffe St.
PO Box R12
Fredericton, NB E3A 0A1

Brian Keirstead
Constituency: Albert, Electoral District 24 *No. of Constituents:* 12,320, Progressive Conservative
Tel: 506-856-3006; *Fax:* 506-856-3000
Keirstead.Brian@gnb.ca
pcnb.ca/brian-keirstead
Social Media: twitter.com/BrianKeirstead
Constituency Office
1037 Rte. 114
Lower Cloverdale, NB E1J 1A1

Minister, Education & Early Childhood Development, Hon. Brian Kenny
Constituency: Bathurst West-Beresford, Electoral District 4 *No. of Constituents:* 11,079, Liberal
brian.kenny@gnb.ca
nbliberal.ca/support/brian-kenny
Other Communications: Constituency Phone: 506-549-5355; Fax: 506-549-5261
Social Media: twitter.com/BathurstBrian, ca.linkedin.com/pub/brian-kenny/23/825/433
Constituency Office
#5, 325 Vanier Blvd.
Bathurst, NB E2A 3N1

Minister, Justice & Public Safety, Hon. Denis Landry
Constituency: Bathurst East-Nepisiguit-Saint-Isidore, Electoral District 5 *No. of Constituents:* 11,298, Liberal
denis.landry2@gnb.ca
nbliberal.ca/support/denis-landry
Constituency Office
1040-4, rue du Parc
Paquetville, NB E8R 1J7

Minister, Economic Development; Minister Responsible, La Francophonie & Opportunities NB., Hon. Francine Landry
Constituency: Madawaska Les Lacs-Edmundston, Electoral District 49 *No. of Constituents:* 11,677, Liberal
Francine.Landry@gnb.ca
nbliberal.ca/support/francine-landry
Social Media: twitter.com/FrancineLandry
Constituency Office
174, rue de L'Église
Edmundston, NB E3V 1K2

Deputy Speaker, Bernard LeBlanc
Constituency: Memramcook-Tantramar, Electoral District 16 *No. of Constituents:* 11,626, Liberal
Tel: 506-453-2506; *Fax:* 506-453-7154
bernard.leblanc@gnb.ca
nbliberal.ca/support/bernard-leblanc
Other Communications: Constituency Phone: 506-758-4088; Fax: 506-758-4089
Social Media: twitter.com/BLeblancNB
Constituency Office
488 Centrale St.
Memramcook, NB E4K 3S6

Bertrand LeBlanc
Constituency: Kent North, Electoral District 12 *No. of Constituents:* 12,459, Liberal
Tel: 506-876-3592; *Fax:* 506-876-3590
bertrand.leblanc@gnb.ca
nbliberal.ca/support/bertrand-leblanc-2
Constituency Office
10511 Principale St.
Saint-Louis-de-Kent, NB E1A 1E6

Chair, Government Caucus, Monique LeBlanc
Constituency: Moncton East, Electoral District 18 *No. of Constituents:* 12,221, Liberal
Tel: 506-453-2548; *Fax:* 506-453-3956
Monique.A.LeBlanc@gnb.ca
nbliberal.ca/support/monique-leblanc
Other Communications: Constituency Phone: 506-386-2014
Social Media: twitter.com/leblanmo, www.facebook.com/MoniqueAnneLeBlanc
Constituency Office
459A Elmwood Rd.
Moncton, NB E1A 4X2

Gilles LePage
Constituency: Restigouche West, Electoral District 1 *No. of Constituents:* 11,761, Liberal
Tel: 506-826-6120; *Fax:* 506-826-6122
Gilles.LePage@gnb.ca
nbliberal.ca/support/gilles-lepage
Constituency Office
512 Des Pionniers Ave.
Balmoral, NB E8E 1E3

Caucus Chair, Official Opposition, Pam Lynch
Constituency: Fredericton-Grand Lake, Electoral District 38 *No. of Constituents:* 11,835, Progressive Conservative
Tel: 506-453-7494; *Fax:* 506-453-3461
pam.lynch@gnb.ca
pcnb.ca/pam-lynch
Social Media: twitter.com/PamLynchMLA, www.facebook.com/pamela.lynch.752
Constituency Office
121 Gibson St.
Fredericton, NB E3A 4E1

Brian MacDonald
Constituency: Fredericton West-Hanwell, Electoral District 43 *No. of Constituents:* 12,146, Progressive Conservative
Tel: 506-453-8461; *Fax:* 506-453-4135
brian.t.macdonald@gnb.ca
pcnb.ca/brian-macdonald
Constituency Office
1757 Hanwell Rd.
Hanwell, NB E3C 2B9

Kirk Douglas MacDonald
Constituency: Fredericton-York, Electoral District 42 *No. of Constituents:* 12,024, Progressive Conservative
Tel: 506-453-7494; *Fax:* 506-453-3461
kirk.macdonald@gnb.ca
pcnb.ca/kirk-macdonald
Social Media: twitter.com/KirkDMacDonald
Constituency Office, Keswick Landing Mall
#7, 9 Yerxa Lane
Keswick, NB E6L 1N7

President, Treasury Board; Minister responsible, Trade Policy, Hon. Roger Melanson
Constituency: Dieppe, Electoral District 17 *No. of Constituents:* 11,175, Liberal
roger.l.melanson@gnb.ca
nbliberal.ca/support/roger-melanson-2
Social Media: twitter.com/RogerMelanson, www.facebook.com/votevotezroger
Constituency Office
#203, 650 Champlain St.
Dieppe, NB E1A 1P5

Bruce Northrup
Constituency: Sussex-Fundy-St. Martins, Electoral District 26 *No. of Constituents:* 12,022, Progressive Conservative
Tel: 506-432-2686; *Fax:* 506-432-2647
bruce.northrup@gnb.ca
pcnb.ca/bruce-northrup
Constituency Office
12 Marble St.
Sussex, NB E4E 3P9

Bill Oliver
Constituency: Kings Centre, Electoral District 34 *No. of Constituents:* 11,357, Progressive Conservative
Tel: 506-738-6586
Bill.Oliver@gnb.ca
pcnb.ca/bill-oliver
Social Media: www.linkedin.com/pub/bill-oliver/3b/107/649
Constituency Office
#2, 241 River Valley Dr.
Grand Bay-Westfield, NB E5K 1A7

Minister, Finance; Minister responsible, Literacy, Hon. Cathy Rogers
Constituency: Moncton South, Electoral District 20 *No. of Constituents:* 11,650, Liberal
Cathy.Rogers@gnb.ca
nbliberal.ca/support/cathy-rogers
Social Media: twitter.com/ROGERSatMoncton, www.facebook.com/CathyRogersLiberal, ca.linkedin.com/pub/cathy-rogers/4b/33a/4ab
Constituency Office
23 High St.
Moncton, NB E1C 6B4

Wilfred Roussel
Constituency: Shippagan-Lamèque-Miscou, Electoral District 7 *No. of Constituents:* 11,387, Liberal
Tel: 506-336-9169
Wilfred.Roussel@gnb.ca
nbliberal.ca/support/wilfred-roussel
Social Media: www.facebook.com/wilfred.roussel
Constituency Office
#7, 1295 Principale St.
PO Box 4001
Le Goulet, NB E8S 3H5

Attorney General; Minister, Environment & Local Government, Hon. Serge Rousselle, Q.C.
Constituency: Tracadie-Sheila, Electoral District 8 *No. of Constituents:* 11,943, Liberal
Serge.Rousselle@gnb.ca
nbliberal.ca/support/serge-rousselle
Other Communications: Constituency Phone: 506-394-4038; Fax: 506-394-4037
Social Media: www.facebook.com/serge.rousselle1965
Constituency Office
4104, rue Principale
Tracadie-Sheila, NB E1X 1B8

Glen Savoie
Constituency: Saint John East, Electoral District 30 *No. of Constituents:* 11,526, Progressive Conservative
Tel: 506-453-7494; *Fax:* 506-453-3461
glensavoie.ca
Social Media: twitter.com/glen_savoie, www.facebook.com/GlenSavoieNB
Note: MLA-elect Gary Keating resigned on October 14, 2014, citing strain on his health & family. Glen Savoie won the seat in a by-election held November 17, 2014.

Dorothy Shephard
Constituency: Saint John Lancaster, Electoral District 33 *No. of Constituents:* 10,696, Progressive Conservative
Tel: 506-453-7494; *Fax:* 506-453-3461
dorothy.shephard@gnb.ca
pcnb.ca/dorothy-shephard
Other Communications: Constituency Phone: 506-643-2900; Fax: 506-643-2999
Social Media: twitter.com/ShephardDorothy
Constituency Office
649 Manawagonish Rd., #A
Saint John, NB E2M 3W5

Ernie Steeves
Constituency: Moncton Northwest, Electoral District 21 *No. of Constituents:* 12,038, Progressive Conservative
Tel: 506-453-7494; *Fax:* 506-453-3461
Ernie.Steeves@gnb.ca
pnb.ca/ernie-steeves
Other Communications: Constituency Phone: 506-383-2164; Fax: 506-383-3045
Social Media: www.facebook.com/erniesteeves
Constituency Office
#3B, 1888 Mountain Rd.
Moncton, NB E1G 1A9

Jake Stewart
Constituency: Southwest Miramichi-Bay du Vin, Electoral District 11 *No. of Constituents:* 11,382, Progressive Conservative
Tel: 506-453-7494
Toll-free: 855-849-7729; *Fax:* 506-453-3461
jake.stewart@gnb.ca
pcnb.ca/jake-stewart
Other Communications: Constituency Phone: 506-843-7729; 506-843-7726
Social Media: twitter.com/jakestewartnb, www.facebook.com/JakeStewartNB
Constituency Office
137 Main St.
Blackville, NB E9B 1B9

Whip, Official Opposition, Carl Urquhart
Constituency: Carleton-York, Electoral District 44 *No. of*

Constituents: 12,117, Progressive Conservative
Tel: 506-457-7878; *Fax:* 506-457-7865
carl.urquhart@gnb.ca
pcnb.ca/carl-urquhart
Other Communications: Constituency Phone: 506-457-7878; Fax: 506-457-7865
Constituency Office
1757 Hanwell Rd.
Hanwell, NB E3C 2B9

Ross Wetmore
Constituency: Gagetown-Petitcodiac, Electoral District 25 *No. of Constituents:* 11,879, Progressive Conservative
Tel: 506-453-7494; *Fax:* 506-453-3461
ross.wetmore@gnb.ca
pcnb.ca/ross-wetmore
Other Communications: Constituency Phone: 506-488-3577; Fax: 506-488-3511
Social Media: www.facebook.com/voterosswetmore
Constituency Office
56 Front St.
Gagetown, NB E5M 1A1

Sherry Wilson
Constituency: Moncton Southwest, Electoral District 22 *No. of Constituents:* 11,919, Progressive Conservative
Tel: 506-453-7494; *Fax:* 506-453-3461
sherry.wilson@gnb.ca
pcnb.ca/sherry-wilson
Other Communications: Constituency Phone: 506-382-6567; Fax: 506-382-7232
Constituency Office
3118 Main St.
Salisbury, NB E4J 2L6

New Brunswick Government Departments & Agencies / Ministères et organismes du gouvernement du Nouveau-Brunswick

New Brunswick Department of Agriculture, Aquaculture & Fisheries / Agriculture, Aquaculture et Pêches

Agricultural Research Station (Experimental Farm), PO Box 6000 Fredericton, NB E3B 5H1
Tel: 506-453-2666; *Fax:* 506-453-7170
Toll-Free: 888-622-4742
DAAF-MAAP@gnb.ca
www.gnb.ca/agriculture

Minister, Agriculture, Aquaculture, & Fisheries, Hon. Rick Doucet
Tel: 506-755-4200; *Fax:* 506-755-4207
rick.doucet@gnb.ca
Deputy Minister, Jean Finn
Tel: 506-453-2666
jean.finn@gnb.ca
Director, Communications, Vicky Deschenes
Tel: 506-453-2666
vicky.deschenes@gnb.ca

Associated Agencies, Boards & Commissions:

•New Brunswick Agricultural Insurance Commission / Commission de L'assurance Agricole du Nouveau-Brunswick
c/o Department of Agriculture, Aquaculture & Fisheries
PO Box 6000
Fredericton, NB E3B 5H1
Tel: 506-453-2666; *Fax:* 506-453-7406
DAAF-MAAP@gnb.ca
Agricultural Insurance Commission is responsible for administering the delivery to producers of an agricultural insurance plan to provide insurance protection against losses of production. This plan is funded through producer premiums & through contributions from the Province of New Brunswick & the Government of Canada.

•New Brunswick Farm Products Commission / Commission des produits de ferme du Nouveau-Brunswick
c/o Department of Agriculture, Aquaculture & Fisheries
PO Box 6000
Fredericton, NB E3B 5H1
Tel: 506-453-3647; *Fax:* 506-444-5969
DAAF-MAAP@gnb.ca
Provides management/administrative support to the Commission in the monitoring of commodity boards under the provisions of the Natural Products Act.

•New Brunswick Grain Commission / Commission des grains du Nouveau-Brunswick
c/o Department of Agriculture, Aquaculture & Fisheries
PO Box 6000
Fredericton, NB E3B 5H1
Tel: 506-859-3309; *Fax:* 506-856-2092
DAAF-MAAP@gnb.ca
Under the New Brunswick Grain Act, the NB Grain Commission promotes production & marketing of grain & maintains standards of quality for grain & grain handling.

Corporate Services / Services généraux
Acting Executive Director & Director, Information & Technology, Giovanna MacLeod
Tel: 506-457-6766
giovanna.macleod@gnb.ca
Director, Financial Services, Ryan Bourgeois
Tel: 506-453-2185
Ryan.Bourgeois@gnb.ca
Advisor, Human Resources, Karolina Gehres
Tel: 506-453-6766
karolina.gehres@gnb.ca

Industry Programs & Policy / Programmes de l'industrie et politiques
Assistant Deputy Minister, Cathy Larochelle
Tel: 506-453-2366
Cathy.Larochelle@gnb.ca
Director, Strategic Planning & Program Development, Joseph Labelle
Tel: 506-453-2252
Joseph.Labelle@gnb.ca
Director, Industry Financial Programs, Ryan Bourgeois
Tel: 506-453-2185
Ryan.Bourgeois@gnb.ca
Director, Sector Specialist Services, Kevin McCully
Tel: 506-453-2108
Kevin.McCully@gnb.ca
Director, Innovation & Market Development, Pierre Rioux
Tel: 506-453-2108
Pierre.Rioux@gnb.ca
Acting Director, Strategic Planning & Program Development, Shirley Stuible
Tel: 506-453-2252
Shirley.Stuible@gnb.ca
Director, Leasing & Licensing, Andrew Sullivan
Tel: 506-453-2252
andrew.sullivan@gnb.ca

Regional Development / Développment régional
Assistant Deputy Minister, Roger Robichaud
Tel: 506-453-2366
roger.robichaud@gnb.ca
Executive Director, Animal Health Services, Sandi McGeachy
Tel: 506-453-2109
Sandi.McGeachy@gnb.ca

Fisheries Resource Management / Gestion des ressources en pêches
Hédard Robichaud Bldg., 22 St-Pierre Blvd. East, Caraquet, NB E1W 1B6
Tel: 506-726-2400; *Fax:* 506-726-2419
Director, Fisheries Resource Management, Mario Gaudet
Mario.Gaudet@gnb.ca

Regional Offices
Bathurst
Bathurst Agriculture Building, 1425 King Ave., Bathurst, NB E2A 1S7
Tel: 506-547-2088; *Fax:* 506-547-2064
DAAF-MAAP@gnb.ca
Supervisor, Jean Marc Clavette
Tel: 506-547-2088
jean-marc.clavette@gnb.ca

Bon Accord
Bon Accord Elite Seed Potato Centre, 790 Kincardine Rd., Bon Accord, NB E7H 2K8
Tel: 506-273-4741; *Fax:* 506-273-4742
DAAF-MAAP@gnb.ca
Agrologist, Shaun Pelkey
Tel: 506-273-4536
Shaun.Pelkey@gnb.ca

Edmundston
36 Court St., Edmundston, NB E3V 1S3
Tel: 506-735-2060; *Fax:* 506-735-2754
DAAF-MAAP@gnb.ca
Supervisor, Jason Cleghorn
Tel: 506-453-2219
jason.cleghorn@gnb.ca

Grand Falls
PO Box 5001 Grand Falls, NB E3Z 1G1
Tel: 506-473-7755; *Fax:* 506-473-6641
DAAF-MAAP@gnb.ca
Specialist, Jacques Lavoie
Tel: 506-473-7755
Jacques.Lavoie@gnb.ca

Miramichi
Chatham Town Centre, 1780 Water St., Miramichi, NB E1N 1B6
Tel: 506-778-6030; *Fax:* 506-778-6679
DAAF-MAAP@gnb.ca

Moncton
381 Killam Dr., Moncton, NB E1C 3T1
Tel: 506-856-2277; *Fax:* 506-856-2092
DAAF-MAAP@gnb.ca

Wicklow
Potato Development Centre, 39 Barker Lane, Wicklow, NB E7L 3S4
Tel: 506-392-5101; *Fax:* 506-392-5089
Toll-Free: 888-622-4742
DAAF-MAAP@gnb.ca
Supervisor, Werner Debertin
Tel: 506-392-5101
Werner.Debertin@gnb.ca

Departmental Offices
Southeast Branch
26 Acadie St., Bouctouche, NB E4S 2T2
Tel: 506-743-7222; *Fax:* 506-743-7229
DAAF-MAAP@gnb.ca
Regional Director, Abel Noël
Tel: 506-743-7330
Abel.Noel@gnb.ca

Caraquet
22 St-Pierre Blvd. East, Caraquet, NB E1W 1B6
Tel: 506-755-4000; *Fax:* 506-755-4001
DAAF-MAAP@gnb.ca
Regional Director, Mario Gaudet
Tel: 506-726-2400
Mario.Gaudet@gnb.ca

Northeast Region
100 Aquarium St., Shippagan, NB E8S 1H9
Tel: 506-336-3751; *Fax:* 506-336-3057
DAAF-MAAP@gnb.ca
Regional Director, Christian Noris
Tel: 506-336-3751
Christian.Noris@gnb.ca

Office of the Attorney General / Cabinet du procureur général

Chancery Place, PO Box 6000 Fredericton, NB E3B 5H1
Tel: 506-462-5100; *Fax:* 506-453-3651
justice.comments@gnb.ca
www2.gnb.ca/content/gnb/en/departments/attorney_general.html
The Office is mandated to promote the impartial administration of justice & to ensure protection of the public interest.

Attorney General, Hon. Serge Rousselle
serge.rousselle@gnb.ca
Deputy Attorney General, Johanne Bray
johanne.bray@gnb.ca
Public Intervener, Heather Black
Tel: 506-643-6263
heather.black@gnb.ca
Director, Communications, Dave McLean
Tel: 506-462-5100
dave.mclean@gnb.ca
Director, Policy & Planning Branch, Monique Drapeau-Miles
Tel: 506-453-2023
monique.drapeau-miles@gnb.ca

Administrative Services Division / Services administratifs
Tel: 506-453-2719; *Fax:* 506-453-8718
Director, Human Resources Services, Julie Comeau
Tel: 506-444-2191
Julie.M.COMEAU@gnb.ca
Director, Financial Services, Gayle Howard
Tel: 506-444-4015
gayle.howard@gnb.ca
Director, Information Management & Technology, Lachlan MacQuarrie-McLeod
Tel: 506-453-6072
lachlan.macquarrie-mcleod@gnb.ca

Legal Services Branch / Services juridiques
Tel: 506-453-2222; *Fax:* 506-453-3275
Assistant Deputy Attorney General, Guy Daigle
guy.daigle@gnb.ca
Executive Director, Litigation Group, Nancy Forbes
Tel: 506-457-3552
nancy.forbes@gnb.ca
Director, Legal Advice Services Group, Diane Audet Leger
Diane.Audet-Leger@gnb.ca
Director, Employment & Administrative Law Group, Andrea Folster
Tel: 506-444-5595
andrea.folster@gnb.ca

Director, Corporate, Commercial & Property Law Group, Stephen Leavitt
Tel: 506-453-2222
Stephen.Leavitt@gnb.ca

Legislative Services Branch / Services législatifs
Tel: 506-453-2855; *Fax:* 506-457-7342
Assistant Deputy Attorney General, Kim Poffenroth
Kim.Poffenroth@gnb.ca
Registrar of Regulations & Director, Legislative Drafting (Anglophone), Susan Burns
Susan.Burns@gnb.ca
Acting Executive Director, Legislative Development, Elizabeth Strange
Elizabeth.Strange@gnb.ca
Director, Legislative Drafting (Francophone), Elena Bosi
Tel: 506-453-2544
elena.bosi@gnb.ca

Public Legal Education & Information Service of New Brunswick (PLEIS-NB) / Service public d'éducation et d'information juridiques du Nouveau-Brunswick (SPEIJ-NB)
Tel: 506-453-5369; *Fax:* 506-462-5193
pleisnb@web.ca
www.legal-info-legale.nb.ca
twitter.com/PLEIS_NB
www.facebook.com/PLEISNB

The mission of the Public Legal Education & Information Service is to assist the public by developing bilingual educational projects & services about the law. The service promotes access to the legal system & improves citizens' abilities to handle legal issues.

Executive Director, Deborah Doherty, Ph.D.
Tel: 506-453-5369

Public Prosecutions Branch / Poursuites publiques
Tel: 506-453-2784; *Fax:* 506-453-5364
Under the Public Prosecutions Branch, family & youth justice crown services are located in the following places:
Bathurst (506-547-2160);
Campbellton (506-789-2308);
Edmundston (506-735-2027);
Fredericton (506-453-2819);
Miramichi (506-627-4015);
Moncton (506-869-6211);
Saint John (506-658-2580).
Also operating under the Public Prosecutions Branch are the following offices that offer crown prosecutor services:
Bathurst (506-547-2160);
Campbellton (506-789-2308);
Caraquet (506-726-2794);
Edmundston (506-735-2027);
Fredericton (506-453-2819);
Grand Falls (506-473-7702);
Miramichi (506-627-4015);
Moncton (506-856-2310);
Oromocto / Burton (506-357-4033);
Richibucto (506-523-7990);
Saint John (506-658-2580);
St. Stephen (506-466-7397);
Tracadie-Sheila (506-394-3727);
Woodstock (506-325-4416).
Sheriff services are available at the following locations:
Bathurst (506-547-2163);
Campbellton (506-789-2100);
Edmundston (506-735-2032);
Fredericton (506-453-2801);
Miramichi (506-627-4026);
Moncton (506-856-2315);
Saint John (506-658-2569);
Woodstock (506-325-4426).
Assistant Deputy Attorney General, Public Prosecutions, Luc Labonté
Tel: 506-453-2784
Luc.Labonte@gnb.ca
Director, Specialized Prosecutions, Cameron Gunn
Tel: 506-453-2784
cameron.gunn@gnb.ca
Director, Specialized Prosecutions, Jeffrey Mockler
Tel: 506-453-2784
jeff.mockler@gnb.ca

Office of the Auditor General / Bureau du Vérificateur général

HSBC Place, 520 King St., Fredericton, NB E3B 6G3
Tel: 506-453-2243; *Fax:* 506-453-3067
www.agnb-vgnb.ca

The role of the Office of the Auditor General is the promotion of accountability. On behalf of the Legislative Assembly, the Office of the Auditor General audits the accounts of the province & certain Crown agencies. Objective information is provided to the citizens of New Brunswick through the Legislative Assembly.

Auditor General, Kim MacPherson, C.A.
Tel: 506-453-2465; *Fax:* 506-453-3067
Kim.MacPherson@gnb.ca
Deputy Auditor General, Janice Leahy, C.A., C.I.A.
Tel: 506-453-6751; *Fax:* 506-453-3067
janice.leahy@gnb.ca
Director, Financial Audit, Nicholas Hoben
Tel: 506-453-6756
nick.hoben@gnb.ca
Director, Performance Audit, Eric Hopper
Tel: 506-453-6741; *Fax:* 506-453-3067
Eric.Hopper@gnb.ca
Director, Information Technology Audit, Peggy Isnor
Tel: 506-453-2243
Peggy.Isnor@gnb.ca

Office of the Comptroller / Bureau du Contrôleur

Chancery Place, 3rd Fl., PO Box 6000 Fredericton, NB E3B 5H1
Tel: 506-453-2451; *Fax:* 506-457-6878
wwwooc@gnb.ca
www.gnb.ca/0087/index-e.asp

The Office of the Comptroller provides leadership in accounting & internal auditing services to clients & encourages the effective management of the resources of the province.

Comptroller, Paul Martin
Tel: 506-457-4959
paul.martin@gnb.ca
Director, Accounting Services, David Nowlan
Tel: 506-453-2451
David.Nowlan@gnb.ca
Director, Audit & Consulting Services, Lee Mitchell
Tel: 506-453-8975
lee.mitchell@gnb.ca

Premier's Council on the Status of Disabled Persons / Conseil du Premier ministre sur la condition des personnes handicapées

#648, 440 King St., Fredericton, NB E3B 5H8
Tel: 506-444-3000; *Fax:* 506-444-3001
Toll-Free: 800-442-4412
pcsdp@gnb.ca
www2.gnb.ca/content/gnb/en/departments/pcsdp.html
twitter.com/nbPCSDP
www.facebook.com/190814814281727

The role of the Premier's Council on the Status of Disabled Persons is to provide advice to the provincial government of New Brunswick & the public about issues of interest & concern that affect the status of persons with disabilities.

Premier, Hon. Brian Gallant
Tel: 506-453-2548; *Fax:* 506-453-2144
Brian.Gallant@gnb.ca
Chair, Jeff Sparks
Executive Director, Christyne Allain

Economic & Social Inclusion Corporation / Société d'inclusion économique et sociale

Kings Place, PO Box 6000 Fredericton NB E3B 5H1
Tel: 506-444-2977; *Fax:* 506-444-2978
Toll-Free: 888-295-4545
esic-sies@gnb.ca
www2.gnb.ca/content/gnb/en/departments/esic.html

Develops, oversees, coordinates & implements initiatives to reduce poverty & assist New Brunswickers in need.

Minister Responsible, Hon. Ed Doherty
Tel: 506-643-2001
Ed.Doherty@gnb.ca
Executive Director, Stéphane Leclair
stephane.leclair@gnb.ca

New Brunswick Department of Education & Early Childhood Development / Éducation et Développement de la petite enfance

Place 2000, PO Box 6000 Fredericton, NB E3B 5H1
Tel: 506-453-3678; *Fax:* 506-453-4810
edcommunication@gnb.ca
www.gnb.ca/education

The Department of Education & Early Childhood Development consists of an Early Learning & Child Care Sector, an Anglophone Sector, & a Francophone Sector.
The Early Learning & Child Care Sector oversees the following programs & services: Prenatal Benefit Program; the Postnatal Benefit Program; the Infant Parent Attachment Program; Excellence in Parenting; the Pay Equity Program for Child Care Staff; early intervention standards; child day care; Early Childhood Development Centers; the Early Childhood Strategy; the Early Learning & Child Care Trust Fund; the curriculum for early learning & child care; & services for preschool children with autism.
The English Educational Services Division is responsible for curriculum development, student services, e-learning, & student evaluation & assessment.
The Francophone Educational Services Division oversees curriculum development & implementation, special education, psychology, guidance counselling, professional development, & assessment & evaluation.

Minister, Education & Early Childhood Development, Hon. Brian Kenny
Brian.Kenny@gnb.ca
Deputy Minister, John McLaughlin
Tel: 506-453-2529
john.mclaughlin@gnb.ca
Sous-ministre, Gérald Richard
Tél: 506-453-2409
gerald.richard@gnb.ca
Director, Strategic Communications, Robert Duguay
Tel: 506-453-2039
Robert.Duguay@gnb.ca

Corporate Services / Services généraux
Tel: 506-453-2085; *Fax:* 506-457-4810
edcommunication@gnb.ca
Assistant Deputy Minister, Robert Penney
Tel: 506-453-2085
Robert.Penney@gnb.ca
Acting Director, Human Resources, Adrienne Dean
Tel: 506-444-4914
adrienne.dean@gnb.ca
Director, Educational Facilities & Pupil Transportation, Thomas Weber
Tel: 506-453-2242
thomas.weber@gnb.ca
Director, Finance & Services, Audra McKnight
Tel: 506-453-6533
audra.mcknight@gnb.ca

Early Childhood Development / Développement de la petite enfance
Tel: 506-453-2950; *Fax:* 506-453-5629
Executive Director, Nicole Gervais
Tel: 506-457-7893
nicole.gervais@gnb.ca

Educational Services (Anglophone)
Tel: 506-453-3678; *Fax:* 506-457-4810
Assistant Deputy Minister, Nancy Boucher
Tel: 506-453-3326; *Fax:* 506-457-4810
nancy.boucher@gnb.ca
Executive Director, Educational Services (Anglophone) & Director, Curriculum Development & Implementation K-12, Darlene Whitehouse-Sheehan
Tel: 506-444-4672
darlene.whitehouse-sheehan@gnb.ca
Director, Integrated Services, Bob Eckstein
Tel: 506-444-2618
bob.eckstein@gnb.ca
Director, Professional Learning Services, Inga Boehler
Tel: 506-453-2040
inga.boehler@gnb.ca
Director, Confucius Institute, Teng Jing
Tel: 506-871-4855
teng.jing@gnb.ca
Director, Student Services, Brian Kelly
Tel: 506-453-2816
brian.kelly@gnb.ca
Director, Assessment & Evaluation, Sandra MacKinnon
Tel: 506-453-2744
sandra.mackinnon@gnb.ca
Director, First Nation Perspectives, Donna Wahienha:wi Lahache
Tel: 506-462-5013
donna.lahache@gnb.ca
Manager, District Education Councils, Stacey Brown
Tel: 506-453-2618
stacey.brown@gnb.ca

Policy & Planning / Politiques et planification
Tel: 506-453-3090; *Fax:* 506-453-3111
Executive Director, Policy & Planning, Christine Gilbert Estabrooks
Tel: 506-453-3090
christine.gilbertestabrooks@gnb.ca
Acting Director, Policy & Legislative Affairs, Rachel Dion
Tel: 506-444-5250
rachel.dion@gnb.ca
Director, Corporate Data Management & Analysis, Monica LeBlanc
Tel: 506-453-6124
monica.leblanc@gnb.ca

Secteur des services éducatifs francophones
Tél: 506-453-2409; *Téléc:* 506-457-4810

Sous-ministre adjoint, Marcel Lavoie
Tél: 506-453-2409
Marcel.LAVOIE@gnb.ca
Directrice par intérim, Initiatives et relations stratégiques, Sophie Lacroix
Tél: 506-453-8882
sophie.lacroix@gnb.ca
Directeur, Services intégrées, Bob Eckstein
Tél: 506-444-2618
bob.eckstein@gnb.ca
Directrice, Programmes d'études et de l'évaluation, Mireille Fontane-Vautour
Tél: 506-453-2743
mireille.fontaine-vautour@gnb.ca
Directeur, Initiatives et relations stratégiques, Sophie Lacroix
Tél: 506-453-8882
sophie.lacroix@gnb.ca
Directrice, Services d'appui à l'éducation, Tanya Roy
Tél: 506-453-2750
tanya.roy@gnb.ca

Office of the Chief Electoral Officer / Bureau de la directrice générale des élections

#102, Sartain MacDonald Building, PO Box 6000
Fredericton, NB E3B 5H1
Tel: 506-453-2218; *Fax:* 506-457-4926
Toll-Free: 800-308-2922
TTY: 888-718-0544
info@electionsnb.ca
www.electionsnb.ca
twitter.com/ElectionsNB
www.facebook.com/110758452300716

Chief Electoral Officer, Michael Quinn
michael.quinn@electionsnb.ca
Assistant Chief Electoral Officer, David Owens
David.Owens@electionsnb.ca
Director, Operations, Craig Astle
craig.astle@electionsnb.ca
Director, Communications, Paul Harpelle
Paul.Harpelle@gnb.ca
Manager, Voter Information Systems, Ronald Armitage
ron.armitage@electionsnb.ca

New Brunswick Department of Energy & Resource Development / Énergie et des Ressouces

Hugh John Flemming Forestry Centre, 1350 Regent St., Fredericton, NB E3C 2G6
Tel: 506-453-3826; *Fax:* 506-444-4367
dnr_mrnweb@gnb.ca
www.gnb.ca/naturalresources

The department was created in 2016 after the combination of the department of Natural Resources & the department of Energy & Mines.

Minister, Energy & Resource Development, Hon. Rick Doucet
Rick.Doucet@gnb.ca
Deputy Minister, Vacant
Acting Assistant Deputy Minister, Resource/Exploration/Development/Management, Keith Endresen
Tel: 506-444-2683
keith.endresen@gnb.ca
Director, Energy Division, Heather Quinn
Tel: 506-977-2329
Heather.Quinn@gnb.ca

Associated Agencies, Boards & Commissions:

•New Brunswick Forest Products Commission
Hugh John Flemming Forestry Centre
PO Box 6000
Fredericton, NB E3B 5H1
Tel: 506-453-2196; *Fax:* 506-457-4966
dnr_mrnweb@gnb.ca

Corporate Services / Services Généraux
Assistant Deputy Minister, Joanne Walker
Tel: 506-453-2501
joanne.walker@gnb.ca
Director, Information Services & Systems, Lesley Aussant
Tel: 506-292-1869
lesley.aussant@gnb.ca
Director, Financial Services, Louise Girouard
Tel: 506-453-3826
Louise.G.Girouard@gnb.ca
Director, Policy & Strategic Initiatives, Martha O'Sullivan
Tel: 506-440-1730
Martha.OSullivan@gnb.ca
Director, Human Resource Services, Julie Smith
Tel: 506-444-2827
Julie.P.Smith@gnb.ca

Renewable Resources & Operations / Ressources renouvelables et des Opérations
Assistant Deputy Minister, Thomas MacFarlane
Tel: 506-453-2684
Tom.MacFarlane@gnb.ca
Executive Director, Regional Operations & Support Services, Kristian J. Moore
Tel: 506-453-6171
Kristian.Moore@gnb.ca
Director, Crown Lands, Cade Libby
Tel: 506-453-3826
Cade.Libby@gnb.ca

Fish & Wildlife Branch / Direction du poisson et de la faune
fw_pfweb@gnb.ca

Manages the province's fisheries & wildlife. By managing fish populations & habitats the Branch develops sport fisheries. Over 160 species of birds, mammals, reptiles & amphibians live in New Brunswick's forests. A Branch goal is to conserve the habitat to support these species. The staff develops environmental protection plans to ensure these resources are protected & maintained.
Director, Vacant

Forest Management Branch / Gestion des forêts
To manage Crown timber resource in accordance with Government Policy.
Director, Michael Bartlett
Tel: 506-444-2193
Mike.Bartlett@gnb.ca

Energy & Mines / Énergie et Mines
Tel: 506-453-3826; *Fax:* 506-444-4367
DEM@gnb.ca

Business Development & Community Relations / Développement des affaires et relations communautaires
Tel: 506-658-3180; *Fax:* 506-658-3191
geoscience@gnb.ca
Assistant Deputy Minister, Bill Breckenridge
Tel: 506-453-5233
bill.breckenridge@gnb.ca

Resource/Exploration/Development/Management / Exploration, exploitation et gestion des ressources
geoscience@gnb.ca
www.gnb.ca/0078/minerals/index-e.asp
Assistant Deputy Minister, Samuel McEwan
Tel: 506-453-6637
Sam.McEwan@gnb.ca
Director, Geological Surveys, Leslie Fyffe
Tel: 506-444-5005
Les.Fyffe@gnb.ca

New Brunswick Department of Environment & Local Government / Environnement et Gouvernements locaux

Marysville Place, PO Box 6000 Fredericton, NB E3B 5H1
Tel: 506-453-2690; *Fax:* 506-457-4994
elg/egl-info@gnb.ca
www.gnb.ca/environment
Other Communication: Toll-free phone to report pesicide, oil, chemical spills, & other environmental emergencies: 1-800-565-1633

The Departmemt of Environment & Local Government is responsible for environmental stewardship & consultation with municipal governments & Local Service Districts concerning governance issues.

Minister, Environment & Local Government, Hon. Serge Rousselle
serge.rousselle@gnb.ca
Deputy Minister, Kelli Simmonds
Tel: 506-453-3256
Kelli.Simmonds@gnb.ca

Associated Agencies, Boards & Commissions:

•Assessment & Planning Appeal Board
City Centre
435 King St.
PO Box 6000
Fredericton, NB E3B 5H1
Tel: 506-453-2126; *Fax:* 506-444-4881
lg/gl-info@gnb.ca
www2.gnb.ca/content/gnb/en/departments/local_government.html

The Assessment & Planning Appeal Board hears property assessment appeals, appeals of land use & planning decisions, & appeals of local heritage review board decisions. The board consists of 11 regional panels from across New Brunswick.

Corporate Services, Community Funding & Performance Excellence Process Division / La Division des services généraux, du financement communautaire et les processus d'excellence du rendement
The division oversees human resources & administrative services, information management, corporate finance, & community funding.
Assistant Deputy Minister, Deidre Green
Tel: 506-453-6285
deidre.green@gnb.ca
Director, Community Funding, André Chenard
Tel: 506-457-4947
Andre.Chenard@gnb.ca
Director, Corporate Finance, Sara Degrace
Tel: 506-453-2020
sara.degrace@gnb.ca
Director, Communications, Jennifer Graham
Tel: 506-444-2179
jennifer.graham@gnb.ca
Director, Information & Technology Management, Laurie Robichaud
Tel: 506-453-2020
Laurie.Robichaud@gnb.ca
Director, Human Resources & Administration, Mary Ellen Somerville
Tel: 506-453-2020
MaryEllen.Somerville@gnb.ca

Environment Division / Environnement
Tel: 506-444-5119; *Fax:* 506-457-7333
The division oversees human resources & administrative services, information management, corporate finance, & community funding.
Assistant Deputy Minister, Perry Haines
Perry.Haines@gnb.ca
Director, Impact Management, Mike Cormier
Tel: 506-453-7945
Mike.Cormier@gnb.ca
Director, Surface Water Protection, Peter McLaughlin
Tel: 506-457-4850
Peter.McLaughlin@gnb.ca
Director, State of the Environment, Darryl Pupek
Tel: 506-457-4844
Darryl.Pupek@gnb.ca
Director, Sustainable Development & Impact Evaluation, Paul Vanderlaan
Tel: 506-444-5382
Paul.Vanderlaan@gnb.ca

Climate Change Secretariat / Secrétariat des changements climatiques
Tel: 506-457-4844; *Fax:* 506-453-2265
The Climate Change Secretariat is concerned with greenhouse gas emission reductions & adaptations. The secretariat also manages engagement with federal, provincial, territorial, & international jurisdictions on climate change issues. Public awareness & education programs are also produced.
Executive Director, Climate Change Secretariat, Darwin Curtis
Tel: 506-457-4844
Darwin.Curtis@gnb.ca
Director, Mitigation, Susan Atkinson
Tel: 506-457-4844
susan.atkinson@gnb.ca

Program Operations & Enforcement Branch / Direction de l'exécution des programmes et services d'exécution
Tel: 506-444-3635; *Fax:* 506-453-3688
Executive Director, Program Operations & Enforcement Branch, David Schellenberg
Tel: 506-444-3635
dave.schellenberg@gnb.ca

Regional Program Delivery Section
Bathurst Regional Office
PO Box 5001 Bathurst, NB E2A 3Z9
Tel: 506-547-2092; *Fax:* 506-547-7655
Regional Director, Paul Fournier
Tel: 506-547-2092
Paul.Fournier@gnb.ca
Engineer, Gaétan Landry
Tel: 506-547-2092
Gaetan.Landry@gnb.ca

Fredericton Regional Office
Priestman Centre, PO Box 6000 Fredericton, NB E3B 5H1
Tel: 506-444-5149; *Fax:* 506-453-2893
Director, Serge Gagnon
Tel: 506-444-5149
Serge.Gagnon@gnb.ca
Engineer, Jennifer Bishop
Tel: 506-444-5149
jennifer.bishop@gnb.ca

Grand Falls Regional Office
PO Box 5001 Grand Falls, NB E3Z 1G1
Tel: 506-473-7744; *Fax:* 506-475-2510
Regional Director, Richard Keeley
Tel: 506-473-7744
Richard.Keeley@gnb.ca
Engineer, Roger Bélanger
Tel: 506-473-7744
Roger.Belanger@gnb.ca
Miramichi Regional Office
Industrial Park, 316 Dalton Ave., Miramichi, NB E1V 3N9
Tel: 506-778-6032; *Fax:* 506-778-6796
Regional Director, Denis Daigle
Tel: 506-778-6032
Denis.Daigle@gnb.ca
Moncton Regional Office
PO Box 5001 Moncton, NB E1C 8R3
Tel: 506-856-2374; *Fax:* 506-856-2370
Regional Director, Laurie Collette
Tel: 506-856-2374
Laurie.Collette@gnb.ca
Saint John Regional Office
PO Box 5001 Saint John, NB E2L 4Y9
Tel: 506-658-2558; *Fax:* 506-658-3046
Director, Patrick Stull
Tel: 506-658-2558
patrick.stull@gnb.ca
Engineer, Barry Leger
Tel: 506-658-2558
Barry.Leger@gnb.ca

Local Government Division / Gouvernement locaux
Tel: 506-453-6285; *Fax:* 506-457-4994
The Local Government Division provides liaison services, financial support, & assistance with municipal functions. Examples of activities include overseeing the restructuring of municipalities & rural communities, & assisting Business Improvement Areas to improve downtown cores.
Assistant Deputy Minister, Rob Kelly
Tel: 506-453-6285
Rob.Kelly@gnb.ca
Director, Local Government Support Services, Ryan Donaghy
Tel: 506-444-4423
ryan.donaghy@gnb.ca
Director, Community Finances, Alexandra Ferris
Tel: 506-444-4423
Ali.Ferris@gnb.ca
Director, Provincial & Community Planning, Joanne Glynn
Tel: 506-453-2171
Joanne.Glynn@gnb.ca

Policy & Planning Division / Politiques et planification
Tel: 506-453-3700; *Fax:* 506-453-7128
The division is responsible for ensuring that policies & strategic planning intitiatives are developed & implemented to support the Department of Environment & Local Government.
Executive Director, Lesley Rogers
Tel: 506-453-3700
Lesley.Rogers@gnb.ca
Director, Policy, Kim Hughes
Tel: 506-453-3700
kim.hughes@gnb.ca
Director, Legislative Renewal & Legal Affairs, Denyse Smart
Tel: 506-453-3700
Denyse.Smart@gnb.ca
Manager, Education & Engagement, Michelle Daigle
Tel: 506-453-3700
Michelle.Daigle@gnb.ca

New Brunswick Department of Finance / Finances

Chancery Place, 675 King St., PO Box 6000 Fredericton, NB E3B 5H1
Tel: 506-453-2451; *Fax:* 506-457-4989
wwwfin@gnb.ca
www.gnb.ca/finance
The Department of Finance manages the public finances of New Brunswick.
Minister, Finance, Hon. Cathy Rogers
Cathy.Rogers@gnb.ca
Deputy Minister, Gordon Gilman
Tel: 506-453-2534
gordon.gilman@gnb.ca
Chief Operating Officer, New Brunswick Lotteries & Gaming Corporation, Patricia Steeves
Tel: 506-444-3629; *Fax:* 506-444-5818
Patricia.steeves@gnb.ca

Associated Agencies, Boards & Commissions:

•New Brunswick Investment Management Corporation (NBIMC) / Société de gestion des placements du Nouveau-Brunswick
York Tower
#581, 440 King St.
Fredericton, NB E3B 5H8
Tel: 506-444-5800; *Fax:* 506-444-5025
comments@nbimc.com
www.nbimc.com
The New Brunswick Investment Management Corporation assists in the development of the financial services industry & capital markets in the province of New Brunswick.

•New Brunswick Lotteries & Gaming Corporation
Chancery Place, 4th Fl.
PO Box 6000
Fredericton, NB E3B 5H1
Tel: 506-453-2451; *Fax:* 506-453-2053
The name of the Lotteries Commission of New Brunswick, which was established as a Crown corporation under the Lotteries Act, was changed to the New Brunswick Lotteries & Gaming Corporation.

Budget & Financial Affairs / Bureau des affaires budgétaires et financières
Tel: 506-453-2451; *Fax:* 506-457-6456
The Budget & Financial Affairs Division has the following responsibilities: implementation of multi-year expenditure plans; development & monitoring of budgets; & offering options for the government to consider.
Acting Director, Board of Management Operations, Jennifer Sherwood
Tel: 506-453-2451
jennifer.sherwood@gnb.ca
Director, Budget and Expenditure Monitoring, Ben Mersereau
Tel: 506-453-8019
ben.mersereau@gnb.ca
Financial Services Officer, Rose Savage
Tel: 506-453-8039
Rose.Savage@gnb.ca

Communications & Strategic Policy / Communications et politique stratégique
Tel: 506-453-2451; *Fax:* 506-462-5056
Director, Communications, Véronique Taylor
Tel: 506-453-2451; *Fax:* 506-462-5056
veronique.taylor@gnb.ca

Corporate Services / Services généraux
Tel: 506-453-2451; *Fax:* 506-444-5056
Director, Human Resources, Petra Bergner
Tel: 506-444-5099
petra.bergner@gnb.ca
Director, Human Resources Services, Petra Bergner
Tel: 506-444-5099
petra.bergner@gnb.ca
Director, Financial Services, Brenda Waye
Tel: 506-453-6904; *Fax:* 506-462-5056
brenda.waye@gnb.ca

Fiscal Policy / Politiques fiscales
Tel: 503-453-2451; *Fax:* 506-457-6456
The Fiscal Policy Division provides the following services: Advice & analysis in the areas of fiscal & budget policy, federal-provincial fiscal relations, & the economy; Statistical services for the government; & Forecasting & monitoring of government revenues & the economy.
Assistant Deputy Minister, Fiscal Policy, Peter Kieley
Tel: 506-453-6921; *Fax:* 506-453-2281
Peter.Kieley@gnb.ca
Executive Director, Tax Policy, George McAllister
Tel: 506-453-6920
George.McAllister@gnb.ca
Director, Economic & Statistical Analysis, Todd Selby
Tel: 506-453-2451
todd.selby@gnb.ca

Fiscal Policy & Revenue / Direction des Politique fiscale et revenus
Tel: 506-453-2451; *Fax:* 506-457-6456

Revenue Administration / Division de l'administration du revenu
Tel: 506-453-2451; *Fax:* 506-444-4920
Provision of effective, efficient & fair administration of assigned revenue acts. In addition, provides policy & administration support to the Lotteries Commission.
Assistant Deputy Minister, Dany Couillard
Tel: 506-453-2451
dany.couillard@gnb.ca
Director, Research & Tax Administration Policy, Michelle Smith
Tel: 506-453-2451
Michelle.Smith@gnb.ca

Treasury / Trésorerie
Tel: 506-453-2451; *Fax:* 506-453-2053
The Treasury Division is responsible for financing the Province's cash requirements, cash management, administration of outstanding debt, investment management & administration of pension, sinking & special purpose trust funds, financial policy analysis & advice & Crown corporation & municipal financing.
Assistant Deputy Minister, Leonard Lee-White
Tel: 506-444-5141
Leonard.lee-white@gnb.ca

New Brunswick Department of Health / Santé

HSBC Place, PO Box 5100 Fredericton, NB E3B 5G8
Tel: 506-457-4800; *Fax:* 506-453-5243
Health.Sante@gnb.ca
www.gnb.ca/health
twitter.com/NBHealth
www.youtube.com/playlist?list=PLA8D47F3CEFB8D4B6
The mission of New Brunswick's Department of Health is to work with New Brunswickers in achieving well-being, by promoting self-sufficiency & personal responsibility, & providing approved services as required.
The development & delivery of health programs & services to New Brunswick residents is supported by a range of internal department functions, such as administration, planning & evaluation, & program support. The department provides services to prevent illness & disability. Education & awareness-raising initiatives promote the health & well-being of New Brunswickers of all ages, so that they can achieve their best potential, while enjoying an independent & healthy lifestyle for as long as possible.
Public Health services are delivered through the province's seven health regions, under the management of Regional Directors. A Chief Medical Officer of Health & a Deputy Chief Medical Officer of Health oversee the development of policy & regulations, & provide medical operational support to the regional Medical Officers of Health. Public Health Services support healthy growth & development, foster healthy lifestyles, control communicable diseases, & protect the public from adverse health consequences of exposure to chemical, physical & biological agents.
Minister, Health, Hon. Victor Éric Boudreau
Tel: 506-457-4800; *Fax:* 506-453-5442
victor.boudreau@gnb.ca
Deputy Minister, Tom Maston
Tel: 506-453-2542
Tom.Maston@gnb.ca
Director, Communications, Bruce MacFarlane
Tel: 506-453-2536
bruce.macfarlane@gnb.ca
Director, Human Resources, Joanne Stone
Tel: 506-444-2521
Joanne.Stone@gnb.ca

Associated Agencies, Boards & Commissions:

•Psychiatric Patient Advocate Services Review Board
c/o Dept. of Health, Psychiatric Patient Advocate Services
#505, 860 Main St.
Moncton, NB E1C 1G2
Tel: 506-869-6818; *Fax:* 506-869-6101
Toll-free: 888-350-4133
www.gnb.ca/0055/advocate-e.asp
A senior lawyer, a psychiatrist (or a physician, if a psychiatrist is unavailable), & a lay person serve on the Psychiatric Patient Advocate Services Review Board, as required under section 30(2) of the Mental Health Act.
The Review Board is engaged in the following activities: granting certificates of detention; delivering an order to administer a treatment; reviewing a treatment; reviewing the status of an involuntary patient; reviewing a patient's competence to give consent; reviewing the patient's access to information regarding his treatment; reviewing a transfer to another jurisdiction; & reviewing the ability of an involuntary patient to manage his estate

•Psychiatric Patient Advocate Services Tribunal
c/o Dept. of Health, Psychiatric Patient Advocate Services
#505, 860 Main St.
Moncton, NB E1C 1G2
Tel: 506-869-6818; *Fax:* 506-869-6101
Toll-free: 888-350-4133
www.gnb.ca/0055/advocate-e.asp
The Psychiatric Patient Advocate Services Tribunal is made up of a lawyer & two members of the public. The tribunal authorizes involuntary admission according to the Mental Health Act. It also authorize the treatment of involuntary patients.

Community & Institutional Services Division / Services communautaires et en établissement
Assistant Deputy Minister, Claude Allard
Tel: 506-457-4800
Claude.Allard2@gnb.ca

Acting Assistant Deputy Minister, Kathy Perrin
Tel: 506-457-4800
Kathy.Perrin@gnb.ca
Acting Assistant Deputy Minister, Nancy Roberts
Tel: 506-457-4800
Nancy.Roberts@gnb.ca
Director, New Brunswick Extra-Mural Program, Jean Bustard
Tel: 506-444-5360
jean.bustard@gnb.ca
Acting Director, Hospital Services & Operations, Daniel Coulombe
Tel: 506-444-4182
Dan.Coulombe@gnb.ca
Acting Director, Emergency Health Services, John Estey
Tel: 506-444-5360
john.estey@gnb.ca
Director, Chronic Disease Prevention & Management, Beverly Greene
Tel: 506-444-4174
Beverly.Greene@gnb.ca
Acting Director, Health System Standards & Performance, Jane Stafford
Tel: 506-453-6349
Jane.Stafford@gnb.ca

Addiction & Mental Health Services / Services de traitement des dépendances et de santé mentale
Tel: 506-444-4442; *Fax:* 506-453-8711
Executive Director, Gisèle Maillet
Tel: 506-381-0854
gisele.maillet@gnb.ca
Director, Child & Youth Services, Yvette Doiron
Tel: 506-869-6118
yvette.doiron-brun@gnb.ca
Director, Adult Services, Sylvie Martin
Tel: 506-473-7588
sylvie.martin@gnb.ca

New Brunswick Cancer Network / Réseau du cancer du Nouveau-Brunswick
Fax: 506-453-5522
www.gnb.ca/0051/cancer/index-e.asp
Co-Chief Executive Officer, S. Eschwar Kumar
Tel: 506-457-7259
Eshwar.Kumar@gnb.ca
Co-Chief Executive Officer, Réjean Savoie
Tel: 506-453-5521
Rejean.Savoie@gnb.ca

Corporate Services Division / Services ministériels
Tel: 506-453-2745; *Fax:* 506-444-4698
Acting Assistant Deputy Minister, Renée Laforest
Tel: 506-453-2745
dh-ms@gnb.ca
Executive Director, Health Business & Technology Solutions, Cheryl Hansen
Tel: 506-444-6782
cheryl.hansen@gnb.ca
Acting Executive Director, Financial Services, Patsy Mackinnon
Tel: 506-453-2117
Patsy.MacKinnon@gnb.ca
Director, Emergency Preparedness & Response, Cathy Goodfellow
Tel: 506-444-4788
cathy.goodfellow@gnb.ca
Director, Enterprise Solutions, Dawn O'Donnell
Tel: 506-453-2279
dawn.o'donnell@gnb.ca
Director, Corporate Support Services, Mark Thompson
Tel: 506-453-2745
mark.thompson@gnb.ca

Francophone Services, Medicare & Pharmaceutical Services Division / Services aux francophones, Assurance-maladie et Services pharmaceutiques
Tel: 506-453-2582; *Fax:* 506-453-5523
Associate Deputy Minister, Lyne St-Pierre-Ellis
Tel: 506-453-2582
lyne.st-pierre-ellis@gnb.ca
Executive Director, Pharmaceutical Services, Leanne Jardine
Tel: 506-453-3884
leanne.jardine@gnb.ca
Director, Health Workforce Information & Analysis, James Ayles
Tel: 506-453-2793
james.ayles@gnb.ca
Director, Pharmaceutical Services, Hugh Ellis
Tel: 506-444-4932
Hugh.Ellis@gnb.ca
Director, Medicare - Insured Services & Physician Remuneration, Michel Léger
Tel: 506-453-2793
Michel.Leger@gnb.ca
Director, Health Workforce Planning, Eric Levesque
Tel: 506-453-2793
Eric.Levesque2@gnb.ca
Director, Pharmaceutical Services, Heidi Liston
Tel: 506-444-3326
heidi.liston@gnb.ca
Director, Pharmaceutical Services, Kevin Pothier
Tel: 506-444-5961
Kevin.Pothier@gnb.ca
Director, Medicare - Eligibility & Claims, Carole Sharpe
Tel: 506-453-8275
Carole.Sharpe@gnb.ca

Health Intelligence, Policy & Planning Division / Planification, politiques et données du secteur de la santé
Fax: 506-453-5523
Assistant Deputy Minister, Gérin Girouard
Tel: 506-453-2775
gerin.girouard@gnb.ca
Executive Director, Policy, Legislation & Intergovernmental Relations, Mark Wies
Tel: 506-453-2013
Mark.Wies@gnb.ca
Director, Health Information Management, John Boyne
Tel: 506-444-3222
john.boyne@gnb.ca
Director, Federal-Provincial Relations & Atlantic Collaboration, Policy, Legislation & Intergovernmental Relations, Dave Dell
Tel: 506-444-6760
dave.dell@gnb.ca
Acting Director, Health Information Management, Debbie Peters
Tel: 506-453-4079
debbie.peters@gnb.ca

Office of the Chief Medical Officer of Health Division / Bureau du médecin-hygiéniste en chef
Fax: 506-453-5243
Chief Medical Officer, Vacant
Acting Chief Medical Officer & Deputy Chief Medical Officer of Health, Jennifer Russell
Tel: 506-453-2280
jennifer.russell@gnb.ca
Executive Director, Planning & Operations, Janique Robichaud-Savoie
Tel: 506-453-6962
Janique.Robichaud-savoie@gnb.ca
Director, Public Health Practice & Population Health, Kimberly Blinco
Tel: 506-453-6874
kimberley.blinco@gnb.ca
Director, Communicable Disease & Control, Shelley Landsburg
Tel: 506-444-3044
Shelley.Landsburg@gnb.ca
Director, Healthy Environments, Karen White Masry
Tel: 506-453-2427
karen.white-masry@gnb.ca

New Brunswick Department of Human Resources / Ressources humaines

Chancery Place, 675 King St., Fredericton, NB E3B 1E9
Tel: 506-453-2264; *Fax:* 506-453-7195
Ohr-brh@gnb.ca
www.gnb.ca/0163/index-e.asp

This department has been merged with the Treasury Board as of June 6, 2016 as a part of the cabinet shuffle made by Premier Gallant. The Department of Human Resources has responsibility for the policies which govern the following human resources issues: recruitment; compensation; & staff development for the provision of quality public services.

Minister, Human Resources, Hon. Denis Landry
Tel: 506-453-3036; *Fax:* 506-453-7195
denis.landry2@gnb.ca
Deputy Minister, Kelly Cain
Tel: 506-453-3036; *Fax:* 506-453-7195
kelly.cain@gnb.ca
Director, Corporate Relations, Natalie Hartford
Tel: 506-453-4450
Natalie.Hartford@gnb.ca

Employee Relations & Organizational Health / Relations avec les employés et Santé organisationnelle
Tel: 506-453-2264; *Fax:* 506-444-5786
Assistant Deputy Minister, Frédéric Finn
Tel: 506-453-2264
Frederic.Finn@gnb.ca
Director, Compensation, Classification & Corporate Research, Amy Beswarick
Tel: 506-444-4817
amy.beswarick@gnb.ca
Director, Healthy Workplaces, Lynn Noel
Tel: 506-453-2141
Lynn.Noel@gnb.ca
Director, Labour Relations, Luc Sirois
Tel: 506-453-2115
Luc.Sirois@gnb.ca

Human Resource Talent, Policy & Programs / Division des politiques et des programmes en ressources humaines et de la gestion des talents
Tel: 506-453-2141; *Fax:* 506-453-4225
Executive Director, Shannon Ferris
Tel: 506-444-4912
shannon.ferris@gnb.ca
Director, HR Programs & Official Languages, Lori Anne McCracken
Tel: 506-453-2141
LoriAnne.MCCRACKEN@gnb.ca
Director, HR Policy & Development Branch, Jennifer Wilkins
Tel: 506-453-2141; *Fax:* 506-453-4225
Jennifer.Wilkins@gnb.ca

Pensions & Employee Benefits / Pensions et avantages sociaux des employés
Kings Place, #680, 440 King St., PO Box 6000 Fredericton, NB E3B 5H1
Tel: 506-453-2296; *Fax:* 506-457-7388
Toll-Free: 800-561-4012
Assistant Deputy Minister, Pensions & Employee Benefits, Troy Mann
Tel: 506-453-2296; *Fax:* 506-457-7388
Troy.Mann@gnb.ca
Director, Client Services, Marilyn McConnell
Tel: 506-453-2296; *Fax:* 506-457-7388
marilyn.mcconnell@gnb.ca
Director, Finance, Administration & Information Technology Services, Jennie Noel-Theriault
Tel: 506-453-2296
Jennie.NOEL-theriault@gnb.ca
Director, Communications, Pension Policy & Client Communications, Dan Toner
Tel: 506-453-2296
Dan.Toner@gnb.ca

New Brunswick Human Rights Commission / Commission des droits de la personne

Barry House, PO Box 6000 Fredericton, NB E3B 5H1
Tel: 506-453-2301; *Fax:* 506-453-2653
Toll-Free: 888-471-2233
TTY: 506-453-2911
hrc.cdp@gnb.ca
www.gnb.ca/hrc-cdp/index-e.asp

The Human Rights Commission is a provincial government agency. It promotes equality & investigates & tries to settle complaints of discrimination & harassment. The Commission also works to prevent discrimination by promoting human rights & offering educational opportunities to employers, service providers, & the general public.

Minister Responsible, Hon. Francine Landry
Tel: 506-735-7222; *Fax:* 506-735-7226
Francine.Landry@gnb.ca
Chair, Nathalie Chiasson
hrc.cdp@gnb.ca
Director, Marc-Alain Mallet
marc-alain.mallet@gnb.ca
Legal Counsel, Sarina Mckinnon
sarina.mckinnon@gnb.ca

New Brunswick Department of Justice & Public Safety / Justice et sécurité publique

Argyle Place, PO Box 6000 Fredericton, NB E3B 5H1
Tel: 506-453-3992
DPS-MSP.Information@gnb.ca
www.gnb.ca/publicsafety

This department has merged with the Department of Public Safety as of June 6, 2016 as a result of the cabinet shuffle by Premier Gallant. It is renamed the Department of Justice & Public Safety. The Department of Justice promotes the impartial administration of justice & ensures protection of the public interest.

Minister, Justice & Public Safety, Hon. Denis Landry
denis.landry2@gnb.ca
Attorney General, Hon. Serge Rousselle, Q.C.
Tel: 506-453-3678; *Fax:* 506-457-4810
Serge.Rousselle@gnb.ca
Deputy Minister; Deputy Attorney General, Johanne Bray
Tel: 506-453-3992
johanne.bray@gnb.ca
Communications Officer, Elaine Bell
Tel: 506-444-3323
elaine.bell@gnb.ca
Director, Office of the Provincial Advisor, Andrew Easton
Tel: 506-457-7535
sei@gnb.ca

Associated Agencies, Boards & Commissions:

•New Brunswick Legal Aid Services Commission
#501, 500 Beaverbrook Ct.
Fredericton, NB E3B 5X4
Tel: 506-444-2776; *Fax:* 506-444-2290
info@legalaid.nb.ca
www.legalaid.nb.ca
Local legal aid offices are located in the following places:
Baththurst (506-546-5010);
Campbellton (506-753-6453);
Edmundston (506-735-4213);
Fredericton (506-444-2777);
Miramichi (506-622-1061);
Moncton (506-853-7300);
Saint John (506-633-6030);
Tracadie-Sheila (506-395-1507);
Woodstock (506-328-8127.

•Financial & Consumer Services Commission (FCNB) / Commission des services financiers et des services aux consommateurs
#300, 85 Charlotte St.
Saint John, NB E2L 2J2
Tel: 506-658-3060; *Fax:* 506-658-3059
Toll-free: 866-933-2222
info@fcnb.ca
www.fcnb.ca
The New Brunswick Securities Commission adminsters the province's Securities Statute. Staff of the commission are responsible for the following services: review of prospectuses; registration of companies & persons operating in the province's securities industry; consideration of exemption applications; & enforcement of securities laws.

Community, Corrections & Corporate Services / Services communautaires, correctionnels et généraux
Tel: 506-453-5975; *Fax:* 506-453-3311
Assistant Deputy Minister, Michael Comeau
Tel: 506-453-5975
michael.comeau@gnb.ca
Director, Information Management & Technology, Virender Ambwani
Tel: 506-444-4433
vic.ambwani@gnb.ca
Director, Human Resources, Andrew Currie
Tel: 506-453-3903
andrew.currie@gnb.ca
Director, Strategic Policy & Planning, Karen Hughson
Tel: 506-457-7318
Karen.Hughson@gnb.ca
Director, Finance & Administration, Dan MacLean
Tel: 506-238-4693
Dan.Maclean@gnb.ca
Director, Community Services, Gail McDonald
Tel: 506-444-5274
Gail.McDonald@gnb.ca

Justice Branch
Tel: 519-462-5100; *Fax:* 506-453-3651
justice.info@gnb.ca

Administrative Services Division / Services administratifs
Tel: 506-453-2719; *Fax:* 506-453-8718
The Administrative Services Division supports the operations of the Department of Justice & Attorney General by providing the following services: expropriation advisory services; human resources; information management & technology; financial services; & facilities management.
Director, Human Resources Services, Julie Comeau
Tel: 506-444-2191
Julie.M.Comeau@gnb.ca
Director, Financial Services, Gayle Howard
Tel: 506-444-4015
gayle.howard@gnb.ca

Court Services Division / Services aux tribunaux
Tel: 506-453-2933; *Fax:* 506-453-3651
The Court Services Division ensures uniform access for all citizens to criminal & civil courts.
Court services are located in the following regions:
Bathurst / Campbellton / Tracadie (506-547-2150);
Edmundston / Grand Falls (506-735-2029);
Fredericton / Oromocto / Woodstock (506-453-2015);
Miramichi (506-627-4023);
Moncton / Richibucto (506-856-2305);
Saint John / Hampton / St. Stephen (506-658-2400).
Assistant Deputy Minister, Court Services Division, Natalie LeBlanc
Tel: 506-453-3992
Natalie.LeBlanc@gnb.ca
Executive Director, Program Support Services, Joanne Higgins
Tel: 506-453-3992
joanne.higgins@gnb.ca
Registrar, Registrar Services, Caroline Lafontaine
Tel: 506-453-2452
caroline.lafontaine@gnb.ca
Regional Director, Saint John / St. Stephen Court Services, Donald Higgins
Tel: 506-658-2400
donald.higgins@gnb.ca
Regional Director, Bathurst Court Services, Donald Boudreau
Tel: 506-547-2150
donald.boudreau@gnb.ca
Regional Director, Miramichi Court Services, Matthew Cripps
Tel: 506-627-4023
matthew.cripps@gnb.ca
Regional Director, Fredericton Court Services, Andrea Hull
Tel: 506-453-2015
Andrea.Hull@gnb.ca

Public Security & Emergency Services / Sécurité publique et des services d'urgence
Tel: 506-453-7142; *Fax:* 506-453-2307
Fire Marshal, Douglas Browne
Tel: 506-453-2004
Douglas.Browne@gnb.ca
Director, Crime Prevention & Policing Standards, John Jurcina
Tel: 506-478-2785
John.Jurcina@gnb.ca
Director, Emergency Measures Organization, Greg MacCallum
Tel: 506-453-2133
Greg.MacCallum@gnb.ca
Director, NB 911 Bureau, Diane Pelletier
Tel: 506-453-5307
diane.b.pelletier@gnb.ca

Safety Services / Services de sécurité
Tel: 506-453-7142; *Fax:* 506-453-2370
Provides leadership in the areas of law enforcement & community safety in order to preserve & enhance the quality of life in New Brunswick.
Acting Assistant Deputy Minister, Barbara Whitenect
Tel: 506-453-7142; *Fax:* 506-453-3870
BARBARA.WHITENECT@gnb.ca
Executive Director, Inspection & Enforcement, Michael Johnston
Tel: 506-453-3992
Mike.Johnston@gnb.ca
Director, Provincial Firearms Office, Derek Eardley
Tel: 506-453-3775
Derek.Eardley@gnb.ca
Director, Gaming Control, Rosemary Goodridge
Tel: 506-453-7472
Rosemary.goodridge@gnb.ca
Director, Technical Inspection Services, Tim Wiebe
Tel: 506-453-2336
Tim.Wiebe@gnb.ca
Registrar, Gaming Control, Michael Comeau
Tel: 506-453-7142
Michael.Comeau@gnb.ca
Registrar, Motor Vehicle Branch, Chris O'Connell
Tel: 506-453-2410
Chris.O'Connell@gnb.ca
Chief Inspector, Boiler Inspection Program, Eben Creaser
Tel: 506-470-0645
Eben.Creaser@gnb.ca
Chief Inspector, Plumbing Inspection Program, William Fallow
Tel: 506-470-8396
william.fallow@gnb.ca
Chief Coroner, Coroner Services, Gregory J. Forestell
Tel: 506-453-3604
Greg.Forestell@gnb.ca
Chief Inspector, Electrical Inspection Program, Gérald LeBlanc
Tel: 506-874-0697
Jake.LeBlanc@gnb.ca

New Brunswick Liquor Corporation (Alcool NB Liquor) / Société des alcools du Nouveau-Brunswick

170 Wilsey Rd., PO Box 20787 Fredericton, NB E3B 5B8
Tel: 506-452-6826; *Fax:* 506-462-2024
Receptionist@anbl.com
www.anbl.com
Other Communication: Public Affairs Phone: 506-452-6453
www.facebook.com/nbliquor
The Crown corporation manufactures, buys, imports, & sells liquor of every kind.
Minister, Finance, Hon. Cathy Rogers
Cathy.Rogers@gnb.ca
Chairperson, Ron Lindala
Tel: 506-452-6826
ron.lindala@anbl.com
President & CEO, Brian Harriman
Tel: 506-452-6522
Brian.Harriman@anbl.com
Senior Vice-President & Secretary of the Board, Richard A. Smith
Tel: 506-452-6826
rick.smith@anbl.com
Vice-President, Finance & Chief Financial Officer, Chris Evans
Tel: 506-452-6460
Chris.Evans@anbl.com
Vice-President, Supply Chain & Property Management, Mike O'Brien
Tel: 506-452-6505
mike.o'brien@anbl.com
Vice-President, Customer Service & Retail Operations, Brad Cameron
Tel: 506-452-6511
brad.cameron@anbl.com
Vice-President, Category Management & Marketing, Gary von Richter
Tel: 506-452-6546
Gary.vonRichter@anbl.com

Office of the Ombudsman / Bureau de l'ombudsman

PO Box 6000 Fredericton, NB E3B 5H1
Tel: 506-453-2789; *Fax:* 506-453-5599
Toll-Free: 888-465-1100
nbombud@gnb.ca
www.ombudnb.ca
The Ombudsman is independent of government, & is an officer of the Legislative Assembly, with responsibilities under the Ombudsman Act, the Civil Service Act, & the Archives Act. In 1994, the Civil Service Commission was amalgamated with the Office of the Ombudsman, which hears appeals & investigates complaints regarding selections for appointment in the Civil Service.
Ombudsman, Charles Murray
Tel: 506-453-2789; *Fax:* 506-453-5599
nbombud@gnb.ca
Director, Investigations, François Levert
Tel: 506-453-2789
Francois.Levert@gnb.ca
Director, Legal & Corporate Services, Jennifer Murray
Tel: 506-453-2789; *Fax:* 506-453-5599
jennifer.murray@gnb.ca

Opportunities New Brunswick / Opportunités Nouveau-Brunswick

Place 2000, PO Box 6000 Fredericton, NB E3B 5H1
Tel: 506-453-5471; *Fax:* 506-444-5277
Toll-Free: 855-746-4662
info@onbcanada.ca
opportunitiesnb.ca
twitter.com/OpportunitiesNB
www.facebook.com/OpportunitiesNB
Opportunities NB was created in 2015 to replace Invest NB & the Department of Economic Development. Its mandate is to support business development inside New Brunswick; pursue growth opportunities outside the province; & work with economic departments, other public sector partners & stakeholders to construct a portfolio of growth opportunities both inside & outside the province.
Minister, Economic Development; Minister Responsible, Hon. Francine Landry
francine.landry@gnb.ca
President & CEO, Stephen Lund
Tel: 506-453-2794
stephen.lund@onbcanada.ca
Vice-President, Special Projects, Serge Doucet
Tel: 506-453-5471
Serge.Doucet@onbcanada.ca
Director, Communications, Carolyn McCormack
Tel: 506-453-5471
carolyn.mccormack@onbcanada.ca

Business Growth Division / Croissance des entreprises
Tel: 506-453-5471; *Fax:* 506-444-4277
Toll-Free: 855-746-4662
The Business Development Division assists businesses in New Brunswick to become more innovative & competitive.
Vice-President, Serge Doucet
Tel: 506-453-5471
Serge.Doucet@onbcanada.ca
Director, Keith Melvin
Tel: 506-658-5678
Keith.Melvin@onbcanada.ca
Director, Trade & Exports, Suzanne Turmel
Tel: 506-444-5107
suzanne.turmel@gnb.ca

Deal Structuring & CFO / Structuration d'opérations commerciales et chef des services financiers
Tel: 506-453-5471; *Fax:* 506-444-4277

The Corporate Services & Programs Division assists the department through records management, financial administration, & information technology management.
Vice-President, Paul Fudge
Tel: 506-453-3420
Paul.Fudge@onbcanada.ca
Director, Special Accounts & Monitoring, Jean-Bernard Guignard
Tel: 506-444-4421
jean-bernard.guignard@onbcanada.ca
Director, Valuations & Credit, Michel Landry
Tel: 506-478-7365
Michel.Landry@onbcanada.ca
Director, Financial Assistance to Industry, Daniel Seems
Tel: 506-453-6291
Dan.Seems@onbcanada.ca
Manager, Corporate Accounting & Claims, Amy Wesenberg
Tel: 506-453-3021
amy.wesenberg@onbcanada.ca

Investment Attraction Division / Attraction des investissements
Tel: 506-453-5471; *Fax:* 506-444-4277
Toll-Free: 855-746-4662
The Local Development Division supports businesses across the province with growth, innovation & exporting objectives through financial assistance programs & business counselling services.
Assistant Vice-President, Jean Paul Robicheau
Tel: 506-453-2413
JeanPaul.Robicheau@onbcanada.ca
Senior Director, Steve Milbury
Tel: 506-658-5585
Steve.Milbury@onbcanada.ca

Organizational Culture & Services Division / Culture organisationnelle et services
Tel: 506-453-5471; *Fax:* 506-444-4277
Toll-Free: 855-746-4662
The Policy, Strategy & Innovation Division assists in research, development & reporting related to policy & programs that support the economic objectives of the province.
Chief Culture Officer, Heather Libbey
Tel: 506-470-8927
Heather.Libbey@onbcanada.ca

New Brunswick Police Commission (NBPC) / Commission de police du Nouveau-Brunswick

Fredericton City Centre, #202, 435 King St., Fredericton, NB E3B 1E5
Tel: 506-453-2069; *Fax:* 506-457-3542
Toll-Free: 888-389-1777
nbpc@gnb.ca
www.nbpolicecommission.ca
The New Brunswick Police Commission is engaged in the following activities: investigating & determining complaints alleging misconduct by municipal & regional police officers; investigating any matter relating to any aspect of policing in any area of the province; determining the adequacy of municipal, regional, & RCMP police forces within the province.
Acting Chair, Robert M. Stoney
Tel: 506-453-2069; *Fax:* 506-457-3542
robert.stoney@gnb.ca
Acting Vice-Chair, Ronald Cormier
Tel: 506-453-2069; *Fax:* 506-457-3542
Executive Director, Steve Roberge
Tel: 506-453-2069; *Fax:* 506-457-3542
steve.roberge@gnb.ca

New Brunswick Department of Post-Secondary Education, Training & Labour / Éducation postsecondaire, Formation et Travail

Chestnut Complex, PO Box 6000 Fredericton, NB E3B 5H1
Tel: 506-453-2597; *Fax:* 506-453-3618
dpetlinfo@gnb.ca
www.gnb.ca/post-secondary
New Brunswick's Department of Post-Secondary Education, Training, & Labour consists of the following divisions: Adult Learning & Employment; Communications; Corporate Services; Labour & Planning; Population Growth; & Post-Secondary Education.
Minister, Post-Secondary Education, Training & Labour, Hon. Donald Arseneault
Donald.Arseneault@gnb.ca
Deputy Minister, Tom Mann
Tel: 506-453-2343
Tom.Mann@gnb.ca
Director, Performance Excellence Alignment Champion, Jane Breckenridge
Tel: 506-461-4897
jane.breckenridge@gnb.ca

Communications Officer, Molly Cormier
Tel: 506-444-3194
Molly.Cormier2@gnb.ca

Adult Learning & Employment Division / Apprentissage pour adultes et emploi
Tel: 506-453-2587; *Fax:* 506-453-3038
Assistant Deputy Minister, Daniel Mills
Tel: 506-476-2556
daniel.mills@gnb.ca
Executive Director, Employment & Continuous Learning Services, Guy Lamarche
Tel: 506-462-5935
guy.lamarche@gnb.ca
Executive Director, Provincial Office, Sylvie Nadeau
Tel: 506-453-2354
sylvie.nadeau@gnb.ca
www.gnb.ca/publiclibraries
Director, Apprenticeship & Occupational Certification, Michael Barnett
Tel: 506-444-3657
michael.barnett@gnb.ca
Director, Employment Programs, Paul Graham
Tel: 506-643-6963
paul.graham@gnb.ca

Corporate Services Division / Services ministériels
Tel: 506-453-2587; *Fax:* 506-453-3038
Executive Director, Corporate Services, Michael Murray
Tel: 506-453-7129
michael.murray@gnb.ca
Director, Information Management & Technology Services, Suzanne Bourgeois
Tel: 506-453-2588
suzanne.bourgeois@gnb.ca
Manager, Human Resource Strategy & Programs, Melanie Gautreau-Miles
Tel: 506-453-8209
melanie.gautreau-miles@gnb.ca
Acting Director, Departmental Coordination, Roseline Pelletier
Tel: 506-453-8132
roseline.pelletier@gnb.ca
Director, Finance & Administration, Shauna Woodside
Tel: 506-453-3877
Shauna.Woodside@gnb.ca

Labour & Policy Division / Travail et Politique
Tel: 506-453-2592; *Fax:* 506-453-3038
Acting Assistant Deputy Minister, Dianne Nason
Tel: 506-444-2071
dianne.nason@gnb.ca
Assistant Director, Strategic Services, Hope Brewer
Tel: 506-457-7891
Hope.Brewer@gnb.ca

Population Growth Division / Croissance démographique
#500, Beaverbrook Bldg., PO Box 6000 Fredericton, E3B 5H1
Tel: 506-453-3981; *Fax:* 506-444-6729
Issues such as immigration, attraction & repatriation, settlement & multiculturalism, & retention are handled by the Population Growth Division.
Assistant Deputy Minister, Charles Ayles
Tel: 506-444-5663
charles.ayles@gnb.ca
Director, Immigration, Settlement & Multiculturalism, Ashraf Ghanem
Tel: 506-457-7644
ashraf.ghanem@gnb.ca

Post-Secondary Education Division / Éducation Postsecondaire
Tel: 506-444-5732; *Fax:* 506-453-3038
Assistant Deputy Minister, France Haché
Tel: 506-457-4891
france.hache@gnb.ca
Director, New Brunswick College of Craft & Design, Donna Boudreau
Tel: 506-444-2435
donna.boudreau@gnb.ca
Acting Director, College Admissions Service, Debbie Cormier
Tel: 506-789-2016
debbie.cormier@gnb.ca
Director, Student Financial Services, Chris Ferguson
Tel: 506-453-3399
chris.ferguson@gnb.ca
Director, Research & Strategic Initiatives, Peter French
Tel: 506-457-6782
peter.french@gnb.ca
Director, University Relations, Giselle Goguen
Tel: 506-462-5135
giselle.goguen@gnb.ca
Director, New Brunswick College of Craft & Design, Keith McAlpine
Tel: 506-444-4056
keith.mcalpine@gnb.ca
Dean, New Brunswick College of Craft & Design, Harriet Taylor
Tel: 506-444-3735
harriet.taylor@gnb.ca

Regional Development Corporation (RDC) / Société d'aménagement régional (SAR)

Chancery Place, PO Box 6000 Fredericton, NB E3B 5H1
Tel: 506-453-2277; *Fax:* 506-453-7988
www.gnb.ca/rdc
The Regional Development Corporation is a Crown corporation which carries out its mandate in accordance with the Regional Development Corporation Act. The following are responsibilities of the Corporation: administration & management of development agreements between the Province of New Brunswick & the federal government; assistance in the establishment & development of enterprises & institutions; assistance to municipalities in the planning & development of projects to benefit the public; assistance in the development of tourism & recreational facilities; planning, coordinating, & guiding regional development; & performing duties assigned by the Lieutenant-Governor-in-Council.
Minister Responsible, Hon. Donald Arseneault
Donald.Arseneault@gnb.ca
President, Bill Levesque
Tel: 506-453-2277
bill.levesque@gnb.ca
Vice-President, Financial Services & Program Support, Ann Marie Wood-Seems
Tel: 506-453-8526
annmarie.wood-seems@gnb.ca
Vice-President, Regional Development, Hélène Bouchard
Tel: 506-453-5686
helene.bouchard@gnb.ca
Corporate Secretary, Bruce Macfarlane
Tel: 506-444-4583
bruce.macfarlane@gnb.ca

New Brunswick Research & Productivity Council (RPC) / Conseil de la recherche et de la productivité du Nouveau-Brunswick (RPC)

921 College Hill Rd., Fredericton, NB E3B 6Z9
Tel: 506-452-1212; *Fax:* 506-452-1395
Toll-Free: 800-563-0844
info@rpc.ca
www.rpc.ca
Other Communication: Alt. E-mails: accounting@rpc.ca; careers@rpc.ca
www.linkedin.com/company/1414186
The New Brunswick Research & Productivity Council's vision is to excel in technological innovation, enabling its partners in business & industry to create wealth & high quality employment opportunities in New Brunswick.
The council works to steadily improve its capacity to develop & apply new technology, in partnership with firms in the private sector. It provides an expanding range of high quality technical services to clients in the global marketplace.
The Research & Productivity Council is registered to the ISO 9001:2000 International Standard.
Executive Director, Eric Cook
Tel: 506-452-1212
eric.cook@rpc.ca
Department Head, Mechanical Systems & Diagnostics, John Aikens
Tel: 506-452-1212
john.aikens@rpc.ca
Department Head, Food, Fisheries & Aquaculture, Ben Forward
Tel: 506-452-1212
ben.forward@rpc.ca
Department Head, Inorganic Analytical Services, Ross Kean
Tel: 506-452-1212
ross.kean@rpc.ca
Department Head, Organic Analytical Services, Bruce Phillips
Tel: 506-452-1212
bruce.phillips@rpc.ca

Senior & Healthy Aging Secretariat / Secrétariat des aînés en santé

Sartain MacDonald Bldg., 4th Fl., PO Box 6000 Fredericton, NB E3B 5H1
Tel: 506-453-2001; *Fax:* 506-453-2164
seniors@gnb.ca
www.gnb.ca/seniors
The Senior & Healthy Aging Secretariat has the following responsibilities: promoting the healthy aging & wellness of seniors; supporting the Minister Responsible for Seniors; overseeing initiatives under the Renewed Long Term Care Strategy; coordinating strategies that increase support for

informal caregivers; producing & disseminating information for seniors; coordinating the Senior Goodwill Ambassador Program; & working with organizations related to seniors.

Service New Brunswick / Service Nouveau Brunswick

Westmorland Pl., PO Box 1998 Fredericton, NB E3B 5G4
Tel: 506-457-3581; *Fax:* 506-444-2850
snb@snb.ca
www.snb.ca
Other Communication: SNB TeleServices Within NB: 1-888-762-8600; Outside NB: 506-684-7901

Service New Brunswick provides the following services to the public: Service New Brunswick TeleServices (Call Centre); delivery of federal, provincial & municipal government services; Land Registry; Personal Property Registry; Corporate Registry; Property Assessment & Taxation System; & maintaining land information infrastructure.

On Oct. 1, 2015, the new Service New Brunswick was launched, bringing together the former Service New Brunswick, Department of Government Services, FacilicorpNB & New Brunswick Internal Services Agency under one organization.

Minister Responsible, Hon. Ed Doherty
Tel: 506-453-6100
ed.doherty@snb.ca
Chair, Elizabeth Webster
Chief Executive Officer, Gordon Gilman
Tel: 506-444-2897
Gordon.Gilman@snb.ca
Chief Operating Officer, Derrick Jardine
Tel: 506-663-2510
derrick.jardine@snb.ca
Chief Integration Officer, Jill Ritchie
Tel: 506-457-3581
jill.ritchie@snb.ca

Enterprise Services / Services organisationnels

Tel: 506-444-4600; *Fax:* 506-453-5384

Vice-President, Cheryl Hansen
Tel: 506-457-3582
cheryl.hansen@snb.ca
Director, Accounts Payable & Collection Services, Michel Albert
Tel: 506-444-4600
michel.albert@snb.ca
Director, Translation Bureau, Pascale Bergeron
Tel: 506-453-2920
pascale.bergeron@gnb.ca
Director, Corporate Operations, Craig Chouinard
Tel: 506-453-6191
craig.chouinard@snb.ca
Director, Corporate Marketing Services, Rob MacLeod
Tel: 506-474-3452
rob.macleod@snb.ca
Director, Payroll & Benefits, Monica Ward
Tel: 506-444-3279
Monica.Ward@gnb.ca

Finance, Human Resources & Strategy / Finances, Ressources humaines et Stratégie

Tel: 506-457-3581; *Fax:* 506-444-5239

Vice-President, Dan Rae
Tel: 506-457-4805
dan.rae@snb.ca
Corporate Director, Financial Services, Lise Chiasson
Tel: 506-457-4805
lise.chiasson2@snb.ca
Corporate Director, Financial Systems Integration, Kathy Greenbank
Tel: 506-663-2508
kathy.greenbank@snb.ca
Director, Policy & RTIPPA, Liane MacFarlane
Tel: 506-470-0980
liane.macfarlane@snb.ca
Director, Strategy & Corporate Client Relationship Management, Nick McCann
Tel: 506-453-2113
nick.mccann@snb.ca
Director, Finance, James Culligan
Tel: 506-457-4805
james.culligan@snb.ca
Director, External Communications, Bonnie Doyle Creber
Tel: 506-453-2113
bonnie.doylecreber@gnb.ca
Director, Information Management & Compliance, Jodi Hayes
Tel: 506-457-4805
jodi.hayes@snb.ca
Director, Internal Communications, Chantal Poulin
Toll-free: 888-480-4404
chantal.poulin@snb.ca
Corporate Director, Strategy & Organizational Performance, Judy Ross
Tel: 506-453-2113
judy.ross@snb.ca
Chief Privacy Officer & Director, Risk Management, Kelly Steeves
Tel: 506-856-2490
kelly.steeves@snb.ca

Strategy & Organizational Performance Division / Stratégie et rendement organisationnel

Tel: 506-457-3581; *Fax:* 506-453-5384

Corporate Director, Judy Ross
Tel: 506-453-2113
judy.ross@snb.ca
Chief Privacy Officer & Director, Risk Management, Kelly Steeves
Tel: 506-856-2490
kelly.steeves@snb.ca
Chief Information Access & Privacy Officer, Joanne Fletcher
Tel: 506-453-2113
joanne.fletcher@snb.ca
Director, Policy & RTIPPA, Liane MacFarlane
Tel: 506-470-0980
liane.macfarlane@snb.ca
Director, Strategy & Corporate Client Relationship Management, Nick McCann
Tel: 506-453-2113
nick.mccann@snb.ca
Director, Continuous Improvement, Amber Sare
Tel: 506-238-5662
amber.sare@snb.ca

Health Services / Services de santé

Tel: 506-457-3581; *Fax:* 506-444-2850

Vice-President, David Dumont
Tel: 506-663-2510
david.dumont@snb.ca
Executive Director, Clinical Engineering, Charles Beaulieu
Tel: 506-737-5781
Charles.Beaulieu@snb.ca
Executive Director, Strategic Procurement (Health), Ann Dolan
Tel: 506-457-3581
ann.dolan@snb.ca
Executive Director, Supply Chain, Michel Levesque
Tel: 506-869-6140
Michel.Levesque@snb.ca
Executive Director, Laundry & Linen Services, Terry Watters
Tel: 506-457-3581
Terry.Watters@snb.ca
Director, Maintenance - Linen Services, James Belliveau
Tel: 506-457-3581
James.Belliveau@snb.ca
Director, Sourcing Renewal, Nancy Butler-Rioux
Tel: 506-544-2505
Nancy.Butlerrioux@snb.ca
Director, Logistics, Greg Demerchant
Tel: 506-457-3581
greg.demerchant@snb.ca
Director, Procurement (Vitalité), Annick Godin-Bourque
Tel: 506-457-3581
Annick.GodinBourque@snb.ca
Director, Procurement (Horizon), Jana Kirkpatrick
Tel: 506-457-3581
Jana.Kirkpatrick@snb.ca

Technology Services / Services technologiques

Brookside Mall, 435 Brookside Dr., Fredericton, NB E3A 8V4
Tel: 506-444-4600; *Fax:* 506-444-3784
NBISA-ASINB@gnb.ca

Vice-President, Pam Gagnon
Tel: 506-457-3582
Pam.Gagnon@gnb.ca
Director, Infrastructure Operations, Rob Hill
Tel: 506-663-2500
robert.hill@gnb.ca
Executive Director, Health Application Services, Rachel Wilson
Tel: 506-452-5620
Rachel.Wilson@snb.ca
Director, Enterprise Services, Jean-Roger Comeau
Tel: 506-663-2500
Jean-Roger.Comeau@snb.ca
Director, Vitalité Health Network Application Services, Anne Desroches
Tel: 506-862-4977
Anne.DesRoches@snb.ca
Director, Client Support Services, Tracy Gulliver
Tel: 506-444-4600
tracy.gulliver@snb.ca
Director, Horizon Health Network Application Services, Sharon Jamer
Tel: 506-375-2743
Sharon.Jamer@snb.ca
Director, Shared Application Services, Joanne Jury
Tel: 506-443-2601
Joanne.Jury@snb.ca
Director, Enterprise Network, Jean Lajoie
Tel: 506-663-2500
Jean.Lajoie@snb.ca
Director, Corporate Application Services, Trevor MacDonald
Tel: 506-444-4600
trevor.macdonald@snb.ca
Director, Desktop & Application Services, Angie Milbury
Tel: 506-663-2500
Angie.Milbury@snb.ca
Director, Vitalité Health Network Application Services, Ghislain Roy
Tel: 506-444-4600
Ghislain.Roy@snb.ca
Director, Enterprise Storage, Stewart Steele
Tel: 506-663-2500
Stewart.Steele@snb.ca

Public Services & Smart Government / Services publics et Gouvernement intelligent

Tel: 506-457-7838; *Fax:* 506-453-5384

Vice-President, Alan Roy
Tel: 506-457-7838
alan.roy@gnb.ca
Registrar General & Director, Vital Statistics, Josée Dubé
Tel: 506-453-2385
josee.dube@snb.ca
Registrar General, Land Registry, Serge Gauvin
Tel: 506-457-6933
serge.gauvin@snb.ca
Chief Rentalsman, Roger Poirier
Tel: 506-856-2330
irent@snb.ca
Executive Director, Property Assessment Services, Charles Boulay
Tel: 506-453-2658
charles.boulay@snb.ca
Director, Personal Property Registry, Patrick Windle
Toll-free: 855-324-2265
patrick.windle@snb.ca
Director, Land Information Infrastructure Secretariat, Business Opportunities & Digital Services, Andrew MacNeil
Tel: 506-647-7211
andrew.macneil@snb.ca
Director, Customer Care Projects, Louise Rabinovitch
Tel: 506-457-7838
louise.rabinovitch@snb.ca

Strategic Procurement / Approvisionnement stratégique

Marysville Pl., PO Box 6000 Fredericton, NB E3B 5H1
Tel: 506-453-3742; *Fax:* 506-453-7462
Other Communication: Reception: 506-453-4371

Vice-President, Steve Hart
Tel: 506-453-4371
steve.hart@snb.ca
Director, Strategic Sourcing, Robert Boyle
Tel: 506-471-7439
robert.boyle@snb.ca
Director, Procurement Enablement, Joanne Lynch
Tel: 506-444-3280
joanne.lynch@snb.ca

New Brunswick Department of Social Development / Développement social

Sartain MacDonald Bldg., 551 King St., PO Box 6000 Fredericton, NB E3B 5H1
Tel: 506-453-2001; *Fax:* 506-453-2164
sd-ds@gnb.ca
www.gnb.ca/socialdevelopment

The Department of Social Development oversees services to the following citizens of New Brunswick: seniors & persons with disabilities who need long-term care & nursing home services; children who require assistance to prepare for school; abused & neglected children & adults; families in need of affordable day care; & persons in need of affordable housing & social assistance. As of June 6, 2016 the department will be managed by both the minister of families & children as well as the minister of seniors & long term care. However, there remains to be a single deputy minister & mangement team.

Minister, Families & Children, Hon. Stephen Horsman
Stephen.Horsman@gnb.ca
Minister, Seniors & Long-Term Care, Hon. Lisa Harris
lisa.harris@gnb.ca
Deputy Minister, Craig Dalton
Tel: 506-453-2590
craig.dalton@gnb.ca
Director, Wellness Branch, Marlien McKay
Tel: 506-444-4633
marlien.mckay@gnb.ca

Corporate Services / Services ministériels
Tel: 506-453-2379; *Fax:* 506-453-2164
Assistant Deputy Minister, Kim Embleton
Tel: 506-453-2379
Kim.Embleton@gnb.ca
Director, Human Resource Services, Manon Daigle
Tel: 506-444-6715
manon.daigle@gnb.ca
Director, Policy, Legislation & Intergovernmental Relations, Denise Galley-Horncastle
Tel: 506-453-2571
Denise.Galley-Horncastle@gnb.ca
Director, Information Technology Services, Carol LaChapelle
Tel: 506-453-2033
carol.lachapelle@gnb.ca
Director, Integrated Planning, Reporting & Accountabilities, Kelly Rodgers-Sturgeon
Tel: 506-453-2571
kelly.rodgers-sturgeon@gnb.ca
Director, Client Business System Support, Yvonne Samson
Tel: 506-453-2312
Yvonne.Samson@gnb.ca

Program Delivery / Prestation des programmes
Tel: 506-453-2379; *Fax:* 506-453-2164
Assistant Deputy Minister, Jean Rioux
Tel: 506-453-2379
jean.rioux@gnb.ca
Director, Provincial Program Delivery, Marc Gagnon
Tel: 506-856-3364
Marc.Gagnon@gnb.ca

Program Design & Quality Management / Division de la conception des programmes et de gestion de la qualité
Tel: 506-453-2181; *Fax:* 506-453-2164
Director, Community & Individual Development, Amélie Deschenês
Tel: 506-444-4213
Amélie.Deschênes@gnb.ca
Director, Child & Youth Services, William Innes
Tel: 506-453-3622
bill.innes@gnb.ca
Director, Long Term Care & Disability Support Services, Joan McGowan
Tel: 506-457-6811
joan.mcgowan@gnb.ca
Director, Nursing Homes Services, Janet Thomas
Tel: 506-453-3821
janet.thomas@gnb.ca

Wellness
Sartain MacDonald Bldg., PO Box 6000 Fredericton, NB E3B 5H1
Tel: 506-453-4217; *Fax:* 506-444-5722
mieux-etre.wellness@gnb.ca
www.gnb.ca/0131/index-e.asp
twitter.com/WellnessNB
www.facebook.com/WellnessNBMieuxEtreNB
Director, Marlien McKay
Tel: 506-444-4633

New Brunswick Department of Tourism, Heritage & Culture / Tourisme, Patrimoine et Culture

Centennial Building, PO Box 6000 Fredericton, NB E3B 5H1
Tel: 506-453-3115; *Fax:* 506-457-4984
thctpcinfo@gnb.ca
www2.gnb.ca/content/gnb/en/departments/thc.html
www.twitter.com/seenewbrunswick
www.facebook.com/DestinationNB
www.youtube.com/tourismnb
The Department of Tourism, Heritage & Culture is engaged in facilitating community cultural development throughout New Brunswick & maximizing the profile of the province's tourism industry.
Minister, Tourism, Heritage & Culture, Hon. John Ames
John.Ames@gnb.ca
Deputy Minister, Kelly Cain
Tel: 506-453-3261
kelly.cain@gnb.ca
Director, Finance & Administration, Jo-Anne Bradley
Tel: 506-292-1715
jo-anne.bradley@gnb.ca
Director, Communications, Jason Hoyt
Tel: 506-444-5185
jason.hoyt@gnb.ca
Director, Human Resources, Carrie Miles
Tel: 506-470-6632
carrie.miles2@gnb.ca

Associated Agencies, Boards & Commissions:

•Kings Landing Historical Settlement / Village historique de Kings Landing
5804 Rte 102
Prince William, NB E6K 0A5
Tel: 506-363-4999; *Fax:* 506-363-4989
info.kingslanding@gnb.ca
kingslanding.nb.ca

•New Brunswick Arts Board / Conseil des arts Nouveau-Brunswick
649 Queen St., 2nd Fl.
Fredericton, NB E3B 1C3
Tel: 506-444-4444; *Fax:* 506-444-5543
Toll-free: 866-460-2787
www.artsnb.ca
The New Brunswick Arts Board promotes the creation of art. The arts funding agency also administers funding programs for professional artists throughout New Brunswick.

•New Brunswick Museum / Musée du Nouveau-Brunswick
Exhibition Centre, Market Square
Saint John, NB E2L 4Z6
Tel: 506-643-2300; *Fax:* 506-643-6081
Toll-free: 888-268-9595
nbmuseum@nbm-mnb.ca
www.nbm-mnb.ca

Tourism & Culture / Tourisme et Culture
Tel: 506-453-3115; *Fax:* 506-444-5760
Cultural responsibilities include development of the arts, heritage, cultural industries, & the New Brunswick Museum.
Director, Sales, Media & Visitor Experience, Cindy Creamer-Rouse
Tel: 506-444-4097
cindy.creamer-rouse@gnb.ca
Director, Arts & Cultural Industries, Nathalie Dubois
Tel: 506-447-8171
nathalie.dubois@gnb.ca
Director, Marketing & Visitor Information, Kim Matthews
Tel: 506-453-4284
kim.matthews@gnb.ca

Tourism & Parks / Tourisme et Parcs
Fax: 506-453-2854
Assistant Deputy Minister, Alain Basqué
Tel: 506-476-0169
alain.basque@gnb.ca
Director, Heritage, William Hicks
Tel: 506-444-5320
Bill.Hicks@gnb.ca
Director, Active Communities, Ryan Jacobson
Tel: 506-453-2928
ryan.jacobson@gnb.ca
Acting Director, Programs, Jeffrey LeBlanc
Tel: 506-457-4842
Jeffrey.LeBlanc@gnb.ca
Director, Policy & Planning Branch, Susan Morell
Tel: 506-453-5896
susan.morell@gnb.ca

Parks & Attractions / Parcs et attractions
Tourism Operations oversees the following provincial parks & historical sites: De la République, Sugarloaf, Mactaquac, New River Beach, Herring Cove, Parlee Beach, Murray Beach, The Ancorage, Mount Carleton, Hopewell Rocks, Village Historique Acadien, Kings Landing, & Miscou.
Director, Parks & Attractions, Andrew Foster
Tel: 506-453-2170
andrew.foster@gnb.ca

New Brunswick Department of Transportation & Infrastructure / Transports et Infrastructure

Kings Place, PO Box 6000 Fredericton, NB E3B 5H1
Tel: 506-453-3939; *Fax:* 506-453-7987
Transportation.Web@gnb.ca
www.gnb.ca/0113/index-e.asp
The mission of the Department of Transportation & Infrastructure is the maintenance of a safe transportation system & infrastructure within the province of New Brunswick's jurisdiction. The department also monitors & advises on transportation & infrastructure issues of federal jurisdiction.
Minister, Transportation & Infrastructure, Hon. Bill Fraser
bill.fraser@gnb.ca
Deputy Minister, Kelly Cain
Tel: 506-453-2549
Kelly.Cain@gnb.ca
Director, Communications, Judy Cole
Tel: 506-453-5634
judy.cole@gnb.ca
Director, Communications, Veronique Taylor
Tel: 506-453-5634
Veronique.Taylor@gnb.ca

Associated Agencies, Boards & Commissions:

•Vehicle Management Agency
Vehicle Management Centre
PO Box 6000
Fredericton, NB E3B 5H1
Tel: 506-453-3939; *Fax:* 506-453-3628
Transportation.Web@gnb.ca
The Vehicle Management Agency provides vehicle maintenance & fleet management services to the Government of New Brunswick.

Buildings Division / Édifices
Tel: 506-453-3742; *Fax:* 506-462-2072
The Buildings Division oversees the construction & maintenance of New Brunswick's provincial government buildings & leased premises. The division is also responsible for the acquisition & sale of government property.
Assistant Deputy Minister, Robert Martin
Tel: 506-453-2228
bob.martin@gnb.ca
Executive Director, Design & Construction, Bob Daigle
Tel: 506-453-6118
Bob.Daigle@gnb.ca
Executive Director, Special Projects Development, Scott Gibson
Tel: 506-444-4135
Scott.Gibson@gnb.ca
Executive Director, Facilities Management, Gary Lynch
Tel: 506-453-2228
Gary.Lynch@gnb.ca
Director, Planning & Project Development, Pam Barteaux
Tel: 506-453-2362
Pam.Barteaux@gnb.ca
Director, Design Services, Joel Bragdon
Tel: 506-444-5519
Joel.Bragdon@gnb.ca
Director, Construction Services, Wayne Larochelle
Tel: 506-453-2239
wayne.larochelle@gnb.ca

Chief Engineer Division / Ingénieur en chef
Tel: 506-453-3939; *Fax:* 506-453-7987
Responsibilities of the Chief Engineer Division are as follows: offering technical expertise; supporting the design of highway & bridge projects; & coordinating technical transportation research.
Assistant Deputy Minister, Dale Forster
dale.forster@gnb.ca
Director, Property Services, Colleen Brown
Colleen.Brown@gnb.ca
Director, Construction, Carol MacQuarrie
Carol.MacQuarrie@gnb.ca
Director, Design, Robert Sharpe
Robert.Sharpe@gnb.ca

Corporate Services & Fleet Management Division / Services ministériels et Gestion du parc de véhicules
Tel: 506-453-3939; *Fax:* 506-453-7987
The following services are provided by the Corporate Services & Fleet Management Division: administration; financial services; human resources; information technology services; & fleet management for the Government of New Brunswick.
Assistant Deputy Minister, Mark Gaudet
Mark.Gaudet@gnb.ca
Director, Human Resources, Myrna Belyea-Tracy
Tel: 506-444-5531
Myrna.Belyea-Taccy@gnb.ca
Director, Information Management & Technology, Colleen Boldon
Tel: 506-453-4498
colleen.boldon@gnb.ca
Director, Financial & Administrative Services, Charlotte Valley
Tel: 506-453-3389
Charlotte.Valley@gnb.ca

Operations Division / Opérations
Tel: 506-453-3939; *Fax:* 506-462-2072
Responsibilities of the Facilities Management Division include the following: negotiating & administering leases; operating provincially-owned buildings; inspecting buildings; & offering technical support services to government departments, hospitals, & schools.
Executive Director, Operations, David Cogswell
David.Cogswell@gnb.ca
Director, Projects Group, Duane Clowater
Duane.Clowater@gnb.ca
Director, Maintenance & Traffic, Kevin MacLean
Tel: 506-444-2134
Kevin.Maclean@gnb.ca

Policy, Planning & Strategic Development Division / Politiques, planification et développement stratégique
Tel: 506-453-3939; *Fax:* 506-453-5859
Transportation plans & policies are developed in consultation with provincial & federal governments, the transporation industry, & stakeholders.

Assistant Deputy Minister, Sadie Perron
sadie.perron@gnb.ca
Director, Transportation Policy, Nancy Lynch
Nancy.Lynch@gnb.ca
Director, Policy, Shannon Sanford
Shannon.Sanford@gnb.ca

WorkSafeNB (WHSCC) / Travail sécuritaire NB

1 Portland St., PO Box 160 Saint John, NB E2L 3X9
Tel: 506-632-2200; *Fax:* 506-632-4999
Toll-Free: 800-222-9775
communications@ws-ts.nb.ca
www.worksafenb.ca
Other Communication: Toll free fax: 888-629-4722

WorkSafeNB is a crown corporation, responsible for the application of the New Brunswick Occupational Health & Safety Act, the Workers' Compensation Act of New Brunswick, & the Workplace Health, Safety & Compensation Commission Act of New Brunswick on behalf of the workers & employers of this province. WorkSafeNB provides insurance for the workers it represents.

Chair, Dorine Pirie
President & CEO, Gerard M. Adams
Vice-President, WorkSafe Services, Shelly Dauphinee
Tel: 506-632-2320
Acting Vice-President, Corporate Services, Tim Peterson
Tel: 506-633-3555
Corporate Secretary & General Counsel, Michael McGovern
Tel: 506-633-3988
Director, Human Resources, Edith Savoie
Tel: 506-633-4658

Government of Newfoundland & Labrador

Seat of Government: Confederation Bldg., St. John's, NL A1B 4J6
info@gov.nl.ca
www.gov.nl.ca
twitter.com/GovNl
www.youtube.com/govnl; www.flickr.com/govnl

The Province of Newfoundland & Labrador entered Confederation March 31, 1949. It has a land area of 370,494.89 sq km, & the StatsCan census population in 2011 was 514,536.

Office of the Lieutenant Governor

Government House, 50 Military Rd., PO Box 5517 St. John's, NL A1C 5W4
Tel: 709-729-4494; *Fax:* 709-729-2234
governmenthouse@gov.nl.ca
www.govhouse.nl.ca

Lieutenant Governor, The Hon. Frank F. Fagan, CM, ONL, MBA
Tel: 709-729-4019
FrankFagan@gov.nl.ca
Private Secretary, Peter Noel
peternoel@gov.nl.ca

Office of the Premier

East Block, Confederation Bldg., PO Box 8700 St. John's, NL A1B 4J6
Tel: 709-729-3570; *Fax:* 709-729-5875
premier@gov.nl.ca
www.premier.gov.nl.ca

Kathy Dunderdale, the province's first female Premier & tenth Premier overall, resigned on January 22, 2014. She had been Premier since December 3, 2010, having been re-elected in the general election of October 11, 2011. After her resignation, she retained her seat in the district of Virginia Waters until February 2014. Thomas W. Marshall became Acting Premier on January 24, 2014. Paul Davis won the PC leadership on Sept. 13, 2014, becoming the Premier-designate. He was sworn-in on Sept. 26, 2014. Davis lost in the 2015 general election to Liberal Leader Dwight Ball, who became the province's new Premier.

Premier; President, Executive Council, Hon. Dwight Ball
Tel: 709-729-3570; *Fax:* 709-729-5875
premier@gov.nl.ca
Parliamentary Assistant, Mark Browne
Tel: 709-729-3400; *Fax:* 709-729-5202
markbrowne@gov.nl.ca
Chief of Staff, Greg Mercer

Executive Council

c/o Communications Branch, East Block, Confederation Building, 10th Fl., St. John's, NL A1B 4J6
info@gov.nl.ca
www.exec.gov.nl.ca/exec

The mailing address for all Ministers of the Government of Newfoundland & Labrador is as follows: Confederation Building, PO Box 8700, St. John's NL A1B 4J6.
The following is the list of Cabinet Ministers:

Premier; President, Executive Council; Minister, Intergovernmental Affairs; Minister, Labrador & Aboriginal Affairs, Hon. Dwight Ball
Tel: 709-729-3570; *Fax:* 709-729-5875
premier@gov.nl.ca
www.premier.gov.nl.ca/premier
Minister, Finance; President, Treasury Board; Minister Responsible, Human Resource Secretariat, Newfoundland & Labrador Liquor Corporation, Office of the Chief Information Officer, Public Service Commission & Status of Women, Hon. Cathy Bennett
Tel: 709-729-3775; *Fax:* 709-729-2232
cbennett@gov.nl.ca
www.fin.gov.nl.ca/fin/department/minister.html
Minister, Advanced Education & Skills, Hon. Gerry Byrne, P.C.
Tel: 709-729-3580; *Fax:* 709-729-6996
gerrybyrne@gov.nl.ca
www.aes.gov.nl.ca/department/minister.html
Minister, Natural Resources; Minister Responsible, Office of Public Engagement; Deputy Government House Leader, Hon. Siobhan Coady
Tel: 709-729-2920; *Fax:* 709-729-0059
siobhancoady@gov.nl.ca
www.nr.gov.nl.ca/nr/department/minister.html
Minister, Fisheries, Forestry & Agrifood, Hon. Steve Crocker
Tel: 709-729-3705; *Fax:* 709-729-0360
stevecrocker@gov.nl.ca
www.fishaq.gov.nl.ca/department/minister.html
Minister, Children, Seniors & Social Development; Minister Reponsible, Newfoundland & Labrador Housing Corporation & Status of Persons with Disabilities, Hon. Sherry Gambin-Walsh
Tel: 709-729-0659; *Fax:* 709-729-0062
sherrygambinwalsh@gov.nl.ca
www.gov.nl.ca/cyfs/department/minister.html
Minister, Health & Community Services, Hon. Dr. John Haggie
Tel: 709-729-3124; *Fax:* 709-729-0121
johnhaggie@gov.nl.ca
www.health.gov.nl.ca/health/department/minister.html
Minister, Transportation & Works, Hon. Allan Hawkins
Tel: 709-729-3679; *Fax:* 709-729-4285
allanhawkins@gov.nl.ca
www.tw.gov.nl.ca/department/minister.html
Minister, Municipal Affairs; Minister, Service Newfoundland & Labrador; Minister Responsible, Government Purchasing Agency & WorkplaceNL; Registrar General, Hon. Eddie Joyce
Tel: 709-729-3048; *Fax:* 709-729-0943
ejoyce@gov.nl.ca
www.miga.gov.nl.ca/department/minister.html
Minister, Education & Early Childhood Development, Hon. Dale Kirby
Tel: 709-729-5040; *Fax:* 709-729-0414
dalekirby@gov.nl.ca
www.ed.gov.nl.ca/edu/department/minister.html
Minister, Business, Tourism, Culture & Rural Development; Minister Responsible, Research & Development Corporation, Hon. Christopher Mitchelmore
Tel: 709-729-4729; *Fax:* 709-729-0654
cmitchelmore@gov.nl.ca
www.btcrd.gov.nl.ca/department/minister.html
Minister, Justice & Public Safety; Attorney General; Government House Leader, Hon. Andrew Parsons
Tel: 709-729-2869; *Fax:* 709-729-0469
andrewparsons@gov.nl.ca
www.justice.gov.nl.ca/just/department/minister.html
Minister, Environment & Climate Change; Minister Responsible, Francophone Affairs, & Multi-Materials Stewardship Board, Hon. Perry Trimper
Tel: 709-729-2574; *Fax:* 709-729-0112
perrytrimper@gov.nl.ca
www.env.gov.nl.ca/env/department/minister.html

Cabinet Secretariat

East Block, Confederation Building, 4th Fl., PO Box 8700 St. John's, NL A1B 4J6
Tel: 709-729-3490; *Fax:* 709-729-5218
clerkofexecutivecoun@gov.nl.ca

Clerk, Executive Council & Secretary to the Cabinet, Bernard Coffey
Deputy Clerk, Executive Council & Associate Secretary to the Cabinet, Paula Burt
Tel: 709-729-2844; *Fax:* 709-729-5218
paulaburt@gov.nl.ca
Assistant Deputy Clerk, Cindy Hussey
Tel: 709-729-1118
CindyHussey@gov.nl.ca
Associate Secretary to Cabinet, Social Policy, Elizabeth Day
Tel: 709-729-2850
ElizabethDay@gov.nl.ca
Associate Secretary to Cabinet, Communications Branch, Carla Foote
Tel: 709-729-4781
carlafoote@gov.nl.ca
Assistant Deputy Minister, Government Renewal Initiative, Tracy King
Tel: 709-729-2243
tracyking@gov.nl.ca

Office of the Chief Information Officer (OCIO)

40 Higgins Line, PO Box 8700 St. John's, NL A1B 4J6
Tel: 709-729-4000; *Fax:* 709-729-6767
ocio@gov.nl.ca
www.ocio.gov.nl.ca

The OCIO provides a professional Information Technology & Information Management capability aligned to support the business of government & the citizens of Newfoundland & Labrador.

Minister Responsible, Hon. Cathy Bennett
Tel: 709-729-3775; *Fax:* 709-729-2232
cbennett@gov.nl.ca
Chief Information Officer, Ellen MacDonald
Tel: 709-729-2617; *Fax:* 709-729-1464
ellenmacdonald@gov.nl.ca
Executive Director, Application Services, Craig Harding
Tel: 709-729-4329
CraigHarding@gov.nl.ca
Executive Director, Corporate & Information Management, Julie Moore
Tel: 709-729-6260
JulieMoore@gov.nl.ca
Executive Director, Operations, Randy Mouland
Tel: 709-729-5227
randymouland@gov.nl.ca
Executive Director, Solution Delivery, Natalie Templeman
Tel: 709-729-1981
nataliet@gov.nl.ca

Office of Climate Change & Energy Efficiency (CCEE)

PO Box 8700 St. John's, NL A1B 4J6
Tel: 709-729-1210; *Fax:* 709-729-1119
climatechange@gov.nl.ca
www.exec.gov.nl.ca/exec/ccee

Has lead responsibility within Government for strategy & policy development on climate change, energy efficiency & emissions trading. CCEEET is a central agency located within Executive Council. In August 2016 Premier Ball announced the Department of Environment & Conservation & the Office of Climate Change & Energy Efficiency will combine to become the Department of Environment & Climate Change.

Minister Responsible, Hon. Perry Trimper
Tel: 709-729-2574; *Fax:* 709-729-0112
perrytrimper@gov.nl.ca
Assistant Deputy Minister, Jackie Janes
Tel: 709-729-7971; *Fax:* 709-729-1119
jackiejanes@gov.nl.ca
Director, Government Relations, Chad Blundon
Tel: 709-729-7955
ChadBlundon@gov.nl.ca
Director, Research & Evidence, Gerald Crane
Tel: 709-729-0379; *Fax:* 709-729-1119
geraldcrane@gov.nl.ca

Human Resource Secretariat

Confederation Bldg., Main Fl., East Block, PO Box 8700 St. John's, NL A1B 4J6
Tel: 709-729-2476
hrsinfo@gov.nl.ca
www.exec.gov.nl.ca/exec/hrs

Minister Responsible, Hon. Cathy Bennett
Tel: 709-729-3775; *Fax:* 709-729-2232
cbennett@gov.nl.ca
Deputy Minister & Deputy Secretary to Treasury Board, Geoff Williams
Assistant Deputy Minister, Compensation, Staffing & Benefits, Tina Follett
Tel: 709-729-4050; *Fax:* 709-729-1746
tfollett@gov.nl.ca
Assistant Deputy Minister, Labour Relations, Classification, Organization & Management, Brian Miller
Tel: 709-729-1585; *Fax:* 709-729-1746
brianmiller@gov.nl.ca
Assistant Deputy Minister, Client Services, Wanda Penney
Tel: 709-729-3559; *Fax:* 709-729-1746
wandapenney@gov.nl.ca
Director, Communications, Jennifer Tulk
Tel: 709-729-6830
JenniferTulk@gov.nl.ca

Labrador & Aboriginal Affairs Office

Labrador Affairs, 21 Broomfield St., PO Box 3014 Happy Valley - Goose Bay, NL A0P 1E0

Tel: 709-896-1780; *Fax:* 709-896-0045
Toll-Free: 888-435-8111
laa@gov.nl.ca
www.laa.gov.nl.ca
Secondary Address: 6th Fl. Aboriginal Affairs, East Block, Confederation Bldg.PO Box 8700 B Sta.
St. John's, NL A1B 4J6
Alt. Fax: 709-729-4900

Minister, Labrador & Aboriginal Affairs, Hon. Dwight Ball
Tel: 709-729-3570; *Fax:* 709-729-5875
dwightball@gov.nl.ca

Deputy Minister, Aboriginal Affairs, Aubrey Gover
Tel: 709-729-4665; *Fax:* 709-729-4900
aubreygover@gov.nl.ca

Assistant Deputy Minister, Ron Bowles
Tel: 709-896-4449; *Fax:* 709-896-4748
rabowles@gov.nl.ca

Executive Director, Labrador Affairs Office - Labrador West, Janice Barnes
Tel: 709-944-7940; *Fax:* 709-944-7961
janicebarnes@gov.nl.ca

Director, Communications, Kevin Guest
Tel: 709-729-1495
KevinJGuest@gov.nl.ca

Director, Aboriginal Affairs, Brian Harvey
Tel: 709-729-1487; *Fax:* 709-729-4900
brianharvey@gov.nl.ca

Director, Labrador Affairs, Michelle Watkins
Tel: 709-896-1780; *Fax:* 709-896-0045
michellewatkins@gov.nl.ca

Office of Public Engagement

Confederation Bldg., 4th Fl., West Block, PO Box 8700 St. John's, NL A1B 4J6

Tel: 709-729-1125; *Fax:* 709-729-2226
ope@gov.nl.ca
www.ope.gov.nl.ca

Minister Responsible, Hon. Siobhan Coady
Tel: 709-729-2920; *Fax:* 709-729-0059
siobhancoady@gov.nl.ca

Deputy Minister, Judith Hearn
Tel: 709-729-2233
judithhearn@gov.nl.ca

Assistant Deputy Minister, Bruce Gilbert
Tel: 709-729-1611
BruceGilbert@gov.nl.ca

Director, Policy & Research, Jeff Butt
Tel: 709-729-6961
jeffkbutt@gov.nl.ca

Director, Access to Information & Protection of Privacy Office, Victoria Woodworth-Lynas
Tel: 709-729-7073
vwlynas@gov.nl.ca

Women's Policy Office

Confederation Bldg., 4th Fl., West Block, PO Box 8700 St. John's, NL A1B 4J6

Tel: 709-729-5009; *Fax:* 709-729-1418
www.exec.gov.nl.ca/exec/wpo

Minister Responsible, Hon. Cathy Bennett
Tel: 709-729-3775; *Fax:* 709-729-2232
cbennett@gov.nl.ca

Deputy Minister, Donna Ballard, Q.C.
Tel: 709-729-5098
dballard@gov.nl.ca

Director, Violence Prevention, Michelle Smith
Tel: 709-729-5730
michellesmith@gov.nl.ca

House of Assembly

c/o Clerk's Office, Confederation Bldg., PO Box 8700 St. John's, NL A1B 4J6

Tel: 709-729-3405
www.assembly.nl.ca
Other Communication: Legislative Library, Phone: 709-729-3604, E-mail: legislativelibrary@gov.nl.ca
twitter.com/NL_HOA

Clerk, Sandra Barnes
Tel: 709-729-3405
sbarnes@gov.nl.ca
Other Communications: Alternate E-mail: clerkhoa@gov.nl.ca

Speaker, Hon. Tom Osborne
Tel: 709-729-3404; *Fax:* 709-729-4820
speakerhoa@gov.nl.ca

Deputy Speaker; Chair, Committees, Lisa Dempster
Tel: 709-729-3400; *Fax:* 709-729-5202
lisadempster@gov.nl.ca

Deputy Chair, Committees, Paul Lane
Tel: 709-729-2231; *Fax:* 709-729-5202
paullane@gov.nl.ca

Sergeant-at-Arms, Wayne Harnum

Auditor General, Terry Paddon, CPA, CA
Tel: 709-753-2700
Toll-free: 877-753-3888
oagmail@oag.nl.ca
www.ag.gov.nl.ca/ag

Chief Electoral Officer; Commissioner for Legislative Standards, Victor Powers
Tel: 709-729-0712; *Fax:* 709-729-0679
vpowers@gov.nl.ca
www.elections.gov.nl.ca
Social Media: twitter.com/NLElections
Note: Legislative Standards URL: www.legislativestandardscomm.gov.nl.ca

Child & Youth Advocate, Carol A. Chafe
Tel: 709-753-3888
Toll-free: 877-753-3888; *Fax:* 709-753-3988
office@ocya.nl.ca
www.childandyouthadvocate.nl.ca
TTY: 709-753-4366

Citizens' Representative, Barry Fleming, Q.C.
Tel: 709-729-7647; *Fax:* 709-729-7696
citrep@gov.nl.ca
www.citizensrep.nl.ca
Social Media: www.facebook.com/171628062894528

Information & Privacy Commissioner, Donovan Molloy, Q.C.
Tel: 709-729-6309
Toll-free: 877-729-6309; *Fax:* 709-729-6500
commissioner@oipc.nl.ca
www.oipc.nl.ca
Social Media: twitter.com/OIPCNL

Government Caucus Office (Liberal Party)

East Block, 5th Fl., PO Box 8700 St. John's, NL A1B 4J6

nlliberals.ca
twitter.com/nlliberals
www.facebook.com/nlliberals

Premier; President, Executive Council; Minister, Intergovernmental Affairs; Minister, Labrador & Aboriginal Affairs, Hon. Dwight Ball
Tel: 709-729-3570; *Fax:* 709-729-5875
dwightball@gov.nl.ca
Social Media: twitter.com/DwightBallMHA, www.facebook.com/dwightballmha

Government House Leader, Hon. Andrew Parsons
Tel: 709-729-2869; *Fax:* 709-729-0469
andrewparsons@gov.nl.ca

Caucus Whip, Carol Anne Haley
Tel: 709-729-3400; *Fax:* 709-729-5202
carolannehaley@gov.nl.ca

Caucus Chair, Randy Edmunds
Tel: 709-729-3400; *Fax:* 709-729-5202
randyedmunds@gov.nl.ca

Deputy Government House Leader, Hon. Siobhan Coady
Tel: 709-729-2920; *Fax:* 709-729-0059
siobhancoady@gov.nl.ca

Caucus Office of the Official Opposition (Progressive Conservative Party)

PO Box 8700 St. John's, NL A1B 4J6

www.pcpartynl.ca
www.twitter.com/PCpartyNL
www.facebook.com/pcpartynl
www.youtube.com/user/PCNLchannel

PC Leader, Hon. Paul Davis
Tel: 709-729-6670; *Fax:* 709-729-6244
padavis@gov.nl.ca
Social Media: www.facebook.com/pauldavistopsail

Opposition House Leader, Keith Hutchings
Tel: 709-729-1390
Toll-free: 800-634-5504; *Fax:* 709-729-5774
keithhutchings@gov.nl.ca

Caucus Chair, Official Opposition, Kevin Parsons
Tel: 709-729-6979; *Fax:* 709-729-5774
kevinparsons@gov.nl.ca

Caucus Whip, Official Opposition, Tracey Perry
Tel: 709-538-3112; *Fax:* 709-538-3079
traceyperry@gov.nl.ca

Deputy Opposition House Leader, Steve Kent
Tel: 709-729-1526; *Fax:* 709-364-1639
stevekent@gov.nl.ca

Caucus Office of the Third Party (New Democratic Party)

Confederation Building, PO Box 8700 St. John's, NL A1B 4J6

Tel: 709-729-0270; *Fax:* 709-576-1443
Toll-Free: 855-729-0270
ndpinfo@gov.nl.ca
www.nlndpcaucus.ca
twitter.com/NLNDPCaucus
www.facebook.com/NLNDP
www.youtube.com/user/NLNDPCaucus

In the 2011 general election, five members of the New Democratic Party were elected to the House of Assembly. This was the largest Newfoundland & Labrador New Democratic Party Caucus in history. As of the 2015 general election, there were two NDP members left in the House.

Leader, New Democratic Party, Earle McCurdy
Social Media: twitter.com/earlemccurdy, www.facebook.com/earlemccurdy

Third Party House Leader; Third Party Caucus Whip, Lorraine Michael
Tel: 709-729-0270
lorrainemichael@gov.nl.ca

Third Party Caucus Chair, Gerry Rogers
Tel: 709-729-2638; *Fax:* 709-729-1443
gerryrogers@gov.nl.ca

Standing Committees of the House of Assembly

www.assembly.nl.ca/business/committees/ga48session1/default.htm

A five-member committee known as the Striking Committee prepares lists of Members to compose the Standing Committees of the House. The current Standing Committees are as follows: Government Services; Miscellaneous & Private Bills; Privileges & Elections; Public Accounts; Resource; Social Services; & Standing Orders.

Forty-eighth House of Assembly - Newfoundland & Labrador

Confederation Building, PO Box 8700 St. John's, NL A1B 4J6

Tel: 709-729-3405
ClerkHOA@gov.nl.ca
www.assembly.nl.ca
Other Communication: Speaker's Office, Phone: 709-729-3404; Legislative Library, Phone: 709-729-3604; Tours, Phone: 709-729-3670

Last General Election, November 30, 2015.
Party Standings (Sept. 2016)
Liberal 30;
Progressive Conservative 7;
New Democratic Party 2;
Independent 1;
Total 40.
Authorized Salaries & Committee Allowance for Members of the House of Assembly (December 2009): Member, Base Salary $95,357.
In addition to this base salary are the following salaries for office holders:
Speaker $54,072;
Leader of the Opposition $54,072;
Deputy Speaker & Chair of Committees $27,033;
Opposition House Leader $27,033;
Leader of a Third Party $18,918;
Deputy Opposition House Leader $18,457;
Deputy Chair of Committees $13,517;
Chair, Public Accounts Committee $13,517;
Party Whip $13,517;
Caucus Chair $13,517.
All members of the House of Assembly may be reached by including the member's name, the member's district, plus the following address: Confederation Building, PO Box 8700, St. John's NL, A1B 4J6.
The following is an alphabetical list of the members of the House of Assembly, with their electoral district, the total number of registered electors in their district for the 2015 election, plus the members' contact information:

Members of the House of Assembly of Newfoundland & Labrador

Premier; Leader, Liberal Pary of Newfoundland & Labrador; Minister, Intergovernmental Affairs; Minister, Labrador & Aboriginal Affairs, Hon. Dwight Ball
Constituency: Humber — Gros Morne *No. of Constituents:* 9,305, Liberal
Tel: 709-729-3570
Toll-free: 877-635-0132; *Fax:* 70- 72- 587
dwightball@gov.nl.ca
nlliberals.ca/dwight-ball
Other Communications: Constituency Phone: 709-635-0132; Fax: 709-635-0133
Social Media: twitter.com/DwightBallMHA, www.facebook.com/dwightballmha
Constituency Office

#1, 20 Wellon Dr.
Deer Lake, NL A8A 2G5
Minister, Finance; President, Treasury Board; Minister Responsible, Human Resource Secretariat, Newfoundland & Labrador Liquor Corporation, Office of the Chief Information Officer, Public Service Commission & Status of Women, Hon. Cathy Bennett
Constituency: Windsor Lake *No. of Constituents:* 9,088, Liberal
Tel: 709-729-3775; *Fax:* 709-729-2232
cbennett@gov.nl.ca
cathybennett.ca
Other Communications: Constituency Phone: 709-729-3529
Social Media: twitter.com/CathyBennettNL, www.facebook.com/CathyBennettNL
Government Members' Office, East Block, Confederation Bldg., Main Fl.
PO Box 8700
St. John's, NL A1B 4J6
Derek Bennett
Constituency: Lewisporte — Twillingate *No. of Constituents:* 10,291, Liberal
Tel: 709-729-0795
Toll-free: 877-585-0515; *Fax:* 709-729-0662
derekbennett@gov.nl.ca
Other Communications: Constituency Phone: 709-535-2131; Fax: 709-535-2138
Constituency Office, Old Ferry Terminal Bldg.
122 Main St.
Lewisporte, NL A0G 3A0
Derrick Bragg
Constituency: Fogo Island — Cape Freels *No. of Constituents:* 10,456, Liberal
Tel: 709-729-3400
Toll-free: 888-783-9990; *Fax:* 709-729-5202
derrickbragg@gov.nl.ca
Other Communications: Constituency Phone: 709-536-2678; Fax: 709-536-5652
Social Media: twitter.com/derrickbragg
Constituency Office
53 Quay Rd.
PO Box 159
New-Wes-Valley, NL A0G 1C0
David Brazil
Constituency: Conception Bay East — Bell Island *No. of Constituents:* 10,515, Progressive Conservative
Tel: 709-729-0334; *Fax:* 709-729-5774
davidbrazil@gov.nl.ca
Government Members' Office, East Block, Confederation Bldg., 5th Fl.
PO Box 8700
St. John's, NL A1B 4J6
Mark Browne
Constituency: Placentia West — Bellevue *No. of Constituents:* 9,668, Liberal
Tel: 709-729-3400
Toll-free: 800-423-3301; *Fax:* 709-729-5202
markbrowne@gov.nl.ca
Other Communications: Constituency Phone: 709-891-5607; Fax: 709-891-5624
Social Media: twitter.com/markdbrowne
Constituency Office, Father Berney Memorial Bldg.
PO Box 479
Burin Bay Arm, NL A0E 1G0
Minister, Advanced Education, Skills & Labour, Hon. Gerry Byrne, P.C.
Constituency: Corner Brook *No. of Constituents:* 10,397, Liberal
Tel: 709-729-3580; *Fax:* 709-729-6996
gerrybyrne@gov.nl.ca
Other Communications: Constituency Phone: 709-637-4056; Fax: 709-637-4058
Social Media: twitter.com/gerry_byrne, www.facebook.com/MPGerryByrne
Constituency Office, Sir Richard Squires Bldg., 10th Fl.
PO Box 2006
Corner Brook, NL A2H 6J8
Minister, Natural Resources; Deputy Government House Leader, Hon. Siobhan Coady
Constituency: St. John's West *No. of Constituents:* 9,181, Liberal
Tel: 709-729-2920; *Fax:* 709-729-0059
siobhancoady@gov.nl.ca
Other Communications: Constituency Phone: 709-729-2449; Fax: 709-729-0059
Social Media: twitter.com/SiobhanCoadyNL, www.facebook.com/30705872767, ca.linkedin.com/in/siobhan-coady-456a0714
Government Members' Office, Confederation Bldg., 7th Fl.
PO Box 8700
St. John's, NL A1B 4J6
Minister, Fisheries, Forestry & Agrifoods, Hon. Steve Crocker
Constituency: Carbonear — Trinity — Bay de Verde *No. of Constituents:* 11,839, Liberal
Tel: 709-729-3705
Toll-free: 84- 58- 069; *Fax:* 709-729-0360
stevecrocker@gov.nl.ca
Other Communications: Constituency Phone: 709-596-8194; Fax: 709-596-8196
Social Media: twitter.com/stevecrockerlib, www.facebook.com/SteveCrockerLib
Constituency Office
#3, 27 Goff Ave.
Carbonear, NL A1Y 1A6
Bernard Davis
Constituency: Virginia Waters — Pleasantville *No. of Constituents:* 9,832, Liberal
Tel: 709-729-3335; *Fax:* 709-729-0121
bernarddavis@gov.nl.ca
bernarddavis.ca
Other Communications: Constituency Phone: 709-729-5980; Fax: 709-729-0121
Social Media: twitter.com/bernardjdavis, www.facebook.com/bernarddavisnl
Government Members' Office, West Block, Confederation Bldg., 1st Fl.
PO Box 8700
St. John's, NL A1B 4J6
Leader, PC Party; Leader, Official Opposition, Paul Davis
Constituency: Topsail — Paradise *No. of Constituents:* 9,963, Progressive Conservative
Tel: 709-729-6670; *Fax:* 709-729-6244
padavis@gov.nl.ca
Social Media: www.facebook.com/pauldavistopsail
Government Members' Office, East Block, Confederation Building, 5th Fl.
PO Box 8700
St. John's, NL A1B 4J6
Jerry Dean
Constituency: Exploits *No. of Constituents:* 9,381, Liberal
Tel: 709-729-3400
Toll-free: 888-554-7799; *Fax:* 709-729-5202
jerrydean@gov.nl.ca
Constituency Office
6 Dominic St.
Bishop's Falls, NL A0H 1C0
Deputy Speaker; Chair, Committees, Lisa Dempster
Constituency: Cartwright — L'Anse au Clair *No. of Constituents:* 3,056, Liberal
Tel: 709-729-3400
Toll-free: 800-286-9118; *Fax:* 709-729-5202
lisadempster@gov.nl.ca
Other Communications: Constituency Phone: 709-931-2118; Fax: 709-931-2520
Social Media: twitter.com/LisaVDempster, www.facebook.com/lisa.powelldempster
Constituency Office
32 Main St.
PO Box 130
Forteau, NL A0K 2P0
Government Caucus Chair, Randy Edmunds
Constituency: Torngat Mountains *No. of Constituents:* 2,126, Liberal
Tel: 709-729-3400
Toll-free: 877-923-2471; *Fax:* 709-729-5202
randyedmunds@gov.nl.ca
Other Communications: Constituency Phone: 709-923-2471; Fax: 709-923-2473
Social Media: twitter.com/EdmundsMHA, www.facebook.com/randy.edmunds.5
Constituency Office
PO Box 133
Makkovik, NL A0P 1J0
John Finn
Constituency: Stephenville — Port au Port *No. of Constituents:* 9,777, Liberal
Tel: 709-729-3400; *Fax:* 709-729-5202
johnfinn@gov.nl.ca
Other Communications: Constituency Phone: 709-643-0813; Fax: 709-643-0814
Social Media: twitter.com/johnmichaelfinn, www.facebook.com/john.finn.90857
Constituency Office
143 Main St.
PO Box 386
Stephenville, NL A2N 2Z5
Minister, Children, Seniors & Social Development; Minister Reponsible, Newfoundland & Labrador Housing Corporation & Status of Persons with Disabilities, Hon. Sherry Gambin-Walsh
Constituency: Plantia - St. Mary's *No. of Constituents:* 9,305, Liberal
Tel: 709-729-0659
Toll-free: 877-898-0898; *Fax:* 709-729-0662
sherrygambinwalsh@gov.nl.ca
Other Communications: Constituency Phone: 709-227-1304; Fax: 709-227-1307
Social Media: twitter.com/Sgambin, ca.linkedin.com/in/sherry-gambin-walsh-b56b8840
Constituency Office
61 Blockhouse Rd.
PO Box 515
Placentia, NL A0B 2Y0
Minister, Health & Community Services, Hon. Dr. John Haggie
Constituency: Gander *No. of Constituents:* 9,729, Liberal
Tel: 709-729-3124
Toll-free: 80- 81- 685; *Fax:* 709-729-0121
johnhaggie@gov.nl.ca
johnhaggie.ca
Other Communications: Constituency Phone: 709-256-3729; Fax: 709-256-1410
Social Media: twitter.com/johnrockdoc, www.facebook.com/Dr-John-Haggie-626828230729985
Constituency Office
133 Airport Blvd.
Gander, NL A1V 1T5
Government Caucus Whip, Carol Anne Haley
Constituency: Burin — Grand Bank *No. of Constituents:* 9,321, Liberal
Tel: 709-729-3400; *Fax:* 709-729-5202
carolannehaley@gov.nl.ca
Other Communications: Constituency Phone: 709-832-2530
Constituency Office
26 Water St.
PO Box 490
Grand Bank, NL A0E 1W0
Minister, Transportation & Works, Hon. Allan Hawkins
Constituency: Grand Falls — Windsor — Buchans *No. of Constituents:* 8,964, Liberal
Tel: 709-729-3679
Toll-free: 888-610-4440; *Fax:* 709-729-4285
allanhawkins@gov.nl.ca
Other Communications: Constituency Phone: 709-489-3409; Fax: 709-489-5480
Constituency Office
3 Cromer Ave.
Grand Falls-Windsor, NL A2A 1W9
Colin Holloway
Constituency: Terra Nova *No. of Constituents:* 9,794, Liberal
Tel: 709-729-5110
Toll-free: 800-514-9073; *Fax:* 709-729-0654
colinholloway@gov.nl.ca
Other Communications: Constituency Phone: 709-466-4165; Fax: 709-466-4178
Social Media: twitter.com/spruceridgeboy, www.facebook.com/100010298502041
Constituency Office
#208, 86 Manitoba Dr.
Clarenville, NL A5A 1K7
Opposition House Leader, Keith Hutchings
Constituency: Ferryland *No. of Constituents:* 9,924, Progressive Conservative
Tel: 709-729-1390
Toll-free: 800-634-5504; *Fax:* 709-729-5774
keithhutchings@gov.nl.ca
Other Communications: Constituency Phone: 709-729-1390; Fax: 709-729-5774
Social Media: twitter.com/keith_hutchings, www.facebook.com/keithhutchings.ferrylanddistrict
Government Members' Office, East Block, Confederation Bldg., 5th Fl.
PO Box 8700
St. John's, NL A1B 4J6
Minister, Municipal Affairs; Minister, Service Newfoundland & Labrador; Minister Responsible, Government Purchasing Agency & WorkplaceNL; Registrar General, Hon. Eddie Joyce
Constituency: Humber — Bay of Islands *No. of Constituents:* 10,315, Liberal
Tel: 709-729-3048; *Fax:* 709-729-0943
ejoyce@gov.nl.ca
www.eddiejoyce.com
Other Communications: Constituency Phone: 709-634-7883; Fax: 709-634-7885
Constituency Office, Sir Richard Squires Bldg.
PO Box 2006
Corner Brook, NL A2H 6J8
Deputy Opposition House Leader, Steve Kent
Constituency: Mount Pearl North *No. of Constituents:* 9,519, Progressive Conservative
Tel: 709-729-1526; *Fax:* 709-364-1639
stevekent@gov.nl.ca
www.stevekent.ca
Social Media: twitter.com/stephenkent, www.facebook.com/stevekentpc, www.linkedin.com/in/stephenpkent
Neil King
Constituency: Bonavista *No. of Constituents:* 9,172, Liberal
Tel: 709-729-3400
Toll-free: 800-600-4875; *Fax:* 709-729-5202
neilking@gov.nl.ca
Other Communications: Constituency Phone: 709-468-2132; Fax: 709-468-2134

Social Media: twitter.com/kingernl33
Constituency Office
134 Confederation Dr.
Bonavista, NL A0C 1B0

Minister, Education & Early Childhood Development, Hon. Dale Kirby
Constituency: Mount Scio *No. of Constituents:* 8,601, Liberal
Tel: 709-729-5040; *Fax:* 709-729-0414
dalekirby@gov.nl.ca
www.dalekirby.com
Other Communications: Constituency Phone: 709-729-6921; Fax: 709-729-0414
Social Media: twitter.com/dalegkirby, www.facebook.com/dale.kirby
Government Members' Office, West Block, Confederation Bldg., 3rd Fl.
PO Box 8700
St. John's, NL A1B 4J6

Deputy Chair, Committees, Paul Lane
Constituency: Mount Pearl — Southlands *No. of Constituents:* 9,483, Independent
Tel: 709-729-2231; *Fax:* 709-729-5202
paullane@gov.nl.ca
Social Media: twitter.com/PaulLaneMHA, www.facebook.com/paul.lane.5811
Government Members' Office, East Block, Confederation Bldg., 5th Fl.
PO Box 8700
St. John's, NL A1B 4J6

Graham Letto
Constituency: Labrador West *No. of Constituents:* 6,183, Liberal
Tel: 709-729-3048; *Fax:* 709-729-0943
grahamletto@gov.nl.ca
Other Communications: Constituency Phone: 709-944-4881; Fax: 709-944-4880
Social Media: twitter.com/grahamletto
Constituency Office
217 Drake Ave.
Labrador City, NL A2V 2B6

Third Party House Leader; Third Party Caucus Whip, Lorraine Michael
Constituency: St. John's East — Quidi Vidi *No. of Constituents:* 10,178, NDP
Tel: 709-729-0270
lorrainemichael@gov.nl.ca
Other Communications: Constituency Phone: 709-729-3709
Social Media: twitter.com/lorrainemichael, www.facebook.com/lorraine.michael.9
Government Members' Office, East Block, Confederation Bldg., 5th Fl.
PO Box 8700
St. John's, NL A1B 4J6

Minister, Business, Tourism, Culture & Rural Development; Minister Responsible, Research & Development Corporation, Hon. Christopher Mitchelmore
Constituency: St. Barbe — L'Anse Aux Meadows *No. of Constituents:* 9,267, Liberal
Tel: 709-729-4729
Toll-free: 888-729-6091; *Fax:* 709-729-0654
cmitchelmore@gov.nl.ca
christophermitchelmore.com
Other Communications: Constituency Phone: 709-454-2633; Fax: 709-454-2652
Social Media: twitter.com/mitchelmoremha, www.facebook.com/mhachris
Constituency Office
#279, 290 West St.
PO Box 620
St. Anthony, NL A0K 4S0

Speaker, Hon. Tom Osborne
Constituency: Waterford Valley *No. of Constituents:* 9,827, Liberal
Tel: 709-729-3404; *Fax:* 709-729-4820
tosborne@gov.nl.ca
Other Communications: Constituency Phone: 709-729-4882; Fax: 709-729-4820
Government Members' Office, East Block, Confederation Bldg., Main Fl.
PO Box 8700
St. John's, NL A1B 4J6

Betty Parsley
Constituency: Harbour Main *No. of Constituents:* 9,995, Liberal
Tel: 709-729-3400
Toll-free: 877-787-0707; *Fax:* 709-729-5202
bettyparsley@gov.nl.ca
Other Communications: Constituency Phone: 709-229-0160; Fax: 709-229-0169
Social Media: www.facebook.com/1438756219785023
Constituency Office
402 Conception Bay Hwy.
PO Box 129
Holyrood, NL A0A 2R0

Minister, Justice & Public Safety; Attorney General; Government House Leader, Hon. Andrew Parsons
Constituency: Burgeo — La Poile *No. of Constituents:* 7,142, Liberal
Tel: 709-729-2869
Toll-free: 800-518-9479; *Fax:* 709-729-0469
andrewparsons@gov.nl.ca
Other Communications: Constituency Phone: 709-695-3585; Fax: 709-695-5800
Social Media: twitter.com/Andrew_Parsons1, www.facebook.com/andrewkparsons
Constituency Office
PO Box 2263
Port aux Basques, NL A0M 1C0

Caucus Chair, Official Opposition, Kevin Parsons
Constituency: Cape St. Francis *No. of Constituents:* 8,499, Progressive Conservative
Tel: 709-729-6979; *Fax:* 709-729-5774
kevinparsons@gov.nl.ca
Social Media: www.facebook.com/kevinparsonspc, ca.linkedin.com/pub/kevin-parsons/43/100/280
Government Members' Office, East Block, Confederation Bldg., 5th Fl.
PO Box 8700
St. John's, NL A1B 4J6

Pam Parsons
Constituency: Harbour Grace — Port de Grave *No. of Constituents:* 10,613, Liberal
Tel: 709-729-3400
Toll-free: 866-729-1594; *Fax:* 709-729-5202
pamparsons@gov.nl.ca
pamparsons.com
Other Communications: Constituency Phone: 709-786-1372
Social Media: twitter.com/PamNParsons, www.facebook.com/pamforthepeople
Constituency Office
#4, 1 Excel Pl.
PO Box 960
Bay Roberts, NL A0A 1G0

Caucus Whip, Official Opposition, Tracey Perry
Constituency: Fortune Bay — Cape La Hune *No. of Constituents:* 5,516, Progressive Conservative
Tel: 709-538-3112; *Fax:* 709-538-3079
traceyperry@gov.nl.ca
Constituency Office
101 Main St.
PO Box 429
St. Alban's, NL A0H 2E0

Barry Petten
Constituency: Conception Bay South *No. of Constituents:* 8,991, Progressive Conservative
Tel: 709-834-6180; *Fax:* 709-834-6182
barrypetten@gov.nl.ca
Social Media: twitter.com/BarryPetten, www.facebook.com/BarryPettenCBS
Constituency Office
#118, 120 Conception Bay Hwy.
Conception Bay South, NL A1W 3A6

Scott Reid
Constituency: St. George's — Humber *No. of Constituents:* 9,400, Liberal
Tel: 709-729-3400
Toll-free: 866-838-5620; *Fax:* 709-729-5202
ScottReid@gov.nl.ca
Other Communications: Constituency Phone: 709-643-8663; Fax: 709-643-8677
Social Media: twitter.com/scottreidLib_nl, www.facebook.com/ScottReidLibNL
Constituency Office, Harmon Bldg.
58 Oregon Dr., 2nd Fl.
Stephenville, NL A2N 2Y1

Third Party Caucus Chair, Gerry Rogers
Constituency: St. John's Centre *No. of Constituents:* 9,711, NDP
Tel: 709-729-2638; *Fax:* 709-729-1443
gerryrogers@gov.nl.ca
Other Communications: Constituency Phone: 709-576-1443
Social Media: twitter.com/GerryRogersMHA, www.facebook.com/GerryRogersMHA
Government Members' Office, East Block, Confederation Bldg., 3rd Fl.
PO Box 8700
St. John's, NL A1B 4J6

Minister, Environment & Climate Change; Minister Responsible, Francophone Affairs, & Multi-Materials Stewardship Board, Hon. Perry Trimper
Constituency: Lake Melville *No. of Constituents:* 6,173, Liberal
Tel: 709-729-2574
Toll-free: 866-996-5670; *Fax:* 709-729-0112
perrytrimper@gov.nl.ca
www.perrytrimper.com
Other Communications: Constituency Phone: 709-869-7975; Fax: 709-869-7977
Social Media: twitter.com/PerryTrimper, www.facebook.com/107579049607109
Constituency Office
PO Box 2582 B Sta.
Happy Valley-Goose Bay, NL A0P 1E0

Brian Warr
Constituency: Baie Verte — Green Bay *No. of Constituents:* 9,954, Liberal
Tel: 709-729-3400
Toll-free: 800-598-1806; *Fax:* 709-729-5202
brianwarr@gov.nl.ca
brianwarr.ca
Other Communications: Constituency Phone: 709-673-3654; Fax: 709-673-2836
Constituency Office
142 Little Bay Rd.
PO Box 1733
Springdale, NL A0J 1T0

Newfoundland & Labrador Government Departments & Agencies

Newfoundland & Labrador Department of Advanced Education & Skills

Confederation Building, West Block, 3rd Fl., PO Box 8700 St. John's, NL A1B 4J6
Tel: 709-729-2480
aesweb@gov.nl.ca
www.aes.gov.nl.ca
Other Communication: Communications, Phone: 709-729-0753; Employment Supports & Services, Toll-Free: 1-800-563-6600

To meet the needs of a growing economy, Newfoundland & Labrador's Department of Advanced Education & Skills works to ensure that the province has highly educated graduates & skilled workers.

The department focuses upon the following tasks: assisting youth in the development of leadership skills; helping employers by providing access to needed workers; assisting people to find employment; improving the inclusion of persons with disabilities in society; supporting communities to attract & welcome immigrants; supporting persons during disasters; providing financial support for people with little or no income; & reducing poverty.

Income & financial services are available at the following locations: Avalon Region (1-877-729-7888); Central Region (1-888-632-4555); Labrador Region (1-888-773-9311); & Western Region (1-866-417-4753). In August 2016 Premier Ball announced the Labour Relations Agency would be combined with the Department of Advanced Education & Skills to create the Department of Advanced Education, Skills & Labour.

Minister, Hon. Gerry Byrne, P.C.
Tel: 709-729-3580; *Fax:* 709-729-6996
gerrybyrne@gov.nl.ca

Deputy Minister, Genevieve Dooling
Tel: 709-729-3582
gdooling@gov.nl.ca

Director, Communications, John Tompkins
Tel: 709-729-0753

Associated Agencies, Boards & Commissions:

•Income & Employment Support Appeal Board
Confederation Bldg.
PO Box 8700
St. John's, NL A1B 4J6
Tel: 709-729-2479; *Fax:* 709-729-5139

•Labour Relations Board
Beothuck Bldg.
20 Crosbie Pl., 5th Fl.
PO Box 8700
St. John's, NL A1B 4J6
Tel: 709-729-2707; *Fax:* 709-729-5738
lrb@gov.nl.ca
www.hrle.gov.nl.ca/lrb

•Standing Fish Price Setting Panel
Beothuck Bldg.
20 Crosbie Pl., 3rd Fl.
PO Box 8700
St. John's, NL A1B 4J6
Tel: 709-729-2711; *Fax:* 709-729-5905
www.hrle.gov.nl.ca/fishpanel/index.html

Corporate Services Branch

The Corporate Services Branch handles policy planning & evaluation, human resources, information technology services, & financial operations for the provincial office & regions.

Assistant Deputy Minister, Debbie Dunphy
Tel: 709-729-3594
ddunphy@gov.nl.ca

Director, Skills & Labour Market Research, Paul Dinn
Tel: 709-729-2649
pauldinn@gov.nl.ca

Director, Service Improvement & Quality Assurance Division, Sharon Knott
Tel: 709-729-2084; *Fax:* 709-729-5560
sharonknott@gov.nl.ca
Director, Information Management Division, David Moore
Tel: 709-729-5152
davemoore@gov.nl.ca
Director, Policy & Strategic Planning Division, Alicia Sutton
Tel: 709-729-5054
Departmental Coordinator, Finance & General Operations Division, Brendan Hanlon
Tel: 709-729-5140
brenhanlon@gov.nl.ca

Post-Secondary Education Branch

The Post-Secondary Education Branch consists of the following divisions: Apprenticeship & Trade Certification; Literacy & Institutional Services; & Student Financial Services.
The following are some services provided by the branch: providing student financial assistance; regulating private training institutions; administering Red Seal examinations; developing curriculum for adult basic education, & apprenticeship training; registering apprentices; & analyzing post-secondary data.
Assistant Deputy Minister, Bob Gardiner
Tel: 709-729-3026; *Fax:* 709-729-2828
bobgardiner@gov.nl.ca
Director, Literacy & Institutional Services Division, Jacqueline Power
Tel: 709-729-3100; *Fax:* 709-729-0243
JPower@gov.nl.ca
Director, Student Financial Services Division, Robert Feaver
Tel: 709-729-5849
Toll-free: 888-657-0800; *Fax:* 709-729-2298
studentaid@gov.nl.ca
Director, Apprenticeship & Trades Certification Division, Sandra Bishop
Tel: 709-729-2350; *Fax:* 709-729-5878
SandraEBishop@gov.nl.ca

Regional Service Delivery Branch

The Regional Service Delivery Branch is responsible for eligibility assessment for programs, issuing & monitoring benefits to clients, & providing other services such as career counseling, social work & community/business partnership development. Income & Social Supports is the policy division.
Regional contacts are as follows: Avalon: 1-877-729-7888, TTY: 1-888-380-2299; Central: 1-888-632-4555, TTY: 1-877-292-4205; Western: 1-866-417-4753, TTY: 1-888-445-8585; Labrador: 1-888-773-9311; TTY: 1-866-443-4046.
Assistant Deputy Minister, Roxie Wheaton
Tel: 709-729-2320
roxiewheaton@gov.nl.ca

Workforce Development & Immigration Branch

The Workforce Development & Immigration Branch consists of the following divisions: Employment & Training Programs; Immigration & Multiculturalism; Skills & Labour Market Research; & Workforce Development Secretariat.
Assistant Deputy Minister, Dennis Hogan
Tel: 709-729-0217
dhogan@gov.nl.ca
Acting Director, Employment & Training Programs Division, Walt Mavin
Tel: 709-729-0939; *Fax:* 709-729-1129
waltmavin@gov.nl.ca
Director, Workforce Development Secretariat, Candice Ennis-Williams
Tel: 709-729-0541
candiceennis-williams@gov.nl.ca

Office of Immigration & Multiculturalism (OIM)
c/o Department of Advanced Education & Skills, 100 Prince Phillip Dr., PO Box 8700 St. John's, NL A1B 4J6
Tel: 709-729-6607; *Fax:* 709-729-7381
Toll-Free: 888-632-4555
TTY: 877-292-4205
immigration@gov.nl.ca
www.nlimmigration.ca
Other Communication: Provincial Nominee Program, E-mail: pnp@gov.nl.ca; URL: www.nlpnp.ca
www.facebook.com/nlimmigration
www.youtube.com/user/IMMNL

The Office of Immigration & Multiculturalism is engaged in the implementation of the Provincial Immigration Strategy, which involves attracting & retaining immigrants to Newfoundland & Labrador.
Acting Director, Debbie Sheppard
Tel: 709-729-6607; *Fax:* 709-729-7381
Senior Specialist, Provincial Nominee Program (Bilingual), MaryAnn Scanlon
Tel: 709-729-1332; *Fax:* 709-729-7381
MaryAnnScanlon@gov.nl.ca

Office of the Auditor General

PO Box 8700 St. John's, NL A1B 4J6
Tel: 709-729-2695; *Fax:* 709-729-5970
oagmail@oag.nl.ca
www.ag.gov.nl.ca

The Auditor General's fundamental role is to bring an independent audit and reporting process to bear upon the manner in which Government and its various entities discharge their responsibilities, report on their planned programs and their use of public resources.
Auditor General, Terry Paddon, CPA, CA
Deputy Auditor General, Sandra Russell
Tel: 709-729-4999
srussell@oag.nl.ca
Director, Administration, Gregg Griffin
Tel: 709-729-4381
ggriffin@oag.nl.ca
Secretary to the Auditor General, Gertrude Critch
Tel: 709-729-2700
gcritch@oag.nl.ca

Newfoundland & Labrador Department of Business, Tourism, Culture & Rural Development

Confederation Bldg., West Block, 2nd Fl., PO Box 8700 St. John's, NL A1B 4J6
Tel: 709-729-7000
btcrd@gov.nl.ca
www.btcrd.gov.nl.ca

The Department was created in 2004 to reflect the enhanced empasis placed on the innovation aspect of the provincial economic agenda. It is the lead agency for economic development in the province & in each of its regions.
In September 2014, Premier Paul Davis created a new department called Business, Tourism, Culture & Rural Development. It absorbed responsibilities formerly held by Tourism, Culture & Recreation, including: conserving, preserving & protecting natural & cultural resources & promoting the resources for economic benefit, sport & recreation in the province. Programs assist in transforming the province's natural & cultural attractions into opportunities for employment & revenue generation.
Minister, Hon. Christopher Mitchelmore
Tel: 709-729-4729; *Fax:* 709-729-0654
cmitchelmore@gov.nl.ca
Acting Deputy Minister, Daryl Genge
Tel: 709-729-4732
DarylGenge@gov.nl.ca
Parliamentary Secretary, Colin Holloway
Tel: 709-729-5110; *Fax:* 709-729-0654
colinholloway@gov.nl.ca
Director, Policy & Strategic Planning, Terry Johnstone
Tel: 709-729-4771; *Fax:* 709-729-0870
tjohnsto@gov.nl.ca
Director, Communications, Tansy Mundon
Tel: 709-729-4570; *Fax:* 709-729-0654
TansyMundon@gov.nl.ca

Associated Agencies, Boards & Commissions:

•Heritage Foundation of Newfoundland & Labrador (HFNL)
The Newman Bldg.
1 Springdale St.
PO Box 5171
St. John's, NL A1C 5V5
Tel: 709-739-1892; *Fax:* 709-739-5413
Toll-free: 888-739-1892
info@heritagefoundation.ca
www.heritagefoundation.ca

•Marble Mountain Development Corporation
PO Box 947
Corner Brook, NL A2H 6J2
Tel: 709-637-7601; *Fax:* 709-634-1702
Toll-free: 888-462-7253
www.skimarble.com
Other Communication: Villa Reservations, Phone: 709-637-7666; Toll-Free Phone: 1-800-636-2725; Snowline, Phone: 709-637-7669

•Newfoundland & Labrador Arts Council (NLAC)
The Newman Bldg.
1 Springdale St.
PO Box 98
St. John's, NL A1C 5H5
Tel: 709-726-2212; *Fax:* 709-726-0619
Toll-free: 866-726-2212
nlacmail@nlac.ca
www.nlac.ca

•Newfoundland & Labrador Film Development Corporation (NLFDC)
12 King's Bridge Rd.
St. John's, NL A1C 3K3
Tel: 709-738-3456; *Fax:* 709-739-1680
Toll-free: 877-738-3456
info@nlfdc.ca
www.nlfdc.ca

•The Rooms Corporation
9 Bonaventure Ave.
PO Box 1800 C
St. John's, NL A1C 5P9
Tel: 709-757-8000; *Fax:* 709-757-8017
information@therooms.ca
www.therooms.ca
Other Communication: Archives, E-mail: archives@therooms.ca

Arts & Heritage Branch

The department administers archeology permits, the Art Procurement Program, the Heritage Foundation of Newfoundland & Labrador, provides grants to artists, arts organizations, museums & archives through the Newfoundland & Labrador Arts Council, provides grants to assists the Newfoundland & Labrador Film Development Corporation & administers provincial historic sites.
Director, Arts, Eleanor Dawson
Tel: 709-729-7397; *Fax:* 709-729-0870
eleanordawson@gov.nl.ca
Acting Director, Heritage, Jerry Dick
Tel: 709-729-7393; *Fax:* 709-729-0870
jerrydick@gov.nl.ca
Director, Arts & Culture Centres Division, Doreen McCarthy
Tel: 709-729-3453; *Fax:* 709-729-5952
mccarthyd@artsandculturecentres.com
Manager, Provincial Historic Sites, Gerry Osmond
Tel: 709-729-7212; *Fax:* 709-729-7989
gerryosmond@gov.nl.ca
Provincial Archeologist, Martha Drake
Tel: 709-729-2462; *Fax:* 709-729-0870
mdrake@gov.nl.ca
Confederation Bldg.
PO Box 8700
St. John's, NL A1B 4J6

Innovation & Strategic Industries Branch

Supports industry, labour, academic & other research & development institutions & businesses involved in innovation projects.
Assistant Deputy Minister, Brian Burke
Tel: 709-729-2831; *Fax:* 709-729-0654
BrianGBurke@gov.nl.ca
Director, Innovation & Advanced Technology, Doriann Coombs
Tel: 709-729-4887
DoriannCoombs@gov.nl.ca
Director, Information Management, Ruth Parsons
Tel: 709-729-1940
ruthparsons@gov.nl.ca
Director, Innovation & Advanced Technology, Sharon Tiller
Tel: 709-729-7068
stiller@gov.nl.ca
Director, Sector Development, Kirk Tilley
Tel: 709-729-7080
ktilley@gov.nl.ca

Ocean Technology & Arctic Opportunities Branch

Advances New Brunswick's ocean technology cluster through improved business supports & oversees the Arctic Opportunities Initiative.
Assistant Deputy Minister, Brian Burke
Tel: 709-729-2820
BrianGBurke@gov.nl.ca
Director, Diane Taylor
Tel: 709-729-1684
dianetaylor@gov.nl.ca

Regional & Business Development Branch

Promotes & coordinates regional economic planning & development programs & services.
Assistant Deputy Minister, Rita Malone
Tel: 709-637-2977; *Fax:* 709-639-7713
rmalone@gov.nl.ca
Director, Portfolio Management Division, Guy Edwards
Tel: 709-279-0213; *Fax:* 709-279-0218
gedwards@gov.nl.ca
Acting Director, Business Analysis, Liane Price
Tel: 709-729-7108; *Fax:* 709-729-4858
LianePrice@gov.nl.ca
Director, Regional Economic Development, Gillian Skinner
Tel: 709-729-7451; *Fax:* 709-729-5124
gskinner@gov.nl.ca
Director, Industry Adjustment, Fisheries Adjustment Division, Larry Weatherbie

Tel: 709-729-7125
lweather@gov.nl.ca

Regional Offices

Avalon
28 Pippy Place, St. John's, NL A1B 3X4
Tel: 709-729-7124; *Fax:* 709-729-7135
Regional Director, James Antsey
jkantsey@gov.nl.ca

Central
230 Airport Blvd., PO Box 2222 Gander, NL A1V 2N9
Tel: 709-256-1483; *Fax:* 709-256-1490
Regional Director, Percy Farwell
pfarwell@gov.nl.ca

Eastern
211B Memorial Drive, Clarenville, NL A5A 1R3
Tel: 709-466-4171; *Fax:* 709-466-1306
Regional Director, Denis Sullivan
sullivan@gov.nl.ca

Labrador
2 Hillcrest Rd., PO Box 3014 Stn. B, Happy Valley-Goose Bay, NL A0P 1E0
Tel: 709-896-0306; *Fax:* 709-896-0234
Regional Director, Reg Kean
rkean@gov.nl.ca

Western
2 Herald Ave., PO Box 2006 Corner Brook, NL A2H 6J8
Tel: 709-637-2981; *Fax:* 709-639-7713
Regional Director, John Davis
jdavis@gov.nl.ca

Tourism Branch

Markets the province as a travel destination & develops products, facilities & services in partnership with the tourism industry.

Assistant Deputy Minister, Carmela Murphy
Tel: 709-729-2821
carmelamurphy@gov.nl.ca

Manager, Tourism Product Development, Scott Andrews
Tel: 709-729-2413; *Fax:* 709-729-0474
ScottWAndrews@gov.nl.ca

Acting Director, Tourism Marketing Division, Andrea Peddle
Tel: 709-729-2831; *Fax:* 709-729-0057
apeddle@gov.nl.ca

Director, Tourism Research Division, Michaela Roebothan
Tel: 709-729-6024
michaelaroebothan@gov.nl.ca

Trade & Investment Branch

Specializes in assisting provincial businesses develop an export plan to enter new markets, find export business partners & research national & international market opportunities.

Director, Marketing, Sheila Fudge
Tel: 709-729-7019
sfudge@gov.nl.ca

Director, International Business Development, Carolann Harding
Tel: 709-729-4617
carolannharding@gov.nl.ca

Director, Air Access, Fraser Howell
Tel: 709-729-6183
fraserhowell@gov.nl.ca

Director, Policy & Strategic Planning, Terry Johnstone
Tel: 709-729-4771; *Fax:* 709-729-5124
tjohnsto@gov.nl.ca

Director, Trade Policy, Jeff Loder
Tel: 709-729-2789
jeffloder@gov.nl.ca

Newfoundland & Labrador Department of Child, Youth & Family Services

PO Box 8700 St. John's, NL A1B 4J6
Tel: 709-729-0760
www.gov.nl.ca/cyfs
Other Communication: Adoption Services Phone: 709-752-4406; Youth Corrections Program: 709-729-2794

In August 2016 Premier Ball announced the combination of the Department of Child, Youth & Family Services & the Department of Seniors, Wellness and Social Development to create the Department of Children, Seniors and Social Development.

Minister, Hon. Sherry Gambin-Walsh
Tel: 709-729-0659; *Fax:* 709-729-0662
sherrygambinwalsh@gov.nl.ca

Deputy Minister, Rachelle Cochrane
Tel: 709-729-0958
RachelleCochrane@gov.nl.ca

Parliamentary Secretary, Derek Bennett
Tel: 709-729-0795; *Fax:* 709-729-0662
derekbennett@gov.nl.ca

Assistant Deputy Minister, Policies & Programs, Rick Healey
Tel: 709-729-0088
rhealey@gov.nl.ca

Assistant Deputy Minister, Corporate Services, Julie Moore
Tel: 709-729-0656
juliemoore@gov.nl.ca

Assistant Deputy Minister, Services Delivery & Regional Operations, Donna O'Brien
Tel: 709-729-3473
donnaobrien@gov.nl.ca

Director, Information Management & Protection, Ali Askary
Tel: 709-729-1898; *Fax:* 709-729-6382
AliAskary@gov.nl.ca

Acting Director, Strategic Policy & Planning, Krista Connolly
Tel: 709-729-1898; *Fax:* 709-729-6382

Director, Policy & Strategic Planning, Sara Dow
Tel: 709-729-7529; *Fax:* 709-729-1853
saradow@gov.nl.ca

Director, Youth Corrections, Gina Eisenhaur
Tel: 709-729-2794; *Fax:* 709-729-6382
ginaeisenhaur@gov.nl.ca

Director, Quality Assurance, Sandra Evans
Tel: 709-292-4525
sandraevans@gov.nl.ca

Director, Financial & General Operations, Paul Grandy
Tel: 709-729-0276
paulgrandy@gov.nl.ca

Director, Family & Child Development, Jason Higgins
Tel: 709-729-4055; *Fax:* 709-729-6382
jasonhiggins@gov.nl.ca

Director, Communications, Michelle Hunt
Tel: 709-729-5148
michellehunt@gov.nl.ca

Director, Youth Corrections, Child Protection & In-Care, Paul Ludlow
Tel: 709-729-2794; *Fax:* 709-729-6382
pludlow@gov.nl.ca

Director, Adoptions, Child Protection & In-Care, Christine Osmond
Tel: 709-729-3527; *Fax:* 709-729-1853
christineosmond@gov.nl.ca

Director, Child Protection & In-Care, Michelle Shallow
Tel: 709-729-6078
mshallow@gov.nl.ca

Newfoundland & Labrador Department of Education & Early Childhood Development

West Block, Confederation Bldg., 100 Prince Philip Dr., 3rd Fl., PO Box 8700 St. John's, NL A1B 4J6
Tel: 709-729-5097; *Fax:* 709-729-5896
education@gov.nl.ca
www.ed.gov.nl.ca/edu

Responsible for the K-12 & post-secondary school system, literacy & library services; comprises four executive branches: Primary, Elementary & Secondary Education, Corporate Services Branch; Post-Secondary Branch; International Education & Planning Branch; Literacy School Services; reporting to the department through their various boards are the Provincial Information & Library Resources Board, the Literacy Development Council, 4 geographical school boards & a Francophone school board.
In October 2011, a separate Department called Advanced Education & Skills was created by then-Premier Kathy Dunderdale.
In September 2014, Premier Paul Davis expanded the ministry to include Early Childhood Development, which included educational functions previously administered by the Department of Child, Youth & Family Services.

Minister, Hon. Dale Kirby

Deputy Minister, Janet Vivian-Walsh
Tel: 709-729-5086
janetvivianwalsh@gov.nl.ca

Director, Communications, Blair Medd
Tel: 709-729-0048
blairmedd@gov.nl.ca

Associated Agencies, Boards & Commissions:

•Provincial Information & Library Resources Board
48 St. George's Ave.
Stephenville, NL A2H 1K9
Tel: 709-643-0900; *Fax:* 709-643-0925
www.nlpl.ca
To establish & operate those public libraries in the province that it considers necessary & provide support to ensure that library materials, information & programs are available to meet the needs of the public.

Corporate Services Branch

Assistant Deputy Minister, Joan Morris
Tel: 709-729-3025; *Fax:* 709-729-1400
jmorris@gov.nl.ca

Director, Information Management & Special Projects Division, Brian Evans
Tel: 709-729-1841
brianevans@gov.nl.ca

Director, Policy, Planning, & Accountability Division, Amanda Garland
Tel: 709-729-7425
amandagarland@gov.nl.ca

Director, Financial Services, Don Stapleton
Tel: 709-729-5168; *Fax:* 709-729-1400
donjstapleton@gov.nl.ca

Infrastructure Branch

Assistant Deputy Minister, Ingrid Clarke
Tel: 709-729-3025; *Fax:* 709-729-1330
ingridclarke@gov.nl.ca

Director, Design & Construction Division, Natalie Hallett
Tel: 709-729-4988; *Fax:* 709-729-1400
nataliehallett@gov.nl.ca

K-12 Education & Early Childhood Development

Assistant Deputy Minister, Ed Walsh
Tel: 709-729-5720; *Fax:* 709-729-1400
edwalsh@gov.nl.ca

Director, Program Development, Bradley Clarke
Tel: 709-729-3004; *Fax:* 709-729-1400
bradclarke@gov.nl.ca

Director, Early Childhood Learning, Paula Hennessey
Tel: 709-729-5128
paulahennessey@gov.nl.ca

Director, School Services, Georgina Lake
Tel: 709-729-3034; *Fax:* 709-729-1400
georginalake@gov.nl.ca

Director, Student Support Services, Bernie Ottenheimer
Tel: 709-729-3023; *Fax:* 709-729-1400
BernieOttenheimer@gov.nl.ca

Director, Evaluation & Research Division, Ron Smith
Tel: 709-729-3000; *Fax:* 709-729-1400
ronsmith@gov.nl.ca

Director, Centre for Distance Learning & Innovation, Jim Tuff
Tel: 709-729-7614; *Fax:* 709-729-1400
jimtuff@gov.nl.ca
www.cdli.ca

Office of the Chief Electoral Officer

39 Hallett Cr., St. John's, NL A1B 4C4
Tel: 709-729-0712; *Fax:* 709-729-0679
Toll-Free: 877-729-7987
enl@gov.nl.ca
www.elections.gov.nl.ca/elections
twitter.com/NLElections

Chief Electoral Officer, Victor Powers
Tel: 702-729-0712
vpowers@gov.nl.ca

Assistant Chief Electoral Officer & Director, Election Finance, Bruce Chaulk
Tel: 709-729-4116
brucechaulk@gov.nl.ca

Director, Elections Operations & Special Ballot Administrator, Isabel Collins
Tel: 709-729-0713
icollins@gov.nl.ca

Newfoundland & Labrador Department of Environment & Conservation

Confederation Bldg., West Block, 4th Fl., PO Box 8700 St. John's, NL A1B 4J6
Tel: 709-729-2664; *Fax:* 709-729-6639
Toll-Free: 800-563-6181
envcinquires@gov.nl.ca
www.env.gov.nl.ca

To protect, conserve & enhance the Province's environment through the management of water resources, the environmental assessment of undertakings & the control & management of substances & activities that may pollute the environment. The Department is actively working towards reducing the number of landfill sites & implementing the Provincial Waste Management Strategy. In August 2016 Premier Ball announced the Department of Environment & Conservation & the Office of Climate Change & Energy Efficiency will combine to become the Department of Environment & Climate Change.

Minister, Hon. Perry Trimper
Tel: 709-729-2574; *Fax:* 709-729-0112
perrytrimper@gov.nl.ca

Deputy Minister, Colleen Janes
Tel: 709-729-2572
cjanes@gov.nl.ca

Assistant Deputy Minister, Natural Heritage (Corner Brook), Ross Firth
Tel: 709-637-2135; *Fax:* 709-637-2180
rossfirth@gov.nl.ca

Assistant Deputy Minister, Environment, Martin Goebel
Tel: 709-729-2559; *Fax:* 709-729-7413
mgoebel@gov.nl.ca
Director, Policy & Planning Division, Dana Spurrell
Tel: 709-729-1090; *Fax:* 709-729-5818
DanaSpurrell@gov.nl.ca
Director, Communications, Deborah Thomas
Tel: 709-729-2575; *Fax:* 709-729-0112
moneill@gov.nl.ca

Associated Agencies, Boards & Commissions:

•C.A. Pippy Park Commission
Mount Scio House
15 Mount Scio Rd.
St. John's, NL A1B 3T2
Tel: 709-737-3655
info@pippypark.com
www.pippypark.com
C.A. Pippy Park was established by an Act of the Newfoundland Legislature in 1968. The Act created the C.A. Pippy Park Commission, a semi-autonomous Crown Corporation under the laws of the Province of Newfoundland & Labrador. The Commission currently reports to the Minister of Environment & Conservation.

•Multi-Materials Stewardship Board (MMSB)
PO Box 8131 A
St. John's, NL A1B 3M9
Tel: 709-753-0948; *Fax:* 709-753-0974
Toll-free: 800-901-6672
inquiries@mmsb.nl.ca
www.mmsb.nl.ca
The Multi-Materials Stewardship Board is jointly run with the Department of Municipal Affairs.

Environment Branch
Other Communication: Spill Reporting (24 hours): 709-772-2083; Environmental Assessment: 1-800-563-6181
Assistant Deputy Minister, Martin Goebel
Tel: 709-729-2559; *Fax:* 709-729-7413
mgoebel@gov.nl.ca
Director, Environmental Assessment Division, Bas Cleary
Tel: 709-729-0673; *Fax:* 709-729-5518
clearyb@gov.nl.ca
Director, Water Resources, Hassen Khan
Tel: 709-729-2535; *Fax:* 709-729-0320
hkhan@gov.nl.ca
Director, Pollution Prevention, Derrick Maddocks
Tel: 709-729-5782; *Fax:* 709-729-6969
dmaddocks@gov.nl.ca

Natural Heritage
Assistant Deputy Minister, Ross Firth
Tel: 709-637-2135; *Fax:* 709-637-2180
rossfirth@gov.nl.ca
Director, Wildlife Division, John Blake
Tel: 709-637-2008; *Fax:* 709-637-2180
johnblake@gov.nl.ca
Director, Parks & Natural Areas, Sian French
Tel: 709-637-4520; *Fax:* 709-635-4541
sianfrench@gov.nl.ca

Sustainable Development & Strategic Science Branch
Executive Director, Policy & Legislation, Shane P. Mahoney
Tel: 709-729-2542; *Fax:* 709-729-7677
shanemahoney@gov.nl.ca
Director, Science, Monitoring & Data Synthesis, & Contact, Institute for Biodiversity, Ecosystem Science, & Sustainability, Rob Otto
Tel: 709-637-2425
rotto@gov.nl.ca

Newfoundland & Labrador Department of Finance

Confederation Bldg., PO Box 8700 St. John's, NL A1B 4J6
Tel: 709-729-3166; *Fax:* 709-729-2232
finance@gov.nl.ca
www.fin.gov.nl.ca

Minister; President, Treasury Board, Hon. Cathy Bennett
Tel: 709-729-3775; *Fax:* 709-729-2232
cbennett@gov.nl.ca
Deputy Minister, Donna Brewer
Tel: 709-729-2946
dbrewer@gov.nl.ca
Director, Policy, Planning, Accountability & Information Management, K. Gail Boland
Tel: 709-729-2950; *Fax:* 709-729-2070
gailboland@gov.nl.ca
Director, Communications, Jennifer Tulk
Tel: 709-729-6830
jennifertulk@gov.nl.ca

Associated Agencies, Boards & Commissions:

•Atlantic Lottery Corporation (ALC)
922 Main St.
PO Box 5500
Moncton, NB E1C 8W6
Toll-free: 800-561-3942
info@alc.ca
www.alc.ca
Other Communication: Corporate URL: corp.alc.ca
The ALC manages the gaming businesses of the four Atlantic provinces. The board of directors is made up of an independent, non-voting chair & two representatives from each Atlantic Province. The Newfoundland & Labrador office can be contacted as follows: 30 Hallett Cres., St. John's, NL A1B 4C5. The Nova Scotia office can be contacted as follows: 7 Mellor Ave., Dartmouth, NS B3B 0E8.

•Newfoundland & Labrador Government Money Purchase Pension Plan Committee
Confederation Bldg.
PO Box 8700
St. John's, NL A1B 4J6
www.fin.gov.nl.ca/fin/department/agencies.html#2
The Government Money Purchase Pension Plan Committee is responsible for overseeing the Government Money Purchase Pension Plan.

•Newfoundland & Labrador Government Sinking Fund - Board of Trustees
www.fin.gov.nl.ca/fin/department/agencies.html#3
The Board of Trustees consolidates & administers sinking funds established by the Financial Administration Act for the repayment of the Province's debenture debt.

•Newfoundland & Labrador Industrial Development Corporation (NIDC)
Confederation Bldg.
PO Box 8700
St. John's, NL A1B 4J6
www.fin.gov.nl.ca/fin/department/agencies.html#4
The NIDC provides long-term financing to industrial & resource-based projects, but has been largely inactive in recent years as investments have been undertaken by the Province or through other Crown Corporations.

•Newfoundland & Labrador Liquor Corporation
90 Kenmount Rd.
PO Box 8750 A
St. John's, NL A1B 3V1
Tel: 709-724-1100; *Fax:* 709-754-0321
info@nfliquor.com
www.nfliquor.com
The Newfoundland Labrador Liquor Corporation (NLC) is a provincial crown corporation responsible for managing the importation, sale & distribution of beverage alcohol within the province.

•Newfoundland & Labrador Municipal Financing Corporation (NMFC)
Confederation Bldg.
PO Box 8700
St. John's, NL A1B 4J6
Tel: 709-729-6686; *Fax:* 709-729-2095
www.fin.gov.nl.ca/fin/department/agencies.html#6
Newfoundland & Labrador Municipal Financing Corporation is a Crown Corporation established to consolidate the long-term borrowing programs of all municipalities in one central agency. Since the majority of municipalities are now able to finance their own capital programs through financial institutions, the NMFC has discontinued its borrowing program & will wind up its operations once it has collected all outstanding loans.

•Newfoundland Government Fund Limited - Board of Directors (NGFL)
www.fin.gov.nl.ca/fin/department/agencies.html#7
The Board of Directors oversees the investments of the NGFL, a Government-run venture capital fund established under the Immigration Act (Canada).

•Pension Investment Committee (PIC)
Confederation Bldg.
PO Box 8700
St. John's, NL A1B 4J6
www.fin.gov.nl.ca/fin/department/agencies.html#7
The PIC provides the Minister of Finance with advice regarding the operation & investment of the Province of Newfoundland & Labrador Pooled Pension Fund.

Economics & Statistics
Assistant Deputy Minister, Alton Hollett
Tel: 709-729-3255
ahollett@gov.nl.ca
Director, Economic Research & Analysis, Rod Forsey
rforsey@gov.nl.ca
Director, Newfoundland & Labrador Statistics Agency, Robert Reid
Tel: 709-729-0158; *Fax:* 709-729-0393
robertr@gov.nl.ca

Financial Planning & Benefits Administration
Assistant Deputy Minister, Denise Hanrahan
Tel: 709-729-4039
hanrahand@gov.nl.ca
Director, Treasury Board Support Division, Sharlene Jones
Tel: 709-729-4407
SharleneJones@gov.nl.ca
Director, Pensions Administration, Maureen McCarthy
Tel: 709-729-5983; *Fax:* 709-729-6790
mccarthym@gov.nl.ca

Office of the Comptroller General
Comptroller General, Anne Marie Miller
Tel: 709-729-4866
millera@gov.nl.ca
Director, Corporate Services Division, Janice Butt, C.M.A.
Tel: 709-729-1414; *Fax:* 709-729-6900
jbutt@gov.nl.ca
Director, Government Accounting, David Drover
Tel: 709-729-4202; *Fax:* 709-729-2098
droverd@gov.nl.ca
Director, Financial Systems Control Division, Sonya Noble
Tel: 709-729-6530; *Fax:* 709-729-2098
sonyanoble@gov.nl.ca
Director, Professional Services & Internal Audit Division, Brian O'Neill, C.A.
Tel: 709-729-0702
brianoneill@gov.nl.ca

Taxation & Fiscal Policy Branch
Assistant Deputy Minister, Peter Au
Tel: 709-729-2944; *Fax:* 709-729-2070
peterau@gov.nl.ca
Director, Fiscal Policy, Chris Butt
Tel: 709-729-6714
cbutt@gov.nl.ca
Director, Tax Policy, Jay Griffin
Tel: 709-729-6847
jgriffin@gov.nl.ca
Director, Project Analysis, Brian Hurley
Tel: 709-729-3664
bhurley@gov.nl.ca
Director, Debt Management, Paul Myrden
Tel: 709-729-6848
Director, Tax Administration, Cathy M. Whalen
Tel: 709-729-6307; *Fax:* 709-729-2277
cathywhalen@gov.nl.ca

Newfoundland & Labrador Department of Fisheries & Aquaculture

Petten Bldg., 30 Strawberry Marsh Rd., PO Box 8700 St. John's, NL A1B 4J6
Tel: 709-729-3723; *Fax:* 709-729-6082
fisheries@gov.nl.ca
www.fishaq.gov.nl.ca
Other Communication: Aquaculture Phone: 709-292-4100; Fax: 709-292-4113; Email: aquaculture@gov.nl.ca
twitter.com/FA_GovNL

Contributes to economic & community growth in the province by encouraging sustainable growth & development of the harvesting, processing, & distribution sectors; includes providing support for the marketing of fish & aquaculture products produced in Newfoundland & Labrador for domestic & export markets. Responsible for: setting & enforcing standards for the processing & sale of fish products in the province; licensing fish processing establishments; undertaking developmental initiatives in the harvesting, processing, & marketing sectors of the fishing industry; developing, promoting & licensing of aquaculture facilities; developing & maintaining strategic fisheries infrastructure; articulating policies & providing advice for the management & development of fisheries & aquaculture; providing statistical information. In August 2016 Premier Ball announced that the Forestry & Agrifoods Agency & the Department of Fisheries & Aquaculture have combined to create the Department of Fisheries, Forestry & Agrifoods.

Minister, Hon. Steve Crocker
Tel: 709-729-3705; *Fax:* 709-729-0360
stevecrocker@gov.nl.ca
Acting Deputy Minister, David B. Lewis
Tel: 709-729-3707; *Fax:* 790-729-0360
DavidLewis@gov.nl.ca
Director, Communications, Vanessa Colman-Sadd
Tel: 709-729-3733
vanessacolmansadd@gov.nl.ca

Associated Agencies, Boards & Commissions:

•Fish Processing Licensing Board (FPLB)
c/o Fish Processing Licensing Board Secretariat
30 Strawberry Marsh Rd.
St. John's, NL A1B 4J6
fplbsecretariat@gov.nl.ca

•Professional Fish Harvesters Certification Board (PFHCB)
368 Hamilton Ave.
PO Box 8541
St. John's, NL A1B 3P2
Tel: 709-722-8170; *Fax:* 709-722-8201
pfh@pfhcb.com
www.pfhcb.com

Aquaculture Branch

58 Hardy Ave., PO Box 679 Grand Falls-Windsor, NL A2A 2K2
Tel: 709-292-4100; *Fax:* 709-292-4113
aquaculture@gov.nl.ca

The Branch is responsible for licensing & aquaculture development.

Assistant Deputy Minister, Brian Meaney
Tel: 709-729-3710; *Fax:* 709-729-1882
bmeaney@gov.nl.ca

Director & Provincial Aquaculture Veterinarian, Dr. Daryl Whelan
Tel: 709-729-6872; *Fax:* 709-729-1882
darylswhelan@gov.nl.ca

Fisheries Branch

Fax: 709-729-0360
fisheries@gov.nl.ca

This branch is responsible for fish processing operations, inspections, compliance & regulatory programs.

Acting Assistant Deputy Minister, Krista Quinlan
Tel: 709-729-1725; *Fax:* 709-729-1884
KristaQuinlan@gov.nl.ca

Director, Licensing & Quality Assurance, Ian Burford
Tel: 709-729-3736; *Fax:* 709-729-5995
iburford@gov.nl.ca

Director, Innovation & Development, Mark Rumboldt
Tel: 709-729-3714; *Fax:* 709-729-1884
mrumboldt@gov.nl.ca

Marketing & Development Branch

Fax: 709-729-1884
fisheries@gov.nl.ca

This branch is responsible for promoting & supporting the diversification & development of the harvesting, processing, & marketing sectors of the seafood industry through public & private sector partnerships.

Director, Seafood Marketing & Support Services, Sean Barry
Tel: 709-729-3390; *Fax:* 709-729-1884
seanbarry@gov.nl.ca

Policy & Planning Branch

Fax: 709-729-0360
fisheries@gov.nl.ca

Provides policy & program planning services to the Department. Through the Sustainable Fisheries & Oceans Policy Division participates in oceans policy & governance issues, in addition to the resource assessment & management process of the federal Department of Fisheries & Oceans, including local, national, & international bodies responsible for fisheries conservation & management.

Director, Sustainable Fisheries & Oceans Policy, Tom Dooley
Tel: 709-729-0335; *Fax:* 709-729-6082

Director, Planning Services, Wandalee Wiseman
Tel: 709-729-3765; *Fax:* 709-729-6082
wandaleewiseman@gov.nl.ca

Regional Offices

Eastern

PO Box 880 Grand Bank, NL A0E 1W0
Tel: 709-832-2860; *Fax:* 709-832-1669

Regional Director, Ron Brown
Tel: 709-729-1143
RonBrown@gov.nl.ca

Northern

PO Box 3014 Stn. B, Happy Valley-Goose Bay, NL A0P 1E0
Tel: 709-896-3412; *Fax:* 709-896-3483

Regional Director, Craig Taylor
Tel: 709-896-3412; *Fax:* 709-896-3483
craigtaylor@gov.nl.ca

Western

PO Box 2006 Corner Brook, NL A2H 6J8
Tel: 709-637-2955; *Fax:* 709-637-2908

Regional Director, Wilson Goosney
Tel: 709-637-2565; *Fax:* 709-637-2908

Newfoundland & Labrador Department of Health & Community Services (HCS)

West Block, Confederation Bldg., PO Box 8700 St. John's, NL A1B 4J6
Tel: 709-729-4984
healthinfo@gov.nl.ca
www.health.gov.nl.ca
Other Communication: Immunization Records, Phone: 709-729-0724; Medical Care Plan, Toll-Free: 1-800-563-1557; Avalon: 1-866-449-4459

Provides a leadership role in health & community service programs & policy development for the Province. This involves working in partnership with a number of key stakeholders including regional boards, community organizations, professional associations, post-secondary educational institutions, unions, consumer & other government departments.

Minister, Hon. Dr. John Haggie
Tel: 709-729-3124; *Fax:* 709-729-0121
johnhaggie@gov.nl.ca

Deputy Minister, Health, Beverley Clarke
Tel: 709-729-3125
BeverleyClarke@gov.nl.ca

Parliamentary Assistant, Bernard Davis
Tel: 709-729-3335; *Fax:* 709-729-0121
bernarddavis@gov.nl.ca

Associate Deputy Minister, Medical Services, Dr. Cathi Bradbury
Tel: 709-729-1574; *Fax:* 709-729-0121
cathibradbury@gov.nl.ca

Assistant Deputy Minister, Michelle Jewer
Tel: 709-729-0620; *Fax:* 709-729-0640
michellejewer@gov.nl.ca

Assistant Deputy Minister, Denise Tubrett
Tel: 709-729-0580; *Fax:* 709-729-0640
dtubrett@gov.nl.ca

Director, Communications, John Tompkins
Tel: 709-729-1377; *Fax:* 709-728-7762
jtompkins@gov.nl.ca

Associated Agencies, Boards & Commissions:

•Central Regional Health Authority
21 Carmelite Rd.
Grand Falls-Windsor, NL A2A 1Y4
Toll-free: 888-799-2272
client.relations@centralhealth.nl.ca
www.centralhealth.nl.ca

•Eastern Regional Health Authority
Health Sciences Centre
#1345, Prince Philip Dr., Level 1
St. John's, NL A1B 3V6
Tel: 709-777-6500; *Fax:* 709-364-6460
Toll-free: 877-444-1399
client.relations@easternhealth.ca
www.easternhealth.ca
Other Communication: Toll-Free Healthline: 1-888-709-2929

•Health Research Ethics Authority (HREA)
#200, 95 Bonaventure Ave., 2nd Fl.
St. John's, NL A1B 2X5
Tel: 709-777-6974; *Fax:* 709-777-8776
info@hrea.ca
www.hrea.ca

The HREA is responsible for supervising all health research involving human subjects conducted in Newfoundland & Labrador.

•Labrador-Grenfell Regional Health Authority
Administration Bldg.
PO Box 7000 C
Happy Valley-Goose Bay, NL A0P 1C0
Tel: 709-897-2267; *Fax:* 709-896-4032
www.lghealth.ca

•Newfoundland & Labrador Centre for Health Information (NLCHI)
70 O'Leary Ave.
St. John's, NL A1B 2C7
Tel: 709-752-6000; *Fax:* 709-752-6011
Toll-free: 877-752-6006
communications@nlchi.nl.ca
www.nlchi.nl.ca
Other Communication: Information: InfoRequests@nlchi.nl.ca; Privacy: privacy@nlchi.nl.ca; Employment: employment@nlchi.nl.ca; Supply Chain: procurement@nlchi.nl.ca

•Newfoundland & Labrador Health Boards Association (NLHBA)
Beothuck Bldg.
20 Crosbie Pl., 2nd Fl.
St. John's, NL A1B 3Y8
Tel: 709-364-7701; *Fax:* 709-364-6460

•Western Regional Health Authority
Corporate Office
1 Brookfield Ave.
Corner Brook, NL A2H 6J7
Tel: 709-637-5000
westernhealth.nl.ca

Corporate Services Branch

Regional Director, Audit & Claims Integrity, Glenn Budgell
Tel: 709-292-4009; *Fax:* 709-292-4052
gbudgell@gov.nl.ca

Director, Information Management, Michael Bannister
Tel: 709-729-3421
michaelbannister@gov.nl.ca

Policy & Planning Branch

Assistant Deputy Minister, Karen Stone
Tel: 709-729-3103
karens@gov.nl.ca

Acting Director, Planning & Evaluation, Andrea Kearley
Tel: 709-729-6866
AndreaKearley@gov.nl.ca

Director, Policy Development, Wanda Legge
Tel: 709-729-5249
wlegge@gov.nl.ca

Population Health Branch

Assistant Deputy Minister, Elaine Chatigny
Tel: 709-729-3103
ElaineChatigny@gov.nl.ca

Acting Assistant Deputy Minister, Colleen Stockley
Tel: 709-729-3103
cstockley@gov.nl.ca

Chief Medical Officer of Health, Dr. Faith Stratton
Tel: 709-729-3430
fstratton@gov.nl.ca

Director, Environmental Public Health, Darryl Johnson
Tel: 709-729-3422; *Fax:* 709-729-0730
djohnson@gov.nl.ca

Director, Disease Control, Cathy O'Keefe
Tel: 709-729-5019; *Fax:* 709-729-5824
cokeefe@gov.nl.ca

Professional Services

Assistant Deputy Minister, Colleen Janes
Tel: 709-729-1716; *Fax:* 709-729-5218
cjanes@gov.nl.ca

Chief Nurse & Director, Vacant
Tel: 709-729-4018

Provincial Director, Physician Services, Dr. Larry Alteen
Tel: 709-729-3531
LarryAlteen@gov.nl.ca

Provincial Director, Pathology & Laboratory Medicine, Beverly Carter
Tel: 709-729-7652
beverlycarter@gov.nl.ca

Acting Director, Pharmaceutical Services Division, Keith Sheppard
Tel: 709-758-7977
keithsheppard@gov.nl.ca

Director, Dental Services, Dr. Ed Williams
Tel: 709-758-1503
edwilliams@gov.nl.ca

Regional Services Branch

Acting Director, Long-Term Care & Community Supports, Angela Batstone
Tel: 709-729-7686
angelabatstone@gov.nl.ca

Director, Acute Health Services, Emergency Management & Nursing Policy, Beverly Griffiths
Tel: 709-729-0717
bgriffiths@gov.nl.ca

Newfoundland & Labrador Housing Corporation (NLHC)

Sir Brian Dunfield Bldg., 2 Canada Dr., PO Box 220 St. John's, NL A1C 5J2
Tel: 709-724-3000; *Fax:* 709-724-3250
www.nlhc.nf.ca
twitter.com/nlhousing
www.facebook.com/NewfoundlandLabradorHousing
www.linkedin.com/company/newfoundland-&-labrador-housing
www.youtube.com/NLHousingCorp

An agency of the Department of Seniors, Wellness & Social Development, mandated to develop & administer housing assistance policy & programs for low to moderate income households.

Minister Responsible, Hon. Sherry Gambin-Walsh
Tel: 709-729-0659; *Fax:* 709-729-0662
sherrygambinwalsh@gov.nl.ca

Interim Chair & Chief Executive Officer; Chief Financial Officer, Finance & Quality Assurance & Evaluation, Tom

Lawrence
tflawrence@nlhc.nl.ca
Executive Director, Human Resources & Engineering, Glenn Goss
Tel: 709-724-3043
gagoss@nlhc.nl.ca
Executive Director, Regional Operations, Dennis Kendell
Tel: 709-724-3408
dmkendell@nlhc.nl.ca
Executive Director, Program Delivery & Policy, Research & Marketing, Kate Moffatt
Tel: 709-724-3053
camoffatt@nlhc.nl.ca
Executive Director, IT & Administration, Clyde Thornhill
Tel: 709-724-3153
cgthornhill@nlhc.nl.ca

Regional Offices

St. John's - Avalon
Sir Brian Dunfield Bldg., 2 Canada Dr., PO Box 220 St. John's, NL A1C 5J2
Tel: 709-724-3000; *Fax:* 709-724-3007
Other Communication: Maintenance Division, Phone: 709-724-3400; Fax: 709-724-3037

Corner Brook
34 Boone's Rd., PO Box 826 Corner Brook, NL A2H 6H6
Tel: 709-639-5201; *Fax:* 709-639-5206

Gander
5 Garrett Dr., PO Box 410 Gander, NL A1V 1W8
Tel: 709-256-1300; *Fax:* 709-256-1320

Goose Bay
8 Royal St., PO Box 299 Stn. B, Happy Valley-Goose Bay, NL A0P 1E0
Tel: 709-896-1920; *Fax:* 709-896-9208

Grand Falls-Windsor
5 Hardy Ave., Grand Falls-Windsor, NL A2A 2P8
Tel: 709-292-1000; *Fax:* 709-292-1028

Labrador City
#105, 1021 Cavendish Sq., Labrador City, NL A2V 2W5
Tel: 709-944-7474; *Fax:* 709-944-3298

Marystown
60 Atlantic Cres., PO Box 338 Marystown, NL A0E 2M0
Tel: 709-279-5375; *Fax:* 709-279-5387

Stephenville
58 Oregon Dr., Stephenville, NL A2N 2Y1
Tel: 709-643-6826; *Fax:* 709-643-6843
Other Communication: Maintenance Division, Fax: 709-643-6844

Newfoundland & Labrador Human Rights Commission

The Beothuk Bldg., 21 Crosbie Pl., PO Box 8700 St. John's, NL A1B 4J6
Tel: 709-729-2709; *Fax:* 709-729-0790
Toll-Free: 800-563-5808
humanrights@gov.nl.ca
www.justice.gov.nl.ca/hrc

Chair, Remzi Cej
Vice-Chair, Stephanie Newell, Q.C.
Chief Adjudicator, James Merrigan
Executive Director, Carey Majid
careymajid@gov.nl.ca

Newfoundland & Labrador Hydro

Hydro Place, 500 Columbus Dr., PO Box 12400 St. John's, NL A1B 4K7
Tel: 709-737-1400; *Fax:* 709-737-1800
Toll-Free: 888-737-1296
hydro@nlh.nl.ca
www.nlh.nl.ca
Other Communication: Vendor Information, Phone; 709-737-1335; Fax: 709-737-1795; E-Mail: tenders@nlh.nl.ca; Customer Service, E-Mail: customerservices@nlh.nl.ca

Crown corporation, owned by the Province of Newfoundland & Labrador, & a subsidiary of Nalcor Energy. Hydro generates, transmits & distributes electrical power & energy to utility, residential & industrial customers throughout the province. Hydro is the parent company of the Hydro Group of Companies (Hydro Group), comprising Newfoundland & Labrador Hydro, Churchill Falls (Labrador) Corporation Limited (CF(L)Co), Lower Churchill Development Corporation Limited (LCDC), Gull Island Power Company Limited (GIPCo), & Twin Falls Power Corporation Limited (TwinCo). The Hydro Group's installed generating capacity is the fourth largest of all utility companies in Canada, consisting of ten hydroelectric plants, including the Churchill Falls hydraulic plant, which is the largest underground powerhouse in the world with a rated capacity of 5,428 megawatts (MW) of power, one oil-fired plant, four gas turbines & 26 diesel plants.

President & Chief Executive Officer, Ed Martin
Chief Financial Officer & Vice-President, Finance, Derrick Sturge
Vice-President, Newfoundland & Labrador Hydro, Rob Henderson
Vice-President, System Operations & Planning, Paul Humphries
Vice-President, Asset Management, Project Execution & Engineering Services, John MacIsaac
Vice-President, Human Resources & Organzational Effectiveness, Gerard McDonald

Churchill Falls (Labrador) Corporation Limited (CF(L)Co)
Hydro Place, 500 Columbus Dr., PO Box 12500 St. John's, NL A1B 4K7
Tel: 709-737-1859; *Fax:* 709-737-1816
Churchill Falls (Labrador) Corporation operates a hydroelectric generating plant & transmission facilities.

Gull Island Power Co. Ltd. (GIPCo)

Lower Churchill Development Corporation Ltd. (LCDC)
PO Box 12700 St. John's, NL A1B 3T5
Tel: 709-737-1400; *Fax:* 709-737-1400
The corporation seeks to develop the hydroelectric potential of the Lower Churchill basin. It is 49 per cent owned by the federal government.

Twin Falls Power Corporation (TwinCo)
PO Box 12500 St. John's, NL A1B 3T5
Twin Falls Power Corporation has developed a hydroelectric generating plant on the Unknown River in Labrador. The plant has been inoperative since 1974.

Newfoundland & Labrador Department of Justice & Public Safety

Confederation Bldg., East Block, 4th Fl., PO Box 8700 St. John's, NL A1B 4J6
Tel: 709-729-2869; *Fax:* 709-729-0469
justice@gov.nl.ca
www.justice.gov.nl.ca

In September 2014, Premier Paul Davis created the new Department of Public Safety, which assumed the duties of the former Justice department — to ensure the impartial administration of justice & the protection of the public interest — & included Fire & Emergency Services - Newfoundland & Labrador. However, the name was changed again in October 2014 to Justice & Public Safety, in order to avoid confusion about the department's purpose.

Minister & Attorney General, Hon. Andrew Parsons
Tel: 709-729-2869; *Fax:* 709-729-0469
andrewparsons@gov.nl.ca
Acting Deputy Minister; Deputy Attorney General, Heather Jacobs
Tel: 709-729-2872; *Fax:* 709-729-2129
heatherj@gov.nl.ca
Director, Communications, Luke Joyce
Tel: 709-729-6985; *Fax:* 709-729-0469
lukejoyce@gov.nl.ca
Acting Director, Public Prosecutions, Frances Knickle, Q.C.

Associated Agencies, Boards & Commissions:

•Child Death Review Committee
Established by amendments to the Fatalities Investigations Act in 2012, the Committee reviews cases involving the deaths of children under 19 years, which have been provided by the Chief Medical Examiner.

•Commissioner of Lobbyists
Bally Rou Place
#E160, Torbay Rd.
St. John's, NL A1A 3W8
Tel: 709-729-2918; *Fax:* 709-729-1302
www.servicenl.gov.nl.ca/registries/lobby/lobby_commissioner.html

•Consumer Advocate
www.justice.gov.nl.ca/just/department/consumeradvocate.html

•Criminal Code Mental Disorder Review Board
www.justice.gov.nl.ca/just/department/criminalcode.html
The Board's mandate is to issue dispositions related to the management of persons accused of committing a crime who have been found not criminally responsible or unfit to stand trial due to a mental disorder. Three dispositions are at the Board's disposal: absolute discharge, conditionl discharge, or detention with or without conditions.

•Electoral Districts Boundaries Commission
83 Thorburn Rd.
PO Box 8700 C
St. John's, NL A1B 4J6
Tel: 709-729-2605; *Fax:* 709-729-2724
info@nledbc.ca
www.nledbc.ca
Other Communication: Recorded Submission Line: 1-844-411-7410
Mandated by the Electoral Boundaries Act, the Commission was responsible for dividing the province into 48 proposed one-member districts in 2006. The Commission was tasked with dividing the province into 40 proposed one-member districts in 2015.

•Office of the Public Trustee
The Viking Bldg.
#401, 136 Crosbie Rd.
St. John's, NL A1B 3K3
Tel: 709-729-0850; *Fax:* 709-729-3063
justice.gov.nl.ca/just/department/branches/division/trustee.html

•Fire & Emergency Services - Newfoundland & Labrador (FES-NL)
25 Hallett Cres.
PO Box 8700
St. John's, NL A1B 4J6
Tel: 709-729-1608; *Fax:* 709-729-2524
www.gov.nl.ca/fes
Other Communication: Emergency Management, Phone: 709-729-3703; Fax: 709-729-3757

•Human Rights Commission
See Entry Name Index for detailed listing.

•Newfoundland & Labrador Board of Commissioners of Public Utilities
See Entry Name Index for detailed listing.

•Newfoundland & Labrador Legal Aid Commission
#300, 251 Empire Ave.
St. John's, NL A1C 5J9
Tel: 709-753-7860; *Fax:* 709-753-7851
Toll-free: 800-563-9911
nlac@legalaid.nl.ca
www.legalaid.nl.ca
The Legal Aid Commission ensures that persons with limited financial means have access to legal counsel.

•NL 911 Bureau Inc.
c/o Fire & Emergency Services - NL
25 Hallett Cres.
PO Box 8700
St. John's, NL A1B 4J6
www.gov.nl.ca/fes/911/index.html
Created with the proclamation of the Emergency 911 Act in February 2015, the board is responsible for the operation of the province-wide basic 911 service as well as the future development of Next Generation 911.

•Office of the Chief Medical Examiner
#1562, Health Sciences Centre, Level 1
St. John's, NL A1B 3V6
Tel: 709-737-6402
ocme@gov.nl.ca

•Royal Newfoundland Constabulary Public Complaints Commission
689 Topsail Rd.
PO Box 8700
St. John's, NL A1B 4J6
Tel: 709-729-0950; *Fax:* 709-729-1302
rnccomplaintscommission@gov.nl.ca
www.justice.gov.nl.ca/rncpcc
The Royal Newfoundland Constabulary Public Complaints Commission is an independent review authority established under Statute to hear & investigate complaints against members of the Royal Newfoundland Constabulary &, when appropriate, to conduct public hearings in respect of particular complaints.

Courts & Legal Services
Assistant Deputy Minister, Todd Stanley
Tel: 709-729-0288; *Fax:* 709-729-2129
toddstanley@gov.nl.ca
Director, Legal Information Services, Sean Dawe
Tel: 709-729-2861; *Fax:* 709-729-1370
seand@gov.nl.ca
Director, Family Justice Services, Wilma MacInnis
Tel: 709-729-1146
Director, Civil Law, Rolf Pritchard
Tel: 709-729-2597
rolfpritchard@gov.nl.ca

Office of the Legislative Counsel
Assistant Deputy Minister & Chief Legislative Counsel, Kimberly Hawley-George
Tel: 709-729-2881; *Fax:* 709-729-2129
kimhawle@gov.nl.ca

Legislative Counsel & Registrar of Subordinate Legislation, Susan King
Tel: 709-729-4559; *Fax:* 709-729-2129
SusanKing@gov.nl.ca
Legislative Counsel, Angela Whitehead
Tel: 709-729-2877; *Fax:* 709-729-2129

Public Prosecutions Division
Assistant Deputy Minister & Director, Donovan Molloy
Tel: 709-729-2868; *Fax:* 709-729-2129
donovanmolloy@gov.nl.ca
Acting Assistant Director, Elaine Reid
Tel: 709-729-1179; *Fax:* 709-729-2129
emreid@gov.nl.ca

Public Safety & Enforcement
Assistant Deputy Minister, Jacqueline Lake-Kavanagh
Tel: 709-729-7364; *Fax:* 709-729-2129
jackiekavanagh@gov.nl.ca
Chief, Royal Newfoundland Constabulary, William J. Janes
Tel: 709-729-8151
contactrnc@rnc.gov.nl.ca
www.rnc.gov.nl.ca
High Sheriff, Ernest Boone
Tel: 709-729-4607
ErnestBoone@gov.nl.ca
Superintendent, Prisons, Graham Rogerson
Tel: 709-729-2978; *Fax:* 709-729-4312
grahamrogerson@gov.nl.ca
Director, Quality Management & Support Services, Dan Chafe
Tel: 709-729-1078; *Fax:* 709-729-5100
DanChafe@gov.nl.ca
Director, Corrections & Community Services, Dean Gambin
Tel: 709-729-2327

Strategic & Corporate Services
Acting Assistant Deputy Minister, Debbie Dunphy
Tel: 709-729-2880; *Fax:* 709-729-2129
ddunphy@gov.nl.ca

Labour Relations Agency

Beothuck Bldg., 20 Crosbie Pl., 3rd Fl., PO Box 8700 St. John's, NL A1B 4J6
Tel: 709-729-2715; *Fax:* 709-729-1759
Toll-Free: 877-563-1063
labour@gov.nl.ca
www.gov.nl.ca/lra

Works with employers & employees to facilitate positive employment relations throughout the province. In August 2016 Premier Ball announced the Labour Relations Agency would be combined with the Department of Advanced Education & Skills to create the Department of Advanced Education, Skills & Labour.
Minister Responsible, Hon. Perry Trimper
Tel: 709-729-2574; *Fax:* 709-729-0112
perrytrimper@gov.nl.ca
Chief Operating Officer, Bruce Cooper
Assistant Deputy Minister, John Phillips
Tel: 709-729-2242
johnphillips@gov.nl.ca
Director, Labour Standards, Ken Clements
Tel: 709-729-2742; *Fax:* 709-729-3528
kclements@gov.nl.ca
Director, Policy & Planning, Deanne Howe
Tel: 709-729-5551
deannehowe@gov.nl.ca
Director, Labour Relations, Yvonne Scott
yscott@gov.nl.ca

Newfoundland & Labrador Department of Municipal & Intergovernmental Affairs

West Block, Main Fl., Confederation Bldg., PO Box 8700 St. John's, NL A1B 4J6
Tel: 709-729-3046; *Fax:* 709-729-0943
mainfo@gov.nl.ca
www.miga.gov.nl.ca

Works with municipalities to ensure communities are properly managed & planned to ensure residents have a high standard of living in a clean, healthy & safe environment.
Minister, Municipal Affairs, Hon. Eddie Joyce
Tel: 709-729-3048; *Fax:* 709-729-0943
ejoyce@gov.nl.ca
Minister, Intergovernmental Affairs, Hon. Dwight Ball
Tel: 709-729-3570; *Fax:* 709-729-5875
dwightball@gov.nl.ca
Deputy Minister, Municipal Affairs, Jamie Chippett
Tel: 709-729-3049
JamieChippett@gov.nl.ca
Deputy Minister, Intergovernmental Affairs & CEO Fire & Emergency Services, Sean Dutton
Tel: 709-729-6794
sdutton@gov.nl.ca
Assistant Deputy Minister, Intergovernmental Affairs, Paul Scott
Tel: 709-729-5030; *Fax:* 709-729-5038
paulscott@gov.nl.ca
Director, Communications, Heather May
Tel: 709-729-1983; *Fax:* 709-729-0943
heathermay@gov.nl.ca

Associated Agencies, Boards & Commissions:

•Burin Peninsula Waste Management Corporation
PO Box 510
Burin Bay Arm, NL A0E 1G0
Tel: 709-891-1717; *Fax:* 709-891-1727
info@burinpenwaste.com
burinpenwaste.com

•Central Newfoundland Waste Management Authority (CNMW)
Route 3-1-09
PO Box 254
Norris Arm, NL A0G 3M0
Tel: 709-653-2900; *Fax:* 709-653-2920
www.cnwmc.com

•Eastern Waste Management Commission
#3, 255 Majors Path
St. John's, NL A1A 0L5
Tel: 709-579-7960; *Fax:* 709-579-5392
info@easternwaste.ca
easternwaste.ca

•Green Bay Waste Authority Inc.
160 Robert's Arm Rd.
South Brook, NL A0J 1S0
Tel: 709-657-2233; *Fax:* 709-657-2133
Toll-free: 877-657-2233
info@greenbaywaste.com
greenbaywaste.com

•Northern Peninsula Regional Service Board
#171, 173 West St.
PO Box 130
St. Anthony, NL A0K 4S0
Tel: 709-454-3110; *Fax:* 709-454-3818
www.norpenservices.ca

Employment Support & Corporate Services
Assistant Deputy Minister, Dana Spurrell
Tel: 709-729-3016; *Fax:* 709-729-0943
DanaSpurrell@gov.nl.ca
Departmental Controller, Robyn Hayes
Tel: 709-729-0851; *Fax:* 709-729-5535
robynhayes@gov.nl.ca
Director, Community Enhancement & Employment Support, Sandy Hounsell
Tel: 709-729-3016; *Fax:* 709-729-2019
SandyHounsell@gov.nl.ca
Director, Policy & Strategic Planning, Tara Kelly
Tel: 709-729-2787; *Fax:* 709-729-4475
tarakelly@gov.nl.ca

Lands Branch
Assistant Deputy Minister, Peter Howe
Tel: 709-729-3236; *Fax:* 709-729-0112
phowe@gov.nl.ca
Director, Crown Lands Administration Division, Robert Dicks
Tel: 709-729-3174; *Fax:* 709-729-4361
rdicks@gov.nl.ca
Acting Director, Surveys & Mapping Division & Land Management Division, Darren Moore
Tel: 709-729-3844; *Fax:* 709-729-3923
dmoore@gov.nl.ca

Municipal Engineering
Assistant Deputy Minister, Cluney Mercer
Tel: 709-729-3051; *Fax:* 709-729-0477
mercercg@gov.nl.ca
Director, Waste Management, Frank Huxter
Tel: 709-729-0891; *Fax:* 709-729-0477
fhuxter@gov.nl.ca

Municipal Support
Assistant Deputy Minister, Heather Tizzard
Tel: 709-729-3066; *Fax:* 709-729-2109
HeatherTizzard@gov.nl.ca
Secretary, Sherry Auchinleck
Tel: 709-729-3016; *Fax:* 709-729-2019
sauchinleck@gov.nl.ca
Director, Municipal Finance, Paul Tucker
Tel: 709-729-5381; *Fax:* 709-729-4475
Director, Local Governance, Andy Morgans
Tel: 709-729-5539; *Fax:* 709-729-4475
andymorgans@gov.nl.ca
Director, Community Enhancement & Employment Support, Sandy Hounsell
Tel: 709-729-3016; *Fax:* 709-729-2019
SandyHounsell@gov.nl.ca
Director, Policy & Strategic Planning, Tara Kelly
Tel: 709-729-2787; *Fax:* 709-729-4475
tarakelly@gov.nl.ca
Manager, Information Services, Ali Askary
Tel: 709-729-5846
aliaskary@gov.nl.ca
Departmental Controller, Robyn Hayes
Tel: 709-729-0851; *Fax:* 709-729-5535
RobynHayes@gov.nl.ca

Municipal Assessment Agency Inc.

75 O'Leary Ave., St. John's, NL A1B 2C9
Tel: 709-724-1532
Toll-Free: 877-777-2807
info@maa.ca
www.maa.ca

The agency provides property assessment & valuation services. The head office location is also the Eastern Regional Office.
Chair, Dean Ball

Regional Offices

Corner Brook - Western
PO Box 20051 Corner Brook, NL A2H 7J5
Tel: 709-637-7150

Gander - Central
165 Roe Ave., PO Box 570 Gander, NL A1V 2E1
Tel: 709-651-4460

Happy Valley-Goose Bay - Labrador
Elizabeth Goudie Bldg., PO Box 3014 Stn. B, Happy Valley-Goose Bay, NL A0P 1E0
Tel: 709-896-5393

Nalcor Energy

500 Columbus Dr., St. John's, NL A1E 2B2
Tel: 709-737-1400; *Fax:* 709-737-1800
info@nalcorenergy.com
www.nalcorenergy.com
twitter.com/NalcorEnergy
www.facebook.com/NalcorEnergy
www.youtube.com/user/NalcorEnergy

Crown corporation, founded in 2008 & owned by the Province of Newfoundland & Labrador. Nalcor is the parent company of Newfoundland & Labrador Hydro, which in turn is the parent of the Hydro Group of Companies. Nalcor's subsidiaries include: Newfoundland & Labrador Hydro, The Churchill Falls Generating Station, Lower Churchill Project, Oil & Gas & Bull Arm Fabrication.
Interim Chair, John Green, Q.C.
President & Chief Executive Officer, H. Stanley Marshall
Chief Financial Officer & Vice-President, Finance, Derrick Sturge
Vice-President, Lower Churchill Project, Gilbert Bennett
Vice-President, Corporate Relations & Customer Service, Dawn Dalley
Vice-President, Transition to Operations, Rob Henderson
Vice-President, Oil & Gas, Jim Keating
Vice-President, Strategic Planning & Business Development, Chris Kieley

Newfoundland & Labrador Department of Natural Resources

Natural Resources Bldg., 50 Elizabeth Ave., 7th Fl., PO Box 8700 St. John's, NL A1B 4J6
Tel: 709-729-2920; *Fax:* 709-729-0059
www.nr.gov.nl.ca

Responsible for the management of the province's mineral, energy, land, forest & wildlife resources in a manner that will ensure optimum benefits for the people of the province.
Minister, Hon. Siobhan Coady
Tel: 709-729-2920; *Fax:* 709-729-0059
siobhancoady@gov.nl.ca
Deputy Minister, Charles Bown
Tel: 709-729-2766; *Fax:* 709-729-0059
cbown@gov.nl.ca
Assistant Deputy Minister, Agriculture, Keith Deering
Tel: 709-729-2488; *Fax:* 709-637-2461
keithdeering@gov.nl.ca
Executive Director, Policy & Strategic Planning, Tanya Noseworthy
Tel: 709-729-1466
tanyanoseworthy@gov.nl.ca
Executive Director, Iron Ore Industry, Walter Parsons
Tel: 709-729-6760
walterparsons@gov.nl.ca

Director, Information Manangement, Renée Pendergast
Tel: 709-729-1651
reneependergast@gov.nl.ca
Director, Communications, Diana Quinton
Tel: 709-729-5282
dianaquinton@gov.nl.ca
Departmental Controller, Finance & General Operations Division, Philip Ivimey
Tel: 709-729-7009
philipivimey@gov.nl.ca

Associated Agencies, Boards & Commissions:

•Agricultural Land Consolidation Review Committee
The Committee administers the Agricultural Land Consolidation Program, which allows retiring farmers & non-farmer landowners to sell their granted land to the provincial government.

•Canada-Newfoundland & Labrador Offshore Petroleum Board (C-NLOPB)
TD Place
140 Water St., 5th Fl.
St. John's, NL A1C 6H6
Tel: 709-778-1400; *Fax:* 709-778-1473
information@cnlopb.ca
www.cnlopb.ca
Other Communication: Core Storage & Research Centre, Phone: 709-778-1500, E-mail: csrc@cnlopb.nl.ca
Established in 1985, the Canada - Newfoundland & Labrador Offshore Petroleum Board applies the provisions of the *Atlantic Accord* & the *Atlantic Accord Implementation Acts*.
The Board regulates the oil & gas industrr for the Newfoundland & Labrador Offshore Area. Operator activity is overseen for legislative & regulatory compliance in the areas of environmental protection, resource management, offshore safety, & industrial benefits.
The role of the Canada - Newfoundland & Labrador Offshore Petroleum Board facilitates the exploration for & development of hydrocarbon resources.

•Chicken Farmers of Newfoundland & Labrador (CFNL)
Agriculture Canada Bldg. 6
308 Brookfield Rd.
PO Box 8098
St. John's, NL A1B 3M9
Tel: 709-747-1493; *Fax:* 709-747-0544
www.nlchicken.com

•Farm Industry Review Board (FIRB)
Fortis Bldg.
PO Box 2006
Corner Brook, NL A2H 6J8
Tel: 709-637-0806; *Fax:* 709-637-2365
www.nr.gov.nl.ca/NR/agrifoods/ic/firb
FIRB is responsible for controlling & directing the operations of the province's commodity boards, as well as providing farmers with protection against nuisance suits (as long as the farm in question is operating according to acceptable farm practices).

•Forest Land Tax Appeal Board
The Forest Land Tax Appeal Board carried out its responsibilities under Part III of the Forestry Act as of March 31, 2008.

•Mineral Rights Adjudication Board
PO Box 5955
St. John's, NL A1C 5X4
Tel: 709-726-3524; *Fax:* 709-726-9600
The Board is responsible for hearing & determining the outcome of questions, disputes & matters arising out of the application of the Minieral Act & the Mining Act & associated regulations.

•Nalcor Energy
See Entry Name Index for detailed listing.

•Newfoundland & Labrador Crop Insurance Agency
www.nr.gov.nl.ca/nr/agrifoods/crops/prodinsur.html

•Newfoundland & Labrador Farm Products Corporation
The Farm Products Corporation was mandated to establish buildings & establishments necessary for the handling, preparation, processing & storage of farm products, both animal & vegetable. It is currently inactive, but can be reactivated in order to assist the Minister of Natural Resources with provincial sustainable development initiatives.

•Newfoundland & Labrador Livestock Owners Compensation Board

•St. John's Land Development Advisory Authority

•St. John's Urban Region Agricultural Appeal Board

•Timber Scalers Board
The Timber Scalers Board is currently inactive, with its mandate being fulfilled internally within the Department of Natural Resources. Its members remain on standby in the event the Minister required the board re-activated.

•Wooddale Land Development Advisory Authority
The Authority considers applications for development in the Wooddale Agriculture Development Area.

Energy Branch
Associate Deputy Minister, Energy Resources, Tracy English
Tel: 709-729-2349; *Fax:* 709-729-2871
tenglish@gov.nl.ca
Assistant Deputy Minister, Royalties & Benefits, Paul Carter
Tel: 709-729-1644; *Fax:* 709-729-2871
pcarter@gov.nl.ca
Assistant Deputy Minister, Petroleum Development, Wes Foote
Tel: 709-729-2206; *Fax:* 709-729-2508
wesfoote@gov.nl.ca
Director, Regulatory Affairs, Fred Allen
Tel: 709-729-2778
fredallen@gov.nl.ca
Director, Energy Economics, Wayne Andrews
Tel: 709-729-5899
wayneandrews@gov.nl.ca
Acting Director, Electricity & Alternative Energy, & Director, Energy Policy, Planning & Coordination, John Cowan
Tel: 709-729-3906
jcowan@gov.nl.ca
Director, Petroleum Engineering, Keith Hynes
Tel: 709-729-7188; *Fax:* 709-729-2508
keithhynes@gov.nl.ca
Director, Royalties Administration & Monitoring, Craig Martin
Tel: 709-729-0463; *Fax:* 709-729-2508
cmartin@gov.nl.ca
Director, Industrial Benefits, Rob McGrath
Tel: 709-729-1421
robmcgrath@gov.nl.ca
Director, Petroleum Marketing & Promotion, Darrell Spurrell
Tel: 709-729-0579; *Fax:* 709-729-4011
darrellspurrell@gov.nl.ca
Director, Petroleum Geoscience, Vacant

Forestry & Agrifoods Agency
Fortis Bldg., PO Box 2006 Corner Brook, NL A2H 6J8
Tel: 709-637-2349; *Fax:* 709-637-2403
In August 2016 Premier Ball announced that the Forestry & Agrifoods Agency & the Department of Fisheries & Aquaculture have combined to create the Department of Fisheries, Forestry & Agrifoods.
Minister Responsible, Hon. Christopher Mitchelmore
Tel: 709-729-4729; *Fax:* 709-729-0654
cmitchelmore@gov.nl.ca
Assistant Deputy Minister, Agrifoods, Keith Deering
Tel: 709-637-2339
keithdeering@gov.nl.ca
Chief Executive Officer, James Evans
Tel: 709-637-2339; *Fax:* 709-637-2461
jamesevans@gov.nl.ca
Director, Policy & Planning, Dena Parsons
Tel: 709-729-5029; *Fax:* 709-729-0973
denaparsons@gov.nl.ca

Agrifoods Development Branch
Tel: 709-729-2046; *Fax:* 709-637-2591
To contribute to economic & rural development throughout the province by promoting the continued development, expansion & diversification of competitive & sustainable primary & value-added agrifood businesses.
Director, Land Resource Stewardship Division, Richard Carey
Tel: 709-637-2081
rcarey@gov.nl.ca
Director, Agriculture Business Development Division, Cynthia MacDonald
Tel: 709-637-2097; *Fax:* 709-637-2589
cindymacdonald@gov.nl.ca
Director, Animal Health Division & Chief Veterinary Officer, Dr. Hugh Whitney
Tel: 709-729-6879; *Fax:* 709-729-0055
hughwhitney@gov.nl.ca

Forestry Services Branch
Tel: 709-637-2284; *Fax:* 709-634-4378
The Forestry Services Branch is responsible for managing & regulating the forest resources of the Province.
Director, Forest Engineering & Industry Services, Eric Young
Tel: 709-637-2350; *Fax:* 709-637-2403
emyoung@gov.nl.ca
Manager, Ecosystem, William M. Clarke
Tel: 709-729-0884
williamclarke@gov.nl.ca

Forestry Regional Services
Eastern
PO Box 2222 Gander, NL A1V 5T4
Tel: 709-256-1450; *Fax:* 709-256-1459
Director, Special Projects, David Cheeks
Tel: 709-256-1462; *Fax:* 709-256-1459

Labrador
Elizabeth Goudie Bldg., PO Box 3014 Stn. B, Happy Valley-Goose Bay, NL A0P 1E0
Tel: 709-896-3405; *Fax:* 709-896-3747
Other Communication: Wildlife, Phone: 709-896-5107; Fax: 709-896-0188
Regional Compliance Manager, Derek J. LeBoubon
Tel: 709-896-3405 ext: 228; *Fax:* 709-896-3747
derekleboubon@gov.nl.ca

Western
Massey Drive Bldg., PO Box 2006 Corner Brook, NL A2H 6J8
Tel: 709-637-2409; *Fax:* 709-639-1377
Special Projects Officer, Gord Fifield
Tel: 709-637-2298
gfifield@gov.nl.ca

Mines Branch
Promotes & facilitates the sustainable development of the province's mineral & energy resources through its resource assessment, management & development activities for the overall benefit of the citizens of Newfoundland & Labrador.
Assistant Deputy Minister, David Liverman
Tel: 709-729-2768; *Fax:* 709-729-2871
dliverman@gov.nl.ca
Director, Geological Survey Division, Martin Batterson
Tel: 709-729-3419
martinbatterson@gov.nl.ca
Director, Geochemical Laboratory, Chris Finch
Tel: 709-729-3312
chrisfinch@gov.nl.ca
Director, Mineral Lands Division, Jim Hinchey
Tel: 709-729-6425; *Fax:* 709-729-6782
jimhinchey@gov.nl.ca
Director, Mineral Development Division, Alex Smith
Tel: 709-729-6379; *Fax:* 709-729-3493
asmith@gov.nl.ca
Senior Geologist & Section Manager, Geochemistry/Geophysics & Terrain Sciences, Stephen Amor
Tel: 709-729-1161
stephenamor@gov.nl.ca
Senior Geologist & Section Manager, Regional Geology, Alana Hinchey
Tel: 709-729-7725
alanahinchey@gov.nl.ca
Senior Geologist & Section Manager, Mineral Deposits, Andrew Kerr
Tel: 709-729-2164
andykerr@gov.nl.ca
Senior Geologist & Section Manager, Geoscience Data Management, Larry Nolan
Tel: 709-729-2168
larrynolan@gov.nl.ca
Senior Geologist & Section Manager, Geoscience Publications & Information, Sean O'Brien
Tel: 709-729-2775
seanobrien@gov.nl.ca

Newfoundland & Labrador Public Service Commission

50 Mundy Pond Rd., PO Box 8700 St. John's, NL A1B 4J6
Tel: 709-729-5810; *Fax:* 709-729-6234
Toll-Free: 855-330-5810
contactpsc@gov.nl.ca
www.gov.nl.ca/psc

Minister Responsible, Hon. Cathy Bennett
Tel: 709-729-3775; *Fax:* 709-729-2232
cbennett@gov.nl.ca
Chair & Chief Executive Officer, Bruce Hollett
Tel: 709-729-2650; *Fax:* 709-729-3178
brucehollett@gov.nl.ca
Commissioner, Ann Chafe
Tel: 709-729-2659; *Fax:* 709-729-3178
annchafe@gov.nl.ca
Director, Employee Assistance & Respectful Workplace, Ian Shortall
Tel: 709-729-5804
nshortall@gov.nl.ca
Director, Appeal & Investigation, Raelene Thomas
Tel: 709-729-2581
raelenethomas@gov.nl.ca

Newfoundland & Labrador Board of Commissioners of Public Utilities

Prince Charles Bldg., #E-210, 120 Torbay Rd., PO Box 21040 St. John's, NL A1A 5B2
Tel: 709-726-8600; *Fax:* 709-726-9604
Toll-Free: 866-782-0006
ito@pub.nf.ca
www.pub.nf.ca
Regulates electrical utilities in Newfoundland & Labrador.

Chair & CEO, Andy Wells
Tel: 709-726-1133
awells@pub.nl.ca
Vice-Chair, Darlene Whalen
Tel: 709-726-0955
dwhalen@pub.nl.ca
Director, Corporate Services & Board Secretary, G. Cheryl Blundon
Tel: 709-726-8600; *Fax:* 709-726-9604
cblundon@pub.nl.ca
Director, Regulatory & Advisory Services, Robert Byrne
Tel: 709-726-0742
rbyrne@pub.nl.ca

Newfoundland & Labrador Research & Development Corporation (RDC)

68 Portugal Cove Rd., St. John's, NL A1B 2L9
Tel: 709-758-0913; *Fax:* 709-758-0927
info@rdc.org
www.rdc.org
Other Communication: Alternate E-mails: programs@rdc.org; application@rdc.org; careers@rdc.org
twitter.com/RDCNL
www.facebook.com/rdcnl
www.youtube.com/user/RDCNL

The RDC is a provincial Crown corporation established in 2009 to improve Newfoundland & Labrador's research & development capabilities.

Minister Responsible, Hon. Christopher Mitchelmore
Tel: 709-729-4729; *Fax:* 709-729-0654
cmitchelmore@gov.nl.ca
Chair, Fraser H. Edison
Acting Chief Executive Officer, Mark Ploughman
markbploughman@rdc.org
Chief Financial Officer, Levi May
levimay@rdc.org
Vice-President, R&D Opportunities, Doug Trask
dougtrask@rdc.org
Vice-President, R&D Solutions, Nancy Winchester
nancywinchester@rdc.org
Director, Business Development, Steve Mercer
stevemercer@rdc.org
Director, Human Resources, Kimberly Spencer
kimberlyspencer@rdc.org
Director, Financial Operations, Joanne Whelan
joannewhelan@rdc.org

Newfoundland & Labrador Department of Seniors, Wellness & Social Development

PO Box 8700 St. John's, NL A1B 4J6
Tel: 709-729-0862; *Fax:* 709-729-0870
SWSDInfo@gov.nl.ca
www.swsd.gov.nl.ca
Other Communication: Adult Protection: 1-855-376-4957; Seniors & Aging: 1-888-494-2266

Created in September 2014, the Department's main areas of focus are seniors & aging, health promotion, wellness & sport, as well as the Disability Policy Office & the Poverty Reduction Strategy. In August 2016 Premier Ball announced the combination of the Department of Child, Youth & Family Services & the Department of Seniors, Wellness and Social Development to create the Department of Children, Seniors and Social Development.

Minister, Seniors, Wellness & Social Development; Minister Responsible, Newfoundland & Labrador Housing Corporation & Status of Persons with Disabilities, Hon. Sherry Gambin-Walsh
Tel: 709-729-0659; *Fax:* 709-729-0662
sherrygambinwalsh@gov.nl.ca
Deputy Minister, Brent Meade
Tel: 709-729-3555
BMeade@gov.nl.ca
Assistant Deputy Minister, Culture & Recreation, Mark Jones
Tel: 709-729-3609
markjones@gov.nl.ca
Director, Communications, Heather May
Tel: 709-729-0928
heathermay@gov.nl.ca

Associated Agencies, Boards & Commissions:

•Newfoundland & Labrador Housing Corporation
See Entry Name Index for detailed listing.

•Newfoundland & Labrador Sports Centre Inc. (NLSC)
c/o Sport NL
1296A Kenmount Rd.
PO Box 8700
St. John's, NL A1B 4J6
Tel: 709-576-4932; *Fax:* 709-576-7493
sportnl@sportnl.ca
www.nlsportscentre.ca
A venue for athlete training, & a host to provincial, national & international competitions for members of Sport Newfoundland & Labrador (SNL).

•Ministerial Council on Aging & Seniors
c/o Department of Seniors, Wellness & Social Development
PO Box 8700
St. John's, NL A1B 4J6
www.swsd.gov.nl.ca/seniors/focus/ministerialcouncil.html
Develops legislation, policies & programs that affect an aging population, & oversees the implementation of the Provincial Healthy Aging Policy Framework.

•Provincial Advisory Council for the Inclusion of Persons with Disabilities
c/o Department of Seniors, Wellness & Social Development
PO Box 8700
St. John's, NL A1B 4J6
www.swsd.gov.nl.ca/disabilities/advisory_council.html
Advises the Minister Responsible for the Status of Persons with Disabilities on current issues & ways to make improvements.

•Provincial Wellness Advisory Council
c/o Department of Seniors, Wellness & Social Development
PO Box 8700
St. John's, NL A1B 4J6
swsd.gov.nl.ca/healthyliving/provincialwellness_advcouncil.html
Provides strategic advice on wellness issues, & implements & evaluates the Provincial Wellness Plan.

Disability Policy Office

Tel: 709-729-6279; *Fax:* 709-729-6237
Toll-Free: 888-729-6279
TTY: 888-729-5440
disability.policy.office@gov.nl.ca

Director, Mary Reid
Tel: 709-729-6208

Healthy Living Division

Tel: 709-729-6243

Director, Linda Carter
Tel: 709-729-3117
lindacarter@gov.nl.ca

Poverty Reduction Strategy

Fax: 709-729-5139
Toll-Free: 866-883-6600
povertyreduction@gov.nl.ca

Director, Aisling Gogan
Tel: 709-729-1287
aislinggogan@gov.nl.ca

Recreation & Sport

Tel: 709-729-2829; *Fax:* 709-729-5293

Director, Michelle Healey
Tel: 709-729-5241
MichelleHealey@gov.nl.ca
Manager, Programs & Strategic Initiatives, Jaime Collins
Tel: 709-729-0855
Jaimecollins@gov.nl.ca

Seniors & Aging Division

Toll-Free: 888-494-2266
Other Communication: Seniors of Distinction Awards: E-mail: seniorsofdistinction@gov.nl.ca

Newfoundland & Labrador Department of Service NL

PO Box 8700 St. John's, NL A1B 4J6
Tel: 709-729-4834
servicenlinfo@gov.nl.ca
www.servicenl.gov.nl.ca

Service NL provides a great range of services to the people of Newfoundland & Labrador. Areas of attention include public health, public safety, environmental protection, vital statistics, motor vehicles, printing services, provincially regulated financial institutions, the operation of Government Service Centres, consumer & commercial affairs, & occupational health & safety. The department works in accordance with more than 150 pieces of legislation, regulations, standards, & codes of practice. Service NL operates as a single access point for the public to common government services, such as licencing, permitting, & inspecting. The department handles the following responsibilities: issuing birth, marriage, & death certificates; testing & issuing driver licenses; issuing vehicle registrations; mediating landlord & tenant issues; registering companies, deeds, & lobbyists; investigating workplace incidents; issuing charitable gaming licences; & protecting the interests of consumers.
Service NL strives to provide services with a staff of more than 500 people at over 30 locations throughout Newfoundland & Labrador.

Minister; Registrar General, Hon. Eddie Joyce
Tel: 709-729-3048; *Fax:* 709-729-0943
ejoyce@gov.nl.ca
Deputy Minister, Leigh Puddester
Tel: 709-729-4752; *Fax:* 709-729-4754
leighpuddester@gov.nl.ca
Parliamentary Secretary, Graham Letto
Tel: 709-729-3048; *Fax:* 709-729-0943
grahamletto@gov.nl.ca
Director, Strategic Human Resources Management, Marsha Hiscock
Tel: 709-729-5102; *Fax:* 709-729-6661
MarshaHiscock@gov.nl.ca
Director, Communications, Jason Card
Tel: 709-729-4860; *Fax:* 709-729-4754
jasoncard@gov.nl.ca
Director, Policy & Strategic Planning, Megan Collins
Tel: 709-729-6470; *Fax:* 709-729-4754
megancollins@gov.nl.ca
Director, Information Management, Susanna Duke
Tel: 709-729-2544; *Fax:* 709-729-4754
susannaduke@gov.nl.ca

Associated Agencies, Boards & Commissions:

•Credit Union Deposit Guarantee Corporation
PO Box 340
Marystown, NL A0E 2M0
Tel: 709-279-0170; *Fax:* 709-279-0177
Toll-free: 877-279-0170
www.cudgcnl.com
The Credit Union Deposit Guarantee Corporation is a provincial Crown corporation. The corporation administers the Credit Union Act & Regulations. The Credit Union Deposit Guarantee Corporation is responsible for ensuring compliance with the Credit Union Act & Regulations by credit unions, & insuring deposits of credit union members & associate members in Newfoundland & Labrador.

•Government Purchasing Agency
30 Strawberry Marsh Rd.
St. John's, NL A1B 4R4
Tel: 709-729-3348; *Fax:* 709-729-5817
tenders@gov.nl.ca
www.gpa.gov.nl.ca
The Government Purchasing Agency is the Government of Newfoundland & Labrador's central procurement unit. The agency manages the procurement process for goods & services for all government departments. It administers the the Agreement on Internal Trade & the Atlantic Procurement Agreement.

Consumer & Commercial Affairs Branch

Tel: 709-729-2570; *Fax:* 709-729-4151
gsinfo@gov.nl.ca
Other Communication: Commercial Registrations: 709-729-3317

The Consumer & Commercial Affairs Branch of Service NL carries out its functions through the Commercial Registrations Division, the Financial Services Regulation Division, & the Consumer Affairs Division.
The Commercial Registrations Division is involved in administering the registries of deeds, personal property, condominiums, mechanics liens, co-operatives, limited partnerships, companies, & lobbyists.
In the area of financial services, responsibilities include the regulation of industries such as the following: insurance, securities, real estate, mortgage broker, & pension. The Financial Services Regulation Division also administers the Consumer Protection Fund for Prepaid Funerals.
The Consumer Affairs Division strives to safeguard the consumer interests of Newfoundlanders & Labradorians. In the area of consumer protection, the division operates under the authority of the following acts: Architects Act; Business Electronic Filing Act; Certified General Accountants Act; Certified Management Accountants Act; Chartered Accountants Act; Collections Act; Consumer Protection & Business Practices Act; Electronic Commerce Act; Embalmers & Funeral Directors Act; Engineers & Geoscientists Act; Public Accountancy Act; & Sale of Goods Act. Associated regulations include the following: Collections Regulations; Embalmers & Funeral Directors Regulations; Engineers & Geoscientists Regulations; & Lottery Licensing Regulations. The Consumer Affairs Division also handles mediation of disputes between landlords & tenants.
Other services include regulation of the licencing of the following: charitable & non-profit oranganizations' lottery fundraising activities; corporations & individuals who provide private investigation & security services; direct sales contracts between business entities & consumers; & corporations & individuals who facilitate the collection of outstanding debts.

Assistant Deputy Minister, Julian McCarthy
Tel: 709-729-2570; *Fax:* 709-729-4151
jmccarth@gov.nl.ca
Director, Consumer Affairs, Gerry Burke
Tel: 709-729-2660; *Fax:* 709-729-6998
gburke@gov.nl.ca
Director, Commercial Registrations, Dean Doyle
Tel: 709-729-4043; *Fax:* 709-729-0232
doyled@gov.nl.ca

Superintendent, Pensions, Michael Delaney
Tel: 709-729-6014
michaelpdelaney@gov.nl.ca
Director, Financial Services Regulation Division; Superintendent, Insurance, Real Estate, Mortgage Brokers, Securities and Pre-Paid Funerals, John O'Brien
Tel: 709-729-4909; *Fax:* 709-729-3205
JohnOBrien@gov.nl.ca
Other Communications: Securities Fax: 709-729-6187
Insurance Examiner, Frances Hearn
Tel: 709-729-0959
franceshearn@gov.nl.ca

Government Services Branch
Other Communication: Engineering & Inspection Services, Phone: 709-729-2747

The Government Services Branch oversees the following: Government Service Centres; motor vehicle registration; the Office of the Queen's Printer; vital statistics; engineering & inspections; & program & support services. Government services staff handle matters related to vital statistics, public health & safety, environmental issues, accessibility, highway safety, as well as the processing of permits, licences, approvals, & inspections.

Assistant Deputy Minister, Donna Kelland
Tel: 709-729-3056; *Fax:* 709-729-4151
dkelland@gov.nl.ca
Registrar, Vital Statistics, Ken Mullaly
Tel: 709-729-3311; *Fax:* 709-729-1402
kmullaly@gov.nl.ca
Queen's Printer, Office of the Queen's Printer, John Over
Tel: 709-729-3210; *Fax:* 709-729-1900
johnover@gov.nl.ca
Director, Program & Support Services, Rick Curran
Tel: 709-729-3767
Director, Engineering & Inspections, Dennis Eastman
Tel: 709-729-2747; *Fax:* 709-729-2071
deastman@gov.nl.ca

Occupational Health & Safety Branch
Other Communication: Safety Bulletins & Recalls, Toll-Free: 1-563-5471

The Occupational Health & Safety Branch of Service NL works to ensure the health & safety of employees in the workplace in Newfoundland & Labrador.
The branch oversees administration of the Occupational Health & Safety Act, the Radiation Health & Safety Act, & the Workplace Health, Safety, & Compensation Act. Related regulations include the following: Asebestos Abatement Regulations; the Asbestos Exposure Code Regulations; the Occupational Health & Safety Regulations; the Occupational Health & Safety First Aid Regulations; the Radiation Health & Safety Regulations; the Workplace Hazardous Materials Information System (WHMIS) Regulations; & the Workplace Health, Safety, & Compensation Regulations.
Responsibilities of the Occupational Health & Safety Branch are as follows: development of health & safety legislation; compliance inspections of provincially regulated workplaces; hygiene assessments in workplaces; inspection of radiation control measures in workplaces; investigation of workplace incidents; & enforcement of health & safety legislation.

Assistant Deputy Minister, Kim Dunphy
Tel: 709-729-5544; *Fax:* 709-729-4151
kdunphy@gov.nl.ca
Director, Occupational Health & Safety Division, Loyola Power
Tel: 709-729-3275; *Fax:* 709-729-3445
LoyolaPower@gov.nl.ca

Provincial Advisory Council on the Status of Women (PACSW)

#103, 15 Hallett Cres., St. John's, NL A1B 4C4
Tel: 709-753-7270; *Fax:* 709-753-2606
Toll-Free: 877-753-7270
info@pacsw.ca
www.pacsw.ca
twitter.com/PACSWNL

Minister Responsible, Hon. Cathy Bennett
Tel: 709-729-3775; *Fax:* 709-729-2232
cbennett@gov.nl.ca
President & CEO, Linda Ross
Tel: 709-753-7270
lindaross@pacsw.ca
Director, Public Engagement, Dana Aylward
danaaylward@pacsw.ca
Executive Administrator, Michelle Brown
michellebrown@pacsw.ca

Newfoundland & Labrador Department of Transportation & Works

Confederation Bldg., Prince Philip Dr., PO Box 8700 St. John's, NL A1B 4J6
Tel: 709-729-2300
tw@gov.nl.ca
www.tw.gov.nl.ca

To provide a safe, efficient & sustainable transportation system & to provide landlord services & support services such as leasing & mail services for all government departments. The department liaises with other agencies & the federal government to ensure the overall public works & transportation needs & interest of the province are fully provided & protected.

Minister, Hon. Allan Hawkins
Tel: 709-729-3679; *Fax:* 709-729-4285
allanhawkins@gov.nl.ca
Deputy Minister, Lori Anne Companion
Tel: 709-729-3676; *Fax:* 709-729-4285
LoriAnneCompanion@gov.nl.ca
Director, Communications, Jacquelyn Howard
Tel: 709-729-3015; *Fax:* 709-729-4285
ScottBarfoot@gov.nl.ca
Legal Advisor, David Jones
Tel: 709-729-1966; *Fax:* 709-729-6934
davidj@gov.nl.ca

Marine Services Branch
440 Main St., PO Box 97 Lewisporte, NL A0G 3A0
Fax: 709-535-6245
Toll-Free: 888-638-5454
TWMarine@gov.nl.ca
www.gov.nl.ca/FerryServices

Assistant Deputy Minister, Max Harvey
Tel: 709-729-2767
maxharvey@gov.nl.ca
Director, Maintenance & Engineering, Greg Cuff
Tel: 709-535-6210; *Fax:* 709-535-6245
gregcuff@gov.nl.ca
Acting Director, Vessel Replacement, Stephen Mulrooney
Tel: 709-729-3278; *Fax:* 709-729-3440
mulrooneys@gov.nl.ca
Director, Ferry Operations, Walter Pumphrey
Tel: 705-535-6220; *Fax:* 709-535-6245
pumphrey@gov.nl.ca

Transportation Branch
www.roads.gov.nl.ca

Assistant Deputy Minister, Gary Gosse
Tel: 709-729-3796; *Fax:* 709-729-0283
gosseg@gov.nl.ca
Chief Bridge Engineer, Highway Design & Construction, Doug Power
Tel: 709-729-6508; *Fax:* 709-729-0283
Manager, Equipment Support, Murray Adams
Tel: 709-729-5308; *Fax:* 709-729-6934
adamsm@gov.nl.ca
Manager, Highway Design & Traffic Engineering, John Morrissey
Tel: 709-729-5493; *Fax:* 709-729-0283
Senior Bridge & Marine Design Engineer, Garfield Au
Tel: 709-729-6880; *Fax:* 709-729-0283

Strategic & Corporate Services Branch
Assistant Deputy Minister, Paul Smith
Tel: 709-729-6882; *Fax:* 709-729-5934
Director, Financial Operations, Kevin Antle
Tel: 709-729-5356; *Fax:* 709-729-0703
kantle@gov.nl.ca
Director, Policy, Planning & Evaluation, Lynn Bryant
Tel: 709-729-5344; *Fax:* 709-729-3418
lbryant@gov.nl.ca

Works Branch
Assistant Deputy Minister, Cory Grandy
Tel: 709-729-5672; *Fax:* 709-729-5934
corygrandy@gov.nl.ca
Acting Director, Planning & Accommodations, Andrea McKenna
Tel: 709-729-4422; *Fax:* 709-729-4658
AndreaMckenna@gov.nl.ca
Director, Building Design & Construction, Paul Lahey
Tel: 709-729-3342; *Fax:* 709-729-0646
laheyp@gov.nl.ca

Regional Offices
Deer Lake - Western
74 Old Bonne Bay Rd., Deer Lake, NL A8H 3H4
Tel: 709-635-4127; *Fax:* 709-635-2549
Gander - Central
Fraser Mall, PO Box 2222 Gander, NL A1V 2N9
Tel: 709-256-1000; *Fax:* 709-256-1013
Happy Valley-Goose Bay - Labrador
PO Box 3014 Stn. B, Happy Valley-Goose Bay, NL A0P 1E0
Tel: 709-896-7840; *Fax:* 709-896-5513
St. John's - Avalon
West Block, Confederation Complex, PO Box 8700 St. John's, NL A1B 4J6
Tel: 709-729-3362; *Fax:* 709-729-0036

Newfoundland & Labrador Workplace Health, Safety & Compensation Commission (WorkplaceNL)

146 - 148 Forest Rd., PO Box 9000 St. John's, NL A1A 3B8
Tel: 709-778-1000; *Fax:* 709-738-1714
Toll-Free: 800-563-9000
general.inquiries@whscc.nl.ca
www.whscc.nf.ca
Other Communication: Grand Falls toll-free: 800-563-3448; Corner Brook toll-free: 800-563-2772
www.facebook.com/127058107367289
www.youtube.com/user/safeworknl

Utilizing skilled, professional employees, in partnership with workplace parties, the commission facilitates safe & healthy workplaces by assisting employers & workers to prevent accidents, & manage workplace injuries/illnesses & return-to-work processes. Operating as the administrator of the workers' compensation insurance program, the commission provides a reasonable level of benefits to injured workers & their dependents based on reasonable assessment rates for employers, while maintaining or exceeding service level performance when compared to other jurisdictions in Canada.

Minister Responsible, WorkplaceNL, Hon. Eddie Joyce
Tel: 709-729-3048; *Fax:* 709-729-0943
ejoyce@gov.nl.ca
Chair, Ralph Tucker
Chief Executive Officer, Leslie Galway
Chief Financial & Information Officer, Paul Kavanagh
General Counsel & Corporate Secretary, Ann Martin
Executive Director, Employer Services, Brenda Greenslade
Executive Director, Workers Services, Tom Mahoney
Director, Human Resources, Glenda Peet
Director, Communications, Carla Riggs

Regional Offices
Corner Brook
Millbrook Mall, #201B, 2 Herald Ave., Corner Brook, NL A2H 6E6
Tel: 709-637-2700; *Fax:* 709-639-1018
Toll-Free: 800-563-2772
Grand Falls-Windsor
26 High St., PO Box 850 Grand Falls-Windsor, NL A2A 2P7
Tel: 709-489-1600; *Fax:* 709-489-1616
Toll-Free: 800-563-3448

Government of the Northwest Territories

Seat of Government: PO Box 1320 Yellowknife, NT X1A 2L9
Tel: 867-873-7500
www.gov.nt.ca
Other Communication: Devolution Information, URL: devolution.gov.nt.ca; E-mail: devolution@gov.nt.ca

The Northwest Territories was reconstituted September 1, 1905. It has a land area of 1,140,834.90 sq km, & the StatsCan census in 2011 showed the population was 41,462. On April 1, 1999, the Northwest Territories was divided into two new territories: Nunavut Territories and the as yet unnamed territory (known as the Northwest Territories). The Northwest Territories is governed by a fully elected Legislative Assembly of 19 members elected for a four-year term. Government is by consensus rather than party politics. The Legislature elects the Premier & a seven-member Executive Council, which is charged with the operation of government & the establishment of program & spending priorities. The Commissioner of the Northwest Territories is appointed by the Federal Government, & serves a role similar to that of a Lieutenant Governor in provincial jurisdictions. With the implementation of the Northwest Territories Devolution Act on April 1, 2014, the government of the Northwest Territories gained power over its land & resources from the federal government.

Office of the Commissioner

803 Northwest Tower, PO Box 1320 Yellowknife, NT X1A 2L9
Tel: 867-873-7400; *Fax:* 867-873-0223
Toll-Free: 888-270-3318
commissioner@gov.nt.ca
www.commissioner.gov.nt.ca

Acting Commissioner; Deputy Commissioner, Gerald W. Kisoun

Office of the Premier

Legislative Assembly Bldg., PO Box 1320 Yellowknife, NT X1A 2L9
Tel: 867-669-2311; *Fax:* 867-873-0385
www.premier.gov.nt.ca

Premier, Hon. Bob McLeod
Tel: 867-767-9141 ext: 110
bob_mcleod@gov.nt.ca
Executive Secretary, Charlotte Digness
Tel: 867-767-9140 ext: 110
Principal Secretary, Gary Bohnet
Tel: 867-767-9140 ext: 110

Executive Council

PO Box 1320 Yellowknife, NT X1A 2L9
executive_communications@gov.nt.ca
www.executive.gov.nt.ca
Other Communication: Protocol: executive_protocol@gov.nt.ca; Corporate Services: executive_services@gov.nt.ca

Coordination & advisory functions are performed for the Government of the Northwest Territories.

Premier; Minister, Executive; Minister, Aboriginal Affairs & Intergovernmental Relations, Hon. Bob McLeod
Tel: 867-767-9141 ext: 110
bob_mcleod@gov.nt.ca
Deputy Premier; Minister, Finance; Minister, Environment & Natural Resources; Minister, Human Resources; Minister, Lead Responsibilty for Infrastructure, Hon. Robert C. McLeod
Tel: 867-767-9141 ext: 111
robert_c_mcleod@gov.nt.ca
Government House Leader; Minister, Health & Social Services; Minister Responsible, Workers' Safety & Compensation Commission, Public Utilities Board, Persons with Disabilities, Seniors, Hon. Glen Abernethy
Tel: 867-767-9141 ext: 111
glen_abernethy@gov.nt.ca
Minister, Education, Culture & Employment; Minister Responsible, Youth, Hon. Alfred Moses
Tel: 867-767-9141 ext: 111
alfred_moses@gov.nt.ca
Minister, Municipal & Community Affairs; Minister Responsible, Northwest Territories Housing Corporation, Minister Responsible, Status of Women; Minister Responsible, Addressing Homelessness, Hon. Caroline Cochrane
Tel: 867-767-9141 ext: 111
caroline_cochrane@gov.nt.ca
Minister, Industry, Tourism & Investment; Minister, Transportation; Minister, Public Works & Services, Hon. Wally Schumann
Tel: 867-767-9141 ext: 111
wally_schumann@gov.nt.ca
Minister, Justice; Minister, Lands; Minister Responsible, Northwest Territories Power Corporation, Minister Responsible, Public Engagement & Transparency, Hon. Louis Sebert
Tel: 867-767-9142 ext: 111; *Fax:* 867-873-0274
louis_sebert@gov.nt.ca

Department of the Executive

PO Box 1320 Yellowknife, NT X1A 2L9
executive_communications@gov.nt.ca
www.executive.gov.nt.ca
Other Communication: Protocol, E-mail: executive_protocol@gov.nt.ca

Premier; Minister, Executive; Minister, Aboriginal Affairs & Intergovernmental Relations, Minister, Industry, Tourism & Investment; Minister Responsible, Public Utilities Board, Hon. Bob McLeod
Tel: 867-767-9141 ext: 110
bob_mcleod@gov.nt.ca
Secretary to Cabinet & Deputy Minister, Executive, Mike Aumond
Chief of Protocol, Carmen Moore
Tel: 867-767-9140 ext: 110
Assistant Deputy Minister & Deputy Secretary to Cabinet, Alan Cash
Tel: 867-767-9149 ext: 110
Deputy Secretary to Cabinet, Priorities & Planning, David Brock
Tel: 867-767-9156 ext: 111
Director, Cabinet Communications, Shaun Dean
Tel: 867-767-9140 ext: 110
Director, Planning & Communications, Zoe Raemer
Tel: 867-767-9144 ext: 110

NWT Legislative Assembly

4570 - 48 St., PO Box 1320 Yellowknife, NT X1A 2L9
Tel: 867-669-2200
Toll-Free: 800-661-0784
www.assembly.gov.nt.ca
Other Communication: Officer on Duty, Phone: 867-669-2226

Clerk, Tim Mercer
Tel: 867-767-9130
Speaker, Hon. Jackson Lafferty
Tel: 867-767-9133 ext: 120
Jackson_Lafferty@gov.nt.ca
Sergeant-At-Arms, Brian Thagard
Tel: 867-767-9131 ext: 120
Deputy Clerk, Doug Schauerte
Tel: 867-767-9130 ext: 120
Deputy Sergeant-At-Arms, Derek Edjericon
Tel: 867-767-9131 ext: 120
Equal Pay Commissioner, Nitya Iyer
Tel: 867-669-5583
Director, Corporate Services, Darrin Ouellette
Tel: 867-767-9131 ext: 120
Director, Research & Library Services, Lee Selleck
Tel: 867-767-9132 ext: 120
Legislative Librarian, Vera Raschke
Tel: 867-767-9132 ext: 120

Elections NWT/Plebiscite Office

YK Centre East, #7, 4915-48th St., 3rd Fl., Yellowknife, NT X1A 3S4
Tel: 867-767-9100; *Fax:* 867-920-9100
Toll-Free: 844-767-9100
electionsnwt@gov.nt.ca
www.electionsnwt.com
Other Communication: Toll-Free Fax: 1-844-973-9100
www.facebook.com/ElectionsNWT

Chief Electoral Officer, Nicole Latour
Nicole_Latour@gov.nt.ca
Deputy Chief Electoral Officer, Vacant

Standing Committees of the Legislature

www.assembly.gov.nt.ca/documents-proceedings/committees

The following are the Standing Committees of the 18th Legislative Assembly of the Northwest Territories: Priorities & Planning; Economic Development & Infrastructure; Social Development; Government Operations; & Rules & Procedures.

Chair, Standing Committee on Priorities & Planning, Tom Beaulieu
Constituency: Tu Nedhe — Wiilideh
Tel: 867-767-9143 ext: 121
tom_beaulieu@gov.nt.ca
Chair, Standing Committee on Economic Development & Environment, Cory Vanthuyne
Constituency: Yellowknife North
Tel: 867-767-9143 ext: 121
Cory_Vanthuyne@gov.nt.ca
Chair, Standing Committee on Social Development, Shane Thompson
Constituency: Nahendeh
Tel: 867-767-9143 ext: 121
Shane_Thompson@gov.nt.ca
Chair, Standing Committee on Government Operations, Kieron Testart
Constituency: Kam Lake
Tel: 867-767-9143 ext: 121
Kieron_Testart@gov.nt.ca
Chair, Standing Committee on Rules & Procedures, Kevin O'Reilly
Constituency: Frame Lake
Tel: 867-767-9143 ext: 121
Kevin_O'Reilly@gov.nt.ca

Office of the Languages Commissioner

Capital Suites - Zheh Gwizu', PO Box 2096 Inuvik, NT X0E 0T0
Tel: 867-678-2200; *Fax:* 867-678-2201
Toll-Free: 800-661-0889
www.nwtlanguagescommissioner.ca
Other Communication: Alt. Fax: 867-920-2511

Languages Commissioner, Shannon Gullberg
Tel: 867-920-6500

Office of the Conflict of Interest Commissioner

PO Box 1320 Yellowknife, NT X1A 2L9
Tel: 780-433-9000; *Fax:* 780-733-9780
Other Communication: Regina Office, Phone: 306-787-0693

Conflict of Interest Commissioner, David Phillip Jones

Eighteenth Legislative Assembly - Northwest Territories

4570 - 48 St., PO Box 1320 Yellowknife, NT X1A 2L9
Tel: 867-669-2200; *Fax:* 867-920-4735
Toll-Free: 800-661-0784
www.assembly.gov.nt.ca
twitter.com/AssemblyNWT
www.facebook.com/LegislativeAssemblyNWT

Last General Election: October 23, 2015.
Maximum Duration: Four years.
Salaries, Indemnities & Allowances (2014):
Members of the Legislative Assembly are entitled to an annual salary of $101,815. Members are entitled to a non-taxable annual expense allowance of $7,337 for a Minister or for Members living within commuting distance of the capital. Members, who are not Ministers, & who do not live within commuting distance of the capital, are entitled to an additional non-taxable non-accountable allowance of $7,337 for expenses incurred while in the capital while on constituency business or business as a Member. Up to $30,572 annually is paid to Members for capital accommodation, when their residence is not within 80 km of Yellowknife, & when they are attending sittings of the Legislature, committee meetings & performing constituency duties in Yellowknife. Members are provided with a set operating budget to defray the expenses of working on behalf of their constituents. In addition are the following remunerations:
Premier $77,438;
Minister $54,493;
Speaker $44,316;
Deputy Speaker $7,170;
Deputy Chairperson of Committee of the Whole $4,303.
The address for all contacts is as follows: PO Box 1320, Yellowknife, NT, X1A 2L9. The following is a list of Members of the Legislative Assembly, with their constituency, the number of electors on the voting list for the the most recent election, plus contact information:

Members of the Legislative Assembly of the Northwest Territories

Government House Leader; Minister, Health & Social Services; Minister Responsible, Workers' Safety & Compensation Commission, Minister Responsible, Seniors; Minister Responsible, Persons with Disabilities, Hon. Glen Abernethy
Constituency: Great Slave *No. of Constituents:* 2,388
Tel: 867-767-9141 ext: 111
glen_abernethy@gov.nt.ca
Social Media: twitter.com/GlenAbernethy, www.linkedin.com/pub/glen-abernethy/43/679/867
Tom Beaulieu
Constituency: Tu Nedhe — Wiilideh *No. of Constituents:* 814
Tel: 867-767-9143 ext: 121
tom_beaulieu@gov.nt.ca
Frederick Blake Jr.
Constituency: Mackenzie Delta *No. of Constituents:* 996
Tel: 867-767-9143 ext: 121
frederick_blake@gov.nt.ca
Constituency Office
441 Tetlit Gwichin Rd.
PO Box 340
Fort McPherson, NT X0E 0J0
Minister, Municipal & Community Affairs; Minister Responsible, Northwest Territories Housing Corporation, Minister Responsible, Status of Women; Minister Responsible, Addressing Homelessness, Hon. Caroline Cochrane
Constituency: Range Lake *No. of Constituents:* 2,089
Tel: 867-767-9141 ext: 111
caroline_cochrane@gov.nt.ca
Caucus Chair, Julie Green
Constituency: Yellowknife Centre *No. of Constituents:* 2,316
Tel: 867-767-9143 ext: 121
Julie_Green@gov.nt.ca
Speaker, Hon. Jackson Lafferty
Constituency: Monfwi
Tel: 867-767-9133 ext: 120
Jackson_Lafferty@gov.nt.ca
Other Communications: Constituency Phone: 867-392-2586; Fax: 867-392-2584
Note: Jackson Lafferty was acclaimed in the 2015 general election.
Constituency Office, Rae-Edzo Friendship Centre, Donna Tili Bldg. #124
PO Box 85
Behchoko, NT X0E 0Y0
Deputy Premier; Minister, Finance; Minister, Environment & Natural Resources; Minister, Human Resources, Minister, Lead Responsibilty for Infrastructure, Hon. Robert C. McLeod
Constituency: Inuvik Twin Lakes *No. of Constituents:* 1,014
Tel: 867-767-9141 ext: 111
robert_c_mcleod@gov.nt.ca
Other Communications: Constituency Phone: 867-678-2429; Fax: 867-678-2431
Social Media: www.linkedin.com/pub/robert-mcleod/50/120/b23

Constituency Office
#107, 107 Mackenzie Rd.
PO Box 3130
Inuvik, NT X0E 0T0

Premier; Minister, Executive; Minister, Aboriginal Affairs & Intergovernmental Relations, Hon. Bob McLeod
Constituency: Yellowknife South *No. of Constituents:* 2,097
Tel: 867-767-9141 ext: 110
bob_mcleod@gov.nt.ca
bobmcleod.ca

Daniel Mark McNeely
Constituency: Sahtu *No. of Constituents:* 1,592
Tel: 867-767-9143 ext: 121
Daniel_McNeely@gov.nt.ca

Minister, Education, Culture & Employment; Minister Responsible, Youth, Hon. Alfred Moses
Constituency: Inuvik Boot Lake *No. of Constituents:* 971
Tel: 867-767-9141 ext: 111
alfred_moses@gov.nt.ca
Other Communications: Constituency Phone: 867-777-4693
Constituency Office, Mackenzie Hotel
#102, 185 Mackenzie Rd.
PO Box 1998
Inuvik, NT X0E 0T0

Michael M. Nadli
Constituency: Deh Cho *No. of Constituents:* 776
Tel: 867-767-9143 ext: 121
michael_nadli@gov.nt.ca
Other Communications: Constituency Phone: 867-699-4003; Fax: 867-699-4005
Social Media: www.facebook.com/MichaelMNadli
Constituency Office
PO Box 252
Fort Providence, N X0E 0L0

Herbert Nakimayak
Constituency: Nunakput *No. of Constituents:* 991
Tel: 867-767-9143 ext: 121
Herbert_Nakimayak@gov.nt.ca

Kevin O'Reilly
Constituency: Frame Lake *No. of Constituents:* 1,980
Tel: 867-767-9143 ext: 121
Kevin_O'Reilly@gov.nt.ca

Minister, Industry, Tourism & Investment; Minister, Public Works & Services; Minister, Transportation, Hon. Wally Schumann
Constituency: Hay River South *No. of Constituents:* 1,374
Tel: 867-767-9141 ext: 111
wally_schumann@gov.nt.ca
Other Communications: Constituency Phone: 867-874-6141
#3, 66 Woodland Dr.
PO Box 4220
Hay River, NT X0E 1G2

Minister, Justice; Minister, Lands; Minister Responsible, Northwest Territories Power Corporation, Minister Responsible, Public Engagement & Transparency, Hon. Louis Sebert
Constituency: Thebacha *No. of Constituents:* 1,832
Tel: 867-767-9141 ext: 111
louis_sebert@gov.nt.ca

Rocky (R.J.) Simpson
Constituency: Hay River North *No. of Constituents:* 1,377
Tel: 867-767-9143 ext: 121
RJ_Simpson@gov.nt.ca
Other Communications: Constituency Phone: 867-874-6301
Constituency Office, Wright Centre
#104, 62 Woodland Dr., Main Fl.
Hay River, NT X0E 1G1

Kieron Testart
Constituency: Kam Lake *No. of Constituents:* 1,923
Tel: 867-767-9143 ext: 121
Kieron_Testart@gov.nt.ca

Shane Thompson
Constituency: Nahendeh *No. of Constituents:* 1,610
Tel: 867-767-9143 ext: 121
Shane_Thompson@gov.nt.ca
Other Communications: Constituency Phone: 867-695-3780
Constituency Office
9807 - 100 St.
PO Box 466
Fort Simpson, NT X0E 0N0

Cory Vanthuyne
Constituency: Yellowknife North *No. of Constituents:* 2,448
Tel: 867-767-9143 ext: 121
Cory_Vanthuyne@gov.nt.ca

Northwest Territories Government Departments & Agencies

Northwest Territories Department of Aboriginal Affairs & Intergovernmental Relations (DAAIR)

4910 - 52nd St., PO Box 1320 Yellowknife, NT X1A 2L9
Tel: 867-767-9025; *Fax:* 867-873-0233
www.daair.gov.nt.ca
Other Communication: General Inquiries: 867-767-9025, ext. 18000

The Department of Aboriginal Affairs & Intergovernmental Relations is charged with the following responsibilities: to negotiate, implement, & monitor land, resource & self-government agreements; to manage governmental relationships with Aboriginal, federal, provincial, & territorial governments, & with circumpolar countries; to provide advice on federal-provincial-territorial-Aboriginal relations; & to contribute to the political & constitutional development of the Northwest Territories.

Minister, Hon. Bob McLeod
Tel: 867-767-9141 ext: 110
bob_mcleod@gov.nt.ca
Deputy Minister, Shaleen Woodward
Assistant Deputy Minister, Shaleen Woodward
Tel: 867-767-9025 ext: 180
Director, Implementation, Sue Bowie
Tel: 867-767-9136 ext: 180
Director, Policy, Planning & Communications, Richard Robertson
Tel: 867-767-9134 ext: 180
richard_robertson@gov.nt.ca
Director, Negotiations, Fred Talen
Tel: 867-767-9135 ext: 180
fred_talen@gov.nt.ca

Aurora Research Institute (ARI)

191 MacKenzie Rd., PO Box 1450 Inuvik, NT X0E 0T0
Tel: 867-777-3298; *Fax:* 867-777-4264
www.nwtresearch.com
twitter.com/nwtresearch
www.facebook.com/Aurora-Research-Institute-124567754290093

A division of Aurora College that is dedicated to excellence, leadership & innovations in Northern education & research. Administers the research licencing provisions of the Northwest Territories Scientists Act & provides year round logistical assistance for researchers.

Director, Pippa Seccombe-Hett
Tel: 867-777-3298
pseccombe-hett@auroracollege.nt.ca

Northwest Territories Business Development & Investment Corporation (BDIC)

#701, 5201 - 50th Ave., Yellowknife, NT X1A 3S9
Tel: 867-920-6455; *Fax:* 867-765-0652
Toll-Free: 800-661-0599
www.bdic.ca

The BDIC provides access to business financing, support & development assistance to communities throughout the Northwest Territories. Their focus is the small & mid-sized business sector.

Chair, Darrell Beaulieu
Chief Executive Officer, Pawan Chugh
Tel: 867-767-9075 ext: 860
Director, Finance & Subsidiaries, Leonard Kwong
Tel: 867-767-9075 ext: 860

Northwest Territories Department of Education, Culture & Employment (ECE)

PO Box 1320 Yellowknife, NT X1A 2L9
ecepublicaffairs@gov.nt.ca
www.ece.gov.nt.ca

The Ministry's responsibilities cover the following areas: Early Childhood; Kindergarten to Grade 12; Adult & Post-Secondary Education; Career Development & Employment; Apprenticeship & Occupational Certification; Culture, Heritage & Languages; Income Security; & Labour Services.

Minister, Education, Culture & Employment; Minister Responsible, Youth, Hon. Alfred Moses
Tel: 867-767-9141 ext: 111
alfred_moses@gov.nt.ca
Deputy Minister, Sylvia Haener
sylvia_haener@gov.nt.ca
Assistant Deputy Minister, Labour & Income Security, Andy Bevan
Tel: 867-767-9065 ext: 714
Assistant Deputy Minister, Education & Culture, Rita Mueller
Tel: 867-767-9065 ext: 714
Registrar, Teacher Certification, Simon LePage
Tel: 867-874-2084
Executive Director, Secretariat aux affaires francophones / Francophone affairs secreatariat, Benoit Boutin
Tel: 867-767-9343 ext: 710
benoit_boutin@gov.nt.ca
Director, Aboriginal Languages, Angela James
Tel: 867-767-9346 ext: 710
Director, Instructional & School Services, John Stewart
Tel: 867-767-9342 ext: 712

Associated Agencies, Boards & Commissions:

•Aboriginal Languages Revitalization Board
PO Box 1320
Yellowknife, NT X1A 2L9
Tel: 867-920-6484; *Fax:* 867-873-0185

•Apprenticeship, Trade & Occupations Certification Board (ATOCB)
PO Box 1320
Yellowknife, NT X1A 2L9
Tel: 867-873-7357; *Fax:* 867-873-0200

•Northwest Territories Arts Council
PO Box 1320 Main
Yellowknife, NT X1A 2L9
Tel: 867-920-6370; *Fax:* 867-873-0205
nwtartscouncil@gmail.com
www.nwtartscouncil.ca
Other Communication: Alternate E-mail: boris_atamanenko@gov.nt.ca

•Northwest Territories Social Assistance Appeal Board
PO Box 1320
Yellowknife, NT X1A 2L9
Tel: 867-920-8921; *Fax:* 867-873-0443

•Official Languages Board
PO Box 1320
Yellowknife, NT X1A 2L9
Tel: 867-920-6484; *Fax:* 867-873-0185

•Student Financial Assistance Appeal Board
PO Box 1320
Yellowknife, NT X1A 2L9
Tel: 867-873-7194; *Fax:* 867-873-0336

Culture & Heritage
Director, Culture & Heritage, Sarah Carr-Locke
Tel: 867-767-9347 ext: 711

Early Childhood & School Services
Director, Early Childhood Development & Learning, Shelly Kapraelian
Tel: 867-767-9354 ext: 712

Education Operations & Development
Director, Education Operations & Development, Joanne McGrath
Tel: 867-767-9353 ext: 712

Finance & Capital Planning
Director, Finance & Capital Planning, Marissa Martin
Tel: 867-767-9350 ext: 714

Income Security Programs Division
Director, Income Security Programs, Jolene Saturnino
Tel: 867-767-9355 ext: 713

Labour Development & Standards
Director, Labour Development & Standards, & Apprenticeship, Trade & Occupation Certification, Laurie Morton
Tel: 867-767-9351 ext: 711

Planning, Research & Evaluation
Director, Planning, Research & Evaluation, Jennifer Young
Tel: 867-767-9349 ext: 710
Chief Information Officer, Information Systems, Stuart A. Ridgely
Tel: 867-767-9349 ext: 710

Policy, Legislation & Communications
Director, Policy, Legislation & Communications, Sam Shannon
Tel: 867-767-9352 ext: 710

Northwest Territories Department of Environment & Natural Resources (ENR)

#600, 5102 - 50 Ave., Yellowknife, NT X1A 3S8
Tel: 867-767-9231
www.enr.gov.nt.ca

Operations cover a broad spectrum of activities directed at promoting a healthy environment that supports traditional lifestyles within a modern economy. The wise use & protection of natural resources are encouraged. The Department's activities are carried out through the following divisions: Environmental Protection, Forest Management, Policy, Legislation & Communications, Protected Areas Strategy, Informatics, & Wildlife.

Minister, Hon. Robert C. McLeod
Tel: 867-767-9141 ext: 111
robert_c_mcleod@gov.nt.ca
Deputy Minister, Ernie Campbell
Tel: 867-767-9055 ext: 530
ernie_campbell@gov.nt.ca
Acting Assistant Deputy Minister, Operations, Fred Mandeville
Tel: 867-767-9055 ext: 530

Associated Agencies, Boards & Commissions:

•Natural Resources Conservation Trust Fund Board of Trustees
PO Box 1320
Yellowknife, NT X1A 2L9
Tel: 867-873-7401; *Fax:* 867-873-0638

•Waste Reduction & Recovery Advisory Committee
PO Box 1320
Yellowknife, NT X1A 2L9
Tel: 867-873-7654; *Fax:* 867-873-0221
nwtrecycle@gov.nt.ca
icarenwt.ca

•Deh Cho Land Use Planning Committee
PO Box 199
Fort Providence, NT X0E 0L0
Tel: 867-699-3162; *Fax:* 867-699-3166
www.dehcholands.org

Regional Offices

Dehcho
PO Box 240 Fort Simpson, NT X0E 0N0
Tel: 867-695-7450; *Fax:* 867-695-2381
Regional Superintendent, Carl Lafferty
Tel: 867-695-7451
carl_lafferty@gov.nt.ca

Inuvik
PO Box 2749 Shell Lake, NT X0E 0T0
Tel: 867-678-6650; *Fax:* 867-678-6699
Regional Superintendent, Judy Francey
Tel: 867-678-6650
judy_francey@gov.nt.ca

North Slave
PO Box 2668 Yellowknife, NT X1A 2P9
Tel: 867-873-7184; *Fax:* 867-873-6230
Regional Superintendent, Shelley Acton
Tel: b67-920-6114
shelly_acton@gov.nt.ca

Sahtu
PO Box 130 Norman Wells, NT X0E 0V0
Tel: 867-587-3500; *Fax:* 867-587-3516
Regional Superintendent, Jeffrey Walker
Tel: 867-587-3532
jeff_walker@gov.nt.ca

South Slave
Sweetgrass Bldg., PO Box 900 Fort Smith, NT X0E 0P0
Tel: 867-872-6400; *Fax:* 867-872-4250
Regional Superintendent, Terrence Campbell
Tel: 867-872-6417
terrence_campbell@gov.nt.ca

Environment

Fax: 867-873-0221
Other Communication: Environment Main Line: 873-767-9236, ext. 53456

To protect & enhance the environmental quality in the North. Departmental programs are designed to control the discharge of contaminants & reduce their impacts on the natural environment. This is a shared responsibility with federal, territorial, Aboriginal & municipal agencies, as well as every resident of the Northwest Territories. To promote energy conservation & the use of energy efficient technology in the Northwest Territories, identify & facilitate the development of alternative, local energy sources which strengthen community economies, & promote & facilitate energy planning.
Director, Environment, Lisa Dyer
Tel: 867-767-9236 ext: 531

Forest Management

Tel: 867-872-7700; *Fax:* 867-872-2148

Provides the policy, planning & regulatory framework for the stewardship, protection & sustainable management of forest resources on 33 million hectares of land in the Northwest Territories, eight per cent of Canada's entire forested area. Working with First Nations governments, communities, other governments & non-governmental agencies on such a vast land mass presents unique & complex challenges for forest managers. The FMD coordinates & facilitates the implementation of forest management programs & services among the five administrative regions of ENR. The regional offices have the primary responsibility for delivery of programs. Regional staff implement forest resource & fire management programs for the Department. Regional personnel receive applications for approval to harvest, supervise harvesting activities, ensure compliance with standards, support community protection planning efforts & carry out fire management activities under the direction of the Forest Management Division.
Director, Forest Management, Frank Lepine
Tel: 867-872-7725

Policy & Strategic Planning

Provides services in the area of policy, legislation, environmental assessment, land claims & self-government, resource management & public affairs & communications.
Director, Policy & Strategic Planning, Doris Eggers
Tel: 867-767-9231 ext: 530

Water Resources

Director, Water Resources, Robert Jenkins
Tel: 867-767-9234 ext: 531

Wildlife

Fax: 867-873-0293
www.nwtwildlife.com
Other Communication: Wildlife General Inquiries: 873-767-9237, ext. 53468

Activities are directed towards maintaining productive populations of all native wildlife in their natural habitats, encouraging the wise use of wildlife populations within the limits of sustainable yield & encouraging the active participation of northern residents in the management of wildlife resources. In addition to assistance programs that are designed to support the hunting & trapping economy, the division provides support to organizations of resource users to allow them to become more involved in wildlife management.
Director, Wildlife, Lynda Yonge
Tel: 873-767-9237 ext: 532

Northwest Territories Department of Finance

PO Box 1320 Yellowknife, NT X1A 2L9

Tel: 867-873-7500
www.fin.gov.nt.ca

The government of the Northwest Territories has a budget of over $700,000,000 (including federal government transfers of over $500,000,000). The Department of Finance obtains the financial resources to carry on the functions of government & for intergovernmental fiscal negotiations & arrangements.
Minister, Hon. Robert C. McLeod
Tel: 867-767-9141 ext: 111
robert_c_mcleod@gov.nt.ca
Deputy Minister, David Stewart
Chief Information Officer, Dave Heffernan
Tel: 867-767-9170 ext: 154
Territorial Statistician, Vishni Peeris
Tel: 867-767-9169 ext: 150

Associated Agencies, Boards & Commissions:

•Northwest Territories Liquor Commission
#201, 31 Capital Dr.
Hay River, NT X0E 1G2
Tel: 867-874-8700; *Fax:* 867-874-8720
www.fin.gov.nt.ca/liquor

•Northwest Territories Liquor Licensing Board
#204, 31 Capital Dr.
Hay River, NT X0E 1G2
Tel: 867-874-8715; *Fax:* 867-874-8722
Toll-free: 800-351-7770
www.fin.gov.nt.ca/llb

Budget, Treasury & Debt Management

Fax: 867-873-0414

Treasury is responsible for managing the government's cash position; conducting banking, borrowing & investment activities; protecting the government's activities & assets from risk of loss by means of appropriate insurance coverage & risk management activities; & regulating insurance companies, agents, brokers & adjusters operating in the NWT.
Deputy Secretary of the Financial Management Board, Sandy Kalgutkar
Tel: 867-767-9020 ext: 150
Director, Treasury & Superintendent, Insurance, Doug Doak
Tel: 867-767-9177 ext: 152
Director, Program Review, Michael Kalnay
Tel: 867-767-9178 ext: 152

Fiscal Policy

Responsible for developing policies & providing research, analysis & recommendations on the fiscal policies of government. The Division also administers the Formula Financing Agreement with Canada & is responsible for intergovernmental fiscal relations.
Director, Fiscal Policy, Kelly Bluck
Tel: 867-767-9158 ext: 150

Office of the Comptroller General

Fax: 867-873-0414

Comptroller General, Jamie Koe
Tel: 867-767-9020 ext: 150
Assistant Comptroller General, Accounting Services Management, Louise Lavoie
Tel: 867-767-9171 ext: 150
Executive Director, Financial Shared Services, Thomas Beard
Tel: 867-767-9174 ext: 151
Director, Internal Audit Bureau, Bob Shahi
Tel: 867-767-9175 ext: 152

Financial Management Board Secretariat (FMBS)

c/o Secretary of the FMB / Comptroller General, 5003 - 49 St., PO Box 1320 Yellowknife, NT X1A 2L9

Fax: 867-873-0414

Coordinating & promoting the efficient use of the Government's financial & information resources are the chief responsibilities of the Financial Management Board Secretariat. The central agency, that supports the Minister of Finance, provides leadership in functions related to governmental business planning, information management, & program & service evaluation. The FMBS also supports sustainable resource development, self-government development, & the improvement of programs & services.
Minister, Finance, Hon. Robert C. McLeod
Tel: 867-767-9141 ext: 111
robert_c_mcleod@gov.nt.ca
Secretary, David Stewart
Comptroller General, Jamie Koe
Tel: 867-767-9020 ext: 150
Deputy Secretary, Sandy Kalgutkar
Tel: 867-767-9020 ext: 150
Director, Laura Gareau
Tel: 867-767-9176 ext: 152

Northwest Territories Department of Health & Social Services (HSS)

5015 - 49th St., PO Box 1320 Yellowknife, NT X1A 2L9

Fax: 867-873-0306
www.hss.gov.nt.ca
Other Communication: Media Relations, Phone: 867-920-8927; Health Care Coverage/Vital Statistics: 1-800-661-0830
www.youtube.com/user/HSSCommunications

The Department of Health & Social Services is mandated to provide a broad range of health & social programs & services to the residents of the NWT. Seven regional Health & Social Services Authorities plan, manage & deliver a full spectrum of community & facility-based services for health care & social services. Community health programs include daily sick clinics, public health clinics, home care, school health programs & educational programs. Visiting physicians & specialists routinely visit the communities.
Minister, Health & Social Services; Minister Responsible, Seniors & Persons with Disabilities, Hon. Glen Abernethy
Tel: 867-767-9141 ext: 111
glen_abernethy@gov.nt.ca
Deputy Minister, Debbie DeLancey
Tel: 867-767-9060 ext: 490
debbie_delancey@gov.nt.ca
Assistant Deputy Minister, Corporate Services, Derek Elkin
Tel: 867-767-9050 ext: 490
Chief Public Health Officer, Dr. André Corriveau
Tel: 867-767-9063 ext: 492
Deputy Chief Public Health Officer, Dr. Kami Kandola
Tel: 867-767-9063 ext: 492
Director, Corporate Planning, Reporting & Evaluation, Lisa Cardinal
Tel: 867-767-9053 ext: 490; *Fax:* 867-873-0484
Director, Infrastructure Planning, Perry Heath
Tel: 867-767-9057 ext: 491
Director, Strategic Human Resource Planning Division, Beth Collinson
Tel: 867-767-9059 ext: 491
Director, Shared Services & Innovation, Kevin Taylor
Tel: 867-767-9058 ext: 491

Associated Agencies, Boards & Commissions:

•Dental Registration Committee
PO Box 1320
Yellowknife, NT X1A 2L9
Tel: 867-920-8058; *Fax:* 867-873-0484

•Medical Registration Committee
PO Box 1320
Yellowknife, NT X1A 2L9
Tel: 867-920-8058; *Fax:* 867-873-0484

Aboriginal Health & Community Wellness

Fax: 867-873-3585

Director, Aboriginal Health & Community Wellness, Sabrina Broadhead
Tel: 867-876-0640
Territorial Nutritionist, Elsie De Roose
Tel: 867-767-9064 ext: 492

Finance
Director, Finance, Jeannie Mathison
Tel: 867-767-9056 ext: 491
Assistant Director, Financial Planning & Analysis, Elizabeth Johnson
Tel: 867-767-9056 ext: 491

Health Services Administration
Fax: 867-777-3197
Toll-Free: 800-661-0830
Other Communication: Boardroom, Phone: 867-777-7428
Director, Health Services Administration, Nick Saturnino
Tel: 867-777-7400
Registrar General, Janetta Day
Tel: 867-777-7422
jenetta_day@gov.nt.ca

Health & Social Services Authorities
Beaufort-Delta Health & Social Services Authority
#285, 289 Mackenzie Rd., PO Box 2 Inuvik, NT X0E 0T0
Tel: 867-777-8000; *Fax:* 867-777-8049
bdhssa_info@gov.nt.ca
www.bdhssa.hss.gov.nt.ca
Chief Executive Officer, Arlene Jorgensen
Tel: 867-777-8146
Medical Director, Nadia Salvaterra
Tel: 867-777-8108

Dehcho Health & Social Services Authority
PO Box 246 Fort Simpson, NT X0E 0N0
Tel: 867-695-3815; *Fax:* 867-695-2920
www.dhssa.hss.gov.nt.ca
Chief Executive Officer, Ruth Robertson
Tel: 867-695-3815

Fort Smith Health & Social Services Authority
41 Breynat St., PO Box 1080 Yellowknife, NT X0E 0P0
Tel: 867-872-6204; *Fax:* 867-872-6276
www.fshssa.ca
Chief Executive Officer, Phyllis Mawdsley
Tel: 867-872-6201

Hay River Health & Social Services Authority
3 Gaetz Dr., Hay River, NT X0E 0R8
Tel: 867-874-7100; *Fax:* 867-874-7109
www.hrhssa.org
Other Communication: Health Centre Switchboard: 867-874-8000
Chief Executive Officer, Al Woods
Tel: 867-874-7110
al_woods@gov.nt.ca

Sahtu Health & Social Services Authority
Heritage House, 27 MacKenzie Dr., 2nd Fl., PO Box 340 Norman Wells, NT X0E 0V0
Tel: 867-587-3650; *Fax:* 867-587-3436
www.shssa.hss.gov.nt.ca
Chief Executive Officer, Patricia Kyle
Tel: 867-587-3651

Stanton Territorial Health Authority
550 Byrne Rd., PO Box 10 Yellowknife, NT X1A 2N1
Tel: 867-669-4111
sthainfo@gov.nt.ca
www.stha.hss.gov.nt.ca
Other Communication: Administration Office, Phone: 867-669-4361
Acting Chief Executive Officer & Chief Financial Officer, Gloria Badari
Tel: 867-669-4361
Medical Director, Bing Guthrie
Tel: 867-669-4151

Tlicho Community Services Agency
Complex, 2nd Fl., Bag #5, Behchoko, NT X0E 0Y0
Tel: 867-392-3000; *Fax:* 867-392-3001
tcsa@tlicho.net
www.tlicho.ca
Other Communication: Health After-Hours Emergency: 867-392-6075; Child & Family Services After-Hours Emergency: 867-392-3336
Chief Executive Officer, Kevin Armstrong
Tel: 867-392-3011

Yellowknife Health & Social Services Authority
Goga Cho Bldg., 4916 - 47th St., 2nd Fl., PO Box 608 Yellowknife, NT X1A 2N5
Tel: 867-873-7224; *Fax:* 867-873-0161
yhssa@gov.nt.ca
www.yhssa.org
Chief Executive Officer, Les Harrison
Tel: 867-873-7224
Medical Director, Sarah Cook
Tel: 867-873-7609

Information Services
Chief Information Officer, Michele Herriot
Tel: 867-767-9054 ext: 490

Policy, Legislation & Communications
Director, Policy, Legislation & Communications, Denise Canuel
Tel: 867-767-9052 ext: 490

Population Health
Fax: 867-873-0442
Director, Population Health, Laura Seddon
Tel: 867-767-9066 ext: 492
Chief Environmental Health Officer, Peter Workman
Tel: 867-767-9066 ext: 492
Territorial Epidemiologist & Manager, Epidemiology & Disease Registries, Heather Hannah
Tel: 867-767-9066 ext: 492

Territorial Health Services
Fax: 867-873-0196
Director, Territorial Health Services, Kim Riles
Tel: 867-767-9062 ext: 491

Territorial Social Programs
Executive Director, Territorial Social Programs, Andy Langford
Tel: 867-767-9061 ext: 491
Public Guardian, Office of the Public Guardian, Beatrice Raddi
Tel: 867-767-9155 ext: 494

Northwest Territories Housing Corporation

Scotia Centre, 5102 - 50th Ave., PO Box 2100 Yellowknife, NT X1A 2P6
Tel: 867-767-9080; *Fax:* 867-873-9426
Toll-Free: 844-698-4663
www.nwthc.gov.nt.ca
www.facebook.com/NWTHC

The mandate of the Northwest Territories Housing Corporation is to ensure, where necessary, a sufficient supply of affordable, adequate & suitable housing to meet the needs of residents. To accomplish this mandate, the corporation works with citizens, communities, Local Housing Organizations, aboriginal organizations, the business community, non-government organizations, & other governments. Through Housing Choices, the following four programs are available: Providing Assistance for Territorial Homeownership (PATH); Contributing Assistance for Repairs and Enhancements (CARE); Homeowner Entry Level Program (HELP); & Solutions to Educate People (STEP).

Minister Responsible, Hon. Caroline Cochrane
Tel: 867-767-9141 ext: 111
caroline_cochrane@gov.nt.ca
President & CEO, Jeff Anderson
Tel: 867-767-9080 ext: 850
Vice-President, Finance & Infrastructure Services, Jim Martin
Tel: 867-767-9080 ext: 850
Vice-President, Programs & District Operations, Franklin Carpenter
Tel: 867-767-9080 ext: 851
Chief Information Officer, Stephen Murphy
Tel: 867-767-9093 ext: 850
Director, Finance & Administration, Tara Clowes
Tel: 867-767-9329 ext: 850
Director, Infrastructure Services, Scott Reid
Tel: 867-767-9330 ext: 850

Northwest Territories Department of Human Resources

PO Box 1320 Yellowknife, NT X1A 2L9
Tel: 867-678-6625; *Fax:* 867-873-0282
Toll-Free: 866-475-8162
jobsyk@gov.nt.ca
www.hr.gov.nt.ca
Other Communication: Current Employment Opportunites: careers.hr.gov.nt.ca; Client Services, Phone: 867-767-9154
twitter.com/GNWT_Jobs
www.facebook.com/GNWTHumanResources
www.linkedin.com/company/gnwt

The Department services the people of the Northwest Territories & supports the development of employees in the northern public service. Services are provided through the following divisions: Management & Recruitment Services; Corporate Human Resource Services; Human Resource Strategy & Policy; & Employee Services.

Minister, Hon. Robert C. McLeod
Tel: 867-767-9142 ext: 111
robert_c_mcleod@gov.nt.ca
Deputy Minister, Bronwyn Watters
Tel: 867-767-9015 ext: 140

Corporate Affairs & Strategic Human Resources
Director, Michelle Simpson
Tel: 867-767-9151 ext: 140

Labour Relations
Director, Kim Wickens
Tel: 867-767-9153 ext: 140

Management & Recruitment Services Management
Director, Tara Hunter
Tel: 867-767-9154 ext: 141

Northwest Territories Department of Industry, Tourism & Investment (ITI)

PO Box 1320 Yellowknife, NT X1A 2L9
Tel: 867-767-9002
www.iti.gov.nt.ca

The Department of Industry, Tourism & Investment promotes & supports economic prosperity & community self-reliance in the Northwest Territories by providing programs & services. Programs & services are available through the following departmental divisions: Diamonds; Energy Planning; Industrial Initiatives; Informatics; Investment & Economic Analysis; Mackenzie Valley Pipeline Office; Minerals, Oil & Gas; Policy, Legislation & Communications; & Tourism & Parks.

Minister, Hon. Wally Schumann
Tel: 867-767-9142 ext: 111
wally_schumann@gov.nt.ca
Deputy Minister, Tom Jensen
Assistant Deputy Minister, Kelly Kaylo
Tel: 867-767-9060 ext: 630
Director, Policy, Legislation & Communications, Paula MacFadyen
Tel: 867-767-9202 ext: 630

Associated Agencies, Boards & Commissions:

•Agricultural Products Marketing Council
Scotia Centre, 8th Fl.
PO Box 1320
Yellowknife, NT X1A 2L9
Tel: 867-873-7115; *Fax:* 867-873-0563

•Northwest Territories Egg Producers Board
#2, 4 Courtoreille
Hay River, NT X0E 1G2
Tel: 867-874-6820; *Fax:* 867-874-6840

Investment & Economic Analysis
With general responsibilities for strategies, plans & programs to develop the NWT business community, the division provides expert advice & support in the production & marketing of arts & crafts, & acts as a link to national & international businesses & organizations.
Director, Kevin Todd
Tel: 867-767-9205 ext: 630

Mackenzie Valley Petroleum Planning Office
Coordinates the territorial government's planning & response related to the Mackenzie Gas Project, including the regulatory review & environmental assessment processes. Also handles the territorial government's communications with respect to the Mackenzie Gas Project, & will manage selective funding programs to help Aboriginal groups & communities to prepare for the project.
Manager, Ravi Annavarapu
Tel: 867-874-5405

Mineral Resources
The Minerals Resources division develops & implements strategies to encourage & attract non-renewable resource investment in the Northwest Territories. It also provides advice on the geological potential, industrial activity & potential opportunities associated with mineral exploration in the Territory.
Director, Mineral Resources, Pamela Strand
Tel: 867-767-9209 ext: 631

Northwest Territories Geological Survey (NTGS)
4601B - 52 Ave., PO Box 1320 Yellowknife, NT X1A 2L9
Tel: 867-767-9211; *Fax:* 867-873-2652
ntgs@gov.nt.ca
www.nwtgeoscience.ca
Northwest Territories Geological Survey (NTGS) advances the geoscience knowledge of the Northwest Territories for the benefit of northerners through: delivery of geoscience research; analysis of mineral & petroleum resources; excellence in data management. In collaboration with its partners, NTGS provides analysis, information & advice to individuals, communities, governments, & the mining & petroleum industry

Tourism & Parks
Tel: 867-767-9206; *Fax:* 867-873-0163
Develops, operates & maintains facilities that include parks, visitor centres & interpretive displays. The division is also responsible for implementing the Protected Areas Strategy for

the Northwest Territories, in conjunction with Canada's Federal Government & other stakeholders. The division also provides support for tourism marketing, research & product development.

Inuvialuit Water Board (IWB)

Professional Bldg., #302, 125 Mackenzie Rd., PO Box 2531 Yellowknife, NT X0E 0T0

Tel: 867-678-2942; *Fax:* 867-678-2943
info@inuvwb.ca
www.inuvwb.ca

Formerly known as the Northwest Territories Water Board, the board is responsible for licensing water use & waste disposal in the Inuvialuit Settlement Region located within the Northwest Territories, under the Waters Act.

Chair, Roger Connelly
Executive Director, Mardy Semmler
semmlerm@inuvwb.ca

Northwest Territories Department of Justice

4903 - 49th St., PO Box 1320 Yellowknife, NT X1A 2L9

Tel: 867-767-9256
www.justice.gov.nt.ca

The following are some of the services offered by the Department of Justice: Aboriginal Rights Court Challenges Program; Access to Information & Protection of Privacy; Commissioner for Oaths/Notary Public; Coroner; Corporate Registries; Land Titles Office; Legal Aid; Maintenance Enforcement; Mental Disorder Review Board; Personal Property Registry; Public Trustee; Rental Office; Securities Registry; Victim Services; Witness Expense Assistance Program; & Youth Justice.

Minister, Hon. Louis Sebert
Tel: 867-767-9141 ext: 111
louis_sebert@gov.nt.ca
Deputy Minister, Martin Goldney
martin_goldney@gov.nt.ca
Assistant Deputy Minister & Attorney General, Mark Aitken
Tel: 867-767-9070 ext: 820
Assistant Deputy Minister & Solicitor General, Charlene Doolittle
Tel: 867-767-9070 ext: 820
Chief Coroner, Coroner's Office, Cathy Menard
Tel: 867-767-9251 ext: 820
Chief Information Officer, Norm Embleton
Tel: 867-767-9255 ext: 824
norm_embleton@gov.nt.ca
Public Trustee, Public Trustee's Office, Brian Asmundson
Tel: 867-767-9252 ext: 824
Children's Lawyer, Ken Kinnear
Tel: 867-767-9253 ext: 820; *Fax:* 867-873-0184
Deputy Chief Coroner, Adriana Zibolenova
Tel: 867-767-9251 ext: 820; *Fax:* 867-873-0426

Associated Agencies, Boards & Commissions:

•Aboriginal Rights Courts Challenges Committee
PO Box 1320
Yellowknife, NT X1A 2L9
Tel: 867-920-6197; *Fax:* 867-873-0307

•Legal Services Board of the Northwest Territories
4915 - 48th St.
PO Box 1320
Yellowknife, NT X1A 2L9
Tel: 867-873-7450; *Fax:* 867-873-5320
lsb@gov.nt.ca
www.justice.gov.nt.ca/LegalServicesBoard/index.shtml

•Northwest Territories Judicial Renumeration Commission
5204 Lundquist Rd.
Yellowknife, NT X1A 3G2
Tel: 867-873-6024

•Northwest Territories Maintenance Enforcement Program (MEP)
PO Box 1770
Yellowknife, NT X1A 2P3
Tel: 867-920-3378; *Fax:* 867-873-0106
Toll-free: 800-661-0798
mep@gov.nt.ca
www.justice.gov.nt.ca/mep

•Victims Assistance Committee
c/o Community Justice & Community Policing Division
PO Box 1320
Yellowknife, NT X1A 2L9
Tel: 867-920-6911; *Fax:* 867-873-0199
www.justice.gov.nt.ca/VictimsAssistanceCommittee/index.shtml

Community Justice & Community Policing
Fax: 867-873-0199
Director, Community Justice & Community Policing, Blake Wade
Tel: 867-767-9261 ext: 822

Corrections Service
Director, Corrections Service, Robert Riches
Tel: 867-767-9263 ext: 824
Assistant Director, Community Corrections, Parker Kennedy
Tel: 867-767-9263 ext: 822
Assistant Director, Facility Operations, Blair Van Metre
Tel: 867-767-9262 ext: 922
blair_vanmetre@gov.nt.ca

Court Services
Fax: 867-873-0307
www.justice.gov.nt.ca/CourtServices/courtservices.shtml
Other Communication: Family Law Mediation Program, Toll Free Phone: 1-866-217-8923
Director, Court Services, Anne Mould
Tel: 867-920-8852
Chief Court Reporter, Lois Hewitt
Tel: 867-920-8995

NWT Courts
4903 - 49th St., PO Box 550 Yellowknife, NT X1A 2N4
Tel: 867-920-8760; *Fax:* 867-873-0291
Toll-Free: 866-822-5864
www.nwtcourts.ca
Other Communication: Alternate Phone: 867-873-7602
Administrator, Denise Bertolini
Tel: 867-873-7643

Finance
Director, Finance, Kim Schofield
Tel: 867-767-9250 ext: 820
kim_schofield@gov.nt.ca

Legal Division
Fax: 867-873-0234
Director, Legal Division, Brad Patzer
Tel: 867-767-9257 ext: 821

Legal Registries
Fax: 867-873-0243
Director & Registrar, Corporate Registries, Tom Hall
Tel: 867-767-9260 ext: 821

Legislation Division
Fax: 867-920-8898
www.justice.gov.nt.ca/en/browse/laws-and-legislation
Director, Legislation Division, Kelly McLaughlin
Tel: 867-767-9259 ext: 821

Policy & Planning
Fax: 867-873-0659
Director, Policy & Planning, Janice Laycock
Tel: 867-767-9256 ext: 820

Northwest Territories Department of Lands

Gallery Bldg., 4923 - 52nd St., 1st & 2nd Fl., PO Box 1320 Yellowknife, NT X1A 2L9

Tel: 867-767-9185; *Fax:* 867-669-0905
NWTLands@gov.nt.ca
www.lands.gov.nt.ca

The Department of Lands manages, administers & plans for the sustainable use of public land in the Northwest Territories.

Minister, Hon. Louis Sebert
Tel: 867-767-9142 ext: 111
louis_sebert@gov.nt.ca
Deputy Minister, Willard Hagen
Acting Assistant Deputy Minister, Planning & Coordination; Director, Land Use & Sustainability, Terry Hall
Tel: 867-767-9183 ext: 240
Acting Assistant Deputy Minister, Operations, Annette Hopkins
Tel: 867-767-9035 ext: 240
Executive Director, SSC - Informatics, Rick Wind
Tel: 867-767-9186 ext: 241
Director, Lands Administration (Commissioner's Land), Blair Chapman
Tel: 867-767-9184 ext: 240
Director, Lands Administration (Territorial Land), Carla Conkin
Tel: 867-767-9180 ext: 240
Director, Policy, Legislation & Communication, Paula Harker
Tel: 867-767-9182 ext: 240
Director, Finance & Administration, Brenda Hilderman
Tel: 867-767-9181 ext: 240
Acting Director, Liabilities & Financial Assurances, Lorraine Seale
Tel: 867-767-9183 ext: 240

Northwest Territories Department of Municipal & Community Affairs

PO Box 1320 Yellowknife, NT X1A 2L9

Tel: 867-767-9160; *Fax:* 867-873-0309
www.maca.gov.nt.ca

Supports capable, accountable & self-directed community governments providing a safe, sustainable & healthy environment for community residents. Works with community governments & other partners in supporting community residents as they organize & manage democratic, responsible & accountable community governments. The Department assists municipalities with administrative services & infrastructure project management, provides expertise in engineering to communities & arranges for debentures on behalf of communities which are undertaking public works programs. Advisory services are supplied to community councils for the planning, development & administration of public lands within municipal boundaries. Technical expertise is provided for mapping, surveying & air photography & zoning by-law administration.

Minister, Hon. Caroline Cochrane
Tel: 867-767-9142 ext: 111
caroline_cochrane@gov.nt.ca
Deputy Minister, Tom R. Williams
Tel: 867-767-9160 ext: 210
Tom_R_Williams@gov.nt.ca
Assistant Deputy Minister, Regional Operations, Eleanor Young
Tel: 867-767-9160 ext: 210
eleanor_young@gov.nt.ca
Director, Corporate Affairs, Gary Schauerte
Tel: 867-767-9162 ext: 210; *Fax:* 867-873-0309

Associated Agencies, Boards & Commissions:

•Assessment Appeal Tribunal
#600, 5201 - 50th Ave.
PO Box 1320
Yellowknife, NT X1A 3S9
Tel: 867-873-7125; *Fax:* 867-873-0609

•Territorial Board of Revision
#600, 5201 - 50th Ave.
Yellowknife, NT X1A 3S9
Tel: 867-873-7125; *Fax:* 867-873-0609

Community Operations
Director, Community Operations, Grace Lau-a
Tel: 867-767-9164 ext: 210
Manager, Asset Management, Olivia Lee
Tel: 867-767-9164 ext: 210

Corporate Affairs
Tel: 867-767-9162; *Fax:* 867-873-0309
Director, Gary Schauerte
Tel: 867-767-9162 ext: 210

Public Safety
Tel: 867-767-9161; *Fax:* 867-873-0206
Other Communication: 24/7 Emergency Measures Office, Phone: 867-920-2303
Director, Kevin Brezinski
Tel: 867-767-9161 ext: 210
Fire Marshal, Chucker Dewar
Tel: 867-767-9161 ext: 210; *Fax:* 867-873-0206

School of Community Government
Tel: 867-767-9163; *Fax:* 867-873-0584
Director, Dan Schofield
Tel: 867-767-9163 ext: 210
dan_schofield@gov.nt.ca

Sport, Recreation & Youth
Tel: 867-767-9166; *Fax:* 867-920-6467
Director, Ian Legaree
Tel: 867-767-9166 ext: 211

Northwest Territories Power Corporation

4 Capital Dr., Hay River, NT X0E 1G2

Tel: 867-874-5200
info@ntpc.com
www.ntpc.com
twitter.com/NTPC_News
www.facebook.com/591764887576712

Made up of 28 separate power systems, the NWT Power Corporation serves approximately 43,000 people in communities across the Northwest Territories. Facilities include hydro-electric, diesel & natural gas generation plants, transmission systems, & several isolated electrical distribution systems. The Corporation works to provide environmentally sound, safe, reliable, cost-effective energy & related services in the territories.

Minister Responsible, Hon. Louis Sebert
Tel: 867-767-9141 ext: 111
louis_sebert@gov.nt.ca

Chair, David Tucker
President & CEO, Emanuel DaRosa
Chief Financial Officer, Judith Goucher

Public Utilities Board of the Northwest Territories (PUB)

#203, 62 Woodland Dr., PO Box 4211 Hay River, NT X0E 1G1
Tel: 867-874-3944; *Fax:* 867-874-3639
www.nwtpublicutilitiesboard.ca

The independent, quasi-judicial agency of the Government of the Northwest Territories is responsible for the regulation of public utilities in the territory. Its authority is from the Public Utilities Act. Issues are handled by an application & decision process.

Minister Responsible, Hon. Glen Abernethy
Tel: 867-767-9142 ext: 111
glen_abernethy@gov.nt.ca
Chair, Gordon Van Tighem
Vice-Chair, Sandra Jaque
Board Secretary, Louise-Ann Larocque
louise-ann_larocque@gov.nt.ca

Northwest Territories Department of Public Works & Services

Stuart M. Hodgson Bldg., 5009 - 49th St., PO Box 1320 Yellowknife, NT X1A 2L9
www.pws.gov.nt.ca

Designs, constructs, maintains & operates territorial buildings; implements energy efficiency projects; provides essential petroleum products to the public where they are not available from the private sector; provides data systems & communication services to government departments.

Minister, Hon. Wally Schumann
Tel: 867-767-9142 ext: 111
wally_schumann@gov.nt.ca
Deputy Minister, Paul Guy
Tel: 867-767-9045 ext: 320
paul_guy@gov.nt.ca

Asset Management

Estimates the cost of building construction & renovation; consults in the plan of buildings so they meet program needs; reviews consultant designs of buildings & works; implements the Safe Drinking Water Initiatives.

Assistant Deputy Minister, Mike Burns
Tel: 867-767-9048 ext: 320; *Fax:* 867-873-0226
mike_burns@gov.nt.ca
Chief Electrical Inspector, Electrical/Mechanical Safety, Ron Hiscock
Tel: 867-767-9043 ext: 320
Chief Boiler Inspector, Electrical/Mechanical Safety, Matthias Mailman
Tel: 867-767-9043 ext: 320; *Fax:* 867-873-0117
Director, Design & Technical Services, Mark Cronk
Tel: 867-767-9048 ext: 320
Director, Procurement Shared Services, Bill Kaip
Tel: 867-767-9044 ext: 321
bill_kaip@gov.nt.ca
Director, Infrastructure Operations & Accommodation Services, Brian Nagel
Tel: 867-767-9048 ext: 320; *Fax:* 867-873-0226

Corporate Information Management

Fax: 867-873-0212
Director, Corporate Information Management, Steve Hagerman
Tel: 867-767-9046 ext: 321

Corporate Services

Fax: 867-873-0100
Director, Corporate Services, Vince McCormick
Tel: 867-767-9047 ext: 320

Energy

Fax: 867-873-0100
Assistant Deputy Minister, Energy, John Vandenberg
Tel: 867-767-9045 ext: 320
Director, Energy, Policy & Planning, Dave Nightingale
Tel: 867-767-9021 ext: 320
Director, Energy Solutions, Derrick Briggs
Tel: 867-767-9021 ext: 320

Technology Service Centre

Tel: 867-920-4408
Toll-Free: 866-380-6777
Director, Technology Service Centre, Laurie Gault
Tel: 867-767-9024 ext: 322
laurie_gault@gov.nt.ca

Status of Women Council of the Northwest Territories

Northwest Tower, 4th Fl., PO Box 1320 Yellowknife, NT X1A 2L9
Tel: 867-920-6177; *Fax:* 867-873-0285
Toll-Free: 888-234-4485
council@statusofwomen.nt.ca
www.statusofwomen.nt.ca
twitter.com/StatusofWomenNT
www.facebook.com/113623588652526

To work towards the equality of women through advice to the government; research; public education; advocacy on behalf of women; & workshops & other support for the development of women's groups, & other groups working on issues of concern to women.

Minister Responsible, Hon. Caroline Cochrane
Tel: 867-767-9141 ext: 111
caroline_cochrane@gov.nt.ca
Acting President, Georgina Jacobson Masuzumi
Executive Director, Lorraine Phaneuf
Tel: 867-920-8929
lorraine@statusofwomen.nt.ca
Manager, Programs & Research, Annemieke Mulders
Tel: 867-920-8994
am@statusofwomen.nt.ca

Northwest Territories Department of Transportation

New Government Bldg., 5015 - 49 St., 4th Fl., PO Box 1320 Yellowknife, NT X1A 2L9
Tel: 867-767-9089; *Fax:* 867-873-0606
www.dot.gov.nt.ca

Minister, Hon. Wally Schumann
Tel: 867-767-9141 ext: 111
wally_schumann@gov.nt.ca
Deputy Minister, Russell Neudorf
Tel: 867-767-9040 ext: 310
russell_neudorf@gov.nt.ca
Assistant Deputy Minister, Jayleen Robertson
Tel: 867-767-9040 ext: 310
Director, Planning, Policy & Communications, Sonya Saunders
Tel: 867-767-9082 ext: 310
Director, Corporate Services, Joyce Taylor
Tel: 867-767-9081 ext: 310; *Fax:* 867-873-0283

Airports

Tel: 867-767-9084
Director, Airports, Delia Chesworth
Tel: 867-767-9084 ext: 310
Assistant Director, Airport Facilities, Terry Brookes
Tel: 867-767-9084 ext: 310
Assistant Director, Programs & Standards, Ben Webber
Tel: 867-767-9084 ext: 310; *Fax:* 867-873-0297

Highways

Tel: 867-767-9086; *Fax:* 867-873-0288
Director, Highways & Marine, Kevin McLeod
Tel: 867-767-9086 ext: 311; *Fax:* 867-673-0288
Assistant Director, Marine Services, Tom Maher
Tel: 867-874-5023

Road Licensing & Safety

Tel: 867-767-9088; *Fax:* 867-873-0120
Director, Road Licensing & Safety - Yellowknife, Steve Loutitt
Tel: 867-767-9088 ext: 311

Northwest Territories & Nunavut Workers' Safety & Compensation Commission (WSCC)

Centre Square Tower, 5022 - 49th St., 5th Fl., PO Box 8888 Yellowknife, NT X1A 2R3
Tel: 867-920-3888; *Fax:* 867-873-4596
Toll-Free: 800-661-0792
www.wscc.nt.ca
Other Communication: Toll Free Fax: 1-866-277-3677
twitter.com/WSCCNTNU
www.facebook.com/WSCCNTNU

The Workers' Safety & Compensation Commission is engaged in the following activities: ensuring compensation & pensions are awarded to injured workers or their dependents; assessing sufficiently & fairly to meet obligations; maintaining balance in providing benefits to injured workers, while keeping costs to employers as low as possible; & promoting safe workplaces through education & enforcement.

Minister Responsible (Northwest Territories), Hon. Glen Abernethy
Tel: 867-767-9142 ext: 111
glen_abernethy@gov.nt.ca
Minister Responsible (Nunavut), Hon. Keith Peterson
Tel: 867-975-5028; *Fax:* 867-975-5095
kpeterson@gov.nu.ca
Chair, Dave Tucker
President & CEO, Dave Grundy
Tel: 867-669-4442
Vice-President, Prevention Services & Stakeholder Services, Kim Collins Riffel
Tel: 867-920-3821
Vice-President, Corporate Services, Harmeet Jagpal
Tel: 867-669-4446
Vice-President, Financial Services, Len MacDonald
Tel: 867-920-3824
Chief Inspector of Mines, Fred Bailey
Tel: 867-669-4430
General Counsel, Shirley Walsh
Tel: 867-920-3895

Government of Nova Scotia

Seat of Government: Province House, 1726 Hollis St., Halifax, NS B3J 2Y3
Toll-Free: 800-670-4357
TTY: 877-404-0867
novascotia.ca
twitter.com/nsgov

The Province of Nova Scotia entered Confederation July 1, 1867. It has a land area of 52,917,46 sq km, & the StatsCan census population in 2011 was 921,727.

Office of the Lieutenant Governor

Government House, 1451 Barrington St., Halifax, NS B3J 1Z2
Tel: 902-424-7001; *Fax:* 902-424-1790
lgoffice@novascotia.ca
www.lt.gov.ns.ca
Other Communication: Invitation to the Lieutenant Governor: invite-lg@novascotia.ca
twitter.com/LtGovNS
www.facebook.com/LtGovNS
www.flickr.com/photos/lieutenantgovernor/sets

On April 12, 2012, Brigadier-General The Honourable J.J. Grant, CMM, ONS, CD (Ret'd) was installed as Her Majesty's representative in Nova Scotia.

Lieutenant Governor of Nova Scotia, Hon. John James Grant, CMM, ONS, CD (Ret'd)
Note: On February 16, 2012, the Right Honourable Stephen Harper announced the appointment of Brigadier-General Grant as the thirty-second Lieutenant Governor of Nova Scotia.
Executive Director, Government House; Private Secretary to the Lieutenant Governor, Dr. Christopher McCreery, MVO
Chief Aide-de-Camp, SSG Dianne Stairs, AdeC
Chief Commissionaire, Brian Graves, C.W.O.
Coordinator, In-house Events, Kelly Clelland

Office of the Premier

One Government Place, 1700 Granville St., 7th Fl., PO Box 726 Halifax, NS B3J 2T3
Tel: 902-424-6600; *Fax:* 902-424-7648
Toll-Free: 800-267-1993
premier@novascotia.ca
premier.novascotia.ca

The Honorable Stephen McNeil became Premier of Nova Scotia in the General Election of Oct. 8, 2013.

Premier & President, Executive Council, Hon. Stephen McNeil
Tel: 902-424-6600; *Fax:* 902-424-7648
premier@novascotia.ca
Deputy Premier & Deputy President, Executive Council, Hon. Diana C. Whalen
Tel: 902-424-4044; *Fax:* 902-424-0510
justmin@novascotia.ca
Chief of Staff, Kristan Hines
Chief Regulatory Officer, Office of Regulatory Affairs & Service Effectiveness, Fred Crooks
Director, Communications, Stephen Moore
Principal Secretary to the Premier, Laurie Graham

Executive Council Office (ECO)

One Government Place, 1700 Granville St., 5th Fl., PO Box 2125 Halifax, NS B3J 3B7
Tel: 902-424-5970; *Fax:* 902-424-0667
TTY: 866-206-6844
execounc@gov.ns.ca
www.novascotia.ca/exec_council
Other Communication: 902-424-6611 (General Inquiries)

The Executive Branch of government consists of ministers/Members of the Executive Council, who collectively form the Cabinet. Under the Executive Council Act, ministers are chosen by the Premier & appointed by the Lieutenant Governor. Led by the Premier/President of the Executive Council, The Executive Council Office (ECO) serves the Cabinet & its committees. In January 2016, the Office of Planning & Priorities was merged into the ECO.

Premier & President, Executive Council; Leader, Nova Scotia Liberal Party; Minister, Intergovernmental Affairs; Minister, Regulatory Affairs & Service Effectiveness; Minister, Aboriginal Affairs; Minister responsible, Military Relations, Hon. Stephen McNeil
Tel: 902-424-6600; *Fax:* 902-424-7648
premier@gov.ns.ca
Other Communications: Aboriginal Affairs: oaa@gov.ns.ca

Deputy Premier & Deputy President, Executive Council; Attorney General & Minister, Justice; Minister responsible, NS Police Complaints Commissioner, NS Police Review Board & Elections, Human Rights, Regulations, Workers' Comp. & Uniform Closing Day Acts, Hon. Diana C. Whalen
Tel: 902-424-4044; *Fax:* 902-424-0510
justmin@novascotia.ca

Minister, Agriculture; Minister, Fisheries & Aquaculture; Minister responsible, Maritime Provinces Harness Racing Commission Act, Hon. Keith Colwell
Tel: 902-424-4388; *Fax:* 902-424-0699
min_dag@gov.ns.ca
Other Communications: Fisheries & Aquaculture: mindfa@gov.ns.ca

Minister, Energy; Minister, Acadian Affairs; Minister responsible, Part I of the Gaming Control Act, Hon. Michel Samson, ECNS
Tel: 902-424-7793; *Fax:* 902-424-3265
energyminister@novascotia.ca
Other Communications: Acadian Affairs: min-oaa@gov.ns.ca

Minister, Health & Wellness; Minister, Seniors; Chair, Senior Citizens' Secretariat, Hon. Leo A. Glavine
Tel: 902-424-3377; *Fax:* 902-424-0559
health.minister@gov.ns.ca
Other Communications: Seniors: seniorsmin@novascotia.ca

Minister, Education & Early Childhood Development; Chair, Treasury & Policy Board, Hon. Karen Lynn Casey
Tel: 902-424-4236; *Fax:* 902-424-0680
educmin@novascotia.ca
Other Communications: Treasury: tbenquiries@gov.ns.ca

Minister, Labour & Advanced Education; Minister responsible, Apprenticeship & Trades Qualifications Act, the Workers' Compensation Act (except Part II) & Youth, Hon. Kelly Regan
Tel: 902-424-6647; *Fax:* 902-424-0575
min_lae@novascotia.ca

Minister, Transportation & Infrastructure Renewal; Minister responsible, Sydney Tar Ponds Agency (NS), Hon. Geoff MacLellan
Tel: 902-424-5875; *Fax:* 902-424-0171
tirmin@novascotia.ca
Other Communications: Sydney Tar Ponds Agency Phone: 902-567-1035

Minister, Municipal Affairs; Minister, Communications Nova Scotia, Hon. Zach Churchill
Tel: 902-424-5550; *Fax:* 902-424-0581
dmamin@novascotia.ca
Other Communications: Communications NS: cnsminister@novascotia.ca

Minister, Finance & Treasury Board; Minister, Gaelic Affairs; Minister responsible, Credit Union Act, Insurance Act, Liquor Control Act, Nova Scotia Liquor Corporation, Securities Act & Utility & Review Board Act, Hon. Randy Delorey
Tel: 902-424-5720; *Fax:* 902-424-0635
FinanceMinister@novascotia.ca
Other Communications: Gaelic Affairs: gaelicinfo@gov.ns.ca

Minister, Communities, Culture & Heritage; Minister, African Nova Scotian Affairs; Minister responsible, Heritage Property Act, Hon. Tony Ince
Tel: 902-424-4889; *Fax:* 902-424-4872
min_cch@novascotia.ca
Other Communications: ANSA: ansa_newsletter@gov.ns.ca

Minister, Community Services; Minister, Voluntary Sector; Minister responsible, Advisory Council on the Status of Women Act, & Disabled Persons' Commission Act, Hon. Joanne Bernard
Toll-free: 877-424-1177; *Fax:* 902-424-3287
dcsmin@gov.ns.ca
Other Communications: Status of Women: women@novascotia.ca

Minister, Immigration, Hon. Lena M. Diab
Tel: 902-424-5230; *Fax:* 902-424-3178
ImmigrationMinister@novascotia.ca

Minister, Public Service Commission; Minister, Internal Services; Minister responsible, Sydney Steel Corporation Act, Hon. Labi Kousoulis
Tel: 902-424-5465; *Fax:* 902-424-0555
min_psc@gov.ns.ca
Other Communications: Internal Services: MIN_InternalServices@novascotia.ca

Minister, Business; Minister, Service Nova Scotia; Minister responsible, Nova Scotia Business Incorporated, Innovation Corporation Act, Part II of the Gaming Control Act & Residential Tenancies Act, Hon. Mark Furey
Tel: 902-424-5790; *Fax:* 902-424-0514
BusinessMinister@novascotia.ca
Other Communications: Service Nova Scotia: snsmininster@novascotia.ca

Minister, Natural Resources, Hon. Lloyd Hines
Tel: 902-424-4037; *Fax:* 902-424-0594
mindnr@novascotia.ca

Minister, Environment, Hon. Margaret Miller
Tel: 902-424-3600; *Fax:* 902-424-0501
Minister.Environment@novascotia.ca

Legislative House of Assembly

c/o Clerk's Office, Province House, 1st Fl., PO Box 1617 Halifax, NS B3J 2Y3
Tel: 902-424-5978; *Fax:* 902-424-0632
nslegislature.ca
Other Communication: 902-424-0526 (Fax, Office of the Speaker)

Chief Clerk of the House, Neil R. Ferguson
Tel: 902-424-8941

Speaker, House of Assembly, Hon. Kevin Murphy
Tel: 902-424-5707; *Fax:* 902-424-0632
Hon.Kevin.Murphy@novascotia.ca
Speaker's Administration Office
1724 Granville St.
PO Box 1617
Halifax, NS B3J 1X5

Deputy Speaker, Keith Irving
Tel: 902-424-8637; *Fax:* 902-424-0539
keith@irvingmla.ca

Deputy Speaker, Gordon Wilson
Tel: 902-424-8637; *Fax:* 902-424-0539
info@claredigby.ca

Sergeant-at-Arms, David Fraser
Tel: 902-424-4603

Chief Legislative Counsel, Gordon D. Hebb
Tel: 902-424-8941; *Fax:* 902-424-0547
Legc.office@novascotia.ca
Office of the Legislative Counsel, CIBC Building
#802, 1809 Barrington St.
PO Box 1116
Halifax, NS B3J 2X1

Commissioner, Conflict of Interest, Hon. D. Merlin Nunn
Tel: 902-424-5345; *Fax:* 902-424-0632
One Government Place, Barrington Level
1700 Granville St.
PO Box 1617
Halifax, NS B3J 1X5

Legislative Librarian, David McDonald
Tel: 902-424-5932; *Fax:* 902-424-0220
leglib@novascotia.ca
Legislative Library, Province House
1726, Hollis St.
PO Box 396
Halifax, NS B3J 2P8

Editor, Hansard, Robert Kinsman
Tel: 902-424-5706; *Fax:* 902-424-0593
publications@novascotia.ca
Note:
www.nslegislature.ca/index.php/people/offices/hansard-reporting-services
1800 Argyle St.
PO Box 600
Halifax, NS B3J 3N8

Assistant Clerk, Annette M. Boucher, Q.C.

Director, Administration, Speaker's Office, Deborah Lusby
Tel: 902-424-4479; *Fax:* 902-424-2404
Deborah.Lusby@novascotia.ca

Government Caucus Office (Liberal Party)

Nova Scotia Liberal Caucus Office, #1402, 5151 George St., PO Box 741 Halifax, NS B3J 2T3
Tel: 902-424-8637; *Fax:* 902-424-0539
Toll-Free: 877-778-1917
info@nsliberalcaucus.ca
www.nsliberalcaucus.ca
Other Communication: Nova Scotia Liberal Party, URL: www.liberal.ns.ca
twitter.com/NSLiberal
www.youtube.com/nsliberalparty

Premier; Leader, Nova Scotia Liberal Party, Hon. Stephen McNeil, ECNS
Tel: 902-825-2093; *Fax:* 902-825-6306
stephenmcneil@ns.aliantzinc.ca
Social Media: twitter.com/StephenMcNeil, www.facebook.com/StephenMcNeilLiberal

Chair, Liberal Caucus, Iain Rankin
Tel: 902-404-7036; *Fax:* 902-404-7056
info@iainrankin.ca

Government House Leader, Hon. Michel Samson, ECNS
Tel: 902-424-7793; *Fax:* 902-424-3265
energyminister@novascotia.ca
Social Media: twitter.com/msamsonliberal, www.facebook.com/michel.samson.mla

Chief of Staff, Kristan Hines

Executive Director, Linda Tweedie
Social Media: twitter.com/lindatweedie1

Office of the Official Opposition (Progressive Conservative Party)

PC Caucus Office, #1001, 1660 Hollis St., Halifax, NS B3J 1V7
Tel: 902-424-2731; *Fax:* 902-424-7484
Toll-Free: 800-363-1998
pcmlas@gov.ns.ca
www.pccaucus.ns.ca
Other Communication: PC Party of Nova Scotia, URL: www.pcparty.ns.ca
www.youtube.com/user/pcnovascotia

Leader, Official Opposition; Leader, Progressive Conservative Party of Nova Scotia, Jamie Baillie
Tel: 902-424-2731; *Fax:* 902-424-7484
jamiebaillie@novascotia.ca
Social Media: twitter.com/jamiebaillie, www.facebook.com/jamie.baillie.nspc, www.linkedin.com/profile/view?id=18182112

House Leader, Progressive Conservative Party, Chris d'Entremont
Tel: 902-424-2731; *Fax:* 902-424-7484
info@chrisdentremont.com
Social Media: twitter.com/ChrisMLA, www.facebook.com/ChrisMLA

President, Nova Scotia Progressive Conservative Party, Tara Miller
tara.miller@pcparty.ns.ca

Office of the New Democratic Party

New Democratic Party Caucus Office, Centennial Building, #603, 5151 George St., Halifax, NS B3J 1M5
Tel: 902-424-4134; *Fax:* 902-423-9618
Toll-Free: 888-247-0448
nsndp.ca
twitter.com/nsndp
www.facebook.com/nsndp
www.youtube.com/user/NSNDP

Leader, New Democratic Party of Nova Scotia, Gary Burrill
gary@garyburrill.ca
Social Media: twitter.com/garyburrill, www.facebook.com/democracyandjustice
Note: Gary Burrill became the new Leader of the Nova Scotia NDP on Feb. 27, 2016. He was unelected at the time.

Caucus Chair, New Democratic Party of Nova Scotia, Lenore Zann
Tel: 902-424-4134; *Fax:* 902-424-0504
lenorezannmla@bellaliant.com
Social Media: www.facebook.com/LenoreZannMLA

House Leader, New Democratic Party, Dave Wilson
Tel: 902-424-4134; *Fax:* 902-424-0504
davewilsonmla@eastlink.ca

Leader in the House, New Democratic Party of Nova Scotia, Marian Mancini
Tel: 902-424-4134; *Fax:* 902-424-0504
MLAMancini@eastlink.ca

Caucus Whip, New Democratic Party of Nova Scotia, Sterling Belliveau
Tel: 902-424-4134; *Fax:* 902-424-0504
mlaqueens-shelb@eastlink.ca
Social Media: www.facebook.com/sterlingbelliveaumla

Deputy House Leader, New Democratic Party of Nova Scotia, Denise P. Peterson-Rafuse
Tel: 902-424-4134; *Fax:* 902-424-0504
denisepetersmla@bellaliant.com
Social Media: twitter.com/deniseprafuse, www.facebook.com/DeniseMLA

President, New Democratic Party of Nova Scotia, Paula Simon

Standing Committees of the House

Committee Room, One Government Place, 1700 Granville St., 2nd Fl., PO Box 2630 Stn. M, Halifax, NS B3J 3P7
Tel: 902-424-4432; *Fax:* 902-424-0513
legcomm@gov.ns.ca
www.nslegislature.ca/index.php/committees

Legislative committees are appointed by the Nova Scotia House of Assembly & are comprised of Members of the House. The committee system allows for detailed examination of matters in a manner which would not be possible in the larger House & also allows members of the public to have direct input into the parliamentary process by making submissions & attending public hearings.
The following are the Standing Committees of the Legislative

House of Assembly of Nova Scotia: Assembly Matters; Community Services; Economic Development; Human Resources; Internal Affairs; Law Amendments; Private & Local Bills; Public Accounts; Resources; & Veterans Affairs.
Committee Clerk, Kim Langille
Tel: 902-424-5247
Kim.Langille@novascotia.ca
Committee Clerk, Monica Morrison
Tel: 902-424-4494
Monica.Morrison@novascotia.ca
Chair, Standing Committee on Assembly Matters, Hon. Kevin Murphy
Constituency: Eastern Shore, Liberal
Tel: 902-424-5707; *Fax:* 902-424-0632
Hon.Kevin.Murphy@novascotia.ca
Chair, Standing Committee on Community Services, Patricia Arab
Constituency: Fairview-Clayton Park, Liberal
Tel: 902-424-8637; *Fax:* 902-424-0539
info@patriciaarab.com
Chair, Standing Committee on Economic Development, Joachim Stroink
Constituency: Halifax Chebucto, Liberal
Tel: 902-424-8637; *Fax:* 902-424-0539
info@joachimstroink.ca
Chair, Standing Committee on Human Resources, Chuck Porter
Constituency: Hants West, Liberal
Tel: 902-424-8637; *Fax:* 902-424-0539
chuck@chuckporter.ca
Chair, Standing Committee on Internal Affairs, Hon. Stephen McNeil, ECNS
Constituency: Annapolis, Liberal
Tel: 902-424-6600; *Fax:* 902-424-7648
premier@gov.ns.ca
Chair, Standing Committee on Law Amendments, Hon. Diana C. Whalen
Constituency: Clayton Park West, Liberal
Tel: 902-424-4044; *Fax:* 902-424-0510
justmin@novascotia.ca
Chair, Standing Committee on Private & Local Bills, Stephen Gough
Constituency: Sackville-Beaver Bank, Liberal
Tel: 902-424-8637; *Fax:* 902-424-0539
Stephen.Gough@novascotia.ca
Chair, Standing Committee on Public Accounts, Allan MacMaster
Constituency: Inverness, Progressive Conservative
Tel: 902-424-2731; *Fax:* 902-424-7484
mlamacmaster@bellaliant.com
Chair, Standing Committee on Resources, Suzanne Lohnes-Croft
Constituency: Lunenburg, Liberal
Tel: 902-424-8637; *Fax:* 902-424-0539
lunenburgmla@eastlink.ca
Chair, Standing Committee on Veterans Affairs, Derek Mombourquette
Constituency: Sydney-Whitney Pier, Liberal
Tel: 902-424-8637; *Fax:* 902-424-0539
info@mombourquette.ca

Sixty-second General Assembly - Nova Scotia

Province House, 1726 Hollis St., Halifax, NS B3J 2Y3
Tel: 902-424-4661; *Fax:* 902-424-0574
nslegislature.ca

Last General Election, October 8, 2013.
Maximum Duration, 5 years.
Next General Election, 2018.
Party Standings (Sept. 2016):
Liberal 34;
Progressive Conservative 10;
New Democratic Party 6;
Independent 1;
Total: 51.
MLA Remuneration (January 2013):
MLA Indemnity $89,234.90;
Additional Indemnity:
Premier $112,791.20;
Speaker $49,046.51;
Deputy Speaker $24,523.25;
Minister with portfolio $49,046.51;
Minister without portfolio $49,046.51;
Leader of the Opposition $49,046.51;
Leader of a Recognized Opposition Party $24,523.25.
The following list features members, with their constituency, the number of electors on the official list for the 2013 provincial general election, party affiliation, & contact information:

Members of the Legislative Assembly of Nova Scotia

Patricia Arab
Constituency: Fairview-Clayton Park *No. of Constituents:* 15,855, Liberal
Tel: 902-424-8637; *Fax:* 902-424-0539
info@patriciaarab.com
nsliberalcaucus.ca/team/view/38
Other Communications: Constituency Phone: 902-329-8683; Fax: 902-444-7530
Social Media: twitter.com/patriciaarab, www.facebook.com/PatriciaArabMLA
Constituency Office
#203, 3845 Joseph Howe Dr.
Halifax, NS B3I 4H9
Leader, Official Opposition; Leader, Progressive Conservative Party of Nova Scotia, Jamie Baillie
Constituency: Cumberland South *No. of Constituents:* 10,759, Progressive Conservative
Tel: 902-424-2731; *Fax:* 902-424-7484
jamiebaillie@bellaliant.com
www.pccaucus.ns.ca
Other Communications: Constituency Phone: 902-597-1998; Fax: 902-597-8080
Social Media: twitter.com/JamieBaillie, www.facebook.com/jamie.baillie.nspc, www.linkedin.com/profile/view?id=18182112
Constituency Office
6 McFarlane St.
Springhill, NS B0M 1X0
Caucus Whip, New Democratic Party, Sterling Belliveau
Constituency: Queens-Shelburne *No. of Constituents:* 13,686, New Democratic Party
Tel: 902-424-4134; *Fax:* 902-424-0504
mlaqueens-shelb@eastlink.ca
www.sterlingbelliveau.ca
Other Communications: Shelburne: 902-265-3010; Liverpool: 902-356-3073
Social Media: www.facebook.com/sterlingbelliveaumla
Constituency Office
170 Water St.
Shelburne, NS B0T 1W0
Minister, Community Services; Minister, Voluntary Sector; Minister responsible, Advisory Council on the Status of Women Act, & Disabled Persons' Commission Act, Hon. Joanne Bernard
Constituency: Dartmouth North *No. of Constituents:* 14,851, Liberal
Toll-free: 877-424-1177; *Fax:* 902-424-3287
dcsmin@gov.ns.ca
joannebernard.ca
Other Communications: Constituency Phone: 902-444-9693; Fax: 902-444-9694
Social Media: twitter.com/JoanneDNLIB, www.facebook.com/120390951418197
Constituency Office
#102, 260 Wyse Rd.
Dartmouth, NS B3A 1N2
Minister, Education & Early Childhood Development; Chair, Treasury & Policy Board, Hon. Karen Lynn Casey
Constituency: Colchester North *No. of Constituents:* 13,813, Liberal
Tel: 902-424-4236; *Fax:* 902-424-0680
educmin@gov.ns.ca
www.karencasey.ca
Other Communications: Constituency Phone: 902-893-2180; Fax: 902-893-3064
Constituency Office
#10, 30 Duke St.
Truro, NS B2N 2A1
Minister, Municipal Affairs; Minister, Communications Nova Scotia, Hon. Zach Churchill
Constituency: Yarmouth *No. of Constituents:* 13,289, Liberal
Tel: 902-424-5550; *Fax:* 902-424-0581
dmamin@novascotia.ca
nsliberalcaucus.ca/team/view/25
Other Communications: Constituency Phone: 902-742-4444; Fax: 902-742-7391
Social Media: twitter.com/zachchurchill, www.facebook.com/130216460347628
Constituency Office
#100, 396 Main St.
Yarmouth, NS B5A 1E9
Minister, Agriculture; Minister, Fisheries & Aquaculture; Minister responsible, Maritime Provinces Harness Racing Commission Act, Hon. Keith Colwell
Constituency: Preston-Dartmouth *No. of Constituents:* 10,677, Liberal
Tel: 902-424-4388; *Fax:* 902-424-0699
min_dag@gov.ns.ca
nsliberalcaucus.ca/team/view/22
Other Communications: Constituency Phone: 902-433-1494, Fax: 902-435-1712
Social Media: www.facebook.com/keithcolwellNS
Constituency Office
PO Box 1, Comp. 4, 2345 Hwy. 7
East Preston, NS B2Z 1G6
Minister, Finance & Treasury Board; Minister, Gaelic Affairs; Minister responsible, Credit Union Act, Insurance Act, Liquor Control Act, Nova Scotia Liquor Corporation, Securities Act & Utility & Review Board Act, Hon. Randy Delorey
Constituency: Antigonish *No. of Constituents:* 13,653, Liberal
Tel: 902-424-5720; *Fax:* 902-424-0635
FinanceMinister@novascotia.ca
nsliberalcaucus.ca/team/view/27
Other Communications: Constituency Phone: 902-870-5899
Social Media: twitter.com/randydelorey, www.facebook.com/randydeloreyml, ca.linkedin.com/in/randydelorey
Constituency Office
#202, 155 Main St.
Antigonish, NS B2G 2B6
Opposition House Leader, Chris d'Entremont
Constituency: Argyle-Barrington *No. of Constituents:* 6,474, Progressive Conservative
Tel: 902-424-2731; *Fax:* 902-424-7484
info@chrisdentremont.com
www.chrisdentremont.com
Other Communications: Constituency Phone: 902-648-2020, Fax: 902-648-2001
Social Media: twitter.com/ChrisMLA, www.facebook.com/ChrisMLA
Constituency Office
#6, 4200 Hwy. 308
PO Box 94
Tusket, NS B0W 3M0
Minister, Immigration, Hon. Lena M. Diab
Constituency: Halifax Armdale *No. of Constituents:* 11,487, Liberal
Tel: 902-424-5230; *Fax:* 902-424-3178
ImmigrationMinister@novascotia.ca
nsliberalcaucus.ca/team/view/28
Other Communications: Constituency Phone: 902-455-1610; Fax: 902-455-2998
Social Media: twitter.com/LenaDiabMLA, www.facebook.com/lenadiabmla, www.linkedin.com/pub/hon-lena-m-diab-ecns/17/429/218
Constituency Office
#101, 1 Craigmore Dr.
Halifax, NS B3N 0C6
Caucus Chair, Progressive Conservative Party, Hon. Pat Dunn
Constituency: Pictou Centre *No. of Constituents:* 12,896, Progressive Conservative
Tel: 902-424-2731; *Fax:* 902-424-7484
patdunnmla@bellaliant.com
www.pccaucus.ns.ca/member/pat-dunn
Other Communications: Constituency Phone: 902-752-3646
Social Media: www.linkedin.com/pub/pat-dunn/7/678/a9
Constituency Office
#3, 342 Stewart St.
New Glasgow, NS B2H 5E1
Pam Eyking
Constituency: Victoria-The Lakes *No. of Constituents:* 11,670, Liberal
Tel: 902-424-8637; *Fax:* 902-424-0539
Pamela.Eyking@novascotia.ca
nsliberalcaucus.ca/team/view/48
Other Communications: Constituency Phone: 902-736-7263; Fax: 902-736-1930
Social Media: www.facebook.com/pam.eyking
Constituency Office
#7, 15 Alder Point Rd.
Bras d'Or, NS B1Y 2K2
Terry Farrell
Constituency: Cumberland North *No. of Constituents:* 12,585, Liberal
Tel: 902-424-8637; *Fax:* 902-424-0539
terry.farrell@live.com
nsliberalcaucus.ca/team/view/35
Other Communications: Constituency Phone: 902-660-3144; Fax: 902-660-3149
Social Media: twitter.com/TerryEFarrell, www.facebook.com/TerryFarrellCumberlandNorthLiberal
Constituency Office
10B Havelock St.
Amherst, NS B4H 3J7
Minister, Business; Minister, Service Nova Scotia; Minister responsible, Nova Scotia Business Incorporated, Innovation Corporation Act, Part II of the Gaming Control Act & Residential Tenancies Act, Hon. Mark Furey
Constituency: Lunenburg West *No. of Constituents:* 15,592, Liberal
Tel: 902-424-5790; *Fax:* 902-424-0514
BusinessMinister@novascotia.ca
www.markfurey.ca
Other Communications: Constituency Phone: 902-530-3883; Fax: 902-530-3919
Social Media: twitter.com/MarkFurey1, www.facebook.com/MarkFureyLiberal
Constituency Office
425 King St.
Bridgewater, NS B4V 1B1
Minister, Health & Wellness; Minister, Seniors; Chair, Senior Citizens' Secretariat, Hon. Leo A. Glavine
Constituency: Kings West *No. of Constituents:* 14,443, Liberal

Tel: 902-424-3377; *Fax:* 902-424-0559
health.minister@gov.ns.ca
nsliberalcaucus.ca/team/view/18
Other Communications: Constituency Phone: 902-765-4083; Fax: 902-765-4176
Social Media: www.facebook.com/214777192012267
Constituency Office, GW Sampson Bldg.
694 Main St.
PO Box 250
Kingston, NS B0P 1R0

Stephen Gough
Constituency: Sackville-Beaver Bank *No. of Constituents:* 12,437, Liberal
Tel: 902-424-8637; *Fax:* 902-424-0539
Stephen.Gough@novascotia.ca
nsliberalcaucus.ca/team/view/46
Other Communications: Constituency Phone: 902-252-9900; Fax: 902-252-9257
Social Media: twitter.com/StephenAGough
Constituency Office
1000 Sackville Dr.
Sackville, NS B4E 0C2

Larry Harrison
Constituency: Colchester-Musquodoboit Valley *No. of Constituents:* 13,469, Progressive Conservative
Tel: 902-424-2731; *Fax:* 902-424-7484
larryharrisonmla@gmail.com
www.pccaucus.ns.ca/member/larry-harrison
Other Communications: Constituency Phone: 902-639-1010; Fax: 902-639-2598
Social Media: twitter.com/LarryHarrisonPC, www.facebook.com/ElectLarryHarrison
Constituency Office
87 Main St. West
PO Box 219
Stewiacke, NS B0N 2J0

Minister, Natural Resources; Chair, Liberal Caucus, Hon. Lloyd Hines
Constituency: Guysborough-Eastern Shore-Tracadie *No. of Constituents:* 10,142, Liberal
Tel: 902-424-4037; *Fax:* 902-424-0594
mindnr@novascotia.ca
nsliberalcaucus.ca/team/view/39
Other Communications: Constituency Phone: 902-533-2280; Fax: 902-533-3039
Social Media: www.facebook.com/1567347540156289
Constituency Office, Chedabucto Centre
#P-1, 9996 Hwy. 16
PO Box 259
Guysborough, NS B0H 1N0

Bill Horne
Constituency: Waverley-Fall River-Beaverbank *No. of Constituents:* 13,936, Liberal
Tel: 902-424-8637; *Fax:* 902-424-0539
billhornemla@gmail.com
www.billhorne.ca
Other Communications: Constituency Phone: 902-576-3411; Fax: 902-576-3413
Social Media: twitter.com/Bill_Horne_MLA, www.facebook.com/bill.horne.336
Constituency Office
29 Blue Hill Rd.
Fall River, NS B2T 1E6

Tim Houston
Constituency: Pictou East *No. of Constituents:* 11,573, Progressive Conservative
Tel: 902-424-2731; *Fax:* 902-424-7484
tim.houston@mail.com
www.pccaucus.ns.ca/member/tim-houston
Other Communications: Constituency Phone: 902-695-3582
Social Media: twitter.com/TimHouston_, www.facebook.com/houston.timothy
Constituency Office
2042 Queen St.
Westville, NS B0K 2A0

Minister, Communities, Culture & Heritage; Minister, African Nova Scotian Affairs; Minister responsible, Heritage Property Act, Hon. Tony Ince
Constituency: Cole Harbour-Portland Valley *No. of Constituents:* 17,075, Liberal
Tel: 902-424-4889; *Fax:* 902-424-4872
min_cch@novascotia.ca
nsliberalcaucus.ca/team/view/30
Other Communications: Constituency Phone: 902-406-3288
Social Media: twitter.com/rtonyince, www.facebook.com/TonyInceMLA
Constituency Office
#6, 1081 Cole Harbour Rd.
Dartmouth, NS B2V 1E8

Deputy Speaker, Keith Irving
Constituency: Kings South *No. of Constituents:* 16,809, Liberal
Tel: 902-424-8637; *Fax:* 902-424-0539
keith@irvingmla.ca
Other Communications: Constituency Phone: 902-542-0050; Fax: 902-542-3423
Social Media: twitter.com/IrvingMLA, www.facebook.com/IrvingMLA
Constituency Office
#3, 24 Harbourside Dr.
PO Box 2455
Wolfville, NS B4P 2C1

Ben Jessome
Constituency: Hammonds Plains-Lucasville *No. of Constituents:* 11,297, Liberal
Tel: 902-424-8637; *Fax:* 902-424-0539
jessomeben@gmail.com
nsliberalcaucus.ca/team/view/42
Other Communications: Constituency Phone: 902-404-9900; Fax: 902-404-8415
Social Media: twitter.com/BenJessome, www.facebook.com/LiberalsHPL
Constituency Office
#3, 2120 Hammonds Plains Rd.
Hammonds Plains, NS B4B 1P3

Minister, Public Service Commission; Minister, Internal Services; Minister responsible, Sydney Steel Corporation Act, Hon. Labi Kousoulis
Constituency: Halifax Citadel-Sable Island *No. of Constituents:* 12,901, Liberal
Tel: 902-424-5465; *Fax:* 902-424-0555
min_psc@gov.ns.ca
nsliberalcaucus.ca/team/view/32
Other Communications: Constituency Phone: 902-444-8200; Fax: 902-444-8222
Social Media: twitter.com/LabiKousoulis, www.facebook.com/LabiMLA, www.linkedin.com/pub/labi-kousoulis/32/91/a50
Constituency Office, Halifax Professional Centre
#365, 5991 Spring Garden Rd.
Halifax, NS B3H 1Y6

Suzanne Lohnes-Croft
Constituency: Lunenburg *No. of Constituents:* 13,426, Liberal
Tel: 902-424-8637; *Fax:* 902-424-0539
lunenburgmla@eastlink.ca
nsliberalcaucus.ca/team/view/45
Other Communications: Constituency Phone: 902-531-3095; Fax: 902-531-3094
Social Media: www.facebook.com/liberalcandidatelunenburgconstituency, www.linkedin.com/pub/suzanne-lohnes-croft/70/6b1/15
Constituency Office
125A Cornwall Rd.
PO Box 136
Blockhouse, NS B0J 1E0

John A. Lohr
Constituency: Kings North *No. of Constituents:* 15,142, Progressive Conservative
Tel: 902-424-2731; *Fax:* 902-424-7484
johnlohrmla@gmail.com
www.pccaucus.ns.ca/lohr-sworn-mla-kings-north
Other Communications: Constituency Phone: 902-365-3420; Fax: 902-365-3422
Social Media: twitter.com/JohnLohrMLA, www.facebook.com/JohnLohrKingsNorth
Constituency Office
401 Main St., #A
Kentville, NS B4N 1X7

Karla MacFarlane
Constituency: Pictou West *No. of Constituents:* 10,752, Progressive Conservative
Tel: 902-424-2731; *Fax:* 902-424-7484
pictouwestmla@bellaliant.com
www.pccaucus.ns.ca/member/karla-macfarlane
Other Communications: Constituency Phone: 902-485-8958; Fax: 902-485-5135
Social Media: twitter.com/karla_macf_pc, www.facebook.com/VoteKarlaMacFarlane
Constituency Office
25B Front St.
PO Box 310
Pictou, NS B0K 1H0

Minister, Transportation & Infrastructure Renewal; Minister responsible, Sydney Tar Ponds Agency (NS), Hon. Geoff MacLellan
Constituency: Glace Bay *No. of Constituents:* 12,441, Liberal
Tel: 902-424-5875; *Fax:* 902-424-0171
tirmin@novascotia.ca
www.geoffmaclellan.ca
Other Communications: Constituency Phone: 902-842-4390; Fax: 902-842-4389
Social Media: twitter.com/GeoffMacLellan, www.facebook.com/geoffmaclellan
Constituency Office, Peoples Mall
219 Commercial St., #D
Glace Bay, NS B1A 3B9

Whip, Progressive Conservative Party & Deputy Caucus Chair, Alfie MacLeod
Constituency: Sydney River-Mira-Louisbourg *No. of Constituents:* 15,018, Progressive Conservative
Tel: 902-424-2731; *Fax:* 902-424-7484
alfiemacleodmla@ns.aliantzinc.ca
www.pccaucus.ns.ca/member/alfie-macleod
Other Communications: Constituency Phone: 902-564-8679; Fax: 902-564-1204
Social Media: www.facebook.com/ElectAlfieMacLeod
Constituency Office
1990 Kings Rd.
Sydney River, NS B1L 1C4

Allan MacMaster
Constituency: Inverness *No. of Constituents:* 10,796, Progressive Conservative
Tel: 902-424-2731; *Fax:* 902-424-7484
mlamacmaster@bellaliant.com
www.pccaucus.ns.ca/member/allan-macmaster
Other Communications: Constituency Phone: 902-258-2216; Fax: 902-258-3231
Social Media: twitter.com/AllanMacMaster, www.facebook.com/ElectMacMaster
Constituency Office
15759 Central Ave.
Inverness, NS B0E 1N0

Brendan Maguire
Constituency: Halifax Atlantic *No. of Constituents:* 14,104, Liberal
Tel: 902-424-8637; *Fax:* 902-424-0539
brendan@brendanmaguire.ca
nsliberalcaucus.ca/team/view/40
Other Communications: Constituency Phone: 902-444-0147
Social Media: twitter.com/brendanmagu, www.facebook.com/liberalBrendan
Constituency Office
349 Herring Cove Rd., #C
Halifax, NS B3V 1R9

Leader in the House, New Democratic Party of Nova Scotia, Marian Mancini
Constituency: Dartmouth South *No. of Constituents:* 15,845, New Democratic Party
Tel: 902-424-4134; *Fax:* 902-424-0504
MLAMancini@eastlink.ca
Other Communications: Constituency Phone: 902-406-2301; Fax: 902-406-2275
Note: Marian Mancini was elected in a by-election held July 14, 2015.
Constituency Office
#120, 33 Ochterloney St.
Dartmouth, NS B2Y 4R3

Premier & President, Executive Council; Leader, Nova Scotia Liberal Party; Minister, Intergovernmental Affairs; Minister, Planning & Priorities; Minister, Aboriginal Affairs; Minister responsible for Military Relations, Hon. Stephen McNeil, ECNS
Constituency: Annapolis *No. of Constituents:* 15,593, Liberal
Tel: 902-424-6600
Toll-free: 800-317-8533; *Fax:* 902-424-7648
premier@gov.ns.ca
www.liberal.ns.ca/stephen-mcneil
Other Communications: Constituency Phone: 902-825-2093; Fax: 902-825-6306
Social Media: twitter.com/StephenMcNeil, www.facebook.com/StephenMcNeilLiberal
Constituency Office
#2, 291 Marshall St.
PO Box 1420
Middleton, NS B0S 1P0

Minister, Environment, Hon. Margaret Miller
Constituency: Hants East *No. of Constituents:* 17,885, Liberal
Tel: 902-424-8637
Toll-free: 855-383-3465; *Fax:* 902-424-0539
margaretmillermla@bellaliant.net
www.margaretmiller.net
Other Communications: Constituency Phone: 902-883-3465; Fax: 902-883-3293
Social Media: twitter.com/mmillershubie, www.facebook.com/votemargaretmiiller
Constituency Office
#1, 693 Hwy. 2
Elmsdale, NS B2S 1A8

Derek Mombourquette
Constituency: Sydney-Whitney Pier, Liberal
Tel: 902-424-8637; *Fax:* 902-424-0539
info@mombourquette.ca
nsliberalcaucus.ca/team/view/50
Other Communications: Constituency Phone: 902-562-8870; Fax: 902-562-5220
Note: Derek Mombourquette was elected in a by-election held July 14, 2015.
Constituency Office
710 Victoria Rd.
Sydney, NS B1N 1J2

Speaker of the House of Assembly, Hon. Kevin Murphy
Constituency: Eastern Shore *No. of Constituents:* 11,797,

Liberal
Tel: 902-424-5707; *Fax:* 902-424-0632
murphyke@gov.ns.ca
www.kevinmurphy.ca
Other Communications: Constituency Phone: 902-281-3005; Fax: 902-281-3006
Social Media: www.facebook.com/KevinMurphyMLAEasternShore
Constituency Office, Porters Lake Shopping Centre
#9, 5228 Hwy. 7
Porters Lake, NS B3E 1J8

Whip, Progressive Conservative Party, Eddie Orrell
Constituency: Northside-Westmount *No. of Constituents:* 16,367, Progressive Conservative
Tel: 902-424-2731; *Fax:* 902-424-7484
eddieorrell@bellaliant.com
www.pccaucus.ns.ca/member/eddie-orrell
Other Communications: Constituency Phone: 902-794-4847; Fax: 902-794-1815
Social Media: twitter.com/eddieorrell, www.facebook.com/eddie.orrell.9
Constituency Office
#5, 309 Commercial St.
North Sydney, NS B2A 1B9

Deputy House Leader, New Democratic Party, Denise P. Peterson-Rafuse
Constituency: Chester-St. Margaret's *No. of Constituents:* 14,613, New Democratic Party
Tel: 902-424-4134
Toll-free: 877-740-3378; *Fax:* 902-424-0504
denisepetersmla@bellaliant.com
www.denisepetersonrafusemla.ca
Other Communications: Constituency Phone: 902-857-3378, Fax: 902-857-3386
Social Media: twitter.com/deniseprafuse, www.facebook.com/DeniseMLA
Constituency Office
#4, 3794 Hwy. 3, RR1
Chester, NS B0J 1J0

Chuck Porter
Constituency: Hants West *No. of Constituents:* 14,726, Liberal
Tel: 902-424-8637; *Fax:* 902-424-0539
chuck@chuckporter.ca
www.chuckporter.ca
Other Communications: Constituency Phone: 902-798-5779; Fax: 902-798-4093
Social Media: www.facebook.com/chuck.porter.102
Constituency Office
58 Gerrish St.
PO Box 3873
Windsor, NS B0N 2T0

Iain Rankin
Constituency: Timberlea-Prospect *No. of Constituents:* 14,811, Liberal
Tel: 902-424-8637; *Fax:* 902-424-0539
info@iainrankin.ca
iainrankin.ca
Other Communications: Constituency Phone: 902-404-7036; Fax: 902-404-7056
Social Media: twitter.com/IainTRankin, www.facebook.com/IainRankinMLA, www.linkedin.com/pub/iain-rankin/10/a72/925
Constituency Office
#100, 1268 St. Margaret's Bay Rd.
Beechville, NS B3T 1A7

Minister, Labour & Advanced Education; Minister responsible, Apprenticeship & Trades Qualifications Act, the Workers' Compensation Act (except Part II) & Youth, Hon. Kelly Regan
Constituency: Bedford *No. of Constituents:* 17,719, Liberal
Tel: 902-424-6647; *Fax:* 902-424-0575
min_lae@novascotia.ca
www.kellyregan.ca
Other Communications: Constituency Phone: 902-407-3777, Fax: 902-407-3779
Social Media: twitter.com/KellyReganNS, www.facebook.com/kellyreganns
Constituency Office
#555, 1550 Bedford Hwy.
Bedford, NS B4A 1E6

Lisa Roberts
Constituency: Halifax Needham, NDP
Tel: 902-424-4131; *Fax:* 902-424-0504
Social Media: twitter.com/lisarobertshfx, www.facebook.com/lisarobertshalifax
Note: Lisa Roberts won a by-election on August 30, 2016.

Minister, Energy; Minister, Acadian Affairs; Minister responsible, Part I of the Gaming Control Act; Government House Leader, Hon. Michel Samson, ECNS
Constituency: Cape Breton-Richmond *No. of Constituents:* 10,882, Liberal
Tel: 902-424-7793; *Fax:* 902-424-3265
energyminister@novascotia.ca
nsliberalcaucus.ca/team/view/20
Other Communications: Constituency Phone: 902-345-0778, Fax: 902-345-0779
Social Media: twitter.com/msamsonliberal, www.facebook.com/michel.samson.mla
Note: Hon. Michel Samson also assumed the portfolios of Energy, Communications Nova Scotia & Part I of the Gaming Control Act after Andrew Younger took a leave of absence on Dec. 23, 2014.
Constituency Office, Richmond Industrial Mall, 2nd Fl.
PO Box 57
Louisdale, NS B0E 1V0

Joachim Stroink
Constituency: Halifax Chebucto *No. of Constituents:* 15,719, Liberal
Tel: 902-424-8637; *Fax:* 902-424-0539
info@joachimstroink.ca
www.joachimstroink.com
Other Communications: Constituency Phone: 902-405-7802; Fax: 902-405-7804
Social Media: twitter.com/joachimstroink, www.facebook.com/JoachimStroink
Constituency Office
6270 Quinpool Rd.
Halifax, NS B3L 1A3

Joyce Treen
Constituency: Cole Harbour-Eastern Passage *No. of Constituents:* 13,892, Liberal
Tel: 902-424-8637; *Fax:* 902-424-0539
joycetreen@bellaliant.com
nsliberalcaucus.ca/team/view/34
Other Communications: Constituency Phone: 902-465-1888; Fax: 902-465-1890
Constituency Office
1515 Main Rd.
PO Box 371
Eastern Passage, NS B3G 1M7

Deputy Premier & Deputy President, Executive Council; Attorney General & Minister, Justice; Minister responsible, NS Police Complaints Commissioner, NS Police Review Board & Elections, Human Rights, Regulations, Workers' Comp. & Uniform Closing Day Acts, Hon. Diana C. Whalen
Constituency: Clayton Park West *No. of Constituents:* 16,578, Liberal
Tel: 902-424-4044; *Fax:* 902-424-0510
justmin@novascotia.ca
www.dianawhalen.com
Other Communications: Constituency Phone: 902-443-8318; Fax: 902-445-9287
Social Media: twitter.com/dianawhalenNS, www.facebook.com/dianawhalenNS
Constituency Office
#303, 287 Lacewood Dr.
Halifax, NS B3M 3Y7

House Leader, New Democratic Party, Dave Wilson
Constituency: Sackville-Cobequid *No. of Constituents:* 14,732, New Democratic Party
Tel: 902-424-4134; *Fax:* 902-424-0504
davewilsonmla@eastlink.ca
www.davidawilsonmla.ca
Other Communications: Constituency Phone: 902-864-0396; Fax: 902-864-8409
Social Media: www.facebook.com/davidawilsonmla
Constituency Office
#105, 51 Cobequid Rd.
Lower Sackville, NS B4C 2N1

Deputy Speaker, Gordon L. Wilson
Constituency: Clare-Digby *No. of Constituents:* 13,913, Liberal
Tel: 902-424-8637; *Fax:* 902-424-0539
info@claredigby.ca
nsliberalcaucus.ca/team/view/33
Other Communications: Little Brook: 902-769-6683; Conway: 902-245-5300
Social Media: twitter.com/gordonwilsonlns, www.facebook.com/GordonWilsonLiberal
Constituency Office
PO Box 111
Church Point, NS B01 1M0

David Wilton
Constituency: Cape Breton Centre, Liberal
Tel: 902-424-8637; *Fax:* 902-424-0539
davidwiltonmla@bellaliant.com
nsliberalcaucus.ca/team/view/51
Other Communications: Constituency Phone: 902-862-3338; Fax: 902-862-2665
Note: David Wilton was elected in a by-election held July 14, 2015.
Constituency Office
3372 Plummer Ave.
New Waterford, NS B1H 1Y7

Andrew Younger
Constituency: Dartmouth East *No. of Constituents:* 14,411, Independent
www.andrewyounger.ca
Other Communications: Constituency Phone: 902-406-4420; Fax: 902-406-4421
Social Media: twitter.com/AndrewMLA, www.facebook.com/NSYounger
Note: Andrew Younger was removed from cabinet & caucus on Nov. 5, 2015, due to issues surrounding his testimony in the trial of a woman accused of assaulting him. He now sits as an Independent.
Constituency Office
#600, 73 Tacoma Dr.
Dartmouth, NS B2W 376

Caucus Chair, New Democratic Party, Lenore Zann
Constituency: Truro-Bible Hill-Millbrook-Salmon River *No. of Constituents:* 15,424, New Democratic Party
Tel: 902-424-4134; *Fax:* 902-424-0504
lenorezannmla@bellaliant.com
www.mlalenorezann.ca
Other Communications: Constituency Phone: 902-897-9266; Fax: 902-897-1841
Social Media: www.facebook.com/LenoreZannMLA
Constituency Office, BMO Bldg.
#212, 35 Commercial St.
Truro, NS B2N 3H9

Nova Scotia Government Departments & Agencies

Office of Aboriginal Affairs

5251 Duke St., 5th Fl., PO Box 1617 Halifax, NS B3J 2Y3
Tel: 902-424-7409; *Fax:* 902-424-4225
oaa@gov.ns.ca
www.novascotia.ca/abor

The Office undertakes activities that increase the level of pubic awareness of Aboriginal people & the issues they face. It also works collaboratively with Aboriginal communities & organizations & other levels of government to coordinate Aboriginal & tri-partite initiatives, develop strategies, & build & maintain a sustainable foundation for Aboriginal-Government relations. As of April 2015, the Office oversees the Aboriginal Community Development Fund.

Minister, Hon. Stephen McNeil
Tel: 902-424-6600; *Fax:* 902-424-7648
Deputy Minister/Chief Executive Officer, Julie Towers
Tel: 902-424-7662
Executive Director, Justin Huston
Tel: 902-424-4214
Director, Negotiations, Owen Everts-Lind
Tel: 902-424-5967
Director, Consultation, Heather Potter
Tel: 902-424-4174
Director, Policy, Clary Reardon
Tel: 902-424-4931

Office of Acadian Affairs / Affaires acadiennes

Dennis Building, 1741 Brunswick St., PO Box 682 Halifax, NS B3J 2T3
Tel: 902-424-0497; *Fax:* 902-428-0124
Toll-Free: 866-382-5811
bonjour@novascotia.ca
acadien.novascotia.ca
twitter.com/GouvNE
www.facebook.com/Affairesacadiennes

The mission of the Office of Acadian Affairs is to offer advice & support to departments, offices, agencies, & Crown corporations so they can develop & adapt policies, programs, & services that reflect the needs of the Acadian & francophone community of Nova Scotia.

Minister, Hon. Michel Samson, ECNS
Tel: 902-424-0497; *Fax:* 902-428-0124
min-oaa@gov.ns.ca
Executive Director, Mark Bannerman

Office of African Nova Scotian Affairs (ANSA)

1741 Brunswick St., 3rd Fl., PO Box 456 Stn. Central, Halifax, NS B3J 2R5
Tel: 902-424-5555; *Fax:* 902-424-7189
Toll-Free: 866-580-2672
ansa_newsletter@novascotia.ca
ansa.novascotia.ca
twitter.com/OfficeofANSA
www.facebook.com/AfricanNSAffairs

The mission of the Office of African Nova Scotian Affairs is to serve as a broker between community members & government, & to advocate for cross-cultural understanding.

Minister, Hon. Tony Ince
Tel: 902-424-5555; *Fax:* 902-424-7189
Chief Executive Officer, Wayn Hamilton
Tel: 902-424-6643

Regional Offices

Sydney - Cape Breton

Sydney Commerce Towers, #501, 15 Dorchester St., Sydney, NS B1P 5Y9

Tel: 902-563-3735; *Fax:* 902-563-2700

Nova Scotia Department of Agriculture

1800 Argyle St., 6th Fl., PO Box 2223 Halifax, NS B3J 3C4

Tel: 902-424-4560; *Fax:* 902-424-4671
www.novascotia.ca/agri
twitter.com/NSAgriculture

The Department of Agriculture has a legislated mandate to support & develop the agriculture & food industries, recognizing that these sectors are economic engines of Nova Scotia's rural communities. Fosters prosperous & sustainable agriculture & food industries through the delivery of quality public services for the betterment of rural communities in Nova Scotia.

Minister, Hon. Keith Colwell
Tel: 902-424-4388; *Fax:* 902-424-0699
min_dag@gov.ns.ca

Deputy Minister, Kim MacNeil
Tel: 902-424-2386
Kim.MacNeil@novascotia.ca

Director, Communications, Michael Noonan
Tel: 902-424-0192
Michael.Noonan@novascotia.ca

Secretary to Minister, Yvelle Poirier
Tel: 902-424-4388
Yvelle.Poirier@novascotia.ca

Associated Agencies, Boards & Commissions:

•Agricultural Marshland Conservation Commission
nslegislature.ca/legc/statutes/agricmar.htm
The Commission advises the Minister of Agriculture on the conservation & protection of marshland, its development & use in agriculture.

•Crop & Livestock Arbitration Board
The Board deals with loss disputes between the Nova Scotia Crop & Livestock Insurance Commission & insured persons.

•Farm Practices Board
www.novascotia.ca/just/regulations/regs/fprbrd.htm
The Board makes decisions on normal farm practices, as well as conducting studies & preparing reports on the matter.

•Farm Registration Appeal Board
The Board hears appeals under the Farm Registration Act & decides whether an organization meets the criteria for a general farm organization.

•Livestock Health Services Board
nslegislature.ca/legc/statutes/livstkhs.htm
The Board advises the minister on livestock health policies.

•Maritime Provinces Harness Racing Commission
5 Gerald McCarville Dr.
PO Box 128
Kensington, PE C0B 1M0
Tel: 902-836-5500; *Fax:* 902-836-5320
www.mphrc.ca
The Commission governs, regulates, & supervises harness racing in all of its forms relevant & related to pari-mutuel betting.

•Natural Products Marketing Council
179 College Rd.
PO Box 890
Truro, NS B2N 5G6
Tel: 902-893-6511; *Fax:* 902-893-6573
The Council, an agency of the NS Government, is responsible for the administration of the Natural Products Act & the Dairy Industry Act. Ten marketing boards are established under the Natural Products Act & the Dairy Farmers of Nova Scotia is established under the Dairy Industry Act. These boards are producer elected & the Council delegates or regulates authority to them specific to their farm product. The Council is a regulatory & supervisory body, a major role of which is to balance industry interests with teh broader public interest.

•Nova Scotia Crop & Livestock Insurance Commission
60 Research Dr., #A
PO Box 1092
Truro, NS B2N 5G9
Tel: 902-893-6370
Toll-free: 800-565-6371
nsclic@gov.ns.ca
Under the Crop & Livestock Insurance Act, the Commission is responsible for administering the program under the direction, supervision, & control of the Minister of Agriculture.

•Nova Scotia Farm Loan Board
PO Box 890
Truro, NS B2N 5G6
Tel: 902-893-6506; *Fax:* 902-895-7693
FLBNS@gov.ns.ca
novascotia.ca/farmloan
Other Communication: Kentville location: Phone: 902-679-6009, Fax: 902-679-4997
The Nova Scotia Farm Loan Board operates as a Corporation of the Crown & supports the development of sustainable agriculture & agri-rural business in Nova Scotia through responsible lending.

Agriculture & Food Operations Branch

The Agriculture & Food Operations branch is responsible for advisory services & outreach, regional services, provincial programming & protection services.

Executive Director, Vacant
Tel: 902-893-6591

Director, Agriculture, Food & Advisory Services, Loretta Robichaud
Tel: 902-893-7534

Policy & Corporate Services Branch

Responsible for procurement, leasing, building management & occupational health & safety; planning, policy & legislative development; research & analytics; Crown agencies; & programs & business risk management.

Executive Director, Policy & Corporate Services, Vacant

Director, Programs & Business Risk Management, Vacant
Tel: 902-893-4518

Director, Policy & Planning, Ernest Walker
Tel: 902-896-4870
Ernest.Walker@novascotia.ca

Acting Manager, Corporate Services, Chris Hamilton
Tel: 902-896-4878

Office of the Auditor General

Royal Centre, #400, 5161 George St., Halifax, NS B3J 1M7

Tel: 902-424-5907; *Fax:* 902-424-4350
www.oag-ns.ca

The mission of the Auditor General is to make a significant contribution to enhanced accountability & performance in the provincial sector. The Auditor General serves the public interest as the House of Assembly's primary source of assurance on government performance.

Auditor General, Michael Pickup, CPA, CA
Tel: 902-424-4046
Michael.Pickup@novascotia.ca

Deputy Auditor General, Terry M. Spicer, CPA, CMA
Tel: 902-424-8565
Terry.Spicer@novascotia.ca

Nova Scotia Department of Business

Centennial Building, #600, 1660 Hollis St., PO Box 2311 Halifax, NS B3J 3C8

Tel: 902-424-0377; *Fax:* 902-424-0500
business@novascotia.ca
novascotia.ca/business
twitter.com/ns_dob

The Department of Business was created with the 2015-2016 Budget, absorbing responsibilities formerly held by the Department of Economic & Rural Development & Tourism. Aligned with the Office of Regulatory & Service Effectiveness, the Department has three main focus areas: business strategy & planning; strategic projects & investments; & operational leadership, coordination & alignment. Its main objective is economic growth.

Minister, Hon. Mark Furey
Tel: 902-424-5790; *Fax:* 902-424-0514
BusinessMinister@novascotia.ca

Deputy Minister, Business; Deputy Minister, Energy, Murray Coolican
Tel: 902-424-2901; *Fax:* 902-424-0619
Murray.Coolican@novascotia.ca

Director, Regional Development, Jeannie Chow
Tel: 902-424-2904

Director, Issues Management, Jennifer L'Esperance
Tel: 902-424-8604

Director, Sector Development, Gregory Landry
Tel: 902-424-4446

Associated Agencies, Boards & Commissions:

•Canada-Nova Scotia Offshore Petroleum Board (CNSOPB)
TD Centre
1791 Barrington St., 8th Fl.
Halifax, NS B3J 3K9
Tel: 902-422-5588; *Fax:* 902-422-1799
info@cnsopb.ns.ca
www.cnsopb.ns.ca
Created in 1990, the Canada - Nova Scotia Offshore Petroleum Board regulates petroleum activities in the Nova Scotia Offshore Area.
The following are some of the responsibilities of the Board: protecting the environment; overseeing the health & safety of offshore workers; managing the conservation of offshore petroleum resources; issuing licences for offshore exploration & development; collecting & distributing data; & complying with provisions of the *Accord Acts* that deal with employment & industrial benefits.

•Halifax Convention Centre Corporation
Tel: 902-421-8686
sales@halifaxconventioncentre.com
www.halifaxconventioncentre.com

•Innovacorp
#1400, 1801 Hollis St.
Halifax, NS B3J 3N4
Tel: 902-424-8670; *Fax:* 902-424-4679
Toll-free: 800-565-7051
info@innovacorp.ca
www.innovacorp.ns.ca
A network of business resources for the early stage technology entrepreneur. Key services include research & development support, business advice, investment & partnership advice. Focuses on two main growth sectors: life sciences & information technology. In April 2015, Innovacorp assumed responsibility for the following programs after the dissolution of Economic & Rural Development & Tourism: Innovation & Business Competitiveness Fund; Production & Innovation Voucher; & Early Stage Commercialization.

•Nova Scotia Business Inc. (NSBI)
World Trade & Convention Centre
#701, 1800 Argyle St.
PO Box 2374
Halifax, NS B3J 3N8
Tel: 902-424-6650; *Fax:* 902-424-5739
Toll-free: 800-260-6682
info@nsbi.ca
www.novascotiabusiness.com
NSBI is the first point of contact for local companies that want to grow in Nova Scotia, & for international companies that have heard about the province & want to know more. As of April 2015, NSBI is responsible for International Commerce Programs & the Small Business Program Development Program, formerly overseen by Economic & Rural Development & Tourism. It also absorbed the mandate of Film & Creative Industries Nova Scotia (formerly Film Nova Scotia).

•Nova Scotia Utility & Review Board
See Entry Name Index for detailed listing.

•Tourism Nova Scotia (TNS)
See Entry Name Index for detailed listing.

•Trade Centre Limited (TCL)
1800 Argyle St.
PO Box 955
Halifax, NS B3J 2V9
Tel: 902-421-8686; *Fax:* 902-422-2922
www.tradecentrelimited.com
Trade Centre Limited attracts & hosts meetings, conventions, entertainment, cultural & sporting events.

•Waterfront Development Corporation Ltd.
The Cable Wharf
1751 Lower Water St., 2nd Fl.
Halifax, NS B3J 1S5
Tel: 902-422-6591; *Fax:* 902-422-7582
info@wdcl.ca
www.my-waterfront.ca
Coordinates the commercial & recreational development of the downtown waterfront of Halifax & Dartmouth.

Regional/Service Offices

Amherst
35 Church St., Amherst, NS B4H 4A1
Tel: 902-667-3233; *Fax:* 902-667-1452

Antigonish
#4, 149 Church St., Antigonish, NS B2G 2E2
Tel: 902-863-7539; *Fax:* 902-863-7477

Bridgewater
Lunenburg Queens Economic Centre, 373 King St., Bridgewater, NS B4V 1B1
Tel: 902-530-3117

Halifax
Centennial Building, #600, 1660 Hollis St., PO Box 2311 Halifax, NS B3J 1V7
Tel: 902-424-2720; *Fax:* 902-424-0508

Kentville
#103, 35 Webster St., Kentville, NS B4N 1H4
Tel: 902-679-6116; *Fax:* 902-679-6094

New Glasgow
980 East River Rd., New Glasgow, NS B3H 3S8
Tel: 902-755-7040; *Fax:* 902-755-4018

Port Hawkesbury
#3, 32 Paint St., PO Box 219 Port Hawkesbury, NS B9A 3J8
Tel: 902-625-3200; *Fax:* 902-625-3069

Shelburne
Loyalist Plaza, #5, 218 Water St., Shelburne, NS B0T 1W0
Tel: 902-875-7425

Sydney
#207, 275 Charlotte St., Sydney, NS B1P 1C6
Tel: 902-563-2070; *Fax:* 902-563-0500

Truro
#3, 80 Walker St., Truro, NS B2N 4A7
Tel: 902-893-6212; *Fax:* 902-893-6108

Windsor
80 Water St., PO Box 488 Windsor, NS B0N 2T0
Tel: 902-798-6961; *Fax:* 902-798-6962

Yarmouth
Pier One Complex, 103 Water St., Yarmouth, NS B5A 4P4
Tel: 902-742-8404; *Fax:* 902-742-0019

Communications Nova Scotia

1723 Hollis St., 3rd Fl., PO Box 608 Halifax, NS B3J 2R7
Tel: 902-424-7690; *Fax:* 902-424-0515
novascotia.ca/cns

Communications Nova Scotia strives to help Nova Scotians understand what their government is doing & why. They provide a complete range of professional communications services to provincial government departments, agencies, boards & commissions.

Minister, Hon. Zach Churchill
Tel: 902-424-5550; *Fax:* 902-424-0581
cnsminister@novascotia.ca

Deputy Minister, Laura Lee Langley
Tel: 902-424-8940; *Fax:* 902-424-0667
LauraLee.Langley@novascotia.ca

Director, Communications, Wendy Barnable
Tel: 902-424-4536

Director, Communications, Carla Burns
Tel: 902-424-2876

Director, Policy & Corporate Services, Angela Campbell
Tel: 902-424-2878

Director, Communications, Daniel Davis
Tel: 902-424-8978

Director, Communications, Carla Grant
Tel: 902-424-6282

Director, Communications, Tina Thibeau
Tel: 902-424-2727

Director, Communications, Mary Anna Jollymore
Tel: 902-424-2354

Director, Production, Catherine MacIsaac
Tel: 902-424-6283

Director, Communications, Michelle Lucas
Tel: 902-424-3731

Director, Communications, Catherine MacIsaac
Tel: 902-424-6283

Director, Communications, Susan McKeage
Tel: 902-424-7942

Director, Image Services, Brian Murray
Tel: 902-424-6695

Director, Communications, Kristen Tynes-MacEachern
Tel: 902-424-4038

Director, Communications, Natalie Joy Webster
Tel: 902-424-7280

Director, Communications, William Westheuser
Tel: 902-424-4977

Nova Scotia Department of Communities, Culture & Heritage

1741 Brunswick St., 3rd Fl., PO Box 456 Stn. Central, Halifax, NS B3J 2R5
Tel: 902-424-2170
cch@novascotia.ca
cch.novascotia.ca
twitter.com/NS_CCH/cch

The Department of Communities, Culture & Heritage is responsible for contributing to the well-being & prosperity of Nova Scotia's diverse & creative communities through the promotion, development, preservation & celebration of culture, heritage, identity & languages, & by providing leadership, expertise, & innovation to stakeholders. As of April 2015, the Department oversees the Community Access Program.

Minister, Hon. Tony Ince
Tel: 902-424-4889; *Fax:* 902-424-4872
min_cch@novascotia.ca

Deputy Minister, Tracey Taweel
Tel: 902-424-4938; *Fax:* 902-424-4872
Tracey.Taweel@novascotia.ca

Director, Communities Nova Scotia, Natasha Jackson
Tel: 902-424-3480

Director, Innovations & Collections, Stephanie Smith
Tel: 902-424-6523

Director, Strategic Planning, Peggy Tibbo-Cameron
Tel: 902-424-4378

Associated Agencies, Boards & Commissions:

•Art Gallery of Nova Scotia (AGNS)
1723 Hollis St.
PO Box 2262
Halifax, NS B3J 3C8
Tel: 902-424-5280; *Fax:* 902-424-7359
infodesk@gov.ns.ca
www.artgalleryofnovascotia.ca
Other Communication: Security Desk, Phone: 902-424-8459; E-mail: security@gov.ns.ca

•Nova Scotia Museum (NSM)
1747 Summer St.
Halifax, NS B3H 3A6
Fax: 902-424-0560
museum@gov.ns.ca
museum.novascotia.ca
Operates a family of 27 museums throughout the province.

•Nova Scotia Provincial Lotteries & Casino Corporation (NSPLCC)
Summit Place
1601 Lower Water St., 5th Fl.
PO Box 1501
Halifax, NS B3J 2Y3
Tel: 902-424-2203; *Fax:* 902-424-0724
www.gamingns.ca
The Corporation monitors the gaming industry in Nova Scotia along with Atlantic Lottery Corporation & Great Canadian Gaming Corporation, ensuring that it is economically & socially responsible.

NS Archives

6016 University Ave., Halifax, NS B3H 1W4
Tel: 902-424-6060; *Fax:* 902-424-0628
nsarm@gov.ns.ca
novascotia.ca/archives
twitter.com/NS_Archives
www.facebook.com/novascotiaarchives
www.youtube.com/NSArchives

As a documentary heritage institution for the province, the NS Archives serves as the permanent repository for the archival records of the government of Nova Scotia; acquires & preserves provincially significant archival records from the private sector; delivers a range of professional, client-centred reference services; develops & maintains two websites; & provides strategic support & financial assistance to strengthen the provincial archival community.

Provincial Archivist, Lois Yorke
Tel: 902-424-6068

Heritage Division

The mission of Heritage Division is to protect, enhance, & celebrate heritage for all Nova Scotians & for future generations.

Executive Director, Culture & Heritage Development, Marcel McKeough
Tel: 902-424-6393
marcel.mckeough@novascotia.ca

Executive Director, Archives, Museums & Libraries, Rhonda Walker
Tel: 902-424-4986
rhonda.walker@novascotia.ca

Nova Scotia Department of Community Services

Nelson Place, 5675 Spring Garden Rd., 8th Fl., PO Box 696 Halifax, NS B3J 2T7
Toll-Free: 877-424-1177
www.novascotia.ca/coms
twitter.com/NS_DCS

The Department of Community Services is committed to a sustainable social service system that promotes the independence, self-reliance & security of the people it serves.

Minister; Minister, Voluntary Sector, Hon. Joanne Bernard;
Fax: 902-424-3287
dcsmin@gov.ns.ca

Deputy Minister, Lynn Carey Hartwell
Tel: 902-424-3224

Associate Deputy Minister, Nancy MacLellan
Tel: 902-424-5181

Director, Policy, Planning & Research, Brenda Murray
Tel: 902-424-2623

Executive Director, Children & Family Services, Victoria Wood
Tel: 902-424-5653

Director, Accounting & Control, Brian Holley
Tel: 902-424-6156

Project Director, Community Services, Katherine Isnor
Tel: 902-424-4260

Director, Policy, Planning & Strategic Intiatives, Patricia Gorham
Tel: 902-424-3306

Associated Agencies, Boards & Commissions:

•Cape Breton Island Housing Authority
18 Dolbin St.
PO Box 1372
Sydney, NS B1P 6K3
Tel: 902-539-8520; *Fax:* 902-539-0330
Toll-free: 800-565-3135
The Authority oversees Cape Breton, Richmond, Inverness & Victoria Counties.

•Cobequid Housing Authority
114 Victoria East
PO Box 753
Amherst, NS B4H 4B9
Tel: 902-667-8757; *Fax:* 902-667-1686
Toll-free: 800-934-2445
Other Communication: Truro Office Phone: 902-893-7235; Fax: 902-897-1149; Toll-Free Phone: 1-877-846-0440
The Authority oversees Cumberland & Colchester Counties.

•Eastern Mainland Housing Authority
161 Terra Cotta Dr.
New Glasgow, NS B2H 6B6
Tel: 902-752-1225; *Fax:* 902-752-1315
Toll-free: 800-933-2101
The Authority oversees Antigonish, Guysborough & Pictou Counties.

•Metropolitan Regional Housing Authority
MacDonald Bldg.
2131 Gottingen St., 5th Fl.
Halifax, NS B3K 5Z7
Tel: 902-420-6000; *Fax:* 902-420-6020
Toll-free: 800-565-8859
Other Communication: Applications Phone: 902-420-6017
The Authority oversees all of Halifax Regional Municipality.

•Nova Scotia Disabled Persons Commission (NSDPC)
Dartmouth Professional Center
#104, 277 Pleasant St.
Dartmouth, NS B2Y 4B7
Tel: 902-424-8280
Toll-free: 800-565-8280
TTY: 877-996-9954
www.gov.ns.ca/disa
The NSDPC gives people with disabilities a way to participate in the provincial government policy-making process. Its mission is to champion the social & economic inclusion of citizens with disabilities.

•Western Regional Housing Authority
25 Kentucky Ct.
New Minas, NS B4N 4N1
Tel: 902-681-3179; *Fax:* 902-681-0806
Toll-free: 800-441-0447
Other Communication: Middleton Phone: 902-825-3481; Bridgewater Phone: 902-543-8200; Yarmouth Phone: 902-742-4369
The Authority oversees the Counties of Annapolis, Kings, part of Hants, Lunenburg & Queens Regional Municipality, as well as the Counties of Digby, Yarmouth & Shelburne. It is responsible for the areas previously covered by the South Shore Housing Authority, the Annapolis Valley Housing Authority &d the Tri-County Housing Authority.

Children, Youth & Families

www.novascotia.ca/coms/families

Director, Child Protection Services, Wendy Marie Leiper
Tel: 902-424-7433

Employment Support & Income Assistance

www.novascotia.ca/coms/employment

The Employment Support & Income Assistance (ESIA) program helps by giving money for living costs, or providing other kinds of help, when individuals are unable to support themselves or their family.

Director, Income Assistance, Denise MacDonald-Billard
Tel: 902-679-4394

Director, Employment Support Services, Randall Acker
Tel: 902-541-1270

Housing Nova Scotia

#3, 3770 Kempt Rd., Halifax, NS B3K 4X8
Tel: 902-424-8445
housing.novascotia.ca

A provincial corporation that oversees the five Housing Authorities within the province. The corporation's mandate is to ensure all residents of Nova Scotia have access to affordable housing in communities that offer needed services, supports & opportunities.

Chief Executive Officer, Dan MacDougall

Director, Properties & Facilities, Charles E. Lake
Tel: 902-424-6028
Director, Housing, Neil MacDonald
Tel: 902-424-2409

Services for Persons with Disabilities
www.novascotia.ca/coms/disabilities
The SPD Program serves children, youth & adults with intellectual disabilities, long-term mental illness, & physical disabilities in a range of community-based, residential & vocational/day programs.
Director, Lorna McPherson
Tel: 902-424-3787

Regional Offices
Central
PO Box 2561 Halifax, NS B3J 3N5
Tel: 902-424-5110; *Fax:* 902-424-2091
Toll-Free: 800-774-5130
Eastern
Provincial Bldg., #25, 360 Prince St., Sydney, NS B1P 5L1
Tel: 902-563-3302; *Fax:* 902-563-5693
Regional Administrator, Cyril Leblanc
Tel: 902-563-2125
Northern
161 Terra Cotta Dr., New Glasgow, NS B2H 6B6
Tel: 902-755-7023; *Fax:* 902-752-5088
Western
460 Main St., Kentville, NS B4N 1L2
Tel: 902-679-6715; *Fax:* 902-679-6127

Council of Atlantic Premiers (CAP)

Council Secretariat, #1006, 5161 George St., PO Box 2044 Halifax, NS B3J 2Z1
Tel: 902-424-7590; *Fax:* 902-424-8976
info@cap-cpma.ca
www.cap-cpma.ca
The Premiers of New Brunswick, Newfoundland & Labrador, Nova Scotia & Prince Edward Island constitute the Council. It was established by memorandum of understanding to: promote unity of purpose among their respective Governments; ensure maximum coordination of the activities of the Governments & their agencies; & establish a framework for joint action & undertakings. The Council meets up to four times annually to discuss matters of mutual interest or concern to the four Atlantic governments. A Secretariat acts as the focal point for coordinating the efforts of the four Governments in identifying potential benefits that could result from a regional approach to policy formulation & program development.
Secretary to Council, Tim Porter
Tel: 902-424-7600
tporter@cap-cpma.ca
Chief Financial Officer, Rod Casey
Tel: 902-424-5078
rcasey@cap-cpma.ca

Associated Agencies, Boards & Commissions:
•Council of Atlantic Ministers of Education & Training
PO Box 2044
Halifax, NS B3J 2Z1
Tel: 902-424-5352; *Fax:* 902-424-8976
camet-camef@cap-cpma.ca
www.camet-camef.ca
•Maritime Provinces Higher Education Commission (MPHEC) / Commission de l'engseignement supérieur des Provinces Maritimes (CESPM)
#401, 82 Westmorland
PO Box 6000
Fredericton, PE E3B 5H1
Tel: 506-453-2844; *Fax:* 506-453-2106
mphec@mphec.ca
www.mphec.ca
As an Agency of the Council of Atlantic Premiers that provides advice to Ministers responsible for Post-Secondary Education in the Maritimes, the Commission assists institutions & governments in enhancing a post-secondary learning environment that reflects quality, accessibility, mobility, relevance, accountability, scholarship & research.

Nova Scotia Department of Education & Early Childhood Development

Trade Mart Bldg., 2021 Brunswick St., PO Box 578 Halifax, NS B3J 2S9
Tel: 902-424-5168; *Fax:* 902-424-0511
Toll-Free: 888-825-7770
www.ednet.ns.ca
Other Communication: Early Years URL:
www.ednet.ns.ca/earlyyears
twitter.com/nseducation
The mission of the Department of Education is to provide excellence in education & training for personal fulfillment & for a productive, prosperous society.
Minister, Hon. Karen Lynn Casey
Tel: 902-424-4236; *Fax:* 902-424-0680
educmin@novascotia.ca
Deputy Minister, Sandra McKenzie
Tel: 902-424-2912
Director, Finance, Jan Jollymore
Tel: 902-424-8602

Associated Agencies, Boards & Commissions:
•Annapolis Valley Regional School Board (AVRSB)
121 Orchard St.
PO Box 340
Berwick, NS B0P 1E0
Tel: 902-538-4600; *Fax:* 902-538-4630
Toll-free: 800-850-3887
www.avrsb.ca
•Cape Breton-Victoria Regional School Board (CB-VRSB)
275 George St.
Sydney, NS BIP IJ7
Tel: 902-564-8293; *Fax:* 902-564-0123
www.cbv.ns.ca
•Chignecto-Central Regional School Board (CCRSB)
60 Lorne St.
Truro, NS B2N 3K3
Toll-free: 800-770-0008
www.ccrsb.ca
•Conseil scolaire acadien provincial (CSAP)
CP 88
Saulnierville, NS B0W 2Z0
Tél: 902-769-5458; *Téléc:* 902-769-5459
Ligne sans frais: 888-533-2727
csap.ednet.ns.ca
•Halifax Regional School Board (HRSB)
33 Spectacle Lake Dr.
Dartmouth, NS B3B 1X7
Tel: 902-464-2000
www.hrsb.ca
•South Shore Regional School Board (SSRSB)
69 Wentzell Dr.
Bridgewater, NS B4V 0A2
Tel: 902-543-2468; *Fax:* 902-541-3051
Toll-free: 888-252-2217
receptionist@ssrsb.ca
www.ssrsb.ca
•Strait Regional School Board (SRSB)
16 Cemetery Rd.
Port Hastings, NS B9A 1K6
Tel: 902-625-2191; *Fax:* 902-625-2281
Toll-free: 800-650-4448
srsb@srsb.ca
www.srsb.ca
•Tri-County Regional School Board (TCRSB)
79 Water St.
Yarmouth, NS B5A 1L4
Tel: 902-749-5696; *Fax:* 902-749-5697
Toll-free: 800-915-0113
tcrsb.ca

Centre for Learning Excellence
Tel: 902-424-5829
This branch is responsible for student assessment and evaluation, student achievement, educational research and partnerships, and teacher education and certification.
Executive Director, Monica Williams
Tel: 902-424-1711

Early Years
Tel: 902-424-3673
The mandate of this branch is to provide improved support to families with young children.
Executive Director, Nathalie Blanchet

Education Innovation Programs & Serivces
Tel: 902-424-5745
The Education Innovation Programs & Services branch is responsible for creating courses & programs, as well as evaluting their effectiveness & impact on students.
Executive Director, Ann Power
Tel: 902-424-7454

Finance & Operations
Tel: 902-424-7366
The division is responsible for the financial management of the department as well as the facilities management.
Director, Finance, Jan Jollymore

French Programs & Services
Tel: 902-424-3927
The French Programs & Services Branch monitors & approves curriculum development for French first language education, collaborates with other branches of the department to ensure common services are available in French for first language schools, coordinates activities related to federal-provincial funding agreements for French minority language education and French language instruction, & coordinates & manages implementation of national official language programs in Nova Scotia.
Coordinator, French Program Partnerships, Tim Brown
Coordinator, French Language Services, Harold Rennie
Officer, National Programs & Student/Teacher Bursary, Robert McNutt

Strategic Policy & Research
Tel: 902-424-4740
This branch comprises policy, planning, legislation, research coordination, and information and publishing services to all areas of the department.

Student Equity & Support Services
Tel: 902-424-7454
The Student Equity & Support Services branch is responsible for designing the student support programs & services implemented in all public schools.

Elections Nova Scotia

#6, 7037 Mumford Rd., PO Box 2246 Halifax, NS B3J 3C8
Tel: 902-424-8584; *Fax:* 902-424-6622
Toll-Free: 800-565-1504
TTY: 866-774-7074
www.electionsnovascotia.ca
twitter.com/electionsns
www.youtube.com/user/electionsNS
Elections Nova Scotia is independent of any political affiliation, including the government in power. It ensures that every election, by-election, & liquor plebiscite is held in a fair & impartial manner (according to the Elections Act and other relevant laws) & that all political parties & candidates act within the rules.
Chief Electoral Officer, Richard P. Temporale
Director, Operations, Sandra Little
Tel: 902-424-7672

Nova Scotia Department of Energy

Joseph Howe Bldg., 1690 Hollis St., PO Box 2664 Halifax, NS B3J 3J9
Tel: 902-424-4575; *Fax:* 902-424-0528
enerinfo@novascotia.ca
energy.novascotia.ca
To serve as the government's focal point in the development of the province's energy resources, as outlined in the Energy Strategy. Responsible for a wide range of initiatives in the following areas: energy transportation & utilization policy & analysis; resource assessment & royalties; climate change; business & technology; communications & public education.
Minister, Hon. Michel Samson, ECNS
Tel: 902-424-7793; *Fax:* 902-424-0514
energyminister@novascotia.ca
Deputy Minister, Energy; Deputy Minister, Business, Murray Coolican
Tel: 902-424-1710
Murray.Coolican@novascotia.ca

Business & Technology
Director, Toby Balch
Tel: 902-424-8709

Communications & Public Education

Fiscal & Economic Affairs
Director, Fiscal & Economic Affairs, Andrew Childs
Tel: 902-424-8159

Electricity & Renewable Energy, Technical Policy
Director, Reginald McCoombs
Tel: 902-424-7305

Petroleum Resources
Director, Kimberly Ann Doane
Tel: 902-424-7146

Sustainable & Renewable Energy
novascotia.ca/energy/what-we-do.asp#resource-assessment
Executive Director, Sustainable & Renewable Energy, D. Bruce Cameron
Tel: 902-424-2288
Director, Sustainable & Renewable Energy, Sandra Farwell
Tel: 902-424-1700

Regulatory & Strategic Policy
Director, Regulatory & Strategic Policy, Kimberly A. Himmelman
Tel: 902-424-7131

Nova Scotia Department of Environment

#1800, 1894 Barrington St., PO Box 442 Halifax, NS B3J 2P8
Tel: 902-424-3600; *Fax:* 902-424-0501
Toll-Free: 877-936-8476
www.novascotia.ca/nse
Secondary Address: #2085, 1903 Barrington St. Barrington PlacePO Box 442 Sta. Halifax, NS B3J 2P8
Alt. Fax: 902-424-6925

Major program responsibilities for Nova Scotia Environment are environmental & natural areas management, environmental monitoring & compliance, & climate change. Pollution prevention, the NS Youth Conservation Corps., solid waste reduction & recycling, & environmental trade & innovation are all part of the new Nova Scotia Environment.

Minister, Hon. Margaret Miller
Tel: 902-424-3600; *Fax:* 902-424-0501
Minister.Environment@novascotia.ca

Deputy Minister, Frances Martin
Tel: 902-424-2080
Frances.Martin@novascotia.ca

Associated Agencies, Boards & Commissions:

•Advisory Committee on the Protection of Special Places

•Environmental Assessment Review Panel
www.novascotia.ca/just/regulations/regs/envreviewpanel.htm

•Environmental Trust Advisory Board

•On-Site Services Advisory Board
www.novascotia.ca/just/regulations/regs/envsvcbd.htm

•Resource Recovery Fund Board Inc. (RRFB)
#400, 35 Commercial St.
Truro, NS B2N 3H9
Tel: 902-895-7732; *Fax:* 902-897-3256
Toll-free: 877-313-7732
info@rrfb.com
www.rrfb.com

•Round Table on the Environment & Sustainable Prosperity
novascotia.ca/nse/dept/minister.roundtable.asp

Communications

Tel: 902-424-4790; *Fax:* 902-424-0501
novascotia.ca/nse/dept/media.asp

The Communications Division provides strategic communications planning & advice for the department. It is responsible for all external communications functions carried out for the department, including issues management, advertising, & media relations, & shares responsibility within the department for internal communications.

Director, Mary Anna T. Jollymore
Tel: 902-424-2575
MaryAnna.Jollymore@novascotia.ca

Regional Offices

Central - HRM, East Hants, West Hants
Bedford Commons, #115, 30 Damascus Rd., Bedford, NS B4A 0C1
Tel: 902-424-7773; *Fax:* 902-424-0597

Eastern - Port Hawkesbury, Sydney
#2, 1030 Upper Prince St., Sydney, NS B1P 5P6
Tel: 902-563-2100; *Fax:* 902-563-2387

Eastern - Richmond Co., Southern Inverness, Mulgrave, Auld's Cove
#12, 218 MacSween St., Port Hawkesbury, NS B9A 2J9
Tel: 902-625-0791; *Fax:* 902-625-3722

Northern - Amherst, Antigosh, Truro, Pictou
36 Inglis Place, Truro, NS B2N 4B4
Tel: 902-893-5880; *Fax:* 902-893-0282

Northern - Antigosh, Guysborough Counties
#205, 155 Main St., Antigosh, NS B2N 2B6
Tel: 902-863-7389; *Fax:* 902-863-7411

Northern - Colchester County
36 Inglis Place, Truro, NS B2N 4B4
Tel: 902-893-5880; *Fax:* 902-893-0282

Northern - Cumberland County
71 East Victoria St., Amherst, NS B4H 1X7
Tel: 902-667-6205; *Fax:* 902-667-6214

Northern - Pictou County
20 Pumphouse Rd., RR#3, New Glasgow, NS B2H 5C6
Tel: 902-396-4194; *Fax:* 902-396-4765

Western - Bridgewater, Kentville, Yarmouth
136 Exhibition St., Kentville, NS B4N 4E5
Tel: 902-679-6086; *Fax:* 902-679-6186

Western - Digby, Yarmouth & Shelburne Counties
#5, 55 Starrs Rd., Yarmouth, NS B5A 2T2
Tel: 902-742-8985; *Fax:* 902-742-7796

Western - Lunenberg & Queens Counties
60 Logan Rd., Bridgewater, NS B4V 3J8
Tel: 902-543-4685; *Fax:* 902-527-5480

Policy Division

www.novascotia.ca/nse/dept/division.pcs.asp

Founded in 2009, this division combines former divisions (Competitiveness & Compliance, Environmental Assessment, Information & Business Services, & Policy).

Director, Policy & Planning, Peter Geddes

Sustainability & Applied Science

The Division aims to provide leadership & coordination of community engagement activities in Environment (and more broadly) is responsible for delivery of major environmental service contracts with the private sector.

Director, Protected Areas & Ecosystems, Peter Labor
Tel: 902-424-5071

Director, Air Quality & Resource Management Branch, Andrew Murphy
Tel: 902-424-2177

Director, Water & Wastewater, David Briggins
Tel: 902-424-2571

Nova Scotia Department of Finance & Treasury Board

Provincial Bldg., 1723 Hollis St., 7th Fl., PO Box 187 Halifax, NS B3J 2N3
Tel: 902-424-5554; *Fax:* 902-424-0635
FinanceWeb@novascotia.ca
www.novascotia.ca/finance
twitter.com/NSFinance

The Department of Finance & Treasury Board's vision is to provide financial leadership that strengthens Nova Scotia; & their mission is to provide corporate financial services & manage the province's financial affairs & policies in the interests of Nova Scotians.

Minister, Hon. Randy Delorey
Tel: 902-424-5720; *Fax:* 902-424-0635
FinanceMinister@novascotia.ca

Chair, Treasury & Policy Board, Hon. Karen Lynn Casey
Tel: 902-424-4236; *Fax:* 902-424-0680
educmin@gov.ns.ca

Deputy Minister, Laura Lee Langley
Tel: 902-424-8940; *Fax:* 902-424-0667
LauraLee.Langley@novascotia.ca

Deputy Minister, Byron Rafuse
Tel: 902-424-4168; *Fax:* 902-424-0635
Byron.Rafuse@novascotia.ca

Associate Deputy Minister & Controller, Geoff Gatien
Tel: 902-424-4168; *Fax:* 902-424-0635
Geoffrey.Gatien@novascotia.ca

Associated Agencies, Boards & Commissions:

•Nova Scotia Pension Agency
Purdy's Landing
#400, 1949 Upper Water St.
PO Box 371
Halifax, NS B3J 2P8
Tel: 902-424-5070; *Fax:* 902-424-0662
Toll-free: 800-774-5070
pensionsinfo@gov.ns.ca
www.novascotiapension.ca

Capital Markets Administration

The Capital Markets Administration division provides all post trade settlement & accounting functions for the Nova Scotia Pension Agency investment & the Province's debt portfolio activities.

Director, Vicki Dimick
dimickvc@gov.ns.ca

Communications

The Communications division promotes the Department of Finance's programs & policies to the public, primarily Nova Scotians.

Acting Director, Dan Harrison
harrisdj@gov.ns.ca

Finance & Treasury Board Corporate Services Unit (CSU)

The Finance & Treasury Board CSU supplies support in all aspects of financial management to other government departments.

Director, Laurie Bennett

Financial Institutions

Tel: 902-424-6331; *Fax:* 902-424-1298

The Financial Institutions Division regulates the operations of credit unions, trust & loan companies & insurance companies, agents, brokers & adjusters in the Province. The Division also provides a complaint & enquiry service to the public relating to financial institutions & the insurance industry & collects & verifies the insurance premiums tax.

Fiscal & Economic Policy

Director, Taxation & Fiscal Policy, Paul Davies
Tel: 902-424-4655
daviespb@gov.ns.ca

Director, Economics & Statistics, Thomas Storring
Tel: 902-424-2410
storrith@gov.ns.ca

Government Accounting

Executive Director, Suzanne Wile, CA
Tel: 902-424-7021
wilesm@gov.ns.ca

Director, Financial Accounting, Robert Bourgeois, CA
Tel: 902-424-2079
bourgere@gov.ns.ca

Liability Management & Treasury Services

Responsible for ensuring effective money management, maximizing return on investments & minimizing debt servicing costs within risk tolerances acceptable to government.

Executive Director, Peter Urbanc
Tel: 902-424-2435
urbancpv@gov.ns.ca

Director, Treasurey Services & Liability Management, Roy Spence
Tel: 902-424-8634

Middle Office Compliance & Reporting

Ensures that the investment & debt management activities are compliant with legislature as well as Finance's objectives & policy limits by guaranteeing that best-in-class practices/policies/processes are in place to adequately control activities, such as monitoring & reporting ongoing investment & debt activities to management & Governance Committees.

Director, Vicki Dimick
dimickvc@gov.ns.ca

Policy & Advisory Services

Director & Senior Advisor, David Perry
perryde@gov.ns.ca

Nova Scotia Department of Fisheries & Aquaculture

1800 Argyle St., 6th fl., Halifax, NS B3J 2R5
Tel: 902-424-4560; *Fax:* 902-424-4671
aquaculture@novascotia.ca
novascotia.ca/fish
twitter.com/NSFisheries

The Department of Fisheries & Aquaculture's mission is to foster prosperous & sustainable fisheries, aquaculture & food industries through the delivery of quality public services for the betterment of coastal communities & of all Nova Scotians.

Minister, Hon. Keith Colwell
Tel: 902-424-8953; *Fax:* 902-428-3145
min_dag@novascotia.ca

Deputy Minister, Kim MacNeil
Tel: 902-424-4439; *Fax:* 902-424-0698
Kim.MacNeil@novascotia.ca

Associated Agencies, Boards & Commissions:

•Fisheries & Aquaculture Loan Board
MacRae Library
PO Box 890
Truro, NS B2N 2P2
Tel: 902-896-4800; *Fax:* 902-896-4812
novascotia.ca/fish/programs-and-services/funding-programs

Aquaculture Division

Director, Bruce Hancock
Tel: 902-875-7433; *Fax:* 902-875-7430

Inland Fisheries Division

Marine & Coastal Division

Director, Karen Wong-Petrie
Tel: 902-679-6011

Office of Gaelic Affairs (OGA)

1741 Brunswick St., 3rd Fl., PO Box 456 Stn. Central, Halifax, NS B3J 2R5
Tel: 902-424-4298; *Fax:* 902-424-0171
Toll-Free: 888-842-3542
gaelicinfo@gov.ns.ca
gaelic.novascotia.ca
Other Communication: Alternate E-mail: fiosgaidhlig@gov.ns.ca

The OGA's mission is to renew the Gaelic language through its work with Nova Scotians across the province.

Minister, Hon. Randy Delorey
Tel: 902-424-4298; *Fax:* 902-424-0710
gaelicinfo@novascotia.ca

Regional Offices

Antigonish

155 Main St., 2nd Fl., Antigonish, NS B2G 2B6
Tel: 902-863-7578; *Fax:* 902-863-7428

Mabou

11485 Hwy. 19, PO Box 261 Mabou, NS B0E 1X0
Tel: 902-945-2114
Toll-Free: 888-842-3542

Nova Scotia Department of Health & Wellness

Barrington Tower., 1894 Barrington St., PO Box 488 Halifax, NS B3J 2R8
Tel: 902-424-5818
Toll-Free: 800-387-6665
TTY: 800-670-8888
novascotia.ca/dhw
Other Communication: TeleHealth Network: 1-800-889-5949

Mission: Working together to empower individuals, families, partners, & communities to promote, improve, & maintain the health of Nova Scotians through a proactive & sustainable health care system.

Minister, Hon. Leo Glavine
Tel: 902-424-3377; *Fax:* 902-424-0559
health.minister@gov.ns.ca
Deputy Minister, Dr. Peter Vaughan
Associate Deputy Minister, Tracey Barbrick
Tel: 902-424-7337
Executive Director, Strategic Financial Operations, Abram James Almeda
Tel: 902-424-7931
Executive Director, EHS & Primary Health Care, Ian Bower
Tel: 902-464-6098
Executive Director, Continuing Care, Ruby Knowles
Tel: 902-424-3221
Director, Acute & Tertiary Care, Lewis Bedford
Director, Health Intergovernmental Affairs, Vijay Bhashyakarla
Tel: 902-424-2842
Director, Health Workforce Policies, Cynthia Cruickshank
Tel: 902-424-8838
Director, Addiction Services, Carolyn Davison
Tel: 902-424-7218
Director, Population Health Assessment, Mary Anne Finlayson
Tel: 902-424-2051
Director, Acute Care, Katherine Fraser
Tel: 902-424-4878
Director, Financial & Administrative Services, Shelley Bonang
Tel: 902-424-7256
Director, Primary Health Care, Lisa Ruth Grandy
Tel: 902-424-4617
Director, Accountability & Performance Management, Barbara Harvie
Tel: 902-424-0059
Director, Legislative Policy, Dean Hirtle
Tel: 902-424-1797
Director, Chronic Disease & Injury Prevention, Nancy Hoddinott
Tel: 902-424-5840
Director, Healthy Development, Kathryn Inkpen
Tel: 902-424-4391
Director, Health Economics, Michael Joyce
Tel: 902-427-6879
Director, Insured Services, Harold McCarthy
Tel: 902-424-7538
Director, AIDS Commission, Michelle Proctor-Simms
Tel: 902-424-4741
Director, Physician Services MA/FSS, Angela Purcell
Director, Mental Health Services, Kenneth Scott
Director, Formulary & Clinical Practice, Kathleen Shipp
Director, Emergency Managment Centre, Russell Stuart
Tel: 902-424-0000

Associated Agencies, Boards & Commissions:

•Nova Scotia Advisory Commission on AIDS
Barrington Tower
1894 Barrington St.
PO Box 31
Halifax, NS B3J 2L4
Tel: 902-424-5730
aids@gov.ns.ca
www.gov.ns.ca/aids

Health Services

Director, Suzanne Rhodenizer, RN, BScN, CIC
Tel: 902-722-1244
Suzanne.RhodenizerRose@novascotia.ca

Office of the Chief Public Health Officer
PO Box 488 Halifax, NS B3J 2R8
Tel: 902-424-2358; *Fax:* 902-424-4716

The Office of the Chief Public Health Officer is responsible for the Department of Health's legislated responsibility to protect & promote the public's health in the following areas: communicable disease control, environmental health, emergency preparedness & response. In addition, staff in the Office of the Chief Public Health Officer, in collaboration with academic expertise at Dalhousie University, function as an expert resource in community health science & an epidemiological resource for the department, the health districts, & other relevant government & community groups.

Chief Public Health Officer/Chief Medical Officer of Health, Dr. Robert Strang
Tel: 902-424-2358; *Fax:* 902-424-4716

Nova Scotia Human Rights Commission

Park Lane Terraces, #305, 5657 Spring Garden Rd., PO Box 2221 Halifax, NS B3J 3C4
Tel: 902-424-4111; *Fax:* 902-424-0596
Toll-Free: 877-269-7699
hrcinquiries@novascotia.ca
humanrights.novascotia.ca
twitter.com/NSHumanRights
www.facebook.com/164443166946022

Minister Responsible, Hon. Diana C. Whalen
Tel: 902-424-4044; *Fax:* 902-424-0510
justmin@novascotia.ca
Director & CEO, Christine Hanson

Regional Offices

Digby

Provincial Bldg., 84 Warwick St., PO Box 1029 Digby, NS B0V 1A0
Tel: 902-245-4791; *Fax:* 902-245-7103

Sydney

Provincial Bldg., 360 Prince St., Sydney, NS B1P 5L1
Tel: 902-563-2142; *Fax:* 902-563-5613

Office of Immigration

#110A, 1741 Brunswick St., PO Box 1535 Halifax, NS B3J 2Y3
Tel: 902-424-5230; *Fax:* 902-424-7936
Toll-Free: 877-292-9597
nsnp@novascotia.ca
www.novascotiaimmigration.com
twitter.com/nsimmigration
www.facebook.com/NovaScotiaImmigration
www.linkedin.com/groups/Nova-Scotia-Immigration-3807228
www.youtube.com/nsimmigration

Minister, Hon. Lena M. Diab
Tel: 902-424-5230; *Fax:* 902-428-3178
ImmigrationMinister@novascotia.ca
Chief Executive Officer, Julie Towers
Tel: 902-424-5230; *Fax:* 902-424-7936
Julie.Towers@novascotia.ca
Director, Communications, Brett Loney
Tel: 902-424-4312
bretton.loney@novascotia.ca

Office of the Information & Privacy Commissioner (OIPC)

Centennial Bldg., #1002, 1660 Hollis St., PO Box 181 Halifax, NS B3J 2M4
Tel: 902-424-4684; *Fax:* 902-424-8303
Toll-Free: 866-243-1564
oipcns@novascotia.ca
foipop.ns.ca
twitter.com/NSInfoPrivacy

Nova Scotia was the first province in Canada to enact Freedom of Information legislation, in 1977. The Freedom of Information & Protection of Privacy Review of Privacy Office, now the Office of the Information & Privacy Commissioner, was established in 1994.

Information & Privacy Commissioner, Catherine Tully, B.Sc., B.A., LL.B., LL.M.

Nova Scotia Department of Intergovernmental Affairs

Duke Tower, 5251 Duke St., 5th Fl., PO Box 1617 Halifax, NS B3J 2Y3
Tel: 902-424-5153; *Fax:* 902-424-0728
novascotia.ca/iga

Provides leadership in the development of corporate strategies for Nova Scotia's relations with governments & organizations. Assumed responsibility for Trade Policy & Negotiations after Economic & Rural Development & Tourism was dissolved in 2015.

Minister, Hon. Stephen McNeil
Tel: 902-424-5153; *Fax:* 902-424-0728
premier@novascotia.ca
Deputy Minister, Kelliann Dean
Tel: 902-424-7128; *Fax:* 902-424-4225
Kelliann.Dean@novascotia.ca
Director, Regional Relations, Tatiana Morren Fraser
Tel: 902-424-3448
Director, Strategic Policy, Angela Houston
Tel: 902-424-0909
Director, Economic Policy & Analysis, André C. Moore
Tel: 902-424-7728
Director, Environmental & Social Affairs, Albert Walzak
Tel: 902-424-1289

Nova Scotia Department of Internal Services

World Trade & Convention Centre, 1800 Argyle St., 5th Fl., PO Box 943 Halifax, NS B3J 2V9
Tel: 902-424-5465; *Fax:* 902-424-0555
novascotia.ca/is
twitter.com/NSInternalSvcs

Created on April 1, 2014, when government services from seven departments were realigned.

Minister, Hon. Labi Kousoulis
Tel: 902-424-5465; *Fax:* 902-424-0555
MIN_InternalServices@novascotia.ca
Deputy Minister, Jeff Conrad
Tel: 902-424-3825
jeffrey.conrad@novascotia.ca
Executive Director, Glenn Bishop
Tel: 902-424-7066
Director, Client Services, David Bell
Tel: 902-424-2975
Director, CIS, Kevin Ronald Briand
Tel: 902-424-2284
Director, Strategic Relations, Richard Doucet
Tel: 902-424-3637
Director, Emerging & Specialized Service, David McCurdy
Tel: 902-424-5974
Director, Operational Support, Natalie Webb
Tel: 902-424-1504

Associated Agencies, Boards & Commissions:

•Nova Scotia Lands Inc.
See Entry Name Index for detailed listing.

Financial Services Delivery Branch
Provincial Bldg., 1723 Hollis St., 5th Fl., PO Box 187 Halifax, NS B3J 2N3

Serves government departments & government agencies, school boards & pensioners through managing corporate accounting & financial reporting, payroll transaction & processing, payment transactions & processing services.

Executive Director, Government Accounting, Suzanne Wile
Tel: 902-424-7021
Suzanne.Wile@novascotia.ca
Director, Financial Accounting, Robert Bourgeois
Tel: 902-424-2079
Robert.Bourgeois@novascotia.ca
Director, Payroll Client Relations, Donna Hendy
Tel: 902-424-6672
Director, Operational Accounting, Blair McNaughton
Tel: 902-424-6626
mcnaugbn@gov.ns.ca

Information Communication & Technology Services
Royal Bank Building, 5161 George St., Halifax, NS B3J 2Y1
ICTSenquiries@novascotia.ca
novascotia.ca/cio

Provides technical, functional & business support for the public sector application of Systems Applications Products (SAP); assists in the application of the Freedom of Information Protection of Privacy (FOIPOP) Act & the Personal Information International Disclosure Protection Act (PIIDPA) Act; & promotes best practices regarding information access & privacy throughout the government.

Chief Information Officer, Sandra Cascadden, P. Eng
Tel: 902-424-4838
Chief Information Access & Privacy Officer, Maria Lasheras
Tel: 902-424-8214
Executive Director, Infrastructure Service Management, Carolyn McKenzie
Tel: 902-424-0448

Internal Audit
One Government Place, 1700 Granville St., Halifax, NS B3J 1X5
Tel: 902-424-6102; *Fax:* 902-424-3191

Provides assurance & advisory services to government.

Director, Audit, Carey Bohan
Tel: 902-424-7290

Procurement Services
#502, 1660 Hollis St., Halifax, NS B3J 1V7
Tel: 902-424-3333; *Fax:* 902-424-0622
Toll-Free: 866-399-3377
procure@novascotia.ca
novascotia.ca/tenders
twitter.com/ns_procure

Manages major purchases for departments, agencies, boards & commissions. Also includes the Queen's Printer, which supplies, produces & distributes both regular & confidential documents.
Chief Procurement Officer, Chris Mitchell
Director, Procurement Enablement, Natalie McLean
Tel: 902-424-3635
Natalie.McLean@novascotia.ca
Contact, Queen's Printer, Tim Blanchette
Tel: 902-424-8066
blanctx@gov.ns.ca

Public Works
Johnston Bldg., 1672 Granville St., PO Box 186 Halifax, NS B3J 2N2
Provides corporate & technical support for provincial infrastructure & environmental remediation projects.
Director, Public Safety & Field Communications, Todd Brown
Tel: 902-424-7678
Director, Risk Management & Security Services, Bruce Langille
Tel: 902-424-4440
Director, Building Services, Neil Whyte
Tel: 902-424-2883

Nova Scotia Department of Justice

1690 Hollis St., PO Box 7 Halifax, NS B3J 2L6
Tel: 902-424-4030
justweb@gov.ns.ca
novascotia.ca/just

Minister & Attorney General, Hon. Diana C. Whalen
Tel: 902-424-4044; *Fax:* 902-424-0510
justmin@novascotia.ca
Deputy Minister, Karen Hudson, Q.C.

Associated Agencies, Boards & Commissions:

•Criminal Code Review Board (CCRB)
novascotia.ca/just/ccrb/ccrb_overview.asp

•Serious Incident Response Team (SiRT)
#203, 1256 Barrington St.
Halifax, NS B3J 1Y6
Tel: 902-424-2010
Toll-free: 855-450-2010
sirt@gov.ns.ca
sirt.novascotia.ca

•Human Rights Commission
See Entry Name Index for detailed listing.

•Nova Scotia Legal Aid Commission
Office of the Executive Director
#920, 1701 Hollis St.
Halifax, NS B3J 3M8
Tel: 902-420-6578
Toll-free: 877-420-6578
www.nslegalaid.ca

•Office of the Chief Medical Examiner
Dr. William D. Finn Centre for Forensic Medicine
51 Garland Ave.
Dartmouth, NS B3B 0J2
Tel: 902-424-2722; *Fax:* 902-424-0607
Toll-free: 888-424-4336
novascotia.ca/just/cme
Other Communication: Toll-Free Fax: 1-866-603-4074

•Office of the Police Complaints Commissioner (OPCC)
#720, 1550 Bedford Hwy.
PO Box 1573
Halifax, NS B3J 2Y3
Tel: 902-424-3246; *Fax:* 902-424-1777
polcom@gov.ns.ca
novascotia.ca/opcc

•Public Trustee Office
#405, 5670 Spring Garden Rd.
PO Box 685
Halifax, NS B3J 2T3
Tel: 902-424-7760; *Fax:* 902-424-0616
publictrustee@gov.ns.ca
novascotia.ca/just/pto
Other Communication: Health Care Decisions Division, Phone: 902-424-4454; Fax: 902-428-2159; E-mail: publictrusteehcd@gov.ns.ca

•Workers' Compensation Appeals Tribunal
#1002, 5670 Spring Garden Rd.
Halifax, NS B3J 1H6
Tel: 902-424-2250; *Fax:* 902-424-2321
Toll-free: 800-274-8281
www.novascotia.ca/wcat

Communications
Director, Peter McLaughlin
Tel: 902-424-6282; *Fax:* 902-424-0510
Peter.McLaughlin@novascotia.ca

Correctional Services
1690 Hollis St., PO Box 7 Halifax, NS B3J 2L6
Tel: 902-424-7640; *Fax:* 902-424-0693
Director, Correctional Services, Diana MacKinnon
Tel: 902-424-5661
Director, Correctional Services, Chris Collett
Tel: 902-893-5995
Director, Sean Kelly
Tel: 902-424-5342

Court Services
1690 Hollis St., 4th Fl., PO Box 7 Halifax, NS B3J 2L6
Tel: 902-424-4030
justweb@gov.ns.ca
Director, William Clancey
Tel: 902-424-6414
Director, Peter James
Tel: 902-543-0816
Director, Pamela Kachafanas
Tel: 902-563-3757

Finance & Administration
Director, Finance, Lisa MacKinnon
Tel: 902-424-6530
Director & Administrator, Finance, Beverly Whittaker-Taggart
Tel: 902-424-2699

Maintenance Enforcement Program
PO Box 803 Halifax, NS B3J 2V2
Tel: 902-424-0050; *Fax:* 902-428-2166
Toll-Free: 800-357-9248
nsmep@gov.ns.ca

Public Safety
Executive Director, Robert Purcell
Tel: 902-424-2504
Director, Crime Prevention, Donald Spicer
Tel: 902-424-8356
Director, Victim Services, John Joyce-Robinson
Tel: 902-424-3309

Nova Scotia Department of Labour & Advanced Education

5151 Terminal Rd., 6th Fl., PO Box 697 Halifax, NS B3J 2T8
Tel: 902-424-5301; *Fax:* 902-424-2203
novascotia.ca/lae

Focuses on labour issues, employment rights & responsibilities, adult learning, apprenticeship training & trade qualification, skill development, public & workplace safety, industry regulation, licensing & pensions. In April 2015, the Department gained responsibility for the following programs after the dissolution of Economic & Rural Development & Tourism: Strategic Cooperative Education Incentive; Workplace Innovation Productivity Skills Incentive; Student Career Development Program; & Graduate to Opportunity.
Minister, Hon. Kelly Regan
Tel: 902-424-6647; *Fax:* 902-424-0575
min_lae@novascotia.ca
Deputy Minister, Duff Montgomerie
Tel: 902-424-3095
Associate Deputy Minister, Lora MacEachern
Tel: 902-424-6654
Senior Executive Director, L. Elizabeth Mills
Tel: 902-424-4993
Director, Strategic Initiatives, Richard Alexander
Tel: 902-424-1719
Director, Program, Kenneth Byron
Tel: 902-424-8420
Director, Linda Higgins
Tel: 902-471-3265

Associated Agencies, Boards & Commissions:

•Community Sector Council of Nova Scotia
1697 Brunswick St.
Halifax, NS B3J 2G3
Tel: 902-424-4585
information@csc-ns.ca
csc-ns.ca
The Council was established in December 2012 & seeks to to develop organizational capacity within the non-profit sector, with funds from the Department of Labour & Advanced Education.

•Crane Operators Appeal Board
5151 Terminal Rd., 7th Fl.
PO Box 697
Halifax, NS B3J 2T8
Tel: 902-424-8595; *Fax:* 902-424-0217
fernanfs@gov.ns.ca
www.gov.ns.ca/lae/coab
The Crane Operators Appeal Board was created pursuant to the Crane Operators & Power Engineers Act, which came into force on September 1, 2001. It is an independent adjudicative tribunal charged with considering appeals filed under Part I of the Act.

•Elevators & Lifts Appeal Board
5151 Terminal Rd., 7th Fl.
PO Box 697
Halifax, NS B3J 2T8
Tel: 902-424-8595; *Fax:* 902-424-0217
novascotia.ca/lae/elab

•Labour Board of Nova Scotia
5151 Terminal Rd., 7th Fl.
PO Box 697
Halifax, NS B3J 2T8
Tel: 902-424-6730; *Fax:* 902-424-1744
Toll-free: 877-424-6730
labourboard@gov.ns.ca
novascotia.ca/lae/abct/lmrc.asp

•Labour-Management Review Committee
Tel: 902-424-8466; *Fax:* 902-424-1744
novascotia.ca/lae/abct/lmrc.asp

•Nova Scotia Apprenticeship Agency (NSAA)
2021 Brunswick St.
PO Box 578
Halifax, NS B3J 2S9
Tel: 902-424-5651; *Fax:* 902-424-0717
apprenticeship@gov.ns.ca
nsapprenticeship.ca
Established on July 1, 2014, to manage the trades training & certification system in Nova Scotia. Operates under the authority of the Apprenticeship & Trades Qualifications Act.

•Nova Scotia Apprenticeship Board
2021 Brunswick St.
PO Box 578
Halifax, NS B3J 2S9
Tel: 902-424-0872; *Fax:* 902-424-0717
Toll-free: 800-494-5651
nsapprenticeship.ca/agency/board
Other Communication: General Inquiries, Phone: 902-424-5651
The Nova Scotia Apprenticeship Board, which is linked with the Nova Scotia Apprenticeship Agency as of 2014, is the voice of industry to the Minister of Labour & Advanced Education. The primary role of the board is to consult with industry on apprenticeship matters & to make recommendations to the Minister. In particular, the Board reviews current trade regulations & recommends proposed trades for designation & compulsory certification.

•Occupational Health & Safety Advisory Council
PO Box 697
Halifax, NS B3J 2T8
Tel: 902-424-2484; *Fax:* 902-424-5640
novascotia.ca/lae/abct/ohsadvisory.asp

•Pay Equity Commission
5151 Terminal Rd., 6th Fl.
PO Box 697
Halifax, NS B3J 2T8
Tel: 902-424-8466; *Fax:* 902-424-0575
novascotia.ca/lae/payequity
The Pay Equity Commission is responsible for administrating the Pay Equity Act. In addition to monitoring the pay equity process, the Commission has the power to resolve disputes when employers and employees cannot agree, conducts research, maintains statistics, and advises the Minister of Labour on matters relating to pay equity.

•Power Engineers & Operators Appeal Committee
5151 Terminal Rd., 7th Fl.
PO Box 697
Halifax, NS B3J 2T8
Tel: 902-424-8595; *Fax:* 902-424-0217
novascotia.ca/lae/peoac

•Workers' Advisers Program
#502, 5670 Spring Garden Rd.
PO Box 1063
Halifax, NS B3J 2X1
Fax: 902-424-0530
Toll-free: 800-774-4712
www.gov.ns.ca/lwd/wap
The Workers' Advisers Program is a legal clinic that is funded by the provincial government offering services to injured workers. Our purpose is to provide legal assistance when an injured worker has been denied Workers' Compensation Board benefits.

Corporate Policy & Services Branch

novascotia.ca/lae/policy
Other Communication: Professional Services, URL: novascotia.ca/lae/ProfessionalServices.asp

Consists of Planning, Research & Accountability, Policy & Planning & Professional Services.

Director, Professional Services, Stewart Sampson
Tel: 902-424-8055

Higher Education Branch

5151 Terminal Rd., 6th Fl., PO Box 697 Halifax, NS B3J 2T8

novascotia.ca/lae/highereducation

Consists of Post-Secondary Disability Services, Private Career Colleges, Student Assistance & Universities & Colleges.

Executive Director, Universities & Colleges, Gregory Ells
Tel: 902-424-3758

Executive Director, Student Assistance, Carol Lowthers
Tel: 902-424-5189

Director, Universities & Colleges, Theodore Vaughan
Tel: 902-424-3755

Labour Services Branch

Consists of Conciliation & Labour Tribunals, Labour Standards, Pension Regulation & Workers' Advisers Program.

Executive Director, Labour Services, Flavia Fernandis
Tel: 902-424-5673

Executive Officer, Labour Services, Cynthia Yazbek
Tel: 902-424-4588

Director, Labour Standards, Evelyn Hartley
Tel: 902-424-3345

Safety Branch

novascotia.ca/lae/publicsafety
Other Communication: novascotia.ca/lae/ohs

Consists of Technical Safety, Office of the Fire Marshall & Occupational Health & Safety.

Executive Director, Occupational Health & Safety, Harold Carroll
Tel: 902-662-3030

Fire Marshal, Harold James Pothier
Tel: 902-538-4112
Harold.Pothier@novascotia.ca

Director, Technical Safety, David Wigmore
Tel: 902-424-5434
David.Wigmore@novascotia.ca

Skills & Learning Branch

Consists of Adult Education, Employment Nova Scotia & Skill Development. Apprenticeship functions are now handled by the Nova Scotia Apprenticeship Agency, created on July 1, 2014.

Director, Adult Education, Candida Gordon
Tel: 902-424-0959

Volunteerism & Non-Profit Sector Division

#3, 60 Lorne St., Truro, NS B2N 3K3

Fax: 902-893-5609
novascotia.ca/lae/volunteerism

Nova Scotia Lands Inc.

Harbourside Pl., 45 Wabana Ct., PO Box 430 Stn. A, Sydney, NS B1P 6H2

Fax: 902-564-7903
www.nslands.ca

Crown corporation responsible for remediating & redeveloping crown-owned property in Nova Scotia, including land located in Sydney Mines, Sydney River, Grand Lake area, Catalone, Pictou, New Glasgow & Grand Narrows. The former Sydney Steel Plant property is currently undergoing remediation. NS Lands also manages the Harbourside Commercial Park in Sydney. Associated with the Department of Internal Services.

President, Gary Campbell
Tel: 902-424-2800
Gary.Campbell@novascotia.ca

Chief Operating Officer, Joel MacLean, P.Eng
Tel: 902-564-7959
Joel.MacLean@novascotia.ca

Executive Director, Frank Potter
Tel: 902-564-0037
Frank.Potter@novascotia.ca

Nova Scotia Liquor Corporation (NSLC)

Bayers Lake Business Park, 93 Chain Lake Dr., Halifax, NS B3S 1A3

Tel: 902-450-5874
Toll-Free: 800-567-5874
www.mynslc.com
twitter.com/theNSLC
www.facebook.com/theNSLC
www.youtube.com/mynslc

Minister Responsible, Hon. Randy Delorey
Tel: 902-424-5720; *Fax:* 902-424-0635
FinanceMinister@novascotia.ca

Chair, Sherry Porter

President & Chief Executive Officer, Bret Mitchell

Nova Scotia Department of Municipal Affairs

Maritime Centre, 14 North, 1505 Barrington St., PO Box 216 Halifax, NS B3J 3K5

Tel: 902-424-6642
Toll-Free: 800-670-4357
TTY: 877-404-0867
www.novascotia.ca/dma

Provides programs, grants & funding opportunities for municipalities & community groups, as well as services & guidance to municipalities in areas such as budget planning & finance, land use planning & infrastructure development, & policy & program development. In April 2015, the Department gained responsibility for the Regional Enterprise Networks formerly overseen by Economic & Rural Development & Tourism.

Minister, Hon. Zach Churchill
Tel: 902-424-5550; *Fax:* 902-424-0581
dmamin@novascotia.ca

Deputy Minister, Kelliann Dean
Tel: 902-424-7128; *Fax:* 902-424-4225
Kelliann.Dean@novascotia.ca

Director, Provincial Operations, Sean Irvine
Tel: 902-427-0486

Director, Communications, Roy Jamieson
Tel: 902-424-6336

Associated Agencies, Boards & Commissions:

•Nova Scotia Municipal Finance Corporation (NSMFC)
Maritime Centre
1505 Barrington St., 10th Fl. South
PO Box 850 M
Halifax, NS B3J 2V2
Tel: 902-424-4590; *Fax:* 902-424-0525
gharding@gov.ns.ca
www.gov.ns.ca/nsmfc

NSMFC issues pooled debentures that provide low-cost, long-term capital financing for municipal capital projects. The NSMFC issues in capital markets twice a year, generally in the spring & fall. On occasion the NSMFC will do a single issue, provided the size is large enough.

Emergency Management Office (EMO)

PO Box 2581 Halifax, NS B3J 3N5

Tel: 902-424-5620; *Fax:* 902-424-5376
Toll-Free: 866-424-5620
emo@gov.ns.ca
novascotia.ca/dma/emo
Secondary Address: 33 Acadia St. Dartmouth, NS B2Y 2N1
twitter.com/nsemo
www.facebook.com/EmergencyManagementOfficeNovaScotia

Now a branch of the Department of Municipal Affairs, the EMO has the responsibility of assisting municipalities in planning & preparing for emergencies; is also responsible for the implementation of the province-wide 911 service. Coordinates emergency efforts of provincial & federal departments & agencies, as well as private health & social services, to provide assistance to disaster areas; sponsors the Ground Search & Rescue Program; maintains a professional planner at all offices. Coordinates all emergency preparedness training for municipal staff at the Emergency Preparedness College (Arnprior, ON) & through the Joint Emergency Preparedness Program (JEPP), which provides a federal government cost-sharing formula for emergency equipment for first-response agencies.

Executive Director, Andrew Lathem
Tel: 902-424-5620

Office of the Fire Marshal

Tel: 902-424-5721; *Fax:* 902-424-3239
Toll-Free: 800-559-3473
novascotia.ca/dma/firesafety

Fire Marshal, Harold Pothier
Harold.Pothier@novascotia.ca

Nova Scotia Department of Natural Resources

Founder's Square, 1701 Hollis St., 3rd Fl., PO Box 698 Halifax, NS B3J 2T9

Tel: 902-424-5935; *Fax:* 902-424-7735
Toll-Free: 800-565-2224
novascotia.ca/natr
twitter.com/DNRNovaScotia

Responsible for the administration & management of provincial Crown lands, development of mineral & energy resources, protection & sustainable development of forest resources & operation & maintenance of parks system, & promoting the conservation & sustainable use of wildlife populations, habitat & ecosystems. Initiatives include: a State of the Forest report; working with other departments on State of the Environment report; leading the development of a provincial climate change strategy; implementing recovery plans for endangered & threatened wildlife species; & developing strategic land use plans for Crown lands using an integrated resource management planning process.

Minister, Hon. Lloyd Hines
Tel: 902-424-4037; *Fax:* 902-424-0594
mindnr@novascotia.ca

Deputy Minister, Frank Dunn
Tel: 902-424-7366
Frank.Dunn@novascotia.ca

Associate Deputy Minister, J. Allan Eddy
Tel: 902-424-4121

Director, Communications, Bruce Nunn
Tel: 902-424-5239
nunnbx@gov.ns.ca

Director, Financial Services, Weldon Myers
Tel: 902-424-3288

Associated Agencies, Boards & Commissions:

•Crown Land Information Management Centre (CLIMC)
Founders Square
1701 Hollis St.
PO Box 698
Halifax, NS B3J 2T9
Tel: 902-424-7068; *Fax:* 902-424-3171
crownland@gov.ns.ca
novascotia.ca/natr/land/grantmap.asp

•Nova Scotia Primary Forest Products Marketing Board
#202, 1256 Barrington St.
Halifax, NS B3J 1Y6
Tel: 902-424-7598; *Fax:* 902-424-6965
nspfpmb@gov.ns.ca
www.novascotia.ca/pfpmb

Geoscience & Mines Branch

novascotia.ca/natr/meb

Implements policies & programs dealing with the exploration, development, management & efficient use of energy & mineral resources, promotes scientific studies of the geology of the province for use by government, industry & the public, provides a mineral rights tenure system to establish legal rights to minerals for exploration & development. Promotes concepts of environmental responsibility & sustainability.

Executive Director, Don James
Tel: 902-424-2523

Director, Geological Services, Rob Naylor
Tel: 902-424-8119

Land Services Branch

novascotia.ca/natr/thedepartment/landservices.asp

The Land Services Branch management oversees, coordinates & approves all activities within the Branch relating to the administration of Crown land. The Branch provides advice on legislative revisions & advises & drafts policies relating to the administration of Crown land.

Executive Director, Gretchen Pohlkamp
Tel: 902-424-4267
pohlkagg@gov.ns.ca

Director, Land Services Renewal, Eli Elias
Tel: 902-424-1190

Director, Surveys, Bruce Albert MacQuarrie
Tel: 902-424-3144

Policy, Planning & Support Services

Provides planning & policy coordination support to the Department, ensures that policies & plans developed in the Department are coordinated, supports the integrated management of natural resources. Also provides a range of administrative, planning, research, information management, information distribution, graphics, cartographic, communication, & occupational health & safety-related services.

Executive Director, Patricia MacNeil
Tel: 902-424-4988

Regional Services Branch

Delivers departmental programs & services through a field office network, responsible for forest protection & planning, forest nurseries, research & development, enforcement, coordination of the hunter safety program, regional geological services, Crown land surveys, operation & maintenance of provincial parks, resource conservation, forest fire prevention & monitoring of forest insects & diseases.

Executive Director, Walter Fanning
Tel: 902-424-4445

Director, Operations, Linda Redmond
Tel: 902-424-6307

Regional Offices

Central

PO Box 68 Truro, NS B2N 5B8

Tel: 902-893-6350; *Fax:* 902-893-5613
Secondary Address: #7, 15 Arlington Place Truro, NS B2N 5B8

Regional Director, Central, Gordon Delano
Gordon.Delano@novascotia.ca

Eastern
300 Mountain Rd., Sydney, NS B1L 1A9
Tel: 902-563-3370; *Fax:* 902-567-2535
Other Communication: Alternate Phone: 902-563-3372

Western
PO Box 6000 Lunenberg, NS B0J 2C0
Tel: 902-634-7555; *Fax:* 902-634-7577
Secondary Address: 312 Green St.
Lunenburg, NS B0J 2C0

Renewable Resources
Executive Director, Jonathan Porter
Tel: 902-424-4103
Jon.Porter@novascotia.ca
Director, Forestry, Jonathan Kierstead
Tel: 902-893-5673
Director, Program Development, Peter MacQuarrie
Tel: 902-424-7708
Director, Wildlife, Robert Petrie
Tel: 902-679-6139

Office of the Ombudsman

#700, 5670 Spring Garden Rd., PO Box 2152 Halifax, NS B3J 3B7
Tel: 902-424-6780; *Fax:* 902-424-6675
Toll-Free: 800-670-1111
ombudsman@gov.ns.ca
www.novascotia.ca/ombu
Other Communication: Youth Services, Toll-Free Phone: 1-888-839-6884; Disclosure of Wrongdoing Inquiries, Toll-Free Phone: 1-877-670-1100
twitter.com/NS_Ombudsman
www.facebook.com/107686089866
Ombudsman, William (Bill) Smith

Nova Scotia Public Service Commission (NSPSC)

1800 Argyle St., 5th Fl., PO Box 943 Halifax, NS B3J 2V9
Tel: 902-424-7660
novascotia.ca/psc
Minister, Hon. Labi Kousoulis
Tel: 902-424-5465; *Fax:* 902-424-0555
min_psc@novascotia.ca
Public Service Commissioner, Laura Lee Langley
Tel: 902-424-4886
Executive Director, Client Service Delivery, Steven Feindel
Tel: 902-497-3416
Director, Labour Relations & Compensation, Alexandra Smith
Tel: 902-424-0066
Director, Audit & Evaluation, Katharine Cox-Brown
Tel: 902-424-8383
Director, Organizational Effectiveness, Pamela Matheson
Tel: 902-424-5604

Nova Scotia Securities Commission (NSSC)

Duke Tower, #400, 5251 Duke St., PO Box 458 Halifax, NS B3J 2P8
Tel: 902-424-7768; *Fax:* 902-424-4625
Toll-Free: 855-424-2499
NSSCinquiries@novascotia.ca
nssc.novascotia.ca
twitter.com/NSSCommission
Established to provide investors with protection in accordance with Nova Scotia's securities laws from practices & activities that tend to undermine investor confidence in the fairness & efficiency of capital markets.
Acting Chair, Paul E. Radford
Director, Enforcement, Randy Gass
Tel: 902-424-6179
Director, Corporate Finance, Kevin G. Redden
Tel: 902-424-7379
Director, Securities, J. William Slattery
Tel: 902-424-7355

Nova Scotia Department of Seniors

Barrington Tower, 1894 Barrington St., 15th Fl., Halifax, NS B3J 2R8
Tel: 902-424-0770; *Fax:* 902-424-0561
Toll-Free: 844-277-0770
seniors@NovaScotia.ca
novascotia.ca/seniors
twitter.com/NSSeniors
Committed to ensuring the inclusion, well-being, & independence of seniors in Nova Scotia by facilitating the development of policies on aging & programs for seniors across government & through the provision & coordination of strategic planning, support, services, programs & information.
Minister, Hon. Leo A. Glavine
Tel: 902-424-0065; *Fax:* 902-424-0561
seniorsmin@novascotia.ca
Deputy Minister, Simon d'Entremont
Director, Corporate Strategy & Policy, Faizal Nanji
Tel: 902-424-7933

Service Nova Scotia

c/o Public Enquiries - Service Nova Scotia, PO Box 2734 Halifax, NS B3J 3K5
Tel: 902-424-5200; *Fax:* 902-424-0720
Toll-Free: 800-670-4357
TTY: 877-404-0867
novascotia.ca/sns
twitter.com/ns_servicens
Provides assessment services, business licensing & registration, vehicle registration & driver licensing, taxation & revenue collection & vital statistics. As of April 1, 2015, a new structure was implemented in order to focus on improving service & modernizing programs & reducing red tape.
Minister, Hon. Mark Furey
Tel: 902-424-5550; *Fax:* 902-424-0581
snsminister@novascotia.ca
Chief Executive Officer, Joanne Munro
Tel: 902-424-4089; *Fax:* 902-424-5510
Executive Director, John MacDonald
Tel: 902-424-6413
Director, Client Relations & Support, Paul Benoit
Tel: 902-424-1285
Director, Collection Services, Sharon Glazebrook
Tel: 902-424-6711
Director, Communications, Elizabeth MacDonald
Tel: 902-424-6315
Director, Licensing & Registration, Jonpaul Landry
Tel: 902-483-9454

Associated Agencies, Boards & Commissions:
•Motor Vehicle Appeal Board
Maritime Centre
1505 Barrington St., 9th Fl. North
Halifax, NS B3J 3K5
Tel: 902-424-4256
Toll-free: 855-424-4256
novascotia.ca/snsmr/access/drivers/motor-vehicle-appeal-board.asp

Access Nova Scotia
PO Box 2734 Halifax, NS B3J 3K5
Tel: 902-424-5200; *Fax:* 902-424-0720
Toll-Free: 800-670-4357
askus@gov.ns.ca
www.novascotia.ca/snsmr/access

Co-operatives Branch
15 Alderbrook Dr., Truro Heights, NS B6L 0C4
Tel: 902-893-6190; *Fax:* 902-893-6264
nscoop@gov.ns.ca
Other Communication: URL: www.novascotia.ca/snsmr/access/business/registry-joint-stock-companies/co-operatives.asp

Geomatics Centre
160 Willow St., Amherst, NS B4H 3W5
Tel: 902-667-7231; *Fax:* 902-667-6008
geoinfo@novascotia.ca
geonova.novascotia.ca
twitter.com/NSGeoNOVA
Director, Geographic Information Services, Colin Wade MacDonald
Tel: 902-424-5281

Information Management Services
Director, Project & Portfolio Technology, Chad Joseph MacDonald
Tel: 902-424-8439

Land Programs
#14S, 1505 Barrington St., Halifax, NS B3J 2Y3
Fax: 902-424-0639
Toll-Free: 800-670-4357
propertyonline@gov.ns.ca
Other Communication: URL: www.novascotia.ca/snsmr/access/land/land-services-information/land-registry.asp
Registrar General & Director, Norman Hill
Tel: 902-722-5079
Director, Land Programs & Registrar General, Mark Coffin
Tel: 902-424-8899

Property Online (POL)
RGLandTitles@gov.ns.ca
www.novascotia.ca/snsmr/access/land/property-online.asp
Director, Property Registry, Donna MacRury
Tel: 902-563-2234

Provincial Tax Commission
Maritime Centre, 1505 Barrington St., 9th Fl., PO Box 1003 Halifax, NS B3J 2X1
Tel: 902-424-6300; *Fax:* 902-424-7434
Toll-Free: 800-565-2336
taxcommission@gov.ns.ca
www.novascotia.ca/snsmr/access/business/tax-commission.asp
Other Communication: Tax Info, Phone: 902-424-6538; E-mail: taxcommission@novascotia.ca
Associate Deputy Minister & Provincial Tax Commissioner, Scott Farmer
Director, Audit & Enforcement, Bernard Meagher
Tel: 902-424-3192
Director, Appeals; Senior Policy Advisor, Robert Newcomb
Tel: 902-424-1709

Registry of Joint Stock Companies
Maritime Centre, 1505 Barrington St., 9th Fl., PO Box 1529 Halifax, NS B3J 2Y4
Tel: 902-424-7770; *Fax:* 902-424-4633
Toll-Free: 800-225-8227
joint-stocks@gov.ns.ca
Other Communication: URL: www.novascotia.ca/snsmr/access/business/registry-joint-stock-companies.asp
Registrar, Hayley Clarke
Tel: 902-424-7742

Registry of Motor Vehicles
Tel: 902-424-5851
Toll-Free: 800-898-7668
www.novascotia.ca/snsmr/rmv
Registrar & Director, Paul Arsenault
Tel: 902-424-7801
Director, Metro Service, David McCarthy
Tel: 902-424-1285

Service Delivery
Programs & services include e-Service, Operations Centre, Northeast Region, South & Western Valley Region, Service Integration, Access to Business & Access for Citizens.

Vital Statistics
300 Horseshoe Lake Dr., PO Box 157 Halifax, NS B3J 2M9
Tel: 902-424-4381; *Fax:* 902-450-7311
Toll-Free: 877-848-2578
vstat@gov.ns.ca
www.novascotia.ca/snsmr/access/vitalstats.asp

Access Nova Scotia Centres
Amherst
144 Robert Angus Dr., Amherst, NS B4H 4R7
Toll-Free: 800-670-4357

Antigonish
Antigosh Mall Annex, #3, 149 Church St., Antigonish, NS B2G 2E2
Toll-Free: 800-670-4357

Bridgewater
80 Logan Rd., Bridgewater, NS B4V 3J8
Toll-Free: 800-670-4357

Dartmouth
Russell Lake West, #134, 250 Baker Dr., Dartmouth, NS B2W 6L4
Tel: 902-424-5200
Toll-Free: 800-670-4357

Digby
338 Hwy. 303, Digby, NS B0V 1A0
Tel: 902-837-5111
Toll-Free: 800-670-4357

Halifax
Bayers Lake Business Park, 300 Horseshoe Lake Drive, Halifax, NS B3S 0B7
Tel: 902-424-5200
Toll-Free: 800-670-4357

Kentville
5 Shylah Drive, Kentville, NS B4N 0H2
Toll-Free: 800-670-4357

Lower Sackville
486 Sackville Dr., Lower Sackville, NS B4C 2R8
Tel: 902-424-5200
Toll-Free: 800-670-4357

Port Hawkesbury
Provincial Building, #22, 218 MacSween St., Port Hawkesbury, NS B9A 2J9
Toll-Free: 800-670-4357

Stellarton
94 Lawrence Blvd., Stellarton, NS B0K 1S0
Toll-Free: 800-670-4357

Sydney
Moxam Centre, 380 King's Rd., Sydney, NS B1S 1A8
Toll-Free: 800-670-4357

Truro
15 Alderbrooke Dr., Truro, NS B6L 0C4
Toll-Free: 800-670-4357

Yarmouth
Provincial Bldg., #127, 10 Starrs Rd., Yarmouth, NS B5A 2T1
Toll-Free: 800-670-4357

Program Management & Corporate Services
Director, Finance, Marianne Hakkert-Lebel
Tel: 902-424-0310
Director, Consumer & Business Policy, Dean Johnson
Tel: 902-722-1322

Nova Scotia Advisory Council on the Status of Women

Quinpool Centre, #202, 6169 Quinpool Rd., PO Box 745 Halifax, NS B3J 2T3
Tel: 902-424-8662; *Fax:* 902-424-0573
Toll-Free: 800-565-8662
women@gov.ns.ca
www.women.gov.ns.ca
twitter.com/StatusofWomenNS
www.facebook.com/112218661874

The agency advocates for improved legislation, policies & programs for women, & provides research & policy advice to government on ways in which public policies & programs could better serve women.
Minister Responsible, Hon. Joanne Bernard
Tel: 902-424-8662; *Fax:* 902-424-0573
Executive Director, Stephanie MacInnis-Langley
Tel: 902-424-7548

Tourism Nova Scotia (TNS)

8 Water St., PO Box 667 Windsor, NS B0N 2T0
Tel: 902-798-6700; *Fax:* 902-798-6610
Toll-Free: 800-565-0000
TNS@gov.ns.ca
www.tourismns.ca
Other Communication: Travel Information: explore@novascotia.ca
twitter.com/VisitNovaScotia
www.facebook.com/novascotia
instagram.com/visitnovascotia

Formerly known as the Nova Scotia Tourism Agency (NSTA), Tourism Nova Scotia is reponsible for designing a tourism strategy for Nova Scotia & creates sustainable gowth in the industry.
Chair, Ben Cowan-Dewar
Vice-Chair, Irene d'Entremont
Chief Executive Officer, Michele Saran

Nova Scotia Department of Transportation & Infrastructure Renewal

Johnston Bldg., 1672 Granville St., 2nd Fl., PO Box 186 Halifax, NS B3J 2N2
Tel: 902-424-2297; *Fax:* 902-424-0532
Toll-Free: 888-432-3233
tpwpaff@novascotia.ca
novascotia.ca/tran

Provides a transportation network for the safe & efficient movement of people & goods; serves the building, property & accommodation needs of government departments & agencies; employs professional, dedicated people & offers a high level of customer service.
Minister, Hon. Geoff MacLellan
Tel: 902-424-5875; *Fax:* 902-424-0171
tirmin@novascotia.ca
Deputy Minister, Paul T. LaFleche
Tel: 902-424-4036; *Fax:* 902-424-2014
Paul.LaFleche@novascotia.ca
Executive Director, Government Services, John Bernard O'Connor
Tel: 902-424-2756
Director, Vehicle Compliance, Raymond Beaton
Tel: 902-631-0772
Director, Darrell MacDonald
Tel: 902-424-6586
Director, Road Safety, Janice Harland
Tel: 902-424-4206
Director, Highway Engineering & Capital Programs, Brian Ward
Tel: 902-860-5600
Director, Financial Services, D. Brent Pero
Tel: 902-424-5018
Associated Agencies, Boards & Commissions:

•Sydney Tar Ponds Agency
1 Inglis St.
PO Box 1028 A
Sydney, NS B1P 6J7
Tel: 902-567-1035; *Fax:* 902-567-1037
www.tarpondscleanup.ca

Highway Operations
novascotia.ca/tran/highways

This division provides for provincial highway & bridge maintenance, as well as the operation of the Department's fleet management & a strategic planning section. District Services provides general services on primary & secondary roads & works with private sector contractors to provide the public with enhanced road systems.
Executive Director, Highway Maintenance & Operations, Barbara Baillie
Tel: 902-563-2255
Executive Director, Highway Engineering & Construction, Peter Hackett
Tel: 902-860-5600
Director, Highway Engineering & Capital Progress, Brian Ward
Tel: 902-860-5600

Public Works
novascotia.ca/tran/works

This division provides technical expertise & services required by the Department's highway, building & property divisions. The Highway Engineering Services section provides delivery of highway planning, geometric & structural design, traffic engineering, capital program maintenance & asset management business functions. The Engineering & Design section provides engineering, architectural, environmental & technical services & project management services for projects that are related to maintaining & constructing highway & building infrastructure. The Building Services & Operations section oversees the management, operation, maintenance & renovation of government buildings, infrastructure & properties, as well as the provision of trade & contract services in both leased & owned premises.
Executive Director, Building Project Services, Thomas Gouthro
Tel: 902-860-2999

Nova Scotia Utility & Review Board (NSUARB)

Summit Place, 1601 Lower Water St., 3rd Fl., PO Box 1692 Stn. M, Halifax, NS B3J 3S3
Tel: 902-424-4448; *Fax:* 902-424-3919
Toll-Free: 855-442-4448
board@novascotia.ca
nsuarb.novascotia.ca

The Board has a very broad mandate encompassing a number of Acts. Operations fall into two categories, regulatory & adjudicative. The regulatory category includes the regulation of public utilities, licensing of public passenger carriers, monitoring of automobile insurance rates, the approval of Halifax-Dartmouth bridge fares, & the regulation of natural gas distribution & pipelines. The Board conducts hearings relating to gaming control, liquor control & film classification. The adjudicative category includes appeals or applications relating to property assessments, expropriation compensation claims, planning & subdivisions, heritage properties, criminal injury compensation claims, municipal boundaries, municipal & school board electoral boundaries, as well as gasoline, diesel oil & tobacco taxes. The Board receives its authority from the Public Inquiries Act & the Utility & Review Board Act.
Chair, Peter W. Gurnham, Q.C.
Executive Director, Paul G. Allen, CA
Chief Clerk, Elaine Wagner
Tel: 902-424-4448 ext: 236

Workers' Compensation Board of Nova Scotia

5668 South St., PO Box 1150 Halifax, NS B3J 2Y2
Tel: 902-491-8999
Toll-Free: 800-870-3331
info@wcb.gov.ns.ca
www.wcb.ns.ca
Other Communication: Injury Reporting, Fax: 902-491-8001
twitter.com/worksafeforlife

Coordinates the workers' compensation system to assist injured workers & their employers by providing timely medical & rehabilitative support to help injured workers return to work. Also, to provide appropriate compensation for work-related injuries & illnesses.
Chair, Rodney Burgar
Chief Executive Officer, Stuart MacLean
Tel: 902-491-8304
Chief Financial Officer, Leo McKenna, CA
Tel: 902-491-8402

Government of Nunavut

Seat of Government: PO Box 1000 Stn. 200, Iqaluit, NU X0A 0H0
Tel: 867-975-6000; *Fax:* 867-975-6099
Toll-Free: 877-212-6438
info@gov.nu.ca
www.gov.nu.ca
twitter.com/GovofNunavut
www.facebook.com/244924798918807
www.youtube.com/user/GovernmentofNunavut

On April 1, 1999, Nunavut Territory was created as part of the Nunavut Land Claims Agreement signed in 1993. It has a land area of 1,877,787.62 sq km, & the StatsCan census in 2011 showed the population was 31,906. Nunavut Territory is governed by a fully elected Legislative Assembly of 22 members elected for a five-year term. Government is by consensus rather than party politics. The Legislature elects the Premier & a seven-member Executive Council, which is charged with the operation of government & the establishment of program & spending priorities. Nunavut Territory acts under the same conditions as other territories in Canada. For an explanation of the difference between provinces & territories please see the Yukon Territory listing. The Commissioner of Nunavut Territory is appointed by the Federal Government, & serves a role similar to that of the Lieutenant Governor in provincial jurisdictions.

Office of the Commissioner

PO Box 2379 Iqaluit, NU X0A 0H0
Tel: 867-975-5120; *Fax:* 867-975-5123
commissionerofnunavut@gov.nu.ca
www.commissioner.gov.nu.ca
Secondary Address: House 2554
Commissioner's Residence
Iqaluit, NU
Commissioner, Nellie T. Kusugak
Note: Commissioner Edna Elias finished her term on May 12, 2015.

Office of the Premier

PO Box 2410 Iqaluit, NU X0A 0H0
Tel: 867-975-5050; *Fax:* 867-975-5051
www.premier.gov.nu.ca
Premier; Minister, Executive & Intergovernmental Affairs; Minister Responsible, Aboriginal Affairs, Senior's Advocate & Immigration, Hon. Peter Taptuna
Tel: 867-975-5050; *Fax:* 867-975-5016
premier.taptuna@gov.nu.ca
Note: Peter Taptuna was elected as Premier at a leadership forum held onNovember 15, 2013.
Principal Secretary, Ed Picco
epicco@gov.nu.ca

Executive Council

PO Box 2410 Iqaluit, NU X0A 0H0
www.gov.nu.ca/cabinet
Premier; Minister, Executive & Intergovernmental Affairs; Minister Responsible, Aboriginal Affairs, Immigration, & Senior's Advocate, Hon. Peter Taptuna
Tel: 867-975-5050; *Fax:* 867-975-5016
premier.taptuna@gov.nu.ca
Deputy Premier; Minister, Economic Development & Transportation; Minister Responsible, Mines, Nunavut Business Credit Corporation, Nunavut Development Corporation, Status of Women & Utility Rates Review Council, Hon. Monica Ell-Kanayuk
Tel: 867-975-5075; *Fax:* 867-975-5095
mell@gov.nu.ca
Minister, Culture & Heritage; Minister, Languages; Minister Responsible, Nunavut Housing Corporation, Hon. George Kuksuk
Tel: 867-975-5018; *Fax:* 867-975-5095
gkuksuk@gov.nu.ca
Minister, Family Services; Minister Responsible, Poverty Reduction, Homelessness & Qulliq Energy Corporation, Hon. Johnny Mike
Tel: 867-975-5024; *Fax:* 867-975-5095
jmike@gov.nu.ca
Minister, Finance; Minister, Justice; Chair, Financial Management Board; Minister Responsible, Nunavut Liquor Commission, Liquor Licensing Board, Human Rights Tribunal, Labour Standards Board & Workers' Safety & Compensation Commission, Hon. Keith Peterson
Tel: 867-975-5028; *Fax:* 867-975-5095
kpeterson@gov.nu.ca
Government House Leader; Minister, Education; Minister Responsible, Nunavut Arctic College, Hon. Paul Aarulaaq Quassa
Tel: 867-975-5023; *Fax:* 867-975-5095
pquassa@gov.nu.ca

Minster, Health; Minister Responsible, suicide prevention, Hon. George Hickes
Tel: 867-975-5074; *Fax:* 867-975-2034
ghickes@gov.nu.ca

Minister, Community & Government Services; Minister, Evironment; Minister, Energy; Nunavut Chair, Hudson Bay Roundtable, Hon. Joe Savikataaq
Tel: 867-975-5026; *Fax:* 867-975-5042
jsavikataaq@gov.nu.ca

Nunavut Legislative Assembly

926 Federal Rd., PO Box 1200 Iqaluit, NU X0A 0H0
Tel: 867-975-5000; *Fax:* 867-975-5190
Toll-Free: 877-334-7266
leginfo@assembly.nu.ca
www.assembly.nu.ca
Other Communication: Security, Phone: 867-975-5111

Speaker, Hon. George Qulaut
Tel: 867-975-5017
gqulaut@assembly.nu.ca

Clerk of the Assembly, John Quirke
Tel: 867-975-5100
jquirke@assembly.nu.ca

Deputy Clerk, Nancy Tupik
Tel: 867-975-5115
ntupik@assembly.nu.ca

Clerk Assistant, Stephen Innuksuk
Tel: 867-975-5163
sinnuksuk@assembly.nu.ca

Director, Research, Policy & Library Services, Alex Baldwin
Tel: 867-975-5130
abaldwin@assembly.nu.ca

Director, Corporate Services, Michael Rafter
Tel: 867-975-5104
mrafter@assembly.nu.ca

Legislative Librarian, Yvonne Earle
Tel: 867-975-5134
yearle@assembly.nu.ca
PO Box 1200
Iqaluit, NU X0A 0H0 Canada

Standing & Special Committees

www.assembly.nu.ca/standing-and-special-committees

Standing Committees provide an opportunity to study legislation, examine policy issues & review government spending proposals. Special Committees investigate specific issues & policy areas. The current Standing Committees are: Government Estimates & Operations; Legislation; Public Accounts, Independent Officers & Other Entities; & Rules, Procedures & Privileges.

Chair, Standing Committee on Government Estimates & Operations, David Joanasie
Constituency: South Baffin
Tel: 867-975-5047; *Fax:* 867-975-5124
djoanasie@assembly.nu.ca

Chair, Standing Committee on Legislation, Tom Sammurtok
Constituency: Rankin Inlet North-Chesterfield Inlet
Tel: 867-975-5045; *Fax:* 967-975-5046
tsammurtok@assembly.nu.ca

Chair, Standing Committee on Public Accounts, Independent Officers & Other Entities, Pat Angnakak
Constituency: Iqaluit-Niaqunnguu
Tel: 867-975-5025; *Fax:* 867-975-5061
pangnakak@assembly.nu.ca

Chair, Standing Committee on Rules, Procedures & Privileges, Joe Enook
Constituency: Tununiq
Tel: 867-975-5035; *Fax:* 867-975-5107
jenook@assembly.nu.ca

Fourth Legislative Assembly - Nunavut

PO Box 1200 Iqaluit, NU X0A 0H0
www.assembly.nu.ca

Last General Election: Oct. 28, 2013.
Maximum Duration, 5 years.
Salaries, Indemnities & Allowances (effective 2011):
MLAs $90,396 including $1,000 tax free allowance;
Premier $179,683 total;
Deputy Premier $167,094 total;
Ministers & Speaker $160,505 total;
Deputy Speaker $108,475 total.
A taxable Northern allowance ranging between $15,000 & $34,500 is paid to all Members & is dependent upon the community & residence of the Member.
The address for all members of the Legislative Assembly is as follows: Legislative Assembly of Nunavut, PO Box 1200, Iqaluit NU X0A OHO. The following is a list of members, their constituency, the number of persons on the official voters list for the most recent election, & contact information:

Members of the Legislative Assembly of Nunavut

Tony Akoak
Constituency: Gjoa Haven *No. of Constituents:* 628
Tel: 867-975-5014; *Fax:* 867-975-5117
takoak@assembly.nu.ca
Other Communications: Constituency Phone: 867-360-6337; Fax: 867-360-6819

Pat Angnakak
Constituency: Iqaluit-Niaqunnguu *No. of Constituents:* 741
Tel: 867-975-5025; *Fax:* 867-975-5061
pangnakak@assembly.nu.ca
Other Communications: Constituency Phone: 867-979-0410; Fax: 867-979-0415

Deputy Premier; Minister, Economic Development & Transportation; Minister Responsible, Mines, Nunavut Business Credit Corporation, Nunavut Development Corporation, Status of Women & Utility Rates Review Council, Hon. Monica Ell-Kanayuk
Constituency: Iqaluit-Manirajak *No. of Constituents:* 709
Tel: 867-975-5075; *Fax:* 867-975-5095
mell@gov.nu.ca
Other Communications: Constituency Phone: 867-979-5807; Fax: 867-979-2226

Joe Enook
Constituency: Tununiq *No. of Constituents:* 729
Tel: 867-975-5035; *Fax:* 867-975-5107
jenook@assembly.nu.ca
Other Communications: Constituency Phone: 867-899-8999; Fax: 975-899-8713

Minister, Health; Minister Responsible, suicide prevention, Hon. George Hickes
Constituency: Iqaluit-Tasiluk *No. of Constituents:* 856
Tel: 867-975-5074; *Fax:* 867-975-2034
ghickes@gov.nu.ca
Other Communications: Constituency Phone: 867-979-6923; Fax: 867-979-4604

David Joanasie
Constituency: South Baffin *No. of Constituents:* 854
Tel: 867-975-5047; *Fax:* 867-975-5124
djoanasie@assembly.nu.ca
Other Communications: Constituency Phone: 867-897-8753; Fax: 867-897-8645

Pauloosie Keyootak
Constituency: Uqqummiut *No. of Constituents:* 738
Tel: 867-975-5027; *Fax:* 867-975-5121
pkeyootak@assembly.nu.ca
Other Communications: Constituency Phone: 867-927-8004; Fax: 867-927-8005
Note: Pauloosie Keeyootak was elected in a by-election held February 9, 2015.

Minister, Culture & Heritage; Minister, Languages; Minister Responsible, Nunavut Housing Corporation, Hon. George Kuksuk
Constituency: Arviat North-Whale Cove *No. of Constituents:* 616
Tel: 867-975-5018; *Fax:* 867-975-5095
gkuksuk@gov.nu.ca
Other Communications: Constituency Phone: 867-857-4201, Fax: 867-857-4205

Steve Mapsalak
Constituency: Aivilik *No. of Constituents:* 709
Tel: 867-975-5031; *Fax:* 867-975-5037
smapsalak@assembly.nu.ca
Other Communications: Constituency Phone: 867-462-4363; Fax: 867-462-4364

Minister, Family Services; Minister Responsible, Poverty Reduction, Homelessness & Qulliq Energy Corporation, Hon. Johnny Mike
Constituency: Pangnirtung *No. of Constituents:* 666
Tel: 867-975-5024; *Fax:* 867-975-5095
jmike@gov.nu.ca
Other Communications: Constituency Phone: 867-473-8220; Fax: 867-473-8227

Simeon Mikkungwak
Constituency: Baker Lake *No. of Constituents:* 936
Tel: 867-975-5019; *Fax:* 867-975-5112
smikkungwak@assembly.nu.ca
Other Communications: Constituency Phone: 867-793-4949; Fax: 867-793-4950

Paul Okalik
Constituency: Iqaluit-Sinaa *No. of Constituents:* 771
Tel: 867-975-5048; *Fax:* 867-975-5049
pokalik@assembly.nu.ca
Other Communications: Constituency Phone: 867-979-2210; Fax: 867-979-2211

Minister, Finance; Minister, Justice; Chair, Financial Management Board; Minister Responsible, Nunavut Liquor Commission, Liquor Licensing Board, Human Rights Tribunal, Labour Standards Board & Workers' Safety & Compensation Commission, Hon. Keith Peterson
Constituency: Cambridge Bay *No. of Constituents:* 644
Tel: 867-975-5028; *Fax:* 867-975-5095
kpeterson@gov.nu.ca
Other Communications: Constituency Phone: 867-983-3777; Fax: 867-983-3778

Emiliano Qirngnuq
Constituency: Netsilik *No. of Constituents:* 751
Tel: 867-975-5021; *Fax:* 867-975-5116
EQirngnuq@assembly.nu.ca
Note: Emiliano Qirngnuq won the riding in a by-election held Feb. 8, 2016.

Government House Leader; Minister, Education; Minister Responsible, Nunavut Arctic College, Hon. Paul Aarulaaq Quassa
Constituency: Aggu *No. of Constituents:* 457
Tel: 867-975-5023; *Fax:* 867-975-5095
pquassa@gov.nu.ca
Other Communications: Constituency Phone: 867-934-4070; Fax: 867-934-4071

Speaker of the Legislative Assembly, Hon. George Quviq Qulaut
Constituency: Amittuq *No. of Constituents:* 588
Tel: 867-975-5017; *Fax:* 867-975-5035
gqulaut@assembly.nu.ca
Other Communications: Constituency Phone: 867-934-4070; Fax: 867-934-4071

Allan Rumbolt
Constituency: Hudson Bay *No. of Constituents:* 423
Tel: 867-975-5032; *Fax:* 867-975-5113
arumbolt@assembly.nu.ca
Other Communications: Constituency Phone: 867-266-8518; Fax: 867-266-8315

Alexander Sammurtok
Constituency: Rankin Inlet South *No. of Constituents:* 615
Tel: 867-975-5015; *Fax:* 867-975-5109
asammurtok@assembly.nu.ca
Other Communications: Constituency Phone: 867-645-4866; Fax: 867-645-4865
Note: Alexander Sammurtok won Rankin Inlet South after a by-election held February 11, 2014.

Tom Sammurtok
Constituency: Rankin Inlet North-Chesterfield Inlet *No. of Constituents:* 535
Tel: 867-975-5045; *Fax:* 967-975-5046
tsammurtok@assembly.nu.ca
Other Communications: Constituency Phone: 867-645-4900; Fax: 867-645-4981

Minister, Community & Government Services; Minister, Environment; Minister, Energy; Nunavut Chair, Hudson Bay Roundtable, Hon. Joe Savikataaq
Constituency: Arviat South *No. of Constituents:* 592
Tel: 867-975-5026; *Fax:* 867-975-5042
jsavikataaq@gov.nu.ca
Other Communications: Constituency Phone: 867-857-4485; Fax: 867-857-4486

Isaac Shooyook
Constituency: Quttiktuq *No. of Constituents:* 532
Tel: 867-975-5030; *Fax:* 867-975-5108
ishooyook@assembly.nu.ca
Other Communications: Constituency Phone: 867-439-8050; Fax: 867-439-8051

Premier; Minister, Executive & Intergovernmental Affairs; Minister Responsible, Aboriginal Affairs, Immigration, & Senior's Advocate, Hon. Peter Taptuna
Constituency: Kugluktuk
Tel: 867-975-5050; *Fax:* 867-975-5016
premier.taptuna@gov.nu.ca
Other Communications: Constituency Phone: 867-982-4232; Fax: 867-982-5733
Note: Peter Taptuna was acclaimed in the October 2013 general election, & was elected as Premier at a leadership forum held on November 15, 2013.

Nunavut Territory Government Departments & Agencies

Nunavut Territory Department of Community & Government Services

W.G. Brown Bldg., 4th Fl., PO Box 1000 Stn. 700, Iqaluit, NU X0A 0H0
Tel: 867-975-5400; *Fax:* 867-975-5305
cgs.gov.nu.ca
Other Communication: 867-975-5306

To support the development, provision & maintenance of programs & services which affect the communities in all areas of municipal responsibility & transportation.

Minister; Nunavut Chair, Hudson Bay Roundtable, Hon. Joe Savikataaq
Tel: 867-975-5026; *Fax:* 867-975-5042
jsavikataaq@gov.nu.ca

Deputy Minister, Lori Kimball

Assistant Deputy Minister, Darren Flynn
Tel: 867-645-8106; *Fax:* 867-645-8141

Corporate Chief Information Officer, Dean Wells
Tel: 867-975-6439
dwells@gov.nu.ca

Executive Director, Municipal Training Organization (MTO), Matthew Ayres

Tel: 867-975-5346
mayres@gov.nu.ca
Executive Director, NCIAC, Catherine Foo
Tel: 867-975-5336
cfoo@gov.nu.ca
Director, Community Infrastructure, Bu Lam
Tel: 867-975-5462
blam@gov.nu.ca
Director, Corporate Affairs & Support Services, Carmen Levi
Tel: 867-975-5332
clevi@gov.nu.ca
Director, Policy & Procedures, Lucy Magee
Tel: 867-975-5309; *Fax:* 867-975-5351
lmagee@gov.nu.ca
Director, Protection Services, Ed Zebedee
Tel: 867-975-5319; *Fax:* 867-975-5453
ezebedee@gov.nu.ca
Senior Manager, Operations & Networks, Jeff Bisson
Tel: 867-975-6474
jbisson@gov.nu.ca
Senior Consumer Affairs Officer, Leah Aupaluktuq
Tel: 867-793-3303; *Fax:* 867-793-3321
Administrative Officer, Dorothy Kaludjak
Tel: 867-975-5306; *Fax:* 867-975-5305
dkaludjak@gov.nu.ca

Regional Offices

Baffin
PO Box 330 Cape Dorset, NU X0A 0C0
Regional Director, Timoon Toonoo
Tel: 867-897-3607
ttoonoo@gov.nu.ca

Kitikmeot
PO Box 200 Cambridge Bay, NU X0B 0C0
Regional Director, Kevin Niptanatiak
Tel: 867-983-4138; *Fax:* 867-983-4026

Kivalliq
PO Box 490 Rankin Inlet, NU X0C 0G0
Regional Director, Jason Tologanak
Tel: 867-645-8150; *Fax:* 867-645-8197

Nunavut Territory Department of Culture & Heritage

PO Box 1000 Stn. 800, Iqaluit, NU X0A 0H0
Tel: 867-975-5500; *Fax:* 867-975-5504
Toll-Free: 866-934-2035
www.ch.gov.nu.ca

Responsible for the protection, preservation & promotion of Inuit languages. Cultural initiatives & departmental goals are reached in coordination with & in support of elder & youth groups. Acts in respect to issues concerning women & people with disabilities. The government is dedicated to preserving & promoting elements that make up the Inuit identity.

Minister; Minister, Languages, Hon. George Kuksuk
Tel: 867-975-5018; *Fax:* 867-975-5095
gkuksuk@gov.nu.ca
Deputy Minister, Pauloosie Suvega
psuvega@gov.nu.ca
Assistant Deputy Minister, Irene Tanuyak
Tel: 867-975-5532
itanuyak@gov.nu.ca
Chair, Inuit Uqausinginnik Taiguusiliuqtiit, Elijah Erkloo
Tel: 867-975-5545
eerkloo@gov.nu.ca
Director, Corporate Services, Regilee Adla
Tel: 867-975-5514
radla@gov.nu.ca
Director, Official Languages, Stephanie Clouter
Tel: 867-975-5507
scloutier1@gov.nu.ca
Director, Policy & Planning, Gideonie Joamie
Tel: 867-975-5505
gjoamie@gov.nu.ca
Director, Inuit Quajimajatuqangit, Shuvinai Mike
Tel: 867-975-5525; *Fax:* 867-975-5504
smike@gov.nu.ca
Director, Elders & Youth, Joanna Quassa
Tel: 867-934-2032
jquassa@gov.nu.ca
Director, Heritage, Douglas Stenton
Tel: 867-975-5524
dstenton1@gov.nu.ca
Acting Manager, Nunavut Public Library Services, Dan Galway
Tel: 867-979-5401
dgalway@gov.nu.ca

Nunavut Territory Department of Economic Development & Transportation

Inuksugait Plaza, Bldg. 1104A, PO Box 1000 Stn. 1500, Iqaluit, NU X0A 0H0
Tel: 867-975-7800; *Fax:* 867-975-7870
Toll-Free: 888-975-5999
edt@gov.nu.ca
www.edt.gov.nu.ca

Deputy Premier; Minister, Hon. Monica Ell-Kanayuk
Tel: 867-975-5075; *Fax:* 867-975-5095
mell@gov.nu.ca
Deputy Minister, Sherri Rowe
Tel: 867-975-7800
Director, Policy, Planning & Communications, Matthew Bowler
Tel: 867-975-7808
mbowler@gov.nu.ca
Director, Community Operations, Rhoda Katsak
Tel: 867-899-7339
RKatsak@gov.nu.ca
Director, Finance & Administration, Tanya Winmill
Tel: 867-975-7816
twinmill@gov.nu.ca
Executive Coordinator, Nunavummi Nangminiqaqtunik Ikajuuti (NNI) Secretariat, Ron Dewar
Tel: 867-975-7835
RDewar@gov.nu.ca

Associated Agencies, Boards & Commissions:

•Nunavut Business Credit Corporation (NBCC)
Parnaivak Bldg.
#100
PO Box 2548
Iqaluit, NU X0A 0H0
Tel: 867-975-7891; *Fax:* 867-975-7897
Toll-free: 800-758-0038
credit@nbcc.nu.ca
www.nbcc.nu.ca

Economic Development

Assistant Deputy Minister, Bernie MacIsaac
Tel: 867-975-7823
bmacisaac@gov.nu.ca
Director, Community Operations, Kitikmeot, Vacant
Director, Tourism & Cultural Industries, Nancy Guyon
Tel: 867-975-7856
NGuyon@gov.nu.ca
Director, Community Operations, Qikiqtaaluk, Rhoda Katsak
Tel: 867-899-7339
rkatsak@gov.nu.ca
Director, Community Operations, Kivalliq, Laura MacKenzie
Tel: 867-645-8458
lmackenzie@gov.nu.ca
Director, Minerals & Petroleum Resources, David Kunuk
Tel: 867-975-7892
DKunuk@gov.nu.ca

Transportation

Assistant Deputy Minister, Jim Stevens
Tel: 867-975-7831
jstevens@gov.nu.ca
Director, Motor Vehicles, Lorna Gee
Tel: 867-360-4614
lgee@gov.nu.ca
Director, Iqaluit International Airport, John Graham
Tel: 867-979-5224
jgraham@gov.nu.ca
Director, Nunavut Airports, Shawn Maley
Tel: 867-645-8203
smaley@gov.nu.ca
Interim Director, Transportation Policy & Planning, Art Stewart
Tel: 867-975-7826

Nunavut Territory Department of Education

Bldg. 1107, 2nd Fl., PO Box 1000 Stn. 900, Iqaluit, NU X0A 0H0
Tel: 867-975-5600; *Fax:* 867-975-5605
info.edu@gov.nu.ca
www.edu.gov.nu.ca

Government House Leader; Minister, Hon. Paul Aarulaaq Quassa
Tel: 867-975-5023; *Fax:* 867-975-5095
pquassa@gov.nu.ca
Deputy Minister, Kathy Okpik
Tel: 867-975-5600
kokpik@gov.nu.ca
Director, French Education Services, Martine St-Louis
Tel: 867-975-5627
mstlouis@gov.nu.ca
Director, Policy & Planning, Kuthula Matshazi
Tel: 867-975-5606
kmatshazi@gov.nu.ca
Director, Corporate Services, Heather Moffett
Tel: 867-975-5616; *Fax:* 867-975-5605
hmoffett@gov.nu.ca

Adult Learning, Career & Early Childhood Services
Fax: 867-857-3090

Asst. Deputy Minister, Irene Tanuyak
Tel: 867-975-5604; *Fax:* 867-975-5635
itanuyak@gov.nu.ca
Director, Income Support, Sandy Teiman
Tel: 867-975-5685; *Fax:* 867-975-5690
steiman@gov.nu.ca
Acting Director, Adult Learning & Post-Secondary Services, Edward Duru
Tel: 867-857-3056
eduru@gov.nu.ca
Director, Career Development Services & Adult Special Project, David Lloyd
Tel: 867-975-5648
dlloyd@gov.nu.ca

Regional Offices
Tel: 867-983-7214; *Fax:* 867-983-2004

Kitikmeot
Kitikmeot Career & Early Childhood Services, PO Box 20 Cambridge Bay, NU X0B 0C0
Tel: 867-983-4031; *Fax:* 867-983-4025
Toll-Free: 800-661-0845
Regional Director, Brenda Jancke
bjancke@gov.nu.ca

Kivalliq
Kivalliq Career & Early Childhood Services, Bag 002, Tapariit Bldg., Rankin Inlet, NU X0C 0G0
Tel: 867-645-5040; *Fax:* 867-645-2148
Toll-Free: 800-953-8516
Regional Director, Richard MacKenzie
rmackenzie@gov.nu.ca

Qikiqtani
Qikiqtani Career & Early Childhood Services, PO Box 204 Pangnirtung, NU X0A 0R0
Tel: 867-473-2600; *Fax:* 867-473-2647
Toll-Free: 800-567-1514
Regional Director, John MacDonald
jmacdonald@gov.nu.ca

Curriculum & School Services

Assistant Deputy Minister, Peter Geikie
Tel: 867-975-5630
pgeikie@gov.nu.ca
Executive Director, Curriculum Development, Cathy McGregor
Tel: 867-975-5641; *Fax:* 867-975-5635
cmcgregor@gov.nu.ca
Director, French, Leonie Leduc Aissaoui
Tel: 867-975-5627
laissaoui@gov.nu.ca

Nunavut Emergency Management

PO Box 1000 Stn. 700, Iqaluit, NU X0A 0H0
Tel: 867-975-5403; *Fax:* 867-979-4221
Toll-Free: 800-693-1666
cgs.gov.nu.ca/en/commemergency.aspx
Other Communication: Headquarters Phone: 867-979-6262; Kitikmeot: 867-983-2542; Kivalliq: 867-645-3625; Qikiqtaaluk: 1-888-624-4043

Fire Marshall, Robert Prima
Tel: 867-975-5310
rprima@gov.nu.ca
Fire Marshal Trainee, Jerry Anilniliak
Tel: 867-975-5319
janilniliak1@gov.nu.ca
Manager, Emergency Response & Recovery, Steven Baillie
Tel: 867-975-5403
sbailliecgs@gov.nu.ca
Senior Emergency Preparedness Planner, Glen Higgins
Tel: 867-975-5764
ghiggins@gov.nu.ca

Nunavut Territory Department of Environment

PO Box 1000 Stn. 1300, Iqaluit, NU X0A 0H0
Tel: 867-975-7700; *Fax:* 867-975-7742
environment@gov.nu.ca
env.gov.nu.ca

Minister, Hon. Joe Savikataaq
Tel: 867-975-5026; *Fax:* 867-975-5042
jsavikataaq@gov.nu.ca
Deputy Minister, David Akeeagok

Assistant Deputy Minister, Earle Baddaloo
Tel: 867-975-7704
ebaddaloo@gov.nu.ca
Chief Federal Negotiator for Nunavut Devolution, Fred Caron
Director, Fisheries & Sealing, Wayne Lynch
Tel: 867-975-7750; *Fax:* 867-975-7742
cegeni@gov.nu.ca
Director, Corporate Services, Nikki Nweze
Tel: 867-975-7708
nnweze@gov.nu.ca
Director, Policy, Planning & Legislation, Steve Pinksen
Tel: 867-975-7718; *Fax:* 867-975-7740
spinksen@gov.nu.ca
Executive Secretary, Lena Hughes
Tel: 867-975-7705; *Fax:* 867-975-7740
lhughes@gov.nu.ca

Regional Offices

Baffin
PO Box 569 Pond Inlet, NU X0A 0S0
Acting Regional Wildlife Manager, Robert Arsenault
Tel: 867-266-8098
rarsenault@gov.nu.ca

Kitikmeot
PO Box 377 Kugluktuk, NU X0B 0E0

Kivalliq
PO Box 120 Arviat, NU X0C 0E0

Nunavut Territory Department of Executive & Intergovernmental Affairs

1084 Aeroplex bldg., PO Box 1000 Stn. 200, Iqaluit, NU X0A 0H0
Tel: 867-975-6000; *Fax:* 867-975-6099
www.gov.nu.ca/executive-and-intergovernmental-affairs

The department provides advice & administrative support to Cabinet & the government, works to ensure that the Nunavut Land Claims Agreement & Nunavut's relationships with other governments in Canada & the circumpolar world are used to support common goals. The department compiles & communicates information & evaluates government programs & data.The Intergovernmental Affairs Division is responsible for the management & development of government strategies, policies & initiatives relating to federal, provincial, territorial, circumpolar & aboriginal affairs. This office participates in preparations for Intergovernmental activities such as the Western & Annual Premiers Conferences, First Ministers meetings & the Social Union Framework Agreement, the Arctic Council, the Nunavut Implementation Panel & the Clyde River Protocol.

Premier; Minister, Hon. Peter Taptuna
Tel: 867-975-5050; *Fax:* 867-975-5016
premier.taptuna@gov.nu.ca
Deputy Minister; Cabinet Secretary; Secretary to Senior Personnel Secretariat, Chris D'Arcy
Commissioner, Nellie Kusugak
Tel: 867-975-5122
nkusugakcom@gov.nu.ca
Deputy Commissioner, Vacant
Director, Communications, Catriona Macleod
Tel: 867-975-6049
CMacleod@gov.nu.ca
Director, Government Liaison Office, David Akoak
Tel: 867-975-6050
Director, Policy, Planning & Evaluation, Rachel Mark
Tel: 867-975-6029; *Fax:* 867-975-6029
rmark@gov.nu.ca
Director, Aboriginal & Circumpolar Affairs, Letia Obed
Tel: 867-975-6036; *Fax:* 867-975-6091
lobed@gov.nu.ca
Director, Corporate Services, Les Hickey
Tel: 867-975-6026
LHickey@gov.nu.ca
Director, Devolution Division, Mark Thompson
Tel: 867-975-6070
mthompson1@gov.nu.ca
Manager, Access Information, Jessica Bell
Tel: 867-975-6044
jessica.bell@gov.nu.ca
Manager, Administrative Services, Johnny Issaluk
Tel: 867-975-6051
jissaluk@gov.nu.ca
Manager, Administrative Services, Johnny Issaluk
Tel: 867-975-6051
jissaluk@gov.nu.ca
Manager, Finance, Angela Kabvitok
Tel: 867-975-6002
akabvitok@gov.nu.ca

Nunavut Territory Department of Family Services

PO Box 1000 Stn. 950, Iqaluit, NU X0A 0H0
Tel: 867-975-6038; *Fax:* 867-975-6091
www.fs.gov.nu.ca
Other Communication: Qikiqtani, Toll-Free: 1-800-567-1514; Kivalliq, Toll-Free: 1-800-953-8516; Kitikmeot, Toll-Free: 1-800-661-0845

The department began operations in 2013-14 & was created by uniting resources from the Departments of Education, Health & Social Services, Executive & Intergovernmental Affairs, Economic Development & Transportation, Human Resources & the Nunavut Housing Corporation. Its goal is to provide access to social safety services, protect vulnerable members of the community, to improve standards of living & assist the Territory with becoming more self-reliant. Matters of concern to the department include child welfare, adoptions, social advocacy, poverty reduction initiatives, family violence prevention, income assistance, career development & financial assistance for post-secondary students.

Minister; Minister Responsible, Poverty Reduction & Homelessness, Hon. Johnny Mike
Tel: 867-975-5024; *Fax:* 867-975-5095
jmike@gov.nu.ca
Deputy Minister, Rebekah Williams
Tel: 867-975-5204
rwilliams@gov.nu.ca
Assistant Deputy Minister, Irene Tanuyak
Tel: 867-975-5224
itanuyak@gov.nu.ca
Executive Director, Lynn Ryan MacKenzie
Tel: 867-975-5776
lmackenzie1@gov.nu.ca
Director, Social Services, Mark Arnold
Tel: 867-975-5750
marnold@gov.nu.ca
Director, Children & Family Services, Peter Dudding
Tel: 867-975-5750
pdudding@gov.nu.ca
Director, Income Assistance, Brandon Grant
Tel: 867-975-5682
bgrant@gov.nu.ca
Director, Career Development, John MacDonald
Tel: 867-975-5655
jmacdonald@gov.nu.ca
Director, Poverty Reduction, Ed McKenna
Tel: 867-975-7817
emckenna@gov.nu.ca
Director, Policy & Planning, Sherry McNeil-Mulak
Tel: 867-975-6022
smcneil-mulak@gov.nu.ca

Nunavut Territory Department of Finance

Bldg. 1079, 1st Fl., PO Box 1000 Stn. 430, Iqaluit, NU X0A 0H0
Tel: 867-975-5800; *Fax:* 867-975-5805
www.finance.gov.nu.ca

The Department of Finance is committed to provide direction and leadership to ensure fiscal responsibility and to create a secure base for Nunavut's economic growth, while promoting and maintaining public confidence in the prudence, propriety and integrity of government financial operations and respecting the principles of Inuit Qaujimajatuqangit (IQ).

Minister; Chair, Financial Management Board, Hon. Keith Peterson
Tel: 867-975-5028; *Fax:* 867-975-5095
kpeterson@gov.nu.ca
Deputy Minister, Finance; Secretary to the Financial Management Board, Jeffery Chown
jchown@gov.nu.ca
Assistant Deputy Minister, Peter Tumilty
Tel: 867-975-6865
ptumilty@gov.nu.ca
Director, Fiscal Policy, Dan Carlson
Tel: 867-975-6813
dcarlson@gov.nu.ca
Director, Expenditure Management, Camilius Egeni
Tel: 867-975-5835; *Fax:* 867-975-6825
cegeni@gov.nu.ca
Director, Corporate Services, Christine Ellsworth
Tel: 867-975-6812
cellsworth@gov.nu.ca
Director, Employee Relations & Job Evaluation, Cheryl Ramsay
Tel: 867-975-6211
cramsay@gov.nu.ca
Director, Liquor Management, Marion Love
Tel: 867-645-8478
mlove@gov.nu.ca
Director, Corporate Services, Scott Mariott
Tel: 867-975-6803; *Fax:* 867-975-6868
smarriott@gov.nu.ca
Director, Recruiting & Staffing, Jessa Chupik
Tel: 867-975-6223
jchupik@gov.nu.ca
Director, Financial Reporting & Controls, Susan Nichols
Tel: 867-975-5840
snichols@gov.nu.ca
Director, Financial Operations, Michael Pringle
Tel: 867-975-5829
mpringle@gov.nu.ca
Director, Compensation & Benefits, Tracey Moyles
Tel: 867-975-6870
tmoyles@gov.nu.ca
Director, Financial Systems Management, Suzanne Wilkes
Tel: 867-975-5870
swilkes@gov.nu.ca
Director, Corporate Policy, Jo-Anne Falkiner
Tel: 867-975-5831
jfalkiner@gov.nu.ca

Associated Agencies, Boards & Commissions:

•Nunavut Liquor Commission
Rankin Inlet, NU
The Commission oversees the operation of liquor stores, as well as the purchasing, selling, classifying, & distributing of liquor in Nunavut.

Regional Offices
Tel: 867-983-4043; *Fax:* 867-983-4041

Kitikmeot
Director, Regional Financial Services, Sandra Peterson
Tel: 867-983-4042
speterson@gov.nu.ca

Kivalliq

Qikiqtaaluk
Tel: 867-934-2056; *Fax:* 867-934-8677

Nunavut Territory Department of Health

PO Box 1000 Stn. 1000, Iqaluit, NU X0A 0H0
Tel: 867-975-5700; *Fax:* 867-975-5705
Toll-Free: 800-661-0833
www.gov.nu.ca/health

The Environmental Health Specialist provides recommendations & direction, consultation, development of standards, monitoring, maintenance & evaluation of all environmental health programs within Nunavut. Reviews the Public Health Act & Regulations & environmental health standards & policies & makes recommendations for revisions. Guides the regional environmental health officers in development & implementation of programs & policies in prevention of diseases caused by environmental factors, including food, water, waste disposal, housing & the sanitation of public places, including schools, day cares & other institutional facilities. Guides the Regional Environmental Health Officers in water & food-borne related illness investigations & food recalls. Guides the regions in the monitoring of drinking water supplies. Assists with development of health education & promotional materials & activities related to environmental health.

Minister; Minister Responsible, Suicide Prevention, Hon. George Hickes
Tel: 867-975-5074; *Fax:* 867-975-2034
ghickes@gov.nu.ca
Deputy Minister, Colleen Stockley
Tel: 867-975-5702
cstockley@gov.nu.ca
Assistant Deputy Minister, Rosemary Keenainak
Tel: 867-975-5798
rkeenainak@gov.nu.ca
Assistant Deputy Minister, Operations, Monita O'Connor
Tel: 867-975-5704
mo'connor@gov.nu.ca
Assistant Deputy Minister, Operations, Kathy Perrin
Tel: 867-975-5708
kperrin@gov.nu.ca
Chief Medical Officer of Health, Dr. Kim Barker
Tel: 867-975-5769
kbarker@gov.nu.ca
Deputy Chief Medical Officer of Health, Dr. Maureen Baikie
Tel: 867-975-5743
mbaikie@gov.nu.ca
Territorial Director, Medical Affairs, Kevin Compton
Tel: 867-975-7146
kcompton@gov.nu.ca
Executive Director, Corporate Services, Johan Glaudemans
Tel: 867-975-5742
jglaudemanshss@gov.nu.ca
Executive Director, Population Health, Gogi Greeley
Tel: 867-975-5709
ggreeley@gov.nu.ca
Executive Director, Lynn Ryan MacKenzie
Tel: 867-975-5992
lmackenzie1@gov.nu.ca

Executive Director, Iqaluit Health Services, Darlene McPherson
Tel: 867-975-7103
dmcpherson@gov.nu.ca
Acting Director, Support Services QGH, Katrina Burt
Tel: 867-975-7104
kburt@gov.nu.ca
Director, Medical Education, Dr. Madeleine Cole
Tel: 867-979-7300
mcole@gov.nu.ca
Director, Mental Health, Victoria Madsen
Tel: 867-979-7648
vmadsen@gov.nu.ca
Director, Medical Affairs & Telehealth, Dr. William MacDonald
Tel: 867-979-7117
wmacdonald2@gov.nu.ca
Director, Policy & Planning, Jacquie Pepper-Journal
Tel: 867-975-5956
jpepper-journal@gov.nu.ca
Director, Operations OHSNI, Judy Plourde
Director, Human Resources, Lisa Richter
Tel: 867-975-5738
lrichter@gov.nu.ca

Regional Offices
Tel: 867-983-4043; *Fax:* 867-983-4041

Baffin
Regional Director, Roy Inglangasuk
Tel: 867-473-2638
ringlangas@gov.nu.ca
Kitikmeot
Executive Director, Clara Evalik
Tel: 867-983-4075
cevalik@gov.nu.ca
Kivalliq
Acting Director, Kivalliq Health Centre, Andrea Sateana
Tel: 867-645-8374
asateana@gov.nu.ca

Nunavut Housing Corporation

PO Box 480 Arviat, NU X0C 0E0
Tel: 867-857-3000; *Fax:* 867-857-3040
www.nunavuthousing.ca

Minister Responsible, Hon. George Kuksuk
Tel: 867-975-5018; *Fax:* 867-975-5095
gkuksuk@gov.nu.ca
President & CEO, Terry Audla
Chief Operating Officer, Adam Gordon
Tel: 867-975-7200 ext: 724; *Fax:* 867-979-4194
agordon@gov.nu.ca
Vice-President, Operations, Patsy Kuksuk
Tel: 867-857-3001; *Fax:* 867-857-3040
pkuksuk@gov.nu.ca
Director, Project Management Office, Stephen Hooey
shooey@gov.nu.ca
Director, Technical Services, Christine Klazinga
Tel: 867-975-7200 ext: 723
cklazinga@gov.nu.ca

Nunavut Territory Department of Justice

Sivummut, 1st Fl., PO Box 1000 Stn. 500, Iqaluit, NU X0A 0H0
Tel: 867-975-6170; *Fax:* 867-975-6195
justice@gov.nu.ca
www.justice.gov.nu.ca

Minister, Hon. Keith Peterson
Tel: 867-975-5028; *Fax:* 867-975-5095
kpeterson@gov.nu.ca
Deputy Minister, William MacKay
Tel: 867-975-6180
WMackay@gov.nu.ca

Associated Agencies, Boards & Commissions:

•Baffin Correctional Centre
PO Box 1000
Iqaluit, NU X0A 0H0
Tel: 867-979-8100; *Fax:* 867-979-4646

•Labour Standards Board
PO Box 1269
Iqaluit, NU X0A 0H0
Tel: 867-975-6159; *Fax:* 867-975-6376
nlsb@gov.nu.ca

•Legal Services Board of Nunavut
1104-B Inuksugait Plaza
PO Box 29
Iqaluit, NU X0A 0H0
Tel: 867-975-6395
nulas.ca

•Nunavut Criminal Code Review Board
PO Box 1269
Iqaluit, NU X0A 0H0
Tel: 867-975-6532; *Fax:* 867-975-6511
nccrb@gov.nu.ca

•Liquor Licensing Board
PO Box 1269
Iqaluit, NU X0A 0H0
Tel: 867-975-6533; *Fax:* 867-975-6511
nllb@gov.nu.ca

•Young Offenders Facility
1548 Federal Rd.
PO Box 1439
Iqaluit, NU X0A 0H0
Tel: 867-979-4452; *Fax:* 867-979-5506

•Office of the Chief Coroner
c/o Court Services Division
PO Box 297
Iqaluit, NU X0A 0H0
Tel: 867-975-6100; *Fax:* 867-975-6168
theofficeofthechiefcoroner@gov.nu.ca

Community Justice

PO Box 1000 Stn. 500, Iqaluit, NU X0A 0H0
Tel: 867-975-6363; *Fax:* 867-975-6160
communityjustice@gov.nu.ca

Promotes community justice, family abuse intervention, & victim services development, as well as crime prevention programs.

Director, Sunday Thomas
Tel: 867-975-6176
sthomas@gov.nu.ca
Sentence Administrator, Community Corrections, Patricia Melanson
Tel: 867-979-4452 ext: 3
pmelanson@gov.nu.ca

Corporate Services

PO Box 1000 Stn. 520, Iqaluit, NU X0A 0H0
Tel: 867-975-6170; *Fax:* 867-975-6188
justice.corporate@gov.nu.ca

Provides financial support services to the department, including the negotiation of financial agreements between Nunavut & the federal government.

Director, Edward Dingle
Tel: 867-975-6181
edingle@gov.nu.ca

Corrections

PO Box 1000 Stn. 580, Iqaluit, NU X0A 0H0
Tel: 867-975-6500; *Fax:* 867-975-6515
justice.corrections@gov.nu.ca

Provides security & management services, & promotes healing through the rehabilitation of inmates & young offenders.

Director, J.P. Deroy
Tel: 867-975-6501
jpderoy@gov.nu.ca
Assistant Director, Jackie Simpson
Tel: 867-975-6502
jsimpson@gov.nu.ca
Corrections Psychologist, Wayne Podmoroff
Tel: 867-979-8132
wpodmoroff@gov.nu.ca

Court Services

PO Box 297 Iqluit, NU X0A 0H0
Tel: 867-975-6100; *Fax:* 867-975-6168
ncj.criminal@gov.nu.ca; ncj.civil@gov.nu.ca
www.nucj.ca
Other Communication: Judge's Chambers, E-mail: ncj.judgeschambers@gov.nu.ca; Residential Tenancy Office, E-mail: rentaloffice@gov.nu.ca

Responsibilities include: support services for the Nunavut Court of Justice; assistance for the public, judiciary, counsel, RCMP, & other officials; Sheriff's office; Justice of the Peace Program; Coroner's Program; Family Support Program; Commissioners for Oaths & Notaries Public Program; Labour Standards Administration; support for the Labour Standards Board & Nunavut Criminal Code Review Board; administration of the Residential Tenancies Act; & access to legal research through the courthouse law library.

Director, Lou Hall
Tel: 867-975-6131; *Fax:* 867-975-6511
lhall@gov.nu.ca
Acting Director, Lucy Wilson
Tel: 867-975-6130
lwilson@gov.nu.ca
Sheriff of Nunavut, Chris Kennedy
Tel: 867-975-6119; *Fax:* 867-975-6168
ckennedy@gov.nu.ca
Senior Justice of the Peace, Alexina Kublu
Tel: 867-975-6120
akublu@gov.nu.ca
Chief Coroner, Tim Neily
Tel: 867-975-7292
tneily@gov.nu.ca
Chief Coroner, Padma Suramala
Tel: 867-975-7292
psuramala@gov.nu.ca

Legal & Constitutional Law

PO Box 1000 Stn. 540, Iqaluit, NU X0A 0H0
Tel: 867-975-6320; *Fax:* 867-975-6349
justice.legal@gov.nu.ca

Provides legal services &d advice to Cabinet, government departments, & certain boards & public agencies; also responsible for constitutional matters, such as the Nunavut Land Claims Agreement, Devolution, & the Canadian Charter of Rights & Freedoms.

Public Trustee, Esmeralda Bautista
Tel: 867-975-6311; *Fax:* 867-975-6343
ebautista@gov.nu.ca

Legal Registries

PO Box 1000 Stn. 570, Iqaluit, NU X0A 0H0
Tel: 867-975-6590; *Fax:* 867-975-6594
Legal.Registries@gov.nu.ca
Other Communication: Corporate Search & Filings, E-mail: corporatesearches@gov.nu.ca, corporateregistrations@gov.nu.ca; Superintendent of Securities, E-mail: securities@gov.nu.ca

Contains the following registries & offices: Corporate Registries; Personal Property Registry; Land Titles Office; Office of the Superintendent of Securities; & Commissioner for Oaths & Notary Public.

Director, Jeff Mason
Tel: 867-975-6591
jmason@gov.nu.ca
Deputy Civil Registrar, Allasua Knickelbein
Tel: 867-975-6525
AAningmiuq@gov.nu.ca

Legislation

PO Box 1000 Stn. 550, Iqaluit, NU X0A 0H0
Tel: 867-975-6335; *Fax:* 867-975-6189
territorial.printer@gov.nu.ca

Responsible for drafting all bills, regulations & appointments; prints the Nunavut Gazette, & provides annual volumes of statutes.

Director & Registrar, Regulations, Susan Hardy
Tel: 867-975-6334
shardy@gov.nu.ca
Nunavut Official Editor & Territorial Printer, Danielle Lepage
Tel: 867-975-6305
dlepage@gov.nu.ca
Manager, Legal Translation - Inuktitut & Inuinnaqtun, Betty Brewster
Tel: 867-975-6164
bbrewster@gov.nu.ca

Policy & Planning

PO Box 1000 Stn. 500, Iqaluit, NU X0A 0H0
Tel: 867-975-6170; *Fax:* 867-975-6151
justice.policy@gov.nu.ca

Responsible for policies & briefings, consultations with other governments, access to information & protection of privacy, negotiating & managing grants & contribution funds, & responses to justice issues.

Senior Policy Counsel, Marc Noreau
Tel: 867-975-6158
mnoreau@gov.nu.ca

Northwest Territories & Nunavut Workers' Safety & Compensation Commission (WSCC)

For a detailed listing please see Northwest Territories.

Government of Ontario

Seat of Government: Queen's Park, Toronto, ON M7A 1A2
Tel: 416-326-1234
Toll-Free: 800-267-8097
TTY: 800-268-7095
www.ontario.ca
twitter.com/ongov
www.facebook.com/ONgov
www.youtube.com/ONgov

The Province of Ontario entered Confederation July 1, 1867. It has a land area of 908,607.67 sq km, & the StatsCan census population in 2011 was 12,851,821.

Office of the Lieutenant Governor

Legislative Bldg., Queen's Park, Toronto, ON M7A 1A1
Tel: 416-325-7780; *Fax:* 416-325-7787
TTY: 416-325-5003
lt.gov@ontario.ca
www.lgontario.ca
twitter.com/LGLizDowdeswell
www.facebook.com/LGLizDowdeswell
www.youtube.com/OntarioLG

Represents Her Majesty The Queen in Ontario. The Office coordinates, supports & promotes the activities of the Lieutenant Governor. In her constitutional role, the Lieutenant Governor swears-in the Executive Council, outlines the Government's plans in the Speech from the Throne, provides the Royal Assent needed for bills to become laws, approves orders-in-council & appointments recommended by Cabinet, & prorogues or dissolves each session of Parliament. In her community role, she represents the people of Ontario & acts as the Province's official host, welcoming world leaders & diplomats. She hosts or attends hundreds of community events throughout Ontario & presents honours & awards to outstanding Ontarians. Elizabeth Dowdeswell was appointed as the 29th Lieutenant-Governor on June 26, 2014. She replaces David Onley, who held the position for seven years - the longest term for a Lieutenant Governor of Ontario since WWII.

Lieutenant Governor of Ontario, Hon. Elizabeth Dowdeswell, OC, OOnt

Chief of Staff/Private Secretary to the Lieutenant Governor, Anthony Hylton
Tel: 416-325-7781
anthony.hylton@ontario.ca

Chief Steward, Robert Adams
Tel: 416-325-7794
robert.adams@ontario.ca

Office of the Premier

Legislative Building, Queen's Park, Toronto, ON M7A 1A1
Tel: 416-325-1941; *Fax:* 416-325-3745
TTY: 800-387-5559
www.premier.gov.on.ca
www.youtube.com/user/premierofontario

Premier; Leader, Liberal Party of Ontario; Minister, Intergovernmental Affairs, Hon. Kathleen O. Wynne
kwynne.mpp@liberal.ola.org

Deputy Premier; Chair, Cabinet, Hon. Deborah Matthews
Tel: 416-326-9500; *Fax:* 416-326-2497
dmatthews.mpp@liberal.ola.org

Government House Leader, Hon. Yasir Naqvi
Tel: 416-325-0408; *Fax:* 416-325-6067
ynaqvi.mpp.co@liberal.ola.org

Chief Government Whip; Deputy Government House Leader, James J. Bradley
Tel: 416-325-1162; *Fax:* 416-325-1389
jbradley.mpp@liberal.ola.org

Chief of Staff & Principal Secretary to the Premier, Andrew Bevan
Tel: 416-325-2228; *Fax:* 416-325-9895

Deputy Chief of Staff, Planning & Administration, Shelley Potter
Tel: 416-327-2637; *Fax:* 416-325-0803

Chief Operating Officer & Deputy Chief of Staff, Operations, Patricia Sorbara
Tel: 416-212-0401; *Fax:* 416-327-1170

Parliamentary Assistant, Dr. Shafiq Qaadri
Tel: 416-327-2295; *Fax:* 416-314-7421
sqaadri.mpp.co@liberal.ola.org

Executive Director, Issues Management & Legislative Affairs, Bill Killorn
Tel: 416-325-0289

Executive Director, Communications, Rebecca MacKenzie
Tel: 416-325-6734; *Fax:* 416-325-0803

Executive Director, Caucus Relations, Carol Price
Tel: 416-325-2491; *Fax:* 416-314-5189

Executive Director, External Relations & Operations, Chad Walsh
Tel: 416-325-7254
chad.walsh@ontario.ca

Cabinet of Ontario

Legislative Building, Queen's Park, Toronto, ON M7A 1A1
news.ontario.ca/cabinet/en

Premier; Minister, Intergovernmental Affairs; President of the Executive Council; Leader, Government; Leader, Liberal Party of Ontario, Hon. Kathleen O. Wynne
Tel: 416-325-1941; *Fax:* 416-325-9895
kwynne.mpp@liberal.ola.org
www.ontarioliberal.ca/leader/Biography.aspx
Social Media: twitter.com/Kathleen_Wynne, www.facebook.com/WynneFans, www.linkedin.com/in/kathleenwynne
Note: Web Site: www.ontario.ca/ministry-intergovernmental-affairs (Intergovernmental Affairs)
Queen's Park
#281, Main Legislative Building
Toronto, ON M7A 1A1

Deputy Premier; Chair, Cabinet; Minister, Advanced Education & Skills Development; Minister Responsible, Digital Government, Hon. Deborah Matthews
Tel: 416-326-9500; *Fax:* 416-326-2497
dmatthews.mpp@liberal.ola.org
Social Media: twitter.com/Deb_Matthews
Note: Web Sites: debmatthews.onmpp.ca (MPP); www.tcu.gov.on.ca (Advanced Education & Skills Development)
Ministry of Advanced Education & Skills Development, Mowat Block
900 Bay St., 3rd Fl.
Toronto, ON M7A 1N3

Minister, Citizenship & Immigration; Chair, Government Caucus, Hon. Laura Albanese
Tel: 416-325-0400; *Fax:* 416-325-0374
lalbanese.mpp@liberal.ola.org
Social Media: twitter.com/Laura_Albanese, www.facebook.com/lauraalbanese.mpp
Note: Web Sites: lauraalbanese.onmpp.ca (MPP); www.citizenship.gov.on.ca (Citizenship & Immigration)
Ministry of Citizenship & Immigration
400 University Ave., 6th Fl.
Toronto, ON M7A 1T7

Minister, Housing; Minister Responsible, Poverty Reduction Strategy, Hon. Chris Ballard
cballard.mpp.co@liberal.ola.org
Social Media: twitter.com/ChrisBallardMPP, www.facebook.com/ChrisBallardMPP
Note: Web Sites: chrisballard.onmpp.ca (MPP); www.mah.gov.on.ca (Housing)
Ministry of Housing
777 Bay St., 17th Fl.
Toronto, ON M5G 2E5

Minister, International Trade, Hon. Michael Chan
Tel: 416-325-6200; *Fax:* 416-325-6195
mchan.mpp@liberal.ola.org
Social Media: twitter.com/Michael_KC_Chan, www.facebook.com/MichaelChanMarkhamUnionville
Note: Web Sites: michaelchan.onmpp.ca (MPP); www.citizenship.gov.on.ca (International Trade)
Ministry of International Trade
777 Bay St., 18th Fl.
Toronto, ON M7A 1N3

Minister, Infrastructure, Hon. Bob Chiarelli
bchiarelli.mpp.co@liberal.ola.org
Social Media: twitter.com/Bob_Chiarelli, www.facebook.com/BobChiarelliMPP
Note: Web Site: www.bobchiarelli.com (MPP)

Minister, Children & Youth Services; Minister Responsible, Anti-Racism, Hon. Michael Coteau
Tel: 416-212-7432; *Fax:* 416-212-7431
mcoteau.mpp@liberal.ola.org
Social Media: twitter.com/coteau, www.facebook.com/michaelcoteau
Note: Web Sites: michaelcoteau.onmpp.ca (MPP); www.children.gov.on.ca (Children & Youth Services)
Ministry of Children & Youth Services
56 Wellesley St. West, 14th Fl.
Toronto, ON M5S 2S3

Minister Responsible, Seniors Affairs, Hon. Dipika Damerla
ddamerla.mpp@liberal.ola.org
Social Media: twitter.com/DipikaDamerla, www.facebook.com/dipika.damerla.mpp
Note: Web Sites: dipikadamerla.onmpp.ca (MPP); www.seniorsinfo.ca (Seniors)
Ministry Responsible for Seniors, Ferguson Block
77 Wellesley St., 12th Fl.
Toronto, ON M7A 1N3

Minister, Transportation, Hon. Steven Del Duca
Tel: 416-327-9200; *Fax:* 416-327-9188
sdelduca.mpp.co@liberal.ola.org
Social Media: twitter.com/stevendelduca, www.facebook.com/StevenDelDucaMPP
Note: Web Sites: stevendelduca.onmpp.ca (MPP); www.mto.gov.on.ca (Transportation)
Ministry of Transportation, Ferguson Block
77 Wellesley St. West, 3rd Fl.
Toronto, ON M7A 1Z8

Minister, Economic Development & Growth, Hon. Brad Duguid
Tel: 416-325-6900; *Fax:* 416-325-6918
bduguid.mpp@liberal.ola.org
Social Media: twitter.com/BradDuguid, www.linkedin.com/pub/brad-duguid/3/b01/6a3
Note: Web Sites: bradduguid.onmpp.ca (MPP); www.ontario.ca/page/ministry-economic-development-and-growth (Economic Development & Growth)
Ministry of Economic Development & Growth, Hearst Block
900 Bay St., 8th Fl.
Toronto, ON M7A 2E1

Minister, Labour, Hon. Kevin Daniel Flynn
Tel: 416-325-5200; *Fax:* 416-325-5215
kflynn.mpp@liberal.ola.org
Social Media: twitter.com/MPPKevinFlynn, www.facebook.com/KevinFlynnOakville
Note: Web Sites: kevinflynn.onmpp.ca (MPP); www.labour.gov.on.ca (Labour)
Ministry of Labour
400 University Ave., 14th Fl.
Toronto, ON M7A 1T7

Minister, Northern Development & Mines, Hon. Michael Gravelle
Tel: 416-327-0633; *Fax:* 416-327-0665
mgravelle.mpp.co@liberal.ola.org
Social Media: twitter.com/MichaelGravelle
Note: Web Sites: michaelgravelle.onmpp.ca (MPP); www.mndm.gov.on.ca (Northern Development & Mines)
Ministry of Northern Development & Mines, Whitney Block
#5630, 99 Wellesley St. West, 5th Fl.
Toronto, ON M7A 1W3

Minister, Health & Long-Term Care, Hon. Dr. Eric Hoskins
Tel: 416-327-4300; *Fax:* 416-326-1571
ehoskins.mpp@liberal.ola.org
Social Media: twitter.com/DrEricHoskins, www.facebook.com/drerichoskins
Note: Web Sites: erichoskins.onmpp.ca (MPP); www.health.gov.on.ca (Health & Long-Term Care)
Ministry of Health & Long-Term Care, Hepburn Block
80 Grosvenor St., 10th Fl.
Toronto, ON M7A 2C4

Minister, Education, Hon. Mitzie Hunter
Tel: 416-325-2600; *Fax:* 416-325-2608
mhunter.mpp.co@liberal.ola.org
Social Media: twitter.com/MitzieHunter, www.facebook.com/mitzie.hunter
Note: Web Sites: mitziehunter.onmpp.ca (MPP); www.edu.gov.on.ca (Education)
Ministry of Education, Mowat Block
900 Bay St., 22nd Fl.
Toronto, ON M7A 1L2

Minister, Community & Social Services, Hon. Dr. Helena Jaczek
Tel: 416-325-5225
Toll-free: 888-789-4199; *Fax:* 416-325-3347
hjaczek.mpp@liberal.ola.org
Social Media: twitter.com/helenajaczek, www.facebook.com/helenajaczek, www.linkedin.com/pub/helena-jaczek/4/6a5/b77
Note: Web Sites: helenajaczek.onmpp.ca (MPP); www.mcss.gov.on.ca (Community & Social Services)
Ministry of Community & Social Services, Hepburn Block
80 Grosvenor St., 6th Fl.
Toronto, ON M7A 1E9

Minister, Government & Consumer Services; Minister Responsible, Francophone Affairs, Hon. Marie-France Lalonde
Tel: 416-327-8300; *Fax:* 416-326-1947
mflalonde.mpp.co@liberal.ola.org
Social Media: twitter.com/mflalonde, www.facebook.com/LalondeMF, ca.linkedin.com/pub/marie-france-lalonde/55/805/23a
Note: Web Sites: mariefrancelalonde.onmpp.ca (MPP); www.ontario.ca/page/ministry-government-and-consumer-services (Government & Consumer Services)
Ministry of Government & Consumer Services, Mowat Block
900 Bay St., 6th Fl.
Toronto, ON M7A 1L2

Minister, Agriculture, Food & Rural Affairs, Hon. Jeff Leal
Tel: 416-326-3074; *Fax:* 416-326-3083
jleal.mpp@liberal.ola.org
Social Media: twitter.com/JeffLeal_MPP, www.facebook.com/JeffLealMPP
Note: Web Sites: jeffleal.onmpp.ca (MPP); www.omafra.gov.on.ca (Agriculture, Food & Rural Affairs)
Ministry of Agriculture, Food & Rural Affairs
77 Grenville St., 11th Fl.
Toronto, ON M7A 1B3

Minister Responsible, Women's Issues; Minister Responsible, Accessibility, Hon. Tracy MacCharles
tmaccharles.mpp.co@liberal.ola.org
Social Media: twitter.com/TracyMacCharles, www.facebook.com/votemaccharles
Note: Web Sites: tracymaccharles.onmpp.ca (MPP); www.women.gov.on.ca (Women's Issues)

Minister, Municipal Affairs, Hon. Bill Mauro
Tel: 416-585-7000; *Fax:* 416-585-6470
bmauro.mpp.co@liberal.ola.org
Social Media: twitter.com/BillMauroMPP, www.facebook.com/bill.mauro
Note: Web Sites: billmauro.onmpp.ca (MPP); www.mah.gov.on.ca (Municipal Affairs)

Ministry of Municipal Affairs
777 Bay St., 17th Fl.
Toronto, ON M5G 2E5

Minister, Natural Resources & Forestry, Hon. Kathryn McGarry
Tel: 416-314-2301; *Fax:* 416-325-1564
kmcgarry.mpp.co@liberal.ola.org
Social Media: twitter.com/Kathryn_McGarry, ca.linkedin.com/pub/kathryn-mcgarry/36/821/7b7
Note: Web Sites: kathrynmcgarry.onmpp.ca (MPP); www.ontario.ca/page/ministry-natural-resources-and-forestry (Natural Resources & Forestry)
Ministry of Natural Resources & Forestry, Whitney Block
#6630, 99 Wellesley St. West, 6th Fl.
Toronto, ON M7A 1W3

Minister, Tourism, Culture & Sport, Hon. Eleanor McMahon
Tel: 416-326-9326; *Fax:* 416-326-9338
emcmahon.mpp.co@liberal.ola.org
Social Media: www.linkedin.com/in/eleanor-mcmahon-7287146
Note: Web Sites: eleanormcmahon.onmpp.ca (MPP); www.mtc.gov.on.ca (Tourism, Culture & Sport)
Ministry of Tourism, Culture & Sport, Hearst Block
900 Bay St., 9th Fl.
Toronto, ON M7A 2E1

Minister, Research, Innovation & Science, Hon. Reza Moridi
Tel: 416-326-9500; *Fax:* 416-326-2497
rmoridi.mpp@liberal.ola.org
Social Media: twitter.com/rezamoridi, www.facebook.com/rmoridi, www.linkedin.com/pub/reza-moridi-mpp/6/673/bb4
Note: Web Sites: rezamoridi.onmpp.ca (MPP); www.ontario.ca/page/ministry-research-innovation-and-science (Research, Innovation & Science)
Ministry of Research, Innovation & Science, Ferguson Block
77 Wellesley St. West, 12th Fl.
Toronto, ON M7A 1N3

Minister, Environment & Climate Change, Hon. Glen R. Murray
Tel: 416-314-6790; *Fax:* 416-314-6748
gmurray.mpp@liberal.ola.org
Social Media: twitter.com/Glen4ONT, www.facebook.com/MPPGlenMurray, www.linkedin.com/in/glenmurraympp
Note: Web Sites: glenmurray.onmpp.ca (MPP); www.ontario.ca/ministry-environment (Environment & Climate Change)
Ministry of the Environment & Climate Change, Ferguson Block
77 Wellesley St. West, 11th Fl.
Toronto, ON M7A 2T5

Associate Minister, Finance (Ontario Retirement Pension Plan), Hon. Indira Naidoo-Harris
Tel: 416-325-0400; *Fax:* 416-325-0374
inaidoo-harris.mpp.co@liberal.ola.org
Social Media: twitter.com/IndiraNHarris, www.facebook.com/indira.naidooharris, ca.linkedin.com/pub/indira-naidoo-harris/4/b15/421
Note: Web Sites: indiranaidooharris.onmpp.ca (MPP); www.fin.gov.on.ca (Finance)
Ministry of Finance, Frost Bldg. South
7 Queen's Park Cres., 6th Fl.
Toronto, ON M7A 1Y7

Attorney General; Government House Leader, Hon. Yasir Naqvi
Tel: 416-326-2220; *Fax:* 416-326-4016
ynaqvi.mpp@liberal.ola.org
Social Media: twitter.com/Yasir_Naqvi, www.facebook.com/YasirNaqviMPP, www.linkedin.com/in/yasirnaqvimpp
Note: Web Sites: yasirnaqvi.onmpp.ca (MPP); www.attorneygeneral.jus.gov.on.ca (Attorney General)
Ministry of the Attorney General
720 Bay St., 11th Fl.
Toronto, ON M7A 2S9

Minister, Community Safety & Correctional Services, Hon. David Orazietti
Tel: 416-325-0408; *Fax:* 416-325-6067
dorazietti.mpp@liberal.ola.org
Social Media: twitter.com/DavidOrazietti, www.facebook.com/davidorazietti
Note: Web Sites: davidorazietti.onmpp.ca (MPP); www.mcscs.jus.gov.on.ca (Community Safety & Correctional Services)
Ministry of Community Safety & Correctional Services, George Drew Bldg.
25 Grosvenor St., 18th Fl.
Toronto, ON M7A 1Y6

President, Treasury Board, Hon. Liz Sandals
Tel: 416-327-2333; *Fax:* 416-327-3790
lsandals.mpp@liberal.ola.org
Social Media: www.facebook.com/lizsandalsmpp
Note: Web Sites: lizsandals.onmpp.ca (MPP); www.canada.ca/en/treasury-board-secretariat.html (Treasury Board Secretariat)
Treasury Board Secretariat, Whitney Block
#4320, 99 Wellesley St. West, 4th Fl.
Toronto, ON M7A 1W3

Minister, Finance, Hon. Charles Sousa
Tel: 416-325-0400; *Fax:* 416-325-0374
csousa.mpp@liberal.ola.org
Social Media: twitter.com/SousaCharles, www.facebook.com/charles.sousa.121, www.linkedin.com/in/charlessousa
Note: Web Sites: charlessousa.onmpp.ca (MPP); www.fin.gov.on.ca (Finance)
Ministry of Finance, Frost Bldg. South
7 Queen's Park Cres., 7th Fl.
Toronto, ON M7A 1Y7

Minister, Energy, Hon. Glenn Thibeault
Tel: 416-327-6758; *Fax:* 416-327-6754
gthibeault.mpp.co@liberal.ola.org
Note: Web Sites: glennthibeault.onmpp.ca (MPP); www.energy.gov.on.ca (Energy)
Ministry of Energy, Hearst Block
900 Bay St., 4th Fl.
Toronto, ON M7A 2E1

Minister, Indigenous Relations & Reconciliation, Hon. David Zimmer
Tel: 416-325-5110; *Fax:* 416-314-2701
dzimmer.mpp@liberal.ola.org
Social Media: twitter.com/DavidZimmerMPP, www.facebook.com/teamzimmer
Note: Web Sites: davidzimmer.onmpp.ca (MPP); www.ontario.ca/page/ministry-indigenous-relations-and-reconciliation (Indigenous Relations & Reconciliation)
Ministry of Indigenous Relations & Reconciliation
#400, 160 Bloor St. East
Toronto, ON M7A 2E6

Cabinet Office

Whitney Block, Queen's Park, 99 Wellesley St. West, 6th Fl., Toronto, ON M7A 1A1
Tel: 416-325-7635; *Fax:* 416-325-3004
TTY: 416-314-5721

Secretary of the Cabinet, Clerk of the Executive Council & Head of the Ontario Public Service, Steve Orsini
Tel: 416-325-7641
steve.orsini@ontario.ca

Secretary, Management Board of Cabinet; Deputy Minister, Government Services; Secretary, Treasury Board, Greg Orencsak
Tel: 416-325-1607; *Fax:* 416-325-1612
greg.orencsak@ontario.ca

Deputy Minister, Communications & Intergovernmental Affairs; Associate Secretary of Cabinet, Lynn Betzner
Tel: 416-325-9698
lynn.betzner@ontario.ca

Deputy Minister, Policy & Delivery & Associate Secretary of the Cabinet, Steven Davidson
Tel: 416-325-3759
steven.davidson@ontario.ca

Assistant Deputy Minister & Chief Administrative Officer, Corporate Planning & Services, Blair Dunker
Tel: 416-314-0817; *Fax:* 416-325-2388
Blair.E.Dunker@ontario.ca

Assistant Deputy Minister, Economic, Environment, Justice & Intergovernmental Policy, Martha Greenberg
Tel: 416-325-5836
martha.greenberg@ontario.ca

Assistant Deputy Minister, Health, Social, Education & Children's Policy, Shamira Madhany
Tel: 416-325-4902; *Fax:* 416-325-6747
shamira.madhany3@ontario.ca

Assistant Deputy Minister, Communications, Rhonda McMichael
Tel: 416-325-4597; *Fax:* 416-325-1979
rhonda.mcmichael@ontario.ca

Assistant Deputy Minister, Community Hub Secretariat, Nancy Mudrinic
Tel: 416-327-4370
nancy.mudrinic2@ontario.ca

Associated Agencies, Boards & Commissions:

•Executive Development Committee
Queen's Park
Toronto, ON M5G 2K1
Tel: 416-325-1750

Anti-Racism Directorate

Ferguson Block, Queen's Park, 77 Wellesley St. West, 13th Fl., Toronto, ON M7A 1N3

The Anti-Racism Directorate was established in 2016, with the mandate to address racism in all forms.

Minister Responsible, Hon. Michael Coteau
Tel: 416-212-7432; *Fax:* 416-212-7431
mcoteau.mpp@liberal.ola.org

Assistant Deputy Minister, Sam Erry
Tel: 416-327-9223
sam.erry@ontario.ca

Ontario Legislative Assembly

c/o Clerk of the Legislative Assembly, #104, Legislative Bldg., Queen's Park, Toronto, ON M7A 1A2
Tel: 416-325-7500; *Fax:* 416-325-7489
TTY: 416-325-9426
web@ola.org
www.ontla.on.ca
Other Communication: Hansard Email: hansard@ontla.ola.org

Speaker; Chair of the Board of Internal Economy, Hon. Dave Levac
Tel: 416-325-6261; *Fax:* 416-325-6358
dlevac.mpp@liberal.ola.org

Deputy Speaker & Chair, Committee of the Whole House, Soo Wong
Tel: 416-212-5841; *Fax:* 416-325-3347
swong.mpp.co@liberal.ola.org

Clerk, Deborah Deller
Tel: 416-325-7341; *Fax:* 416-325-7344
ddeller@ola.org

Sergeant-at-Arms & Executive Director, Precinct Properties Division, Dennis M. Clark
Tel: 416-325-7446; *Fax:* 416-325-7154
dclark@ola.org
#411, North Wing, Legislative Bldg., Queen's Park
Toronto, ON M7A 1A2 Canada

Deputy Clerk & Executive Director, Legislative Services, Todd Decker
Tel: 416-325-3502; *Fax:* 416-325-5848
tdecker@ola.org
#1640, Whitney Block, Queen's Park
99 Wellesley St. W
Toronto, ON M7A 1A2 Canada

Executive Director, Administrative Services; Director, Human Resources (Acting), Nancy Marling
Tel: 416-325-3557
nmarling@ola.org
#2501, Whitney Block, Queen's Park
Toronto, ON M7A 1A2 Canada

Executive Director & Legislative Librarian, Information & Technology Services, Vicki Whitmell
Tel: 416-325-3939; *Fax:* 416-325-3909
vwhitmell@ola.org
Other Communications: Reference Inquiries: 416-325-3900
#1413, Whitney Block
Toronto, ON M7A 1A9 Canada

Government Caucus Office

#251, Legislative Bldg., Queen's Park, Toronto, ON M7A 1A4
Tel: 416-325-7200; *Fax:* 416-325-9898

Government House Leader, Hon. Yasir Naqvi
Tel: 416-325-0408; *Fax:* 416-325-6067
ynaqvi.mpp@liberal.ola.org

Chief Government Whip; Deputy Government House Leader, James J. Bradley
Tel: 416-325-1162; *Fax:* 416-325-1389
jbradley.mpp@liberal.ola.org

Chair, Government Caucus, Hon. Laura Albanese
Tel: 416-325-0400; *Fax:* 416-325-0374
lalbanese.mpp@liberal.ola.org

Office of the Opposition (PC)

#381, Legislative Bldg., Queen's Park, Toronto, ON M7A 1A8
Tel: 416-325-0445; *Fax:* 416-325-0491
TTY: 416-325-5771
www.ontariopc.com
twitter.com/ontariopcparty
www.facebook.com/ProgressiveConservativePartyofOntario
www.youtube.com/ontariopcparty

Leader, Official Opposition, Patrick Brown
Constituency: Simcoe North
Tel: 416-325-3855; *Fax:* 416-325-9035
patrick.brown@pc.ola.org
www.servingbarrie.com
Social Media: twitter.com/brownbarrie, www.facebook.com/votepatrickbrown
Note: Former Barrie MP Patrick Brown was elected as the new Ontario PC Leader by the party membership on May 9, 2015.

Deputy Leader, Official Opposition, Steve Clark
Tel: 416-325-1522; *Fax:* 416-325-1493
steve.clark@pc.ola.org

Deputy Leader, Official Opposition, Sylvia Jones
Tel: 416-325-1898; *Fax:* 416-325-1936
sylvia.jones@pc.ola.org

Official Opposition House Leader, Jim Wilson
Tel: 416-325-2069; *Fax:* 416-325-2079
jim.wilsonco@pc.ola.org
Official Opposition Whip, John Yakabuski
Tel: 416-325-2170; *Fax:* 416-325-2196
john.yakabuski@pc.ola.org
Caucus Chair, Toby Barrett
Tel: 416-325-8404; *Fax:* 416-325-8408
toby.barrettco@pc.ola.org

Office of the Third Party (NDP)
Legislative Bldg., #113, Queen's Park, Toronto, ON M7A 1A5
Tel: 416-325-7116; *Fax:* 416-325-8222
TTY: 416-325-6564
www.ontariondp.com
www.youtube.com/user/OntarioNewDemocrat

Leader, Third Party, Andrea Horwath
Tel: 416-325-7116; *Fax:* 416-325-8222
ahorwath-qp@ndp.on.ca
Social Media: twitter.com/andreahorwath,
www.facebook.com/AndreaHorwathONDP
Deputy Leader, Third Party, Jagmeet Singh
Tel: 416-325-1784; *Fax:* 416-325-1790
jsingh-qp@ndp.on.ca
Third Party House Leader, Gilles Bisson
Tel: 416-325-7122; *Fax:* 416-325-7181
gbisson@ndp.on.ca
Third Party Whip, John Vanthof
Tel: 416-325-2000; *Fax:* 416-325-1999
jvanthof-co@ndp.on.ca
Deputy Third Party Whip, Teresa J. Armstrong
Tel: 416-325-1872; *Fax:* 416-325-1912
tarmstrong-qp@ndp.on.ca

Standing Committees of the Legislative Assembly
www.ontla.on.ca/lao/en/committees

Estimates Committee
Chair, Cheri DiNovo
Constituency: Parkdale-High Park, New Democratic Party
Tel: 416-325-0244; *Fax:* 416-325-0305
dinovoc-qp@ndp.on.ca
Clerk, Eric Rennie
Tel: 416-325-3506
erennie@ola.org

Finance & Economic Affairs Committee
Chair, Peter Milczyn
Constituency: Etobicoke—Lakeshore, Liberal
Tel: 416-325-7815; *Fax:* 416-325-6918
Pmilczyn.mpp.co@liberal.ola.org
Clerk, Eric Rennie
Tel: 416-325-3506
erennie@ola.org

General Government Committee
Chair, Grant Crack
Constituency: Glengarry-Prescott-Russell, Liberal
Tel: 416-325-5494; *Fax:* 416-325-9295
gcrack.mpp@liberal.ola.org
Clerk, Sylwia Przezdziecki
Tel: 416-325-3515
sprzezdzieckl@ola.org

Government Agencies Committee
Chair, Cristina Martins
Constituency: Davenport, Liberal
Tel: 416-325-6002; *Fax:* 416-212-1812
cmartins.mpp.co@liberal.ola.org
Clerk, Sylwia Przezdziecki
Tel: 416-325-3515
sprzezdzieckl@ola.org

Justice Policy Committee
Chair, Shafiq Qaadri
Constituency: Etobicoke North, Liberal
Tel: 416-327-2295; *Fax:* 416-314-7421
sqaadri.mpp@liberal.ola.org
Clerk, Christopher Tyrell
Tel: 416-325-3883
ctyrell@ola.org

Legislative Assembly Committee
Chair, Monte McNaughton
Constituency: Lambton-Kent-Middlesex, Progressive Conservative
Tel: 416-325-3362; *Fax:* 416-325-3275
monte.mcnaughtonco@pc.ola.org
Clerk, Trevor Day
Tel: 416-325-3509
tday@ola.org

Public Accounts Committee
Chair, Ernie Hardeman
Constituency: Oxford, Progressive Conservative
Tel: 416-325-1239; *Fax:* 416-325-1259
ernie.hardeman@pc.ola.org
Clerk, Valerie Quioc Lim
Tel: 416-325-7352
vquioc@ola.org

Regulations & Private Bills Committee
Chair, Hon. Ted McMeekin
Constituency: Ancaster-Dundas-Flamborough-Westdale, Liberal
Tel: 416-314-0143
tmcmeekin.mpp@liberal.ola.org
Clerk, Christopher Tyrell
Tel: 416-325-3883
ctyrell@ola.org

Social Policy Committee
Chair, Peter Tabuns
Constituency: Toronto-Danforth, New Democratic Party
Tel: 416-325-3250; *Fax:* 416-325-3252
tabunsp-qp@ndp.on.ca
Clerk, Katch Koch
Tel: 416-325-3526
kkoch@ola.org

Forty-first Provincial Parliament - Ontario

Clerk's Office, #104, Legislative Building, Queen's Park, Toronto, ON M7A 1A2
Tel: 416-325-7500; *Fax:* 416-325-7489
TTY: 416-325-9426
web@ola.org
www.ontla.on.ca

Last General Election, June 12, 2014.
Maximum Duration, 5 years.
Party Standings (Sept. 2016):
Liberal Party 57;
Progressive Conservative Party 29;
New Democratic Party 20;
Vacant 1;
Total Seats 107.
Salary Disclosure for 2013:
Premier $198,521.29;
Leader, Official Opposition $180,885.96;
Leader, Third Party $158,157.96;
Minister, Finance $160,275.33;
Speaker $152,913.96;
Chief Government Whip $135,781.14;
Chief Whip, Official Opposition $132,867;
Chief Whip, Third Party $131,235;
House Leader, Official Opposition $137,879.04;
House Leader, Third Party $134,732.04.
The following list features information about members after the 2014 election, with their constituency, party affiliation, & contact information:

Members of Provincial Parliament

Minister, Citizenship & Immigration; Chair, Government Caucus, Hon. Laura Albanese
Constituency: York South-Weston *No. of Constituents:* 71,860, Liberal
Tel: 416-325-0400; *Fax:* 416-325-0374
lalbanese.mpp@liberal.ola.org
www.lauraalbanese.onmpp.ca
Other Communications: Constituency Phone: 416-243-7984; Fax: 416-243-0327
Social Media: twitter.com/Laura_Albanese,
www.facebook.com/lauraalbanese.mpp
Note: Web Site: www.citizenship.gov.on.ca (Citizenship & Immigration)
Constituency Office
99 Ingram Dr.
Toronto, ON M6M 2L7

Parliamentary Assistant to the Minister of Children & Youth Services, Granville Anderson
Constituency: Durham *No. of Constituents:* 99,404, Liberal
Tel: 416-326-0820
Toll-free: 800-661-2433; *Fax:* 416-326-3951
ganderson.mpp.co@liberal.ola.org
granvilleanderson.onmpp.ca
Other Communications: Constituency Phone: 905-697-1501; Fax: 905-697-1506
Social Media: twitter.com/GranvilleMPP,
www.facebook.com/GranvilleMPP,
ca.linkedin.com/pub/granville-anderson/47/844/57a
Constituency Office
23 King St. West
Bowmanville, ON L1C 1R2

Deputy Third Party Whip, Teresa J. Armstrong
Constituency: London-Fanshawe *No. of Constituents:* 77,524, New Democratic Party
Tel: 416-325-1872; *Fax:* 416-325-1912
tarmstrong-qp@ndp.on.ca
www.teresaarmstrong.ca
Other Communications: Constituency Phone: 519-668-1104; Fax: 519-668-1941
Social Media: twitter.com/TArmstrongNDP,
www.facebook.com/teresaarmstrong.ndp
Constituency Office
155 Clarke Rd.
London, ON N5W 5C9

Ted Arnott
Constituency: Wellington-Halton Hills *No. of Constituents:* 88,349, Progressive Conservative
Tel: 416-325-3880
Toll-free: 800-265-2366; *Fax:* 416-325-6649
ted.arnottco@pc.ola.org
www.tedarnottmpp.com
Other Communications: Constituency Phone: 519-787-5247; Fax: 519-787-5249
Social Media: twitter.com/TedArnottMPP,
www.facebook.com/ted.arnott.ont
Constituency Office
181 St. Andrew St. East, 2nd Fl.
Fergus, ON N1M 1P9

Robert (Bob) Bailey
Constituency: Sarnia-Lambton *No. of Constituents:* 80,669, Progressive Conservative
Tel: 416-325-1715; *Fax:* 416-325-1852
bob.baileyco@pc.ola.org
www.bobbaileympp.com
Other Communications: Constituency Phone: 519-337-0051; Fax: 519-337-3246
Social Media: twitter.com/BobBaileyPC,
www.facebook.com/BobBaileyPC
Constituency Office
836 Upper Canada Dr.
Sarnia, ON N7W 1A4

Parliamentary Assistant to the President of the Treasury Board, Yvan Baker
Constituency: Etobicoke Centre *No. of Constituents:* 85,192, Liberal
Tel: 416-327-6611
ybaker.mpp.co@liberal.ola.org
yvanbaker.onmpp.ca
Other Communications: Constituency Phone: 416-234-2800; Fax: 416-234-2276
Social Media: twitter.com/Yvan_Baker,
www.facebook.com/yvanbaker,
ca.linkedin.com/pub/yvan-baker/6/5ba/267
Constituency Office
#200, 4800 Dundas St. West
Toronto, ON M9A 1B1

Minister, Housing; Minister Responsible, Poverty Reduction Strategy, Hon. Chris Ballard
Constituency: Newmarket-Aurora *No. of Constituents:* 99,407, Liberal
cballard.mpp.co@liberal.ola.org
chrisballard.onmpp.ca
Other Communications: Constituency Phone: 905-750-0019; Fax: 905-750-0050
Social Media: twitter.com/ChrisBallardMPP,
www.facebook.com/ChrisBallardMPP
Note: Web Site: www.mah.gov.on.ca (Housing)
Constituency Office, Hunters Gate Plaza
#201, 14845 Yonge St.
Aurora, ON L4G 6H8

Caucus Chair, Official Opposition, Toby Barrett
Constituency: Haldimand-Norfolk *No. of Constituents:* 80,907, Progressive Conservative
Tel: 416-325-8404; *Fax:* 416-325-8408
toby.barrettco@pc.ola.org
www.tobybarrett.com
Other Communications: Constituency Phone: 519-428-0446; Fax: 519-428-0835
Social Media: twitter.com/tobybarrettmpp,
www.facebook.com/tobybarrett.mpp
Constituency Office
39 Norfolk St. North
Simcoe, ON N3Y 3N6

Parliamentary Assistant to the Attorney General, Lorenzo Berardinetti
Constituency: Scarborough Southwest *No. of Constituents:* 74,333, Liberal
Tel: 416-325-1008; *Fax:* 416-325-1219
lberardinetti.mpp.co@liberal.ola.org
www.lorenzoberardinetti.onmpp.ca
Other Communications: Constituency Phone: 416-261-9525; Fax: 416-261-0381
Social Media: twitter.com/LBerardinetti,
www.facebook.com/berardinetti
Constituency Office
#403B, 3090 Kingston Rd.
Toronto, ON M1M 1P2

Third Party House Leader, Gilles Bisson
Constituency: Timmins-James Bay *No. of Constituents:* 51,398, New Democratic Party
Tel: 416-325-7122
Toll-free: 800-461-9878; *Fax:* 416-325-7181
gbisson@ndp.on.ca
www.gillesbisson.ca
Other Communications: Timmins: 705-268-6400;

Kapuskasing: 705-335-6400
Social Media: twitter.com/bissongilles, www.facebook.com/GillesBissonONDP, www.linkedin.com/pub/gilles-bisson/32/42b/363
Constituency Office
#202, 60 Wilson Ave.
Timmins, ON P4N 2S7

Chief Government Whip; Deputy Government House Leader, James J. Bradley
Constituency: St Catharines *No. of Constituents:* 86,198, Liberal
Tel: 416-325-1162; *Fax:* 416-325-1389
jbradley.mpp.co@liberal.ola.org
www.jimbradley.onmpp.ca
Other Communications: Constituency Phone: 905-935-0018; Fax: 905-935-0191
Constituency Office
#2, 2 Secord Dr.
St Catharines, ON L2N 1K8

Leader, Progressive Conservative Party of Ontario (Official Opposition), Patrick Brown
Constituency: Simcoe North, Progressive Conservative
Tel: 416-325-3855; *Fax:* 416-325-9035
patrick.brownco@pc.ola.org
www.servingbarrie.com
Other Communications: Constituency Phone: 705-526-8671; Fax: 705-526-8600
Social Media: twitter.com/brownbarrie, www.facebook.com/votepatrickbrown
Note: Garfield Dunlop resigned his seat in order to provide a vacancy for PC Leader Patrick Brown to run. He won the seat in a by-election held Sept. 3, 2015.
Constituency Office
482 Elizabeth St.
Midland, ON L4R 1Z8

Sarah Campbell
Constituency: Kenora-Rainy River *No. of Constituents:* 49,912, New Democratic Party
Tel: 416-325-2750
Toll-free: 800-465-8501; *Fax:* 416-325-1645
scmpp@ndp.on.ca
www.sarah4nwo.ca
Other Communications: Dryden: 807-223-6456; Fort Frances: 807-274-7619
Social Media: twitter.com/Sarah4NWO, www.facebook.com/sarah4nwo
Constituency Office
34 G King St.
Dryden, ON P8N 1B3

Minister, International Trade, Hon. Michael Chan
Constituency: Markham-Unionville *No. of Constituents:* 95,367, Liberal
Tel: 416-325-6200; *Fax:* 416-325-6195
mchan.mpp.co@liberal.ola.org
www.michaelchan.onmpp.ca
Other Communications: Constituency Phone: 905-305-1935; Fax: 905-305-1938
Social Media: twitter.com/Michael_KC_Chan, www.facebook.com/MichaelChanMarkhamUnionville
Note: Web Site: www.citizenship.gov.on.ca (International Trade)
Constituency Office
#5, 450 Alden Rd.
Markham, ON L3R 5H4

Minister, Infrastructure, Hon. Bob Chiarelli
Constituency: Ottawa West-Nepean *No. of Constituents:* 85,125, Liberal
bchiarelli.mpp.co@liberal.ola.org
www.bobchiarelli.com
Other Communications: Constituency Phone: 613-721-8075; Fax: 613-721-5756
Social Media: twitter.com/Bob_Chiarelli, www.facebook.com/BobChiarelliMPP
Constituency Office
#201, 2249 Carling Ave.
Ottawa, ON K2B 7E9

Raymond Cho
Constituency: Scarborough-Rouge River, Progressive Conservative
Note: Raymond Cho won a by-election for the riding held on September 1st, 2016.

Deputy Leader, Official Opposition, Steve Clark
Constituency: Leeds-Grenville *No. of Constituents:* 79,415, Progressive Conservative
Tel: 416-325-1522
Toll-free: 800-267-4408; *Fax:* 416-325-1493
steve.clark@pc.ola.org
www.steveclarkmpp.com
Other Communications: Constituency Phone: 613-342-9522; Fax: 613-342-2501
Social Media: twitter.com/SteveClarkpc, www.facebook.com/steveclarkmpp, www.linkedin.com/pub/steve-clark/44/a0b/4a
Constituency Office
#101, 100 Strowger Blvd.
Brockville, ON K6V 5J9

Lorne Coe
Constituency: Whitby-Oshawa, Progressive Conservative
Tel: 416-325-1331; *Fax:* 416-325-1423
lorne.coe@pc.ola.org
Other Communications: Constituency Phone: 905-430-1141; Fax: 905-430-1840
Social Media: twitter.com/lornecoe, www.facebook.com/Lorne-Coe-511552075645442
Note: Lorne Coe won the riding in a by-election held Feb. 11, 2016.
Constituency Office
#101, 114 Dundas St. East
Whitby, ON L1N 2H7

Deputy Government Whip; Parliamentary Assistant to the Minister of Labour, Mike Colle
Constituency: Eglinton-Lawrence *No. of Constituents:* 77,946, Liberal
Tel: 416-325-1404; *Fax:* 416-325-1447
mcolle.mpp.co@liberal.ola.org
www.mikecolle.com
Other Communications: Constituency Phone: 416-781-2395; Fax: 416-781-4116
Social Media: twitter.com/mikecolleMPP, www.facebook.com/miketcolle, www.linkedin.com/pub/mike-colle-mpp/15/55a/748
Constituency Office
2882 Dufferin St.
Toronto, ON M6B 3S6

Minister, Children & Youth Services; Minister Responsible, Anti-Racism, Hon. Michael Coteau
Constituency: Don Valley East *No. of Constituents:* 73,070, Liberal
Tel: 416-212-7432; *Fax:* 416-212-7431
mcoteau.mpp.co@liberal.ola.org
www.michaelcoteau.onmpp.ca
Other Communications: Constituency Phone: 416-494-6856; Fax: 416-494-9937
Social Media: twitter.com/coteau, www.facebook.com/michaelcoteau
Note: Web Site: www.children.gov.on.ca (Children & Youth Services)
Constituency Office
2062 Sheppard Ave. East
Toronto, ON M2J 5B3

Parliamentary Assistant to the Minister of Education, Grant Crack
Constituency: Glengarry-Prescott-Russell *No. of Constituents:* 89,741, Liberal
Tel: 416-325-5494
Toll-free: 800-355-9666; *Fax:* 416-325-9295
gcrack.mpp.co@liberal.ola.org
www.grantcrack.onmpp.ca
Other Communications: Rockland: 613-446-4010; Alexandria: 613-525-4605
Social Media: twitter.com/GrantCrack, www.facebook.com/GrantCrack
Constituency Office
345 Laurier St.
PO Box 339
Rockland, ON K4K 1K4

Minister Responsible, Seniors Affairs, Hon. Dipika Damerla
Constituency: Mississauga East-Cooksville *No. of Constituents:* 92,402, Liberal
ddamerla.mpp.co@liberal.ola.org
www.dipikadamerla.onmpp.ca
Other Communications: Constituency Phone: 905-238-1751; Fax: 905-238-4918
Social Media: twitter.com/DipikaDamerla, www.facebook.com/dipika.damerla.mpp
Note: Web Site: www.seniorsinfo.ca (Seniors)
Constituency Office
#315, 1420 Burnamthorpe Rd. East
Mississauga, ON L4X 2Z9

Parliamentary Assistant to the Minister of Energy, Bob Delaney
Constituency: Mississauga-Streetsville *No. of Constituents:* 92,937, Liberal
Tel: 416-325-4140; *Fax:* 416-325-0818
bdelaney.mpp.co@liberal.ola.org
www.bobdelaney.com
Other Communications: Constituency Phone: 905-569-1643; Fax: 905-569-6416
Social Media: twitter.com/BobDelaneyMPP, www.facebook.com/BobDelaneyMPP, www.linkedin.com/in/bobdelaneympp
Constituency Office, Meadowvale Corporate Centre, Plaza IV
#220, 2000 Argentia Rd.
Mississauga, ON L5N 1W1

Minister, Transportation, Hon. Steven Del Duca
Constituency: Vaughan *No. of Constituents:* 136,426, Liberal
Tel: 416-327-9200; *Fax:* 416-327-9188
sdelduca.mpp.co@liberal.ola.org
www.stevendelduca.onmpp.ca
Other Communications: Constituency Phone: 905-832-6630; Fax: 905-832-3375
Social Media: twitter.com/stevendelduca, www.facebook.com/StevenDelDucaMPP
Note: Web Site: www.mto.gov.on.ca (Transportation)
Constituency Office
#9, 9587 Weston Rd.
Woodbridge, ON L4H 3A5

Parliamentary Assistant to the Minister of Aboriginal Affairs, Vic Dhillon
Constituency: Brampton West *No. of Constituents:* 131,434, Liberal
Tel: 416-325-0241; *Fax:* 416-325-0272
vdhillon.mpp.co@liberal.ola.org
www.vicdhillon.onmpp.ca
Other Communications: Constituency Phone: 905-796-8669; Fax: 905-796-8069
Social Media: twitter.com/dhillonvic, www.facebook.com/dhillonvic
Constituency Office
#304, 37 George St. North
Brampton, ON L6X 1R5

Parliamentary Assistant to the Minister of Northern Development & Mines, Joe Dickson
Constituency: Ajax-Pickering *No. of Constituents:* 103,629, Liberal
Tel: 416-327-0653; *Fax:* 416-327-0617
jdickson.mpp.co@liberal.ola.org
www.joedickson.onmpp.ca
Other Communications: Constituency Phone: 905-427-2060; Fax: 905-427-6976
Social Media: twitter.com/mppjoedickson, www.facebook.com/MPPJoeDickson
Constituency Office
#201A, 50 Commercial Ave.
Ajax, ON L1S 2H5

Caucus Chair, New Democratic Party, Cheri DiNovo
Constituency: Parkdale-High Park *No. of Constituents:* 80,122, New Democratic Party
Tel: 416-325-0244; *Fax:* 416-325-0305
dinovoc-qp@ndp.on.ca
www.cheridinovo.ca
Other Communications: Constituency Phone: 416-763-5630; Fax: 416-763-5640
Social Media: twitter.com/cheridinovo, www.facebook.com/CheriDiNovoParkdaleHighPark
Constituency Office
2849 Dundas St. West
Toronto, ON M6P 2A1

Parliamentary Assistant to the Minister of Training, Colleges & Universities, Han Dong
Constituency: Trinity-Spadina *No. of Constituents:* 117,804, Liberal
Tel: 416-326-1600; *Fax:* 416-326-2807
hdong.mpp.co@liberal.ola.org
handong.onmpp.ca
Other Communications: Constituency Phone: 416-603-9664; Fax: 416-603-1241
Social Media: twitter.com/HanDongMPP, www.facebook.com/HanDongMPP, www.linkedin.com/pub/han-dong/93/3ba/a40
Constituency Office
808 Dundas St. West
Toronto, ON M6J 1V3

Minister, Economic Development & Growth, Hon. Brad Duguid
Constituency: Scarborough Centre *No. of Constituents:* 74,190, Liberal
Tel: 416-325-6900; *Fax:* 416-325-6918
bduguid.mpp@liberal.ola.org
www.bradduguid.onmpp.ca
Other Communications: Constituency Phone: 416-615-2183; Fax: 416-615-2011
Social Media: twitter.com/BradDuguid, www.linkedin.com/pub/brad-duguid/3/b01/6a3
Note: Web Site: www.ontario.ca/page/ministry-economic-development-and-growth (Economic Development & Growth)
Constituency Office
2063 Lawrence Ave. East
Scarborough, ON M1R 2Z4

Victor Fedeli
Constituency: Nipissing *No. of Constituents:* 60,422, Progressive Conservative
Tel: 416-325-3434; *Fax:* 416-325-3437
vic.fedelico@pc.ola.org
www.fedeli.com
Other Communications: Constituency Phone: 705-474-8340; Fax: 705-474-9747
Social Media: twitter.com/VicFedeliMPP, www.facebook.com/VictorFedeli, www.linkedin.com/in/victorfedeli
Constituency Office
165 Main St. East
North Bay, ON P1B 1A9

Catherine Fife
Constituency: Kitchener-Waterloo *No. of Constituents:* 100,972, New Democratic Party
Tel: 416-325-6913; *Fax:* 416-325-6942
cfife-co@ndp.on.ca
www.catherinefife.com
Other Communications: Constituency Phone: 519-725-3477; Fax: 519-725-3667
Social Media: twitter.com/CfifeKW, www.facebook.com/catherinefifeNDP
Note: Catherine Fife won Kitchener-Waterloo for the first time in NDP history in a Sept. 2012 by-election, & was re-elected in the 2014 General Election.
Constituency Office
#401, 22 King St. South
Waterloo, ON N2J 1N8

Minister, Labour, Hon. Kevin Daniel Flynn
Constituency: Oakville *No. of Constituents:* 90,006, Liberal
Tel: 416-325-5200; *Fax:* 416-325-5215
kflynn.mpp.co@liberal.ola.org
www.kevinflynn.onmpp.ca
Other Communications: Constituency Phone: 905-827-5141; Fax: 905-827-3786
Social Media: twitter.com/MPPKevinFlynn, www.facebook.com/KevinFlynnOakville
Note: Web Site: www.labour.gov.on.ca (Labour)
Constituency Office
#2, 2318 Lakeshore Rd. West
Oakville, ON L6L 1H3

Cindy Forster
Constituency: Welland *No. of Constituents:* 87,263, New Democratic Party
Tel: 416-325-7106; *Fax:* 416-325-7067
cforster-co@ndp.on.ca
www.cindyforster.ca
Other Communications: Constituency Phone: 905-732-6884; Fax: 905-732-9782
Social Media: twitter.com/cindyforster, www.facebook.com/cindyforster
Constituency Office
#103, 60 King St.
Welland, ON L3B 6A4

Parliamentary Assistant to the Minister of Health & Long-Term Care (Health), John Fraser
Constituency: Ottawa South *No. of Constituents:* 89,150, Liberal
Tel: 416-327-0205; *Fax:* 416-325-3862
jfraser.mpp.co@liberal.ola.org
johnfraser.onmpp.ca
Other Communications: Constituency Phone: 613-736-9573; Fax: 613-736-7374
Social Media: www.facebook.com/JohnFraserOttawaSouth
Constituency Office
1795 Kilborn Ave.
Ottawa, ON K1H 6N1

Jennifer K. French
Constituency: Oshawa *No. of Constituents:* 96,154, New Democratic Party
Tel: 416-325-0117; *Fax:* 416-325-0084
jfrench-co@ndp.on.ca
www.jenniferfrench.ca
Other Communications: Constituency Phone: 905-723-2411; Fax: 905-723-1054
Social Media: twitter.com/jennkfrench, www.facebook.com/jenniferfrenchNDP
Constituency Office
#2, 78 Centre St. North
Oshawa, ON L1G 4B6

Wayne Gates
Constituency: Niagara Falls *No. of Constituents:* 100,698, New Democratic Party
Tel: 416-212-6102; *Fax:* 416-212-6106
wgates-co@ndp.on.ca
Other Communications: Niagara Falls: 905-357-0681; Fort Erie: 905-871-8868
Social Media: twitter.com/Wayne_Gates, www.facebook.com/waynegatesniagara
Note: Wayne Gates won the riding of Niagara Falls in a by-election held February 13, 2014, & was re-elected in the 2014 General Election.
Constituency Office
#1, 6746 Morrison St.
Niagara Falls, ON L2E 6Z8

France Gélinas
Constituency: Nickel Belt *No. of Constituents:* 64,910, New Democratic Party
Tel: 416-325-9203; *Fax:* 416-325-9185
fgelinas-co@ndp.on.ca
www.francegelinas.ca
Other Communications: Constituency Phone: 705-969-3621; Fax: 705-969-3538
Social Media: twitter.com/NickelBelt, www.facebook.com/france.gelinas.92
Constituency Office, Hanmer Valley Shopping Plaza
#15, 5085 Hwy. 69 North
Hanmer, ON P3P 1P7

Minister, Northern Development & Mines, Hon. Michael Gravelle
Constituency: Thunder Bay-Superior North *No. of Constituents:* 55,436, Liberal
Tel: 416-327-0633; *Fax:* 416-327-0665
mgravelle.mpp.co@liberal.ola.org
www.michaelgravelle.onmpp.ca
Other Communications: Constituency Phone: 807-345-3647; Fax: 807-345-2922
Social Media: twitter.com/MichaelGravelle
Note: Web Site: www.mndm.gov.on.ca (Ministry of Northern Development & Mines)
Constituency Office
179 Algoma St. South
Thunder Bay, ON P7B 3C1

Lisa Gretzky
Constituency: Windsor West *No. of Constituents:* 86,285, New Democratic Party
Tel: 416-325-0235; *Fax:* 416-325-0873
lgretzky-co@ndp.on.ca
Other Communications: Constituency Phone: 519-977-7191; Fax: 519-977-7029
Social Media: twitter.com/LGretzky, www.facebook.com/LisaGretzky
Constituency Office
#5, 321 Tecumseh Rd. East
Windsor, ON N8X 2R5

Ernie Hardeman
Constituency: Oxford *No. of Constituents:* 80,398, Progressive Conservative
Tel: 416-325-1239
Toll-free: 800-265-4046; *Fax:* 416-325-1259
ernie.hardemanco@pc.ola.org
www.erniehardemanmpp.com
Other Communications: Constituency Phone: 519-537-5222; Fax: 519-537-3577
Social Media: www.facebook.com/ernie.hardeman, www.linkedin.com/pub/ernie-hardeman/2b/18a/37a
Constituency Office
12 Perry St., 2nd Fl.
Woodstock, ON N4S 3C2

Michael Harris
Constituency: Kitchener-Conestoga *No. of Constituents:* 94,886, Progressive Conservative
Tel: 416-325-3130; *Fax:* 416-325-3214
michael.harris@pc.ola.org
michaelharrismpp.ca
Other Communications: Constituency Phone: 519-954-8679; Fax: 519-650-7006
Social Media: twitter.com/Michaelharrispc, www.facebook.com/michaelharrispc, www.linkedin.com/pub/michael-harris/26/267/ab2
Constituency Office
#4, 4281 King St. East
Kitchener, ON N2P 2E9

Percy Hatfield
Constituency: Windsor-Tecumseh *No. of Constituents:* 87,108, New Democratic Party
Tel: 416-325-6773; *Fax:* 416-325-6795
phatfield-co@ndp.on.ca
Other Communications: Constituency Phone: 519-251-5199; Fax: 519-251-5299
Social Media: twitter.com/PercyHatfield, www.facebook.com/PercyHatfieldNDP
Constituency Office
#1, 5452 Tecumseh Rd. East
Windsor, ON N8T 1C7

Randy Hillier
Constituency: Lanark-Frontenac-Lennox & Addington *No. of Constituents:* 94,674, Progressive Conservative
Tel: 416-325-2244; *Fax:* 416-325-2166
randy.hillierco@pc.ola.org
www.randyhilliermpp.com
Other Communications: Constituency Phone: 613-267-8239; Fax: 613-267-7398
Social Media: twitter.com/randyhillier, www.facebook.com/randy.hillier, www.linkedin.com/pub/randy-hillier/34/496/41b
Constituency Office
#1, 105 Dufferin St.
Perth, ON K7H 3A5

Parliamentary Assistant to the Minister of Labour, Ann Hoggarth
Constituency: Barrie *No. of Constituents:* 101,169, Liberal
Tel: 416-212-9790
ahoggarth.mpp.co@liberal.ola.org
annhoggarth.onmpp.ca
Other Communications: Constituency Phone: 705-726-5538; Fax: 705-726-2880
Social Media: twitter.com/AnnHoggarthMPP
Constituency Office
#14, 20 Bell Farm Rd.
Barrie, ON L4M 6E4

Leader, New Democratic Party of Ontario, Andrea Horwath
Constituency: Hamilton Centre *No. of Constituents:* 82,062, New Democratic Party
Tel: 416-325-7116; *Fax:* 416-325-8222
ahorwath-co@ndp.on.ca
www.ontariondp.com
Other Communications: Constituency Phone: 905-544-9644; Fax: 905-544-5152
Social Media: twitter.com/andreahorwath, www.facebook.com/AndreaHorwathONDP
Constituency Office
#200, 20 Hughson St. South
Hamilton, ON L8N 2A1

Minister, Health & Long-Term Care, Hon. Dr. Eric Hoskins
Constituency: St. Paul's *No. of Constituents:* 88,905, Liberal
Tel: 416-327-4300; *Fax:* 416-326-1571
ehoskins.mpp.co@liberal.ola.org
www.erichoskins.onmpp.ca
Other Communications: Constituency Phone: 416-656-0943; Fax: 416-656-0875
Social Media: twitter.com/DrEricHoskins, www.facebook.com/drerichoskins
Note: Web Site: www.health.gov.on.ca (Health & Long-Term Care)
Constituency Office
803 St. Clair Ave. West
Toronto, ON M6C 1B9

Minister, Education, Hon. Mitzie Hunter
Constituency: Scarborough-Guildwood *No. of Constituents:* 71,311, Liberal
Tel: 416-325-2600; *Fax:* 416-325-2608
mhunter.mpp.co@liberal.ola.org
www.mitziehunter.onmpp.ca
Other Communications: Constituency Phone: 416-281-2787; Fax: 416-281-2360
Social Media: twitter.com/MitzieHunter, www.facebook.com/mitzie.hunter
Note: Web Site: www.edu.gov.on.ca (Education)
Constituency Office
#109, 4117 Lawrence Ave. East
Toronto, ON M1E 2S2

Minister, Community & Social Services, Hon. Dr. Helena Jaczek
Constituency: Oak Ridges-Markham *No. of Constituents:* 177,255, Liberal
Tel: 416-325-5225
Toll-free: 866-531-9551; *Fax:* 416-325-3347
hjaczek.mpp.co@liberal.ola.org
www.helenajaczek.onmpp.ca
Other Communications: Constituency Phone: 905-294-4931; Fax: 905-294-0014
Social Media: twitter.com/helenajaczek, www.facebook.com/helenajaczek, www.linkedin.com/pub/helena-jaczek/4/6a5/b77
Note: Web Site: www.mcss.gov.on.ca (Community & Social Services)
Constituency Office
#204, 137 Main St. North
Markham, ON L3P 1Y2

Deputy Leader, Official Opposition, Sylvia Jones
Constituency: Dufferin-Caledon *No. of Constituents:* 89,024, Progressive Conservative
Tel: 416-325-1898; *Fax:* 416-325-1936
sylvia.jonesco@pc.ola.org
www.sylviajonesmpp.ca
Other Communications: Orangeville: 519-941-7751; Bolton: 905-951-9382
Social Media: twitter.com/SylviaJonesMPP, www.linkedin.com/pub/sylvia-jones/47/b82/922
Constituency Office
244 Broadway Ave.
Orangeville, ON L9W 1K5

Parliamentary Assistant to the Minister of Tourism, Culture & Sport, Sophie Kiwala
Constituency: Kingston & the Islands *No. of Constituents:* 97,188, Liberal
Tel: 416-327-0185; *Fax:* 416-212-7155
skiwala.mpp.co@liberal.ola.org
sophiekiwala.onmpp.ca
Other Communications: Constituency Phone: 613-547-2385; Fax: 613-547-5001
Social Media: twitter.com/SophieKiwala, www.facebook.com/SKiwala, ca.linkedin.com/pub/sophie-kiwala/51/15b/88
Constituency Office, The LaSalle Mews
#2, 303 Bagot St.
Kingston, ON K7K 5W7

Parliamentary Assistant to the Minister of Citizenship, Immigration & International Trade, & Chair, Ontario Investment & Trade Advisory Council, Monte Kwinter
Constituency: York Centre *No. of Constituents:* 76,714, Liberal
Tel: 416-325-0036; *Fax:* 416-325-0316
mkwinter.mpp.co@liberal.ola.org
montekwinter.onmpp.ca

Other Communications: Constituency Phone: 416-630-0080; Fax: 416-630-8828
Social Media: twitter.com/MonteKwinter, www.facebook.com/MonteKwinter
Constituency Office
539 Wilson Heights Blvd.
Toronto, ON M3H 2V7

Minister, Government & Consumer Services; Minister Responsible, Francophone Affairs, Hon. Marie-France Lalonde
Constituency: Ottawa-Orléans *No. of Constituents:* 95,258, Liberal
Tel: 416-327-8300; *Fax:* 416-326-1947
mflalonde.mpp.co@liberal.ola.org
mariefrancelalonde.onmpp.ca
Other Communications: Constituency Phone: 613-834-8679; Fax: 613-834-7647
Social Media: twitter.com/mflalonde, www.facebook.com/LalondeMF, ca.linkedin.com/pub/marie-france-lalonde/55/805/23a
Note: Web Site: www.ontario.ca/page/ministry-government-and-consumer-services (Government & Consumer Services)
Constituency Office
#206, 260 Centrum Blvd.
Orléans, ON K1E 3J1

Minister, Agriculture, Food & Rural Affairs, Hon. Jeff Leal
Constituency: Peterborough *No. of Constituents:* 94,167, Liberal
Tel: 416-326-3074; *Fax:* 416-326-3083
jleal.mpp.co@liberal.ola.org
www.jeffleal.onmpp.ca
Other Communications: Constituency Phone: 705-742-3777; Fax: 705-742-1822
Social Media: twitter.com/JeffLeal_MPP, www.facebook.com/JeffLealMPP
Note: Web Site: www.omafra.gov.on.ca (Agriculture, Food & Rural Affairs)
Constituency Office
236 King St.
Peterborough, ON K9J 7L8

Speaker; Chair of the Board of Internal Economy, Hon. Dave Levac
Constituency: Brant *No. of Constituents:* 99,564, Liberal
Tel: 416-325-6261; *Fax:* 416-325-6358
dlevac.mpp.co@liberal.ola.org
www.davelevac.onmpp.ca
Other Communications: Constituency Phone: 519-759-0361, Fax: 519-759-6439
Social Media: twitter.com/DaveLevac, www.facebook.com/davelevacmpp
Constituency Office
#101, 96 Nelson St.
Brantford, ON N3T 2N1

Minister Responsible, Women's Issues; Minister Responsible, Accessibility, Hon. Tracy MacCharles
Constituency: Pickering-Scarborough East *No. of Constituents:* 82,518, Liberal
tmaccharles.mpp.co@liberal.ola.org
www.tracymaccharles.onmpp.ca
Other Communications: Constituency Phone: 905-509-0336; Fax: 905-509-0334
Social Media: twitter.com/TracyMacCharles, www.facebook.com/tracymaccharles1
Note: Web Sites: www.women.gov.on.ca (Women's Issues)
Constituency Office
#7, 300 Kingston Rd.
Pickering, ON L1V 6Z9

Jack MacLaren
Constituency: Carleton-Mississippi Mills *No. of Constituents:* 116,047, Progressive Conservative
Tel: 416-314-7900
Toll-free: 800-267-1020; *Fax:* 416-314-7966
jack.maclarenco@pc.ola.org
www.jackmaclarenmpp.com
Other Communications: Constituency Phone: 613-599-3000; Fax: 613-599-8183
Social Media: www.facebook.com/181470968553829
Constituency Office
#100, 240 Michael Cowpland Dr.
Katana, ON K2M 1P6

Lisa MacLeod
Constituency: Nepean-Carleton *No. of Constituents:* 120,669, Progressive Conservative
Tel: 416-325-6351; *Fax:* 416-325-6364
lisa.macleod@pc.ola.org
lisamacleod.com
Other Communications: Constituency Phone: 613-823-2116; Fax: 613-823-8284
Social Media: twitter.com/MacLeodLisa, www.facebook.com/LisaMacLeodMPP, www.linkedin.com/pub/lisa-macleod/13/675/163
Constituency Office
#10, 3500 Fallowfield Rd.
Nepean, ON K2J 4A7

Parliamentary Assistant to the Minister Responsible for Women's Issues, Harinder Malhi
Constituency: Brampton-Springdale *No. of Constituents:* 94,424, Liberal
Tel: 416-212-1645
hmalhi.mpp.co@liberal.ola.org
harindermalhi.onmpp.ca
Other Communications: Constituency Phone: 905-495-8030; Fax: 905-495-1041
TTY: 90- 49- 431
Social Media: twitter.com/Harindermalhi, www.facebook.com/harinder.malhi.5
Constituency Office
#515, 2250 Bovaird Dr. East
Brampton, ON L6R 0W3

Parliamentary Assistant to the Minister of the Environment & Climate Change, Amrit Mangat
Constituency: Mississauga-Brampton South *No. of Constituents:* 101,010, Liberal
Tel: 416-325-7188; *Fax:* 416-325-7293
amangat.mpp.co@liberal.ola.org
www.amritmangat.onmpp.ca
Other Communications: Constituency Phone: 905-696-0367; Fax: 905-696-7545
Social Media: www.facebook.com/265148843495306
Constituency Office
#203, 7045 Edwards Blvd.
Mississauga, ON L5S 1X2

Michael Mantha
Constituency: Algoma-Manitoulin *No. of Constituents:* 54,395, New Democratic Party
Tel: 416-325-1938
Toll-free: 800-831-1899; *Fax:* 416-325-1976
mmantha-co@ndp.on.ca
Other Communications: Constituency Phone: 705-461-9710, Fax: 705-461-9720
Social Media: www.facebook.com/MichaelMantha
Constituency Office, Lester B Pearson Civic Ctr.
#310, 255 Highway 108 North
Elliot Lake, ON P5A 2L9

Parliamentary Assistant to the Minister of Citizenship, Immigration & International Trade (Citizenship & Immigration), Cristina Martins
Constituency: Davenport *No. of Constituents:* 72,851, Liberal
Tel: 416-325-6002; *Fax:* 416-212-1812
cmartins.mpp.co@liberal.ola.org
cristinamartins.onmpp.ca
Other Communications: Constituency Phone: 416-535-3158; Fax: 416-535-6587
Social Media: twitter.com/CMartinsMPP
Constituency Office
1674 St. Clair Ave. West
Toronto, ON M6N 1H8

Gila Martow
Constituency: Thornhill *No. of Constituents:* 105,139, Progressive Conservative
Tel: 416-325-1415; *Fax:* 416-325-1485
gila.martowco@pc.ola.org
thornhill.ontariopc.com
Other Communications: Constituency Phone: 905-731-8462; Fax: 905-731-2984
Social Media: twitter.com/GilaMartow, www.facebook.com/gila.martow
Note: Gila Martow won the riding of Thornill in a by-election held February 13, 2014, & was re-elected in the 2014 General Election. Her 2014 win was declared after a recount, as Liberal candidate Sandra Yeung Racco was initially named the winner.
Constituency Office, Centre Street Square
#4, 1136 Centre St.
Thornhill, ON L4J 3M8

Deputy Premier; Chair, Cabinet; Minister, Advanced Education & Skills Development; Minister Responsible, Digital Government, Hon. Deborah Matthews
Constituency: London North Centre *No. of Constituents:* 91,997, Liberal
Tel: 416-326-9500; *Fax:* 416-326-2497
dmatthews.mpp@liberal.ola.org
Other Communications: Constituency Phone: 519-432-7339; Fax: 519-432-0613
Social Media: twitter.com/Deb_Matthews
Note: Web Site: www.tcu.gov.on.ca (Advanced Education & Skills Development)
Constituency Office
242 Piccadilly St., 1st Fl.
London, ON N6A 1S4

Minister, Municipal Affairs, Hon. Bill Mauro
Constituency: Thunder Bay-Atikokan *No. of Constituents:* 58,908, Liberal
Tel: 416-585-7000; *Fax:* 416-585-6470
bmauro.mpp.co@liberal.ola.org
www.billmauro.onmpp.ca
Other Communications: Atikokan: 807-597-2629; Thunder Bay: 807-623-9237
Social Media: twitter.com/BillMauroMPP, www.facebook.com/bill.mauro
Note: Web Site: www.mah.gov.on.ca (Municipal Affairs)
Constituency Office
240 South Syndicate Ave.
Thunder Bay, ON P7E 1C8

Jim McDonell
Constituency: Stormont-Dundas-South Glengarry *No. of Constituents:* 77,544, Progressive Conservative
Tel: 416-325-2910; *Fax:* 416-325-2917
jim.mcdonellco@pc.ola.org
jimmcdonellmpp.ca
Other Communications: Constituency Phone: 613-933-6513; Fax: 613-933-6449
Social Media: twitter.com/JimMcDonell
Constituency Office, Time Square
120 Second St. West
Cornwall, ON K6J 1G5

Minister, Natural Resources & Forestry, Hon. Kathryn McGarry
Constituency: Cambridge *No. of Constituents:* 100,130, Liberal
Tel: 416-314-2301; *Fax:* 416-325-1564
kmcgarry.mpp.co@liberal.ola.org
kathrynmcgarry.onmpp.ca
Other Communications: Constituency Phone: 519-623-5852; Fax: 519-650-3918
Social Media: twitter.com/Kathryn_McGarry, ca.linkedin.com/pub/kathryn-mcgarry/36/821/7b7
Note: Web Site: www.ontario.ca/page/ministry-natural-resources-and-forestry (Natural Resources & Forestry)
Constituency Office
498 Eagle St. North
Cambridge, ON N3H 1C2

Minister, Tourism, Culture & Sport, Hon. Eleanor McMahon
Constituency: Burlington *No. of Constituents:* 95,504, Liberal
Tel: 416-326-9326; *Fax:* 416-326-9338
emcmahon.mpp.co@liberal.ola.org
eleanormcmahon.onmpp.ca
Other Communications: Constituency Phone: 905-639-7924; Fax: 905-639-3284
Social Media: www.linkedin.com/in/eleanor-mcmahon-7287146
Note: Web Site: www.mtc.gov.on.ca (Tourism, Culture & Sport)
Constituency Office
#44, 760 Brant St.
Burlington, ON L7R 4B7

Ted McMeekin
Constituency: Ancaster-Dundas-Flamborough-Westdale *No. of Constituents:* 92,833, Liberal
Tel: 416-585-7000
Toll-free: 888-566-6614; *Fax:* 416-585-6470
tmcmeekin.mpp.co@liberal.ola.org
www.tedmcmeekin.onmpp.ca
Other Communications: Constituency Phone: 905-690-6552; Fax: 905-690-6562
Social Media: twitter.com/TedMcMeekin, www.facebook.com/ted.mcmeekin
Constituency Office
299 Dundas St. East
PO Box 1240
Waterdown, ON L0R 2H0

Monte McNaughton
Constituency: Lambton-Kent-Middlesex *No. of Constituents:* 81,678, Progressive Conservative
Tel: 416-325-3362; *Fax:* 416-325-3275
monte.mcnaughtonco@pc.ola.org
montemcnaughtonmpp.ca
Other Communications: Strathroy: 519-245-8696; Wallaceburg: 519-627-1015
Social Media: twitter.com/MonteMcNaughton, www.facebook.com/MonteMcNaughtonMPP
Constituency Office
81 Front St. West
Strathroy, ON N0L 1M0

Madeleine Meilleur
Constituency: Ottawa-Vanier *No. of Constituents:* 81,412, Liberal
Tel: 416-326-2220
Toll-free: 800-518-7901; *Fax:* 416-326-4016
mmeilleur.mpp.co@liberal.ola.org
www.madeleinemeilleur.onmpp.ca
Other Communications: Constituency Phone: 613-744-4484; Fax: 613-744-0889
Social Media: twitter.com/m_meilleur, www.facebook.com/madeleine.meilleur
Constituency Office
237 Montreal Rd.
Vanier, ON K1L 6C7

Parliamentary Assistant to the Minister of Economic Development, Employment & Infrastructure (Infrastructure),

Peter Z. Milczyn
Constituency: Etobicoke-Lakeshore *No. of Constituents:* 96,304, Liberal
Tel: 416-325-7815; *Fax:* 416-314-7906
pmilczyn.mpp.co@liberal.ola.org
Other Communications: Constituency Phone: 416-259-2249; Fax: 416-259-3704
Social Media: twitter.com/PeterMilczyn, www.facebook.com/peter.milczyn
Constituency Office
933 The Queensway
Toronto, ON M8Z 1P3

Norm Miller
Constituency: Parry Sound-Muskoka *No. of Constituents:* 75,153, Progressive Conservative
Tel: 416-325-1012
Toll-free: 888-267-4826; *Fax:* 416-325-1153
norm.miller@pc.ola.org
www.normmillermpp.ca
Other Communications: Bracebridge: 705-645-8538; Parry Sound: 705-746-4266
Social Media: twitter.com/normmillermpp, www.facebook.com/normmillercampaign
Constituency Office
#1, 165 Manitoba St.
Bracebridge, ON P1L 1S3

Paul Miller
Constituency: Hamilton East-Stoney Creek *No. of Constituents:* 88,782, New Democratic Party
Tel: 416-325-0707; *Fax:* 416-325-0853
pmiller-co@ndp.on.ca
paulmiller.ca
Other Communications: Constituency Phone: 905-545-0114; Fax: 905-545-9024
Social Media: twitter.com/PaulMillerMPP, www.facebook.com/PaulMillerHamilton
Constituency Office
289 Queenston Rd.
Hamilton, ON L8K 1H2

Minister, Research, Innovation & Science, Hon. Reza Moridi
Constituency: Richmond Hill *No. of Constituents:* 94,977, Liberal
Tel: 416-326-9500; *Fax:* 416-326-2497
rmoridi.mpp.co@liberal.ola.org
www.rezamoridi.onmpp.ca
Other Communications: Constituency Phone: 905-884-8080; Fax: 905-884-1040
Social Media: twitter.com/rezamoridi, www.facebook.com/rmoridi, www.linkedin.com/pub/reza-moridi-mpp/6/673/bb4
Note: Web Site: www.ontario.ca/page/ministry-research-innovation-and-science (Research, Innovation & Science)
Constituency Office
#311, 9555 Yonge St.
Richmond Hill, ON L4C 9M5

Julia Munro
Constituency: York-Simcoe *No. of Constituents:* 100,744, Progressive Conservative
Tel: 416-325-3392
Toll-free: 866-206-1373; *Fax:* 416-325-3466
julia.munro@pc.ola.org
www.juliamunrompp.com
Other Communications: Constituency Phone: 905-895-1555; Fax: 905-895-0337
Social Media: twitter.com/juliamunropc
Constituency Office
#8, 45 Grist Mill Rd.
Holland Landing, ON L9N 1M7

Minister, Environment & Climate Change, Hon. Glen R. Murray
Constituency: Toronto Centre *No. of Constituents:* 101,741, Liberal
Tel: 416-314-6790; *Fax:* 416-314-6748
gmurray.mpp@liberal.ola.org
www.glenmurray.onmpp.ca
Other Communications: Constituency Phone: 416-972-7683; Fax: 416-972-7686
Social Media: twitter.com/Glen4ONT, www.facebook.com/MPPGlenMurray, www.linkedin.com/in/glenmurraympp
Note: Web Site: www.ontario.ca/ministry-environment (Environment & Climate Change)
Constituency Office
#318, 120 Carlton St.
Toronto, ON M5A 4K2

Associate Minister, Finance (Ontario Retirement Pension Plan), Hon. Indira Naidoo-Harris
Constituency: Halton *No. of Constituents:* 149,633, Liberal
Tel: 416-325-0400; *Fax:* 416-325-0374
inaidoo-harris.mpp.co@liberal.ola.org
indiranaidooharris.onmpp.ca
Other Communications: Constituency Phone: 905-878-1729; Fax: 905-878-5144
Social Media: twitter.com/IndiraNHarris, www.facebook.com/indira.naidooharris, ca.linkedin.com/pub/indira-naidoo-harris/4/b15/421
Note: Web Site: www.fin.gov.on.ca (Finance)
Constituency Office
#1, 174 Mill St.
Milton, ON L9T 1S2

Attorney General; Government House Leader, Hon. Yasir Naqvi
Constituency: Ottawa Centre *No. of Constituents:* 94,777, Liberal
Tel: 416-326-2220; *Fax:* 416-326-4016
ynaqvi.mpp.co@liberal.ola.org
www.yasirnaqvi.onmpp.ca
Other Communications: Constituency Phone: 613-722-6414; Fax: 613-722-6703
Social Media: twitter.com/Yasir_Naqvi, www.facebook.com/YasirNaqviMPP, www.linkedin.com/in/yasirnaqvimpp
Note: Web Site: www.attorneygeneral.jus.gov.on.ca (Attorney General)
Constituency Office
109 Catherine St.
Ottawa, ON K2P 0P4

Taras Natyshak
Constituency: Essex *No. of Constituents:* 94,008, New Democratic Party
Tel: 416-325-0714
Toll-free: 800-265-3909; *Fax:* 416-325-0980
tnatyshak-co@ndp.on.ca
Other Communications: Constituency Phone: 519-776-6420; Fax: 519-776-6980
Social Media: twitter.com/TarasNatyshak, www.linkedin.com/pub/taras-natyshak/11/540/432
Constituency Office
316 Talbot St. North
Essex, ON N8M 2E1

Rick Nicholls
Constituency: Chatham-Kent-Essex *No. of Constituents:* 74,559, Progressive Conservative
Tel: 416-325-9099; *Fax:* 416-325-9000
rick.nichollsco@pc.ola.org
ricknichollsmpp.ca
Other Communications: Chatham: 519-351-0510; Leamington: 519-326-3367
Social Media: twitter.com/RickNicholls, www.facebook.com/RickNichollsPCofCKEX, www.linkedin.com/pub/rick-nicholls/10/280/b05
Constituency Office
#100, 111 Heritage Rd.
Chatham, ON N7M 5W7

Minister, Community Safety & Correctional Services, Hon. David Orazietti
Constituency: Sault Ste. Marie *No. of Constituents:* 59,385, Liberal
Tel: 416-325-0408; *Fax:* 416-325-6067
dorazietti.mpp@liberal.ola.org
www.davidorazietti.onmpp.ca
Other Communications: Constituency Phone: 705-949-6959; Fax: 705-946-6269
Social Media: twitter.com/DavidOrazietti, www.facebook.com/davidorazietti
Note: Web Site: www.mcscs.jus.gov.on.ca (Community Safety & Correctional Services)
Constituency Office
#202, 432 Great Northern Rd., 2nd Fl.
Sault Ste Marie, ON P6B 4Z9

Randy Pettapiece
Constituency: Perth-Wellington *No. of Constituents:* 74,914, Progressive Conservative
Tel: 416-325-3400; *Fax:* 416-325-3430
randy.pettapiececo@pc.ola.org
pettapiece.ca
Other Communications: Constituency Phone: 519-272-0660; Fax: 519-272-1064
Social Media: twitter.com/randypettapiece, www.facebook.com/randypettapiece
Constituency Office
55 Lorne Ave. East
Stratford, ON N5A 6S4

Parliamentary Assistant to the Minister of Agriculture, Food & Rural Affairs, Arthur Potts
Constituency: Beaches-East York *No. of Constituents:* 77,381, Liberal
Tel: 416-326-3057; *Fax:* 416-326-3119
apotts.mpp.co@liberal.ola.org
arthurpotts.onmpp.ca
Other Communications: Constituency Phone: 416-690-1032; Fax: 416-690-8420
Social Media: twitter.com/arthurpottsmpp, www.linkedin.com/pub/arthur-potts/6/9b6/452
Constituency Office
1821 Danforth Ave.
Toronto, ON M4C 1J2

Parliamentary Assistant to the Premier, Dr. Shafiq Qaadri
Constituency: Etobicoke North *No. of Constituents:* 64,284, Liberal
Tel: 416-327-2295; *Fax:* 416-314-7421
sqaadri.mpp.co@liberal.ola.org
shafiqqaadri.onmpp.ca
Other Communications: Constituency Phone: 416-745-2859; Fax: 416-745-4601
Social Media: twitter.com/ReElectQaadri, www.linkedin.com/in/doctorqca
Constituency Office
823 Albion Rd.
Etobicoke, ON M9V 1A3

Parliamentary Assistant to the Minister of Municipal Affairs & Housing, Lou Rinaldi
Constituency: Northumberland-Quinte West *No. of Constituents:* 98,945, Liberal
Tel: 416-585-6768; *Fax:* 416-585-4035
lrinaldi.mpp.co@liberal.ola.org
www.lourinaldi.onmpp.ca
Other Communications: Cobourg: 905-372-4000; Brighton: 613-475-1040
Social Media: twitter.com/RinaldiLou
Constituency Office
#7, 513 Division St.
Cobourg, ON K9A 5G6

President, Treasury Board, Hon. Liz Sandals
Constituency: Guelph *No. of Constituents:* 96,599, Liberal
Tel: 416-327-2333; *Fax:* 416-327-3790
lsandals.mpp.co@liberal.ola.org
www.lizsandals.onmpp.ca
Other Communications: Constituency Phone: 519-836-4190; Fax: 519-836-4191
Social Media: www.facebook.com/lizsandalsmpp
Note: Web Site: www.canada.ca/en/treasury-board-secretariat.html (Treasury Board Secretariat)
Constituency Office
173 Woolwich St.
Guelph, ON N1H 3V4

Peggy Sattler
Constituency: London West *No. of Constituents:* 99,472, New Democratic Party
Tel: 416-325-6908; *Fax:* 416-325-7030
psattler-co@ndp.on.ca
www.peggysattler.ca
Other Communications: Constituency Phone: 519-657-3120; Fax: 519-657-0368
Social Media: twitter.com/PeggySattlerNDP, www.facebook.com/PeggySattlerONDP
Constituency Office
#106, 240 Commissioners Rd. West
London, ON N6J 1Y1

Deputy Opposition Whip, Laurie Scott
Constituency: Haliburton-Kawartha Lakes-Brock *No. of Constituents:* 96,029, Progressive Conservative
Tel: 416-325-2771
Toll-free: 800-424-2490; *Fax:* 416-325-2904
laurie.scottco@pc.ola.org
www.lauriescottmpp.com
Social Media: www.facebook.com/199126813450886
Constituency Office
14 Lindsay St. North
Lindsay, ON K9V 1T4

Mario Sergio
Constituency: York West *No. of Constituents:* 61,054, Liberal
Tel: 416-314-9710; *Fax:* 416-325-4787
msergio.mpp@liberal.ola.org
www.mariosergio.onmpp.ca
Other Communications: Constituency Phone: 416-743-7272; Fax: 416-743-3292
Social Media: twitter.com/mariosergiompp, www.linkedin.com/pub/mario-sergio/18/b65/28
Constituency Office
#38, 2300 Finch Ave. West
Toronto, ON M9M 2Y3

Deputy Leader, Third Party, Jagmeet Singh
Constituency: Bramalea-Gore-Malton *No. of Constituents:* 119,534, New Democratic Party
Tel: 416-325-1784; *Fax:* 416-325-1790
jsingh-qp@ndp.on.ca
www.jagmeetsingh.ca
Other Communications: Constituency Phone: 905-799-3939; Fax: 905-799-9505
Social Media: twitter.com/jagmeetNDP, www.facebook.com/jagmeetndp
Constituency Office
#18, 470 Chrysler Dr.
Brampton, ON L6S 0C1

Todd Smith
Constituency: Prince Edward-Hastings *No. of Constituents:* 90,761, Progressive Conservative
Tel: 416-325-2702
Toll-free: 877-536-6248; *Fax:* 416-325-2675
todd.smithco@pc.ola.org
toddsmithmpp.ca

Other Communications: Belleville: 613-962-1144; Bancroft: 613-332-5850
Social Media: twitter.com/toddsmithpc, www.facebook.com/183429548412185
Constituency Office
#3, 81 Millennium Pkwy.
PO Box 575
Belleville, ON K8N 5B2

Minister, Finance, Hon. Charles Sousa
Constituency: Mississauga South *No. of Constituents:* 82,480, Liberal
Tel: 416-325-0400; *Fax:* 416-325-0374
csousa.mpp.co@liberal.ola.org
www.charlessousa.onmpp.ca
Other Communications: Constituency Phone: 905-274-8228; Fax: 905-274-8552
Social Media: twitter.com/SousaCharles, www.facebook.com/charles.sousa.121, www.linkedin.com/in/charlessousa
Note: Web Site: www.fin.gov.on.ca (Finance)
Constituency Office
#1 & 2, 120 Lakeshore Rd. West
Mississauga, ON L5H 1E8

Peter Tabuns
Constituency: Toronto-Danforth *No. of Constituents:* 78,787, New Democratic Party
Tel: 416-325-3250; *Fax:* 416-325-3252
tabunsp-qp@ndp.on.ca
petertabuns.ca
Other Communications: Constituency Phone: 416-461-0223; Fax: 416-461-9542
Social Media: twitter.com/Peter_Tabuns, www.facebook.com/peter.tabuns
Constituency Office
923 Danforth Ave.
Toronto, ON M4J 1L8

Harinder S. Takhar
Constituency: Mississauga-Erindale *No. of Constituents:* 111,690, Liberal
Tel: 416-325-4265; *Fax:* 416-325-4289
htakhar.mpp@liberal.ola.org
www.hstakhar.com
Other Communications: Constituency Phone: 905-897-8815; Fax: 905-897-6960
Social Media: twitter.com/harindertakhar, www.facebook.com/HarinderTakharMPPCandidate, linkedin.com/pub/hon-harinder-takhar/34/a2a/58
Note: Harinder Takhar resigned from his cabinet post of Minister of Government Services on May 8, 2013, due to health reasons. However, he remained the MPP for Mississauga-Erindale, & was re-elected in the 2014 General Election.
Constituency Office
#1 & 2, 3413 Wolfedale Rd.
Mississauga, ON L5C 1V8

Monique Taylor
Constituency: Hamilton Mountain *No. of Constituents:* 94,360, New Democratic Party
Tel: 416-325-1796; *Fax:* 416-325-1863
mtaylor-co@ndp.on.ca
www.moniquetaylormpp.ca
Other Communications: Constituency Phone: 905-388-9734; Fax: 905-388-7862
Social Media: twitter.com/MoniqueONDP, www.facebook.com/151616944893613
Constituency Office
#2, 952 Concession St.
Hamilton, ON L8V 1G2

Minister, Energy, Hon. Glenn Thibeault
Constituency: Sudbury, Liberal
Tel: 416-327-6758; *Fax:* 416-327-6754
gthibeault.mpp.co@liberal.ola.org
Other Communications: Constituency Phone: 705-675-1914; Fax: 705-675-1456
Note: Web Site: www.energy.gov.on.ca (Energy)
Constituency Office
#4B, 555 Barrydowne Rd.
Sudbury, ON P3A 3T4

Lisa Thompson
Constituency: Huron-Bruce *No. of Constituents:* 80,428, Progressive Conservative
Tel: 416-325-3467
Toll-free: 866-396-3007; *Fax:* 416-325-3490
lisa.thompsonco@pc.ola.org
www.lisathompsonmpp.ca
Other Communications: Blyth: 519-523-4251; Kincardine: 519-396-3007
Social Media: twitter.com/LisaThompsonMPP, www.facebook.com/lisathompsonmpp
Constituency Office
408 Queen St.
PO Box 426
Blyth, ON N0M 1H0

Third Party Whip, John Vanthof
Constituency: Timiskaming-Cochrane *No. of Constituents:* 52,572, New Democratic Party
Tel: 416-325-2000; *Fax:* 416-325-1999
jvanthof-co@ndp.on.ca
johnvanthof.com
Other Communications: New Lisk.: 705-647-5995; Kirkland Lake: 705-567-4650
Social Media: twitter.com/john_vanthof, www.facebook.com/JohnVanthof
Constituency Office, Pinewoods Centre
#5, 247 Whitewood Ave.
PO Box 398
New Liskeard, ON P0J 1P0

Parliamentary Assistant to the Minister of Research & Innovation, Daiene Vernile
Constituency: Kitchener Centre *No. of Constituents:* 83,170, Liberal
Tel: 416-326-9437; *Fax:* 416-326-2497
dvernile.mpp.co@liberal.ola.org
daienevernile.onmpp.ca
Other Communications: Constituency Phone: 519-579-5460; Fax: 519-579-2121
Social Media: twitter.com/DaieneVernile, www.facebook.com/daienevernile, ca.linkedin.com/pub/daiene-vernile/21/a/904
Constituency Office
#3, 379 Queen St. South
Kitchener, ON N2G 1W6

Bill Walker
Constituency: Bruce-Grey-Owen Sound *No. of Constituents:* 80,646, Progressive Conservative
Tel: 416-325-6242
Toll-free: 800-461-2664; *Fax:* 416-325-6248
bill.walkerco@pc.ola.org
billwalkermpp.com
Other Communications: Constituency Phone: 519-371-2421; Fax: 519-371-0953
Social Media: twitter.com/billwalkermpp, www.facebook.com/BillWalkerMPP, www.linkedin.com/pub/bill-walker-mpp/54/594/19
Constituency Office
#100, 920 - 1st Ave. West
Owen Sound, ON N4K 4K5

House Leader, Official Opposition, Jim Wilson
Constituency: Simcoe-Grey *No. of Constituents:* 107,762, Progressive Conservative
Tel: 416-325-2069
Toll-free: 800-268-7542; *Fax:* 416-325-2079
jim.wilsonco@pc.ola.org
www.jimwilsonmpp.com
Other Communications: Alliston: 705-435-4087; Collingwood: 705-446-1090
Social Media: twitter.com/jwilsonmpp
Constituency Office
50 Hume St.
Collingwood, ON L9Y 1V2

Deputy Speaker & Chair, Committee of the Whole House; Parliamentary Assistant to the Minister of Community & Social Services, Soo Wong
Constituency: Scarborough-Agincourt *No. of Constituents:* 76,549, Liberal
Tel: 416-212-5841; *Fax:* 416-325-3347
swong.mpp.co@liberal.ola.org
www.soowong.onmpp.ca
Other Communications: Constituency Phone: 416-297-6568; Fax: 416-297-4962
Social Media: twitter.com/SooWongMPP, www.facebook.com/SooWongSA, www.linkedin.com/pub/soo-wong/97/382/100
Constituency Office
#3, 2245 Kennedy Rd.
Toronto, ON M1T 3G8

Premier; Minister, Intergovernmental Affairs; President, Executive Council; Leader, Government; Leader, Liberal Party of Ontario, Hon. Kathleen O. Wynne
Constituency: Don Valley West *No. of Constituents:* 86,092, Liberal
Tel: 416-325-1941; *Fax:* 416-325-9895
kwynne.mpp@liberal.ola.org
www.ontarioliberal.ca/leader/Biography.aspx
Other Communications: Constituency Phone: 416-425-6777; Fax: 416-425-0350
Social Media: twitter.com/Kathleen_Wynne, www.facebook.com/WynneFans, www.linkedin.com/in/kathleenwynne
Note: Web Site: www.ontario.ca/ministry-intergovernmental-affairs (Ministry of Intergovernmental Affairs)
Constituency Office
#101, 795 Eglinton Ave. East
Toronto, ON M4G 4E4

Chief Whip, Official Opposition, John Yakabuski
Constituency: Renfrew-Nipissing-Pembroke *No. of Constituents:* 76,956, Progressive Conservative
Tel: 416-325-2170; *Fax:* 416-325-2196
john.yakabuskico@pc.ola.org
www.johnyakabuski.com
Other Communications: Constituency Phone: 613-735-6627; Fax: 613-735-6692
Constituency Office, The Victoria Centre
#6, 84 Isabella St.
Pembroke, ON K8A 5S5

Jeff Yurek
Constituency: Elgin-Middlesex-London *No. of Constituents:* 84,970, Progressive Conservative
Tel: 416-325-3965
Toll-free: 800-265-7638; *Fax:* 416-325-3988
jeff.yurekco@pc.ola.org
www.jeffyurekmpp.com
Other Communications: Constituency Phone: 519-631-0666; Fax: 519-631-9478
Social Media: twitter.com/JeffYurekMPP
Constituency Office
#201, 750 Talbot St., West Wing
St. Thomas, ON N5P 1E2

Minister, Indigenous Relations & Reconciliation, Hon. David Zimmer
Constituency: Willowdale *No. of Constituents:* 99,726, Liberal
Tel: 416-325-5110; *Fax:* 416-314-2701
dzimmer.mpp.co@liberal.ola.org
www.davidzimmer.ca
Other Communications: Constituency Phone: 416-733-7878; Fax: 416-733-7709
Social Media: twitter.com/DavidZimmerMPP, www.facebook.com/teamzimmer
Note: Web Site: www.ontario.ca/page/ministry-indigenous-relations-and-reconciliation (Indigenous Relations & Reconciliation)
Constituency Office, Newtonbrook Plaza
#3, 5801 Yonge St.
Toronto, ON M2M 3T9

Vacant
Constituency: Niagara West-Glanbrook
Note: Tim Hudak resigned as Leader of the PC Party of Ontario after his party's defeat in the 2014 General Election. He remained as an MPP until Sept. 2016, when he resigned to become the CEO of the Ontario Real Estate Association.

Ontario Government Departments & Agencies

Ontario Ministry of Advanced Education & Skills Development

Mowat Block, 900 Bay St., 14th Fl., Toronto, ON M7A 1L2
Tel: 416-326-1600; *Fax:* 416-325-6348
Toll-Free: 800-387-5514
TTY: 800-268-7095
information.met@ontario.ca
www.tcu.gov.on.ca
twitter.com/OntarioTCU
www.facebook.com/OntTCU
www.youtube.com/user/OntarioTCU

Together with the Ministry of Education, the Ministry of Advanced Education & Skills Development (formerly Training, Colleges & Universities) is responsible for the administration of laws relating to education & skills training. It operates Employment Ontario & is responsible for postsecondary education in the province.

Minister; Minister Responsible, Digital Government, Hon. Deborah Matthews
Tel: 416-326-1600; *Fax:* 416-326-1656
deb.matthews@ontario.ca

Deputy Minister, Sheldon Levy
Tel: 416-314-9244; *Fax:* 416-314-7117
sheldon.levy@ontario.ca

Parliamentary Assistant, Han Dong
Tel: 416-314-3295; *Fax:* 416-326-2807
han.dong@ontario.ca

Director, Communications Branch, Heather Wright
Tel: 416-325-2944
heather.wright@ontario.ca

Associated Agencies, Boards & Commissions:

•College of Trades Appointments Council
Mowat Block
900 Bay St., 23rd Fl.
Toronto, ON M7A 1L2
Tel: 416-326-5629; *Fax:* 416-326-5653
appointments.council@ontario.ca
www.cot-appointments.ca
Other Communication: Alt. Phones: 416-326-5638; 416-212-9521

•Higher Education Quality Council of Ontario (HEQCO)
#2402, 1 Yonge St.
Toronto, ON M5E 1E5
Tel: 416-212-3893; *Fax:* 416-212-3899
info@heqco.ca
www.heqco.ca

•Ontario Graduate Scholarship Program Selection Board
189 Red River Rd., 4th Fl.
PO Box 4500
Thunder Bay, ON P7B 6G9
Tel: 807-343-7257; *Fax:* 807-343-7278
Toll-free: 800-465-3957
Provides advice & recommendations to the minister concerning the policies & administration of the Ontario Graduate Scholarship program & selects successful candidates for funding under the program.

•Ontario Student Assistance Program Financial Eligibility Advisory Committee
77 Wellesley St. West
PO Box 276
Toronto, ON M7A 1N3
Tel: 416-314-0714; *Fax:* 416-325-3096
osap.gov.on.ca

•Post-secondary Education Quality Assessment Board
Mowat Block
900 Bay St., 23rd Fl.
Toronto, ON M7A 1L2
Tel: 416-212-1230; *Fax:* 416-212-6620
peqab@ontario.ca
peqab.ca

•Training Completion Assurance Fund Advisory Board
Mowat Block
900 Bay St., 9th Fl.
Toronto, ON M7A 1L2
Tel: 416-314-0500; *Fax:* 416-314-0499
www.tcu.gov.on.ca/pepg/audiences/pcc/tcaf.html

Corporate Management & Services Division
Mowat Block, #342, 900 Bay St., Toronto, ON M7A 1L2
Tel: 416-325-2772; *Fax:* 416-325-2778

Assistant Deputy Minister & Chief Administrative Officer, Bohodar Rubashewsky
Tel: 416-325-2773; *Fax:* 416-325-2778
Bohodar.I.Rubashewsky@ontario.ca

Director, Strategic Human Resources, Lisa Brisebois
Tel: 416-327-2731; *Fax:* 416-327-9043
Lisa.Brisebois@ontario.ca

Director, Organizational Renewal Project, Lisa Alfieri Sladen
Tel: 416-314-1195
lisa.alfierisladen@ontario.ca

Acting Director, Corporate Finance & Service, Susan Flanagan
Tel: 416-325-7677; *Fax:* 416-325-1835
susan.flanagan@ontario.ca

Acting Director, Corporate Coordination Branch, Sarah Truscott
Tel: 416-326-6662; *Fax:* 416-314-0558
sarah.truscott@ontario.ca

Director, Legal Services, Karen Inselsbacher
Tel: 416-325-4021; *Fax:* 416-325-2410
karen.inselsbacher@ontario.ca

Employment & Training Division
Mowat Block, 900 Bay St., 3rd Fl., Toronto, ON M7A 1L2
Fax: 416-325-2995
Toll-Free: 888-562-4769

Assistant Deputy Minister, David Fulford
Tel: 416-325-2989
david.fulford@ontario.ca

Director, Program Delivery Support Branch, Teresa Damaso
Tel: 416-314-4268; *Fax:* 416-325-6162
teresa.damaso@ontario.ca

Director, Organizational & Business Excellence Branch, Sandra DiProspero
Tel: 416-325-4511; *Fax:* 416-325-6162
sandra.diprospero@ontario.ca

Director, Finance, Analysis & Systems Support Branch, Todd Kilpatrick
Tel: 416-325-2751
todd.kilpatrick@ontario.ca

Director, Service Standards & Management, Vacant
Other Communications: JobGrow Hotline: 416-326-5656; Fax: 416-326-5868

Project Director, ETD Regional Review Project, Jan Hughes
Tel: 416-327-5883; *Fax:* 416-327-1958
jan.hughes@ontario.ca

French-Language, Aboriginal Learning & Research Division
Mowat Block, 900 Bay St., 22nd Fl., Toronto, ON M7A 1L2
Tel: 416-325-2132; *Fax:* 416-327-1182

Assistant Deputy Minister, Janine Griffore
Tel: 416-325-2132
janine.griffore@ontario.ca

Director, Aboriginal Education Office, Shirley Carder
Tel: 416-325-8561
Shirley.Carder@ontario.ca

Director, French Language Education Policy & Programs, Denys Giguere
Tel: 416-327-9072
denys.giguere@ontario.ca

Post-secondary Education Division
Mowat Block, 900 Bay St., 7th Fl., Toronto, ON M7A 1L2
Tel: 416-325-2199; *Fax:* 416-326-3256

Assistant Deputy Minister, David Carter-Whitney
Tel: 416-325-2199
david.carter-whitney@ontario.ca

Lead Director, Post-secondary Financial Information System Project, Barry McCartan
Tel: 416-325-9231
barry.mccartan@ontario.ca

Director, Post-secondary Accountability, Linda Hawke
Tel: 416-325-1815
linda.hawke@ontario.ca

Director, Student Financial Assistance, Noah Morris
Tel: 416-325-2853; *Fax:* 416-325-3096
noah.morris@ontario.ca

Director, Post-secondary Finance & Information Management Branch, Kelly Shields
Tel: 416-325-1952
kelly.shields@ontario.ca

Director & Superintendent, Private Career Colleges, Carol Strachan
Tel: 416-325-5859; *Fax:* 416-314-0499
carol.strachan@ontario.ca

Strategic Policy & Programs Division
#1747, 900 Bay St., 17th Fl., Toronto, ON M7A 1L2

Acting Assistant Deputy Minister, Patricia Buckley
Tel: 416-212-5420
paddy.buckley@ontario.ca

Acting Director, Strategic Policy & Initiatives, Fiona Foster
Tel: 416-212-6597; *Fax:* 416-314-3864
fiona.foster@ontario.ca

Director, Programs, Jen Liptrot
Tel: 416-326-5849; *Fax:* 416-326-5505
jen.liptrot@ontario.ca

Director, Labour Market Negotiations, Vacant
Tel: 416-326-0832

Acting Director, Research & Planning, Bill Praamsma
Tel: 416-325-4034; *Fax:* 416-326-0601
bill.praamsma@ontario.ca

Chief Executive Officer & Director, Postsecondary Education Quality Assessment Board, James Brown
Tel: 416-325-2422; *Fax:* 416-212-6620
james.brown@ontario.ca

Ontario Ministry of Agriculture, Food & Rural Affairs

Ontario Government Bldg., 1 Stone Rd. West, Guelph, ON N1G 4Y2
Tel: 519-826-3100; *Fax:* 519-826-4335
Toll-Free: 888-466-2372
about.omafra@ontario.ca
www.omafra.gov.on.ca
Other Communication: Rural Affairs, URL: www.omafra.gov.on.ca/english/rural
Secondary Address: 77 Grenville St., 11th Fl. Toronto, ON M5S 1B3
twitter.com/atomafra
www.youtube.com/user/atomafra

The Ministry works in partnership with an industry that employs over 640,000 people & contributes over $25 billion annually to the provincial economy. The Ministry plays a key role in bringing a strong agricultural & rural perspective to provincial policies. The Ministry works with other Ministries to resolve local economic issues & assists rural communities in retaining & attracting business. Staff at the Ministry's Guelph headquarters & across the province provide a wide range of agri-food & rural economic development programs & services to clients. The Rural Affairs section seeks to strengthen Ontario's rural communities through funding programs, economic development programs, infrastructure & broadband internet access.

Minister, Hon. Jeff Leal
Tel: 416-326-3074; *Fax:* 416-326-3083
jleal.mpp.co@liberal.ola.org

Deputy Minister, Deb Stark
Tel: 416-326-3101
deb.stark@ontario.ca

Parliamentary Assistant, Arthur Potts
Tel: 416-326-3057; *Fax:* 416-326-3119
apotts.mpp.co@liberal.ola.org

Director, Communications Branch, Diane Gumbs
Tel: 416-326-5196; *Fax:* 519-826-4253
diane.gumbs@ontario.ca

Director, Legal Services, Jeff Schelling
Tel: 519-826-3422; *Fax:* 519-826-3385
jeff.schelling@ontario.ca

Associated Agencies, Boards & Commissions:

•Agricorp
1 Stone Rd. West, 3rd Fl.
PO Box 3660 Central
Guelph, ON N1H 8M4
Fax: 519-826-4118
Toll-free: 888-247-4999
TTY: 877-275-1380
contact@agricorp.com
www.agricorp.com
Other Communication: AgriStability Fax: 519-826-4334
Responsible for delivering government & non-government priority products & services that assist Ontario's agri-food industry in managing risks.

•Agricultural Research Institute of Ontario (ARIO)
1 Stone Rd. West, 2nd Fl.
Guelph, ON N1G 4Y2
Tel: 519-826-4554
Toll-free: 888-466-2372
research.omafra@ontario.ca
www.omafra.gov.on.ca/english/research/ario/institute.htm
The role of ARIO is to enquire into programs of research with respect to agriculture, veterinary medicine & consumer studies, select & recommend areas of research for the betterment of agriculture, veterinary medicine & consumer studies, & stimulate interest in research as a means of developing a high degree of efficiency in the production & marketing of agricultural products in Ontario.

•Agriculture, Food & Rural Affairs Tribunal & Board of Negotiation
1 Stone Rd. West, 2nd Fl.
Guelph, ON N1G 4Y2
Tel: 519-826-3433; *Fax:* 519-826-4232
Toll-free: 888-466-2372
appeals.tribunal.omafra@ontario.ca
www.omafra.gov.on.ca/english/tribunal/index.html

•College of Veterinarians of Ontario
2106 Gordon St.
Guelph, ON N1L 1G6
Tel: 519-824-5600; *Fax:* 519-824-6497
Toll-free: 800-424-2856
inquiries@cvo.org
www.cvo.org
Other Communication: Toll-Free Fax: 1-888-662-9479

•Grain Financial Protection Board
1 Stone Rd. West, 1st Fl. Northeast
PO Box 3660 Central
Guelph, ON N1H 8M4
Tel: 519-826-3949; *Fax:* 519-826-3367

•Livestock Financial Protection Board
1 Stone Rd. West, 5th Fl. Northwest
Guelph, ON N1G 4Y2
Tel: 519-826-3886; *Fax:* 519-826-4375
Toll-free: 888-466-2372

•Livestock Medicines Advisory Committee
1 Stone Rd. West, 3rd Fl. Northeast
Guelph, ON N1G 4Y2
Tel: 519-826-4110; *Fax:* 519-826-3254
ag.info.omafra@ontario.ca

•Normal Farm Practices Protection Board
1 Stone Rd. West, 3rd Fl.
Guelph, ON N1G 4Y2
Tel: 519-826-4047; *Fax:* 519-826-3259
Toll-free: 877-424-1300
ag.info.omafra@ontario.ca

•Ontario Farm Products Marketing Commission
1 Stone Rd. West, 5th Fl. Southwest
Guelph, ON N1G 4Y2
Tel: 519-826-4220; *Fax:* 519-826-3400
ontariofarm.productsmarketing.omafra@ontario.ca
www.omafra.gov.on.ca/english/farmproducts

•Ontario Food Terminal Board
165 The Queensway
Toronto, ON M8Y 1H8
Tel: 416-259-5479; *Fax:* 416-259-4303
oftboard@interlog.com
www.oftb.com

•Ontario Racing Commission (ORC)
#400, 10 Carlson Crt.
Toronto, ON M9W 6L2
Tel: 416-213-0520; *Fax:* 416-213-7827
inquiry@ontarioracingcommission.ca
www.ontarioracingcommission.ca

•Rural Economic Development (RED) Panel
1 Stone Rd. West, 4th Fl.
Guelph, ON N1G 4Y2
Fax: 519-826-4336
Toll-free: 888-588-4111
red.omafra@ontario.ca
www.ontario.ca/rural

Economic Development Division
Fax: 519-826-3567
Toll-Free: 877-424-1300
Other Communication: Northern Ontario, Toll-Free Phone: 1-800-461-6132

Assistant Deputy Minister, Randy Jackiw
Tel: 519-826-3528
Randy.Jackiw@ontario.ca
Director, Business Development, George Borovilos
Tel: 519-826-4452
george.borovilos@ontario.ca
omafra.gov.on.ca/english/food
Director, Rural Programs, Brent Kennedy
Tel: 519-826-3419; *Fax:* 519-826-4336
brent.kennedy@ontario.ca
Director, Agriculture Development, Aileen MacNeil
Tel: 519-826-6588; *Fax:* 519-826-3254
aileen.macneil@ontario.ca
Director, Regional Economic Development, Douglas Reddick
Tel: 519-826-4167; *Fax:* 519-826-3567
douglas.reddick@ontario.ca

Regional Offices

Central Region
Elora Resource Centre, #10, 6484 Wellington Rd. 7, Elora, ON N0B 1S0
Tel: 519-846-0941; *Fax:* 519-846-8178
Regional Administrative Coordinator, Wanda Martin-Koch
Tel: 519-846-3387
wanda.martin-koch@ontario.ca
East Region, Kemptville District Office
59 Ministry Dr., PO Box 2004 Kemptville, ON K0G 1J0
Tel: 613-258-8295; *Fax:* 613-258-8392
North Region
Caldwell Township Hall Bldg., Hwy. 64, PO Box 521 Verner, ON P0H 2M0
Tel: 705-594-2312; *Fax:* 705-594-9675
Toll-Free: 800-461-6132
Southwest Region
London Resource Centre, 667 Exeter Rd., London, ON N6E 1L3
Tel: 519-873-4070; *Fax:* 519-873-4062

Food Safety & Environment Division
Tel: 519-826-4304; *Fax:* 519-826-4416
Assistant Deputy Minister, Debra Sikora
Tel: 519-826-4301
debra.sikora@ontario.ca
Director, Animal Health & Welfare/Office of the Chief Veterinarian for Ontario, Dr. Greg Douglas
Tel: 519-826-3577; *Fax:* 519-826-4375
greg.b.douglas@ontario.ca
Acting Director, Food Inspection Branch, Gavin Downing
Tel: 519-826-4366; *Fax:* 519-826-4375
gavin.downing@ontario.ca
Acting Director, Food Safety & Traceability Programs, George McCaw
Tel: 519-826-3112
george.mccaw@ontario.ca
Director, Environmental Management, Jim Richardson
Tel: 519-826-4975; *Fax:* 519-826-3259
jim.richardson@ontario.ca

Office of the Chief Information Officer, Land & Resources I & IT Cluster
99 Wellesley St. West, Toronto, ON M7A 1W3
Fax: 416-314-6091
Chief Information Officer, John DiMarco
Tel: 416-326-6954
john.dimarco@ontario.ca

Policy Division
Tel: 519-826-4020; *Fax:* 519-826-3492
Responsible for the ministry's policy processes, the administration & delivery of several farm business risk management programs & the management of the ministry's strategic partnership with Agricorp.
Assistant Deputy Minister, Phil Malcolmson
Tel: 519-326-6463; *Fax:* 519-826-3492
phil.malcolmson@ontario.ca
Director, Food Safety & Environmental Policy Branch, Sharon Bailey
Tel: 519-826-6800; *Fax:* 519-826-3492
sharon.bailey@ontario.ca
Director, Farm Finance, David Hagarty
Tel: 519-826-3244; *Fax:* 519-826-3170
david.hagarty@ontario.ca
Director, Economic Development Policy, Thom Hagerty
Tel: 519-826-3918; *Fax:* 519-826-4328
thom.hagerty@ontario.ca
Director, Strategic Policy, Brendan McKay
Tel: 519-400-1832
brendan.mckay@ontario.ca

Research & Corporate Services Division
Tel: 519-826-4152; *Fax:* 519-826-3390
Assistant Deputy Minister & Chief Administrative Officer, Christine Primeau
Tel: 519-826-6599
christine.primeau@ontario.ca
Director, Strategic Solutions, Alan Hogan
Tel: 519-826-3739
alan.hogan@ontario.ca
Director, Transportation & Agriculture Audit Services Team, Nancy Lavoie
Tel: 905-704-2879; *Fax:* 905-704-2333
nancy.lavoie@ontario.ca
Director, Business Services Branch, Ramneet Aujla
Tel: 519-826-4698
ramneet.aujla@ontario.ca
Acting Manager, Horse Racing Industry, Heather Harrison
Tel: 519-826-4129
heather.harrison@ontario.ca
Director, Research & Innovation, Michael Toombs
Tel: 519-826-4172; *Fax:* 519-826-4211
michael.toombs@ontario.ca
Acting Director, Business Planning & Financial Management, Shelley Tapp
Tel: 519-826-3336; *Fax:* 519-826-4130
shelley.tapp@ontario.ca
Director, Strategic Solutions, Alan Hogan
Tel: 519-826-3739; *Fax:* 519-826-3160
alan.hogan@ontario.ca

Ontario Ministry of the Attorney General

McMurtry-Scott Bldg., 720 Bay St., 11th Fl., Toronto, ON M7A 2S9
Tel: 416-326-2220; *Fax:* 416-326-4007
Toll-Free: 800-518-7901
TTY: 877-425-0575
attorneygeneral@ontario.ca
www.attorneygeneral.jus.gov.on.ca
twitter.com/ontmag
www.flickr.com/photos/ontmag

Justice services are delivered to Ontarians by the Ministry of the Attorney General. The Ministry is engaged in the following activities: supporting victims of crime; providing justice support services to vulnerable people in the province; ensuring the availability of effective & efficient criminal, civil & family courts, plus related justice services; prosecuting crime; & giving legal advice & services to government.

Attorney General, Hon. Yasir Naqvi
Tel: 416-326-2220; *Fax:* 416-326-4016
ynaqvi.mpp@liberal.ola.org
Deputy Attorney General/Deputy Minister, Patrick Monahan
Tel: 416-326-2640
patrick.monahan@ontario.ca
Parliamentary Assistant, Lorenzo Berardinetti
Tel: 416-325-1008; *Fax:* 416-325-1219
lberardinetti.mpp@liberal.ola.org
Director, Communications Branch, Marianne Summers
Tel: 416-326-2604; *Fax:* 416-326-4007
marianne.summers@ontario.ca

Associated Agencies, Boards & Commissions:

•Alcohol & Gaming Commission of Ontario (AGCO)
90 Sheppard Ave. East
Toronto, ON M2N 0A4
Tel: 416-326-8700; *Fax:* 416-326-5555
Toll-free: 800-522-2876
customer.service@agco.ca
www.agco.on.ca

•Animal Care Review Board (ACRB)
#530, 20 Dundas St. West
Toronto, ON M5G 2C2
Tel: 416-212-0334; *Fax:* 416-314-4270
Toll-free: 855-444-7454
acrb.registrar@ontario.ca
slasto.gov.on.ca/en/Pages/Animal-Care-Review-Board.aspx
Other Communication: Toll-Free Fax: 1-800-720-5292
Part of Safety, Licensing Appeals & Standards Tribunals Ontario (SLASTO)

•Assessment Review Board (ARB)
#1500, 655 Bay St.
Toronto, ON M5G 1E5
Tel: 416-212-6349; *Fax:* 416-314-3717
Toll-free: 866-448-2248
TTY: 877-849-2066
assessment.review.board@ontario.ca
www.arb.gov.on.ca
Part of Environment & Land Tribunals Ontario (ELTO)

•Chief Inquiry Officer - Expropriations Act
McMurtry-Scott Bldg.
720 Bay St., 8th Fl.
Toronto, ON M7A 2S9
Tel: 416-314-2226

•Child & Family Services Review Board/Custody Review Board (CFSRB/CRB)
1075 Bay St., 7th Fl.
Toronto, ON M5S 2B1
Tel: 416-327-4673; *Fax:* 416-327-4379
Toll-free: 888-728-8823
www.cfsrb.ca; www.cfsrb.ca/en/crb
Part of Social Justice Tribunals Ontario (SJTO)

•Conservation Review Board (CRB)
#1500, 655 Bay St.
Toronto, ON M5G 1E5
Tel: 416-212-6349; *Fax:* 416-326-6209
Toll-free: 866-448-2248
conservation.review.board@ontario.ca
www.crb.gov.on.ca
Part of Environment & Land Tribunals Ontario (ELTO)

•Criminal Injuries Compensation Board (CICB)
439 University Ave., 4th Fl.
Toronto, ON M5G 1Y8
Tel: 416-326-2900; *Fax:* 416-326-2883
Toll-free: 800-372-7463
info.cicb@ontario.ca
www.cicb.gov.on.ca
Other Communication: Victim Support Line: 1-888-579-2888

•Environment & Land Tribunals Ontario (ELTO)
#1500, 655 Bay St.
Toronto, ON M5G 1E5
Tel: 416-212-6349; *Fax:* 416-314-3717
Toll-free: 866-448-2248
www.elto.gov.on.ca
Other Communication: Toll-Free Fax: 1-877-849-2066
The ELTO cluster contains the following tribunals: Assessment Review Board; Board of Negotiation; Conservation Review Board; Environmental Review Tribunal; & Ontario Municipal Board.

•Environmental Review Tribunal (ERT)
#1500, 655 Bay St.
Toronto, ON M5G 1E5
Tel: 416-212-6349; *Fax:* 416-314-4506
Toll-free: 800-855-1155
erttribunalsecretary@ontario.ca
www.ert.gov.on.ca
Part of Environment & Land Tribunals Ontario (ELTO)

•Fire Safety Commission
Place Nouveau Bldg.
5775 Yonge St., 7th Fl.
Toronto, ON M2M 4J1
Tel: 416-325-3100; *Fax:* 416-314-1217
Part of Safety, Licensing Appeals & Standards Tribunals Ontario (SLASTO)

•Human Rights Tribunal of Ontario (HRTO)
655 Bay St., 14th Fl.
Toronto, ON M7A 2A3
Tel: 416-326-1312; *Fax:* 416-326-2199
Toll-free: 866-598-0322
TTY: 416-326-2027
hrto.tdpo@ontario.ca
www.hrto.ca
Other Communication: Toll-Free TTY: 1-866-607-1240; Fax: 1-866-355-6099
Part of Social Justice Tribunals Ontario (SJTO)

•Judicial Appointments Advisory Committee (JAAC)
c/o Ministry of Government Services Mail Delivery
77 Wellesley St. West, #M2B-88
Toronto, ON M7A 1N3
Tel: 416-326-4060; *Fax:* 416-212-7316
www.ontariocourts.ca/ocj/jaac

•Landlord & Tenant Board (LTB)
College Park
777 Bay St., 12th Fl.
Toronto, ON M5G 2E5
Tel: 416-645-8080; *Fax:* 416-585-6363
Toll-free: 888-332-3234
www.ltb.gov.on.ca

Part of Social Justice Tribunals Ontario (SJTO)

•Legal Aid Ontario (LAO)
Atrium on Bay
#200, 40 Dundas St. West
Toronto, ON M5G 2H1
Tel: 416-979-1446; *Fax:* 416-979-8669
Toll-free: 800-668-8258
TTY: 866-641-8867
info@lao.on.ca
www.legalaid.on.ca
Other Communication: Toll-Free TTY: 1-866-641-8867; Media, E-mail: media@lao.on.ca

•Licence Appeal Tribunal (LAT)
#530, 20 Dundas St. West
Toronto, ON M5G 2C2
Tel: 416-314-4260; *Fax:* 416-314-4270
Toll-free: 800-255-2214
www.lat.gov.on.ca
Other Communication: Toll Free Fax: 1-800-720-5292
The LAT hears appeals when a decision or order to suspend or a proposal is made to cancel or to refuse to grant or renew a registration, certificate or a licence, or when a claim for compensation has been denied. As of 2013, it is part of Safety, Licensing Appeals & Standards Tribunals Ontario (SLASTO).

•Office for Victims of Crime (OVC)
700 Bay St., 3rd Fl.
Toronto, ON M5G 1Z6
Tel: 416-326-1682; *Fax:* 416-326-4497
Toll-free: 887-435-7661
TTY: 416-325-9341
ovc@ontario.ca
www.ovc.gov.on.ca

•Office of Consolidated Hearings
#1500, 655 Bay St.
Toronto, ON M5G 1E5
Tel: 416-212-6349; *Fax:* 416-314-4506
www.ert.gov.on.ca/english/About/OCH/index.htm
Under the Consolidated Hearings Act, the Environmental Assessment Board holds public hearings in conjunction with the Ontario Municipal Board. This occurs when a proposal requires more than one tribunal hearing under more than one of the acts set out in the schedule to the Consolidated Hearings Act, 1981. The hearings registrar must receive written notice from the person proposing the undertaking, specifying the nature of the undertaking, required hearings & governing acts. The matter is then referred to the chairs of the two boards, who establish a joint board for the hearing. The board's decision can be varied or rescinded only by the Lieutenant-Governor-in-Council or, on a question of law, may be appealed to the Divisional Court.

•Office of the Independent Police Review Director (OIPRD)
655 Bay St., 10th Fl.
Toronto, ON M7A 2T4
Tel: 416-246-7071; *Fax:* 416-327-8332
Toll-free: 877-411-4773
TTY: 877-414-4773
oiprd@ontario.ca
www.oiprd.on.ca
Other Communication: Toll-Free Fax: 877-415-4773

•Ontario Civilian Police Commission (OCPC)
#605, 250 Dundas St. West
Toronto, ON M7A 2T3
Tel: 416-314-3004; *Fax:* 416-314-0198
Toll-free: 888-515-5005
www.ocpc.ca
Other Communication: Complaints (GTA): 416-326-1189; Toll-Free Fax: 1-888-311-7555
Part of Safety, Licensing Appeals & Standards Tribunals Ontario (SLASTO)

•Ontario Human Rights Commission (OHRC)
See Entry Name Index for detailed listing.

•Ontario Municipal Board & Board of Negotiation (OMB/BON)
#1500, 655 Bay St.
Toronto, ON M5G 1E5
Tel: 416-212-6349; *Fax:* 416-326-5370
Toll-free: 866-448-2248
ontario.municipal.board@ontario.ca
www.omb.gov.on.ca
Other Communication: Board of Negotiation, E-mail: board.of.negotiation@ontario.ca; URL: www.bon.gov.on.ca
Part of Environment & Land Tribunals Ontario (ELTO)

•Ontario Parole Board (OPB)
#1803, 415 Yonge St.
Toronto, ON M5B 2E7
Tel: 416-325-4480; *Fax:* 416-325-4485
Toll-free: 888-579-2888
www.opb.gov.on.ca
Part of Safety, Licensing Appeals & Standards Tribunals Ontario (SLASTO)

•Ontario Special Education Tribunals (OSET)
655 Bay St., 7th Fl.
Toronto, ON M7A 2A3
Tel: 416-326-1356; *Fax:* 416-326-2199
Toll-free: 866-355-6099
TTY: 866-607-1240
oset@ontario.ca
www.oset-tedo.ca
Other Communication: French E-mail: tedo@ontario.ca
Part of Social Justice Tribunals Ontario (SJTO)

•Safety, Licensing Appeals & Standards Tribunals Ontario (SLASTO)
#5230, 20 Dundas St. West
Toronto, ON M5G 2C2
Tel: 416-212-0334; *Fax:* 416-314-4270
Toll-free: 855-444-7454
slastoinfo@ontario.ca
www.slasto.gov.on.ca
Other Communication: Toll-Free Fax: 1-800-720-5292
Safety, Licensing Appeals & Standards Tribunals Ontario was created in 2013, clustering the following tribunals: Animal Care Review Board (ACRB); Fire Safety Commission (FSC); Licence Appeal Tribunal (LAT); Ontario Civilian Police Commission (OCPC); & Ontario Parole Board (OPB).

•Social Benefits Tribunal (SBT)
1075 Bay St., 7th Fl.
Toronto, ON M5S 2B1
Tel: 416-326-0978; *Fax:* 416-326-5135
Toll-free: 800-753-3895
TTY: 800-268-7095
www.sbt.gov.on.ca
Other Communication: Ottawa TTY: 613-566-2235
Part of Social Justice Tribunals Ontario (SJTO)

•Social Justice Tribunals Ontario (SJTO)
#421, 40 Dundas St. West
Toronto, ON M7A 0A9
Tel: 416-212-8000; *Fax:* 416-212-8024
Toll-free: 855-558-2514
sjtoinfo@ontario.ca
www.sjto.gov.on.ca
The SJTO cluster includes the following tribunals: Child & Family Services Review Board; Custody Review Board; Human Rights Tribunal of Ontario; Landlord & Tenant Board; Ontario Special Education (English) Tribunal; Ontario Special Education (French) Tribunal; & Social Benefits Tribunal.

•Special Investigations Unit (SIU) / Unité des Enquêtes Spéciales (UTS)
5090 Commerce Blvd.
Mississauga, ON L4W 5M4
Tel: 416-622-0748; *Fax:* 416-622-2455
Toll-free: 800-787-8529
www.siu.on.ca
Other Communication: Shift Supervisor Phone: 416-641-1879

Agency & Tribunal Relations Division
Assistant Deputy Attorney General, Ali Arlani
Tel: 416-212-9721
ali.arlani@ontario.ca
Director, Agency Relations, Ana Kapralos
Tel: 416-212-4061
ana.kapralos@ontario.ca

Civil Law Division
Tel: 416-325-0826; *Fax:* 416-326-6996
Assistant Deputy Attorney General, Malliha Wilson
Tel: 416-326-2505; *Fax:* 416-326-6996
malliha.wilson@ontario.ca
Director, Education & Development Branch, Jane Price
Tel: 416-326-2153
jane.price@ontario.ca
Director, Crown Law Office - Civil, Troy Harrison
Tel: 416-326-4100; *Fax:* 416-326-4181
troy.harrison@ontario.ca
Director, Constitutional Law, Michel Y. Hélie
Tel: 416-326-4454; *Fax:* 416-326-4015
michel.helie@ontario.ca
Acting Director, Civil Remedies for Illicit Activities Office, Tom Schneider
Tel: 416-326-4188; *Fax:* 416-314-3714
tom.schneider@ontario.ca
Director, Strategic Business Management Branch, Suzanna Birchwood
Tel: 416-326-4173; *Fax:* 416-326-6996
suzanna.birchwood@ontario.ca

Corporate Services Management Division
Tel: 416-326-4431; *Fax:* 416-326-4441
Assistant Deputy Attorney General & Chief Administrative Officer, Dante Pontone
Tel: 416-326-9844
dante.pontone@ontario.ca
Director, Business & Fiscal Planning, Jatinder Singh
Tel: 416-326-4020; *Fax:* 416-326-6955
jatinder.singh@ontario.ca
Director, Justice Audit Service Team, David Horie
Tel: 705-329-6747; *Fax:* 705-329-6762
david.horie@ontario.ca
Director, Human Resources Strategic Business Unit, Barbara Ross
Tel: 416-326-3283; *Fax:* 416-326-2298
barbara.ross@ontario.ca
Director, Facilities Management Branch, Susan Patterson
Tel: 416-212-7949; *Fax:* 416-326-4029
susan.patterson@ontario.ca

Court Services Division
Tel: 416-326-4263; *Fax:* 416-326-2652
Assistant Deputy Attorney General, Lynne Wagner
Tel: 416-326-2609; *Fax:* 416-326-2652
lynne.wagner@ontario.ca
Director, Criminal/POA Policy & Programs Branch, Diana Hunt
Tel: 416-326-2531; *Fax:* 416-326-1869
diana.hunt@ontario.ca
Acting Director, Divisional Support Branch, Sheila Bristo
Tel: 416-326-0887
sheila.bristo@ontario.ca
Director, Civil Policy & Programs Branch, Susan Charendoff
Tel: 416-326-2511; *Fax:* 416-326-4289
susan.charendoff@ontario.ca
Director, Family Policy & Programs, Anne Marie Predko
Tel: 416-326-7867
annemarie.predko@ontario.ca

Regional Court Services Offices
Central East
#201, 1091 Gorham St., Newmarket, ON L3Y 8X7
Tel: 905-836-5621; *Fax:* 905-836-5620
Director, Court Operations, Sarina Kashak
Tel: 905-836-5484; *Fax:* 905-836-5620
sarina.kashak@ontario.ca
Central West
John Sopinka Courthouse, #518B, 45 Main St. East, Hamilton, ON L8N 2B7
Tel: 905-645-5333; *Fax:* 905-645-5375
Acting Director, Court Operations, Cathy Hiuser
Tel: 905-645-5335; *Fax:* 905-645-5375
joanne.spriet@ontario.ca
East
#100, 343 Preston St., Ottawa, ON K1S 1N4
Tel: 613-239-1551; *Fax:* 613-239-1273
Other Communication: Information Technology Toll-Free: 1-866-494-3000
Acting Director, Court Operations, Viviane Carpentier
Tel: 613-239-1597
viviane.carpentier@ontario.ca
Northeast
#501, 159 Cedar St., Sudbury, ON P3E 6A5
Tel: 705-564-7671; *Fax:* 705-564-4158
Acting Director, Court Operations, Jo Dee Kamm
Tel: 807-343-2701
jodee.kamm@ontario.ca
Northwest
277 Camelot St., Thunder Bay, ON P7A 4B3
Tel: 807-343-2747; *Fax:* 807-345-6383
Acting Director, Court Operations, Jo Dee Kamm
Tel: 807-343-2701
jodee.kamm@ontario.ca
Toronto
#1601, 700 Bay St., Toronto, ON M5G 1Z6
Tel: 416-326-4249; *Fax:* 416-326-2073
Director, Court Operations, Beverly Leonard
Tel: 416-326-4250
beverly.leonard@ontario.ca
West
80 Dundas St., #D, London, ON N6A 6A4
Tel: 519-660-3090; *Fax:* 519-660-3098
Director, Court Operations, Paul Langlois
Tel: 519-660-3094
paul.langlois@ontario.ca

Courts of Justice
Osgoode Hall, 130 Queen St. West, Toronto, ON M5H 2N5
Tel: 416-327-5020
Other Communication: Fax: 416-327-6256 (Appeal Scheduling), 416-327-5032 (Intake Office)
Chief Justice, Superior Court of Justice, Hon. Heather Smith
Tel: 416-327-5111; *Fax:* 416-327-5417
Other Communications: Judges' Reception: 416-327-5101
Chief Justice, Court of Appeal for Ontario, Hon. George R. Strathy

Regional Senior Justices' Offices

Central East

50 Eagle St. West, 2nd Fl., Newmarket, ON L3Y 6B1

Fax: 905-853-4826

Regional Senior Justice, Superior Court of Justice, Hon. Michael F. Brown
Tel: 905-853-4827

Central South

John Sopinka Courthouse, #762, 45 Main St. East, Hamilton, ON L8N 2B7

Fax: 905-645-5374
Secondary Address: #100, 7755 Hurontario St.
A. Grenville & William Davis Courthouse
Brampton, ON L6W 4T6

Regional Senior Justice, Superior Court of Justice, Hon. Stephen Glithero
Tel: 905-645-5323

Central West

A Grenville & William Davis Courthouse, #100, 7755 Hurontario St., Brampton, ON L6W 4T6

Fax: 905-456-4836

Regional Senior Justice, Superior Court of Justice, Hon. Francine Van Melle
Tel: 905-456-4837

East

161 Elgin St., 6th Fl., Ottawa, ON K2P 2L1

Fax: 613-239-1067

Regional Senior Justice, Superior Court of Justice, Hon. Charles Hackland
Tel: 613-239-1527; *Fax:* 613-239-1067

Northeast

155 Elm St., 2nd Fl., Sudbury, ON P3C 1T9

Fax: 705-564-7902
Secondary Address: 155 Elm St., 2nd Fl.
Sudbury, ON P3C 1T9

Regional Senior Justice, Superior Court of Justice, Hon. Louise Gauthier
Tel: 705-564-7814

Northwest

277 Camelot St., 3rd Fl., Thunder Bay, ON P7A 4B3

Fax: 807-343-2713
Secondary Address: 277 Camelot St., 3rd Fl.
Thunder Bay, ON P7A 4B3

Regional Senior Justice, Superior Court of Justice, Hon. Helen Pierce
Tel: 807-343-2712

Southwest

80 Dundas St. East, London, ON N6A 2P3

Fax: 519-660-2294

Regional Senior Justice, Superior Court of Justice, Hon. Edward Ducharme
Tel: 519-660-2291

Toronto

361 University Ave., Toronto, ON M5G 1T3

Tel: 416-327-5284
Other Communication: Trial Scheduling, Fax: 416-325-2872; Judicial Scheduling, Fax: 416-327-9931
Secondary Address: 361 University Ave., 6th Fl.
Toronto, ON M5G 1T3

Regional Senior Justice, Superior Court of Justice, Hon. Edward Then
Tel: 416-327-5000

Criminal Law Division

Tel: 416-326-2615; *Fax:* 416-326-2063

Assistant Deputy Attorney General, James Cornish
Tel: 416-326-2616

Senior Counsel & Executive Director, Education, Alexander Smith
Tel: 416-212-1166
alexander.smith@ontario.ca

Director, Strategic Operations & Management Centre, Tammy Browes-Bugden
Tel: 416-326-2099; *Fax:* 416-326-2423
tammy.browes-bugden@ontario.ca

Director, Crown Law Office - Criminal, Howard Leibovich
Tel: 416-326-4600; *Fax:* 416-326-4619
howard.leibovich@ontario.ca

Director, The Office of Crown Strategic Initiatives, Mark Saltmarsh
Tel: 416-326-2419; *Fax:* 416-326-2063
mark.saltmarsh@ontario.ca

Directors of Crown Operations, Regional Offices

Central East

150 Bond St. East, 3rd Fl., Oshawa, ON L1G 0A2

Tel: 905-836-5624; *Fax:* 905-836-6299

Director, Crown Operations, John Sotirakos
john.sotirakos@ontario.ca

Central West

#400, 45 Main St. East, Hamilton, ON L8N 2B7

Tel: 905-645-5338; *Fax:* 905-645-5376

Assistant Crown Attorney, Victoria Reid
Tel: 905-645-5262
victoria.reid@ontario.ca

East

#3225, 161 Elgin St., Ottawa, ON K2P 2K1

Tel: 613-239-1222; *Fax:* 613-239-1420

Regional Director, Hilary McCormack
Tel: 613-239-1200
hilary.mccormack@ontario.ca

North

#501, 159 Cedar St., Sudbury, ON P3E 6A5

Tel: 705-564-7674; *Fax:* 705-564-7664

Director, Crown Operations, John Luczak
john.luczak@ontario.ca

Toronto

McMurtry-Scott Bldg., #2101, 700 Bay St., Toronto, ON M7A 2B1

Tel: 416-326-4487; *Fax:* 416-326-4488

Crown Attorney, Michael Cantlon
Tel: 416-327-6369
michael.cantlon@ontario.ca

West

#202, 150 Dufferin Ave., London, ON N6A 5N6

Tel: 519-660-2400; *Fax:* 519-661-2887

Director, Crown Operations, Marc Garson
marc.garson@ontario.ca

Justice Technology Services

#300, 21 College St., Toronto, ON M5G 2B3

Tel: 416-314-1841; *Fax:* 416-326-1104

Chief Information Officer, Robin M. Thompson
Tel: 416-326-2338
robin.m.thompson@ontario.ca

Legislative Counsel

Whitney Block, #3600, 99 Wellesley St. West, Toronto, ON M7A 1A2

Tel: 416-326-2841; *Fax:* 416-326-2806

Chief Legislative Counsel, Mark Spakowski
Tel: 416-326-2740
mark.spakowski@ontario.ca

Acting Associate Chief Legislative Counsel, Legislative Council Services, Cornelia Schuh
Tel: 416-326-2741
cornelia.schuch@ontario.ca

Director, French Legislative Services, Gerard Hernando
Tel: 416-326-2793
gerard.hernando@ontario.ca

Policy & Adjudicative Tribunals Division

Tel: 416-326-2500; *Fax:* 416-326-2699

Assistant Deputy Attorney General, Irwin Glasberg
Tel: 416-326-0190
irwin.glasberg@ontario.ca

Director, Corporate Policy & Tribunal Relations, Robin Dafoe
Tel: 416-326-2336; *Fax:* 416-326-2699
robin.dafoe@ontario.ca

Director, Jury Review, David Didluck
Tel: 416-326-4932
david.didluck@ontario.ca

Director, Justice Policy Development Branch, Andrea Storm
Tel: 416-326-2482
andrea.strom@ontario.ca

Victims & Vulnerable Persons Division

18 King St. E, 7th Fl., Toronto, ON M5C 1C4

Tel: 416-325-3265; *Fax:* 416-212-1091

Assistant Deputy Attorney General, Louise Stratford
Tel: 416-212-5059
louise.stratford@ontario.ca

Director, Programs & Community Development, Linda D. Haldenby
Tel: 416-326-2428; *Fax:* 416-212-1091
linda.d.haldenby@ontario.ca

Director, Policy & Program Development, Danielle Racine
Tel: 416-325-3695; *Fax:* 416-212-1091

Office of the Children's Lawyer

393 University Ave., 14th Fl., Toronto, ON M5G 1W9

Tel: 416-314-8000; *Fax:* 416-314-8050
www.attorneygeneral.jus.gov.on.ca/english/family/ocl

Children's Lawyer for Ontario, Lucy McSweeney
Tel: 416-314-8011
lucy.mcsweeney@ontario.ca

Chief Administrative Officer, Margaret-Jean Morandin
Tel: 416-314-8038
margaretjean.morandin@ontario.ca

Office of the Public Guardian & Trustee (OPGT)

Atrium on Bay, #800, 595 Bay St., 8th Fl., Toronto, ON M5G 2M6

Tel: 416-314-2800; *Fax:* 416-326-1366
Toll-Free: 800-366-0335
TTY: 416-314-2687
www.attorneygeneral.jus.gov.on.ca/english/family/pgt

Public Guardian & Trustee, Kenneth R. Goodman
Tel: 416-314-2988
ken.goodman@ontario.ca

Deputy Public Guardian & Trustee, & General Counsel, Legal Services, Laurie Redden
Tel: 416-314-2777
laurie.redden@ontario.ca

Deputy Public Guardian & Trustee, Program Policy, Trudy Spinks
Tel: 416-314-3957
trudy.spinks@ontario.ca

Office of the Auditor General

20 Dundas St. West, 15th Fl., PO Box 105 Toronto, ON M5G 2C2

Tel: 416-327-2381; *Fax:* 416-327-9862
TTY: 416-327-6123
comments@auditor.on.ca
www.auditor.on.ca

Auditor General, Bonnie Lysyk, MBA, CPA, CA, LPA
Tel: 416-327-1326
bonnie.lysyk@auditor.on.ca

Deputy Auditor General, Gary Peall
Tel: 416-327-1658
gary.peall@auditor.on.ca

Director, Crown Agencies (2) Portfolio, Laura Bell
Tel: 416-327-2377
laura.bell@auditor.on.ca

Director, Infrastructure, Environment & Economic Development Portfolio, Gus Chagani
Tel: 416-327-2395
gus.chagani@auditor.on.ca

Director, Health & Long-term Care (2) Portfolio, Rudolph Chiu
Tel: 416-327-1663
rudolph.chiu@auditor.on.ca

Director, Education, Training, Colleges & Universities Portfolio, Gerard Fitzmaurice
Tel: 416-327-1371
gerard.fitzmaurice@auditor.on.ca

Director, Community, Social Services & Other Portfolio, Vanna Gotsis
Tel: 416-327-1679
vanna.gotsis@auditor.on.ca

Director, Health & Long-term Care (1) Portfolio, Susan Klein
Tel: 416-327-1668
susan.klein@auditor.on.ca

Director, Justice & Regulatory Portfolio, Vince Mazzone
Tel: 416-327-1669
vince.mazzone@auditor.on.ca

Director, Crown Agencies (1) Portfolio, John McDowell
Tel: 416-327-1656
john.mcdowell@auditor.on.ca

Director, Public Accounts, Bill Pelow
Tel: 416-327-4631
bill.pelow@auditor.on.ca

Ontario Ministry of Children & Youth Services

Macdonald Block, #M-1B114, 900 Bay St., Toronto, ON M7A 1N3

Fax: 416-212-1977
Toll-Free: 866-821-7770
TTY: 800-387-5559
mcsinfo@mcys.gov.on.ca
www.children.gov.on.ca
twitter.com/OntYouth

Working collaboratively with community partners, as well as the Ministries of Education, Health & Long-Term Care, Community & Social Services, Citizenship, Immigration & International Trade, & Tourism, Culture & Sport, to integrate a number of Ontario's children & youth programs & services. By bringing these programs under one roof, the government seeks to make children a top priority & to make it easier for families to access services at all stages of a child's development.

Minister, Hon. Michael Coteau
Tel: 416-212-7432; *Fax:* 416-212-7431
mcoteau.mpp@liberal.ola.org

Deputy Minister, Alexander Bezzina
Tel: 416-212-2280
alexander.bezzina@ontario.ca

Parliamentary Assistant, Granville Anderson
Tel: 416-326-0820; *Fax:* 416-326-3951
ganderson.mpp.co@liberal.ola.org

Director, Feathers & Hope Initiative, Bruce Leslie
Tel: 905-521-7585; *Fax:* 416-325-5335
bruce.leslie@ontario.ca
Director, Communications & Marketing, Wendy Seed
Tel: 416-326-3512; *Fax:* 416-212-1977
wendy.seed@ontario.ca
Legal Director, Legal Services Branch, Diane Zimnica
Tel: 416-314-5173; *Fax:* 416-327-0568
diane.zimnica@ontario.ca

Business Planning & Corporate Services
Hepburn Block, 80 Grosvenor St., 6th Fl., Toronto, ON M7A 1E9
Tel: 416-325-5595; *Fax:* 416-325-5615
Assistant Deputy Minister & Chief Administrative Officer, Lorraine Graham-Watson
Tel: 416-325-5588
lorraine.graham-watson@ontario.ca
Director, Human Resources Strategic Business Unit, Frank Caccia
Tel: 416-327-4753
frank.caccia@ontario.ca
Director, Capital & Accommodation Services, Nadia Cornacchia
Tel: 416-327-7454
nadia.cornacchia@ontario.ca
Acting Director, Financial Planning & Business Management, Blair Dunker
Tel: 416-325-5139
blair.dunker@ontario.ca
Director, Corporate Services, Michelle Gittens
Tel: 416-327-3950
michelle.gittens@ontario.ca
Director, Ontario Internal Audit, Community Services Audit Team, Gordon Nowlan
Tel: 416-585-6550
gordon.nowlan@ontario.ca

Children, Youth & Social Services Cluster, I & IT
Hepburn Block, 80 Grosvenor St., 6th Fl., Toronto, ON M7A 1E9
Tel: 416-314-9694; *Fax:* 416-314-0266
Chief Information Officer, Corbin Kerr
Tel: 416-326-4330
corbin.kerr@ontario.ca
Executive Lead, Child Protection Information Network (CPIN), Alex Sarchuk
Tel: 416-226-4358
alex.sarchuk@ontario.ca
Director, Child Protection Information Network (CPIN), Kevin Byrnes
Tel: 416-226-4400

Organizational Renewal Division
Hepburn Block, 80 Grosvenor St., 6th Fl., Toronto, ON M7A 1E9
Tel: 416-212-8218
Assistant Deputy Minister, Denise Cole
Tel: 416-212-4893
denise.cole@ontario.ca
Director, Strategy & Organizational Renewal, Maxine Daley
Tel: 416-326-3302
maxine.daley@ontario.ca
Director, Regional Modernization Strategy Unit, Karen Eisler
Tel: 905-567-7171 ext: 313
karen.eisler@ontario.ca

Policy Development & Program Design Division
56 Wellesley St. West, 14th Fl., Toronto, ON M5S 2S3
Tel: 416-212-1961; *Fax:* 416-314-1862
Assistant Deputy Minister, Aryeh Gitterman
Tel: 416-212-1961
aryeh.gitterman@ontario.ca
Director, System Transition Team, Cynthia Abel
Tel: 416-314-5147
cynthia.abel@ontario.ca
Director, Specialized Services & Supports, Jane Cleve
Tel: 416-325-5331; *Fax:* 416-212-2021
jane.cleve@ontario.ca
Director, Children & Youth at Risk, Marian Mlakar
Tel: 416-212-5205; *Fax:* 416-212-2021
marian.mlakar@ontario.ca
Director, Child Welfare Secretariat, Jennifer Morris
Tel: 416-325-3560; *Fax:* 416-326-8098
jennifer.morris@ontario.ca

Service Delivery Division
56 Wellesley St. West, 14th Fl., Toronto, ON M5S 2S3
Tel: 416-212-5663; *Fax:* 416-314-1862
Assistant Deputy Minister, Rachel Kampus
Tel: 416-212-3141
rachel.kampus@ontario.ca
Acting Director, Resource Management, Dorothy Cheung
Tel: 416-212-8480
dorothy.cheung@ontario.ca
Director, Client Services, Greg Douglas
Tel: 416-326-3170; *Fax:* 416-325-9631
greg.douglas@ontario.ca
Director, CAS Amalgamation, Sally Johnson
Tel: 416-327-2531; *Fax:* 416-326-5359
sally.johnson@ontario.ca
Director, Children's Facilities, Child & Parent Resource Institute, Anne Stark
Tel: 519-858-2774 ext: 201; *Fax:* 519-858-3913
anne.stark@ontario.ca

Regional Offices

Central East
#1, 17310 Yonge St., Newmarket, ON L3Y 7R8
Tel: 905-868-8900

Central West
#200, 6733 Mississauga Rd., Mississauga, ON L5N 6J5
Tel: 905-567-7177; *Fax:* 905-567-3215
Toll-Free: 877-832-2818
Other Communication: Serious Occurrence Toll-Free Phone: 1-877-708-2896

Eastern
347 Preston St., 3rd Fl., Ottawa, ON K1S 2T7
Tel: 613-234-1188; *Fax:* 613-787-5284
Toll-Free: 800-267-5111
Other Communication: Alternate Faxes: 613-787-5283, 613-787-5252 (7th Fl.), 613-787-4090 (6th Fl.), 613-788-2382

Hamilton/Niagara
Ellen Fairclough Bldg., 119 King St. West, Hamilton, ON L8P 4Y7
Tel: 905-521-7280; *Fax:* 905-546-8277
TTY: 905-546-8276
Other Communication: Human Resources Fax: 905-521-7736; Best Start/Early Years Fax: 905-521-7684; Business Services & IT Fax: 905-521-7442; Municipal & First Nations Fax: 905-546-8247

North East
621 Main St. West, North Bay, ON P1B 2V6
Tel: 705-474-3540; *Fax:* 705-474-5815
Toll-Free: 800-461-6977
TTY: 705-474-7665
Other Communication: Community Programs & Busines Services Fax: 705-474-3825; Administration, Municipal, Planning & Child Care Fax: 705-474-5446

Northern
#1002, 199 Larch St., Sudbury, ON P3E 5P9
Tel: 705-564-6699; *Fax:* 705-564-3099
Toll-Free: 800-265-1222
Other Communication: Northern Bursary Program Toll-Free Phone: 1-800-263-3347

South East
11 Beechgrove Lane, Kingston, ON K7M 9A6
Tel: 613-545-0539; *Fax:* 613-536-7272
Toll-Free: 800-646-3209
TTY: 613-536-7304

South West
#203, 217 York St., PO Box 5217 London, ON N6A 5R1
Tel: 519-438-5111; *Fax:* 519-672-9510
Toll-Free: 800-265-4197
TTY: 519-663-5276

Toronto
477 Mount Pleasant Rd., 3rd Fl., Toronto, ON M7A 1G1
Tel: 416-325-0500; *Fax:* 416-325-0541
TTY: 416-325-3600

Strategic Policy & Planning Division
56 Wellesley St., 14th Fl., Toronto, ON M5S 2S3
Tel: 416-327-9460; *Fax:* 416-314-1862
Assistant Deputy Minister, Darryl Sturtevant
Tel: 416-327-9481; *Fax:* 416-314-1862
darryl.sturtevant@ontario.ca
Director, Child & Youth Development, Esther Levy
Tel: 416-212-9887; *Fax:* 416-326-0478
esther.levy@ontario.ca
Director, Strategic Information & Business Intelligence, Anne Premi
Tel: 416-325-5944; *Fax:* 416-327-0570
anne.premi@ontario.ca
Director, Strategic Policy & Aboriginal Relationships, Rachel Simeon
Tel: 416-314-1489; *Fax:* 416-327-0570
rachel.simeon@ontario.ca
Director, Youth Strategies, Sean Twyford
Tel: 416-325-4699; *Fax:* 416-327-0570
sean.twyford@ontario.ca

Youth Justice Services
56 Wellesley St. W, 14th fl., Toronto, ON M5S 2S3
Tel: 416-314-3502; *Fax:* 416-327-0478
Assistant Deputy Minister, JoAnn Miller-Reid
Tel: 416-327-9910
joann.miller-reid@ontario.ca
Director, Divisional Services, Madeleine Davidson
Tel: 416-314-6576; *Fax:* 416-327-2418
madeleine.davidson@ontario.ca
Director, Operational Support, Trish Moloughney
Tel: 416-212-7609; *Fax:* 416-327-0944
robert.burkholder@ontario.ca
Director, Planning & Program Development, Paul Wheeler
Tel: 416-212-7610; *Fax:* 416-327-0944
paul.wheeler@ontario.ca

Regional Offices

Central
Bldg. C, 171 Judson St., Etobicoke, ON M8Z 1A4
Tel: 416-314-0520; *Fax:* 416-314-8388
TTY: 416-326-8703

Eastern
23 Beechgrove Lane, Kingston, ON K7M 9A6
Tel: 613-531-5740; *Fax:* 613-536-7377
Toll-Free: 877-345-5622
TTY: 613-536-7285

Northern
200 First Ave. West, 4th Fl., North Bay, ON P1B 3B9
Tel: 705-494-3642; *Fax:* 705-494-3212

Western
Morgan Bldg., 600 Sanatorium Rd., London, ON N6H 3W7
Tel: 519-858-2774; *Fax:* 519-858-8745
TTY: 519-858-0257

Ontario Ministry of Citizenship & Immigration

400 University Ave., 6th Fl., Toronto, ON M7A 2R9
Tel: 416-327-2422; *Fax:* 416-327-1061
Toll-Free: 800-267-7329
TTY: 866-853-2137
info.mci@ontario.ca
www.citizenship.gov.on.ca
Other Communication: Ontario Immigration URL: www.ontarioimmigration.ca
twitter.com/OntMCIIT
www.facebook.com/studyworkstay

The Ministry seeks to help newcomers successfully integrate into life in Ontario, both economically & socially, as well as securing future investment, trade & immigration in Ontario. In June 2016, the Ministry was divided into two portfolios: Citizenship & Immigration, & International Trade.

Minister, Citizenship & Immigration, Hon. Laura Albanese
Tel: 416-325-0400; *Fax:* 416-325-0374
lalbanese.mpp@liberal.ola.org
Acting Deputy Minister, Shirley Phillips
Tel: 416-325-6220
shirley.phillips@ontario.ca
Parliamentary Assistant, Shafiq Qaadri
Tel: 416-325-6002; *Fax:* 416-212-1812
shafiq.qaadri@ontario.ca
Operations & Policy Advisor, Gianluca Ferrari
Tel: 416-325-6216
gianluca.ferrari@ontario.ca
Director, Communications Branch, Deborah Swain
Tel: 416-314-7606; *Fax:* 416-314-1061
deborah.swain@ontario.ca

Associated Agencies, Boards & Commissions:

•Office of the Fairness Commissioner
#1201, 595 Bay St.
Toronto, ON M7A 2B4
Tel: 416-325-9380; *Fax:* 416-326-6081
Toll-free: 877-727-5365
TTY: 416-326-6080
ofc@ontario.ca
www.fairnesscommissioner.ca

Citizenship & Immigration Division
400 University Ave., 3rd Fl., Toronto, ON M7A 2R9
Tel: 416-314-7541; *Fax:* 416-314-7599
Acting Assistant Deputy Minister, Cindy Lam
Tel: 416-212-2783; *Fax:* 416-314-7599
cindy.lam@ontario.ca
Director, Citizenship Branch, Rick Beaver
Tel: 416-314-7523; *Fax:* 416-314-6050
rick.beaver@ontario.ca
Director, Immigration Programs Branch, Doug Dixon
Tel: 416-212-4290; *Fax:* 416-326-6265
doug.dixon@ontario.ca
Acting Director, Projects, Debbie Strauss
Tel: 416-212-3285
debbie.strauss@ontario.ca
Director, Immigration Policy Branch, Alice Young
Tel: 416-326-8595
alice.young@ontario.ca

Executive Director, Refugee Resettlement Program, Yvonne Ferrer
Tel: 416-326-2597
yvonne.ferrer@ontario.ca

Ontario Seniors' Secretariat
#601C, 777 Bay St., 6th Fl., Toronto, ON M7A 2J4
Tel: 416-326-7076; *Fax:* 416-326-7078
infoseniors@ontario.ca
www.seniors.gov.on.ca
Minister Responsible, Hon. Dipika Damerla
dipika.damerla@ontario.ca
Assistant Deputy Minister, Abby Katz Starr
Tel: 416-326-7069
abby.katzstarr@ontario.ca
Director, Strategic Policy & Stakeholder Relations, Vacant

Ontario Women's Directorate (OWD)
College Park, 777 Bay St., 6th Fl., Toronto, ON M7A 2J4
Tel: 416-314-0300; *Fax:* 416-314-0247
Toll-Free: 866-510-5902
TTY: 416-314-0258
owd@ontario.ca
www.women.gov.on.ca
Other Communication: www.flickr.com/photos/OntWomen
twitter.com/OntWomen
www.youtube.com/playlist?list=PLC6D18DF2A03D61CB
A division of the Ministry of Citizenship & Immigration, the OWD focuses upon the following issues related to women: social, economic & justice-related concerns. The main activities of the OWD are preventing violence against women & promoting women's economic independence.
Minister Responsible; Minister Responsible, Accessibility, Hon. Tracy MacCharles
Tel: 416-212-3180
tracy.maccharles@ontario.ca
Parliamentary Assistant, Amrit Mangat
Tel: 416-212-0409
amrit.mangat@ontario.ca
Executive Director, Vacant
Tel: 416-314-1850

Regional & Corporate Services Division
400 University Ave., 2nd fl., Toronto, ON M7A 2R9
Tel: 416-314-7311; *Fax:* 416-314-7313
Acting Assistant Deputy Minister & Chief Administration Officer, Maureen Buckley
Tel: 416-314-7311; *Fax:* 416-314-7313
maureen.buckley@ontario.ca
Director, Regional Services & Corporate Support Branch, Tom Chrzan
Tel: 416-314-6680; *Fax:* 416-314-6686
tom.chrzan@ontario.ca
Director, Corporate Resources, Tony Marzotto
Tel: 416-325-6135; *Fax:* 416-325-6387
tony.marzotto@ontario.ca

Central Area Regional Offices
Hamilton
Ellen Fairclough Bldg., 119 King St. West, 14th Fl., Hamilton, ON L8P 4Y7
Fax: 905-521-7398
Toll-Free: 877-998-9927

Huntsville
207 Main St. West, Huntsville, ON P1H 1Z9
Tel: 705-789-4448; *Fax:* 705-789-9533

Midhurst
2284 Nursery Rd., Midhurst, ON L0L 1X0
Fax: 705-739-6697
Toll-Free: 877-395-4105

Toronto
400 University Ave., 4th Fl., Toronto, ON M7A 2R9
Tel: 416-314-6044; *Fax:* 416-314-2024
Toll-Free: 877-395-4105

Eastern Area Regional Offices
Kingston
Ontario Government Bldg./Beechgrove Complex, 51 Heakes Lane, Kingston, ON K7M 9B1
Tel: 613-531-5580; *Fax:* 613-531-5585
Toll-Free: 800-293-7543

Ottawa
347 Preston St., 4th Fl., Ottawa, ON K1S 3J4
Tel: 613-742-3360; *Fax:* 613-742-5300
Toll-Free: 800-267-9340

Peterborough
Robinson Pl. South, 300 Water St., 2nd Fl., Peterborough, ON K9J 8M5
Tel: 705-755-2624; *Fax:* 705-755-2631
Toll-Free: 800-461-7629

Northern Area Regional Offices
Dryden
Ontario Government Bldg., 479 Government Rd., PO Box 3 Dryden, ON P8N 3B3
Fax: 807-223-4964
Toll-Free: 800-525-8785

Kenora
810 Robertson St., Kenora, ON P9N 4J4
Tel: 807-468-2450; *Fax:* 807-468-2788
Toll-Free: 800-465-1108

North Bay
447 McKeown Ave., North Bay, ON P1B 9S9
Tel: 705-494-4182; *Fax:* 705-494-4069
Toll-Free: 800-461-9563

Sault Ste. Marie
Roberta Bondar Place, #200, 70 Foster Dr., Sault Ste Marie, ON P6A 6V8
Tel: 705-945-5885; *Fax:* 705-541-2175
Toll-Free: 800-461-7284

Sioux Lookout
62 Queen St., PO Box 267 Sioux Lookout, ON P8T 1A3
Fax: 807-737-4112
Toll-Free: 800-529-6619

Sudbury
Ontario Government Bldg., #401, 199 Larch St., Sudbury, ON P3E 5P9
Tel: 705-564-3035; *Fax:* 705-564-3043
Toll-Free: 800-461-4004

Thunder Bay
#334, 435 James St. South, Thunder Bay, ON P7E 6S7
Tel: 807-475-1683; *Fax:* 807-475-1297
Toll-Free: 800-465-6861

Timmins
Ontario Government Complex, Hwy. 101 East, PO Box 3085 South Porcupine, ON P0N 1H0
Tel: 705-235-1550; *Fax:* 705-235-1553
Toll-Free: 800-305-4442

Western Area Regional Offices
Kitchener
4275 King St., 2nd Fl., Kitchener, ON N2P 2E9
Tel: 519-650-0200; *Fax:* 519-650-3425
Toll-Free: 800-265-2189

London
Exeter Rd. Complex, 659 Exeter Rd., 2nd Fl., London, ON N6A 1L3
Fax: 519-873-4061
Toll-Free: 800-265-4730

St Catharines
301 St Paul St., 9th Fl., St Catharines, ON L2R 7R4
Fax: 905-704-3955
Toll-Free: 800-263-2441

Walkerton
Bldg. 3, #103, 200 McNab St., Walkerton, ON N0G 2V0
Fax: 519-881-0525
Toll-Free: 800-265-5520

Windsor
221 Mill St., Windsor, ON N9C 2R1
Fax: 519-252-3476
Toll-Free: 800-265-1330

Syrian Refugee Resettlement Secretariat
Whitney Block, #4600, 99 Wellesley St. West, Toronto, ON M7A 1A1
Tel: 416-325-5375
The Secretariat was created in 2016 as a way to support & provide guidance to Syrian refugees.
Acting Assistant Deputy Minister, Melissa Thomson
Tel: 416-325-5512
melissa.thomson@ontario.ca
Acting Directory, Hannah Evans
Tel: 416-325-5355
hannah.evans2@ontario.ca

Ontario Ministry of Community & Social Services

Hepburn Block, 80 Grosvenor St., 6th Fl., Toronto, ON M7A 1E9
Tel: 416-325-5666; *Fax:* 416-325-3347
Toll-Free: 888-789-4199
TTY: 800-387-5559
www.mcss.gov.on.ca
Other Communication: Welfare Fraud Hotline: 1-800-394-7867
twitter.com/onsocialservice
www.facebook.com/ontariosocialservices
www.youtube.com/ontariosocialservice
The Ministry is responsible for social assistance, programs for adults with a developmental disability, community services & child & spousal support orders.
Minister, Hon. Dr. Helena Jaczek
Tel: 416-325-5225; *Fax:* 416-325-3347
hjaczek.mpp@liberal.ola.org
Deputy Minister, Janet Menard
Tel: 416-325-5233
Janet.Menard@ontario.ca
Parliamentary Assistant, Soo Wong
Tel: 416-212-5841; *Fax:* 416-325-3347
swong.mpp.co@liberal.ola.org
Chief Information Officer, Children, Youth & Social Services I&IT Cluster, Corbin Kerr
Tel: 416-326-4330; *Fax:* 416-325-0266
corbin.kerr@ontario.ca
Director, Communications & Marketing, Garth Cramer
Tel: 416-325-5203; *Fax:* 416-325-5191
garth.cramer@ontario.ca
Legal Director, Legal Services, Diane Zimnica
Tel: 416-314-5173; *Fax:* 416-327-0568
diane.zimnica@ontario.ca

Associated Agencies, Boards & Commissions:
•Commission for the Review of Social Assistance in Ontario
#400, 2 Bloor St. West, 4th Fl.
Toronto, ON M4W 3E2
Tel: 416-212-8029; *Fax:* 416-212-0413
Toll-free: 855-269-6250

Business Planning & Corporate Services Division
Tel: 416-325-5595; *Fax:* 416-325-5615
Assistant Deputy Minister & Chief Administrative Officer, Lorraine Graham-Watson
Tel: 416-325-5588
lorraine.graham-watson@ontario.ca
Director, Human Resources Strategic Business Unit, Frank Caccia
Tel: 416-327-4753; *Fax:* 416-325-0561
frank.caccia@ontario.ca
Director, Capital & Accommodation Services, Nadia Cornacchia
Tel: 416-327-7454; *Fax:* 416-327-0554
nadia.cornacchia@ontario.ca
Director, Financial Planning & Business Management Branch, Blair Dunker
Tel: 416-325-5139; *Fax:* 416-325-5125
blair.dunker@ontario.ca
Director, Ontario Internal Audit, Gordon Nowlan
Tel: 416-585-6550; *Fax:* 416-585-7377
gordon.nowlan@ontario.ca

Community & Developmental Services Division
Assistant Deputy Minister, Karen D. Chan
Tel: 416-325-5579; *Fax:* 416-325-5432
karen.d.chan@ontario.ca
Director, Program Policy Implementation Branch, Christine Kuepfer
Tel: 416-314-9741; *Fax:* 416-325-5554
christine.kuepfer@ontario.ca
Director, Service Delivery & Supports Branch, Sal Marrello
Tel: 416-325-5446; *Fax:* 416-212-1499
sal.marrello@ontario.ca
Acting Director, Controllership & Accountability Branch, Lourdes Valenton
Tel: 416-325-4401; *Fax:* 416-325-7854
lourdes.valenton@ontario.ca

Regional Offices
Central East
#1, 17310 Yonge St., Newmarket, ON L3Y 7R8
Tel: 905-868-8900; *Fax:* 905-895-4330
Toll-Free: 877-669-6658
TTY: 905-715-7759

Central West
#200, 6733 Mississauga Rd., Mississauga, ON L5N 6J5
Tel: 905-567-7177; *Fax:* 905-567-3215
Toll-Free: 877-832-2818
TTY: 905-567-3219
Other Communication: Serious Occurrence Reporting, Toll-Free Phone: 1-877-708-2896

Eastern
347 Preston St., 2nd & 3rd fl., Ottawa, ON K1S 3H8
Tel: 613-234-1188; *Fax:* 613-788-2382
Toll-Free: 800-267-5111
TTY: 613-787-5264
Other Communication: ODSP Intake Line: 613-787-3951

Hamilton/Niagara
Ellen Fairclough Bldg., 119 King St. West, 7th Fl., Hamilton, ON L8P 4Y7
Tel: 905-521-7280; *Fax:* 905-546-8277
TTY: 866-221-2229

Northern
Provincial Bldg., #1002, 199 Larch St., Sudbury, ON P3E 5P9
Tel: 705-564-6699; *Fax:* 705-564-3099
Toll-Free: 800-265-1222

North East
621 Main St. West, North Bay, ON P1B 2V6
Tel: 705-474-3540; *Fax:* 705-474-5815
Toll-Free: 800-461-6977
TTY: 705-474-7665

South East
11 Beechgrove Lane, Kingston, ON K7M 9A6
Tel: 613-545-0539; *Fax:* 613-536-7272
Toll-Free: 800-646-3209
TTY: 613-536-7304

South West
#203, 217 York St., PO Box 5217 London, ON N6A 5R1
Tel: 519-483-5111; *Fax:* 519-672-9510
Toll-Free: 800-265-4197
TTY: 519-663-5276

Toronto
477 Mount Pleasant Rd., 3rd Fl., Toronto, ON M7A 1G1
Tel: 416-325-0500; *Fax:* 416-325-0541
TTY: 416-325-3600

Family Responsibility Office
PO Box 220 Stn. Downsview, Toronto, ON M3M 3A3
Tel: 416-326-1817; *Fax:* 416-240-2401
Toll-Free: 800-267-4330
TTY: 416-240-2414
Other Communication: Automated Information, Phone: 416-326-1818; Toll-Free: 1-800-267-7263

Acting Assistant Deputy Minister, Jeff Butler
Tel: 416-240-2477
jeff.butler@ontario.ca

Director, Support Services, Bani Bawa
Tel: 416-246-2591
bani.bawa@ontario.ca

Director, Strategic & Operational Effectiveness Branch, Sylva McCormick
Tel: 416-240-2456
sylva.mccormick@ontario.ca

Acting Director, Finance & Administration, Sandra Yee
Tel: 416-240-2422
sandra.yee@ontario.ca

Acting Director, Client Services, Mena Zaffino
Tel: 416-240-4622
mena.zaffino@ontario.ca

Organizational Renewal Division
Tel: 416-212-8218

Assistant Deputy Minister, Denise Cole
Tel: 416-212-4893
denise.cole@ontario.ca

Director, Regional Modernization Strategy Unit, Karen Eisler
Tel: 905-567-7171 ext: 313
karen.eisler@ontario.ca

Social Assistance Operations Division

Assistant Deputy Minister, Richard Steele
Tel: 416-325-5374

Director, Social Assistance & Municipal Operations, Jeffrey Bowen
Tel: 416-212-1246; *Fax:* 416-212-1257
jeffrey.bowen@ontario.ca

Director, Social Assistance Services & Innovation, Patti Redmond
Tel: 416-314-1122
Patti.Redmond@ontario.ca

Director, Social Assistance Services Delivery Branch, Susan Waring
Tel: 416-212-2096
susan.waring@ontario.ca

Social Policy Development Division
Tel: 416-325-5421; *Fax:* 416-325-9408

Acting Assistant Deputy Minister, Erin Hannah
Tel: 416-325-3592

Acting Director, Ontario Works, Anna Cain
Tel: 416-325-6203; *Fax:* 416-326-9777
anna.cain@ontario.ca

Director, Planning & Strategic Policy, Erin Hannah
Tel: 416-325-5550
erin.hannah@ontario.ca

Director, Ontario Disability Support Program, Patti Redmond
Tel: 416-314-1122; *Fax:* 416-326-1735
patti.redmond@ontario.ca
www.mcss.gov.on.ca/en/mcss/programs/social/odsp

Director, Community & Developmental Services, Barbara Simmons
Tel: 416-325-5359; *Fax:* 416-325-8865
barbara.simmons@ontario.ca

Director, Policy Research & Analysis, Aklilu Tefera
Tel: 416-325-1171; *Fax:* 416-325-8764
aklilu.tefera@ontario.ca

Divisional Coordinator, Claire Maharaj
Tel: 416-325-5344
claire.maharaj@ontario.ca

Ontario Ministry of Community Safety & Correctional Services

George Drew Bldg., 25 Grosvenor St., 18th Fl., Toronto, ON M7A 1Y6
Tel: 416-326-5000; *Fax:* 416-326-0498
Toll-Free: 866-517-0571
TTY: 416-326-5511
mcscs.feedback@ontario.ca
www.mcscs.jus.gov.on.ca
Other Communication: TTY: 1-866-517-0572; Ministry Programs Information, Phone: 416-326-5010

The Ministry ensures that communities across the province are protected by safe, effective & accountable law enforcement & public safety systems. General responsibilities of the Ministry are as follows: correctional services; public safety & security; & policing services.

Minister, Hon. David Orazietti
Tel: 416-325-0408; *Fax:* 416-325-6067
dorazietti.mpp@liberal.ola.org

Deputy Minister, Community Safety, Matthew Torigian
Tel: 416-326-5060; *Fax:* 416-327-0469
matt.torigian@ontario.ca

Director, Communications, Minister's Office, Jonathan Rose
Tel: 416-325-8282; *Fax:* 416-325-6067
jonathan.rose@ontario.ca

Associated Agencies, Boards & Commissions:

•Death Investigation Oversight Council (DIOC)
George Drew Bldg.
25 Grosvenor St., 1st Fl.
Toronto, ON M7A 1Y6
Tel: 416-212-8443
Toll-free: 855-240-3414
dioc@ontario.ca
www.sse.gov.on.ca/mcscs/dioc

•Fire Marshal's Public Fire Safety Council
Place Nouveau Bldg.
5775 Yonge St., 7th Fl.
Toronto, ON M2M 4J1
Tel: 416-325-3152; *Fax:* 416-325-3162
info@firesafetycouncil.com
www.firesafetycouncil.com
Other Communication: Order Information, E-mail: orders@firesafetycouncil.com

•Ontario Police Arbitration Commission (OPAC)
George Drew Bldg.
25 Grosvenor St., 1st Fl.
Toronto, ON M7A 1Y6
Tel: 416-314-3520; *Fax:* 416-314-3522
Toll-free: 866-517-0571
TTY: 416-326-5511
www.policearbitration.on.ca
Other Communication: Toll-Free TTY: 1-866-517-0572

Communications Branch
George Drew Bldg., 25 Grosvenor St., 10th fl., Toronto, ON M7A 1Y6
Tel: 416-314-7868; *Fax:* 416-326-0498

Director, Stuart McGetrick
Tel: 416-326-5004
stuart.mcgetrick@ontario.ca

Legal Services Branch
#501, 655 Bay St., Toronto, ON M7A 0A8
Tel: 416-314-3509; *Fax:* 416-314-3518
Other Communication: Orillia Fax: 705-329-6882
Secondary Address: 777 Memorial Ave., 3rd Fl. Orillia, ON L3V 7V3

Acting Director, Brian Loewen
Tel: 416-326-5044
brian.loewen@ontario.ca

Commissioner for Community Safety
George Drew Bldg., North Side, 25 Grosvenor St., 11th fl., Toronto, ON M7A 1Y6
Tel: 416-212-7656; *Fax:* 416-327-0469

Ontario Commissioner for Community Safety, Daniel Hefkey
dan.hefkey@ontario.ca

Assistant Deputy Minister, Public Safety Training Division, Denise R. Dwyer
Tel: 416-326-4108
denise.dwyer@ontario.ca

Director, Public Safety Modernization, Connie Forrest
Tel: 416-212-5345
connie.forrest@ontario.ca

Director, Business Operations & Training Support Services, dianne Kasias
Tel: 416-325-5591
dianne.kasias@ontario.ca

Ontario Fire College
1495 Muskoka Rd. North, Gravenhurst, ON P1P 1R8
Tel: 705-687-2294; *Fax:* 705-687-7911
Toll-Free: 800-565-0613
Other Communication: Registration Phone: 705-687-9653; Fax: 705-687-4611

Acting Principal, Guy Degagne
Tel: 705-687-9650

Registrar, Vacant
Tel: 705-687-9653

Assistant Registrar, Tracey Sylvester
Tel: 705-687-9652
tracey.sylvester@ontario.ca

Ontario Police College
10716 Hacienda Rd., PO Box 1190 Aylmer West, ON N5H 2T2
Tel: 519-773-5361; *Fax:* 519-773-5762
www.opconline.ca
Other Communication: Registration Fax: 519-765-1519; Training Office Fax: 519-773-8225; Library E-mail: opclibrary@ontario.ca

Director, Bruce Herridge
Tel: 519-773-4200
bruce.herridge@ontario.ca

Acting Deputy Director, Transformation & Distance Learning, Jon Schmidt
Tel: 519-773-4560
jon.schmidt@ontario.ca

Acting Deputy Director, Allan B. Phibbs
Tel: 519-773-4471
allan.phibbs@ontario.ca

Deputy Director, Peter Sherriff
Tel: 519-773-4286
peter.sherriff@ontario.ca

Registrar, Nicole Adams
Tel: 519-773-4203
nicole.adams@ontario.ca

Corporate Services Division
George Drew Bldg., North Side, 25 Grosvenor St., 18th fl., Toronto, ON M7A 1Y6
Tel: 416-325-3257; *Fax:* 416-326-3149

Assistant Deputy Minister & Chief Administration Officer, David Lynch
Tel: 416-325-9208
david.lynch@ontario.ca

Director, Ontario Internal Audit, Justice Audit Service Team, David Horie
Tel: 705-329-6747
david.horie@ontario.ca

Acting Director, HR-Strategic Business Unit, Kevin Sawicki
Tel: 416-212-3555; *Fax:* 416-314-5559
kevin.sawicki@ontario.ca

Acting Director, Business & Financial Planning & Director, Procurement & Business Improvement Branch, Drew Vanderduim
Tel: 416-326-1016; *Fax:* 416-325-3465
drew.vanderduim@ontario.ca

Director, Facilities & Capital Planning, Ali Veshkini
Tel: 416-314-6683; *Fax:* 416-327-1470
ali.veshkini@ontario.ca

Correctional Services

Assistant Deputy Minister, Operational Support, Curt Arthur
Tel: 416-327-0099
curt.arthur@ontario.ca

Assistant Deputy Minister, Institutional Services, Steven F. Small
Tel: 416-327-9992; *Fax:* 416-314-6669
steve.small@ontario.ca

Assistant Deputy Minister, Community Services, Marg Welch
Tel: 519-661-1773
marg.welch@ontario.ca

Chief, Oversight & Investigations, Stephen Rooke
Tel: 905-279-1882; *Fax:* 905-279-1295
steve.rooke@ontario.ca

Director, Management & Operational Support Branch, Lynn Kenn
Tel: 416-327-9918; *Fax:* 416-314-5987
lynn.kenn@ontario.ca

Director, Strategic & Operational Initiatives, Jennifer Oliver
Tel: 416-327-2329; *Fax:* 416-314-5987
jennifer.oliver@ontario.ca

Regional Offices

Central Region
Other Communication: Community Services Phone: 416-212-6714; Fax: 416-327-4468; Institutional Services Phone: 905-279-6997; Fax: 905-279-6710

Acting Regional Director, Institutional Services, David Hatt
Tel: 905-279-6366
david.hatt@ontario.ca
Regional Director, Community Services, David Mitchell
Tel: 416-212-6708
david.mitchell@ontario.ca
Eastern Region
25 Heakes Lane, Kingston, ON K7M 9B1
Tel: 613-536-7350
Other Communication: Fax: 613-531-8496 (Community Services), 613-544-6460 (Institutional Services)
Acting Regional Director, Community Services, Lori Potter
Tel: 613-536-7390
lori.potter@ontario.ca
Regional Director, Institutional Services, Marilyn Tomkinson
Tel: 613-536-7353
marilyn.tomkinson@ontario.ca
Northern Region
200 First Ave. W., 4th Fl., North Bay, ON P1B 3B9
Other Communication: Institutional Services Phone 705-494-3430; Fax 705-494-3435; Community Services Phone: 807-343-7521 Thunder Bay); Fax: 705-494-3459
Regional Director, Institutional Services, Kathy Kinger
Tel: 705-494-3426
katherine.kinger@ontario.ca
Regional Director, Community Services, Mary-Jo Knappett
Tel: 705-494-3645
maryjo.knappett@ontario.ca
Western Region
#704, 150 Dufferin Ave., London, ON N6A 5N6
Tel: 519-675-7757; *Fax:* 519-679-0699
Acting Regional Director, Institutional Services, Christina Danylchenko
Tel: 519-661-1693
christina.danylchenko@ontario.ca
Regional Director, Community Services, Emelie Milloy
Tel: 519-661-1694
emelie.milloy@ontario.ca

Emergency Management Ontario (EMO)
77 Wellesley St. West, PO Box 222 Toronto, ON M7A 1N3
Tel: 416-314-3723; *Fax:* 416-314-3758
Toll-Free: 877-314-3723
www.emergencymanagementontario.ca
twitter.com/ontariowarnings
www.facebook.com/EmergencyManagementOntario
www.youtube.com/EmergMgtON
For executive listings, please see Office of the Fire Marshal & Emergency Management.

Justice Technology Services
#300, 21 College St., 3rd Fl., Toronto, ON M5G 2B3
Tel: 416-314-1841; *Fax:* 416-326-6987
Assistant Deputy Minister & Chief Information Officer, Robin M. Thompson
Tel: 416-326-2338
robin.m.thompson@ontario.ca
Director, Integrated Business Services, Supriya Mahimkar-Patrick
Tel: 416-326-1631
supriya.mahimkar-patrick@ontario.ca
Head, MAG Solutions Branch, Catherine Emile
Tel: 416-326-6898; *Fax:* 416-212-4981
catherine.emile@ontario.ca
Head, Common Cluster Solutions, Serge Fournier
Tel: 416-326-3303
serge.fournier@ontario.ca
Head, MCSCS Solutions Branch, Irene McGlashen
Tel: 416-325-0999
irene.mcglashan@ontario.ca
Head, Service Management Branch, Chris Walpole
Tel: 416-326-4267; *Fax:* 416-326-6628
chris.walpole@ontario.ca

Office of the Chief Coroner & Ontario Forensic Pathology Service
25 Morton Shulman Ave., Toronto, ON M3M 0B1
Tel: 416-314-4000; *Fax:* 416-314-4030
Toll-Free: 877-991-9959
Chief Coroner for Ontario, Dr. Dirk Huyer
Tel: 647-329-1814
dirk.huyer@ontario.ca
Chief Forensic Pathologist for Ontario, Dr. Michael Pollanen
Tel: 416-329-1914; *Fax:* 416-314-4060
michael.pollanen@ontario.ca
Chief Legal Counsel, Michael Blain
Tel: 647-329-1850; *Fax:* 416-314-4030
michael.blain@ontario.ca
Deputy Chief Coroner, Investigations, Dr. Dan Cass
Tel: 647-329-1830; *Fax:* 416-314-4030
dan.cass@ontario.ca
Deputy Chief Coroner, Inquests, Bill Lucas
Tel: 647-329-1834; *Fax:* 416-314-4030
william.lucas@ontario.ca
Deputy Chief Forensic Pathologist, Dr. Toby Rose
Tel: 647-329-1922; *Fax:* 647-329-1389
toby.rose@ontario.ca
Director, Operational Services, Forensic Pathology Unit, Melanie Fraser
Tel: 647-329-1880; *Fax:* 416-314-4060
melanie.fraser@ontario.ca
Medical Director, Provincial Forensic Pathology Unit, Dr. Jayantha Herath
Tel: 647-329-1926; *Fax:* 647-329-1389
jayantha.herath@ontario.ca

Regional Supervising Coroners
Central Region
#700, 24 Queen St. East, Brampton, ON L6V 1A3
Tel: 905-874-3972; *Fax:* 905-874-3976
Regional Supervising Coroner, Dr. Lucas William
lucas.william@ontario.ca
Central West Region
25 Morton Shulman Ave., Toronto, ON M3M 0B1
Tel: 519-837-6330; *Fax:* 519-837-6329
Regional Supervising Coroner, Dr. Roger Skinner
Tel: 647-329-1838
roger.skinner@ontario.ca
Eastern Region
#440, 366 King St. East, Kingston, ON K7M 6Y3
Tel: 613-544-1596; *Fax:* 613-544-3473
Acting Regional Supervising Coroner, Dr. Peter Clark
Tel: 613-544-1596
peter.clark@ontario.ca
Northeast Region
270 George St. North, PO Box D Peterborough, ON K9J 3H1
Tel: 705-755-5265; *Fax:* 705-755-5266
Regional Supervision Coroner, Dr. Peter Clark
Tel: 705-745-9887
peter.clark@ontario.ca
Northwestern Region
Ontario Government Bldg., 189 Red River Rd., 4th Fl., PO Box 4500 Thunder Bay, ON P7B 6G9
Tel: 807-343-7663; *Fax:* 807-343-7665
Regional Supervising Coroner, Dr. Michael B. Wilson
Tel: 807-343-7664
michael.b.wilson@ontario.ca
Southwestern Region
#303, 235 North Centre Rd., London, ON N5X 4E7
Tel: 519-661-6624; *Fax:* 519-661-6617
Regional Supervising Coroner, Dr. Rick Mann
rick.mann@ontario.ca
Toronto East Region
25 Morton Shulman Ave., Toronto, ON M3M 0B1
Tel: 416-314-1013; *Fax:* 416-314-4030
Regional Supervising Coroner, Dr. Jim N. Edwards
Tel: 647-329-1823
jim.n.edwards@ontario.ca
Toronto West Region
25 Morton Shulman Ave., Toronto, ON M3M 0B1
Tel: 416-314-4105; *Fax:* 416-314-4030
Deputy Chief Coroner of Investigations, Dr. Dan Cass
Tel: 647-329-1830
dan.cass@ontario.ca
West Region
119 King St. West, 13th Fl., Hamilton, ON L8P 4Y7
Tel: 905-546-8204; *Fax:* 905-546-8210
Regional Supervising Coroner, Dr. David Eden
Tel: 807-343-7663
david.eden@ontario.ca
Regional Supervising Coroner, Dr. Jack Stanborough
Tel: 905-546-8201
jack.stanborough@ontario.ca

Office of the Fire Marshal & Emergency Management
Place Nouveau, 5775 Yonge St., 7th Fl., Toronto, ON M2M 4J1
Tel: 416-325-3100; *Fax:* 416-325-3119
www.mcscs.jus.gov.on.ca/english/FireMarshal/OFM_main.html
Fire Marshal of Ontario & Chief of Emergency Management, Ted Wieclawek
Tel: 416-325-3101
ted.wieclawek@ontario.ca
Interim Deputy Fire Marshal & Director, Operations, Response, Barney Owens
Tel: 416-314-2393
barney.owens@ontario.ca
Deputy Chief, Planning & Programming Development, Prevention & Risk Assessment, Tom Kontra
Tel: 416-212-3472
tom.kontra@ontario.ca
Deputy Chief, Business & Support Services, Administration & Business Services, Edward Unger
Tel: 416-314-3135
edward.unger@ontario.ca
Acting Assistant Deputy Fire Marshal/Executive Officer, Executive Strategies & Relations, Jeff Dick
Tel: 705-725-7616
jeff.dick@ontario.ca
Acting Assistant Deputy Fire Marshal, Technical Services, Mary Prencipe
Tel: 416-325-3208
mary.prencipe@ontario.ca
Assistant Deputy Fire Marshal, Fire Investigation Services, Christopher Williams
Tel: 416-325-3233
chris.williams@ontario.ca
Acting Assistant Deputy Fire Marshal, Field Fire Protection Services, Pierre Yelle
Tel: 705-725-8681
pierre.yelle@ontario.ca
Acting Director, Administration & Business Services, Troy Fernandes
Tel: 416-325-3111
troy.fernandes@ontario.ca
Director, Field & Advisory Services, Jim Jessop
Tel: 416-325-3239
jim.jessop@ontario.ca
Director/Deputy, Prevention & Risk Management, Al Suleman
Tel: 416-325-3230
al.suleman@ontario.ca

Ontario Provincial Police
Lincoln M. Alexander Bldg., 777 Memorial Ave., 3rd Fl., Orillia, ON L3V 7V3
Tel: 705-329-6111
Toll-Free: 888-310-1122
TTY: 888-310-1133
www.opp.ca
twitter.com/OPP_News
www.facebook.com/ontarioprovincialpolice
www.youtube.com/user/OPPCorpComm
Commissioner, Vince D. Hawkes
Tel: 705-329-6199
vince.hawkes@ontario.ca
Chief Superintendent, Brad Blair
Tel: 705-329-7401
brad.blair@ontario.ca
Chief Adjudicator (Inspector), Robin Mcelary-Downer
Tel: 705-329-6411
chris.d.lewis@ontario.ca

Corporate Services
Tel: 705-329-7500; *Fax:* 705-329-6317
Chief Superintendent, Career Development Bureau, Angie Howe
Tel: 705-329-6276
angie.howe@ontario.ca
Corporate Advisor/Chief Superintendent, Strategic Initiatives Office, Nora Skelding
Tel: 705-329-6389
nora.skelding@ontario.ca
Acting Superintendent, Human Resources Director's Office, Dave Quigley
Tel: 705-329-6614; *Fax:* 705-329-6188
dave.quigley@ontario.ca

Investigations/Organized Crime
Tel: 705-329-7500; *Fax:* 705-329-6317
Executive Officer, Investigation & Support Bureau, & Organized Crime Enforcement Bureau, Randy Craig
Tel: 705-329-6359; *Fax:* 705-329-6318
randy.craig@ontario.ca
Commander, Organized Crime Enforcement Bureau (North East), Ken Leppert
Tel: 705-329-6321
ken.leppert@ontario.ca
Commander, Organized Crime Enforcement Bureau (Central West), Tim Millar
Tel: 905-671-6820
tim.millar@ontario.ca
Director/Superintendent, Behavioural Forensic Electronic Services, Evan Evans
Tel: 705-329-6355; *Fax:* 705-329-6318
evan.evans@ontario.ca

Traffic Safety & Operational Support
Tel: 705-329-7500; *Fax:* 705-329-6317
Deputy Commissioner & Provincial Commander, Larry Beechey
larry.beechey@ontario.ca
Director/Superintendent, Operations, Dave Farrar
Tel: 705-329-7462; *Fax:* 705-329-7593
dave.farrar@ontario.ca

Policy & Strategic Planning Division
George Drew Bldg., 25 Grosvenor St., 9th Fl., Toronto, ON M7A 1Y6
Tel: 416-212-4437; *Fax:* 416-212-4020
Assistant Deputy Minister, Karen Maxwell
Tel: 416-314-8789
karen.maxwell@ontario.ca
Director, Strategic Planning & Research Branch, Michael McBain
Tel: 416-325-3426
michael.mcbain@ontario.ca
Acting Director, Policy Development & Coordination, Rebecca Ramsarran
Tel: 416-212-4025

Public Safety Division
George Drew Bldg., 25 Grosvenor St., 12th Fl., Toronto, ON M7A 2H3
Tel: 416-314-3377; *Fax:* 416-314-4037
Assistant Deputy Minister, Glenn Murray
Tel: 416-325-3454
glenn.murray@ontario.ca
Registrar & Director, Private Security & Investigative Services, Lisa Kool
Tel: 416-326-0817
lisa.kool@ontario.ca
Director, External Relations, Stephen Waldie
Tel: 416-325-3132; *Fax:* 416-314-3092
stephen.waldie@ontario.ca

Centre of Forensic Sciences
25 Morton Shulman Ave., Toronto, ON M3M 1J8
Tel: 647-329-1320; *Fax:* 647-329-1361
www.mcscs.jus.gov.on.ca/english/centre_forensic/CFS_intro.htm l
Director, Tony Tessarolo
Tel: 416-314-3224; *Fax:* 416-314-3225
tony.tessarolo@ontario.ca
Deputy Director, Support Services, Colette Blair
Tel: 647-329-1323
colette.blair@ontario.ca
Deputy Director, Scientific Services, Jonathan Newman
Tel: 416-314-3280
jonathan.newman@ontario.ca
Assistant Section Head, Northern Regional Forensic Laboratory, Andrew Greenfield
Tel: 416-314-3268
andrew.greenfield@ontario.ca

Ontario Ministry of Economic Development & Growth

Hearst Block, 900 Bay St., 8th Fl., Toronto, ON M7A 2E1
Tel: 416-325-6666
Toll-Free: 800-268-7095
TTY: 416-325-3408
www.ontario.ca/page/ministry-economic-development-and-growt h
Other Communication: Toll-Free TTY: 1-800-268-7095
twitter.com/Onteconomy
www.youtube.com/user/OntarioEconomy

Promotes economic development & job creation in Ontario by creating a climate for business to prosper & eliminate red tape as well as stimulating trade. This Ministry markets the province as a desirable place to live, work, invest & raise a family. It works with its private sector partners to ensure that its core responsibilities of employment & business development, investment & trade continue to help Ontario businesses compete globally; contribute to a highly-skilled, well-educated workforce; & generate prosperity for all Ontarians. In Northern Ontario, the Ministry is represented by the Northern Development Division of the Ministry of Northern Development & Mines.

Minister, Hon. Brad Duguid
Tel: 416-325-6900; *Fax:* 416-325-6918
Deputy Minister, Giles Gherson
Tel: 416-325-6927
Giles.Gherson@ontario.ca
Director, Communications Marketing Branch, Clare Barnett
Tel: 416-325-8058; *Fax:* 416-325-6688
clare.barnett@ontario.ca
Legal Director, Legal Services Branch, Carolyn Calwell
Tel: 416-212-8392; *Fax:* 416-326-1021
carolyn.calwell@ontario.ca
Director, Policy, Minister's Office, Alyssa Brierley
Tel: 416-325-6907; *Fax:* 416-325-6918
alyssa.brierley@ontario.ca
Director, Stakeholder Relations, Guy Bethell
Tel: 416-325-6706; *Fax:* 416-325-6918
guy.bethell@ontario.ca
Director, Operations, Trish Dyl
Tel: 416-325-6992
trish.dyl@ontario.ca

Associated Agencies, Boards & Commissions:

•Infrastructure Ontario
College Park
777 Bay St., 6th Fl.
Toronto, ON M5G 2C8
Tel: 416-212-7289; *Fax:* 416-325-4646
info@infrastructureontario.ca
www.infrastructureontario.ca
Management of complex infrastructure projects identified in the government's mulit-year capital plan as alternative financing & procurement projects.

•Waterfront Toronto
#1310, 20 Bay St.
Toronto, ON M5J 2N8
Tel: 416-241-1344; *Fax:* 416-214-4591
info@waterfronttoronto.ca
www.waterfronttoronto.ca

Accessibility Directorate of Ontario
College Park, #601A & 601B, 777 Bay St., 6th Fl., Toronto, ON M7A 2J4
Tel: 416-849-8276; *Fax:* 416-325-9620
Toll-Free: 866-515-2025
TTY: 800-268-7095
www.ontario.ca/page/accessibility-laws
twitter.com/ONAccessibility
www.facebook.com/AccessON
www.youtube.com/accessontario
Assistant Deputy Minister, Ann Hoy
Tel: 416-325-5247
ann.hoy@ontario.ca
Director, Standards, Policy & Compliance Branch, Mary Bartolomucci
Tel: 416-327-1509
mary.bartolomucci@ontario.ca
Director, Outreach & Strategic Initiatives Branch, Alfred Spencer
Tel: 416-314-7289
alfred.spencer@ontario.ca

Corporate Services Division
56 Wellesley St., 4th Fl., Toronto, ON M7A 2E7
Tel: 416-325-6866; *Fax:* 416-314-7014
TTY: 888-664-6008
Assistant Deputy Minister & Chief Executive Officer, Robert Burns
Tel: 416-327-3682
robert.burns@ontario.ca
Director, Investment Funding & Coordination Branch, Richard Kikuta
Tel: 416-325-6849
richard.kikuta@ontario.ca
Director, Strategic Human Resources Business Unit, Dan Keating
Tel: 416-325-6598; *Fax:* 416-325-6715
dan.keating@ontario.ca
Director, Service Management & Facilities Branch, Betty Morgan
Tel: 416-314-3309; *Fax:* 416-325-1118
betty.morgan@ontario.ca
Director, Business Planning & Finance, Kevin Perry
Tel: 416-327-1137; *Fax:* 416-327-4239
kevin.perry@ontario.ca

Corporate Services Division (Infrastructure)
77 Grenville St., 10th Fl., Toronto, ON M7A 2C1
Tel: 416-325-6866; *Fax:* 416-314-3354
Assistant Deputy Minister & Chief Administrative Officer, Robert Burns
Tel: 416-327-3682
Robert.Burns@ontario.ca
Director, Service Management, Betty Morgan
Tel: 416-314-3309; *Fax:* 416-314-6654
betty.morgan@ontario.ca
Acting Director & Controller, Business & Resource, Shella Salazar
Tel: 416-327-7227
shella.salazar4@ontario.ca

Infrastructure Policy Division
Mowat Block, 900 Bay St., 5th Fl., Toronto, ON M7A 1C2
Assistant Deputy Minister, Karen Maxwell
Tel: 416-314-8789
karen.maxwell@ontario.ca
Director, Strategic Initiatives, Planning & Analytics, Sarah McQuarrie
Tel: 416-325-7966
sarah.mcquarrie@ontario.ca
Director, Inter-Governmental Policy Branch, Elizabeth Doherty
Tel: 416-212-8757
elizabeth.doherty@ontario.ca
Manager, Infrastructure Finance Policy, Trevor Fleck
Tel: 416-325-8559
trevor.fleck@ontario.ca
Manager, Project Design & Implementation, Kristi Kelly
Tel: 416-212-8665
kristi.kelly@ontario.ca

Investment & Industry Division
56 Wellesley St. West, 7th Fl., Toronto, ON M7A 2E7
Fax: 416-212-3658
Acting Assistant Deputy Minister, Gregory Wootton
Tel: 416-325-6623
gregory.wootton@ontario.ca
Manager, Business Development, Robert Crabtree
Tel: 416-325-6864; *Fax:* 416-325-6757
robert.crabtree@ontario.ca
Acting Director, Infotech, Life Sciences & Services Branch, Joanne Anderson
Tel: 416-212-7469; *Fax:* 416-325-6799
joanne.anderson2@ontario.ca
Director, Business Advisory Services Branch, Brian Love
Tel: 416-325-6522; *Fax:* 416-325-6757
brian.love@ontario.ca
Manager, Aerospace & Materials Unit, Joseph Veloce
Tel: 416-325-6767; *Fax:* 416-325-6534
joe.veloce@ontario.ca

Open for Business
250 Yonge St., 35th Fl., Toronto, ON M5B 2L7
Tel: 416-326-5540; *Fax:* 416-212-3288
Assistant Deputy Minister, John Marshall
Tel: 416-212-3283
john.ofb.marshall@ontario.ca
Acting Director, Open for Business, Anne Bermonte
Tel: 416-212-3284
anne.bermonte@ontario.ca
Director, Social Enterprise, Katie Gibson
Tel: 416-314-5525
Katie.Gibson@ontario.ca

Policy & Strategy Division
Hearst Block, 900 Bay St., 7th Fl., Toronto, ON M7A 2E7
Tel: 416-212-6653; *Fax:* 416-326-6393
Assistant Deputy Minister, Victor Severino
Tel: 416-325-4655
victor.severino@ontario.ca
Director, Trade Policy Branch, Hugo Cameron
Tel: 416-325-6930
hugo.cameron@ontario.ca
Acting Director, Sector Strategy Branch, Akin Alaga
Tel: 416-212-6280; *Fax:* 416-325-6534
akin.alaga@ontario.ca
Acting Director, Research & Analysis Branch, Karen Paquin
Tel: 416-325-6938
karen.paquin@ontario.ca
Director, Strategic Policy, Steve Romanyshyn
Tel: 416-325-8554; *Fax:* 416-325-6825
steve.romanyshyn@ontario.ca

Realty Division
College Park, 777 Bay St., 4th Fl., Toronto, ON M5G 2E5
Tel: 416-327-5596; *Fax:* 416-325-4920
Assistant Deputy Minister, Bruce Singbush
Tel: 416-326-1766
bruce.singbush2@ontario.ca
Director, Realty Management, Maggie Allan
Tel: 416-212-1167; *Fax:* 416-212-4941
maggie.allan@ontario.ca
Director, Realty Policy, Trevor Bingler
Tel: 416-327-2900; *Fax:* 416-212-4941
trevor.bingler@ontario.ca

Research, Commercialization & Entrepreneurship Division
56 Wellesley St. West, 11th Fl., Toronto, ON M7A 2E7
Tel: 416-314-8474; *Fax:* 416-314-4344
Assistant Deputy Minister, Bill Mantel
Tel: 416-327-2889
bill.mantel@ontario.ca
Director, Research Branch, Allison Barr
Tel: 416-212-6990; *Fax:* 416-314-8224
allison.barr@ontario.ca
Director, Entrepreneurship Branch, Carrie Burd
Tel: 416-314-3809
carrie.burd@ontario.ca
Director, Commercialization Branch, Rachel Simeon
Tel: 416-314-0670; *Fax:* 416-314-0680
rachel.simeon@ontario.ca

Ontario Capital Growth Corporation
250 Yonge St., 35th Fl., Toronto, ON M5B 2L7
Tel: 416-325-6874; *Fax:* 416-212-0794
Toll-Free: 877-422-5818
www.ocgc.gov.on.ca
The OCGC was established by the Ontario Capital Growth Corporation Act, 2008. The Corporation's main focus is the management of the Government of Ontario's interests in the

Ontario Venture Capital Fund LP & the Ontario Emerging Technologies Fund.
President & CEO, John W. Marshall
Tel: 416-325-6644
john.w.marshall@ontario.ca
Chief Financial Officer, George Loo
Tel: 416-326-9623
george.loo@ontario.ca

Ontario Ministry of Education

Mowat Block, 900 Bay St., 22nd Fl., Toronto, ON M7A 1L2
Tel: 416-325-2929; *Fax:* 416-325-6348
Toll-Free: 800-387-5514
TTY: 416-325-3408
information.met@ontario.ca
www.edu.gov.on.ca
Other Communication: Toll-Free TTY: 1-800-268-7095
twitter.com/OntarioEDU
www.youtube.com/user/OntarioEDU

The Ministry focuses on three priority areas: Attaining high levels of student achievement; reducing gaps in student achievement; & increasing public confidence in publicly funded education.

Minister, Hon. Mitzie Hunter
Tel: 613-325-2600; *Fax:* 416-325-2608
mhunter.mpp.co@liberal.ola.org
Deputy Minister, George Zegarac
Tel: 416-325-2600; *Fax:* 416-327-9063
george.zegarac@ontario.ca
Parliamentary Assistant, Grant Crack
Tel: 416-325-5496
gcrack.mpp.co@liberal.ola.org
Assistant Deputy Minister, Unregulated Child Care Realignment, Karen D. Chan
Tel: 416-314-7987
karen.chan@ontario.ca
Director, Communications Branch, Murray Leaning
Tel: 416-325-2742; *Fax:* 416-212-4158
murray.leaning@ontario.ca

Associated Agencies, Boards & Commissions:

•Education Quality & Accountability Office (EQAO)
#1200, 2 Carlton St.
Toronto, ON M5B 2M9
Tel: 416-314-0146; *Fax:* 416-325-2956
Toll-free: 888-327-7377
www.eqao.com

•Languages of Instruction Commission of Ontario
Mowat Block
900 Bay St., 8th Fl.
Toronto, ON M7A 1L2
Tel: 416-314-3500; *Fax:* 416-325-2979

•Minister's Advisory Council on Special Education (MACSE)
900 Bay St., 18th Fl.
Toronto, ON M7A 1L2
Tel: 416-314-2333; *Fax:* 416-314-0637
Toll-free: 877-699-5431
macse@ontario.ca
www.edu.gov.on.ca/eng/general/abcs/acse/acse_eng.html

•Ontario Educational Communications Authority (TVO)
2180 Yonge St.
PO Box 200 Q
Toronto, ON M4T 2T1
Tel: 416-484-2600
Toll-free: 800-613-0513
ww3.tvo.org

•Ontario French-Language Education Communications Authority
21 College St.
Toronto, ON MRY 2M5
Tel: 416-968-3536; *Fax:* 416-968-8203
TTY: 800-387-8435
www3.tfo.org

•Provincial Schools Authority (PSA)
c/o Leadership Development Branch, Mowatt Block
900 Bay St., 13th Fl.
Toronto, ON M7A 1L2
www.psbnet.ca/eng/about_us/psa.html

Corporate Management & Services Division

Mowat Block, #342, 900 Bay St., Toronto, ON M7A 1L2
Tel: 416-325-2772; *Fax:* 416-325-2778
Assistant Deputy Minister & Chief Administrative Officer, Bohodar Rubashewsky
Tel: 416-325-2773
Bohodar.I.Rubashewsky@ontario.ca
Director, Strategic Human Resources Branch, Lisa Brisebois
Tel: 416-327-2731; *Fax:* 416-327-9043
Lisa.Brisebois@ontario.ca
Director, Internal Audit Services, Education Audit Service Team, Warren McCay
Tel: 416-212-4814; *Fax:* 416-325-1120
warren.mccay@ontario.ca
Acting Director, Corporate Finance & Services Branch, Susan Flanagan
Tel: 416-325-7677; *Fax:* 416-325-1835
susan.flanagan@ontario.ca
Acting Director, Corporate Coordination Branch, Sarah Truscott
Tel: 416-326-6662; *Fax:* 416-314-0558
sarah.truscott@ontario.ca
Director, Legal Services, Prabhu Rajan
Tel: 416-326-5045 ext: 650; *Fax:* 416-325-2410
prabhu.rajan@ontario.ca

Early Years Division

Mowat Block, 900 Bay St., 24th Fl., Toronto, ON M7A 1L2
Tel: 416-314-8277; *Fax:* 416-314-7836
Assistant Deputy Minister, Jim Grieve
Tel: 416-314-9393
jim.grieve@ontario.ca
Director, Business Planning, Outcomes & Assessments Branch, Shannon Fuller
Tel: 416-314-0903
shannon.fuller@ontario.ca
Director, Early Years Policy & Program Branch, Rupert Gordon
Tel: 416-314-8241
rupert.gordon@ontario.ca
Director, Early Years Implementation Branch, Pam Musson
Tel: 416-314-8192
pam.musson@ontario.ca
Director, Child Care Quality Assurance & Licensing Branch, Jill Vienneau
Tel: 416-314-2190
jill.vienneau@ontario.ca

Education Labour Relations Division

Mowat Block, 900 Bay St., 12th Fl., Toronto, ON M7A 1L2
Acting Assistant Deputy Minister, Andrew Davis
Tel: 416-326-6939
andrew.davis@ontario.ca
Director, Labour Relations Policy Branch, Stephanie Donaldson
Tel: 416-212-6971
Stephanie.Donaldson@ontario.ca
Director, Labour Relations Operations Branch, Brian Blakeley
Tel: 416-325-2836
brian.blakeley@ontario.ca

Financial Policy & Business Division

Mowat Block, 900 Bay St., 20th fl., Toronto, ON M7A 1L2
Tel: 416-325-6127; *Fax:* 416-325-9560
Assistant Deputy Minister, Gabriel Sékaly
Tel: 416-325-6127
gabriel.sekaly@ontario.ca
Executive Director, Andrew Davis
Tel: 416-327-9356
andrew.davis@ontario.ca
Director, Financial Analysis & Accountability Branch, Med Ahmadoun
Tel: 416-326-0201; *Fax:* 416-325-2007
med.ahmadoun@ontario.ca
Director, School Business Support Branch, Cheri Hayward
Tel: 416-327-7503; *Fax:* 416-212-3990
cheri.hayward@ontario.ca
Director, Capital Policy & Programs Branch, Grant Osborn
Tel: 416-325-1705; *Fax:* 416-326-9959
grant.osborn@ontario.ca
Director, Education Finance Branch, Joshua Paul
Tel: 416-327-9060; *Fax:* 416-325-6370
joshua.paul@ontario.ca

French-Language, Aboriginal Learning & Research Division

Mowat Block, 900 Bay St., 22nd Fl., Toronto, ON M7A 1L2
Tel: 416-325-2132; *Fax:* 416-327-1182
Assistant Deputy Minister, Janine Griffore
Tel: 416-325-2132
janine.griffore@ontario.ca
Acting Director, Aboriginal Education Office, Shirley Carder
Tel: 416-314-6194
Shirley.Carder@ontario.ca
Director (Bilingual), French-Language Education Policy & Programs, Denys Giguere
Tel: 416-327-9072; *Fax:* 416-325-2156
denys.giguere@ontario.ca
Director, Education Statistics & Analysis, Taddesse Haile
Tel: 416-325-9122; *Fax:* 416-325-2373
taddesse.haile@ontario.ca
Director, Education Research & Evaluation Strategy Branch, Doris McWhorter
Tel: 416-314-3819; *Fax:* 416-325-3734
doris.mcwhorter@ontario.ca
Director, Field Services Branch, Steven Reid
Tel: 416-314-8679
Acting Director, Aboriginal Education Office, Shirley Carder
Tel: 416-314-6194
Shirley.Carder@ontario.ca

Leadership & Learning Environment Division

Mowat Block, 900 Bay St., 13th fl., Toronto, ON M7A 1L2
Assistant Deputy Minister, Denise Dwyer
Tel: 416-326-4108
denise.dwyer@ontario.ca
Director, Leadership Development & School Board Governance Branch, Bruce Drewett
Tel: 416-325-1079; *Fax:* 416-325-7019
bruce.drewett@ontario.ca
Director, Inclusive Education Branch, Ruth Flynn
Tel: 416-326-7597; *Fax:* 416-325-7019
ruth.flynn@ontario.ca
Director, Teaching Policy & Standards, Demetra Saldaris
Tel: 416-325-7744; *Fax:* 416-326-1113
demetra.saldaris@ontario.ca
Acting Director, Safe Schools & Student Well-being Branch, Eileen Silver
Tel: 416-325-7645; *Fax:* 416-325-2664
eileen.silver@ontario.ca

Learning & Curriculum Division

Mowat Block, 900 Bay St., 22nd fl., Toronto, ON M7A 1L2
Tel: 416-325-2135; *Fax:* 416-327-1182
Assistant Deputy Minister, Grant Clarke
Tel: 416-314-5788
grant.clarke@ontario.ca
Director, Special Education Policy & Programs Branch, Barry Finlay
Tel: 416-325-2889; *Fax:* 416-314-0637
barry.finlay@ontario.ca
Director, Curriculum & Assessment Policy, Karen Gill
Tel: 416-325-2576; *Fax:* 416-325-2575
karen.gill@ontario.ca

Provincial Schools Branch

255 Ontario St. South, Milton, ON L9T 2M5
Tel: 905-878-2851; *Fax:* 905-878-1354
TTY: 905-878-7195
Other Communication: Alternate Fax: 905-878-5405
Director, June Rogers
Tel: 905-878-2851 ext: 214
june.rogers@ontario.ca
Superintendent, Deaf Programs & Learning Disabilities, Cheryl Zinszer
Tel: 905-878-2851 ext: 230
cheryl.zinszer@ontario.ca

Office of the Chief Information Officer, Community Services I & IT Cluster

Mowat Block, 900 Bay St., 3rd Fl., Toronto, ON M7A 1L2
Tel: 416-325-4598; *Fax:* 416-325-8371
This office works in conjunction with the Ministry of Advanced Education & Skills Development.
Chief Information Officer & Assistant Deputy Minister, Soussan Tabari
Tel: 416-326-8216
soussan.tabari@ontario.ca
Director, Case & Grants Management Solutions, Sanaul Haque
Tel: 416-314-4954
sanaul.haque@ontario.ca
Director, IAccess Solutions, Sanjay Madan
Tel: 416-325-2264
sanjay.madan@ontario.ca
Director, Strategic Planning & Business Relationship Management, Lolita Singh
Tel: 416-326-7942

Student Achievement Division

Mowat Block, 900 Bay St., 10th Fl., Toronto, ON M7A 1L2
Fax: 416-325-8565
Chief Student Achievement Officer of Ontario & Assistant Deputy Minister, Mary Jean Gallagher
Tel: 416-325-9964
maryjean.gallagher@ontario.ca
Director, Student Success/Learning to 18 Implementation, Innovation & Support, Rob J. Andrews
Tel: 416-326-9369
rob.j.andrews@ontario.ca
Director, Research, Evaluation & Capacity Building, Literacy & Numeracy Secretariat, Richard Franz
Tel: 416-325-9963
richard.franz@ontario.ca
Acting Director, Student Success/Learning to 18 Strategic Policy, Pauline McNaughton
Tel: 416-325-2564; *Fax:* 416-325-2552
pauline.mcnaughton@ontario.ca
Director, Leadership & Implementation, Literacy & Numeracy Secretariat, Bruce Shaw
Tel: 416-325-9979
bruce.shaw@ontario.ca

Elections Ontario

51 Rolark Dr., Toronto, ON M1R 3B1
Tel: 416-326-6300; *Fax:* 416-326-6200
Toll-Free: 888-668-8683
TTY: 866-479-1118
info@elections.on.ca
www.elections.on.ca
Other Communication: Election Finances 416-325-9401 or 866-566-9066; Fax: 416-325-9466; Toll-Free: 1-866-566-9066
twitter.com/ElectionsON
www.facebook.com/ElectionsON
www.youtube.com/ElectionsON

Chief Electoral Officer, Greg Essensa
Tel: 416-326-6383; *Fax:* 416-326-6201
greg.essensa@elections.on.ca
Deputy Chief Electoral Officer, Loren A. Wells
Tel: 416-326-6387; *Fax:* 416-326-6201
loren.wells@elections.on.ca
Director, Compliance & General Counsel, Jonathan Batty
Tel: 416-212-3367
jonathan.batty@elections.on.ca
Director, Operations, Lalitha Flach
Tel: 416-326-5688
lalitha.flach@elections.on.ca
Director, Chief Electoral Office & Communications, Lisa Forte
Tel: 416-326-4394
lisa.forte@elections.on.ca
Director, Technology Services, Shawn Pollock
Tel: 416-212-1183
shawn.pollock@elections.on.ca

Corporate Services
Acting Director, Pam Reel
Tel: 416-326-6303
pam.reel@elections.on.ca

Election Finances
Acting Deputy Director, Renee English
Tel: 416-325-9456
renee.english@elections.on.ca

Ontario Ministry of Energy

Hearst Block, 900 Bay St., 4th Fl., Toronto, ON M7A 2E1
Fax: 416-325-8440
Toll-Free: 888-668-4636
TTY: 800-387-5559
www.energy.gov.on.ca
twitter.com/OntMinEnergy

The Ministry of Energy is responsible for ensuring that Ontario's electricity system functions at a high level of reliability, security & productivity. The Ministry also focuses on promoting ingenuity & innovation in the energy sector, by encouraging the development of new ideas & technologies. Protecting the environment is also a top priority for the Ministry, as it strives to develop renewable sources of energy, cleaner forms of fuel, & foster a conservation culture.

Minister, Hon. Glenn Thibeault
Tel: 416-327-6758; *Fax:* 416-327-6754
gthibeault.mpp.co@liberal.ola.org
Deputy Minister, Serge Imbrogno
Tel: 416-327-6734; *Fax:* 416-327-6755
serge.imbrogno@ontario.ca
Parliamentary Assistant, Bob Delaney
Tel: 416-325-4140; *Fax:* 416-325-0818
bdelaney.mpp.co@liberal.ola.org
Director, Legal Services Branch, Halyna Perun
Tel: 416-325-6681; *Fax:* 416-325-1781
halyna.perun2@ontario.ca
Director, Communications Branch, John Whytock
Tel: 416-327-6541; *Fax:* 416-326-3947
john.whytock@ontario.ca

Associated Agencies, Boards & Commissions:

•Hydro One Inc.
See Entry Name Index for detailed listing.

•Independent Electricity System Operator
See Entry Name Index for detailed listing.

•Ontario Energy Board (OEB)
#2700, 2300 Yonge St.
PO Box 2319
Toronto, ON M4P 1E4
Tel: 416-481-1967; *Fax:* 416-440-7656
Toll-free: 888-632-6273
www.ontarioenergyboard.ca
Other Communication: Regulatory Information, E-mail: boardsec@ontarioenergyboard.ca

•Ontario Power Generation
See Entry Name Index for detailed listing.

Conservation & Renewable Energy Division
77 Grenville St., Toronto, ON M7A 2C1
Tel: 416-314-6216; *Fax:* 416-325-3438

The branch provides analysis, advice & policy development on issues relating to energy efficiency, demand management & conservation as well as administering the Energy Efficiency Act.

Assistant Deputy Minister, Kaili Sermat-Harding
Tel: 416-327-5555
kaili.sermat-harding@ontario.ca
Director, Conservation & Energy Efficiency, Barry Beale
Tel: 416-326-4551
barry.beale@ontario.ca
Director, Partnerships & Strategic Initiatives, Jennifer Block
Tel: 416-212-9267
jennifer.block@ontario.ca
Director, Renewables & Energy Facilitation, Mirrun Zaveri
Tel: 416-327-3868
mirrun.zaveri@ontario.ca

Corporate Services Division
880 Bay St., 5th Fl., Toronto, ON M7A 2C1
Tel: 416-325-6866; *Fax:* 416-314-3354

Provides a structure to identify strategic issues, to coordinate policy & program development; & to coordinate & integrate action by the Ministry & other governments.

Assistant Deputy Minister & Chief Administrative Officer, Robert Burns
Tel: 416-327-3682
robert.burns@ontario.ca
Chief Accountant, Business & Resource Planning, Vacant
Tel: 416-314-3323
Director, Service Management Branch, Betty Morgan
Tel: 416-314-3309; *Fax:* 416-314-3354
betty.morgan@ontario.ca
Acting Director & Controller, Business & Resource Planning, Shella Salazar
Tel: 416-327-7227; *Fax:* 416-314-3354
shella.salazar4@ontario.ca

Energy Supply Policy Division
77 Grenville St., 7th Fl., Toronto, ON M7A 2C1
Tel: 416-327-7353; *Fax:* 416-314-6224

Assistant Deputy Minister, Rick Jennings
Tel: 416-314-6190
rick.jennings@ontario.ca
Acting Director, Energy Supply & Economics Branch, Michael England
Tel: 416-325-8627; *Fax:* 416-314-6224
michael.england@ontario.ca
Director, Energy Supply - Nuclear Branch, Cedric Jobe
Tel: 416-325-6545; *Fax:* 416-314-6224
cedric.jobe@ontario.ca
Acting Director, Special Projects, Adrian Nalasco
Tel: 416-325-8627

Strategic, Network & Agency Policy Division
Mowat Block, 77 Grenville St., 6th Fl., Toronto, ON M7A 2C1
Tel: 416-325-6559; *Fax:* 416-325-7041

Provides strategic policy coordination & development for the ministry as well as policy analysis & advice related to energy conservation & efficiency, demand management, & conservation.

Assistant Deputy Minister, Michael Reid
Tel: 416-325-6544
michael.reid@ontario.ca
Acting Director, Strategic Policy Branch, Joanne F. Anderson
Tel: 416-325-6898
joanne.anderson2@ontario.ca
Director, Delivery & Agency Policy Branch, Doug MacCallum
Tel: 416-325-6594
Director, Analytics & Finance Branch, Scott Nelms
Tel: 416-212-6469
scott.nelms@ontario.ca
Director, Transmission & Distribution Policy Branch, Ken Nakahara
Tel: 416-325-6729
ken.nakahara@ontario.ca

Ontario Ministry of Environment & Climate Change

Public Information Centre, Macdonald Block, 900 Bay St., 2nd Fl., Toronto, ON M7A 1N3
Tel: 416-325-4000; *Fax:* 416-314-6713
Toll-Free: 800-565-4923
TTY: 800-515-2759
www.ontario.ca/ministry-environment-and-climate-change
Other Communication: Pollution Hotline: 1-866-MOE-TIPS (1-866-663-8477); Spills or Emergencies: 1-800-268-6060
twitter.com/EnvironmentONT
www.facebook.com/OntarioEnvironment

The Ministry is responsible for protecting clean & safe air, land & water to ensure healthy communities, ecological protection & sustainable development for present & future generations of Ontarians. Using stringent regulations, targeted enforcement & a variety of other programs & initiatives, the Ministry continues to address environmental issues that have local, regional &/or global effects. The Ministry has built a strong foundation of clear laws, regulations, standards & permits & approvals. The Ministry monitors pollution & restoration trends in an effort to determine the effectiveness of its activities & to assess risks to human health & the environment. This information is used to develop & implement environmental legislation, regulations, standards, policies, guidelines & programs to enhance environmental protection.

Minister, Hon. Glen R. Murray
Tel: 416-314-6790; *Fax:* 416-314-6748
gmurray.mpp@liberal.ola.org
Deputy Minister, Paul Evans
Tel: 416-314-6753; *Fax:* 416-314-6791
paul.evans@ontario.ca
Parliamentary Assistant, Amrit Mangat
Tel: 416-325-7188; *Fax:* 416-325-7293
amangat.mpp.co@liberal.ola.org
Acting Director, Legal Services Branch, Jay Lipman
Tel: 416-314-6525; *Fax:* 416-212-0863
jay.lipman@ontario.ca
Other Communications: Southwest Region Counsel Fax: 519-682-9539
Director, Communications Branch, Michael Maddock
Tel: 416-325-9361; *Fax:* 416-314-6711
michael.maddock@ontario.ca
Director, Ontario Internal Audit, Resources & Labour Audit Team, Ray Masse
Tel: 416-314-9208; *Fax:* 416-314-3467
ray.masse@ontario.ca
Director, Policy, Minister's Office, Iain Myrans
Tel: 416-314-6743
Iain.Myrans@ontario.ca
Director, Operations, Minister's Office, Mary Yoannidis
Tel: 416-212-7198
mary.yoannidis@ontario.ca

Associated Agencies, Boards & Commissions:

•Ontario Drinking Water Advisory Council (ODWAC)
40 St. Clair Ave. West, 3rd Fl.
Toronto, ON M4V 1M2
Tel: 416-212-7779; *Fax:* 416-212-7595
www.odwac.gov.on.ca
Also known as the Advisory Council on Drinking Water Quality & Testing Standards

•Ontario Clean Water Agency (OCWA)
1 Yonge St., 17th Fl.
Toronto, ON M5E 1E5
Tel: 416-314-5600
Toll-free: 800-667-6292
ocwa@ocwa.com
www.ocwa.com
The Ontario Clean Water Agency (OCWA) was established as a Provincial Crown Agency in November 1993 & is committed to providing safe & reliable clean water services. The Agency is an established leader in the operation, maintenance & management of water & wastewater treatment facilities & their associated distribution & collection systems. OCWA operates hundreds of water & wastewater facilities, ranging in size from small wells & pumping stations to large-scale urban water & wastewater systems.

•Pesticides Advisory Committee
135 St. Clair Ave. West, 15th Fl.
Toronto, ON M4V 1P5
Tel: 416-314-9230; *Fax:* 416-314-9237
www.opac.gov.on.ca
This committee advises the Minister of the Environment on matters pertaining to pesticides. It annually reviews the Pesticides Act & regulations, & government publications respecting pesticides & control of pests. The committee also recommends classifications for all new pesticide products prior to their marketing & use in Ontario, & publishes an annual report, which is available upon request. For other ministry publications on pests & pest control & information on pesticide licensing, contact the Standards Development Branch, Pesticides Section.

•Walkerton Clean Water Centre
20 Ontario Rd.
PO Box 160
Walkerton, ON N0G 2V0
Tel: 519-881-2003; *Fax:* 519-881-4947
Toll-free: 866-515-0550
inquiry@wcwc.ca
www.wcwc.ca
Other Communication: Bell Relay Service: 1-800-267-6511
The vision of the Walkerton Clean Water Centre is to create a world-class intitute dedicated to safe & secure drinking water for

the people of Ontario. Established by Ontario Regulation 304/04 as a crown agency of the Ministry of the Environment in October 2004, & governed by a 12-member board of directors, the Centre's work will complement & support that of the Ministry with a focus on ensuring that training, education & information is available & accessible to owners, operators & operating authorities of Ontario's drinking water systems, particularly in rural & remote communities.

Corporate Management Division
135 St. Clair Ave. West, 14th Fl., Toronto, ON M4V 1P5
Tel: 416-314-6426; *Fax:* 416-314-6425
Director, Strategic Human Resources, Jacques LeGris
Tel: 416-314-9305; *Fax:* 416-314-9313
jacques.legris@ontario.ca
Director, Business & Fiscal Planning, Kevin Perry
Tel: 416-314-7370; *Fax:* 416-314-7858
kevin.perry@ontario.ca
Director, Transition Office, Becky Taylor
Tel: 416-314-5606; *Fax:* 416-325-7962
becky.taylor@ontario.ca
Director, Information Management & Access Branch, Vacant
Tel: 416-314-3856; *Fax:* 416-314-6872
Senior Divisional Coordinator, Jennifer Borsellino
Tel: 416-212-4578
jennifer.borsellino@ontario.ca

Drinking Water Management Division
135 St. Clair Ave. West, 14th Fl., Toronto, ON M4V 1P5
Tel: 416-314-4475; *Fax:* 416-314-6935
The Drinking Water Management Division, led by the Chief Drinking Water Inspector, has lead responsibility for program & operational activities related to the protection & provision of safe drinking water in Ontario.
Assistant Deputy Minister & Chief Drinking Water Inspector, Sue Lo
Tel: 416-314-4463
sue.lo@ontario.ca
Director, Source Protection Programs Branch, Ling Mark
Tel: 416-212-6459; *Fax:* 416-212-2757
ling.mark@ontario.ca
Director, Safe Drinking Water Branch, Paul Nieweglowski
Tel: 416-314-1977; *Fax:* 416-212-7576
paul.nieweglowski@ontario.ca
Director, Drinking Water Programs Branch, Orna Salamon
Tel: 416-212-2355; *Fax:* 416-314-9477
orna.salamon@ontario.ca

Environmental Programs Division
135 St. Clair Ave. West, 14th Fl., Toronto, ON M4V 1P5
Tel: 416-326-7203; *Fax:* 416-327-8777
Assistant Deputy Minister, Jim Whitestone
Tel: 416-314-9530
jim.whitestone@ontario.ca
Director, Modernization of Approvals Project, Doris Dumais
Tel: 416-327-9466; *Fax:* 416-325-7962
doris.dumais@ontario.ca
Acting Director, Program Planning & Implementation, Jeff Hurdman
Tel: 416-327-9730; *Fax:* 416-325-8475
jeff.hurdman@ontario.ca
Director, Environmental Innovations Branch, Tom Kaszas
Tel: 416-325-8068; *Fax:* 416-314-7919
tom.kaszas@ontario.ca
Director, Aboriginal Affairs Branch, Judy Lynn Malloy
Tel: 416-327-6953; *Fax:* 416-326-8114
judy.lynn.malloy@ontario.ca

Environmental Sciences & Standards Division
135 St. Clair Ave. West, 14th Fl., Toronto, ON M4V 1P5
Fax: 416-314-6358
The Environmental Sciences & Standards Division (ESSD) provides the best available science & technology to support decisions about the natural environment, & implements those decisions by developing & managing programs & partnerships, setting scientifically credible standards, monitoring the environment & providing valuable analytical & scientific expertise. Programs such as Drive Clean, that improve the environment & increase public awareness, are central to the ministry's efforts to strengthen environmental protection.
Assistant Deputy Minister, Anne Neary
Tel: 416-314-6310
anne.neary@ontario.ca

Drive Clean Office
40 St. Clair Ave. West, 4th Fl., Toronto, ON M4V 1M2
Tel: 416-314-5856; *Fax:* 416-314-4160
www.ontario.ca/environment-and-energy/drive-clean-ontario
Director, Garth Napier
Tel: 416-314-3920
garth.napier@ontario.ca
Assistant Director/Manager, Program Design & Evaluation Section, Neera Shukla
Tel: 416-314-5862
neera.shukla@ontario.ca

Environmental Monitoring & Reporting Branch
West Wing, 125 Resources Rd., Toronto, ON M9P 3V6
Tel: 416-235-6300; *Fax:* 416-235-6235
Director, Ian Smith
Tel: 416-235-6160
ian.r.smith@ontario.ca

Laboratory Services Branch
125 Resources Rd., Toronto, ON M9P 3V6
Tel: 416-235-5743; *Fax:* 416-235-5744
Director, Joseph Odumeru
Tel: 416-235-5747
joseph.odumeru@ontario.ca

Standards Development Branch
40 St. Clair Ave. West, 7th Fl., Toronto, ON M4V 1M2
Tel: 416-327-5519; *Fax:* 416-327-2936
Director, Steve Klose
Tel: 416-327-5543
steve.klose@ontario.ca

Integrated Environmental Policy Division
77 Wellesley St. West, 11th Fl., Toronto, ON M7A 2T5
Tel: 416-314-6338; *Fax:* 416-314-6346
Integrated Environmental Planning Division is responsible for integrating the overall policy development & planning functions of the Ministry. This involves integrating & synthesizing all information, data & perspectives on the many aspects of the Ministry's mandate. The division consults extensively on developing policies, strategies & programs that support the Ministry's core business of conservation & environmental protection.
Assistant Deputy Minister, Robert Fleming
Tel: 416-314-6352
rob.fleming@ontario.ca
Director, Environmental Intergovernmental Affairs & Acting Director, Land & Water Policy, Brian Nixon
Tel: 416-212-1340; *Fax:* 416-212-3296
brian.nixon@ontario.ca
Director, Strategic Policy, John Vidan
Tel: 416-314-4157; *Fax:* 416-325-8181
john.vidan@ontario.ca
Acting Director, Air Policy & Climate Change, Karen Clark
Tel: 416-212-2747; *Fax:* 416-314-2979
karen.clark2@ontario.ca
Director, Waste Management Policy, Wendy Ren
Tel: 416-327-9743; *Fax:* 416-325-4233
wendy.ren@ontario.ca
Acting Director, Air Policy Instruments & Programs Design, Heather E. Pearson
Tel: 416-314-6419
heather.e.pearson@ontario.ca

Office of the Chief Information Officer, Land & Resources Cluster
99 Wellesley St. West, Toronto, ON M7A 1W3
Tel: 416-314-5017; *Fax:* 705-755-1599
Chief Information Officer, John DiMarco
Tel: 416-326-6954

Operations Division
135 St. Clair Ave. West, 8th Fl., Toronto, ON M4V 1P5
Tel: 416-314-6378; *Fax:* 416-314-6396
The Operations Division is the operations & program delivery arm of the ministry. It is responsible for delivering programs to protect air quality, to protect surface & ground water quality & quantity, to ensure appropriate management of wastes, to ensure an adequate quality of drinking water & to control the use of pesticides. In addition, the division is responsible for administering the ministry's approvals & licensing programs as well as an investigative & enforcement program to ensure compliance with environmental laws. The division has a province-wide network of regional, district & area offices.
Assistant Deputy Minister, Nancy Matthews
Tel: 416-314-6366
nancy.matthews@ontario.ca
Director, Environmental Approvals Branch, Agatha Garcia-Wright
Tel: 416-314-7288; *Fax:* 416-314-8452
agatha.garciawright@ontario.ca
Director, Northern Environmental Initiatives, Mary Hennessy
Tel: 416-314-7141
mary.hennessy@ontario.ca
Director/Manager, Regional Enforcement, Investigations & Enforcement Branch, Hollee Kew
Tel: 416-326-3444; *Fax:* 416-326-5256
lisa.feldman@ontario.ca
Director, Operations Integration, Jim O'Mara
Tel: 416-314-3994
james.omara@ontario.ca
Director, Environmental Approvals Access & Service Integration, Sarah Paul
Tel: 416-314-8171; *Fax:* 416-314-8452
sarah.paul@ontario.ca
Director, Sector Compliance Branch, Greg Sones
Tel: 416-314-4241; *Fax:* 416-314-4464
greg.sones@ontario.ca

Central District Offices
Toronto
Place Nouveau, 5775 Yonge St., 9th Fl., Toronto, ON M2M 4J1
Tel: 416-326-6700; *Fax:* 416-325-6345
Director, Regional Office, Dolly Goyette
Tel: 416-326-1825
dolly.goyette@ontario.ca

Eastern District Offices
Kingston
#3, 1259 Gardiners Rd., PO Box 22032 Kingston, ON K7M 8S5
Tel: 613-549-4000; *Fax:* 613-548-6908
Toll-Free: 800-267-0974
Director, Regional Office, Richard Raeburn-Gibson
Tel: 613-548-6901; *Fax:* 613-548-6911
richard.raeburngibson@ontario.ca

Northern District Offices
Thunder Bay
#331B, 435 James St. South, Thunder Bay, ON P7E 6S7
Tel: 807-475-1205; *Fax:* 807-475-1754
Toll-Free: 800-875-7772
Other Communication: District Office Phone: 807-475-1315; Alternate Fax: 807-473-3160
Director, Regional Office, John P. Taylor
Tel: 807-475-1690
john.p.taylor@ontario.ca

Southwestern District Offices
London
733 Exeter Rd., London, ON N6E 1L3
Tel: 519-873-5000; *Fax:* 519-873-5020
Toll-Free: 800-265-7672
Acting Director, Regional Office, Mili New
Tel: 519-873-5001
mili.new@ontario.ca

West Central District Offices
Hamilton
Ellen Fairclough Bldg., 119 King St. West, 9th Fl., Hamilton, ON L8P 4Y7
Tel: 905-521-7650; *Fax:* 905-521-7820
Toll-Free: 800-668-4557
Other Communication: Regional Office Phone: 905-521-7640
Director, District Office, Mili New
Tel: 905-521-7680
mili.new@ontario.ca

Environmental Commissioner of Ontario (ECO)

#605, 1075 Bay St., Toronto, ON M5S 2B1
Tel: 416-325-3377; *Fax:* 416-325-3370
Toll-Free: 800-701-6454
commissioner@eco.on.ca
www.eco.on.ca
Other Communication: Media Enquiries: 416-805-7720, media@eco.on.ca; Resource Centre: 416-325-0363
twitter.com/Ont_ECO
facebook.com/OntarioEnvironmentalCommissioner
www.youtube.com/user/EcoComms
An independent officer of the Legislative Assembly of Ontario, the Environmental Commissioner of Ontario promotes the values, goals & purposes of the Environmental Bill of Rights (EBR) to improve the quality of Ontario's natural environment. The ECO monitors & reports on the application of the EBR, provides public education to facilitate Ontario residents' participation in the EBR & reviews government accountability for environmental decision-making.
Commissioner, Dianne Saxe, Ph.D.
Deputy Commissioner, Ellen Schwartzel
Director, Operations, Tyler Schulz

Ontario Ministry of Finance

Frost Bldg. South, 7 Queen's Park Cres., 7th Fl., Toronto, ON M7A 1Y7
Fax: 866-888-3850
Toll-Free: 866-668-8297
TTY: 800-263-7776
financecommunications.fin@ontario.ca
www.fin.gov.on.ca
Other Communication: Toll-Free (French): 1-800-668-5821
Secondary Address: 33 King St. West
Oshawa OfficePO Box 627 Sta.
Oshawa, ON L1H 8H5
twitter.com/OntMinFinance
www.youtube.com/OntarioFinance

The Ministry of Finance recommends taxation, fiscal & economic policies. Other responsibilities include the management of provincial finances & the development & allocation of Ontario's budget.

Minister, Hon. Charles Sousa
Tel: 416-325-0400; *Fax:* 416-325-0374
csousa.mpp@liberal.ola.org

Associate Minister, Ontario Retirement Pension Plan, Hon. Indira Naidoo-Harris
Tel: 416-325-0400; *Fax:* 416-325-1775
inaidoo-harris.mpp.co@liberal.ola.org

Deputy Minister, Scott Thompson
Tel: 416-325-1590
scott.thompson@ontario.ca

Director, Communications Services Branch, Dianne Lone
Tel: 416-212-1440; *Fax:* 416-325-0339
dianne.lone@ontario.ca

Director, Operations, Minister's Office, Kent Emerson
Tel: 416-212-7486
kent.emerson@ontario.ca

Director, Policy, Minister's Office, Cara O'Hagan
Tel: 416-325-7333
cara.o'hagan@ontario.ca

General Counsel, Ontario Securities Commission, James D. Sinclair
Tel: 416-263-3870; *Fax:* 416-593-3662
jsinclair@osc.gov.on.ca

Associated Agencies, Boards & Commissions:

•Deposit Insurance Corporation of Ontario (DICO)
#700, 4711 Yonge St.
Toronto, ON M2N 6K8
Tel: 416-325-9444; *Fax:* 416-325-9722
Toll-free: 800-268-6653
info@dico.com
www.dico.com
The Deposit Insurance Corporation of Ontario provides deposit insurance, to the extent provided under the Credit Unions & Caisses Populaires Act, on deposits of members of credit unions & caisses populaires.

•Financial Services Commission of Ontario (FSCO)
New York City Ctr.
5160 Yonge St., 17th Fl.
PO Box 85
Toronto, ON M2N 6L9
Tel: 416-250-7250; *Fax:* 416-590-7070
Toll-free: 800-668-0128
TTY: 800-387-0584
contactcentre@fsco.gov.on.ca
www.fsco.gov.on.ca
Other Communication: Contact Centre Fax: 416-590-2040
Regulates insurance, pensions plans, credit unions, caisses populaires, mortgage brokers, cooperative corporations & loan & trust companies in Ontario. FSCO provides regulatory services that protect financial services consumers & pension plan beneficiaries & support a healthy & competitive financial services industry.

•Liquor Control Board of Ontario (LCBO)
55 Lake Shore Blvd. East
Toronto, ON M5E 1A4
Tel: 416-365-5900; *Fax:* 416-864-2476
Toll-free: 800-668-5226
infoline@lcbo.com
www.lcbo.com
The Liquor Control Board of Ontario (LCBO) is a provincial Crown corporation in Ontario, Canada established in 1927 by Lieutenant Governor William Donald Ross, on the advice of his Premier, Howard Ferguson, to sell liquor, wine, and beer through a chain of retail stores. In July 2016, the LCBO launched an online shopping platform.

•Ontario Electricity Financial Corporation (OEFC)
#1400, 1 Dundas St. West
Toronto, ON M7A 1Y7
Tel: 416-325-8000; *Fax:* 416-325-8005
www.oefc.on.ca

•Ontario Financing Authority (OFA)
#1400, 1 Dundas St. West
Toronto, ON M7A 1Y7
Tel: 416-325-8000; *Fax:* 416-204-3391
investor@ofina.on.ca
www.ofina.on.ca
Other Communication: Meetings, E-mail: irmanager@ofina.on.ca
The Ontario Financing Authority (OFA) is an agency of the Province of Ontario that manages the Province's debt and borrowing program. The OFA is governed by a Board of Directors that reports to the Minister of Finance.

•Ontario Lottery & Gaming Corporation (OLG)
Roberta Bondar Pl.
#800, 70 Foster Dr.
Sault Ste. Marie, ON P6A 6V2
Tel: 705-946-6464; *Fax:* 416-224-7000
Toll-free: 800-387-0098
TTY: 800-563-5357
www.olg.ca
Created on April 1, 2000 under the Ontario Lottery and Gaming Corporation Act, 1999, the Ontario Lottery & Gaming Corporation (OLG) is a provincial agency operating & managing province-wide lotteries, casinos & slots facilities at horse racing tracks.

•Ontario Retirement Pension Plan Administration Corporation (ORPP AC)
375 University Ave.
Toronto, ON M5G 2J5
This professional, independent organization is responsible for administering the Ontario Retirement Pension Plan.

•Ontario Securities Commission (OSC)
#1903, 20 Queen St. West
Toronto, ON M5H 3S8
Tel: 416-593-8314; *Fax:* 416-593-8122
Toll-free: 877-785-1555
TTY: 866-827-1295
inquiries@osc.gov.on.ca
www.osc.gov.on.ca
Other Communication: Public Records Phone: 416-593-3735; TTY: 1-866-827-1295; E-mail: record@osc.gov.on.ca
The mandate of the Ontario Securities Commission (OSC) is to protect investors while fostering capital formation & the efficiency & integrity of Ontario's & Canada's capital markets.
The Office of the Whistleblower was created in July 2016, making it the first paid whistleblower program by a securities regulator in Canada. Toll-Free Phone: 1-888-672-5553; URL: www.osc.gov.on.ca/en/whistleblower.htm.

Corporate & Quality Service Division
Michael Starr Bldg., 33 King St. West, 6th Fl., Toronto, ON L1H 8H5
Fax: 905-433-6688

Assistant Deputy Minister & Chief Administrative Officer, Helmut Zisser
Tel: 416-314-5158
helmut.zisser@ontario.ca

Director, Corporate Planning & Finance, Linda Gibney
Tel: 905-433-5637
linda.gibney@ontario.ca

Director, Business Services, Vacant

Financial Services Policy Division
Frost Bldg. North, 95 Grosvenor St., 4th Fl., Toronto, ON M7A 1Z1
Fax: 416-325-1187

Acting Assistant Deputy Minister, Financial Services Policy, Alvaro del Castillo
Tel: 416-325-0928
alvaro.delcastillo@ontario.ca

Acting Director, Financial Institutions Policy Branch, Maria Cece
Tel: 416-326-9086
maria.cece@ontario.ca

Acting Executive Lead, Cooperative Capital Markets Regulatory System & Securities, Colin Nickerson
Tel: 416-327-0940; *Fax:* 416-325-1187
colin.nickerson@ontario.ca

Income Security & Pension Policy Division
Frost Bldg. South, 7 Queen's Park Cres., Toronto, ON M7A 1Y7
Tel: 416-327-0133; *Fax:* 416-327-0160

Assistant Deputy Minister, Leah Myers
Tel: 416-212-5983
leah.myers@ontario.ca

Director, Income Security Policy Branch, Norman Helfand
Tel: 416-325-5722
norman.helfand@ontario.ca

Director, BPS Pensions Branch, Alex Killoch
Tel: 416-325-5724
alex.killoch@ontario.ca

Director, Pension Policy Branch, Jennifer Rook
Tel: 416-212-7535
jennifer.rook@ontario.ca

Office of Economic Policy
Frost Bldg. North, 95 Grosvenor St., 5th Fl., Toronto, ON M7A 1Z1

Assistant Deputy Minister & Chief Economist, Brian Lewis
Tel: 416-325-0850
Brian.Lewis@ontario.ca

Director, Economic Policy Branch, Ambaye Kidane
Tel: 416-325-0801; *Fax:* 416-325-0841
ambaye.kidane@ontario.ca

Director, Economic & Revenue Forecasting & Analysis, Paul D. Lewis
Tel: 416-325-0754
paul.d.lewis@ontario.ca

Director, Statistical & Quantitative Research Branch, Charles Whitfield
Tel: 416-327-0143
charles.whitfield@ontario.ca

Office of the Budget
Frost Bldg. South, 7 Queen's Park Cres., 7th Fl., Toronto, ON M7A 1Y7

Assistant Deputy Minister, Chris Giannekos
Tel: 416-325-5621
Chris.Giannekos@ontario.ca

Ontario Retirement Pension Plan Implementation Secretariat
375 University Ave., Toronto, ON M5G 2J5
Fax: 416-327-6606

Associate Deputy Minister, Mahmood Nanji
Tel: 416-326-9524

Assistant Deputy Minister, Delivery & Operations, Jennifer Brown
Tel: 416-327-2865
jennifer.brown3@ontario.ca

Provincial-Local Finance Division
College Park, 777 Bay St., 10th Fl., Toronto, ON M5G 2C8
Tel: 416-327-0264; *Fax:* 416-325-7644

Assistant Deputy Minister, Allan Doheny
Tel: 416-327-9592
allan.doheny@ontario.ca

Acting Director, Property Tax Policy, Chris Broughton
Tel: 416-314-3801; *Fax:* 416-314-3853
chris.broughton@ontario.ca

Director, Municipal Funding Policy Branch, Robert Lowry
Tel: 416-325-4056
robert.lowry@ontario.ca

Director, Assessment Policy & Legislation Branch, Diane Ross
Tel: 416-327-0266; *Fax:* 416-212-8406
diane.ross@ontario.ca

Acting Manager, Provincial Land Tax Policy Unit, Ashley McCall
Tel: 416-212-1450

Revenue Agencies Oversight Division
Frost Bldg. South, 7 Queen's Park Cres., 2nd Fl., Toronto, ON M7A 1Y7
Tel: 416-325-0400

Assistant Deputy Minister, Revenue Agencies Oversight Division, Nancy Kennedy
Tel: 416-325-2880
nancy.kennedy@ontario.ca

Director, Alcohol Policy Branch, Allison Rickaby
Tel: 416-314-4288
allison.rickaby@ontario.ca

Director, Gaming Policy Branch, Elizabeth Yeigh
Tel: 416-212-7401
elizabeth.yeigh@ontario.ca

Tax & Benefits Administration
Michael Starr Bldg., 33 King St. West, PO Box 623 Oshawa, ON L1H 8H5
Toll-Free: 866-668-8297

Acting Associate Deputy Minister, Agatha Garcia-Wright
Tel: 905-433-2292
Agatha.Garcia-Wright@ontario.ca

Strategy, Stewardship & Program Policy Division
Fax: 905-433-6686

Assistant Deputy Minister, Maria Mavroyannis
Tel: 416-325-7830
maria.mavroyannis@ontario.ca

Director, Benefits Transformation Branch, Mashood Mirza
Tel: 905-436-4519
mashood.mirza@ontario.ca

Director, Strategy, Stewardship & Risk Management, Kevin O'Grady
Tel: 905-433-4942
kevin.ogrady@ontario.ca

Acting Director, Program Policy & Analytics Branch, Paul Devnich

Tel: 905-433-6992
paul.devnich@ontario.ca

Tax Compliance & Benefits Division
Toll-Free: 866-668-8297
Assistant Deputy Minister, Agatha Garcia-Wright
Tel: 905-433-5275
Agatha.Garcia-Wright@ontario.ca
Director, Objections, Appeals & Services Branch, Victoria Chiodi
Tel: 905-435-2040; *Fax:* 905-435-2000
victoria.chiodi@ontario.ca
Director, Account Management & Collections Branch, Maureen Kelly
Tel: 905-433-5640
maureen.e.kelly@ontario.ca

Taxation Policy Division
7 Queen's Park Cres., Toronto, ON M7A 1Y7
Tel: 416-314-0700
Assistant Deputy Minister, Sriram Subrahmanyan
Tel: 416-327-7294
sriram.subrahmanyan@ontario.ca
Director, Corporate & Commodity Taxation Branch, Ann Langleben
Tel: 416-327-0222
ann.langleben@ontario.ca
Director, Personal Tax Policy & Design Branch, Kostas Plainos
Tel: 416-327-0246
kostas.plainos@ontario.ca

Office of Francophone Affairs

#200, 700 Bay St., 2nd Fl., Toronto, ON M7A 0A2
Tel: 416-325-4949; *Fax:* 416-325-4980
Toll-Free: 800-268-7507
TTY: 416-325-0017
ofa@ontario.ca
www.ontario.ca/page/office-francophone-affairs

A central agency that assists the Government of Ontario in its delivery of services in French, & in the development of policies & programs that meet the needs of the province's francophones.

Minister Responsible, Hon. Marie-France Lalonde
Tel: 416-327-8300; *Fax:* 416-326-1947
mflalonde.mpp.co@liberal.ola.org
Deputy Minister, Marie-Lison Fougère
Tel: 416-212-2320; *Fax:* 416-212-2459
marie-lison.fougere@ontario.ca
Assistant Deputy Minister, Kelly Burke
Tel: 416-325-4936
kelly.burke@ontario.ca
Director, Strategic Communications, Charles Jean Sucsan
Tel: 416-325-4968
charlesjean.sucsan@ontario.ca

Ontario Ministry of Government & Consumer Services

Mowat Block, 900 Bay St., 6th Fl., Toronto, ON M7A 1L2
Tel: 416-212-2665
Toll-Free: 844-286-8404
TTY: 416-915-0001
www.ontario.ca/ministry-government-services
Other Communication: Consumer Protection Branch Phone: 416-326-8800; Fax: 416-326-8665; TTY: 416-229-6086; E-mail: consumer@ontario.ca
twitter.com/ontarioconsumer
www.facebook.com/ontarioconsumer

The Ministry seeks to educate, protect & serve consumers in Ontario by maintaining a fair, safe & informed marketplace; providing modern information services; & regulating practices that serve the interests of Ontarians. In 2014 the existing Ministry of Consumer Services was combined with Government Services, bringing the two mandates together. That includes responsibility for the delivery of government services, the government workforce, procurement & technology resources. The Ministry is engaged in the following main activities: providing government information to individuals & businesses, including distribution through Publications Ontario; protecting consumers through information about frauds & scams & mediating complaints about businesses; & issuing birth, death & marriage certificates, & managing Land Registry Offices throughout the province.

Minister, Hon. Marie-France Lalonde
Tel: 416-327-8300; *Fax:* 416-326-1947
mflalonde.mpp.co@liberal.ola.org
Deputy Minister, Angela Coke
Tel: 416-314-1957
angela.coke@ontario.ca
Acting Director, Integration Project Office, Debbie Farr
Tel: 416-212-2985
debbie.farr@ontario.ca
Director, Communications Branch, Laurie Menard
Tel: 416-327-4995
laurie.menard@ontario.ca
Director, Legal Services Branch, Fateh Salim
Tel: 416-314-7022; *Fax:* 416-326-8456
fateh.salim@ontario.ca
Advisor, Communications, Minister's Office, Lauren Souch
Tel: 416-212-3721; *Fax:* 416-326-1947
Lauren.Souch@ontario.ca
Director, Government & Consumer Services Audit Service Team, Allyson McKeever
Tel: 416-314-9501
allyson.mckeever@ontario.ca

Associated Agencies, Boards & Commissions:

•Advertising Review Board
Macdonald Block
#M2-56, 900 Bay St., 2nd Fl.
Toronto, ON M7A 1N3
Tel: 416-327-2183; *Fax:* 416-327-2179

•Ontario Film Review Board (OFRB)
#101B, 4950 Yonge St.
Toronto, ON M1N 6K1
Tel: 416-314-3626; *Fax:* 416-314-3632
Toll-free: 800-268-6024
www.ofrb.gov.on.ca

Consumer Services Operations Division
5775 Yonge St., 15th Fl., Toronto, ON M7A 2E5
Tel: 416-326-8800; *Fax:* 416-327-8461
Assistant Deputy Minister, Renu Kulendran
Tel: 416-325-5976
renu.kulendran@ontario.ca
Director, Licensing, Inspections & Investigations Branch, Barbara Duckitt
Tel: 416-326-8598
barbara.duckitt@ontario.ca

Corporate Services Division
College Park, 777 Bay St., 15th Fl., Toronto, ON M7A 2J3
Assistant Deputy Minister & Chief Administrative Officer, Clare McMillan
Tel: 416-326-1895
clare.mcmillan@ontario.ca
Acting Director, Strategic Human Resources Branch, Diane MacNeill
Tel: 416-327-3874
diane.macneill@ontario.ca
Director, Organizational Development Branch, Trevor Sparrow
Tel: 416-326-7156
trevor.sparrow@ontario.ca
Acting Director, Revenue Management Branch, Debbie Strauss
Tel: 416-314-0803; *Fax:* 416-314-5111
debbie.strauss@ontario.ca
Director, Corporate Financial Services Branch, Beverley Thomas-Barnes
Tel: 416-326-0211
beverley.thomas-barnes@ontario.ca

Government Services Integration Cluster
Tel: 416-246-7171; *Fax:* 416-326-9424
Chief Information Officer, Robert Devries
Tel: 416-327-2561
robert.devries@ontario.ca
Head, Contact Centre Modernization, Franca Aquila
Tel: 416-326-1286
Franca.Aquila@ontario.ca
Director, Integrated Business Services, Susan McIntosh
Tel: 416-327-7867
susan.mcintosh@ontario.ca

Information, Privacy & Archives Division
134 Ian Macdonald Blvd., Toronto, ON M7A 2C5
Tel: 416-327-1600; *Fax:* 416-327-1999
Toll-Free: 800-668-9933
www.archives.gov.on.ca
Other Communication: Circulation Desk: 416-327-1016; Main Reading Room: 416-327-1582
twitter.com/ArchivesOntario
www.youtube.com/ArchivesOfOntario
Chief Privacy Officer & Archivist of Ontario, John Roberts
Tel: 416-327-1603; *Fax:* 416-327-1992
john.roberts@ontario.ca
Director, Archives Management & Information Storage, Mary Anne Courtney
Tel: 416-327-1577; *Fax:* 416-327-1999
maryanne.courtney@ontario.ca
Acting Director, Policy & Planning, Violeta Quintanilla-Webb
Tel: 416-327-1467; *Fax:* 416-327-1999
violeta.quintanilla-webb@ontario.ca

Ontario Shared Services
222 Jarvis St., 7th Fl., Toronto, ON M7A 0B6
Tel: 416-326-9300
Toll-Free: 866-979-9300
Associate Deputy Minister, Kevin French
Tel: 416-325-5065
kevin.french@ontario.ca
Director, Strategy & Resource Management, Jackie Korecki
Tel: 416-314-4324; *Fax:* 416-327-4246
jackie.korecki@ontario.ca

Enterprise Business Services Division
222 Jarvis St., 8th Fl., Toronto, ON M7A 0B6
Tel: 416-326-9300
Assistant Deputy Minister, Glen Medeiros
Tel: 416-212-6569
glen.medeiros@ontario.ca
Acting Director, Customer Relationship Management Branch, Jim Barclay
Tel: 416-314-2229
Jim.Barclay@ontario.ca
Acting Director, Risk Management & Insurance Services Branch, Jim Kalpakis
Tel: 416-314-3439
jim.kalpakis@ontario.ca
Acting Director, Business Development & Services Branch, Nelson Janicas
Tel: 416-212-6852
nelson.janicas@ontario.ca
Acting Director, Forms Print & Distribution Services Branch, Nella Puntillo
Tel: 416-314-3656
nella.puntillo@ontario.ca

Enterprise Financial Services & Systems
222 Jarvis St., 9th Fl., Toronto, ON M7A 0B6
Tel: 416-326-4400
Toll-Free: 866-979-9300
Other Communication: OSS Contact Centre (GTA), Phone: 416-326-9300
Assistant Deputy Minister & Chief Information Officer, David W. Clifford
Tel: 416-327-2022
david.clifford@ontario.ca
Acting Director, Operations & Transformation Support Branch, Alex Goncharenko
Tel: 416-325-6424
alex.goncharenko@ontario.ca
Director, Financial Processing Operations Branch, Ken Sheldon
Tel: 705-494-3104
ken.sheldon@ontario.ca
Director, Client Services Management Branch, Mano Sharma
Tel: 416-325-5782
mano.sharma@ontario.ca
Director, Business & Divisional Support Services Branch, Lillian Duda
Tel: 416-326-0124
lillian.duda@ontario.ca
Director, Business Application Solutions Support Branch, Robert Tee
Tel: 416-325-9477
robert.tee@ontario.ca

HR Service Delivery Division
#3440, 99 Wellesley St., Toronto, ON M7A 1W3
Tel: 416-325-4789
Assistant Deputy Minister, Donna Holmes
Tel: 416-325-7612
Director, HR Program Management Branch, Stephen Brown
Tel: 416-212-7592
stephen.brown1@ontario.ca
Director, Transformation Consulting Services Branch, Mike Tedesco
Tel: 416-326-5620
mike.tedesco@ontario.ca
Acting Director, Centre for Employee Health, Safety & Wellness, Stephen Boyd
Tel: 705-755-5680
steve.boyd@ontario.ca
Acting Director, Job Evaluation Initiatives, Angela Sullivan
Tel: 416-327-8308
angela.sullivan@ontario.ca

Pay & Benefits Services Division
222 Jarvis St., 7th Fl., Toronto, ON M7A 0B6
Tel: 416-326-9300; *Fax:* 416-325-1165
Assistant Deputy Minister, Kristen Delorme
Tel: 416-212-6731; *Fax:* 416-327-4246
kristen.delorme@ontario.ca
Director, Pay & Benefits Support Branch, Hatem Belhi
Tel: 416-212-2402; *Fax:* 416-212-2916
hatem.belhi@ontario.ca
Director, Pay & Benefits Business Solutions Branch, George Karlos
Tel: 416-212-2933
george.karlos@ontario.ca
Director, Pay & Benefits Operations Branch, Rob Gagne
Tel: 705-494-3176; *Fax:* 705-494-3141
rob.gagne@ontario.ca

Supply Chain Ontario
222 Jarvis St., 8th Fl., Toronto, ON M7A 0B6
Fax: 416-327-3573
Develops & implements an integrated corporate procurement strategy to: leverage & optimize government procurement of goods & services; identify and implement procurement process improvements; enhance procurement controllership; provide strategic advice on large scale procurements; develop innovative policy frameworks to support service delivery through third party service providers.
Assistant Deputy Minister, Marian Macdonald
Tel: 416-327-7508
marian.macdonald@ontario.ca
Director, Program & Policy Enablement Branch, Susan Hoyle-Howieson
Tel: 416-327-8765
susan.hoyle-howieson@ontario.ca
Director, BPS Supply Chain Program Branch, Christopher Gonsalves
Tel: 416-314-1919
christopher.gonsalves@ontario.ca
Director, Enterprise Procurement Branch, Wes Lapish
Tel: 416-327-3518
wes.lapish@ontario.ca
Acting Director, Strategic Procurement Services Branch, Jim Hadjiyianni
Tel: 416-212-1055
jim.hadjiyianni@ontario.ca
Director, Continuous Improvement & Strategic Planning Branch, Ben Sopel
Tel: 416-325-7553; *Fax:* 416-327-3573
ben.sopel@ontario.ca

Ontario Public Service Diversity Office
375 University Ave., 5th Fl., Toronto, ON M5G 2J5
Tel: 416-325-2114; *Fax:* 416-326-8461
TTY: 416-327-1459
Acting Chief Officer, Diversity & Accessibility, Yvonne Defoe
Tel: 416-314-6989
yvonne.defoe@ontario.ca
Acting Director, Inclusion Transformation, Rae Williams
Tel: 416-325-9012
rae.williams@ontario.ca
Acting Director, Inclusion Program Design & Delivery Branch, Debbie Burke-Benn
Tel: 416-325-2925
debbie.burke-benn@ontario.ca
Acting Director, Accessibility Program Design & Delivery Branch, Debbie Strauss
Tel: 416-212-6279
debbie.strauss@ontario.ca

Policy, Planning & Oversight Division
College Park, 777 Bay St., 5th Fl., Toronto, ON M7A 2J3
Fax: 416-325-6192
Assistant Deputy Minister, Frank Denton
Tel: 416-326-2826
frank.denton@ontario.ca
Director, Consumer Policy & Liaison, Glen Padassery
Tel: 416-326-8868; *Fax:* 416-326-8885
glen.padassery@ontario.ca
Actor Director, Public Safety, Elizabeth Kay-Zorowski
Tel: 416-326-8877; *Fax:* 416-326-8885
elizabeth.kay-zorowski@ontario.ca

ServiceOntario
College Park, 777 Bay St., 15th fl., Toronto, ON M7A 2J3
Fax: 416-326-1313
Toll-Free: 800-267-8097
TTY: 800-268-7095
www.ontario.ca/welcome-serviceontario
twitter.com/serviceontario
www.facebook.com/ServiceOntario
www.youtube.com/user/serviceontario
Associate Deputy Minister & Chief Executive Officer, David Denault
Tel: 416-314-3709
david.denault@ontario.ca

Business Development Division
Fax: 416-326-1313
Assistant Deputy Minister, David Ward
Tel: 416-325-8804
david.ward@ontario.ca
Director, Partnerships & Business Development Branch, Steve Burnett
Tel: 416-325-8783
steve.burnett@ontario.ca
Director, Strategic Planning & Policy Branch, Rakhi Lad
Tel: 416-314-1201
rakhi.lad@ontario.ca
Acting Director, Digital Planning Branch, Lisa Vescio
Tel: 416-212-1976
lisa.vescio@ontario.ca
Director, Regulatory Services Branch, Bill Snell
Tel: 416-314-4886; *Fax:* 905-372-4758
bill.snell@ontario.ca
Other Communications: Alternate Faxes: 519-675-7771; 705-564-4354

Business Improvement Division
Assistant Deputy Minister, Bev Hawton
Tel: 416-326-6062
bev.hawton@ontario.ca
Director, Business Effectiveness Branch, Chris McAlpine
Tel: 416-326-1717; *Fax:* 416-326-3392
chris.mcalpine@ontario.ca
Other Communications: Thunder Bay, Fax: 807-343-7360
Director, Citizen Services Transformation, Asim Hussain
Tel: 416-326-4897
asim.hussain@ontario.ca
Director, Business Services Transformation Branch, Mario Tarsitano
Tel: 416-326-8573
mario.tarsitano@ontario.ca

Central Services Division
Fax: 416-326-5550
Acting Assistant Deputy Minister, Robert Mathew
Tel: 416-325-2857
robert.mathew@ontario.ca
Branch Coordinator, Logistics Services Branch, Vacant
Director, Central Production & Verification Services Branch, Robert Mathew
Tel: 416-314-4879
robert.mathew@ontario.ca
Director, Thunder Bay Production & Verification Services Branch, Alexandra Schmidt
Tel: 807-343-7408
alexandra.schmidt@ontario.ca
Director, Kingston Production & Verification Services Branch, Karen Harry
Tel: 613-545-4631
Karen.Harry@ontario.ca

Customer Care Division
Assistant Deputy Minister, Helga Iliadis
Tel: 416-326-2784; *Fax:* 416-326-1313
helga.iliadis@ontario.ca
Acting Director, Eastern Contact Centre Services Branch, Christina Snider
Tel: 613-547-8344
christina.snider@ontario.ca
Director, Central Region Contact Centre Services Branch, Mary Ben Hamoud
Tel: 416-212-5377
mary.benhamoud@ontario.ca
Director, Private Service Providers Branch, Vacant
Acting Director, East Retail Offices Branch, Christine Levin
Tel: 613-548-6767 ext: 355; *Fax:* 705-755-5249
christine.levin@ontario.ca
Director, North Retail Offices Branch, Louise R. Larocque
Tel: 705-564-4485; *Fax:* 705-564-7372
louise.larocque@ontario.ca
Director, West Retail Offices Branch, Tara Meagher
Tel: 519-826-4531; *Fax:* 519-826-6363
tara.meagher@ontario.ca
Acting Director, Central Retail Offices Branch, Nadine Rhodd
Tel: 416-294-4424
nadine.rhodd@ontario.ca

Land Registrars

Algoma
420 Queen St. East, Sault Ste Marie, ON P6A 1Z7
Tel: 705-253-8887; *Fax:* 705-253-9245

Brant
Court House, 80 Wellington St., Brantford, ON N3T 2L9
Tel: 519-752-8321; *Fax:* 519-752-0273

Bruce
203 Cayley St., PO Box 1690 Walkerton, ON N0G 2V0
Tel: 519-881-2259; *Fax:* 519-881-2322

Cochrane
143 - 4th Ave., PO Box 580 Cochrane, ON P0L 1C0
Tel: 705-272-5791; *Fax:* 705-272-2951

Dufferin
#7, 41 Briadway Ave., Orangeville, ON L9W 1J7
Tel: 519-941-1481; *Fax:* 519-941-6444

Dundas
8 - 5th St. West, PO Box 645 Morrisburg, ON K0C 1X0
Tel: 613-543-2583; *Fax:* 613-543-4541

Durham
590 Rossland Rd. East, Whitby, ON L1N 9G5
Tel: 416-665-4007; *Fax:* 416-665-5247

Elgin
#36, 1010 Talbot St., St Thomas, ON N5P 4N2
Tel: 519-631-3015; *Fax:* 519-631-8182

Essex
#100, 949 McDougall St., Windsor, ON N9A 1L9
Tel: 519-971-9980; *Fax:* 519-971-9937

Frontenac
1201 Division St., Kingston, ON K7K 6X4
Tel: 613-548-6767; *Fax:* 613-548-6766

Glengarry
101 Main St. North, PO Box 668 Alexandria, ON K0C 1A0
Tel: 613-525-1315; *Fax:* 613-525-0509

Grenville
499 Centre St., PO Box 1660 Prescott, ON K0E 1T0
Tel: 613-925-3177; *Fax:* 613-925-0302

Grey
East Court Plaza, #1-2, 1555 - 16th St. East, Owen Sound, ON N4K 5N3
Tel: 519-376-1637; *Fax:* 519-376-1639

Haldimand
10 Echo St. West, PO Box 310 Cayuga, ON N0A 1E0
Tel: 905-772-3531; *Fax:* 905-772-0105

Haliburton
12 Newcastle St., PO Box 270 Minden, ON K0M 2K0
Tel: 705-286-1391; *Fax:* 705-286-4324

Halton
2800 Highpoint Dr., 2nd Fl., Milton, ON L9T 6P4
Tel: 905-864-3500; *Fax:* 905-864-3549

Hastings
Cenutry Place, #109, 199 Front St., Belleville, ON K8N 5H5
Tel: 613-968-4597; *Fax:* 613-968-3606

Huron
38 North St., Goderich, ON N7A 2T4
Tel: 519-524-9562; *Fax:* 519-524-2482

Kenora
220 Main St. South, Kenora, ON P9N 1T2
Tel: 807-468-2794; *Fax:* 807-468-2796

Kent
40 William St. North, Chatham, ON N7M 4L2
Tel: 519-352-5520; *Fax:* 519-352-3222

Lambton
#102, 700 Christina St. North, Sarnia, ON N7V 3C2
Tel: 519-337-2393; *Fax:* 519-337-8371

Lanark
2 Industrial Dr., PO Box 1180 Almonte, ON K0A 1A0
Tel: 613-256-1577; *Fax:* 613-256-0940

Leeds
7 King St. West, Brockville, ON K6V 3P7
Tel: 613-345-5751; *Fax:* 613-345-7390

Lennox
#2, 7 Snow Rd., Napanee, ON K7R 0A2
Tel: 613-354-3751; *Fax:* 613-354-1474

Manitoulin
Courthouse, 27 Phipps St., PO Box 619 Gore Bay, ON P0P 1H0
Tel: 705-282-2442; *Fax:* 705-282-2131

Middlesex
100 Dundas St., Ground Fl., London, ON N6A 5B6
Tel: 519-675-7600; *Fax:* 519-675-7611

Muskoka
15 Dominion St., Bracebridge, ON P1L 2E7
Tel: 705-645-4415; *Fax:* 705-645-7826

Niagara North & South
59 Church St., St. Catharines, ON L2R 3C3
Tel: 905-684-6351; *Fax:* 905-684-5874

Nipissing
360 Plouffe St., North Bay, ON P1B 9L5
Tel: 705-474-2270; *Fax:* 705-495-8511

Norfolk
Court House, #201, 50 Frederick Hobson VC Dr., Simcoe, ON N3Y 4K8
Tel: 519-426-2216; *Fax:* 519-426-9627

Northumberland
#105, 1005 Elgin St. West, Cobourg, ON K9A 5J4
Tel: 905-372-3813; *Fax:* 905-372-4758

Ottawa-Carleton
Court House, 161 Elgin St., 4th Fl., Ottawa, ON K2P 2K1
Tel: 613-239-1230; *Fax:* 613-239-1422

Oxford
480 Peel St., Woodstock, ON N4S 1K2
Tel: 519-537-6287; *Fax:* 519-537-3107

Parry Sound
28 Miller St., Parry Sound, ON P2A 1T1
Tel: 705-746-5816; *Fax:* 705-746-6517

Peel
1 Gateway Blvd., Brampton, ON L6T 0G3
Tel: 905-874-4008; *Fax:* 905-874-4012

Perth
5 Huron St., Stratford, ON N5A 5S4
Tel: 519-271-3343; *Fax:* 519-271-2550

Peterborough
North Tower, 300 Water St., 1st Fl., PO Box 7000 Peterborough, ON K9J 8M5
Tel: 705-755-1342; *Fax:* 705-755-1343

Prescott
179 Main St. East, Hawkesbury, ON K6A 1A1
Tel: 613-636-0314; *Fax:* 613-636-0772

Prince Edward
1 Pitt St., PO Box 1310 Picton, ON K0K 2T0
Tel: 613-476-3219; *Fax:* 613-476-7908

Rainy River
353 Church St., Fort Frances, ON P9A 1C9
Tel: 807-274-5451; *Fax:* 807-274-1704

Renfrew
400 Pembroke St. East, Pembroke, ON K8A 3K8
Tel: 613-732-8331; *Fax:* 613-732-0297

Russell
#3, 717 Notre Dame St., Embrun, ON K0A 1W1
Tel: 613-443-7852; *Fax:* 613-443-2377

Simcoe
Court House, 114 Worsley St., Barrie, ON L4M 1M1
Tel: 705-725-7232; *Fax:* 705-725-7246

Stormont
#2, 720 - 14th St. West, Cornwall, ON K6J 5T9
Tel: 613-932-4522; *Fax:* 613-932-4524

Sudbury
#300, 199 Larch St., Sudbury, ON P3E 5P9
Tel: 705-675-4300; *Fax:* 705-675-4148

Thunder Bay
#201, 189 Red River Rd., Thunder Bay, ON P7B 1A2
Tel: 807-343-7436; *Fax:* 807-343-7439

Timiskaming
375 Main St., PO Box 159 Haileybury, ON P0J 1K0
Tel: 705-672-3332; *Fax:* 705-672-3906

Toronto
Atrium on Bay, #420, 20 Dundas St. West, PO Box 117 Toronto, ON M5G 2C2
Tel: 416-314-4430; *Fax:* 416-314-4435

Victoria
322 Kent St. West, Lindsay, ON K9V 4T7
Tel: 705-324-4912; *Fax:* 705-324-6290

Waterloo
30 Duke St. West, 2nd Fl., Kitchener, ON N2H 3W5
Tel: 519-571-6043; *Fax:* 519-571-6067

Wellington
1 Stone Rd. West, Guelph, ON N1G 4Y2
Tel: 519-826-3372; *Fax:* 519-826-3373

Wentworth
119 King St. West, 4th Fl., Hamilton, ON L8P 4Y7
Tel: 905-521-7561; *Fax:* 905-521-7505

York Region
50 Bloomington Rd. West, 3rd Fl., Aurora, ON L4G 0L8
Tel: 905-713-7798; *Fax:* 905-713-7799

Ontario Ministry of Health & Long-Term Care

Hepburn Block, 80 Grosvenor St., 10th Fl, Toronto, ON M7A 2C4
Tel: 416-327-4327
Toll-Free: 800-268-1153
TTY: 800-387-5559
www.health.gov.on.ca
twitter.com/ONThealth
www.facebook.com/217753654940869
www.youtube.com/user/ontariomohltc

The Ministry is responsible for administering the health care system & providing services to the Ontario public through such programs as health insurance, drug benefits, assistive devices, care for the mentally ill, long-term care, home care, community & public health, & health promotion & disease prevention. It also regulates hospitals & nursing homes, operates psychiatric hospitals & medical laboratories, & co-ordinates emergency health services.

Minister, Hon. Dr. Eric Hoskins
Tel: 416-327-4300; *Fax:* 416-326-1571
ehoskins.mpp@liberal.ola.org

Deputy Minister, Dr. Bob Bell
Tel: 416-327-4496; *Fax:* 416-326-1570
bob.bell@ontario.ca

Parliamentary Assistant (Health), John Fraser
Tel: 416-327-0205; *Fax:* 416-325-3862
jfraser.mpp.co@liberal.ola.org

Associate Deputy Minister, Policy & Transformation, Sharon Lee Smith
Tel: 416-212-4030
sharonlee.smith@ontario.ca

Associate Deputy Minister, Health System DSelivery & Implementation, Susan Fitzpatrick
Tel: 416-326-0232; *Fax:* 416-327-5186
susan.fitzpatrick@ontario.ca

Assistant Deputy Minister, Communications & Marketing, Jean-Claude Camus
Tel: 416-327-4352
jean-claude.camus@ontario.ca

Chief Health Innovation Strategist, William Charnetski
Tel: 416-326-2121
William.Charnetski@ontario.ca

Director, Health Quality Branch, L. Miin Alikhan
Tel: 416-325-2658; *Fax:* 416-327-5186
Miin.Alikhan@ontario.ca

Director, Stakeholder Relations, Derrick Araneda
Tel: 416-212-3763

Director, Legal Services Branch, Janice B. Crawford
Tel: 416-327-8565; *Fax:* 416-327-8605
janice.b.crawford@ontario.ca

Director, Policy & Delivery, Deputy Minister's Office, Patrick Dicerni
Tel: 416-325-7999; *Fax:* 416-326-1570
Patrick.Dicerni@ontario.ca

Director, Transformation Secretariat, Martha Greenberg
Tel: 416-327-7615
martha.greenberg@ontario.ca

Director, Health Capital Investment Branch, Peter Kaftarian
Tel: 416-314-0402
Peter.Kaftarian@ontario.ca

Director, Policy, Minister's Office, Jacob Mksyartinian
Tel: 416-327-4329
jacob.mksyartinian@ontario.ca

Acting Director, Health System Funding Policy, Brian Pollard
Tel: 416-314-0036
brian.pollard@ontario.ca

Director, Strategic Planning & Integrated Marketing Branch, Naomi Rose
Tel: 416-326-3912
naomi.rose@ontario.ca

Associated Agencies, Boards & Commissions:

•Cancer Care Ontario (CCO)
620 University Ave., 15th Fl.
Toronto, ON M5G 2L7
Tel: 416-971-9800; *Fax:* 416-971-6888
TTY: 416-217-1815
www.cancercare.on.ca

•Chiropody Review Committee
#2102, 180 Dundas St. West
Toronto, ON M5G 1Z8
Tel: 416-542-1333; *Fax:* 416-542-1666
Toll-free: 877-232-7653
A committee of the College of Chiropodists of Ontario that reviews accounts of podiatrists referred to it by the General Manager of the Ontario Health Insurance Plan.

•Consent & Capacity Board (CCB)
151 Bloor St. West, 10th Fl.
Toronto, ON M5S 2T5
Tel: 416-327-4142; *Fax:* 416-924-8873
Toll-free: 866-777-7391
TTY: 877-301-0889
ccb@ontario.ca
www.ccboard.on.ca
Other Communication: Toll-Free Fax: 1-866-777-7273
Hears appeals relating to involuntary placement in a psychiatric facility, capacity to make personal care & financial decisions & access to personal records from a psychiatric facility.

•Dentistry Review Committee
350 Rumsey Rd.
Toronto, ON M4G 1R8
Tel: 416-961-6555
A committee of the Royal College of Dental Surgeons that reviews accounts of dentists referred to it by the General Manager of the Ontario Health Insurance Plan.

•eHealth Ontario
College Park
#701, 777 Bay St.
PO Box 148
Toronto, ON M5G 2C8
Tel: 416-586-6500; *Fax:* 416-586-4363
Toll-free: 888-411-7742
TTY: 855-645-3390
info@ehealthontario.on.ca
www.ehealthontario.on.ca
Other Communication: Privacy Office, Phone: 416-946-4767; E-mail: privacy@ehealthontario.on.ca

•Health Boards Secretariat
151 Bloor St. West, 9th Fl.
Toronto, ON M5S 2T5
Tel: 416-327-8512; *Fax:* 416-327-8524
Toll-free: 866-282-2179

•HealthForceOntario
163 Queen St. East
Toronto, ON M5A 1S1
Tel: 416-862-2200
Toll-free: 800-596-4046
TTY: 416-862-4817
opportunity@healthforceontario.ca
www.healthforceontario.ca
Other Communication: International Toll-Free: 1-800-596-4046, ext. 4
HealthForceOntario seeks to identify & address the province's health human resource needs on behalf of the Ministry of Health & Long-Term Care, & the Ministry of Training, Colleges & Universities.

•Health Quality Ontario (HQO)
#702, 130 Bloor St. West
Toronto, ON M5S 1N5
Tel: 416-323-6868; *Fax:* 416-323-9261
Toll-free: 866-623-6868
info@hqontario.ca
www.hqontario.ca

•Medical Eligibility Committee (MEC)
370 Select Dr.
PO Box 168
Kingston, ON K7M 8T4
Tel: 613-536-3058
Deals with the eligibility of insured services as well as other matters assigned to it by the act or the regulation or by the minister; makes recommendations to the general manager with respect to these decisions.

•Ontario Mental Health Foundation (OMHF)
180 Bloor St. West, #UC 101
Toronto, ON M5S 2V6
Tel: 416-920-7721; *Fax:* 416-920-0026
grants@omhf.on.ca
www.omhf.on.ca

•Ontario Review Board (ORB)
151 Bloor St. West, 10th Fl.
Toronto, ON M5S 2T5
Tel: 416-327-8866; *Fax:* 416-327-8867
TTY: 877-301-0889
orb@ontario.ca
www.orb.on.ca

•Optometry Review Committee
6 Crescent Rd, 3rd Fl.
Toronto, ON M4W 1T1
Tel: 416-962-4071
A committee of the College of Optometrists of Ontario that reviews accounts of optometrists referred to it by the General Manager of the Ontario Health Insurance Plan.

•Public Health Ontario (PHO)
#300, 480 University Ave.
Toronto, ON M5G 1V2
Tel: 647-260-7100; *Fax:* 647-260-7600
Toll-free: 877-543-8931
info@oahpp.ca
www.publichealthontario.ca

•Trillium Gift of Life Network
#900, 522 University Ave.
Toronto, ON M5G 1W7
Tel: 416-363-4001; *Fax:* 416-363-4002
Toll-free: 800-263-2833
www.giftoflife.on.ca
Other Communication: Healthcare Professionals Organ & Tissue Referral: 416-363-4438; Toll-Free: 1-877-363-8456

Chief Medical Officer of Health

Hepburn Block, 80 Grosvenor St., 11th Fl., Toronto, ON M7A 1R3
Tel: 416-212-3831; *Fax:* 416-325-8412
health.gov.on.ca/en/common/ministry/cmoh.aspx

Chief Medical Officer of Health; Associate Chief Medical Officer of Health, Infrastructure & System (Transition), Dr. Robin Williams
Tel: 416-325-7672
dr.robin.williams@ontario.ca
Associate Chief Medical Officer of Health, Environmental Health, Vacant
Associate Chief Medical Officer of Health, Health Promotion, Chronic Diseases & Injury Prevention, Vacant
Associate Chief Medical Officer of Health, Health Protection & Prevention, Vacant
Executive Director, Public Health Division, Roselle Martino
Tel: 416-327-9555; *Fax:* 416-325-8412
roselle.martino@ontario.ca
Director, Public Health Policy & Programs, Nina Arron
Tel: 416-212-4873
nina.arron@ontario.ca
Acting Director, Public Health Standards, Practice & Accountability, Paulina Salamo
Tel: 416-327-7423
paulina.salamo@ontario.ca
Acting Director, Emergency Management, Clint Shingler
Tel: 416-327-8865
clint.shingler@ontario.ca
Director, Public Health Planning & Liaison, Elizabeth S. Walker
Tel: 416-212-6359
elizabeth.walker@ontario.ca

Corporate Services Division
Hepburn Block, 80 Grosvenor St., 11th Fl., Toronto, ON M7A 1R3
Tel: 416-327-4266; *Fax:* 416-314-5915
Assistant Deputy Minister & Chief Administrative Officer, Mike Weir
Tel: 416-327-4266
mike.weir@ontario.ca
Director, Accounting Policy & Financial Reporting, Charles Brown
Tel: 416-327-7350; *Fax:* 416-327-7364
charles.brown@ontario.ca
Director, HR Strategic Business Unit, Kristen Delorme
Tel: 416-327-8747; *Fax:* 416-327-7580
kristen.delorme@ontario.ca
Director, Financial Management, Pier Faltico
Tel: 416-212-0723; *Fax:* 416-212-0683
pier.falotico@ontario.ca
Director, Supply Chain & Facilities Branch, Shelley Gibson
Tel: 416-327-0782; *Fax:* 416-327-7312
shelley.gibson@ontario.ca
Director, Health Audit Service Team, Charles Meehan
Tel: 416-327-7786; *Fax:* 416-327-7809
charles.meehan@ontario.ca
Acting Director, Fiscal Oversight & Performance, Eva Roszuk
Tel: 416-327-8674; *Fax:* 416-325-9017
eva.roszuk@ontario.ca
Director, Corporate Management Branch, Michele Sanborn
Tel: 416-326-5725; *Fax:* 416-327-2714
michele.sanborn@ontario.ca
Director, Ministry Project Management & Process Improvement Office, Simon Trevarthen
Tel: 416-327-2299
simon.trevarthen@ontario.ca

Direct Services Division
56 Wellesley St. West, 2nd Fl., Toronto, ON M5S 2S3
Fax: 416-212-9710
Assistant Deputy Minister, Patricia Li
Tel: 416-327-4845
patricia.li@ontario.ca
Director, Psychiatric Patient Advocate Office, Nancy Dickson
Tel: 613-532-1702; *Fax:* 416-327-7008
nancy.dickson@ontario.ca
www.ppao.gov.on.ca
Director, Claims Services, Josephine Fuller
Tel: 613-548-6333; *Fax:* 416-548-6320
josephine.fuller@ontario.ca
Director, Emergency Health Services (Land & Air), & Air Ambulance Program Oversight, Richard Jackson
Tel: 416-327-7909; *Fax:* 416-327-7879
richard.jackson@ontario.ca
Director, Assistive Devices Program, Susan Picarello
Tel: 416-212-5906
Toll-free: 800-268-6021; *Fax:* 416-327-8192
susan.picarello@ontario.ca
www.health.gov.on.ca/adp
TTY: 800-387-5559

Health Human Resources Strategy Division
Macdonald Block, #M2-61, 900 Bay St., 2nd Fl., Toronto, ON M7A 1R3
Tel: 416-212-6115; *Fax:* 416-314-3751
Assistant Deputy Minister, Suzanne McGurn
Tel: 416-212-7688; *Fax:* 416-314-3751
suzanne.mcgurn@ontario.ca
Provincial Chief Nursing Officer, Debra Bournes
Tel: 416-212-4835; *Fax:* 416-327-1878
debra.bournes@ontario.ca
Director, Health System Labour Relations & Regulatory Policy, John Amodeo
Tel: 416-212-0873; *Fax:* 416-325-9827
john.amodeo@ontario.ca
Acting Director, Health Workforce Policy, Tim Blakley
Tel: 416-326-6000; *Fax:* 416-327-0167
tim.blakley@ontario.ca

Health Promotion Division
College Park, #1903, 777 Bay St., 19th Fl., Toronto, M7A 1S5
Acting Assistant Deputy Minister, Olha Dobush
Tel: 416-326-4790
olha.dobush@ontario.ca
Acting Director, Strategic Initiatives Branch, Sherene Lindsay
Tel: 416-212-7785
sherene.lindsay@ontario.ca
Director, Health Promotion Implementation Branch, Laura Pisko
Tel: 416-327-7445; *Fax:* 416-314-5497
laura.pisko@ontario.ca

Health Services Information & Information Technology Cluster
56 Wellesley St. West, 10th Fl., Toronto, ON M5S 2S3
Tel: 416-314-0234; *Fax:* 416-314-4182
Chief Information Officer, Lorelle Taylor
Tel: 416-314-1279; *Fax:* 416-314-0234
lorelle.taylor@ontario.ca
Project Director, Ontario Public Health Intregrated Solutions, Karen McKibbin
Tel: 416-326-7169
Karen.McKibbin@ontario.ca
Director, Business & Financial Services, Raj Sharda
Tel: 416-327-6962; *Fax:* 416-314-4182
raj.sharda@ontario.ca
Head, Business Consulting Branch, Joan Berry
Tel: 416-326-7133; *Fax:* 416-315-4182
joan.berry@ontario.ca
Head, Integrated Health Solutions, Cathy Bulych
Tel: 416-314-2146
cathy.bulych@ontario.ca
Head, Technology Management & Solutions Integration, Shelley Edworthy
Tel: 613-548-6688; *Fax:* 416-327-4429
Shelley.Edworthy@ontario.ca
Head, Health Solutions Delivery, Kevan Malden
Tel: 613-548-6395; *Fax:* 613-548-6539
kevan.malden@ontario.ca
Head, I&IT Strategy & Architecture, Evan Woodhead
Tel: 416-327-1002
evan.woodhead@ontario.ca

Health System Accountability & Performance Division
Hepburn Block, 80 Grosvenor St., 5th Fl., Toronto, ON M7A 1R3
Fax: 416-212-1859
Assistant Deputy Minister, Nancy Naylor
Tel: 416-212-1134
nancy.naylor@ontario.ca
Director, Implementation, Tamara Gilbert
Tel: 416-327-7056
Tamara.Gilbert@ontario.ca
Director, LHIN Liaison, Kathryn McCulloch
Tel: 416-314-1864; *Fax:* 416-326-0018
kathryn.mcculloch@ontario.ca
Director, X-Ray Safety & Long-Term Care Homes, Nancy Lytle
Tel: 416-212-2362
nancy.lytle@ontario.ca

Health System Information Management & Investment Division
1075 Bay St., 13th Fl., Toronto, ON M5S 2B1
Tel: 416-212-1852; *Fax:* 416-327-8835
Interim Assistant Deputy Minister, Lorelle Taylor
Tel: 416-327-8854
lorelle.taylor@ontario.ca
Director, Information Management Strategy & Policy, Alison Blair
Tel: 416-212-4433; *Fax:* 416-314-6731
alison.blair@ontario.ca
Director, Special Projects, Aileen Chan
Tel: 416-325-2311; *Fax:* 416-212-3542
aileen.chan@ontario.ca
Director, Health Analytic Branch, Ashif Damji
Tel: 416-327-6483; *Fax:* 416-326-6560
ashif.damji@ontario.ca
Director, E-Health Liaison, Greg Hein
Tel: 416-325-9075; *Fax:* 416-326-9967
greg.hein@ontario.ca
Director, Capacity Building & Sector Support, Christina Hoy
Tel: 416-327-7305
christina.hoy@ontario.ca
Director, Health Data, Jeanette Munshaw
Tel: 416-212-9163; *Fax:* 416-327-8951
jeanette.munshaw@ontario.ca

Health System Strategy & Policy Division
Hepburn Block, 80 Grosvenor St., 8th Fl., Toronto, ON M7A 1R3
Tel: 416-327-8295; *Fax:* 416-327-5109
Assistant Deputy Minister, Nancy Kennedy
Tel: 416-327-7261
nancy.kennedy@ontario.ca
Senior Medical Scientific & Health Technology Advisor, Dr. Leslie Levin
Tel: 416-314-0249
les.levin@ontario.ca
Director, Strategy, Relations & Productivity Branch, Louis Dimitracopoulos
Tel: 416-327-8850
louis.dimitracopoulos@ontario.ca
Director, Community & Population Health, Anna Greenberg
Tel: 416-327-8319; *Fax:* 416-314-8275
anna.greenberg@ontario.ca
Director, Planning, Research & Analysis, Michael Hillmer
Tel: 416-327-3314; *Fax:* 416-327-3200
Michael.Hillmer@ontario.ca
Acting Director, System Policy & Strategy, Joanne Plaxton
Tel: 416-212-5218
Joanne.Plaxton@ontario.ca
Manager, Intergovernmental Relations Unit, Karen Moore
Tel: 416-212-4366
karen.moore2@ontario.ca

Negotiations & Accountability Management Division
Hepburn Block, 80 Grosvenor St., 5th Fl., Toronto, ON M7A 1R3
Tel: 416-212-7012; *Fax:* 416-327-5186
Interim Assistant Deputy Minister, Pauline Ryan
Tel: 416-314-0129
pauline.ryan@ontario.ca
Director, Negotiations, David W. Clarke
Tel: 613-212-4904; *Fax:* 416-327-7519
david.w.clarke@ontario.ca
Acting Director, Primary Health Care, Phil Graham
Tel: 416-212-1791
Toll-free: 866-766-0266
phil.graham@ontario.ca
Director, Program Development & Delivery, Pearl Ing
Tel: 416-327-0848
Pearl.Ing@ontario.ca
Acting Director, Provincial Programs, Miriam Johnston
Tel: 416-326-3834
miriam.johnston@ontario.ca
Acting Director, Health Services, Dr. Garry Salisbury
Tel: 613-536-3078; *Fax:* 613-536-3188
garry.salisbury@ontario.ca

Ontario Public Drug Programs Division
Hepburn Block, 80 Grosvenor St., 9th Fl., Toronto, ON M7A 1R3
Tel: 416-212-4724; *Fax:* 416-325-6647
www.health.gov.on.ca/en/public/programs/drugs
Acting Assistant Deputy Minister & Executive Officer, Diane McArthur
Tel: 416-327-0902
suzanne.mcgurn@ontario.ca
Director, Exceptional Access Program, Rob W. Campbell
Tel: 416-327-8118; *Fax:* 416-327-8912
rob.w.campbell@ontario.ca
Director, Drug Program Services, Brent Fraser
Tel: 416-327-8315
brent.fraser@ontario.ca

Ontario Ministry of Housing

College Park, 777 Bay St., 17th Fl., Toronto, ON M5G 2E5
Tel: 416-585-6500; *Fax:* 416-585-4035
TTY: 416-585-6991
mininfo@ontario.ca
www.mah.gov.on.ca
The ministry was created in 2016 after Premier Wynne split the Ministry of Municipal Affairs & Housing into two.
Minister, Hon. Chris Ballard
Tel: 416-585-6500
Minister.MOH@ontario.ca
Deputy Minister, Laurie LeBlanc
Tel: 416-585-7100
laurie.leblanc@ontario.ca
Director, Communications, Mary Anne Covelli
Tel: 416-585-6900
maryanne.covelli@ontario.ca

Legal Director, Joanne Davies
Tel: 416-585-6551
joanne.davies@ontario.ca

Business Management Division

College Park, 777 Bay St., 17th Fl., Toronto, ON M5G 2E5
Tel: 416-585-7062; *Fax:* 416-585-6191

Assistant Deputy Minister & Chief Administrative Officer, Jim Cassimatis
Tel: 416-585-6670; *Fax:* 416-585-6191
Jim.Cassimatis@ontario.ca

Director, Controllership & Financial Planning, Jason Arandjelovic
Tel: 416-585-7448; *Fax:* 416-585-7328
jason.arandjelovic@ontario.ca

Acting Executive Coordinator, Human Resources Strategies Branch, Andrea Ubeysekera
Tel: 416-585-7358
andrea.ubeysekera@ontario.ca

Director, Corporate Services Branch, Jim D. Lewis
Tel: 416-585-7321; *Fax:* 416-585-7643
jim.d.lewis@ontario.ca

Housing Division

College Park, 777 Bay St., 16th Fl., Toronto, ON M5G 2E5
Tel: 416-585-6738; *Fax:* 416-585-6800

Assistant Deputy Minister, Janet Hope
Tel: 416-585-6755
janet.hope@ontario.ca

Director, Housing Programs, Jim Adams
Tel: 416-585-7021
jim.adams@ontario.ca

Director, Housing Funding & Risk Management, Keith Extrance
Tel: 416-585-7524
keith.extance@ontario.ca

Director, Housing Policy, Carol Latimer
Tel: 416-585-6400; *Fax:* 416-585-7607
carol.latimer@ontario.ca

Municipal Services Division

College Park, 777 Bay St., 16th Fl., Toronto, ON M5G 2E5
Fax: 416-585-6445

Assistant Deputy Minister, Elizabeth Harding
Tel: 416-585-6427
liz.harding@ontario.ca

Acting Director, Municipal Programs & Education, Andrew Tang
Tel: 416-585-7226
andrew.tang@ontario.ca

Ontario Human Rights Commission (OHRC)

#900, 180 Dundas St. West, Toronto, ON M7A 2R9
Tel: 416-326-9511; *Fax:* 416-314-4494
Toll-Free: 800-387-9080
TTY: 800-308-5561
info@ohrc.on.ca
www.ohrc.on.ca
twitter.com/OntHumanRights
www.facebook.com/the.ohrc

Chief Commissioner, Renu Mandhane

Chief Administrative Officer, Karen Pereira
Tel: 416-314-4480; *Fax:* 416-314-4494
karen.pereira@ohrc.on.ca

Executive Director, Dianne Carter
Tel: 416-326-0567; *Fax:* 416-325-2004
dianne.carter@ohrc.on.ca

Director, Policy, Education, Monitoring & Outreach, Shaheen Azmi
Tel: 416-314-4532; *Fax:* 416-314-4533
shaheen.azmi@ohrc.on.ca

Hydro One Inc.

North Tower, 483 Bay St., 15th Fl., Toronto, ON M5G 2P5
Tel: 416-345-5000; *Fax:* 905-944-3251
Toll-Free: 877-955-1155
customercommunications@hydroone.com
www.hydroone.comPO Box 5700 Sta. Markham, ON L3R 1C8
twitter.com/HydroOne

Subsidiaries are: Hydro One Networks Inc.; Hydro One Remote Communities Inc.; Hydro One Telecom Inc.; Hydro One Brampton Inc.; & Norfolk Power Distribution Inc.
The Ontario government began the process of privitizing Hydro One in Nov. 2015 with an initial public offering of 13.6 percent of the company, with a goal of eventually selling 60 percent.

Chair, David Denison

President & Chief Executive Officer, Mayo Schmidt

President & Chief Executive Officer, Hydro One Telecom Inc., Paul Marchant

President & Chief Executive Officer, Hydro One Brampton Inc., Paul Tremblay

Director, Hydro One Remote Communities Inc., Kraemer Coulter

Chief Operating Officer & Executive Vice-President, Strategic Planning, Sandy Struthers

Chief Financial Officer, Michael Vels

Chief Investment & Pension Officer & Senior Vice-President, Robert Cultraro

Chief Risk Officer & Vice-President, Frank D'Andrea

Chief Information Officer & Senior Vice-President, Technology, Colin Penny

Senior Vice-President, Customer & Corporate Relations, Laura Cooke

Senior Vice-President, People & Culture, Judy McKeller

Vice-President, Shared Services, Gary Schneider

General Counsel, Joe Agostino

Independent Electricity System Operator (IESO)

#1600, 120 Adelaide St. West, Toronto, ON M5H 1T1
Tel: 905-403-6900; *Fax:* 905-403-6921
Toll-Free: 888-448-7777
customer.relations@ieso.ca
www.ieso.ca
Other Communication: Reception: 905-855-6100; Conservation Programs, Toll-Free Phone: 1-877-797-9473
twitter.com/ieso_tweets
www.facebook.com/OntarioIESO
www.linkedin.com/company/ieso

The IESO was established in 1998 by the Electricity Act of Ontario. It is a not-for-profit organization engaged in the following activities: balancing energy supply & demand & directing energy flow; planning Ontario's medium- & long-term energy needs & finding clean sources of energy; overseeing the electricity wholesale market; & encouraging energy conservation through programs such as saveONenergy.
On Jan. 1, 2015, the IESO absorbed the activites of the Ontario Power Authority (OPA).

Chair, Tim O'Neill

President & CEO, Bruce Campbell

Chief Financial Officer & Vice-President, Corporate Services, Kimberly Marshall

Chief Operating Officer & Vice-President, Market & System Operations, Kim Warren

Chief Information Officer & Vice-President, Information & Technology Serivces, Doug Thomas

Vice-President, Market & Resource Development, JoAnne Butler

Vice-President, Planning, Law & Aboriginal Relations, Michael Lyle

Vice-President, Conservation & Corporate Relations, Terry Young

Ontario Ministry of Indigenous Relations & Reconciliation

160 Bloor St. East, 4th Fl., Toronto, ON M7A 2E6
Tel: 416-326-4740; *Fax:* 416-326-4017
Toll-Free: 866-381-5337
TTY: 866-686-6072
Other Communication: URL: www.ontario.ca/page/ministry-indigenous-relations-and-reconciliation
twitter.com/IndigenousON
www.facebook.com/IndigenousON

Ministry of Indigenous Relations & Reconciliation (formerly Aboriginal Affairs) was created in 2007 to replace the Ontario Secretariat of Aboriginal Affairs. The Ministry focuses on: coordination of Aboriginal policy & programs across ministries; overseeing the province's Aboriginal agenda; enhancing government awareness of Aboriginal people & issues; partnering with the federal government on Aboriginal funding; assisting Aboriginal people with accessing government programs, services & information; addressing historical grievances through reforming the land claims process; & promoting the representation of Aboriginal people in the Ontario Public Service.

Minister, Hon. David Zimmer
Tel: 416-327-4464; *Fax:* 416-314-2701
david.zimmer@ontario.ca

Deputy Minister, Deborah Richardson
Tel: 416-314-1141; *Fax:* 416-314-1165

Parliamentary Assistant, Sophie Kiwala
Tel: 416-212-2592

Acting Director, Communications Services, Ian Ross
Tel: 416-314-5383
Ian.Ross@ontario.ca

Acting Director, Legal Services, Raj Dhir
Tel: 416-326-2372
raj.dhir@ontario.ca

Director, Programs & Services Branch, Nadia Temple
Tel: 416-314-6133
nadia.temple@ontario.ca

Indigenous Relations & Programs Division
Tel: 416-326-4740; *Fax:* 416-325-1066

Assistant Deputy Minister, Hillary Thatcher
Tel: 416-325-0304
hillary.thatcher@ontario.ca

Director, Programs & Services Branch, Nadia Temple
Tel: 416-314-6133
nadia.temple@ontario.ca

Acting Director, Indigenous Relations Branch, Heather Levecque
Tel: 416-325-7032
heather.levecque@ontario.ca

Negotiations & Reconciliation
Tel: 416-326-4740; *Fax:* 416-326-4710

The branch carries out the following responsibilities: researching & conducting land claim negotiations; managing & coordinating negotiations; representing the province for federally-led governance negotiations; & implementing settlements.

Assistant Deputy Minister, Shawn Batise
Tel: 416-326-4741
shawn.batise@ontario.ca

Acting Director, Negotiations, Greg Coleman
Tel: 416-326-6330; *Fax:* 416-326-4017
greg.coleman@ontario.ca

Director, Community Intiatives, Bruce Leslie
Tel: 416-212-2755
bruce.leslie@ontario.ca

Office of the Chief Administrative Officer - Corporate Management Division

Whitney Block, #6540, 99 Wellesley St. W., Toronto, ON M7A 1W3
Tel: 416-314-1939; *Fax:* 416-314-1901

Chief Administrative Officer, Paula Reid
Tel: 416-314-1939
paula.reid@ontario.ca

Director, Strategic Human Resources, Amanda Holmes
Tel: 705-755-3131
amanda.holmes@ontario.ca

Acting Director, Corporate Management, Esther Laquer
Tel: 416-212-1277
esther.laquer@ontario.ca

Strategic Policy & Planning
Tel: 416-326-4740; *Fax:* 416-326-4777

The branch is engaged in the following key activities: developing & coordinating government-wide Aboriginal policy; providing corporate planning & policy advice on Aboriginal matters; & developing & maintaining positive relationships with Aboriginal leaders.

Assistant Deputy Minister, Alison Pilla
Tel: 416-212-2302
alison.pilla@ontario.ca

Director, Strategic Planning & Economic Policy, Matt Garrow
Tel: 416-314-1607
Matt.Garrow@ontario.ca

Information & Privacy Commissioner of Ontario (IPC)

#1400, 2 Bloor St. East, Toronto, ON M4W 1A8
Tel: 416-326-3333; *Fax:* 416-325-9195
Toll-Free: 800-387-0073
TTY: 416-325-7539
info@ipc.on.ca
www.ipc.on.ca
twitter.com/IPCinfoprivacy

The IPC is the oversight body for Ontario's three provincial freedom of information & protection of privacy statues, & is responsible for resolving appeals when government organizations refuse to grant access to information; investigating privacy complaints related to government-held information; ensuring government compliance with the acts; conducting research on access & privacy issues & providing advice on proposed government legislation & programs; educating the public on Ontario's access, privacy & personal health information laws & access & privacy issues; investigating complaints related to personal health information; reviewing policies & procedures, & ensuring compliance with the Personal Health Information Protection Act.

Commissioner, Brian Beamish
Tel: 416-326-3333
commissioner@ipc.on.ca

Acting Assistant Commissioner, Sherry Liang
Tel: 416-326-3333
sherry.liang@ipc.on.ca

Director, Policy, Renee Barrette
Tel: 416-326-3461
renee.barrette@ipc.on.ca

Director, Legal Services, Manuela Di Re
Tel: 416-326-8809
manuela.dire@ipc.on.ca

Director, Corporate Services, Janet Geisberger
Tel: 416-326-3937
janet.geisberger@ipc.on.ca

Registrar, Tribunal Services, Robert Binstock
Tel: 416-326-0008
robert.binstock@ipc.on.ca

Office of the Integrity Commissioner (OICO)

#2100, 2 Bloor St. East, Toronto, ON M4W 3E2
Tel: 416-314-8983; *Fax:* 416-314-8987
integrity.mail@oico.on.ca
www.oico.on.ca

The Commissioner administers the Member's Integrity Act, 1994 as it applies to members of the Legislative Assembly & Executive Council in Ontario, including the filing of Public Disclosure Statements, & the right to conduct an inquiry if there are reasonable & probable grounds to believe that the Act has been contravened. The Commissioner also has responsibility under the MPP Compensation Reform Act (Arm's Length Process), 2001 & the Accountability for Expenses Act (Cabinet Ministers & Opposition Leaders), 2002

Commissioner, Hon. J. David Wake
Director, Cathryn Motherwell
cathryn.motherwell@oico.on.ca
Counsel, Daman Thable
daman.thable@oico.on.ca

Lobbyists Registration Office
#2101, 2 Bloor St. E., Toronto, ON M4W 1A8
Tel: 416-327-4053; *Fax:* 416-327-4017
lobbyist.mail@oico.on.ca
lobbyist.oico.on.ca

Under the Lobbyists Registration Act, 1998, the Registrar is responsible for administering the lobbyist registration process, ensuring paid lobbyists report their lobbying of public office holders by filing a return; & ensuring public accessibility to the information contained in the lobbyist's registry.

Registrar, Lynn Morrison
Tel: 416-327-4053
lynn.morrison@oico.on.ca

Ontario Ministry of Infrastructure

Hearst Block, 900 Bay St., 8th Fl., Toronto, ON M7A 2E1
Tel: 416-325-6666
Toll-Free: 800-268-7095
TTY: 416-325-3408
www.ontario.ca/page/ministry-infrastructure

The ministry was created in 2016 after Premier Wynne divided the Ministry of Economic Growth, Development & Infrastructure.

Minsiter, Hon. Bob Chiarelli
bob.chiarelli@ontario.ca
Deputy Minsiter, George Zegarac
Tel: 416-326-3880
george.zegarac@ontario.ca

Corporate Services Division
54 Wellesley St., 4th Fl., Toronto, ON M7A 2E7
Tel: 416-325-6866; *Fax:* 416-314-7014
Toll-Free: 888-664-6008
TTY: 416-325-6707

Chief Administrative Officer & Assistant Deputy Minister, Robert Burns
Tel: 416-327-3682
robert.burns@ontario.ca
Director, Business Planning & Finance, Kevin Perry
Tel: 416-327-1137
kevin.perry@ontario.ca
Director, Investment Funding & Coordination, Richard Kikuta
Tel: 416-325-6849
richard.kikuta@ontario.ca
Director, Service Management & Facilities, Betty Morgan
Tel: 416-314-3309
betty.morgan@ontario.ca
Director, Strategic Human Resources Business Unit, Dan Keating
Tel: 416-325-6598
dan.keating@ontario.ca

Ontario Ministry of Intergovernmental Affairs

Ferguson Block, 77 Wellesley St. West, 12th Fl., Toronto, ON M7A 1N3
Tel: 416-326-1234
www.ontario.ca/ministry-intergovernmental-affairs
www.youtube.com/ongov

Minister, Hon. Kathleen O. Wynne
Tel: 416-325-1941
kwynne.mpp@liberal.ola.org
Deputy Minister & Associate Secretary of the Cabinet, Communications & Intergovernmental Affairs, Lynn Betzner
Tel: 416-325-4631
lynn.betzner@ontario.ca
Assistant Deputy Minister, Economic & Justice, Craig McFadyen
Tel: 416-325-4603
craig.mcfadyen@ontario.ca
Assistant Deputy Minister, Health, Social, Environment & National Institutions, Ernie Bartucci
Tel: 416-325-4804
ernie.bartucci@ontario.ca
Acting Assistant Deputy Minister & Chief of Protocol, Office of International Relations & Protocol, Craig McFadyen
Tel: 416-325-8545; *Fax:* 416-325-8550
craig.mcfadyen@ontario.ca

Ontario Ministry of International Trade

College Park, #1836, 777 Bay St., Toronto, ON M5G 2E5
www.ontario.ca/page/ministry-international-trade

The ministry was created in 2016, after Premier Wynne split the ministry of Citizenship, Immigration & International Trade. Its goal is to increase Ontario's exports.

Minister, Hon. Michael Chan
Tel: 416-326-8475
Michael.Chan@ontario.ca
Deputy Minister, Helen Angus
helen.angus@ontario.ca
Parliamentary Assistant, Monte Kwinter
Tel: 416-325-0036
monte.kwinter@ontario.ca
Director, Policy, Jerry Khouri
Tel: 416-327-2736
jerry.khouri@ontario.ca
Executive Director, Operations, Herman Ng
Tel: 416-327-2807
herman.ng@ontario.ca

International Trade & Representation Division
Hearst Block, 900 Bay St., 5th Fl., Toronto, ON M7A 2E1
Tel: 416-325-9802; *Fax:* 416-325-5617
Toll-Free: 877-468-7233

Assistant Deputy Minister, Cameron Sinclair
Tel: 416-325-9801
cameron.sinclair@ontario.ca
Director, International Representation, David Barnes
Tel: 416-326-8886
david.barnes@ontario.ca
Director, International Trade, Enrico Di Nino
Tel: 416-326-5660
enrico.dinino@ontario.ca
Director, Business Engagement & Outreach, Margaret Steeves
Tel: 416-325-6690
margaret.steeves@ontario.ca

Ontario Ministry of Labour

400 University Ave., 14th Fl., Toronto, ON M7A 1T7
Tel: 416-326-7160
Toll-Free: 800-531-5551
TTY: 866-567-8893
www.labour.gov.on.ca
Other Communication: Health & Safety Contact Centre: 1-877-202-0008
twitter.com/OntMinLabour
www.facebook.com/OntarioMinistryofLabour

Advances safe, fair & harmonious workplace practices that are essential to the social & economic well-being of the people of Ontario. Through the Ministry's key areas of occupational health & safety, employment rights & responsibilities, labour relations & internal administration, the ministry's mandate is to set, communicate & enforce workplace standards while encouraging greater workplace self-reliance. A range of specialized agencies, boards & commissions assist the Ministry in its work.

Minister, Hon. Kevin Daniel Flynn
Tel: 416-325-5200; *Fax:* 416-325-5215
kflynn.mpp@liberal.ola.org
Deputy Minister, Sophie Dennis
Tel: 416-326-7576; *Fax:* 416-326-0507
sophie.dennis@ontario.ca
Parliamentary Assistant, Mike Colle
Tel: 416-325-1404; *Fax:* 416-325-1447
mcolle.mpp.co@liberal.ola.org
Parliamentary Assistant, Ann Hoggarth
Tel: 416-212-9790
ahoggarth.mpp.co@liberal.ola.org
Chief Information Officer, Labour & Transportation I&IT Cluster, Howard Bertrand
Tel: 416-327-1955; *Fax:* 416-327-3755
howard.bertrand@ontario.ca
Director, Legal Services, Bridget Lynett
Tel: 416-326-7953; *Fax:* 416-326-7985
bridget.lynett@ontario.ca
Director, Ontario Internal Audit, Resources & Labour Audit Service Team, Ray Masse
Tel: 416-314-9208; *Fax:* 416-314-9220
ray.masse@ontario.ca
Director, Communications & Marketing, Tom Zach
Tel: 416-326-7404; *Fax:* 416-314-5809
tom.zach@ontario.ca

Associated Agencies, Boards & Commissions:

•Grievance Settlement Board (GSB)
Dundas/Edward Ctr.
#600, 180 Dundas St. West
Toronto, ON M5G 1Z8
Tel: 416-326-1388; *Fax:* 416-326-1396
gsb.gsb@ontario.ca
www.psab.gov.on.ca/english/gsb/index.htm

•Office of the Employer Advisor (OEA)
#704, 151 Bloor St. West.
Toronto, ON M5S 1S4
Tel: 416-327-0020; *Fax:* 416-327-0726
Toll-free: 800-387-0774
www.employeradviser.ca
Advise & represent employers with fewer than 100 employees in relation to worker's compensation issues at no cost to the employer.

•Office of the Worker Advisor (OWA)
#1300, 123 Edward St.
Toronto, ON M5G 1E2
Tel: 416-325-8570; *Fax:* 416-325-4830
Toll-free: 800-660-6769
TTY: 866-455-3092
owaweb@ontario.ca
www.owa.gov.on.ca
Other Communication: Toll-Free French: 1-800-661-6365

•Ontario Labour Relations Board (OLRB)
505 University Ave., 2nd Fl.
Toronto, ON M5G 2P1
Tel: 416-326-7500; *Fax:* 416-326-7531
Toll-free: 877-339-3335
TTY: 416-212-7036
www.olrb.gov.on.ca

•Pay Equity Commission
#300, 180 Dundas St. West
Toronto, ON M7A 2S6
Tel: 416-314-1896; *Fax:* 416-314-8741
Toll-free: 800-387-8813
TTY: 855-253-8333
www.payequity.gov.on.ca

•Workplace Safety & Insurance Appeals Tribunal (WSIAT)
505 University Ave., 7th Fl.
Toronto, ON M5G 2P2
Tel: 416-314-8800; *Fax:* 416-326-5164
Toll-free: 888-618-8846
TTY: 416-314-1787
www.wsiat.on.ca
Formerly known as the Workers' Compensation Appeals Tribunal.

•Workplace Safety & Insurance Board
See Entry Name Index for detailed listing.

Internal Administrative Services Division
Tel: 416-326-7586; *Fax:* 416-326-5809

Assistant Deputy Minister & Chief Administrative Officer, Mike Anderson
Tel: 416-326-7305; *Fax:* 416-326-5809
Mike.Anderson@ontario.ca
Director, Organizational Effectiveness, Janis Bartley
Tel: 416-326-7215; *Fax:* 416-326-7241
janis.bartley@ontario.ca
Director, Finance & Administration, Susan Flanagan
Tel: 416-326-7271; *Fax:* 416-326-9069
susan.flanagan@ontario.ca

Labour Relations Solutions Division
Tel: 416-326-0660; *Fax:* 416-326-5809

Assistant Deputy Minister, Peter Simpson
Tel: 416-325-3608
Director, Dispute Resolution Services, Peter Simpson
Tel: 416-326-7322
peter.simpson@ontario.ca

Operations Division
Tel: 416-326-7606; *Fax:* 416-212-4455

Acting Assistant Deputy Minister, Cara Martin
Tel: 416-326-7665
Cara.Martin@ontario.ca
Chief Physician, Health Care & Occupational Medicine Unit, Dr. Leon Genesove
Tel: 416-326-2913
leon.genesove@ontario.ca
Director Lead, Divisional Learning Unit, Ken Fox
Tel: 647-777-5112
ken.fox@ontario.ca

Acting Director, Employment Practices, Stephen McDonald
Tel: 416-326-7004
stephen.mcdonald@ontario.ca
Director, Operations Integration Unit, Laura Orlandi
Tel: 416-212-1132
laura.orlandi@ontario.ca
Acting Director, Occupational Health & Safety, Carol Sackville-Duyvelshoff
Tel: 416-326-7866; *Fax:* 416-326-7242
carol.sackville-duyvelshoff@ontario.ca

Regional Offices

Central East
#1600, 5001 Yonge St., Toronto, ON M7A 0A3
Tel: 647-777-5005; *Fax:* 647-777-5010
Regional Director, Ken Fox
Tel: 647-777-5112
ken.fox@ontario.ca

Central West
#400, 1290 Central Pkwy. West, Mississauga, ON L5C 4R3
Tel: 905-273-7800; *Fax:* 905-615-7191
Toll-Free: 800-991-7454
TTY: 866-567-8893
Regional Director, Jody Young
Tel: 905-615-6543
jody.young@ontario.ca

Eastern
Preston Sq., 347 Preston St., 4th Fl., Ottawa, ON K1S 3J4
Tel: 613-228-8050; *Fax:* 613-727-2900
Toll-Free: 800-267-1916
TTY: 866-567-8893
Regional Director, Sandra Lawson
Tel: 613-727-2844; *Fax:* 613-727-2900
sandra.lawson@ontario.ca

Northern
#301, 159 Cedar St., Sudbury, ON P3E 6A5
Tel: 705-564-7400; *Fax:* 705-670-7435
Toll-Free: 800-461-6325
TTY: 866-567-8893
Regional Director, Peter Augruso
Tel: 705-564-7433
peter.augruso@ontario.ca

Western
119 King St. West, 13th Fl., Hamilton, ON L8P 4Y7
Tel: 905-577-6221; *Fax:* 905-577-1200
Toll-Free: 800-263-6906
Regional Director, Filomena Savoia
Tel: 905-577-1238
filomena.savoia@ontario.ca

Policy Division

Assistant Deputy Minister, Marcelle Crouse
Tel: 416-326-7555
marcelle.crouse@ontario.ca
Director, Employment, Labour & Corporate Policy, David Beaulieu
Tel: 416-326-7641; *Fax:* 416-326-7650
david.beaulieu@ontario.ca
Director, Health & Safety Policy, Maria Papoutsis
Tel: 416-326-7628; *Fax:* 416-326-7650
maria.papoutsis@ontario.ca

Prevention Office

Tel: 416-212-3960; *Fax:* 416-314-5809
Chief Prevention Officer, George Gritziotis
Tel: 416-314-6342
george.gritziotis@ontario.ca
Director, Stakeholder & Partner Relations, Ayumi Bailly
Tel: 416-212-5321
ayumi.bailly@ontario.ca
Director, Training & Safety Programs, Cordelia Clarke-Julien
Tel: 416-212-5301
cordelia.clarkejulien@ontario.ca
Director, Mining Health, Safety & Prevention Review, Wayne De L'Orme
Tel: 416-212-7870
wayne.del'orme@ontario.ca
Director, Strategy & Integration, Brian Lewis
Tel: 416-327-6427
brian.lewis@ontario.ca

Ontario Ministry of Municipal Affairs

College Park, 777 Bay St., 17th Fl., Toronto, ON M5G 2E5
Tel: 416-585-7000; *Fax:* 416-585-6470
TTY: 866-220-2290
mininfo@ontario.ca
www.mah.gov.on.ca
Other Communication: TTY: 416-585-6991
twitter.com/OntMMAH
www.youtube.com/user/ontariommah

Responsible for providing provincial leadership in defining the framework for governance, finances & management for the local government systems; as well as leadership in the development & administration of the legislative & policy framework for land use planning. In June 2016 the Ministry was divided into two portfolios: Ministry of Municipal Affairs, & Ministry of Housing.

Minister, Municipal Affairs, Hon. Bill Mauro
Tel: 416-585-7000; *Fax:* 416-585-6470
Minister.MAH@ontario.ca
Deputy Minister, Laurie LeBlanc
Tel: 416-585-7100; *Fax:* 416-585-7211
Laurie.LeBlanc@ontario.ca
Parliamentary Assistant, Lou Rinaldi
Tel: 416-585-7000
lou.rinaldi@ontario.ca
Director, Communications, Mary Anne Covelli
Tel: 416-585-6900; *Fax:* 416-585-6227
maryanne.covelli@ontario.ca

Associated Agencies, Boards & Commissions:

•Building Code Commission (BCC)
777 Bay St., 2nd Fl.
Toronto, ON M5G 2E5
Tel: 416-585-6666; *Fax:* 416-585-7531
codeinfo@ontario.ca
www.mah.gov.on.ca/Page7394.aspx
Works with the municipal & building sectors & consumer groups to improve & streamline the building regulatory system. This leads to efficient development & more construction jobs, while protecting public safety. The Branch administers the Building Code Act (BCA) & the Ontario Building Code (OBC), which govern the construction of new buildings & the renovation & maintenance of existing buildings. It provides enforcement officials & other building code users with advice & information so that they can apply building code requirements more consistently.

•Building Materials Evaluation Commission (BMEC)
777 Bay St., 2nd Fl.
Toronto, ON M5G 2E5
Tel: 416-585-4234; *Fax:* 416-585-7531
www.mah.gov.on.ca/Page8295.aspx

Business Management Division

College Park, 777 Bay St., 17th Fl., Toronto, ON M5G 2E5
Tel: 416-585-7062; *Fax:* 416-585-6191
Assistant Deputy Minister & Chief Administrative Officer, Jim Cassimatis
Tel: 416-585-6670; *Fax:* 416-585-6191
Jim.Cassimatis@ontario.ca
Director, Controllership & Financial Planning, Jason Arandjelovic
Tel: 416-585-7448; *Fax:* 416-585-7328
jason.arandjelovic@ontario.ca
Acting Executive Coordinator, Human Resources Strategies Branch, Andrea Ubeysekera
Tel: 416-585-7358
andrea.ubeysekera@ontario.ca
Director, Corporate Services Branch, Jim D. Lewis
Tel: 416-585-7321; *Fax:* 416-585-7643
jim.d.lewis@ontario.ca

Local Government & Planning Policy Division

College Park, 777 Bay St., 13th Fl., Toronto, ON M5G 2E5
Tel: 416-585-6321; *Fax:* 416-585-6463
Assistant Deputy Minister, Kate Manson-Smith
Tel: 416-585-6320
kate.manson-smith@ontario.ca
Director, Provincial Planning Policy, Audrey Bennett
Tel: 416-585-6072; *Fax:* 416-585-6870
audrey.bennett@ontario.ca
Director, Municipal Finance Policy, Oliver Jerschow
Tel: 416-585-6951; *Fax:* 416-585-6315
Oliver.Jerschow@ontario.ca
Director, Intergovernmental Relations & Partnerships, Diane McArthur-Rodgers
Tel: 416-585-6047
diane.mcarthur-rodgers@ontario.ca
Director, Local Government Policy, Jonathan Lebi
Tel: 416-585-7260
jonathan.lebi@ontario.ca

Municipal Services Division

777 Bay St., 16th Fl., Toronto, ON M5G 2E5
Fax: 416-585-6445
Assistant Deputy Minister, Elizabeth Harding
Tel: 416-585-6427
liz.harding@ontario.ca
Acting Director, Municipal Programs & Education, Andrew Tang
Tel: 416-585-7226; *Fax:* 416-585-7292
andrew.tang@ontario.ca
Director, Building & Development, Brenda Lewis
Tel: 416-585-6656
brenda.lewis@ontario.ca
www.ontario.ca/buildingcode

Municipal Services Offices

Central
777 Bay St., 2nd Fl., Toronto, ON M5G 2E5
Tel: 416-585-6226; *Fax:* 416-585-6882
Toll-Free: 800-668-0230
Regional Director, Marcia Wallace
Tel: 416-585-7264; *Fax:* 416-585-6882
Marcia.Wallace@ontario.ca

Eastern
Rockwood House, 8 Estate Lane, Kingston, ON K7M 9A8
Tel: 613-545-2100; *Fax:* 613-548-6822
Toll-Free: 800-267-9438
Regional Director, Allan Scott
Tel: 613-545-2133; *Fax:* 613-548-6822
allan.scott@ontario.ca

North (Sudbury)
#401, 159 Cedar St., Sudbury, ON P3E 6A5
Tel: 705-564-0120; *Fax:* 705-564-6863
Toll-Free: 800-461-1193
Regional Director, Lynn Buckham
Tel: 705-564-6858; *Fax:* 705-564-6863
lynn.buckham@ontario.ca

North (Thunder Bay)
#223, 435 James St. South, Thunder Bay, ON P7E 6S7
Regional Director, Lynn Buckingham
Tel: 807-475-1187
lynn.buckham@ontario.ca

Western
Exeter Road Complex, 659 Exeter Rd., 2nd Fl., London, ON N6E 1L3
Tel: 519-873-4020; *Fax:* 519-873-4018
Toll-Free: 800-265-4736
Regional Director, Ginette Brindle
Tel: 519-873-4037
ginette.brindle@ontario.ca

Office of the Provincial Land & Development Facilitator

College Park, #2704, 777 Bay St., 27th Fl., Toronto, ON M7A 2J8
Tel: 416-325-0835; *Fax:* 416-325-0209
www.moi.gov.on.ca
Provincial Development Facilitator, Paula Dill
Tel: 416-325-9764
paula.dill@ontario.ca

Ontario Growth Secretariat

College Park, #425, 777 Bay St., Toronto, ON M5G 2E5
Tel: 416-325-1210; *Fax:* 416-325-7405
Toll-Free: 866-479-9781
www.placestogrow.ca
Assistant Deputy Minister, Larry Clay
Tel: 416-325-5803
larry.clay@ontario.ca
Director, Partnerships & Consultation, Tanzeel Merchant
Tel: 416-325-5799; *Fax:* 416-325-7403
Tanzeel.Merchant@ontario.ca
Director, Growth Policy, Planning & Analysis, Adam Redish
Tel: 416-314-1548; *Fax:* 416-325-7403
Adam.Redish@ontario.ca

Ontario Ministry of Natural Resources & Forestry

300 Water St., PO Box 7000 Peterborough, ON K9J 8M5
Toll-Free: 800-667-1940
TTY: 866-686-6072
www.ontario.ca/ministry-natural-resources-forestry
twitter.com/MNRFcentral
www.facebook.com/MNRFcentral

The Ministry manages & protects natural resources in the province for wise use. Working with environmental organizations, private industries, fish & game associations, researchers, & other government agencies, the Ministry is responsible for the following areas: science & information resources; forest management; fish & wildlife management; land & waters management; Ontario Parks; aviation & forest fire management; & geographic information.

Minister, Hon. Kathryn McGarry
Tel: 416-314-2301; *Fax:* 416-325-1564
kmcgarry.mpp.co@liberal.ola.org
Other Communications: Alt. E-mail: minister.mnr@ontario.ca
Deputy Minister, Bill Thornton
Tel: 416-314-2150; *Fax:* 416-314-2159
bill.thornton@ontario.ca
Commissioner, Mining & Lands, Linda Kamerman
Tel: 416-314-2322; *Fax:* 416-314-2327
linda.kamerman@ontario.ca
Acting Director, Communications Services, Jenna LeBlanc
Tel: 416-314-2119; *Fax:* 416-314-2102
jenna.leblanc@ontario.ca

Director, Legal Services, Leith Hunter
Tel: 416-314-2025; *Fax:* 416-314-2030
leith.hunter@ontario.ca

Director, Ontario Internal Audit, Resources & Labour Audit Service Team, Ray Masse
Tel: 416-314-9208; *Fax:* 416-314-9220
ray.masse@ontario.ca

Director, Transformation Secretariat, Rebecca Ramsarran
Tel: 416-212-9592
rebecca.ramsarran@ontario.ca

Associated Agencies, Boards & Commissions:

•Academic & Experience Requirements Committee of the Association of Ontario Land Surveyors (AERC)
1043 McNicoll Ave.
Toronto, ON M1W 3W6
Tel: 416-491-9020; *Fax:* 416-491-2576

•Algonquin Forestry Authority - Huntsville
222 Main St. West
Huntsville, ON P1H 1Y1
Tel: 705-789-9647; *Fax:* 705-789-3353
info@algonquinforestry.on.ca
www.algonquinforestry.on.ca
Ensures the viability of the local forest industry while preserving the soil & water resources, fish & wildlife habitat & recreational areas in the park.

•Algonquin Forestry Authority - Pembroke
Victoria Centre
84 Isabella St., 2nd Fl.
Pembroke, ON K8A 5S5
Tel: 613-735-0173; *Fax:* 613-735-4192
info@algonquinforestry.on.ca
www.algonquinforestry.on.ca

•Association of Ontario Land Surveyors
1043 McNicoll Ave.
Toronto, ON M1W 3W6
Tel: 416-491-9020; *Fax:* 416-491-2576
Toll-free: 800-268-0718
www.aols.org

•Ontario Fish & Wildlife Heritage Commission
Robinson Pl.
300 Water St.
PO Box 7000
Peterborough, ON K9J 8M5
Tel: 705-755-1905; *Fax:* 705-755-1900

•Ontario Geographic Names Board
Robinson Place
300 Water St., 2nd Fl.
PO Box 7000
Peterborough, ON K9J 8M5
Tel: 705-755-2132
The Board investigates the background of geographic names & recommends names to be used on maps.

•Ontario Moose & Bear Allocation Advisory Committee
PO Box 964
Sioux Lookout, ON P8T 1B3
Tel: 807-737-2615; *Fax:* 807-737-4173
An independent advisory committee to allocate moose & bear hunting opportunities provided by the Ministry of Natural Resources within the tourism industry in a manner which is ecologically sustainable & supports the economic viability of the industry in general & specific tourist establishments.

•Ottawa River Regulation Planning Board / Commission de planification de la régularisation de la rivière des Outaouais
c/o Ottawa River Regulation Secretariat, Block E1
373 Sussex Dr.
Ottawa, ON K1A 0H3
Tel: 613-995-3443
Toll-free: 800-778-1246
secretariat@ottawariver.ca
www.ottawariver.ca
Established under the terms of a Canada-Ontario-Québec Agreement, it is responsible for the preparation & continuing review of policies, guidelines & criteria for the integrated management of the principal reservoirs of the Ottawa River Basin in order to reduce flood damages along the river, its tributaries & in the Montréal area; it is also responsible for the operation & coordination of inflow forecasting, flow routing & optimization models that will reduce flood damages while having the least possible impact on users of the basin.

•Rabies Advisory Committee
DNA Bldg, Trent University
2140 East Bank Dr.
PO Box 4840
Peterborough, ON K9J 7B8
Tel: 705-755-2270
Established in 1979 it advises the Minister on the development of suitable vaccines against rabies & an effective system for vaccinating wild animals.

•Shibogama Interim Planning Board
PO Box 105
Wunnumin, ON P0V 2Z0
Tel: 807-442-2559; *Fax:* 807-442-2627
Advises the province on land use & resource development in an 11,131-square-kilometre area south of Big Trout Lake in northwestern Ontario.

•Windigo Interim Planning Board
PO Box 299
Sioux Lookout, ON P8T 1A3
Tel: 807-737-1585; *Fax:* 807-737-3133
Advises the province on land use & resource development in two areas totalling 15,959 square kilometres south of Big Trout Lake.

Niagara Escarpment Commission (NEC)
232 Guelph St., Georgetown, ON L7G 4B1
Tel: 905-877-5191; *Fax:* 905-873-7452
www.escarpment.org
twitter.com/Escarpment_NEC
Responsible for implementing the Niagara Escarpment Planning & Development Act, which is designed to maintain the escarpment & surrounding area as a continuous natural environment & to ensure that all new development in the escarpment area is compatible with provincial goals of environmental protection & conservation. The commission is also the main source of information on the Niagara Escarpment & the Niagara Escarpment Plan.

Chair, Don Scott
Tel: 905-877-5594; *Fax:* 905-873-7452
don.scott@ontario.ca

Director, Deb Pella Keen
Tel: 905-877-4810
deb.pellakeen@ontario.ca

Corporate Management & Information Division
Whitney Block, #6540, 99 Wellesley St., 6th Fl., Toronto, ON M7A 1W3
Tel: 416-314-1900; *Fax:* 416-314-1994
Other Communication: Peterborough Fax: 705-755-5369

Assistant Deputy Minister, Paula Reid
Tel: 416-314-1939; *Fax:* 416-314-1994
paula.reid@ontario.ca

Director, Services & Infrastructure Management, Phil Cooke
Tel: 705-755-2532; *Fax:* 705-755-2508
phil.cooke@ontario.ca
300 Water St., 3rd Fl.
PO Box 7000
Peterborough, ON K9J 8M5 Canada

Director, Corporate Finance & Controllership, Andrew Flynn
Tel: 705-755-1857
andrew.flynn@ontario.ca

Director, Mapping & Information Resources Branch, Steve Gregory
Tel: 705-755-2204; *Fax:* 705-755-2149
steve.gregory@ontario.ca
300 Water St., 3rd Fl.
PO Box 7000
Peterborough, ON K9J 8M5 Canada

Director, Strategic Human Resources Business, Amanda Holmes
Tel: 705-755-3131; *Fax:* 705-755-3120
amanda.holmes@ontario.ca
300 Water St., 3rd Fl.
PO Box 7000
Peterborough, ON K9J 8M5 Canada

Forest Industry Division
Roberta Bondar Pl., #400, 70 Foster Dr., Sault Ste. Marie, ON P6A 6V5
Fax: 705-945-5977
Toll-Free: 800-667-1940

Assistant Deputy Minister, Kathleen McFadden
Tel: 705-945-6767
kathleen.mcfadden@ontario.ca

Director, Business Development, Wayne Barnes
Tel: 705-945-6795; *Fax:* 705-945-6796
wayne.barnes@ontario.ca

Director, Operations, David Hayhurst
Tel: 705-945-5733; *Fax:* 705-945-6667
david.hayhurst@ontario.ca

Director, Forest Tenure & Economics, Faye Johnson
Tel: 705-945-6636
faye.johnson@ontario.ca

Office of the Chief Information Officer, Land & Resources I & IT Cluster
Whitney Block, #6601, 99 Wellesley, 6th Fl., Toronto, ON M7A 1W3
Fax: 416-314-6091
The department works in collaboration with the Ministry of Indigenous Relations & Reconciliation.

Chief Information Officer, John DiMarco
Tel: 416-326-6954
john.dimarco@ontario.ca

Acting Head, Business Solutions Services, Igor Solesa
Tel: 416-314-4786
igor.solesa@ontario.ca

Head, Service Management, Uwe Helmer
Tel: 519-826-5160
uwe.helmer@ontario.ca

Head, Strategy, Information & Program Management, Doug Green
Tel: 519-826-3236; *Fax:* 705-755-5552
doug.green@ontario.ca

Policy Division
Whitney Block, #6540, 99 Wellesley St. West, Toronto, ON M7A 1W3
Fax: 416-314-1994
Toll-Free: 800-667-1940
Provides assistance, advice & direction to ministry staff at all levels, on a variety of compliance & law enforcement matters. The branch is responsible for the development, coordination & delivery of an Integrated Provincial Compliance Program which focuses on the promotion, monitoring & enforcement aspects of compliance.

Assistant Deputy Minister, Rosalyn Lawrence
Tel: 416-314-6131
rosalyn.lawrence@ontario.ca

Director, Aboriginal Policy, Karan Aquino
Tel: 705-755-1996; *Fax:* 705-755-1372
karan.aquino@ontario.ca

Director, Biodiversity Branch, Eric Boysen
Tel: 705-755-5999; *Fax:* 705-755-2901
eric.boysen@ontario.ca

Director, Strategic Policy & Economics, Craig Brown
Tel: 416-314-1923; *Fax:* 416-314-1948
craig.brown@ontario.ca

Director, Species at Risk, Leith Hunter
Tel: 416-314-1819; *Fax:* 705-755-5483
leith.hunter@ontario.ca

Director, Natural Heritage, Lands & Protected Spaces, Ray Pichette
Tel: 705-755-1241; *Fax:* 705-755-1971
ray.pichette@ontario.ca

Director, Forests, Chris M. Walsh
Tel: 705-945-6653; *Fax:* 705-945-6667
chris.m.walsh@ontario.ca

Provincial Services Division
#6540, 99 Wellesley St. West, Toronto, ON M7A 1W3
Tel: 416-326-9504
The ministry's local presence in communities across the province, delivering integrated programs on resource management through 3 regions & 25 districts. The division delivers programs on provincial enforcement, native affairs, fisheries, forests & provincial lands, in addition to resources such as finance, facilities & engineering infrastructure, equipment & vehicles.

Acting Assistant Deputy Minister, Al Tithecott
Tel: 416-326-9502
al.tithecott@ontario.ca

Director, Enforcement, Lois Deacon
Tel: 705-755-1750; *Fax:* 705-755-1757
lois.deacon@ontario.ca

Managing Director, Ontario Parks, Bradley Fauteux
Tel: 705-755-1702
Toll-free: 800-667-1940; *Fax:* 705-755-1701
bradley.fauteux@ontario.ca
www.ontarioparks.com

Acting Director, Fish & Wildlife Services, Bruce Bateman
Tel: 705-755-5603; *Fax:* 705-755-1901
bruce.bateman@ontario.ca

Acting Director, Aviation, Forest Fire & Emergency Services, Mike O'Brien
Tel: 705-541-5118; *Fax:* 705-945-5785
mike.obien@ontario.ca

Science & Research Branch
Roberta Bondar Pl., 300 Water St., 4th Fl., Peterborough, ON K9J 8M5
Tel: 705-755-2809; *Fax:* 705-755-2802

Director, Eileen Forestall
Tel: 705-755-2807
eileen.forestell@ontario.ca

Regional Operations Division
Whitney Block, #6610, 99 Wellesley St. West, Toronto, ON M7A 1W3
Fax: 416-314-2629
Toll-Free: 800-667-1940
Other Communication: Peterborough Fax: 705-755-5073

Assistant Deputy Minister, Carrie Hayward
Tel: 416-314-2621
carrie.hayward@ontario.ca

Director, Far North Branch (South Porcupine), Dianne Corbett
Tel: 705-235-1284; *Fax:* 705-235-1106
dianne.corbett@ontario.ca
Director, Integration Branch, Monique Rolf von den Baumen-Clark
Tel: 705-755-1620; *Fax:* 705-755-1201
monique.rolfvondenbaumen@ontario.ca

Regional Offices

Northeast Region
Ontario Government Complex, 5520 Hwy. 101 East, PO Box 3020 South Porcupine, ON P0N 1H0
Tel: 705-235-1157; *Fax:* 705-235-1246
Acting Regional Director, Dianne Corbett
Tel: 705-235-1153; *Fax:* 705-235-1226
dianne.corbett@ontario.ca

Northwest Region
Ontario Government Bldg., #221A, 435 James St. South, Thunder Bay, ON P7E 6S8
Tel: 807-475-1261; *Fax:* 807-473-3023
Regional Director, Allan Willcocks
Tel: 807-475-1264
allan.willcocks@ontario.ca
District Manager, Jim Fry
Tel: 807-887-5013
jim.fry@ontario.ca

Southern Region
Robinson Place, South Tower, 300 Water St., 4th Fl. South, Peterborough, ON K9J 8M5
Tel: 705-755-2000; *Fax:* 705-755-3233
Regional Director, Jane Ireland
Tel: 705-755-3235
jane.ireland@ontario.ca
District Manager, Debbie Pella Keen
Tel: 905-713-7372
debbie.pellakeen@ontario.ca
District Manager, Kenneth Durst
Tel: 613-258-8201
ken.durst@ontario.ca
District Manager, Bruce Mighton
Tel: 613-732-5520
bruce.mighton@ontario.ca

Ontario Ministry of Northern Development & Mines

159 Cedar St., Sudbury, ON P3E 6A5
Tel: 705-670-5755; *Fax:* 705-670-5818
Toll-Free: 888-415-9845
TTY: 866-349-1388
ndmminister@ontario.ca
www.mndm.gov.on.ca
Secondary Address: #5630, 99 Wellesley St. West, 5th Fl. Whitney Block
Toronto, ON M7A 1W3
twitter.com/OntarioMNDM
www.facebook.com/OntarioMNDM
www.youtube.com/user/OntarioMNDM

The Ministry of Northern Development & Mines is the only regional Ministry within the government & plays a central role in northern affairs. It supports the mineral industry by providing it with valuable information about the province's geology. It also delivers & administers Ontario's Mining Act to improve the investment climate for mineral development. The Ministry has a two-fold mandate, to promote northern economic development & support mineral sector competitiveness. The Ministry is developing an initiative to help Ontario's Far North communities attract environmentally sound development, work with First Nation communities, partner ministries, the federal government, the mineral sector & private sector stakeholders to create opportunities for residents to help First Nation communities become more self-reliant. The Ministry works with the Northern Ontario Heritage Fund Corporation & with the Ontario Northland Transportation Commission to bring much-needed service improvements to the northeast.

Minister, Hon. Michael Gravelle
Tel: 416-327-0633; *Fax:* 416-327-0665
mgravelle.mpp.co@liberal.ola.org
Deputy Minister, David de Launay
Tel: 416-327-0647; *Fax:* 416-327-0634
david.delaunay@ontario.ca
Parliamentary Assistant, Joe Dickson
Tel: 416-327-0615; *Fax:* 416-327-0617
jdickson.mpp.co@liberal.ola.org
Director, Communication Services, Nina Chairelli
Tel: 416-327-0687; *Fax:* 416-327-0664
Director, Corporate Policy Secretariat, Priya Tandon
Tel: 416-327-0302; *Fax:* 647-723-2126
priya.tandon@ontario.ca
Director, Legal Services, Andrew Macdonald
Tel: 416-327-0640; *Fax:* 416-327-0646
andrew.macdonald@ontario.ca

Director, Resources & Labour Audit Service Team, Ray Masse
Tel: 416-314-9208; *Fax:* 416-314-9220
ray.masse@ontario.ca

Associated Agencies, Boards & Commissions:

•Ontario Northland Transportation Commission (ONTC)
555 Oak St. East
North Bay, ON P1B 8L3
Tel: 705-472-4500; *Fax:* 705-476-5598
Toll-free: 800-363-7512
info@ontarionorthland.ca
www.ontarionorthland.ca
Other Communication: Marketing & Media E-mail: pr@ontarionorthland.ca
Provides motor coach, rail transportation (including the Polar Bear Express), & refurbishment services to northeastern Ontario.

•Owen Sound Transportation Company Ltd. (OSTC)
717875, Hwy. 6
Owen Sound, ON N4K 5N7
Tel: 519-376-8740
Toll-free: 800-265-3163
www.ontarioferries.com

Corporate Management Division
#704, 159 Cedar St., Sudbury, ON P3E 6A5
Tel: 705-564-7443; *Fax:* 705-564-7447
Assistant Deputy Minister & Chief Adminstrative Officer, Scott Mantle
Tel: 705-564-7949; *Fax:* 705-564-7447
scott.mantle@ontario.ca
Acting Director, Human Resources Business Branch, Caroline Savarie
Tel: 705-564-7931; *Fax:* 705-564-7447
caroline.savarie@ontario.ca
Director, Business Planning, Lisa Zanetti
Tel: 705-564-7016; *Fax:* 705-564-7447
lisa.zanetti@ontario.ca

Mines & Minerals Division
Willet Green Miller Centre, 933 Ramsey Lake Rd., Level B6, Sudbury, ON P3E 6B5
Tel: 705-670-5755; *Fax:* 705-670-5818
Toll-Free: 888-415-9845
The Mines & Minerals Division works to generate new wealth & benefits for the residents of Ontario by providing basic geological information gathering & interpretation in support of Ontario's exploration, mine development & mining sectors & the administration of Ontario's Mining Act in a fair & consistent fashion. Collects, analyzes & publishes valuable information about the state of the mining & mineral industries, as well as specific information about the location & quality of mineral deposits. The field staff throughout the province provide consultative services to the industry through all phases of the mining sequence, & include resident geologists, mining recorders & mineral development officers.
Assistant Deputy Minister, Cindy Blancher-Smith
Tel: 705-670-5820; *Fax:* 705-670-5818
cindy.blancher-smith@ontario.ca
Director, Aboriginal Relations, Bernie Hughes
Tel: 705-670-5743; *Fax:* 705-670-5818
bernie.hughes@ontario.ca
Acting Director, Strategic Services Branch, Jamesene King
Tel: 705-670-3003; *Fax:* 705-670-5818
jamesene.king@ontario.ca

Mineral Development & Lands Branch
Willet Green Miller Centre, 933 Ramsey Lake Rd., Level B6, Sudbury, ON P3E 6B5
Tel: 705-670-5787; *Fax:* 705-670-5803
Toll-Free: 888-415-9845
Director, Gordon MacKay
Tel: 705-670-5784
gordon.mackay@ontario.ca

Ontario Geological Survey
Willet Green Miller Centre, 933 Ramsey Lake Rd., Level B6, Sudbury, ON P3E 6B5
Tel: 705-670-5758; *Fax:* 705-670-5818
Toll-Free: 888-415-9845
Director, Dr. J. Andy Fyon
Tel: 705-670-5924
andy.fyon@ontario.ca
Senior Manager, Resident Geologist Program, Robert Ferguson
Tel: 705-235-1622; *Fax:* 705-670-5905
rob.ferguson@ontario.ca

Northern Development Division
Roberta Bondar Place, #200, 70 Foster Dr., Sault Ste. Marie, ON P6A 6V8
Tel: 705-945-5900; *Fax:* 705-945-5931
Toll-Free: 800-461-2287
Responsible for promoting business, industrial, community & regional economic development & diversification; improving access to social & health services for northerners; planning & coordinating an integrated transportation system to meet private & commercial transportation needs at local, regional & provincial levels; coordinating the policies & programs of other ministries to ensure the special needs of northerners are addressed by government.
Assistant Deputy Minister, Helen Mulc
Tel: 705-945-6733; *Fax:* 705-945-5932
helen.mulc@ontario.ca
Executive Director, Northern Ontario Heritage Fund Corporation, Bruce Strapp
Tel: 705-945-6734; *Fax:* 705-564-7447
bruce.strapp@ontario.ca
Director, Transportation, Trade & Investment, Mark Speers
Tel: 705-945-6636
mark.speers@ontario.ca
Executive Director, Northern Ontario Heritage Fund Corporation, Bruce Strapp
Tel: 705-945-6734
bruce.strapp@ontario.ca

Area Offices

Kenora
#104, 810 Robertson St., Kenora, ON P9N 4J2
Tel: 807-468-2937; *Fax:* 807-468-2930
Manager, Christine Hansen
Tel: 807-468-2938
christine.hansen@ontario.ca

North Bay
#203, 447 McKeown Ave., North Bay, ON P1B 9S9
Tel: 705-494-4045; *Fax:* 705-494-4069
Manager, Moe Dorie
Tel: 705-494-4176
moe.dorie@ontario.ca

Sault Ste. Marie
Roberta Bondar Place, #200, 70 Foster Dr., Sault Ste Marie, ON P6A 6V8
Tel: 705-945-5914; *Fax:* 705-945-5931
Acting Manager, Marl Melisek
Tel: 705-945-5839
mark.melisek@ontario.ca

Sudbury
#601, 159 Cedar St., Sudbury, ON P3E 6A5
Tel: 705-564-7517; *Fax:* 705-564-7583
Acting Manager, Denis Rochon
Tel: 705-564-7513
denis.rochon@ontario.ca

Thunder Bay
Ontario Government Bldg., #332, 435 James St. South, Thunder Bay, ON P7E 6L3
Tel: 807-475-1648; *Fax:* 807-475-1589
Manager, John Guerard
Tel: 807-475-1573
john.guerard@ontario.ca

Timmins
Ontario Government Complex, East Wing, 5520 Hwy. 101 East, PO Box 3060 South Porcupine, ON P0N 1H0
Tel: 705-235-1664; *Fax:* 705-235-1660
Manager, Brian Pountney
Tel: 705-235-1654
brian.pountney@ontario.ca

Office of the Chief Information Officer, Land & Resources I & IT Cluster
Whitney Block, #6601, 99 Wellesley St. West, 6th Fl., Toronto, ON M7A 1W3
Chief Information Officer, John DiMarco
Tel: 416-326-6954
john.dimarco@ontario.ca
Head, Strategy, Information & Program Management, Doug Green
Tel: 519-826-3236
doug.green@ontario.ca
Head, Service Management, Uwe Helmer
Tel: 519-826-5160
uwe.helmer@ontario.ca
Acting Head, Business Solutions Services, Igor Solesa
Tel: 416-314-4786
igor.solesa@ontario.ca

Ring of Fire Secretariat
Willet Green Miller Centre, 933 Ramsey Lake Rd., Level B2, Sudbury, ON P3E 6B5
Tel: 705-670-5819; *Fax:* 705-670-5626
Toll-Free: 888-415-9845
Assistant Deputy Minister, Christine Kaszycki
Tel: 705-670-5877
christine.kaszycki@ontario.ca

Director, Aboriginal Community & Stakeholder Relations, Lori Churchill
Tel: 705-670-5767
lori.churchill@ontario.ca
Acting Director, Toronto Office, Fiona Mackintosh
Tel: 416-212-8207
fiona.mackintosh@ontario.ca

Office of the Ombudsman

Bell Trinity Sq., South Tower, 483 Bay St., 10th Fl., Toronto, ON M5G 2C9
Tel: 416-586-3300; *Fax:* 416-586-3485
Toll-Free: 800-263-1830
TTY: 866-411-4211
info@ombudsman.on.ca
www.ombudsman.on.ca
Other Communication: www.flickr.com/photos/ont_ombudsman; Ligne sans frais: 1-800-387-2620 (Français)
twitter.com/ont_ombudsman
www.facebook.com/OntarioOmbudsman
www.youtube.com/user/OntarioOmbudsman

An impartial body independent of government that investigates & resolves complaints about the administrative actions & decisions of provincial government organizations such as ministries, boards, agencies, commissions & tribunals. The Ombudsman is an Officer of the provincial Legislature & has jurisdiction over all provincial government organizations as an office of last resort. All available complaint & appeal procedures whenever possible should be used before the Ombudsman conducts an investigation. The Ombudsman decides cases based on independent investigations & works to find solutions that are acceptable to everyone involved. Services are free & confidential & are available in English, French or any other language.

Ombudsman, Paul Dubé

Communications & Media Relations
Director, Linda Williamson
Tel: 416-586-3426
lwilliamson@ombudsman.on.ca

Corporate
Director, Miller Scott
Tel: 416-586-3425

Operations
Deputy Ombudsman/Director, Barbara Finley
Tel: 416-586-3300
Director, Investigations, Sue Haslam
Tel: 416-586-3415

Special Ombudsman Response Team (SORT)
Director, Gareth Jones
Tel: 416-586-3329

Ontario Power Generation (OPG)

700 University Ave., Toronto, ON M5G 1X6
Tel: 416-592-2555
Toll-Free: 877-592-2555
webmaster@opg.com
www.opg.com
Other Communication: Media Relations Email: media@opg.com; Investor Relations Email: investor.relations@opg.com
twitter.com/OntarioPowerGen
www.youtube.com/opgvideos

Mandate is to meet Ontario's requirements for electricity so as to result in the greatest overall benefit to the community & the lowest cost to the consumer, while operating in a safe & environmentally responsible manner. Assets include 2 nuclear generating stations, 5 thermal power stations, 65 hydroelectric stations & 2 wind generating stations.

Chair, Bernard Lord
President & Chief Executive Officer, Jeffrey Lyash
President, OPG Nuclear & Chief Nuclear Officer, Glenn Jager
Chief Financial Officer, Beth Summers
Senior Vice-President, Commercial Operations & Environment, Bruce Boland
Senior Vice-President & Chief Risk Officer, Corporate Business Development, Carlo Crozzoli
Senior Vice-President, Law & General Counsel & Chief Ethics Officer, Christopher Ginther
Senior Vice-President, People & Culture, Barb Keenan
Senior Vice-President, Business & Administrative Services, Scott Martin
Senior Vice-President, Hydro-Thermal Operations, Mike Martelli
Senior Vice-President, Nuclear Projects, Dietmar Reiner
Vice-President, Corporate Relations & Communications, Ted Gruetzner
Vice-President & Corporate Secretary, Executive Operations, Catriona King

Office of the Provincial Advocate for Children & Youth

#2200, 401 Bay St., Toronto, ON M7A 0A6
Tel: 416-325-5669; *Fax:* 416-325-5681
Toll-Free: 800-263-2841
TTY: 416-325-2648
advocacy@provincialadvocate.on.ca
www.provincialadvocate.on.ca
Secondary Address: 435 Balmoral St.
Thunder Bay, ON P7C 5N4
Alt. Fax: 807-625-6351
twitter.com/OntarioAdvocate

The Office's mandate is to provide an independent voice for children & youth (including those with special needs & First Nations children) by reporting directly to the Legislature.

Provincial Advocate, Irwin Elman
Director, Advocacy Service, Laura Arndt
Director, Investigation, Diana Cooke
Director, Strategic Development, Liviu Georgescu

Ontario Ministry of Research, Innovation & Science

Hearst Block, 900 Bay St., 8th Fl., Toronto, ON M7A 2E1
Tel: 416-325-6666; *Fax:* 416-325-6688
Toll-Free: 866-668-4249
TTY: 416-325-3408
www.ontario.ca/page/ministry-research-innovation-and-science
Other Communication: Toll-Free TTY: 1-800-268-7095
twitter.com/OntInnovation
www.facebook.com/ontarioinnovation
www.youtube.com/OntarioInnovation

The Ministry (formerly known as Research & Innovation) supports research, commercialization & innovation in Ontario through programs & services such as the Ontario Research Fund, Innovation Demonstration Fund & Ontario Venture Capital Fund. The Ministry partners with universities, colleges, hospitals, entrepreneurs & business leaders in order to foster new scientific & technological discoveries that can be marketed to the world.

Minister, Hon. Reza Moridi
Tel: 416-326-9500; *Fax:* 416-326-2497
Deputy Minister, Giles Gherson
Tel: 416-325-6927; *Fax:* 416-325-6999
Giles.Gherson@ontario.ca

Corporate Services Division
54 Wellesley St., 4th Fl., Toronto, ON M7A 2E7
Tel: 416-325-6866; *Fax:* 416-314-7014
Toll-Free: 888-664-6008
TTY: 416-325-6707

Chief Administrative Officer & Assistant Deputy Minister, Robert Burns
Tel: 416-327-3682
robert.burns@ontario.ca
Director, Business Planning & Finance, Kevin Perry
Tel: 416-327-1137
kevin.perry@ontario.ca
Director, Investment Funding & Coordination, Richard Kikuta
Tel: 416-325-6849
richard.kikuta@ontario.ca
Director, Service Management & Facilities, Betty Morgan
Tel: 416-314-3309
betty.morgan@ontario.ca
Director, Strategic Human Resources Business Unit, Dan Keating
Tel: 416-325-6598
dan.keating@ontario.ca

Ontario Ministry of Tourism, Culture & Sport

Hearst Block, 900 Bay St., 9th Fl., Toronto, ON M7A 2E1
Tel: 416-326-9326; *Fax:* 416-314-7854
Toll-Free: 888-997-9015
TTY: 416-325-5807
www.mtc.gov.on.ca
Other Communication: Ontario Travel Information: 1-800-668-2746; Toll-Free TTY: 1-866-700-0040
twitter.com/ExploreON

The Ministry's mandate includes promoting a sustainable tourism industry in Ontario as a means of improving quality of life, increasing community pride, & increasing economic growth; encouraging & supporting the arts & culture industries; protecting Ontario's heritage & furthering the public library system; promoting sport & recreation activities; & working with Ministry agencies, attractions, boards & commissions, the tourism industry, other Ministries, other levels of government & the private sector to achieve these goals.

Minister, Hon. Eleanor McMahon
Tel: 416-326-9326; *Fax:* 416-326-9338
emcmahon.mpp.co@liberal.ola.org
Deputy Minister, Maureen Adamson
Tel: 416-314-7846
maureen.adamson@ontario.ca
Parliamentary Assistant, Sophie Kiwala
Tel: 416-212-2592; *Fax:* 416-212-7155
skiwala.mpp.co@liberal.ola.org
Director, Communications, Jennifer Lang
Tel: 416-212-3929; *Fax:* 416-325-5968
jennifer.lang@ontario.ca

Associated Agencies, Boards & Commissions:

•Art Gallery of Ontario (AGO)
317 Dundas St. West
Toronto, ON M5T 1G4
Tel: 416-977-0414; *Fax:* 416-979-6669
Toll-free: 877-225-4246
www.ago.net
Other Communication: Art Rental & Sales: 416-977-4654; Donations: 416-979-6619; membership Information: 416-979-6620: Resource Centres: 416-979-6642; Image Resources: 416-979-6674

•McMichael Canadian Art Collection
10365 Islington Ave.
Kelinburg, ON L0J 1C0
Tel: 905-893-1121; *Fax:* 905-893-0692
Toll-free: 888-213-1121
info@mcmichael.com
www.mcmichael.com

•Metro Toronto Convention Centre Corporation (MTCC)
255 Front St. West
Toronto, ON M5V 2W6
Tel: 416-585-8120; *Fax:* 416-585-8198
info@mtccc.com
www.mtccc.com
Other Communication: Sales, E-mail: sales@mtccc.com

•Minister's Advisory Council for Arts & Culture
400 University Ave., 5th Fl.
Toronto, ON M7A 2R9
Tel: 416-314-7621; *Fax:* 416-314-7635
Toll-free: 866-888-5829
macac@ontario.ca

•Niagara Parks Commission
Oak Hall Administration Bldg.
7400 Portage Rd. South
PO Box 150
Niagara Falls, ON L2E 6T2
Tel: 905-356-2241; *Fax:* 905-354-6041
Toll-free: 877-642-7275
www.niagaraparks.com

•Ontario Arts Council
151 Bloor St. West, 5th Fl.
Toronto, ON M5S 1T6
Tel: 416-961-1660; *Fax:* 416-961-7796
Toll-free: 800-387-0058
info@arts.on.ca
www.arts.on.ca

•Ontario Heritage Trust (OHT)
10 Adelaide St. East
Toronto, ON M5C 1J3
Tel: 416-325-5000; *Fax:* 416-325-5071
www.heritagetrust.on.ca
Other Communication: TTY: 711-416-325-5000

For more than three decades, the Ontario Heritage Trust has preserved, protected & promoted Ontario's rich & varied heritage. The Trust celebrates the people, places & events that have influenced & continue to shape our culture. As Ontario's lead heritage agency, the Trust's work extends to every corner of the province.

•Ontario Library Service - North (OLSN) / Service des bibliothèques de l'Ontario - Nord
334 Regent St.
Sudbury, ON P3C 4E2
Tel: 705-675-6467; *Fax:* 705-675-2285
Toll-free: 800-461-6348
www.olsn.ca
Other Communication: Toll-Free Fax: 1-800-461-6348

•Ontario Media Development Corporation (OMDC)
South Tower
#501, 175 Bloor St. East
Toronto, ON M4W 3R8
Tel: 416-314-6858; *Fax:* 416-314-6876
reception@omdc.on.ca
www.omdc.on.ca
Formerly the Ontario Film Development Corporation (OFDC).

•Ontario Place Corporation
955 Lake Shore Blvd. West
Toronto, ON M6K 3B9
Tel: 416-314-9900; *Fax:* 416-314-9989
Toll-free: 866-663-4386
www.ontarioplace.com

•Ontario Science Centre
770 Don Mills Rd.
Toronto, ON M3C 1T3
Tel: 416-696-1000; *Fax:* 416-696-3166
Toll-free: 888-696-1110
TTY: 416-696-3202
www.ontariosciencecentre.ca

•Ontario Tourism Marketing Partnership Corporation
#900, 10 Dundas St. East
Toronto, ON M7A 2A1
Tel: 416-212-0757; *Fax:* 416-325-6004
Toll-free: 800-668-2746
www.ontariotravel.net

•Ontario Trillium Foundation (OTF)
800 Bay St., 5th Fl.
Toronto, ON M5S 3A9
Tel: 416-963-4927; *Fax:* 416-963-8781
Toll-free: 800-263-2887
TTY: 416-963-7905
otf@otf.ca
www.otf.ca
The Ontario Trillium Foundation is an agency of the Ministry of Culture. Grants are provided to eligible not-for-profit & charitable organizations in the areas of arts & culture, sports and recreation, human & social services, & the environment.

•Ottawa Convention Centre (OCC)
55 Colonel By Dr.
Ottawa, ON K1N 9J2
Tel: 613-563-1984; *Fax:* 613-563-7646
Toll-free: 800-450-0077
info@ottawaconventioncentre.com
www.ottawaconventioncentre.com

•Royal Botanical Gardens (RBG)
680 Plains Rd. West
Burlington, ON L7T 4H4
Tel: 905-527-1158; *Fax:* 905-577-0375
Toll-free: 800-694-4769
info@rbg.ca
www.rbg.ca
Other Communication: GTA Toll-Free: 905-825-5040

•Royal Ontario Museum (ROM)
100 Queen's Park Cres.
Toronto, ON M5S 2C6
Tel: 416-586-5549; *Fax:* 416-586-5685
info@rom.on.ca
www.rom.on.ca

•Science North
100 Ramsey Lake Rd.
Sudbury, ON P3E 5S9
Tel: 705-522-3701; *Fax:* 705-522-4954
Toll-free: 800-461-4898
contactus@sciencenorth.ca
www.sciencenorth.ca
Other Communication: Exhibit Fax: 705-522-1283

•Southern Ontario Library Service (SOLS)
#902, 111 Peter St.
Toronto, ON M5V 2H1
Tel: 416-961-1669; *Fax:* 416-961-5122
Toll-free: 800-387-5765
www.sols.org

•St. Lawrence Parks Commission
13740 County Rd. 2
Morrisburg, ON K0C 1X0
Tel: 613-543-3704; *Fax:* 613-543-2847
Toll-free: 800-437-2233
TTY: 613-543-4181
getaway@parks.on.ca
www.parks.on.ca
The St. Lawrence Parks Commission is an Ontario provincial agency established in 1955 to provide recreation, tourism, cultural & educational opportunities for residents of Ontario & visitors to the province through the presentation & interpretation of historical attractions & the development & operation of parks, campgrounds, scenic parkways & recreational areas.

Culture Division
#1800, 401 Bay St., Toronto, ON M7A 0A7
Tel: 416-314-7265; *Fax:* 416-314-7461
Assistant Deputy Minister, Kevin Finnerty
Tel: 416-314-7262
kevin.finnerty@ontario.ca
Director, Programs & Services, Peter Armstrong
Tel: 416-314-7342; *Fax:* 416-212-1802
peter.armstrong@ontario.ca
Acting Director, Culture & Strategic Policy, Dawn Landry
Tel: 416-212-7646; *Fax:* 416-314-7635
dawn.landry@ontario.ca
Director, Culture Agencies, Diane Wise
Tel: 416-327-4305
diane.wise@ontario.ca

Office of the Chief Information Officer, Community Services I & IT Cluster
Mowat Block, 900 Bay St., 3rd Fl., Toronto, ON M7A 1L2
Assistant Deputy Minister & Chief Information Officer, Soussan Tabari
Tel: 416-326-8216
soussan.tabari@ontario.ca
Director, Case & Grants Management Solutions, Sanaul Haque
Tel: 416-314-4954; *Fax:* 416-585-7394
sanaul.haque@ontario.ca
Director, IAccess Solutions, Sanjay Madan
Tel: 416-325-2264
sanjay.madan@ontario.ca
Director, Strategic Planning & Business Relationship Management, Lolita Singh
Tel: 416-326-7942

Culture & Innovation Audit Service Team
College Park, 777 Bay St., 25th Fl., Toronto, ON M5G 2E5
Tel: 416-326-0800; *Fax:* 416-326-1712
Director, Sonia Gigliotti
Tel: 416-325-5983
sonia.gigliotti@ontario.ca

Regional & Corporate Services Division
400 University Ave., 2nd Fl., Toronto, ON M7A 2R9
Tel: 416-314-7311; *Fax:* 416-314-7313
Assistant Deputy Minister & Chief Administrative Officer, Cindy Lam
Tel: 416-314-7311
cindy.lam@ontario.ca
Director, Regional Services, Tom Chrzan
Tel: 416-314-6680; *Fax:* 416-314-6686
tom.chrzan@ontario.ca
Director, Corporate Resources, Tony Marzotto
Tel: 416-325-6135
tony.marzotto@ontario.ca
Director, Legal Services, Vacant
Director, Human Resources/Strategic Business Unit, Liborio Campisi
Tel: 416-325-6108; *Fax:* 416-325-6371
liborio.campisi@ontario.ca

Regional Offices
Central Region
400 University Ave., 4th Fl., Toronto, ON M7A 2R9
Tel: 416-314-6044; *Fax:* 416-314-2024
Toll-Free: 877-395-4105
Manager, Chris Rosati
Tel: 416-314-6682
chris.rosati@ontario.ca
East Region
347 Preston St., 4th Fl., Ottawa, ON K1S 3J4
Tel: 613-742-3360; *Fax:* 613-742-5300
Toll-Free: 800-267-9340
Manager, Valerie Andrews
Tel: 613-742-3366
valerie.andrews@ontario.ca
North Region
#334, 435 James St. South, Thunder Bay, ON P7E 6S7
Tel: 807-475-1683; *Fax:* 807-475-1297
Toll-Free: 800-465-6861
Manager, Elaine Lynch
Tel: 807-475-1635
elaine.lynch@ontario.ca
West Region
4275 King St., 2nd Fl., Kitchener, ON N2P 2E9
Fax: 519-650-3425
Toll-Free: 800-265-2189
Manager, Chris Stack
Tel: 519-650-3421
chris.stack@ontario.ca

Sport, Recreation & Community Programs
College Park, 777 Bay St., 23rd Fl., Toronto, ON M7A 1S5
Tel: 416-326-4371; *Fax:* 416-314-7458
Assistant Deputy Minister, Steve Harlow
Tel: 416-212-8995
steve.harlow@ontario.ca
Director, Sport, Recreation & Community Programs, Susan Golets
Tel: 416-314-7696; *Fax:* 416-314-7458
susan.golets@ontario.ca
Director, Policy Branch, Anna Ilnyckyj
Tel: 416-326-0825
anna.ilnyckyj@ontario.ca

Tourism Planning & Operations Division
Hearst Block, 900 Bay St., 10th Fl., Toronto, ON M7A 2E2
Tel: 416-325-6961
Assistant Deputy Minister, Richard McKinnell
Tel: 416-325-2861
richard.mckinnell@ontario.ca
Acting Director, Tourism Agencies & Manager, Agency Relations Unit, Kathleen Henschel
Tel: 416-325-6411; *Fax:* 416-314-7003
kathleen.henschel@ontario.ca
Director, Ontario Place Revitalization, Sandeep Persaud
Tel: 416-325-3936; *Fax:* 416-212-9628
sandeep.persaud@ontario.ca
Coordinator, Divisional Operations, Daniela Davidson
Tel: 416-325-7809
daniela.davidson@ontario.ca

Fort William Historical Park
1350 King Rd., Thunder Bay, ON P7K 1L7
Tel: 807-577-8461; *Fax:* 807-473-2327
info@fwhp.ca
www.fwhp.ca
Other Communication: Admissions: 807-473-2347; Admissions Fax: 807-473-2312; Reservations: 807-473-2344; Event Hotline: 807-473-2333; Emergency After Hours: 807-473-9750
twitter.com/FWHPtweets
www.facebook.com/fortwilliamhistoricalpark
General Manager, Sergio Buonocore
Tel: 807-473-2341; *Fax:* 807-473-2336
sergio.buonocore@ontario.ca

Huronia Historical Parks
16164 Hwy. 12, PO Box 160 Midland, ON L4R 4K8
Tel: 705-526-7838; *Fax:* 705-526-9193
TTY: 705-528-7697
www.hhp.on.ca
General Manager, Jan Gray
Tel: 705-528-7690
jan.gray@ontario.ca

Tourism Policy & Development Division
Hearst Block, 900 Bay St., 10th Fl., Toronto, ON M7A 2E1
Tel: 416-326-9326; *Fax:* 416-325-6985
Assistant Deputy Minister, Richard McKinnell
Tel: 416-325-6961
richard.mckinnell@ontario.ca
Acting Director, Investment & Development Office, Debbie Jewell
Tel: 416-314-7553; *Fax:* 416-327-2506
debbie.jewell@ontario.ca
Acting Director, Tourism Policy & Research, Jodi Melnychuk
Tel: 416-325-6055; *Fax:* 416-314-7341
Jodi.Melnychuk@ontario.ca

Ontario Ministry of Transportation

Ferguson Block, 77 Wellesley St. West, 3rd Fl., Toronto, ON M7A 1Z8
Tel: 416-327-9200; *Fax:* 416-327-9185
Toll-Free: 800-268-4686
TTY: 866-471-8929
www.mto.gov.on.ca
Other Communication: Driver & Vehicle Licensing: 1-800-387-3445; Road Test Booking: 1-888-570-6110
The Ministry performs the following functions: planning, designing & building highways; performing environmental assessments; rehabilitating existing highways to increase their efficiency & safety; performing ongoing highway maintenance; developing standards, operational guidelines & policies relating to highways; & researching & introducing new technologies for more effective highway management. The Ministry commits to providing & promoting transportation services in a way that sustains a healthful environment through the Ministry's Statement of Environmental Values. The Ministry applies & integrates environmental concerns, along with prevailing social, economic, scientific & other considerations when conducting its business activities.
Minister, Hon. Steven Del Duca
Tel: 416-327-9200; *Fax:* 416-327-9188
sdelduca.mpp.co@liberal.ola.org
Deputy Minister, Stephen Rhodes
Tel: 416-327-9162; *Fax:* 416-327-9185
stephen.rhodes@ontario.ca
Director, Communications Branch, Kimberley Bates
Tel: 416-327-2117; *Fax:* 416-327-2591
kimberley.bates@ontario.ca
Director, Legal Services, Mary Gersht
Tel: 416-235-4406; *Fax:* 416-235-4924
mary.gersht@ontario.ca

Director, Ontario Internal Audit, Transportation & Agriculture Service Team, Nancy Lavoie
Tel: 905-704-2870; *Fax:* 905-704-2333
nancy.lavoie@ontario.ca

Associated Agencies, Boards & Commissions:

•Metrolinx
97 Front St. West
Toronto, ON M5J 1E6
Tel: 416-874-5900; *Fax:* 416-869-1755
www.metrolinx.com
Metrolinx serves the Greater Toronto Area & Hamilton, & operates the following companies & programs: GO Transit; Union Pearson Express; PRESTO; Smart Commute; & the Transit Procurement Initiative (TPI).

•Ontario Highway Transport Board (OHTB)
151 Bloor St. West, 10th Fl.
Toronto, ON M5S 2T5
Tel: 416-326-6732; *Fax:* 416-326-6738
ohtb@mto.gov.on.ca
www.ohtb.gov.on.ca

Corporate Services Division
Garden City Tower, 301 St. Paul St., 6th Fl., St Catharines, ON L2R 7R4
Tel: 905-704-2693; *Fax:* 905-704-2445
Divisional Lead, Marketing & Communications, Klari Kalkman
Tel: 905-704-2460
Klari.Kalkman@ontario.ca
Director, Finance Branch, Ian Freeman
Tel: 905-704-2702; *Fax:* 905-704-2515
Ian.Freeman@ontario.ca
Director, Corporate Business Services Branch, Shelley Tapp
Tel: 905-704-2608; *Fax:* 905-704-2833
shelley.tapp@ontario.ca
Director, Strategic Human Resources, Maria Tejeda
Tel: 905-704-2043; *Fax:* 905-704-2747
maria.tejeda@ontario.ca

Labour & Transportation I & IT Cluster
400 University Ave., 9th Fl., Toronto, ON M7A 1T7
Tel: 416-327-3754; *Fax:* 416-327-3755
Chief Information Officer, Howard Bertrand
Tel: 416-327-1955
howard.bertrand@ontario.ca
Director, Service Management, Dani Danyluk
Tel: 905-704-2834; *Fax:* 905-704-2666
dani.danyluk@ontario.ca
Director, RUS Modernization IT Branch, George Jazvac
Tel: 416-235-6798
george.jazvac@ontario.ca
Director, OPS Net Solutions Delivery Centre of Excellence, Wynnann Rose
Tel: 905-704-2488
wynnann.rose@ontario.ca
Director, Road User Safety Solutions, Bob Stephens
Tel: 416-235-5209; *Fax:* 416-235-5658
bob.stephens@ontario.ca
Director, Information Management, Project Advisor & Labour Solutions, Daniel Young
Tel: 416-326-3181; *Fax:* 416-325-0000
daniel.young@ontario.ca

Policy & Planning Division
Ferguson Block, 77 Wesley St., 3rd Fl., Toronto, ON M7A 1Z8
Tel: 416-327-8521; *Fax:* 416-327-8746
Assistant Deputy Minister, John Lieou
Tel: 416-327-8521
john.lieou@ontario.ca
Executive Director, Transportation Pan/Parapan Am Games, Andrew Posluns
Tel: 416-212-4842; *Fax:* 416-212-7840
andrew.posluns@ontario.ca
Director, Transportation Planning, Tija Dirks
Tel: 416-585-7238; *Fax:* 416-585-7324
tija.dirks@ontario.ca
Director, Transportation Policy, Jill Hughes
Tel: 416-585-7177; *Fax:* 416-585-7204
jill.hughes@ontario.ca
Acting Director, Transit Policy, Christopher Langford
Tel: 416-585-7352; *Fax:* 416-585-7343
christopher.langford@ontario.ca
Director, Transportation Pan/Parapan Am Games Branch, Teresa Marando
Tel: 416-326-5969; *Fax:* 416-212-7840
teresa.marando@ontario.ca
Acting Director, Aboriginal Relations, Greg Tokarz
Tel: 416-585-7315; *Fax:* 416-585-6876
greg.tokarz@ontario.ca
Director, Strategic Policy & Transportation, Economics, David Ward
Tel: 416-212-1893; *Fax:* 416-212-2351
david.ward@ontario.ca

Provincial Highways Management Division
Ferguson Block, 77 Wellesley St. West, 3rd Fl., Toronto, ON M7A 1Z8
Tel: 416-327-9044; *Fax:* 416-327-9226
Assistant Deputy Minister, Gerry Chaput
Tel: 416-327-9044; *Fax:* 416-327-9226
gerry.chaput@ontario.ca
Executive Director, Asset Management, Suzanne Beale
Tel: 905-704-2299; *Fax:* 905-704-2562
suzanne.beale@ontario.ca
Director, Highway Standards, Dino Bagnariol
Tel: 905-704-2194; *Fax:* 905-704-2055
dino.bagnariol@opntario.ca
Acting Director, Investment Strategies, Paul Botelho
Tel: 905-704-2092; *Fax:* 905-704-2044
paul.botelho@ontario.ca
Director, Contract Management & Operations, Paul Y. Leocoarer
Tel: 905-704-2601; *Fax:* 905-704-2030
paul.lecoarer@ontario.ca
Director, Windsor Border Initiatives Implementation Group (BIIG), Vacant
Tel: 416-326-6876; *Fax:* 416-326-7056

Regional Offices

Central
Atrium Tower, 1201 Wilson Ave., Downsview, ON M3M 1J8
Tel: 416-235-5412; *Fax:* 416-235-5266
Regional Director, Lou Politano
Tel: 416-235-5400; *Fax:* 416-235-5266
lou.politano@ontario.ca

Eastern
1355 John Counter Blvd., PO Box 4000 Kingston, ON K7L 5A3
Tel: 613-545-4711; *Fax:* 613-545-4786
Toll-Free: 800-267-0295
Regional Director, Kathryn Moore
Tel: 613-545-4600
kathryn.moore@ontario.ca

Northeastern
Ontario Government Bldg., 447 McKeown Ave., 1st Fl., North Bay, ON P1B 9S9
Tel: 705-472-7900; *Fax:* 705-497-5422
Toll-Free: 800-461-9547
Regional Director, Eric Doidge
Tel: 705-497-5500
eric.doidge@ontario.ca

Northwestern
615 James St. South, Thunder Bay, ON P7E 6P6
Tel: 807-473-2000; *Fax:* 807-473-2157
Toll-Free: 800-465-5034
Regional Director, Ian Smith
Tel: 807-473-2050; *Fax:* 807-473-2165
ian.smith@ontario.ca

Western
659 Exeter Rd., 4th Fl., London, ON N6E 1L3
Tel: 519-873-4335; *Fax:* 519-873-4236
Toll-Free: 800-265-6072
Regional Director, Ann Baldwin
Tel: 519-873-4333; *Fax:* 519-873-4236
ann.baldwin@ontario.ca

Road User Safety Division
Bldg A, #191, 1201 Wilson Ave., Downsview, ON M3M 1J8
Tel: 416-235-2999; *Fax:* 416-235-4153
The division sets safety standards, develops policies, legislation & regulation, & educates road users about road user safety. Responsibilities include evaluating the effectiveness of safety measures, inspecting, monitoring & enforcing compliance with standards, testing, licenses & drivers, & registering vehicles. Through public education, legislation & enforcement, the government strives to ensure all motorists take responsibility for their driving behaviour. The Assistant Deputy Minister, Road User Safety, is responsible for the co-ordination of all Road User Safety activities for the province & acts as the Registrar of Motor Vehicles for Ontario.
Acting Assistant Deputy Minister, Heidi Francis
Tel: 416-235-4453; *Fax:* 416-235-4153
heidi.francis@ontario.ca
Director, Licencing Services, Paul Brown
Tel: 416-235-4392; *Fax:* 416-235-4378
paul.h.brown@ontario.ca
Director, Program Development & Evaluation, Paul Harbottle
Tel: 416-235-4199; *Fax:* 416-235-4111
paul.harbottle@ontario.ca
Director, Regional Operations, Jeff Hudebine
Tel: 416-235-3526; *Fax:* 416-235-4670
jeff.hudebine@ontario.ca
Director, Carrier Safety & Enforcement, Peter Hurst
Tel: 416-235-2501; *Fax:* 905-704-2530
paul.harbottle@ontario.ca
Acting Director, Safety Policy & Education; Manager, Road Safety Policy Office - Road Users, Teepu Khawja
Tel: 416-235-4050; *Fax:* 416-235-5139
teepu.khawja@ontario.ca
Director, Service Delivery Partnerships, Kim Lambert
Tel: 416-235-3570; *Fax:* 416-235-4433
kim.lambert@ontario.ca
Director, Oranizational Development & Controllership, Barbara Maher
Tel: 416-235-4864; *Fax:* 416-235-3939
barbara.maher@ontario.ca

Treasury Board Secretariat

Ferguson Block, 77 Wellesley St. West, 8th Fl., Toronto, ON M7A 1N3
Tel: 416-326-8525; *Fax:* 416-327-3790
Toll-Free: 800-268-1142
TTY: 416-326-8566
www.ontario.ca/treasury-board-secretariat
The Treasury Board Secretariat is involved in the following: decision-making related to capital; labour relations between the government, the Ontario Public Service & the public sector; corporate policy & agency governance; internal audit; internal human resources; & information & information technology.
President, Treasury Board, Hon. Liz Sandals
Tel: 416-327-2333; *Fax:* 416-327-3790
lsandals.mpp@liberal.ola.org
Deputy Minister; Secretary, Treasury Board; Secretary, Management Board of Cabinet, Greg Orencsak
Tel: 416-325-1607; *Fax:* 416-325-1612
greg.orencsak@ontario.ca
Parliamentary Assistant to the President of the Treasury Board, Yvan Baker
Tel: 416-327-6611
ybaker.mpp.co@liberal.ola.org
Director, Policy, Minister's Office, James Alberding
Tel: 416-327-6619
james.alberding2@ontario.ca
Director, Operations, Deputy Minister's Office, Kyle MacIntyre
Tel: 416-325-9084
Director, Legal Services Branch, Sean Kearney
Tel: 416-327-6396; *Fax:* 416-325-9404
sean.kearney@ontario.ca
Director, Communications Branch, Anne Matthews
Tel: 416-325-1376; *Fax:* 416-327-2817
anne.matthews@ontario.ca
Director, Operations, Minister's Office, Josie Verrilli
Tel: 416-327-0943
Josie.Verrilli3@ontario.ca

Associated Agencies, Boards & Commissions:

•Case Management Masters Remuneration Commission
Makes recommendations about the renumeration of case management masters.

•Deputy Judges Remuneration Commission
Makes recommendations about the per diem rate to be paid to Deputy Judges, as well as the payment of reasonable expenses related to carrying out their duties.

•Justices of the Peace Remuneration Commission
Makes recommendations about the salaries, pensions & benefits of Ontario's justices of the peace.

•Conflict of Interest Commissioner
#1802, 2 Bloor St. East
Toronto, ON M4W 3J5
Tel: 416-325-1571; *Fax:* 416-325-4330
Toll-free: 866-956-1191
coicommissioner@ontario.ca
www.coicommissioner.gov.on.ca

•Ontario Pension Board (OPB)
Sun Life Bldg.
#2200, 200 King St. West
Toronto, ON M5H 3X6
Tel: 416-364-8558; *Fax:* 416-364-7578
Toll-free: 800-668-6203
clientservice@opb.ca
www.opb.on.ca
Administrator of the Public Service Pension Plan

•OPSEU Pension Trust (OPTrust)
#1200, 1 Adelaide St. East
Toronto, ON M5C 3A7
Tel: 416-681-6161; *Fax:* 416-681-6175
Toll-free: 800-637-0024
www.optrust.com
Other Communication: Member & Pensioner Services, Phone: 416-681-6100

•Provincial Judges Pension Board
c/o Ontario Pension Board
#2200, 200 King St. West
Toronto, ON M5H 3X6
Tel: 416-601-3923; *Fax:* 416-364-9094
Administers pension benefits associated with the pension plan established for provincial judges.

•Provincial Judges Remuneration Commission
Ferguson Block
77 Wellesley St. West, 13th Fl.
Toronto, ON M7A 1N3
Tel: 416-325-4141; *Fax:* 416-327-8402
Makes recommendations about the salaries, pensions & benefits of Ontario provincial judges.

•Public Service Commission
Whitney Block
99 Wellesley St. West, 5th Fl.
Toronto, ON M7A 1W4
Tel: 416-325-1750

•Public Service Grievance Board (PSGB)
#600, 180 Dundas St. West
Toronto, ON M5G 1Z8
Tel: 416-326-1388; *Fax:* 416-326-1396
psgb.psgb@ontario.ca
www.psab.gov.on.ca/english/psgb/index.htm

Bargaining & Compensation
77 Wellesley St. West, 5th Fl., Toronto, ON M7A 1N3
Associate Deputy Minister, Reg Pearson
Tel: 416-327-0132
reg.pearson@ontario.ca
Acting Director, HR Policy & Planning, Janet O'Grady
Tel: 416-325-0222
Director, Labour Relations Secretariat, Michael Uhlmann
Tel: 416-326-3865
michael.uhlmann@ontario.ca

Employee Relations Division
77 Wellesley St. West, 7th Fl., Toronto, ON M7A 1N3
Tel: 416-325-1475; *Fax:* 416-325-1483
Assistant Deputy Minister, Marc Rondeau
Tel: 416-325-4545
marc.rondeau@ontario.ca
Director, Total Compensation Strategy Branch, Janette Jozefacki
Tel: 416-327-8306
janette.jozefacki@ontario.ca
Acting Director, Negotiations & Security Branch, Matt Siple
Tel: 416-325-4117
matt.siple@ontario.ca
Director, Centre for Employee Relations, Vacant
Tel: 416-325-1490; *Fax:* 416-325-1483

Central Agencies I&IT Cluster
222 Jarvis St., 2nd Fl., Toronto, ON M7A 0B6
Tel: 416-326-2700; *Fax:* 416-327-3347
Chief Information Officer, Ron Huxter
Tel: 905-433-6890
ron.huxter@ontario.ca

Centre for Leadership & Learning
#5320, 99 Wellesley St. West, 5th Fl., Toronto, ON M7A 1W4
Tel: 416-325-1768; *Fax:* 416-325-6317
Chief Talent Officer, Diane McArthur
Tel: 416-325-1777
diane.mcarthur@ontario.ca
Director, Talent Management Branch, Chettie Legaspi
Tel: 416-325-1617; *Fax:* 416-325-4996
chettie.legaspi@ontario.ca
Director, Corporate Leadership & Learning Branch, Judi Hartman
Tel: 416-325-2802
judi.hartman@ontario.ca
Director, Executive Programs & Services, Janet Hannah
Tel: 416-325-8816
janet.hannah@ontario.ca

Corporate Policy, Agency Governance & Open Government Division
77 Wellesley St. West, 13th Fl., Toronto, ON M7A 1N3
Tel: 416-327-9262; *Fax:* 416-325-9577
Acting Assistant Deputy Minister, Brian Fior
Tel: 416-325-8320
Director, Public Appointments Secretariat, Neil Downs
Tel: 416-327-2632; *Fax:* 416-327-2633
neil.downs@ontario.ca
www.pas.gov.on.ca
Director, Agency Governance Branch, Scot Weeres
Tel: 416-325-1345
Scot.Weeres@ontario.ca

Corporate Services Division
Whitney Block, 99 Wellesley St. West, 5th Fl., Toronto, ON M7A 1W3
Tel: 416-212-7807; *Fax:* 416-327-2866
Toll-Free: 888-745-8888
Assistant Deputy Minister & Chief Administrative Officer, Melanie Fraser
Tel: 416-325-3821
melanie.fraser@ontario.ca
Director, Enterprise Services Strategic Business Unit, Mary Kostic
Tel: 416-326-8914
Mary.kostic@ontario.ca
Director, Service Management & Service Delivery Branch, Karl Cunningham
Tel: 416-326-8896; *Fax:* 416-326-8932
karl.cunningham@ontario.ca
Director, Business Planning & Financial Management, Anna Di Misa
Tel: 416-327-2526; *Fax:* 416-327-3794
anna.dimisa@ontario.ca

Office of the Corporate Chief Information Officer (OCCIO)
Ferguson Block, 77 Wellesley St. West, 8th Fl., Toronto, ON M7A 1N3
Tel: 416-327-3442; *Fax:* 416-327-3264
Corporate Chief Information & Information Technology Officer, David Nicholl
Tel: 416-327-9696
david.nicholl@ontario.ca
Executive Lead & Assistant Deputy Minister, Infrastructure Technology Services, Rocco Passero
Tel: 416-326-3398
rocco.passero@ontario.ca
Corporate Chief Strategist, I&IT Strategy & Cyber Security, Fred Pitt
Tel: 416-212-1624; *Fax:* 416-314-7710
fred.pitt@ontario.ca
Director, Service Management, Michael Amato
Tel: 416-327-9274
michael.amato@ontario.ca
Director, Telecommunications Branch, Conrad Brown
Tel: 416-327-5505
conrad.brown@ontario.ca
Director, I&IT Development & Performance Branch, Jasmine Kanga
Tel: 416-212-7924; *Fax:* 416-326-1374
jasmine.kanga@ontario.ca
Director, Infrastructure Project Delivery, Deborah Hendriks
Tel: 905-433-5358
deborah.hendriks2@ontario.ca
Director, Desktop Services/Field Services, Zelko Holjevac
Tel: 416-212-2259
zelko.holjevac@ontario.ca
Director, I&IT Development & Performance Branch, Jasmine Kanga
Tel: 416-212-7924; *Fax:* 416-326-1374
jasmine.kanga@ontario.ca
Director, Enterprise Planning & Project Delivery Services, Rick Provenzano
Tel: 416-212-4702
rick.provenzano@ontario.ca
Director, Data Centre Operations, Mark Elliot
Tel: 416-325-8673
mark.elliott@ontario.ca
Director, Corporate Services, Martin Thumm
Tel: 416-327-3049; *Fax:* 647-723-2034
Martin.Thumm@ontario.ca

Office of the Treasury Board
7 Queens Park Cres., 7th Fl., Toronto, ON M7A 1Y7
Tel: 416-325-7620; *Fax:* 416-212-7767
Division Coordinator, Mandi Doris
Tel: 416-327-2062
mandi.doris@ontario.ca

Capital Planning Division
7 Queens Park Cres., 6th Fl., Toronto, ON M7A 1Y7
Tel: 416-325-9411; *Fax:* 416-325-8851
Assistant Deputy Minister, Artur Arruda
Tel: 416-325-3359
artur.arruda@ontario.ca
Director, Capital Planning Branch, Raj Sharda
Tel: 416-325-8640
Director, Economic Infrastructure & Analytics Branch, Dorothy Cheung
Tel: 416-325-3391
dorothy.cheung@ontario.ca
Director, Social Infrastructure & Infrastructure Finance Branch, Gladys Miu
Tel: 416-325-5311
gladys.miu@ontario.ca

Office of the Provincial Controller Division
7 Queens Park Cres., 2nd Fl., Toronto, ON M7A 1Y7
Tel: 416-325-0535; *Fax:* 416-325-2029
Acting Assistant Deputy Minister & Provincial Controller, Sanjeev Batra
Tel: 416-325-8017
sanjeev.batra@ontario.ca
Director, Operations Control & Management Reporting Branch, Joe Liscio
Tel: 416-327-3273
joe.liscio@ontario.ca
Director, Accounting Policy & Financial Reporting Branch, Nadine Petsche
Tel: 416-325-8027
nadine.petsche@ontario.ca
Director, Financial Management & Control Policy Branch, Gary Wuschnakowski
Tel: 416-212-5545
gary.wuschnakowski@ontario.ca

Planning & Expenditure Management Division
Frost Bldg. North, 95 Grosvenor St., 4th Fl., Toronto, ON M7A 1Y7
Tel: 416-325-7620
Acting Assistant Deputy Minister, Maria Duran-Schneider
Tel: 416-326-1213
maria.duran-schneider@ontario.ca
Acting Director, Education, Justice & Quantitative Management Branch, Tim Cook
Tel: 416-212-9693
Tim.Cook@ontario.ca
Director, General Government, Planning & Resources Branch, Andrea Dutton
Tel: 416-327-0206
andrea.dutton@ontario.ca
Director, Management Board of Cabinet Support Branch, Lisa Sherin
Tel: 416-326-9302
lisa.sherin@ontario.ca
Health, Social & Coordination Branch, Vacant
Tel: 416-325-8244

Ontario Internal Audit Division
777 Bay St., 25th Fl., Toronto, ON M5G 2E5
Tel: 416-327-9512; *Fax:* 416-327-9486
Chief Internal Auditor & Assistant Deputy Minister, Richard Kennedy
Tel: 416-327-9319
richard.kennedy@ontario.ca
Executive Lead & Strategic Advisor, Audit Centre for Excellence, Marisa Fernandez
Tel: 416-212-6357
marisa.fernandez@ontario.ca

Workplace Safety & Insurance Board (WSIB)

200 Front St. West, Ground Fl., Toronto, ON M5V 3J1
Tel: 416-344-1000; *Fax:* 416-344-4684
Toll-Free: 800-387-0750
TTY: 800-387-0050
www.wsib.on.ca
Other Communication: eServices Inquiries, Phone: 1-888-243-1569; Collections, Phone: 1-800-268-0929
twitter.com/wsib
www.linkedin.com/company/wsib
www.youtube.com/ontariowsib
The Workplace Safety & Insurance Board is involved in Ontario's occupational health & safety system. The Board's responsibilities are as follows: administering no-fault workplace insurance in Ontario for employers & workers; providing disability benefits; monitoring the quality of healthcare; & assisting workers who have been injured on the job or persons who have contracted an occupational disease in an early & safe return to work.
Chair, Elizabeth Witmer
President & CEO, Thomas Teahen

Government of Prince Edward Island

Seat of Government: Island Information Service, PO Box 2000
Charlottetown, PE C1A 7N8
Tel: 902-368-4000
island@gov.pe.ca
www.gov.pe.ca
Other Communication: Tourism Information, Toll-Free Phone: 1-800-463-4734
twitter.com/infopei
www.facebook.com/govpe
youtube.com/user/govpeca; flickr.com/photos/peigov
The Province of Prince Edward Island entered Confederation on July 1, 1873. It has a land area of 5,685.73 sq km, with a population of 140,204, according to the 2011 StatsCan census.

Office of the Lieutenant Governor

Government House, PO Box 846 Charlottetown, PE C1A 7L9
Tel: 902-368-5480; *Fax:* 902-368-5481
www.gov.pe.ca/olg

The Honourable H. Frank Lewis was sworn in as the 41st Lieutenant Governor of Prince Edward Island by the Chief Justice of the Supreme Court of Prince Edward Island at Province House on August 15, 2011.

Lieutenant Governor, Hon. H. Frank Lewis, OPEI
Tel: 902-368-5480; *Fax:* 902-368-5481
hflewis@gov.pe.ca

Office of the Premier

Shaw Bldg., 95 Rochford St. South, 5th Fl., PO Box 2000 Charlottetown, PE C1A 7N8
Tel: 902-368-4400; *Fax:* 902-368-4416
premier@gov.pe.ca
www.gov.pe.ca/premier

Honourable H. Wade MacLauchlan is the thirty-second Premier of Prince Edward Island. He was acclaimed Leader of the PEI Liberal Party on Feb. 21, 2015, & was sworn in as Premier on Feb. 23, 2015. He then won the general election held May 4, 2015.

Premier; President, Executive Council; Minister, Justice & Public Safety & Attorney General; Minister Responsible, Aboriginal Affairs, Acadian & Francophone Affairs & Intergovernmental Affairs, & Labour, Hon. H. Wade MacLauchlan
Tel: 902-368-4400; *Fax:* 902-386-4416
premier@gov.pe.ca
Social Media: twitter.com/wadepeiliberal, www.facebook.com/WadePEI

Deputy Minister, Policy & Priorities; Intergovernment & Public Affairs, Paul Ledwell
Tel: 902-368-4407; *Fax:* 902-368-6118
ptledwell@gov.pe.ca

Ethics & Integrity Commissioner, Shauna Sullivan-Curley, QC

Chief of Staff, Robert Vessey
Tel: 902-368-4400; *Fax:* 902-368-4416
rsvessey@gov.pe.ca

Executive Council

Shaw Bldg., 5th Fl., PO Box 2000 Charlottetown, PE C1A 7N8
Tel: 902-368-4502; *Fax:* 902-368-6118
www.gov.pe.ca/eco

The Executive Council of Prince Edward Island is made up of Ministers of the Crown. The role of the Executive Council is to decide upon the policy & direction that the government will take & to advise the Lieutenant Governor.

President, Executive Council; Premier; Minister, Justice & Public Safety & Attorney General; Minister Responsible, Intergovernmental Affairs, Aboriginal Affairs & Acadian & Francophone Affairs, & Labour; Leader, Liberal Party of Prince Edward Island, Hon. H. Wade MacLauchlan
Tel: 902-368-4400; *Fax:* 902-368-4416
premier@gov.pe.ca
Social Media: twitter.com/wadepeiliberal, www.facebook.com/WadePEI
Note: Web Sites: www.gov.pe.ca/premier (Office of the Premier); www.gov.pe.ca/jps (Department of Justice & Safety)
Office of the Premier of Prince Edward Island, Shaw Bldg.
95 Rochford St. South, 5th Fl.
PO Box 2000
Charlottetown, PE C1A 7N8

Minister, Workforce & Advanced Learning, Hon. Richard E. Brown
Tel: 902-368-5956; *Fax:* 902-368-5277
rebrown@gov.pe.ca
Note: Web Site: www.gov.pe.ca/ial (Department of Workforce & Advanced Learning)
Department of Workforce & Advanced Learning, Shaw Bldg.
105 Rochford St., 3rd Fl.
PO Box 2000
Charlottetown, PE C1A 7N8

Minister, Education, Early Learning & Culture, Hon. Doug W. Currie
Tel: 902-438-4130; *Fax:* 902-438-4062
dwcurrie@gov.pe.ca
Social Media: twitter.com/DougCurrie, www.facebook.com/doug.w.currie
Note: Web Sites: www.gov.pe.ca/eecd (Department of Education, Early Learning & Culture); www.dougcurrie.ca (Personal Website)
Department of Education, Early Learning & Culture, Holman Centre
#101, 250 Water St.
Summerside, PE C1N 1B6

Minister, Agriculture & Fisheries; Government House Leader, Hon. J. Alan McIsaac
Tel: 902-368-4880; *Fax:* 902-368-4857
jamcisaac@gov.pe.ca
Social Media: www.facebook.com/alan.mcisaac.3
Note: Web Sites: www.gov.pe.ca/agriculture (Department of Agriculture & Fisheries)
Department of Agriculture & Fisheries, Jones Bldg.
11 Kent St.
PO Box 2000
Charlottetown, PE C1A 7N8

Minister, Finance, Hon. Allen F. Roach
Tel: 902-368-4050; *Fax:* 902-368-6575
afroach@gov.pe.ca
Social Media: www.facebook.com/allen.roach.127
Note: Web Sites: www.gov.pe.ca/finance (Department of Finance)
Department of Finance, Shaw Bldg.
95 Rochford St., 2nd Fl. South
PO Box 2000
Charlottetown, PE C1A 7N8

Minister, Health & Wellness, Hon. Robert L. Henderson
Tel: 902-368-6414; *Fax:* 902-368-4121
rlhenderson@gov.pe.ca
Social Media: www.facebook.com/robert.henderson.92317
Note: Web Sites: www.gov.pe.ca/health (Department of Health & Wellness)
Department of Health & Wellness, Shaw Bldg.
105 Rochford St.
PO Box 2000
Charlottetown, PE C1A 7N8

Minister, Transportation, Infrastructure & Energy; Minister Responsible, Status of Women, Hon. Paula J. Biggar
Tel: 902-368-5100; *Fax:* 902-368-5395
pjbiggar@gov.pe.ca
Note: Web Site: www.gov.pe.ca/tir (Department of Transportation, Infrastructure & Energy)
Department of Transportation, Infrastructure & Energy, Jones Bldg.
11 Kent St., 3rd Fl.
PO Box 2000
Charlottetown, PE C1A 7N8

Minister, Communities, Land & Environment, Hon. Robert J. Mitchell
Tel: 902-620-3646; *Fax:* 902-368-5542
rjmitchell@gov.pe.ca
Social Media: twitter.com/robmitchellpei
Note: Web Site: www.gov.pe.ca/cle (Department of Communities, Land & Environment)
Department of Communities, Land & Environment, Jones Bldg.
11 Kent St.
PO Box 2000
Charlottetown, PE C1A 7N8

Minister, Economic Development & Tourism, Hon. J. Heath MacDonald
Tel: 902-368-4230; *Fax:* 902-368-3726
hmacdonald@gov.pe.ca
Note: Web Site: www.gov.pe.ca/tourism (Department of Economic Development & Tourism)
Department of Economic Development & Tourism, Shaw Bldg.
105 Rochford St.
PO Box 2000
Charlottetown, PE C1A 7N8

Minister, Family & Human Services, Hon. Tina M. Mundy
Tel: 902-620-3777; *Fax:* 902-894-0242
tmmundy@gov.pe.ca
Social Media: twitter.com/tinamundy, www.facebook.com/tinamundyforegmont
Note: Web Site: www.gov.pe.ca/sss (Department of Family & Human Services)
Department of Family & Human Services, Jones Bldg.
11 Kent St., 2nd Fl.
PO Box 2000
Charlottetown, PE C1N 1B6

Executive Council Office

Shaw Bldg., 5th Fl., PO Box 2000 Charlottetown, PE C1A 7N8
Tel: 902-368-4000
www.gov.pe.ca/eco

It is the responsibility of the Executive Council Office to provide administrative services & advice to the Executive Council. Advice & support are also offered to the government's departments & agencies.
An important activity of the Executive Council Office is the provision of research & analysis on intergovernmental affairs. Advice is given related to social & economic policies.
The Executive Office is also involved in the coordination of traditional ceremonial or legal requirements, such as the swearing into office of Members of Cabinet or the Lieutenant Governor.

Premier; President, Executive Council; Minister, Justice & Public Safety & Attorney General; Minister Responsible, Intergovernmental Affairs & Aboriginal Affairs & Acadian & Francophone Affairs, & Labour, Hon. H. Wade MacLauchlan
Tel: 902-368-4400; *Fax:* 902-368-4416
premier@gov.pe.ca
Social Media: twitter.com/wadepeiliberal, www.facebook.com/WadePEI
Note: Web Site: www.gov.pe.ca/premier (Office of the Premier)

Clerk of the Executive Council; Secretary to Cabinet, Paul Ledwell
Tel: 902-368-4502; *Fax:* 902-368-5385

Deputy Minister, Intergovernmental & Public Affairs; Deputy Minister of Policy & Priorities, Paul Ledwell
Tel: 902-368-4407; *Fax:* 902-368-6118
ptledwell@gov.pe.ca

Chief of Protocol, Rhonda Sexton
Tel: 902-368-4605; *Fax:* 902-368-6118
rmsexton@gov.pe.ca

Director, Acadian & Francophone Affairs Secretariat, Diane Arsenault
Tel: 902-368-4872; *Fax:* 902-368-4857
dianearsenault@gov.pe.ca

Director, Intergovernmental Affairs Secretariat, Rochelle Gallant
Tel: 902-368-4415; *Fax:* 902-368-6118
rgallant@gov.pe.ca

Cabinet Committee on Priorities

Chair, Hon. J. Alan McIsaac
Tel: 902-368-4820; *Fax:* 902-368-4846
jamcisaac@gov.pe.ca

Vice-Chair, Hon. Doug W. Currie
Tel: 902-368-5250; *Fax:* 902-368-4121
dwcurrie@gov.pe.ca

Deputy Minister, Policy & Priorities, Hon. Paul Ledwell
Tel: 902-368-4407; *Fax:* 902-368-6118
ptlwdwell@gov.pe.ca

Clerk Assistant & Coordinating Secretary, Wendy MacDonald
Tel: 902-620-3457; *Fax:* 902-368-6118
wimacdonald@gov.pe.ca

Operations Committee

Shaw Bldg., 5th Fl., PO Box 2000 Charlottetown, PE C1A 7N8
Tel: 902-368-4305; *Fax:* 902-368-6118

The Operations Committee coordinates the legislative development process. All proposed legislation, regulations, & amendments to regulations are reviewed & analyzed prior to submission to the Executive Council for approval.

Chair, Hon. Allen F. Roach
Tel: 902-368-4050
afroach@gov.pe.ca

Vice-Chair, Hon. Robert L. Henderson
Tel: 902-368-6414; *Fax:* 902-368-4121
rlhenderson@gov.pe.ca

Secretary, Operations Committee, Allan Campbell
Tel: 902-368-4400; *Fax:* 902-368-4416
avcampbell@gov.pe.ca

Treasury Board

Shaw Bldg., 95 Rochford St. South, 3rd Fl., PO Box 2000 Charlottetown, PE C1A 7N8
www.gov.pe.ca/finance/tb-info/dg.inc.php3

The Executive Council Act established the Treasury Board as a committee of the Executive Council. The Board advises the Executive Council about budgeting & financial matters & the management of the Public Service.

Chair, Hon. Allen F. Roach
Tel: 902-368-4050
afroach@gov.pe.ca

Vice-Chair, Hon. Richard E. Brown
Tel: 902-368-5956; *Fax:* 902-368-5277
rebrown@gov.pe.ca

Secretary to Treasury Board, Dan Campbell, CFA
Tel: 902-368-4201; *Fax:* 902-368-6661
dmcampbell@gov.pe.ca

Prince Edward Island Legislative Assembly

197 Richmond St., PO Box 2000 Charlottetown, PE C1A 7N8
Tel: 902-368-5970; *Fax:* 902-368-5175
Toll-Free: 877-315-5518
legislativelibrary@assembly.pe.ca
www.assembly.pe.ca

The Legislative Assembly of Prince Edward Island consists of the lawmakers & the offices & officials who support their work.

Office of the Clerk

197 Richmond St., 2nd Fl., PO Box 2000 Charlottetown, PE C1A 7N8
Tel: 902-368-5970; *Fax:* 902-368-5175

The Clerk of the Legislative Assembly is responsible for providing administrative support to the Speaker, the House, & its members. Decisions of the House are recorded by the Clerk & published in the Journals of the Legislative Assembly of Prince Edward Island.

Clerk of the Legislative Assembly, Charles MacKay
Tel: 902-368-5970; *Fax:* 902-368-5175
chmackay@assembly.pe.ca

Clerk of Committees & Clerk Assistant, Marian Johnston
Tel: 902-368-5972; *Fax:* 902-368-5175
majohnston@assembly.pe.ca

Director, Communications & External Relations, JoAnne Holden
Tel: 902-368-4316; *Fax:* 902-368-5175
jdholden@assembly.pe.ca

Director, Corporate Services, Joey Jeffrey
Tel: 902-368-5525; *Fax:* 902-368-5175
jajeffrey@assembly.pe.ca

Sergeant-at-Arms & Director, Security, W/O Al J. McDonald
Tel: 902-368-5976; *Fax:* 902-368-5175
ajmcdonald@assembly.pe.ca

Office of the Conflict of Interest Commissioner

197 Richmond St., 1st Fl., PO Box 2000 Charlottetown, PE C1A 7N8

Tel: 902-368-5970; *Fax:* 902-368-5175

The Conflict of Interest Commissioner is an independent officer of the Legislative Assembly who administers the Conflict of Interest Act. To enhance public confidence in the Legislative Assembly, the Conflict of Interest Act ensures that Ministers & Members reconcile their private & public interests & conduct their responsibilities with integrity.

Commissioner, Conflict of Interest, Hon. John A. McQuaid
jamcquaid@assembly.pe.ca

Government Members' Office (Liberal)

Coles Bldg., 175 Richmond St., 2nd Fl., PO Box 2890 Charlottetown, PE C1A 8C5

Tel: 902-368-4330; *Fax:* 902-368-4348
www.assembly.pe.ca/GMO

Administrative support to government backbenchers is provided by the Government Members' Office.

Premier, Prince Edward Island; Leader, Liberal Party of Prince Edward Island; President, Executive Council; Minister Responsible, Intergovernmental Affairs; Minister Responsible, Aboriginal, Acadian & Francophone Affairs, Hon. H. Wade MacLaughlan
Tel: 902-368-4400; *Fax:* 902-368-4416
premier@gov.pe.ca
Note: Web Site: www.gov.pe.ca/premier (Office of the Premier)

Government House Leader, Hon. J. Alan McIsaac
Tel: 902-368-4820; *Fax:* 902-368-4846
jamcisaac@gov.pe.ca

Government Whip, Jordan Brown
Tel: 902-368-4330; *Fax:* 902-368-4348
jbrown@assembly.pe.ca

Caucus Chair, Kathleen Casey
Tel: 902-620-3851; *Fax:* 902-368-4348
kmcasey@assembly.pe.ca

Office of the Information & Privacy Commissioner

J. Angus MacLean Bldg., 180 Richmond St., 2nd Fl., PO Box 2000 Charlottetown, PE C1A 7N8

Tel: 902-368-4099; *Fax:* 902-368-5947

The Information & Privacy Commissioner is appointed by the Legislature for a five year term. The Commissioner, who is an independent officer of the Legislative Assembly, reports annually to the Speaker of the Legislative Assembly about the work of the Office.

The Commissioner accepts Requests for Review from persons who are not satisfied with responses as a result of access to information requests made under the Freedom of Information & Protection of Privacy Act. Upon conclusion of a review, the order of the Information & Privacy Commissioner is final. Applicants, the public body, or a third party may only apply to the Supreme Court of Prince Edward Island for judicial review.

The Commissioner also conducts investigations related to privacy complaints.

Commissioner, Information & Privacy, Karen A. Rose
karose@gov.pe.ca

Legislative Library & Research Service

J. Angus MacLean Bldg., 94 Great George St., PO Box 2000 Charlottetown, PE C1A 7N8

Tel: 902-620-3765; *Fax:* 902-620-3975
legislativelibrary@assembly.pe.ca
www.assembly.pe.ca/libraryresearch

Opened in 2008, the Legislative Library supports members, committees, & house officers in their work. Non-partisan reports are provided by the research service.

Librarian, Research, Web Services & Design, Laura Morrell
lemorrell@assembly.pe.ca

Office of the Official Opposition (Progressive Conservative)

Coles Bldg., 175 Richmond St., 3rd Fl., PO Box 338 Charlottetown, PE C1A 7K7

Tel: 902-368-4360; *Fax:* 902-368-4377
www.assembly.pe.ca/oppositionoffice
Other Communication: Party URL: peipc.ca
twitter.com/PEIPCParty
www.facebook.com/peipcparty

The Official Opposition raises concerns of Islanders & holds the government accountable for its policies & promises.

Leader, Official Opposition; Interim Leader, Progressive Conservative Party of PEI, Jamie Fox
Tel: 902-368-4360; *Fax:* 902-368-4377
jdfox@assembly.pe.ca
Social Media: twitter.com/jamiedfox

Opposition House Leader, Matthew MacKay
Tel: 902-368-4360; *Fax:* 902-368-4377
mmackay@assembly.pe.ca

Opposition Whip, Sidney MacEwen
Tel: 902-368-4360; *Fax:* 902-368-4377
smacewen@assembly.pe.ca

Chief of Staff, Ernie Hudson

Parliamentary Publications & Services

J. Angus MacLean Bldg., 180 Richmond St., 2nd Fl., PO Box 2000 Charlottetown, PE C1A 7N8

Tel: 902-368-5371; *Fax:* 902-368-5175

The published daily debates of Members in the House & in committees are known as Hansard. Staff of the Hansard office transcribe, publish, & indexe the debates.

Manager, Jeff Bursey
jrbursey@assembly.pe.ca

Office of the Speaker

197 Richmond St., 1st Fl., PO Box 2000 Charlottetown, PE C1A 7N8

Tel: 902-368-4310; *Fax:* 902-368-4473
www.assembly.pe.ca/speaker

At the beginning of each new General Assembly, a Speaker of the Legislative Assembly is elected by secret ballot. The following Members of the Legislative Assembly are ineligible to be the Speaker: the Premier, the Leader of the Opposition & leaders of other political parties in the Assembly, & Members of the Executive Council.

Speaker, Hon. Buck Watts
Constituency: District #8 - Tracadie - Hillsborough Park, Liberal
Tel: 902-620-3850; *Fax:* 902-368-4348
fdwatts@assembly.pe.ca

Deputy Speaker, Sonny Gallant
Constituency: District #24 - Evangeline - Miscouche, Liberal
Tel: 902-368-4345; *Fax:* 902-368-4348
sjgallant@assembly.pe.ca

Office of the Third Party (Green)

Basement, Coles Bldg., 175 Richmond St., PO Box 2000 Charlottetown, PE C1A 7N8

Tel: 902-620-3977
www.assembly.pe.ca/thirdparty
Other Communication: Party URL: greenparty.pe.ca
twitter.com/PEIgreens
www.facebook.com/GreenPartyPEI

Leader, Third Party, Peter Bevan-Baker
Tel: 902-368-4339
psbevanbaker@assembly.pe.ca

Legislative Committees

www.assembly.pe.ca/committees/index.php

The Standing Committees of the Legislative Assembly of Prince Edward Island are as follows: Agriculture & Fisheries; Communities, Land & Environment; Education & Economic Development; Health & Wellness; Infrastructure & Energy; Legislative Management; Public Accounts; Rules, Regulations, Private Bills & Privileges.

Chair, Agriculture & Fisheries, Pat Murphy
Constituency: District #26 - Alberton - Roseville, Liberal
Tel: 902-368-4367; *Fax:* 902-368-4348
pwmurphy@assembly.pe.ca

Chair, Communities, Land & Environment, Kathleen Casey
Constituency: District #14 - Charlottetown - Lewis Point, Liberal
Tel: 902-620-3851; *Fax:* 902-368-4348
kmcasey@assembly.pe.ca

Chair, Education & Economic Development, Bush Dumville
Constituency: District #15 - West Royalty - Springvale, Liberal
Tel: 902-368-4380; *Fax:* 902-368-4348
sfdumville@assembly.pe.ca

Chair, Health & Wellness, Jordan Brown
Constituency: District #13 - Charlottetown - Brighton, Liberal
Tel: 902-368-4330; *Fax:* 902-368-4348
jbrown@assembly.pe.ca

Chair, Infrastructure & Energy, Sonny Gallant
Constituency: District #24 - Evangeline - Miscouche, Liberal
Tel: 902-368-4345; *Fax:* 902-368-4348
sjgallant@assembly.pe.ca

Chair, Legislative Management, Hon. Buck Watts
Constituency: District #8 - Tracadie - Hillsborough Park, Liberal
Tel: 902-620-3850; *Fax:* 902-368-4348
fdwatts@assembly.pe.ca

Chair, Public Accounts, James Aylward
Constituency: District #6 - Stratford - Kinlock, Progressive Conservative
Tel: 902-368-4360; *Fax:* 902-368-4377
jsjaylward@assembly.pe.ca

Chair, Rules, Regulations, Private Bills & Privileges, Kathleen Casey
Constituency: District #14 - Charlottetown - Lewis Point, Liberal
Tel: 902-620-3851; *Fax:* 902-368-4348
kmcasey@assembly.pe.ca

Sixty-fifth General Assembly - Prince Edward Island

Province House, 165 Richmond St., 1st Fl., PO Box 2000 Charlottetown, PE C1A 7N8

Tel: 902-368-5970; *Fax:* 902-368-5175
Toll-Free: 877-315-5518
www.assembly.pe.ca
twitter.com/peileg

Last Provincial General Election: May 4, 2015.
Next Provincial General Election (scheduled under the province's fixed-date legislation): October 2019.
Party Standings (Sept. 2016):
Liberal: 17;
Progressive Conservative 8;
Green Party: 1;
Vacant 1;
Total: 27.
Salaries, Indemnities & Allowances (April 2010):
A Member of the Legislative Assembly's salary is $65,344. In addition to this basic salary for each Member of the Legislative Assembly are the following additional salaries:
Premier $71,094 (total $136,438);
Ministers $45,688 (total $111,032);
Speaker $38,474 (total $103,818);
Deputy Speaker $19,237 (total $84,581);
Leader of the Opposition $45,688 (total $111,032);
Government House Leader $12,337 (total $77,681);
Opposition House Leader $4,339 (total $69,683);
Government Whip & Opposition Whip $3,659 (total $69,003);
Non-Ministerial Members of Executive Council Committees $5,996 (total $71,340);
Leader of a Third Party $16,764 (total $82,108).
The following is a list of Members of the Legislative Assembly, with their electoral district number & name, number of persons enumerated in the district for the 2011 provincial general election, party affiliation, & contact information. The general address for all Members of the Legislative Assembly is as follows: PO Box 2000, Charlottetown PE, C1A 7N8.

Members of the Legislative Assembly of Prince Edward Island

James Aylward
Constituency: District #6 - Stratford - Kinlock, Progressive Conservative
Tel: 902-368-4360; *Fax:* 902-368-4377
jsjaylward@assembly.pe.ca
Social Media: twitter.com/jsjaylward, www.linkedin.com/profile/view?id=111998898
Coles Bldg.
175 Richmond St., 3rd Fl.
PO Box 338
Charlottetown, PE C1A 7K7

Leader, Third Party; Leader, Green Party of Prince Edward Island, Peter Bevan-Baker
Constituency: District #17 - Kellys Cross - Cumberland, Green Party of Canada
Tel: 902-368-4339
psbevanbaker@assembly.pe.ca
Social Media: twitter.com/thehappydentist, www.facebook.com/102385486513276
Note: Peter Bevan-Baker is the first member of the Green Party to be elected to the PEI legislature.

Minister, Transportation, Infrastruture & Energy; Minister Responsible, Status of Women, Hon. Paula J. Biggar
Constituency: District #23 - Tyne Valley - Linkletter, Liberal
Tel: 902-368-5120; *Fax:* 902-368-5385
pjbiggar@gov.pe.ca
Social Media: twitter.com/pjbiggar, www.facebook.com/paula.biggar, www.linkedin.com/pub/paula-biggar/17/13a/392
Department of Transportation, Infrastructure & Energy, Jones Bldg.
11 Kent St., 3rd Fl.
PO Box 2000
Charlottetown, PE C1A 7N8

Government Whip, Jordan Brown
Constituency: District #13 - Charlottetown - Brighton, Liberal
Tel: 902-368-4330; *Fax:* 902-368-4348
jbrown@assembly.pe.ca
Social Media: twitter.com/jordanbrownpei
Coles Bldg.
175 Richmond St.
PO Box 2890
Charlottetown, PE C1A 8C5

Minister, Workforce & Advanced Learning, Hon. Richard E. Brown
Constituency: District #12 - Charlottetown - Victoria Park, Liberal
Tel: 902-368-4801; *Fax:* 902-368-5277
rebrown@gov.pe.ca
Social Media: twitter.com/richardbrownpei
Department of Workforce & Advanced Learning, Shaw Bldg.
105 Richford St., 3rd Fl.
PO Box 2000
Charlottetown, PE C1A 7N8

Caucus Chair, Kathleen Casey
Constituency: District #14 - Charlottetown - Lewis Point, Liberal
Tel: 902-620-3851; *Fax:* 902-368-4348
kmcasey@assembly.pe.ca
Social Media: www.facebook.com/kathleen.casey.96, www.linkedin.com/pub/kathleen-casey/9/a84/134
Coles Bldg.
175 Richmond St., 2nd Fl.
PO Box 2890
Charlottetown, PE C1A 8C5

Darlene Compton
Constituency: District #4 - Belfast - Murray River, Progressive Conservative
Tel: 902-368-4360; *Fax:* 902-368-4377
dcompton@assembly.pe.ca
darlenecompton.ca
Social Media: twitter.com/darlene_compton, www.facebook.com/pcdarlenecompton4
Coles Bldg.
175 Richmond St., 3rd Fl.
PO Box 338
Charlottetown, PE C1A 7K7

Minister, Education, Early Learning & Culture, Hon. Doug W. Currie
Constituency: District #11 - Charlottetown - Parkdale, Liberal
Tel: 902-438-4130; *Fax:* 902-438-4062
dwcurrie@gov.pe.ca
www.dougcurrie.ca
Social Media: twitter.com/DougCurrie, www.facebook.com/doug.w.currie
Department of Education, Early Learning & Culture
#101, 250 Water St.
Summerside, PE C1N 1B6

Bush Dumville
Constituency: District #15 - West Royalty - Springvale, Liberal
Tel: 902-368-4380; *Fax:* 902-368-4348
sfdumville@assembly.pe.ca
Social Media: www.facebook.com/bush.dumville
Coles Bldg.
175 Richmond St., 2nd Fl.
PO Box 2890
Charlottetown, PE C1A 8C5

Interim Leader, Progressive Conservative Party of PEI; Leader, Official Opposition, Jamie Fox
Constituency: District #19 - Borden - Kinkora, Progressive Conservative
Tel: 902-368-4360; *Fax:* 902-368-4377
jdfox@assembly.pe.ca
Social Media: twitter.com/jamiedfox

Deputy Speaker, Sonny Gallant
Constituency: District #24 - Evangeline - Miscouche, Liberal
Tel: 902-368-4345; *Fax:* 902-368-4348
sjgallant@assembly.pe.ca
Social Media: www.facebook.com/sonny.gallant
Coles Bldg.
175 Richmond St., 2nd Fl.
PO Box 2890
Charlottetown, PE C1A 8C5

Minister, Health & Wellness, Hon. Robert L. Henderson
Constituency: District #25 - O'Leary - Inverness, Liberal
Tel: 902-368-6414; *Fax:* 902-368-4121
rlhenderson@gov.pe.ca
Social Media: www.facebook.com/robert.henderson.92317
Department of Health & Wellness, Shaw Bldg.
105 Rochford St.
PO Box 2000
Charlottetown, PE C1A 7N8

Colin LaVie
Constituency: District #1 - Souris - Elmira, Progressive Conservative
Tel: 902-368-4360; *Fax:* 902-368-4377
crlavie@assembly.pe.ca
Social Media: www.facebook.com/crlavie
Coles Bldg.
175 Richmond St., 3rd Fl.
PO Box 338
Charlottetown, PE C1A 7K7

Minister, Economic Development & Tourism, Hon. J. Heath MacDonald
Constituency: District #16 - Cornwall - Meadowbank, Liberal
Tel: 902-368-4230; *Fax:* 902-368-3726
hmacdonald@gov.pe.ca
Social Media: twitter.com/CornwallMeadowb
Department of Economic Development & Tourism, Shaw Bldg.
105 Rochford St.
PO Box 2000
Charlottetown, PE C1A 7N8

Opposition Whip, Sidney MacEwen
Constituency: District #7 - Morell - Mermaid, Progressive Conservative
Tel: 902-368-4360; *Fax:* 902-368-4377
smacewen@assembly.pe.ca
Social Media: twitter.com/sidneymacewen, www.facebook.com/809886662433716
Coles Bldg.
175 Richmond St., 3rd Fl.
PO Box 338
Charlottetown, PE C1A 7K7

Opposition House Leader, Matthew MacKay
Constituency: District #20 - Kensington - Malpeque, Progressive Conservative
Tel: 902-836-4360; *Fax:* 902-368-4377
mmackay@assembly.pe.ca
Social Media: twitter.com/matthewmackaypc
Coles Bldg.
175 Richmond St., 3rd Fl.
PO Box 338
Charlottetown, PE C1A 7K7

President, Executive Council; Premier; Minister, Justice & Public Safety & Attorney General; Minister Responsible, Intergovernmental Affairs, Aboriginal Affairs & Acadian & Francophone Affairs, & Labour; Leader, Liberal Party of Prince Edward Island, Hon. H. Wade MacLauchlan
Constituency: District #9 - York - Oyster Bed, Liberal
Tel: 902-368-4400; *Fax:* 902-386-4416
premier@gov.pe.ca
Social Media: twitter.com/WadePEILiberal, www.facebook.com/WadePEI
Office of the Premier of Prince Edward Island, Shaw Bldg.
95 Rochford St. South, 5th Fl.
PO Box 2000
Charlottetown, PE C1A 7N8

Minister, Agriculture & Fisheries; Government House Leader, Hon. J. Alan McIsaac
Constituency: District #5 - Vernon River - Stratford, Liberal
Tel: 902-368-4820; *Fax:* 902-368-4846
jamcisaac@gov.pe.ca
Social Media: www.facebook.com/alan.mcisaac.3
Department of Agriculture & Fisheries, Jones Bldg.
11 Kent St., 5th Fl.
PO Box 2000
Charlottetown, PE C1A 7N8

Minister, Communities, Land & Environment, Hon. Robert J. Mitchell
Constituency: District #10 - Charlottetown - Sherwood, Liberal
Tel: 902-620-3646; *Fax:* 902-368-5542
rjmitchell@gov.pe.ca
Social Media: www.facebook.com/robert.mitchell.75054689
Department of Communities, Land & Environment, Jones Bldg.
11 Kent St.
PO Box 2000
Charlottetown, PE C1A 7N8

Minister, Family & Human Services, Hon. Tina M. Mundy
Constituency: District #22 - Summerside - St. Eleanors, Liberal
Tel: 902-620-3777; *Fax:* 902-894-0242
tmmundy@gov.pe.ca
Social Media: twitter.com/tinamundy, www.facebook.com/tinamundyforegmont
Department of Family & Human Services, Jones Bldg.
11 Kent St., 2nd Fl.
PO Box 2000
Charlottetown, PE C1N 1B6

Pat Murphy
Constituency: District #26 - Alberton - Roseville, Liberal
Tel: 902-368-4367; *Fax:* 902-368-4348
pwmurphy@assembly.pe.ca
Social Media: www.facebook.com/pwmurphy
Coles Bldg.
175 Richmond St., 2nd Fl.
PO Box 2890
Charlottetown, PE C1A 8C5

Steven Myers
Constituency: District #2 - Georgetown - St. Peters, Progressive Conservative
Tel: 902-368-4360; *Fax:* 902-368-4377
samyers@assembly.pe.ca
Coles Bldg.
175 Richmond St., 3rd Fl.
PO Box 338
Charlottetown, PE C1A 7K7

Hal Perry
Constituency: District #27 - Tignish - Palmer Road, Liberal
Tel: 902-368-4330; *Fax:* 902-368-4348
jhperry@gov.pe.ca

Minister, Finance, Hon. Allen F. Roach
Constituency: District #3 - Montague - Kilmuir, Liberal
Tel: 902-368-4000; *Fax:* 902-368-5544
afroach@gov.pe.ca
Social Media: www.facebook.com/allen.roach.127
Department of Finance, Shaw Bldg.
95 Rochford St., 2nd Fl. South
PO Box 2000
Charlottetown, PE C1A 7N8

Brad Trivers
Constituency: District #18 - Rustico - Emerald, Progressive Conservative
Tel: 902-368-4360; *Fax:* 902-368-4377
bgtrivers@assembly.pe.ca
bradtrivers.com
Social Media: twitter.com/bradtrivers, www.facebook.com/BradTriversPC, www.linkedin.com/in/bradtrivers
Coles Bldg.
175 Richmond St., 3rd Fl.
PO Box 338
Charlottetown, PE C1A 7K7

Speaker, Hon. Buck Watts
Constituency: District #8 - Tracadie - Hillsborough Park, Liberal
Tel: 902-620-3850; *Fax:* 902-368-4348
fdwatts@assembly.pe.ca
Social Media: twitter.com/BuckWatts1
Coles Bldg.
175 Richmond St., 2nd Fl.
PO Box 2890
Charlottetown, PE C1A 8C5

Vacant
Constituency: District #21 - Summerside - Wilmot
Note: Janice Sherry retired from politics on Aug. 1, 2016, to return to private life.

Prince Edward Island Government Departments & Agencies

Prince Edward Island Department of Agriculture & Fisheries

Jones Bldg., 11 Kent St., 5th Fl., PO Box 2000
Charlottetown, PE C1A 7N8
Tel: 902-368-4880; *Fax:* 902-368-4857
www.gov.pe.ca/agriculture
twitter.com/AgInfoPEI
www.facebook.com/FishWildlifePEI

Prince Edward Island's Department of Agriculture & Fisheries provides programs & services to farmers & the fishing industry. Programs are developed within the context of the Sustainable Resource Policy, which protects the province's land, water, & air. The following are some examples of program categories: AgriFlexibility; Buy PEI; Crop Production; Food Safety, Biosecurity, & Traceability; Forestry; Innovation & Applied Research; Laboratory Services; Livestock; Organic; & Training.

Minister, Hon. J. Alan McIsaac
Tel: 902-368-4880; *Fax:* 902-368-4857
jamcisaac@gov.pe.ca

Deputy Minister, John Jamieson
Tel: 902-368-4830; *Fax:* 902-368-4846
jdjamieson@gov.pe.ca

Associated Agencies, Boards & Commissions:

•Agricultural Insurance Corporation
29 Indigo Cres.
PO Box 1600
Charlottetown, PE C1A 7N3
Tel: 902-368-4842; *Fax:* 902-368-6677
www.gov.pe.ca/growingforward
Production insurance is administered by the Prince Edward Island Agricultural Insurance Corporation. It provides production risk protection to producers who may sustain crop losses due to natural hazards.
Programs administered by the Corporation are as follows: AgriStability, AgriInvest, AgriInsurance, & AgriRecovery.

•Agricultural Insurance Corporation Appeal Board

•Animal Health Advisory Committee

•Farm Practices Review Board
The Farm Practices Review Board is responsible for reviewing concerns from the public about farm practices.

•Grain Elevators Corporation
7 Gerald McCarville Dr.
PO Box 250
Kensington, PE C0B 1M0
Tel: 902-836-8935; *Fax:* 902-836-8926
www.peigec.com
The Prince Edward Island Grain Elevators Corporation is a leader in the province's cereal & protein sector.
For growers who want the pooled return, the Corporation operates grain marketing pools. Producers may also sell part of their crop to the Corporation at daily market prices.
Grain & products marketed throughout Prince Edward Island & Atlantic Canada.

•Marketing Council

•Natural Products Appeals Tribunal

•Pesticides Advisory Committee

•Veterinary College Advisory Council

•Veterinary Medical Association Licensing Board

Agriculture Policy & Regulatory
Jones Bldg., 11 Kent St., 5th Fl., Charlottetown, PE C1A 7N8
The Agriculture Policy & Regulatory Division oversees areas such as the following: research; administration of industry development programs; community pastures; on-farm food safety; food quality; marketing legislation; domestic & foreign trade; traceability; foreign animal disease; & emergency preparedness.
Director, Agriculture Policy & Regulatory Division, Brian Matheson
Tel: 902-368-5087; *Fax:* 902-368-4857
bgmatheson@gov.pe.ca
Executive Director, Women's Institute, Ellen D. MacPhail
Tel: 902-368-4860; *Fax:* 902-368-4439
edmacphail@gov.pe.ca
Administrative Director, 4-H, Kelly Mullaly
Tel: 902-368-4836; *Fax:* 902-368-6289
kjmullaly@gov.pe.ca
Other Communications: URL: www.pei4h.pe.ca

Agriculture Resource
Jones Bldg., 11 Kent St., PO Box 2000 Charlottetown, PE C1A 7N8
Tel: 902-368-4145; *Fax:* 902-368-4857
Toll-Free: 866-734-3276
The Agriculture Resource Division delivers sustainable resource & farm extension programs & services.
Director, Tracy Wood
Tel: 902-368-5645; *Fax:* 902-368-4857
tmwood@gov.pe.ca
Manager, Agriculture Information, Sandra MacKinnon
Tel: 902-368-5647; *Fax:* 902-368-4857
sjmackinnon@gov.pe.ca
Manager, Agriculture Innovation, Lynda MacSwain
Tel: 902-368-4815; *Fax:* 902-368-4857
lemacswain@gov.pe.ca
Manager, Sustainable Agriculture Resources, Barry Thompson
Tel: 902-368-6366; *Fax:* 902-368-4857
blthompson@gov.pe.ca

Aquaculture
548 Main St., PO Box 1180 Charlottetown, PE C0A 1R0
Tel: 902-838-0910; *Fax:* 902-838-0975
Toll-Free: 877-407-0187
The Aquaculture Division delivers the following services: advice & information to the provinces's aquaculture industry; financial programs to assist in aquaculture development; & biological & technical services to the shellfish & finfish sectors on the Island.
Director, Aquaculture, Neil MacNair
Tel: 902-838-0685; *Fax:* 902-368-0975
ngmacnair@gov.pe.ca

Corporate & Financial Services
Jones Bldg., 11 Kent St., 5th Fl., PO Box 2000 Charlottetown, PE C1A 7N8
Tel: 902-368-4880; *Fax:* 902-368-4857
Financial, administrative, & human resources services are provided by the Corporate & Financial Services Division.
Director, Mary Kinsman
Tel: 902-368-5741; *Fax:* 902-368-4857
makinsman@gov.pe.ca
Manager, Human Resource Services, Kelly Drummond
Tel: 902-368-6694; *Fax:* 902-368-4857
ktdrummond@gov.pe.ca

Marine Fisheries & Seafood Services
548 Main St., PO Box 1180 Montague, PE C0A 1R0
Tel: 902-838-0910; *Fax:* 902-838-0975
Toll-Free: 877-407-0187
The Marine Fisheries & Seafood Services Division is engaged in the following activities: advocating for Prince Edward Island's fishing industry; offering programs to support new technology & value-added processing of seafood; supporting development of emerging species; undertaking biological research in support of major fish species; issuing licences for fish buying, fish peddling, & fish processing; managing & maintaining shellfish launching sites around the province; enforcing regulations under Prince Edward Island's Fish Inspection Act & Fisheries Act; overseeing the dead mammal removal program from the province's shore line; & compiling statistics about the fishing industry.
Director, Bob Creed
Tel: 902-838-0625
Toll-free: 877-407-0187; *Fax:* 902-838-0975
bdcreed@gov.pe.ca
Manager, Marine Fisheries, David MacEwen
Tel: 902-838-0635
Toll-free: 877-407-0187; *Fax:* 902-838-0975
dgmacewen@gov.pe.ca
Manager, Seafood Services, David McGuire
Tel: 902-838-0691
Toll-free: 877-407-0187; *Fax:* 902-838-0975
dpmcguire@gov.pe.ca

Prince Edward Island Analytical Laboratories
23 Innovation Way, Charlottetown, PE C1E 0B7
Tel: 902-368-4190
Prince Edward Island Analytical Laboratories include the Dairy Laboratory, the Soil, Feed, & Water Chemistry Testing Laboratory, & the Water Microbiology Laboratory.
The Dairy Laboratory works in support of the Prince Edward Island Dairy Industry Act & Regulations. It also provides services to VALACTA in Prince Edward Island, Nova Scotia, & New Brunswick.
The Soil, Feed, & Water Chemistry Testing Laboratory provides analytical information for farmers & the public.
Director, Tracy Wood
Acting Laboratory Manager, Anna Marie MacFarlane
Tel: 902-368-4190; *Fax:* 902-569-7778
ammacfarlane@gov.pe.ca
Supervisor, Soil, Feed, & Water Chemistry Testing Laboratory, Lori C. Connolly-Brine
Tel: 902-368-3300; *Fax:* 902-368-6299
lconnolly@gov.pe.ca
Acting Supervisor, Dairy Lab, Plant Health Diagnostic Laboratory & Water Microbiology Laboratory, April M. Driscoll
Tel: 902-368-5701
amdriscoll@gov.pe.ca

Office of the Auditor General

Shaw Bldg., 105 Rochford St. North, 2nd Fl., PO Box 2000 Charlottetown, PE C1A 7N8
Tel: 902-368-4520; *Fax:* 902-368-4598
www.assembly.pe.ca/auditorgeneral
Accountability & best practices in government operations are promoted by the Office of the Auditor General. Independent audits & examinations are conducted by the Office of the Auditor General for the Legislative Assembly of Prince Edward Island.
Auditor General, B. Jane MacAdam, CA
bjmacadam@gov.pe.ca
Audit Director, Scott Messervey, CA, CPA, MPA
Tel: 902-368-4524; *Fax:* 902-368-4598
dsmesservey@gov.pe.ca
Audit Director, Gerri Russell, CA, CPA
Tel: 902-368-4526; *Fax:* 902-368-4598
gfrussell@gov.pe.ca
Audit Director, Barbara Waite, CA, CPA
Tel: 902-368-4522; *Fax:* 902-368-4598
bawaite@gov.pe.ca

Prince Edward Island Department of Communities, Land & Environment

Aubin-Arsenault Bldg., 3 Brighton Rd., Charlottetown, PE C1A 7N8
Tel: 902-620-3558; *Fax:* 902-569-7545
www.gov.pe.ca/cle
The Department of Communities, Land & Environment is oversees areas such as: acting as a liaison between the municipal & provincial govnerment; implementing & developing acts having to do with the environment. The following divisions have been assumed by the Department: the Environment Division of the former Department of Environment, Labour & Justice; the Municipal Affairs & Provincial Planning Division of the former Department of Finance, Energy & Municipal Affairs; the Forests, Fish & Wildlife Division of the former Department of Agriculture & Forestry.
Minister, Hon. Robert J. Mitchell
Tel: 902-620-3646; *Fax:* 902-368-5542
rjmitchell@gov.pe.ca
Deputy Minister, Michele Dorsey, Q.C.
Tel: 902-620-3646
Assistant Deputy Minister, Environment, Todd Dupuis

Associated Agencies, Boards & Commissions:

•Boilers & Pressure Vessels Advisory Board

•Commission on the Land & Local Governance
Aubin Arsenault Bldg.
3 Brighton Rd.
Charlottetown, PE C1A 7N8
Tel: 902-620-3558; *Fax:* 902-569-7545
landuse@gov.pe.ca
www.gov.pe.ca/landandlocalgovernance

•Environmental Advisory Council
www.gov.pe.ca/environment/eac
The Environmental Advisory Council advises the Minister responsible for the environment about environmental concerns. Members of the council are appointed by the Lieutenant Governor in Council.

•Natural Areas Advisory Committee

•Power Engineers Board of Examiners

•Species at Risk Advisory Committee
The Species at Risk Advisory Committee performs the following tasks: assessing the province's wildlife resources; advising the Minister of Environment, Energy, & Forestry about the species that should be listed at risk; analyzing the effects of land use on wildlife & their habitat; & making recommendations about the conservation of wildlife & its habitat.

•Wildlife Conservation Fund Advisory Committee

•Public Forest Council (PFC)
The Public Forest Council is made up of six private sector members & three public sector members, who are appointed by the Lieutenant Governor in Council. Council members foster discussion about the potential for provincial woodlands. The council is especially interested in non-traditional, non-consumptive uses of public forests.

Environment
Jones Bldg., 11 Kent St., 4th Fl., PO Box 2000 Charlottetown, PE C1A 7N8
Tel: 902-368-5028; *Fax:* 902-368-5830
Toll-Free: 866-368-5044
The Environment Division oversees programs that protect the province's environement, including the following elements: groundwater; inland surface water & coastal estuaries; drinking water; the ozone layer; & air quality.
The division is also involved in waste management activities, such as the handling of litter, beverage containers, hazardous wastes, used oil, petroleum storage tanks, lead-acid batteries, tires, & derelict vehicles.
Director, Jim Young
Tel: 902-368-5034; *Fax:* 902-368-5830
jjyoung@gov.pe.ca
Director, Special Projects, Beverage Container Program Management, John Hughes
Tel: 902-368-5884; *Fax:* 902-368-5830
jshughes@gov.pe.ca
Director, Policy Development, Tony Sturz
Tel: 902-569-7529; *Fax:* 902-368-5830
avsturz@gov.pe.ca
Acting Laboratory Manager, PEI Analytical Laboratories, Anna Marie MacFarlane
Tel: 902-368-4190; *Fax:* 902-569-7778
ammacfarlane@gov.pe.ca
Manager, Inspection Services, Glenda MacKinnon-Peters, P.Eng.
Tel: 902-368-4874; *Fax:* 902-368-5526
gcmackinnon-peters@gov.pe.ca
Manager, Watershed & Subdivision Planning, Bruce Raymond
Tel: 902-368-5054; *Fax:* 902-368-5830
bgraymond@gov.pe.ca
Manager, Drinking Water & Wastewater Management, George Somers
Tel: 902-368-5046; *Fax:* 902-368-5830
ghsomers@gov.pe.ca
Manager, Climate Change & Air Management, Erin Taylor
Tel: 902-368-6111; *Fax:* 902-368-5830
eotaylor@gov.pe.ca
Manager, Environmental Land Management, Greg Wilson
Tel: 902-368-5274; *Fax:* 902-368-5830
gbwilson@gov.pe.ca

Finance & Corporate Services
Jones Bldg., 11 Kent St., 4th Fl., PO Box 2000 Charlottetown, PE C1A 7N8
Tel: 902-368-5273; *Fax:* 902-368-5830
Administrative services, human resources, & finances are the responsibilities of this division.
Director, George W. Mason
Tel: 902-620-3351; *Fax:* 902-368-5830
gwmason@gov.pe.ca
Manager, Human Resource Management, Michael Ready

Forests, Fish, & Wildlife
J. Frank Gaudet Tree Nursery, 183 Upton Rd., PO Box 2000 Charlottetown, PE C1A 7N8
Tel: 902-368-4700; *Fax:* 902-368-4713
The Forests, Fish, & Wildlife Division oversees the following programs & services: the provincial forests; the private forest program; production development; resource inventory & modelling; & wildlife & fish.
Director, Kate E. MacQuarrie
Tel: 902-368-4705; *Fax:* 902-368-4713
kemacquarrie@gov.pe.ca
Manager, Private Forest, Brian Brown
Tel: 902-368-6431; *Fax:* 902-368-4713
bmbrown@gov.pe.ca
Manager, Fish & Wildlife, Brad Potter
Tel: 902-368-5111; *Fax:* 902-368-4713
bdpotter@gov.pe.ca
Manager, Nursery, Mary N. Myers
Tel: 902-368-4711; *Fax:* 902-368-4713
mnmyers@gov.pe.ca

Municipal Affairs & Provincial Planning
Aubin-Arsenault Bldg., 3 Brighton Rd., PO Box 2000 Charlottetown, PE C1A 7N8
Tel: 902-620-3558; *Fax:* 902-569-7545
Municipal Affairs acts as the liaison with municipalities & municipal interest groups on municipal matters. Consulting services are available regarding governance, administration, operations, & municipal land use planning.
Provincial Planning works in accordance with Prince Edward Island's Planning Act & Lands Protection Act related to land use & development in the province. Efforts are made to achieve sustainable development in the province.
Acting Director, Municipal Affairs & Provincial Planning; Director, Implementation, Christine MacKinnon
Tel: 902-368-5282; *Fax:* 902-569-7545
cgmackinnon@gov.pe.ca
Manager, Municipal Affairs, Samantha J. Murphy
Acting Manager, Provincial Planning, Dale McKeigan
Tel: 902-620-3634; *Fax:* 902-569-7545
dfmckeigan@gov.pe.ca

Prince Edward Island Department of Economic Development & Tourism

PO Box 2000 Charlottetown, PE C1A 7N8
Tel: 902-368-5540; *Fax:* 902-368-5277
tpswitch@gov.pe.ca
www.gov.pe.ca/tourism
Prince Edward Island's Department of Economic Development & Tourism is engaged in the following activities: promoting tourism & special events; facilitating product development; managing infrastructure projects such as parks & golf courses; providing library services; promoting historic preservation & documentation; & encouraging cultural development.
Minister, Hon. J. Heath MacDonald
Tel: 902-368-4230; *Fax:* 902-368-3726
hmacdonald@gov.pe.ca
Deputy Minister; CEO, Tourism PEI, Neil Stewart, C.A.
Tel: 902-368-4250
nmstewart@gov.pe.ca

Associated Agencies, Boards & Commissions:

•Anne of Green Gables Licensing Authority Inc.
94 Euston St.
PO Box 910
Charlottetown, PE C1A 7L9
Tel: 902-368-5961
Other Communication: Toronto Office, Phone: 416-971-7473
The Anne of Green Gables Licensing Authority Inc. controls the use of Anne of Green Gables & related trademarks, protects the integrity of Anne images, & preserves the legacy of L.M. Montgomery & her works. The authority is jointly owned by the Province of Prince Edward Island, Ruth Macdonald, & David Macdonald.

•BIO|FOOD|TECH
101 Belvedere Ave.
PO Box 2000
Charlottetown, PE C1A 7N8
Tel: 902-368-5548; *Fax:* 902-368-5549
Toll-free: 877-368-5548
biofoodtech@biofoodtech.ca
www.biofoodtech.ca
Formerly known as the PEI Food Technology Centre, BIO|FOOD|TECH operates as a contract research & analytical services company. It serves companies & entrepreneurs in the food & bioprocessing sectors.

•Charlottetown Area Development Corporation (CADC)
4 Pownal St.
PO Box 786
Charlottetown, PE C1A 7L9
Tel: 902-892-5341; *Fax:* 902-368-1935
www.cadcpei.com
The Charlottetown Area Development Corporation operates as a self-financed entity that aims to attract private sector development to the Greater Charlottetown area. To carry out its work, the Charlottetown Area Development Corporation partners with the Province of Prince Edward Island, the City of Charlottetown, & the Town of Stratford.

•Eastlink Centre Charlottetown
46 Kensington Rd.
Charlottetown, PE C1A 5H7
Tel: 902-629-6600; *Fax:* 902-629-6650
www.eastlinkcentrepei.com
The Eastlink Centre Charlottetown is a multi-purpose facility.

•Finance PEI
98 Fitzroy St., 2nd Fl.
Charlottetown, PE C1A 1R7
Tel: 902-368-6200; *Fax:* 902-368-6201
financepei@gov.pe.ca
financepei.ca
Finance PEI administers business financing programs for the provincial government.

•Innovation PEI
94 Euston St.
PO Box 910
Charlottetown, PE C1A 7L9
Tel: 902-368-6300; *Fax:* 902-368-6301
Toll-free: 800-563-3734
innovation@gov.pe.ca
www.innovationpei.com
Innovation PEI strives to advance economic development in Prince Edward Island. It promotes small business development, business improvement, employment creation, research, innovation, market access, & trade. Through the Island Prosperity Strategy, Innovation PEI focuses upon the following sectors: renewable energy, aerospace, information technology, & bioscience.

•Island Investment Development Inc. (IIDI)
94 Euston St., 2nd Fl.
PO Box 1176
Charlottetown, PE C1A 7M8
Tel: 902-620-3628; *Fax:* 902-368-5886
opportunitiespei@gov.pe.ca
The Island Investment Development Inc. is a crown corporation. Its business name is Immigration Services. The organization oversees the Prince Edward Island Provincial Nominee Program.

•Tourism Advisory Council of Prince Edward Island (TAC)
Shaw Bldg., 3rd Fl.
Rochford St.
PO Box 2000
Charlottetown, PE C1A 7N8
Tel: 902-368-5907
peitac@peitac.com
www.peitac.com
An industry advisory board to the Minister of Tourism & Culture, Prince Edward Island's Tourism Advisory Council features nineteen members. Members include senior provincial & federal government members & industry stakeholders who discuss the challenges of the tourism industry.
The Tourism Advisory Council works to ensure growing revenues in the tourism industry. To achieve this goal, the council partners with the Tourism Industry Association of PEI, Tourism PEI, & the Atlantic Canada Opportunities Agency.
The Minister of Tourism & Culture receives advice from the council about research initiatives, product development, & marketing.

•Tourism Arbitration Board

•Tourism PEI Board

Corporate Services
PO Box 2000 Charlottetown, PE C1A 7N8
Activities of the Corporate Services Division include financial services, administration, human resources, insurance matters, records management, & the operation of provincial parks & golf courses.
Director, Kevin Jenkins, CA
Tel: 902-368-5874; *Fax:* 902-894-0342
wkjenkin@gov.pe.ca
General Manager, Provincial Golf Courses, Ryan Garrett
Tel: 902-368-4238; *Fax:* 902-894-0342
ragarrett@gov.pe.ca
Manager, Provincial Parks, Shane Arbing
Tel: 902-368-4404; *Fax:* 902-894-0342
sdarbing@gov.pe.ca
Manager, Financial Services, Beecher D. Gillis, CMA
Tel: 902-368-5932; *Fax:* 902-894-0342
bdgillis@gov.pe.ca
Controller, Jennifer DeCoursey, CA
Tel: 902-368-4084; *Fax:* 902-894-0342
jbdecourse@gov.pe.ca

Economic, Trade, Policy & Strategy
Shaw Bldg., 105 Rochford St., 5th Fl., PO Box 2000 Charlottetown, PE C1A 7N8
Secretary, Sandy Stewart
Tel: 902-368-4505; *Fax:* 902-368-4242
swstewart@gov.pe.ca
Director, Policy & Strategy, Jane Mallard
Tel: 902-569-7556; *Fax:* 902-368-4252
jmallard@gov.pe.ca

Economic Research & Trade Negotiations
Shaw Bldg., 105 Rochford St., 5th Fl., PO Box 2000 Charlottetown, PE C1A 7N8
Senior Director, Kal Whitnell
Tel: 902-368-4228; *Fax:* 902-368-4242
kbwhitnell@gov.pe.ca

Marketing Communications, Sales & Customer Relationship Management
Shaw Bldg., PO Box 2000 Charlottetown, PE C1A 7N8
The role of the Marketing Communications, Sales & CRM Division is the promotion of Prince Edward Island as a tourist destination.
Director, Brenda Gallant
Tel: 902-368-6066; *Fax:* 902-368-4438
bgallant@gov.pe.ca
Manager, Digital Marketing, Brian Fleming
Tel: 902-368-6316; *Fax:* 902-368-4438
bdfleming@gov.pe.ca
Manager, Visitor Services, Heather Pollard
Tel: 902-368-4441; *Fax:* 902-368-4438
hlpollard@gov.pe.ca
Manager, Call Centre, Jennifer Bernard
Tel: 902-368-5556; *Fax:* 902-368-4438
jfbernard@gov.pe.ca
Acting Manager, Advertising & Publicity, Robert Ferguson
Tel: 902-368-5522; *Fax:* 902-368-4438
rnfergus@gov.pe.ca
Manager, Trade & Sales, Craig Sulis
Tel: 902-368-5754; *Fax:* 902-368-4438
cdsulis@gov.pe.ca

Rural Development
548 Main St., PO Box 1180 Montague, PE C0A 1R0
Tel: 902-838-0910; *Fax:* 902-838-0975
Toll-Free: 877-407-0187
The responsibilities of the Rural Development Division are as follows: implementing action items in the Rural Action Plan; overseeing the delivery of the Island Community Fund; & ensuring the effectiveness of the Seasonal Hiring Centre & the Employment Development Agency.
Director, Amie Swallow MacDonald
Tel: 902-838-0662
Toll-free: 877-407-0187; *Fax:* 902-838-0975
aswallowmacdonald@gov.pe.ca
Community Development Officer, Giselle Bernard
Tel: 902-854-3680; *Fax:* 902-854-3099
gbbernard@gov.pe.ca
Community Development Officer, Chris Blaisdell
Tel: 902-687-7083
Toll-free: 877-407-0187; *Fax:* 902-687-7091
cwblaisdell@gov.pe.ca
Community Development Officer, Southern Kings, Stephen Lewis
Tel: 902-838-0618
Toll-free: 877-407-0187; *Fax:* 902-838-0975
sjlewis@gov.pe.ca
Community Development Officer, East Prince, Kellie Mulligan
Tel: 902-887-3975
Toll-free: 877-407-0187; *Fax:* 902-887-2400
kamulligan@gov.pe.ca
Community Development Officer, Brenda O'Meara
Tel: 902-853-0104; *Fax:* 902-853-3839
bfomeara@gov.pe.ca

Strategic Initiatives
Shaw Bldg., PO Box 2000 Charlottetown, PE C1A 7N8
The Strategic Initiatives Division works with regional tourism associations to help them prosper. Overseeing the development of support programs is a key activity.
The division is also responsible for the management of regulatory affairs related to the Highway Signage Act & the Tourism Industry Act. Examples of these responsibilities include special event signage, on-premise signage, licensing, & occupancy reports.
Advocating for the interests of the tourism industry is another part of the mandate for the Strategic Initiatives Division. The

division has represented the tourism industry in areas such as the Atlantic Gateway Initiative & land use issues.
Director, Chris K. Jones
Tel: 902-368-6342; *Fax:* 902-368-4438
ckjones@gov.pe.ca
Manager, Evaluation, Measurement, & Business Intelligence Unit, Brian Dunn
Tel: 902-368-4237; *Fax:* 902-368-4438
bjdunn@gov.pe.ca
Manager, Product Development, Investment, & Regulatory Affairs Unit; Manager, Cultural Affairs, Janet Wood
Tel: 902-368-5508; *Fax:* 902-368-4438
jewood@gov.pe.ca

Prince Edward Island Department of Education, Early Learning & Culture

Holman Centre, #101, 250 Water St., Summerside, PE C1N 1B6
Tel: 902-438-4130; *Fax:* 902-438-4062
www.gov.pe.ca/eecd
Other Communication: Charlottetown Phone: 902-368-4600
www.youtube.com/playlist?list=PL43AED4EF5801598F&
Prince Edward Island's Department of Education, Early Learning & Culture offers programs & services for children from birth to the conclusion of grade 12. In Nov. 2015, it was announced that the department would absorb the functions of the English Language School Board, which represented 56 schools in the province.
Minister, Hon. Doug W. Currie
Tel: 902-438-4130; *Fax:* 902-438-4062
dwcurrie@gov.pe.ca
Deputy Minister, Susan Willis
Tel: 902-438-4876
eswillis@gov.pe.ca

Associated Agencies, Boards & Commissions:

•Atlantic Provinces Special Education Authority (APSEA)
5940 South St.
Halifax, NS B3H 1S6
Tel: 902-424-8500; *Fax:* 902-423-8700
apsea@apsea.ca
www.apsea.ca
The APSEA serves children & youth who are deaf, hard of hearing, deafblind, blind, or visually impaired. It is a cooperative agency between the Provincial Departments of Education of New Brunswick, Nova Scotia, & Prince Edward Island.

•Certification & Standards Board
www.gov.pe.ca/eecd/index.php3?number=1028331&
The APSEA serves children & youth who are deaf, hard of hearing, deafblind, blind, or visually impaired. It is a cooperative agency between the Provincial Departments of Education of New Brunswick, Nova Scotia, & Prince Edward Island.

•Child Care Facilities Board
Responsible for providing safe, good quality, & appropriate child care facilities.

•Child & Youth Services Commissioner
Homan Bldg.
#101, 250 Water St.
Summerside, PE C1N 1B6
Tel: 902-438-4872; *Fax:* 902-438-4874
www.gov.pe.ca/childandyouth
The Child & Youth Services Commissioner deals with issues that affect children & youth in Prince Edward Island. The following legislation in Prince Edward Island affects children & youth: Child Protection Act; Mental Health Act; School Act; & Youth Justice Act.

•Education Negotiation Agency

•Fathers of Confederation Buildings Trust

•French Language School Board / La Commission scolaire de langue française de l'ilw-du-Prince-Édouard
1596, rte 124
Abram-Village, PE C0B 2E0
Tel: 902-854-2975; *Fax:* 902-854-2981
cslf@edu.pe.ca
www.edu.pe.ca/cslf
Prince Edward Island's French Language School Board administers six schools.

•Heritage Places Advisory Board

•Island Regulatory & Appeals Commission (IRAC)
See Entry Name Index for detailed listing.

•Lucy Maud Montgomery Foundation

•Prince Edward Island School Athletic Association (PEISAA)
#101, 250 Water St.
Summerside, PE C1N 1B6
Tel: 902-438-4846; *Fax:* 902-438-4884
www.peisaa.pe.ca
The Prince Edward Island Athletic Association was established as the governing body for all school sports in the province. The association is a member of the Canadian School Sport Federation & is affiliated with the National Federation of State High School Athletic Associations.

•Teachers' Superannuation Commission
c/o Pensions & Benefits
PO Box 2000
Charlottetown, PE C1A 7N8
www.peitsf.ca/index.php3?number=1017189

Administration & Corporate Services

#101, 250 Water St., Summerside, PE C1N 1B6
Tel: 902-438-4819; *Fax:* 902-438-4874
The Administration & Corporate Services Division oversees the following areas: finance & school board operations; program evaluation & student assessment; research & corporate services; technology in education; human resources; & the Office of the Registrar.
Senior Director, Terry Keefe
Tel: 902-438-4880; *Fax:* 902-438-4874
tekeefe@gov.pe.ca
Director, Finance & School Board Operations, Chris DesRoche
Tel: 902-438-4882; *Fax:* 902-438-4874
cmdesroche@edu.pe.ca
Manager, Research & Corporate Services, Robin Phillips
Tel: 902-438-4837; *Fax:* 902-438-4874
Manager, Human Resources, Rebecca Gill
Tel: 902-438-4881; *Fax:* 902-438-4874
rjgill@gov.pe.ca
Registrar, Nancy Desrosiers
Tel: 902-438-4827; *Fax:* 902-438-4062
ndesrosiers@gov.pe.ca

Learning & Early Childhood Development Division

Tel: 902-438-4130; *Fax:* 902-438-4062
The Public Education Branch is responsible for the following services: early childhood development & kindergarten; child & student services; & English & French programs.
Senior Director, Imelda Arsenault
Tel: 902-438-4879; *Fax:* 902-438-4150
imarsenault@edu.pe.ca
Director, French Curriculum, René Hurtubise
Tel: 902-438-4155; *Fax:* 902-438-4884
rvhurtubise@edu.pe.ca
Director, Instructional Development & Achievement, Elizabeth Costa
Tel: 902-438-4820; *Fax:* 902-438-4874
eecosta@edu.pe.ca
Director, English Curriculum, Derek McEwen
Tel: 902-438-4870; *Fax:* 902-438-4884
dpmcewan@edu.pe.ca
Director, Early Childhood Development, Carolyn Simpson
Tel: 902-438-4883; *Fax:* 902-438-4884
cesimpson@edu.pe.ca

Libraries & Archives

Shaw Bldg., 105 Rochford St., 3rd Fl., PO Box 2000 Charlottetown, PE C1A 7N8
Tel: 902-368-4784; *Fax:* 902-894-0342
The Libraries & Archives Division acts as a liaison between the Prince Edward Island provincial government & organizations that represent the library, heritage, & cultural sectors.
Director, Kathleen Eaton
Tel: 902-368-4784; *Fax:* 902-894-0342
keeaton@gov.pe.ca
Provincial Archivist, Public Archives & Records Offices, Jill MacMicken-Wilson
Tel: 902-368-4351; *Fax:* 902-368-6327
jswilson@gov.pe.ca
French Library Services Coordinator, Lori MacAdam
Tel: 902-368-5967
lamacadam@gov.pe.ca

Museum & Heritage Foundation

Beaconsfield, 2 Kent St., Charlottetown, PE C1A 1M6
Tel: 902-368-6600; *Fax:* 902-368-6608
mhpei@gov.pe.ca
www.peimuseum.com
twitter.com/PEIMUSEUM
www.facebook.com/124989037532122
www.flickr.com/photos/pei_museum
Governed by the Museum Act, the Prince Edward Island Museum & Heritage Foundation operates as a Schedule B Provincial Crown Corporation. The mandate of the registered charitable corporation is to collect, preserve, & interpret Prince Edward Island's human & natural heritage.
The following seven provincial museums & heritage sites across Prince Edward Island are administered by the organization for the benefit & enjoyment of the people of the province & tourists: Elmira Railway Museum; Basin Head Fisheries Museum; Orwell Corner Historic Village & Agricultural Museum; Beaconsfield Historic House; Eptek Art & Culture Centre; The Acadian Museum of Prince Edward Island; & Green Park Shipbuilding Museum & Yeo House. There are more than 90,000 artifacts in the Provincial Collection, which are the responsibility of the Foundation.
Chair, Harry Kielly
Tel: 902-368-6600; *Fax:* 902-368-6608
Executive Director, Dr. David Keenlyside
Tel: 902-368-6601; *Fax:* 902-368-6608
dlkeenlyside@gov.pe.ca
Heritage Officer, Charlotte Stewart
Tel: 902-368-5940; *Fax:* 902-368-4663
clstewart@gov.pe.ca

Elections Prince Edward Island

Atlantic Technology Centre, #160, 176 Great George St., Charlottetown, PE C1A 4K3
Tel: 902-368-5895; *Fax:* 902-368-6500
Toll-Free: 888-234-8783
www.electionspei.ca
Elections Prince Edward Island provides information to electors & candidates. Guided by the Canadian Charter of Rights & Freedoms, Elections Prince Edward Island works to ensure that electors & candidates have the opportunity to exercise their democratic right.
Chief Electoral Officer, Gary McLeod
Tel: 902-368-5898
gbmcleod@electionspei.ca
Deputy Chief Electoral Officer, Judy Richard
Tel: 902-368-5895; *Fax:* 902-368-6500
jgrichard@electionspei.ca

Prince Edward Island Department of Family & Human Services

Jones Bldg., 11 Kent St., 2nd Fl., PO Box 2000 Charlottetown, PE C1A 7N8
Tel: 902-620-3777; *Fax:* 902-894-0242
Toll-Free: 866-594-3777
www.gov.pe.ca/sss
The Department of Family & Human Services strives to develop healthy & self-reliant individuals & to support vulnerable members of the province. Programs & services are offered to promote social & economic prosperity & the creation of work environments that contribute to a safe, healthy & engaged workforce.
Minister, Hon. Tina M. Mundy
Tel: 902-620-3777; *Fax:* 902-894-0242
tmmundy@gov.pe.ca
Deputy Minister, Teresa Hennebery
Tel: 902-368-6520
tahennebery@gov.pe.ca

Associated Agencies, Boards & Commissions:

•Alberton Housing Authority

•Charlottetown Area Housing Authority

•Disability Action Council
The 19 member Council is responsible for consulting with & advising the provincial government on legislation, policies, programs & services that affect people with disabilities.

•Georgetown Housing Authority

•Montague Housing Authority

•Mount Stewart Housing Authority

•O'Leary Housing Authority

•PEI Social Work Registration Board (PEISWRB)
81 Prince St.
Charlottetown, PE C1A 4R3
Tel: 902-368-7337; *Fax:* 902-368-7180
registrar@socialworkpei.ca
socialworkpei.ca
Regulatory body for the social work profession on Prince Edward Island, seeking to protect the public from preventable harm.

•Premier's Action Committee on Family Violence Prevention
c/o Child and Family Services Division
161 St. Peters Rd.
PO Box 2000
Charlottetown, PE C1A 7N8
Tel: 902-368-6712; *Fax:* 902-368-6186
werhoekoftedahl@gov.pe.ca
www.stopfamilyviolence.pe.ca

- •Seniors' Secretariat
- •Social Assistance Appeals Panel
- •Souris Housing Authority
- •Summerside Housing Authority
- •Tignish Housing Authority

Child & Family Services
Jones Bldg., 11 Kent St., 2nd Fl., PO Box 2000
Charlottetown, PE C1A 7N8
Tel: 902-368-5294

The Child & Family Services Division offers a wide range of programs & services to care for Prince Edward Island's children & families. Examples of programs include child protection, foster care, & adoption services.

Director, Child & Family Services, Rona Smith
Tel: 902-368-5396; *Fax:* 902-368-4258
ronasmith@gov.pe.ca

Director, Child Protection, Wendy L. McCourt
Tel: 902-368-6515; *Fax:* 902-620-3776
wlmccourt@gov.pe.ca

Provincial Coordinator, Residential Services, Barry L. Chandler
Tel: 902-368-6180; *Fax:* 902-620-3362
blchandler@ihis.org

Provincial Coordinator, Child Protection, Maureen G. MacEwen
Tel: 902-368-6161; *Fax:* 902-620-3362
mgmacewen@gov.pe.ca

Corporate Support & Seniors
Jones Bldg., 11 Kent St., 2nd Fl., PO Box 2000
Charlottetown, PE C1A 7N8
Tel: 902-620-3777; *Fax:* 902-894-0242

Corporate Support & Seniors has responsibility for the Senior's Secretariat / the Office of Seniors, records information management, French Language Services, intergovernmental & external relations, & emergency social services.

Director, Jennifer Burgess
Tel: 902-368-5199; *Fax:* 902-894-0242
jmburgess@gov.pe.ca

Housing Services
Jones Bldg., 11 Kent St., 2nd Fl., PO Box 2000
Charlottetown, PE C1A 7N8
Tel: 902-620-3777; *Fax:* 902-894-0242

The Housing Services Division is responsible for the following areas: finance, administration, human resources, communications, French language services, intergovernmental & external relations, records information management, & emergency social services.

Director, Sonya L. Cobb
Tel: 902-620-3408; *Fax:* 902-894-0242
slcobb@gov.pe.ca

Director, Financial Services & Audit, Lane E. Pineau

Manager, Human Resources, Barb J. Stewart
Tel: 902-368-5529; *Fax:* 902-894-0242
bjstewart@gov.pe.ca

Social Programs
Jones Bldg., 11 Kent St., 2nd Fl., PO Box 2000
Charlottetown, PE C1A 7N8

The Social Programs Division provides services related to social assistance & disability support.

Director, Social Programs; Coordinator, Social Assistance & Disability Support Programs (East), Rhea M. Jenkins
Tel: 902-368-6446; *Fax:* 902-620-3553
rmjenkins@gov.pe.ca

Coordinator, Social Assistance & Disability Support Programs (West), Pat W. MacDonald
Tel: 902-888-8149; *Fax:* 902-888-8398
pwmacdonald@ihis.org

Prince Edward Island Department of Finance

Shaw Bldg., 95 Rochford St. South, 2nd Fl., PO Box 2000
Charlottetown, PE C1A 7N8
Tel: 902-368-4000; *Fax:* 902-368-5544
www.gov.pe.ca/finance

The Department of Finance facilitates the management of the Government of Prince Edward Island's human & financial resources.

Minister, Hon. Allen F. Roach
Tel: 902-368-4050; *Fax:* 902-368-6575
afroach@gov.pe.ca

Deputy Minister, David Arsenault
Tel: 902-368-4053; *Fax:* 902-368-6575
davidarsenault@gov.pe.ca

Associated Agencies, Boards & Commissions:

- •Classification Appeal Committee
- •Lotteries Commission
- •Maritime Geomatics Committee
- •Maritime Provinces Harness Racing Commission
  5 Gerald McCarville Dr.
  PO Box 128
  Kensington, PE C0B 1M0
  Tel: 902-836-5500; *Fax:* 902-836-5320
  www.mphrc.ca
- •Northumberland Strait Crossing Advisory Group
- •Prince Edward Island Liquor Control Commission
  See Entry Name Index for detailed listing.
- •Prince Edward Island Master Trust Advisory Board
- •Public Service Commission (PSC)
  Shaw Bldg. North
  105 Rochford St., 1st Fl.
  PO Box 2000
  Charlottetown, PE C1A 7N8
  Tel: 902-368-4080; *Fax:* 902-368-4383
  www.gov.pe.ca/psc
  The independent & impartial agency coordinates human resources in the public sector of Prince Edward Island. All government departments & agencies, health authorities, & other public sector employers are served by Prince Edward Island's Public Service Commission. Examples of services include recruitment, selection, occupational health & safety, payroll & benefits administration, & the employee assistant program.
- •Self-Insurance & Risk Management Fund Advisory Committee

Administration
Jones Bldg., 11 Kent St., 2nd Fl., PO Box 2000
Charlottetown, PE C1A 7N8

The Administration Division carries out the following responsibilities: human resources & payment processing.

Manager, Lane Pineau
Tel: 902-569-7559; *Fax:* 902-620-3503
lepineau@gov.pe.ca

Administrator, Finance Section, Harold Lee
Tel: 902-368-6626; *Fax:* 902-368-4152
hmlee@gov.pe.ca

Manager, Human Resources Section, Alana Sobey
Tel: 902-620-3079; *Fax:* 902-368-6575
avsobey@gov.pe.ca

Debt, Investment & Pension Management
Shaw Bldg. South, 95 Rochford St., 3rd Fl., PO Box 2000
Charlottetown, PE C1A 7N8
Fax: 902-368-4077

The Debt, Investment & Pension Management Division carries out the following responsibilities: provincial banking; sinking fund asset management; supervision of the pension fund managers; financial research; investment & debt management strategies; project financing; asset/liability management of crown corporations; & coordinating insurance of public debt.

Budget Analyst & Accountant, Alan Silliker
Tel: 902-569-7666; *Fax:* 902-368-4077
agsilliker@gov.pe.ca

Officer, Investment, Ryan Bradley, MBA
Tel: 902-368-4167; *Fax:* 902-368-4077
rxbradley@gov.pe.ca

Economics, Statistics, & Federal Fiscal Relations
Shaw Bldg., 95 Rochford St., 2nd Fl., PO Box 2000
Charlottetown, PE C1A 7N8
Tel: 902-368-4030; *Fax:* 902-368-4034

The Economics, Statistics, & Federal Fiscal Relations Division is engaged in the following activities: offering economic policy, statistical, tax, & fiscal advice; providing a liaison with the federal government & the other provinces on fiscal arrangements; & responding to queries regarding statistical information.

Director, Nigel Burns
Tel: 902-368-4181; *Fax:* 902-368-4034
ndburns@gov.pe.ca

Fiscal Management
Shaw Bldg., 95 Rochford St. South, 3rd Fl., PO Box 2000
Charlottetown, PE C1A 7N8
Tel: 902-368-5802; *Fax:* 902-368-4077

The Fiscal Management Division has the following roles: administering pensions & benefits; offering administrative support & financial analysis to the Treasury Board, & ensuring that public funds are budgeted & monitored properly.

Assistant Secretary to Treasury Board, Jim Miles, CA
Tel: 902-368-6278; *Fax:* 902-368-4077
jamiles@gov.pe.ca

Senior Budget Analyst, Budgement Management Section, Vaughn Smith
Tel: 902-620-3352; *Fax:* 902-368-4077
wvsmith@gov.pe.ca

Information Technology Shared Services
Sullivan Bldg., 5th Fl., PO Box 2000 Charlottetown, PE C1A 7N8
Tel: 902-620-3470

Information Technology Shared Services consists of the following sections: Client Services; Information Technology Infrastructure Support; Corporate, Operations, Finance & Policy Planning; Business Systems; & Enterprise Architecture Services.

Chief Operating Officer, Norman MacDonald
ncmacdonald@gov.pe.ca

Director, Enterprise Architecture Services, Scott Cudmore
Tel: 902-569-7510; *Fax:* 902-569-7632
fscudmore@gov.pe.ca

Director, Infrastructure, Business Infrastructure Services, Edmund Malone
Tel: 902-368-4111; *Fax:* 902-368-4716
emmalone@gov.pe.ca

Director, Business Application Services, Carol A. Mayne
Tel: 902-368-4126; *Fax:* 902-368-5444
camayne@gov.pe.ca

Office of the Comptroller
Shaw Bldg., 95 Rochford St., 2nd Fl., PO Box 2000
Charlottetown, PE C1A 7N8
Tel: 902-368-4040; *Fax:* 902-368-6661

The Office of the Comptroller carries out the following responsibilities: operating the government's corporate accounting system; providing advice related to financial management; administering the corporate procurement service for departments & agencies; managing a corporate fleet information system; & producing the province's public accounts.

Comptroller, Gordon MacFadyen, CA
Tel: 902-368-4201; *Fax:* 902-368-6661
gsmacfadyen@gov.pe.ca

Manager, Procurement, Ian K. Burge
Tel: 902-368-4041; *Fax:* 902-368-5171
ikburge@gov.pe.ca

Manager, Accounting, Doug H. Carr, FCGA
Tel: 902-368-4014; *Fax:* 902-368-6661
dhcarr@gov.pe.ca

Administrator, Financial System Administrator, Helen Clow
Tel: 902-368-4225; *Fax:* 902-368-6661
mhclow@gov.pe.ca

Pensions & Benefits
Sullivan Bldg., 16 Fitzroy St., 3rd Fl., PO Box 2000
Charlottetown, PE C1A 7N8

The Pension & Benefits Division carries out the following responsibilities: financial management and policy development of pension and group insurance programs; & administering the pension program to retired employees.

Manager, Terry Hogan
Tel: 902-368-4002; *Fax:* 902-620-3096
tmhogan@gov.pe.ca

Senior Officer, Pensions & Benefits, Elmer Ramsay
Tel: 902-368-4164; *Fax:* 902-620-3096
erramsay@gov.pe.ca

Risk Management & Insurance
Shaw Bldg., 95 Rochford St., PO Box 2000 Charlottetown, PE C1A 7N8
Tel: 902-368-6170; *Fax:* 902-368-6243

The Risk Management & Insurance Division carries out the following responsibilities: insurance requirement for all government agencies & most crown corporations; settling insurance losses; & risk management issues.

Risk Manager, Vacant

Taxation & Property Records
Shaw Bldg., 95 Rochford St., 1st Fl., PO Box 2000
Charlottetown, PE C1A 7N8
Tel: 902-368-4070; *Fax:* 902-368-6164
www.taxandland.pe.ca

The role of the Taxation & Property Records Division is to ensure equity in the collection of provincial tax revenues & in the production of both provincial & municipal real property assessment rolls. Services are coordinated with federal, provincial, & municipal governments.

Provincial Tax Commissioner, Elizabeth (Beth) Gaudet
Tel: 902-368-4060; *Fax:* 902-368-6584
eagaudet@gov.pe.ca

Manager, Compliance & Tax Administration Services, Lorne Bay, CA
Tel: 902-368-5137; *Fax:* 902-368-6164
lwbay@gov.pe.ca

Manager, Real Property Services, Vacant

Prince Edward Island Department of Health & Wellness

105 Rochford St. North, 4th Fl., PO Box 2000 Charlottetown, PE C1A 7N8

Tel: 902-368-6414; *Fax:* 902-368-4121
www.gov.pe.ca/health

The Department of Health & Wellness carries out the following responsibilities: ensuring quality health care to the citizens of Prince Edward Island; providing leadership in policy, programs, & operations; maintaining & improving the health of citizens; playing a leadership role in innovation; coordinating the implementation of the Healthy Living Strategy; providing regulatory services to the health system; acting as a central contact for Aboriginal organizations; & promoting cooperation on governmental matters related to Aboriginal affairs.

Minister, Hon. Robert L. Henderson
Tel: 902-368-6414; *Fax:* 902-368-4121
rlhenderson@gov.pe.ca

Deputy Minister, Dr. Kim Critchley

Associated Agencies, Boards & Commissions:

•Community Care Facilities & Nursing Homes Board
PO Box 2000
Charlottetown, PE C1A 7N8
Tel: 902-368-4953
The Board issues licenses to community care facilities & nursing homes.

•Council of the Association of Registered Nurses of PEI (ARNPEI)
#6, 161 Maypoint Rd.
Charlottetown, PE C1E 1X6
Tel: 902-368-3764; *Fax:* 902-368-1430
www.arnpei.ca

•Council of the College of Physicians & Surgeons of PEI (CPSPEI)
14 Paramount Dr.
Charlottetown, PE C1E 0C7
Tel: 902-566-3861; *Fax:* 902-566-3986
cpspei.ca

•Council of the Denturist Society of PEI

•Council of the PEI Chiropractic Association

•Council of the PEI College of Physiotherapists (PEICPT)
PO Box 20078
Charlottetown, PE C1A 9E3
www.peicpt.com

•Dental Council of PEI
184 Belvedere Ave.
Charlottetown, PE C1A 2Z1
Tel: 902-892-4470; *Fax:* 902-892-4470

•Dietitians Registration Board (PEIDRB)
PO Box 362
Charlottetown, PE C1A 7K7
www.peidietitians.ca

•Dispensing Opticians Board

•Emergency Medical Services Board

•Financial Assistance Appeal Panel

•Health PEI
See Entry Name Index for detailed listing.

•Licensed Practical Nurses Registration Board (LPNA)
#204, 155 Belvedere Ave.
Charlottetown, PE C1A 2Y9
Tel: 902-566-1512; *Fax:* 902-892-6315
info@lpna.ca
www.lpna.ca

•Medical Advisory Committee

•Mental Health Review Board

•Nurse Practitioner Diagnostic & Therapeutics Committee

•Prince Edward Island College of Optometrists
15 Ellis Rd.
Charlottetown, PE C1A 9B3
Tel: 902-368-3001; *Fax:* 902-628-6604
info@ideologic.net
www.peico.ca

•Prince Edward Island Occupational Therapists Registration Board
PO Box 2248 Central
Charlottetown, PE C1A 8B9
Tel: 902-626-8323
www.peiot.org

•Prince Edward Island College of Pharmacists
375 Trans Canada Hwy.
PO Box 208
Cornwall, PE C0A 1H0
Tel: 902-628-3561; *Fax:* 902-628-6946
info@pepharmacists.ca
www.pepharmacists.ca
The Prince Edward Island College of Pharmacists regulates the practice of pharmacy in Prince Edward Island. Its goal is to promote high standards of pharmaceutical service for the welfare of the public.

•Prince Edward Island Psychologists Registration Board (PEIPRB)
c/o Dept. of Psychology, UPEI
550 University Ave.
Charlottetown, PE C1A 4P3
Tel: 902-566-0549
www.peipsychology.org/peiprb

•Prince Edward Island Sports Hall of Fame & Museum, Inc. Board
40 Enman Cres.
Charlottetown, PE C1E 1E6
Tel: 902-368-4547
publicrelations@sportpei.pe.ca

•Pharmaceutical Information Program Advisory Committee

•Physician Resource Planning Committee

Chief Public Health Office

Sullivan Bldg., 16 Fitzroy St., PO Box 2000 Charlottetown, PE C1A 7N8

The Chief Health Office administers & enforces the Public Health Act. The office also delivers services in the following areas: environmental health, epidemiology, reproductive care, & vital statistics.

Chief Public Health Officer, Dr. Heather G. Morrison
Tel: 902-368-4996; *Fax:* 902-620-3354
hgmorrison@gov.pe.ca

Deputy Chief Public Health Officer, Dr. David S. Sabapathy
Tel: 902-368-4996; *Fax:* 902-620-3354
dsabapathy@gov.pe.ca

Manager, Environmental Health, Joe Bradley
Tel: 902-368-4792; *Fax:* 902-368-6468
joebradley@gov.pe.ca

Manager, Health Promotion, Laura Lee Noonan
Tel: 902-620-3517
lanoonan@gov.pe.ca

Provincial Epidemiologist, Dr. Carolyn J. Sanford
Tel: 902-368-4964; *Fax:* 902-620-3354
cjsanford@gov.pe.ca

Finance & Corporate Management

Shaw Bldg., 105 Rochford St. North, 4th Fl., PO Box 2000 Charlottetown, PE C1A 7N8

The Finance & Corporate Management Division supports the Department of Health & Wellness in the areas of finances, human resources, communications, & the administration of the Freedom of Information & Protection of Privacy Act.

Director, Kevin Barnes, CA
Tel: 902-368-4865; *Fax:* 902-368-4224
kcbarnes@gov.pe.ca

Manager, Finance & Administration, Kelli Bulger
Tel: 902-368-4897; *Fax:* 902-368-4224
kcspence@gov.pe.ca

Manager, Human Resources, Kelly Drummond
Tel: 902-368-6694
ktdrummond@gov.pe.ca

Health Policy & Programs

Shaw Bldg. North, 105 Rochford St., 4th Fl., PO Box 2000 Charlottetown, PE C1A 7N8

The Health Policy & Programs Division supports the Department of Health & Wellness. It includes the Health Recruitment & Retention section.

Acting Director, Kevin Barnes, CA
Tel: 902-368-4865; *Fax:* 902-368-4224
kcbarnes@gov.pe.ca

Manager, Health Recruitment & Retention, Marney MacKinnon
Tel: 902-620-3874; *Fax:* 902-620-3875
mjmackinnon@gov.pe.ca

Chief Mental Health & Addiction Officer, Dr. Rhonda Matters
Tel: 902-368-4926; *Fax:* 902-620-3081
rkmatters@gov.pe.ca

Manager, Policy & Planning, FPT Relations & FOIPP Coordinator, Shaun MacNeill
Tel: 902-368-6117; *Fax:* 902-368-4224
smacneill@gov.pe.ca

Sport & Recreation

Sullivan Bldg., 16 Fitzroy St., 3rd Fl., PO Box 2000 Charlottetown, PE C1A 7N8

Tel: 902-368-4789; *Fax:* 902-368-4224
www.teampei.ca

The main role of the Sport & Recreation Division is to encourage citizens of Prince Edward Island to be active. Sport, recreation, & other physical activities are promoted.
Consultation services & grants are available for community, regional, & provincial groups.

Director, John Morrison
Tel: 902-894-0283; *Fax:* 902-368-4224
jwmorris@gov.pe.ca

Health PEI

16 Garfield St., PO Box 2000 Charlottetown, PE C1A 7N8

Tel: 902-368-6130; *Fax:* 902-368-6136
healthinput@gov.pe.ca
www.healthpei.ca
twitter.com/Health_PEI

When the Health Services Act was proclaimed in 2010, Health PEI took on responsibility for the operation & delivery of health services in the province.
The main goals of Health PEI are to improve access to quality health care across Prince Edward Island & to develop more consistent standards & practices for health services

Chair, Phyllis Horne
Tel: 902-368-4637; *Fax:* 902-368-4974
phorne@gov.pe.ca

Chief Executive Officer, Dr. Michael Mayne
mbmayne@gov.pe.ca

Acute Care, Mental Health & Addictions

16 Garfield St., 3rd Fl., PO Box 2000 Charlottetown, PE C1A 7N8

Tel: 902-569-7768; *Fax:* 902-368-5444

Executive Director, Pamela Trainor
Tel: 902-569-7768; *Fax:* 902-620-3072
pjtrainor@gov.pe.ca

Director, Mental Health & Addictions, Verna Ryan
Tel: 902-368-6197; *Fax:* 902-569-0579
vryan@gov.pe.ca

Director, Emergency Health & Planning Services, James Sullivan
Tel: 902-368-6719; *Fax:* 902-620-3072
jasullivan@gov.pe.ca

Manager, Provincial Organ & Tissue Donation & Transplant, Angela Carpenter
Tel: 902-368-5920; *Fax:* 902-620-3072
adcarpenter@ihis.org

Prince County Hospital, Community Hospitals West & Provincial Renal Program (PCH)

65 Roy Boates Ave., PO Box 3000 Summerside, PE C1N 2A9

Tel: 902-438-4200

Executive Director, Prince County Hospital, Community Hospitals West & Provincial Renal Program, Arlene Gallant-Bernard
Tel: 902-438-4514; *Fax:* 902-438-4381
algallant-bernard@gov.pe.ca

Director, Hospital Services, Cheryl Banks
Tel: 902-438-4519
cabanks@gov.pe.ca

Director, Support Services, Marsha Pyke
Tel: 902-438-4530; *Fax:* 902-438-4381
mlpyke@gov.pe.ca

Acting Director, Nursing Services, Kelley Wright
Tel: 902-438-4516; *Fax:* 902-438-4381
kmwright@gov.pe.ca

Director, Medical Services, Vacant

Queen Elizabeth Hospital & Community Hospitals East

60 Riverside Dr., PO Box 6600 Charlottetown, PE C1A 8T5

Tel: 902-894-2351

Chief Administrative Officer, Jamie MacDonald
Tel: 902-894-2350; *Fax:* 902-894-2416
jamiemacdonald@gov.pe.ca

Director, Support Services, Terry Campbell
Tel: 902-894-2353; *Fax:* 902-894-2416
tscampbell@gov.pe.ca

Director, Medical Services, Dr. Tom Dorran
Tel: 902-894-2411; *Fax:* 902-894-2416
tjdorran@gov.pe.ca

Director, Nursing Services, Marion H. Dowling
Tel: 902-894-2356; *Fax:* 902-894-2416
mhdowling@gov.pe.ca

Director, Hospital Services, Kelley Rayner
Tel: 902-894-2364; *Fax:* 902-894-2416
kjrayner@gov.pe.ca

Acting Administrator, Community Hospitals East, Edna Miller
Tel: 902-687-7150; *Fax:* 902-687-7175
emiller@ihis.org

Chief Nursing Office & Laboratory Services

16 Garfield St., 1st Fl., PO Box 2000 Charlottetown, PE C1A 7N8

Tel: 902-368-5375; *Fax:* 902-368-4969

Provincial Chief Nursing Officer & Executive Director, Brenda Worth
Tel: 902-620-3010; *Fax:* 902-368-4969
baworth@gov.pe.ca
Director, Laboratory Services & Manager, QEH Lab Services, Brian Timmons
Tel: 902-569-7647; *Fax:* 902-894-2385
bdtimmons@ihis.org
Manager, PCH Laboratory Services, Sharlene Fennell
Tel: 902-438-4290; *Fax:* 902-438-4281
smfennell@ihis.org
Manager, KCMH & Souris Diagnostic Services, Vacant

Community Health
16 Garfield St., 1st Fl., PO Box 2000 Charlottetown, PE C1A 7N8
Tel: 902-368-6157; *Fax:* 902-569-0579
Executive Director, Deborah Bradley
Tel: 902-368-6157; *Fax:* 902-569-0579
mdbradley@gov.pe.ca
Director, Primary Care Networks & Chronic Desease, Marilyn A. Barrett
Tel: 902-569-7640; *Fax:* 902-569-0579
mabarrett@gov.pe.ca
Director, Public Health & Children's Developmental Services, Kathy Jones
Tel: 902-894-0247; *Fax:* 902-569-0579
kljones@gov.pe.ca
Director, Home Care, Palliative & Geriatric Care, Mary Sullivan
Tel: 902-569-7646; *Fax:* 902-368-6136
mksullivan@gov.pe.ca

Corporate Services & Long-Term Care
16 Garfield St., 2nd Fl., PO Box 2000 Charlottetown, PE C1A 7N8
Tel: 902-368-4927; *Fax:* 902-368-4969
Executive Director, Rick Adams
Tel: 902-368-5804; *Fax:* 902-368-4969
radams@gov.pe.ca
Chief Nursing Officer, Long-Term Care, Shelley Woods
Tel: 902-894-0359; *Fax:* 902-368-6136
slwoods@gov.pe.ca
Director, Quality & Access Management, Joanne Donahoe
Tel: 902-368-5815; *Fax:* 902-368-4969
jmdonahoe@gov.pe.ca
Director, Strategy & Performance, Jennifer LaRosa
Tel: 902-368-5831; *Fax:* 902-368-4969
jnlarosa@gov.pe.ca
Director, Human Resources, Tanya Tynski
Tel: 902-368-6257; *Fax:* 902-368-4969
tmtynski@gov.pe.ca

Financial Services & Pharmacare
16 Garfield St., 1st Fl., PO Box 2000 Charlottetown, PE C1A 7N8
Tel: 902-368-6196; *Fax:* 902-368-6136
Executive Director, Denise Lewis Fleming
Tel: 902-368-6125; *Fax:* 902-368-6136
dmlewis@gov.pe.ca
Director, Fiscal Planning, Analysis, & Audit, Kellie C. Hawes
Tel: 902-569-0506; *Fax:* 902-368-6136
kchawes@ihis.org
Director, Materials Management, Todd Gillis
Tel: 902-894-2097; *Fax:* 902-894-2384
gtgillis@ihis.org
Director, Provincial Pharmacy Services, Iain Smith
Tel: 902-894-0292; *Fax:* 902-894-2911
idsmith@gov.pe.ca
Comptroller, Business Office, Pat G. Ryan
Tel: 902-368-4921; *Fax:* 902-368-6136
pgryan@gov.pe.ca

Health Information Management
16 Garfield St., 1st Fl., PO Box 2000 Charlottetown, PE C1A 7N8
Tel: 902-620-3052; *Fax:* 902-368-6136
The Health Information Management Division oversees the following areas: eHealth implementation; eHealth operations; eHealth strategy; health information; IM & IT planning; & privacy & information access.
Acting Chief Information Officer; Director, Health Information, Privacy & Records Management, Mark Spidel
Tel: 902-620-3052; *Fax:* 902-368-6136
maspidel@gov.pe.ca
Director, eHealth Clinical Operations, Robin Laird
Tel: 902-620-3869; *Fax:* 902-620-3388
rlaird@ihis.org
Manager, Privacy & Information Access, Jeanne MacDougall
Tel: 902-368-4602; *Fax:* 902-368-6136
jnmacdougall@ihis.org

Medical Affairs & Diagnostic Imaging
16 Garfield St., 2nd Fl., PO Box 2000 Charlottetown, PE C1A 7N8
Tel: 902-368-6261; *Fax:* 902-620-3072
Executive Director, Dr. Nadeem Dada
Tel: 902-368-6261; *Fax:* 902-620-3072
nadada@ihis.org
PHC Medical Director, Summerside & West Prince (Acting), Dr. Andre Celliers
acelliers@ihis.org
PHC Medical Director, Kings, Dr. David Hambly
jdhambly@ihis.org
PHC Medical Director, Queens (East & West), Dr. Alf Morais
jamorais@ihis.org
Director, Provincial Diagnostic Imaging Services, Theresa Callaghan
Tel: 902-894-2277; *Fax:* 902-894-2510
tkcallaghan@gov.pe.ca
Director, Laboratory Services Medical, Dr. Humaira Khanam
Tel: 902-894-2304
hkhanam@ihis.org
Manager, Physician Services, Lauren Kelly
Tel: 902-368-6736
lekelly@gov.pe.ca

Prince Edward Island Human Rights Commission

53 Water St., PO Box 2000 Charlottetown, PE C1A 7N8
Tel: 902-368-4180; *Fax:* 902-368-4236
Toll-Free: 800-237-5031
contact@peihumanrights.ca
www.gov.pe.ca/humanrights
The Prince Edward Island Human Rights Act is administered & enforced by the Prince Edward Island Human Rights Commission.
The Commission receives, investigates, & settles & makes rulings on complaints. Other tasks of the Commission include the development of public information & educational programs & the provision of advice to the government about human rights issues.
Chair, John G. Rogers
Commissioner, Alcide J. Bernard
Commissioner, George Lyle
Commissioner, Ellen M. Macdonald
Commissioner, Carmen de Pontbriand
Commissioner, Maurice H.J. Rio
Executive Director, Brenda J. Picard, Q.C.
Tel: 902-368-4134; *Fax:* 902-368-4236
bpicard@peihumanrights.ca
Human Rights Legal Officer, Wendy M. Baker
Tel: 902-368-4180; *Fax:* 902-368-4236
wbaker@peihumanrights.ca
Mediator/Intake Officer, R. Lorraine Buell
Tel: 902-368-4180; *Fax:* 902-368-4236
lbuell@peihumanrights.ca
Education Project Officer, Thomas V. Hilton
Tel: 902-368-5021; *Fax:* 902-368-4236

Prince Edward Island Department of Justice & Public Safety

Shaw Bldg. South, 95 Rochford St., 4th Fl., PO Box 2000 Charlottetown, PE C1A 7N8
Tel: 902-368-6410; *Fax:* 902-368-6488
www.gov.pe.ca/jps
Other Communication: Corporations: 902-368-4550
Minister; Attorney General; Premier, Hon. H. Wade MacLauchlan
Tel: 902-368-4400; *Fax:* 902-368-4416
premier@gov.pe.ca
Deputy Minister & Deputy Attorney General, Erin Mitchell
Tel: 902-368-5152; *Fax:* 902-368-4910

Associated Agencies, Boards & Commissions:

•Court Transcribers Examining Board

•Credit Union Deposit Insurance Corporation (CUDIC)
#209, 281 University Ave.
Charlottetown, PE C1A 4M3
Tel: 902-628-6280; *Fax:* 902-628-8147
info@peicudic.com
www.peicudic.com

•Employment Standards Board
The Employment Standards Board listens to appeals from employers regarding alleged violations of the Employment Standards Act. The Employment Standards Board is also responsible for presenting recommendations about the Minimum Wage Order to the Lieutenant Governor in Council.

•Judicial Remuneration Review Commission

•Labour Relations Board
Sherwood Business Centre
161 St. Peters Rd.
PO Box 2000
Charlottetown, PE C1A 7N8
Tel: 902-368-5550; *Fax:* 902-368-5476
Toll-free: 800-333-4362
www.gov.pe.ca/sss
The Labour Relations Board works to resolve applications received from labour or management, in accordance with Prince Edward Island's Labour Act.

•Law Society of Prince Edward Island Council (LSPEI)
49 Water St.
PO Box 128
Charlottetown, PE C1A 7K2
Tel: 902-566-1666; *Fax:* 902-368-7557
lawsociety@lspei.pe.ca
www.lspei.pe.ca/council.php

•Prince Edward Island Criminal Code Review Board

•Prince Edward Island Human Rights Commission
See Entry Name Index for detailed listing.

•Prince Edward Island Workers Compensation Board
See Entry Name Index for detailed listing.

•Office of the Police Commissioner
114 Kent St.
PO Box 427
Charlottetown, PE C1A 7K7
Tel: 902-368-7200; *Fax:* 902-368-1123
Toll-free: 877-541-7204
www.policecommissioner.pe.ca
The Office of the Police Commissioner investigates & resolves complaints about the unprofessional conduct of police, other than the RCMP. Under the Police Act, a person who is 18 years of age & over, who has been directly affected by the conduct of municipal police officer, may make a complaint. The Office of the Police Commissioner also handles complaints about a chief of a municipal police service, a director or instructing officer at the Atlantic Police Academy, or a security police officer at the University of Prince Edward Island. The independent statutory office works to carry out its mission in a timely & impartial manner.
Persons must call the Office of the Police Commissioner to book an appointment.

•Public Trustee Advisory Committee

•Supreme Court Finance Committee

•Victim Services Advisory Committee

•Workers Compensation Appeal Tribunal (WCAT)
161 St. Peters Rd., 1st Fl.
PO Box 2000
Charlottetown, PE C1A 7N8
Tel: 902-894-0278; *Fax:* 902-620-3477
Established under Prince Edward Island's Worker's Compensation Act, the Workers Compensation Appeal Tribunal operates as an independent quasi-judicial administrative tribunal. Workers or employers who are dissatisfied with a decision made by the Internal Reconsideration Officer can appeal it through the Workers Compensation Appeal Tribunal. The appeal body is the last level of appeal for workers' compensation matters.
The Office of the Workers Compensation Appeal Tribunal Coordinator is responsible for administrative duties related to the tribunal. The coordinator attends all hearings, but is not part of the decision making process.

Community & Correctional Services
109 Water St., Summerside, PE C1N 1A8
Tel: 902-432-2847; *Fax:* 902-432-2851
The Community & Correctional Services Division provides community & custody programs to contribute to the rehabilitation of youth & adult offenders. The division also offers the following services: research; policy development; support services to the courts & victims of crime; crime prevention programs; & public education.
The work of the Community & Correctional Services Division is conducted by the following sections: Community Programs; Correctional Programs; Victim Services; & Clinical Services.
Director, Karen MacDonald
Tel: 902-620-3124; *Fax:* 902-368-5283
karenmacdonald@gov.pe.ca
Provincial Manager, Community Programs, Gary Trainor
Tel: 902-368-5295; *Fax:* 902-368-4579
gjtrainor@gov.pe.ca
Provincial Manager, Victim Services, Susan Maynard
Tel: 902-368-4584; *Fax:* 902-368-4514
smaynard@gov.pe.ca
Provincial Manager, Custody Programs, Donna Myers
Tel: 902-569-7680; *Fax:* 902-569-7711
dfmyers@gov.pe.ca

Manager, Prince Edward Island Youth Centre, Allan J. Curley
Tel: 902-569-7763; *Fax:* 902-569-7711
ajcurley@gov.pe.ca
Manager, Probation Services, Darlene Dawson
Tel: 902-368-4697; *Fax:* 902-368-4579
dndawson@gov.pe.ca
Acting Manager, Youth Justice Services, Philip Duffy
Tel: 902-368-4578; *Fax:* 902-368-4579
pvduffy@gov.pe.ca
Manager, Provincial Correctional Centre, Kim Kempton
Tel: 902-368-4885; *Fax:* 902-368-5834
kjkempton@gov.pe.ca
Manager, Prince Correctional Centre, Gordon Roche
Tel: 902-888-8209; *Fax:* 902-888-8464
gmroche@gov.pe.ca
Manager, Corporate Services, Denise M. Spenceley
Tel: 902-569-7681; *Fax:* 902-569-7711
dmspenceley@gov.pe.ca

Consumer, Labour, & Financial Services
Shaw Bldg., 95 Rochford St., 4th Fl., PO Box 2000 Charlottetown, PE C1A 7N8
Tel: 902-368-4550; *Fax:* 902-368-5283
The Consumer, Labour, & Financial Services Division consists of the following sections: Consumer Affairs; Corporations; Securities; Firearms Office; & Insurance & Real Estate.
The Consumer Affairs section administers the Lottery Schemes Order. It also responds to complaints & inquiries from consumers.
The Corporations section handles the registration of partnerships & business names. It also oversees the incorporation of companies, non-profit corporations, co-operatives, & credit unions.
The Securities Act is administered & enforced by the Securities Division.
The Gun Control Program is administered by the Firearms Office, in accordance with the Criminal Code of Canada & the federal Firearms Act. The Firearms Office is also responsible for the administration of the Private Investigators & Security Guards Act.
Under the supervision of the Superintendent of Insurance, the Insurance & Real Estate section administers the Fire Prevention Act, the Insurance Act, the Premium Tax Act, & the Real Estate Trading Act.
Acting Director & General Counsel, Steve Dowling
Tel: 902-368-4551; *Fax:* 902-368-5283
sddowling@gov.pe.ca
Superintendent, Insurance, Robert Bradley
Tel: 902-368-6478; *Fax:* 902-368-5283
rabradley@gov.pe.ca
Manager, Labour & Industrial Relations; Chief Conciliation Officer, Faye M. Martin
Tel: 902-569-0545
Toll-free: 866-333-4362; *Fax:* 902-368-5476
fmmartin@gov.pe.ca
Corporations Officer, Corporation Section, Joan MacKay
Tel: 902-368-4509; *Fax:* 902-368-5283
jmmakday@gov.pe.ca
Compliance Officer, Consumer Affairs Section, Adam Peters
Tel: 902-368-5653; *Fax:* 902-368-5283
ajpeters@gov.pe.ca

Coroner's Office
www.gov.pe.ca/jps/coroner
Chief Coroner, Dr. Desmond Colohan
Deputy Coroner, Dr. Charles Trainor

Crown Attorneys Office
50 Water St., Charlottetown, PE C1A 1A3
Tel: 902-368-4595; *Fax:* 902-368-5812
It is the responsibility of the Crown Attorneys Office to prosecute criminal cases under provincial statutes & the Criminal Code of Canada.
Director, Cyndria L. Wedge, Q.C.
Tel: 902-368-5073; *Fax:* 902-368-5812
clwedge@gov.pe.ca
Senior Crown Attorney, Summerside Location, David P. O'Brien, Q.C.
Tel: 902-888-8047; *Fax:* 902-888-8224
dpobrien@gov.pe.ca
243 Harbour Dr.
Summerside, PE C1N 5R1
Senior Crown Attorney, Charlottetown Location, Gerald Quinn, Q.C.
Tel: 902-368-5076; *Fax:* 902-368-5812
gkquinn@gov.pe.ca

Justice Policy & Privacy Services
Shaw Bldg., 105 Rochford St., 4th Fl., Charlottetown, PE C1A 7N8
Tel: 902-368-6620; *Fax:* 902-368-5283
The Justice Policy & Privacy Services Division is comprised of the following sections: Justice Policy; & Access & Privacy Services.
The Access & Privacy Services Section offers advice regarding the operation of the Freedom of Information & Protection of Privacy (FOIPP) Act & its regulations.
Director, Vacant
Tel: 902-368-6619; *Fax:* 902-368-5335
Provincial Manager, Access & Privacy Services, Kathryn Dickson
Tel: 902-569-0568
kedickson@gov.pe.ca

Legal Aid
40 Great George St., PO Box 2000 Charlottetown, PE C1A 7N8
The Legal Aid program in Prince Edward Island is staffed by lawyers who offer direct assistance to legal aid clients in the areas of family & criminal law. In order to be eligible for these legal services, potential clients are required to take a financial means test.
Funding of the family legal aid program is provided by the province of Prince Edward Island & the Prince Edward Island Law Foundation. Prince Edward Island & Canada fund the criminal legal aid program.
Director, W. Kent Brown, Q.C.
Tel: 902-368-6043; *Fax:* 902-368-6122
wkbrown@gov.pe.ca
Lawyer, Family Legal Aid, Summerside Location, Michelle L. Arsenault
Tel: 902-888-8066; *Fax:* 902-438-4071
miarsenault@gov.pe.ca
Manager/Lawyer, Criminal Legal Aid, Summerside Location, Patricia L. Cheverie, Q.C.
Tel: 902-888-8219; *Fax:* 902-438-4071
tlcheverie@gov.pe.ca
Lawyer, Family Legal Aid, Charlottetown Location, Leslie A. Collins, Q.C.
Tel: 902-368-6540; *Fax:* 902-620-3083
lacollins@gov.pe.ca
Lawyer, Criminal Legal Aid, Charlottetown Location, Thane A. MacEachern, Q.C.
Tel: 902-368-6043; *Fax:* 902-368-6122
tamaceachern@gov.pe.ca

Legal & Court Services
Shaw Bldg., 95 Rochford St., 4th Fl., PO Box 2000 Charlottetown, PE C1A 7N8
Tel: 902-368-6522; *Fax:* 902-368-4563
The Legal & Court Services Division consists of the following sections: Office of the Public Trustee & Public Guardian; Court Services; Legal Services; Law Enforcement; & Family Law.
The Office of the Public Trustee & Public Guardian administers the Provincial Administrator of Estates Act & the Public Trustee Act.
The Court Services Section oversees court personnel & services, while the Legal Services Section handles legal services to the provincial government's departments & agencies.
The Law Enforcement Section is headed by the Commanding Officer of the RCMP, the Provincial Police Force. Police protection throughout the province is handled by the RCMP, except for the areas of Borden-Carleton, Charlottetown, Kensington, St. Eleanors, & Summerside which have municipal police forces.
The following programs & services are administered by the Family Law Section: Parent Education Program, Family Court Counsellors' Office, Child Support Guidelines Office, Administrative Recalculation Office, & the Maintenance Enforcement Program.
Acting Director; Manager, Legal Services Section, Terri MacPherson, Q.C.
Tel: 902-368-5145; *Fax:* 902-368-4563
tamacpherson@gov.pe.ca
Public Trustee & Guardian, Office of the Public Trustee & Public Guardian, Mark L. Gallant, LLB
Tel: 902-368-4552; *Fax:* 902-368-5335
mlgallant@gov.pe.ca
Prothonotary & Registrar, Court Services Section, Charles P. Thompson, Q.C.
Tel: 902-368-6669; *Fax:* 902-368-0266
cpthompson@gov.pe.ca
Chief Superintendent & Commanding Officer, RCMP, Law Enforcement Section, Craig Gibson
Tel: 902-566-7133; *Fax:* 902-566-7235
craig.gibson@rcmp-grc.gc.ca
Chief Sheriff, Court Services Section, Ron Dowling
Tel: 902-368-6055; *Fax:* 902-368-6571
rjdowling@gov.pe.ca
Chief Provincial Court Clerk, Court Services Section, Laura Littlewood
Tel: 902-368-6040; *Fax:* 902-368-6220
littlewood@gov.pe.ca
Director, Maintenance Enforcement Program, Family Law Section, Norma Reardon
Tel: 902-368-6499; *Fax:* 902-368-6934
nireardon@gov.pe.ca
Manager, Family Law Section, Loretta Coady MacAulay, Q.C.
Tel: 902-368-4886; *Fax:* 902-368-6474
llmacaulay@gov.pe.ca
Manager, Court Services & Deputy Registrar, Court Services Section, Judy A. Turpin
Tel: 902-368-6005; *Fax:* 902-368-6210
jaturpin@gov.pe.ca

Legislative Counsel
J. Angus MacLean Bldg., 180 Richmond St., PO Box 2000 Charlottetown, PE C1A 7N8
www.gov.pe.ca/jps/index.php3?number=1027247&
The Legislative Counsel is responsible for the following duties: drafting statutes & regulations; revising statutes, & producing loose-leaf updates of the consolidations of statutes & regulations.
Chief Legislative Counsel, Peter F. Allison
Tel: 902-368-4553; *Fax:* 902-368-5176
pfallison@gov.pe.ca

Public Safety
National Bank Tower, #600, 134 Kent St., Charlottetown, PE C1A 8R8
Tel: 902-894-0385; *Fax:* 902-368-6362
www.gov.pe.ca/jps/index.php3?number=1004340&
twitter.com/PEIPublicSafety
www.facebook.com/PEIPublicSafety
The Public Safety Division includes the following sections: 911 Administration Office; Emergency Measures Organization; Fire Marshal's Office; & the Office for Business Continuity Management Planning.
Director, Aaron Campbell
Tel: 902-894-0385; *Fax:* 902-368-6362
acampbell@gov.pe.ca
Fire Marshal, Fire Marshal's Office, David Rossiter
Tel: 902-368-4869; *Fax:* 902-368-5526
derossiter@gov.pe.ca
Deputy Fire Marshal, Fire Marshal's Office, Robert Arsenault
Tel: 902-368-4893; *Fax:* 902-368-5526
robarsenault@gov.pe.ca
Chief Firearms Officer, Vivian Hayward
Tel: 902-368-4585; *Fax:* 902-368-5198
vdhayward@gov.pe.ca
Acting Provincial Coordinator, 911 Administration, Pat J. Kelly
Tel: 902-894-0299; *Fax:* 902-368-6362
pjkelly@gov.pe.ca
Provincial Emergency Management Coordinator, Emergency Measures Organization, Tanya Mullally
Tel: 902-368-5980; *Fax:* 902-368-6362
tlmullally@gov.pe.ca
Manager, Policing Services, Gardon Garrison
Tel: 902-368-4823; *Fax:* 902-368-5335
gagarrison@gov.pe.ca
Manager, Investigation & Enforcement, Wade MacKinnon
Tel: 902-368-4808; *Fax:* 902-368-5198
wjmackinnon@gov.pe.ca

Prince Edward Island Liquor Control Commission (PEILCC)

3 Garfield St., PO Box 967 Charlottetown, PE C1A 7M4
Tel: 902-368-5710; *Fax:* 902-368-5735
www.peilcc.ca
Under the authority of the Liquor Control Act & Regulations, the Prince Edward Island Liquor Control Commission is responsible for managing the distribution of alcohol & regulating the sale & purchase of all alcoholic beverages. The crown corporation also administers the operation of nineteen retail liquor stores across the province. Licenses are issued by the commission for dining rooms, clubs, lounges, special premises, military canteens, & caterers & waiters.
Chair, Hector MacLeod
Chief Executive Officer; Director, Marketing & Retail, Andrew MacMillan
Chief Financial Officer, Carl Adams
Director, Corporate Services, James C. MacLeod
Tel: 902-368-5714; *Fax:* 902-368-5735
jcmacleod@gov.pe.ca
Director, Purchasing & Distribution, David Stewart
Tel: 902-368-5721; *Fax:* 902-368-5735
dlstewart@gov.pe.ca

Prince Edward Island Regulatory & Appeals Commission (IRAC) / Commission de réglementation et d'appels

National Bank Tower, #501, 134 Kent St., PO Box 577 Charlottetown, PE C1A 7L1
Tel: 902-892-3501; *Fax:* 902-566-4076
Toll-Free: 800-501-6268
info@irac.pe.ca
www.irac.pe.ca

Prince Edward Island's Regulatory & Appeals Commission was established in 1991, with the amalgamation of the Office of the Director of Residential Property, the Public Utilities Commission, & the Land Use Commission.
Operating under the authority of the Island Regulatory & Appeals Commission Act, the Regulatory & Appeals Commission works at arms-length from the provincial government to administer statutes dealing with economic regulation. The quasi-judicial tribunal also listens to appeals dealing with property & revenue sales tax, land use, & unsightly premises.
The Regulatory & Appeals Commission reports to the Legislative Assembly of Prince Edward Island through the Minister of Education & Early Childhood Development.

Chair & Chief Executive Officer, J. Scott MacKenzie, Q.C.
Vice-Chair, Doug Clow
Full-time Commissioner, John Broderick
Director, Corporate Services & Appeals, Mark Lanigan
jmlanigan@irac.pe.ca
Director, Residential Rental Property, Cathy Flanagan
cflanagan@irac.pe.ca
Director, Regulatory Services, Allison MacEwen
amacewen@irac.pe.ca

Prince Edward Island Department of Transportation, Infrastructure & Energy

Jones Bldg., 11 Kent St., 3rd Fl., PO Box 2000 Charlottetown, PE C1A 7N8
Tel: 902-368-5100; *Fax:* 902-368-5395
www.gov.pe.ca/tir

Prince Edward Island's Department of Transportation, Infrastructure & Energy maintains & enhances transportation systems & services throughout the province to ensure the safe & efficient movement of people, goods, & services.
The department also works to provide necessary infrastructure for the efficient operation of government. The department is therefore involved in crown land management & building construction & maintenance.

Minister, Hon. Paula J. Biggar
Tel: 902-368-5100; *Fax:* 902-368-5395
pjbiggar@gov.pe.ca
Deputy Minister, John MacQuarrie
Tel: 902-368-5130
jamacquarrie@gov.pe.ca

Associated Agencies, Boards & Commissions:

•100099 P.E.I. Inc.

•Advisory Council on the Status of Women
Sherwood Business Centre
161 St. Peter's Rd., Main Level
PO Box 2000
Charlottetown, PE C1A 7N8
Tel: 902-368-4510; *Fax:* 902-368-3269
info@peistatusofwomen.ca
www.gov.pe.ca/acsw
The Prince Edward Island Advisory Council on the Status of Women consists of nine members. Members are appointed by government to serve on the government advisory agency. The Council advises the Minister Responsible for the Status of Women & works to support equality & the participation of women in economic, political, legal, & cultural activities.

•C.V.C. Management Inc.

•Crown Building Corporation

•Island Waste Management Corporation (IWMC)
110 Watts Ave.
Charlottetown, PE C1E 2C1
Tel: 902-894-0330; *Fax:* 902-894-0331
Toll-free: 888-280-8111
info@iwmc.pe.ca
www.iwmc.pe.ca
Other Communication: Customer Service Fax: 902-882-0520
The Island Waste Management Corporation is a provincial Crown Corporation that was formed in 1999, according to the Environmental Act R.S.P.E.I. 1988, Cap. E-9. Conducting business throughout Prince Edward Island, the corporation administers & provides solid waste management services to both commercial & residential sectors.
One of the Island Waste Management Corporation's successful environmental programs is Waste Watch. Everyone in Prince Edward Island must separate waste into one of three categories: compost, marketable recyclable material, & waste. Waste Watch Drop-Off Centres also accept household hazardous waste free of charge.
In addition to operating the Waste Watch Drop-Off Centres, the Island Waste Management Corporation also operates or oversees the following facilities: Central Compost Facility, East Prince Waste Management Facility, & the Energy from Waste Facility.

•Land Surveyors Board of Examiners

•Prince Edward Island Energy Corporation
Sullivan Bldg.
16 Fitzroy St.
PO Box 2000
Charlottetown, PE C1A 7N8
The Prince Edward Island Energy Corporation promotes the development, generation, transmission, & distribution of energy in an economic & efficient manner.

Access PEI / Single Window Service

548 Main St., PO Box 1180 Montague, PE C0A 1R0
Tel: 902-838-0910; *Fax:* 902-838-0975
Toll-Free: 877-407-0187
www.gov.pe.ca/accesspei

Prince Edward Island Provincial Government services are available at government service centres, known as Access PEI locations. At the eight Access PEI centres across Prince Edward Island, citizens obtain information about the Provincial Government & its programs.
The Access PEI Centres are situated in the following places:
Alberton (902-853-8622);
Charlottetown (902-368-5200);
Montague (902-838-0600);
O'Leary (902-859-8800);
Souris' Johnny Ross Young Service Centre (902-687-7000);
Summerside (902-888-8000);
Tignish (902-882-7351); &
Wellington (902-854-7250).

Director, Tim G. Garrity
Tel: 902-838-0651; *Fax:* 902-838-0975
tggarrity@gov.pe.ca
Manager, Access PEI Summerside & PEI Wellington, Leah Smallwood
Tel: 902-888-8001; *Fax:* 902-888-8306
Other Communications: Access PEI Wellington: accesspeiwellington@gov.pe.ca
Access PEI Summerside
120 Heather Moyse Dr.
Summerside, PE C1N 5Y8
Manager, Access PEI Montague & Access PEI Souris, Lori Deveaux-MacKinnon
Tel: 902-687-7050; *Fax:* 902-687-7091
lmdeveaux@gov.pe.ca
Other Communications: Access PEI Souris, E-mail: accesspeisouris@gov.pe.ca
Access PEI Souris, Johnny Ross Young Services Centre
15 Green St.
PO Box 550
Souris, PE C0A 2B0
Manager, Access PEI Alberton, Access PEI O'Leary, & Access PEI Tignish, Martha Dawson
Tel: 902-859-8801; *Fax:* 902-859-8709
accesspeialberton@gov.pe.ca
Other Communications: Access PEI Tignish E-mail: accesspeitignish@gov.pe.ca
Access PEI O'Leary
45 East Dr.
PO Box 8
O'Leary, PE C0B 1V0
Manager, Access PEI Charlottetown, Paulette Gallant
Tel: 902-368-6847; *Fax:* 902-569-7560
plgallant@gov.pe.ca
Other Communications: Access PEI Charlottetown, Fax: 902-569-7560
Access PEI Charlottetown, Highway Safety Bldg.
33 Riverside Dr.
PO Box 2000
Charlottetown, PE C1A 7N8

Capital Projects

Jones Bldg., 11 Kent St., 3rd Fl., Charlottetown, PE C1A 7N8
Tel: 902-368-5180; *Fax:* 902-368-5425

The following sections make up the Capital Projects Division: Engineering Services; Highway Construction; Materials Lab; & Planning & Design. Staff take care of the design & construction of highways & building infrastructure.

Director & Chief Engineer, Stephen J. Yeo, P.Eng.
Tel: 902-368-5105; *Fax:* 902-368-5425
sjyeo@gov.pe.ca
Senior Manager, Materials Lab, Terry Kelly, P.Eng.
Tel: 902-676-7979; *Fax:* 902-676-7994
jtkelly@gov.pe.ca
Manager, Design & Bridge Maintenance, Darrell Evans, P.Eng.
Tel: 902-569-0578; *Fax:* 902-368-5395
djevans@gov.pe.ca
Manager, Engineering Services, Dan MacDonald
Tel: 902-368-5158; *Fax:* 902-368-5425
wdmacdonald@gov.pe.ca
Manager, Traffic Data Collection & Analysis, Orooba H. Mohammed
Tel: 902-368-5107; *Fax:* 902-368-5425
ohmohammed@gov.pe.ca

Energy & Minerals

Jones Bldg., 4th Fl., PO Box 2000 Charlottetown, PE C1A 7N8
Tel: 902-894-0288; *Fax:* 902-894-0290

The Energy & Minerals Division is engaged in the following activities: developing & managing energy policies & programs; overseeing the development of mineral resources; & supporting gas exploration.

Director, Kim Horrelt, P.Eng.
Tel: 902-894-0289; *Fax:* 902-894-0290
kdhorrelt@gov.pe.ca
Manager, Office of Energy Efficiency, Mike Proud
Tel: 902-620-3792; *Fax:* 902-620-3796
mpproud@gov.pe.ca
Other Communications: URL: www.gov.pe.ca/oee

Finance & Human Resources

Jones Bldg., 11 Kent St., 2nd Fl., Charlottetown, PE C1A 7N8
Tel: 902-368-5100; *Fax:* 902-368-5395

The fiscal matters & human resources issues of the Department of Transportation, Infrastructure & Energy are handled by the Finance & Human Resources Division.

Director, Wendy L. MacDonald, CA
Tel: 902-368-5126; *Fax:* 902-368-5395
wlmacdonald@gov.pe.ca
Manager, Finance, Vacant

Highway Maintenance

Park St. & Riverside Dr. Provincial Headquarters, PO Box 2000 Charlottetown, PE C1A 7N8
Tel: 902-368-5090; *Fax:* 902-368-6244

The Highway Maintenance Division is responsible for the upkeep of the total provincial highway system.

Director, Darren Chaisson, P.Eng
Tel: 902-368-5103; *Fax:* 902-368-6244
ddchaisson@gov.pe.ca
Manager, Light Fleet, Mechanical Branch, Tina L. Lowther
Tel: 902-368-4758; *Fax:* 902-368-5994
tllowther@gov.pe.ca
Manager, Fleet, Mechanical Branch, Wilfred J. MacDonald
Tel: 902-368-5222; *Fax:* 902-368-5994
wjmacdonald@gov.pe.ca
Manager, Inventory Control, Provincial Headquarters, Robert A. MacKinnon
Tel: 902-368-4746; *Fax:* 902-368-6244
ramackinnon@gov.pe.ca

Highway Safety

33 Riverside Dr., Charlottetown, PE C1A 9R9
Tel: 902-368-5228; *Fax:* 902-368-5236

Safety issues from the province's highways are handled by the Highway Safety Division.

Acting Director & Registrar, Graham L. Miner
Tel: 902-368-5223; *Fax:* 902-368-5236
glminer@gov.pe.ca
Manager, International Registration, Cyndie F. Cunneyworth
Tel: 902-368-5202; *Fax:* 902-368-6269
cfcunneyworth@gov.pe.ca
Coordinator, Safety, Doug J. MacEwen
Tel: 902-368-5219; *Fax:* 902-368-5236
djmacewen@gov.pe.ca

Interministerial Women's Secretariat

Jones Bldg., 11 Kent St., 2nd Fl., PO Box 2000 Charlottetown, PE C1A 7N8
Tel: 902-368-6494; *Fax:* 902-892-0242

The role of the Interministerial Women's Secretariat is to assist the Minister Responsible for the Status of Women to protect & promote gender equality.

Director, Michelle Harris-Genge
Tel: 902-368-5557; *Fax:* 902-892-0242
mdharris-genge@gov.pe.ca

Land & Environment

Jones Bldg., 11 Kent St., 3rd Fl., PO Box 2000 Charlottetown, PE C1A 7N8
Tel: 902-368-5221; *Fax:* 902-368-5395

The Land & Environment Division is responsible for provincial lands. Environmental services are also provided by the Land & Environment Division for projects related to transportation & public works. Staff members ensure compliance with provincial & federal environmental legislation & regulations during highway construction & maintenance projects.

Director; Manager, Environmental Management, Brian F. Thompson, P.Eng.
Tel: 902-368-5185; *Fax:* 902-368-5395
bfthompson@gov.pe.ca
Chief Surveyor, Wayne Tremblay
Tel: 902-368-5143; *Fax:* 902-620-3033
wltremblay@gov.pe.ca
Manager, Provincial Lands, Carol Craswell, BBA
Tel: 902-368-6119; *Fax:* 902-368-5395
cmcraswell@gov.pe.ca

Public Works & Planning

Jones Bldg., 11 Kent St., 3rd Fl., Charlottetown, PE C1A 7N8
Tel: 902-368-5100; *Fax:* 902-368-5395

The Public Works & Planning Division is engaged in the following activities: analyzing long term transportation requirements; planning & designing construction projects; implementing major projects; & maintaining buildings.

Director, Alan Maynard, P.Eng.
Tel: 902-368-5147; *Fax:* 902-569-0590
aemaynard@gov.pe.ca
Manager, Policy & Planning, Paul Godfrey, P.Eng.
Tel: 902-368-4849; *Fax:* 902-569-0590
jpgodfrey@gov.pe.ca
Manager, General Services, Shawn Heron
Tel: 902-368-5116; *Fax:* 902-368-5395
sjheron@gov.pe.ca
Manager, Building Maintenance & Accommodation, Holly Hinds
Tel: 902-368-4854; *Fax:* 902-368-5395
hahinds@gov.pe.ca
Manager, Building Construction Contract Administration, Kevin Kennedy
Tel: 902-368-5148; *Fax:* 902-368-5395
kjkennedy@gov.pe.ca
Manager, Building Design & Construction, Tyler Richardson, P.Eng.
Tel: 902-368-4249; *Fax:* 902-569-0590
ttrichardson@gov.pe.ca

Infrastructure Secretariat

#303, 75 Fitzroy St., PO Box 2000 Charlottetown, PE C1A 7N8
Fax: 902-620-3383
Toll-Free: 888-240-4411
cpei-infrastructure@gov.pe.ca

Infrastructure is a joint initiative between the Government of Prince Edward Island & the Government of Canada.

Provincial Manager, Darlene Rhodenizer
Tel: 902-368-6213; *Fax:* 902-620-3383
dlrhodenizer@gov.pe.ca
Director, Infrastructure, Paul Godfrey, P. Eng.
Tel: 902-368-4849; *Fax:* 902-569-0590
jpgodfrey@gov.pe.ca

Prince Edward Island Workers Compensation Board (WCB)

14 Weymouth St., PO Box 757 Charlottetown, PE C1A 7L7
Tel: 902-368-5680; *Fax:* 902-368-5696
Toll-Free: 800-237-5049
www.wcb.pe.ca
Other Communication: Customer Liaison Service, Toll-Free Phone: 1-866-460-3074; Employer Services, Fax: 902-368-5705

The Workers Compensation Board of Prince Edward Island operates as an independent, non-profit organization. Prince Edward Island employers provide funding for the board. Both workers & employers are served by the Workers Compensation Board through the promotion of workplace health & safety & the provision of workplace injury & illness insurance.

Chair, Stuart Affleck
Chief Executive Officer, Luanne Gallant
Tel: 902-368-6352
lmgallant@wcb.pe.ca
Director, Corporate Services, Tory Kennedy
Tel: 902-894-0315
tkennedy@wcb.pe.ca
Director, Workplace Services, Kate Marshall
Tel: 902-368-6358
kmarshall@wcb.pe.ca
Acting Director, Occupational Health & Safety, Danny Miller
Tel: 902-368-5562
jdmiller@wcb.pe.ca
Director, Finance, Tammy Turner
Tel: 902-368-4102
teturner@wcb.pe.ca

Prince Edward Island Department of Workforce & Advanced Learning

Shaw Bldg., 105 Rochford St., 5th Fl., PO Box 2000 Charlottetown, PE C1A 7N8
Tel: 902-368-5956; *Fax:* 902-368-5277
www.gov.pe.ca/ial

The role of Prince Edward Island's Department of Workforce & Advanced Learning is to manage the implementation of The Island Prosperity Strategy, A Focus for Change. This is the provincial government's economic strategy. It is the goal of the government to improve post-secondary opportunities for Islanders to ensure a strong workforce prepared for the present economy.

Minister, Hon. Richard E. Brown
Tel: 902-368-5956; *Fax:* 902-368-5277
rebrown@gov.pe.ca
Deputy Minister, Sharon Cameron
Tel: 902-368-5956; *Fax:* 902-368-5277
secameron@gov.pe.ca
Chief Financial Officer, Brad Colwill, CPA, CA
Tel: 902-368-5360; *Fax:* 902-368-6114
bccolwill@gov.pe.ca
Manager, Human Resources, Michael Ready
Tel: 902-569-0549; *Fax:* 902-368-4224
mcready@gov.pe.ca

Associated Agencies, Boards & Commissions:

•Employment Development Agency
548 Main St.
PO Box 1180
Montague, PE C0A 1R0
Tel: 902-838-0910; *Fax:* 902-838-0975
Toll-free: 877-407-0187

•Prince Edward Island Lending Agency
Homburg Financial Tower
98 Fitzroy St., 2nd Fl.
Charlottetown, PE C1A 1R7
Tel: 902-368-6200; *Fax:* 902-368-6201
Assistance is provided by the Lending Agency to new & growing businesses. Loans are available for organizations with export potential in the following industries: agriculture, fisheries & aquaculture, tourism, manufacturing & processing, information technology, & small business.

Labour Market Research

Atlantic Technology Centre, #228, 176 Great George St., Charlottetown, PE C1A 4K9

Acting Director, Mary Hunter
Tel: 902-368-4005; *Fax:* 902-368-6580
mehunter@gov.pe.ca
Senior Manager, Scot MacDonald
Tel: 902-368-6521
dsmacdonald@gov.pe.ca

Post-Secondary & Continuing Education

Atlantic Technology Centre, #212, 176 Great George St., Charlottetown, PE C1A 4K9
Tel: 902-368-4670; *Fax:* 902-368-6144

Executive Director, Susan A. MacKenzie
Tel: 902-368-4615; *Fax:* 902-368-6144
samackenzie@gov.pe.ca
Controller, PEI Student Financial Assistance Corporation, Brad Colwill
Tel: 902-894-0343; *Fax:* 902-368-6580
bccolwill@gov.pe.ca
Director, Training, Grant Sweet
Tel: 902-620-3980; *Fax:* 902-368-6144
glsweet@gov.pe.ca
Manager, GED, Literacy & Essential Skills, Barbara Macnutt
Tel: 902-368-6286; *Fax:* 902-368-6144
bemacnutt@edu.pe.ca
Manager, Apprenticeship Harmonization Initiative, Roger MacInnis
Tel: 902-368-4461; *Fax:* 902-368-6144
rjmacinnis@edu.pe.ca

Office of Recruitment & Settlement

Atlantic Technology Centre, #228, 176 Great George St., PO Box 2000 Charlottetown, PE C1A 4K9
Tel: 902-894-0353; *Fax:* 902-368-6144

Acting Director, Mary Hunter
Tel: 902-620-3940; *Fax:* 902-368-6340
mehunter@gov.pe.ca
Senior Manager, Philip Muise
Tel: 902-368-5899
pamuise@gov.pe.ca

SkillsPEI

Atlantic Technology Centre, #212, 176 Great George St., Charlottetown, PE C1A 4K9
Tel: 902-368-6290; *Fax:* 902-368-6340
Toll-Free: 877-491-4766
www.skillspei.com

SkillsPEI manages the delivery of training & skills development programs. The programming is funded by the Labour Market Agreement & the Canada-Prince Edward Island Labour Market Development Agreement. Examples of programs include Training PEI, Employ PEI, Self Employ PEI, Community Internship, Immigrant Work Experience, & Labour Market Partnerships. SkillsPEI offices are located across Prince Edward Island.

Director, Richard Gallant
Tel: 902-620-4244; *Fax:* 902-368-6340
rkgallant@gov.pe.ca
Manager, Service Delivery, Kings & Queens County, Blair Aitken
Tel: 902-368-4178; *Fax:* 902-368-6580
abaitken@gov.pe.ca
Manager, Service Delivery, Prince County, Nelda Praught
Tel: 902-438-4110; *Fax:* 902-438-4096
ndpraught@gov.pe.ca

Gouvernement du Québec / Government of Québec

Siege du gouvernement: Hôtel du Parlement, 1045, rue des Parlementaires, Québec, QC G1A 1A3
Tél: 418-644-4545
Ligne sans frais: 877-644-4545
TTY: 800-361-9596
www.gouv.qc.ca
Autres nombres: Montréal, Tél: 514-644-4545

La Province de Québec est entrée dans la Confédération le 1ère juillet, 1867. Terre: 1,356,366.78 kilomètres carrés. Population: 7,903,001 (2011)

Cabinet du Lieutenant-gouverneur / Office of the Lieutenant Governor

Édifice André-Laurendeau, 1050, rue des Parlementaires R.C., Québec, QC G1A 1A1
Tél: 418-643-5385; *Téléc:* 418-644-4677
Ligne sans frais: 866-791-0766
www.lieutenant-gouverneur.qc.ca

Rôles constitutionnels et cérémoniels: le lieutenant-gouverneur a des pouvoirs constitutionnels d'un chef d'État et est le fonctionnaire exécutif en chef de la province; il/elle donne une suite légale à la politique déterminée par le gouvernement en ce qui concerne la nomination du premier ministre, et les membres du Conseil exécutif, la convocation, la prorogation et la dissolution de l'Assemblée nationale, la ratification des décrets du gouvernement, et la nomination des juges des cours de la province; il/elle occupe le plus haut rang protocolaire du Québec et il/elle a préséance sur tous les membres de la famille royale, à l'exception de Sa Majesté qu'il/elle représente

Lieutenant-gouverneur, L'hon. J. Michel Doyon
Secrétaire général et aide de camp principal, Michel Demers, Col. (Ret'd)

Cabinet du premier ministre / Office of the Premier

Édifice Honoré-Mercier, 835, boul René-Lévesque est, 3e étage, Québec, QC G1A 1B4
Tél: 418-643-5321; *Téléc:* 418-643-3924
www.premier-ministre.gouv.qc.ca
Autres nombres: Alt. Tél: 514-873-3411; Téléc: 514-873-6769

Premier ministre, L'hon. Philippe Couillard, P.C.
Tél: 418-643-5321; *Téléc:* 418-643-3924
commentaires-pm@mce.gouv.qc.ca
Autres numéros: Alt. Tél: 514-873-3411
Les réseaux sociaux: twitter.com/phcouillard, www.facebook.com/phcouillard
Secrétaire général, Juan Roberto Iglesias
Tél: 418-643-7355; *Téléc:* 418-528-9552
Adjoint parlementaire du premier ministre pour la région du Saguenay-Lac-Saint-Jean, Serge Simard
Tél: 418-263-0615; *Téléc:* 418-643-0183
Serge.Simard.DUBU@assnat.qc.ca
Adjoint parlementaire du premier ministre (volet jeunesse), Karine Vallières
Tél: 418-263-0546; *Téléc:* 418-643-2929
kvallieres-ricm@assnat.qc.ca

Ministère du Conseil exécutif / Executive Council

875, Grande Allée est, Québec, QC G1R 4Y8
Tél: 418-643-2001; *Téléc:* 418-528-9242
www.mce.gouv.qc.ca
Autres nombres: Montréal: 514-873-7029

Premier ministre; Ministre responsable de la région du Saguenay-Lac-Saint-Jean; Ministre responsable des dossiers jeunesse, L'hon. Philippe Couillard, P.C.
Tél: 418-643-5321; *Téléc:* 418-646-1854
commentaires-pm@mce.gouv.qc.ca
Autres numéros: Alt. Tél: 514-873-3411
Les réseaux sociaux: twitter.com/phcouillard, www.facebook.com/phcouillard
Vice-première ministre; Ministre de la Condition féminine; Ministre responsable de la région de Lanaudière, Ministre responsable, Petites et Moyennes Entreprises, l'Allègement réglementaire et Développement économique régional, L'hon. Lise Thériault

Tél: 418-691-5650; *Téléc:* 418-643-8553
Les réseaux sociaux: www.facebook.com/LiseTheriaultplq
Ministre responsable des Relations canadiennes et de la Francophonie canadienne; Leader parlementaire du gouvernement, L'hon. Jean-Marc Fournier
Tél: 418-646-5950; *Téléc:* 418-528-0981
ministre.saic@mce.gouv.qc.ca
Autres numéros: Alt. Tél: 418-643-3804; Téléc: 418-643-2514
Les réseaux sociaux: facebook.com/JeanMarcFournier.SaintLaurent
Ministre de la Justice; Ministre responsable de la région de l'Outaouais, L'hon. Stéphanie Vallée
Tél: 418-643-4210; *Téléc:* 418-646-0027
ministre@justice.gouv.qc.ca
Autres numéros: Alt. Tél: 514-873-3317; Téléc: 514-873-7174
Les réseaux sociaux: twitter.com/ValleeStephanie, www.facebook.com/stephanie.vallee.96
Ministre des Finances; Ministre responsable de l'Administration gouvernementale et de la Révision permanente des programmes, et Président du Conseil du trésor, L'hon. Carlos J. Leitao
Tél: 418-643-5270; *Téléc:* 418-646-1574
ministre@finances.gouv.qc.ca
Autres numéros: Alt. Tél: 514-873-5363; Téléc: 514-873-4728
Les réseaux sociaux: twitter.com/CarlosLeitaoPLQ, www.facebook.com/carlosleitaoplq
Ministre délégué aux Finances, L'hon. Pierre Moreau
Tél: 418-643-5270; *Téléc:* 418-643-8553
ministre@education.gouv.qc.ca
Les réseaux sociaux: twitter.com/PierreMoreauPLQ, www.facebook.com/pierre.moreau.plq
Ministre de l'Économie, de la Science et de l'Innovation; Ministre responsable de la Stratégie numérique, L'hon. Dominique Anglade
Tél: 514-499-2552
ministre@economie.gouv.qc.ca
Les réseaux sociaux: twitter.com/domanglade, ca.linkedin.com/in/dominique-anglade-568935
Ministre de l'Énergie et des Ressources naturelles; Ministre responsable du Plan Nord, et Ministre responsable de la région de Côte-Nord, L'hon. Pierre Arcand
Tél: 418-643-7295; *Téléc:* 418-643-4318
ministre@mern.gouv.qc.ca
Autres numéros: Alt. Tél: 514-864-7222; Téléc: 514-864-7695
Les réseaux sociaux: twitter.com/PierreArcand, www.facebook.com/arcand.pierre
Ministre de la Santé et des Services sociaux, L'hon. Gaétan Barrette
Tél: 418-266-7171; *Téléc:* 418-266-7197
ministre@msss.gouv.qc.ca
Autres numéros: Alt. Tél: 514-873-3700; Téléc: 514-873-7488
Les réseaux sociaux: www.facebook.com/Gaetanbarretteplq
Ministre de l'Éducation, du Loisir et du Sport; Ministre de la Famille; Ministre responsable, région de la Gaspésie-Iles-de-la-Madeleine, L'hon. Sébastien Proulx
Tél: 418-643-2181; *Téléc:* 418-643-2640
ministre.famille@mfa.gouv.qc.ca
Autres numéros: Alt. Tél: 514-873-9342; Téléc: 514-873-9395
Les réseaux sociaux: twitter.com/sebastienproulx, www.facebook.com/SebastienProulxPLQ
Ministre responsable de l'Enseignement supérieur, L'hon. Hélène David
Tél: 514-482-0199; *Téléc:* 514-482-9985
ministre@mcc.gouv.qc.ca
Les réseaux sociaux: www.facebook.com/plq.helenedavid
Ministre des Affaires municipales et de l'Occupation du territoire; Ministre de la Sécurité publique, et Ministre responsable de la région de Montréal, L'hon. Martin Coiteux
Tél: 418-691-2050; *Téléc:* 418-643-1795
ministre@mamot.gouv.qc.ca
Ministre de l'Emploi et de la Solidarité sociale; Ministre responsable de la région de la Capitale-Nationale, L'hon. François Blais
Tél: 418-643-4810; *Téléc:* 418-643-2802
ministre@mess.gouv.qc.ca
Autres numéros: Alt. Tél: 514-873-0638; Téléc: 514-873-0004
Les réseaux sociaux: www.facebook.com/francois.blais.plq2014
Ministre des Relations internationales et de la Francophonie; Ministre responsable de la région des Laurentides, L'hon. Christine St-Pierre
Tél: 418-649-2319; *Téléc:* 418-643-4804
acadie@mri.gouv.qc.ca
Autres numéros: Alt. Tél: 514-864-2252; Téléc: 514-873-7257
Les réseaux sociaux: twitter.com/stpierre_ch, www.facebook.com/145662342147329, ca.linkedin.com/pub/christine-st-pierre/53/b00/345
Ministre du Développement durable, de l'Environnement et de la Lutte contre les changements climatiques, L'hon. David Heurtel
Tél: 418-521-3911; *Téléc:* 418-643-4143
ministre@mddelcc.gouv.qc.ca
Autres numéros: Alt. Tél: 514-864-8500; Téléc: 514-864-8503
Les réseaux sociaux: twitter.com/Heurtel, www.facebook.com/david.heurtel, www.linkedin.com/pub/david-heurtel/5/631/517
Ministre de la Culture et des Communications; Ministre responsable de la Protection et de la Promotion de la langue française, Ministre responsable de la région de l'Estrie, L'hon. Luc Fortin
Tél: 418-380-2310; *Téléc:* 418-380-2311
ministre@mcc.gouv.qc.ca
Ministre des Transports, de la Mobilité durable et de l'Électrification des transports, Ministre responsable de la région du Centre-du-Québec, L'hon. Laurent Lessard
Tél: 418-643-6980; *Téléc:* 418-643-2033
Les réseaux sociaux: twitter.com/Laurentplq, www.facebook.com/laurentlessard.plq
Ministre de l'Agriculture, des Pêcheries et de l'Alimentation, L'hon. Pierre Paradis
Tél: 418-380-2525; *Téléc:* 418-380-2184
ministre@mapaq.gouv.qc.ca
Les réseaux sociaux: www.facebook.com/494150353945963
Ministre de l'Immigration, de la Diversité et de l'Inclusion, L'hon. Kathleen Weil
Tél: 418-644-2128; *Téléc:* 418-528-0829
cabinet@midi.gouv.qc.ca
Autres numéros: Alt. Tél: 514-873-9940; Téléc: 514-864-2899
Les réseaux sociaux: twitter.com/Kathleen_Weil, www.facebook.com/KathleenWeilNDG
Ministre du Tourisme; Ministre responsable de la région de la Mauricie, L'hon. Julie Boulet
Tél: 418-528-8063; *Téléc:* 418-528-8066
ministre@tourisme.gouv.qc.ca
Autres numéros: Alt. Tél: 514-864-3419; Téléc: 514-864-6988
Ministre responsable des Affaires autochtones, L'hon. Geoffrey Kelley
Tél: 418-646-9131; *Téléc:* 418-646-9487
ministre.autochtones@mce.gouv.qc.ca
Les réseaux sociaux: twitter.com/MNAgeoffkelley, www.facebook.com/129616153783851
Ministre responsable du Travail; Ministre responsable de la région de la Chaudière-Appalaches, et Leader parlementaire adjointe du gouvernement, L'hon. Dominique Vien
Tél: 418-643-7623; *Téléc:* 418-643-8098
ministre@travail.gouv.qc.ca
Les réseaux sociaux: twitter.com/Dominique_Vien, www.facebook.com/197888626915062
Ministre responsable des Aînés et de la Lutte contre l'intimidation; Ministre responsable de la région de Laval, L'hon. Francine Charbonneau
Tél: 418-643-2181; *Téléc:* 418-643-2640
ministre.aines@mfa.gouv.qc.ca
Les réseaux sociaux: twitter.com/mille_iles, ca.linkedin.com/pub/francine-charbonneau/63/a86/744
Ministre responsable de l'Accès à l'information et de la Réforme des institutions démocratiques, L'hon. Rita de Santis
Tél: 418-780-4345; *Téléc:* 418-643-8109
ministre.sridaministre@mce.gouv.qc.ca
Ministre déléguée à la Réadaptation, à la Protection de la jeunesse et à la Santé publique et aux Saines habitudes de vie, et Ministre responsable de la région de la Montérégie, L'hon. Lucie Charlebois
Tél: 418-266-7181; *Téléc:* 41- 26- 719
ministre.deleguee@msss.gouv.qc.ca
Les réseaux sociaux: twitter.com/luciecharlebois, www.facebook.com/lucie.charlebois.9, ca.linkedin.com/pub/lucie-charlebois/1b/ba2/b6
Ministre délégué aux Affaires maritimes; Ministre responsable de la région du Bas-Saint-Laurent, L'hon. Jean D'Amour
Tél: 418-691-5650; *Téléc:* 418-691-5800
ministre.maritimes@economie.gouv.qc.ca
Les réseaux sociaux: www.facebook.com/60265923724
Ministre des Forêts, de la Faune et des Parcs; Ministre responsable de la région de l'Abitibi-Témiscamingue, et de la région du Nord-du-Québec, L'hon. Luc Blanchette
Tél: 418-643-7295; *Téléc:* 418-643-4318
Ministre.delegue.mines@mern.gouv.qc.ca
Les réseaux sociaux: www.facebook.com/lucblanchette.plq
Whip en chef du gouvernement, L'hon. Stéphane Billette
Tél: 418-643-6018; *Téléc:* 418-643-3325
sbillette-hunt@assnat.qc.ca
Les réseaux sociaux: twitter.com/stephanbillette, www.facebook.com/stephane.billette
Président du caucus du parti du gouvernement, L'hon. Nicole Ménard
Tél: 418-263-0548; *Téléc:* 418-643-2895
nmenard-lapo@assnat.qc.ca
Les réseaux sociaux: twitter.com/Nicole_Menard, www.facebook.com/nicole.menard.90

Cabinet du Conseil exécutif / Cabinet Office
Édifice Honoré-Mercier, #2.12A, 835, boul René-Lévesque est, Québec, QC G1A 1B4
Tél: 418-643-7355; *Téléc:* 418-528-9552
www.mce.gouv.qc.ca/ministere/ministere.htm
Secrétaire général et greffier du Conseil exécutif, Juan Roberto Iglesias
Tél: 418-643-7355; *Téléc:* 418-528-9552
Secrétaire général associé, Secrétariat du Conseil exécutif, Marc-Antoine Adam
Secrétaire général associé, Secrétariat aux priorités et aux projets stratégiques, Pierre Hamelin
Secrétaire général associé, Secrétariat du comité ministériel de l'économie, de la création d'emplois et du développement durable, Pietro Perrino
Secrétaire générale associée, Secrétariat à la législation, Anne Trotier

Comités ministériels / Cabinet Committees
Secrétariat général, Édifice Honoré-Mercier, #2.12A, 835, boul René-Lévesque est, Québec, QC G1A 1B4
Tél: 418-643-7355; *Téléc:* 418-528-9552
mce.gouv.qc.ca/comites_ministeriels/comites.htm
Président, Conseil du trésor, L'hon. Carlos J. Leitao
Tel: 418-643-5270; *Fax:* 418-646-1574
ministre@finances.gouv.qc.ca
Président, Comité ministériel des priorités et des projets stratégiques, L'hon. Philippe Couillard, P.C.
Tel: 418-643-5321; *Fax:* 418-643-3924
commentaires-pm@mce.gouv.qc.ca
Other Communications: Alt. Tél: 514-873-3411
Président, Comité ministériel du développement social, éducatif et culturel, L'hon. François Blais
Tel: 418-643-4810; *Fax:* 418-643-2802
ministre@mess.gouv.qc.ca
Président, Comité ministériel de l'économie, de la création d'emplois et du développement durable, L'hon. Pierre Arcand
Tel: 418-643-7295; *Fax:* 418-643-4318
ministre@mern.gouv.qc.ca
Président, Comité de législation, L'hon. Stéphanie Vallée
Tel: 418-643-4210; *Fax:* 418-646-0027
ministre@justice.gouv.qc.ca
Président, Comité ministériel de l'implantation de la stratégie maritime, L'hon. Jean D'Amour
Tel: 418-691-5650; *Fax:* 418-643-8553
ministre.maritimes@economie.gouv.qc.ca

L'Assemblée nationale / National Assembly

Hôtel du Parlement, 1045, rue des Parlementaires, Québec, QC G1A 1A3
Tél: 418-643-7239; *Téléc:* 418-646-4271
Ligne sans frais: 866-337-8837
responsable.contenu@assnat.qc.ca
www.assnat.qc.ca
Président de l'Assemblée nationale, Président de la Commission de l'Assemblée nationale, et la Sous-commission de la réforme parlementaire, L'hon. Jacques Chagnon
Tél: 418-643-2820; *Téléc:* 418-643-3423
presidentcabinet@assnat.qc.ca
Première vice-président, François Ouimet
Tél: 418-643-2750; *Téléc:* 418-643-2942
fouimet-marq@assnat.qc.ca
Deuxième vice-présidente, Maryse Gaudreault
Tél: 418-643-2810; *Téléc:* 418-643-3688
mgaudreault-hull@assnat.qc.ca
Troisième vice-président, François Gendron
Tél: 418-644-1007; *Téléc:* 418-644-1368
Francois.Gendron.ABOU@assnat.qc.ca
Leader parlementaire du gouvernement, L'hon. Jean-Marc Fournier
Tél: 418-646-5950; *Téléc:* 418-528-0981
jean-marc.fournier-sala@assnat.qc.ca
Autres numéros: Alt. Tél: 418-643-3804; Téléc: 418-643-1906
Les réseaux sociaux: facebook.com/JeanMarcFournier.SaintLaurent
Leader parlementaire adjoint du gouvernement, Gerry Sklavounos
Tél: 418-644-5987; *Téléc:* 418-644-5977
gsklavounos-lado@assnat.qc.ca
Leader parlementaire adjointe du gouvernement, L'hon. Dominique Vien
Tél: 418-528-8063; *Téléc:* 418-528-8066
ministre@tourisme.gouv.qc.ca
Les réseaux sociaux: twitter.com/Dominique_Vien, www.facebook.com/197888626915062
Whip en chef du gouvernement, L'hon. Stéphane Billette
Tél: 418-643-6018; *Téléc:* 418-643-3325
sbillette-hunt@assnat.qc.ca
Les réseaux sociaux: twitter.com/stephanbillette, www.facebook.com/stephane.billette

Whip adjoint du gouvernement, Patrick Huot
Tél: 418-643-7719; *Téléc:* 418-643-2939
Patrick.Huot.VANI@assnat.qc.ca
Les réseaux sociaux: twitter.com/patrickhuot

Présidente du caucus du parti du gouvernement, L'hon. Nicole Ménard
Tél: 418-263-0548; *Téléc:* 418-643-2895
nmenard-lapo@assnat.qc.ca
Les réseaux sociaux: twitter.com/Nicole_Menard, www.facebook.com/nicole.menard.90

Cabinet du chef de l'opposition officielle / Office of the Leader of the Official Opposition

Hôtel du Parlement, #2.89, 1045, rue des Parlementaires, Québec, QC G1A 1A4

pq.org
twitter.com/partiquebecois
www.facebook.com/lepartiquebecois
www.youtube.com/user/LePartiQuebecois

Chef de l'opposition officielle (par intérim), Sylvain Gaudreault
Tél: 418-263-0670; *Téléc:* 418-644-9697
Sylvain.Gaudreault.JONQ@assnat.qc.ca

Leader parlementaire de l'opposition officielle, Vacant

Leader parlementaire adjointe de l'opposition officielle, Gaétan Lelièvre
Gaetan.Lelievre.GASP@assnat.qc.ca

Whip en chef de l'opposition officielle, Stéphane Bergeron
Tél: 418-263-0664; *Téléc:* 418-528-0416
Stephane.Bergeron.VERC@assnat.qc.ca

Présidente du caucus de l'opposition officielle, Lorraine Richard
Tél: 418-643-2446; *Téléc:* 418-644-3219
lorrainerichard-dupl@assnat.qc.ca

Cabinet du chef du deuxième groupe d'opposition / Office of the Leader of the Second Opposition Group

Hôtel du Parlement, #3.157, 1045, rue des Parlementaires, Québec, QC G1A 1A4

coalitionavenirquebec.org
twitter.com/coalitionavenir
fr-fr.facebook.com/coalitionavenir

Chef du deuxième groupe d'opposition, François Legault
Tel: 418-644-9318; *Fax:* 418-528-9479
flegault-asso@assnat.qc.ca

Leader parlementaire du deuxième groupe d'opposition, François Bonnardel
Tel: 418-644-1467; *Fax:* 418-643-0237
fbonnardel-gran@assnat.qc.ca

Leader parlementaire adjoint du deuxième groupe d'opposition, Éric Caire
Tel: 418-644-0185; *Fax:* 418-643-0237
ecaire-lape@assnat.qc.ca

Whip du deuxième groupe d'opposition, Donald Martel
Tel: 418-644-1444; *Fax:* 418-528-6935
donaldmartel-nico@assnat.qc.ca

Présidente du caucus du deuxième groupe d'opposition, Natalie Roy
Tel: 418-644-0655; *Fax:* 418-643-0237
nroy-mota@assnat.qc.ca

Direction de l'Assemblée nationale du Québec / Directorate of the National Assembly of Québec

Secrétaire général, Michel Bonsaint
sec.general@assnat.qc.ca

Directeur et adjoint du secrétaire général, Secrétariat du Bureau, Marc Painchaud
Tél: 418-643-2724

Directrice générale, Affaires juridiques et parlementaries, Ariane Mignolet
Tél: 418-528-0020

Directeur, Travaux parlementaires, François Arsenault
Tél: 418-643-2722
seance@assnat.qc.ca

Directeur, Service de l'édition des lois, Jean-Pierre Drapeau
Tél: 418-643-2840
trad.ed.lois@assnat.qc.ca

Directrice, Service du Journal des débats, Carole Lessard
journal.debats@assnat.qc.ca

Directrice, Traduction et de l'édition des lois, Catherine Morin
trad.ed.lois@assnat.qc.ca

Directrice, Service de la traduction, Evelyn Wever
trad.ed.lois@assnat.qc.ca

Administration

Directeur général, Administration, Serge Bouchard
Tél: 418-643-6000

Directeur, Service des systèmes informationnels et des réseaux, François Asselin
Tél: 418-643-2725
informatique@assnat.qc.ca

Directrice, Ressources financières, de l'approvisionnement et de la vérification, Lyne Bergeron
Tél: 418-643-3022
res.financieres@assnat.qc.ca

Directeur, Sécurité, Yves Bouchard
securite@assnat.qc.ca

Directrice, Centre de services et bureautique, Catherine Grétas
informatique@assnat.qc.ca

Directrice, Service de la télédiffusion des débats, Dominique Drouin
informatique@assnat.qc.ca

Directeur, Informatique, de la télédiffusion et des télécommunications, Claude Dugas
Tél: 418-643-2725
informatique@assnat.qc.ca

Directeur, Gestion immobilière et des ressources matérielles, Guy L. Huot
Tél: 418-643-1828
gestion.immobiliere@assnat.qc.ca

Directeur, Ressources humaines, Claudia Rousseau
Tél: 418-644-5444
res.humaines@assnat.qc.ca

Affaires institutionnelles et de la Bibliothéque de l'Assemblée nationale / Institutional Affairs & the Library of the National Assembly

bibliotheque@assnat.qc.ca

Directeur général, Frédéric Fortin
Tél: 418-646-2383

Directeur, Relations interparlementaires et internationales et du protocole, Daniel Cloutier
Tél: 418-643-4206
rel.interparlementaires@assnat.qc.ca

Directeur, Service de la recherche, Jacques Gagnon
Tél: 418-643-4567

Directrice, Communications, des programmes éducatifs et de l'accueil, Isabelle Giguère
Tél: 418-643-1992
communications@assnat.qc.ca

Les Régions administratives au Québec - Les ministres responsables / Ministers Responsible for the Administrative Regions of Québec

Abitibi-Témiscamingue, L'hon. Luc Blanchette
Bas-Saint-Laurent, L'hon. Jean D'Amour
Capitale-Nationale, L'hon. François Blais
Centre-du-Québec, L'hon. Laurent Lessard
Chaudière-Appalaches, L'hon. Dominique Vien
Côte-Nord, L'hon. Pierre Arcand
Estrie (par intérim), L'hon. Pierre Paradis
Gaspésie—Iles-de-la-Madeleine, L'hon. Sébastien Proulx
Lanaudière, L'hon. Lise Thériault
Laurentides, L'hon. Christine St-Pierre
Laval, L'hon. Francine Charbonneau
Mauricie, L'hon. Julie Boulet
Montérégie, L'hon. Lucie Charlebois
Montréal, L'hon. Martin Coiteux
Nord-du-Québec, L'hon. Luc Blanchette
Outaouais, L'hon. Stéphanie Vallée
Saguenay—Lac-Saint-Jean, L'hon. Philippe Couillard, P.C.

Le travail en commission / Committees

www.assnat.qc.ca/fr/abc-assemblee/travail-commission.html

Commission de l'administration publique (CAP) / Committee on Public Administration

Président, Carole Poirier
Circonscription électorale: Hochelaga-Maisonneuve, Parti Québécois
Tél: 418-263-0707; *Téléc:* 418-643-7127
cpoirier-homa@assnat.qc.ca

Secrétaire, Pierre-Luc Turgeon
Tél: 418-643-2722; *Téléc:* 418-643-0248
cap@assnat.qc.ca

Commission de l'agriculture, des pêcheries, de l'énergie et des ressources naturelles (CAPERN) / Committee on Agriculture, Fisheries, Energy & Natural Resources

Président, Sylvain Pagé
Circonscription électorale: Labelle, Parti Québécois
Tél: 418-528-1349; *Téléc:* 418-528-7185
spage@assnat.qc.ca

Secrétaire, Stéphanie Pinault-Reid
Tél: 418-643-2722; *Téléc:* 418-643-0248
capa@assnat.qc.ca

Commission de l'aménagement du territoire (CAT) / Committee on Planning & the Public Domain

Président, Pierre-Michel Auger
Circonscription électorale: Champlain, Liberal
Tél: 418-644-2499; *Téléc:* 418-528-5668
Pierre-Michel.Auger.CHMP@assnat.qc.ca

Secrétaire, Anne-Marie Larochelle
Tél: 418-643-2722; *Téléc:* 418-643-0248
cat@assnat.qc.ca

Commission de l'Assemblée nationale (CAN) / Committee on the National Assembly

Président, L'hon. Jacques Chagnon
Circonscription électorale: Westmount—Saint-Louis, Liberal
Tél: 418-643-2820; *Téléc:* 418-643-3423
presidentcabinet@assnat.qc.ca

Secrétaire, François Arsenault
Tél: 418-643-2722; *Téléc:* 418-643-0248
can@assnat.qc.ca

Commission de la culture et de l'éducation (CCE) / Committee on Culture & Education

Présidente, Filomena Rotiroti
Circonscription électorale: Jeanne-Mance-Viger, Liberal
Tél: 418-646-5743; *Téléc:* 418-644-5990
frotiroti-jmv@assnat.qc.ca

Secrétaire, Pierre-Luc Turgeon
Tél: 418-643-2722; *Téléc:* 418-643-0248
cce@assnat.qc.ca

Commission de l'économie et du travail (CET) / Committee on Labour & the Economy

Président, Claude Cousineau
Circonscription électorale: Bertrand, Parti Québécois
Tél: 418-263-0682; *Téléc:* 418-643-7127
ccousineau-berr@assnat.qc.ca

Secrétaire, Anik Laplante
Tél: 418-643-2722; *Téléc:* 418-643-0248
cet@assnat.qc.ca

Commission des finances publiques (CFP) / Committee on Public Finance

Président, Raymond Bernier
Circonscription électorale: Montmorency, Liberal
Tél: 418-644-9600; *Téléc:* 418-646-8169
Raymond.Bernier.MONT@assnat.qc.ca

Secrétaire, Mathew Lagacé
Tél: 418-643-2722; *Téléc:* 418-643-0248
cfp@assnat.qc.ca

Commission des institutions (CI) / Committee on Institutions

Président, Guy Ouellette
Circonscription électorale: Chomedey, Liberal
Tél: 418-644-4050; *Téléc:* 418-646-7385
gouellette-chom@assnat.qc.ca

Secrétaire, Maxime Perreault
Tél: 418-643-2722; *Téléc:* 418-643-0248
ci@assnat.qc.ca

Commission des relations avec les citoyens (CRC) / Committee on Citizen Relations

Président, Marc Picard
Circonscription électorale: Chutes-de-la-Chaudière, CA
Tél: 418-528-1694; *Téléc:* 418-528-6935
mpicard-cdlc@assnat.qc.ca

Secrétaire, Anne-Marie Larochelle
Tél: 418-643-2722; *Téléc:* 418-643-0248
crc@assnat.qc.ca

Commission de la santé et des services sociaux (CSSS) / Committee on Health & Social Services

Président, Marc Tanguay
Circonscription électorale: LaFontaine, Liberal
Tél: 418-528-7413; *Téléc:* 418-528-1650
marc.tanguay-lafo@assnat.qc.ca

Secrétaire, Dany Hallé
Circonscription électorale: LaFontaine, Liberal
Tél: 418-643-2722; *Téléc:* 418-643-0248
csss@assnat.qc.ca

Commission des transports et de l'environnement (CTE) / Committee on Transportation & the Environment

Président, Pierre Reid
Circonscription électorale: Orford, Liberal
Tél: 418-644-3944; *Téléc:* 418-528-5668
preid-orfo@assnat.qc.ca

Secrétaire, Louisette Cameron
Tél: 418-643-2722; *Téléc:* 418-643-0248
cte@assnat.qc.ca

Quarante-et-unième assemblée nationale / Forty-first National Assembly - Québec

Hôtel du Parlement, 1045, rue des Parlementaires, Québec, QC G1A 1A4

Tél: 418-643-7239; *Téléc:* 418-646-4271
Ligne sans frais: 866-337-8837
www.assnat.qc.ca
twitter.com/AssnatQc
www.facebook.com/AssnatQc
www.youtube.com/user/quebecassnat

La dernière élection générale: le 7 avril 2014.
Depuis le septembre 2016, la composition de l'Assemblée est la suivante:
Parti Libéral du Québec (PLQ) 70;
Parti québécois (PQ) 28;
Coalition Avenir Québec (CAQ) 20;

Québec solidaire 3;
Vacant 4;
Total 125.
Salaires, indemnités, allocations: indemnité annuelle: $89,950 et une allocation de dépenses de $16,226. En plus, le Premier ministre reçoit $94,448, les ministres $67,463, le Leader parlementaire du gouvernement et le Président $67,463, le Chef de l'Opposition officielle $67,463.
Par la suite: membre, circonscription, allégeance politique, téléphone & télécopieur, courriel, (Adresse: Hôtel du Parlement, Québec, QC G1A 1A4)

Députés de l'Assemblée nationale

Ministre de l'Économie, de la Science et de l'Innovation; Ministre responsable de la Stratégie numérique, L'hon. Dominique Anglade
Circonscription électorale: Saint-Henri—Sainte-Anne *Nombre de constituants:* 55 999, Liberal
Tél: 514-499-2552
ministre@economie.gouv.qc.ca
Autres numéros: Circ. Tél: 514-933-8796; Téléc: 514-933-4986
Bureau de circonscription
3269, rue Saint-Jacques
Montréal, QC H4C 1G8

Ministre de l'Énergie et des Ressources naturelles; Ministre responsable du Plan Nord, et Ministre responsable de la région de Côte-Nord, L'hon. Pierre Arcand
Circonscription électorale: Mont-Royal *Nombre de constituants:* 43 154, Liberal
Tél: 418-643-7295; *Téléc:* 418-643-4318
ministre@mern.gouv.qc.ca
www.plq.org/fr/equipe/pierrearcand
Autres numéros: Circ. Tél: 514-341-1151; Téléc: 514-341-4777
Les réseaux sociaux: twitter.com/PierreArcand, www.facebook.com/arcand.pierre
Bureau de circonscription
5005, Jean-Talon ouest
Montréal, QC H4P 1W7

Pierre-Michel Auger
Circonscription électorale: Champlain *Nombre de constituants:* 48 978, Liberal
Tél: 418-644-2499; *Téléc:* 418-528-0427
Pierre-Michel.Auger.CHMP@assnat.qc.ca
www.plq.org/fr/equipe/pierre-michel-auger
Autres numéros: Circ. Tél: 819-694-4600; Téléc: 819-694-4606
Les réseaux sociaux: www.facebook.com/pierremichel.auger.3, ca.linkedin.com/pub/pierre-michel-auger-asc/38/67b/818
Bureau de circonscription, Rez-de-chaussée
278, rue Saint-Laurent
Trois-Rivières, QC G8T 6G7

Ministre de la Santé et des Services sociaux, L'hon. Gaétan Barrette
Circonscription électorale: La Pinière *Nombre de constituants:* 60 247, Liberal
Tél: 418-266-7171; *Téléc:* 418-266-7197
ministre@msss.gouv.qc.ca
www.plq.org/fr/equipe/gaetanbarrette
Autres numéros: Circ. Tél: 450-678-0611; Téléc: 450-678-1758
Les réseaux sociaux: www.facebook.com/Gaetanbarretteplq
Bureau de circonscription
#254, 7005, boul Taschereau
Brossard, QC J4Z 1A7

Whip en chef de l'opposition officielle, Stéphane Bergeron
Circonscription électorale: Verchères *Nombre de constituants:* 57 448, Parti Québécois
Tél: 418-263-0664
Ligne sans frais: 800-652-4419; *Téléc:* 418-528-0416
Stephane.Bergeron.VERC@assnat.qc.ca
stephanebergeron.org
Autres numéros: Circ. Tél: 450-652-4419; Téléc: 450-652-3713
Les réseaux sociaux: twitter.com/sbergeron, www.facebook.com/stephanebergeronvercheres
Bureau de circonscription, Complexe Biarritz
#1A, 100, boul de la Marine
Varennes, QC J3X 2B1

Raymond Bernier
Circonscription électorale: Montmorency *Nombre de constituants:* 55 950, Liberal
Tél: 418-644-9600; *Téléc:* 418-646-8169
Raymond.Bernier.MONT@assnat.qc.ca
www.plq.org/fr/equipe/raymondbernier
Autres numéros: Circ. Tél: 418-660-6870; Téléc: 418-660-8988
Les réseaux sociaux: twitter.com/BernierRaymond, www.facebook.com/raymond.bernier.92
Bureau de circonscription
#203, 2400 boul Louis-XIV
Québec, QC G1C 5Y8

Pascal Bérubé
Circonscription électorale: Matane-Matapédia *Nombre de constituants:* 47 356, Parti Québécois
Tél: 418-263-0695
Ligne sans frais: 877-462-0371; *Téléc:* 418-643-6264
Pascal.Berube.MATN@assnat.qc.ca
pq.org/depute/pascal-berube
Autres numéros: Circ. Tél: 418-562-0371; Téléc: 418-562-7806
Les réseaux sociaux: twitter.com/PascalBerube, www.facebook.com/PascalBerubeDepute, ca.linkedin.com/pub/pascal-bérubé/36/437/943
Bureau de circonscription
121, av Fraser
Matane, QC G4W 3G8

Whip en chef du gouvernement, L'hon. Stéphane Billette
Circonscription électorale: Huntingdon *Nombre de constituants:* 42 056, Liberal
Tél: 418-643-6018
Ligne sans frais: 866-540-9097; *Téléc:* 418-643-5462
sbillette-hunt@assnat.qc.ca
www.plq.org/fr/equipe/stephanebillette
Autres numéros: Circ. Tél: 450-247-3474; Téléc: 450-247-2083
Les réseaux sociaux: twitter.com/stephanbillette, www.facebook.com/stephane.billette
Bureau de circonscription
528, rue Frontière
Hemmingford, QC J0L 1H0

David Birnbaum
Circonscription électorale: D'Arcy-McGee *Nombre de constituants:* 40 892, Liberal
Tél: 418-528-1960; *Téléc:* 418-643-0183
David.Birnbaum.DMG@assnat.qc.ca
www.plq.org/fr/equipe/davidbirnbaum
Autres numéros: Circ. Tél: 514-488-7028; Téléc: 514-488-1713
Bureau de circonscription
#403, 5800, boul Cavendish
Côte-Saint-Luc, QC H4W 2T5

Ministre de l'Emploi et de la Solidarité sociale; Ministre responsable de la région de la Capitale-Nationale, L'hon. François Blais
Circonscription électorale: Charlesbourg *Nombre de constituants:* 52 879, Liberal
Tél: 418-643-4810; *Téléc:* 418-643-2802
ministre@mess.gouv.qc.ca
www.plq.org/fr/equipe/francoisblais
Autres numéros: Circ. Tél: 418-644-9240; Téléc: 418-644-9266
Les réseaux sociaux: www.facebook.com/francois.blais.plq2014
Bureau de circonscription, Carrefour Charlesbourg
#213, 8500, boul Henri-Bourassa
Québec, QC G1G 5X1

Ministre responsable de la région de l'Abitibi-Témiscamingue et de la région du Nord-du-Québec, Ministre des Forêts, de la Faune et des Parcs, L'hon. Luc Blanchette
Circonscription électorale: Rouyn-Noranda—Témiscamingue *Nombre de constituants:* 44 587, Liberal
Tél: 418-643-7295
Ligne sans frais: 866-268-4685; *Téléc:* 418-643-4318
www.plq.org/fr/equipe/lucblanchette
Autres numéros: Circ. Tél: 819-763-3047; Téléc: 819-763-3050
Les réseaux sociaux: www.facebook.com/lucblanchette.plq
Bureau de circonscription
#103, 170, av Principale
Rouyn-Noranda, QC J9X 4P7

Ghislain Bolduc
Circonscription électorale: Mégantic *Nombre de constituants:* 38 589, Liberal
Tél: 418-644-0711; *Téléc:* 418-528-5668
gbolduc-mega@assnat.qc.ca
www.plq.org/fr/equipe/ghislainbolduc
Autres numéros: Circ. Tél: 819-583-4500; Téléc: 819-583-0926
Les réseaux sociaux: twitter.com/GhislainBolduc, www.facebook.com/ghyslainvaillancourtplq, ca.linkedin.com/pub/ghislain-bolduc/88/a15/b9
Bureau de circonscription
4315, rue Laval
Lac-Mégantic, QC G6B 1B7

Leader parlementaire du deuxième groupe d'opposition, François Bonnardel
Circonscription électorale: Granby *Nombre de constituants:* 50 650, CA
Tél: 418-644-1467; *Téléc:* 418-643-0237
fbonnardel-gran@assnat.qc.ca
www.francoisbonnardel.ca
Autres numéros: Circ. Tél: 450-372-9152; Téléc: 450-372-3040
Les réseaux sociaux: twitter.com/fbonnardelCAQ, www.facebook.com/Bonnardel.coalition, ca.linkedin.com/pub/françois-bonnardel/6a/464/773
Bureau de circonscription
#4, 398, rue Principale
Granby, QC J2G 2W6

Jean Boucher
Circonscription électorale: Ungava *Nombre de constituants:* 26 786, Liberal
Tél: 418-644-1363
Ligne sans frais: 800-463-7122; *Téléc:* 418-643-7133
Jean.Boucher.UNGA@assnat.qc.ca
www.plq.org/fs/equipe/jeanboucher
Autres numéros: Circ. Téléc: 418-748-3255
Les réseaux sociaux: www.facebook.com/jeanboucherplq
Bureau de circonscription
#12, 462, 3e rue
Chibougamau, QC G8P 1N7

Ministre du Tourisme; Ministre responsable de la région de la Mauricie, L'hon. Julie Boulet
Circonscription électorale: Laviolette *Nombre de constituants:* 35 771, Liberal
Tél: 418-528-8063
Ligne sans frais: 800-567-2996; *Téléc:* 418-528-8066
ministre@tourisme.gouv.qc.ca
www.plq.org/fr/equipe/julieboulet
Autres numéros: Circ. Tél: 819-538-3349; Téléc: 819-538-0887
Bureau de circonscription
570, 6e av
Grand-Mère, QC G9T 2H2

Guy Bourgeois
Circonscription électorale: Abitibi-Est *Nombre de constituants:* 33 638, Liberal
Tél: 418-263-0662; *Téléc:* 418-528-7447
Guy.Bourgeois.ABES@assnat.qc.ca
www.plq.org/fr/equipe/guybourgeois
Autres numéros: Circ. Tél: 819-824-3333; Téléc: 819-824-4300
Bureau de circonscription
#202, 888, 3e av
Val-d'Or, QC J9P 5E6

Paul Busque
Circonscription électorale: Beauce-Sud *Nombre de constituants:* 48 193, Liberal
Tél: 418-263-0645; *Téléc:* 418-528-7447
Paul.Busque.BESU@assnat.qc.ca
Autres numéros: Circ. Tél: 418-226-4570; Téléc: 418-227-9664
Bureau de circonscription
#102, 11287, 1re Av
Saint-Georges, QC G5Y 2C2

Leader parlementaire adjoint du deuxième groupe d'opposition, Éric Caire
Circonscription électorale: La Peltrie *Nombre de constituants:* 55 695, CA
Tél: 418-644-0185; *Téléc:* 418-643-0237
ecaire-lape@assnat.qc.ca
www.ericcaire.qc.ca
Autres numéros: Circ. Tél: 418-877-5260; Téléc: 418-877-6533
Les réseaux sociaux: twitter.com/ericcaire, www.facebook.com/caire.coalition
Bureau de circonscription
#201, 5121 boul Chauveau ouest
Québec, QC G2E 5A6

Marc Carrière
Circonscription électorale: Chapleau *Nombre de constituants:* 54 814, Liberal
Tél: 418-528-0390; *Téléc:* 418-643-9164
mcarriere-chap@assnat.qc.ca
www.plq.org/fr/equipe/marccarriere
Autres numéros: Circ. Tél: 819-246-4558; Téléc: 819-246-2970
Les réseaux sociaux: twitter.com/plqcarriere, www.facebook.com/marc.carriere.39
Bureau de circonscription
#503, 160, boul de l'Hôpital
Gatineau, QC J8T 8J1

Président de l'Assemblée nationale, L'hon. Jacques Chagnon
Circonscription électorale: Westmount—Saint-Louis *Nombre de constituants:* 39 736, Liberal
Tél: 418-643-2820; *Téléc:* 418-643-3423
jchagnon-wsl@assnat.qc.ca
www.plq.org/fr/equipe/jacqueschagnon
Autres numéros: Circ. Tél: 514-395-2929; Téléc: 514-395-2955
Bureau de circonscription
#1312, 1155, rue University
Montréal, QC H3B 3A7

Ministre responsable des Aînés et de la Lutte contre l'intimidation, et Ministre responsable de la région de Laval, L'hon. Francine Charbonneau
Circonscription électorale: Mille-Îles *Nombre de constituants:* 42 804, Liberal
Tél: 418-643-2181; *Téléc:* 418-643-2640

ministre.aines@mfa.gouv.qc.ca
francinecharbonneau.ca
Autres numéros: Circ. Tél: 450-661-3595; Téléc: 450-661-6093
Les réseaux sociaux: twitter.com/mille_iles, ca.linkedin.com/pub/francine-charbonneau/63/a86/744
Bureau de circonscription
#11, 3095, boul de la Concorde est
Laval, QC H7E 2C1

Benoit Charette
Circonscription électorale: Deux-Montagnes *Nombre de constituants:* 47 612, CA
Tél: 418-528-0765; *Téléc:* 418-643-0237
Benoit.Charette.DEMO@assnat.qc.ca
coalitionavenirquebec.org/equipe/benoit
Autres numéros: Circ. Tél: 450-623-4963; Téléc: 450-623-7178
Les réseaux sociaux: twitter.com/CharetteB, www.facebook.com/Charette.Coalition
Bureau de circonscription
#230, 477, 25e av
Saint-Eustache, QC J7P 4Y1

Ministre déléguée à la Réadaptation, à la Protection de la jeunesse, à la Santé publique et aux Saines habitudes de vie;, Ministre responsable de la région de la Montérégie, L'hon. Lucie Charlebois
Circonscription électorale: Soulanges *Nombre de constituants:* 48 340, Liberal
Tél: 418-266-7181
Ligne sans frais: 866-268-3607; *Téléc:* 418-266-7199
ministre.deleguee@msss.gouv.qc.ca
www.luciecharlebois.org
Autres numéros: Circ. Tél: 450-456-3816; Téléc: 450-456-3930
Les réseaux sociaux: twitter.com/luciecharlebois, www.facebook.com/lucie.charlebois.9, ca.linkedin.com/pub/lucie-charlebois/1b/ba2/b6
Bureau de circonscription
607, route 201
Saint-Clet, QC J0P 1S0

Germain Chevarie
Circonscription électorale: Îles-de-la-Madeleine *Nombre de constituants:* 10 855, Liberal
Tél: 418-644-1454; *Téléc:* 418-643-0183
Germain.Chevarie.IDLM@assnat.qc.ca
www.plq.org/fr/equipe/germainchevarie
Autres numéros: Circ. Tél: 418-986-4140; Téléc: 418-986-2577
Les réseaux sociaux: www.facebook.com/germainchevarie2014
Bureau de circonscription
210, ch Principal
Cap-aux-Meules, QC G4T 1C7

Alexandre Cloutier
Circonscription électorale: Lac-Saint-Jean *Nombre de constituants:* 43 027, Parti Québécois
Tél: 418-263-0697; *Téléc:* 418-643-7126
Alexandre.Cloutier.LSJ@assnat.qc.ca
alexandrecloutier.org
Autres numéros: Circ. Tél: 418-668-6149; Téléc: 418-668-0684
Les réseaux sociaux: twitter.com/alexcloutier, www.facebook.com/AlexandreCloutierPQ
Bureau de circonscription
510-A, rue Sacré-Coeur ouest
Alma, QC G8B 1L9

Ministre des Affaires municipales et de l'Occupation du territoire; Ministre de la Sécurité publique;, Ministre responsable de la région de Montréal, L'hon. Martin Coiteux
Circonscription électorale: Nelligan *Nombre de constituants:* 58 147, Liberal
Tél: 418-691-2050; *Téléc:* 41- 64- 179
ministre@mamot.gouv.qc.ca
www.plq.org/fr/equipe/martincoiteux
Autres numéros: Circ. Tél: 514-695-2440; Téléc: 514-695-8648
Bureau de circonscription
#400, 3535, boul Saint-Charles
Kirkland, QC H9H 5B9

Premier ministre; Ministre responsable de la région du Saguenay-Lac-Saint-Jean; Responsable des dossiers jeunesse, L'hon. Philippe Couillard, P.C.
Circonscription électorale: Roberval *Nombre de constituants:* 45 143, Liberal
Tél: 418-643-5321; *Téléc:* 418-643-3924
commentaires-pm@mce.gouv.qc.ca
www.plq.org/fr/le-chef
Autres numéros: Circ. Tél: 418-679-8070; Téléc: 418-679-3648
Les réseaux sociaux: twitter.com/phcouillard, www.facebook.com/phcouillard

Claude Cousineau
Circonscription électorale: Bertrand *Nombre de constituants:* 58 161, Parti Québécois
Tél: 418-263-0682
Ligne sans frais: 800-882-4757; *Téléc:* 418-643-7127
ccousineau-berr@assnat.qc.ca
claudecousineau.org
Autres numéros: Circ. Tél: 819-321-1676; Téléc: 819-321-1680
Les réseaux sociaux: www.facebook.com/claudecousineau
Bureau de circonscription
#101, 197, rue Principale
Sainte-Agathe-des-Monts, QC J8C 1K5

Ministre délégué aux Affaires maritimes; Ministre responsable de la région du Bas-Saint-Laurent, L'hon. Jean D'Amour
Circonscription électorale: Rivière-du-Loup-Témiscouata *Nombre de constituants:* 50 688, Liberal
Tél: 418-691-5650; *Téléc:* 418-691-5800
ministre.maritimes@economie.gouv.qc.ca
www.jeandamour.com
Autres numéros: Circ. Tél: 418-868-0822; Téléc: 418-868-0826
Les réseaux sociaux: www.facebook.com/60265923724
Bureau de circonscription
#102, 320, boul. de l'Hôtel-de-Ville
Rivière-du-Loup, QC G5R 5C6

Sylvie D'Amours
Circonscription électorale: Mirabel *Nombre de constituants:* 60 386, CA
Tél: 418-644-1543; *Téléc:* 418-643-0237
Sylvie.DAmours.MIRA@assnat.qc.ca
coalitionavenirquebec.org/equipe/sylvie-damours
Autres numéros: Circ. Tél: 418-851-1748; Téléc: 418-851-2103
Les réseaux sociaux: twitter.com/SylvieDAmours, www.facebook.com/DAmoursS.coalition
Bureau de circonscription
#200, 2871, boul des Promenades
Sainte-Marthe-sur-le-Lac, QC J0N 1P0

Françoise David
Circonscription électorale: Gouin *Nombre de constituants:* 43 831, QS
Tél: 418-644-1367; *Téléc:* 418-643-0624
fdavid-goui@assnat.qc.ca
www.quebecsolidaire.net/equipe/francoise-david
Autres numéros: Circ. Tél: 514-864-6133; Téléc: 514-873-8998
Les réseaux sociaux: twitter.com/FrancoiseDavid, www.facebook.com/FrancoiseDavid.QS
Bureau de circonscription
1453, rue Beaubien est
Montréal, QC H2G 3C6

Ministre responsable de l'Enseignement supérieur, L'hon. Hélène David
Circonscription électorale: Outremont *Nombre de constituants:* 39 580, Liberal
Tél: 418-266-3255
ministre.enseignement.superieur@education.gouv.qc.ca
www.plq.org/fr/equipe/helenedavid
Autres numéros: Circ. Tél: 514-482-0199; Téléc: 514-482-9985
Les réseaux sociaux: www.facebook.com/plq.helenedavid
Bureau de circonscription
#115, 5450, ch de la Côte-des-Neiges
Montréal, QC H3T 1Y6

Ministre responsable de l'Accès à l'information et de la Réforme des institutions démocratiques, Hon. Rita de Santis
Circonscription électorale: Bourassa-Sauvé *Nombre de constituants:* 47 769, Liberal
Tél: 418-780-4345; *Téléc:* 418-643-8109
ministre.sridaministre@mce.gouv.qc.ca
www.plq.org/fr/equipe/rita_desantis
Autres numéros: Circ. Tél: 514-328-6006; Téléc: 514-328-0763
Les réseaux sociaux: www.facebook.com/RitaDeSantisPLQ
Bureau de circonscription
#305, 5879, boul Henri-Bourassa est
Montréal-Nord, QC H1G 2V1

André Drolet
Circonscription électorale: Jean-Lesage *Nombre de constituants:* 46 643, Liberal
Tél: 418-646-7635; *Téléc:* 418-528-0425
adrolet-jele@assnat.qc.ca
www.plq.org/fr/equipe/andredrolet
Autres numéros: Circ. Tél: 418-648-6221; Téléc: 418-648-2061
Les réseaux sociaux: twitter.com/andredrolet
Bureau de circonscription
#303, 1750, ave De Vitré
Québec, QC G1J 1Z6

André Fortin
Circonscription électorale: Pontiac *Nombre de constituants:* 50 103, Liberal
Tél: 418-644-0679
Ligne sans frais: 866-988-7070; *Téléc:* 418-528-5668
Andre.Fortin.PONT@assnat.qc.ca
www.avecandrefortin.ca
Autres numéros: Circ. Tél: 819-648-7070; Téléc: 819-648-2448
Les réseaux sociaux: twitter.com/AvecAndreFortin, www.facebook.com/AvecAndreFortin
Bureau de circonscription
1226, rte 148
PO Box 100
Campbell's Bay, QC J0X 1K0

Ministre de la Culture et des Communications; Ministre responsable de la Protection et de la Promotion de la langue française, Ministre responsable de la région de l'Estrie, L'Hon. Luc Fortin
Circonscription électorale: Sherbrooke *Nombre de constituants:* 49 255, Liberal
Tél: 41- 38- 231; *Téléc:* 418-380-2311
ministre@mcc.gouv.qc.ca
www.plq.org/fr/equipe/lucfortin
Autres numéros: Circ. Tél: 819-569-5646; Téléc: 819-569-0229
Les réseaux sociaux: twitter.com/SherbrookePLQ, www.facebook.com/1478020959086646
Bureau de circonscription
#05, 1650, rue King Ouest
Sherbrooke, QC J1J 2C3

Ministre responsable des Affaires intergouvernementales canadiennes et de la Francophonie canadienne;, Leader parlementaire du gouvernement, L'hon. Jean-Marc Fournier
Circonscription électorale: Saint-Laurent *Nombre de constituants:* 55 083, Liberal
Tél: 418-643-3804; *Téléc:* 418-643-2514
jean-marc.fournier-sala@assnat.qc.ca
www.plq.org/fr/equipe/jeanmarcfournier
Autres numéros: Circ. Tél: 514-747-4050; Téléc: 514-747-5605
Les réseaux sociaux: facebook.com/JeanMarcFournier.SaintLaurent
Bureau de circonscription
#312, 5255, boul Henri-Bourassa ouest
Saint-Laurent, QC H4R 2M6

Deuxième vice-présidente de l'Assemblée nationale, Maryse Gaudreault
Circonscription électorale: Hull *Nombre de constituants:* 52 542, Liberal
Tél: 418-643-2810; *Téléc:* 418-643-3688
mgaudreault-hull@assnat.qc.ca
marysegaudreault.com
Autres numéros: Circ. Tél: 819-772-3000; Téléc: 819-772-3265
Les réseaux sociaux: twitter.com/MGaudreaultHull, www.facebook.com/maryse.gaudreault.14
Bureau de circonscription
#207, 259, boul Saint-Joseph
Gatineau, QC J8Y 6T1

Chef de l'opposition officielle (par intérim), Sylvain Gaudreault
Circonscription électorale: Jonquière *Nombre de constituants:* 45 648, Parti Québécois
Tél: 418-263-0670; *Téléc:* 418-644-9697
Sylvain.Gaudreault.JONQ@assnat.qc.ca
sylvaingaudreault.org
Autres numéros: Circ. Tél: 418-547-0666; Téléc: 418-547-1166
Les réseaux sociaux: twitter.com/SylvainGaudrea2, www.facebook.com/Sylvain.Gaudreault.Jonquiere
Bureau de circonscription
2240, rue Montpetit, rez-de-chaussée
Jonquière, QC G7X 6A3

Troisième vice-président de l'Assemblée nationale, François Gendron
Circonscription électorale: Abitibi-Ouest *Nombre de constituants:* 35 382, Parti Québécois
Tél: 418-644-1007; *Téléc:* 418-644-1368
François.Gendron.ABOU@assnat.qc.ca
www.francoisgendron.qc.ca
Autres numéros: Circ. Tél: 819-339-7707; Téléc: 819-339-7711
Les réseaux sociaux: www.facebook.com/FrancoisGendronPQ
Bureau de circonscription
258, 2e rue est
La Sarre, QC J9Z 2H2

Pierre Giguère
Circonscription électorale: Saint-Maurice *Nombre de constituants:* 36 712, Liberal
Tél: 418-528-1277; *Téléc:* 418-528-5668
Pierre.Giguere.SAMA@assnat.qc.ca
www.plq.org/fr/equipe/pierregiguere
Autres numéros: Circ. Tél: 819-539-7292; Téléc: 819-539-8441
Bureau de circonscription
#101, 695, av de la Station
Shawinigan, Q G9N 1V9

Jean-Denis Girard
Circonscription électorale: Trois-Rivières *Nombre de constituants:* 43 721, Liberal

Tél: 581-628-1007; *Téléc:* 418-643-7838
Jean-Denis.Girard.TRRI@assnat.qc.ca
www.plq.org/fr/equipe/jeandenisgirard
Autres numéros: Circ. Tél: 819-371-6901; Téléc: 819-371-6648
Les réseaux sociaux: twitter.com/girardjd, www.facebook.com/GirardJD, ca.linkedin.com/pub/jean-denis-girard/71/316/436
Bureau de circonscription
#180, 1500, rue Royale
Trois-Rivières, QC G9A 6E6

Jean Habel
Circonscription électorale: Sainte-Rose *Nombre de constituants:* 50 826, Liberal
Tél: 418-263-0619; *Téléc:* 418-644-1872
Jean.Habel.SARO@assnat.qc.ca
www.plq.org/fr/equipe/jeanhabel
Autres numéros: Circ. Tél: 819-963-8272; Téléc: 450-963-7318
Les réseaux sociaux: twitter.com/JeanHabel, www.facebook.com/jeanhabelplq
Bureau de circonscription
132, boul Sainte-Rose
Laval, QC H7L 1K4

Sam Hamad
Circonscription électorale: Louis-Hébert *Nombre de constituants:* 44 887, Liberal
Tél: 418-643-5926; *Téléc:* 418-643-7824
www.plq.org/fr/equipe/samhamad
Autres numéros: Circ. Tél: 418-528-0483; Téléc: 418-644-1253
Les réseaux sociaux: twitter.com/SamHamad, www.facebook.com/ministre.samhamad
Bureau de circonscription
#202, 810, rue Jean-Gauvin
Québec, QC G1X 0B6

Guy Hardy
Circonscription électorale: Saint-François *Nombre de constituants:* 55 945, Liberal
Tél: 418-263-0703; *Téléc:* 418-643-0183
Guy.Hardy.SAFR@assnat.qc.ca
www.plq.org/fr/equipe/guyhardy
Autres numéros: Circ. Tél: 819-565-3667; Téléc: 819-565-8779
Bureau de circonscription
220, 12e av nord
Sherbrooke, QC J1E 2W3

Ministre du Développement durable, de l'Environnement et de la Lutte contre les changements climatiques, L'hon. David Heurtel
Circonscription électorale: Viau *Nombre de constituants:* 41 161, Liberal
Tél: 418-521-3911; *Téléc:* 418-643-4143
dheurtel-viau@assnat.qc.ca
www.plq.org/fr/equipe/davidheurtel
Autres numéros: Circ. Tél: 514-728-2474; Téléc: 514-728-2759
Les réseaux sociaux: twitter.com/Heurtel, www.facebook.com/david.heurtel, www.linkedin.com/pub/david-heurtel/5/631/517
Bureau de circonscription
#402, 3750, boul Crémazie est
Montréal, QC H2A 1B6

Véronique Hivon
Circonscription électorale: Joliette *Nombre de constituants:* 57 591, Parti Québécois
Tél: 418-263-0666; *Téléc:* 418-644-9697
Veronique.Hivon.JOLI@assnat.qc.ca
veroniquehivon.org
Autres numéros: Circ. Tél: 450-752-6929; Téléc: 450-752-6935
Les réseaux sociaux: twitter.com/vhivon, www.facebook.com/veroniquehivon, ca.linkedin.com/pub/véronique-hivon/4/967/b22
Bureau de circonscription
970, rue Saint-Louis
Joliette, QC J6E 3A4

Whip adjoint du gouvernement, Patrick Huot
Circonscription électorale: Vanier-Les Rivières *Nombre de constituants:* 56 404, Liberal
Tél: 418-643-7719; *Téléc:* 418-643-2939
Patrick.Huot.VANI@assnat.qc.ca
www.plq.org/fr/equipe/patrickhuot
Autres numéros: Circ. Tél: 418-644-3107; Téléc: 418-643-9258
Les réseaux sociaux: twitter.com/patrickhuot
Bureau de circonscription
#311, 1170, boul Lebourgneuf
Québec, QC G2K 2E3

Alexandre Iracà
Circonscription électorale: Papineau *Nombre de constituants:* 57 999, Liberal
Tél: 418-263-0369
Ligne sans frais: 866-971-7974; *Téléc:* 418-528-0421
airaca-papi@assnat.qc.ca
www.plq.org/fr/equipe/alexandreiraca
Autres numéros: Circ. Tél: 819-986-9300; Téléc: 819-986-8629
Les réseaux sociaux: twitter.com/Alexandre_Iraca, www.facebook.com/alexandre.iraca
Bureau de circonscription
564, av de Buckingham
Gatineau, QC J8L 2H1

Mireille Jean
Circonscription électorale: Chicoutimi *Nombre de constituants:* 46,626, Parti Québécois
Tél: 418-263-0720
Mireille.Jean.CHIC@assnat.qc.ca
www.mireillejean.com
Autres numéros: Circ. Tél: 418-543-7797; Téléc: 418-543-1355
Les réseaux sociaux: twitter.com/mireillejean, www.facebook.com/mireille.jean.184, ca.linkedin.com/pub/mireille-jean/19/67/77b
Note: Mireille Jean won the riding in a by-election held April 11, 2016.
Bureau de circonscription
#300, 267, rue Racine est
Chicoutimi, QC G7H 1S5

Simon Jolin-Barrette
Circonscription électorale: Borduas *Nombre de constituants:* 56 663, CA
Tél: 418-263-0684; *Téléc:* 418-643-0237
sjb.BORD@assnat.qc.ca
coalitionavenirquebec.org/equipe/brouillon
Autres numéros: Circ. Tél: 450-464-5505; Téléc: 450-464-4335
Les réseaux sociaux: www.facebook.com/JolinBarrette.coalition
Bureau de circonscription
#304, 535, boul Sir-Wilfrid-Laurier
Beloeil, Q J3G 5E9

Ministre responsable des Affaires autochtones, L'hon. Geoffrey Kelley
Circonscription électorale: Jacques-Cartier *Nombre de constituants:* 44 612, Liberal
Tél: 418-646-9131; *Téléc:* 418-646-9487
ministre.autochtones@mce.gouv.qc.ca
www.plq.org/fr/equipe/geoffreykelley
Autres numéros: Circ. Tél: 514-697-7663; Téléc: 514-697-6499
Les réseaux sociaux: twitter.com/MNAgeoffkelley, www.facebook.com/129616153783851
Bureau de circonscription, Place Scotia
#206, 620, boul Saint-Jean
Pointe-Claire, QC H9R 3K2

Amir Khadir
Circonscription électorale: Mercier *Nombre de constituants:* 40 052, QS
Tél: 418-644-1430; *Téléc:* 418-643-0624
akhadir-merc@assnat.qc.ca
www.quebecsolidaire.net/equipe/amir-khadir
Autres numéros: Circ. Tél: 514-525-8877; Téléc: 514-521-0147
Les réseaux sociaux: twitter.com/amirkhadir, www.facebook.com/AmirKhadir
Bureau de circonscription
#102, 1012, av du Mont-Royal est
Montréal, QC H2J 1X6

Maka Kotto
Circonscription électorale: Bourget *Nombre de constituants:* 49 334, Parti Québécois
Tél: 418-263-0691; *Téléc:* 418-646-6640
Maka.Kotto.BOUR@assnat.qc.ca
makakotto.org
Autres numéros: Circ. Tél: 514-251-8126; Téléc: 514-251-1064
Les réseaux sociaux: twitter.com/Maka_Kotto, www.facebook.com/KottoMaka, ca.linkedin.com/pub/maka-kotto/83/8a5/8a3
Bureau de circonscription
#105, 6070, rue Sherbrooke est
Montréal, QC H1N 1C1

Mario Laframboise
Circonscription électorale: Blainville *Nombre de constituants:* 58 968, CA
Tél: 418-263-0613; *Téléc:* 418-643-0237
Mario.Laframboise.BLAI@assnat.qc.ca
coalitionavenirquebec.org/equipe/mario-laframboise
Autres numéros: Circ. Tél: 450-430-8086; Téléc: 450-430-9795
Les réseaux sociaux: www.facebook.com/Mario.Laframboise.Coallition
Bureau de circonscription
#211, 369, boul Adolphe-Chapleau
Bois-des-Filion, QC J6Z 1H1

Diane Lamarre
Circonscription électorale: Taillon *Nombre de constituants:* 51 736, Parti Québécois
Tél: 418-263-0668; *Téléc:* 418-643-7128
Diane.Lamarre.TAIL@assnat.qc.ca
dianelamarre.org
Autres numéros: Circ. Tél: 450-463-3772; Téléc: 450-463-1527
Les réseaux sociaux: www.facebook.com/843157719033918
Bureau de circonscription
498, boul Roland-Therrien
Longueuil, QC J4H 3V9

André Lamontagne
Circonscription électorale: Johnson *Nombre de constituants:* 57 123, CA
Tél: 418-263-0677; *Téléc:* 418-643-0237
Andre.Lamontagne.JOHN@assnat.qc.ca
coalitionavenirquebec.org/equipe/andre-lamontagne
Autres numéros: Circ. Tél: 819-474-7770; Téléc: 819-474-4492
Les réseaux sociaux: www.facebook.com/andrelamontagnecaq
Bureau de circonscription
641, rue Saint-Pierre
Drummondville, QC J2C 3W6

Lise Lavallée
Circonscription électorale: Repentigny *Nombre de constituants:* 51 484, CA
Tél: 418-263-0612; *Téléc:* 418-643-0237
Lise.Lavallee.REPE@assnat.qc.ca
coalitionavenirquebec.org/equipe/lise-lavallee
Autres numéros: Circ. Tél: 450-581-6102; Téléc: 450-581-9173
Les réseaux sociaux: www.facebook.com/lise.lavallee.9655
Bureau de circonscription
#102, 522, rue Notre-Dame
Repentigny, QC J6A 2T8

Harold Lebel
Circonscription électorale: Rimouski *Nombre de constituants:* 44 687, Parti Québécois
Harold.Lebel.RIMO@assnat.qc.ca
Autres numéros: Circ. Tél: 418-722-9787; Téléc: 418-725-0526
Les réseaux sociaux: www.facebook.com/haroldrimouski
Bureau de circonscription
#400, 320, rue Saint-Germain est
Rimouski, QC G5L 1C2

Guy Leclair
Circonscription électorale: Beauharnois *Nombre de constituants:* 46 006, Parti Québécois
Tél: 418-644-7844; *Téléc:* 418-528-7410
guy.leclair-beau@assnat.qc.ca
guyleclair.deputes.pq.org
Autres numéros: Circ. Tél: 450-377-3131; Téléc: 450-373-5272
Les réseaux sociaux: www.facebook.com/GuyLeclair2012
Bureau de circonscription
#135, 157, rue Victoria
Salaberry-de-Valleyfield, QC J6T 1A5

Chef du deuxième groupe d'opposition, François Legault
Circonscription électorale: L'Assomption *Nombre de constituants:* 52 567, CA
Tél: 418-644-9318; *Téléc:* 418-528-9479
flegault-asso@assnat.qc.ca
coalitionavenirquebec.org/equipe/francois-legault
Autres numéros: Circ. Tél: 450-589-0226; Téléc: 450-589-3457
Les réseaux sociaux: twitter.com/francoislegault, www.facebook.com/FrancoisLegaultPageOfficielle
Bureau de circonscription
#208, 831, boul de l'Ange-Gardien nord
L'Assomption, QC J5W 1P5

Nicole Léger
Circonscription électorale: Pointe-aux-Trembles *Nombre de constituants:* 40 905, Parti Québécois
Tél: 418-263-0672; *Téléc:* 418-646-7815
Nicole.Leger.PAT@assnat.qc.ca
nicoleleger.org
Autres numéros: Circ. Tél: 514-640-9085; Téléc: 514-640-0857
Les réseaux sociaux: twitter.com/nicolelegerPAT, www.facebook.com/nicoleleger.pat
Bureau de circonscription
#101, 3715, boul Saint-Jean-Baptiste
Montréal, QC H1B 5V4

Ministre des Finances; Ministre responsable de l'Administration gouvernementale et de la Révision permanente des programmes, et Président du Conseil du trésor, L'hon. Carlos J. Leitao
Circonscription électorale: Robert-Baldwin *Nombre de constituants:* 54 979, Liberal
Tél: 41- 64- 527; *Téléc:* 418-646-1574
ministre@finances.gouv.qc.ca
www.plq.org/fr/equipe/carlosleitao
Autres numéros: Circ. Tél: 514-684-9000; Téléc: 514-683-7271

Les réseaux sociaux: twitter.com/CarlosLeitaoPLQ, www.facebook.com/carlosleitaoplq
Bureau de circonscription
#203, 3869, boul des Sources
Dollard-des-Ormeaux, QC H9B 2A2

Leader parlementaire adjoint de l'opposition officielle, Gaétan Lelièvre
Circonscription électorale: Gaspé *Nombre de constituants:* 30 850, Parti Québécois
Ligne sans frais: 855-368-5827
Gaetan.Lelievre.GASP@assnat.qc.ca
pq.org/depute/gaetan-lelievre
Autres numéros: Circ. Tél: 418-368-5827; 418-763-2389; 418-385-3791
Les réseaux sociaux: www.facebook.com/gaetanlelievre.pq
Bureaux de circonscription
153, Grande Allée Est
Grande Rivière, QC G0C 1V0

Mathieu Lemay
Circonscription électorale: Masson *Nombre de constituants:* 50 840, CA
Tél: 418-643-5771; *Téléc:* 418-643-0237
Mathieu.Lemay.MASS@assnat.qc.ca
coalitionavenirquebec.org/equipe/mathieu-lemay
Autres numéros: Circ. Tél: 450-966-0111; Téléc: 450-966-0115
Les réseaux sociaux: www.facebook.com/246420318894371
Bureaux de circonscription
#108, 3101, ch Sainte-Marie
Mascouche, QC J7K 1P2

Ministre des Transports, de la Mobilité durable et de l'Électrification des transports, Ministre responsable de la région du Centre-du-Québec, L'hon. Laurent Lessard
Circonscription électorale: Lotbinière-Frontenac *Nombre de constituants:* 54 278, Liberal
Tél: 418-643-7295
Ligne sans frais: 855-718-3444; *Téléc:* 418-643-4318
laurentlessardplq.com
Autres numéros: Circ. Tél: 418-332-3444; Téléc: 418-332-3445
Les réseaux sociaux: twitter.com/Laurentplq, www.facebook.com/laurentlessard.plq
Bureaux de circonscription, Édifice Place 309
#200, 309, boul Frontenac ouest
Thetford Mines, QC G6G 6K2

Jean-François Lisée
Circonscription électorale: Rosemont *Nombre de constituants:* 51 819, Parti Québécois
Tél: 418-263-0674; *Téléc:* 418-646-4098
Jean-Francois.Lisee.ROSE@assnat.qc.ca
jflisee.org
Autres numéros: Circ. Tél: 514-593-7495; Téléc: 514-593-4264
Les réseaux sociaux: twitter.com/JFLisee, www.facebook.com/jflisee
Bureaux de circonscription
3308, boul Rosemont
Montréal, QC H1X 1K2

Agnès Maltais
Circonscription électorale: Taschereau *Nombre de constituants:* 49 582, Parti Québécois
Tél: 418-643-1275; *Téléc:* 418-643-1906
Agnes.Maltais.TASC@assnat.qc.ca
agnesmaltais.org
Autres numéros: Circ. Tél: 418-646-6090; Téléc: 418-646-6088
Les réseaux sociaux: twitter.com/AgnesMaltais, www.facebook.com/261596713873754
Bureau de circonscription
#209, 320, rue Saint-Joseph est
Québec, QC G1K 8G5

Nicolas Marceau
Circonscription électorale: Rousseau *Nombre de constituants:* 63 181, Parti Québécois
Tél: 418-263-0688
Ligne sans frais: 800-889-4401; *Téléc:* 418-643-0616
Nicolas.Marceau.ROUS@assnat.qc.ca
nicolasmarceau.deputes.pq.org
Autres numéros: Circ. Tél: 450-831-8979; Téléc: 450-831-2093
Bureau de circonscription
#2, 2450, rue Victoria
Sainte-Julienne, QC J0K 2T0

Whip du deuxième groupe d'opposition, Donald Martel
Circonscription électorale: Nicolet-Bécancour *Nombre de constituants:* 39 638, CA
Tél: 418-644-1444
Ligne sans frais: 855-333-3521; *Téléc:* 418-528-6935
donaldmartel-nico@assnat.qc.ca
coalitionavenirquebec.org/equipe/donald-martel
Autres numéros: Circ. Tél: 819-233-3521; Téléc: 819-233-3529
Les réseaux sociaux: twitter.com/domartell, www.facebook.com/MartelD.coalition
Bureau de circonscription
#202, 625, av Godefroy
Bécancour, QC G9H 1S3

Manon Massé
Circonscription électorale: Sainte-Marie—Saint-Jacques *Nombre de constituants:* 42 287, QS
Tél: 418-644-1632; *Téléc:* 418-643-0624
Manon.Masse.SMSJ@assnat.qc.ca
www.quebecsolidaire.net/equipe/manon-masse
Autres numéros: Circ. Tél: 514-525-2501; Téléc: 514-525-5637
Les réseaux sociaux: twitter.com/ManonMasse_Qs, www.facebook.com/QS.ManonMasse
Bureau de circonscription
#330, 533, rue Ontario est
Montréal, QC H2L 1N8

Michel Matte
Circonscription électorale: Portneuf *Nombre de constituants:* 41 239, Liberal
Tél: 418-644-1473
Ligne sans frais: 855-383-0712; *Téléc:* 418-646-6684
Michel.Matte.PORT@assnat.qc.ca
www.plq.org/fr/equipe/michelmatte
Autres numéros: Circ. Tél: 418-268-4670; Téléc: 418-268-4823
Les réseaux sociaux: www.facebook.com/175611139176078
Bureau de circonscription
#154, 1780, boul Bona-Dussault
Saint-Marc-des-Carrières, QC G0A 4B0

Président du caucus du parti du gouvernement, L'hon. Nicole Ménard
Circonscription électorale: Laporte *Nombre de constituants:* 45 988, Liberal
Tél: 418-263-0548; *Téléc:* 418-643-2895
nmenard-lapo@assnat.qc.ca
www.plq.org/fr/equipe/nicolemenard
Autres numéros: Circ. Tél: 450-672-1885; Téléc: 450-465-6046
Les réseaux sociaux: twitter.com/Nicole_Menard, www.facebook.com/nicole.menard.90
Bureau de la circonscription
228, rue de Woodstock
Saint-Lambert, QC J4P 3R5

Richard Merlini
Circonscription électorale: La Prairie *Nombre de constituants:* 42 419, Liberal
Tél: 418-644-1489; *Téléc:* 418-644-1872
Richard.Merlini.LAPR@assnat.qc.ca
www.plq.org/fr/equipe/richardmerlini
Autres numéros: Circ. Tél: 450-619-7313; Téléc: 450-619-7519
Les réseaux sociaux: twitter.com/richmerlini, www.facebook.com/richardmerliniplq, ca.linkedin.com/pub/richard-merlini/19/3b7/533
Bureau de la circonscription
#212, 30, boul Taschereau
La Prairie, QC J5R 5H7

Marie Montpetit
Circonscription électorale: Crémazie *Nombre de constituants:* 46 596, Liberal
Tél: 418-263-0705; *Téléc:* 418-643-2893
Marie.Montpetit.CREM@assnat.qc.ca
www.plq.org/fr/equipe/mariemontpetit
Autres numéros: Circ. Tél: 514-387-6314; Téléc: 514-387-6462
Les réseaux sociaux: twitter.com/Marie_Montpetit, www.facebook.com/MarieMontpetitPLQ
Bureau de la circonscription
1421, rue Fleury est
Montréal, QC H2C 1R9

Ministre délégué aux Finances, L'hon. Pierre Moreau
Circonscription électorale: Châteauguay *Nombre de constituants:* 50 370, Liberal
Tél: 418-643-5270; *Téléc:* 418-643-8553
www.pierremoreau.ca
Autres numéros: Circ. Tél: 450-699-4136; Téléc: 450-699-9056
Les réseaux sociaux: twitter.com/PierreMoreauPLQ, www.facebook.com/pierre.moreau.plq
Bureau de la circonscription
#98, 22, boul Saint-Jean-Baptiste
Châteauguay, QC J6K 3C3

Norbert Morin
Circonscription électorale: Côte-du-Sud *Nombre de constituants:* 50 550, Liberal
Tél: 418-644-0513
Ligne sans frais: 866-774-1893; *Téléc:* 418-643-0163
nmorin-cds@assnat.qc.ca
www.plq.org/fr/equipe/norbertmorin
Autres numéros: Circ. Tél: 418-234-1893; Téléc: 418-234-1659
Les réseaux sociaux: twitter.com/norbertmorin
Bureau de la circonscription
#101, 144, av de la Gare
Montmagny, QC G5V 2T3

Marie-Claude Nichols
Circonscription électorale: Vaudreuil *Nombre de constituants:* 58 822, Liberal
Tél: 418-646-7623; *Téléc:* 418-528-5668
Marie-Claude.Nichols.VAUD@assnat.qc.ca
www.plq.org/fr/equipe/marieclaudenichols
Autres numéros: Circ. Tél: 450-424-6666; Téléc: 450-424-9274
Les réseaux sociaux: www.facebook.com/1386941401579023
Bureau de la circonscription
416, boul Harwood
Vaudreuil-Dorion, QC J7V 7H4

Martine Ouellet
Circonscription électorale: Vachon *Nombre de constituants:* 49 226, Parti Québécois
Tél: 418-263-0686; *Téléc:* 418-646-7811
Martine.Ouellet.VACHON@assnat.qc.ca
martineouellet.org
Autres numéros: Circ. Tél: 450-676-5086; Téléc: 450-676-0709
Les réseaux sociaux: twitter.com/martineouellet, www.facebook.com/101541096562158
Bureau de circonscription
5610, ch de Chambly
Saint-Hubert, QC J3Y 7E5

Martin Ouellet
Circonscription électorale: René-Lévesque *Nombre de constituants:* 34 459, Progressive Conservative
Tél: 581-628-1002
Martin.Ouellet.RELE@assnat.qc.ca
Autres numéros: Circ. Tél: 418-295-4001; Téléc: 418-295-4028
Bureau de circonscription
965, rue de Parfondeval
Baie-Comeau, QC G5C 2W8

Guy Ouellette
Circonscription électorale: Chomedey *Nombre de constituants:* 58 464, Liberal
Tél: 418-644-4050; *Téléc:* 418-646-7385
gouellette-chom@assnat.qc.ca
www.plq.org/fr/equipe/guyouellette
Autres numéros: Circ. Tél: 450-686-0166; Téléc: 450-686-7153
Les réseaux sociaux: twitter.com/Guy0uellette, www.facebook.com/guy.ouellette.chomedey, ca.linkedin.com/pub/guy-ouellette/2b/75a/752
Bureau de circonscription
#201, 4599, boul Samson
Laval, QC H7W 2H2

Première vice-président de l'Assemblée nationale, François Ouimet
Circonscription électorale: Marquette *Nombre de constituants:* 46 167, Liberal
Tél: 418-643-2750; *Téléc:* 418-643-2942
fouimet-marq@assnat.qc.ca
www.plq.org/fr/equipe/francoisouimet
Autres numéros: Circ. Tél: 514-634-9720; Téléc: 514-634-1653
Les réseaux sociaux: twitter.com/FrancoisOuimet_, www.facebook.com/33886048663
Bureau de circonscription
#202, 655, 32e av
Lachine, QC H8T 3G6

Sylvain Pagé
Circonscription électorale: Labelle *Nombre de constituants:* 47 641, Parti Québécois
Tél: 418-528-1349; *Téléc:* 418-528-7185
spage@assnat.qc.ca
www.sylvainpagedepute.org
Autres numéros: Circ. Tél: 819-623-1277; Téléc: 819-623-6838
Les réseaux sociaux: twitter.com/spage_pag, www.facebook.com/sylvainpagedepute
Bureau de circonscription
472, rue Mercier
Mont-Laurier, QC J9L 2W1

François Paradis
Circonscription électorale: Lévis *Nombre de constituants:* 47,006, CA
Tél: 418-646-7673; *Téléc:* 418-643-0237
Francois.Paradis.LEVI@assnat.qc.ca
coalitionavenirquebec.org/equipe/francois-paradis
Autres numéros: Circ. Tél: 418-833-5550; Téléc: 418-833-0999
Les réseaux sociaux: twitter.com/francoisparadis, www.facebook.com/francois.paradis.coalition
Note: François Paradis was elected in a by-election held Oct. 20, 2014.
Bureau de circonscription
#210, 5955, rue Saint-Laurent
Lévis, QC G6V 3P5

Ministre de l'Agriculture, des Pêcheries et de l'Alimentation, L'hon. Pierre Paradis
Circonscription électorale: Brome-Missisquoi *Nombre de constituants:* 56 480, Liberal
Tél: 418-380-2525; *Téléc:* 418-380-2184
ministre@mapaq.gouv.qc.ca
www.plq.org/fr/equipe/pierreparadis
Autres numéros: Circ. Tél: 450-248-3343; Téléc: 450-248-4500
Les réseaux sociaux: www.facebook.com/494150353945963
Bureau de circonscription
49, rue du Pont
Bedford, QC J0J 1A0

Marc Picard
Circonscription électorale: Chutes-de-la-Chaudière *Nombre de constituants:* 55 587, CA
Tél: 418-528-1694; *Téléc:* 418-528-6935
mpicard-cdlc@assnat.qc.ca
marcpicard.com
Autres numéros: Circ. Tél: 418-834-0015; Téléc: 418-834-0368
Les réseaux sociaux: twitter.com/MarcPicardQc, www.facebook.com/marcpicard01
Bureau de circonscription
#202, 880, rue Commerciale
Saint-Jean-Chrysostome, QC G6Z 2E2

Marc H. Plante
Circonscription électorale: Maskinongé *Nombre de constituants:* 47 793, Liberal
Tél: 418-644-0617
Ligne sans frais: 877-528-9722; *Téléc:* 418-528-5668
Marc.HPlante.MASK@assnat.qc.ca
www.plq.org/fr/equipe/marchplante
Autres numéros: Circ. Tél: 819-228-9722; Téléc: 819-228-0040
Les réseaux sociaux: twitter.com/MhPlante, www.facebook.com/1407540566148921
Bureau de circonscription
264, av Saint-Laurent
Louiseville, QC J5V 1J9

L'hon. Robert Poëti
Circonscription électorale: Marguerite-Bourgeoys *Nombre de constituants:* 52 371, Liberal
Tél: 581-628-1007; *Téléc:* 418-643-7839
Robert.Poeti.MABO@assnat.qc.ca
www.plq.org/fr/equipe/robertpoeti
Autres numéros: Circ. Tél: 514-368-1818; Téléc: 514-368-1844
Les réseaux sociaux: twitter.com/robertpoeti, www.facebook.com/robertpoetiplq, ca.linkedin.com/pub/robert-poeti/18/226/78a
Bureau de circonscription
#311, 7655, boul Newman
Lasalle, QC H8N 1X7

Carole Poirier
Circonscription électorale: Hochelaga-Maisonneuve *Nombre de constituants:* 41 405, Parti Québécois
Tél: 418-263-0707; *Téléc:* 418-643-7127
cpoirier-homa@assnat.qc.ca
carolepoirier.org
Autres numéros: Circ. Tél: 514-873-9309; Téléc: 514-873-5415
Les réseaux sociaux: twitter.com/CPoirierHM, www.facebook.com/carole.poirier
Bureau de circonscription
#102, 2065, av Jeanne-d'Arc
Montréal, QC H1W 3Z4

Saul Polo
Circonscription électorale: Laval-des-Rapides *Nombre de constituants:* 54 691, Liberal
Tél: 418-263-0617; *Téléc:* 418-528-7447
Saul.Polo.LDR@assnat.qc.ca
www.plq.org/fr/equipe/saulpolo
Les réseaux sociaux: twitter.com/Saul_Polo, www.facebook.com/SaulJPolo, ca.linkedin.com/in/saulpolo

Ministre de l'Éducation, du Loisir et du Sport; Ministre de la Famille;, Ministre responsable de la région de la Gaspésie-Iles-de-la-Madeleine, Hon. Sébastien Proulx
Circonscription électorale: Jean-Talon, Liberal
Tél: 418-643-2181; *Téléc:* 418-643-2640
ministre.famille@mfa.gouv.qc.ca
Autres numéros: Circ Tél: 418-682-8167; Téléc: 418-682-0794
Circonscription
#305, 1040, av Belvédère
Québec, QC G1S 3G3

Pierre Reid
Circonscription électorale: Orford *Nombre de constituants:* 41 195, Liberal
Tél: 418-644-3944
Ligne sans frais: 855-547-3911; *Téléc:* 418-528-5668
preid-orfo@assnat.qc.ca
www.plq.org/fr/equipe/pierrereid
Autres numéros: Circ. Tél: 819-847-3911; Téléc: 819-847-4099
Bureau de circonscription
618, rue Sherbrooke
Magog, QC J1X 2S6

Présidente du caucus de l'opposition officielle, Lorraine Richard
Circonscription électorale: Duplessis *Nombre de constituants:* 38 784, Parti Québécois
Tél: 418-643-2446
Ligne sans frais: 800-463-1644; *Téléc:* 418-644-3219
lorrainerichard-dupl@assnat.qc.ca
pq.org/depute/lorraine-richard
Autres numéros: Circ. Tél: 418-968-5044; Téléc: 418-968-2541
Bureau de circonscription
#227, 700, boul Laure
Sept-Iles, QC G4R 1Y1

Jean-François Roberge
Circonscription électorale: Chambly *Nombre de constituants:* 46 866, CA
Tél: 418-263-0679; *Téléc:* 418-643-0237
Jean-Francois.Roberge.CHMB@assnat.qc.ca
coalitionavenirquebec.org/equipe/jean-francois-roberge
Autres numéros: Circ. Tél: 418-658-5452; Téléc: 418-658-4417
Les réseaux sociaux: twitter.com/jfrcaq, www.facebook.com/roberge.coalition
Bureau de circonscription
2028, av Bourgogne
Chambly, QC J3L 1Z6

Sylvain Rochon
Circonscription électorale: Richelieu *Nombre de constituants:* 44,356, Parti Québécois
Tél: 418-263-0660
Ligne sans frais: 866-649-8832; *Téléc:* 418-646-7798
Sylvain.Rochon.RICL@assnat.qc.ca
Autres numéros: Circ. Tél: 450-742-3781; Téléc: 450-742-7744
Note: Sylvain Rochon won Richelieu in a by-election held March 9, 2015.
Bureau de circonscription
#101, 71, rue de Ramezay
Sorel-Tracy, QC J3P 3Z1

Filomena Rotiroti
Circonscription électorale: Jeanne-Mance-Viger *Nombre de constituants:* 48 925, Liberal
Tél: 418-646-5743; *Téléc:* 418-644-5990
frotiroti-jmv@assnat.qc.ca
www.plq.org/fr/equipe/filomenarotiroti
Autres numéros: Circ. Tél: 514-326-0491; Téléc: 514-326-9837
Les réseaux sociaux: twitter.com/FiloRotiroti, www.facebook.com/355163211170530, ca.linkedin.com/pub/filomena-rotiroti/5b/91b/734
Bureau de circonscription
#100, 5450, rue Jarry est
Saint-Léonard, QC H1P 1T9

Jean Rousselle
Circonscription électorale: Vimont *Nombre de constituants:* 44 955, Liberal
Tél: 418-644-0877; *Téléc:* 418-643-2889
jrousselle-vimo@assnat.qc.ca
www.plq.org/fr/equipe/jeanrousselle
Autres numéros: Circ. Tél: 450-628-9269; Téléc: 450-963-7547
Les réseaux sociaux: www.facebook.com/jean.rousselle.73
Bureau de circonscription
#415, 4650, boul des Laurentides
Laval, QC H7K 2J4

Présidente du caucus du deuxième groupe d'opposition, Nathalie Roy
Circonscription électorale: Montarville *Nombre de constituants:* 52 071, CA
Tél: 418-644-0655; *Téléc:* 418-643-0237
nroy-mota@assnat.qc.ca
nathalieroy.org
Autres numéros: Circ. Tél: 450-641-2748; Téléc: 450-641-0689
Les réseaux sociaux: twitter.com/NathalieRoyCAQ, facebook.com/Roy.Coalition
Bureau de circonscription
#500, 1570, rue Ampère
Boucherville, QC J4B 7L4

Sylvain Roy
Circonscription électorale: Bonaventure *Nombre de constituants:* 36 179, Parti Québécois
Tél: 418-263-0359
Ligne sans frais: 800-490-3511; *Téléc:* 418-643-0616
sylvainroy-bona@assnat.qc.ca
sylvainroy.org
Autres numéros: Circ. Tél: 418-364-6153; Téléc: 418-364-7906
Les réseaux sociaux: www.facebook.com/SylvainRoyPQ
Bureau de circonscription
314E, boul Perron
Carleton, QC G0C 1J0

Claire Samson
Circonscription électorale: Iberville *Nombre de constituants:* 46 739, CA
Tél: 418-644-1475
Ligne sans frais: 866-877-8522; *Téléc:* 418-643-0237
Claire.Samson.IBER@assnat.qc.ca
coalitionavenirquebec.org/equipe/claire-samson
Autres numéros: Circ. Tél: 450-346-1123; Téléc: 450-346-9068
Bureau de circonscription
327, 2e av
Saint-Jean-sur-Richelieu, QC J2X 2B5

Monique Sauvé
Circonscription électorale: Fabre *Nombre de constituants:* 48 972, Liberal
Tél: 418-263-0554; *Téléc:* 418-643-2953
Monique.Sauve.FABR@assnat.qc.ca
Autres numéros: Circ. Tél: 450-689-5516; Téléc: 450-689-7842
Bureau de circonscription
538, rue Principale
Laval, QC H7X 1C8

Sébastien Schneeberger
Circonscription électorale: Drummond-Bois-Francs *Nombre de constituants:* 50 041, CA
Tél: 418-644-1052; *Téléc:* 418-643-0237
sschneeberger-drum@assnat.qc.ca
coalitionavenirquebec.org/equipe/sebastien-schneeberger
Autres numéros: Circ. Tél: 819-475-4343; Téléc: 819-475-2354
Les réseaux sociaux: www.facebook.com/Schneeberger.coalition
Bureau de circonscription
#203, 228, rue Hériot
Drummondville, QC J2C 1K1

Caroline Simard
Circonscription électorale: Charlevoix-Côte-de-Beaupré *Nombre de constituants:* 51 165, Liberal
Tél: 418-263-0701; *Téléc:* 418-643-9127
Caroline.Simard.CHCB@assnat.qc.ca
www.plq.org/fr/equipe/carolinesimard
Autres numéros: Circ. Tél: 418-435-0395; Téléc: 418-435-6625
Les réseaux sociaux: www.facebook.com/686573054738903
Bureau de circonscription
#201, 11, rue Saint-Jean-Baptiste
Baie-Saint-Paul, QC G3Z 1M1

Serge Simard
Circonscription électorale: Dubuc *Nombre de constituants:* 40 081, Liberal
Tél: 418-263-0615
Ligne sans frais: 877-380-8106; *Téléc:* 418-643-0183
Serge.Simard.DUBU@assnat.qc.ca
www.plq.org/fr/equipe/sergesimard
Autres numéros: Circ. Tél: 418-544-8106; Téléc: 418-544-8167
Bureau de circonscription
439, rue Albert
La Baie, QC G7B 3L5

Leader parlementaire adjoint du gouvernement, Gerry Sklavounos
Circonscription électorale: Laurier-Dorion *Nombre de constituants:* 47 011, Liberal
Tél: 418-644-5987; *Téléc:* 418-644-5977
gsklavounos-lado@assnat.qc.ca
www.gerrysklavounos.com
Autres numéros: Circ. Tél: 514-273-1412; Téléc: 514-273-3150
Les réseaux sociaux: twitter.com/GerrySklavounos, www.facebook.com/22634974355, ca.linkedin.com/pub/gerry-sklavounos/41/584/971
Bureau de circonscription
#200, 7665, boul Saint-Laurent
Montréal, QC H2R 1W9

Chantal Soucy
Circonscription électorale: Saint-Hyacinthe *Nombre de constituants:* 57 803, CA
Tél: 418-644-5283; *Téléc:* 418-643-0237
Chantal.Soucy.SAHY@assnat.qc.ca
coalitionavenirquebec.org/equipe/chantal-soucy
Autres numéros: Circ. Tél: 450-773-0550; Téléc: 450-773-6092
Les réseaux sociaux: www.facebook.com/1374287322846942
Bureau de circonscription
1970, rue des Cascades
Saint-Hyacinthe, QC J2S 3J5

André Spénard
Circonscription électorale: Beauce-Nord *Nombre de constituants:* 42 229, CA
Tél: 418-643-5016
Ligne sans frais: 800-463-2544; *Téléc:* 418-643-0237

aspenard-beno@assnat.qc.ca
coalitionavenirquebec.org/equipe/andre-spenard
Autres numéros: Circ. Tél: 418-387-2044; Téléc: 418-387-4250
Les réseaux sociaux: twitter.com/AndreSpenard, www.facebook.com/spenard.coalition
Bureau de circonscription
700, rue Notre-Dame Nord, #E
Sainte-Marie, QC G6E 2K9

Yves St-Denis
Circonscription électorale: Argenteuil *Nombre de constituants:* 44 931, Liberal
Tél: 418-528-6379
Ligne sans frais: 800-870-7964; *Téléc:* 418-643-0183
Yves.St-Denis.ARGE@assnat.qc.ca
www.plq.org/fr/equipe/yvesstdenis
Autres numéros: Circ. Tél: 450-562-0785; Téléc: 450-562-0650
Les réseaux sociaux: www.facebook.com/argenteuilplq
Bureau de circonscription
512, rue Principale
Lacute, QC J8H 1Y3

Ministre des Relations internationales et de la Francophonie; Ministre responsable de la région des Laurentides, L'hon. Christine St-Pierre
Circonscription électorale: Acadie *Nombre de constituants:* 49 413, Liberal
Tél: 418-649-2319; *Téléc:* 418-643-4804
acadie@mri.gouv.qc.ca
www.plq.org/fr/equipe/christinestpierre
Autres numéros: Circ. Tél: 514-337-4278; Téléc: 514-337-0987
Les réseaux sociaux: twitter.com/stpierre_ch, www.facebook.com/145662342147329, ca.linkedin.com/pub/christine-st-pierre/53/b00/345
Bureau de circonscription
#540, 1600, boul Henri-Bourassa ouest
Montréal, QC H3M 3E2

Claude Surprenant
Circonscription électorale: Groulx *Nombre de constituants:* 57 216, CA
Tél: 418-644-0958; *Téléc:* 418-643-0237
Claude.Surprenant.GROU@assnat.qc.ca
coalitionavenirquebec.org/equipe/claude-surprenant
Autres numéros: Circ. Tél: 450-430-7890; Téléc: 450-430-4587
Bureau de circonscription
#210, 204, boul du Curé-Labelle
Sainte-Thérèse, QC J7E 2X7

Marc Tanguay
Circonscription électorale: LaFontaine *Nombre de constituants:* 41 609, Liberal
Tél: 418-528-7413; *Téléc:* 418-528-1650
marc.tanguay-lafo@assnat.qc.ca
www.plq.org/fr/equipe/marctanguay
Autres numéros: Circ. Tél: 514-648-1007; Téléc: 514-648-4559
Les réseaux sociaux: twitter.com/marc_tanguay
Bureau de circonscription
11977, av Alexis-Carrel
Montréal, QC H1E 5K7

Vice-première ministre; Ministre responsable de la Condition féminine; Ministre responsable de la région de Lanaudière;, Ministre responsable des Petites et Moyennes Entreprises, de l'Allègement réglementaire et du Développement économique régional, L'hon. Lise Thériault
Circonscription électorale: Anjou-Louis-Riel *Nombre de constituants:* 43 718, Liberal
Tél: 418-691-5650; *Téléc:* 418-643-8553
ministre.pme@economie.gouv.qc.ca
www.plq.org/fr/equipe/lisetheriault
Autres numéros: Circ. Tél: 514-493-9630; Téléc: 514-493-9633
Les réseaux sociaux: www.facebook.com/LiseTheriaultplq
Bureau de circonscription
#205, 7077, rue Beaubien est
Anjou, QC H1M 2Y2

Alain Therrien
Circonscription électorale: Sanguinet *Nombre de constituants:* 39 658, Parti Québécois
Tél: 418-263-0543; *Téléc:* 418-643-0616
atherrien-sagu@assnat.qc.ca
alaintherrien.org
Autres numéros: Circ. Tél: 450-632-1164; Téléc: 450-632-2145
Les réseaux sociaux: www.facebook.com/AlainTherrienSanguinet
Bureau de circonscription
#115, 55, rue Saint-Pierre
Saint-Constant, QC J5A 1B9

Mathieu Traversy
Circonscription électorale: Terrebonne *Nombre de constituants:* 54 874, Parti Québécois
Tél: 418-644-1616; *Téléc:* 418-644-5976
mtraversy-terr@assnat.qc.ca
www.mathieutraversy.com
Autres numéros: Circ. Tél: 450-964-3553; Téléc: 450-964-4634
Les réseaux sociaux: twitter.com/mathieutraversy, www.facebook.com/mathieutraversy
Bureau de circonscription
#201, 180, rue Sainte-Marie
Terrebonne, QC J6W 3E1

Véronyque Tremblay
Circonscription électorale: Chauveau, Liberal
Tél: 418-263-0681; *Téléc:* 418-643-7142
Veronyque.Tremblay.CHAU@assnat.qc.ca
Autres numéros: Circ. Tél: 418-842-3330; Téléc: 418-842-6444
Circonscription
359, rue Racine
Québec, QC G2B 1E9

Dave Turcotte
Circonscription électorale: Saint-Jean *Nombre de constituants:* 59 296, Parti Québécois
Tél: 418-644-1463; *Téléc:* 418-646-7798
dave.turcotte-saje@assnat.qc.ca
daveturcotte.org
Autres numéros: Circ. Tél: 450-346-3040; Téléc: 450-346-3340
Les réseaux sociaux: twitter.com/daveturcotte, www.facebook.com/daveturcotte.depute, ca.linkedin.com/in/daveturcotte
Bureau de circonscription
#235, 100, rue Richelieu
Saint-Jean-sur-Richelieu, QC J3B 6X3

Ministre de la Justice; Ministre responsable de la région de l'Outaouais, L'hon. Stéphanie Vallée
Circonscription électorale: Gatineau *Nombre de constituants:* 57 670, Liberal
Tél: 418-643-4210
Ligne sans frais: 866-315-0237; *Téléc:* 418-646-0027
ministre@justice.gouv.qc.ca
stephanievallee.com
Autres numéros: Circ. Tél: 819-441-2626; Téléc: 819-441-1793
Les réseaux sociaux: twitter.com/ValleeStephanie, www.facebook.com/stephanie.vallee.96
Bureau de circonscription
224, rue Principale sud
Maniwaki, QC J9E 1Z9

Karine Vallières
Circonscription électorale: Richmond *Nombre de constituants:* 58 296, Liberal
Tél: 418-263-0546
Ligne sans frais: 800-567-3596; *Téléc:* 418-643-2929
kvallieres-ricm@assnat.qc.ca
www.plq.org/fr/equipe/karinevallieres
Autres numéros: Circ. Tél: 819-839-3326; Téléc: 819-839-3325
Les réseaux sociaux: twitter.com/kavalcom, www.facebook.com/karine.vallieres.5817, ca.linkedin.com/pub/karine-vallières/21/775/923
Bureau de circonscription
50, rue Daniel-Johnson
PO Box 160
Danville, QC J0A 1A0

Ministre responsable du Travail; Ministre responsable de la région de la Chaudière-Appalaches, et Leader parlementaire adjointe du gouvernement, L'hon. Dominique Vien
Circonscription électorale: Bellechasse *Nombre de constituants:* 43 158, Liberal
Tél: 418-643-7623
Ligne sans frais: 866-504-3294; *Téléc:* 418-643-8098
ministre@travail.gouv.qc.ca
www.plq.org/fr/equipe/dominiquevien
Autres numéros: Circ. Tél: 418-642-1343; Téléc: 418-642-1331
Les réseaux sociaux: twitter.com/Dominique_Vien, www.facebook.com/197888626915062
Bureau de circonscription
640, route Henderson
Saint-Malachie, QC G0R 3N0

André Villeneuve
Circonscription électorale: Berthier *Nombre de constituants:* 56 312, Parti Québécois
Tél: 418-644-1399
Ligne sans frais: 866-256-3898; *Téléc:* 418-646-7801
avilleneuve-berh@assnat.qc.ca
andrevilleneuve.org
Autres numéros: Circ. Tél: 450-886-3171; Téléc: 450-886-2305
Les réseaux sociaux: www.facebook.com/AndreVilleneuveDeputeDeBerthier
Bureau de circonscription
L-204, rue Principale
Saint-Jean-de-Matha, QC J0K 2S0

Ministre de l'Immigration, de la Diversité et de l'Inclusion, L'hon. Kathleen Weil
Circonscription électorale: Notre-Dame-de-Grâce *Nombre de constituants:* 40 476, Liberal
Tél: 418-644-2128; *Téléc:* 418-528-0829
cabinet@midi.gouv.qc.ca
www.plq.org/fr/equipe/kathleenweil
Autres numéros: Circ. Tél: 514-489-7581; Téléc: 514-489-5426
Les réseaux sociaux: twitter.com/Kathleen_Weil, www.facebook.com/KathleenWeilNDG
Bureau de circonscription
#210, 5252, de Maisonneuve ouest
Montréal, QC H4A 3S5

Vacant
Circonscription électorale: Marie-Victorin

Vacant
Circonscription électorale: Saint-Jérôme

Vacant
Circonscription électorale: Verdun

Vacant
Circonscription électorale: Arthabaska

Ministères et organismes du gouvernement du Québec / Québec Government Departments & Agencies

Secrétariat aux affaires autochtones / Aboriginal Affairs

905, av Honoré-Mercier, 1er étage, Québec, QC G1R 5M6
Tél: 418-643-3166; *Téléc:* 418-646-4918
www.autochtones.gouv.qc.ca

Ministre responsable, L'hon. Geoffrey Kelley
Tél: 418-646-9131; *Téléc:* 418-646-9487
ministre.autochtones@mce.gouv.qc.ca
Secrétaire général associé, Michel Létourneau
Secrétaire générale associée, Marie-José Thomas
Secrétaire exécutif et greffier, Jean-Daniel Thériault
Directeur général, Relations avec les Autochtones et des initiatives économiques, Marie-José Thomas

Secrétariat aux affaires intergouvernementales canadiennes / Canadian Intergovernmental Affairs Secretariat

875, Grande Allée est, 3e étage, Québec, QC G1R 4Y8
Tél: 418-643-4011; *Téléc:* 418-528-0052
www.saic.gouv.qc.ca

Ministre responsable, L'hon. Jean-Marc Fournier
Tél: 418-646-5950; *Téléc:* 418-528-0981
ministre.saic@mce.gouv.qc.ca
Autres numéros: Alt. Tél: 418-643-3804; Téléc: 418-643-1906
Secrétaire général associé, Yves Castonguay
Tél: 418-646-9562
Secrétaire adjointe, Suzanne Lévesque
Tél: 418-528-2931
Secrétaire adjointe, Francophonie canadienne, Sylvie Lachance
Tél: 418-643-4060
Responsable, Centre de la francophonie des Amériques, Denis Desgagné
Responsable, Bureau du Secrétaire général associé/Responsable de l'accès à l'information, Cynthia Jean
Tél: 418-646-5948
Directeur, Réflexion stratégique, Simon Carmichael
Tél: 418-646-2483
Directeur, Politiques institutionnelles et constitutionnelles, Michel Frédérick
Tél: 418-528-0919
Directeur, Affaires économiques, culturelles et sociales, Vacant
Directeur, Francophonie et des Bureaux du Québec au Canada, Christiane Morin
Tél: 418-643-1645

Bureaux du Quebec au Canada/Regional Offices

Moncton
Bureau du Québec dans les Provinces atlantiques, #510, 777, rue Main, 5e étage, Moncton, NB E1C 1E9
Tél: 506-857-9851; *Téléc:* 506-857-9883
bqmoncton@mce.gouv.qc.ca
Chef de poste, Richard Barrette

Ottawa
Bureau du Québec à Ottawa, #300, 81 rue Metcalfe, 3e étage, Ottawa, ON K1P 6K7
Tél: 613-238-5322; *Téléc:* 613-563-9137
bqottawa@mce.gouv.qc.ca
Chef de poste, Richard Yves Le Lay

Toronto
Bureau du Québec à Toronto, #1504, 20 rue Queen ouest, CP 13 Toronto, ON M5H 3S3
Tél: 416-977-6060; *Téléc:* 416-596-1407
bqtoronto@mce.gouv.qc.ca
Chef de poste, Nicole Lemieux

Vancouver
Antenne de Vancouver, #780, 789 rue Pender ouest, Vancouver, BC V6C 1H2
Tél: 604-682-3500; *Téléc:* 604-682-6670
vancouver@mce.gouv.qc.ca
Sous la responsabilité du Bureau du Québec à Toronto
Responsable, Vicky Trépanier

Ministère des Affaires municipales et Occupation du territoire / Municipal Affairs & Land Occupancy

Aile Chaveau, 10, rue Pierre-Olivier-Chauveau, Québec, QC G1R 4J3
Tél: 418-691-2015; *Téléc:* 418-643-7385
communications@mamrot.gouv.qc.ca
www.mamrot.gouv.qc.ca

A la charge de conseiller le gouvernement & d'assurer la coordination interministérielle dans ces domaines; a pour mission de favoriser la mise en place & le maintien d'un cadre de vie & de services municipaux de qualité pour des citoyens/citoyennes; le développement des régions & des milieux ruraux; & le progrès & le rayonnement de la métropole; intervient auprès des municipalités locales, régionales de comté, des communautés métropolitaines de Montréal & de Québec, & de l'administration régionale Kativik

Ministre, L'hon. Martin Coiteux
Tél: 418-691-2050; *Téléc:* 418-643-1795
ministre@mamrot.gouv.qc.ca
Sous-ministre, Marc Croteau
Tél: 418-691-2040; *Téléc:* 418-643-7708
Adjoint parlementaire, Norbert Morin
Tél: 418-644-0513; *Téléc:* 418-643-0163
nmorin-cds@assnat.qc.ca
Sous-ministre adjoint, Projets spéciaux, Martin Arsenault
Tél: 418-691-2040
Sous-ministre adjoint, Manon Lecours
Sous-ministre adjoint, Daniel Gaudreau
Commissaire aux plaintes, Richard Villeneuve
Tél: 418-691-2071
Directeur, Affaires juridiques, Nicolas Paradis
Tél: 418-691-2022
Directrice, Vérification interne et de l'évaluation de programmes, Danielle Tremblay
Tél: 418-691-2057

Agences, Conseils et Commissions Associés/ Associated Agencies, Boards & Commissions:

•Commission municipale du Québec (CMQ) / Québec Municipal Commission
Mezzanine, aile Chauveau
10, rue Pierre-Olivier-Chauveau
Québec, QC G1R 4J3
Tél: 418-691-2014; *Téléc:* 418-644-4676
Ligne sans frais: 866-353-6767
www.cmq.gouv.qc.ca
CMQ est un tribunal et un organisme administratif, d'enquête et de conseil, spécialisé en matière municipale.

•Régie du logement du Québec / Québec Rental Board
Village Olympique
#2360, 5199, rue Sherbrooke est
Montréal, QC H1T 3X1
Tél: 514-873-2245; *Téléc:* 514-864-8077
Ligne sans frais: 800-683-2245
www.rdl.gouv.qc.ca
Autres numéros: Montréal, Laval & Longueuil: 514-873-2245

•Société d'habitation du Québec (SHQ) / Housing Québec
Aile St-Amable
1054, rue Louis-Alexandre-Taschereau, 3e étage
Québec, QC G1R 5E7
Téléc: 418-643-2533
Ligne sans frais: 800-463-4315
www.habitation.gouv.qc.ca

Communications
Directeur, Stéphanie Jourdain
Tél: 418-691-2019

Gouvernance des technologies de l'information / Information Technology
Secrétariat général, Gouvernance des technologies de l'information; Directeur (par intérim), Technologies de l'information et systèmes et de la coordination des projets, Dominique Jodoin
Tél: 418-691-2027

Services à la gestion / Administrative Services
Directeur général, Raymond Sarrazin
Tél: 418-691-2040
Directrice (par intérim), Ressources humaines/Performance organisationnelle, Kathleen Dumont
Tél: 418-691-2025
Directrice, Ressources financières et matérielles, Sylvie Plante
Tél: 418-691-2001

Infrastructures et finances municipales / Infrastructures & Municipal Financing
Sous-ministre adjoint, Frédéric Guay
Tél: 418-691-2040
Directeur général (par intérim), Infrastructures, Jean-François Bellemare
Tél: 418-691-2005
Directeur général, Finances municipales, Jean Villeneuve
Tél: 418-691-2007

Politiques / Policy
Sous-ministre adjoint, Jérôme Unterberg
Tél: 418-691-2040
Directrice générale (par interim), Urbanisme/Aménagement du territoire, Stéphane Bouchard
Tél: 418-691-2015
Directeur général, Fiscalité et de l'évaluation foncière, Bernard Guay
Tél: 418-691-2035
Directrice générale, Politiques, Jocelyn Savoie
Tél: 418-691-2015 ext: 352
Directeur (par interim), Affaires métropolitaines, Nicolas Froger
Tél: 514-873-8246

Territoires / Regions
Sous-ministre adjointe, Louise Lambert
Tél: 418-691-2040
Directrice générale, Affaires territoriales, Bertrand Caouette
Tél: 418-691-2015 ext: 339
Directeur, Développement régional, rural et de l'économie sociale, Yannick Routhier
Tél: 418-691-2078

Secrétariat à la région métropolitaine / Secretariat of the Metropolitan Area
Sous-ministre associé; Director (par intérim), Développement économique, culturel et social, André Lavallée
Tel: 514-873-8395
Other Communications: Alt. tél: 514-873-3860
Directrice, Développement territorial, Lucie Tremblay
Tel: 514-873-3860

Directions régionales/Regional Offices
Abitibi-Témiscamingue
#105, 170, av Principale, 1er étage, Rouyn-Noranda, QC J9X 4P7
Tél: 819-763-3582; *Téléc:* 819-763-3803
dr.abitibi-temis@mamrot.gouv.qc.ca
Directeur, Denis Moffet
Tél: 519-763-3582

Bas-Saint-Laurent
337, rue Moreault, 2e étage, Rimouski, QC G5L 1P4
Tél: 418-727-3629; *Téléc:* 418-727-3537
dr.bas-st-laur@mamrot.gouv.qc.ca
Directeur, Gilles Julien
Tél: 418-727-3629

Capitale-Nationale
Aile Chauveau, 10, rue Pierre-Olivier-Chauveau, 3e étage, Québec, QC G1R 4J3
Tél: 418-691-2016; *Téléc:* 418-643-2206
dr.capnat@mamrot.gouv.qc.a
Directeur, Jean Dionne
Tél: 418-691-2060

Centre-du-Québec
le Chauveau, 62, rue Saint-Jean-Baptiste, #S-05, Québec, QC G6P 4E3
Tél: 819-752-2453; *Téléc:* 819-795-3673
dr.centre-quebec@mamrot.gouv.qc.a
Directeur, Gaétan Désilets
Tél: 819-752-2453

Chaudière-Appalaches
#102, 1100, boul Frontenac est, Thetford Mines, QC G6G 6H1
Tél: 418-338-4624; *Téléc:* 418-338-1908
dr.chaud-app@mamrot.gouv.qc.ca
Directrice, Danie Croteau
Tél: 418-338-4624

Côte-Nord
#RC 708, 625, boul Laflèche, Baie-Comeau, QC G5C 1C5
Tél: 418-295-4241; *Téléc:* 418-295-4955
dr.cotenord@mamrot.gouv.qc.ca
Directeur, Gaétan Gauthier
Tél: 418-295-4241

Estrie
#4.04, 200, rue Belvédère nord, Sherbrooke, QC J1H 4A9
Tél: 819-820-3244; *Téléc:* 819-820-3979
dr.estrie@mamrot.gouv.qc.ca
Directeur, Pierre Poulin
Tél: 819-820-3244

Gaspésie—Iles-de-la-Madeleine
#10B, 500, av Daigneault, Chandler, QC G0C 1K0
Tél: 418-689-5024; *Téléc:* 418-689-4823
dr.gaspe-ilesmad@mamrot.gouv.qc.ca
Directeur, Michel Gionest
Tél: 418-689-5024

Lanaudière
#3200, 40, rue Gauthier sud, Joliette, QC J6E 4J4
Tél: 450-752-8080; *Téléc:* 450-752-8087
dr.lanaudiere@mamrot.gouv.qc.ca
Directeur (par intérim), Jessy Baron
Tél: 450-752-8060

Laurentides
#210, 161, rue de la Gare, Saint-Jérôme, QC J7Z 2B9
Tél: 450-569-7646; *Téléc:* 450-569-3131
dr.laurentides@mamrot.gouv.qc.ca
Directrice, Claudette Larouche
Tél: 450-569-7646

Mauricie
#321, 100, rue Laviolette, 3e étage, Trois-Rivières, QC G9A 5S9
Tél: 819-371-6653; *Téléc:* 819-371-6953
dr.mauricie@mamrot.gouv.qc.ca
Directeur, Pierre Robert
Tél: 819-371-6653

Montérégie
#403, 201, place Charles-Le Moyne, Longueuil, QC J4K 2T5
Tél: 450-928-5670; *Téléc:* 450-928-5673
dr.monteregie@mamrot.gouv.qc.ca
Directeur, Robert Sabourin
Tél: 450-926-5670

Nord-du-Québec
#1, 215, 3e Rue, Chibougamau, QC G8P 1N3
Tél: 418-748-7737; *Téléc:* 418-748-7841
nord-du-quebec@mamrot.gouv.qc.ca
Directeur, Richard Leclerc
Tél: 418-748-7738

Outaouais
#9.300, 170, rue de l'Hôtel-de-Ville, Gatineau, QC J8X 4C2
Tél: 819-772-3006; *Téléc:* 819-772-3989
dr.outaouais@mamrot.gouv.qc.ca
Directeur, Gisèle Demers
Tél: 819-772-3006

Saguenay—Lac-Saint-Jean
#RC.03, 227, rue Racine est, Chicoutimi, QC G7H 7B4
Tél: 418-698-3523; *Téléc:* 418-698-3526
dr.sag-lac@mamrot.gouv.qc.ca
Directeur, Jean Dionne
Tél: 418-698-3523

Ministère de l'Agriculture, des Pêcheries et de l'Alimentation (MAPAQ) / Agriculture, Fisheries & Food

200, ch Sainte-Foy, Québec, QC G1R 4X6
Tél: 418-380-2110
Ligne sans frais: 888-222-6272
www.mapaq.gouv.qc.ca
twitter.com/mapaquebec
www.youtube.com/user/mapaquebec

Le Ministère influence et appuie l'essor de l'industrie bioalimentaire québécoise dans une perspective de développement durable; réalise des interventions en production, transformation, commercialisation & consommation des produits agricoles, marins & alimentaires; & joue un rôle important en matière de recherche & de développement, d'enseignement & de formation

Ministre, L'hon. Pierre Paradis
Tél: 418-380-2525; *Téléc:* 418-380-2184
ministre@mapaq.gouv.qc.ca
Sous-ministre, Fernand Archambault
Adjoint parlementaire, Germain Chevarie
Tél: 418-644-1454; *Téléc:* 418-643-0183
Germain.Chevarie.IDLM@assnat.qc.ca
Sous-ministre adjointe, Christine Barthe
Sous-ministre adjointe, Gisèle Pagé

Agences, Conseils et Commissions Associés/ Associated Agencies, Boards & Commissions:

•Commission de protection du territoire agricole du Québec (CPTAQ) / Agricultural Land Preservation Commission
200, ch Ste-Foy, 2e étage
Québec, QC G1R 4X6
Tél: 418-643-3314; *Téléc:* 418-643-2261
Ligne sans frais: 800-667-5294
info@cptaq.gouv.qc.ca
www.cptaq.gouv.qc.ca

•La financière agricole de Québec (FADQ) / Farm Financial Québec
1400, boul Guillaume-Couture
Lévis, QC G6W 8K7
Tél: 418-838-5602; *Téléc:* 418-833-3871
Ligne sans frais: 800-749-3646
financiereagricole@fadq.qc.ca
www.fadq.qc.ca

•Régie des marchés agricoles et alimentaires du Québec (RMAAQ) / Québec Agriculture & Food Marketing Board
201, boul Crémazie est, 5e étage
Montréal, QC H2M 1L3
Tél: 514-873-4024; *Téléc:* 514-873-3984
rmaaqc@rmaaq.gouv.qc.ca
www.rmaaq.gouv.qc.ca

Développement régional et développement durable / Regional Development/Sustainable Development
Sous-ministre adjoint, Hélène Doddridge
Directeur général, Coordination des opérations régionales, Sylvain Tremblay
Directrice (par interim), Appui au développement des entreprises et de l'aménagement du territoire, Bernard Racine
Directeur, Agroenvironnement et développement durable, Linda Guy
Directeur (par interim), Soutien à l'enregistrement & remboursement des taxes, Sylvie Tremblay

Directions régionales/Regional Offices

Abitibi-Témiscamingue - Nord-du-Québec
#2.01, 180, boul Rideau, Rouyn-Noranda, QC J9X 1N9
Tél: 819-763-3287; *Téléc:* 819-763-3359
Directeur régionale, Alain Sarrazin

Bas-Saint-Laurent
335, rue Moreault, Rimouski, QC G5L 9C8
Tél: 418-727-3615; *Téléc:* 418-727-3967
Directeur régionale, Michel Riendeau

Capitale Nationale
#RC.22, 1685, boul Wilfrid-Hamel ouest, Québec, QC G1N 3Y7
Tél: 418-643-0033; *Téléc:* 418-644-8263
Directrice régionale (par interim), Renée Poirier

Centre-du-Québec
460, boul Louis-Fréchette, 2e étage, Québec, QC J3T 1Y2
Tél: 819-293-8501; *Téléc:* 819-293-8446
Directeur régional, Luc Couture

Chaudière-Appalaches
#100, 675, route Cameron, Sainte-Marie, QC G6E 3V7
Tél: 418-386-8116; *Téléc:* 418-386-8345
castemarie@mapaq.gouv.qc.ca
Directrice régionale, Renée Caron

Estrie
Directeur régional, Alain Roy

Gaspésie—Îles-de-la-Madeleine
34, boul Perron ouest, CP 524 Caplan, QC G0C 1H0
Tél: 418-388-2282; *Téléc:* 418-388-2834
Ligne sans frais: 877-221-7038
dr11@mapaq.gouv.qc.ca
Directeur régional, Louis Bigaouette

Laurentides
#100, 617, boul Labelle, Blainville, QC J7C 2J1
Tél: 450-971-5110; *Téléc:* 450-971-5069
blainville@mapaq.gouv.qc.ca
Directeur régional, Michel Boisclair

Mauricie
#102, 5195, boul des Forges, Trois-Rivières, QC G8Y 4Z3
Tél: 819-371-6761; *Téléc:* 819-371-6976
Ligne sans frais: 866-943-3012
dr04m@mapaq.gouv.qc.ca
Directeur régional, Norman Houle

Montérégie Est
#3300, 1355, rue Johnson ouest, Saint-Hyacinthe, QC J2S 8W7
Tél: 450-778-6530; *Téléc:* 450-778-6540
Directeur régional, Jean-Pierre Lessard

Montérégie Ouest
#201, 177, rue Saint-Joseph, Sainte-Martine, QC J0S 1V0
Tél: 450-427-2000; *Téléc:* 450-427-0407
Directeur régional (par interim), Jean-Pierre Lessard

Montréal-Laval-Lanaudière
#1.01, 867, boul de l'Ange-Gardien, L'Assomption, QC J5W 1T3
Tél: 450-589-5781; *Téléc:* 450-589-7812
bureau.assomption@mapaq.gouv.qc.ca
Directeur régional (par interim), Norman Houle

Outaouais
Galeries de Buckingham, 999, rue Dollard, Local 01, Gatineau, QC J8L 3E6
Tél: 819-986-8544; *Téléc:* 819-986-9299
Directeur régional, Yves Lévesque

Saguenay—Lac-Saint-Jean
801, ch du Pont-Taché nord, Alma, QC G8B 5W2
Tél: 418-662-6457; *Téléc:* 418-668-8694
Ligne sans frais: 866-727-6584
Directeur régional, Sylvie Denis

Formation Bioalimentaire / Bio-food Training
www.ita.qc.ca
www.facebook.com/Institut.technologie.agroalimentaire.ITA
Sous-ministre associé, Christian Dubois
Directrice, Main-d'ouvre et relève bioalimentaire, Hélène Brassard

Pêches et aquaculture commerciales / Commercial Fishing & Aquaculture
Sous-ministre adjointe, Abdoul Aziz Niang
Directeur, Analyses et politiques des peches et de l'aquaculture, Denis Desrosiers

Directions régionales/Regional Offices

Côte-Nord
466, av Arnaud, Sept-Îles, QC G4R 3B1
Tél: 418-964-8521; *Téléc:* 418-964-8744
drcn@mapag.gouv.qc.ca
Directeur régional, Alain Côté

Estuaire et eaux intérieures
460, boul Louis-Fréchette, RC, Nicolet, QC J3T 1Y2
Tél: 819-293-5677; *Téléc:* 819-293-8519
dreei@mapaq.gouv.qc.ca
Directeur régional, Denis Lacerte

Gaspésie
#205, 96, montée de Sandy Beach, Gaspé, QC G4X 2V6
Tél: 418-368-7630; *Téléc:* 418-360-8851
drg@mapaq.gouv.qc.ca
Directeur régional, Marcel Roussy

Îles-de-la-Madeleine
Édifice Réjean-Richard, 101-125, ch du Parc, Cap-aux-Meules, QC G4T 1B3
Tél: 418-986-2098; *Téléc:* 418-986-4421
drim@mapaq.gouv.qc.ca
Directeur régional, Donald Arseneau

Politiques agroalimentaires / Food Policy
Sous-ministre adjoint, Bernard Verret

Santé animale & inspection des aliments / Animal Health & Food Inspection
dgsaia@mapaq.gouv.qc.ca
Directeur général, Inspection des aliments, Guy Caron
Directrice générale, Services aux clientèles, Michelle Lavoie
Directeur général, Laboratoire d'expertises, Claude Rivard
#C 2.105, 2700, rue Einstein
Sainte-Foy, QC G1P 3W8 Canada
Directeur général, Inspection des viandes, Daniel Tremblay
Directeur, Laboratoire d'épidémiosurveillance animale du Québec, Sophie Beaulieu
Directeur, Coordination administrative, Jean Bergeron
Directeur, Réglementation et Centre ministériel de sécurité civile, Laurent Bolduc
Directeur (par intérim), Opérations régionales, Alain Fournier
Directrice (par intérim), Santé et bien-être des animaux, Geneviève Godbout
Directeur, Soutien à l'inspection, Michel Houle
Directeur, Laboratoire d'expertises et d'analyses alimentaires, Geneviève Rousseau
Directeur, Laboratoire d'expertise en pathologie animale du Québec, Chantal Vincent

Transformation Alimentaire et des Marchés / Food Processing Québec
Sous-ministre adjointe, Manon Boucher
Directeur, Développement des entreprises et des produits, Alain Fournier
Directrice (par interim), Développement des entreprises, Marie-Christine Boucher
Directeur, Accès aux marchés, François Gaudreau

Secrétariat à la Capitale-Nationale / National Capital Affairs

700, boul René-Lévesque est, 31e étage, Québec, QC G1R 5H1
Tél: 418-528-8549; *Téléc:* 418-528-8558
www.scn.gouv.qc.ca
Ministre responsable, L'hon. François Blais
Tel: 418-643-4810; *Fax:* 418-643-2802
ministre@mess.gouv.qc.ca
Sous-ministre associé, Alain Kirouac
Tel: 418-528-0784

Ministère de la Culture et Communications / Culture & Communications

225, Grande Allée est, Québec, QC G1R 5G5
Ligne sans frais: 888-380-8882
www.mcc.gouv.qc.ca
twitter.com/mccquebec
www.facebook.com/mccquebec
www.youtube.com/user/MCCQuebec
Ministre; Ministre responsable de la Protection et de la Promotion de la langue française, L'hon. Luc Fortin
ministre@mcc.gouv.qc.ca
Sous-ministre, Marie-Claude Champoux
Adjoint parlementaire, Luc Fortin
Tél: 418-643-2301
Directeur général, Administration et immobilisations, Denis Charland
Tél: 418-380-2355 ext: 715
Directrice, Secrétariat général et bureau de projet, Pascale Demers
Tél: 418-380-2393 ext: 639; *Téléc:* 418-380-2349
pascale.demers@mcc.gouv.qc.ca
Directrice, Communications & affaires publiques, Colette Duval
Tél: 418-380-2363; *Téléc:* 418-380-2364
colette.duval@mcccf.gouv.qc.ca
Directeur, Technologies de l'information et gestion documentaire, Louis Guilbault
Tél: 418-380-2312; *Téléc:* 418-380-2314
louis.guilbault@mcccf.gouv.qc.ca
Directeur, Immobilisations, Dominique Malack
Tél: 418-380-2356
Directeur, Affaires juridiques, Daniel Morin
Tél: 418-643-3747
daniel.morin@mcc.gouv.qc.ca
Directeur, Financement des sociétés d'État, Patrick Tessier
Tél: 418-380-2301 ext: 728
Directrice, Ressources humaines et gestion immobilière, Marc Tremblay
Tél: 418-380-2358; *Téléc:* 418-380-2364
Directeur, Ressources financières et matérielles, Geneviève Vézina
Tél: 418-380-2301; *Téléc:* 418-380-2302
genevieve.vezina@mcccf.gouv.qc.ca

Développement culturel, au patrimoine et aux institutions muséales / Cultural Development, Heritage, and Museums
Sous-ministre adjoint, Jean Bissonnette
Tél: 418-380-2330; *Téléc:* 418-380-2392
jean.bissonnette@mcc.gouv.qc.ca
Directeur général, Bureau du chantier du réseau muséal, Daniel Cloutier
Tél: 418-380-2348 ext: 700
Directrice général, Patrimoine et des institutions muséales, Danielle Dubé
Tél: 418-380-2352 ext: 635; *Téléc:* 418-380-2336
danielle.dube@mcc.gouv.qc.ca
Directeur, Archéologie et institutions muséales, Jean-Jacques Adjizian
Tél: 418-380-2352 ext: 743; *Téléc:* 418-380-2336
jean-jacques.adjizian@mcc.gouv.qc.ca
Directeur, Coordination des programmes, Dany Gilbert
Tél: 418-380-2304 ext: 630; *Téléc:* 418-380-2324
dany.gilbert@mcc.gouv.qc.ca

Directions régionales/Regional Offices

Abitibi-Témiscamingue et Nord-du-Québec
145, av Québec, Rouyn-Noranda, QC J9X 6M8
Tél: 819-763-3517; *Téléc:* 819-763-3382
dratnq@mcc.gouv.qc.ca
Directrice, Monik Duhaime

Bas-Saint-Laurent
337, rue Moreault, # RC-12, Rimouski, QC G5L 1P4
Tél: 418-727-3650; *Téléc:* 418-727-3824
drbsl@mcc.gouv.qc.ca
Directeur (par intérim), Louis Landry

Capitale-Nationale
Bloc C, RC, 225, Grande-Allée est, Québec, QC G1R 5G5
Tél: 418-380-2346; *Téléc:* 418-380-2347
dcn@mcc.gouv.qc.ca
Directeur, Martin Pineault

Chaudière-Appalaches
51, rue du Mont-Marie, Lévis, QC G6V 0C3
Tél: 418-838-9886; *Téléc:* 418-838-1485
drca@mcc.gouv.qc.ca
Directrice, Nicole Champagne

Côte-Nord
#1.806, 625, boul Laflèche, Baie-Comeau, QC G5C 1C5
Tél: 418-295-4979; *Téléc:* 418-295-4070
drcn@mcc.gouv.qc.ca
Directrice (par intérim), Élizabeth Carmichael

Estrie
#410, 225, rue Frontenac, Sherbrooke, QC J1H 1K1
Tél: 819-820-3007; *Téléc:* 819-820-3930
dre@mcc.gouv.qc.ca
Directrice, Jocelyne Jacques

Gaspésie—Iles-de-la-Madeleine
146, av de Grand-Pré, Bonaventure, QC G0C 1E0
Tél: 418-534-4431; *Téléc:* 418-534-4564
drgim@mcc.gouv.qc.ca
Directrice, Hélène Latérière

Laval, de Lanaudière et des Laurentides
#200, 300, rue Sicard, Sainte-Thérèse, QC J7E 3X5
Tél: 450-430-3737; *Téléc:* 450-430-2475
drlll@mcc.gouv.qc.ca
Directeur, Gilbert Lepage

Mauricie et Centre-du-Québec
#315, 100, rue Laviolette, Trois-Rivières, QC G9A 5S9
Tél: 819-387-6001; *Téléc:* 819-371-6984
drmcq@mcc.gouv.qc.ca
Directrice, Claire Pépin

Montérégie
#500, 2, boul Desaulniers, Saint-Lambert, QC J4P 1L2
Tél: 450-671-1231; *Téléc:* 450-671-3884
drmonter@mcc.gouv.qc.ca
Directrice, Annie Goudreault

Montréal
#600, 480, boul St-Laurent, Montréal, QC H2Y 3Y7
Tél: 514-873-2255; *Téléc:* 514-864-2448
dm@mcc.gouv.qc.ca
Directrice, Hélène Binette

Outaouais
#4.140, 170, rue de l'Hôtel-de-Ville, 4e étage, Gatineau, QC J8X 4C2
Tél: 819-772-3002; *Téléc:* 819-772-3950
dro@mcc.gouv.qc.ca
Directrice, Anne-Marie Gendron
Tél: 819-772-3282
anne-marie.gendron@mcccf.gouv.qc.ca

Saguenay—Lac-Saint-Jean
202, rue Jacques-Cartier est, Chicoutimi, QC G7H 6R8
Tél: 418-698-3500; *Téléc:* 418-698-3522
drslstj@mcc.gouv.qc.ca
Directeur, Réjean Goudreault

Politiques de culture et de communications
Sous-ministre adjoint, Jacques Laflamme
Tél: 418-380-2330; *Téléc:* 418-380-2392
jacques.laflamme@mcc.gouv.qc.ca
Directeur générale, Politiques de culture et de communications, Gilles Simard
Tél: 418-380-2365; *Téléc:* 418-380-2340
gilles.simard@mcc.gouv.qc.ca
Directeur générale, Centre de conservation du Québec, René Bouchard
Tél: 418-643-7001; *Téléc:* 418-646-5419
rene.bouchard@mcc.gouv.qc.ca
Directeur, Affaires internationales et des relations intergouvernementales, Julie Bissonnette
Tél: 418-380-2335 ext: 726
Directrice, Politiques de culture, de la recherche et de l'évaluation, Sophie Magnan
Tél: 418-380-2360 ext: 636; *Téléc:* 418-380-2345
sophie.magnan@mcc.gouv.qc.ca
Directrice, Politiques de communications et de l'audiovisuel, Louise Gingras
Tél: 418-380-2307 ext: 636; *Téléc:* 418-380-2316
louise.gingras@mcc.gouv.qc.ca
Directrice, Politiques gouvernementales et du suivi législatif, Josée Blackburn
Tél: 418-380-2322 ext: 632; *Téléc:* 418-380-2345
josee.blackburn@mcc.gouv.qc.ca
Coordonnatrice, Sociétés d'État, Suzanne Gobeille
Tél: 418-380-2362 ext: 709
suzanne.gobeille@mcc.gouv.qc.ca
Coordonnatrice, Planification stratégique, Brigitte Ricard
Tél: 418-380-2362 ext: 725; *Téléc:* 418-380-2345
brigitte.ricard@mcc.gouv.qc.ca
Coordonnatrice, Intégration des arts à l'architecture, Maryline Tremblay
Tél: 418-380-2323 ext: 705

Organismes et Sociétés d'État/Associated Agencies, Boards & Commissions

Bibliothèque et Archives nationales du Québec (BAnQ) / National Library & Archives of Québec
2275, rue Holt, Montréal, QC H2G 3H1
Tél: 514-873-1100; *Téléc:* 514-873-9312
Ligne sans frais: 800-363-9028
www.banq.qc.ca
twitter.com/_BAnQ
www.facebook.com/banqweb20
www.youtube.com/user/BAnQweb20
Président-directeur générale, Guy Berthiaume
Secrétaire générale et directrice, Carole Payen

Commission des biens culturels du Québec (CBCQ) / Québec Cultural Property Commission
Bloc A-RC, 225, Grande Allée est, Québec, QC G1R 5G5
Tél: 418-643-8378; *Téléc:* 418-643-8591
info@cbcq.gouv.qc.ca
www.cbcq.gouv.qc.ca
Président, Yves Lefebvre
Vice-présidente, Ann Mundy

Conseil des arts et des lettres du Québec (CALQ)
79, boul René-Lévesque est, 3e étage, Québec, QC G1R 5N5
Tél: 418-643-1707; *Téléc:* 418-643-4558
Ligne sans frais: 800-897-1707
info@calq.gouv.qc.ca
www.calq.gouv.qc.ca
Secondary Address: 500, Place d'Armes, 15e étage
Montréal, QC H2Y 2W2
Alt. Téléc: 514 864-4160
twitter.com/LeCALQ
www.facebook.com/12468994038
www.youtube.com/user/LeCALQ
Présidente-directrice générale, Anne-Marie Jean

Musée d'art contemporain de Montréal (MACM) / Montréal Museum of Contemporary Art
185, rue Ste-Catherine ouest, Montréal, QC H2X 3X5
Tél: 514-847-6226; *Téléc:* 514-847-6292
info@macm.org
www.macm.org
twitter.com/macmtl
www.facebook.com/macmontreal
pinterest.com/macmontreal; youtube.com/macmvideos
Directrice Générale, Paulette Gagnon

Musée de la civilisation (MCQ) / Museum of Civilisation
85, rue Dalhousie, CP 155 Succ B, Québec, QC G1K 8R2
Tél: 418-643-2158; *Téléc:* 418-646-9705
Ligne sans frais: 866-710-8031
mcqweb@mcq.org
www.mcq.org
Autres nombres: www.flickr.com/photos/museedelacivilisation;
www.ustream.tv/channel/participe-present
twitter.com/mcqorg
www.facebook.com/museedelacivilisation
youtube.com/mcqpromo
Présidente, Margaret Delisle
Directeur général, Michel Côté

Musée national des beaux-arts du Québec (MNBA)
Parc des Champs-de-Bataille, 1, av Wolfe-Montcalm, Québec, QC G1R 5H3
Tél: 418-643-2150
Ligne sans frais: 866-220-2150
info@mnba.qc.ca
www.mnba.qc.ca
twitter.com/mnbaq
www.facebook.com/mnbaq
Président, Conseil d'administration, Pierre Lassonde
Directrice générale, Line Ouellet

Régie du cinéma (RCQ) / Film Board
#100, 390, rue Notre-Dame ouest, Montréal, QC H2Y 1T9
Tél: 514-873-2371; *Téléc:* 514-873-8874
Ligne sans frais: 800-463-2463
www.rcq.gouv.qc.ca
www.facebook.com/regieducinema
Présidente, Michel Létourneau
Directeur, Planification stratégique, Lise A. Lambert

Société de développement des entreprises culturelles (SODEC) / Arts & Cultural Enterprise Development Commission
#800, 215, rue Saint-Jacques, Montréal, QC H2Y 1M6
Tél: 514-841-2200; *Téléc:* 514-841-8606
Ligne sans frais: 800-363-0401
info@sodec.gouv.qc.ca
www.sodec.gouv.qc.ca
Secondary Address: 36 1/2, rue St-Pierre
Québec, QC G1K 3Z6
Alt. Téléc: 418-643-8918
twitter.com/la_SODEC
www.facebook.com/SODEC.gouv.qc.ca
Présidente, Conseil d'administration, Doris Girard
Tél: 514-841-2273
Président et chef de la direction, François Macerola
Tél: 514-841-2250
Directrice générale, Contrôle & gestion financière, Carole Hamelin
Directeur des affaires juridiques & Secrétaire, Jean Valois

Société de la Place des Arts de Montréal / Montréal Place des Arts Corporation
260, boul de Maisonneuve ouest, Montréal, QC H2X 1Y9
Tél: 514-285-4200; *Téléc:* 514-285-1968
info@pda.qc.ca
www.pda.qc.ca
twitter.com/Place_des_Arts
www.facebook.com/placedesarts
Président-Directeur général, Marc Blondeau

Société de télédiffusion du Québec (Télé-Québec)
1000, rue Fullum, Montréal, QC H2K 3L7
Tél: 514-521-2424; *Téléc:* 514-864-1970
info@telequebec.tv
www.telequebec.tv
twitter.com/telequebec
www.facebook.com/TeleQc
Présidente-directrice générale, Michèle Fortin

Société du Grand Théâtre de Québec / Grand Theatre of Québec
269, boul René-Lévesque est, Québec, QC G1R 2B3
Tél: 418-643-8111
gtq@grandtheatre.qc.ca
www.grandtheatre.qc.ca
twitter.com/GrandTheatreQc
www.facebook.com/grandtheatre
Président-directeur général, Marcel Dallaire

Ministère du Développement durable, de l'Environnement et de la Lutte contre les changements climatiques / Sustainable Development, Environment & the Fight Against Climate Change

Édifice Marie-Guyart, 675, boul René-Lévesque est, 29e étage, Québec, QC G1R 5V7
Tél: 418-521-3830; *Téléc:* 418-646-5974
Ligne sans frais: 800-561-1616
info@mddefp.gouv.qc.ca
www.mddelcc.gouv.qc.ca
twitter.com/MDDELCC
www.facebook.com/MDDEFP
www.linkedin.com/company/mddep
www.youtube.com/user/MDDEPQuebec

A pour mission d'assurer la protection de l'environnement & des écosystèmes naturels; de promouvoir le développement durable & d'assurer à la population un environnement sain en harmonie avec le développement économique & le progrès social du Québec

Ministre, L'hon. David Heurtel
Tél: 418-521-3911; *Téléc:* 418-643-4143
dheurtel-viau@assnat.qc.ca
Autres numéros: Alt. Tél: 514-864-8500; Téléc: 514-864-8503
Sous-ministre, Marie-Renée Roy
Tél: 418-521-3860
Adjoint parlementaire, Marc H. Plante
Tél: 418-644-0617; *Téléc:* 418-528-5668
Marc.HPlante.MASK@assnat.qc.ca
Directeur, Bureau des renseignements, de l'accès à l'information et des plaintes sur la qualité des services, Pascale Porlier
Directeur, Communications, Pauline Boissinot
Tél: 418-521-3823 ext: 416
Directrice du Cabinet, Gabriela Quiroz
Directrice, Vérification interne et du réexamen des sanctions administratives pécuniaires, Julie Parent
Tél: 418-521-3861 ext: 435
Directrice, Affaires juridiques, Monique Rousseau
Tél: 418-521-3816 ext: 454

Agences, Conseils et Commissions Associés/ Associated Agencies, Boards & Commissions:

•Bureau d'audiences publiques sur l'environnement (BAPE) / Environmental Public Hearing Board
Édifice Lomer-Gouin
#2.10, 575, rue Saint-Amable
Québec, QC G1R 6A6
Tél: 418-643-7447; *Téléc:* 418-643-9474
Ligne sans frais: 800-463-4732
communication@bape.gouv.qc.ca
www.bape.gouv.qc.ca

•Comité consultatif de l'environnement Kativik (CCEK) / Kativik Environmental Advisory Committee (KEAC)
CP 930
Kuujjuaq, QC J0M 1C0
Tél: 819-964-2961; *Téléc:* 819-964-0694
keac-ccek@krg.ca
www.keac-ccek.ca

•Société des établissements en plein air du Québec (SÉPAQ)
Place de la Cité, Tour Cominar
#250, 2640, boul Laurier, 2e étage
Québec, QC G1V 5C2
Tel: 418-686-4875; *Fax:* 418-643-8177
Toll-free: 800-665-6527
inforeservation@sepaq.com
www.sepaq.com

•Société québécoise de récupération et de recyclage (RECYC-QUÉBEC)
#411, 300, rue Saint-Paul
Québec, QC G1K 7R1
Tél: 418-643-0394; *Téléc:* 418-643-6507
Ligne sans frais: 866-523-8290
info@recyc-quebec.gouv.qc.ca
www.recyc-quebec.gouv.qc.ca
Autres numéros: Infoline: 1-800-807-0678; Montréal: 514-351-7835; Relations médias: medias@recyc-quebec.gouv.qc.ca

Contrôle environnemental et à la sécurité des barrages / Environmental Control & Dam Safety
Sous-ministre adjoint, Michel Rousseau
Tél: 418-521-3860
Directeur, Sécurité des barrages, Michel Rhéaume

Centre de contrôle environnemental du Québec / Québec Centre for Environmental Control

Directions régionales/Regional Offices

Baie-Comeau - Côte-Nord
20, boulevard Comeau, Baie-Comeau, QC G4Z 3A8
Tél: 418-294-8888; *Téléc:* 418-294-8018
cote-nord@mddelcc.gouv.qc.ca
Directrice, Nathalie Chouinard

Gatineau - Outaouais
#7.340, 170, rue de l'Hôtel-de-Ville, Gatineau, QC J8X 4C2
Tél: 819-772-3434; *Téléc:* 819-772-3952
outaouais@mddelcc.gouv.qc.ca
Directrice, Valérie Grandmont

Montréal - Montréal, Laval, Lanaudière et Laurentides
#3860, 5199, rue Sherbrooke est, Montréal, QC H1T 3X9
Tél: 514-873-3636; *Téléc:* 514-873-5662
montreal@mddelcc.gouv.qc.ca
Directeur, Luc St-Martin

Nicolet - Mauricie et Centre-du-Québec
1579, boul Louis-Fréchette, Nicolet, QC J3T 2A5
Tél: 819-293-4122; *Téléc:* 819-293-8322
centre-du-quebec@mddelcc.gouv.qc.ca
Directeur, Pierre Boucher

Rimouski - Bas-Saint-Laurent, Gaspésie et Iles-de-la-Madeleine
212, av Belzile, Rimouski, QC G5L 3C3
Tél: 418-727-3511; *Téléc:* 418-727-3849
bas-saint-laurent@mddelcc.gouv.qc.ca
Directeur, Jules Boulanger

Rouyn-Noranda - Abitibi-Témiscamingue et Nord-du-Québec
180, boul Rideau, 1er étage, Rouyn-Noranda, QC J9X 1N9
Tél: 819-763-3333; *Téléc:* 819-763-3202
abitibi-temiscamingue@mddelcc.gouv.qc.ca
Directrice, Hélène Iracà

Saguenay - Saguenay-Lac-Saint-Jean
3950, boul Harvey, 4e étage, Saguenay, QC G7X 8L6
Tél: 418-695-7883; *Téléc:* 418-695-7897
saguenay-lac-saint-jean@mddelcc.gouv.qc.ca
Directeur, Daniel Labrecque

Sainte-Marie - Capitale-Nationale et Chaudière-Appalaches
#200, 675, rte Cameron, Sainte-Marie, QC G6E 3V7
Tél: 418-386-8000; *Téléc:* 418-386-8080
chaudiere-appalaches@mddelcc.gouv.qc.ca
Directeur, Jean-Marc Lachance

Sherbrooke
770, rue Goretti, Sherbrooke, QC J1E 3H4
Tél: 819-820-3882; *Téléc:* 819-820-3958
estrie@mddelcc.gouv.qc.ca
Directeur, Daniel Savoie

Développement durable et à la qualité de l'environnement / Sustainable Development & Environmental Quality
Sous-ministre adjoint, Patrick Beauchesne
Tél: 418-521-3860
Directeur général, Politiques du milieu terrestre, Mario Bérubé
Directrice générale, Suivi de l'état de l'environnement, Linda Tapin

Évaluations et aux autorisations environnementales / Assessments & Environmental Permits
Sous-ministre adjointe, Marie-Josée Lizotte
Tél: 418-521-3861
Directeur général (par intérim), Évaluation environnementale et stratégique, Yves Rochon

Analyse et de l'expertise régionales / Regional Analysis & Expertise
La mission est d'assurer l'analyse & la délivrance d'autorisations environnementales & d'offrir une expertise professionnelle en matière d'environnement

Directions régionales/Regional Offices

Baie-Comeau - Côte-Nord
20, boul Comeau, Baie-Comeau, QC G4Z 3A8
Tél: 418-294-8888; *Téléc:* 418-294-8018
cote-nord@mddelcc.gouv.qc.ca
Directeur, Alain Gaudreault

Gatineau - Outaouais
#7.340, 170, rue de l'Hôtel-de-Ville, Gatineau, QC J8X 4C2
Tél: 819-772-3434; *Téléc:* 819-772-3952
outaouais@mddelcc.gouv.qc.ca

Laval - Montréal, Laval, Lanaudière et Laurentides
850, boul Vanier, Laval, QC H7C 2M7
Tél: 450-661-2008; *Téléc:* 450-661-2217
laval@mddelcc.gouv.qc.ca
Directrice, Hélène Proteau

Longueuil - Estrie et Montérégie
201, Place Charles-Le Moyne, 2e étage, Longueuil, QC J4K 2T5
Tél: 450-928-7607; *Téléc:* 450-928-7625
monteregie@mddelcc.gouv.qc.ca
Directrice, Nathalie Provost

Montréal - Montréal, Laval, Lanaudière et Laurentides
#3860, 5199, rue Sherbrooke est, Montréal, QC H1T 3X9
Tél: 514-873-3636; *Téléc:* 514-873-5662
montreal@mddelcc.gouv.qc.ca
Directeur, Hélène Proteau

Nicolet - Mauricie et Centre-du-Québec
1579, boul Louis-Fréchette, Nicolet, QC J3T 2A5
Tél: 819-293-4122; *Téléc:* 819-293-8322
centre-du-quebec@mddelcc.gouv.qc.ca
Directeur, Céline Tremblay

Québec - Capitale-Nationale et Chaudière-Appalaches
#100, 1175, boul Lebourgneuf, Québec, QC G2K 0B7
Tél: 418-644-8844; *Téléc:* 418-646-1214
capitale-nationale@mddelcc.gouv.qc.ca
Directrice, Isabelle Olivier

Repentigny - Montréal, Laval, Lanaudière et Laurentides
100, boul Industriel, Repentigny, QC J6A 4X6
Tél: 450-654-4355; *Téléc:* 450-654-6131
lanaudiere@mddelcc.gouv.qc.ca
Directeur, Hélène Proteau

Rimouski - Bas-Saint-Laurent, Gaspésie et Iles-de-la-Madeleine
212, av Belzile, Rimouski, QC G5L 3C3
Tél: 418-727-3511; *Téléc:* 418-727-3849
bas-saint-laurent@mddelcc.gouv.qc.ca
Directeur, Jean-Marie Dionne

Rouyn-Noranda - Abitibi-Témiscamingue et Nord-du-Québec
180, boul Rideau, 1er étage, Rouyn-Noranda, QC J9X 1N9
Tél: 819-763-3333; *Téléc:* 819-763-3202
abitibi-temiscamingue@mddelcc.gouv.qc.ca
Directrice, Anick Lavoie

Saguenay - Saguenay-Lac-Saint-Jean
3950, boul Harvey, 4e étage, Saguenay, QC G7X 8L6
Tél: 418-695-7883; *Téléc:* 418-695-7897
saguenay-lac-saint-jean@mddelcc.gouv.qc.ca
Directrice, Édith Tremblay

Sainte-Anne-des-Monts - Bas-Saint-Laurent, Gaspésie et Iles-de-la-Madeleine
124, 1re av ouest, Sainte-Anne-des-Monts, QC G4V 1C5
Tél: 418-763-3301; *Téléc:* 418-763-7810
gaspesie-iles-de-la-madeleine@mddelcc.gouv.qc.ca
Directeur, Jean-Marie Dionne

Sainte-Marie - Capitale-Nationale et Chaudière-Appalaches
#200, 675, rte Cameron, Sainte-Marie, QC G6E 3V7
Tél: 418-386-8000; *Téléc:* 418-386-8080
chaudiere-appalaches@mddelcc.gouv.qc.ca
Directrice, Isabelle Olivier

Sainte-Thérèse - Montréal, Laval, Lanaudière et Laurentides
#80, 300, rue Sicard, Sainte-Thérèse, QC J7E 3X5
Tél: 450-433-2220; *Téléc:* 450-433-1315
laurentides@mddelcc.gouv.qc.ca
Directeur, Hélène Proteau

Sept-Îles - Côte-Nord
818, boul Laure, Sept-Îles, QC G4R 1Y8
Tél: 418-964-8888; *Téléc:* 418-964-8023
cote-nord@mddelcc.gouv.qc.ca
Directeur, Alain Gaudreault

Sherbrooke - Estrie et Montérégie
770, rue Goretti, Sherbrooke, QC J1E 3H4
Tél: 819-820-3882; *Téléc:* 819-820-3958
estrie@mddelcc.gouv.qc.ca
Directrice, Nathalie Provost

Trois-Rivières - Mauricie et Centre-du-Québec
#102, 100, rue Laviolette, Trois-Rivières, QC G9A 5S9
Tél: 819-371-6581; *Téléc:* 819-371-6987
mauricie@mddelcc.gouv.qc.ca
Directrice, Céline Tremblay

Expertise et aux politiques de l'eau et de l'air / Water & Air Policies & Expertise
Sous-ministre adjoint, Jacques Dupont
Tel: 418-521-3861
Directeur général, Centre d'expertise en analyse environnementale du Québec, Claude Denis
Directeur général, Politiques de l'eau, Marcel Gaucher

Lutte contre les changements climatiques / Fight Against Climate Change
Sous-ministre adjointe, Geneviève Moisan
Tél: 418-521-3861 ext: 411
Directrice générale, Expertise climatique et des partenariats, Guylaine Bouchard
Directrice générale (par intérim), Réglementation Carbone et des données d'émission, France Delisle

Services à la gestion / Administrative Services
Sous-ministre adjointe, Lise Lallemand
Tél: 418-521-3860
Directeur général, Technologies de l'information, Yvan Déry
Directrice générale adjointe, Ressources financières et matérielles, Joëlle Jobin

Commission des droits de la personne et des droits de la jeunesse (CDPDJ) / Commission for Human Rights & the Rights of Youth

360, rue Saint-Jacques, 2e étage, Montréal, QC H2Y 1P5
Tél: 514-873-5146; *Téléc:* 514-873-6032
Ligne sans frais: 800-361-6477
accueil@cdpdj.qc.ca
www.cdpdj.qc.ca
Autres nombres: TTY: 514-873-2648; Relations avec les médias: communications@cdpdj.qc.ca
twitter.com/CDPDJ1
www.facebook.com/171258630277

A pour mission d'assurer la promotion et la respect des droits et libertés affirmés par la Charte des droits et libertés de la personne, par la Loi sur la protection de la jeunesse, et par la Loi sur les jeunes contrevenants.

Président (par intérim) et Vice-président responsable du mandat jeunesse, Camil Picard
Vice-présidente responsable du mandat Charte, Renée Dupuis
Secrétariat général et administration, Véronique Emond

Ministère de l'Économie, de la Science et de l'Innovation / Economy, Science & Innovation

710, place D'Youville, 3e étage, Québec, QC G1R 4Y4
Tél: 418-691-5950; *Téléc:* 418-644-0118
Ligne sans frais: 866-680-1884
www.economie.gouv.qc.ca
Secondary Address: 380, rue Saint-Antoine Ouest, 5e étage
Montréal, QC H2Y 3X7
twitter.com/economie_quebec
www.youtube.com/user/MDEIEQuebec

Ministre; Ministre responsable, Stratégie Numérique, L'hon. Dominique Anglade
Tel: 418-691-5650; *Fax:* 418-643-8553
Ministre responsable, Petites et Moyennes Entreprises, l'Allègement réglementaire et Développement économique régional, et Ministre responsable, Condition féminine, L'hon. Lise Thériault
Tel: 418-691-5650; *Fax:* 418-643-8553
Ministre délégué aux Affaires maritimes, L'hon. Jean D'Amour
Tel: 418-691-5650; *Fax:* 418-691-5800
ministre.maritimes@economie.gouv.qc.ca
Sous-ministre, Jocelin Dumas
Adjoint parlementaire de la ministre de l'Économie, de la Science et de l'Innovation, Saul Polo
Tel: 418-263-0617; *Fax:* 418-644-6828
Saul.Polo-LDR@assnat.qc.ca
Adjoint parlementaire de la ministre responsable des Petites et Moyennes Entreprises, de l'Allègement réglementaire, et du Développement économique régional, André Drolet
Tel: 418-646-7635; *Fax:* 418-528-0425
adrolet-jele@assnat.qc.ca
Directrice, Communications, Nancy Carignan
Tel: 418-691-5698 ext: 565
Directrice, Audit interne, Natalie Desjardins
Directrice, Bureau du sous-ministre et Secrétariat général, Marie-Claude Lajoie

Agences, Conseils et Commissions Associés/ Associated Agencies, Boards & Commissions:

•Centre de recherche industrielle du Québec (CRIQ) / Industrial Research Centre of Québec
333, rue Franquet
Québec, QC G1P 4C7
Tél: 418-659-1550; *Téléc:* 418-652-2251
Ligne sans frais: 800-667-2386
infocriq@criq.qc.ca
www.criq.qc.ca
Recherche industrielle appliquée; services de RD pour des entreprises

•Commission de l'éthique en science et en technologie (CEST) / Ethics of Science & Technology Commission
1150, Grande Allée ouest, 1er étage
Québec, QC G1S 4Y9
Tél: 418-691-5989; *Téléc:* 418-646-0920
ethique@ethique.gouv.qc.ca
www.ethique.gouv.qc.ca

•Coopérative régionale d'électricité de Saint-Jean-Baptiste-de-Rouville / Electric Cooperative of Saint-Jean-Baptiste-de-Rouville
3113, rue Principale
Saint-Jean-Baptiste, QC J0L 1B0
Tél: 450-467-5583; *Téléc:* 450-467-0092
Ligne sans frais: 800-267-5583
info@coopsjb.com
www.coopsjb.com

•Fonds de recherche du Québec / Québec Research Funds
#800, 500, rue Sherbrooke Ouest
Montréal, QC H3A 3C6
Tél: 514-873-2114
www.frq.gouv.qc.ca

•Investissement Québec / Investment Québec
#500, 1200, rte de l'Église
Québec, QC G1V 5A3
Tél: 418-643-5172; *Téléc:* 418-528-2063
Ligne sans frais: 866-870-0437
www.investquebec.com

•Société du parc industriel et portuaire de Bécancour (SPIPB) / Industrial Park & Port Society of Bécancour
1000, boul Arthur-Sicard
Bécancour, QC G9H 2Z8
Tél: 819-294-6656; *Téléc:* 819-294-9020
spipb@spipb.com
www.spipb.com

Services à la gestion / Administrative Services
Directrice générale, Francis Mathieu

Commerce extérieur et Export Québec / Foreign Trade & Export Québec
Sous-ministre adjoint, Jean Séguin
Directeur, Marchés de l'Europe, Julien Cormier
Directrice, Marchés de l'Asie-Pacifique et de l'Océanie, Marie-Ève Jean
Directeur, Marchés de l'Amérique du Nord, Yves Lafortune
Directeur, Coordination et stratégies commerciales, Isabelle Phaneuf
Directeur, Marchés de l'Amérique latine, de l'Afrique et du Moyen-Orient, Rafael Sanchez

Industries stratégiques, projets économiques majeurs et sociétés d'État / Strategic Industries, Major Economic Projects & Crown Corporations
Sous-ministre adjoint, Mario Bouchard
Directeur général, Interventions stratégiques, Pierre Dupont
Directeur général, Développement des industries, Bernard Lauzon
Directeur, Transport et logistique, Martin Aubé
Directrice, Biens de consommation, commerce et services, Marie-Annick Drouin
Directrice, Technologies de l'information et des communications, Diane Hastie
Directrice, Sciences de la vie et technologies vertes, Michèle Houpert
Directeur, Projets économiques majeurs, Raymond Jeudi
Directrice, Fonds du développement économique et programmes, Lise Mathieu
Directrice, Produits industriels, Marie-Hélène Savard
Directrice, Coordination, analyse sectorielle et sociétés d'État, Listte Seyer
Directeur, Programmes et interventions financières, Frédéric Simard

Innovation
Sous-ministre adjoint, Vacant
Directrice générale, Marie-Josée Blais
Directrice, Partenariats internationaux, Barbara Béliveau
Directeur, Maillages et partenariats industriels, Marco Blouin
Directrice, Bureau de gestion des projets d'infrastructure, Marie-Noëlle Perron
Directrice, Intelligence économique, Mélanie Pomerleau
Directrice, Développement de la relève, Nancy-Sonia Trudelle
Directrice, Soutien aux organisations, Frédérique-Myriam Villemure

Politiques économiques / Economic Policies
Sous-ministre associé, Philippe Dubuisson
Directeur, Allègement réglementaire et administratif, Yves Blouin
Directeur, Entrepreneuriat collectif, Michel Jean
Directrice, Coordination, évaluation et planification, et Bureau de coordination du développement durable (par intérim), François Maxime Langlois
Directeur (par intérim), Développement de l'entrepreunariat, Louis-Pierre Légaré
Directeur, Politiques et analyse économiques, Mawana Pongo
Directeur, Politique commerciale, Jean-François Raymond

Secrétariat à la condition féminine / Status of Women Commission
905, avenue Honoré-Mercier, 3e étage, Québec, QC G1R 5M6
Tél: 418-643-9052; *Téléc:* 418-643-4991
www.scf.gouv.qc.ca
Sous-ministre associée, Catherine Ferembach
Directrice (par intérim), Régionalisation, Abdelouaheb Baalouch

Services aux entreprises et affaires territoriales / Business Services & Regional Affairs
Sous-ministre adoint, Mario Limoges
Directeur général, Affaires économiques métropolitaines et régionales, Bertrand Verbruggen
Directrice, Coordination régionale, Monique Asselin
Directrice, Bannière Entreprises Québec, Jocelyn Bianki
Directeur, Développement des entreprises, Pierre Hébert
Directeur, Pôles et créneaux d'excellence, Alexandre Vézina

Bureaux régionaux/Regional Offices

Abitibi-Témiscamingue
#202, 170, av Principale, Rouyn-Noranda, QC J9X 4P7
Tél: 819-763-3561; *Téléc:* 819-763-3462
Ligne sans frais: 866-463-6642

Bas-Saint-Laurent
#RC 04, 337, rue Moreault, Rimouski, QC G5L 1P4
Tél: 418-727-3577; *Téléc:* 418-727-3640
Ligne sans frais: 866-463-6642

Capitale-Nationale
900, place D'Youville, 3e étage, Québec, QC G1R 3P7
Tél: 418-691-5824; *Téléc:* 418-643-4099
Ligne sans frais: 866-463-6642

Centre-du-Québec
Édifice provincial, #1.03, 62, rue Saint-Jean-Baptiste, Victoriaville, QC G6P 4E3
Tél: 819-752-9781; *Téléc:* 819-758-4306
Ligne sans frais: 866-463-6642

Chaudière-Appalaches à Montmagny - Centre de services
116, rue Saint-Jean-Baptiste ouest, Montmagny, QC G5V 3B9
Tél: 418-248-3331; *Téléc:* 418-248-4098
Ligne sans frais: 866-463-6642

Chaudière-Appalaches à Sainte-Marie
#1, 1055, boul Vachon nord, Sainte-Marie, QC G6E 1M4
Tél: 418-386-8677; *Téléc:* 418-386-8037
Ligne sans frais: 866-463-6642

Côte-Nord à Baie-Comeau
#RC 711, 625, boul Laflèche, Baie-Comeau, QC G5C 1C5
Tél: 418-295-4349; *Téléc:* 418-295-4199
Ligne sans frais: 866-463-6642

Côte-Nord - Le Centre d'affaires regroupé de Sept-Îles
454, rue Arnaud, Sept-îles, QC G4R 3A9
Tél: 418-964-8160; *Téléc:* 418-964-8164
Ligne sans frais: 866-463-6642

Estrie
#4.05, 200, rue Belvédère nord, Sherbrooke, QC J1H 4A9
Tél: 819-820-3731; *Téléc:* 819-820-3929
Ligne sans frais: 866-463-6642

Gaspésie-Iles-de-la-Madeleine à Chandler
#10-A, 500, av Daignault, CP 1360 Chandler, QC G0C 1K0
Tél: 418-689-1200; *Téléc:* 418-689-4108
Ligne sans frais: 866-463-6642

Gaspésie-Iles-de-la-Madeleine à New Carlisle - Centre de services
224, boul Gérard-D.-Lévesque, CP 579 New Carlisle, QC G0C 1Z0
Tél: 418-752-2220; *Téléc:* 418-752-2902
Ligne sans frais: 866-463-6642

Gaspésie-Iles-de-la-Madeleine à Gaspé - Centre de services
167, rue de la Reine, CP 8 Gaspé, QC G4X 2W6
Tél: 418-361-3815; *Téléc:* 418-368-3104
Ligne sans frais: 866-463-6642

Lanaudière
#3300, 40, rue Gauthier sud, Joliette, QC J6E 4J4
Tél: 450-752-8050; *Téléc:* 450-752-8064
Ligne sans frais: 866-463-6642

Laurentides
85, rue de Martigny ouest, #C-3.35, Saint-Jérôme, QC J7Y 3R8
Tél: 450-569-3031; *Téléc:* 450-569-3039
Ligne sans frais: 866-463-6642

Laval
705, ch du Trait-Carré, Laval, QC H7N 1B3
Tél: 450-680-6175; *Téléc:* 450-972-3090
Ligne sans frais: 866-463-6642

Mauricie
Édifice Capitanal, #114, 100, rue Laviolette, Trois-Rivières, QC G9A 5S9
Tél: 450-680-6175; *Téléc:* 450-972-3090
Ligne sans frais: 866-463-6642

Montérégie
#101, 201, place Charles-Le Moyne, Longueuil, QC J4K 2T5
Tél: 450-928-7645; *Téléc:* 450-928-7465
Ligne sans frais: 866-463-6642

Montréal
380, rue Saint-Antoine ouest, 5e étage, Montréal, QC H2Y 3X7
Tél: 514-499-2550; *Téléc:* 514-873-9913
Ligne sans frais: 866-463-6642

Nord-du-Québec
333, 3e Rue, Chibougamau, QC G8P 1N4
Tél: 418-748-6681; *Téléc:* 418-748-6698
Ligne sans frais: 866-463-6642

Outaouais
#7.200, 170, rue de l'Hôtel-de-Ville, Gatineau, QC J8X 4C2
Tél: 819-772-3219; *Téléc:* 819-772-3968
Ligne sans frais: 866-463-6642

Saguenay-Lac-Saint-Jean
#2.05, 3950, boul Harvey, Saguenay, QC G7X 8L6
Tél: 418-695-7971; *Téléc:* 418-695-7870
Ligne sans frais: 866-463-6642

Ministère de l'Éducation et de l'Enseignement supérieur / Education & Higher Education

1035, rue De La Chevrotière, 28e étage, Québec, QC G1R 5A5
Tél: 418-643-7095; *Téléc:* 418-646-6561
Ligne sans frais: 866-747-6626
www.education.gouv.qc.ca
Ministre de l'Éducation, du Loisir et du Sport, L'hon. Sébastien Proulx
Tél: 418-643-2181; *Téléc:* 418-643-2640
ministre.famille@mfa.gouv.qc.ca
Autres numéros: Alt. Tél: 514-873-9342; Téléc: 514-873-9395
Ministre responsable de l'Enseignement supérieur, L'hon. Hélène David

Tél: 514-482-0199; *Téléc:* 514-482-9985
ministre@mcc.gouv.qc.ca
Sous-ministre, Sylvie Barcelo
Adjoint parlementaire du ministre de l'Éducation, du Loisir et du Sport (volet éducation primaire et secondaire), et Adjoint parlementaire de la ministre responsable de l'Enseignement supérieur (volet enseignement collégial et universitaire), David Birnbaum
David.Birnbaum.DMG@assnat.qc.ca
Adjoint parlementaire du ministre de l'Éducation, du Loisir et du Sport (volets infrastructures, loisir et sport), et Adjoint parlementaire de la ministre responsable de l'Enseignement supérieur (volet infrastructures), Marc Carrière
mcarriere-chap@assnat.qc.ca
Directrice générale, Politiques et performance ministérielle, Francis Gauthier
Directrice (par intérim), Accès à l'information et plaintes, Ingrid Barakatt
Directeur, Vérification interne, Christian Boivin
Directeur, Communications, Robert Demers
Directeur, Affaires juridiques, Nicolas Paradis
Directrice, Coordination ministérielle et Secrétariat général, Stéphanie Vachon

Agences, Conseils et Commissions Associés/ Associated Agencies, Boards & Commissions:

•Commission consultative de l'enseignement privé (CCEP) / Advisory Committee on Private Education (ACPE)
1035, rue de la Chevrotière, 14e étage
Québec, QC G1R 5A5
Tél: 418-646-1249; *Téléc:* 418-643-7752
commission.consultative@mels.gouv.qc.ca
www.mels.gouv.qc.ca/organismes-relevant-de-la-ministre/ccep
Autres numéros: Téléphone poste: 2503

•Commission d'évaluation de l'enseignement collégial (CEEC) / College Teachers Assessment Commission
800, place d'Youville, 18e étage
Québec, QC G1R 5P4
Tél: 418-643-9938; *Téléc:* 418-643-9019
info@ceec.gouv.qc.ca
www.ceec.gouv.qc.ca

•Commission de l'éducation en langue anglaise (CELA) / Advisory Board on English Education (ABEE)
600, rue Fullum, 11e étage
Montréal, QC H2K 4L1
Tél: 514-873-5656; *Téléc:* 514-864-4181
cela-abee@mels.gouv.qc.ca
www.mels.gouv.qc.ca/cela/anglais.htm

•Comité-conseil sur les programmes d'études (CCPE)
1035, de la Chevrotière, 17e étage
Québec, QC G1R 5A5
Tél: 418-646-0133; *Téléc:* 418-643-0056
ccpe@mels.gouv.qc.ca
www.ccpe.gouv.qc.ca

•Conseil supérieur de l'éducation / Superior Council of Education
#180, 1175, av Lavigerie
Québec, QC G1V 5B2
Tél: 418-643-3850; *Téléc:* 418-644-2530
panorama@cse.gouv.qc.ca
www.cse.gouv.qc.ca

•Fonds de la recherche en santé du Québec / Québec Health Research Fund
#800, 500, rue Sherbrooke ouest
Montréal, QC H3A 3C6
Tél: 514-873-2114; *Téléc:* 514-873-8768
www.frsq.gouv.qc.ca

•Fonds québécois de la recherche sur la nature et les technologies (FQRNT) / Québec Fund for Research on Nature and Technologies
#450, 140, Grande Allée est
Québec, QC G1R 5M8
Tél: 418-643-8560; *Téléc:* 418-643-1451
info.nt@frq.gouv.qc.ca
www.frqnt.gouv.qc.ca

•Fonds québécois de la recherche sur la société et la culture (FQRSC) / Québec Fund for Research on Society & Culture
#470, 140, Grande Allée est
Québec, QC G1R 5M8
Tél: 418-643-7582; *Téléc:* 418-644-5248
frq.sc@frq.gouv.qc.ca
www.frqsc.gouv.qc.ca

Aide financière aux études et relations extérieures / Student Financial Aid & External Relations
Sous-ministre adjoint, Raymond Lesage
Directeur (par intérim), Planification et programmes, Simon Boucher-Doddridge
Directeur, Relations extérieures, Yvon Doyle
Directeur, Attribution et pilotage des systèmes, Mario Godin
Directeur, Gestion des prêts, Chantale Tremblay

Éducation préscolaire, enseignement primaire et secondaire / Preschool, Elementary & Secondary Education
Sous-ministre adjoint, Yves Sylvain
Directrice, Operations financières aux réseaux, Nathalie Bussière
Directeur, Formation professionnelle, Jean-Sébastien Drapeau
Directrice, Évaluation des apprentissages, Linda Drouin
Directrice, Formation générale des jeunes, Catherine Dupont
Directeur (par intérim), Sanction des études, Daniel Desbiens
Directrice, Éducation des adultes et action communautaire, Geneviève LeBlanc
Directeur, Adaptation scolaire et services éducatifs complémentaires, Paule Mercier
Directrice, Financement, Nathalie Parenteau
Directeur (par intérim), Ressources didactiques, Pierre-Luc Pouliot

Enseignement supérieur / Higher Education
Sous-ministre adjointe, Ginette Legault
Directrice générale, Enseignement collégial, Esther Blais
Directeur général, Affaires universitaires et interordres, Jean-François Lehoux
Directeur général, Financement, Jean Leroux
Directeur (par intérim), Programmes de formation technique, Ronald Bisson
Directeur (par intérim), Affaires étudiantes et institutionnelles, Jean-François Constant
Directeur, Planification de l'offre et formation continue, Jean-Pierre Forgues
Directrice (par intérim), Programmation budgétaire et financement, Lucille Johnson
Directrice, Recherche et enseignement universitaires, Marie-Josée Larocque
Directeur, Planification et politiques, Jean-François Noël
Directrice, Contrôles financiers et systèmes, Catherine Tremblay

Infrastructures, relations du travail dans les réseaux et partenariats / Infrastructure, Labour Relations in Networks & Partnerships
Sous-ministre adjoint, Normand Légaré
Directeur général, Relations du travail, formation et titularisation du réseau scolaire, Éric Bergeron
Directeur général, Infrastructures de l'enseignement supérieur, Bernard Buteau
Directeur général, Relations du travail du réseau collégial, Richard Bernier
Directrice générale, Infrastructures scolaires, Hélène Gauthier
Directeur, Personnel enseignant, Pascal Poulin

Loisir et sport / Sport & Recreation
Sous-ministre adjoint, Robert Bédard
Directeur, Promotion de la sécurité, Michel Fafard
Directeur, Gestion administrative et contrôles des programmes, Normand Fauchon
Directrice, Sport, loisir et activité physique, France Vigneault

Gouvernance interne des ressources / Internal Resource Governance
Sous-ministre adjoint, Éric Thibault
Directeur général, Ressources informationnelles, Stéphane Lehoux
Directrice générale, Statistiques, Valérie Saysset
Directrice, Ressources humaines, Catherine Bédard
Directeur (par intérim), Gouvernance des solutions d'affaires, Stéphane Lehoux
Directrice, Assistance aux utilisateurs, Hélène Fournier
Directeur, Soutien à la clientèle et technologies, Simon Gauvin
Directrice, Ressources financières et matérielles, Katlyn Langlais
Directeur, Systèmes d'information, Jean Lauzier

Services aux anglophones, aux autochtones et à la diversité culturelles / Anglophone Services, Aboriginal Affairs & Cultural Diversity
Sous-ministre adjointe, Anne-Marie Lepage
Directrice, Services à la communauté anglophone, Lise Langlois
Directeur, Accueil et éducation interculturelle, Christian Rousseau
Directeur (par intérim), Services aux autochtones et développement nordique, Martin Quirion

Directeur général des Élections du Québec / Chief Electoral Officer of Québec

Édifice René-Lévesque, 3460, rue de La Pérade, Québec, QC G1X 3Y5
Tél: 418-528-0422; *Téléc:* 418-643-7291
Ligne sans frais: 888-353-2846
TTY: 418-646-0644
info@electionsquebec.qc.ca
www.electionsquebec.qc.ca
Autres nombres: plus.google.com/111667190553912284339
twitter.com/electionsquebec
www.facebook.com/electionsquebec
www.youtube.com/user/electionsquebec

Directeur général, Président de la commission de la représentation électorale, Jacques Drouin
Tél: 418-646-3569
Secrétaire général, Catherine Lagacé
Tél: 418-646-6072

Agences, Conseils et Commissions Associés/ Associated Agencies, Boards & Commissions:

•Commission de la représentation électorale (CRE)
Édifice René-Lévesque
3460, rue de La Pérade
Québec, QC G1X 3Y5
Tél: 418-528-0422; *Téléc:* 418-643-7291
Ligne sans frais: 888-353-2846
TTY: 800-537-0644
info@electionsquebec.qc.ca
www2.electionsquebec.qc.ca/lacartechange

Ministère des Énergie et des Ressources naturelles (MERN) / Energy & Natural Resources

Service à la clientèle, #A409, 5700, 4e av ouest, Québec, QC G1H 6R1
Téléc: 418-644-6513
Ligne sans frais: 866-248-6936
services.clientele@mern.gouv.qc.ca
www.mern.gouv.qc.ca
twitter.com/MERN_Quebec
www.facebook.com/MinistereRessourcesNaturellesQuebec
youtube.com/mrnfquebec; flickr.com/photos/mrnfquebec

Ministre, L'hon. Pierre Arcand
Tél: 418-643-7295; *Téléc:* 418-643-4318
ministre@mern.gouv.qc.ca
Autres numéros: Alt. Tél: 514-864-7222; Téléc: 514-864-7695
Ministre délégué aux Mines, L'hon. Luc Blanchette
Tél: 418-643-7295; *Téléc:* 418-643-4318
Ministre.delegue.mines@mern.gouv.qc.ca
Sous-ministre, Line Drouin
Tél: 418-627-8658 ext: 405
Adjoint parlementaire, Guy Bourgeois
Tél: 418-263-0662; *Téléc:* 418-528-7447
Guy.Bourgeois.ABES@assnat.qc.ca
Secrétariat général du MERN, Lynda Roy
Directeur, Affaires juridiques, Christian Caron
Directrice, Gouvernance, évaluation et vérification interne, Isabelle Godbout
Tél: 418-627-6383 ext: 272
Directrice, Accès à l'information, plaintes et relations internationales, Nicole McKinnon
Tél: 418-627-6370
Directeur, Communications, Terry McKinnon
Tél: 418-627-8609 ext: 303; *Téléc:* 418-643-0720

Agences, Conseils et Commissions Associés/ Associated Agencies, Boards & Commissions:

•Agence de l'efficacité énergétique / Energy Efficiencies Agency
#B406, 5700, 4e av ouest
Québec, QC G1H 6R1
Tél: 418-627-6379; *Téléc:* 418-643-5828
Ligne sans frais: 877-727-6655
efficaciteenergetique@mern.gouv.qc.ca
www.efficaciteenergetique.gouv.qc.ca
Promotes the efficient use of all forms of energy, in all sectors of activity, for the benefit of the people of Québec. The Agency achieves this through demonstration projects, which highlight new technologies, new approaches or new applications that save energy; design, management & evaluation of energy efficient programs; information, training & educational materials; technical & organizational support for export of products & services; review, commentary on proposed amendments to applicable laws & regulations.

•Hydro Québec
See Entry Name Index for detailed listing.

•Régie de l'énergie / Energy Regulation Board
Tour de la Bourse
#2.55, 800, Place Victoria
Montréal, QC H4Z 1A2
Tél: 514-873-2452; *Téléc:* 514-873-2070
Ligne sans frais: 888-873-2452
secretariat@regie-energie.qc.ca
www.regie-energie.qc.ca
Autres numéros: Greffe, Courriel: greffe@regie-energie.qc.ca
An economic regulation agency, its mission is to reconcile the public interest, consumer protection, & fair treatment of the electricity carrier & distributors.

•Société de développement de la Baie James (SDBJ) / James Bay Development Society
#10, 462, 3e rue
Chibougamau, QC G8P 1N7
Tél: 418-748-7777; *Téléc:* 418-748-6868
chi@sdbj.gouv.qc.ca
www.sdbj.gouv.qc.ca
Autres numéros: Matagami, Tél: 819-739-4717; Téléc: 819-739-4329; Courriel: mat@sdbj.gouv.qc.ca; Radisson, Tél: 819 638-8411; Téléc: 819 638-8838; Courriel: rad@sdbj.gouv.qc.ca
Developed in 1971, this organization uses its resources & vast knowledge of the territory, contributors, & development projects to promote & maintain activities in the James Bay area, with a perspective of integrated economic development & harmonious cohabitation with territorial residents.

Mandats stratégiques / Strategic Manadates
Directeur général, Marc Leduc
Tél: 418-627-6370 ext: 469

Ressources financières et matérielles et gestion contractuelle / Financial & Material Resources & Contract Management
Directeur général, Marc Gagné
Tel: 418-627-6264 ext: 378
Directrice générale adjointe, Ressources matérielles et gestion contractuelle, Julie Falardeau
Tel: 418-627-6280 ext: 344

Ressources humaines et ressources informationnelles / Human Resources & Information Resources
Directrice générale, Mylène Martel
Tel: 418-627-6268 ext: 340
Directeur général adjoint, Gilles Rousseau
Tel: 418-627-6266 ext: 320

Énergie / Energy
#A407, 5700, 4e av ouest, Québec, QC G1H 6R1
Tél: 418-627-6377; *Téléc:* 418-643-0701
www.mern.gouv.qc.ca/energie
Le gouvernement québécois prévoit le lancement des projets hydoélectriques représentant 4,500 MW, qui susciteront des investissements de l'ordre de 25m de dollars, et la création d'environ 70,000 emplois sur six ans. Il mise sur le développement du potentiel existant d'énergie éolienne, avec l'objectif de 4,000 MW d'ici 2015, et prend plusieurs moyens afin de renforcer la sécurité des approvisionnements en pétrole et gaz naturel
Sous-ministre associée, Luce Asselin
Tél: 418-627-6377 ext: 817
Directeur général, Hydrocarbures et bioarburants, Roger Ménard
Directeur général, Électricité, Louis Germain
Directeur général, Bureau de l'efficacité et innovation énergétiques, Renaud Raymond
Tél: 418-627-6380 ext: 805
Directeur (par intérim), Approvisionnements et biocombustibles, Xavier Brosseau
Directeur, Développement des énergies renouvelables, Denis Careau
Tél: 418-627-6386 ext: 835
Directeur, Secteurs transport, industrie et innovation technologique, Dominique Deschênes
Directeur, Affaires stratégiques, Gilles Lavoie
Tél: 418-627-6380 ext: 811
Directeur, Secteurs résidentiel institutionnel et affaires, Pierre Lessard
Tél: 418-627-6379 ext: 804
Directeur, Grands projets et réglementation, Philippe-Pierre Nazon
Tél: 418-627-6386 ext: 830
Directeur (par intérim), Bureau des hydrocarbures, Mathieu Roy
hydrocarbures@mern.gouv.qc.ca

Mines
Centre de service des Mines, #100, 1300, rue du Blizzard, Québec, QC G2K 0G9
Tél: 418-627-6278; *Téléc:* 418-644-8960
Ligne sans frais: 800-363-7233
service.mines@mern.gouv.qc.ca
Sous-ministre associé, Mines, Line Drouin
Tél: 418-627-8658 ext: 405
Directeur général, Développement de l'industrie minérale, Renée Garon
Tél: 418-627-6292 ext: 560
Directeur général, Géologie Québec, Robert Giguère
Tél: 418-627-6276 ext: 553
Directrice générale, Gestion du milieu minier, Lucie Ste-Croix
Tél: 418-627-6292 ext: 538
Directeur, Titres miniers et systémes, Roch Gaudreau
Tél: 418-627-6292 ext: 546
Directrice, Imposition minière, Jocelyne Lamothe
Tél: 418-627-6292 ext: 530
Directeur, Information géologique de Québec, Charles Roy
Tél: 418-627-6269 ext: 523
Directeur, Bureau de la connaissance géoscientifique du Québec, Patrice Roy
Tél: 819-354-4514 ext: 245
Directrice, Restauration des sites miniers, Sophie Trudel
Tél: 418-627-6292 ext: 560

Territoire
#A313, 5700, 4e av ouest, Québec, QC G1H 6R1
Tél: 418-627-6256; *Téléc:* 418-528-2075
Autres nombres: Géoboutique Québec, Tél: 418-627-6356; Ligne sans frais: 1-877-803-0613; Courriel: geoboutique@mern.gouv.qc.ca
Le Ministère favorise une utilisation du territoire qui rejoint les préoccupations économiques, sociales & environnementales des Québécois
Sous-ministre associé, Mario Gosselin
Tél: 418-627-6252 ext: 308
Directeur général, Arpentage et cadastre, Julien Arsenault
Tél: 418-627-6267 ext: 288
Directeur général, Registre foncier, Stéphanie Cashman-Pelletier
Tél: 418-627-6350 ext: 227
Directeur général, Politiques et intégité du territoire; Directeur (par intérim), Politiques territoriales, Sébastien Desrochers
Tél: 418-627-6362 ext: 260
Directeur général, Technologies d'affaires, Karl Gosselin
Tél: 418-627-6282 ext: 272
Directeur général, Information géographique, Mario Perron
Tél: 418-627-6285 ext: 211
information.geographique@mern.gouv.qc.ca
Directeur, Admissibilité, inscription et publicité des droits et Centre d'admissibilité et d'inscription St-Jérôme, Pierre Brunet
Tél: 418-569-3155
Directeur, Évolution et des services de mission, Guy Cantin
Tél: 418-627-6374 ext: 232
Directrice, Bureau de la coordination du modèle d'affaires, Caroline Davoine
Tél: 418-627-6383 ext: 281
Directeur, Prestation services à la clientèle, Marc Desgagné
Tél: 418-266-8176 ext: 225
Directeur, Cartographie topographique, Serge Fortin
Directeur, Cartographie générale et administrative, Mario Hinse
Tél: 418-627-6284 ext: 211
Directeur, Intégration, planification et exploitation, Jacques Lafond
Tél: 418-627-6282 ext: 229
Directeur, Bureau de l'arpenteur général du Québec, Annie Langlois
Tél: 418-627-6263 ext: 241
Directeur, Géodésie et levés géospatiaux, Luc Lapointe
Tél: 418-627-6281 ext: 207
Directeur, Enregistrement cadastral, Marc Lasnier
Tél: 418-627-6298 ext: 240
Directrice, Bureau de l'officier de la publicité foncière, Marie-Josée Pelchat
Tél: 418-627-6350 ext: 226
Directeur (par intérim), Systèmes, Karl Gosselin
Directrice, Rénovation cadastrale, Jean Thibault
Tél: 418-627-6299 ext: 282

Foncier / Lands
Tél: 418-643-3582; *Téléc:* 418-528-8721
Ligne sans frais: 866-226-0977
info.foncier@mern.gouv.qc.ca
Autres nombres: Propriétaires touchés par la réforme du cadastre québécois, Tél: 418-627-8600; Ligne sans frais: 1-888-733-3720

Réseau régional / Regional Network
www.mern.gouv.qc.ca/regions
Directrice générale, Linda Tremblay

Abitibi-Témiscamingue
70, av Québec, Rouyn-Noranda, QC J9X 6R1

Bas-Saint-Laurent
#207, 92, 2e rue ouest, Rimouski, QC G5L 8B3
Tél: 418-727-3710; *Téléc:* 418-727-3735
bas-saint-laurent@mffp.gouv.qc.ca

Capitale-Nationale et de la Chaudière-Appalaches
#101, 1300, rue du Blizzard, Québec, QC G2K 0G9
Tél: 418-643-4680; *Téléc:* 418-644-8960
capitale-nationale@mffp.gouv.qc.ca

Côte-Nord
625, boul Laflèche, Baie-Comeau, QC G5C 1C5
Tél: 418-295-4676; *Téléc:* 418-295-4682
cote-nord@mffp.gouv.qc.ca

Estrie-Montréal-Montérégie
545, boul Crémazie est, 8e étage, Montréal, QC H2M 2V1
Tél: 514-873-2140; *Téléc:* 514-873-8983
estrie@mffp.gouv.qc.ca

Gaspésie-Iles-de-la-Madeleine
195, boul Perron est, Caplan, QC G0C 1H0
Tél: 418-388-2125; *Téléc:* 418-388-2444
gaspesie-iles-de-la-madeleine@mffp.gouv.qc.ca

Laval-Lanaudière-Laurentides
545, boul Crémazie est, 8e étage, Montréal, QC H2M 2V1
Tél: 514-873-2140; *Téléc:* 514-873-8983
lanaudiere@mffp.gouv.qc.ca

Mauricie-Centre-du-Québec
#207, 100, rue Laviolette, Trois-Rivières, QC G9A 5S9
Tél: 819-371-6151; *Téléc:* 819-371-6978
Ligne sans frais: 866-821-4625
mauricie@mffp.gouv.qc.ca

Nord-du-Québec
1121, boul Industriel, CP 159 Lebel-sur-Quévillon, QC J0Y 1X0
Tél: 819-755-4838; *Téléc:* 819-755-3541
Nord-du-Quebec@mffp.gouv.qc.ca

Outaouais
#RC 100, 16, impasse de la Gare-Talon, Gatineau, QC J8T 0B1
Tél: 819-246-4827; *Téléc:* 819-246-5049
outaouais@mffp.gouv.qc.ca

Saguenay-Lac-Saint-Jean
3950, boul Harvey, 3e étage, Jonquière, QC G7X 8L6
Tél: 418-695-8125; *Téléc:* 418-695-8133
saguenay-lac-saint-jean@mffp.gouv.qc.ca

Ministère de la Famille / Family

425, rue Saint-Amable, 1er étage, Québec, QC G1R 4Z1
Ligne sans frais: 877-216-6202
www.mfa.gouv.qc.ca
www.youtube.com/user/mfaquebec
A la suite de la formation du nouveau Conseil des ministres, le 19 septembre 2012, le volet Aînés relève désormais du ministère de la Santé et des Services sociaux.
Ministre de la Famille, L'hon. Sébastien Proulx
Tél: 514-873-9342; *Téléc:* 514-873-9395
ministre.famille@mfa.gouv.qc.ca
Autres numéros: Alt. Tél: 418-643-2181; Téléc: 418-643-2640
Sous-ministre, Line Bérubé
Secretaire générale, Sylvain Pelletier
Tél: 418-528-6689

Agences, Conseils et Commissions Associés/ Associated Agencies, Boards & Commissions:

•Comité national d'éthique sur le vieillissement et les changements démographiques / National Ethics Committee on Aging & Demographic Changes
#700, 875, Grande Allée est, 5e étage
Québec, QC G1R 5W5
Tél: 418-643-0098; *Téléc:* 418-643-0082
aines.gouv.qc.ca/forum-partenaires/comite_national_ethique

•Curateur public du Québec / Québec Public Trustee
600, boul René-Lévesque ouest
Montréal, QC H3B 4W9
Tél: 514-873-4074
Ligne sans frais: 800-363-9020
www.curateur.gouv.qc.ca

•Secrétariat aux aînés / Seniors' Secretariat
#4.09, 930, ch Sainte-Foy, 4e étage
Québec, QC G1S 2L4
aines.gouv.qc.ca

Administration
Sous-ministre adjointe, Doris Paradis

Opérations régionales
Sous-ministre adjointe, Pierre Robert

Politiques
Sous-ministre adjointe, Brigitte Thériault

Services de garde éducatifs à l'enfance
Sous-ministre adjointe, Jacques Robert

Ministère des Finances / Finance

12, rue Saint-Louis, Québec, QC G1R 5L3
Tél: 418-528-9323; *Téléc:* 418-646-1631
info@finances.gouv.qc.ca
www.finances.gouv.qc.ca

Ministre, L'hon. Carlos J. Leitao
Tél: 418-643-5270; *Téléc:* 418-646-1574
ministre@finances.gouv.qc.ca
Sous-ministre, Luc Monty
Tél: 418-643-5738; *Téléc:* 418-528-5546
Adjointe parlementaire, André Fortin
Tél: 418-644-0679; *Téléc:* 418-528-5668
Andre.Fortin.PONT@assnat.qc.ca
Directrice générale, Administration, Claire Massé
Directeur principale, Systèms d'information, Rénald Bergeron
Directeur, Sécurité de l'information et de l'audit interne, Yvan Alie
Directeur, Développement des systèms, Michel Bergeron
Directeur, Santé des personnes au travail, Danielle Boisvert
Directeur, Ressources humaines, Chantal Brunet
Directeur, Communications, Nathalie Foster
Directeur, Ressources financières, Martine Gélinas
Directrice, de la gestion de la main-d'oeuvre, des relations du travail et du développement, Lyne Pilon
Directeur, Affaires juridiques, Jean-François Lord
Directeur, Secrétariat général et de la coordination ministérielle, David St-Martin
Directrice, Coordination de l'administration et des ressources matérielles, Sophie Tremblay

Agences, Conseils et Commissions Associés/ Associated Agencies, Boards & Commissions:

•Autorité des marchés financiers (AMF)
Tour de la Bourse
800, Square Victoria, 22e étage
Montréal, QC H4Z 1G3
Tél: 514-395-0337; *Téléc:* 514-873-3090
Ligne sans frais: 877-525-0337
information@lautorite.qc.ca
www.lautorite.qc.ca

•Bureau de décision et de révision (BDRQ)
#16.40, 500, boul Réné-Lévesque ouest
Montréal, QC H2Z 1W7
Tél: 514-873-2211; *Téléc:* 514-873-2162
Ligne sans frais: 877-873-2211
secretariatBDR@bdr.gouv.qc.ca
www.bdr.gouv.qc.ca

•Caisse de dépôt et placement du Québec
1000, place Jean-Paul-Riopelle
Montréal, QC H2Z 2B3
Tél: 514-842-3261; *Téléc:* 514-842-4833
Ligne sans frais: 866-330-3936
TTY: 514-847-2190
www.lacaisse.com

•Financement-Québec
12, rue Saint-Louis, 3e étage
Québec, QC G1R 5L3
Tél: 418-691-2203; *Téléc:* 418-644-6214
financement.regroupe@finances.gouv.qc.ca
www.finances.gouv.qc.ca

•Institut de la statistique du Québec (BSQ) / Québec Statistics Office
200, ch Ste-Foy, 1er étage
Québec, QC G1R 5T4
Tél: 418-691-2401; *Téléc:* 418-643-4129
Ligne sans frais: 800-463-4090
www.stat.gouv.qc.ca

•Société de financement des infrastructures locales / Local Infrastructure Financing Corporation
12, rue Saint-Louis
Québec, QC G1R 5L3
www.sofil.gouv.qc.ca

•Société des alcools du Québec (SAQ) / Québec Liquor Corporation
905, av De Lorimier
Montréal, QC H2K 3V9
Tél: 514-254-2020
Ligne sans frais: 866-873-2020
info@saq.com
www.saq.com

•Société des loteries du Québec / Québec Lotteries Corporation
500, rue Sherbrooke ouest
Montréal, QC H3A 3G6
Tél: 514-282-8000; *Téléc:* 514-873-8999
lotoquebec.com

Contrôleur des finances / Financial Controller
Contrôleur des finances, Simon-Pierre Falardeau
Contrôleur adjoint, Richard Gagnon
Directeur générale, Relations avec les ministères et les organismes, Gilles Couturier
Directeur générale, Comptes publics, Richard Gagnon
Directeur générale, Pratique professionnelle, Lucie Pageau
Directeur générale, Intégrité et de l'évolution des systèmes, Jean Ricard
Directeur principale, Intégrité des systèmes et des opérations SAGIR, Denis Aubé
Directeur principale, Analyse de l'information financière et des revenus fiscaux, Gilles Boulianne
Directrice principale, Réalisation des états financiers du gouvernement, Nathalie Giroux
Directrice principale, Production des données financières, Stéphane Jacob
Directrice principale, Analyse de l'information financière et des réseaux, Gaétan Marcotte
Directrice principale, Analyse de l'information financière, François Martel
Directrice principale, Évolution des systèmes et des processus, Marie-Claude Rheault

Droit fiscal et aux politiques locales et autochtones / Fiscal Law & Aboriginal & Local Affairs
Sous-ministre adjoint, Marc Grandisson
Directeur, Impôts des entreprises et de l'intégrité, Luc Bilodeau
Directrice, Taxes, Lyne Dussault
Directrice, Impôts des particuliers, Lyse Gauthier
Directrice, Politiques locales et autochtones, Étienne Paré
Directeur adjointe, Impôts des entreprises et de l'intégrité, Alain Ross

Financement, à la gestion de la dette et opérations financières / Financing, Debt Management & Financial Transactions
Sous-ministre associé, Bernard Turgeon
Directeur général, Financement et gestion de la dette, Alain Bélanger
Directeur général, Régimes de retraite et des projets spéciaux, Guy Émond
Directeur général, Opérations bancaires et financières et des relations avec les agences de notation, Gino Ouellet

Politiques aux particuliers, aux relations fédérales-provinciales et à l'économique / Social Policy, Federal-Provincial Relations & Economy
Sous-ministre adjoint, Pierre Côté
Directeur général, Analyse et de la prévision économiques, Daneil Floréa
Directeur général, Politiques aux particuliers, Jean-Pierre Simard

Politique budgétaire / Budgetary Policy
Sous-ministre adjoint, Simon Bergeron
Directrice générale, Revenus autonomes et de l'organisation financière, Julie Gingras
Directeur général, Politique budgétaire, Marc Sirois

Politiques fiscales aux enterprises, au développement économique et aux sociétés d'État / Tax Policies for Businesses, Economic Development & Crown Corporations
Sous-ministre adjoint, David Bahan
Directeur, Mesures fiscales aux entreprises, Mathieu Gervais
Directeur, Développement économique, Jonathan Gignac
Directeur, Sociétés d'État et des projets économiques, Richard Masse
Directeur, Taxation des entreprises, Nicolas Tremblay

Politiques relatives aux institutions financières et au droit corporatif / Policy Regarding Financial Institutions & Corporations
Sous-ministre adjoint, Richard Boivin
Directeur général, Droit corporatif et des politiques relatives au secteur financie, Pierre Rhéaume
Directeur, Droit corporatif et de la solvabilité, François Bouchard
Directeur, Pratiques commerciales et du developpement du secteur financier, Veerle Braeken

Commission de la fonction publique / Public Service Commission

800, place D'Youville, 7e étage, Québec, QC G1R 3P4
Tél: 418-643-1425; *Téléc:* 418-643-7264
Ligne sans frais: 800-432-0432
cfp@cfp.gouv.qc.ca
www.cfp.gouv.qc.ca

Présidente, Christiane Barbe
Secrétaire général et directeur, Services administratifs, Richard Saint-Pierre
Directrice générale, Activités de surveillance et du renseignement, Lucie Robitaille

Ministère des Forêts, de la Faune et des Parcs / Forestry, Wildlife & Parks

Service à la clientèle, #A409, 5700, 4e av ouest, Québec, QC G1H 6R1
Téléc: 418-644-6513
Ligne sans frais: 844-523-6738
services.clientele@mrnf.gouv.qc.ca
www.mffp.gouv.qc.ca
Autres nombres: SOS Braconnage, Tél: 1-800-463-2191; Courriel: centralesos@mffp.gouv.qc.ca
twitter.com/MFFP_Quebec

Ministre, L'hon. Laurent Lessard
Tel: 418-643-7295; *Fax:* 418-643-4318
ministre-mffp@mffp.gouv.qc.ca
Sous-ministre, Sylvain Boucher
Tel: 418-627-6370
Adjoint parlementaire, Jean Boucher
Tel: 418-644-1363; *Fax:* 418-643-7133
Jean.Boucher.UNGA@assnat.qc.ca
Directeur général, Mandats stratégiques, André Auclair
Tel: 418-627-6256 ext: 312
Directeur général, Ressources financières et matérielles et gestion contractuelle, Marc Gagné
Tel: 418-627-6264 ext: 378
Directrice générale, Ressources humaines et ressources informationnelles, Mylène Martel
Tel: 418-627-6268 ext: 340
Directeur, Affaires juridiques, Christian Caron
Directeur, Bureau du sous-ministre et du secrétariat, Démosthène Blasi
Tel: 418-627-6370 ext: 441
Directrice, Évaluation et vérification, Renée Brassard
Tel: 418-627-6251 ext: 316
Directeur, Communications, Jean Dumas
Tel: 418-627-8609 ext: 301
Directeur, Planification et coordination, Marcel Grenier
Tel: 418-627-6256 ext: 312
Directeur, Relations avec les nations autochtones, Hugo Jacqmain
Tel: 418-627-8666 ext: 498

Agences, Conseils et Commissions Associés/ Associated Agencies, Boards & Commissions:

•Comité conjoint de chasse, de pêche et de piégeage / Hunting, Fishing & Trapping Joint Committee
#C220, 383 rue Saint-Jacques
Montréal, QC H2Y 1N9
Tél: 514-284-2151; *Téléc:* 514-284-0039
cccppinfo@cccpp-hftcc.com
www.cccpp-hftcc.com

•Fondation de la faune du Québec / Québec Wildlife Foundation
Place Iberville II
#420, 1175, av Lavigerie
Québec, QC G1V 4P1
Tél: 418-644-7926; *Téléc:* 418-643-7655
Ligne sans frais: 877-639-0742
ffq@fondationdelafaune.qc.ca
www.fondationdelafaune.qc.ca
Non-profit organization whose mission is to enhance the value & promote the conservation of wildlife & its habitats.

Faune et des parcs / Wildlife & Parks
Autres nombres: Faune: www.mffp.gouv.qc.ca/faune; Parcs: www.mffp.gouv.qc.ca/parcs
Sous-ministre associée, Julie Grignon
Directeur général, Expertise sur la faune et ses habitats, Pierre Bérubé
Directeur général, Développement de la faune, Jacob Martin-Malus
Tél: 418-627-8691 ext: 736
Directeur général, Protection de la faune, Réjean Rioux
Directeur, Parcs nationaux, Serge Alain
Directeur, Affaires législatives et des permis, Martin Bourgeois
Tél: 418-521-3888 ext: 739

Bureau de la faune / Regional Wildlife Offices
www.mffp.gouv.qc.ca/regions

Abitibi-Témiscamingue
70, av Québec, Rouyn-Noranda, QC J9X 6R1
Tél: 819-763-3388; *Téléc:* 819-763-3186
abitibi-temiscamingue@mffp.gouv.qc.ca
Directeur, Gestion de la faune, Marc Deschesnes
Directeur, Protection de la faune, Danny Dumont

Bas-Saint-Laurent
#207, 92, 2e rue ouest, Rimouski, QC G5L 8B3
Tél: 418-727-3710; *Téléc:* 418-727-3735
bas-saint-laurent@mffp.gouv.qc.ca
Directeur, Gestion de la faune, Nelson Fournier
Directeur, Protection de la faune, Dominic Gagnon

Capitale-Nationale—Chaudière-Appalaches
8400, av Sous-le-Vent, Charny, QC G6X 3S9
Tél: 418-832-7222; *Téléc:* 418-832-1827
Directeur, Protection de la faune, André Jutras
Directeur, Gestion de la faune, Serge Tremblay

Mauricie—Centre-du-Québec
#207, 100 rue Laviolette, Trois-Rivières, QC G9A 5S9
Tél: 819-371-6151; *Téléc:* 819-371-6978
Ligne sans frais: 866-821-4625
mauricie@mffp.gouv.qc.ca
Directeur, Protection de la faune, Gérald Desharnais
Directrice, Gestion de la faune, Stéphanie Lachance

Côte-Nord
#RC 702, 625, boul Laflèche, Baie-Comeau, QC G5C 1C5
Tél: 418-295-4676; *Téléc:* 418-295-4682
cote-nord@mffp.gouv.qc.ca
Directeur, Gestion de la faune, Sylvain Boulianne
Directeur, Protection de la faune, Denis Moisan

Estrie—Montréal—Montérégie
770, rue Goretti, Sherbrooke, QC J1E 3H4
Tél: 514-873-2140; *Téléc:* 514-873-8983
estrie@mffp.gouv.qc.ca
Directeur (par intérim), Gestion de la faune, Pierre Bilodeau
Directeur, Protection de la faune, Pierre Fortin

Gaspésie—Iles-de-la-Madeleine
124, 1re Avenue ouest, Sainte-Anne-des-Monts, QC G4V 1C5
Tél: 418-763-3302; *Téléc:* 418-764-2378
Directeur, Protection de la faune, Dominic Gagnon
Directeur, Gestion de la faune, Claudel Pelletier

Laval—Lanaudière—Laurentides
#1.50B, 999, rue Nobel, Saint-Jérôme, QC J7Z 7A3
Tél: 450-569-3113; *Téléc:* 450-469-7568
Directeur, Gestion de la faune, Donald Jean
Directeur (par intérim), Protection de la faune, Pierre Raymond

Nord-du-Québec
1121, boul Industriel, CP 159 Lebel-sur-Quévillon, QC J0Y 1X0
Tél: 819-755-4838; *Téléc:* 819-755-3541
Nord-du-Quebec@mffp.gouv.qc.ca
Directeur, Protection de la faune, Michel Bergeron
Directrice, Gestion de la faune, Élizabeth Harvey

Outaouais
#RC 100, 16, impasse de la Gare-Talon, Gatineau, QC J8T 0B1
Tél: 819-246-4827; *Téléc:* 819-246-5049
outaouais@mffp.gouv.qc.ca
Directrice, Gestion de la faune, Simona Motnikar
Directeur (par intérim), Protection de la faune, Pierre Raymond

Saguenay—Lac-Saint-Jean
3950, boul Harvey, 4e étage, Jonquière, QC G7X 8L6
Tél: 418-695-8125; *Téléc:* 418-695-8436
saguenay-lac-saint-jean@mffp.gouv.qc.ca
Directeur (par intérim), Gestion de la faune, Claude Dussault
Directrice, Protection de la faune, Jasmin Larouche

Forestier en chef / Chief Forester
845, boul Saint-Joseph, Roberval, QC G8H 2L4
Tél: 418-275-7770; *Téléc:* 418-275-8884
bureau@forestierenchef.gouv.qc.ca
www.forestierenchef.gouv.qc.ca
twitter.com/Forestierenchef
Forestier en chef, Louis Pelletier
Directeur, Calcul et des analyses, Jean Girard

Forêts / Forests
Tél: 418-627-8652; *Téléc:* 418-528-1278
foretquebec@mffp.gouv.qc.ca
www.mffp.gouv.qc.ca/forets
Autres nombres: Alt. Courriel: forets@mffp.gouv.qc.ca
Sous-ministre associé, Ronald Brizard
Tél: 418-627-8652 ext: 442
Directeur général, Bureau de mise en marché des bois; Directeur (par intérim), Évaluations économiques et opérations financières, Jean-Pierre Adam
Tél: 418-627-8640 ext: 437
Directeur général (par intérim), Connaissance et aménagement durable des forêts, Ronald Brizard
Directeur général, Coordination, Yves Robertson
Directeur général (par intérim), Attribution des bois et développement industriel; Directeur, Gestion des stocks ligneux, Alain Sénéchal
Tél: 418-627-8657 ext: 412

Opérations régionales / Regional Operations
Sous-ministre associé, Jean-Sylvain Lebel
Tél: 418-627-6354
Directeur générale, Coordination de la gestion des forêts, François Provost
Tél: 418-627-8638 ext: 205
Directeur générale, Production de semences et de plants forestiers, Daniel Richard
Tél: 418-627-8660 ext: 465
Directeur générale, Coordination de la gestion de la faune, Serge Tremblay

Abitibi-Témiscamingue
70, av Québec, Rouyn-Noranda, QC J9X 6R1
Tél: 819-763-3388; *Téléc:* 819-763-3216
abitibi-temiscamingue@mffp.gouv.qc.ca
Directeur général, Martin Gingras

Bas-Saint-Laurent
#207, 92, 2e Rue ouest, Rimouski, QC G5L 8B3
Tél: 418-727-3710; *Téléc:* 418-727-3735
bas-saint-laurent@mffp.gouv.qc.ca
Directeur général, Paul St-Laurent

Capitale-Nationale—Chaudières-Appalaches
#101, 1300, rue du Blizzard, Québec, QC G2K 0G9
Tél: 418-643-4680; *Téléc:* 418-644-8960
capitale-nationale@mffp.gouv.qc.ca
Directrice générale, Cécile Tremblay

Côte-Nord
#RC 702, 625, boul Laflèche, Baie-Comeau, QC G5C 1C5
Tél: 418-295-4676; *Téléc:* 418-295-4682
cote-nord@mffp.gouv.qc.ca
Directeur général, Mathieu Cyr

Gaspésie—Iles-de-la-Madeleine
195, boul Perron est, Caplan, QC G0C 1H0
Tél: 418-388-2125; *Téléc:* 418-388-2444
gaspesie-iles-de-la-madeleine@mffp.gouv.qc.ca
Directeur général, Marc Lauzon

Mauricie—Centre-du-Québec
#207, 100, rue Laviolette, Trois-Rivières, QC G9A 5S9
Tél: 418-371-6151; *Téléc:* 418-371-6978
Ligne sans frais: 866-821-4625
mauricie@mffp.gouv.qc.ca
Directeur général, Alain Simard

Estrie—Montréal—Montérégie et Laval—Lanaudière—Laurentides
545, boul Crémazie est, 8e étage, Montréal, QC H2M 2V1
Tél: 514-873-2140; *Téléc:* 514-873-8983
estrie@mffp.gouv.qc.ca
Autres nombres: Alt. Courriel: lanaudiere@mffp.gouv.qc.ca
Directeur général (par intérim), Jean-Philippe Détolle

Nord-du-Québec
1121, boul Industriel, CP 159 Lebel-sur-Quévillon, QC J0Y 1X0
Tél: 819-755-4838; *Téléc:* 819-755-3541
Nord-du-Quebec@mffp.gouv.qc.ca
Directeur général, Guy Hétu

Outaouais
#RC 100, 16, impasse de la Gare-Talon, Gatineau, QC J8T 0B1
Tél: 819-246-4827; *Téléc:* 819-246-5049
outaouais@mffp.gouv.qc.ca
Directeur général, Pierre Ménard

Saguenay—Lac-Saint-Jean
3950, boul Harvey, 3e étage, Jonquière, QC G7X 8L6
Tél: 418-695-8125; *Téléc:* 418-695-8133
saguenay-lac-saint-jean@mffp.gouv.qc.ca
Directeur général, Alain Thibeault

Hydro-Québec

75, boul René-Lévesque ouest, 19e étage, Montréal, QC H2Z 1A4
Tél: 514-289-2211
www.hydroquebec.com
Autres nombres: Développement durable: www.hydroquebec.com/developpement-durable; Innovation technologique: www.hydroquebec.com/innovation/fr/index.html
twitter.com/hydroquebec
Président, Conseil d'administration, Michael D. Penner
Président-directeur général, Eric Martel
Vice-présidente exécutive, Affaires corporatives & Secrétaire générale, Marie-José Nadeau
Vice-président exécutif, Technologie, Élie Saheb
Président, Hydro-Québec TransÉnergie, André Boulanger
Président, Hydro-Québec Production, Richard Cacchione
Président, Hydro-Québec Équipement & services partagés, Réal Laporte
Président, Hydro-Québec Distribution, Daniel Richard
Vice-présidente, Comptabilité et contrôle, Lise Croteau

Filiales/Subsidiaries

Société d'énergie de la Baie-James (SEBJ) / James Bay Energy
#1200, 800, de Maisonneuve est, Montréal, QC H2L 4L8
Tél: 514-286-2020
www.hydroquebec.com/sebj
Président Hydro-Québec Équipement et services partagés; Président-directeur général de la SEBJ, Réal Laporte
Directeur, Projets de l'Eastmain, Denis Groleau

Ministère de l'Immigration, de la Diversité et de l'Inclusion / Immigration, Diversity & Inclusion

Édifice Gérald-Godin, 360, rue McGill, Montréal, QC H2Y 2E9
Tél: 514-864-9191; *Téléc:* 514-864-2899
Ligne sans frais: 877-864-9191
TTY: 514-864-8158
www.immigration-quebec.gouv.qc.ca
Autres nombres: Téléscripteur: 1-866-227-5968
Ministre, L'hon Kathleen Weil
Tél: 418-644-2128; *Téléc:* 418-528-0829
cabinet@midi.gouv.qc.ca
Autres numéros: Alt. Tél: 514-873-9940; Téléc: 514-864-2899
Sous-ministre, Robert Baril
Tél: 514-873-9450
Adjointe parlementaire, Filomena Rotiroti
Tél: 418-646-5743; *Téléc:* 418-644-5990
frotiroti-jmv@assnat.qc.ca
Secrétaire général, Paul Rémillard
Tél: 514-873-3464; *Téléc:* 514-864-2255
Directrice générale, Énoncé de politique, Martine Faille
Tél: 514-864-3404
Directeur, Audit interne et enquête, Manon Beauregard
Tél: 514-864-9896; *Téléc:* 514-864-2255
Directeur, Affaires publiques et communications, Alain Dupont
Tél: 514-873-8624; *Téléc:* 514-873-7349
Directrice, Affaires juridiques, Anne-Marie Wilson
Tél: 514-873-7484; *Téléc:* 514-873-2354

Agences, Conseils et Commissions Associés/ Associated Agencies, Boards & Commissions:

•Secrétariat à la politique linguistique (SPL) / French Language Board
225 Grande-Allée est, 4e étage
Québec, QC G1R 5G5
Tél: 418-643-4248; *Téléc:* 418-646-7832
www.spl.gouv.qc.ca

Administration et transformation / Administration & Processing
Sous-ministre adjoint et Directeur général (par interim), Transformation et technologies de l'information, Younes Mihoubi
Tél: 514-873-5942
Directrice générale, Administration, Charlotte Poirier
Directeur, Technologies de l'information, Manon Doray
Directrice, Recherche et analyse prospective, Anne-Marie Fadel
Tél: 514-864-9812
Directrice, Développement des solutions d'affaires, Odette Guertin
Tél: 514-873-2324
Directrice, Soutien aux utilisateurs, Stéphanie Laliberté
Tél: 514-873-1533; *Téléc:* 514-873-8180
Directrice, Planification, Anne-Michèle Meggs
Tél: 514-873-2324
Directrice (par interim), Ressources humaines, Suzie Melançon
Tél: 514-873-7172
Directeur (par interim), Ressources financières et matérielles, Denis Williams
Tél: 514-873-1565

Immigration / Immigration
Sous-ministre adjointe, Lucie Latulippe
Tél: 514-873-0706; *Téléc:* 514-873-0453
Directeur général, Opérations, Éric Gervais
Tél: 514-873-2446
Directeur, Courrier, encaissement et de l'évaluations comparative, Gilles Boileau
Directrice (par interim), Prospection et promotion, Mélissa Caron
Tél: 514-873-5945
Directrice, Immigration familiale & humanitaire, Chantal Drolet
Tél: 514-864-9305
Directrice, Authentification, évaluation professionnelle et révision administrative, Lyn Fleury
Tél: 514-873-5914

Directrice, Politiques et programmes d'immigration, Marie-Josée Lemay
Tél: 514-873-5914
Directeur (par intérim), Immigration économique — Québec, Fanny Marcoux
Tél: 514-864-1165
Directeur, Immigration économique — International, Owen-John Peate
Tél: 514-873-2812

Francisation et intégration / French Language & Integration
Sous-ministre adjoint (par intérim), Jacques Leroux
Tél: 514-864-3511
Directeur général (par intérim), Services de francisation et d'intégration, Bernard Roy
Directeur, Registraire et services en ligne, Luc Boisvert
Directeur, Politiques et programmes de francisation et d'intégration, Hubert de Nicolini
Tél: 514-873-9393
Directrice, Assurance qualité des services de francisation et d'intégration, Jacinthe Michaud
Tél: 514-873-6440
Directrice, Coordination des partenariats, Thérèse Trottier
Tél: 514-873-3280
Directeur, Enseignement du français, langue d'intégration, Siham Zouali

Services Immigration-Québec

Immigration-Québec - Capitale-Nationale/Est-de-Québec
Édifice Bois-Fontaine, 930, ch Sainte-Foy, RC, Québec, QC G1S 2L4
Directeur régionale, Michel-André Roy
Tél: 418-646-1605

Immigration-Québec - Estrie/Mauricie/Centre-du-Québec
202, rue Wellington nord, Sherbrooke, QC J1H 5C6
Directrice régionale, Chantal Lussier
Tél: 819-820-3600

Immigration-Québec - Ile de Montréal
#301, 800, boulevard De Maisonneuve est, Montréal, QC H2L 4L8
Directrice régionale, Johanne Côté-Galarneau
Tél: 514-940-1501

Immigration-Québec - Laval, Laurentides et Lanaudière
1438, boul Daniel-Johnson, Laval, QC H7N 4B5
Directeur régional, Serge Tétreault
Tél: 450-687-9080

Immigration-Québec - Montérégie
2, boul Desaulniers, 3e étage, Saint-Lambert, QC J4P 1L2
Directeur régional, Sylvain Lacroix
Tél: 450-466-4025

Immigration-Québec - Outaouais/Abitibi-Témiscamingue/Nord-du-Québec
Édifice Jos-Montferrand, #9.600, 170, rue de l'Hôtel-de-Ville, Gatineau, QC J8X 4C2
Directrice régionale, Dominic Vaillancourt
Tél: 819-246-3212

Ministère de la Justice / Justice

Édifice Louis-Philippe-Pigeon, 1200, rte de l'Église, Québec, QC G1V 4M1
Tél: 418-643-5140
Ligne sans frais: 866-536-5140
informations@justice.gouv.qc.ca
www.justice.gouv.qc.ca
Ministre, L'hon. Stéphanie Vallée
Tél: 418-643-4210; *Téléc:* 418-646-0027
ministre@justice.gouv.qc.ca
Sous-ministre, Nathalie G. Drouin
Directrice, Vérification interne, Francine Asselin
Tél: 418-643-8372 ext: 202
Directeur, Orientations et politiques, Renée Madore
Directeur, Communications, Pierre Tessier
Responsable, Bureau de lutte contre l'homophobe, Roger Noël

Agences, Conseils et Commissions Associés/ Associated Agencies, Boards & Commissions:

•Commission des droits de la personne et des droits de la jeunesse (CDPDJ) / Commission for Human Rights & the Rights of Youth
See Entry Name Index for detailed listing.

•Commission des services juridiques (CSJ) / Legal Services Commission
Tour de l'Est
#1404, 2, Complexe Desjardins
CP 123
Montréal, QC H5B 1B3
Tél: 514-873-3562; *Téléc:* 514-864-2351
info@csj.qc.ca
www.csj.qc.ca

•Conseil de la justice administrative (CJA) / Administrative Justice Council
#RC-01, 575, rue Saint-Amable
Québec, QC G1R 2G4
Tél: 418-644-6279; *Téléc:* 418-528-8471
Ligne sans frais: 888-848-2581
president@cja.gouv.qc.ca
www.cja.gouv.qc.ca

•Conseil de la magistrature
#RC.01, 300, boul Jean-Lesage
Québec, QC G1K 8K6
Tél: 418-644-2196; *Téléc:* 418-528-1581
information@cm.gouv.qc.ca
www.conseildelamagistrature.qc.ca

•Conseil du statut de la femme / Status of Women Council
#300, 800, place D'Youville, 3e étage
Québec, QC G1R 6E2
Tél: 418-643-4326; *Téléc:* 418-643-8926
Ligne sans frais: 800-463-2851
csf@csf.gouv.qc.ca
www.csf.gouv.qc.ca

•Directeur des poursuites criminelles et pénales (DPCP) / Criminal & Penal Prosecutions
Tour 1
#500, 2828, boul Laurier
Québec, QC G1V 0B9
Tél: 418-643-4085; *Téléc:* 418-643-7462
info@dpcp.gouv.qc.ca
www.dpcp.gouv.qc.ca

•Fonds d'aide aux recours collectifs
#10.30, 1, rue Notre-Dame est
Montréal, QC H2Y 1B6
Tél: 514-393-2087
www.farc.justice.gouv.qc.ca

•Office de la protection du consommateur (OPC) / Consumer Protection Board
#450, 400, boul Jean-Lesage
Québec, QC G1K 8W4
Tél: 418-643-1484; *Téléc:* 418-528-0979
Ligne sans frais: 888-672-2556
www.opc.gouv.qc.ca

•Office des professions du Québec / Occupations Board
See Entry Name Index for detailed listing.

•Société québécoise d'information juridique (SOQUIJ) / Judicial Information Society of Québec
#600, 715, carré Victoria
Montréal, QC H2Y 2H7
Tél: 514-842-8741; *Téléc:* 514-844-8984
www.soquij.qc.ca

•Tribunal administratif du Québec / Administrative Tribunal of Québec
575, rue Saint-Amable
Québec, QC G1R 5R4
Tél: 418-643-3418; *Téléc:* 418-643-5335
Ligne sans frais: 800-567-0278
tribunal.administratif@taq.gouv.qc.ca
www.taq.gouv.qc.ca

Affaires juridiques et législatives / Judicial & Legislative Affairs
Sous-ministre associé, Pierre Vigneault
Tél: 418-643-4228; *Téléc:* 418-644-0420
Directrice générale adjointe, Affaires économiques et territoriales, France Fradette
Directrice générale adjointe, Activités juridiques, Vacant
Tél: 418-643-4228 ext: 207
Directeur général associé, Affaires contentieuses, Jean-Yves Bernard
Directrice générale associée, Litige et droit public, Judith Sauvé
Directeur, Réseaux et affaires gouvernementales, François Bélanger

Services à l'organisation / Administrative Services
Sous-ministre associée, Lyne Bouchard
Tél: 418-643-4314
Directeur général associé, Ressources informationnelles, Lison Dubé
Directeur général associé, Personnel et administration, Sylvie St-Pierre

Services de justice et des registres / Judicial Services & Registries
Sous-ministre associée, France Lynch
Tél: 418-644-7700 ext: 202; *Téléc:* 418-528-9539
Directeur générale associée, Services de gestion et de l'administration judiciaire, Andrée Blanchet
Directrice générale associée, Services judiciaires de la Capitale-Nationale et des régions, Chantal Couturier
Directrice générale associée, Registres et la certification, Suzanne Potvin Plamondon
Directeur général associée, Services judiciaires de la Métropole, Christian G. Sirois

Office des professions du Québec (OPQ) / Occupations Board

800, place D'Youville, 10e étage, Québec, QC G1R 5Z3
Tél: 418-643-6912; *Téléc:* 418-643-0973
Ligne sans frais: 800-643-6912
courrier@opq.gouv.qc.ca
www.opq.gouv.qc.ca
Président, Jean Paul Dutrisac
Tél: 418-643-6912
Vice-présidente, Christiane Gagnon
Directeur et secrétaire, Affaires juridiques, Jean-François Paquet
Directrice, Recherche & analyse, Hélène Beaulieu
Tél: 418-643-6912 ext: 358
Directeur, Services administratifs, Jacques Laflamme
Tél: 418-643-6912 ext: 342

Le Protecteur du Citoyen / Ombudsman

#1.25, 525, boul René-Lévesque est, Québec, QC G1R 5Y4
Tél: 418-643-2688; *Téléc:* 418-643-8759
Ligne sans frais: 800-463-5070
TTY: 866-410-0901
protecteur@protecteurducitoyen.qc.ca
www.protecteurducitoyen.qc.ca
Secondary Address: #1000, 1080, côte du Beaver Hull, 10e étage
Montréal, QC H2Z 1S8
Alt. Téléc: 514-873-4640
twitter.com/PCitoyen
www.facebook.com/592335790831343
plus.google.com/u/0/114137425993281713965
Protectrice du citoyen, Raymonde Saint-Germain
Tél: 418-643-2688
Vice-protecteur, Affaires institutionnelles et prévention, Jean-François Bernier
Tél: 418-643-2688
Directeur, Ressources humaines & l'administration, Marcel Domingue
Tél: 418-646-2623
Directeur, Communications, Joanne Trudel
Tél: 418-643-2688

Ministère des Relations internationales et Francophonie / International Relations & La Francophonie

Édifice Hector-Fabre, 525, boul Réne-Lévesque est, Québec, QC G1R 5R9
Tél: 418-649-2300; *Téléc:* 418-649-2656
www.mrif.gouv.qc.ca
Autres nombres:
www.linkedin.com/company/minist-re-des-relations-internationales-de-la-francophonie-et-du-commerce-ext-rieur
Secondary Address: 380, rue St-Antoine ouest
Montréal, QC H2Y 3X7
Alt. Téléc: 514-873-7468
twitter.com/MRIF_Quebec
www.facebook.com/MRIQuebec
Ministre, L'hon. Christine St-Pierre
Tél: 418-649-2319; *Téléc:* 418-643-4804
acadie@mri.gouv.qc.ca
Sous-ministre, Jean-Stéphane Bernard
Secrétaire général, Relations fédérales-provinciales, Bernard Denault
Tél: 418-649-2400 ext: 563
Directrice, Audit interne et évaluation de programmes, Marie-Josée Blanchette
Tél: 418-649-2400 ext: 570
Directrice, Performance et planification stratégique, Henriette Dumont
Tél: 418-649-2400 ext: 579
Directrice, Affaires juridiques, Manon Godin
Tél: 418-649-2400 ext: 570

Directrice, Communications & affaires publiques, Michèle St-Jean
Tél: 418-649-2333

Administration / Administration

Directeur général, Bernard Dubois
Tél: 418-649-2400 ext: 566
Director, Technologies; Directeur (par intérim), Ressources informationnelles, Denis Bilodeau
Tél: 418-649-2400 ext: 570
Directeur, Ressources financières, Daniel Cloutier
Tél: 418-649-2400 ext: 573
Directrice, Gestion immobilière, Renée Delisle
Tél: 418-649-2400 ext: 570
Directrice, Dotation, relations professionelles et conditions de travail, Méliza Deschènes
Tél: 418-649-2400 ext: 571
Directeur, Ressources humaines, Anouk Gagné
Tél: 418-649-2400 ext: 574

Affaires bilatérales / Bilateral Affairs

Sous-ministre adjoint, Jean-Stéphane Bernard
Tél: 418-649-2400 ext: 563
Directeur général, Europe, Afrique et Moyen-Orient, Michel Lafleur
Tél: 418-649-2400 ext: 570
Directeur général, Amériques et Asie-Pacifique, Jean Saintonge
Tél: 418-649-2400 ext: 572
Directeur, Afrique et Moyen-Orient, Yvan Bédard
Tél: 418-649-2400 ext: 571
Directeur, France, Luc Bergeron
Tél: 418-649-2400 ext: 573
Directrice (par intérim), Europe et institutions européennes, Françoise Cloutier
Tél: 418-649-2400 ext: 560
Directeur, Asie-Pacifique, Donald Leblanc
Tél: 418-649-2400 ext: 571
Directeur, États-Unis, Marc-André Thivierge
Tél: 418-649-2400 ext: 571
Directrice, Amérique latine et Antilles, Elisa Valentin
Tél: 418-649-2400 ext: 571

Amérique du Nord - Bureaux à l'étranger / North America - Offices Abroad

Atlanta, GA, USA
Délégation du Québec à Atlanta, #3240, 191 Peachtree St. NE, Atlanta, GA 30303 USA
Tél: 404-584-2995; *Téléc:* 404-584-2089
qc.atlanta@mri.gouv.qc.ca
www.international.gouv.qc.ca/en/atlanta
Chef de poste, Louise Fortin
Louise.Fortin@mri.gouv.qc.ca

Boston, MA, USA
One Boston Place, #3850, 201 Washington St., Boston, MA 02108 USA
Tél: 617-482-1193; *Téléc:* 617-482-1195
qc.boston@mri.gouv.qc.ca
www.international.gouv.qc.ca/en/boston
twitter.com/QuebecBoston
www.facebook.com/QuebecBoston
Chef de poste, Marie-Claude Francoeur

Chicago, IL, USA
Délégation du Québec à Chicago, #3650, 444 N Michigan Ave., Chicago, IL 60611 USA
Tél: 312-645-0932; *Téléc:* 312-645-0542
qc.chicago@mri.gouv.qc.ca
www.international.gouv.qc.ca/en/chicago
twitter.com/QcChicago
www.facebook.com/QuebecChicago
Chef de poste, Éric Marquis

Los Angeles, CA, USA
Délégation du Québec à Los Angeles, #720, 10940 Wilshire Blvd., Los Angeles, CA 90024 USA
Tél: 310-824-4173; *Téléc:* 310-824-7759
qc.losangeles@mri.gouv.qc.ca
www.international.gouv.qc.ca/en/los-angeles
twitter.com/QuebecLA
www.facebook.com/QuebecLosAngeles
Chef de poste, Alain Houde

Mexico City, Mexico
Délégation générale du Québec, Avenida Taine 411, Colonia Bosques de Chapultepec, Mexico, DF 11580 Mexico
qc.mexico@mri.gouv.qc.ca
www.international.gouv.qc.ca/es/mexico
Autres nombres: Téléphone: 52-55-1100-4330; Téléc: 52-55-1100-4339
twitter.com/QuebecMX
www.facebook.com/QuebecMX
Chef de poste, Eric R. Mercier

New York, NY, USA
Délégation générale du Québec, One Rockefeller Plaza, 26the Fl., New York, NY 10020-2102 USA
Tél: 212-843-0950; *Téléc:* 212-757-4753
qc.newyork@mri.gouv.qc.ca
www.international.gouv.qc.ca/en/new-york
twitter.com/quebecnewyork
www.facebook.com/QuebecNewYork
Chef de poste, Dominique Poirier

Washington, DC, USA
Bureau du Québec à Washington, #450, 805 15th St. NW, Washington, DC 20005 USA
Tél: 202-659-8990; *Téléc:* 202-659-5654
qc.washington@mri.gouv.qc.ca
www.international.gouv.qc.ca/en/washington
twitter.com/QcWashington
www.facebook.com/QuebecWashington

Amérique du Sud - Bureaux à l'étranger / South America - Offices Abroad

Sao Paulo, Brésil
Avenida Engenheiro Luis Carlos Berrini, 1511, CJ 151 e 152, 15e Andar, Sao Paulo, 04571-011 Brésil
qc.saopaulo@mri.gouv.qc.ca
www.international.gouv.qc.ca/pt/sao-paulo
Autres nombres: Télé: +55 11 5505 0444; Téléc: +55 11 5505 0445
twitter.com/QuebecBrasil
www.facebook.com/QuebecnoBrasil
Chef de poste, Élise Racicot

Asie - Bureaux à l'étranger / Asia - Offices Abroad

Directrice, Asie-Pacifique, Juliette Champagne
Tél: 418-649-2662

Beijing, Chine
Ambassade du Canada, 19, Dongzhimenwai Dajie, Dist. de Chaoyang, Beijing, 100600 China
qc.beijing@mri.gouv.qc.ca
www.international.gouv.qc.ca/zh/beijing
Autres nombres: Tél: 86 10 5139 4000; Téléc: 86 10 5139 4445
Chef de poste, Maud-Andrée Lefebvre

Hong Kong, Chine
Bureau d'immigration, Consulat général du Canada, 7/F, 25 Westlands Road, Quarry Bay, Hong Kong
biq.hkong@micc.gouv.qc.ca
www.international.gouv.qc.ca/zh/hong-kong
Autres nombres: Téléphone: 852 2810 7183; Télécopieur: 852 2845 3889
Chef de poste, Louis Bélanger

Mumbai, Inde
Indiabulls Finance Centre, Tour 2, 21ème étage, Rue Senapati Bapat, Elphinstone Road (West), Mumbai, MH 400 013 India
qc.mumbai@mri.gouv.qc.ca
www.international.gouv.qc.ca/en/mumbai
Autres nombres: Téléphone: 91-22-6749-4444; Télécopieur: 91-22-6749-4454

Séoul, Korea
Antenne du Québec, 5F, Leema Bldg., 146-1, Soosong-dong, Jongno-gu, Séoul, 110-755 Korea
qc.seoul@mri.gouv.qc.ca
www.international.gouv.qc.ca/ko/seoul
Autres nombres: Téléphone: 82-2-3703-7700; Télécopieur: 82-2-732-5175
Chef de poste, Chungyoll Yoo

Shanghai, Chine
a/s Consulat général du Canada, Eco City Bldg., 8e étage, 1788 Nanjing Xi Lu, Shanghai, 200040 Chine
qc.shanghai@mri.gouv.qc.ca
www.international.gouv.qc.ca/zh/shanghai
Autres nombres: Téléphone: 86-21-3279-2800; Télécopieur: 86-21-3279-2801
Chef de poste, Maud-Andrée Lefebvre

Tokyo, Japon
Délégation générale du Québec, Shiroyama Trust Tower, 32e étage, 4-3-1 Toranomon, Minato-Ku, Tokyo, 105-6032 Japan
qc.tokyo@mri.gouv.qc.ca
www.international.gouv.qc.ca/ja/tokyo
Autres nombres: Téléphone: 81-3-5733-4001; Télécopieur: 81-3-5472-6721
Chef de poste, Claire Deronzier

Europe - Bureaux à l'étranger / Europe - Offices Abroad

Directrice (par intérim), Europe de l'Ouest & du Nord -Institutions européennes, Élisa Valentin
Tél: 418-649-2669; *Téléc:* 418-649-2421
Directrice, Solidarité internationale/Haïti et Afrique subsaharienne, Marjolaine Ricard
Tél: 418-649-2341
Directeur, Europe méditerranéenne et est/Maghreb et Moyen-Orient, Bernard Denault
Tél: 418-649-2343

Barcelone, Espagne
Bureau du Québec, Avinguda Diagonal, 420, 3er 1a, Barcelone, 08037 Espagne
qc.barcelone@mri.gouv.qc.ca
www.international.gouv.qc.ca/ca/barcelone
Autres nombres: Téléphone: 34-93-476-42-58; Télécopieur: 34-93-476-47-74
twitter.com/QuebecEspana
www.facebook.com/quebecenbarcelona
Chef de poste (par intérim), Alfons Calderon Riera

Berlin, Allemagne
Bureau du Québec, Pariser Platz 6A, Berlin, 10117 Allemagne
qc.berlin@mri.gouv.qc.ca
www.international.gouv.qc.ca/de/allemagne
Autres nombres: Téléphone: 49-30-5900646-0; Télécopieur: 49-30-5900646-29

Bruxelles, Belgique
Délégation générale du Québec, 46, av des Arts, 7e étage, Bruxelles, 1000 Belgique
qc.bruxelles@mri.gouv.qc.ca
www.international.gouv.qc.ca/nl/bruxelles
Autres nombres: Téléphone: 32-2-512-00-36; Télécopieur: 32-2-514-26-41
twitter.com/QuebecEuropeBe
www.facebook.com/QuebecEuropeBe
Chef de poste, Caroline Emond

Londres, Angleterre
Délégation générale du Québec, 59 Pall Mall, Londres, SW1Y 5JH Royaume-Uni
qc.londres@mri.gouv.qc.ca
www.international.gouv.qc.ca/en/londres
Autres nombres: Téléphone: 44-207-766-5900; Télécopieur: 44-207-930-7938
twitter.com/quebec_uk
www.facebook.com/QuebecUK
Chef de poste, Stéphane Paquet

Milan, Italie
Antenne économique du Québec, Via San Clemente, 1, Milan, 20122 Italie
qc.milan@mri.gouv.qc.ca
www.international.gouv.qc.ca/it/rome
Autres nombres: Téléphone: 39-02-8052-210; Télécopieur: 39-02-72016399

Munich, Allemagne
Délégation générale du Québec, Karl-Scharnagl-Ring 6, Munich, 80539 Allemagne
qc.munich@mri.gouv.qc.ca
www.international.gouv.qc.ca/de/allemagne
Autres nombres: Téléphone: 49-89-2554931-0; Télécopieur: 49-89-21019473
Chef de poste, Claude Trudelle

Paris, France
Délégation générale du Québec, 66, rue Pergolèse, Paris, 75116 France
qc.paris@mri.gouv.qc.ca
www.international.gouv.qc.ca/fr/paris
Autres nombres: Téléphone: 33-1-40-67-85-00; Télécopieur: 33-1-40-67-85-09
twitter.com/Quebec_Fr
www.facebook.com/QuebecFrance
Chef de poste, Michel Robitaille

Rome, Italie
Délégation du Québec, #5, 16 via Delle Quattro Fontane, 2e étage, Rome, 00184 Italie
qc.rome@mri.gouv.qc.ca
www.international.gouv.qc.ca/it/rome
Autres nombres: Téléphone: 39-06-4203-4501; Télécopieur: 39-06-4203-4502
Chef de poste, Amalia Daniela Renosto

Stockholm, Suède
Bureau d'Investissement Québec à Stockholm, Klarabergsgatan 23, 6e étage, CP 16129 Stockholm, 103 23 Suède
www.international.gouv.qc.ca/en/stockholm
Autres nombres: Téléphone: 46-8-453-30-37; Télécopieur: 46-8-453-30-16

Politiques et affaires francophones et multilatérales / Policy & Francophone & Multilateral Affairs

Sous-ministre adjoint, Éric Théroux
Tél: 418-649-2400 ext: 563
Directeur, Organisations internationales et enjeux globaux, Daniel Lacroix
Tél: 418-649-2400 ext: 563

Directeur, Analyses économiques et politiques, Roger Ménard
Tél: 418-649-2400 ext: 570
Directeur (par intérim), Engagements internationaux, Pierre Noël
Tél: 418-649-2400 ext: 573
Directrice, Francophonie, Christina Vigna
Tél: 418-649-2400 ext: 571

Protocole / Protocol
Sous-ministre associée, Marie Claire Ouellet
Directeur, Gestion des évènements officiels, Nicolas Boulanger
Tél: 418-649-2400 ext: 574
Directeur, Correspondance officielle, privilèges et immunités, Steeve Harbour
Tél: 418-649-2400 ext: 572
Directeur, Visites, missions et cérémonial d'État, Dominic Toupin
Tél: 418-649-2400 ext: 571

Revenu Québec / Revenue Québec

Direction des relations publiques/Communications, 3800, rue de Marly, Québec, QC G1X 4A5
Tél: 418-652-6831; *Téléc:* 418-646-0167
cabinet@revenuquebec.ca
www.revenuquebec.ca
Secondary Address: 150, rue Ste-Catherine ouest
Complexe Desjardins
Montréal, QC H5B 1A7
Alt. Téléc: 514-873-7502

Ministre des Finances; Président du Conseil du trésor, L'hon. Carlos J. Leitao
Tél: 418-643-5270; *Téléc:* 418-646-1574
ministre@finances.gouv.qc.ca
Président du conseil d'administration, Florent Gagné
Vice-président du conseil d'administration, Pierre Roy

Bureau de président-directeur général / Office of the President/Director General
Président-directeur général, Éric Ducharme
Vice-présidente et directrice générale, Traitement des plaintes et de l'éthique, Josée Morin
Vice-présidente et directrice générale, Ressources humaines, Line Paulin

Centre de perception fiscale et des biens non réclamés / Tax Collection
Le rôle du Centre est de recouvrer les créances de la clientèle de Revenu Québec
Vice-président et directeur général, Recouvrement, François T. Tremblay
Directeur principal, Services administratifs et techniques, Marcel Turgeon

Entreprises / Businesses Directorate
Vice-président & Directeur général, Hajib Amachi
Directeur principal, Relations avec la clientèle des entreprises, Denis Gendron
Directeur principal, Vérification des entreprises - Sud-Ouest du Québec, Jean Jenkins
Directeur principal, Vérification des entreprises - Centre du Québec, Serge Lamothe
Directeur principal, Vérification des entreprises - Montréal, Pierre Leclerc
Directrice principal, Vérification des entreprises - Capitale-Nationale et autres régions, Pierre Montreuil
Directeur principal, Soutien opérationnel et du développement des compétences, Danny Pagé
Directrice principale, Vérification des entreprises - Laval, Lucie Veilleux

Innovation et de l'administration / Innovation & Administration
Vice-président & Directeur général, Daniel Prud'homme
Directeur principal, Recherche et Innovation, Gilles Bernard
Directeur principal, Statistiques, de l'administration et de la gestion des renseignements, Alain Gagnon
Directeur principal, Finances et des contrats, Éric Maranda
Chef du Service, Expertise et de la qualité du registre, Valérie Dran

Législation et du Registraire des entreprises / Legislation & Businesses Directorate
Vice-président & Directeur général, René Martineau
Directeur général, Enquêtes, de l'inspection et des poursuites pénales, Yves Trudel
Directrice principale, Services administratifs & informatiques, Nathalie Dionne
Directeur, Oppositions de Québec, Denis Morin

Particuliers / Individuals Directorate
Vice-présidente & Directrice générale, Particuliers, Nicole Bourget
Directeur principal, Programmes sociofiscaux, Normand Bilodeau
Directeur principal, Relations avec la clientèle des particuliers, Benoit Côté
Directeur principal du contrôle fiscal des particuliers - Québec, Marc Simard

Traitement et des Technologies / Data Processing & Technologies
Vice-président & Directeur général, Patrice Alain
Directeur principal, Planification et du conseil à la gestion, Marco Beaulieu
Directeur principal, Système de gestion intégrée des ressources humaines et solutions organisationnelles, Daniel Forest
Directeur général associé, Traitement massif, Olivier Blondeau

Ministère de la Santé et des Services sociaux / Health & Social Services

Direction des communications, 1075, ch Sainte-Foy, 16e étage, Québec, QC G1S 2M1
Tél: 418-643-9395; *Téléc:* 418-643-4768
regisseur.web@msss.gouv.qc.ca
www.msss.gouv.qc.ca

Ministre, L'hon. Gaétan Barrette
Tél: 418-266-7171; *Téléc:* 418-266-7197
ministre@msss.gouv.qc.ca
Ministre déléguée, Réadaptation, à la Protection de la jeunesse et à la Santé publique, L'hon. Lucie Charlebois
Tél: 418-266-7181; *Téléc:* 418-266-7199
ministre.deleguee@msss.gouv.qc.ca
Sous-ministre, Michel Fontaine
Adjointe parlementaire, Marie Montpetit
Tél: 418-643-6018
Adjointe parlementaire de la ministre déléguée à la Réadaptation, à la Protection de la jeunesse, à la Santé publique et aux Saines habitudes de vie, Véronyque Tremblay
Tél: 418-263-0681; *Téléc:* 418-643-7142
Veronyque.Tremblay.CHAU@assnat.qc.ca
Directeur, Cabinet du ministre, Daniel Desharnais
Tél: 418-266-7171
Directrice, Cabinet du ministre délégué, Natacha Joncas-Boudreau
Tél: 418-266-7181

Agences, Conseils et Commissions Associés/ Associated Agencies, Boards & Commissions:

•Institut national d'excellence en santé et en services sociaux (INESSS) / National Institute for Excellence in Health & Social Services
2535, boul Laurier, 5e étage
Québec, QC G1V 4M3
Tél: 418-643-1339; *Téléc:* 418-646-8349
inesss@inesss.qc.ca
www.inesss.qc.ca

•Institut national de santé publique du Québec (INSPQ) / National Public Health Institute of Québec
945, av Wolfe
Québec, QC G1V 5B3
Tél: 418-650-5115; *Téléc:* 418-646-9328
info@inspq.qc.ca
www.inspq.qc.ca
Autres numéros: Poste: 5336

•Modernisation des centres hospitaliers universitaires de Montréal, CHUM, CUSM, CHU Sainte-Justine / Modernization of Montréal's University Health Centres CHUM, MUHC & Sainte-Justine UHC
#10.049, 2021, rue Union
Montréal, QC H3A 2S9
Tél: 514-864-9883; *Téléc:* 514-873-7362
info.construction3chu@msss.gouv.qc.ca
construction3chu.msss.gouv.qc.ca

•Office des personnes handicapées du Québec / Office for Handicapped Persons
309, rue Brock
Drummondville, QC J2B 1C5
Téléc: 819-475-8753
Ligne sans frais: 800-567-1465
TTY: 800-567-1477
aide@ophq.gouv.qc.ca
www.ophq.gouv.qc.ca

•Régie de l'assurance maladie du Québec (RAMQ) / Québec Health Insurance Board
1125, Grande Allée ouest
Québec, QC G1S 1E7
Tél: 418-646-4636
Ligne sans frais: 800-561-9749
www.ramq.gouv.qc.ca

•Secrétariat à l'accès aux services en langue anglaise et aux communautés ethnoculturelles / English Language & Ethnocultural Communities Services Secretariat
#840, 2021, av Union
Montréal, QC H3A 2S9
Tél: 514-873-5163; *Téléc:* 514-873-9876
www.msss.gouv.qc.ca/ministere/saslacc

•Urgences-santé Québec / Emergency Health Services Québec
3232, rue Bélanger
Montréal, QC H1Y 3H5
Tél: 514-723-5600
info@urgences-sante.qc.ca
www.urgences-sante.qc.ca

Cabinet du Sous-ministre / Office of the Deputy Minister
Sous-ministre, Lise Verreault
Tél: 418-266-8989
Directrice, Domonique Breton
Tél: 418-266-8989
Directeur (par intérim), Secrétariat général, Jean-François Boudreau
Tél: 418-266-8989
Directeur, Communications, Robert Demers
Tél: 418-266-8905
Directeur, Service de l'accès à l'information et de la propriété intellectuelle, Claude Lamarre
Tél: 418-266-7005
Directeur, Direction québécoise de cancéroogie, Jean Latreille
Tél: 418-266-6940
Directeur, Affaires juridiques, Danielle Parent
Tél: 418-266-8950
Directrice, Audit interne, Isabelle Savard
Tél: 418-266-8989

Coordination, financement, immobilisations et budget / Coordination, funding & capital budget
Sous-ministre associé, François Dion
Tél: 418-266-5965
Sous-ministre adjoint (par intérim), Financement, immobilisations et budget, François Dion
Tél: 418-266-5965
Sous-ministre adjoint (par intérim), Coordination, Pierre Lafleur
Tél: 418-266-8850
Directeur général adjointe (par intérim), Gestion financière et des politiques de financement, Guylaine Lajoie
Tél: 418-266-5920
Directeur général adjointe, Investissements, Sylvain Périgny
Tél: 418-266-5830
Directeur général adjointe (par intérim), Coordination, Alain Saucier
Tél: 418-266-6822
Directrice, Ressources matérielles, Marie-Claude Beauchamp
Tél: 418-266-8760
Directeur, Expertise et de la normalisation, Céline Drolet
Tél: 418-266-5956
Directrice, Logistique et des équipements, Caroline Imbeau
Tél: 418-266-5835
Directeur, Secrétariat à l'accès aux services pour les communautés culturelles, Pierre Lafleur
Tél: 514-266-5812
Directeur (par intérim), Allocation des ressources, Normand Latagne
Tél: 418-266-7111
Directeur (par intérim), Gestion financière - réseau, Pierre Martin
Tél: 418-266-5940
Directrice, Affaires autochtones et régions nordiques, Louise Rondeau
Tél: 418-266-6811
Directeur, Gestion intégrée de l'information, Alain Saucier
Tél: 418-266-8399
Directeur, Relations institutionnelles et de la sécurité civile, Martin Simard
Tél: 418-266-5800
Directrice, Investissements du financement, Marlène Sinclair
Tél: 418-266-5850
Directeur, Inspection et des enquêtes, Jean-François Therrien
Tél: 418-643-6084
Directrice, Gestion intégrée de l'information, Sylvie Vézina
Tél: 418-266-8399
Directeur, Ententes de gestion et d'imputabilité, Yves Villeneuve
Tél: 418-266-6822

Planification, performance et qualité / Planning, Performance and Quality
Sous-ministre adjoint, Luc Castonguay
Tél: 418-266-5990
Directeur général adjointe, Performance, Éric Fournier
Tél: 418-266-7025
Directrice (par intérim), Affaires pharmaceutiques et du médicament, Dominic Bélanger
Tél: 418-266-8810

Directeur (par interim), Études et des analyses, Vivian Cantin
Tél: 418-266-7025
Directeur, Évaluation, Harold Côté
Tél: 418-266-7025
Directrice, Éthique et de la qualité, Nathalie Desrosiers
Tél: 418-266-7707
Directrice, Planification et orientations stratégiques, Lynda Fortin
Tél: 418-266-7088
Directrice, Affaires intergouvernementales et de la coopération internationale, Anne Marcoux
Tél: 418-266-8740
Directrice, Recherche, innovation et transfert des connaissances, Manon St-Pierre
Tél: 418-266-7056

Personnel réseau et ministériel / Personal & Corporate Network

Sous-ministre adjointe, Marco Thibault
Tél: 418-266-8400
Directeur général adjointe, Relations de travail et professionnelles, Alexandre Hubert
Tél: 418-266-8408
Directeur, Personnel horsétablissement et de la classification réseau, Luc Bouchard
Tél: 418-266-8410
Directrice, Ressources humaines ministérielles, Josée Doyon
Tél: 418-266-8710
Directeur, Professionels de la santé et personnel d'encadrement, Yves Lapointe
Tél: 418-266-8420
Directeur, Planification de la main-d'oeuvre et du soutien au changement, Gilles Le Beau
Tél: 418-266-8835
Directrice, Analyse et du soutien informationnel, Marie-Pierre Legault
Tél: 418-266-8457
Directeur, Personnel syndiqué, Pascal Pedneault
Tél: 514-266-8408

Santé publique / Public Health

Sous-ministre adjoint, Horacio Arruda
Tél: 514-873-1587
Directrice générale adjointe, Lyne Jobin
Tél: 418-266-6780
Directrice, Protection de la santé publique, Danielle Auger
Tél: 514-864-2755
Directeur, Prévention et de la promotion de la santé, André Dontigny
Tél: 418-266-6714

Services de santé et médecine universitaire / Health Services & Academic Medicine

Sous-ministre adjoint, Louis Couture
Tél: 418-266-6930
Directeur, Santé mentale, André Delorme
Tél: 418-266-6835
Directeur, Soins infirmiers, Danielle Fleury
Tél: 418-266-8485
Directeur, Organisation des services de première ligne intégrés, Antoine Groulx
Tél: 418-266-6976
Directeur, Accès, des technologies et de la biologie médicales, Yves Jalbert
Tél: 418-266-6946
Directeur nationale, Urgences, services de traumatologie & services préhospitaliers d'urgence, Daniel Lefrançois
Tél: 418-266-5811
Directeur, Services mère-enfant, Daniel Riverin
Tél: 418-266-5827
Directeur, Services hospitaliers et des affaires universitaires, Monique St-Pierre
Tél: 418-266-7500
Directrice, Main d'oeuvre médicale, Isabelle Savard
Tél: 418-266-6975

Services sociaux / Social Services

Sous-ministre associé, Sylvain Gagnon
Tél: 418-266-6800
Directrice générale adjointe, Services aux aînés, Natalie Rosebush
Tél: 418-266-6855
Directrice, Operations des services aux aînés, Danielle Benoit
Tél: 418-266-6860
Directrice, Dépendances et de l'itinérance, Lynne Duguay
Tél: 418-266-6830
Directeur, Services sociaux généraux et des activités communautaires, Mario Fréchette
Tél: 418-266-6936
Directeur (par intérim), Jeunes et des familles, Sylvain Gagnon
Tél: 418-226-6840
Directrice, Secrétariat à l'adoption internationale, Josée-Anne Goupil
Tél: 514-873-4747
Directrice, Presonnes ayant une déficience, Renée Lecours
Tél: 418-266-6874
Directeur, Soutien à domicile, Renée Moreau
Tél: 418-266-6876

Technologies de l'information / Information Technology

Sous-ministre associée, Richard Audet
Tél: 418-266-8770
Directeur général adjoint, Systèmes aux services de santé et administratifs, Alain Chouinard
Tél: 418-266-2287
Directeur général adjoint, Systèmes aux services sociaux et administratifs, Denis Deslauriers
Tél: 514-597-2066
Directeur général adjoint, DSQ, Renald Lemieux
Tél: 514-597-2066
Directrice générale adjointe, Orientations et de la planification, Nathalie Surprenant
Tél: 418-266-5890
Directrice générale adjointe, Opérations technologiques, Agathe Tremblay
Tél: 418-527-5211
Directrice, Systèmes aux services sociaux et administratifs, Lynda Bergeron
Tél: 514-527-5211
Directeur, Gestion des licenses et de l'assurance qualité, Stéphane Brossard
Tél: 514-597-2066
Directrice, Pilotage, France Émond
Tél: 418-266-8779
Directrice, Soutien à la gouvernance, Danielle Lavoie
Tél: 418-266-5879
Directrice, Infrastructures technologiques, Nathalie Lemay
Tél: 418-527-5211
Directrice, Planification et du suivi des projets, Caroline Martin
Tél: 418-266-6266
Directeur, Systèmes aux services de santé et administratifs, Alexandre Poirier
Tél: 418-266-5880
Directeur, Sécurité, Dave Roussy
Tél: 418-527-5211
Directrice (par interim), Orientations et de l'architecture, Nathalie Surprenant
Tél: 418-266-5890
Directeur, Exploitation et des services aux utilisateurs, Roger Villeneuve
Tél: 418-527-5211

Commission de la santé et de la sécurité du travail du Québec (CSST) / Québec Occupational Health & Safety Commission

524, rue Bourdages, CP 1200 Succ Terminus, Québec, QC G1K 7E2

Téléc: 418-266-4015
Ligne sans frais: 866-302-2778
www.csst.qc.ca
Autres nombres:
www.linkedin.com/company/commission-de-la-sant-et-s-curit-du-travail-csst-
twitter.com/laCSST
www.facebook.com/laCSST
www.youtube.com/user/LaCSST

A pour mission de soutenir aux travailleurs & aux employeurs dans leurs démarches pour éliminer les dangers présents dans leur milieu de travail, inspecter des lieux de travail, & promouvoir la santé & sécurité du travail

Président & Chef de la direction, Michel Després
Vice-président, Opérations, Josée Dupont
Vice-présidente, Administration, Sylvain Gagnon
Vice-président, Finances, Carl Gauthier
Vice-présidente, Partenariat et l'expertise-conseil, Claude Sicard

Ministère de la Sécurité publique / Public Security

Tour des Laurentides, 2525, boul Laurier, 5e étage, Québec, QC G1V 2L2

Tél: 418-646-6777; *Téléc:* 418-643-0275
Ligne sans frais: 866-644-6826
www.securitepublique.gouv.qc.ca
Secondary Address: #11.39, 10, rue Saint-Antoine est
Bureau de Montréal
Montréal, QC H2Y 1A2
Alt. Téléc: 514-873-6597

A pour mission d'assurer la sécurité publique au Québec

Ministre, L'hon. Martin Coiteux
Tél: 418-643-2112; *Téléc:* 418-646-6168
ministre@msp.gouv.qc.ca
Sous-ministre, Liette Larrivée
Adjoint parlementaire, Jean Rousselle
Tél: 418-644-0877; *Téléc:* 418-643-2889
jrousselle-vimo@assnat.qc.ca
Sous-ministre associé, Louis Morneau
Directrice de cabinet, Louise Bédard
Directeur, Vérification interne, enquêtes & inspection, Sylvain Ayotte
Tél: 418-644-6777
Directeur, Laboratoire de sciences juridiciaires et de médecine légale, Yves (Bob) Dufour
Directrice, Secrétariat général, Katia Petit
Directeur, Affaires juridiques, Marilyn Thibault

Agences, Conseils et Commissions Associés/ Associated Agencies, Boards & Commissions:

•Bureau du coroner / Office of the Coroner
Édifice le Delta 2
#390, 2875, boul Laurier
Québec, QC G1V 5B1
Tél: 418-643-1845; *Téléc:* 418-643-6174
Ligne sans frais: 866-312-7051
clientele.coroner@msp.gouv.qc.ca
www.coroner.gouv.qc.ca

•Comité de déontologie policière / Police Ethics Committee
Tour du Saint-Laurent
#A-200, 2525, boul Laurier, 2e étage
Québec, QC G1V 4Z6
Tél: 418-646-1936; *Téléc:* 418-528-0987
comite.deontologie@msp.gouv.qc.ca
www.deontologie-policiere.gouv.qc.ca

•Commissaire à la déontologie policière / Police Ethics Commissioner
#1-40, 1200, rte de l'Église
Québec, QC G1V 4Y9
Tél: 418-643-7897; *Téléc:* 418-528-9473
Ligne sans frais: 877-237-7897
deontologie-policiere.quebec@msp.gouv.qc.ca
www.deontologie-policiere.gouv.qc.ca

•Commissaire à la lutte contre la corruption (Unité permanente anticorruption) (UPAC) / Commissioner in the Fight Against Corruption
#UA8010, 600, rue Fullum
Montréal, QC H2K 3L6
Tél: 514-228-3098; *Téléc:* 514-873-0177
Ligne sans frais: 855-567-8722
www.upac.gouv.qc.ca

•Commissariat des incendies / Fire Commissioner
455, rue Dupont
Québec, QC G1K 6N2
Tél: 418-529-5706; *Téléc:* 418-529-9922
securitepublique.gouv.qc.ca/securite-incendie.html

•Commission québecoise des libérations conditionnelles (CQLC) / Parole Board
#1.32A, 300, boul Jean-Lesage
Québec, QC G1K 8K6
Tél: 418-646-8300; *Téléc:* 418-643-7217
cqlc@cqlc.gouv.qc.ca
www.cqlc.gouv.qc.ca

•École nationale de police du Québec (ENPQ) / National Police School of Québec
350, rue Marguerite-d'Youville
Nicolet, QC J3T 1X4
Tél: 819-293-8631; *Téléc:* 819-293-8630
courriel@enpq.qc.ca
www.enpq.qc.ca

•École nationale des pompiers du Québec (ENPQ) / Québec National Fire Fighters School
Palais de justice de Laval
#3.08, 2800, boul Saint-Martin ouest
Laval, QC H7T 2S9
Tél: 450-680-6800; *Téléc:* 450-680-6818
Ligne sans frais: 866-680-3677
enpq@enpq.gouv.qc.ca
www.enpq.gouv.qc.ca

•Régie des alcools, des courses et des jeux (RACJ) / Liquor, Gaming & Racing Board
560, boul Charest est
Québec, QC G1K 3J3
Tél: 418-643-7667; *Téléc:* 418-643-5971
Ligne sans frais: 800-363-0320
www.racj.gouv.qc.ca

Affaires policières / Police Services

Sous-ministre associée, Marie Gagnon
Directrice générale adjointe, Sylvie Tousignant
Tél: 418-646-6777 ext: 601; *Téléc:* 418-644-0132
Directeur principale, Sécurité dans les palais de justice et des affaires autochtones et du nord, Richard Coleman

Directeur (par interim), Sécurité dans les palais de justice, Josée Bilodeau
Directeur, Prévention et de l'organisation policière, Catherine Fournier
Directeur, Intégrité de l'état, et sécurité de l'état (par intérim), Jérôme Gagnon
Directeur, Protection des personnalités, Martin Maranda

Services à la gestion / Administrative Services

Directeur, Ressources humaines, Luc Gadbois
Directeur, Gestion immobilière, Jean Leclerc
Directrice, Ressources financières et matérielles, Lucie Picard

Sécurité civile et sécurité incendie / Public Safety & Fire Services

Tél: 418-643-3500; *Téléc:* 418-643-0275

Sous-ministre associé, Guy Laroche
Tél: 418-643-3500; *Téléc:* 418-643-0275
Directeur, Prévention et de la planification, Raynald Chassé
Directeur, Opérations, Éric Houde
Tél: 418-646-6777 ext: 400; *Téléc:* 418-646-5426
Directeur, Rétablissement, Denis Landry
Tél: 418-646-6638; *Téléc:* 418-646-6628
Directeur (par intérim), Service de l'analyse et des politiques, Marc Morin
2525, boul Laurier, 6e etage
Sainte-Foy, QC G1V 2L2 Canada

Directions régionales/Regional Offices

Bas-Saint-Laurent, Gaspésie et Iles-de-la-Madeleine
#60, 70, rue Saint-Germain est, Rimouski, QC G5L 7J9
Tel: 418-727-3589; *Fax:* 418-727-3643
securite.civile01@msp.gouv.qc.ca

Directeur, Jacques Bélanger

Capitale-Nationale, Chaudière Appalaches et Nunavik
#200, 1122, Grande-Allée ouest, Québec, QC G1S 1E5
Tél: 418-643-3244; *Téléc:* 418-644-2080
securite.civile03@msp.gouv.qc.ca

Directrice, France-Sylvie Loisel

Estrie et Montérégie
165, rue Jacques-Cartier nord, Saint-Jean-sur-Richelieu, QC J3B 6S9
Tél: 450-346-3200; *Téléc:* 450-346-5856
securite.civile16@msp.gouv.qc.ca

Directrice, Christine Savard

Mauricie et Centre-du-Québec
4000, rue Louis-Pinard, Trois-Rivières, QC G8Y 4L9
Tel: 819-371-6703; *Fax:* 819-371-6983
securite.civile04@msp.gouv.qc.ca

Directeur, Sébastien Doire

Montréal, Laval, Lanaudière et Laurentides
RC #23, 5100, rue Sherbrooke est, Montréal, QC H1V 3R9
Tél: 514-873-1300; *Téléc:* 514-864-8654
securite.civile06@msp.gouv.qc.ca
Autres nombres: securite.civile13@msp.gouv.qc.ca; securite.civile14@msp.gouv.qc.ca; securite.civile15@msp.gouv.qc.ca

Directeur, Gilles Desgagnés

Outaouais, Abitibi-Témiscamingue et Nord-du-Québec
817, boul St-René ouest, Gatineau, QC J8T 8M3
Tel: 819-772-3737; *Fax:* 819-772-3954
securite.civile07@msp.gouv.qc.ca

Directeur (par intérim), Gaëtan L. Lessard

Saguenay-Lac-Saint-Jean et Côte-Nord
RC #01, 3950, boul Harvey, Saguenay, QC G7X 8L6
Tel: 418-695-7872; *Fax:* 418-695-7875
securite.civile02@msp.gouv.qc.ca

Directeur, Pierre Dassylva

Services correctionnels / Correctional Services

Sous-ministre associé, Johanne Beausoleil
Directrice générale adjointe, Programmes, à la sécurite et à l'administration, Élaine Raza
Directrice principale (par intérim), Programmes et à la sécurité, Josée Desjardins
Directeur principale, Administration, Louis Robitaille
Tél: 418-646-6777 ext: 500; *Téléc:* 418-643-3426
Directrice, Sécurité, Chantal Robert
Directrice (par intérim), Conseil à l'organisation, Marie-Annick Côté
Directrice, Programmes, Marlène Langlois
Adjointe de la Sous-ministre associée, Brigette Robert

Directions régionales/Regional Offices

Abitibi-Témiscamingue, Nord-du-Québec
851, 3e Rue est, Amos, QC J9T 2T4
Tel: 819-444-5222; *Fax:* 819-444-5298

Directrice (par intérim), Isabel Brodeur

Bas-Saint-Laurent
200, rue des Négociants, Rimouski, QC G5M 1B6
Tel: 418-727-3534; *Fax:* 418-727-3799

Directeur, Michel Levasseur

Côte-Nord
73, av Mance, Baie-Comeau, QC G4Z 1N1
Tel: 418-294-8646; *Fax:* 418-294-8853
Toll-Free: 866-640-3026

Directrice (par intérim), Marie-Josée Dumont

Estrie
1055, rue Talbot, Sherbrooke, QC J1G 2P3
Tel: 819-820-3100; *Fax:* 819-820-3964

Directrice, Kathleen Carroll

Gaspésie-Iles-de-la-Madeleine
#206, 484, Hôtel-de-Ville, Chandler, QC G0C 1K0
Tel: 418-689-4947; *Fax:* 418-689-2478

Directrice, Suzanne Bourget
suzanne.bourget@msp.gouv.qc.ca

Mauricie—Centre-du-Québec
7 600, boul Parent, Trois-Rivières, QC G9A 5E1
Tel: 819-372-1311; *Fax:* 819-371-6979
Toll-Free: 866-292-6281

Directeur (par intérim), Daniel Vivers

Montérégie
75, boul Poliquin, Sorel-Tracy, QC J3P 7Z5
Tel: 450-742-0471; *Fax:* 450-742-8399

Directrice, Stéphanie Smith

Montréal
#11.87, 10, rue Saint-Antoine est, Montréal, QC H2Y 1A2
Tel: 514-864-1800; *Fax:* 514-873-9362

Directeur, Pierre Couture

Outaouais
75, rue Saint-François, Gatineau, QC J9A 1B4
Tel: 819-772-3065; *Fax:* 819-772-3076
Toll-Free: 866-466-7603

Directeur (par intérim), Gérard Murray-Chevrier

Saguenay—Lac-Saint-Jean
237, rue Price est, Saguenay, QC G7H 2E5
Tel: 418-698-3841; *Fax:* 418-690-8560

Directrice (par intérim), Julie Besson

Sûreté du Québec / Québec Provincial Police
1701, rue Parthenais, Montréal, QC H2K 3S7
Tél: 514-598-4141; *Téléc:* 514-598-4242
www.sq.gouv.qc.ca
twitter.com/sureteduquebec
www.facebook.com/policesureteduquebec
www.youtube.com/user/sureteduquebecvideo

Directeur général, Martin Prud'homme
Chef de cabinet, Liette Abel-Normandin
Président, Comité de disipline, Gaston Bellemare
Directeur, Grande fonction de la surveillance du territoire, Sylvain Caron
Directeur, Audit, François Charpentier
Directeur, Grande fonction corporative, Luc Fillion
Directeur, Grande fonction des enquêtes criminelles, et Grande fonction de l'intégrité de l'état, Jocelyn Latulippe
Directeur, Grande fonction de l'administration, Yves Morency

Ministère du Tourisme / Tourism

#400, 900, boul René-Lévesque est, Québec, QC G1R 2B5
Tél: 418-643-5959; *Téléc:* 418-646-8723
Ligne sans frais: 800-482-2433
www.tourisme.gouv.qc.ca

Ministre, L'hon. Julie Boulet
Tél: 418-528-8063; *Téléc:* 418-528-8066
ministre@tourisme.gouv.qc.ca
Sous-ministre par intérim, Patrick Dubé
Tél: 418-643-5959 ext: 341
Adjointe parlementaire, Caroline Simard
Tél: 418-263-0701; *Téléc:* 418-643-9127
Caroline.Simard.CHCB@assnat.qc.ca
Directeur, Affaires institutionnelles et secrétariat, David Belgue
Tél: 418-643-5959 ext: 349
Directeur, Communications, Jean Guay
Tél: 418-643-5959

Agences, Conseils et Commissions Associés/ Associated Agencies, Boards & Commissions:

•Régie des installations olympiques/Parc olympique Québec / Québec Olympic Park
4141, av Pierre-De Coubertin
Montréal, QC H1V 3N7
Tél: 514-252-4141; *Téléc:* 514-252-0372
Ligne sans frais: 877-997-0919
rio@rio.gouv.qc.ca
www.parcolympique.qc.ca

•Société du Centre des congrès de Québec / Québec City Convention Centre
900, boul René-Lévesque est, 2e étage
Québec, QC G1R 2B5
Tél: 418-644-4000; *Téléc:* 418-644-6455
Ligne sans frais: 888-679-4000
www.convention.qc.ca

•Société du Palais des congrès de Montréal / Montréal City Convention Centre
159, rue Saint-Antoine ouest, 9é étage
Montréal, QC H2Z 1H2
Tél: 514-871-8122; *Téléc:* 514-871-9389
Ligne sans frais: 800-268-8122
info@congresmtl.com
congresmtl.com

Développement de l'industrie touristique / Development of the Tourism Industry

Directeur général, Patrick Dubé
Directeur, Conseil, François Belzile
Directeur, Accompagnement des entreprises et de l'aide financière, François Côté
Directeur, Connaissances stratégiques en tourisme, Christian Desbiens
Directeur (par intérim), Planification et de la coordination, Denis Dutilly
Directeur, Interventions stratégiques en tourisme, Steeve Martel

Services à la gestion / Administrative Services

Directrice générale, Clémence Verret
Tél: 418-643-5959 ext: 330
Directeur, Ressources informationelles, Denis Archambault
Directeur, Ressources financières & matérielles, Maryse Chabot
Directrice, Ressources humaines, Valérie Lévesque

Services d'accueil et aux projets majeurs / Services & Major Projects

Sous-ministre adjoint, Martin-Philippe Côté
Directeur exécutive, Coordination des projets majeurs, François Belzile
Directrice, Accueil et de l'hébergement touristiques, Suzanne Asselin
Directrice, Renseignements par téléphone et par internet, Brigitte Hernando

Sous-ministériat au marketing / Marketing

Sous-ministre adjoint, Johanne Dumont
Tél: 514-873-7977 ext: 560
Directeur, Accueil touristique et de l'animation numérique, Julien Cormier
Directeur, Promotion et de la mise en marché, Sylvain Lacombe
Directrice, Centre d'affaires électroniques, Michèle Morel

Ministère des Transports, de la Mobilité durable et de l'Électrification des transports / Ministry of Transport, Sustainable Mobility & Transportation Electrification

700, boul René-Lévesque est, 29e étage, Québec, QC G1R 5H1
Tél: 418-643-6980; *Téléc:* 418-643-2033
Ligne sans frais: 888-355-0511
communications@mtq.gouv.qc.ca
www.transports.gouv.qc.ca
Autres nombres: Au Québec: 5-1-1
Secondary Address: 500, boul René-Lévesque ouest, 16e étage
Montréal, QC H4Z 1W7
Alt. Téléc: 514-873-7886

Ministre, L'hon. Laruent Lessard
Tél: 418-643-6980; *Téléc:* 418-643-2033
Sous-ministre, Denis Marsolais
Tél: 418-643-6740
Adjoint parliamentaire, Ghislain Bolduc
Tél: 418-644-0711; *Téléc:* 418-528-5668
gbolduc-mega@assnat.qc.ca
Directeur, Cabinet du ministre, Pierre Ouellet
Tél: 418-643-6980

Agences, Conseils et Commissions Associés/ Associated Agencies, Boards & Commissions:

•Agence métropolitaine de transport (AMT)
700, rue de la Gauchetière ouest, 26e étage
Montréal, QC H3B 5M2
Tél: 514-287-2464
www.amt.qc.ca

•Commission des transports du Québec / Québec Transport Commission
200, ch Sainte-Foy, 7e étage
Québec, QC G1R 5V5
Tél: 514-873-6424; *Téléc:* 418-644-8034
Ligne sans frais: 888-461-2433
courier@ctq.gouv.qc.ca
www.ctq.gouv.qc.ca

•Société de l'assurance automobile du Québec (SAAQ)
333, boul Jean-Lesage
CP 19600 Terminus
Québec, QC G1K 8J6
Tél: 418-643-7620; *Téléc:* 418-644-0339
Ligne sans frais: 800-361-7620
TTY: 800-565-7763
www.saaq.gouv.qc.ca

•Société des traversiers du Québec / Ferries Québec
250, rue Saint-Paul
Québec, QC G1K 9K9
Tél: 418-643-2019; *Téléc:* 418-643-7308
Ligne sans frais: 877-787-7483
stq@traversiers.gouv.qc.ca
traversiers.com

•Société du port ferroviaire Baie-Comeau-Haute-Rive / Baie-Comeau-Haute-Rive Railway Station
18, rte Maritime
Baie-Comeau, QC G4Z 2L6
Tél: 418-296-6785; *Téléc:* 418-296-2377
societeduport@globetrotter.net
www.sopor.ca

Bureau de la sous-ministre / Office of the Deputy Minister

Sous-ministre, Dominique Savoie
Tél: 418-643-6740
Directrice, Révision des programmes, Louise Boily
Tél: 418-643-6591
Directeur, Centre de gestion de l'équipement roulant, Paul-Yvan Deschênes
Tél: 418-643-5430
Directrice, Bureau de la sous-ministre, Mélanie Drainville
Tél: 418-643-6740
Directeur, Exploitation et services à la clientèle, Carl Gauthier
Tél: 418-643-5430
Directeur, Communications, Yolaine Morency
Tél: 418-644-1537
Directrice, Affaires juridiques, Lise Proulx
Tél: 418-643-6937

Infrastructures et technologies / Infrastructure & Technologies

Directrice générale et sous-ministre adjointe, Anne-Marie Leclerc
Tél: 418-528-0808
Directeur, Structures, Daniel Bouchard
Tél: 418-643-6906
Directeur, Soutien aux opérations, Éric Breton
Tél: 418-643-9298
Directeur, Environnement et recherche, Danielle Fleury
Tél: 418-643-8326
Directeur, Laboratoire des chaussées, Guy Tremblay
Tél: 418-643-6618

Surveillance des marchés et de l'administration / Market Supervision & Administration

Directrice générale et sous-ministre adjointe, Danièle Cantin
Tél: 418-528-0808
Directeur général adjoint, Ressources humaines, financières et informationnelles, Martin Fortier
Tél: 418-266-8086
Directeur, Soutien à la gestion des ressources, Jean-Sébastien Dumont
Tél: 418-643-6993
Directeur, Contrats, Donald Desjardins
Tél: 418-643-5473
Directrice, Ressources humaines, Brigitte Duchesne
Tél: 418-646-4157
Directeur (par intérim), Technologies de l'information, Martin Fortier
Tél: 418-643-4431
Directrice, Surveillance des marchés et observation des règles contractuelles, Nathalie Noël
Tél: 418-266-8084
Directrice, Gestion financière et expertise immobilière, Lise Roberge
Tél: 418-644-2182

Territoires / Territories

Directeur général et sous-ministre associé, André Caron
Tél: 418-528-0808
Directrice générale adjointe et sous-ministre adjointe, Projet Turcot et du suivi des projets routiers, Chantal Gingras
Tél: 514-864-1850
Directrice générale adjointe et sous-ministre adjointe, Projets stratégiques, Marie-France Bérard
Tél: 514-864-1850
Directeur général adjoint, Coordination des ressources territoriales, Richard Dionne
Tél: 514-529-0808
Directrice, Programmation et ressources territoriales, Odile Béland
Tél: 418-643-7726
Directeur, Projet Turcot, Stéphan Deschênes
Tél: 514-873-3838
Directeur, Suivi des projets routiers, Jean Douville
Tél: 514-864-1730
Directeur, Opérations d'exploitation routière et aéroportuaire, Jean-François Harvey
Tél: 418-643-1490
Directrice, Ile-de-Montréal, Fadi Moubayed
Tél: 514-873-7781
Directeur, Projets routiers stratégiques, Maroun Shaneen
Tél: 514-940-2960

Directions régionales/Regional Offices

Abitibi-Témiscamingue
80, av Québec, Rouyn-Noranda, QC J9X 6R1
Tél: 819-763-3271; *Téléc:* 819-763-3493
dat@mtq.gouv.qc.ca

Directeur régional, Yves Coutu
Tél: 819-763-3237

Bas-Saint-Laurent—Gaspésie—Îles-de-la-Madeleine
#101, 92, 2e rue ouest, Rimouski, QC G5L 8E6
Tél: 418-727-3674; *Téléc:* 418-727-3673
dtbgi@mtq.gouv.qc.ca

Directeur régional, Richard Dionne
Tél: 418-727-3674

Capitale-Nationale
475, boul de l'Atrium, 2e étage, Québec, QC G1H 7H9
Tél: 418-643-1911; *Téléc:* 418-646-0003
dcnat@mtq.gouv.qc.ca

Directeur régional, Jean-François Saulnier
Tél: 418-380-2003

Chaudière-Appalaches
1156, boul de la Rive-Sud, Saint-Romuald, QC G6W 5M6
Tél: 418-839-5581; *Téléc:* 418-834-7338
dtca@mtq.gouv.qc.ca

Directeur régional, Richard Charpentier
Tél: 418-839-5581

Côte-Nord
#110, 625, boul Laflèche, Baie-Comeau, QC G5C 1C5
Tél: 418-295-4765; *Téléc:* 418-295-4766
cotenord@mtq.gouv.qc.ca

Directeur régional, Michel Bérubé
Tél: 418-295-4778

Est-de-la-Montérégie
201, place Charles-Lemoyne, 5e étage, Longueuil, QC J4K 2T5
Tél: 450-677-3413; *Téléc:* 450-442-1317
dtem@mtq.gouv.qc.ca

Directeur régional, Daniel Donais
Tél: 450-677-8974

Estrie
#2.02, 200, rue Belvédère nord, Sherbrooke, QC J1H 4A9
Tél: 819-820-3280; *Téléc:* 819-820-3118
dte@mtq.gouv.qc.ca

Directeur régional, Gilles Bourque
Tél: 819-820-3280

Île-de-Montréal
500, boul René-Lévesque ouest, 12e étage, CP 5 Montréal, QC H2Z 1W7
Tél: 514-873-7781; *Téléc:* 514-864-3867
dtim@mtq.gouv.qc.ca

Directeur régional (par intérim), Maroun Shaneen
Tél: 514-873-7781

Laurentides-Lanaudière
222, rue Saint-Georges, 2e étage, Saint-Jérôme, QC J7Z 4Z9
Tél: 450-569-3057; *Téléc:* 450-569-3072
dll@mtq.gouv.qc.ca

Directrice régional, Sylvie Laroche
Tél: 450-569-7414

Laval—Mille-Îles
1725, boul Le Corbusier, Laval, QC H7S 2K7
Tél: 450-680-6330; *Téléc:* 450-973-4959
dtlmi@mtq.gouv.qc.ca

Directrice régionale, Odile Béland
Tél: 450-680-6333

Mauricie—Centre-du-Québec
100, rue Laviolette, 4e étage, Trois-Rivières, QC G9A 5S9
Tél: 819-371-6896; *Téléc:* 819-371-6136
dmcq@mtq.gouv.qc.ca

Directeur régional, Carl Bélanger
Tél: 819-371-6896

Ouest-de-la-Montérégie
#200, 180, boul d'Anjou, Châteauguay, QC J6K 1C4
Tél: 450-698-3400; *Téléc:* 450-698-3452
dtom@mtq.gouv.qc.ca

Directrice régional, Joceline Béland
Tél: 450-698-3400

Outaouais
#5.110, 170, rue de l'Hôtel-de-Ville, Gatineau, QC J8X 4C2
Tél: 819-772-3849; *Téléc:* 819-772-3338
dto@mtq.gouv.qc.ca

Directeur général, Jacques Henry
Tél: 819-772-3107

Saguenay—Lac-Saint-Jean—Chibougamau
3950, boul Harvey, Jonquière, QC G7X 8L6
Tél: 418-695-7916; *Téléc:* 418-695-7926
dt.slsjc@mtq.gouv.qc.ca

Directeur régional, Donald Turgeon
Tél: 418-695-7916

Transport collectif, des politiques et de la sécurité / Transit, Politics & Security

Directeur général et sous-ministre adjoint, André Meloche
Tél: 418-528-0808
Directeur général adjoint, Parcs routiers et des relations extérieures; Directeur principale (par intérim), Service aérien gouvernemental, Claude Morin
Tél: 418-266-6648
Directeur, Parcs routiers, Paul Bergeron
Tél: 418-646-8301
Directeur, Transport routier des marchandises, Yanick Blouin
Tél: 418-528-0631
Directeur, Opérations aériennes, Benoît Bouchard
Tél: 418-528-8320
Directeur, Transport terrestre des personnes, Martin Breault
Tél: 418-644-0324
Directrice, Sécurité en transport, France Dompierre
Tél: 418-643-1564
Directrice, Transport maritime, aérien et ferroviaire, Josée Hallé
Tél: 418-643-1864
Directeur, Aéronefs, Jean-François Lachance
Tél: 418-528-8350
Directrice, Planification, Évangéline Lévesque
Tél: 418-644-0447
Directrice, Optimisation et relations avec les partenaires, Valérie Perron
Tél: 418-528-8385

Ministère du Travail, de l'Emploi et de la Solidarité sociale / Labour, Employment & Social Solidarity

200, ch Sainte-Foy, 5e étage, Québec, QC G1R 5S1
Tél: 418-644-4545; *Téléc:* 418-528-0559
Ligne sans frais: 877-644-4545
www.travail.gouv.qc.ca
Autres nombres: Emploi et de la Solidarité sociale: www.mess.gouv.qc.ca
twitter.com/TravailQuebec

Ministre de l'Emploi et de la Solidarité sociale, L'hon. François Blais
Tél: 418-643-4810; *Téléc:* 418-643-2802
ministre@mess.gouv.qc.ca
Ministre responsable du Travail, L'hon. Dominique Vien
Tél: 418-643-7623; *Téléc:* 418-643-8098
ministre@travail.gouv.qc.ca
Sous-ministre, Bernard Matte
Adjointe parlementaire du ministre de l'Emploi et de la Solidarité sociale, Monique Sauvé
Tél: 418-263-0554; *Téléc:* 418-643-2953
Monique.Sauve.FABR@assnat.qc.ca
Adjoint parlementaire de la ministre responsable du Travail, Yves St-Denis
Tél: 418-528-6379; *Téléc:* 418-643-0183
Yves.St-Denis.ARGE@assnat.qc.ca
Sous-ministre adjoint, Normand Pelletier
Sous-ministre adjoint, Jean Poirier
Directeur, Comité consultatif du travail et de la main-d'oeuvre, François Lamoureux
Directeur, Cabinet, Steeve LeBlanc
Directeur, Vérification interne et enquêtes administratives, Sylvain Massé
Directrice, Bureau du sous-ministre et Secrétarie générale, Anne Moore

Directrice, Affaires juridiques, Mélanie Paradis
Directrice, Ressources humaines, Nathalie Tremblay

Agences, Conseils et Commissions Associés/ Associated Agencies, Boards & Commissions:

•Comité consultatif de lutte contre la pauvreté et l'exclusion sociale (CCLP) / Advisory Committee on the Fight Against Poverty & Social Exclusion
425, rue Saint-Amable, RC 145
Québec, QC G1R 4Z1
Tél: 418-528-9866; *Téléc:* 418-643-6623
infocclp@mess.gouv.qc.ca
www.cclp.gouv.qc.ca

•Commission de la construction du Québec (CCQ) / Québec Construction Commission
8485, av Christophe-Colomb
Montréal, QC H2M 0A7
Tél: 514-341-7740
Ligne sans frais: 888-842-8282
www.ccq.org

•Commission de la santé et de la sécurité du travail (CSST) / Occupational Health & Safety Commission
See Entry Name Index for detailed listing.

•Commission de l'équité salariale (CES) / Pay Equity Commission
200, ch Ste-Foy, 4e étage
Québec, QC G1R 6A1
Tél: 418-528-8765; *Téléc:* 418-528-6999
Ligne sans frais: 888-528-8765
equite.salariale@ces.gouv.qc.ca
www.ces.gouv.qc.ca

•Commission des lésions professionnelles (CLP) / Work-Related Injuries Commission
#700, 900, Place d'Youville
Québec, QC G1R 3P7
Tél: 418-644-7777; *Téléc:* 418-644-6443
Ligne sans frais: 800-463-1591
www.clp.gouv.qc.ca
Administrative tribunal that is the last recourse for employers or workers who contest a decision made by the Commission de la santé et de la sécurité du travail.

•Commission des normes du travail (CNT) / Labour Standards Commission
Hall Est
400, boul Jean-Lesage, 7e étage
Québec, QC G1K 8W1
Tél: 514-873-7061; *Téléc:* 418-646-3678
Ligne sans frais: 800-265-1414
www.cnt.gouv.qc.ca

•Commission des partenaires du marché du travail / Labour Market Partnerships Commission
Tour de la Place-Victoria
800, rue du Square-Victoria, 28e étage
CP 100
Montréal, QC H4Z 1B7
Tél: 514-873-5252
Ligne sans frais: 800-334-6728
partenaires@mess.gouv.qc.ca
www.cpmt.gouv.qc.ca

•Commission des relations du travail (CRT) / Labour Relations Commission
Hall est
900, boul René-Lévesque est, 5e étage
Québec, QC G1R 6C9
Tél: 418-643-3208; *Téléc:* 418-643-8946
Ligne sans frais: 866-864-3646
crtq@crt.gouv.qc.ca
www.crt.gouv.qc.ca

•Conseil consultatif du travail et de la main d'oeuvre (CCTM) / Advisory Council on Labour & Manpower
#17.100, 500, boul René-Lévesque ouest
Montréal, QC H2Z 1W7
Tél: 514-873-2880; *Téléc:* 514-873-1129
cctm@cctm.gouv.qc.ca
www.cctm.gouv.qc.ca

•Conseil de gestion de l'assurance parentale (CGAP) / Management Board of Parental Insurance
#104, 1122, Grande Allée ouest
Québec, QC G1S 1E5
Tél: 418-643-1009; *Téléc:* 418-643-6738
Ligne sans frais: 888-610-7727
www.cgap.gouv.qc.ca
Autres numéros: Régime fédéral d'assurance-emploi: 1-800-808-6352

•Directeur de l'état civil / Vital Statistics
2535, boul Laurier
Québec, QC G1V 5C5
Tél: 418-644-4545
Ligne sans frais: 877-644-4545
TTY: 800-361-9596
etatcivil@dec.gouv.qc.ca
www.etatcivil.gouv.qc.ca
Autres numéros: Montréal: 514-644-4545

•Office de la sécurité du revenu des chasseurs et piègeurs cris / Cree Hunters & Trappers Income Security Board
Édifice Champlain
#1100, 2700, boul Laurier
Québec, QC G1V 4K5
Tél: 418-643-7300; *Téléc:* 418-643-6803
Ligne sans frais: 800-363-1560
courrier@osrcpc.ca
www.osrcpc.ca

•Régie des rentes du Québec (RRQ) / Québec Pension Board
CP 5200
Sainte-Foy, QC G1K 7S9
Tél: 418-643-5185
Ligne sans frais: 800-463-5185
www.rrq.gouv.qc.ca
Autres numéros: Montréal: 514-873-2433

•Régie du bâtiment du Québec (RBQ) / Québec Construction Companies Board
545, boul Crémazie est, 4e étage
Montréal, QC H2M 2V2
Tél: 514-873-0976; *Téléc:* 866-315-0106
Ligne sans frais: 800-361-0761
crc@rbq.gouv.qc.ca
www.rbq.gouv.qc.ca

Développement des services aux citoyens et gouvernance / Development of Citizen & Government Services
Sous-ministre adjoint, Patrick Grenier
Tel: 418-644-0425 ext: 357
Directeur, Communications, Thierry Audin
Tel: 418-646-0425 ext: 672
Directeur, État civil, Reno Bernier
Tél: 418-643-1447 ext: 230
Directeur, Mandats stratégiques et amélioration continue, Daniel Guay
Tel: 418-646-0425 ext: 380
Directeur, Orientations et partenariat de Services Québec, Guy Larose
Tel: 418-646-0425 ext: 663
Directeur, Plaintes et relations avec la clientèle, Laurence Mosseray
Tel: 418-646-0425 ext: 422

Régime québécois d'assurance parentale (RQAP) / Québec Parental Insurance Plan
19, rue Perreault ouest, 1er étage, Rouyn-Noranda, QC J9X 0A1
Tél: 418-643-7246
Ligne sans frais: 888-610-7727
www.rqap.gouv.qc.ca
Directeur général, Martin Bouchard
Tél: 418-528-7727 ext: 891

Emploi-Québec / Employment Québec
Direction du Centre de communication avec la clientèle, 150, rue Monseigneur-Ross, 5e étage, Gaspé, QC G4X 2S7
Tél: 514-873-4000
Ligne sans frais: 877-767-8773
emploiquebec.gouv.qc.ca
twitter.com/emploi_quebec
www.facebook.com/emploiquebec
www.youtube.com/user/promomess
Sous-ministre associé et secrétaire générale de la CPMT, Johanne Bourassa
Tél: 514-365-4543 ext: 262
Directeur générale adjointe, Budget d'Emploi-Québec, Johanne Blanchette
Tél: 514-873-0800 ext: 351
Directeur générale adjointe, Planification et du marché du travail, Richard St-Pierre
Tél: 514-864-3660

Mesures, services et soutien / Measures, Services & Support
Directrice générale adjointe, Guylaine Larose
Tél: 418-646-0425 ext: 340

Opérations territoriales / Regional Operations
Sous-ministre adjointe, Martine Bégin
Tél: 418-646-0425 ext: 484
Directrice générale adjointe, Île-de-Montréal, Johanne Beaulieu
Tél: 514-725-5221 ext: 210
Directeur générale adjointe, Enquêtes et conformité, Denis Laporte
Tél: 418-644-0575 ext: 463
Directrice générale adjointe, Déploiement territorial, Marie-Andrée Matte
Tél: 418-646-0800 ext: 135
Directeur générale adjointe, Opérations du Sud et de l'Ouest, Lorraine St-Cyr
Tél: 514-873-0800 ext: 387
Directeur générale adjointe, Opérations du Nord et de l'Est, Roger Tremblay
Tél: 418-646-0425 ext: 886

Politiques, analyse stratégique et action communautaire / Policy, Strategic Analysis & Community Action
Sous-ministre adjointe, Chantal Maltais
Tél: 418-646-0425 ext: 355
Directeur générale adjointe, Solidarité et action communautaire, Daniel Jean
Tél: 418-646-9270 ext: 657
Directrice générale adjointe, Statistique, information de gestion et suivi de la performance, Brigitte Mercier
Tél: 418-646-0425 ext: 499
Directeur, Secrétariat à l'action communautaire autonome et aux initiatives sociales, Lucie Goulet
Tél: 418-646-0425 ext: 867

Politiques et recherche / Policy & Research
Sous-ministre adjoint, Anne Parent
Tél: 418-643-7458
Directeur, Politiques du travail, Steeve Audet
Tél: 418-644-1639
Directeur, Information sur le travail, Charles Bélanger
Tél: 418-643-7572
Directeur, Recherche et innovation en milieu de travail, Louis Tremblay
Tél: 418-646-1893

Relations avec la clientèle / Client Relations
Sous-ministre adjoint, Jean Audet
Tél: 418-646-0425 ext: 427
Directrice générale adjointe, Recouvrement, révision et recours administratifs, Esther Quirion
Tél: 418-646-0425 ext: 617
Directrice générale adjointe, Relations avec la clientèle, Yves Pepin
Tél: 418-644-0425 ext: 891

Relations du travail / Labour Relations
Sous-ministre adjointe, Suzanne Thérien
Tél: 514-873-4678
Directeur, Relations du travail, Sylvain Gonthier
Tél: 514-873-1999
Directeur (par intérim), Bureau d'évaluation médicale, Dr Rémi Côté
Tél: 418-643-5899
Directeur, Médiation-conciliation & prévention (Montréal), Robert Dupuis
Tél: 514-873-0516
Directeur (par intérim), Médiation-conciliation, prévention & arbitrage (Québec), Jean Nolin
Tél: 418-643-8792

Secrétariat du Travail / Labour Secretariat
Sous-ministre associée, Manuelle Oudar
Tel: 418-643-5127
Directeur, Bureau de la sous-ministre associée, Robert Bédard
Tel: 418-643-2795
Directeur, Comité consultatif du travail et de la main-d'ouvre, François Lamoureux
Tel: 514-873-2880

Services à la gestion et ressources informationnelles / Administrative Services & Information Resources
Sous-ministre adjoint, Pierre E. Rodrigue
Tél: 418-646-0425 ext: 668
Directrice, Technologies de l'information, Nicole Boucher
Tél: 418-646-0425 ext: 652
Directeur, Ressources matérielles, Richard Dumais
Tél: 418-646-0425 ext: 354
Directrice, Portefeuille de projets, Denise Latulippe
Tél: 418-646-0800 ext: 133
Directrice, Conception et architecture, Nathalie Levasseur
Tél: 418-646-0425 ext: 660
Directeur, Services à la gestion, Etienne Sabourin
Tél: 418-646-0800 ext: 149

Services Québec
Bureau de la qualité, 800, place D'Youville, 20e étage, Québec, QC G1R 3P4
www.mess.gouv.qc.ca/services-quebec
twitter.com/servicesquebec
www.facebook.com/ServicesQuebec
www.linkedin.com/company/services-qu-bec
www.youtube.com/servicesquebec

Les Publications du Québec
1000 rte de l'Église, 5e étage, Québec, QC G1V 3V9
Tél: 418-643-5150; *Téléc:* 418-643-6177
Ligne sans frais: 800-463-2100
publicationsduquebec@cspq.gouv.qc.ca
www.publicationsduquebec.gouv.qc.ca
Autres nombres: Téléc sans frais: 1-800-561-3479
www.facebook.com/PublicationsQuebec

Secrétariat du Conseil du trésor / Treasury Board

875, Grande Allée est, 5e étage, secteur 500, Québec, QC G1R 5R8
Tél: 418-643-1529; *Téléc:* 418-643-9226
Ligne sans frais: 866-552-5158
communication@sct.gouv.qc.ca
www.tresor.gouv.qc.ca

Ministre des Finances; Ministre responsable de l'Administration gouvernementale et de la Révision permanente des programmes, et Président du Conseil du trésor, L'hon. Carlos J. Leitao
Tél: 418-643-5270; *Téléc:* 418-646-1574
ministre@finances.gouv.qc.ca
Secrétaire, Yves Ouellet
Tél: 418-643-1977; *Téléc:* 418-643-6494
communication@sct.gouv.qc.ca
Greffière, Marie-Claude Rioux
Tél: 418-643-0875 ext: 420
Adjoint parlementaire du ministre responsable de l'Administration gouvernementale et de la Révision permanente des programmes, et président du Conseil du trésor, Richard Merlini
Tél: 418-644-1489; *Téléc:* 418-644-1872
Richard.Merlini.LAPR@assnat.qc.ca
Directeur (par intérim), Vérification interne, Marc Samson
Tél: 418-643-0875 ext: 493
Directrice, Affaires juridiques, Josée De Bellefeuille
Tél: 418-643-0875 ext: 426
Directrice, Communications, Colette Duval

Agences, Conseils et Commissions Associés/ Associated Agencies, Boards & Commissions:

•Centre du services partagés du Québec (CSPQ) / Québec Shared Services Centre
875, Grande Allée est, 4e étage, section 4.751
Québec, QC G1R 5W5
Tél: 418-644-2777; *Téléc:* 418-644-0462
Ligne sans frais: 855-644-2777
cspq@cspq.gouv.qc.ca
www.cspq.gouv.qc.ca
Autres numéros: Alt. Courriel: commentaires-plaintes@cspq.gouv.qc.ca

•Commission administrative des régimes de retraite et d'assurances (Québec) (CARRA) / Retirement & Insurance Planning Commission
475, rue Saint-Amable
Québec, QC G1R 5X3
Tél: 418-643-4881; *Téléc:* 418-644-3839
Ligne sans frais: 800-463-5533
www.carra.gouv.qc.ca

•Commission de la capitale nationale du Québec (CCNQ)
Edifice Hector-Fabre
525 boul René-Lévesque Est, RC
Québec, QC G1R 5S9
Tél: 418-528-0773; *Téléc:* 418-528-0833
Ligne sans frais: 800-442-0773
commission@capitale.gouv.qc.ca
www.capitale.gouv.qc.ca

•Commission de la fonction publique (Québec) / Public Service Commission
800, Place d'Youville, 7e étage
Québec, QC G1R 3P4
Tél: 418-643-1425; *Téléc:* 418-643-7264
Ligne sans frais: 800-432-0432
cfp@cfp.gouv.qc.ca
www.cfp.gouv.qc.ca
The Commission works towards the following goals: to ensure equal access for all citizens to the public service; to ensure the competence of persons recruited & promoted; & to guarantee the fairness of decisions in human resources management.

•Société québécoise des infrastructures / Infrastructure
Édifice Marie-Fitzbach
1075, rue de l'Amérique-Française, 1er étage
Québec, QC G1R 5P8
Tél: 418-646-1766; *Téléc:* 418-646-6911
courrier@sqi.gouv.qc.ca
www.sqi.gouv.qc.ca
Autres numéros: Bureau des plaintes, Tél: 418-644-4542; Téléc: 418-528-2999; Courrier: plainte@sqi.gouv.qc.ca

Administration
Directeur général, Yvan Bouchard
Directrice, Opérations financières et matérielles, Suzanne Dorval
Directeur, Ressources humaines, France Normand
Directeur, Ressources financières et de l'information de gestion, Guillaume Quirion

Ressources informationnelles / Information Resources
Directrice générale, Alexandre Mailhot

Bureau de la gouvernance en gestion des ressources humaines / Office of Governance & Human Resources Management
Directrice principale, Jocelyne Tremblay
Directrice générale, Gouvernance des systèmes en ressources humaines, Michelle Rhéaume
Directrice, Stratégies d'évaluation et de planification de la main-d'ouvre, Marie-Claude Corbeil-Gravel
Directrice, Gestion de la main-d'ouvre, Francine Massé
Directrice, Maîtrise d'ouvrage des systèmes en ressources humaines, Carolle Nolin
Directrice, Développement des personnes et des organisations, Claire Villeneuve

Bureau de la révision permanente des programmes / Office of Ongoing Program Review
Secrétaire associée, Brigitte Portelance
Directeur général, Révision des programmes; Directeur (par intérim), Évaluation et de la révision des programmes, Renée Berger
Directrice, Application de la Loi sur l'administration publique, Isabelle Desbiens

Sous-secrétariat à la négociation intersectorielle et aux relations de travail fonction publique / Secretariat for Intersectoral Negotiation & Public Service Labour Relations
Secrétaire associée, Édith Lapointe
Tel: 418-643-0875 ext: 460
Directeur général, Relations de travail, secteur fonction publique, Jean-Philippe Day

Sous-secrétariat aux infrastructures publiques / Public Infrastructure
Secrétaire associé, Jacques Caron

Sous-secrétariat aux marchés publics / Public Markets
Tél: 418-643-1529; *Téléc:* 418-643-9226
marches.publics@sct.gouv.qc.ca
Secrétaire associée, Julie Blackburn
Tél: 418-643-0875 ext: 490
Directrice générale, Encadrement des contrats publics, Marie-Josée Fournier
Tél: 418-643-0875 ext: 497
Directeur général, Politiques de marchés publics, Marc Samson
Tél: 418-643-0875 ext: 493

Sous-secrétariat aux politiques budgétaires et aux programmes / Budget Policies & Programs
Secrétaire associée, Jean-François Lachaine
Tél: 418-643-0875 ext: 450
Directrice générale, Programmes économiques, éducatifs et culturels, Anne Boucher
Tél: 418-643-0875 ext: 455
Directeur général (par intérim), Programmes administratifs, sociaux & de santé, Serge Garon
Tél: 418-643-0875 ext: 453
Directeur général, Politiques & opérations budgétaires, Carl Lessard
Tél: 418-643-0875 ext: 451

Sous-secrétariat à la coordination intersectorielle des négociations et à la rémunération globale / Secretariat for Intersectoral Coordination of Negotiations & Overall Compensation
Secrétaire associée, Dominique Gauthier
Tél: 418-643-0875 ext: 460
Directeur général, Rémunération globale, René Dufresne
Directeur général, Coordination des négociations, Jean-Olivier Ferron
Tél: 418-643-0875 ext: 487
Directrice principale, Rémunération directe, Caroline Beauregard

Sous-secrétariat du dirigeant principal de l'information / Office of the Chief Information Officer
Secrétaire associé, Benoît Boivin
Tél: 418-643-0875 ext: 500
Directrice générale (par intérim), Performance gouvernementale des ressources informationnelles; Directrice (par intérim), Qualité des données et soutien aux DI; Directrice, Optimisation des ressources informationnelles et de la performance en projet, Jenny Côté
Tél: 418-643-0875 ext: 515
Directeur général, Orientations gouvernementales en ressources informationnelles, Bertrand Lauzon
Tél: 418-643-0875 ext: 514

Vérificateur général du Québec / Auditor General

750, boulevard Charest est, 3e étage, Québec, QC G1K 9J6
Tél: 418-691-5900; *Téléc:* 418-644-4460
verificateur.general@vgq.gouv.qc.ca
www.vgq.gouv.qc.ca
Secondary Address: #1910, 770, rue Sherbrooke ouest
Montréal, QC H3A 1G1
Alt. Téléc: 514-873-7665
Le Vérificateur général du Québec a pour mission de favoriser par la vérification le contrôle parlementaire sur les fonds et autres biens publics.
Vérificatrice générale, Guylaine Leclerc, FCPA auditrice, FCA
Vérificateur général adjoint, Commissaire au développement durable, Jean Cinq-Mars, B.Sc. (Hons.) M.A.P.
Vérificateur général adjoint, Marcel Couture, CPA auditeur, CA
Vérificateur général adjoint, Jean-Pierre Fiset, CPA auditeur, CA
Vérificateur général adjoint, Serge Giguère, CPA auditeur, CA
Vérificateur général adjoint, Michel Samson, FCPA auditeur, FCA

Government of Saskatchewan

Seat of Government: 2405 Legislative Dr., Regina, SK S4S 0B3
www.saskatchewan.ca
twitter.com/SKGov
www.facebook.com/SKGov
The Province of Saskatchewan entered Confederation on September 1, 1905. It has a land area of 588,276.09 sq km, & the StatsCan census population in 2011 was 1,033,381.

Office of the Lieutenant Governor

Government House, 4607 Dewdney Ave., Regina, SK S4T 1B7
Tel: 306-787-4070; *Fax:* 306-787-7716
lgo@ltgov.sk.ca
ltgov.sk.ca
Other Communication: Authentication of Documents, Phone: 306-787-2951
twitter.com/vaughnschofield
www.facebook.com/LtGovSk
The position of the Lieutenant Governor is apolitical & non-partisan. Her Honour the Honourable Vaughn Solomon Schofield, Lieutenant Governor of Saskatchewan, is the representative of The Queen in Saskatchewan.
Some responsibilities of the Lieutenant Governor are as follows: presiding over the swearing in of the Premier, cabinet ministers, & the Chief Justice of Saskatchewan; delivering the Speech from the Throne; giving Royal Assent to acts of the Legislative Assembly; participating in commemorative ceremonies & provincial celebrations; & honouring achievements.
Lieutenant Governor of Saskatchewan, Hon. Vaughn Solomon Schofield, SOM, SVM
Note: The Lieutenant Governor's full title is Her Honour the Honourable Vaughn Solomon Schofield, Lieutenant Governor of Saskatchewan
Executive Director & Private Secretary, Heather Salloum
Tel: 306-787-4070
hsalloum@ltgov.sk.ca

Office of the Premier

Legislative Building, #226, 2405 Legislative Dr., Regina, SK S4S 0B3
Tel: 306-787-9433; *Fax:* 306-787-0885
www.premier.gov.sk.ca
www.youtube.com/user/SaskPremier
In November 2011, Brad Wall was re-elected Premier of Saskatchewan.
Premier; President, Executive Council; Minister, Intergovernmental Affairs, Hon. Brad Wall
Tel: 306-787-9433; *Fax:* 306-787-0885
premier@gov.sk.ca
Social Media: twitter.com/PremierBradWall, www.facebook.com/PremierBradWall

Executive Council

Communications Services, Executive Council, #130, 3085 Albert St., Regina, SK S4S 0B1

Tel: 306-787-6276; *Fax:* 306-787-6123
Other Communication: Cabinet URL: www.saskatchewan.ca/government/government-structure/cabinet

Appointed by the Premier of Saskatchewan, each cabinet minister is responsible for a ministry or portfolio.

Premier; President, Executive Council; Minister, Intergovernmental Affairs, Hon. Brad Wall
Tel: 306-787-9433; *Fax:* 306-787-0885
premier@gov.sk.ca
www.premier.gov.sk.ca
Social Media: twitter.com/PremierBradWall, www.facebook.com/PremierBradWall
#226, 2405 Legislative Dr.
Regina, SK S4S 0B3

Deputy Premier; Minister, Education; Minister, Labour Relations & Workplace Safety; Minister Responsible, Saskatchewan Workers' Compensation Board, Hon. Don Morgan, Q.C.
Tel: 306-787-0613; *Fax:* 306-787-6946
minister.edu@gov.sk.ca
Office of the Minister of Education / Labour Relation & Workplace Safety, Legislative Bldg.
#361, 2405 Legislative Dr.
Regina, SK S4S 0B3

Minister, Energy & Resources; Minister Responsible, SaskEnergy Incorporated; Saskatchewan Telecommunications, Hon. Dustin Duncan
Tel: 306-787-0804; *Fax:* 306-798-2009
Office of the Minister of Economy, Legislative Building
#340, 2405 Legislative Dr.
Regina, SK S4S 0B3

Minister, Crown Investments Corporation; Minister, Saskatchewan Government Insurance; Minister, Saskatchewan Transportation Corporation, Hon. Joe Hargrave
minister.cc@gov.sk.ca
Office of the Minister of Crown Investments, Legislative Building
#302, 2405 Legislative Dr.
Regina, SK S4S 0B3

Minister, Government Relations; Minister Responsible, First Nations, Métis & northern affairs, Hon. Donna Harpauer
Tel: 306-787-3661; *Fax:* 306-787-0656
Social Media: www.facebook.com/60494388240
Office of the Minister of Social Services, Legislative Building
#303, 2405 Legislative Dr.
Regina, SK S4S 0B3

Minister, Finance, Hon. Kevin Doherty
Tel: 306-787-0341; *Fax:* 306-798-0263
fin.minister@gov.sk.ca
Social Media: www.linkedin.com/in/dmaniii
Office of the Minister of Finance, Legislative Building
#312, 2405 Legislative Dr.
Regina, SK S4S 0B3

Minister, Health, Hon. Jim Reiter
he.minister@gov.sk.ca
Office of the Minister of Health, Legislative Building
#204, 2405 Legislative Dr.
Regina, SK S4S 0B3

Minister, Justice & Attorney General; Minister Responsible, SaskBuilds, Saskatchewan Power Corporation, Hon. Gordon Wyant, Q.C.
Tel: 306-787-5353; *Fax:* 306-787-1232
jus.minister@gov.sk.ca
Social Media: twitter.com/GordWyant
Office of the Minister of Justice & Attorney General, Legislative Building
#355, 2405 Legislative Dr.
Regina, SK S4S 0B3

Minister, Agriculture; Minister Responsible, Saskatchewan Crop Insurance Corporation, Hon. Lyle Stewart
Tel: 306-787-0338; *Fax:* 306-787-0630
minister.ag@gov.sk.ca
Office of the Minister of Agriculture, Legislative Building
#334, 2405 Legislative Dr.
Regina, SK S4S 0B3

Minister, Highways & Infrastructure, Hon. David Marit
hi.minister@gov.sk.ca
Office of the Minister of Highways & Infrastructure, Legislative Building
#302, 2405 Legislative Dr.
Regina, SK S4S 0B3

Minister, Central Services; Minister responsible, Provincial Capital Commission, Saskatchewan Gaming Corporation, Hon. Christine Tell
Tel: 306-787-0942; *Fax:* 306-787-8677
Social Media: www.facebook.com/christinetellsp
Office of the Minister Responsible, Corrections & Policing, Legislative Building
#345, 2405 Legislative Dr.
Regina, SK S4S 0B3

Minister, Economy; Minister responsible, Global Transportation Hub, Saskatchewan Liquor & Gaming Authority, Hon. Jeremy Harrison
Tel: 306-787-4300; *Fax:* 306-787-3174
Jeremy.Harrison@gov.sk.ca
Office of the Minister Responsible for Immigration, Legislative Building
#346, 2405 Legislative Dr.
Regina, SK S4S 0B3

Minister, Social Services; Minister Responsible, Status of Women, Hon. Tina Beaudry-Mellor
Office of the Minister of Central Services, Legislative Building
#306, 2405 Legislative Dr.
Regina, SK S4S 0B3

Minister, Parks, Culture & Sport; Minister Responsible, Public Service Commission, Hon. Ken Cheveldayoff
minister.pcs@gov.sk.ca
Office of the Minister of Parks, Culture & Sport, Legislative Building
#315, 2405 Legislative Dr.
Regina, SK S4S 0B3

Minister, Advanced Education, Hon. Bronwyn Eyre
Office of the Minister of Finance, Legislative Building
#38, 2405 Legislative Dr.
Regina, SK S4S 0B3

Minister, Environment; Minister responsible, Saskatchewan Water Corporation, Saskatchewan Water Security Agency, Hon. Scott Moe
Tel: 306-787-0341; *Fax:* 306-798-0263
Office of the Minister of Advanced Education, Legislative Building
#307, 2405 Legislative Dr.
Regina, SK S4S 0B3

Minister Responsible, Rural & Remote Health; Government Whip, Hon. Greg Ottenbreit
Tel: 306-798-9014; *Fax:* 306-798-9013
minister.rrhe@gov.sk.ca
Office of the Minister of Rural & Remote Health, Legislative Building
#208, 2405 Legislative Dr.
Regina, SK S4S 0B3

Cabinet Secretariat

Legislative Building, #145, 2405 Legislative Dr., Regina, SK S4S 0B3

Tel: 306-787-6343; *Fax:* 306-787-8299
cabsec@ec.gov.sk.ca

The Cabinet Secretariat has the following responsibilities: supporting the Premier & President of the Executive Council; offering administrative support to the Cabinet; maintaining public records & employment contracts.

Assistant Cabinet Secretary & Clerk of the Executive Council, Paul Crozier
Tel: 306-787-9630; *Fax:* 306-787-8299
paul.crozier@gov.sk.ca

Office of the Chief of Staff to the Premier

Legislative Building, #110, 2405 Legislative Dr., Regina, SK S4S 0B3

Tel: 306-787-9433; *Fax:* 306-787-0883

Includes the Correspondence Unit, which handles daily correspondence to & from the Premier. The unit also processes requests for photographs of the Premier.

Chief of Staff to the Premier, Joe Donlevy
Tel: 306-787-0064
joe.donlevy@gov.sk.ca

Executive Director, House Business & Research, Jarret Coels
Tel: 306-787-0866
jarret.coels@gov.sk.ca

Executive Coordinator, Communications, Kimberly Levesque
Tel: 306-787-6276
kimberly.levesque@gov.sk.ca

Director, Saskatoon Cabinet Office, Ed Carleton
Tel: 306-933-8299; *Fax:* 306-933-5831
ed.carleton@gov.sk.ca
#315 - 22nd St. East
Saskatoon, SK S7K 0G6

Director, Correspondence Unit, Bonnie Krajewski-Riel
Tel: 306-787-0492; *Fax:* 306-787-0885
bonnie.krajewski-riel@gov.sk.ca
www.gov.sk.ca/executive-council/correspondence-unit

Acting Director, Communications Services, Ashley Gayton
Tel: 306-787-9976
Ashley.Gayton@gov.sk.ca

Director, Human Resources, Sheree Ruller
Tel: 306-787-2059; *Fax:* 306-787-8337
sheree.ruller@gov.sk.ca

Communications Services

#110, 2405 Legislative Dr., Regina, SK S4S 0B3

Tel: 306-787-0425; *Fax:* 306-787-0883

The Communications Services branch administers the Communications Procurement Policy to government ministries, agencies, & Crowns. The Executive Director of Communications oversees communications to ensure information is provided to the media & the public in a timely & effective manner. Media relations staff provide assistance in the preparation & distribution of news releases.

Chief, Operations & Communications, Kathy Young
Tel: 306-787-0425; *Fax:* 306-787-0883
kathy.young@gov.sk.ca
Legislative Building
#110, 2405 Legislative Dr.
Regina, SK S4S 0B3

Director, Interactive Communications, Derek Robinson
Tel: 306-787-0906
derek.robinson@gov.sk.ca

Office of the Deputy Minister to the Premier

Legislative Building, #135, 2405 Legislative Dr., Regina, SK S4S 0B3

Tel: 306-787-6337; *Fax:* 306-787-8338

The Office of the Deputy Minister to the Premier carries out the following key functions: supporting the Premier; providing coordination between the Cabinet, ministries, agencies, & Crown corporations; & handling appointments of senior executives for ministries.

Deputy Minister to the Premier & Cabinet Secretary, Alanna Koch
Tel: 306-787-6338
Alanna.Koch@gov.sk.ca

Director, Executive Education, Winter Fedyk
Tel: 306-787-3115
winter.fedyk@gov.sk.ca

Cabinet Planning

Legislative Building, #37, 2405 Legislative Dr., Regina, SK S4S 0B3

Tel: 306-787-6344; *Fax:* 306-787-0012

The Cabinet Planning branch is involved in the following activities: offering research & advice about ministry & sectoral plans & policy proposals; providing policy analysis & secretariat support to the Premier, members of the Executive Council, & the Committee on Planning & Priorities; & participating in inter-ministry & inter-agency working groups.

Associate Deputy Minister, James Saunders
Tel: 306-787-6339
james.saunders@gov.sk.ca

Corporate Services

Legislative Building, #34, 2405 Legislative Dr., Regina, SK S4S 0B3

Tel: 306-787-7448; *Fax:* 306-787-0097

The Corporate Services branch of the Executive Council oversees the following areas: the ministry's budget; expense claims of cabinet ministers & ministry staff; human resource services; & information technology.

Executive Director, Corporate Services, Bonita Cairns
Tel: 306-787-6351; *Fax:* 306-787-0097
bonita.cairns@gov.sk.ca

Intergovernmental Affairs

#303, 3085 Albert St., Regina, SK S4S 0B1

Tel: 306-787-8003

The Government of Saskatchewan's Intergovernmental Affairs manages the province's relationships with Canadian provincial & territorial governments, federal governments, & international jurisdictions.

The mission of Intergovernmental Affairs involves promoting the province's interests, securing access to markets for products from Saskatchewan, handling official protocol, managing the provincial honours & awards program, & overseeing Francophone affairs.

Deputy Minister, Kent Campbell
Tel: 306-787-4220; *Fax:* 306-787-0973
kent.campbell@gov.sk.ca
Legislative Building
#14, 2405 Legislative Dr.
Regina, SK S4S 0B3

Assistant Deputy Minister, International Relations & Protocol, Kari Harvey
Tel: 306-787-0306; *Fax:* 306-787-0973
kari.harvey@gov.sk.ca
Legislative Building
#14, 2405 Legislative Dr.
Regina, SK S4S 0B3

Chief of Protocol, Jason Quilliam
Tel: 306-787-3109
Toll-free: 877-427-5505; *Fax:* 306-787-1269
jason.quilliam@gov.sk.ca
1831 College Ave.
Regina, SK S4P 4V5

Executive Director, International Relations, Renata Bereziuk
Tel: 306-787-0527; *Fax:* 306-787-7317
renata.bereziuk@gov.sk.ca
Executive Director, Trade Policy, Robert Donald
Tel: 306-787-8910; *Fax:* 306-787-7317
robert.donald@gov.sk.ca
Executive Director, Canadian Intergovernmental Relations, Ashley Metz
Tel: 306-787-7962; *Fax:* 306-787-7317
ashley.metz@gov.sk.ca
Executive Director, Francophone Affairs, Charles-Henri Warren
Tel: 306-787-8035; *Fax:* 306-787-6352
charleshenri.warren@gov.sk.ca
Other Communications: Alt. E-mail: fab-daf@gov.sk.ca

Provincial Secretary

Legislative Building, #349, 2405 Legislative Dr., Regina, SK S4S 0B3

Tel: 306-787-1636; *Fax:* 306-787-0012

The Provincial Secretary reports to the Premier. The work of the Provincial Secretary is to assist the Premier with protocol, events, & French language services.

Provincial Secretary, Hon. Nadine Wilson
Tel: 306-787-1636; *Fax:* 306-787-0012
nadine.wilson@gov.sk.ca

Legislative Assembly of Saskatchewan

Office of the Clerk, Legislative Building, #239, 2405 Legislative Dr., Regina, SK S4S 0B3

info@legassembly.sk.ca
www.legassembly.sk.ca
Other Communication: Library Reference Questions, E-mail: reference@legassembly.sk.ca
twitter.com/SKLegAssembly
www.facebook.com/SKLegAssembly

The Legislative Assembly oversees the government & performs three major roles: a legislative role, an inquiry role, & a financial role.
Members of the Assembly may include the Premier, the Leader of the Opposition, House Leaders, & Whips. Officers of the House include the Speaker, Clerks, & the Sargeant-at-Arms. Some major legislative services are legislative library services, visitor services, the production of parliamentary publications, & communication & technology services.

Speaker, Legislative Assembly, Hon. Corey Tochor
Tel: 306-787-2282; *Fax:* 306-787-2283
speaker@legassembly.sk.ca
Legislative Building
#203, 2405 Legislative Dr.
Regina, SK S4S 0B3

Deputy Speaker, Legislative Assembly, Glen Hart
Tel: 306-787-4300; *Fax:* 306-787-3174
ghart.mla@sasktel.net

Clerk, Greg Putz
Tel: 306-787-2335; *Fax:* 306-787-0408
gputz@legassembly.sk.ca

Law Clerk; Parliamentary Counsel, Kenneth S. Ring, Q.C.
Tel: 306-787-2298; *Fax:* 306-787-1246
kring@legassembly.sk.ca
Legislative Building
#225, 2405 Legislative Dr.
Regina, SK S4S 0B3

Sergeant-at-Arms, Terry Quinn
Tel: 306-787-8798
tquinn@legassembly.sk.ca
Legislative Building
#128, 2405 Legislative Dr.
Regina, SK S4S 0B3

Chief Technology Officer, Darcy Hislop
Tel: 306-787-8071; *Fax:* 306-787-4278
dhislop@legassembly.sk.ca
Legislative Building
#33, 2405 Legislative Dr.
Regina, SK S4S 0B3

Executive Director, Member & Corporate Services, Lynn Jacobson
Tel: 306-787-6477; *Fax:* 306-787-1558
ljacobson@legassembly.sk.ca
Legislative Building
#123, 2405 Legislative Dr.
Regina, SK S4S 0B3

Director, Financial Services, Brad Gurash
Tel: 306-787-2338; *Fax:* 306-798-2085
bgurash@legassembly.sk.ca
Legislative Building
#123, 2405 Legislative Dr.
Regina, SK S4S 0B3

Director, Visitor Services, Lorraine DeMontigny
Tel: 306-787-5357; *Fax:* 306-787-8217
ldemontigny@legassembly.sk.ca
Legislative Building
#122, 2405 Legislative Dr.
Regina, SK S4S 0B3

Director, Parliamentary Publications, Lenni Frohman
Tel: 306-787-1924; *Fax:* 306-787-1556
lfrohman@legassembly.sk.ca
Walter Scott Building
#110, 3085 Albert St.
Regina, SK S4S 0B1

Director, Member Services, Mike Halayka
Tel: 306-787-2384; *Fax:* 306-798-2085
Legislative Building
#119, 2405 Legislative Dr.
Regina, SK S4S 0B3

Director, Human Resources, Ginette Michaluk
Tel: 306-787-1734; *Fax:* 306-787-1558
gmichaluk@legassembly.sk.ca
Legislative Building
#123, 2405 Legislative Dr.
Regina, SK S4S 0B3

Legislative Librarian, Melissa Bennett
Tel: 306-787-2277; *Fax:* 306-787-1772
mbennett@legassembly.sk.ca
www.legassembly.sk.ca/LegLibrary
Other Communications: Alt. E-mail: reference@legassembly.sk.ca
Office of the Legislative Librarian, Legislative Building
#234, 2405 Legislative Dr.
Regina, SK S4S 0B3

Government Caucus Office (Saskatchewan Party)

Legislative Building, #141, 2405 Legislative Dr., Regina, SK S4S 0B3

Tel: 306-787-4300; *Fax:* 306-787-3174
Toll-Free: 888-708-7780
info@skcaucus.com
www.skcaucus.com
twitter.com/SaskParty
www.facebook.com/SaskParty

Hon. Brad Wall was first elected Premier of Saskatchewan in the 2007 provincial election. The Saskatchewan Party was re-elected in the November 2011 provincial election.

Premier; President, Executive Council; Minister, Intergovernmental Affairs; Leader, Saskatchewan Party, Hon. Brad Wall
Tel: 306-787-9433; *Fax:* 306-787-0885
bradwallmla@sasktel.net
www.premier.gov.sk.ca
Social Media: twitter.com/PremierBradWall, www.facebook.com/PremierBradWall
Minister, Crown Investments; Minister Saskatchewan Government Insurance; Minister, Saskatchewan Transportation Corporation, Hon. Joe Hargrave
Caucus Chair, Saskatchewan Party, Randy Weekes
Tel: 306-787-1479; *Fax:* 306-798-9013
randyweekes.mla@accesscomm.ca
Government House Leader, Ken Cheveldayoff
Tel: 306-787-4232; *Fax:* 306-787-3174
ken.cheveldayoff.mla@sasktel.net
Chief of Staff, John Saltasuk
Tel: 306-787-4300; *Fax:* 306-787-3174
jsaltasuk@skcaucus.com

Opposition Caucus Office (New Democratic Party)

Legislative Building, #265, 2405 Legislative Dr., Regina, SK S4S 0B3

Tel: 306-787-7388; *Fax:* 306-787-6247
caucus@ndpcaucus.sk.ca
www.ndpcaucus.sk.ca

Dwain Lingenfelter resigned as the leader of Saskatchewan's New Democratic Party after he lost his seat in the November 2011 provincial election. John Nilson, a veteran Member of the Legislative Assembly, took over as the interim leader of the party. Cam Broten became the new leader in March 2013, but lost his seat in the 2016 general election. Following the election, Trent Wotherspoon became the party's Interim Leader.

Interim Leader, Official Opposition; Interim Leader, Saskatchewan New Democratic Party, Trent Wotherspoon
Tel: 306-787-0077; *Fax:* 306-787-6247
reginarosemont@ndpcaucus.sk.ca
Deputy Leader, Official Opposition, Buckley Belanger
Tel: 306-787-0394; *Fax:* 306-787-6247
athabasca@ndpcaucus.sk.ca
Caucus Chair, New Democratic Party, David Forbes
Tel: 306-787-0975; *Fax:* 306-787-6247
saskatooncentre@ndpcaucus.sk.ca
Deputy Caucus Chair, New Democratic Party, Cathy Sproule
Tel: 306-787-9999; *Fax:* 306-787-6247
saskatoonnutana@ndpcaucus.sk.ca
House Leader, Opposition, Warren McCall
Tel: 306-787-8276; *Fax:* 306-787-6247
reginaelphinstonecentre@ndpcaucus.sk.ca
Opposition Whip, Doyle Vermette
Tel: 306-787-6340; *Fax:* 306-787-6247
cumberland@ndpcaucus.sk.ca
Deputy Opposition Whip, Carla Beck
Tel: 306-787-7388
Director, Human Resources & Administration, Cheryl Stecyk
Tel: 306-787-7389; *Fax:* 306-787-6247
cstecyk@ndpcaucus.sk.ca

Standing Committees of the Legislative Assembly of Saskatchewan

Legislative Building, #7, 2405 Legislative Dr., Regina, SK S4S 0B3

Tel: 306-787-9930
committees@legassembly.sk.ca
www.legassembly.sk.ca/legislative-business/legislative-committees

Standing committees are established according to the permanent Rules of the Legislative Assembly. There are three categories of Standing Committees: Policy Field, House, & Scrutiny. The committees function for the duration of the legislature. The following are the Standing Committees of the Legislative Assembly of Saskatchewan: Crown & Central Agencies; Economy; House Services; Human Services; Intergovernmental Affairs & Justice; Private Bills; Privileges; & Public Accounts.

Principal Clerk, Iris Lang
Tel: 306-787-1743; *Fax:* 306-798-9650
ilang@legassembly.sk.ca
Clerk Assistant, Committees, Kathy Burianyk
Tel: 306-787-4989; *Fax:* 306-798-9650
kburianyk@legassembly.sk.ca
Chair, Standing Committee on Crown & Central Agencies, Colleen Young
Constituency: Carrot River Valley, Saskatchewan Party
Tel: 306-787-0007; *Fax:* 306-787-3174
colleen.young@sasktel.net
Chair, Standing Committee on the Economy, Gene Makowsky
Constituency: Regina Gardiner Park, Saskatchewan Party
Tel: 306-787-4300; *Fax:* 306-798-3174
gmakowsky.mla@sasktel.net
Chair, Standing Committee on House Services & Standing Committee on Privileges, Hon. Corey Tochor
Constituency: Saskatoon Eastview, Saskatchewan Party
Tel: 306-787-2282; *Fax:* 306-787-2283
ctochormlasaskatooneastview@gmail.com
Chair, Standing Committee on Human Services, Greg Lawrence
Constituency: Moose Jaw Wakamow, Saskatchewan Party
Tel: 306-787-4300; *Fax:* 306-787-3174
greglawrencemla@sasktel.net
Chair, Standing Committee on Intergovernmental Affairs & Justice, Greg Brkich
Constituency: Regina Rochdale, Saskatchewan Party
Tel: 306-787-9036; *Fax:* 306-787-3174
gregpbrkich@sasktel.net
Chair, Standing Committee on Public Accounts, Danielle Chartier
Constituency: Saskatoon Riversdale, New Democratic Party
Tel: 306-787-1900; *Fax:* 306-787-6247
saskatoonriversdale@ndpcaucus.sk.ca

Twenty-eighth Legislature - Saskatchewan

2405 Legislative Dr., Regina, SK S4S 0B3

www.legassembly.sk.ca
Other Communication: Legislative Library, Phone: 306-787-2276
twitter.com/SKLegAssembly
www.facebook.com/SKLegAssembly

Last General Election: April 4, 2016.
Party Standings (Sept. 2016):
Saskatchewan Party: 50;
New Democratic Party: 10;
Independent: 1;
Total 61.
Salaries & Allowances of Members (May 2014):
Member of the Legislative Assembly, Annual Indemnity $94,668.
Additional Allowances:
Premier $68,852 (total $163,520);
Deputy Premier $55,083 (total $149,751);
Speaker $48,198 (total $142,866);
Minister $48,198 (total $142,866);
Leader of the Opposition $48,198 (total $142,866);
Leader of the Third Party $24,098 (total $118,766;
Government House Leader $14,086 (total $108,754);
Opposition House Leader $14,086 (total $108,754);
Third Party House Leader $7,043 (total $101,711);
Government Whip $14,086 (total $108,754);
Opposition Whip $14,086 (total $108,754);
Third Party Whip $7,043 (total $101,711);
Government Caucus Chair $14,086 (total $108,754);
Opposition Caucus Chair $14,086 (total $108,754);
Third Party Caucus Chair $7,043 (total $101,711).
The following is a list of members, with their constituency, the

number of electors in the constituency for the 2016 general election, party affiliation, & contact information:
Minister, Social Services; Minister responsible, Status of Women, Hon. Tina Beaudry-Mellor
Constituency: Regina University *No. of Constituents:* 10,743, Saskatchewan Party
Tel: 306-787-7550; *Fax:* 306-787-3174
www.saskparty.com/beaudrymellor
Social Media: twitter.com/tbeaudrymellor, www.facebook.com/TBMstratgies
Deputy Opposition Whip, Carla Beck
Constituency: Regina Lakeview *No. of Constituents:* 11,928, New Democratic Party
Tel: 306-787-7388
www.sasknpd.ca/beck
Social Media: www.facebook.com/carla4lakeview, ca.linkedin.com/in/carla-beck-35989858
Deputy Leader, Official Opposition, Buckley Belanger
Constituency: Athabasca *No. of Constituents:* 7,604, New Democratic Party
Tel: 306-787-0394; *Fax:* 306-787-6247
athabasca@ndpcaucus.sk.ca
www.ndpcaucus.sk.ca/belanger
Other Communications: Constituency Phone: 306-833-3200; Fax: 306-833-2622
Constituency Office
PO Box 310
Ile-A-La-Crosse, SK S0M 1C0
Steven Bonk
Constituency: Moosomin *No. of Constituents:* 12,345, Saskatchewan Party
Tel: 306-787-9088
www.saskparty.com/bonk
Bill Boyd
Constituency: Kindersley *No. of Constituents:* 11,518, Saskatchewan Party
Tel: 306-787-0497; *Fax:* 306-787-0395
boyd.mla@sasktel.net
www.saskparty.com/boyd
Other Communications: Constituency Phone: 306-463-4480; Fax: 306-463-6873
Constituency Office
116C Main St.
PO Box 490
Kindersley, SK S0L 1S0
Fred Bradshaw
Constituency: Carrot River Valley *No. of Constituents:* 11,739, Saskatchewan Party
Tel: 306-787-0540; *Fax:* 306-787-3174
fbradshaw.mla@sasktel.net
fredbradshaw.ca
Other Communications: Constituency Phone: 306-768-3977; Fax: 306-768-3979
Constituency Office
29 Main St.
PO Box 969
Carrot River, SK S0E 0L0
Greg Brkich
Constituency: Arm River *No. of Constituents:* 12,140, Saskatchewan Party
Tel: 306-787-9036; *Fax:* 306-787-3174
gregpbrkich@sasktel.net
www.gregbrkich.ca
Other Communications: Constituency Phone: 306-567-2843; Fax: 306-567-3259
Constituency Office
102 Washington St.
PO Box 1077
Davidson, SK S0G 1A0
David Buckingham
Constituency: Saskatoon Westview *No. of Constituents:* 14,286, Saskatchewan Party
Tel: 306-787-9434
www.saskparty.com/buckingham
Social Media: www.facebook.com/855162971231224
Note: NDP Leader Cam Broten lost his seat to Saskatchewan Party candidate David Buckingham by 232 votes in the 2016 general election.
Jennifer Campeau
Constituency: Saskatoon Fairview *No. of Constituents:* 12,156, Saskatchewan Party
Tel: 306-787-0942; *Fax:* 306-787-8677
casaskatoonfairview@shaw.ca
www.saskparty.com/campeau
Other Communications: Constituency Phone: 306-974-4125; Fax: 306-974-4128
Constituency Office
#16, 15 Worobetz Pl.
Saskatoon, SK S7L 6R4
Lori Carr
Constituency: Estevan *No. of Constituents:* 11,772, Saskatchewan Party
Tel: 306-787-4300; *Fax:* 306-787-3174
loricarrmla@sasktel.net
www.saskparty.com/carr
Other Communications: Constituency Phone: 306-634-7311; Fax: 306-634-7332
Constituency Office
1108 - 4th St.
Estevan, SK S4A 0W7
Danielle Chartier
Constituency: Saskatoon Riversdale *No. of Constituents:* 11,769, New Democratic Party
Tel: 306-787-1900; *Fax:* 306-787-6247
saskatoonriversdale@ndpcaucus.sk.ca
www.daniellechartier.ca
Other Communications: Constituency Phone: 306-244-5167; 306-244-6070
Social Media: twitter.com/RiversdaleMLA
Constituency Office
1030 Ave. L South
Saskatoon, SK S7M 2J5
Minister, Parks, Culture & Sport; Minister responsible, Public Service Commission; Government House Leader, Hon. Ken Cheveldayoff
Constituency: Saskatoon Willowgrove *No. of Constituents:* 15,295, Saskatchewan Party
Tel: 306-787-4232; *Fax:* 306-787-3174
ken.cheveldayoff.mla@sasktel.net
www.cheveldayoff.com
Other Communications: Constituency Phone: 306-651-7100; Fax: 306-651-6008
Social Media: twitter.com/kencheveld, www.facebook.com/52760912740
Constituency Office
1106A Central Ave.
Saskatoon, SK S7N 2H1
Herb Cox
Constituency: The Battlefords *No. of Constituents:* 13,213, Saskatchewan Party
Tel: 306-787-9639; *Fax:* 306-787-3174
herbcox@sasktel.net
www.skcaucus.com/herb_cox
Other Communications: Constituency Phone: 306-445-5195; Fax: 306-445-5196
Constituency Office
1991 - 100th St. North
North Battleford, SK S9A 0X2
Dan D'Autremont
Constituency: Cannington *No. of Constituents:* 11,855, Saskatchewan Party
Tel: 306-787-2282; *Fax:* 306-787-2283
cannington.mla@sasktel.net
www.dandautremont.ca
Other Communications: Constituency Phone: 306-443-2420; Fax: 306-443-2269
Constituency Office
303 Hwy. 361
PO Box 130
Alida, SK S0C 0B0
Terry Dennis
Constituency: Canora-Pelly *No. of Constituents:* 11,001, Saskatchewan Party
Tel: 306-787-4300; *Fax:* 306-787-3174
Canora.PellyMLA@sasktel.net
www.saskparty.com/dennis
Other Communications: Constituency Phone: 306-563-1363; Fax: 306-563-1365
Constituency Office
106 - 1st Ave. East
PO Box 838
Canora, SK S0A 0L0
Mark Docherty
Constituency: Regina Coronation Park *No. of Constituents:* 12,004, Saskatchewan Party
Tel: 306-787-9408; *Fax:* 306-798-0264
markdoc@sasktel.net
www.skcaucus.com/mark_docherty
Other Communications: Constituency Phone: 306-359-3624; Fax: 306-359-3630
Social Media: twitter.com/dochertymark
Constituency Office
3120 Avonhurst Dr.
Regina, SK S4R 3J7
Minister, Finance, Hon. Kevin Doherty
Constituency: Regina Northeast *No. of Constituents:* 12,466, Saskatchewan Party
Tel: 306-787-0341; *Fax:* 306-798-0263
kevindohertymla@sasktel.net
www.skcaucus.com/kevin_doherty
Other Communications: Constituency Phone: 306-525-5568; Fax: 306-525-5680
Social Media: www.linkedin.com/in/dmaniii
Constituency Office
1010 Winnipeg St.
Regina, SK S4R 8P8
Larry Doke
Constituency: Cut Knife-Turtleford *No. of Constituents:* 12,219, Saskatchewan Party
Tel: 306-787-4300; *Fax:* 306-787-3174
larrydoke@sasktel.net
www.skcaucus.com/larry_doke
Other Communications: Constituency Phone: 306-893-2619; Fax: 306-893-2660
Constituency Office
#6, 116 - 1st Ave. West
PO Box 850
Maidstone, SK S0M 1M0
Minister, Energy & Resources; Minister responsible, SaskEnergy Incorporated & Saskatchewan Telecommunications, Hon. Dustin Duncan
Constituency: Weyburn-Big Muddy *No. of Constituents:* 12,106, Saskatchewan Party
Tel: 306-787-7345; *Fax:* 306-787-0237
dduncan.mla@accesscomm.ca
www.skcaucus.com/dustin_duncan
Other Communications: Constituency Phone: 306-842-4810; Fax: 306-842-4811
Constituency Office
28 - 4th St. NE
Weyburn, SK S4H 0X7
Minister, Advanced Education, Hon. Bronwyn Eyre
Constituency: Saskatoon Stonebridge-Dakota *No. of Constituents:* 15,215, Saskatchewan Party
Tel: 306-787-7527
www.saskparty.com/eyre
Social Media: twitter.com/bronwyneyre, www.facebook.com/electbronwyneyre
Muhammad Fiaz
Constituency: Regina Pasqua *No. of Constituents:* 15,078, Saskatchewan Party
Tel: 306-787-4277
www.saskparty.com/fiaz
Social Media: twitter.com/fiazregina, www.facebook.com/muhammad.fiaz.338
Note: Muhammad Fiaz is the first Muslim MLA in Saskatchewan history.
Caucus Chair, New Democratic Party, David Forbes
Constituency: Saskatoon Centre *No. of Constituents:* 12,260, New Democratic Party
Tel: 306-787-0975; *Fax:* 306-787-6247
saskatooncentre@ndpcaucus.sk.ca
www.davidforbesmla.ca
Other Communications: Constituency Phone: 306-244-3555; Fax: 306-244-3602
Social Media: www.facebook.com/DavidForbesMLA
Constituency Office
904D - 22nd St. West
Saskatoon, SK S7M 0S1
Minister, Crown Investments Corporation; Minister, Saskatchewan Government Insurance; Minister, Saskatchewan Transportation Company, Joe Hargrave
Constituency: Prince Albert Carlton *No. of Constituents:* 12,622, Saskatchewan Party
Tel: 306-787-4300; *Fax:* 306-787-3174
pacarltonmla@sasktel.net
www.saskparty.com/hargrave
Other Communications: Constituency Phone: 306-922-2828; Fax: 306-922-0261
Constituency Office
#4, 406 South Industrial Dr.
Prince Albert, SK S6V 7L8
Minister, Government Relations; Minister Responsible, First Nations, Métis & northern affairs, Hon. Donna Harpauer
Constituency: Humboldt-Watrous *No. of Constituents:* 12,016, Saskatchewan Party
Tel: 306-787-3661; *Fax:* 306-787-0656
humboldtmla@sasktel.net
www.donnaharpauer.ca
Other Communications: Constituency Phone: 306-682-5141; Fax: 306-683-5144
Social Media: www.facebook.com/60494388240
Constituency Office
632 - 9th St.
PO Box 2950
Humboldt, SK S0K 2A0
Minister, Economy; Minister responsible, Global Transportation Hub, Saskatchewan Liquor & Gaming Authority, Hon. Jeremy Harrison
Constituency: Meadow Lake *No. of Constituents:* 13,047, Saskatchewan Party
Tel: 306-787-4300; *Fax:* 306-787-3174
jharrisonmla@sasktel.net
www.jeremyharrison.ca
Other Communications: Constituency Phone: 306-236-6669; Fax: 306-236-6744
Constituency Office, North Entrance
201 - 2nd St. West
PO Box 848
Meadow Lake, SK S9X 1Y6

Deputy Speaker, Legislative Assembly, Glen Hart
Constituency: Last Mountain-Touchwood *No. of Constituents:* 11,227, Saskatchewan Party
Tel: 306-787-4300; *Fax:* 306-787-3174
ghart.mla@sasktel.net
www.glenhart.ca
Other Communications: Constituency Phone: 306-723-4421; Fax: 306-723-4654
Constituency Office
402 Stanley St.
PO Box 309
Cupar, SK S0G 0Y0

Nancy Heppner
Constituency: Martensville-Warman *No. of Constituents:* 15,066, Saskatchewan Party
Tel: 306-787-6447; *Fax:* 306-787-8677
mail@nancyheppner.com
www.nancyheppner.com
Other Communications: Constituency Phone: 306-975-0284; Fax: 306-975-0283
Constituency Office
#3G, 520 Central St. West
PO Box 2270
Hague, SK S0K 4S0

Warren Kaeding
Constituency: Melville-Saltcoats *No. of Constituents:* 12,083, Saskatchewan Party
Tel: 306-787-4300; *Fax:* 306-787-3174
warrenkaedingmla@sasktel.net
www.saskparty.com/kaeding
Other Communications: Constituency Phone: 306-728-3882; Fax: 306-728-3884
Social Media: twitter.com/wkaeding, ca.linkedin.com/in/warren-kaeding-35583165
Constituency Office
113 - 3rd Ave. West
PO Box 3215
Melville, SK S0A 2P0

Delbert Kirsch
Constituency: Batoche *No. of Constituents:* 10,608, Saskatchewan Party
Tel: 306-787-4300; *Fax:* 306-787-3174
batochemla@sasktel.net
www.saskparty.com/kirsch
Other Communications: Constituency Phone: 306-256-3930; Fax: 306-256-3924
Constituency Office
115 Main St.
PO Box 308
Cudworth, SK S0K 1B0

Lisa Lambert
Constituency: Saskatoon Churchill-Wildwood *No. of Constituents:* 12,278, Saskatchewan Party
Tel: 306-787-9173
lisalambert.mla@sasktel.net
www.saskparty.com/lambert
Other Communications: Constituency Phone: 306-373-7373
Social Media: twitter.com/lisalambert88, www.facebook.com/lisa.lambert.3538, ca.linkedin.com/in/lisa-lambert-75a7478a
Constituency Office
#1B, 270 Acadia Dr.
Saskatoon, SK S7H 3V4

Greg Lawrence
Constituency: Moose Jaw Wakamow *No. of Constituents:* 12,559, Saskatchewan Party
Tel: 306-787-4300; *Fax:* 306-787-3174
greglawrencemla@sasktel.net
www.skcaucus.com/greg_lawrence
Other Communications: Constituency Phone: 306-694-1001; Fax: 306-691-0486
Social Media: www.linkedin.com/pub/greg-lawrence/54/854/499
Constituency Office
404B Lillooet St. West
Moose Jaw, SK S6H 7T1

Gene Makowsky
Constituency: Regina Gardiner Park *No. of Constituents:* 11,736, Saskatchewan Party
Tel: 306-787-4300; *Fax:* 306-787-3174
gmakowsky.mla@sasktel.net
www.genemakowsky.ca
Other Communications: Constituency Phone: 306-545-4363; Fax: 306-545-4370
Social Media: www.facebook.com/GeneAMakowsky
Constituency Office
#105, 438 Victoria Ave. East
Regina, SK S4N 0N7

Minister, Highways & Infrastructure, David Marit
Constituency: Wood River *No. of Constituents:* 11,337, Saskatchewan Party
Tel: 306-787-0250
www.saskparty.com/marit
Other Communications: Constituency Phone: 306-642-4200
Social Media: twitter.com/david_marit, ca.linkedin.com/pub/david-marit/81/a94/817
Constituency Office
#3, 100 - 1st Ave. West
Assiniboia, SK S0H 0B0

House Leader, Opposition, Warren McCall
Constituency: Regina Elphinstone-Centre *No. of Constituents:* 11,549, New Democratic Party
Tel: 306-787-8276; *Fax:* 306-787-6247
reginaelphinstonecentre@ndpcaucus.sk.ca
www.ndpcaucus.sk.ca/mccall
Other Communications: Constituency Phone: 306-352-2002; Fax: 306-352-2065
Social Media: www.linkedin.com/pub/warren-mccall/19/2a7/672
Constituency Office
2900 - 5th Ave.
Regina, SK S4T 0L6

Don McMorris
Constituency: Indian Head-Milestone *No. of Constituents:* 12,462, Independent
mcmorris.mla@sasktel.net
www.donmcmorris.ca
Other Communications: Constituency Phone: 306-771-2733; Fax: 306-771-2574
Social Media: twitter.com/dmcmorrissp
Constituency Office
125 Railway St.
PO Box 720
Balgonie, SK S0G 0E0

Paul Merriman
Constituency: Saskatoon Silverspring-Sutherland *No. of Constituents:* 12,864, Saskatchewan Party
Tel: 306-787-4300; *Fax:* 306-787-3174
office@paulmerriman.ca
www.skcaucus.com/paul_merriman
Other Communications: Constituency Phone: 306-244-5623; Fax: 306-244-5626
Constituency Office
#211, 3521 - 8th St. East
Saskatoon, SK S7H 0W5

Warren Michelson
Constituency: Moose Jaw North *No. of Constituents:* 12,377, Saskatchewan Party
Tel: 306-787-4300; *Fax:* 306-798-3174
moosejawnorthmla@shaw.ca
www.warrenmichelson.ca
Other Communications: Constituency Phone: 306-692-8884; Fax: 306-692-8872
Constituency Office
326B High St. West
Moose Jaw, SK S6H 1S9

Minister, Environment; Minister responsible, Saskatchewan Water Corporation, Saskatchewan Water Security Agency, Hon. Scott Moe
Constituency: Rosthern-Shellbrook *No. of Constituents:* 11,131, Saskatchewan Party
Tel: 306-787-0341; *Fax:* 306-798-0263
scottmoe.mla@sasktel.net
www.scott-moe.com
Other Communications: Constituency Phone: 306-747-3422; Fax: 306-747-3472
Social Media: www.facebook.com/182365048474566
Constituency Office
34 Main St.
PO Box 115
Shellbrook, SK S0J 2E0

Deputy Premier; Minister, Education; Minister, Labour Relations & Workplace Safety; Minister Responsible, Saskatchewan Workers' Compensation Board, Hon. Don Morgan, Q.C.
Constituency: Saskatoon Southeast *No. of Constituents:* 13,083, Saskatchewan Party
Tel: 30- 78- 061; *Fax:* 306-787-6946
mla@donmorgan.ca
www.donmorgan.ca
Other Communications: Constituency Phone: 306-955-4755; Fax: 306-955-4765
Social Media: twitter.com/saskmla
Constituency Office
#109, 3502 Taylor St. East
Saskatoon, SK S7H 5H9

Hugh Nerlien
Constituency: Kelvington-Wadena *No. of Constituents:* 11,653, Saskatchewan Party
Tel: 306-787-0868
nerlien.mla@sasktel.net
www.saskparty.com/nerlien
Other Communications: Constituency Phone: 306-278-2200
Social Media: twitter.com/hughnerlien, www.facebook.com/273135516207511
Constituency Office
#102, 302 Pine St. West
Porcupine Plain, SK S0E 1H0

Eric Olauson
Constituency: Saskatoon University *No. of Constituents:* 10,753, Saskatchewan Party
Tel: 306-787-0797
ca@saskatoonuniversity.ca
www.saskparty.com/olauson
Other Communications: Constituency Phone: 306-244-4004
Constituency Office
#1B, 270 Acadia Dr.
Saskatoon, SK S7H 3V4

Minister Responsible, Rural & Remote Health; Government Whip, Hon. Greg Ottenbreit
Constituency: Yorkton *No. of Constituents:* 12,296, Saskatchewan Party
Tel: 306-798-9014; *Fax:* 306-798-9013
yorkton.mla@sasktel.net
www.gregottenbreit.ca
Other Communications: Constituency Phone: 306-783-7275; Fax: 306-783-7273
Social Media: twitter.com/GregOttenbreit
Constituency Office
#29A Broadway St. East
Yorkton, SK S3N 0K4

Roger Parent
Constituency: Saskatoon Meewasin *No. of Constituents:* 11,998, Saskatchewan Party
Tel: 306-787-4300; *Fax:* 306-787-3174
rogerparentmla@gmail.com
www.skcaucus.com/roger_parent
Other Communications: Constituency Phone: 306-652-4607; Fax: 306-652-4614
Social Media: www.facebook.com/rogerparentmla
Constituency Office
96 - 33rd St. East, Bay C
Saskatoon, SK S7K 0S1

Kevin Phillips
Constituency: Melfort *No. of Constituents:* 12,052, Saskatchewan Party
Tel: 306-787-4300; *Fax:* 306-787-3174
mail@melfortconstituency.ca
www.skcaucus.com/kevin_phillips
Other Communications: Constituency Phone: 306-752-9500; Fax: 306-752-9005
Constituency Office, Melfort Mall
1121 Main St., Bay 14
PO Box 2800
Melfort, SK S0E 1A0

Nicole Rancourt
Constituency: Prince Albert Northcote *No. of Constituents:* 12,994, New Democratic Party
Tel: 306-787-7388
princealbertnorthcote@ndpcaucus.sk.ca
www.sasknde.ca/rancourt
Other Communications: Constituency Phone: 306-763-4400
Constituency Office
#203, 1100 - 1st Ave. East
Prince Albert, SK S6V 2A7

Minister, Health, Hon. Jim Reiter
Constituency: Rosetown-Elrose *No. of Constituents:* 10,906, Saskatchewan Party
Tel: 306-787-7345; *Fax:* 306-787-0237
jimreitermla@sasktel.net
www.jimreiter.ca
Other Communications: Constituency Phone: 306-882-4105; Fax: 306-882-4108
Social Media: twitter.com/jim_reiter
Constituency Office
215 Main St.
PO Box 278
Rosetown, SK S0L 2V0

Laura Ross
Constituency: Regina Rochdale *No. of Constituents:* 15,744, Saskatchewan Party
Tel: 306-787-4300; *Fax:* 306-787-3174
laurarossmla@sasktel.net
www.lauraross.ca
Other Communications: Constituency Phone: 306-545-6333; Fax: 306-545-6112
Social Media: www.linkedin.com/pub/laura-ross/46/174/285
Constituency Office
4519 Rochdale Blvd.
Regina, SK S4X 4R3

Nicole Sarauer
Constituency: Regina Douglas Park *No. of Constituents:* 11,867, New Democratic Party
Tel: 306-787-7388
www.saskndp.ca/sarauer
Social Media: twitter.com/nicolesarauer, ca.linkedin.com/in/nicole-sarauer-a2594346

Deputy Caucus Chair, Opposition, Cathy Sproule
Constituency: Saskatoon Nutana *No. of Constituents:* 12,323, New Democratic Party
Tel: 306-787-9999; *Fax:* 306-787-6247
saskatoonnutana@ndpcaucus.sk.ca

www.cathysproule.com
Other Communications: Constituency Phone: 306-664-6101; Fax: 306-665-5633
Social Media: twitter.com/cathysproule, www.facebook.com/173288332783856, www.linkedin.com/pub/cathy-sproule/16/ab8/7b3
Constituency Office
621A Main St.
Saskatoon, SK S7H 0J8

Douglas Steele
Constituency: Cypress Hills *No. of Constituents:* 11,644, Saskatchewan Party
Tel: 306-787-4300; *Fax:* 306-787-3174
steelemla@sasktel.net
www.saskparty.com/steele
Other Communications: Constituency Phone: 306-672-1756; Fax: 306-672-1755
Constituency Office
4671 Price Ave.
Gull Lake, SK S0N 1A0

Warren Steinley
Constituency: Regina Walsh Acres *No. of Constituents:* 11,880, Saskatchewan Party
Tel: 306-787-4300; *Fax:* 306-787-3174
walshacresmla@sasktel.net
www.warrensteinley.com
Other Communications: Constituency Phone: 306-565-3881; Fax: 306-565-3893
Social Media: twitter.com/WSteinley_SP, www.facebook.com/102220736527442
Constituency Office
6845 Rochdale Blvd.
Regina, SK S4X 2Z2

Minister, Agriculture; Minister Responsible, Saskatchewan Crop Insurance Corporation, Hon. Lyle Stewart
Constituency: Lumsden-Morse *No. of Constituents:* 12,492, Saskatchewan Party
Tel: 306-787-0338; *Fax:* 306-787-0630
thundercreek.mla@sasktel.net
www.lylestewart.ca
Other Communications: Constituency Phone: 306-693-3229; Fax: 306-693-3251
Constituency Office
#207, 310 Main St. North
Moose Jaw, SK S6H 3K1

Minister, Central Services; Minister responsible, Provincial Capital Commission, Saskatchewan Gaming Corporation, Hon. Christine Tell
Constituency: Regina Wascana Plains *No. of Constituents:* 14,154, Saskatchewan Party
Tel: 306-787-0942; *Fax:* 306-787-8677
christinetellmla@accesscomm.ca
www.christinetell.com
Other Communications: Constituency Phone: 306-205-2126; Fax: 306-205-2127
Social Media: www.facebook.com/christinetellsp
Constituency Office
2318B Assiniboine Ave. East
Regina, SK S4V 2P5

Speaker, Legislative Assembly, Hon. Corey Tochor
Constituency: Saskatoon Eastview *No. of Constituents:* 12,474, Saskatchewan Party
Tel: 306-787-4300; *Fax:* 306-787-3174
ctochormlasaskatooneastview@gmail.com
www.coreytochormla.com
Other Communications: Constituency Phone: 306-384-2011; Fax: 306-384-2229
Social Media: www.facebook.com/corey.tochor
Constituency Office
#1, 3012 Louise St.
Saskatoon, SK S7J 3L8

Opposition Whip, Doyle Vermette
Constituency: Cumberland *No. of Constituents:* 13,326, New Democratic Party
Tel: 306-787-6340; *Fax:* 306-787-6247
cumberland@ndpcaucus.sk.ca
www.ndpcaucus.sk.ca/vermette
Other Communications: Constituency Phone: 306-425-2525; Fax: 306-425-2885
Social Media: www.facebook.com/doyle.vermette
Constituency Office
251 La Ronge Ave.
PO Box 192
La Ronge, SK S0J 1L0

Premier; President, Executive Council; Minister, Intergovernmental Affairs, Hon. Brad Wall
Constituency: Swift Current *No. of Constituents:* 12,204, Saskatchewan Party
Tel: 306-787-9433; *Fax:* 306-787-0885
bradwallmla@sasktel.net
www.bradwall.ca
Other Communications: Constituency Phone: 306-778-2429; Fax: 306-778-3614
Social Media: twitter.com/PremierBradWall, www.facebook.com/PremierBradWall
Constituency Office
233 Central Ave. North
Swift Current, SK S9H 0L3

Randy Weekes
Constituency: Biggar-Sask Valley *No. of Constituents:* 12,536, Saskatchewan Party
Tel: 306-787-1479; *Fax:* 306-798-9013
randyweekes.mla@accesscomm.ca
www.randyweekes.ca
Other Communications: Constituency Phone: 306-948-4880; Fax: 306-948-4882
Social Media: www.facebook.com/randy.weekes.1
Constituency Office
106 - 3rd Ave. West
PO Box 1413
Biggar, SK S0K 0M0

Provincial Secretary, Hon. Nadine Wilson
Constituency: Saskatchewan Rivers *No. of Constituents:* 11,449, Saskatchewan Party
Tel: 306-787-4300; *Fax:* 306-798-3174
saskatchewanrivers@sasktel.net
www.nadinewilson.ca
Other Communications: Constituency Phone: 306-763-0615; Fax: 306-763-2503
Social Media: www.facebook.com/49297133345
Constituency Office
Box 4, Site 16, RR#5
Prince Albert, SK S6V 5R3

Interim Leader, Official Opposition; Interim Leader, Saskatchewan New Democratic Party, Trent Wotherspoon
Constituency: Regina Rosemont *No. of Constituents:* 12,587, New Democratic Party
Tel: 306-787-0077; *Fax:* 306-787-6247
reginarosemont@ndpcaucus.sk.ca
www.trentwotherspoon.com
Other Communications: Constituency Phone: 306-565-2444; Fax: 306-565-2952
Social Media: twitter.com/WotherspoonT
Constituency Office
#700E, 4400 - 4th Ave.
Regina, SK S4T 0H8

Minister, Justice & Attorney General; Minister Responsible, SaskBuilds, Saskatchewan Power Corporation, Hon. Gordon Wyant, Q.C.
Constituency: Saskatoon Northwest *No. of Constituents:* 11,547, Saskatchewan Party
Tel: 306-787-5353; *Fax:* 306-787-1232
g.wyant.mla@sasktel.net
gordonwyant.ca
Other Communications: Constituency Phone: 306-934-2847; Fax: 306-934-2867
Social Media: twitter.com/GordWyant
Constituency Office
75B Lenore Dr.
Saskatoon, SK S7K 7Y1

Colleen Young
Constituency: Lloydminster *No. of Constituents:* 13,257, Saskatchewan Party
Tel: 306-787-0007; *Fax:* 306-787-3174
colleen.young@sasktel.net
www.saskparty.com/young
Other Communications: Constituency Phone: 306-825-5550; Fax: 306-825-5552
Social Media: www.facebook.com/222841891386875
Constituency Office
#2, 4304 - 40th Ave.
Lloydminster, SK S9V 2H1

Saskatchewan Government Departments & Agencies

Saskatchewan Advanced Education (AE)

#1120, 2010 - 12 Ave., Regina, SK S4P 0M3
Tel: 306-787-9478
aeeinquiry@gov.sk.ca
ae.gov.sk.ca

The Ministry strives to create a vital, educated & skilled workforce by focussing on the following areas: retaining educated & skilled workers in Saskatchewan; providing educational & training programs to develop a skilled workforce; & promoting the province's opportunities to attract educated & skilled workers from outside Saskatchewan & Canada. In November 2007, a new provincial government resulted in the reorganization of provincial government ministries. An expanded Ministry of Advanced Education, Employment & Labour was formed, & was subsequently changed to Advanced Education, Employment & Immigration, then simply to Advanced Education.

Minister, Hon. Bronwyn Eyre
minister.ae@gov.sk.ca
Minister's Office, Ministry of Advanced Education, Legislative Building
#307, 2405 Legislative Dr.
Regina, SK S4S 0B3

Deputy Minister, Louise Greenberg
Tel: 306-787-7071; *Fax:* 306-798-0975
louise.greenberg@gov.sk.ca

Associated Agencies, Boards & Commissions:

•Saskatchewan Apprenticeship & Trade Certification Commission
2140 Hamilton St.
Regina, SK S4P 2E3
Tel: 306-787-2444; *Fax:* 306-787-5105
Toll-free: 877-363-0536
apprenticeship@gov.sk.ca
www.saskapprenticeship.ca

Communications
Tel: 306-787-9478; *Fax:* 306-798-5021

Acting Executive Director, David Horth
Tel: 306-787-0926
david.horth@gov.sk.ca

Corporate Services & Accountability Division
Tel: 306-787-3920; *Fax:* 306-787-7392

Assistant Deputy Minister, David Boehm
Tel: 306-787-0835; *Fax:* 306-787-7392
david.boehm@gov.sk.ca

Executive Director, Corporate Finance, Scott Giroux
Tel: 306-787-3501; *Fax:* 306-787-7392
scott.giroux@gov.sk.ca

Executive Director, Business Systems & Risk Management, Duane Rieger
Tel: 306-787-1421; *Fax:* 306-798-0016
duane.rieger@gov.sk.ca

Executive Director, Planning, Strategy & Evaluation Branch, Linda Smith
Tel: 306-787-2984
linda.smith@gov.sk.ca

Sector Relations & Student Services

Executive Director, Student Services & Program Development Branch, Rikki Bote
Tel: 306-787-4156; *Fax:* 306-787-7537
Rikki.Bote@gov.sk.ca
www.saskatchewan.ca/studentloans
Other Communications: Alt. E-mail: studentservices@gov.sk.ca

Executive Director, Universities & Private Vocational Schools, Ann Lorenzen
Tel: 306-787-2267; *Fax:* 306-798-3379
ann.lorenzen@gov.sk.ca

Executive Director, Technical & Trades Branch, Mike Pestill
Tel: 306-787-2189; *Fax:* 306-798-3159
mike.pestill@gov.sk.ca

Director, Capital Planning, Todd Godfrey
Tel: 306-787-3369; *Fax:* 306-798-3159
todd.godfrey@gov.sk.ca

Saskatchewan Agriculture (AG)

Walter Scott Bldg., 3085 Albert St., Regina, SK S4S 0B1
Toll-Free: 866-457-2377
www.saskatchewan.ca/agriculture

The Ministry's mandate is to foster, in partnership with individuals, communities, industry, & government, a commercially viable, self-sufficient, & sustainable agricultural sector in Saskatchewan. The Ministry addresses needs of individual farmers & ranchers, encourages & develops higher value production & processing, & promotes sustainable economic development in rural areas of the province. Some responsibilities are as follows: agri-business development through provision of agriculture-based business experts & technical support; agricultural research to promote development & diversification; corporate services to support the Information Technology Office & the Rural Economic Co-operative Development; crop development; financial programs; inspection & administration of regulations for food & crop protection, animal disease surveillance, environmental reviews, licenses, registrations, & complaint resolution; irrigation development; promotion of sustainable use of Crown land; livestock development; provision of food safety, quality, policy, regulatory, market & business development programs; policy analysis, strategies, & agricultural information services; & delivery of Saskatchewan Crop Insurance Corporation programs & services.

Minister, Hon. Lyle Stewart
Tel: 306-787-0338; *Fax:* 306-787-0630
minister.ag@gov.sk.ca
Office of the Minister of Agriculture, Legislative Bldg.
#334, 2405 Legislative Dr.
Regina, SK S4S 0B3

Deputy Minister, Alanna Koch
Tel: 306-787-5170; *Fax:* 306-787-2393
alanna.koch@gov.sk.ca

Assistant Deputy Minister, Programs, Lee Auten
Tel: 306-787-3121; *Fax:* 306-787-2393
lee.auten@gov.sk.ca
Assistant Deputy Minister, Policy, Rick Burton
Tel: 306-787-8077; *Fax:* 306-787-2393
rick.burton@gov.sk.ca
Assistant Deputy Minister, Regulatory & Innovation, William Greuel
Tel: 306-787-5247; *Fax:* 306-787-2393
william.greuel@gov.sk.ca
Executive Director, Corporate Services, Raymond Arscott
Tel: 306-787-5211; *Fax:* 306-787-0600
raymond.arscott@gov.sk.ca
Executive Director, Livestock Branch, Jodi Banks
Tel: 306-787-6395; *Fax:* 306-787-1315
jodi.banks@gov.sk.ca
Executive Director, Policy, Jonathan Greuel
Tel: 306-787-5834; *Fax:* 306-787-5134
jonathan.greuel2@gov.sk.ca
Executive Director, Lands Branch, Wally Hoehn
Tel: 306-787-1045; *Fax:* 306-787-5180
wally.hoehn@gov.sk.ca
Executive Director, Agriculture Research Branch, Abdul Jalil
Tel: 306-787-5960; *Fax:* 306-787-2654
abdul.jalil@gov.sk.ca
Executive Director, Crops & Irrigation Branch, Penny McCall
Tel: 306-787-8061; *Fax:* 306-787-0428
penny.mccall@gov.sk.ca
Executive Director, Communications, Tiffany Stephenson
Tel: 306-787-4031; *Fax:* 306-787-0216
Executive Director, Financial Programs Branch, Vacant
Tel: 306-787-8510; *Fax:* 306-798-3042

Associated Agencies, Boards & Commissions:

•Agri-Food Council
#302, 3085 Albert St.
Regina, SK S4S 0B1
Tel: 306-787-5978; *Fax:* 306-787-5134
corey.ruud@gov.sk.ca
www.agriculture.gov.sk.ca/Agri-Food-Council
The Agri-Food Council is an independent board appointed by the provincial government. The Council is accountable to the Minister of Agriculture for the supervision of all agencies established under The Agri-Food Act, 2004.

•Agricultural Implements Board
#315, 3085 Albert St.
Regina, SK S4S 0B1
Tel: 306-787-8861; *Fax:* 306-787-8599

•Farm Stress Unit
3085 Albert St.
Regina, SK S4S 0B1
Toll-free: 800-667-4442

•Farmland Security Board
#315, 3988 Albert St.
Regina, SK S4S 3R1
Tel: 306-787-5047; *Fax:* 306-787-8599
www.farmland.gov.sk.ca

•Prairie Agricultural Machinery Institute (PAMI)
2215 - 8th Ave.
PO Box 1150
Humboldt, SK S0K 2A0
Tel: 306-682-5033; *Fax:* 306-682-5080
Toll-free: 800-567-7264
humboldt@pami.ca
www.pami.ca
PAMI works for the advancement of technology in agriculture through research & development. Satellite offices are located in Winnipeg, Saskatoon & Ottawa.

•Saskatchewan Crop Insurance Corporation (SCIC)
484 Prince William Dr.
PO Box 3000
Melville, SK S0A 2P0
Tel: 306-728-7200; *Fax:* 306-728-7202
Toll-free: 888-935-0000
customer.service@scic.gov.sk.ca
www.saskcropinsurance.com
Other Communication: AgriStability Call Centre, Toll-Free: 1-866-270-8450, Toll-Free Fax: 1-888-728-0440, Email: agristability@scic.gov.sk.ca
The provincial Crown Corporation provides responsive & flexible risk management tools. Crop insurance programs are as follows: Multi-Peril Insurance; Organic Insurance; Forage Insurance; & Weather Based Insurance.

•Saskatchewan Egg Producers (SEP)
496 Hoffer Dr.
Regina, SK S4N 7A1
Tel: 306-924-1505; *Fax:* 306-924-1515
www.saskegg.ca

•Saskatchewan Lands Appeal Board (SLAB)
#315, 3085 Albert St.
Regina, SK S4S 0B1
Tel: 306-787-8861

•Saskatchewan Milk Marketing Board (SMMB)
444 McLeod St.
Regina, SK S4N 4Y1
Tel: 306-949-6999; *Fax:* 306-949-2605
info@saskmilk.ca
www.saskmilk.ca

•Saskatchewan Sheep Development Board (SSDB)
2213C Hanselman Crt.
Saskatoon, SK S7L 6A8
Tel: 306-933-5200; *Fax:* 306-933-7182
sheepdb@sasktel.net
www.sksheep.com

•Saskatchewan Turkey Producers' Marketing Board (STP)
1438 Fletcher Rd.
Saskatoon, SK S7M 5T2
Tel: 306-931-1050
saskaturkey@sasktel.net
www.saskturkey.com
The STP manages the supply management system in Saskatchewan & raises levies in order to submit their own levy to the Canadian Turkey Marketing Agency (CTMA). The STP negotiates the province's quota levels with the CTMA, negotiates price levels with local processors, & develops a long-term strategy for the turkey industry in Saskatchewan.

Saskatchewan Archives Board

#401, 1870 Albert St., PO Box 1665 Regina, SK S4P 3C6
Tel: 306-787-4068; *Fax:* 306-787-1197
www.saskarchives.com
Secondary Address: 3 Campus Dr.
Murray Bldg., University of Saskatchewan
Saskatoon, SK S7N 5A4
Alt. Fax: 306-933-7305
info.saskatoon@archives.gov.sk.ca

The Saskatchewan Archives is a joint university-government agency, which was established under legislation. The Archives collects official records of the Government of Saskatchewan, as well as documentary material from local government & private sources.

Minister-in-charge, Hon. Christine Tell
Tel: 306-787-0942
minister.cs@gov.sk.ca
Chair, Trevor Powell
Tel: 306-585-0390; *Fax:* 306-787-1975
Provincial Archivist, Linda B. McIntyre
Tel: 306-798-4018; *Fax:* 306-787-1975
lmcintyre@archives.gov.sk.ca
Executive Director, Archival Programs & Information Management, Lenora Toth
Tel: 306-787-4741
ltoth@archives.gov.sk.ca
Manager, Preservation Management Unit; Digital Records Program, Curt Campbell
Tel: 306-933-8819
ccampbell@archives.gov.sk.ca
Manager, Reference Services Unit, Saskatoon, Nadine Charabin
Tel: 306-933-8321
ncharabin@archives.gov.sk.ca
Manager, Appraisal & Acquisition Unit, Trina Gillis
Tel: 306-787-0452
tgillis@archives.gov.sk.ca
Manager, Records Processing Unit, Jeremy Mohr
Tel: 306-787-5803; *Fax:* 306-798-0333
jmohr@archives.gov.sk.ca
Manager, Information Management Unit; Legislative Compliance & Access Unit, Anna Stoszek
Tel: 306-787-0700
astoszek@archives.gov.sk.ca
Manager, Information Technology Unit, Warren Weber
Tel: 306-787-0705; *Fax:* 306-787-1975
wweber@archives.gov.sk.ca

Saskatchewan Assessment Management Agency (SAMA)

#200, 2201 - 11th Ave., Regina, SK S4P 0J8
Tel: 306-924-8000; *Fax:* 306-924-8070
Toll-Free: 800-667-7262
info.request@sama.sk.ca
www.sama.sk.ca
Other Communication: Alt. E-mails: roll.confn@sama.sk.ca (Quality Assurance); revaluation.unit@sama.sk.ca (Revaluation); industrial.unit@sama.sk.ca (Industrial)
plus.google.com/+SamaSkCa

SAMA is an independent agency with responsibility to develop & maintain the province's assessment policies, standards & procedures, audit assessments, & review & confirm municipal assessment rolls & provide property valuation services to local governments (municipalities & school boards).
Chair, Neal Hardy
Chief Executive Officer, Irwin Blank

SaskBuilds

#720, 1855 Victoria Ave., Regina, SK S4P 3T2
Tel: 306-798-8014; *Fax:* 306-798-0626
saskbuilds@gov.sk.ca
www.saskbuilds.ca

SaskBuilds is a Crown corporation created in October 2012. Its mandate is to plan & manage large-scale infrastructure projects that are high-cost ($100 million or more), & that are high-priority for the province. These projects will likely be candidates for alternative financing.
Minister Responsible; Chair, Hon. Gordon Wyant, Q.C.
Tel: 306-787-5353; *Fax:* 306-787-1232
jus.minister@gov.sk.ca
President & Chief Executive Officer, Rupen Pandya
Tel: 306-798-8015
rupen.pandya@gov.sk.ca
Chief Financial Officer, Teresa Florizone
Tel: 306-798-1228
teresa.florizone@gov.sk.ca
Vice-President, Strategy & Engagement, Sarah Harrison
Tel: 306-798-1213
sarah.harrison@gov.sk.ca
Acting Vice-President, Priority Saskatchewan, Greg Lusk
Tel: 306-787-7842
greg.lusk2@gov.sk.ca

Saskatchewan Central Services (CS)

1920 Rose St., Regina, SK S4P 0A9
Tel: 306-787-6911; *Fax:* 306-787-1061
GSReception@gs.gov.sk.ca
www.cs.gov.sk.ca

In May 2012, Central Services replaced the Ministry of Government Services in Saskatchewan. The new organization manages government operations, including human resources, accommodations, transportation & IT services.
Minister, Hon. Christine Tell
minister.cs@gov.sk.ca
Office of the Minister Central Services, Legislative Building
#306, 2405 Legislative Dr.
Regina, SK S4S 0B3
Deputy Minister, Richard Murray
Tel: 306-787-6520; *Fax:* 306-787-6547
richard.murray@gov.sk.ca
Executive Director, Project Management & Delivery, Harlan Kennedy
Tel: 306-787-6495; *Fax:* 306-798-0043
harlan.kennedy@gov.sk.ca

Associated Agencies, Boards & Commissions:

•Public Service Commission (PSC)
2350 Albert St.
Regina, SK S4P 4A6
Tel: 306-787-7853
Toll-free: 866-319-5999
csinquiry@gov.sk.ca
www.cs.gov.sk.ca/HRServices
The human resource agency for the Government of Saskatchewan is the Public Service Commission.
The following are some services delivered by the Commission: classifying positions; recruiting & selecting employees; providing a mentorship program & professional development opportunities; offering anti-harassment resources & information about ethics & conduct; participating in labour relations; providing payroll tasks; offering an employee & family assistance program; & providing a long service recognition program.
The Commission is guided by The Public Service Act, 1998 & The Public Service Regulations 1999, as it serves more than 12,000 government employees.

Corporate Services
Tel: 306-787-6945; *Fax:* 306-798-0700
Executive Director, Troy Smith
Tel: 306-787-2433; *Fax:* 306-798-0700
troy.smith@gov.sk.ca

Digital Strategy & Operations
Walter Scott Bldg., #130, 3085 Albert St., Regina, SK S4S 0B1
Tel: 306-787-0909
csweb@gov.sk.ca
Chief Digital Officer, Lisa Raddysh
Tel: 306-787-0936
lisa.raddysh@gov.sk.ca

Planning, Performance & Communications
Fax: 306-787-1061

Executive Director, Planning, Performance & Communications, Robin Campese
Tel: 306-787-5959; *Fax:* 306-798-0371
robin.campese@gov.sk.ca
Executive Director, Communications, Laur'Lei Silzer
Tel: 306-787-0280; *Fax:* 306-798-0371
laurlei.silzer@gov.sk.ca

Commercial Services Division
Fax: 306-787-1061
Executive Director, Commercial Services Division, Greg Lusk
Tel: 306-787-7842; *Fax:* 306-787-1061
greg.lusk@gov.sk.ca
Executive Director, Air Services, Chris Oleson
Tel: 306-787-7717; *Fax:* 306-787-1424
chris.oleson@gov.sk.ca
Hangar 4, Regina Airport
2710 Airport Rd.
Regina, SK S4W 1A3
Director, Central Vehicle Agency (CVA), Derek Collins
Tel: 306-798-7103
Toll-free: 877-787-6902; *Fax:* 306-787-1625
derek.collins@gov.sk.ca
www.employeeservices.gov.sk.ca/CVA
500 McLeod St.
Regina, SK S4N 4Y1

Information Technology Division
2101 Scarth St., 8th Fl., Regina, SK S4P 2H9
Tel: 306-787-4586; *Fax:* 306-787-5718
inquiries@ito.gov.sk.ca
www.cs.gov.sk.ca/ITServices
Other Communication: ITO Service Desk, Phone: 306-787-5000
The work of the Information Technology Office is guided by The Information Technology Office Regulations, December 2004 & The Canadian Information Processing Society of Saskatchewan Act, 2005.
The following are some of the programs & services of the Information Technology Office: the procurement of information technology goods & services; corporate services, such as planning & communications; customer support; leadership on issues related to enterprise architecture; application management services; & operations such as the help desk.
Chief Information Officer, Bonnie Schmidt
Tel: 306-798-2307; *Fax:* 306-798-0700
bonnie.schmidt@gov.sk.ca
Executive Director, Application Management Services, Atiq Ahmad
Tel: 306-787-1447; *Fax:* 306-787-5454
atiq.ahmad@gov.sk.ca
Acting Executive Director, Infrastructure Management Services, Operations, Kelly Fuessel
Tel: 306-787-7894; *Fax:* 306-798-1048
kelly.fuessel@gov.sk.ca
Acting Executive Director, Support Services, Operations, Michele Rousseau
Tel: 306-798-1660
Michele.Rousseau@gov.sk.ca

Property Management
Fax: 306-798-0371
property.gov.sk.ca/accommodation
Acting Executive Director, Property Management, Andre Laberge
Tel: 306-787-7592; *Fax:* 306-798-0371
andre.laberge@gov.sk.ca
Director, Pricing & Services, Garth Belanger
Tel: 306-787-9680; *Fax:* 306-787-1980
garth.belanger@gov.sk.ca
Director, Infrastructure Support, Juan Garzon
Tel: 306-787-8023; *Fax:* 306-787-2019
juan.garzon@gov.sk.ca
Director, Property Management, Loreen Porter
Tel: 306-787-4241; *Fax:* 306-787-1061
loreen.porter@gov.sk.ca

Technical Services
Fax: 306-787-1061
Executive Director, Rob Clarke
Tel: 306-787-6332; *Fax:* 306-787-1980
rob.clarke@gov.sk.ca
Director, Major Provincial Projects, Adam Fehler
Tel: 306-787-6968; *Fax:* 306-787-1061
adam.fehler@gov.sk.ca
Director, Engineering & Sustainability, Jared Kleisinger
Tel: 306-798-1312; *Fax:* 306-787-1980
jared.kleisinger@gov.sk.ca
Acting Director, Infrastructure Renewal & Data Management, Darrell Toth
Tel: 306-787-4416; *Fax:* 306-787-1980
darrell.toth@gov.sk.ca

Crown Investments Corporation of Saskatchewan (CIC)

#400, 2400 College Ave., Regina, SK S4P 1C8
Tel: 306-787-6851; *Fax:* 306-787-8125
www.cicorp.sk.ca
The holding company for the commercial Crown corporations of Saskatchewan is the Crown Investments Corporation.
The key functions of the Corporation are as follows: assisting the boards of Crown corporations to strengthen governance; overseeing the direction of Crown corporations to improve performance & acountability; managing CIC Asset Management Inc. & the Gradworks program; & overseeing funds established with the administrative coordination or financial assistance of the government.
Minister Responsible, Hon. Joe Hargrave
minister.cc@gov.sk.ca
Office of the Minister of Crown Investments, Legislative Building
#322, 2405 Legislative Dr.
Regina, SK S4S 0B3
President & Chief Executive Officer, Blair Swystun
Tel: 306-787-9085; *Fax:* 306-787-8125
bswystun@cicorp.sk.ca
Vice-President, Special Projects, Ron Dedman
Tel: 306-798-4469
ron.dedman@gov.sk.ca
Executive Director, Communications, Cole Goertz
Tel: 306-787-5889; *Fax:* 306-787-8125
cgoertz@cicorp.sk.ca
Executive Director, Human Resources, Brian Gyoerick
Tel: 306-787-1257; *Fax:* 306-787-8125
bgyoerick@cicorp.sk.ca

Saskatchewan Development Fund Corporation
Tel: 306-787-7264
www.cicorp.sk.ca/funds/saskatchewan_development_fund_corp
The Saskatchewan Development Fund is a low risk investment fund that provides income & long-term investment growth to Saskatchewan residents. The Fund is administered by the Saskatchewan Development Fund Corporation. Since 1983, the Fund no longer sells new shares to the public, & instead serves the needsof existing clients & focuses on the winding down of its assets.

Finance & Administration Division
Tel: 306-787-5937; *Fax:* 306-787-8030
Chief Financial Officer & Senior Vice-President, Cindy Ogilvie
Tel: 306-787-6246; *Fax:* 306-787-8030
cogilvie@cicorp.sk.ca
Director, Performance Management & Financial Analysis, Pam Haubrich
Tel: 306-787-2714; *Fax:* 306-787-8030
phaubrich@cicorp.sk.ca
Director, Performance Management & Financial Analysis, Kyla Hillmer
Tel: 306-787-7286; *Fax:* 306-787-8030
khillmer@cicorp.sk.ca

Human Resource Policy, Governance & Legal Division
Tel: 306-787-5915; *Fax:* 306-787-0294
Senior Vice-President & General Counsel, Doug Kosloski
Tel: 306-787-5892
dkosloski@cicorp.sk.ca
Executive Director, Crown Sector Human Resources, Brian Gyoerick
Tel: 306-787-1257; *Fax:* 306-787-8125
bgyoerick@cicorp.sk.ca

Saskatchewan Economy (ECON)

#300, 2103 - 11th Ave., Regina, SK S4P 3Z8
webmasterECON@gov.sk.ca
economy.gov.sk.ca
Saskatchewan's Ministry of the Economy was created in May 2012 to reflect the provincial government's economic growth agenda. The new ministry incoporates economic functions of the government such as energy & resources, Enterprise Saskatchewan, & Tourism Saskatchewan.
Minister, Economy, Hon. Jeremy Harrison
minister.econ@gov.sk.ca
Minister's Office, Ministry of Economy, Legislative Building
#340, 2405 Legislative Dr.
Regina, SK S4S 0B3
Deputy Minister, Laurie Pushor
Tel: 306-787-9580; *Fax:* 306-787-2159
laurie.pushor@gov.sk.ca

Associated Agencies, Boards & Commissions:

•**Surface Rights Board of Arbitration**
113 - 2nd Ave. East
PO Box 1597
Kindersley, SK S0L 1S0
Tel: 306-463-5447; *Fax:* 306-463-5449
surfacerightsboard@gov.sk.ca
economy.gov.sk.ca/surfacerights
Governed by The Surface Rights Acquisition & Compensation Act, the Surface Rights Board of Arbitration is a last resort when an occupant or landowner & an oil, gas or potash operator are unable to reach an agreement.

Marketing & Communications
2103 - 11th Ave., 5th Fl., Regina, SK S4P 3Z8
Fax: 306-787-8447
Executive Director, Joanne Johnson
Tel: 306-787-7967; *Fax:* 306-787-8447
joanne.johnson@gov.sk.ca

Economic Development
2103 - 11th Ave., 4th Fl., Regina, SK S4P 3Z8
Tel: 306-933-7200; *Fax:* 306-933-7726
Assistant Deputy Minister & Senior Strategic Lead, Mineral Development, Kirk Westgard
Tel: 306-787-0370; *Fax:* 306-787-7559
Kirk.Westgard@gov.sk.ca
Director, International Engagement, Gavin Conacher
Tel: 306-787-0910; *Fax:* 306-787-7559
gavin.conacher@gov.sk.ca
Director, First Nations & Metis Economic Development, Peter Gosselin
Tel: 306-798-0489; *Fax:* 306-787-7559
peter.gosselin@gov.sk.ca
Director, Northern Economic Development, Doug Howorko
Tel: 306-798-5167; *Fax:* 306-787-7559
doug.howorko@gov.sk.ca
Director, Lead & Prospect Generation, Bill Spring
Tel: 306-787-2225; *Fax:* 306-787-7559
bill.spring@gov.sk.ca

Energy & Resources (ER)
2101 Scarth St., Regina, SK S4P SH9
Tel: 306-787-2528
To build an innovative, diversified, & sustainable economy for Saskatchewan, the Energy & Resources unit develops, implements, & promotes policies & programs related to the province's energy, mineral, & forestry sectors.
The following mineral resource databases are available: Saskatchewan Mineral Assessment Database; Saskatchewan Mineral Deposit Index; & Saskatchewan Kimberlite Indicator Minerals.
Minister, Hon. Dustin Duncan
er.minister@gov.sk.ca
Office of the Minister, Legislative Building
#340, 2405 Legislative Dr.
Regina, SK S4S 0B3
Deputy Minister, Laurie Pushor
Tel: 306-787-9580; *Fax:* 306-787-2159
laurie.pushor@gov.sk.ca

Minerals, Lands & Resource Policy
Tel: 306-787-8178; *Fax:* 306-787-2198
Assistant Deputy Minister, Hal Sanders
Tel: 306-787-3524; *Fax:* 306-787-2198
hal.sanders@gov.sk.ca
Chief Geologist, Gary Delaney
Tel: 306-787-1160; *Fax:* 306-787-1284
gary.delaney@gov.sk.ca
Executive Director, Mineral Policy, Cory Hughes
Tel: 306-787-3628; *Fax:* 306-787-2198
cory.hughes@gov.sk.ca
Executive Director, Lands & Mineral Tenure, Paul Mahnic
Tel: 306-787-5385; *Fax:* 306-798-0047
Paul.Mahnic@gov.sk.ca
Executive Director, Forestry Development - Prince Albert, Shane Vermette
Tel: 306-953-3797; *Fax:* 306-953-3733
shane.vermette@gov.sk.ca
Executive Director, Energy Policy, Floyd Wist
Tel: 306-787-2477; *Fax:* 306-787-2198
floyd.wist@gov.sk.ca

Petroleum & Natural Gas Division
Tel: 306-787-2592; *Fax:* 306-787-2478
Assistant Deputy Minister, Doug MacKnight
Tel: 306-787-2082; *Fax:* 306-787-2478
Doug.Macknight@gov.sk.ca
Executive Director, Field Services, Bert West
Tel: 306-787-2318; *Fax:* 306-787-2478
Bert.West@gov.sk.ca
Director, Field Operations, Ken Kowal
Tel: 306-798-3085; *Fax:* 306-787-2478
Ken.Kowal@gov.sk.ca

Director, Data Management, Bruce Lerner
Tel: 306-798-9507; *Fax:* 306-787-8236
bruce.lerner@gov.sk.ca
Director, Client Services, Janice Loseth
Tel: 306-798-9509; *Fax:* 306-787-3872
Janice.Loseth@gov.sk.ca
Director, Liability Management, Brad Wagner
Tel: 306-787-2348; *Fax:* 306-787-2478
Brad.Wagner@gov.sk.ca
Director, Resource Conservation, Debby Westerman
Tel: 306-798-4210; *Fax:* 306-787-2478
Debby.Westerman@gov.sk.ca

Labour Market Development
1945 Hamilton St., 12th Fl., Regina, SK S4P 2C8
Tel: 306-787-2495; *Fax:* 306-787-7182
economy.gov.sk.ca/labourmarketservices
Assistant Deputy Minister, Alastair MacFadden
Tel: 306-787-6846; *Fax:* 306-787-7182
alastair.macfadden2@gov.sk.ca
Executive Director, Labour Market Planning & Systems Support, Leah Goodwin
Tel: 306-798-0476; *Fax:* 306-787-8122
leah.goodwin@gov.sk.ca
Executive Director, Labour Market Services, Jan Kot
Tel: 306-787-8458; *Fax:* 306-798-5022
Jan.Kot@gov.sk.ca
Executive Director, Immigration Services, Christa Ross
Tel: 306-787-3099; *Fax:* 306-787-0713
christa.ross@gov.sk.ca
Other Communications: Alt. E-mail: christa.ross@gov.sk.ca
Executive Director, Apprenticeship & Workforce Skills, Darcy Smycniuk
Tel: 306-787-5984; *Fax:* 306-787-7182
darcy.smycniuk@gov.sk.ca

Performance & Strategic Initiatives
2103 - 11th Ave., 4th Fl., Regina, SK S4P 3Z8
Fax: 306-787-3989
Assistant Deputy Minister, Michael Mitchell
Tel: 306-787-0572; *Fax:* 306-787-3989
michael.mitchell@gov.sk.ca
Director, Regulatory Modernization, Joe Carson
Tel: 306-787-8865; *Fax:* 306-787-8865
joe.carson@gov.sk.ca
Director, Strategic Planning & Performance, Bryan Dilling
Tel: 306-933-7599; *Fax:* 306-933-8244
bryan.dilling@gov.sk.ca
Director, Greater China, William Wang
Tel: 306-798-1276; *Fax:* 306-787-7559
william.wang@gov.sk.ca
Director, Strategic Policy & Initiatives, Vacant

Revenue & Corporate Services
2103 - 11th Ave., 3rd Fl., Regina, SK S4P 3Z8
Tel: 306-787-9878; *Fax:* 306-787-3872
Chief Financial Officer, Denise Haas
Tel: 306-787-2756; *Fax:* 306-787-3872
denise.haas@gov.sk.ca
Executive Director, Financial Services, Andrea Terry Munro
Tel: 306-787-9694; *Fax:* 306-787-8702
andrea.terrymunro@gov.sk.ca
Director, Financial & Administration, Neil Cooke
Tel: 306-787-7874; *Fax:* 306-787-8702
neil.cooke@gov.sk.ca
Director, Audit & Collections, Beverly Deglau
Tel: 306-787-5347; *Fax:* 306-798-2158
beverly.deglau@gov.sk.ca
Director, IRIS Management Services, Danette Flegel
Tel: 306-798-3068; *Fax:* 306-798-0599
Danette.Flegel@gov.sk.ca
Director, Financial Programs, Gerry Holland
Tel: 306-798-1277; *Fax:* 306-798-0796
gerry.holland@gov.sk.ca
Director, Legislative, Information & Technology Services, Cam Pelzer
Tel: 306-787-2378; *Fax:* 306-787-2198
cam.pelzer@gov.sk.ca

Saskatchewan Education (ED)

2220 College Ave., Regina, SK S4P 4V9
linquiry@gov.sk.ca
www.education.gov.sk.ca
The Ministry provides programs & services in the following key areas: early learning & child care, the pre-kindergarten to grade 12 education system, & the Provincial Library. In November 2007, a new provincial government resulted in the reorganization of provincial government ministries. The work of Saskatchewan Learning was merged into the newly named Ministry of Education.
Minister, Hon. Don Morgan, Q.C.
Tel: 306-787-0613; *Fax:* 306-787-6946
minister.edu@gov.sk.ca
Minister's Office, Ministry of Education, Legislative Building #361, 2405 Legislative Dr.
Regina, SK S4S 0B3
Deputy Minister, Julie MacRae
Tel: 306-787-2471; *Fax:* 306-787-1300
Assistant Deputy Minister, Donna Johnson
Tel: 306-787-6056; *Fax:* 306-787-1300
donna.johnson@gov.sk.ca
Assistant Deputy Minister, Greg Miller
Tel: 306-787-3222; *Fax:* 306-787-1300
greg.miller@gov.sk.ca
Executive Director, Communications & Sector Relations, Jill Welke
Tel: 306-787-5609; *Fax:* 306-798-2045
jill.welke@gov.sk.ca
Executive Director, Corporate Services, Robert Spelliscy
Tel: 306-787-3520; *Fax:* 306-798-5042
rob.spelliscy@gov.sk.ca

Associated Agencies, Boards & Commissions:
·Teachers' Superannuation Commission
#129, 3085 Albert St.
Regina, SK S4S 0B1
Tel: 306-787-6440; *Fax:* 306-787-1939
Toll-free: 877-364-8202
mail@stsc.gov.sk.ca
www.stsc.gov.sk.ca

Early Years
Tel: 306-787-2004; *Fax:* 306-787-0277
Executive Director, Lynn Allan
Tel: 306-787-0765; *Fax:* 306-787-0277
lynn.allan@gov.sk.ca
Director, Early Years Planning, Education & Evaluation, Kathy Abernethy
Tel: 306-787-6158; *Fax:* 306-787-0277
kathy.abernethy@gov.sk.ca
Director, Early Childhood Program, Policy & Design, Brenda Dougherty
Tel: 306-787-3858; *Fax:* 306-787-0277
brenda.dougherty@gov.sk.ca
Director, Early Learning & Child Care Service Delivery, Cindy Jeanes
Tel: 306-787-3750; *Fax:* 306-798-3146
cindy.jeanes@gov.sk.ca
Director, Early Years, Janet Mitchell
Tel: 306-798-4738; *Fax:* 306-787-0277
janet.mitchell@gov.sk.ca

Education Funding
Fax: 306-787-5059
Acting Executive Director, Angela Chobanik
Tel: 306-787-6042
angela.chobanik@gov.sk.ca
Director, Education Financial Policy, Tracey McMurchy
Tel: 306-787-5192
tracey.mcmurchy@gov.sk.ca
Director, Financial Analyst & Reporting, Doug Schell
Tel: 306-787-6634
doug.schell@gov.sk.ca

Information Management & Support
#128, 1621 Albert St., Regina, SK S4P 2S5
Tel: 306-787-2494; *Fax:* 306-787-0035
Executive Director, Gerry Craswell
Tel: 306-787-6053
gerry.craswell@gov.sk.ca
Director & Registrar, Student & Educator Services, Shelley Lowes
Tel: 306-787-6039
shelley.lowes@gov.sk.ca

Infrasturcture
Tel: 306-798-3071; *Fax:* 306-798-5042
Executive Director, Sheldon Ramstead
Tel: 306-787-7856; *Fax:* 306-798-0787
sheldon.ramstead@gov.sk.ca
Director, School Bundle Project, Phil Pearson
Tel: 306-787-9505; *Fax:* 306-798-5042
phil.pearson@gov.sk.ca

Provincial Library & Literacy Office
409A Park St., Regina, SK S4N 5B2
Tel: 306-787-2976; *Fax:* 306-787-2029
srp.adm@prov.lib.sk.ca
www.education.gov.sk.ca/Provincial-Library
Other Communication: Literacy Office: www.education.gov.sk.ca/literacy
Provincial Librarian, Brett Waytuck
Tel: 306-787-2972; *Fax:* 306-787-2029
brett.waytuck@gov.sk.ca
Director, Public Library Planning, Julie Arie
Tel: 306-787-3005; *Fax:* 306-787-2029
julie.arie@gov.sk.ca
Director, Library Accountability & Administration, Barbara Bulat
Tel: 306-787-6032; *Fax:* 306-787-2029
barbara.bulat@gov.sk.ca
Director, Literacy Office, Maureen Johns
Tel: 306-787-8020; *Fax:* 306-787-2029
maureen.johns@gov.sk.ca

Strategic Policy
Tel: 306-787-6769; *Fax:* 306-787-6319
Executive Director, Rosanne Glass
Tel: 306-787-3897; *Fax:* 306-787-6139
Rosanne.Glass@gov.sk.ca

Student Achievement & Supports
Tel: 306-787-9256
Executive Director, Tim Caleval
Tel: 306-787-5632; *Fax:* 306-787-3164
tim.caleval@gov.sk.ca
Director, Curriculum Unit, Susan Nedelcov-Anderson
Tel: 306-787-6089; *Fax:* 306-787-2223
susan.nedelcovanderson@gov.sk.ca
Director, Assessment Unit, Michelle Belisle
Tel: 306-787-2370; *Fax:* 306-787-9178
michelle.belisle@gov.sk.ca
Director, Instruction, Kevin Kleisinger
Tel: 306-787-9042; *Fax:* 306-787-2223
kevin.kleisinger@gov.sk.ca
Director, Programs, Kevin Gabel
Tel: 306-787-1843; *Fax:* 306-787-2223
kevin.gabel@gov.sk.ca
Senior Program Manager, English as an Additional Language & Languages, Nadia Prokopchuk
Tel: 306-933-8497; *Fax:* 306-787-2223
nadia.prokopchuk@gov.sk.ca

Regional Offices
Southern Region
1831 College Ave., 3rd Fl., Regina, SK S4P 4V5
Fax: 306-787-6139
Central Region
122 - 3rd Ave. North, 8th Fl., Saskatoon, SK S7K 2H6
Fax: 306-933-7469
Northern Region
Mistasinihk Place, #2200, 1328 La Ronge Ave., PO Box 5000 La Ronge, SK S0J 1L0
Tel: 306-425-4380; *Fax:* 306-425-4383
Toll-Free: 800-667-4380
Regional Director, Daryl Arnott
Tel: 306-425-4382
daryl.arnott@gov.sk.ca

Elections Saskatchewan

1702 Park St., Regina, SK S4N 6B2
Tel: 306-787-4000; *Fax:* 306-787-4052
Toll-Free: 877-958-8683
info@elections.sk.ca
www.elections.sk.ca
Other Communication: Toll-Free Fax: 1-866-678-4052
twitter.com/ElectionsSask
www.facebook.com/242710365081
Chief Electoral Officer, Michael Boda
Tel: 306-787-4027
Deputy Chief Electoral Officer, Jennifer Colin
Tel: 306-787-4061
jcolin@elections.sk.ca
Electoral Operations Officer, Maureen Matthew
Tel: 306-787-9656
mmatthew@elections.sk.ca
Senior Director, Outreach, Policy & Communications, Tim Kydd
Tel: 306-787-7355
tkydd@elections.sk.ca
Director, Information Technology, Jordan Arendt
Tel: 306-531-2373
jarendt@elections.sk.ca
Director, Finance, Brent Nadon
Tel: 306-787-4017
bnadon@elections.sk.ca
Director, Electoral Operations, Bonnie Schenher
Tel: 306-787-0156
bschenher@elections.sk.ca

Saskatchewan Environment (ENV)

3211 Albert St., 2nd Fl., Regina, SK S4S 5W6
Tel: 306-787-2584; *Fax:* 306-787-9544
Toll-Free: 800-567-4224
Centre.Inquiry@gov.sk.ca
www.environment.gov.sk.ca
Other Communication: Parkwatch Line: 1-800-667-1788; Firewatch Line: 1-800-667-9660; Spill Control Centre: 1-800-667-7525; TIP (Turn in Poachers: 1-800-667-7561

Saskatchewan Environment protects & mananges the province's environmental & natural resources by offering the following programs & services: compliance & enforcement to protect the public's interests in the management of air, land, water & natural resources; protection & management of forest ecosystems; wildfire management; Green Strategy; environmental assessment; legislation, & policies to ensure that Crown land is used in ways that respect environmental, economic & social values; fishing & fisheries management; hunting management; licensing & guiding the trapping industry; protection of wildlife; recycling; waste management; & water resource & treatment plant operations management.

Minister, Hon. Scott Moe
Tel: 306-787-0393; *Fax:* 306-787-1669
env.minister@gov.sk.ca
Office of the Minister of the Environment, Legislative Building #38, 2405 Legislative Dr.
Regina, SK S4S 0B3

Deputy Minister, Cam Swan
Tel: 306-787-2930; *Fax:* 306-787-2947
cam.swan@gov.sk.ca

Director, Communications Services Branch, Wayne Wark
Tel: 306-787-2770; *Fax:* 306-787-3941
wayne.wark@gov.sk.ca

Associated Agencies, Boards & Commissions:

•Saskatchewan Conservation Data Centre (SKCDC)
Fish & Wildlife Branch, Ministry of Environment
3211 Albert St.
Regina, SK S4S 5W6
Tel: 306-787-7196; *Fax:* 306-787-9544
www.biodiversity.sk.ca

The SKCDC was formed as a co-operative venture between the province, The Nature Conservancy USA & The Nature Conservancy of Canada. The SKCDC gathers, interprets & distributes scientific information on the ecological status of provincial wild species & communities. The SKCDC is committed to conserving biological diversity; producing scientific reports & being the provincial clearinghouse for threatened & endangered species information.

•Water Appeal Board
#217, 3085 Albert St.
Regina, SK S4S 0B1
Tel: 306-798-7462; *Fax:* 306-787-8558

Environmental Protection & Audit Division

3211 Albert St., 5th Fl., Regina, SK S4S 5W6
Fax: 306-787-2947

Protects human health & ecosystem integrity.

Assistant Deputy Minister, Erika Ritchie
Tel: 306-787-5419; *Fax:* 306-787-2947
erika.ritchie@gov.sk.ca

Chief Engineer, Technical Resources Branch, Kevin McCullum
Tel: 306-787-2739; *Fax:* 306-787-2947
kevin.mccullum@gov.sk.ca

Executive Director, Environmental Protection Branch, Wes Kotyk
Tel: 306-933-6542; *Fax:* 306-933-8442
wes.kotyk@gov.sk.ca

Executive Director, RBR & Code Management Branch, Thon Phommavong
Tel: 306-787-9986; *Fax:* 306-787-1513
thon.phommavong@gov.sk.ca

Acting Director, Climate Change Branch, Ed Dean
Tel: 306-787-7812; *Fax:* 306-787-0024
ed.dean@gov.sk.ca

Director, Environmental Assessment Branch, Sharla Hordenchuk
Tel: 306-787-1023; *Fax:* 306-787-0930
sharla.hordenchuk@gov.sk.ca

Wildfire Management Branch

Provincial Wildfire Centre, Hwy. #2 North, PO Box 3003 Prince Albert, SK S6V 6G1
Tel: 306-953-3473; *Fax:* 306-953-3575

Executive Director, Steve Roberts
Tel: 306-953-2206
steve.roberts@gov.sk.ca

Environmental Support Division

3211 Albert St., 5th Fl., Regina, SK S4S 5W6
Fax: 306-787-2947

Assistant Deputy Minister, Lori Uhersky
Tel: 306-787-5737; *Fax:* 306-787-2947
lori.uhersky@gov.sk.ca

Executive Director, Strategic Planning & Performance Improvement, Troy Metz
Tel: 306-787-5194; *Fax:* 306-787-0024
troy.metz@gov.sk.ca

Executive Director, Finance & Administration, Laurel Welsh
Tel: 306-787-2484; *Fax:* 306-787-8441
laurel.welsh@gov.sk.ca

Director, Budget & Fiscal Planning Section, Kristen Fry
Tel: 306-787-9315; *Fax:* 306-787-8441
kristen.fry@gov.sk.ca

Acting Director, Financial Management, Cheryl Jansen
Tel: 306-787-1259; *Fax:* 306-787-8441
cheryl.jansen@gov.sk.ca

Director, Financial & Property Management, Zachery Solomon
Tel: 306-798-3904; *Fax:* 306-787-8441
zachery.solomon@gov.sk.ca

Resource Management & Compliance Division

3211 Albert St., 5th fl., Regina, SK S4S 5W6
Fax: 306-787-2947

Assistant Deputy Minister, Kevin Murphy
Tel: 306-787-8567; *Fax:* 306-787-2947
kevin.murphy@gov.sk.ca

Executive Director, Compliance & Field Services, Kevin Callele
Tel: 306-787-3388; *Fax:* 306-787-3913
kevin.callele@gov.sk.ca

Executive Director, Landscape Stewardship Branch, Jennifer McKillop
Tel: 306-787-9643; *Fax:* 306-787-0197
jennifer.mckillop@gov.sk.ca

Executive Director, Fish & Wildlife, Lyle Saigeon
Tel: 306-787-2309; *Fax:* 306-787-9544
lyle.saigeon@gov.sk.ca

Executive Director, Forest Service, Bob Wynes
Tel: 306-953-2491; *Fax:* 306-953-2360
bob.wynes@gov.sk.ca

Director, Compliance & Enforcement Section, Ken Aube
Tel: 306-953-2993; *Fax:* 306-953-2999
ken.aube@gov.sk.ca

Acting Director, Aboriginal Affairs Section, Roger Brown
Tel: 306-787-1990; *Fax:* 306-787-0197
roger.brown@gov.sk.ca

Director, Client Service, Kim Clark
Tel: 306-953-2786; *Fax:* 306-953-2684
kim.clark@gov.sk.ca

Acting Director, Lands, Todd Olexson
Tel: 306-953-2586; *Fax:* 306-953-2684
todd.olexson@gov.sk.ca

Director, Field Services, Brent Webster
Tel: 306-446-7424; *Fax:* 306-446-7464
brent.webster@gov.sk.ca

Regional Operations

Beauval Compliance Area
Lavoie St., PO Box 280 Beauval, SK S0M 0G0
Tel: 306-288-4710; *Fax:* 306-288-4717

Compliance Manager, Dennis Daigneault
Tel: 306-288-4713; *Fax:* 306-288-4717
Dennis.Daigneault@gov.sk.ca

La Ronge Compliance Area
Mistasinihk Place, #1100 - 1328 La Ronge Ave., PO Box 5000 La Ronge, SK S0J 1L0
Tel: 306-425-4234; *Fax:* 306-425-2580

Compliance Manager, Daryl Minster
Tel: 306-425-4244; *Fax:* 306-425-2580
Daryl.Minter@gov.sk.ca

Meadow Lake Compliance Area
#1, 101 Railway Pl., Meadow Lake, SK S9X 1X6
Tel: 306-236-7557; *Fax:* 306-236-7677

Compliance Manager, Marc Painchaud
Tel: 306-236-9833; *Fax:* 306-236-7677
Marc.Painchaud@gov.sk.ca

Prince Albert Compliance Area
800 Central Ave., PO Box 3003 Prince Albert, SK S6V 6G1
Tel: 306-953-2322; *Fax:* 306-953-2321

Compliance Manager, Bill Zimmer
Tel: 306-953-2945; *Fax:* 306-953-2999
Bill.Zimmer@gov.sk.ca

Saskatoon Compliance Area
112 Research Dr., Saskatoon, SK S7N 3R3
Tel: 306-933-6240; *Fax:* 306-933-5773

Compliance Manager, Kerry Wrishko
Tel: 306-933-7416; *Fax:* 306-933-5773

Swift Current Compliance Area
350 Cheadle St. West, PO Box 5000 Swift Current, SK S9H 4G3
Tel: 306-778-8205; *Fax:* 306-778-8212

Compliance Manager, Bob Roberts
Tel: 306-778-8644; *Fax:* 306-778-8212
bob.roberts@gov.sk.ca

Yorkton Compliance Area
120 Smith St. East, Yorkton, SK S3N 3V3
Fax: 306-786-5716

Compliance Manager, Phil Decker
Tel: 306-786-1692; *Fax:* 306-786-5716
Phil.Decker@gov.sk.ca

SaskEnergy Incorporated

1777 Victoria Ave., Regina, SK S4P 4K5
Tel: 306-777-9225
Toll-Free: 800-567-8899
www.saskenergy.com
Other Communication: Emergency & safety Line: 1-888-700-0427; Line Locates: 1-866-828-4888

The provincial Crown corporation provides natural gas to residential, farm, commercial, & industrial customers in 92% of Saskatchewan's communities. Subsidiaries include the following: TransGas Limited; Bayhurst Gas Limited (including Bayhurst Energy Services Corporation & BG Storage Inc.); Many Islands Pipe Lines (Canada) Limited; Swan Valley Gas Corporation; & Saskatchewan First Call Corporation.

Minister Responsible, Hon. Dustin Duncan
Tel: 306-787-0804; *Fax:* 306-798-2009
Office of the Minister Responsible Energy & Resources / SaskEnergy Incorporated
#348, 2405 Legislative Dr.
Regina, SK S4S 0B3

Chair, Susan Barber
Tel: 306-777-9901

President & Chief Executive Officer, Doug Kelin
Tel: 306-777-9901; *Fax:* 306-522-2217
presidentsoffice@saskenergy.com

Vice-President, General Counsel & Corporate Secretary, Mark Guillet
Tel: 306-777-9427; *Fax:* 306-565-3332
mguillet@saskenergy.com

Corporate Support

Fax: 306-777-9561

Vice-President, Colleen Huber
Tel: 306-777-9660
chuber@saskenergy.com

Distribution Engineering & Construction

Tel: 306-777-9994; *Fax:* 306-522-2217

Executive Director, Distribution Engineering & Construction, Perry Blazic
Tel: 306-975-8567; *Fax:* 306-975-8698
pblazic@saskenergy.com

Distribution Utility & Gas Supply

Tel: 306-777-9354; *Fax:* 306-569-3522

Executive Vice-President, Distribution Utility, Dean Reeve
Tel: 306-777-9402; *Fax:* 306-525-3488

Executive Director, Gas Supply, Marketing & Rates, Lori Christie
Tel: 306-777-9361; *Fax:* 306-569-3522
lchristie@saskenergy.com

Executive Director, Customer Service, Randy Greggains
Tel: 306-777-9994; *Fax:* 306-522-2217
rgreggains@saskenergy.com

Executive Director, Business & Customer Solutions, Jacquie Kerr
Tel: 306-777-9049; *Fax:* 306-522-2217

Finance

Fax: 306-777-9070

Vice-President & Chief Financial Officer, Christine Short
Tel: 306-777-9428
cshort@saskenergy.com

Human Resources & Corporate Affairs

Fax: 306-781-7050

Vice-President, Robert Haynes
Tel: 306-777-9405
rhaynes@saskenergy.com

Director, Government & Media Relations, Dave Burdeniuk
Tel: 306-777-9842; *Fax:* 306-352-4438
dburdeniuk@saskenergy.com

Director, Compensation & Strategic Initiatives, Trish Deck
Tel: 306-777-9406
tdeck@saskenergy.com

Director, Safety, Health & Employee Well-being, Harvey Fedyk
Tel: 306-777-9166
hfedyk@saskenergy.com

Director, Organizational Development, Margot Johnson
Tel: 306-777-9498
mjohnson@saskenergy.com

Director, Labour Relations & Staffing, Maria McCullough
Tel: 306-777-9398
mmccullough@saskenergy.com

Saskatchewan Finance (FI)

2350 Albert St., Regina, SK S4P 4A6
Tel: 306-787-6768; *Fax:* 306-787-0241
communications@finance.gov.sk.ca
www.finance.gov.sk.ca
Other Communication: General Tax Inquiries: 1-800-667-6102

The Ministry of Finance manages the financing, revenue, & expenses of the provincial government. The following are some of the duties performed by the department: administering provincial taxes, grant, & refund programs; managing banking, investment, & public debt functions; providing financial & policy analysis; offering economic forecasting & economic & social statistics; producing the provincial budget; assisting the government in the management of public monies; & managing governmental pension & benefit plans.

Minister, Hon. Kevin Doherty
Tel: 306-787-0341; *Fax:* 306-798-0263
fin.minister@gov.sk.ca
Legislative Building
#312, 2405 Legislative Dr.
Regina, SK S4S 0B3

Deputy Minister, Clare Isman
Tel: 306-787-6621; *Fax:* 306-787-7155
clare.isman@gov.sk.ca

Executive Director, Communications, Jeff Welke
Tel: 306-787-6046; *Fax:* 306-787-7155
jeff.welke@gov.sk.ca

Executive Director, Personnel Policy Secretariat, Don Zerr
Tel: 306-787-3101; *Fax:* 306-798-0386
don.zerr@gov.sk.ca

Director, Communications, Debbie Clark
Tel: 306-787-6578; *Fax:* 306-787-7155
deb.clark@gov.sk.ca

Associated Agencies, Boards & Commissions:

•Board of Revenue Commissioners
#480, 2151 Scarth St.
Regina, SK S4P 2H8
Tel: 306-787-6221; *Fax:* 306-787-1610
www.gov.sk.ca/BRC
The Board hears & determines appeals regarding taxes & other monies claimed to be due & payable to the Crown, where the right of taking appeal to the Board is given by any statute.

•Municipal Employees' Pension Commission
#1000, 1801 Hamilton St.
Regina, SK S4P 4W3
Fax: 306-787-8822
www.peba.gov.sk.ca/pensions/mepp/about/commission.html
The Municipal Employees' Pension Commission is responsible for the administration of the Municipal Employees' Pension Fund.

•Municipal Financing Corporation of Saskatchewan (MFC)
2350 Albert St., 6th Fl.
Regina, SK S4P 4A6
Tel: 306-787-8150; *Fax:* 306-787-8493
www.gov.sk.ca/mfc
The MFC, established in 1969 under the authority of The Municipal Financing Corporation Act, makes capital funds available to the financing of sewer & water, school, hospital, & other vital municipal construction projects.

•Saskatchewan Pension Plan (SPP)
608 Main St.
PO Box 5555
Kindersley, SK S0L 1S0
Tel: 306-463-5410; *Fax:* 306-463-3500
Toll-free: 800-667-7153
TTY: 888-213-1311
info@saskpension.com
www.saskpension.com

Budget Analysis Division
Tel: 306-787-6742

Associate Deputy Minister, Treasury Board & Treasury Management, Denise Macza
Tel: 306-787-6780; *Fax:* 306-787-3982
Denise.Macza@gov.sk.ca

Executive Director, Planning, Accountability & Reporting Branch, Deanna Bergbusch
Tel: 306-787-2572; *Fax:* 306-787-3982
deanna.bergbusch@gov.sk.ca

Executive Director, Economic & Fiscal Policy Branch, Joanne Brockman
Tel: 306-787-6743; *Fax:* 306-787-1426
joanne.brockman@gov.sk.ca

Executive Director, Cash & Debt Management, Jim Fallows
Tel: 306-787-3923; *Fax:* 306-787-8493
Jim.Fallows@gov.sk.ca

Executive Director, Estimates, Jeannette Lowe
Tel: 306-787-6726; *Fax:* 306-787-3982
jeannette.lowe@gov.sk.ca

Executive Director, Taxation & Intergovernmental Affairs Branch, Arun Srinivas
Tel: 306-787-6731; *Fax:* 306-787-7003
arun.srinivas@gov.sk.ca

Corporate Services Division
2350 Albert St., 5th Fl., Regina, SK S4P 4A6
Fax: 306-787-6576

Assistant Deputy Minister, Karen Allen
Tel: 306-787-6530
karen.allen@gov.sk.ca

Director, Planning & Accountability, Jessica Broda
Tel: 306-787-6744
jessica.broda2@gov.sk.ca

Director, Business Systems Branch, Jeremy Phillips
Tel: 306-787-6658
jeremy.phillips@gov.sk.ca

Provincial Comptroller's Division
2350 Albert St., 8th Fl., Regina, SK S4P 4A6
Tel: 306-787-6353; *Fax:* 306-787-9720

Provincial Comptroller, Terry Paton
Tel: 306-787-9254; *Fax:* 306-787-9720
Terry.Paton@gov.sk.ca

Executive Director, Financial Management, & Internal Audit, Chris Bayda
Tel: 306-787-6848; *Fax:* 306-787-9720
Chris.Bayda@gov.sk.ca

Public Employees Benefits Agency
1000 - 1801 Hamilton St., Regina, SK S4P 4W3
Tel: 306-787-2992; *Fax:* 306-787-8822
peba@peba.gov.sk.ca
www.peba.gov.sk.ca

Assistant Deputy Minister, Dave Wild
Tel: 306-787-6757; *Fax:* 306-798-0065
dave.wild@peba.gov.sk.ca

Executive Director, Pension Programs, Ann Mackrill
Tel: 306-787-3293; *Fax:* 306-787-8822
ann.mackrill@peba.gov.sk.ca

Revenue Division
2350 Albert St., 5th Fl., PO Box 200 Regina, SK S4P 2Z6
Tel: 306-787-6645; *Fax:* 306-787-0776
Toll-Free: 800-667-6102

Assistant Deputy Minister, Brent Hebert
Tel: 306-787-6685; *Fax:* 306-787-0241
brent.hebert@gov.sk.ca

Director, Tax Information & Compliance Branch, Larry Jacobson
Tel: 306-787-7773; *Fax:* 306-798-3045
larry.jacobson@gov.sk.ca

Director, Audit Branch, Garth Herbert
Tel: 306-787-7784; *Fax:* 306-798-3045
garth.herbert@gov.sk.ca

Director, Revenue Operations Branch, Kelly Laurans
Tel: 306-787-7788; *Fax:* 306-787-6653
kelly.laurans@gov.sk.ca

Director, Revenue Administration Modernization Project (RAMP), Nancy Perras
Tel: 306-787-7785; *Fax:* 306-787-0776
nancy.perras@gov.sk.ca

Saskatchewan Gaming Corporation (SaskGaming)

1880 Saskatchewan Dr., 3rd Fl., Regina, SK S4P 0B2
Tel: 306-787-1590
Toll-Free: 800-555-3189
contact@casinoregina.com
www.casinoregina.com/corporate
twitter.com/casinoregina
www.facebook.com/casinoregina
www.linkedin.com/company/saskatchewan-gaming-corporation

SaskGaming was created by The Saskatchewan Gaming Corporation Act in 1994, in order to establish & operate casinos across the province. It owns & operates Casinos Regina & Moose Jaw.

Minister Responsible, Hon. Christine Tell
Legislative Building
#322, 2405 Legislative Dr.
Regina, SK S4S 0B3

President & Chief Executive Officer, Susan Flett
susan.flett@saskgaming.com

Senior Vice-President, Finance & Information Technology, John Amundson, FCPA, FCA
Tel: 306-798-0998; *Fax:* 306-798-0824
john.amundson@saskgaming.com

Senior Vice-President, Marketing & Business Planning, Gerry Fischer
gerry.fischer@saskgaming.com

Vice-President, Risk & Compliance, Bob Arlint
Tel: 306-787-2353; *Fax:* 306-787-0639
bob.arlint@saskgaming.com

Vice-President, Corporate Services, Blaine Pilatzke
Tel: 306-798-0720; *Fax:* 306-798-0449
blaine.pilatzke@saskgaming.com

Director, Communications, Shanna Schulhauser
Tel: 306-787-8515; *Fax:* 306-787-0639
shanna.schulhauser@saskgaming.com

Saskatchewan Government Insurance (SGI)

2260 - 11th Ave., Regina, SK S4P 0J9
Tel: 306-751-1200; *Fax:* 306-787-7477
Toll-Free: 800-667-8015
sgiinquiries@sgi.sk.ca
www.sgi.sk.ca
Other Communication: Customer Service Centre: 1-800-667-9868
twitter.com/SGItweets
www.facebook.com/SGIcommunity
www.linkedin.com/company/sgi_5
www.youtube.com/user/SGICommunications

Operating in 21 claims centres in Saskatchewan communities, SGI sells property & casualty insurance products. One of SGI's operations is The Saskatchewan Auto Fund, the province's compulsory auto insurance program. The Auto Fund administers the driver's licensing & vehicle registration system.

Minister Responsible, Hon. Joe Hargrave
minister.cc@gov.sk.ca
Legislative Building
#302, 2405 Legislative Dr.
Regina, SK S4S 0B3

Chair, Board of Directors, Arlene Wiks

President & Chief Executive Officer, Andrew Cartmell
Tel: 306-751-1683; *Fax:* 306-525-6040
acartmell@sgi.sk.ca

Chief Financial Officer, Jeff Stepan
Tel: 306-775-6004
jstepan@sgi.sk.ca

Vice-President, Auto Fund, Earl Cameron
Tel: 306-751-1705
ecameron@sgi.sk.ca

Vice-President, Human Resources & Corporate Services, Tamara Erhardt
Tel: 306-775-6994; *Fax:* 306-347-0089
terhardt@sgi.sk.ca

Vice-President, Customer & Marketing Strategy, Penny McCune
Tel: 306-751-1510
pmccune@sgicanada.ca

Vice-President, Product Management, Don Thompson
Tel: 306-751-1585
dthompson@sgi.sk.ca

Vice-President, Systems & Facilities, Dwain Wells
Tel: 306-775-6093
dwells@sgi.sk.ca

Vice-President, Claims & Salvage, Sherry Wolf
Tel: 306-751-1646
swolf@sgi.sk.ca

Saskatchewan Government Relations (GR)

1855 Victoria Ave., Regina, SK S4P 3T2
Tel: 306-787-8885
www.saskatchewan.ca

Municipal relations, public safety, & First Nations, Métis & northern affairs are the main responsibilities of the Ministry of Government Relations. The Ministry aims to ensure effective governance, to provide emergency management programs & to fulfill obligations under Treaty Land Entitlement.

Minister; Minister Responsible, First Nations, Métis & Northern Affairs, Hon. Donna Harpauer
Tel: 306-787-6100; *Fax:* 306-787-0399
minister.gr@gov.sk.ca
Office of the Minister of Government Relations, Legislative Building
#348, 2405 Legislative Dr.
Regina, SK S4S 0B3

Deputy Minister, Alan Hilton
Tel: 306-787-1925; *Fax:* 306-787-1987
alan.hilton@gov.sk.ca

Assistant Deputy Minister, Municipal Relations & Northern Engagement, Keith Comstock
Tel: 306-787-5765; *Fax:* 306-787-1987
keith.comstock@gov.sk.ca

Assistant Deputy Minister, Corporate Services, Public Safety Standards & Disaster Recovery, Laurier Donais
Tel: 306-787-8081; *Fax:* 306-798-0270
laurier.donais@gov.sk.ca

Associated Agencies, Boards & Commissions:

•Saskatchewan Municipal Board (SMB)
#480, 2151 Scarth St.
Regina, SK S4P 2H8
Tel: 306-787-6221; *Fax:* 306-787-1610
info@smb.gov.sk.ca
www.smb.gov.sk.ca

Advisory Services & Municipal Relations
#1010, 1855 Victoria Ave., Regina, SK S4P 3T2
Fax: 306-798-2568
www.municipal.gov.sk.ca

Executive Director, Sheldon Green
Tel: 306-787-7883; *Fax:* 306-798-2568
sheldon.green@gov.sk.ca
Director, Randy McAfee
Tel: 306-787-9641; *Fax:* 306-798-2568
randy.mcafee@gov.sk.ca

Building Standards & Licensing Branch
#100, 1855 Victoria Ave., Regina, SK S4P 3T2
building.standards@gov.sk.ca

Executive Director, William Hawkins
Tel: 306-787-4517; *Fax:* 306-798-4172
william.hawkins@gov.sk.ca
Director, Construction Codes, Building Standards, Margaret Ball
Tel: 306-787-4520; *Fax:* 306-798-4172
margaret.ball@gov.sk.ca
www.gr.gov.sk.ca/Building-Standards
Director, Gas & Electrical Licensing, Gary Gehring
Tel: 306-787-8418; *Fax:* 306-798-4172
gary.gehring@gov.sk.ca

Communications
#220, 1855 Victoria Ave., Regina, SK S4P 3T2
Fax: 306-787-4181

Executive Director, Michael Harrison
Tel: 306-787-6156; *Fax:* 306-787-4181
michael.harrison@gov.sk.ca
Co-Director, Bob Ellis
Tel: 306-787-2709; *Fax:* 306-787-4181
bob.ellis@gov.sk.ca
Co-Director, Cathe Offet
Tel: 306-787-5701; *Fax:* 306-798-0083
cathe.offet@gov.sk.ca

Community Planning
#420, 1855 Victoria Ave., Regina, SK S4P 3T2
Tel: 306-787-2725; *Fax:* 306-798-0194

Executive Director, Community Planning, Ralph Leibel
Tel: 306-787-7672; *Fax:* 306-798-0194
ralph.leibel@gov.sk.ca
Director, Community Planning (Regina), Barry Braitman
Tel: 306-787-2893; *Fax:* 306-798-0194
barry.braitman@gov.sk.ca
Director, Community Planning (Saskatoon), Len Kowalko
Tel: 306-933-6118; *Fax:* 306-933-7720
len.kowalko@gov.sk.ca
#978, 122 - 3rd Ave. North, 9th Fl.
Saskatoon, SK S7K 2H6

Corporate Services
#1410, 1855 Victoria Ave., Regina, SK S4P 3T2
Tel: 306-787-0325; *Fax:* 306-787-4161

Acting Executive Director, Jeff Markewich
Tel: 306-787-9415; *Fax:* 306-787-4161
jeff.markewich@gov.sk.ca
Director, Corporate Administration, Marj Abel
Tel: 306-787-4172; *Fax:* 306-787-4161
marj.abel@gov.sk.ca
Acting Director, Financial Planning, Heather Evans
Tel: 306-787-1682; *Fax:* 306-787-4161
heather.evans@gov.sk.ca
Director, Financial Services, Bev Hungle
Tel: 306-787-6408; *Fax:* 306-787-4161
Bev.Hungle@gov.sk.ca
Director, Corporate Planning, Garett Murray
Tel: 306-798-6093; *Fax:* 306-787-4161
garett.murray@gov.sk.ca
Director, Gaming, Trusts & Grants, Sam Swan
Tel: 306-787-1695; *Fax:* 306-787-4161
sam.swan@gov.sk.ca

Emergency Management & Fire Safety
1855 Victoria Ave., 5th Fl., Regina, SK S4P 3T2
Tel: 306-787-3774; *Fax:* 306-787-7107
Toll-Free: 866-757-5911
Other Communication: Fire Loss Reporting, Toll-Free Phone: 1-800-739-3473; Fax: 306-787-7107

Commissioner & Executive Director, Duane McKay
Tel: 306-787-4516
duane.mckay@gov.sk.ca
www.gr.gov.sk.ca/OFC
Executive Coordinator, Veronica Criddle
Tel: 306-798-3906
veronica.criddle@gov.sk.ca
Deputy Commissioner/Director, Planning, Mieka Cleary
Tel: 306-787-9012; *Fax:* 306-787-1694
mieka.cleary@gov.sk.ca
Deputy Commissioner & Director, PPSTN/Logistics, Prince Albert Office, Howard Georgeson
Tel: 306-953-3691
Toll-free: 866-757-5911; *Fax:* 306-953-3697
howard.georgeson@gov.sk.ca
Other Communications: Alternate Phone: 306-953-3763
1084 Central Ave.
Prince Albert, SK S6V 7P3
Deputy Commissioner, Operations, Colin King
Tel: 306-787-9568
colin.king@gov.sk.ca
Acting Deputy Commissioner/Director, Saskatoon Office, Charlene Luskey
Tel: 306-964-2000
Toll-free: 866-757-5911; *Fax:* 306-964-1094
charlene.luskey@gov.sk.ca
Other Communications: Alternate Phone: 306-787-3774; Fax: 306-933-5013
#964, 122 - 3rd Avenue North
Saskatoon, SK S7K 2H6
Deputy Commissioner, 700 MHz Project, Maureen Schmidt
Tel: 306-798-3082
maureen.schmidt@gov.sk.ca

Lands & Consultation
#610, 1855 Victoria Ave., Regina, SK S4P 3T2
Tel: 306-787-5722; *Fax:* 306-787-6336

Executive Director, Trisha Delormier-Hill
Tel: 306-787-6681
trisha.delormier-hill@gov.sk.ca
Director, Aboriginal Consultation, Karen Bolton
Tel: 306-798-5166
karen.bolton@gov.sk.ca
Director, Land Claims, Susan Carani
Tel: 306-787-9706
susan.carani@gov.sk.ca

Municipal Infrastructure & Finance
#410, 1855 Victoria Ave., Regina, SK S4P 3T2
Tel: 306-787-1262; *Fax:* 306-787-3641
www.municipal.gov.sk.ca

Executive Director, Kathy Rintoul
Tel: 306-787-8887; *Fax:* 306-787-3641
kathy.rintoul@gov.sk.ca
Director, Grants Administration, John Billington
Tel: 306-787-7994; *Fax:* 306-787-3641
John.Billington@gov.sk.ca
Director, Gas Tax Program & Financial Management, Cathy Moberly
Tel: 306-787-9699; *Fax:* 306-787-3641
cathy.moberly@gov.sk.ca

Northern Engagement
#210, 1855 Victoria Ave., Regina, SK S4P 3T2
Tel: 306-787-2906; *Fax:* 306-787-6014

Executive Director, Richard Turkheim
Tel: 306-787-2143; *Fax:* 306-787-6014
richard.turkheim@gov.sk.ca

Northern Municipal Services
Mistasinihk Pl., #2700, 1328 La Ronge Ave., PO Box 5000 La Ronge, SK S0J 1L0
Tel: 306-425-4320; *Fax:* 306-425-2401
Toll-Free: 800-663-1555
www.municipal.gov.sk.ca

Northern Municipal Services administers the Northern Municipal Account. Administrative support & operational assistance are given to Saskatchewan's northern municipalities through municipal management functions, training, & advisory services.
Executive Director, Brad Henry
Tel: 306-425-4322; *Fax:* 306-425-2401
brad.henry@gov.sk.ca

Office of the Provincial Interlocutor
#210, 1855 Victoria Ave., Regina, SK S4P 3T2
Tel: 306-798-0183; *Fax:* 306-787-5832
interlocutor@gov.sk.ca

Provincial Interlocutor, James Froh
Tel: 306-787-7405; *Fax:* 306-787-1987
james.froh@gov.sk.ca

Policy & Program Services
#1540, 1855 Victoria Ave., Regina, SK S4P 3T2
Tel: 306-787-2653; *Fax:* 306-787-5822

Executive Director, John Edwards
Tel: 306-787-2665; *Fax:* 306-787-5822
john.edwards2@gov.sk.ca
Director, Policy & Program Analysis, Ryan Cossitt
Tel: 306-787-2780; *Fax:* 306-787-5822
Ryan.Cossitt@gov.sk.ca
Director, Property Assessment & Taxation, Norm Magnin
Tel: 306-787-2895; *Fax:* 306-787-5822
Norm.Magnin@gov.sk.ca
Director, Legislation & Regulations, Rod Nasewich
Tel: 306-798-7048; *Fax:* 306-787-5822
Rod.Nasewich@gov.sk.ca

Provincial Disaster Assistance Program (PDAP)
PO Box 227 Regina, SK S4P 2Z6
Tel: 306-787-7800; *Fax:* 306-798-2318
Toll-Free: 866-632-4033

Assistance is provided to recover from natural disasters such as tornadoes, plow winds, flooding, & other severe weather. The Provincial Disaster Assistance Program serves the following people & organizations of Saskatchewan: residents, communal organizations, agricultural operations, nonprofit organizations, small businesses, parks, & communities.
Executive Director, Margaret Anderson
Tel: 306-798-8470
margaret.anderson@gov.sk.ca
Director, Program & Customer Service, Tamie Folwark
Tel: 306-798-0590
tamie.folwark@gov.sk.ca
Director, Finance & Accountability, Kerry Gray
Tel: 306-787-2123
kerry.gray@gov.sk.ca
Director, Policy, Kevin Roche
Tel: 306-798-8020
kevin.roche@gov.sk.ca

Saskatchewan Health (HE)

T.C. Douglas Bldg., 3475 Albert St., Regina, SK S4S 6X6
Tel: 306-787-0146
Toll-Free: 800-667-7766
info@health.gov.sk.ca
www.health.gov.sk.ca
Other Communication: Family Health Benefits: 1-800-266-0695; HealthLine: 1-877-800-0002; Health Registration / Health Card: 1-800-667-7551; Prescription Drug Plan: 1-800-667-7581

Saskatchewan Health offers the following programs & services: continuing care to help people live independently; e-health & information systems for access to medical information; emergency services; health benefits; recruitment & retention of healthcare providers; promotion of mental health & treatment for mental illness & addictions; personal health services; prescription drug coverage; public health programs; privacy of health information; services for people with long term disabilities or illnesses; surgery & diagnostics initiatives; & vital statistics.

Minister, Health, Hon. Jim Reiter
Tel: 306-787-7345; *Fax:* 306-787-0237
Office of the Minister of Health, Legislative Building
#204, 2405 Legislative Dr.
Regina, SK S4S 0B3
Minister Responsible, Rural & Remote Health, Hon. Greg Ottenbreit
Tel: 306-798-9014; *Fax:* 306-798-9013
minister.rrhe@gov.sk.ca
Office of the Minister Responsible for Rural & Remote Health, Legislative Building
#208, 2405 Legislative Dr.
Regina, SK S4S 0B3
Deputy Minister, Max Hendricks
Tel: 306-787-3041; *Fax:* 306-787-4533
max.hendricks@health.gov.sk.ca
Chief of Staff, Morgan Bradshaw
Tel: 306-787-9091; *Fax:* 306-787-0237
Acting Assistant Deputy Minister, Mark Wyatt
Tel: 306-787-4695; *Fax:* 306-787-4533
mark.wyatt@health.gov.sk.ca
Executive Director, Physician Leadership & Organizational Development, Brad Havervold
Tel: 306-787-0716; *Fax:* 306-787-2974
Bhavervold@health.gov.sk.ca
Executive Director, Saskatchewan Surgical Initiative, Mark Wyatt
Tel: 306-787-3153; *Fax:* 306-798-3367
mark.wyatt@gov.sk.ca
Director, Patient Safety Unit, Valerie Phillips
Tel: 306-787-3542
vphillips@health.gov.sk.ca

Associated Agencies, Boards & Commissions:

•Health Quality Council
Atrium Bldg., Innovation Place
241, 111 Research Dr.
Saskatoon, SK S7N 3R2
Tel: 306-668-8810; *Fax:* 306-668-8820
info@hqc.sk.ca
www.hqc.sk.ca

•eHealth Saskatchewan
2130 - 11th Ave.
Regina, SK S4P 0J5
Tel: 306-337-0600
Toll-free: 855-347-5465
www.ehealthsask.ca
Other Communication: Vital Statistics, Fax: 306-787-2288; E-mail: vitalstatistics@ehealthsask.ca
eHealth Saskatchewan is mandated to develop & implement the provincial electronic health record. Vital Statistics services were transferred from the Information Services Corporation of Saskatchewan after it became a public company in 2013.

•Saskatchewan Health Research Foundation (SHRF)
Atrium Bldg., Innovation Place
#253, 111 Research Dr.
Saskatoon, SK S7N 3R2
Tel: 306-975-1680; *Fax:* 306-975-1688
Toll-free: 800-975-1699
www.shrf.ca

Acute & Emergency Services
Tel: 306-787-3204; *Fax:* 306-787-6113
www.health.gov.sk.ca/acute-emergency
Executive Director, Deborah Jordan
Tel: 306-787-7854; *Fax:* 306-787-6113
djordan@health.gov.sk.ca
Director, Cancer Services & EMS, Doug Line
Tel: 306-787-1101; *Fax:* 306-787-6113
dline@health.gov.sk.ca
Director, Hospitals & Specialized Services, Patrick O'Byrne
Tel: 306-787-3219; *Fax:* 306-787-6113
paobyrne@health.gov.sk.ca

Communications Branch
Tel: 306-787-3696; *Fax:* 306-787-8310
Toll-Free: 800-667-7766
www.health.gov.sk.ca/communications
Executive Director, Kimberly Kratzig
Tel: 306-787-8433; *Fax:* 306-787-8310
kimberly.kratzig@gov.sk.ca
Director, Program Services, Carolyn Hamilton
Tel: 306-787-2743; *Fax:* 306-787-8310
carolyn.hamilton@gov.sk.ca
Correspondence & Internal Communications, Karen Prokopetz
Tel: 306-787-2036; *Fax:* 306-787-8310
karen.prokopetz@gov.sk.ca
Director, Regional Services, Lorri Thacyk
Tel: 306-787-7296; *Fax:* 306-787-8310
lorri.thacyk@gov.sk.ca

Community Care Branch
Tel: 306-787-7239; *Fax:* 306-787-7095
www.health.gov.sk.ca/community-care
Executive Director, Roger Carriere
Tel: 306-787-6092; *Fax:* 306-787-7095
rcarriere@health.gov.sk.ca
Director, Continuing Care & Rehabilitation, Linda Restau
Tel: 306-787-7901; *Fax:* 306-787-7095
lrestau@health.gov.sk.ca
Director, Research, Evaluation & Central Support, Heather Murray
Tel: 306-787-3236; *Fax:* 306-787-7095
Director, Mental Health & Addictions, Kathy Willerth
Tel: 306-787-5020; *Fax:* 306-787-7095
kwillerth@health.gov.sk.ca
Director, Licensing, Dawn Skalicky-Souliere
Tel: 306-787-1718; *Fax:* 306-787-7095

Drug Plan & Extended Benefits Branch
Tel: 306-787-3317; *Fax:* 306-787-8679
www.health.gov.sk.ca/drugplan-extendedbenefits
Executive Director, Kevin Wilson
Tel: 306-787-3301; *Fax:* 306-787-8679
kwilson@health.gov.sk.ca
Director, Business Unit, Morley Machin
Tel: 306-787-3031
mmachin@health.gov.sk.ca
Director, Pharmaceutical Services, Tracey Smith
Tel: 306-787-3305; *Fax:* 306-787-8679
tsmith@health.gov.sk.ca
Acting Director, Operations Unit, Susan Yee
Tel: 306-787-9268; *Fax:* 306-787-8679
syee@health.gov.sk.ca
Acting Director, Extended Benefits, Cheri Kellington
Tel: 306-787-6970; *Fax:* 306-787-8679

Financial Services Branch
Tel: 306-787-4923; *Fax:* 306-787-0218
www.health.gov.sk.ca/financial-services
Acting Executive Director, Budget & Financial Planning, Brenda Russell
Tel: 306-787-5025; *Fax:* 306-787-0218
brussell@health.gov.sk.ca

Medical Services Branch
Tel: 306-787-3475; *Fax:* 306-787-3761
Toll-Free: 800-667-7523
www.health.gov.sk.ca/medical-services
Executive Director, Shaylene Salazar
Tel: 306-787-3423; *Fax:* 306-787-3761
ssalazar@health.gov.sk.ca
Director, Strategic Financial Planning & Support, Joy Vanstone
Tel: 306-787-2982; *Fax:* 306-787-3761
jvanstone@health.gov.sk.ca
Director, Insured Services, Lori St. Dennis
Tel: 306-787-3425; *Fax:* 306-787-3761
lstdennis@health.gov.sk.ca
Director, Fee For Service and Statistics, Policy, Research & Negotiations, June Schultz
Tel: 306-798-2655; *Fax:* 306-787-3761
jschultz@health.gov.sk.ca
Director, Non-Fee For Service, Policy, Research & Negotiations, Ingrid Kirby
Tel: 306-787-8938; *Fax:* 306-787-3761
ikirby@health.gov.sk.ca

Primary Health Services Branch
Fax: 306-787-0890
www.health.gov.sk.ca/primary-health-services
Executive Director, Donna Magnusson
Tel: 306-787-0875; *Fax:* 306-787-0890
dmagnusson@health.gov.sk.ca
Director, Margaret Baker
Tel: 306-787-0670; *Fax:* 306-787-8697
mbaker@health.gov.sk.ca
Director, Andrea Wagner
Tel: 306-798-7491; *Fax:* 306-787-0890
awagner1@health.gov.sk.ca

Population Health Branch
Tel: 306-787-8847; *Fax:* 306-787-3237
www.health.gov.sk.ca/population-health
Chief Medical Health Officer, Dr. Saqib Shahab
Tel: 306-787-4722; *Fax:* 306-787-3237
Chief Population Health Epidemiologist, Dr. Valerie Mann
Tel: 306-787-4086; *Fax:* 306-787-3823
vmann@health.gov.sk.ca
Executive Director, Rick Trimp
Tel: 306-787-8847; *Fax:* 306-787-3237
rtrimp@health.gov.sk.ca
Executive Director, Health Promotion, Ron Knaus
Tel: 306-787-3329; *Fax:* 306-787-3823
ron.knaus@health.gov.sk.ca
Director, Health Promotion, Tami Denomie
Tel: 306-787-7110; *Fax:* 306-787-3823
tami.denomie@health.gov.sk.ca
Director, Epidemiology & Research, Winanne Downey
Tel: 306-787-7625; *Fax:* 306-787-3237
Director, Corporate Services, Paul Leech
Tel: 306-787-6544; *Fax:* 306-787-3237
pleech@health.gov.sk.ca
Director, Environmental Health, Tim Macaulay
Tel: 306-787-7128; *Fax:* 306-787-3237
tmacaulay@health.gov.sk.ca
Director, Disease Prevention, Jim Myres
Tel: 306-787-1580; *Fax:* 306-787-3823
jim.myres@health.gov.sk.ca

Risk & Relationship Management
Tel: 306-787-3143; *Fax:* 306-787-2974
www.health.gov.sk.ca/risk-and-relationship-management
Other Communication: Alternate Phone: 306-787-3150
Executive Director, Lori Hutchison Hunter
Tel: 306-787-7954; *Fax:* 306-787-4534
Director, Intergovernmental, First Nations & Métis Relations, Randy Passmore
Tel: 306-787-3155; *Fax:* 306-787-4534
randy.passmore@health.gov.sk.ca
Director, Regional Support, Planning & Labour Relations, Jim McIlmoyl
Tel: 306-787-0219; *Fax:* 306-787-4534
jmcilmoyl@health.gov.sk.ca
Director, Operations, Health & Emergency Management, Garnet Matchett
Tel: 306-787-3179; *Fax:* 306-798-3093
gmatchett@health.gov.sk.ca
Acting Director, Health & Emergency Management, Carey Cooney
Tel: 306-798-3091; *Fax:* 306-798-3093
ccooney@health.gov.sk.ca
Director, Governance, Policy & Legislation, David Smith
Tel: 306-787-0297; *Fax:* 306-787-2974
David.Smith@gov.sk.ca
Other Communications: Alt E-mail: david.smith@saskatoonhealthregion.ca
Director, Health Information Policy, Susan Hawryluk
Tel: 306-787-2137; *Fax:* 306-787-4534

Saskatchewan Disease Control Laboratory
5 Research Dr., Regina, SK S4S 0A4
Tel: 306-787-3131; *Fax:* 306-787-1525
www.health.gov.sk.ca/lab
Executive Director, Rick Trimp
Tel: 306-787-3129; *Fax:* 306-787-1525
rtrimp@health.gov.sk.ca
Associate Executive Director, Niki Coffin
Tel: 306-787-1522; *Fax:* 306-787-1525
ncoffin@health.gov.sk.ca
Medical Director, Dr. Greg Horsman
Tel: 306-787-8316; *Fax:* 306-787-1525
ghorsman@health.gov.sk.ca
Director, Environmental Services, Dr. Phillip Bailey
Tel: 306-787-3140; *Fax:* 306-787-1525
pbailey@health.gov.sk.ca
Director, Screening & Reference Testing, Jeff Eichhorst
Tel: 306-787-3284; *Fax:* 306-798-0955
jeichhorst@health.gov.sk.ca
Director, Operations, Joyce Kirsch
Tel: 306-787-9404; *Fax:* 306-787-1525
joyce.kirsch@health.gov.sk.ca
Acting Director, Bacteriology, Dr. David Alexander
Tel: 306-798-4154; *Fax:* 306-787-1525
dalexander@health.gov.sk.ca
Director, Administration, Debra Ulrich
Tel: 306-787-3033; *Fax:* 306-787-1525
dulrich@health.gov.sk.ca

Strategy & Innovation Branch
Tel: 306-787-0769; *Fax:* 306-787-2974
www.health.gov.sk.ca/strategic-planning-branch
Executive Director, Pauline M. Rousseau
Tel: 306-787-3951; *Fax:* 306-787-2974
Director, Health System Planning, Kathleen Peterson
Tel: 306-787-3163; *Fax:* 306-787-2974
kpeterson@health.gov.sk.ca
Director, Kaizen Promotion Office, Trish Livingstone
Tel: 306-787-3146; *Fax:* 306-787-2974

Workforce Planning Branch
Tel: 306-787-3152; *Fax:* 306-798-0023
www.health.gov.sk.ca/workforce-planning
Executive Director, Brad Havervold
Tel: 306-787-6672; *Fax:* 306-798-0023
Chief Nursing Officer, Lynn Digney-Davis
Tel: 306-787-7195; *Fax:* 306-798-0023
ldigneydavis@health.gov.sk.ca
Director, Planning & Provincial Recruitment Projects, Andy Churko
Tel: 306-787-3072; *Fax:* 306-798-0023
achurko@health.gov.sk.ca
Director, Programs & Resource Development, Sandra Cripps
Tel: 306-787-5693; *Fax:* 306-798-0023
scripps@health.gov.sk.ca

Saskatchewan Highways & Infrastructure (HI)

Victoria Tower, 1855 Victoria Ave., Regina, SK S4P 3T2
Tel: 306-787-4800
communications@highways.gov.sk.ca
www.highways.gov.sk.ca
Other Communication: Road Information Hotline: 306-933-8333
twitter.com/skgovhwyhotline
www.facebook.com/SaskatchewanHighwayHotline
The Ministry of Highways & Infrastructure is concerned with transportation in Saskatchewan as it relates to the social & economic development of the province. Business areas include ministry services & standards information, plning & policy development, & regional services.
The following are some programs & services offered through the Ministry: Urban Highway Connector Program; Adopt a Highway; Assistance to Motorists; Preservation Program; & Community Airport Partnership Program.
Minister, Hon. David Marit
hi.minister@gov.sk.ca
Minister's Office, Legislative Building
#302, 2405 Legislative Dr.
Regina, SK S4S 0B3
Deputy Minister, Nithi Govindasamy
Tel: 306-787-4949; *Fax:* 306-787-9777
nithi.govindasamy@gov.sk.ca

Associated Agencies, Boards & Commissions:

•Global Transportation Hub Authority
#350, 1777 Victoria Ave.
Regina, SK S4P 4K5
Tel: 306-787-4842; *Fax:* 306-798-4600
www.thegth.com
The Hub Authority was created in June 2009, & is the primary agency in charge of planning, developing, constructing & promoting the Global Transportation Hub - a transportation & logistics centre encompassing 2,000 acres of serviced land.

•Highway Traffic Board (HTB)
1621A McDonald St.
Regina, SK S4N 5R2
Tel: 306-775-8336; *Fax:* 306-775-6618
contactus@highwaytrafficboard.sk.ca
www.highwaytrafficboard.sk.ca
The Highway Traffic Board's mandate is to establish & to administer legislation relating to the safe & legal operations of private vehicles, the bus-truck industry & the short line rail industry in Saskatchewan, where specifically legislated to do so.

•Saskatchewan Grain Car Corporation (SGCC)
#1210, 1855 Victoria Ave.
Regina, SK S4P 3T2
Tel: 306-787-1137; *Fax:* 306-798-0931
www.sgcc.gov.sk.ca
The SGCC works with farmers, community groups, shippers, & railroads to maximize the efficiency and effectiveness of transporting grain across the province.

Ministry Services & Standards Division
Victoria Tower, #1200, 1855 Victoria Ave., Regina, SK S4P 3T2
Tel: 306-787-4904
Responsibilities of the Ministry Services & Standards Division include budgeting, financial reporting, information management, technical standards, enterprise risk management, performance management, & administrative services related to land management.

Assistant Deputy Minister, Ministry Services & Standards, Jennifer Ehrmantraut
Tel: 306-787-4859; *Fax:* 306-787-9777
Jennifer.Ehrmantraut@gov.sk.ca
Executive Director, Technical Standards, Dave Stearns
Tel: 306-787-2295; *Fax:* 306-787-4836
Director, Earth Sciences & Research, Magdy Beshara
Tel: 306-787-4922; *Fax:* 306-787-4582
Magdy.Beshara@gov.sk.ca
Director, Financial Services, Gary Diebel
Tel: 306-787-4794; *Fax:* 306-787-8700
Gary.Diebel@gov.sk.ca
Director, Corporate Support, Wayne Gienow
Tel: 306-787-1355; *Fax:* 306-787-8700
wayne.gienow@gov.sk.ca
Director, Design & Traffic Engineering, Sukhy Kent
Tel: 306-787-4945; *Fax:* 306-787-4836
Sukhy.Kent@gov.sk.ca
Director, Preservation & Operations Standards, Frass Len
Tel: 306-933-5226; *Fax:* 306-933-7090
Director, Construction Standards, Bill Pacholka
Tel: 306-787-4917; *Fax:* 306-787-4836
Bill.Pacholka@gov.sk.ca
Director, Bridge Standards, Howard Yea
Tel: 306-787-4830; *Fax:* 306-787-4836
Howard.Yea@gov.sk.ca
Manager, Forecasting, Judy A. Adams
Tel: 306-787-4796; *Fax:* 306-787-8700
Judy.Adams@gov.sk.ca
Manager, Property Rights & Registration, Neil Daku
Tel: 306-787-4884; *Fax:* 306-787-4100
Neil.Daku@gov.sk.ca
Manager, IT Systems, Robert Gee
Tel: 306-787-4824; *Fax:* 306-787-8700
Robert.Gee@gov.sk.ca
Manager, TLE & Property Preservation, Peter Gennutt
Tel: 306-787-4045; *Fax:* 306-787-4100
Peter.Gennutt@gov.sk.ca

Planning & Policy Division
Tel: 306-787-4904
Assistant Deputy Minister, George Stamatinos
Tel: 306-787-5028; *Fax:* 306-787-9777
george.stamatinos@gov.sk.ca
Executive Director, Systems Planning & Management, Miranda Carlberg
Tel: 306-787-0825; *Fax:* 306-787-3963
Miranda.Carlberg@gov.sk.ca
Executive Director, Strategic Planning & Policy, Harold Hugg
Tel: 306-787-5311; *Fax:* 306-787-3963
Harold.Hugg@gov.sk.ca
Director, Legislation & Administration, Reg Cox
Tel: 306-964-9241; *Fax:* 306-787-3963
Director, Trucking Policy & Regulation, Andrew Cipywnyk
Tel: 306-787-6998; *Fax:* 306-787-3963
Director, Transportation Infrastructure, Andrew Liu
Tel: 306-787-4784; *Fax:* 306-787-3963
Andrew.Liu@gov.sk.ca
Director, Strategic Business Planning, Cathy Lynn Borbely
Tel: 306-787-4787; *Fax:* 306-787-3963
CathyLynn.Borbely@gov.sk.ca
Director, Multimodal, Trade & Logistics, Michael Makowsky
Tel: 306-787-7664; *Fax:* 306-787-3963
Michael.Makowsky@gov.sk.ca
Director, Rail Services, Ed Zsombor
Tel: 306-787-5847; *Fax:* 306-787-3963
Ed.Zsombor@gov.sk.ca
Director, Systems Management, Ben Liu
Tel: 306-787-4121; *Fax:* 306-787-3963
Director, Transportation Planning, Harold Retzlaff
Tel: 306-787-4758; *Fax:* 306-787-3963

Saskatchewan Human Rights Commission (SHRC)

Saskatoon Office, Sturdy Stone Bdg., #816, 122 - 3 Ave. North, 8th Fl., Saskatoon, SK S7K 2H6
Tel: 306-933-5952; *Fax:* 306-933-7863
Toll-Free: 800-667-9249
TTY: 306-373-2119
shrc@gov.sk.ca
saskatchewanhumanrights.ca
Secondary Address: #301, 1942 Hamilton St.
Regina, SK S4P 2C5
Alt. Fax: 306-787-0454
shrc@shrc.gov.sk.ca
Other Communication: Toll Free Phone: 1-800-667-8577; Telewriter: 306-787-8550
The Saskatchewan Human Rights Commission promotes & protects individual dignity & equal rights by discouraging & eliminating discrimination. The Commission's guide is The Saskatchewan Human Rights Code. The following are the principle functions of the Commission: approving equity programs; educating people & promoting human rights laws in Saskatchewan; & investigating complaints of discrimination.

Minister Responsible, Hon. Gordon Wyant, Q.C.
Tel: 306-787-5353; *Fax:* 306-787-1232
jus.minister@gov.sk.ca
Social Media: twitter.com/GordWyant
Chief Commissioner, Hon. David M. Arnot
Tel: 306-933-7796; *Fax:* 306-933-7863
david.arnot@gov.sk.ca
Executive Director, Norma Gunningham-Kapphahn
Tel: 306-933-8284; *Fax:* 306-933-7863
norma.gunningham-kapphahn@gov.sk.ca
Manager, Finance & Administration, Regina Office, Sue Lake
Tel: 306-787-2704; *Fax:* 306-787-0454
sue.lake@gov.sk.ca
Manager, Human Resources, Brenda Rorke
Tel: 306-933-8285; *Fax:* 306-933-7863
brenda.rorke@gov.sk.ca

Information & Privacy Commissioner of Saskatchewan

#503, 1801 Hamilton St., Regina, SK S4P 4B4
Tel: 306-787-8350; *Fax:* 306-798-1603
Toll-Free: 877-748-2298
webmaster@oipc.sk.ca
www.oipc.sk.ca
twitter.com/saskipc
Information & Privacy Commissioner, Ron Kruzeniski
Tel: 306-798-1601; *Fax:* 306-798-1603
rkruzeniski@oipc.sk.ca
Director, Operations, Pam Scott
Tel: 306-798-2261; *Fax:* 306-798-1603
pscott@oipc.sk.ca

Saskatchewan Justice & Attorney General (JU)

1874 Scarth St., Regina, SK S4P 4B3
Tel: 306-787-7872
www.justice.gov.sk.ca
Minister & Attorney General, Hon. Gordon Wyant, Q.C.
Tel: 306-787-5353; *Fax:* 306-787-1232
jus.minister@gov.sk.ca
Office of the Minister of Justice & Attorney General, Legislative Buiding
#355, 2405 Legislative Dr.
Regina, SK S4S 0B3
Deputy Minister, Justice; Deputy Attorney General, Kevin Fenwick, Q.C.
Tel: 306-787-5352; *Fax:* 306-787-3874
kevin.fenwick@gov.sk.ca
Executive Director, Communications, Linsay Rabyj
Tel: 306-787-0775; *Fax:* 306-787-3874
linsay.rabyj@gov.sk.ca
Executive Director, Civil Law Division, Linda Zarzeczny, Q.C.
Tel: 306-787-8387; *Fax:* 306-787-0581
linda.zarzeczny@gov.sk.ca
www.justice.gov.sk.ca/civillaw

Associated Agencies, Boards & Commissions:

•Automobile Injury Appeal Commission
#504, 2400 College Ave.
Regina, SK S4P 1C8
Tel: 306-798-5545; *Fax:* 306-798-5540
Toll-free: 866-798-5544
aiac@gov.sk.ca
www.autoinjuryappeal.sk.ca

•Financial & Consumer Affairs Authority (FCAA)
#601, 1919 Saskatchewan Dr.
Regina, SK S4P 4H2
Tel: 306-787-5645; *Fax:* 306-787-5899
Toll-free: 877-880-5550
consumerprotection@gov.sk.ca
www.fcaa.gov.sk.ca
Other Communication: Film Classification Board Inquiries, E-mail: skfilmclass@gov.sk.ca
The Financial & Consumer Affairs Authority (formerly known as the Saskatchewan Financial Services Commission (SFSC)) protects consumer & public interests & supports economic well-being through responsive financial marketplace regulation. The SFSC enhances consumer protection through licensing, registration, audit, complaint handling & enforcement activities pursuant to various provincial statutes.

•Law Reform Commission of Saskatchewan
c/o University of Saskatchewan, College of Law
#185, 15 Campus Dr.
Saskatoon, SK S7N 5A6
Tel: 306-966-1625; *Fax:* 306-966-5900
www.lawreformcommission.sk.ca
The Law Reform Commission of Saskatchewan was established by An Act to Establish a Law Reform Commission, proclaimed in force in November, 1973, & began functioning in February of 1974.

•Legal Aid Saskatchewan
#502, 201 - 21 St. East
Saskatoon, SK S7K 0B8
Tel: 306-933-5300; *Fax:* 306-933-6764
Toll-free: 800-667-3764
www.legalaid.sk.ca
The Saskatchewan Legal Aid Commission provides legal services to persons & organizations for criminal & civil matters where those persons & organizations are financially unable to secure these services from their own resources. The organization has been in existence since 1974.

•Office of Residential Tenancies (ORT)
#304, 1855 Victoria Ave.
Regina, SK S4P 3T2
Tel: 306-787-2699; *Fax:* 306-787-5574
Toll-free: 888-215-2222
ort@gov.sk.ca
www.justice.gov.sk.ca/ort
Other Communication: Toll-Free Fax: 1-888-867-7776

•Provincial Mediation Board
#120, 2151 Scarth St.
Regina, SK S4P 2H8
Tel: 306-787-5408; *Fax:* 306-787-5574
Toll-free: 877-787-5408
pmb@gov.sk.ca
www.justice.gov.sk.ca/PMB
The Provincial Mediation Board provides budgeting advice & counselling to individuals with personal debt problems. It may be able to arrange repayment plans with creditors. The Board also deals with problems of debtors related to property tax arrears, eviction of commercial tenants & residential mortgage foreclosures.

•Public & Private Rights Board
#23, 3085 Albert St.
Regina, SK S4S 0B1
Tel: 306-787-4071; *Fax:* 306-787-0088
www.justice.gov.sk.ca/publicandprivaterightsboard

•Saskatchewan Film & Video Classification Board
#500, 1919 Saskatchewan Dr.
Regina, SK S4P 4H2
Tel: 306-787-5550; *Fax:* 306-787-9779
Toll-free: 888-374-4636
www.fcaa.gov.sk.ca/CPD-SK-FCB
While the Saskatchewan Film & Video Classification Board still provides administrative duties, an agreement between the province of British Columbia & Saskatchewan was reached on October 1, 1997, under which the British Columbia Film Classification Office gained responsibility for classifying all new theatrical releases & adult videos on behalf of the Saskatchewan Film & Video Classification Board.

•Saskatchewan Human Rights Commission (SHRC)
See Entry Name Index for detailed listing.

•Saskatchewan Police College (SkPC)
College West Bldg., University of Regina
#217, 3737 Wascana Pkwy.
Regina, SK S4S 0A2
Tel: 306-787-9292
www.saskpolicecollege.ca

•Saskatchewan Police Commission
#1850, 1881 Scarth St.
Regina, SK S4P 4K9
Tel: 306-787-9292; *Fax:* 306-798-4908
www.justice.gov.sk.ca/pcs-commission
The Commission promotes crime prevention, improved police relationships with communities, & effective policing throughout Saskatchewan by working closely with police services & Boards of Police Commissioners.

•Saskatchewan Public Complaints Commission (PCC)
#300, 1919 Saskatchewan Dr.
Regina, SK S4P 4H2
Tel: 306-787-6519; *Fax:* 306-787-6528
Toll-free: 866-256-6194
www.publiccomplaintscommission.ca
The Public Complaints Commission is a five-person, non-police body appointed by the government. It is mandated to investigate complaints against the police or of possible criminal offences by police officers, & to ensure that investigations are fair & thorough.

•Saskatchewan Review Board
188 - 11th St. West
Prince Albert, SK S6V 6G1
Tel: 306-953-2812; *Fax:* 306-953-3342
lbutton-rowe@skprovcourt.ca
www.justice.gov.sk.ca/saskatchewanreviewboard
The Saskatchewan Review Board was established under the Criminal Code of Canada to review decisions & orders regarding an accused person, where a verdict of not criminally responsible by reason of mental disorder or unfit to stand trial on account of mental disorder has been made.

Office of the Minister of Corrections & Policing
Legislative Bldg., #345, 2405 Legislative Dr., Regina, SK S4S 0B3
Tel: 306-787-4983; *Fax:* 306-787-5331
www.justice.gov.sk.ca/CP
Corrections & Policing promotes safe communities in Saskatchewan. Adult correction & young offender programs & services are delivered that serve individuals in conflict with the law. Public safety is also addressed through the following programs & services: protection & emergency planning & communication; monitoring of building standards; fire prevention & disaster assistance programs; & licensing & inspections services.

Minister Responsible, Hon. Gordon Wyant
Tel: 306-787-5353; *Fax:* 306-787-1232
minister.cp@gov.sk.ca
Deputy Minister, Dale McFee
Tel: 306-787-8065; *Fax:* 306-798-0270
dale.mcfee@gov.sk.ca
Executive Director, Strategic Systems & Innovation, Monica Field
Tel: 306-798-1309; *Fax:* 306-798-0270
monica.field@gov.sk.ca
Executive Director, Research & Evidence-based Excellence, Brian Rector
Tel: 306-787-3892; *Fax:* 306-798-0270
brian.rector@gov.sk.ca

Community Justice Division
#610, 1874 Scarth St., Regina, SK S4P 4B3
Tel: 306-787-5096; *Fax:* 306-787-0078
www.justice.gov.sk.ca/communityservicesdivision
Executive Director, Pat Thiele
Tel: 306-787-6707; *Fax:* 306-787-0078
Pat.Thiele@gov.sk.ca
Executive Director, Aboriginal Courtworker Program, Chris LaFontaine
Tel: 306-787-6470; *Fax:* 306-787-0078
chris.lafontaine@gov.sk.ca

Office of the Chief Coroner
#920, 1801 Hamilton St., Regina, SK S4P 4B4
Tel: 306-787-5541; *Fax:* 306-787-5503
Toll-Free: 866-592-7845
ocoroner@gov.sk.ca
www.justice.gov.sk.ca/officeofthechiefcoroner
Secondary Address: #3, 2345 Ave. C North
Saskatoon, SK S7L 5Z5
Alt. Fax: 306-964-1896
ocoronernorthern@gov.sk.ca
Other Communication: Toll-Free Phone: 1-888-824-0491

Chief Coroner, R. Kent Stewart
Tel: 306-787-5541; *Fax:* 306-787-5503
kent.stewart@gov.sk.ca
Chief Forensic Pathologist, Dr. Shaun Ladham
Tel: 306-964-1677; *Fax:* 306-655-8399
shaun.ladham@saskatoonhealthregion.ca
Regional Coroner, Northern Region, Maureen Laurie
Tel: 306-964-1891; *Fax:* 306-964-1896
maureen.laurie@gov.sk.ca

Community Safety Outcomes & Corporate Supports
#1200, 1874 Scarth St., Regina, SK S4P 4B3
Tel: 306-787-0493; *Fax:* 306-798-0270
Assistant Deputy Minister, Ron Anderson
Tel: 306-787-0397; *Fax:* 306-798-0270
ronald.anderson@gov.sk.ca
Acting Executive Director, Strategic Engagement, Rae Gallivan
Tel: 306-787-3572; *Fax:* 306-787-0078
Rae.Gallivan@gov.sk.ca
Director, Strategic Engagement, Peter Braun
Tel: 306-787-6290; *Fax:* 306-787-0078
Peter.Braun@gov.sk.ca
Director, Healthy Families, Jeffrey Dudar
Tel: 306-798-8066; *Fax:* 306-787-0078
Jeffrey.Dudar@gov.sk.ca
Director, Continuous Improvement, Raequel Giles
Tel: 306-787-8060; *Fax:* 306-798-0270
Raequel.Giles@gov.sk.ca
Director, BPRC, Matthew Gray
Tel: 306-798-1051; *Fax:* 306-787-0078
matthew.gray@gov.sk.ca
Director, Occupational Health & Safety, Garry Thompson
Tel: 306-798-1357; *Fax:* 306-787-0078
garry.thompson@gov.sk.ca

Corporate Affairs
#1200, 1874 Scarth St., Regina, SK S4P 4B3
Tel: 306-787-7100; *Fax:* 306-798-0270
communicationsCPJU@gov.sk.ca
Executive Director, Drew Wilby
Tel: 306-787-5883
drew.wilby@gov.sk.ca

Corporate Services Branch
#1100, 1874 Scarth St., Regina, SK S4P 4B3
Tel: 306-787-2583; *Fax:* 306-787-5830
Executive Director, Dave Tulloch
Tel: 306-787-5472; *Fax:* 306-787-5830
dave.tulloch@gov.sk.ca
Executive Director, Capital Planning & Enterprise Projects Unit, Kim Gurnsey
Tel: 306-787-3065; *Fax:* 306-787-5830
Kim.Gurnsey@gov.sk.ca

Courts & Tribunals Division
#1010, 1874 Scarth St., Regina, SK S4P 4B3
Tel: 306-787-5359; *Fax:* 306-787-8737
Assistant Deputy Minister, Jan Turner
Tel: 306-787-5112; *Fax:* 306-787-8737
jan.turner@gov.sk.ca
Registrar, Court of Appeal, Melanie Baldwin, Q.C.
Tel: 306-787-5382; *Fax:* 306-787-5815
lschwann@sasklawcourts.ca
Court House
2425 Victoria Ave.
Regina, SK S4P 4W6
Director, Enforcement of Money Judgment Unit, Debbie Barker
Tel: 306-787-4108; *Fax:* 306-787-8737
debbie.barker@gov.sk.ca
Director, Provincial Court Security, Ralph Martin
Tel: 306-787-4729; *Fax:* 306-787-8737
ralph.martin@gov.sk.ca
Director, HR Services & Employee Development, Donna Mitchell
Tel: 306-787-5386; *Fax:* 306-787-8737
donna.mitchell@gov.sk.ca

Custody, Supervision & Rehabilitation Services
#700, 1874 Scarth St., Regina, SK S4P 4B3
Tel: 306-787-8958; *Fax:* 306-787-0676
www.justice.gov.sk.ca/cp-cr
Assistant Deputy Minister, Dennis Cooley
Tel: 306-787-4701; *Fax:* 306-787-0676
dennis.cooley@gov.sk.ca
Executive Director, Strategic Support, Judy Orthner
Tel: 306-787-9378; *Fax:* 306-787-0676
Judy.Orthner@gov.sk.ca
Director, Recruiting & Staffing, Organizational Improvement, Paul Blain
Tel: 306-953-3166; *Fax:* 306-953-2832
Paul.Blain@gov.sk.ca
Director, Legislation, Policy & Planning, Fred Burch
Tel: 306-787-3242; *Fax:* 306-787-0676
fred.burch@gov.sk.ca
Director, Operational Support, Rick Davis
Tel: 306-787-3640; *Fax:* 306-787-0676
rick.davis@gov.sk.ca
Director, Organizational Improvement, Terry Hawkes
Tel: 306-787-1150; *Fax:* 306-787-0676
terry.hawkes@gov.sk.ca
Director, Saskatchewan Impaired Driver Treatment Centre, Michelle Ketzmerick
Tel: 306-922-8333; *Fax:* 306-922-8815
Director, Business Strategy & Risk Management, Kathleen Wilde
Tel: 306-787-3599; *Fax:* 306-787-0676
kathleen.wilde@gov.sk.ca

Community
Acting Executive Director, Caroline Graves
Tel: 306-798-1409; *Fax:* 306-787-0676
Caroline.Graves@gov.sk.ca

Custody
Executive Director, Heather Scriver
Tel: 306-787-3571; *Fax:* 306-787-0676
heather.scriver@gov.sk.ca

Offender Services
Executive Director, Doris Schnell
Tel: 306-787-5467; *Fax:* 306-787-0676
doris.schnell@gov.sk.ca
Chief Clinical Director, Clinical Services, Ross Keele
Tel: 306-933-5039; *Fax:* 306-933-5044
Ross.Keele@gov.sk.ca

Freedom of Information & Privacy
#1510, 1855 Victoria Ave., Regina, SK S4P 3T2
Fax: 306-798-9007
Executive Director, Tom Young
Tel: 306-787-3316
tom.young@gov.sk.ca
Director, Privacy, Access & Risk Management, Tanessa Boutin
Tel: 306-798-0334; *Fax:* 306-798-9007
tanessa.boutin@gov.sk.ca
Acting Director, Records Manager, Bonnie Caven
Tel: 306-798-3299
bonnie.caven@gov.sk.ca
Director, Program Priorities & Strategic Alignment, Anita Ingram
Tel: 306-787-0391
Anita.Ingram@gov.sk.ca

Innovation Division
#1020, 1874 Scarth St., Regina, SK S4P 4B3
Fax: 306-798-4064
Assistant Deputy Minister, J. Glen Gardner
Tel: 306-787-5651
glen.gardner@gov.sk.ca
Public Guardian & Trustee, Rod Cook
Tel: 306-787-5427; *Fax:* 306-787-5065
rod.crook@gov.sk.ca
Executive Director, Innovation & Strategic Initiatives, Kylie Head
Tel: 306-787-8220; *Fax:* 306-787-9008
kylie.head@gov.sk.ca
Executive Director, Access & Privacy Branch, Aaron Orban
Tel: 306-787-6428; *Fax:* 306-787-6979
aaron.orban@gov.sk.ca

Policing & Community Safety Services
#1200, 1874 Scarth St., Regina, SK S4P 4B3
Tel: 306-787-0493; *Fax:* 306-798-0270
www.justice.gov.sk.ca/policing
Assistant Deputy Minister, Dale Larsen
Tel: 306-787-5903; *Fax:* 306-798-0270
dale.larsen@gov.sk.ca
Registrar, Private Investigators & Security Guards Program, Bill Blanshard
Tel: 306-787-0402; *Fax:* 306-787-0136
bill.blanshard@gov.sk.ca
Director, Saskatchewan Witness Protection Program, Randy Koroluk
Tel: 306-798-0262
Toll-free: 888-798-0262; *Fax:* 306-798-7700
randy.koroluk@gov.sk.ca
Director, Financial Policy & Controls, Cindy Mak
Tel: 306-787-8608; *Fax:* 306-787-0136
cindy.mak@gov.sk.ca
Director, Policing & Community Safety Services, Dan Pooler
Tel: 306-787-1978; *Fax:* 306-787-0136
dan.pooler@gov.sk.ca

Public Law
#800, 1874 Scarth St, Regina, SK S4P 4B3
Tel: 306-787-8389; *Fax:* 306-787-9111
Executive Director, Susan Amrud, Q.C.
Tel: 306-787-8990
susan.amrud@gov.sk.ca
Chief Legislative Crown Counsel, Legislative Drafting, Ian Brown, Q.C.

Tel: 306-787-9346; *Fax:* 306-787-9111
ian.brown@gov.sk.ca
Director, Office of Public Registry Administration, Catherine Benning
Tel: 306-787-8391; *Fax:* 306-787-5830
catherine.benning@gov.sk.ca
Director, Aboriginal Law & Constitutional Law, Mitch McAdam, Q.C.
Tel: 306-787-7846; *Fax:* 306-787-9111
mitch.mcadam@gov.sk.ca
Director, Legislative Services, Darcy McGovern, Q.C.
Tel: 306-787-5662; *Fax:* 306-787-9111
darcy.mcgovern@gov.sk.ca
Manager, Queen's Printer, Marilyn Lustig-McEwen
Tel: 306-787-9345
Toll-free: 800-226-7302; *Fax:* 306-798-0835
marilyn.lustig-mcewen@gov.sk.ca
www.qp.gov.sk.ca
Other Communications: Alternate E-mail: qprinter@gov.sk.ca
3085 Albert St., #B19
Regina, SK S4S 0B1

Public Prosecutions
#300, 1874 Scarth St., Regina, SK S4P 4B3
Tel: 306-787-5490; *Fax:* 306-787-8878
www.justice.gov.sk.ca/publicprosecutionsdivision
Executive Director, Daryl Rayner, Q.C.
Tel: 306-787-5490; *Fax:* 306-787-8878
Director, High Risk Violent Offender Unit, Roger DeCorby
Tel: 306-787-5490; *Fax:* 306-787-8878
Director, Financial & Information Services, Shari Parisian
Tel: 306-787-8943; *Fax:* 306-787-8878
Director, Appeals, Dean Sinclair, Q.C.
Tel: 306-787-5490; *Fax:* 306-787-8878

Saskatchewan Labour Relations & Workplace Safety (LRWS)

#300, 1870 Albert St., Regina, SK S4P 4W1
Tel: 306-787-7404
webmaster@lab.gov.sk.ca
www.lrws.gov.sk.ca
The Ministry is responsible for labour standards, labour support services, labour relations, mediation, occupational health & safety, & workers' advocacy.
Minister, Hon. Don Morgan, Q.C.
Tel: 306-787-0613; *Fax:* 306-787-6946
minister.edu@gov.sk.ca
Office of the Minister of Education / Labour Relation & Workplace Safety, Legislative Bldg.
#361, 2405 Legislative Dr.
Regina, SK S4S 0B3
Deputy Minister, Mike Carr
Tel: 306-787-7424; *Fax:* 306-798-5190
Mike.Carr@gov.sk.ca
Executive Director, Corporate Finance, Corporate Services & Accountability Division (Shared Services), Scott Giroux
Tel: 306-787-3501; *Fax:* 306-787-7392
scott.giroux@gov.sk.ca
Executive Director, Central Services, Louise Usick
Tel: 306-787-8078; *Fax:* 306-798-5190
louise.usick@gov.sk.ca
Executive Director, Labour Relations & Mediation, Pete Suderman
Tel: 306-787-9106; *Fax:* 306-787-1064
pete.suderman@gov.sk.ca
Executive Director, Communications (Shared Services), Rikki Bote
Tel: 306-787-4156; *Fax:* 306-798-5021
rikki.bote@gov.sk.ca

Associated Agencies, Boards & Commissions:

•Labour Relations Board
#1600, 1920 Broad St.
Regina, SK S4P 3V2
Tel: 306-787-2406; *Fax:* 306-787-2664
www.sasklabourrelationsboard.com
An independent, quasi-judicial tribunal charged with the responsibility of adjudicating disputes that arise under The Trade Union Act, The Construction Industry Labour Relations Act, 1992 & The Health Labour Relations Reorganization Act

•Minimum Wage Board
#400, 1870 Albert St.
Regina, SK S4P 4W1
www.lrws.gov.sk.ca/minimum-wage-board-review-reporting
Makes recommendations respecting minimum employment standards including: the minimum wage, minimum age, maximum work periods, maximum rates for room & board & minimum rest periods.

•Office of the Worker's Advocate
#300, 1870 Albert St.
Regina, SK S4P 4W1
Tel: 306-787-2456; *Fax:* 306-787-0249
Toll-free: 877-787-2456
www.lrws.gov.sk.ca/office-workers-advocate
The Office of the Worker's Advocate provides free assistance to workers who are experiencing difficulties with workers' compensation claims. The Office offers information about the following programs & services: wage loss, benefits, survivor's benefits, medical aid, rehabilitation, & retraining. Working with advocacy groups & unions, The Office of the Worker's Advocate strives to improve service to injured workers. Workers' Compensation Board (WCB) decisions about claims can be reviewed & appealed.

•Saskatchewan Workers' Compensation Board
See Entry Name Index for detailed listing.

Labour Standards
Tel: 306-787-2438; *Fax:* 306-787-4780
Toll-Free: 800-667-1783
www.lrws.gov.sk.ca/labour-standards
Executive Director, Greg Tuer
Tel: 306-787-2432; *Fax:* 306-787-4780
greg.tuer@gov.sk.ca
Director, Compliance & Investigations (Saskatoon), Glen McRorie
Tel: 306-933-5087; *Fax:* 306-787-4780
glen.mcrorie@gov.sk.ca
Director, Legal & Education Services, Daniel Parrott
Tel: 306-787-9454; *Fax:* 306-787-4780
daniel.parrott@gov.sk.ca

Occupational Health & Safety Division
Tel: 306-787-4496; *Fax:* 306-787-2208
Toll-Free: 800-567-7233
www.lrws.gov.sk.ca/ohs
Executive Director, Glennis Bihun
Tel: 306-787-4481; *Fax:* 306-787-2208
glennis.bihun@gov.sk.ca
Chief Mines Inspector, Mines Safety, Neil Crocker
Tel: 306-933-5106; *Fax:* 306-933-7339
neil.crocker@gov.sk.ca
Director, Health Services, Rita Coshan
Tel: 306-787-4539; *Fax:* 306-787-2208
rita.coshan@gov.sk.ca
Director, Safety Services, Ray Anthony
Tel: 306-787-4502; *Fax:* 306-787-2208
ray.anthony@gov.sk.ca

Saskatchewan Liquor & Gaming Authority (SLGA)

2500 Victoria Ave., PO Box 5054 Regina, SK S4P 3M3
Tel: 306-787-5563
Toll-Free: 800-667-7565
inquiry@slga.gov.sk.ca
www.slga.gov.sk.ca
The Treasury Board Crown Corporation is responsible for the distribution, control, & regulation of liquor & most gaming across Saskatchewan.
Minister Responsible, Hon. Jeremy Harrison
Legislative Building
#302, 2405 Legislative Dr.
Regina, SK S4S 0B3
President & Chief Executive Officer, Barry Lacey
Tel: 306-787-1737; *Fax:* 306-787-8439
blacey@slga.gov.sk.ca
Registrar, Licensing Commission, Kathie Schumann
Tel: 306-787-1799; *Fax:* 306-798-0653
kschumann@slga.gov.sk.ca
Director, Financial Services, Performance Management Division, Val Banilevic
Tel: 306-787-4215; *Fax:* 306-787-8468
vbanilevic@slga.gov.sk.ca
Director, Communications, Stephanie Choma
Tel: 306-787-1799; *Fax:* 306-787-8468
schoma@slga.gov.sk.ca
Director, Strategy & Corporate Performance, Performance Management Division, Jason Grossman
Tel: 306-526-7631
jgrossman@slga.gov.sk.ca
Director, Enterprise Initiatives, Raynelle Wilson
Tel: 306-787-8163
rwilson@slga.gov.sk.ca

Corporate Services
Tel: 306-787-9902; *Fax:* 306-787-8439
Vice-President, Jim Engel
Tel: 306-787-2977
jengel@slga.gov.sk.ca

Liquor Store Operations Division
Vice-President, Greg Gettle
Tel: 306-787-8027; *Fax:* 306-787-8201
ggettle@slga.gov.sk.ca
Senior Director, Greg Mildenberger
Tel: 306-787-1222
gmildenberger@slga.gov.sk.ca

Partnerships & Supply Management Division
Vice-President, Vacant
Tel: 306-787-4211
Senior Director, Liquor & Gaming Partnerships, Warren Fry
Tel: 306-787-5360
wfry@slga.gov.sk.ca

Regulatory Compliance Division
Tel: 306-787-1780; *Fax:* 306-787-8981
Vice-President, Fiona Cribb
Tel: 306-787-4705
fcribb@slga.gov.sk.ca

Ombudsman Saskatchewan

#150, 2401 Saskatchewan Dr., Regina, SK S4P 4H8
Tel: 306-787-6211; *Fax:* 306-787-9090
Toll-Free: 800-667-7180
ombreg@ombudsman.sk.ca
www.ombudsman.sk.ca
Secondary Address: #500, 350 - 3rd Ave. North
Saskatoon, SK S7K 6G7
Alt. Fax: 306-933-8406
ombsktn@ombudsman.sk.ca
Other Communication: Toll-Free Phone: 1-800-667-9787
The Ombudsman is an Officer of the Legislative Assembly with the authority to investigate complaints received from members of the public who believe the government administration has dealt with them unfairly. Government administration includes any department, branch, board, agency or commission responsible to the Crown & any public servant in Saskatchewan. The Ombudsman was established by the Ombudsman & Children's Advocate Act.
Ombudsman, Mary McFadyen, B.A., LL.B., LL.M.
Tel: 306-787-6211; *Fax:* 306-787-9090
ombreg@ombudsman.sk.ca
Deputy Ombudsman, Regina Office, Janet Mirwaldt
Tel: 306-787-6142
jmirwaldt@ombudsman.sk.ca
Acting Deputy Ombudsman, Saskatoon Office, Renee Gavigan
Tel: 306-933-6767; *Fax:* 306-933-8406
rgavigan@ombudsman.sk.ca

Saskatchewan Opportunities Corporation (SOCO)

Innovation Place, #114, 14 Innovation Blvd., Saskatoon, SK S7N 2X8
Tel: 306-933-6295; *Fax:* 306-933-8215
saskatoon@innovationplace.com
www.soco.sk.ca
The Opportunities Corporation aims to support Saskatchewan's technology sector through the development & operation of research parks. The corporation operates under the business name Innovation Place.
Minister Responsible, Hon. Joe Hargrave
minister.cc@gov.sk.ca
President & Chief Executive Officer, Van Isman
Tel: 306-933-6258; *Fax:* 306-933-8215
visman@innovationplace.com
Chief Financial Officer, Brent Sukenik
Tel: 306-787-8576; *Fax:* 306-787-8601
bsukenik@innovationplace.com
Chief Operating Officer & Vice-President, Research Park Operations, Ken Loeppky
Tel: 306-787-5706; *Fax:* 306-787-8601
kloeppky@innovationplace.com
Vice-President, Corporate Services & Initiatives, Trevor Cross
Tel: 306-361-7565; *Fax:* 306-787-8601
tcross@innovationplace.com

Saskatchewan Parks, Culture & Sport (PCS)

3211 Albert St., 1st Fl., Regina, SK S4S 5W6
Tel: 306-787-5729; *Fax:* 306-798-0033
Toll-Free: 800-205-7070
info@tpcs.gov.sk.ca
www.pcs.gov.sk.ca
Other Communication: Park Watch (Emergency & Security Issues), Toll-Free Phone: 1-800-667-1788
The Ministry is concerned with Saskatchewan's quality of life, tourism, & economic growth.
The following are some of the goals of the Ministry of Parks, Culture, & Sport: to enhance the province's parks by offering

recreational activities & focussing upon natural resources that appeal to residents & visitors; to conserve heritage resources & ecosystems; to protect the province's history & culture; to promote Saskatchewan's cultural & artistic communities; & to encourage residents to be healthy & active through participation in sports & recreational events.
Some of the programs & services available through the Ministry include the Developers' Online Screening Tool, the provision of Archaeological/Palaeontological Permits, the maintenance of the Saskatchewan Register of Heritage Property, the operation of the Royal Saskatchewan Museum, competitive games information, the operation of the Canadian Sport Centre Saskatchewan, & the Active Families Benefit.
Ministry publications available through the provincial government's publication centre include the annual *Parks GuideA Physically Active Saskatchewan: A Strategy to get Saskatchewan People in Motion*& *Conserving Your Historic Places.*

Minister, Hon. Ken Cheveldayoff
minister.pcs@gov.sk.ca
Office of the Minister, Parks, Culture, & Sport, Legislative Building
#38, 2405 Legislative Dr.
Regina, SK S4S 0B3

Deputy Minister, Lin Gallagher
Tel: 306-787-5050
lin.gallagher@gov.sk.ca

Associated Agencies, Boards & Commissions:

•Conexus Arts Centre
200A Lakeshore Dr.
Regina, SK S4S 7L3
Tel: 306-565-4500; *Fax:* 306-565-3274
Toll-free: 800-667-8497
reception@conexusartscentre.ca
www.conexusartscentre.ca
Other Communication: Box Office, Phone: 306-525-9999
Formerly known as the Saskatchewan Centre of the Arts, the Conexus Arts Centrs is a performing arts & theatre complex. The Centre's mandate is to provide facilities, services, & programs to educate & entertain the people of Saskatchewan.

•Provincial Capital Commission (PCC)
4607 Dewdney Ave.
Regina, SK S4T 1B7
Tel: 306-787-9261
www.opcc.gov.sk.ca
The Provincial Capital Commission aims to provide education about the history of Saskatchewan. The Commission creates tourism & economic development opportunities, through the preservation & promotion of the province's heritage & culture.
The following Acts & Regulations guide the work of the Provincial Capital Commission:
Air, Army, Sea, & Navy League Cadets Recognition Day Act;
Archives Act, 2004;
Culture & Recreation Act, 1993;
Government House Foundation Regulations;
Heritage Property Act;
Historic Properties Foundations Act;
Provincial Capital Commission Regulations;
National Peacekeepers Recognition Day Act;
Recognition of John George Diefenbaker Day Act;
Recognition of Telemiracle Week Act;
Saskatchewan Centre of the Arts Act, 2000;
Saskatchewan Heritage Foundation Act;
Tartan Day Act;
Tommy Douglas Day Act;
Wascana Centre Act.

•Royal Saskatchewan Museum (RSM)
2445 Albert St.
Regina, SK S4P 4W7
Tel: 306-787-2815; *Fax:* 306-787-2820
rsminfo@gov.sk.ca
www.royalsaskmuseum.ca
The Royal Saskatchewan Museum in Regina presents Saskatchewan's geological & natural history, as well as a look at First Nations' cultures of the past& present.

•Saskatchewan Archives Board
See Entry Name Index for detailed listing.

•Saskatchewan Arts Board
1355 Broad St.
Regina, SK S4R 7V1
Tel: 306-787-4056; *Fax:* 306-787-4199
Toll-free: 800-667-7526
info@artsboard.sk.ca
www.artsboard.sk.ca

•Saskatchewan Heritage Foundation
3211 Albert St., 1st Fl.
Regina, SK S4S 5W6
Tel: 306-787-8600; *Fax:* 306-787-0069
www.pcs.gov.sk.ca/SHF
The Saskatchewan Heritage Foundation was established by provincial legislation as an agent of the Crown. Its mission is to conserve heritage resources for the benefit of present & future generations.

•Saskatchewan Science Centre
2903 Powerhouse Dr.
Regina, SK S4N 0A1
Tel: 306-522-4629
Toll-free: 800-667-6300
info@sasksciencecentre.com
www.sasksciencecentre.com
Other Communication: Administration: 306-791-7900; Media: 306-791-7917

•Wanuskewin Heritage Park
RR#4 Penner Rd.
Saskatoon, SK S7K 3J7
Tel: 306-931-6767; *Fax:* 306-931-4522
www.wanuskewin.com

•Wascana Centre Authority
2900 Wascana Dr.
PO Box 7111
Regina, SK S4P 3S7
Tel: 306-522-3661; *Fax:* 306-565-2742
wca@wascana.ca
www.wascana.ca
The Wascana Centre is committed to the conservation of the environment, the enhancement of educational & research opportunities, the improvement of recreational facilities, & the advancement of cultural arts. The Centre's vision, mission, & mandate are guided by The Wascana Centre Act.

•Western Development Museum (WDM)
Curatorial Centre
2935 Lorne Ave.
Saskatoon, SK S7J 0S5
Tel: 306-934-1400; *Fax:* 306-934-4467
Toll-free: 800-363-6345
info@wdm.ca
www.wdm.ca
There are locations in Moose Jaw (50 Diefenbaker Dr., Moose Jaw, SK S6J 1L9), North Battleford (PO Box 183, Hwy. 16 & 40, North Battleford SK S9A 2Y1), Saskatoon (2610 Lorne Ave. South, Saskatoon, SK S7J 0S6), & Yorkton (PO Box 98, Hwy. 16 West, Yorkton, SK S3N 2V6).

Communications Branch
Tel: 306-787-0346; *Fax:* 306-798-0033
Other Communication: Inquiry Line: 306-787-5729; Marketing, Phone: 306-787-7828, Fax: 306-798-0033

Executive Director, Jennifer Johnson
Tel: 306-787-0619
jennifer.johnson@gov.sk.ca

Corporate Services Branch
Tel: 306-787-1702; *Fax:* 306-798-0033

Director, Lynette Halvorsen
Tel: 306-787-5896
lynette.halvorsen@gov.sk.ca

Parks Division
Tel: 306-798-0697; *Fax:* 306-798-0033
www.pcs.gov.sk.ca/parks
Other Communication: Sask Parks, URL: www.saskparks.net
www.facebook.com/saskparks
Responsibilities of the Parks division include planning, managing & operating the provincial park system.
Saskatchewan has a provincial parks & protected areas network encompassing 1.4 million hectares, in 34 provincial parks, 8 historic sites, 24 protected areas & 129 recreation sites. The Ministry provides programs & services to conserve, protect, & enhance the province's natural & cultural resources in its parks & protected areas.

Assistant Deputy Minister, Nancy Cherney
Tel: 306-798-3905
nancy.cherney@gov.sk.ca

Acting Executive Director, Parks Services - Operations, Bob McEachern
Tel: 306-787-2948; *Fax:* 306-787-7000
bob.mceachern@gov.sk.ca

Director, Facilities Branch, Byron Davis
Tel: 306-787-3035; *Fax:* 306-787-4218
byron.davis@gov.sk.ca
Other Communications: Alternate Phone: 306-787-3035

Acting Director, Park Management Services; Manager, Business Development & Leasing, Kevin Engel
Tel: 306-787-1285; *Fax:* 306-787-7000
kevin.engel@gov.sk.ca

Director, Southern Park Operations & Planning, Marty Halpape
Tel: 306-787-7621
Toll-free: 800-205-7070; *Fax:* 306-787-7000
marty.halpape@gov.sk.ca
Other Communications: Alternate Phone: 306-787-7031

Director, Visitor Experiences, Mary-Anne Wihak
Tel: 306-787-7826
Toll-free: 800-205-7070; *Fax:* 306-787-7000
mary-anne.wihak@gov.sk.ca
Other Communications: Alternate Phone: 306-787-7031

Director, Northern Park Operations & Planning, Randy Zielke
Tel: 306-953-2884
Toll-free: 800-205-7070; *Fax:* 306-953-2502
randy.zielke@gov.sk.ca
Northern Park Operations & Planning, L.F. McIntosh Building
800 Central Ave., 6th Fl.
PO Box 3003
Prince Albert, SK S6V 6G1

Manager, Landscape Protection & Planning, Southern Park Operations & Planning, Glen Longpre
Tel: 306-787-0846; *Fax:* 306-787-7000

Policy, Planning, & Evaluation
Tel: 306-787-0346; *Fax:* 306-798-0033
The Policy, Planning, & Evaluation unit carries out the following functions: provision of professional development activities to assist in the policy & program decision-making process; performance of primary research & evaluation studies; provision of technical assistance to external consultants; & analysis of secondary data to support policy & program development.

Executive Director, Leanne Thera
Tel: 306-798-8762
leanne.thera@gov.sk.ca

Director, Strategic Alignment, Nancy Martin
Tel: 306-787-2834
nancy.martin@gov.sk.ca

Stewardship Division
Tel: 306-798-0697; *Fax:* 306-798-0033
The Stewardship Division is responsible for advancing sport, recreation & heritage conservation, oversight of the Saskatchewan Heritage Foundation & the Royal Saskatchewan Museum.
Heritage conservation involves the protection of the province's heritage legacy, through inventories, research, & consultative services. Resources are available to help municipalities manage their historic places. One program is known as Main Street Saskatchewan, which works to revitalize historic downtown commercial districts.

Assistant Deputy Minister, Twyla MacDougall
Tel: 306-787-6717
twyla.macdougall@gov.sk.ca

Executive Director, Sport, Recreation, & Stewardship, Darin Banadyga
Tel: 306-787-0685; *Fax:* 306-787-0069
darin.banadyga@gov.sk.ca

Executive Director, Cultural Planning & Development Branch, Gerald Folk
Tel: 306-787-8527; *Fax:* 306-798-3177
gerry.folk@gov.sk.ca
www.pcs.gov.sk.ca/culture
Other Communications: Alternate Phone: 306-787-5877

Director, Heritage Conservation Branch, Carlos Germann
Tel: 306-787-5772; *Fax:* 306-787-0069
carlos.germann@gov.sk.ca
www.pcs.gov.sk.ca/heritage
Other Communications: Alternate Phone: 306-787-2817

Physician Recruitment Agency of Saskatchewan (SaskDocs)

309 - 4th Ave. North, Saskatoon, SK S7K 2L8
Tel: 306-933-5000; *Fax:* 306-933-5115
Toll-Free: 888-415-3627
info@saskdocs.ca
www.saskdocs.ca
twitter.com/saskdocs
www.facebook.com/saskdocs
linkedin.com/company/physician-recruitment-agency-of-saskatchewan
The Physician Recruitment Agency of Saskatchewan is a Crown corporation established in 2009. Its mandate is to provide resources for physicians & their families wanting to live & work in Saskatchewan. It partners with students, medical trainees, physicians, international medical graduates, communities, health facilities & others, & aims to match communities with the right physicians.

Chair; Deputy Minister, Health, Max Hendricks
Tel: 306-787-3041; *Fax:* 306-787-4533
max.hendricks@health.gov.sk.ca

Chief Executive Officer, Edward Mantler
Tel: 306-933-5061
edward.mantler@saskdocs.ca

Director, Corporate Operations, Erin Brady
Tel: 306-933-5074
erin.brady@saskdocs.ca

Manager, Communications, James Winkel
Tel: 306-933-5094
james.winkel@saskdocs.ca

Saskatchewan Power Corporation (SaskPower)

2025 Victoria Ave., Regina, SK S4P 0S1
Tel: 306-566-2121
Toll-Free: 888-757-6937
www.saskpower.com
Other Communication: Media phone: 306-536-2886
twitter.com/SaskPower
www.facebook.com/saskpower
www.linkedin.com/company/saskpower
www.youtube.com/user/Poweringthefuture

A Crown Corporation which provides services to over 490,000 customers over 652,000 square kilometres of diverse terrain in Saskatchewan; operates 18 generating facilities including three coal-fired power stations, seven hydroelectric stations, six natural gas stations, & two wind facilities; capacity of 3,513 megawatts. The SaskPower Environmental policy maintains a commitment to environmental responsibility. The policy includes compliance with relevant environmental legislation, regulations & corporate environmental committees; continual improvement of environmental management systems & prevention of pollution. SaskPower's management system is ISO 14001 registered.

Minister Responsible, Hon. Gord Wyant
President & Chief Executive Officer, Mike Marsh
President, Carbon Capture & Storage Initiatives, Mike Monea
Tel: 306-566-3132
mmonea@saskpower.com
Chief Financial Officer & Vice-President, Finance, Sandeep Kalra
Tel: 306-566-2620
skalra@saskpower.com
Chief Information Officer & Vice-President, Information Technology & Security, Tom Kindred
Tel: 306-566-2146
tkindred@saskpower.com
Vice-President, Customer Services, Diane Avery
Vice-President, Resource Planning; Acting Vice-President, Properties & Project Delivery, Guy Bruce
Tel: 306-566-2386
gbruce@saskpower.com
Acting Vice-President, Human Resources, Environment & Safety, Judy May
Vice-President, Business Development, Grant Ring
Tel: 306-566-3577
gring@northpointenergy.com
Vice-President, Law, Land & Regulatory Affairs; General Counsel & Assistant Secretary, Rachelle Verret Morphy
Tel: 306-566-3139
rverretmor@saskpower.com

NorthPoint Energy Solutions Inc.
2025 Victoria Ave., Regina, SK S4P 0S1
Tel: 306-566-2103; *Fax:* 306-566-3364
info@northpointenergy.com
www.northpointenergy.com

NorthPoint Energy is the wholly owned marketing subsidiary of SaskPower, & operates a 24/7 electrical energy trading desk.

President & Chief Executive Officer; Acting Vice-President, Fuel & Cross-Crown Collaboration, Kory Hayko
khayko@northpointenergy.com
Director, Power Marketing & Contract Management, Dean Krauss
Tel: 306-566-2977
dkrauss@northpointenergy.com

Provincial Auditor Saskatchewan

Chateau Tower, #1500, 1920 Broad St., Regina, SK S4P 3V2
Tel: 306-787-6398; *Fax:* 306-787-6383
info@auditor.sk.ca
auditor.sk.ca

The Provincial Auditor is the auditor of public money managed by the Government of Saskatchewan. The Provincial Auditor Act gives the Provincial Auditor the responsibility, authority & independence to audit & publicly report on all government organizations.

Provincial Auditor, Judy Ferguson
Tel: 306-787-6372
ferguson@auditor.sk.ca
Deputy Provincial Auditor & Chief Operating Officer, Angèle Borys
Tel: 306-787-6326
borys@auditor.sk.ca
Deputy Provincial Auditor, Tara Clemett
Tel: 306-787-6313
clemett@auditor.sk.ca
Deputy Provincial Auditor, Kelly Deis
Tel: 306-787-0027
deis@auditor.sk.ca
Deputy Provincial Auditor, Carolyn O'Quinn
Tel: 306-787-9686
oquinn@auditor.sk.ca
Deputy Provincial Auditor, Regan Sommerfeld
Tel: 306-787-8249
sommerfeld@auditor.sk.ca

Saskatchewan Research Council (SRC)

#125, 15 Innovation Blvd., Saskatoon, SK S7N 2X8
Tel: 306-933-5400; *Fax:* 306-933-7446
info@src.sk.ca
www.src.sk.ca
twitter.com/srcnews
www.facebook.com/saskresearchcouncil
www.linkedin.com/company/saskatchewan-research-council-src
wwww.youtube.com/user/saskresearchcouncil

Research activities include: gas emissions testing; indoor environment testing; groundwater pesticides testing; indoor air quality & source testing for rayon & asbestos; spray drift research; vegetation studies for range, forestry, conservation; aquatic monitoring & assessment methods; climate impact assessment for environmental economic & urban stormwater management; development of plant bioassays for assessing the effects of hazardous materials in aquatic ecosystems; radiochemistry, chromatographic analysis, water analysis; parenting verification centre for the Canadian livestock industry; develops the optimum engine & fuel system for natural gas operation; bioprocessing technology; emulsions research; studies to support mineral exploration; analyses various sample material used in mineral exploration; geoenvironmental research. SRC's Biofuels Test Centre opened in September, 2006.

President & Chief Executive Officer, Dr. Laurier Schramm
Tel: 306-933-5402
schramm@src.sk.ca
Vice-President, Organizational Effectiveness, Toby Arnold
Tel: 306-933-5479; *Fax:* 306-933-7896
arnold@src.sk.ca
Vice-President, Energy, Michael Crabtree
Tel: 306-933-8131; *Fax:* 306-933-7446
mike.crabtree@src.sk.ca
Vice-President, Environment, Joe Muldoon
Tel: 306-933-5439; *Fax:* 306-933-7299
muldoon@src.sk.ca
Vice-President, Mining & Minerals, Craig Murray
Tel: 306-933-5482; *Fax:* 306-933-7446
murray@src.sk.ca
Vice-President, Business Ventures & Communications, Wanda Nyirfa
Tel: 306-933-5400; *Fax:* 306-933-7519
advertising@src.sk.ca
Vice-President, Agriculture & Biotechnology, Phillip Stephan
Tel: 306-933-8199; *Fax:* 306-933-7662
stephan@src.sk.ca

Saskatchewan Social Services (SS)

1920 Broad St., Regina, SK S4P 3V6
Tel: 306-787-3700
Toll-Free: 866-221-5200
TTY: 306-787-7283
socialservicesinquiry@gov.sk.ca
www.socialservices.gov.sk.ca
Other Communication: Income Assistance: 306-798-0660; Media inquiries: 306-787-3686; Staus of Women Office: 306-787-7401

The Ministry works with citizens in the following areas: income support; child & family services; supports for persons with disabilities; affordable housing; economic independence; & active involvement in the labour market & the community. In November 2007, a new provincial government resulted in the reorganization of provincial government ministries. The work of Saskatchewan Community Resources was merged into the newly named Ministry of Social Services.

Minister, Hon. Tina Beaudry-Mellor
Minister's Office, Ministry of Social Services, Legislative Building
#303, 2405 Legislative Dr.
Regina, SK S4S 0B3
Deputy Minister, Greg Miller
Tel: 306-787-3491; *Fax:* 306-787-1032
greg.miller2@gov.sk.ca
Executive Director, Communications, Trish Alcorn
Tel: 306-787-0916; *Fax:* 306-787-8669
trish.alcorn@gov.sk.ca

Corporate Services Division
Tel: 306-787-3984; *Fax:* 306-787-1032
Executive Director, Enterprise Projects & Risk Management, Lorne Brown
Tel: 306-787-3940; *Fax:* 306-798-2118
Lorne.Brown@gov.sk.ca
Executive Director, Status of Women Office, Pat Faulconbridge
Tel: 306-787-7423; *Fax:* 306-787-2058
pat.faulconbridge@gov.sk.ca
www.socialservices.gov.sk.ca/swo
Other Communications: Alternate E-mail: status.women@gov.sk.ca
Executive Director, Strategic Management Branch, Ken Kolb
Tel: 306-787-1338; *Fax:* 306-787-3650
ken.kolb@gov.sk.ca
Executive Director, Finance, Miriam Myers
Tel: 306-787-8666; *Fax:* 306-787-6825
miriam.myers@gov.sk.ca
Executive Director, Program Support, Beverly Smith
Tel: 306-787-1951; *Fax:* 306-787-6825
beverly.smith@gov.sk.ca
Executive Director, Linkin Enterprise Office, Lynn Tulloch
Tel: 306-787-1967; *Fax:* 306-787-1886
lynn.tulloch@gov.sk.ca
Director, Information Technology Services, Sharon Amorth
Tel: 306-787-4173; *Fax:* 306-798-2118
sharon.amorth@gov.sk.ca
Director, Financial Planning, Leanne Forgie
Tel: 306-787-1911; *Fax:* 306-787-6825
leanne.forgie@gov.sk.ca
Director, Legislation & Intergovernmental Affairs, Leeane Gherasim
Tel: 306-787-3615; *Fax:* 306-787-3650
leeane.gherasim@gov.sk.ca
Director, Risk Management & Business Improvement, Maury Harvey
Tel: 306-787-6097; *Fax:* 306-798-5550
maury.harvey@gov.sk.ca
Director, Enterprise Projects, Ron MacLeod
Tel: 306-787-5241; *Fax:* 306-798-2118
ron.macleod@gov.sk.ca
Director, Housing Finance, Scott Joyce
Tel: 306-787-4961; *Fax:* 306-787-8571
scott.joyce@gov.sk.ca
Director, Community-Based Organization Contract Management, Gail Stuermer
Tel: 306-787-9105; *Fax:* 306-787-8203
gail.stuermer@gov.sk.ca
Director, Children & Families Policy, Tara Truemner
Tel: 306-787-3621; *Fax:* 306-787-3650
tara.truemner@gov.sk.ca
Director, Accommodation Services, Dale Von Hagen
Tel: 306-787-1383; *Fax:* 306-798-0077
dale.vonhagen@gov.sk.ca

Child & Family Services
Tel: 306-787-7010; *Fax:* 306-787-0925
Executive Director, Program & Service Design, Natalie Huber
Tel: 306-787-2245; *Fax:* 306-787-0925
natalie.huber@gov.sk.ca
Acting Executive Director, Child & Family Service Delivery, Garry Prediger
Tel: 306-787-3652; *Fax:* 306-787-0925
garry.prediger@gov.sk.ca
Executive Director, Community Services, Wayne Phaneuf
Tel: 306-787-5481; *Fax:* 306-787-0925
wayne.phaneuf@gov.sk.ca
Director, Linkin, Nicole Adams
Tel: 306-787-7356; *Fax:* 306-787-0925
nicole.adams@gov.sk.ca
Director, Residential Services, Greg MacLean
Tel: 306-787-3643; *Fax:* 306-787-0925
greg.maclean@gov.sk.ca
Acting Director, Service Delivery Support, Ellen McGuire
Tel: 306-787-5698
ellen.mcguire@gov.sk.ca
Director, First Nations & Métis Services, Kim Taylor
Tel: 306-787-3949; *Fax:* 306-787-0925
kim.taylor@gov.sk.ca

Income Assistance & Disability Services Division
Fax: 306-787-1032
Assistant Deputy Minister, Bob Wihidal
Tel: 306-787-7357; *Fax:* 306-787-1032
bob.wihlidal@gov.sk.ca
Executive Director, Income Assistance Service Delivery, Jeff Redekop
Tel: 306-787-9013; *Fax:* 306-787-4450
jeff.redekop@gov.sk.ca
Executive Director, Community Living Service Delivery, Bob Martinook
Tel: 306-787-1348; *Fax:* 306-787-4450
bob.martinook@gov.sk.ca
www.socialservices.gov.sk.ca/community-living
Executive Director, Program & Service Design, Gord Tweed
Tel: 306-787-0015; *Fax:* 306-787-3650
gord.tweed@gov.sk.ca
Director, Disability Services Program Design & Operational Policy, Joel Kilbride

Tel: 306-787-4717; *Fax:* 306-787-2134
joel.kilbride@gov.sk.ca
Director, Office of Disability Issues, Daryl Stubel
Tel: 306-787-3670
Toll-free: 877-915-7468; *Fax:* 306-798-4450
daryl.stubel@gov.sk.ca
www.socialservices.gov.sk.ca/office-disability
Other Communications: Alternate E-mail: odi@gov.sk.ca
TTY: 306-787-7283

Housing Division
Tel: 306-787-4177; *Fax:* 306-798-3110
Toll-Free: 800-667-7567
www.socialservices.gov.sk.ca/housing
Executive Director, Program & Service Design, Patrick Cooper
Tel: 306-787-7288; *Fax:* 306-798-3110
patrick.cooper@gov.sk.ca
Executive Director, Housing Network, Dianne Baird
Tel: 306-787-8569; *Fax:* 306-798-3110
dianne.baird@gov.sk.ca
Executive Director, Housing Development, Tim Gross
Tel: 306-787-1008; *Fax:* 306-798-3110
tim.gross@gov.sk.ca
Director, Housing Network, Grant Tofte
Tel: 306-798-0932; *Fax:* 306-798-3110
grant.tofte@gov.sk.ca

Saskatchewan Telecommunications (SaskTel)

2121 Saskatchewan Dr., Regina, SK S4P 3Y2
Tel: 306-777-3737
Toll-Free: 800-727-5835
corporate.comments@sasktel.sk.ca
www.sasktel.com
twitter.com/sasktel
www.facebook.com/SaskTel
www.youtube.com/user/SaskTelOfficial

The provincial Crown Corporation delivers full service telecommunications to the people of Saskatchewan. Services are as follows: competitive voice, data, dial-up, & high speed internet; entertainment & multimedia services; security; web hosting; text & messaging services; & cellular & wireless data services.

Minister, Hon. Dustin Duncan
Tel: 306-787-0804; *Fax:* 306-798-2009
Legislative Building
#348, 2405 Legislative Dr.
Regina, SK S4S 0B3
Chair, Grant Kook
Tel: 306-777-2201
President & Chief Executive Officer, Ron Styles
ron.styles@sasktel.sk.ca
Chief Financial Officer, Mike Anderson
Chief Technology Officer, Daryl Godfrey
Chief Information Officer, John Hill
Chief Marketing Officer, Stacey Sandison
Tel: 306-777-3670
Vice-President, Human Resources & Corporate Services, Doug Burnett
Vice-President, Customer Service (Sales), Ken Keesey
Vice-President, Corporate Communications, Darcee MacFarlane
Tel: 306-777-4441
Vice-President, Corporate Counsel & Regulatory Affairs, John Meldrum
Tel: 306-777-2223

Saskatchewan Transportation Company (STC)

1717 Saskatchewan Dr., Regina, SK S4P 2E2
Tel: 306-787-3347; *Fax:* 306-787-1633
info@stcbus.com
www.stcbus.com
www.facebook.com/STCbus
www.linkedin.com/company/saskatchewan-transportation-company

The STC was established in 1946 to provide safe, affordable & accessible freight & passenger bus service throughout Saskatchewan.

Minister Responsible, Hon. Joe Hargrave
minister.cs@gov.sk.ca
Legislative Building
#306, 2405 Legislative Dr.
Regina, SK S4S 0B3
President & Chief Executive Officer, Shawn Grice
Tel: 306-787-2116; *Fax:* 306-798-4755
sgrice@stcbus.com
Chief Operating Officer, Customer Services/Maintenance, Phil Bohay
Tel: 306-787-7302; *Fax:* 306-787-1633
pbohay@stcbus.com
Chief Financial Officer, Jason Sherwin
Tel: 306-787-8189; *Fax:* 306-787-3429
jsherwin@stcbus.com

Tourism Saskatchewan

#189, 1621 Albert St., Regina, SK S4P 2S5
Tel: 306-787-9600; *Fax:* 306-787-2866
Toll-Free: 877-237-2273
travel.info@sasktourism.com
www.tourismsaskatchewan.com
twitter.com/Saskatchewan
www.facebook.com/TourismSaskatchewan
www.youtube.com/user/TourismSaskatchewan

Tourism Saskatchewan is a Crown corporation responsible for promoting & developing tourism in the province of Saskatchewan. Tourism training opportunities are available through the Saskatchewan Tourism Education Council (STEC).

Chief Executive Officer, Mary Taylor-Ash
Tel: 306-787-0570
mary.taylor-ash@tourismsask.com
Chief Financial Officer & Executive Director, Corporate Services, Veronica Gelowitz
Tel: 306-787-1535
veronica.gelowitz@tourismsask.com
Executive Director, Industry & Community Development, Ken Dueck
Tel: 306-787-3016
ken.dueck@tourismsask.com
Executive Director, Marketing & Communications, Jonathan Potts
Tel: 306-787-2313
jonathan.potts@tourismsask.com
Director, Saskatchewan Tourism Education Council (STEC), Carol Lumb
Tel: 306-933-5905
Toll-free: 800-331-1529; *Fax:* 306-933-6250
carol.lumb@tourismsask.com
www.stec.com
#102, 202 - 4th Ave. North
Saskatoon, SK S7K 0K1

Saskatchewan Water Corporation (SaskWater)

#200, 111 Fairford St. East, Moose Jaw, SK S6H 1C8
Fax: 306-694-3207
Toll-Free: 888-230-1111
comm@saskwater.com
www.saskwater.com

SaskWater, a provincial Crown corporation, is Saskatchewan's water utility service provider. Lines of business are as follows: supply of potable & non-potable water; treatment & management of wastewater; & certified operations & maintenance. SaskWater is responsible for designing, building, & operating transmission, regional, & stand-alone water supply & wastewater systems. All systems must meet regulatory requirements.

Minister Responsible, Hon. Scott Moe
Tel: 306-787-0393; *Fax:* 306-787-1669
env.minister@gov.sk.ca
Office of the Minister, Legislative Building
#38, 2405 Legislative Dr.
Regina, SK S4S 0B3
President, Doug Matthies
Tel: 306-694-3903; *Fax:* 306-694-3207
doug.matthies@saskwater.com
Vice-President, Business Development & Corporate Services Division, Marie Alexander
Tel: 306-694-3916; *Fax:* 306-694-3207
marie.alexander@saskwater.com
Vice-President, Operations & Engineering, Jeff Mander
Tel: 306-694-3880; *Fax:* 306-694-3207
jeff.mander@saskwater.com

Saskatchewan Water Security Agency (WSA)

#400, 111 Fairford St. East, Moose Jaw, SK S6H 7X9
Tel: 306-694-3900; *Fax:* 306-694-3105
comm@wsask.ca
www.wsask.ca

Saskatchewan Water Security Agency (formerly known as Saskatchewan Watershed Authority) was created in 2012 to coincide with the release of the 25 Year Saskatchewan Water Security Plan. The agency is a Crown corporation that is responsible for managing water resources in Saskatchewan, & to work to ensure reliable water supplies & safe drinking water sources.
The following regulations are administered by the Saskatchewan Watershed Authority: Conservation & Development; Drainage Control; Ground Water; & Reservoir Development Area.

Minister Responsible, Hon. Scott Moe
Tel: 306-787-0393; *Fax:* 306-787-1669
env.minister@gov.sk.ca
Office of the Minister, Legislative Building
#38, 2405 Legislative Dr.
Regina, SK S4S 0B3
President, Wayne Dybvig
Tel: 306-694-7739; *Fax:* 306-694-3991
wayne.dybvig@swa.ca
Vice-President, Legal, Regulatory & Aboriginal Affairs, & General Counsel, Susan Ross
Executive Director, Engineering & Geoscience, Bill Duncan
Tel: 306-694-3990; *Fax:* 306-694-3944
bill.duncan@swa.ca
Executive Director, Environmental & Municipal Management Services, Sam Ferris
Tel: 306-787-6193; *Fax:* 306-787-0780
sam.ferris@wsask.ca
Executive Director, Integrated Water Services, Jim Gerhart
Tel: 306-694-3952; *Fax:* 306-694-3944
jim.gerhart@swa.ca
Executive Director, Policy & Communications, Dale Hjertaas
Tel: 306-787-0726; *Fax:* 306-787-0780
dale.hjertaas@swa.ca
Executive Director, Corporate Services, Irene Hrynkiw
Tel: 306-694-3960; *Fax:* 306-694-3465
irene.hrynkiw@wsask.ca

Saskatchewan Workers' Compensation Board

#200, 1881 Scarth St., Regina, SK S4P 4L1
Tel: 306-787-4370; *Fax:* 306-787-4311
Toll-Free: 800-667-7590
webmaster@wcbsask.com
www.wcbsask.com
Other Communication: Injury Reports: 1-800-787-9288; Health Care Provider Inquiries: internet_healthcare@wcbsask.com; Appeal Fax: 306-787-1116
Secondary Address: 115 - 24th St. East
Saskatoon, SK S7K 1L5
twitter.com/saskwcb
www.facebook.com/SaskWCB
www.youtube.com/channel/UCkf1lQhS90NnJxx4AFFuKyQ

The Saskatchewan's Workers' Compensation Board was created by the following provincial legislation in Saskatchewan: the Workers' Compensation Act 1979, General Regulations, & Exclusion Regulations. The Board is an independent body that administers a no-fault compensation system to protect employers and workers against the result of work injuries. The WCB provides financial protection, medical benefits. & rehabilitation services to injured workers & their dependents in cases of injury or death arising from, & in the course of, employment.

Minister Responsible, Hon. Don Morgan, Q.C.
Tel: 306-787-0613; *Fax:* 306-787-6946
minister.edu@gov.sk.ca
Office of the Minister of Education / Labour Relation & Workplace Safety, Legislative Bldg.
#361, 2405 Legislative Dr.
Regina, SK S4S 0B3
Chairman, Gordon Dobrowolsky
Tel: 306-787-4379; *Fax:* 306-787-0213
Chief Executive Officer, Peter Federko
Tel: 306-787-7398; *Fax:* 306-787-0213
pfederko@wcbsask.com
Vice-President, Human Resources & Team Support, Donna Kane
Tel: 306-787-4440; *Fax:* 306-787-0213
dkane@wcbsask.com
Chief Information Officer, Bruce D'Sena
Tel: 306-787-0522
bdsena@wcbsask.com
Vice-President, Operations, Graham Topp
Tel: 306-787-4371; *Fax:* 306-787-7582
gtopp@wcbsask.com

Government of the Yukon Territory

Seat of Government: PO Box 2703 Whitehorse, YT Y1A 2C6
Tel: 867-667-5811
Toll-Free: 800-661-0408
TTY: 867-393-7460
www.gov.yk.ca
twitter.com/yukongov
www.facebook.com/yukongov
www.linkedin.com/company/yukon-government
www.youtube.com/user/yukongovernment

The Yukon was created as a separate territory June 13, 1898. It has an area of 474,711.02 sq km, & StatsCan's census in 2011 showed the population was 32,897. A federally appointed commissioner (similar to a provincial lieutenant-governor) oversees federal interests in the territory, but the day-to-day operation of the government rests with the wholly elected executive council (cabinet). The territorial legislature has power to make acts on generally all matters of a local nature in the territory, including the imposition of local taxes, property & civil rights & the administration of justice, education & health & social services. Legislative powers vested in the provinces but not available to the territory include control of unoccupied Crown land, renewable & non-renewable resources (except wildlife & sport fisheries) & the power to amend the Yukon Act, a federal statute.

Office of the Commissioner of Yukon

Taylor House, 412 Main St., Whitehorse, YT Y1A 2B7
Tel: 867-667-5121; *Fax:* 867-393-6201
commissioner@gov.yk.ca
www.commissioner.gov.yk.ca

The Yukon Territory is governed by a commissioner appointed for a 5-year term by the federal government, a government leader, an executive council which functions as a cabinet, & a legislative assembly. The Yukon Act provides for the establishment of a commissioner & the elected legislative assembly.

Commissioner of Yukon, Hon. Doug Phillips
Douglas.Phillips@gov.yk.ca

Office of the Premier

2071 - 2nd Ave., PO Box 2703 Whitehorse, YT Y1A 2C6
Tel: 867-667-8660; *Fax:* 867-393-6252
premier@gov.yk.ca
www.yukonpremier.ca
twitter.com/YukonPremier

Darrell Pasloski was elected Leader of the Yukon Party on May 28, 2011. He was first sworn in as Premier on June 11, 2011. In the general election of October 11, 2011, The Honourable Darrell Pasloski was elected to the Yukon Legislative Assembly.

Premier, Yukon Territory; Leader, Yukon Party; Minister Responsible, Executive Council Office; Minister, Finance; Member, Legislative Assembly, Hon. Darrell Pasloski, Yukon Party
Tel: 867-393-7053; *Fax:* 867-393-6252
darrell.pasloski@gov.yk.ca
Social Media: twitter.com/YukonPremier, www.facebook.com/TeamYukon, ca.linkedin.com/pub/darrell-pasloski/18/943/975

Principal Secretary, Gordon Steele
Tel: 867-667-5842
gordon.steele@gov.yk.ca

Chief of Staff, Michael Hale
Tel: 867-667-8660
Michael.Hale@gov.yk.ca

Executive Council

2071 Second Ave., PO Box 2703 Whitehorse, YT Y1A 2C6
Tel: 867-667-5393; *Fax:* 867-393-6214
eco@gov.yk.ca
www.yukonpremier.ca/premiersteam.html

The Executive Council of Yukon Territory is selected by the Honourable Darrell Pasloski, Premier. Members of Yukon's cabinet are members of the Yukon Party, following its victory in the October 2011 general election.

Premier, Yukon Territory; Leader, Yukon Party; Minister Responsible, Executive Council Office; Minister, Finance, Hon. Darrell Pasloski
Tel: 867-393-7053; *Fax:* 867-393-6252
darrell.pasloski@gov.yk.ca
www.yukonpremier.ca
Social Media: twitter.com/YukonPremier, www.facebook.com/TeamYukon, ca.linkedin.com/pub/darrell-pasloski/18/943/975

Deputy Premier; Minister, Tourism & Culture; Minister Responsible for the Women's Directorate, Minister responsible for the French Language Services Directorate, Hon. Elaine Taylor
Tel: 867-667-8641; *Fax:* 867-393-6252
elaine.taylor@gov.yk.ca
Social Media: www.facebook.com/135880316425564

Government House Leader; Minister, Justice; Minister Responsible for the Yukon Development Corporation, Minister Responsible for the Yukon Energy Corporation, Hon. Brad Cathers
Tel: 867-667-5806; *Fax:* 867-393-6252
brad.cathers@gov.yk.ca
Social Media: twitter.com/BradCathers, www.facebook.com/BradCathers.MLAforLakeLaberge

Minister, Education, Hon. Doug Graham
Tel: 867-667-8629; *Fax:* 867-393-6252
doug.graham@gov.yk.ca

Minister, Energy, Mines & Resources; Minister, Highways & Public Works, Hon. Scott Kent
Tel: 867-667-8643; *Fax:* 867-393-7400
scott.kent@gov.yk.ca
Social Media: www.facebook.com/287536247929989

Minister, Community Services; Minister Responsible for the Public Service Commission, Hon. Currie Dixon
Tel: 867-667-8628; *Fax:* 867-393-7400
currie.dixon@gov.yk.ca
Social Media: twitter.com/curriedixon

Minister, Environment, Hon. Wade Istchenko
Tel: 867-667-8644; *Fax:* 867-393-7400
wade.istchenko@gov.yk.ca
Social Media: www.facebook.com/wade.istchenko

Minister, Health & Social Services; Minister Responsible for the Yukon Workers' Compensation Health & Safety Board, Hon. Mike Nixon
Tel: 867-633-7973; *Fax:* 867-393-6252
mike.nixon@gov.yk.ca
Social Media: twitter.com/nixon_mike, www.facebook.com/264844376862257

Minister, Economic Development; Minister Responsible for the Yukon Housing Corporation, Yukon Liquor Corporation, & Yukon Lottery Commission, Hon. Stacey Hassard
Tel: 867-456-6509; *Fax:* 867-393-7400
stacey.hassard@gov.yk.ca

Executive Council Office

2071 - 2nd Ave., Whitehorse, YT Y1A 2C6
Tel: 867-667-5393; *Fax:* 897-393-6214
www.eco.gov.yk.ca

Deputy Minister, Kelvin Leary
Kelvin.Leary@gov.yk.ca

Assistant Deputy Minister, Corporate Programs & Intergovernmental Relations, Andrea Buckley
Tel: 867-939-6323
Andrea.Buckley@gov.yk.ca

Acting Assistant Deputy Minister, Aboriginal Relations, Al Jones
Tel: 867-667-8127
Al.Jones@gov.yk.ca

Assistant Deputy Minister, Strategic Corporate Services, Pamela Muir
Tel: 867-667-5421
Pamela.Muir@gov.yk.ca

Chief of Protocol, Pamela Bangart
Tel: 867-667-5875; *Fax:* 867-563-9602
pamela.bangart@gov.yk.ca

Director, Intergovernmental Relations, Mark Roberts
Tel: 867-667-5744
Mark.Roberts@gov.yk.ca

Director, Yukon Bureau of Statistics, Bishnu Saha
Tel: 867-667-5463; *Fax:* 867-393-6203
saha.bushnu@gov.yk.ca

Government Inquiry Office

Government of Yukon Administration Bldg., 2071 - 2nd Ave., PO Box 2703 Whitehorse, YT Y1A 2C6
Tel: 867-667-5811
Toll-Free: 800-661-0408
inquiry.desk@gov.yk.ca
www.gov.yk.ca/contactus.html
Other Communication: Alternate Phone: 867-667-5812
twitter.com/yukongov
www.facebook.com/yukongov

Yukon Legislative Assembly

2071 - 2nd Ave., PO Box 2703 Whitehorse, YT Y1A 2C6
Tel: 867-667-5498
yla@gov.yk.ca
www.legassembly.gov.yk.ca

Speaker, Hon. Patti McLeod
Tel: 867-667-8646; *Fax:* 867-393-6252
patti.mcleod@gov.yk.ca

Clerk (Deputy Minister), Floyd McCormick
Tel: 867-667-5498; *Fax:* 867-393-6280
floyd.mccormick@gov.yk.ca

Sergeant-at-Arms, Rudy Couture

Deputy Sergeant-at-Arms, Doris McLean

Deputy Speaker; Chair, Committee of the Whole, Darius Elias
Tel: 867-456-6710; *Fax:* 867-393-6252
darius.elias@gov.yk.ca

Deputy Clerk, Linda Kolody
Tel: 867-667-5499
linda.kolody@gov.yk.ca

Hansard Administrator, Deana Lemke

Acting Director, Administration, Finance & Systems, Patrick Michael
Tel: 867-667-5618
Patrick.Michael@gov.yk.ca

Government Caucus Office (Yukon Party)

PO Box 31113 Whitehorse, YT Y1A 5P7
Tel: 867-668-6505
info@yukonparty.ca
www.yukonparty.ca
Other Communication: Caucus URL: www.yukonpartycaucus.ca

Leader, Yukon Party; Premier, Yukon Territory; Minister Responsible, Executive Council Office; Minister, Finance; Member, Legislative Assembly, Hon. Darrell Pasloski
Tel: 867-393-7053; *Fax:* 867-393-6252
darrell.pasloski@gov.yk.ca
Social Media: twitter.com/YukonPremier, www.facebook.com/TeamYukon, ca.linkedin.com/pub/darrell-pasloski/18/943/975

Government House Leader, Hon. Brad Cathers
Tel: 867-667-5806; *Fax:* 867-393-6252
brad.cathers@gov.yk.ca

President, Pat McInroy

Office of the Official Opposition (New Democratic Party)

PO Box 2703 A-10 Whitehorse, YT Y1A 2C6
Tel: 867-668-2203
Toll-Free: 800-661-0408
reception.ndp@yla.gov.yk.ca
www.yukonndp.ca
Other Communication: Caucus URL: www.yukonndpcaucus.ca
twitter.com/YukonNDPCaucus
www.facebook.com/YukonNDP

In September 2009, Elizabeth Hanson became the leader of Yukon's New Democratic Party. After the New Democratic Party won six seats in the general election of October 11, 2011, Hanson became Leader of the Official Opposition.

Leader, Official Opposition, Liz Hanson
Tel: 867-393-7059; *Fax:* 867-393-6499
elizabeth.hanson@yla.gov.yk.ca
www.yukonndp.ca/liz
Social Media: twitter.com/lizhansonndp, www.facebook.com/lizhansonMLA, www.linkedin.com/pub/elizabeth-hanson/59/4b8/a8a

Official Opposition House Leader, Jan Stick
Tel: 867-393-7021; *Fax:* 867-393-6499
jan.stick@yla.gov.yk.ca
Other Communications: Toll-Free Phone: 1-800-661-0408, ext. 7021

Official Opposition Caucus Chair, Kevin Barr
Tel: 867-393-7015; *Fax:* 867-393-6499
kevin.barr@yla.gov.yk.ca
Other Communications: Toll-Free Phone: 1-800-661-0408, ext. 7015

Official Opposition Caucus Whip, Lois Moorcroft
Tel: 867-393-6999; *Fax:* 867-393-6499
lois.moorcroft@yla.gov.yk.ca
Other Communications: Toll-Free Phone: 1-800-661-0408, ext. 6999

Official Opposition Deputy Caucus Chair, Kate White
Tel: 867-393-7001; *Fax:* 867-393-6499
kate.white@yla.gov.yk.ca
Other Communications: Toll-Free Phone: 1-800-661-0408, ext. 7001

Official Opposition Deputy Caucus Whip & Deputy First Nations Liaison, Jim Tredger
Tel: 867-393-7023; *Fax:* 867-393-6499
jim.tredger@yla.gov.yk.ca
Other Communications: Toll-Free Phone: 1-800-661-0408, ext. 7023

Office of the Leader of the Third Party (Liberal Party)

#183, 108 Elliott St., Whitehorse, YT Y1A 6C4
Tel: 867-667-4748
info@ylp.ca
www.ylp.ca
twitter.com/YukonLiberal
www.facebook.com/yukonliberalparty

Following the general election of October 2011, Darius Elias was named the interim leader of the Yukon Liberal party. When Elias resigned from the Liberal Party in 2012, Sandy Silver became the new Interim Leader. He was acclaimed as permanent Leader in February 2014. He is the MLA for Klondike, & one of two Liberals elected in the October 2011 election.

Leader, Yukon Liberal Party, Sandy Silver, Liberal
Tel: 867-393-7007; *Fax:* 867-393-7444
sandy.silver@yla.gov.yk.ca
Yukon Legislative Assembly
PO Box 2703
Whitehorse, YT Y1A 2C6

President, Yukon Liberal Party, Devin Bailey
President@ylp.ca

Standing Committees of the Yukon Legislative Assembly

www.legassembly.gov.yk.ca/committees.html

The following are the Standing Committees of the Yukon Legislative Assembly: Members' Services Board; Rules, Elections & Privileges; Public Accounts; Statuatory Instruments; & Appointments to Major Government Boards & Committees.

Clerk of Committees, Allison Lloyd
Tel: 867-667-5494
Allison.Lloyd@gov.yk.ca

Chair, Members' Services Board, Hon. Patti McLeod
Constituency: Watson Lake, Yukon Party
Tel: 867-667-8646; *Fax:* 867-393-6252
patti.mcleod@gov.yk.ca

Chair, Standing Committee on Rules, Elections & Privileges, Vacant

Chair, Standing Committee on Public Accounts, Liz Hanson
Constituency: Whitehorse Centre, New Democratic Party
Tel: 867-393-7059; *Fax:* 867-393-6499
liz.hanson@yla.gov.yk.ca
Chair, Standing Committee on Appointments to Major Government Boards & Committees, Hon. Stacey Hassard
Constituency: Pelly-Nisutlin, Yukon Party
Tel: 867-456-6509; *Fax:* 867-393-7400
stacey.hassard@gov.yk.ca

Thirty-third Legislative Assembly - Yukon Territory

Yukon Legislative Assembly Office, 2071 Second Ave., PO Box 2703 Whitehorse, YT Y1A 2C6
Tel: 867-667-5498
www.legassembly.gov.yk.ca

Last General Election: October 11, 2011.
Percentage of eligible voters who cast a ballot in the October 2011 general election: 76.2%.
Party Standings (Sept. 2016):
Yukon Party 11;
New Democratic Party 6;
Liberal Party 1;
Independent 1;
Total Seats 19.
Party Leaders: Yukon Party Hon. Darrell Pasloski, Premier; New Democratic Party Elizabeth Hanson, Official Opposition Leader;
Liberal Party Sandy Silver, Third Party Leader.
Salaries, Indemnities, & Allowances (2012-2013):
Members' indemnity $71,200, plus $13,692 expense allowances for both Whitehorse & rural members;
Minister's salary $38,338;
Premier's salary $16,431;
Leader of the Official Opposition's salary $38,338;
Leader of the Third Party's salary $16,431;
Speaker's salary $27,385;
Deputy Speaker's salary $10,954.
Members of the 33rd Legislative Assembly are listed with their constituency, number of electors on the list for the most recent election, party affiliation, & contact information. The address for all Members of the Yukon Legislative Assembly is as follows: PO Box 2703, Whitehorse, YT, Y1A 2C6.

Members of the Legislative Assembly of Yukon Territory

Kevin Barr
Constituency: Mount Lorne - Southern Lakes *No. of Constituents:* 1,374, New Democratic Party
Tel: 867-393-7015; *Fax:* 867-393-6499
kevin.barr@yla.gov.yk.ca
www.yukonndp.ca/kevin
Social Media: www.facebook.com/KevinBarrYNDP
Government House Leader; Minister, Justice; Minister Responsible for the Yukon Development Corporation, Minister Responsible for the Yukon Energy Corporation, Hon. Brad Cathers
Constituency: Lake Laberge *No. of Constituents:* 1,272, Yukon Party
Tel: 867-667-5806; *Fax:* 867-393-6252
brad.cathers@gov.yk.ca
www.bradcathers.ca
Social Media: twitter.com/BradCathers, www.facebook.com/BradCathers.MLAforLakeLaberge
Minister, Community Services; Minister Responsible for the Public Service Commission, Hon. Currie Dixon
Constituency: Copperbelt North *No. of Constituents:* 1,543, Yukon Party
Tel: 867-667-8628; *Fax:* 867-393-7400
currie.dixon@gov.yk.ca
Social Media: twitter.com/curriedixon
Deputy Speaker; Chair, Committee of the Whole, Darius Elias
Constituency: Vuntut Gwitchin *No. of Constituents:* 154, Yukon Party
Tel: 867-456-6710; *Fax:* 867-393-6252
darius.elias@gov.yk.ca
www.northyukon.ca
Minister, Education, Hon. Doug Graham
Constituency: Porter Creek North *No. of Constituents:* 1,289, Yukon Party
Tel: 867-667-8629; *Fax:* 867-393-6252
doug.graham@gov.yk.ca
Leader, Official Opposition, Liz Hanson
Constituency: Whitehorse Centre *No. of Constituents:* 1,249, New Democratic Party
Tel: 867-393-7059; *Fax:* 867-393-6499
liz.hanson@yla.gov.yk.ca
www.yukonndp.ca/liz
Social Media: twitter.com/lizhansonndp, www.facebook.com/lizhansonMLA, www.linkedin.com/pub/elizabeth-hanson/59/4b8/a8a
Minister, Economic Development; Minister Responsible for the Yukon Housing Corporation, Yukon Liquor Corporation, & Yukon Lottery Commission, Hon. Stacey Hassard
Constituency: Pelly-Nisutlin *No. of Constituents:* 748, Yukon Party
Tel: 86- 45- 650; *Fax:* 867-393-7400
stacey.hassard@gov.yk.ca
Minister, Highways & Public Works, Hon. Wade Istchenko
Constituency: Kluane *No. of Constituents:* 888, Yukon Party
Tel: 867-667-8644; *Fax:* 867-393-7400
wade.istchenko@gov.yk.ca
Social Media: www.facebook.com/wade.istchenko
Minister, Energy, Mines & Resources; Minister, Highways & Public Works, Hon. Scott Kent
Constituency: Riverdale North *No. of Constituents:* 1,313, Yukon Party
Tel: 867-667-8643; *Fax:* 867-393-7400
scott.kent@gov.yk.ca
Social Media: www.facebook.com/287536247929989
David Laxton
Constituency: Porter Creek Centre *No. of Constituents:* 1,055, Independent
Tel: 867-667-5800; *Fax:* 867-393-6252
david.laxton@gov.yk.ca
Speaker; Chair, Committee of the Whole, Hon. Patti McLeod
Constituency: Watson Lake *No. of Constituents:* 845, Yukon Party
Tel: 867-667-8646; *Fax:* 867-393-6252
patti.mcleod@gov.yk.ca
Lois Moorcroft
Constituency: Copperbelt South *No. of Constituents:* 1,283, New Democratic Party
Tel: 867-393-6999; *Fax:* 867-393-6499
lois.moorcroft@yla.gov.yk.ca
www.yukonndp.ca/lois
Social Media: www.facebook.com/LoisMoorcroftNDP
Minister, Health & Social Services; Minister Responsible for the Yukon Workers' Compensation Health & Safety Board, Hon. Mike Nixon
Constituency: Porter Creek South *No. of Constituents:* 810, Yukon Party
Tel: 867-633-7973; *Fax:* 867-393-6252
mike.nixon@gov.yk.ca
Social Media: twitter.com/nixon_mike, www.facebook.com/264844376862257
Premier; Minister, Finance; Minister Responsible for the Executive Council Office; Leader, Yukon Party, Hon. Darrell Pasloski
Constituency: Mountainview *No. of Constituents:* 1,382, Yukon Party
Tel: 867-393-7053; *Fax:* 867-393-6252
darrell.pasloski@gov.yk.ca
www.yukonpremier.ca
Other Communications: Office, Phone: 867-667-8660; Fax: 867-393-6252
Social Media: twitter.com/YukonPremier, www.facebook.com/TeamYukon, ca.linkedin.com/pub/darrell-pasloski/18/943/975
Leader, Third Party; Third Party House Leader, Sandy Silver
Constituency: Klondike *No. of Constituents:* 1,319, Liberal
Tel: 867-393-7007; *Fax:* 867-393-7444
sandy.silver@yla.gov.yk.ca
Social Media: twitter.com/klondike_silver, www.linkedin.com/pub/sandy-silver/43/80b/b09
Official Opposition House Leader, Jan Stick
Constituency: Riverdale South *No. of Constituents:* 1,387, New Democratic Party
Tel: 867-393-7021; *Fax:* 867-393-6499
jan.stick@yla.gov.yk.ca
www.yukonndp.ca/jan
Social Media: twitter.com/janstickndp, www.facebook.com/janstickYNDP
Deputy Premier; Minister, Tourism & Education; Minister responsible for the Women's Directorate, Minister responsible for the French Language Services Directorate, Hon. Elaine Taylor
Constituency: Whitehorse West *No. of Constituents:* 961, Yukon Party
Tel: 867-667-8641; *Fax:* 867-393-6252
elaine.taylor@gov.yk.ca
Social Media: www.facebook.com/135880316425564
Jim Tredger
Constituency: Mayo-Tatchun *No. of Constituents:* 916, New Democratic Party
Tel: 867-393-7050; *Fax:* 867-393-6499
jim.tredger@yla.gov.yk.ca
www.yukonndp.ca/jim
Social Media: www.facebook.com/JimTredgerNDP
Kate White
Constituency: Takhini-Kopper King *No. of Constituents:* 1,552, New Democratic Party
Tel: 867-393-7001; *Fax:* 867-393-6499
kate.white@yla.gov.yk.ca
www.yukonndp.ca/kate
Social Media: twitter.com/MsKateWhite, www.facebook.com/KateWhiteNDP

Yukon Territory Government Departments & Agencies

Yukon Child & Youth Advocate Office

#19, 2071 Second Ave., Whitehorse, YT Y1A 1B1
Tel: 867-456-5575; *Fax:* 867-456-5574
Toll-Free: 800-661-0408
www.ycao.ca
www.facebook.com/116941835050317
www.youtube.com/user/YukonChildAdvocate

Yukon Child & Youth Advocate, Annette King
Deputy Child & Youth Advocate, Bengie Clethero
bengie.clethero@ycao.ca
Office Adminstrator, Tina Dickson
tina.dickson@gov.yk.ca

Yukon Community Services

PO Box 2703 Whitehorse, YT Y1A 2C6
Tel: 867-667-5811; *Fax:* 867-393-6295
Toll-Free: 800-661-0408
TTY: 867-393-7460
inquiry@gov.yk.ca
www.community.gov.yk.ca
www.facebook.com/YGCommunityServices

The main purpose of the department is to serve Yukoners & their communities by providing access to services to strengthen communities. The department focuses on community affairs & municipal relations within government on behalf of Yukon communities & acts as a liaison between community groups & government departments.

Minister, Hon. Currie Dixon
Tel: 867-667-8628; *Fax:* 867-393-7400
currie.dixon@gov.yk.ca
Deputy Minister, Paul Moore
Tel: 867-456-6512; *Fax:* 867-633-7957
Paul.Moore@gov.yk.ca
Acting Director, Human Resources, Stephanie Chapman
Tel: 867-667-5667; *Fax:* 867-393-6933
stephanie.chapman@gov.yk.ca
Director, Corporate Policy, Caitlin Kerwin
Tel: 867-667-5865; *Fax:* 867-393-6404
caitlin.kerwin@gov.yk.ca
Director, Finance, Systems & Administration, Karen Mason
Tel: 867-667-5311; *Fax:* 867-393-6264
karen.mason@gov.yk.ca
Director, Communications, Ben Yu Schott
Tel: 867-456-6580; *Fax:* 867-393-6404
ben.yuschott@gov.yk.ca

Associated Agencies, Boards & Commissions:

•Yukon Lottery Commission/Lotteries Yukon
#101, 205 Hawkins St.
Whitehorse, YT Y1A 1X3
Tel: 867-633-7890; *Fax:* 867-668-7561
Toll-free: 800-661-0555
lotteriesyukon@gov.yk.ca
www.lotteriesyukon.com

Community Development Division
Fax: 867-393-6258

The branch assists, advises & organizes municipal & unincorporated communities, provides funding by administering the comprehensive municipal grants & grants in lieu of taxes, assesses properties, collects property taxes & administers the Rural Electrification & Telecommunication program & the Home Owner Grant program. The branch collaborates with communities for the planning, design, & construction of land development projects & includes residential, rural residential, commercial, industrial, & cottage lots. The branch is responsible for regulatory approvals & design, managing construction capital works projects, such as upgrading roads, water & sewage treatment facilities & solid waste disposal sites & assists communities in developing land use plans, working closely with the Yukon Municipal Board & the Association of Yukon Communities. The branch is responsible for the operation of Yukon Government owned facilities for water supply & distribution, sewage treatment & solid waste disposal.

Assistant Deputy Minister, Paul Moore
Tel: 867-667-3534; *Fax:* 867-393-6216
paul.moore@gov.yk.ca
Director, Infrastructure Development, Jennifer MacGillivray
Tel: 867-393-6954; *Fax:* 867-393-6216
jennifer.macgillivray@gov.yk.ca
Director, Operations & Programs, Dwayne Muckosky
Tel: 867-667-6191; *Fax:* 867-393-6258
dwayne.muckosky@gov.yk.ca
Director, Public Libraries, Julie Ourom
Tel: 867-667-5447; *Fax:* 867-393-6333
julie.ourom@gov.yk.ca

Director, Community Affairs, Christine Smith
Tel: 867-667-8684; *Fax:* 867-393-6258
christine.smith@gov.yk.ca
Director, Sport & Recreation Branch, Karen Thompson
Tel: 867-667-5608; *Fax:* 867-393-6416
karen.thomson@gov.yk.ca

Corporate Policy & Consumer Affairs Division
Berska Bldg., 307 Black St., 2nd Fl., Whitehorse, YT Y1A 2N1
Fax: 867-393-6943
Assistant Deputy Minister, Charlene Beauchemin
Tel: 867-667-5486
charlene.beauchemin@gov.yk.ca
Director, Professional Licensing & Regulatory Affairs, Fiona Charbonneau
Tel: 867-667-5257
fiona.charbonneau@gov.yk.ca
Director, Property Assessment & Taxation Branch, Kelly Eby
Tel: 867-667-5234
kelly.eby@gov.yk.ca
Director, Corporate Policy, Caitlin Kerwin
Tel: 867-667-5865
caitlin.kerwin@gov.yk.ca
Director, Employment Standards & Residential Tenancies, Michael Noseworthy
Tel: 867-667-5944; *Fax:* 867-393-6317
micheal.noseworthy@gov.yk.ca
Director, Corporate Affairs, Fred Pretorius
Tel: 867-667-5225
fred.pretorius@gov.yk.ca

Protective Services
91790 Alaska Hwy., Whitehorse, YT Y1A 5X7
Fax: 867-456-6589
Assistant Deputy Minister, Rick Smith
Tel: 867-393-7409
rick.smith@gov.yk.ca
Chief Mechanical Inspector, Paul Christensen
Tel: 867-667-5765
paul.christensen@gov.yk.ca
Chief Building/Plumbing Inspector, Stan Dueck
Tel: 867-667-5445
stan.dueck@gov.yk.ca
Acting Chief Electrical Inspector, Hector Lang
Tel: 867-667-5485
hector.lang@gov.yk.ca
Director, Building Safety, Doug Badry
Tel: 867-456-6596
doug.badry@gov.yk.ca

Emergency Measures Organization (EMO)
Whitehorse Airport, Combined Services Bldg., 2nd Fl., 60 Norseman Rd., Whitehorse, YT Y1A 2C6
Tel: 867-667-5220; *Fax:* 867-393-6266
Toll-Free: 800-661-0408
emo.yukon@gov.yk.ca
www.community.gov.yk.ca/emo
Other Communication: Toll-Free Phone: 1-800-661-0408, ext. 5220
twitter.com/YukonAlerts
www.facebook.com/yukonemo

Responsible for coordinating the Territory's preparedness for, response to, & recovery from, major emergencies & disasters. EMO provides authority to ensure that contingency plans are in place to deal with foreseeable risks & hazards. The Yukon EMO is divided into 13 geographical preparedness areas, mirroring the RCMP detachment boundaries. Eight of these areas have incorporated Municipalities that have appointed a Municipal EMO Coordinator to chair the local Emergency Planning Committee. In the remaining areas, the Emergency Measures Branch appoints a co-ordinator.

Manager, Michael Templeton
michael.templeton@gov.yk.ca

Emergency Medical Services (EMS)
Yukon Electrical Bldg., #200, 1100 First Ave., Whitehorse, YT Y1A 6K6
www.community.gov.yk.ca/ems
Director, Michael McKeage
Tel: 867-456-6591
michael.mckeage@gov.yk.ca

Fire & Life Safety/Fire Marshal's Office
91790 Alaska Hwy., PO Box 2703 C-20 Whitehorse, YT Y1A 2C6
Fax: 867-667-3165
Toll-Free: 800-661-0408
inquiry@gov.yk.ca
www.community.gov.yk.ca/fireprotection/contact.html
www.facebook.com/159594500729337

The Fire Marshal's Office works to reduce the loss of life & property due to fire & is responsible for public education & fire fighter training, as well as for funding & administering volunteer fire departments in Yukon unincorporated communities. Staff carry out fire & life safety inspections on hotels, motels, public assembly buildings, schools, day care centers, homes for special care, restaurants, etc. throughout Yukon. The Office inspects & permits underground fuel storage tank installations.

Director, Fire & Life Safety/Fire Marshal, Dennis Berry
Tel: 867-667-5217
dennis.berry@gov.yk.ca

Wildland Fire Management
91790 Alaska Hwy., Whitehorse, YT Y1A 5X7
Tel: 867-456-3845; *Fax:* 867-667-3191
Toll-Free: 800-826-4750
www.community.gov.yk.ca/firemanagement
Other Communication: Fire Information, Phone: 867-393-7415; Report Wildfires, Toll-Free: 1-888-798-3473
twitter.com/YukonWildFire
www.facebook.com/148976218447555
Director, Wildland Fire Management, Mike Etches
Tel: 867-456-3904
mike.etches@gov.yk.ca
Fire Information Officer, George Maratos
Tel: 867-667-3013
colin.urquhart@gov.yk.ca

Yukon Development Corporation (YDC)

PO Box 2703 D-1 Whitehorse, YT Y1A 2C6
Tel: 867-456-3837; *Fax:* 867-393-7167
www.ydc.yk.ca

The Yukon Development Corporation (YDC) assists with implementation of energy policies from the Department of Energy, Mines & Resources, by designing & delivering related energy programs. YDC facilitates the generation, production, transmission & distribution of energy in a manner consistent with sustainable development. YDC has investments in electricity & related energy infrastructure & acts as the primary vehicle for delivery of territorial energy programs & services. YDC owns two subsidiary corporations, Yukon Energy Corporation, YEC, & the Energy Solutions Centre Inc., ESC. YEC is the primary producer & transmitter of electrical energy in the territory & operates under the Yukon Utilities Board & the Public Utilities Act. ESC provides technical services, promotes efficiency & renewable energy technologies, co-ordinates & delivers federal & territorial energy programs to households, businesses, institutions, First Nation & public governments.

Minister responsible, Hon. Brad Cathers
Tel: 867-667-5806; *Fax:* 867-393-6252
brad.cathers@gov.yk.ca
Chair, Joanne Fairlie
Tel: 867-456-3837
joanne.fairlie@gov.yk.ca
Corporate Secretary, Lisa Jarvis
lisa.jarvis@gov.yk.ca
Chief Executive Officer / Deputy Minister, George Ross
Tel: 867-667-5417
george.ross@gov.yk.ca

Yukon Economic Development

#209, 212 Main St., F-1, Whitehorse, YT Y1A 2A9
Tel: 867-393-7191; *Fax:* 867-393-6412
Toll-Free: 800-661-0408
ecdev@gov.yk.ca
www.economicdevelopment.gov.yk.ca

The Department works with the Yukon business community & with other governments to support business development, trade & investment opportunities, & partnerships for the development of the Yukon economy. It co-ordinates & facilitates the Yukon Government's economic development agenda. The Department is focused on creating a positive business climate in Yukon & is committed to First Nation business development in the territory. Economic Development markets Yukon as a great place to do business.

Minister, Hon. Stacey Hassard
Tel: 867-456-6509; *Fax:* 867-393-7400
stacey.hassard@gov.yk.ca
Deputy Minister, Vacant
Assistant Deputy Minister, Steve Rose
Tel: 867-667-8416
steve.rose@gov.yk.ca
Director, Finance & Information Management Branch, Jessica Schultz
Tel: 867-667-5933
jessica.schultz@gov.yk.ca

Business & Economic Research
economics@gov.yk.ca
www.economics.gov.yk.ca

Provides research, analysis & reports to support a broad understanding of the economy & the assessment of its impacts on Yukon's fiscal position, budgetary projections & financial decision making.

Director, Derrick Hynes
Tel: 867-667-8011
derrick.hynes@gov.yk.ca

Business & Industry Development
PO Box 2703 F-2 Whitehorse, YT Y1A 2C6
Tel: 867-393-7014; *Fax:* 867-393-6944
investyukon@gov.yk.ca
www.economicdevelopment.gov.yk.ca/bidb.html
Other Communication: Alt. E-mail: business.trade@gov.yk.ca
Director, Barbara Dunlop
Tel: 867-667-3430; *Fax:* 867-393-6944
barbara.dunlop@gov.yk.ca

Technology & Telecommunications Development
#201, 208 Main St., Whitehorse, YT Y1A 2A9
www.economicdevelopment.gov.yk.ca/t2d2.html

The directorate works with the Information & Communications Technology sector in the Yukon in order to develop & promote availability, reliability & affordability of telecommunications services in the Territory.

Director, Steve Sorochan, P. Eng.
Tel: 867-667-8073
steve.sorochan@gov.yk.ca

Coporate Policy, Planning & Research Branch
#209, 212 Main St., Whitehorse, YT
Tel: 867-456-3914; *Fax:* 867-393-6412
www.economicdevelopment.gov.yk.ca/cpepb.html

Film & Sound Commission
Closeleigh Manor, 101 Elliott St., PO Box 2703 Whitehorse, YT Y1A 2C6
Tel: 867-667-5400; *Fax:* 867-393-7040
info@reelyukon.com
www.reelyukon.com
Film & Sound Commissioner, Nova Alberts
Tel: 867-667-8302
nova.alberts@gov.yk.ca
Film Officer, Iris Merritt
Tel: 867-667-5678
iris.merritt@gov.yk.ca
Sound Officer, Vacant
Tel: 867-667-5400

Regional Economic Development
308 Wood St., 2nd Fl., Whitehorse, YT
Tel: 867-456-3991
Toll-Free: 800-661-0408
red@gov.yk.ca
www.economicdevelopment.gov.yk.ca/redb.html
Director, Andrew Gaule
Tel: 867-667-8853
andrew.gaule@gov.yk.ca

Yukon Education

PO Box 2703 Whitehorse, YT Y1A 2C6
Tel: 867-667-5141; *Fax:* 867-393-6339
contact.education@gov.yk.ca
www.education.gov.yk.ca
Other Communication: Toll-Free Phone: 1-800-661-0408, ext. 5141

The Yukon has 28 public schools (14 in Whitehorse, 14 in other communities) & two private schools. The public schools are administered directly by the Department of Education, although elected school council officials are gradually assuming more powers under the 1990 Education Act, & may evolve into school boards in the near future. In 1996, the Yukon Francophone School Board was created, becoming Yukon's first school board. Curriculum is largely based on that of British Columbia, with flexibility for locally developed courses, particularly from a First Nations perspective (approximately one-third of the Yukon's students are of First Nations ancestry). Instruction is English-based for the majority of students. French & Aboriginal languages are widely offered as second language instruction. French Immersion & French First Language education is offered in Whitehorse.

Minister, Hon. Doug Graham
Tel: 867-667-8629; *Fax:* 867-393-6252
doug.graham@gov.yk.ca
Deputy Minister, Judy Arnold
Tel: 867-667-5126
Judy.Arnold@gov.yk.ca

Advanced Education
PO Box 2703 Whitehorse, YT Y1A 2C6
Tel: 867-667-5131; *Fax:* 867-667-8555
contact.education@gov.yk.ca
www.education.gov.yk.ca/advanceded
Other Communication: Toll-Free Phone: 1-800-661-0408, ext. 5131
Assistant Deputy Minister, Shawn Kitchen
Tel: 867-667-5129
shawn.kitchen@gov.yk.ca

Director, Labour Market Programs & Services, Anton Solomon
Tel: 867-667-5727
anton.solomon@gov.yk.ca
Director, Training Programs, Judy Thrower
Tel: 867-456-6748
judy.thrower@gov.yk.ca

Education Support Services
1000 Lewes Blvd., Whitehorse, YT Y1A 3H9
Fax: 867-393-6254
www.education.gov.yk.ca/ess

Director, Finance & Administration, Cyndy Dekuysscher
Tel: 867-667-5701
cyndy.dekuysscher@gov.yk.ca
Director, Human Resources, Peggy Dorosz
Tel: 867-667-5808
peggy.dorosz@gov.yk.ca
Director, Policy, Planning & Evaluation, Michael McBride
Tel: 867-332-7065
michael.mcbride@gov.yk.ca

Public Schools Branch
PO Box 2703 Whitehorse, YT Y1A 2C6
Tel: 867-667-5068; *Fax:* 867-393-6339
www.education.gov.yk.ca/psb
Other Communication: Toll-Free Phone: 1-800-661-0408, ext. 5068

Assistant Deputy Minister, Albert Trask
Tel: 867-667-5127
albert.trask@gov.yk.ca
President, Yukon College, Dr. Karen Barnes
Tel: 867-668-8704
kbarnes@yukoncollege.yk.ca
500 College Dr.
PO Box 2799
Whitehorse, YT Y1A 5K4
Superintendent of Schools, Penny Prysnuk
Tel: 867-667-3747
penny.prysnuk@gov.yk.ca
Superintendent of Schools, Greg Storey
Tel: 867-667-3722
greg.storey@gov.yk.ca
Superintendent of Schools, Mike Woods
Tel: 867-667-5180
mike.woods@gov.yk.ca
Director, Student Achievment & Systems Accountability, Judith Arnold
Tel: 867-667-5609
judith.arnold@gov.yk.ca
Director, Programs & Services, Elizabeth Lemay
Tel: 867-667-8238
elizabeth.lemay@gov.yk.ca
Director, First Nations Programs & Partnerships, Janet McDonald
Tel: 867-393-6905
janet.mcdonald@gov.yk.ca
Director, Native Language Centre, John Ritter
Tel: 867-668-8820
Toll-free: 877-414-9652; *Fax:* 867-668-8825
john.ritter@gov.yk.ca
PO Box 2799
Whitehorse, YT Y1A 5K4
Director, Student Support Services, Trish Smillie
Tel: 867-667-5986
trish.smillie@gov.yk.ca
Coordinator, Francophone Partnerships, Yann Herry
Tel: 867-667-8610
yann.henry@gov.yk.ca
Coordinator, Primary Programs, Jeanette McCrie
Tel: 867-667-5186
jeanette.mccrie@gov.yk.ca

Elections Yukon

Yukon Government Bldg., PO Box 2703 Whitehorse, YT Y1A 2C6
Tel: 867-667-8683; *Fax:* 867-393-6977
Toll-Free: 866-668-8683
elections.yukon@gov.yk.ca
www.electionsyukon.gov.yk.ca

Elections Yukon is responsible for the administration of elections of members to the Yukon Legislative Assembly.

Chief Electoral Officer, Lori McKee
Tel: 867-667-8777
lori.mckee@gov.yk.ca

Yukon Energy, Mines & Resources (EMR)

PO Box 2703 Whitehorse, YT Y1A 2C6
Tel: 867-667-3130; *Fax:* 867-456-3965
Toll-Free: 800-661-0408
TTY: 867-393-7460
emr@gov.yk.ca
www.emr.gov.yk.ca
twitter.com/EMRYukon

The territory has extensive mineral deposits, oil & gas potential, with two producing gas wells, which rank among the top producing wells in Canada, forest reserves & local manufacturing of wood products, such as furniture, wood laminate stock & lumber. The territory has abundant & diverse energy resources due to the presence of fossil fuel reserves, numerous lakes & rivers, windy & mountainous terrain, broad forest cover & sunny conditions. The Yukon is one of the few places left in Canada where Crown land can be obtained for agricultural purposes.

Minister, Hon. Scott Kent
Tel: 867-667-8643; *Fax:* 867-393-7400
scott.kent@gov.yk.ca
Deputy Minister, Stephen Mills
Tel: 867-667-5417
Stephen.Mills@gov.yk.ca
Director, Human Resources, Ingrid Fawcus
Tel: 867-667-3549
ingrid.fawcus@gov.yk.ca

Client Services & Inspections Branch
Elijah Smith Bldg., #330, 300 Main St., PO Box 2703 Whitehorse, YT Y1A 2C6
Tel: 867-456-3882; *Fax:* 867-667-3193
www.emr.gov.yk.ca/csi

Director, Robert Thomson
Tel: 867-667-3136
robert.thomson@gov.yk.ca
Chief Mining Inspector, Terry Anderson
Tel: 867-456-6812
terry.anderson@gov.yk.ca
Chief Inspector, Sustainable Resources, Richard Potvin
Tel: 867-667-3160
richard.potvin@gov.yk.ca
Chief, Water Quality Research & Laboratory Services, Mark Nowosad
Tel: 867-667-3211
mark.nowosad@gov.yk.ca

Corporate Services
PO Box 2703 Whitehorse, YT Y1A 2C6
Fax: 867-456-3965

Director, Corporate Services, Ross McLachlan
Tel: 867-456-3960
ross.mclachlan@gov.yk.ca

Library
Elijah Smith Building, #335, 300 Main St., Whitehorse, YT Y1A 2B5
Tel: 867-667-3111; *Fax:* 867-456-3888
emrlibrary@gov.yk.ca
www.emr.gov.yk.ca/library

Manager, Aimee Ellis
Tel: 867-667-3108
aimee.ellis@gov.yk.ca

Energy, Corporate Policy & Communications
PO Box 2703 Whitehorse, YT Y1A 2C6
Tel: 867-667-5015; *Fax:* 867-667-8601
energy@gov.yk.ca
Other Communication: Toll-Free Phone: 1-800-661-0408, ext. 5015

Assistant Deputy Minister, Shirley Abercrombie
Tel: 867-667-3187
shirley.abercrombie@gov.yk.ca
Director, Communications, Michele Royle
Tel: 867-667-5307
michele.royle@gov.yk.ca

Human Resources
PO Box 2703 Whitehorse, YT Y1A 2C6
Tel: 867-667-3007; *Fax:* 867-393-7422
www.emr.gov.yk.ca/hr
Other Communication: Toll-Free Phone: 1-800-661-0408, ext. 3007

Director, Ingrid Fawcus
Tel: 867-667-3549
ingrid.fawcus@gov.yk.ca

Sustainable Resources
PO Box 2703 Whitehorse, YT Y1A 2C6
Fax: 867-393-6340

Assistant Deputy Minister, Lyle Henderson
Tel: 867-456-3827
lyle.henderson@gov.yk.ca

Agriculture
Tel: 867-667-5838; *Fax:* 867-393-6222
agriculture@gov.yk.ca
www.emr.gov.yk.ca/agriculture
Other Communication: Toll-Free Phone: 1-800-661-0408, ext. 5838

Director, Tony Hill
tony.hill@gov.yk.ca

Forest Management Branch
Mile 918 Alaska Hwy., PO Box 2703 Whitehorse, YT Y1A 2C6
Tel: 867-456-3999; *Fax:* 867-667-3138
forestry@gov.yk.ca
www.emr.gov.yk.ca/forestry
Other Communication: Toll-Free Phone: 1-800-661-0408, ext. 3999

Oversees the development & management of Yukon's forest resources. The services & responsibilities include: taking inventory of & managing Yukon forests, conduct environmental assessments of proposed timber harvesting projects, forest renewal, forest management planning, identifying & allocating timber harvesting areas, issuing permits to harvest timber, conducting environmental assessments of proposed forest activities, collecting stumpage revenues; auditing activities, consultation, forestry legislations, forest practices planning & liaison, & maintaining & improving forestry GIS & mapping capabilities.

Director, Lyle Dinn
Tel: 867-456-3813
lyle.dinn@gov.yk.ca

Land Management Branch
#320, 300 Main St., PO Box 2703 Whitehorse, YT Y1A 2C6
Tel: 867-667-5215; *Fax:* 867-667-3214
land.disposition@gov.yk.ca
www.emr.gov.yk.ca/lands
Other Communication: Toll-Free Phone: 1-800-661-0408, ext. 5215; Alt. E-mail: land.use@gov.yk.ca

Director, Colin McDowell
Tel: 867-667-3150
colin.mcdowell@gov.yk.ca
Director, Land Planning Branch, Jerome McIntyre
Tel: 867-667-3530
jerome.mcintyre@gov.yk.ca

Oil & Gas Mineral Resources Division
PO Box 2703 Whitehorse, YT Y1A 2C6
Tel: 867-667-5087; *Fax:* 867-393-6262
oilandgas@gov.yk.ca
www.emr.gov.yk.ca/oilandgas
Other Communication: Toll-Free Phone: 1-800-661-0408, ext. 5087

Assistant Deputy Minister, Brian Love
Tel: 867-667-3011
brian.love@gov.yk.ca
Director, Oil & Gas Resources, Ron Sumanik
Tel: 867-667-5026
ron.sumanik@gov.yk.ca

Assessment & Abandoned Mines Branch
PO Box 2703 Stn. K-419, Whitehorse, YT Y1A 2C6
Tel: 867-393-7098; *Fax:* 867-456-6780
yukonabandonedmines@gov.yk.ca
www.emr.gov.yk.ca/aam
Other Communication: Toll-Free Phone: 1-800-661-0408, ext. 7098

Director, Stephen Mead
Tel: 867-393-6904
stephen.mead@gov.yk.ca

Mineral Resources Branch
Shoppers Plaza, #400, 211 Main St., Whitehorse, YT Y1A 2B2
Tel: 867-633-7952; *Fax:* 867-456-3899
mining@gov.yk.ca
www.emr.gov.yk.ca/mining
Other Communication: 1-800-661-0408

Director, Mineral Resources, Bob Holmes
Tel: 867-667-3126
robert.holmes@gov.yk.ca

Yukon Geological Survey
Elijah Smith Building, #102 & 230, 300 Main St., Whitehorse, YT Y1A 2B5
Tel: 867-455-2800
geology@gov.yk.ca
www.geology.gov.yk.ca
Other Communication: Toll-Free Phone: 1-800-661-0408, ext. 5087

Also located at the H.S. Bostock Core Library, 91807 Alaska Hwy., Whitehorse, YT.

Director, Carolyn Relf
Tel: 867-667-8892
carolyn.relf@gov.yk.ca

Yukon Environment

10 Burns Rd., PO Box 2703 V-3A Whitehorse, YT Y1A 2C6
Tel: 867-667-5652; *Fax:* 867-393-7197
environment.yukon@gov.yk.ca
www.env.gov.yk.ca
Other Communication: Toll-Free Phone: 1-800-661-0408, ext. 5652
twitter.com/ENV_Yukon
www.facebook.com/getoutyukon
www.youtube.com/user/environmentyukon

The department is responsible for legislation, regulations licensing, management, policies, programs, services, education & information regarding the natural environment in three program areas: fish & wildlife, environmental protection & assessment & parks & protection areas. The department's branches educate resource users & the general public, develop & enforce policies, regulations, & legislation & assist other departments in the sustainable use & management of the territory's natural resources. The department supports land claims negotiations & assists in implementing land claims agreements. The department represents the Yukon government at national & global environmental forums on issues such as climate change & biodiversity conservation.Through the Environmental Awareness Fund the government provides funding to assist registered non-government organizations to promote environmental education or awareness, resource planning & sustainable development in the Yukon.

Minister, Hon. Wade Istchenko
Tel: 867-667-8644; *Fax:* 867-393-7400
wade.istchenko@gov.yk.ca

Deputy Minister, Joe MacGillivray
joe.macgillivray@gov.yk.ca

Director, Finance & Administration, Bonnie Love
Tel: 867-667-5160; *Fax:* 867-393-6219
bonnie.love@gov.yk.ca

Associated Agencies, Boards & Commissions:

•Alsek Renewable Resource Council (ARRC)
180 Alaska Hwy.
PO Box 2077
Haines Junction, YT Y0B 1L0
Tel: 867-634-2524; *Fax:* 867-634-2527
admin@alsekrrc.ca
www.alsekrrc.ca
Renewable Resource Councils provide a voice for local community members in managing renewable resources, such as fish, wildlife & forests. The ARRC was formed in 1995 with the signing of the Champagne & Aishihik First Nations (CAFN) Final Agreement.

•Carcross / Tagish Renewable Resource Council (CTRRC)
PO Box 70
Tagish, YT Y0B 1T0
Tel: 867-399-4923; *Fax:* 867-399-4978
carcrosstagishrrc@gmail.com
www.yfwmb.ca/rrc/carcrosstagish

•Carmacks Renewable Resource Council (CRRC)
PO Box 122
Carmacks, YT Y0B 1C0
Tel: 867-863-6838; *Fax:* 867-863-6429
carmacksrrc@northwestel.net
www.yfwmb.ca/rrc/carmacks

•Dan Keyi Renewable Resource Council (DKRRC)
PO Box 50
Burwash Landing, YT Y0B 1V0
Tel: 867-841-5820; *Fax:* 867-841-5821
dankeyirrc@northwestel.net
www.yfwmb.ca/rrc/dankeyi

•Dawson District Renewable Resource Council (DDRRC)
PO Box 1380
Dawson City, YT Y0B 1G0
Tel: 867-993-6976; *Fax:* 867-993-6093
dawsonrrc@northwestel.net
www.yfwmb.ca/rrc/dawson

•Laberge Renewable Resource Council (LRRC)
102 Copper Rd.
Whitehorse, YT Y1A 2Z7
Tel: 867-393-3940; *Fax:* 867-393-3940
labergerrc@northwestel.net
www.yfwmb.ca/rrc/laberge

•Mayo District Renewable Resources Council (MDRRC)
PO Box 249
Mayo, YT Y0B 1M0
Tel: 867-996-2942; *Fax:* 867-996-2948
mayorrc@northwestel.net
www.yfwmb.ca/rrc/mayo

•North Yukon Renewable Resources Council (NYRRC)
PO Box 80
Old Crow, YT Y0B 1N0
Tel: 867-966-3034; *Fax:* 867-966-3036
nyrrc@northwestel.net
www.yfwmb.ca/rrc/northyukon

•Selkirk Renewable Resources Council (SRRC)
PO Box 32
Pelly Crossing, YT Y0B 1P0
Tel: 867-537-3937; *Fax:* 867-537-3939
selkirkrrc@northwestel.net
www.yfwmb.ca/rrc/selkirk

•Teslin Renewable Resource Council (TRRC)
PO Box 186
Teslin, YT Y0A 1B0
Tel: 867-390-2323; *Fax:* 867-390-2919
teslinrrc@northwestel.net
www.yfwmb.ca/rrc/teslin

•Yukon Fish & Wildlife Management Board (YFWMB)
106 Main St., 2nd Fl.
PO Box 31104
Whitehorse, YT Y1A 5P7
Tel: 867-667-3754; *Fax:* 867-393-6947
officemanager@yfwmb.ca
www.yfwmb.ca
The Board focuses its efforts on territorial policies, legislation & other measures to help guide management of fish & wildlife, conserve habitat & enhance the renewable resources economy. The Board influences management decisions through public education & by making recommendations to Yukon, Federal and First Nations governments. Recommendations & positions are based on the best technical, traditional & local information available.

•Yukon Land Use Planning Council
#201, 307 Jarvis St.
Whitehorse, YT Y1A 2H3
Tel: 867-667-7397; *Fax:* 867-667-4624
ylupc@planyukon.ca
www.planyukon.ca
The Yukon Land Use Planning Council assists government & Yukon First Nationsto co-ordinate efforts to conduct community based regional land use planning. This planning is necessary to resolve land use & resource conflicts. The plans ensure that use of lands & resources is consistent with social, cultural, economic & environmental values. These plans build upon traditional knowledge & experience of the residents of each region.

Animal Health Branch

Fax: 867-667-7197

Chief Veterinary Officer, Mary Vanderkop
Tel: 867-456-5582
mary.vanderkop@gov.yk.ca

Climate Change Secretariat

Tel: 867-456-5544; *Fax:* 867-456-5543
climatechange@gov.yk.ca
Other Communication: Toll-Free Phone: 1-800-661-0408, ext. 5544

The Secretariat has the lead role in ensuring Yukon government actions support a healthy & resilient Yukon in a changing climate. It strives to identify needs, opportunities & priorities; promote & support action; & monitor & report on progress.

Director, Rebecca World
Tel: 867-456-5522
rebecca.world@gov.yk.ca

Conservation Officer Services

Tel: 867-667-8005; *Fax:* 867-393-6206
coservicesgov.yk.ca
Other Communication: Toll-Free Phone: 1-800-661-0408, ext. 8005; T.I.P.P. Line: 1-800-661-0525

The Branch provides environmental education, environmental youth camps & projects, provides hunting, fishing & trapping licences, provides hunter & trapper education, resource management support, wildlife safety for the public & provides enforcement & compliance.

Director, John Russell
Tel: 867-667-5786
john.russell@gov.yk.ca

Environmental Programs Branch

Tel: 867-667-5683; *Fax:* 867-393-6213
envprot@gov.yk.ca
Other Communication: Toll-Free Phone: 1-800-661-0408, ext. 5683

Formed in 1994, the Branch is responsible for development of regulations & standards under the Environment Act & programs associated with everyday waste management, contaminated sites, air quality & pesticides. The Branch is also responsible for monitoring & inspection of permits, spill cleanup & environmental assessments of development projects, recycling education & promotion, public education & awareness.

Director, Kevin McDonnell
Tel: 867-667-8177
kevin.mcdonnell@gov.yk.ca

Fish & Wildlife Branch

Tel: 867-667-5715; *Fax:* 867-393-6263
fish.wildlife@gov.yk.ca
Other Communication: Toll-Free Phone: 1-800-661-0408, ext. 5715

The Branch maintains the ecosystem based on sound management of fish, wildlife & their habitats, preserves the sustainability of fish & wildlife populations, works with First Nations & community relations to preserve & enhance the ecosystem, develops management plans, provides policy & planning, collects, assesses & disseminates natural resource data & provides public education for resource users.

Director, Dan Lindsey
Tel: 867-667-5715
dan.lindsey@gov.yk.ca

Human Resources Branch

Fax: 867-393-7012

Director, Mindy Crayford
Tel: 867-667-8486

Policy, Planning & Aboriginal Affairs

Fax: 867-393-6213

Director, Policy & Planning, Dan Paleczny
Tel: 867-667-3028
dan.paleczny@gov.yk.ca

Water Resources Branch

Tel: 867-667-3171; *Fax:* 867-667-3195
water.resources@gov.yk.ca
Other Communication: Toll-Free Phone: 1-800-661-0408, ext. 3171

Director, Jon Bowen
Tel: 867-667-3145
kevin.mcdonnell@gov.yk.ca

Yukon Parks Branch

Tel: 867-667-5648; *Fax:* 867-393-6223
Toll-Free: 800-661-0408
yukon.parks@gov.yk.ca
Other Communication: Toll-Free Phone: 1-800-661-0408, ext. 5648

Director, Eric Schroff
Tel: 867-667-5639
eric.schroff@gov.yk.ca

Yukon Finance

PO Box 2703 Whitehorse, YT Y1A 2C6
Tel: 867-667-5343; *Fax:* 867-393-6217
fininfo@gov.yk.ca
www.finance.gov.yk.ca

Premier; Minister, Hon. Darrell Pasloski
Tel: 867-393-7053; *Fax:* 867-393-6252
darrell.pasloski@gov.yk.ca

Deputy Minister, Katherine White
Tel: 867-667-3571
Katherine.White@gov.yk.ca

Director, Finance & Administration, Bill Curtis
Tel: 867-667-5276; *Fax:* 867-393-6217
bill.curtis@gov.yk.ca

Financial Operations & Revenue Services

Fax: 867-393-6217

Assistant Deputy Minister, Clarke Laprarie
Tel: 867-667-5355
clarke.laprarie@gov.yk.ca

Comptroller, Accounting & Policy, Christina Frisch
Tel: 867-667-5996
tina.frisch@gov.yk.ca

Director, Investments & Debt Services, Elaine Carlyle
Tel: 867-667-5346
elaine.carlyle@gov.yk.ca

Director, Taxation, Gerald Gagnon
Tel: 867-667-3074; *Fax:* 867-456-6709
gerald.gagnon@gov.yk.ca

Director, Financial Systems, Alan Houston
Tel: 867-667-5278
alan.houston@gov.yk.ca

Fiscal Relations & Management Board Secretariat

Fax: 867-393-6355

Director, Management Board Secretariat, Kimberly Brant
Tel: 867-667-3542
kimberly.brant@gov.yk.ca

Director, Budgets, Eugene Ritz
Tel: 867-667-5277; *Fax:* 867-393-6217
eugene.ritz@gov.yk.ca

Director, Fiscal Relations, Tim Shoniker
Tel: 867-667-5303
tim.shoniker@gov.yk.ca

Deputy Secretary to Management Board, Mark Tubman
Tel: 867-667-5821; *Fax:* 867-393-6217
mark.tubman@gov.yk.ca

Yukon French Language Services Directorate

305 Jarvis St., 3rd Fl., PO Box 2703 Whitehorse, YT Y1A 2C6
Tel: 867-667-8260; *Fax:* 867-393-6226
www.flsd.gov.yk.ca
Other Communication: Toll-Free Phone: 1-800-661-0408, ext. 8260

The French Language Services Directorate does not provide services directly to the public; rather, it supports the Yukon's government departments & corporations in meeting the Languages Act requirements.

Minister responsible, Hon. Elaine Taylor
Tel: 867-667-8641; *Fax:* 867-393-6252
elaine.taylor@gov.yk.ca
Director, Patrice Tremblay
Tel: 867-667-3735

Yukon Health & Social Services

PO Box 2703 Whitehorse, YT Y1A 2C6
Tel: 867-667-3673; *Fax:* 867-667-3096
Toll-Free: 800-661-0408
hss@gov.yk.ca
www.hss.gov.yk.ca
twitter.com/HSSYukon
www.facebook.com/yukonhss
www.youtube.com/user/hssyukongovernment

Committed to quality health & social services for Yukoners by helping individuals acquire the skills to live responsible, healthy & independent lives; & providing a range of accessible, affordable services that assist individuals, families & communities to reach their full potential.

Minister, Hon. Mike Nixon
Tel: 867-633-7973; *Fax:* 867-393-6252
mike.nixon@gov.yk.ca
Deputy Minister, Bruce McLennan
Tel: 867-667-5770
Bruce.McLennan@gov.yk.ca
Medical Officer of Health, Brendan Hanley
Tel: 867-456-6136
brendan.hanley@gov.yk.ca
Director, Human Resources, Brian Farrell
Tel: 867-667-3031
brian.farrell@gov.yk.ca
Director, Communications & Social Marketing, Pat Living
Tel: 867-667-3673
patricia.living@gov.yk.ca

Associated Agencies, Boards & Commissions:

•Health & Social Service Council
c/o Yukon Health & Social Services Council Secretariat
PO Box 2703 H-1
Whitehorse, YT Y1A 2C6
Tel: 867-667-5770; *Fax:* 867-667-3096
www.hss.gov.yk.ca/hssc.php
Other Communication: Toll-Free Phone: 1-800-661-0408, ext. 5770

This advisory body makes recommendations to the government relating to issues of health, social services, education & justice.

•Yukon Child Care Board
PO Box 31117
Whitehorse, YT Y1A 5P7

This advisory body makes recommendations to the Minister of Health & Social Services, on any issues that pertain to child care.

Continuing Care

#201, 1 Hospital Rd., Whitehorse, YT Y1A 3H7
Tel: 867-667-5945
www.hss.gov.yk.ca/continuing.php
Other Communication: Toll-Free Phone: 800-661-0408, ext. 5945 (toll-free)

Provides residential, home care & regional therapy services for the citizens of the Yukon Territory.

Assistant Deputy Minister, Cathy Morton-Bielz
Tel: 867-667-8922; *Fax:* 867-456-6545
cathy.morton-bielz@gov.yk.ca
Director, Safety & Clinical Excellence, Nancy Kidd
Tel: 867-667-8750; *Fax:* 867-393-6953
nancy.kidd@gov.yk.ca
Director, Extended Care, Willy Shippey
Tel: 867-393-7574
willy.shippey@gov.yk.ca
Director, Care & Community, Liris Smith
Tel: 867-456-6839
liris.smith@gov.yk.ca
Director, Clinical Psychology, Reagan Gale
Tel: 867-667-5968

Corporate Services

Fax: 867-393-6457
www.hss.gov.yk.ca/corporate.php

Plays a key role in ensuring that Yukon residents have accurate, up-to-date information about the territory's health & social programs, services & systems.

Assistant Deputy Minister, Birgitte Hunter
Tel: 867-667-8309
birgitte.hunter@gov.yk.ca
Director, Corporate Planning & Risk Management, Kathy Fredrickson
Tel: 867-667-5943
kathy.fredrickson@gov.yk.ca
Director, Policy & Program Development, Brian Kitchen
Tel: 867-667-5688; *Fax:* 867-667-3096
brian.kitchen@gov.yk.ca

Health Services

Financial Plaza, 204 Lambert St., 4th Fl., Whitehorse, YT Y1A 3T2
Fax: 867-393-6486
www.hss.gov.yk.ca/healthservices.php

Responsible for a variety of health care, disease prevention & treatment services which assist eligible Yukon residents in attaining maximum individual independence within their community.

Assistant Deputy Minister, Health Services, Sherri Wright
Tel: 867-667-5689; *Fax:* 867-667-3096
sherri.wright@gov.yk.ca
Deputy Registrar, Vital Statistics, Sylvia Kitching
Tel: 867-667-5207; *Fax:* 867-393-6486
sylvia.kitching@gov.yk.ca
Director, Insured Health & Hearing Services, Shauna Demers
Tel: 867-667-5202
shauna.demers@gov.yk.ca
Director, Community Nursing, Karen Archbell
Tel: 867-667-8325; *Fax:* 867-667-8338
karen.archbell@gov.yk.ca
Director, Community Health Programs, Cathy Stannard
Tel: 867-667-8340; *Fax:* 867-456-6502
cathy.stannard@gov.yk.ca

Social Services

www.hss.gov.yk.ca/socialservices.php

Consists of Adult Community Services, Alcohol & Drug Services, Family & Children's Services, Regional Services, Senior Services, Seniors & Elder Abuse, Services for People With Disabilities, & Social Assistance.

Assistant Deputy Minister, Dorothea Warren
Tel: 867-667-3702
dorothea.warren@gov.yk.ca
Director, Family & Children's Services Branch, Elaine Schroeder
Tel: 867-667-3471; *Fax:* 867-393-6239
elaine.schroeder@gov.yk.ca
Director, Adult Services Branch, Michele McDonnell
Tel: 867-667-3705; *Fax:* 867-667-5815
michele.mcdonnell@gov.yk.ca
Manager, Seniors' Services / Adult Protection Unit, Kelly Cooper
Tel: 867-456-3948; *Fax:* 867-393-6926
kelly.cooper@gov.yk.ca
Manager, Program Management, Michael Hanson
Tel: 867-667-5056; *Fax:* 867-667-8471
michael.hanson@gov.yk.ca
Supervisor, Services to Persons with Disabilities, Marg Render
Tel: 867-667-5669; *Fax:* 867-667-5819
marg.render@gov.yk.ca

Yukon Highways & Public Works

PO Box 2703 Whitehorse, YT Y1A 2C6
Tel: 867-393-7193; *Fax:* 867-393-6218
Toll-Free: 800-661-0408
TTY: 867-393-7460
hpw-info@gov.yk.ca
www.hpw.gov.yk.ca

The Department of Highways & Public Works is responsible for ensuring safe & efficient public highways, airstrips, buildings & information systems.

Minister, Hon. Scott Kent
Tel: 867-667-8643; *Fax:* 867-393-7400
scott.kent@gov.yk.ca
Deputy Minister, Angus Robertson
Tel: 867-667-3732
Angus.Robertson@gov.yk.ca
Director, Policy & Communications, Kendra Black
Tel: 867-667-5436; *Fax:* 867-393-6218
kendra.black@gov.yk.ca
Director, Finance, Jacqueline McBride-Dickson
Tel: 867-667-5410; *Fax:* 867-667-8231
jackie.mcbride-dickson@gov.yk.ca
Director, Human Resources, Jeananne Lindstrom
Tel: 867-667-5156; *Fax:* 867-667-3685
jeananne.lindstrom@gov.yk.ca

Associated Agencies, Boards & Commissions:

•Driver Control Board
#102, 211 Hawkins St.
PO Box 2703
Whitehorse, YT Y1A 2C6
Tel: 867-667-5623; *Fax:* 867-667-5799
dcb@gov.yk.ca
www.hpw.gov.yk.ca/dcb
Other Communication: Toll-Free Phone: 1-800-661-0408, ext. 5623

Corporate Services

Tel: 867-667-3732; *Fax:* 867-393-6218
hpw-info@gov.yk.ca
www.hpw.gov.yk.ca/csb/corporateservices.html
Other Communication: Toll-Free Phone: 1-800-661-0408, ext. 5128

Assistant Deputy Minister, Martha Kenney
Tel: 867-667-5128
martha.kenney@gov.yk.ca
Director, Catherine Harwood
Tel: 867-456-6574
catherine.harwood@gov.yk.ca

Information & Communications Technology

Tel: 867-667-5397; *Fax:* 867-667-5304
Other Communication: Toll-Free 1-800-661-0408, ext. 5397

Assistant Deputy Minister & Chief Information Officer, Sean McLeish
Tel: 867-667-3712
sean.mcleish@gov.yk.ca
Deputy Chief Information Officer, Chris Bookless
Tel: 867-456-6781; *Fax:* 867-667-5304
chris.bookless@gov.yk.ca
Project Director, Records Program Improvement Initiative, David Downing
Tel: 867-667-8329; *Fax:* 867-633-5188
david.downing@gov.yk.ca
Director, Technology Infrastructure & Operations, Shane Horsnell
Tel: 867-667-5396; *Fax:* 867-393-6200
shane.horsnell@gov.yk.ca
Director, Information Management, George Harvey
Tel: 867-332-1756; *Fax:* 867-393-6490

Property Management Division (PMD)

9010 Quartz Rd., Whitehorse, YT Y1A 2Z5
Tel: 867-667-5879; *Fax:* 867-667-5349
www.hpw.gov.yk.ca/pm
Other Communication: Toll-Free Phone: 1-800-661-0408, ext. 5879

Assistant Deputy Minister, Cynthia Tucker
Tel: 867-667-8191
cynthia.tucker@gov.yk.ca
Superintendent of Operations, Facilities Management, Jody Fobe
Tel: 867-667-8882; *Fax:* 867-393-7039
jody.fobe@gov.yk.ca
Acting Chief Security Guard, Facilities Management, Chris Schneider
Tel: 867-334-5898; *Fax:* 867-393-7039
chris.schneider@gov.yk.ca
Director, Realty Capital Asset Planning, Scott Milton
Tel: 867-456-3820; *Fax:* 867-667-5349
Director, Capital Development, Haider Rajab
Tel: 867-456-6153; *Fax:* 867-393-6319
Director, Facilities Management & Regional Services, Ryan Parry
Tel: 867-667-3589; *Fax:* 867-393-7039
Manager, Finance & Administration, Faye Doiron
Tel: 867-667-3706
faye.doiron@gov.yk.ca

Supply Services

Tel: 867-667-5385; *Fax:* 867-393-6245
contracts@gov.yk.ca
www.hpw.gov.yk.ca/ssb
Other Communication: Toll-Free Phone: 1-800-661-0408, ext. 5385

Director, Debra Thibodeau
Tel: 867-667-5289; *Fax:* 867-393-6463
debra.thibodeau@gov.yk.ca

Transportation

Tel: 867-667-5196; *Fax:* 867-393-6218
hpw-info@gov.yk.ca
www.hpw.gov.yk.ca/trans
Other Communication: Toll-Free Phone: 1-800-661-0408, ext. 5196

Assistant Deputy Minister, Allan Nixon
Tel: 867-667-5196
allan.nixon@gov.yk.ca
Director, Transportation Maintenance, Clint Ireland
Tel: 867-667-5644; *Fax:* 867-393-7002
clint.ireland@gov.yk.ca
Director, Transport Services Branch, Vern Janz
Tel: 867-667-5833; *Fax:* 867-667-5799
vern.janz@gov.yk.ca
Director, Transportation Engineering, Paul Murchison
Tel: 867-633-7930; *Fax:* 867-393-6447
paul.murchison@gov.yk.ca

Aviation
PO Box 2129 Haines Junction, YT Y0B 1L0
Tel: 867-634-2450; *Fax:* 867-634-2131
aviation@gov.yk.ca
www.hpw.gov.yk.ca/airports
Other Communication: Toll-Free Phone: 1-800-661-0408, ext. 2450

The Aviation branch operates 4 airports & 25 aerodromes, & manages the NAV CANADA's Yukon Community Aerodrome Radio Station (CARS) program.
Director, Branch Management, Bill Blahitka
Tel: 867-634-2440
bill.blahitka@gov.yk.ca
Superintendent of Airports, Mark Ritchie
Tel: 867-634-2948; *Fax:* 867-634-2131
mark.ritchie@gov.yk.ca

Yukon Housing Corporation

410G Jarvis St., PO Box 2703 Whitehorse, YT Y1A 2H5
Tel: 867-667-5759; *Fax:* 867-667-3664
Toll-Free: 800-661-0408
ykhouse@housing.yk.ca
www.housing.yk.ca

Links families, communities & the housing industry with programs & services that work to support the housing needs of Yukoners.
Minister responsible, Hon. Stacey Hassard
Tel: 867-456-6509; *Fax:* 867-393-7400
stacey.hassard@gov.yk.ca
President, Pamela Hine
Tel: 867-667-5155; *Fax:* 867-393-6274
pamela.hine@gov.yk.ca
Vice-President, Operations, Matt King
Tel: 867-667-5155; *Fax:* 867-393-6274
matt.king@gov.yk.ca
Director, Community & Industry Partnering, Mary Cameron
Tel: 867-667-3773; *Fax:* 867-393-6441
mary.cameron@gov.yk.ca
Director, Systems & Administration, Mark Davey
Tel: 867-667-8773; *Fax:* 867-393-6399
mark.davey@gov.yk.ca
Acting Director, Capital Development, Bill Greer
Tel: 867-456-6190; *Fax:* 867-393-6441
bill.greer@gov.yk.ca
Director, Policy & Communications, JoAnne Harach
Tel: 867-456-6802; *Fax:* 867-393-6274
joanne.harach@gov.yk.ca
Director, Program Delivery, Marc Perreault
Tel: 867-393-7154; *Fax:* 867-667-3664
marc.perreault@gov.yk.ca
Director, Human Resources, Sue Richards
Tel: 867-667-8272; *Fax:* 867-393-6274
sue.richards@gov.yk.ca

Yukon Justice

Andrew Philipsen Law Centre, 2134 Second Ave., PO Box 2703 Whitehorse, YT Y1A 2C6
Tel: 867-667-3033; *Fax:* 867-393-5790
justice@gov.yk.ca
www.justice.gov.yk.ca
Other Communication: Toll-Free Phone: 1-800-661-0408, ext. 3033

Minister, Hon. Brad Cathers
Tel: 867-667-5806; *Fax:* 867-393-6252
brad.cathers@gov.yk.ca
Deputy Minister, Thomas Ullyett
Tel: 867-667-5959; *Fax:* 867-667-5200
thomas.ullyett@gov.yk.ca
Director, Finance, Systems & Administration, Luda Ayzenberg
Tel: 867-667-5615; *Fax:* 867-393-6301
luda.ayzenberg@gov.yk.ca
Director, Policy & Communications, Dan Cable
Tel: 867-667-3508; *Fax:* 867-677-5790
dan.cable@gov.yk.ca
Director, Human Resources, Tracey Maher
Tel: 867-667-3414
tracey.maher@gov.yk.ca

Associated Agencies, Boards & Commissions:

•Law Society of Yukon - Executive
#202, 302 Steele St.
Whitehorse, YT Y1A 2C5
Tel: 867-668-4231; *Fax:* 867-667-7556
www.lawsocietyyukon.com
This regulatory society serves & protects the public interest in the administration of justice.

•Law Society of Yukon - Discipline Committee
#202, 302 Steele St.
Whitehorse, YT Y1A 3W8
Tel: 867-668-4231; *Fax:* 867-667-7556
www.lawsocietyyukon.com/discipline.php
This adjudicative committee conducts inquiries/investigations into matters regarding the conduct of a member or a student-at-law.

•Yukon Human Rights Commission
#101, 9010 Quartz St.
Whitehorse, YT Y1A 2Z5
Tel: 867-667-6226; *Fax:* 867-667-2662
Toll-free: 800-661-0535
humanrights@yhrc.yk.ca
www.yhrc.yk.ca
The Commission administers the Human Rights Act, hears complaints & arranges for adjudication if required. Promotes & coordinates public education & research programs in the area of human rights.

•Yukon Judicial Council
PO Box 31222
Whitehorse, YT Y1A 5P7
Tel: 867-667-5438; *Fax:* 867-393-6400
courtservices@gov.yk.ca
www.yukoncourts.ca/courts/territorial/judicialcouncil.html
Other Communication: Toll-Free Phone: 1-800-661-0408, ext. 5438
The Council makes recommendations respecting appointments of judges& justices, & deals with formal complaints respecting judges & justices. It makes recommendations respecting the efficiency, uniformity & quality of judicial services provided by the Territorial Court or the Justice of the Peace Court. It also performs other duties requested by the Minister.

•Yukon Law Foundation
PO Box 31789
Whitehorse, YT Y1A 6L3
Tel: 867-667-7500; *Fax:* 867-393-3904
www.yukonlawfoundation.com

•Yukon Legal Services Society/Legal Aid
#203, 2131 - 2nd Ave.
Whitehorse, YT Y1A 1C3
Tel: 867-667-5210; *Fax:* 867-667-8649
administration@legalaid.yk.ca
www.legalaid.yk.ca
Other Communication: Toll-Free Phone: 1-800-661-0408, ext. 5210

•Yukon Utilities Board
#19, 1114 - 1st Ave.
PO Box 31728
Whitehorse, YT Y1A 6L3
Tel: 867-667-5058; *Fax:* 867-667-5059
yub@utilitiesboard.yk.ca
www.yukonutilitiesboard.yk.ca
This regulatory board consists of three to five members appointed by the Government of Yukon. It receives its mandate from the Public Utilities Act & Regulations.

Community Justice & Public Safety Branch
Prospector Building, 301 Jarvis St., 2nd Fl., PO Box 2703 Whitehorse, YT Y1A 2C6
Tel: 867-393-7077; *Fax:* 867-393-6326
justice@gov.yk.ca
www.justice.gov.yk.ca/prog/cjps
Other Communication: Toll-Free Phone: 1-800-661-0408, ext. 7077

Assistant Deputy Minister, Robert Riches
Tel: 867-393-7077
robert.riches@gov.yk.ca
Chief Coroner, Coroner's Service, Kirsten MacDonald
Tel: 867-667-5317; *Fax:* 867-456-6826
kirsten.macdonald@gov.yk.ca
Director, Public Safety & Investigations Services, Jeff Ford
Tel: 867-667-5868
jeff.ford@gov.yk.ca
Director, Victim Services & Community Justice, Annette King
Tel: 867-667-5962
annette.king@gov.yk.ca
Director, Community & Correctional Services, Tricia Ratel
Tel: 867-667-8294
tricia.ratel@gov.yk.ca

Court Services
Andrew A. Philipsen Law Centre, 2134 Second Ave., 1st Fl., PO Box 2703 J-3 Whitehorse, YT Y1A 2C6
Tel: 867-667-5441; *Fax:* 867-393-6212
courtservices@gov.yk.ca
www.justice.gov.yk.ca/csindex.html
Other Communication: Toll-Free Phone: 1-800-661-0408, ext. 5441
Assistant Deputy Minister, Courts & Regulatory Services, Lesley McCullough
Tel: 867-667-5942
lesley.mccullough@gov.yk.ca
Clerk of the Supreme Court & Registry Officer, Federal Court, Edwige Graham
Tel: 867-667-5938
edwige.graham@gov.yk.ca
Clerk, Small Claims Court, Jackie Davis
Tel: 867-667-5619
jackie.davis@gov.yk.ca
Registrar, Court of Appeal, Sharon Kerr
Tel: 867-667-3429
sharon.kerr@gov.yk.ca
Sheriff, Navhreet Nijhar
Tel: 867-667-5365
navhreet.nijhar@gov.yk.ca
Director, Court Services, Sheri Blaker
Tel: 867-667-3440
sheri.blaker@gov.yk.ca

Family & Regulatory Services
PO Box 2703 Whitehorse, YT Y1A 2C6
Fax: 867-393-6212
www.justice.gov.yk.ca/1215.html
Public Guardian & Trustee, Lori Whitson
Tel: 867-667-5807; *Fax:* 867-393-6246
Manager & Registrar of Land Titles, Denise Dollin
Tel: 867-667-5611; *Fax:* 867-393-6358
denise.dollin@gov.yk.ca
Manager, Maintenance Enforcement & Family Law Information Centre, Lori Zazulak
Tel: 867-667-3038
Toll-free: 877-617-5347; *Fax:* 867-393-6989
lori.zazulak@gov.yk.ca

Legal Services
PO Box 2703 Whitehorse, YT Y1A 2C6
Tel: 867-667-5764; *Fax:* 867-393-6379
legalservices@gov.yk.ca
www.justice.gov.yk.ca/prog/ls
Other Communication: Toll-Free Phone: 1-800-661-0408, ext. 5764
Assistant Deputy Minister, Thomas Ullyett
Tel: 867-667-3469
thomas.ullyett@gov.yk.ca
Chief Legislative Counsel, Pamela Muir
Tel: 867-667-8254
pamela.muir@gov.yk.ca

Yukon Liquor Corporation

9031 Quartz Rd., Whitehorse, YT Y1A 4P9
Tel: 867-667-5245; *Fax:* 867-393-6306
yukon.liquor@gov.yk.ca
www.ylc.yk.ca
Other Communication: Toll-Free Phone: 1-800-661-0408, ext. 5245

Minister responsible, Hon. Stacey Hassard
Tel: 867-456-6509; *Fax:* 867-393-7400
stacey.hassard@gov.yk.ca
President, Pamela Hine
Tel: 867-667-5155; *Fax:* 867-393-6274
pamela.hine@gov.yk.ca
Vice-President, Operations, Mark Hill
Tel: 867-667-5708; *Fax:* 867-393-6306
mark.hill@gov.yk.ca
Director, Finance, Systems & Administration, Mark Davey
Tel: 867-667-8773; *Fax:* 867-393-6399
mark.davey@gov.yk.ca
Director, Purchasing & Distribution, Geoff Dixon
Tel: 867-667-5244
geoff.dixon@gov.yk.ca
Director, Policy & Communications, JoAnne Harach
Tel: 867-456-6802
joanne.harach@gov.yk.ca
Director, Licensing & Social Responsibility, Ken Howard
Tel: 867-667-8926
ken.howard@gov.yk.ca
Director, Retail Sales & Territorial Agent Services, Bonnie Palamar
Tel: 867-667-8924
bonnie.palamar@gov.yk.ca

Director, Human Resources, Sue Richards
Tel: 867-667-8272
sue.richards@gov.yk.ca

Yukon Ombudsman & Privacy Commissioner

#201, 211 Hawkins St., Whitehorse, YT Y1A 2C6
Tel: 867-667-8468; *Fax:* 867-667-8469
info@ombudsman.yk.ca
www.ombudsman.yk.ca/ombudsman
Other Communication: Toll-Free Phone: 1-800-661-0408, ext. 8468

Ombudsman/Information & Privacy Commissioner, Diane McLeod-McKay
diane.mcleod-mckay@ombudsman.yk.ca

Yukon Public Service Commission

Yukon Government Administration Bldg., 2071 Second Ave., PO Box 2703 Whitehorse, YT Y1A 2C6
Tel: 867-667-5653; *Fax:* 867-667-5755
TTY: 867-667-5864
PSCWebsite@gov.yk.ca
www.psc.gov.yk.ca
Other Communication: Toll-Free Phone: 1-800-661-0408, ext. 5653

This central agency has a mandate to provide human resource advice & support services to Yukon government departments & employees, to act as the employer on behalf of the Yukon government & to establish & maintain human resource legislation, policies & collective agreements.

Minister responsible, Hon. Currie Dixon
Tel: 867-667-8628; *Fax:* 867-393-7400
currie.dixon@gov.yk.ca

Public Service Commissioner, Jim Connell
jim.connell@gov.yk.ca

Director, Health, Safety & Disability Management, Les Hudson
Tel: 867-667-5197; *Fax:* 867-456-3977
les.hudson@gov.yk.ca

Director, Policy & Planning Branch, David Krocker
Tel: 867-667-8420; *Fax:* 867-667-6705
david.krocker@gov.yk.ca

Director, Finance & Administration, Catherine Marangu
Tel: 867-667-5861; *Fax:* 867-667-6705

Director, Respectful Workplace Services, Cheryl McLean
Tel: 867-667-3536; *Fax:* 867-393-7009
cheryl.mclean@gov.yk.ca

Director, Corporate Human Resource Staffing, Renée Paquin
Tel: 867-667-5024; *Fax:* 867-667-5755
renee.paquin@gov.yk.ca

Director, Staff Relations, Mark Pindera
Tel: 867-667-5201; *Fax:* 867-393-6919
mark.pindera@gov.yk.ca

Director, Compensation & Classification, Kim Runions
Tel: 867-667-5250; *Fax:* 867-667-6705
kim.runions@gov.yk.ca

Director, Staff Development, Megan Slobodin
Tel: 867-667-8267; *Fax:* 867-393-6920
megan.slobodin@gov.yk.ca

Director, Human Resource Management, Felix Vogt
Tel: 867-667-8222; *Fax:* 867-667-6705
felix.vogt@gov.yk.ca

Yukon Tourism & Culture

100 Hanson St., PO Box 2703 Whitehorse, YT Y1A 2C6
Tel: 867-667-5036; *Fax:* 867-667-3546
www.tc.gov.yk.ca
twitter.com/insideyukon

The department focuses on business, tourism, cultural industries & technology/telecommunications to develop & promote economic capacity & entrepreneurial skills to stimulate economy. The department works with the Yukon's diverse arts communities to foster creativity & quality of life & with heritage interests to preserve & interpret heritage resources.

Minister, Hon. Elaine Taylor
Tel: 867-667-8641; *Fax:* 867-393-6252
elaine.taylor@gov.yk.ca

Deputy Minister, Murray Arsenault
murray.arsenault@gov.yk.ca

Corporate Services

Fax: 867-667-8844

Provides a range of central support services within the Department of Tourism & Culture. These include human resources, information technology, administration, information management, & finance.

Director, Beth Fricke
Tel: 867-667-3009
beth.fricke@gov.yk.ca

Cultural Services

Tel: 867-667-8589; *Fax:* 867-393-6456

Dedicated to the preservation, development, interpretation of Yukon's heritage resources & to fostering the growth & mpact of the territory's visual, literary, & performing arts.

Director, Rick Lemaire
Tel: 867-667-8592
Rick.Lemaire@gov.yk.ca

Yukon Archeologist, Ruth Gotthardt
Tel: 867-667-5983
ruth.gotthardt@gov.yk.ca

Territorial Archivist, Ian Burnett
Tel: 867-667-5275

Yukon Paleontologist, Grant Zazula
Tel: 867-667-8089
grant.zazula@gov.yk.ca

Private Records Archivist, Yukon Archives, Lesley Buchan
Tel: 867-667-5641; *Fax:* 867-393-6253
lesley.buchan@gov.yk.ca

Policy & Communications

Fax: 867-393-8844

Provides legislative & policy support for Tourism & Culture & coordinates the communications efforts of the department.

Director, Mark Roberts
Tel: 867-667-3016
mark.roberts@gov.yk.ca

Tourism & Culture

Tel: 867-667-3053; *Fax:* 867-667-3546

Engages in tourism marketing, product development, & research in order to bring the scenic natural beauty and rich & diverse cultural heritage of Yukon to the attention of potential visitors.

Director, Pierre Germain
Tel: 867-667-3087
pierre.germain@gov.yk.ca

Yukon Women's Directorate

#1, 404 Hason St., PO Box 2703 Whitehorse, YT Y1A 2C6
Tel: 867-667-3030; *Fax:* 867-393-6270
www.womensdirectorate.gov.yk.ca
Other Communication: Toll-Free Phone: 1-800-661-0408, ext. 3030
www.facebook.com/163944003626045

Minister responsible, Hon. Elaine Taylor
Tel: 867-667-8641; *Fax:* 867-393-6252
elaine.taylor@gov.yk.ca

Director, Jennifer England
Tel: 867-667-5182
jennifer.england@gov.yk.ca

Yukon Workers' Compensation Health & Safety Board (YWCHSB)

401 Strickland St., Whitehorse, YT Y1A 5N8
Tel: 867-667-5645; *Fax:* 867-393-6279
Toll-Free: 800-661-0443
worksafe@gov.yk.ca
wcb.yk.ca
Other Communication: 24-Hour Emergency Line: 867-667-5450

The Yukon Workers' Compensation Health & Safety Board (YWCHSB) administers workers' compensation & occupational health & safety in the Yukon.

Minister responsible, Hon. Mike Nixon
Tel: 867-633-7973; *Fax:* 867-393-6252
mike.nixon@gov.yk.ca

President & CEO, Joy Waters
Tel: 867-667-8983; *Fax:* 867-393-6419
joy.waters@gov.yk.ca

Vice-President & Chief Financial Officer, Jim Stephens
Tel: 867-667-8210
jim.stephens@gov.yk.ca

Acting Chief Mine Safety Officer, Michael Henney
Tel: 867-667-8739
michael.henney@gov.yk.ca

Director, Claimant Services, Karen Branigan
Tel: 867-667-8186
karen.branigan@gov.yk.ca

Director, Corporate Services, Kurt Dieckmann
Tel: 867-667-8695
kurt.dieckmann@gov.yk.ca

Acting Director, Occupational Health & Safety, Bruce Milligan
Tel: 867-667-3726
bruce.milligan@gov.yk.ca

Director, Human Resources, Karen Pearson
Tel: 867-667-8190
karen.pearson@gov.yk.ca

Director, Assessments, Clarence Timmons
Tel: 867-667-5831
clarence.timmons@gov.yk.ca

The Queen & Royal Family

The House of Windsor

In 1917 the late King George V, by Proclamation, changed the House name of the Royal Family from Saxe-Coburg-Gotha to the House of Windsor.

THE QUEEN. - Elizabeth the Second, (Elizabeth Alexandra Mary, of Windsor) by the Grace of God, of the United Kingdom, Canada and Her other Realms and Territories Queen; Head of the Commonwealth, Defender of the Faith, Succeeded to the throne February 6th, 1952 , and was crowned June 2nd, 1953, at Westminster Abbey. Her Majesty, the elder daughter of the late King George VI and Queen Elizabeth The Queen Mother, was born at 17 Bruton St., London, W.1, on April 21st, 1926, married November 20th, 1947, H.R.H. The Prince Philip, Duke of Edinburgh, K.G., K.T., O.M., G.B.E., A.C., Q.S.O.

THE CHILDREN of Queen Elizabeth and H.R.H. The Prince Philip, Duke of Edinburgh are:

H.R.H. Prince Charles Philip Arthur George, Prince of Wales and Earl of Chester, Duke of Cornwall and Duke of Rothesay, Earl of Carrick and Baron Renfrew, Lord of the Isles, and Great Steward of Scotland, K.G., K.T., G.C.B., O.M., A.K., Q.S.O., A.D.C., born November 14th, 1948. Married July 29th, 1981. Marriage dissolved 1996. The Lady Diana Spencer (died August 31st, 1997) and has issue. Prince William, Prince of Wales and Duke of Cambridge, born June 21st, 1982 (married April 29, 2011, Kate Middleton, H.R.H. Duchess of Cambridge and has issue, Prince George of Cambridge, born July 22, 2013); and Prince Henry of Wales, born September 15th, 1984. Prince Charles married April 9th, 2005 Mrs. Camilla Parker Bowles (H.R.H. The Duchess of Cornwall).

H.R.H. The Princess Royal, Anne Elizabeth Alice Louise, K.G., K.T., G.C.V.O., Q.S.O., born August 15th, 1950. Married 1st November 14th, 1973 Captain Mark Anthony Peter Phillips, C.V.O., A.D.C. and has issue. Peter Phillips born November 15th, 1977 and Zara Phillips born May 15th, 1981. Marriage dissolved 1992. Married 2nd December 12th, 1993 Commodore Timothy James Hamilton Laurence, M.V.O., R.N.

H.R.H. The Prince Andrew Albert Christian Edward, K.C.V.O., A.D.C., Duke of York, Earl of Inverness and Baron Killyleagh, born February 19th, 1960, married July 23rd, 1986 Miss Sarah Margaret Ferguson and has issue, Princess Beatrice of York, born August 8th, 1988, and Princess Eugenie of York, born March 23rd, 1990. Marriage dissolved 1996.

H.R.H. The Prince Edward Antony Richard Louis, K.C.V.O., Earl of Wessex, and Viscount Severn, born March 10th, 1964, married June 19, 1999 Miss Sophie Rhys-Jones.

THE LATE GEORGE VI. - George VI succeeded to the Throne December 11th, 1936; and was crowned at Westminster Abbey, May 12th, 1937. Second son of King George V and Queen Mary, he was born at York Cottage, Sandringham, on December 14th, 1895, married, April 26th, 1923, Lady Elizabeth Bowes-Lyon, daughter of the Earl and Countess of Strathmore and Kinghorne. As Heir Presumptive succeeded to the Throne on the abdication of Edward VIII.

QUEEN ELIZABETH, THE QUEEN MOTHER - born August 4th, 1900, daughter of the 14th Earl of Strathmore and Kinghorne; married, April 26th, 1923. Died March 30th, 2002.

THE ISSUE of the late King George VI and Queen Elizabeth are:

The reigning Sovereign, Elizabeth the Second (elder daughter).

The Princess Margaret (Rose), Countess of Snowdon, C.I., G.C.V.O., born August 21st, 1930, married Antony Charles Robert Armstrong-Jones, G.C.V.O., (since created Earl of Snowdon) May 6th, 1960, and has issue, Viscount Linley, born November 3rd, 1961 and the Lady Sarah Frances Elizabeth Armstrong-Jones, born May 1st, 1964. Marriage dissolved 1978. Died February 9th, 2002.

SUCCESSION-The order stands:

The Prince of Wales
The Duke of Cambridge
Prince George of Cambridge
Princess Charlotte of Cambridge
Prince Henry of Wales
The Duke of York, Prince Andrew
Princess Beatrice of York
Princess Eugenie of York
The Earl of Wessex, Prince Edward
The Lady Louise Mountbatten-Windsor
The Princess Royal, Princess Anne
Mr. Peter Phillips
Miss Savannah Phillips
Miss Isla Phillips
Miss Zara Tindall
Miss Mia Grace Tindall
Viscount Linley
The Hon. Charles Armstrong-Jones
The Hon. Margarita Armstrong-Jones
The Lady Sarah Chatto
Master Samuel Chatto
Master Arthur Chatto
The Duke of Gloucester, Prince Richard
Earl of Ulster, Alexander Windsor
Lord Culloden (Xan Windsor)
Lady Cosima Windsor
The Lady Davina Lewis
Miss Senna Lewis
Miss Tane Lewis
The Lady Rose Gilman
Miss Lyla Gilman
Master Rufus Gilman
The Duke of Kent, Prince Edward
The Earl of St. Andrews, George Windsor
The Lady Amelia Windsor
The Lady Helen Taylor
Master Columbus Taylor
Master Cassius Taylor
Miss Eloise Taylor
Miss Estella Taylor
Prince Michael of Kent
The Lord Frederick Windsor
Miss Maud Windsor
The Lady Gabriella Windsor
Princess Alexandra, The Hon. Lady Ogilvy
Mr. James Ogilvy
Master Alexander Ogilvy
Miss Flora Ogilvy
Mrs. Marina Ogilvy
Master Christian Mowatt
Miss Zenouska Mowatt

NOTES

1. The Sucession was governed by the Act of Settlement 1701 (12 & 13 Will 3 c 2) which limited the succession to the Throne to the heirs, being Protestants, of Princess Sophia of Hanover, granddaughter of King James I. Section 6 (4) of the Legitimacy Act of 1959 (Nothing in this Act affects the succession to the Throne) was also relevant.
2. The Bill of Rights and the Act of Settlement were amended by the Succession to the Crown Act (2003), ending the system of male primogeniture, and applying to those born after Oct. 28, 2011. The Act also ended provisions stating that those who marry Roman Catholics are ineligible for inclusion in the line of succession.

HER MAJESTY'S HOUSEHOLD

Lord Chamberlain, The Earl Peel, G.C.V.O.
Private Secretary to The Queen, The Rt. Hon. Sir Christopher Geidt, K.C.B., K.C.V.O., O.B.E.
Keeper of the Privy Purse, Sir Alan Reid
The Lord Chamberlain has the general supervision of the Royal Household.

The Commonwealth

The Commonwealth of Nations is a voluntary association of 53 independent member countries representing over 1.8 billion people around the world - in Africa, the Americas, Asia, the Caribbean, Europe & the Pacific. It promotes good governance, democracy, sustainable economic & social development, the rule of law & human rights. These & other principles are enshrined in the Harare Commonwealth Declaration of 1991.

There are three principal international organizations of the Commonwealth:

THE COMMONWEALTH SECRETARIAT
Marlborough House, Pall Mall, London SW1Y 5HX, UK, +44 (0)20 7747 6500; Fax: +44 (0)20 7930 0827, Email: info@commonwealth.int, URL: www.thecommonwealth.org
Patricia Scotland, Q.C. (Dominica), Commonwealth Secretary-General
Gary Dunn, Commonwealth Deputy Secretary-General
Deodat Maharaj, Commonwealth Deputy Secretary-General
Josephine Ojiambo,Commonwealth Deputy Secretary-General
Neil Ford, Official Spokesperson, Director, Communicaitons & Public Affairs, 44 (0)20 7747 6380, n.ford@commonwealth.int

THE COMMONWEALTH FOUNDATION
Marlborough House, Pall Mall, London SW1Y 5HY, UK, +44 (0)20 7830 3783; Fax: +44 (0)20 7839 8157, URL: www.commonwealthfoundation.com

THE COMMONWEALTH OF LEARNING (COL)
#2500, 4710 Kingsway, Burnaby BC V5H 4M2, 604-775-8200; Fax: 604-775-8210, Email: info@col.org, URL: www.col.org
The Commonwealth of Learning's focus is in strengthening institutions in developing Commonwealth countries that are striving to provide affordable education to larger numbers of their citizens.

Member States

(showing capital, population (2013) & date of membership. Dates for Australia, Canada & New Zealand are those on which Dominion Status was acquired):

Antigua & Barbuda - St. John's; 90,000; Nov. 1, 1981
Australia - Canberra; 23,343,000; Jan. 1, 1901
- External territories: Norfolk Island, Coral Sea Islands Territory, Australian Antarctic Territory, Heard Island & McDonald Islands, Cocos (Keeling) Islands, Christmas Island, Territory of Ashmore & Cartier Islands

The Bahamas - Nassau; 377,000; July 10, 1973
Bangladesh - Dhaka; 156,595,000; Mar. 26, 1972
Barbados - Bridgetown; 285,000; Nov. 30, 1966
Belize - Belmopan; 332,000; Sept. 21, 1981
Botswana - Gaborone; 2,021,000; Sept. 30, 1966
Brunei Darussalam - Bandar Seri Begawan; 418,000; Feb. 23, 1984
Cameroon - Yaoundé; 22,254,000; May 20, 1995
Canada - Ottawa; 35,182,000; July 1, 1867
Cyprus - Nicosia; 1,141,000; Oct. 1, 1961
Dominica - Roseau; 72,000; Nov. 3, 1978
Fiji Islands - Suva; 881,000; Oct. 10, 1997 N.B. Fiji Islands was suspended from the councils of the Commonwealth in May 2000 following the overthrow of its democratically elected government.It was suspended again in 2006 after another coup, but reinstated in 2014 after elections were held.
Ghana - Accra; 25,905,000; Mar. 6, 1957
Grenada - St. George's; 106,000; Feb. 7, 1974
Guyana - Georgetown; 800,000; Feb. 23, 1966
India - New Delhi; 1,252,140,000; Jan. 26, 1947
Jamaica - Kingston; 2,784,000; Aug. 6, 1962
Kenya - Nairobi; 44,354,000; Dec. 12, 1963
Kiribati - Tarawa; 102,000; July 12, 1979
Lesotho - Maseru; 2,074,000; Oct. 4, 1966
Malawi - Lilongwe; 16,363,000; July 6, 1964
Malaysia - Kuala Lumpur; 29,717,000; Aug. 31, 1957
Maldives - Malé; 345,000; July 26, 1982
Malta - Valletta; 429,000; Mar. 31, 1964
Mauritius - Port Louis; 1,244,000; Mar. 12, 1968
Mozambique - Maputo; 25,834,000; June 25, 1995
Namibia - Windhoek; 2,303,000; Mar. 21, 1990
Nauru - Nauru; 10,000; Jan. 31, 1968 N.B. Member in Arrears until 2011.
New Zealand - Wellington; 4,506,000; Sept. 26, 1907 - Includes the territories of Tokelau & the Ross Dependency (Antarctic). Self-governing countries in free association with New Zealand: Cook Islands & Niue.
Nigeria - Abuja; 173,615,000; Oct. 1, 1960
Pakistan - Islamabad; 182,143,000; Mar. 23, 1989 (previously member 1947-1972; rejoined in 1989) N.B. Pakistan was suspended from participation in the councils of the Commonwealth in October 1999 following a military coup, but was reinstated in 2004.
Rwanda - Kigali; 11,777,000; Nov. 2009
Papua New Guinea - Port Moresby; 7,321,000; Sept. 16, 1975
Saint Lucia - Castries; 182,000; Feb. 22, 1979
St. Kitts & Nevis - Basseterre; 54,000; Sept. 19, 1983
St. Vincent & The Grenadines - Kingstown; 109,000; Oct. 27, 1979
Samoa - Apia; 190,000; June 1, 1970
Seychelles - Victoria; 93,000; June 18, 1976
Sierra Leone - Freetown; 6,092,000; Apr. 27, 1961
Singapore - Singapore; 5,412,000; Aug. 9, 1965
Solomon Islands - Honiara; 561,000; July 7, 1978
South Africa - Pretoria; 52,776,000; 1931 - Left Commonwealth 1961, rejoined 1994
Sri Lanka - Colombo; 21,273,000; Feb. 4, 1948
Swaziland - Mbabane; 1,250,000; Sept. 6, 1968
Tonga - Nuku'alofa; 105,000; June 4, 1970
Trinidad & Tobago - Port of Spain; 1,341,000; Aug. 31, 1962
Tuvalu - Funafuti; 10,000; Oct. 1, 1978
Uganda - Kampala; 37,579,000; Oct. 9, 1962
United Kingdom - London; 63,136,000
- Overseas territories: Anguilla, Bermuda, British Antarctic Territory, British Indian Ocean Territory, British Virgin Islands, Cayman Islands, Falkland Islands, Gibraltar, Montserrat, Pitcairn (incl. Henderson, Ducie & Oeno Islands), St. Helena & St. Helena Dependencies (Ascension & Tristan da Cunha), South Georgia & the South Sandwich Islands, & Turks & Caicos Islands

United Republic of Tanzania - Dodoma; 49,253,000; Dec. 9, 1961
Vanuatu - Port Vila; 253,000; July 30, 1980
Zambia - Lusaka; 14,539,000; Oct. 24, 1964

La Francophonie

ORGANISATION INTERNATIONALE DE LA FRANCOPHONIE
Secrétariat général, 19-21, av Bosquet, 75007 Paris, France 1-44-37-33-00; Téléc: 1-45-79-14-98; URL: www.francophonie.org
Michaëlle Jean (Canada), Secrétaire général

Member States

(showing member name, population (2010-2013), national holiday):

Albanie (République d'), 3,169 M, 11 janvier et 28 novembre
Andorre (Principauté), 0,870 M, 8 septembre
Arménie (République d'), 3,090 M, 23 août

Belgique (Royaume de), 10,698 M, 21 juillet
Bénin (République du), 9,212 M, 1er août
Bulgarie (République de), 7,497 M, 3 mars
Burkina Faso, 16,287 M, 11 décembre
Burundi (République du), 8,519 M, 1er juillet
Cambodge (Royaume du), 15,053 M, 7 janvier - 17 avril
Cameroun (République du), 19,958 M, 20 mai
Canada, 34,483 M, 1er juillet
Canada - Nouveau-Brunswick (Province du), 0,751 M, 15 août
Canada - Québec (Province du), 7,903 M, 24 juin
Cap-Vert (République du), 0,513 M, 5 juillet
Centrafricaine (République), 4,506 M, 1er décembre
Chypre, 0,880 M, 1er octobre
Communauté française de Belgique (Wallonie-Bruxelles), 4,505 M, 27 septembre
Comores (Union des), 0,691 M, 6 juillet
Congo (République du), 3,759 M, 15 août
Congo (République démocratique du Congo), 67,827 M, 30 juin
Côte d'Ivoire (République de), 21,571 M, 7 août
Djibouti (République de), 0,879 M, 27 juin
Dominique (Commonwealth de la), 0,067 M, 3 novembre
Égypte (République arabe d'), 84,474 M, 23 juillet
France (République française), 62,637 M, 14 juillet
Gabon (République gabonaise), 1,501 M, 17 août
Ghana, 24,333 M, 6 mars
Grèce, 11,183 M, 25 mars
Guinée (République de), 10,324 M, 2 octobre
Guinée-Bissau (République de), 1,647 M, 24 septembre
Guinée-équatoriale (République de), 0,693 M, 12 octobre
Haïti (République d'), 10,188 M, 1er janvier
Laos (République démocratique populaire Lao), 6,436 M, 2 décembre
Liban (République libanaise), 4,255 M, 22 novembre
Luxembourg (Grand-Duché de), 0,492 M, 23 juin
Macédonie (ARY), 2,043 M, 8 septembre
Madagascar (République de), 20,146 M, 26 juin
Mali (République du), 13,323 M, 22 septembre
Maroc (Royaume du), 32,381 M, 30 juillet
Maurice (République de), 1,297 M, 12 mars
Mauritanie (République islamique de), 3,366 M, 28 novembre
Moldavie, 3,576 M, 27 août
Monaco (Principauté de), 0,033 M, 19 novembre
Niger (République du), 15,891 M, 18 décembre
Qatar (État du), 2,100 M, 18 décembre
Roumanie, 21,190 M, 1er décembre
Rwanda (République rwandaise), 10,943 M, 1er juillet
Sainte-Lucie, 0,174 M, 22 février
Sao Tomé et Principe (République démocratique de), 0,165 M, 12 juillet
Sénégal (République du), 12,861 M, 4 avril
Seychelles (République des), 0,085 M, 18 juin
Suisse (Confédération), 7,597 M, 1er août
Tchad (République du), 11,506 M, 11 janvier
Togo (République du), 6,780 M, 13 janvier et 27 avril
Tunisie (République tunisienne), 10,374 M, 20 mars
Vanuatu (République de), 0,246 M, 30 juillet
Vietnam (République socialiste du), 89,029 M, 2 septembre

Canadian Permanent Missions Abroad

Canadian Delegation to the Organization for Security & Cooperation in Europe
Laurenzerberg 2, Vienna, Austria
011 43 1 531-38-3000, Fax: 011 43 1 531-38-3915
vosce@international.gc.ca
Her Excellency Isabelle Poupart, Ambassador & Permanent Representative

Canadian Joint Delegation to NATO (North Atlantic Treaty Organization)
Léopold III Blvd., Brussels, 1110 Belgium
11-322-707-7100, Fax: 11-322-707-7148
bnato@international.gc.ca
www.europe.forces.gc.ca/sites/page-eng.asp?page=7777
His Excellency Kerry Buck, Ambassador & Permanent Representative of Canada
Vice-Admiral Robert Davidson, Military Representative of Canada CMM, MSC, CD

Mission of Canada to the European Union, Brussels
2, av de Tervuren, Brussels, 1040 Belgium
322-741-06-60, Fax: 322-741-06-29
breu@international.gc.ca
www.canadainternational.gc.ca/eu-ue/index.aspx
His Excellency Daniel J. Costello, Ambassador
Alan Bowman, Minister-Counsellor & Deputy Head of Mission
Lorraine Diguer, Counsellor, Foreign Policy, Diplomacy & Public Affairs

NORAD (North American Aerospace Defense Command)
NORAD Public Affairs, Peterson AFB, #B-016, 250 Vandenberg, Colorado Springs, 80914-3808 USA
719-554-6889
noradpa@norad.mil, pa@forces.gc.ca
www.norad.mil
Bill Gortney, Commander, Adm. USA
Pierre St-Amand, Deputy Commander-in-Chief, Lt. Gen. Cdn. Forces CMM, CD

Organization for Economic Cooperation & Development
2, rue André Pascal, Paris, F-75775 France
331-45-24-82-00, Fax: 331-45-24-85-00
www.oecd.org
Angel Gurría, Secretary-General
Gabriela Ramos, Chief of Staff

Permanent Mission of Canada to the Organization of American States
501 Pennsylvania Ave. NW, Washington, DC 20001 USA
202-682-1768, Fax: 202-682-7264
wshdc-prmoas@international.gc.ca
www.international.gc.ca/oas-oea/permanent_mission_permanent e.aspx
Her Excellency Jennifer Loten, Ambassador & Permanent Representative of Canada
Brett Maitland, Head of Cooperation, Counselor & Alternate Representative

UN: Permanent Delegation of Canada to the UN Educational, Scientific & Cultural Organization (UNESCO)
5, rue Constantine, Paris, 75007 France
331-44-43-25-71, Fax: 331-44 43-25-79
pesco@international.gc.ca
www.canadainternational.gc.ca/unesco/index.aspx
Her Excellency Élaine Ayotte, Ambassador & Permanent Delegate
Line Beauchamp, Counsellor & Representative of the Quebec Government

UN: Permanent Mission of Canada to the Food & Agriculture Organization (FAO)
FAO, Via Zara 30, Rome, 00198 Italy
39-06-854-441, Fax: 39-06-85444-2930
www.fao.org
Peter McGovern, Permanent Representative

UN: Permanent Mission of Canada to the International Civil Aviation Organization
ICAO, 999, boul Robert-Bourassa, Montréal, QC H3C 5H7 Canada
514-954-8219, Fax: 514-954-6077
icaohq@icao.int, library@icao.int
www.icao.int
Fang Liu, Secretary General
Olumuyiwa Benard Aliu, President of the Council
Jean Benoît Leblanc, Permanent Representative

UN: Permanent Mission of Canada to the International Organizations in Vienna
United Nations Office at Vienna, Vienna International Centre, PO Box 500, Wagramer Strasse 5, 1400 Vienna, Austria
43-1-26060, Fax: 43-1-263-3389
www.unvienna.org/unov
His Excellency John Barrett, Permanent Representative & Ambassador

UN: Permanent Mission of Canada to the Office of the UN, The Conference on Disarmament
5, av de l'Ariana, Geneva, 1202 Switzerland
41-22-919-9200, Fax: 41-22-919-9233
genev@international.gc.ca
www.international.gc.ca/genev/index.aspx
His Excellency Jonathan T. Fried, Permanent Representative & Ambassador to the World Trade Organization
Her Excellency Elissa Golberg, Permanent Representative & Ambassador to the United Nations & the Conference on Disarmament

UN: Permanent Mission of Canada to the United Nations
One Dag Hammarskjold Plaza, 885 Second Ave., 14th Fl., New York, NY 10017 USA
212-848-1100, Fax: 212-848-1195
canada.un@international.gc.ca
www.canadainternational.gc.ca/prmny-mponu/index.aspx
His Excellency Marc-André Blanchard, Permanent Representative & Ambassador
His Excellency Michael Grant, Ambassador & Deputy Permanent Representative

UN: Permanent Mission of Canada to the United Nations Centre for Human Settlements (Habitat)
PO Box 1013, Nairobi, 00621 Kenya
254-20-366-3000, Fax: 254-20-366-3900
nrobi@international.gc.ca
www.unhabitat.org

UN: Permanent Mission of Canada to the United Nations Environment Programme
PO Box 1013, Nairobi, 00621 Kenya
254-20-366-3000, Fax: 254-20-366-3900
nrobi@international.gc.ca
www.unep.org

Diplomatic & Consular Representatives in Canada

Islamic State of Afghanistan
Embassy of the Islamic Republic of Afghanistan, 240 Argyle Ave.
Ottawa, ON K2P 1B9
Tel: 613-563-4223; *Fax:* 613-563-4962
contact@afghanembassy.ca
www.afghanembassy.ca
www.facebook.com/afghani stan.embassyottawa
Mohmmad Dawood Qayomi, Counsellor & Chargé d'affaires, a.i.
Laila Ayan, First Secretary
Wahid Sheerzuy, First Secretary
Najibullah Safi, Second Secretary

Republic of Albania
Embassy of Albania (to Canada), #302, 130 Albert St.
Ottawa, ON K1P 5G4
Tel: 613-236-3053; *Fax:* 613-236-0804
embassy.ottawa@mfa.gov.al
www.ambasadat.gov.al/canada/en
Her Excellency Elida Petoshati, Ambassador
Virgjil Muci, Counsellor
Marvin Vokopola, First Secretary

People's Democratic Republic of Algeria
Embassy of Algeria, 500 Wilbrod St.
Ottawa, ON K1N 6N2
Tel: 613-789-8505; *Fax:* 613-789-1406
info@embassyalgeria.ca
www.ambalgott.com
His Excellency Hocine Meghar, Ambassador
Cherif Hacene, Minister-Counsellor
Mohamed Yahia Helali, Counsellor
Ali Saidi, Counsellor
El Khier Rouabhi, Counsellor
Salem Bousnadji, Secretary, Transmissions
Fatiha Naouiri, Secretary, Administrative & Financial Affairs

Principality of Andorra
Two United Nations Plaza, 25th Fl.
New York, NY 10017 USA
Tel: 212-750-8064; *Fax:* 212-750-6630
andorra@un.int
Her Excellency Elisenda Vives Balmana, Ambassador
Gemma Raduan Corrius, Third Secretary & Chargé d'Affaires, a.i.

Republic of Angola
Embassy of the Republic of Angola, 189 Laurier Ave. East
Ottawa, ON K1N 6P1
Tel: 613-234-1152; *Fax:* 613-234-1179
info@embangola-can.org
www.embangola-can.org
His Excellency Edgar Augusto Brandao G. Martins, Ambassador
José Maria Capon Duarte Silva, Minister-Counsellor
Destineza Adelina Pedro De Almeida, First Secretary
Adriano Fernandes Fortunato, First Secretary
Matilde Pedro Zeferino Antonio, Second Secretary
Joao Maria Dos Santos De Carvalho, Second Secretary

Anguilla
***See:* Organization of the Eastern Caribbean States**

Antigua & Barbuda
***See:* Organization of the Eastern Caribbean States**

Argentine Republic
Embassy of the Argentine Republic, 81 Metcalfe St., 7th Fl.
Ottawa, ON K1P 6K7
Tel: 613-236-2351; *Fax:* 613-235-2659
ecana@mrecic.gov.ar
www.ecana.mrecic.gob.ar/en
Her Excellency Norma Ester Nascimbene, Ambassador
Gerardo E. Bompadre, Minister, Political & Cultural Section

Sebastian Molteni, Counsellor, Political & Education Section
Cecilia Ines Silberberg, Second Secretary
Emiliano Montagna, Attaché

Republic of Armenia
Embassy of the Republic of Armenia, 7 Delaware Ave.
Ottawa, ON K2P 0Z2
Tel: 613-234-3710; *Fax:* 613-234-3444
armcanadaembassy@mfa.am
www.canada.mfa.am
His Excellency Armen Yeganian, Ambassador
Susan Hovhannisyan, Attaché

Aruba
***See:* Republic of Venezuela**

Commonwealth of Australia
Australian High Commission, #710, 50 O'Connor St.
Ottawa, ON K1P 6L2
Tel: 613-236-0841; *Fax:* 613-786-7621
www.canada.embassy.gov.au
twitter.com/AusHCCanada
www.facebook.com/Aus traliaInCanada
His Excellency Tony William Negus, High Commissioner
Adrian Hugh Morrison, Deputy High Commissioner
David John Sharpe, Minister-Counsellor
Bill Noble, First Secretary
Ken Smith, First Secretary
Damon Rhys Keogh, First Secretary
Melissa Gaye Stenfors, First Secretary & Consul
Louise Murray, Second Secretary & Consul
David Reid, Second Secretary
Cmdr. Bradley John Vizard, Defence Adviser

Republic of Austria
Embassy of Austria, 445 Wilbrod St.
Ottawa, ON K1N 6M7
Tel: 613-789-1444; *Fax:* 613-789-3431
ottawa-ob@bmaa.gv.at
www.bmeia.gv.at/botschaft/ottawa.html
His Excellency Arno Riedel, Ambassador
Bernhard Faustenhammer, Minister & Deputy Head of Mission
Sigrid Kodym, First Secretary & Consul

Republic of Azerbaijan
Embassy of Azerbaijan (to Canada), #1203, 275 Slater St.
Ottawa, ON K1P 5H9
Tel: 613-288-0497; *Fax:* 613-230-8089
azerbaijan@azembassy.ca
www.azembassy.ca
twitter.com/AzEmbCanada
www .facebook.com/185253704851295
Ramil Huseynli, Counsellor & Chargé d'Affaires, a.i.
Arif Mammadov, Second Secretary

Autonomous Region of the Azores
***See:* Portuguese Republic**

Commonwealth of the Bahamas
High Commission for the Commonwealth of The Bahamas, #1313, 50 O'Connor St.
Ottawa, ON K1P 6L2
Tel: 613-232-1724; *Fax:* 613-232-0097
www.bahighco.ca
His Excellency Calsey Willmore Johnson, High Commissioner
Roselyn Danielle Dorsett-Horton, Minister-Counsellor & Consul
Marjorie Julien, Second Secretary & Vice-Consul

Kingdom of Bahrain
Embassy of Bahrain (to Canada), 3502 International Dr. NW
Washington, DC 20008 USA
Tel: 202-342-1111; *Fax:* 202-362-2192
ambsecretary@bahrainembassy.org
www.bahrainembassy.org
www.youtube.com/bahrainvideo
twitter.com/bahdiplomatic
His Excellency Shaikh Abdulla Mohamed Al-Khalifa, Ambassador

People's Republic of Bangladesh
Bangladesh High Commission, #1100, 350 Sparks St.
Ottawa, ON K1R 7S8
Tel: 613-236-0138; *Fax:* 613-567-3213
bangla@rogers.com
www.bdhcottawa.ca
His Excellency Kamrul Ahsan, High Commissioner
Dewan Mahmudul Haque, First Secretary, Commerce
Muhammed Muksud Khan, First Secretary, Consular
Alauddin Vuian, First Secretary
Aparna Rani Paul, First Secretary

Barbados
High Commission for Barbados, #470, 55 Metcalfe St.
Ottawa, ON K1P 6L5
Tel: 613-236-9517; *Fax:* 613-230-4362
Her Excellency Yvonne Veronica Walkes, High Commissioner
Christobelle Elaine Reece, Counsellor
Joanna Esme N. Benn-Griffith, First Secretary

Republic of Belarus
Embassy of the Republic of Belarus, #600, 130 Albert St.
Ottawa, ON K1P 5G4
Tel: 613-233-9994; *Fax:* 613-233-8500
canada@mfa.gov.by
canada.mfa.gov.by
www.youtube.com/user/BelarusMFA
twitter.com/BelarusMFA
www.facebook.co m/BelarusEmbassy.Canada
Dimitry Basik, Counsellor & Chargé d'affaires, a.i.
Timofei Demin, Second Secretary & Consul

Kingdom of Belgium
Embassy of Belgium, #820, 360 Albert St.
Ottawa, ON K1R 7X7
Tel: 613-236-7267; *Fax:* 613-236-7882
ottawa@diplobel.fed.be
diplomatie.belgium.be/canada
www.facebook.com/B elEmbassyOttawa
His Excellency Raoul Roger Delcorde, Ambassador
Julien Pierre Francois Lecomte, Counsellor
Patrick Hubert M. Stevens, Counsellor
Jonas Valerius Juliana De Meyer, First Secretary
Brig. Gen. Johan Maria J. Andries, Defence Attaché

Belize
High Commission for Belize (to Canada), 2535 Massachusetts Ave. NW
Washington, DC 20008 USA
Tel: 202-332-9636; *Fax:* 202-332-6888
www.embassyofbelize.org
www.facebook.com/belizeembassydc
Ardelle Sabido, Chargé d'Affaires a.i.

Republic of Benin
Embassy of Benin, 58 Glebe Ave.
Ottawa, ON K1S 2C3
Tel: 613-233-4429; *Fax:* 613-233-8952
amba.benin@yahoo.ca
www.benin.ca
His Excellency Comlan Pamphile Goutondji, Ambassador

Kingdom of Bhutan
Royal Bhutanese Embassy (to Canada), 343 East 43rd St.
New York, NY 10017 USA
Tel: 212-682-2268; *Fax:* 212-661-0551
Her Excellency Kunzang Choden Namgyel, Ambassador

Plurinational State of Bolivia
Embassy of Bolivia, #416, 130 Albert St.
Ottawa, ON K1P 5G4
Tel: 613-236-5730; *Fax:* 613-236-8237
www.emboliviacanada.com
Claudia Maria Alexis Rocabado Mrden, First Secretary & Chargé d'Affaires, a.i.
Stael Angelica Rodriguez Romero, First Secretary

Bosnia & Herzegovina
Embassy of Bosnia & Herzegovina, 17 Blackburn Ave.
Ottawa, ON K1N 8A2
Tel: 613-236-0028; *Fax:* 613-236-1139
info@bhembassy.ca
www.ambasadabih.ca
twitter.com/AmbasadaBiH
Her Excellency Koviljka Spiric, Ambassador
Fuad Didic, Counsellor

Republic of Botswana
High Commission for Botswana (to Canada), 1531 - 1533 New Hampshire Ave. NW
Washington, DC 20036 USA
Tel: 202-244-4990; *Fax:* 202-244-4164
info@botswanaembassy.org
www.botswanaembassy.org
His Excellency David John Newman, High Commissioner
Col. Conrad Otsile Isaacs, Defence, Military & Air Attaché

Federative Republic of Brazil
Embassy of Brazil, 450 Wilbrod St.
Ottawa, ON K1N 6M8
Tel: 613-237-1090; *Fax:* 613-237-6144
consular.ottawa@itamaraty.gov.br
ottawa.itamaraty.gov.br/en-us
His Excellency Pedro Fernando Bretas Bastos, Ambassador
Pedro Miguel Da Costa E Silva, Minister-Counsellor
Pablo Duarte Cardoso, Counsellor
Ricardo Edgard Rolf Lima Bernhard, Third Secretary
MajGen. Ricardo Pucci Magalhaes, Defence & Air Attaché

British Virgin Islands
***See:* Organization of the Eastern Caribbean States**

Brunei Darussalam
High Commission of Brunei Darussalam, 395 Laurier Ave. East
Ottawa, ON K1N 6R4
Tel: 613-234-5656; *Fax:* 613-234-4397
His Excellency PG Kamal Bashah PG Ahmad, High Commissioner
Sukri Sharbini, Second Secretary
Faadzilah Raheemah Safri Mohdzar, Third Secretary

Republic of Bulgaria
Embassy of the Republic of Bulgaria, 325 Stewart St.
Ottawa, ON K1N 6K5
Tel: 613-789-3215; *Fax:* 613-789-3524
Embassy.Ottawa@mfa.bg
www.mfa.bg/embassies/canada
His Excellency Nikolay Milkov Milkov, Ambassador
Svetlana Sashova Stoycheva-Etropolski, First Secretary, Political Section
Kamen Valentinov Dikov, Second Secretary, Consular Section
Desislava Petrova Dragneva, Second Secretary, Commercial Section

Burkina-Faso
Embassy of Burkina-Faso, 48 Range Rd.
Ottawa, ON K1N 8J4
Tel: 613-238-4796; *Fax:* 613-238-3812
contact@ambabf-ca.org
ambabf-ca.org
His Excellency Amadou Adrien Koné, Ambassador
Hortense Marie Louise Tanga, Counsellor
Ibrahim Ben Harouna Zarani, Counsellor
Michel Sawadogo, First Counsellor
Ketokata Roselyne E. Kamboi Sanou, Second Counsellor

Republic of Burundi
Embassy of Burundi, #410, 350 Albert St.
Ottawa, ON K1R 1A4
Tel: 613-234-9000; *Fax:* 613-234-4030
ambabottawa@yahoo.ca
ambassadeduburundi.ca
Emmanuel Niyonzima, Second Counsellor & Chargé d'Affaires, a.i

Kingdom of Cambodia
c/o Permanent Mission of the Kingdom of Cambodia to the UN, 327 East 58 St.
New York, NY 10022 USA
Tel: 212-336-0777; *Fax:* 212-759-7672
cambodia@un.int
His Excellency Tuy Ry, Ambassador

Republic of Cameroon
Cameroon High Commission, 170 Clemow Ave.
Ottawa, ON K1S 2B4
Tel: 613-236-1522; *Fax:* 613-236-3885
cameroun@rogers.com
www.hc-cameroon-ottawa.org
His Excellency Solomon Azoh-Mbi Anu'A-Gheyle, High Commissioner
Labarang Abdoullahi, First Secretary, Financial Affairs
Ntaribo Ashu Agborngah, First Secretary, Administrative & Consular Affairs
Col. Elie Banbara, Defence Attaché
L.Col. André Hubert Onana Mfege, Air Attaché

Republic of Cabo Verde
Embassy of Cabo Verde (to Canada), 3415 Massachusetts Ave. NW
Washington, DC 20007 USA
Tel: 202-965-6820; *Fax:* 202-965-1207
www.virtualcapeverde.net

Central African Republic
Embassy of Central African Republic (to Canada), 2704 Ontario Rd. NW
Washington, DC 20009 USA
His Excellency Stanislas Moussa-Kembe, Ambassador

Republic of Chad
Embassy of Chad, #802, 350 Sparks St.
Ottawa, ON K1R 7S8
Tel: 613-680-3322; *Fax:* 613-695-6622
Other contact information: Alt. Phone: 613-421-1189
His Excellency Mahamat Ali Adoum, Ambassador
Naimbaye Yelke Dasnan, Defence Attaché

Republic of Chile
Embassy of Chile, #1413, 50 O'Connor St.
Ottawa, ON K1P 6L2
Tel: 613-235-4402; *Fax:* 613-235-1176
chileabroad.gov.cl/canada
His Excellency Oscar Alfonso Sebastian Silva Navarro, Ambassador
Elena Del Carmen Bornand Perez, First Secretary & Chargé d'Affaires, a.i.
Marta Evelyn Vargas Diaz, Second Secretary & Consul
Rodrigo Andrés Meza Gotor, Second Secretary
Paola Andrea Palma Pérez, Second Secretary

People's Republic of China
Embassy of China, 515 St. Patrick St.
Ottawa, ON K1N 5H3
Tel: 613-789-3434; *Fax:* 613-789-1911
chineseembassy.ca@gmail.com
ca.china-embassy.org
twitter.com/ChinaEmbO ttawa
His Excellency Zhaohui Luo, Ambassador
Wentian Wang, Minister & Deputy Head of Mission
Tao Han, Minister-Counsellor
Xinyu Yang, Minister-Counsellor
Xiang Xia, Minister-Counsellor
Haisheng Zhao, Minister-Counsellor
Liping Zhao, Minister-Counsellor
Senior Col. Haitao Zhu, Military, Naval & Air Attaché

Republic of Colombia
Embassy of Colombia, #1002, 360 Albert St.
Ottawa, ON K1R 7X7
Tel: 613-230-3760; *Fax:* 613-230-4416
embajada@embajadacolombia.ca
www.embajadacolombia.ca
www.youtube.com/CancilleriaCol
twitter.com/CancilleriaCol
www.facebook.com/CancilleriaCol
His Excellency Nicolas Lloreda Ricaurte, Ambassador
Juan Carlos Rojas Arango, First Secretary

Union of the Comoros
c/o Permanent Mission of the Comoros to the UN, #418, 866 UN Plaza
New York, NY 10017 USA
Tel: 212-750-1637; *Fax:* 212-750-1657
comoros@un.int
www.un.int/comoros
His Excellency Soilih Mohamed Soilih, Ambassador

Republic of the Congo
Embassy of the Congo (to Canada), 1720 - 16th St. NW
Washington, DC 20009 USA
Tel: 202-726-5500; *Fax:* 202-726-1860
info@ambacongo-us.org
www.ambacongo-us.org
His Excellency Serge Mombouli, Ambassador

Democratic Republic of the Congo
Embassy of the Democratic Republic of the Congo, 18 Range Rd.
Ottawa, ON K1N 8J3
Tel: 613-230-6391; *Fax:* 613-230-1945
www.ambardcongocanada.ca
Jean-Claude Kalelwa Kalimasi, Attaché & Chargé d'Affaires a.i.

Republic of Costa Rica
Embassy of Costa Rica, #701, 350 Sparks St.
Ottawa, ON K1R 7S8
Tel: 613-562-2855; *Fax:* 613-562-2582
embcr@costaricaembassy.com
www.costaricaembassy.com
www.facebook.com/1 31158646950387
Roberto Carlos Dormond Cantu, Ambassador
Monica Cruz Bolaños, Minister-Counsellor & Consul General
Jorge Eduardo Umana Vargas, Counsellor & Consul

Republic of Côte d'Ivoire
Embassy of Côte d'Ivoire, 9 Marlborough Ave.
Ottawa, ON K1N 8E6
Tel: 613-236-9919; *Fax:* 613-563-8287
info@canada.diplomatie.gouv.ci
www.canada.diplomatie.gouv.ci
His Excellency N'Goran Kouame, Ambassador
Lydie Yao, First Secretary
Marie-Ange Flore Elloh Nee Aouely, First Secretary
Aminata Kone, First Secretary
Adama Oulai, First Secretary

Republic of Croatia / Hrvatska
Embassy of Croatia, 229 Chapel St.
Ottawa, ON K1N 7Y6
Tel: 613-562-7820; *Fax:* 613-562-7821
croemb.ottawa@mvep.hr
ca.mvep.hr
www.youtube.com/mvephr
twitter.com/MVEP_hr
www.facebook.com/5064537260 37312
Her Excellency Marica Matkovic, Ambassador
Ljubica Beric, First Secretary
Martina Mihovilic Vracaric, First Secretary
Maj. Gen. Vlado Sindler, Defence, Military, Naval & Air Attaché

Republic of Cuba
Embassy of Cuba, 388 Main St.
Ottawa, ON K1S 1E3
Tel: 613-563-0141; *Fax:* 613-563-0068
cuba@embacubacanada.net
www.cubadiplomatica.cu/canada
His Excellency Julio Antonio Garmendia Pena, Ambassador
Deborah Leticia Ojeda Valedon, Minister-Counsellor
Ofelia Perera Ibanez, Counsellor
Jose Antonio Roget Cuenca, Counsellor

Republic of Cyprus
High Commission for the Repulic of Cyprus (to Canada), 2211 R St. NW
Washington, DC 20008 USA
Tel: 202-462-5772; *Fax:* 202-483-6710
www.cyprusembassy.net
Other contact information: Phone, Press Office: 202-232-8993; Fax, Press Room: 202-234-1936
His Excellency Pavlos Anastasiades, High Commissioner

Czech Republic
Embassy of the Czech Republic, 251 Cooper St.
Ottawa, ON K2P 0G2
Tel: 613-562-3875; *Fax:* 613-562-3878
ottawa@embassy.mzv.cz
www.mzv.cz/ottawa
His Excellency Pavel Hrncír, Ambassador
Jiri Borcel, Deputy Head of Mission
Vladimir Hejduk, Second Secretary
Josef Dvoracek, Counsellor

Kingdom of Denmark
Royal Danish Embassy, #450, 47 Clarence St.
Ottawa, ON K1N 9K1
Tel: 613-562-1811; *Fax:* 613-562-1812
ottamb@um.dk
canada.um.dk
twitter.com/denmarkincanada
His Excellency Niels Boel Abrahamsen, Ambassador
Maja Sverdrup, Minister-Counsellor

Republic of Djibouti
Embassy of the Republic of Djibouti (to Canada), #515, 1156 - 15th St. NW
Washington, DC 20005 USA
Tel: 202-331-0270; *Fax:* 202-331-0302
His Excellency Roble Olhaye, Ambassador
Issa Daher Bouraleh, Counsellor

Commonwealth of Dominica
See: **Organization of the Eastern Caribbean States**

Dominican Republic
Embassy of the Dominican Republic, #1605, 130 Albert St.
Ottawa, ON K1P 5G4
Tel: 613-569-9893; *Fax:* 613-569-8673
www.drembassy.org
His Excellency Hector Virgilio Alcantara Mejia, Ambassador
Dulce Ileana E. Rosario de la Maza, Minister-Counsellor & Deputy Head of Mission
Ricardo Alberto Almonte Arias, Minister-Counsellor
Glenis Regina Guzman Felipe, Minister-Counsellor
Ana Melba Rosario de Arias, Minister-Counsellor
Teofilo Antonio Alcantara Mercado, Counsellor
Wendy Teresa Goico Campagna, Counsellor
Orly David Perez Medina, Counsellor
Gretchen Purisima Pockels Saneaux, Counsellor
Julio Alejandro Rodriguez Velez, Counsellor
Marien Judisa Santana Rosa, Counsellor

Republic of Ecuador
Embassy of the Republic of Ecuador, #230, 99 Bank St.
Ottawa, ON K1P 6B9
Tel: 613-563-8206; *Fax:* 613-235-5776
embassy@embassyecuador.ca
www.embassyecuador.ca
His Excellency Nicolás Trujillo-Newlin, Ambassador
Hilda Josefina Sisalema Hidalgo, Minister
Luis Fernando Fiallos Pazmino, Second Secretary
Oscar Ismael Ramirez Lama, Second Secretary
Ingrid Susana Villafuerte Holguin, Second Secretary

Arab Republic of Egypt
Embassy of the Arab Republic of Egypt, 454 Laurier Ave. East
Ottawa, ON K1N 6R3
Tel: 613-234-4931; *Fax:* 613-234-9347
Egyptemb@sympatico.ca
www.mfa.gov.eg/english/embassies/Egyptian_Embassy_ Ottawa
His Excellency Moataz Mounir Moharram Zahran, Ambassador
Yasser Mahmoud Abed, Minister & Deputy Head of Mission
Ahmed Mamdouh Madian Elbuckley, Second Secretary
Amr Mohammed F. M.S. Koraiem, Second Secretary
Mahmoud Abdelhakim A. Ahmed, Third Secretary
RDML Mohamed M. Abdelaziz Elsayed, Military, Air, Naval & Defence Attaché

Republic of El Salvador
Embassy of El Salvador, 209 Kent St.
Ottawa, ON K2P 1Z8
Tel: 613-238-2939; *Fax:* 613-238-6940
elsalvadorottawa@rree.gob.sv
embajadacanada.rree.gob.sv
www.youtube.com/user/cancilleria1
twitter.com/cancilleriasv
www.facebo ok.com/EmbajadaES
Xochitl Guadalupe Zelaya Gomez, Minister-Counsellor & Chargé d'affaires, a.i.

Republic of Equatorial Guinea
c/o Permanent Mission of the Republic of Equatorial Guinea to the UN, 242 East 51st St.
New York, NY 10022 USA
Tel: 212-223-2324; *Fax:* 212-223-2366
equatorialguineamission@yahoo.com
www.un.int/equatorialguinea
His Excellency Anatolio Ndong Mba, Permanent Representative

State of Eritrea
Embassy of Eritrea (to Canada), 1708 New Hampshire Ave. NW
Washington, DC 20009 USA
Tel: 202-319-1991; *Fax:* 202-319-1304

Republic of Estonia
Embassy of Estonia, #210, 260 Dalhousie St.
Ottawa, ON K1N 7E4
Tel: 613-789-4222; *Fax:* 613-789-9555
embassy.ottawa@mfa.ee
www.estemb.ca
www.facebook.com/estemb.ottawa
Her Excellency Gita Kalmet, Ambassador

Federal Democratic Republic of Ethiopia
Embassy of Federal Democratic Republic of Ethiopia, #1501, 275 Slater St.
Ottawa, ON K1P 5H9
Tel: 613-235-6637; *Fax:* 613-565-9175
info@ethioembassycanada.org
ethioembassycanada.org
Her Excellency Birtukan Ayano Dadi, Ambassador
Nebiat Getachew Assegid, Minister-Counsellor & Deputy Head of Mission
Kenasa Mekonnen Gura, Minister-Counsellor
Almaw Atnafu Muluneh, Second Counsellor

European Union
Delegation of the European Union to Canada, #1900, 150 Metcalfe St.
Ottawa, ON K2P 1P1
Tel: 613-238-6464; *Fax:* 613-238-5191
Delegation-Canada@eeas.europa.eu
eeas.europa.eu/delegations/canada/index _en.htm
www.facebook.com/EUinCanada
Her Excellency Maria Anne E.L.L.G. Coninsx, Ambassador & Head of Delegation
Manfred Edgar G. Auster, Minister-Counsellor
Karsten Mecklenburg, Counsellor

Republic of the Fiji Islands
High Commission for the Republic of the Fiji Islands (to Canada), #200, 1707 L St. NW
Washington, DC 20036 USA
Tel: 202-337-8320; *Fax:* 202-466-8325
info@fijiembassydc.com
www.fijiembassydc.com
Sakiusa Rabuka, Counsellor

Republic of Finland
Embassy of Finland, #850, 55 Metcalfe St.
Ottawa, ON K1P 6L5
Tel: 613-288-2233; *Fax:* 613-288-2244
embassy@finland.ca
www.finland.ca
www.facebook.com/FinnishEmbassyOttawa
His Excellency Kaarlo Arnold M. Murto, Ambassador
Veli-Pekka Jalmari Kaivola, Minister-Counsellor
Capt. Timo Uuri Stahlhammar, Military, Air, Naval & Defence Attaché

French Republic
Embassy of France, 42 Sussex Dr.
Ottawa, ON K1M 2C9
Tel: 613-789-1795; *Fax:* 613-562-3735
webmestre@ambafrance-ca.org
www.ambafrance-ca.org
www.youtube.com/user/Ambafracanada
twitter.com/franceaucanada
www.face book.com/ambassadefrance.canada
His Excellency Nicolas Marcel Jacques Chapuis, Ambassador
Florence Vanessa Sophie Ferrari, Minister-Counsellor & Deputy Head of Mission
Philippe Ferdinand Huberdeau, Minister-Counsellor
Jean-Christophe D. Auffray, Counsellor
Catherine Madeleine C. Briat, Counsellor
Jean-Marc Capdevila, Counsellor
Karine Gonnet, Counsellor
Pascal Charles F. Helwaser, Counsellor
Stephane Emmanuel Schorderet, Counsellor

Gabonese Republic
Embassy of Gabon, PO Box 368, 4 Range Rd.
Ottawa, ON K1N 8J5
Tel: 613-232-5301; *Fax:* 613-232-6916
info@ambassadegabon.ca
www.ambassadegabon.ca
His Excellency Sosthene Ngokila, Ambassador
François Ebibi Mba, Minister-Counsellor
Johanna Rose Mamiaka, Counsellor

Republic of the Gambia
High Commission for Gambia (to Canada), Georgetown Plaza, #240, 2233 Wisconsin Ave. NW
Washington, DC 20007 USA
Tel: 202-785-1399; *Fax:* 202-785-1430
info@gambiaembassy.us
www.gambiaembassy.us
Baboucarr Jallow, Minister-Counsellor & Deputy Chief of Mission

Georgia
Embassy of Georgia, #2010, 350 Albert St.
Ottawa, ON K1R 1A4
Tel: 613-421-0460; *Fax:* 613-680-0394
ottawa.emb@mfa.gov.ge
canada.mfa.gov.ge
His Excellency Alexander Latsabidze, Ambassador
Ilia Imnadze, Minister-Counsellor

Federal Republic of Germany
Embassy of the Federal Republic of Germany, 1 Waverley St.
Ottawa, ON K2P 0T8
Tel: 613-232-1101; *Fax:* 613-594-9330
www.canada.diplo.de
twitter.com/GermanyInCanada
www.facebook.com/Germa nyInCanada
His Excellency Werner Franz Wnendt, Ambassador
Jörn Rosenberg, Minister-Counsellor
Martin Ingolf Bierbach, First Secretary
Martin Schurig, First Secretary
Marcus Stadthaus, First Secretary
Bernhard Wille, First Secretary
L.Col. Ralf Heimrich, Defence Attaché

Republic of Ghana
High Commission for Ghana, 1 Clemow Ave.
Ottawa, ON K1S 2A9
Tel: 613-236-0871; *Fax:* 613-236-0874
ghanacom@ghc-ca.com
www.ghc-ca.com
His Excellency Dr. Sulley Gariba, High Commissioner
Florence Buerki Akonor, Minister & Deputy High Commissioner
Elizabeth Nyantakyi, Minister-Counsellor
Ernest Nana Adjei, First Secretary
Rita Akyaa Agyekum, First Secretary
Norman Johnson, First Secretary
Celestine Patience Smith, First Secretary
Brig. Gen. Seidu Mumuni Adams, Defence Adviser

Grenada
***See:* Organization of the Eastern Caribbean States**

Republic of Guatemala
Embassy of Guatemala, #1010, 130 Albert St.
Ottawa, ON K1P 5G4
Tel: 613-233-7237; *Fax:* 613-233-0135
embassy1@embaguate-canada.com
www.canada.minex.gob.gt
Her Excellency Blanca Rita Josefina Claverie Diaz de Sciolli, Ambassador
Martha Aida Rogelia Argueta Molina, First Secretary & Consul, margueta@minex.gob.gt
Sandra Refugio Cruz Ordonez, Third Secretary, scruz@minex.gob.gt

Republic of Guinea
Embassy of Guinea, 483 Wilbrod St.
Ottawa, ON K1N 6N1
Tel: 613-789-8444; *Fax:* 613-789-7560
ambassadedeguinee@bellnet.ca
ambaguinee-canada.org
His Excellency Saramady Touré, Ambassador
Adama Kouyate, First Secretary, Consular & Financial Affairs
Brig. Gen. Bachir Diallo, Defence Attaché

Republic of Guinea-Bissau
c/o Permanent Mission of the Republic of Guinea-Bissau to the UN, 336 East 45th St., 13th Fl.
New York, NY 10017 USA
Tel: 212-896-8311; *Fax:* 212-896-8313
guinea-bissau@un.int
www.un.int/guineabissau
His Excellency Joao Soares Da Gama, Permanent Representative

Co-operative Republic of Guyana
High Commission for the Republic of Guyana, #800, 151 Slater St.
Ottawa, ON K1P 5H3
Tel: 613-235-7249; *Fax:* 613-235-1447
guyanahcott@rogers.com
www.guyanamissionottawa.org
Her Excellency Sabita Riehl, High Commissioner

Republic of Haiti
Embassy of Haiti, #1110, 85 Albert St.
Ottawa, ON K1P 6A4
Tel: 613-238-1628; *Fax:* 613-238-2986
info@ambassade-haiti.ca
ambassade-haiti.ca
www.facebook.com/3719436795 43938
His Excellency O. Andre Frantz Liautaud, Ambassador
Marie Michel Geralde Carre Alerte, Minister-Counsellor
Ann-Kathryne Lassegue, Minister-Counsellor
Marie Jose Justinvil, Counsellor
Marjorie Latortue Presume, First Secretary
Emmanuelle Jean-Louis, First Secretary

Hellenic Republic
Embassy of Greece, 80 MacLaren St.
Ottawa, ON K2P 0K6
Tel: 613-238-6271; *Fax:* 613-238-5676
gremb.otv@mfa.gr
www.mfa.gr/canada/en/the-embassy
twitter.com/Greeceln Canada
www.facebook.com/Greeceincanada
His Excellency George L. Marcantonatos, Ambassador
Pelagia Sousiopoulou, First Secretary
Col. Ioannis Birmpilis, Air Attaché

Holy See
Apostolic Nunciature, 724 Manor Ave.
Ottawa, ON K1M 0E3
Tel: 613-746-4914; *Fax:* 613-746-4786
nuntiatura@nuntiatura.ca
www.nuntiatura.ca
His Excellency Most Rev. Luigi Bonazzi, Apostolic Nuncio
Monsignor Sosa Rodriguez Fermin Emilio, Counsellor

Republic of Honduras
Embassy of Honduras, #805A, 151 Slater St.
Ottawa, ON K1P 5H3
Tel: 613-233-8900; *Fax:* 613-232-0193
ambassador@embassyhonduras.hn
embajadahondurasencanada.hn
www.facebook .com/embajada.encanada
Her Excellency Sofia Lastenia Cerrato Rodriguez, Ambassador
Luis Francisco Bogran Moncada, Minister-Counsellor

Hungary
Embassy of Hungary, 302 Metcalfe St.
Ottawa, ON K2P 1S2
Tel: 613-230-8215; *Fax:* 613-230-8887
consulate.ott@mfa.gov.hu
www.mfa.gov.hu/emb/ottawa
www.facebook.com/14 98404670420877
His Excellency Balint David Odor, Ambassador
Lajos Olah, Counsellor
Peter Orosz, Third Secretary
Eva Simon, Third Secretary & Consul

Iceland
Embassy of Iceland, #710, 360 Albert St.
Ottawa, ON K1R 7X7
Tel: 613-482-1944; *Fax:* 613-482-1945
icemb.ottawa@utn.stjr.is
www.iceland.is/iceland-abroad/ca
twitter.com/ iceincan
www.facebook.com/IcelandInCanada
His Excellency Sturla Sigurjónsson, Ambassador

Republic of India
High Commission of India, 10 Springfield Rd.
Ottawa, ON K1M 1C9
Tel: 613-744-3751; *Fax:* 613-744-0913
hicomind@hciottawa.ca
www.hciottawa.ca
www.youtube.com/user/Indiandiplomacy
www.facebook.com/MEAINDIA
His Excellency Vishnu Prakash, High Commissioner, hc@hciottawa.ca
Arun Kumar Sahu, Deputy High Commissioner
Parag Jain, Counsellor, Coordination & Community Affairs, cca@hciottawa.ca
Rajesh Agarwal, Counsellor, Commercial, commercial@hciottawa.ca
Vishwa Nath Goel, Second Secretary, HOC, hoc@hciottawa.ca

Republic of Indonesia / Republik Indonesia
55 Parkdale Ave.
Ottawa, ON K1Y 1E5
Tel: 613-724-1100; *Fax:* 613-724-1105
publicaffairs@indonesia-ottawa.org
www.indonesia-ottawa.org
www.youtube.com/user/kbriottawa
twitter.com/KBRI_Ottawa
www.facebook.com/kbri.ottawa.5
His Excellency Teuku Faizasyah, Ambassador
Suwartini Wirta, Deputy Head of Mission
Kartika Candra Negara, Minister-Counsellor, Economic Affairs
Rezal Akbar Nasrun, Minister-Counsellor, Political Affairs
Andy Aron, First Secretary
Erry Kananga, Second Secretary
Nova Maulani, Third Secretary

Islamic Republic of Iran
Embassy of the Islamic Republic of Iran, 245 Metcalfe St.
Ottawa, ON K2P 2K2
Canada suspended diplomatic relations with Iran in September 2012.

Republic of Iraq
Embassy of Iraq, 215 McLeod St.
Ottawa, ON K2P 0Z8
Tel: 613-236-9177; *Fax:* 613-236-9641
media@iqemb.ca
mofamission.gov.iq/ab/CanadaOt
His Excellency Abdul Kareem Toma M. Kaab, Ambassador
Yasmin Yarub Mohammed H. Al-Sabaa, Second Secretary
Haider Rasim Hussein A-Lawadi, Third Secretary

Republic of Ireland
Embassy of Ireland, #1105, 130 Albert St.
Ottawa, ON K1P 5G4
Tel: 613-233-6281; *Fax:* 613-233-5835
www.embassyofireland.ca
twitter.com/IrlEmbCanada
His Excellency John Raymond Bassett, Ambassador
Michael Declan Hurley, First Secretary
Elizabeth Anne Keogh, Second Secretary

State of Israel
Embassy of Israel, #1005, 50 O'Connor St.
Ottawa, ON K1P 6L2
Tel: 613-750-7500; *Fax:* 613-750-7555
info@ottawa.mfa.gov.il
embassies.gov.il/ottawa/AboutTheEmbassy
twitter .com/IsraelinCanada
www.facebook.com/IsraelinCanada
His Excellency Rafael Raul Barak, Ambassador
Shlomit Sufa, Minister-Counsellor
Adir Rubin, Minister-Counsellor & Consul
Benjamin Paul Finn, Counsellor

Eitan Weiss, First Secretary, Public Diplomacy
Moshe Elimelech, Second Secretary
Col. Adam Susman, Defence Attaché

Italian Republic
Embassy of Italy, 275 Slater St., 21st Fl.
Ottawa, ON K1P 5H9
Tel: 613-232-2401; *Fax:* 613-233-1484
ambasciata.ottawa@esteri.it
www.ambottawa.esteri.it/ambasciata_ottawa
www.flickr.com/photos/ambitaliaottawa
twitter.com/AmbItaliaOttawa
www.facebook.com/ambottawa
His Excellency Gian Lorenzo Cornado, Ambassador
Fabrizio Nava, Minister-Counsellor & Deputy Chief of Mission
Giorgio Taborri, Counsellor
Francesco Corsaro, First Secretary
Maj. Gen. Luca Goretti, Defence & Air Attaché

Ivory Coast
***See:* Republic of Côte d'Ivoire**

Jamaica
Jamaican High Commission, The Burnside Bldg., #1000, 151 Slater St.
Ottawa, ON K1P 5H3
Tel: 613-233-9311; *Fax:* 613-233-0611
jamaica@jhcottawa.ca
www.jhcottawa.ca
Her Excellency Janice Avonne Miller, High Commissioner
Cyeth Cylonia Allison Denton-Watts, Counsellor

Japan
Embassy of Japan, 255 Sussex Dr.
Ottawa, ON K1N 9E6
Tel: 613-241-8541; *Fax:* 613-241-4261
infocul@ot.mofa.go.jp
www.ca.emb-japan.go.jp
twitter.com/JapaninCanada
www.facebook.com/infoculEmbassyofJapanCA
His Excellency Kenjiro Monji, Ambassador
Hiroshi Karube, Minister & Deputy Head of Mission
Hiroyuki Minami, Minister
Hiroshi Honjo, Counsellor
Osamu Iwasa, Counsellor
Tetsu Shiraishi, Counsellor
Keishi Suzuki, Counsellor
Col. Yasuhiro Ogawa, Air Attaché

Hashemite Kingdom of Jordan
Embassy of Jordan, #701, 100 Bronson Ave.
Ottawa, ON K1R 6G8
Tel: 613-238-8090; *Fax:* 613-232-3341
ottawa@fm.gov.jo
www.embassyofjordan.ca
His Excellency Basheer Fawwaz Zoubi, Ambassador
Mo'ath Bassam Youssif Al-Tall, First Secretary & Consul

Republic of Kazakhstan
Embassy of the Republic of Kazakhstan, #1603-1064, 150 Metcalfe St.
Ottawa, ON K2P 1P1
Tel: 613-695-8055; *Fax:* 613-695-8755
kazakhembassy@gmail.com
www.kazembassy.ca
www.youtube.com/channel/UCqRrK986Hn6Z3KsQ6WZXKOQ
twitter.com/KZEmbassyCA
www.facebook.com/232463933540282
His Excellency Konstantin V. Zhigalov, Ambassador
Daniyar Seidaliyev, Counsellor
Rustem Belgibayev, First Secretary
Nurzhan Aitmakhanov, First Secretary
Artem Kuzmin, First Secretary
Gulanz Altynbayeva, Third Secretary
Almas Makulbekov, Third Secretary

Republic of Kenya
High Commission for Kenya, 415 Laurier Ave. East
Ottawa, ON K1N 6R4
Tel: 613-563-1773; *Fax:* 613-233-6599
www.kenyahighcommission.ca
www.facebook.com/kenyahighcommissionottawa
His Excellency John Lepi Lanyasunya, High Commissioner
John Kipkoech Cheruiyot, First Counsellor
Edwin Afande, First Counsellor
Isaiah Kiprotich Koech, First Secretary
James Muthii Karani, Second Secretary

Republic of Korea
Embassy of Korea, 150 Boteler St.
Ottawa, ON K1N 5A6
Tel: 613-244-5010; *Fax:* 613-244-5034
canada@mofa.go.kr
can-ottawa.mofa.go.kr
www.youtube.com/user/koreanembassycanada
twitter.com/koremb_canada
www .facebook.com/embassyofkorea.canada
His Excellency DaeShik Jo, Ambassador
Janghoi Kim, Minister-Counsellor
In Kyu Park, Minister
Yungjoon Jo, Counsellor
Tok Won Lee, Counsellor
Yongpil Lee, Counsellor
Col. Jang Min Choi, Defence Attaché

Democratic People's Republic of Korea
Permanent Mission of Democratic People's Republic of Korea to the UN, 820 - 2 Ave., 13th Fl.
New York, NY 10017 USA
Tel: 212-972-3105; *Fax:* 212-972-3154
His Excellency Ja Song Nam, Permanent Representative

Republic of Kosovo
Embassy of the Republic of Kosovo (to Canada), 200 Elgin St.
Ottawa, ON K2P 1L5
Tel: 613-569-2828; *Fax:* 613-569-2828
embassy.canada@rks.gov.net
Lulzim Hiseni, Chargé d'affaires, a.i.

State of Kuwait
Embassy of Kuwait, 333 Sussex Dr.
Ottawa, ON K1N 1J9
Tel: 613-780-9999; *Fax:* 613-780-9905
His Excellency Ali Hussain S.H. Alsammak, Ambassador
Hamad Buhadedah, First Secretary
Hadi M.M.F. Alsubaie, Second Secretary
Ahmad Alsurayei, Second Secretary
Husain Ebrahim, Third Secretary

Kyrgyz Republic
Embassy of the Kyrgyz Republic (to Canada), 2360 Masachussets. Ave. NW
Washington, DC 20008 USA
Tel: 202-449-9822; *Fax:* 202-386-7550
info@kgembassy.org
www.kyrgyzembassy.org
www.youtube.com/user/KGEMBASSYUSA
www.facebook.com/kgembassyusa
His Excellency Kadyr M. Toktogulov, Ambassador
Mukhamed Lou, Minister-Counsellor, Political & Security Issues, m.lou@kgembassy.org
Zhanybek Eraliev, First Secretary, Economic Cooperation & Cooperation With Canada, j.eraliev@kgembassy.org

Lao People's Democratic Republic
Embassy of the Lao People's Democratic Republic (to Canada), 2222 S St. NW
Washington, DC 20008 USA
Tel: 202-332-6416; *Fax:* 202-332-4923
embasslao@gmail.com
www.laoembassy.com
His Excellency Mai Sayavongs, Ambassador
Khen Sombandith, Counsellor & Deputy Chief of Mission
Bounthala Panyavichith, First Secretary, Political, Economic, Culture
Heuankeo Sangsomsak, Second Secretary
Kedmany Zouphonetheva, Third Secretary

Republic of Latvia
Embassy of the Republic of Latvia, #1200, 350 Sparks St.
Ottawa, ON K1R 7S8
Tel: 613-238-6014; *Fax:* 613-238-7044
embassy.canada@mfa.gov.lv
www.ottawa.mfa.gov.lv
www.flickr.com/photos/latvianmfa
twitter.com/LV_EmbassyCA
www.facebook .com/EmbassyOfLatviaInCanada
His Excellency Juris Audarins, Ambassador
Sanita Ulmane, First Secretary

Lebanese Republic
Embassy of Lebanon, 640 Lyon St.
Ottawa, ON K1S 3Z5
Tel: 613-236-5825; *Fax:* 613-232-1609
info@lebanonembassy.ca
www.lebanonembassy.ca
Sami Haddad, Counsellor & Chargé d'affaires, a.i., consul@lebanonembassy.ca

Kingdom of Lesotho
High Commission for the Kingdom of Lesotho, #1820, 130 Albert St.
Ottawa, ON K1P 5G4
Tel: 613-234-0770; *Fax:* 636-234-5665
lesotho.ottawa@bellnet.ca
www.lesothocanada.gov.ls
Her Excellency Dr. Mathabo Theresia Tsepa, High Commissioner
Liteboho Kutloano Mahlakeng, Counsellor
Jacob Malefetsane Nhlapo, First Secretary

Republic of Liberia
Embassy of the Republic of Liberia (to Canada), 5201 - 16th St. NW
Washington, DC 20011 USA
Tel: 202-723-0437; *Fax:* 202-723-0436
www.liberianembassyus.org
www.facebook.com/346327728855982
His Excellency Jeremiah C. Sulunteh, Ambassador

State of Libya
Embassy of the State of Libya, #1000, 81 Metcalfe St.
Ottawa, ON K1P 6K7
Tel: 613-842-7519; *Fax:* 613-842-8627
info@Libyanembassy.ca
libyanembassy.ca
His Excellency Fathi Baja, Ambassador
Mohamed Abdulnaser, Minister
Murad Abudina, Counsellor
Mohamed Algamodi, Counsellor
Abdalla S.A. Bgar, Counsellor
Khaled Elsahli, Counsellor

Liechtenstein
***See:* Swiss Confederation**

Republic of Lithuania
Embassy of Lithuania, #1600, 150 Metcalfe St.
Ottawa, ON K2P 1P1
Tel: 613-567-5458; *Fax:* 613-567-5315
amb.ca@urm.lt
ca.mfa.lt
His Excellency Vytautas Zalys, Ambassador
Jonas Skardinskas, Minister

Grand Duchy of Luxembourg
Embassy of Luxembourg (to Canada), 2200 Massachusetts Ave. NW
Washington, DC 20008 USA
Tel: 202-265-4171; *Fax:* 202-328-8270
luxembassy.was@mae.etat.lu
washington.mae.lu
His Excellency Jean-Louis Wolzfeld, Ambassador
Olivier Christian Baldauff, Deputy Head of Mission

Republic of Macedonia
Embassy of the Republic of Macedonia, #1006, 130 Albert St.
Ottawa, ON K1P 5G4
Tel: 613-234-3882; *Fax:* 613-233-1852
ottawa@mfa.gov.mk
www3.sympatico.ca/emb.macedonia.ottawa
His Excellency Toni Dimovski, Ambassador

Republic of Madagascar
Embassy of Madagascar, 3 Raymond St.
Ottawa, ON K1R 1A3
Tel: 613-537-0505; *Fax:* 613-537-2882
ambamadcanada@bellnet.ca
www.madagascar-embassy.ca
His Excellency Simon Constant Horace, Ambassador
Tsitohaina Hasina A. Randrianarizao, Counsellor
Philippe Velo, Counsellor

Republic of Malawi
High Commission for Malawi (to Canada), 2408 Massachussets Ave. NW
Washington, DC 20008 USA
Tel: 202-721-0270; *Fax:* 202-721-0288
www.malawiembassy-dc.org
His Excellency Necton Darlington Mhura, Ambassador

Malaysia
High Commission for Malaysia, 60 Boteler St.
Ottawa, ON K1N 8Y7
Tel: 613-241-5182; *Fax:* 613-241-5214
mwottawa@kln.gov.my
www.kln.gov.my/web/can_ottawa
www.facebook.com/Mal awakil.Ottawa
Her Excellency Aminahtun Binti HJ A. Karim, High Commissioner
Dzulkefly Bin Abdullah, Minister-Counsellor

Deddy Faisal Bin Ahmad Salleh, First Secretary, deddy@kln.gov.my
Mohd Nasir Bin Aris, Second Secretary
Brig. Gen. Jaafar Bin Kasim, Defence Adviser

Republic of Maldives
c/o Permanent Mission of the Republic of Maldives to the UN, #202E, 801 - 2 Ave.
New York, NY 10017 USA
Tel: 212-599-6194; *Fax:* 212-661-6405
maldivesmission.com
twitter.com/MVPMNY
His Excellency Ahmed Sareer, Ambassador
Jeffrey Salim Waheed, Minister & Deputy Permanent Representative

Republic of Mali
Embassy of Mali, 50 Goulburn Ave.
Ottawa, ON K1N 8C8
Tel: 613-232-1501; *Fax:* 613-232-7429
ambassade@ambamali.ca
www.ambamali.ca
Cherif Mohamed Kanoute, First Counsellor & Chargé d'Affaires, a.i.
Amadou Ba, Second Counsellor

Republic of Malta
High Commission for Malta (to Canada), 2017 Connecticut Ave. NW
Washington, DC 20008 USA
Tel: 202-462-3611; *Fax:* 202-387-5470
maltaembassy.washington@gov.mt
www.foreign.gov.mt/default.aspx?MDIS=504
Her Excellency Marisa Maria-Louise Micallef, Ambassador
Patricia Borg, First Secretary & Deputy High Commissioner

Republic of the Marshall Islands
Embassy of the Republic of the Marshall Islands (to Canada), 2433 Massachusetts Ave. NW
Washington, DC 20008 USA
Tel: 202-234-5414; *Fax:* 202-232-3236
info@rmiembassyus.org
www.rmiembassyus.org
His Excellency Charles R. Paul, Ambassador

Islamic Republic of Mauritania
c/o Permanent Mission of the Islamic Republic of Mauritania to the UN, 116 East 38th St.
New York, NY 10016 USA
Tel: 212-252-0113; *Fax:* 212-252-0175
mauritaniamission@gmail.com
www.un.int/mauritania
Other contact information: Canadian URL: www.mauritania-canada.ca
His Excellency Sidi Mohamed Boubacar, Ambassador
Maata Ould Mohamed, First Counsellor

Republic of Mauritius
High Commission for Mauritius (to Canada), 1709 N St. NW
Washington, DC 20036 USA
Tel: 202-244-1491; *Fax:* 202-966-0983
His Excellency Sooroojdev Phokeer, High Commissioner
Hans Irvin Antish Bhugun, First Secretary
Mohammad Kayoum Safee, Second Secretary

United Mexican States
Embassy of Mexico, #1000 & #1030, 45 O'Connor St.
Ottawa, ON K1P 1A4
Tel: 613-233-8988; *Fax:* 613-235-9123
info@embamexcan.com
embamex.sre.gob.mx/canada
www.flickr.com/photos/embamexcan
twitter.com/embamexcan
www.facebook.c om/115560035126811
His Excellency Agustin Garcia Lopez Loaeza, Ambassador
Julian Juarez Cadenas, Minister
Cesar Manuel Remis Santos, Minister
Iker Reyes Godelmann, Minister
Mae Helen Yvonne Stinson Ortiz, Minister
Edgar Zurita Borja, Minister
Brig. Gen. Luis Martinez Dominguez, Military & Air Attaché

Republic of Moldova
Embassy of the Republic of Moldova, #801, 275 Slater St.
Ottawa, ON K1P 5H9
Tel: 613-695-6167; *Fax:* 613-695-6164
moldovaconsulate.ca/moldova-embassy
Her Excellency Ala Beleavschi, Ambassador
Corneliu Bobeica, Counsellor

Principality of Monaco
Embassy of the Principality of Monaco (to Canada), #2K-100, 3400 International Dr. NW
Washington, DC 20008 USA
Tel: 202-234-1530; *Fax:* 202-244-7656
info@monacodc.org
monacodc.org/canadahome.html
Her Excellency Maguy Maccario-Doyle, Ambassador

Mongolia
Embassy of Mongolia, #503, 151 Slater St.
Ottawa, ON K1P 5H3
Tel: 613-569-3830; *Fax:* 613-569-3916
ottawa@mfa.gov.mn
ottawa.embassy.mn
www.facebook.com/mfamongoliaMN
His Excellency Radnaabazar Altangerel, Ambassador
Munkh-Ulzii Tserendorj, Counsellor & Deputy Head of Mission
Zorigtbaatar Tserenchimed, First Secretary
Delgerjargal Ganbold, Third Secretary

Montenegro
Embassy of Montenegro (to Canada), 1610 New Hampshire Ave. NW
Washington, DC 20009
Tel: 202-234-6108; *Fax:* 202-234-6109
His Excellency Srdan Darmanovic, Ambassador
Dubravka Lalovic, Minister-Counsellor
Marija Petrovic, First Secretary
L.Col. Velibor Bakrac, Military, Naval & Air Attaché

Montserrat
See: Organization of the Eastern Caribbean States

Kingdom of Morocco
Embassy of Morocco, 38 Range Rd.
Ottawa, ON K1N 8J4
Tel: 613-236-7391; *Fax:* 613-236-6164
sifamaot@bellnet.ca
www.ambamaroc.ca
Her Excellency Nouzha Chekrouni, Ambassador
Abdollah Lkahya, Minister-Counsellor, Political Service
Amina Rabhi, Minister, Culture & Social Service
Houda Ayouch, Counsellor, Economic Service
Ahmed Amine Bahnini, Counsellor, Economic Service & Communication
Lamya Mohandis, Second Secretary, Cultural & Administrative Affairs

Republic of Mozambique
High Commission of the Republic of Mozambique (to Canada), 1525 New Hampshire Ave. NW
Washington, DC 20036 USA
Tel: 202-293-7146; *Fax:* 202-835-0245
embamoc@aol.com
www.embamoc-usa.org
His Excellency Carlos Dos Santos, Ambassador
Eduardo Candido Albino Zaqueu, Minister-Counsellor
Ana Maria R. D'Assunçao Alberto, Counsellor

Republic of the Union of Myanmar
Embassy of the Republic of the Union of Myanmar, 336 Island Park Dr.
Ottawa, ON K1Y 0A7
Tel: 613-232-9990
meottawa@rogers.com
www.meottawa.org
His Excellency Hau Do Suan, Ambassador
U Soe Myint, Counsellor
Daw Khine Nyein Su, First Secretary

Republic of Namibia
High Commission for Namibia (to Canada), 1605 New Hampshire Ave. NW
Washington, DC 20009 USA
Tel: 202-986-0540; *Fax:* 202-986-0443
info@namibianembassyusa.org
www.namibianembassyusa.org
His Excellency Martin Andjaba, High Commissioner
Ulrich Freddie Gaoseb, Counsellor, Trade & Investment, gaoseb@namibianembassyusa.org
Aino Stella Kuume, First Secretary, Economic & Social, akuume@namibianembassyusa.org

Federal Democratic Republic of Nepal
Embassy of Nepal, 408 Queen St.
Ottawa, ON K1R 5A7
Tel: 613-680-5513; *Fax:* 613-422-5149
www.nepalembassy.ca
His Excellency Kali Prasad Pokhrel, Ambassador
Dilip Kumar Paudel, Counsellor & Deputy Head of Mission

Kingdom of the Netherlands
Embassy of the Netherlands, #2020, 350 Albert St.
Ottawa, ON K1R 1A4
Fax: 613-237-6471
Toll-Free: 877-388-2443
ottawa.the-netherlands.org
twitter.com/NLinCanada
www.facebook.com/the netherlandsincanada
His Excellency Cornelis Johannes Kole, Ambassador
Rochus Johannes Pieter Pronk, Minister & Deputy Head of Mission
Regina Maria Alida T. Aalders, Counsellor
Peter John Van Mechelen, Counsellor
L.Col. Christa Oppers-Beumer, Defence, Military, Naval & Air Attaché

New Zealand
New Zealand High Commission, #1401, 150 Elgin St.
Ottawa, ON K2P 1L4
Tel: 613-238-5991; *Fax:* 613-238-5707
info@nzhcottawa.org
www.nzembassy.com/canada
twitter.com/NZinOttawa
www.facebook.com/219970494714908
His Excellency Daniel John Mellsop, High Commissioner
Elizabeth Katherine H. Haliday, Deputy High Commissioner
Micaela Marie-Therese Buckley, Counsellor
Neil David Hallett, Counsellor
Chrisopher Gerard Howley, Counsellor
Charlotte Louise Kempthorne, Second Secretary

Republic of Nicaragua
Embassy of Nicaragua (to Canada), 1627 New Hamphire Ave. NW
Washington, DC 20009 USA
Tel: 202-939-6570; *Fax:* 202-939-6545
consuladodenicaragua.com
His Excellency Francisco Obadiah Campbell Hooker, Ambassador

Republic of Niger
Embassy of Niger (to Canada), 2204 R St. NW
Washington, DC 20008 USA
Tel: 202-483-4224; *Fax:* 202-483-9052
www.embassyofniger.org
Her Excellency Hassana Alidou, Ambassador

Federal Republic of Nigeria
High Commission for the Federal Republic of Nigeria, 295 Metcalfe St.
Ottawa, ON K2P 1R9
Tel: 613-236-0521; *Fax:* 613-236-0529
chancery@nigeriahcottawa.ca
www.nigeriahcottawa.ca
Ja'afar Mahmoud Balarabe, Minister & Chargé d'affaires, a.i.
Augustine Ndubuisi Ekeanyanwu, Minister
Oluremi Olutayo Oliyide, Minister

Kingdom of Norway
Embassy of the Kingdom of Norway, #1300, 130 Albert St.
Ottawa, ON K2P 1P1
Tel: 613-238-6571; *Fax:* 613-238-2765
emb.ottawa@mfa.no
www.emb-norway.ca
www.facebook.com/377624805683166
Her Excellency Anne Kari Hansen Ovind, Ambassador
Else Kveinen, Minister-Counsellor
Alf Hakon Hoel, Counsellor
Olafr Rosnes, Counsellor

Sultanate of Oman
Embassy of Oman (to Canada), 2535 Belmont Rd. NW
Washington, DC 20008 USA
Tel: 202-387-1980; *Fax:* 202-745-4933
inquiries@mofa.gov.om
www.culturaloffice.info
Her Excellency Hunaina Sultan Ahmed Al Mughairy, Ambassador
Silvana Bolocan, Second Secretary

Organization of the Eastern Caribbean States (OECS)
Eastern Caribbean Liaison Service in Toronto, #409, 200 Consumers Rd.
Toronto, ON M2J 4R4
Tel: 416-222-1988
ecls@oecs.org
www.oecs.org
The Organization of the Eastern Caribbean States includes Anguilla, Antigua & Barbuda, the British Virgin Islands, the Commonwealth of Dominica, Grenada, Montserrat, Federation of Saint Christopher & Nevis (Saint Kitts & Nevis), Saint Lucia, & Saint Vincent & the Grenadines.
The High Commission office in Ottawa closed permanently in

2011 & was replaced with the Eastern Caribbean Liaison Service, which is affiliated with the Canada/Caribbean Seasonal Agricultural Workers Programme.

Islamic Republic of Pakistan
High Commission for Pakistan, 10 Range Rd.
Ottawa, ON K1N 8J3
Tel: 613-238-7881; *Fax:* 613-238-7296
pahicottawa@mofa.gov.pk
www.mofa.gov.pk/ottawa
His Excellency Tariq Azim Khan, High Commissioner
Muhammad Saleem, Minister
Abrar Hussain Hashmi, Counsellor

Republic of Panama
Embassy of Panama, #300, 130 Albert St.
Ottawa, ON K1P 5G4
Tel: 613-236-7177; *Fax:* 613-236-5775
info@embassyofpanama.ca
www.embassyofpanama.ca
twitter.com/EmbPanamaCa nada
www.facebook.com/EmbPty
His Excellency Alberto Aristides Arosemena Medina, Ambassador

Papua New Guinea
High Commission of Papua New Guinea (to Canada), #805, 1779 Massachusetts Ave. NW
Washington, DC 20036 USA
Tel: 202-745-3680; *Fax:* 202-745-3679
info@pngembassy.org
www.pngembassy.org
His Excellency Rupa Abraham Mulina, Ambassador

Republic of Paraguay
Embassy of Paraguay, #501, 151 Slater St.
Ottawa, ON K1P 5H3
Tel: 613-567-1283; *Fax:* 613-567-1679
embassy@embassyofparaguay.ca
www.embassyofparaguay.ca
His Excellency Julio Cesar Arriola Ramirez, Ambassador
Alberto Esteban Caballero Gennari, Counsellor
Jose Antonio Giret Soto, Second Secretary

Republic of Peru
Embassy of Peru, #1901, 130 Albert St.
Ottawa, ON K1P 5G4
Tel: 613-238-1777; *Fax:* 613-232-3062
emperuca@bellnet.ca
www.embassyofperu.ca
Her Excellency Doraliza Marcela Lopez Bravo, Ambassador
Carlos Manuel Gil de Montes Molinari, Deputy Head of Mission
Cristian Steve Cordova Bocanegra, Counsellor
Bruno Mario Iriarte Noriega, Counsellor
Col. Eduardo Narcisho Malca Valverde, Assistant Military & Defence Attaché

Republic of the Philippines
Embassy of the Philippines, #900, 130 Albert St.
Ottawa, ON K1P 5G4
Tel: 613-233-1121; *Fax:* 613-233-4165
embassyofphilippines@rogers.com
philembassy.ca
twitter.com/PHembassyOt tawa
www.facebook.com/philippineembassy.ottawa
Her Excellency Petronila P. Garcia, Ambassador
Uriel Norman Garibay, Deputy Chief of Mission
Eric Gerardo Tamayo, Minister & Consul General
Flerida Ann Camille Mayo, Minister & Consul
Porfirio Jr. Mayo, Minister & Consul

Republic of Poland
Embassy of Poland, 443 Daly Ave.
Ottawa, ON K1N 6H3
Tel: 613-789-0468; *Fax:* 613-789-1218
ottawa.info@msz.gov.pl
ottawa.msz.gov.pl
www.youtube.com/user/PolishEmbassyCA
twitter.com/PLinCanada
www.facebo
ok.com/pages/Embassy-of-Poland-Ottawa/182626731781483
His Excellency Marcin Rafal Bosacki, Ambassador
Zbigniew Chmura, First Counsellor, Public & Cultural Diplomacy, zbigniew.chmura@msz.gov.pl
Lukasz Weremiuk, First Counsellor & Head, Political Unit, andrzej.fafara@msz.gov.pl
Olga Jablonska, First Secretary, Press & Protocol, olga.jablonska@msz.gov.pl
Tomasz Pawel Kijewski, Third Secretary, Economic Affairs, tomasz.kijewski@msz.gov.pl

Portuguese Republic
Embassy of Portugal, 645 Island Park Dr.
Ottawa, ON K1Y 0B8
Tel: 613-729-0883; *Fax:* 613-729-4236
ottawa@mne.pt
embportugalotava.blogspot.ca
twitter.com/embportugal_ca
www.facebook.com/embaixadadeportugal.otava
His Excellency Jose Fernando Moreira da Cunha, Ambassador
Manuel Filipe Pinhao Ramalheira, Counsellor

State of Qatar
Embassy of the State of Qatar, 150 Metcalfe St., 8th Fl.
Ottawa, ON K2P 1P1
Tel: 613-241-4917; *Fax:* 613-241-3304
ottawa@mofa.gov.qa
www.facebook.com/Qatarembassycanada
His Excellency Fahad Mohamed Y. Kafoud, Ambassador
Hussain Ali S. Al-Fadhala, First Secretary
Mirdef Ali M.A. Al-Qashouti, Second Secretary

Romania
Embassy of Romania, 655 Rideau St.
Ottawa, ON K1N 6A3
Tel: 613-789-3709; *Fax:* 613-789-4365
ottawa@mae.ro
ottawa.mae.ro/en
Her Excellency Maria Ligor, Ambassador
Adrian Ligor, Minister-Counsellor
Gabriel Petric, Counsellor
Silvana Bolocan, Second Secretary

Russian Federation
Embassy of the Russian Federation, 285 Charlotte St.
Ottawa, ON K1N 8L5
Tel: 613-235-4341; *Fax:* 613-236-6342
info@rusembassy.ca
www.rusembassy.ca
www.youtube.com/user/midrftube
twitter.com/russianembassyc
His Excellency Alexander N. Darchiev, Ambassador
Petr Plikhin, Minister-Counsellor
Yury Petrenko, Senior Counsellor
Oleg Pozdnyakov, Senior Counsellor
Alexander Ermishin, Counsellor
Sergey Strokov, Counsellor, Agricultural Division
Anton Vannovskiy, Counsellor, Science & Education Division

Republic of Rwanda
High Commission for the Republic of Rwanda, #404, 294 Albert St.
Ottawa, ON K1P 6E6
Tel: 613-569-5420; *Fax:* 613-569-5421
ambaottawa@minaffet.gov.rw
www.rwandahighcommission.ca
Shakilla K. Umutoni Umutoni, First Counsellor & Chargé d'Affaires
Eric Rutsindintwarane, First Secretary, erutsindintwarane@minaffet.gov.rw

Federation of Saint Kitts & Nevis
High Commission for the Federation of Saint Kitts & Nevis, 421 Besner St.
Ottawa, ON K1N 6H4
Her Excellency Shirley Rosemary Skerritt-Andrew, High Commissioner

Saint Lucia
See: **Organization of the Eastern Caribbean States**

Saint Vincent & the Grenadines
See: **Organization of the Eastern Caribbean States**

Independent State of Samoa
Samoa High Commission (to Canada), #400J, 800 - 2nd Ave.
New York, NY 10017 USA
Tel: 212-599-6196; *Fax:* 212-599-0797
samoa@un.int
His Excellency Ali'ioaiga Feturi Elisaia, High Commissioner

Republic of San Marino
c/o Permanent Mission of the Republic of San Marino to the UN, 327 East 50th St.
New York, NY 10022 USA
Tel: 212-751-1234; *Fax:* 212-751-1436
sanmarinoun@gmail.com
www.un.int/sanmarino
His Excellency Daniele D. Bodini, Permanent Representative

Democratic Republic of Sao Tomé & Principe
Embassy of the Democratic Republic of Sao Tomé & Principe, #1807, 675 - 3rd Ave.
New York, NY 10017 USA
pmstpun@gmail.com
Domingos Ferreira, First Secretary

Kingdom of Saudi Arabia
Royal Embassy of Saudi Arabia, 201 Sussex Dr.
Ottawa, ON K1N 1K6
Tel: 613-237-4100; *Fax:* 613-237-0567
caemb@mofa.gov.sa
embassies.mofa.gov.sa/sites/canada/AR/Pages/default.as px
His Excellency Naif Bandir A. Alsudairy, Ambassador & Consul General
Ali Abdullah O. Bahitham, Minister
Bandar Talal M. Al Rashid, Counsellor
Zaid Mukhlid Z. Alharbi, Counsellor
Salem Almansour, Counsellor
Khalid Youssef M. Alselmi, Counsellor
Nabeel A.S. Najjar, Counsellor

Republic of Senegal
Embassy of Senegal, 57 Marlborough Ave.
Ottawa, ON K1N 8E8
Tel: 613-238-6392; *Fax:* 613-238-2695
www.ambsencanada.org
His Excellency Ousmane Paye, Ambassador
Zaccaria Coulibaly, Minister-Counsellor
Babacar Matar Ndiaye, Minister-Counsellor
Saiba Sylla, First Counsellor
Aliou Diouf, Second Counsellor

Republic of Serbia
Embassy of the Republic of Serbia, 21 Blackburn Ave.
Ottawa, ON K1N 8A2 Canada
Tel: 613-233-6280; *Fax:* 613-233-7850
diplomat@serbianembassy.ca
www.ottawa.mfa.gov.rs
His Excellency Mihailo Papazoglu, Ambassador
Miodrag Sekulic, Counsellor, diaspora@serbianembassy.ca
Mirjana Sesum-Curcic, Counsellor, counsellor@serbianembassy.ca

Republic of Seychelles
High Commission for Seychelles (to Canada), #400C, 800 - 2nd Ave.
New York, NY 10017 USA
Tel: 212-972-1785; *Fax:* 212-972-1786
seychelles@un.int
Her Excellency Marie-Louise C. Potter, High Commissioner

Republic of Sierra Leone
High Commission for Sierra Leone (to Canada), 1701 - 19th St. NW
Washington, DC 20009 USA
Tel: 202-939-9261; *Fax:* 202-483-1793
info@embassyofsierraleone.net
embassyofsierraleone.net
twitter.com/sle mbassy_usa
www.facebook.com/sierraleoneembassy
His Excellency Bockari Kortu Stevens, Chief of Mission
Ibrahim Sorie Conteh, Deputy Chief of Mission
Edward Kawa, Second Secretary
Fatmatta Dao, Third Secretary

Republic of Singapore
c/o Ministry of Foreign Affairs, Tanglin
Tanglin, 248163 Singapore
Other contact information: Tel: 65-6379-8000; Fax: 65-6474-7885
His Excellency Heng Nee Philip Eng, High Commissioner

Slovak Republic / Slovenská Republika
Embassy of the Slovak Republic, 50 Rideau Terrace
Ottawa, ON K1M 2A1
Tel: 613-749-4442; *Fax:* 613-749-4989
emb.ottawa@mzv.sk
www.mzv.sk/ottawa
His Excellency Andrej Droba, Ambassador
Adriana Kolarikova, First Secretary

Republic of Slovenia
Embassy of Slovenia, #2200, 150 Metcalfe St.
Ottawa, ON K2P 1P1
Tel: 613-565-5781; *Fax:* 613-565-5783
sloembassy.ottawa@gov.si
ottawa.embassy.si
twitter.com/SLOinCAN
www. facebook.com/SlovenianEmbassyCanada
His Excellency Marjan Cencen, Ambassador
Irena Gril, Minister

Solomon Islands
High Commission c/o Permanent Mission to the UN, #400L, 800 - 2 Ave.
New York, NY 10017 USA
Tel: 212-599-6192; *Fax:* 212-661-8925
simun@solomons.com
www.un.int/solomonislands
His Excellency Collin David Beck, High Commissioner

Republic of South Africa
High Commission for the Republic of South Africa, 15 Sussex Dr.
Ottawa, ON K1M 1M8
Tel: 613-744-0330; *Fax:* 613-741-1639
rsafrica@southafrica-canada.ca
www.southafrica-canada.ca
twitter.com/S outhAfricanHC
www.facebook.com/214329748587991
His Excellency Membathisi Mphumzi S. Mdladlana, High Commissioner
Diedre Viljoen, Minister
Anesh Maistry, Counsellor
Wida Cloete, First Secretary
Tamara Ndaba, First Secretary

Republic of South Sudan
Embassy of South Sudan (to Canada), #300, 1015 - 31st St. NW
Washington, DC 20007 USA
Tel: 202-293-7940; *Fax:* 202-293-7941
www.southsudanembassydc.org
www.youtube.com/user/southsudanembassyDC
twitter.com/SSudanEmbassyDC
w ww.facebook.com/135992466585944
His Excellency Akec Khoc Aciew, Ambassador

Kingdom of Spain
Embassy of Spain, 74 Stanley Ave.
Ottawa, ON K1M 1P4
Tel: 613-747-2252; *Fax:* 613-744-1224
emb.ottawa@maec.es
www.exteriores.gob.es/embajadas/ottawa/en/Pages/inici o.aspx
His Excellency Carlos Gómez-Múgica Sanz, Ambassador
Sara Eugenia Ciriza Beortegui, Counsellor
Maria Jose Fabre Gonzalez, Counsellor
Miguel Angel Feito Hernandez, Counsellor
Francisco Xavier Gisbert da Cruz, Counsellor
David Gonzalez Vera, Counsellor

Democratic Socialist Republic of Sri Lanka
High Commission of the Democratic Socialist Republic of Sri Lanka, #1204, 333 Laurier Ave. West
Ottawa, ON K1P 1C1
Tel: 613-233-8449; *Fax:* 613-238-8448
slhcit@rogers.com
www.srilankahcottawa.org
His Excellency Ahmed Aflel Jawad, High Commissioner
Aratchige Don L. G. Kalansuriya, Minister
Saddha Waruna Wilpatha, Minister

Republic of The Sudan
Embassy of The Sudan, 354 Stewart St.
Ottawa, ON K1N 6K8
Tel: 613-235-4000; *Fax:* 613-235-6880
sudanembassy-canada@rogers.com
www.sudanembassy.ca/embassy_e.htm
Mahmoud Fadl A. Mohammed, Chargé d'affaires
Osman Abufatima Adam Mohammed, Deputy Head of Mission
Nura Osman M. Suleiman, First Secretary

Republic of Suriname
Embassy of Suriname (to Canada), Van Ness Center, #460, 4301 Connecticut Ave. NW
Washington, DC 20008 USA
Tel: 202-244-7488; *Fax:* 202-244-5878
www.surinameembassy.org
Humbert Ewald Eersel, Counsellor

Kingdom of Swaziland
High Commission for Swaziland (to Canada), 1712 New Hampshire Ave. NW
Washington, DC 20009 USA
Tel: 202-234-5002; *Fax:* 202-234-8254
His Excellency Abednego Mandla Ntshangase, High Commissioner
Lindiwe Cynthia Trizah Kunene, First Secretary

Kingdom of Sweden
Embassy of Sweden, #305, 377 Dalhousie St.
Ottawa, ON K1N 9N8
Tel: 613-244-8200; *Fax:* 613-241-2277
sweden.ottawa@gov.se
www.swedishembassy.ca
His Excellency Per Ola Sjögren, Ambassador
Jessica Hedin, Counsellor
Annica White, First Secretary, Administration & Consular Affairs

Swiss Confederation
Embassy of Switzerland, 5 Marlborough Ave.
Ottawa, ON K1N 8E6
Tel: 613-235-1837; *Fax:* 613-563-1394
ott.vertretung@eda.admin.ch
www.eda.admin.ch/canada
His Excellency Beat Walter Nobs, Ambassador
Barbara Schedler Fischer, Deputy Head of Mission
Annette Bettina Moser, First Secretary

Syrian Arab Republic
Embassy of Syria, 46 Cartier St.
Ottawa, ON K2P 1J3

Republic of China (ROC)
Also Known As: Taiwan
Taipei Economic & Cultural Office in Canada, World Exchange Plaza, #1960, 45 O'Connor St.
Ottawa, ON K1P 1A4
Tel: 613-231-5080; *Fax:* 613-231-7235
teco@taiwan-canada.org
www.roc-taiwan.org/CA
Represents the government of the Republic of China (Taiwan); offers consular services, as well as promoting bilateral trade, investment, culture, science & technology exchanges.
Frank Lin, Acting Representative

United Republic of Tanzania
High Commission of the United Republic of Tanzania, 50 Range Rd.
Ottawa, ON K1N 8J4
Tel: 613-232-1509; *Fax:* 613-232-5184
contact@tzrepottawa.ca
www.tzrepottawa.ca
His Excellency Jack Mugendi Zoka, High Commissioner
Paul James Makelele, Second Secretary

Kingdom of Thailand
Royal Thai Embassy, 180 Island Park Dr.
Office of Commercial Affairs: 31 Gloucester St., Toronto ON M4Y 1L8
Ottawa, ON K1Y 0A2
Tel: 613-722-4444; *Fax:* 613-722-6624
contact@thaiembassy.ca
www.thaiembassy.ca
His Excellency Vijavat Isarabhakdi, Ambassador
Nantana Sivakua, Minister & Deputy Chief of Mission
Benjamin Sukanjanajtee, Minister-Counsellor
Aidsada Sundaramani, Counsellor, Consular Affairs
Adisak Jantatum, First Secretary, Int'l Organizations, Political & Economic Affairs
Chalatip Apiwattananon, Second Secretary, Administrative & Accounting

Democratic Republic of Timor-Leste
Embassy of the Democratic Republic of Timor-Leste (to Canada), #504, 4201 Connecticut Ave. NW
Washington, DC 20008 USA
Tel: 202-966-3202; *Fax:* 202-966-3202
info@timorlesteembassy.org
www.timorlesteembassy.org
His Excellency Domingos Sarmento Alves, Ambassador

Togolese Republic
Embassy of the Togolese Republic, 12 Range Rd.
Ottawa, ON K1N 8J3
Tel: 613-238-5916; *Fax:* 613-235-6425
His Ecxellency Kokou Kpayedo, Ambassador
Ayite Alexis Ange Atayi, First Secretary

Kingdom of Tonga
High Commission for the Kingdom of Tonga (to Canada), 250 East 51st St.
New York, NY 10022 USA
Tel: 917-369-1025; *Fax:* 917-369-1024
His Excellency Mahe Uliuli Sandhurst Tupouniua, High Commissioner

Republic of Trinidad & Tobago
High Commission for the Republic of Trinidad & Tobago, 200 - 1st Ave.
Ottawa, ON K1S 2G6
Tel: 613-232-2418; *Fax:* 613-232-4349
ottawa@ttmissions.com
www.ttmissions.com
Venessa Ramhit-Ramroop, First Secretary & Acting High Commissioner
Liana Elizabeth Sukhbir, Second Secretary

Republic of Tunisia
Embassy of the Republic of Tunisia, 515 O'Connor St.
Ottawa, ON K1S 3P8
Tel: 613-237-0330; *Fax:* 613-237-7939
ambtun13@bellnet.ca
His Excellency Riadh Essid, Ambassador
Borhene El Kamel, Minister
Kadri Mahmoudi, Counsellor
Lotfi Trabelsi, Counsellor

Republic of Turkey
Embassy of the Republic of Turkey, 197 Wurtemburg St.
Ottawa, ON K1N 8L9
Tel: 613-244-2470; *Fax:* 613-789-3442
embassy.ottawa@mfa.gov.tr
ottava.be.mfa.gov.tr
twitter.com/TurkEmbOtta wa
www.facebook.com/TurkishEmbassyInOttawa
His Excellency Selcuk Unal, Ambassador
Gulcan Akoguz, Minister-Counsellor
Muammer Hakan Cengiz, Counsellor
Serdar Ulker, Counsellor
Emir Polat Ogun, First Secretary
Ali Murat Akpinar, Second Secretary
Fulya Kucukdag Ozen, Second Secretary
Serkan Ozdemir, Second Secretary
Erim Ozen, Second Secretary

Republic of Turkmenistan
Embassy of the Republic of Turkmenistan, 2207 Massachussets Ave. NW
Washington, DC 20008 USA
Tel: 202-588-1500; *Fax:* 202-588-0697

Tuvalu
c/o Permanent Mission of Tuvalu to the UN, #400D, 800 - 2nd Ave.
New York, NY 10017 USA
Tel: 212-490-0534; *Fax:* 212-808-4975
tuvalu.un@gmail.com
www.un.int/tuvalu
His Excellency Aunese Makoi Simati, Permanent Representative

Republic of Uganda
High Commission for Uganda, #1210, 350 Sparks St.
Ottawa, ON K1R 7S8
Tel: 613-789-7797; *Fax:* 613-789-8909
uhc@ugandahighcommission.com
www.ugandahighcommission.com
His Excellency John Chrysostom Alintuma Nsambu, High Commissioner
Margaret Lucy Kyogire, Deputy Head of Mission
Elizabeth Beatrice Wamanga, Minister-Counsellor
Tazenya Allan, Second Secretary

Ukraine
Embassy of Ukraine, 310 Somerset St. West
Ottawa, ON K2P 0J9
Tel: 613-230-2961; *Fax:* 613-230-2400
emb_ca@ukremb.ca
canada.mfa.gov.ua
His Excellency Andrii Shevchenko, Ambassador
Marko Shevchenko, Counsellor
Oleksandr Bunisevych, First Secretary
Zoriana Stsiban, Second Secretary

United Arab Emirates
Embassy of the United Arab Emirates, 125 Boteler St.
Ottawa, ON K1N 0A4
Tel: 613-565-7272; *Fax:* 613-565-8007
www.uae-embassy.ae/Embassies/ca
His Excellency Mohammed Saif Helal M. Al shehhi, Ambassador
Hamad A. Yousef Ali Alawadi, Counsellor
Ibtisam Saleh A. A. Alali, Second Secretary

United Kingdom
British High Commission, 80 Elgin St.
Ottawa, ON K1P 5K7
Tel: 613-237-1530; *Fax:* 613-232-0738
ukincanada@fco.gov.uk
www.gov.uk/government/world/organisations/british-high-commission-ottawa
www.flickr.com/ukincanada
twitter.com/ukincanada
www.facebook.com/ukincanada
His Excellency Howard Ronald Drake, High Commissioner OBE
Thomas Barry, Deputy Head of Mission
Anthony Julian Coulter, Counsellor
Christian Michael Cook, First Secretary
Sarah Lucy Horton, First Secretary
Julia Elizabeth Nolan, First Secretary
Beth Dyson, Second Secretary
Marc James Leslie, Second Secretary
Jacqueline Susanna Richards, Second Secretary

Brig. Jonathan David Calder-Smith, Defence Adviser

United States of America
Embassy of the United States of America, 490 Sussex Dr.
Ottawa, ON K1N 1G8
Tel: 613-238-5335; *Fax:* 613-688-3082
canada.usembassy.gov
www.youtube.com/user/USEmbassyOttawa
twitter.com/usembassyottawa
www.f acebook.com/canada.usembassy
His Excellency Bruce Alan Heyman, Ambassador
Richard M. Sanders, Deputy Chief of Mission
Matthew Gordon Boyse, Minister-Counsellor
Russel John Brown, Minister-Counsellor
Thomas Raymond Favret, Minister-Counsellor
Holly Sue Higgins, Minister-Counsellor
Elizabeth Kay Mayfield, Minister-Counsellor
Christopher Ronald Quinlivan, Minister-Counsellor
Steven Edward Zate, Minister-Counsellor

Eastern Republic of Uruguay
Embassy of Uruguay, #901, 350 Sparks St.
Ottawa, ON K1R 7S8
Tel: 613-234-2727; *Fax:* 613-233-4670
urucanada@mrree.gub.uy
www.embassyofuruguay.ca
Trilce Gervaz Muniz, Second Secretary & Chargé d'Affaires a.i.

Republic of Uzbekistan
Embassy of the Republic of Uzbekistan, 1746 Massachusetts Ave. NW
Washington, DC 20036 USA
Tel: 202-887-5300; *Fax:* 202-293-6804
info@uzbekistan.org
www.uzbekistan.org
His Excellency Bakhtiyar Gulyamov, Ambassador

Republic of Venezuela
Embassy of Venezuela, 32 Range Rd.
Ottawa, ON K1N 8J4
Tel: 613-235-5151; *Fax:* 613-235-3205
embve.caotw@mppre.gob.ve
www.misionvenezuela.org
His Excellency Wilmer Omar Barrientos Barrientos Fernandez, Ambassador
Angel Herrera, Second Secretary, Commercial & Political Section
Andrés Useche, Second Secretary, Consular & Administrative Section
Jissette Abreu, Second Secretary, Cultural Section

Socialist Republic of Vietnam
Embassy of Vietnam, 55 Mackay St.
Ottawa, ON K1M 2B2
Tel: 613-236-0772; *Fax:* 613-236-2704
vietem-inter@uniserve.com
vietem-ca.com
His Excellency To Anh Dung, Ambassador
Hung Son Nguyen, Minister-Counsellor, Political & Economic
Dung Hoang Anh, Counsellor
Duc Thien Le, First Secretary, Consular
Dang Huy Nguyen, Second Secretary

Republic of Yemen
Embassy of the Republic of Yemen, 54 Chamberlain Ave.
Ottawa, ON K1S 1V9
Tel: 613-729-6627; *Fax:* 613-729-8915
yeminfo@yemenembassy.ca
www.yemenembassy.ca
www.facebook.com/205072892 918967
Ahmed Ali Yahya Al-Enad, Chargé d'Affaires, a.i., Ambassador@yemenembassy.ca
Radowan Ahmed A. Alfutini, Third Secretary

Republic of Zambia
High Commission for Zambia (to Canada), #205, 151 Slater St.
Ottawa, ON K1B 5H3
Tel: 613-232-4400; *Fax:* 613-232-4410
zhc.ottawa@bellnet.ca
www.zambiahighcommission.ca
Evaristo D. Kasunga, Chargé d'affaires, a.i.
Grace Chintu Ng'andu, First Secretary
Chrispin Nchimunya Chibawe, First Secretary
Musata Kaunda Banda, Second Secretary
Winstone Bwalya, Second Secretary
Jennifer Konjela Manda, Third Secretary

Republic of Zimbabwe
Embassy for the Republic of Zimbabwe, 332 Somerset St. West
Ottawa, ON K2P 0J9
Tel: 613-421-1242; *Fax:* 613-422-7403
www.zimottawa.com
Her Excellency Florence Zano Chideya, Ambassador
Barbra Chimhandamba, Counsellor
Admire Hwata, Counsellor
Epiphania Kwari, Second Secretary
Dorcas Mugadza, Third Secretary

Diplomatic & Consular Representatives Abroad

Islamic State of Afghanistan
Embassy of Canada, House 256, St. 15, Wazir-Akbar-Khan
Kabul, Afghanistan
kabul@international.gc.ca
www.afghanistan.gc.ca
twitter.com/CanEmbAFG
Other contact information: Tel: 93 (0) 701 108 800; Fax: 93 (0) 701 108 805
Kenneth Neufeld, Ambassador

Republic of Albania
***See:* Italian Republic**

People's Democratic Republic of Algeria
Embassy of Canada, PO Box 464 Ben Aknon, 18 Mustapha Khalef St.
Algiers, 16306 Algeria
alger@international.gc.ca
www.algerie.gc.ca
twitter.com/CanadaAlgeria
www.facebook.com/CanadaAlgeria
Other contact information: Phone: 213 (0) 770-083-000; Fax: 213 (0) 770-083-070
Isabelle Roy, Ambassador
Rachid Benhacine, Trade Commissioner, Environmental Industries

American Samoa
Australian High Commission, PO Box 704, Beach Rd.
Apia, Samoa
samoa.embassy.gov.au/apia/home.html
Other contact information: Tel: 68 5 23 411; Fax: 68 5 23 159
Under the Canada-Australia Consular Services Sharing Agreement, the High Commission of Australia will serve Canadians abroad.
Sue Langford, High Commissioner

Principality of Andorra
***See:* Kingdom of Spain**

People's Republic of Angola
***See:* Republic of Zimbabwe**

Anguilla
***See:* Barbados**

Antigua & Barbuda
***See:* Barbados**

Argentine Republic
Canadian Embassy, Tagle 2828
Buenos Aires, C1425EEH Argentine
bairs-webmail@international.gc.ca
www.argentina.gc.ca
twitter.com/CanadaArgentina
www.facebook.com/CanadainArgentina
Other contact information: Tel: 54 (11) 4808-1000; Fax: 54 (11) 4808-1111
Robert Fry, Ambassador
Alejandro D'Agostino, Trade Commissioner, Environmental Industries

Republic of Armenia
***See:* Russian Federation**

Aruba
***See:* Republic of Venezuela**

Commonwealth of Australia
High Commission of Canada, Commonwealth Ave.
Canberra, ACT 2600 Australia
cnbra@international.gc.ca
www.australia.gc.ca
twitter.com/CanHCAustralia
Other contact information: Phone: (02) 6270-4000; Fax: (02) 6270-4081
Paul Maddison, High Commissioner
Charles Reeves, Deputy High Commissioner
Justin Wallace, Counsellor
Louis-Martin Aumais, Counsellor
Dean Barry, Counsellor, Immigration
Christian Dussault, Counsellor
Michael Lazaruk, Counsellor, Commercial
Peter Lambertucci, Counsellor, RCMP
Steve Gagné, Counsellor, Management & Consul
David Ingham, Trade Commissioner, Environmental Industries, david.ingham@international.gc.ca

Republic of Austria
Embassy of Canada, Laurenzerberg 2
Vienna, A-1010 Austria
vienn@international.gc.ca
www.austria.gc.ca
twitter.com/CanAmbAustria
www.facebook.com/CanadainAustria
Mark Bailey, Ambassador
Susanne Knobloch, Trade Commissioner, Environmental Industries, vienn-td@international.gc.ca

Republic of Azerbaijan
***See:* Republic of Turkey**

Autonomous Region of the Azores
***See:* Portuguese Republic**

Commonwealth of the Bahamas
***See:* Jamaica**

Kingdom of Bahrain
***See:* Kingdom of Saudi Arabia**

People's Republic of Bangladesh
Canadian High Commission, United Nations Road, Baridhara
Dhaka, 1212 Bangladesh
dhakag@international.gc.ca
www.bangladesh.gc.ca
www.facebook.com/CanadaInBangladesh
Other contact information: Phone: 880 2 5566 8444; Fax: 880 2 5566 8423
Benoît-Pierre Laramée, High Commissioner
Kamal Uddin, Trade Commissioner, Environmental Industries, kamal.uddin@international.gc.ca

Barbados
Canadian High Commission, PO Box 404, Bishop's Court Hill
Bridgetown, BB11000 Barbados
Tel: 246-429-3550
bdgtn@international.gc.ca
www.barbados.gc.ca
twitter.com/CanHCBarbados
www.facebook.com/Canadain Barbados
Marie Legault, High Commissioner
Marc Parisien, Senior Trade Commissioner, Environmental Industries, marc.parisien@international.gc.ca

Republic of Belarus
***See:* Republic of Poland**

Kingdom of Belgium
Embassy of Canada, 2, av de Tervuren
Brussels, 1040 Belgium
bru@international.gc.ca
www.belgium.gc.ca
Other contact information: Phone: 32 2 741 0611; Fax: 32 2 741 0643
Olivier Nicoloff, Ambassador
Fabienne De Kimpe, Trade Commissioner, Environmental Industries, fabienne.de-kimpe@international.gc.ca

Belize
***See:* Republic of Guatemala**

Republic of Benin
***See:* Burkina Faso**

Bermuda
***See:* United States of America**

Kingdom of Bhutan
***See:* Republic of India**

Republic of Bolivia
***See:* Republic of Peru**

Bonaire
***See:* Republic of Venezuela**

Bosnia & Herzegovina
***See:* Republic of Austria**

Republic of Botswana
***See:* Republic of Zimbabwe**

Federative Republic of Brazil
Canadian Embassy, SES-Av. das Naçeõs - Qd. 803 - Lote 16
Brasilia, D.F., 70410-900 Brazil
brsla@international.gc.ca
www.brazil.gc.ca
twitter.com/canadabrazil
www.facebook.com/CanadainBrazil
Other contact information: Tel: (5561) 3424-5400; Fax: (5561) 3424-5490
Rick Savone, Ambassador
Stéphane Larue, Consul-General
Evelyne Coulombe, Consul-General
Angela Santos, Trade Commissioner, Environmental Industries, commerce.br@international.gc.ca

British Virgin Islands
***See:* Barbados**

Brunei Darussalam
Canadian High Commission, PO Box 2808
Located at Jalan McArthur Building, No. 1, Jalan McArthur, 5th Fl., Bandar Seri Begawan BS 8711
Bandar Seri Begawan, BS8675 Brunei Darussalam
bsbgn@international.gc.ca
www.brunei.gc.ca
www.facebook.com/313058828859778
Other contact information: Tel: 673 (2) 22-00-43; Fax: 673 (2) 22-00-40
Marina Laker, High Commissioner
Eva Eng Chin Ng, Trade Commissioner, EvaEngChin.Ng@international.gc.ca

Republic of Bulgaria
***See:* Republic of Romania**

Republic of Burundi
***See:* Republic of Kenya**

Kingdom of Cambodia
***See:* Thailand**

Republic of Cameroon
High Commission of Canada, PO Box 572
Yaoundé, Cameroon
yunde@international.gc.ca
www.canadainternational.gc.ca/cameroon-cameroun
Other contact information: Phone: 237 222-203-900; Fax: 237 222-503-904
René Cremonese, High Commissioner
Jude Bijingsi, Trade Commissioner, Environmental Industries, yunde-td@international.gc.ca

Canary Islands
***See:* Kingdom of Spain**

Republic of Cabo Verde
***See:* Republic of Senegal**

Cayman Islands
***See:* Jamaica**

Central African Republic
***See:* Republic of Cameroon**

Republic of Chad
***See:* Republic of The Sudan**

Republic of Chile
Canadian Embassy, Cassilla 139, Correo 10
Santiago, Chile
stago@international.gc.ca
www.chile.gc.ca
twitter.com/CanEmbChile
www.facebook.com/CanadainChile
Other contact information: Tel: 56 (2) 2652-3800; Fax: 56 (2) 2652-3912
Marcel Lebleu, Ambassador
Geoff White, Counsellor, Commercial
Gonzalo Munoz, Trade Commissioner, Environmental Industries, santiago.commerce@international.gc.ca

People's Republic of China
Canadian Embassy, 19 Dong Zhi Men Wai St., Chao Yang Dist.
Beijing, 100600 China
beijing-pa@international.gc.ca
www.beijing.gc.ca
Other contact information: Tel: 86 (10) 5139-4000; Fax: 86 (10) 5139-4448
Guy Saint-Jacques, Ambassador
Melanie Klingbeil, Trade Commissioner, Environmental Industries, infocentrechina@international.gc.ca

Republic of Colombia
Canadian Embassy, Carrera 7, No. 114-33
Bogota, Colombia
bgota@international.gc.ca
www.colombia.gc.ca
twitter.com/CanadaColombia
www.facebook.com/CanadainColombia
Other contact information: Tel: 57 (1) 657-9800; Fax: 57 (1) 657-9912
Donald Bobiash, Ambassador
Nancy Duran, Trade Commissioner, Environmental Industries, bogotatd@international.gc.ca

Union of the Comoros
***See:* United Republic of Tanzania**

Democratic Republic of the Congo
Canadian Embassy to the Democratic Republic of the Congo, PO Box 8341
Street Address: 17, av Pumbu, Commune de la Gambe, Kinshasa, Democratic Republic of Congo
Kinshasa, 1 Congo (Kinshasa)
knsha@international.gc.ca
www.canadainternational.gc.ca/congo
Other contact information: Tel: 243-996-021-500; Fax: 243-996-021-510
Ginette Martin, Ambassador
Guy-Olivier Mantomina, Trade Commissioner

Cook Islands
***See:* New Zealand**

Republic of Costa Rica
Canadian Embassy, PO Box 351-1007 Centro Colón
San José, Costa Rica
sjcra@international.gc.ca
www.costarica.gc.ca
twitter.com/CanEmbChile
www.facebook.com/233889133466393
Other contact information: Tel: 506 2242-4400; Fax: 506 2242-4410
Michael Gort, Ambassador
Adolfo Quesada, Trade Commissioner, Environmental Industries, adolfo.quesada@international.gc.ca

Republic of Côte d'Ivoire
Canadian Embassy, Immeuble Trade Centre, 23, av Nogues, 6th & 7th Fls., Le Plateau
Abidjan, Ivory Coast
abdjn@international.gc.ca
www.canadainternational.gc.ca/cotedivoire
Other contact information: Tel: 225-20 30 07 00; Fax: 225-20 30 07 20
Patricia McCullagh, Ambassador

Republic of Croatia
Canadian Embassy, Prilaz Gjure Dezelica 4
Zagreb, 10 000 Croatia
zagrb@international.gc.ca
www.canadainternational.gc.ca/croatia-croatie
twitter.com/CanadaCroatia
www.facebook.com/CanadainCroatia
Other contact information: Tel: 385-1-488-1200; Fax: 385-1-488-1230
Daniel Maksymiuk, Ambassador
Synthia Dodig, Trade Commissioner, Environmental Industries, synthia.dodig@international.gc.ca

Republic of Cuba
Canadian Embassy, Calle 30, No. 518, Esquina 7a, Miramar
Havana, Cuba
havan@international.gc.ca
www.canadainternational.gc.ca/cuba
twitter.com/CanEmbCuba
Other contact information: Tel: 53-7-204-2516; Fax: 53-7-204-2044
Patrick Parisot, Ambassador
David Verbiwski, Counsellor & Senior Trade Commissioner, david.verbiwski@international.gc.ca
Francisco Rodriguez, Trade Commissioner, Environmental Industries, francisco.rodriguez@international.gc.ca

Republic of Cyprus
***See:* Hellenic Republic**

Czech Republic
Canadian Embassy, Ve Struhach 95/2
Prague, 160 00 Czech Republic
canada@canada.cz
www.canadainternational.gc.ca/czech-tcheque
twitter.com/canembcz
www.f acebook.com/KanadaCZ
Other contact information: Tel: 420 272 101 800; Fax: 420 272 101 890

Barbara Richardson, Ambassador
Martina Taxova, Trade Commissioner, Environmental Industries, martina.taxova@international.gc.ca

Kingdom of Denmark
Canadian Embassy, Kristen Bernikowsgade 1
Copenhagen, K-1105 Denmark
copen@international.gc.ca
www.canadainternational.gc.ca/denmark-danemark
twitter.com/CanadaDenmark
Other contact information: Tel: 45-33-48-32-00; Fax: 45-33-48-32-20
Emi Furuya, Ambassador
David Horup, Trade Commissioner, Environmental Industries, NordiCommerce@international.gc.ca

Republic of Djibouti
***See:* Federal Democratic Republic of Ethiopia**

Commonwealth of Dominica
***See:* Barbados**

Dominican Republic
Torre Citigroup en Acrópolis Center, Av. Winston Churchill 1099, piso 18
Santo Domingo, Dominican Republic
Tel: 809-262-3100; *Fax:* 809-262-3155
sdmgo@international.gc.ca
www.canadainternational.gc.ca/dominican_republic-republique_dominicaine
twitter.com/CanEmbDR
www.facebook.com/285332 761634064
Steve Côté, Ambassador
Regis Batista-Lemaire, Trade Commissioner, Environmental Industries, sdmgotd@international.gc.ca

Republic of Ecuador
PO Box 17-11-6512
Street Address: Av. Amazonas 4153 y Union Nacional de Periodistas, Edificio Eurocenter, 3 piso, Quito, Ecuador
Quito, Ecuador
quito@international.gc.ca
www.canadainternational.gc.ca/ecuador-equateur
twitter.com/CanadaEcuador
www.facebook.com/CanadainEcuador
Other contact information: Tel: (011 593 2) 2455-499; Fax: (011 593 2) 2277-672
Marianick Tremblay, Ambassador
Ricardo Valdez, Trade Commissioner, Environmental Industries, ricardo.valdez@international.gc.ca

Arab Republic of Egypt
Nile City Towers, South Tower, 2005 (A) Corniche El Nile, 18th Fl.
Cairo, 11221 Egypt
cairo@international.gc.ca
www.canadainternational.gc.ca/egypt-egypte
twitter.com/CanEmbEgypt
www .facebook.com/727169163982678
Other contact information: Tel: 20 2 2461-2200; Fax: 20 2 2461-2201
Troy Lulashnyk, Ambassador
Joseph Tadros, Trade Commissioner, Environmental Industries, cairo-td@international.gc.ca

Republic of El Salvador
Canadian Embassy, Edificio Centro Financiero Gigante, Alameda Roosevelt y 63 Avenida Sur, Nivel Lobby 2, Loca
San Salvador, El Salvador
ssal@international.gc.ca
www.canadainternational.gc.ca/el_salvador-salvador
twitter.com/CanEmbSV
www.facebook.com/CanadainElSalvador
Other contact information: Tel: 503-2279-4655; Fax: 503-2279-0765
Maryse Guilbeault, Ambassador
Romeo Calderón, Trade Commisioner

England
***See:* United Kingdom of Great Britain & Northern Ireland**

Republic of Equatorial Guinea
***See:* Federal Republic of Nigeria**

Eritrea
***See:* Republic of The Sudan**

Republic of Estonia
Office of the Canadian Embassy, Toom Kooli 13
Tallinn, 15186 Estonia
Tel: 372-627-3311; *Fax:* 372-627-3312
tallinn@canada.ee
www.canada.ee
twitter.com/CanadaEstonia
Alain Hausser, Ambassador

Federal Democratic Republic of Ethiopia
Canadian Embassy, PO Box 1130
Street Address: Old Airport Area, Nefas Silk Lafto Sub City, Kebele 04, #122, Addis Ababa, Ethiopia
Addis Ababa, Ethiopia
addis@international.gc.ca
www.canadainternational.gc.ca/ethiopia-ethiopie
www.facebook.com/1603079 529915945
Other contact information: Tel: 251-11-317-0000; Fax: 251-11-317-0040
Philip Baker, Ambassador
Barnesh Mesfin Teshome, Trade Commissioner, Environmental Industries

European Union
The Mission of Canada to the European Union, 2, av de Tervuren
Brussels, 1040 Belgium
breu@international.gc.ca
www.canadainternational.gc.ca/eu-ue
Other contact information: Tel: 32 0(2) 741 0660; Fax: 32 0(2) 741 0629
Daniel Costello, Ambassador
Alan Bowman, Minister-Counsellor & Deputy Head of Mission
Michelle Cooper, Counsellor & Section Head, Agriculture
Lorraine Diguer, Counsellor & Section Head, Foreign Policy, Diplomacy & Public Affairs
Duncan de Lugt, First Secretary, Trade Policy & Commercial Affairs

Republic of the Fiji Islands
***See:* New Zealand**

Republic of Finland
Canadian Embassy, PO Box 779
Street Address: Pohjoisesplanadi 27C, 00100 Helsinki, Finland
Helsinki, 00101 Finland
hsnki@international.gc.ca
www.canadainternational.gc.ca/finland-finlande
twitter.com/CanEmbFinland
Other contact information: Tel: 358-9-228-530; Fax: 358-9-2285-3385
Andrée Noëlle Cooligan, Ambassador
Seppo Vihersaari, Trade Commissioner, Environmental Industries, NordiCommerce@international.gc.ca

French Republic
Canadian Embassy, 35, av Montaigne
Paris, 75008 France
www.canadainternational.gc.ca/france
twitter.com/CanEmbFrance
Other contact information: Tel: 33-1-44-43-29-00; Fax: 33-1-44-43-29-99
Lawrence Cannon, Ambassador
Denis Trottier, Trade Commissioner, Environmental Industries, france-td@international.gc.ca

Gabonese Republic
***See:* Republic of Cameroon**

Republic of the Gambia
***See:* Republic of Senegal**

Georgia
***See:* Republic of Turkey**

Federal Republic of Germany
Canadian Embassy, Leipziger Platz 17
Berlin, D-10117 Germany
www.canadainternational.gc.ca/germany-allemagne
twitter.com/CanEmbGermany
www.facebook.com/795153663847541
Other contact information: Tel: 49-30-20-312-0
Marie Gervais-Vidricaire, Ambassador
Richard Tarasofsky, Commercial Counsellor & Trade Commissioner, Environmental Industries, deutschland.commerce@international.gc.ca

Republic of Ghana
Canadian High Commission, PO Box 1639, 42 Independence Ave.
Accra, Ghana
accra@international.gc.ca
www.canadainternational.gc.ca/ghana
Other contact information: Tel: 011 233 302 211521; Fax: 011 233 302 211523
Heather Cameron, High Commissioner
Peter Fiamor, Trade Commissioner, Environmental Industries, peter.fiamor@international.gc.ca

Grenada
***See:* Barbados**

Saint Vincent & the Grenadines
***See:* Barbados**

Republic of Guatemala
Canadian Embassy, PO Box 400
Street Address: Edificio Edyma Plaza, 13 Calle 8-44, Zone 10, Guatemala City, Guatamala
Guatemala City, Guatemala
gtmla@international.gc.ca
www.canadainternational.gc.ca/guatemala
www.facebook.com/CanadainGuatema la
Other contact information: Tel: 502 2363-4348; Fax: 502 2365-1210
Deborah Chatsis, Ambassador
Christine Luttmann, Trade Commissioner, Environmental Industries, christine.luttmann@international.gc.ca

Republic of Guinea-Bissau
***See:* Republic of Senegal**

Co-operative Republic of Guyana
Canadian High Commission, PO Box 10880
Street Address: High & Young Sts., Kingston, Georgetown, Guyana
Georgetown, Guyana
Tel: 592-227-2081; *Fax:* 592-225-8380
grgtn@international.gc.ca
www.canadainternational.gc.ca/guyana
twitter .com/canambguyana
www.facebook.com/CanadainGuyanaandSuriname
Pierre Giroux, High Commissioner

Republic of Haiti
Delmas Rd.
Port-au-Prince, Haiti
prnce@international.gc.ca
www.canadainternational.gc.ca/haiti
twitter.com/CanEmbHaiti
www.facebo ok.com/CanadainHaiti
Other contact information: Tel: 011 (509) 2249-9000; Fax: 011 (509) 2249-9920
Paula Caldwell St. Onge, Ambassador
Emmanuel Choute, Trade Commissioner, Environmental Industries, emmanuel.choute@international.gc.ca

Hellenic Republic
Canadian Embassy, 48 Ethnikis Antistaseos St.
Chalandri, 152 31 Athens Greece
athns@international.gc.ca
www.canadainternational.gc.ca/greece-grece
www.facebook.com/CanadainGree ce
Other contact information: Tel: 30-210-727-3400; Fax: 30-210-727-3480
Keith Morrill, Ambassador
David Mallette, Senior Trade Commissioner

Holy See
Canadian Embassy, Via della Conciliazione 4/D
Rome, 00193 Italy
vatcn@international.gc.ca
www.canadainternational.gc.ca/holy_see-saint_siege
twitter.com/CanadaHol ySee
Other contact information: Tel: 39-06-6830-7316; Fax: 39-06-6880-6283
Dennis Savoie, Ambassador

Republic of Honduras
Canadian Embassy, PO Box 3552
Tegucigalpa, Honduras
tglpa@international.gc.ca
www.canadainternational.gc.ca/costa_rica
www.facebook.com/23388913346639 3
Other contact information: Tel: 504 2232 4551; Fax: 504 2239 7767
Michael Gort, Ambassador
Adolfo Quesada, Trade Commissioner, Environmental Industries, adolfo.quesada@international.gc.ca

Hungary
Canadian Embassy, Ganz U. 12-14
Budapest, 1027 Hungary
bpest@international.gc.ca
www.canadainternational.gc.ca/hungary-hongrie
Other contact information: Tel: 36-1-392-3360; Fax: 36-1-392-3390
Isabelle Poupart, Ambassador
Gergely Morvai, Trade Commissioner, Environmental Industries, gergely.morvai@international.gc.ca

Iceland
Túngata 14
Reykjavik, 101 Iceland
Tel: 354-575-6500; *Fax:* 354-575-6501
rkjvk@international.gc.ca
www.canadainternational.gc.ca/iceland-islande
twitter.com/CanadaIceland
www.facebook.com/CanadaIceland
Anne-Tamara Lorre, Ambassador
Saemundur Finnbogason, Trade Commissioner, Environmental Industries

Republic of India
Canadian High Commission, 7/8 Shantipath, Chanakyapuri
New Delhi, 110021 India
delhi@international.gc.ca
www.canadainternational.gc.ca/india-inde
www.youtube.com/user/CanadaInIndia
twitter.com/CanadaInIndia
www.faceb ook.com/CanadaInIndia
Other contact information: Tel: 91-11-4178-2000; Fax: 91-11-4178-2020
Nadir Patel, High Commissioner
Saibal Ghosh, Trade Commissioner, Environmental Industries, india.commerce@international.gc.ca

Republic of Indonesia
Canadian Embassy, PO Box 8324/JKS.MP
Street Address: World Trade Centre I, 6th Fl., Jalan Jenderal Sudirman Kav. 29-31, Jakarta 12920, Indonesia
Jakarta, 12083 Indonesia
canadianembassy.jkrta@international.gc.ca
www.canadainternational.gc.ca/indonesia-indonesie
twitter.com/CanEmbIndo nesia
www.facebook.com/CanadainIndonesia
Other contact information: Tel: 62-21-2550-7800; Fax: 62-21-2550-7811
Peter MacArthur, Ambassador
Irnawati Irnawati, Trade Commissioner, Environmental Industries, irnawati.irnawati@international.gc.ca

Republic of Iraq
***See:* Hashemite Kingdom of Jordan**

Republic of Ireland
Canadian Embassy, 7-8 Wilton Terrace
Dublin, 2 Ireland
dubln@international.gc.ca
www.canadainternational.gc.ca/ireland-irlande
Other contact information: Tel: 353-1-234-4000; Fax: 353-1-234-4001
Kevin Vickers, Ambassador
Noami Gilker, Vice Consul
Gerry Mongey, Trade Commissioner, Environmental Industries, gerry.mongey@international.gc.ca

State of Israel
Canadian Embassy, PO Box 9442
Tel Aviv, 6706038 Israel
taviv@international.gc.ca
www.canadainternational.gc.ca/israel
twitter.com/CanEmbIsrael
www.face book.com/CanadaInIsrael
Other contact information: Tel: (011 972 3) 636-3300; Fax: (011 972 3) 636-3380
Deborah Lyons, Ambassador
Ralph Jansen, Deputy Head of Mission
Rebecca Shafrir, Trade Commissioner, Environmental Industries, rebecca.shafrir@international.gc.ca

Italian Republic
Canadian Embassy, Villa Grazioli, Via Salaria 243
Rome, 00199 Italy
www.canadainternational.gc.ca/italy-italie
twitter.com/CanadaInItaly
www.facebook.com/CanadaInItaly
Other contact information: Tel: (011-39) 06-85444-1; Fax: (011-39) 06-85444-3915
Peter McGovern, Ambassador
Patrizia Giuliotti, Trade Commissioner, Environmental Industries, ital-td@international.gc.ca

Jamaica
Canadian High Commission, PO Box 1500
Street Address: 3 West Kings House Rd., Kingston, Jamaica
Kingston, 10 Jamaica
Tel: 876-926-1500; *Fax:* 876-733-3493
kngtn@international.gc.ca
www.canadainternational.gc.ca/jamaica-jamaique
twitter.com/CanadaJamaica
www.facebook.com/CanadainJamaica
Sylvain Fabi, High Commissioner
Yasmin Chong, Trade Commissioner, Environmental Industries, yasmin.chong@international.gc.ca

Japan
Canadian Embassy, 3-38 Akasaka, 7-chome Minato-ku
Tokyo, 107-8503 Japan
www.canadainternational.gc.ca/japan-japon
twitter.com/CanEmbJapan
Other contact information: Tel: 81-3-5412-6200; Fax: 81-3-5412-6291
Ian Burney, Ambassador
Akira Kajita, Trade Commissioner, Environmental Industries, jpn.commerce@international.gc.ca

Hashemite Kingdom of Jordan
Canadian Embassy, PO Box 815403
Street Address: 133 Zahran St., Amman 11180, Jordan
Amman, 11180 Jordan
amman@international.gc.ca
www.canadainternational.gc.ca/jordan-jordanie
twitter.com/CanadainIraq
www.facebook.com/canadainjordan
Other contact information: Tel: 962-6-590-1500; Fax: 962-6-590-1501
Peter MacDougall, Ambassador
Hala Helou, Trade Commissioner, Environmental Industries, hala.helou@international.gc.ca

Republic of Kazakhstan
Canadian Embassy, 13/1 Kabanbay Batyr St.
Astana, 010000 Kazakhstan
astnag@international.gc.ca
www.canadainternational.gc.ca/kazakhstan
twitter.com/CanEmbKZ
www.face book.com/CanadainKazakhstan
Other contact information: Tel: 7-7172-47-55-77; Fax: 7-7172-47-55-87
Shawn Steil, Ambassador
Jude Pecora, Trade Commissioner, Sustainable Technologies, Jude.Pecora@international.gc.ca
Gaziz Shotanov, Trade Commissioner, Environmental Industries, gaziz.shotanov@international.gc.ca

Republic of Kenya
Canadian High Commission, PO Box 1013
Street Address: Limuru Rd., Gigiri, 00621, Nairobi, Kenya
Nairobi, 00621 Kenya
nrobi@international.gc.ca
www.nairobi.gc.ca
Other contact information: Tel: 254-20-366-3000; Fax: 254-20-366-3900
Sara Hradecky, High Commissioner
Ryan Ward, Counsellor, Commercial
David Mwagiru, Trade Commissioner, Environmental Industries, david.mwagiru@international.gc.ca

Republic of Kiribati
***See:* New Zealand**

Republic of Korea
Canadian Embassy, 21 Jeongdong-gil, Jung-gu
Seoul, 04518 Korea
seoul@international.gc.ca
www.korea.gc.ca
twitter.com/CanEmbKorea
Other contact information: Tel: 82-2-3783-6000; Fax: 82-2-3783-6239
Eric Walsh, Ambassador
Richard Dubuc, Minister-Counsellor & Senior Trade Commissioner
Tommy Couture, Counsellor
Kevin Jo, Trade Commissioner, Environmental Industries, kevin.jo@international.gc.ca

State of Kuwait
Canadian Embassy, PO Box 25281
Street Address: Da'Aiah, Block 4, Al-Mutawakel St., Villa 24, Kuwait City, Kuwait
Kuwait City, 13113 Kuwait
kwait@international.gc.ca
www.kuwait.gc.ca
twitter.com/CanadaKuwait
Other contact information: Tel: 965-2256-3025; Fax: 965-2256-0173
Martine Moreau, Ambassador
Raed Bishara, Trade Commissioner, Environmental Industries, kwait-td@international.gc.ca
Tammy Ames, Counsellor, Commercial

Kyrgyz Republic
***See:* Republic of Kazakhstan**

Republic of Latvia
Canadian Embassy, 20/22 Baznicas St., 6th Fl.
Riga, LV-1010 Latvia
riga@international.gc.ca
www.latvia.gc.ca
twitter.com/CanadaLatvia
Other contact information: Tel: 371-6781-3945; Fax: 371-6781-3960
Alain Hausser, Ambassador

Lebanese Republic
Canadian Embassy, PO Box 60163
Street Address: Coolrite Building, 43 Jal-El-Dib Hwy., 1st Fl., Beirut, Lebanon
Jal El Dib, Lebanon
berut@international.gc.ca
www.lebanon.gc.ca
Other contact information: Tel: 961-4-726-700; Fax: 961-4-726-703
Michelle Cameron, Ambassador
Grace Dib, Trade Commissioner, Environmental Industries, grace.dib@international.gc.ca

Kingdom of Lesotho
***See:* Republic of South Africa**

Republic of Liberia
***See:* Republic of Côte d'Ivoire**

State of Libya
***See:* Republic of Tunisia**
David Sproule, Ambassador

Principality of Liechtenstein
***See:* Swiss Confederation**

Republic of Lithuania
Office of the Canadian Embassy, Business Center 2000, Jogailos St. 4
Vilnius, LT-01116 Lithuania
vilnius@canada.lt
www.balticstates.gc.ca
twitter.com/CanadaLithuania
Other contact information: Tel: 370-5249-0950; Fax: 370-5249-7865
Alain Hausser, Ambassador

Grand Duchy of Luxembourg
***See:* Kingdom of Belgium**

Macao
***See:* People's Republic of China**

Republic of Macedonia
***See:* Serbia**

Democratic Republic of Madagascar
***See:* Republic of South Africa**

Republic of Malawi
***See:* Republic of Mozambique**

Federation of Malaysia
PO Box 10990
Street Address: 17th Fl. Menara Tan & Tan, 207 Jalan Tun Razak, 50400 Kuala Lumpur, Malaysia
Kuala Lumpur, 50732 Malaysia
klmpr@international.gc.ca
www.malaysia.gc.ca
twitter.com/CanadaMalaysia
www.facebook.com/CanadaMalaysia
Other contact information: Tel: 6-03-2718-3333; Fax: 6-03-2718-3399
Judith St. George, High Commissioner
John Nojey, Trade Commissioner, Environmental Industries, john.nojey@international.gc.ca

Republic of Maldives
***See:* Democratic Socialist Republic of Sri Lanka**

Republic of Mali
Canadian Embassy, PO Box 198
Bamako, Mali
bmakog@international.gc.ca
www.mali.gc.ca
twitter.com/CanEmbMali
www.facebook.com/canadainmali
Other contact information: Tel: 223-4498-0450; Fax: 223-4498-0455
Marc-André Fredette, Ambassador

Republic of Malta
***See:* Italian Republic**

Marshall Islands
***See:* Commonwealth of Australia**

Islamic Republic of Mauritania
***See:* Kingdom of Morocco**

Republic of Mauritius
***See:* Republic of South Africa**

United Mexican States
Canadian Embassy, Schiller 529, Col. Bosque de Chapultepec, Del. Miguel H
Mexico City, 11580 Mexico
mex@international.gc.ca
www.mexico.gc.ca
twitter.com/CanEmbMexico
www.facebook.com/CanadainMexico
Other contact information: Tel: 52-57-24-7900; Fax: 52-57-24-7980
Pierre Alarie, Ambassador
François Rivest, Minister Counsellor & Senior Trade Commissioner
Nadin Nanji, Trade Commissioner, Environmental Industries, nadin.nanji@international.gc.ca

Federated States of Micronesia
***See:* Commonwealth of Australia**

Republic of Moldova
***See:* Republic of Romania**

Principality of Monaco
***See:* French Republic**

Mongolia
The Canadian Embassy, PO Box 1028
Street Address: Central Tower, Great Chinggis Khaan's Square 2, Sukhbaatar District, Horoo 8, Ulaanbaatar, Mongolia
Ulaanbaatar, 14200 Mongolia
ulaan@international.gc.ca
www.mongolia.gc.ca
twitter.com/CanadaMongolia
www.facebook.com/CanadaMongolia
Other contact information: Tel: 976-11-332-500; Fax: 976-11-32-515
Ed Jager, Ambassador
Oyundari Galsandorj, Trade Commissioner, Environmental Services

Montenegro
***See:* Serbia**

Montserrat
***See:* Barbados**

Kingdom of Morocco
Canadian Embassy, PO Box 2040
Street Address: 66 Mehdi Ben Barka Ave., Rabat-Souissi, Moroccoo
Rabat-Ryad, 10000 Morocco
rabat@international.gc.ca
www.morocco.gc.ca
twitter.com/CanEmbMorocco
www.facebook.com/CanadaauMaroc
Other contact information: Tel: 212-537-54-4949; Fax: 212-537-54-4853
Her Excellency Nathalie Dubé, Ambassador
Christian Hallé, Senior Trade Commissioner
Zouhair Kanouni, Trade Commissioner, Environmental Industries, rabat-td@international.gc.ca

Republic of Mozambique
Canadian High Commission, 1138 Kenneth Kaunda Ave.
Maputo, Mozambique

mputo@international.gc.ca
www.canadainternational.gc.ca/mozambique
twitter.com/CanHCMozambique
w ww.facebook.com/CanadainMozambique
Other contact information: Tel: 258-21-492-623; Fax: 258-21-492-667

Antoine Chevrier, High Commissioner
Alexandre Côté, Counsellor, Commercial
Lurdes Magneli, Trade Commissioner, Environmental Industries

Republic of the Union of Myanmar
Embassy of Canada, Centrepoint Towers, 9th Fl., 65 Sule Pagoda Rd.
Yangon, Burma

YNGON@international.gc.ca
www.canadainternational.gc.ca/burma-birmanie
www.facebook.com/1421359581 427574
Other contact information: Tel: 95-1-384-805; Fax: 95-1-384-806

Karen MacArthur, Ambassador

Republic of Namibia
***See:* Republic of South Africa**

Nauru
***See:* Commonwealth of Australia**

Federal Democratic Republic of Nepal
***See:* Republic of India**

Kingdom of the Netherlands
Canadian Embassy, Sophialaan 7
The Hague, 2514 JP The Netherlands

info@canada.nl
www.netherlands.gc.ca
twitter.com/CanAmbNL
www.fac ebook.com/CanadainNetherlands
Other contact information: Tel: 31-70-311-1600; Fax: 31-70-311-1620

Sabine Nolke, Ambassador
Diederik Beutener, Trade Commissioner, Environmental Industries, hague-td@international.gc.ca

Netherlands Antilles
***See:* Republic of Venezuela**

New Caledonia
***See:* Commonwealth of Australia**

New Zealand
Canadian High Commission, PO Box 8047
Wellington, 6143 New Zealand

wlgtn@international.gc.ca
www.newzealand.gc.ca
twitter.com/CanHCNZ
Other contact information: Tel: 64-4-473-9577; Fax: 64-4-471-2082

Mario Bot, High Commissioner
Pierre Delorme, Senior Trade Commissioner, Environmental Industries, pierre.delorme@international.gc.ca

Republic of Nicaragua
Canadian Embassy, 25 Nogal St.
Managua, Nicaragua

mngua@international.gc.ca
www.nicaragua.gc.ca
Other contact information: Tel: 505-2268-0433; Fax: 505-2268-0437

Michael Gort, Ambassador (located in Costa Rica)

Republic of Niger
***See:* Republic of Mali**

Federal Republic of Nigeria
Canadian High Commission, Central Business District
Abuja, PO Box 5144, 13010G, Palm close, Diplomatic Dr.
Abuja, Nigeria

abuja@international.gc.ca
www.canadainternational.gc.ca/nigeria
Other contact information: Tel: 234-9-461-2900; Fax: 234-9-461-2901

Christopher Thornley, High Commissioner
Sylvia Koleva, Trade Commissioner, Environmental Industries, sylvia.koleva@international.gc.ca

Northern Ireland
***See:* United Kingdom of Great Britain & Northern Ireland**

Northern Marianas
***See:* Commonwealth of Australia**

Kingdom of Norway
Canadian Embassy, Wergelandsveien 7
Oslo, 0244 Norway

oslo@international.gc.ca
www.norway.gc.ca
Other contact information: Tel: 47-2299-5300; Fax: 47-2299-5301

Artur Wilczynski, Ambassador
John Winterbourne, Trade Commissioner, Environmental Industries, NordiCommerce@international.gc.ca

Sultanate of Oman
***See:* Kingdom of Saudi Arabia**

Islamic Republic of Pakistan
Canadian High Commission, PO Box 1042
Street Address: Diplomatic Enclave, Sector G-5, Islamabad, Pakistan
Islamabad, Pakistan

isbad@internationl.gc.ca
www.pakistan.gc.ca
twitter.com/canhcpakistan
www.facebook.com/CanadainPakistan
Other contact information: Tel: 92-51-208-6000; Fax: 92-51-208-6900

Perry Calderwood, High Commissioner
Ali Khan, Trade Commissioner, Environmental Industries

Republic of Palau
***See:* Commonwealth of Australia**

Republic of Panama
Estafeta World Trade Center, PO Box 0832-2446
Street Address: Torres de Las Americas, Tower A, 11th Floor, Punta Pacifica, Panama City, Panama
Panama City, Panama

panam@international.gc.ca
www.panama.gc.ca
twitter.com/CanEmbPanama
www.facebook.com/canada.pa
Other contact information: Tel: (011 507) 264-2500; Fax: (011 507) 294-2514

Karine Asselin, Ambassador
Luis Cedeno, Trade Commissioner, Environmental Industries, luis.cedeno@international.gc.ca

Papua New Guinea
***See:* Commonwealth of Australia**

Republic of Paraguay
***See:* Argentine Republic**

Republic of Peru
Canadian Embassy, PO Box 18-1126 Miraflores
Lima, Peru

Tel: 511-319-3200; *Fax:* 511-446-4912
lima@international.gc.ca
www.peru.gc.ca
twitter.com/CanadaPeru
www.f acebook.com/CanadaPeruBolivia

Gwyneth Kutz, Ambassador
Alexandra Laverdure, Trade Commissioner, Environmental Industries, lima.commerce@international.gc.ca

Republic of the Philippines
PO Box 2098, Makati Central Post Office
Street Address: Floors 6-8, Tower 2, RCBC Plaza, 6819 Ayala Ave., Makati City, Manila, Philippines1261 Philippines

manil@international.gc.ca
www.philippines.gc.ca
twitter.com/CanEmbPH
www.facebook.com/CanEmbPH
Other contact information: Tel: 63-2-857-9000; Fax: 63-2-843-1082

John Holmes, Ambassador
Ramon Yazon, Trade Commissioner, Environmental Industries, ramon.yazon@international.gc.ca

Republic of Poland
Canadian Embassy, ul. Jana Matejiki 1/5
Warsaw, 00-481 Poland

wsaw@international.gc.ca
www.poland.gc.ca
twitter.com/CanadaPoland
www.facebook.com/Canada-Polska-Connection-12644 3964065449
Other contact information: Tel: 48-22-584-3100; Fax: 48-22-584-3192

Stephen de Boer, Ambassador
Nicholas Lepage, Senior Trade Commissioner

Portuguese Republic
Canadian Embassy, Avenida da Liberdade, 196-200, 3rd Fl.
Lisbon, 1269-121 Portugal

lsbon@international.gc.ca
www.portugal.gc.ca
www.facebook.com/Embassy-of-Canada-to-Portugal-141793602 8487891
Other contact information: Tel: 351-21-316-4600; Fax: 351-21-316-4693

Jeffrey Marder, Ambassador
Michael Wylie, Senior Trade Commissioner, Environmental Industries, michael.wylie@international.gc.ca

Puerto Rico
***See:* United States of America**

State of Qatar
Embassy of Canada, PO Box 24876, Doha Qatar

dohag@international.gc.ca
www.canadainternational.gc.ca/qatar
www.facebook.com/CanadainQatar
Other contact information: Tel: 974-4419-9000; Fax: 974-4419-9035

Adrian Norfolk, Ambassador
John Rodney, Commercial Counsellor & Senior Trade Commissioner, Environmental Industries

Republic of Romania
Canadian Embassy, Sector 1, #1, 3 Tuberozelor St.
Bucharest, 011411 Romania

bucst@international.gc.ca
www.romania.gc.ca
twitter.com/canadaromania
Other contact information: Tel: 40-21-307-5000; Fax: 40-21-307-5010

Kevin Hamilton, Ambassador
Neil Swain, Senior Trade Commissioner, bucst-td@international.gc.ca

Russian Federation
Canadian Embassy, 23 Starokonyushenny Pereulok
Moscow, 119002 Russia

mosco@international.gc.ca
www.russia.gc.ca
twitter.com/CanEmbRussia
Other contact information: Tel: 7-495-925-6000; Fax: 7-495-925-6025

John Kur, Ambassador
Lilya Panova, Trade Commissioner, Environmental Industries, rus.commerce@international.gc.ca

Republic of Rwanda
Canadian Embassy, PO Box 1117
Street Address: 59 KN16 Ave., Kigali, Rwanda
Kigali, Rwanda

kgali@international.gc.ca
www.tradecommissioner.gc.ca/rw
Other contact information: Tel: 250-252-573-210; Fax: 250-252-572-719

Saint Kitts & Nevis
***See:* Barbados**

Saint Lucia
***See:* Barbados**

Saint-Pierre & Miquelon
***See:* French Republic**

Samoa
***See:* New Zealand**

Republic of San Marino
***See:* Italian Republic**

Democratic Republic of Sao Tomé & Principe
***See:* Federal Republic of Nigeria**

Kingdom of Saudi Arabia
Canadian Embassy, PO Box 94321
Street Address: Diplomatic Quarter, Riyadh, Saudi Arabia
Riyadh, 11693 Saudi Arabia

ryadh@international.gc.ca
www.saudiarabia.gc.ca
twitter.com/CanEmbSA
Other contact information: Tel: 966-11-488-2288; Fax: 966-11-482-5670

Dennis Horak, Ambassador
Maya El-Khoury, Trade Commissioner, Environmental Industries, ryadh-td@international.gc.ca

Scotland
See: United Kingdom of Great Britain & Northern Ireland

Republic of Senegal
Canadian Embassy, PO Box 3373
Dakar, Senegal

dakar@international.gc.ca
www.senegal.gc.ca
twitter.com/CanEmbSenegal
www.facebook.com/canadainsenegal
Other contact information: Tel: 221-33-889-4700; Fax: 221-33-889-4720

Lise Filiatrault, Ambassador

Republic of Serbia
Canadian Embassy, Kneza Milosa 75
Belgrade, 111711 Serbia

bgrad@international.gc.ca
www.serbia.gc.ca
twitter.com/CanadaSerbia
www.facebook.com/CanadainSerbia
Other contact information: Tel: 381-11-306-3000; Fax: 381-11-306-3042

Philip Pinnington, Ambassador
Djurdjevka Ceramilac, Trade Commissioner, Enviromental Industries

Republic of Seychelles
See: United Republic of Tanzania

Republic of Sierra Leone
See: Republic of Ghana

Republic of Singapore
Canadian High Commission, PO Box 845
Street Address: #11-01, 1 George St., Singapore 049145901645 Singapore

spore@international.gc.ca
www.singapore.gc.ca
twitter.com/CanHCSingapore
www.facebook.com/HighCommissionOfCanadaToSing apore
Other contact information: Tel: 65-6854-5900; Fax: 65-6854-5930

Nancy Lynn McDonald, High Commissioner
Francis Chan, Trade Commissioner, Environmental Industries, spore-td@international.gc.ca

Slovak Republic
Embassy of Canada, Mostova 2, Carlton Savoy Building
Bratislava, 81102 Slovak Republic

brtsv@international.gc.ca
www.canadainternational.gc.ca/austria-autriche
twitter.com/canadaslovaki a
www.facebook.com/CanadainSlovakia
Other contact information: Tel: 421-259-204-031; Fax: 421-254-434-227

Ambassador resides in Prague, Czech Republic
Kathy Bunka, Chargé d'affaires
Milan Harustiak, Trade Commissioner, Environmental Industries

Republic of Slovenia
See: Republic of Hungary

Solomon Islands
See: Commonwealth of Australia

Somali Democratic Republic
See: Republic of Kenya

Republic of South Africa
Canadian High Commission, Private Bag X13, Hatfield
Street Address: 1103 Arcadia St., Hatfield, Pretoria, South Africa
Pretoria, 0028 South Africa

pret@international.gc.ca
www.canadainternational.gc.ca/southafrica-afriquedusud
twitter.com/CanHC ZA
Other contact information: Tel: 27-12-422-3000; Fax: 27-12-422-3052

Sandra McCardell, High Commissioner
Christophe Bezou, Trade Commissioner, Environmental Industries, christophe.bezou@international.gc.ca

Republic of South Sudan
Canadian Embassy, Former JDO Compound, Airport Ave.
Juba, South Sudan

juba-g@international.gc.ca
www.canadainternational.gc.ca/south_sudan-soudan_du_sud
Other contact information: Tel: 211-955-196-936

Alan W. Hamson, Ambassador

Kingdom of Spain
Canadian Embassy, Torre Espacio, Paseo de la Castellana 259D
Madrid, 28046 Spain

mdrid@international.gc.ca
www.spain.gc.ca
twitter.com/CanEmbSpain
www.facebook.com/CanadainSpain
Other contact information: Tel: 34-91-382-8400; Fax: 34-91-382-8490

Matthew Levin, Ambassador
Isidro Garcia, Trade Commissioner, Environmental Industries, espana@international.gc.ca

Democratic Socialist Republic of Sri Lanka
Canadian High Commission, 33A, 5th Lane, Colpetty
Colombo, 3 Sri Lanka

ColomboConsul@international.gc.ca
www.srilanka.gc.ca
Other contact information: Tel: 94-11-532-6232; Fax: 94-11-532-6296

Shelley Whiting, High Commissioner
Avanthi Coonghe, Trade Commissioner

Republic of The Sudan
Canadian Embassy, PO Box 10503
Khartouom, Sudan

khrtm@international.gc.ca
www.canadainternational.gc.ca/sudan-soudan
www.facebook.com/235198976643 93
Other contact information: Tel: 249-156-550-500; Fax: 249-156-550-501

Salah-Eddine Bendaoud, Ambassador

Republic of Suriname
See: Republic of Guyana

Kingdom of Swaziland
See: Republic of Mozambique

Kingdom of Sweden
Canadian Embassy, PO Box 16129, Klarabergsgatan 23
Street Address: 23 Klarabergsgatan, 6th. Fl., Stockholm, Sweden, 11121
Stockholm, 10323 Sweden

stkhm@international.gc.ca
www.sweden.gc.ca
Other contact information: Tel: 46-8-453-3000; Fax: 46-8-453-3016

Heather Grant, Ambassador
Maria Stenberg, Trade Commissioner, Environmental Industries

Swiss Confederation
Canadian Embassy, PO Box 234
Bern 6, CH-3000 Switzerland

bern@international.gc.ca
www.switzerland.gc.ca
twitter.com/CanSwitzerland
Other contact information: Tel: 41-31-357-3200; Fax: 41-31-357-3210

Jennifer MacIntyre, Ambassador
Dominique Gruhl-Bégin, Trade Commissioner, Environmental Industries

Syrian Arab Republic
See: Lebanon

Taiwan
Canadian Trade Office, #6F Citibank Bldg., 1 SongZhi Rd., Xinyi District
Taipei, 11047 Taiwan

tapei@international.gc.ca
www.canada.org.tw
www.facebook.com/CTOTEnFr
Other contact information: Tel: 886-2-8723-3000; Fax: 886-2-8723-3592

Mario Ste. Marie, Executive Director
Vanessa Chen, Trade Commissioner, Environmental Industries, vanessa.chen@international.gc.ca
Tom Cumming, Trade Commissioner, Environmental Industries, tom.cumming@international.gc.ca

Republic of Tajikistan
See: Republic of Kazakhstan

United Republic of Tanzania
Canadian High Commission, PO Box 1022
Street Address: 38 Mirambo St., Dar-es-Salaam, Tanzania
Dar-es-Salaam, Tanzania

dslam@international.gc.ca
www.tanzania.gc.ca
twitter.com/CanadaTanzania
www.facebook.com/CanadainTanzania
Other contact information: Tel: 255-22-216-3300; Fax: 255-22-211-6897

Ian Myles, High Commissioner
Specioza Lugazia, Trade Commissioner, Environmental Industries, specioza.lugazia@international.gc.ca

Kingdom of Thailand
Canadian Embassy, PO Box 2090
Street Address: Abdulrahim Pl., 990 Rama IV Rd., 15th Fl., 10500, Bangkok, Thailand
Bangkok, 10501 Thailand

bngkk@international.gc.ca
www.thailand.gc.ca
twitter.com/CanadaThailand
Other contact information: Tel: 66-0-2646-4300; Fax: 66-0-2646-4336

Donica Pottie, Ambassador
Dolrawee Akarakupt, Trade Commissioner, Environmental Industries, dolrawee.akarakupt@international.gc.ca

Togolese Republic
See: Republic of Ghana

Kingdom of Tonga
See: New Zealand

Republic of Trinidad & Tobago
Canadian High Commission, PO Box 1246
Street Address: Maple House, #3, 3A Sweet Briar Rd., St. Clair, Port of Spain, Trinidad & Tobago
Port of Spain, Trinidad & Tobago

Tel: 868-622-6232; *Fax:* 868-628-2581
pspan@international.gc.ca
www.trinidadandtobago.gc.ca
twitter.com/Cana daTandT
www.facebook.com/hccanada.tt

Carla Hogan Rufelds, High Commissioner
Debra Boyce, Senior Trade Commissioner, Oil & Gas; Defence & Security
Michaeline Narcisse, Trade Commissioner, Education, Infrastructure, michaeline.narcisse@international.gc.ca

Republic of Tunisia
Canadian Embassy, PO Box 48, 1053 Les Berges du Lac II
Tunis, Tunisia

tunis-cs@international.gc.ca
www.tunis.gc.ca
www.facebook.com/179395175598053
Other contact information: Tel: 216-70-010-200; Fax: 216-70-010-393

Carol McQueen, Ambassador
Ezzeddine Cherni, Trade Commissioner, Environmental Industries, ezzeddine.cherni@international.gc.ca

Republic of Turkey
Canadian Embassy, Cinnah Caddesi 58, Cankaya
Ankara, 06690 Turkey

ankra@international.gc.ca
www.turkey.gc.ca
twitter.com/CanEmbTurkey
Other contact information: Tel: 90-312-409-2700; Fax: 90-312-409-2712

Chris Cooter, Ambassador
Lucie Verreault, Trade Commissioner, Environmental Industries, ankra-td@international.gc.ca

Turkmenistan
See: Republic of Turkey

Turks & Caicos Islands
See: Jamaica

Republic of Tuvalu
See: New Zealand

Republic of Uganda
See: Republic of Kenya

Ukraine
Canadian Embassy, 13A Kostelna St.
Kyiv, 01901 Ukraine

kyiv@international.gc.ca
www.ukraine.gc.ca
twitter.com/CanEmbUkraine
www.facebook.com/270529536435244
Other contact information: Tel: 380-44-590-3100; Fax: 380-44-590-3134

Roman Waschuk, Ambassador
Yury Mardak, Trade Commissioner, Environmental Industries

United Arab Emirates
The Canadian Embassy, PO Box 6970
Street Address: 9th Fl., West Tower, Abu Dhabi Trade Towers (Abu Dhabi Mall), Abu Dhabi, United Arab Emirates
Abu Dhabi, United Arab Emirates

abdbi@international.gc.ca
www.canadainternational.gc.ca/uae-eau
twitter.com/CanadainUAE
www.face book.com/CanadainUAE
Other contact information: Tel: 971-2-694-0300; Fax: 971-2-694-0399

Masud Husain, Ambassador
Hayley Jean Rahman, Trade Commissioner, Environmental Industries

United Kingdom
Canadian High Commission, Canada House, Trafalgar Square
London, SW1Y 5BJ UK

LDN.publicaffairs@international.gc.ca
UnitedKingdom.gc.ca
twitter.c om/CanadianUK
www.facebook.com/CanadaintheUK
Other contact information: Phone: 0207 004 6000

Janice Charette, High Commissioner
Greg Houlahan, Senior Trade Commissioner
Rachel Soares, Trade Commissioner, Environmental Industries, ldn-td@international.gc.ca

United States of America
Canadian Embassy, 501 Pennsylvannia Ave. NW
Washington, DC 20001-2111 USA

Tel: 202-682-1740; *Fax:* 202-682-7726
wshdc.consul@international.gc.ca
www.washington.gc.ca
twitter.com/CanE mbUSA

David MacNaughton, Ambassador
Denis Stevens, Minister & Deputy Head of Mission
Gilles Gauthier, Minister, Economic
Carl Hartill, Counsellor, Science & Technology
Jason LaTorre, Senior Trade Commissioner & Minister-Counsellor, Commerce
Benjamin Eliasoph, Trade Commissioner, Environmental Industries

Eastern Republic of Uruguay
Canadian Embassy, #102, Plaza Independencia 749
Montevideo, 11100 Uruguay

mvdeo@international.gc.ca
www.uruguay.gc.ca
twitter.com/CanEmbUruguay
Other contact information: Tel: 598-2-902-2030; Fax: 598-2-902-2029

Joanne Frappier, Ambassador
Patricia Wilson, Trade Commissioner, Environmental Industries, patricia.wilson@international.gc.ca

Republic of Uzbekistan
***See:* Russian Federation**

Republic of Vanuatu
***See:* Commonwealth of Australia**

Republic of Venezuela
Canadian Embassy, PO Box 62302
Street Address: Av. Francisco de Miranda con Av. Sur de Altamira, Altamira, Caracas 1060, Venezuela
Caracas, 1060A Venezuela

crcas@international.gc.ca
www.venezuela.gc.ca
twitter.com/CanEmbVenezuela
Other contact information: Tel: 58-212-600-3000; Fax: 58-212-263-8326

Ben Rowswell, Ambassador
Daniela Oyague, Trade Commissioner, Environmental Industries, daniela.oyague@international.gc.ca
David Ramirez, Trade Commissioner, Environmental Industries, david.ramirez@international.gc.ca

Socialist Republic of Vietnam
Canadian Embassy, 31 Huong Vuong St.
Hanoi, Vietnam

hanoi@international.gc.ca
www.vietnam.gc.ca
www.facebook.com/canadainvietnam
Other contact information: Tel: 84-4-3734-5000; Fax: 84-4-3734-5049

Ping Kitnikone, Ambassador
Richard Bale, Counsel General
Barbara Nadeau, Commercial Counsellor & Senior Trade Commissioner, Environmental Industries, barbara.nadeau@international.gc.ca

Wales
***See:* United Kingdom of Great Britain & Northern Ireland**

Republic of Yemen
***See:* Kingdom of Saudi Arabia**

Republic of Zambia
Canadian High Commission, PO Box 31313
Street Address: 5199 United Nation Ave., Lusaka, Zambia
Lusaka, Zambia

lusaka@international.gc.ca
www.tanzania.gc.ca
Other contact information: Tel: 260-211-25-08-33; Fax: 260-211-25-41-76

Alexandre Lévêque, High Commissioner

Republic of Zimbabwe
Canadian Embassy, PO Box 1430
Street Address: 45 Baines Ave., Harare, Zimbabwe
Harare, Zimbabwe

hrare-cs@international.gc.ca
www.zimbabwe.gc.ca
twitter.com/CanEmbZimbabwe
www.facebook.com/CanadaZimbabwe
Other contact information: Tel: 263-4-252181-5; Fax: 263-4-252186

Kumar Gupta, Ambassador

SECTION 8
GOVERNMENT: MUNICIPAL

Listings in this section are arranged by province and are as current as possible at time of publication. For appointments made and results of elections held after publication, please refer to Canada's Information Resource Centre (CIRC), if your library subscribes to this online database. Each provincial section includes a district map, notes concerning local government structure and elections, and the following categories:

Counties & Municipal Districts

Major Municipalities

Other Municipalities

MUNICIPAL GOVERNMENTS

ALBERTA

The major legislation concerning municipal government in Alberta is the Municipal Government Act.

Municipal government in Alberta is rural, urban or specialized. Rural municipal governments are organized into Municipal Districts, with Specialized Municipalities created to meet the unique needs of a specific municipality. Elected councils are responsible for the welfare and interests of the municipalities. Two other rural categories are Improvement Districts and Special Areas, which are geographically large, sparsely populated areas for which the provincial government levies and collects all taxes and provides services.

Urban municipalities include Summer Villages, Villages, Towns and Cities. These are fully autonomous municipal units, each with an elected council. They are responsible for providing all municipal services within their corporate limits and for levying taxes and rates.

In addition to the above forms of municipal government there are eight Metis Settlements established under the Metis Settlements Act.

Types of Municipalities that may be formed:

Municipal District: A majority of the buildings used as dwellings are on parcels of land with an area of at least 1,850 square metres and there is a population of 1,000 or more.

Village: A majority of the buildings are on parcels of land smaller than 1,850 square metres and there is a population of 300 or more.

Town: A majority of the buildings are on parcels of land smaller than 1,850 square metres and there is a population of 1,000 or more.

City: A majority of the buildings are on parcels of land smaller than 1,850 square metres and there is a population of 10,000 or more.

Specialized Municipality: An area in which the Minister is satisfied that a type of municipality (as listed above) does not meet the needs of the proposed municipality; to provide for a form of local government that, in the opinion of the Minister, will provide for the orderly development of the municipality to a type of municipality (as listed above), or to another form of specialized municipality; an area in which the Minister is satisfied for any other reason that it is appropriate in the circumstances to form a specialized municipality.

Incorporation and changes in status are determined by the Lieutenant Governor in Council (Provincial Cabinet) on the recommendation of the Minister of Municipal Affairs. It is not necessary to change status by reason of population change. Elections are held in October. As of 2013, terms of office are now four years (2017, 2021, etc.).

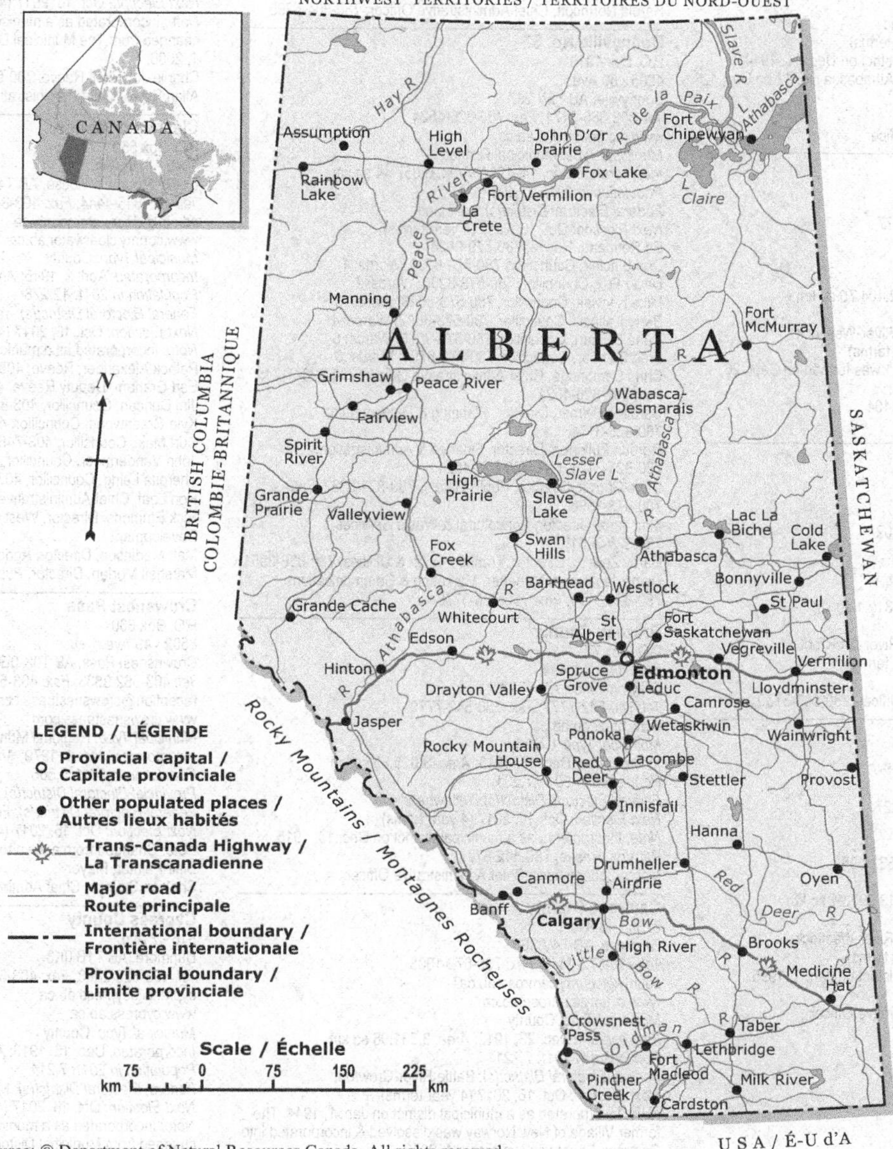

Alberta

Counties & Municipal Districts in Alberta

Acadia No. 34
P.O. Box 30
9 Main St.
Acadia Valley, AB T0J 0A0
Tel: 403-972-3808; *Fax:* 403-972-3833
md34@mdacadia.ab.ca
www.mdacadia.ab.ca
Municipal Type: Municipal District
Incorporated: Dec. 9, 1913; *Area:* 1,076.26 sq km
Population in 2011: 495
Federal Electoral District(s): Battle River-Crowfoot
Next Election: Oct. 16, 2017 (4 year terms)
Peter Rafa, Reeve
Gary E. Peers, Municipal Administrator

Athabasca County
3602 - 48 Ave.
Athabasca, AB T9S 1M8
Tel: 780-675-2273; *Fax:* 780-675-5512
info@athabascacounty.com
www.athabascacounty.com
Municipal Type: County
Incorporated: Dec. 18, 1913; *Area:* 6,126.43 sq km
Population in 2011: 7,662
Federal Electoral District(s): Lakeland
Next Election: Oct. 16, 2017 (4 year terms)
Note: Incorporated as a municipal district on Dec. 14, 1914. Name changed from The County of Athabasca No. 12 on Dec. 1, 2009.
Doris Splane, Reeve
Ryan Maier, Chief Administrative Officer

Barrhead County No. 11
5306 - 49 St.
Barrhead, AB T7N 1N5
Tel: 780-674-3331; *Fax:* 780-674-2777
info@countybarrhead.ab.ca
www.countybarrhead.ab.ca
Municipal Type: County
Incorporated: Dec. 18, 1913; *Area:* 2,404.70 sq km
Population in 2011: 6,096
Federal Electoral District(s): Peace River-Westlock
Next Election: Oct. 16, 2017 (4 year terms)
Note: The County of Barrhead No. 11 was formed on Sept. 26, 1958.
William (Bill) Lee, Reeve, 780-674-4404
Mark Oberg, County Manager

Beaver County
P.O. Box 140
5223 - 46 St.
Ryley, AB T0B 4A0
Tel: 780-663-3730; *Fax:* 780-663-3602
administration@beaver.ab.ca
www.beaver.ab.ca
Municipal Type: County
Incorporated: Feb. 1, 1943; *Area:* 3,319.1 sq km
Population in 2011: 5,689
Federal Electoral District(s): Battle River-Crowfoot
Next Election: Oct. 16, 2017 (4 year terms)
Arnold Hanson, Reeve
Robert Beck, Chief Administrative Officer, 780-663-3730

Big Lakes
P.O. Box 239
5305 - 56 St.
High Prairie, AB T0G 1E0
Tel: 780-523-5955; *Fax:* 780-523-4227
biglakes@mdbiglakes.ca
www.mdbiglakes.ca
Other Information: Toll Free: 1-866-523-5955
Municipal Type: Municipal District
Incorporated: Dec. 18, 1913; *Area:* 13,892.91 sq km
Population in 2011: 5,912
Federal Electoral District(s): Peace River-Westlock
Next Election: Oct. 16, 2017 (4 year terms)
Note: Incorporated as a municipal district on Jan. 1, 1995.
Ken Matthews, Reeve
William (Bill) Kostiw, Chief Administrative Officer

Bighorn No. 8
P.O. Box 310
2 Heart Mountain Drive
Exshaw, AB T0L 2C0
Tel: 403-673-3611; *Fax:* 403-673-3895
bighorn@mdbighorn.ca
www.mdbighorn.ca
Municipal Type: Municipal District
Incorporated: April 1, 1945; *Area:* 2,767.94 sq km
Population in 2011: 1,341
Federal Electoral District(s): Banff-Airdrie; Foothills
Next Election: Oct. 16, 2017 (4 year terms)
Note: Incorporated as a municipal district on Jan. 1, 1988.
Dene Cooper, Reeve, 403-673-3968
Martin Buckley, Chief Administrative Officer

Birch Hills County
P.O. Box 157
4601 - 50 St.
Wanham, AB T0H 3P0
Tel: 780-694-3793; *Fax:* 780-694-3788
cao@birchhillscounty.com
www.birchhillscounty.com
Municipal Type: County
Incorporated: Dec. 18, 1913; *Area:* 2,856.69 sq km
Population in 2011: 1,582
Federal Electoral District(s): Peace River-Westlock
Next Election: Oct. 16, 2017 (4 year terms)
Marvin Doran, Reeve
Harold Northcott, Chief Administrative Officer, 780-864-5295

Bonnyville No. 87
P.O. Box 1010
4905 - 50 Ave.
Bonnyville, AB T9N 2J7
Tel: 888-886-3171; *Fax:* 780-826-4524
www.md.bonnyville.ab.ca
Municipal Type: Municipal District
Incorporated: Dec. 14, 1914; *Area:* 6,057.44 sq km
Population in 2011: 11,191
Federal Electoral District(s): Lakeland
Next Election: Oct. 16, 2017 (4 year terms)
Ed Rondeau, Reeve, 780-579-9624
Don Sinclair, Councillor, 780-573-6029, Wards: 1
David Fox, Councillor, 780-573-3266, Wards: 2
Mike Krywiak, Councillor, 780-573-6093, Wards: 3
Barry Kalinski, Councillor, 780-573-6082, Wards: 4
Dana Swigart, Councillor, 780-573-9095, Wards: 5
Fred Bamber, Councillor, 780-573-6793, Wards: 6
Chris Cambridge, Chief Administrative Officer, 780-826-3171, Fax: 780-826-4524
Caroline Palmer, Director, Planning & Development, 780-826-3171
Gordon Fullerton, Director, Finance & Administration, 780-826-3171, Fax: 780-826-4524
Chris Garner, Director, Public Safety, 780-823-3332, Fax: 780-573-1586
Matt Janz, Director, Agricultural & Waste Services, 780-826-3951
Darcy Zelisko, Director, Transportation & Utilities, 780-826-3951
Diane Jenkinson, Manager, Marketing & Communications, 780-826-3171, Fax: 780-826-3775

Brazeau County
P.O. Box 77
7401 Twp Rd. 494
Drayton Valley, AB T7A 1R1
Tel: 780-542-7777; *Fax:* 780-542-7770
www.brazeau.ab.ca
Municipal Type: County
Incorporated: Dec. 18, 1913; *Area:* 3,015.83 sq km
Population in 2011: 7,201
Federal Electoral District(s): Yellowhead
Next Election: Oct. 16, 2017 (4 year terms)
Note: Incorporated as a municipal district on Dec. 13, 1915.
Pat Vos, Reeve, 780-542-8777
Marco Schoeninger, Chief Administrative Officer

Camrose County
3755 - 43 Ave.
Camrose, AB T4V 3S8
Tel: 780-672-4446; *Fax:* 780-672-1008
county@county.camrose.ab.ca
www.county.camrose.ab.ca
Municipal Type: County
Incorporated: Dec. 23, 1912; *Area:* 3,331.98 sq km
Population in 2011: 7,721
Federal Electoral District(s): Battle River-Crowfoot
Next Election: Oct. 16, 2017 (4 year terms)
Note: Incorporated as a municipal district on Jan. 1, 1944. The former Village of New Norway was dissolved & incorporated into Camrose County on November 1, 2012.
Don L. Gregorwich, Reeve, 780-373-2503
Paul King, County Administrator

Cardston County
P.O. Box 580
1050 Main Street
Cardston, AB T0K 0K0
Tel: 403-653-4977; *Fax:* 403-653-1126
office@cardstoncounty.com
www.cardstoncounty.com
Municipal Type: County
Incorporated: Dec. 18, 1913; *Area:* 3,414.87 sq km
Population in 2011: 4,167
Federal Electoral District(s): Medicine Hat-Cardston-Warner
Next Election: Oct. 16, 2017 (4 year terms)
Note: Incorporated as a municipal district on Jan. 1, 1946.
Fred C. Lacey, Reeve, 403-448-0262
Murray Millward, Chief Administrative Officer, 403-653-4977

Clear Hills County
P.O. Box 240
Worsley, AB T0H 3W0
Tel: 780-685-3925; *Fax:* 780-685-3960
info@clearhillscounty.ab.ca
www.clearhillscounty.ab.ca
Municipal Type: County
Incorporated: Dec. 18, 1913; *Area:* 15,112.69 sq km
Population in 2011: 2,801
Federal Electoral District(s): Grande Prairie-Mackenzie
Next Election: Oct. 16, 2017 (4 year terms)
Note: Incorporated as a municipal district on Jan. 1, 1995. Name changed from The Municipal District of Clear Hills No. 21 on Jan. 1, 2006.
Charlie Johnson, Reeve, 780-596-2187
Allan Rowe, Chief Administrative Officer

Clearwater County
P.O. Box 550
4340 - 47th Ave.
Rocky Mountain House, AB T4T 1A4
Tel: 403-845-4444; *Fax:* 403-845-7330
admin@clearwatercounty.ca
www.county.clearwater.ab.ca
Municipal Type: County
Incorporated: April 1, 1945; *Area:* 18,691.65 sq km
Population in 2011: 12,278
Federal Electoral District(s): Yellowhead
Next Election: Oct. 16, 2017 (4 year terms)
Note: Incorporated as a municipal district on Jan. 1, 1985.
Patrick Alexander, Reeve, 403-729-2399, Wards: 7
Earl Graham, Deputy Reeve, 403-722-2774, Wards: 6
Jim Duncan, Councillor, 403-845-6319, Wards: 1
Kyle Greenwood, Councillor, 403-729-2053, Wards: 2
Curt Maki, Councillor, 403-746-3642, Wards: 3
John Vandermeer, Councillor, 403-722-2186, Wards: 4
Theresa Laing, Councillor, 403-845-7120, Wards: 5
Ron Leaf, Chief Administrative Officer
Rick Emmons, Director, West Country & Planning & Development
Matt Martinson, Director, Agricultural Services
Marshall Morton, Director, Public Works

Crowsnest Pass
P.O. Box 600
8502 - 19 Ave.
Crowsnest Pass, AB T0K 0E0
Tel: 403-562-8833; *Fax:* 403-563-5474
reception@crowsnestpass.com
www.crowsnestpass.com
Municipal Type: Regional Municipality
Incorporated: Jan. 1, 1979; *Area:* 373.07 sq km
Population in 2011: 5,565
Provincial Electoral District(s): Livingstone-Macleod
Federal Electoral District(s): Foothills
Next Election: Oct. 16, 2017 (4 year terms)
Note: Changed from a town to a specialized municipality in 2008.
Blair Painter, Mayor
Sheldon Steinke, Chief Administrative Officer

Cypress County
816 - 2 Ave.
Dunmore, AB T1B 0K3
Tel: 403-526-2888; *Fax:* 403-526-8958
cypress@cypress.ab.ca
www.cypress.ab.ca
Municipal Type: County
Incorporated: Dec. 18, 1913; *Area:* 13,166.13 sq km
Population in 2011: 7,214
Federal Electoral District(s): Medicine Hat-Cardston-Warner
Next Election: Oct. 16, 2017 (4 year terms)
Note: Incorporated as a municipal district on Jan. 1, 1985. Name changed from Municipal District of Cypress on Nov. 1, 1998.

Bob Olson, Reeve, 403-898-2184
Kevin Miner, County Manager

Fairview No. 136
P.O. Box 189
10957 - 91 Ave.
Fairview, AB T0H 1L0
Tel: 780-835-4903; *Fax:* 780-835-3131
mdinfo@mdfairview.ab.ca
www.mdfairview.com
Municipal Type: Municipal District
Incorporated: Dec. 18, 1913; *Area:* 1,390.66 sq km
Population in 2011: 1,673
Federal Electoral District(s): Peace River-Westlock
Next Election: Oct. 16, 2017 (4 year terms)
Note: Incorporated as a municipal district on Dec. 9, 1914.
Ernie Newman, Reeve, 780-835-4482, Wards: 5/6
Sandra Fox, Chief Administrative Officer, 780-835-4903

Flagstaff County
P.O. Box 358
12435 Township Rd. 442
Sedgewick, AB T0B 4C0
Tel: 780-384-4100; *Fax:* 780-384-3635
county@flagstaff.ab.ca
www.flagstaff.ab.ca
Other Information: Toll-Free: 1-877-387-4100
Municipal Type: County
Incorporated: Dec. 9, 1912; *Area:* 4,066.92 sq km
Population in 2011: 3,244
Federal Electoral District(s): Battle River-Crowfoot
Next Election: Oct. 16, 2017 (4 year terms)
Gerald Kuefler, Reeve, 780-583-2208
Shelly Armstrong, Chief Administrative Officer, 780-384-4101

Foothills No. 31
P.O. Box 5605
309 Macleod Trail
High River, AB T1V 1M7
Tel: 403-652-2341; *Fax:* 403-652-7880
mdfthlls@mdfoothills.com
www.mdfoothills.com
Other Information: Emergencies: 1-888-808-3722
Municipal Type: Municipal District
Incorporated: Dec. 23, 1912; *Area:* 3,643.6 sq km
Population in 2011: 21,258
Federal Electoral District(s): Foothills
Next Election: Oct. 16, 2017 (4 year terms)
Note: Incorporated as a municipal district on Jan. 1, 1944.
Larry Spilak, Reeve, 403-233-8577, Wards: 6
Rick Percifield, Councillor, 403-684-3695, Wards: 1
Delilah Miller, Councillor, 403-558-2415, Wards: 2
Jason Parker, Councillor, 403-931-1480, Wards: 3
Suzanne Oel, Councillor, 403-931-2711, Wards: 4
Ron Chase, Councillor, 403-931-3797, Wards: 5
Ted Mills, Councillor, 403-652-2584, Wards: 7
Harry Riva-Cambrin, Municipal Manager

Forty Mile County No. 8
P.O. Box 160
303 Main St.
Foremost, AB T0K 0X0
Tel: 403-867-3530; *Fax:* 403-867-2242
info@fortymile.ab.ca
www.40mile.ca
Municipal Type: County
Incorporated: Dec. 9, 1912; *Area:* 7,229.84 sq km
Population in 2011: 3,336
Federal Electoral District(s): Medicine Hat-Cardston-Warner
Next Election: Oct. 16, 2017 (4 year terms)
Bryne Lengyel, Reeve, 403-867-2407
Dale Brown, Administrator

Grande Prairie County No. 1
10001 - 84 Ave.
Clairmont, AB T0H 0W0
Tel: 780-532-9722; *Fax:* 780-539-9880
info@countygp.ab.ca
www.countygp.ab.ca
Municipal Type: County
Incorporated: Dec. 9, 1912; *Area:* 5,883.92 sq km
Population in 2011: 20,347
Federal Electoral District(s): Grande Prairie-Mackenzie
Next Election: Oct. 16, 2017 (4 year terms)
Note: Incorporated as a county on Jan. 1, 1951.
Leanne Beaupre, Reeve, 780-814-3121, Fax: 780-402-3809, Wards: 3
Harold Bulford, Councillor, 780-876-9009, Fax: 780-567-3620, Wards: 1
Daryl Beeston, Councillor, 780-933-3464, Wards: 2
Ross Sutherland, Councillor, 780-512-5385, Wards: 4
Bob Marshall, Councillor, 780-933-2053, Wards: 5
Peter Harris, Councillor, 780-933-3074, Wards: 6
Brock Smith, Councillor, 780-293-1973, Wards: 7
Richard Harpe, Councillor, 780-831-5156, Fax: 780-356-2867, Wards: 8
Corey Beck, Councillor, 780-831-6394, Wards: 9
Bill Rogan, County Administrator, 780-532-9722
Nick Lapp, Director, Planning & Development, 780-513-3950
Noreen Vavrek, Director, Finance & Systems, 780-532-9722
Everett Cooke, Fire Chief, 780-532-9727, Fax: 780-567-5578
Dale Van Volkinburgh, Director, Public Works, 780-532-7393, Fax: 780-539-9871
Megan Schur, Manager, Parks & Recreation, 780-532-9727, Fax: 780-567-5576
Charlotte Bierman, Coordinator, Human Resources, 780-513-3970, Fax: 780-532-9709

Greenview No. 16
P.O. Box 1079
Valleyview, AB T0H 3N0
Tel: 780-524-7600; *Fax:* 780-524-4307
www.mdgreenview.ab.ca
Other Information: Toll-Free Phone: 1-888-524-7601
Municipal Type: Municipal District
Incorporated: Jan. 1, 1969; *Area:* 32,994.14 sq km
Population in 2011: 5,299
Federal Electoral District(s): Grande Prairie-Mackenzie; Peace River-Westlock; Yellowhead
Next Election: Oct. 16, 2017 (4 year terms)
Note: Incorporated as a municipal district on Jan. 1, 1994.
Dale Gervais, Reeve
Mike Haugen, Chief Administrative Officer

Jasper
P.O. Box 520
303 Pyramid Lake Rd.
Jasper, AB T0E 1E0
Tel: 780-852-3356; *Fax:* 780-852-4019
info@town.jasper.ab.ca
www.jasper-alberta.com
Other Information: After-hours Emergencies: 780-852-6155
Municipal Type: Regional Municipality
Incorporated: Aug. 31, 1995; *Area:* 925.52 sq km
Population in 2011: 4,051
Federal Electoral District(s): Yellowhead
Next Election: Oct. 16, 2017 (4 year terms)
Note: Incorporated as a specialized municipality on July 20, 2001.
Richard Ireland, Mayor
Peter Waterworth, Chief Administrative Officer, 780-852-6501

Kneehill County
P.O. Box 400
232 Main St.
Three Hills, AB T0M 2A0
Tel: 866-443-5541; *Fax:* 403-443-5115
office@kneehillcounty.com
www.kneehillcounty.com
Municipal Type: County
Incorporated: Dec. 9, 1912; *Area:* 3,380.04 sq km
Population in 2011: 4,921
Federal Electoral District(s): Battle River-Crowfoot
Next Election: Oct. 16, 2017 (4 year terms)
R.T. (Bob) Long, Reeve
Al Hoggan, Chief Administrative Officer

Lac La Biche County
P.O. Box 1679
Lac La Biche, AB T0A 2C0
Tel: 780-623-1747; *Fax:* 780-623-2039
main.office@laclabichecounty.com
www.laclabichecounty.com
Other Information: Toll-Free: 1-877-806-5632
Municipal Type: County
Incorporated: Aug. 1, 2007; *Area:* 16,300 sq km
Population in 2011: 8,402
Federal Electoral District(s): Fort McMurray-Cold Lake
Next Election: Oct. 16, 2017 (4 year terms)
Note: The Town of Lac La Biche & Lakeland County amalgamated on August 1, 2007 to create Lac La Biche County.
Omer Moghrabi, Mayor, 780-623-6810
Shadia Amblie, Chief Administrative Officer

Lac Ste. Anne County
P.O. Box 219
4928 Langston St.
Sangudo, AB T0E 2A0
Tel: 780-785-3411; *Fax:* 780-785-2359
lsac@gov.lacsteanne.ab.ca
www.gov.lacsteanne.ab.ca
Other Information: Toll-Free: 1-866-880-5722
Municipal Type: County
Incorporated: Jan. 1, 1944; *Area:* 2,842.46 sq km
Population in 2011: 10,260
Federal Electoral District(s): Sturgeon River-Parkland
Next Election: Oct. 16, 2017 (4 year terms)
Lloyd Giebelhaus, Reeve, 780-785-2095, Wards: 7
Lorne Olsvik, Councillor, 780-967-5360, Wards: 1
Bill Hegy, Councillor, 780-967-2793, Wards: 2
Wayne Borle, Councillor, 780-967-3073, Wards: 3
Dwight Davidson, Councillor, 780-785-3736, Wards: 4
Robert Kohn, Councillor, 780-892-2211, Wards: 5
Ross Bohnet, Councillor, 780-786-4290, Wards: 6
Mike Primeau, County Manager
Trista Court, General Manager, Community & Protective Services
Abid Malik, Manager, Public Works
Carla Callihoo, General Manager, Corporate Services
Cindy Suter, Director, Finance/Economic Development

Lacombe County
RR#3
Lacombe, AB T4L 2N3
Tel: 403-782-6601; *Fax:* 403-782-3820
info@lacombecounty.com
www.lacombecounty.com
Municipal Type: County
Incorporated: Jan. 1, 1944; *Area:* 2,777.26 sq km
Population in 2011: 10,312
Federal Electoral District(s): Red Deer-Lacombe
Next Election: Oct. 16, 2017 (4 year terms)
Note: Incorporated as a county on Jan. 1, 1961.
Paula Law, Reeve, 403-784-3803, Wards: 4
Brenda Knight, Deputy Reeve, 403-788-2168, Wards: 2
Rod McDermand, Councillor, 403-747-2131, Wards: 1
Barb Shepherd, Councillor, 403-885-4097, Wards: 3
Ken Wigmore, Councillor, 403-782-2593, Wards: 5
Keith Stephenson, Councillor, 403-748-2431, Wards: 6
Dana Kreil, Councillor, 403-746-3607, Wards: 7
Terry Hager, County Commissioner, 403-782-6601
Keith Boras, Manager, Environmental & Protective Services, 403-782-6601
Dale Freitag, Manager, Planning Services, 403-782-6601
Tim Timmons, Manager, Corporate Services, 403-782-6601
Phil Lodermeier, Manager, Operations, 403-782-6601

Lamont County
Administration Bldg.
5303 - 50 Ave.
Lamont, AB T0B 2R0
Tel: 780-895-2233; *Fax:* 780-895-7404
info@lamontcounty.ca
www.lamontcounty.ca
Other Information: Toll-Free: 1-877-895-2233
Municipal Type: County
Incorporated: Dec. 23, 1912; *Area:* 2,400.78 sq km
Population in 2011: 3,872
Federal Electoral District(s): Lakeland
Next Election: Oct. 16, 2017 (4 year terms)
Note: Incorporated as a county on Jan. 1, 1968.
Wayne Woldanski, Reeve
Allan Harvey, Chief Administrative Officer

Leduc County
#101, 1101 - 5 St.
Nisku, AB T9E 2X3
Tel: 780-955-3555; *Fax:* 780-955-3444
shaunaf@leduc-county.com
www.leduc-county.com
Other Information: Toll free: 1-800-379-9052
Municipal Type: County
Incorporated: Jan. 1, 1944; *Area:* 2,610.25 sq km
Population in 2011: 13,541
Federal Electoral District(s): Edmonton-Wetaskiwin
Next Election: Oct. 16, 2017 (4 year terms)
Note: Incorporated as a county on Jan. 1, 1964.
John Whaley, Mayor, 780-955-4564, Wards: 4
Rick Smith, Councillor, 780-955-4561, Wards: 1
Clay Stumph, Councillor, 780-955-4562, Wards: 2
John Schonewille, Councillor, 780-955-4563, Wards: 3
Tanni Doblanko, Councillor, 780-955-4565, Wards: 4
Glenn Belozer, Councillor, 780-955-4566, Wards: 6
Audrey Kelto, Councillor, 780-955-4567, Wards: 7
Brian Bowles, County Manager, 780-955-6400
Allan Krasowski, Deputy County Manager, 780-955-6414
Rick Thomas, General Manager, Community Services, 780-955-6415
Grant Bain, Director, Planning & Development, 780-979-2113
Garett Broadbent, Director, Agricultural Services, 780-955-6404
Des Mrygold, Director, Public Works & Engineering, 780-955-6418
Dean Ohnysty, Director, Parks & Recreation, 780-955-4535
Darrell Fleming, Fire Chief, Fire, 780-955-7099

Lesser Slave River No. 124
P.O. Box 722
Slave Lake, AB T0G 2A0
Tel: 780-849-4888; *Fax:* 780-849-4939
md124@md124.ca
www.md124.ca
Other Information: Toll Free: 1-866-449-4888
Municipal Type: Municipal District
Incorporated: Jan. 1, 1969; *Area:* 10,075.88 sq km
Population in 2011: 2,929
Federal Electoral District(s): Peace River-Westlock
Next Election: Oct. 16, 2017 (4 year terms)
Note: Incorporated as a municipal district on Jan. 1, 1995.
Murray Kerik, Reeve
Allan Winarski, Chief Administrative Officer

Lethbridge County
#100, 905 - 4 Ave. South
Lethbridge, AB T1J 4E4
Tel: 403-328-5525; *Fax:* 403-328-5602
mailbox@lethcounty.ca
www.lethcounty.ca
Municipal Type: County
Incorporated: Jan. 1, 1954; *Area:* 2,839.28 sq km
County or District: Lethbridge No. 26; *Population in 2011:* 10,061
Federal Electoral District(s): Lethbridge
Next Election: Oct. 16, 2017 (4 year terms)
Note: Incorporated as a county on Jan 1, 1964.
Lorne Hickey, Reeve, Wards: 1
Henry Doeve, Deputy Reeve, Wards: 3
John Willms, Councillor, Wards: 2
Ken Benson, Councillor, Wards: 4
Steve Campbell, Councillor, Wards: 5
Tom White, Councillor, Wards: 6
Morris Zeinstra, Councillor, Wards: 7
Rick Robinson, Chief Administrative Officer
Tracy Anderson, Director, Corporate Services
Kevin Veirgutz, Director, Municipal Services
Terry Ostrom, Supervisor, Public Works

Mackenzie County
P.O. Box 640
4511 - 46 Ave.
Fort Vermilion, AB T0H 1N0
Tel: 780-927-3718; *Fax:* 780-927-4266
office@mackenziecounty.com
www.mackenziecounty.com
Other Information: Toll Free: 1-877-927-0677
Municipal Type: Regional Municipality
Incorporated: Jan. 1, 1995; *Area:* 80,484.42 sq km
Population in 2011: 10,927
Federal Electoral District(s): Grande Prairie-Mackenzie
Next Election: Oct. 16, 2017 (4 year terms)
Note: Incorporated as a specialized municipality on June 23, 1999. Name changed from The Municipal District of Mackenzie No. 23 to Mackenzie County in 2007.
Bill Neufeld, Reeve, 780-841-1806, Fax: 780-928-4224, Wards: 2
Walter Sarapuk, Deputy Reeve, 780-926-6384, Fax: 780-927-4561, Wards: 8
Josh Knelsen, Councillor, 780-926-7405, Wards: 1
Peter F. Braun, Councillor, 780-926-6238, Fax: 780-928-2683, Wards: 3
John W. Driedger, Councillor, 780-926-9410, Fax: 780-928-2700, Wards: 4
Elmer Derksen, Councillor, 780-926-0451, Fax: 780-928-0181, Wards: 5
Eric Jorgensen, Councillor, 780-826-9605, Wards: 6
Ricky Paul, Councillor, 780-285-4807, Wards: 7
Jacquie Bateman, Councillor, 780-926-3388, Wards: 9
Lisa Wardley, Councillor, 780-841-5799, Wards: 10
Joulia Whittleton, Chief Administrative Officer, 780-927-3718
John Klassen, Director, Environmental Services & Operations, 780-928-3983
Ron Pelensky, Director, Community Services & Operations, 780-927-3718
Byron Peters, Director, Planning & Development, 780-928-3983
Mark Schonken, Interim Director, Finance, 780-927-3718
Grant Smith, Agriculture Fieldman, 780-927-3718
Carol Gabriel, Manager, Legislative & Support Services, 780-927-3718

Minburn County No. 27
P.O. Box 550
4909 - 50 St.
Vegreville, AB T9C 1R6
Tel: 780-632-2082; *Fax:* 780-632-6296
info@minburncounty.ab.ca
www.minburncounty.ab.ca
Municipal Type: County
Incorporated: Jan. 30, 1942; *Area:* 2,911.14 sq km
Population in 2011: 3,278
Federal Electoral District(s): Lakeland
Next Election: Oct. 16, 2017 (4 year terms)
Note: Incorporated as a county on Jan. 1, 1965.
Roger Konieczny, Reeve
David Marynowich, Manager

Mountain View County
P.O. Box 100
1408 Twp Rd. 320
Didsbury, AB T0M 0W0
Tel: 403-335-3311; *Fax:* 403-335-9207
info@mountainviewcounty.com
www.mountainviewcounty.com
Other Information: Toll Free Phone: 1-877-264-9754
Municipal Type: County
Incorporated: Dec. 9, 1912; *Area:* 3,804.43 sq km
Population in 2011: 12,359
Federal Electoral District(s): Red Deer-Mountain View
Next Election: Oct. 16, 2017 (4 year terms)
Note: Incorporated as a county on Jan. 1, 1961.
Bruce Beattie, Reeve, 403-335-3311, Wards: 4
Patricia McKean, Deputy Reeve, 403-875-2969, Wards: 2
Jeremy Sayer, Councillor, 587-223-4554, Wards: 1
Duncan Milne, Councillor, 403-507-3844, Wards: 3
Angela Aalbers, Councillor, 403-507-1057, Wards: 5
Ken Heck, Councillor, 403-559-7896, Wards: 6
Al Kemmere, Councillor, 403-507-3345, Wards: 7
Tony Martens, Chief Administrative Officer, 403-335-3311
Ron Baker, Director, Operational Services, 403-335-3311
Jeff Holmes, Director, Legislative, Community & Agricultural Services, 403-335-3311
Margaretha Bloem, Director, Planning & Development Services, 403-335-3311
Greg Wiens, Director, Corporate Services, 403-335-3311

Newell County
P.O. Box 130
183037 Range Rd. 145
Brooks, AB T1R 1B2
Tel: 403-362-3266; *Fax:* 888-361-7921
administration@newellmail.ca
www.countyofnewell.ab.ca
Municipal Type: County
Incorporated: Feb. 10, 1948; *Area:* 5,903.47 sq km
Population in 2011: 6,786
Federal Electoral District(s): Bow River
Next Election: Oct. 16, 2017 (4 year terms)
Note: Incorporated as a county on Jan. 1, 1953. The Village of Tilley was dissolved on August 31, 2013, & its lands became part of the County of Newell.
Molly Douglass, Reeve, 403-641-2562, Fax: 403-641-2564
Kevin Stephenson, Chief Administrative Officer, 403-794-2325

Northern Lights County
P.O. Box 10
600 - 7th Ave. NW
Manning, AB T0H 2M0
Tel: 780-836-3348; *Fax:* 780-836-3663
countyofnorthernlights@countyofnorthernlights.com
www.countyofnorthernlights.com
Other Information: Toll Free: 1-888-525-3481
Municipal Type: County
Incorporated: Dec. 18, 1913; *Area:* 20,745.45 sq km
Population in 2011: 4,117
Federal Electoral District(s): Grande Prairie-Mackenzie
Next Election: Oct. 16, 2017 (4 year terms)
Note: Incorporated as a municipal district on April 1, 1995.
Cheryl Anderson, Reeve, 780-624-8660
Theresa Van Oort, Chief Administrative Officer, 780-836-3348

Northern Sunrise County
P.O. Box 1300
Peace River, AB T8S 1Y9
Tel: 780-624-0013; *Fax:* 780-624-0023
general@northernsunrise.net
www.northernsunrise.net
Municipal Type: County
Incorporated: Dec. 18, 1913; *Area:* 21,141.25 sq km
Population in 2011: 1,791
Federal Electoral District(s): Peace River-Westlock
Next Election: Oct. 16, 2017 (4 year terms)
Note: Incorporated as a municipal district on April 1, 1994.
Carolyn Kolebaba, Reeve
Peter Thomas, Chief Administrative Officer

Opportunity No. 17
P.O. Box 60
2077 Mistassiniy Rd. North
Wabasca, AB T0G 2K0
Tel: 780-891-3778; *Fax:* 780-891-4283
info@mdopportunity.ab.ca
www.mdopportunity.ab.ca
Other Information: Toll Free: 1-888-891-3778
Municipal Type: Municipal District
Incorporated: Dec. 18, 1913; *Area:* 29,140.78 sq km
Population in 2011: 3,074
Federal Electoral District(s): Fort McMurray-Cold Lake; Peace River-Westlock
Next Election: Oct. 16, 2017 (4 year terms)
Note: Incorporated as a municipal district on Aug. 1, 1995.
Paul Sinclair, Reeve
Helen Alook, Chief Administrative Officer

Paintearth County No. 18
P.O. Box 509
1 Crowfoot Crossing
Castor, AB T0C 0X0
Tel: 403-882-3211; *Fax:* 403-882-3560
www.countypaintearth.ca
Municipal Type: County
Incorporated: Dec. 8, 1913; *Area:* 3,287.24 sq km
Population in 2011: 2,029
Federal Electoral District(s): Battle River-Crowfoot
Next Election: Oct. 16, 2017 (4 year terms)
Note: Incorporated as a county on Jan. 1, 1962.
George Glazier, Reeve, 403-578-2050, Fax: 403-578-4306
Tarolyn Peach, Chief Administrative Officer, 403-741-6203

Parkland County
53109A Hwy. 779
Parkland County, AB T7Z 1R1
Tel: 780-968-8888; *Fax:* 780-968-8413
inquiries@parklandcounty.com
www.parklandcounty.com
Other Information: Toll Free: 1-888-880-0858
Municipal Type: County
Incorporated: March 1, 1918; *Area:* 2,392.61 sq km
Population in 2011: 30,568
Federal Electoral District(s): Sturgeon River-Parkland; Yellowhead
Next Election: Oct. 16, 2017 (4 year terms)
Note: Incorporated as a county on Jan. 1, 1969.
Rodney Shaigec, Mayor, 780-968-8410, Fax: 780-968-8430
AnnLisa Jensen, Councillor, 780-968-8420, Fax: 780-968-8430, Wards: 1
Jackie McCuaig, Councillor, 780-968-8421, Fax: 780-968-8430, Wards: 2
Phyllis Kobasiuk, Councillor, 780-968-8422, Fax: 780-968-8430, Wards: 3
Darrell Hollands, Councillor, 780-968-8423, Fax: 780-968-8150, Wards: 4
John McNab, Councillor, 780-968-8424, Fax: 780-968-8430, Wards: 5
Tracey Melnyk, Councillor, 780-968-8425, Fax: 780-968-8430, Wards: 6
Michael Heck, Chief Administrative Officer

Peace No. 135
P.O. Box 34
5239 - 52 Ave.
Berwyn, AB T0H 0E0
Tel: 780-338-3845; *Fax:* 780-338-2222
mdpeace@wispernet.ca
mdpeace.com
Other Information: Alt. Phone: 780-338-3846
Municipal Type: Municipal District
Incorporated: Dec. 11, 1916; *Area:* 851.92 sq km
Population in 2011: 1,344
Federal Electoral District(s): Peace River-Westlock
Next Election: Oct. 16, 2017 (4 year terms)
Veronica Bliska, Reeve
Lyle McKen, Chief Administrative Officer

Pincher Creek No. 9
P.O. Box 279
1037 Herron Ave.
Pincher Creek, AB T0K 1W0
Tel: 403-627-3130; *Fax:* 403-627-5070
info@mdpinchercreek.ab.ca
www.mdpinchercreek.ab.ca
Municipal Type: Municipal District
Incorporated: Jan. 1, 1944; *Area:* 3,482.26 sq km
Population in 2011: 3,158
Federal Electoral District(s): Foothills
Next Election: Oct. 16, 2017 (4 year terms)
Brian Hammond, Reeve
Wendy Kay, Chief Administrative Officer

Ponoka County
Encana Building
4205 Hwy. 2A
Ponoka, AB T4J 1V9
Tel: 403-783-3333; *Fax:* 403-783-6965
ponokacounty@ponokacounty.com
www.ponokacounty.com
Municipal Type: County
Incorporated: Jan. 1, 1944; *Area:* 2,807.94 sq km
Population in 2011: 8,856
Federal Electoral District(s): Red Deer-Lacombe
Next Election: Oct. 16, 2017 (4 year terms)
Note: Incorporated as a county on July 1, 1999.
Paul McLauchlin, Reeve
Charlie Cutforth, Chief Administrative Officer

Provost No. 52
P.O. Box 300
4504 - 53 Ave.
Provost, AB T0B 3S0
Tel: 780-753-2434; *Fax:* 780-753-6432
mdprovost@mdprovost.ca
www.mdprovost.ca
Other Information: Alt. Phone: 780-857-2434
Municipal Type: Municipal District
Incorporated: Dec. 9, 1912; *Area:* 3,625.2 sq km
Population in 2011: 2,288
Federal Electoral District(s): Battle River-Crowfoot
Next Election: Oct. 16, 2017 (4 year terms)
Allan Murray, Reeve, 780-753-6531
Tyler Lawrason, Administrator

Ranchland No. 66
P.O. Box 1060
Nanton, AB T0L 1R0
Tel: 403-646-3131; *Fax:* 403-646-3141
admin@ranchland66.com
www.mdranchland.ca
Municipal Type: Municipal District
Incorporated: Jan. 1, 1969; *Area:* 2,639.16 sq km
Population in 2011: 79
Federal Electoral District(s): Foothills
Next Election: Oct. 16, 2017 (4 year terms)
Note: Incorporated as a municipal district on Jan. 1, 1995.
Cameron Gardner, Reeve
Gregory Brkich, Chief Administrative Officer

Red Deer County
Red Deer County Centre
38106 Range Rd. 275
Red Deer County, AB T4S 2L9
Tel: 403-350-2150; *Fax:* 403-346-9840
info@rdcounty.ca
rdcounty.ca
Municipal Type: County
Incorporated: Jan. 1, 1944; *Area:* 4,002.58 sq km
Population in 2011: 18,351
Federal Electoral District(s): Red Deer-Lacombe; Red Deer-Mountain View
Next Election: Oct. 16, 2017 (4 year terms)
Note: Incorporated as a county on Jan. 1, 1963.
Jim Wood, Mayor, 403-773-2215
Philip Massier, Deputy Mayor & Councillor, 403-749-2956, Wards: 1
Jean Bota, Councillor, 403-309-2085, Wards: 2
Don Church, Councillor, 403-340-2092, Wards: 3
Connie Huelsman, Councillor, 403-224-3037, Wards: 4
Richard Lorenz, Councillor, 780-728-3285, Wards: 5
Christine Moore, Councillor, 403-314-4084, Wards: 6
Curtis Herzberg, County Manager, 403-350-2152
Marty Campbell, Director, Operations Services, 403-350-2174
Cynthia Cvik, Director, Planning & Development Services, 403-350-2170
Heather Gray, Director, Corporate Services, 403-350-2159
Ric Henderson, Director, Community & Protective Services, 403-357-2371
Tom Metzger, Fire Chief, 403-343-6667
Jana Erichson, Manager, Human Resources, 403-350-2156
Tyler Harke, Manager, Corporate Communications, 406-357-2367
Art Preachuck, Manager, Agriculture, 403-350-2162
Jo-Ann Symington, Manager, Community Services, 403-357-2370
Andrew Treu, Coordinator, Environmental Services, 403-357-2365

Rocky View County
911 - 32 Ave. NE
Calgary, AB T2E 6X6
Tel: 403-230-1401; *Fax:* 403-277-5977
comments@rockyview.ca
www.rockyview.ca
Municipal Type: County
Incorporated: Feb. 1, 1943; *Area:* 4,014.89 sq km
Population in 2011: 36,461
Federal Electoral District(s): Banff-Airdrie; Bow River; Foothills
Next Election: Oct. 16, 2017 (4 year terms)
Margaret Bahcheli, Reeve, Wards: 3
Greg Boehlke, Deputy Reeve, 403-880-7062, Wards: 6
Liz Brakey, Councillor, 403-630-3522, Wards: 1
Jerry Arshinoff, Councillor, 403-542-9789, Wards: 2
Rolly Ashdown, Councillor, 403-999-2722, Wards: 4
Earl Solberg, Councillor, 403-809-7165, Wards: 5
Lois Habberfield, Councillor, 403-461-3298, Wards: 7
Al Sacuta, Councillor, 403-239-4089, Wards: 8
Bruce Kendall, Councillor, 403-835-0762, Wards: 9
Kevin Greig, County Manager
Sherry Baers, Manager, Planning Services
Cole Nelson, Manager, Agricultural & Environmental Services
Rick Wiljamaa, Manager, Engineering Services
Nona Housenga, Manager, Legislative Services, 403-520-1184
David Kalinchuk, Manager, Economic Development, 403-520-8195
Lorraine Wesley-Riley, Manager, Enforcement Services
Stacey McGuire, Communications Coordinator, 403-520-3901

Saddle Hills County
P.O. Box 69
Spirit River, AB T0H 3G0
Tel: 780-864-3760; *Fax:* 780-864-3904
admin@saddlehills.ab.ca
www.saddlehills.ab.ca
Other Information: Toll Free: 1-888-864-3760
Municipal Type: County
Incorporated: April 1, 1945; *Area:* 5,836.94 sq km
Population in 2011: 2,288
Federal Electoral District(s): Grande Prairie-Mackenzie
Next Election: Oct. 16, 2017 (4 year terms)
Note: Incorporated as a municipal district on Jan. 1, 1995.
Alvin Hubert, Reeve
Bob Cardwell, Chief Administrative Officer

St. Paul County No. 19
5015 - 49 Ave.
St. Paul, AB T0A 3A4
Tel: 780-645-3301; *Fax:* 780-645-3104
countysp@county.stpaul.ab.ca
www.county.stpaul.ab.ca
Municipal Type: County
Incorporated: Jan. 30, 1942; *Area:* 3,297.74 sq km
Population in 2011: 5,831
Federal Electoral District(s): Lakeland
Next Election: Oct. 16, 2017 (4 year terms)
Steve Upham, Reeve
Sheila Kitz, Chief Administrative Officer

Smoky Lake County
P.O. Box 310
4612 McDougall Dr.
Smoky Lake, AB T0A 3C0
Tel: 780-656-3730; *Fax:* 780-656-3768
county@smokylakecounty.ab.ca
www.smokylakecounty.ab.ca
Other Information: Toll free: 888-656-3730
Municipal Type: County
Incorporated: May 3, 1922; *Area:* 3,412.81 sq km
Population in 2011: 3,910
Federal Electoral District(s): Lakeland
Next Election: Oct. 16, 2017 (4 year terms)
Cary Smigerowsky, Reeve, 780-656-5370
Cory Ollikka, Chief Administrative Officer

Smoky River No. 130
P.O. Box 210
701 Main St.
Falher, AB T0H 1M0
Tel: 780-837-2221; *Fax:* 780-837-2453
md130adm@telusplanet.net
www.mdsmokyriver.com
Municipal Type: Municipal District
Incorporated: Dec. 18, 1913; *Area:* 2,842.82 sq km
Population in 2011: 2,126
Federal Electoral District(s): Peace River-Westlock
Next Election: Oct. 16, 2017 (4 year terms)
Note: Incorporated as a municipal district on Jan. 1, 1952.
Robert Brochu, Reeve
Lucien G. Turcotte, Municipal Administrator

Spirit River No. 133
P.O. Box 389
4202 - 50 St.
Spirit River, AB T0H 3G0
Tel: 780-864-3500; *Fax:* 780-864-4303
mdsr133@mdspiritriver.ab.ca
www.mdspiritriver.ab.ca
Municipal Type: Municipal District
Incorporated: Dec. 18, 1913; *Area:* 684.14 sq km
Population in 2011: 713
Federal Electoral District(s): Grande Prairie-Mackenzie
Next Election: Oct. 16, 2017 (4 year terms)
Note: Incorporated as a municipal district on Dec. 11, 1916.
Stanley W. Bzowy, Reeve
Kelly Hudson, Chief Administrative Assistant

Starland County
P.O. Box 249
103 Main St.
Morrin, AB T0J 2B0
Tel: 403-772-3793; *Fax:* 403-772-3807
info@starlandcounty.com
www.starlandcounty.com
Municipal Type: County
Incorporated: Dec. 9, 1912; *Area:* 2,557.7 sq km
Population in 2011: 2,057
Federal Electoral District(s): Battle River-Crowfoot
Next Election: Oct. 16, 2017 (4 year terms)
J. Barrie Hoover, Reeve, 403-364-2040
Ross D. Rawlusyk, Chief Administrative Officer, 403-772-3793, Fax: 403-772-3807

Stettler County No. 6
P.O. Box 1270
6602 - 44 Ave.
Stettler, AB T0C 2L0
Tel: 403-742-4441; *Fax:* 403-742-1277
info@stettlercounty.ca
www.stettlercounty.ca
Municipal Type: County
Incorporated: Dec. 9, 1912; *Area:* 4,008.72 sq km
Population in 2011: 5,089
Federal Electoral District(s): Battle River-Crowfoot
Next Election: Oct. 16, 2017 (4 year terms)
Wayne Nixon, Reeve
Tim Fox, Chief Administrative Officer

Strathcona County
2001 Sherwood Dr.
Sherwood Park, AB T8A 3W7
Tel: 780-464-8111; *Fax:* 780-464-8050
info@strathcona.ab.ca
www.strathcona.ab.ca
Municipal Type: Regional Municipality
Incorporated: Jan. 1, 1962; *Area:* 1,179.43 sq km
Population in 2011: 92,490
Federal Electoral District(s): Sherwood Park-Fort Saskatchewan
Next Election: Oct. 16, 2017 (4 year terms)
Note: Incorporated as a specialized municipality on Jan. 1, 1996.
Roxanne Carr, Mayor, 780-646-8000, Fax: 780-646-8051
Vic Bidzinski, Councillor, 780-464-8005, Fax: 780-464-8114, Wards: 1
Dave Anderson, Councillor, 780-464-8002, Fax: 780-464-8114, Wards: 2
Brian Botterill, Councillor, 780-464-8149, Fax: 780-464-8114, Wards: 3
Carla Howatt, Councillor, 780-464-8146, Fax: 780-464-8114, Wards: 4
Paul Smith, Councillor, 780-464-8147, Fax: 780-464-8114, Wards: 5
Linton Delainey, Councillor, 780-464-8206, Fax: 780-464-8114, Wards: 6
Bonnie Riddell, Councillor, 780-464-8003, Fax: 780-464-8114, Wards: 7
Fiona Beland-Quest, Councillor, 780-464-8158, Fax: 780-464-8114, Wards: 8
Rob Coon, Chief Commissioner, 780-464-8100, Fax: 780-464-8050
George Huybregts, Associate Commissioner/Chief Financial Officer, 780-464-8068, Fax: 780-464-8050
Darlene Bouwsema, Associate Commissioner, Corporate Services Division, 780-400-2085, Fax: 780-464-8050
Denise Exton, Associate Commissioner, Community Services Division, 780-464-8291, Fax: 780-464-8050
Kevin Glebe, Associate Commissioner, Infrastructure Planning Services Division, 780-464-8188, Fax: 780-464-8050

Sturgeon County
9613 - 100 St.
Morinville, AB T8R 1L9
Tel: 780-939-4321; *Fax:* 780-939-3003
sturgeonmail@sturgeoncounty.ca
www.sturgeoncounty.ab.ca
Other Information: Toll free: 1-866-939-9303
Municipal Type: County
Incorporated: Feb. 1, 1943; *Area:* 2,108.9 sq km
Population in 2011: 19,578
Federal Electoral District(s): Sturgeon River-Parkland
Next Election: Oct. 16, 2017 (4 year terms)
Tom Flynn, Mayor, 780-718-1411
Ferd Caron, Deputy Mayor & Councillor, 587-873-4671, Wards: 1
Susan Evans, Councillor, 587-879-0208, Wards: 2
Wayne Bokenfohr, Councillor, 587-879-5787, Wards: 3
Jerry Kaup, Councillor, 780-914-1795, Wards: 4
Patrick D. Tighe, Councillor, 587-879-5797, Wards: 5
Karen Shaw, Councillor, 780-999-2381, Wards: 6
Peter Tarnawsky, Chief Administrative Officer, 780-939-8345
Ian McKay, General Manager, Municipal Services, 780-939-8337
Stephane Labonne, General Manager, Integrated Growth, 780-939-8337
Rick Wojtkiw, General Manager, Corporate Support, 780-939-8326
Susan Berry, Manager, Legislative Services, 780-939-8369
Ed Kaemingh, Manager, Financial Services, 780-939-8348

Taber
4900B - 50 St.
Taber, AB T1G 1T2
Tel: 403-223-3541; *Fax:* 403-223-1799
dkrizsan@mdtaber.ab.ca
www.mdtaber.ab.ca
Municipal Type: Municipal District
Incorporated: April 1, 1945; *Area:* 4,204.38 sq km
Population in 2011: 6,851
Federal Electoral District(s): Bow River
Next Election: Oct. 16, 2017 (4 year terms)
Brian Brewin, Reeve, 403-655-2463, Fax: 403-655-2403
Derrick Krizsan, Municipal Administrator

Thorhild County
P.O. Box 10
801 - 1 St.
Thorhild, AB T0A 3J0
Tel: 780-398-3741; *Fax:* 780-398-3748
cao@thorhildcounty.com
www.thorhildcounty.com
Other Information: Toll-Free Phone: 1-877-398-3777
Municipal Type: County
Incorporated: Jan. 1, 1955; *Area:* 1,998.38 sq km
Population in 2011: 3,417
Federal Electoral District(s): Lakeland
Next Election: Oct. 16, 2017 (4 year terms)
Note: Thorhild County No. 7 was changed to Thorhild County on March 20, 2013.

Two Hills County No. 21
P.O. Box 490
4818 - 50 Ave
Two Hills, AB T0B 4K0
Tel: 780-657-3358; *Fax:* 780-657-3504
info@thcounty.ab.ca
www.thcounty.ab.ca
Municipal Type: County
Incorporated: Jan. 1, 1944; *Area:* 2,630.95 sq km
Population in 2011: 3,160
Federal Electoral District(s): Lakeland
Next Election: Oct. 16, 2017 (4 year terms)
Note: Incorporated as a county on Jan. 1, 1963.
Allen Sayler, Reeve
Sally Dary, Chief Administrative Officer

Vermilion River County
P.O. Box 69
4912 - 50 Ave.
Kitscoty, AB T0B 2P0
Tel: 780-846-2244; *Fax:* 780-846-2716
county24@telusplanet.net
www.vermilion-river.com
Municipal Type: County
Incorporated: Jan. 1, 1944; *Area:* 5,518.71 sq km
Population in 2011: 7,905
Federal Electoral District(s): Lakeland
Next Election: Oct. 16, 2017 (4 year terms)
Note: Name changed from Vermilion River No. 24 County on Sept. 13, 2006.
Daryl Watt, Reeve, 780-808-1359
Rhonda King, County Administrator, 780-846-2244

Vulcan County
P.O. Box 180
102 Centre St.
Vulcan, AB T0L 2B0
Tel: 403-485-2241; *Fax:* 403-485-2920
www.vulcancounty.ab.ca
Other Information: Toll Free: 1-877-485-2299
Municipal Type: County
Incorporated: April 1, 1945; *Area:* 5,430.06 sq km
Population in 2011: 3,875
Federal Electoral District(s): Bow River
Next Election: Oct. 16, 2017 (4 year terms)
Note: Incorporated as a county on Jan. 1, 1951.
Derrick Annable, Reeve, 403-331-5587
Leo Ludwig, County Administrator, 403-485-2241

Wainwright No. 61
717 - 14 Ave.
Wainwright, AB T9W 1B3
Tel: 780-842-4454; *Fax:* 780-842-2463
info@mdwainwright.ca
www.mdwainwright.ca
Municipal Type: Municipal District
Incorporated: Jan. 30, 1942; *Area:* 4,154.74 sq km
Population in 2011: 4,138
Federal Electoral District(s): Battle River-Crowfoot
Next Election: Oct. 16, 2017 (4 year terms)
Bob Barss, Reeve, 780-754-2195
Kelly Buchinski, Municipal Administrator, 780-842-4454

Warner County No. 5
P.O. Box 90
300 County Rd.
Warner, AB T0K 2L0
Tel: 403-642-3635; *Fax:* 403-642-3631
ably@warnercounty.ca
www.warnercounty.ca
Other Information: Toll Free: 1-888-642-2241
Municipal Type: County
Incorporated: Dec. 9, 1912; *Area:* 4,517.67 sq km
Population in 2011: 3,841
Federal Electoral District(s): Medicine Hat-Cardston-Warner
Next Election: Oct. 16, 2017 (4 year terms)
Ross Ford, Reeve, 403-344-3053, Fax: 403-344-3055
Shawn Hathaway, Chief Administrative Officer

Westlock County
10336 - 106 St.
Westlock, AB T7P 2G1
Tel: 780-349-3346; *Fax:* 780-349-2012
info@westlockcounty.com
www.westlockcounty.com
Other Information: Toll Free: 1-877-349-5880
Municipal Type: County
Incorporated: Feb. 1, 1943; *Area:* 3,174.6 sq km
Population in 2011: 7,644
Federal Electoral District(s): Peace River-Westlock
Next Election: Oct. 16, 2017 (4 year terms)
Bud Massey, Reeve
Duane Coleman, Chief Administrative Officer, 780-307-0525

Wetaskiwin County No. 10
P.O. Box 6960
Wetaskiwin, AB T9A 2G5
Tel: 780-352-3321; *Fax:* 780-352-3486
www.county.wetaskiwin.ab.ca
Other Information: Toll Free: 1-800-661-4125
Municipal Type: County
Incorporated: Dec. 13, 1915; *Area:* 3,130.9 sq km
Population in 2011: 10,866
Federal Electoral District(s): Edmonton-Wetaskiwin
Next Election: Oct. 16, 2017 (4 year terms)
Note: Incorporated as a county on Jan. 1, 1958.
Kathy Rooyakkers, Reeve, Wards: 6
Pearl Hay, Councillor, 780-352-3157, Wards: 1
Terry Van De Kraats, Councillor, 780-352-2395, Wards: 2
Garry Dearing, Councillor, 780-352-4889, Wards: 3
Keith Johnson, Councillor, 780-387-5543, Wards: 4
Larry McKeever, Councillor, 780-389-3339, Wards: 5
Lyle Seely, Councillor, 780-388-3894, Wards: 7
Frank Coutney, Chief Administrative Officer
Rod Hawken, Assistant Chief Administrative Officer
David Blades, Director, Planning & Economic Development Services
Grace French, Director, Finance

Wheatland County
Hwy. 1, RR#1
Strathmore, AB T1P 1J6
Tel: 403-934-3321; *Fax:* 403-934-4889
admin@wheatlandcounty.ca
www.wheatlandcounty.ca
Municipal Type: County
Incorporated: April 1, 1945; *Area:* 4,550.92 sq km
Population in 2011: 8,285
Federal Electoral District(s): Bow River
Next Election: Oct. 16, 2017 (4 year terms)
Note: Incorporated as a county on Jan. 1, 1961.
Glenn Koester, Reeve, 403-533-2228
Alan Parkin, Chief Administrative Officer

Willow Creek No. 26
P.O. Box 550
Claresholm, AB T0L 0T0
Tel: 403-625-3351; *Fax:* 403-625-3886
md26@mdwillowcreek.com
www.mdwillowcreek.com
Other Information: Toll-Free Phone: 1-888-337-3351
Municipal Type: Municipal District
Incorporated: Jan. 1, 1944; *Area:* 4,560.22 sq km
Population in 2011: 5,107
Federal Electoral District(s): Foothills
Next Election: Oct. 16, 2017 (4 year terms)
Neil Wilson, Reeve, 403-646-3088
Cynthia Vizzutti, Chief Administrative Officer

Wood Buffalo
9909 Franklin Ave.
Fort McMurray, AB T9H 2K4
Tel: 780-743-7000; *Fax:* 780-743-7028
info@woodbuffalo.ab.ca
www.woodbuffalo.ab.ca
Other Information: Toll Free: 1-800-973-9663
Municipal Type: Regional Municipality
Incorporated: April 1, 1995; *Area:* 63,342.89 sq km
Population in 2011: 65,565
Federal Electoral District(s): Fort McMurray-Cold Lake
Next Election: Oct. 16, 2017 (4 year terms)
Note: Incorporated as a specialized municipality on April 1, 1995.
Melissa Blake, Mayor, 780-743-7009, Fax: 780-743-7099
Tyran Ault, Councillor, 780-743-7011, Wards: 1
Guy C. Boutilier, Councillor, 780-743-7011, Wards: 1
Lance Bussieres, Councillor, 780-743-7011, Wards: 1
Sheldon Germain, Councillor, 780-743-7011, Wards: 1
Keith McGrath, Councillor, 780-743-7011, Wards: 1
Phil Meagher, Councillor, 780-799-7900, Wards: 1
Julia Cardinal, Councillor, 780-743-7011, Wards: 2
John H. Chadi, Councillor, 780-743-7011, Wards: 2
Allan Glen Vinni, Councillor, 780-792-7616, Wards: 3
Jane Stroud, Councillor, 780-334-0516, Fax: 780-743-7028, Wards: 4
Marcel Ulliac, Chief Administrative Officer, 780-743-7023, Fax: 780-743-7099
Dianne Batstone, Senior Executive Assistant, 780-743-7023, Fax: 780-743-7028

Woodlands County
P.O. Box 60
1 Woodlands Ln.
Whitecourt, AB T7S 1N3
Tel: 780-778-8400; *Fax:* 780-778-8402
admin@woodlands.ab.ca
www.woodlands.ab.ca
Other Information: Toll free: 1-888-870-6315
Municipal Type: County
Incorporated: Jan. 1, 1969; *Area:* 7,668.11 sq km
Population in 2011: 4,306
Federal Electoral District(s): Peace River-Westlock
Next Election: Oct. 16, 2017 (4 year terms)
Note: Incorporated as a municipal district on Jan. 1, 1994.
Jim Rennie, Mayor, 780-778-0202
Luc Mercier, Chief Administrative Officer, 780-778-8400

Yellowhead County
2716 - 1st Ave.
Edson, AB T7E 1N9
Tel: 780-723-4800; *Fax:* 780-723-5066
info@yellowheadcounty.ab.ca
www.yellowheadcounty.ab.ca
Other Information: Toll Free Phone: 1-800-665-6030
Municipal Type: County
Incorporated: Jan. 1, 1994; *Area:* 22,303.82 sq km
Population in 2011: 10,469
Federal Electoral District(s): Yellowhead
Next Election: Oct. 16, 2017 (4 year terms)
Gerald Soroka, Mayor, 780-727-2101
Fred Prestley-Wright, Deputy Mayor, 780-795-2211, Wards: 3, Nilton/Carrot Creek Area
Sandra Cherniawsky, Councillor, 780-727-2693, Wards: 1, Evansburg & Area
Anthony Giezen, Councillor, 780-325-2459, Wards: 2, Wildwood & Area
David Russell, Councillor, 780-693-2209, Wards: 4, Peers/Rosevear/Shiningbank

Shawn Berry, Councillor, 780-723-2606, Wards: 5, Wolf Creek/Pinedale Area
William (Bill) Velichko, Councillor, 780-723-2216, Wards: 6, Edson Area
Dawn Mitchell, Councillor, 780-725-1174, Wards: 7, Edson West
Jack Williams, Councillor, 780-817-4968, Wards: 8, Hinton/Cadomin/Robb
Jack Ramme, Chief Administrative Officer
Debbie Charest, Director, Community & Protective Services
Barb Lyons, Director, Corporate & Planning Serivces
Don O'Quinn, Director, Infrastructure Services
Brent Shepherd, Manager, Planning & Development
Cory Chegwyn, Fire Chief

Major Municipalities in Alberta

Airdrie
400 Main St. SE
Airdrie, AB T4B 3C3
Tel: 403-948-8800; *Fax:* 403-948-6567
information.systems@airdrie.ca
www.airdrie.ca
Other Information: Toll Free: 1-888-247-3743
Municipal Type: City
Incorporated: Sept. 10, 1909; *Area:* 33.10 sq km
Population in 2011: 42,564
Provincial Electoral District(s): Airdrie
Federal Electoral District(s): Banff-Airdrie
Next Election: Oct. 16, 2017 (4 year terms)
Note: Incorporated as a city on Jan. 1, 1985.
Peter Brown, Mayor, 403-948-8820
Darrell Belyk, Deputy Mayor, 403-862-8643
Fred Burley, Councillor, 403-948-2778
Ron Chapman, Councillor, 403-992-4604
Kelly Hegg, Councillor, 403-862-2035
Allan Hunter, Councillor, 403-540-4616
Candice Kolson, Councillor, 403-828-1448
Paul Schulz, City Manager, 403-948-8800, Fax: 403-948-6567

Beaumont
5600 - 49 St.
Beaumont, AB T4X 1A1
Tel: 780-929-8782; *Fax:* 780-929-8729
admin@town.beaumont.ab.ca
www.town.beaumont.ab.ca
Municipal Type: City
Incorporated: Jan. 1, 1973; *Area:* 10.5 sq km
County or District: Leduc County; *Population in 2011:* 13,284
Provincial Electoral District(s): Leduc-Beaumont
Federal Electoral District(s): Edmonton-Wetaskiwin
Next Election: Oct. 16, 2017 (4 year terms)
Note: Incorporated as a town on Jan 1, 1980.
Camille Bérubé, Mayor, 780-929-8368
Kathy Barnhart, Councillor, 780-721-5504
Kerri Bauer, Councillor, 780-929-2441
Perry Hendriks, Councillor, 780-929-5102
Bruce LeCren, Councillor, 780-709-4431
Bill McNamara, Councillor, 780-929-8215
Louise White-Gibbs, Councillor, 780-929-2233
Marc Landry, Chief Administrative Officer
Brenda Molter, Municipal Clerk

Brooks
P.O. Box 879
201 - 1 Ave. West
Brooks, AB T1R 0Z6
Tel: 403-362-3333; *Fax:* 403-362-4787
admin@brooks.ca
www.brooks.ca
Municipal Type: City
Incorporated: July 14, 1910; *Area:* 17.7 sq km
Population in 2011: 13,676
Provincial Electoral District(s): Strathmore-Brooks
Federal Electoral District(s): Bow River
Next Election: Oct. 16, 2017 (4 year terms)
Note: Incorporated as a city on Sept. 1, 2005.
Martin Shields, Mayor
Cathy Corbett-Schock, Councillor
Norm Gerestein, Councillor
Dan Klein, Councillor
Barry Morishita, Councillor
Bill Prentice, Councillor
Fred Rattai, Councillor
Alan Martens, Chief Administrative Officer
Don Saari, Manager, Public Works, 403-362-3146, Fax: 403-362-5658
Shelley Thomas, Manager, Finance Services
Kevin Swanson, Fire Chief, Fire & Rescue Services
Kelly Attwell, Supervisor, Facilities
Phil Lunn, Supervisor, Parks, 403-362-0271, Fax: 403-363-2356
Rebecca Taylor, Supervisor, Planning & Development Services
Tony Diep, Communications Officer

Calgary
P.O. Box 2100 Stn. M
800 Macleod Trail SE
Calgary, AB T2P 2M5
Tel: 403-268-2489; *Fax:* 403-538-6111
311contactus@calgary.ca
www.calgary.ca
Other Information: TTY: 403-268-4889
Municipal Type: City
Incorporated: Nov. 7, 1884; *Area:* 726.5 sq km
Population in 2011: 1,096,833
Provincial Electoral District(s): Cal.-Acadia; Cal.-Bow; Cal.-Buffalo; Cal.-Cross; Cal.-Currie; Cal.-East; Cal.-Elbow; Cal.-Fish Creek; Cal.-Foothills; Cal.-Fort; Cal.-Glenmore; Cal.-Greenway; Cal.-Hawkwood; Cal.-Hays; Cal.-Klein; Cal.-Lougheed; Cal.-McCall; Cal.-Mackay-Nose Hill; Cal.-Mountain View; Cal.-Northern Hills; Cal.-North West; Cal.-Shaw; Cal.-South East; Cal.-Varsity; Cal.-West
Federal Electoral District(s): Calgary Centre; Calgary Confederation; Calgary Forest Lawn; Calgary Heritage; Calgary Midnapore; Calgary Nose Hill; Calgary Rocky Ridge; Calgary Shepard; Calgary Signal Hill; Calgary Skyview
Next Election: Oct. 16, 2017 (4 year terms)
Note: Incorporated as a city on Jan. 1, 1894.
Naheed K. Nenshi, Mayor, 403-268-5622, Fax: 403-268-8130
Ward Sutherland, Councillor, 403-268-2430, Fax: 403-268-3823, Wards: 1
Joe Magliocca, Councillor, 403-268-2430, Fax: 403-268-3823, Wards: 2
Jim Stevenson, Councillor, 403-268-2430, Fax: 403-268-8091, Wards: 3
Sean Chu, Councillor, 403-268-2430, Fax: 403-268-8091, Wards: 4
Ray Jones, Councillor, 403-268-2430, Fax: 403-268-3823, Wards: 5
Richard Pootmans, Councillor, 403-268-2430, Fax: 403-268-3823, Wards: 6
Druh Farrell, Councillor, 403-268-2430, Fax: 403-268-3823, Wards: 7
Evan Woolley, Councillor, 403-268-2430, Fax: 403-268-3823, Wards: 8
Gian-Carlo Carra, Councillor, 403-268-5330, Fax: 403-268-8091, Wards: 9
Andre Chabot, Councillor, 403-268-2430, Fax: 403-268-3823, Wards: 10
Brian Pincott, Councillor, 403-268-2430, Fax: 403-268-8091, Wards: 11
Shane A. Keating, Councillor, 403-268-2478, Fax: 403-268-8091, Wards: 12
Diane Colley-Urquhart, Councillor, 403-268-1624, Fax: 403-268-8091, Wards: 13
Peter Demong, Councillor, 403-268-1653, Fax: 403-268-3823, Wards: 14
Sue Gray, City Clerk, 403-268-5848
Jeff Fielding, City Manager, 403-268-2109
Brad Stevens, Deputy City Manager, 403-268-2353
Eric Sawyer, Chief Financial Officer, 403-268-5589
Stuart Dalgleish, General Manager, Planning & Development, 403-268-2601
Mac Logan, General Manager, Transportation, 403-268-5637
Rob Pritchard, General Manager, Utilities & Environmental Protection, 403-268-2042
Rolin Stanley, General Manager, Urban Strategy, 403-268-1367
Roger Chaffin, Chief of Police
Steve Dongworth, Fire Chief, 403-287-4255
Christopher Collier, Director, Environmental & Safety Management, 403-268-1012
Mark Lavallee, Director, Human Resources, 403-268-2201
Dan Limacher, Director, Water Services, 403-268-5733
Rob Spackman, Director, Water Resources, 403-268-2572
Rick Valdarchi, Director, Waste & Recycling Services, 403-268-6474

Camrose
City Hall
5204 - 50 Ave.
Camrose, AB T4V 0S8
Tel: 780-672-4426; *Fax:* 780-672-2469
admin@camrose.ca
www.camrose.ca
Municipal Type: City
Incorporated: May 4, 1905; *Area:* 31.14 sq km
Population in 2011: 17,286
Provincial Electoral District(s): Wetaskiwin-Camrose
Federal Electoral District(s): Battle River-Crowfoot
Next Election: Oct. 16, 2017 (4 year terms)
Note: Incorporated as a city on Jan. 1, 1955.
Norman Mayer, Mayor, 780-678-3027
Agnes Hoveland, Councillor, 780-678-3027
Kevin Hycha, Councillor, 780-678-3027
Max Lindstrand, Councillor, 780-678-3027
Ray McIsaac, Councillor, 780-678-3027
Bill Sears, Councillor, 780-678-3027
PJ Stasko, Councillor, 780-678-3027
Wayne Throndson, Councillor, 780-678-3027
Greg Wood, Councillor, 780-678-3027
Malcolm Boyd, City Manager, 780-678-3027, Fax: 780-672-2469
Mark Barrett, Director, Infrastructure Services, 780-672-4428, Fax: 780-672-6316
Kim Isaak, General Manager, Corporate & Protective Services, 780-678-3027, Fax: 780-672-2469
Paul Neilsen, General Manager, Community Services, 780-672-9195
Diane Urkow, General Manager, Financial Services, 780-672-4426, Fax: 780-672-2469
Chris Clarkson, Director, Parks, 780-672-9195, Fax: 780-672-4915
Jim Kupka, Director, Public Works, 780-672-5513
Aaron Leckie, Director, Planning & Development, 780-672-4428
Darrell Kambeitz, Police Chief, 780-672-8300
Peter Krich, Fire Chief/Deputy Director, Emergency Management, 780-672-2906, Fax: 780-672-1384

Canmore
902 - 7 Ave.
Canmore, AB T1W 3K1
Tel: 403-678-1500; *Fax:* 403-678-1524
info@canmore.ca
www.canmore.ca
Municipal Type: City
Incorporated: Jan. 1, 1965; *Area:* 68.9 sq km
Population in 2011: 12,288
Provincial Electoral District(s): Banff-Cochrane
Federal Electoral District(s): Banff-Airdrie
Next Election: Oct. 16, 2017 (4 year terms)
Note: Incorporated as a town on June 1, 1966.
John Barrowman, Mayor, 403-678-1517
Esme Comfort, Councillor
Sean Krausert, Councillor, 403-609-1762
Joanna McCallum, Councillor, 403-678-1500
Vi Sandford, Councillor, 403-678-2370
Rob Seeley, Councillor, 403-678-1535
Ed Russell, Councillor, 403-678-1535
Lisa De Soto, Chief Administrative Officer, 403-678-1535, Fax: 403-678-1524
Andy Esarte, Manager, Engineering Services, 403-678-1545, Fax: 403-678-1534
Stephen Hanus, Manager, Facilities, 403-678-0808, Fax: 406-678-6661
Katherine Van Keimpema, Manager, Financial Services

Chestermere
105 Marina Rd.
Chestermere, AB T1X 1V7
Tel: 403-207-7050; *Fax:* 403-569-0512
town@chestermere.ca
www.chestermere.ca
Municipal Type: City
Incorporated: April 1, 1977; *Area:* 8.91 sq km
County or District: Rocky View County; *Population in 2011:* 14,824
Provincial Electoral District(s): Chestermere-Rocky View
Federal Electoral District(s): Bow River
Next Election: Oct. 16, 2017 (4 year terms)
Note: Incorporated as a town on March 1, 1993.
Patricia Matthews, Mayor, 403-207-7073
Heather Davies, Deputy Mayor, 403-272-6361
Stu Hutchinson, Councillor, 403-248-1952
Jennifer Massig, Councillor, 403-470-2333
Gail Smith, Councillor, 403-207-7050
Christopher Steeves, Councillor, 403-988-5790
Patrick Watson, Councillor, 403-923-0099
Randy Patrick, Chief Administrative Officer, 403-207-7042
Tracy Anderson, Director, Corporate Services
Ann Thai, Manager, Finance

Cochrane
P.O. Box 10
101 RancheHouse Rd.
Cochrane, AB T4C 2K8
Tel: 403-851-2500; *Fax:* 403-932-6032
cochrane@cochrane.ca
www.cochrane.ca
Municipal Type: City
Incorporated: June 17, 1903; *Area:* 30.03 sq km
County or District: Rocky View County; *Population in 2011:* 17,580
Provincial Electoral District(s): Banff-Cochrane
Federal Electoral District(s): Banff-Airdrie

Next Election: Oct. 16, 2017 (4 year terms)
Note: Incorporated as a town on Feb. 15, 1971.
Ivan Brooker, Mayor, 403-851-2506, Fax: 403-851-2581
Mary Lou Davis, Councillor, 403-851-2505, Fax: 403-851-2581
Gaynor Levisky, Councillor, 403-851-2505, Fax: 403-851-2581
Tara McFadden, Councillor, 403-851-2505, Fax: 403-851-2581
Morgan Nagel, Councillor, 403-851-2505, Fax: 403-851-2581
Jeff Toews, Councillor, 403-851-2505, Fax: 403-851-2581
Ross Watson, Councillor, 403-851-2505, Fax: 403-851-2581
Julian deCocq, Chief Adminstrative Officer, 403-851-2505
Mac deBeaudrap, Senior Manager, Protective Services
Jared Kassel, Manager, Planning & Engineering Services, 403-851-2279

Cold Lake
5513 - 48 Ave.
Cold Lake, AB T9M 1A1
Tel: 780-594-4494; *Fax:* 780-594-3480
city@coldlake.com
www.coldlake.com
Municipal Type: City
Incorporated: Dec. 31, 1953; *Area:* 59.3 sq km
Population in 2011: 13,839
Provincial Electoral District(s): Bonnyville-Cold Lake
Federal Electoral District(s): Fort McMurray-Cold Lake
Next Election: Oct. 16, 2017 (4 year terms)
Note: Incorporated as a city on Oct. 1, 2000.
Craig Copeland, Mayor
Bob Buckle, Councillor
Duane Lay, Councillor
Vicky Lefebvre, Councillor
Darrell MacDonold, Councillor
Kevin Plain, Councillor
Chris Vining, Councillor
Kevin Nagoya, Chief Administrative Officer

Edmonton
City Hall
1 Sir Winston Churchill Sq., 3rd Fl.
Edmonton, AB T5J 2R7
Tel: 780-442-5311; *Fax:* 780-496-5618
311@edmonton.ca
www.edmonton.ca
Other Information: Telephone: 311 in Edmonton
Municipal Type: City
Incorporated: Jan. 9, 1892; *Area:* 684.37 sq km
Population in 2011: 812,201
Provincial Electoral District(s): Ed.-Beverly-Clareview; Ed.-Calder; Ed.-Castle Downs; Ed.-Centre; Ed.-Decore; Ed.-Ellerslie; Ed.-Glenora; Ed.-Gold Bar; Ed.-Highlands-Norwood; Ed.-Manning; Ed.-McClung; Ed.-Meadowlark; Ed.-Mill Creek; Ed.-Mill Woods; Ed.-Riverview; Ed.-Rutherford; Ed.-Strathcona; Ed.-Whitemud
Federal Electoral District(s): Edmonton Griesbach; Edmonton Centre; Edmonton Manning; Edmonton Mill Woods; Edmonton Riverbend; Edmonton Strathcona; Edmonton West; Edmonton-Wetaskiwin; St. Albert-Edmonton
Next Election: Oct. 16, 2017 (4 year terms)
Note: Incorporated as a city on Oct. 08, 1904.
Don Iveson, Mayor, 780-496-8100, Fax: 780-496-8113
Andrew Knack, Councillor, 780-496-8122, Fax: 780-496-8113, Wards: 1
Bev Esslinger, Councillor, 780-496-8136, Fax: 780-496-8113, Wards: 2
Dave Loken, Councillor, 780-496-8128, Fax: 780-496-8113, Wards: 3
Ed Gibbons, Councillor, 780-496-8138, Fax: 780-496-8113, Wards: 4
Michael Oshry, Councillor, 780-496-8120, Fax: 780-496-8113, Wards: 5
Scott McKeen, Councillor, 780-496-8140, Fax: 780-496-8113, Wards: 6
Tony Caterina, Councillor, 780-496-8333, Fax: 780-496-8113, Wards: 7
Ben Henderson, Councillor, 780-496-8146, Fax: 780-496-8113, Wards: 8
Bryan Anderson, Councillor, 780-496-8130, Fax: 780-496-8113, Wards: 9
Michael Walters, Councillor, 780-496-8132, Fax: 780-496-8113, Wards: 10
Mike Nickel, Councillor, 780-496-8142, Fax: 780-496-8113, Wards: 11
Mohinder Banga, Councillor, 780-496-8148, Fax: 780-496-8113, Wards: 12
Linda Cochrane, City Manager, 780-496-8231, Fax: 780-496-8220
David Wiun, City Auditor, 780-496-8300, Fax: 780-496-8062
Gary Klassen, General Manager, Sustainable Development
Tracy Williams, Coordinator, Office of Emergency Preparedness, Fax: 780-496-3062
Rod Knecht, Police Chief, 780-421-3333, Fax: 780-421-2187

Fort Saskatchewan
10005 - 102 St.
Fort Saskatchewan, AB T8L 2C5
Tel: 780-992-6200; *Fax:* 780-998-4774
www.fortsask.ca
Municipal Type: City
Incorporated: March 1, 1899; *Area:* 48.12 sq km
Population in 2011: 19,051
Provincial Electoral District(s): Fort Saskatchewan-Vegreville
Federal Electoral District(s): Sherwood Park-Fort Saskatchewan
Next Election: Oct. 16, 2017 (4 year terms)
Note: Incorporated as a city on July 1, 1985.
Gale Katchur, Mayor, 780-992-6232, Fax: 780-998-4774
Birgit Blizzard, Councillor, 780-998-5405, Fax: 780-998-4774
Sheldon Bossert, Councillor, 587-991-6387, Fax: 780-998-4774
Frank Garritsen, Councillor, 780-266-1911, Fax: 780-998-4774
Stew Henning, Councillor, 780-998-9223, Fax: 780-998-4774
Arjun Randhawa, Councillor, 780-904-9988, Fax: 780-998-4774
Ed Sperling, Councillor, 780-719-1150, Fax: 780-998-4774
Kelly Kloss, City Manager, 780-992-6212, Fax: 780-998-4774
Brenda Rauckman, General Manager, Community & Protective Services, 780-992-6580
Wendy Kinsella, Director, Communications & Marketing, 780-992-6155

Grande Prairie
P.O. Box 4000
10205 - 98 St.
Grande Prairie, AB T8V 6V3
Tel: 780-538-0300; *Fax:* 780-539-1056
www.cityofgp.com
Municipal Type: City
Incorporated: April 30, 1914; *Area:* 61.08 sq km
Population in 2011: 55,032
Provincial Electoral District(s): Grande Prairie-Smoky; Grande Prairie-Wapiti
Federal Electoral District(s): Grande Prairie-Mackenzie
Next Election: Oct. 16, 2017 (4 year terms)
Note: Incorporated as a city on Jan. 1, 1958.
Bill Given, Mayor, 780-538-0311
Jackie Clayton, Councillor, 780-814-3118
Dwight Logan, Councillor, 780-538-0963
Kevin Mclean, Councillor, 780-512-9858
Kevin O'Toole, Councillor, 780-933-0925
Lorne Radbourne, Councillor, 780-882-5001
Helen Rice, Councillor, 780-518-0939
Rory Tarant, Councillor, 780-402-9415
Chris Thiessen, Councillor, 780-831-1328
Greg Scerbak, City Manager, 780-538-0312
Ken Anderson, Director, Corporate Services, 780-538-0302
Dan Lemieux, Fire Chief, 780-538-0398

High River
309B MacLeod Trail SW
High River, AB T1V 1Z5
Tel: 403-652-2110; *Fax:* 403-652-2396
info@highriver.ca
www.highriver.ca
Municipal Type: City
Incorporated: Dec. 5, 1901; *Area:* 14.27 sq km
County or District: Municipal District of Foothills No. 31;
Population in 2011: 12,920
Provincial Electoral District(s): Highwood
Federal Electoral District(s): Foothills
Next Election: Oct. 16, 2017 (4 year terms)
Note: Incorporated as a town on Feb. 12, 1906.
Craig Snodgrass, Mayor
Emile Blokland, Councillor
Dragan Brankovich, Councillor
Cathy Couey, Councillor
Peter Loran, Councillor
Bruce Masterman, Councillor
Don Moore, Councillor
Tom Maier, Chief Administrative Officer
Ton Maier, Chief Financial Officer
Sharon Doll, Director, Legislative & Administrative Services
Reiley McKerracher, Director, Engineering, Planning & Operational Services
Robyn Green, Director, Corporate Services
Doug Mann, Director, Community Services

Lacombe
5432 - 56 Ave.
Lacombe, AB T4L 1E9
Tel: 403-782-6666; *Fax:* 403-782-5655
webmaster@lacombe.ca
www.lacombe.ca
Municipal Type: City
Incorporated: July 28, 1896; *Area:* 18.24 sq km
Population in 2011: 11,707
Provincial Electoral District(s): Lacombe-Ponoka
Federal Electoral District(s): Red Deer-Lacombe
Next Election: Oct. 16, 2017 (4 year terms)
Note: Incorporated as a town on May 5, 1902.
Steve Christie, Mayor, 403-782-1271
Wayne Armishaw, Councillor, 403-782-2895
Peter Bouwsema, Councillor, 403-782-4323
Grant Harder, Councillor, 403-350-9958
Reuben Konnik, Councillor, 403-782-1682
W.J. (Bill) McQueesten, Councillor, 403-782-5834
Wayne Rempel, Councillor, 403-782-6811
Norma MacQuarrie, Chief Administrative Officer, 403-782-1259
Michael Minchin, Director, Corporate Services
Brenda Vaughan, Director, Community Service

Leduc
1 Alexandra Park
Leduc, AB T9E 4C4
Tel: 780-980-7177; *Fax:* 780-980-7127
info@leduc.ca
www.leduc.ca
Municipal Type: City
Incorporated: Dec. 15, 1899; *Area:* 36.97 sq km
Population in 2011: 24,279
Provincial Electoral District(s): Leduc-Beaumont
Federal Electoral District(s): Edmonton-Wetaskiwin
Next Election: Oct. 16, 2017 (4 year terms)
Note: Incorporated as a city on Sept. 01, 1983.
Greg Krischke, Mayor
Beverly Beckett, Councillor
Glen Finstad, Councillor
Terry Lazowski, Councillor
David MacKenzie, Councillor
Dana Smith, Councillor
Bob Young, Councillor
Paul Benedetto, City Manager, 780-980-7101
Laura Knoblock, City Clerk, 780-980-7177
Irene Sasyniuk, General Manager, Corporate Services

Lethbridge
City Hall
910 - 4 Ave. South
Lethbridge, AB T1J 0P6
Tel: 403-329-7355; *Fax:* 403-320-7575
info@lethbridge.ca
www.lethbridge.ca
Municipal Type: City
Incorporated: Nov. 29, 1890; *Area:* 121.97 sq km
Population in 2011: 83,417
Provincial Electoral District(s): Lethbridge-East; Lethbridge-West
Federal Electoral District(s): Lethbridge
Next Election: Oct. 16, 2017 (4 year terms)
Note: Incorporated as a city on May 9, 1906.
Chris Spearman, Mayor, 403-320-3823
Jeff Carlson, Councillor, 403-360-7550
Jeff Coffman, Councillor, 403-315-9092, Fax: 403-320-7575
Blaine Hydden, Councillor, 403-320-4080
Liz Iwaskiw, Councillor, 403-360-7771
Joe Mauro, Councillor, 403-330-1522
Bridget Mearns, Councillor-elect, 403-393-3344
Rob Miyashiro, Councillor, 403-360-2039
Ryan Parker, Councillor, 403-360-8880
Garth Sherwin, B.Comm., CA, City Manager
Aleta Neufeld, City Clerk
Tim Jorgensen, City Solicitor
Bary Beck, Director, Community Services
Jeff Greene, Director, Planning & Development
Doug Hawkins, Director, Infrastructure Services
Kathy Hopkins, Director, City Manager's Office
Corey Wight, Director, Corporate Services & City Treasurer
Jason Elliot, Manager, Human Resources

Lloydminster
City Hall
4420 - 50 Ave.
Lloydminster, AB T9V 0W2
Tel: 780-875-6184; *Fax:* 780-871-8345
jkeeley@lloydminster.ca
www.lloydminster.ca
Municipal Type: City
Incorporated: Nov. 25, 1903; *Area:* 24.19 sq km
Population in 2011: 18,032
Provincial Electoral District(s): Vermilion-Lloydminster
Federal Electoral District(s): Lakeland
Next Election: Oct. 26, 2016 (4 year terms)
Note: Population figure represents both the Alberta & Saskatchewan populations. Incorporated as a city on Jan. 1, 1958.
Jeff Mulligan, Mayor
Beth Kembel, City Clerk, 780-871-8328, Fax: 780-871-8346
Glenn Carroll, City Manager, 780-871-8326, Fax: 780-871-8346
Terry Burton, Director, Planning & Engineering, 780-875-8332

Don Stang, Director, Community Services, 780-874-3710, Fax: 780-874-3711
Alan Cayford, Director, Public Works, 780-874-3700, Fax: 780-874-3701
Nicole Reiniger, Director, Finance, 780-875-6184, Fax: 780-871-8345
Brent Stasiuk, Deputy CAO, Protective Services, 780-874-9054
Tara Smith, General Manager, Human Resources, 780-871-8343, Fax: 780-871-8348
Penny Manners, Manager, Communications & Marketing, 780-871-8339, Fax: 780-871-8345

Medicine Hat
City Hall
580 - 1 St. SE
Medicine Hat, AB T1A 8E6
Tel: 403-529-8115; *Fax:* 403-529-8182
clerk@medicinehat.ca
www.medicinehat.ca
Municipal Type: City
Incorporated: May 31, 1894; *Area:* 112.01 sq km
Population in 2011: 60,005
Provincial Electoral District(s): Cypress-Medicine Hat; Medicine Hat
Federal Electoral District(s): Medicine Hat-Cardston-Warner
Next Election: Oct. 16, 2017 (4 year terms)
Note: Incorporated as a city on May 9, 1906.
Ted Clugson, Mayor, 403-529-8181
Bill Cocks, Councillor, 403-952-5855
Robert Dumanowski, Councillor, 403-502-4348
Julie Friesen, Councillor, 403-952-5355
Jamie McIntosh, Councillor, 403-581-8098
Les Pearson, Councillor, 403-504-3325
Celina Symmonds, Councillor, 403-548-4985
Jim Turner, Councillor, 403-502-4435
Brian Varga, Councillor, 403-502-2888
Merete Heggelund, Chief Administrative Officer
Angela Cruickshank, City Clerk, 403-529-8115, Fax: 403-529-8182
Bob Schmitt, City Solicitor, 403-529-8362
Karen Charlton, Commissioner, Public Services, 403-529-8229
Brian Mastel, Commissioner, Corporate Services
Stan Schwartzenberger, Commissioner, Development & Infrastructure
Ron Robinson, Director, Emergency Management, 403-525-8686
Andy McGrogan, Police Chief, 403-529-8410, Fax: 403-529-8444

Okotoks
P.O. Box 20 Main
Okotoks, AB T1S 1K1
Tel: 403-938-4404; *Fax:* 403-938-7387
communications@okotoks.ca
www.okotoks.ca
Municipal Type: City
Incorporated: Oct. 25, 1899; *Area:* 18.55 sq km
County or District: Municipal District of Foothills No. 31;
Population in 2011: 24,511
Provincial Electoral District(s): Highwood
Federal Electoral District(s): Foothills
Next Election: Oct. 16, 2017 (4 year terms)
Note: Incorporated as a town on June 1, 1904.
Bill Robertson, Mayor, 403-938-8904
Carrie Fischer, Councillor, 403-370-2726
Ken Heemeryck, Councillor, 403-512-6985
Matt Rockley, Councillor
Ed Sands, Councillor, 403-938-2065
Tanya Thorn, Councillor, 403-860-7342
Ray Watrin, Councillor, 403-650-9544
Rick Quail, Chief Administrative Officer, 403-938-8900
Linda Turnbull, Municipal Secretary
Wayne Braun, Manager, Financial Services

Red Deer
City Hall
P.O. Box 5008
4914 - 48th Ave.
Red Deer, AB T4N 3T4
Tel: 403-342-8111; *Fax:* 403-346-6195
feedback@reddeer.ca
www.reddeer.ca
Municipal Type: City
Incorporated: May 31, 1894; *Area:* 69.23 sq km
Population in 2011: 90,564
Provincial Electoral District(s): Red Deer-North; Red Deer-South
Federal Electoral District(s): Red Deer-Lacombe; Red Deer-Mountain View
Next Election: Oct. 16, 2017 (4 year terms)
Note: Incorporated as a city on March 25, 1913.
Tara Veer, Mayor, 403-342-8154, Fax: 403-346-6195
Buck Buchanan, Councillor, 403-358-5517, Fax: 403-346-6195
Tanya Handley, Councillor, 403-596-5848, Fax: 403-346-6195
Paul Harris, Councillor, 403-341-3352, Fax: 403-341-5754
Ken Johnston, Councillor, 403-358-8049, Fax: 403-346-6195
Lawrence Lee, Councillor, 403-318-8862, Fax: 403-346-6195
Lynne Mulder, Councillor, 403-341-6418, Fax: 403-346-6195
Frank Wong, Councillor, 403-347-6514, Fax: 403-346-6195
Dianne Wyntjes, Councillor, 403-505-4256, Fax: 403-346-6195
Craig Curtis, City Manager, 403-342-8156, Fax: 403-342-8365
Frieda McDougall, City Clerk
Elaine Vincent, Director, Corporate Services
Dean Krejci, Manager, Financial Services
Andrea Sutherland, Coordinator, Access & Privacy

St. Albert
5 St. Anne St.
St. Albert, AB T8N 3Z9
Tel: 780-459-1500; *Fax:* 780-460-2394
stalbert@st-albert.net
www.stalbert.ca
Municipal Type: City
Incorporated: Dec. 7, 1899; *Area:* 35.04 sq km
Population in 2011: 61,466
Provincial Electoral District(s): Spruce Grove-St. Albert; St. Albert
Federal Electoral District(s): St. Albert-Edmonton
Next Election: Oct. 16, 2017 (4 year terms)
Note: Incorporated as a city on Jan. 1, 1977.
Nolan Crouse, Mayor, 780-459-1606, Fax: 780-459-1591
Wes Broadhead, Councillor, 780-915-9622, Fax: 780-459-1591
Cathy Heron, Councillor, 780-288-6791, Fax: 780-459-1591
Sheena Hughes, Councillor, 780-240-9889, Fax: 780-459-1591
Cam MacKay, Councillor, 780-721-8679, Fax: 780-459-1591
Tim Osborne, Councillor, 587-930-5566, Fax: 780-459-1591
Gilles Prefontaine, Councillor, 780-932-7959, Fax: 780-459-1591
Chris Jardine, Acting City Manager
Brenda Barclay, Manager, Financial Operations & Reporting
Christopher Belke, FOIP Coordinator

Spruce Grove
315 Jespersen Ave.
Spruce Grove, AB T7X 3E8
Tel: 780-962-2611; *Fax:* 780-962-2526
info@sprucegrove.org
www.sprucegrove.org
Municipal Type: City
Incorporated: March 14, 1907; *Area:* 26.4 sq km
Population in 2011: 26,171
Provincial Electoral District(s): Spruce Grove-St. Albert
Federal Electoral District(s): Sturgeon River-Parkland
Next Election: Oct. 16, 2017 (4 year terms)
Note: Incorporated as a city on March 1, 1986.
Stuart Houston, Mayor, 780-962-7604, Fax: 780-962-0149
Louise Baxter, Alderman, 780-962-7604, Fax: 780-962-0149
Bill Kesanko, Alderman, 780-962-7604, Fax: 782-962-0149
Ed McLean, Alderman, 780-962-7604, Fax: 782-962-0149
Wayne Rothe, Alderman, 780-962-7604, Fax: 780-962-0149
Bill Steinburg, Alderman, 780-962-7604, Fax: 780-962-0149
Searle Turton, Alderman, 780-962-7604, Fax: 780-962-0149
Robert Cotterill, Chief Administrative Officer
Tania Shepherd, City Clerk
Glen Jarbeau, Director, Finance

Stony Plain
4905 - 51 Ave.
Stony Plain, AB T7Z 1Y1
Tel: 780-963-2151; *Fax:* 780-963-2197
info@stonyplain.com
www.stonyplain.com
Municipal Type: City
Incorporated: March 14, 1907; *Area:* 35.61 sq km
County or District: Parkland County; *Population in 2011:* 15,051
Provincial Electoral District(s): Stony Plain
Federal Electoral District(s): Sturgeon River-Parkland
Next Election: Oct. 16, 2017 (4 year terms)
Note: Incorporated as a town on Dec. 10, 1908
William Choy, Mayor
Robert Twerdoclib, Deputy Mayor
Judy Bennett, Councillor
Dwight Ganske, Councillor
Russ Graff, Councillor
Pat Hansard, Councillor
Bruce Lloy, Councillor
Thomas Goulden, Town Manager
Louise Frostad, Director, Corporate Services
Karl Hill, Director, Community Services
Janine Peter, Director, Family & Community Support Services
P. Hanlan, General Manager, Planning & Infrastructure

Strathmore
680 Westchester Rd.
Strathmore, AB T1P 1J1
Tel: 403-934-3133; *Fax:* 403-934-4713
webadmin@strathmore.ca
www.strathmore.ca
Municipal Type: City
Incorporated: March 20, 1908; *Area:* 15.59 sq km
County or District: Wheatland County; *Population in 2011:* 12,305
Provincial Electoral District(s): Strathmore-Brooks
Federal Electoral District(s): Bow River
Next Election: Oct. 16, 2017 (4 year terms)
Note: Incorporated as a town on July 6, 1911.
Michael Ell, Mayor, 403-901-9866
Rocky Blokland, Councillor, 403-324-1849
Pat Fule, Councillor, 403-324-3314
Denise Peterson, Councillor, 403-901-5606
John Rempel, Councillor, 403-324-4028
Bob Sobol, Councillor, 403-324-4276
Brad Walls, Councillor, 403-324-4136
James Thackray, Chief Administrative Officer, 403-935-3133
Mike Marko, Contact, Planning & Development, 403-934-3133
Bryce Mackan, Contact, Engineering
Steve Barna, Contact, Public Works, 403-934-3133

Sylvan Lake
5012 - 48th Ave.
Sylvan Lake, AB T4S 1G6
Tel: 403-887-2141; *Fax:* 403-887-3660
tsl@sylvanlake.ca
www.sylvanlake.ca
Municipal Type: City
Incorporated: Dec. 30, 1912; *Area:* 10.83 sq km
County or District: Red Deer County; *Population in 2011:* 12,327
Provincial Electoral District(s): Innisfail-Sylvan Lake
Federal Electoral District(s): Red Deer-Lacombe
Next Election: Oct. 16, 2017 (4 year terms)
Note: Incorporated as a town on May 20, 1946.
Sean McIntyre, Mayor
Megan Chernoff, Councillor
Christine Lust, Councillor
Jas Payne, Councillor
Matt Prete, Councillor
Betty Osmond, Chief Administrative Officer
Darren Moore, Director, Finance
Amber Hennig, Records & Information Clerk

Wetaskiwin
P.O. Box 6210
4705 - 50th Ave.
Wetaskiwin, AB T9A 2E9
Tel: 780-361-4400; *Fax:* 780-361-4402
reception@wetaskiwin.ca
www.wetaskiwin.ca
Other Information: Toll Free Phone: 1-800-989-6899
Municipal Type: City
Incorporated: Dec. 4, 1899; *Area:* 16.74 sq km
Population in 2011: 12,525
Provincial Electoral District(s): Wetaskiwin-Camrose
Federal Electoral District(s): Edmonton-Wetaskiwin
Next Election: Oct. 16, 2017 (4 year terms)
Note: Incorporated as a city on May 9, 1906.
Bill Elliot, Mayor, 780-361-4408
June Boyda, Councillor, 780-312-0928
Joe Branco, Councillor, 780-352-4313
Tyler Gandam, Councillor, 780-361-4409
Bert Horvey, Councillor, 780-361-4409
Patricia MacQuarrie, Councillor, 780-362-2216
Wayne Neilson, Councillor, 780-361-4409
Dave Burgess, City Manager
Therese Myndio, Assistant City Manager & FOIP Contact
Ron Holland, Manager, Economic Development, 780-361-4404
Kevin Lucas, Manager, Recreation, 780-361-4444
Jeff Riege, Manager, Finance, 780-361-4400
Merlin Klassen, Fire Chief, 780-361-4429, Fax: 780-352-6261
Robin Benoit, Director, Engineering & Development, 780-361-4430, Fax: 780-352-8266

Other Municipalities in Alberta

Acme
P.O. Box 299
203 Clarke St.
Acme, AB T0M 0A0
Tel: 403-546-3783; *Fax:* 403-546-3014
clerk@acme.ca
www.acme.ca
Municipal Type: Village
Incorporated: July 7, 1910; *Area:* 2.47 sq km

County or District: Kneehill County; *Population in 2011:* 653
Provincial Electoral District(s): Olds-Didsbury-Three Hills
Federal Electoral District(s): Bow River
Next Election: Oct. 16, 2017 (4 year terms)
Bruce McLeod, Mayor
David Alderdice, Chief Administrative Officer

Alberta Beach
P.O. Box 278
4935 - 50 Ave.
Alberta Beach, AB T0E 0A0
Tel: 780-924-3181; *Fax:* 780-924-3313
abofficea@albertabeach.com
www.albertabeach.com
Municipal Type: Village
Incorporated: Aug. 23, 1920; *Area:* 1.98 sq km
County or District: Lac Ste. Anne County; *Population in 2011:* 865
Provincial Electoral District(s): Whitecourt-Ste. Anne
Federal Electoral District(s): Yellowhead
Next Election: Oct. 16, 2017 (4 year terms)
Note: Status changed to a village on Nov. 25, 1998.
Jim Benedict, Mayor
Kathy Skwarchuck, Chief Administrative Officer

Alix
P.O. Box 87
4849 - 50 St.
Alix, AB T0C 0B0
Tel: 403-747-2495; *Fax:* 403-747-3663
info@villageofalix.ca
www.villageofalix.ca
Municipal Type: Village
Incorporated: June 3, 1907; *Area:* 3.15 sq km
County or District: Lacombe County; *Population in 2011:* 830
Provincial Electoral District(s): Lacombe-Ponoka
Federal Electoral District(s): Red Deer-Lacombe
Next Election: Oct. 16, 2017 (4 year terms)
Curtis Peterson, Mayor, 403-747-2414
Bonnie Cretzman, Chief Administrative Officer

Alliance
P.O. Box 149
Alliance, AB T0B 0A0
Tel: 780-879-3911; *Fax:* 780-879-2235
info@villageofalliance.ca
www.villageofalliance.ca
Municipal Type: Village
Incorporated: Aug. 26, 1918; *Area:* 0.64 sq km
County or District: Flagstaff County; *Population in 2011:* 174
Provincial Electoral District(s): Battle River-Wainwright
Federal Electoral District(s): Battle River-Crowfoot
Next Election: Oct. 16, 2017 (4 year terms)
Sue Thomas, Mayor
Laura Towers, Administrator

Amisk
P.O. Box 72
Amisk, AB T0B 0B0
Tel: 780-856-3980; *Fax:* 780-856-3980
amiskvil@telusplanet.net
www.amisk.ca
Municipal Type: Village
Incorporated: Jan. 1, 1956; *Area:* 0.76 sq km
County or District: Municipal District of Provost No. 52; *Population in 2011:* 207
Provincial Electoral District(s): Battle River-Wainwright
Federal Electoral District(s): Battle River-Crowfoot
Next Election: Oct. 16, 2017 (4 year terms)
Mervin Anholt, Mayor
Kathy Ferguson, Municipal Administrator

Andrew
P.O. Box 180
5021 - 50 St.
Andrew, AB T0B 0C0
Tel: 780-365-3687; *Fax:* 780-365-2061
vandway@mcsnet.ca
www.villageofandrew.ca
Municipal Type: Village
Incorporated: June 24, 1930; *Area:* 1.23 sq km
County or District: Lamont County; *Population in 2011:* 379
Provincial Electoral District(s): Fort Saskatchewan-Vegreville
Federal Electoral District(s): Lakeland
Next Election: Oct. 16, 2017 (4 year terms)
Heather Tait, Mayor
Pat Skoreyko, Chief Administrative Officer

Argentia Beach
P.O. Box 100
605-2 Ave.
Ma-Me-O Beach, AB T0C 1X0
Tel: 780-586-2494; *Fax:* 780-586-3567
information@svofficepl.com
www.argentiabeach.ca
Other Information: Alt. URL: www.svofficepl.com
Municipal Type: Summer Village
Incorporated: Jan. 1, 1967; *Area:* 0.69 sq km
County or District: Wetaskiwin County No. 10; *Population in 2011:* 15
Provincial Electoral District(s): Drayton Valley-Devon
Federal Electoral District(s): Edmonton-Wetaskiwin
Next Election: Summer 2017 (4 year terms)
Donald Oborowsky, Mayor
Sylvia Roy, Chief Administrative Officer

Arrowwood
P.O. Box 36
22 Center St.
Arrowwood, AB T0L 0B0
Tel: 403-534-3821; *Fax:* 403-534-3821
vlgarrw@telusplanet.net
www.villageofarrowwood.ca
Municipal Type: Village
Incorporated: May 13, 1926; *Area:* 0.66 sq km
County or District: Vulcan County; *Population in 2011:* 188
Provincial Electoral District(s): Little Bow
Federal Electoral District(s): Bow River
Next Election: Oct. 16, 2017 (4 year terms)
Matt Crane, Mayor
Cristopher Northcott, Chief Administrative Officer

Athabasca
4705 - 49 Ave.
Athabasca, AB T9S 1B7
Tel: 780-675-2063; *Fax:* 780-675-4242
town@town.athabasca.ab.ca
www.town.athabasca.ab.ca
Municipal Type: Town
Incorporated: May 18, 1905; *Area:* 16.98 sq km
County or District: Athabasca County; *Population in 2011:* 2,990
Provincial Electoral District(s): Athabasca-Sturgeon-Redwater
Federal Electoral District(s): Lakeland
Next Election: Oct. 16, 2017 (4 year terms)
Note: Incorporated as a town on Aug. 4, 1913.
Roger Morrill, Mayor
Ryan Maier, Chief Administrative Officer

Banff
P.O. Box 1260
110 Bear St.
Banff, AB T1L 1A1
Tel: 403-762-1200; *Fax:* 403-762-1260
comments@banff.ca
www.banff.ca
Municipal Type: Town
Incorporated: Jan. 1, 1990; *Area:* 4.85 sq km
County or District: Improvement District No. 9 (Banff); *Population in 2011:* 7,584
Provincial Electoral District(s): Banff-Cochrane
Federal Electoral District(s): Banff-Airdrie
Next Election: Oct. 16, 2017 (4 year terms)
Karen Sorensen, Mayor
Robert Earl, Town Manager

Barnwell
P.O. Box 159
612 Heritage Rd.
Barnwell, AB T0K 0B0
Tel: 403-223-4018; *Fax:* 403-223-2373
barnwell@platinum.ca
www.barnwell.ca
Municipal Type: Village
Incorporated: Jan. 1, 1980; *Area:* 0.9 sq km
County or District: Municipal District of Taber; *Population in 2011:* 771
Provincial Electoral District(s): Cardston-Taber-Warner
Federal Electoral District(s): Bow River
Next Election: Oct. 16, 2017 (4 year terms)
Robin Hansen, Mayor
Wendy Bateman, Chief Administrative Officer

Barons
P.O. Box 129
Barons, AB T0L 0G0
Tel: 403-757-3633; *Fax:* 403-757-2599
barons@figment.ca
www.barons.ca
Municipal Type: Village
Incorporated: May 6, 1910; *Area:* 0.68 sq km
County or District: Lethbridge County; *Population in 2011:* 315
Provincial Electoral District(s): Little Bow
Federal Electoral District(s): Lethbridge
Next Election: Oct. 16, 2017 (4 year terms)
Ronald Gorzitza, Mayor
Laurie Beck, Chief Administrative Officer

Barrhead
P.O. Box 4189
5014 - 50 Ave.
Barrhead, AB T7N 1A2
Tel: 780-674-3301; *Fax:* 780-674-5648
town@barrhead.ca
www.barrhead.ca
Municipal Type: Town
Incorporated: Nov. 14, 1927; *Area:* 8.1 sq km
County or District: Barrhead County No. 11; *Population in 2011:* 4,432
Provincial Electoral District(s): Barrhead-Morinville-Westlock
Federal Electoral District(s): Peace River-Westlock
Next Election: Oct. 16, 2017 (4 year terms)
Note: Proclaimed as a town on Nov. 26, 1946.
Gerry St. Pierre, Mayor
Martin Taylor, Chief Administrative Officer

Bashaw
P.O. Box 510
5011 - 52 Ave.
Bashaw, AB T0B 0H0
Tel: 780-372-3911; *Fax:* 780-372-2335
admin@townofbashaw.com
www.townofbashaw.com
Municipal Type: Town
Incorporated: Aug. 18, 1911; *Area:* 2.84 sq km
County or District: Camrose County; *Population in 2011:* 873
Provincial Electoral District(s): Battle River-Wainwright
Federal Electoral District(s): Battle River-Crowfoot
Next Election: Oct. 16, 2017 (4 year terms)
Note: Incorporated as a town on May 1, 1964.
Penny Shantz, Mayor
Linda Hannah, Chief Administrative Officer

Bassano
P.O. Box 299
502 - 2 Ave.
Bassano, AB T0J 0B0
Tel: 403-641-3788; *Fax:* 403-641-2585
townbass@telus.net
www.bassano.ca
Municipal Type: Town
Incorporated: Dec. 28, 1909; *Area:* 5.16 sq km
County or District: Newell County; *Population in 2011:* 1,282
Provincial Electoral District(s): Strathmore-Brooks
Federal Electoral District(s): Bow River
Next Election: Oct. 16, 2017 (4 year terms)
Note: Incorporated as a town on Jan. 16, 1911.
Tom Rose, Mayor, 403-641-3464
Sabine Nasse, Chief Administrative Officer, 403-641-3788

Bawlf
P.O. Box 40
203 Hanson St.
Bawlf, AB T0B 0J0
Tel: 780-373-3797; *Fax:* 780-373-3798
vilbawlf@syban.net
www.bawlf.com
Municipal Type: Village
Incorporated: Oct. 12, 1906; *Area:* 0.96 sq km
County or District: Camrose County; *Population in 2011:* 403
Provincial Electoral District(s): Battle River-Wainwright
Federal Electoral District(s): Battle River-Crowfoot
Next Election: Oct. 16, 2017 (4 year terms)
John Tessari, Mayor
Tracy Stewart, Acting Chief Administrative Officer

Beaverlodge
P.O. Box 30
1016 - 4 Ave.
Beaverlodge, AB T0H 0C0
Tel: 780-354-2201; *Fax:* 780-354-2207
town@beaverlodge.ca
www.beaverlodge.ca
Municipal Type: Town
Incorporated: July 31, 1929; *Area:* 5.58 sq km
County or District: Grande Prairie County No. 1; *Population in 2011:* 2,365
Provincial Electoral District(s): Grande Prairie-Wapiti
Federal Electoral District(s): Grande Prairie-Mackenzie
Next Election: Oct. 16, 2017 (4 year terms)
Note: Incorporated as a town on Jan. 24, 1956.
Leona Hanson, Mayor, 780-676-7582
Christopher J. Parker, Chief Administrative Officer

Beiseker
P.O. Box 349
700 - 1 Ave.
Beiseker, AB T0M 0G0
Tel: 403-947-3774; *Fax:* 403-947-2146
beiseker@beiseker.com
www.beiseker.com
Municipal Type: Village
Incorporated: Feb. 23, 1921; *Area:* 2.84 sq km
County or District: Rocky View County; *Population in 2011:* 785
Provincial Electoral District(s): Olds-Didsbury-Three Hills
Federal Electoral District(s): Bow River
Next Election: Oct. 16, 2017 (4 year terms)
Ray Courtman, Mayor
Jo-Anne Lambert, Chief Administrative Officer

Bentley
P.O. Box 179
4918 - 50 Ave.
Bentley, AB T0C 0J0
Tel: 403-748-4044; *Fax:* 403-748-3213
vlgben@telusplanet.net
www.town.bentley.ab.ca
Municipal Type: Town
Incorporated: March 17, 1915; *Area:* 2.3 sq km
County or District: Lacombe County; *Population in 2011:* 1,073
Provincial Electoral District(s): Rimbey-Rocky Mountain House-Sundre
Federal Electoral District(s): Red Deer-Lacombe
Next Election: Oct. 16, 2017 (4 year terms)
Note: Incorporated as a town on Jan. 1, 2001.
Lynda Haarstad-Petten, Mayor, 403-748-4922
Elizabeth Smart, Chief Administrative Officer

Berwyn
P.O. Box 250
Berwyn, AB T0H 0E0
Tel: 780-338-3922; *Fax:* 780-338-2224
vberwynadmin@serbernet.com
www.berwyn.govoffice.com
Municipal Type: Village
Incorporated: Nov. 28, 1936; *Area:* 1.66 sq km
County or District: Municipal District of Peace No. 135; *Population in 2011:* 526
Provincial Electoral District(s): Dunvegan-Central Peace-Notley
Federal Electoral District(s): Peace River-Westlock
Next Election: Oct. 16, 2017 (4 year terms)
Ron Longtin, Mayor
Olive Toews, Chief Administrative Officer

Betula Beach
P.O. Box 190
Seba Beach, AB T0E 2B0
Tel: 780-797-3863; *Fax:* 780-797-3800
svseba@telusplanet.net
Municipal Type: Summer Village
Incorporated: Jan. 1, 1960; *Area:* 0.18 sq km
County or District: Parkland County; *Population in 2011:* 10
Provincial Electoral District(s): Stony Plain
Federal Electoral District(s): Yellowhead
Next Election: Summer 2017 (4 year terms)
Rob Dickie, Mayor
Susan Evans, Chief Administrative Officer

Big Valley
P.O. Box 236
29 - 1 Ave. South
Big Valley, AB T0J 0G0
Tel: 403-876-2269; *Fax:* 403-876-2223
info@villagebigvalley.ca
www.villageofbigvalley.ca
Municipal Type: Village
Incorporated: July 28, 1914; *Area:* 1.84 sq km
County or District: Stettler County No. 6; *Population in 2011:* 364
Provincial Electoral District(s): Drumheller-Stettler
Federal Electoral District(s): Battle River-Crowfoot
Next Election: Oct. 16, 2017 (4 year terms)
Gail Knudson, Mayor
Michelle White, Chief Administrative Officer

Birch Cove
P.O. Box 7
#19, RR 1
Gunn, AB T0E 1A0
Tel: 780-446-1426;
www.birchcove.ca
Municipal Type: Summer Village
Incorporated: Dec. 31, 1988; *Area:* 0.29 sq km
County or District: Lac Ste. Anne County; *Population in 2011:* 45
Provincial Electoral District(s): Whitecourt-Ste. Anne
Federal Electoral District(s): Sturgeon River-Parkland
Next Election: Summer 2017 (4 year terms)
Eugene Evans, Mayor
Dennis Evans, Municipal Administrator

Birchcliff
Bay 8, 14 Thevenaz Industrial Tr.
Sylvan Lake, AB T4S 1W2
Tel: 403-887-2822; *Fax:* 403-887-2897
www.sylvansummervillages.ca/location/birchcliff
Municipal Type: Summer Village
Incorporated: Jan. 1, 1972; *Area:* 0.98 sq km
County or District: Lacombe County; *Population in 2011:* 112
Provincial Electoral District(s): Innisfail-Sylvan Lake
Federal Electoral District(s): Red Deer-Lacombe
Next Election: Summer 2017 (4 year terms)
Joyce Megson, Mayor
Phyllis Forsyth, Chief Administrative Officer

Bittern Lake
P.O. Box 5
300 Railway Ave.
Bittern Lake, AB T0C 0L0
Tel: 780-672-7373; *Fax:* 780-672-2353
www.villageofbitternlake.ca
Municipal Type: Village
Incorporated: Nov. 21, 1904; *Area:* 6.64 sq km
County or District: Camrose County; *Population in 2011:* 224
Provincial Electoral District(s): Wetaskiwin-Camrose
Federal Electoral District(s): Battle River-Crowfoot
Next Election: Oct. 16, 2017 (4 year terms)
Clarence Grettum, Mayor
Theresa Fuller, Chief Administrative Officer

Black Diamond
P.O. Box 10
301 Centre Ave. West
Black Diamond, AB T0L 0H0
Tel: 403-933-4348; *Fax:* 403-933-5865
info@town.blackdiamond.ab.ca
www.town.blackdiamond.ab.ca
Municipal Type: Town
Incorporated: May 8, 1929; *Area:* 3.21 sq km
County or District: Municipal District of Foothills No. 31; *Population in 2011:* 2,373
Provincial Electoral District(s): Livingstone-Macleod
Federal Electoral District(s): Foothills
Next Election: Oct. 16, 2017 (4 year terms)
Note: Incorporated as a town on Jan 1, 1956.
Sharlene Brown, Mayor
Joanne Irwin, Chief Administrative Officer

Blackfalds
P.O. Box 220
5018 Waghorn St.
Blackfalds, AB T0M 0J0
Tel: 403-885-4677; *Fax:* 403-885-4610
info@blackfalds.com
www.blackfalds.com
Municipal Type: Town
Incorporated: June 17, 1904; *Area:* 8.4 sq km
County or District: Lacombe County; *Population in 2011:* 6,300
Provincial Electoral District(s): Lacombe-Ponoka
Federal Electoral District(s): Red Deer-Lacombe
Next Election: Oct. 16, 2017 (4 year terms)
Note: Incorporated as a town on April 1, 1980.
Melodie Stol, Mayor, 403-885-2587
Myron Thompson, Chief Administrative Officer

Bon Accord
P.O. Box 779
5025 - 50 Ave
Bon Accord, AB T0A 0K0
Tel: 780-921-3550; *Fax:* 780-921-3585
www.bonaccord.ca
Municipal Type: Town
Incorporated: Jan. 1, 1964; *Area:* 2.11 sq km
County or District: Sturgeon County; *Population in 2011:* 1,488
Provincial Electoral District(s): Athabasca-Sturgeon-Redwater
Federal Electoral District(s): Sturgeon River-Parkland
Next Election: Oct. 16, 2017 (4 year terms)
Note: Incorporated as a town on Nov. 20, 1979.
Randy Boyd, Mayor
Vicky Zinyk, Chief Administrative Officer

Bondiss
724 Baptiste Dr.
West Baptiste, AB T9S 1R8
Tel: 780-675-9270
Municipal Type: Summer Village
Incorporated: Jan. 1, 1983; *Area:* 1.33 sq km
County or District: Athabasca County; *Population in 2011:* 106
Provincial Electoral District(s): Athabasca-Sturgeon-Redwater
Federal Electoral District(s): Lakeland
Next Election: Summer 2017 (4 year terms)
Robert (Bob) Walker, Mayor
Edwin Tomaszyk, Chief Administrative Officer

Bonnyville
P.O. Box 1006
4917 - 49 Ave.
Bonnyville, AB T9N 2J7
Tel: 780-826-3496; *Fax:* 780-826-4806
www.town.bonnyville.ab.ca
Other Information: Toll free: 1-866-826-3496
Municipal Type: Town
Incorporated: Sept. 19, 1929; *Area:* 14.1 sq km
County or District: Municipal District of Bonnyville No. 87; *Population in 2011:* 6,216
Provincial Electoral District(s): Bonnyville-Cold Lake
Federal Electoral District(s): Lakeland
Next Election: Oct. 16, 2017 (4 year terms)
Note: Proclaimed as a town on Feb. 3, 1948.
Gene Sobolewski, Mayor
Mark Power, Chief Administrative Officer

Bonnyville Beach
P.O. Box 6439 Main
Bonnyville, AB T9N 2G9
Tel: 780-826-2925; *Fax:* 780-812-2904
admin@bonnyvillebeach.com
www.bonnyvillebeach.com
Municipal Type: Summer Village
Incorporated: Jan 1, 1958; *Area:* 0.38 sq km
County or District: Municipal District of Bonnyville No. 87; *Population in 2011:* 95
Provincial Electoral District(s): Bonnyville-Cold Lake
Federal Electoral District(s): Lakeland
Next Election: Summer 2017 (4 year terms)
Gail Brosseau, Mayor
Lionel P. Tercier, Chief Administrative Officer

Botha
P.O. Box 160
Botha, AB T0C 0N0
Tel: 403-742-5079; *Fax:* 403-742-6586
vlbotha@xplornet.com
villageofbotha.com
Municipal Type: Village
Incorporated: Sept. 5, 1911; *Area:* 1.09 sq km
County or District: Stettler County No. 6; *Population in 2011:* 175
Provincial Electoral District(s): Drumheller-Stettler
Federal Electoral District(s): Battle River-Crowfoot
Next Election: Oct. 16, 2017 (4 year terms)
Flo Iskiw, Mayor
Eric Jerrard, Chief Administrative Officer

Bow Island
P.O. Box 100
52 Centre St.
Bow Island, AB T0K 0G0
Tel: 403-545-2522; *Fax:* 403-545-6642
townoffice@bowisland.com
www.bowisland.com
Municipal Type: Town
Incorporated: June 14, 1910; *Area:* 5.92 sq km
County or District: Forty Mile County No. 8; *Population in 2011:* 2,025
Provincial Electoral District(s): Cypress-Medicine Hat
Federal Electoral District(s): Medicine Hat-Cardston-Warner
Next Election: Oct. 16, 2017 (4 year terms)
Note: Incorporated as a town on Feb. 1, 1912.
Gordon Reynolds, Mayor
Anna-Marie Bridge, Town Manager

Bowden
P.O. Box 338
2101 - 20 Ave.
Bowden, AB T0M 0K0
Tel: 403-224-3395; *Fax:* 403-224-2244
admin@town.bowden.ab.ca
www.town.bowden.ab.ca
Municipal Type: Town
Incorporated: June 17, 1904; *Area:* 1.9 sq km
County or District: Red Deer County; *Population in 2011:* 1,241
Provincial Electoral District(s): Innisfail-Sylvan Lake
Federal Electoral District(s): Red Deer-Mountain View
Next Election: Oct. 16, 2017 (4 year terms)
Note: Incorporated as a town on Sept. 1, 1981.
Robb Stuart, Mayor
Andy Weiss, Chief Administrative Officer

Boyle
P.O. Box 9
5002 - 3 St.
Boyle, AB T0A 0M0
Tel: 780-689-3643; *Fax:* 780-689-3998
admin@boylealberta.com
www.boylealberta.com
Municipal Type: Village
Incorporated: Dec. 31, 1953; *Area:* 4.1 sq km
County or District: Athabasca County; *Population in 2011:* 916
Provincial Electoral District(s): Athabasca-Sturgeon-Redwater
Federal Electoral District(s): Lakeland
Next Election: Oct. 16, 2017 (4 year terms)
Don Radmanovich, Mayor
Charlie Ashbey, Chief Executive Officer

Breton
P.O. Box 480
4916 - 50 Ave.
Breton, AB T0C 0P0
Tel: 780-696-3636; *Fax:* 780-696-3590
vbreton@telusplanet.net
www.village.breton.ab.ca
Municipal Type: Village
Incorporated: Jan. 1, 1957; *Area:* 1.73 sq km
County or District: Brazeau County; *Population in 2011:* 496
Provincial Electoral District(s): Drayton Valley-Devon
Federal Electoral District(s): Yellowhead
Next Election: Oct. 16, 2017 (4 year terms)
Darren Aldous, Mayor
Terry Molenkamp, Chief Administrative Officer

Bruderheim
P.O. Box 280
5017 Queen St.
Bruderheim, AB T0B 0S0
Tel: 780-796-3731; *Fax:* 780-796-3037
www.bruderheim.ca
Municipal Type: Town
Incorporated: May 29, 1908; *Area:* 4.23 sq km
County or District: Lamont County; *Population in 2011:* 1,155
Provincial Electoral District(s): Fort Saskatchewan-Vegreville
Federal Electoral District(s): Lakeland
Next Election: Oct. 16, 2017 (4 year terms)
Note: Incorporated as a town on Sept. 17, 1980.
Karl Hauch, Mayor
John Dance, Chief Administrative Officer

Burnstick Lake
P.O. Box 501
Caroline, AB T0M 0M0
Tel: 403-304-3591; *Fax:* 403-722-4050
burnstick8@gmail.com
www.burnsticklakesummervillage.ca
Municipal Type: Summer Village
Incorporated: Dec. 31, 1991; *Area:* 0.18 sq km
County or District: Clearwater County; *Population in 2011:* 16
Provincial Electoral District(s): Rimbey-Rocky Mountain House-Sundre
Federal Electoral District(s): Yellowhead
Next Election: Summer 2017 (4 year terms)
Harold Esche, Mayor
Therese Kleeberger, Chief Administrative Officer

Calmar
P.O. Box 750
4901 - 50 Ave.
Calmar, AB T0C 0V0
Tel: 780-985-3604; *Fax:* 780-985-3039
info@calmar.ca
www.calmar.ca
Other Information: Toll free: 1-877-922-5627
Municipal Type: Town
Incorporated: Jan. 1, 1949; *Area:* 4.34 sq km
County or District: Leduc County; *Population in 2011:* 1,970
Provincial Electoral District(s): Drayton Valley-Devon
Federal Electoral District(s): Edmonton-Wetaskiwin
Next Election: Oct. 16, 2017 (4 year terms)
Note: Incorporated as a town on Jan. 19, 1954.
Don Faulkner, Mayor
Kathy Rodberg, Town Manager

Carbon
P.O. Box 249
238 Hillside Ave.
Carbon, AB T0M 0L0
Tel: 403-572-3244; *Fax:* 403-572-3778
www.villageofcarbon.com
Municipal Type: Village
Incorporated: Nov. 18, 1912; *Area:* 2 sq km
County or District: Kneehill County; *Population in 2011:* 592
Provincial Electoral District(s): Olds-Didsbury-Three Hills
Federal Electoral District(s): Bow River
Next Election: Oct. 16, 2017 (4 year terms)
Michael Still, Mayor
Debra Grosfield, Chief Administrative Officer

Cardston
P.O. Box 280
67 - 3 Ave. West
Cardston, AB T0K 0K0
Tel: 403-653-3366; *Fax:* 403-653-2499
info@cardston.ca
www.cardston.ca
Other Information: Toll free: 1-888-434-3366
Municipal Type: Town
Incorporated: Dec. 29, 1898; *Area:* 8.64 sq km
County or District: Cardston County; *Population in 2011:* 3,580
Provincial Electoral District(s): Cardston-Taber-Warner
Federal Electoral District(s): Medicine Hat-Cardston-Warner
Next Election: Oct. 16, 2017 (4 year terms)
Note: Incorporated as a town on July 2, 1901.
Maggie Kronen, Mayor, 403-653-2553
Marian Carlson, Chief Administrative Officer

Carmangay
P.O. Box 130
Carmangay, AB T0L 0N0
Tel: 403-643-3595; *Fax:* 403-643-2007
admin@villageofcarma.ca
Municipal Type: Village
Incorporated: Jan. 20, 1910; *Area:* 1.86 sq km
County or District: Vulcan County; *Population in 2011:* 367
Provincial Electoral District(s): Little Bow
Federal Electoral District(s): Bow River
Next Election: Oct. 16, 2017 (4 year terms)
Kym Nichols, Mayor
Carolyn Erb, Administrator

Caroline
P.O. Box 148
Caroline, AB T0M 0M0
Tel: 403-722-3781; *Fax:* 403-722-4050
info@caroline.ca
www.caroline.ca
Municipal Type: Village
Incorporated: Dec. 31, 1951; *Area:* 1.98 sq km
County or District: Clearwater County; *Population in 2011:* 501
Provincial Electoral District(s): Rimbey-Rocky Mountain House-Sundre
Federal Electoral District(s): Yellowhead
Next Election: Oct. 16, 2017 (4 year terms)
Rachele Peters, Mayor
Melissa Beebe, Chief Administrative Officer

Carstairs
P.O. Box 370
844 Centre St.
Carstairs, AB T0M 0N0
Tel: 403-337-3341; *Fax:* 403-337-3343
www.carstairs.ca
Municipal Type: Town
Incorporated: May 15, 1903; *Area:* 5 sq km
County or District: Mountain View County; *Population in 2011:* 3,442
Provincial Electoral District(s): Olds-Didsbury-Three Hills
Federal Electoral District(s): Red Deer-Mountain View
Next Election: Oct. 16, 2017 (4 year terms)
Note: Incorporated as a town on Sept. 1, 1966.
Lance Colby, Mayor, 403-337-3697
Carl McDonnell, Chief Administrative Officer

Castle Island
7 Delwood Pl.
St. Albert, AB T8N 6Y5
Tel: 780-418-8348; *Fax:* 780-419-2476
svcastle@telus.net
Municipal Type: Summer Village
Incorporated: Jan. 1, 1955; *Area:* 0.05 sq km
County or District: Lac Ste. Anne County; *Population in 2011:* 19
Provincial Electoral District(s): Whitecourt-Ste. Anne
Federal Electoral District(s): Yellowhead
Next Election: Oct. 16, 2017 (4 year terms)
Cornelia Helland, Mayor
Shelley Marsh, Chief Administrative Officer

Castor
P.O. Box 479
4901 - 50 Ave.
Castor, AB T0C 0X0
Tel: 403-882-3215; *Fax:* 403-882-2700
www.castor.ca
Municipal Type: Town
Incorporated: Nov. 26, 1909; *Area:* 2.72 sq km
County or District: Paintearth County No. 18; *Population in 2011:* 932
Provincial Electoral District(s): Drumheller-Stettler
Federal Electoral District(s): Battle River-Crowfoot
Next Election: Oct. 16, 2017 (4 year terms)
Note: Incorporated as a town on June 27, 1910.
Gerry DeVloo, Mayor
Sandra Jackson, Chief Administrative Officer

Cereal
P.O. Box 160
Cereal, AB T0J 2J0
Tel: 403-326-3823; *Fax:* 403-326-3826
vofc@netago.ca
www.samda.ca/cereal.html
Municipal Type: Village
Incorporated: Aug. 19, 1914; *Area:* 0.95 sq km
Population in 2011: 134
Provincial Electoral District(s): Drumheller-Stettler
Federal Electoral District(s): Battle River-Crowfoot
Next Election: Oct. 16, 2017 (4 year terms)
Tami Olds, Mayor
Mary Ann Salik, Municipal Administrator

Champion
P.O. Box 367
Champion, AB T0L 0R0
Tel: 403-897-3833; *Fax:* 403-897-2250
Municipal Type: Village
Incorporated: May 27, 1911; *Area:* 0.88 sq km
County or District: Vulcan County; *Population in 2011:* 378
Provincial Electoral District(s): Little Bow
Federal Electoral District(s): Bow River
Next Election: Oct. 16, 2017 (4 year terms)
James F. Smith, Mayor
Colleen Mayne, Chief Administrative Officer

Chauvin
P.O. Box 160
Chauvin, AB T0B 0V0
Tel: 780-858-3881; *Fax:* 780-858-2125
vchauvin@cciwireless.ca
www.villageofchauvin.ca
Municipal Type: Village
Incorporated: Dec. 30, 1912; *Area:* 2.32 sq km
County or District: Municipal District of Wainwright No. 61;
Population in 2011: 334
Provincial Electoral District(s): Battle River-Wainwright
Federal Electoral District(s): Battle River-Crowfoot
Next Election: Oct. 16, 2017 (4 year terms)
Lance LaPierre, Mayor
Shelly McMann, Chief Administrative Officer

Chipman
P.O. Box 176
4816 - 50 St.
Chipman, AB T0B 0W0
Tel: 780-363-3982; *Fax:* 780-363-2386
info@chipmanab.ca
www.chipmanab.ca
Municipal Type: Village
Incorporated: Oct. 21, 1913; *Area:* 0.62 sq km
County or District: Lamont County; *Population in 2011:* 284
Provincial Electoral District(s): Fort Saskatchewan-Vegreville
Federal Electoral District(s): Lakeland
Next Election: Oct. 16, 2017 (4 year terms)
Jim Palmer, Mayor
Pat Tomkow, Administrator

Claresholm
P.O. Box 1000
221 - 45 Ave. West
Claresholm, AB T0L 0T0
Tel: 403-625-3381; *Fax:* 403-625-3869
www.townofclaresholm.com
Municipal Type: Town
Incorporated: May 30, 1903; *Area:* 8.3 sq km
County or District: Municipal District of Willow Creek No. 26;
Population in 2011: 3,758
Provincial Electoral District(s): Livingstone-Macleod
Federal Electoral District(s): Foothills
Next Election: Oct. 16, 2017 (4 year terms)
Note: Incorporated as a town on Aug. 31, 1905.
Rob Steel, Mayor
Kris Holbeck, Chief Administrative Officer

Clive
P.O. Box 90
5115 - 50 St.
Clive, AB T0C 0Y0
Tel: 403-784-3366; *Fax:* 403-784-2012
admin@clive.ca
www.clive.ca
Municipal Type: Village
Incorporated: Jan. 9, 1912; *Area:* 2.12 sq km
County or District: Lacombe County; *Population in 2011:* 675
Provincial Electoral District(s): Lacombe-Ponoka
Federal Electoral District(s): Red Deer-Lacombe
Next Election: Oct. 16, 2017 (4 year terms)
Anita Gillard, Mayor
Carla Kenney, Chief Administrative Officer

Clyde
P.O. Box 190
4812 - 50 St.
Clyde, AB T0G 0P0
Tel: 780-348-5356; *Fax:* 780-348-5699
www.villageofclyde.ca
Municipal Type: Village
Incorporated: Jan. 28, 1914; *Area:* 1.36 sq km
County or District: Westlock County; *Population in 2011:* 503
Provincial Electoral District(s): Barrhead-Morinville-Westlock
Federal Electoral District(s): Peace River-Westlock
Next Election: Oct. 16, 2017 (4 year terms)
Doug Nyal, Mayor
Garth Bancroft, Chief Administrative Officer

Coaldale
1920 - 17 St.
Coaldale, AB T1M 1M1
Tel: 403-345-1300; *Fax:* 403-345-1311
admin@coaldale.ca
www.coaldale.ca
Municipal Type: Town
Incorporated: Dec. 27, 1919; *Area:* 7.95 sq km
County or District: Lethbridge County; *Population in 2011:* 7,493
Provincial Electoral District(s): Little Bow
Federal Electoral District(s): Lethbridge
Next Election: Oct. 16, 2017 (4 year terms)
Note: Incorporated as a town on Jan. 7, 1952.
Kim Craig, Mayor
Kalen Hastings, Chief Administrative Officer

Coalhurst
P.O. Box 456
100 - 51 Ave.
Coalhurst, AB T0L 0V0
Tel: 403-381-3033; *Fax:* 403-381-2924
main@town.coalhurst.ab.ca
www.town.coalhurst.ab.ca
Municipal Type: Town
Incorporated: Dec. 17, 1913; *Area:* 1.64 sq km
County or District: Lethbridge County; *Population in 2011:* 1,963
Provincial Electoral District(s): Little Bow
Federal Electoral District(s): Lethbridge
Next Election: Oct. 16, 2017 (4 year terms)
Note: Incorporated as a town on June 1, 1995.
Dennis Cassie, Mayor
R. Kim Hauta, Chief Administrative Officer, 403-381-3033

Consort
P.O. Box 490
4901 - 50 Ave.
Consort, AB T0C 1B0
Tel: 403-577-3623; *Fax:* 403-577-2024
consort@netago.ca
www.consort.ca
Municipal Type: Village
Incorporated: Sept. 23, 1912; *Area:* 2.63 sq km
Population in 2011: 689
Provincial Electoral District(s): Drumheller-Stettler
Federal Electoral District(s): Battle River-Crowfoot
Next Election: Oct. 16, 2017 (4 year terms)
Roxanne Stillings, Mayor
Monique Jeffrey, Chief Administrative Officer

Coronation
P.O. Box 219
5015 Victoria Ave.
Coronation, AB T0C 1C0
Tel: 403-578-3679; *Fax:* 403-578-3020
www.town.coronation.ab.ca
Municipal Type: Town
Incorporated: Dec. 16, 1911; *Area:* 3.73 sq km
County or District: Paintearth County No. 18; *Population in 2011:* 947
Provincial Electoral District(s): Drumheller-Stettler
Federal Electoral District(s): Battle River-Crowfoot
Next Election: Oct. 16, 2017 (4 year terms)
Note: Incorporated as a town on April 29, 1912.
Marks Stannard, Mayor
Sandra Kulyk, Chief Administrative Officer

Coutts
P.O. Box 236
Coutts, AB T0K 0N0
Tel: 403-344-3848; *Fax:* 403-344-4360
vilcoutt@telus.net
www.villagecoutts.ab.ca
Municipal Type: Village
Incorporated: Jan. 1, 1960; *Area:* 0.98 sq km
County or District: Warner County No. 5; *Population in 2011:* 277
Provincial Electoral District(s): Cardston-Taber-Warner
Federal Electoral District(s): Medicine Hat-Cardston-Warner
Next Election: Oct. 16, 2017 (4 year terms)
Thomas Butler, Mayor
Lori Rolfe, Chief Administrative Officer

Cowley
P.O. Box 40
Cowley, AB T0K 0P0
Tel: 403-628-3808; *Fax:* 403-628-2807
vilocow@shaw.ca
Municipal Type: Village
Incorporated: Aug. 16, 1906; *Area:* 1.4 sq km
County or District: Municipal District of Pincher Creek No. 9; *Population in 2011:* 236
Provincial Electoral District(s): Livingstone-Macleod
Federal Electoral District(s): Foothills
Next Election: Oct. 16, 2017 (4 year terms)
Linda Findlater, Mayor
Cindy Cornish, Chief Administrative Officer

Cremona
P.O. Box 10
205 - 1 St. East
Cremona, AB T0M 0R0
Tel: 403-637-3762; *Fax:* 403-637-2101
www.village.cremona.ab.ca
Municipal Type: Village
Incorporated: Jan. 1, 1955; *Area:* 0.68 sq km
County or District: Mountain View County; *Population in 2011:* 457
Provincial Electoral District(s): Olds-Didsbury-Three Hills
Federal Electoral District(s): Red Deer-Mountain View
Next Election: Oct. 16, 2017 (4 year terms)
Timothy Hagen, Mayor
Luana G. Smith, Chief Administrative Officer

Crossfield
P.O. Box 500
1005 Ross St.
Crossfield, AB T0M 0S0
Tel: 403-946-5565; *Fax:* 403-946-4523
town@crossfieldalberta.com
Municipal Type: Town
Incorporated: June 3, 1907; *Area:* 4.8 sq km
County or District: Rocky View County; *Population in 2011:* 2,853
Provincial Electoral District(s): Olds-Didsbury-Three Hills
Federal Electoral District(s): Banff-Airdrie
Next Election: Oct. 16, 2017 (4 year terms)
Note: Incorporated as a town on Aug. 1, 1980.
Nathan Anderson, Mayor
Cheryl Skelly, Chief Administrative Officer

Crystal Springs
P.O. Box 100
605 - 2 Ave.
Ma-Me O Beach, AB T0C 1X0
Tel: 780-586-2494; *Fax:* 780-586-3567
www.crystalsprings.ca
Municipal Type: Summer Village
Incorporated: Jan. 1, 1957; *Area:* 0.58 sq km
County or District: Wetaskiwin County No. 10; *Population in 2011:* 90
Provincial Electoral District(s): Drayton Valley-Devon
Federal Electoral District(s): Edmonton-Wetaskiwin
Next Election: Summer 2017 (4 year terms)
Doris Bell, Mayor
Sylvia Roy, Chief Administrative Officer

Czar
P.O. Box 30
Czar, AB T0B 0Z0
Tel: 780-857-3740; *Fax:* 780-857-2353
Municipal Type: Village
Incorporated: Nov. 12, 1917; *Area:* 1.18 sq km
County or District: Municipal District of Provost No. 52; *Population in 2011:* 167
Provincial Electoral District(s): Battle River-Wainwright
Federal Electoral District(s): Battle River-Crowfoot
Next Election: Oct. 16, 2017 (4 year terms)
Angela Large, Mayor
Tricia Strang, Administrator

Daysland
P.O. Box 610
5130 - 50 St.
Daysland, AB T0B 1A0
Tel: 780-374-3767; *Fax:* 780-374-2455
info@daysland.com
www.daysland.com
Municipal Type: Town
Incorporated: April 23, 1906; *Area:* 1.75 sq km
County or District: Flagstaff County; *Population in 2011:* 807
Provincial Electoral District(s): Battle River-Wainwright
Federal Electoral District(s): Battle River-Crowfoot
Next Election: Oct. 16, 2017 (4 year terms)
Note: Incorporated as a town on April 2, 1907.
Gail Watt, Mayor
Rod Krips, Chief Administrative Officer

Delburne
P.O. Box 341
Delburne, AB T0M 0V0
Tel: 403-749-3606; *Fax:* 403-749-2800
village@delburne.ca
www.delburne.ca
Municipal Type: Village
Incorporated: Jan. 17, 1913; *Area:* 1.32 sq km
County or District: Red Deer County; *Population in 2011:* 830
Provincial Electoral District(s): Innisfail-Sylvan Lake
Federal Electoral District(s): Red Deer-Mountain View
Next Election: Oct. 16, 2017 (4 year terms)
Ray Reckseidler, Mayor
Karen Fegan, Chief Administrative Officer

Delia
P.O. Box 206
218 Main St.
Delia, AB T0J 0W0
Tel: 403-364-3787; *Fax:* 403-364-2089
delia@netago.ca
www.delia.ca
Municipal Type: Village
Incorporated: July 20, 1914; *Area:* 1.31 sq km
County or District: Starland County; *Population in 2011:* 186
Provincial Electoral District(s): Drumheller-Stettler
Federal Electoral District(s): Battle River-Crowfoot
Next Election: Oct. 16, 2017 (4 year terms)
Dawn Bancroft, Mayor
Marcia Raymond, Chief Administrative Officer

Devon
1 Columbia Ave. West
Devon, AB T9G 1A1
Tel: 780-987-8300; *Fax:* 780-987-4778
information@devon.ca
www.town.devon.ab.ca
Municipal Type: Town
Incorporated: Dec. 31, 1949; *Area:* 8.63 sq km
Population in 2011: 6,510
Provincial Electoral District(s): Drayton Valley-Devon
Federal Electoral District(s): Edmonton-Wetaskiwin; Yellowhead
Next Election: Oct. 16, 2017 (4 year terms)
Note: Incorporated as a town on Feb. 24, 1950.
Stephen Lindrop, Mayor
Tony Kulbisky, Chief Administrative Officer

Dewberry
P.O. Box 30
22 Centre St.
Dewberry, AB T0B 1G0
Tel: 780-847-3053; *Fax:* 780-847-3057
dewberry@hmsinet.ca
www.villageofdewberry.ca
Municipal Type: Village
Incorporated: Jan. 1, 1957; *Area:* 0.84 sq km
County or District: Vermilion River County; *Population in 2011:* 201
Provincial Electoral District(s): Vermilion-Lloydminster
Federal Electoral District(s): Lakeland
Next Election: Oct. 16, 2017 (4 year terms)
Ken Haney, Mayor
Sherry Johnson, Acting Chief Administrative Officer

Didsbury
P.O. Box 790
2037 - 19 Ave.
Didsbury, AB T0M 0W0
Tel: 403-335-3391; *Fax:* 403-335-9794
inquiries@didsbury.ca
www.didsbury.ca
Municipal Type: Town
Incorporated: Dec. 24, 1901; *Area:* 5.47 sq km
County or District: Mountain View County; *Population in 2011:* 4,957
Provincial Electoral District(s): Olds-Didsbury-Three Hills
Federal Electoral District(s): Red Deer-Mountain View
Next Election: Oct. 16, 2017 (4 year terms)
Note: Incorporated as a town on Sept. 27, 1906.
Rick Mousseau, Mayor
Roy Brown, Chief Administrative Officer

Donalda
P.O. Box 160
5001 Main St.
Donalda, AB T0B 1H0
Tel: 403-883-2345; *Fax:* 403-883-2022
admin@village.donalda.ab.ca
www.village.donalda.ab.ca
Municipal Type: Village
Incorporated: Dec. 30, 1912; *Area:* 0.99 sq km
County or District: Stettler County No. 6; *Population in 2011:* 259
Provincial Electoral District(s): Drumheller-Stettler
Federal Electoral District(s): Battle River-Crowfoot
Next Election: Oct. 16, 2017 (4 year terms)
Bruce Gartside, Mayor
Joan Kapiniak, Chief Administrative Officer

Donnelly
P.O. Box 200
Donnelly, AB T0H 1G0
Tel: 780-925-3835; *Fax:* 780-925-2100
vilofdon@serbernet.com
Municipal Type: Village
Incorporated: Jan. 1, 1956; *Area:* 1.04 sq km
County or District: Municipal District of Smoky River No. 130; *Population in 2011:* 305
Provincial Electoral District(s): Dunvegan-Central Peace
Federal Electoral District(s): Peace River-Westlock
Next Election: Oct. 16, 2017 (4 year terms)
Myrna Lanctot, Mayor
Lilliane Bessette, Chief Administrative Officer

Drayton Valley
P.O. Box 6837
5120 - 52 St.
Drayton Valley, AB T7A 1A1
Tel: 780-514-2200; *Fax:* 780-542-5753
info@draytonvalley.ca
www.draytonvalley.ca
Other Information: Alt. Phone: 780-542-5327
Municipal Type: Town
Incorporated: Jan. 1, 1956; *Area:* 12.27 sq km
County or District: Brazeau County; *Population in 2011:* 7,049
Provincial Electoral District(s): Drayton Valley-Devon
Federal Electoral District(s): Yellowhead
Next Election: Oct. 16, 2017 (4 year terms)
Note: Incorporated as a town on June 1, 1956.
Glenn McLean, Mayor
Manny Deol, Chief Administrative Officer

Drumheller
22 Centre St.
Drumheller, AB T0J 0Y4
Tel: 403-823-6300; *Fax:* 403-823-7739
www.dinosaurvalley.com
Municipal Type: Town
Incorporated: May 15, 1913; *Area:* 107.93 sq km
Population in 2011: 8,029
Provincial Electoral District(s): Drumheller-Stettler
Federal Electoral District(s): Battle River-Crowfoot
Next Election: Oct. 16, 2017 (4 year terms)
Note: Incorporated as a town on March 2, 1916.
Terry Yemen, Mayor, 403-823-1306
Ray Romanetz, Chief Administrative Officer

Duchess
P.O. Box 158
103 - 2 St. East
Duchess, AB T0J 0Z0
Tel: 403-378-4452; *Fax:* 403-378-3860
administration@villageofduchess.com
www.villageofduchess.com
Municipal Type: Village
Incorporated: May 12, 1921; *Area:* 1.89 sq km
County or District: Newell County; *Population in 2011:* 992
Provincial Electoral District(s): Strathmore-Brooks
Federal Electoral District(s): Bow River
Next Election: Oct. 16, 2017 (4 year terms)
Bruce Snape, Mayor
Yvonne Cosh, Chief Administrative Officer

Eckville
P.O. Box 578
5023 - 51 Ave.
Eckville, AB T0M 0X0
Tel: 403-746-2171; *Fax:* 403-746-2900
info@eckville.com
www.eckville.com
Municipal Type: Town
Incorporated: Nov. 3, 1921; *Area:* 1.58 sq km
County or District: Lacombe County; *Population in 2011:* 1,125
Provincial Electoral District(s): Rimbey-Rocky Mountain House-Sundre
Federal Electoral District(s): Red Deer-Lacombe
Next Election: Oct. 16, 2017 (4 year terms)
Note: Incorporated as a town on July 1, 1966.
Helen Posti, Mayor
Jack Ramsden, Chief Administrative Officer

Edberg
P.O. Box 160
Edberg, AB T0B 1J0
Tel: 780-877-3999; *Fax:* 780-877-2562
www.villageofedberg.com
Municipal Type: Village
Incorporated: Feb. 4, 1930; *Area:* 0.36 sq km
County or District: Camrose County; *Population in 2011:* 168
Provincial Electoral District(s): Battle River-Wainwright
Federal Electoral District(s): Battle River-Crowfoot
Next Election: Oct. 16, 2017 (4 year terms)
Colleen Wack, Mayor
Patrick Risk, Chief Administrative Officer

Edgerton
P.O. Box 57
5017 - 50 Ave.
Edgerton, AB T0B 1K0
Tel: 780-755-3933; *Fax:* 780-755-3750
info@edgerton-oasis.ca
www.edgerton-oasis.ca
Municipal Type: Village
Incorporated: Sept. 11, 1917; *Area:* 1.22 sq km
County or District: Municipal District of Wainwright No. 61; *Population in 2011:* 317
Provincial Electoral District(s): Battle River-Wainwright
Federal Electoral District(s): Battle River-Crowfoot
Next Election: Oct. 16, 2017 (4 year terms)
Barbara L. Sjoquist, Mayor
Al Gordon, Chief Administrative Officer

Edson
P.O. Box 6300
605 - 50th St.
Edson, AB T7E 1T7
Tel: 780-723-4401; *Fax:* 780-723-8617
www.townofedson.ca
Municipal Type: Town
Incorporated: Jan. 9, 1911; *Area:* 29.54 sq km
County or District: Yellowhead County; *Population in 2011:* 8,475
Provincial Electoral District(s): West Yellowhead
Federal Electoral District(s): Yellowhead
Next Election: Oct. 16, 2017 (4 year terms)
Note: Incorporated as a town on Sept. 21, 1911.
Greg Pasychny, Mayor
Clarence Joly, Chief Administrative Officer

Elk Point
P.O. Box 448
Elk Point, AB T0A 1A0
Tel: 780-724-3810; *Fax:* 780-724-2762
town@elkpoint.ca
www.elkpoint.ca
Municipal Type: Town
Incorporated: May 31, 1938; *Area:* 4.88 sq km
County or District: St. Paul County No. 19; *Population in 2011:* 1,412
Provincial Electoral District(s): Lac La Biche-St. Paul-Two Hills
Federal Electoral District(s): Lakeland
Next Election: Oct. 16, 2017 (4 year terms)
Note: Incorporated as a town on Jan. 1, 1962.
Parrish Tung, Mayor
Myron J. Goyan, Manager

Elnora
P.O. Box 629
219 Main St.
Elnora, AB T0M 0Y0
Tel: 403-773-3922; *Fax:* 403-773-3173
info@villageofelnora.com
www.villageofelnora.com
Municipal Type: Village
Incorporated: July 22, 1929; *Area:* 0.69 sq km
County or District: Red Deer County; *Population in 2011:* 313
Provincial Electoral District(s): Innisfail-Sylvan Lake
Federal Electoral District(s): Red Deer-Mountain View
Next Election: Oct. 16, 2017 (4 year terms)
Rob Aellen, Mayor
Cindy Armstrong, Chief Administrative Officer

Empress
P.O. Box 159
6 - 3 Ave.
Empress, AB T0J 1E0
Tel: 403-565-3938; *Fax:* 403-565-2010
voe14@villageofempress.com
www.villageofempress.com
Municipal Type: Village
Incorporated: Feb. 5, 1914; *Area:* 1.75 sq km
Population in 2011: 188
Provincial Electoral District(s): Drumheller-Stettler
Federal Electoral District(s): Battle River-Crowfoot
Next Election: Oct. 16, 2017 (4 year terms)
Chad Van Dam, Mayor
Debbie Ross, Chief Administrative Officer

Fairview
P.O. Box 730
10209 - 109 St.
Fairview, AB T0H 1L0
Tel: 780-835-5461; *Fax:* 780-835-3576
reception@fairview.ca
www.fairview.ca
Municipal Type: Town
Incorporated: March 28, 1929; *Area:* 9.65 sq km
County or District: Municipal District of Fairview No. 136; *Population in 2011:* 3,162
Provincial Electoral District(s): Dunvegan-Central Peace-Notley
Federal Electoral District(s): Peace River-Westlock
Next Election: Oct. 16, 2017 (4 year terms)
Note: Incorporated as a town on April 25, 1949.
Gordon MacLeod, Mayor
Larry Davidson, Chief Administrative Officer

Falher
P.O. Box 155
11 Central Ave. SW
Falher, AB T0H 1M0
Tel: 780-837-2247; *Fax:* 780-837-2647
info@town.falher.ab.ca
www.town.falher.ab.ca
Municipal Type: Town
Incorporated: Sept. 05, 1923; *Area:* 2.87 sq km
County or District: Municipal District of Smoky River No. 130; *Population in 2011:* 1,075
Provincial Electoral District(s): Dunvegan-Central Peace-Notley
Federal Electoral District(s): Peace River-Westlock
Next Election: Oct. 16, 2017 (4 year terms)
Note: Incorporated as a town on Jan. 1, 1955.
Donna Buchinski, Mayor
Adele Parker, Chief Administrative Officer

Ferintosh
P.O. Box 160
301 Main St.
Ferintosh, AB T0B 1M0
Tel: 780-877-3767; *Fax:* 780-877-2338
villgfrn@telus.net
www.ferintosh.info
Municipal Type: Village
Incorporated: Jan. 9, 1911; *Area:* 0.62 sq km
County or District: Camrose County; *Population in 2011:* 181
Provincial Electoral District(s): Battle River-Wainwright
Federal Electoral District(s): Battle River-Crowfoot
Next Election: Oct. 16, 2017 (4 year terms)
Marvin Jassman, Mayor
Patrick Risk, Chief Administrative Officer

Foremost
P.O. Box 159
301 Main St.
Foremost, AB T0K 0X0
Tel: 403-867-3733; *Fax:* 403-867-2031
www.foremostalberta.com
Municipal Type: Village
Incorporated: Dec. 31, 1950; *Area:* 1.74 sq km

County or District: Forty Mile County No. 8; *Population in 2011:* 526
Provincial Electoral District(s): Cypress-Medicine Hat
Federal Electoral District(s): Medicine Hat-Cardston-Warner
Next Election: Oct. 16, 2017 (4 year terms)
Kenneth R. Kultgen, Mayor
Kelly Calhoun, Municipal Administrator

Forestburg
P.O. Box 210
Forestburg, AB T0B 1N0
Tel: 780-582-3668; *Fax:* 780-582-2233
forestburg@persona.ca
www.forestburg.ca
Municipal Type: Village
Incorporated: Aug. 21, 1919; *Area:* 2.19 sq km
County or District: Flagstaff County; *Population in 2011:* 831
Provincial Electoral District(s): Battle River-Wainwright
Federal Electoral District(s): Battle River-Crowfoot
Next Election: Oct. 16, 2017 (4 year terms)
Peter V. Miller, Mayor
Debra Moffatt, Chief Administrative Officer

Fort Macleod
P.O. Box 1420
Fort MacLeod, AB T0L 0Z0
Tel: 403-553-4425; *Fax:* 403-553-2426
administration@fortmacleod.com
www.fortmacleod.com
Other Information: Toll free: 1-877-622-5366
Municipal Type: Town
Incorporated: Dec. 31, 1892; *Area:* 23.34 sq km
County or District: Municipal District of Willow Creek No. 26; *Population in 2011:* 3,117
Provincial Electoral District(s): Livingstone-Macleod
Federal Electoral District(s): Foothills
Next Election: Oct. 16, 2017 (4 year terms)
Rene Gendre, Mayor
David Connauton, Chief Administrative Officer, 403-553-4425

Fox Creek
P.O. Box 149
102 Kaybob Drive
Fox Creek, AB T0H 1P0
Tel: 780-622-3896; *Fax:* 780-622-4247
executivesecretary@foxcreek.ca
www.foxcreek.ca
Municipal Type: Town
Incorporated: July 19, 1967; *Area:* 11.54 sq km
County or District: Municipal District of Greenview No. 16; *Population in 2011:* 1,969
Provincial Electoral District(s): Grande Prairie-Smoky
Federal Electoral District(s): Peace River-Westlock
Next Election: Oct. 16, 2017 (4 year terms)
James Ahn, Mayor, 780-622-3896
Roy Dell, Chief Administrative Officer

Gadsby
P.O. Box 80
Gadsby, AB T0C 1K0
Tel: 403-574-3793; *Fax:* 403-574-2369
vgadsby@xplornet.ca
Municipal Type: Village
Incorporated: May 6, 1910; *Area:* 0.82 sq km
County or District: Stettler County No. 6; *Population in 2011:* 25
Provincial Electoral District(s): Drumheller-Stettler
Federal Electoral District(s): Battle River-Crowfoot
Next Election: Oct. 16, 2017 (4 year terms)
Laura Kelly-Stevenson, Mayor
Carla Tuck, Chief Administrative Officer

Galahad
P.O. Box 66
Galahad, AB T0B 1R0
Tel: 780-583-3741; *Fax:* 780-583-2230
office@cable-lynx.net
www.villageofgalahad.ca
Municipal Type: Village
Incorporated: March 5, 1918; *Area:* 0.6 sq km
County or District: Flagstaff County; *Population in 2011:* 119
Provincial Electoral District(s): Battle River-Wainwright
Federal Electoral District(s): Battle River-Crowfoot
Next Election: Oct. 16, 2017 (4 year terms)
Jeanette Herle, Mayor
Shelly Armstrong, Chief Administrative Officer

Ghost Lake
P.O. Box 19554
Calgary, AB T3M 0V4
Tel: 403-554-5515; *Fax:* 403-206-7209
admin@ghostlake.ca
www.ghostlake.ca
Municipal Type: Summer Village
Incorporated: Dec. 31, 1953; *Area:* 0.63 sq km
County or District: Municipal District of Bighorn No. 8; *Population in 2011:* 81
Provincial Electoral District(s): Banff-Cochrane
Federal Electoral District(s): Banff-Airdrie
Next Election: Oct. 16, 2017 (4 year terms)
Brian Oblak, Mayor, 403-275-5007
Sharon Plett, Chief Administrative Officer

Gibbons
P.O. Box 68
4807 - 50 Ave.
Gibbons, AB T0A 1N0
Tel: 780-923-3331; *Fax:* 780-923-3691
webresponse@gibbons.ca
www.gibbons.ca
Municipal Type: Town
Incorporated: Jan. 1, 1959; *Area:* 6.46 sq km
County or District: Sturgeon County; *Population in 2011:* 3,030
Provincial Electoral District(s): Athabasca-Sturgeon-Redwater
Federal Electoral District(s): Sturgeon River-Parkland
Next Election: Oct. 16, 2017 (4 year terms)
Note: Incorporated as a town on April 1, 1977.
Doug J. Horner, Mayor, 780-923-3307
Farrell O'Malley, Chief Administrative Officer, 780-923-3331

Girouxville
P.O. Box 276
Girouxville, AB T0H 1S0
Tel: 780-323-4270; *Fax:* 780-323-4110
girouxvl@serbernet.com
Municipal Type: Village
Incorporated: Dec. 31, 1951; *Area:* 0.58 sq km
County or District: Municipal District of Smoky River No. 130; *Population in 2011:* 266
Provincial Electoral District(s): Dunvegan-Central Peace-Notley
Federal Electoral District(s): Peace River-Westlock
Next Election: Oct. 16, 2017 (4 year terms)
Carmen Ewing, Mayor
Estelle Girard, Municipal Administrator

Glendon
P.O. Box 177
Glendon, AB T0A 1P0
Tel: 780-635-3807; *Fax:* 780-635-2100
www.glendonalberta.ca
Municipal Type: Village
Incorporated: Jan. 1, 1956; *Area:* 1.98 sq km
County or District: Municipal District of Bonnyville No. 87; *Population in 2011:* 486
Provincial Electoral District(s): Bonnyville-Cold Lake
Federal Electoral District(s): Lakeland
Next Election: Oct. 16, 2017 (4 year terms)
Laura Papirny, Mayor
Melody Kwiatkowski, Chief Administrative Officer

Glenwood
P.O. Box 1084
Glenwood, AB T0k 2R0
Tel: 403-626-3233; *Fax:* 403-626-3234
admin@glenwood.ca
glenwood.ca
Municipal Type: Village
Incorporated: Jan. 1, 1961; *Area:* 1.46 sq km
County or District: Cardston County; *Population in 2011:* 287
Provincial Electoral District(s): Cardston-Taber-Warner
Federal Electoral District(s): Foothills
Next Election: Oct. 16, 2017 (4 year terms)
Jordan Koch, Mayor
Kurtis Pratt, Chief Administrative Officer

Golden Days
605 - 2 Ave.
Ma-Me O Beach, AB T0k 1x0
Tel: 780-586-2494; *Fax:* 780-586-3567
www.goldendays.ca
Municipal Type: Summer Village
Incorporated: Jan. 1, 1965; *Area:* 2.27 sq km
County or District: Leduc County; *Population in 2011:* 141
Provincial Electoral District(s): Drayton Valley-Devon
Federal Electoral District(s): Edmonton-Wetaskiwin
Next Election: Summer 2017 (4 year terms)
Randal Kay, Mayor
Sylvia Roy, Chief Administrative Officer

Grande Cache
P.O. Box 300
10001 Hoppe Ave.
Grande Cache, AB T0E 0Y0
Tel: 780-827-3362; *Fax:* 780-827-2406
admin@grandecache.ca
www.grandecache.ca
Municipal Type: Town
Incorporated: Sept. 1, 1966; *Area:* 35.48 sq km
County or District: Municipal District of Greenview No. 16; *Population in 2011:* 4,319
Provincial Electoral District(s): West Yellowhead
Federal Electoral District(s): Yellowhead
Next Election: Oct. 16, 2017 (4 year terms)
Herb Castle, Mayor, 780-827-2800
Loretta Thompson, Chief Administrative Officer

Grandview
P.O. Box 100
605 - 2 Ave.
Ma-Me O Beach, AB T0C 1X0
Tel: 780-586-2494; *Fax:* 780-586-3567
www.grandview.ca
Municipal Type: Summer Village
Incorporated: Jan. 1, 1967; *Area:* 0.8 sq km
County or District: Wetaskiwin County No. 10; *Population in 2011:* 108
Provincial Electoral District(s): Drayton Valley-Devon
Federal Electoral District(s): Edmonton-Wetaskiwin
Next Election: Summer 2017 (4 year terms)
Don Davidson, Mayor
Sylvia Roy, Chief Administrative Officer

Granum
P.O. Box 88
304 Railway Ave.
Granum, AB T0L 1A0
Tel: 403-687-3822; *Fax:* 403-687-2285
www.granum.ca
Municipal Type: Town
Incorporated: July 12, 1904; *Area:* 1.87 sq km
County or District: Municipal District of Willow Creek No. 26; *Population in 2011:* 447
Provincial Electoral District(s): Livingstone-Macleod
Federal Electoral District(s): Foothills
Next Election: Oct. 16, 2017 (4 year terms)
Note: Incorporated as a town on Nov. 7, 1910.
Gerald Brown, Mayor
Ken Anderson, Chief Administrative Officer

Grimshaw
P.O. Box 377
5005 - 53 Ave.
Grimshaw, AB T0H 1W0
Tel: 780-332-4626; *Fax:* 780-332-1250
www.grimshaw.ca
Municipal Type: Town
Incorporated: Feb. 18, 1930; *Area:* 7.21 sq km
County or District: Municipal District of Peace No. 135; *Population in 2011:* 2,515
Provincial Electoral District(s): Dunvegan-Central Peace-Notley
Federal Electoral District(s): Peace River-Westlock
Next Election: Oct. 16, 2017 (4 year terms)
Note: Incorporated as a town on Feb. 2, 1953.
Bob Regal, Mayor
Brian Allen, Chief Administrative Officer

Gull Lake
P.O. Box 5
RR#1, Site 2
Lacombe, AB T4L 2N1
Tel: 403-784-2966; *Fax:* 888-241-6027
admin@summervillageofgulllake.com
www.summervillageofgulllake.com
Municipal Type: Summer Village
Incorporated: Sept. 1, 1993; *Area:* 0.7 sq km
County or District: Lacombe County; *Population in 2011:* 122
Provincial Electoral District(s): Lacombe-Ponoka
Federal Electoral District(s): Red Deer-Lacombe
Next Election: Summer 2017 (4 year terms)
Linda D'Angelo, Mayor
Myra Reiter, Chief Administrative Officer

Half Moon Bay
Bay 8, Thevenaz Indsutrial Trail
Sylvan Lake, AB T4S 2J5
Tel: 403-887-2822; *Fax:* 403-887-2897
info@sylvansummervillages.ca
www.sylvansummervillages.ca/location/half-moon-bay
Municipal Type: Summer Village
Incorporated: Jan. 1, 1978; *Area:* 0.17 sq km
County or District: Lacombe County; *Population in 2011:* 38

Provincial Electoral District(s): Rocky Mountain House
Federal Electoral District(s): Red Deer-Lacombe
Next Election: Summer 2017 (4 year terms)
Edward (Ted) Hiscock, Mayor
Phyllis Forsyth, Village Administrator

Halkirk
P.O. Box 126
Halkirk, AB T0C 1M0
Tel: 403-884-2464; *Fax:* 403-884-2113
halkirk@wildroseinternet.ca
www.halkirk.ca
Municipal Type: Village
Incorporated: Feb. 10, 1912; *Area:* 0.65 sq km
County or District: Paintearth County No. 18; *Population in 2011:* 121
Provincial Electoral District(s): Drumheller-Stettler
Federal Electoral District(s): Battle River-Crowfoot
Next Election: Oct. 16, 2017 (4 year terms)
Dale Kent, Mayor
Doris Cordel, Village Administrator

Hanna
P.O. Box 430
202 - 1 St. West
Hanna, AB T0J 1P0
Tel: 403-854-4433; *Fax:* 403-854-2772
admin@hanna.ca
www.hanna.ca
Municipal Type: Town
Incorporated: Dec. 31, 1912; *Area:* 8.39 sq km
Population in 2011: 2,673
Provincial Electoral District(s): Drumheller-Stettler
Federal Electoral District(s): Battle River-Crowfoot
Next Election: Oct. 16, 2017 (4 year terms)
Note: Incorporated as a town on April 14, 1914.
Chris Warwick, Mayor
Kim Neill, Chief Administrative Officer

Hardisty
P.O. Box 10
4807 - 49 St.
Hardisty, AB T0B 1V0
Tel: 780-888-3623; *Fax:* 780-888-2200
www.hardisty.ca
Other Information: Emergency/after hours phone: 780-888-1747
Municipal Type: Town
Incorporated: Dec. 11, 1906; *Area:* 5.48 sq km
County or District: Flagstaff County; *Population in 2011:* 639
Provincial Electoral District(s): Battle River-Wainwright
Federal Electoral District(s): Battle River-Crowfoot
Next Election: Oct. 16, 2017 (4 year terms)
Note: Incorporated as a town on Nov. 9, 1910.
Anita Miller, Mayor
Kevin Miller, Chief Administrative Officer

Hay Lakes
P.O. Box 40
Hay Lakes, AB T0B 1W0
Tel: 780-878-3200; *Fax:* 780-878-3897
haylakes@syban.net
www.villageofhaylakes.com
Municipal Type: Village
Incorporated: April 17, 1928; *Area:* 0.58 sq km
County or District: Camrose County; *Population in 2011:* 425
Provincial Electoral District(s): Battle River-Wainwright
Federal Electoral District(s): Battle River-Crowfoot
Next Election: Oct. 16, 2017 (4 year terms)
Todd Skaret, Mayor
Heather Nadeau, Municipal Administrator

Heisler
P.O. Box 60
Heisler, AB T0B 2A0
Tel: 780-889-3774; *Fax:* 780-889-2280
administration@villageofheisler.ca
www.villageofheisler.ca
Municipal Type: Village
Incorporated: July 27, 1920; *Area:* 0.75 sq km
County or District: Flagstaff County; *Population in 2011:* 151
Provincial Electoral District(s): Battle River-Wainwright
Federal Electoral District(s): Battle River-Crowfoot
Next Election: Oct. 16, 2017 (4 year terms)
Dennis Steil, Mayor
Amanda Howell, Chief Administrative Officer

High Level
10511 - 103 St.
High Level, AB T0H 1Z0
Tel: 780-926-2201; *Fax:* 780-926-2899
reception@highlevel.ca
www.highlevel.ca
Municipal Type: Town
Incorporated: June 1, 1965; *Area:* 31.99 sq km
County or District: Mackenzie County; *Population in 2011:* 3,641
Provincial Electoral District(s): Peace River
Federal Electoral District(s): Grande Prairie-Mackenzie
Next Election: Oct. 16, 2017 (4 year terms)
Crystal McAteer, Mayor, 780-841-5729
Tom Derreck, Chief Administrative Officer, 780-821-4001

High Prairie
P.O. Box 179
4806 - 53 Ave.
High Prairie, AB T0G 1E0
Tel: 780-523-3388; *Fax:* 780-523-5930
reception@highprairie.ca
www.highprairie.ca
Municipal Type: Town
Incorporated: April 6, 1945; *Area:* 6.39 sq km
County or District: Municipal District of Big Lakes; *Population in 2011:* 2,600
Provincial Electoral District(s): Lesser Slave Lake
Federal Electoral District(s): Peace River-Westlock
Next Election: Oct. 16, 2017 (4 year terms)
Note: Incorporated as a town on Jan. 10, 1950.
Linda Cox, Mayor, 780-536-6363
Keli Tamaklo, Chief Administrative Officer, 780-523-1844

Hill Spring
P.O. Box 40
Hill Spring, AB T0K 1E0
Tel: 403-626-3876; *Fax:* 403-626-2333
office@hillspring.ca
www.hillspring.ca
Municipal Type: Village
Incorporated: Jan. 1, 1961; *Area:* 1.11 sq km
County or District: Cardston County; *Population in 2011:* 186
Provincial Electoral District(s): Cardston-Taber-Warner
Federal Electoral District(s): Foothills
Next Election: Oct. 16, 2017 (4 year terms)
Monte Christensen, Mayor
Kurtis Pratt, Chief Administrative Officer

Hines Creek
P.O. Box 421
212 - 10th St.
Hines Creek, AB T0H 2A0
Tel: 780-494-3690; *Fax:* 780-494-3605
www.hinescreek.com
Other Information: Alt. Phone: 780-494-3760
Municipal Type: Village
Incorporated: Dec. 31, 1951; *Area:* 4.37 sq km
County or District: Clear Hills County; *Population in 2011:* 380
Provincial Electoral District(s): Dunvegan-Central Peace-Notley
Federal Electoral District(s): Grande Prairie-Mackenzie
Next Election: Oct. 16, 2017 (4 year terms)
Hazel Reintjes, Mayor
Leila Sumner, Chief Adminsitrative Officer, 780-434-3690

Hinton
131 Civic Centre Rd., 2nd Fl.
Hinton, AB T7V 2E5
Tel: 780-865-6000; *Fax:* 780-865-5706
www.hinton.ca
Municipal Type: Town
Incorporated: Nov. 1, 1956; *Area:* 25.76 sq km
County or District: Yellowhead County; *Population in 2011:* 9,640
Provincial Electoral District(s): West Yellowhead
Federal Electoral District(s): Yellowhead
Next Election: Oct. 16, 2017 (4 year terms)
Rob Mackin, Mayor
Bernie Kreiner, Town Manager, 780-865-6072

Holden
P.O. Box 357
Holden, AB T0B 2C0
Tel: 780-688-3928; *Fax:* 780-688-2091
vholden@telusplanet.net
www.village.holden.ab.ca
Municipal Type: Village
Incorporated: April 14, 1909; *Area:* 1.7 sq km
County or District: Beaver County; *Population in 2011:* 381
Provincial Electoral District(s): Battle River-Wainwright
Federal Electoral District(s): Battle River-Crowfoot
Next Election: Oct. 16, 2017 (4 year terms)
Don Thompson, Mayor
Katherine Whiteside, Chief Administrative Officer

Horseshoe Bay
P.O. Box 1778
St Paul, AB T0A 3A0
Tel: 780-645-4677; *Fax:* 780-645-4677
svhorseshoebay@gmail.com
www.svhorseshoebay.com
Municipal Type: Summer Village
Incorporated: Jan. 1, 1985; *Area:* 1.04 sq km
County or District: St. Paul County No. 19; *Population in 2011:* 37
Provincial Electoral District(s): Lac La Biche-St. Paul-Two Hills
Federal Electoral District(s): Lakeland
Next Election: Summer 2017 (4 year terms)
Gary Burns, Mayor, 780-645-4609
Norman Briscoe, Chief Administrative Officer

Hughenden
P.O. Box 26
33 McKenzie Ave.
Hughenden, AB T0B 2E0
Tel: 780-856-3830; *Fax:* 780-856-2034
hughenden@xplornet.com
www.hughendenab.ca
Municipal Type: Village
Incorporated: Dec. 27, 1917; *Area:* 0.78 sq km
County or District: Municipal District of Provost No. 52; *Population in 2011:* 230
Provincial Electoral District(s): Battle River-Wainwright
Federal Electoral District(s): Battle River-Crowfoot
Next Election: Oct. 16, 2017 (4 year terms)
Lee Van Koughnett, Mayor
Lawrence Komaranky, Chief Administrative Officer

Hussar
P.O. Box 100
109 - 1 Ave.
Hussar, AB T0J 1S0
Tel: 403-787-3766; *Fax:* 888-800-4937
office@villageofhussar.ca
www.villageofhussar.ca
Municipal Type: Village
Incorporated: April 20, 1928; *Area:* 1.05 sq km
County or District: Wheatland County; *Population in 2011:* 176
Provincial Electoral District(s): Strathmore-Brooks
Federal Electoral District(s): Bow River
Next Election: Oct. 16, 2017 (4 year terms)
Tim Frank, Mayor
Jennifer Pratt, Chief Administrative Officer, 403-361-1934

Hythe
P.O. Box 219
10011 - 100 St.
Hythe, AB T0H 2C0
Tel: 780-356-3888; *Fax:* 780-356-2009
admin@hythe.ca
www.hythe.ca
Municipal Type: Village
Incorporated: Aug. 31, 1929; *Area:* 4.12 sq km
County or District: Grande Prairie County No. 1; *Population in 2011:* 820
Provincial Electoral District(s): Grande Prairie-Wapiti
Federal Electoral District(s): Grande Prairie-Mackenzie
Next Election: Oct. 16, 2017 (4 year terms)
Gary Burgess, Mayor
Greg Gayton, Administrator

Innisfail
4943 - 53 St.
Innisfail, AB T4G 1A1
Tel: 403-227-3376; *Fax:* 403-227-4045
www.innisfail.ca
Municipal Type: Town
Incorporated: Dec. 15, 1899; *Area:* 13.02 sq km
County or District: Red Deer County; *Population in 2011:* 7,876
Provincial Electoral District(s): Innisfail-Sylvan Lake
Federal Electoral District(s): Red Deer-Mountain View
Next Election: Oct. 16, 2017 (4 year terms)
Note: Incorporated as a town on Nov. 20, 1903.
Brian Spiller, Mayor
Helen Dietz, Town Manager

Innisfree
P.O. Box 69
5116 - 50 Ave.
Innisfree, AB T0B 2G0
Tel: 780-592-3886; *Fax:* 780-592-3729
innisfree@telus.net
www.villageofinnisfree.ca
Municipal Type: Village
Incorporated: March 11, 1911; *Area:* 1.27 sq km
County or District: Minburn County No. 27; *Population in 2011:* 220

Provincial Electoral District(s): Vermilion-Lloydminster
Federal Electoral District(s): Lakeland
Next Election: Oct. 16, 2017 (4 year terms)
Deborah McMann, Mayor
Jennifer Hodel, Chief Administrative Officer

Irma
P.O. Box 419
4919 - 50 St.
Irma, AB T0B 2H0
Tel: 780-754-3665; *Fax:* 780-754-3668
info@irma.ca
www.irma.ca
Municipal Type: Village
Incorporated: May 30, 1912; *Area:* 1.11 sq km
County or District: Municipal District of Wainwright No. 61;
Population in 2011: 457
Provincial Electoral District(s): Battle River-Wainwright
Federal Electoral District(s): Battle River-Crowfoot
Next Election: Oct. 16, 2017 (4 year terms)
Douglas Coubrough, Mayor
Neil Loonen, Chief Administrative Officer

Irricana
P.O. Box 100
222 - 2nd St.
Irricana, AB T0M 1B0
Tel: 403-935-4672; *Fax:* 403-935-4270
irricana@irricana.com
www.irricana.com
Municipal Type: Town
Incorporated: June 9, 1911; *Area:* 3.18 sq km
County or District: Rocky View County; *Population in 2011:* 1,162
Provincial Electoral District(s): Olds-Didsbury-Three Hills
Federal Electoral District(s): Bow River
Next Election: Oct. 16, 2017 (4 year terms)
Note: Incorporated as a town on June 9, 2005.
Valerie Squires, Mayor
Dawn Mosondz, Chief Administrative Officer

Island Lake
11318 - 10 Ave. NW
Edmonton, AB T6J 6S9
Tel: 780-431-9712; *Fax:* 780-431-0882
svoffice@telusplanet.net
www.islandlake.ca
Municipal Type: Summer Village
Incorporated: Jan. 1, 1958; *Area:* 1.45 sq km
County or District: Athabasca County; *Population in 2011:* 243
Provincial Electoral District(s): Athabasca-Sturgeon-Redwater
Federal Electoral District(s): Lakeland
Next Election: Summer 2017 (4 year terms)
Bob Yontz, Mayor
Anita Blais, Chief Administrative Officer

Island Lake South
10511 - 109 St.
Westlock, AB T7P 1A9
Tel: 780-349-3651; *Fax:* 780-349-5194
www.myislandlakesouth.com
Municipal Type: Summer Village
Incorporated: Jan. 1, 1983; *Area:* 0.63 sq km
County or District: Athabasca County; *Population in 2011:* 72
Provincial Electoral District(s): Athabasca-Sturgeon-Redwater
Federal Electoral District(s): Lakeland
Next Election: Summer 2017 (4 year terms)
Gary Tym, Mayor
Garth Bancroft, Chief Administrative Officer

Itaska Beach
10 Norwood Cl.
Wetaskiwin, AB T9A 0C8
Tel: 780-312-0928; *Fax:* 780-401-3161
cao@itaska.ca
www.itaska.ca
Municipal Type: Summer Village
Incorporated: June 30, 1953; *Area:* 0.28 sq km
County or District: Leduc County; *Population in 2011:* 20
Provincial Electoral District(s): Drayton Valley-Devon
Federal Electoral District(s): Edmonton-Wetaskiwin
Next Election: Summer 2017 (4 year terms)
Ralph Johnston, Mayor
June Boyda, Chief Administrative Officer

Jarvis Bay
Bay 8, Thevenaz Industrial Trial
Sylvan Lake, AB T4S 1W2
Tel: 403-887-2822; *Fax:* 403-887-2897
info@sylvansummervillages.ca
www.sylvansummervillages.ca/location/jarvis-bay
Municipal Type: Summer Village
Incorporated: Jan. 1, 1986; *Area:* 0.55 sq km
County or District: Red Deer County; *Population in 2011:* 203
Provincial Electoral District(s): Innisfail-Sylvan Lake
Federal Electoral District(s): Red Deer-Lacombe
Next Election: Summer 2017 (4 year terms)
Bob Thomlinson, Mayor
Phyllis Forsyth, Village Administrator

Kapasiwin
P.O. Box 9
Kapasiwin, AB T0E 2Y0
Tel: 780-892-2684;
gckapa@cruzinternet.com
www.kapasiwinalberta.com
Municipal Type: Summer Village
Incorporated: Oct. 25, 1913; *Area:* 0.31 sq km
County or District: Parkland County; *Population in 2011:* 10
Provincial Electoral District(s): Stony Plain
Federal Electoral District(s): Yellowhead
Next Election: Summer 2017 (4 year terms)
Note: Incorporated as a summer village on Sept. 01, 1993.
Kathy Boschma, Mayor
George Jones, Chief Administrative Officer

Killam
P.O. Box 189
4923 - 50 St.
Killam, AB T0B 2L0
Tel: 780-385-3977; *Fax:* 780-385-2120
tkillam@telusplanet.net
www.town.killam.ab.ca
Municipal Type: Town
Incorporated: Dec. 29, 1906; *Area:* 4.53 sq km
County or District: Flagstaff County; *Population in 2011:* 981
Provincial Electoral District(s): Battle River-Wainwright
Federal Electoral District(s): Battle River-Crowfoot
Next Election: Oct. 16, 2017 (4 year terms)
Note: Incorporated as a town on May 1, 1965.
H.L. (Bud) James, Mayor, 780-385-0027
Kimberly Borgel, Chief Administrative Officer

Kitscoty
P.O. Box 128
Kitscoty, AB T0B 2P0
Tel: 780-846-2221; *Fax:* 780-846-2213
info@vokitscoty.ca
www.vokitscoty.ca
Municipal Type: Village
Incorporated: March 22, 1911; *Area:* 1.54 sq km
County or District: Vermilion River County; *Population in 2011:* 846
Provincial Electoral District(s): Vermilion-Lloydminster
Federal Electoral District(s): Lakeland
Next Election: Oct. 16, 2017 (4 year terms)
Daryl Frank, Mayor
Sharon Williams, Chief Administrative Officer

Lakeview
P.O. Box 190
Seba Beach, AB T0E 2B0
Tel: 780-797-3863; *Fax:* 780-797-3800
svseba@telusplanet.net
Municipal Type: Summer Village
Incorporated: Oct. 25, 1913; *Area:* 0.33 sq km
County or District: Parkland County; *Population in 2011:* 26
Provincial Electoral District(s): Stony Plain
Federal Electoral District(s): Yellowhead
Next Election: Oct. 16, 2017 (4 year terms)
Earle Robertson, Mayor
Susan H. Evans, Chief Administrative Officer

Lamont
P.O. Box 330
5307 - 50 Ave.
Lamont, AB T0B 2R0
Tel: 780-895-2010; *Fax:* 780-895-2595
www.lamont.ca
Municipal Type: Town
Incorporated: June 14, 1910; *Area:* 4.59 sq km
County or District: Lamont County; *Population in 2011:* 1,753
Provincial Electoral District(s): Fort Saskatchewan-Vegreville
Federal Electoral District(s): Lakeland
Next Election: Oct. 16, 2017 (4 year terms)
Note: Incorporated as a town on May 31, 1968.
Bill Skinner, Mayor, 780-895-2967
Sandi Maschmeyer, Chief Administrative Officer

Larkspur
10511 - 109 St.
Westlock, AB T2P 1A9
Tel: 780-349-3651; *Fax:* 780-349-5194
www.myislandlakesouth.com
Municipal Type: Summer Village
Incorporated: Jan. 1, 1985; *Area:* 0.22 sq km
County or District: Westlock County; *Population in 2011:* 38
Provincial Electoral District(s): Barrhead-Morinville-Westlock
Federal Electoral District(s): Peace River-Westlock
Next Election: Summer 2017 (4 year terms)
Frank Atkinson, Mayor
Marion Bankroft, Chief Administrative Officer

Legal
P.O. Box 390
5021 - 50 St.
Legal, AB T0G 1L0
Tel: 780-961-3773; *Fax:* 780-961-4133
main@town.legal.ab.ca
www.town.legal.ab.ca
Municipal Type: Town
Incorporated: Feb. 20, 1914; *Area:* 2.55 sq km
County or District: Sturgeon County; *Population in 2011:* 1,225
Provincial Electoral District(s): Barrhead-Morinville-Westlock
Federal Electoral District(s): Sturgeon River-Parkland
Next Election: Oct. 16, 2017 (4 year terms)
Note: Incorporated as a town on Jan. 1, 1998.
Ken Baril, Mayor
Robert Proulx, Chief Administrative Officer

Linden
P.O. Box 213
109 Central Ave. East
Linden, AB T0M 1J0
Tel: 403-546-3888; *Fax:* 403-546-2112
www.linden.ca
Municipal Type: Village
Incorporated: Jan. 1, 1964; *Area:* 2.56 sq km
County or District: Kneehill County; *Population in 2011:* 725
Provincial Electoral District(s): Olds-Didsbury-Three Hills
Federal Electoral District(s): Bow River
Next Election: Oct. 16, 2017 (4 year terms)
Vanessa Van Der Meer, Mayor
Joanne Weller, Chief Administrative Officer

Lomond
P.O. Box 268
Lomond, AB T0L 1G0
Tel: 403-792-3611; *Fax:* 403-792-3300
Municipal Type: Village
Incorporated: Feb. 16, 1916; *Area:* 1.28 sq km
County or District: Vulcan County; *Population in 2011:* 173
Provincial Electoral District(s): Little Bow
Federal Electoral District(s): Bow River
Next Election: Oct. 16, 2017 (4 year terms)
Brad Koch, Mayor
Tracy Doram, Chief Administrative Officer

Longview
P.O. Box 147
128 Morrison Rd.
Longview, AB T0L 1H0
Tel: 403-558-3922; *Fax:* 403-558-3743
info@village.longview.ab.ca
www.village.longview.ab.ca
Municipal Type: Village
Incorporated: Jan. 1, 1964; *Area:* 1.09 sq km
County or District: Municipal District of Foothills No. 31;
Population in 2011: 307
Provincial Electoral District(s): Livingstone-Macleod
Federal Electoral District(s): Foothills
Next Election: Oct. 16, 2017 (4 year terms)
Cliff Ayrey, Mayor
Geraldine Gervais, Chief Administrative Officer

Lougheed
P.O. Box 5
5004 - 50 St.
Lougheed, AB T0B 2V0
Tel: 780-386-3970; *Fax:* 780-386-2136
villageoflougheed@xplorenet.com
www.villageoflougheed.com
Municipal Type: Village
Incorporated: Nov. 7, 1911; *Area:* 1.13 sq km
County or District: Flagstaff County; *Population in 2011:* 233
Provincial Electoral District(s): Battle River-Wainwright
Federal Electoral District(s): Battle River-Crowfoot
Next Election: Oct. 16, 2017 (4 year terms)
Joseph Cameron, Mayor
Kevin Miller, Chief Adminsitrative Officer

Magrath
P.O. Box 520
55 South 1 St. West
Magrath, AB T0K 1J0
Tel: 403-758-3212; *Fax:* 403-758-6333
info@magrath.ca
www.magrath.ca
Municipal Type: Town
Incorporated: Aug. 20, 1901; *Area:* 4.97 sq km
County or District: Cardston County; *Population in 2011:* 2,217
Provincial Electoral District(s): Cardston-Taber-Warner
Federal Electoral District(s): Medicine Hat-Cardston-Warner
Next Election: Oct. 16, 2017 (4 year terms)
Note: Incorporated as a town on July 24, 1907.
Russ Barnett, Mayor
Wade Alston, Chief Administrative Officer

Ma-Me-O Beach
P.O. Box 100
605 - 2 Ave.
Ma-Me-O Beach, AB T0C 1X0
Tel: 780-586-2494; *Fax:* 780-586-3567
information@svofficepl.com
www.mameobeach.ca
Municipal Type: Summer Village
Incorporated: Dec. 31, 1948; *Area:* 0.65 sq km
County or District: Wetaskiwin County No. 10; *Population in 2011:* 113
Provincial Electoral District(s): Drayton Valley-Devon
Federal Electoral District(s): Edmonton-Wetaskiwin
Next Election: Summer 2017 (4 year terms)
Don Fleming, Mayor
Sylvia Roy, Administrator
Sunni-Jeanne Walker, Mayor
Gerald Loewen, Chief Administrative Officer

Manning
P.O. Box 125
413 Main St.
Manning, AB T0H 2M0
Tel: 780-836-3606; *Fax:* 780-836-3570
www.manning.govoffice.com
Municipal Type: Town
Incorporated: Dec. 31, 1951; *Area:* 3.42 sq km
County or District: Northern Lights County; *Population in 2011:* 1,164
Provincial Electoral District(s): Peace River
Federal Electoral District(s): Grande Prairie-Mackenzie
Next Election: Oct. 16, 2017 (4 year terms)
Note: Incorporated as a town on Jan. 1, 1957.

Mannville
P.O. Box 180
5127 - 50th St.
Mannville, AB T0B 2W0
Tel: 780-763-3500; *Fax:* 780-763-3643
info@mannville.com
www.mannville.com
Municipal Type: Village
Incorporated: Dec. 29, 1906; *Area:* 2.15 sq km
County or District: Minburn County No. 27; *Population in 2011:* 803
Provincial Electoral District(s): Vermilion-Lloydminster
Federal Electoral District(s): Lakeland
Next Election: Oct. 16, 2017 (4 year terms)
Sid Hinton, Mayor
Thelma Rogers, Chief Administrative Officer

Marwayne
P.O. Box 113
210 - 2 Ave. South
Marwayne, AB T0B 2X0
Tel: 780-847-3962; *Fax:* 780-847-3324
marwayne@mcsnet.ca
www.marwayne.ca
Municipal Type: Village
Incorporated: Dec. 31, 1952; *Area:* 1.15 sq km
County or District: Vermilion River County; *Population in 2011:* 612
Provincial Electoral District(s): Vermilion-Lloydminster
Federal Electoral District(s): Lakeland
Next Election: Oct. 16, 2017 (4 year terms)
Jenelle Saskiw, Mayor
Joanne Horton, Chief Administrative Officer

Mayerthorpe
P.O. Box 420
4911 Denny Hay Dr.
Mayerthorpe, AB T0E 1N0
Tel: 780-786-2416; *Fax:* 780-786-4590
www.mayerthorpe.ca
Municipal Type: Town
Incorporated: March 5, 1927; *Area:* 4.78 sq km
County or District: Lac Ste. Anne County; *Population in 2011:* 1,398
Provincial Electoral District(s): Whitecourt-Ste. Anne
Federal Electoral District(s): Yellowhead
Next Election: Oct. 16, 2017 (4 year terms)
Note: Incorporated as a town on March 20, 1961.
Kate Patrick, Mayor
Karen St. Martin, Chief Administrative Officer

McLennan
P.O. Box 356
19 - 1st Ave. NW
McLennan, AB T0H 2L0
Tel: 780-324-3065; *Fax:* 780-324-2288
admin@mclennan.ca
mclennan.ca
Municipal Type: Town
Incorporated: Feb. 1, 1944; *Area:* 3.58 sq km
County or District: Municipal District of Smoky River No. 130; *Population in 2011:* 809
Provincial Electoral District(s): Dunvegan-Central Peace-Notley
Federal Electoral District(s): Peace River-Westlock
Next Election: Oct. 16, 2017 (4 year terms)
Note: Incorporated as a town on Feb. 11, 1948.
Donald Regier, Mayor
Lorraine Willier, Chief Administrative Officer

Mewatha Beach
10511 - 109 St.
Westlock, AB T7P 1A9
Tel: 780-349-3651; *Fax:* 780-349-5194
www.mymewathabeach.com
Municipal Type: Summer Village
Incorporated: Jan. 1, 1978; *Area:* 0.78 sq km
County or District: Athabasca County; *Population in 2011:* 79
Provincial Electoral District(s): Athabasca-Sturgeon-Redwater
Federal Electoral District(s): Lakeland
Next Election: Summer 2017 (4 year terms)
Barry J. Walker, Mayor
Garth Bancroft, Chief Administrative Officer

Milk River
P.O. Box 270
240 Main St.
Milk River, AB T0K 1M0
Tel: 403-647-3773; *Fax:* 403-647-3772
main@milkriver.ca
www.milkriver.ca
Municipal Type: Town
Incorporated: July 11, 1916; *Area:* 2.39 sq km
County or District: Warner County No. 5; *Population in 2011:* 811
Provincial Electoral District(s): Cardston-Taber-Warner
Federal Electoral District(s): Medicine Hat-Cardston-Warner
Next Election: Oct. 16, 2017 (4 year terms)
Note: Incorporated as a town on Feb. 7, 1956.
David Hawco, Mayor
Mario Berthiaume, Chief Administrative Officer

Millet
P.O. Box 270
5120 - 50 St.
Millet, AB T0C 1Z0
Tel: 780-387-4554; *Fax:* 780-387-4459
millet@millet.ca
www.millet.ca
Municipal Type: Town
Incorporated: June 17, 1903; *Area:* 3.74 sq km
County or District: Wetaskiwin County No. 10; *Population in 2011:* 2,092
Provincial Electoral District(s): Wetaskiwin-Camrose
Federal Electoral District(s): Edmonton-Wetaskiwin
Next Election: Oct. 16, 2017 (4 year terms)
Note: Incorporated as a town on Sept. 1, 1983.
Robert E. Lorenson, Mayor
Teri Pelletier, Chief Administrative Officer

Milo
P.O. Box 65
Milo, AB T0L 1L0
Tel: 403-599-3883; *Fax:* 403-599-2201
vilmilo@wildroseinternet.ca
villageofmilo.ca
Municipal Type: Village
Incorporated: May 7, 1931; *Area:* 0.48 sq km
County or District: Vulcan County; *Population in 2011:* 122
Provincial Electoral District(s): Little Bow
Federal Electoral District(s): Bow River
Next Election: Oct. 16, 2017 (4 year terms)
Rafael Zea, Mayor
Christopher Northcott, Municipal Administrator

Minburn
c/o Minburn County No. 27
P.O. Box 550
4909 - 50 St.
Vegreville, AB T9C 1R6
Tel: 780-632-2082; *Fax:* 780-632-6296
info@minburncounty.ab.ca
www.minburncounty.ab.ca
Municipal Type: Hamlet
Incorporated: June 24, 1919; *Area:* 0.73 sq km
County or District: Minburn County No. 27; *Population in 2011:* 105
Provincial Electoral District(s): Vermilion-Lloydminster
Federal Electoral District(s): Lakeland
Next Election: Oct. 16, 2017 (4 year terms)
Note: Minburn was dissolved from village status to become a hamlet on July 1, 2015.
Roger Konieczny, Reeve, Minburn County No. 27
David Marynowich, County Manager

Morinville
10125 - 100 Ave.
Morinville, AB T8R 1L6
Tel: 780-939-4361; *Fax:* 780-939-5633
www.morinville.ca
Other Information: Alt. Fax: 780-939-7448
Municipal Type: Town
Incorporated: Aug. 24, 1901; *Area:* 11.34 sq km
County or District: Sturgeon County; *Population in 2011:* 8,569
Provincial Electoral District(s): Barrhead-Morinville-Westlock
Federal Electoral District(s): Sturgeon River-Parkland
Next Election: Oct. 16, 2017 (4 year terms)
Note: Incorporated as a town on April 21, 1911.
Lisa Holmes, Mayor
Debbie Oyarzun, Chief Administrative Officer, 780-939-4361, Fax: 780-939-5633

Morrin
P.O. Box 149
Morrin, AB T0J 2B0
Tel: 403-772-3870; *Fax:* 403-772-2123
morrin@netago.ca
Municipal Type: Village
Incorporated: April 16, 1920; *Area:* 0.82 sq km
County or District: Starland County; *Population in 2011:* 245
Provincial Electoral District(s): Drumheller-Stettler
Federal Electoral District(s): Battle River-Crowfoot
Next Election: Oct. 16, 2017 (4 year terms)
Suzanne Lacher, Mayor
Annette Plachner, Chief Administrative Officer

Mundare
P.O. Box 348
5128 - 50 St.
Mundare, AB T0B 3H0
Tel: 780-764-3929; *Fax:* 780-764-2003
www.mundare.ca
Municipal Type: Town
Incorporated: March 6, 1907; *Area:* 3 sq km
County or District: Lamont County; *Population in 2011:* 855
Provincial Electoral District(s): Fort Saskatchewan-Vegreville
Federal Electoral District(s): Lakeland
Next Election: Oct. 16, 2017 (4 year terms)
Note: Incorporated as a town on Jan. 4, 1951.
Charlie Gargus, Mayor
Colin Zyla, Chief Administrative Officer

Munson
P.O. Box 10
Munson, AB T0J 2C0
Tel: 403-823-6987; *Fax:* 403-823-9883
munson@netago.ca
Municipal Type: Village
Incorporated: May 5, 1911; *Area:* 2.6 sq km
County or District: Starland County; *Population in 2011:* 204
Provincial Electoral District(s): Drumheller-Stettler
Federal Electoral District(s): Battle River-Crowfoot
Next Election: Oct. 16, 2017 (4 year terms)
Kerry McLellan, Mayor
Lyle Cawiezel, Administrator

Myrnam
P.O. Box 278
5007 - 50 St.
Myrnam, AB T0B 3K0
Tel: 780-366-3910; *Fax:* 780-366-2246
admin@myrnam.ca
myrnam.ca
Municipal Type: Village
Incorporated: Aug. 22, 1930; *Area:* 2.76 sq km
County or District: Two Hills County No. 21; *Population in 2011:* 370

Provincial Electoral District(s): Lac La Biche-St. Paul-Two Hills
Federal Electoral District(s): Lakeland
Next Election: Oct. 16, 2017 (4 year terms)
Edward Sosnowski, Mayor, 780-366-3920
Gary Dupuis, Chief Administrative Officer

Nakamun Park
13 Grandin Rd.
St Albert, AB T8N 3B2
Tel: 780-460-7226; *Fax:* 780-419-2476
www.svnakamun.com
Municipal Type: Summer Village
Incorporated: Jan. 1, 1966; *Area:* 0.41 sq km
County or District: Lac Ste. Anne County; *Population in 2011:* 36
Provincial Electoral District(s): Whitecourt-Ste. Anne
Federal Electoral District(s): Sutrgeon River-Parkland
Next Election: Summer 2017 (4 year terms)
Harry Kassian, Mayor
Hilda Marsh, Chief Administrative Officer

Nampa
P.O. Box 69
Nampa, AB T0H 2R0
Tel: 780-322-3852; *Fax:* 780-322-2100
www.nampa.ca
Municipal Type: Village
Incorporated: Jan. 1, 1958; *Area:* 1.86 sq km
County or District: Northern Sunrise County; *Population in 2011:* 362
Provincial Electoral District(s): Peace River
Federal Electoral District(s): Peace River-Westlock
Next Election: Oct. 16, 2017 (4 year terms)
Perry Skrlik, Mayor
Dianne Roshuk, Chief Administrative Officer

Nanton
P.O. Box 609
1907 - 21 Ave.
Nanton, AB T0L 1R0
Tel: 403-646-2029; *Fax:* 403-646-2653
www.nanton.ca
Municipal Type: Town
Incorporated: June 22, 1903; *Area:* 4.25 sq km
County or District: Municipal District of Willow Creek No. 26; *Population in 2011:* 2,132
Provincial Electoral District(s): Livingstone-Macleod
Federal Electoral District(s): Foothills
Next Election: Oct. 16, 2017 (4 year terms)
Note: Incorporated as a town on Aug. 9, 1907.
Rick Everett, Mayor
Kevin Miller, Chief Administrative Officer

Nobleford
P.O. Box 67
906 Highway Ave.
Nobleford, AB T0L 1S0
Tel: 403-824-3555; *Fax:* 403-824-3553
admin@village.nobleford.ab.ca
nobleford.ca
Municipal Type: Village
Incorporated: Feb. 28, 1918; *Area:* 1.17 sq km
County or District: Lethbridge County; *Population in 2011:* 1,000
Provincial Electoral District(s): Little Bow
Federal Electoral District(s): Lethbridge
Next Election: Oct. 16, 2017 (4 year terms)
Don McDowell, Mayor, 403-824-3193
Kirk Hofman, Chief Administrative Officer

Norglenwold
Bay 8, 14 Thevenaz Industrial Trail
Sylvan Lake, AB T4S 2J5
Tel: 403-887-2822; *Fax:* 403-887-2897
info@sylvansummervillages.ca
www.sylvansummervillages.ca/location/norglenwold
Municipal Type: Summer Village
Incorporated: Jan. 1, 1965; *Area:* 0.67 sq km
County or District: Red Deer County; *Population in 2011:* 232
Provincial Electoral District(s): Innisfail-Sylvan Lake
Federal Electoral District(s): Red Deer-Lacombe
Next Election: Summer 2017 (4 year terms)
Carol McMillan, Mayor, 403-887-5792
Phyllis Forsyth, Chief Administrative Officer

Norris Beach
P.O. Box 100
Ma-Me-O Beach, AB T0C 1X0
Tel: 780-586-2494; *Fax:* 780-586-3567
information@svofficepl.com
www.svofficepl.com
Municipal Type: Summer Village
Incorporated: Dec. 31, 1988; *Area:* 0.16 sq km
County or District: Wetaskiwin County No. 10; *Population in 2011:* 46
Provincial Electoral District(s): Drayton Valley-Devon
Federal Electoral District(s): Edmonton-Wetaskiwin
Next Election: Summer 2017 (4 year terms)
Brian Keeler, Mayor
Sylvia Roy, Chief Administrative Officer

Olds
4512 - 46 St.
Olds, AB T4H 1R5
Tel: 403-556-6981; *Fax:* 403-556-6537
admin@olds.ca
www.olds.ca
Municipal Type: Town
Incorporated: May 26, 1896; *Area:* 11.05 sq km
County or District: Mountain View County; *Population in 2011:* 8,235
Provincial Electoral District(s): Olds-Didsbury-Three Hills
Federal Electoral District(s): Red Deer-Mountain View
Next Election: Oct. 16, 2017 (4 year terms)
Note: Incorporated as a town on July 01, 1905.
Judy Dahl, Mayor, 403-507-4114
Norman McInnis, Chief Administrative Officer

Onoway
P.O. Box 540
4812 - 51 St.
Onoway, AB T0E 1V0
Tel: 780-967-5338; *Fax:* 780-967-3226
info@onoway.com
www.onoway.com
Municipal Type: Town
Incorporated: June 25, 1923; *Area:* 3.34 sq km
County or District: Lac Ste. Anne County; *Population in 2011:* 1,039
Provincial Electoral District(s): Whitecourt-Ste. Anne
Federal Electoral District(s): Sturgeon River-Parkland
Next Election: Oct. 16, 2017 (4 year terms)
Note: Incorporated as a town on Sept. 1, 2005.
Donald Harrison, Mayor, 780-967-0125
Wendy Wildman, Chief Administratrive Officer

Oyen
P.O. Box 360
201 Main St.
Oyen, AB T0J 2J0
Tel: 403-664-3511; *Fax:* 403-664-3712
cao@townofoyen.com
www.townofoyen.com
Municipal Type: Town
Incorporated: Jan. 17, 1913; *Area:* 4.93 sq km
Population in 2011: 973
Provincial Electoral District(s): Drumheller-Stettler
Federal Electoral District(s): Battle River-Crowfoot
Next Election: Oct. 16, 2017 (4 year terms)
Note: Incorporated as a town on Sept. 1, 1965.
Douglas A. Jones, Mayor, 403-664-0560
Charmain Snell, Chief Administrative Officer

Paradise Valley
P.O. Box 24
109 Main St.
Paradise Valley, AB T0B 3R0
Tel: 780-745-2287; *Fax:* 780-745-2287
villageofpv@mcsnet.ca
Municipal Type: Village
Incorporated: Jan. 1, 1964; *Area:* 0.57 sq km
County or District: Vermilion River County; *Population in 2011:* 174
Provincial Electoral District(s): Vermilion-Lloydminster
Federal Electoral District(s): Lakeland
Next Election: Oct. 16, 2017 (4 year terms)
Mark Kaese, Mayor
Connie Wilkinson, Municipal Administrator

Parkland Beach
P.O. Box 130
9 Parkland Beach Rd. NW
Rimbey, AB T0C 2J0
Tel: 403-843-2055; *Fax:* 888-470-2762
admin@parklandbeachsv.ca
www.parklandbeachsv.ca
Municipal Type: Summer Village
Incorporated: Jan. 1, 1984; *Area:* 0.93 sq km
County or District: Ponoka County; *Population in 2011:* 124
Provincial Electoral District(s): Rimbey-Rocky Mountain House-Sundre
Federal Electoral District(s): Red Deer-Lacombe
Next Election: Summer 2017 (4 year terms)
Keith B. Nesbitt, Mayor
Marilee Yakunin, Chief Administrative Officer

Peace River
P.O. Box 6600
9911 - 100 St.
Peace River, AB T8S 1S4
Tel: 780-624-2574; *Fax:* 780-624-4664
info@peaceriver.net
peaceriver.net
Municipal Type: Town
Incorporated: June 2, 1914; *Area:* 24.87 sq km
Population in 2011: 6,744
Provincial Electoral District(s): Peace River
Federal Electoral District(s): Peace River-Westlock
Next Election: Oct. 16, 2017 (4 year terms)
Note: Incorporated as a town on Dec. 1, 1919.
Tom Tarpey, Mayor, 780-624-8522
Kelly Bunn, Chief Administrative Officer

Pelican Narrows
P.O. Box 7878
Bonnyville, AB T9N 2J2
Tel: 780-826-5907; *Fax:* 780-826-2804
Municipal Type: Summer Village
Incorporated: July 1, 1979; *Area:* 0.7 sq km
County or District: Municipal District of Bonnyville No. 87; *Population in 2011:* 162
Provincial Electoral District(s): Bonnyville-Cold Lake
Federal Electoral District(s): Lakeland
Next Election: Summer 2017 (4 year terms)
Robert Hornseth, Mayor
Padey Lapointe, Administrator

Penhold
P.O. Box 10
1 Waskasoo Ave.
Penhold, AB T0M 1R0
Tel: 403-886-4567; *Fax:* 403-886-4039
community1@townofpenhold.ca
www.townofpenhold.ca
Municipal Type: Town
Incorporated: May 4, 1904; *Area:* 2.35 sq km
County or District: Red Deer County; *Population in 2011:* 2,375
Provincial Electoral District(s): Innisfail-Sylvan Lake
Federal Electoral District(s): Red Deer-Mountain View
Next Election: Oct. 16, 2017 (4 year terms)
Note: Incorporated as a town on Sept. 1, 1980.
Dennis Cooper, Mayor
Rick Binnendyk, Chief Administrative Officer

Picture Butte
P.O. Box 670
120 - 4 St. North
Picture Butte, AB T0K 1V0
Tel: 403-732-4555; *Fax:* 403-732-4334
info@picturebutte.ca
www.picturebutte.ca
Municipal Type: Town
Incorporated: Feb. 4, 1943; *Area:* 2.9 sq km
County or District: Lethbridge County; *Population in 2011:* 1,650
Provincial Electoral District(s): Little Bow
Federal Electoral District(s): Lethbridge
Next Election: Oct. 16, 2017 (4 year terms)
Note: Incorporated as a town on Jan. 1, 1960.
Wendy Jones, Mayor
Mike Derricott, Chief Administrative Officer

Pincher Creek
P.O. Box 159
962 St. John Ave.
Pincher Creek, AB T0K 1W0
Tel: 403-627-3156; *Fax:* 403-627-4784
reception@pinchercreek.ca
www.pinchercreek.ca
Municipal Type: Town
Incorporated: Aug. 18, 1898; *Area:* 8.84 sq km
County or District: Municipal District of Pincher Creek No. 9; *Population in 2011:* 3,685
Provincial Electoral District(s): Livingstone-Macleod
Federal Electoral District(s): Foothills
Next Election: Oct. 16, 2017 (4 year terms)
Note: Incorporated as a town on May 12, 1906.
Don Anderberg, Mayor
Laurie Wilgosh, Chief Administrative Officer

Point Alison
P.O. Box 221
Wabamun, AB T0E 2K0
Tel: 780-462-6372;
www.pointalison.com
Municipal Type: Summer Village
Incorporated: Dec. 31, 1950; *Area:* 0.16 sq km
County or District: Parkland County; *Population in 2011:* 15
Provincial Electoral District(s): Stony Plain

Federal Electoral District(s): Yellowhead
Next Election: Summer 2017 (4 year terms)
C. Gordon Wilson, Mayor, 780-892-2984
Tom Thompson, Administrator

Ponoka
5102 - 48 Ave.
Ponoka, AB T4J 1P7
Tel: 403-783-4431; *Fax:* 403-783-6745
www.ponoka.org
Municipal Type: Town
Incorporated: Oct. 19, 1900; *Area:* 13.05 sq km
County or District: Ponoka County; *Population in 2011:* 6,773
Provincial Electoral District(s): Lacombe-Ponoka
Federal Electoral District(s): Red Deer-Lacombe
Next Election: Oct. 16, 2017 (4 year terms)
Note: Incorporated as a town on Oct. 15, 1904.
Rick Bonnett, Mayor
Albert Flootman, Chief Administrative Officer, 403-783-0129, Fax: 403-783-4086

Poplar Bay
P.O. Box 100
605 - 2 Ave.
Ma-Me-O Beach, AB T0C 1X0
Tel: 780-586-2494; *Fax:* 780-586-3567
information@svofficepl.com
www.poplarbay.ca
Municipal Type: Summer Village
Incorporated: Jan. 1, 1967; *Area:* 0.76 sq km
County or District: Wetaskiwin County No. 10; *Population in 2011:* 80
Provincial Electoral District(s): Drayton Valley-Devon
Federal Electoral District(s): Edmonton-Wetaskiwin
Next Election: Summer 2017 (4 year terms)
Debra McDaniel, Mayor
Sylvia Roy, Chief Administrative Officer

Provost
P.O. Box 449
4904 - 51 Ave.
Provost, AB T0B 3S0
Tel: 780-753-2261; *Fax:* 780-753-6889
info@townofprovost.ca
www.provost.ca
Municipal Type: Town
Incorporated: Jan. 20, 1910; *Area:* 4.93 sq km
County or District: Municipal District of Provost No. 52; *Population in 2011:* 2,041
Provincial Electoral District(s): Battle River-Wainwright
Federal Electoral District(s): Battle River-Crowfoot
Next Election: Oct. 16, 2017 (4 year terms)
Note: Incorporated as a town on Dec. 29, 1952.
Kenneth E. (Ken) Knox, Mayor
Judy Larson, Administrator

Rainbow Lake
P.O. Box 149
Rainbow Lake, AB T0H 2Y0
Tel: 780-956-3934; *Fax:* 780-956-3570
admin@rainbowlake.ca
www.rainbowlake.ca
Municipal Type: Town
Incorporated: Sept. 1, 1966; *Area:* 11.04 sq km
County or District: Mackenzie County; *Population in 2011:* 870
Provincial Electoral District(s): Peace River
Federal Electoral District(s): Grande Prairie-Mackenzie
Next Election: Oct. 16, 2017 (4 year terms)
Boyd Langford, Mayor, 780-926-3373
Dan Fletcher, Chief Administrative Officer, 780-956-3934, Fax: 780-956-3570

Raymond
P.O. Box 629
15 Broadway St.
Raymond, AB T0K 2S0
Tel: 403-752-3322; *Fax:* 403-752-4379
contact@raymond.ca
www.raymond.ca
Municipal Type: Town
Incorporated: May 30, 1902; *Area:* 4.75 sq km
County or District: Warner County No. 5; *Population in 2011:* 3,743
Provincial Electoral District(s): Cardston-Taber-Warner
Federal Electoral District(s): Medicine Hat-Cardston-Warner
Next Election: Oct. 16, 2017 (4 year terms)
Note: Incorporated as a town on July 1, 1903.
George Bohne, Mayor
J. Scott Barton, Chief Administrative Officer

Redcliff
P.O. Box 40
1 - 3 St. NE
Redcliff, AB T0J 2P0
Tel: 403-548-3618; *Fax:* 403-548-6623
redcliff@redcliff.ca
www.redcliff.ca
Municipal Type: Town
Incorporated: Oct. 29, 1910; *Area:* 10.51 sq km
County or District: Cypress County; *Population in 2011:* 5,588
Provincial Electoral District(s): Cypress-Medicine Hat
Federal Electoral District(s): Medicine Hat-Cardston-Warner
Next Election: Oct. 16, 2017 (4 year terms)
Note: Incorporated as a town on Aug. 5, 1912.
Ernie Reimer, Mayor, 403-548-6455
Arlos Crofts, Municipal Manager

Redwater
P.O. Box 397
4924 - 47 St.
Redwater, AB T0A 2W0
Tel: 780-942-3519; *Fax:* 780-942-4321
redwater@redwater.ca
www.redwater.ca
Municipal Type: Town
Incorporated: Dec. 31, 1949; *Area:* 7.95 sq km
County or District: Sturgeon County; *Population in 2011:* 1,915
Provincial Electoral District(s): Athabasca-Sturgeon-Redwater
Federal Electoral District(s): Sturgeon River-Parkland
Next Election: Oct. 16, 2017 (4 year terms)
Note: Incorporated as a town on Dec. 31, 1950.
Mel Smith, Mayor, 780-942-3519
Debbie Hamilton, Town Manager, 780-942-3519

Rimbey
P.O. Box 350
4938 - 50th Ave.
Rimbey, AB T0C 2J0
Tel: 403-843-2113; *Fax:* 403-843-6599
generalinfo@rimbey.com
www.rimbey.com
Municipal Type: Town
Incorporated: June 13, 1919; *Area:* 11.34 sq km
County or District: Ponoka County; *Population in 2011:* 2,378
Provincial Electoral District(s): Rimbey-Rocky Mountain House-Sundre
Federal Electoral District(s): Red Deer-Lacombe
Next Election: Oct. 16, 2017 (4 year terms)
Note: Incorporated as a town on Dec. 13, 1948.
Rick Pankiw, Mayor
Lori Hills, Chief Administrative Officer, 403-843-2113

Rochon Sands
1 Hall St.
Rochon Sands, AB T0C 3B0
Tel: 403-742-4717; *Fax:* 403-742-4771
info@rochonsands.net
www.rochonsands.net
Municipal Type: Summer Village
Incorporated: May 17, 1929; *Area:* 2.32 sq km
County or District: Stettler County No. 6; *Population in 2011:* 84
Provincial Electoral District(s): Drumheller-Stettler
Federal Electoral District(s): Battle River-Crowfoot
Next Election: Summer 2017 (4 year terms)
Blaine Brinson, Mayor
Carrie Turgeon, Village Administrator

Rocky Mountain House
P.O. Box 1509
5116 - 50 Ave.
Rocky Mountain House, AB T4T 1B2
Tel: 403-845-2866; *Fax:* 403-845-3230
town@rockymtnhouse.com
www.rockymtnhouse.com
Municipal Type: Town
Incorporated: May 15, 1913; *Area:* 12.44 sq km
County or District: Clearwater County; *Population in 2011:* 6,933
Provincial Electoral District(s): Rimbey-Rocky Mountain House-Sundre
Federal Electoral District(s): Yellowhead
Next Election: Oct. 16, 2017 (4 year terms)
Note: Incorporated as a town on Aug. 31, 1939.
Fred Nash, Mayor, 403-845-2866
Todd Becker, Chief Administrative Officer

Rockyford
P.O. Box 294
Rockyford, AB T0J 2R0
Tel: 403-533-3950; *Fax:* 403-533-3744
billr_village@rockyford.ca
www.rockyford.ca
Municipal Type: Village
Incorporated: March 28, 1919; *Area:* 1.05 sq km
County or District: Wheatland County; *Population in 2011:* 325
Provincial Electoral District(s): Strathmore-Brooks
Federal Electoral District(s): Bow River
Next Election: Oct. 16, 2017 (4 year terms)
Darcy J. Burke, Mayor
Lois Mountjoy, Administrator

Rosalind
P.O. Box 181
Rosalind, AB T0B 3Y0
Tel: 780-375-3996; *Fax:* 780-375-3997
rosalindvillage@xplornet.com
www.villageofrosalind.ca
Municipal Type: Village
Incorporated: Jan. 1, 1966; *Area:* 0.59 sq km
County or District: Camrose County; *Population in 2011:* 190
Provincial Electoral District(s): Battle River-Wainwright
Federal Electoral District(s): Battle River-Crowfoot
Next Election: Oct. 16, 2017 (4 year terms)
James McTavish, Mayor
Nancy Friend, Chief Administrative Officer

Rosemary
P.O. Box 128
Rosemary, AB T0J 2W0
Tel: 403-378-4246; *Fax:* 403-378-3144
rosemary.admin@eidnet.org
www.rosemary.ca
Municipal Type: Village
Incorporated: Dec. 31, 1951; *Area:* 0.56 sq km
County or District: Newell County; *Population in 2011:* 342
Provincial Electoral District(s): Strathmore-Brooks
Federal Electoral District(s): Bow River
Next Election: Oct. 16, 2017 (4 year terms)
Don L. Gibb, Mayor
Margaret Loewen, Chief Administrative Officer

Ross Haven
P.O. Box 7
Site 19, RR#1
Gunn, AB T0E 1A0
Tel: 780-446-1426;
www.asva.ca/ross-haven
Municipal Type: Summer Village
Incorporated: Jan. 1, 1962; *Area:* 0.7 sq km
County or District: Lac Ste. Anne County; *Population in 2011:* 137
Provincial Electoral District(s): Whitecourt-Ste. Anne
Federal Electoral District(s): Yellowhead
Next Election: Summer 2017 (4 year terms)
Louis Belland, Mayor
Dennis Evans, Municipal Administrator

Rycroft
P.O. Box 360
Rycroft, AB T0H 3A0
Tel: 780-765-3652; *Fax:* 780-765-2002
rycroft@rycroft.ca
www.rycroft.ca
Municipal Type: Village
Incorporated: March 15, 1944; *Area:* 1.69 sq km
County or District: Municipal District of Spirit River No. 133; *Population in 2011:* 628
Provincial Electoral District(s): Dunvegan-Central Peace-Notley
Federal Electoral District(s): Grande Prairie-Mackenzie
Next Election: Oct. 16, 2017 (4 year terms)
Patricia Sydoruk, Mayor
Ben Boettcher, Chief Administrative Officer

Ryley
P.O. Box 230
5016 - 53 Ave.
Ryley, AB T0B 4A0
Tel: 780-663-3653; *Fax:* 780-663-3541
info@ryley.ca
www.ryley.ca
Municipal Type: Village
Incorporated: April 2, 1910; *Area:* 1.97 sq km
County or District: Beaver County; *Population in 2011:* 497
Provincial Electoral District(s): Battle River-Wainwright
Federal Electoral District(s): Battle River-Crowfoot
Next Election: Oct. 16, 2017 (4 year terms)
Brian Ducherer, Mayor
Janet Winsnes, Chief Administrative Officer

St. Paul
P.O. Box 1480
St. Paul, AB T0A 3A0
Tel: 780-645-4481; *Fax:* 780-645-5076
www.town.stpaul.ab.ca

Municipal Type: Town
Incorporated: June 14, 1912; *Area:* 6.86 sq km
County or District: St. Paul County No. 19; *Population in 2011:* 5,400
Provincial Electoral District(s): Lac La Biche-St. Paul-Two Hills
Federal Electoral District(s): Lakeland
Next Election: Oct. 16, 2017 (4 year terms)
Note: Incorporated as a town on Dec. 15, 1936.
Glenn Andersen, Mayor, 780-614-0260, Fax: 780-645-4988
Ronald O. Boisvert, Chief Administrative Officer

Sandy Beach
RR#1, Site 1, Comp 63
Onoway, AB T0E 1V0
Tel: 780-967-2873; *Fax:* 780-967-2813
summervillageofsandybeach.ca
Municipal Type: Summer Village
Incorporated: Jan. 1, 1956; *Area:* 2.43 sq km
County or District: Lac Ste. Anne County; *Population in 2011:* 223
Provincial Electoral District(s): Whitecourt-Ste. Anne
Federal Electoral District(s): Sturgeon River-Parkland
Next Election: Summer 2017 (4 year terms)
Denise Lambert, Mayor
Wendy Wildman, Chief Administrative Officer

Seba Beach
P.O. Box 190
Seba Beach, AB T0E 2B0
Tel: 780-797-3863; *Fax:* 780-797-3800
svseba@telusplanet.net
www.sebabeach.ca
Municipal Type: Summer Village
Incorporated: Aug. 2, 1920; *Area:* 0.66 sq km
County or District: Parkland County; *Population in 2011:* 143
Provincial Electoral District(s): Stony Plain
Federal Electoral District(s): Yellowhead
Next Election: Summer 2017 (4 year terms)
Doug Thomas, Mayor
Susan H. Evans, Chief Administrative Officer

Sedgewick
P.O. Box 129
Sedgewick, AB T0B 4C0
Tel: 780-384-3504; *Fax:* 780-384-3545
sedgewick@persona.ca
www.sedgewick.ca
Municipal Type: Town
Incorporated: March 6, 1907; *Area:* 2.6 sq km
County or District: Flagstaff County; *Population in 2011:* 857
Provincial Electoral District(s): Battle River-Wainwright
Federal Electoral District(s): Battle River-Crowfoot
Next Election: Oct. 16, 2017 (4 year terms)
Note: Incorporated as town on May 1, 1966.
Perry Robinson, Mayor
Amanda Davis, Chief Administrative Officer

Sexsmith
P.O. Box 420
9927 - 100 St.
Sexsmith, AB T0H 3C0
Tel: 780-568-3681; *Fax:* 780-568-2200
reception@sexsmith.ca
www.sexsmith.ca
Municipal Type: Town
Incorporated: April 12, 1929; *Area:* 3.43 sq km
County or District: Grande Prairie County No. 1; *Population in 2011:* 2,418
Provincial Electoral District(s): Grande Prairie-Smoky
Federal Electoral District(s): Grande Prairie-Mackenzie
Next Election: Oct. 16, 2017 (4 year terms)
Note: Incorporated as a town on Oct. 15, 1979.
Claude Lagace, Mayor, 780-568-3681
Carolyn Gaunt, Chief Administrative Officer

Silver Beach
P.O. Box 619
Thorsby, AB T0C 2P0
Tel: 780-985-2441; *Fax:* 780-401-3251
www.silverbeach.ca
Municipal Type: Summer Village
Incorporated: Dec. 31, 1953; *Area:* 0.66 sq km
County or District: Wetaskiwin County No. 10; *Population in 2011:* 52
Provincial Electoral District(s): Drayton Valley-Devon
Federal Electoral District(s): Edmonton-Wetaskiwin
Next Election: Summer 2017 (4 year terms)
Allan Watt, Mayor
Harold Wynne, Chief Administrative Officer

Silver Sands
P.O. Box 8
Alberta Beach, AB T0E 0A0
Tel: 587-873-5765; *Fax:* 780-924-3025
administration@wildwillowenterprises.com
www.summervillageofsilversands.com
Municipal Type: Summer Village
Incorporated: Jan. 1, 1969; *Area:* 2.35 sq km
County or District: Lac Ste. Anne County; *Population in 2011:* 85
Provincial Electoral District(s): Whitecourt-Ste. Anne
Federal Electoral District(s): Yellowhead
Next Election: Summer 2017 (4 year terms)
Bernie Poulin, Mayor
Wendy Wildman, Chief Administrative Officer

Slave Lake
P.O. Box 1030
10 Main St. SW
Slave Lake, AB T0G 2A0
Tel: 780-849-8000; *Fax:* 780-849-2633
town@slavelake.ca
www.slavelake.ca
Other Information: Toll Free: 1-800-661-2594
Municipal Type: Town
Incorporated: Jan. 1, 1961; *Area:* 14.18 sq km
County or District: Municipal District of Lesser Slave River No. 124; *Population in 2011:* 6,782
Provincial Electoral District(s): Lesser Slave Lake
Federal Electoral District(s): Peace River-Westlock
Next Election: Oct. 16, 2017 (4 year terms)
Note: Incorporated as a town on Aug. 2, 1965.
Tyler Warman, Mayor, 780-805-4045
Brian Vance, Chief Administrative Officer

Smoky Lake
P.O. Box 460
56 Wheatland Ave.
Smoky Lake, AB T0A 3C0
Tel: 780-656-3674; *Fax:* 780-656-3675
www.smokylake.ca
Municipal Type: Town
Incorporated: March 26, 1923; *Area:* 4.2 sq km
County or District: Smoky Lake County; *Population in 2011:* 1,022
Provincial Electoral District(s): Athabasca-Sturgeon-Redwater
Federal Electoral District(s): Lakeland
Next Election: Oct. 16, 2017 (4 year terms)
Note: Incorporated as a town on Feb. 1, 1962.
Ernest Brousseau, Mayor, 780-656-0577
Harvey Prockiw, Chief Administrative Officer

South Baptiste
724 Baptiste Dr.
West Baptiste, AB T9S 1R8
Tel: 780-675-9270;
www.southbaptiste.com
Municipal Type: Summer Village
Incorporated: Jan. 1, 1983; *Area:* 1.05 sq km
County or District: Athabasca County; *Population in 2011:* 52
Provincial Electoral District(s): Athabasca-Sturgeon-Redwater
Federal Electoral District(s): Lakeland
Next Election: Summer 2017 (4 year terms)
Steve Hamilton, Mayor
Edwin Tomaszyk, Chief Administrative Officer

South View
P.O. Box 8
Alberta Beach, AB T0E 0A0
Tel: 587-873-5765; *Fax:* 780-924-3025
administration@wildwillowenterprises.com
www.summervillageofsouthview.com
Municipal Type: Summer Village
Incorporated: Jan. 1, 1970; *Area:* 0.69 sq km
County or District: Lac Ste. Anne County; *Population in 2011:* 35
Provincial Electoral District(s): Whitecourt-Ste. Anne
Federal Electoral District(s): Yellowhead
Next Election: Summer 2017 (4 year terms)
Sandra Benford, Mayor
Wendy Wildman, Chief Administrative Officer

Spirit River
P.O. Box 130
Spirit River, AB T0H 3G0
Tel: 780-864-3998; *Fax:* 780-864-3433
www.townofspiritriver.ca
Municipal Type: Town
Incorporated: June 13, 1916; *Area:* 2.81 sq km
County or District: Municipal District of Spirit River No. 133; *Population in 2011:* 1,025
Provincial Electoral District(s): Dunvegan-Central Peace-Notley
Federal Electoral District(s): Grande Prairie-Mackenzie
Next Election: Oct. 16, 2017 (4 year terms)
Note: Incorporated as a town on Sept. 18, 1951.
Allan J. Georget, Mayor
Deedra Deveau, Chief Administrative Officer

Spring Lake
990 Bauer Ave.
Spring Lake, AB T7Z 2S9
Tel: 780-963-4211; *Fax:* 780-963-4260
villageoffice@springlakealberta.com
www.springlakealberta.com
Municipal Type: Village
Incorporated: Jan. 1, 1959; *Area:* 2.12 sq km
County or District: Parkland County; *Population in 2011:* 533
Provincial Electoral District(s): Stoney Plain
Federal Electoral District(s): Sturgeon River-Parkland
Next Election: Oct. 16, 2017 (4 year terms)
Note: Incorporated as a village on Jan. 1, 1999.
John Roznicki, Mayor
Emily House, Chief Administrative Officer

Standard
P.O. Box 249
Standard, AB T0J 3G0
Tel: 403-644-3968; *Fax:* 403-644-2284
cao@standardab.ca
www.standardab.ca
Municipal Type: Village
Incorporated: April 29, 1922; *Area:* 2.34 sq km
County or District: Wheatland County; *Population in 2011:* 379
Provincial Electoral District(s): Strathmore-Brooks
Federal Electoral District(s): Bow River
Next Election: Oct. 16, 2017 (4 year terms)
Alan Larsen, Mayor
Leah Jensen, Chief Administrative Officer

Stavely
P.O. Box 249
5001 - 50 Ave.
Stavely, AB T0L 1Z0
Tel: 403-549-3761; *Fax:* 403-549-3743
stavely@platinum.ca
www.stavely.ca
Municipal Type: Town
Incorporated: Oct. 16, 1903; *Area:* 1.62 sq km
County or District: Municipal District of Willow Creek No. 26; *Population in 2011:* 505
Provincial Electoral District(s): Livingstone-Macleod
Federal Electoral District(s): Foothills
Next Election: Oct. 16, 2017 (4 year terms)
Note: Incorporated as a town on May 25, 1912.
Gentry Hall, Mayor, 403-549-2031
Clayton Gillespie, Chief Administrative Officer

Stettler
P.O. Box 280
5031 - 50 St.
Stettler, AB T0C 2L0
Tel: 403-742-8305; *Fax:* 403-742-1404
townoffice@stettler.net
www.stettler.net
Municipal Type: Town
Incorporated: June 30, 1906; *Area:* 9.5 sq km
County or District: Stettler County No. 6; *Population in 2011:* 5,748
Provincial Electoral District(s): Drumheller-Stettler
Federal Electoral District(s): Battle River-Crowfoot
Next Election: Oct. 16, 2017 (4 year terms)
Note: Incorporated as a town on Nov. 23, 1906.
Dick Richards, Mayor, 403-742-8321
Greg Switenky, Chief Administrative Officer

Stirling
P.O. Box 360
229 - 4 Ave.
Stirling, AB T0K 2E0
Tel: 403-756-3379; *Fax:* 403-756-2262
office@stirling.ca
stirling.ca
Municipal Type: Village
Incorporated: Sept. 3, 1901; *Area:* 2.64 sq km
County or District: Warner County No. 5; *Population in 2011:* 1,090
Provincial Electoral District(s): Cardston-Taber-Warner
Federal Electoral District(s): Medicine Hat-Cardston-Warner
Next Election: Oct. 16, 2017 (4 year terms)
Ben Nilsson, Mayor
Michael Selk, Chief Administrative Officer

Strome
P.O. Box 179
5025 - 50 St.
Strome, AB T0B 4H0
Tel: 780-376-3558; *Fax:* 780-376-3557
strome@syban.net
www.villageofstrome.com
Municipal Type: Village
Incorporated: Feb. 3, 1910; *Area:* 0.92 sq km
County or District: Flagstaff County; *Population in 2011:* 228
Provincial Electoral District(s): Battle River-Wainwright
Federal Electoral District(s): Battle River-Crowfoot
Next Election: Oct. 16, 2017 (4 year terms)
Bruce Curtis, Mayor
Shelley Armstrong, Chief Administrative Officer

Sunbreaker Cove
Bay 8, 14 Thevenaz Industrial Trail
Sylvan Lake, AB T4S 2J3
Tel: 403-887-2822; *Fax:* 403-887-2897
info@sylvansummervillages.ca
www.sunbreakercove.ca
Municipal Type: Summer Village
Incorporated: Dec. 31, 1990; *Area:* 0.49 sq km
County or District: Lacombe County; *Population in 2011:* 69
Provincial Electoral District(s): Rimbey-Rocky Mountain House-Sundre
Federal Electoral District(s): Red Deer-Lacombe
Next Election: Summer 2017 (4 year terms)
Bill Carr, Mayor, 403-239-1189
Phyllis Forsyth, Administrator

Sundance Beach
P.O. Box 658
Thorsby, AB T0C 2P0
Tel: 780-985-2441; *Fax:* 780-401-3251
www.sundancebeach.ca
Municipal Type: Summer Village
Incorporated: Jan. 1, 1970; *Area:* 0.42 sq km
County or District: Leduc County; *Population in 2011:* 82
Provincial Electoral District(s): Drayton Valley-Devon
Federal Electoral District(s): Edmonton-Wetaskiwin
Next Election: Summer 2017 (4 year terms)
Peter Pellatt, Mayor
Harold Wynne, Chief Administrative Officer

Sundre
P.O. Box 420
717 Main Ave. West
Sundre, AB T0M 1X0
Tel: 403-638-3551; *Fax:* 403-638-2100
townmail@sundre.com
www.sundre.com
Municipal Type: Town
Incorporated: Dec. 31, 1949; *Area:* 7.65 sq km
County or District: Mountain View County; *Population in 2011:* 2,610
Provincial Electoral District(s): Rimbey-Rocky Mountain House-Sundre
Federal Electoral District(s): Red Deer-Mountain View
Next Election: Oct. 16, 2017 (4 year terms)
Note: Incorporated as a town on Jan. 1, 1956.
Terry Leslie, Mayor
David Dubauskas, Chief Administrative Officer

Sunrise Beach
P.O. Box 63
Site 1, RR#1
Onoway, AB T0E 1V0
Tel: 780-967-2873; *Fax:* 780-967-2813
svsandyb@xplornet.ca
www.summervillageofsunrisebeach.ca
Municipal Type: Summer Village
Incorporated: Dec. 31, 1988; *Area:* 1.72 sq km
County or District: Lac Ste. Anne County; *Population in 2011:* 149
Provincial Electoral District(s): Whitecourt-Ste. Anne
Federal Electoral District(s): Sturgeon River-Parkland
Next Election: Summer 2017 (4 year terms)
Glen Usselman, Mayor
Wendy Wildman, Chief Administrative Officer, 780-819-3681

Sunset Beach
724 Baptiste Dr.
West Baptiste, AB T9S 1R8
Tel: 780-675-9270
Municipal Type: Summer Village
Incorporated: May 1, 1977; *Area:* 0.99 sq km
County or District: Athabasca County; *Population in 2011:* 44
Provincial Electoral District(s): Athabasca-Sturgeon-Redwater
Federal Electoral District(s): Lakeland
Next Election: Summer 2017 (4 year terms)
Mark Lindskoog, Mayor
Edwin Tomaszyk, Chief Administrative Officer

Sunset Point
P.O. Box 89
RR#2, Site 202
Onoway, AB T0E 1V0
Tel: 780-717-6843; *Fax:* 780-967-5651
www.sunsetpoint.ca
Municipal Type: Summer Village
Incorporated: Jan. 1, 1959; *Area:* 1.11 sq km
County or District: Lac Ste. Anne County; *Population in 2011:* 221
Provincial Electoral District(s): Whitecourt-Ste. Anne
Federal Electoral District(s): Yellowhead
Next Election: Summer 2017 (4 year terms)
Ann Morrison, Mayor
Paul Hanlan, Chief Administrative Officer

Swan Hills
P.O. Box 149
5536 Main St.
Swan Hills, AB T0G 2C0
Tel: 780-333-4477; *Fax:* 780-333-4547
town@townofswanhills.com
www.townofswanhills.com
Municipal Type: Town
Incorporated: Sept. 1, 1959; *Area:* 25.44 sq km
County or District: Municipal District of Big Lakes; *Population in 2011:* 1,465
Provincial Electoral District(s): Barrhead-Morinville-Westlock
Federal Electoral District(s): Peace River-Westlock
Next Election: Oct. 16, 2017 (4 year terms)
Craig Wilson, Mayor
Douglas Borg, Chief Administrative Officer

Taber
4900A - 50 St.
Taber, AB T1G 1T1
Tel: 403-223-5500; *Fax:* 403-223-5530
town@taber.ca
www.taber.ca
Municipal Type: Town
Incorporated: March 15, 1905; *Area:* 15.09 sq km
County or District: Municipal District of Taber; *Population in 2011:* 8,104
Provincial Electoral District(s): Cardston-Taber-Warner
Federal Electoral District(s): Bow River
Next Election: Oct. 16, 2017 (4 year terms)
Note: Incorporated as a town on July 1, 1907.
Hendrick De Vlieger, Mayor, 403-223-5500
Greg Birch, Chief Administrative Officer, 403-223-5500

Thorsby
P.O. Box 297
4917 Hankin St.
Thorsby, AB T0C 2P0
Tel: 780-789-3935; *Fax:* 780-789-3779
www.thorsby.ca
Municipal Type: Village
Incorporated: Dec. 31, 1949; *Area:* 2.92 sq km
County or District: Leduc County; *Population in 2011:* 797
Provincial Electoral District(s): Drayton Valley-Devon
Federal Electoral District(s): Yellowhead
Next Election: Oct. 16, 2017 (4 year terms)
Barry Rasch, Mayor
Jason Gariepy, Chief Administrative Officer

Three Hills
P.O. Box 610
135 - 2 Ave. SE
Three Hills, AB T0M 2A0
Tel: 403-443-5822; *Fax:* 403-443-2616
info@threehills.ca
www.threehills.ca
Municipal Type: Town
Incorporated: June 14, 1912; *Area:* 5.63 sq km
County or District: Kneehill County; *Population in 2011:* 3,198
Provincial Electoral District(s): Olds-Didsbury-Three Hills
Federal Electoral District(s): Battle River-Crowfoot
Next Election: Oct. 16, 2017 (4 year terms)
Note: Incorporated as a town on Jan. 1, 1929.
Timothy J. Shearlaw, Mayor
Lori Conkin, Chief Administrative Officer

Tofield
P.O. Box 30
5407 - 50 St.
Tofield, AB T0B 4J0
Tel: 780-662-3269; *Fax:* 780-662-3929
tofieldadmin@tofieldalberta.caz
www.tofieldalberta.ca
Municipal Type: Town
Incorporated: Sept. 9, 1907; *Area:* 6.01 sq km
County or District: Beaver County; *Population in 2011:* 2,182
Provincial Electoral District(s): Fort Saskatchewan-Vegreville
Federal Electoral District(s): Battle River-Crowfoot
Next Election: Oct. 16, 2017 (4 year terms)
Note: Incorporated as a town on Sept. 10, 1909.
Harold Neale Conquest, Mayor
Cindy Neufeld, Chief Administrative Officer, 780-662-3269

Trochu
P.O. Box 340
416 Arena Ave.
Trochu, AB T0M 2C0
Tel: 403-442-3085; *Fax:* 403-442-2528
www.town.trochu.ab.ca
Municipal Type: Town
Incorporated: May 5, 1911; *Area:* 2.82 sq km
County or District: Kneehill County; *Population in 2011:* 1,072
Provincial Electoral District(s): Olds-Didsbury-Three Hills
Federal Electoral District(s): Battle River-Crowfoot
Next Election: Oct. 16, 2017 (4 year terms)
Note: Incorporated as a town on Aug. 1, 1962.
Barry Kletke, Mayor
Carl Peterson, Chief Administrative Officer

Turner Valley
P.O. Box 330
514 Windsor Ave. NW
Turner Valley, AB T0L 2A0
Tel: 403-933-4944; *Fax:* 403-933-5377
admin@turnervalley.ca
www.turnervalley.ca
Municipal Type: Town
Incorporated: Feb. 25, 1930
County or District: Municipal District of Foothills No. 31; *Population in 2011:* 2,167
Provincial Electoral District(s): Livingstone-Macleod
Federal Electoral District(s): Foothills
Next Election: Oct. 16, 2017 (4 year terms)
Note: Incorporated as a town on Sept.1, 1977.
Kelly Tuck, Mayor
Barry Williamson, Chief Administrative Officer

Two Hills
P.O. Box 630
4712 - 50 St.
Two Hills, AB T0B 4K0
Tel: 780-657-3395; *Fax:* 780-657-2158
info@townoftwohills.com
townoftwohills.com
Municipal Type: Town
Incorporated: June 4, 1929; *Area:* 3.31 sq km
County or District: Two Hills County No. 21; *Population in 2011:* 1,379
Provincial Electoral District(s): Lac La Biche-St. Paul-Two Hills
Federal Electoral District(s): Lakeland
Next Election: Oct. 16, 2017 (4 year terms)
Note: Incorporated as a town on Jan. 1, 1955.
Henry Neufeld, Mayor
Elsie Howanyk, Chief Administrative Officer

Val Quentin
P.O. Box 7
Site 19, RR#1
Gunn, AB T0E 1A0
Tel: 780-446-1426;
www.valquentin.ca
Municipal Type: Summer Village
Incorporated: Jan. 1, 1966; *Area:* 0.3 sq km
County or District: Lac Ste. Anne County; *Population in 2011:* 157
Provincial Electoral District(s): Whitecourt-Ste. Anne
Federal Electoral District(s): Yellowhead
Next Election: Summer 2017 (4 year terms)
Bob Lehman, Mayor
Dennis Evans, Municipal Administrator

Valleyview
P.O. Box 270
4802 - 50 St.
Valleyview, AB T0H 3N0
Tel: 780-524-5150; *Fax:* 780-524-2727
info@valleyview.ca
www.valleyview.govoffice.com
Municipal Type: Town
Incorporated: Jan. 1, 1955; *Area:* 4.57 sq km
County or District: Municipal District of Greenview No. 16; *Population in 2011:* 1,761
Provincial Electoral District(s): Grande Prairie-Smoky
Federal Electoral District(s): Peace River-Westlock

Next Election: Oct. 16, 2017 (4 year terms)
Note: Incorporated as a town on Feb. 5, 1957.
Vern Lymburner, Mayor
Garry Peterson, Twon Manager

Vauxhall
P.O. Box 509
223 - 5 St. North
Vauxhall, AB T0K 2K0
Tel: 403-654-2174; *Fax:* 403-654-4110
www.town.vauxhall.ab.ca
Municipal Type: Town
Incorporated: Dec. 31, 1949; *Area:* 2.88 sq km
County or District: Municipal District of Taber; *Population in 2011:* 1,288
Provincial Electoral District(s): Little Bow
Federal Electoral District(s): Bow River
Next Election: Oct. 16, 2017 (4 year terms)
Note: Incorporated as a town on Jan. 1, 1961.
Margaret Plumtree, Mayor
Cris Burns, Chief Administrative Officer

Vegreville
P.O. Box 640
4829 - 50 St.
Vegreville, AB T9C 1R7
Tel: 780-632-2606; *Fax:* 780-632-3088
vegtown@vegreville.com
www.vegreville.com
Municipal Type: Town
Incorporated: April 4, 1906; *Area:* 13.49 sq km
County or District: Minburn County No. 27; *Population in 2011:* 5,717
Provincial Electoral District(s): Fort Saskatchewan-Vegreville
Federal Electoral District(s): Lakeland
Next Election: Oct. 16, 2017 (4 year terms)
Note: Incorporated as a town on Aug 15, 1906.
Myron Hayduk, Mayor
Jody Quickstad, Town Manager

Vermilion
5021 - 49th Ave.
Vermilion, AB T9X 1X1
Tel: 780-853-5358; *Fax:* 780-853-4910
townofvermilion@vermilion.ca
www.vermilion.ca
Municipal Type: Town
Incorporated: Feb. 17, 1906; *Area:* 13.69 sq km
County or District: Vermilion River County; *Population in 2011:* 3,930
Provincial Electoral District(s): Vermilion-Lloydminster
Federal Electoral District(s): Lakeland
Next Election: Oct. 16, 2017 (4 year terms)
Note: Incorporated as a town on Aug. 27, 1906.
Bruce MacDuff, Mayor
Dion Pollard, Town Manager

Veteran
P.O. Box 439
Veteran, AB T0C 2S0
Tel: 403-575-3954; *Fax:* 403-575-3954
veteran@veterancable.net
www.villageofveteran.ca
Municipal Type: Village
Incorporated: June 30, 1914; *Area:* 0.84 sq km
Population in 2011: 249
Provincial Electoral District(s): Drumheller-Stettler
Federal Electoral District(s): Battle River-Crowfoot
Next Election: Oct. 16, 2017 (4 year terms)
Pat Gorcak, Mayor
Debbie Johnstone, Chief Administrative Officer

Viking
P.O. Box 369
Viking, AB T0B 4N0
Tel: 780-336-3466; *Fax:* 780-336-2660
info@viking.ca
www.town.viking.ab.ca
Municipal Type: Town
Incorporated: Feb. 5, 1909; *Area:* 3.76 sq km
County or District: Beaver County; *Population in 2011:* 1,041
Provincial Electoral District(s): Vermilion-Lloydminster
Federal Electoral District(s): Battle River-Crowfoot
Next Election: Oct. 16, 2017 (4 year terms)
Note: Incorporated as a town on Nov. 10, 1952.
David Zayonce, Mayor
Jackie Fenton, Chief Administrative Officer, 780-336-3466

Vilna
P.O. Box 10 Mainstreet
Vilna, AB T0A 3L0
Tel: 780-636-3620; *Fax:* 780-636-3022
vilna@mcsnet.ca
www.vilna.ca
Municipal Type: Village
Incorporated: June 23, 1923; *Area:* 0.9 sq km
County or District: Smoky Lake County; *Population in 2011:* 249
Provincial Electoral District(s): Lac La Biche-St. Paul-Two Hills
Federal Electoral District(s): Lakeland
Next Election: Oct. 16, 2017 (4 year terms)
Donald Romanko, Mayor
Loni Leslie, Chief Administrative Officer

Vulcan
P.O. Box 360
321 - 2 St. South
Vulcan, AB T0L 2B0
Tel: 403-485-2417; *Fax:* 403-485-2914
admin@townofvulcan.ca
www.townofvulcan.ca
Municipal Type: Town
Incorporated: Dec. 23, 1912; *Area:* 6.58 sq km
County or District: Vulcan County; *Population in 2011:* 1,836
Provincial Electoral District(s): Little Bow
Federal Electoral District(s): Bow River
Next Election: Oct. 16, 2017 (4 year terms)
Note: Incorporated as a town on Jun 15, 1921.
Tom Grant, Mayor
Kim Fath, Chief Administrative Officer

Wabamun
P.O. Box 240
5217 - 52 St.
Wabamun, AB T0E 2K0
Tel: 780-892-2699; *Fax:* 780-892-2669
www.wabamun.ca
Municipal Type: Village
Incorporated: July 18, 1912; *Area:* 3.24 sq km
County or District: Parkland County; *Population in 2011:* 661
Provincial Electoral District(s): Stony Plain
Federal Electoral District(s): Yellowhead
Next Election: Oct. 16, 2017 (4 year terms)
Fred Lindsay, Mayor
Shawn Patience, Chief Administrative Officer

Wainwright
1018 - 2 Ave.
Wainwright, AB T9W 1R1
Tel: 780-842-3381; *Fax:* 780-842-2898
info@wainwright.ca
www.wainwright.ca
Municipal Type: Town
Incorporated: March 25, 1909; *Area:* 8.55 sq km
County or District: Municipal District of Wainwright No. 61; *Population in 2011:* 5,925
Provincial Electoral District(s): Battle River-Wainwright
Federal Electoral District(s): Battle River-Crowfoot
Next Election: Oct. 16, 2017 (4 year terms)
Note: Incorporated as town on July 14, 1910.
Brian Bethune, Mayor
Ed Chow, Chief Administrative Officer

Waiparous
P.O. Box 19554
RPO South Cranston
Calgary, AB T3M 0V4
Tel: 403-554-5515; *Fax:* 403-206-7209
admin@waiparous.ca
www.waiparous.ca
Municipal Type: Summer Village
Incorporated: Jan. 1, 1986; *Area:* 0.41 sq km
County or District: Municipal District of Bighorn No. 8; *Population in 2011:* 42
Provincial Electoral District(s): Banff-Cochrane
Federal Electoral District(s): Banff-Airdrie
Next Election: Summer 2017 (4 year terms)
Larry Anderson, Mayor, 403-809-9192
Sharon Plett, Administrator

Warburg
P.O. Box 29
5212 - 50 Ave.
Warburg, AB T0C 2T0
Tel: 780-848-2841; *Fax:* 780-848-2296
villageofwarburg@wildroseinternet.ca
www.villageofwarburg.com
Municipal Type: Village
Incorporated: Dec. 31, 1953; *Area:* 2.08 sq km
County or District: Leduc County; *Population in 2011:* 789
Provincial Electoral District(s): Drayton Valley-Devon
Federal Electoral District(s): Yellowhead
Next Election: Oct. 16, 2017 (4 year terms)
Ralph Van Assen, Mayor
Christine Pankewitz, Municipal Administrator

Warner
P.O. Box 88
Warner, AB T0K 2L0
Tel: 403-642-3877; *Fax:* 403-642-2011
vowarner@shockware.com
www.warner.ca
Municipal Type: Village
Incorporated: Nov. 12, 1908; *Area:* 1.15 sq km
County or District: Warner County No. 5; *Population in 2011:* 331
Provincial Electoral District(s): Cardston-Taber-Warner
Federal Electoral District(s): Medicine Hat-Cardston-Warner
Next Election: Oct. 16, 2017 (4 year terms)
Jon Hood, Mayor
Lisa C. Carroll, Chief Administrative Officer

Waskatenau
P.O. Box 99
5008 - 51st St.
Waskatenau, AB T0A 3P0
Tel: 780-358-2208; *Fax:* 780-358-2208
info@waskatenau.ca
www.waskatenau.ca
Municipal Type: Village
Incorporated: May 19, 1932; *Area:* 0.6 sq km
County or District: Smoky Lake County; *Population in 2011:* 255
Provincial Electoral District(s): Athabasca-Sturgeon-Redwater
Federal Electoral District(s): Lakeland
Next Election: Oct. 16, 2017 (4 year terms)
Casey Caron, Mayor
Bernice Macyk, Village Administrator

Wembley
P.O. Box 89
Wembley, AB T0H 3S0
Tel: 780-766-2269; *Fax:* 780-766-2868
admin@wembley.ca
www.wembley.ca
Municipal Type: Town
Incorporated: Jan. 3, 1928; *Area:* 3.63 sq km
County or District: Grande Prairie County No. 1; *Population in 2011:* 1,383
Provincial Electoral District(s): Grande Prairie-Wapiti
Federal Electoral District(s): Grande Prairie-Mackenzie
Next Election: Oct. 16, 2017 (4 year terms)
Note: Incorporated as a town on Aug. 1, 1980.
Chris Turnmire, Mayor
Lori Parker, Chief Administrative Officer

West Baptiste
945 Baptiste Dr.
West Baptiste, AB T9S 1R8
Tel: 780-675-3900; *Fax:* 780-675-4174
svwestbaptiste.ca
Municipal Type: Summer Village
Incorporated: Jan. 1, 1983; *Area:* 0.6 sq km
County or District: Athabasca County; *Population in 2011:* 52
Provincial Electoral District(s): Athabasca-Sturgeon-Redwater
Federal Electoral District(s): Lakeland
Next Election: Summer 2017 (4 year terms)
Keith Wilson, Mayor
Vivian Driver, Administrator

West Cove
11318 - 10 Ave.
Edmonton, AB T0E 1A0
Tel: 780-431-9712;
svoffice@telusplanet.net
www.westcove.ca
Municipal Type: Summer Village
Incorporated: Jan. 1, 1963; *Area:* 1.21 sq km
County or District: Lac Ste. Anne County; *Population in 2011:* 121
Provincial Electoral District(s): Whitecourt-Ste. Anne
Federal Electoral District(s): Yellowhead
Next Election: Summer 2017 (4 year terms)
Brad Londeau, Mayor
Anita Blais, Chief Administrative Officer

Westlock
10003 - 106 St.
Westlock, AB T7P 2K3
Tel: 780-349-4444; *Fax:* 780-349-4436
info@westlock.ca
www.westlock.ca
Other Information: Toll Free: 1-866-349-4445
Municipal Type: Town
Incorporated: March 13, 1916; *Area:* 9.64 sq km

County or District: Westlock County; *Population in 2011:* 4,823
Provincial Electoral District(s): Barrhead-Morinville-Westlock
Federal Electoral District(s): Peace River-Westlock
Next Election: Oct. 16, 2017 (4 year terms)
Note: Incorporated as a town on Jan. 7, 1947.
Ralph Leriger, Mayor
Dean Krause, Chief Administrative Officer, 780-350-2100

Whispering Hills
10511 - 109 St.
Westlock, AB T7P 1A9
Tel: 780-349-3651; *Fax:* 780-349-5194
www.mywhisperinghills.com
Municipal Type: Summer Village
Incorporated: Jan. 1, 1983; *Area:* 1.73 sq km
County or District: Athabasca County; *Population in 2011:* 108
Provincial Electoral District(s): Athabasca-Sturgeon-Redwater
Federal Electoral District(s): Lakeland
Next Election: Summer 2017 (4 year terms)
Dennis Irving, Mayor
Garth Bancroft, Administrator

White Sands
P.O. Box 119
Stettler, AB T0C 2L0
Tel: 403-742-8305; *Fax:* 403-742-1404
townoffice@stettler.net
www.stettler.net
Municipal Type: Summer Village
Incorporated: Jan. 1, 1980; *Area:* 1.6 sq km
County or District: Stettler County No. 6; *Population in 2011:* 91
Provincial Electoral District(s): Drumheller-Stettler
Federal Electoral District(s): Battle River-Crowfoot
Next Election: Summer 2017 (4 year terms)
Lorne Thurston, Mayor
Greg Switenky, Chief Administrative Officer

Whitecourt
P.O. Box 509
5004 - 52 Ave.
Whitecourt, AB T7S 1N6
Tel: 780-778-2273; *Fax:* 780-778-4166
administration@whitecourt.ca
www.whitecourt.ca
Municipal Type: Town
Incorporated: Jan. 1, 1959; *Area:* 26.14 sq km
County or District: Woodlands County; *Population in 2011:* 9,605
Provincial Electoral District(s): Whitecourt-Ste. Anne
Federal Electoral District(s): Peace River-Westlock
Next Election: Oct. 16, 2017 (4 year terms)
Note: Incorporated as a town on Aug. 15, 1961.
Maryann Chichak, Mayor
Peter Smyl, Chief Administrative Officer

Willingdon
P.O. Box 210
Willingdon, AB T0B 4R0
Tel: 780-367-2337; *Fax:* 780-367-2167
vilwil@rjvnet.ca
Municipal Type: Village
Incorporated: Aug. 31, 1928; *Area:* 0.97 sq km
County or District: Two Hills County No. 21; *Population in 2011:* 275
Provincial Electoral District(s): Lac La Biche-St. Paul-Two Hills
Federal Electoral District(s): Lakeland
Next Election: Oct. 16, 2017 (4 year terms)
Marie Zwozdesky, Mayor
Robert Jorgensen, Chief Administrative Officer

Yellowstone
P.O. Box 8
Alberta Beach, AB T0E 0A0
Tel: 587-873-5765; *Fax:* 780-924-3025
administration@wildwillowenterprises.com
www.summervillageofyellowstone.com
Municipal Type: Summer Village
Incorporated: Jan. 1, 1965; *Area:* 0.28 sq km
County or District: Lac Ste. Anne County; *Population in 2011:* 124
Provincial Electoral District(s): Whitecourt-Ste. Anne
Federal Electoral District(s): Yellowhead
Next Election: Summer 2017 (4 year terms)
Alice Solesbury, Mayor
Wendy Wildman, Chief Administrative Officer

Youngstown
P.O. Box 99
Youngstown, AB T0J 3P0
Tel: 403-779-3873; *Fax:* 403-779-3875
ytown@netago.ca
Municipal Type: Village
Incorporated: March 8, 1913; *Area:* 1 sq km
Population in 2011: 178
Provincial Electoral District(s): Drumheller-Stettler
Federal Electoral District(s): Battle River-Crowfoot
Next Election: Oct. 16, 2017 (4 year terms)
Robert Blagen, Mayor
Emma Garlock, Municipal Administrator

Improvement Districts in Alberta

Improvement District No. 12 (Jasper National Park)
Municipal Services Branch
10155 - 102 St., 17th Fl.
Edmonton, AB T5J 4L4
Tel: 780-422-8876; *Fax:* 780-420-1016
lgsmail@gov.ab.ca
Municipal Type: Improvement Districts
Incorporated: April 1, 1945; *Area:* 10,181.58 sq. km
Population in 2011: 34
Federal Electoral District(s): Yellowhead
Darryl Joyce, Chief Administrative Officer

Improvement District No. 13 (Elk Island)
Municipal Services Branch
10155 - 102 St., 17th Fl.
Edmonton, AB T5J 4L4
Tel: 780-422-8876; *Fax:* 780-420-1016
lgsmail@gov.ab.ca
Municipal Type: Improvement Districts
Incorporated: April 1, 1958; *Area:* 165.28 sq. km
Population in 2011: 10
Federal Electoral District(s): Lakeland
Darryl Joyce, Chief Administrative Officer

Improvement District No. 24 (Wood Buffalo)
Municipal Services Branch
10155 - 102 St., 17th Fl.
Edmonton, AB T5J 4L4
Tel: 780-422-8876; *Fax:* 780-420-1016
lgsmail@gov.ab.ca
Municipal Type: Improvement Districts
Incorporated: Jan. 1, 1967; *Area:* 165.28 sq. km.
Population in 2011: 590
Federal Electoral District(s): Peace River-Westlock
Darryl Joyce, Chief Administrative Officer

Improvement District No. 25 (Willmore Wilderness)
Municipal Services Branch
10155 - 102 St., 17th Fl.
Edmonton, AB T5J 4L4
Tel: 780-422-8876; *Fax:* 780-420-1016
lgsmail@gov.ab.ca
Municipal Type: Improvement Districts
Incorporated: Jan. 2, 1994; *Area:* 4,604.97 sq. km
Federal Electoral District(s): Yellowhead
Darryl Joyce, Chief Administrative Officer

Improvement District No. 349
Municipal Services Branch
10155 - 102 St., 17th Fl.
Edmonton, AB T5J 4L4
Tel: 780-422-8876; *Fax:* 780-420-1016
ID349@gov.ab.ca
www.municipalaffairs.alberta.ca/1760.cfm
Municipal Type: Improvement Districts
Incorporated: Jan. 1, 2012
Federal Electoral District(s): Fort McMurray-Cold Lake
Note: Created from land separated from Lac La Biche County & the Regional Municipality of Wood Buffalo.
Darryl Joyce, Chief Administrative Officer

Improvement District No. 4 (Waterton)
Municipal Services Branch
10155 - 102 St., 17th Fl.
Edmonton, AB T5J 4L4
Tel: 403-752-3322; *Fax:* 403-752-4379
lgsmail@gov.ab.ca
Municipal Type: Improvement Districts
Incorporated: Jan. 1, 1944; *Area:* 480.58 sq. km
Population in 2011: 88
Federal Electoral District(s): Foothills
Next Election: Oct. 16, 2017 (4 year terms)
Brian Reeves, Chairperson
J. Scott Barton, Chief Administrative Officer

Improvement District No. 9 (Banff)
Municipal Services Branch
10155 - 102 St., 17th Fl.
Edmonton, AB T5J 4L4
Tel: 403-752-3322; *Fax:* 403-752-4379
lgsmail@gov.ab.ca
Municipal Type: Improvement Districts
Incorporated: April 1, 1945; *Area:* 6,782.26 sq. km
Population in 2011: 1,175
Federal Electoral District(s): Banff-Airdrie
Rick Werner, Chairperson
Ethan Gorner, Chief Administrative Officer

Kananaskis Improvement District
P.O. Box 70
Kananaskis, AB T0L 2H0
Tel: 403-591-7774; *Fax:* 403-591-7123
www.kananaskisid.ca
Municipal Type: Improvement Districts
Incorporated: April 1, 1945; *Area:* 4,210.72 sq km
Population in 2011: 249
Federal Electoral District(s): Banff-Airdrie
Next Election: Oct. 16, 2017 (4 year terms)
Dan DeSantis, Chairperson
Shawn Polley, Chief Administrative Officer

Metis Settlements in Alberta

Buffalo Lake
P.O. Box 16
Caslan, AB T0A 0R0
Tel: 780-689-2170; *Fax:* 780-689-2024
buffalolakems.ca
Municipal Type: Metis Settlements
Area: 336.97 square km
Population in 2011: 492
Provincial Electoral District(s): Battle River-Wainwright
Federal Electoral District(s): Grande Prairie-Mackenzie
Next Election: Oct. 16, 2017 (4 year terms)
Stan Delorme, Chairperson
Lana Howse, Administrator

East Prairie
P.O. Box 1289
High Prairie, AB T0G 1E0
Tel: 780-523-2594; *Fax:* 780-523-2777
Municipal Type: Metis Settlements
Area: 333.87 square km
Population in 2011: 366
Provincial Electoral District(s): Lesser Slave Lake
Federal Electoral District(s): Peace River-Westlock
Next Election: Oct. 16, 2017 (4 year terms)
Gerald Cunningham, Chairperson
Donna Lakey, Administrator

Elizabeth
P.O. Box 420
Cold Lake, AB T9M 1P1
Tel: 780-594-5026; *Fax:* 780-594-5452
ems@jetnet.ab.ca
elizabethms.ca
Other Information: Alt. Phone: 780-594-5028
Municipal Type: Metis Settlements
Federal Electoral District(s): Lakeland
Next Election: Oct. 16, 2017 (4 year terms)
Archie Collins, Chairperson
Anne Turbide, Administrator

Fishing Lake
General Delivery
Fishing Lake, AB T0A 3G0
Tel: 780-943-2202; *Fax:* 780-943-2575
administrator@fishinglakems.ca
www.fishinglakems.ca
Municipal Type: Metis Settlements
Area: 355.74 square km
Population in 2011: 436
Provincial Electoral District(s): Bonnyville-Cold Lake
Federal Electoral District(s): Fort McMurray-Cold Lake
Next Election: Oct. 16, 2017 (4 year terms)
Lorne Dustow, Chairperson
Ryck Chalifoux, Administrator

Gift Lake
P.O. Box 60
Gift Lake, AB T0G 1B0
Tel: 780-767-3794; *Fax:* 780-767-3888
glms@telus.net
Municipal Type: Metis Settlements
Area: 811.30 square km
Population in 2011: 662
Provincial Electoral District(s): Lesser Slave Lake
Federal Electoral District(s): Peace River-Westlock
Next Election: Oct. 16, 2017 (4 year terms)
Dave Lamouche, Chairperson
Gerry Peardon, Administrator

Kikino
General Delivery
Kikino, AB T0A 2B0
Tel: 780-623-7868; *Fax:* 780-623-7080
kiadmin@telus.net
Municipal Type: Metis Settlements
Area: 442.92 square km
Population in 2011: 959
Provincial Electoral District(s): Lac La Biche-St. Paul-Two Hills
Federal Electoral District(s): Lakeland
Next Election: Oct. 16, 2017 (4 year terms)
Floyd Thompson, Chairperson
Roger Littlechilds, Administrator

Paddle Prairie
P.O. Box 58
Paddle Prairie, AB T0H 2W0
Tel: 780-981-2227; *Fax:* 780-981-3737
reception@paddleprairie.com
Municipal Type: Metis Settlements
Area: 1716.72 square km
Population in 2011: 562
Provincial Electoral District(s): Peace River
Federal Electoral District(s): Grande Prairie-Mackenzie
Next Election: Oct. 16, 2017 (4 year terms)
Greg Calliou, Chairperson
Tina St. Germain, Administrator

Peavine
P.O. Box 4
High Prairie, AB T0G 1E0
Tel: 780-523-2557; *Fax:* 780-523-2626
Municipal Type: Metis Settlements
Area: 817.13 square km
Population in 2011: 690
Provincial Electoral District(s): Lesser Slave Lake
Federal Electoral District(s): Peace River-Westlock
Next Election: Oct. 16, 2017 (4 year terms)
Ken Noskey, Chairperson
Judy Hopkins, Interim Administrator

BRITISH COLUMBIA

Incorporated municipalities in British Columbia include Villages, Towns, Cities, and District Municipalities as well as one Indian Government District, one Resort Municipality, two Mountain Resort Municipalities, and one Island Municipality. Twenty-eight regional districts (plus one administered by the provincial government) provide services to unincorporated areas and member municipalities.

Municipal elections in all municipalities are held on the 3rd Saturday of October. Election terms are four years (2014, 2018, etc.).

Legislation: The Local Government Act, excluding the City of Vancouver, which is regulated under the provisions of the Vancouver Charter.

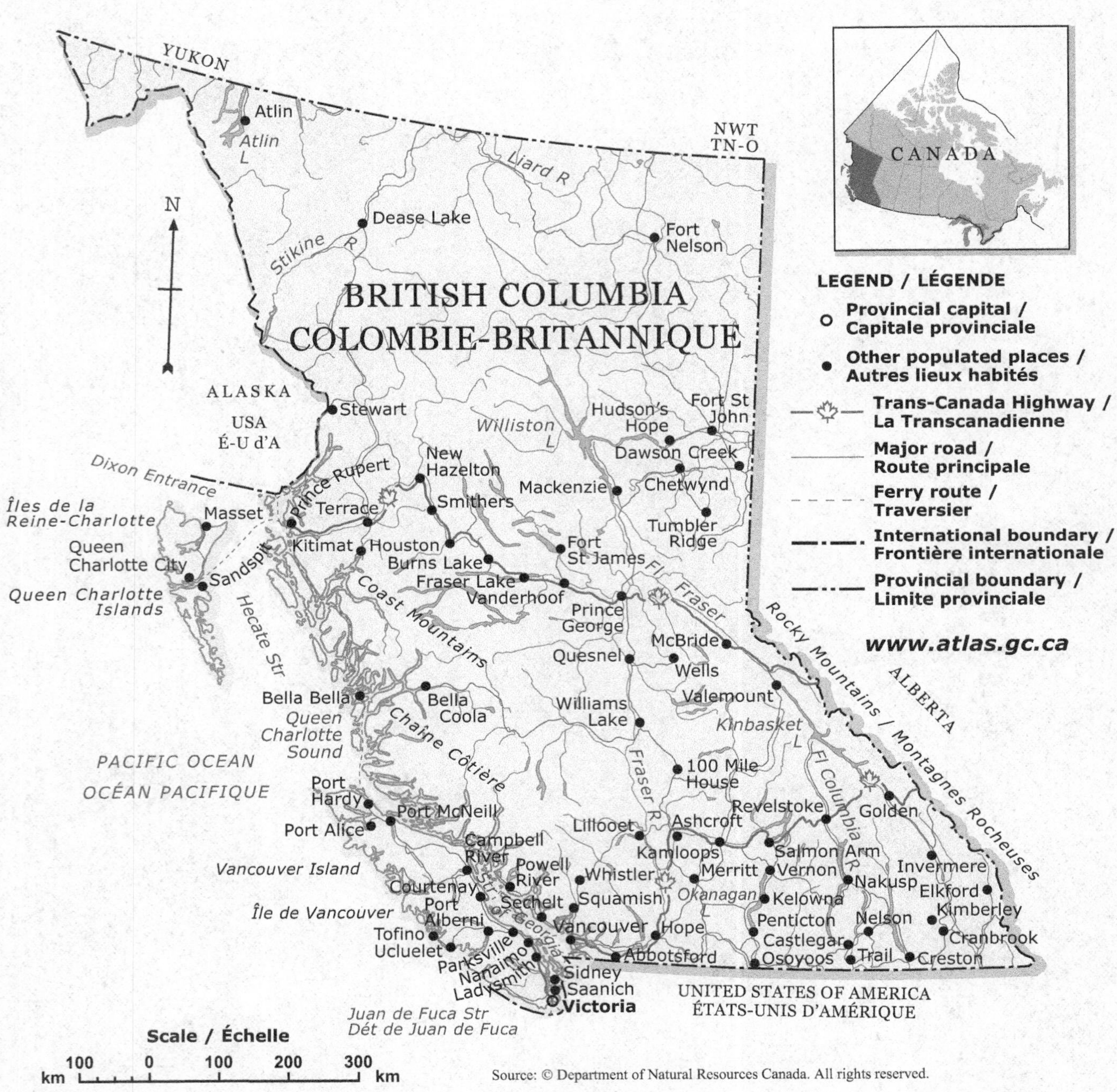

British Columbia

Counties & Municipal Districts in British Columbia

Alberni-Clayoquot
3008 - 5 Ave.
Port Alberni, BC V9Y 2E3
Tel: 250-720-2700; *Fax:* 250-723-1327
mailbox@acrd.bc.ca
www.acrd.bc.ca
Municipal Type: Regional Districts
Incorporated: April 21, 1966; *Area:* 6,596.58 sq km
Population in 2011: 31,061
Federal Electoral District(s): Courtenay-Alberni
Next Election: Oct. 20, 2018 (4-year terms)
Note: Member municipalities: Port Alberni; Tofino; Ucluelet.
Josie Osborne, Chair, 250-725-3229
Russell Dyosn, Chief Administrative Officer, 250-720-2705
Wendy Thompson, Manager, Administrative Services, 250-720-2706
Teri Fong, Manager, Finance, 250-720-2707
Mike Irg, Manager, Planning & Development, 250-720-2710

Bulkley-Nechako
P.O. Box 820
37, 3rd Ave.
Burns Lake, BC V0J 1E0
Tel: 250-692-3195; *Fax:* 250-692-3305
inquiries@rdbn.bc.ca
www.rdbn.bc.ca
Other Information: Toll Free Phone: 1-800-320-3339
Municipal Type: Regional Districts
Incorporated: Feb. 1, 1966; *Area:* 73,440.95 sq km
Population in 2011: 39,208
Federal Electoral District(s): Cariboo-Prince George; Skeena-Bulkley Valley
Next Election: Oct. 20, 2018 (4-year terms)
Note: Member municipalities: Smithers; Fort St. James; Housten; Vanderhoof; Burns Lake; Fraser Lake; Granisle; Telkwa.
Bill Miller, Chair, 250-692-3195
Gail Chapman, Chief Administrative Officer, 250-692-3195, Fax: 250-692-3305
Jason Llewellyn, Director, Planning
Janine Dougall, Director, Environmental Services, 250-692-3195
Hans Berndorff, C.A., Administrator, Financial Services
Richard Wainwright, C.A., Chief Building Inspector
Corrine Swenson, C.A., Manager, Regional Economic Development
Rory McKenzie, Supervisor, Field Operations, Environmental Services
Janette Derksen, Coordinator, Wastewater/Water

Capital Regional District
625 Fisgard St.
Victoria, BC V8W 1R7
Tel: 250-360-3000
www.crd.bc.ca
Other Information: Mailing address: PO Box 1000, Victoria, BC V8W 2S6
Municipal Type: Regional Districts
Incorporated: Feb. 1, 1966; *Area:* 2,341.02 sq km
Population in 2011: 359,991
Federal Electoral District(s): Cowichan-Malahat-Langford; Esquimalt-Saanich-Sooke; Saanish-Gulf Islands
Next Election: Oct. 20, 2018 (4-year terms)
Note: Member municipalities: Central Saanich; Colwood; Esquimalt; Highlands; Langford; Metchosin; North Saanich; Oak Bay; Saanich; Sidney; Sooke; Victoria; View Royal.
Nick Jensen, Chair, 250-598-3311, Fax: 250-598-9108
Bob Lapham, Chief Administrative Officer, 250-360-3125, Fax: 250-360-3232
Diana Lokken, General Manager, Finance & Technology Services, 250-360-3010
Larissa Hutcheson, General Manager, Parks & Environmental Services, 250-360-3085
Ted Robbins, General Manager, Integrated Water Services, 250-360-3000
Kevin Lorette, General Manager, Planning & Protective Services, 250-360-3285
Andy Orr, Senior Manager, Corporate Communications, 250-360-3229
Dan Telford, Senior Manager, Environmental Engineering, 250-360-3064
Glenn Harris, Senior Manager, Environmental Protection, 250-360-3090
Russ Smith, Senior Manager, Environmental Resource Management, 250-360-3083
Peter Sparanese, Senior Manager, Infrasturcture Operations, 250-361-0292
Maurice Rachwalski, Senior Manager, Health & Capital Planning Strategies, 250-360-3114
Ian Hennigar, Senior Manager, Panorama Recreation, 250-655-2170
June Klassen, Senior Manager, Local Area Planning, 250-360-3081
Annette Constabel, Senior Manager, Watershed Protection, 250-391-3556

Cariboo
180 North 3rd Ave., #D
Williams Lake, BC V2G 2A4
Tel: 250-392-3351; *Fax:* 250-392-2812
mailbox@cariboord.bc.ca
www.cariboord.bc.ca
Other Information: Toll Free Phone: 1-800-665-1636
Municipal Type: Regional Districts
Incorporated: July 9, 1968; *Area:* 80,629.34 sq km
Population in 2011: 62,392
Federal Electoral District(s): Cariboo-Prince George; Port Moody-Coquitlam; Skeena-Bulkley Valley
Next Election: Oct. 20, 2018 (4-year terms)
Note: Member municipalities: 100 Mile House; Quesnel; Wells; Williams Lake.
Al Richmond, Chair
Janis Bell, Chief Administrative Officer
Alice Johnston, Corporate Officer
Scott Reid, Chief Financial Officer
Todd Conway, Chief Building Official
Mitch Minchau, Manager, Environmental Services
Karen Moores, Manager, Development Services
Darron Campbell, Manager, Community Services
Rowena Bastien, Manager, Protective Services

Central Coast
P.O. Box 186
626 Cliff St.
Bella Coola, BC V0T 1C0
Tel: 250-799-5291; *Fax:* 250-799-5750
info@ccrd-bc.ca
www.ccrd-bc.ca
Municipal Type: Regional Districts
Incorporated: July 16, 1968; *Area:* 24,556.35 sq km
Population in 2011: 3,206
Federal Electoral District(s): North Island-Powell River; Skeena-Bulkley Valley
Next Election: Oct. 20, 2018 (4-year terms)
Reginald Moody-Humchitt, Chair, 250-799-5291
Darla Blake, Chief Administrative Officer
Donna Mikkelson, Chief Financial Officer
Ken McIlwain, R.P.F., Manager, Public Works
Cheryl Waugh, Transportation & Land Use Coordinator, 250-799-5291

Central Kootenay
P.O. Box 590
202 Lakeside Dr.
Nelson, BC V1L 5R4
Tel: 250-352-6665; *Fax:* 250-352-9300
info@rdck.bc.ca
www.rdck.bc.ca
Other Information: Toll Free Phone: 1-800-268-7325
Municipal Type: Regional Districts
Incorporated: Nov. 30, 1965; *Area:* 22,130.72 sq km
Population in 2011: 58,441
Federal Electoral District(s): Kootenay-Columbia; North Okanagan-Shuswap; South Okanagan-West Kootenay
Next Election: Oct. 20, 2018 (4-year terms)
Note: Member municipalities: Castlegar; Creston; Kaslo; Nakusp; Nelson; New Denver; Salmo; Silverton; Slocan.
Karen Hamling, Chair, 250-265-3689
Stuart Horn, Chief Administrative Officer, 250-352-8184
Heather Smith, Chief Financial Officer, 250-352-8181
Lindsay Gaschnitz, Human Resources Technician, 250-352-1515
Joe Chirico, General Manager, Community Services, 250-352-8158
Anita Winje, General Manager, Administration, 250-352-8166
Uli Wolf, General Manager, Environmental Services, 250-352-8163
Sangita Sudan, General Manager, Development Services, 250-352-8157
David Oosthuizen, Manager, Information Technology Services, 250-352-8188

Central Okanagan
1450 KLO Rd.
Kelowna, BC V1W 3Z4
Tel: 250-763-4918; *Fax:* 250-763-0606
info@cord.bc.ca
www.cord.bc.ca
Municipal Type: Regional Districts
Incorporated: Aug. 24, 1967; *Area:* 2,904.01 sq km
Population in 2011: 179,839
Federal Electoral District(s): Central Okanagan-Similkameen-Nicola; Kelowna-Lake County
Next Election: Oct. 20, 2018 (4-year terms)
Note: Member municipalities: Kelowna; West Kelowna; Lake Country; Peachland.
Gail Given, Chair, 250-469-8677
Brian Reardon, Chief Administrative Officer
Marilyn Rilkoff, Director, Administration & Finance, 250-469-6242
Robert Fine, Director, Economic Development Commission, 250-469-6280
Peter Rotheisler, Manager, Environmental Services, 250-469-6250
Murray Kopp, Director, Parks Services
Dan Wildeman, Manager, Inspection & Fire Services, 250-469-6246, Fax: 250-762-7011
Ron Fralick, Manager, Planning, 250-469-6227, Fax: 250-470-7011

Columbia-Shuswap
P.O. Box 978
781 Marine Park Dr. NE
Salmon Arm, BC V1E 4P1
Tel: 250-832-8194; *Fax:* 250-832-3375
enquiries@csrd.bc.ca
www.csrd.bc.ca
Other Information: Toll Free Phone: 1-888-248-2773
Municipal Type: Regional Districts
Incorporated: Nov. 30, 1965; *Area:* 29,003.97 sq km
Population in 2011: 50,512
Federal Electoral District(s): Kootenay-Columbia; North Okanagan-Shuswap
Next Election: Oct. 20, 2018 (4-year terms)
Note: Member municipalities: Golden; Revelstoke; Sicamous; Salmon Arm.
Rhona Martin, Chair
Charles Hamilton, Chief Administrative Officer, 250-832-8194
Gerald Christie, Manager, Development Services, 250-833-5919
Gary Holte, Manager, Environment & Engineering Services, 250-833-5935
Jodi Kooistra, Manager, Financial Services, 250-833-5907
Kenn Mount, Co-ordinator, Fire Services, 250-833-5945
Hamish Kassa, Co-ordinator, Environment Services, 250-833-5942
Terry Langois, Co-ordinator, Water Systems, 250-833-5941
Ben Van Nostrand, Co-ordinator, Waste Management, 250-833-5940

Comox Valley
600 Comox Rd.
Courtenay, BC V9N 3P6
Tel: 250-334-6000; *Fax:* 250-334-4358
administration@comoxvalleyrd.ca
www.comoxvalleyrd.ca
Other Information: Toll Free Phone: 1-800-331-6007
Municipal Type: Regional Districts
Incorporated: Aug. 19, 1965; *Area:* 20,013.48 sq km
Population in 2011: 63,538
Federal Electoral District(s): Courtenay-Alberni; North Island-Powell River
Next Election: Oct. 20, 2018 (4-year terms)
Note: Member municipalities: Comox; Courtenay; Cumberland.
Bruce Jolliffe, Chair
Debra Oakman, Chief Administrative Officer
Beth Dunlop, Corporate Financial Officer
James Warren, Corporate Legislative Officer
Ian Smith, General Manager, Community Services
Ann MacDonald, General Manager, Planning & Development Services
Leigh Carter, General Manager, Public Affairs/Information Systems Branch
Julie Bradley, Executive Manager, Human Resources
Marc Rutten, General Manager, Engineering Services

Cowichan Valley
175 Ingram St.
Duncan, BC V9L 1N8
Tel: 250-746-2500
cvrd@cvrd.bc.ca
www.cvrd.bc.ca
Other Information: Toll Free Phone: 1-800-665-3955
Municipal Type: Regional Districts
Incorporated: Sept. 26, 1967; *Area:* 3,473.12 sq km
Population in 2011: 80,332
Federal Electoral District(s): Cowichan-Malahat-Langford; Nanaimo-Ladysmith
Next Election: Oct. 20, 2018 (4-year terms)
Note: Member municipalities: Duncan; Ladysmith; Lake Cowichan; North Cowichan.

Jon Lefebure, Chair
Brian Carruthers, Chief Administrative Officer, 250-746-2500
Mark Kueber, General Manager, Corporate Services, 250-746-2571
Hamid Hatami, General Manager, Engineering, 250-746-2538
John Elzinga, General Manager, Recreation & Culture, 250-746-0400
Ross Blackwell, General Manager, Planning & Development
Conrad Cowan, Manager, Public Safety, 250-746-2562

East Kootenay
19 - 24 Ave. South
Cranbrook, BC V1C 3H8
Tel: 250-489-2791; *Fax:* 250-489-3498
info@rdek.bc.ca
www.rdek.bc.ca
Other Information: Toll Free Phone: 1-888-478-7335
Municipal Type: Regional Districts
Incorporated: Nov. 30, 1965; *Area:* 27,560.49 sq km
Population in 2011: 56,685
Federal Electoral District(s): Kootenay-Columbia
Next Election: Oct. 20, 2018 (4-year terms)
Note: Member municipalities: Canal Flats; Cranbrook; Kimberley; Fernie; Sparwood; Elkford; Invermere; Radium Hot Springs.
Rob Gay, Chair
Lee-Ann Crane, Chief Administrative Officer
Shawn Tomlin, Chief Financial Officer
Sanford Brown, Manager, Building & Protective Services
Loree Duczek, Manager, Communications
Shannon Moskal, Corporate Officer
Brian Funke, Manager, Engineering Services
Kevin Paterson, Manager, Environmental Services
Lori Engler, Manager, Human Resources
Andrew McLeod, Manager, Planning & Development Services

Fraser Valley
#1, 45950 Cheam Ave.
Chilliwack, BC V2P 1N6
Tel: 604-702-5000; *Fax:* 604-792-9684
info@fvrd.bc.ca
www.fvrd.bc.ca
Other Information: Toll Free Phone: 1-800-528-0061
Municipal Type: Regional Districts
Incorporated: Dec. 12, 1995; *Area:* 13,361.74 sq km
Population in 2011: 277,593
Next Election: Oct. 20, 2018 (4-year terms)
Note: Member municipalities: Abbotsford; Chilliwack; Hope; Kent; Mission; Harrison Hot Springs.
Sharon Gaetz, Chair, 604-793-2900
Paul Gipps, Chief Administrative Officer, 604-702-5000
Mike Veenbaas, Chief Financial Officer & Manager, Financial Services
Jennifer Kinneman, Manager, Communications, 604-702-5056
Tareq Islam, Director, Engineering & Community Services
Janice Mikuska, Manager, Human Resources
Margaret Thornton, Director, Planning & Development

Fraser-Fort George
155 George St.
Prince George, BC V2L 1P8
Tel: 250-960-4400
district@rdffg.bc.ca
www.rdffg.bc.ca
Other Information: Toll Free Phone: 1-800-667-1959
Municipal Type: Regional Districts
Incorporated: March 8, 1967; *Area:* 50,705.84 sq km
Population in 2011: 91,879
Federal Electoral District(s): Cariboo-Prince George; Prince George-Peace River-Northern Rockies
Next Election: Oct. 20, 2018 (4-year terms)
Note: Member municipalities: McBride; Mackenzie; Prince George; Valemount.
Art Kaehn, Chair
Jim Martin, Chief Administrative Officer
Tery McEachen, General Manager, Development Services
Donna Munt, General Manager, Community Services
Petra Wildauer, General Manager, Environmental Services
Marie St. Laurent, Manager, Human Resources

Kitimat-Stikine
#300, 4545 Lazelle Ave.
Terrace, BC V8G 4E1
Tel: 250-615-6100; *Fax:* 250-635-9222
info@rdks.bc.ca
www.rdks.bc.ca
Other Information: Toll Free Phone: 1-800-663-3208
Municipal Type: Regional Districts
Incorporated: Sept. 14, 1967; *Area:* 91,917.88 sq km
Population in 2011: 37,361
Federal Electoral District(s): Skeena-Bulkley Valley
Next Election: Oct. 20, 2018 (4-year terms)
Note: Member municipalities: Kitimat; Terrace; Stewart; Hazelton; New Hazelton.
Stacey Tyers, Chair
Robert Marcellin, Administrator
Verna Wickie, Treasurer
Margaret Kujat, Coordinator, Environmental Services
Andrew Webber, Manager, Planning & Economic Development
Roger Tooms, Manager, Works & Services
Ted Pellegrino, Planner
Nick Redpath, Planner

Kootenay Boundary
#202, 843 Rossland Ave.
Trail, BC V1R 4S8
Tel: 250-368-9148; *Fax:* 250-368-3990
admin@rdkb.com
rdkb.com
Other Information: Toll Free Phone: 1-800-355-7352 (BC only)
Municipal Type: Regional Districts
Incorporated: Feb. 22, 1966; *Area:* 8,095.63 sq km
Population in 2011: 31,138
Federal Electoral District(s): South Okanagan-West Kootenay
Next Election: Oct. 20, 2018 (4-year terms)
Note: Member municipalities: Fruitvale; Grand Forks; Greenwood; Midway; Montrose; Rossland; Trail; Warfield.
Grace McGregor, Chair
John MacLean, Chief Administrative Officer
Mark Andison, General Manager, Operations
Beth Burget, General Manager, Finance
Al Stanley, General Manager, Environmental Services
Mark Daines, Director, Facilities and Recreation (Greater Trail)
Goran Denkovski, Manager, Infrastructure & Sustainability
Tom Sprado, Manager, Recreation and Facilities (Boundary and City of Grand Forks)
Tim Dueck, Coordinator, Solid Waste Management

Metro Vancouver
4330 Kingsway
Burnaby, BC V5H 4G8
Tel: 604-432-6200; *Fax:* 604-436-6901
icentre@metrovancouver.org
www.metrovancouver.org
Municipal Type: Regional Districts
Incorporated: June 29, 1967; *Area:* 2,877.36 sq km
Population in 2011: 2,313,328
Next Election: Oct. 20, 2018 (4-year terms)
Note: Member municipalities: Anmore; Belcarra; Bowen Island; Burnaby; Coquitlam; Delta; Langley; Lions Bay; New Westminster; North Vancouver; Pitt Meadows; Port Coquitlam; Port Moody; Richmond; Surrey; Vancouver; West Vancouver; White Rock
Greg Moore, Chair
Carol Mason, Chief Administrative Officer/Commissioner
Phil Trotzuk, Chief Financial Officer
Paul Henderson, General Manager, Solid Waste Services
Ralph Hildebrand, Solicitor & General Manager, Corporate Services
Tim Jervis, P.Eng., General Manager, Water Services
Allan Neilson, General Manager, Planning, Policy & Environment
Simon So, General Manager, Liquid Waste Services
Donna Brown, Senior Director, Human Resources
Chris Plagnol, Director, Board & Information Services
Heather Schoemaker, Director, External Relations

Mount Waddington
P.O. Box 729
2044 McNeill Rd.
Port McNeill, BC V0N 2R0
Tel: 250-956-3301; *Fax:* 250-956-3232
info@rdmw.bc.ca
www.rdmw.bc.ca
Other Information: Alternate Phone: 250-956-3161
Municipal Type: Regional Districts
Incorporated: June 13, 1966; *Area:* 20,288.19 sq km
Population in 2011: 11,506
Federal Electoral District(s): North Island-Powell River
Next Election: Oct. 20, 2018 (4-year terms)
Note: Member municipalities: Alert Bay; Port Alice; Port Hardy; Port McNeill.
Dave Rushton, Chair, 250-956-3301
Greg Fletcher, Administrator
Joe MacKenzie, Treasurer
Pat English, Manager, Economic Development/Parks
Patrick Donaghy, Manager, Operations
Jonas Velanskis, Manager, Planning

Nanaimo
6300 Hammond Bay Rd.
Nanaimo, BC V9T 6N2
Tel: 250-390-4111; *Fax:* 250-390-4163
corpsrv@rdn.bc.ca
www.rdn.bc.ca
Other Information: Toll Free Phone: 1-877-607-4111
Municipal Type: Regional Districts
Incorporated: Aug. 24, 1967; *Area:* 2,034.93 sq km
Population in 2011: 146,574
Federal Electoral District(s): Courtenay-Alberni; Nanaimo-Ladysmith
Next Election: Oct. 20, 2018 (4-year terms)
Note: Member municipalities: Nanaimo; Lantzville; Parksville; Qualicum Beach.
Joe Stanhope, Chair, 250-390-4111
Paul Thorkelsson, Chief Administrative Officer
Randy Alexander, General Manager, Regional & Community Utilities, 250-390-4111
Geoff Garbutt, General Manager, Strategic & Community Development, 250-390-4111
Tom Osborne, General Manager, Recreation & Parks, 250-390-4111
Dennis Trudeau, General Manager, Transportation & Solid Waste
Joan Harrison, Manager, Corporate Services

North Okanagan
9848 Aberdeen Rd.
Coldstream, BC V1B 2K9
Tel: 250-550-3700; *Fax:* 250-550-3701
info@nord.ca
www.nord.ca
Municipal Type: Regional Districts
Incorporated: Nov. 9, 1965; *Area:* 7,511.94 sq km
Population in 2011: 81,237
Federal Electoral District(s): North Okanagan-Shuswap
Next Election: Oct. 20, 2018 (4-year terms)
Note: Member municipalities: Enderby; Armstrong; Spallumcheen; Vernon; Coldstream; Lumby.
Rick Fairbairn, Chair
David Sewell, Chief Administrative Officer, 250-550-3760
Stephen Banmen, General Manager, Finance
Dale McTaggart, General Manager, Engineering, 250-550-3700
Leah Mellott, General Manager, Electoral Area Administration
Rob Smailes, General Manager, Planning & Building
Ron Baker, Manager, Community Protective Services
Nicole Kohnert, Regional Manager, Engineering Services, 250-550-3674
Dale Danallanko, Manager, Recycling & Disposal Facilities Operations, 250-550-3744

Northern Rockies
P.O. Box 399
5319 - 50th Ave. South
Fort Nelson, BC V0C 1R0
Tel: 250-774-2541; *Fax:* 250-774-6794
justask@northernrockies.ca
www.northernrockies.ca
Municipal Type: Regional Districts
Incorporated: Oct. 31, 1987; *Area:* 85,148.87 sq km
Population in 2011: 5,578
Federal Electoral District(s): Prince George-Peace River-Northern Rockies
Next Election: Oct. 20, 2018 (4-year terms)
Note: Member municipality: Fort Nelson.
Bill Streeper, Mayor, 250-774-6700
Randy McLean, Chief Administrative Officer, 250-774-2541
Scott Barry, Director, Public Works, 250-774-2541
Erin La Vale, Director, Human Resources, 250-774-2541
Jack Stevenson, Director, Community Development & Planning, 250-774-2541
Harvey Woodland, Director, Recreation, 250-774-2541
Toni Thurbide, Director, Finance, 250-774-2541
Terry Cavaliere, Chief Building Inspector, 250-774-2541
Jaylene Arnold, Economic Development & Tourism Officer, 250-774-2541

Okanagan-Similkameen
101 Martin St.
Penticton, BC V2A 5J9
Tel: 250-492-0237
info@rdos.bc.ca
www.rdos.bc.ca
Other Information: Toll Free Phone: 1-877-610-3737
Municipal Type: Regional Districts
Incorporated: March 4, 1966; *Area:* 10,412.64 sq km
Population in 2011: 80,742
Federal Electoral District(s): Central Okanagan-Similkameen-Nicola; South Okanagan-West Kootenay

Next Election: Oct. 20, 2018 (4-year terms)
Note: Member municipalities: Penticton; Summerland; Oliver; Osoyoos; Princeton; Keremeos.
Mark Pendergraft, Chair
Bill Newell, Chief Administrative Officer, 250-492-0237
Mark Woods, Manager, Community Services, 250-490-4132
Donna Butler, Manager, Development Services, 250-490-4109
Sandy Croteau, Manager, Finance, 250-490-4230
Marnie Manders, Manager, Human Resources, 250-490-4138
Tim Bouwmeester, Manager, Information Services
Doug French, P.Eng., Manager, Public Works, 250-490-4103

Peace River
P.O. Box 810
1981 Alaska Ave.
Dawson Creek, BC V1G 4H8
Tel: 250-784-3200; *Fax:* 250-784-3201
prrd.dc@prrd.bc.ca
prrd.bc.ca
Other Information: Toll-Free Phone: 1-800-670-7773
Municipal Type: Regional Districts
Incorporated: Oct. 31, 1987; *Area:* 117,761.07 sq km
Population in 2011: 60,082
Federal Electoral District(s): Prince George-Peace River-Northern Rockies
Next Election: Oct. 20, 2018 (4-year terms)
Note: Member municipalities: Dawson Creek; Fort St. John; Chetwynd; Hudson's Hope; Tumbler Ridge; Pouce Coupe; Taylor.
Lori Ackerman, Chair, 250-787-8160
Chris Cvik, Chief Administrative Officer
Kim French, Chief Financial Officer, 250-784-3221
Jo-Anne Frank, Corporate Officer
Bruce Simard, General Manager, Development Services, 250-784-3204
Jeff Rahn, General Manager, Environmental Services
Trish Morgan, Manager, Community Services, 250-784-3218

Powell River
5776 Marine Ave.
Powell River, BC V8A 2M4
Tel: 604-483-3231; *Fax:* 604-483-2229
administration@powellriverrd.bc.ca
www.powellriverrd.bc.ca
Municipal Type: Regional Districts
Incorporated: Dec. 19, 1967; *Area:* 5,092.05 sq km
Population in 2011: 19,906
Federal Electoral District(s): Courtenay-Alberni; North Island-Powell River
Next Election: Oct. 20, 2018 (4-year terms)
Note: Member municipality: Powell River.
Patrick Brabazon, Chair
Al Radke, Chief Administrative Officer
Mike Wall, Manager, Community Services
Linda Greenan, Manager, Financial Services
Ryan Thoms, Manager, Emergency Services
Laura Roddan, Manager, Planning Services

Skeena-Queen Charlotte
100 - 1st Ave. East
Prince Rupert, BC V8J 1A6
Tel: 250-624-2002; *Fax:* 250-627-8493
info@sqcrd.bc.ca
www.sqcrd.bc.ca
Other Information: Toll Free Phone: 1-888-301-2002
Municipal Type: Regional Districts
Incorporated: Aug. 17, 1967; *Area:* 19,871.85 sq km
Population in 2011: 18,784
Federal Electoral District(s): Skeena-Bulkley Valley
Next Election: Oct. 20, 2018 (4-year terms)
Note: Member municipalities: Prince Rupert; Port Edward; Queen Charlotte; Port Clemens; Masset.
Barry Pages, Chair, 250-626-3995, Fax: 250-626-5503
Karen Mellor, Chief Administrative Officer, 250-624-2002
Jennifer Robb, Treasurer, 250-624-2002

Squamish-Lillooet
P.O. Box 219
1350 Aster St.
Pemberton, BC V0N 2L0
Tel: 604-894-6371; *Fax:* 604-894-6526
info@slrd.bc.ca
www.slrd.bc.ca
Other Information: Toll Free Phone: 1-800-298-7753
Municipal Type: Regional Districts
Incorporated: Oct. 3, 1968; *Area:* 16,353.66 sq km
Population in 2011: 38,171
Federal Electoral District(s): West Vancouver-Sunshine Coast-Sea to Sky Country
Next Election: Oct. 20, 2018 (4-year terms)
Note: Member municipalities: Squamish; Whistler; Pemberton; Lillooet.
Jack Crompton, Chair, 604-932-5535
Lynda Flynn, Chief Administrative Officer, 604-894-6371
Peter DeJong, Director, Administrative Services, 604-894-6371
Suzanne Lafrance, Director, Finance, 604-894-6371
Angela Barth, Manager, Recreation Services, 604-894-2340
Janis Netzel, Director, Utilities & Environmental Services, 604-894-6371
Kim Needham, Director, Planning & Development Services, 604-894-6371

Strathcona
#301, 990 Cedar St.
Campbell River, BC V9W 7Z8
Tel: 250-830-6700; *Fax:* 250-830-6710
administration@strathconard.ca
www.strathconard.ca
Other Information: Toll Free Phone: 1-877-830-2990
Municipal Type: Regional Districts
Incorporated: Feb. 15, 2008; *Area:* 22,000 sq km
Population in 2011: 43,252
Federal Electoral District(s): Vancouver East
Next Election: Oct. 20, 2018 (4-year terms)
Note: Member municipalities: Campbell River; Gold River; Sayward; Tahsis; Zeballos.
Jim Abram, Chair, 250-830-6700
Russell Hotsenpiller, Chief Administrative Officer, 250-830-6703
Yves Bienvenu, Manager, Facilities, 250-287-9234
Ralda Hansen, Manager, Community Services, 250-830-6709
Dawn Christenson, Manager, Financial Services, 250-830-6705
Lorne Parker, Manager, Operations, 250-287-9234
Susan Bullock, Manager, Programs, 250-287-9234

Sunshine Coast
1975 Field Rd.
Sechelt, BC V0N 3A1
Tel: 604-885-6800; *Fax:* 604-885-7909
info@scrd.ca
www.scrd.ca
Other Information: Toll Free Phone: 1-800-687-5753
Municipal Type: Regional Districts
Incorporated: Jan. 4, 1967; *Area:* 3,778.08 sq km
Population in 2011: 28,619
Federal Electoral District(s): West Vancouver-Sunshine Coast-Sea to Sky Country
Next Election: Oct. 20, 2018 (4-year terms)
Note: Member municipalities: Sechelt; Gibsons.
Garry Nohr, Chair
John France, Chief Administrative Officer
Steve Olmstead, General Manager, Planning & Development
Bryan Shoji, General Manager, Infrastructure Services
Robyn Cooper, Manager, Waste Reduction & Recovery
Angie Legault, Manager, Legislative Services
Dave Crosby, Manager, Utility Services
Paul Preston, Chief Building Inspector
Gary Parker, Manager, Human Resources

Thompson-Nicola
#300, 465 Victoria St.
Kamloops, BC V2C 2A9
Tel: 250-377-8673; *Fax:* 250-372-5048
admin@tnrd.ca
www.tnrd.ca
Other Information: Toll Free Phone: 1-877-377-8673
Municipal Type: Regional Districts
Incorporated: Nov. 24, 1967; *Area:* 44,475.73 sq km
Population in 2011: 128,473
Federal Electoral District(s): Central Okanagan-Similkameen-Nicola; Kamloops-Thompson-Cariboo; Mission-Matsqui-Fraser Canyon; North Okanagan-Shuswap
Next Election: Oct. 20, 2018 (4-year terms)
Note: Member municipalities: Ashcroft; Barriere; Cache Creek; Chase; Clearwater; Clinton; Kamloops; Logan Lake; Lytton; Merritt; Sun Peaks.
John Ranta, Chair
Sukhbinder Gill, Chief Administrative Officer, 250-377-8673
Victoria Weller, Film Commissioner, 250-377-7058
Ron Storie, Director, Community Services, 250-377-8673
Regina Sadilkova, Director, Development Services, 250-377-7060
Peter Hughes, Director, Environmental Services
Doug Rae, Director, Finance, 250-378-7050
Marc Saunders, Director, Libraries, 250-377-8673
Ron Popoff, Manager, Building Inspection Services, 250-377-7062
Jamie Viera, Manager, Environmental Health Services, 250-377-7197
Debbie Sell, Manager, Human Resources, 250-377-8673
Arden Bolton, Manager, Utility Services, 250-377-7056

Major Municipalities in British Columbia

Abbotsford
32315 South Fraser Way
Abbotsford, BC V2T 1W7
Tel: 604-853-2281; *Fax:* 604-853-1934
info@abbotsford.ca
www.abbotsford.ca
Other Information: Toll Free Phone: 1-866-853-2281
Municipal Type: City
Incorporated: Jan. 1, 1995; *Area:* 359.36 sq km
County or District: Fraser Valley; *Population in 2011:* 133,497
Provincial Electoral District(s): Abbotsford-Mission; Abbotsford South; Abbotsford West
Federal Electoral District(s): Abbotsford; Langley-Aldergrove; Mission-Matsqui-Fraser Canyon
Next Election: Oct. 20, 2018 (4-year terms)
Henry Braun, Mayor, 604-864-5500, Fax: 604-853-1934
Les Barkman, Councillor
Sandy Blue, Councillor
Kelly Chahal, Councillor
Brenda Falk, Councillor
Moe Gill, Councillor
Dave Loewengor, Councillor
Patricia Ross, Councillor
Ross Siemens, Councillor
Bill Flitton, City Clerk, 604-864-5603
George Murray, City Manager, 604-864-5584
Susan Bahry, Director, Human Resources, 604-864-5504
Patricia Soanes, General Manager, Finance & Corporate Services, 604-864-5524, Fax: 604-853-7968
Karen Treloar, Director, Communications & Marketing, 604-557-4421
Don Beer, Fire Chief, 604-853-3566
Bob Rich, Chief Constable, Abbotsford Police Department, 604-859-5225, Fax: 604-859-4812

Burnaby
4949 Canada Way
Burnaby, BC V5G 1M2
Tel: 604-294-7944
postmaster@burnaby.ca
www.city.burnaby.bc.ca
Municipal Type: City
Incorporated: Sept. 22, 1892; *Area:* 89.12 sq km
County or District: Metro Vancouver; *Population in 2011:* 223,218
Provincial Electoral District(s): Burnaby-Edmonds; Burnaby North; Burnaby-Willingdon
Federal Electoral District(s): Burnaby North-Seymour; Burnaby South; New Westminster-Burnaby
Next Election: Oct. 20, 2018 (4-year terms)
Derek Corrigan, Mayor, 604-294-7340
Pietro Calendino, Councillor, 604-614-7379
James Wang, Councillor
Sav Dhaliwal, Councillor, 604-420-8188, Fax: 604-420-8133
Dan Johnston, Councillor, 778-228-6714
Colleen Jordan, Councillor, 604-970-8117
Anne Kang, Councillor, 604-346-6732, Fax: 604-439-1576
Paul McDonell, Councillor
Nick Volkow, Councillor, 778-228-6713, Fax: 604-437-1169
Dennis Black, City Clerk, 604-294-7290, Fax: 604-294-7537
Lambert Chu, City Manager, 604-294-7101
Chad Turpin, Deputy City Manager
Leon Gous, Director, Engineering
Dave Ellenwood, Director, Parks, Recreation & Cultural Services
Denise Jorgeonson, Director, Finance
Lou Pelletier, Director, Planning & Building
Pat Tennant, Director, Human Resources
Joe Robertson, Fire Chief

Campbell River
301 St. Ann's Rd.
Campbell River, BC V9W 4C7
Tel: 250-286-5700
info@campbellriver.ca
www.campbellriver.ca
Municipal Type: City
Incorporated: June 24, 1947; *Area:* 143.48 sq km
County or District: Strathcona; *Population in 2011:* 31,186
Provincial Electoral District(s): North Island
Federal Electoral District(s): North Island-Powell River
Next Election: Oct. 20, 2018 (4-year terms)
Andy Adams, Mayor, 250-286-5708
Michele Babchuk, Councillor
Charlie Cornfield, Councillor
Colleen Evans, Councillor
Ron Kerr, Councillor
Larry Samson, Councillor
Marlene Wright, Councillor
Peter Wipper, City Clerk, 250-286-5707

Deborah Sargent, City Manager, 250-286-5740
Ron Bowles, General Manager, Corporate Services
Ross Milnthorp, General Manager, Parks, Recreation & Culture
Dave Morris, General Manager, Facilities & Supply Management
Elle Brovold, Manager, Facilities - Property
Tyler Massee, Manager, Airport
Drew Hadfield, Manager, Transportation, 250-286-5783
Jason Hartley, Manager, Capital Works, 250-286-5790
Warren Kalyn, Manager, Information Services, 250-286-5716
Jennifer Peters, Manager, Utilities, 250-286-5730
Myriah Foort, Manager, Finance
Amber Zirnhelt, Manager, Long Range Planning/Sustainability, 250-286-5742
Carrie Jacobs, RCMP Municipal Manager, 250-286-5611
Ian Baikie, Fire Chief, 250-286-6266

Chilliwack

8550 Young Rd
Chilliwack, BC V2P 8A4
Tel: 604-792-9311; *Fax:* 604-795-8443
info@chilliwack.com
www.chilliwack.com
Municipal Type: City
Incorporated: Jan. 1, 1980; *Area:* 260.19 sq km
County or District: Fraser Valley; *Population in 2011:* 77,936
Provincial Electoral District(s): Chilliwack-Kent, Chilliwack-Sumas
Federal Electoral District(s): Chilliwack-Hope
Next Election: Oct. 20, 2018 (4-year terms)
Sharon Gaetz, Mayor, 604-793-2900, Fax: 604-792-2561
Sue Attrill, Councillor
Chris Kloot, Councillor
Jason Lum, Councillor
Ken Popove, Councillor
Chuck Stam, Councillor
Sam Waddington, Councillor
Peter Monteith, Chief Administrative Officer, 604-793-2903, Fax: 604-792-2561
Heahter Vegh, Manager, Human Resources, 604-793-2752, Fax: 604-793-2715
Tara Friesen, Manager, Environmental Services, 604-792-2907
Erik Leidekker, Manager, Information Technology, 604-793-2912, Fax: 604-793-1812
Ryan Mulligan, Manager, Civic Facilities, 604-793-2704, Fax: 604-792-2583
Karen Stanton, Manager, Long Range Planning, 604-793-2906
Gillian Villeneuve, Manager, Development Planning, 604-793-2779
Holly Vokey, Manager, Purchasing, 604-793-2819, Fax: 604-795-2963
Glen Savard, Director, Finance, 604-793-2738, Fax: 604-793-6047
Robert Carnegie, Director, Corporate Services, 604-793-2986, Fax: 604-793-2715
David Blain, Director, Planning & Engineering, 604-793-2907, Fax: 604-793-2285
Glen MacPherson, Director, Operations, 604-793-2810, Fax: 604-793-2997
Ryan Mulligan, Director, Recreation & Culture, 604-793-2904, Fax: 604-793-8443
Ian Josephson, Fire Chief, 604-792-8713, Fax: 604-702-5087

Colwood

3300 Wishart Rd.
Victoria, BC V9C 1R1
Tel: 250-478-5541; *Fax:* 250-478-7516
generalinquiry@colwood.ca
colwood.ca
Municipal Type: City
Incorporated: June 24, 1985; *Area:* 17.76 sq km
County or District: Capital; *Population in 2011:* 16,093
Provincial Electoral District(s): Esquimalt-Metchosin
Federal Electoral District(s): Esquimalt-Saanich-Sooke
Next Election: Oct. 20, 2018 (4-year terms)
Carol Hamilton, Mayor
Lilja Chong, Councillor, 250-478-5999
Cynthia Day, Councillor, 250-478-5999
Gordie Logan, Councillor, 250-478-5999
Rob Martin, Councillor, 250-478-5999
Jason Nault, Councillor, 250-478-5999
Terry Trace, Councillor, 250-478-5999
Ian Howat, Chief Administrative Officer, 250-478-5999
Ross Myles, Acting Manager, Public Works, 250-474-4133, Fax: 250-474-6977
Michael Baxter, Director, Engineering
Iain Bourhill, Director, Planning, 250-478-5999
Andrea deBucy, Acting Director, Finance, 250-478-5999
Kerry Smith, Fire Chief, 250-478-8321, Fax: 250-478-8032

Comox

Town Hall
1809 Beaufort Ave.
Comox, BC V9M 1R9
Tel: 250-339-2202; *Fax:* 250-339-7110
town@comox.ca
www.comox.ca
Municipal Type: City
Incorporated: Jan. 14, 1946; *Area:* 15.16 sq km
County or District: Comox Valley; *Population in 2011:* 13,627
Provincial Electoral District(s): Comox Valley
Federal Electoral District(s): North Island-Powell River
Next Election: Oct. 20, 2018 (4-year terms)
Paul Ives, Mayor, 250-339-9109
Russ John Arnott, Councillor, 250-218-2001
Marg Grant, Councillor, 250-941-1128
Ken Grant, Councillor, 250-339-2202
Hugh MacKinnon, Councillor, 250-339-0661
Barbara Price, Councillor, 250-339-4037
Maureen Swift, Councillor, 250-339-1211
Richard Kanigan, Chief Administrative Officer
Donald Jacquest, Director, Finance
Mandy Johns, Director, Recreation, 250-339-2255
Allan Fraser, Superintendent, Parks, 250-339-2421
Glenn Westendorp, Superintendent, Public Works, 250-339-5410, Fax: 250-890-0698
Marvin Kamenz, Municipal Planner, 250-339-1118
Gord Schreiner, Fire Chief, 250-339-2432, Fax: 250-339-1988

Coquitlam

3000 Guildford Way
Coquitlam, BC V3B 7N2
Tel: 604-927-3000
feedback@coquitlam.ca
www.coquitlam.ca
Municipal Type: City
Incorporated: July 25, 1891; *Area:* 121.69 sq km
County or District: Metro Vancouver; *Population in 2011:* 126,456
Provincial Electoral District(s): Coquitlam-Maillardville
Federal Electoral District(s): Coquitlam-Port Coquitlam; Port Moody-Coquitlam
Next Election: Oct. 20, 2018 (4-year terms)
Richard Stewart, Mayor, 604-927-3001
Brent Asmundson, Councillor, 604-616-6331
Craig Hodge, Councillor, 604-657-7309
Dennis Marsden, Councillor, 604-306-0686
Terry O'Neil, Councillor
Mae Reid, Councillor, 604-464-0414
Teri Towner, Councillor, 604-617-6042
Chris Wilson, Councillor, 604-927-3000
Bonita Zarrillo, Councillor, 604-927-3000
Jay Gilbert, City Clerk, 604-927-3013
Peter Steblin, City Manager, 604-927-3006
Sheena Macleod, Treasurer & Manager, Financial Services, 604-927-3031
Raul Allueva, General Manager, Parks, Recreation & Culture Services, 604-927-3538
Jim McIntyre, General Manager, Planning & Development, 604-927-3400, Fax: 604-927-3405
Jozsef Dioszeghy, General Manager, Engineering & Public Works, 604-927-3504, Fax: 604-927-3505
Heather Bradfield, Director, Legal & Bylaw Services, 604-927-3097
Deana Trudeau, Manager, Purchasing, 604-927-3034, Fax: 604-927-3015
Ron Price, Director, Human Resources, 604-927-3072

Courtenay

830 Cliffe Ave.
Courtenay, BC V9N 2J7
Tel: 250-334-4441; *Fax:* 250-334-4241
info@courtenay.ca
www.courtenay.ca
Municipal Type: City
Incorporated: Jan. 1, 1915; *Area:* 26.68 sq km
County or District: Comox Valley; *Population in 2011:* 24,099
Provincial Electoral District(s): Comox Valley
Federal Electoral District(s): Courtenay-Alberni; North Island-Powell River
Next Election: Oct. 20, 2018 (4-year terms)
Larry Jangula, Mayor, 250-703-4842, Fax: 250-334-4241
Erik Eriksson, Councillor, 250-218-0568
David Frisch, Councillor, 250-338-3638
Doug Hillan, Councillor, 250-334-0693
Rebecca Lennox, Councillor, 250-650-5582
Manno Theos, Councillor, 250-792-5884
Bob Wells, Councillor, 250-792-1945
David Allen, Chief Administrative Officer, 250-703-4854
Peter Crawford, Director, Development Services
Lesley Hatch, Director, Engineering & Public Works
Tillie Manthey, Director, Financial Services
Mickie Donley, Manager, Human Resources
Bernd Guderjahn, Manager, Purchasing
Randy Wiwchar, Director, Community Services

Cranbrook

40 - 10th Ave. South
Cranbrook, BC V1C 2M8
Tel: 250-426-4211; *Fax:* 250-426-4026
info@cranbrook.ca
www.cranbrook.ca
Other Information: Toll Free Phone: 1-800-728-2726
Municipal Type: City
Incorporated: Nov. 1, 1905; *Area:* 25.14 sq km
County or District: East Kootenay; *Population in 2011:* 19,319
Provincial Electoral District(s): East Kootenay
Federal Electoral District(s): Kootenay-Columbia
Next Election: Oct. 20, 2018 (4-year terms)
Lee Pratt, Mayor, 250-489-0200
Norma Blissett, Councillor, 250-426-4211
Danielle Cardozo, Councillor, 250-426-4211
Wesly Graham, Councillor, 250-426-4211
Isaac Hockley, Councillor, 250-426-4211
Ron Popoff, Councillor, 250-426-4211
Tom Shypitka, Councillor, 250-426-4211
Marnie Dueck, Municipal Clerk/Acting Director, Corporate Services
David Kim, Chief Administrative Officer
Maryse Leroux, Director, Corporate Services
Chris New, Director, Leisure Services
Wayne Price, Director, Fire & Emergency Services
Eric Sharpe, Director, Engineering & Development Services
Chris Zettel, Corporate Communications Officer
Drew Miller, Manager, Human Resources
Wayne Price, Director, Fire & Emergency Services

Dawson Creek

P.O. Box 150
10105 - 12A St.
Dawson Creek, BC V1G 4G4
Tel: 250-784-3600; *Fax:* 250-782-3203
admin@dawsoncreek.ca
www.dawsoncreek.ca
Other Information: General Fax: 250-782-3352
Municipal Type: City
Incorporated: May 26, 1936; *Area:* 22.32 sq km
County or District: Peace River; *Population in 2011:* 11,583
Provincial Electoral District(s): Peace River South
Federal Electoral District(s): Prince George-Peace River-Northern Rockies
Next Election: Oct. 20, 2018 (4-year terms)
Dale Bumstead, Mayor, 250-784-3616, Fax: 250-782-3203
Paul Gevatkoff, Councillor, 250-782-8792
Terry McFadyen, Councillor, 250-782-2237
Charlie Parslow, Councillor, 250-782-1783
Mark Rogers, Councillor, 250-784-4376
Cheryl Shuman, Councillor, 250-782-5323
Shaely Wilbur, Councillor, 250-719-9492
Jim Chute, Chief Administrative Officer, 250-784-3613, Fax: 250-782-3203
Shelly Woolf, Chief Financial Officer, 250-784-3611
Shawn Dahlen, Director, Infrastructure, 250-784-3624
Kara Armitage, Manager, Purchasing, 250-784-3607
Barry Reynard, Director, Community Services, 250-784-3605
Brenda Ginter, Director, Corporate Administration, 250-784-3614
Kevin Henderson, Director, Development Services, 250-784-3622
Gordon Smith, Fire Chief, 250-784-3635

Fort St. John

10631 - 100 St.
Fort St John, BC V1J 3Z5
Tel: 250-787-8150; *Fax:* 250-787-8181
info@fortstjohn.ca
www.fortstjohn.ca
Municipal Type: City
Incorporated: Dec. 31, 1947; *Area:* 22.74 sq km
County or District: Peace River; *Population in 2011:* 18,609
Provincial Electoral District(s): Peace River North
Federal Electoral District(s): Prince George-Peace River-Northern Rockies
Next Election: Oct. 20, 2018 (4-year terms)
Lori Ackerman, Mayor, 250-787-8160
Trevor Bolin, Councillor, 250-262-7334
Bruce Christensen, Councillor, 250-787-2202
Dan Davies, Councillor, 250-787-5847
Larry Evans, Councillor, 250-785-2416
Gord Klassen, Councillor
Bryon Stewart, Councillor
Dianne Hunter, City Manager, 250-787-8150
Wally Ferris, General Manager, Community Services
Victor Shopland, General Manager, Integrated Services
Mindy Smith, General Manager, Corporate Services

Mike Roy, Director, Finance & Corporate Services
Janet Prestley, Director, Legislative & Administrative Services
Fred Burrows, Fire Chief

Kamloops

City Hall
7 Victoria St. West
Kamloops, BC V2C 1A2
Tel: 250-828-3311
info@kamloops.ca
www.kamloops.ca
Municipal Type: City
Incorporated: Oct. 17, 1967; *Area:* 297.3 sq km
County or District: Thompson-Nicola; *Population in 2011:* 85,678
Provincial Electoral District(s): Kamloops; Kamloops-North Thompson
Federal Electoral District(s): Kamloops-Thompson-Cariboo
Next Election: Oct. 20, 2018 (4-year terms)
Peter Milobar, Mayor, 250-828-3495
Donovan Cavers, Councillor, 250-828-3311
Ken Christian, Councillor, 250-828-1030
Deiter Dudy, Councillor, 250-828-3311
Tina Lange, Councillor, 250-372-0902
Arjun Singh, Councillor, 250-828-3311
Marg Spina, Councillor, 250-372-0440
Pat Wallace, Councillor, 778-470-8332
Denis Walsh, Councillor, 250-828-3311
David Trawin, Chief Administrative Officer, 250-828-3498
David Duckworth, Director, Community Safety & Corporate Services, 250-828-3484
Jen Fretz, Director, Public Works & Utilities
Marvin Kwiatkowski, Director, Development & Engineering Services
Byron McCorkell, Director, Parks, Recreation & Culture, 250-828-3580
Lori Rilkoff, Director, Human Resources
W. Dale Maclean, Fire Chief, 250-372-5131

Kelowna

City Hall
1435 Water St.
Kelowna, BC V1Y 1J4
Tel: 250-469-8500; *Fax:* 250-862-3399
ask@kelowna.ca
www.kelowna.ca
Municipal Type: City
Incorporated: May 4, 1905; *Area:* 211.69 sq km
County or District: Central Okanagan; *Population in 2011:* 117,312
Provincial Electoral District(s): Kelowna-Mission; Kelowna-Lake Country; Westside-Kelowna
Federal Electoral District(s): Central Okanagan-Similkameen-Nicola; Kelowna-Lake Country
Next Election: Oct. 20, 2018 (4-year terms)
Colin Basran, Mayor, 250-469-8980
Maxine DeHart, Councillor
Ryan Donn, Councillor
Gail Given, Councillor
Tracy Gray, Councillor
Charlie Hodge, Councillor
Brad Sieben, Councillor
Mohini Singh, Councillor
Luke Stack, Councillor
Stephen Fleming, City Clerk, 250-469-8660
Ron Mattiussi, City Manager, 250-469-8901
Joe Creron, Divisional Director, Civic Operations
Jim Paterson, Divisional Director, Active Living & Culture
Doug Gilchrist, Divisional Director, Community Planning & Real Estate
Stu Leatherdale, Divisional Director, Human Resources & Corporate Performance
Rob Mayne, Divisional Director, Corporate and Protective Services
Mo Bayat, Director, Development Services
Shelley Gambacort, Director, Subdivision, Agriculture & Environment
Genelle Davidson, Director, Financial Services
Ian Wilson, Manager, Parks Services
Jeff Carlisle, Fire Chief

Langford

877 Goldstream Ave., 2nd Fl.
Victoria, BC V9B 2X8
Tel: 250-478-7882
www.cityoflangford.ca
Municipal Type: City
Incorporated: Dec. 8, 1992; *Area:* 39.55 sq km
County or District: Capital; *Population in 2011:* 29,228
Provincial Electoral District(s): Malahat-Juan de Fuca
Federal Electoral District(s): Cowichan-Malahat-Langford
Next Election: Oct. 20, 2018 (4-year terms)
Stewart Young, Mayor
Denise Blackwell, Councillor
Matthew Sahlstrom, Councillor
Lanny Seaton, Councillor
Winnie Sifert, Councillor
Lillian Szpak, Councillor
Roger Wade, Councillor
Lindy Kaercher, Deputy Clerk
Jim Bowden, Administrator
Michelle Mahovlich, Director, Engineering
Matthew Baldwin, City Planner

Langley

20399 Douglas Cres.
Langley, BC V3A 4B3
Tel: 604-514-2800; *Fax:* 604-530-4371
info@langleycity.ca
www.city.langley.bc.ca
Municipal Type: City
Incorporated: March 15, 1955; *Area:* 10.22 sq km
County or District: Metro Vancouver; *Population in 2011:* 25,081
Provincial Electoral District(s): Langley
Federal Electoral District(s): Cloverdale-Langley City; Langley-Aldergrove
Next Election: Oct. 20, 2018 (4-year terms)
Ted Schaffer, Mayor, 604-514-2800
Paul Albrecht, Councillor
Jack Arnold, Councillor
Dave Hall, Councillor
Gayle Martin, Councillor
Rudy Storteboom, Councillor
Val van den Broek, Councillor
Francis Cheung, Chief Administrative Officer

Nanaimo

455 Wallace St.
Nanaimo, BC V9R 5J6
Tel: 250-754-4251
legislativeservices.office@nanaimo.ca
www.nanaimo.ca
Municipal Type: City
Incorporated: Dec. 24, 1874; *Area:* 89.3 sq km
County or District: Nanaimo; *Population in 2011:* 83,810
Provincial Electoral District(s): Nanaimo-Parksville; Nanaimo
Federal Electoral District(s): Courtenay-Alberni; Nanaimo-Ladysmith
Next Election: Oct. 20, 2018 (4-year terms)
Bill McKay, Mayor, 250-755-4400
Bill Bestwick, Councillor
Diane Brennan, Councillor
Gordon Fuller, Councillor
Jerry Hong, Councillor
Jim Kipp, Councillor
Wendy Pratt, Councillor
Ian Thorpe, Councillor
Bill Yoachim, Councillor
Tracy Samra, Chief Administrative Officer, 250-755-4401
Ian Howat, General Manager, Corporate Services, 250-755-4502
Tom Hickey, General Manager, Community Services, 250-756-5346
Suzanne Samborski, Senior Manager, Culture & Heritage, 250-755-7518
Brian Clemens, Director, Finance, 250-755-4431
Guillermo Ferrero, Director, Information Technology & Legislative Services, 250-755-4423
Geoff Goodall, Director, Engineering & Public Works, 250-754-4251
Richard Harding, Director, Parks, Recreation & Environment, 250-755-7516
Terry Hartley, Director, HR & Organizational Planning, 250-755-4427
Dale Lindsay, Director, Community Development, 250-755-4493
Toby Seward, Director, Social & Protective Services, 250-755-4424
John Elliot, Manager, Utilities
Kurtis Felker, Manager, Purchasing & Stores
Gary Franssen, Manager, Sanitation, Recycling, Cemeteries, 250-756-5307
Bruce Labelle, Manager, Fleet
Mark Fisher, Superintendent & Officer-in-Charge, Nanaimo RCMP Detachment, 250-755-3230
Craig Richardson, Fire Chief, 250-755-4557

Nelson

#101, 310 Ward St.
Nelson, BC V1L 5S4
Tel: 250-352-5511; *Fax:* 250-352-2131
www.nelson.ca
Municipal Type: City
Incorporated: March 18, 1897; *Area:* 11.72 sq km
County or District: Central Kootenay; *Population in 2011:* 10,230
Provincial Electoral District(s): Nelson-Creston
Federal Electoral District(s): Kootenay-Columbia
Next Election: Oct. 20, 2018 (4-year terms)
Debra Kozak, Mayor, 250-352-5511
Bob Adams, Councillor, 250-352-5511
Robin Cherbo, Councillor
Michael Dailly, Councillor
Janice Morrison, Councillor
Anna Purcell, Councillor
Valerie Warmington, Councillor
Kevin Cormack, City Manager, 250-352-8203
Colin McClure, Chief Financial Officer, 250-352-8235
Colin Innes, Director, Public Works & Utilities, 250-352-8107
Frances Director, Director, Corporate Services, 250-352-8254
Pam Mierau, Manager, Development Services, 250-352-8217
Len MacCharles, Fire Chief, 250-352-8264
Wayne Holland, Police Chief, 250-354-3919

New Westminster

511 Royal Ave.
New Westminster, BC V3L 1H9
Tel: 604-521-3711; *Fax:* 604-521-3895
postmaster@newwestcity.ca
www.newwestcity.ca
Municipal Type: City
Incorporated: July 16, 1860; *Area:* 15.41 sq km
County or District: Metro Vancouver; *Population in 2011:* 65,976
Provincial Electoral District(s): New Westminster
Federal Electoral District(s): New Westminster-Burnaby
Next Election: Oct. 20, 2018 (4-year terms)
Jonathan Cote, Mayor, 604-527-4523
Bill Harper, Councillor, 604-527-4523
Patrick M. Johnstone, Councillor
Jamie McEvoy, Councillor, 604-522-9114
Betty McIntosh, Councillor, 778-773-0546
Chuck Puchmayr, Councillor
Mary F. Trentadue, Councillor
Lorrie Williams, Councillor
Lisa Spitale, Chief Administrative Officer
Rod Carle, General Manager, Electric Utility
Joan Burgess, Director, Human Resources
Dean Gibson, Director, Parks, Culture & Recreation
Gary Holowatiuk, Director, Finance & Information Technology
Jim Lowrie, Director, Engineering Services
Jan Gibson, Acting Director, Legislative Services
Beverly Grieve, Director, Development Services
Roy Moulder, Manager, Purchasing
Dave Jones, Police Chief, Police Services
Tim Armstrong, Fire Chief, Fire & Rescue Services

North Vancouver

141 - 14 St. West
North Vancouver, BC V7M 1H9
Tel: 604-985-7761; *Fax:* 604-985-9417
info@cnv.org
www.cnv.org
Municipal Type: City
Incorporated: May 13, 1907; *Area:* 11.85 sq km
County or District: Metro Vancouver; *Population in 2011:* 48,196
Provincial Electoral District(s): N. Vancouver-Lonsdale; N. Vancouver-Seymour; W. Vancouver-Capilano; W. Vancouver-Garibaldi
Federal Electoral District(s): North Vancouver; Burnaby North-Seymour
Next Election: Oct. 20, 2018 (4-year terms)
Darrell R. Mussatto, Mayor, 604-998-3280
Holly Janet Back, Councillor
Don Bell, Councillor
Pam Bookham, Councillor
Linda Buchanan, Councillor
Rod Clark, Councillor
Craig Keating, Councillor, Fax: 604-904-7968
Karla Graham, City Clerk, 604-990-4233, Fax: 604-990-4202
Ken Tollstam, Chief Administrative Officer, 604-990-4243, Fax: 604-985-5971
Susan Ney, Director, Human Resources, 604-983-7364
Barbara Pearce, Director, Special Projects, 604-982-3962
Gary Penway, Director, Community Development, 604-983-7382
Ben Themens, Director, Finance, 604-983-7312
Heather Turner, Director, Recreation, 604-983-6309
Brent Mahood, Manager, Operations, 604-983-7388
Connie Rabold, Manager, Communications, 604-983-7383
Doug Pope, City Engineer, 604-983-7337
Richard Charlton, Manager, Public Works, 604-983-7391
Dan Pistilli, Fire Chief, 604-904-5203

Parksville

P.O. Box 1390
100 Jensen Ave. East
Parksville, BC V9P 2H3
Tel: 250-248-6144; *Fax:* 250-248-6650
info@parksville.ca
www.parksville.ca

Municipal Type: City
Incorporated: June 19, 1945; *Area:* 14.6 sq km
County or District: Nanaimo; *Population in 2011:* 11,977
Provincial Electoral District(s): Nanaimo-Parksville
Federal Electoral District(s): Courtenay-Alberni
Next Election: Oct. 20, 2018 (4-year terms)
Marc Lefebvre, Mayor, 250-954-4661
Mary Beil, Councillor, 250-927-4097
Al Greir, Councillor, 250-248-6144
Kirkr Oates, Councillor, 250-802-2059
Teresa Patterson, Councillor
Sue E. Powell, Councillor, 250-951-1082
Leanne Salter, Councillor
Debbie Comis, Chief Administrative Officer, 250-954-3068
Lucy Butterworth, Director, Finance, 250-954-3063
Keeva Kehler, Director, Administrative Services, 250-954-4660
Vaughan Figueira, Director, Engineering, 250-951-2474
Shannon Kleibl, Director, Human Resources, 250-954-4663
Blaine Russell, Director, Community Planning, 250-954-4673
Marc Norris, Fire Chief, 250-954-4695

Penticton
171 Main St.
Penticton, BC V2A 5A9
Tel: 250-490-2400; *Fax:* 250-490-2402
ask@penticton.ca
www.penticton.ca
Municipal Type: City
Incorporated: Jan. 1, 1909; *Area:* 42.02 sq km
County or District: Okanagan-Similkameen; *Population in 2011:* 32,877
Provincial Electoral District(s): Penticton-Okanagan Valley
Federal Electoral District(s): South Okanagan-West Kootenay
Next Election: Oct. 20, 2018 (4-year terms)
Andrew Jakubeit, Mayor, 250-490-2403
Helena Konanz, Councillor
Andre Martin, Councillor
Max Picton, Councillor
Tarik Sayeed, Councillor
Judy Sentes, Councillor
Campbell Watt, Councillor
Eric Sorensen, Chief Administrative Officer, 250-490-2407
Colin Fisher, Chief Financial Officer, 250-490-2480
Lori Mullin, General Manager, Recreation & Culture, 250-490-2432
Cathy Ingram, Manager, Purchasing, 250-490-2555
Gillian Kenny, Manager, Human Resources, 250-490-2470
Len Robson, Manager, Public Works, 250-490-2500
Mitch Moroziuk, Director, Infrastructure, 250-490-2515
Larry Watkinson, Fire Chief, 250-490-2309

Pitt Meadows
Municipal Hall
12007 Harris Rd.
Pitt Meadows, BC V3Y 2B5
Tel: 604-465-5454; *Fax:* 604-465-2404
info@pittmeadows.bc.ca
www.pittmeadows.bc.ca
Municipal Type: City
Incorporated: April 25, 1914; *Area:* 85.38 sq km
County or District: Metro Vancouver; *Population in 2011:* 17,736
Provincial Electoral District(s): Maple Ridge-Pitt Meadows
Federal Electoral District(s): Pitt Meadows-Maple Ridge
Next Election: Oct. 20, 2018 (4-year terms)
Note: Effective Jan. 1, 2007, Pitt Meadows' designation was changed from a district to a city.
John Becker, Mayor, 604-465-2416
Bruce Bell, Councillor
Bill Dingwall, Councillor
Janis Elkerton, Councillor
Tracy Miyashita, Councillor
David Murray, Councillor
Mike Stark, Councillor
Mark Roberts, Chief Administrative Officer, 604-465-2449
Kelly Swift, General Manager, Community Development, Parks & Leisure Services, 604-467-7337
Don Jolley, Fire Chief, 604-465-2401
Lorna Jones, Director, Human Resources, Communications & IT, 604-465-2448
Mark Roberts, Director, Financial Services
Kate Zanon, Director, Operations & Development Services, 604-465-2420

Port Alberni
4850 Argyle St.
Port Alberni, BC V9Y 1V8
Tel: 250-723-2146; *Fax:* 250-723-1003
citypa@portalberni.ca
www.portalberni.ca
Municipal Type: City
Incorporated: Oct. 28, 1967; *Area:* 19.92 sq km
County or District: Alberni-Clayoquot; *Population in 2011:* 17,743
Provincial Electoral District(s): Alberni-Qualicum
Federal Electoral District(s): Courtenay-Alberni
Next Election: Oct. 20, 2018 (4-year terms)
Mike Ruttan, Mayor
Chris Alemany, Councillor
Jack McLeman, Councillor
Sharie Minions, Councillor
Ron Paulson, Councillor
Denis Sauve, Councillor
Dan Washington, Councillor
Davina Sparrow, City Clerk, 250-720-2810
Tim Pley, Fire Chief & Acting City Manager, 250-720-2824
Jacob Colbyn, Supervisor, Horticulture & Parks Operations, 250-720-2516
Wilf Taekema, Manager, Public Works & Infrastructure Operations, 250-720-2845
Cathy Rothwell, Director, Finance, 250-720-2821
Guy Cicon, City Engineer, 250-720-2838
Scott Smith, City Planner, 250-720-2808

Port Coquitlam
2580 Shaughnessy St.
Port Coquitlam, BC V3C 2A8
Tel: 604-927-5411; *Fax:* 604-927-5360
info@portcoquitlam.ca
www.portcoquitlam.ca
Municipal Type: City
Incorporated: March 7, 1913; *Area:* 28.85 sq km
County or District: Metro Vancouver; *Population in 2011:* 56,342
Provincial Electoral District(s): Port Coquitlam-Burke Mountain
Federal Electoral District(s): Coquitlam-Port Coquitlam
Next Election: Oct. 20, 2018 (4-year terms)
Greg Moore, Mayor, 604-927-5410, Fax: 604-927-5331
Laura Dupont, Councillor, 604-328-8026
Michael Forrest, Councillor, 604-942-6289
Darrell Penner, Councillor, 604-941-9823
Glenn Pollock, Councillor, 604-771-4415
Dean Washington, Councillor, 604-317-7045
Brad West, Councillor, 604-313-9185
Susan Rauh, CMC, Corporate Officer/City Clerk, 604-927-5421, Fax: 604-927-5402
John Leeburn, Chief Administrative Officer
Kristen Meersman, Director, Engineering & Public Works
Laura Lee Richard, Director, Development Services
Steve Traviss, Director, Human Resources, 604-927-5417
Robin Wishart, Director, Corporate Support, 604-927-5302
Tim Arthur, Manager, Building Permits & Inspections, 604-927-5444
Karen Laustrup, Manager, Purchasing, 604-927-5430
Brian North, Manager, Revenues & Collections, 604-927-5426
Nick Delmonico, Fire Chief & City Emergency Coordinator

Port Moody
P.O. Box 36
100 Newport Dr.
Port Moody, BC V3H 3E1
Tel: 604-469-4500; *Fax:* 604-469-4550
info@portmoody.ca
www.portmoody.ca
Municipal Type: City
Incorporated: March 11, 1913; *Area:* 25.62 sq km
County or District: Metro Vancouver; *Population in 2011:* 32,975
Provincial Electoral District(s): Port Moody-Westwood
Federal Electoral District(s): Port Moody-Coquitlam
Next Election: Oct. 20, 2018 (4-year terms)
Mike Clay, Mayor, 604-469-4515
Diana Dilworth, Councillor, 604-469-4516
Rick Glumac, Councillor, 604-469-4585
Barbara Junker, Councillor, 604-469-4584
Meghan Lahti, Councillor, 604-469-4586
Zoe Royer, Councillor, 604-469-4518
Robert Vagramov, Councillor, 604-469-4517
Kevin Ramsay, City Manager, 604-469-4519
Ron Higo, General Manager, Community Services, 604-469-4542
Angie Parnell, General Manager, Corporate Services, 604-469-4595
Paul Rockwood, General Manager, Financial Services, 604-469-4504
Remo Faedo, Fire Chief

Powell River
6910 Duncan St.
Powell River, BC V8A 1V4
Tel: 604-485-6291; *Fax:* 604-485-2913
info@cdpr.bc.ca
www.powellriver.ca
Municipal Type: City
Incorporated: Oct. 15, 1955; *Area:* 29.77 sq km
County or District: Powell River; *Population in 2011:* 13,165
Provincial Electoral District(s): Powell River-Sunshine Coast
Federal Electoral District(s): Courtenay-Alberni; North Island-Powell River
Next Election: Oct. 20, 2018 (4-year terms)
Dave Formosa, Mayor, 604-485-8601
Russell Brewer, Councillor
Maggie Hathaway, Councillor
CaroleAnn Leishman, Councillor
Jim Palm, Councillor
Karen Skadsheim, Councillor
Rob Southcott, Councillor
Marie Claxton, City Clerk, 604-485-8601, Fax: 604-485-8628
Mac Fraser, Chief Administrative Officer, 604-485-8601, Fax: 604-485-8628
Shehzad Somji, Chief Financial Officer, 604-485-8639
Tor Birtig, Director, Infrastructure, 604-485-8610
Ray Boogaards, Director, Parks, Recreation, & Culture, 604-485-8907
Thomas Knight, Director, Planning Services, 604-485-8613
Barbara Mohan, Director, Human Resources & Corporate Planning, 604-485-8602
Dan Ouellette, Director, Fire & Emergency Services, 604-485-4431

Prince George
City Hall
1100 Patricia Blvd.
Prince George, BC V2L 3V9
Tel: 250-561-7600
cityclerk@city.pg.bc.ca
princegeorge.ca
Municipal Type: City
Incorporated: March 6, 1915; *Area:* 316 sq km
County or District: Fraser-Fort George; *Population in 2011:* 71,974
Provincial Electoral District(s): Pr. George-Mt. Robson; Pr. George N.; Pr. George-Omineca
Federal Electoral District(s): Cariboo-Prince George; Prince George-Peace River-Northern Rockies
Next Election: Oct. 20, 2018 (4-year terms)
Lyn Hall, Mayor, 250-561-7609
Frank Everitt, Councillor
Garth Frizzell, Councillor, 250-613-2363
Albert Koehler, Councillor
Murry Krause, Councillor
Terri McConnachie, Councillor
Jillian Merrick, Councillor
Susan Scott, Councillor
Brian Skakun, Councillor
Kathleen Soltis, City Manager
Walter Babicz, Director, Legal & Regulatory Services, 250-561-7605, Fax: 250-561-0283
Gina Layte Liston, Director, Engineering & Public Works
Sean LeBrun, Manager, Parks & Solid Waste
Wil Wedel, Manager, Utilities
Ian Wells, Manager, Planning & Development
Frank Blues, Asset Manager, Downtown Projects, 250-561-7503, Fax: 250-561-7721
Rae-Ann Emery, Manager, Human Resources, 250-561-7692
Debbie Deley, Manager, Financial Services, 250-561-7695, Fax: 250-561-7759
Rob Whitwham, Manager, Community Services
John Iverson, Fire Chief

Prince Rupert
424 - 3rd Ave. West
Prince Rupert, BC V8J 1L7
Tel: 250-627-0934; *Fax:* 250-627-0999
cityhall@princerupert.ca
www.princerupert.ca
Municipal Type: City
Incorporated: March 10, 1910; *Area:* 54.9 sq km
County or District: Skeena-Queen Charlotte; *Population in 2011:* 12,508
Provincial Electoral District(s): North Coast
Federal Electoral District(s): Skeena-Bulkley Valley
Next Election: Oct. 20, 2018 (4-year terms)
Lee Brain, Mayor, 250-627-0930
Barry Cunningham, Councillor
Nelson Kinney, Councillor
Blair Mirau, Councillor
Wade Niesh, Councillor
Gurvinder Randhawa, Councillor
Joy Thorkelson, Councillor, 250-624-6048
Robert Long, City Manager
Zeno Krekic, City Planner
Rory Grodecki, Corporate Administrator
Corinne Bomben, Chief Financial Officer, 250-627-0934
Willa Thorpe, Director, Recreation
Richard Pucci, Coordinator, Engineering Operations
Garin Gardiner, Field Manager, Operations
Christine Yew, Manager, Finance, 250-627-0921, Fax: 250-627-0918

Dave Mckenzie, Fire Chief, 250-624-5115

Quesnel
410 Kinchant St.
Quesnel, BC V2J 7J5
Tel: 250-992-2111; *Fax:* 250-992-2206
cityhall@quesnel.ca
www.quesnel.ca
Municipal Type: City
Incorporated: March 21, 1928; *Area:* 35.34 sq km
County or District: Cariboo; *Population in 2011:* 10,007
Provincial Electoral District(s): Cariboo North
Federal Electoral District(s): Cariboo-Prince George
Next Election: Oct. 20, 2018 (4-year terms)
Bob Simpson, Mayor
John Brisco, Councillor
Ed Coleman, Councillor
Scott Elliott, Councillor
Ron Paull, Councillor
Laurey Roodenburg, Councillor
Sushil Thepar, Councillor
Byron Johnson, Chief Administrative Officer
Kari Bolton, Deputy City Manager
Ken Coombs, Director, Infrastructure & Capital Works
Jeff Norburn, Director, Community Services
Tanya Turner, Manager, Development Services
Nancy Coe, Human Resources Advisor
Sylvian Gauthier, Fire Chief & Director, Emergency Services

Richmond
6911 No. 3 Rd.
Richmond, BC V6Y 2C1
Tel: 604-276-4000
cityclerk@richmond.ca
www.richmond.ca
Other Information: TTY: 604-276-4311
Municipal Type: City
Incorporated: Nov. 10, 1879; *Area:* 128.76 sq km
County or District: Metro Vancouver; *Population in 2011:* 190,473
Provincial Electoral District(s): Richmond-Centre; Richmond E.; Richmond-Steveston
Federal Electoral District(s): Richmond Centre; Steveston-Richmond East
Next Election: Oct. 20, 2018 (4-year terms)
Malcolm D. Brodie, Mayor
Chak Kwong Au, Councillor
Derek Dang, Councillor
Carol Day, Councillor
Ken Johnston, Councillor
Alexa Loo, Councillor
Bill McNulty, Councillor
Linda McPhail, Councillor
Harold Steves, Councillor
George Duncan, Chief Administrative Officer, 604-276-4336, Fax: 604-276-4222
David Weber, Director, City Clerk's Office, 604-276-4007, Fax: 604-278-5139
Cathryn Carlile, General Manager, Community Services, 604-276-4068
Phyllis Carlyle, General Manager, Law & Community Safety, 604-276-4104
Joe Erceg, General Manager, Planning & Development, 604-276-4214
Robert Gonzalez, P. Eng., General Manager, Engineering & Public Works, 604-276-4150
Andrew Nazareth, General Manager, Finance & Corporate Services, 604-276-4095
Grant Fengstad, Director, Information Technology, 604-276-4096
Jerry Chong, Director, Finance, 604-276-4064, Fax: 604-276-4162
Jim Tait, Director, Human Resources, 604-276-4312
William (John) McGowan, Fire Chief, 604-303-2719

Salmon Arm
P.O. Box 40
500 - 2nd Ave. NE
Salmon Arm, BC V1E 4N2
Tel: 250-803-4000; *Fax:* 250-803-4041
cityhall@salmonarm.ca
www.salmonarm.ca
Municipal Type: City
Incorporated: May 15, 1905; *Area:* 155.36 sq km
County or District: Columbia-Shuswap; *Population in 2011:* 17,464
Provincial Electoral District(s): Shuswap
Federal Electoral District(s): North Okanagan-Shuswap
Next Election: Oct. 20, 2018 (4-year terms)
Nancy Cooper, Mayor
Chad Eliason, Councillor
Kevin Flynn, Councillor
Alan Harrison, Councillor
Ken Jamieson, Councillor
Tim Lavery, Councillor
Lousie Wallace Richmond, Councillor
Carl Bannister, Chief Administrative Officer
Robert Niewenhuizen, Director, Engineering & Public Works
Monica Dalziel, Chief Financial Officer
Dale Berger, Manager, Shuswap Recreation Society
Rob Hein, Manager, Roads & Parks
Brad Shirley, Fire Chief, 250-803-4060

Surrey
14245 - 56th Ave.
Surrey, BC V3X 3A2
Tel: 604-591-4011; *Fax:* 604-591-8731
clerks@surrey.ca
www.surrey.ca
Municipal Type: City
Incorporated: Nov. 10, 1879; *Area:* 317.19 sq km
County or District: Metro Vancouver; *Population in 2011:* 468,251
Provincial Electoral District(s): Surrey-Cloverdale; Surrey-Green Timbers; Surrey-Newton; Surrey-Panorama Ridge; Surrey-Tynehead; Surrey-Whalley; Surrey-White Rock
Federal Electoral District(s): Cloverdale-Langley City; Fleetwood-Port Kells; South Surrey-White Rock; Surrey Centre; Surrey-Newton
Next Election: Oct. 20, 2018 (4-year terms)
Linda Hepner, Mayor, 604-591-4192
Tom Gill, Councillor, 604-591-4634
Bruce Hayne, Councillor
Vera LeFranc, Councillor, 604-591-4898
Mary Martin, Councillor, 604-591-4622
Mike Starchuk, Councillor, 604-591-5829
Barbara Steele, Councillor, 604-591-4623
Judy Villeneuve, Councillor, 604-591-4625
Dave Woods, Councillor, 604-591-5114
Jane Sullivan, City Clerk, 604-591-4132
Vince Lalonde, City Manager, 604-591-4122, Fax: 604-591-4357
Laurie Cavan, General Manager, Parks, Recreation & Culture, 604-598-5760, Fax: 604-598-5781
Jean Lamontagne, General Manager, Planning & Development, 604-591-4441, Fax: 604-591-2507
Fraser Smith, General Manager, Engineering, 604-591-4042, Fax: 604-591-8693
Nicola Webb, General Manager, Human Resources, 604-591-4660, Fax: 604-591-4517
Vivienne Wilke, General Manager, Finance & Technology, 604-591-4817
Robert Costanzo, Manager, Operations, 604-590-7287
Kam Grewal, Manager, Corporate Audit / Purchasing & AP, 604-591-4880
Donna Jones, Manager, Economic Development, 604-591-4289
Len Garis, Fire Chief, 604-541-4011

Terrace
3215 Eby St.
Terrace, BC V8G 2X8
Tel: 250-635-6311; *Fax:* 250-638-4777
cityhall@terrace.ca
www.terrace.ca
Municipal Type: City
Incorporated: Dec. 31, 1927; *Area:* 41.52 sq km
County or District: Kitimat-Stikine; *Population in 2011:* 11,486
Provincial Electoral District(s): Skeena
Federal Electoral District(s): Skeena-Bulkley Valley
Next Election: Oct. 20, 2018 (4-year terms)
Carol Leclerc, Mayor
Sean Bujtas, Councillor
Lynne Christiansen, Councillor
James Cordeiro, Councillor
Brian Downie, Councillor
Michael Prevost, Councillor
Stacey Tyers, Councillor
Heather Avison, Chief Administrative Officer, 250-638-4722
Phyllis Proteau, Financial Administrator, 250-638-4731
Carmen Didier, Director, Leisure Services, 250-615-3021
Rob Schibli, Director, Public Works, 250-615-4043
Chris Cordts, Supervisor, 250-615-4042
John Klie, Fire Chief, 250-638-4742

Vancouver
453 West 12th Ave.
Vancouver, BC V5Y 1V4
Tel: 604-873-7000
info@vancouver.ca
www.vancouver.ca
Other Information: Telephone locally: 311; TTY: 711
Municipal Type: City
Incorporated: November 15, 2008; *Area:* 114.71 sq km
County or District: Metro Vancouver; *Population in 2011:* 603,502
Provincial Electoral District(s): Vancouver-Fairview; Vanc.-False Creek; Vanc.-Fraserview; Vanc.-Hastings; Vanc. Kensington; Vanc.-Kingsway; Vanc.-Langara; Vanc.-Mount Pleasant; Vanc.-Point Grey; Vanc.-Quilchena; Vanc.-West End
Federal Electoral District(s): Vancouver Centre; Vancouver East; Vancouver Granville; Vancouver Kingsway; Vancouver Quadra; Vancouver South
Next Election: Oct. 20, 2018 (4-year terms)
Gregor Robertson, Mayor, 604-873-7621, Fax: 604-873-7685
George Affleck, Councillor, 604-873-7248, Fax: 604-873-7750
Elizabeth Ball, Councillor, 604-873-7240, Fax: 604-873-7750
Adriane Carr, Councillor, 604-873-7245, Fax: 604-873-7750
Melissa De Genova, Councillor, 604-873-7244, Fax: 604-873-7750
Heather Deal, Councillor, 604-873-7242, Fax: 604-873-7750
Kerry Jang, Councillor, 604-873-7246, Fax: 604-873-7750
Raymond Louie, Councillor, 604-873-7243, Fax: 604-873-7750
Geoff Meggs, Councillor, 604-873-7249, Fax: 604-873-7750
Andrea Reimer, Councillor, 604-873-7241, Fax: 604-873-7750
Tim Stevenson, Councillor, 604-873-7247, Fax: 604-873-7750
Janice MacKenzie, City Clerk, 604-871-6146
Sadhu Johnston, City Manager, 604-873-7627
Patrice Impey, Chief Financial Officer, 604-873-7610
Robert Bartlett, Chief Risk Officer, Risk Management, 604-873-7701
Mukhtar Latif, Chief Housing Officer, 604-871-6939
Malcolm Bromley, General Manager, Parks & Recreation, 604-257-8448
Jerry Dobrovolny, General Manager, Engineering Services, 604-873-7331
Kathleen Llewellyn-Thomas, General Manager, Community Services, 604-871-6858
Jane Pickering, Acting General Manager, Planning & Development Services, 604-873-7456
Richard Newirth, Managing Director, Cultural Services, 604-871-6455
Francie Connell, Director, Legal Services, 604-873-7506
Rena Kendall-Craden, Director, Corporate Communications, 604-673-8121
John McKearney, Fire Chief/General Manager, Vancouver Fire & Rescue Services, 604-665-6051, Fax: 604-654-0623
Adam Palmer, Chief Constable, Vancouver Police Department, 604-717-3321

Vernon
3400 - 30th St.
Vernon, BC V1T 5E6
Tel: 250-545-1361; *Fax:* 250-545-7876
admin@vernon.ca
www.vernon.ca
Municipal Type: City
Incorporated: Dec. 30, 1892; *Area:* 94.2 sq km
County or District: North Okanagan; *Population in 2011:* 38,150
Provincial Electoral District(s): Okanagan-Vernon
Federal Electoral District(s): North Island-Powell River; North Okanagan-Shuswap
Next Election: Oct. 20, 2018 (4-year terms)
Akbal Mund, Mayor
Scott Anderson, Councillor
Juliette unningham, Councillor
Catherine Lord, Councillor
Dalvir Nahal, Councillor
Brian Quiring, Councillor
Bob Spiers, Councillor
Will Pearce, Chief Administrative Officer
Kevin Bertles, Director, Finance
Patti Bridal, Director, Corporate Services
Kim Flick, Director, Community Development
Shirley Koenig, Director, Operation Services
Raeleen Manjak, Director, Human Resources
James Rice, Manager, Public Works
Ed Stranks, Acting Director, Engineering & GIS
Doug Ross, Director, Recreation Services
Keith Green, Fire Chief, 250-550-3561

Victoria
1 Centennial Sq.
Victoria, BC V8W 1P6
Tel: 250-385-5711; *Fax:* 250-361-0214
publicsrv@victoria.ca
www.victoria.ca
Municipal Type: City
Incorporated: Aug. 2, 1862; *Area:* 19.68 sq km
County or District: Capital Regional District; *Population in 2011:* 80,017
Provincial Electoral District(s): Victoria-Beacon Hill; Victoria-Hillside; Oak Bay-Gordon Head. In Greater Victoria: Esquimalt-Metchosin; Saanich South; Saanich North & the Islands; and Malahat-Juan de Fuca
Federal Electoral District(s): Victoria
Next Election: Oct. 20, 2018 (4-year terms)
Lisa Helps, Mayor, 250-361-0200
Marianne Alto, Councillor, 250-361-0216
Chris Coleman, Councillor, 250-361-0223

Ben Isitt, Councillor, 250-361-0222
Jeremy Loveday, Councillor, 250-361-0218
Margaret Lucas, Councillor, 250-361-0217
Pamela Madoff, Councillor, 250-361-0221
Charlayne Thornton-Joe, Councillor, 250-361-0219
Geoff Young, Councillor, 250-361-0220
Chris Coates, City Clerk, Legislative & Regulatory Services, 250-361-0203
Jason Johnson, City Manager, 250-361-0202
Jocelyn Jenkyns, Deputy City Manager, 250-361-0563
Katie Hamilton, Director, Civic Engagement & Strategic Planning, 250-361-0210
Fraser Work, Director, Engineering & Public Works, 250-361-0522
Susanne Thompson, Director, Finance, 250-361-0280
Thomas Soulliere, Director, Parks, Recreation & Facilities, 250-361-0631
Taaj Daliran, Manager, Waste Management & Cleaning Services, 250-361-0459
Brad Dellebuur, Manager, Transporation & Infrastructure Design, 250-361-0325
Mike Frost, Manager, Fleet & Operations, 250-361-0459
Deryk Lee, Manager, Waterworks & Underground Utility Operations, 250-361-0467
David Myles, Manager, Wastewater & Underground Utilities, 250-361-0415
Tom Zworski, City Solicitor, 250-361-0547, Fax: 250-361-0348
Paul Bruce, Fire Chief, 250-920-3380
Frank Elsner, Chief of Police

White Rock

15322 Buena Vista Ave.
White Rock, BC V4B 1Y6
Tel: 604-541-2100; *Fax:* 604-541-2118
webmaster@whiterockcity.ca
www.whiterockcity.ca
Municipal Type: City
Incorporated: April 15, 1957; *Area:* 5.16 sq km
County or District: Metro Vancouver; *Population in 2011:* 19,339
Provincial Electoral District(s): Surrey-White Rock
Federal Electoral District(s): South Surrey-White Rock
Next Election: Oct. 20, 2018 (4-year terms)
Wayne Baldwin, Mayor
David Chesney, Councillor
Helen Fathers, Councillor
Megan Knight, Councillor
Bill Lawrence, Councillor
Grant Meyer, Councillor
Lynne Sinclair, Councillor
Tracey Arthur, City Clerk, 604-541-2212
Dan Bottrill, Chief Administrative Officer, 604-541-2133, Fax: 604-541-9348
Sandra Kurylo, Director, Financial Services, 604-541-2111
Greg St. Louis, Director, Engineering & Municipal Operations, 604-541-2184
Karen Cooper, Director, Planning & Development Services, 604-541-2142
Eric Stepura, Director, Recreation & Culture, 604-787-4902
Jacquie Johnstone, Director, Human Resources, 604-541-2157
Chris Zota, Manager, Information Technology, 604-541-2113
Phil Lemire, Fire Chief, 604-541-2122
Lesli Roseberry, Staff Sergeant RCMP Detachment, 604-541-5101

Williams Lake

450 Mart St.
Williams Lake, BC V2G 1N3
Tel: 250-392-2311; *Fax:* 250-392-4408
corporateservices@williamslake.ca
www.williamslake.ca
Municipal Type: City
Incorporated: March 15, 1929; *Area:* 33.11 sq km
County or District: Cariboo; *Population in 2011:* 10,832
Provincial Electoral District(s): Cariboo North; Cariboo South
Federal Electoral District(s): Cariboo-Prince George
Next Election: Oct. 20, 2018 (4-year terms)
Walt Lloyd Cobb, Mayor, 250-392-2311
Ivan Bonnell, Councillor
Scott Douglas Nelson, Councillor
Jason Ryll, Councillor
Craig Robert Smith, Councillor
Laurie Walters, Councillor
Sue Zacharias, Councillor
Darrell Garceau, Chief Administrative Officer, 250-392-1763
Ashley Williston, Manager, Human Resources, 250-392-1795
Gary Muraca, Director, Municipal Services
Margaret Stewart, Director, Financial Services, 250-392-1762
Des Webster, Fire Chief
Geoff Paynton, Director, Community Services, 250-392-1786
Cindy Bouchard, Manager, Legislative Services
Joe Engelberts, Manager, Water & Waste

Other Municipalities in British Columbia

100 Mile House

P.O. Box 340
385 South Birch Ave.
100 Mile House, BC V0K 2E0
Tel: 250-395-2434; *Fax:* 250-395-3625
district@dist100milehouse.bc.ca
www.100milehouse.com
Municipal Type: District
Incorporated: July 27, 1965; *Area:* 51.34 sq km
County or District: Cariboo; *Population in 2011:* 1,886
Provincial Electoral District(s): Cariboo South
Federal Electoral District(s): Kamloops-Thomson-Cariboo
Next Election: Oct. 20, 2018 (4-year terms)
Mitch Campsall, Mayor
Roy Scott, Chief Administrative Officer, Corporate Administration

Alert Bay

P.O. Box 2800
15 Maple Rd.
Alert Bay, BC V0N 1A0
Tel: 250-974-5213; *Fax:* 250-974-5470
officeclerk@alertbay.ca
www.alertbay.ca
Municipal Type: Village
Incorporated: Jan. 14, 1946; *Area:* 1.78 sq km
County or District: Mount Waddington; *Population in 2011:* 445
Provincial Electoral District(s): North Island
Federal Electoral District(s): North Island-Powell River
Next Election: Oct. 20, 2018 (4-year terms)
Michael Berry, Mayor, 250-974-5213, Fax: 250-974-5470
Heather Nelson-Smith, Chief Administrative Officer
Pete Nelson-Smith, Public Works Superintendent

Anmore

2697 Sunnyside Rd.
Anmore, BC V3H 3C8
Tel: 604-469-9877; *Fax:* 604-469-0537
village.hall@anmore.com
www.anmore.com
Municipal Type: Village
Incorporated: Dec. 7, 1987; *Area:* 27.42 sq km
County or District: Metro Vancouver; *Population in 2011:* 2,092
Provincial Electoral District(s): Port Moody-Westwood
Federal Electoral District(s): Port Moody-Coquitlam
Next Election: Oct. 20, 2018 (4-year terms)
John McEwen, Mayor, 604-461-3384, Fax: 604-469-0537
Tim Harris, Chief Administrative Officer
Kevin Dicken, Manager, Public Works

Armstrong

P.O. Box 40
3570 Bridge St.
Armstrong, BC V0E 1B0
Tel: 250-546-3023; *Fax:* 250-546-3710
info@cityofarmstrong.bc.ca
www.cityofarmstrong.bc.ca
Municipal Type: Town
Incorporated: March 31, 1913; *Area:* 5.24 sq km
County or District: North Okanagan; *Population in 2011:* 4,815
Provincial Electoral District(s): Shuswap
Federal Electoral District(s): North Okanagan-Shuswap
Next Election: Oct. 20, 2018 (4-year terms)
Chris Pieper, Mayor, 250-550-7239
Melinda Stickney, Chief Administrative Officer
Tim Perepolkin, Manager, Public Works

Ashcroft

P.O. Box 129
Ashcroft, BC V0K 1A0
Tel: 250-453-9161; *Fax:* 250-453-9664
admin@ashcroftbc.ca
www.ashcroftbc.ca
Other Information: Toll Free Phone: 1-877-453-9161
Municipal Type: Village
Incorporated: June 27, 1952; *Area:* 51.45 sq km
County or District: Thompson-Nicola; *Population in 2011:* 1,628
Provincial Electoral District(s): Cariboo South
Federal Electoral District(s): Mission-Matsqui-Fraser Canyon
Next Election: Oct. 20, 2018 (4-year terms)
Jack Jeyes, Mayor, 250-453-2259
Michelle Allen, Chief Administrative Officer

Barriere

P.O. Box 219
4936 Barriere Town Rd.
Barriere, BC V0E 1E0
Tel: 250-672-9751; *Fax:* 250-672-9708
inquiry@barriere.ca
www.barriere.ca
Other Information: Toll Free Phone: 1-866-672-9751
Municipal Type: District
Incorporated: Dec. 4 2007; *Area:* 6.17 sq km
County or District: Thompson-Nicola; *Population in 2011:* 1,773
Provincial Electoral District(s): Lower North Thompson
Federal Electoral District(s): Kamloops-Thompson-Cariboo
Next Election: Oct. 20, 2018 (4-year terms)
Virginia Smith, Mayor
Colleen Hannigan, Chief Administrative Officer, 250-672-9751

Belcarra

4084 Bedwell Bay Rd.
Belcarra, BC V3H 4P8
Tel: 604-937-4100; *Fax:* 604-939-5034
belcarra@belcarra.ca
www.belcarra.ca
Municipal Type: Village
Incorporated: Aug. 22, 1979; *Area:* 5.46 sq km
County or District: Metro Vancouver; *Population in 2011:* 644
Provincial Electoral District(s): Port Moody-Westwood
Federal Electoral District(s): Port Moody-Coquitlam
Next Election: Oct. 20, 2018 (4-year terms)
Ralph E. Drew, Mayor, 604-937-0143
Lynda Floyd, Chief Administrative Officer, 604-937-4101

Bowen Island

981 Artisan Lane
Bowen Island, BC V0N 1G0
Tel: 604-947-4255; *Fax:* 604-947-0193
bim@bimbc.ca
www.bimbc.ca
Municipal Type: Island Municipality
Incorporated: Dec. 4, 1999; *Area:* 49.94 sq km
County or District: Metro Vancouver; *Population in 2011:* 3,402
Provincial Electoral District(s): West Vancouver-Garibaldi
Federal Electoral District(s): West Vancouver-Sunshine Coast-Sea to Sky Country
Next Election: Oct. 20, 2018 (4-year terms)
Murray Skeels, Mayor, 604-947-4255
Kathy Lalonde, Chief Administrative Officer, 604-947-4255
Bob Robinson, Superintendent, Public Works, 604-947-4255

Burns Lake

P.O. Box 570
Burns Lake, BC V0J 1E0
Tel: 250-692-7587; *Fax:* 250-692-3059
village@burnslake.org
www.burnslake.org
Other Information: Fire Hall Phone: 250-692-3664
Municipal Type: Village
Incorporated: Dec. 6, 1923; *Area:* 7.17 sq km
County or District: Bulkley-Nechako; *Population in 2011:* 2,029
Provincial Electoral District(s): Bulkley Valley-Stikine
Federal Electoral District(s): Skeena-Bulkley Valley
Next Election: Oct. 20, 2018 (4-year terms)
Note: Mayor Strimbold resigned September 15, 2016. A by-election is planned for December.
Sheryl Worthing, Chief Administrative Officer
Cameron Harthing, City Clerk, 250-692-7587
Rick Martin, Director, Public Works, 250-692-7587
Jim McBride, Director, Protective Services / Fire Chief, 250-692-7587

Cache Creek

P.O. Box 7
Cache Creek, BC V0K 1H0
Tel: 250-457-6237; *Fax:* 250-457-9192
admin@cachecreek.info
www.cachecreekvillage.com
Municipal Type: Village
Incorporated: Nov. 28, 1967; *Area:* 10.57 sq km
County or District: Thompson-Nicola; *Population in 2011:* 1,040
Provincial Electoral District(s): Cariboo South
Federal Electoral District(s): Mission-Matsqui-Fraser Canyon
Next Election: Oct. 20, 2018 (4-year terms)
John Ranta, Mayor
Dan Plamondon, Chief Administrative Officer

Canal Flats

P.O. Box 159
8853 Grainger Rd.
Canal Flats, BC V0B 1B0
Tel: 250-349-5462; *Fax:* 250-349-5460
village@canalflats.ca
www.canalflats.com

Municipal Type: Village
Incorporated: June 29, 2004; *Area:* 10.84 sq km
County or District: East Kootenay; *Population in 2011:* 715
Provincial Electoral District(s): Columbia River-Revelstoke
Federal Electoral District(s): Kootenay-Columbia
Next Election: Oct. 20, 2018 (4-year terms)
Ute Juras, Mayor, 250-349-5462
Brian Woodward, Chief Administrative Officer, 250-349-5462

Castlegar
460 Columbia Ave.
Castlegar, BC V1N 1G7
Tel: 250-365-7227; *Fax:* 250-365-4810
castlegar@castlegar.ca
www.castlegar.ca
Municipal Type: Town
Incorporated: Jan. 1, 1974; *Area:* 19.8 sq km
County or District: Central Kootenay; *Population in 2011:* 7,816
Provincial Electoral District(s): West Kootenay-Boundary
Federal Electoral District(s): South Okanagan-West Kootenay
Next Election: Oct. 20, 2018 (4-year terms)
Lawrence Chernoff, Mayor
John Malcolm, Chief Administrative Officer
Phil Markin, Director, Development Services
Chris Barlow, Director, Transportation & Civic Works
Carolyn Rempel, Director, Corporate Services

Central Saanich
1903 Mt. Newton Cross Rd.
Saanichton, BC V8M 2A9
Tel: 250-652-4444; *Fax:* 250-652-0135
municipalhall@csaanich.ca
www.centralsaanich.ca
Municipal Type: District
Incorporated: Dec. 12, 1950; *Area:* 41.42 sq km
County or District: Capital; *Population in 2011:* 15,936
Provincial Electoral District(s): Saanich North & the Islands
Federal Electoral District(s): Saanich-Gulf Islands
Next Election: Oct. 20, 2018 (4-year terms)
Ryan Windsor, Mayor
Alicia Cormier, Councillor
Christopher R. Graham, Councillor
Carl Jensen, Councillor
Zeb King, Councillor
Niall Paltiel, Councillor
Bob L. Thompson, Councillor
Patrick Robins, Chief Administrative Officer
Paul Hames, Chief Constable, 250-652-4441
David McAllister, Director, Engineering & Public Works, 250-544-4210
Bruce Greig, Director, Planning & Building Services
Ron French, Fire Chief, 250-544-4227

Chase
P.O. Box 440
826 Okanagan Ave.
Chase, BC V0E 1M0
Tel: 250-679-3238; *Fax:* 250-679-3070
chase@chasebc.ca
www.chasebc.ca
Municipal Type: Village
Incorporated: April 22, 1969; *Area:* 3.75 sq km
County or District: Thompson-Nicola; *Population in 2011:* 2,495
Provincial Electoral District(s): Kamloops-North Thompson
Federal Electoral District(s): North Okanagan-Shuswap
Next Election: Oct. 20, 2018 (4-year terms)
Rick Berrigan, Mayor, 250-679-5330
Joni Heinrich, Chief Administrative Officer

Chetwynd
P.O. Box 357
5400 North Access Rd.
Chetwynd, BC V0C 1J0
Tel: 250-401-4100; *Fax:* 250-401-4101
d-chet@gochetwynd.com
www.gochetwynd.com
Municipal Type: District
Incorporated: Sept. 25, 1962; *Area:* 64.32 sq km
County or District: Peace River; *Population in 2011:* 2,635
Provincial Electoral District(s): Peace River South
Federal Electoral District(s): Prince George-Peace River-Northern Rockies
Next Election: Oct. 20, 2018 (4-year terms)
Merlin Nichols, Mayor
Doug Fleming, Chief Administrative Officer, 250-401-4103
Paul Gordon, Director, Engineering & Public Works, 250-401-4111

Clearwater
P.O. Box 157
132 Clearwater Station Rd.
Clearwater, BC V0E 1N0
Tel: 250-674-2257; *Fax:* 250-674-2173
admin@docbc.ca
www.districtofclearwater.com
Municipal Type: District
Incorporated: Dec. 7 2007; *Area:* 60 sq km
County or District: Thompson-Nicola; *Population in 2011:* 2,331
Provincial Electoral District(s): Kamloops-North Thompson
Federal Electoral District(s): Kamloops-Thompson-Cariboo
Next Election: Oct. 20, 2018 (4-year terms)
John Harwood, Mayor, 250-674-3270
Leslie Groulx, Chief Administrative Officer, 250-674-2257
Bruce Forsyth, Superindendent, Public Works

Clinton
P.O. Box 309
1423 Cariboo Hwy.
Clinton, BC V0K 1K0
Tel: 250-459-2261; *Fax:* 250-459-2227
admin@village.clinton.bc.ca
www.village.clinton.bc.ca
Municipal Type: Village
Incorporated: July 16, 1963; *Area:* 4.36 sq km
County or District: Thompson-Nicola; *Population in 2011:* 636
Provincial Electoral District(s): Cariboo South
Federal Electoral District(s): Kamloops-Thompson-Cariboo
Next Election: Oct. 20, 2018 (4-year terms)
Jim Rivett, Mayor
Tom Dall, Chief Administrative Officer, 250-459-2261

Coldstream
9901 Kalamalka Rd.
Coldstream, BC V1B 1L6
Tel: 250-545-5304; *Fax:* 250-545-4733
info@districtofcoldstream.ca
www.districtofcoldstream.ca
Municipal Type: District
Incorporated: Dec. 21, 1906; *Area:* 67.25 sq km
County or District: North Okanagan; *Population in 2011:* 10,214
Provincial Electoral District(s): Okanagan-Vernon
Federal Electoral District(s): North Okanagan-Shuswap
Next Election: Oct. 20, 2018 (4-year terms)
Jim Garlick, Mayor, 250-307-9490
Trevor Seibel, Chief Administrative Officer
Michael Baker, Director, Infrastructure Services, 250-545-5304
Mike Reiley, Director, Development Services, 250-545-5304

Creston
P.O. Box 1339
#238, 10th Ave. North
Creston, BC V0B 1G0
Tel: 250-428-2214; *Fax:* 250-428-9164
info@creston.ca
www.creston.ca
Municipal Type: Town
Incorporated: May 14, 1924; *Area:* 8.48 sq km
County or District: Central Kootenay; *Population in 2011:* 5,306
Provincial Electoral District(s): Nelson-Creston
Federal Electoral District(s): Kootenay-Columbia
Next Election: Oct. 20, 2018 (4-year terms)
Ron Toyota, Mayor, 250-428-2214
Lou Varela, Town Manager, 250-428-2214, Fax: 250-428-9164
Ross Beddoes, Director, Municipal Services, 250-428-2214, Fax: 250-428-9164

Cumberland
P.O. Box 340
2673 Dunsmuir Ave.
Cumberland, BC V0R 1S0
Tel: 250-336-2291; *Fax:* 250-336-2321
info@cumberland.ca
www.cumberlandbc.net
Municipal Type: Village
Incorporated: Jan. 1, 1898; *Area:* 29.13 sq km
County or District: Comox Valley; *Population in 2011:* 3,398
Provincial Electoral District(s): Comox Valley
Federal Electoral District(s): Courtenay-Alberni
Next Election: Oct. 20, 2018 (4-year terms)
Leslie Baird, Mayor, 250-336-3001
Sundance Topham, Chief Administrative Officer, 250-336-3002

Delta
4500 Clarence Taylor Cres.
Delta, BC V4K 3E2
Tel: 604-946-4141
clerks@delta.ca
www.delta.ca
Municipal Type: District
Incorporated: Nov. 10, 1879; *Area:* 183.7 sq km
County or District: Metro Vancouver; *Population in 2011:* 99,863
Provincial Electoral District(s): Delta North; Delta South
Federal Electoral District(s): Delta
Next Election: Oct. 20, 2018 (4-year terms)
Lois E. Jackson, Mayor, 604-946-3210, Fax: 604-946-6055
Sylvia Bishop, Councillor
Robert Campbell, Councillor, 604-948-0623
Jeannie Kanakos, Councillor, 604-591-1995
Heather King, Councillor, 604-943-6468
Bruce McDonald, Councillor, 604-596-8345
Ian L. Paton, Councillor, 604-940-0852
Robyn Anderson, Municipal Clerk, 604-952-3125, Fax: 604-946-3390
George Harvie, Chief Administrative Officer, 604-946-3212, Fax: 604-946-3864
Ken Kuntz, Director, Parks, Recreation & Culture, 604-952-3000, Fax: 604-946-4693
Steven Lan, Director, Engineering
Jeff Day, Director, Community Planning & Development
Sean McGill, Director, Human Resources & Corporate Planning, 604-946-3246
Karl Preuss, CA, Director, Finance, 604-946-3230, Fax: 604-946-3962
Mike Brotherston, Manager, Climate Action & Environment, 604-946-3253
Greg Vanstone, Municipal Solicitor, 604-952-3138
Dan Copeland, Fire Chief, 604-946-8541
Jim Cessford, Chief Constable, 604-946-4411, Fax: 604-946-3729

Duncan
200 Craig St.
Duncan, BC V9L 1W3
Tel: 250-746-6126; *Fax:* 250-746-6129
duncan@duncan.ca
www.duncan.ca
Municipal Type: Town
Incorporated: March 4, 1912; *Area:* 2.05 sq km
County or District: Cowichan Valley; *Population in 2011:* 4,932
Provincial Electoral District(s): Cowichan-Ladysmith
Federal Electoral District(s): Cowichan-Malahat-Langford
Next Election: Oct. 20, 2018 (4-year terms)
Phil Kent, Mayor, 250-709-0186
Peter de Verteuil, Chief Administrative Officer, 250-746-6126
Abbas Farahbakhsh, Director, Public Works, 250-746-6126

Elkford
P.O. Box 340
Elkford, BC V0B 1H0
Tel: 250-865-4000; *Fax:* 250-865-4001
info@elkford.ca
www.elkford.ca
Municipal Type: District
Incorporated: July 16, 1971; *Area:* 101.59 sq km
County or District: East Kootenay; *Population in 2011:* 2,523
Provincial Electoral District(s): East Kootenay
Federal Electoral District(s): Kootenay-Columbia
Next Election: Oct. 20, 2018 (4-year terms)
Dean McKerracher, Mayor, 250-865-4000
Curtis Helgesen, Chief Administrative Officer, 250-865-4004
Bernie Van Tighem, Director, Fire Rescue & Emergency Services, 250-865-4020

Enderby
P.O. Box 400
619 Cliff Ave.
Enderby, BC V0E 1V0
Tel: 250-838-7230; *Fax:* 250-838-6007
enderbycity@sunwave.net
www.cityofenderby.com
Municipal Type: Village
Incorporated: March 1, 1905; *Area:* 4.23 sq km
County or District: North Okanagan; *Population in 2011:* 2,932
Provincial Electoral District(s): Shuswap
Federal Electoral District(s): North Okanagan-Shuswap
Next Election: Oct. 20, 2018 (4-year terms)
Greg McCune, Mayor, 250-838-9874
Tate Bengtson, Chief Administrative Officer, 250-838-7230

Esquimalt
1229 Esquimalt Rd.
Victoria, BC V9A 3P1
Tel: 250-414-7100; *Fax:* 250-414-7111
info@esquimalt.ca
www.esquimalt.ca
Municipal Type: Township
Incorporated: Sept. 1, 1912; *Area:* 7.04 sq km
County or District: Capital; *Population in 2011:* 16,209
Provincial Electoral District(s): Esquimalt-Metchosin
Federal Electoral District(s): Esquimalt-Saanich-Sooke
Next Election: Oct. 20, 2018 (4-year terms)
Barbara Desjardins, Mayor, 250-414-7100

Meagan Brame, Councillor
Beth Burton-Krahn, Councillor
Lynda Hundleby, Councillor
Olga Liberchuk, Councillor
Susan Low, Councillor
Tim Morrison, Councillor
Laurie Hurst, Chief Administrative Officer, 250-414-7133
Ian Irvine, Chief Financial Officer & Director, Financial Services, 250-414-7141
Scott Hartman, Director, Parks & Recreation, 250-412-8509
Bill Brown, Director, Development Services, 250-414-7146
Gina Griffith, Manager, Human Resources, 250-414-7137
Blair McDonald, Director, Community Safety Services

Fernie
P.O. Box 190
#501, 3rd Ave.
Fernie, BC V0B 1M0
Tel: 250-423-6817; *Fax:* 250-423-3034
cityhall@fernie.ca
www.fernie.ca
Municipal Type: Town
Incorporated: July 28, 1904; *Area:* 16.05 sq km
County or District: East Kootenay; *Population in 2011:* 4,448
Provincial Electoral District(s): East Kootenay
Federal Electoral District(s): Kootenay-Columbia
Next Election: Oct. 20, 2018 (4-year terms)
Mary Giuliano, Mayor, 250-423-2233
Jim Hendricks, Chief Administrative Officer, 250-423-2225
Ted Ruiter, Director, 250-423-4226

Fort Nelson
P.O. Box 399
5319 - 50th Ave.
Fort Nelson, BC V0C 1R0
Tel: 250-774-2541
justask@northernrockies.ca
www.northernrockies.ca
Municipal Type: Town
Incorporated: Oct. 31, 1987; *Area:* 13.26 sq km
County or District: Northern Rockies; *Population in 2011:* 3,902
Provincial Electoral District(s): Peace River North
Federal Electoral District(s): Prince George-Peace River-Northern Rockies
Next Election: Oct. 20, 2018 (4-year terms)
Bill Streeper, Mayor
Randy McLean, Chief Administrative Officer

Fort St. James
P.O. Box 640
477 Stuart Dr. West
Fort St James, BC V0J 1P0
Tel: 250-996-8233; *Fax:* 250-996-2248
district@fortstjames.ca
www.stuartnechako.ca/fort-st-james
Municipal Type: District
Incorporated: Dec. 19, 1952; *Area:* 22.1 sq km
County or District: Bulkley-Nechako; *Population in 2011:* 1,691
Provincial Electoral District(s): Prince George-Omineca
Federal Electoral District(s): Skeena-Bulkley Valley
Next Election: Oct. 20, 2018 (4-year terms)
Rob MacDougall, Mayor, 250-996-8233
Kevin Crook, Chief Administrative Officer, 250-996-8233
David Stewart, Public Works Superintendent, 250-996-7161

Fraser Lake
P.O. Box 430
210 Carrier Cres.
Fraser Lake, BC V0J 1S0
Tel: 250-699-6257; *Fax:* 250-699-6469
village@fraserlake.ca
www.fraserlake.ca
Municipal Type: Village
Incorporated: Sept. 27, 1966; *Area:* 3.9 sq km
County or District: Bulkley-Nechako; *Population in 2011:* 1,167
Provincial Electoral District(s): Prince George-Omineca
Federal Electoral District(s): Skeena-Bulkley Valley
Next Election: Oct. 20, 2018 (4-year terms)
Dwayne Lindstrom, Mayor, 250-699-6257
Rodney J. Holland, Chief Administrative Officer & Director, Corporate Services, 250-699-6257
Vern Hilman, Director, Public Works, 250-699-6562

Fruitvale
P.O. Box 370
1947 beaver St.
Fruitvale, BC V0G 1L0
Tel: 250-367-7551; *Fax:* 250-367-9267
info@village.fruitvale.bc.ca
www.village.fruitvale.bc.ca
Municipal Type: Village
Incorporated: Nov. 4, 1952; *Area:* 36.86 sq km
County or District: Kootenay Boundary; *Population in 2011:* 2,016
Provincial Electoral District(s): West Kootenay-Boundary
Federal Electoral District(s): South Okanagan-West Kootenay
Next Election: Oct. 20, 2018 (4-year terms)
Patricia Cecchini, Mayor, 250-367-7691, Fax: 250-367-9267
Lila Cresswell, Chief Administrative Officer, 250-367-7551

Gibsons
P.O. Box 340
474 South Fletcher Rd.
Gibsons, BC V0N 1V0
Tel: 604-886-2274; *Fax:* 604-886-9735
info@gibsons.ca
www.gibsons.ca
Municipal Type: Town
Incorporated: March 4, 1929; *Area:* 4.33 sq km
County or District: Sunshine Coast; *Population in 2011:* 4,437
Provincial Electoral District(s): Powell River-Sunshine Coast
Federal Electoral District(s): West Vancouver-Sunshine Coast-Sea to Sky Country
Next Election: Oct. 20, 2018 (4-year terms)
Wayne Rowe, Mayor, 604-886-2274, Fax: 604-886-9735
Emanuel Machado, Chief Administrative Officer, 604-886-2274
Andre Boel, Director, Planning
Greg Foss, Director, Public Works
Wendy Gilbertson, Director, Parks
Dave Newman, Director, Engineering

Gold River
P.O. Box 610
499 Muchalat Dr.
Gold River, BC V0P 1G0
Tel: 250-283-2202; *Fax:* 250-283-7500
villageofgoldriver@cablerocket.com
www.villageofgoldriver.com
Municipal Type: Village
Incorporated: Aug. 26, 1965; *Area:* 10.51 sq km
County or District: Strathcona; *Population in 2011:* 1,267
Provincial Electoral District(s): North Island
Federal Electoral District(s): North Island-Powell River
Next Election: Oct. 20, 2018 (4-year terms)
Brad Unger, Mayor, 250-283-2615
Larry Plourde, Chief Administrative Officer, 250-283-2202
Mick Mann, Public Works Supervisor & Manager, Parks & Rec

Golden
P.O. Box 350
Golden, BC V0A 1H0
Tel: 250-344-2271; *Fax:* 250-344-6577
enquiries@town.golden.bc.ca
www.golden.ca
Municipal Type: Town
Incorporated: June 26, 1957; *Area:* 11.02 sq km
County or District: Columbia-Shuswap; *Population in 2011:* 3,701
Provincial Electoral District(s): Columbia River-Revelstoke
Federal Electoral District(s): Kootenay-Columbia
Next Election: Oct. 20, 2018 (4-year terms)
Ron Oszust, Mayor, 250-344-2271
Jon Wilsgard, Chief Administrative Officer, 250-344-2271

Grand Forks
P.O. Box 220
7217 - 4th St.
Grand Forks, BC V0H 1H0
Tel: 250-442-8266; *Fax:* 250-442-8000
info@citinfo@grandforks.ca
www.grandforks.ca
Municipal Type: Town
Incorporated: April 15, 1897; *Area:* 10.44 sq km
County or District: Kootenay Boundary; *Population in 2011:* 3,985
Provincial Electoral District(s): West Kootenay-Boundary
Federal Electoral District(s): South Okanagan-West Kootenay
Next Election: Oct. 20, 2018 (4-year terms)
Frank Konrad, Mayor, 250-443-2370
Douglas Allin, Chief Administrative Officer, 250-442-8266

Granisle
P.O. Box 128
Granisle, BC V0J 1W0
Tel: 250-697-2248; *Fax:* 250-697-2306
general@villageofgranisle.ca
www.villageofgranisle.ca
Municipal Type: Village
Incorporated: June 29, 1971; *Area:* 40.21 sq km
County or District: Bulkley-Nechako; *Population in 2011:* 303
Provincial Electoral District(s): Bulkley Valley-Stikine
Federal Electoral District(s): Skeena-Bulkley Valley
Next Election: Oct. 20, 2018 (4-year terms)
Linda McGuire, Mayor, 250-697-2248
Sharon Smith, Chief Administrative Officer, 250-697-2428
Blaine Maughan, Manager, Public Works, 250-697-2429

Greenwood
P.O. Box 129
202 Government Ave.
Greenwood, BC V0H 1J0
Tel: 250-445-6644; *Fax:* 250-445-6441
info@greenwoodcity.com
www.greenwoodcity.com
Municipal Type: Village
Incorporated: July 12, 1897; *Area:* 2.52 sq km
County or District: Kootenay Boundary; *Population in 2011:* 708
Provincial Electoral District(s): West Kootenay-Boundary
Federal Electoral District(s): South Okanagan-West Kootenay
Next Election: Oct. 20, 2018 (4-year terms)
Ed I. Smith, Mayor, 250-445-6644
Robin Dalziel, Chief Administrative Officer, 250-445-6644
Randy Smith, Superintendent of Public Works

Harrison Hot Springs
P.O. Box 160
495 Hot Springs Rd.
Harrison Hot Springs, BC V0M 1K0
Tel: 604-796-2171; *Fax:* 604-796-2192
info@harrisonhotsprings.ca
www.harrisonhotsprings.ca
Municipal Type: Village
Incorporated: May 27, 1949; *Area:* 5.47 sq km
County or District: Fraser Valley; *Population in 2011:* 1,468
Provincial Electoral District(s): Chilliwack-Kent
Federal Electoral District(s): Mission-Matsqui-Fraser Canyon
Next Election: Oct. 20, 2018 (4-year terms)
Leo Facio, Mayor, 604-796-2171
Ian Crane, Chief Administrative Officer, 604-796-2171

Hazelton
P.O. Box 40
Hazelton, BC V0J 1Y0
Tel: 250-842-5991; *Fax:* 250-842-5152
info@hazelton.ca
www.hazelton.ca
Municipal Type: Village
Incorporated: Feb. 15, 1956; *Area:* 2.85 sq km
County or District: Kitimat-Stikine; *Population in 2011:* 270
Provincial Electoral District(s): Bulkley Valley-Stikine
Federal Electoral District(s): Skeena-Bulkley Valley
Next Election: Oct. 20, 2018 (4-year terms)
Alice Maitland, Mayor, 250-842-5991
Tanalee Hesse, Chief Administrative Officer, 250-842-5991

Highlands
1980 Millstream Rd.
Victoria, BC V9B 6H1
Tel: 250-474-1773; *Fax:* 250-474-3677
www.highlands.bc.ca
Municipal Type: District
Incorporated: Dec. 7, 1993; *Area:* 37.87 sq km
County or District: Capital; *Population in 2011:* 2,120
Provincial Electoral District(s): Malahat-Juan de Fuca
Federal Electoral District(s): Cowichan-Malahat-Langford
Next Election: Oct. 20, 2018 (4-year terms)
Ken Williams, Mayor
Christopher D. Coates, Chief Administrative Officer

Hope
325 Wallace St.
Hope, BC V0X 1L0
Tel: 604-869-5671; *Fax:* 604-869-2275
info@hope.ca
www.hope.ca
Municipal Type: District Municipality
Incorporated: April 6, 1929; *Area:* 41.42 sq km
County or District: Fraser Valley; *Population in 2011:* 5,969
Provincial Electoral District(s): Yale-Lillooet
Federal Electoral District(s): Chilliwack-Hope
Next Election: Oct. 20, 2018 (4-year terms)
Wilfried Vicktor, Mayor, 604-869-5671
John Fortoloczky, Chief Administrative Officer, 604-869-5607
Scott Misumi, Director, Community Development, 604-869-5607
Ian Vaughan, Director, Operations, 604-869-2333

Houston
P.O. Box 370
3367 - 12th St.
Houston, BC V0J 1Z0
Tel: 250-845-2238; *Fax:* 250-845-3429
doh@houston.ca
www.houston.ca
Municipal Type: District
Incorporated: March 4, 1957; *Area:* 72.83 sq km
County or District: Bulkley-Nechako; *Population in 2011:* 3,147
Provincial Electoral District(s): Bulkley Valley-Stikine

Federal Electoral District(s): Skeena-Bulkley Valley
Next Election: Oct. 20, 2018 (4-year terms)
Shane Brienen, Mayor, 250-845-8842
Michael D. Gavin, Chief Administrative Officer, 250-845-2238
Ryan Coltura, Director, 250-845-7420

Hudson's Hope
P.O. Box 330
9904 Dudley Dr.
Hudson's Hope, BC V0C 1V0
Tel: 250-783-9901; *Fax:* 250-783-5741
district@hudsonshope.ca
www.hudsonshope.ca
Municipal Type: District
Incorporated: Nov. 16, 1965; *Area:* 869.43 sq km
County or District: Peace River; *Population in 2011:* 970
Provincial Electoral District(s): Peace River North
Federal Electoral District(s): Prince George-Peace River-Northern Rockies
Next Election: Oct. 20, 2018 (4-year terms)
Gwen Johansson, Mayor, 250-783-9901
Tom Matus, Chief Administrative Officer

Invermere
P.O. Box 339
914 - 8th Ave.
Invermere, BC V0A 1K0
Tel: 250-342-9281; *Fax:* 250-342-2934
info@invermere.net
www.invermere.net
Municipal Type: District
Incorporated: May 22, 1951; *Area:* 10.18 sq km
County or District: East Kootenay; *Population in 2011:* 2,955
Provincial Electoral District(s): Columbia River-Revelstoke
Federal Electoral District(s): Kootenay-Columbia
Next Election: Oct. 20, 2018 (4-year terms)
Gerry Taft, Mayor, 250-342-9281
Christopher Prosser, Chief Administrative Officer, 250-342-9281
Rory Hromadnik, Director, Development Services

Kaslo
P.O. Box 576
312 Fourth St.
Kaslo, BC V0G 1M0
Tel: 250-353-2311; *Fax:* 250-353-7767
admin@kaslo.ca
www.kaslo.ca
Municipal Type: Village
Incorporated: Aug. 14, 1893; *Area:* 2.8 sq km
County or District: Central Kootenay; *Population in 2011:* 1,026
Provincial Electoral District(s): Nelson-Creston
Federal Electoral District(s): Kootenay-Columbia
Next Election: Oct. 20, 2018 (4-year terms)
Suzan Hewat, Mayor, 250-353-2311
Neil Smith, Chief Administrative Officer, 250-353-2311

Kent
P.O. Box 70
7170 Cheam Ave.
Agassiz, BC V0M 1A0
Tel: 604-796-2235; *Fax:* 604-796-9854
www.district.kent.bc.ca
Municipal Type: District
Incorporated: Jan. 1, 1895; *Area:* 166.51 sq km
County or District: Fraser Valley; *Population in 2011:* 5,664
Provincial Electoral District(s): Chilliwack-Kent
Federal Electoral District(s): Mission-Matsqui-Fraser Canyon
Next Election: Oct. 20, 2018 (4-year terms)
John Van Laerhoven, Mayor, 604-796-2235
Wallace Mah, Chief Administrative Officer, 604-796-2235
Darcey Kohuch, Director, Development Services
Mick Thiessen, Director, Engineering Services

Keremeos
P.O. Box 160
702 - 4th St.
Keremeos, BC V0X 1N0
Tel: 250-499-2711; *Fax:* 250-499-5477
town@keremeos.ca
www.keremeos.ca
Municipal Type: Village
Incorporated: Oct. 30, 1956; *Area:* 2.11 sq km
County or District: Okanagan-Similkameen; *Population in 2011:* 1,330
Provincial Electoral District(s): Yale-Lillooet
Federal Electoral District(s): Central Okanagan-Similkameen-Nicola
Next Election: Oct. 20, 2018 (4-year terms)
Manfred Bauer, Mayor
Laurie Taylor, Chief Administrative Officer

Kimberley
340 Spokane St.
Kimberley, BC V1A 2E8
Tel: 250-427-5311; *Fax:* 250-427-5252
info@citinfo@kimberley.ca
www.kimberley.ca
Municipal Type: Town
Incorporated: March 29, 1944; *Area:* 58.31 sq km
County or District: East Kootenay; *Population in 2011:* 6,652
Provincial Electoral District(s): Columbia River-Revelstoke
Federal Electoral District(s): Kootenay-Columbia
Next Election: Oct. 20, 2018 (4-year terms)
Don McCormick, Mayor, 250-432-5460
Scott Sommerville, Chief Administrative Officer
Janyce Bampton, Human Resources Officer, 250-427-9656

Kitimat
270 City Centre
Kitimat, BC V8C 2H7
Tel: 250-632-8900; *Fax:* 250-632-4995
feedback@kitimat.ca
www.kitimat.ca
Municipal Type: District
Incorporated: March 31, 1953; *Area:* 242.63 sq km
County or District: Kitimat-Stikine; *Population in 2011:* 8,335
Provincial Electoral District(s): Skeena
Federal Electoral District(s): Skeena-Bulkley Valley
Next Election: Oct. 20, 2018 (4-year terms)
Philip Germuth, Mayor, 250-632-8920
Warren Waycheshen, Chief Administrative Officer, 250-632-8916
Gwendolyn Sewell, Director, 250-632-8912
Brian Krause, Manager, 250-632-8935
Trent Bossence, Fire Chief, 250-632-8942

Ladysmith
Town Hall
P.O. Box 220 Main
410 Esplanade
Ladysmith, BC V9G 1A2
Tel: 250-245-6400; *Fax:* 250-245-6411
info@ladysmith.ca
www.ladysmith.ca
Municipal Type: Town
Incorporated: June 3, 1904; *Area:* 12.18 sq km
County or District: Cowichan Valley; *Population in 2011:* 7,921
Provincial Electoral District(s): Cowichan-Ladysmith
Federal Electoral District(s): Nanaimo-Ladysmith
Next Election: Oct. 20, 2018 (4-year terms)
Aaron Stone, Mayor, 250-245-6400
Ruth E. Malli, City Manager, 250-245-6401
Sandy Bowden, Director, Corporate Services
Felicity Adams, Director, Development Services
John Manson, Director, Infrastructure Services
Clayton Postings, Director, Parks, Recreation & Culture
Karen Cousins, Manager, Human Resources, 250-245-6412

Lake Country
10150 Bottom Wood Lake Rd.
Lake Country, BC V4V 2M1
Tel: 250-766-5650; *Fax:* 250-766-0116
admin@lakecountry.bc.ca
www.lakecountry.bc.ca
Municipal Type: District
Incorporated: May 2, 1995; *Area:* 122.16 sq km
County or District: Central Okanagan; *Population in 2011:* 11,708
Provincial Electoral District(s): Kelowna-Lake Country
Federal Electoral District(s): Kelowna-Lake Country
Next Election: Oct. 20, 2018 (4-year terms)
James Baker, Mayor
Alberto De Feo, Chief Administrative Officer, 250-766-6671
Holly Flinkman, Manager, Human Resources, 250-766-5650
Michael J. Mercer, Director, Engineering & Environmental Services, 250-766-5650

Lake Cowichan
P.O. Box 860
39 South Shore Rd.
Lake Cowichan, BC V0R 2G0
Tel: 250-749-6681; *Fax:* 250-749-3900
general@lakecowichan.ca
www.town.lakecowichan.bc.ca
Municipal Type: Town
Incorporated: Aug. 19, 1944; *Area:* 8.25 sq km
County or District: Cowichan Valley; *Population in 2011:* 2,948
Provincial Electoral District(s): Cowichan-Ladysmith
Federal Electoral District(s): Cowichan-Malahat-Langford
Next Election: Oct. 20, 2018 (4-year terms)
Ross Forrest, Mayor, 250-749-6681
Joseph A. Fernandez, Chief Administrative Officer
Nagi Rizk, Superintendent, Public Works & Engineering Services, 250-749-6244

Langley
20338 - 65 Ave.
Langley, BC V2Y 3J1
Tel: 604-534-3211
info@tol.ca
www.tol.ca
Municipal Type: Township
Incorporated: April 26, 1873; *Area:* 306.93 sq km
County or District: Metro Vancouver; *Population in 2011:* 104,177
Provincial Electoral District(s): Fort Langely-Aldergrove
Federal Electoral District(s): Cloverdale-Langley City; Langley-Aldergrove
Next Election: Oct. 20, 2018 (4-year terms)
Jack Froese, Mayor, 604-533-6000
Petrina Arnason, Councillor
David Davis, Councillor
Charlie Fox, Councillor
Bob Long, Councillor
Angie Quaale, Councillor
Kim Richter, Councillor
Michelle Sparrow, Councillor
Blair Whitmarsh, Councillor
Mark Bakken, Administrator, Legislative Services, 604-533-6002
Christine Blair, Director, Corporate Administration, 604-533-6015
Shannon Harvey-Renner, Director, Human Resources, 604-533-6121
Ramin Seifi, General Manager, Engineering & Development Services, 604-532-7300
Hilary Tsikayi, Director, Finance, 604-533-6156
Stephen Gamble, Fire Chief, 604-534-7500
Murray Power, Superintendent, RCMP, 604-532-3200

Lantzville
P.O. Box 100
7192 Lantzville Rd.
Lantzville, BC V0R 2H0
Tel: 250-390-4006; *Fax:* 250-390-5188
district@lantzville.ca
www.lantzville.ca
Municipal Type: District
Incorporated: June 25, 2003; *Area:* 27.87 sq km
County or District: Nanaimo; *Population in 2011:* 3,601
Provincial Electoral District(s): Nanaimo-Parksville
Federal Electoral District(s): Nanaimo-Ladysmith
Next Election: Oct. 20, 2018 (4-year terms)
Colin Robert Haime, Mayor, 250-390-4131
Twyla Graff, Chief Administrative Officer
Fred Spears, Director, Public Works, 250-390-4006

Lillooet
P.O. Box 610
615 Main St.
Lillooet, BC V0K 1V0
Tel: 250-256-4289; *Fax:* 250-256-4288
cityhall@lillooetbc.com
www.lillooetbc.com
Municipal Type: District
Incorporated: Dec. 31, 1946; *Area:* 27.83 sq km
County or District: Squamish-Lillooet; *Population in 2011:* 2,322
Provincial Electoral District(s): Yale-Lillooet
Federal Electoral District(s): Mission-Matsqui-Fraser Canyon
Next Election: Oct. 20, 2018 (4-year terms)
Margaret Lampman, Mayor
Brad McRae, Chief Administrative Officer
Wayne Robinson, Director, Recreation
Jodi Pawloski, Supervisor, Public Works

Lions Bay
P.O. Box 141
400 Centre Rd.
Lions Bay, BC V0N 2E0
Tel: 604-921-9333; *Fax:* 604-921-6643
reception@lionsbay.ca
www.lionsbay.ca
Municipal Type: Village
Incorporated: Dec. 17, 1970; *Area:* 2.55 sq km
County or District: Metro Vancouver; *Population in 2011:* 1,318
Provincial Electoral District(s): West Vancouver-Garibaldi
Federal Electoral District(s): West Vancouver-Sunshine Coast-Sea to Sky Country
Next Election: Oct. 20, 2018 (4-year terms)
Kari Buhr, Mayor, 604-921-9333
Mandy Koonts, Chief Administrative Officer, 604-921-9333
Nikii Hoglund, Manager, Public Works & Services

Logan Lake
P.O. Box 190
1 Opal Dr.
Logan Lake, BC V0K 1W0
Tel: 250-523-6225; *Fax:* 250-523-6678
districtofloganlake@loganlake.ca
www.loganlake.ca

Municipal Type: District
Incorporated: Nov. 10, 1970; *Area:* 325.4 sq km
County or District: Thompson-Nicola; *Population in 2011:* 2,073
Provincial Electoral District(s): Yale-Lillooet
Federal Electoral District(s): Central Okanagan-Similkameen-Nicola
Next Election: Oct. 20, 2018 (4-year terms)
Robin Smith, Mayor
Randy Diehl, Chief Administrative Officer, 250-523-6225
Jeff Carter, Director, Public Works & Recreation

Lumby
P.O. Box 430
1775 Glencaird St.
Lumby, BC V0E 2G0
Tel: 250-547-2171; *Fax:* 250-547-6894
info@lumby.ca
www.lumby.ca
Municipal Type: Village
Incorporated: Dec. 20, 1955; *Area:* 5.27 sq km
County or District: North Okanagan; *Population in 2011:* 1,731
Provincial Electoral District(s): Okanagan-Vernon
Federal Electoral District(s): North Okanagan-Shuswap
Next Election: Oct. 20, 2018 (4-year terms)
Kevin Acton, Mayor, 250-547-2171
Tom Kadla, Chief Administrative Officer
Dave Manson, Superintendent, Public Works, Parks & Recreation

Lytton
P.O. Box 100
380 Main St.
Lytton, BC V0K 1Z0
Tel: 250-455-2355; *Fax:* 250-455-2142
hotspot@lytton.ca
www.lytton.ca
Municipal Type: Village
Incorporated: May 3, 1945; *Area:* 6.71 sq km
County or District: Thompson-Nicola; *Population in 2011:* 228
Provincial Electoral District(s): Yale-Lillooet
Federal Electoral District(s): Mission-Matsqui-Fraser Canyon
Next Election: Oct. 20, 2018 (4-year terms)
Jessoa Lightfoot, Mayor
Lorna Dysart, Chief Administrative Officer

Mackenzie
P.O. Box 340
1 Mackenzie Blvd.
Mackenzie, BC V0J 2C0
Tel: 250-997-3221; *Fax:* 250-997-5186
info@district.mackenzie.bc.ca
www.district.mackenzie.bc.ca
Municipal Type: District
Incorporated: May 19, 1966; *Area:* 159.09 sq km
County or District: Fraser-Fort George; *Population in 2011:* 3,507
Provincial Electoral District(s): Prince George North
Federal Electoral District(s): Prince George-Peace River-Northern Rockies
Next Election: Oct. 20, 2018 (4-year terms)
Pat Crook, Mayor, 250-997-3221
Peter Weeber, Chief Administrative Officer, 250-997-3221
Gord Petersen, Director, Community Services, 250-997-3221

Maple Ridge
11995 Haney Pl.
Maple Ridge, BC V2X 6A9
Tel: 604-463-5221; *Fax:* 604-467-7329
enquiries@mapleridge.ca
www.mapleridge.ca
Municipal Type: District
Incorporated: Sept. 12, 1874; *Area:* 265.79 sq km
County or District: Metro Vancouver; *Population in 2011:* 76,052
Provincial Electoral District(s): Maple Ridge-Pitt Meadows; Maple Ridge-Mission
Federal Electoral District(s): Pitt Meadows-Maple Ridge
Next Election: Oct. 20, 2018 (4-year terms)
Nicole Read, Mayor
Corisa Bell, Councillor
Kiersten Duncan, Councillor
Bob Masse, Councillor
Gordy Robson, Councillor
Tyler Shymkiw, Councillor
Craig Speirs, Councillor
Ted Swabey, Chief Administrative Officer, 604-463-5221
Paul Gill, General Manager, Corporate & Financial Services, 604-467-7398
David Boag, Director, Parks & Facilities, 604-467-7344
Christine Carter, Director, Planning, 604-467-7469
Laura Benson, Manager, Sustainability & Corporate Planning, 604-466-4338
Liz Holitzki, Director, Licences, Permits & Bylaws, 604-467-7370
Sue Wheeler, Director, Community Services, 604-467-7308
Fred Armstrong, Manager, Corporate Communications
Ceri Marlo, P.Eng., Manager, Legislative Services & Emergency Program, 604-467-7482
Dane Spence, Fire Chief, 604-476-3057

Masset
P.O. Box 68
Masset, BC V0T 1M0
Tel: 250-626-3995; *Fax:* 250-626-3968
vom@mhtv.ca
www.massetbc.com
Municipal Type: Village
Incorporated: May 11, 1961; *Area:* 19.45 sq km
County or District: Skeena-Queen Charlotte; *Population in 2011:* 884
Provincial Electoral District(s): North Coast
Federal Electoral District(s): Skeena-Bulkley Valley
Next Election: Oct. 20, 2018 (4-year terms)
Andrew Merilees, Mayor, 250-626-3995
Trevor Jarvis, Chief Administrative Officer, 250-626-3995
Ralph Lamorie, Supervisor of Works, 250-626-3995

McBride
P.O. Box 519
100 Robson Centre
McBride, BC V0J 2E0
Tel: 250-569-2229; *Fax:* 250-569-3276
mcbride@mcbride.ca
www.mcbride.ca
Municipal Type: Village
Incorporated: April 7, 1932; *Area:* 4.43 sq km
County or District: Fraser-Fort George; *Population in 2011:* 586
Provincial Electoral District(s): Prince George-Mount Robson
Federal Electoral District(s): Prince George-Peace River-Northern Rockies
Next Election: Oct. 20, 2018 (4-year terms)
Loranne Martin, Mayor, 250-569-2229
Eliana Clements, Chief Administrative Officer, 250-569-2229

Merritt
P.O. Box 189
2185 Voght St.
Merritt, BC V1K 1B8
Tel: 250-378-4224; *Fax:* 250-378-2600
info@merritt.ca
www.merritt.ca
Municipal Type: Town
Incorporated: April 1, 1911; *Area:* 24.94 sq km
County or District: Thompson-Nicola; *Population in 2011:* 6,998
Provincial Electoral District(s): Yale-Lillooet
Federal Electoral District(s): Central Okanagan-Similkameen-Nicola
Next Election: Oct. 20, 2018 (4-year terms)
Neil Leonard Menard, Mayor, 250-315-7259
Allan Chabot, Chief Administrative Officer/Clerk, 250-378-4224
Shawn Boven, Manager, Public Works, 250-378-8626
Carole Fraser, Deputy Clerk & Manager, Human Resources, 250-378-8614
Sean O'Flaherty, Manager, Planning & Development Services, 250-378-2503

Metchosin
4450 Happy Valley Rd.
Victoria, BC V9C 3Z3
Tel: 250-474-3167; *Fax:* 250-474-6298
info@metchosin.ca
www.metchosin.ca
Municipal Type: District
Incorporated: Dec. 3, 1984; *Area:* 71.32 sq km
County or District: Capital; *Population in 2011:* 4,803
Provincial Electoral District(s): Esquimalt-Metchosin
Federal Electoral District(s): Esquimalt-Saanich-Sooke
Next Election: Oct. 20, 2018 (4-year terms)
John Ranns, Mayor, 250-474-3167
Lisa Urlacher, Chief Administrative Officer, 250-474-3167

Midway
P.O. Box 160
661 Eighth Ave.
Midway, BC V0H 1M0
Tel: 250-449-2222; *Fax:* 250-449-2258
midwaybc@shaw.ca
www.midwaybc.ca
Municipal Type: Village
Incorporated: May 25, 1967; *Area:* 12.16 sq km
County or District: Kootenay Boundary; *Population in 2011:* 674
Provincial Electoral District(s): West Kootenay-Boundary
Federal Electoral District(s): South Okanagan-West Kootenay
Next Election: Oct. 20, 2018 (4-year terms)
Randy Kappes, Mayor, 250-449-2222
Penny Feist, Chief Administrative Officer, 250-449-2222

Mission
P.O. Box 20
8645 Stave Lake St.
Mission, BC V2V 4L9
Tel: 604-820-3700; *Fax:* 604-820-3715
info@mission.ca
www.mission.ca
Municipal Type: District
Incorporated: June 2, 1892; *Area:* 225.78 sq km
County or District: Fraser Valley; *Population in 2011:* 36,426
Provincial Electoral District(s): Maple Ridge-Mission
Federal Electoral District(s): Mission-Matsqui-Fraser Canyon; Pitt Meadows-Maple Ridge
Next Election: Oct. 20, 2018 (4-year terms)
Randy Hawes, Mayor, 604-820-3702
Pam Alexis, Councillor, 604-820-3703
Carol Hamilton, Councillor, 604-820-3703
Jim Hinds, Councillor, 604-820-3703
Rhett Nicholson, Councillor, 604-820-3703
Danny Plecas, Councillor, 604-820-3703
Jenny Stevens, Councillor, 604-820-3703
Ron Poole, Chief Administrative Officer, 604-820-3704
Tracy Kyle, Director, Engineering & Public Works, 604-820-3739
Gina MacKay, Director, Long Range Planning & Special Projects, 604-820-3730
Bob O'Neal, Director, Forestry, 604-820-3762
Kathryn Bekkering, Manager, Human Resources, 604-820-3707
Michael Boronowski, Manager, Civic Engagement & Corporate Initiatives
Kirsten Hargreaves, Manager, Social Development, 604-820-3752
Dale Unrau, Fire Chief, 604-820-3794
Ted De Jager, Chief of Police, 604-826-7161

Montrose
P.O. Box 510
565 - 11th Ave.
Montrose, BC V0G 1P0
Tel: 250-367-7234; *Fax:* 250-367-7288
admin@montrose.ca
www.montrose.ca
Municipal Type: Village
Incorporated: June 22, 1956; *Area:* 1.53 sq km
County or District: Kootenay Boundary; *Population in 2011:* 1,030
Provincial Electoral District(s): West Kootenay-Boundary
Federal Electoral District(s): South Okanagan-West Kootenay
Next Election: Oct. 20, 2018 (4-year terms)
Joe Danchuk, Mayor, 250-367-7234
Bryan Teasdale, Chief Administrative Officer, 250-367-7234

Nakusp
P.O. Box 280
91 - 1st St. NW
Nakusp, BC V0G 1R0
Tel: 250-265-3689; *Fax:* 250-265-3788
info@nakusp.com
www.nakusp.com
Municipal Type: Village
Incorporated: Nov. 24, 1964; *Area:* 8 sq km
County or District: Central Kootenay; *Population in 2011:* 1,569
Provincial Electoral District(s): Nelson-Creston
Federal Electoral District(s): South Okanagan-West Kootenay
Next Election: Oct. 20, 2018 (4-year terms)
Karen Hamling, Mayor, 250-265-3689
Linda Tynan, Chief Administrative Officer, 250-265-3689

New Denver
P.O. Box 40
115 Slocan Ave.
New Denver, BC V0G 1S0
Tel: 250-358-2316; *Fax:* 250-358-7251
office@newdenver.ca
www.newdenver.ca
Municipal Type: Village
Incorporated: Jan. 12, 1929; *Area:* 1.1 sq km
County or District: Central Kootenay; *Population in 2011:* 504
Provincial Electoral District(s): Nelson-Creston
Federal Electoral District(s): South Okanagan-West Kootenay
Next Election: Oct. 20, 2018 (4-year terms)
Ann Bunka, Mayor, 250-358-2316
Bruce Woodbury, Chief Administrative Officer, 250-358-2316

New Hazelton
P.O. Box 340
3026 Bowser St.
New Hazelton, BC V0J 2J0
Tel: 250-842-6571; *Fax:* 250-842-6077
info@newhazelton.ca
www.newhazelton.ca
Municipal Type: District
Incorporated: Dec. 15, 1980; *Area:* 25.64 sq km

County or District: Kitimat-Stikine; *Population in 2011:* 666
Provincial Electoral District(s): Bulkley Valley-Stikine
Federal Electoral District(s): Skeena-Bulkley Valley
Next Election: Oct. 20, 2018 (4-year terms)
Gail Lowry, Mayor, 250-842-6571
Wendy Hunt, Chief Administrative Officer, 250-842-6571

North Cowichan
P.O. Box 278
7030 Trans Canada Hwy.
Duncan, BC V9L 3X4
Tel: 250-746-3100; *Fax:* 250-746-3133
info@northcowichan.bc.ca
www.northcowichan.bc.ca
Municipal Type: District
Incorporated: June 18, 1873; *Area:* 193.66 sq km
County or District: Cowichan Valley; *Population in 2011:* 28,807
Provincial Electoral District(s): Cowichan-Ladysmith
Federal Electoral District(s): Cowichan-Malahat-Langford
Next Election: Oct. 20, 2018 (4-year terms)
Jon Lefebure, Mayor
Joyce Behnsen, Councillor
Rob Douglas, Councillor
Maeve Maguire, Councillor
Kate Marsh, Councillor
Al Siebring, Councillor
Tom Walker, Councillor
Dave Devana, Chief Administrative Officer, 250-746-3115
Mark O. Ruttan, Deputy Chief Administrative Officer/Director
Mark Frame, Director, Finance
Gaya Laflamme, Director, Human Resources
Scott Mack, Director, Development Services
David Conway, Director, Engineering & Operations, 250-746-3136
Ernie Mansueti, Director, Parks & Recreation

North Saanich
1620 Mills Rd.
North Saanich, BC V8L 5S9
Tel: 250-656-0781; *Fax:* 250-656-3155
admin@northsaanich.ca
www.northsaanich.ca
Municipal Type: District
Incorporated: Aug. 19, 1965; *Area:* 37.14 sq km
County or District: Capital; *Population in 2011:* 11,089
Provincial Electoral District(s): Saanich North & the Islands
Federal Electoral District(s): Saanich-Gulf Islands
Next Election: Oct. 20, 2018 (4-year terms)
Alice Finall, Mayor, 250-656-0781
Heather Gartshore, Councillor, 250-656-0974
Jack McClintock, Councillor, 250-888-4890
Geoff Orr, Councillor, 250-656-4562
Celia Stock, Councillor
Jack Thornburgh, Councillor, 250-665-6314
Murray Weisenberger, Councillor, 778-351-2213
Rob Buchan, Chief Administrative Officer, 250-655-5452
Curt Kingsley, Manager, Corporate Services, 250-655-5453
Mark Brodrick, Director, Planning & Community Services, 250-655-5471
Patrick O'Reilly, Director, Infrastructure Services, 250-655-5461
Theresa Flynn, Director, Financial Services, 250-656-0781
Gary Wilton, Director, Emergency Services, 250-661-0223

North Vancouver
355 West Queens Rd.
North Vancouver, BC V7N 4N5
Tel: 604-990-2311
infoweb@dnv.org
www.dnv.org
Municipal Type: District Municipality
Incorporated: Aug. 10, 1891; *Area:* 160.67 sq km
County or District: Metro Vancouver; *Population in 2011:* 84,412
Provincial Electoral District(s): N. Vancouver-Lonsdale; N. Vancouver-Seymour; W. Vancouver-Capilano; W. Vancouver-Garibaldi
Federal Electoral District(s): North Vancouver; Burnaby North-Seymour
Next Election: Oct. 20, 2018 (4-year terms)
Richard Walton, Mayor, 604-990-2208
Roger Bassam, Councillor
Matthew M. Bond, Councillor
Jim M. Hanson, Councillor
Robin Hicks, Councillor
Doug Mackay-Dunn, Councillor
Lisa Muri, Councillor
David Stuart, Chief Administrative Officer, 604-990-2209
Brian Bydwell, General Manager, Planning, Permits & Bylaws, 604-990-2398
Nicole Deveaux, CFO & General Manager, Financial Services & IT Services, 604-990-2234
Joyce Gavin, General Manager, Engineering, Parks & Facilities, 604-990-3828
Heather Turner, Director, Recreation, 604-983-6309
Jacqueline van Dyk, Director, Library Services, 604-990-5800
Lorn Carter, Manager, Utilities
Cindy Rogers, Manager, Human Resources
Mairi Welman, Manager, Strategic Communications & Community Relations
Allen Lynch, Manager, North Shore Recycling Program, 604-984-9730
Doug Trussler, Fire Chief, 604-990-3651
Tonia Enger, Superintendent, North Vancouver RCMP Detachment, 604-985-1311

Oak Bay
2167 Oak Bay Ave.
Victoria, BC V8R 1G2
Tel: 250-598-3311; *Fax:* 250-598-9108
www.oakbay.ca
Municipal Type: District
Incorporated: July 2, 1906; *Area:* 10.38 sq km
County or District: Capital; *Population in 2011:* 18,015
Provincial Electoral District(s): Oak Bay-Gordon Head
Federal Electoral District(s): Victoria
Next Election: Oct. 20, 2018 (4-year terms)
Nils Jensen, Mayor
Hazel Braithwaite, Councillor
Tom Croft, Councillor
Michelle Kirby, Councillor
Kevin Murdoch, Councillor
Tara Ney, Councillor
Eric Wood Zhelka, Councillor
Loranne Hilton, Clerk
Helen Koning, Chief Administrative Officer
Patricia A. Walker, Treasurer
Ray Herman, Director, Parks, Recreation & Culture, 250-370-7102
David Brozuk, Superintendent, Public Works & Acting Director, Engineering Services, 250-598-4501
Dave Cockle, Fire Chief, 250-592-9121
Andy Brinton, Chief Constable, Police Services, 250-592-2424

Oliver
P.O. Box 638
35016 - 97th St.
Oliver, BC V0H 1T0
Tel: 250-485-6200; *Fax:* 250-498-4466
admin@oliver.ca
www.oliver.ca
Municipal Type: Town
Incorporated: Dec. 31, 1945; *Area:* 4.95 sq km
County or District: Okanagan-Similkameen; *Population in 2011:* 4,824
Provincial Electoral District(s): Penticton-Okanagan Valley
Federal Electoral District(s): South Okanagan-West Kootenay
Next Election: Oct. 20, 2018 (4-year terms)
Ronald Hovanes, Mayor, 250-485-6205
Heidi Frank, Chief Administrative Officer
Carol Sheridan, Director, Recreation & Community Services

Osoyoos
P.O. Box 3010
8707 Main St.
Osoyoos, BC V0H 1V0
Tel: 250-495-6515; *Fax:* 250-495-2400
info@osoyoos.ca
www.osoyoos.ca
Other Information: Toll-Free Phone: 1-888-495-6515
Municipal Type: Town
Incorporated: Jan. 14, 1946; *Area:* 8.76 sq km
County or District: Okanagan-Similkameen; *Population in 2011:* 4,845
Provincial Electoral District(s): Penticton-Okanagan Valley
Federal Electoral District(s): South Okanagan-West Kootenay
Next Election: Oct. 20, 2018 (4-year terms)
Sue McKortoff, Mayor
Barry Romanko, Chief Administrative Officer

Peachland
5806 Beach Ave.
Peachland, BC V0H 1X7
Tel: 250-767-2647; *Fax:* 250-767-3433
info@peachland.ca
www.peachland.ca
Municipal Type: District
Incorporated: Jan. 1, 1909; *Area:* 15.98 sq km
County or District: Central Okanagan; *Population in 2011:* 5,200
Provincial Electoral District(s): Okanagan-Westside
Federal Electoral District(s): Central Okanagan-Similkameen-Nicola
Next Election: Oct. 20, 2018 (4-year terms)
Cindy Fortin, Mayor, 250-212-9416
Elsie Lemke, Chief Administrative Officer, 250-767-2647

Pemberton
P.O. Box 100
7400 Prospect St.
Pemberton, BC V0N 2L0
Tel: 604-894-6135; *Fax:* 604-894-6136
admin@pemberton.ca
www.pemberton.ca
Municipal Type: Village
Incorporated: July 20, 1956; *Area:* 4.45 sq km
County or District: Squamish-Lillooet; *Population in 2011:* 2,369
Provincial Electoral District(s): West Vancouver-Garibaldi
Federal Electoral District(s): West Vancouver-Sunshine Coast-Sea to Sky Country
Next Election: Oct. 20, 2018 (4-year terms)
Mike Richman, Mayor
Nikki Gilmore, Chief Administrative Officer, 604-894-6135
Jeff Westlake, Public Works Supervisor, 604-894-6135

Port Alice
P.O. Box 130
1061 Marine Dr.
Port Alice, BC V0N 2N0
Tel: 250-284-3391; *Fax:* 250-284-3416
info@portalice.ca
www.portalice.ca
Municipal Type: Village
Incorporated: June 16, 1965; *Area:* 7.65 sq km
County or District: Mount Waddington; *Population in 2011:* 805
Provincial Electoral District(s): North Island
Federal Electoral District(s): North Island-Powell River
Next Election: Oct. 20, 2018 (4-year terms)
Jan Allen, Mayor
Madeline McDonald, Chief Administrative Officer

Port Clements
P.O. Box 198
36 Cedar Ave. West
Port Clements, BC V0T 1R0
Tel: 250-557-4295; *Fax:* 250-557-4568
deputy@portclements.ca
www.portclements.com
Municipal Type: Village
Incorporated: Dec. 31, 1975; *Area:* 13.59 sq km
County or District: Skeena-Queen Charlotte; *Population in 2011:* 378
Provincial Electoral District(s): North Coast
Federal Electoral District(s): Skeena-Bulkley Valley
Next Election: Oct. 20, 2018 (4-year terms)
Ian Gould, Mayor
Kim Mushynsky, Chief Administrative Officer
Sean O'Donoghue, Superintendent, Public Works

Port Edward
P.O. Box 1100
770 Pacific Ave.
Port Edward, BC V0V 1G0
Tel: 250-628-3667; *Fax:* 250-628-9225
info@portedward.ca
www.portedward.ca
Municipal Type: District
Incorporated: June 29, 1966; *Area:* 168.12 sq km
County or District: Skeena-Queen Charlotte; *Population in 2011:* 544
Provincial Electoral District(s): North Coast
Federal Electoral District(s): Skeena-Bulkley Valley
Next Election: Oct. 20, 2018 (4-year terms)
Dave MacDonald, Mayor
Bob Payette, Chief Administrative Officer

Port Hardy
P.O. Box 68
7360 Columbia St.
Port Hardy, BC V0N 2P0
Tel: 250-949-6665; *Fax:* 250-949-7433
general@porthardy.ca
www.porthardy.ca
Municipal Type: District
Incorporated: May 5, 1966; *Area:* 40.81 sq km
County or District: Mount Waddington; *Population in 2011:* 4,008
Provincial Electoral District(s): North Island
Federal Electoral District(s): North Island-Powell River
Next Election: Oct. 20, 2018 (4-year terms)
Hank Bood, Mayor, 250-949-6665
Rick Davidge, Chief Administrative Officer, 250-949-6665
Allison McCarrick, Director, Financial Services, 250-949-6665
Jeff Long, Director, Corporate & Development Services, 250-949-6665

Port McNeill
P.O. Box 728
1775 Grenville Pl.
Port McNeill, BC V0N 2R0
Tel: 250-956-3111; *Fax:* 250-956-4300
reception@portmcneill.ca
www.portmcneill.ca
Municipal Type: Town
Incorporated: Feb. 18, 1966; *Area:* 7.74 sq km
County or District: Mount Waddington; *Population in 2011:* 2,505
Provincial Electoral District(s): North Island
Federal Electoral District(s): North Island-Powell River
Next Election: Oct. 20, 2018 (4-year terms)
Shirley Ackland, Mayor
Sue Harvey, Administrator

Pouce Coupé
P.O. Box 190
5011 - 49 Ave.
Pouce Coupe, BC V0C 2C0
Tel: 250-786-5794; *Fax:* 250-786-5257
admin@poucecoupe.ca
www.poucecoupe.ca
Municipal Type: Village
Incorporated: Jan. 5, 1932; *Area:* 2.06 sq km
County or District: Peace River; *Population in 2011:* 738
Provincial Electoral District(s): Peace River South
Federal Electoral District(s): Prince George-Peace River-Northern Rockies
Next Election: Oct. 20, 2018 (4-year terms)
William Plowright, Mayor
Carol Bishop, Chief Administrative Officer

Princeton
P.O. Box 670
169 Bridge St.
Princeton, BC V0X 1W0
Tel: 250-295-3135; *Fax:* 250-295-3477
admin@princeton.ca
www.princeton.ca
Municipal Type: Town
Incorporated: Sept. 11, 1951; *Area:* 10.25 sq km
County or District: Okanagan-Similkameen; *Population in 2011:* 2,724
Provincial Electoral District(s): Yale-Lillooet
Federal Electoral District(s): Central Okanagan-Similkameen-Nicola
Next Election: Oct. 20, 2018 (4-year terms)
Frank Armitage, Mayor
Rick Zerr, Chief Administrative Officer
Kevin Huey, Director, Infrastructure & Parks

Qualicum Beach
P.O. Box 130
#201, 660 Primrose St.
Qualicum Beach, BC V9K 1S7
Tel: 250-752-6921; *Fax:* 250-752-1243
qbtown@qualicumbeach.com
www.qualicumbeach.com
Municipal Type: Town
Incorporated: May 5, 1942; *Area:* 18 sq km
County or District: Nanaimo; *Population in 2011:* 8,687
Provincial Electoral District(s): Alberni-Qualicum
Federal Electoral District(s): Courtenay-Alberni
Next Election: Oct. 20, 2018 (4-year terms)
Teunis Westbroek, Mayor
Daniel Sailland, Chief Administrative Officer, 250-752-6921
Al Cameron, Superintendent, Public Works, Parks & Buildings, 250-752-6921
Luke Sales, Director, Planning & Approving Officer
Bob Weir, Director, Engineering, Utilities & Airport

Queen Charlotte
P.O. Box 580
903A Oceanview Dr.
Queen Charlotte, BC V0T 1S0
Tel: 250-559-4765; *Fax:* 250-559-4742
office@queencharlotte.ca
www.queencharlotte.ca
Municipal Type: Village
Incorporated: Dec. 7, 2005; *Area:* 37.28 sq km
County or District: Skeena-Queen Charlotte; *Population in 2011:* 944
Provincial Electoral District(s): North Coast
Federal Electoral District(s): Skeena-Bulkley Valley
Next Election: Oct. 20, 2018 (4-year terms)
Greg Martin, Mayor, 250-559-4765
Lori Wiedeman, Chief Administrative Officer, 250-559-4765

Radium Hot Springs
P.O. Box 340
Radium Hot Springs, BC V0A 1M0
Tel: 250-347-6455; *Fax:* 250-347-9068
www.radiumhotsprings.ca
Municipal Type: Village
Incorporated: Dec. 10, 1990; *Area:* 6.31 sq km
County or District: East Kootenay; *Population in 2011:* 777
Provincial Electoral District(s): Columbia River-Revelstoke
Federal Electoral District(s): Kootenay-Columbia
Next Election: Oct. 20, 2018 (4-year terms)
Clara Reinhardt, Mayor
Mark Read, Chief Administrative Officer/Clerk/Approving Officer

Revelstoke
P.O. Box 170
216 Mackenzie Ave.
Revelstoke, BC V0E 2S0
Tel: 250-837-2161; *Fax:* 250-837-4930
admin@revelstoke.ca
www.cityofrevelstoke.com
Municipal Type: Town
Incorporated: March 1, 1899; *Area:* 31.9 sq km
County or District: Columbia-Shuswap; *Population in 2011:* 7,139
Provincial Electoral District(s): Columbia River-Revelstoke
Federal Electoral District(s): Kootenay-Columbia
Next Election: Oct. 20, 2018 (4-year terms)
Mark McKee, Mayor
Laurie Donato, Director, Parks, Recreation & Culture
Mike Thomas, Director, Engineering & Development Services

Rossland
P.O. Box 1179
1899 Columbia Ave.
Rossland, BC V0G 1Y0
Tel: 250-362-7396; *Fax:* 250-362-5451
cityhall@rossland.ca
www.rossland.ca
Municipal Type: Town
Incorporated: March 18, 1897; *Area:* 57.97 sq km
County or District: Kootenay Boundary; *Population in 2011:* 3,556
Provincial Electoral District(s): West Kootenay-Boundary
Federal Electoral District(s): South Okanagan-West Kootenay
Next Election: Oct. 20, 2018 (4-year terms)
Kathy Moore, Mayor, 250-362-3319
Tracey Butler, Chief Administrative Officer, 250-362-2321
Darrin Albo, Manager, Public Works, 250-362-2328

Saanich
770 Vernon Ave.
Victoria, BC V8X 2W7
Tel: 250-475-1775
clerksec@saanich.ca
www.saanich.ca
Municipal Type: District Municipality
Incorporated: Dec. 12, 1950; *Area:* 103.44 sq km
County or District: Capital; *Population in 2011:* 109,752
Provincial Electoral District(s): Oak Bay-Gordon Head; Saanich N. & the Islands; Saanich S.
Federal Electoral District(s): Esquimalt-Saanich-Sooke; Saanich-Gulf Islands; Victoria
Next Election: Oct. 20, 2018 (4-year terms)
Richard Atwell, Mayor, 250-475-5510
Susan Brice, Councillor
Judy Brownoff, Councillor
Vic Derman, Councillor
Fred Haynes, Councillor
Dean Murdock, Councillor
Colin Plant, Councillor
Vicki Sanders, Councillor
Leif Wergeland, Councillor
Paul Thorkelsson, Chief Administrative Officer, 250-475-5555, Fax: 250-475-5440
Laura Ciarniello, Director, Corporate Services
Harley Machielse, Director, Engineering, 250-475-5575, Fax: 250-475-5450
Suzanne Samborski, Director, Parks & Recreation, 250-475-5421, Fax: 250-475-5411
Sharon Hvozdanski, Director, Planning, 250-475-5470, Fax: 250-475-5430
Carrie M. MacPhee, Director, Legislative Services
Valia Tinney, Director, Finance, 250-475-5521, Fax: 250-475-5429
Shane Laye, Manager, Facility Operations
Mike Lai, Manager, Transportation, 250-475-7114, Fax: 250-475-5450
David Sparanese, Manager, Public Works, 250-475-5494, Fax: 250-475-5487
Kelli-Ann Armstrong, Sr. Manager, Recreation Services, 250-475-5452, Fax: 250-475-5411
Jim Hemstock, Manager, Capital Works, 250-475-5464, Fax: 250-475-5590
Adriane Pollard, Manager, Environmental Services, 250-475-5494, Fax: 250-475-5430
Cameron Scott, Manager, Community Planning, 250-475-7115, Fax: 250-475-5430
Michael Burgess, Fire Chief
Bob Downie, Chief Constable, 250-475-4321, Fax: 250-475-6138

Salmo
P.O. Box 1000
423 Davies Ave.
Salmo, BC V0G 1Z0
Tel: 250-357-9433; *Fax:* 250-357-9633
salmo.ca
Municipal Type: Village
Incorporated: Oct. 30, 1946; *Area:* 2.38 sq km
County or District: Central Kootenay; *Population in 2011:* 1,139
Provincial Electoral District(s): Nelson-Creston
Federal Electoral District(s): Kootenay-Columbia
Next Election: Oct. 20, 2018 (4-year terms)
Stephen White, Mayor
Diane Kalensukra, Chief Administrative Officer

Sayward
P.O. Box 29
601 Kelsey Way
Sayward, BC V0P 1R0
Tel: 250-282-5512; *Fax:* 250-282-5511
village@saywardvalley.net
www.sayward.ca
Municipal Type: Village
Incorporated: June 27, 1968; *Area:* 4.72 sq km
County or District: Strathcona; *Population in 2011:* 317
Provincial Electoral District(s): North Island
Federal Electoral District(s): North Island-Powell River
Next Election: Oct. 20, 2018 (4-year terms)
John MacDonald, Mayor
Darren Kiedyk, Chief Administrative Officer/Chief Financial Officer

Sechelt
P.O. Box 129
5797 Cowrie St., 2nd Fl.
Sechelt, BC V0N 3A0
Tel: 604-885-1986; *Fax:* 604-885-7591
info@sechelt.ca
www.sechelt.ca
Municipal Type: District Municipality
Incorporated: Feb. 15, 1956; *Area:* 39.71 sq km
County or District: Sunshine Coast; *Population in 2011:* 9,291
Provincial Electoral District(s): Powell River-Sunshine Coast
Federal Electoral District(s): West Vancouver-Sunshine Coast-Sea to Sky Country
Next Election: Oct. 20, 2018 (4-year terms)
Bruce Milne, Mayor
Darren Inkster, Councillor
Alice Lutes, Councillor
Noel Muller, Councillor
Mike Shanks, Councillor
Darnelda Siegers, Councillor
Doug Wright, Councillor
Tim Palmer, Chief Administrative Officer
Mike Vance, Acting Director, Development Services
John Mercer, Superintendent, Parks & Public Works
Susan Sagman, Human Resources Advisor

Sicamous
P.O. Box 219
446 Main St.
Sicamous, BC V0E 2V0
Tel: 250-836-2477; *Fax:* 250-836-4314
cityhall@sicamous.ca
www.sicamous.ca
Municipal Type: District
Incorporated: Dec. 4, 1989; *Area:* 14.68 sq km
County or District: Columbia-Shuswap; *Population in 2011:* 2,441
Provincial Electoral District(s): Shuswap
Federal Electoral District(s): North Okanagan-Shuswap
Next Election: Oct. 20, 2018 (4-year terms)
Terry Rysz, Mayor
Fred Banham, Chief Administrative Officer
Darrell Symbaluk, Public Works Supervisor

Sidney
Municipal Hall
2440 Sidney Ave.
Sidney, BC V8L 1Y7
Tel: 250-656-1184; *Fax:* 250-655-4508
admin@sidney.ca
www.sidney.ca

Municipal Type: Town
Incorporated: Sept. 30, 1952; *Area:* 5.04 sq km
County or District: Capital; *Population in 2011:* 11,178
Provincial Electoral District(s): Saanich N. & the Islands
Federal Electoral District(s): Saanich-Gulf Islands
Next Election: Oct. 20, 2018 (4-year terms)
Steve Price, Mayor, 250-656-1139
Erin Bremner, Councillor
Tim Chad, Councillor
Barbara Fallot, Councillor
Mervyn Lougher-Goodey, Councillor
Cam McLennan, Councillor
Peter Wainwright, Councillor
Randy Humble, Chief Administrative Officer/Corporate Administrator, 250-656-1139
Tim Tanton, Director, Development Services, Engineering, Parks & Works, 250-656-4502
Marlaina Elliott, Director, Development Services, 250-655-5418
Andrew Hicik, Director, Corporate Services, 250-655-5410
Mike van der Linden, Manager, Engineering & Environmental Services, 250-655-5416
Troy Restell, Manager, Finance, 250-655-5409
Brett Mikkelsen, Fire Chief

Silverton
P.O. Box 14
421 Lake Ave.
Silverton, BC V0G 2B0
Tel: 250-358-2472; *Fax:* 250-358-2321
administration@silverton.ca
www.silverton.ca
Municipal Type: Village
Incorporated: May 6, 1930; *Area:* 0.44 sq km
County or District: Central Kootenay; *Population in 2011:* 195
Provincial Electoral District(s): Nelson-Creston
Federal Electoral District(s): South Okanagan-West Kootenay
Next Election: Oct. 20, 2018 (4-year terms)
Jason Clarke, Mayor
Melisa Miles, Chief Administrative Officer
Leonard Casley, Fire Chief & Supervisor, Works

Slocan
P.O. Box 50
503 Slocan Ave.
Slocan, BC V0G 2C0
Tel: 250-355-2277; *Fax:* 250-355-2666
info@villageofslocan.ca
www.slocancity.com
Other Information: Toll Free Phone: 1-866-355-2023
Municipal Type: Village
Incorporated: June 1, 1901; *Area:* 0.75 sq km
County or District: Central Kootenay; *Population in 2011:* 296
Provincial Electoral District(s): Nelson-Creston
Federal Electoral District(s): South Okanagan-West Kootenay
Next Election: Oct. 20, 2018 (4-year terms)
Jessica Lunn, Mayor
Patricia Dehnel, Chief Administrative Officer

Smithers
P.O. Box 879
1027 Aldous St.
Smithers, BC V0J 2N0
Tel: 250-847-1600; *Fax:* 250-847-1601
general@smithers.ca
www.smithers.ca
Municipal Type: Town
Incorporated: Oct. 6, 1921; *Area:* 15.69 sq km
County or District: Bulkley-Nechako; *Population in 2011:* 5,404
Provincial Electoral District(s): Bulkley Valley-Stikine
Federal Electoral District(s): Skeena-Bulkley Valley
Next Election: Oct. 20, 2018 (4-year terms)
Taylor Bachrach, Mayor
Deborah Sargent, Chief Administrative Officer
Mark Allenn, Director, Development Services
Andrew Hillaby, Director, Recreation, Parks & Culture
Roger Smith, Director, Works & Operations

Sooke
2205 Otter Point Rd.
Sooke, BC V9Z 1J2
Tel: 250-642-1634; *Fax:* 250-642-0541
info@sooke.ca
www.sooke.ca
Municipal Type: District
Incorporated: Dec. 7, 1999; *Area:* 50.01 sq km
County or District: Capital; *Population in 2011:* 11,435
Provincial Electoral District(s): Malahat-Juan de Fuca
Federal Electoral District(s): Esquimalt-Saanich-Sooke
Next Election: Oct. 20, 2018 (4-year terms)
Maja Tait, Mayor, 250-642-1634
Gord Howie, Chief Administrative Officer, 250-642-1634

Spallumcheen
4144 Spallumcheen Way
Spallumcheen, BC V0E 1B6
Tel: 250-546-3013; *Fax:* 250-546-8878
mail@spallumcheentwp.bc.ca
www.spallumcheentwp.bc.ca
Municipal Type: Township
Area: 254.9 sq km
County or District: North Okanagan; *Population in 2011:* 5,055
Provincial Electoral District(s): Shuswap
Federal Electoral District(s): North Okanagan-Shuswap
Next Election: Oct. 20, 2018 (4-year terms)
Janice Brown, Mayor
Corey Paiement, Chief Administrative Officer

Sparwood
P.O. Box 520
136 Spruce Ave.
Sparwood, BC V0B 2G0
Tel: 250-425-6271; *Fax:* 250-425-7277
sparwood@sparwood.ca
www.sparwood.ca
Municipal Type: District
Incorporated: Oct. 6, 1964; *Area:* 177.71 sq km
County or District: East Kootenay; *Population in 2011:* 3,667
Provincial Electoral District(s): East Kootenay
Federal Electoral District(s): Kootenay-Columbia
Next Election: Oct. 20, 2018 (4-year terms)
Cal McDougall, Mayor
Terry Melcer, Chief Administrative Officer
Melvin Bohmer, Director, Operations
Danny Dwyer, Director, Engineering
James Jones, Director, Fire Services
Duane Lawrence, Director, Community & Facility Services
Michelle Martineau, Director, Corporate Services

Squamish
P.O. Box 310
37955 Second Ave.
Squamish, BC V0N 3G0
Tel: 604-892-5217; *Fax:* 604-892-1083
admdept@squamish.ca
www.squamish.ca
Municipal Type: District
Incorporated: May 18, 1948; *Area:* 106.11 sq km
County or District: Squamish-Lillooet; *Population in 2011:* 17,158
Provincial Electoral District(s): West Vancouver-Garibaldi
Federal Electoral District(s): West Vancouver-Sunshine Coast-Sea to Sky Country
Next Election: Oct. 20, 2018 (4-year terms)
Patricia Heintzman, Mayor, 604-892-5217
Jason Blackman-Wulff, Councillor
Susan Chapelle, Councillor
Karen Elliott, Councillor
Peter Kent, Councillor
Ted C. Prior, Councillor
Doug Race, Councillor
Linda Glenday, Chief Administrative Officer, 604-815-5034
Robin Arthurs, General Manager, Corporate Services
Gary Buxton, General Manager, Development Services & Public Works, 604-815-5217
Joanne Greenless, General Manager, Financial Services
Tim Hoskin, Director, Recreation Services
Rod MacLeod, Director, Engineering
Bob Smith, Director, Operations
Julie Morris, Manager, Human Resources, 604-892-5217
Bob Fulton, Fire Chief, 604-848-9666

Stewart
P.O. Box 460
705 Brightwell St.
Stewart, BC V0T 1W0
Tel: 250-636-2251; *Fax:* 250-636-2417
info@districtofstewart.com
www.districtofstewart.com
Municipal Type: District
Incorporated: May 16, 1930; *Area:* 571.5 sq km
County or District: Kitimat-Stikine; *Population in 2011:* 494
Provincial Electoral District(s): North Coast
Federal Electoral District(s): Skeena-Bulkley Valley
Next Election: Oct. 20, 2018 (4-year terms)
Galina Durant, Mayor
Maureen Tarrant, Chief Administrative Officer
Chad McKay, Director, Public Works

Summerland
P.O. Box 159
11321 Henry Ave.
Summerland, BC V0H 1Z0
Tel: 250-494-6451; *Fax:* 250-494-1415
info@summerland.ca
www.summerland.ca
Municipal Type: District
Incorporated: Dec. 21, 1906; *Area:* 73.88 sq km
County or District: Okanagan-Similkameen; *Population in 2011:* 11,280
Provincial Electoral District(s): Okanagan-Westside
Federal Electoral District(s): Central Okanagan-Similkameen-Nicola
Next Election: Oct. 20, 2018 (4-year terms)
Peter Waterman, Mayor
Richard H. Barkwill, Councillor
Toni Boot, Councillor
Erin Carlson, Councillor
Doug Holmes, Councillor
Janet Peake, Councillor
Erin Trainer, Councillor
Linda Tynan, Chief Administrative Officer
Kris Johnson, Director, Works & Utilities, 250-404-4096
Jeremy Denegar, Director, Corporate Services
Ian McIntosh, Director, Development Services, 205-404-4048
Lorrie Coates, Director, Finance
Glenn Noble, Fire Chief, 250-404-4092

Sun Peaks
P.O. Box 1002
#106, 3270 Village Way
Sun Peaks, BC V0E 5N0
Tel: 250-578-2020; *Fax:* 250-578-2023
admin@sunpeaksmunicipality.ca
sunpeaksmunicipality.ca
Municipal Type: Mountain Resort Village
Incorporated: June 28, 2010; *Area:* 40.86 sq km
County or District: Thompson-Nicola; *Population in 2011:* 371
Provincial Electoral District(s): Kamloops-North Thompson
Federal Electoral District(s): Kamloops-Thompson-Cariboo
Next Election: Oct. 20, 2018 (4-year terms)
Al Raine, Mayor
Rob Bremmer, Chief Administrative Officer

Tahsis
P.O. Box 219
Tahsis, BC V0P 1X0
Tel: 250-934-6344
reception@villageoftahsis.com
www.villageoftahsis.com
Municipal Type: Village
Incorporated: June 17, 1970; *Area:* 5.73 sq km
County or District: Strathcona; *Population in 2011:* 316
Provincial Electoral District(s): North Island
Federal Electoral District(s): North Island-Powell River
Next Election: Oct. 20, 2018 (4-year terms)
Judith Schooner, Mayor
Doug Chapman, Chief Administrative Officer & Chief Financial Officer, 250-934-6344

Taylor
P.O. Box 300
10007 - 100A St.
Taylor, BC V0C 2K0
Tel: 250-789-3392; *Fax:* 250-789-3543
feedback@districtoftaylor.com
www.districtoftaylor.com
Municipal Type: District
Incorporated: Aug. 23, 1958; *Area:* 16.61 sq km
County or District: Peace River; *Population in 2011:* 1,373
Provincial Electoral District(s): Peace River South
Federal Electoral District(s): Prince George-Peace River-Northern Rockies
Next Election: Oct. 20, 2018 (4-year terms)
Rob Fraser, Mayor
Charlette LcLeod, Administrator
Troy Gould, Director, Parks & Facilities, 250-789-3333

Telkwa
P.O. Box 220
1704 Riverside St.
Telkwa, BC V0J 2X0
Tel: 250-846-5212; *Fax:* 250-846-9572
info@telkwa.com
www.telkwa.com
Municipal Type: Village
Incorporated: July 18, 1952; *Area:* 6.56 sq km
County or District: Bulkley-Nechako; *Population in 2011:* 1,350
Provincial Electoral District(s): Bulkley Valley-Stikine
Federal Electoral District(s): Skeena-Bulkley Valley
Next Election: Oct. 20, 2018 (4-year terms)
Darcy Repen, Mayor
Kim Martinsen, Chief Administrative Officer

Tofino
P.O. Box 9
121 Third St.
Tofino, BC V0R 2Z0
Tel: 250-725-3229; *Fax:* 250-725-3775
office@tofino.ca
www.tofino.ca
Municipal Type: District
Incorporated: Feb. 5, 1932; *Area:* 10.54 sq km
County or District: Alberni-Clayoquot; *Population in 2011:* 1,876
Provincial Electoral District(s): Alberni-Qualicum
Federal Electoral District(s): Courtenay-Alberni
Next Election: Oct. 20, 2018 (4-year terms)
Josie Osborne, Mayor, 250-725-3229
Bob MacPherson, Chief Administrative Officer, 250-725-3229
Bob Schantz, Director, Public Works & Building Inspection, 250-725-3229

Trail
1394 Pine Ave.
Trail, BC V1R 4E6
Tel: 250-364-1262; *Fax:* 250-364-0830
info@trail.ca
www.trail.ca
Municipal Type: Town
Incorporated: June 14, 1901; *Area:* 34.78 sq km
County or District: Kootenay Boundary; *Population in 2011:* 7,681
Provincial Electoral District(s): West Kootenay-Boundary
Federal Electoral District(s): South Okanagan-West Kootenay
Next Election: Oct. 20, 2018 (4-year terms)
Mike Martin, Mayor, 250-364-1262
David Perehudoff, Chief Administrative Officer/Financial Administrator, 250-364-0805
Trisha Davison, Director, Parks & Recreation, 250-364-0852
Larry Abenante, Manager, Public Works, 250-364-0825

Tumbler Ridge
P.O. Box 100
305 Founders St.
Tumbler Ridge, BC V0C 2W0
Tel: 250-242-4242; *Fax:* 250-242-3993
tradmin@dtr.ca
www.tumblerridge.ca
Municipal Type: District
Incorporated: April 9, 1981; *Area:* 1,574.45 sq km
County or District: Peace River; *Population in 2011:* 2,710
Provincial Electoral District(s): Peace River South
Federal Electoral District(s): Prince George-Peace River-Northern Rockies
Next Election: Oct. 20, 2018 (4-year terms)
Don McPherson, Mayor, 250-242-4242
Barry Elliot, Chief Administrative Officer, 250-242-4242
John Seweryn, Director, Community Services, 250-242-4242

Ucluelet
P.O. Box 999
200 Main St.
Ucluelet, BC V0R 3A0
Tel: 250-726-7744; *Fax:* 250-726-7335
info@ucluelet.ca
www.ucluelet.ca
Municipal Type: District
Incorporated: Feb. 26, 1952; *Area:* 6.55 sq km
County or District: Alberni-Clayoquot; *Population in 2011:* 1,627
Provincial Electoral District(s): Alberni-Qualicum
Federal Electoral District(s): Courtenay-Alberni
Next Election: Oct. 20, 2018 (4-year terms)
Dianne St. Jacques, Mayor
Andrew Yeates, Chief Administrative officer
Warren Cannon, Superintendent, Public Works
Karla Robison, Manager, Emergency & Environmental Services

Valemount
P.O. Box 168
735 Cranberry Lake Rd.
Valemount, BC V0E 2Z0
Tel: 250-566-4435; *Fax:* 250-566-4249
office@valemount.ca
www.valemount.ca
Municipal Type: Village
Incorporated: Dec. 13, 1962; *Area:* 4.96 sq km
County or District: Fraser-Fort George; *Population in 2011:* 1,020
Provincial Electoral District(s): Prince George-Mount Robson
Federal Electoral District(s): Prince George-Peace River-Northern Rockies
Next Election: Oct. 20, 2018 (4-year terms)
Jeanette Townsend, Mayor
Anne Yanciw, Chief Administrative Officer, 250-566-4435
Trevor Pelletier, Superintendent, Public Works, 250-566-4435

Vanderhoof
P.O. Box 900
160 Connaught St.
Vanderhoof, BC V0J 3A0
Tel: 250-567-4711; *Fax:* 250-567-9169
info@district.vanderhoof.ca
www.vanderhoof.ca
Municipal Type: District
Incorporated: Jan. 22, 1926; *Area:* 54.85 sq km
County or District: Bulkley-Nechako; *Population in 2011:* 4,480
Provincial Electoral District(s): Prince George-Omineca
Federal Electoral District(s): Cariboo-Prince George
Next Election: Oct. 20, 2018 (4-year terms)
Gerry Thiessen, Mayor
Evan Parliament, Chief Administrative Officer

View Royal
45 View Royal Ave.
Victoria, BC V9B 1A6
Tel: 250-479-6800; *Fax:* 250-727-9551
info@viewroyal.ca
www.viewroyal.ca
Municipal Type: Town
Incorporated: Dec. 5, 1988; *Area:* 14.48 sq km
County or District: Capital; *Population in 2011:* 9,381
Provincial Electoral District(s): Esquimalt-Metchosin
Federal Electoral District(s): Esquimalt-Saanich-Sooke
Next Election: Oct. 20, 2018 (4-year terms)
David Screech, Mayor
Kim Anema, Chief Administrative Officer
Lindsay Chase, Director, Development Services
John Rosenberg, Director, Engineering

Warfield
555 Schofield Hwy.
Trail, BC V1R 2G7
Tel: 250-368-8202; *Fax:* 250-368-9354
warfieldadmin@shawlink.ca
www.warfield.ca
Municipal Type: Village
Incorporated: Dec. 8, 1952; *Area:* 1.9 sq km
County or District: Kootenay Boundary; *Population in 2011:* 1,700
Provincial Electoral District(s): West Kootenay-Boundary
Federal Electoral District(s): South Okanagan-West Kootenay
Next Election: Oct. 20, 2018 (4-year terms)
Ted Pahl, Mayor, 250-368-8202
Vince Morelli, CAO/Clerk/Treasurer
Teresa Mandoli, Director, Parks & Recreation

Wells
P.O. Box 219
Wells, BC V0K 2R0
Tel: 250-994-3330; *Fax:* 250-994-3331
wells@goldcity.net
www.wells.ca
Municipal Type: District
Incorporated: June 29, 1998; *Area:* 159.15 sq km
County or District: Cariboo; *Population in 2011:* 245
Provincial Electoral District(s): Cariboo North
Federal Electoral District(s): Cariboo-Prince George
Next Election: Oct. 20, 2018 (4-year terms)
Robin Sharpe, Mayor, 250-993-3330
Katrina Leckovic, Chief Administrative Officer, 250-994-3330
Dennis Manuel, Fire Chief & Superintendent, Public Works, 250-994-3330

West Kelowna
2760 Cameron Rd.
West Kelowna, BC V1Z 2T6
Tel: 778-797-1000; *Fax:* 778-797-1001
info@districtofwestkelowna.ca
www.districtofwestkelowna.ca
Municipal Type: District
Incorporated: Dec. 6, 2007; *Area:* 121.4 sq km
County or District: Central Okanagan; *Population in 2011:* 30,892
Provincial Electoral District(s): Westside-Kelowna
Federal Electoral District(s): Central Okanagan-Similkameen-Nicola
Next Election: Oct. 20, 2018 (4-year terms)
Doug Findlater, Mayor, 778-797-2210
Rick de Jong, Councillor, 778-797-2210
Rusty Ensign, Councillor, 778-797-2210
Rosalind Neis, Councillor, 778-797-2210
Duane Ophus, Councillor, 250-801-5281
Bryden Winsby, Councillor, 250-801-9557
Carol Zanon, Councillor, 250-801-5937
Tracey Batten, City Clerk, 778-797-2250
Jim Zaffino, Chief Administrative Officer, 778-797-2210
Tanya Garost, General Manager, Finance & Corporate Services, 778-797-8855
Tracey Batten, General Manager, Admin & Protective Services, 778-797-8897
Allen Fillion, General Manager, 778-797-2244
Nancy Henderson, General Manager, Development Services, 778-797-8833
Patty Tracy, Manager, Human Resources, 778-797-8898
Wayne Schnitzler, Fire Chief, 250-769-1640, Fax: 250-769-4800

West Vancouver
750 - 17 St.
West Vancouver, BC V7V 3T3
Tel: 604-925-7000; *Fax:* 604-925-5999
info@westvancouver.ca
www.westvancouver.ca
Municipal Type: District
Incorporated: March 15, 1912; *Area:* 87.13 sq km
County or District: Metro Vancouver; *Population in 2011:* 42,694
Provincial Electoral District(s): N. Vancouver-Lonsdale; W. Vancouver-Capilano; W. Vancouver-Garibaldi
Federal Electoral District(s): West Vancouver-Sunshine Coast-Sea to Sky Country
Next Election: Oct. 20, 2018 (4-year terms)
Michael Smith, Mayor
Mary-Ann Booth, Councillor
Craig Cameron, Councillor
Christine Cassidy, Councillor
Nora Gambioli, Councillor
Michael Lewis, Councillor
Bill Soporovich, Councillor
Nina Leemhuis, Chief Administrative Officer, 604-925-7002
Jeff McDonald, Director, Communications, 604-925-4736
Raymond Fung, Director, Engineering & Environment Services, 604-925-7159
Michael Koke, Chief Financial Officer, 604-925-7086
Anne Mooi, Director, Parks, Culture & Community Services, 604-925-7235
Andrew Banks, Senior Manager, Parks, 604-925-7139
Lauren Hughes, Acting Director, HR & Payroll Services, 604-925-7075
Randy Heath, Fire Chief, 604-925-7375

Whistler
4325 Blackcomb Way
Whistler, BC V0N 1B4
Tel: 604-932-5535; *Fax:* 604-935-8109
info@whistler.ca
www.whistler.ca
Municipal Type: Resort Municipality
Incorporated: Sept. 6, 1975; *Area:* 161.71 sq km
County or District: Squamish-Lillooet; *Population in 2011:* 9,824
Provincial Electoral District(s): West Vancouver-Garibaldi
Federal Electoral District(s): West Vancouver-Sunshine Coast-Sea to Sky Country
Next Election: Oct. 20, 2018 (4-year terms)
Nancy Wilhelm-Morden, Mayor
Mike Furey, Chief Administrative Officer, 604-935-8181
Jan Jansen, General Manager, Resort Experience, 604-932-8177
Norm McPhail, General Manager, Corporate & Community Services
Joe Paul, General Manager, Infrastructure Services & Approving Officer, 604-935-8193
Mike Kirkegaard, Director, Planning, 604-935-8163
Denise Wood, Director, Human Resources, 604-935-8217

Zeballos
P.O. Box 127
Zeballos, BC V0P 2A0
Tel: 250-761-4229; *Fax:* 250-761-4331
adminzeb@recn.ca
www.zeballos.com
Municipal Type: Village
Incorporated: June 27, 1952; *Area:* 130 sq km
County or District: Strathcona; *Population in 2011:* 125
Provincial Electoral District(s): North Island
Federal Electoral District(s): North Island-Powell River
Next Election: Oct. 20, 2018 (4-year terms)
Donnie Cox, Mayor
Eileen Lovestrom, Chief Administrative Officer
Mike Atchison, Fire Chief & Superintendent, Public Works

Indian Government District in British Columbia

Sechelt
P.O. Box 740
5555 Sunshine Coast Hwy.
Sechelt, BC V0N 3A0
Tel: 604-885-2273; *Fax:* 604-885-4324
www.shishalh.com

Municipal Type: Metis Settlements
Incorporated: March 17, 1988; *Area:* 10.95 sq km
Population in 2011: 819

Federal Electoral District(s): West Vancouver-Sunshine Coast-Sea to Sky Country
Next Election: Oct. 20, 2018 (4-year terms)

Calvin Craigon, Chief, 604-885-2273
Nadine Hoehne, Chief Adminsitrative Officer, 604-885-2273

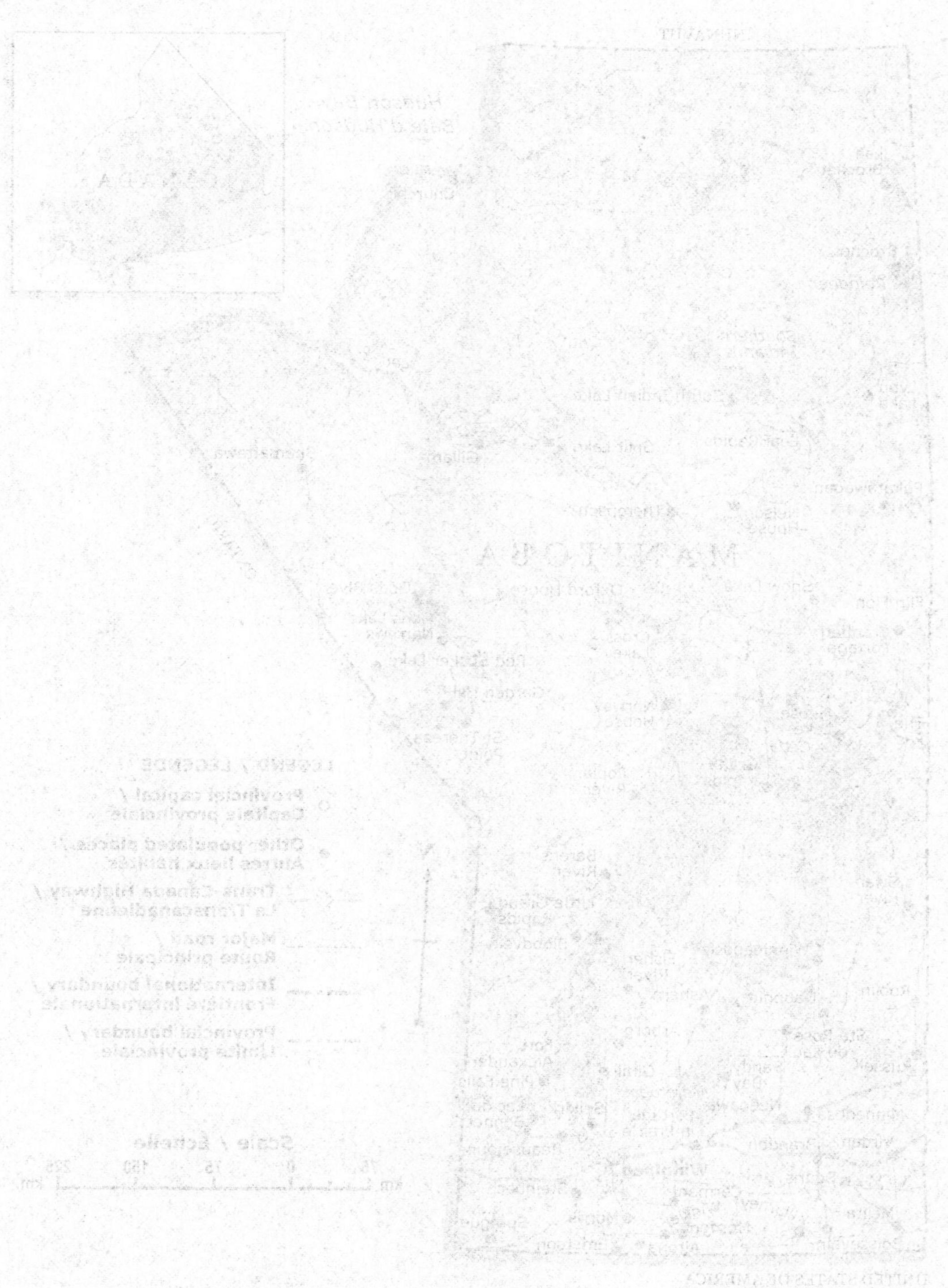

MANITOBA

All municipalities in Manitoba (except Winnipeg, which is governed by the City of Winnipeg Act) come under authority of the Manitoba Municipal Act.

In Manitoba there are no counties or regional governments; there are only urban and rural municipalities. Incorporation of a new municipality requires a population of at least 1,000 residents and a population density of at least 400 residents per square kilometre for an urban municipality and a population density of less than 400 residents per square kilometre for a rural municipality. Urban municipalities may be called cities, towns, villages or urban municipalities. The population requirement for a city is at least 7,500 residents.

Municipal elections are held every four years on the fourth Wednesday of October (2014, 2018, etc.). As of January 1, 2015, the province amalgamated municipalities with populations of fewer than 1,000, merging neighbouring municipalities and reducing the total number of municipalities in the province from 197 to 137.

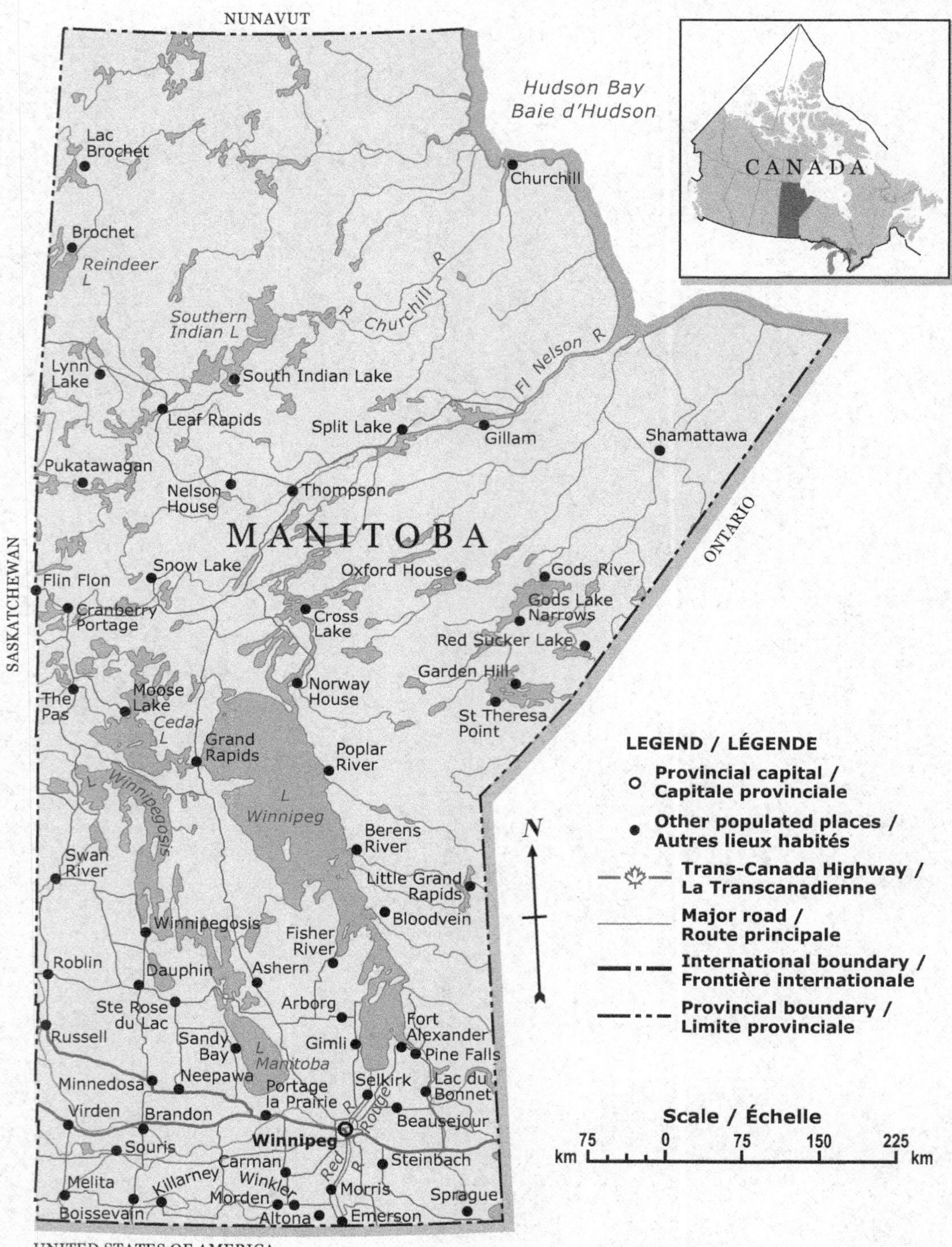

Manitoba

Major Municipalities in Manitoba

Brandon
410 - 9th St.
Brandon, MB R7A 6A2
Tel: 204-729-2186; *Fax:* 204-729-8244
cityclerk@brandon.ca
www.brandon.ca
Municipal Type: City
Incorporated: May 3, 1882; *Area:* 76.89 sq km
Population in 2011: 46,061
Provincial Electoral District(s): Brandon East; Brandon West
Federal Electoral District(s): Brandon-Souris
Next Election: Oct. 2018 (4 year terms)
Rick Chrest, Mayor
Jeff Fawcett, Councillor, Wards: 1. Assiniboine
Kris Desjarlais, Councillor, Wards: 2. Rosser
Barry Cullen, Councillor, Wards: 3. Victoria
Jeff Harwood, Councillor, Wards: 4. University
John LoRegio, Councillor, Wards: 5. Meadows
Lonnie Patterson, Councillor, Wards: 6. South Centre
Shawn Berry, Councillor, Wards: 7. Linden Lanes
Ron W. Brown, Councillor, Wards: 8. Richmond
Vanessa Hamilton, Councillor, Wards: 9. Riverview
Jan Chaboyer, Councillor, Wards: 10. Green Acres
Heather Ewasiuk, City Clerk, 204-729-2206
Scott Hildebrand, City Manager, 204-729-2204
Brent Dane, Fire Chief, 204-729-2404
Ian Christiansen, Director, Engineering Services & Water Resources
Allison Collins, Director, Communications, 204-729-2590
Sandy Trudel, Director, Economic Development, 204-729-2131
L. Hargreaves, Manager, Environmental Initiatives, 204-729-2171
Vivianne Lockerby, CPP, Manager, Purchasing, 204-729-2252, Fax: 204-726-8546

Flin Flon
20 - 1st Ave.
Flin Flon, MB R8A 0T7
Tel: 204-684-7511; *Fax:* 204-681-7530
www.cityofflinflon.ca
Municipal Type: City
Incorporated: Jan. 1, 1933; *Area:* 13.88 sq km
Population in 2011: 5,405
Provincial Electoral District(s): Flin Flon
Federal Electoral District(s): Churchill-Keewatinook Aski
Next Election: Oct. 2018 (4 year terms)
Cal Huntley, Mayor
Mark Kolt, Chief Administrative Officer

Portage la Prairie
97 Saskatchewan Ave. East
Portage la Prairie, MB R1N 0L8
Tel: 204-239-8337; *Fax:* 204-239-1532
info@city-plap.com
www.city-plap.com
Municipal Type: City
Incorporated: Jan. 3, 1907; *Area:* 24.67 sq km
Population in 2011: 12,996
Provincial Electoral District(s): Portage la Prairie
Federal Electoral District(s): Portage-Lisgar
Next Election: Oct. 2018 (4 year terms)
Irvine A. Ferris, Mayor
Brent Budz, Councillor
Melissa Draycott, Councillor
Liz Driedger, Councillor
Ryan Espey, Councillor
Brent Froese, Councillor
Wayne Wall, Councillor
Jean-Marc Nadeau, City Manager
Kelly Braden, Director, Operations, 204-239-8350, Fax: 204-857-7275
N. Neudorf, Director, Finance
Phil Carpenter, Chief, Fire & Emergency, 204-239-8340, Fax: 204-239-5154
K. Friesen, Manager, Wastewater Treatment, 204-239-8359
Dave Green, Manager, Parks, 204-239-8325
M. Sadney, Manager, Water Treatment, 204-239-8373
Brian Taylor, Manager, Public Works, 204-239-8352

Selkirk
200 Eaton Ave.
Selkirk, MB R1A 0W6
Tel: 204-785-4900; *Fax:* 204-482-5448
ea@cityofselkirk.com
www.cityofselkirk.com
Municipal Type: City
Incorporated: June 5, 1882; *Area:* 24.87 sq km
Population in 2011: 9,834
Provincial Electoral District(s): Selkirk
Federal Electoral District(s): Selkirk-Interlake-Eastman
Next Election: Oct. 2018 (4 year terms)
Larry Johannson, Mayor
Duane Nicol, Chief Administrative Officer

Steinbach
225 Reimer Ave.
Steinbach, MB R5G 2J1
Tel: 204-326-9877; *Fax:* 204-346-6235
info@steinbach.ca
www.steinbach.ca
Municipal Type: City
Incorporated: Jan. 3, 1946; *Area:* 25.57 sq km
Population in 2011: 13,524
Provincial Electoral District(s): Steinbach
Federal Electoral District(s): Provencher
Next Election: Oct. 2018 (4 year terms)
Chris Goertzen, Mayor
John Fehr, Councillor
Earl Funk, Councillor
Cari Penner, Councillor
Susan Penner, Councillor
Jac Siemens, Councillor
Michael Zwaagstra, Councillor
Jack Kehler, Chief Administrative Officer

Thompson
226 Mystery Lake Rd.
Thompson, MB R8N 1S6
Tel: 204-677-7910; *Fax:* 204-677-7936
reception@thompson.ca
www.thompson.ca
Municipal Type: City
Incorporated: Jan. 5, 1970; *Area:* 17.18 sq km
Population in 2011: 12,829
Provincial Electoral District(s): Thompson
Federal Electoral District(s): Churchill-Keewatinook Aski
Next Election: Oct. 2018 (4 year terms)
Dennis Fenske, Mayor
Penny Byer, Councillor
Blake Ellis, Councillor
Dennis Foley, Councillor
Judy Kolada, Councillor
Ron Matechuk, Councillor
Colleen Smook, Councillor
Cathy Valentino, Councillor
Duncan Wong, Councillor
Gary Ceppetelli, Chief Administrative Officer
John Maskerine, Fire Chief, 204-677-7916
Wayne Koversky, Director, Public Works
Mike Webb, Technician, Water & Sewer
Joyce Kopp, Agent, Purchasing

Winkler
185 Main St.
Winkler, MB R6W 1B4
Tel: 204-325-9524; *Fax:* 204-325-5915
info@cityofwinkler.ca
www.cityofwinkler.ca
Municipal Type: City
Incorporated: Jan. 6, 1954; *Area:* 17.01 sq km
Population in 2011: 10,670
Provincial Electoral District(s): Pembina
Federal Electoral District(s): Portage-Lisgar
Next Election: Oct. 2018 (4 year terms)
Martin Harder, Mayor
Don Fehr, Councillor
Don Friesen, Councillor
Andrew Froese, Councillor
Michael Grenier, Councillor
Marvin Plett, Councillor
Henry Siemens, Councillor
Dave Burgess, Chief Administrative Officer

Winnipeg
City Hall
510 Main St.
Winnipeg, MB R3B 1B9
311@winnipeg.ca
www.winnipeg.ca
Other Information: Phone or Fax: 311 for information on city services
Municipal Type: City
Incorporated: Nov. 8, 1873; *Area:* 464.01 sq km
Population in 2011: 633,617
Provincial Electoral District(s): Burrows; Charleswood; Concordia; Elmwood; Ft. Garry-Riverview; Ft. Rouge; Ft. Whyte; Inkster; Kildonan; Kirkfield Park; Logan; Minto; Point Douglas; Radisson; Riel; River East; River Heights; Rossmere; Seine River; Southdale; St. Boniface; St. James; St. Johns; St. Norbert; St. Vital; The Maples; Transcona; Tuxedo; Tyndall Park; Wolseley; Assiniboia
Federal Electoral District(s): Charleswood-St. James-Assiniboia-Headingley; Elmwood-Transcona; Kildonan-St. Paul; Saint Boniface-Saint Vital; Winnipeg Centre; Winnipeg North; Winnipeg South; Winnipeg South Centre
Next Election: Oct. 2018 (4 year terms)
Brian Bowman, Mayor
Marty Morantz, Councillor, 204-986-5232, Fax: 204-986-3725, Wards: Charleswood-Tuxedo-Whyte Ridge
Cindy Gilroy, Councillor, 204-986-5951, Fax: 204-986-3725, Wards: Daniel McIntyre
Jason Schreyer, Councillor, 204-986-5195, Fax: 204-986-3725, Wards: Elmwood-East Kildonan
Jenny Gerbasi, Councillor, 204-986-5878, Fax: 204-986-5636, Wards: Fort Rouge-East Fort Garry
Ross Eadie, Councillor, 204-986-5188, Fax: 204-986-3726, Wards: Mynarski
Jeff Browaty, Councillor, 204-986-5196, Fax: 204-986-3725, Wards: North Kildonan
Devi Sharma, Councillor & Speaker, 204-986-5264, Fax: 204-986-7806, Wards: Old Kildonan
Mike Pagtakhan, Councillor & Deputy Mayor, 204-986-8401, Fax: 204-986-3725, Wards: Point Douglas
John Orlikow, Councillor, 204-986-5236, Fax: 204-986-3725, Wards: River Heights-Fort Garry
Matt Allard, Councillor, 204-396-4636, Fax: 204-986-3725, Wards: St. Boniface
Shawn Dobson, Councillor, 204-986-5920, Fax: 204-986-3725, Wards: St. Charles
Scott Gillingham, Councillor, 204-986-5848, Fax: 204-986-4320, Wards: St. James-Brooklands-Weston
Brian Mayes, Councillor, 204-986-5088, Fax: 204-986-3725, Wards: St. Vital
Janice Lukes, Councillor & Acting Deputy Mayor, 204-986-6824, Fax: 204-986-3725, Wards: South Winnipeg-St. Norbert
Russ Wyatt, Councillor, 204-986-8087, Fax: 204-986-8549, Wards: Transcona
Richard Kachur, City Clerk
Doug McNeil, Chief Administrative Officer, 204-986-5104, Fax: 204-949-1174
Michael Jack, Chief Operating Officer, 204-986-2566, Fax: 204-947-9155
Michael P. Ruta, Chief Financial Officer, 204-986-2378, Fax: 204-949-1174
John Lane, Chief, Winnipeg Fire Paramedic Service
Art Stannard, Interim Chief of Police, Winnipeg Police Service
Lester Deane, Director, Public Works
John Kiernan, Director, Planning, Property & Development
Diane Sacher, Director, Water & Waste
Dave Wardrop, Director, Winnipeg Transit
Clive Wightman, Director, Community Services
Dave Domke, Manager, Parks & Open Space

Other Municipalities in Manitoba

Altona
P.O. Box 1630
111 Centre Ave. East
Altona, MB R0G 0B0
Tel: 204-324-6468; *Fax:* 204-324-1550
info@altona.ca
altona.ca
Municipal Type: Town
Incorporated: Jan. 1, 1956; *Area:* 9.39 sq km
Population in 2011: 4,088
Provincial Electoral District(s): Emerson
Federal Electoral District(s): Portage-Lisgar
Next Election: Oct. 2018 (4 year terms)
Melvin H. Klassen, Mayor
Dan Gagne, Chief Administrative Officer

Arborg
P.O. Box 159
337 River Rd.
Arborg, MB R0C 0A0
Tel: 204-376-2647; *Fax:* 204-376-5379
townofarborg@mymts.net
www.townofarborg.com
Municipal Type: Town
Incorporated: 1964; *Area:* 2.26 sq km
Population in 2011: 1,152
Provincial Electoral District(s): Interlake
Federal Electoral District(s): Selkirk-Interlake-Eastman
Next Election: Oct. 2018 (4 year terms)
Randy Sigurdson, Mayor
Lorraine Bardarson, Chief Administrative Officer

Beausejour
P.O. Box 1028
639 Park Ave.
Beausejour, MB R0E 0C0
Tel: 204-268-7550; *Fax:* 204-268-3107
www.ourhomeyourhome.ca
Municipal Type: Town
Incorporated: Jan. 2, 1912; *Area:* 5.35 sq km
Population in 2011: 3,126
Provincial Electoral District(s): Lac du Bonnet
Federal Electoral District(s): Selkirk-Interlake-Eastman
Next Election: Oct. 2018 (4 year terms)
Ed Dubray, Mayor
Jack Douglas, Chief Administrative Officer

Bifrost-Riverton
P.O. Box 70
329 River Rd.
Arborg, MB R0C 0A0
Tel: 204-376-2391; *Fax:* 204-376-2742
bifrost@mymts.net
rmbifrost.com
Municipal Type: Municipality
Incorporated: Jan. 4, 1908; *Area:* 1,643.69 sq km
Population in 2011: 3,514
Provincial Electoral District(s): Interlake
Federal Electoral District(s): Selkirk-Interlake-Eastman
Next Election: Oct. 2018 (4 year terms)
Note: The RM of Bifrost & the Village of Riverton amalgamated to form the new Municipality of Bifrost-Riverton on Jan. 1, 2015.
Harold J. Foster, Reeve
Grant Thorsteinson, Chief Administrative Officer

Boissevain-Morton
P.O. Box 490
420 South Railway Ave.
Boissevain, MB R0K 0E0
Tel: 204-534-2433; *Fax:* 204-534-3710
admin@boissevain.ca
www.boissevain.ca
Municipal Type: Municipality
Incorporated: 1906; *Area:* 1092.65 sq km
Population in 2011: 2,270
Provincial Electoral District(s): Arthur-Virden
Federal Electoral District(s): Brandon-Souris
Next Election: Oct. 2018 (4 year terms)
Note: The Town of Boissevain & the RM of Morton amalgamated to form the new Municipality of Boissevain-Morton on Jan. 1, 2015.
M. Edward Anderson, Mayor
Lloyd Leganchuk, Chief Administrative Officer

Brenda-Waskada
P.O. Box 40
33 Railway Ave.
Waskada, MB R0M 2E0
Tel: 204-673-2401; *Fax:* 204-673-2663
waskadan@mymts.net
Municipal Type: Municipality
Area: 766.77 sq km
Population in 2011: 652
Provincial Electoral District(s): Arthur-Virden
Federal Electoral District(s): Brandon-Souris
Next Election: Oct. 2018 (4 year terms)
Note: The RM of Brenda & the Village of Waskada amalgamated to form the new Municipality of Brenda-Waskada on Jan. 1, 2015.
Gary Williams, Head of Council
Diane Woodworth, Chief Administrative Officer

Carberry
P.O. Box 130
316 - 4th Ave.
Carberry, MB R0K 0H0
Tel: 204-834-6600; *Fax:* 204-834-6604
edo@townofcarberry.ca
www.townofcarberry.ca
Municipal Type: Town
Incorporated: Jan. 1, 1905; *Area:* 4.79 sq km
Population in 2011: 1,669
Provincial Electoral District(s): Turtle Mountain
Federal Electoral District(s): Dauphin-Swan River-Neepawa
Next Election: Oct. 2018 (4 year terms)
Stuart Olmstead, Mayor
Sandra Jones, Chief Administrative Officer

Carman
P.O. Box 160
12 - 2nd Ave. SW
Carman, MB R0G 0J0
Tel: 204-745-2443; *Fax:* 204-745-2903
info@townofcarman.com
www.carmanmanitoba.ca
Municipal Type: Town
Incorporated: Jan. 1, 1905; *Area:* 4.12 sq km
Population in 2011: 3,027
Provincial Electoral District(s): Carman
Federal Electoral District(s): Portage-Lisgar
Next Election: Oct. 2018 (4 year terms)
Bob Mitchell, Mayor
Cheryl Young, Chief Administrative Officer

Cartwright-Roblin
P.O. Box 9
485 Curwen St.
Cartwright, MB R0K 0L0
Tel: 204-529-2363; *Fax:* 204-529-2288
www.cartwrightroblin.ca
Municipal Type: Municipality
Incorporated: Jan. 5, 1948; *Area:* 718.01 sq km
Population in 2011: 1,240
Provincial Electoral District(s): Turtle Mountain
Federal Electoral District(s): Brandon-Souris
Next Election: Oct. 2018 (4 year terms)
Note: The RM of Roblin & the Village of Cartwright amalgamated to form the new Rural Municipality of Cartwright-Roblin on Jan. 1, 2015.
Rod Lovell, Head of Council
Colleen Mullin, Chief Administrative Officer

Churchill
P.O. Box 459
180 LaVerendrye Blvd.
Churchill, MB R0B 0E0
Tel: 204-675-8871; *Fax:* 204-675-2934
townofchurchill@churchill.ca
www.churchill.ca
Municipal Type: Town
Incorporated: Jan. 4, 1997; *Area:* 53.96 sq km
Population in 2011: 813
Provincial Electoral District(s): Rupertsland
Federal Electoral District(s): Churchill-Keewatinook Aski
Next Election: Oct. 2018 (4 year terms)
Michael Spence, Mayor
Cory Young, Chief Executive Officer

Clanwilliam-Erickson
P.O. Box 40
45 Main St.
Erickson, MB R0J 0P0
Tel: 204-636-2431; *Fax:* 204-636-2516
ericksonadmin@ericksonmb.ca
www.townerickson.ca
Municipal Type: Municipality
Incorporated: Jan. 3, 1884; *Area:* 352.08 sq km
Population in 2011: 901
Provincial Electoral District(s): Russell
Federal Electoral District(s): Dauphin-Swan River-Neepawa
Next Election: Oct. 2018 (4 year terms)
Note: The Town of Erickson & the RM of Clanwilliam amalgamated to form the new Municipality of Clanwilliam-Erickson on Jan. 1, 2015.
Elgin A. Hall, Head of Council
William Hildebrand, Chief Administrative Officer

Dauphin
100 Main St. South
Dauphin, MB R7N 1K3
Tel: 204-622-3200; *Fax:* 204-622-3290
info@dauphin.ca
www.dauphin.ca
Municipal Type: Town
Incorporated: Jan. 7, 1898; *Area:* 12.65 sq km
Population in 2011: 8,251
Provincial Electoral District(s): Dauphin-Roblin
Federal Electoral District(s): Dauphin-Swan River-Neepawa
Next Election: Oct. 2018 (4 year terms)
Eric B. Irwin, Mayor
Brad D. Collett, Chief Administrative Officer

Dunnottar
P.O. Box 321
44 Whytewold Rd.
Matlock, MB R0C 2B0
Tel: 204-389-4962; *Fax:* 204-389-4966
info@dunnottar.ca
www.dunnottar.ca
Municipal Type: Resort Village
Area: 2.79 sq km
Population in 2011: 696
Provincial Electoral District(s): Interlake
Federal Electoral District(s): Selkirk-Interlake-Eastman
Next Election: July 2018 (4 year terms)
Richard Gamble, Mayor
Kristine Shields, Chief Administrative Officer

Emerson-Franklin
P.O. Box 66
115 Waddell Ave.
Dominion City, MB R0A 0H0
Tel: 204-427-2557; *Fax:* 204-427-2224
rmfrank@mymts.net
www.rmfranklin.com
Municipal Type: Municipality
Area: 975.62 sq km
Population in 2011: 2,439
Provincial Electoral District(s): Emerson
Federal Electoral District(s): Provencher
Next Election: Oct. 2018 (4 year terms)
Note: The RM of Franklin & the Town of Emerson amalgamated to form the new Municipality of Emerson-Franklin on Jan. 1, 2015.
Greg Janzen, Reeve
Tracey French, Chief Administrative Officer

Ethelbert
P.O. Box 115
56 - 2nd Ave.
Ethelbert, MB R0L 0T0
Tel: 204-742-3212; *Fax:* 204-742-3642
rmethelbert@inetlink.ca
Municipal Type: Municipality
Incorporated: Jan. 1, 1905; *Area:* 1,134.5 sq km
Population in 2011: 629
Provincial Electoral District(s): Swan River
Federal Electoral District(s): Dauphin-Swan River-Neepawa
Next Election: Oct. 2018 (4 year terms)
Note: The RM of Ethelbert & the Village of Ethelbert amalgamated to form the new Municipality of Ethelbert on Jan. 1, 2015.
Art Potoroka, Head of Council
Loretta Woytkiewicz, Chief Administrative Officer

Gilbert Plains
P.O. Box 220
201 Main St. North
Gilbert Plains, MB R0L 0X0
Tel: 204-548-2326; *Fax:* 204-548-2564
gilbertplainsmunicipality@mymts.net
www.gilbertplains.com
Municipal Type: Municipality
Incorporated: Jan. 3, 1901; *Area:* 1,049.14 sq km
Population in 2011: 1,623
Provincial Electoral District(s): Dauphin-Roblin
Federal Electoral District(s): Dauphin-Swan River-Neepawa
Next Election: Oct. 2018 (4 year terms)
Note: The RM of Gilbert Plains & the Town of Gilbert Plains amalgamated to form the new Municipality of Gilbert Plains on Jan. 1, 2015.
Blake Price, Head of Council
Susan Boyachek, Chief Administrative Officer

Gillam
P.O. Box 100
323 Railway Ave.
Gillam, MB R0B 0L0
Tel: 204-652-3150; *Fax:* 204-652-3199
information@townofgillam.com
www.townofgillam.com
Municipal Type: Town
Area: 1,996.35 sq km
Population in 2011: 1,704
Provincial Electoral District(s): Rupertsland
Federal Electoral District(s): Churchill-Keewatinook Aski
Next Election: Oct. 2018 (4 year terms)
Tom Zelenesky, Mayor
Jackie Clayton, Chief Administrative Officer

Glenboro-South Cypress
P.O. Box 219
618 Railway Ave.
Glenboro, MB R0K 0X0
Tel: 204-827-2252; *Fax:* 204-827-2123
caormsc@mts.net
glenboro.com
Municipal Type: Municipality
Incorporated: Jan. 7, 1881; *Area:* 1,095.08 sq km
Population in 2011: 1,483
Provincial Electoral District(s): Turtle Mountain

Federal Electoral District(s): Brandon-Souris
Next Election: Oct. 2018 (4 year terms)
Note: The Village of Glenboro & the RM of South Cypress amalgamated to form the new Municipality of Glenboro-South Cypress on Jan. 1, 2015.
Earl E. Malyon, Mayor
Darren Myers, Chief Administrative Officer

Glenella-Lansdowne
P.O. Box 10
50 Main St. North
Glenella, MB R0J 0V0
Tel: 204-352-4281; *Fax:* 204-352-4100
rmofglen@inetlink.ca
glenella.ca
Municipal Type: Municipality
Incorporated: Jan. 5, 1920; *Area:* 1263.43 sq km
Population in 2011: 1,245
Provincial Electoral District(s): Ste. Rose
Federal Electoral District(s): Dauphin-Swan River-Neepawa
Next Election: Oct. 2018 (4 year terms)
Note: The RM of Glenella & the RM of Lansdowne amalgamated to form the new Municipality of Glenella-Lansdowne on Jan. 1, 2015.
Richard Funk, Reeve
Wendy Wutzke, Chief Administrative Officer

Grand Rapids
P.O. Box 301
200 Grand Rapids Dr.
Grand Rapids, MB R0C 1E0
Tel: 204-639-2260; *Fax:* 204-639-2475
towngra@xplornet.ca
Municipal Type: Town
Incorporated: Jan. 2, 1962; *Area:* 85.95 sq km
Population in 2011: 239
Provincial Electoral District(s): Swan River
Federal Electoral District(s): Churchill-Keewatinook Aski
Next Election: Oct. 2018 (4 year terms)
Robert Buck, Mayor
Karen Turner, Chief Administrative Officer

Grandview
P.O. Box 219
531 Main St.
Grandview, MB R0L 0Y0
Tel: 204-546-5250; *Fax:* 204-546-5269
townofgv@mymts.net
www.grandviewmanitoba.com
Municipal Type: Municipality
Incorporated: Jan. 3, 1901; *Area:* 1,152.5 sq km
Population in 2011: 1,508
Provincial Electoral District(s): Dauphin-Roblin
Federal Electoral District(s): Dauphin-Swan River-Neepawa
Next Election: Oct. 2018 (4 year terms)
Note: The RM of Grandview & the Town of Grandview amalgamated to form the new Municipality of Grandview on Jan. 1, 2015.
Lyle Morran, Mayor
Sharon Dalgleish, Chief Administrative Officer

Grassland
P.O. Box 399
209 Airdrie St.
Hartney, MB R0M 0X0
Tel: 204-858-2590; *Fax:* 204-858-2681
hartney@mts.net
Municipal Type: Municipality
Incorporated: Jan. 6, 1897
Population in 2011: 1,480
Provincial Electoral District(s): Arthur-Virden
Federal Electoral District(s): Brandon-Souris
Next Election: Oct. 2018 (4 year terms)
Note: The RM of Cameron, the Town of Hartney & the RM of Whitewater amalgamated to form the new Municipality of Grassland on Jan. 1, 2015.
Blair Woods, Reeve
Brad Coe, Chief Administrative Officer

Hamiota
P.O. Box 100
75 Maple Ave. East
Hamiota, MB R0M 0T0
Tel: 204-764-3050; *Fax:* 204-764-3055
info@hamiota.com
www.hamiota.com
Municipal Type: Municipality
Incorporated: 1907; *Area:* 3.38 sq km
Population in 2011: 1,288
Provincial Electoral District(s): Russell
Federal Electoral District(s): Dauphin-Swan River-Neepawa
Next Election: Oct. 2018 (4 year terms)
Note: The RM of Hamiota & the Town of Hamiota amalgamated to form the new Municipality of Hamiota on Jan. 1, 2015.
Larry Oakden, Reeve
Tom Mollard, Chief Administrative Officer

Harrison Park
P.O. Box 190
43 Gateway St.
Onanole, MB R0J 1N0
Tel: 204-848-7614; *Fax:* 204-848-2082
admin@rmofpark.ca
www.rmofpark.ca
Municipal Type: Municipality
Incorporated: Jan. 6, 1954; *Area:* 793.38 sq km
Population in 2011: 1,799
Provincial Electoral District(s): Dauphin-Roblin; Russell
Federal Electoral District(s): Dauphin-Swan River-Neepawa
Next Election: Oct. 2018 (4 year terms)
Note: The RM of Harrison & the RM of Park amalgamated to form the new Municipality of Harrison Park on Jan. 1, 2015.
Lloyd Ewashko, Reeve
Chad Davies, Chief Administrative Officer

Hillsburg-Roblin-Shell River
P.O. Box 998
213 - 2nd Ave. NW
Roblin, MB R0L 1P0
Tel: 204-937-4430; *Fax:* 204-937-8496
toroblin@mts.net
Municipal Type: Municipality
Incorporated: Jan. 3, 1884; *Area:* 735.12 sq km
Population in 2011: 3,284
Provincial Electoral District(s): Dauphin-Roblin
Federal Electoral District(s): Dauphin-Swan River-Neepawa
Next Election: Oct. 2018 (4 year terms)
Note: The RM of Hillsburg, the RM of Shell River & the Town of Roblin amalgamated to form the new Municipality of Hillsburg-Roblin-Shell River on Jan. 1, 2015.
Wade Schott, Mayor
Twyla Ludwig, Chief Administrative Officer

Killarney-Turtle Mountain
P.O. Box 10
415 Broadway Ave.
Killarney, MB R0K 1G0
Tel: 204-523-7247; *Fax:* 204-523-4637
info@killarney.ca
www.killarney.ca
Municipal Type: Municipality
Incorporated: Jan. 1, 1882; *Area:* 925.13 sq km
Population in 2011: 3,233
Provincial Electoral District(s): Turtle Mountain
Federal Electoral District(s): Brandon-Souris
Next Election: Oct. 2018 (4 year terms)
Note: The municipalities of Killarney & Turtle Mountain amalgamated to form one entity effective Jan. 1, 2007.
Rick Pauls, Mayor
Jim Dowsett, Chief Administrative Officer

Lac du Bonnet
P.O. Box 339
84 - 2nd St.
Lac du Bonnet, MB R0E 1A0
Tel: 204-345-8693; *Fax:* 204-345-8694
townldb@mts.net
www.lacdubonnet.com
Municipal Type: Town
Incorporated: Jan. 4, 1947; *Area:* 2.25 sq km
Population in 2011: 1,328
Provincial Electoral District(s): Lac du Bonnet
Federal Electoral District(s): Selkirk-Interlake-Eastman
Next Election: Oct. 2018 (4 year terms)
Gordon Peters, Mayor
Michelle Wazny, Chief Administrative Officer

Leaf Rapids
Town Centre Complex
P.O. Box 340
Leaf Rapids, MB R0B 1W0
Tel: 204-473-2436; *Fax:* 204-473-2566
administrator@townofleafrapids.ca
www.townofleafrapids.com
Municipal Type: Town
Incorporated: Jan. 5, 1976; *Area:* 1,272.87 sq km
Population in 2011: 453
Provincial Electoral District(s): Flin Flon
Federal Electoral District(s): Churchill-Keewatinook Aski
Next Election: Oct. 2018 (4 year terms)
Leslie Baker, Mayor
Christina Stanford, Chief Administrative Officer

Lorne
P.O. Box 10
307 - 3rd St.
Somerset, MB R0G 2L0
Tel: 204-744-2133; *Fax:* 204-744-2349
rmlorne@mymts.net
www.rmoflorne.ca
Municipal Type: Municipality
Incorporated: Jan. 5, 1880; *Area:* 906.82 sq km
Population in 2011: 3,006
Provincial Electoral District(s): Carman
Federal Electoral District(s): Portage-Lisgar
Next Election: Oct. 2018 (4 year terms)
Note: The RM of Lorne, the Village of Notre Dame de Lourdes & the Village of Somerset amalgamated to form the new Municipality of Lorne on Jan. 1, 2015.
Aurel Pantel, Reeve
Shannon Gaultier, Chief Administrative Officer

Louise
P.O. Box 310
26 South Railway Ave. East
Crystal City, MB R0K 0N0
Tel: 204-873-2591; *Fax:* 204-873-2459
rmlouise@inetlink.ca
Municipal Type: Municipality
Incorporated: Jan. 5, 1880; *Area:* 932.67 sq km
Population in 2011: 1,932
Provincial Electoral District(s): Turtle Mountain
Federal Electoral District(s): Brandon-Souris
Next Election: Oct. 2018 (4 year terms)
Note: The RM of Louise, the Town of Pilot Mound & the Village of Crystal City amalgamated to form the new Municipality of Louise on Jan. 1, 2015.
Kenneth S. Buchanan, Head of Council
Doris Heaver, Chief Administrative Officer

Lynn Lake
P.O. Box 100
503 Sherritt Ave.
Lynn Lake, MB R0B 0W0
Tel: 204-356-2418; *Fax:* 204-356-8297
info@lynnlake.ca
www.lynnlake.ca
Municipal Type: Town
Incorporated: 1950; *Area:* 910.23 sq km
Population in 2011: 482
Provincial Electoral District(s): Flin Flon
Federal Electoral District(s): Churchill-Keewatinook Aski
Next Election: Oct. 2018 (4 year terms)
James Lindsay, Mayor
Ric Stryde, Chief Administrative Officer

McCreary
P.O. Box 338
432 - 1st Ave.
McCreary, MB R0J 1B0
Tel: 204-835-2309; *Fax:* 204-835-2649
municipalityofmccreary@inetlink.ca
www.exploremccreary.com
Municipal Type: Municipality
Incorporated: Jan. 6, 1909; *Area:* 522.69 sq km
Population in 2011: 948
Provincial Electoral District(s): Ste. Rose
Federal Electoral District(s): Dauphin-Swan River-Neepawa
Next Election: Oct. 2018 (4 year terms)
Note: The RM of McCreary & the Village of McCreary amalgamated to form the new Municipality of McCreary on Jan. 1, 2015.
Larry McLauchlan, Reeve
Wendy Turko, Chief Administrative Officer

Melita
P.O. Box 364
79 Main St.
Melita, MB R0M 1L0
Tel: 204-522-3413; *Fax:* 204-522-3587
meladmin@mymts.net
www.melitamb.ca
Municipal Type: Town
Incorporated: Jan. 2, 1906; *Area:* 2.96 sq km
Population in 2011: 1,069
Provincial Electoral District(s): Arthur-Virden
Federal Electoral District(s): Brandon-Souris
Next Election: Oct. 2018 (4 year terms)
William Holden, Mayor
Sandra Anderson, Chief Administrative Officer

Minitonas-Bowsman
P.O. Box 9
311 Main St.
Minitonas, MB R0L 1G0
Tel: 204-525-4461; *Fax:* 204-525-4857
rmmin@minitonas.ca
Municipal Type: Municipality
Incorporated: Jan. 3, 1901; *Area:* 1,197.67 sq km
Population in 2011: 1,816
Provincial Electoral District(s): Swan River
Federal Electoral District(s): Dauphin-Swan River-Neepawa
Next Election: Oct. 2018 (4 year terms)
Note: The RM of Minitonas, the Town of Minitonas & the Village of Bowsman amalgamated to form the new Municipality of Minitonas-Bowsman on Jan. 1, 2015.
Clint Eisner, Reeve
Kasey Chartrand, Chief Administrative Officer

Minnedosa
P.O. Box 426
103 Main St. South
Minnedosa, MB R0J 1E0
Tel: 204-867-2727; *Fax:* 204-867-2686
minnedosa@mymts.net
Municipal Type: Town
Incorporated: Jan. 5, 1948; *Area:* 15.26 sq km
Population in 2011: 2,587
Provincial Electoral District(s): Minnedosa
Federal Electoral District(s): Dauphin-Swan River-Neepawa
Next Election: Oct. 2018 (4 year terms)
Ray Orr, Mayor
Ken Jenkins, Chief Administrative Officer

Morden
#100, 195 Stephen St.
Morden, MB R6M 1V3
Tel: 204-822-4434; *Fax:* 204-822-6494
info@mordenmb.com
www.mordenmb.com
Municipal Type: Town
Incorporated: Jan. 1, 1882; *Area:* 16.39 sq km
Population in 2011: 7,812
Provincial Electoral District(s): Pembina
Federal Electoral District(s): Portage-Lisgar
Next Election: Oct. 2018 (4 year terms)
Ken Wiebe, Mayor
John Scarce, Chief Administrative Officer

Morris
P.O. Box 28
#1, 380 Stampede Grounds
Morris, MB R0G 1K0
Tel: 204-746-2531; *Fax:* 204-746-6009
cao@townofmorris.ca
townofmorris.ca
Municipal Type: Town
Incorporated: Jan. 2, 1883; *Area:* 6.1 sq km
Population in 2011: 1,797
Provincial Electoral District(s): Morris
Federal Electoral District(s): Portage-Lisgar
Next Election: Oct. 2018 (4 year terms)
Gavin van der Linde, Mayor
Brigitte Doerksen, Chief Administrative Officer

Neepawa
P.O. Box 339
275 Hamilton St.
Neepawa, MB R0J 1H0
Tel: 204-476-7600; *Fax:* 204-476-7624
neepawa@wcgwave.ca
www.neepawa.ca
Municipal Type: Town
Incorporated: Jan. 2, 1883; *Area:* 17.57 sq km
Population in 2011: 3,629
Provincial Electoral District(s): Ste. Rose
Federal Electoral District(s): Dauphin-Swan River-Neepawa
Next Election: Oct. 2018 (4 year terms)
Adrian De Groot, Mayor
Colleen Synchyshyn, Chief Administrative Officer

Niverville
P.O. Box 267
86 Main St.
Niverville, MB R0A 1E0
Tel: 204-388-4600; *Fax:* 204-388-6110
www.whereyoubelong.ca
Municipal Type: Town
Incorporated: Jan. 4, 1969; *Area:* 8.79 sq km
Population in 2011: 3,540
Provincial Electoral District(s): Steinbach
Federal Electoral District(s): Provencher
Next Election: Oct. 2018 (4 year terms)
Myron Dyck, Mayor
G. Jim Buys, Chief Administrative Officer

Norfolk Treherne
P.O. Box 30
215 Broadway St.
Treherne, MB R0G 2V0
Tel: 204-723-2044; *Fax:* 204-723-2719
info@treherne.ca
www.treherne.ca
Municipal Type: Municipality
Area: 726.76 sq km
Population in 2011: 1,741
Provincial Electoral District(s): Carman
Federal Electoral District(s): Portage-Lisgar
Next Election: Oct. 2018 (4 year terms)
Note: The Town of Treherne & the RM of South Norfolk amalgamated to form the new Municipality of Norfolk-Treherne on Jan. 1, 2015.
Craig Spencer, Reeve
Jackie Jenkinson, Chief Administrative Officer

North Cypress-Langford
P.O. Box 130
316 - 4th Ave.
Carberry, MB R0K 0H0
Tel: 204-834-6600; *Fax:* 204-834-6604
ncl@rmofnorthcypress.ca
www.rmofnorthcypress.ca
Municipal Type: Municipality
Incorporated: Jan. 1, 1882; *Area:* 1,199.92 sq km
Population in 2011: 2,627
Provincial Electoral District(s): Turtle Mountain
Federal Electoral District(s): Dauphin-Swan River-Neepawa
Next Election: Oct. 2018 (4 year terms)
Note: The RM of Langford & the RM of North Cypress amalgamated to form the new RM of North Cypress-Langford on Jan. 1, 2015.
Robert Adriaansen, Reeve
Sandra Jones, Chief Administrative Officer

North Norfolk
P.O. Box 190
27 Hampton St. East
MacGregor, MB R0H 0R0
Tel: 204-685-2211; *Fax:* 204-685-2616
office@macgregor.ca
www.macgregor.ca
Municipal Type: Municipality
Incorporated: Jan. 4, 1947; *Area:* 1,160.76 sq km
Population in 2011: 3,762
Provincial Electoral District(s): Turtle Mountain
Federal Electoral District(s): Dauphin-Swan River-Neepawa
Next Election: Oct. 2018 (4 year terms)
Note: The RM of North Norfolk & the Town of MacGregor amalgamated to form the new Municipality of North Norfolk on Jan. 1, 2015.
Neil Christoffersen, Mayor
Valorie Unrau, Chief Administrative Officer

Oakland-Wawanesa
P.O. Box 28
54 Main St.
Nesbitt, MB R0K 1P0
Tel: 204-824-2666; *Fax:* 204-824-2374
oakwawa@outlook.com
oaklandrm.ca
Municipal Type: Municipality
Incorporated: Jan. 2, 1883; *Area:* 575.21 sq km
Population in 2011: 1,618
Provincial Electoral District(s): Minnedosa
Federal Electoral District(s): Brandon-Souris
Next Election: Oct. 2018 (4 year terms)
Note: The RM of Oakland & the Village of Wawanesa amalgamated to form the new Municipality of Oakland-Wawanesa on Jan. 1, 2015.
David B. Inkster, Head of Council
Marlene Biles, Chief Administrative Officer

The Pas
P.O. Box 870
81 Edwards Ave.
The Pas, MB R9A 1K8
Tel: 204-627-1100; *Fax:* 204-623-5506
info@townofthepas.ca
www.townofthepas.com
Municipal Type: Town
Incorporated: Jan. 2, 1912; *Area:* 47.83 sq km
Population in 2011: 5,513
Provincial Electoral District(s): The Pas
Federal Electoral District(s): Churchill-Keewatinook Aski
Next Election: Oct. 2018 (4 year terms)
Jim Scott, Mayor
Randi Salamanowicz, Chief Administrative Officer

Pembina
P.O. Box 189
360 PTH 3
Manitou, MB R0G 1G0
Tel: 204-242-2838; *Fax:* 204-242-2798
admin@pembina.ca
www.rmofpembina.com
Municipal Type: Municipality
Incorporated: Jan. 4, 1890; *Area:* 1,114.76 sq km
Population in 2011: 2,369
Provincial Electoral District(s): Pembina
Federal Electoral District(s): Portage-Lisgar
Next Election: Oct. 2018 (4 year terms)
Note: The RM of Pembina & the Town of Manitou amalgamated to form the new Municipality of Pembina on Jan. 1, 2015.
Glenn Shiskoski, Head of Council
Wes Unrau, Chief Administrative Officer

Powerview-Pine Falls
P.O. Box 220
277B Main St.
Powerview, MB R0E 1P0
Tel: 204-367-8483; *Fax:* 204-367-4747
caopvpf@mts.net
www.powerview-pinefalls.com
Municipal Type: Town
Incorporated: Jan. 2, 1951; *Area:* 5.05 sq km
Population in 2011: 1,314
Provincial Electoral District(s): Lac du Bonnet
Federal Electoral District(s): Selkirk-Interlake-Eastman
Next Election: Oct. 2018 (4 year terms)
Beverley Dube, Mayor
Margaret Bonekamp, Chief Administrative Officer

Prairie View
P.O. Box 70
678 Main St.
Birtle, MB R0M 0C0
Tel: 204-842-3403; *Fax:* 204-842-3496
www.birtle.ca
Municipal Type: Municipality
Incorporated: Jan. 3, 1884
Population in 2011: 2,167
Provincial Electoral District(s): Russell
Federal Electoral District(s): Dauphin-Swan River-Neepawa
Next Election: Oct. 2018 (4 year terms)
Note: The Town of Birtle, the RM of Birtle & the RM of Miniota amalgamated to form the new Prairie View Municipality on Jan. 1, 2015.
Linda Clark, Reeve
Debbie Jensen, Chief Administrative Officer

Rhineland
P.O. Box 270
72 - 2nd St. NE
Altona, MB R0G 0B0
Tel: 204-324-5357; *Fax:* 204-324-1516
rhineland@mts.net
www.rmofrhineland.com
Municipal Type: Municipality
Incorporated: Jan. 3, 1884; *Area:* 953.42 sq km
Population in 2011: 5,772
Provincial Electoral District(s): Emerson
Federal Electoral District(s): Portage-Lisgar
Next Election: Oct. 2018 (4 year terms)
Note: The RM of Rhineland, the Town of Gretna & the Town of Plum Coulee amalgamated to form the new Municipality of Rhineland on Jan. 1, 2015.
Don Wiebe, Reeve
Michael Rempel, Chief Administrative Officer

Riverdale
P.O. Box 520
670 - 2nd Ave.
Rivers, MB R0K 1X0
Tel: 204-328-5250; *Fax:* 204-328-5374
rivers@mymts.net
riversdaly.ca
Municipal Type: Municipality
Area: 570.42 sq km
Population in 2011: 2,019
Provincial Electoral District(s): Minnedosa
Federal Electoral District(s): Dauphin-Swan River-Neepawa
Next Election: Oct. 2018 (4 year terms)
Note: The Town of Rivers & the RM of Daly amalgamated to form the new Riverdale Municipality on Jan. 1, 2015.
Todd Gill, Mayor
Kat Bridgeman, Chief Administrative Officer

Rossburn
P.O. Box 70
43 Main St. North
Rossburn, MB R0J 1V0
Tel: 204-859-2779; *Fax:* 204-859-2959
municipaloffice@rossburn.ca
www.rossburn.ca
Municipal Type: Municipality
Incorporated: Jan. 4, 1913; *Area:* 3.43 sq km
Population in 2011: 1,046
Provincial Electoral District(s): Russell
Federal Electoral District(s): Dauphin-Swan River-Neepawa
Next Election: Oct. 2018 (4 year terms)
Note: The RM of Rossburn & the Town of Rossburn amalgamated to form the new Rossburn Municipality on Jan. 1, 2015.
Brian Brown, Head of Council
Cheryl Melnyk, Chief Administrative Officer

Russell-Binscarth
P.O. Box 10
178 Main St. North
Russell, MB R0J 1W0
Tel: 204-773-2253; *Fax:* 204-773-3370
info@mrbgov.com
www.russellmb.com
Municipal Type: Municipality
Incorporated: Jan. 4, 1913; *Area:* 3.15 sq km
Population in 2011: 2,553
Provincial Electoral District(s): Russell
Federal Electoral District(s): Dauphin-Swan River-Neepawa
Next Election: Oct. 2018 (4 year terms)
Note: The RM of Russell, Town of Russell & Village of Binscarth amalgamated to form the new Municipality of Russell-Binscarth on Jan. 1, 2015.
Len Derkach, Mayor
Wally R. Melnyk, Chief Administrative Officer

Ste. Anne
30 Dawson Rd., Unit B
Ste. Anne, MB R5H 1B5
Tel: 204-422-5293; *Fax:* 204-422-5459
town@steannemb.ca
www.steannemb.ca
Municipal Type: Town
Incorporated: Jan. 3, 1963; *Area:* 4.19 sq km
Population in 2011: 1,626
Provincial Electoral District(s): La Verendrye
Federal Electoral District(s): Provencher
Next Election: Oct. 2018 (4 year terms)
Richard Pelletier, Mayor
Nicole Champagne, Chief Administrative Officer

Ste. Rose
P.O. Box 30
722 Central Ave.
Ste. Rose du Lac, MB R0L 1S0
Tel: 204-447-2229; *Fax:* 204-447-2875
sterose@mts.net
www.sterose.ca
Municipal Type: Municipality
Incorporated: Jan. 5, 1920; *Area:* 2.53 sq km
Population in 2011: 1,794
Provincial Electoral District(s): Ste. Rose
Federal Electoral District(s): Dauphin-Swan River-Neepawa
Next Election: Oct. 2018 (4 year terms)
Note: The Town of Ste. Rose du Lac & the RM of St. Rose amalgamated to form the new Municipality of Ste. Rose on Jan. 1, 2015.
Robert Brunel, Mayor
Marlene M. Bouchard, Chief Administrative Officer

St. Pierre-Jolys
P.O. Box 218
555 Hébert St.
St. Pierre-Jolys, MB R0A 1V0
Tel: 204-433-7832; *Fax:* 204-433-7053
info@villagestpierrejolys.ca
www.stpierrejolys.com
Municipal Type: Village
Incorporated: Jan. 4, 1947; *Area:* 2.6 sq km
Population in 2011: 1,099
Provincial Electoral District(s): Morris
Federal Electoral District(s): Provencher
Next Election: Oct. 2018 (4 year terms)
Mona Fallis, Mayor
Janine Wiebe, Chief Administrative Officer

Snow Lake
P.O. Box 40
113 Elm St.
Snow Lake, MB R0B 1M0
Tel: 204-358-2551; *Fax:* 204-358-2112
snowlake@mts.net
snowlake.com
Municipal Type: Town
Incorporated: 1947; *Area:* 1,211.89 sq km
Population in 2011: 723
Provincial Electoral District(s): Flin Flon
Federal Electoral District(s): Churchill-Keewatinook Aski
Next Election: Oct. 2018 (4 year terms)
Kim Stephens, Mayor
Charles Boulet, Chief Administrative Officer

Souris-Glenwood
P.O. Box 518
100 - 2nd St. South
Souris, MB R0K 2C0
Tel: 204-483-5200; *Fax:* 204-483-5203
tnsouris@mymts.net
www.sourismanitoba.com
Municipal Type: Municipality
Incorporated: Jan. 6, 1904; *Area:* 3.64 sq km
Population in 2011: 2,439
Provincial Electoral District(s): Minnedosa
Federal Electoral District(s): Brandon-Souris
Next Election: Oct. 2018 (4 year terms)
Note: The RM of Glenwood & the Town of Souris amalgamated to form the new Municipality of Souris-Glenwood on Jan. 1, 2015.
Darryl Jackson, Mayor
Charlotte Parham, Chief Administrative Officer

Stonewall
P.O. Box 250
293 Main St.
Stonewall, MB R0C 2Z0
Tel: 204-467-7979; *Fax:* 204-467-7999
info@stonewall.ca
www.stonewall.ca
Municipal Type: Town
Incorporated: Jan. 4, 1908; *Area:* 6.02 sq km
Population in 2011: 4,536
Provincial Electoral District(s): Lakeside
Federal Electoral District(s): Selkirk-Interlake-Eastman
Next Election: Oct. 2018 (4 year terms)
Lockie McLean, Mayor
Robert Potter, Chief Administrative Officer

Swan River
P.O. Box 879
135 - 5th Ave. North
Swan River, MB R0L 1Z0
Tel: 204-734-4586; *Fax:* 204-734-5166
cao@townsr.ca
www.swanrivermanitoba.ca
Municipal Type: Town
Incorporated: Jan. 4, 1908; *Area:* 6.78 sq km
Population in 2011: 3,907
Provincial Electoral District(s): Swan River
Federal Electoral District(s): Dauphin-Swan River-Neepawa
Next Election: Oct. 2018 (4 year terms)
Glen McKenzie, Mayor
Shirley Bateman, Chief Administrative Officer

Swan Valley West
P.O. Box 610
216 Main St. West
Swan River, MB R0L 1Z0
Tel: 204-734-3344; *Fax:* 204-734-3701
rmswanriver@gmail.com
www.rmofswanriver.com
Municipal Type: Municipality
Incorporated: Jan. 3, 1901; *Area:* 1,719.58 sq km
Population in 2011: 2,923
Provincial Electoral District(s): Swan River
Federal Electoral District(s): Dauphin-Swan River-Neepawa
Next Election: Oct. 2018 (4 year terms)
Note: The RM of Swan River & the Village of Benito amalgamated to form the new Municipality of Swan Valley West on Jan. 1, 2015.
Verne Scouten, Reeve
Debbie Reich, Chief Administrative Officer

Teulon
P.O. Box 69
44 - 4 Ave. SE
Teulon, MB R0C 3B0
Tel: 204-886-2314; *Fax:* 204-886-3918
teulon@mymts.net
www.teulon.ca
Municipal Type: Town
Incorporated: Jan. 4, 1919; *Area:* 3.2 sq km
Population in 2011: 1,124
Provincial Electoral District(s): Lakeside
Federal Electoral District(s): Selkirk-Interlake-Eastman
Next Election: Oct. 2018 (4 year terms)
Bert Campbell, Mayor
Jeff Precourt, Chief Administrative Officer

Two Borders
P.O. Box 429
138 Main St.
Melita, MB R0M 1L0
Tel: 204-522-3263; *Fax:* 204-522-8706
info@twoborders.ca
Municipal Type: Municipality
Area: 2,304.46 sq km
Population in 2011: 1,310
Provincial Electoral District(s): Arthur-Virden
Federal Electoral District(s): Brandon-Souris
Next Election: Oct. 2018 (4 year terms)
Note: The RM of Albert, the RM of Arthur & the RM of Edward amalgamated to form the new Municipality of Two Borders on Jan. 1, 2015.
Debbie McMechan, Reeve
Marion Grogan, Chief Administrative Officer

Victoria Beach
#303, 960 Portage Ave.
Winnipeg, MB R3G 0R4
Tel: 204-774-4263; *Fax:* 204-774-9834
vicbeach@mymts.net
rmofvictoriabeach.ca
Municipal Type: Resort Village
Incorporated: Jan. 4, 1902; *Area:* 20.28 sq km
Population in 2011: 374
Provincial Electoral District(s): Selkirk
Federal Electoral District(s): Selkirk-Interlake-Eastman
Next Election: July 2018 (4 year terms)
Brian Hodgson, Reeve
Shelley Jensen, Chief Administrative Officer

Virden
P.O. Box 310
236 Wellington St. West
Virden, MB R0M 2C0
Tel: 204-748-2440; *Fax:* 204-748-2501
virden_cao@mymts.net
www.virden.ca
Municipal Type: Town
Incorporated: Jan. 6, 1904; *Area:* 8.56 sq km
Population in 2011: 3,114
Provincial Electoral District(s): Arthur-Virden
Federal Electoral District(s): Brandon-Souris
Next Election: Oct. 2018 (4 year terms)
Jeff McConnell, Mayor
Rhonda Stewart, Chief Administrative Officer

West Interlake
P.O. Box 10
10 Main St.
Eriksdale, MB R0C 0W0
Tel: 204-739-2666; *Fax:* 204-739-2073
cao@rmofwestinterlake.com
Municipal Type: Municipality
Incorporated: Jan. 6, 1904; *Area:* 784.76 sq km
Population in 2011: 2,206
Provincial Electoral District(s): Interlake
Federal Electoral District(s): Selkirk-Interlake-Eastman
Next Election: Oct. 2018 (4 year terms)
Note: The RM of Eriksdale & the RM of Siglunes amalgamated to form the new RM of West Interlake on Jan. 1, 2015.
Randy Helgason, Reeve
Arlene Brandson Darknell, Chief Administrative Officer

Westlake-Gladstone
P.O. Box 25
14 Dennis St.
Gladstone, MB R0J 0T0
Tel: 204-385-2332; *Fax:* 204-385-2391
info@westlake-gladstone.ca
www.gladstone.ca
Municipal Type: Municipality
Incorporated: Jan. 1, 1882; *Area:* 2.43 sq km
Population in 2011: 3,068

Provincial Electoral District(s): Ste. Rose
Federal Electoral District(s): Dauphin-Swan River-Neepawa
Next Election: Oct. 2018 (4 year terms)
Note: The Town of Gladstone, the RM of Lakeview & the RM of Westbourne amalgamated to form the new Municipality of WestLake-Gladstone on Jan. 1, 2015.
David Single, Mayor
Eileen Peters, Chief Administrative Officer

Winnipeg Beach
P.O. Box 160
29 Robinson Ave.
Winnipeg Beach, MB R0C 3G0
Tel: 204-389-2698; *Fax:* 204-389-2019
info@winnipegbeach.ca
www.winnipegbeach.ca
Municipal Type: Resort Village
Incorporated: Jan. 5, 1914; *Area:* 3.88 sq km
Population in 2011: 1,011
Provincial Electoral District(s): Gimli
Federal Electoral District(s): Selkirk-Interlake-Eastman
Next Election: July 2018 (4 year terms)
Tony Pimentel, Mayor
Doreen Steg, Chief Administrative Officer

Rural Municipalities in Manitoba

Alexander
P.O. Box 100
104058 Provincial Trunk Hwy. 11
St Georges, MB R0E 1V0
Tel: 204-367-6170; *Fax:* 204-367-2257
info@rmalexander.com
Municipal Type: Rural Municipalities
Incorporated: Jan. 2, 1945; *Area:* 1,568.66 sq km
Population in 2011: 2,983
Provincial Electoral District(s): Lac du Bonnet; Selkirk
Federal Electoral District(s): Brandon-Souris; Selkirk-Interlake-Eastman
Next Election: Oct. 2018 (4 year terms)
Raymond Garand, Reeve
Scott Spicer, Chief Administrative Officer

Alonsa
P.O. Box 127
20 Railway Ave.
Alonsa, MB R0H 0A0
Tel: 204-767-2054; *Fax:* 204-767-2044
rmalonsa@inetlink.ca
Municipal Type: Rural Municipalities
Area: 2,977.50 sq km
Population in 2011: 1,270
Provincial Electoral District(s): Ste. Rose
Federal Electoral District(s): Dauphin-Swan River-Neepawa
Next Election: Oct. 2018 (4 year terms)
Stan Asham, Reeve
Pamela Sul, Chief Administrative Officer

Argyle
P.O. Box 40
132 - 2nd St. North
Baldur, MB R0K 0B0
Tel: 204-535-2176; *Fax:* 204-535-2505
rmofargyle@mymts.net
Municipal Type: Rural Municipalities
Incorporated: Jan. 1, 1882; *Area:* 770.44 sq km
Population in 2011: 1,071
Provincial Electoral District(s): Turtle Mountain
Federal Electoral District(s): Selkirk-Interlake-Eastman
Next Election: Oct. 2018 (4 year terms)
Daniel Martens, Reeve
Barbara Bramwell, Chief Administrative Officer

Armstrong
P.O. Box 69
55 Hwy. 17
Inwood, MB R0C 1P0
Tel: 204-278-3377; *Fax:* 204-278-3437
rmofarmstrong@highspeedcrow.ca
Municipal Type: Rural Municipalities
Incorporated: Dec. 5, 1944; *Area:* 1,864.96 sq km
Population in 2011: 1,835
Provincial Electoral District(s): Interlake
Federal Electoral District(s): Selkirk-Interlake-Eastman
Next Election: Oct. 2018 (4 year terms)
Jack Cruise, Head of Council
John Livingstone, Chief Administrative Officer

Brokenhead
P.O. Box 490
72013 Rd. 42 East
Beausejour, MB R0E 0C0
Tel: 204-268-6700; *Fax:* 204-268-1504
www.ourhomeyourhome.ca/rm-of-brokenhead
Municipal Type: Rural Municipalities
Incorporated: Jan. 2, 1900; *Area:* 750.54 sq km
Population in 2011: 4,635
Provincial Electoral District(s): Lac du Bonnet
Federal Electoral District(s): Selkirk-Interlake-Eastman
Next Election: Oct. 2018 (4 year terms)
Brad Saluk, Reeve
Kate Moir, Chief Administrative Officer

La Broquerie
P.O. Box 130
123 Simard St.
La Broquerie, MB R0A 0W0
Tel: 204-424-5251; *Fax:* 204-424-5193
www.labroquerie.com
Municipal Type: Rural Municipalities
Incorporated: Jan. 2, 1883; *Area:* 578.2 sq km
Population in 2011: 5,198
Provincial Electoral District(s): Emerson
Federal Electoral District(s): Provencher
Next Election: Oct. 2018 (4 year terms)
Lewis Weiss, Reeve
Roger Bouvier, Chief Administrative Officer

Cartier
P.O. Box 117
28 Provincial Rd. 248 South
Elie, MB R0H 0H0
Tel: 204-353-2214; *Fax:* 204-353-2335
anne@rm-cartier.mb.ca
www.rm-cartier.mb.ca
Municipal Type: Rural Municipalities
Incorporated: Jan. 5, 1914; *Area:* 553.42 sq km
Population in 2011: 3,153
Provincial Electoral District(s): Morris
Federal Electoral District(s): Portage-Lisgar
Next Election: Oct. 2018 (4 year terms)
Dale Fossay, Reeve
Virginia Beckwith, Chief Administrative Officer

Coldwell
P.O. Box 90
35 Main St.
Lundar, MB R0C 1Y0
Tel: 204-762-5421; *Fax:* 204-762-5177
coldwell@mymts.net
Municipal Type: Rural Municipalities
Incorporated: Jan. 4, 1913; *Area:* 901.84 sq km
Population in 2011: 1,351
Provincial Electoral District(s): Lakeside
Federal Electoral District(s): Selkirk-Interlake-Eastman
Next Election: Oct. 2018 (4 year terms)
Brian Sigfusson, Reeve
Nicole Christensen, Chief Administrative Officer

Cornwallis
P.O. Box 10 500
RR#5
Brandon, MB R7A 5Y5
Tel: 204-725-8686; *Fax:* 204-725-3659
info@gov.cornwallis.mb.ca
www.gov.cornwallis.mb.ca
Municipal Type: Rural Municipalities
Incorporated: Jan. 3, 1884; *Area:* 500.82 sq km
Population in 2011: 4,378
Provincial Electoral District(s): Minnedosa
Federal Electoral District(s): Brandon-Souris
Next Election: Oct. 2018 (4 year terms)
Heather Dalgleish, Reeve
Donna Anderson, Chief Administrative Officer

Dauphin
P.O. Box 574
Hwy. 20A East
Dauphin, MB R7N 2V4
Tel: 204-638-4531; *Fax:* 204-638-7598
rmofdphn@mymts.net
Municipal Type: Rural Municipalities
Area: 1,516.1 sq km
Population in 2011: 2,200
Provincial Electoral District(s): Dauphin-Roblin
Federal Electoral District(s): Dauphin-Swan River-Neepawa
Next Election: Oct. 2018 (4 year terms)
Dennis Forbes, Reeve
Laura Murray, Chief Administrative Officer

De Salaberry
P.O. Box 40
466 Sabourin St.
St Pierre Jolys, MB R0A 1V0
Tel: 204-433-7406; *Fax:* 204-433-7063
info@rmdesalaberry.mb.ca
www.rmdesalaberry.mb.ca
Municipal Type: Rural Municipalities
Incorporated: Jan. 2, 1883; *Area:* 670.29 sq km
Population in 2011: 3,450
Provincial Electoral District(s): Morris
Federal Electoral District(s): Provencher
Next Election: Oct. 2018 (4 year terms)
Marc Marion, Reeve
Larissa Bodz, Chief Administrative Officer

Deloraine-Winchester
P.O. Box 387
129 Broadway St.
Deloraine, MB R0M 0M0
Tel: 204-747-2572; *Fax:* 204-747-2883
admin@delowin.ca
www.deloraine.org
Municipal Type: Rural Municipalities
Incorporated: Jan. 6, 1904; *Area:* 727.83 sq km
Population in 2011: 1,485
Provincial Electoral District(s): Arthur-Virden
Federal Electoral District(s): Brandon-Souris
Next Election: Oct. 2018 (4 year terms)
Note: The RM of Winchester & the Town of Deloraine amalgamated to form the new Rural Municipality of Deloraine-Winchester on Jan. 1, 2015.
Gordon Weidenhamer, Head of Council
Pamela Hainsworth, Chief Administrative Officer

Dufferin
P.O. Box 100
12 - 2nd Ave. SW
Carman, MB R0G 0J0
Tel: 204-745-2301; *Fax:* 204-745-6348
info@rmofdufferin.com
Municipal Type: Rural Municipalities
Incorporated: Feb. 7, 1880; *Area:* 915.72 sq km
Population in 2011: 2,394
Provincial Electoral District(s): Carman
Federal Electoral District(s): Portage-Lisgar
Next Election: Oct. 2018 (4 year terms)
George Gray, Reeve
Sharla Murray, Chief Administrative Officer

East St. Paul
#1, 3021 Bird's Hill Rd.
East St Paul, MB R2E 1A7
Tel: 204-668-8112; *Fax:* 204-668-1987
info@eaststpaul.com
www.eaststpaul.com
Municipal Type: Rural Municipalities
Incorporated: May 2, 1916; *Area:* 42.1 sq km
Population in 2011: 9,046
Provincial Electoral District(s): Springfield
Federal Electoral District(s): Kildonan-St. Paul
Next Election: Oct. 2018 (4 year terms)
Shelley Hart, Reeve
Bruce Schmidt, Chief Administrative Officer

Ellice-Archie
P.O. Box 67
318 Railway Ave.
McAuley, MB R0M 1H0
Tel: 204-722-2053; *Fax:* 204-722-2027
rmarchie@mts.net
www.rmarchie.com
Municipal Type: Rural Municipalities
Incorporated: Jan. 2, 1883; *Area:* 1153.33 sq km
Population in 2011: 971
Provincial Electoral District(s): Russell
Federal Electoral District(s): Dauphin-Swan River-Neepawa
Next Election: Oct. 2018 (4 year terms)
Note: The RM of Archie, the RM of Ellis & the Village of St. Lazare amalgamated to form the new Rural Municipality of Ellice-Archie on Jan. 1, 2015.
Barry Lowes, Reeve
Trisha Coleman, Chief Administrative Officer

Elton
Forest, MB R0K 0W0
Tel: 204-728-7834; *Fax:* 204-725-1865
elton@inetlink.ca
Municipal Type: Rural Municipalities
Incorporated: Jan. 2, 1883; *Area:* 571.85 sq km
Population in 2011: 1,257
Provincial Electoral District(s): Minnedosa

Federal Electoral District(s): Dauphin-Swan River-Neepawa
Next Election: Oct. 2018 (4 year terms)
Ross Farley, Reeve
Kathleen E.I. Steele, Chief Administrative Officer

Fisher
P.O. Box 280
30 Tache St.
Fisher Branch, MB R0C 0Z0
Tel: 204-372-6393; *Fax:* 204-372-8470
rmoffisher@mts.net
Municipal Type: Rural Municipalities
Incorporated: Jan. 2, 1945; *Area:* 1,481.35 sq km
Population in 2011: 1,704
Provincial Electoral District(s): Interlake
Federal Electoral District(s): Selkirk-Interlake-Eastman
Next Election: Oct. 2018 (4 year terms)
Shannon Pyziak, Reeve
Linda Podaima, Chief Administrative Officer

Gimli
P.O. Box 1246
62 - 2nd St.
Gimli, MB R0C 1B0
Tel: 204-642-6650; *Fax:* 204-642-6660
gimli@rmgimli.com
www.gimli.ca
Municipal Type: Rural Municipalities
Incorporated: Jan. 7, 1887; *Area:* 319.25 sq km
Population in 2011: 5,845
Provincial Electoral District(s): Gimli
Federal Electoral District(s): Selkirk-Interlake-Eastman
Next Election: Oct. 2018 (4 year terms)
Randy Woroniuk, Reeve
Joann King, Chief Administrative Officer

Grahamdale
P.O. Box 160
23 Government Rd.
Moosehorn, MB R0C 2E0
Tel: 204-768-2858; *Fax:* 204-768-3374
info@grahamdale.ca
www.grahamdale.ca
Municipal Type: Rural Municipalities
Incorporated: Jan. 2, 1945; *Area:* 2,384.62 sq km
Population in 2011: 1,354
Provincial Electoral District(s): Interlake
Federal Electoral District(s): Selkirk-Interlake-Eastman
Next Election: Oct. 2018 (4 year terms)
Clifford Halaburda, Reeve
Shelly Schwitek, Chief Administrative Officer

Grey
P.O. Box 99
27 Church Ave. East
Elm Creek, MB R0G 0N0
Tel: 204-436-2014; *Fax:* 204-436-2543
info@rmofgrey.ca
www.rmofgrey.ca
Municipal Type: Rural Municipalities
Incorporated: Jan. 2, 1906; *Area:* 958.49 sq km
Population in 2011: 2,615
Provincial Electoral District(s): Carman
Federal Electoral District(s): Portage-Lisgar
Next Election: Oct. 2018 (4 year terms)
Note: The RM of Grey & the Village of St. Claude amalgamated to form the new RM of Grey on Jan. 1, 2015.
Raymond Franzmann, Reeve
Kim Arnal, Chief Administrative Officer

Hanover
P.O. Box 1720
28 Westland Dr.
Steinbach, MB R5G 1N4
Tel: 204-326-4488; *Fax:* 204-326-4830
www.hanovermb.ca
Municipal Type: Rural Municipalities
Incorporated: Jan. 7, 1881; *Area:* 740.31 sq km
Population in 2011: 14,026
Provincial Electoral District(s): Steinbach
Federal Electoral District(s): Provencher
Next Election: Oct. 2018 (4 year terms)
Stan Toews, Reeve
Luc Lahaie, Chief Administrative Officer

Headingley
#1, 126 Bridge Rd.
Headingley, MB R4H 1G9
Tel: 204-837-5766; *Fax:* 204-831-7207
rmofheadingley@rmofheadingley.ca
www.rmofheadingley.ca
Municipal Type: Rural Municipalities
Incorporated: Jan. 4, 1992; *Area:* 106.96 sq km
Population in 2011: 3,215
Provincial Electoral District(s): Morris
Federal Electoral District(s): Charleswood-St. James-Assiniboia-Headingley
Next Election: Oct. 2018 (4 year terms)
Wilfred R. Taillieu, Reeve
Chris Fulsher, Chief Administrative Officer

Kelsey
P.O. Box 578
264 Fischer Ave.
The Pas, MB R9A 1K6
Tel: 204-623-7474; *Fax:* 204-623-4546
rmkelsey@mts.net
Municipal Type: Rural Municipalities
Incorporated: Jan. 7, 1944; *Area:* 867.64 sq km
Population in 2011: 2,272
Provincial Electoral District(s): Flin Flon; The Pas
Federal Electoral District(s): Churchill-Keewatinook Aski
Next Election: Oct. 2018 (4 year terms)
Rod Berezowecki, Reeve
Jerry Hlady, Chief Administrative Officer

Lac du Bonnet
P.O. Box 100
4187 Provincial Trunk Hwy. 317
Lac du Bonnet, MB R0E 1A0
Tel: 204-345-2619; *Fax:* 204-345-6716
rmldb@lacdubonnet.com
www.lacdubonnet.com
Municipal Type: Rural Municipalities
Incorporated: Jan. 2, 1917; *Area:* 1,100.17 sq km
Population in 2011: 2,671
Provincial Electoral District(s): Lac du Bonnet
Federal Electoral District(s): Selkirk-Interlake-Eastman
Next Election: Oct. 2018 (4 year terms)
Cathie Brereton, Mayor
Tannis Lodge, Chief Administrative Officer

Lakeshore
P.O. Box 220
714 Main St.
Rorketon, MB R0L 1R0
Tel: 204-732-2333; *Fax:* 204-732-2557
Municipal Type: Rural Municipalities
Incorporated: Jan. 5, 1914; *Area:* 761.64 sq km
Population in 2011: 1,401
Provincial Electoral District(s): Dauphin-Roblin
Federal Electoral District(s): Dauphin-Swan River-Neepawa
Next Election: Oct. 2018 (4 year terms)
Note: The RM of Lawrence & the RM of Ochre River amalgamated to form the new RM of Lakeshore on Jan. 1, 2015.
Clinton Cleave, Reeve
Donna Ainscough, Chief Administrative Officer

Macdonald
P.O. Box 100
161 Mandan Dr.
Sanford, MB R0G 2J0
Tel: 204-736-2255; *Fax:* 204-736-4335
info@rmofmacdonald.com
rmofmacdonald.com
Municipal Type: Rural Municipalities
Incorporated: Jan. 7, 1881; *Area:* 1,156.62 sq km
Population in 2011: 6,280
Provincial Electoral District(s): Morris
Federal Electoral District(s): Portage-Lisgar
Next Election: Oct. 2018 (4 year terms)
Bradley Erb, Reeve
W. Tom Raine, Chief Administrative Officer

Minto-Odanah
P.O. Box 1197
49 Main St. South
Minnedosa, MB R0J 1E0
Tel: 204-867-3282; *Fax:* 204-867-1937
mintoodanah@wcgwave.ca
Municipal Type: Rural Municipalities
Incorporated: Jan. 5, 1903; *Area:* 363.65 sq km
Population in 2011: 1,177
Provincial Electoral District(s): Minnedosa
Federal Electoral District(s): Dauphin-Swan River-Neepawa
Next Election: Oct. 2018 (4 year terms)
Note: The RM of Minto & the RM of Odanah amalgamated to form the new RM of Minto-Odanah on Jan. 1, 2015.
James A. Andersen, Reeve
Aaren Robertson, Chief Administrative Officer

Montcalm
P.O. Box 300
46 - 1st St. East
Letellier, MB R0G 1C0
Tel: 204-737-2271; *Fax:* 204-737-2326
caomontcalm@mymts.net
Municipal Type: Rural Municipalities
Incorporated: Jan. 1, 1882; *Area:* 469.41 sq km
Population in 2011: 1,309
Provincial Electoral District(s): Emerson
Federal Electoral District(s): Provencher
Next Election: Oct. 2018 (4 year terms)
Derek Sabourin, Reeve
Michelle Robert, Chief Administrative Officer

Morris
P.O. Box 518
207 Main St. North
Morris, MB R0G 1K0
Tel: 204-746-2642; *Fax:* 204-746-8801
info@rmofmorris.ca
Municipal Type: Rural Municipalities
Incorporated: Jan. 5, 1880; *Area:* 1,041.15 sq km
Population in 2011: 2,999
Provincial Electoral District(s): Morris
Federal Electoral District(s): Portage-Lisgar
Next Election: Oct. 2018 (4 year terms)
Ralph Groening, Reeve
Larry Driedger, Chief Administrative Officer

Mossey River
P.O. Box 370
130 - 2nd St.
Winnipegosis, MB R0L 2G0
Tel: 204-656-4791; *Fax:* 204-656-4751
vofwinnipegosis@mts.net
Municipal Type: Rural Municipalities
Incorporated: Jan. 6, 1915; *Area:* 2.5 sq km
Population in 2011: 1,186
Provincial Electoral District(s): Swan River
Federal Electoral District(s): Dauphin-Swan River-Neepawa
Next Election: Oct. 2018 (4 year terms)
Note: The RM of Mossey River & the Village of Winnipegosis amalgamated to form the new RM of Mossey River on Jan. 1, 2015.
Kate Basford, Head of Council
Kevin Drewniak, Chief Administrative Officer

Mountain
P.O. Box 155
200 Drury Ave.
Birch River, MB R0L 0E0
Tel: 204-236-4222; *Fax:* 204-236-4773
rmmountn@mymts.net
Municipal Type: Rural Municipalities
Area: 2607.69 sq km
Population in 2011: 1,104
Provincial Electoral District(s): Swan River
Federal Electoral District(s): Dauphin-Swan River-Neepawa
Next Election: Oct. 2018 (4 year terms)
Marvin Kovachik, Reeve
Robin Wiebe, Chief Administrative Officer

Mystery Lake
Thompson Airport Terminal Bldg.
P.O. Box 189 Main
Airport Rd. South
Thompson, MB R8N 1N1
Tel: 204-677-4075; *Fax:* 204-778-7642
lgdml@mymts.net
Municipal Type: Local Goverment District
Incorporated: Jan. 1, 1956; *Area:* 3,464.06 sq km
Population in 2011: 10
Corinne Stewart, Resident Administrator & Chief Administrative Officer

Oakview
P.O. Box 179
10 Cochrane St.
Oak River, MB R0K 1T0
Tel: 204-566-2146; *Fax:* 204-566-2126
blanshardrm@inetlink.ca
www.rmofblanshard.ca
Municipal Type: Rural Municipalities
Incorporated: Jan. 3, 1884
Population in 2011: 1,513
Provincial Electoral District(s): Russell
Federal Electoral District(s): Dauphin-Swan River-Neepawa
Next Election: Oct. 2018 (4 year terms)
Note: The RM of Blanshard, the RM of Saskatchewan & the Town of Rapid City amalgamated to form the new Rural Municipality of Oakview on Jan. 1, 2015.

Brent Fortune, Reeve
Diane Kuculym, Chief Administrative Officer

Pinawa
P.O. Box 100
36 Burrows Rd.
Pinawa, MB R0E 1L0
Tel: 204-753-5100; *Fax:* 204-753-2770
info@pinawa.com
www.pinawa.com
Municipal Type: Local Goverment District
Incorporated: Jan. 3, 1963; *Area:* 128.47 sq km
Population in 2011: 1,444
Federal Electoral District(s): Selkirk-Interlake-Eastman
Next Election: Oct. 2018 (4 year terms)
Blair Skinner, Mayor
Jenny Petersen, Chief Administrative Officer

Piney
P.O. Box 48
6092 Boundary St.
Vassar, MB R0A 2J0
Tel: 204-437-2284; *Fax:* 204-437-2556
rmofpiney@wiband.ca
www.rmofpiney.mb.ca
Municipal Type: Rural Municipalities
Area: 2,433.77 sq km
Population in 2011: 1,720
Provincial Electoral District(s): Emerson
Federal Electoral District(s): Provencher
Next Election: Oct. 2018 (4 year terms)
Wayne Anderson, Reeve
Martin Van Osch, Chief Administrative Officer

Pipestone
P.O. Box 99
401 - 3rd Ave.
Reston, MB R0M 1X0
Tel: 204-877-3327; *Fax:* 204-877-3999
admin@rmofpipestone.com
www.rmofpipestone.com
Municipal Type: Rural Municipalities
Incorporated: Jan. 6, 1897; *Area:* 1,147.35 sq km
Population in 2011: 1,447
Provincial Electoral District(s): Arthur-Virden
Federal Electoral District(s): Brandon-Souris
Next Election: Oct. 2018 (4 year terms)
Archie McPherson, Reeve
June Greggor, Chief Administrative Officer

Portage la Prairie
35 Tupper St. South
Portage la Prairie, MB R1N 1W7
Tel: 204-857-3821; *Fax:* 204-239-0069
info@rmofportage.ca
www.rmofportage.ca
Municipal Type: Rural Municipalities
Incorporated: Jan. 4, 1879; *Area:* 1,964.32 sq km
Population in 2011: 6,525
Provincial Electoral District(s): Portage la Prairie; Carman
Federal Electoral District(s): Portage-Lisgar
Next Election: Oct. 2018 (4 year terms)
Kameron W. Blight, Reeve
Daryl Hrehirchuk, Chief Administrative Officer

Prairie Lakes
P.O. Box 100
211 - 3rd St.
Belmont, MB R0K 0C0
Tel: 204-537-2241; *Fax:* 204-537-2364
caostrathcona@inethome.ca
Municipal Type: Rural Municipalities
Incorporated: Jan. 2, 1906; *Area:* 485.56 sq km
Population in 2011: 1,423
Provincial Electoral District(s): Turtle Mountain
Federal Electoral District(s): Brandon-Souris
Next Election: Oct. 2018 (4 year terms)
Note: The RM of Strathcona & the RM of Riverside amalgamated to form the new RM of Prairie Lakes on Jan. 1, 2015.
Lonn Dunlop, Reeve
Carolyn Davies, Chief Administrative Officer

Reynolds
P.O. Box 46
46044 Hwy. 11
Hadashville, MB R0E 0X0
Tel: 204-426-5305; *Fax:* 204-426-5552
rmreynol@mymts.net
www.rmofreynolds.com
Municipal Type: Rural Municipalities
Incorporated: Jan. 2, 1945; *Area:* 3,573.31 sq km
Population in 2011: 1,285
Provincial Electoral District(s): La Verendrye; Lac du Bonnet
Federal Electoral District(s): Provencher
Next Election: Oct. 2018 (4 year terms)
David Turchyn, Reeve
Trudy Turchyn, Chief Administrative Officer

Riding Mountain West
P.O. Box 110
118 Main St.
Inglis, MB R0J 0X0
Tel: 204-564-2589; *Fax:* 204-564-2643
rmosb@mts.net
Municipal Type: Rural Municipalities
Incorporated: Jan. 6, 1999; *Area:* 1,622.55 sq km
Population in 2011: 1,390
Provincial Electoral District(s): Russell
Federal Electoral District(s): Dauphin-Swan River-Neepawa
Next Election: Oct. 2018 (4 year terms)
Note: The RM of Shellmouth-Boulton & the RM of Silver Creek amalgamated to form the new RM of Riding Mountain West on Jan. 1, 2015.
Barry Chescu, Reeve
Cindy Marzoff, Chief Administrative Officer

Ritchot
352 Main St.
St. Adolphe, MB R5A 1B9
Tel: 204-883-2293; *Fax:* 204-883-2674
municipaloffice@ritchot.com
www.ritchot.com
Municipal Type: Rural Municipalities
Incorporated: Jan. 4, 1890; *Area:* 333.53 sq km
Population in 2011: 5,478
Provincial Electoral District(s): La Verendrye; Morris
Federal Electoral District(s): Provencher; Winnipeg South
Next Election: Oct. 2018 (4 year terms)
Jackie Hunt, Mayor
Mitch Duval, Chief Administrative Officer

Rockwood
P.O. Box 902
285 Main St.
Stonewall, MB R0C 2Z0
Tel: 204-467-2272; *Fax:* 204-467-5329
info@rockwood.ca
www.rockwood.ca
Municipal Type: Rural Municipalities
Incorporated: Jan. 7, 1881; *Area:* 1,199.76 sq km
Population in 2011: 7,964
Provincial Electoral District(s): Lakeside
Federal Electoral District(s): Selkirk-Interlake-Eastman
Next Election: Oct. 2018 (4 year terms)
Jim Campbell, Reeve
L. Grant Thorsteinson, Chief Administrative Officer

Roland
P.O. Box 119
45 - 3rd St.
Roland, MB R0G 1T0
Tel: 204-343-2061; *Fax:* 204-343-2001
rmroland@pmcnet.ca
Municipal Type: Rural Municipalities
Incorporated: Jan. 4, 1908; *Area:* 485.06 sq km
Population in 2011: 1,058
Provincial Electoral District(s): Carman
Federal Electoral District(s): Portage-Lisgar
Next Election: Oct. 2018 (4 year terms)
John Hughes, Reeve
Kristi Olson, Chief Administrative Officer

Rosedale
P.O. Box 100
282 Hamilton St.
Neepawa, MB R0J 1H0
Tel: 204-476-5414; *Fax:* 204-476-5431
rosedale@mts.net
Municipal Type: Rural Municipalities
Incorporated: Jan. 3, 1884; *Area:* 865.58 sq km
Population in 2011: 1,627
Provincial Electoral District(s): Ste. Rose
Federal Electoral District(s): Dauphin-Swan River-Neepawa
Next Election: Oct. 2018 (4 year terms)
Bill Martin, Reeve
Karen McDonald, Chief Administrative Officer

Rosser
P.O. Box 131
0077E - PR #221
Rosser, MB R0H 1E0
Tel: 204-467-5711; *Fax:* 204-467-5958
info@rmofrosser.com
www.rmofrosser.com
Municipal Type: Rural Municipalities
Incorporated: Jan. 1, 1893; *Area:* 441.43 sq km
Population in 2011: 1,352
Provincial Electoral District(s): Lakeside
Federal Electoral District(s): Selkirk-Interlake-Eastman
Next Election: Oct. 2018 (4 year terms)
Frances Smee, Reeve
Beverley Wells, Chief Administrative Officer

St. Andrews
P.O. Box 130
500 Railway Ave.
Clandeboye, MB R0C 0P0
Tel: 204-738-2264; *Fax:* 204-738-2500
office@rmofstandrews.com
www.rmofstandrews.com
Municipal Type: Rural Municipalities
Incorporated: Jan. 5, 1880; *Area:* 752.7 sq km
Population in 2011: 11,875
Provincial Electoral District(s): Gimli
Federal Electoral District(s): Selkirk-Interlake-Eastman
Next Election: Oct. 2018 (4 year terms)
George Pike, Mayor
Andrew Weremy, Chief Administrative Officer

St. Clements
P.O. Box 2
1043 Kittson Rd., Grp 35, RR# 1
East Selkirk, MB R0E 0M0
Tel: 204-482-3300; *Fax:* 204-482-3098
info@rmofstclements.com
www.rmofstclements.com
Municipal Type: Rural Municipalities
Incorporated: July 7, 1883; *Area:* 728.67 sq km
Population in 2011: 10,505
Provincial Electoral District(s): Selkirk
Federal Electoral District(s): Selkirk-Interlake-Eastman
Next Election: Oct. 2018 (4 year terms)
Debbie Fiebelkorn, Mayor
DJ Sigmundson, Chief Administrative Officer

Ste. Anne
P.O. Box 6
395 Traverse St., Grp 50, RR# 1
Ste. Anne, MB R5H 1R1
Tel: 204-422-5929; *Fax:* 204-422-9723
info@rmofsteanne.com
www.rmofsteanne.com
Municipal Type: Rural Municipalities
Incorporated: Feb. 3, 1881; *Area:* 477.65 sq km
Population in 2011: 4,686
Provincial Electoral District(s): La Verendrye
Federal Electoral District(s): Provencher
Next Election: Oct. 2018 (4 year terms)
Art Bergmann, Reeve
Jennifer Blatz, Chief Administrative Officer

St. François Xavier
1060 Hwy. 26
St François Xavier, MB R4L 1A5
Tel: 204-864-2092; *Fax:* 204-864-2390
info@rm-stfrancois.mb.ca
www.rm-stfrancois.mb.ca
Municipal Type: Rural Municipalities
Incorporated: Jan. 5, 1880; *Area:* 204.55 sq km
Population in 2011: 1,240
Provincial Electoral District(s): Morris
Federal Electoral District(s): Portage-Lisgar
Next Election: Oct. 2018 (4 year terms)
Dwayne Clark, Reeve
Robert Poirier, Chief Administrative Officer

St. Laurent
P.O. Box 220
Lot 825, Provincial Trunk Hwy. 6
St Laurent, MB R0C 2S0
Tel: 204-646-2259; *Fax:* 204-646-2705
rmstlaur@mymts.net
www.rmofstlaurent.ca
Municipal Type: Rural Municipalities
Incorporated: Jan. 1, 1882; *Area:* 462.51 sq km
Population in 2011: 1,305
Provincial Electoral District(s): Lakeside
Federal Electoral District(s): Selkirk-Interlake-Eastman
Next Election: Oct. 2018 (4 year terms)

Cheryl Smith, Reeve
Diana Friesen, Chief Administrative Officer

Sifton
P.O. Box 100
293 - 2nd Ave. West
Oak Lake, MB R0M 1P0
Tel: 204-855-2423; *Fax:* 204-855-2836
cao_sifton@mymts.net
Municipal Type: Rural Municipalities
Incorporated: Jan. 3, 1884; *Area:* 768.11 sq km
Population in 2011: 1,172
Provincial Electoral District(s): Arthur-Virden
Federal Electoral District(s): Dauphin-Swan River-Neepawa; Brandon-Souris
Next Election: Oct. 2018 (4 year terms)
Note: The RM of Sifton & the RM of Oak Lake amalgamated to form the new RM of Sifton on Jan. 1, 2015.
Rick Plaisier, Reeve
Mary Smith, Chief Administrative Officer

Springfield
P.O. Box 219
100 Springfield Centre Dr.
Oakbank, MB R0E 1J0
Tel: 204-444-3321; *Fax:* 204-444-2137
www.rmofspringfield.ca
Municipal Type: Rural Municipalities
Incorporated: Jan. 4, 1873; *Area:* 1,100.81 sq km
Population in 2011: 14,069
Provincial Electoral District(s): Springfield
Federal Electoral District(s): Provencher
Next Election: Oct. 2018 (4 year terms)
Bob Bodnaruk, Reeve
Russell Phillips, Chief Administrative Officer

Stanley
P.O. Box 1600
23111 Provincial Trunk Hwy. 14W
Morden, MB R6W 4B5
Tel: 204-325-4101; *Fax:* 204-325-4008
info@rmofstanley.ca
www.rmofstanley.ca
Municipal Type: Rural Municipalities
Incorporated: Nov. 7, 1890; *Area:* 835.59 sq km
Population in 2011: 8,256
Provincial Electoral District(s): Pembina
Federal Electoral District(s): Portage-Lisgar
Next Election: Oct. 2018 (4 year terms)
Morris Olafson, Reeve
Dale Toews, Chief Administrative Officer

Stuartburn
P.O. Box 59
108 Main St. North
Vita, MB R0A 2K0
Tel: 204-425-3218; *Fax:* 204-425-3513
inquiries@rmofstuartburn.com
Municipal Type: Rural Municipalities
Incorporated: Jan. 4, 1997; *Area:* 1,161.65 sq km
Population in 2011: 1,535
Provincial Electoral District(s): Emerson
Federal Electoral District(s): Provencher
Next Election: Oct. 2018 (4 year terms)
Jim Swidersky, Reeve
Lucie Maynard, Chief Administrative Officer

Taché
P.O. Box 100
1294 Dawson Rd.
Lorette, MB R0A 0Y0
Tel: 204-878-3321; *Fax:* 204-878-9977
info@rmtache.ca
rmtache.ca
Municipal Type: Rural Municipalities
Incorporated: Jan. 5, 1880; *Area:* 581.52 sq km
Population in 2011: 10,284
Provincial Electoral District(s): La Verendrye
Federal Electoral District(s): Provencher
Next Election: Oct. 2018 (4 year terms)
Robert Rivard, Mayor
Dan Poersch, Chief Administrative Officer

Thompson
P.O. Box 190
531 Norton Ave.
Miami, MB R0G 1H0
Tel: 204-435-2114; *Fax:* 204-435-2067
rmthomp@mts.net
Municipal Type: Rural Municipalities
Incorporated: Jan. 6, 1909; *Area:* 528.57 sq km
Population in 2011: 1,397
Provincial Electoral District(s): Carman
Federal Electoral District(s): Portage-Lisgar
Next Election: Oct. 2018 (4 year terms)
Brian Callum, Reeve
Jody Oakes, Chief Administrative Officer

Victoria
P.O. Box 40
130 Broadway St.
Holland, MB R0G 0X0
Tel: 204-526-2423; *Fax:* 204-526-2028
rm.office@rmofvictoria.com
rmofvictoria.com
Municipal Type: Rural Municipalities
Incorporated: Jan. 4, 1902; *Area:* 697.63 sq km
Population in 2011: 1,119
Provincial Electoral District(s): Carman
Federal Electoral District(s): Brandon-Souris
Next Election: Oct. 2018 (4 year terms)
Harold W. Purkess, Reeve
Ivan Bruneau, Chief Administrative Officer

Wallace-Woodworth
P.O. Box 2200
154023-PR 257
Virden, MB R0M 2C0
Tel: 204-748-1239; *Fax:* 204-748-3450
info@wallace-woodworth.com
www.wallace-woodworth.com
Municipal Type: Rural Municipalities
Incorporated: Jan. 6, 1909; *Area:* 1,148.75 sq km
Population in 2011: 2,857
Provincial Electoral District(s): Arthur-Virden
Federal Electoral District(s): Brandon-Souris; Dauphin-Swan River-Neepawa
Next Election: Oct. 2018 (4 year terms)
Note: The RM of Wallace, the RM of Woodworth & the Village of Elkhorn amalgamated to form the new RM of Wallace-Woodworth on Jan. 1, 2015.
Denis Carter, Reeve
Garth Mitchell, Chief Administrative Officer

West St. Paul
3550 Main St.
West St Paul, MB R4A 5A3
Tel: 204-338-0306; *Fax:* 204-334-9362
info@weststpaul.com
www.weststpaul.com
Municipal Type: Rural Municipalities
Incorporated: Jan. 7, 1916; *Area:* 87.66 sq km
Population in 2011: 4,932
Provincial Electoral District(s): Gimli
Federal Electoral District(s): Kildonan-St. Paul
Next Election: Oct. 2018 (4 year terms)
Bruce Henley, Reeve
Brent Olynyk, Chief Administrative Officer

Whitehead
P.O. Box 107
517 - 2nd Ave.
Alexander, MB R0K 0A0
Tel: 204-752-2261; *Fax:* 204-752-2129
rmwhitehead@mymts.net
Municipal Type: Rural Municipalities
Incorporated: Jan. 2, 1883; *Area:* 562.82 sq km
Population in 2011: 1,533
Provincial Electoral District(s): Minnedosa
Federal Electoral District(s): Brandon-Souris
Next Election: Oct. 2018 (4 year terms)
Heather Curle, Reeve
Cindy Izzard, Chief Administrative Officer

Whitemouth
P.O. Box 248
47 Railway Ave.
Whitemouth, MB R0E 2G0
Tel: 204-348-2221; *Fax:* 204-348-2576
rmwhite@mymts.net
www.rmwhitemouth.com
Municipal Type: Rural Municipalities
Incorporated: Jan. 1, 1905; *Area:* 703.02 sq km
Population in 2011: 1,548
Provincial Electoral District(s): Lac du Bonnet
Federal Electoral District(s): Provencher
Next Election: Oct. 2018 (4 year terms)
Bill Dowbyhuz, Reeve
Laurie Kjartanson, Chief Administrative Officer

Woodlands
P.O. Box 10
57 Railway Ave.
Woodlands, MB R0C 3H0
Tel: 204-383-5679; *Fax:* 204-383-5169
rmwdlds1@mts.net
www.rmwoodlands.info
Municipal Type: Rural Municipalities
Incorporated: Jan. 5, 1880; *Area:* 1,160.45 sq km
Population in 2011: 3,521
Provincial Electoral District(s): Lakeside
Federal Electoral District(s): Selkirk-Interlake-Eastman
Next Election: Oct. 2018 (4 year terms)
Trevor King, Reeve
Lynn Kauppila, Chief Administrative Officer

Yellowhead
P.O. Box 278
306 Elm St.
Shoal Lake, MB R0J 1Z0
Tel: 204-759-2565; *Fax:* 204-759-2740
shoalake@goinet.ca
Municipal Type: Rural Municipalities
Area: 1,110.72 sq km
Population in 2011: 1,973
Provincial Electoral District(s): Russell
Federal Electoral District(s): Dauphin-Swan River-Neepawa
Next Election: Oct. 2018 (4 year terms)
Note: The Municipality of Shoal Lake & the RM of Strathclair amalgamated to form the new RM of Yellowhead on Jan. 1, 2015.
Donald Yanick, Reeve
Nadine Gapka, Chief Administrative Officer

NEW BRUNSWICK

The provincial government of New Brunswick provides all services of a municipal nature for the rural area of the province, while municipalities provide these services to their residents. For the rural area, an advisory committee may be elected at public meetings biennially to assist and advise the Minister. Municipal councils are elected to look after the affairs of the municipalities.

Acts of the legislature governing municipalities are the Municipalities Act, the Municipal Assistance Act, the Community Planning Act, the Assessment Act, the Municipal Capital Borrowing Act, the Municipal Elections Act, the Municial Debentures Act, the Municipal Capital Borrowing Act, and the New Brunswick Municipal Finance Corporation Act.

Population requirements for incorporation of municipalities are 10,000 for cities and 1,500 for towns. There are no specified requirements for villages.

Municipal elections are held every four years on the second Monday in May (2016, 2020, etc.).

New Brunswick

Major Municipalities in New Brunswick

Bathurst
150 St. George St.
Bathurst, NB E2A 1B5
Tel: 506-548-0400; *Fax:* 506-548-0581
city@bathurst.ca
www.bathurst.ca
Municipal Type: City
Area: 91.55 sq km
County or District: Gloucester; *Population in 2011:* 12,275
Provincial Electoral District(s): Bathurst West-Beresford; Bathurst East-Nepisiguit-Saint-Isidore
Federal Electoral District(s): Acadie-Bathurst
Next Election: May 2020 (4 year terms)
Paolo Fongemie, Mayor
Penny Anderson, Councillor
Kim Chamberlain, Councillor
Bernard (Bernie) Cormier, Councillor
Samuel Daigle, Councillor
Rickey Hondas, Councillor
Katherine Lanteigne, Councillor
Lee Stever, Councillor
Hugh L. Comeau, Councillor, 506-548-2255
André Doucet, City Manager, 506-548-0733
Susan Doucet, City Clerk, 506-548-0417
Matthew Abernethy, Director of Engineering Services, Public Works
Donald McLaughlin, Planning Technician, 506-548-0444, Fax: 506-548-0581

Dieppe
333, av Acadie
Dieppe, NB E1A 1G9
Tel: 506-877-7900
info@dieppe.ca
www.dieppe.ca
Municipal Type: City
Incorporated: Jan. 1, 1952; *Area:* 51.17 sq km
County or District: Westmorland; *Population in 2011:* 23,310
Provincial Electoral District(s): Shediac Bay-Dieppe; Dieppe
Federal Electoral District(s): Moncton-Riverview-Dieppe; Beauséjour
Next Election: May 2020 (4 year terms)
Yvon Lapierre, Mayor
Daniel Allain, Councillor-at-Large
Jordan Nowlan, Councillor-at-Large
Patricia Thomas-Arseneault, Councillor-at-Large
Jean-Marc Brideau, Councillor, Wards: 1
Jean-Claude Cormier, Councillor, Wards: 2
Ted Gaudet, Councillor, Wards: 3
Ernest Thibodeau, Councillor, Wards: 4
Roger J. LeBlanc, Councillor, Wards: 5
Marc Melanson, Chief Administrative Officer
Jacques LeBlanc, Director, Public Works
Charles LeBlanc, Fire Chief, Fire Department, 506-877-7970

Edmundston
7 Canada Rd.
Edmundston, NB E3V 1T7
Tel: 506-739-2115; *Fax:* 506-737-6820
communication@edmundston.ca
edmundston.ca
Municipal Type: City
Area: 106.92 sq km
County or District: Madawaska; *Population in 2011:* 16,032
Provincial Electoral District(s): Edmundston-Madawaska Centre; Madawaska Les Lacs-Edmundston
Federal Electoral District(s): Madawaska-Restigouche
Next Election: May 2020 (4 year terms)
Cyrille Simard, Mayor
Lise Ouellette, Councillor, Wards: 1
Michel Maxime Serry, Councillor, Wards: 1
Éric Doiron, Councillor, Wards: 2
Camille Roy, Councillor, Wards: 2
Eric Marquis, Councillor, Wards: 3
Gérald G. Morneault, Councillor, Wards: 3
Eric Fournier, Councillor, Wards: 4
Eric McGuire, Councillor, Wards: 4
Marc Michaud, Chief Administrative Officer
Paul Dionne, Director, Public Works and Environment, 506-739-2103

Fredericton
City Hall
P.O. Box 130
397 Queen St.
Fredericton, NB E3B 4Y7
Tel: 506-460-2020; *Fax:* 506-460-2042
www.fredericton.ca
Municipal Type: City
Incorporated: 1848; *Area:* 130.68 sq km
County or District: York; *Population in 2011:* 56,224
Provincial Electoral District(s): Oromocto-Lincoln; Fredericton-Grand Lake; New Maryland-Sunbury; Fredericton South; Fredericton North; Fredericton-York; Fredericton West-Hanwell
Federal Electoral District(s): Fredericton;Tobique-Mactaquac
Next Election: May 2020 (4 year terms)
Mike O'Brien, Mayor, 506-460-2085, Fax: 506-460-2134
Kate Rogers, Deputy Mayor & Councillor, Wards: 11
Daniel R. Keenan, Councillor, 506-472-6046, Fax: 506-460-2905, Wards: 1
Mark Peters, Councillor, Wards: 2
Bruce Grandy, Councillor, Wards: 3
Eric D. Price, Councillor, Wards: 4
Steven Hicks, Councillor, 506-458-1973, Fax: 506-460-2905, Wards: 5
Eric Megarity, Councillor, Wards: 6
Kevin Darrah, Councillor, Wards: 7
Greg Ericson, Councillor, Wards: 8
Stephen A. Chase, Councillor, 506-455-0711, Fax: 506-460-2905, Wards: 9
John MacDermid, Councillor, Wards: 10
Henri Mallet, Councillor, Wards: 12
Brenda Knight, City Clerk
Tina Tapley, City Treasurer & Director, Financial Services
Chris MacPherson, Chief Administrative Officer
Leanne Fitch, Police Chief
Paul Fleming, Fire Chief
Wayne Tallon, Director, Public Safety
Ken Forrest, Director, Growth & Community Planning
Darren Charters, Manager, Transit

Miramichi
141 Henry St.
Miramichi, NB E1V 2N5
Tel: 506-623-2200; *Fax:* 506-623-2201
www.miramichi.org
Municipal Type: City
Incorporated: Jan. 1, 1995; *Area:* 179.84 sq km
County or District: Northumberland; *Population in 2011:* 17,811
Provincial Electoral District(s): Miramichi Bay-Neguac; Miramichi; Southwest Miramichi-Bay du Vin
Federal Electoral District(s): Miramichi-Grand Lake
Next Election: May 2020 (4 year terms)
Gerry Cormier, Mayor
Adam Lordon, Deputy Mayor & Councillor
Chad Duplessie, Councillor
Billy Fleiger, Councillor, 506-773-6508
Brian J. King, Councillor, 506-773-6543
Tom King, Councillor
Tara Ross-Robinson, Councillor
Tony (Bucket) Walsh, Councillor, 506-622-4612
Shelly A. Williams, Councillor, 506-622-6548
Cathy Goguen, City Clerk, 506-623-2212
Ian Gavet, Fire Chief, 506-623-2225, Fax: 506-623-2226
Csaba Kazamer, Director, Engineering, 506-623-2021, Fax: 506-623-2201
Suzanne Watters, Director, Community Wellness & Recreation, 506-623-2300, Fax: 506-623-2306

Moncton / Ville de Moncton
655 Main St.
Moncton, NB E1C 1E8
Tel: 506-853-3333; *Fax:* 506-389-5904
info@moncton.ca
www.moncton.ca
Municipal Type: City
Incorporated: 1890; *Area:* 141.17 sq km
County or District: Westmorland; *Population in 2011:* 69,074
Provincial Electoral District(s): Moncton East; Moncton Centre; Moncton South; Moncton Northwest; Moncton Southwest
Federal Electoral District(s): Moncton-Riverview-Dieppe; Beauséjour; Fundy Royal
Next Election: May 2020 (4 year terms)
Dawn Arnold, Mayor
Pierre A. Boudreau, Councillor at Large
Greg Turner, Councillor at Large
Shawn Crossman, Deputy Mayor, Councillor, Wards: 1
Paulette Thériault, Councillor, Wards: 1
Blair Lawrence, Councillor, Wards: 2
Charles Léger, Councillor, Wards: 2
Bryan David Butler, Councillor, Wards: 3
Rob McKee, Councillor, Wards: 3
René (Pepsi) Landry, Councillor, Wards: 4
Paul A. Pellerin, Councillor, Wards: 4
Don MacLellan, Acting City Manager & General Manager, Community Safety Services, 506-843-3498, Fax: 506-859-4225
Maurice Belliveau, General Manager, Economic Development & Events
Catherine Dallaire, General Manager, Corporate Services
Laurann Hanson, General Manager, Human Resources
Jack MacDonald, General Manager, Engineering & Environmental Services
John Martin, General Manager & CFO, Finance & Administration, 506-383-6703
Eric Arsenault, Fire Chief, 506-857-8800, Fax: 506-856-4353
Bill Budd, Director, Urban Planning, 506-853-3533
Claude Despres, Director, Strategic Initiatives, 506-856-4309
Isabelle LeBlanc, Director, Corporate Communications
Alcide Richard, Director, Design & Construction
Kevin Silliker, Director, Economic Development, 506-853-3516
Sherry Sparks, Director, Building Inspection
Tanya Carter, Manager, Purchasing, 506-853-3535

Quispamsis
P.O. Box 21085
12 Landing Ct.
Quispamsis, NB E2E 4Z4
Tel: 506-849-5778; *Fax:* 506-849-5799
quispamsis@quispamsis.ca
www.quispamsis.ca
Municipal Type: City
Area: 57.06 sq km
County or District: Kings; *Population in 2011:* 17,886
Provincial Electoral District(s): Hampton; Quispamsis
Federal Electoral District(s): Fundy Royal
Next Election: May 2020 (4 year terms)
Gary Clark, Mayor
Lisa Loughery, Councillor, 506-849-6165
Sean Luck, Councillor
Kirk R. Miller, Councillor, 506-847-9571
Libby O'Hara, Deputy Mayor, Councillor, 506-847-3800
Emil T. Olsen, Councillor, 506-847-5197
J. Pierre Rioux, Councillor, 506-847-4925
Beth Thompson, Councillor, 506-849-2852
Susan Deuville, Chief Administrative Officer, 506-849-5763
Jo-Anne McGraw, Treasurer, 506-849-5739
Chris Vriezen, Superintendent, Utility, 506-849-5734
Michael Stephen, Superintendent, Public Works, 506-849-5742
Dwight Colbourne, Municipal Planning Officer, 506-849-5749
Gary Losier, Director, Engineering & Works, 506-849-5749

Riverview
30 Honour House Ct.
Riverview, NB E1C3Y9
Tel: 506-387-2020
www.townofriverview.ca
Municipal Type: City
Area: 33.88 sq km
County or District: Albert; *Population in 2011:* 19,128
Provincial Electoral District(s): Riverview; Albert
Federal Electoral District(s): Moncton-Riverview-Dieppe; Fundy Royal
Next Election: May 2020 (4 year terms)
Ann Seamans, Mayor, 506-386-1703
Lana Hansen, Councillor, Wards: 1
John Coughlan, Councillor, Wards: 2
Jeremy Thorne, Councillor, Wards: 3
Wayne Bennett, Councillor, 506-386-3295, Wards: 4
Cecile Cassista, Councillor at Large
Andrew J. Leblanc, Councillor at Large
Tammy Rampersaud, Councillor at Large
Colin Smith, Chief Administrative Officer, 506-387-2021
Denyse Richard, Deputy Town Clerk, 506-387-2043
Denis Pleau, Chief, Fire & Rescue, 506-387-2201

Rothesay
70 Hampton Rd.
Rothesay, NB E2E 5L5
Tel: 506-848-6600; *Fax:* 506-848-6677
rothesay@rothesay.ca
www.rothesay.ca
Municipal Type: City
Incorporated: Jan. 1, 1998; *Area:* 34.73 sq km
County or District: Kings; *Population in 2011:* 11,947
Provincial Electoral District(s): Rothesay
Federal Electoral District(s): Saint John-Rothesay; Fundy Royal
Next Election: May 2020 (4 year terms)
Nancy Grant, Mayor
Matt Alexander, Councillor
Grant Brenan, Councillor
Tiffany MacKay French, Councillor
Bill McGuire, Councillor
Peter Lewis, Councillor

Don Shea, Councillor
Miriam Wells, Councillor
Mary Jane Banks, Clerk
Doug MacDonald, Treasurer
Brian White, Director, Development Services

Saint John
City Hall
P.O. Box 1971
15 Market Sq.
Saint John, NB E2L 4L1
Tel: 506-649-6000
www.saintjohn.ca
Municipal Type: City
Incorporated: May 18, 1785; *Area:* 315.49 sq km
County or District: Saint John; *Population in 2011:* 70,063
Provincial Electoral District(s): Hampton; Saint John East; Portland-Simonds; Saint John Harbour; Saint John Lancaster; Fundy-The Isles-Saint John West
Federal Electoral District(s): Saint John-Rothesay
Next Election: May 2020 (4 year terms)
Don Darling, Mayor
Shirley McAlary, Councillor at Large
H. Gary Sullivan, Councillor at Large
Blake Armstrong, Councillor, Wards: 1
Greg J. Norton, Councillor, Wards: 1
Sean Casey, Councillor, Wards: 2
John Mackenzie, Councillor, Wards: 2
Gerry Lowe, Councillor, Wards: 3
Donna Reardon, Councillor, Wards: 3
David Merrithew, Councillor, Wards: 4
Ray Strowbridge, Councillor, Wards: 4
Jeff Trail, City Manager, 506-658-2913, Fax: 506-658-2802
Cathy Graham, Comptroller, Finance & Administrative Services, 506-658-2951, Fax: 506-649-7901
Jacqueline Hamilton, Commissioner, Growth & Community Development, 506-658-2835, Fax: 506-658-2837
William Edwards, Commissioner, Transportation & Environment Services; Water, 506-658-4455
Neil Jacobsen, Commissioner, Strategic Services
Victoria Clarke, Executive Director, Discover Saint John
John Nugent, City Solicitor, 506-658-2860, Fax: 506-649-7939
John Bates, Police Chief
Kevin Clifford, Fire Chief, 506-658-2910, Fax: 506-658-2916
David Logan, Manager, Material & Fleet Management, 506-658-2930, Fax: 506-658-4742

Other Municipalities in New Brunswick

Alma
8 School St.
Alma, NB E4H 1L2
Tel: 506-887-6123; *Fax:* 506-887-6124
villageofalma@gmail.com
www.villageofalma.ca
Municipal Type: Village
Area: 47.64 sq km
County or District: Albert; *Population in 2011:* 232
Provincial Electoral District(s): Albert
Federal Electoral District(s): Fundy Royal
Next Election: May 2020 (4 year terms)
Kirstin H. Shortt, Mayor
Louise Butland, Clerk-Treasurer

Aroostook
383 Main St.
Aroostook, NB E7H 2Z4
Tel: 506-273-6443; *Fax:* 506-273-3025
Municipal Type: Village
Area: 2.24 sq km
County or District: Victoria; *Population in 2011:* 351
Provincial Electoral District(s): Carleton-Victoria
Federal Electoral District(s): Tobique-Mactaquac
Next Election: May 2020 (4 year terms)
Marven Demmings, Mayor

Atholville
247, rue Notre-Dame
Atholville, NB E3N 4T1
Tél: 506-789-2944; *Téléc:* 506-789-2925
www.atholville.net
Entité municipal: Village
Incorporation: 1966; *Area:* 10.25 sq km
Comté ou district: Restigouche; *Population au 2011:* 1,237
Circonscription(s) électorale(s) provinciale(s): Restigouche West
Circonscription(s) électorale(s) fédérale(s): Madawaska-Restigouche
Prochaines élections: May 2020 (4 year terms)
Michel Soucy, Mayor
Nicole LeBrun, Clerk-Administrator

Baker Brook
3677, rue Principale, #A
Baker Brook, NB E7A 1V3
Tél: 506-258-3030; *Téléc:* 506-258-3017
villagebakerbrook@nb.aibn.com
Entité municipal: Village
Area: 12.4 sq km
Comté ou district: Madawaska; *Population au 2011:* 645
Circonscription(s) électorale(s) provinciale(s): Madawaska Les Lacs-Edmundston
Circonscription(s) électorale(s) fédérale(s): Madawaska-Restigouche
Prochaines élections: May 2020 (4 year terms)
Francine Caron, Mayor

Balmoral
CP 2531
1447, av des Pionniers
Balmoral, NB E8E 2W7
Tél: 506-826-6060; *Téléc:* 506-826-6037
vilbal@nbnet.nb.ca
www.balmoralnb.com
Entité municipal: Village
Incorporation: 1972; *Area:* 43.51 sq km
Comté ou district: Restigouche; *Population au 2011:* 1,719
Circonscription(s) électorale(s) provinciale(s): Restigouche West
Circonscription(s) électorale(s) fédérale(s): Madawaska-Restigouche
Prochaines élections: May 2020 (4 year terms)
Charles Bernard, Mayor

Bas-Caraquet
8185, rue St-Paul
Bas-Caraquet, NB E1W 6C4
Tél: 506-726-2776; *Téléc:* 506-726-2770
municipalite@bascaraquet.com
www.bascaraquet.com
Entité municipal: Village
Area: 31 sq km
Comté ou district: Gloucester; *Population au 2011:* 1,380
Circonscription(s) électorale(s) provinciale(s): Caraquet
Circonscription(s) électorale(s) fédérale(s): Acadie-Bathurst
Prochaines élections: May 2020 (4 year terms)
Agnès Doiron, Mairesse
Richard Frigault, Directeur général

Bath
161 School St.
Bath, NB E7J 1C3
Tel: 506-278-5293; *Fax:* 506-278-5932
bath@nbnet.nb.ca
www.villageofbath.ca
Municipal Type: Village
Area: 2.03 sq km
County or District: Carleton; *Population in 2011:* 532
Provincial Electoral District(s): Carleton-Victoria
Federal Electoral District(s): Tobique-Mactaquac
Next Election: May 2020 (4 year terms)
Troy F.J. Stone, Mayor

Belledune
P.O. Box 1006
2330 Main St.
Belledune, NB E8G 2X9
Tel: 506-522-3700; *Fax:* 506-522-3704
bell001@nbnet.nb.ca
www.belledune.com
Municipal Type: Village
Incorporated: Jan. 1, 1968; *Area:* 189.03 sq km
County or District: Gloucester; *Population in 2011:* 1,548
Provincial Electoral District(s): Restigouche-Chaleur
Federal Electoral District(s): Acadie-Bathurst
Next Election: May 2020 (4 year terms)
Joe Noel, Mayor
Paul Arseneault, Councillor
Tracy Culligan, Councillor
Nick Duivenvoorden, Councillor
David Hughes, Chief Administrative Officer

Beresford
#2, 855, rue Principale
Beresford, NB E8K 1T3
Tél: 506-542-2727; *Téléc:* 506-542-2702
info@beresford.ca
beresford.ca
Entité municipal: Town
Area: 19.2 sq km
Comté ou district: Gloucester; *Population au 2011:* 4,351
Circonscription(s) électorale(s) provinciale(s): Bathurst West-Beresford
Circonscription(s) électorale(s) fédérale(s): Acadie-Bathurst
Prochaines élections: May 2020 (4 year terms)

Jean Guy Grant, Mayor
Marc-André Godin, General Manager

Bertrand
#1, 651, boul des Acadiens
Bertrand, NB E1W 1G5
Tél: 506-726-2442; *Téléc:* 506-726-2449
bertrand@nb.aibn.com
Entité municipal: Village
Area: 46.45 sq km
Comté ou district: Gloucester; *Population au 2011:* 1,137
Circonscription(s) électorale(s) provinciale(s): Caraquet
Circonscription(s) électorale(s) fédérale(s): Acadie-Bathurst
Prochaines élections: May 2020 (4 year terms)
Yvon Godin, Maire
Joël Thibodeau, Directeur général

Blacks Harbour
65 Wallace Cove Rd.
Blacks Harbour, NB E5H 1G9
Tel: 506-456-4870; *Fax:* 506-456-4872
info@blacksharbour.ca
www.blacksharbour.ca
Municipal Type: Village
Area: 8.9 sq km
County or District: Charlotte; *Population in 2011:* 982
Provincial Electoral District(s): Fundy-The Isles-Saint John West
Federal Electoral District(s): New Brunswick Southwest
Next Election: May 2020 (4 year terms)
Terry James, Mayor
Heather Chase, Chief Administrative Officer

Blackville
12 South Bartholomew Rd.
Blackville, NB E9B 1N2
Tel: 506-843-6337; *Fax:* 506-843-6043
www.villageofblackville.com
Municipal Type: Village
Area: 21.73 sq km
County or District: Northumberland; *Population in 2011:* 990
Provincial Electoral District(s): Southwest Miramichi-Bay du Vin
Federal Electoral District(s): Miramichi-Grand Lake
Next Election: May 2020 (4 year terms)
Christopher David Hennessy, Mayor

Bouctouche
30, rue Évangéline
Bouctouche, NB E4S 3E4
Tél: 506-743-7260; *Téléc:* 506-743-7261
ville@bouctouche.ca
www.bouctouche.ca
Entité municipal: Town
Area: 18.34 sq km
Comté ou district: Kent; *Population au 2011:* 2,423
Circonscription(s) électorale(s) provinciale(s): Kent South
Circonscription(s) électorale(s) fédérale(s): Beauséjour
Prochaines élections: May 2020 (4 year terms)
Roland Fougère, Maire
Denny Richard, Directeur général

Cambridge-Narrows
Municipal Bldg.
6 Municipal Lane
Cambridge-Narrows, NB E4C 4P4
Tel: 506-488-3155; *Fax:* 506-488-1018
office@nbnet.nb.ca
www.cambridge-narrows.ca
Municipal Type: Village
Area: 106.94 sq km
County or District: Queens; *Population in 2011:* 620
Provincial Electoral District(s): Gagetown-Petitcodiac
Federal Electoral District(s): New Brunswick Southwest
Next Election: May 2020 (4 year terms)
Blair C. Cummings, Mayor

Campbellton
Campbellton City Centre
P.O. Box 100
76 Water St.
Campbellton, NB E3N 3G1
Tel: 506-789-2700; *Fax:* 506-759-7403
info@campbellton.org
www.campbellton.org
Municipal Type: Town
Incorporated: 1889; *Area:* 18.66 sq km
County or District: Restigouche; *Population in 2011:* 7,385
Provincial Electoral District(s): Campbellton-Dalhousie
Federal Electoral District(s): Madawaska-Restigouche
Next Election: May 2020 (4 year terms)
Stephanie Angleheart-Paulin, Mayor
Manon Cloutier, Chief Administrative Officer

Canterbury
199 Main St.
Canterbury, NB E6H 1M6
Tel: 506-279-6248; *Fax:* 506-279-9019
Municipal Type: Village
Area: 5.34 sq km
County or District: York; *Population in 2011:* 331
Provincial Electoral District(s): Carleton-York
Federal Electoral District(s): Tobique-Mactaquac
Next Election: May 2020 (4 year terms)
Elaine B. English, Mayor
Susan Patterson, Clerk

Cap-Pelé
33, ch St-André
Cap-Pelé, NB E4N 1Z4
Tél: 506-577-2030; *Téléc:* 506-577-2035
cappele@nb.aibn.com
www.cap-pele.com
Entité municipal: Village
Incorporation: 1969; *Area:* 23.78 sq km
Comté ou district: Westmorland; *Population au 2011:* 2,256
Circonscription(s) électorale(s) provinciale(s): Shediac-Beaubassin-Cap-Pelé
Circonscription(s) électorale(s) fédérale(s): Beauséjour
Prochaines élections: May 2020 (4 year terms)
Serge J. Léger, Maire
Stéphane Dallaire, Directeur général

Caraquet
CP 5695
10, rue du Colisée
Caraquet, NB E1W 1B7
Tél: 506-726-2727; *Téléc:* 506-726-2660
ville@caraquet.ca
www.caraquet.ca
Entité municipal: Town
Incorporation: Nov. 15, 1961; *Area:* 68.26 sq km
Comté ou district: Gloucester; *Population au 2011:* 4,169
Circonscription(s) électorale(s) provinciale(s): Caraquet
Circonscription(s) électorale(s) fédérale(s): Acadie-Bathurst
Prochaines élections: May 2020 (4 year terms)
Kevin J. Haché, Maire
Marc Duguay, Directeur général

Centreville
836 Central St.
Centreville, NB E7K 2E7
Tel: 506-276-3671; *Fax:* 506-276-9891
clerk@nbnet.nb.ca
www.villageofcentreville.ca
Municipal Type: Village
Area: 2.69 sq km
County or District: Carleton; *Population in 2011:* 542
Provincial Electoral District(s): Carleton-Victoria
Federal Electoral District(s): Tobique-Mactaquac; New Brunswick Southwest
Next Election: May 2020 (4 year terms)
Michael John Stewart, Mayor
Andrea Callahan, Administrator

Charlo
614, rue Chaleur
Charlo, NB E8E 2G6
Tél: 506-684-7850; *Téléc:* 506-684-7855
www.villagecharlo.com
Entité municipal: Village
Incorporation: 1966; *Area:* 30.75 sq km
Comté ou district: Restigouche; *Population au 2011:* 1,324
Circonscription(s) électorale(s) provinciale(s): Campbellton-Dalhousie
Circonscription(s) électorale(s) fédérale(s): Madawaska-Restigouche
Prochaines élections: May 2020 (4 year terms)
Denis McIntyre, Maire
Johanne McIntyre Levesque, Administratrice

Chipman
#1, 10 Civic Ct.
Chipman, NB E4A 2H9
Tel: 506-339-6601; *Fax:* 506-339-6197
www.chipmannb.org
Municipal Type: Village
Area: 19.58 sq km
County or District: Queens; *Population in 2011:* 1,236
Provincial Electoral District(s): Fredericton-Grand Lake
Federal Electoral District(s): Miramichi-Grand Lake
Next Election: May 2020 (4 year terms)
Carson Atkinson, Mayor
Susan Kennedy, Clerk

Clair
809E, rue Principale
Clair, NB E7A 2H7
Tél: 506-992-6030; *Téléc:* 506-992-6041
vgeclair@nbnet.nb.ca
www.villagedeclair.com
Entité municipal: Village
Area: 10.46 sq km
Comté ou district: Madawaska; *Population au 2011:* 857
Circonscription(s) électorale(s) provinciale(s): Madawaska Les Lacs-Edmundston
Circonscription(s) électorale(s) fédérale(s): Madawaska-Restigouche
Prochaines élections: May 2020 (4 year terms)
Pierre Michaud, Maire

Dalhousie
#1, 111 Hall St.
Dalhousie, NB E8C 1X2
Tel: 506-684-7600; *Fax:* 506-684-7613
reception@dalhousie.ca
www.dalhousie.ca
Municipal Type: Town
Incorporated: 1905; *Area:* 14.51 sq km
County or District: Restigouche; *Population in 2011:* 3,512
Provincial Electoral District(s): Campbellton-Dalhousie
Federal Electoral District(s): Madawaska-Restigouche
Next Election: May 2020 (4 year terms)
Normand Gerard Pelletier, Mayor
Christy Arseneau, Chief Administrative Officer

Doaktown
8 Miramichi St.
Doaktown, NB E9C 1C8
Tel: 506-365-7970; *Fax:* 506-365-7111
doaktown@nb.aibn.com
www.discoverdoaktown.com
Municipal Type: Village
Area: 28.74 sq km
County or District: Northumberland; *Population in 2011:* 793
Provincial Electoral District(s): Southwest Miramichi-Bay du Vin
Federal Electoral District(s): Miramichi-Grand Lake
Next Election: May 2020 (4 year terms)
Beverly K. Gaston, Mayor
Marilyn E. Price, Clerk-Administrator

Dorchester
4984 Main St.
Dorchester, NB E4K 2Z1
Tel: 506-379-3030; *Fax:* 506-379-3033
www.dorchester.ca
Municipal Type: Village
Area: 5.74 sq km
County or District: Westmorland; *Population in 2011:* 1,167
Provincial Electoral District(s): Memramcook-Tantramar
Federal Electoral District(s): Beauséjour
Next Election: May 2020 (4 year terms)
Jerome Simon Bear, Mayor

Drummond
1413, ch Tobique
Drummond, NB E3Y 1H7
Tél: 506-475-4000; *Téléc:* 506-475-4010
drummond@mins.ca
www.drummondnb.com
Entité municipal: Village
Area: 8.91 sq km
Comté ou district: Victoria; *Population au 2011:* 775
Circonscription(s) électorale(s) provinciale(s): Victoria-La Vallée
Circonscription(s) électorale(s) fédérale(s): Tobique-Mactaquac
Prochaines élections: May 2020 (4 year terms)
France Roussel, Maire
Annie Gagné, Administratrice

Eel River Crossing
20, rue Savoie
Eel River Crossing, NB E8E 1T8
Tél: 506-826-6080; *Téléc:* 506-826-6088
erc@ercvillage.com
www.ercvillage.com
Entité municipal: Village
Area: 17.43 sq km
Population au 2011: 1,209
Circonscription(s) électorale(s) provinciale(s): Campbellton-Dalhousie
Circonscription(s) électorale(s) fédérale(s): Madawaska-Restigouche
Prochaines élections: May 2020 (4 year terms)
Denis D. Savoie, Maire
Kim Bujold, Directrice générale

Florenceville-Bristol
19 Station Rd.
Florenceville-Bristol, NB E7L 3J8
Tel: 506-392-6763; *Fax:* 506-392-5211
office@florencevillebristol.ca
www.florencevillebristol.ca
Municipal Type: Village
Incorporated: 2008
County or District: Carleton; *Population in 2011:* 1,639
Provincial Electoral District(s): Carleton-Victoria
Federal Electoral District(s): Tobique-Mactaquac
Next Election: May 2020 (4 year terms)
Note: The villages of Florenceville & Bristol amalgamated to create the municipality of Florenceville-Bristol.
Karl E. Curtis, Mayor
Nancy Shaw, Chief Administrative Officer

Fredericton Junction
102 Wilsey Rd.
Fredericton Junction, NB E5L 1W7
Tel: 506-368-2628; *Fax:* 506-368-1900
fredjct@nb.aibn.com
www.frederictonjunction.ca
Municipal Type: Village
Area: 23.86 sq km
County or District: Sunbury; *Population in 2011:* 752
Provincial Electoral District(s): New Maryland-Sunbury
Federal Electoral District(s): New Brunswick Southwest
Next Election: May 2020 (4 year terms)
Gary W. Mersereau, Mayor
Cindy Ogden, Chief Administrative Officer

Gagetown
68 Babbit St.
Gagetown, NB E5M 1C8
Tel: 506-488-3567; *Fax:* 506-488-3543
gagetnvl@nbnet.nb.ca
www.villageofgagetown.ca
Municipal Type: Village
Incorporated: 1966; *Area:* 49.48 sq km
County or District: Queens; *Population in 2011:* 698
Provincial Electoral District(s): Gagetown-Petitcodiac
Federal Electoral District(s): New Brunswick Southwest
Next Election: May 2020 (4 year terms)
Michael Blaney, Mayor
Connie May, Clerk-Administrator

Le Goulet
1295, rue Principale
Le Goulet, NB E8S 2E9
Tél: 506-336-3272; *Téléc:* 506-336-3281
www.legoulet.ca
Entité municipal: Village
Incorporation: May 12, 1986; *Area:* 5.46 sq km
Comté ou district: Gloucester; *Population au 2011:* 817
Circonscription(s) électorale(s) provinciale(s): Lamèque-Shippagan-Miscou
Circonscription(s) électorale(s) fédérale(s): Acadie-Bathurst
Prochaines élections: May 2020 (4 year terms)
Paul-Aimé Mallet, Maire
Alvine Bulger, Directeur général

Grand Bay-Westfield
P.O. Box 3001
609 River Valley Dr.
Grand Bay-Westfield, NB E5K 4V3
Tel: 506-738-6400; *Fax:* 506-738-6424
www.town.grandbay-westfield.nb.ca
Municipal Type: Town
Incorporated: 1998; *Area:* 59.73 sq km
County or District: Kings; *Population in 2011:* 5,117
Provincial Electoral District(s): Kings Centre
Federal Electoral District(s): New Brunswick Southwest
Next Election: May 2020 (4 year terms)
Grace Losier, Mayor
Sandra M. Gautreau, Town Manager

Grand Falls / Grand-Sault
#200, 131, rue Pleasant
Grand-Sault, NB E3Z 1G6
Tel: 506-475-7777; *Fax:* 506-475-7779
vgs-tgf@nb.aibn.com
www.grandfalls.com
Municipal Type: Town
Area: 18.06 sq km
County or District: Victoria; *Population in 2011:* 5,706
Provincial Electoral District(s): Victoria-La Vallée
Federal Electoral District(s): Tobique-Mactaquac
Next Election: May 2020 (4 year terms)
Marcel Deschenes, Mayor
Peter Michaud, Chief Administrative Officer-Clerk

Grand Manan
#4, 1021 rte 776
Grand Manan, NB E5G 4E5
Tel: 506-662-7059; *Fax:* 506-662-7060
office@villageofgrandmanan.com
www.villageofgrandmanan.com
Municipal Type: Village
Incorporated: May 8, 1995; *Area:* 150.78 sq km
County or District: Charlotte; *Population in 2011:* 2,377
Provincial Electoral District(s): Fundy-The Isles-Saint John West
Federal Electoral District(s): New Brunswick Southwest
Next Election: May 2020 (4 year terms)
Dennis Clifton Greene, Mayor
Rob MacPherson, Chief Administrative Officer
Ami Petrovics, Clerk/Assistant Treasurer

Grande-Anse
393, rue Acadie
Grande-Anse, NB E8N 1E2
Tél: 506-732-3242; *Téléc:* 506-732-3217
village@grande-anse.net
www.grande-anse.net
Entité municipal: Village
Incorporation: 1968; *Area:* 24.42 sq km
Comté ou district: Gloucester; *Population au 2011:* 738
Circonscription(s) électorale(s) provinciale(s): Caraquet
Circonscription(s) électorale(s) fédérale(s): Acadie-Bathurst
Prochaines élections: May 2020 (4 year terms)
Réginald Boudreau, Maire
Rhéal Paulin, Administrateur

Hampton
P.O. Box 1066
27 Centennial Rd.
Hampton, NB E5N 8H1
Tel: 506-832-6065; *Fax:* 506-832-6098
info@townofhampton.ca
www.townofhampton.ca
Municipal Type: Town
Area: 21 sq km
County or District: Kings; *Population in 2011:* 4,292
Provincial Electoral District(s): Hampton
Federal Electoral District(s): Fundy Royal
Next Election: May 2020 (4 year terms)
Kenneth A. Chorley, Mayor
Richard Malone, Town Manager

Hartland
#1, 31 Orser St.
Hartland, NB E7P 1R4
Tel: 506-375-4357; *Fax:* 506-375-8265
www.town.hartland.nb.ca
Municipal Type: Town
Area: 9.63 sq km
County or District: Carleton; *Population in 2011:* 947
Provincial Electoral District(s): Carleton
Federal Electoral District(s): Tobique-Mactaquac
Next Election: May 2020 (4 year terms)
J. Craig Melanson, Mayor
Linda Brown, Chief Administrative Officer

Harvey
58 Hanselpacker Rd.
Harvey, NB E6K 1A3
Tel: 506-366-6240; *Fax:* 506-366-6242
village.harvey@rogers.com
www.village.harvey-station.nb.ca
Municipal Type: Village
Incorporated: Nov. 9, 1966; *Area:* 2.46 sq km
County or District: York; *Population in 2011:* 363
Provincial Electoral District(s): Carleton-York
Federal Electoral District(s): New Brunswick Southwest; Fundy Royal
Next Election: May 2020 (4 year terms)
Winston Gamblin, Mayor
Amber Binney, Clerk, 506-366-6240, Fax: 506-366-6242

Hillsborough
#1, 2849 Main St.
Hillsborough, NB E4H 2X7
Tel: 506-734-3733; *Fax:* 506-734-3711
hillsboroughnb@rogers.com
www.villageofhillsborough.ca
Municipal Type: Village
Incorporated: 1966; *Area:* 12.98 sq km
County or District: Albert; *Population in 2011:* 1,350
Provincial Electoral District(s): Albert
Federal Electoral District(s): Fundy Royal
Next Election: May 2020 (4 year terms)
Barry Snider, Mayor
Shari Kaster, Administrator-Clerk

Kedgwick
114, rue Notre-Dame
Kedgwick, NB E8B 1H8
Tél: 506-284-2160; *Téléc:* 506-284-2859
crkedgwick@bellaliant.com
Entité municipal: Village
Area: 4.28 sq km
Comté ou district: Restigouche; *Population au 2011:* 993
Circonscription(s) électorale(s) provinciale(s): Restigouche West
Circonscription(s) électorale(s) fédérale(s): Madawaska-Restigouche
Prochaines élections: May 2020 (4 year terms)
Jean Paul (JP) Savoie, Maire
Francis Bérubé, Directeur général

Lac-Baker
5442, rue Centrale
Lac Baker, NB E7A 1H7
Tel: 506-992-6060; *Fax:* 506-992-6061
lacbaker.ca
Municipal Type: Village
Area: 4.02 sq km
County or District: Madawaska; *Population in 2011:* 719
Provincial Electoral District(s): Madawaska Les Lacs-Edmundston
Federal Electoral District(s): Madawaska-Restigouche
Next Election: May 2020 (4 year terms)
Louis Chouinard, Mayor

Lamèque
28, rue de l'Hôpital
Lamèque, NB E8T 3N4
Tél: 506-344-3222; *Téléc:* 506-344-3266
info@lameque.ca
www.lameque.ca
Entité municipal: Town
Area: 12.45 sq km
Comté ou district: Gloucester; *Population au 2011:* 1,432
Circonscription(s) électorale(s) provinciale(s): Shippagan-Lamèque-Miscou
Circonscription(s) électorale(s) fédérale(s): Acadie-Bathurst
Prochaines élections: May 2020 (4 year terms)
Jules Haché, Maire
Dave Brown, Directeur général

Maisonnette
1512, rue Châtillon
Maisonnette, NB E8N 1S4
Tél: 506-726-2717; *Téléc:* 506-726-2718
www.maisonnette.ca
Entité municipal: Village
Incorporation: May 12, 1986; *Area:* 12.88 sq km
Comté ou district: Gloucester; *Population au 2011:* 573
Circonscription(s) électorale(s) provinciale(s): Caraquet
Circonscription(s) électorale(s) fédérale(s): Acadie-Bathurst
Prochaines élections: May 2020 (4 year terms)
Viviane Baldwin, Mairesse
Carole Frigault, Greffière

McAdam
146 Saunders Rd.
McAdam, NB E6J 1L2
Tel: 506-784-2293; *Fax:* 506-784-1402
villageofmcadam@nb.aibn.com
www.mcadamnb.com
Municipal Type: Village
Area: 14.47 sq km
County or District: York; *Population in 2011:* 1,284
Provincial Electoral District(s): Charlotte-Campobello
Federal Electoral District(s): New Brunswick Southwest
Next Election: May 2020 (4 year terms)
Kenneth Stannix, Mayor
Ann Donahue, Clerk-Treasurer

Meductic
320 Rte. 165
Meductic, NB E6H 1J5
Tel: 506-272-2098; *Fax:* 506-272-1883
villageofmeductic@nb.aibn.com
Municipal Type: Village
Area: 5.57 sq km
County or District: York; *Population in 2011:* 270
Provincial Electoral District(s): Carleton-York
Federal Electoral District(s): Tobique-Mactaquac
Next Election: May 2020 (4 year terms)
Lance Royden Graham, Mayor
Pamela Grant, Clerk-Treasurer

Memramcook
540, rue Centrale
Memramcook, NB E4K 3S6
Tél: 506-758-4078; *Téléc:* 506-758-4079
village@memramcook.com
www.memramcook.com
Entité municipal: Village
Incorporation: 1995; *Area:* 185.71 sq km
Comté ou district: Westmorland; *Population au 2011:* 4,831
Circonscription(s) électorale(s) provinciale(s): Memramcook-Tantramar
Circonscription(s) électorale(s) fédérale(s): Beauséjour
Prochaines élections: May 2020 (4 year terms)
Michel (Mike) Gaudet, Maire
Yves Leger, Directeur général

Millville
39 Howland Ridge Rd.
Millville, NB E6E 1Y3
Tel: 506-463-2719; *Fax:* 506-463-8262
villageofmillville@nb.aibn.com
www.villageofmillville.com
Municipal Type: Village
Area: 12.16 sq km
County or District: York; *Population in 2011:* 307
Provincial Electoral District(s): Carleton-York
Federal Electoral District(s): Tobique-Mactaquac
Next Election: May 2020 (4 year terms)
Beverly Herbert Forbes, Mayor
Natalie Hill, Clerk-Treasurer

Minto
420 Pleasant Dr.
Minto, NB E4B 2T3
Tel: 506-327-3383; *Fax:* 506-327-3041
www.villageofminto.ca
Municipal Type: Village
Area: 31.53 sq km
County or District: Sunbury-Queens; *Population in 2011:* 2,505
Provincial Electoral District(s): Fredericton-Grand Lake
Federal Electoral District(s): Miramichi-Grand Lake
Next Election: May 2020 (4 year terms)
Donald Gould, Mayor
Trila McKenelley, Clerk-Administrator

Nackawic
115 Otis Dr.
Nackawic, NB E6G 2P1
Tel: 506-575-2241; *Fax:* 506-575-2035
townhall@nackawic.com
www.nackawic.com
Municipal Type: Town
Area: 8.4 sq km
County or District: York; *Population in 2011:* 1,049
Provincial Electoral District(s): Carleton-York
Federal Electoral District(s): Tobique-Mactaquac
Next Election: May 2020 (4 year terms)
Ian Kitchen, Mayor
Kathryn Clark, Secretary-Treasurer, 506-575-2241

Néguac
#1, 1175, rue Principale
Néguac, NB E9G 1T1
Tél: 506-776-3950; *Téléc:* 506-776-3975
info@neguac.com
www.neguac.com
Entité municipal: Village
Incorporation: Aug. 23, 1967; *Area:* 26.69 sq km
Comté ou district: Northumberland; *Population au 2011:* 1,678
Circonscription(s) électorale(s) provinciale(s): Miramichi Bay-Neguac
Circonscription(s) électorale(s) fédérale(s): Miramichi-Grand Lake
Prochaines élections: May 2020 (4 year terms)
Georges Rhéal Savoie, Maire
Daniel Hachey, Directeur général

New Maryland
584 New Maryland Hwy.
New Maryland, NB E3C 1K1
Tel: 506-451-8508; *Fax:* 506-450-1605
www.vonm.ca
Municipal Type: Village
Incorporated: 1991; *Area:* 21.23 sq km
County or District: York; *Population in 2011:* 4,232
Provincial Electoral District(s): New Maryland-Sunbury
Federal Electoral District(s): Fredericton; New Brunswick Southwest
Next Election: May 2020 (4 year terms)
Judy E. Wilson-Shee, Mayor
Cynthia Geldart, Chief Administrative Officer-Clerk

Nigadoo
#1, 385, rue Principale
Nigadoo, NB E8K 3R6
Tél: 506-542-2626; *Téléc:* 506-542-2678
nigadoov@nbnet.nb.ca
Entité municipal: Village
Incorporation: 1967; *Area:* 7.69 sq km
Comté ou district: Gloucester; *Population au 2011:* 952
Circonscription(s) électorale(s) provinciale(s): Restigouche-Chaleur
Circonscription(s) électorale(s) fédérale(s): Acadie-Bathurst
Prochaines élections: May 2020 (4 year terms)
Charles Henri Doucet, Maire

Norton
201 Rte. 24
Norton, NB E5T 1B7
Tel: 506-839-3011; *Fax:* 506-839-3015
Municipal Type: Village
Area: 75.35 sq km
County or District: Kings; *Population in 2011:* 1,301
Provincial Electoral District(s): Kings Centre
Federal Electoral District(s): Fundy Royal
Next Election: May 2020 (4 year terms)
Juliana Catherine Booth, Mayor
Anita Pollock, Clerk-Treasurer

Oromocto
4 Doyle Dr.
Oromocto, NB E2V 2V3
Tel: 506-357-4400; *Fax:* 506-357-2266
gengov@oromocto.ca
www.oromocto.ca
Municipal Type: Town
Area: 22.37 sq km
County or District: Sunbury; *Population in 2011:* 8,932
Provincial Electoral District(s): Oromocto-Lincoln
Federal Electoral District(s): Fredericton
Next Election: May 2020 (4 year terms)
Robert (Bob) Edward Powell, Mayor
Richard Isabelle, Chief Administrative Officer-Clerk

Paquetville
1094, rue du Parc
Paquetville, NB E8R 1J4
Tél: 506-764-2500; *Téléc:* 506-764-2504
www.villagepaquetville.com
Entité municipal: Village
Incorporation: 1966; *Area:* 9.4 sq km
Comté ou district: Gloucester; *Population au 2011:* 706
Circonscription(s) électorale(s) provinciale(s): Caraquet
Circonscription(s) électorale(s) fédérale(s): Acadie-Bathurst
Prochaines élections: May 2020 (4 year terms)
Luc Robichaud, Maire
Ghislain Comeau, Directeur général

Perth-Andover
1131 West Riverside Dr.
Perth-Andover, NB E7H 5G5
Tel: 506-273-4958
www.perth-andover.com
Municipal Type: Village
Incorporated: 1966; *Area:* 8.89 sq km
County or District: Victoria; *Population in 2011:* 1,778
Provincial Electoral District(s): Carleton-Victoria
Federal Electoral District(s): Tobique-Mactaquac
Next Election: May 2020 (4 year terms)
Marianne Bell, Mayor
Daniel Dionne, Chief Administrative Officer

Petitcodiac
P.O. Box 2507
63 Main St.
Petitcodiac, NB E4Z 6H4
Tel: 506-756-3140; *Fax:* 506-756-3142
vop@nbnet.nb.ca
www.petitcodiac.ca
Municipal Type: Village
Area: 17.22 sq km
County or District: Westmorland; *Population in 2011:* 1,429
Provincial Electoral District(s): Gagetown-Petitcodiac
Federal Electoral District(s): Fundy Royal
Next Election: May 2020 (4 year terms)
Gerald A.W. Gogan, Mayor

Petit-Rocher
582, rue Principale
Petit-Rocher, NB E8J 1S5
Tél: 506-542-2686; *Téléc:* 506-542-2708
petit-rocher@nb.aibn.com
www.petit-rocher.ca
Entité municipal: Village
Area: 4.49 sq km
Comté ou district: Gloucester; *Population au 2011:* 1,908
Circonscription(s) électorale(s) provinciale(s): Restigouche-Chaleur
Circonscription(s) électorale(s) fédérale(s): Acadie-Bathurst
Prochaines élections: May 2020 (4 year terms)
Luc Desjardins, Maire
Michael Roy, Administrateur municipal

Plaster Rock
159 Main St.
Plaster Rock, NB E7G 2H2
Tel: 506-356-6070; *Fax:* 506-356-6081
vilprock@nb.aibn.com
www.plasterrockvillage.com
Municipal Type: Village
Area: 3.09 sq km
County or District: Victoria; *Population in 2011:* 1,135
Provincial Electoral District(s): Carleton-Victoria
Federal Electoral District(s): Tobique-Mactaquac
Next Election: May 2020 (4 year terms)
Alexis D. Fenner, Mayor
Patty St. Peter, Clerk-Manager, 506-356-6071

Pointe-Verte
375, rue Principale
Pointe-Verte, NB E8J 2S8
Tél: 506-542-2606; *Téléc:* 506-542-2638
info@pointeverte.net
pointe-verte.ca
Entité municipal: Village
Area: 13.79 sq km
Comté ou district: Gloucester; *Population au 2011:* 976
Circonscription(s) électorale(s) provinciale(s): Restigouche-Chaleur
Circonscription(s) électorale(s) fédérale(s): Acadie-Bathurst
Prochaines élections: May 2020 (4 year terms)
Normand Doiron, Maire
Vincent Poirier, Directeur général

Port Elgin
41 East Main St.
Port Elgin, NB E4M 2X8
Tel: 506-538-2120; *Fax:* 506-538-2126
www.villageofportelgin.com
Municipal Type: Village
Incorporated: 1922; *Area:* 2.61 sq km
County or District: Westmorland; *Population in 2011:* 418
Provincial Electoral District(s): Memramcook-Tantramar
Federal Electoral District(s): Beauséjour
Next Election: May 2020 (4 year terms)
Judy E. Scott, Mayor
Angela Grant, Clerk-Treasurer

Rexton
82 Main St.
Rexton, NB E4W 5N4
Tel: 506-523-6921; *Fax:* 506-523-7383
villageofrexton@nb.aibn.com
www.villageofrexton.com
Municipal Type: Village
Incorporated: Nov. 9, 1966; *Area:* 6.14 sq km
County or District: Kent; *Population in 2011:* 818
Provincial Electoral District(s): Kent North
Federal Electoral District(s): Beauséjour
Next Election: May 2020 (4 year terms)
Randy Warman, Mayor
Ashley Jones, General Manager

Richibucto
#1, 9235, rue Main
Richibucto, NB E4W 4B4
Tél: 506-523-7870; *Téléc:* 506-523-7850
vtrcto@nbnet.nb.ca
www.richibucto.org
Entité municipal: Town
Incorporation: 1967; *Area:* 11.83 sq km
Comté ou district: Kent; *Population au 2011:* 1,286
Circonscription(s) électorale(s) provinciale(s): Kent North
Circonscription(s) électorale(s) fédérale(s): Beauséjour
Prochaines élections: May 2020 (4 year terms)
Roger Doiron, Maire
Pamela Robichaud, Directrice générale

Riverside-Albert
5823 King St.
Riverside-Albert, NB E4H 4B4
Tel: 506-882-3022
villra@nbnet.nb.ca
www.riverside-albert.ca
Municipal Type: Village
Area: 3.41 sq km
County or District: Albert; *Population in 2011:* 353
Provincial Electoral District(s): Albert
Federal Electoral District(s): Fundy Royal
Next Election: May 2020 (4 year terms)
Jim Campbell, Mayor
Deborah Murray-Butland, Clerk

Rivière-Verte
78, rue Principale
Rivière-Verte, NB E7C 2T8
Tél: 506-263-1060; *Téléc:* 506-263-1065
www.riviere-verte.ca
Entité municipal: Village
Area: 7 sq km
Comté ou district: Madawaska; *Population au 2011:* 744
Circonscription(s) électorale(s) provinciale(s): Edmundston-Madawaska Centre
Circonscription(s) électorale(s) fédérale(s): Madawaska-Restigouche
Prochaines élections: May 2020 (4 year terms)
Michel Leblond, Maire
Evelyne Therrien, Secrétaire municipale

Rogersville
10989, rue Principale
Rogersville, NB E4Y 2L6
Tél: 506-775-2080; *Téléc:* 506-775-2090
rogervil@nbnet.nb.ca
www.rogersvillenb.com
Entité municipal: Village
Incorporation: Nov. 9, 1966; *Area:* 7.23 sq km
Comté ou district: Kent; *Population au 2011:* 1,170
Circonscription(s) électorale(s) provinciale(s): Kent North
Circonscription(s) électorale(s) fédérale(s): Miramichi-Grand Lake
Prochaines élections: May 2020 (4 year terms)
Pierrette F. Robichaud, Mairesse
Angèle McCaie, Directrice générale

Sackville
P.O. Box 6191
31C Main St.
Sackville, NB E4L 1G6
Tel: 506-364-4930; *Fax:* 506-364-4976
www.sackville.com
Municipal Type: Town
Incorporated: Jan. 1903; *Area:* 74.32 sq km
County or District: Westmorland; *Population in 2011:* 5,558
Provincial Electoral District(s): Memramcook-Tantramar
Federal Electoral District(s): Beauséjour
Next Election: May 2020 (4 year terms)
John Higham, Mayor
Phil Handrahan, Chief Administrative Officer

Saint-André
492, ch de l'Église
Saint-André, NB E3Y 2Y6
Tél: 506-473-7580; *Téléc:* 506-473-7585
vilstand@nb.aibn.com
www.saintandrenb.ca
Entité municipal: Village
Area: 3.72 sq km
Comté ou district: Madawaska; *Population au 2011:* 819
Circonscription(s) électorale(s) provinciale(s): Victoria-La Vallée
Circonscription(s) électorale(s) fédérale(s): Tobique-Mactaquac
Prochaines élections: May 2020 (4 year terms)
Allain Desjardins, Maire
John Morrisey, Greffier/Secrétaire municipal/Directeur général

St. Andrews
212 Water St.
St. Andrews, NB E5B 1B4
Tel: 506-529-5120; *Fax:* 506-529-5183
town@townofstandrews.ca
www.townofstandrews.ca
Municipal Type: Town
Area: 8.35 sq km
County or District: Charlotte; *Population in 2011:* 1,889
Provincial Electoral District(s): Charlotte-Campobello
Federal Electoral District(s): New Brunswick Southwest
Next Election: May 2020 (4 year terms)
Doug Naish, Mayor
Chris Spear, Interim Chief Administrative Officer/Treasurer/Deputy Clerk

Saint-Antoine
300, 4556, rue Principale
Saint-Antoine, NB E4V 1P8
Tél: 506-525-4020; *Téléc:* 506-525-4027
village@saint-antoine.ca
saint-antoine.ca
Entité municipal: Village
Area: 6.43 sq km
Comté ou district: Kent; *Population au 2011:* 1,770
Circonscription(s) électorale(s) provinciale(s): Kent South
Circonscription(s) électorale(s) fédérale(s): Beauséjour
Prochaines élections: May 2020 (4 year terms)
Ricky Gautreau, Maire
Bernadine Maillet-LeBlanc, Directrice générale

Sainte-Anne-de-Madawaska
75, rue Principale
Sainte-Anne-de-Madawaska, NB E7E 1A8
Tél: 506-445-2449; *Téléc:* 506-445-2405
ste-anne@nb.aibn.com
Entité municipal: Village
Area: 9.21 sq km
Comté ou district: Madawaska; *Population au 2011:* 1,002
Circonscription(s) électorale(s) provinciale(s):
Edmundston-Madawaska Centre
Circonscription(s) électorale(s) fédérale(s):
Madawaska-Restigouche
Prochaines élections: May 2020 (4 year terms)
Roger Levesque, Maire
Lise Deschênes, Clerk-Très.

Sainte-Marie-Saint-Raphaël
1541, boul de la Mer
Sainte-Marie-Saint-Raphaël, NB E8T 1P5
Tél: 506-344-3210; *Téléc:* 506-344-3213
info@ste-marie-st-raphael.ca
www.ste-marie-st-raphael.ca
Entité municipal: Village
Incorporation: May 12, 1986; *Area:* 15.61 sq km
Comté ou district: Gloucester; *Population au 2011:* 955
Circonscription(s) électorale(s) provinciale(s):
Lamèque-Shippagan-Miscou
Circonscription(s) électorale(s) fédérale(s): Acadie-Bathurst
Prochaines élections: May 2020 (4 year terms)
Conrad Godin, Maire
Susie Godin, Secrétaire municipale adjointe

Saint-François-de-Madawaska
2033, rue Commerciale
Saint-François-de-Madawaska, NB E7A 1B3
Tél: 506-992-6050; *Téléc:* 506-992-6049
munstf@nb.aibn.com
Entité municipal: Village
Area: 6.34 sq km
Comté ou district: Madawaska; *Population au 2011:* 630
Circonscription(s) électorale(s) provinciale(s): Madawaska Les Lacs-Edmundston
Circonscription(s) électorale(s) fédérale(s):
Madawaska-Restigouche
Prochaines élections: May 2020 (4 year terms)
Robert Bonenfant, Maire

St. George
1 School St.
St George, NB E5C 3N2
Tel: 506-755-4320; *Fax:* 506-755-4329
www.town.stgeorge.nb.ca
Municipal Type: Town
Incorporated: Oct. 17, 1904; *Area:* 16.13 sq km
County or District: Charlotte; *Population in 2011:* 1,543
Provincial Electoral District(s): Fundy-The Isles-Saint John West
Federal Electoral District(s): New Brunswick Southwest
Next Election: May 2020 (4 year terms)
Crystal D. Cook, Mayor
Penny Henneberry, Chief Administration Officer

Saint-Hilaire
2190, rue Centrale
Saint-Hilaire, NB E3V 4W1
Tél: 506-258-3307; *Téléc:* 506-258-1802
Entité municipal: Village
Area: 5.67 sq km
Comté ou district: Madawaska; *Population au 2011:* 290
Circonscription(s) électorale(s) provinciale(s): Madawaska Les Lacs-Edmundston
Circonscription(s) électorale(s) fédérale(s):
Madawaska-Restigouche
Prochaines élections: May 2020 (4 year terms)
Roland Dubé, Maire
Oscar Roussel, Maire
Dave Cowan, Directeur général

Saint-Isidore
3906, boul des Fondateurs
Saint-Isidore, NB E8M 1C2
Tel: 506-358-6005; *Fax:* 506-358-6010
www.saintisidore.ca
Municipal Type: Village
Incorporated: June 1, 1991; *Area:* 22.58 sq km
Population in 2011: 748
Provincial Electoral District(s): Bathurst East-Nepisiguit-Saint-Isidore
Federal Electoral District(s): Acadie-Bathurst
Next Election: May 2020 (4 year terms)

Saint-Léolin
117, rue des Prés
Saint-Léolin, NB E8N 2P9
Tél: 506-732-3266; *Téléc:* 506-732-3267
www.villagesaintleolin.ca
Entité municipal: Village
Area: 19.78 sq km
Comté ou district: Gloucester; *Population au 2011:* 488
Circonscription(s) électorale(s) provinciale(s): Caraquet
Circonscription(s) électorale(s) fédérale(s): Acadie-Bathurst
Prochaines élections: May 2020 (4 year terms)
Mathieu Chayer, Maire
Gérard Battah, Administrateur

Saint-Léonard
564, rue St-Jean
Saint-Léonard, NB E7E 2B5
Tél: 506-423-3111; *Téléc:* 506-423-3115
info@saint-leonard.ca
www.saint-leonard.ca
Entité municipal: Town
Incorporation: 1920; *Area:* 5.2 sq km
Comté ou district: Madawaska; *Population au 2011:* 1,343
Circonscription(s) électorale(s) provinciale(s): Victoria-La Vallée
Circonscription(s) électorale(s) fédérale(s):
Madawaska-Restigouche
Prochaines élections: May 2020 (4 year terms)
Carmel St-Amand, Maire
Bernard Violette, Directeur général

Saint-Louis-de-Kent
10511, rue Principale
Saint-Louis-de-Kent, NB E4X 1A6
Tél: 506-876-3420; *Téléc:* 506-876-3477
info@st-louis-de-kent.ca
www.st-louis-de-kent.ca
Entité municipal: Village
Area: 2 sq km
Comté ou district: Kent; *Population au 2011:* 930
Circonscription(s) électorale(s) provinciale(s): Kent North
Circonscription(s) électorale(s) fédérale(s): Beauséjour
Prochaines élections: May 2020 (4 year terms)
Danielle Andrée Dugas, Mairesse
Marie-Paul Robichaud, Administrateur

St. Martins
#2, 73 Main St.
St Martins, NB E5R 1B4
Tel: 506-833-2010; *Fax:* 506-833-2008
vilstmar@nbnet.nb.ca
www.stmartinscanada.com
Municipal Type: Village
Incorporated: Nov. 9, 1967; *Area:* 2.29 sq km
County or District: Saint John; *Population in 2011:* 314
Provincial Electoral District(s): Sussex-Fundy-St. Martins
Federal Electoral District(s): Fundy Royal
Next Election: May 2020 (4 year terms)
Bette Ann M. Chatterton, Mayor
Darcy Hutchinson, Clerk

Saint-Quentin
10, rue Deschênes
Saint-Quentin, NB E8A 1M1
Tél: 506-235-2425; *Téléc:* 506-235-1952
ville@saintquentin.nb.ca
www.saintquentin.nb.ca
Entité municipal: Town
Incorporation: 1947; *Area:* 4.3 sq km
Comté ou district: Restigouche; *Population au 2011:* 2,095
Circonscription(s) électorale(s) provinciale(s): Restigouche West
Circonscription(s) électorale(s) fédérale(s):
Madawaska-Restigouche
Prochaines élections: May 2020 (4 year terms)
Note: Proclaimed as a town in 1992.
Nicole Somers, Maire
Suzanne Coulombe, Directrice générale

St. Stephen
#112, 73 Milltown Blvd.
St Stephen, NB E3L 1G5
Tel: 506-466-7700; *Fax:* 506-466-7701
info@town.ststephen.nb.ca
www.town.ststephen.nb.ca
Municipal Type: Town
County or District: Charlotte; *Population in 2011:* 4,817
Provincial Electoral District(s): Charlotte-Campobello
Federal Electoral District(s): New Brunswick Southwest
Next Election: May 2020 (4 year terms)
Allan L. MacEachern, Mayor
Derek O'Brien, Chief Administrative Officer

Salisbury
56, rue Douglas
Salisbury, NB E4J 3E3
Tel: 506-372-3230; *Fax:* 506-372-3225
vilsalisbury@nb.aibn.com
www.salisburynb.ca
Municipal Type: Village
Incorporated: 1966; *Area:* 13.68 sq km
County or District: Westmorland; *Population in 2011:* 2,208
Provincial Electoral District(s): Albert
Federal Electoral District(s): Fundy Royal
Next Election: May 2020 (4 year terms)
Terry A. Keating, Mayor
Pamela Cochrane, Clerk-Administrator

Shediac
#300, 290, rue Main
Shediac, NB E4P 2E3
Tél: 506-532-7000; *Téléc:* 506-532-6156
info@shediac.org
www.shediac.ca
Entité municipal: Town
Area: 11.97 sq km
Comté ou district: Westmorland; *Population au 2011:* 6,053
Circonscription(s) électorale(s) provinciale(s): Shediac Bay-Dieppe; Shediac-Beaubassin-Cap-Pelé
Circonscription(s) électorale(s) fédérale(s): Beauséjour
Prochaines élections: May 2020 (4 year terms)
Jacques Leblanc, Maire
Gilles Belleau, Directeur général, 506-532-7000

Shippagan
200, av Hôtel de Ville
Shippagan, NB E8S 1M1
Tél: 506-336-3900; *Téléc:* 506-336-3901
info@shippagan.ca
www.shippagan.ca
Entité municipal: Town
Incorporation: 1947; *Area:* 9.94 sq km
Comté ou district: Gloucester; *Population au 2011:* 2,603
Circonscription(s) électorale(s) provinciale(s):
Lamèque-Shippagan-Miscou
Circonscription(s) électorale(s) fédérale(s): Acadie-Bathurst
Prochaines élections: May 2020 (4 year terms)
Note: Proclaimed as a town in 1958.
Anita Savoie Robichaud, Maire
Joanne Richard, Directrice générale

Stanley
20 Main St.
Stanley, NB E6B 1A2
Tel: 506-367-3245; *Fax:* 506-367-0006
vstanley@nbnet.nb.ca
www.thevillageofstanley.ca
Municipal Type: Village
Area: 17.34 sq km
County or District: York; *Population in 2011:* 419
Provincial Electoral District(s): Fredericton-York
Federal Electoral District(s): Tobique-Mactaquac
Next Election: May 2020 (4 year terms)
Mark A.J. Foreman, Mayor
Bethany Ryan, Clerk

Sussex
524 Main St.
Sussex, NB E4E 3E4
Tel: 506-432-4540; *Fax:* 506-432-4566
townofsussex@sussex.ca
www.sussex.ca
Municipal Type: Town
Incorporated: 1904; *Area:* 9.03 sq km
County or District: Kings; *Population in 2011:* 4,312
Provincial Electoral District(s): Sussex-Fundy-St. Martins
Federal Electoral District(s): Fundy Royal
Next Election: May 2020 (4 year terms)
Marc Thorne, Mayor
Scott Hatcher, Chief Administrative Officer

Sussex Corner
1067 Main St.
Sussex Corner, NB E4E 3A1
Tel: 506-433-5184; *Fax:* 506-433-3785
village@sussexcorner.com
www.sussexcorner.com
Municipal Type: Village
Incorporated: 1966; *Area:* 9.43 sq km
County or District: Kings; *Population in 2011:* 1,495
Provincial Electoral District(s): Sussex-Fundy-St. Martins
Federal Electoral District(s): Fundy Royal
Next Election: May 2020 (4 year terms)
Mark Knowlton Flewwelling, Mayor
Don Smith, Clerk-Treasurer

Tide Head
6 Mountain St.
Tide Head, NB E3N 4J9
Tel: 506-789-6550
viltide@nb.sympatico.ca
www.tidehead.ca
Municipal Type: Village
Area: 19.57 sq km
County or District: Restigouche; *Population in 2011:* 1,036
Provincial Electoral District(s): Restigouche West
Federal Electoral District(s): Madawaska-Restigouche
Next Election: May 2020 (4 year terms)
Randy Hunter, Mayor

Angie Irvine, Clerk-Administrator

Tracadie-Sheila
CP 3600 Main
3620, rue Principale
Tracadie-Sheila, NB E1X 1G5
Tél: 506-394-4020; *Téléc:* 506-394-4025
info@tracadie-sheila.ca
www.tracadie-sheila.ca
Entité municipal: Town
Incorporation: Jan. 1, 1992; *Area:* 24.64 sq km
Comté ou district: Gloucester; *Population au 2011:* 4,933
Circonscription(s) électorale(s) provinciale(s): Tracadie-Sheila
Circonscription(s) électorale(s) fédérale(s): Acadie-Bathurst
Prochaines élections: May 2020 (4 year terms)
Denis Losier, Maire
Denis Poirier, Directeur général

Tracy
4435 Heritage Dr.
Tracy, NB E5L 1C1
Tel: 506-368-2878; *Fax:* 506-368-1014
Municipal Type: Village
Area: 29.36 sq km
County or District: Sunbury; *Population in 2011:* 611
Provincial Electoral District(s): New Maryland-Sunbury
Federal Electoral District(s): New Brunswick-Southwest
Next Election: May 2020 (4 year terms)
Dale W. Mowry, Mayor

Upper Miramichi
6094 Route 8
Boiestown, NB E6A 1M7
Tel: 506-369-9810; *Fax:* 506-369-8180
uppermiramichi1@nb.aibn.com
www.uppermiramichi.ca
Municipal Type: Community
County or District: Northumberland; *Population in 2011:* 2,373
Provincial Electoral District(s): Southwest Miramichi-Bay du Vin
Federal Electoral District(s): Miramichi-Grand Lake
Next Election: May 2020 (4 year terms)
M A Douglas Munn, Mayor
Mary Hunter, Clerk

Woodstock
824 Main St.
Woodstock, NB E7M 2E8
Tel: 506-325-4600; *Fax:* 506-325-4308
townhall@town.woodstock.nb.ca
www.town.woodstock.nb.ca
Municipal Type: Town
Incorporated: 1856; *Area:* 13.41 sq km
County or District: Carleton; *Population in 2011:* 5,254
Provincial Electoral District(s): Carleton
Federal Electoral District(s): Tobique-Mactaquac
Next Election: May 2020 (4 year terms)
Arthur L. Slipp, Mayor
Ken Harding, Chief Administrative Officer

NEWFOUNDLAND & LABRADOR

The provincial government of Newfoundland and Labrador exercises control over the activities of all municipalities in accordance with the Executive Council Act and the Municipal Affairs Act. Under the provisions of the Municipalities Act, the Department exercises a certain degree of financial and administrative control over all municipalities with the exception of the cities of St. John's, Corner Brook and Mount Pearl. The towns incorporated under the Municipalities Act do not require ministerial approval of their annual budgets, but the Department employs Municipal Analysts to oversee municipal activities. The province assumes responsibility for public health, welfare and law enforcement which are elsewhere generally considered to be municipal functions.

The cities and towns incorporated in Newfoundland are authorized to levy taxes and to provide a wide range of municipal services and to make appropriate bylaws or regulations for the implementation and administration of these services.

City and town councils in Newfoundland are elected on the last Tuesday in September every four years (2017, 2021, etc.).

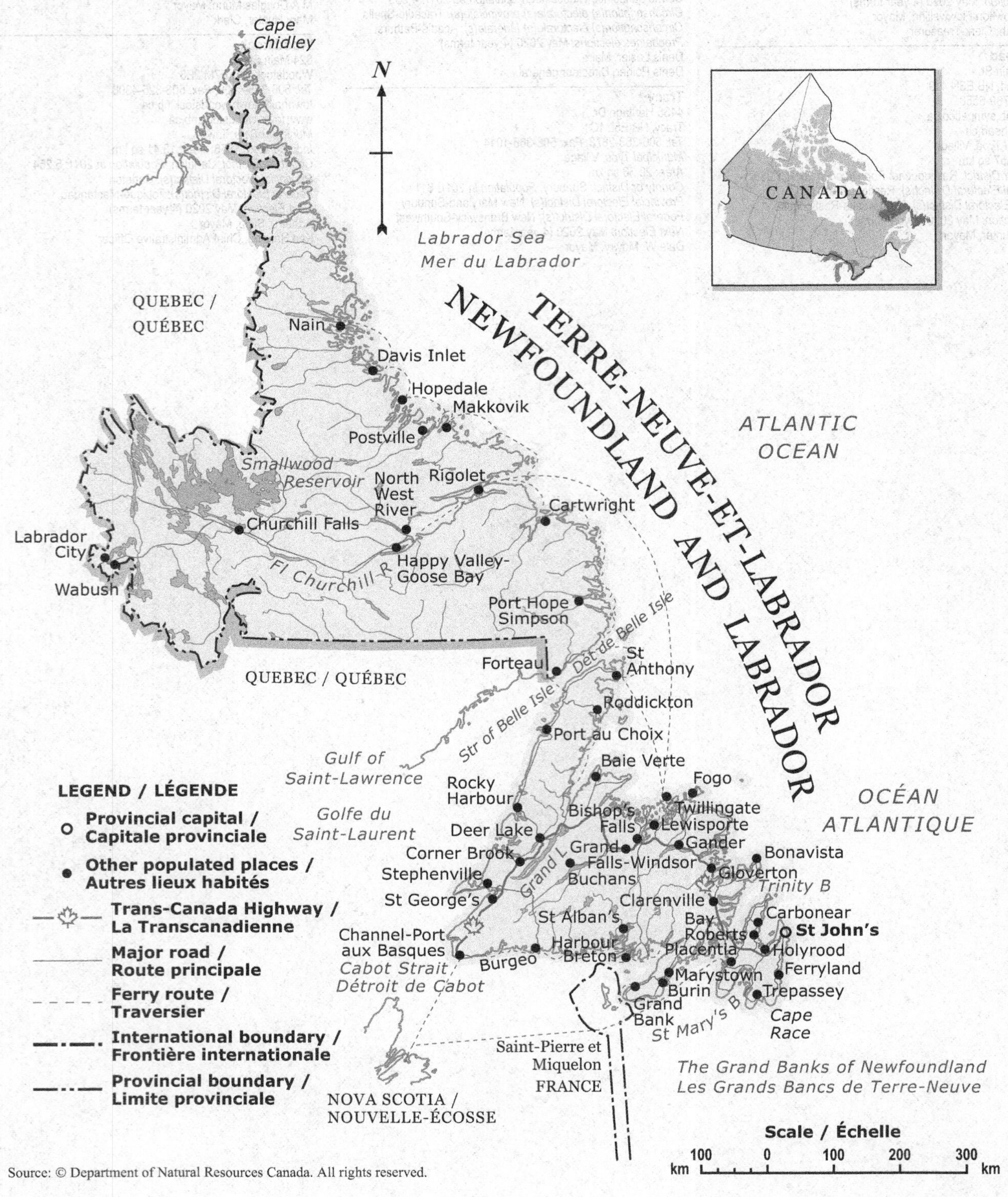

Newfoundland & Labrador

Major Municipalities in Newfoundland & Labrador

Conception Bay South
P.O. Box 14040 Stn. Manuels
11 Remembrance Sq.
Conception Bay South, NL A1W 3J1
Tel: 709-834-6500; *Fax:* 709-834-8337
www.conceptionbaysouth.ca
Municipal Type: City
Incorporated: Sept. 1, 1971; *Area:* 59.27 sq km
Population in 2011: 24,848
Provincial Electoral District(s): Conception Bay South; Topsail
Federal Electoral District(s): Avalon
Next Election: Sept. 26, 2017 (4 year terms)
Stephen Tessier, Mayor, 709-834-6500
Kenneth George, Deputy Mayor, 709-834-3013
Darrin Bent, Councillor, 709-834-7168, Wards: 1
Evan Bursey, Councillor, 709-834-6500, Wards: 1
Gerard Tilley, Councillor, 709-834-6418, Wards: 3
Richard Murphy, Councillor, 709-744-2188, Wards: 4
Beverly Rowe, Councillor at Large, 709-834-9619
Kirk Youden, Councillor at Large, 709-744-2004
Paul Connors, Councillor at Large, 709-834-9009
Gail Pomroy, Clerk, 709-834-6500
Dan Noseworthy, Chief Administrative Officer, 709-834-6500
Jennifer Manuel, Director, Engineering & Public Works, 709-834-6500
Elaine Mitchell, Director, Planning, 709-834-6500
Dave Tibbo, Director, Recreation & Leisure Services, 709-834-6500
John Heffernan, Fire Chief, Fire Department, 709-834-6500

Corner Brook
City Hall
P.O. Box 1080
5 Park St.
Corner Brook, NL A2H 6E1
Tel: 709-637-1500; *Fax:* 709-637-1625
city.hall@cornerbrook.com
www.cornerbrook.com
Other Information: tourism@cornerbrook.com; business@cornerbrook.com
Municipal Type: City
Incorporated: April 27, 1955; *Area:* 148.27 sq km
Population in 2011: 19,886
Provincial Electoral District(s): Humber East; Humber West
Federal Electoral District(s): Long Range Mountains
Next Election: Sept. 26, 2017 (4 year terms)
Charles Pender, Mayor
Bernd Staeben, Deputy Mayor & Councillor
Tony Buckle, Councillor
Josh Carey, Councillor
Linda Chaisson, Councillor
Keith Cormier, Councillor
Mary Ann Murphy, Councillor
Marina Redmond, City Clerk, 709-637-1534
Melissa Wiklund, City Manager, 709-637-1532
Paul Barnable, Director, Community, Development & Planning, 709-637-1548, Fax: 709-637-1514
Steve May, Director, Infrastructure & Public Works, 709-637-1541, Fax: 709-637-1502
Dale Park, Director, Finance & Administration, 709-637-1563
James Warford, P.Eng., Manager, Engineering Services, 709-637-1626
Keith Costello, Superintendent, Water & Sewer, 709-637-1595
Craig Kennedy, Superintendent, Public Works, 709-637-1607
Colleen Humphries, Supervisor, Planning, 709-637-1553
Jessica Parsons, Supervisor, Recreational Services, 709-637-1232
Jonathan Pynn, Supervisor, Land Management, 709-637-1544
Deon Rumbolt, Supervisor, Development & Inspection, 709-637-1552

Grand Falls-Windsor
P.O. Box 439
5 High St.
Grand Falls-Windsor, NL A2A 2J8
Tel: 709-489-0407; *Fax:* 709-489-0465
jrowsell@grandfallswindsor.com
www.grandfallswindsor.com
Municipal Type: City
Incorporated: Jan. 1, 1991; *Area:* 54.48 sq km
Population in 2011: 13,725
Provincial Electoral District(s): Grand Falls-Buchans; Windsor-Springdale
Federal Electoral District(s): Coast of Bays-Central-Notre Dame
Next Election: Sept. 26, 2017 (4 year terms)
Barry Manuel, Mayor
Darren Finn, Deputy Mayor & Councillor
Mike Browne, Councillor
Peggy Bartlett, Councillor
Amy Coady-Davis, Councillor
Bruce Moores, Councillor
Tom Pinsent, Councillor
Michael Pinsent, Town Manager, 709-487-0407, Fax: 709-292-0018
Vince J. MacKenzie, Fire Chief, 709-489-0431, Fax: 709-489-0885
Keith Antle, Director, Parks & Recreation, 709-489-0452, Fax: 709-489-0454
Jeff Saunders, Director, Engineering Works, 709-489-0427, Fax: 709-489-0465
Susanne Hillier, Officer, Purchasing, 709-489-0422, Fax: 709-489-0465

Mount Pearl
3 Centennial St.
Mount Pearl, NL A1N 1G4
Tel: 709-748-1000; *Fax:* 709-748-1150
info@mountpearl.ca
www.mountpearl.ca
Municipal Type: City
Incorporated: Jan. 11, 1955; *Area:* 15.75 sq km
Population in 2011: 24,284
Provincial Electoral District(s): Mount Pearl; Waterford Valley
Federal Electoral District(s): St. John's South-Mount Pearl
Next Election: Sept. 26, 2017 (4 year terms)
Randy Simms, Mayor
Jim Locke, Deputy Mayor
Dave Aker, Councillor
Andrew Ledwell, Councillor
Lucy Stoyles, Councillor
Paula Tessier, Councillor
John Walsh, Councillor
Michele Peach, Chief Administrative Officer, 709-748-1025
Mona Lewis, Deputy City Clerk, 709-748-1032
Gerry Antle, Director, Infrastructure & Public Works, 709-748-1028
Jason Collins, Director, Community Services, 709-748-1027
Stephen Jewczyk, Director, Planning & Development, 709-748-1029
Jason Silver, Director, Corporate Services, 709-748-1026
Colleen Butler, Manager, Human Resources, 709-748-1095
Norm Snelgrove, Manager, Finance, 709-748-1159
Blair Tilley, Superintendent, Municipal Enforcement, 709-748-1068
Steve Butler, Economic Development Officer, 709-748-1117

Paradise
28 McNamara Dr.
Paradise, NL A1L 0A6
Tel: 709-782-1400; *Fax:* 709-782-3603
info@townofparadise.ca
www.townofparadise.ca
Municipal Type: City
Incorporated: Feb. 1, 1992; *Area:* 29.24 sq km
Population in 2011: 17,695
Provincial Electoral District(s): Conception Bay East & Bell Island; Topsail
Federal Electoral District(s): Avalon; Coast of Bays-Central-Notre Dame; Labrador; St. John's East
Next Election: Sept. 26, 2017 (4 year terms)
Dan Bobbett, Mayor
Paul Dinn, Deputy Mayor, Councillor
Vince Burton, Councillor
Elizabeth Laurie, Councillor
Patrick Martin, Councillor
Deborah Quilty, Councillor
Sterling Willis, Councillor
Rodney Cumby, CAO, 709-782-1400
Conrad Freake, Director, Recreation & Leisure Services, 709-782-6290
Alton Glenn, Director, Planning & Protective Services, 709-782-3558
Terrilynn Smith, Director, Corporate Services, 709-782-1400

St. John's
City Hall
P.O. Box 908
10 New Gower St.
St. John's, NL A1C 5M2
Tel: 709-754-2489; *Fax:* 709-576-8474
accessstjohns@stjohns.ca
www.stjohns.ca
Other Information: 311 for city services
Municipal Type: City
Incorporated: Aug. 7, 1921; *Area:* 446.04 sq km
Population in 2011: 106,172
Provincial Electoral District(s): Kilbride; Signal Hill-Quidi Vidi; St. J. Centre; St. J. East; St. J. North; St. J. South; St. J. West; Virginia Waters; Mount Pearl North; Cape St. Francis
Federal Electoral District(s): St. John's East; St. John's South-Mount Pearl
Next Election: Sept. 26, 2017 (4 year terms)
Dennis O'Keefe, Mayor, 709-576-8477
Ron Ellsworth, Deputy Mayor, 709-576-8363
Danny Breen, Councillor, 709-576-2332, Wards: 1
Jonathan Galgay, Councillor, 709-576-7144, Wards: 2
Bruce Tilley, Councillor, 709-576-8643, Wards: 3
Sheilagh O'Leary, Councillor, 709-576-8217, Wards: 4
Wally Collins, Councillor, 709-576-8584, Wards: 5
Tom Hann, Councillor at Large, 709-576-8219, Wards: 5
Sandy Hickman, Councillor at Large, 709-576-8045, Wards: 5
Dave Lane, Councillor at Large, 709-576-8243, Wards: 5
Art Puddister, Councillor at Large, 709-576-8286, Wards: 5
Elaine Henley, City Clerk, Corporate Services, 709-576-8202
Kevin Breen, City Manager, 709-576-8207
Robert Bishop, C.A., Deputy City Manager, Financial Management, 709-576-8696, Fax: 709-576-8564
Tanya Haywood, Deputy City Manager, Community Services, 709-576-8020, Fax: 709-576-8469
Lynnann Winsor, Deputy City Manager/Director, Public Works & Parks
Ken O'Brien, Chief Municipal Planner, Planning, Development & Engineering, 709-576-8220
David Blackmore, Director, Building & Property Management, 709-576-8701, Fax: 709-576-8160
Elizabeth Lawrence, Director, Strategy & Engagement, 709-576-8107
Robin King, Transportation Engineer, 709-576-8232, Fax: 709-576-8625

Other Municipalities in Newfoundland & Labrador

Admiral's Beach
P.O. Box 196
Admiral's Beach, NL A0B 3A0
Tel: 709-521-2671; *Fax:* 709-521-2671
Municipal Type: Town
Incorporated: Jan. 16, 1968; *Area:* 24.42 sq km
Population in 2011: 153
Provincial Electoral District(s): Placentia & St. Mary's
Federal Electoral District(s): Avalon
Next Election: Sept. 26, 2017 (4 year terms)
Keith Guitar, Mayor
Mary Dobbin, Clerk

Anchor Point
P.O. Box 117
Anchor Point, NL A0K 1A0
Tel: 709-456-2011; *Fax:* 709-456-2364
anchorpoint@nf.aibn.com
Municipal Type: Town
Incorporated: Sept. 10, 1974; *Area:* 2.41 sq km
Population in 2011: 326
Provincial Electoral District(s): St. Barbe
Federal Electoral District(s): Long Range Mountains
Next Election: Sept. 26, 2017 (4 year terms)
Gerry Gros, Mayor
Sharon Gaulton, Clerk

L'Anse au Clair
P.O. Box 83
L'Anse au Clair, NL A0K 3K0
Tel: 709-931-2481; *Fax:* 709-931-2488
townoflanseauclair@hotmail.com
www.lanseauclair.ca
Municipal Type: Town
Incorporated: June 2, 1970; *Area:* 61.92 sq km
Population in 2011: 264
Provincial Electoral District(s): Cartwright-L'Anse au Clair
Federal Electoral District(s): Labrador
Next Election: Sept. 26, 2017 (4 year terms)
Nath Moores, Mayor
Loretta Griffin, Clerk

L'Anse au Loup
P.O. Box 101
L'Anse au Loup, NL A0K 3L0
Tel: 709-927-5573; *Fax:* 709-927-5263
lanseauloup@nf.aibn.com
www.lanseauloup.ca
Municipal Type: Town
Incorporated: April 11, 1975; *Area:* 3.48 sq km
Population in 2011: 600
Provincial Electoral District(s): Cartwright-L'Anse au Clair
Federal Electoral District(s): Labrador; Bonavista-Burin-Trinity
Next Election: Sept. 26, 2017 (4 year terms)
Headley Ryland, Mayor
Janice Normore, Clerk

Appleton
PO Box 31, Site 4
Appleton, NL A0G 2K0
Tel: 709-679-2289; *Fax:* 709-679-5552
townofappleton@personainternet.com
Municipal Type: Town
Incorporated: Feb. 27, 1962; *Area:* 6.39 sq km
Population in 2011: 622
Provincial Electoral District(s): Gander
Federal Electoral District(s): Coast of Bays-Central-Notre Dame
Next Election: Sept. 26, 2017 (4 year terms)
Derm Flynn, Mayor
Pat Barnes, Clerk

Aquaforte
General Delivery
Aquaforte, NL A0A 1A0
Tel: 709-363-2618
aquafortecouncil@bellaliant.com
Municipal Type: Town
Incorporated: April 25, 1972; *Area:* 6.82 sq km
Population in 2011: 83
Provincial Electoral District(s): Ferryland
Federal Electoral District(s): Avalon
Next Election: Sept. 26, 2017 (4 year terms)
Carol Ann Cose, Mayor
Kathleen Hayes, Clerk

Arnold's Cove
P.O. Box 70
Arnolds Cove, NL A0B 1A0
Tel: 709-463-2323; *Fax:* 709-463-2326
townofarnoldscove@nf.aibn.com
www.townofarnoldscove.com
Municipal Type: Town
Incorporated: June 3, 1967; *Area:* 4.93 sq km
Population in 2011: 990
Provincial Electoral District(s): Bellevue
Federal Electoral District(s): Bonavista-Burin-Trinity
Next Election: Sept. 26, 2017 (4 year terms)
Basil Daley, Mayor
Angela Gale, Clerk

Avondale
P.O. Box 59
Avondale, NL A0A 1B0
Tel: 709-229-4201; *Fax:* 709-229-4446
townofavondale@persona.ca
Municipal Type: Town
Incorporated: Nov. 26, 1974; *Area:* 29.93 sq km
Population in 2011: 636
Provincial Electoral District(s): Harbour Main-Whitbourne
Federal Electoral District(s): Avalon
Next Election: Sept. 26, 2017 (4 year terms)
Owen Mahoney, Mayor
Linda Bourgeois-Fraser, Clerk

Badger
P.O. Box 130
Badger, NL A0H 1A0
Tel: 709-539-2406; *Fax:* 709-539-5262
townofbadger@gmail.com
Municipal Type: Town
Incorporated: Sept. 24, 1963; *Area:* 1.96 sq km
Population in 2011: 793
Provincial Electoral District(s): Grand Falls-Buchans
Federal Electoral District(s): Coast of Bays-Central-Notre Dame
Next Election: Sept. 26, 2017 (4 year terms)
Michael Patey, Mayor
Pansy Hurley, Clerk

Baie Verte
P.O. Box 218
Baie Verte, NL A0K 1B0
Tel: 709-532-8222; *Fax:* 709-532-4134
info@townofbaieverte.ca
www.townofbaieverte.ca
Municipal Type: Town
Incorporated: Cpril 29, 1958; *Area:* 371.07 sq km
Population in 2011: 1,370
Provincial Electoral District(s): Baie Verte
Federal Electoral District(s): Coast of Bays-Central-Notre Dame
Next Election: Sept. 26, 2017 (4 year terms)
Clar Brown, Mayor
Angela Furey, Clerk

Baine Harbour
General Delivery
Baine Harbour, NL A0E 1A0
Tel: 709-443-2980; *Fax:* 709-443-2355
bhrtc@bellaliant.net
Municipal Type: Town
Incorporated: Dec. 1, 1970; *Area:* 4.82 sq km
Population in 2011: 137
Provincial Electoral District(s): Burin-Placentia West
Federal Electoral District(s): Bonavista-Burin-Trinity
Next Election: Sept. 26, 2017 (4 year terms)
Harold Kenway, Mayor
Dinah Smith, Clerk

Bauline
2 Brook Path
Bauline, NL A1K 1E9
Tel: 709-335-2483; *Fax:* 709-335-2053
baulinetowncouncil@nf.aibn.com
Municipal Type: Town
Incorporated: July 1, 1988; *Area:* 15.95 sq km
Population in 2011: 397
Provincial Electoral District(s): Cape St. Francis
Federal Electoral District(s): St. John's East
Next Election: Sept. 26, 2017 (4 year terms)
Christopher Dredge, Mayor
Craig Drover, Clerk

Bay Bulls
P.O. Box 70
Bay Bulls, NL A0A 1C0
Tel: 709-334-3454; *Fax:* 709-334-3477
townofbaybulls@nf.aibn.com
www.townofbaybulls.com
Municipal Type: Town
Incorporated: Jan. 1, 1986; *Area:* 30.74 sq km
Population in 2011: 1,283
Provincial Electoral District(s): Ferryland
Federal Electoral District(s): St. John's South-Mount Pearl
Next Election: Sept. 26, 2017 (4 year terms)
Patrick D'Driscoll, Mayor
Janet O'Brien, Clerk

Bay de Verde
P.O. Box 10
Bay de Verde, NL A0A 1E0
Tel: 709-587-2260; *Fax:* 709-587-2049
info@baydeverde.com
www.baydeverde.com
Municipal Type: Town
Incorporated: Aug. 22, 1950; *Area:* 13.28 sq km
Population in 2011: 398
Provincial Electoral District(s): Trinity-Bay de Verde
Federal Electoral District(s): Bonavista-Burin-Trinity
Next Election: Sept. 26, 2017 (4 year terms)
Gerald Murphy, Mayor
Molly Walsh, Clerk

Bay L'Argent
P.O. Box 29
Bay L'Argent, NL A0E 1B0
Tel: 709-461-2606; *Fax:* 709-461-2608
townofbaylargent@nf.aibn.com
Municipal Type: Town
Incorporated: July 13, 1971; *Area:* 3.56 sq km
Population in 2011: 285
Provincial Electoral District(s): Bellevue
Federal Electoral District(s): Bonavista-Burin-Trinity
Next Election: Sept. 26, 2017 (4 year terms)
Rhonda Baker, Mayor
Viola Pardy, Clerk

Bay Roberts
P.O. Box 114
Bay Roberts, NL A0A 1G0
Tel: 709-786-2126; *Fax:* 709-786-2128
www.bayroberts.com
Municipal Type: Town
Incorporated: Feb. 17, 1951; *Area:* 23.92 sq km
Population in 2011: 5,818
Provincial Electoral District(s): Port de Grave
Federal Electoral District(s): Avalon
Next Election: Sept. 26, 2017 (4 year terms)
Philip Wood, Mayor
Christine Bradbury, Clerk

Baytona
P.O. Box 29
Baytona, NL A0G 2J0
Tel: 709-659-6101; *Fax:* 709-659-6101
thetownofbaytona@eastlink.ca
Municipal Type: Town
Incorporated: Aug. 1, 1975; *Area:* 15.38 sq km
Population in 2011: 264
Provincial Electoral District(s): Lewisporte
Federal Electoral District(s): Coast of Bays-Central-Notre Dame
Next Election: Sept. 26, 2017 (4 year terms)
Rex Quinlan, Mayor
Angie Burt, Clerk

Beachside
112 Bayview Rd.
Beachside, NL A0J 1T0
Tel: 709-267-5251; *Fax:* 709-267-5251
Municipal Type: Town
Incorporated: July 7, 1961; *Area:* 2.61 sq km
Population in 2011: 150
Provincial Electoral District(s): Baie Verte
Federal Electoral District(s): Coast of Bays-Central-Notre Dame
Next Election: Sept. 26, 2017 (4 year terms)
Ward Verge, Mayor
Linda Grothe, Clerk

Bellburns
General Delivery
Bellburns, NL A0K 1H0
Tel: 709-898-2468; *Fax:* 709-898-2442
bellburns.tripod.com
Municipal Type: Town
Incorporated: May 13, 1969; *Area:* 7.39 sq km
Population in 2011: 62
Provincial Electoral District(s): St. Barbe
Federal Electoral District(s): Long Range Mountains
Next Election: Sept. 26, 2017 (4 year terms)
Denise House, Mayor
Pauline House, Clerk

Belleoram
P.O. Box 29
Belleoram, NL A0H 1B0
Tel: 709-881-6161; *Fax:* 709-881-6161
belloeam1946@yahoo.ca
Municipal Type: Town
Incorporated: March 19, 1946; *Area:* 2.1 sq km
Population in 2011: 409
Provincial Electoral District(s): Fortune Bay-Cape La Hune
Federal Electoral District(s): Coast of Bays-Central-Notre Dame
Next Election: Sept. 26, 2017 (4 year terms)
Steward May, Mayor
Janice Keeping, Clerk

Birchy Bay
P.O. Box 40
Birchy Bay, NL A0G 1E0
Tel: 709-659-3221; *Fax:* 709-659-2121
office@birchybay.ca
Municipal Type: Town
Incorporated: Aug. 27, 1974; *Area:* 49.52 sq km
Population in 2011: 566
Provincial Electoral District(s): Lewisporte
Federal Electoral District(s): Coast of Bays-Central-Notre Dame
Next Election: Sept. 26, 2017 (4 year terms)
Seymour Quinlan, Mayor
Cynthia Baker, Clerk

Bird Cove
67 Michael's Dr.
Bird Cove, NL A0K 1L0
Tel: 709-247-2256; *Fax:* 709-247-2254
Municipal Type: Town
Incorporated: April 15, 1977; *Area:* 9.39 sq km
Population in 2011: 182
Provincial Electoral District(s): St. Barbe
Federal Electoral District(s): Long Range Mountains
Next Election: Sept. 26, 2017 (4 year terms)
Andre Myers, Mayor
Irene Myers, Clerk

Bishop's Cove
P.O. Box 36
Bishop's Cove, NL A0A 3X0
Tel: 709-594-3001; *Fax:* 709-594-3002
bishopscove@eastlink.ca
Municipal Type: Town
Incorporated: June 24, 1969; *Area:* 1.89 sq km
Population in 2011: 275
Provincial Electoral District(s): Port de Grave
Federal Electoral District(s): Avalon
Next Election: Sept. 26, 2017 (4 year terms)
Josiah Clarke, Mayor
Irene Menchions, Clerk

Bishop's Falls
P.O. Box 310
Bishops Falls, NL A0H 1C0
Tel: 709-258-6581; *Fax:* 709-258-6346
info@bishopsfalls.com
Municipal Type: Town
Incorporated: Nov. 1, 1961; *Area:* 28.12 sq km
Population in 2011: 3,341

Provincial Electoral District(s): Exploits
Federal Electoral District(s): Coast of Bays-Central-Notre Dame
Next Election: Sept. 26, 2017 (4 year terms)
Robert Hobbs, Mayor
Dan Oldford, Clerk

Bonavista
P.O. Box 279
Bonavista, NL A0C 1B0
Tel: 709-468-7816; *Fax:* 709-468-2495
town.bonavista@nf.sympatico.ca
Municipal Type: Town
Incorporated: Nov. 24, 1964; *Area:* 31.5 sq km
Population in 2011: 3,589
Provincial Electoral District(s): Bonavista South
Federal Electoral District(s): Bonavista-Burin-Trinity
Next Election: Sept. 26, 2017 (4 year terms)
Betty Fitzgerald, Mayor
David Hiscock, Clerk

Botwood
P.O. Box 490
Botwood, NL A0H 1E0
Tel: 709-257-2839; *Fax:* 709-257-3330
botwoodtowncouncil@nf.aibn.com
town.botwood.nl.ca
Municipal Type: Town
Incorporated: June 21, 1960; *Area:* 15.05 sq km
Population in 2011: 3,008
Provincial Electoral District(s): Exploits
Federal Electoral District(s): Coast of Bays-Central-Notre Dame
Next Election: Sept. 26, 2017 (4 year terms)
Jerry Dean, Mayor
Audrey Rowsell, Clerk

Branch
P.O. Box 129
Branch, NL A0B 1E0
Tel: 709-338-2920; *Fax:* 709-338-2921
townofbranch@xplornet.ca
Municipal Type: Town
Incorporated: May 17, 1966; *Area:* 16.15 sq km
Population in 2011: 247
Provincial Electoral District(s): Placentia & St. Mary's
Federal Electoral District(s): Avalon
Next Election: Sept. 26, 2017 (4 year terms)
Kelly Power, Mayor
Augustus Power, Clerk

Brent's Cove
General Delivery
Brents Cove, NL A0K 1R0
Tel: 709-661-5301; *Fax:* 709-661-5216
Municipal Type: Town
Incorporated: April 12, 1966; *Area:* 1.02 sq km
Population in 2011: 181
Provincial Electoral District(s): Baie Verte
Federal Electoral District(s): Coast of Bays-Central-Notre Dame
Next Election: Sept. 26, 2017 (4 year terms)
Richard Andrews, Mayor
Ellen Butler, Clerk

Brighton
General Delivery
Brighton, NL A0J 1B0
Tel: 709-263-7391; *Fax:* 709-263-7391
townofbrighton@hotmail.com
Municipal Type: Town
Incorporated: Jan. 1, 1986; *Area:* 2.23 sq km
Population in 2011: 171
Provincial Electoral District(s): Windsor-Springdale
Federal Electoral District(s): Coast of Bays-Central-Notre Dame
Next Election: Sept. 26, 2017 (4 year terms)
Stewart Fillier, Mayor
Gloria Fudge, Clerk

Brigus
P.O. Box 220
Brigus, NL A0A 1K0
Tel: 709-528-4588; *Fax:* 709-528-4588
brigus@eastlink.ca
www.brigus.net
Municipal Type: Town
Incorporated: July 21, 1964; *Area:* 11.57 sq km
Population in 2011: 750
Provincial Electoral District(s): Harbour Main-Whitbourne
Federal Electoral District(s): Avalon
Next Election: Sept. 26, 2017 (4 year terms)
Byron Rodway, Mayor, 709-528-3201
Wayne Rose, Town Clerk & Manager

Bryant's Cove
PO Box 5, Site 3
Bryant's Cove, NL A0A 3P0
Tel: 709-596-2291; *Fax:* 709-596-0015
bryantscove@eastlink.ca
Municipal Type: Town
Incorporated: July 29, 1977; *Area:* 4.87 sq km
Population in 2011: 396
Provincial Electoral District(s): Port de Grave
Federal Electoral District(s): Avalon
Next Election: Sept. 26, 2017 (4 year terms)
Kim Sheppard, Mayor
Michelle Antle, Clerk

Buchans
P.O. Box 190
Buchans, NL A0H 1G0
Tel: 709-672-3972; *Fax:* 709-672-3702
townofbuchans@nf.aibn.com
www.townofbuchans.nf.ca
Municipal Type: Town
Incorporated: April 24, 1963; *Area:* 4.88 sq km
Population in 2011: 696
Provincial Electoral District(s): Grand Falls-Buchans
Federal Electoral District(s): Coast of Bays-Central-Notre Dame
Next Election: Sept. 26, 2017 (4 year terms)
Derm Corbett, Mayor
David Whalen, Clerk

Burgeo
P.O. Box 220
Burgeo, NL A0N 2H0
Tel: 709-886-2250; *Fax:* 709-886-2166
townofburgeo@gmail.com
www.burgeonl.com
Municipal Type: Town
Incorporated: June 17, 1950; *Area:* 31.34 sq km
Population in 2011: 1,464
Provincial Electoral District(s): Burgeo & La Poile
Federal Electoral District(s): Long Range Mountains
Next Election: Sept. 26, 2017 (4 year terms)
Barbara G. Barter, Mayor
Blaine Marks, Clerk

Burin
P.O. Box 370
Burin, NL A0E 1E0
Tel: 709-891-1760; *Fax:* 709-891-2069
townofburin@persona.ca
www.townofburin.com
Municipal Type: Town
Incorporated: July 18, 1950; *Area:* 34.05 sq km
Population in 2011: 2,424
Provincial Electoral District(s): Burin-Placentia West; Grand Bank
Federal Electoral District(s): Bonavista-Burin-Trinity
Next Election: Sept. 26, 2017 (4 year terms)
Kevin Lundrigan, Mayor
Joanne Jackman, Clerk

Burlington
General Delivery
Burlington, NL A0K 1S0
Tel: 709-252-2607; *Fax:* 709-252-2161
mbartlett@townofburlington.ca
Municipal Type: Town
Incorporated: Oct. 20, 1953; *Area:* 4.1 sq km
Population in 2011: 349
Provincial Electoral District(s): Baie Verte
Federal Electoral District(s): Coast of Bays-Central-Notre Dame
Next Election: Sept. 26, 2017 (4 year terms)
George Kelly, Mayor
Mary Lou Bartlett, Clerk

Burnt Islands
P.O. Box 39
Burnt Islands, NL A0M 1B0
Tel: 709-698-3512; *Fax:* 709-698-3512
townofburntislands@hotmail.com
www.burntislandsnl.ca
Municipal Type: Town
Incorporated: Oct. 31, 1975; *Area:* 9.52 sq km
Population in 2011: 651
Provincial Electoral District(s): Burgeo & La Poile
Federal Electoral District(s): Long Range Mountains
Next Election: Sept. 26, 2017 (4 year terms)
Paul Strickland, Mayor
Linda Thorne, Clerk

Campbellton
P.O. Box 70
Campbellton, NL A0G 1L0
Tel: 709-261-2300; *Fax:* 709-261-2375
townofcampbellton@nf.aibn.com
Municipal Type: Town
Incorporated: Oct. 21, 1972; *Area:* 35.71 sq km
Population in 2011: 520
Provincial Electoral District(s): Lewisporte
Federal Electoral District(s): Coast of Bays-Central-Notre Dame
Next Election: Sept. 26, 2017 (4 year terms)
Maisie Clarke, Mayor
Gail Osmond, Clerk

Cape Broyle
P.O. Box 69
Cape Broyle, NL A0A 1P0
Tel: 709-432-2288; *Fax:* 709-432-2794
townofcapebroyle@nf.aibn.com
Municipal Type: Town
Incorporated: Jan. 1, 1990; *Area:* 10.05 sq km
Population in 2011: 506
Provincial Electoral District(s): Ferryland
Federal Electoral District(s): Avalon
Next Election: Sept. 26, 2017 (4 year terms)
Donald Graham, Mayor
Wendy Duggan, Clerk

Cape St. George
876 Oceanview Drive
Cape St George, NL A0N 1T1
Tel: 709-644-2290; *Fax:* 709-644-2291
townofcapestgeorge@eastlink.ca
Municipal Type: Town
Incorporated: June 24, 1969; *Area:* 33.46 sq km
Population in 2011: 949
Provincial Electoral District(s): Port au Port
Federal Electoral District(s): Long Range Mountains
Next Election: Sept. 26, 2017 (4 year terms)
Peter Fenwick, Mayor
Ina Renouf, Clerk

Carbonear
P.O. Box 999
Carbonear, NL A1Y 1C5
Tel: 709-596-3831; *Fax:* 709-596-5021
info@carbonear.ca
www.carbonear.ca
Municipal Type: Town
Incorporated: July 13, 1948; *Area:* 11.81 sq km
Population in 2011: 4,739
Provincial Electoral District(s): Carbonear-Harbour Grace
Federal Electoral District(s): Avalon
Next Election: Sept. 26, 2017 (4 year terms)
George Butt Jr., Acting Mayor
Cathy Somers, Clerk

Carmanville
P.O. Box 239
Carmanville, NL A0G 1N0
Tel: 709-534-2814; *Fax:* 709-534-2425
townofcarmanville@nf.aibn.com
carmanville.canadianwebs.com
Municipal Type: Town
Incorporated: March 29, 1955; *Area:* 43.08 sq km
Population in 2011: 737
Provincial Electoral District(s): Bonavista North
Federal Electoral District(s): Bonavista-Burin-Trinity
Next Election: Sept. 26, 2017 (4 year terms)
Keith Howell, Mayor
Dianne Goodyear, Clerk

Cartwright
P.O. Box 129
Cartwright, NL A0K 1V0
Tel: 709-938-7259; *Fax:* 709-938-7454
twcouncil@bellaliant.com
Municipal Type: Town
Incorporated: Oct. 10, 1956; *Area:* 3.27 sq km
Population in 2011: 516
Provincial Electoral District(s): Cartwright-L'Anse au Clair
Federal Electoral District(s): Labrador
Next Election: Sept. 26, 2017 (4 year terms)
Blair Gillis, Mayor
Shirley Hopkins, Clerk

Centreville-Wareham-Trinity
P.O. Box 130
Centreville, NL A0G 4P0
Tel: 709-678-2840; *Fax:* 709-678-2536
townofcwt@bellaliant.com
www.townofcwt.com

Municipal Type: Town
Incorporated: Jan. 1, 1992; *Area:* 37.25 sq km
Population in 2011: 1,161
Provincial Electoral District(s): Bonavista North
Federal Electoral District(s): Bonavista-Burin-Trinity
Next Election: Sept. 26, 2017 (4 year terms)
Churence Rogers, Mayor
Michelle Lane, Clerk

Chance Cove
P.O. Box 133
Chance Cove, NL A0B 1K0
Tel: 709-460-4151; *Fax:* 709-460-5580
townofchancecove@nf.aibn.com
Municipal Type: Town
Incorporated: Feb. 8, 1972; *Area:* 18.2 sq km
Population in 2011: 282
Provincial Electoral District(s): Bellevue
Federal Electoral District(s): Bonavista-Burin-Trinity
Next Election: Sept. 26, 2017 (4 year terms)
Edgar Crann, Mayor
Glenys Rowe, Clerk

Change Islands
P.O. Box 67
Change Islands, NL A0G 1R0
Tel: 709-621-4181; *Fax:* 709-621-4181
townclerk@changeislands.ca
www.changeislands.ca
Municipal Type: Town
Incorporated: Oct. 16, 1951; *Area:* 5.31 sq km
Population in 2011: 257
Provincial Electoral District(s): Twillingate & Fogo
Federal Electoral District(s): Coast of Bays-Central-Notre Dame
Next Election: Sept. 26, 2017 (4 year terms)
Stephen Brinson, Mayor, 709-621-3401
Sherry Diamond, Clerk

Channel-Port aux Basques
P.O. Box 67
Port aux Basques, NL A0G 1R0
Tel: 709-621-4181; *Fax:* 709-695-9852
townchannelpab@nf.aibn.com
www.portauxbasques.ca
Municipal Type: Town
Incorporated: Nov. 6, 1945; *Area:* 38.77 sq km
Population in 2011: 4,170
Provincial Electoral District(s): Burgeo & La Poile
Federal Electoral District(s): Long Range Mountains
Next Election: Sept. 26, 2017 (4 year terms)
Lloyd Mushrow, Mayor
Julia Ingram, Clerk

Chapel Arm
68 Main Rd.
Chapel Arm, NL A0B 1L0
Tel: 709-592-2720; *Fax:* 709-592-2800
townofchapelarm@eastlink.ca
Municipal Type: Town
Incorporated: Nov. 24, 1970; *Area:* 28.17 sq km
Population in 2011: 468
Provincial Electoral District(s): Bellevue
Federal Electoral District(s): Bonavista-Burin-Trinity
Next Election: Sept. 26, 2017 (4 year terms)
Shawn Reid, Mayor
Tracy Smith, Clerk

Charlottetown
P.O. Box 151
Charlottetown, NL A0K 5Y0
Tel: 709-949-0299; *Fax:* 709-949-0377
ctown@nf.aibn.com
Municipal Type: Town
Incorporated: March 4, 1988; *Area:* 30.53 sq km
Population in 2011: 308
Provincial Electoral District(s): Cartwright-L'Anse au Clair
Federal Electoral District(s): Bonavista-Burin-Trinity; Labrador
Next Election: Sept. 26, 2017 (4 year terms)
Ina Jefferies, Mayor
Stewart Macnab, Clerk

Clarenville
99 Pleasant St.
Clarenville, NL A5A 1V9
Tel: 709-466-7937; *Fax:* 709-466-2276
info@clarenville.net
www.clarenville.net
Municipal Type: Town
Incorporated: June 12, 1951; *Area:* 140.79 sq km
Population in 2011: 6,036
Provincial Electoral District(s): Trinity North
Federal Electoral District(s): Bonavista-Burin-Trinity
Next Election: Sept. 26, 2017 (4 year terms)
Frazer Russell, Mayor
Marie Blackmore, Clerk

Clarke's Beach
P.O. Box 159
113 Conception Bay Hwy.
Clarkes Beach, NL A0A 1W0
Tel: 709-786-3993; *Fax:* 709-786-4065
Municipal Type: Town
Incorporated: Aug. 24, 1965; *Area:* 12.71 sq km
Population in 2011: 1,396
Provincial Electoral District(s): Harbour Main-Whitbourne
Federal Electoral District(s): Avalon
Next Election: Sept. 26, 2017 (4 year terms)
Betty Moore, Mayor, 709-786-0614
Joan Wilcox, Clerk

Coachman's Cove
General Delivery
Coachmans Cove, NL A0K 1X0
Tel: 709-253-5161; *Fax:* 709-253-5161
Municipal Type: Town
Incorporated: Nov. 24, 1970; *Area:* 18.15 sq km
Population in 2011: 92
Provincial Electoral District(s): Baie Verte
Federal Electoral District(s): Coast of Bays-Central-Notre Dame
Next Election: Sept. 26, 2017 (4 year terms)
Martin Breen Sr., Mayor
Johanna Breen, Clerk

Colinet
P.O. Box 8
Colinet, NL A0B 1M0
Tel: 709-521-2300; *Fax:* 709-521-2300
Municipal Type: Town
Incorporated: Sept. 24, 1974; *Area:* 6.23 sq km
Population in 2011: 110
Provincial Electoral District(s): Placentia & St. Mary's
Federal Electoral District(s): Avalon
Next Election: Sept. 26, 2017 (4 year terms)
William Gambin, Mayor
Maureen Didham, Clerk

Colliers
P.O. Box 84
Colliers, NL A0A 1Y0
Tel: 709-229-4333; *Fax:* 709-229-4033
townofcolliers@eastlink.ca
Municipal Type: Town
Incorporated: Oct. 31, 1972; *Area:* 26.16 sq km
Population in 2011: 651
Provincial Electoral District(s): Harbour Main-Whitbourne
Federal Electoral District(s): Avalon
Next Election: Sept. 26, 2017 (4 year terms)
Michael Moriarity, Mayor
Mariette Holly, Clerk

Come By Chance
P.O. Box 89
Come By Chance, NL A0B 1N0
Tel: 709-542-3240; *Fax:* 709-542-3121
townofcbc@eastlink.ca
www.townofcomebychance.ca
Municipal Type: Town
Incorporated: July 22, 1969; *Area:* 41.16 sq km
Population in 2011: 265
Provincial Electoral District(s): Bellevue
Federal Electoral District(s): Bonavista-Burin-Trinity
Next Election: Sept. 26, 2017 (4 year terms)
Joan Cleary, Mayor
Stephanie Eddy, Clerk

Comfort Cove-Newstead
P.O. Box 10
Comfort Cove, NL A0G 3K0
Tel: 709-244-4125; *Fax:* 709-244-4122
ccntown@eastlink.ca
Municipal Type: Town
Incorporated: Oct. 24, 1967; *Area:* 29.83 sq km
Population in 2011: 451
Provincial Electoral District(s): Lewisporte
Federal Electoral District(s): Coast of Bays-Central-Notre Dame
Next Election: Sept. 26, 2017 (4 year terms)
Randy White, Mayor
Lloyd Brenton, Clerk

Conception Harbour
P.O. Box 128
Conception Harbour, NL A0A 1Z0
Tel: 709-229-4781; *Fax:* 709-229-0432
charbour@eastlink.ca
Municipal Type: Town
Incorporated: Oct. 31, 1972; *Area:* 21.62 sq km
Population in 2011: 697
Provincial Electoral District(s): Harbour Main-Whitbourne
Federal Electoral District(s): Avalon
Next Election: Sept. 26, 2017 (4 year terms)
Craig Williams, Mayor
Lillian Connors, Clerk

Conche
P.O. Box 59
Conche, NL A0K 1Y0
Tel: 709-622-4531; *Fax:* 709-622-4491
townofconche@nf.aibn.com
Municipal Type: Town
Incorporated: Sept. 13, 1960; *Area:* 9.09 sq km
Population in 2011: 181
Provincial Electoral District(s): The Straits & White Bay North
Federal Electoral District(s): Long Range Mountains
Next Election: Sept. 26, 2017 (4 year terms)
Doris Carroll, Mayor
Alice Flynn, Clerk

Cook's Harbour
P.O. Box 69
Cooks Harbour, NL A0K 1Z0
Tel: 709-249-3111; *Fax:* 709-249-4105
r.short@nf.aibn.com
Municipal Type: Town
Incorporated: Oct. 10, 1956; *Area:* 1.95 sq km
Population in 2011: 76
Provincial Electoral District(s): The Straits & White Bay North
Federal Electoral District(s): Long Range Mountains
Next Election: Sept. 26, 2017 (4 year terms)
Barry Decker, Mayor
Regina Short, Clerk

Cormack
280 Veteran'S Dr.
Cormack, NL A8A 2R4
Tel: 709-635-7025; *Fax:* 709-635-7363
townofcormack@nf.aibn.com
townofcormack.ca
Municipal Type: Town
Incorporated: April 14, 1964; *Area:* 135.23 sq km
Population in 2011: 605
Provincial Electoral District(s): Humber Valley
Federal Electoral District(s): Long Range Mountains
Next Election: Sept. 26, 2017 (4 year terms)
Melvin Rideout Sr., Mayor
Tracey Hewitt, Clerk

Cottlesville
P.O. Box 10
Cottlesville, NL A0G 1S0
Tel: 709-629-3505; *Fax:* 709-629-7411
towncottlesville@eastlink.ca
www.cottlesville.com
Municipal Type: Town
Incorporated: Oct. 24, 1972; *Area:* 11.17 sq km
Population in 2011: 272
Provincial Electoral District(s): Twillingate & Fogo
Federal Electoral District(s): Coast of Bays-Central-Notre Dame
Next Election: Sept. 26, 2017 (4 year terms)
Rodney Wheeler, Mayor
Shelly Abbott, Clerk

Cow Head
P.O. Box 40
Cow Head, NL A0K 2A0
Tel: 709-243-2446; *Fax:* 709-243-2590
townofcowhead@bellaliant.com
www.cowhead.ca
Municipal Type: Town
Incorporated: Feb. 1, 1964; *Area:* 17.84 sq km
Population in 2011: 475
Provincial Electoral District(s): St. Barbe
Federal Electoral District(s): Long Range Mountains
Next Election: Sept. 26, 2017 (4 year terms)
Garland Hutchings, Mayor
Terri-Lynn Payne, Clerk

Cox's Cove
P.O. Box 100
Coxs Cove, NL A0L 1C0
Tel: 709-688-2900; *Fax:* 709-688-2929
coxcove@eastlink.ca
Municipal Type: Town
Incorporated: Nov. 11, 1969; *Area:* 7.21 sq km
Population in 2011: 660
Provincial Electoral District(s): Bay of Islands

Federal Electoral District(s): Long Range Mountains
Next Election: Sept. 26, 2017 (4 year terms)
Tony Oxford, Mayor
Tina Sheppard, Clerk

Crow Head
P.O. Box 250
Crow Head, NL A0G 4M0
Tel: 709-884-5651; *Fax:* 709-884-2344
Municipal Type: Town
Incorporated: Sept. 13, 1960; *Area:* 2.98 sq km
Population in 2011: 203
Provincial Electoral District(s): Twillingate & Fogo
Federal Electoral District(s): Coast of Bays-Central-Notre Dame
Next Election: Sept. 26, 2017 (4 year terms)
John Hamlyn, Mayor
Meta J. Hamlyn, Clerk

Cupids
P.O. Box 99
Cupids, NL A0A 2B0
Tel: 709-528-4428; *Fax:* 709-528-4430
townofcupids@eastlink.ca
Municipal Type: Town
Incorporated: April 13, 1965; *Area:* 11.02 sq km
Population in 2011: 761
Provincial Electoral District(s): Harbour Main-Whitbourne
Federal Electoral District(s): Avalon
Next Election: Sept. 26, 2017 (4 year terms)
Harold Akerman, Mayor
Ivy King, Clerk

Daniel's Harbour
P.O. Box 68
Daniels Harbour, NL A0K 2C0
Tel: 709-898-2300; *Fax:* 709-898-2311
townofdanielsharbour@nf.aibn.com
Municipal Type: Town
Incorporated: March 9, 1965; *Area:* 8.19 sq km
Population in 2011: 265
Provincial Electoral District(s): St. Barbe
Federal Electoral District(s): Long Range Mountains
Next Election: Sept. 26, 2017 (4 year terms)
Ross Humber, Mayor
Melda Hann, Clerk

Deer Lake
6 Crescent St.
Deer Lake, NL A8A 1E9
Tel: 709-635-2451; *Fax:* 709-635-5857
deerlake@nf.aibn.com
www.town.deerlake.nf.ca
Municipal Type: Town
Incorporated: May 27, 1950; *Area:* 73.23 sq km
Population in 2011: 4,995
Provincial Electoral District(s): Humber Valley
Federal Electoral District(s): Long Range Mountains
Next Election: Sept. 26, 2017 (4 year terms)
Dean Ball, Mayor
Lori Humphrey, Clerk

Dover
P.O. Box 10
Dover, NL A0G 1X0
Tel: 709-537-2139; *Fax:* 709-537-2190
townofdover@persona.ca
Municipal Type: Town
Incorporated: July 13, 1971; *Area:* 11.55 sq km
Population in 2011: 673
Provincial Electoral District(s): Terra Nova
Federal Electoral District(s): Bonavista-Burin-Trinity
Next Election: Sept. 26, 2017 (4 year terms)
Tony R. Keats, Mayor
Yvonne Collins, Clerk

Duntara
P.O. Box 6
Duntara, NL A0C 1M0
Municipal Type: Town
Incorporated: Nov. 14, 1961; *Area:* 17.78 sq km
Population in 2011: 46
Provincial Electoral District(s): Bonavista South
Federal Electoral District(s): Bonavista-Burin-Trinity
Next Election: Sept. 26, 2017 (4 year terms)
Crystal Martin, Clerk

Eastport
P.O. Box 119
Eastport, NL A0G 1Z0
Tel: 709-677-2161; *Fax:* 709-677-2144
info@eastport.ca
www.eastport.ca
Municipal Type: Town
Incorporated: Oct. 20, 1959; *Area:* 18.64 sq km
Population in 2011: 482
Provincial Electoral District(s): Terra Nova
Federal Electoral District(s): Bonavista-Burin-Trinity
Next Election: Sept. 26, 2017 (4 year terms)
Genevieve Squire, Mayor
Cynthia Bull, Clerk

Elliston
P.O. Box 115
Elliston, NL A0C 1N0
Tel: 709-468-2649; *Fax:* 709-468-2867
town_elliston@yahoo.ca
www.townofelliston.ca
Municipal Type: Town
Incorporated: June 15, 1965; *Area:* 10.05 sq km
Population in 2011: 337
Provincial Electoral District(s): Bonavista South
Federal Electoral District(s): Bonavista-Burin-Trinity
Next Election: Sept. 26, 2017 (4 year terms)
Derek Martin, Mayor
Donna Chaulk, Clerk

Embree
P.O. Box 81
General Delivery
Embree, NL A0G 2A0
Tel: 709-535-8712; *Fax:* 709-535-8716
Municipal Type: Town
Incorporated: Sept. 28, 1971; *Area:* 18.16 sq km
Population in 2011: 691
Provincial Electoral District(s): Lewisporte
Federal Electoral District(s): Coast of Bays-Central-Notre Dame
Next Election: Sept. 26, 2017 (4 year terms)
Wayne Purchase, Mayor
Maxine Lane, Clerk

Englee
P.O. Box 160
Englee, NL A0K 2J0
Tel: 709-866-2711; *Fax:* 709-866-2357
www.engleenl.ca
Municipal Type: Town
Incorporated: Dec. 23, 1948; *Area:* 28.76 sq km
Population in 2011: 583
Provincial Electoral District(s): The Straits & White Bay North
Federal Electoral District(s): Long Range Mountains
Next Election: Sept. 26, 2017 (4 year terms)
Rudy Porter, Mayor
Doris Randell, Clerk

English Harbour East
P.O. Box 21
General Delivery
English Harbour East, NL A0E 1M0
Tel: 709-245-4556; *Fax:* 709-245-4556
Municipal Type: Town
Incorporated: Feb. 5, 1974; *Area:* 3.2 sq km
Population in 2011: 147
Provincial Electoral District(s): Bellevue
Federal Electoral District(s): Bonavista-Burin-Trinity
Next Election: Sept. 26, 2017 (4 year terms)
Maxine Hackett, Mayor
Barbara Byrd, Clerk

Fermeuse
General Delivery
Fermeuse, NL A0A 2G0
Tel: 709-363-2400; *Fax:* 709-363-2308
townoffermeuse@gmail.com
Municipal Type: Town
Incorporated: Nov. 28, 1967; *Area:* 38.73 sq km
Population in 2011: 323
Provincial Electoral District(s): Ferryland
Federal Electoral District(s): Avalon
Next Election: Sept. 26, 2017 (4 year terms)
Perry Oates, Mayor
Marsha Kenny, Clerk

Ferryland
P.O. Box 75
Ferryland, NL A0A 2H0
Tel: 709-432-2127; *Fax:* 709-432-2209
town.ferryland@nf.aibn.com
Municipal Type: Town
Incorporated: Oct. 19, 1971; *Area:* 13.62 sq km
Population in 2011: 465
Provincial Electoral District(s): Ferryland
Federal Electoral District(s): Avalon
Next Election: Sept. 26, 2017 (4 year terms)
Roddy Paul, Mayor
Doris Kavanagh, Clerk

Flatrock
663 Wind Gap Rd.
Flatrock, NL A1K 1C7
Tel: 709-437-6312; *Fax:* 709-437-6311
info@townofflatrock.com
www.townofflatrock.com
Municipal Type: Town
Incorporated: Oct. 31, 1975; *Area:* 18.12 sq km
Population in 2011: 1,457
Provincial Electoral District(s): Cape St. Francis
Federal Electoral District(s): St. John's East
Next Election: Sept. 26, 2017 (4 year terms)
Darin Thorne, Mayor
Diane Stamp, Clerk

Fleur de Lys
General Delivery
Fleur de Lys, NL A0K 2M0
Tel: 709-253-3131; *Fax:* 709-253-2146
fleurdelys@xplonet.ca
Municipal Type: Town
Incorporated: April 18, 1967; *Area:* 39.77 sq km
Population in 2011: 265
Provincial Electoral District(s): Baie Verte
Federal Electoral District(s): Coast of Bays-Central-Notre Dame
Next Election: Sept. 26, 2017 (4 year terms)
Millie Walsh, Mayor
Ester Lewis, Clerk

Flower's Cove
P.O. Box 149
Flowers Cove, NL A0K 2N0
Tel: 709-456-2124; *Fax:* 709-456-2124
townofflowerscove@nf.aibn.net
Municipal Type: Town
Incorporated: Dec. 12, 1961; *Area:* 7.64 sq km
Population in 2011: 308
Provincial Electoral District(s): The Straits & White Bay North
Federal Electoral District(s): Long Range Mountains
Next Election: Sept. 26, 2017 (4 year terms)
Keith Billard, Mayor
Bruce Way, Clerk

Fogo Island
P.O. Box 2
6 Centre Island Rd. South, Hwy. 333
Fogo Island Centre, NL A0G 2X0
Tel: 709-266-1320; *Fax:* 709-266-1323
info@townoffogoisland.ca
www.townoffogoisland.ca
Municipal Type: Town
Incorporated: March 1, 2011; *Area:* 237.65 sq km
Population in 2011: 2,395
Provincial Electoral District(s): The Isles of Notre Dame
Federal Electoral District(s): Coast of Bays-Central-Notre Dame
Next Election: Sept. 27, 2017 (4 year terms)
Note: Effective Dec. 2010, the towns of Fogo, Joe Batt's Arm-Barr'd Islands-Shoal Bay, Seldom-Little Seldom, Tilting & Fogo Island Region amalgamated to form the new Town of Fogo Island.
Andrew Shea, Mayor
Blanche Bennett, Clerk

Forteau
P.O. Box 99
Forteau, NL A0K 2P0
Tel: 709-931-2241; *Fax:* 709-931-2037
gflynn2006@hotmail.com
Municipal Type: Town
Incorporated: Dec. 7, 1971; *Area:* 7.44 sq km
Population in 2011: 429
Provincial Electoral District(s): Cartwright-L'Anse au Clair
Federal Electoral District(s): Labrador
Next Election: Sept. 26, 2017 (4 year terms)
Wilson Belbin, Mayor
Gail Flynn, Clerk

Fortune
P.O. Box 159
Fortune, NL A0E 1P0
Tel: 709-832-2810; *Fax:* 709-832-2210
fortune@nf.aibn.com
www.townoffortune.ca
Municipal Type: Town
Incorporated: Sept. 3, 1946; *Area:* 54.85 sq km
Population in 2011: 1,442
Provincial Electoral District(s): Grand Bank
Federal Electoral District(s): Bonavista-Burin-Trinity
Next Election: Sept. 26, 2017 (4 year terms)
Charles Penwell, Mayor

Debbie Hillier, Clerk

Fox Cove-Mortier
PO Box 17, Site 25, RR#1
Fox Cove-Mortier, NL A0E 1E0
Tel: 709-891-1500; *Fax:* 709-891-1999
Municipal Type: Town
Incorporated: June 2, 1970; *Area:* 25.6 sq km
Population in 2011: 333
Provincial Electoral District(s): Burin-Placentia West
Federal Electoral District(s): Bonavista-Burin-Trinity
Next Election: Sept. 26, 2017 (4 year terms)
Wanda Antle, Mayor
Gladys Kavanagh, Clerk

Fox Harbour
P.O. Box 64
Fox Harbour PB, NL A0B 1V0
Tel: 709-227-2271; *Fax:* 709-227-2271
Municipal Type: Town
Incorporated: Oct. 13, 1964; *Area:* 19.78 sq km
Population in 2011: 270
Provincial Electoral District(s): Placentia & St. Mary's
Federal Electoral District(s): Avalon
Next Election: Sept. 26, 2017 (4 year terms)
John Whiffen, Mayor
Audrey Rolls, Clerk

Frenchman's Cove
P.O. Box 20
Frenchman's Cove, NL A0E 1R0
Tel: 709-826-2190; *Fax:* 709-826-2190
townoffrenchmanscove@persona.ca
Municipal Type: Town
Incorporated: May 28, 1974; *Area:* 68.55 sq km
Population in 2011: 172
Provincial Electoral District(s): Grand Bank; Bay of Islands
Federal Electoral District(s): Bonavista-Burin-Trinity; Long Range Mountains
Next Election: Sept. 26, 2017 (4 year terms)
Donna Cluett, Mayor
Marsha Anderson, Clerk

Gallants
General Delivery
Gallants, NL A0L 1G0
Tel: 709-646-5353; *Fax:* 709-646-2840
Municipal Type: Town
Incorporated: Aug. 16, 1966; *Area:* 6.34 sq km
Population in 2011: 59
Provincial Electoral District(s): Humber West
Federal Electoral District(s): Long Range Mountains
Next Election: Sept. 26, 2017 (4 year terms)
Todd Brake, Mayor
Georgina Robinson, Clerk

Gambo
P.O. Box 250
Gambo, NL A0G 1T0
Tel: 709-674-4476; *Fax:* 709-674-5399
www.townofgambo.com
Municipal Type: Town
Incorporated: July 10, 1962; *Area:* 92.07 sq km
Population in 2011: 1,984
Provincial Electoral District(s): Terra Nova
Federal Electoral District(s): Bonavista-Burin-Trinity
Next Election: Sept. 26, 2017 (4 year terms)
Peter Lush, Mayor
Jean Blackwood, Clerk

Gander
100 Elizabeth Dr.
Gander, NL A1V 1G7
Tel: 709-651-2930; *Fax:* 709-256-5809
info@gandercanada.com
www.gandercanada.com
Municipal Type: Town
Incorporated: Dec. 28, 1954; *Area:* 104.25 sq km
Population in 2011: 11,054
Provincial Electoral District(s): Gander
Federal Electoral District(s): Coast of Bays-Central-Notre Dame
Next Election: Sept. 27, 2017 (4 year terms)
Claude Elliott, Mayor
Dermot Chafe, Chief Administrative Officer
Stephen Burbridge, Director, Municipal Works

Garnish
P.O. Box 70
Garnish, NL A0E 1T0
Tel: 709-826-2330; *Fax:* 709-826-2173
townclerk@eastlink.ca
www.townofgarnish.com
Municipal Type: Town
Incorporated: Aug. 25, 1971; *Area:* 39.11 sq km
Population in 2011: 545
Provincial Electoral District(s): Grand Bank
Federal Electoral District(s): Bonavista-Burin-Trinity
Next Election: Sept. 26, 2017 (4 year terms)
Reuben Noseworthy, Mayor
Ruth Cluett, Clerk

Gaskiers-Point La Haye
P.O. Box 434
St Marys, NL A0B 3B0
Tel: 709-525-2430; *Fax:* 709-525-2431
townofgaskiers@nf.aibn.com
Municipal Type: Town
Incorporated: Aug. 25, 1970; *Area:* 23.81 sq km
Population in 2011: 233
Provincial Electoral District(s): Placentia & St. Mary's
Federal Electoral District(s): Avalon
Next Election: Sept. 26, 2017 (4 year terms)
Pearl Kielly, Mayor
Jeanette Critch, Clerk

Gaultois
P.O. Box 101
Gaultois, NL A0H 1N0
Tel: 709-841-6546; *Fax:* 709-841-3521
townofgaultois@hotmail.com
Municipal Type: Town
Incorporated: Jan. 1, 1962; *Area:* 4.33 sq km
Population in 2011: 179
Provincial Electoral District(s): Fortune Bay-Cape La Hune
Federal Electoral District(s): Coast of Bays-Central-Notre Dame
Next Election: Sept. 26, 2017 (4 year terms)
Gordon Hunt, Mayor
Marcella Drover, Clerk

Gillams
P.O. Box 3968
RR#2
Corner Brook, NL A2H 6B9
Tel: 709-783-2800; *Fax:* 709-783-2671
townofgillams@nf.aibn.com
www.gillams.net
Municipal Type: Town
Incorporated: Aug. 17, 1971; *Area:* 6.7 sq km
Population in 2011: 407
Provincial Electoral District(s): Bay of Islands
Federal Electoral District(s): Long Range Mountains
Next Election: Sept. 26, 2017 (4 year terms)
Joy Burt, Mayor
Shelly Penney, Clerk

Glenburnie-Birchy Head-Shoal Brook
General Delivery
Birchy Head, NL A0K 1K0
Tel: 709-453-7220; *Fax:* 709-453-7220
gbstownoffice@eastlink.ca
Municipal Type: Town
Incorporated: Sept. 1, 1978; *Area:* 6.57 sq km
Population in 2011: 258
Provincial Electoral District(s): Humber Valley
Federal Electoral District(s): Long Range Mountains
Next Election: Sept. 26, 2017 (4 year terms)
Clarice Bursey, Mayor
Myrna Hynes, Clerk

Glenwood
P.O. Box 130
Glenwood, NL A0G 2K0
Tel: 709-679-2159; *Fax:* 709-679-5470
townofglenwood@hotmail.com
Municipal Type: Town
Incorporated: June 12, 1962; *Area:* 6.92 sq km
Population in 2011: 791
Provincial Electoral District(s): Gander
Federal Electoral District(s): Coast of Bays-Central-Notre Dame
Next Election: Sept. 26, 2017 (4 year terms)
Darren Bursey, Mayor
Susan Gillingham, Clerk

Glovertown
P.O. Box 224
Glovertown, NL A0G 2L0
Tel: 709-533-2351; *Fax:* 709-533-2225
glovertowncounc@eastlink.ca
www.glovertown.net
Municipal Type: Town
Incorporated: Dec. 28, 1954; *Area:* 70.33 sq km
Population in 2011: 2,122
Provincial Electoral District(s): Terra Nova
Federal Electoral District(s): Bonavista-Burin-Trinity
Next Election: Sept. 26, 2017 (4 year terms)
Douglas Churchill, Mayor
Joanne Perry, Clerk

Goose Cove East
P.O. Box 8
St. Anthony, NL A0K 4S0
Tel: 709-454-8393; *Fax:* 709-454-8393
Municipal Type: Town
Incorporated: Oct. 19, 1971; *Area:* 2.69 sq km
Population in 2011: 211
Provincial Electoral District(s): The Straits & White Bay North
Federal Electoral District(s): Long Range Mountains
Next Election: Sept. 26, 2017 (4 year terms)
Marie Reardon, Mayor
Patricia Reardon, Clerk

Grand Bank
P.O. Box 640
56 Main St.
Grand Bank, NL A0E 1W0
Tel: 709-832-1600; *Fax:* 709-832-1636
townofgrandbank@townofgrandbank.net
www.townofgrandbank.com
Municipal Type: Town
Incorporated: Dec. 28, 1943; *Area:* 16.97 sq km
Population in 2011: 2,415
Provincial Electoral District(s): Grand Bank
Federal Electoral District(s): Bonavista-Burin-Trinity
Next Election: Sept. 26, 2017 (4 year terms)
Rex Matthews, Mayor
Cathy Follett, Clerk

Grand Le Pierre
P.O. Box 35
Grand Le Pierre, NL A0E 1Y0
Tel: 709-662-2702; *Fax:* 709-662-2076
towncouncilglp@hotmail.ca
Municipal Type: Town
Incorporated: June 17, 1969; *Area:* 153.59 sq km
Population in 2011: 260
Provincial Electoral District(s): Bellevue
Federal Electoral District(s): Bonavista-Burin-Trinity
Next Election: Sept. 26, 2017 (4 year terms)
Willoughby Bolt, Mayor
Rhonda Bolt, Clerk

Greenspond
P.O. Box 100
Greenspond, NL A0G 2N0
Tel: 709-269-3111; *Fax:* 709-269-3191
greenspond@eastlink.ca
Municipal Type: Town
Incorporated: Aug. 15, 1951; *Area:* 2.85 sq km
Population in 2011: 305
Provincial Electoral District(s): Bonavista North
Federal Electoral District(s): Bonavista-Burin-Trinity
Next Election: Sept. 26, 2017 (4 year terms)
Kevin Blackwood, Mayor
Derrick Bragg, Clerk

Hampden
P.O. Box 9
Hampden, NL A0K 2Y0
Tel: 709-455-4212; *Fax:* 709-455-2117
townofhampden@eastlink.ca
Municipal Type: Town
Incorporated: Dec. 8, 1959; *Area:* 32.97 sq km
Population in 2011: 457
Provincial Electoral District(s): Humber Valley
Federal Electoral District(s): Long Range Mountains
Next Election: Sept. 26, 2017 (4 year terms)
Jamie Goodyear, Mayor
Ruth Jenkins, Clerk

Hant's Harbour
P.O. Box 40
Hants Harbour, NL A0B 1Y0
Tel: 709-586-2741; *Fax:* 709-586-2680
townofhantsharbour@hotmail.ca
Municipal Type: Town
Incorporated: Oct. 13, 1970; *Area:* 32.31 sq km
Population in 2011: 346
Provincial Electoral District(s): Trinity-Bay de Verde
Federal Electoral District(s): Bonavista-Burin-Trinity
Next Election: Sept. 26, 2017 (4 year terms)
Judy King, Mayor
Betty Tuck, Clerk

Happy Adventure
PO Box 1, Site 2
Happy Adventure, NL A0G 1Z0
Tel: 709-677-2593; *Fax:* 709-677-2594
happyadventure@nf.aibn.com
Municipal Type: Town
Incorporated: May 10, 1960; *Area:* 9.62 sq km
Population in 2011: 219
Provincial Electoral District(s): Terra Nova
Federal Electoral District(s): Bonavista-Burin-Trinity
Next Election: Sept. 26, 2017 (4 year terms)
James Warren, Mayor
Judy Powell, Clerk

Happy Valley-Goose Bay
P.O. Box 40 B
Happy Valley-Goose Bay, NL A0P 1E0
Tel: 709-896-3321; *Fax:* 709-896-9454
www.happyvalley-goosebay.com
Municipal Type: Town
Incorporated: March 15, 1955; *Area:* 305.85 sq km
Population in 2011: 7,552
Provincial Electoral District(s): Lake Melville
Federal Electoral District(s): Labrador
Next Election: Sept. 26, 2017 (4 year terms)
Jamie Snook, Mayor
Wyman Jacque, Town Manager

Harbour Breton
P.O. Box 130
Harbour Breton, NL A0H 1P0
Tel: 709-885-2354; *Fax:* 709-885-2095
bernice@harbourbreton.com
www.harbourbreton.com
Municipal Type: Town
Incorporated: Dec. 16, 1952; *Area:* 13.74 sq km
Population in 2011: 1,711
Provincial Electoral District(s): Fortune Bay-Cape La Hune
Federal Electoral District(s): Coast of Bays-Central-Notre Dame
Next Election: Sept. 26, 2017 (4 year terms)
Roy G. Drake, Mayor
Bernice Herritt, Clerk

Harbour Grace
P.O. Box 310
Harbour Grace, NL A0A 2M0
Tel: 709-596-3631; *Fax:* 709-596-1991
thg@nf.sympatico.ca
www.hrgrace.ca
Municipal Type: Town
Incorporated: July 10, 1945; *Area:* 33.71 sq km
Population in 2011: 3,131
Provincial Electoral District(s): Carbonear-Harbour Grace
Federal Electoral District(s): Avalon
Next Election: Sept. 26, 2017 (4 year terms)
Terry Barnes, Mayor
Michael Saccary, Clerk

Harbour Main-Chapel Cove-Lakeview
P.O. Box 40
362 Conception Bay Hwy.
Harbour Main, NL A0A 2P0
Tel: 709-229-6822; *Fax:* 709-229-6234
hmcouncil@eastlink.ca
Municipal Type: Town
Incorporated: June 1, 1965; *Area:* 21.05 sq km
Population in 2011: 1,083
Provincial Electoral District(s): Harbour Main-Whitbourne
Federal Electoral District(s): Avalon
Next Election: Sept. 26, 2017 (4 year terms)
Raymond Parsley, Mayor
Marian Hawco, Clerk

Hare Bay
P.O. Box 130
Hare Bay BB, NL A0G 2P0
Tel: 709-537-2187; *Fax:* 709-537-2987
harebaytowncouncil@bellaliant.com
Municipal Type: Town
Incorporated: Oct. 20, 1964; *Area:* 34.06 sq km
Population in 2011: 1,031
Provincial Electoral District(s): Terra Nova
Federal Electoral District(s): Bonavista-Burin-Trinity
Next Election: Sept. 26, 2017 (4 year terms)
James Payne, Mayor
George R. Collins, Clerk

Hawke's Bay
P.O. Box 58
Hawkes Bay, NL A0K 3B0
Tel: 709-248-5216; *Fax:* 709-248-5201
hbcouncil@nf.aibn.com
Municipal Type: Town
Incorporated: Aug. 21, 1956; *Area:* 46.55 sq km
Population in 2011: 338
Provincial Electoral District(s): St. Barbe
Federal Electoral District(s): Long Range Mountains
Next Election: Sept. 26, 2017 (4 year terms)
Lloyd Bennett, Mayor
Emily Smith, Clerk

Heart's Content
P.O. Box 31
Hearts Content, NL A0B 1Z0
Tel: 709-583-2491; *Fax:* 709-583-2226
heartscontent@persona.ca
www.heartscontent.ca
Municipal Type: Town
Incorporated: Aug. 25, 1967; *Area:* 62.81 sq km
Population in 2011: 375
Provincial Electoral District(s): Trinity-Bay de Verde
Federal Electoral District(s): Bonavista-Burin-Trinity
Next Election: Sept. 26, 2017 (4 year terms)
Fred Cumby, Mayor
Alice Cumby, Clerk

Heart's Delight-Islington
P.O. Box 129
Hearts Delight, NL A0B 2A0
Tel: 709-588-2708; *Fax:* 709-588-2235
heartsdelightislington@persona.ca
Municipal Type: Town
Incorporated: Oct. 24, 1972; *Area:* 27.27 sq km
Population in 2011: 704
Provincial Electoral District(s): Trinity-Bay de Verde
Federal Electoral District(s): Bonavista-Burin-Trinity
Next Election: Sept. 26, 2017 (4 year terms)
Denzil Sheppard, Mayor
Emily Harnum, Clerk

Heart's Desire
P.O. Box 10
Hearts Desire, NL A0B 2B0
Tel: 709-588-2280; *Fax:* 709-588-2343
townofheartsdesire@persona.ca
Municipal Type: Town
Incorporated: Sept. 28, 1971; *Area:* 17.27 sq km
Population in 2011: 223
Provincial Electoral District(s): Trinity-Bay de Verde
Federal Electoral District(s): Bonavista-Burin-Trinity
Next Election: Sept. 26, 2017 (4 year terms)
Francis St. George, Mayor
Eleanor Andrews, Clerk

Hermitage-Sandyville
P.O. Box 160
Hermitage, NL A0H 1S0
Tel: 709-883-2343; *Fax:* 709-883-2150
jsimms@nf.aibn.com
www.hermitage-sandyville.ca
Municipal Type: Town
Incorporated: Oct. 22, 1960; *Area:* 28.91 sq km
Population in 2011: 450
Provincial Electoral District(s): Fortune Bay-Cape La Hune
Federal Electoral District(s): Coast of Bays-Central-Notre Dame
Next Election: Sept. 26, 2017 (4 year terms)
Stephen Crewe, Mayor
Josephine (Josie) Rideout Simms, Clerk

Holyrood
P.O. Box 100
Holyrood, NL A0A 2R0
Tel: 709-229-7252; *Fax:* 709-229-7269
holyrood.ca
Municipal Type: Town
Incorporated: March 23, 1969; *Area:* 125.57 sq km
Population in 2011: 1,995
Provincial Electoral District(s): Conception Bay South
Federal Electoral District(s): Avalon
Next Election: Sept. 26, 2017 (4 year terms)
Gary Goobie, Mayor
Marie Searle, Clerk

Hopedale
P.O. Box 189
Hopedale, NL A0P 1G0
Tel: 709-933-3864; *Fax:* 709-933-3800
towncouncilhopedale@nf.aibn.com
Municipal Type: Town
Incorporated: Sept. 30, 1969; *Area:* 3.36 sq km
Population in 2011: 556
Provincial Electoral District(s): Torngat Mountains
Federal Electoral District(s): Labrador
Next Election: Sept. 26, 2017 (4 year terms)
Wayne Piercey, Mayor
Jullian Mistuk, Clerk

Howley
P.O. Box 40
Howley, NL A0K 3E0
Tel: 709-635-5555; *Fax:* 709-635-5850
howleynewfoundland.com
Municipal Type: Town
Incorporated: Feb. 4, 1958; *Area:* 19.91 sq km
Population in 2011: 221
Provincial Electoral District(s): Humber Valley
Federal Electoral District(s): Long Range Mountains
Next Election: Sept. 26, 2017 (4 year terms)
Calvin Samms, Mayor
Blanche Gilley, Clerk

Hughes Brook
P.O. Box 2527
RR#2
Corner Brook, NL A2H 6B9
Tel: 709-783-2921; *Fax:* 709-783-3039
info@hughesbrook.com
www.hughesbrook.com
Municipal Type: Town
Incorporated: July 25, 1975; *Area:* 1.6 sq km
Population in 2011: 231
Provincial Electoral District(s): Bay of Islands
Federal Electoral District(s): Long Range Mountains
Next Election: Sept. 26, 2017 (4 year terms)
Vaughan Hefford, Mayor
Gloria Loder, Clerk

Humber Arm South
P.O. Box 10
Benoits Cove, NL A0L 1A0
Tel: 709-789-2981; *Fax:* 709-789-2918
info@humberarmsouth.com
www.humberarmsouth.com
Municipal Type: Town
Incorporated: June 15, 1971; *Area:* 65.05 sq km
Population in 2011: 1,681
Provincial Electoral District(s): Bay of Islands
Federal Electoral District(s): Long Range Mountains
Next Election: Sept. 26, 2017 (4 year terms)
Arch Mitchell, Mayor
Marion Evoy, Clerk

Indian Bay
10-18 Municipal Cres.
Indian Bay, NL A0G 2V0
Tel: 709-678-2727; *Fax:* 709-678-2727
townofindianbay@hotmail.com
Municipal Type: Town
Incorporated: Oct. 19, 1971; *Area:* 86.24 sq km
Population in 2011: 174
Provincial Electoral District(s): Bonavista North
Federal Electoral District(s): Bonavista-Burin-Trinity
Next Election: Sept. 26, 2017 (4 year terms)
Maxwell Pickett, Mayor
Elaine Feltham, Clerk

Irishtown-Summerside
P.O. Box 2795
RR#2
Corner Brook, NL A2H 6B9
Tel: 709-783-2146; *Fax:* 709-783-3220
irishtownsummerside@persona.ca
Municipal Type: Town
Incorporated: Jan. 1, 1991; *Area:* 11.89 sq km
Population in 2011: 1,428
Provincial Electoral District(s): Bay of Islands
Federal Electoral District(s): Long Range Mountains
Next Election: Sept. 26, 2017 (4 year terms)
Tony Blanchard, Mayor
Rita Blanchard, Clerk

Isle aux Morts
P.O. Box 110
11 Legallais St.
Isle-aux-Morts, NL A0M 1J0
Tel: 709-698-3441; *Fax:* 709-698-3449
info@isleauxmorts.ca
www.isleauxmorts.ca
Municipal Type: Town
Incorporated: Nov. 5, 1956; *Area:* 7.66 sq km
Population in 2011: 619
Provincial Electoral District(s): Burgeo & La Poile
Federal Electoral District(s): Long Range Mountains
Next Election: Sept. 26, 2017 (4 year terms)
Steven LeFrense, Mayor
Lydia Francis, Clerk

Jackson's Arm
P.O. Box 10
Jacksons Arm, NL A0K 3H0
Tel: 709-459-5151; *Fax:* 709-459-3173
townofjackson@explornet.ca
Municipal Type: Town
Incorporated: June 19, 1982; *Area:* 7.02 sq km
Population in 2011: 323
Provincial Electoral District(s): Humber Valley
Federal Electoral District(s): Long Range Mountains
Next Election: Sept. 26, 2017 (4 year terms)
Vincent Parsons, Mayor
Carmel Wicks, Clerk

Keels
P.O. Box 30
Keels, NL A0C 1R0
Tel: 709-447-3127; *Fax:* 709-447-6186
Municipal Type: Town
Incorporated: June 14, 1966; *Area:* 6.54 sq km
Population in 2011: 61
Provincial Electoral District(s): Bonavista South
Federal Electoral District(s): Bonavista-Burin-Trinity
Next Election: Sept. 26, 2017 (4 year terms)
Annie Fitzgerald, Mayor
Crystal Taylor, Clerk

King's Cove
General Delivery
Kings Cove, NL A0C 1S0
Municipal Type: Town
Incorporated: June 14,1966; *Area:* 21.48 sq km
Population in 2011: 111
Provincial Electoral District(s): Bonavista South
Federal Electoral District(s): Bonavista-Burin-Trinity; Coast of Bays-Central-Notre Dame; Labrador
Next Election: Sept. 26, 2017 (4 year terms)
Tom Maddox, Mayor
Nora Ricketts, Clerk

King's Point
P.O. Box 10
Kings Point, NL A0J 1H0
Tel: 709-268-3838; *Fax:* 709-268-3856
kpcouncil@eastlink.ca
Municipal Type: Town
Incorporated: Oct. 1, 1957; *Area:* 46.31 sq km
Population in 2011: 675
Provincial Electoral District(s): Baie Verte
Federal Electoral District(s): Coast of Bays-Central-Notre Dame
Next Election: Sept. 26, 2017 (4 year terms)
Perry Gillingham, Mayor
Marie Cumming, Clerk

Kippens
2 Juniper Ave.
Kippens, NL A2N 3H8
Tel: 709-643-5281; *Fax:* 709-643-9773
kippens@nf.aibn.com
www.kippens.ca
Municipal Type: Town
Incorporated: Dec. 31, 1968; *Area:* 14.32 sq km
Population in 2011: 1,815
Provincial Electoral District(s): Port au Port
Federal Electoral District(s): Long Range Mountains
Next Election: Sept. 26, 2017 (4 year terms)
Paul Noseworthy, Mayor
Debbie Cormier, Clerk

Labrador City
P.O. Box 280
Labrador City, NL A2V 2K5
Tel: 709-944-5537; *Fax:* 709-944-2810
www.labradorwest.com
Municipal Type: Town
Incorporated: June 27, 1961; *Area:* 38.83 sq km
Population in 2011: 7,367
Provincial Electoral District(s): Labrador West
Federal Electoral District(s): Labrador
Next Election: Sept. 26, 2017 (4 year terms)
Karen Oldford, Mayor
Cathy Coish, Clerk

Lamaline
P.O. Box 40
Lamaline, NL A0E 2C0
Tel: 709-857-2341; *Fax:* 709-857-2210
barbking70@hotmail.com
Municipal Type: Town
Incorporated: April 24, 1963; *Area:* 81.69 sq km
Population in 2011: 286
Provincial Electoral District(s): Grand Bank
Federal Electoral District(s): Bonavista-Burin-Trinity
Next Election: Sept. 26, 2017 (4 year terms)
Maureen Fleming, Mayor
Barbara King, Clerk

Lark Harbour
P.O. Box 40
Lark Harbour, NL A0L 1H0
Tel: 709-681-2270; *Fax:* 709-681-2900
larkharbourtowncouncil@nf.aibn.com
yorkharbourlarkharbour.com
Municipal Type: Town
Incorporated: Jan. 22, 1974; *Area:* 12.92 sq km
Population in 2011: 510
Provincial Electoral District(s): Bay of Islands
Federal Electoral District(s): Long Range Mountains
Next Election: Sept. 26, 2017 (4 year terms)
John Parsons, Mayor
Joanne Pot, Co-Clerk
Peggy Sheppard, Co-Clerk

Lawn
P.O. Box 29
Lawn, NL A0E 2E0
Tel: 709-873-2439; *Fax:* 709-873-3006
townoflawn@eastlink.ca
Municipal Type: Town
Incorporated: Sept. 30, 1952; *Area:* 3.61 sq km
Population in 2011: 672
Provincial Electoral District(s): Grand Bank
Federal Electoral District(s): Bonavista-Burin-Trinity
Next Election: Sept. 26, 2017 (4 year terms)
John Strang, Mayor
Wendy Jarvis, Clerk

Leading Tickles
P.O. Box 39
Leading Tickles West, NL A0H 1T0
Tel: 709-483-2180; *Fax:* 709-483-2185
leadingtickles@nf.aibn.com
Municipal Type: Town
Incorporated: July 11, 1961; *Area:* 26.73 sq km
Population in 2011: 337
Provincial Electoral District(s): Exploits
Federal Electoral District(s): Coast of Bays-Central-Notre Damed
Next Election: Sept. 26, 2017 (4 year terms)
Fabian Chippett, Mayor
Doreen Haggett, Clerk

Lewin's Cove
P.O. Box 40
Lewins Cove, NL A0E 2G0
Tel: 709-894-4777; *Fax:* 709-894-4952
townoflewinscove@bellaliant.com
Municipal Type: Town
Incorporated: May 1, 1973; *Area:* 6.52 sq km
Population in 2011: 555
Provincial Electoral District(s): Grand Bank
Federal Electoral District(s): Bonavista-Burin-Trinity
Next Election: Sept. 26, 2017 (4 year terms)
John Moore, Mayor
Barbara Mullett, Clerk

Lewisporte
P.O. Box 219
Lewisporte, NL A0G 3A0
Tel: 709-535-2737; *Fax:* 709-535-2695
info@lewisportecanada.com
www.lewisportecanada.com
Municipal Type: Town
Incorporated: July 2, 1946; *Area:* 36.91 sq km
Population in 2011: 3,483
Provincial Electoral District(s): Lewisporte
Federal Electoral District(s): Coast of Bays-Central-Notre Dame
Next Election: Sept. 26, 2017 (4 year terms)
Brian Sceviour, Mayor
Elaine Bursey, Clerk

Little Bay
P.O. Box 40
Little Bay, NL A0J 1J0
Tel: 709-267-3200; *Fax:* 709-267-3200
Municipal Type: Town
Incorporated: April 19, 1966; *Area:* 1.45 sq km
Population in 2011: 108
Provincial Electoral District(s): Baie Verte
Federal Electoral District(s): Bonavista-Burin-Trinity; Coast of Bays-Central-Notre Dame
Next Election: Sept. 26, 2017 (4 year terms)
Phyllis Simms, Mayor
Linda Grothe, Clerk

Little Bay East
P.O. Box 15
Little Bay East, NL A0E 2J0
Tel: 709-461-2724; *Fax:* 709-461-2724
Municipal Type: Town
Incorporated: April 27, 1979; *Area:* 1.48 sq km
Population in 2011: 130
Provincial Electoral District(s): Bellevue
Federal Electoral District(s): Bonavista-Burin-Trinity
Next Election: Sept. 26, 2017 (4 year terms)
William Bungay, Mayor
Gail Clarke, Clerk
Donna Simon, Supervisor, Accounting

Little Bay Islands
P.O. Box 64
Little Bay Islands, NL A0J 1K0
Tel: 709-626-3511; *Fax:* 709-626-3512
lbtowncouncil@eastlink.ca
Municipal Type: Town
Incorporated: Oct. 25, 1955; *Area:* 7.16 sq km
Population in 2011: 70
Provincial Electoral District(s): Baie Verte
Federal Electoral District(s): Coast of Bays-Central-Notre Dame
Next Election: Sept. 26, 2017 (4 year terms)
Maxine Oxford, Clerk

Little Burnt Bay
P.O. Box 40
Little Burnt Bay, NL A0G 3B0
Tel: 709-535-6415; *Fax:* 709-535-6490
lbbtowncouncil@bellaliant.com
Municipal Type: Town
Incorporated: Sept. 19, 1975; *Area:* 8.5 sq km
Population in 2011: 294
Provincial Electoral District(s): Lewisporte
Federal Electoral District(s): Coast of Bays-Central-Notre Dame
Next Election: Sept. 26, 2017 (4 year terms)
Laverne Suppa, Mayor
Maisie Wells, Clerk

Logy Bay-Middle Cove-Outer Cove
744 Logy Bay Rd.
Logy Bay, NL A1K 3B5
Tel: 709-726-7930; *Fax:* 709-726-2178
office@lbmcoc.ca
Municipal Type: Town
Incorporated: Sept. 1, 1986; *Area:* 16.98 sq km
Population in 2011: 2,098
Provincial Electoral District(s): Cape St. Francis
Federal Electoral District(s): St. John's East
Next Election: Sept. 26, 2017 (4 year terms)
John Kennedy, Mayor
Richard Roache, Clerk

Long Harbour-Mount Arlington Heights
P.O. Box 40
Long Harbour, NL A0B 2J0
Tel: 709-228-2920; *Fax:* 709-228-2900
towncouncil@longharbour.net
Municipal Type: Town
Incorporated: Oct. 22, 1968; *Area:* 18.41 sq km
Population in 2011: 298
Provincial Electoral District(s): Bellevue
Federal Electoral District(s): Avalon
Next Election: Sept. 26, 2017 (4 year terms)
Gary Keating, Mayor
Kathleen Griffiths, Clerk

Lord's Cove
PO Box 21, Site 11
Lord's Cove, NL A0E 2C0
Tel: 709-857-2316
Municipal Type: Town
Incorporated: May 17, 1966; *Area:* 30.91 sq km
Population in 2011: 175
Provincial Electoral District(s): Grand Bank
Federal Electoral District(s): Bonavista-Burin-Trinity
Next Election: Sept. 26, 2017 (4 year terms)
Natasha Fitzpatrick, Mayor
Eileen Harnett, Clerk

Lourdes
P.O. Box 29
Lourdes, NL A0N 1R0
Tel: 709-642-5812; *Fax:* 709-642-5558
townoflourdes@yahoo.ca
Municipal Type: Town
Incorporated: July 17, 1969; *Area:* 8.1 sq km
Population in 2011: 532
Provincial Electoral District(s): Port au Port

Federal Electoral District(s): Long Range Mountains
Next Election: Sept. 26, 2017 (4 year terms)
Henry Gaudon, Mayor
Angela Young, Clerk

Lumsden
P.O. Box 100
Lumsden, NL A0G 3E0
Tel: 709-530-2309; *Fax:* 709-530-2144
townoflumsden@nf.aibn.com
www.lumsdennl.ca
Municipal Type: Town
Incorporated: April 16, 1968; *Area:* 20.43 sq km
Population in 2011: 545
Provincial Electoral District(s): Bonavista North
Federal Electoral District(s): Bonavista-Burin-Trinity
Next Election: Sept. 26, 2017 (4 year terms)
Rosalind Gibbons, Mayor
Jeanie Stokes, Clerk

Lushes Bight-Beaumont-Beaumont North
P.O. Box 40
Beaumont, NL A0J 1A0
Tel: 709-264-3271; *Fax:* 709-264-3191
beaumont@xplornet.ca
Municipal Type: Town
Incorporated: Oct. 15, 1968; *Area:* 34.38 sq km
Population in 2011: 220
Provincial Electoral District(s): Windsor-Springdale
Federal Electoral District(s): Coast of Bays-Central-Notre Dame
Next Election: Sept. 26, 2017 (4 year terms)
Barbara Colbourne, Mayor
Jacqueline Morgan, Clerk

Main Brook
P.O. Box 130
Main Brook, NL A0K 3N0
Tel: 709-865-6561; *Fax:* 709-865-3279
townofmainbrook@nf.aibn.com
Municipal Type: Town
Incorporated: June 1, 1948; *Area:* 28.51 sq km
Population in 2011: 265
Provincial Electoral District(s): The Straits & White Bay North
Federal Electoral District(s): Long Range Mountains
Next Election: Sept. 26, 2017 (4 year terms)
Leander Pilgrim, Mayor
Sherry Reid, Clerk

Makkovik
P.O. Box 132
Makkovik, NL A0P 1J0
Tel: 709-923-2221; *Fax:* 709-923-2126
info@makkovik.ca
www.makkovik.ca
Municipal Type: Town
Incorporated: April 7, 1970; *Area:* 1.97 sq km
Population in 2011: 361
Provincial Electoral District(s): Torngat Mountains
Federal Electoral District(s): Labrador
Next Election: Sept. 26, 2017 (4 year terms)
Herbert R. Jacque, Mayor
Doreen Winters, Clerk

Mary's Harbour
P.O. Box 134
Mary's Harbour, NL A0K 3P0
Tel: 709-921-6281; *Fax:* 709-921-6255
maryshbr@nf.aibn.com
Municipal Type: Town
Incorporated: April 11, 1975; *Area:* 38.16 sq km
Population in 2011: 383
Provincial Electoral District(s): Cartwright-L'Anse au Clair
Federal Electoral District(s): Labrador
Next Election: Sept. 26, 2017 (4 year terms)
Larry Rumbolt, Mayor
Glenys Rumbolt, Clerk

Marystown
P.O. Box 1118
Marystown, NL A0E 2M0
Tel: 709-279-1661; *Fax:* 709-279-2862
www.townofmarystown.com
Municipal Type: Town
Incorporated: Dec. 18, 1951; *Area:* 61.97 sq km
Population in 2011: 5,506
Provincial Electoral District(s): Burin-Placentia West
Federal Electoral District(s): Bonavista-Burin-Trinity
Next Election: Sept. 26, 2017 (4 year terms)
Sam Synard, Mayor
Dennis P. Kelly, Clerk & Manager

Massey Drive
85 Massey Dr.
Massey Drive, NL A2H 7A2
Tel: 709-634-2742; *Fax:* 709-634-2899
info@masseydrive.com
www.masseydrive.com
Municipal Type: Town
Incorporated: Sept. 28, 1971; *Area:* 2.48 sq km
Population in 2011: 1,412
Provincial Electoral District(s): Humber East
Federal Electoral District(s): Long Range Mountains
Next Election: Sept. 26, 2017 (4 year terms)
Gordon Davis, Mayor
Rodger Hunt, Town Manager/Clerk

McIvers
P.O. Box 4375
RR#2
Corner Brook, NL A2H 6B9
Tel: 709-688-2603; *Fax:* 709-688-2680
mciverscouncil@eastlink.ca
Municipal Type: Town
Incorporated: June 15, 1971; *Area:* 12.06 sq km
Population in 2011: 546
Provincial Electoral District(s): Bay of Islands
Federal Electoral District(s): Long Range Mountains
Next Election: Sept. 26, 2017 (4 year terms)
Warren Blanchard, Mayor
Bernice E. Parsons, Clerk

Meadows
P.O. Box 3529
RR#2
Corner Brook, NL A2H 6B9
Tel: 709-783-2339; *Fax:* 709-783-2501
townofmeadows@nf.aibn.com
Municipal Type: Town
Incorporated: Jan. 13, 1970; *Area:* 3.79 sq km
Population in 2011: 649
Provincial Electoral District(s): Bay of Islands
Federal Electoral District(s): Long Range Mountains
Next Election: Sept. 26, 2017 (4 year terms)
Kenneth March, Mayor
Joy Taylor, Clerk

Middle Arm
P.O. Box 51
Middle Arm, NL A0K 3R0
Tel: 709-252-2521; *Fax:* 709-252-2400
townofmiddlearm@nf.aibn.com
townofmiddlearm.com
Municipal Type: Town
Incorporated: Nov. 29, 1966; *Area:* 25.19 sq km
Population in 2011: 476
Provincial Electoral District(s): Baie Verte
Federal Electoral District(s): Avalon; Coast of Bays-Central-Notre Dame
Next Election: Sept. 26, 2017 (4 year terms)
Neville Robinson, Mayor, 709-252-2136
Loretta Budgell, Clerk

Miles Cove
General Delivery
Miles Cove, NL A0J 1L0
Tel: 709-652-3685; *Fax:* 709-652-3695
mctownhall@hotmail.com
milescove.tripod.com
Municipal Type: Town
Incorporated: Sept. 22, 1970; *Area:* 4.03 sq km
Population in 2011: 137
Provincial Electoral District(s): Windsor-Springdale
Federal Electoral District(s): Coast of Bays-Central-Notre Dame
Next Election: Sept. 26, 2017 (4 year terms)
Melvin Morey, Mayor
Grace Burton, Clerk

Millertown
P.O. Box 56
Millertown, NL A0H 1V0
Tel: 709-852-6216; *Fax:* 709-852-5431
townofmillertown@nf.aibn.com
www.communityofmillertown.ca
Municipal Type: Town
Incorporated: Dec. 15, 1959; *Area:* 3.24 sq km
Population in 2011: 99
Provincial Electoral District(s): Grand Falls-Buchans
Federal Electoral District(s): Coast of Bays-Central-Notre Dame
Next Election: Sept. 26, 2017 (4 year terms)
Charlie Fost, Mayor
Bonnie Warr, Clerk

Milltown-Head of Bay d'Espoir
P.O. Box 70
Milltown, NL A0H 1W0
Tel: 709-882-2232; *Fax:* 709-882-2636
townofmill@bellaliant.com
Municipal Type: Town
Incorporated: Dec. 16, 1952; *Area:* 25.02 sq km
Population in 2011: 789
Provincial Electoral District(s): Fortune Bay-Cape La Hune
Federal Electoral District(s): Coast of Bays-Central-Notre Dame
Next Election: Sept. 26, 2017 (4 year terms)
Jerry Kearley, Mayor
Kimberly Kendell, Clerk

Ming's Bight
PO Box 61, Site 1
Mings Bight, NL A0K 3S0
Tel: 709-254-6516; *Fax:* 709-254-7461
townmingsbight@xplornet.ca
Municipal Type: Town
Incorporated: June 6, 1970; *Area:* 3.78 sq km
Population in 2011: 333
Provincial Electoral District(s): Baie Verte
Federal Electoral District(s): Coast of Bays-Central-Notre Dame
Next Election: Sept. 26, 2017 (4 year terms)
Danny Regular, Mayor
Lacey Sacrey, Clerk

Morrisville
P.O. Box 19
Morrisville, NL A0H 1W0
Tel: 709-538-3138; *Fax:* 709-882-2831
Municipal Type: Town
Incorporated: June 1, 1971; *Area:* 14.26 sq km
Population in 2011: 117
Provincial Electoral District(s): Fortune Bay-Cape La Hune
Federal Electoral District(s): Coast of Bays-Central-Notre Dame
Next Election: Sept. 26, 2017 (4 year terms)
Shawn Nash, Mayor
Karl Kendell, Clerk

Mount Carmel-Mitchell's Brook-St. Catherines
General Delivery
Mount Carmel, NL A0B 2M0
Tel: 709-521-2040; *Fax:* 709-521-2258
mountcarmeltowncouncil@hotmail.com
Municipal Type: Town
Incorporated: Oct. 6, 1970; *Area:* 61.55 sq km
Population in 2011: 358
Provincial Electoral District(s): Placentia & St. Mary's
Federal Electoral District(s): Avalon
Next Election: Sept. 26, 2017 (4 year terms)
David Sorenson, Mayor
Susan Parrott, Clerk

Mount Moriah
P.O. Box 31
Mount Moriah, NL A0L 1J0
Tel: 709-785-5232; *Fax:* 709-785-5332
mtmoriahtowncouncil@nf.aibn.com
Municipal Type: Town
Incorporated: Oct. 12, 1971; *Area:* 15.71 sq km
Population in 2011: 785
Provincial Electoral District(s): Bay of Islands
Federal Electoral District(s): Long Range Mountains
Next Election: Sept. 26, 2017 (4 year terms)
James Park, Mayor
Carol Skeard, Clerk

Musgrave Harbour
P.O. Box 159
Musgrave Harbour, NL A0G 3J0
Tel: 709-655-2119; *Fax:* 709-655-2064
musgravetowncouncil@nf.aibn.com
www.musgraveharbour.com
Municipal Type: Town
Incorporated: Jan. 1, 1954; *Area:* 69.94 sq km
Population in 2011: 1,053
Provincial Electoral District(s): Bonavista North
Federal Electoral District(s): Bonavista-Burin-Trinity
Next Election: Sept. 26, 2017 (4 year terms)
Raymond Stokes, Mayor
Kim Osbourne, Clerk

Musgravetown
P.O. Box 129
Musgravetown, NL A0C 1Z0
Tel: 709-467-2726; *Fax:* 709-467-2109
townofmusg@nf.aibn.com
Municipal Type: Town
Incorporated: March 1, 1974; *Area:* 13.63 sq km
Population in 2011: 556

Provincial Electoral District(s): Terra Nova
Federal Electoral District(s): Bonavista-Burin-Trinity
Next Election: Sept. 26, 2017 (4 year terms)
Jim Brown, Mayor
Linda Fitzgerald, Clerk

Nain
P.O. Box 400
Nain, NL A0P 1L0
Tel: 709-922-2842; *Fax:* 709-922-2295
nainicg@nf.aibn.com
Municipal Type: Town
Incorporated: Nov. 24, 1970; *Area:* 94.58 sq km
Population in 2011: 1,188
Provincial Electoral District(s): Torngat Mountains
Federal Electoral District(s): Labrador
Next Election: Sept. 26, 2017 (4 year terms)
Tony Andersen, Mayor
Karen Dicker, Clerk

New Perlican
P.O. Box 130
New Perlican, NL A0B 2S0
Tel: 709-583-2500; *Fax:* 709-583-2554
townofnewperlican@persona.ca
Municipal Type: Town
Incorporated: Sept. 28, 1971; *Area:* 24.47 sq km
Population in 2011: 210
Provincial Electoral District(s): Trinity-Bay de Verde
Federal Electoral District(s): Bonavista-Burin-Trinity
Next Election: Sept. 26, 2017 (4 year terms)
Linda Moyles, Mayor
Shelley Burrage, Temporary Clerk

New-Wes-Valley
P.O. Box 64
Badgers Quay, NL A0G 1B0
Tel: 709-536-2010; *Fax:* 709-536-3481
new-wes-valley@nf.aibn.com
www.townofnewwesvalley.com
Municipal Type: Town
Incorporated: Jan. 1, 1992; *Area:* 133.59 sq km
Population in 2011: 2,265
Provincial Electoral District(s): Bonavista North
Federal Electoral District(s): Bonavista-Burin-Trinity
Next Election: Sept. 26, 2017 (4 year terms)
Grant Burry, Mayor, 709-536-3492
Harry Winter, Clerk & Manager

Nipper's Harbour
P.O. Box 10
Nippers Harbour, NL A0K 3T0
Tel: 709-255-4583; *Fax:* 709-255-4583
towncouncil@aibn.nf.com
Municipal Type: Town
Incorporated: Nov. 10, 1964; *Area:* 1.93 sq km
Population in 2011: 128
Provincial Electoral District(s): Baie Verte
Federal Electoral District(s): Coast of Bays-Central-Notre Dame
Next Election: Sept. 26, 2017 (4 year terms)
Ted Noble, Mayor
Beth Prole, Clerk

Norman's Cove-Long Cove
P.O. Box 70
Normans Cove, NL A0B 2T0
Tel: 709-592-2490; *Fax:* 709-592-2106
townofnclc@eastlink.ca
Municipal Type: Town
Incorporated: June 2, 1970; *Area:* 19.98 sq km
Population in 2011: 720
Provincial Electoral District(s): Bellevue
Federal Electoral District(s): Bonavista-Burin-Trinity
Next Election: Sept. 26, 2017 (4 year terms)
Barry Drake, Mayor
Dianne Hudson, Clerk

Norris Arm
P.O. Box 70
Norris Arm, NL A0G 3M0
Tel: 709-653-2519; *Fax:* 709-653-2163
townofnorrisarm@gmail.com
www.norrisarm.net
Municipal Type: Town
Incorporated: April 20, 1971; *Area:* 41.49 sq km
Population in 2011: 912
Provincial Electoral District(s): Lewisporte
Federal Electoral District(s): Coast of Bays-Central-Notre Dame
Next Election: Sept. 26, 2017 (4 year terms)
Chris Manuel, Mayor
Beverly Peyton, Clerk

Norris Point
P.O. Box 119
Norris Point, NL A0K 3V0
Tel: 709-458-2896; *Fax:* 709-458-2883
info@norrispoint.ca
www.norrispoint.ca
Municipal Type: Town
Incorporated: Oct. 25, 1960; *Area:* 4.91 sq km
Population in 2011: 685
Provincial Electoral District(s): St. Barbe
Federal Electoral District(s): Long Range Mountains
Next Election: Sept. 26, 2017 (4 year terms)
Joseph Reid, Mayor
Regina Organ, Clerk

North River
P.O. Box 104
North River, NL A0A 3C0
Tel: 709-786-6216; *Fax:* 709-786-1955
townofnorthriver@persona.ca
Municipal Type: Town
Incorporated: Aug. 11, 1964; *Area:* 4.32 sq km
Population in 2011: 562
Provincial Electoral District(s): Harbour Main-Whitbourne
Federal Electoral District(s): Avalon; Labrador
Next Election: Sept. 26, 2017 (4 year terms)
Blair Hurley, Mayor
Sheila Hall, Clerk

North West River
P.O. Box 100
North West River, NL A0P 1M0
Tel: 709-497-8533; *Fax:* 709-497-8228
manager@townofnwr.ca
www.townofnwr.ca
Municipal Type: Town
Incorporated: March 11, 1958; *Area:* 3.2 sq km
Population in 2011: 553
Provincial Electoral District(s): Lake Melville
Federal Electoral District(s): Labrador
Next Election: Sept. 26, 2017 (4 year terms)
Arthur Williams, Mayor
Alicia Penashue, Clerk

Northern Arm
P.O. Box 2006
Northern Arm, NL A0H 1E0
Tel: 709-257-3482; *Fax:* 709-257-3482
ella@townofnorthernarm.ca
www.townofnorthernarm.ca
Municipal Type: Town
Incorporated: July 18, 1972; *Area:* 25.64 sq km
Population in 2011: 397
Provincial Electoral District(s): Exploits
Federal Electoral District(s): Coast of Bays-Central-Notre Dame
Next Election: Sept. 26, 2017 (4 year terms)
Peter Chayter, Mayor
Valie Pelley, Clerk

Old Perlican
P.O. Box 39
Old Perlican, NL A0A 3G0
Tel: 709-587-2266; *Fax:* 709-587-2261
info@townofoldperlican.ca
www.townofoldperlican.ca
Municipal Type: Town
Incorporated: March 30, 1971; *Area:* 14.47 sq km
Population in 2011: 661
Provincial Electoral District(s): Trinity-Bay de Verde
Federal Electoral District(s): Bonavista-Burin-Trinity
Next Election: Sept. 26, 2017 (4 year terms)
Bruce Button, Mayor
Margie Hopkins, Clerk

Pacquet
97 Main St.
Pacquet, NL A0K 3X0
Tel: 709-251-5496; *Fax:* 709-251-5497
pacquet@eastlink.ca
Municipal Type: Town
Incorporated: June 12, 1962; *Area:* 14.48 sq km
Population in 2011: 184
Provincial Electoral District(s): Baie Verte
Federal Electoral District(s): Coast of Bays-Central-Notre Dame
Next Election: Sept. 26, 2017 (4 year terms)
Morris Geenham, Mayor
Janet Sacrey, Clerk

Parker's Cove
General Delivery
Parker's Cove, NL A0E 1H0
Tel: 709-443-2216; *Fax:* 709-443-2216
council@eatlink.ca
www.parkerscove.com
Municipal Type: Town
Incorporated: Jan. 25, 1966; *Area:* 4.85 sq km
Population in 2011: 301
Provincial Electoral District(s): Burin-Placentia West
Federal Electoral District(s): Bonavista-Burin-Trinity
Next Election: Sept. 26, 2017 (4 year terms)
Harold Murphy, Mayor
Jennifer Murphy, Clerk

Parson's Pond
P.O. Box 39
Parsons Pond, NL A0K 3Z0
Tel: 709-243-2564; *Fax:* 709-243-2500
towncouncilpp@nf.aibn.com
Municipal Type: Town
Incorporated: March 29, 1966; *Area:* 12.63 sq km
Population in 2011: 383
Provincial Electoral District(s): St. Barbe
Federal Electoral District(s): Long Range Mountains
Next Election: Sept. 26, 2017 (4 year terms)
Brenda Biggin, Mayor
Stephanie Keough, Clerk

Pasadena
18 Tenth Ave.
Pasadena, NL A0L 1K0
Tel: 709-686-2075; *Fax:* 709-686-2507
info@pasadena.ca
www.pasadena.ca
Municipal Type: Town
Incorporated: Oct. 25, 1955; *Area:* 49.16 sq km
Population in 2011: 3,352
Provincial Electoral District(s): Humber East
Federal Electoral District(s): Long Range Mountains
Next Election: Sept. 26, 2017 (4 year terms)
Otto Goulding, Mayor
Brian Hudson, Clerk & Manager

Peterview
P.O. Box 10
Peterview, NL A0H 1Y0
Tel: 709-257-2926; *Fax:* 709-257-2926
townofpeterview@nf.aibn.com
www.peterview.ca
Municipal Type: Town
Incorporated: June 12, 1962; *Area:* 6.72 sq km
Population in 2011: 809
Provincial Electoral District(s): Exploits
Federal Electoral District(s): Coast of Bays-Central-Notre Dame
Next Election: Sept. 26, 2017 (4 year terms)
James Samson, Mayor, 709-257-4223
Venus Samson, Clerk

Petty Harbour-Maddox Cove
P.O. Box 434
35 Main Rd.
Petty Harbour, NL A0A 3H0
Tel: 709-368-3959; *Fax:* 709-368-3994
www.pettyharbourmaddoxcove.ca
Municipal Type: Town
Incorporated: March 25, 1969; *Area:* 4.51 sq km
Population in 2011: 924
Provincial Electoral District(s): Ferryland
Federal Electoral District(s): St. John's South-Mount Pearl
Next Election: Sept. 26, 2017 (4 year terms)
Nat Hutchings, Mayor
Stephanie Stack, Clerk

Pilley's Island
P.O. Box 70
Pilleys Island, NL A0J 1M0
Tel: 709-652-3555; *Fax:* 709-652-3852
pilleysisland@eastlink.ca
Municipal Type: Town
Incorporated: April 11, 1975; *Area:* 34.67 sq km
Population in 2011: 301
Provincial Electoral District(s): Windsor-Springdale
Federal Electoral District(s): Coast of Bays-Central-Notre Dame
Next Election: Sept. 26, 2017 (4 year terms)
Dennis Vincent, Mayor
Heather Ivany, Clerk

Pinware
P.O. Box 37
Pinware, NL A0K 5S0
Municipal Type: Town
Incorporated: May 18, 1978; *Area:* 4.37 sq km
Population in 2011: 107
Provincial Electoral District(s): Cartwright-L'Anse au Clair
Federal Electoral District(s): Labrador
Next Election: Sept. 26, 2017 (4 year terms)
Joanne Dorey, Mayor
Barbara Tracey, Clerk

Placentia
P.O. Box 99
Placentia, NL A0B 2Y0
Tel: 709-227-2151; *Fax:* 709-227-2323
townofplacentia@placentia.ca
www.placentia.ca
Municipal Type: Town
Incorporated: Nov. 6, 1945; *Area:* 58.05 sq km
Population in 2011: 3,643
Provincial Electoral District(s): Placentia & St. Mary's
Federal Electoral District(s): Avalon
Next Election: Sept. 26, 2017 (4 year terms)
Wayne D. Power, Mayor
Ed O'Keefe, Clerk

Point au Gaul
PO Box 30, Site 8
Point au Gaul, NL A0E 2C0
Tel: 709-857-2021
Municipal Type: Town
Incorporated: Jan. 4, 1966; *Area:* 3.84 sq km
Population in 2011: 97
Provincial Electoral District(s): Grand Bank
Federal Electoral District(s): Bonavista-Burin-Trinity
Next Election: Sept. 26, 2017 (4 year terms)
Paul Lockyear, Mayor
Candy Lockyear, Clerk

Point Lance
P.O. Box 15
Point Lance, NL A0B 1E0
Tel: 709-338-2186; *Fax:* 709-338-2186
Municipal Type: Town
Incorporated: Dec. 7, 1971; *Area:* 29.14 sq km
Population in 2011: 120
Provincial Electoral District(s): Placentia & St. Mary's
Federal Electoral District(s): Avalon
Next Election: Sept. 26, 2017 (4 year terms)
Melvin Careen, Mayor
Jane Power, Clerk

Point Leamington
P.O. Box 39
Point Leamington, NL A0H 1Z0
Tel: 709-484-3421; *Fax:* 709-484-3556
ptleamington@nf.aibn.com
Municipal Type: Town
Incorporated: Aug. 25, 1970; *Area:* 28.81 sq km
Population in 2011: 619
Provincial Electoral District(s): Exploits
Federal Electoral District(s): Coast of Bays-Central-Notre Dame
Next Election: Sept. 26, 2017 (4 year terms)
Wilf Mercer, Mayor
Wanda Ryan, Clerk

Point May
P.O. Box 19
Point May, NL A0E 2C0
Tel: 709-857-2640; *Fax:* 709-857-2640
Municipal Type: Town
Incorporated: Dec. 4, 1962; *Area:* 64.89 sq km
Population in 2011: 233
Provincial Electoral District(s): Grand Bank
Federal Electoral District(s): Bonavista-Burin-Trinity
Next Election: Sept. 26, 2017 (4 year terms)
Muriel Cousins, Mayor
Janice Haley, Clerk

Point of Bay
P.O. Box 9
Point of Bay, NL A0H 2A0
Tel: 709-257-3171; *Fax:* 709-257-3192
Municipal Type: Town
Incorporated: April 18, 1967; *Area:* 21.94 sq km
Population in 2011: 159
Provincial Electoral District(s): Exploits
Federal Electoral District(s): Coast of Bays-Central-Notre Dame
Next Election: Sept. 26, 2017 (4 year terms)
Edward Cameron, Mayor
Sybil Boone, Clerk

Pool's Cove
P.O. Box 10
Pools Cove, NL A0H 2B0
Tel: 709-665-3371; *Fax:* 709-665-3372
Municipal Type: Town
Incorporated: Nov. 25, 1969; *Area:* 2.64 sq km
Population in 2011: 182
Provincial Electoral District(s): Fortune Bay-Cape La Hune
Federal Electoral District(s): Coast of Bays-Central-Notre Dame
Next Election: Sept. 26, 2017 (4 year terms)
Dwayne Williams, Mayor
Branda Williams, Clerk

Port Anson
General Delivery
Port Anson, NL A0J 1N0
Tel: 709-652-3683; *Fax:* 709-652-3680
townofportanson@hotmail.com
Municipal Type: Town
Incorporated: Dec. 12, 1961; *Area:* 7.69 sq km
Population in 2011: 165
Provincial Electoral District(s): Windsor-Springdale
Federal Electoral District(s): Coast of Bays-Central-Notre Dame
Next Election: Sept. 26, 2017 (4 year terms)
Shawn Burton, Mayor
Grace Burton, Clerk

Port au Choix
P.O. Box 89
Port au Choix, NL A0K 4C0
Tel: 709-861-3409; *Fax:* 709-861-3061
portauchoix@nf.aibn.com
Municipal Type: Town
Incorporated: July 26, 1966; *Area:* 35.61 sq km
Population in 2011: 839
Provincial Electoral District(s): St. Barbe
Federal Electoral District(s): Long Range Mountains
Next Election: Sept. 26, 2017 (4 year terms)
Carolyn Lavers, Mayor
Annette Payne, Clerk

Port au Port East
P.O. Box 160
Port au Port East, NL A0N 1T0
Tel: 709-648-2731; *Fax:* 709-648-9481
townofpape@hotmail.com
Municipal Type: Town
Incorporated: Dec. 16, 1952; *Area:* 24.76 sq km
Population in 2011: 598
Provincial Electoral District(s): Port au Port
Federal Electoral District(s): Long Range Mountains
Next Election: Sept. 26, 2017 (4 year terms)
Eileen Hann, Mayor
Joanne Ryan, Clerk

Port au Port West-Aguathuna-Felix Cove
P.O. Box 89
Aguathuna, NL A0N 1T0
Tel: 709-648-2891; *Fax:* 709-648-9292
papwaf@nf.aibn.com
Municipal Type: Town
Incorporated: Oct. 6, 1970; *Area:* 16.72 sq km
Population in 2011: 447
Provincial Electoral District(s): Port au Port
Federal Electoral District(s): Long Range Mountains
Next Election: Sept. 26, 2017 (4 year terms)
Melina Bennett, Mayor
Vanessa Glasgow, Clerk

Port Blandford
P.O. Box 70
Port Blandford, NL A0C 2G0
Tel: 709-543-2170; *Fax:* 709-543-2153
vgreening@nf.aibn.com
www.portblandford.com
Municipal Type: Town
Incorporated: Sept. 28, 1971; *Area:* 50.56 sq km
Population in 2011: 483
Provincial Electoral District(s): Terra Nova
Federal Electoral District(s): Bonavista-Burin-Trinity
Next Election: Sept. 26, 2017 (4 year terms)
Chad Holloway, Mayor
Vida Greening, Town Clerk & Manager

Port Hope Simpson
P.O. Box 130
Port Hope Simpson, NL A0K 4E0
Tel: 709-960-0236; *Fax:* 709-960-0387
porthopesimpson@nf.aibn.com
Municipal Type: Town
Incorporated: May 1, 1973; *Area:* 32.52 sq km
Population in 2011: 441
Provincial Electoral District(s): Cartwright-L'Anse au Clair
Federal Electoral District(s): Labrador
Next Election: Sept. 26, 2017 (4 year terms)
Margaret Burden, Mayor
Joyce Clarke, Clerk

Port Kirwan
PO Box 40, Site 2
Port Kirwan, NL A0A 2G0
Fax: 709-363-2114
Municipal Type: Town
Incorporated: June 15, 1965; *Area:* 9.19 sq km
Population in 2011: 65
Provincial Electoral District(s): Ferryland
Federal Electoral District(s): Avalon
Next Election: Sept. 26, 2017 (4 year terms)
Eugene Brothers, Mayor
Dana Boland, Clerk

Port Rexton
P.O. Box 55
Port Rexton, NL A0C 2H0
Tel: 709-464-2006; *Fax:* 709-464-2581
portrexton@bellaliant.com
Municipal Type: Town
Incorporated: April 22, 1969; *Area:* 11.78 sq km
Population in 2011: 338
Provincial Electoral District(s): Trinity North
Federal Electoral District(s): Bonavista-Burin-Trinity
Next Election: Sept. 26, 2017 (4 year terms)
Alvin Piercey, Mayor
Lois Long, Clerk

Port Saunders
P.O. Box 39
Port Saunders, NL A0K 4H0
Tel: 709-861-3105; *Fax:* 709-861-2137
townofportsaunders@nf.aibn.com
www.townofportsaunders.ca
Municipal Type: Town
Incorporated: Aug. 21, 1956; *Area:* 38.81 sq km
Population in 2011: 697
Provincial Electoral District(s): St. Barbe
Federal Electoral District(s): Long Range Mountains
Next Election: Sept. 26, 2017 (4 year terms)
Tony Ryan, Mayor
Judy Quinlan, Co-Clerk
Helen Hamlyn, Co-Clerk

Portugal Cove South
PO Box 8, Site 11
Trepassey, NL A0A 4B0
Tel: 709-438-2092; *Fax:* 709-438-2090
townofpcs@live.ca
Municipal Type: Town
Incorporated: Aug. 6, 1963; *Area:* 1.14 sq km
Population in 2011: 160
Provincial Electoral District(s): Ferryland
Federal Electoral District(s): Avalon
Next Election: Sept. 26, 2017 (4 year terms)
Clarence Molloy, Mayor
Ida Perry, Clerk

Portugal Cove-St Philip's
1119 Thorburn Rd.
Portugal Cove-St Philips, NL A1M 1T6
Tel: 709-895-8000; *Fax:* 709-895-3780
pcsp@pcsp.ca
www.pcsp.ca
Municipal Type: Town
Incorporated: Feb. 1, 1992; *Area:* 57.35 sq km
Population in 2011: 7,366
Provincial Electoral District(s): Conception Bay East & Bell Island
Federal Electoral District(s): St. John's East
Next Election: Sept. 26, 2017 (4 year terms)
Moses Tucker, Mayor
Judy Squires, Town Clerk & Treas.

Postville
P.O. Box 74
Postville, NL A0P 1N0
Tel: 709-479-9830; *Fax:* 709-479-9888
communitycouncil@nf.aibn.com
Municipal Type: Town
Incorporated: Aug. 1, 1975; *Area:* 1.96 sq km
Population in 2011: 206
Provincial Electoral District(s): Torngat Mountains
Federal Electoral District(s): Labrador
Next Election: Sept. 26, 2017 (4 year terms)
Diane Gear, Mayor
Melanie Gear, Clerk

Pouch Cove
P.O. Box 59
Pouch Cove, NL A0A 3L0
Tel: 709-335-2848; *Fax:* 709-335-2840
pouchcove@nf.aibn.com
www.pouchcove.ca
Municipal Type: Town
Incorporated: Dec. 22, 1970; *Area:* 58.34 sq km
Population in 2011: 1,866
Provincial Electoral District(s): Cape St. Francis
Federal Electoral District(s): St. John's East
Next Election: Sept. 26, 2017 (4 year terms)
Joedy Wall, Mayor
Jacqueline Berkshire, Clerk

Raleigh
P.O. Box 119
Raleigh, NL A0K 4J0
Tel: 709-452-4461; *Fax:* 709-452-2135
townofraleigh@nf.aibn.com
Municipal Type: Town
Incorporated: Oct. 2, 1973; *Area:* 11.12 sq km
Population in 2011: 201
Provincial Electoral District(s): The Straits & White Bay North
Federal Electoral District(s): Long Range Mountains
Next Election: Sept. 26, 2017 (4 year terms)
Millicent Taylor, Mayor
Angela Taylor, Clerk

Ramea
P.O. Box 69
Ramea, NL A0N 2J0
Tel: 709-625-2280; *Fax:* 709-625-2010
rameatowncouncil@gmail.com
Municipal Type: Town
Incorporated: March 20, 1951; *Area:* 1.89 sq km
Population in 2011: 280
Provincial Electoral District(s): Fortune Bay-Cape La Hune
Federal Electoral District(s): Long Range Mountains
Next Election: Sept. 26, 2017 (4 year terms)
Clyde Dominie, Mayor
Minnie Organ, Clerk

Red Bay
P.O. Box 108
Red Bay, NL A0K 4K0
Tel: 709-920-2197; *Fax:* 709-920-2103
redbaytowncouncil@nf.aibn.com
Municipal Type: Town
Incorporated: May 22, 1973; *Area:* 1.58 sq km
Population in 2011: 194
Provincial Electoral District(s): Cartwright-L'Anse au Clair
Federal Electoral District(s): Labrador
Next Election: Sept. 26, 2017 (4 year terms)
Wanita Stone, Mayor
Liz Yetman, Clerk

Red Harbour
P.O. Box 5
Red Harbour PB, NL A0E 2R0
Tel: 709-443-2599; *Fax:* 709-443-2599
townofredharbour@yahoo.ca
townofredharbour.webspawner.com
Municipal Type: Town
Incorporated: Nov. 9, 1969; *Area:* 11.35 sq km
Population in 2011: 191
Provincial Electoral District(s): Burin-Placentia West
Federal Electoral District(s): Bonavista-Burin-Trinity
Next Election: Sept. 26, 2017 (4 year terms)
Patsy Badcock, Mayor
Kevin Paddle, Clerk

Reidville
2 Community Sq.
Reidville, NL A8A 2V7
Tel: 709-635-5232; *Fax:* 709-635-4498
townofreidville@nf.aibn.com
Municipal Type: Town
Incorporated: Oct. 3, 1975; *Area:* 58.41 sq km
Population in 2011: 474
Provincial Electoral District(s): Humber Valley
Federal Electoral District(s): Long Range Mountains
Next Election: Sept. 26, 2017 (4 year terms)
Roger Barrett, Mayor
Connie Reid, Clerk

Rencontre East
P.O. Box 33
Rencontre East, NL A0H 2C0
Tel: 709-848-3171; *Fax:* 709-848-4194
rencontreeast.com
Municipal Type: Town
Incorporated: Feb. 8, 1972; *Area:* 2.62 sq km
Population in 2011: 141
Provincial Electoral District(s): Fortune Bay-Cape La Hune
Federal Electoral District(s): Coast of Bays-Central-Notre Dame
Next Election: Sept. 26, 2017 (4 year terms)
Tom Caines, Mayor
Barbara Caines, Clerk

Renews-Cappahayden
P.O. Box 40
Renews, NL A0A 3N0
Tel: 709-363-2500; *Fax:* 709-363-2143
townofrenewscappahayden@nf.aibn.com
www.townofrenewscappahayden.com
Municipal Type: Town
Incorporated: Sept. 19, 1967; *Area:* 127.84 sq km
Population in 2011: 310
Provincial Electoral District(s): Ferryland
Federal Electoral District(s): Avalon
Next Election: Sept. 26, 2017 (4 year terms)
Donna Dinn, Mayor
Susan Sheehan, Clerk

Rigolet
P.O. Box 69
Rigolet, NL A0P 1P0
Tel: 709-947-3382; *Fax:* 709-947-3360
townmanager@rigolet.ca
www.townofrigolet.com
Municipal Type: Town
Incorporated: Jan. 7, 1977; *Area:* 3.61 sq km
Population in 2011: 306
Provincial Electoral District(s): Torngat Mountains
Federal Electoral District(s): Labrador
Next Election: Sept. 26, 2017 (4 year terms)
Charlotte Wolfrey, Mayor
Sherry Wolfrey, Clerk

River of Ponds
P.O. Box 10
River of Ponds, NL A0K 4M0
Tel: 709-225-3161; *Fax:* 709-225-3162
townofriverofponds@nf.aibn.com
Municipal Type: Town
Incorporated: May 26, 1970; *Area:* 4.69 sq km
Population in 2011: 228
Provincial Electoral District(s): St. Barbe
Federal Electoral District(s): Long Range Mountains
Next Election: Sept. 26, 2017 (4 year terms)
Eric Patey, Mayor
Valerie House, Clerk

Riverhead
PO Box 14, Site 5
St Marys, NL A0B 3B0
Tel: 709-525-2600; *Fax:* 709-525-2106
Municipal Type: Town
Incorporated: Dec. 20, 1966; *Area:* 105.6 sq km
Population in 2011: 212
Provincial Electoral District(s): Placentia & St. Mary's
Federal Electoral District(s): Avalon; Bonavista-Burin-Trinity
Next Election: Sept. 26, 2017 (4 year terms)
Sheila Lee, Mayor
Janet Barron, Clerk

Robert's Arm
P.O. Box 10
Roberts Arm, NL A0J 1R0
Tel: 709-652-3331; *Fax:* 709-652-3079
townofrobertsarm@eastlink.ca
www.robertsarm.com
Municipal Type: Town
Incorporated: Sept. 7, 1954; *Area:* 35.79 sq km
Population in 2011: 807
Provincial Electoral District(s): Windsor-Springdale
Federal Electoral District(s): Coast of Bays-Central-Notre Dame
Next Election: Sept. 26, 2017 (4 year terms)
Lloyd Coulbourne, Mayor
Stephanie Ryan, Part-time Clerk

Rocky Harbour
P.O. Box 24
Rocky Harbour, NL A0K 4N0
Tel: 709-458-2376; *Fax:* 709-458-2293
rockyharbour@msn.com
www.rockyharbour.ca
Municipal Type: Town
Incorporated: April 5, 1966; *Area:* 12.08 sq km
Population in 2011: 979
Provincial Electoral District(s): St. Barbe
Federal Electoral District(s): Long Range Mountains
Next Election: Sept. 26, 2017 (4 year terms)
Walter Nicolle, Mayor
Debbie Reid, Clerk

Roddickton-Bide Arm
P.O. Box 10
Roddickton, NL A0K 4P0
Tel: 709-457-2413; *Fax:* 709-457-2663
roddickton@nf.aibn.com
Municipal Type: Town
Incorporated: April 7, 1953; *Area:* 47.71 sq km
Population in 2011: 1,057
Provincial Electoral District(s): The Straits & White Bay North
Federal Electoral District(s): Long Range Mountains
Next Election: Sept. 26, 2017 (4 year terms)
Sheila Fitzgerald, Mayor
Denise Adams, Clerk

Rose Blanche-Harbour Le Cou
P.O. Box 159
Rose Blanche, NL A0M 1P0
Tel: 709-956-2540; *Fax:* 709-956-2541
townofroseblanche@nf.aibn.com
Municipal Type: Town
Incorporated: Aug. 25, 1971; *Area:* 4.44 sq km
Population in 2011: 118
Provincial Electoral District(s): Burgeo & La Poile
Federal Electoral District(s): Long Range Mountains
Next Election: Sept. 26, 2017 (4 year terms)
Clayton Durnford, Mayor
Tammy Farrell, Clerk

Rushoon
P.O. Box 25
Rushoon, NL A0E 2S0
Tel: 709-443-2572; *Fax:* 709-443-2572
townofrushoon@bellaliant.com
Municipal Type: Town
Incorporated: Jan. 18, 1966; *Area:* 6.15 sq km
Population in 2011: 288
Provincial Electoral District(s): Burin-Placentia West
Federal Electoral District(s): Bonavista-Burin-Trinity
Next Election: Sept. 26, 2017 (4 year terms)
Jill Mulrooney, Mayor
Jackie Gaulton, Clerk

St. Alban's
P.O. Box 10
St Albans, NL A0H 2E0
Tel: 709-538-3132; *Fax:* 709-538-3683
st.albans@nf.aibn.com
www.stalbans.ca
Municipal Type: Town
Incorporated: Sept. 1, 1953; *Area:* 20.85 sq km
Population in 2011: 1,233
Provincial Electoral District(s): Fortune Bay-Cape La Hune
Federal Electoral District(s): Coast of Bays-Central-Notre Dame
Next Election: Sept. 26, 2017 (4 year terms)
Jamie LeRoux, Mayor
Genevieve Tremblett, Clerk & Manager

St. Anthony
P.O. Box 430
St Anthony, NL A0K 4S0
Tel: 709-454-3454; *Fax:* 709-454-4154
stanthony@nf.aibn.com
www.town.stanthony.nf.ca
Municipal Type: Town
Incorporated: July 18, 1945; *Area:* 37.02 sq km
Population in 2011: 2,418
Provincial Electoral District(s): The Straits & White Bay North
Federal Electoral District(s): Long Range Mountains
Next Election: Sept. 26, 2017 (4 year terms)
Ernest Simms, Mayor
Judy Patey, Clerk

St. Bernard's-Jacques Fontaine
P.O. Box 70
St Bernards, NL A0E 2T0
Tel: 709-461-2257; *Fax:* 709-461-2179
townofsbjf@eastlink.ca
Municipal Type: Town
Incorporated: Nov. 21, 1967; *Area:* 16.44 sq km
Population in 2011: 470
Provincial Electoral District(s): Bellevue
Federal Electoral District(s): Bonavista-Burin-Trinity
Next Election: Sept. 26, 2017 (4 year terms)
Clifford Allen, Mayor
Pauline Smith, Clerk

St. Brendan's
P.O. Box 54
St Brendans, NL A0G 3V0
Tel: 709-669-4271; *Fax:* 709-669-4271
Municipal Type: Town
Incorporated: Sept. 1, 1953; *Area:* 10.14 sq km
Population in 2011: 147
Provincial Electoral District(s): Terra Nova
Federal Electoral District(s): Bonavista-Burin-Trinity
Next Election: Sept. 26, 2017 (4 year terms)
Veronica Broomfield, Mayor
Rita White, Clerk

St. Bride's
37 Main St.
St Brides, NL A0B 2Z0
Tel: 709-337-2160; *Fax:* 709-337-2160
Municipal Type: Town
Incorporated: May 2, 1972; *Area:* 5.84 sq km
Population in 2011: 308
Provincial Electoral District(s): Placentia & St. Mary's
Federal Electoral District(s): Avalon
Next Election: Sept. 26, 2017 (4 year terms)
Eugene Manning, Mayor
Joan Morrissey, Clerk

St. George's
P.O. Box 250
St Georges, NL A0N 1Z0
Tel: 709-647-3283; *Fax:* 709-647-3180
townofstgeorges@nf.aibn.com
www.townofstgeorges.com
Municipal Type: Town
Incorporated: May 18, 1965; *Area:* 25.83 sq km
Population in 2011: 1,207
Provincial Electoral District(s): St. George's-Stephenville East
Federal Electoral District(s): Long Range Mountains
Next Election: Sept. 26, 2017 (4 year terms)
Fintan Alexander, Mayor
Debbie Woolridge, Clerk

St. Jacques-Coomb's Cove
P.O. Box 102
English Harbour West, NL A0H 1M0
Tel: 709-888-6141; *Fax:* 709-888-6102
sjcctc@gmail.com
Municipal Type: Town
Incorporated: Nov. 15, 1971; *Area:* 83.76 sq km
Population in 2011: 618
Provincial Electoral District(s): Fortune Bay-Cape La Hune
Federal Electoral District(s): Coast of Bays-Central-Notre Dame
Next Election: Sept. 26, 2017 (4 year terms)
Hubert Langdon, Mayor
Joan Sheppard, Clerk

St. Joseph's
P.O. Box 9
St Josephs, NL A0B 3A0
Tel: 709-521-2440; *Fax:* 709-521-2440
Municipal Type: Town
Incorporated: Aug. 18, 1970; *Area:* 32.31 sq km
Population in 2011: 115
Provincial Electoral District(s): Placentia & St. Mary's
Federal Electoral District(s): Avalon; Bonavista-Burin-Trinity
Next Election: Sept. 26, 2017 (4 year terms)
Mary Moyland, Mayor
Tony Reardon, Clerk

St. Lawrence
P.O. Box 128
St Lawrence, NL A0E 2V0
Tel: 709-873-2222; *Fax:* 709-873-3352
townofstlawrence@nf.aibn.com
www.townofstlawrence.com
Municipal Type: Town
Incorporated: Nov. 15, 1949; *Area:* 35.5 sq km
Population in 2011: 1,244
Provincial Electoral District(s): Grand Bank
Federal Electoral District(s): Bonavista-Burin-Trinity
Next Election: Sept. 26, 2017 (4 year terms)
Paul Pike, Mayor
Gregory Quirke, Clerk

St. Lewis
P.O. Box 106
St. Lewis, NL A0K 4W0
Tel: 709-939-2282; *Fax:* 709-939-2210
stlewistownoffice@nf.aibn.com
Municipal Type: Town
Incorporated: July 17, 1981; *Area:* 9.25 sq km
Population in 2011: 207
Provincial Electoral District(s): Cartwright-L'Anse au Clair
Federal Electoral District(s): Labrador
Next Election: Sept. 26, 2017 (4 year terms)
Gerald Chubbs, Mayor
Lorraine Poole, Clerk

St. Lunaire-Griquet
P.O. Box 9
St Lunaire-Griquet, NL A0K 2X0
Tel: 709-623-2323; *Fax:* 709-623-2170
stlunaire.griquet@nf.aibn.com
Municipal Type: Town
Incorporated: June 10, 1958; *Area:* 16.68 sq km
Population in 2011: 661
Provincial Electoral District(s): The Straits & White Bay North
Federal Electoral District(s): Long Range Mountains
Next Election: Sept. 26, 2017 (4 year terms)
Dale Colbourne, Mayor
Linda Hillier, Clerk

St. Mary's
P.O. Box 348
St Marys, NL A0B 3B0
Tel: 709-525-2586
townofstmarys@nf.aibn.com
Municipal Type: Town
Incorporated: Dec. 13, 1966; *Area:* 37.05 sq km
Population in 2011: 439
Provincial Electoral District(s): Placentia & St. Mary's
Federal Electoral District(s): Avalon
Next Election: Sept. 26, 2017 (4 year terms)
Keith Bowen, Mayor
Patricia Walsh, Clerk

St. Pauls
P.O. Box 9
St Pauls, NL A0K 4Y0
Tel: 709-243-2279; *Fax:* 709-243-2299
townofstpauls@nf.aibn.com
Municipal Type: Town
Incorporated: July 30, 1968; *Area:* 5.35 sq km
Population in 2011: 258
Provincial Electoral District(s): St. Barbe
Federal Electoral District(s): Long Range Mountains
Next Election: Sept. 26, 2017 (4 year terms)
Cyril Hutchings, Mayor
Monica Pittman, Clerk

St. Shott's
General Delivery
St Shotts, NL A0A 3R0
Fax: 709-438-2617
Municipal Type: Town
Incorporated: May 21, 1963; *Area:* 1.14 sq km
Population in 2011: 81
Provincial Electoral District(s): Placentia & St. Mary's
Federal Electoral District(s): Avalon
Next Election: Sept. 26, 2017 (4 year terms)
Elizabeth Molloy, Mayor
Elizabeth Hewitt, Clerk

St. Vincent's-St. Stephen's-Peter's River
P.O. Box 39
St Vincents, NL A0B 3C0
Tel: 709-525-2540; *Fax:* 709-525-2110
svstpr@nf.aibn.com
Municipal Type: Town
Incorporated: Aug. 1, 1971; *Area:* 87.5 sq km
Population in 2011: 340
Provincial Electoral District(s): Placentia & St. Mary's
Federal Electoral District(s): Avalon
Next Election: Sept. 26, 2017 (4 year terms)
Daniel St. Croix, Mayor
Marilyn Gibbons, Clerk

Salmon Cove
P.O. Box 240
Salmon Cove, NL A0A 3S0
Tel: 709-596-2101; *Fax:* 709-596-1170
townofsalmoncove@nf.aibn.com
Municipal Type: Town
Incorporated: Aug. 27, 1974; *Area:* 4.21 sq km
Population in 2011: 695
Provincial Electoral District(s): Carbonear-Harbour Grace
Federal Electoral District(s): Avalon; Bonavista-Burin-Trinity
Next Election: Sept. 26, 2017 (4 year terms)
Nathan Graham, Mayor
Donette Morris, Clerk

Salvage
General Delivery
Salvage, NL A0G 3X0
Tel: 709-677-3535; *Fax:* 709-677-3535
Municipal Type: Town
Incorporated: Oct. 24, 1972; *Area:* 15.86 sq km
Population in 2011: 136
Provincial Electoral District(s): Terra Nova
Federal Electoral District(s): Bonavista-Burin-Trinity
Next Election: Sept. 26, 2017 (4 year terms)
Gordon Janes, Mayor
Beverly Hunter, Clerk

Sandringham
43-47 Main St.
Sandringham, NL A0G 3Y0
Tel: 709-677-2317; *Fax:* 709-677-3836
townofsandringham@yahoo.ca
Municipal Type: Town
Incorporated: April 30, 1968; *Area:* 9.6 sq km
Population in 2011: 274
Provincial Electoral District(s): Terra Nova
Federal Electoral District(s): Bonavista-Burin-Trinity
Next Election: Sept. 26, 2017 (4 year terms)
Glenn Arnold, Mayor
Audrey Penney, Clerk

Sandy Cove
PO Box 37, Site 8
Eastport, NL A0G 1Z0
Tel: 709-677-2731; *Fax:* 709-677-2731
sandycove@bellaliant.com
sandycovenl.com
Municipal Type: Town
Incorporated: Sept. 18, 1956; *Area:* 9.01 sq km
Population in 2011: 132
Provincial Electoral District(s): Terra Nova; The Straits & White Bay North
Federal Electoral District(s): Bonavista-Burin-Trinity; Labrador; Long Range Mountains
Next Election: Sept. 26, 2017 (4 year terms)
Tony Parsons, Mayor
Anne Benger, Clerk

La Scie
P.O. Box 130
La Scie, NL A0K 3M0
Tel: 709-675-2266; *Fax:* 709-675-2168
townoflascie@eastlink.ca
Municipal Type: Town
Incorporated: May 25, 1955; *Area:* 29.14 sq km
Population in 2011: 899
Provincial Electoral District(s): Baie Verte
Federal Electoral District(s): Coast of Bays-Central-Notre Dame
Next Election: Sept. 26, 2017 (4 year terms)
Paul Toms, Mayor
Chasity Andrews, Clerk

Seal Cove Fortune Bay
P.O. Box 156
Seal Cove Fortune Bay, NL A0H 2G0
Tel: 709-851-4431; *Fax:* 709-851-6174
sealcovecc@nf.aibn.com
Municipal Type: Town
Incorporated: Jan. 25, 1972; *Area:* 2.42 sq km
Population in 2011: 263
Provincial Electoral District(s): Fortune Bay-Cape La Hune
Federal Electoral District(s): Coast of Bays-Central-Notre Dame
Next Election: Sept. 26, 2017 (4 year terms)
Junior Abbott, Mayor
Emily Loveless, Clerk

Seal Cove White Bay
P.O. Box 119
Seal Cove White Bay, NL A0K 5E0
Tel: 709-531-2550; *Fax:* 709-531-2551
sealcovewb@nf.aibn.com
Municipal Type: Town
Incorporated: Dec. 16, 1958; *Area:* 10.79 sq km
Population in 2011: 304
Provincial Electoral District(s): Baie Verte
Federal Electoral District(s): Coast of Bays-Central-Notre Dame
Next Election: Sept. 26, 2017 (4 year terms)
Elizabeth Rice, Mayor
Patricia Rice, Clerk

Small Point-Adam's Cove-Blackhead-Broad Cove
P.O. Box 160
Broad Cove, NL A0A 1L0
Tel: 709-598-2610; *Fax:* 709-598-2618
towncouncil@eastlink.ca
Municipal Type: Town
Incorporated: Oct. 24, 1972; *Area:* 22.22 sq km
Population in 2011: 389
Provincial Electoral District(s): Tinity-Bay de Verde

Federal Electoral District(s): Bonavista-Burin-Trinity
Next Election: Sept. 26, 2017 (4 year terms)
Ernest Gosney, Mayor
Dana Fagner, Clerk

South Brook
P.O. Box 63
South Brook, NL A0J 1S0
Tel: 709-657-2206; *Fax:* 709-657-2202
townofsbrk@yahoo.ca
southbrook.tripod.com
Municipal Type: Town
Incorporated: July 6, 1965; *Area:* 9.07 sq km
Population in 2011: 487
Provincial Electoral District(s): Windsor-Springdale
Federal Electoral District(s): Coast of Bays-Central-Notre Dame; Long Range Mountains
Next Election: Sept. 26, 2017 (4 year terms)
Paul Mills, Mayor
Michelle Kelly, Clerk

South River
P.O. Box 40
South River, NL A0A 3W0
Tel: 709-786-6761; *Fax:* 709-786-6760
townofsouthriver@persona.com
www.townofsouthriver.ca
Municipal Type: Town
Incorporated: June 7, 1966; *Area:* 6.06 sq km
Population in 2011: 655
Provincial Electoral District(s): Harbour Main-Whitbourne
Federal Electoral District(s): Avalon
Next Election: Sept. 26, 2017 (4 year terms)
Arthur Petten, Mayor
Terrie Lynn Hussey-Aisien, Town Clerk & Manager

Southern Harbour
P.O. Box 10
Southern Harbour PB, NL A0B 3H0
Tel: 709-463-2329; *Fax:* 709-463-2208
twnsouthernhr@nf.aibn.com
Municipal Type: Town
Incorporated: Aug. 20, 1968; *Area:* 5.41 sq km
Population in 2011: 534
Provincial Electoral District(s): Bellevue
Federal Electoral District(s): Bonavista-Burin-Trinity
Next Election: Sept. 26, 2017 (4 year terms)
Joseph Brewer, Mayor
Renee Hickey, Clerk

Spaniard's Bay
P.O. Box 190
Spaniards Bay, NL A0A 3X0
Tel: 709-786-3568; *Fax:* 709-786-7273
spaniardsbay@persona.ca
www.townofspaniardsbay.ca
Municipal Type: Town
Incorporated: June 8, 1965; *Area:* 65.73 sq km
Population in 2011: 2,622
Provincial Electoral District(s): Port de Grave
Federal Electoral District(s): Avalon
Next Election: Sept. 26, 2017 (4 year terms)
Wayne Smith, Mayor
Tony Ryan, Clerk & Manager

Springdale
P.O. Box 57
Springdale, NL A0J 1T0
Tel: 709-673-3439; *Fax:* 709-673-4969
info@townofspringdale.ca
www.townofspringdale.ca
Municipal Type: Town
Incorporated: Oct. 23, 1961; *Area:* 17.6 sq km
Population in 2011: 2,907
Provincial Electoral District(s): Windsor-Springdale
Federal Electoral District(s): Coast of Bays-Central-Notre Dame
Next Election: Sept. 26, 2017 (4 year terms)
Harvey Tizzard, Mayor
Daphne Earle, Clerk & Manager

Steady Brook
P.O. Box 117
Steady Brook, NL A2H 2N2
Tel: 709-634-7601; *Fax:* 709-634-7547
townoffice@steadybrook.com
www.steadybrook.com
Municipal Type: Town
Incorporated: April 7, 1953; *Area:* 1.22 sq km
Population in 2011: 408
Provincial Electoral District(s): Humber East
Federal Electoral District(s): Long Range Mountains
Next Election: Sept. 26, 2017 (4 year terms)

Peter Rowsell, Mayor
Tracey Caines, Clerk & Manager

Stephenville
P.O. Box 420
Stephenville, NL A2N 2Z5
Tel: 709-643-8360; *Fax:* 709-643-2770
www.townofstephenville.com
Municipal Type: Town
Incorporated: Oct. 1, 1952; *Area:* 35.69 sq km
Population in 2011: 6,719
Provincial Electoral District(s): St. George's-Stephenville East; Port au Port
Federal Electoral District(s): Long Range Mountains
Next Election: Sept. 26, 2017 (4 year terms)
Tom O'Brien, Mayor
Carolyn Lindstone, Clerk

Stephenville Crossing
P.O. Box 68
Stephenville Crossing, NL A0N 2C0
Tel: 709-646-2600; *Fax:* 709-646-2065
www.townofstephenvillecrossing.com
Municipal Type: Town
Incorporated: Oct. 20, 1958; *Area:* 31.2 sq km
Population in 2011: 1,875
Provincial Electoral District(s): St. George's-Stephenville East
Federal Electoral District(s): Long Range Mountains
Next Election: Sept. 26, 2017 (4 year terms)
Brian Joy, Mayor
Yvonne Young, Clerk

Summerford
P.O. Box 59
Summerford, NL A0G 4E0
Tel: 709-629-3419; *Fax:* 709-629-7532
townofsummerford@nf.aibn.com
Municipal Type: Town
Incorporated: Sept. 28, 1971; *Area:* 16.06 sq km
Population in 2011: 853
Provincial Electoral District(s): Twillingate & Fogo
Federal Electoral District(s): Coast of Bays-Central-Notre Dame
Next Election: Sept. 26, 2017 (4 year terms)
Kevin Barnes, Mayor
Vicky Anstey, Clerk

Sunnyside
P.O. Box 89
10 Post Office Rd.
Sunnyside, NL A0B 3J0
Tel: 709-472-4506; *Fax:* 709-472-4182
townofsunnyside@eastlink.ca
Municipal Type: Town
Incorporated: March 10, 1970; *Area:* 37.95 sq km
Population in 2011: 452
Provincial Electoral District(s): Bellevue
Federal Electoral District(s): Coast of Bays-Central-Notre Dame; Bonavista-Burin-Trinity; Labrador
Next Election: Sept. 26, 2017 (4 year terms)
Robert Snook, Mayor
G. Philip Smith, Clerk

Terra Nova
1 River Road
Terra Nova, NL A0C 1L0
Tel: 709-265-6543; *Fax:* 709-265-6533
townofterranova@nf.aibn.com
Municipal Type: Town
Incorporated: Sept. 13, 1960; *Area:* 2.46 sq km
Population in 2011: 83
Provincial Electoral District(s): Terra Nova
Federal Electoral District(s): Bonavista-Burin-Trinity
Next Election: Sept. 26, 2017 (4 year terms)
Grant Barnes, Mayor
Thelma Greening, Clerk

Terrenceville
P.O. Box 100
Terrenceville, NL A0E 2X0
Tel: 709-662-2204; *Fax:* 709-662-2071
terrencevilletownoffice@nf.aibn.com
Municipal Type: Town
Incorporated: Aug. 15, 1972; *Area:* 14.5 sq km
Population in 2011: 530
Provincial Electoral District(s): Bellevue
Federal Electoral District(s): Bonavista-Burin-Trinity
Next Election: Sept. 26, 2017 (4 year terms)
Cornelius Clarke, Mayor
Jessica Baker, Clerk

Tilt Cove
P.O. Box 22
Tilt Cove, NL A0K 3M0
Tel: 709-675-2641
Municipal Type: Town
Incorporated: March 4, 1969; *Area:* 3.1 sq km
Population in 2011: 5
Provincial Electoral District(s): Baie Verte
Federal Electoral District(s): Coast of Bays-Central-Notre Dame
Next Election: Sept. 26, 2017 (4 year terms)
Donald Collins, Mayor
Margaret Collins, Clerk

Torbay
P.O. Box 1160
1288 Torbay Rd.
Torbay, NL A1K 1K4
Tel: 709-437-6532; *Fax:* 709-437-1309
torbay.ca
Municipal Type: Town
Incorporated: Oct. 24, 1972; *Area:* 34.88 sq km
Population in 2011: 7,397
Provincial Electoral District(s): Cape St. Francis
Federal Electoral District(s): St. John's East
Next Election: Sept. 26, 2017 (4 year terms)
Ralph Tapper, Mayor
Dawn Chaplin, CAO-Clerk

Traytown
1 Poplar Lane
Traytown, NL A0G 4K0
Tel: 709-533-2156; *Fax:* 709-533-2155
townoftraytown@yahoo.ca
Municipal Type: Town
Incorporated: June 15, 1971; *Area:* 13.31 sq km
Population in 2011: 283
Provincial Electoral District(s): Terra Nova
Federal Electoral District(s): Bonavista-Burin-Trinity
Next Election: Sept. 26, 2017 (4 year terms)
John Baird, Mayor
Sarah Patten, Clerk

Trepassey
P.O. Box 129
Trepassey, NL A0A 4B0
Tel: 709-438-2641; *Fax:* 709-438-2749
townoftrepassey@hotmail.com
Municipal Type: Town
Incorporated: Aug. 1, 1967; *Area:* 55.81 sq km
Population in 2011: 570
Provincial Electoral District(s): Ferryland
Federal Electoral District(s): Avalon
Next Election: Sept. 26, 2017 (4 year terms)
Con Finlay, Mayor
Sharon Topping, Clerk

Trinity
P.O. Box 42
Trinity, NL A0C 2S0
Tel: 709-464-3836; *Fax:* 709-464-3836
counciltrinity@netscape.net
www.townoftrinity.com
Municipal Type: Town
Incorporated: May 13, 1969; *Area:* 12.92 sq km
Population in 2011: 137
Provincial Electoral District(s): Trinity North; Bonavista North
Federal Electoral District(s): Bonavista-Burin-Trinity
Next Election: Sept. 26, 2017 (4 year terms)
Jim Miller, Mayor
Linda Sweet, Clerk

Trinity Bay North
P.O. Box 91
Port Union, NL A0C 2J0
Tel: 709-469-2571; *Fax:* 709-469-3444
tbn@personainternet.com
www.trinitybaynorth.com
Municipal Type: Town
Incorporated: Jan. 1, 2005; *Area:* 14.28 sq km
Population in 2011: 1,827
Provincial Electoral District(s): Bonavista South
Federal Electoral District(s): Bonavista-Burin-Trinity
Next Election: Sept. 26, 2017 (4 year terms)
Note: Effective Jan. 1, 2005, the towns of Catalina, Port Union, & Melrose amalgamated to form the new town of Trinity Bay North. Little Catalina was included on Oct. 1, 2010.
Donald Burt, Mayor
Valerie Rogers, Clerk

Triton
P.O. Box 10
Triton, NL A0J 1V0
Tel: 709-263-2264; *Fax:* 709-263-2381
townoftriton@eastlink.ca
www.townoftriton.ca
Municipal Type: Town
Incorporated: March 11, 1958; *Area:* 7.55 sq km
Population in 2011: 998
Provincial Electoral District(s): Windsor-Springdale
Federal Electoral District(s): Coast of Bays-Central-Notre Dame
Next Election: Sept. 26, 2017 (4 year terms)
Jason Roberts, Mayor
Marcus Vincent, Clerk

Trout River
P.O. Box 89
Trout River, NL A0K 5P0
Tel: 709-451-5376; *Fax:* 709-451-2127
townoftroutriver@nf.aibn.com
Municipal Type: Town
Incorporated: April 12, 1966; *Area:* 5.91 sq km
Population in 2011: 576
Provincial Electoral District(s): Humber Valley
Federal Electoral District(s): Long Range Mountains
Next Election: Sept. 26, 2017 (4 year terms)
Paul Matthews, Mayor
Shelly Emily Butler, Clerk

Twillingate
P.O. Box 220
Twillingate, NL A0G 4M0
Tel: 709-884-2438; *Fax:* 709-884-5278
townoftwillingate@bellaliant.com
Municipal Type: Town
Incorporated: Jan. 1, 1992; *Area:* 25.74 sq km
Population in 2011: 2,268
Provincial Electoral District(s): Twillingate & Fogo
Federal Electoral District(s): Coast of Bays-Central-Notre Dame
Next Election: Sept. 26, 2017 (4 year terms)
Gordon Noseworthy, Mayor
David Burton, Clerk

Upper Island Cove
P.O. Box 149
Upper Island Cove, NL A0A 4E0
Tel: 709-589-2503; *Fax:* 709-589-2522
townoffice@upperislandcove.ca
www.upperislandcove.ca
Municipal Type: Town
Incorporated: Oct. 19, 1965; *Area:* 7.85 sq km
Population in 2011: 1,594
Provincial Electoral District(s): Port de Grave
Federal Electoral District(s): Avalon
Next Election: Sept. 26, 2017 (4 year terms)
George Adams, Mayor
Dorothy Mercer, Clerk

Victoria
P.O. Box 130
Victoria, NL A0A 4G0
Tel: 709-596-3783; *Fax:* 709-596-5020
townofvictoria@nf.aibn.com
Municipal Type: Town
Incorporated: July 1, 1971; *Area:* 17.64 sq km
Population in 2011: 1,764
Provincial Electoral District(s): Carbonear-Harbour Grace
Federal Electoral District(s): Avalon
Next Election: Sept. 26, 2017 (4 year terms)
Barry Dooley, Mayor
Shelly Butt, Clerk

Wabana
P.O. Box 1229
Wabana, NL A0A 4H0
Tel: 709-488-2990; *Fax:* 709-488-3181
info@townofwabana.net
www.townofwabana.net
Municipal Type: Town
Incorporated: Aug. 28, 1950; *Area:* 14.5 sq km
Population in 2011: 2,346
Provincial Electoral District(s): Conception Bay East & Bell Island
Federal Electoral District(s): St. John's East
Next Election: Sept. 26, 2017 (4 year terms)
Gary Gosine, Mayor
Ben Noseworthy, Clerk

Wabush
P.O. Box 190
Wabush, NL A0R 1B0
Tel: 709-282-5696; *Fax:* 709-282-5142
info@wabush.ca
www.labradorwest.com
Municipal Type: Town
Incorporated: April 11, 1967; *Area:* 46.25 sq km
Population in 2011: 1,861
Provincial Electoral District(s): Labrador West
Federal Electoral District(s): Labrador
Next Election: Sept. 26, 2017 (4 year terms)
Colin Vardy, Mayor
Charlie Perry, Town Manager

West St. Modeste
P.O. Box 78
West St Modeste, NL A0K 5S0
Tel: 709-927-5583; *Fax:* 709-927-5898
townofweststmodeste@hotmail.ca
Municipal Type: Town
Incorporated: Aug. 1, 1975; *Area:* 7.78 sq km
Population in 2011: 120
Provincial Electoral District(s): Cartwright-L'Anse au Clair
Federal Electoral District(s): Labrador
Next Election: Sept. 26, 2017 (4 year terms)
Agnes Pike, Mayor
Sandra O'Dell, Clerk

Westport
P.O. Box 29
Westport, NL A0K 5R0
Tel: 709-224-5501; *Fax:* 709-224-5501
Municipal Type: Town
Incorporated: July 18, 1967; *Area:* 5.13 sq km
Population in 2011: 220
Provincial Electoral District(s): Baie Verte
Federal Electoral District(s): Coast of Bays-Central-Notre Dame
Next Election: Sept. 26, 2017 (4 year terms)
Maxwell Warren, Mayor
Peggy Randell, Clerk

Whitbourne
P.O. Box 119
Whitbourne, NL A0B 3K0
Tel: 709-759-2780; *Fax:* 709-759-2016
whit.towncouncil@eastlink.ca
Municipal Type: Town
Incorporated: April 16, 1968; *Area:* 21.41 sq km
Population in 2011: 916
Provincial Electoral District(s): Harbour Main-Whitbourne
Federal Electoral District(s): Bonavista-Burin-Trinity
Next Election: Sept. 26, 2017 (4 year terms)
Hilda Whalen, Mayor
Crystal Peddle, Clerk

Whiteway
420 Main St.
Whiteway, NL A0B 3L0
Tel: 709-588-2948; *Fax:* 709-588-2985
townofwhiteway@eastlink.ca
Municipal Type: Town
Incorporated: Oct. 3, 1975; *Area:* 22.64 sq km
Population in 2011: 293
Provincial Electoral District(s): Trinity-Bay de Verde
Federal Electoral District(s): Bonavista-Burin-Trinity
Next Election: Sept. 26, 2017 (4 year terms)
Craig Whalen, Mayor
Erica Jackson, Clerk

Winterland
P.O. Box 10
Winterland, NL A0E 2Y0
Tel: 709-279-3701; *Fax:* 709-279-3702
townofwinterland@hotmail.com
Municipal Type: Town
Incorporated: Nov. 24, 1970; *Area:* 54.34 sq km
Population in 2011: 363
Provincial Electoral District(s): Grand Bank
Federal Electoral District(s): Bonavista-Burin-Trinity
Next Election: Sept. 26, 2017 (4 year terms)
Ches Kenway, Mayor
Marlyese Simms, Clerk

Winterton
P.O. Box 59
Winterton, NL A0B 3M0
Tel: 709-583-2010; *Fax:* 709-583-2099
info@winterton.ca
www.winterton.ca
Municipal Type: Town
Incorporated: April 15, 1964; *Area:* 10.52 sq km
Population in 2011: 484
Provincial Electoral District(s): Trinity-Bay de Verde
Federal Electoral District(s): Bonavista-Burin-Trinity
Next Election: Sept. 26, 2017 (4 year terms)
Mark Sheppard, Mayor
Stephanie Crocker, Clerk

Witless Bay
P.O. Box 130
Witless Bay, NL A0A 4K0
Tel: 709-334-3407; *Fax:* 709-334-2377
townofwitlessbay@nl.rogers.com
www.townofwitlessbay.com
Municipal Type: Town
Incorporated: Jan. 1, 1986; *Area:* 17.49 sq km
Population in 2011: 1,179
Provincial Electoral District(s): Ferryland
Federal Electoral District(s): St. John's South-Mount Pearl
Next Election: Sept. 26, 2017 (4 year terms)
Sebastien Despres, Mayor
Geraldine Caul, Clerk

Woodstock
19 Park St.
Woodstock, NL A0K 5X0
Tel: 709-251-3176; *Fax:* 709-251-3176
townofwoodstock@nf.aibn.com
Municipal Type: Town
Incorporated: Sept. 29, 1970; *Area:* 10.09 sq km
Population in 2011: 190
Provincial Electoral District(s): Baie Verte
Federal Electoral District(s): Avalon; Coast of Bays-Central-Notre Dame
Next Election: Sept. 26, 2017 (4 year terms)
Rosalyn Arnaldo, Mayor
Tracey Decker, Clerk

Woody Point
P.O. Box 100
Woody Point, NL A0K 1P0
Tel: 709-453-2273; *Fax:* 709-453-2270
www.woodypoint.ca
Municipal Type: Town
Incorporated: March 27, 1956; *Area:* 2.91 sq km
Population in 2011: 281
Provincial Electoral District(s): Humber Valley
Federal Electoral District(s): Long Range Mountains
Next Election: Sept. 26, 2017 (4 year terms)
Ken Thomas, Mayor
Jacqueline Blanchard, Clerk

York Harbour
P.O. Box 179
136-138 Main St.
York Harbour, NL A0L 1L0
Tel: 709-681-2280; *Fax:* 709-681-2799
yorkharbourcouncil@nf.aibn.com
yorkharbourlarkharbour.com
Municipal Type: Town
Incorporated: June 27, 1972; *Area:* 3.9 sq km
Population in 2011: 347
Provincial Electoral District(s): Bay of Islands
Federal Electoral District(s): Long Range Mountains
Next Election: Sept. 26, 2017 (4 year terms)
Florence Lombard, Mayor
Michelle Sheppard, Clerk

NORTHWEST TERRITORIES

The Department of Municipal and Community Affairs is responsible for the following legislation regarding municipalities in the Territory: Business License Act; Charter Communities Act; Cities, Towns and Villages Act; Civil Emergency Measures Act; Community Employees Benefits Act; Community Planning and Development Act; Consumer Protection Act; Cost of Credit Disclosure Act; Dog Act; Film Classification Act; Fire Prevention Act; Hamlets Act; Home Owner's Property Tax Rebate Act; Local Authorities Elections Act; Lotteries Act; Property Assessment and Taxation Act; Real Estate Agent's Licensing Act; Senior Citizens and Disabled Persons Property Tax Relief Act; Tłı̨chǫ Community Government Act; Western Canada Lottery Act.

Incorporation as a city, town or village is determined by the value of all assessable land. Incorporation values: Village, $10 million; Town, $50 million; City, $200 million. All tax-based. Hamlets and Charter Communities may request tax-based status.

Local Authorities Elections: three years for cities, towns and villages; two years/staggered terms for hamlets and settlements; two to three years for charter communities. The Minister may extend or shorten terms on applications. Except for settlement councils, heads of councils are elected by separate ballot. First Nations conduct their own electoral process.

Heads of Councils: Mayor, K'wati, Ehk'Wahtide, Chief, Chairperson.

First Nations provide municipal services as the main governing authority in several communities. On March 13, 2014, the Charter Community of Déline voted in favour of self-government. The Déline Gotine Government began operating in September 2016, and is responsible for matters such as health care, justice and adoption.

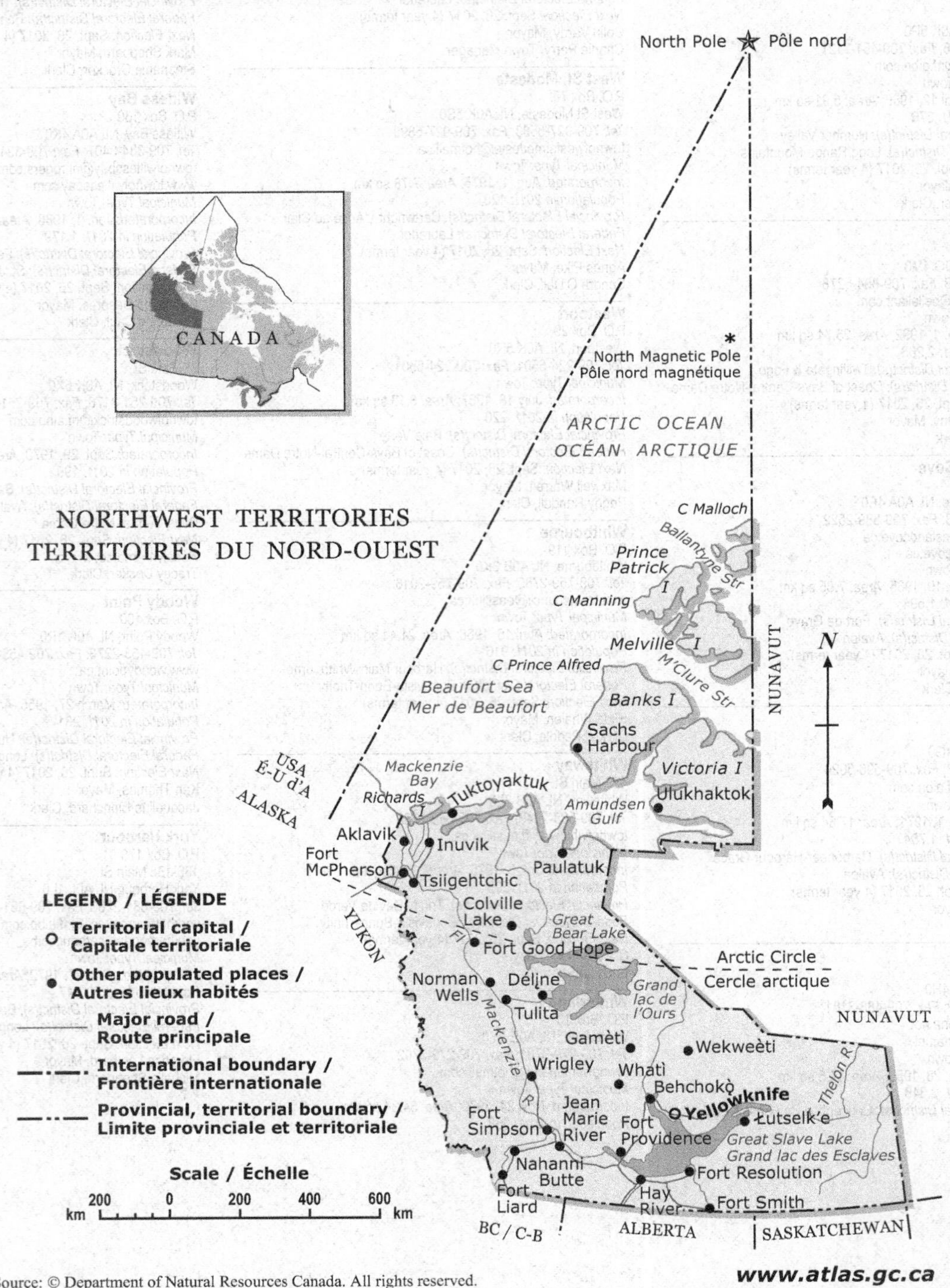

Northwest Territories

Major Municipalities in Northwest Territories

Yellowknife
P.O. Box 580
4807 - 52 St.
Yellowknife, NT X1A 2N4
Tel: 867-920-5600; *Fax:* 867-920-5649
cityclerk@yellowknife.ca
www.yellowknife.ca
Other Information: Alt. E-mail: council@yellowknife.ca
Municipal Type: City
Incorporated: Jan. 1, 1970; *Area:* 105.22 sq km
Population in 2011: 19,234
Provincial Electoral District(s): Yellowknife South; Yellowknife Centre; Frame Lake; Great Slave; Weledeh; Kam Lake, Range Lake
Federal Electoral District(s): Northwest Territories
Next Election: Oct. 15, 2018 (3 year terms)
Mark Heyck, Mayor
Rebecca Alty, City Councillor
Adrian Bell, City Councillor
Linda Bussey, City Councillor
Niels Konge, City Councillor
Shauna Morgan, City Councillor
Julian Morse, City Councillor
Steve Payne, City Councillor
Rommel Silverio, City Councillor
Debbie Gillard, City Clerk, 867-920-5646
Dennis Kefalas, Senior Administrative Officer, 867-920-5685, Fax: 867-920-5649
Darcy Hernblad, Fire Chief, 867-766-5501
Chris Greencorn, Director, Public Works & Engineering, 867-920-5624
Jeffrey Humble, Director, Planning & Development, 867-920-5685
Dennis Marchiori, Director, Public Safety, 867-920-5685
Nalini Naidoo, Director, Communications & Economic Development, 867-920-5660
Clem Hand, Manager, Corporate Services & Risk Assessment, 867-920-5617
Carl Grabke, Supervisor, Solid Waste Management Facility, 867-669-3406

Other Municipalities in Northwest Territories

Aklavik
P.O. Box 88
Aklavik, NT X0E 0A0
Tel: 867-978-2351; *Fax:* 867-978-2434
www.aklavik.ca
Other Information: Alternate Phone: 867-978-2361
Municipal Type: Hamlet
Incorporated: Jan. 1, 1974; *Area:* 8.16 sq km
Population in 2011: 633
Provincial Electoral District(s): Mackenzie Delta
Federal Electoral District(s): Northwest Territories
Charles Furlong, Mayor
Fred Behrens, Senior Administrative Officer

Behchokò
P.O. Box 68
Behchokò, NT X0E 0Y0
Tel: 867-392-6500; *Fax:* 867-392-6139
www.tlicho.ca/community/behchoko
Other Information: Alt. Phone 867-392-6561
Municipal Type: Tłı̨chǫ Community Government
Area: 75.08 sq km
Population in 2011: 1,926
Provincial Electoral District(s): Monfwi
Federal Electoral District(s): Northwest Territories
Clifford Daniels, Chief
John Hazenberg, Senior Administrative Officer

Colville Lake
Behdzi Ahda First Nation
P.O. Box 53
Colville Lake, NT X0E 0L0
Tel: 867-709-2200; *Fax:* 867-709-2202
Municipal Type: Settlement Corporation
Incorporated: Nov. 30, 1995; *Area:* 128.3 sq km
Population in 2011: 149
Provincial Electoral District(s): Sahtu
Federal Electoral District(s): Northwest Territories
Wilbert Kochon, Chief
Joseph Kochon, Band Manager

Déline
P.O. Box 180
Deline, NT X0E 0G0
Tel: 867-589-4800; *Fax:* 867-589-4106
www.deline.ca
Other Information: Alternate Phone: 867-589-3604
Municipal Type: Charter Community
Incorporated: April 1, 1993; *Area:* 79.33 sq km
Population in 2011: 472
Provincial Electoral District(s): Sahtu
Federal Electoral District(s): Northwest Territories
Note: Déline sets its election date through its community charter. On March 13, 2014, the community voted in favour of self-government. Once approved, the Deline Gotine Government will be formed.
Leonard Kenny, Chief
Kirk Dolphus, Senior Administrative Officer

Dettah
Yellowknives Dene First Nation
P.O. Box 2514
Yellowknife, NT X1A 2P8
Tel: 867-873-4307; *Fax:* 867-873-5969
dettahadmin@ykdene.com
www.ykdene.com
Municipal Type: First Nations/Governing Authority
Area: 1.34 sq km
Population in 2011: 210
Provincial Electoral District(s): Weledeh
Federal Electoral District(s): Northwest Territories
Edward Sangris, Chief
Ernest Betsina, Chief
Michael Cheeks, Chief Executive Officer

Enterprise
526 Robin Rd.
Enterprise, NT X0E 0R1
Tel: 867-984-3491; *Fax:* 867-984-3400
Municipal Type: Hamlet
Incorporated: July 1, 1988; *Area:* 286.9 sq km
Population in 2011: 87
Provincial Electoral District(s): Deh Cho
Federal Electoral District(s): Northwest Territories
Craig McMaster, Mayor
Tammy Neal, Senior Administrative Officer

Fort Good Hope
K'asho Got'ine Charter Community
P.O. Box 80
Fort Good Hope, NT X0E 0H0
Tel: 867-598-2231; *Fax:* 867-598-2024
Other Information: Alternate Phone: 867-598-2232
Municipal Type: Charter Community
Incorporated: April 1, 1995; *Area:* 52.82 sq km
Population in 2011: 515
Provincial Electoral District(s): Sahtu
Federal Electoral District(s): Northwest Territories
Note: Fort Good Hope sets its election date through its community charter.
Wilfred Glenn McNeely Jr., Chief
Wilbert Cook, Senior Administrative Officer

Fort Liard
General Delivery
Fort Liard, NT X0G 0A0
Tel: 867-770-4104; *Fax:* 867-770-4004
www.fortliard.com
Municipal Type: Hamlet
Incorporated: April 1, 1987; *Area:* 67.96 sq km
Population in 2011: 536
Provincial Electoral District(s): Nahendeh
Federal Electoral District(s): Northwest Territories
Steven Steeves, Mayor
Mark Misquitta, Senior Administrative Officer

Fort McPherson
P.O. Box 57
Fort McPherson, NT X0E 0J0
Tel: 867-952-2428; *Fax:* 867-952-2725
supervisor@fortmcpherson.ca
www.fortmcpherson.ca
Municipal Type: Hamlet
Incorporated: Nov. 1, 1986; *Area:* 53.06 sq km
Population in 2011: 792
Provincial Electoral District(s): Mackenzie Delta
Federal Electoral District(s): Northwest Territories
Note: Governing powers were revoked from the hamlet on July 22, 2014, & given to a municipal administrator. A new municipal election will likely be held within one to two years.
Bill Buckle, Municipal Administrator

Fort Providence
P.O. Box 290
Fort Providence, NT X0E 0L0
Tel: 867-699-3441; *Fax:* 867-699-3360
Municipal Type: Hamlet
Incorporated: Jan. 1, 1987; *Area:* 256.33 sq km
Population in 2011: 734
Provincial Electoral District(s): Deh Cho
Federal Electoral District(s): Northwest Territories
Sam Gargan, Mayor
Susan Christie, Senior Administrative Officer

Fort Resolution
General Delivery
P.O. Box 197
Fort Resolution, NT X0E 0M0
Tel: 867-394-4556; *Fax:* 867-394-5415
Municipal Type: Settlement Corporation
Incorporated: April 1, 1988; *Area:* 455.06 sq km
Population in 2011: 474
Provincial Electoral District(s): Tu Nedhe
Federal Electoral District(s): Northwest Territories
Garry Bailey, Mayor
Tausia Kaitu'u-Lal, Senior Administrative Officer

Fort Simpson
P.O. Box 438
Fort Simpson, NT X0E 0N0
Tel: 867-695-2253; *Fax:* 867-695-2005
adminasst@vofs.ca
www.fortsimpson.com
Municipal Type: Village
Incorporated: Jan. 1, 1973; *Area:* 78.32 sq km
Population in 2011: 1,238
Provincial Electoral District(s): Nahendeh
Federal Electoral District(s): Northwest Territories
Next Election: Oct. 15, 2018 (3 year terms)
Darlene Sibbeston, Mayor
Beth Jumbo, Senior Administrative Officer, 867-695-2253

Fort Smith
P.O. Box 147
174 McDougal Rd.
Fort Smith, NT X0E 0P0
Tel: 867-872-8400; *Fax:* 867-872-8401
townoffortsmith@fortsmith.ca
www.fortsmith.ca
Municipal Type: Town
Incorporated: Oct. 1, 1966; *Area:* 92.79 sq km
Population in 2011: 2,093
Provincial Electoral District(s): Thebacha
Federal Electoral District(s): Northwest Territories
Next Election: Oct. 15, 2018 (3 year terms)
Lynn Napier Buckley, Mayor
Keith Morrison, Senior Administrative Officer, 867-872-8400

Gamèti
Gameti First Nation
P.O. Box 1
Gameti, NT X0E 1R0
Tel: 867-997-3441; *Fax:* 867-997-3411
Municipal Type: Tłı̨chǫ Community Government
Incorporated: Aug. 4, 2005; *Area:* 9.18 sq km
Population in 2011: 253
Provincial Electoral District(s): Monfwi
Federal Electoral District(s): Northwest Territories
David Wedawin, Chief
Judal Dominicata, Senior Administrative Officer

Hay River
73 Woodland Dr.
Hay River, NT X0E 1G1
Tel: 867-874-6522; *Fax:* 867-874-3237
townhall@hayriver.com
www.hayriver.com
Municipal Type: Town
Incorporated: June 16, 1963; *Area:* 132.58 sq km
Population in 2011: 3,606
Provincial Electoral District(s): Hay River North; Hay River South
Federal Electoral District(s): Northwest Territories
Next Election: Oct. 15, 2018 (3 year terms)
Bradley Mapes, Mayor
Scotty Edgerton, Senior Administrative Officer

Inuvik
P.O. Box 1160
2 Firth St.
Inuvik, NT X0E 0T0
Tel: 867-777-8600; *Fax:* 867-777-8601
www.inuvik.ca
Municipal Type: Town
Incorporated: Jan. 1, 1979; *Area:* 49.76 sq km

Population in 2011: 3,463
Provincial Electoral District(s): Inuvik Twin Lakes; Inuvik Boot Lake
Federal Electoral District(s): Northwest Territories
Next Election: Oct. 15, 2018 (3 year terms)
Jim McDonald, Mayor
Steven Baryluk, Deputy Mayor & Councillor
Joseph Lavoie, Assistant Deputy Mayor & Councillor
Darell Christie, Councillor
Natasha Kulikowski, Councillor
Alana Mero, Councillor
Vince Sharpe, Councillor
Kurt Wainman, Councillor
Clarence Wood, Councillor
Grant Hood, Senior Administrator Officer, 867-777-8608

Jean Marie River
TthedzedK'edili First Nation
General Delivery
Jean Marie River, NT X0E 0N0
Tel: 867-809-2000; *Fax:* 867-809-2002
www.jmrfn.com
Municipal Type: First Nations/Governing Authority
Area: 37.26 sq km
Population in 2011: 64
Provincial Electoral District(s): Nahendeh
Federal Electoral District(s): Northwest Territories
Gladys Norwegian, Chief
Pamela Norwegian, Senior Administrative Officer

K'atlodeeche
K'atlodeeche First Nation
P.O. Box 3060
Hay River, NT X0E 1G4
Tel: 867-874-6701; *Fax:* 867-874-3229
www.katlodeeche.com
Municipal Type: Reserve
Area: 134.21 sq km
Population in 2011: 292
Provincial Electoral District(s): Deh Cho
Federal Electoral District(s): Northwest Territories
Note: Also known as Hay River Reserve or Hay River Dene 1.
Roy Fabian, Chief
Peter Groenen, Senior Administrative Officer

Kakisa
Ka'a'gee Tu First Nation
P.O. Box 4428
Hay River, NT X0E 1G4
Tel: 867-825-2000; *Fax:* 867-825-2002
Municipal Type: First Nations/Governing Authority
Area: 94.82 sq km
Population in 2011: 45
Provincial Electoral District(s): Deh Cho
Federal Electoral District(s): Northwest Territories
Lloyd Chicot, Chief
Ruby Landry, Council Manager

Lutsel K'e
Lutsel K'e Dene Band
P.O. Box 28
Lutselk'e, NT X0E 1A0
Tel: 867-370-7000; *Fax:* 867-370-3010
Municipal Type: First Nations/Governing Authority
Area: 43.01 sq km
Population in 2011: 295
Provincial Electoral District(s): Tu Nedhe
Federal Electoral District(s): Northwest Territories
Felix Lockhart, Chief
Agatha Laboucan, Senior Administrative Officer

Nahanni Butte
Nahanni Butte Dene Band
General Delivery
Fort Simpson, NT X0E 0N0
Tel: 867-602-2900; *Fax:* 867-602-2910
Municipal Type: First Nations/Governing Authority
Area: 78.96 sq km
Population in 2011: 102
Provincial Electoral District(s): Nahendeh
Federal Electoral District(s): Northwest Territories
Mike Matou, Chief
Frank Moretti, Senior Administrative Officer

Norman Wells
P.O. Box 5
Norman Wells, NT X0E 0V0
Tel: 867-587-3700; *Fax:* 867-587-3701
info@normanwells.com
www.normanwells.com
Municipal Type: Town
Incorporated: April 12, 1992; *Area:* 93.28 sq km
Population in 2011: 727
Provincial Electoral District(s): Sahtu
Federal Electoral District(s): Northwest Territories
Next Election: Oct. 15, 2018 (3 year terms)
Nathan Watson, Mayor, 867-587-6741, Fax: 867-587-2718
Catherine Mallon, Town Manager, 867-587-3703, Fax: 867-587-3701

Paulatuk
P.O. Box 98
Paulatuk, NT X0E 1N0
Tel: 867-580-3531; *Fax:* 867-580-3703
hopaulatuk@gmail.com
Municipal Type: Hamlet
Incorporated: April 1, 1987; *Area:* 66.76 sq km
Population in 2011: 313
Provincial Electoral District(s): Nunakput
Federal Electoral District(s): Northwest Territories
Ray Ruben, Sr., Mayor
Greg Morash, Senior Administrative Officer

Sachs Harbour
General Delivery
P.O. Box 90
Sachs Harbour, NT X0E 0Z0
Tel: 867-690-4351; *Fax:* 867-690-4802
Municipal Type: Hamlet
Incorporated: April 1, 1986; *Area:* 290.94 sq km
Population in 2011: 112
Provincial Electoral District(s): Nunakput
Federal Electoral District(s): Northwest Territories
Lloyd Acheson, Mayor
Stephen Wylie, Senior Administrative Officer, 897-960-4351, Fax: 897-690-4802

Trout Lake
Sambaa K'e Dene Band
P.O. Box 10
Trout Lake, NT X0E 1Z0
Tel: 867-206-2800; *Fax:* 867-206-2828
Municipal Type: First Nations/Governing Authority
Area: 119.42 sq km
Population in 2011: 92
Provincial Electoral District(s): Nahendeh
Federal Electoral District(s): Northwest Territories
Dolphus Jumbo, Chief
Ruby Jumbo, Band Manager

Tsiigehtchic
General Delivery
Tsiigehtchic, NT X0E 0B0
Tel: 867-953-3201; *Fax:* 867-953-3302
Municipal Type: Charter Community
Incorporated: June 21, 1993; *Area:* 48.98 sq km
Population in 2011: 143
Provincial Electoral District(s): Mackenzie Delta
Federal Electoral District(s): Northwest Territories
Note: Tsiigehtchic sets its election date through its community charter.
Phillip Blake, Chief
Marjorie Dobson, Senior Administrative Officer

Tuktoyaktuk
P.O. Box 120
Tuktoyaktuk, NT X0E 1C0
Tel: 867-977-2286; *Fax:* 867-977-2110
Municipal Type: Hamlet
Incorporated: April 1, 1970; *Area:* 11.07 sq km
Population in 2011: 854
Provincial Electoral District(s): Nunakput
Federal Electoral District(s): Northwest Territories
Darrel Nasogaluak, Mayor
William Beamish, Senior Administrative Officer

Tulita
General Delivery
P.O. Box 91
Tulita, NT X0E 0K0
Tel: 867-588-4471; *Fax:* 867-588-4908
Municipal Type: Hamlet
Incorporated: April 1, 1984; *Area:* 51.74 sq km
Population in 2011: 478
Provincial Electoral District(s): Sahtu
Federal Electoral District(s): Northwest Territories
Rocky Norwegian Sr., Mayor
Roberto Moretti, Senior Administrative Officer

Ulukhaktok
P.O. Box 157
Ulukhaktok, NT X0E 0S0
Tel: 867-396-8000; *Fax:* 867-396-8001
Municipal Type: Hamlet
Incorporated: April 1, 1984; *Area:* 124.43 sq km
Population in 2011: 402
Provincial Electoral District(s): Nunakput
Federal Electoral District(s): Northwest Territories
Note: Formerly known as Holman.
Laverna Klengenberg, Mayor
Judi Wall, Senior Administrative Officer

Wekweeti
Community Government of Wekweeti
P.O. Box 69
Wekweeti, NT X0E 1W0
Tel: 867-713-2010; *Fax:* 867-713-2030
Municipal Type: Tlîchô Community Government
Incorporated: Aug. 4, 2005; *Area:* 14.66 sq km
Population in 2011: 141
Provincial Electoral District(s): Monfwi
Federal Electoral District(s): Northwest Territories
Johnny Arrowmaker, Chief
Grace Angel, Senior Administrative Officer

Whatì
Community Government of Whatì
P.O. Box 71
Whatì, NT X0E 1P0
Tel: 867-573-3401; *Fax:* 867-573-3018
www.tlicho.ca/community/whati
Municipal Type: Tlîchô Community Government
Incorporated: Aug. 4, 2005; *Area:* 15.18 sq km
Population in 2011: 492
Provincial Electoral District(s): Monfwi
Federal Electoral District(s): Western Arctic
Alfonz Nitsiza, Chief
Larry Baran, Senior Administrative Officer

Wrigley
Pehdzeh Ki First Nation
General Delivery
Wrigley, NT X0E 1E0
Tel: 867-581-3321; *Fax:* 867-581-3229
pklands@northwestel.net
Municipal Type: First Nations/Governing Authority
Area: 55.83 sq km
Population in 2011: 133
Provincial Electoral District(s): Nahendeh
Federal Electoral District(s): Northwest Territories
Darcy E. Moses, Chief
Tim Lennie, Acting Senior Administrative Official

NOVA SCOTIA

Nova Scotia is geographically divided into 18 counties. Twelve of these constitute separate municipalities (three are regional municipalities). The remaining six are each divided into two districts and each of these constitutes a separate municipality. Thus there are 21 rural municipalities. Within each of these areas are 31 autonomous incorporated towns and other local organizations with limited jurisdiction, including school boards, boards of school trustees, village commissions, local service commissions, rural fire districts and other special purpose forms.

Incorporation of a town is governed by the Municipal Government Act, Sections 383 to 393 (dissolution is governed by Sections 394 to 402).

The organization of municipalities and villages is governed by the Municipal Government Act. Additional regulation is provided by the Municipal Finance Corporation Act.

All general and special municipal elections, including elections for school board members, are governed by the Municipal Elections Act, 1979. The term of office for mayors, councillors, aldermen, and elective school board members is four years. Elections take place on the third Saturday in October in every four years (2016, 2020, etc.).

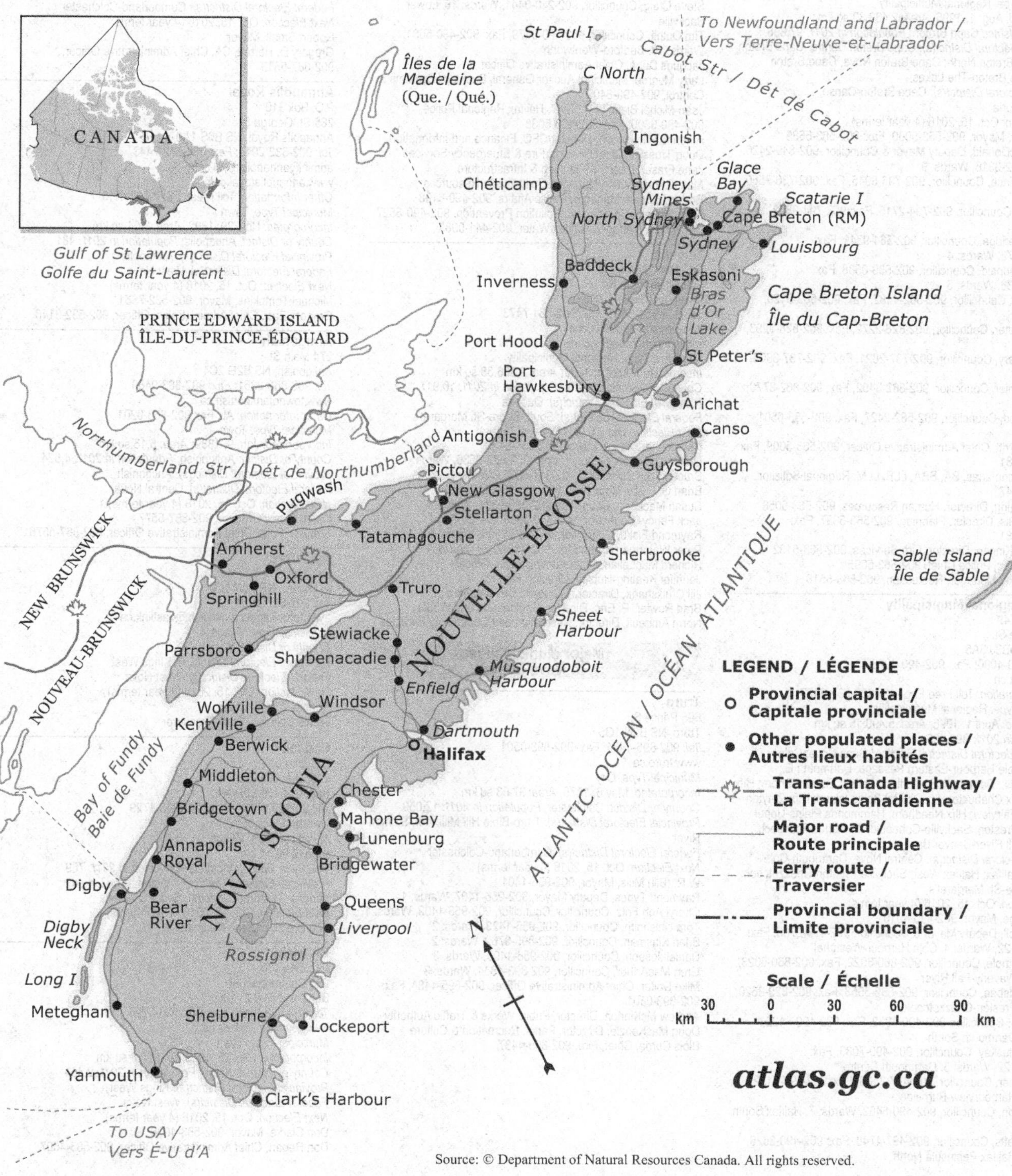

Source: © Department of Natural Resources Canada.

Nova Scotia

Counties & Municipal Districts in Nova Scotia

Cape Breton
320 Esplanade
Sydney, NS B1P 7B9
Tel: 902-563-5080; *Fax:* 902-564-0481
cbrm@cbrm.ns.ca
www.cbrm.ns.ca
Municipal Type: Regional Municipality
Incorporated: Aug. 1, 1995; *Area:* 2,433.33 sq km
County or District: Cape Breton; *Population in 2011:* 97,398
Provincial Electoral District(s): Cape Breton Centre; Cape Breton East; Cape Breton North; Cape Breton Nova; Cape Breton South; Cape Breton-The Lakes
Federal Electoral District(s): Cape Breton-Canso; Sydney-Victoria
Next Election: Oct. 15, 2016 (4 year terms)
Cecil Clarke, Mayor, 902-563-5000, Fax: 902-563-5585
George MacDonald, Deputy Mayor & Councillor, 902-849-2426, Fax: 902-842-3316, Wards: 9
Clarence Prince, Councillor, 902-736-8045, Fax: 902-736-7580, Wards: 1
Mae Rowe, Councillor, 902-794-2715, Fax: 902-794-9362, Wards: 3
Claire Detheridge, Councillor, 902-564-9341, Fax: 902-563-5179, Wards: 4
Eldon MacDonald, Councillor, 902-539-0588, Fax: 902-564-1036, Wards: 5
Ray Paruch, Councillor, 902-562-4482, Fax: 902-563-5129, Wards: 6
Ivan Doncaster, Councillor, 902-828-2272, Fax: 902-828-3293, Wards: 7
Kevin Saccary, Councillor, 902-737-2821, Fax: 902-737-3003, Wards: 8
Lowell Cormier, Councillor, 902-862-3462, Fax: 902-862-3770, Wards: 11
Jim MacLeod, Councillor, 902-562-2427, Fax: 902-563-5501, Wards: 12
Michael Merritt, Chief Administrative Officer, 902-563-5009, Fax: 902-564-0481
Demetri Kachafanas, BA, BBA, LLB, LLM, Regional Solicitor, 902-563-5047
Angus Fleming, Director, Human Resources, 902-563-5058
Malcolm Gillis, Director, Planning, 902-563-5027, Fax: 902-564-0481
Bernie MacKinnon, Director, Fire Services, 902-563-5132
Peter McIsaac, Police Chief, 902-563-5095
Christa Dicks, Manager, Recreation, 902-563-5510

Halifax Regional Municipality
P.O. Box 1749
1841 Argyle St.
Halifax, NS B3J 3A5
Tel: 902-490-4000; *Fax:* 902-490-4208
www.halifax.ca
Other Information: Toll Free Phone: 1-800-835-6428
Municipal Type: Regional Municipality
Incorporated: April 1, 1996; *Area:* 5,490.18 sq km
Population in 2011: 390,096
Provincial Electoral District(s): Bedford-Birch Cove; Cole Harbour; Cole Harbour-Eastern Passage; Dartmouth E.; Dartmouth N.; Dartmouth S.-Portland Valley; Eastern Shore; Hlfx Atlantic; Hlfx Chebucto; Hlfx Citadel-Sable Island; Hlfx-Clayton Park; Hlfx Fairview; Hlfx Needham; Hammonds Plains-Upper Sackville; Preston; Sackville-Cobequid; Timberlea-Prospect; Waverly-Fall River-Beaver Bank
Federal Electoral District(s): Central Nova; Dartmouth-Cole Harbour; Halifax; Halifax West; Sackville-Preston-Chezzetcook; South Shore-St. Margaret's
Next Election: Oct. 15, 2016 (4 year terms)
Mike Savage, Mayor, 902-490-4010
Lorelei Nicoll, Deputy Mayor & Councillor, 902-478-2705, Fax: 902-490-4122, Wards: 4. Cole Harbour-Westphal
Barry Dalrymple, Councillor, 902-860-6022, Fax: 902-860-6023, Wards: 1. Waverly-Fall River
David Hendsbee, Councillor, 902-889-3553, Fax: 902-829-3620, Wards: 2. Preston-Chezzetcook
Bill Karsten, Councillor, 902-490-7032, Fax: 902-490-4122, Wards: 3. Dartmouth South
Gloria McCluskey, Councillor, 902-490-7033, Fax: 902-490-4122, Wards: 5. Dartmouth Centre
Darren Fisher, Councillor, 902-497-7166, Fax: 902-490-4122, Wards: 6. Harbourview-Burnside
Waye Mason, Councillor, 902-490-8462, Wards: 7. Halifax South Downtown
Jennifer Watts, Councillor, 902-497-4748, Fax: 902-490-2626, Wards: 8. Halifax Peninsula North
Linda Mosher, Councillor, 902-477-8618, Wards: 9. Halifax West Armdale
Russell Walker, Councillor, 902-443-8010, Fax: 902-443-6513, Wards: 10. Halifax-Bedford Basin West
Stephen Adams, Councillor, 902-477-0627, Fax: 902-490-4122, Wards: 11. Spyfield-Sambro Loop
Reg Rankin, Councillor, 902-499-3744, Fax: 902-876-4304, Wards: 12. Timberlea-Beechville
Matt Whitman, Councillor, 902-240-3330, Fax: 902-490-4122, Wards: 13. Hammonds Plains
Brad Johns, Councillor, 902-476-1234, Fax: 902-869-4749, Wards: 14. Middle/Upper Sackville
Steve Craig, Councillor, 902-240-0441, Wards: 15. Lower Sackville
Tim Outhit, Councillor, 902-490-5679, Fax: 902-490-5681, Wards: 16. Bedford-Wentworth
Jacques Dubé, Chief Administrative Officer
Larry Munroe, Municipal Auditor General, Business Systems & Control, 902-490-8407
Jean-Michel Blais, LLB, Chief, Halifax Regional Police, 902-490-6500, Fax: 902-490-5038
Amanda Whitewood, Director/CFO, Finance and Information
Doug Trussler, Chief Director, Fire & Emergency Services
Jane Fraser, Director, Planning & Infrastructure
Matt Keliher, Acting Manager, Solid Waste Resources
Breton Murphy, Manager, Public Affairs, 902-490-6198
John Sibbald, Coordinator, Pollution Prevention, 902-490-5527
Carl Yates, Manager, Halifax Water, 902-441-0985

Queens
P.O. Box 1264
249 White Point Rd.
Liverpool, NS B0T 1K0
Tel: 902-354-3453; *Fax:* 902-354-7473
info@regionofqueens.com
www.regionofqueens.com
Municipal Type: Regional Municipality
Incorporated: April 1, 1996; *Area:* 2,386.58 sq km
County or District: Queens; *Population in 2011:* 10,917
Provincial Electoral District(s): Queens
Federal Electoral District(s): South Shore-St. Margaret's
Next Election: Oct. 15, 2016 (4 year terms)
Christopher Clarke, Mayor, 902-354-3453
Darlene Norman, Deputy Mayor, 902-683-2530, Wards: 1
Bruce Inglis, Councillor, 902-354-5075, Wards: 2
Brian G. Fralic, Councillor, 902-354-5308, Wards: 3
Susan MacLeod, Councillor, 902-350-0334, Wards: 4
Jack Fancy, Councillor, 902-350-3905, Wards: 5
Raymond Fiske, Councillor, 902-685-2990, Wards: 6
Peter Waterman, Councillor, 902-212-2239, Wards: 7
Richard MacLellan, Chief Administrative Officer
Jennifer Keating-Hubley, Director, Finance
Jill Cruikshank, Director, Economic Development
Brad Rowter, P. Eng, Director, Engineering and Works
Norm Amirault, Director, Recreation and Community Facilities

Major Municipalities in Nova Scotia

Truro
695 Prince St.
Truro, NS B2N 1G5
Tel: 902-895-4484; *Fax:* 902-893-0501
www.truro.ca
Municipal Type: City
Incorporated: May 6, 1875; *Area:* 37.63 sq km
County or District: Colchester; *Population in 2011:* 12,059
Provincial Electoral District(s): Truro-Bible Hill-Millbrook-Salmon River
Federal Electoral District(s): Cumberland-Colchester
Next Election: Oct. 15, 2016 (4 year terms)
W.R. (Bill) Mills, Mayor, 902-956-1401
Raymond Tynes, Deputy Mayor, 902-956-1407, Wards: 1
Cheryl Ann Fritz, Councillor, Councillor, 902-956-1402, Wards: 1
Tom Chisholm, Councillor, 902-956-1423, Wards: 2
Brian Kinsman, Councillor, 902-895-9762, Wards: 2
Daniel Joseph, Councillor, 902-956-1403, Wards: 3
Greg MacArthur, Councillor, 902-893-4834, Wards: 3
Mike Dolter, Chief Administrative Officer, 902-895-4484, Fax: 902-893-0501
Andrew McKinnon, Director, Public Works & Traffic Authority
Doug MacKenzie, Director, Parks, Recreation & Culture
Blois Currie, Chief, Fire, 902-895-4437

Other Municipalities in Nova Scotia

Amherst
98 East Victoria Street
Amherst, NS B4H 1X6
Tel: 902-667-3352; *Fax:* 902-667-3356
www.amherst.ca
Municipal Type: Town
Incorporated: Dec. 18, 1889; *Area:* 12.02 sq km
County or District: Cumberland; *Population in 2011:* 9,717
Provincial Electoral District(s): Cumberland North
Federal Electoral District(s): Cumberland-Colchester
Next Election: Oct. 15, 2016 (4 year terms)
Robert Small, Mayor
Gregory D. Herrett, CA, Chief Administrative Officer, 902-667-6513

Annapolis Royal
P.O. Box 310
285 St. George St.
Annapolis Royal, NS B0S 1A0
Tel: 902-532-2043; *Fax:* 902-532-7443
admin@annapolisroyal.com
www.annapolisroyal.com
Other Information: Toll Free: 1-877-522-1110
Municipal Type: Town
Incorporated: Nov. 29, 1892; *Area:* 2.04 sq km
County or District: Annapolis; *Population in 2011:* 481
Provincial Electoral District(s): Annapolis
Federal Electoral District(s): West Nova
Next Election: Oct. 15, 2016 (4 year terms)
Michael Tompkins, Mayor, 902-532-7551
Gregory Barr, Chief Administrative Officer, 902-532-3146

Antigonish
274 Main St.
Antigonish, NS B2G 2C4
Tel: 902-863-2351; *Fax:* 902-863-0460
www.townofantigonish.ca
Other Information: Alt. Fax 902-863-9201
Municipal Type: Town
Incorporated: Jan. 9, 1889; *Area:* 5.15 sq km
County or District: Antigonish; *Population in 2011:* 4,524
Provincial Electoral District(s): Antigonish
Federal Electoral District(s): Central Nova
Next Election: Oct. 15, 2016 (4 year terms)
Carl Chisholm, Mayor, 902-867-5577
Stephen Feist, Chief Administrative Officer, 902-867-5576

Aylesford
P.O. Box 91
Aylesford, NS B0P 1C0
Tel: 902-847-0827
aylesfordvillagecommission@eastlink.ca
Municipal Type: Village
County or District: Kings
Provincial Electoral District(s): Kings West
Federal Electoral District(s): West Nova
Next Election: Oct. 15, 2016 (4 year terms)
Rhonda Carey, Chair
Trudie Spinney, Clerk-Treasurer

Baddeck
P.O. Box 63
495 Chebucto St.
Baddeck, NS B0E 1B0
Tel: 902-295-3666; *Fax:* 902-295-1729
www.baddeck.com
Municipal Type: Village
Area: 2.08 sq km
County or District: Victoria; *Population in 2011:* 769
Provincial Electoral District(s): Victoria-The Lakes
Federal Electoral District(s): Sydney-Victoria
Next Election: Oct. 15, 2016 (4 year terms)
Erin Bradley, Clerk-Treasurer

Berwick
P.O. Box 130
236 Commercial St.
Berwick, NS B0P 1E0
Tel: 902-538-8068; *Fax:* 902-538-3724
www.town.berwick.ns.ca
Municipal Type: Town
Incorporated: May 25, 1923; *Area:* 6.8 sq km
County or District: Kings; *Population in 2011:* 2,454
Provincial Electoral District(s): Kings West
Federal Electoral District(s): West Nova
Next Election: Oct. 15, 2016 (4 year terms)
Don Clarke, Mayor, 902-583-4008
Don Regan, Chief Administrative Officer, 902-583-4007

Bible Hill
67 Pictou Rd.
Bible Hill, NS B2N 2R9
Tel: 902-893-8083
clerk@biblehill.ca
www.biblehill.ca
Municipal Type: Village
County or District: Colchester; *Population in 2011:* 5,500
Provincial Electoral District(s): Truro-Bible Hill-Millbrook-Salmon River
Federal Electoral District(s): Cumberland-Colchester
Next Election: Oct. 15, 2016 (4 year terms)
Tom Burke, Chair, 902-893-8083
Robert Christianson, Clerk/Treasurer

Bridgewater
60 Pleasant St.
Bridgewater, NS B4V 3X9
Tel: 902-543-4651; *Fax:* 902-543-6876
www.bridgewater.ca
Municipal Type: Town
Incorporated: Feb. 13, 1899; *Area:* 13.6 sq km
County or District: Lunenburg; *Population in 2011:* 8,241
Provincial Electoral District(s): Lunenburg West
Federal Electoral District(s): South Shore-St. Margaret's
Next Election: Oct. 15, 2016 (4 year terms)
David Walker, Mayor, 902-541-4364
Ken Smith, Chief Administrative Officer, 902-541-4363, Fax: 902-543-4651

Canning
P.O. Box 9
2229 North Ave.
Canning, NS B0P 1H0
Tel: 902-582-3768; *Fax:* 902-582-3068
village.canning@xcountry.tv
www.canningnovascotia.ca
Municipal Type: Village
Area: 1.86 sq km
County or District: Kings; *Population in 2011:* 761
Provincial Electoral District(s): Kings North
Federal Electoral District(s): Kings-Hants
Next Election: Oct. 15, 2016 (4 year terms)
Everett MacPherson, Chair
Ruth Pearson, Clerk/Treasurer

Clark's Harbour
P.O. Box 260
2648 Main St.
Clarks Harbour, NS B0W 1P0
Tel: 902-745-2390; *Fax:* 902-745-1772
www.clarksharbour.com
Municipal Type: Town
Incorporated: March 4, 1919; *Area:* 2.9 sq km
County or District: Shelburne; *Population in 2011:* 820
Provincial Electoral District(s): Shelburne
Federal Electoral District(s): South Shore-St. Margaret's
Next Election: Oct. 15, 2016 (4 year terms)
Leigh Stoddart, Mayor, 902-745-2390
Jennifer Jones, Clerk, 902-745-2390

Cornwallis Square
P.O. Box 129
1415 County Home Rd.
Waterville, NS B0P 1VO
Tel: 902-538-0325; *Fax:* 902-538-1683
Municipal Type: Village
County or District: Kings
Provincial Electoral District(s): Kings North
Federal Electoral District(s): Kings-Hants
Next Election: Oct. 15, 2016 (4 year terms)
George Foote, Chair
William Farrell, Clerk, 902-538-0325

Digby
P.O. Box 579
147 First Ave.
Digby, NS B0V 1A0
Tel: 902-245-4769; *Fax:* 902-245-2121
townhall@digby.ca
www.digby.ca
Municipal Type: Town
Incorporated: Feb. 28, 1890; *Area:* 3.14 sq km
County or District: Digby; *Population in 2011:* 2,152
Provincial Electoral District(s): Digby-Annapolis
Federal Electoral District(s): West Nova
Next Election: Oct. 15, 2016 (4 year terms)
Ben Cleveland, Mayor, 902-247-0484
Tom Ossinger, Chief Administrative Officer, 902-245-4769, Fax: 902-245-2121

Freeport
P.O. Box 31
Freeport, NS B0V 1B0
Tel: 902-839-2144
Municipal Type: Village
County or District: Digby
Provincial Electoral District(s): Digby-Annapolis
Federal Electoral District(s): West Nova
Next Election: Oct. 15, 2016 (4 year terms)
Peter Morehouse, Chair

Greenwood
P.O. Box 1068
904 Central Ave.
Greenwood, NS B0P 1N0
Tel: 902-765-8788; *Fax:* 902-765-4369
villageoffice@greenwoodns.ca
www.greenwoodnovascotia.com
Municipal Type: Village
County or District: Kings
Provincial Electoral District(s): Kings West
Federal Electoral District(s): Central Nova; West Nova
Next Election: Oct. 15, 2016 (4 year terms)
Note: As of 2011, Statistics Canada shows that the Designated Place known as Kingston - Greenwood has an area of 14.50 sq km, & a population of 6,595.
Brian Banks, Chair
Marian Elsworth, Clerk-Treasurer, 902-765-8788

Hantsport
P.O. Box 399
20 Main St.
Hantsport, NS B0P 1P0
Tel: 902-684-3211; *Fax:* 902-684-3227
town@hantsportnovascotia.com
www.hantsportnovascotia.com
Municipal Type: Town
Incorporated: April 1, 1895; *Area:* 2.13 sq km
County or District: Hants; *Population in 2011:* 1,159
Provincial Electoral District(s): Hants West
Federal Electoral District(s): Kings-Hants
Next Election: Oct. 15, 2016 (4 year terms)
Note: On July 1st 2015, Hantsport dissolved and folded into West Hants. Residents will be represented by their current mayor until General Election of 2016.
H. Robbie Zwicker, Mayor, 902-684-1360, Fax: 902-684-3227

Havre Boucher
1318 Catejack Rd.
Havre Boucher, NS B0P 1P0
hbcdra@hotmail.com
www.havreboucher.com
Municipal Type: Village
County or District: Antigonish
Provincial Electoral District(s): Antigonish
Federal Electoral District(s): Cape Breton-Canso
Next Election: Oct. 15, 2016 (4 year terms)
Sylvester Landry, Chair
Raymond Carpenter, Clerk

Hebbville
47 Catidian Pl., RR#4
Bridgewater, NS B4V 2W3
Tel: 902-543-5786; *Fax:* 902-543-7006
www.villageofhebbville.ca
Municipal Type: Village
County or District: Lunenburg
Provincial Electoral District(s): Lunenburg West
Federal Electoral District(s): South Shore-St. Margaret's
Next Election: Oct. 15, 2016 (4 year terms)
Russell Barrier, Chair, 902-543-1155

Kentville
354 Main St.
Kentville, NS B4N 1K6
Tel: 902-679-2500; *Fax:* 902-679-2375
info@town.kentville.ns.ca
www.kentville.ca
Municipal Type: Town
Incorporated: May 1, 1886; *Area:* 17.35 sq km
County or District: Kings; *Population in 2011:* 6,094
Provincial Electoral District(s): Kings North
Federal Electoral District(s): Kings-Hants
Next Election: Oct. 15, 2016 (4 year terms)
David Corkum, Mayor
Mark Phillips, Chief Administrative Officer, 902-679-2501

Kingston
P.O. Box 254
671 Main St.
Kingston, NS B0P 1R0
Tel: 902-765-2800; *Fax:* 902-765-0807
info@kingstonnovascotia.ca
www.kingstonnovascotia.ca
Municipal Type: Village
Incorporated: 1957
County or District: Kings
Provincial Electoral District(s): Kings West
Federal Electoral District(s): West Nova
Next Election: Oct. 15, 2016 (4 year terms)
Note: As of 2011, Statistics Canada shows that the Designated Place known as Kingston - Greenwood has an area of 14.50 sq km, & a population of 6,595.
Martha Armstrong, Chair
Mike McCleave, Clerk-Treasurer

Lawrencetown
P.O. Box 38
12 Prince St.
Lawrencetown, NS B0S 1M0
Tel: 902-584-3082; *Fax:* 902-584-3878
villagelawrencetown@ns.aliantzinc.ca
www.lawrencetownnovascotia.ca
Municipal Type: Village
Area: 5.62 sq km
County or District: Annapolis; *Population in 2011:* 625
Provincial Electoral District(s): Annapolis
Federal Electoral District(s): West Nova
Next Election: Oct. 15, 2016 (4 year terms)
Jaki Fraser, Chair, 902-840-1079
Lisa Taylor, Clerk-Treasurer, 902-584-3082, Fax: 902-584-3878

Lockeport
P.O. Box 189
26 North St.
Lockeport, NS B0T 1L0
Tel: 902-656-2216; *Fax:* 902-656-2935
townoflockeport@ns.sympatico.ca
www.lockeport.ns.ca
Municipal Type: Town
Incorporated: Feb. 26, 1907; *Area:* 2.32 sq km
County or District: Shelburne; *Population in 2011:* 588
Provincial Electoral District(s): Queens-Shelburne
Federal Electoral District(s): South Shore-St. Margaret's
Next Election: Oct. 15, 2016 (4 year terms)
Darian Huskilson, Mayor, 902-875-7747
Joyce Y. Young, Clerk-Treasurer

Lunenburg
P.O. Box 129
119 Cumberland St.
Lunenburg, NS B0J 2C0
Tel: 902-634-4410; *Fax:* 902-634-4416
explorelunenburg@ns.sympatico.ca
www.explorelunenburg.ca
Municipal Type: Town
Incorporated: Oct. 29, 1888; *Area:* 4.01 sq km
County or District: Lunenburg; *Population in 2011:* 2,313
Provincial Electoral District(s): Lunenburg
Federal Electoral District(s): South Shore-St. Margaret's
Next Election: Oct. 15, 2016 (4 year terms)
Rachel Bailey, Mayor, 902-634-4410, Fax: 902-634-4416
Beatrice Renton, Chief Administrative Officer, 902-634-4410

Mahone Bay
P.O. Box 530
493 Main St.
Mahone Bay, NS B0J 2E0
Tel: 902-624-8327; *Fax:* 902-624-8069
clerk@townofmahonebay.ca
www.townofmahonebay.ca
Municipal Type: Town
Incorporated: March 31, 1919; *Area:* 3.13 sq km
County or District: Lunenburg; *Population in 2011:* 943
Provincial Electoral District(s): Lunenburg
Federal Electoral District(s): South Shore-St. Margaret's
Next Election: Oct. 15, 2016 (4 year terms)
C. Joseph Feeney, Mayor, 902-624-8327, Fax: 902-624-8069
Jim Wentzell, Chief Administrative Officer, 902-624-8327, Fax: 902-624-8069

Middleton
P.O. Box 340
131 Commercial St.
Middleton, NS B0S 1P0
Tel: 902-825-4841; *Fax:* 902-825-6460
billingclerk@town.middleton.ns.ca
www.discovermiddleton.ca

Municipal Type: Town
Incorporated: May 31, 1909; *Area:* 5.44 sq km
County or District: Annapolis; *Population in 2011:* 1,749
Provincial Electoral District(s): Annapolis
Federal Electoral District(s): West Nova
Next Election: Oct. 15, 2016 (4 year terms)
Calvin Eddy, Mayor, 902-825-6809
Rachel Turner, Chief Administrative Officer, 902-825-3559, Fax: 902-825-6460

Mulgrave
P.O. Box 129
457 MacLeod St.
Mulgrave, NS B0E 2G0
Tel: 902-747-2243; *Fax:* 902-747-2585
kathy.hearn@townofmulgrave.ca
www.townofmulgrave.ca
Municipal Type: Town
Incorporated: Dec. 1, 1923; *Area:* 17.81 sq km
County or District: Guysborough; *Population in 2011:* 794
Provincial Electoral District(s): Guysborough-Eastern Shore-Tracadie
Federal Electoral District(s): Cape Breton-Canso
Next Election: Oct. 15, 2016 (4 year terms)
Lorne MacDonald, Mayor, 902-747-3424
Kevin Matheson, Acting Chief Administrative Officer, 902-747-2243

New Glasgow
P.O. Box 7
111 Provost St.
New Glasgow, NS B2H 5E1
Tel: 902-755-7788; *Fax:* 902-755-6242
cheryl.young@newglasgow.ca
www.newglasgow.ca
Municipal Type: Town
Incorporated: May 6, 1875; *Area:* 9.93 sq km
County or District: Pictou; *Population in 2011:* 9,562
Provincial Electoral District(s): Pictou Centre
Federal Electoral District(s): Central Nova
Next Election: Oct. 15, 2016 (4 year terms)
Barrie MacMillan, Mayor, 902-755-8333, Fax: 902-755-6242
Lisa M. MacDonald, Chief Administrative Officer, 902-755-8333

New Minas
9489 Commercial St.
New Minas, NS B4N 3G3
Tel: 902-681-6972; *Fax:* 902-681-0779
newminas@ns.aliantzinc.ca
www.newminas.com
Municipal Type: Village
Incorporated: Sept. 1, 1968
County or District: Kings; *Population in 2011:* 4,000
Provincial Electoral District(s): Kings South
Federal Electoral District(s): Kings-Hants
Next Election: Oct. 15, 2016 (4 year terms)
Dave Chaulk, Chair, 902-681-2387
Terry Silver, Clerk-Treasurer, 902-681-0292

Oxford
P.O. Box 338
105 Lower Main St.
Oxford, NS B0M 1P0
Tel: 902-447-2170; *Fax:* 902-447-2485
townhall@town.oxford.ns.ca
www.town.oxford.ns.ca
Municipal Type: Town
Incorporated: April 19, 1904; *Area:* 10.76 sq km
County or District: Cumberland; *Population in 2011:* 1,151
Provincial Electoral District(s): Cumberland South
Federal Electoral District(s): Cumberland-Colchester
Next Election: Oct. 15, 2016 (4 year terms)
Trish Stewart, Mayor
Darrell White, Chief Administrative Officer

Parrsboro
P.O. Box 400
4030 Eastern Ave.
Parrsboro, NS B0M 1S0
Tel: 902-254-2036; *Fax:* 902-254-2313
town@town.parrsboro.ns.ca
www.town.parrsboro.ns.ca
Municipal Type: Town
Incorporated: July 15, 1889; *Area:* 14.88 sq km
County or District: Cumberland; *Population in 2011:* 1,305
Provincial Electoral District(s): Cumberland South
Federal Electoral District(s): Cumberland-Colchester
Next Election: Oct. 15, 2016 (4 year terms)
Lois Smith, Mayor, 902-254-2280
Ray Hickey, Chief Administrative Officer, 902-254-2036, Fax: 902-254-2313

Pictou
P.O. Box 640
40 Water St.
Pictou, NS B0K 1H0
Tel: 902-485-4372; *Fax:* 902-485-8110
info@townofpictou.ca
www.townofpictou.com
Municipal Type: Town
Incorporated: May 4, 1874; *Area:* 7.94 sq km
County or District: Pictou; *Population in 2011:* 3,437
Provincial Electoral District(s): Pictou West
Federal Electoral District(s): Central Nova
Next Election: Oct. 15, 2016 (4 year terms)
Joseph F. Hawes, Mayor, 902-485-6025
Scott Conrod, Chief Administrative Officer, 902-485-4372

Port Hawkesbury
606 Reeves St.
Port Hawkesbury, NS B9A 2R7
Tel: 902-625-0116; *Fax:* 902-625-0040
www.townofporthawkesbury.ca
Municipal Type: Town
Incorporated: Jan. 22, 1889; *Area:* 8.11 sq km
County or District: Inverness; *Population in 2011:* 3,366
Provincial Electoral District(s): Cape Breton-Richmond
Federal Electoral District(s): Cape Breton-Canso
Next Election: Oct. 15, 2016 (4 year terms)
W.J. (Billy Joe) MacLean, Mayor, 902-625-1800, Fax: 902-625-0040
Maris Freimanis, Chief Administrative Officer, 902-625-7890, Fax: 902-625-0040

Port Williams
P.O. Box 153
1045 Main St.
Port Williams, NS B0P 1T0
Tel: 902-542-4411; *Fax:* 902-542-4566
villageoffice@portwilliams.com
www.portwilliams.com
Municipal Type: Village
County or District: Kings
Provincial Electoral District(s): Kings North
Federal Electoral District(s): Kings-Hants
Next Election: Oct. 15, 2016 (4 year terms)
Lewis Benedict, Chairperson, 902-542-9519
Darlene Robertson, Clerk, 902-542-4411, Fax: 902-542-4566

Pugwash
P.O. Box 220
124 Water St.
Pugwash, NS B0K 1L0
Tel: 902-243-2946; *Fax:* 902-243-2126
villagecommission@pugwashvillage.com
www.pugwashvillage.com
Municipal Type: Village
Area: 9.83 sq km
County or District: Cumberland; *Population in 2011:* 744
Provincial Electoral District(s): Cumberland North
Federal Electoral District(s): Cumberland-Colchester
Next Election: Oct. 15, 2016 (4 year terms)
Kathy Redmond, Chair, 902-243-2606
Lisa Betts, Clerk-Treasurer, 902-243-2946

River Hebert
2724 Taylor Rd.
River Hebert, NS B0L 1G0
Tel: 902-251-2250
Municipal Type: Village
County or District: Cumberland
Provincial Electoral District(s): Cumberland South
Federal Electoral District(s): Cumberland-Colchester
Next Election: Oct. 15, 2016 (4 year terms)
Dale Porter, Chair
Judy Jollymore, Clerk-Treas.

St. Peter's
P.O. Box 452
60 Denys St.
St. Peters, NS B0E 3B0
Tel: 902-535-2155; *Fax:* 902-535-2330
stpeters.village@stpeterscable.com
www.visitstpeters.com
Municipal Type: Village
County or District: Richmond; *Population in 2011:* 800
Provincial Electoral District(s): Cape Breton-Richmond
Federal Electoral District(s): Cape Breton-Canso
Next Election: Oct. 15, 2016 (4 year terms)
Esther McDonnell, Chair
Rena Burke, Clerk-Treasurer

Shelburne
P.O. Box 670
168 Water St.
Shelburne, NS B0T 1W0
Tel: 902-875-2991; *Fax:* 902-875-3932
lrobinson@town.shelburne.ns.ca
www.town.shelburne.ns.ca
Municipal Type: Town
Incorporated: April 4, 1907; *Area:* 9 sq km
County or District: Shelburne; *Population in 2011:* 1,686
Provincial Electoral District(s): Shelburne
Federal Electoral District(s): South Shore-St. Margaret's
Next Election: Oct. 15, 2016 (4 year terms)
Karen Mattatall, Mayor, 902-875-2991, Fax: 902-875-3932
Dylan Heide, Chief Administrative Officer, 902-875-2991

Stellarton
P.O. Box 2200
250 Foord St.
Stellarton, NS B0K 1S0
Tel: 902-752-2114; *Fax:* 902-755-4105
townoffice@town.stellarton.ns.ca
www.stellarton.ca
Municipal Type: Town
Incorporated: Oct. 22, 1889; *Area:* 8.99 sq km
County or District: Pictou; *Population in 2011:* 4,485
Provincial Electoral District(s): Pictou Centre
Federal Electoral District(s): Central Nova
Next Election: Oct. 15, 2016 (4 year terms)
Joe Gennoe, Mayor, 902-752-6152
Joyce Eaton, Clerk-Treasurer, 902-752-2114

Stewiacke
P.O. Box 8
295 George St.
Stewiacke, NS B0N 2J0
Tel: 902-639-2231; *Fax:* 902-639-2221
town@stewiacke.net
www.stewiacke.net
Municipal Type: Town
Incorporated: Aug. 30, 1906; *Area:* 17.67 sq km
County or District: Colchester; *Population in 2011:* 1,438
Provincial Electoral District(s): Colchester-Musqodoboit Valley
Federal Electoral District(s): Cumberland-Colchester
Next Election: Oct. 15, 2016 (4 year terms)
Wendy Robinson, Mayor
Sheldon Dorey, Chief Administrative Officer, 902-639-2231

Tatamagouche
P.O. Box 119
423 Main St.
Tatamagouche, NS B0K 1V0
Tel: 902-657-3696
tata.village@ns.sympatico.ca
Municipal Type: Village
Area: 8.04 sq km
County or District: Colchester; *Population in 2011:* 752
Provincial Electoral District(s): Colchester North
Federal Electoral District(s): Cumberland-Colchester
Next Election: Oct. 15, 2016 (4 year terms)
Jim Baird, Chair, 902-956-1938
Marilyn Ebsary, Clerk-Treasurer

Tiverton
P.O. Box 16
RR#1
Tiverton, NS B0V 1G0
Tel: 902-839-2369
Municipal Type: Village
County or District: Digby
Provincial Electoral District(s): Digby-Annapolis
Federal Electoral District(s): West Nova
Next Election: Oct. 15, 2016 (4 year terms)

Trenton
P.O. Box 328
120 Main St.
Trenton, NS B0K 1X0
Tel: 902-752-5311; *Fax:* 902-752-0090
trenton@town.trenton.ns.ca
www.town.trenton.ns.ca
Municipal Type: Town
Incorporated: March 18, 1911; *Area:* 6 sq km
County or District: Pictou; *Population in 2011:* 2,616
Provincial Electoral District(s): Pictou Centre
Federal Electoral District(s): Central Nova
Next Election: Oct. 15, 2016 (4 year terms)
Glen MacKinnon, Mayor, 902-752-5311
Cathy MacGillivary, Chief Administrative Officer, 902-752-5311

Westport
The Spouter Inn
P.O. Box 1192
263 Water St.
Westport, NS B0V 1H0
Tel: 902-839-2219; *Fax:* 902-839-2219
Municipal Type: Village
County or District: Digby
Provincial Electoral District(s): Clare-Digby
Federal Electoral District(s): West Nova
Next Election: Oct. 15, 2016 (4 year terms)
James Outhouse, Chair
Caroline Norwood, Clerk-Treasurer

Westville
P.O. Box 923
2042 Queen St.
Westville, NS B0K 2A0
Tel: 902-396-1500; *Fax:* 902-396-3986
www.westville.ca
Municipal Type: Town
Incorporated: Aug. 20, 1894; *Area:* 14.39 sq km
County or District: Pictou; *Population in 2011:* 3,798
Provincial Electoral District(s): Pictou East
Federal Electoral District(s): Central Nova
Next Election: Oct. 15, 2016 (4 year terms)
Roger MacKay, Mayor, 902-396-1437
Kelly Rice, Chief Administrative Officer, 902-396-1500

Weymouth
P.O. Box 121
5108 Hwy. 1
Weymouth, NS B0W 3T0
Tel: 902-837-4976; *Fax:* 902-837-5397
village@weymouthnovascotia.com
www.weymouthnovascotia.com
Municipal Type: Village
County or District: Digby
Provincial Electoral District(s): Digby-Annapolis
Federal Electoral District(s): West Nova
Next Election: Oct. 15, 2016 (4 year terms)
Murray Betts, Clerk, 902-837-4976
Suzanne MacLean, Co-Chair, 902-837-4976
Barry Faulner, Co-Chair, 902-837-4976

Windsor
P.O. Box 158
100 King St.
Windsor, NS B0N 2T0
Tel: 902-798-2275; *Fax:* 902-798-5679
info@town.windsor.ns.ca
www.town.windsor.ns.ca
Municipal Type: Town
Incorporated: April 4, 1878; *Area:* 9.06 sq km
County or District: Hants; *Population in 2011:* 3,785
Provincial Electoral District(s): Hants West
Federal Electoral District(s): Kings-Hants
Next Election: Oct. 15, 2016 (4 year terms)
Paul Beazley, Mayor, 902-798-2275
Louis Coutinho, Chief Administrative Officer, 902-798-6675

Wolfville
359 Main St.
Wolfville, NS B4P 1A1
Tel: 902-542-5767; *Fax:* 902-542-4789
www.town.wolfville.ns.ca
Municipal Type: Town
Incorporated: March 4, 1893; *Area:* 6.45 sq km
County or District: Kings; *Population in 2011:* 4,269
Provincial Electoral District(s): Kings South
Federal Electoral District(s): Kings-Hants
Next Election: Oct. 15, 2016 (4 year terms)
Jeff Cantwell, Mayor, 902-542-4008, Fax: 902-542-4789
Erin Beaudin, Chief Administrative Officer, 902-542-4494, Fax: 902-542-4789

Yarmouth
400 Main St.
Yarmouth, NS B5A 1G2
Tel: 902-742-2521; *Fax:* 902-742-6244
www.yarmouth-town.com
Municipal Type: Town
Incorporated: Aug. 6, 1890; *Area:* 10.56 sq km
County or District: Yarmouth; *Population in 2011:* 6,761
Provincial Electoral District(s): Yarmouth
Federal Electoral District(s): West Nova
Next Election: Oct. 15, 2016 (4 year terms)
Pam Mood, Mayor, 902-742-8565, Fax: 902-742-6244
Jeffrey Gushue, Chief Administrative Officer, 902-742-8565, Fax: 902-742-6244

Rural Municipalities in Nova Scotia

Annapolis County
P.O. Box 100
752 St. George St.
Annapolis Royal, NS B0S 1A0
Tel: 902-532-2331; *Fax:* 902-532-2096
info@annapoliscounty.ns.ca
www.annapoliscounty.ca
Other Information: Alt. Phone: 902-825-2005
Municipal Type: Rural Municipalities
Incorporated: April 17, 1879; *Area:* 3,184.97 sq km
County or District: Annapolis; *Population in 2011:* 21,705
Provincial Electoral District(s): Annapolis; Digby-Annapolis
Federal Electoral District(s): West Nova
Next Election: Oct. 15, 2016 (4 year terms)
Note: The Town of Bridgetown dissolved on April 1, 2015 and was folded into Annapolis County.
Reg Ritchie, Warden/Councillor, 902-532-5470, Wards: 8
Marilyn Wilkins, Deputy Warden/Councillor, 902-765-8158, Wards: 1
Brian Connell, Councillor, 902-532-2331, Wards: 2
R. Wayne Fowler, Councillor, 902-584-3702, Wards: 3
Paul McDonald, Councillor, 902-532-2975, Wards: 4
Gregory Heming, Councillor, 902-532-7189, Wards: 5
Alex Morrison, Councillor, 902-638-3416, Wards: 6
Timothy Habinski, Deputy Warden/Councillor, 902-955-0258, Wards: 7
Frank Chipman, Councillor, 902-825-6421, Wards: 9
Martha Roberts, Councillor, 902-825-8345, Wards: 10
Diane LeBlanc, Councillor, 902-765-2403, Wards: 11
John Ferguson, Chief Administrative Officer, 902-532-3130
Horace Hurlburt, Councillor, 902-588-2016, Wards: Bridgetown
Carolyn Young, Municipal Clerk, 902-532-3136
Stephen McInnis, Director of Municipal Operations/Deputy CAO, 902-665-4543

Antigonish County
285 Beech Hill Rd. RR #6
Antigonish, NS B2G 0B4
Tel: 902-863-1117; *Fax:* 902-863-5751
www.antigonishcounty.ns.ca
Municipal Type: Rural Municipalities
Incorporated: April 17, 1879; *Area:* 1,457.82 sq km
County or District: Antigonish; *Population in 2011:* 19,589
Provincial Electoral District(s): Antigonish
Federal Electoral District(s): Central Nova
Next Election: Oct. 15, 2016 (4 year terms)
Russell Boucher, Warden & Councillor, Wards: 9.Havre Boucher
Owen McCarron, Deputy Warden & Councillor, Wards: 6. St. Andrew's
Mary MacLellan, Councillor, Wards: 1. Arisaig
Donnie MacDonald, Councillor, Wards: 2. North Grant/Colverville
Hugh Stewart, Councillor, Wards: 3. St. Joseph's
Vaughan Chisholm, Councillor, Wards: 4. Fringe Area West
Remi Deveau, Councillor, Wards: 5. Pomquet
Angus Bowie, Councillor, Wards: 7. Heatherton/Afton
Pierre Boucher, Councillor, Wards: 8. Tracadie/Monestary
Bill MacFarlane, Councillor, Wards: 10. Fringe Area South
Glenn Horne, Clerk/Treasurer
Daryl Myers, Director, Public Works, 902-863-5004
Jim Davis, Director, Finance
Marlene Melanson, Director, Recreation

Argyle District
P.O. Box 10
27 Courthouse Road
Tusket, NS B0W 3M0
Tel: 902-648-2311; *Fax:* 902-648-0367
admin@munargyle.com
www.munargyle.com
Municipal Type: Rural Municipalities
Incorporated: April 17, 1879; *Area:* 1,527.1 sq km
County or District: Yarmouth; *Population in 2011:* 8,252
Provincial Electoral District(s): Argyle
Federal Electoral District(s): West Nova
Next Election: Oct. 15, 2016 (4 year terms)
Aldric D'Entremont, Warden & Councillor, 902-762-2195, Wards: 8. West Pubnico
Alain Muise, Chief Administrative Officer, 902-648-3293

Barrington District
P.O. Box 100
2447 Hwy. 3
Barrington, NS B0W 1E0
Tel: 902-637-2015; *Fax:* 902-637-2075
www.barringtonmunicipality.com
Municipal Type: Rural Municipalities
Incorporated: April 17, 1879; *Area:* 631.94 sq km
County or District: Shelburne; *Population in 2011:* 6,994
Provincial Electoral District(s): Argyle-Barrington
Federal Electoral District(s): South Shore-St. Margaret's
Next Election: Oct. 15, 2016 (4 year terms)
Eddie Nickerson, Warden/Councillor, 902-745-3250, Wards: 4
Brian Holland, Clerk/Treasurer, 902-637-2015, Fax: 902-637-2075

Chester District
P.O. Box 369
151 King St.
Chester, NS B0J 1J0
Tel: 902-275-3554; *Fax:* 902-275-4771
administration@district.chester.ns.ca
www.chester.ca
Municipal Type: Rural Municipalities
Incorporated: April 17, 1879; *Area:* 1,120.75 sq km
County or District: Lunenburg; *Population in 2011:* 10,599
Provincial Electoral District(s): Chester-St. Margaret's
Federal Electoral District(s): South Shore-St. Margaret's
Next Election: Oct. 15, 2016 (4 year terms)
Allen Webber, Warden, 902-275-2536, Wards: 4
Floyd Shatford, Deputy Warden, 902-857-9817, Wards: 2
Andre Veinotte, Councillor, 902-277-1409, Wards: 1
Brad Armstrong, Councillor, 902-275-3121, Wards: 3
Robert Myra, Councillor, 902-627-2470, Wards: 5
Tina Connors, Councillor, 902-679-4461, Wards: 6
Sharon Church-Cornelius, Councillor, 902-277-1301, Wards: 7
Tammy Wilson, Chief Administrative Officer, 902-275-3554, Fax: 902-275-4771
Pam Myra, Municipal Clerk, 902-275-3554, Fax: 902-275-4771
Matthew Davidson, Director, Engineering & Public Works, 902-275-1312, Fax: 902-275-3673
Bruce Forest, Director, Solid Waste, 902-275-2330
Cliff Gall, Director, Information Services, 902-275-3554
Steve Graham, Treasurer/Director of Finance, Finance, 902-275-3554
Chad Haughn, Director, Recreation & Parks, 902-275-3490, Fax: 902-275-3630
Tara Maguire, Director, Community Development, 902-275-2599, Fax: 902-275-2598

Clare District
P.O. Box 458
1185 Hwy. 1
Little Brook, NS B0W 1Z0
Tel: 902-769-2031; *Fax:* 902-769-3773
www.clarenovascotia.com
Municipal Type: Rural Municipalities
Incorporated: April 17, 1879; *Area:* 852.82 sq km
County or District: Digby; *Population in 2011:* 8,319
Provincial Electoral District(s): Clare
Federal Electoral District(s): West Nova
Next Election: Oct. 15, 2016 (4 year terms)
Ronnie LeBlanc, Warden & Councillor, 902-769-8006, Wards: 7
Connie Saulnier, Chief Administrative Officer, 902-769-2031, Fax: 902-769-3773

Colchester County
P.O. Box 697
1 Church St.
Truro, NS B2N 5E7
Tel: 902-897-3160; *Fax:* 902-843-4066
www.colchester.ca
Other Information: Toll Free: 1-866-728-5144
Municipal Type: Rural Municipalities
Incorporated: April 17, 1879; *Area:* 3,627.69 sq km
County or District: Colchester; *Population in 2011:* 50,968
Provincial Electoral District(s): Colchester North; Truro-Bible Hill-Millbrook-Salmon River
Federal Electoral District(s): Cumberland-Colchester
Next Election: Oct. 15, 2016 (4 year terms)
Bob Taylor, Mayor, 902-897-3160, Fax: 902-843-4066
Bill Masters, Deputy Mayor & Councillor, 902-895-0877, Fax: 902-893-7603, Wards: 2
Christine Blair, Councillor, 902-895-6537, Wards: 1
Geoff Stewart, Councillor, 902-673-3039, Wards: 3
Mike Cooper, Councillor, 902-671-2854, Wards: 4
Lloyd Gibbs, Councillor, 902-897-4050, Wards: 5
Karen MacKenzie, Councillor, 902-895-8930, Wards: 6
Michael Gregory, Councillor, 902-305-4002, Wards: 7
Ron Cavanaugh, Councillor, 902-895-7305, Wards: 8
Doug MacInnes, Councillor, 902-895-2242, Wards: 9
Tom Taggart, Councillor, 902-647-2025, Wards: 10
Wade Parker, Councillor, 902-893-5448, Wards: 11
Rob Simonds, Chief Administrative Officer, 902-897-3184
Michelle Newell, Director, Public Works, 902-897-3175
Crawford Macpherson, Director, Community Development, 902-897-3170
Scott Fraser, Director, Corporate Services, 902-897-3165
Wayne Wamboldt, Director, Solid Waste, 902-897-0450

Cumberland County
E.D. Fullerton Municipal Bldg.
1395 Blair Lake Rd., RR#6
Amherst, NS B4H 3Y4
Tel: 902-667-2313; *Fax:* 902-667-1352
info@cumberlandcounty.ns.ca
www.cumberlandcounty.ns.ca
Other Information: Toll Free: 1-888-756-6262
Municipal Type: Rural Municipalities
Incorporated: April 17, 1879; *Area:* 4,271.14 sq km
County or District: Cumberland; *Population in 2011:* 31,353
Provincial Electoral District(s): Cumberland North; Cumberland South
Federal Electoral District(s): Cumberland-Colchester
Next Election: Oct. 15, 2016 (4 year terms)
Note: The town of Springhill dissolved on April 1st 2015 and was folded into the Municipality of Cumberland County.
Keith Hunter, Warden & Councillor, 902-661-4315, Wards: 3
Donald Smith, Councillor, 902-667-1247, Wards: 1
John Kellegrew, Councillor, 902-667-2094, Wards: 2
Allison Gillis, Councillor, 902-243-3313, Wards: 4
Lynne Welton, Councillor, 902-257-1137, Wards: 5
William Baker, Councillor, 902-548-2496, Wards: 6
Daniel Rector, Councillor, 902-447-3120, Wards: 7
Ernest Gilbert, Councillor, 902-545-2022, Wards: 8
Michael McLellan, Councillor, 902-251-2202, Wards: 9
Donald Fletcher, Councillor, 902-392-2727, Wards: 10
Doug Williams, Councillor, 902-694-8854, Wards: 11
Maryanne Jackson, Councillor, 902-763-2294, Wards: 12
Brenda Moore, Clerk
Rennie Bugley, Chief Administrative Officer
Justin Waugh-Cress, Director, Engineering and Operations, 902-667-2313
Andrew MacDonald, Director, Finance
Steve Ferguson, Director, Social Capital & Special Projects

Digby District
P.O. Box 429
Digby, NS B0V 1A0
Tel: 902-245-4777; *Fax:* 902-245-5748
administration@municipality.digby.ns.ca
www.digbydistrict.ca
Municipal Type: Rural Municipalities
Incorporated: April 17, 1879; *Area:* 1,655.93 sq km
County or District: Digby; *Population in 2011:* 7,463
Provincial Electoral District(s): Digby-Annapolis
Federal Electoral District(s): West Nova
Next Election: Oct. 15, 2016 (4 year terms)
Linda Gregory, Warden & Councillor, 902-245-2616, Wards: 3
Linda Fraser, Chief Administrative Officer

Guysborough District
Municipal Bldg.
P.O. Box 79
33 Pleasant St.
Guysborough, NS B0H 1N0
Tel: 902-533-3705; *Fax:* 902-533-2749
www.municipality.guysborough.ns.ca
Other Information: Alt. Phone: 902-533-3508
Municipal Type: Rural Municipalities
Incorporated: April 17, 1879; *Area:* 2,111.42 sq km
County or District: Guysborough; *Population in 2011:* 8,143
Provincial Electoral District(s): Guysborough-Eastern Shore-Tracadie
Federal Electoral District(s): Cape Breton-Canso
Next Election: Oct. 15, 2016 (4 year terms)
Vernon Pitts, Warden, 902-533-3705
Barry Carroll, Chief Administrative Officer, 902-533-3705

Hants East District
P.O. Box 190
230-15 Commerce Ct.
Elmsdale, NS B2S 3K5
Tel: 902-883-2299; *Fax:* 888-684-5912
info@easthants.ca
www.easthants.ca
Other Information: Toll Free: 1-866-758-2299
Municipal Type: Rural Municipalities
Incorporated: April 17, 1879; *Area:* 1,787.64 sq km
County or District: Hants; *Population in 2011:* 22,111
Provincial Electoral District(s): Hants East
Federal Electoral District(s): Kings-Hants
Next Election: Oct. 15, 2016 (4 year terms)
Jim Smith, Warden & Councillor, 902-883-8503, Wards: 10. Enfield/Horne Settlement
Cecil Dixon, Councillor, 902-883-9764, Wards: 1. Enfield
Norval Mitchell, Councillor, 902-883-9167, Wards: 2. Elmsdale
Willy Versteeg, Councillor, 902-758-2456, Wards: 3. Milford
Albert Flemming, Councillor, 902-758-3919, Wards: 4. Shubenacadie
Keith Ryno, Councillor, 902-261-2533, Wards: 5. Maitland
Wayne Greene, Councillor, 902-369-2629, Wards: 6. Noel
John A. MacDonald, Councillor, 902-483-7382, Wards: 7. Lantz
Greg Grant, Deputy Warden & Councillor, 902-362-2896, Wards: 8. Gore
Eldon Hebb, Councillor, 902-883-2047, Wards: 9. Nine Mile River
Eleanor Roulston, Councillor, 902-632-2573, Wards: 11. Rawdon
Rosanne Bland, Councillor, 902-452-0603, Wards: 12. Mount Uniacke/East Uniacke
Cyril McDonald, Councillor, 902-866-3302, Wards: 13. Mount Uniacke/Lakelands
Connie Nolan, Chief Administrative Officer, 902-883-7098
Jesse Hulsman, Director, Infrastructure & Operations
Kate Friars, Director, Parks, Recreation & Culture
John Woodford, Director, Planning and Development, 902-883-7098

Inverness County
Municipal Bldg.
P.O. Box 179
375 Main St.
Port Hood, NS B0E 2W0
Tel: 902-787-2274; *Fax:* 902-787-3110
www.invernesscounty.ca
Municipal Type: Rural Municipalities
Incorporated: April 17, 1879; *Area:* 3,830.4 sq km
County or District: Inverness; *Population in 2011:* 17,947
Provincial Electoral District(s): Inverness
Federal Electoral District(s): Cape Breton-Canso; Sydney-Victoria
Next Election: Oct. 15, 2016 (4 year terms)
Duart MacAulay, Warden & Councillor, 902-295-7890, Wards: 4
Dwayne MacDonald, Deputy Warden, 902-631-0002, Wards: 6
Alfred Poirier, Deputy Warden & Councillor, 902-224-0097, Wards: 1
Gloria Leblanc, Councillor, 902-235-2348, Wards: 2
James Mustard, Councillor, 902-295-0974, Wards: 3
Betty Ann MacQuarrie, Councillor, 902-227-8796, Wards: 5
Joe O'Connor, Chief Administrative Officer, 902-787-3500, Fax: 902-787-3110
Garett Beaton, Director, Public Works, 902-787-3502, Fax: 902-787-2339

Kings County
P.O. Box 100
87 Cornwallis St.
Kentville, NS B4N 3W3
Tel: 902-678-6141; *Fax:* 902-678-9279
inquiry@county.kings.ns.ca
www.countyofkings.ns.ca
Other Information: Toll Free: 1-888-337-2999
Municipal Type: Rural Municipalities
Incorporated: April 17, 1879; *Area:* 2,122.18 sq km
County or District: Kings; *Population in 2011:* 60,589
Provincial Electoral District(s): Kings North; Kings South; Kings West
Federal Electoral District(s): Kings-Hants; West Nova
Next Election: Oct. 15, 2016 (4 year terms)
Diana Brothers, Warden, 902-765-8609
Mike Ennis, Deputy Warden/Councillor, 902-542-5217, Wards: District 12
Kim MacQuarrie, Councillor, 902-582-1342, Wards: District 1
Pauline Raven, Councillor, 902-670-2949, Wards: District 3
Brian Hirtle, Councillor, 902-538-7192, Wards: District 4
Wayne Atwater, Councillor, 902-847-9179, Wards: District 5
Dale Lloyd, Councillor, 902-538-8144, Wards: District 8
Bob Best, Councillor, 902-698-2125, Wards: District 9
Patricia Bishop, Councillor, 902-542-3277, Wards: District 10
Jim Winsor, Councillor, 902-678-7776, Wards: District 11
Tom MacEwan, Chief Administrative Officer
Nichole Gilbert, Coordinator, Recreation, 902-690-6124

Lunenburg District
P.O. Box 200
210 Aberdeen Rd.
Bridgewater, NS B4V 4G8
Tel: 902-543-8181; *Fax:* 902-543-7123
info@modl.ca
www.modl.ca
Municipal Type: Rural Municipalities
Incorporated: April 17, 1879; *Area:* 1,759.14 sq km
County or District: Lunenburg; *Population in 2011:* 25,118
Provincial Electoral District(s): Chester-St. Margaret's Lunenburg; Lunenburg West
Federal Electoral District(s): South Shore-St. Margaret's
Next Election: Oct. 15, 2016 (4 year terms)
Don Downe, Mayor, 902-543-5357
Lee Nauss, Deputy Mayor & Councillor, 902-543-2756, Wards: 10
Errol Knickle, Councillor, 902-634-9180, Wards: 1
Donald Zwicker, Councillor, 902-766-4016, Wards: 2
Michael Ernst, Councillor, 902-624-8864, Wards: 4
Claudette Garland, Councillor, 902-543-1029, Wards: 5
Terry Dorey, Councillor, 902-644-2061, Wards: 6
Cathy Moore, Councillor, 902-644-2922, Wards: 7
John Veinot, Councillor, 902-685-2924, Wards: 8
Carolyn Bolivar-Getson, Councillor, 902-685-2416
Martin Bell, Councillor, 902-543-7090, Wards: 11
Eric Hustvedt, Councillor, 902-677-2794
Kevin Malloy, Chief Administrative Officer, 902-541-1337
Satu Peori, P. Eng, Acting Director, Engineering & Public Works, 902-541-1339
Jeff Merrill, Director, Planning & Development, 902-541-1340

Pictou County
46 Municipal Dr.
Pictou, NS B0K 1H0
Tel: 902-485-4311; *Fax:* 902-485-6475
carolyn.macintosh@munpict.ca
www.county.pictou.ns.ca
Other Information: Alt. Phone: 902-485-6475
Municipal Type: Rural Municipalities
Incorporated: April 17, 1879; *Area:* 2,845.26 sq km
County or District: Pictou; *Population in 2011:* 45,643
Provincial Electoral District(s): Pictou Centre; Pictou East; Pictou West
Federal Electoral District(s): Central Nova
Next Election: Oct. 15, 2016 (4 year terms)
Ronald Baillie, Warden & Councillor, 902-351-2764, Wards: 4
Andy Thompson, Deputy Warden & Councillor, 902-695-2356, Wards: 11
Sally Fraser, Councillor, 902-926-2155, Wards: 1
Deborah Wadden, Councillor, 902-752-1303, Wards: 2
Edward MacMaster, Councillor, 902-485-6241, Wards: 3
Robert Parker, Councillor, 902-925-2240, Wards: 5
Jim Turple, Councillor, 902-485-6901, Wards: 6
David Parker, Councillor, 902-396-3481, Wards: 7
Leonard Fraser, Councillor, 902-396-3137, Wards: 8
Larry Turner, Councillor, 902-921-1227, Wards: 9
Jamie Davidson, Councillor, 902-928-8826, Wards: 10
Chester Dewar, Councillor, 902-923-2931, Wards: 12
Randy Palmer, Councillor, 902-922-2277, Wards: 13
Scott Johnston, Councillor, 902-923-2574, Wards: 14
Brian Cullen, Chief Administrative Officer, 902-485-4311, Fax: 902-485-6475

Richmond County
P.O. Box 120
2357 Hwy. 206
Arichat, NS B0E 1A0
Tel: 902-226-2400; *Fax:* 902-226-1510
www.richmondcounty.ca
Other Information: Toll Free: 1-800-567-2600
Municipal Type: Rural Municipalities
Incorporated: April 17, 1879; *Area:* 1,244.24 sq km
County or District: Richmond; *Population in 2011:* 9,293
Provincial Electoral District(s): Cape Breton-Richmond
Federal Electoral District(s): Cape Breton-Canso
Next Election: Oct. 15, 2016 (4 year terms)
Victor David, Warden, 902-226-2151, Fax: 902-226-0153, Wards: 1
Warren Olsen, Chief Adminstrative Officer, 902-226-3970

St. Mary's District
P.O. Box 296
8296 Hwy #7
Sherbrooke, NS B0J 3C0
Tel: 902-522-2049; *Fax:* 902-522-2309
www.saint-marys.ca
Other Information: Alt. Phone: 902-522-2496
Municipal Type: Rural Municipalities
Incorporated: April 17, 1879; *Area:* 1,909.59 sq km
County or District: Guysborough; *Population in 2011:* 2,354
Provincial Electoral District(s): Guysborough-Eastern Shore-Tracadie
Federal Electoral District(s): Central Nova
Next Election: Oct. 15, 2016 (4 year terms)
Michael Mosher, Warden, 902-347-2784, Fax: 902-522-2309
David Gillis, Clerk, 902-522-2049, Fax: 902-522-2309
Marvin MacDonald, Chief Administrative Officer, 902-522-2049, Fax: 902-522-2309

Shelburne District
P.O. Box 280
136 Hammond St.
Shelburne, NS B0T 1W0
Tel: 902-875-3544; *Fax:* 902-875-1278
www.municipalityofshelburne.ca
Other Information: Alt. Phone: 902-875-3083
Municipal Type: Rural Municipalities
Incorporated: April 17, 1879; *Area:* 1,818.49 sq km
County or District: Shelburne; *Population in 2011:* 4,408
Provincial Electoral District(s): Shelburne

Federal Electoral District(s): South Shore-St. Margaret's
Next Election: Oct. 15, 2016 (4 year terms)
Roger Taylor, Warden, 902-874-0160, Wards: 7
Kirk Cox, Chief Administrative Officer, 902-875-3544

Victoria County

495 Chebucto St.
Baddeck, NS B0E 1B0
Tel: 902-295-3659; *Fax:* 902-295-3331
www.victoriacounty.com
Municipal Type: Rural Municipalities
Incorporated: April 17, 1879; *Area:* 2,870.85 sq km
County or District: Victoria; *Population in 2011:* 7,115
Provincial Electoral District(s): Victoria-The Lakes
Federal Electoral District(s): Sydney-Victoria
Next Election: Oct. 15, 2016 (4 year terms)
Bruce Morrison, Warden, 902-565-8229, Fax: 902-295-1311, Wards: 3
Sandy W. Hudson, Chief Administrative Officer, 902-295-3660, Fax: 902-295-3331

West Hants

P.O. Box 3000
76 Morison Dr.
Windsor, NS B0N 2T0
Tel: 902-798-8391; *Fax:* 902-798-8553
westhants@westhants.ca
www.westhants.ca
Municipal Type: Rural Municipalities
Incorporated: April 17, 1879; *Area:* 1,238.12 sq km
County or District: Hants; *Population in 2011:* 14,165
Provincial Electoral District(s): Hants West
Federal Electoral District(s): Kings-Hants
Next Election: Oct. 15, 2016 (4 year terms)
Richard Dauphinee, Warden & Councillor, 902-798-4908, Wards: 6. Three Mile Plains
Gary Cochrane, Deputy Warden, 902-798-5186, Wards: 5. Wentworth-Newport
Reed W. Allen, Councillor, 902-790-1080, Wards: 1. Summerville-Kempt
Shirley Pineo, Councillor, 902-757-2003, Wards: 2. Avondale-The Burlingtons
Randall Matheson, Councillor, 302-757-2508, Wards: 3. Brooklyn-Scotch Village
Thomas Brown, Councillor, Wards: 4. St. Croix-Ellershouse
Jennifer Daniels, Councillor, 902-792-8253, Wards: 7. Three Mile Plains-Martock
Paul Morton, Councillor, 902-684-9415, Wards: 8
Robbie Zwicker, Councillor, 902-684-0029, Wards: 10
Rhonda Brown, Clerk, 902-798-6908, Fax: 902-798-8553
Cathie Osborne, Chief Administrative Officer
Rick Sherrard, Director, Public Works
Karen Dempsey, Director, Planning
Kathy Kehoe, Director, Recreation

Yarmouth District

932 Hwy 1
Hebron, NS B5A 5Z5
Tel: 902-742-7159; *Fax:* 902-742-3164
admin@district.yarmouth.ns.ca
www.district.yarmouth.ns.ca
Municipal Type: Rural Municipalities
Incorporated: April 17, 1879; *Area:* 585.27 sq km
County or District: Yarmouth; *Population in 2011:* 10,105
Provincial Electoral District(s): Yarmouth
Federal Electoral District(s): West Nova
Next Election: Oct. 15, 2016 (4 year terms)
Murray Goodwin, Warden & Councillor, 902-742-7159, Fax: 902-742-3164, Wards: 2
Stephen Paquette, Deputy Warden & Councillor, 902-742-7159, Fax: 902-742-3164, Wards: 4
John Cunningham, Councillor, 902-742-7159, Fax: 902-742-3164, Wards: 1
Gerard LeBlanc, Councillor, 902-761-7159, Fax: 902-742-3164, Wards: 3
Trevor Cunningham, Councillor, 902-742-7159, Fax: 902-742-3164, Wards: 5
Rich Churchill, Councillor, 902-742-7159, Fax: 902-742-3164, Wards: 6
Leland Anthony, Councillor, 902-742-7159, Fax: 902-742-3164, Wards: 7
Kenneth Moses, Chief Administrative Officer

NUNAVUT

The Department of Community and Government Services has legislative responsibility for Territorial Acts and Regulations. Some of these include: Area Development; Business Licenses; Cities, Towns and Villages; Civil Emergency Measures; Commissioner's Land; Community Employees Benefits Program Transfer; Conflict of Interest; Consumer Protection; Curfew; Dog; Film Classification; Fire Prevention; Hamlet; Homeowners Property; Local Authorities Election; Lotteries; Pawnbrokers and Second-hand Dealers; Planning; Property Assessments and Taxation; Real Estate Agents Licensing; Religious Societies; Residential Tenancies; Technical Standards and Safety; Senior Citizens and Disabled Persons Property Tax Relief Act; Settlement; Western Canada Lottery.

Incorporation as a city, town or village is determined by the value of all assessable land. Incorporation values: Village, $10 million; Town, $50 million; City, $200 million, all tax-based. Hamlets may request tax-based status. There are 24 hamlets and one city in Nunavut.

There is no fixed schedule for elections, but they are typically held every two to three years.

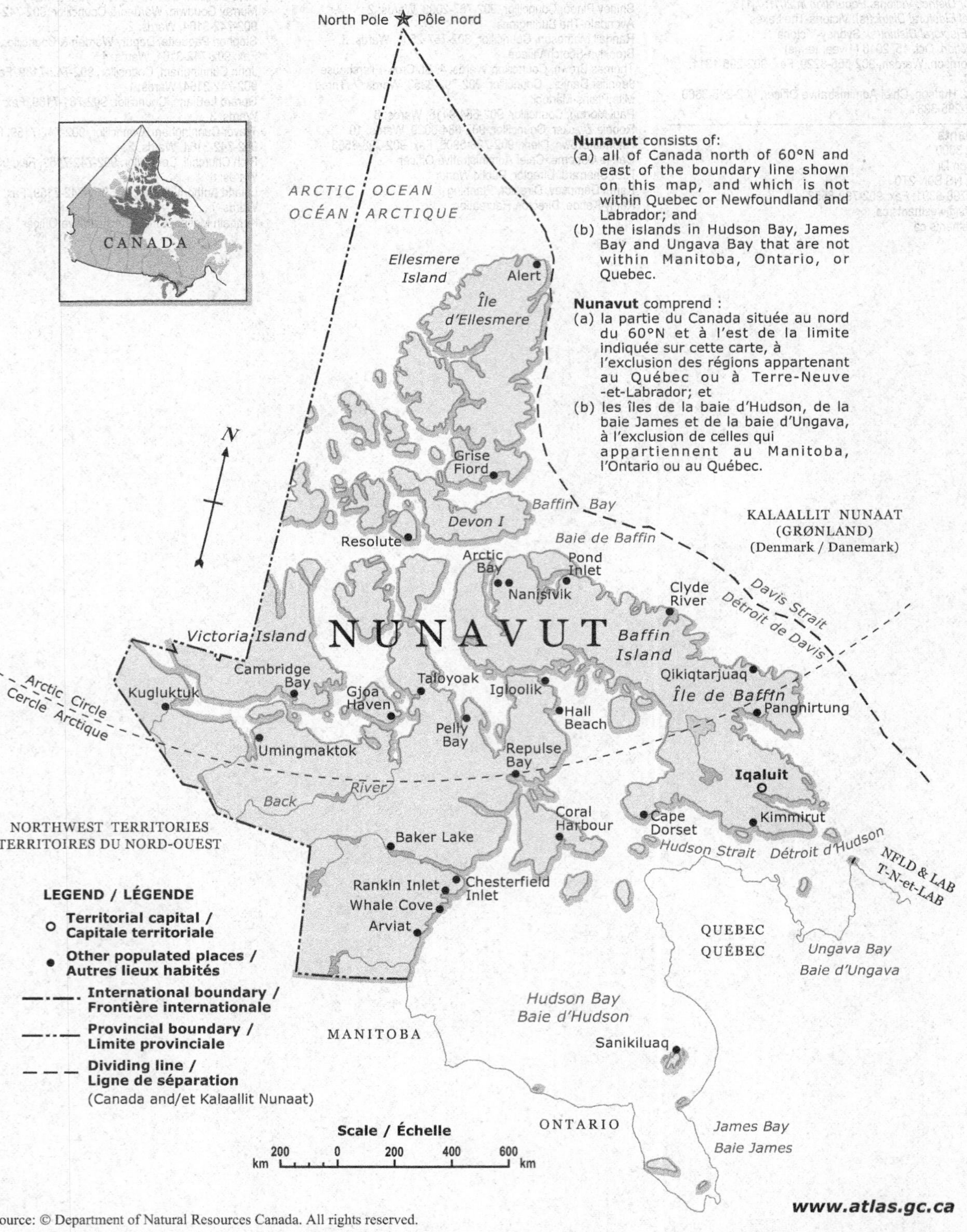
North Pole ☆ Pôle nord
CANADA
ARCTIC OCEAN
OCÉAN ARCTIQUE
Nunavut consists of:
(a) all of Canada north of 60°N and east of the boundary line shown on this map, and which is not within Quebec or Newfoundland and Labrador; and
(b) the islands in Hudson Bay, James Bay and Ungava Bay that are not within Manitoba, Ontario, or Quebec.
Nunavut comprend :
(a) la partie du Canada située au nord du 60°N et à l'est de la limite indiquée sur cette carte, à l'exclusion des régions appartenant au Québec ou à Terre-Neuve-et-Labrador; et
(b) les îles de la baie d'Hudson, de la baie James et de la baie d'Ungava, à l'exclusion de celles qui appartiennent au Manitoba, l'Ontario ou au Québec.
Ellesmere Island
Alert
Île d'Ellesmere
N
Grise Fiord
Baffin Bay
Devon I
Resolute
Baie de Baffin
KALAALLIT NUNAAT
(GRØNLAND)
(Denmark / Danemark)
Arctic Bay
Pond Inlet
Nanisivik
Clyde River
Davis Strait
Détroit de Davis
Victoria Island
NUNAVUT
Baffin Island
Cambridge Bay
Taloyoak
Igloolik
Qikiqtarjuaq
Île de Baffin
Arctic Circle
Cercle Arctique
Kugluktuk
Gjoa Haven
Pelly Bay
Hall Beach
Pangnirtung
Umingmaktok
Repulse Bay
Iqaluit
Back River
Coral Harbour
Cape Dorset
Kimmirut
NORTHWEST TERRITORIES
TERRITOIRES DU NORD-OUEST
Baker Lake
Hudson Strait
Détroit d'Hudson
NFLD & LAB
T-N-et-LAB
Rankin Inlet
Chesterfield Inlet
Whale Cove
Arviat
QUEBEC
QUÉBEC
Ungava Bay
Baie d'Ungava
LEGEND / LÉGENDE
Territorial capital / Capitale territoriale
Other populated places / Autres lieux habités
International boundary / Frontière internationale
Provincial boundary / Limite provinciale
Dividing line / Ligne de séparation
(Canada and/et Kalaallit Nunaat)
Hudson Bay
Baie d'Hudson
MANITOBA
Sanikiluaq
ONTARIO
James Bay
Baie James
Scale / Échelle
200 0 200 400 600
km km
www.atlas.gc.ca

Nunavut

Major Municipalities in Nunavut

Iqaluit
P.O. Box 460
Iqaluit, NU X0A 0H0
Tel: 867-979-5600; *Fax:* 867-979-5922
info@city.iqaluit.nu.ca
www.city.iqaluit.nu.ca
Municipal Type: City
Incorporated: 2001; *Area:* 52.34 sq km
Population in 2011: 6,699
Provincial Electoral District(s): Iqaluit East; Iqaluit West; Iqaluit Centre
Federal Electoral District(s): Nunavut
Next Election: Oct. 15, 2018 (3 year terms)
Note: Formerly known as Frobisher Bay.
Madeleine Redfern, Mayor
Joanasie Akumalik, Councillor
Terry Dobbin, Councillor
Simon Nattaq, Alternate Deputy Mayor
Romeyn Stevenson, Deputy Mayor
Gideonie Joamie, Councillor
Megan Pizzo Lyall, Councillor
Jason Rochon, Councillor
Kuthula Matshazi, Councillor
Muhamud Hassan, Chief Administration Officer, 867-979-5667, Fax: 867-979-0228
Tracy Cooke, City Clerk, 867-979-5634, Fax: 867-979-0228
John Mabberi-Mudonyi, Senior Director, Corporate Services & Finance, 867-979-5675, Fax: 867-979-0866
Luc Grandmaison, Director, Emergency & Protective Services, 867-979-5657, Fax: 867-979-0680
Matthew Hamp, Director, Engineering & Sustainability, 867-979-5653
Robyn Mackey, Director, Human Resources, 867-975-8506, Fax: 867-979-5210
Mélodie Simard, Director, Planning & Development, 867-979-6363
Amy Elgersma, Director, Recreation, 867-979-5616
Joamie Eegeesiak, Community Economic Development Officer, Community Economic Development, 867-979-6363, Fax: 867-979-6383

Other Municipalities in Nunavut

Arctic Bay
P.O. Box 150
Arctic Bay, NU X0A 0A0
Tel: 867-439-9917; *Fax:* 867-439-8767
sao_ab@qiniq.com
Other Information: Alternate: 867-439-9918; recep_ap@qiniq.com
Municipal Type: Hamlet
Area: 247.5 sq km
Population in 2011: 823
Provincial Electoral District(s): Quttiktuq
Federal Electoral District(s): Nunavut
Geela Arnauyumayuq, Mayor
Joeli Qamanirq, Senior Administrative Officer

Arviat
P.O. Box 150
613 3rd Avenue
Arviat, NU X0C 0E0
Tel: 867-857-2841
arviatclerk@gmail.com
www.arviat.ca
Municipal Type: Hamlet
Incorporated: 1977; *Area:* 132 sq km
Population in 2011: 2,318
Provincial Electoral District(s): Arviat
Federal Electoral District(s): Nunavut
Note: Formerly known as Eskimo Point.
Bob Leonard, Mayor
Steve England, Senior Administrative Officer

Baker Lake
P.O. Box 149
Baker Lake, NU X0C 0A0
Tel: 867-793-2874; *Fax:* 867-793-2509
www.bakerlake.ca
Municipal Type: Hamlet
Incorporated: 1977; *Area:* 182.22 sq km
Population in 2011: 1,872
Provincial Electoral District(s): Baker Lake
Federal Electoral District(s): Nunavut
Joedee Joedee, Mayor
Dennis Zettler, Senior Administrative Officer

Cambridge Bay
P.O. Box 16
16 Omingmak Street
Cambridge Bay, NU X0B 0C0
Tel: 867-983-4650; *Fax:* 867-983-2193
www.cambridgebay.ca
Municipal Type: Hamlet
Incorporated: 1984; *Area:* 202.2 sq km
Population in 2011: 1,608
Provincial Electoral District(s): Cambridge Bay
Federal Electoral District(s): Nunavut
Jeannie Ehaloak, Mayor
Stephen King, Senior Administrative Officer, 867-983-4650

Cape Dorset
P.O. Box 30
Cape Dorset, NU X0A 0C0
Tel: 867-897-8943; *Fax:* 867-897-8030
info@capedorset.ca
www.capedorset.ca
Municipal Type: Hamlet
Incorporated: 1982; *Area:* 9.74 sq km
Population in 2011: 1,363
Provincial Electoral District(s): South Baffin
Federal Electoral District(s): Nunavut
Padlaya Qiatsuk, Mayor
Ed Devereaux, Senior Administrative Officer

Chesterfield Inlet
P.O. Box 10
Chesterfield Inlet, NU X0C 0B0
Tel: 867-898-9951
www.chesterfieldinlet.net
Municipal Type: Hamlet
Incorporated: 1980; *Area:* 141.08 sq km
Population in 2011: 313
Provincial Electoral District(s): Nanulik
Federal Electoral District(s): Nunavut
Barney Aggark, Mayor, 867-898-9951
Greg Holitzki, Senior Administrative Officer, 867-898-9926

Clyde River
P.O. Box 89
Clyde River, NU X0A 0E0
Tel: 867-924-6220; *Fax:* 867-924-6293
saoclyde2005@qiniq.com
Municipal Type: Hamlet
Area: 106.48 sq km
Population in 2011: 934
Provincial Electoral District(s): Uqqummiut
Federal Electoral District(s): Nunavut
Jerry Qillaq, Mayor
John Ivey, Senior Administrative Officer

Coral Harbour
P.O. Box 30
Coral Harbour, NU X0C 0C0
Tel: 867-925-8867; *Fax:* 867-925-8233
coraledo@qiniq.com
www.coralharbour.ca
Municipal Type: Hamlet
Area: 137.83 sq km
Population in 2011: 834
Provincial Electoral District(s): Nanulik
Federal Electoral District(s): Nunavut
Willie Nakoolaak, Mayor
Leonie Pameolik, Senior Administrative Officer

Gjoa Haven
P.O. Box 200
Gjoa Haven, NU X0B 1J0
Tel: 867-360-7141
saogjoa@qiniq.com
www.gjoahaven.net
Municipal Type: Hamlet
Incorporated: 1981; *Area:* 28.47 sq km
Population in 2011: 1,279
Provincial Electoral District(s): Nattilik
Federal Electoral District(s): Nunavut
Allen Aglukkaq, Mayor
Shawn Stuckey, Senior Administrative Officer

Grise Fiord
P.O. Box 77
Grise Fiord, NU X0A 0J0
Tel: 867-980-9959; *Fax:* 867-980-9052
www.grisefiord.ca
Municipal Type: Hamlet
Incorporated: 1987; *Area:* 332.7 sq km
Population in 2011: 130
Provincial Electoral District(s): Quttiktuq
Federal Electoral District(s): Nunavut
Meeka Kigutak, Mayor
Marty Kuluguaqtuq, Senior Administrative Officer

Hall Beach
P.O. Box 3
Hall Beach, NU X0A 0K0
Tel: 867-928-8829; *Fax:* 867-928-8871
sao_hbhamlet@qiniq.com
Other Information: Alternate Phone: 867-928-8945
Municipal Type: Hamlet
Area: 16.52 sq km
Population in 2011: 546
Provincial Electoral District(s): Amittuq
Federal Electoral District(s): Nunavut
Peter Siakuluk, Mayor
Hailie MacNeil-Smith, Senior Administrative Officer

Igloolik
P.O. Box 30
Igloolik, NU X0A 0L0
Tel: 867-934-8940; *Fax:* 867-934-8757
igloolik@magma.ca
Other Information: Alternate Phone: 867-934-8830
Municipal Type: Hamlet
Incorporated: 1976; *Area:* 102.87 sq km
Population in 2011: 1,454
Provincial Electoral District(s): Amittuq
Federal Electoral District(s): Nunavut
Peter Ivalu, Mayor
Brian Fleming, Senior Administrative Officer, 867-934-8429, Fax: 867-934-8228

Kimmirut
P.O. Box 120
Kimmirut, NU X0A 0N0
Tel: 867-939-2247; *Fax:* 867-939-2045
cedkimm@qiniq.com
www.kimmirut.ca
Municipal Type: Hamlet
Area: 2.27 sq km
Population in 2011: 455
Provincial Electoral District(s): South Baffin
Federal Electoral District(s): Nunavut
Maliktoo Lyta, Mayor
Mike Richards, Acting Senior Administrative Officer

Kugaaruk
P.O. Box 205
Kugaaruk, NU X0B 1K0
Tel: 867-769-6281; *Fax:* 867-769-6069
sao_kug@qiniq.com
Municipal Type: Hamlet
Incorporated: 1972; *Area:* 4.97 sq km
Population in 2011: 771
Provincial Electoral District(s): Akulliq
Federal Electoral District(s): Nunavut
Note: Formerly known as Pelly Bay.
Stephan Inaksajak, Mayor

Kugluktuk
P.O. Box 271
Kugluktuk, NU X0B 0E0
Tel: 867-982-6500; *Fax:* 867-982-3060
Other Information: Alternate Phone: 867-982-6505
Municipal Type: Hamlet
Incorporated: 1981; *Area:* 549.61 sq km
Population in 2011: 1,450
Provincial Electoral District(s): Kugluktuk
Federal Electoral District(s): Nunavut
Note: Formerly known as Coppermine.
Red Pedersen, Mayor
Don LeBlanc, Senior Administrative Officer

Naujaat
P.O. Box 10
Naujaat, NU X0C 0H0
Tel: 867-462-9952; *Fax:* 867-462-4411
www.repulsebay.ca/hamlet.html
Municipal Type: Hamlet
Incorporated: 1978; *Area:* 423.74 sq km
Population in 2011: 945
Provincial Electoral District(s): Aivilik
Federal Electoral District(s): Nunavut
Note: Residents of Repulse Bay voted on May 12, 2014, to change the Hamlet's name to Naujaat, which is the community's Inuktitut name, meaning "Nesting place for seagulls."
Solomon Malliki, Mayor
Clayton Croucher, Interim Senior Administrative Officer

Pangnirtung
P.O. Box 253
Pangnirtung, NU X0A 0R0
Tel: 867-473-8953; *Fax:* 867-473-8832
pang_reception@qiniq.com
www.pangnirtung.ca
Municipal Type: Hamlet
Incorporated: 1972; *Area:* 7.54 sq km
Population in 2011: 1,425
Provincial Electoral District(s): Pangnirtung
Federal Electoral District(s): Nunavut
Mosesee Qappik, Mayor
Shawn Trepanier, Senior Administrative Officer, 867-473-8953

Pond Inlet
P.O. Box 180
Pond Inlet, NU X0A 0S0
Tel: 867-899-8934; *Fax:* 867-899-8940
info@pondinlet.ca
www.pondinlet.ca
Other Information: Alternate Phone: 867-899-8935
Municipal Type: Hamlet
Area: 173.36 sq km
Population in 2011: 1,549
Provincial Electoral District(s): Tunnuniq
Federal Electoral District(s): Nunavut
Charlie Inuarak, Mayor
Rikki Butt, Senior Administrative Officer, 867-889-8934, Fax: 867-889-8940

Qikiqtarjuaq
P.O. Box 4
Qikiqtarjuaq, NU X0A 0B0
Tel: 867-927-8832; *Fax:* 867-927-8178
munqik@qiniq.com
Other Information: Alternate Phone: 867-927-8178
Municipal Type: Hamlet
Area: 130.65 sq km
Population in 2011: 520
Provincial Electoral District(s): Uqqummiut
Federal Electoral District(s): Nunavut
Note: Formerly Broughton Island.
Mary Killiktee, Mayor

Rankin Inlet
P.O. Box 310
Rankin Inlet, NU X0C 0G0
Tel: 867-645-2895; *Fax:* 867-645-2146
www.rankininlet.net
Municipal Type: Hamlet
Incorporated: 1975; *Area:* 20.24 sq km
Population in 2011: 2,266
Provincial Electoral District(s): Rankin Inlet North; Rankin Inlet South/Whale Cove
Federal Electoral District(s): Nunavut
Robert Janes, Mayor
Tom Ng, Senior Administrative Officer

Resolute Bay
P.O. Box 60
Resolute Bay, NU X0A 0V0
Tel: 867-252-3616; *Fax:* 867-252-3749
Municipal Type: Hamlet
Incorporated: 1987; *Area:* 116.89 sq km
Population in 2011: 214
Provincial Electoral District(s): Quttiktuq
Federal Electoral District(s): Nunavut
Note: Also called Resolute.
Ross Pudlat, Mayor
Angela Idlout, Senior Administrative Officer

Sanikiluaq
P.O. Box 157
Sanikiluaq, NU X0A 0W0
Tel: 867-266-7900; *Fax:* 867-266-7924
www.sanikiluaq.ca
Municipal Type: Hamlet
Incorporated: 1976; *Area:* 114.98 sq km
Population in 2011: 812
Provincial Electoral District(s): Hudson Bay
Federal Electoral District(s): Nunavut
Elijassie Sala, Mayor
Daryl Dibblee, Senior Administrative Officer, 867-266-7910

Taloyoak
P.O. Box 8
Taloyoak, NU X0B 1B0
Tel: 867-561-6341; *Fax:* 867-561-5057
Municipal Type: Hamlet
Incorporated: 1981; *Area:* 37.65 sq km
Population in 2011: 899
Provincial Electoral District(s): Nattilik
Federal Electoral District(s): Nunavut
Note: Formerly known as Spence Bay.
Joe Ashevak, Mayor
Greg Holitzki, Senior Administrative Officer, 867-561-6341, Fax: 897-561-5057

Whale Cove
P.O. Box 120
Whale Cove, NU X0C 0J0
Tel: 867-896-9961; *Fax:* 867-896-9109
www.whalecove.ca
Municipal Type: Hamlet
Incorporated: 1976; *Area:* 283.65 sq km
Population in 2011: 407
Provincial Electoral District(s): Rankin Inlet South/Whale Cove
Federal Electoral District(s): Nunavut
Stanley Adjuk, Sr., Mayor
Paul Kaludjak, Senior Administrative Officer

ONTARIO

There are two types of municipal government structures in Ontario: two-tier municipalities, which consist of upper-tier municipalities, known as either regions or counties, plus their constituent lower-tier municipalities; and single-tier municipalities.

One-half of Ontario's population lives in the single-tier cities of Toronto, Ottawa and Hamilton and in areas with a regional system of government. The regional system was created for the more densely populated areas of this province. Regions have more servicing responsibilities than a county, and while there are variations, services usually provided by regions include arterial roads, transit, policing, sewer and water systems, waste disposal, region-wide land use planning and development, health and social services. Lower-tier municipalities within regions are generally responsible for local roads, fire protection, tax collection, garbage collection, recreation and local land use planning. All municipalities in a region participate in the regional system.

Counties exist only in southern Ontario. Lower-tier municipalities (known as cities, towns, villages, townships) within counties provide the majority of municipal services to their residents. The services provided by county governments are usually limited to arterial roads, health and social services and county land use planning. Local municipalities raise taxes for their own purposes, as well as for upper-tier and school board purposes.

Generally, membership of the upper-tier council comprises representatives from the lower tiers, although heads of council can be directly elected.

Single-tier municipalities exist across Ontario and include separated municipalities that are located within a county but are not part of the county for municipal purposes (e.g. City of Windsor, Town of Smiths Falls, Township of Pelee). Single-tier municipalities also include all northern municipalities (e.g. City of Thunder Bay, Town of Blind River, Township of Cockburn Island). Single-tier municipalities also include those former counties or regional municipalities that have amalgamated into single-tier municipalities (e.g. Municipality of Chatham-Kent, County of Prince Edward, County of Brant, City of Kawartha Lakes, City of Toronto, City of Hamilton, City of Ottawa, City of Greater Sudbury, Haldimand County, Norfolk County). Single-tier municipalities have responsibilibities for their residents.

The more populated areas are incorporated into municipalitites; only 40,000 people (not including aboriginal peoples on reserves) live in areas not incorporated as municipalities. Services in the northern regions have been structured to optimize efficiencies in service delivery. District Social Service Administration Boards deliver core services in social assistance, child care and social housing, and may also provide optional health services, land ambulances and public health. Some services in a limited number of unincorporated areas are provided by local service boards and local roads which are funded by the province.

Under the Municipal Elections Act, local government elections are held on the fourth Monday in October, for a four-year term (2014, 2018, etc.).

Ontario

Counties & Municipal Districts in Ontario

Brant
P.O. Box 160
26 Park Ave.
Burford, ON N0E 1A0
Tel: 519-449-2451; *Fax:* 519-449-2454
brant@county.brant.on.ca
www.brant.ca
Other Information: Toll Free Phone: 1-888-250-2295
Municipal Type: County
Incorporated: Jan. 1, 1999; *Area:* 843.1 sq km
Population in 2011: 35,638
Provincial Electoral District(s): Brant
Federal Electoral District(s): Brantford-Brant
Next Election: Oct. 2018 (4 year terms)
Ron Eddy, Mayor
Willem Bouma, Councillor, Wards: 1
John Wheat, Councillor, Wards: 1
Don H. Cardy, Councillor, Wards: 2
Shirley Simons, Councillor, Wards: 2
John Peirce, Councillor, Wards: 3
Murray Powell, Councillor, Wards: 3
Robert Chambers, Councillor, Wards: 4
David Miller, Councillor, Wards: 4
Brian Coleman, Councillor, Wards: 5
Joan Gatward, Councillor, Wards: 5
Heather Boyd, Clerk & Manager, Council Services
Paul Emerson, Chief Administrative Officer
Heather Mifflin, Treasurer & Director, Finance
Michael Bradley, Deputy CAO & General Manager, Operations
Kathy Ballantyne, Director, Parks & Facilities, 519-442-1818
Alex Davidson, Director, Water
Mark Pomponi, Director, Development Services, 519-442-6324
Lee Robinson, Director, Engineering
Mike Tout, Director, Roads
Paul Boissonneault, Fire Chief, 519-442-4500

Bruce
P.O. Box 70
30 Park St.
Walkerton, ON N0G 2V0
Tel: 519-881-1291;
www.brucecounty.on.ca
Municipal Type: County
Area: 4,079.17 sq km
Population in 2011: 66,102
Next Election: Oct. 2018 (4 year terms)
Mitch Twolan, Warden, Wards: Huron-Kinloss
Paul Eagleson, Councillor, Wards: Arran-Elderslie
David Inglis, Councillor, Wards: Brockton
Anne Eadie, Councillor, Wards: Kincardine
Mike Smith, Councillor, Wards: Saugeen Shores
Milt McIver, Councillor, Wards: Northern Bruce Peninsula
Janice Jackson, Councillor, Wards: South Bruce
Kelley Coulter, Chief Administrative Officer
Bettyanne Cobean, C.M.O., Clerk-Treasurer & Head, Corporate Services
Marianne Nero, Director, Human Resources
Chris LaForest, Director, Planning
Christine MacDonald, Director, Social Services & Social Housing
Doug Smith, Director, Emergency Services
Brian Knox, County Engineer

Dufferin
55 Zina St.
Orangeville, ON L9W 1E5
Tel: 519-941-2816; *Fax:* 519-941-4565
info@dufferincounty.ca
www.dufferincounty.ca
Other Information: Toll-Free Phone: 1-877-941-6991
Municipal Type: County
Incorporated: Jan. 24, 1881; *Area:* 1,485.58 sq km
Population in 2011: 56,881
Next Election: Oct. 2018 (4 year terms)
Warren Maycock, Warden, Wards: Orangeville
Don MacIver, Councillor, Wards: Amaranth
Jane Aultman, Councillor, Wards: Amaranth
Guy Gardhouse, Councillor, Wards: East Garafraxa
Steve Soloman, Councillor, Wards: Grand Valley
Darren White, Councillor, Wards: Melancthon
Laura Ryan, Councillor, Wards: Mono
Ken McGhee, Councillor, Wards: Mono
Paul Mills, Councillor, Wards: Mulmur
Heather Hayes, Councillor, Wards: Mulmur
Jeremy Williams, Councillor, Wards: Orangeville
Ken Bennington, Councillor, Wards: Shelburne
Geoff Dunlop, Councillor, Wards: Shelburne
Pam Hillock, Clerk & Director, Corporate Services
Sonya Pritchard, Chief Administrative Officer
Alan Selby, Treasurer
Michael A. Giles, Chief Building Official
Scott Burns, Director, Public Works
Keith Palmer, Director, Community Services
Caroline Mach, Manager, Forest
Scott Martin, Manager, Operations
Steven Piercey, Manager, Facilities

Durham
P.O. Box 623
605 Rossland Rd. East
Whitby, ON L1N 6A3
Tel: 905-668-7711;
info@durham.ca
www.durham.ca
Other Information: Toll-Free Phone: 1-800-372-1102
Municipal Type: Regional Municipality
Incorporated: Jan. 1, 1974; *Area:* 2,523.15 sq km
Population in 2011: 608,124
Next Election: Oct. 2018 (4 year terms)
Note: Durham Region elected its first chair in 2014.
Roger Anderson, Regional Chair & Chief Executive Officer, Councillor, Fax: 905-668-1567
Steve Parish, Councillor, Wards: Ajax Mayor
Shaun Collier, Councillor, Wards: Ajax 1 & 2
Colleen Jordan, Councillor, Wards: Ajax 3 & 4
John Grant, Councillor, Wards: Brock Mayor
Ted Smith, Councillor, Wards: Brock
Adrian Foster, Councillor, Wards: Clarington Mayor
Joe Neal, Councillor, Wards: Clarington 1 & 2
Willie Woo, Councillor, Wards: Clarington 3 & 4
John Henry, Councillor, Wards: Oshawa Mayor
John Aker, Councillor, Wards: Oshawa
Dan Carter, Councillor, Wards: Oshawa
Bob Chapman, Councillor, Wards: Oshawa
Nancy Diamond, Councillor, Wards: Oshawa
Amy England, Councillor, Wards: Oshawa
John Neal, Councillor, Wards: Oshawa
Nester Pidwerbecki, Councillor, Wards: Oshawa
Dave Ryan, Councillor, Wards: Pickering Mayor
Jennifer O'Connell, Councillor, Wards: Pickering 1
Bill McLean, Councillor, Wards: Pickering 2
David Pickles, Councillor, Wards: Pickering 3
Tom Rowett, Councillor, Wards: Scugog Mayor
Bobbie Drew, Councillor, Wards: Scugog
Gerri-Lynn O'Connor, Councillor, Wards: Uxbridge Mayor
Jack Ballinger, Councillor, Wards: Uxbridge
Don Mitchell, Councillor, Wards: Whitby Mayor
Lorne Earl Coe, Councillor, Wards: Whitby
Joe Drumm, Councillor, Wards: Whitby
Elizabeth Roy, Councillor, Wards: Whitby
Debi Wilcox, Regional Clerk, Fax: 905-668-9963
Garry H. Cubitt, M.S.W., Chief Administrative Officer
R. Jim Clapp, Treasurer/Commissioner, Finance Department, Fax: 905-666-6256
Cliff Curtis, Commissioner, Works Department, Fax: 905-668-2051
Hugh A. Drouin, Commissioner, Social Services Department, Fax: 905-666-6219
Alex L. Georgieff, Commissioner, Planning Department, Fax: 905-666-6208
Matthew L. Gaskell, Commissioner, Corporate Services
Robert J. Kyle, Commissioner, Health Department & Medical Officer of Health, Fax: 905-666-3327
Pat W. Olive, Commissioner, Economic Development & Tourism, 800-413-0017, Fax: 905-666-6228
Warren Leonard, Director, Durham Emergency Management Office, 905-430-2792, Fax: 905-430-8635
Sherri Munns-Audet, Director, Corporate Communications, Fax: 905-668-1468
Ted Galinis, General Manager, Durham Region Transit, Fax: 905-666-6193

Elgin
450 Sunset Dr.
St Thomas, ON N5R 5V1
Tel: 519-631-1460;
www.elgincounty.ca
Municipal Type: County
Incorporated: 1852; *Area:* 1,880.84 sq km
Population in 2011: 87,461
Next Election: Oct. 2018 (4 year terms)
Note: Restructuring of the county occurred in 1998.
Paul Ens, Warden, Wards: Bayham
Greg Currie, Councillor, Wards: Aylmer
David Marr, Councillor, Wards: Central Elgin
Sally Martyn, Councillor, Wards: Central Elgin
Cameron McWilliam, Councillor, Wards: Dutton/Dunwich
Dave Mennill, Councillor, Wards: Malahide
Mike Wolfe, Councillor, Wards: Malahide
Grant Jones, Councillor, Wards: Southwold
Bernie Wiehle, Councillor, Wards: West Elgin
Mark G. McDonald, Chief Administrative Officer
Rob Bryce, Director, Human Resources
Jim Bundschuh, Director, Financial Services
Brian Masschaele, Director, Community & Cultural Services
Clayton Watters, Director, Engineering Services

Essex
360 Fairview Ave. West
Essex, ON N8M 1Y6
Tel: 519-776-6441; *Fax:* 519-776-4455
www.countyofessex.on.ca
Municipal Type: County
Incorporated: 1999; *Area:* 1,851.34 sq km
Population in 2011: 388,782
Next Election: Oct. 2018 (4 year terms)
Tom Bain, Warden, Wards: Lakeshore
Ken Antaya, Deputy Warden, Wards: LaSalle
Aldo DiCarlo, Councillor, Wards: Amherstburg
Bart DiPasquale, Councillor, Wards: Amerstburg
Ron McDermott, Councillor, 519-776-8150, Wards: Essex
Richard Meloche, Councillor, Wards: Essex
Nelson Santos, Councillor, 519-733-9936, Wards: Kingsville
Gord Queen, Councillor, Wards: Kingsville
Al Fazio, Councillor, Wards: Lakeshore
Marc Bondy, Councillor, Wards: LaSalle
John Paterson, Councillor, Wards: Leamington
Hilda MacDonald, Councillor, Wards: Leamington
Gary McNamara, Councillor, Wards: Tecumseh
Joe Bachetti, Councillor, Wards: Tecumseh
Mary S. Brennan, Clerk & Director, Council Services
Brian Gregg, Chief Administrative Officer
Robert Maisonville, Director, Corporate Services & Treasurer
Greg Schlosser, Director, Human Resources
Bill King, Manager, Planning Services
Tom Bateman, County Engineer
Phillip Berthiaume, Planner, Emergency Measures

Frontenac
2069 Battersea Rd., RR#1
Glenburnie, ON K0H 1S0
Tel: 613-548-9400; *Fax:* 613-546-8460
www.frontenaccounty.ca
Municipal Type: County
Incorporated: Jan. 1, 1998; *Area:* 3,672.49 sq km
Population in 2011: 149,738
Next Election: Oct. 2018 (4 year terms)
Denis Doyle, Warden, Wards: Frontenac Islands
Frances Smith, Deputy Warden, Wards: Central Frontenac
Tom Dewey, Councillor, Wards: Central Frontenac
Natalie Nossal, Councillor, Wards: Frontenac Islands
John Inglis, Councillor, Wards: North Frontenac
Ron Higgins, Councillor, Wards: North Frontenac
Ron Vandewal, Councillor, Wards: South Frontenac
John McDougall, Councillor, Wards: South Frontenac
Kelly Pender, Chief Administrative Officer
Marian Van Bruinessen, Treasurer
Paul Charbonneau, Director, Emergency & Transportation Services & Chief, Paramedics
Joe Gallivan, Director, Planning & Economic Development
Anne Marie Young, Manager, Economic Development

Grey
County Administration Bldg.
595 - 9th Ave. East
Owen Sound, ON N4K 3E3
Tel: 519-376-2205;
www.grey.ca
Other Information: Toll-Free Phone: 1-800-567-4739
Municipal Type: County
Incorporated: Jan. 1, 1852; *Area:* 4,508.12 sq km
Population in 2011: 92,568
Next Election: Oct. 2018 (4 year terms)
Kevin Eccles, Warden, Wards: West Grey
Bob Pringle, Councillor, Wards: Chatsworth
Scott McKay, Councillor, Wards: Chatsworth
Alan Barfoot, Councillor, Wards: Georgian Bluffs
Dwight Burley, Councillor, Wards: Georgian Bluffs
Paul McQueen, Councillor, Wards: Grey Highlands
Stewart Halliday, Councillor, Wards: Grey Highlands
Sue Paterson, Councillor, Wards: Hanover
Selwyn Hicks, Councillor, Wards: Hanover
Barb Clumpus, Councillor, Wards: Meaford
Harley Greenfield, Councillor, Wards: Meaford
Ian Boddy, Councillor, Wards: Owen Sound
Arlene Wright, Councillor, Wards: Owen Sound
Anna-Marie Fosbrooke, Councillor, Wards: Southgate
Norman Jack, Councillor, Wards: Southgate
John F. McKean, Councillor, Wards: The Blue Mountains
Gail Ardiel, Councillor, Wards: The Blue Mountains

John Bell, Councillor, Wards: West Grey
Sharon Vokes, C.M.O., County Clerk & Director, Council Services
Kim Wingrove, Chief Administrative Officer
Kevin Weppler, Director, Finance
Barb Fedy, BA, Director, Social Services
Geoff Hogan, BSc, Director, Information Technology
Randy Scherzer, BES, MCIP, RPP, Director, Planning & Development
Grant McLevy, Director, Human Resources

Haldimand
Cayuga Administration Bldg.
P.O. Box 400
45 Munsee St. North
Cayuga, ON N0A 1E0
Tel: 905-318-5932; *Fax:* 905-772-3542
www.haldimandcounty.on.ca
Municipal Type: County
Incorporated: Jan. 1, 2001; *Area:* 1,251.58 sq km
Population in 2011: 44,876
Provincial Electoral District(s): Haldimand-Norfolk
Federal Electoral District(s): Haldimand-Norfolk
Next Election: Oct. 2018 (4 year terms)
Ken Hewitt, Mayor
Leroy Bartlett, Councillor, Wards: 1
Fred Morison, Councillor, Wards: 2
Craig Grice, Councillor, Wards: 3
Tony Dalimonte, Councillor, Wards: 4
Rob Shirton, Councillor, Wards: 5
Bernie Corbett, Councillor, Wards: 6
Evelyn Eichenbaum, Clerk
Donald Boyle, Chief Administrative Officer
Karen General, General Manager, Corporate Services
Hugh Hanly, General Manager, Community Services
Craig Manley, General Manager, Planning & Economic Development
Paul Mungar, General Manager, Public Works

Haliburton
P.O. Box 399
11 Newcastle St.
Minden, ON K0M 2K0
Tel: 705-286-1333; *Fax:* 705-286-4829
info@county.haliburton.on.ca
www.haliburtoncounty.ca
Municipal Type: County
Incorporated: Jan. 1, 2001; *Area:* 4,025.27 sq km
Population in 2011: 17,026
Next Election: Oct. 2018 (4 year terms)
Murray Fearrey, Warden, Wards: Dysart et al
Carol Moffatt, Councillor, Wards: Algonquin Highlands
Liz Danielsen, Councillor, Wards: Algonquin Highlands
Andrea Roberts, Councillor, Wards: Dysart et al
Dave Burton, Councillor, Wards: Highlands East
Suzanne Patridge, Councillor, Wards: Highlands East
Brent Devolin, Councillor, Wards: Minden Hills
Cheryl Murdoch, Councillor, 705-286-1701, Wards: Minden Hills
Mike Rutter, County Clerk & Chief Administrative Officer
Laura Janke, Treasurer
Craig Jones, Director, Paramedic Services
Craig Douglas, Director, Public Works
Amanda Virtanen, Director, Tourism
Charlsey White, Director, Planning
Sylvin Cloutier, Manager, Operations

Halton
1151 Bronte Rd.
Oakville, ON L6M 3L1
Tel: 905-825-6000; *Fax:* 905-825-9010
accesshalton@halton.ca
www.halton.ca
Other Information: Toll-Free Phone: 1-866-442-5866; TTY: 905-827-9833
Municipal Type: Regional Municipality
Incorporated: Jan. 1, 1974; *Area:* 967.17 sq km
Population in 2011: 501,669
Next Election: Oct. 2018 (4 year terms)
Gary Carr, Regional Chair, Councillor, 905-825-6115, Fax: 905-825-8273
Rick Goldring, Councillor, Wards: Burlington Mayor
Rick Craven, Councillor, Wards: Burlington 1
Marianne Meed Ward, Councillor, Wards: Burlington 2
John Taylor, Councillor, Wards: Burlington 3
Jack Dennison, Councillor, Wards: Burlington 4
Paul Sharman, Councillor, Wards: Burlington 5
Blair Lancaster, Councillor, Wards: Burlington 6
Rick Bonnette, Councillor, Wards: Halton Hills Mayor
Clark Somerville, Councillor, Wards: Halton Hills 1 & 2
Jane Fogal, Councillor, Wards: Halton Hills 3 & 4
Gordon A. Krantz, Councillor, Wards: Milton Mayor
Mike Cluett, Councillor, Wards: Milton 1, 6, 7, 8
Colin Best, Councillor, Wards: Milton 2, 3, 4, 5
Rob Burton, Councillor, Wards: Oakville Mayor
Sean O'Meara, Councillor, Wards: Oakville 1
Cathy Duddeck, Councillor, Wards: Oakville 2
Dave Gittings, Councillor, Wards: Oakville 3
Allan Elgar, Councillor, Wards: Oakville 4
Jeff Knoll, Councillor, Wards: Oakville 5
Tom Adams, Councillor, Wards: Oakville 6
Karyn Bennett, Regional Clerk & Director, Council Services
Jane MacCaskill, Chief Administrative Officer
Mark Scinocca, Regional Treasurer & Commissioner, Corporate Services
Hamidah Meghani, Commissioner & Medical Officer of Health
Mark Meneray, Commissioner, Legislative & Planning Services & Corporate Counsel
Sheldon Wolfson, Commissioner, Social & Community Services
Jim Harnum, Commissioner, Public Works

Hastings
County Administration Bldg.
P.O. Box 4400
235 Pinnacle St.
Belleville, ON K8N 3A9
Tel: 613-966-1319; *Fax:* 613-966-2574
www.hastingscounty.com
Other Information: Toll-Free Phone: 1-800-510-3306
Municipal Type: County
Incorporated: 1850; *Area:* 5,977.64 sq km
Population in 2011: 134,934
Next Election: Oct. 2018 (4 year terms)
Rick Phillips, Warden, Wards: Tyendinaga
Bernice Jenkins, Councillor, Wards: Bancroft
Bonnie Adams, Councillor, Wards: Carlow/Mayo
Tom Deline, Councillor, Wards: Centre Hastings
Norm Clark, Councillor, Wards: Deseronto
Carl Tinney, Councillor, Wards: Faraday
Vivian Bloom, Councillor, Wards: Hastings Highlands
Sharon Carson, Councillor, Wards: Limerick
Bob Sager, Councillor, Wards: Madoc
Terry Clemens, Councillor, Wards: Marmora & Lake
Rodney Cooney, Councillor, Wards: Stirling-Rawdon
Wanda Donaldson, Councillor, Wards: Tudor & Cashel
Jo-Anne Albert, Councillor, Wards: Tweed
Graham Blair, Councillor, Wards: Wollaston
James Pine, Chief Administrative Officer & Clerk
Jim Duffin, Deputy Clerk
Sue Horwood, Treasurer, Director, Finance, Asset Management & Services
Shaune Lightfoot, Director, Human Resources
Brian McComb, Director, Planning

Huron
1 Courthouse Sq.
Goderich, ON N7A 1M2
Tel: 519-524-8394; *Fax:* 519-524-2044
huronadmin@huroncounty.ca
www.huroncounty.ca
Other Information: Toll-Free Phone: 1-888-524-8394 (in 519 area)
Municipal Type: County
Area: 3,396.68 sq km
Population in 2011: 59,100
Next Election: Oct. 2018 (4 year terms)
Paul Gowing, Warden, Wards: Morris-Turnberry
Ben Van Diepenbeek, Councillor, Wards: Ashfield-Colborne-Wawanosh
Roger Watt, Councillor, Wards: Ashfield-Colborne-Wawanosh
Tyler Hessel, Councillor, Wards: Bluewater
Jim Ferguson, Councillor, Wards: Bluewater
Jim Ginn, Councillor, Wards: Central Huron
David Jewitt, Councillor, Wards: Central Huron
Kevin Morrison, Councillor, Wards: Goderich
Jim Donnelly, Councillor, Wards: Goderich
Art Versteeg, Councillor, Wards: Howick
Bernie MacLellan, Councillor, Wards: Huron East
Joe Steffler, Councillor, Wards: Huron East
Neil Vincent, Councillor, Wards: North Huron
Maureen Cole, Councillor, Wards: South Huron
David Frayne, Councillor, Wards: South Huron
Brenda Orchard, Chief Administrative Officer
Susan Cronin, Clerk
Steve Lund, Director, Public Works
Scott Tousaw, Director, Planning & Development
Jeff Horseman, Acting Chief, Emergency Services

Lambton
P.O. Box 3000
789 Broadway St.
Wyoming, ON N0N 1T0
Tel: 519-845-0801; *Fax:* 519-845-3160
administration@county-lambton.on.ca
www.lambtononline.com
Other Information: Toll-Free Phone: 1-866-324-6912
Municipal Type: County
Incorporated: 1853; *Area:* 3,001.7 sq km
Population in 2011: 126,199
Next Election: Oct. 2018 (4 year terms)
Bev MacDougal, Warden, Wards: Sarnia
Ian Veen, Deputy Warden, Wards: Oil Springs
Don McGugan, Councillor, Wards: Brooke-Alvinston
Alan Broad, Councillor, Wards: Dawn-Euphemia
Kevin Marriott, Councillor, Wards: Enniskillen
Bill Weber, Councillor, Wards: Lambton Shores
Doug Cook, Councillor, Wards: Lambton Shores
John McCharles, Councillor, Wards: Petrolia
Lonny Napper, Councillor, Wards: Plympton-Wyoming
Larry MacKenzie, Councillor, Wards: Point Edward
Mike Bradley, Councillor, Wards: Sarnia
Dave Boushy, Councillor, Wards: Sarnia
Andy Bruziewicz, Councillor, Wards: Sarnia
Anne Marie Gillis, Councillor, Wards: Sarnia
Steve Arnold, Councillor, Wards: St. Clair
Peter Giilliland, Councillor, Wards: St. Clair
Todd Case, Councillor, Wards: Warwick
Ronald G. Van Horne, Chief Administrative Officer
Andrew Taylor, General Manager, Public Health Services
Jim Kutyba, P.Eng., General Manager, Infrastructure & Development Services
Robert Tremain, General Manager, Cultural Services
Jason Cole, P.Eng., Manager, Public Works

Lanark
County Administration Bldg.
99 Christie Lake Rd.
Perth, ON K7H 3C6
Tel: 613-267-4200; *Fax:* 613-267-2964
info@lanarkcounty.ca
www.county.lanark.on.ca
Other Information: Toll-Free Phone: 1-888-952-6275
Municipal Type: County
Incorporated: Jan. 1st 1998; *Area:* 2,979.14 sq km
Population in 2011: 65,667
Next Election: Oct. 2018 (4 year terms)
Keith Kerr, Warden, Wards: Tay Valley
Richard Kidd, Councillor, Wards: Beckwith
Sharon Mousseau, Councillor, Wards: Beckwith
Louis Antonakos, Councillor, Wards: Carleton Place
Jerry Flynn, Councillor, Wards: Carleton Place
Aubrey Churchill, Councillor, Wards: Drummond/North Elmsley
Gail Code, Councillor, Wards: Drummond/North Elmsley
Brian Stewart, Councillor, Wards: Lanark Highlands
John Hall, Councillor, Wards: Lanark Highlands
Shaun McLaughlin, Councillor, Wards: Mississippi Mills
Jane Torrance, Councillor, Wards: Mississippi Mills
Bill Dobson, Councillor, Wards: Montague
Klaas Van Der Meer, Councillor, Wards: Montague
John Fenik, Councillor, Wards: Perth
John Gemmell, Councillor, Wards: Perth
Brian Campbell, Councillor, Wards: Tay Valley
Leslie Drynan, Deputy Clerk
Kurt Greaves, Chief Administrative Officer
Nancy Green, Director, Social Services
Terry McCann, Director, Public Works

Lennox & Addington
97 Thomas St. East
Napanee, ON K7R 3S9
Tel: 613-354-4883; *Fax:* 613-354-3112
www.lennox-addington.on.ca
Municipal Type: County
Area: 2,776.48 sq km
Population in 2011: 41,824
Next Election: Oct. 2018 (4 year terms)
Gordon Schermerhorn, Warden, Wards: Greater Napanee
Henry Hogg, Councillor, 613-336-0227, Wards: Addington Highlands
Helen Yanch, Councillor, Wards: Addington Highlands
Marg Isbester, Councillor, Wards: Greater Napanee
Bill Lowry, Councillor, 613-583-2412, Wards: Loyalist
Ric Bresee, Councillor, 613-634-5544, Wards: Loyalist
Clarence Kennedy, Councillor, 613-358-2720, Wards: Stone Mills
Eric Smith, Councillor, 613-379-2366, Wards: Stone Mills
Larry Keech, Chief Administrative Officer & Clerk
Mark Schjerning, Chief, Emergency Services
Bill Bishop, Director, Human Resources

Stephen Fox, Director, Financial & Physical Services
Stephen Paul, Director, Community & Development Services

Middlesex
399 Ridout St. North
London, ON N6A 2P1
Tel: 519-434-7321; *Fax:* 519-434-0638
www.middlesex.ca
Municipal Type: County
Area: 3,317.15 sq km
Population in 2011: 439,151
Next Election: Oct. 2018 (4 year terms)
Vance Blackmore, Warden, Wards: Southwest Middlesex
Kurtis Smith, Councillor, Wards: Adelaide Metcalfe
Cathy Burghardt-Jesson, Councillor, Wards: Lucan Biddulph
Al Edmondson, Councillor, Wards: Middlesex Centre
Clare Bloomfield, Councillor, Wards: Middlesex Centre
Don Shipway, Councillor, Wards: North Middlesex
Brian Ropp, Councillor, Wards: North Middlesex
Marigay Wilkins, Councillor, Wards: Southwest Middlesex
Joanne Vanderheyden, Councillor, Wards: Strathroy Caradoc
Brad Richards, Councillor, Wards: Strathroy Caradoc
Jim Maudsley, Councillor, Wards: Thames Centre
Marcel Meyer, Councillor, Wards: Thames Centre
Kathy Bunting, Clerk
Bill Rayburn, Chief Administrative Officer
Jim Gates, Treasurer
Cindy Howard, Director, Social Services
Cara Finn, Manager, Economic Development
Morgan Calvert, Manager, Information Technology
Chris Traini, County Engineer
Doug Spettigue, Human Resource Officer
Durk Vanderwerff, Manager, Planning

Muskoka
70 Pine St.
Bracebridge, ON P1L 1N3
Tel: 705-645-2231; *Fax:* 705-645-5319
info@muskoka.on.ca
www.muskoka.on.ca
Other Information: Toll-Free Phone: 1-800-461-4210 (In 705 area code)
Municipal Type: Regional Municipality
Incorporated: Jan. 1, 1971; *Area:* 3,890.24 sq km
Population in 2011: 57,047
Next Election: Oct. 2018 (4 year terms)
John Klinck, Disctrict Chair
Lori-Lynn Giaschi-Pacini, Councillor, Wards: Bracebridge
Graydon Smith, Councillor, Wards: Bracebridge Mayor
Steve Clement, Councillor, Wards: Bracebridge
Don Smith, Councillor, Wards: Bracebridge
Larry Braid, Councillor, Wards: Georgian Bay Mayor
Paul Wiancko, Councillor, Wards: Georgian Bay 1 & 3
Peter Cooper, Councillor, Wards: Georgian Bay 2 & 4
Paisley Donaldson, Councillor, Wards: Gravenhurst Mayor
Sandy Cairns, Councillor, Wards: Gravenhurst
Paul Kelly, Councillor, Wards: Gravenhurst
Terry Pilger, Councillor, Wards: Gravenhurst
Scott Aitchison, Councillor, Wards: Huntsville Mayor
Nancy Alcock, Councillor, Wards: Huntsville
Karin Terziano, Councillor, Wards: Huntsville
Brian Thompson, Councillor, Wards: Huntsville
Bob Young, Councillor, Wards: Lake of Bays Mayor
Shane Baker, Councillor, Wards: Lake of Bays Franklin/Sinclair
Bob Lacroix, Councillor, Wards: Lake of Bays Ridout/McLean
Don Furniss, Councillor, Wards: Muskoka Lakes Mayor
Ruth-Ellen Nishikawa, Councillor, Wards: Muskoka Lakes A
Allen Edwards, Councillor, Wards: Muskoka Lakes B
Phil Harding, Councillor, Wards: Muskoka Lakes C
Debbie Crowder, District Clerk
Michael Duben, Chief Administrative Officer
Samantha Hastings, Commissioner, Planning Economic Development
Fred Jahn, Commissioner, Engineering & Public Works, 705-645-6764
Julie Stevens, Commissioner, Finance & Corporate Services
Rick Williams, Commissioner, Community Services, 705-645-2100
Terri Burton, Director, Emergency Services
Marcus Firman, Director, Water & Sewer Operations
Anna Landry, Director, Human Resources

Niagara
P.O. Box 1042
2201 St. David's Rd.
Thorold, ON L2V 4T7
Tel: 905-980-6000;
www.niagararegion.ca
Other Information: Toll-Free Phone: 1-800-263-7215; TTY: 905-984-3613
Municipal Type: Regional Municipality
Incorporated: Jan. 1, 1970; *Area:* 1,854.17 sq km
Population in 2011: 431,346
Next Election: Oct. 2018 (4 year terms)
Alan Caslin, Regional Chair, Wards: St Catharines
Wayne H. Redekop, Councillor, Wards: Fort Erie Mayor
Sandy Annunziata, Councillor, Wards: Fort Erie
Bob Bentley, Councillor, Wards: Grimsby Mayor
Tony Quirk, Councillor, Wards: Grimsby
Sandra Easton, Councillor, Wards: Lincoln Mayor
Bill Hodgson, Councillor, Wards: Lincoln
Jim Diodati, Councillor, Wards: Niagara Falls Mayor
Bob Gale, Councillor, Wards: Niagara Falls
Bart Maves, Councillor, Wards: Niagara Falls
Selina Volpeti, Councillor, Wards: Niagara Falls
Patrick Darte, Councillor, Wards: Niagara-on-the-Lake Mayor
Gary Burroughs, Councillor, Wards: Niagara-on-the-Lake
Dave Augustyn, Councillor, Wards: Pelham Mayor
Brian Baty, Councillor, Wards: Pelham
John Maloney, Councillor, Wards: Port Colborne Mayor
David Barrick, Councillor, Wards: Port Colborne
Walter Sendzik, Councillor, Wards: St Catharines Mayor
Brian Heit, Councillor, Wards: St Catharines
Debbie MacGregor, Councillor, Wards: St Catharines
Andrew (Andy) Petrowski, Councillor, Wards: St Catharines
Tim Rigby, Councillor, Wards: St Catharines
Bruce Timms, Councillor, Wards: St Catharines
Kelly Edgar, Councillor, Wards: St Catharines
Ted Luciani, Councillor, Wards: Thorold Mayor
Henry D'Angela, Councillor, Wards: Thorold
April Jeffs, Councillor, Wards: Wainfleet Mayor
Frank Campion, Councillor, Wards: Welland Mayor
Paul Grenier, Councillor, Wards: Welland
George H. Marshall, Councillor, Wards: Welland
Douglas Joyner, Councillor, Wards: West Lincoln Mayor
Maurice Lewis, Treasurer & Commissioner, Corporate Services, & Acting CAO
Katherine Chislett, Commissioner, Community Services
Valerie Jaeger, Commissioner, Public Health & Medical Officer of Health
Rino Mostacci, Commissioner, Planning & Development Services
Ron Tripp, Commissioner, Public Works
Catherine Habermebl, Director, Waste Management Services
Matt Robinson, Associate Director, Corporate Communications

Norfolk
50 Colborne St. South
Simcoe, ON N3Y 4N5
Tel: 519-426-5870; *Fax:* 519-426-8573
www.norfolkcounty.on.ca
Other Information: Delhi Customer Service Ctr., Phone: 519-582-2100
Municipal Type: County
Incorporated: Jan. 1, 2001; *Area:* 1,606.91 sq km
Population in 2011: 62,175
Provincial Electoral District(s): Haldimand-Norfolk
Federal Electoral District(s): Haldimand-Norfolk
Next Election: Oct. 2018 (4 year terms)
Charlie Luke, Mayor
Noel Haydt, Councillor, Wards: 1
Roger Geysens, Councillor, Wards: 2
Michael J. Columbus, Councillor, Wards: 3
Jim Oliver, Councillor, Wards: 4
Peter Black, Councillor, Wards: 5
Doug Brunton, Councillor, Wards: 5
John Wells, Councillor, Wards: 6
Harold Sonnenberg, Councillor, Wards: 7
Andy Grozelle, Clerk & Manager, Council Services
Keith Robicheau, County Manager
John Ford, General Manager, Financial Services
Christopher D. Baird, General Manager, Development & Cultural Services
Lee Robinson, General Manager, Public Works & Environmental Services
Kandy Webb, General Manager, Employee & Business Services
Kevin Lichach, General Manager, Community Services
Marlene Miranda, General Manager, Health & Social Services
Bob Fields, Manager, Environmental Services
Gary Houghton, Manager, Engineering
Terry Dicks, Fire Chief

Northumberland
555 Courthouse Rd.
Cobourg, ON K9A 5J6
Tel: 905-372-3329; *Fax:* 905-372-1746
www.northumberlandcounty.ca
Other Information: Toll-Free Phone: 1-800-354-7050
Municipal Type: County
Area: 1,902.97 sq km
Population in 2011: 82,126
Next Election: Oct. 2018 (4 year terms)
Marc Coombs, Warden, Wards: Cramahe
John Logel, Councillor, Wards: Alnwick/Haldimand
Mark Walas, Councillor, Wards: Brighton
Gil Brocanier, Councillor, Wards: Cobourg
Bob Sanderson, Councillor, Wards: Port Hope
Mark Lovshin, Councillor, Wards: Hamilton
Hector Macmillan, Councillor, Wards: Trent Hills
Cathie Ritchie, CMO, County Clerk
Jennifer Moore, Chief Administrative Officer
Ben Walters, Forest Manager
Ken Stubbings, Manager, Emergency Planning, Health & Safety

Peel
10 Peel Centre Dr.
Brampton, ON L6T 4B9
Tel: 905-791-7800;
www.peelregion.ca
Other Information: Toll-Free Phone: 1-888-919-7800
Municipal Type: Regional Municipality
Incorporated: Oct. 15, 1973; *Area:* 1,242.40 sq km
Population in 2011: 1,296,814
Next Election: Oct. 2018 (4 year terms)
Frank Dale, Regional Chair, Wards: Mississauga 4
Linda Jeffrey, Councillor, Wards: Brampton Mayor
Grant Gibson, Councillor, Wards: Brampton 1 & 5
Elaine Moore, Councillor, Wards: Brampton 1 & 5
Michael P. Palleschi, Councillor, Wards: Brampton 2 & 6
Martin Medeiros, Councillor, Wards: Brampton 3 & 4
Gael Miles, Councillor, Wards: Brampton 7 & 8
John Sprovieri, Councillor, Wards: Brampton 9 & 10
Allan Thompson, Councillor, Wards: Caledon Mayor
Barb Shaughnessy, Councillor, Wards: Caledon 1
Johanna Downey, Councillor, Wards: Caledon 2
Jennifer Innis, Councillor, Wards: Caledon 3 & 4
Annette Groves, Councillor, Wards: Caledon 5
Bonnie Crombie, Councillor, Wards: Mississauga Mayor
Jim Tovey, Councillor, Wards: Mississauga 1
Karen Ras, Councillor, Wards: Mississauga 2
Chris Fonseca, Councillor, Wards: Mississauga 3
John Kovac, Councillor, Wards: Mississauga 4
Carolyn Parrish, Councillor, Wards: Mississauga 5
Ron Starr, Councillor, Wards: Mississauga 6
Nando Iannicca, Councillor, Wards: Mississauga 7
Matt Mahoney, Councillor, Wards: Mississauga 8
Pat Saito, Councillor, Wards: Mississauga 9
Sue McFadden, Councillor, Wards: Mississauga 10
George Carlson, Councillor, Wards: Mississauga 11
Kathryn Lockyer, Regional Clerk
David Szwarc, Chief Administrative Officer
Stephen VanOfwegen, Chief Financial Officer & Commissioner, Finance
Lorraine Graham-Watson, Commissioner, Corporate Services
Dan Labrecque, Commissioner, Public Works
Gayle Bursey, Acting Commissioner, Human Services
Gilbert Sabat, Commissioner, Service Innovation, Information & Technology
Janette Smith, Commissioner, Health Services
David Mowat, Medical Officer of Health
Norman Lee, Director, Waste Management
Arvin Prasad, Director, Planning Policy & Research

Perth
Courthouse
1 Huron St.
Stratford, ON N5A 5S4
Tel: 519-271-0531; *Fax:* 519-271-6265
www.perthcounty.ca
Other Information: Toll-free: 800-463-8275
Municipal Type: County
Incorporated: Jan. 1850; *Area:* 2,218.41 sq km
Population in 2011: 75,112
Next Election: Oct. 2018 (4 year terms)
Note: Restructuring occurred in Jan. 1998.
Robert Wilhelm, Warden, 519-225-2304, Wards: Perth South
Julie Behrns, Councillor, Wards: North Perth
Doug Kellum, Councillor, Wards: North Perth
Meredith Schneider, Councillor, Wards: North Perth
Bob McMillan, Councillor, Wards: Perth East
Rhonda Ehgoetz, Councillor, Wards: Perth East
Helen Dowd, Councillor, Wards: Perth East
James Aitcheson, Councillor, Wards: Perth South
Walter McKenzie, Councillor, 519-348-4236, Wards: West Perth
Douglas Eidt, Councillor, Wards: West Perth
Jillene Bellchamber-Glazier, Clerk
Bill Arthur, Chief Administrative Officer
Renato Pullia, Treasurer & Director, Corporate Services
Calana Hinnegan, Administration Clerk, Public Works
Allan Rothwell, Director, Planning & Development
Linda Rockwood, Director, Emergency Services
Cliff Eggleton, Manager, EMS Operations

Peterborough
County Court House
470 Water St.
Peterborough, ON K9H 3M3
Tel: 705-743-0380; *Fax:* 705-876-1730
info@county.peterborough.on.ca
www.county.peterborough.on.ca
Other Information: Toll-Free Phone: 1-800-710-9586
Municipal Type: County
Area: 3,805.71 sq km
Population in 2011: 134,933
Next Election: Oct. 2018 (4 year terms)
James Murray Jones, Warden, Wards: Douro-Dummer
Terry Low, Councillor, Wards: Asphodel-Norwood
Rodger Bonneau, Councillor, Wards: Asphodel-Norwood
Scott McFadden, Councillor, Wards: Cavan Monaghan
John Fallis, Councillor, Wards: Cavan Monaghan
Karl Moher, Councillor, Wards: Douro-Dummer
Bev Matthews, Councillor, Wards: Trent Lakes
Ronald Windover, Councillor, Wards: Trent Lakes
Ron Gerow, Councillor, Wards: Havelock-Belmont-Methuen
Jim Martin, Councillor, Wards: Havelock-Belmont-Methuen
Rick Woodcock, Councillor, Wards: North Kawartha
Doug Hutton, Councillor, Wards: North Kawartha
David Nelson, Councillor, Wards: Otonabee-South Monaghan
Joe Taylor, Councillor, Wards: Otonabee-South Monaghan
Mary Smith, Councillor, Wards: Selwyn
Sherry Senis, Councillor, Wards: Selwyn
Sally Saunders, Clerk
Gary King, Chief Administrative Officer & Deputy Clerk
Christine Lang, Secretary-Treasurer
Chris Bradley, Director, Public Works
Patti Kraft, Director, Human Resources
Bryan Weir, Director, Planning
Sheridan Graham, Director, Corporate Projects & Services
Bill Linnen, Manager, Operations
Randy Mellow, Chief, Paramedics

Prince Edward
332 Main St.
Picton, ON K0K 2T0
Tel: 613-476-2148; *Fax:* 613-476-8356
info@pecounty.on.ca
www.pecounty.on.ca
Municipal Type: County
Incorporated: Jan. 1, 1998; *Area:* 1,050.14 sq km
Population in 2011: 25,258
Provincial Electoral District(s): Prince Edward-Hastings
Federal Electoral District(s): Bay of Quinte
Next Election: Oct. 2018 (4 year terms)
Robert Quaiff, Mayor
Lenny Epstein, Councillor, Wards: 1 - Picton
Treat Hull, Councillor, Wards: 1 - Picton
Barry Turpin, Councillor, Wards: 2 - Bloomfield
Jim Dunlop, Councillor, Wards: 3 - Wellington
Roy Pennell, Councillor, Wards: 4 - Ameliasburgh
Dianne O'Brien, Councillor, Wards: 4 - Ameliasburgh
Janice Maynard, Councillor, Wards: 4 - Ameliasburgh
Jamie Forrester, Councillor, Wards: 5 - Athol
Gordon Fox, Councillor, Wards: 6 - Hallowell
Brad Nieman, Councillor, Wards: 6 - Hallowell
Steven Graham, Councillor, Wards: 7 - Hillier
David Harrison, Councillor, Wards: 8 - North Marysburgh
Steve Ferguson, Councillor, Wards: 9 - South Marysburgh
Kevin Gale, Councillor, Wards: 10 - Sophiasburgh
Bill Roberts, Councillor, Wards: 10 - Sophiasburgh
Kim White, Clerk
James Hepburn, Chief Administrative Officer
Wanda Thissen, Manager of Revenue & Deputy Treasurer
Neil Carbone, Director, Community Development
Robert McAuley, Commissioner, Engineering, Development & Works
Susan Turnbull, Commissioner, Corporate Services & Finance
Kimberly Pierce, Manager, Human Resources
Scott Manlow, Fire Chief

Renfrew
9 International Dr.
Pembroke, ON K8A 6W5
Tel: 613-735-7288; *Fax:* 613-735-2081
info@countyofrenfrew.on.ca
www.countyofrenfrew.on.ca
Other Information: Toll-Free Phone: 1-800-273-0183
Municipal Type: County
Incorporated: June 8, 1861; *Area:* 7,403.46 sq km
Population in 2011: 101,326
Next Election: Oct. 2018 (4 year terms)
Peter Emon, Warden, Wards: Renfrew
Michael Donohue, Councillor, Wards: Admaston/Bromley
Walter Stack, Councillor, Wards: Arnprior
Jennifer Murphy, Councillor, 613-628-3101, Wards: Bonnechere Valley
Garry Gruntz, Councillor, Wards: Brudenell, Lyndoch, & Raglan
Glenn Doncaster, Councillor, Wards: Deep River
Glenda McKay, Councillor, Wards: Greater Madawaska
Jim Gibson, Councillor, Wards: Head, Clara & Maria
Robert Kingsbury, Councillor, Wards: Horton
Janice Visneskie Moore, Councillor, 613-757-2300, Wards: Killaloe, Hagarty & Richards
John Reinwald, Councillor, Wards: Laurentian Hills
Debbie Robinson, Councillor, Wards: Laurentian Valley
Kim Love, Councillor, Wards: Madawaska Valley
Tom Peckett, Councillor, Wards: McNab/Braeside
Deborah Farr, Councillor, Wards: North Algona Wilberforce
Bob Sweet, Councillor, Wards: Petawawa
Terry Millar, Councillor, Wards: Whitewater Region
Jim Hutton, Chief Administrative Officer & Clerk
James D. Kutschke, CA, Treasurer & Deputy Clerk
Bruce Beakley, Director, Human Resources
Steven Boland, Director, Public Works & Engineering
Michael Nolan, Director, Emergency Services

Simcoe
County of Simcoe Administration Centre
1110 Hwy. 26
Midhurst, ON L0L 1X0
Tel: 705-726-9300; *Fax:* 705-719-4626
info@simcoe.ca
www.simcoe.ca
Other Information: Toll-Free Phone: 1-866-893-9300
Municipal Type: County
Incorporated: Jan. 1, 1850; *Area:* 4,840.56 sq km
Population in 2011: 446,063
Next Election: Oct. 2018 (4 year terms)
Gerry Marshall, Warden, Wards: Penetanguishene
Terry Dowdall, Deputy Warden, Wards: Essa
Mary Small Brett, Councillor, Wards: Adjala-Tosorontio
Doug Little, Councillor, Wards: Adjala-Tosorontio
Rob Keffer, Councillor, Wards: Bradford West Gwillimbury
James Leduc, Councillor, Wards: Bradford West Gwillimbury
Christopher Vanderkruys, Councillor, Wards: Clearview
Barry Burton, Councillor, Wards: Clearview
Sandra Cooper, Councillor, Wards: Collingwood
Brian Saunderson, Councillor, Wards: Collingwood
Sandie Macdonald, Councillor, Wards: Essa
Gord Wauchope, Councillor, Wards: Innisfil
Lynn Dollin, Councillor, Wards: Innisfil
Gord McKay, Councillor, Wards: Midland
Mike Ross, Councillor, Wards: Midland
Rick Milne, Councillor, Wards: New Tecumseth
Jamie Smith, Councillor, Wards: New Tecumseth
Harry Hughes, Councillor, Wards: Oro-Medonte
Ralph Hough, Councillor, Wards: Oro-Medonte
Anita Dubeau, Councillor, Wards: Penetanguishene
Basil Clarke, Councillor, Wards: Ramara
John O'Donnell, Councillor, Wards: Ramara
Mike Burkett, Councillor, Wards: Severn
Judith Cox, Councillor, Wards: Severn
Bill French, Councillor, Wards: Springwater
Don Allen, Councillor, Wards: Springwater
Scott Warnock, Councillor, Wards: Tay
Bill Rawson, Councillor, Wards: Tay
George Cornell, Councillor, Wards: Tiny
Steffen Walma, Councillor, Wards: Tiny
Brian Smith, Councillor, Wards: Wasaga Beach
Nina Bifolchi, Councillor, Wards: Wasaga Beach
Brenda Clark, Clerk
Mark Aitken, Chief Administrative Officer
Lealand Sibbick, Treasurer
David Parks, Director, Planning, Development & Tourism
Cathy Clark, Manager, 911 & Emergency Planning
Terry Talon, General Manager, Social & Community Services
Christian Meile, Director, Transportation Maintenance
Michael Moffatt, Director, Human Resources

Waterloo
Regional Administration Bldg.
P.O. Box 9051 C
150 Frederick St.
Kitchener, ON N2G 4J3
Tel: 519-575-4400; *Fax:* 519-575-4481
regionalinquiries@regionofwaterloo.ca
www.regionofwaterloo.ca
Other Information: Phone, Regional Councillors: 519-575-4581
Municipal Type: Regional Municipality
Incorporated: Jan. 1, 1973; *Area:* 1,368.64 sq km
Population in 2011: 507,096
Next Election: Oct. 2018 (4 year terms)
Ken Seiling, Regional Chair & Councillor, 519-575-4585, Fax: 519-575-4440
Doug Craig, Councillor, Wards: Cambridge
Helen Jowett, Councillor, Wards: Cambridge
Karl Kiefer, Councillor, Wards: Cambridge
Berry Vrbanovic, Councillor, Wards: Kitchener
Karen Redman, Councillor, Wards: Kitchener
Tom Galloway, Councillor, Wards: Kitchener
Elizabeth Clarke, Councillor, Wards: Kitchener
Geoff Lorentz, Councillor, Wards: Kitchener
Sue Foxton, Councillor, Wards: North Dumfries
Dave Jaworsky, Councillor, Wards: Waterloo
Sean Strickland, Councillor, Wards: Waterloo
Jane Mitchell, Councillor, Wards: Waterloo
Joe Nowak, Councillor, Wards: Wellesley
Les Armstrong, Councillor, Wards: Wilmot
Sandy Shantz, Councillor, Wards: Woolwich
Kris Fletcher, Regional Clerk & Director, Council & Administrative Services
Mike Murray, Chief Administrative Officer
Craig Dyer, Chief Financial Officer
Rob Horne, Commissioner, Planning, Housing & Community Services
Thomas Schmidt, Commissioner, Transportation & Environmental Services
Michael Schuster, Commissioner, Social Services
Penny Smiley, Commissioner, Human Resources
Gary Sosnoski, Commissioner, Corporate Resources
Jon Arsenault, Director, Waste Management
Debra Arnold, Director, Legal Services & Regional Solicitor
Lucille Bish, Director, Cultural Services
Amanda Kutler, Director, Community Planning
Eric Gillespie, Director, Transit Services
Nancy Kodousek, Director, Water Services
Ellen McGaghey, Director, Facilities Management & Fleet Services
Liana Nolan, Medical Officer of Health

Wellington
74 Woolwich St.
Guelph, ON N1H 3T9
Tel: 519-837-2600; *Fax:* 519-837-1909
www.wellington.ca
Other Information: Toll-Free Phone: 1-800-663-0750
Municipal Type: County
Incorporated: Jan. 1, 1852; *Area:* 2,656.66 sq km
Population in 2011: 208,360
Next Election: Oct. 2018 (4 year terms)
Note: The council of the County of Wellington is comprised of the mayors of its seven municipalities, plus nine elected county ward councillors.
George Bridge, Warden, Wards: Minto
Kelly Linton, Councillor, Wards: Centre Wellington
Allan Alls, Councillor, Wards: Erin
Chris White, Councillor, Wards: Guelph/Eramosa
S. Neil Driscoll, Councillor, Wards: Mapleton
Dennis Lever, Councillor, Wards: Puslinch
Andy Lennox, Councillor, Wards: Wellington North
David Anderson, Councillor, Wards: 1
Gregg Davidson, Councillor, Wards: 2
Gary Williamson, Wards: 3
Lynda White, Councillor, Wards: 4
Rob Black, Councillor, Wards: 5
Shawn Watters, Councillor, Wards: 6
Don McKay, Councillor, Wards: 7
Doug Breen, Councillor, Wards: 8
Pieere Brianceau, Councillor, Wards: 9
Donna Bryce, County Clerk
Scott Wilson, Chief Administrative Officer
Kenneth DeHart, Treasurer
Andrea Lawson, Director, Human Resources
Harry Blinkhorn, Manager, Housing Operations
Gary Cousins, Director, Planning
Luisa Artuso, Director, Child Care Services
Linda Dickson, Coordinator, Community Emergency Management
Rob Johnson, Manager, Green Lagacy

York
17250 Yonge St.
Newmarket, ON L3Y 6Z1
Tel: 905-895-1231;
info@york.ca
www.york.ca
Other Information: Toll-Free Phone: 1-877-464-9675
Municipal Type: Regional Municipality
Incorporated: Jan. 1, 1971; *Area:* 1,761.84 sq km
Population in 2011: 1,032,524
Next Election: Oct. 2018 (4 year terms)
Wayne Emmerson, Regional Chair & CEO
Geoffrey Dawe, Councillor, Wards: Aurora
Virginia Hackson, Councillor, Wards: East Gwillimbury
Margaret Quirk, Councillor, Wards: Georgina
Danny Wheeler, Councillor, Wards: Georgina

Steve Pellegrini, Councillor, Wards: King
Frank Scarpitti, Councillor, Wards: Markham
Jack Heath, Councillor, Wards: Markham
Jim Jones, Councillor, Wards: Markham
Nirmala Armstrong, Councillor, Wards: Markham
Joe Li, Councillor, Wards: Markham
A.J. (Tony) Van Bynen, Councillor, Wards: Newmarket
John Taylor, Councillor, Wards: Newmarket
David Barrow, Councillor, Wards: Richmond Hill
Brenda Hogg, Councillor, Wards: Richmond Hill
Vito Spatafora, Councillor, Wards: Richmond Hill
Maurizio Bevilacqua, Councillor, Wards: Vaughan
Michael Di Biase, Councillor, Wards: Vaughan
Mario Ferri, Councillor, Wards: Vaughan
Gino Rosati, Councillor, Wards: Vaughan
Justin Altmann, Councillor, Wards: Whitchurch-Stouffville
Denis Kelly, Regional Clerk
Bruce Macgregor, Chief Administrative Officer
Bill Hughes, Regional Treasurer & Commissioner, Finance
Dino Basso, Commissioner, Corporate Services
Daniel Kostopoulos, Commissioner, Transportation
Erin Mahoney, Commissioner, Environmental Services
Adelina Urbanski, Commissioner, Community & Health Services
Valerie Shuttleworth, Chief Planner, Planning & Economic Development
Patrick Casey, Director, Corporate Communications
Karen Close, Director, Human Resources
Karim Kurji, Medical Officer of Health & Director, Public Health Programs

Major Municipalities in Ontario

Ajax

65 Harwood Ave. South
Ajax, ON L1S 2H9
Tel: 905-683-4550; *Fax:* 905-683-1061
contactus@ajax.ca
www.townofajax.com
Other Information: TTY: 1-866-460-4489
Municipal Type: City
Incorporated: 1955; *Area:* 67.09 sq km
County or District: Durham Regional Municipality; *Population in 2011:* 109,600
Provincial Electoral District(s): Ajax-Pickering
Federal Electoral District(s): Ajax
Next Election: Oct. 2018 (4 year terms)
Steve Parish, Mayor, 905-619-2529, Fax: 905-683-9450
Shaun Collier, Regional Councillor, 905-409-6891, Fax: 905-683-8207, Wards: 1 & 2
Colleen Jordan, Regional Councillor, 905-626-3639, Fax: 905-683-8207, Wards: 3 & 4
Marilyn Crawford, Councillor, 905-550-1133, Fax: 905-683-8207, Wards: 1
Renrick Ashby, Councillor, 905-627-6062, Fax: 905-683-8207, Wards: 2
Joanne Dies, Councillor, Councillor, 905-626-1916, Fax: 905-683-8207, Wards: 3
Pat Brown, Councillor, 905-626-2301, Fax: 905-683-8207, Wards: 4
Rob Ford, Chief Administrative Officer
Dave Meredith, Director, Operations & Environmental Services
Tracey Vaughan, Director, Recreation & Culture
David Sheen, Fire Chief

Amherstburg

271 Sandwich St. South
Amherstburg, ON N9V 2A5
Tel: 519-736-0012; *Fax:* 519-736-5403
www.amherstburg.ca
Other Information: TTY: 519-736-9860
Municipal Type: City
Incorporated: 1851; *Area:* 185.65 sq km
County or District: Essex; *Population in 2011:* 21,556
Provincial Electoral District(s): Essex
Federal Electoral District(s): Essex
Next Election: Oct. 2018 (4 year terms)
Note: Incorporated as a town in 1878.
Aldo DiCarlo, Mayor
Bart DiPasquale, Deputy Mayor
Joan Courtney, Councillor
Richard (Rick) Fryer, Councillor
Jason Lavigne, Councillor
Leo Meloche, Councillor
Diane Pouget, Councillor
Giovanni (John) Miceli, Chief Administrative Officer, 519-736-0012
Dean Collver, Director, Recreation & Culture, 519-736-5712
Rebecca Belanger, Manager, Planning Services, 519-736-5408
Justin Rousseau, Director, Financial Services
Dwayne Grondin, Manager, Environmental Services, 519-736-3664
Todd Hewitt, Manager, Engineering & Operations, 519-736-3664

Aurora

P.O. Box 1000
100 John Way West
Aurora, ON L4G 6J1
Tel: 905-727-1375; *Fax:* 905-726-4732
info@aurora.ca
www.aurora.ca
Other Information: Alternative Phone: 905-727-3123; TTY: 905-726-4766
Municipal Type: City
Area: 49.62 sq km
County or District: York Regional Municipality; *Population in 2011:* 53,203
Provincial Electoral District(s): Newmarket-Aurora
Federal Electoral District(s): Newmarket-Aurora; Aurora-Oak Ridges-Richond Hill
Next Election: Oct. 2018 (4 year terms)
Geoffrey Dawe, Mayor, 905-727-3123
John Abel, Councillor, 905-727-3123
Wendy Gaertner, Councillor, 905-727-3123
Sandra Humfryes, Councillor
Harold Kim, Councillor
Tom Mrakas, Councillor
Paul Pirri, Councillor, 905-727-3123
Jeff Thom, Councillor
Michael Thompson, Councillor, 905-727-3212
Doug Nadorozny, Chief Administrative Officer
Dan Elliot, Treasurer, 905-727-1375, Fax: 905-727-1953
Allan Downey, Director, Parks & Recreation, 905-727-3123
Marco Ramunno, Director, Planning & Development Services, 905-727-1375, Fax: 905-726-4736
Ilmar Simanovskis, Director, Infrastructure & Environmental Services, 902-727-1375, Fax: 905-841-7119
Techa Van Leeuwen, Director, Building & By-Law Services, 905-727-1375, Fax: 905-726-4731
Ian Laing, Fire Chief

Barrie

P.O. Box 400
70 Collier St.
Barrie, ON L4M 4T5
Tel: 705-726-4242; *Fax:* 705-739-4243
cityinfo@barrie.ca
www.barrie.ca
Other Information: TTY: 705-792-7910; Council Info: 705-739-4204
Municipal Type: City
Incorporated: 1853; *Area:* 76.99 sq km
County or District: Simcoe; *Population in 2011:* 135,711
Provincial Electoral District(s): Barrie
Federal Electoral District(s): Barrie-Innisfil; Barrie-Springwater-Oro-Medonte
Next Election: Oct. 2018 (4 year terms)
Jeff Lehman, Mayor, 705-792-7900
Bonnie J. Ainsworth, Councillor, Wards: 1
Rose Romita, Councillor, Wards: 2
Doug Shipley, Councillor, Wards: 3
Barry J. Ward, Councillor, Wards: 4
Peter Silveira, Councillor, Wards: 5
Michael Prowse, Councillor, Wards: 6
John Brassard, Councillor, Wards: 7
Arif Khan, Councillor, Wards: 8
Sergio Morales, Councillor, Wards: 9
Mike McCann, Councillor, Wards: 10
Dawn McAlpine, City Clerk, 705-739-4204
Carla Ladd, Chief Administrative Officer
Patricia Elliott-Spencer, General Manager, Community & Corporate Services
Richard Forward, M.Sc., P.Eng., General Manager, Infrastructure & Growth Management, 705-739-4220
Dave Friary, Director, Roads, Parks & Fleet Operations
Hany Kirolos, Director, Strategy & Economic Development, Business Development Department
Debbie McKinnon, Director, Finance, 705-739-4232, Fax: 705-739-4237
Bill Boyes, Fire Chief
Sandy Coulter, B.Sc., Manager, Environmental Operations, 705-739-4220
Bob Kahle, Manager, Engineering Design & Construction
Steve Lee Young, Manager, Recreation

Belleville

City Hall
169 Front St.
Belleville, ON K8N 2Y8
Tel: 613-968-6481; *Fax:* 613-967-3206
www.belleville.ca
Other Information: TTY: 613-967-3768; Toll Free:1-877-968-6481
Municipal Type: City
Area: 246.76 sq km
County or District: Hastings; *Population in 2011:* 49,454
Provincial Electoral District(s): Prince Edward-Hastings
Federal Electoral District(s): Bay of Quinte; Hastings-Lennox and Addington
Next Election: Oct. 2018 (4 year terms)
Taso Christopher, Mayor
Egerton Boyce, Councillor, 613-849-1066, Wards: 1
Mike Graham, Councillor, Wards: 1
Mitch McCaw, Councillor, Wards: 1
Jack Miller, Councillor, 613-968-8343, Wards: 1
Mitch Panciuk, Councillor, Wards: 1
Garnet Thompson, Councillor, 613-962-4442, Wards: 1
Paul Carr, Councillor, Wards: 2
Jackie Denyes, Councillor, 613-477-2970, Fax: 613-477-1522, Wards: 2
Matt MacDonald, City Clerk, 613-967-3256
Rick Kester, Chief Administrative Officer, 613-968-6481, Fax: 613-967-3209
Rod Bovay, Director, Engineering & Development Services, 613-968-6481, Fax: 613-967-3262
Brian Cousins, Director, Finance, 613-967-3242
Mark Fluhrer, Director, Recreation, Culture & Community Services, 613-967-3217
Mark MacDonald, Fire Chief, 613-771-3075
Matt Coffey, Manager, Transit Services, 613-962-4344
Art MacKay, Manager, Policy Planning, 613-968-6481
Tim Osborne, Manager, Human Resources, 613-968-6481, Fax: 613-967-3225
Richard Reinert, Manager, Environmental Services, 613-966-3657

Bracebridge

1000 Taylor Ct.
Bracebridge, ON P1L 1R6
Tel: 705-645-5264; *Fax:* 705-645-1262
www.bracebridge.ca
Other Information: Fax, Public Works: 705-645-7525
Municipal Type: City
Area: 617.42 sq km
County or District: Muskoka Dist. Mun.; *Population in 2011:* 15,409
Provincial Electoral District(s): Parry Sound-Muskoka
Federal Electoral District(s): Parry Sound-Muskoka
Next Election: Oct. 2018 (4 year terms)
Graydon Smith, Mayor, 705-644-3253
Chris Wilson, Councillor, Wards: Bracebridge
Archie Buie, Councillor, Wards: Draper
Rick Maloney, Councillor, 705-645-0874, Wards: Macaulay
Mark Quemby, Councillor, 705-646-7676, Wards: Monck/Muskoka
Barb McMurray, Councillor, 705-645-3706, Wards: Oakley
Steve Clement, District Councillor, 705-645-5325
Lori-Lynn Giaschi-Pacini, District Councillor, 705-646-8122
Don Smith, District Councillor
Lori McDonald, Clerk/Director, Corporate Services, 705-645-5264
John R. Sisson, Chief Administrative Officer, 705-645-6319, Fax: 705-645-1262
Cheryl Kelley, Director, Planning & Development, 705-645-6319
Stephen Rettie, Director, Finance, 519-645-5264
Walt Schmid, Director, Public Works, 705-645-6319
Murray Medley, Fire Chief, 705-465-8258

Bradford West Gwillimbury

Administration Centre
P.O. Box 100
#7 & #8, 100 Dissette St.
Bradford, ON L3Z 2A7
Tel: 905-775-5366; *Fax:* 905-775-0153
www.townofbwg.com
Municipal Type: City
Incorporated: 1857; *Area:* 201.03 sq km
County or District: Simcoe; *Population in 2011:* 28,077
Provincial Electoral District(s): York-Simcoe
Federal Electoral District(s): York-Simcoe
Next Election: Oct. 2018 (4 year terms)
Note: Incorporated as a town in 1960.
Rob Keffer, Mayor, 905-775-5366
James Leduc, Deputy Mayor & Councillor, 905-775-5366
Raj Sandhu, Councillor, 905-775-5366, Wards: 1
Gary Baynes, Councillor, 905-775-5366, Wards: 2

Gary R. Lamb, Councillor, 905-775-5366, Wards: 3
Ron Orr, Councillor, 905-775-5366, Wards: 4
Peter Ferragine, Councillor, 905-775-5366, Wards: 5
Mark Contois, Councillor, 905-775-5366, Wards: 6
Peter Dykie, Jr., Councillor, 905-775-5366, Wards: 7
Rebecca Murphy, Clerk & Director, Legal Services, 905-775-5366
Geoff McKnight, Chief Administrative Officer, 905-775-5366
Ian Goodfellow, Director, Finance, 905-775-5303
Ryan Windle, Manager, Community Planning, 905-778-2055
Kevin Gallant, Fire Chief, 905-775-7311
Edward O'Donnell, Manager, Water, 905-778-2055
Paul Feehely, Superintendent, Public Works

Brampton
2 Wellington St. West
Brampton, ON L6Y 4R2
Tel: 905-874-2000; *Fax:* 905-874-2119
city.hall@brampton.ca
www.brampton.ca
Other Information: E-mail, Economic Development: edo@brampton.ca
Municipal Type: City
Incorporated: Jan. 1, 1974; *Area:* 266.71 sq km
County or District: Peel Reg. Mun.; *Population in 2011:* 523,911
Provincial Electoral District(s): Bramalea-Gore-Malton; Brampton Springdale; Brampton West; Brampton South-Mississauga
Federal Electoral District(s): Brampton Centre; Brampton East, Brampton North; Brampton West; Brampton South
Next Election: Oct. 2018 (4 year terms)
Linda Jeffrey, Mayor, 905-874-2600
Grant Gibson, City Councillor, 905-874-2605, Wards: 1 & 5
Doug Whillans, City Councillor, 905-874-2606, Wards: 2 & 6
Jeff Bowman, City Councillor, 905-874-2603, Wards: 3 & 4
Pat Fortini, City Councillor, 905-874-2611, Wards: 7 & 8
Gurpreet S. Dhillon, City Councillor, 905-874-2609, Wards: 9 & 10
Elaine Moore, Regional Councillor, 905-874-2601, Wards: 1 & 5
Michael P. Palleschi, Regional Councillor, 902-874-2661, Wards: 2 & 6
Martin Medeiros, Regional Councillor, 905-874-2634, Wards: 3 & 4
Gael Miles, Regional Councillor, 905-874-2671, Wards: 7 & 8
John Sprovieri, Regional Councillor, 905-874-2610, Wards: 9 & 10
Harry Schlange, Chief Administrative Officer
Marilyn Ball, Chief Planning & Inrastructure Services Officer
Dennis Cutajar, Chief Operating Officer
Julian Patteson, Chief Public Services Officer
Peter Simmons, Chief Corporate Services Officer

Brantford
City Hall
P.O. Box 818
100 Wellington Sq.
Brantford, ON N3T 5R7
Tel: 519-759-4150;
webmaster@brantford.ca
www.brantford.ca
Municipal Type: City
Incorporated: May 31, 1877; *Area:* 72.47 sq km
County or District: Brant; *Population in 2011:* 93,650
Provincial Electoral District(s): Brant
Federal Electoral District(s): Brantford-Brant
Next Election: Oct. 2018 (4 year terms)
Chris Friel, Mayor
Larry M. Kings, Councillor, Wards: 1
Rick Weaver, Councillor, Wards: 1
John Sless, Councillor, Wards: 2
John K. Utley, Councillor, Wards: 2
Greg Martin, Councillor, Wards: 3
Dan McCreary, Councillor, Wards: 3
Cheryl Lynn Antoski, Councillor, Wards: 4
Richard Carpenter, Councillor, Wards: 4
David E. Neumann, Councillor, Wards: 5
Brian Van Tilborg, Councillor, Wards: 5
Lori Wolfe, City Clerk, 519-759-4150, Fax: 519-759-7840
Geoff Rae, Chief Administrative Officer
Greg Dworak, General Manager, Community Services
Darryl Lee, General Manager, Corporate Services
Beth Goodger, General Manager, Public Works Commission
Josephine Atanas, General Manager, Public Health, Safety, & Social Services

Brighton
P.O. Box 189
35 Alice St.
Brighton, ON K0K 1H0
Tel: 613-475-0670; *Fax:* 613-475-3453
general@brighton.ca
www.brighton.ca
Other Information: Phone, Public Works & Planning: 613-475-1162
Municipal Type: City
Area: 222.52 sq km
County or District: Northumberland; *Population in 2011:* 10,928
Provincial Electoral District(s): Northumberland-Quinte West
Federal Electoral District(s): Northumberland-Peterborough South
Next Election: Oct. 2018 (4 year terms)
Mark Walas, Mayor, 613-475-0670
Steven R. Baker, Councillor
John Martinello, Councillor, 613-475-5120
Roger McMurray, Councillor
Brian Ostrander, Councillor
Mary Tadman, Councillor, 613-475-0888
Laura Vink, Councillor
Bill Watson, Chief Administrative Officer, 613-475-0670
Scott Hodgson, Supervisor, Public Works Operations, 613-475-1162
Jim Millar, Director, Parks & Recreation, 613-475-0302
Linda Widdifield, Director, Finance & Administrative Services, 613-475-0670
Lloyd Hutchinson, Fire Chief, 613-475-1744, Fax: 613-475-1385

Brockville
Victoria Bldg.
P.O. Box 5000
1 King St. West
Brockville, ON K6V 7A5
Tel: 613-342-8772; *Fax:* 613-342-8780
info@brockville.com; tourism@brockvillechamber.com
www.brockville.com
Municipal Type: City
Area: 20.74 sq km
County or District: Leeds & Grenville; *Population in 2011:* 21,870
Provincial Electoral District(s): Leeds-Grenville
Federal Electoral District(s): Leeds-Grenville-Thousand Islands and Rideau Lakes
Next Election: Oct. 2018 (4 year terms)
David L. Henderson, Mayor, 613-342-2549
Jason Baker, Councillor, 613-246-0473
Tom Blanchard, Councillor, 613-345-2579
Leigh Z. Bursey, Councillor, 613-342-7712
Philip Deery, Councillor, 613-342-3950
Jeffery Earle, Councillor, 613-498-1429
Jane Fullerton, Councillor, 613-345-3410
Mike Kalivas, Councillor, 613-345-0453
David D. LeSueur, Councillor, 613-342-7869
Sandra M. MacDonald, City Clerk, 613-342-8772
Bob Casselman, City Manager, 613-342-8772
David Dick, Treasurer & Director, Corporate Services, 613-342-8772
Maureen Pascoe Merkley, Director, Planning, 613-342-8772
David C. Paul, Director, Economic Development, 613-342-8772
Peter Raabe, Director, Environmental Services, 613-342-8772
Ghislain Pigeon, Fire Chief, 613-498-1261
Debra Neilson, Manager, Human Resources, 613-342-8772

Burlington
City Hall
P.O. Box 5013
426 Brant St.
Burlington, ON L7R 3Z6
Tel: 905-335-7600; *Fax:* 905-335-7881
cob@burlington.ca
www.burlington.ca
Other Information: Toll Free: 1-877-213-3609
Municipal Type: City
Incorporated: 1914; *Area:* 185.74 sq km
County or District: Halton Regional Municipality; *Population in 2011:* 175,779
Provincial Electoral District(s): Ancaster-Dundas-Flamborough-Westdale; Burlington; Halton
Federal Electoral District(s): Burlington; Milton; Oakville North-Burlington
Next Election: Oct. 2018 (4 year terms)
Note: Incorporated as a city in 1974.
Rick Goldring, Mayor, 905-335-7607, Fax: 905-335-7708
Rick Craven, Councillor, 905-335-7600, Fax: 905-335-7881, Wards: 1
Marianne Meed Ward, Councillor, 905-335-7600, Fax: 905-335-7881, Wards: 2
John Taylor, Councillor, 905-335-7600, Fax: 905-335-7881, Wards: 3
Jack Dennison, Councillor, 905-632-4800, Fax: 905-632-4041, Wards: 4
Paul Sharman, Councillor, 905-335-7600, Fax: 905-335-7881, Wards: 5
Blair Lancaster, Councillor, 905-335-7600, Fax: 905-335-7881, Wards: 6
James Ridge, City Manager
Kim Phillips, General Manager, Community & Corporate Services, 905-335-7600

Caledon
Town Hall
6311 Old Church Rd.
Caledon, ON L7C 1J6
Tel: 905-584-2272; *Fax:* 905-584-4325
www.caledon.ca
Other Information: Toll Free: 1-888-225-3366
Municipal Type: City
Incorporated: Jan. 1, 1974; *Area:* 687.17 sq km
County or District: Peel Regional Municipality; *Population in 2011:* 59,460
Provincial Electoral District(s): Dufferin-Caledon
Federal Electoral District(s): Dufferin-Caledon
Next Election: Oct. 2018 (4 year terms)
Allan Thompson, Mayor
Barb Shaughnessy, Regional Councillor, Wards: 1
Johanna Downey, Regional Councillor, Wards: 2
Jennifer Innis, Regional Councillor, Wards: 3 & 4
Annette Groves, Regional Councillor, Wards: 5
Doug Beffort, Area Councillor, 519-927-5365, Fax: 905-584-4325, Wards: 1
Gord McClure, Area Councillor, 905-843-9797, Fax: 905-584-4325, Wards: 2
Nick deBoer, Area Councillor, 905-880-1370, Fax: 905-880-1168, Wards: 3 & 4
Rob Mezzapelli, Area Councillor, 905-533-0209, Fax: 905-584-4325, Wards: 5
Carey deGorter, Town Clerk & Director, Administration
Fuwing Wong, Chief Financial Officer & Director, Corporate Services
Mike Galloway, Chief Administrative Officer

Cambridge
P.O. Box 669
50 Dickson St.
Cambridge, ON N1R 5W8
Tel: 519-623-1340; *Fax:* 519-740-3011
questions@cambridge.ca
www.cambridge.ca
Other Information: TTY: 519-623-6691
Municipal Type: City
Incorporated: Jan. 1973; *Area:* 112.86 sq km
County or District: Waterloo Regional Municipality; *Population in 2011:* 126,748
Provincial Electoral District(s): Cambridge
Federal Electoral District(s): Cambridge
Next Election: Oct. 2018 (4 year terms)
Doug Craig, Mayor, 519-740-4517
Donna Reid, City Councillor, 519-740-4517, Fax: 519-740-4663, Wards: 1
Mike Devine, City Councillor, Wards: 2
Mike Mann, City Councillor, Wards: 3
Jan Liggett, City Councillor, Wards: 4
Pam Wolf, City Councillor, 519-740-4517, Fax: 519-740-4663, Wards: 5
Shannon Adshade, City Councillor, Wards: 6
Frank Monteiro, City Councillor, 519-740-4517, Fax: 519-740-4663, Wards: 7
Nicholas Ermeta, City Councillor, 519-740-4517, Fax: 519-740-4663, Wards: 8
Helen Jowett, Regional Councillor
Karl Kiefer, Regional Councillor
Alex Mitchell, City Clerk, 519-740-4680
Gary Dyke, City Manager, 519-740-4683
Steven Fairweather, Treasurer
Hardy Bromberg, Commissioner, Planning & Development, 519-740-4650
George Elliott, Commisssioner, Transportation & Public Works, 519-621-0740
Kent McVittie, Commissioner, Community Services, 519-740-4681
Neil Main, Fire Chief, 519-627-6001

Clarence-Rockland
1560 Laurier St.
Rockland, ON K4K 1P7
Tel: 613-446-6022; *Fax:* 613-446-1497
www.clarence-rockland.com
Municipal Type: City
Incorporated: Jan. 1, 1998; *Area:* 296.53 sq km
County or District: Prescott & Russell; *Population in 2011:* 23,185

Provincial Electoral District(s): Glengarry-Prescott-Russell
Federal Electoral District(s): Glengarry-Prescott-Russell
Next Election: Oct. 2018 (4 year terms)
Note: Amalgamation of the Town of Rockland and the Township of Clarence.
Guy Desjardins, Mayor
Jean-Marc Lalonde, Councillor, Wards: 1
Mario Zanth, Councillor, Wards: 2
Carl Grimard, Councillor, Wards: 3
Yvon Simoneau, Councillor, Wards: 4
André J. Lalonde, Councillor, Wards: 5
Krysta Simard, Councillor, Wards: 6
Michel Levert, Councillor, Wards: 7
Diane Choinière, Councillor, Wards: 8
Monique Ouellet, Clerk
Helen Collier, Chief Administrative Officer
Thérèse Lefaivre, Director, Community Services
Michael Michaud, Director, Planning
Yves Rivard, Director, By-law Enforcement
Yves Rousselle, Director, Physical Services
Pierre Sabourin, Fire Chief
Denis Longpré, Manager, Environment

Cobourg
55 King St. West
Cobourg, ON K9A 2M2
Tel: 905-372-4301; *Fax:* 905-372-7421
webmaster@cobourg.ca
www.cobourg.ca
Other Information: Toll Free: 1-888-262-6874
Municipal Type: City
Area: 22.37 sq km
County or District: Northumberland; *Population in 2011:* 18,519
Provincial Electoral District(s): Northumberland-Quinte West
Federal Electoral District(s): Northumberland-Peterborough South
Next Election: Oct. 2018 (4 year terms)
Gil Brocanier, Mayor
John Henderson, Deputy Mayor & Councillor
Brian F. Darling, Councillor
Debra McCarthy, Councillor
Theresa Rickerby, Councillor
Forrest Rowden, Councillor
Larry E. Sherwin, Councillor, 905-373-0337
Lorraine Brace, Municipal Clerk, 905-372-4301, Fax: 905-372-7421
Stephen E. Peacock, P.Eng., Chief Administrative Officer, 905-372-4301, Fax: 905-372-2910
Ian Davey, Director, Corporate Services, 905-372-8944, Fax: 905-372-7421
Glenn J. McGlashon, Director, Planning & Development Services, 905-372-1005, Fax: 905-372-1533
Barry Thrasher, Director, Public Works

Collingwood
P.O. Box 157
97 Hurontario St.
Collingwood, ON L9Y 3Z5
Tel: 705-445-1030; *Fax:* 705-445-2448
www.collingwood.ca
Municipal Type: City
Incorporated: 1858; *Area:* 33.46 sq km
County or District: Simcoe; *Population in 2011:* 19,241
Provincial Electoral District(s): Simcoe-Grey
Federal Electoral District(s): Simcoe-Grey
Next Election: Oct. 2018 (4 year terms)
Sandra Cooper, Mayor, 705-445-8451
Brian Saunderson, Deputy Mayor & Councillor
Deb Doherty, Councillor
Cam Ecclestone, Councillor
Mike Edwards, Councillor, 705-441-5037
Tim Fryer, Councillor
Kathy Jeffery, Councillor
Kevin Lloyd, Councillor, 705-444-4207
Bob Madigan, Councillor
Sara J. Almas, Clerk, 705-445-1030
John Brown, Chief Administrative Officer, 705-445-1030
Marjory Leonard, Treasurer, 705-445-1030
Bill Plewes, Chief Building Official & Director, Building Services, 705-445-1030
Nancy Farrer, Director, Planning Services, 705-445-1290
Brian MacDonald, Director, Public Works & Engineering, 705-445-1292
Trent Elyea, Fire Chief, 705-445-3920
Jody Livingstone, Manager, Public Works, 705-445-1351
Wendy Martin, Manager, Parks, 705-444-2500

Cornwall
P.O. Box 877
360 Pitt St.
Cornwall, ON K6H 5T9
Tel: 613-930-2787; *Fax:* 613-932-8145
www.cornwall.ca
Municipal Type: City
Incorporated: 1834; *Area:* 61.52 sq km
County or District: Stormont, Dundas & Glengarry; *Population in 2011:* 46,340
Provincial Electoral District(s): Stormont-Dundas-South Glengarry
Federal Electoral District(s): Stormont-Dundas-South Glengarry
Next Election: Oct. 2018 (4 year terms)
Note: Incorporated as a city in 1945.
Leslie O'Shaughnessy, Mayor
Bernadette Clément, Councillor, 613-932-2703
Maurice Dupelle, Councillor, 613-662-2597
Brock Frost, Councillor
Carilyne Hebert, Councillor
Elaine MacDonald, Councillor
Mark A. MacDonald, Councillor
Claude E. McIntosh, Councillor
David Murphy, Councillor
Justin Towndale, Councillor
Andre Rivette, Councillor
Helen Finn, City Clerk
Maureen Adams, Chief Administrative Officer, 613-932-6252
Maureen Adams, General Manager, Financial Services
James Fawthrop, Manager, Parks & Recreation
Bill de Wit, Manager, Municipal Works
Morris McCormick, Manager, Environmental Division
Pierre Voisine, Fire Chief
Mark Boileau, Manager, Economic Development
Patrick Carrière, Supervisor, Waste Water Treatment Facility

East Gwillimbury
19000 Leslie St.
Sharon, ON L0G 1V0
Tel: 905-478-4282; *Fax:* 905-478-2808
customerservice@eastgwillimbury.ca
www.eastgwillimbury.ca
Other Information: Alternate Fax: 905-478-8545
Municipal Type: City
Incorporated: 1850; *Area:* 245.06 sq km
County or District: York Regional Municipality; *Population in 2011:* 22,473
Provincial Electoral District(s): York-Simcoe
Federal Electoral District(s): Newmarket-Aurora; York-Simcoe
Next Election: Oct. 2018 (4 year terms)
Virginia Hackson, Mayor
Marlene Johnston, Councillor
Joe Persechini, Councillor
Tara Roy-Diclemente, Councillor
James R. Young, Councillor
Fernando Lamanna, Municipal Clerk
Thomas R. Webster, Chief Administrative Officer
Don Sinclair, Town Solicitor
Carolyn Kellington, General Manager, Development Services
Mike Molinari, General Manager, Community Infrastructure & Environmental Services
Mark Valcic, General Manager, Corporate & Financial Services & Treasurer
Larry Hollett, Manager, Environmental Services
Steve Krystal, Manager, Capital Programs & Traffic Engineering Branch
Gary Shropshire, Manager, Community Parks & Programs Branch

Elliot Lake
45 Hillside Dr. North
Elliot Lake, ON P5A 1X5
Tel: 705-848-2287;
www.cityofelliotlake.com
Municipal Type: City
Area: 698.12 sq km
County or District: Algoma District; *Population in 2011:* 11,348
Provincial Electoral District(s): Algoma-Manitoulin
Federal Electoral District(s): Algoma-Manitoulin-Kapuskasing
Next Election: Oct. 2018 (4 year terms)
Al Collett, Mayor
Luc Cyr, Councillor
Candace Martin Scott, Councillor
Connie Nykyforak, Councillor
Ed Pearce, Councillor
Scot Reinhardt, Councillor
Tammy Vanroon, Councillor
Lesley Sprague, City Clerk
Jeff Renaud, Chief Administrative Officer
Dawn Halcrow, Director, Finance
John Thomas, Fire Chief

Erin
5684 Trafalgar Rd.
Hillsburgh, ON N0B 1Z0
Tel: 519-855-4407; *Fax:* 519-855-4821
info@erin.ca
www.erin.ca
Other Information: Toll-Free Phone: 1-877-818-2888
Municipal Type: City
Incorporated: 1997; *Area:* 296.98 sq km
County or District: Wellington; *Population in 2011:* 10,770
Provincial Electoral District(s): Wellington-Halton Hills
Federal Electoral District(s): Wellington-Halton Hills
Next Election: Oct. 2018 (4 year terms)
Allan Alls, Mayor
John Brennan, Councillor
Jeff Duncan, Councillor
Matt Sammut, Councillor
Rob Smith, Councillor
Pierre Brianceau, County Councillor
Dina Lundy, Clerk
Kathryn Ironmonger, CAO/Town Manager
Sharon Marshall, Director, Finance
Dan Callaghan, Fire Chief
Andrew Hartholt, Chief Building Official
Larry Van Wyck, Superintendent, Roads
Louise Warn, Administrator, Water Compliance

Essex
33 Talbot St. South
Essex, ON N8M 1A8
Tel: 519-776-7336; *Fax:* 519-776-8811
www.essex.ca
Municipal Type: City
Incorporated: 1883; *Area:* 277.95 sq km
County or District: Essex; *Population in 2011:* 19,600
Provincial Electoral District(s): Essex
Federal Electoral District(s): Essex
Next Election: Oct. 2018 (4 year terms)
Note: Incorporated as a town in 1890. Restructuring occurred in 1999.
Ron McDermott, Mayor, 519-776-8150
Steve Bjorkman, Councillor, Wards: 1
Randy Voakes, Councillor, Wards: 1
Richard Meloche, Councillor, Wards: 2
Bill Caixeiro, Councillor, Wards: 3
Larry Snively, Councillor, Wards: 3
Sherry Bondy, Councillor, Wards: 4
Cheryl Bondy, Clerk & Deputy-Treasurer
Russell Phillips, Chief Administrative Officer
Donna Hunter, Director, Corporate Services
Chris Nepszy, Director, Infastructure & Development
Ed Pillon, Fire Chief, 519-776-6476, Fax: 519-776-7171
Heather Jablonski, Town Planner
Dan Boudreau, Superintendent, Drainage
Andy Graf, Manager, Environmental Services

Fort Erie
1 Municipal Centre Dr.
Fort Erie, ON L2A 2S6
Tel: 905-871-1600; *Fax:* 905-871-4022
www.forterie.on.ca
Other Information: Fax, Corporate Services: 905-871-9984
Municipal Type: City
Incorporated: 1857; *Area:* 166.35 sq km
County or District: Niagara Regional Municipality; *Population in 2011:* 29,960
Provincial Electoral District(s): Niagara Falls
Federal Electoral District(s): Niagara Falls
Next Election: Oct. 2018 (4 year terms)
Wayne H. Redekop, Mayor
George P. McDermott, Councillor, Wards: 1
Rick Shular, Councillor, Wards: 2
Kimberly Zanko, Councillor, Wards: 3
Marina Butler, Councillor, Wards: 4
Don Lubberts, Councillor, Wards: 5
Chris Knutt, Councillor, Wards: 6
Sandy Annunziata, Regional Councillor
Tom Kuchyt, Chief Administrative Officer
Jonathan Janzen, Treasuer & Director, Financial Services
Richard Brady, Director, Community & Development Services
Larry Coplen, Fire Chief & Coordinator, Community Emergency Management

Georgina
Georgina Civic Centre
26557 Civic Centre Rd., RR#2
Keswick, ON L4P 3G1
Tel: 905-476-4301; *Fax:* 905-476-8100
info@georgina.ca
www.georgina.ca
Other Information: Alternative Phones: 905-722-6516; 705-437-2210
Municipal Type: City
Area: 287.72 sq km
County or District: York Reg. Mun.; *Population in 2011:* 43,517
Provincial Electoral District(s): York-Simcoe
Federal Electoral District(s): York-Simcoe
Next Election: Oct. 2018 (4 year terms)
Note: Amalgamation of the Village of Keswick, the Township of Georgina & Village of Sutton.
Margaret Quirk, Mayor
Danny Wheeler, Regional Councillor
Naomi Davison, Councillor, Wards: 1
Dan Fellini, Councillor, Wards: 2
Dave Neeson, Councillor, Wards: 3
Frank A. Sebo, Councillor, Wards: 4
David A. Harding, Councillor, Wards: 5
Winanne Grant, Chief Administrative Officer, 905-476-4301
Rebecca Mathewson, C.G.A., Treasurer & Director, Administrative Services, 905-476-4301
Harold Lenters, M.Sc.Pl., MCIP, RPP, Director, Planning & Building, 905-476-4301
Robin McDougall, B.A. KINE, DPA, Director, Recreation & Culture, 905-476-4301
Dan Pisani, P.Eng., Director, Operations & Engineering, 905-476-4301
Steve Richardson, C.M.M. III, Director, Emergency Services & Fire Chief, 905-476-4301
Tricia Quinlan, CHRP, Manager, Human Resources, 905-476-4301

Gravenhurst
3 - 5 Pineridge Gate
Gravenhurst, ON P1P 1Z3
Tel: 705-687-3412; *Fax:* 705-687-7016
reception@gravenhurst.ca
www.gravenhurst.ca
Municipal Type: City
Area: 517.99 sq km
County or District: Muskoka District Municipality; *Population in 2011:* 11,640
Provincial Electoral District(s): Parry Sound-Muskoka
Federal Electoral District(s): Parry Sound-Muskoka
Next Election: Oct. 2018 (4 year terms)
Paisley Donaldson, Mayor, 705-689-5659
Sandy Cairns, District Councillor
Paul Kelly, District Councillor
Terry Pilger, District Councillor
Heidi Lorenz, Councillor, Wards: 1
Erin Eiter, Councillor, Wards: 2
Bob Colhoun, Councillor, Wards: 3
Randy Jorgensen, Councillor, Wards: 4
Jeff Watson, Councillor, Wards: 5
Candace Thwaites, Clerk
Glen Davies, Chief Administrative Officer, 705-687-6774
Kenneth Watson, Treasurer
Scott Lucas, Director, Development Services, 705-687-3412
Marta Proctor, Director, Recreation, Arts & Culture
Andrew Stacey, Director, Infrastructure Services, 705-687-2230

Greater Napanee
P.O. Box 97
124 John St.
Napanee, ON K7R 3L4
Tel: 613-354-3351; *Fax:* 613-354-6545
info@greaternapanee.com
www.greaternapanee.com
Other Information: E-mail, Programs: recreation@greaternapanee.com
Municipal Type: City
Area: 459.71 sq km
County or District: Lennox-Addington; *Population in 2011:* 15,511
Provincial Electoral District(s): Lanark-Frontenac-Lennox & Addington
Federal Electoral District(s): Hastings-Lennox & Addington
Next Election: Oct. 2018 (4 year terms)
Gord Schermerhorn, Mayor, 613-354-0429
Marg Isbester, Deputy Mayor & Councillor
Michael Schenk, Councillor, Wards: 1
Max Kaiser, Councillor, Wards: 2
Roger Cole, Councillor, Wards: 3
Carol Harvey, Councillor, Wards: 4
Shaune Lucas, Councillor, Wards: 5
Susan Beckel, Clerk, 613-354-3351
Raymond Callery, Chief Administrative Officer, 613-354-3351
Mark Day, Director, Finance & Treasurer, 613-354-3351
Jeff Cuthill, Director, Utilities & Public Works, 613-354-5931
Charles McDonald, Director, Operational Audits & Chief Building Officer, 613-354-3351
Terry Gervais, Fire Chief, 613-354-3415
Dan Macdonald, Manager, Facilities, 613-354-4423
Ron Vankoughnet, Supervisor, Public Works

Greater Sudbury / Grand Sudbury
Tom Davies Square
P.O. Box 5000 A
200 Brady St.
Sudbury, ON P3A 5P3
Tel: 705-671-2489; *Fax:* 705-671-8118
311@greatersudbury.ca
www.greatersudbury.ca
Other Information: Phone, Local Calls: 311; TTY: 705-688-3919
Municipal Type: City
Incorporated: Jan. 1, 2001; *Area:* 3,200.56 sq km
Population in 2011: 160,274
Provincial Electoral District(s): Nickel Belt; Sudbury
Federal Electoral District(s): Nickel Belt; Sudbury
Next Election: Oct. 2018 (4 year terms)
Brian Bigger, Mayor
Mark Signoretti, Councillor, Wards: 1
Michael Vagnini, Councillor, Wards: 2
Gerry Montpellier, Councillor, Wards: 3
Evelyn Dutrisac, Councillor, Wards: 4
Robert Kirwan, Councillor, Wards: 5
René Lapierre, Councillor, Wards: 6
Mike Jakubo, Councillor, Wards: 7
Al Sizer, Councillor, Wards: 8
Deb McIntosh, Councillor, Wards: 9
Fern Cormier, Councillor, Wards: 10
Lynne Reynolds, Councillor, Wards: 11
Joscelyne Landry-Altmann, Councillor, Wards: 12
Caroline Hallsworth, City Clerk & Executive Director, 705-674-4455
Ed Archer, Chief Administrative Officer
Lorella M. Hayes, B.Comm., CA, Chief Financial Officer & Treasurer
Bruno Mangiardi, Chief Information Officer
Paul Baskcomb, General Manager, Growth & Development
Tony Cecutti, P. Eng, General Manager, Infrastructure Services
Ron Henderson, General Manager, Citizen & Leisure Services
Guido Mazza, Director & Chief Building Official, Building Services

Grimsby
160 Livingston Ave.
Grimsby, ON L3M 4G3
Tel: 905-945-9634; *Fax:* 905-945-5010
www.town.grimsby.on.ca
Municipal Type: City
Area: 68.94 sq km
County or District: Niagara Reg. Mun.; *Population in 2011:* 25,325
Provincial Electoral District(s): Niagara West-Glanbrook
Federal Electoral District(s): Niagara West
Next Election: Oct. 2018 (4 year terms)
Robert N. Bentley, Mayor, 905-945-2710
Steve Berry, Alderman, 905-945-2578, Wards: 1
Dave Wilson, Alderman, Wards: 1
Dave Kadwell, Alderman, 905-945-8259, Wards: 2
Michelle Seaborn, Alderman, 905-945-7963, Wards: 2
John Dunstall, Alderman, Wards: 3
Joanne Johnston, Alderman, 905-945-9851, Wards: 3
Nick DiFlavio, Alderman, 905-309-4133, Wards: 4
Carolyn Mullins, Alderman, 289-235-9460, Wards: 4
Tony Quirk, Regional Councillor
Hazel Soady-Easton, Town Clerk, 905-309-2003
Derik Brandt, Town Manager, 905-945-9634
Stephen Gruninger, CGA, Town Treasurer & Director, Finance
Bruce Atkinson, CGA, Director, Recreation, Facilities, & Culture
Robert LeRoux, P.Eng., Director, Public Works
Michael Seaman, Director, Planning
Michael Cain, Fire Chief
Brandon Wartman, Manager, EHS Compliance, 905-309-2016

Guelph
City Hall
1 Carden St.
Guelph, ON N1H 3A1
Tel: 519-822-1260; *Fax:* 519-763-1269
info@guelph.ca
www.guelph.ca
Other Information: TTY: 519-826-9771
Municipal Type: City
Incorporated: 1879; *Area:* 86.72 sq km
County or District: Wellington; *Population in 2011:* 121,688
Provincial Electoral District(s): Guelph; Wellington-Halton Hills
Federal Electoral District(s): Guelph; Wellington-Halton Hills
Next Election: Oct. 2018 (4 year terms)
Cam Guthrie, Mayor
Bob Bell, Councillor, Wards: 1
Dan Gibson, Councillor, Wards: 1
James Gordon, Councillor, Wards: 2
Andy Van Hellemond, Councillor, Wards: 2
Phil Allt, Councillor, Wards: 3
June Hofland, Councillor, Wards: 3
Christine Billings, Councillor, Wards: 4
Mike Salisbury, Councillor, Wards: 4
Cathy Downer, Councillor, Wards: 5
Leanne Piper, Councillor, Wards: 5
Mark MacKinnon, Councillor, Wards: 6
Karl Wettstein, Councillor, Wards: 6
Stephen O'Brien, City Clerk
Derrick Thomson, Chief Administrative Officer, 519-822-1260
Albert Horsman, Chief Financial Officer & Executive Director, Finance & Enterprise Services
Mark Amorosi, Executive Director, Corporate & Human Resources
Janet Laird, Executive Director, Planning, Building, Engineering & Environment
Derek McCaughan, Executive Director, Operations, Transit & Emergency Services
Derrick Thomson, Executive Director, Community & Social Services

Halton Hills
1 Halton Hills Dr.
Georgetown, ON L7G 5G2
Tel: 905-873-2600; *Fax:* 905-873-2347
www.haltonhills.ca
Other Information: TTY: 905-873-0644
Municipal Type: City
Area: 276.26 sq km
County or District: Halton Reg. Mun.; *Population in 2011:* 59,008
Provincial Electoral District(s): Wellington-Halton Hills
Federal Electoral District(s): Wellington-Halton Hills
Next Election: Oct. 2018 (4 year terms)
Rick Bonnette, Mayor
Clark Somerville, Regional Councillor, Wards: 1 & 2
Jane Fogal, Regional Councillor, Wards: 3 & 4
Jon Hurst, Councillor, Wards: 1
Mike O'Leary, Councillor, Wards: 1
Ted Brown, Councillor, Wards: 2
Bryan Lewis, Councillor, Wards: 2
Moya Johnson, Councillor, Wards: 3
David Kentner, Councillor, Wards: 3
Bob Inglis, Councillor, Wards: 4
Ann Lawlor, Councillor, Wards: 4
Suzanne Jones, Town Clerk
Brent Marshall, Chief Administrative Officer & Fire Chief, 905-873-2601
Ed DeSousa, Treasurer & Director, Corporate Services
Kevin Okimi, Manager, Parks & Open Space, 905-873-2601
Damian Szybalski, Manager, Sustainability, 905-873-2601

Hamilton
71 Main St. West
Hamilton, ON L8P 4Y5
Tel: 905-546-2489; *Fax:* 905-546-2095
askCITY@hamilton.ca
www.hamilton.ca
Municipal Type: City
Incorporated: 1846; *Area:* 1,117.21 sq km
Population in 2011: 519,949
Provincial Electoral District(s): Ancaster-Dundas-Flamborough-Westdale; Hamilton Centre; Hamilton East-Stoney Creek; Hamilton Mountain; Niagara West-Glanbrook
Federal Electoral District(s): Flamborough-Glanbrook; Hamilton Centre; Hamilton East-Stoney Creek; Hamilton Mountain; Hamilton West-Ancaster-Dundas; Northumberland-Peterborough South
Next Election: Oct. 2018 (4 year terms)
Note: Incorporated as a city on Jan. 1, 2001.
Fred Eisenberger, Mayor
Aidan Johnson, Councillor, Wards: 1 - Chedoke-Cootes
Jason Farr, Councillor, Wards: 2 - Downtown
Matthew Green, Councillor, Wards: 3 - Hamilton Centre
Sam Merulla, Councillor, Wards: 4 - East Hamilton
Chad Collins, Councillor, Wards: 5 - Redhill
Tom Jackson, Councillor, Wards: 6 - East Mountain
Donna Skelly, Councillor, Wards: 7 - Central Mountain
Terry Whitehead, Councillor, Wards: 8 - West Mountain
Doug Conley, Councillor, Wards: 9 - Heritage Stoney Creek
Maria Pearson, Councillor, Wards: 10 - Stoney Creek
Brenda Johnson, Councillor, Wards: 11 Glan., Stoney Crk., Winona
Lloyd Ferguson, Councillor, Wards: 12 - Ancaster

Arlene Vanderbeek, Councillor, Wards: 13 - Community of Dundas
Robert Pasuta, Councillor, Wards: 14 - Wentworth
Judi Partridge, Councillor, Wards: 15 - Flamborough
Rose Caterini, City Clerk
Chris Murray, City Manager
Joe-Anne Priel, General Manager, Community Services
Mike Zegarac, General Manager, Finance & Corporate Services
John Verbeek, Assistant Deputy Fire Chief

Hawkesbury
600 Higginson St.
Hawkesbury, ON K6A 1H1
Tel: 613-632-0106;
www.hawkesbury.ca
Municipal Type: City
Area: 9.46 sq km
County or District: Prescott & Russell; *Population in 2011:* 10,551
Provincial Electoral District(s): Glengarry-Prescott-Russell
Federal Electoral District(s): Glengarry-Prescott-Russell
Next Election: Oct. 2018 (4 year terms)
Jeanne Charlebois, Mayor
André Chamaillard, Councillor
Daniel Lalonde, Councillor
Pierre Ouellet, Councillor
Yves Paquette, Councillor
Johanne Portelance, Councillor
Michel Thibodeau, Councillor
Christine Groulx, Clerk
Jean-Yves Carrier, Chief Administrative Officer
Richard Guertin, Superintendent, Water Treatment Plant
Alan Lavoie, Superintendent, Public Works
Roger Champagne, Acting Fire Chief, 613-632-1105
Élise Larocque, Manager, Human Resources
Denise Robitaille, Administrative Secretary, Recreation & Culture

Huntsville
37 Main St. East
Huntsville, ON P1H 1A1
Tel: 705-789-1751; *Fax:* 705-789-6689
www.huntsville.ca
Other Information: TTY: 705-789-1768
Municipal Type: City
Area: 703.23 sq km
County or District: Muskoka Dist. Mun.; *Population in 2011:* 19,056
Provincial Electoral District(s): Parry Sound-Muskoka
Federal Electoral District(s): Parry Sound-Muskoka
Next Election: Oct. 2018 (4 year terms)
Scott Aitchison, Mayor
Nancy Alcock, District Councillor
Karin Terziano, District Councillor
Brian Thompson, District Councillor
Daniel Armour, Councillor, Wards: Brunel
Jonathan Wiebe, Councillor, Wards: Chaffey
Bob Stone, Councillor, Wards: Huntsville
Det Schumacher, Councillor, Wards: Stisted/Stephenson/Port Sydney
Chris Zanetti, Councillor, Wards: Stisted/Stephenson/Port Sydney
Denise Corry, CAO & Clerk
Julia Finch, Treasurer
Mike Gooch, Executive Director, Development Services
Lisa Smith, Executive Director, Human Resources & Corporate Information
Steve Hernen, Director, Protective Services & Fire Chief
Steve Keeley, Director, Public Works
Colleen MacDonald, Manager, Parks & Cemeteries
Brian Crozier, Property Manager, Canada Summit Centre

Ingersoll
130 Oxford St., 2nd Fl.
Ingersoll, ON N5C 2V5
Tel: 519-485-0120; *Fax:* 519-485-3543
www.ingersoll.ca
Other Information: info@ingersoll.ca
Municipal Type: City
Area: 12.9 sq km
County or District: Oxford; *Population in 2011:* 12,146
Provincial Electoral District(s): Oxford
Federal Electoral District(s): Oxford
Next Election: Oct. 2018 (4 year terms)
Ted J. Comiskey, Mayor
Fred Freeman, Deputy Mayor & Councillor
Michael Bowman, Councillor
Gord Lesser, Councillor
Brian Petrie, Councillor
Kristy Van Kooten-Bossence, Councillor
Reagan Warnick-Franklin, Councillor
Michael Graves, Clerk
William Tigert, Chief Administrative Officer, 519-485-0120

Jim Brown, Treasurer & Director, Finance
Sandra Lawson, Director, Engineering
Bonnie Ward, Director, Recreation
John Holmes, Fire Chief

Innisfil
2101 Innisfil Beach Rd.
Innisfil, ON L9S 1A1
Tel: 705-436-3710; *Fax:* 705-436-7120
www.innisfil.ca
Municipal Type: City
Incorporated: 1850; *Area:* 284.18 sq km
County or District: Simcoe; *Population in 2011:* 33,079
Provincial Electoral District(s): York Simcoe
Federal Electoral District(s): Barrie-Innisfil
Next Election: Oct. 2018 (4 year terms)
Gord Wauchope, Mayor
Lynn Dollin, Deputy Mayor & Councillor
Doug Lougheed, Councillor, Wards: 1
Richard Simpson, Councillor, Wards: 2
Donna Orsatti, Councillor, Wards: 3
Stan J. Daurio, Councillor, Wards: 4
Bill Loughead, Councillor, Wards: 5
Carolyn Payne, Councillor, Wards: 6
Rob Nicol, Councillor, Wards: 7
Jason Reynar, Chief Administrative Officer
Jason Reynar, Deputy CAO & Town Solicitor
Lockie Davis, Chief Financial Officer & Director, Finance & Customer Service
Michelle Collette, Director, Human Resources
Danny Rodgers, Chief Building Official
R. Wayne Young, Manager, Roads
Steven Montgomery, Senior Planner
Jon Pegg, Fire Chief

Kawartha Lakes
P.O. Box 9000
26 Francis St.
Lindsay, ON K9V 5R8
Tel: 705-324-9411; *Fax:* 705-324-8110
info@city.kawarthalakes.on.ca
www.city.kawarthalakes.on.ca
Other Information: Toll-Free Phone: 1-888-822-2225
Municipal Type: City
Incorporated: Jan. 1, 2001; *Area:* 3,059.47 sq km
Population in 2011: 73,214
Provincial Electoral District(s): Haliburton-Kawartha Lakes-Brock
Federal Electoral District(s): Haliburton-Kawartha Lakes-Brock
Next Election: Oct. 2018 (4 year terms)
Note: Formerly the County of Victoria.
Andy Letham, Mayor
Rob Macklem, Councillor, Wards: 1
Emmett Yeo, Councillor, Wards: 2
Gord Miller, Councillor, Wards: 3
Andrew Veale, Councillor, Wards: 4
Stephen Strangway, Councillor, Wards: 5
Doug Elmslie, Councillor, Wards: 6
Brian Junkin, Councillor, Wards: 7
John Pollard, Councillor, Wards: 8
Isaac Breadner, Councillor, Wards: 9
Pat Dunn, Councillor, Wards: 10
Patrick O'Reilly, Councillor, Wards: 11
Gord James, Councillor, Wards: 12
Kathleen Seymour-Fagan, Councillor, Wards: 13
Gerard Jilesen, Councillor, Wards: 14
Mary Ann Martin, Councillor, Wards: 15
Heather Stauble, Councillor, Wards: 16
Judy Currins, City Clerk
Ron Taylor, Chief Administrative Officer
Mary-Anne Dempster, Director, Corporate Services
Bryan Robinson, Director, Public Works
Craig Shanks, Acting Director, Community Services
Rod Sutherland, Acting Director, Health & Social Services
Mark Pankhurst, Fire Chief

Kenora
1 Main St. South
Kenora, ON P9N 3X2
Tel: 807-467-2000; *Fax:* 807-467-2009
www.kenora.ca
Municipal Type: City
Area: 210.91 sq km
County or District: Kenora District; *Population in 2011:* 15,348
Provincial Electoral District(s): Kenora-Rainy River
Federal Electoral District(s): Kenora
Next Election: Oct. 2018 (4 year terms)
David S. Canfield, Mayor
Mort Goss, Councillor
Rory McMillan, Councillor
Dan Reynard, Councillor
Louis Roussin, Councillor
Sharon L. Smith, Councillor

Colin Wasacase, Councillor
Heather Kasprick, Clerk
Karen Brown, Chief Administrative Officer
Charlotte Edie, Treasurer
Warren Brinkman, Manager, Emergency Services
Sharen McDowall, Manager, Human Resources
Colleen Neil, Manager, Recreation
Rick Perchuk, Manager, Operations
Mike Mostow, Supervisor, Fleet & Solid Waste
Biman Paudel, Supervisor, Sewer & Water
Kevin Robertson, Chief Building Official
Marco Vogrig, Municipal Engineer

Kingston
City Hall
216 Ontario St.
Kingston, ON K7L 2Z3
Tel: 613-546-0000; *Fax:* 613-546-5232
www.cityofkingston.ca
Other Information: TTY: 613-546-4889
Municipal Type: City
Incorporated: Jan. 1, 1998; *Area:* 450.39 sq km
County or District: Frontenac; *Population in 2011:* 123,363
Provincial Electoral District(s): Kingston & the Islands
Federal Electoral District(s): Kingston & the Islands; Lanark-Frontenac-Kingston
Next Election: Oct. 2018 (4 year terms)
Bryan Paterson, Mayor
Richard Allen, Councillor, Wards: 1 - Countryside
Kevin George, Councillor, Wards: 2 - Loyalist-Cataraqui
Lisa Osanic, Councillor, Wards: 3 - Collins-Bayridge
Laura Turner, Councillor, Wards: 4 - Lakeside
Liz Schell, Councillor, Wards: 5 - Portsmouth
Adam Candon, Councillor, Wards: 6 - Trillium
Mary Rita Holland, Councillor, Wards: 7 - Kingscourt-Rideau
Jeff McLaren, Councillor, Wards: 8 - Meadowbrook-Strathcona
Jim Neill, Councillor, Wards: 9 - Williamsville
Peter Stroud, Councillor, Wards: 10 - Sydenham
Rob Hutchinson, Councillor, Wards: 11 - King's Town
Ryan Boehme, Councillor, Wards: 12 - Pittsburgh
John Bolognone, City Clerk
Gerard Hunt, Chief Administrative Officer
Desiree Kennedy, Treasurer & Director, Financial Services
Cynthia Beach, Commissioner, Corporate & Strategic Initiatives
Denis Leger, Commissioner, Transportation, Facilities & Emergency Services
Lanie Hurdle, Commissioner, Community Services & Director, Recreation & Leisure Services
Paul MacLatchy, Director, Environment & Sustainability
Mark Van Buren, Director, Engineering
Damon Wells, Director, Public Works
Shawn Armstrong, Fire Chief
John Giles, Manager, Solid Waste

Kingsville
2021 Division Rd. North
Kingsville, ON N9Y 2Y9
Tel: 519-733-2305; *Fax:* 519-733-8108
www.kingsville.ca
Other Information: kingsvilleworks@kingsville.ca
Municipal Type: City
Incorporated: 1874; *Area:* 246.84 sq km
County or District: Essex; *Population in 2011:* 21,362
Provincial Electoral District(s): Essex
Federal Electoral District(s): Essex
Next Election: Oct. 2018 (4 year terms)
Note: Incorporated as a town in 1901. Restructuring occurred in 1999.
Nelson Santos, Mayor
Gord Queen, Deputy Mayor & Councillor
Susanne Coghill, Councillor
Tony Gaffan, Councillor
Sandy McIntyre, Councillor
Thomas Neufeld, Councillor
Larry Patterson, Councillor
Ruth Orton, Clerk & Director, Corporate Services
Peggy Van-Mierlo West, Chief Administrative Officer
Sandra Ingratta, Director, Financial Services
Andy Coghill, Manager, Public Works
Maggie Durocher, Program Manager, Parks & Recreation
Bob Kissner Jr., Fire Chief

Kitchener
City Hall
P.O. Box 1118
200 King St. West
Kitchener, ON N2G 4G7
Tel: 519-741-2345;
www.kitchener.ca
Other Information: TTY: 1-866-969-9994
Municipal Type: City
Incorporated: June 9, 1912; *Area:* 136.89 sq km

County or District: Waterloo Regional Municipality; *Population in 2011:* 219,153
Provincial Electoral District(s): Kitchener Centre; Kitchener-Waterloo; Waterloo-Wellington
Federal Electoral District(s): Kitchener Centre; Kitchener-Conestoga; Kitchener South-Hespeler; Waterloo
Next Election: Oct. 2018 (4 year terms)
Berry Vrbanovic, Mayor, 519-741-2300
Scott Davey, Councillor, Wards: 1
Dave Schnider, Councillor, Wards: 2
John Gazzola, Councillor, Wards: 3
Yvonne Fernandes, Councillor, Wards: 4
Kelly Galloway-Sealock, Councillor, Wards: 5
Paul Singh, Councillor, Wards: 6
Bil Ioannidis, Councillor, Wards: 7
Zyg Janecki, Councillor, Wards: 8
Frank Etherington, Councillor, Wards: 9
Sarah Marsh, Councillor, Wards: 10
Jeff Willmer, Chief Administrative Officer
Dan Chapman, Deputy CAO, Finance & Corporate Services
Pauline Houston, Deputy CAO & Head, Infrastructure Services
Rod Regier, Executive Director, Economic Development
Alain Pinard, Director, Planning
Mike Seiling, Director, Building
Jon Rehill, Fire Chief

LaSalle
5950 Malden Rd.
Lasalle, ON N9H 1S4
Tel: 519-969-7770; *Fax:* 519-969-4469
www.town.lasalle.on.ca
Municipal Type: City
Incorporated: 1924; *Area:* 65.25 sq km
County or District: Essex; *Population in 2011:* 28,643
Provincial Electoral District(s): Essex
Federal Electoral District(s): Essex
Next Election: Oct. 2018 (4 year terms)
Note: Dissolved into Township of Sandwich West in 1959. Status & name change to Town of LaSalle in 1991.
Ken Antaya, Mayor
Marc Bondy, Deputy Mayor & Councillor
Michael Akpata, Councillor
Terry Burns, Councillor
Sue Desjarlais, Councillor
Crystal B. Meloche, Councillor
Jeff Renaud, Councillor
Brenda Andreatta, Clerk
Kevin Miller, Chief Administrative Officer, 519-969-7770
Joe Milicia, Treasurer
Peter Marra, Director, Public Works, 519-969-7770
Larry Silani, Director, Development & Strategic Initiatives, 519-969-7770
Dave Sutton, Fire Chief, 519-966-0744

Lincoln
4800 South Service Rd.
Beamsville, ON L0R 1B1
Tel: 905-563-8205; *Fax:* 905-563-6566
info@lincoln.ca
www.lincoln.ca
Municipal Type: City
Incorporated: Jan. 1, 1970; *Area:* 162.86 sq km
County or District: Niagara Reg. Mun.; *Population in 2011:* 22,487
Provincial Electoral District(s): Niagara West-Glanbrook
Federal Electoral District(s): Niagara West
Next Election: Oct. 2018 (4 year terms)
Note: Amalgamation of the Town of Beamsville, the Township of Clinton, & part of the Township of Louth.
Sandra Easton, Mayor
Robert Foster, Councillor, Wards: 1
Dianne Rintjema, Councillor, Wards: 1
Tony G. Brunet, Councillor, Wards: 2
John D. Pachereva, Councillor, Wards: 2
Paul MacPherson, Councillor, Wards: 3
Dave A. Thomson, Councillor, Wards: 3
Wayne MacMillan, Councillor, Wards: 4
Lynn Timmers, Councillor, Wards: 4
Bill Hodgson, Regional Councillor
William J. Kolasa, Clerk & Director, Corporate Services
Michael Kirkopoulos, Chief Administrative Officer
Kathleen Dale, Director, Planning & Development
Dave Graham, Director, Public Works
Judy Pease, Director, Community Services
Robert Spadoni, Director, Finance
Greg Hudson, Fire Chief
Chuck Judson, Manager, Facilities & Parks

London
City Hall
P.O. Box 5035
300 Dufferin Ave.
London, ON N6A 4L9
Tel: 519-661-4500; *Fax:* 519-661-4892
webmaster@london.ca
www.london.ca
Municipal Type: City
Incorporated: 1855; *Area:* 420.57 sq km
County or District: Middlesex; *Population in 2011:* 366,151
Provincial Electoral District(s): London-Fanshawe; Elgin-Middlesex-London; London North Centre; London West
Federal Electoral District(s): Elgin-Middlesex-London; Lambton-Kent-Middlesex; London North Centre; London West; London-Fanshawe
Next Election: Oct. 2018 (4 year terms)
Matt Brown, Mayor
Michael Van Holst, Councillor, Wards: 1
Bill Armstrong, Councillor, Wards: 2
Mo Mohamed Salih, Councillor, Wards: 3
Jesse Helmer, Councillor, Wards: 4
Maureen Cassidy, Councillor, Wards: 5
Phil Squire, Councillor, Wards: 6
Josh Morgan, Councillor, Wards: 7
Paul Hubert, Councillor, Wards: 8
Anna Hopkins, Councillor, Wards: 9
Virginia Ridley, Councillor, Wards: 10
Stephen Turner, Councillor, Wards: 11
Harold Usher, Councillor, Wards: 12
Tanya Park, Councillor, Wards: 13
Jared Zaifman, Councillor, Wards: 14
Cathy Saunders, City Clerk
Art Zuidema, City Manager
Martin Hayward, City Treasurer & Chief Financial Officer
Veronica McAlea Major, Chief Human Resources Officer
William Coxhead, Managing Director, Parks & Recreation
John M. Fleming, City Planner & Managing Director, Planning
Mat Daley, Interim Director, Information Technology Services
John Braam, City Engineer & Managing Director
John W. Kobarda, Fire Chief

Markham
Markham Civic Centre
101 Town Centre Blvd.
Markham, ON L3R 9W3
Tel: 905-477-7000; *Fax:* 905-479-7771
customerservice@markham.ca
www.markham.ca
Other Information: Customer Service: 905-477-5530
Municipal Type: City
Incorporated: Jan. 1, 1971; *Area:* 212.58 sq km
County or District: York Reg. Mun.; *Population in 2011:* 301,709
Provincial Electoral District(s): Markham-Unionville; Oak Ridges-Markham; Thornhill
Federal Electoral District(s): Markham-Stouffville; Markham-Thornhill; Markham-Unionville; Richmond Hill; Thornhill
Next Election: Oct. 2018 (4 year terms)
Frank Scarpitti, Mayor, 905-475-4702
Nirmala Armstrong, Regional Councillor
Jack Heath, Regional Councillor, 905-475-4872
Jim Jones, Regional Councillor, 905-479-7757
Joe Li, Regional Councillor, 905-479-7749
Valerie Burke, Councillor, Wards: 1
Alan Ho, Councillor, Wards: 2
Don Hamilton, Councillor, Wards: 3
Karen Rea, Councillor, Wards: 4
Colin Campbell, Councillor, Wards: 5
Amanda Yeung Collucci, Councillor, Wards: 6
Logan Kanapathi, Councillor, Wards: 7
Alex Chiu, Councillor, Wards: 8
Kimberly Kitteringham, Town Clerk, 905-475-4729
Andy Taylor, Chief Administrative Officer
Joel Lustig, Treasurer, 905-475-4715
Jim Baird, Commissioner, Development Services
Trinela Cane, Commissioner, Corporate Services
Nasir Kenea, Chief Information Officer, 905-475-4733
Dave Decker, Fire Chief
Sharon Laing, Director, Human Resources, 905-475-4725
Peter Loukes, Director, Environmental Services

Midland
575 Dominion Ave.
Midland, ON L4R 1R2
Tel: 705-526-4275; *Fax:* 705-526-9971
clerks@midland.ca
www.midland.ca
Other Information: TTY: 705-526-4276, ext. 2824
Municipal Type: City
Area: 29.09 sq km
County or District: Simcoe; *Population in 2011:* 16,572
Provincial Electoral District(s): Simcoe North
Federal Electoral District(s): Simcoe North
Next Election: Oct. 2018 (4 year terms)
James M. Downer, Mayor
Mike Ross, Deputy Mayor & Councillor
Patricia A. File, Councillor, Wards: 1
George J. MacDonald, Councillor, Wards: 1
Jonathan G. Main, Councillor, Wards: 1
Glen Canning, Councillor, Wards: 2
Jack Contin, Councillor, Wards: 2
Cody Oschefski, Councillor, Wards: 2
Stewart Strathearn, Councillor, Wards: 3
Andrea Fay, Clerk & Deputy Chief Administrative Officer
Marc Villeneuve, Treasurer & Director, Finance
Shawn Berriault, Director, Public Works
Pat Leclair, Manager, Water & Wastewater Operations
Paul Ryan, Fire Chief

Milton
150 Mary St.
Milton, ON L9T 6Z5
Tel: 905-878-7252; *Fax:* 905-878-6995
www.milton.ca
Municipal Type: City
Incorporated: 1857; *Area:* 366.61 sq km
County or District: Halton Regional Municipality; *Population in 2011:* 84,362
Provincial Electoral District(s): Halton
Federal Electoral District(s): Milton
Next Election: Oct. 2018 (4 year terms)
Gordon A. Krantz, Mayor
Mike Cluett, Local & Regional Councillor, Wards: 1, 6, 7, 8
Colin Best, Local & Regional Councillor, Wards: 2, 3, 4, 5
Robert Duvall, Councillor, Wards: 1
Mike Boughton, Councillor, Wards: 2
Cindy Lunau, Councillor, Wards: 3
Rick Malboeuf, Councillor, Wards: 4
Arnold Huffman, Councillor, Wards: 5
John Pollard, Councillor, Wards: 6
Rick Di Lorenzo, Councillor, Wards: 7
Zeeshan Hamid, Councillor, Wards: 8
Troy McHarg, Clerk
Bill Mann, Chief Administrative Officer
Linda Leeds, Treasurer & Director, Corporate Services
Jennifer Reynolds, Director, Community Services
Brian Ellsworth, P.Eng., Fire Chief

Mississauga
Civic Centre
300 City Centre Dr.
Mississauga, ON L5B 3C1
Tel: 905-615-4311; *Fax:* 905-615-4081
public.info@mississauga.ca
www.mississauga.ca
Other Information: TTY: 905-896-5151
Municipal Type: City
Incorporated: Jan. 1, 1974; *Area:* 288.53 sq km
County or District: Peel Reg. Mun.; *Population in 2011:* 713,443
Provincial Electoral District(s): Bramalea-Gore-Malton; Mississauga-Brampton South; Mississauga-Erindale; Mississauga East-Cooksville; Mississauga South; Mississauga-Streetsville
Federal Electoral District(s): Mississauga Centre; Mississauga East-Cooksville; Mississauga-Erin Mills; Mississauga-Lakeshore; Mississauga-Malton; Mississauga-Streetsville
Next Election: Oct. 2018 (4 year terms)
Bonnie Crombie, Mayor
Jim Tovey, Councillor, 905-896-5100, Wards: 1
Karen Ras, Councillor, 905-896-5200, Wards: 2
Chris Fonseca, Councillor, 905-896-5300, Wards: 3
John Kovac, Councillor, 905-896-5400, Wards: 4
Carolyn Parrish, Councillor, 905-896-5500, Wards: 5
Ron Starr, Councillor, 905-896-5600, Wards: 6
Nando Iannicca, Councillor, 905-896-5700, Wards: 7
Matt Mahoney, Councillor, 905-896-5800, Wards: 8
Pat Saito, Councillor, 905-896-5900, Wards: 9
Sue McFadden, Councillor, 905-896-5010, Wards: 10
George Carlson, Councillor, 905-896-5011, Wards: 11
Crystal Greer, City Clerk, Legislative Services
Janice Baker, FCPA, FCA, City Manager & Chief Administrative Officer
Brenda Breault, Commissioner, Corporate Services, & Treasurer
Paul Mitcham, Commissioner, Community Services
Martin Powell, P. Eng., Commissioner, Transportation & Works
Ed Sajecki, Commissioner, Planning & Building
Tim Beckett, Fire Chief

Mississippi Mills
P.O. Box 400
3131 Old Perth Rd., RR#2
Almonte, ON K0A 1A0
Tel: 613-256-2064; *Fax:* 613-256-4887
town@mississippimills.ca
www.mississippimills.ca
Municipal Type: City
Incorporated: Jan. 1, 1998; *Area:* 509.05 sq km
County or District: Lanark; *Population in 2011:* 12,385
Provincial Electoral District(s): Carleton-Mississippi Mills
Federal Electoral District(s): Lanark-Frontenac-Kingston
Next Election: Oct. 2018 (4 year terms)
Note: Merger of the Town of Almonte with the townships of Ramsay & Pakenham.
Shaun McLaughlin, Mayor, 613-256-2064
Alex Gillis, Councillor, Wards: Almonte
Jill McCubbin, Councillor, Wards: Almonte
Amanda Pulker-Mok, Councillor, Wards: Almonte
Jane Torrance, Councillor, Wards: Almonte
Duncan A. Abbott, Councillor, Wards: Pakenham
Denzil Ferguson, Councillor, Wards: Pakenham
John H. Edwards, Councillor, Wards: Ramsay
Christa Lowry, Councillor, Wards: Ramsay
Paul J. Watters, Councillor, Wards: Ramsay
Val Wilkinson, Councillor, Wards: Ramsay
Shawna Stone, Town Clerk, 613-256-2064
Diane Smithson, Chief Administrative Officer, 613-256-2064
Rhonda Whitmarsh, Treasurer, 613-256-2064
Pascal Meunier, Fire Chief, 613-256-1589
Lennox Smith, Chief Building Official, 613-256-2064
Cindy Hartwick, Administrative Assistant, Roads & Public Works, 613-256-2064
Bonnie Hawkins, Administrative Assistant, Recreation & Culture, 613-256-1077

New Tecumseth
Town Administration Centre
P.O. Box 910
10 Wellington St. East
Alliston, ON L9R 1A1
Tel: 705-435-6219; *Fax:* 705-435-2873
newtecumseth.ca
Other Information: Alternative Phone: 905-729-0057
Municipal Type: City
Incorporated: Jan. 1991; *Area:* 274.18 sq km
County or District: Simcoe; *Population in 2011:* 30,234
Provincial Electoral District(s): Simcoe-Grey
Federal Electoral District(s): Simcoe-Grey
Next Election: Oct. 2018 (4 year terms)
Rick Milne, Mayor
Jamie Smith, Deputy Mayor & Councillor
Marc Biss, Councillor, Wards: 1
Michael Beattie, Councillor, Wards: 2
J.J. Paul Whiteside, Councillor, Wards: 3
Fran Sainsbury, Councillor, Wards: 4
Donna Jebb, Councillor, Wards: 5
Richard Norcross, Councillor, Wards: 6
Shira Harrison McIntyre, Councillor, Wards: 7
Chris Ross, Councillor, Wards: 8
Cindy Maher, Clerk & Manager, Administration
Brendan Holly, Chief Administrative Officer, 705-435-3900
Mark Sirr, Treasurer & Director, Finance
Bruce Hoppe, Director, Planning & Development
Chad Horan, Director, Public Works
Hilary McCormack, Director, Human Resources
Rick Vatri, Director, Engineering
Patrick D'Almada, Director, Parks, Recreation & Culture
Dan Heydon, Fire Chief
John Miller, Chief Building Official & Manager, Building Standards

Newmarket
P.O. Box 328
395 Mulock Dr.
Newmarket, ON L3Y 4X7
Tel: 905-895-5193; *Fax:* 905-953-5100
info@newmarket.ca
www.newmarket.ca
Municipal Type: City
Incorporated: 1857; *Area:* 38.08 sq km
County or District: York Regional Municipality; *Population in 2011:* 79,978
Provincial Electoral District(s): Newmarket-Aurora
Federal Electoral District(s): Newmarket-Aurora
Next Election: Oct. 2018 (4 year terms)
Note: Incorporated as a town in 1880.
Tony Van Bynen, Mayor, 905-898-2876, Fax: 905-953-5102
John Taylor, Regional Councillor
Tom Vegh, Councillor, Wards: 1
Dave Kerwin, Councillor, Wards: 2
Jane Twinney, Councillor, Wards: 3
Tom Hempen, Councillor, Wards: 4
Joe Sponga, Councillor, Wards: 5
Kelly Broome-Plumley, Councillor, Wards: 6
Christina Bisanz, Councillor, Wards: 7
Andrew Brouwer, Clerk & Director, Legislative Services
Robert N. Shelton, Chief Administrative Officer
Mike Mayes, Treasurer & Director, Financial Services
Ian McDougall, Commissioner, Community Services
Anita Moore, Commissioner, Corporate & Financial Services
Peter Noehammer, Commissioner, Development & Infrastructure
Lynn Georgeff, Director, Human Resources
Chris Kalimootoo, Director, Public Works Services
Rick Nethery, Director, Planning & Building Services
Rachel Prudhomme, Director, Engineering Services
Ian Laing, Fire Chief

Niagara Falls
City Hall
P.O. Box 1023
4310 Queen St.
Niagara Falls, ON L2E 6X5
Tel: 905-356-7521; *Fax:* 905-356-9083
www.niagarafalls.ca
Municipal Type: City
Incorporated: Jan. 1, 1904; *Area:* 209.58 sq km
County or District: Niagara Reg. Mun.; *Population in 2011:* 82,997
Provincial Electoral District(s): Niagara Falls
Federal Electoral District(s): Niagara Falls
Next Election: Oct. 2018 (4 year terms)
Jim Diodati, Mayor
Wayne Campbell, City Councillor
Kim Craitor, City Councillor
Carolynn Ioannoni, City Councillor
Vince A. Kerrio, City Councillor
Joyce Morocco, City Councillor
Victor Pietrangelo, City Councillor
Mike Strange, City Councillor
Wayne Thomson, City Councillor
Bob Gale, Regional Councillor
Bart Maves, Regional Councillor
Selina Volpatti, Regional Councillor
Dean Iorfida, City Clerk & Director, Council Services
Ken Todd, Chief Administrative Officer
Serge Felicetti, Director, Business Development
Alex Herlovich, Director, Planning, Building & Development
Geoffrey Holman, Director, Municipal Works

Niagara-on-the-Lake
P.O. Box 100
1593 Four Mile Creek Rd.
Virgil, ON L0S 1T0
Tel: 905-468-3266; *Fax:* 905-468-2959
info@notl.org
www.notl.org
Municipal Type: City
Area: 132.83 sq km
County or District: Niagara Reg. Mun.; *Population in 2011:* 15,400
Provincial Electoral District(s): Niagara Falls
Federal Electoral District(s): Niagara Falls
Next Election: Oct. 2018 (4 year terms)
Patrick Darte, Lord Mayor
Gary Burroughs, Regional Councillor
Maria Bau-Coote, Councillor
Jim Collard, Councillor
Betty Disero, Councillor
Terry Flynn, Councillor
Jamie R. King, Councillor
Martin Mazza, Councillor
Paolo Miele, Councillor
John Wiens, Councillor
Holly Dowd, Town Clerk & Acting Director, Corporate Services
Milena Avramovic, Chief Administrative Officer
John Henricks, Director, Community & Development Services
Sheldon Randall, Director, Operations
Alex Burbidge, Fire Chief
Doug Kerr, Deputy Director, Public Works

North Bay
City Hall
P.O. Box 360
200 McIntyre St. East
North Bay, ON P1B 8H8
Tel: 705-474-0400; *Fax:* 705-495-4353
customerservice@cityofnorthbay.ca
www.cityofnorthbay.ca
Other Information: Toll-Free Phone: 1-800-465-1882
Municipal Type: City
Incorporated: 1925; *Area:* 314.91 sq km
County or District: Nipissing District; *Population in 2011:* 53,651
Provincial Electoral District(s): Nipissing
Federal Electoral District(s): Nipissing-Timiskaming
Next Election: Oct. 2018 (4 year terms)
Al McDonald, Mayor
Mike Anthony, Councillor
Mac Bain, Councillor
Sheldon Forgette, Councillor
Mark R. King, Councillor
George Maroosis, Councillor
Chris Mayne, Councillor
Jeff J. Serran, Councillor
Derek Shogren, Councillor
Daryl Vaillancourt, Councillor
Tanya G. Vrebosch, Councillor
Cathy Conrad, City Clerk
Margaret Karpenko, Chief Financial Officer & Treasurer
David Euler, Managing Director, Engineering, Environmental & Works
John Severino, Managing Director, Community Services
Lea Janisse, Director, Human Resources
Ian Kilgour, Director, Parks, Recreation, & Leisure Services
Peter Leckie, City Solicitor
Grant Love, Fire Chief
Beverley Hillier, Manager, Planning Services

North Perth
330 Wallace Ave. North
Listowel, ON N4W 1L3
Tel: 519-291-2950;
town@northperth.ca
www.northperth.ca
Other Information: Toll-Free Phone: 1-888-714-1993
Municipal Type: City
Incorporated: 1998; *Area:* 493.18 sq km
County or District: Perth; *Population in 2011:* 12,631
Provincial Electoral District(s): Perth-Wellington
Federal Electoral District(s): Perth-Wellington
Next Election: Oct. 2018 (4 year terms)
Note: Amalgamation of Elma Township, Town of Listowel & Wallace Township.
Julie Behrns, Mayor
Doug Kellum, Deputy Mayor & Councillor
Kenneth Buchanan, Councillor, Wards: Elma
Matt Duncan, Councillor, Wards: Elma
David Ludington, Councillor, Wards: Elma
Vince Judge, Councillor, Wards: Listowel
Matt Richardson, Councillor, Wards: Listowel
Terry Siler, Councillor, Wards: Listowel
Paul Horn, Councillor, Wards: Wallace
Meredith Schneider, Councillor, Wards: Wallace
Patricia Berfelz, Clerk, 519-292-2062
Kriss Snell, Chief Administrative Officer
Frances Hale, Treasurer & Director, Finance, 519-292-2045
Steve Hardie, Director, Parks & Recreation, 519-292-2055
Ed Podniewicz, Chief Building Official & Administrator, Zoning, 519-292-2058
Ed Smith, Fire Chief, 519-291-6825
Mark Hackett, Manager, Environmental Services, 519-292-2069

Oakville
1225 Trafalgar Rd.
Oakville, ON L6J 5A6
Tel: 905-845-6601; *Fax:* 905-815-2025
serviceoakville@oakville.ca
www.oakville.ca
Other Information: TTY: 905-338-4200
Municipal Type: City
Incorporated: May 27, 1857; *Area:* 138.56 sq km
County or District: Halton Regional Municipality; *Population in 2011:* 182,520
Provincial Electoral District(s): Halton; Oakville
Federal Electoral District(s): Oakville; Oakville North-Burlington
Next Election: Oct. 2018 (4 year terms)
Rob Burton, Mayor, 905-845-6601, Fax: 905-815-2001
Sean O'Meara, Town & Regional Councillor, Wards: 1
Ralph Robinson, Town Councillor, Wards: 1
Cathy Duddeck, Town & Regional Councillor, Wards: 2
Pam Damoff, Town Councillor, Wards: 2
Dave Gittings, Town & Regional Councillor, Wards: 3
Nick Hutchins, Town Councillor, Wards: 3
Allan Elgar, Town & Regional Councillor, Wards: 4
Roger Lapworth, Town Councillor, Wards: 4
Jeff Knoll, Town & Regional Councillor, Wards: 5
Marc Grant, Town Councillor, Wards: 5
Tom Adams, Regional Councillor, Wards: 6
Natalia Lishchyna, Town Councillor, Wards: 6
Ray Green, Chief Administrative Officer
Gord Lalonde, Treasurer & Commissioner, Corporate Services Commission
Jane Clohecy, Commissioner, Community Development
Elizabeth Bourns, Director, Human Resources

Barry Cole, Director, Transit Services
Chris Mark, Director, Parks & Open Space
Cindy Toth, Director, Environmental Policy
Brian Durdin, Fire Chief

Orangeville

87 Broadway St.
Orangeville, ON L9W 1K1
Tel: 519-941-0440; *Fax:* 519-941-9033
info@orangeville.ca
www.orangeville.ca
Other Information: Toll-Free Phone: 1-866-941-0440; TTY: 519-943-0782
Municipal Type: City
Incorporated: Dec. 22, 1863; *Area:* 15.57 sq km
County or District: Dufferin; *Population in 2011:* 27,975
Provincial Electoral District(s): Dufferin-Caledon
Federal Electoral District(s): Dufferin-Caledon
Next Election: Oct. 2018 (4 year terms)
Note: Incorporated as a town on Dec. 15, 1873.
Jeremy Williams, Mayor
Warren Maycock, Deputy Mayor & Councillor
Sylvia Bradley, Councillor
Gail Campbell, Councillor
Nick Garisto, Councillor
Don Kidd, Councillor
Scott Wilson, Councillor
Susan Greatrix, Clerk
Ed Brennan, Interim Chief Administrative Officer, 519-941-0440
Brian Parrott, Treasurer
Charles Cosgrove, Manager, Facilities & Parks
Doug Jones, Director, Public Works, 519-941-0440
Nancy Tuckett, Director, Economic Development, Planning & Innovation
Ron Morden, Fire Chief, 519-941-3083
Jennifer Gohn, Manager, Human Resources

Orillia

Administration Office
#300, 50 Andrew St. South
Orillia, ON L3V 7T5
Tel: 705-325-1311; *Fax:* 705-325-5178
info@orillia.ca
www.orillia.ca
Municipal Type: City
Incorporated: 1867; *Area:* 28.61 sq km
County or District: Simcoe; *Population in 2011:* 30,586
Provincial Electoral District(s): Simcoe North
Federal Electoral District(s): Simcoe North
Next Election: Oct. 2018 (4 year terms)
Note: Incorporated as a town in 1875 & as a city in 1969.
Steve Clarke, Mayor
Ted Edmond, Councillor, Wards: 1
Sarah Valiquette, Councillor, Wards: 1
Ralph Cipolla, Councillor, Wards: 2
Rob Kloostra, Councillor, Wards: 2
Mason Ainsworth, Councillor, Wards: 3
Jeff Clark, Councillor, Wards: 3
Pat Hehn, Councillor, Wards: 4
Tim Lauer, Councillor, Wards: 4
Gayle Jackson, City Clerk & Chief Administrative Officer, 705-329-7232
Bob Ripley, Chief Financial Officer
Lori Bolton, Director, Human Resources
George Bowa, Director, Public Works, 705-329-7246
Ray Merkley, Director, Parks, Recreation & Culture, 705-325-2045
Andrew Schell, Director, Environmental Services, 705-325-7551
Ian Sugden, Director, Development Service, 705-329-7256
Ralph Dominelli, Fire Chief, 705-325-2412
Kelly Smith, Chief Building Official, 705-325-2214
Jack Green, Manager, Transportation, 705-329-7255
Percival Thomas, Manager, Water & Wastewater Systems, 705-325-2212

Oshawa

City Hall
50 Centre St. South
Oshawa, ON L1H 3Z7
Tel: 905-436-3311; *Fax:* 905-436-5642
service@oshawa.ca
www.oshawa.ca
Other Information: Toll-Free Phone: 1-800-667-4292; TTY: 905-436-5627
Municipal Type: City
Incorporated: March 8, 1924; *Area:* 145.67 sq km
County or District: Durham Reg. Mun.; *Population in 2011:* 149,607
Provincial Electoral District(s): Whitby-Oshawa; Oshawa
Federal Electoral District(s): Durham; Oshawa
Next Election: Oct. 2018 (4 year terms)
John Henry, Mayor
John Aker, Regional & City Councillor
Dan Carter, Regional & City Councillor
Bob Chapman, Regional & City Councillor
Nancy Diamond, Regional & City Councillor
Amy England, Regional & City Councillor
John Neal, Regional & City Councillor
Nester Pidwerbecki, Regional & City Councillor
Rick Kerr, City Councillor
Doug Sanders, City Councillor
John Shields, City Councillor
Sandra Kranc, City Clerk, Fax: 905-436-5697
Jag Sharma, City Manager, 905-436-3311, Fax: 905-436-5623
Tony Tollis, Interim Treasurer & Director, Finance Services
Beverly Hendry, Commissioner, Corporate Services Department
Tom Hodgins, Commissioner, Development Services Department
Tracy Adams, Director, Corporate Communications & Marketing
Gary Carroll, Director, Engineering Services
Ron Diskey, Director, Recreation & Culture Services
Jacqueline Long, Director, Human Resource Services
Paul Ralph, Director, Planning Services
Glenn Simmonds, Director, Operations
Steve Meringer, Fire Chief

Ottawa

City Hall
110 Laurier Ave. West
Ottawa, ON K1P 1J1
Tel: 613-580-2400; *Fax:* 613-560-1380
info@ottawa.ca
www.ottawa.ca
Other Information: Toll Free Phone: 1-866-261-9799; or 311
Municipal Type: City
Incorporated: Jan. 1, 1855; *Area:* 2,778.13 sq km
Population in 2011: 883,391
Provincial Electoral District(s): Glengarry-Prescott-Russell; Nepean-Carleton; Ottawa Centre; Ottawa South; Ottawa-Vanier; Ottawa West-Nepean; Ottawa-Orléans; Carleton-Mississippi Mills
Federal Electoral District(s): Carleton; Glengarry-Prescott-Russell; Kanata-Carleton; Nepean; Orléans; Ottawa Centre; Ottawa South; Ottawa West-Nepean; Ottawa-Vanier
Next Election: Oct. 2018 (4 year terms)
Jim Watson, Mayor, 613-580-2496
Bob Monette, Councillor, 613-580-2471, Wards: 1 - Orléans
Jody Mitic, Councillor, 613-580-2472, Wards: 2 - Innes
Jan Harder, Councillor, 613-580-2473, Wards: 3 - Barrhaven
Marianne Wilkinson, Councillor, 613-580-2474, Wards: 4 - Kanata North
Eli El-Chantiry, Councillor, 613-580-2475, Wards: 5 - West Carleton-March
Shad Qadri, Councillor, 613-580-2476, Wards: 6 - Stittsville
Mark Taylor, Councillor, 613-580-2477, Wards: 7 - Bay
Rick Chiarelli, Councillor, 613-580-2478, Wards: 8 - College
Keith Egli, Councillor, 613-580-2479, Wards: 9 - Knoxdale-Merivale
Diane Deans, Councillor, 613-580-2480, Wards: 10 - Gloucester-Southgate
Tim Tierney, Councillor, 613-580-2481, Wards: 11 - Beacon Hill-Cyrville
Mathieu Fleury, Councillor, 613-580-2482, Wards: 12 - Rideau-Vanier
Tobi Nussbaum, Councillor, 613-580-2483, Wards: 13 - Rideau-Rockcliffe
Catherine McKenney, Councillor, 613-580-2484, Wards: 14 - Somerset
Jeff Leiper, Councillor, 613-580-2485, Wards: 15 - Kitchissippi
Riley Brockington, Councillor, 613-580-2486, Wards: 16 - River
David Chernushenko, Councillor, 613-580-2487, Wards: 17 - Capital
Jean Cloutier, Councillor, 613-580-2488, Wards: 18 - Alta Vista
Stephen Blais, Councillor, 613-580-2489, Wards: 19 - Cumberland
George Darouze, Councillor, 613-580-2490, Wards: 20 - Osgoode
Scott Moffatt, Councillor, 613-580-2491, Wards: 21 - Rideau-Goulbourn
Michael Qaqish, Councillor, 613-580-2751, Wards: 22 - Gloucester-South Nepean
Allan Hubley, Councillor, 613-580-2752, Wards: 23 - Kanata South
M. Rick O'Connor, City Clerk & Solicitor, 613-580-2424
Steve Kanellakos, City Manager, 613-580-2424
Marian Simulik, City Treasurer, 613-580-2424
Susan Jones, Acting Deputy City Manager, City Operations Portfolio, 613-580-2424
John Moser, Acting Deputy City Manager, Planning & Infrastructure Portfolio, 613-580-2424
Charles Duffett, Director & Chief Information Officer, Information Technology, 613-580-2424
Marianne Phillips, Director, Human Resources, 613-580-2424
Aaron Burry, General Manager, Community & Social Services, 613-580-2424
Dan Chenier, General Manager, Parks, Recreation & Cultural Services, 613-580-2424
John Manconi, General Manager, Transit Services, 613-842-3636
Michael Mizzi, Acting General Manager, Planning & Growth Management, 613-580-2424
Wayne Newell, General Manager, Infrastructure Services, 613-580-2424
Dixon A. Weir, General Manager, Environmental Services, 613-580-2424
Kevin Wylie, General Manager, Public Works, 613-580-2424
Isra Levy, Medical Officer of Health, 613-580-6744
Lisa Allaire, Chief, Corporate Communications, 613-580-2424
Michel Chevalier, Manager, Wastewater Services, 613-580-2424
Marilyn Journeaux, Manager, Solid Waste Systems, 613-580-2424
John Kukalis, Manager, Surface Water Management Services Branch, 613-580-2424
Shelley McDonald, Manager, Environmental Engineering, 613-580-2424
Sally McIntyre, Manager, Environmental Business Services, 613-580-2424
Tammy Rose, Manager, Drinking Water Services, 613-580-2424

Owen Sound

City Hall
808 - 2nd Ave. East
Owen Sound, ON N4K 2H4
Tel: 519-376-1440;
cityadmin@owensound.ca
www.owensound.ca
Municipal Type: City
Incorporated: Jan. 1, 2001; *Area:* 24.22 sq km
County or District: Grey; *Population in 2011:* 21,688
Provincial Electoral District(s): Bruce-Grey-Owen Sound
Federal Electoral District(s): Bruce-Grey-Owen Sound
Next Election: Oct. 2018 (4 year terms)
Ian Boddy, Mayor
Arlene Wright, Deputy Mayor
Travis Dodd, Councillor
Scott Greig, Councillor
Marion Koepke, Councillor
Peter Lemon, Councillor
Jim McManaman, Councillor
Brian O'Leary, Councillor
Richard Thomas, Councillor
Kristen Van Alphen, City Clerk, 519-376-4440
Wayne Ritchie, City Manager, 519-376-4440
Pam Coulter, Director, Community Services, Community Services, 519-376-4440
Doug Barfoot, Fire Chief, 519-376-2512
Steve Furness, Manager, Economic Development

Pelham

P.O. Box 400
20 Pelham Town Sq.
Fonthill, ON L0S 1E0
Tel: 905-892-2607;
www.pelham.ca
Municipal Type: City
Incorporated: 1970; *Area:* 126.42 sq km
County or District: Niagara Reg. Mun.; *Population in 2011:* 16,598
Provincial Electoral District(s): Niagara West-Glanbrook
Federal Electoral District(s): Niagara West
Next Election: Oct. 2018 (4 year terms)
Dave Augustyn, Mayor
Marvin Junkin, Councillor, Wards: 1
Richard Rybiak, Councillor, Wards: 1
Gary Accursi, Councillor, Wards: 2
Catherine King, Councillor, Wards: 2
John Durley, Councillor, Wards: 3
Peter Papp, Councillor, Wards: 3
Brian Baty, Regional Councillor, Councillor
Nancy J. Bozzato, Clerk & Secretary-Treasurer
Darren Ottaway, Chief Administrative Officer, 905-892-2607
Cari Pupo, Treasurer
Barb Wiens, Director, Planning & Development, 905-892-2607
Andrea Clemencio, Director, Public Works, 905-892-2607
Bob Lymburner, Fire Chief, 905-892-2607

Pembroke

1 Pembroke St. East
Pembroke, ON K8A 3J5
Tel: 613-735-6821; *Fax:* 613-735-3660
pembroke@pembroke.ca
www.pembroke.ca
Municipal Type: City
Incorporated: 1877; *Area:* 14.35 sq km

County or District: Renfrew; *Population in 2011:* 14,360
Provincial Electoral District(s): Renfrew-Nipissing-Pembroke
Federal Electoral District(s): Renfrew-Nipissing-Pembroke
Next Election: Oct. 2018 (4 year terms)
Note: Incorporated as a city in 1971.
Mike LeMay, Mayor
Ronald Gervais, Councillor, Councillor
Patricia Lafreniere, Councillor
John McCann, Councillor
Andrew Plummer, Councillor
Christine Reavie, Councillor
Les Scott, Councillor
Terry Lapierre, Chief Administrative Officer, 613-735-6821
LeeAnn McIntyre, Treasurer
Susan Ellis, Manager, Economic Development, Recreation, & Tourism
Douglas Sitland, Manager, Operations
Daniel Herback, Fire Chief

Petawawa
1111 Victoria St.
Petawawa, ON K8H 2E6
Tel: 613-687-5536; *Fax:* 613-687-5973
www.petawawa.ca
Municipal Type: City
Incorporated: July 1, 1997; *Area:* 164.68 sq km
County or District: Renfrew; *Population in 2011:* 15,988
Provincial Electoral District(s): Renfrew-Nipissing-Pembroke
Federal Electoral District(s): Renfrew-Nipissing-Pembroke
Next Election: Oct. 2018 (4 year terms)
Note: Amalgamation of Petawawa Village & Petawawa Township.
Robert Sweet, Mayor
James Carmody, Councillor
Treena Lemay, Councillor
Tom Mohns, Councillor
Murray Rutz, Councillor
Theresa Sabourin, Councillor
Gary Serviss, Councillor
Daniel Scissons, Chief Administrative Officer & Clerk
Annette Mantifel, Treasurer
Randy Mohns, Chief Building Official
Steve Knott, Fire Chief
Tom Renaud, Supervisor, Public Works
Karen Cronier, Coordinator, Planning
Cyndy Phillips McCann, Coordinator, Economic Development

Peterborough
500 George St. North
Peterborough, ON K9H 3R9
Tel: 705-742-7777; *Fax:* 705-742-4138
cityptbo@peterborough.ca
www.peterborough.ca
Other Information: E-mail, Human Resources: hr@peterborough.ca
Municipal Type: City
Incorporated: 1850; *Area:* 58.40 sq km
County or District: Peterborough; *Population in 2011:* 78,698
Provincial Electoral District(s): Peterborough
Federal Electoral District(s): Northumberland-Peterborough South; Peterborough-Kawartha
Next Election: Oct. 2018 (4 year terms)
Daryl Bennett, Mayor
Dan McWilliams, Councillor, Wards: 1 - Otonabee
Lesley Parnell, Councillor, Wards: 1 - Otonabee
Henry Clarke, Councillor, Wards: 2 - Monaghan
Don Vassiliadis, Councillor, Wards: 2 - Monaghan
Dean Pappas, Councillor, Wards: 3 - Town
Diane Therrien, Councillor, Wards: 3 - Town
Gary Baldwin, Councillor, Wards: 4 - Ashburnham
Keith G. Riel, Councillor, Wards: 4 - Ashburnham
Andrew Beamer, Councillor, Wards: 5 - Northcrest
Dave Haacke, Councillor, Wards: 5 - Northcrest
John Kennedy, City Clerk
Sandra Clancy, Treasurer / Director, Corporate Services
Ken Doherty, Director, Community Services
Malcolm Hunt, Director, Planning & Development Services
Wayne Jackson, Director, Utility Services & Deputy CAO
Chris Snetsinger, Fire Chief

Pickering
1 The Esplanade
Pickering, ON L1V 6K7
Tel: 905-420-2222;
www.cityofpickering.com
Other Information: Toll-Free Phone: 1-866-683-2760; TTY: 905-420-1739
Municipal Type: City
Incorporated: 1849; *Area:* 231.59 sq km
County or District: Durham Reg. Mun.; *Population in 2011:* 88,721
Provincial Electoral District(s): Ajax-Pickering; Pickering-Scarborough East
Federal Electoral District(s): Ajax; Pickering-Uxbridge
Next Election: Oct. 2018 (4 year terms)
Note: Incorporated as a town in 1974 & as a city in 2000.
Dave Ryan, Mayor, 905-420-4600, Fax: 905-420-6064
Jennifer O'Connell, Regional Councillor, Wards: 1
Kevin Ashe, City Councillor, Wards: 1
Bill McLean, Regional Councillor, Wards: 2
Ian Cumming, City Councillor, Wards: 2
David Pickles, Regional Councillor, Wards: 3
Rick Johnson, City Councillor, Wards: 3
Debbie Shields, City Clerk, 905-420-4660
Tony Prevedel, Chief Administrative Officer, 905-420-4648
Paul Bigioni, City Solicitor & Director, Corporate Services, 905-420-4660
Marisa Carpino, Director, Culture & Recreation, 905-420-4660
Richard W. Holborn, Director, Engineering & Public Works, 905-420-4660
Thomas E. Melymuk, Director, City Development, 902-420-4660
Jennifer Eddy, Division Head, Human Resources, 905-420-4660
Kyle Bentley, Chief Building Official, 905-420-4660
Catherine Rose, Chief Planner, 905-420-4660
John Hagg, Fire Chief, 905-420-4660

Port Colborne
66 Charlotte St.
Port Colborne, ON L3K 3C8
Tel: 905-835-2900; *Fax:* 905-834-5746
www.portcolborne.ca
Municipal Type: City
Incorporated: 1870; *Area:* 121.97 sq km
County or District: Niagara Reg. Mun.; *Population in 2011:* 18,424
Provincial Electoral District(s): Welland
Federal Electoral District(s): Niagara Centre
Next Election: Oct. 2018 (4 year terms)
Note: Incorporated as a town in 1918 & as a city in 1966.
John Maloney, Mayor
David Barrick, Regional Councillor
David B. Elliott, Councillor, Wards: 1
John Mayne, Councillor, Wards: 1
Angie Desmarais, Councillor, Wards: 2
Yvon A. Doucet, Councillor, Wards: 2
Frank M. Danch, Councillor, Wards: 3
Bea Kenny, Councillor, Wards: 3
Ron Bodner, Councillor, Wards: 4
Barbara Butters, Councillor, Wards: 4
Ashley Grigg, City Clerk
Scott Luey, Chief Administrative Officer, 905-835-2900
Dan Aquilina, Director, Planning & Development, 905-835-2900
Ron Hanson, Director, Engineering & Operations, 905-835-2900
Peter Senese, Director, Community & Corporate Services
Thomas Cartwright, Fire Chief, 905-834-4512
Lyle Merritt, Chief Building Official, 905-835-2900
Darlene Suddard, Supervisor, Environmental Compliance, 905-835-5079
Carrie Stone, Coordinator, Human Resources
Evan Acs, Economic Development Officer

Quinte West
P.O. Box 490
7 Creswell Dr.
Trenton, ON K8V 5R6
Tel: 613-392-2841; *Fax:* 613-392-5608
www.city.quintewest.on.ca
Other Information: Toll-Free Phone: 1-866-485-2841
Municipal Type: City
Incorporated: Jan. 1, 1998; *Area:* 493.85 sq km
County or District: Hastings; *Population in 2011:* 43,086
Provincial Electoral District(s): Northumberland-Quinte West
Federal Electoral District(s): Bay of Quinte
Next Election: Oct. 2018 (4 year terms)
Note: Amalgamation of the former municipalities of Trenton, Sidney, Murray & Frankford.
Jim Harrison, Mayor
Duncan Armstrong, Councillor, Wards: 1 - Trenton
Sally Freeman, Councillor, 613-965-6769, Wards: 1 - Trenton
Michael Kotsovos, Councillor, Wards: 1 - Trenton
Fred Kuypers, Councillor, 613-392-8588, Wards: 1 - Trenton
Douglas Whitney, Councillor, Wards: 1 - Trenton
Allan DeWitt, Councillor, Wards: 2 - Sidney
Don Kuntze, Councillor, 613-962-6122, Wards: 2 - Sidney
Rob MacIntosh, Councillor, Wards: 2 - Sidney
Karen Sharpe, Councillor, Wards: 2 - Sidney
Jim Alyea, Councillor, 613-475-1519, Wards: 3 - Murray
David McCue, Councillor, Wards: 3 - Murray
Keith Reid, Councillor, 613-398-7991, Wards: 4 - Frankford
Kevin Heath, Clerk & Manager, Corporate Services
Charlie Murphy, Chief Administrative Officer
David Clazie, Treasurer & Director, Corporate & Financial Services
Chris Angelo, Director, Public Works & Environmental Services
Brian Jardine, Director, Planning & Development Services
Phillip Lappan, Chief Building Official
John Whelan, Fire Chief
Tim Colasante, Manager, Engineering Services
Matt Tracey, Manager, Water & Wastewater

Richmond Hill
225 East Beaver Creek Rd.
Richmond Hill, ON L4B 3P4
Tel: 905-771-8800; *Fax:* 905-771-2500
www.richmondhill.ca
Municipal Type: City
Incorporated: 1873; *Area:* 100.89 sq km
County or District: York Reg. Mun.; *Population in 2011:* 185,541
Provincial Electoral District(s): Richmond Hill; Oak Ridges-Markham
Federal Electoral District(s): Aurora-Oak Ridges-Richmond Hill; Richmond Hill
Next Election: Oct. 2018 (4 year terms)
Dave Barrow, Mayor
Brenda Hogg, Regional & Local Councillor
Vito Spatafora, Regional & Local Councillor
Greg Beros, Councillor, Wards: 1
Tom Muench, Councillor, Wards: 2
Castro Liu, Councillor, Wards: 3
David West, Councillor, Wards: 4
Karen Cilevitz, Councillor, Wards: 5
Godwin Chan, Councillor, Wards: 6
Donna McLarty, Town Clerk
Neil Garbe, Chief Administrative Officer
David Dexter, Treasurer & Director, Financial Services, 905-771-8800
Ana Bassios, Commissioner, Planning & Regulatory Services
Italo Brutto, Commissioner, Environment & Infrastructure Services
Dean Miller, Commissioner, Corporate & Financial Services, 905-771-2497
Darlene Joslin, Director, Recreation & Culture
Patrick Lee, Director, Policy Planning

St. Catharines
City Hall
P.O. Box 3012
50 Church St.
St Catharines, ON L2R 7C2
Tel: 905-688-5600; *Fax:* 905-682-3631
info@stcatharines.ca
www.stcatharines.ca
Other Information: TTY: 905-688-4889
Municipal Type: City
Incorporated: 1876; *Area:* 96.11 sq km
County or District: Niagara Reg. Mun.; *Population in 2011:* 131,400
Provincial Electoral District(s): St. Catharines; Welland
Federal Electoral District(s): Niagara Centre; Niagara West; St. Catharines
Next Election: Oct. 2018 (4 year terms)
Walter Sendzik, Mayor
David Haywood, Councillor, Wards: 1 - Merritton
Jennifer Stevens, Councillor, Wards: 1 - Merritton
Matthew J. Harris, Councillor, Wards: 2 - St. Andrew's
Joseph Kushner, Councillor, Wards: 2 - St. Andrew's
Mike Britton, Councillor, Wards: 3 - St. Georges
Sal Sorrento, Councillor, Wards: 3 - St. Georges
Mark Elliott, Councillor, Wards: 4 - St. Patricks
Mathew D. Siscoe, Councillor, Wards: 4 - St. Patricks
Sandie Bellows, Councillor, Wards: 5 - Grantham
Bill Phillips, Councillor, Wards: 5 - Grantham
Carlos Garcia, Councillor, Wards: 6 - Port Dalhousie
Bruce Williamson, Councillor, Wards: 6 - Port Dalhousie
Alan Caslin, Regional Councillor
Brian Heit, Regional Councillor
Debbie MacGregor, Regional Councillor
Andrew (Andy) Petrowski, Regional Councillor
Tim Rigby, Regional Councillor
Bruce Timms, Regional Councillor
Bonnie Nistico-Dunk, City Clerk
Dan Carnegie, Chief Administrative Officer
Dan Dillon, P. Eng., Director, Transportation & Environmental Services
Kristine Douglas, Director, Financial Management Services
Jim Riddell, Director, Planning & Building Services
Dave Wood, Fire Chief
Nicole Auty, City Solicitor

St. Thomas
City Hall
P.O. Box 520
545 Talbot St.
St Thomas, ON N5P 3V7
Tel: 519-631-1680;
stthomas.ca
Other Information: TTY: 519-631-3836
Municipal Type: City
Incorporated: March 4, 1881; *Area:* 35.48 sq km
County or District: Elgin; *Population in 2011:* 37,905
Provincial Electoral District(s): Elgin-Middlesex-London
Federal Electoral District(s): Elgin-Middlesex-London
Next Election: Oct. 2018 (4 year terms)
Heather Jackson, Mayor
Mark Burgess, Alderman
Gary Clarke, Alderman
Jeff Kohler, Alderman
Joan Rymal, Alderman
Linda Stevenson, Alderman
Mark Tinlin, Alderman
Steve Wookey, Alderman
Wendell Graves, CAO & City Clerk, 519-631-1680
David Aristone, City Treasurer
Graham Dart, Director, Human Resources
Justin Lawrence, City Engineer & Director, Environmental Services, 529-631-1680
Patrick Keenan, Director, Planning & Building Services, 519-633-2560
Ross Tucker, Director, Parks & Recreation, 519-633-7112
Rob Broadbent, Fire Chief
Nathan Bokma, Manager, Development & Compliance, 519-631-1680

Sarnia
City Hall
P.O. Box 3018
255 North Christina St.
Sarnia, ON N7T 7N2
Tel: 519-332-0330;
www.sarnia.ca
Other Information: TTY: 519-332-2664
Municipal Type: City
Incorporated: May 7, 1914; *Area:* 164.63 sq km
County or District: Lambton; *Population in 2011:* 72,366
Provincial Electoral District(s): Sarnia-Lambton
Federal Electoral District(s): Sarnia-Lambton
Next Election: Oct. 2018 (4 year terms)
Mike Bradley, Mayor
Dave Boushy, City / County Councillor
Andy Bruziewicz, City / County Councillor
Anne Marie Gillis, City / County Councillor
Bev MacDougall, City / County Councillor
Mike Kelch, City Councillor
Matt Mitro, City Councillor
Cindy Scholten, City Councillor
Brian White, City Councillor
Nancy Wright-Laking, City Clerk
Margaret Misek-Evans, City Manager, 519-332-0330
Brian McKay, Director, Finance
Beth Gignac, Director, Parks & Recreation, 519-332-0330
Jim Stevens, Director, Transit, 519-332-0330
Al Shaw, Acting Director, Planning & Building, 519-332-0330
John Kingyens, Fire Chief, 519-332-0330
Andre Morin, City Engineer, 519-332-0330
Chris Armstrong, Manager, Human Resources
Peter Hungerford, Manager, Economic Development & Corporate Planning

Saugeen Shores
P.O. Box 820
600 Tomlinson Dr.
Port Elgin, ON N0H 2C0
Tel: 519-832-2008; *Fax:* 519-832-2140
www.saugeenshores.ca
Municipal Type: City
Area: 170.58 sq km
County or District: Bruce; *Population in 2011:* 12,661
Provincial Electoral District(s): Huron-Bruce
Federal Electoral District(s): Huron-Bruce
Next Election: Oct. 2018 (4 year terms)
Mike Smith, Mayor
Diane Huber, Vice Deputy Mayor & Councillor
Neil Menage, Wards: Port Elgin
John Rich, Councillor, Wards: Port Elgin
Mike Myatt, Councillor, Wards: Saugeen
Dave Myette, Councillor, Wards: Saugeen
Cheryl Grace, Councillor, Wards: Southampton
Don Matheson, Councillor, Wards: Southampton
Linda White, Clerk, 519-832-2008
Larry Allison, Chief Administrative Officer, 519-832-2008
Kate Allan, Director, Finance, 519-832-2008
Adam Stanley, Director, Engineering Services, 519-832-2008
Len Purdue, Acting Director, Public Works, 519-832-2008
Jayne Jagelewski, Director, Community Services, 519-832-2008
Phil Eagleson, Fire Chief, 519-389-6120
Bart Toby, Chief Building Official & Manager, Development Services, 519-832-2008
Lynn Worsley, Officer, Human Resources, 519-832-2008

Sault Ste. Marie
Civic Centre
P.O. Box 580
99 Foster Dr.
Sault Ste Marie, ON P6A 5N1
Tel: 705-759-2500; *Fax:* 705-759-2310
info@cityssm.on.ca
www.cityssm.on.ca
Other Information: TTY: 877-688-5528
Municipal Type: City
Incorporated: 1912; *Area:* 221.71 sq km
County or District: Algoma District; *Population in 2011:* 75,141
Provincial Electoral District(s): Sault Ste. Marie
Federal Electoral District(s): Sault Ste. Marie
Next Election: Oct. 2018 (4 year terms)
Christian Provenzano, Mayor
Steve Butland, Councillor, Wards: 1
Paul Christian, Councillor, Wards: 1
Susan Myers, Councillor, Wards: 2
Terry Sheehan, Councillor, Wards: 2
Judy Hupponen, Councillor, Wards: 3
Matthew Shoemaker, Councillor, Wards: 3
Rick Niro, Councillor, Wards: 4
Lou Turco, Councillor, Wards: 4
Marchy Bruni, Councillor, Wards: 5
Frank Fata, Councillor, Wards: 5
Joe Krmpotich, Councillor, Wards: 6
Ross Romano, Councillor, Wards: 6
Malcolm White, City Clerk, 705-759-5388
Al Horsman, Chief Administrative Officer, 705-759-5347
William Freiburger, Treasurer & Commissioner, Finance, 705-759-5349
Nicholas J. Apostle, Commissioner, Community Services, 705-759-5310
Jerry Dolcetti, Commissioner, Engineering & Planning, 705-759-5384
Larry Girardi, Commissioner, Public Works & Transportation, 705-759-5206
Mike Nadeau, Commissioner, Social Services
Peter Niro, Commissioner, Human Resources
Nuala Kenny, City Solicitor
Mike Figliola, Fire Chief, 705-759-5273

Stratford
City Hall
P.O. Box 818
1 Wellington St.
Stratford, ON N5A 6W1
Tel: 519-271-0250; *Fax:* 519-273-5041
www.stratfordcanada.ca
Other Information: TTY: 519-271-5241
Municipal Type: City
Incorporated: 1854; *Area:* 25.28 sq km
County or District: Perth; *Population in 2011:* 30,886
Provincial Electoral District(s): Perth-Wellington
Federal Electoral District(s): Perth-Wellington
Next Election: Oct. 2018 (4 year terms)
Note: Incorporated as a city in 1886.
Daniel Mathieson, Mayor
Brad Beatty, Councillor
George Brown, Councillor
Graham Bunting, Councillor
Tom Clifford, Councillor
Bonnie Henderson, Councillor
Danielle Ingram, Councillor
Frank Mark, Councillor
Kerry McManus, Councillor
Martin Ritsma, Councillor
Kathy Vassilakos, Councillor
Joan Thomson, Clerk, 519-271-0250
Andre Morin, Chief Administrative Officer, 519-271-0250
Ed Dujlovic, Director, Infrastructure & Development Services, 519-271-0250
David St. Louis, Director, Community Services
Bill Tigert, Director, Social Services
David Carroll, Chief Building Official, 519-271-0250
John Paradis, Fire Chief
Jeff Bannon, City Planner, 519-271-0250
Jennifer Barnell-Wise, Clerk, Economic Development, 519-271-0250

Tecumseh
917 Lesperance Rd.
Tecumseh, ON N8N 1W9
Tel: 519-735-2184; *Fax:* 519-735-6712
www.tecumseh.ca
Municipal Type: City
Incorporated: 1921; *Area:* 94.71 sq km
County or District: Essex; *Population in 2011:* 23,610
Provincial Electoral District(s): Windsor-Tecumseh
Federal Electoral District(s): Windsor-Tecumseh
Next Election: Oct. 2018 (4 year terms)
Note: Restructuring occurred in 1999.
Gary McNamara, Mayor
Joe Bachetti, Deputy Mayor & Councillor
Andrew Dowie, Councillor, Wards: 1
Rita Ossington, Councillor, 519-735-8251, Wards: 1
Mike Rohrer, Councillor, Wards: 2
Brian Houston, Councillor, Wards: 3
Tania C. Jobin, Councillor, 519-791-4213, Wards: 4
Laura Moy, Clerk & Director, Staff Services
Tony Haddad, Chief Administrative Officer, 519-735-2184
Luc Gagnon, Treasurer & Director, Financial Services
Paul Anthony, Director, Parks & Recreation, 519-735-4756
Shaun Fuerth, Director, Information Systems
Brian Hillman, Director, Planning & Building Services, 519-735-2184
Dan Piescic, Director, Public Works & Environmental Services, 519-735-2184
Doug Pitre, Fire Chief, 519-979-4941
Phil Bartnik, Manager, Engineering Services, 519-735-2184
Denis Berthiume, Manager, Water & Wastewater, 519-735-2184
Kerri Rice, Manager, Recreation Programs & Events

Temiskaming Shores
Temiskaming Shores Administration Office
P.O. Box 2050
325 Farr Ave.
Haileybury, ON P0J 1K0
Tel: 705-672-3363; *Fax:* 705-672-2911
www.temiskamingshores.ca
Municipal Type: City
Incorporated: Jan. 1, 2004; *Area:* 177 sq km
County or District: Timiskaming District; *Population in 2011:* 10,400
Provincial Electoral District(s): Timiskaming-Cochrane
Federal Electoral District(s): Nipissing-Timiskaming
Next Election: Oct. 2018 (4 year terms)
Note: Amalgamation of the Town of Haileybury, the Town of New Liskeard & the Township of Dymond.
Carman Kidd, Mayor
Jesse Foley, Councillor
Patricia Hewitt, Councillor
Doug Jelly, Councillor
Jeff Laferriere, Councillor
Mike McArthur, Councillor
Danny Whalen, Councillor
David Treen, Clerk
Christopher W. Oslund, City Manager
Laura Lee McLeod, Treasurer
Tammie Caldwell, Director, Recreation
Doug Walsh, Director, Public Works
Tim Uttley, Fire Chief
Paul Allair, Superintendent, Parks & Facilities
Robert Beaudoin, Superintendent, Environmental Services
James Sheppard, Superintendent, Transportation Services

Thorold
Thorold City Hall
P.O. Box 1044
3540 Schmon Pkwy.
Thorold, ON L2V 4A7
Tel: 905-227-6613; *Fax:* 905-227-5590
secr@thorold.com (Administrative Assistant)
www.thorold.com
Other Information: E-mail, Deputy City Clerk: depclerk@thorold.com
Municipal Type: City
Incorporated: 1798; *Area:* 83 sq km
County or District: Niagara Reg. Mun.; *Population in 2011:* 17,931
Provincial Electoral District(s): Welland
Federal Electoral District(s): Niagara Centre
Next Election: Oct. 2018 (4 year terms)
Note: Incorporated as a village in 1850, as a town in 1875, as a new town (amalgamating the Township of Thorold & the Town of Thorold) in 1970, & as a city in 1975.
Ted Luciani, Mayor
Henry D'Angela, Regional Councillor
Michael Charron, Councillor
David (Jim) Handley, Councillor
Anthony Longo, Councillor

Fred Neale, Councillor
Sergio Paone, Councillor
Tim Whalen, Councillor
Shawn Wilson, Councillor
Terry Ugulini, Councillor
Susan M. Daniels, AMCT, City Clerk
Frank A. Fabiano, Chief Administrative Officer
Adele Arbour, Director, Planning & Building Services
Maria J. Mauro, Director, Finance
Mike Sauchuk, Director, Operations, Parks & Recreation, 905-227-3535
Martin Wild, Chief Building Official
Dave Akrigg, Manager, Parks, Cemetery & Arena Operations, 905-227-1911

Thunder Bay
City Hall
P.O. Box 800
500 Donald St. East
Thunder Bay, ON P7C 5K4
Tel: 807-625-2230; *Fax:* 807-623-5468
www.thunderbay.ca
Other Information: TTY: 807-622-2225
Municipal Type: City
Incorporated: Jan 1, 1970; *Area:* 328.48 sq km
County or District: Thunder Bay District; *Population in 2011:* 108,359
Provincial Electoral District(s): Thunder Bay-Superior North; Thunder Bay-Atikokan
Federal Electoral District(s): Thunder Bay-Rainy River; Thunder Bay-Superior North
Next Election: Oct. 2018 (4 year terms)
Keith Hobbs, Mayor, 807-625-3600, Fax: 807-623-1164
Iain Angus, Councillor at Large
Larry Hebert, Councillor at Large
Rebecca Johnson, Councillor at Large
Aldo. V. Ruberto, Councillor at Large
Frank Pullia, Councillor at Large
Andrew Foulds, Councillor, Wards: Current River
Trevor Giertuga, Councillor, Wards: McIntyre
Paul Pugh, Councillor, Wards: McKellar
Linda Rydholm, Councillor, Wards: Neebing
Shelby Ch'ng, Councillor, Wards: Northwood
Brian McKinnon, Councillor, Wards: Red River
Joe Virdiramo, Councillor, Wards: Westfort
John S. Hannam, City Clerk, 807-623-2238, Fax: 807-623-5468
Norm Gale, City Manager
Carol Busch, C.G.A., Treasurer & General Manager, Corporate Services & Long Term Care, 807-625-2242
Nadia Koltun, City Solicitor, 807-625-2405, Fax: 807-623-2256
Mark Smith, General Manager, Community Services & Development & Emergency Services, 807-684-3119, Fax: 807-623-3258
Karen Lewis, Director, Corporate Strategic Services, 807-625-3859, Fax: 807-625-0181
John Hay, Fire Chief, 807-625-2101
Bernie Edwards, Manager, Energy & Support Services, 807-684-2409
Brad Loroff, Manager, Transit Services, 807-684-2187
Kerri Marshall, Manager, Infrastructure & Operations, 807-625-2836, Fax: 807-625-3588

Tillsonburg
Customer Service Centre
10 Lisgar Ave.
Tillsonburg, ON N4G 5A5
Tel: 519-842-9200; *Fax:* 519-688-0759
www.tillsonburg.ca
Municipal Type: City
Incorporated: 1872; *Area:* 22.34 sq km
County or District: Oxford; *Population in 2011:* 15,301
Provincial Electoral District(s): Oxford
Federal Electoral District(s): Oxford
Next Election: Oct. 2018 (4 year terms)
Stephen Molnar, Mayor
Dave Beres, Deputy Mayor & Councillor
Macwell (Max) Adam, Councillor
Penny Esseltine, Councillor
Jim Hayes, Councillor
Chris (Chrissy) Rosehart, Councillor
Brian Stephenson, Councillor
Donna Wilson, Clerk
David Calder, Chief Administrative Officer
Darrell Eddington, Director, Finance
Steve Lund, Director, Operations
Kelly Batt, Manager, Parks & Facilities
Peter Fung, Manager, Engineering
Geno Vanhaelewyn, Chief Building Official
Randy White, Deputy Fire Chief

Timmins
220 Algonquin Blvd. East
Timmins, ON P4N 1B3
Tel: 705-264-1331; *Fax:* 705-360-2674
www.timmins.ca
Municipal Type: City
Incorporated: 1973; *Area:* 2,961.58 sq km
County or District: Cochrane District; *Population in 2011:* 43,165
Provincial Electoral District(s): Timmins-James Bay
Federal Electoral District(s): Timmins-James Bay
Next Election: Oct. 2018 (4 year terms)
Steve Black, Mayor
Andre Grzela, Councillor, Wards: 1
Walter Wawrzaszek, Councillor, Wards: 2
Joe Campbell, Councillor, Wards: 3
Pat Bamford, Councillor, Wards: 4
Michael J.J. Doody, Councillor, Wards: 5
Rick Dubeau, Councillor, Wards: 5
Andrew Marks, Councillor, Wards: 5
Noella Rinaldo, Councillor, Wards: 5
Steph Palmateer, City Clerk
Joe Torlone, Chief Administrative Officer
Bernie Christian, City Treasurer
Luc Duval, Director, Public Works & Engineering
David Laneville, Director, Information Technology
Mike Pintar, Fire Chief

Toronto
City Hall
100 Queen St. West
Toronto, ON M5H 2N2
Tel: 416-392-2489; *Fax:* 416-338-0685
311@toronto.ca
www.toronto.ca
Other Information: In Toronto: 311; TTY: 416-338-0889
Municipal Type: City
Incorporated: March 6, 1834; *Area:* 630.18 sq km
Population in 2011: 2,615,060
Provincial Electoral District(s): Beaches-East York; To.-Danforth; Davenport; Don V. East; Don V. West; Eglinton-Lawrence; Etob. Centre; Etob.-Lakeshore; Etob. North; Parkdale-High Park; St. Paul's; Scarb.-Agincourt; Scarb. Centre; Scarb. Southwest; Scarb.-Guildwood; Scarb.-Rouge River; To. Centre; Trinity-Spadina; Willowdale; York Centre; York South-Weston; York West
Federal Electoral District(s): Beaches-East York; Davenport; Don V. W.; Don.V.N.; Eglinton-Lawrence; Etob. Centre; Etob. N.; Etob.-Lakeshore; Humber River-Black Creek; Parkdale-High Park; Scarb. Ctr.; Scarb.N.; Scarb. SW.; Scarb.-Agincourt; Scarb.-Guildwood; Scarb.-Rouge Park; Spadina-Ft. York; Tor. Ctr.; Tor.-Danforth; To.-St.Paul's; University-Rosedale; Willowdale, York Ctr.; York S.-Weston
Next Election: Oct. 2018 (4 year terms)
Note: Incorporated as a city on Jan. 1, 1998, & comprising the 6 former municipalities of: Etobicoke; North York; York; East York; Scarborough; & Old Toronto
John Tory, Mayor
Denzil Minnan-Wong, Deputy Mayor, Councillor, 416-397-9256, Fax: 416-397-4100, Wards: 34 - Don Valley East
Vincent Crisanti, Regional Deputy Mayor, West, Councillor, 416-392-0205, Fax: 416-696-4207, Wards: 1 - Etobicoke North
Glenn De Baeremaeker, Regional Deputy Mayor, East, Councillor, 416-392-0204, Fax: 416-392-7428, Wards: 38 - Scarborough Centre
Pam McConnell, Regional Deputy Mayor, South, Councillor, 416-392-7916, Fax: 416-392-7296, Wards: 28 - Toronto Centre-Rosedale
Michael Ford, Councillor, 416-397-9255, Fax: 416-397-9238, Wards: 2 - Etobicoke North
Stephen Holyday, Councillor, 416-392-4002, Wards: 3 - Etobicoke Centre
John Campbell, Councillor, 416-392-1369, Wards: 4 - Etobicoke Centre
Justin Di Ciano, Councillor, 416-392-4040, Wards: 5 - Etobicoke-Lakeshore
Mark Grimes, Councillor, 416-397-9273, Fax: 416-397-9279, Wards: 6 - Etobicoke-Lakeshore
Giorgio Mammoliti, Councillor, 416-395-6401, Fax: 416-397-9282, Wards: 7 - York West
Anthony Perruzza, Councillor, 416-338-5335, Fax: 416-696-4144, Wards: 8 - York West
Maria Augimeri, Councillor, 416-392-4021, Fax: 416-392-7109, Wards: 9 - York Centre
James Pasternak, Councillor, 416-392-1371, Fax: 416-392-7299, Wards: 10 - York Centre
Frances Nunziata, Councillor, 416-392-4091, Fax: 416-392-4118, Wards: 11 - York South-Weston
Frank Di Giorgio, Councillor, 416-392-4066, Fax: 416-392-1675, Wards: 12 - York South-Weston
Sarah Doucette, Councillor, 416-392-4072, Fax: 416-696-3667, Wards: 13 - Parkdale-High Park
Gord Perks, Councillor, 416-392-7919, Fax: 416-392-0398, Wards: 14 - Parkdale-High Park
Josh Colle, Councillor, 416-392-4027, Fax: 416-392-4191, Wards: 15 - Eglinton-Lawrence
Christin Carmichael Greb, Councillor, 416-392-4090, Fax: 416-392-4129, Wards: 16 - Eglinton-Lawrence
Cesar Palacio, Councillor, 416-392-7011, Fax: 416-392-0212, Wards: 17 - Davenport
Ana Bailao, Councillor, 416-392-7012, Fax: 416-392-7957, Wards: 18 - Davenport
Mike Layton, Councillor, 416-392-4009, Fax: 416-392-4100, Wards: 19 - Trinity-Spadina
Joe Cressy, Councillor, 416-392-4044, Wards: 20 - Trinity-Spadina
Joe Mihevc, Councillor, 416-392-0208, Fax: 416-392-7466, Wards: 21 - St. Paul's
Josh Matlow, Councillor, 416-392-7906, Fax: 416-392-0124, Wards: 22 - St. Paul's
John Filion, Councillor, 416-392-0210, Fax: 416-392-7388, Wards: 23 - Willowdale
David Shiner, Councillor, 416-395-6413, Fax: 416-397-9290, Wards: 24 - Willowdale
Jaye Robinson, Councillor, 416-395-6408, Fax: 416-395-6439, Wards: 25 - Don Valley West
John Burnside, Councillor, 416-392-0215, Wards: 26 - Don Valley West
Kristyn Wong-Tam, Councillor, 416-392-7903, Fax: 416-696-4300, Wards: 27 - Toronto Centre-Rosedale
Mary Fragedakis, Councillor, 416-392-4032, Fax: 416-392-4123, Wards: 29 - Toronto-Danforth
Paula Fletcher, Councillor, 416-392-4060, Fax: 416-397-5200, Wards: 30 - Toronto-Danforth
Janet Davis, Councillor, 416-392-4035, Fax: 416-397-9289, Wards: 31 - Beaches-East York
Mary-Margaret McMahon, Councillor, 416-392-1376, Fax: 416-392-7444, Wards: 32 - Beaches-East York
Shelley Carroll, Councillor, 416-392-4038, Fax: 416-392-4101, Wards: 33 - Don Valley East
Michelle Holland, Councillor, 416-392-0213, Fax: 416-392-7394, Wards: 35 - Scarborough Southwest
Gary Crawford, Councillor, 416-392-4052, Wards: 36 - Scarborough Southwest
Michael Thompson, Councillor, 416-397-9274, Fax: 416-397-9280, Wards: 37 - Scarborough Centre
Jim Karygiannis, Councillor, 416-392-1374, Fax: 416-392-7431, Wards: 39 - Scarborough-Agincourt
Norm Kelly, Councillor, 416-392-4047, Fax: 416-696-4172, Wards: 40 - Scarborough-Agincourt
Chin Lee, Councillor, 416-392-1375, Fax: 416-392-7433, Wards: 41 - Scarborough-Rouge River
Raymond Cho, Councillor, 416-392-4076, Fax: 416-696-4159, Wards: 42 - Scarborough-Rouge River
Paul Ainslie, Councillor, 416-392-4008, Fax: 416-392-4006, Wards: 43 - Scarborough East
Ron Moeser, Councillor, 416-392-1373, Fax: 416-392-7429, Wards: 44 - Scarborough East
Ulli S. Watkiss, City Clerk, 416-392-8010, Fax: 416-392-2980
Peter Wallace, City Manager, 416-392-3551, Fax: 416-392-1827
Roberto Rossini, Deputy City Manager & Chief Financial Officer, 416-392-8773, Fax: 416-397-5236
John Livey, Deputy City Manager, 416-338-7200, Fax: 416-392-4540
Giuliana Carbone, Deputy City Manager, 416-338-7205, Fax: 416-395-0388
Rob Meikle, Chief Information Officer, 416-392-8421, Fax: 416-696-4244
Ann Borooah, Executive Director, Toronto Building, & Chief Building Official, 416-397-4446, Fax: 416-397-4383
Tracey Cook, Executive Director, Municipal Licensing & Standards, 416-392-8445, Fax: 416-397-5463
Jennifer Keesmaat, Executive Director, City Planning, & Chief Planner, 416-392-8772, Fax: 416-392-8115
Kerry Pond, Executive Director, Human Resources, 416-397-4112, Fax: 416-392-1524
Elaine Baxter-Trahair, General Manager, Children's Services, 416-392-8134, Fax: 416-392-4576
Stephen Buckley, General Manager, Transportation Services, 416-392-8431, Fax: 416-392-4455
Rob Cressman, General Manager, Shelter, Support, & Housing Administration, 416-392-0054, Fax: 416-392-0548
Lou Di Gironimo, General Manager, Toronto Water, 416-392-8200, Fax: 416-302-4540
Jim McKay, General Manager, Solid Waste Management Services, 416-392-4715, Fax: 416-392-4754
Paul Raftis, General Manager & Chief, Toronto Paramedic Services, 416-397-9240, Fax: 416-392-2115
Janie Romoff, General Manager, Parks, Forestry, & Recreation, 416-392-8182, Fax: 416-392-8565
J.W. (Jim) Sales, General Manager, Fire Services & Fire Chief, 416-338-9051, Fax: 416-338-9060

Patricia Walcott, General Manager, Employment & Social Services, 416-392-8952, Fax: 416-392-4214
Michael H. Williams, General Manager, Economic Development & Culture, 416-397-1970, Fax: 416-397-5314
Anna Kinastowski, City Solicitor, 416-392-0080, Fax: 416-397-5624
David McKeown, Medical Officer of Health, 416-338-7820, Fax: 416-392-0713
Mark Saunders, Chief of Police

Uxbridge
P.O. Box 190
51 Toronto St. South
Uxbridge, ON L9P 1T1
Tel: 905-852-9181; *Fax:* 905-852-9674
info@town.uxbridge.on.ca
www.town.uxbridge.on.ca
Municipal Type: City
Incorporated: 1872; *Area:* 420.65 sq km
County or District: Durham Reg. Mun.; *Population in 2011:* 20,623
Provincial Electoral District(s): Durham
Federal Electoral District(s): Pickering-Uxbridge
Next Election: Oct. 2018 (4 year terms)
Note: Incorporated as a town in 1885, & town became part of Uxbridge Township in 1973.
Gerri-Lynn O'Connor, Mayor, 905-852-9181
Jack Ballinger, Regional Councillor, 416-320-0585
Pamela Beach, Councillor, Wards: 1
Patrick Molloy, Councillor, 905-852-9181, Wards: 2
Pat Mikuse, Councillor, 905-852-0206, Wards: 3
Fred Bryan, Councillor, Wards: 4
Gordon Highet, Councillor, 905-852-9181, Wards: 5
Debbie Leroux, Clerk, 905-852-9181, Fax: 905-852-9674
Ingrid Svelnis, Chief Administrative Officer, 905-852-9181, Fax: 905-852-9674
Alan Shultz, Treasurer
Ben Kester, C.E.T., Director, Public Works, 905-852-9181, Fax: 905-852-9674
Amanda Ferraro, Manager, Recreation, Culture, & Tourism, 905-852-0095
Richard Vandezand, Manager, Development Services, 905-852-9181, Fax: 905-852-9674
Brian Pigozzo, Chief Building Official, 905-852-9181, Fax: 905-852-9674
Scott Richardson, Fire Chief
Andre Gratton, MLEO (C), C.P.S.O., Supervisor, Municipal Law Enforcement, 905-852-9181, Fax: 905-852-9674

Vaughan
2141 Major Mackenzie Dr.
Vaughan, ON L6A 1T1
Tel: 905-832-2281; *Fax:* 905-832-8535
accessvaughan@vaughan.ca
www.vaughan.ca
Other Information: Automated Tel: 905-832-8585; TTY: 1-866-534-0545
Municipal Type: City
Incorporated: Jan. 1, 1971; *Area:* 273.58 sq km
County or District: York Regional Municipality; *Population in 2011:* 288,201
Provincial Electoral District(s): Vaughan; Thornhill
Federal Electoral District(s): King-Vaughan; Thornhill; Vaughan-Woodbridge
Next Election: Oct. 2018 (4 year terms)
Maurizio Bevilacqua, Mayor
Michael Di Biase, Deputy Mayor & Regional Councillor
Mario Ferri, Regional Councillor
Gino Rosati, Regional Councillor
Marilyn Iafrate, Councillor, Wards: 1
Tony Carella, Councillor, Wards: 2
Rosanna Defrancesca, Councillor, Wards: 3
Sandra Yeung Racco, Councillor, Wards: 4
Alan Shefman, Councillor, Wards: 5
Jeffrey A. Abrams, City Clerk
Daniel Kostopoulos, City Manager, 905-832-8585
Laura Mirabella-Siddall, CFO & City Treasurer
Heather Wilson, City Solicitor, 905-832-8585
Paul Jankowski, Deputy City Manager, Public Works
John MacKenzie, Deputy City Manager, Planning & Growth Management
Mary Reali, Deputy City Manager, Community Services, 905-832-8585
Jamie Bronsema, Director, Parks Development
Paul Compton, Acting Director, Recreation Services
Jack Graziosi, Director, Infrastructure Delivery
Andrew D. Pearce, Director, Development & Transportation Engineering
Gary Williams, Director, Corporate Communications
Larry Bentley, Fire Chief

Wasaga Beach
30 Lewis St.
Wasaga Beach, ON L9Z 1A1
Tel: 705-429-3844; *Fax:* 705-429-7603
www.wasagabeach.com
Municipal Type: City
Incorporated: 1947; *Area:* 58.43 sq km
County or District: Simcoe; *Population in 2011:* 17,537
Provincial Electoral District(s): Simcoe-Grey
Federal Electoral District(s): Simcoe-Grey
Next Election: Oct. 2018 (4 year terms)
Note: Incorporated as a village in 1951 & as a town in 1974.
Brian Smith, Mayor
Nina Bifolchi, Deputy Mayor & Councillor
Ron Anderson, Councillor
Sylvia Bray, Councillor
Ron Ego, Councillor
Bonnie Smith, Councillor
Bill Stockwell, Councillor
Twyla Nicholson, Clerk
George Vadeboncoeur, Chief Administrative Officer
Monica Quinlan, Treasurer
Kevin Lalonde, Director, Public Works
Gerry Reinders, Manager, Parks & Facilities
Mike McWilliam, Fire Chief
Jenny Legget, Economic Development Officer

Waterloo
City Hall
P.O. Box 337 Waterloo
100 Regina St. South
Waterloo, ON N2J 4A8
Tel: 519-886-1550; *Fax:* 519-747-8500
www.waterloo.ca
Other Information: TTY Toll Free: 1-866-786-3941
Municipal Type: City
Incorporated: Jan. 15, 1857; *Area:* 64.1 sq km
County or District: Waterloo Regional Municipality; *Population in 2011:* 98,780
Provincial Electoral District(s): Kitchener-Waterloo
Federal Electoral District(s): Waterloo
Next Election: Oct. 2018 (4 year terms)
Note: Incorporated as a town in 1876 & as a city on Jan 1, 1948.
Dave Jaworsky, Mayor
Bob Mavin, Councillor, Wards: 1
Brian Bourke, Councillor, Wards: 2
Angela Veith, Councillor, Wards: 3
Diane Freeman, Councillor, Wards: 4
Mark Whaley, Councillor, Wards: 5
Jeff Henry, Councillor, Wards: 6
Melissa Durrell, Councillor, Wards: 7
Olga Smith, City Clerk, 519-747-8705, Fax: 519-747-8510
Tim Anderson, Chief Administrative Officer, 519-747-8702, Fax: 519-747-8500
Keshwer Patel, Chief Financial Officer, 519-747-8722
Cameron Rapp, Commissioner, Integrated Planning & Public Works
Megan Harris, Director, Communications & Marketing, 519-747-8513
Steve Heldman, Director, Recreation & Facility Services
Eckhard Pastrik, Director, Environment & Parks Services
Sunda Siva, Director, Facilities & Fleet
Richard Hepditch, Fire Chief
Mary Thorpe, Manager, Volunteer Services

Welland
60 East Main St.
Welland, ON L3B 3X4
Tel: 905-735-1700; *Fax:* 905-732-1919
www.welland.ca
Municipal Type: City
Incorporated: July 24, 1858; *Area:* 81.09 sq km
County or District: Niagara Regional Municipality; *Population in 2011:* 50,631
Provincial Electoral District(s): Welland
Federal Electoral District(s): Niagara Centre
Next Election: Oct. 2018 (4 year terms)
Note: Incorporated as a town on Jan. 1, 1878 & as a city on July 1, 1917.
Frank Campion, Mayor
Mark Carl, Councillor, Wards: 1
Mary Ann Grimaldi, Councillor, Wards: 1
David McLeod, Councillor, Wards: 2
Leo Van Vliet, Councillor, Wards: 2
John Chiocchio, Councillor, Wards: 3
John Mastroianni, Councillor, Wards: 3
Pat Chiocchio, Councillor, Wards: 4
Tony Dimarco, Councillor, Wards: 4
Rocky G. Létourneau, Councillor, Wards: 5
Michael Petrachenko, Councillor, Wards: 5
Bonnie Fokkens, Councillor, Wards: 6
Jim Larouche, Councillor, Wards: 6
Paul Grenier, Regional Councillor
George H. Marshall, Regional Councillor
Christine Raby, City Clerk
Kristine Douglas, Treasurer & General Manager, Financial & Corporate Services
Sal Iannello, General Manager, Infrastructure Services & City Engineer
Rosanne Mantesso, General Manager, Human Resources
Mike Mantesso, Chief Building Official
Denys Prevost, Fire Chief
Dan Degazio, Manager, Economic Development
Rose Di Felice, Manager, Policy Planning

Whitby
575 Rossland Rd. East
Whitby, ON L1N 2M8
Tel: 905-668-5803; *Fax:* 905-686-7005
info@whitby.ca
www.whitby.ca
Other Information: TTY: 905-430-1942
Municipal Type: City
Incorporated: 1855; *Area:* 146.52 sq km
County or District: Durham Reg. Mun.; *Population in 2011:* 122,022
Provincial Electoral District(s): Whitby-Oshawa
Federal Electoral District(s): Whitby
Next Election: Oct. 2018 (4 year terms)
Don Mitchell, Mayor
Derrick Gleed, Councillor, Wards: 1 - North
Chris Leahy, Councillor, Wards: 2 - West
Michael G. Emm, Councillor, Wards: 3 - Centre
Steve Yamada, Councillor, Wards: 4 - East
Lorne Earl Coe, Regional Councillor
Joe Drumm, Regional Councillor
Elizabeth Roy, Regional Councillor
Debi A. Wilcox, Town Clerk
Bob Petrie, Chief Administrative Officer
Peter LeBel, Commissioner, Community & Marketing Services, 905-430-4319
Dave Speed, Fire Chief
Sheila McGrory, Manager, Economic Development, 905-430-4312

Whitchurch-Stouffville
111 Sandiford Dr.
Stouffville, ON L4A 0Z8
Tel: 905-640-1900; *Fax:* 905-640-7957
www.townofws.com
Other Information: Toll-Free Phone: 1-855-642-8696
Municipal Type: City
Incorporated: 1877; *Area:* 206.74 sq km
County or District: York Reg. Mun.; *Population in 2011:* 37,628
Provincial Electoral District(s): Oak Ridges-Markham
Federal Electoral District(s): Markham-Stouffville
Next Election: Oct. 2018 (4 year terms)
Note: Incorporated as a town in 1971, with the amalgamation of Whitchurch Township & the Village of Stouffville.
Justin Altmann, Mayor
Ken Ferdinands, Councillor, Wards: 1
Maurice Smith, Councillor, Wards: 2
Hugo T. Kroon, Councillor, Wards: 3
Rick Upton, Councillor, Wards: 4
Iain Lovatt, Councillor, Wards: 5
Rob Hargrave, Councillor, Wards: 6
Michele Kennedy, Clerk
Andrew McNeely, Chief Administrative Officer
Marc J. Pourvahidi, Treasurer & Director, Finance
Rob Flindall, Director, Public Works
Steve Kemp, Director, Planning & Development Services
Rob Raycroft, Director, Leisure & Community Services
Rob McKenzie, Fire Chief

Windsor
City Hall
350 City Hall Sq. West
Windsor, ON N9A 6S1
Tel: 519-255-2489; *Fax:* 519-256-3311
311@city.windsor.on.ca
www.citywindsor.ca
Other Information: Phone: 311; Toll Free Phone: 1-877-746-4311
Municipal Type: City
Incorporated: 1854; *Area:* 146.91 sq km
County or District: Essex; *Population in 2011:* 210,891
Provincial Electoral District(s): Windsor-Tecumseh; Windsor-West
Federal Electoral District(s): Windsor-Tecumseh; Windsor-West
Next Election: Oct. 2018 (4 year terms)
Note: Incorporated as a town in 1858 & as a city in 1892.
Drew Dilkens, Mayor
Fred Francis, Councillor, Wards: 1
John Elliott, Councillor, Wards: 2

Rino Bortolin, Councillor, Wards: 3
Chris Holt, Councillor, Wards: 4
Ed Sleiman, Councillor, Wards: 5
Jo-Anne Gignac, Councillor, Wards: 6
Irek Kusmierczyk, Councillor, Wards: 7
Bill (Biagio) Marra, Councillor, Wards: 8
Hilary Payne, Councillor, Wards: 9
Paul Borrelli, Councillor, Wards: 10
Valerie Critchley, City Clerk, 519-255-6211, Fax: 519-255-6868
Onorio Colucci, Chief Administrative Officer, 519-255-6349, Fax: 519-255-1861
Thom Hunt, MCIP, RPP, City Planner
Shelby Askin Hager, City Solicitor
Mark Winterton, P. Eng., City Engineer & Corporate Leader, Environmental Protection & Infrastructure Services
Bruce Montone, Fire Chief, 519-253-6573

Woodstock

City Hall
P.O. Box 1539
500 Dundas St.
Woodstock, ON N4S 7W5
Tel: 519-539-1291;
info@cityofwoodstock.ca
www.cityofwoodstock.ca
Other Information: TTY: 519-539-7268
Municipal Type: City
Incorporated: Jan. 1, 1851; *Area:* 43.79 sq km
County or District: Oxford; *Population in 2011:* 37,754
Provincial Electoral District(s): Oxford
Federal Electoral District(s): Oxford
Next Election: Oct. 2018 (4 year terms)
Note: Incorporated as a city on July 1, 1901.
Trevor T. Birtch, Mayor
Deb A. Tait, City & County Councillor, 519-421-7449
Sandra J. Talbot, City & County Councillor, 519-788-0639
Jerry Acchione, City Councillor
Connie Lauder, City Councillor
Todd Poetter, City Councillor
Shawn Shapton, City Councillor
Louise Gartshore, City Clerk
David Creery, Chief Administrative Officer
Patrice Hilderley, Treasurer
Len Magyar, Commissioner, Development
Harold deHaan, City Engineer
Scott Tegler, Fire Chief
Filippo D'Emilio, Engineer, Development, 519-539-2382
Laird Crooks, Manager, Human Resources
Karen Houston, Manager, Culture
Alex Piggott, Superintendent, Works
Chris Kern, Supervisor, Parks

Other Municipalities in Ontario

Addington Highlands

P.O. Box 89
Flinton, ON K0H 1P0
Tel: 613-336-2286; *Fax:* 613-336-2847
www.addingtonhighlands.ca
Municipal Type: Township
Area: 1,288.47 sq km
County or District: Lennox & Addington; *Population in 2011:* 2,532
Provincial Electoral District(s): Lanark-Frontenac-Lennox & Addington
Federal Electoral District(s): Hastings-Lennox and Addington
Next Election: Oct. 2018 (4 year terms)
Henry Hogg, Reeve
Jack Pauhl, Clerk

Adelaide Metcalfe

2340 Egremont Dr., RR#5
Strathroy, ON N7G 3H6
Tel: 519-247-3687; *Fax:* 519-247-3411
info@adelaidemetcalfe.on.ca
www.adelaidemetcalfe.on.ca
Other Information: Toll Free: 1-866-525-8878
Municipal Type: Township
Incorporated: Jan. 1, 2001; *Area:* 331.26 sq km
County or District: Middlesex; *Population in 2011:* 3,028
Provincial Electoral District(s): Lambton-Kent-Middlesex
Federal Electoral District(s): Lambton-Kent-Middlesex
Next Election: Oct. 2018 (4 year terms)
Note: Amalgamation of the former Township of Adelaide & the Township of Metcalfe.
Kurtis Smith, Reeve
Fran Urbshott, Clerk/Administrator

Adjala-Tosorontio

7855 Sideroad 30, RR#1
Alliston, ON L9R 1V1
Tel: 705-434-5055; *Fax:* 705-434-5051
www.adjtos.ca
Municipal Type: Township
Incorporated: Jan. 1, 1994; *Area:* 372.33 sq km
County or District: Simcoe; *Population in 2011:* 10,603
Provincial Electoral District(s): Simcoe-Grey
Federal Electoral District(s): Simcoe-Grey
Next Election: Oct. 2018 (4 year terms)
Note: Amalgamation of the former Township of Adjala & the former Township of Tosorontio.
Mary Small Brett, Mayor
Doug Little, Deputy Mayor & Councillor
Floyd Pinto, Councillor, Wards: 1
Ambrose J. Keenan, Councillor, Wards: 2
Bob Meadows, Councillor, Wards: 3
Dave Rose, Councillor, Wards: 4
Eric Wargel, Chief Administrative Officer, 705-434-5055, Fax: 705-434-5051
Barbara Kane, Clerk, 705-434-5055, Fax: 705-434-5051
Ralph Snyder, Fire Chief & Management Coordinator, Community Emergency, 705-434-5055, Fax: 705-434-5051
Jim Moss, Superintendent, Public Works, 705-434-5055, Fax: 705-434-5051
Jacquie Tschekalin, Director, Planning, 705-434-5055, Fax: 705-434-5051

Admaston/Bromley

477 Stone Rd., RR#2
Renfrew, ON K7V 3Z5
Tel: 613-432-2885; *Fax:* 613-432-4052
info@admastonbromley.com
www.admastonbromley.com
Municipal Type: Township
Incorporated: Jan. 1, 2000; *Area:* 520.5 sq km
County or District: Renfrew; *Population in 2011:* 2,844
Provincial Electoral District(s): Renfrew-Nipissing-Pembroke
Federal Electoral District(s): Renfrew-Nipissing-Pembroke
Next Election: Oct. 2018 (4 year terms)
Note: Amalgamation of Admaston Township & Bromley Township.
Michael Donohue, Mayor
Annette Louis, Clerk-Treasurer, 613-432-2885

Alberton

#B2, RR#1
Fort Frances, ON P9A 3M2
Tel: 807-274-6053; *Fax:* 807-274-8449
alberton@jam21.net
www.alberton.ca
Municipal Type: Township
Area: 115.3 sq km
County or District: Rainy River District; *Population in 2011:* 864
Provincial Electoral District(s): Kenora-Rainy River
Federal Electoral District(s): Thunder Bay-Rainy River; Flamborough-Glanbrook
Next Election: Oct. 2018 (4 year terms)
Michael Hammond, Reeve
Dawn Hayes, Chief Administrative Officer & Clerk-Treasurer

Alfred & Plantagenet

P.O. Box 350
205 Old Hwy. 17
Plantagenet, ON K0B 1L0
Tel: 613-673-4797; *Fax:* 613-673-4812
www.alfred-plantagenet.com
Municipal Type: Township
Incorporated: Jan. 1, 1997; *Area:* 391.68 sq km
County or District: Prescott & Russell; *Population in 2011:* 9,196
Provincial Electoral District(s): Glengarry-Prescott-Russell
Federal Electoral District(s): Glengarry-Prescott-Russell
Next Election: Oct. 2018 (4 year terms)
Note: Amalgamation of the Township of Alfred, the Village of Alfred, the Township of North Plantagenet & the Village of Plantagenet.
Fernand Dicaire, Mayor
Marc Daigneault, Chief Administrative Officer & Clerk, 613-673-4797

Algoma

c/o Algoma District Svs. Administration Bd.
1 Collver Rd., RR#1
Thessalon, ON P0R 1L0
Tel: 705-842-3370; *Fax:* 705-842-3747
www.adsab.on.ca
Municipal Type: District
Area: 48,734.66 sq km
Population in 2011: 115,870
Provincial Electoral District(s): Algoma-Manitoulin
Federal Electoral District(s): Algoma-Manitoulin-Kapuskasing
Keith Bell, Chief Administrative Officer, 705-842-3370

Algonquin Highlands

1123 North Shore Rd., RR#2
Minden, ON K0M 1J1
Tel: 705-489-2379; *Fax:* 705-489-3491
info@algonquinhighlands.ca
www.algonquinhighlands.ca
Other Information: Phone, Dorset Satellite Office: 705-766-2211
Municipal Type: Township
Area: 1,002.12 sq km
County or District: Haliburton; *Population in 2011:* 2,156
Provincial Electoral District(s): Haliburton-Kawartha Lakes-Brock
Federal Electoral District(s): Haliburton-Kawartha Lakes-Brock
Next Election: Oct. 2018 (4 year terms)
Carol Moffat, Reeve
Angela Bird, Clerk & Chief Administrative Officer

Alnwick-Haldimand

P.O. Box 70
10836 County Rd. No. 2
Grafton, ON K0K 2G0
Tel: 905-349-2822; *Fax:* 905-349-3259
alnhald@alnwickhaldimand.ca
www.alnwickhaldimand.ca
Other Information: Phone, Roseneath Satellite Office: 905-352-3949
Municipal Type: Township
Area: 398.08 sq km
County or District: Northumberland; *Population in 2011:* 6,617
Provincial Electoral District(s): Northumberland-Quinte West
Federal Electoral District(s): Northumberland-Peterborough South
Next Election: Oct. 2018 (4 year terms)
John Logel, Mayor
Terry Korotki, Chief Administrative Officer, 905-349-2822

Amaranth

374028 - 6th Line
Amaranth, ON L9W 2Z3
Tel: 519-941-1007; *Fax:* 519-941-1802
township@amaranth-eastgary.ca
www.amaranth-eastgary.ca
Municipal Type: Township
Incorporated: Jan. 2, 1854; *Area:* 264.35 sq km
County or District: Dufferin; *Population in 2011:* 3,963
Provincial Electoral District(s): Dufferin-Caledon
Federal Electoral District(s): Dufferin-Caledon
Next Election: Oct. 2018 (4 year terms)
Don MacIver, Mayor, 519-925-3457
Susan M. Stone, A.M.C.T., Chief Administrative Officer & Clerk-Treasurer, 519-941-1007

The Archipelago

9 James St.
Parry Sound, ON P2A 1T4
Tel: 705-746-4243; *Fax:* 705-746-7301
www.thearchipelago.on.ca
Municipal Type: Township
Incorporated: April 1, 1980; *Area:* 602.3 sq km
County or District: Parry Sound District; *Population in 2011:* 566
Provincial Electoral District(s): Parry Sound-Muskoka
Federal Electoral District(s): Parry Sound-Muskoka
Next Election: Oct. 2018 (4 year terms)
Note: Amalgamation of the Township of Georgian Bay South Archipelago & the Township of Georgian Bay North Archipelago.
Peter Ketchum, Reeve, 416-944-1116
Stephen Kaegi, Chief Administrative Officer & Clerk, 705-746-4243

Armour

Municipal Office
P.O. Box 533
56 Ontario St.
Burks Falls, ON P0A 1C0
Tel: 705-382-3332; *Fax:* 705-382-2068
info@armourtownship.ca
www.armourtownship.ca
Other Information: Alternative Phone: 705-382-2954
Municipal Type: Township
Area: 164.1 sq km
County or District: Parry Sound District; *Population in 2011:* 1,372
Provincial Electoral District(s): Parry Sound-Muskoka
Federal Electoral District(s): Parry Sound-Muskoka
Next Election: Oct. 2018 (4 year terms)
Bob MacPhail, Reeve, 705-636-7678
Wendy Whitwell, Clerk-Administrator

Armstrong
P.O. Box 546
35 10 St.
Earlton, ON P0J 1E0
Tel: 705-563-2375; *Fax:* 705-563-2093
www.armstrongtownship.com
Municipal Type: Township
Area: 90.33 sq km
County or District: Timiskaming District; *Population in 2011:* 1,216
Provincial Electoral District(s): Timiskaming-Cochrane
Federal Electoral District(s): Timmins-James Bay
Next Election: Oct. 2018 (4 year terms)
Robert Éthier, Mayor
Reynald Rivard, Clerk-Treasurer, 705-563-2375

Arnprior
P.O. Box 130
105 Elgin St. West
Arnprior, ON K7S 0A8
Tel: 613-623-4231; *Fax:* 613-623-8091
arnprior@arnprior.ca
www.arnprior.ca
Municipal Type: Town
Area: 13.04 sq km
County or District: Renfrew; *Population in 2011:* 8,114
Provincial Electoral District(s): Renfrew-Nipissing-Pembroke
Federal Electoral District(s): Renfrew-Nipissing-Pembroke
Next Election: Oct. 2018 (4 year terms)
David Reid, Mayor, 613-623-7259
Michael Wildman, Chief Administrative Officer

Arran-Elderslie
P.O. Box 70
1925 Bruce Rd. 10
Chesley, ON N0G 1L0
Tel: 519-363-3039; *Fax:* 519-363-2203
areld@bmts.com
www.arran-elderslie.com
Municipal Type: Municipality
Area: 460.13 sq km
County or District: Bruce; *Population in 2011:* 6,810
Provincial Electoral District(s): Bruce-Grey-Owen Sound
Federal Electoral District(s): Bruce-Grey-Owen Sound
Next Election: Oct. 2018 (4 year terms)
Paul Eagleson, Mayor, 519-363-3559
Peggy Rouse, Clerk

Ashfield-Colborne-Wawanosh
82133 Council Line, RR#5
Goderich, ON N7A 3Y2
Tel: 519-524-4669; *Fax:* 519-524-1951
www.acwtownship.ca
Municipal Type: Township
Area: 587.07 sq km
County or District: Huron; *Population in 2011:* 5,582
Provincial Electoral District(s): Huron-Bruce
Federal Electoral District(s): Huron-Bruce
Next Election: Oct. 2018 (4 year terms)
Ben Van Diepenbeek, Reeve, 519-529-7830
Mark Becker, Administrator/Clerk, 519-524-4669

Asphodel-Norwood
P.O. Box 29
2357 County Rd. 45
Norwood, ON K0L 2V0
Tel: 705-639-5343; *Fax:* 705-639-1880
www.asphodelnorwood.com
Municipal Type: Township
Incorporated: 1998; *Area:* 160.85 sq km
County or District: Peterborough; *Population in 2011:* 4,041
Provincial Electoral District(s): Peterborough
Federal Electoral District(s): Northumberland-Peterborough South
Next Election: Oct. 2018 (4 year terms)
Note: Amalgamation of the Village of Norwood & the Township of Asphodel.
Terry Low, Mayor
Joe van Koeverden, Chief Administrative Officer

Assiginack
P.O. Box 238
25B Spragge St.
Manitowaning, ON P0P 1N0
Tel: 705-859-3196; *Fax:* 705-859-3010
info@assiginack.ca
www.assiginack.ca
Other Information: Toll-Free Phone: 1-800-540-0179
Municipal Type: Township
Area: 227.44 sq km
County or District: Manitoulin District; *Population in 2011:* 960
Provincial Electoral District(s): Algoma-Manitoulin
Federal Electoral District(s): Algoma-Manitoulin-Kapuskasing
Next Election: Oct. 2018 (4 year terms)
Paul Moffatt, Reeve
Alton Hobbs, Clerk-Treasurer

Athens
P.O. Box 189
1 Main St. West
Athens, ON K0E 1B0
Tel: 613-924-2044; *Fax:* 613-924-2091
athens@ripnet.com
www.athenstownship.ca
Municipal Type: Township
Incorporated: 2001; *Area:* 126.46 sq km
County or District: Leeds & Grenville; *Population in 2011:* 3,118
Provincial Electoral District(s): Leeds-Grenville
Federal Electoral District(s): Leeds-Grenville-Thousand Islands and Rideau Lakes
Next Election: Oct. 2018 (4 year terms)
Herb Scott, Mayor, 613-924-2133
Darlene Noonan, Chief Administrative Officer & Clerk Treasurer, 613-924-2044, Fax: 613-924-2091

Atikokan
P.O. Box 1330
120 Marks St.
Atikokan, ON P0T 1C0
Tel: 807-597-1234; *Fax:* 807-597-6186
info@atikokan.ca
www.atikokan.ca
Municipal Type: Township
Area: 316.75 sq km
County or District: Rainy River District; *Population in 2011:* 2,787
Provincial Electoral District(s): Thunder Bay-Atikokan
Federal Electoral District(s): Thunder Bay-Rainy River
Next Election: Oct. 2018 (4 year terms)
Dennis Brown, Mayor, 807-597-2540
Angela Sharbot, Chief Administrative Officer, 801-597-1234

Augusta
3560 County Rd. 26, RR#2
Prescott, ON K0E 1T0
Tel: 613-925-4231; *Fax:* 613-925-3499
www.augusta.ca
Municipal Type: Township
Area: 314.06 sq km
County or District: Leeds & Grenville; *Population in 2011:* 7,430
Provincial Electoral District(s): Leeds-Grenville
Federal Electoral District(s): Leeds-Grenville-Thousand Islands and Rideau Lakes
Next Election: Oct. 2018 (4 year terms)
Doug Malanka, Reeve
Pierre Mercier, Chief Administrative Officer & Clerk, 613-825-4234

Aylmer
46 Talbot St. West
Aylmer, ON N5H 1J7
Tel: 519-773-3164; *Fax:* 519-765-1446
www.aylmer.ca
Municipal Type: Town
Area: 6.22 sq km
County or District: Elgin; *Population in 2011:* 7,151
Provincial Electoral District(s): Elgin-Middlesex-London
Federal Electoral District(s): Elgin-Middlesex-London
Next Election: Oct. 2018 (4 year terms)
Greg Currie, Mayor
Jennifer Reynaert, Chief Administrative Officer, 519-773-3146, Fax: 519-765-1446

Baldwin
P.O. Box 7095
11 Spooner St.
McKerrow, ON P0P 1M0
Tel: 705-869-0225;
baldwin.ca
Municipal Type: Township
Area: 81.82 sq km
County or District: Sudbury District; *Population in 2011:* 551
Provincial Electoral District(s): Algoma-Manitoulin
Federal Electoral District(s): Algoma-Manitoulin-Kapuskasing
Next Election: Oct. 2018 (4 year terms)
Vern Gorham, Reeve
Peggy Young-Lovelace, Clerk & Treasurer

Bancroft
P.O. Box 790
24 Flint Ave.
Bancroft, ON K0L 1C0
Tel: 613-332-3331; *Fax:* 613-332-0384
bancroft@town.bancroft.on.ca
www.town.bancroft.on.ca
Municipal Type: Town
Incorporated: 1904; *Area:* 227.84 sq km
County or District: Hastings; *Population in 2011:* 3,888
Provincial Electoral District(s): Prince Edward-Hastings
Federal Electoral District(s): Hastings-Lennnox and Addington
Next Election: Oct. 2018 (4 year terms)
Bernice Jenkins, Mayor, 613-332-1041
Hazel Lambe, Chief Administrative Officer & Clerk

Bayham
P.O. Box 160
9344 Plank Rd.
Straffordville, ON N0J 1Y0
Tel: 519-866-5521; *Fax:* 519-866-3884
bayham@bayham.on.ca
www.bayham.on.ca
Municipal Type: Municipality
Area: 244.99 sq km
County or District: Elgin; *Population in 2011:* 6,989
Provincial Electoral District(s): Elgin-Middlesex-London
Federal Electoral District(s): Elgin-Middlesex-London
Next Election: Oct. 2018 (4 year terms)
Paul Ens, Mayor
Lynda Millard, Clerk

Beckwith
1702 - 9 Line Beckwith, RR#2
Carleton Place, ON K7C 3P2
Tel: 613-257-1539; *Fax:* 613-257-8996
www.twp.beckwith.on.ca
Other Information: Toll Free: 1-800-535-4532 (in 613 area code)
Municipal Type: Township
Area: 240.12 sq km
County or District: Lanark; *Population in 2011:* 6,986
Provincial Electoral District(s): Lanark-Frontenac-Lennox & Addington
Federal Electoral District(s): Lanark-Frontenac-Kingston
Next Election: Oct. 2018 (4 year terms)
Richard Kidd, Reeve, 613-257-5409
Cynthia Moyle, Chief Administrative Officer

Billings
Municipal Office
P.O. Box 34
15 Old Mill Rd.
Kagawong, ON P0P 1J0
Tel: 705-282-2611; *Fax:* 705-282-3199
billingsadmin@billingstwp.ca
www.billingstwp.ca
Municipal Type: Township
Incorporated: 1884; *Area:* 209.15 sq km
County or District: Manitoulin District; *Population in 2011:* 506
Provincial Electoral District(s): Algoma-Manitoulin
Federal Electoral District(s): Algoma-Manitoulin-Kapuskasing
Next Election: Oct. 2018 (4 year terms)
Austin Hunt, Reeve, 705-282-2684
Katherine McDonald, Clerk-Treasurer, 705-282-2611

Black River-Matheson
P.O. Box 601
429 Park Lane
Matheson, ON P0K 1N0
Tel: 705-273-2313;
reception@blackriver-matheson.com
www.blackriver-matheson.com
Municipal Type: Township
Area: 1,161.67 sq km
County or District: Cochrane District; *Population in 2011:* 2,410
Provincial Electoral District(s): Timiskaming-Cochrane
Federal Electoral District(s): Timmins-James Bay
Next Election: Oct. 2018 (4 year terms)
Edwards Garry, Mayor
Heather Smith, Clerk & Treasurer, 705-273-2313

Blandford-Blenheim
P.O. Box 100
47 Wilmot St. South
Drumbo, ON N0J 1G0
Tel: 519-463-5347; *Fax:* 519-463-5881
generalmail@blandfordblenheim.ca
www.blandfordblenheim.ca
Municipal Type: Township
Area: 382.34 sq km
County or District: Oxford; *Population in 2011:* 7,359
Provincial Electoral District(s): Oxford
Federal Electoral District(s): Oxford
Next Election: Oct. 2018 (4 year terms)
Marion Wearn, Mayor
Fran Bell, Chief Administrative Officer & Clerk, 519-463-5347, Fax: 519-463-5881

Blind River
P.O. Box 640
11 Hudson St.
Blind River, ON P0R 1B0
Tel: 705-356-2251; *Fax:* 705-356-7343
www.blindriver.ca
Municipal Type: Town
Incorporated: 1906; *Area:* 520.59 sq km
County or District: Algoma District; *Population in 2011:* 3,549
Provincial Electoral District(s): Algoma-Manitoulin
Federal Electoral District(s): Algoma-Manitoulin-Kapuskasing
Next Election: Oct. 2018 (4 year terms)
Sue Jensen, Mayor, 705-227-1559
Kathryn Scott, Clerk Administrator, 705-356-2251, Fax: 705-356-7343

The Blue Mountains
P.O. Box 310
32 Mill St.
Thornbury, ON N0H 2P0
Tel: 519-599-3131; *Fax:* 519-599-7723
info@town.thebluemountains.on.ca
www.thebluemountains.ca
Other Information: Toll-Free Phone: 1-888-258-6867
Municipal Type: Town
Incorporated: Jan. 1, 2001; *Area:* 286.78 sq km
County or District: Grey; *Population in 2011:* 6,453
Provincial Electoral District(s): Simcoe-Grey
Federal Electoral District(s): Simcoe-Grey
Next Election: Oct. 2018 (4 year terms)
Note: Amalgamation of Collingwood & Thornbury.
John F. McKean, Mayor
Corrina Giles, Town Clerk, 519-599-3131

Bluewater, Municipality of
P.O. Box 250
14 Mill Ave.
Zurich, ON N0M 2T0
Tel: 519-236-4351; *Fax:* 519-236-4329
www.town.bluewater.on.ca
Other Information: Toll-Free: 1-877-236-4351
Municipal Type: Town
Area: 416.99 sq km
County or District: Huron; *Population in 2011:* 7,044
Provincial Electoral District(s): Huron-Bruce
Federal Electoral District(s): Huron-Bruce
Next Election: Oct. 2018 (4 year terms)
Tyler Hessel, Mayor
Gary Long, Chief Administrative Officer

Bonfield
365 Hwy. 531
Bonfield, ON P0H 1E0
Tel: 705-776-2641; *Fax:* 705-776-1154
www.ebonfield.org
Municipal Type: Township
Incorporated: 1975; *Area:* 205.75 sq km
County or District: Nipissing District; *Population in 2011:* 2,016
Provincial Electoral District(s): Nipissing
Federal Electoral District(s): Nipissing-Timiskaming
Next Election: Oct. 2018 (4 year terms)
Randall McLaren, Mayor
Lise B. McMillan, Administrator, Clerk & Treasurer

Bonnechere Valley
P.O. Box 100
49 Bonnechere St. East
Eganville, ON K0J 1T0
Tel: 613-628-3101; *Fax:* 613-628-1336
admin@eganville.com
www.bonnecherevalleytwp.com
Municipal Type: Township
Incorporated: Jan. 1, 2001; *Area:* 589.87 sq km
County or District: Renfrew; *Population in 2011:* 3,763
Provincial Electoral District(s): Renfrew-Nipissing-Pembroke
Federal Electoral District(s): Renfrew-Nipissing-Pembroke
Next Election: Oct. 2018 (4 year terms)
Note: Amalgamation of Eganville Village, Grattan Township, Sebastopol Township & Algona South Township.
Jennifer Murphy, Mayor, 613-628-3295
Bryan Martin, Chief Administrative Officer

Brethour
P.O. Box 537
51476 Brethour Rd.
Belle Vallee, ON P0J 1A0
Tel: 705-647-1712; *Fax:* 705-647-6851
brethour@parolink.net
Municipal Type: Township
Area: 82.05 sq km
County or District: Timiskaming District; *Population in 2011:* 129
Provincial Electoral District(s): Timiskaming-Cochrane
Federal Electoral District(s): Timmins-James Bay
Next Election: Oct. 2018 (4 year terms)
Arla West, Reeve
Pam Bennewies, Clerk-Treasurer

Brock
P.O. Box 10
1 Cameron St. East
Cannington, ON L0E 1E0
Tel: 705-432-2355; *Fax:* 705-432-3487
brock@townshipofbrock.ca
www.townshipofbrock.ca
Other Information: Toll Free: 1-866-223-7668
Municipal Type: Township
Incorporated: 1973; *Area:* 423.31 sq km
County or District: Durham Reg. Mun.; *Population in 2011:* 11,341
Provincial Electoral District(s): Haliburton-Kawartha Lakes-Brock
Federal Electoral District(s): Haliburton-Kawartha Lakes-Brock
Next Election: Oct. 2018 (4 year terms)
John Grant, Mayor, 705-426-1296
Joe Allin, Regional Coucillor, 705-357-3969
Gord Lodwick, Councillor, 705-426-4670, Wards: 1
Randy Skinner, Councillor, 705-426-7022, Wards: 2
Mike Parliament, Councillor, 705-432-2488, Wards: 3
Therese Miller, Councillor, 705-437-1358, Wards: 4
Lynn Campbell, Councillor, 705-357-0013, Wards: 5
Thomas G. Gettinby, MA, MCIP, RPP, CMO, Chief Administrative Officer & Municipal Clerk, 705-432-2355
Laura Barta, CMA, Treasurer, 705-432-2355
Nick Colucci, P.Eng., Director, Public Works, 705-432-2355
Joseph J. Bonura, Chief Building Offical, 705-432-2355
Rick Harrison, Fire Chief, 705-432-2355

Brockton
P.O. Box 68
100 Scott St.
Walkerton, ON N0G 2V0
Tel: 519-881-2223;
info@brockton.ca
www.brockton.ca
Other Information: Toll-Free Phone: 1-877-885-8084
Municipal Type: Municipality
Incorporated: Jan. 1, 1999; *Area:* 565.07 sq km
County or District: Bruce; *Population in 2011:* 9,432
Provincial Electoral District(s): Huron-Bruce
Federal Electoral District(s): Huron-Bruce
Next Election: Oct. 2018 (4 year terms)
Note: Amalgamation of the Town of Walkerton, Township of Brant, & the Township of Greenock.
David Inglis, Mayor
Debra Roth, Clerk

Brooke-Alvinston
P.O. Box 28
3236 River St.
Alvinston, ON N0N 1A0
Tel: 519-898-2173; *Fax:* 519-898-5653
info@brookealvinston.com
www.brookealvinston.com
Other Information: Toll-Free Phone, Enforcement Unit: 1-866-344-9119
Municipal Type: Township
Area: 311.3 sq km
County or District: Lambton; *Population in 2011:* 2,548
Provincial Electoral District(s): Lambton-Kent-Middlesex
Federal Electoral District(s): Lambton-Kent-Middlesex
Next Election: Oct. 2018 (4 year terms)
Don McGugan, Mayor, 519-847-5606, Fax: 519-847-5607
Janet Denkers, Clerk-Administrator, 519-898-2173, Fax: 519-878-5653

Bruce Mines
P.O. Box 220
9126 Hwy. 17 East
Bruce Mines, ON P0R 1C0
Tel: 705-785-3493; *Fax:* 705-785-3170
brucemines@bellnet.ca
www.brucemines.ca
Municipal Type: Town
Incorporated: 1903; *Area:* 6.13 sq km
County or District: Algoma District; *Population in 2011:* 566
Provincial Electoral District(s): Algoma-Manitoulin
Federal Electoral District(s): Algoma-Manitoulin-Kapuskasing
Next Election: Oct. 2018 (4 year terms)
Lory Patteri, Mayor, 780-785-3493, Fax: 705-785-3170
Donna Brunke, Town Clerk, 905-785-3493, Fax: 905-785-3170

Brudenell, Lyndoch & Raglan
P.O. Box 40
42 Burnt Bridge Rd.
Palmer Rapids, ON K0J 2E0
Tel: 613-758-2061; *Fax:* 613-758-2235
blrtownship@xplornet.com
www.countyofrenfrew.on.ca
Municipal Type: Township
Incorporated: Jan. 1, 1999; *Area:* 702.77 sq km
County or District: Renfrew; *Population in 2011:* 1,658
Provincial Electoral District(s): Renfrew-Nipissing-Pembroke
Federal Electoral District(s): Renfrew-Nipissing-Pembroke
Next Election: Oct. 2018 (4 year terms)
Garry Gruntz, Reeve
Michelle Mantifel, Clerk-Treasurer

Burk's Falls
P.O. Box 160
172 Ontario St.
Burks Falls, ON P0A 1C0
Tel: 705-382-3138; *Fax:* 705-382-2273
villofbf@bellnet.ca
www.burksfalls.net
Municipal Type: Village
Incorporated: 1890; *Area:* 3.12 sq km
County or District: Parry Sound District; *Population in 2011:* 967
Provincial Electoral District(s): Parry Sound-Muskoka
Federal Electoral District(s): Parry Sound-Muskoka
Next Election: Oct. 2018 (4 year terms)
Cathy Still, Reeve
Kim Dunnett, Clerk

Burpee & Mills
RR#1
Evansville, ON P0P 1E0
Tel: 705-282-0624; *Fax:* 705-282-0624
burpeemills@xplornet.com
www.burpeemills.com
Municipal Type: Township
Area: 218.48 sq km
County or District: Manitoulin District; *Population in 2011:* 308
Provincial Electoral District(s): Algoma-Manitoulin
Federal Electoral District(s): Algoma-Manitoulin-Kapuskasing
Next Election: Oct. 2018 (4 year terms)
Ken Noland, Reeve
Bonnie J. Bailey, Clerk-Treasurer

Callander, Municipality of
P.O. Box 100
280 Main St. North
Callander, ON P0H 1H0
Tel: 705-752-1410; *Fax:* 705-752-3116
www.callander.ca
Municipal Type: Township
Area: 100.96 sq km
County or District: Parry Sound District; *Population in 2011:* 3,864
Provincial Electoral District(s): Nipissing
Federal Electoral District(s): Nipissing-Timiskaming
Next Election: Oct. 2018 (4 year terms)
Note: Formerly North Himsworth Township.
Hector Lavigne, Mayor, 705-845-5010
Mike Purcell, Chief Administration Officer

Calvin
1355 Peddlers Dr., RR#2
Mattawa, ON P0H 1V0
Tel: 705-744-2700; *Fax:* 705-744-0309
administration@calvintownship.ca
www.calvintownship.ca
Municipal Type: Township
Area: 139.17 sq km
County or District: Nipissing District; *Population in 2011:* 568
Provincial Electoral District(s): Nipissing
Federal Electoral District(s): Nipissing-Timiskaming
Next Election: Oct. 2018 (4 year terms)
Wayne Brown, Mayor
Lynda Kovacs, Clerk-Treasurer

Carleton Place
175 Bridge St.
Carleton Place, ON K7C 2V8
Tel: 613-257-6200; *Fax:* 613-257-8170
info@carletonplace.ca; bylaw@carletonplace.ca (Bylaws)
www.carletonplace.ca
Other Information: E-mail, Public Works: dyoung@carletonplace.ca
Municipal Type: Town
Area: 8.83 sq km
County or District: Lanark; *Population in 2011:* 9,809
Provincial Electoral District(s): Lanark-Frontenac-Lennox & Addington

Federal Electoral District(s): Lanark-Frontenac-Kingston
Next Election: Oct. 2018 (4 year terms)
Louis Antonakos, Mayor
Paul Knowles, Chief Administrative Officer, 613-257-6207

Carling
2 West Carling Bay Rd., RR#1
Nobel, ON P0G 1G0
Tel: 705-342-5856; *Fax:* 705-342-9527
www.carlingtownship.ca
Municipal Type: Township
Area: 243.94 sq km
County or District: Parry Sound District; *Population in 2011:* 1,248
Provincial Electoral District(s): Parry Sound-Muskoka
Federal Electoral District(s): Parry Sound-Muskoka
Next Election: Oct. 2018 (4 year terms)
Mike Konoval, Mayor
Stephen Kaegi, Chief Administrative Officer & Clerk, 705-342-5856

Carlow/Mayo
General Delivery, 3987 Boulter Rd.
Boulter, ON K0L 1G0
Tel: 613-332-1760; *Fax:* 613-332-2175
clerk@carlowmayo.ca
www.carlowmayo.ca
Municipal Type: Township
Incorporated: Jan. 1, 2001; *Area:* 388.36 sq km
County or District: Hastings; *Population in 2011:* 892
Provincial Electoral District(s): Prince Edward-Hastings
Federal Electoral District(s): Hastings-Lennox and Addington
Next Election: Oct. 2018 (4 year terms)
Note: Amalgamation of the former townships of Carlow & Mayo.
Bonnie Adams, Reeve
Arlene Cox, Clerk-Administrator, 613-332-1760

Casey
P.O. Box 460
Belle Vallee, ON P0J 1A0
Tel: 705-647-7257; *Fax:* 705-647-6373
harlytwp@parolink.net
harley.ca/casey/index.html
Municipal Type: Township
Incorporated: 1909; *Area:* 80.75 sq km
County or District: Timiskaming District; *Population in 2011:* 374
Provincial Electoral District(s): Timiskaming-Cochrane
Federal Electoral District(s): Timmins-James Bay
Next Election: Oct. 2018 (4 year terms)
Guy Labonté, Reeve
Michel Lachapelle, Clerk-Treasurer

Casselman
P.O. Box 710
751 St. Jean St.
Casselman, ON K0A 1M0
Tel: 613-764-3139; *Fax:* 613-764-5709
info@casselman.ca
www.casselman.ca
Municipal Type: Village
Area: 5.15 sq km
County or District: Prescott & Russell; *Population in 2011:* 3,626
Provincial Electoral District(s): Glengarry-Prescott-Russell
Federal Electoral District(s): Glengarry-Prescott-Russell
Next Election: Oct. 2018 (4 year terms)
Conrad Lamadeleine, Mayor
Marc Chénier, Chief Administrative Officer, 613-764-3139

Cavan Monaghan
988 County Rd. 10, RR#3
Millbrook, ON L0A 1G0
Tel: 705-932-2929; *Fax:* 705-932-3458
info@cavanmonaghan.net
www.cavanmonaghan.net
Other Information: Toll-Free Phone: 1-877-906-5556
Municipal Type: Township
Area: 306.13 sq km
County or District: Peterborough; *Population in 2011:* 8,601
Provincial Electoral District(s): Haliburton-Kawartha Lakes-Brock
Federal Electoral District(s): Haliburton-Kawartha Lakes-Brock
Next Election: Oct. 2018 (4 year terms)
Note: Formerly The Corporation of the Township of Cavan-Millbrook-North Monaghan.
Scott McFadden, Mayor
Elana Arthurs, Clerk, 705-932-9326

Central Elgin
450 Sunset Dr.
St Thomas, ON N5R 5V1
Tel: 519-631-4860; *Fax:* 519-631-4036
www.centralelgin.org
Municipal Type: Municipality
Area: 280.22 sq km
County or District: Elgin; *Population in 2011:* 12,743
Provincial Electoral District(s): Elgin-Middlesex-London
Federal Electoral District(s): Elgin-Middlesex-London
Next Election: Oct. 2018 (4 year terms)
David Marr, Mayor
Sally Martyn, Deputy Mayor & Councillor
Dan McNeil, Councillor, Wards: 1
Dennis Crevits, Councillor, Wards: 2
Stephen Carr, Councillor, Wards: 3
Harold Winkworth, Councillor, Wards: 4
Fiona Roberts, Councillor, Wards: 5
Donald N. Leitch, Chief Administrative Officer & Clerk
Karen DePrest, Treasurer & Director, Financial Services
Donald Crocker, Director, Fire & Rescue Services
Lloyd Perrin, Director, Physical Services

Central Frontenac
P.O. Box 89
1084 Elizabeth S.
Sharbot Lake, ON K0H 2P0
Tel: 613-279-2935; *Fax:* 613-279-2422
township@centralfrontenac.com
www.centralfrontenac.com
Municipal Type: Township
Incorporated: Jan. 1, 1998; *Area:* 970.07 sq km
County or District: Frontenac; *Population in 2011:* 4,556
Provincial Electoral District(s): Lanark-Frontenac-Lennox & Addington
Federal Electoral District(s): Lanark-Frontenac-Kingston
Next Election: Oct. 2018 (4 year terms)
Frances Smith, Mayor
Larry Donaldson, Chief Administrative Officer & Clerk

Central Huron, Municipality of
P.O. Box 400
23 Albert St.
Clinton, ON N0M 1L0
Tel: 519-482-3997; *Fax:* 519-482-9183
www.centralhuron.com
Municipal Type: Township
Incorporated: Jan. 1, 2001; *Area:* 447.6 sq km
County or District: Huron; *Population in 2011:* 7,591
Provincial Electoral District(s): Huron-Bruce
Federal Electoral District(s): Huron-Bruce
Next Election: Oct. 2018 (4 year terms)
Note: Amalgamation of the Town of Clinton, the Township of Hullett, & the Township of Goderich.
Jim Ginn, Mayor, 519-524-2522, Fax: 519-524-2755
Peggy Van Mierlo-West, Chief Administrative Officer, 519-482-3997

Central Manitoulin
P.O. Box 187
6020 Hwy. 542
Mindemoya, ON P0P 1S0
Tel: 705-377-5726; *Fax:* 705-377-5585
centralm@amtelecom.net; centralinspections@amtelecom.net
www.centralmanitoulin.ca
Other Information: E-mail, Economic Dev.: centralecdev@amtelecom.net
Municipal Type: Township
Area: 431.53 sq km
County or District: Manitoulin District; *Population in 2011:* 1,958
Provincial Electoral District(s): Algoma-Manitoulin
Federal Electoral District(s): Algoma-Manitoulin-Kapuskasing
Next Election: Oct. 2018 (4 year terms)
Richard Stephens, Reeve
Ruth Frawley, Chief Administrative Officer & Clerk, 705-377-5726

Centre Hastings
P.O. Box 900
7 Furnace St.
Madoc, ON K0K 2K0
Tel: 613-473-4030; *Fax:* 613-473-5444
www.centrehastings.com
Municipal Type: Municipality
Area: 222.09 sq km
County or District: Hastings; *Population in 2011:* 4,543
Provincial Electoral District(s): Prince Edward-Hastings
Federal Electoral District(s): Hastings-Lennox and Addington
Next Election: Oct. 2018 (4 year terms)
Tom Deline, Mayor
Pat Pilgrim, Chief Administrative officer & Clerk

Centre Wellington
P.O. Box 10
1 MacDonald Sq.
Elora, ON N0B 1S0
Tel: 519-846-9691; *Fax:* 519-846-2190
www.centrewellington.ca
Municipal Type: Township
Area: 407.33 sq km
County or District: Wellington; *Population in 2011:* 26,693
Provincial Electoral District(s): Wellington-Halton Hills
Federal Electoral District(s): Wellington-Halton Hills
Next Election: Oct. 2018 (4 year terms)
Kelly Linton, Mayor
Don Fisher, Councillor, Wards: 1
Kirk McElwain, Councillor, Wards: 2
Mary Lloyd, Councillor, Wards: 3
Fred Morris, Councillor, Wards: 4
Stephen Kitras, Councillor, Wards: 5
Steven VanLeeuwen, Councillor, Wards: 6
Kerri O'Kane, Clerk
Andy Goldie, Chief Administrative Officer
Mark Bradey, Financial Manager/Deputy Treasurer
Matt Tucker, Manager, Parks & Facilities
Brett Salmon, Managing Director, Planning & Development
Brad Patton, Fire Chief
Rob Rosoo, Superintendent, Public Works

Chamberlain
467501 Chamberlain Rd. 5, RR#3
Englehart, ON P0J 1H0
Tel: 705-544-8088; *Fax:* 705-544-1118
ctchamberlain@ontera.net
www.twpofchamberlain.com
Municipal Type: Township
Incorporated: 1908; *Area:* 110.13 sq km
County or District: Timiskaming District; *Population in 2011:* 297
Provincial Electoral District(s): Timiskaming-Cochrane
Federal Electoral District(s): Timmins-James Bay
Next Election: Oct. 2018 (4 year terms)
Shirley Blackburn, Reeve
Michelle Nelson, Clerk-Deputy Treasurer, 705-544-8088, Fax: 705-544-1188

Champlain
948 Pleasant Corners Rd. East
Vankleek Hill, ON K0B 1R0
Tel: 613-678-3003; *Fax:* 613-678-3363
info@champlain.com
www.champlain.ca
Municipal Type: Township
Incorporated: Jan. 1, 1998; *Area:* 207.15 sq km
County or District: Prescott & Russell; *Population in 2011:* 8,573
Provincial Electoral District(s): Glengarry-Prescott-Russell
Federal Electoral District(s): Glengarry-Prescott-Russell
Next Election: Oct. 2018 (4 year terms)
Note: Amalgamation of the Village of L'Orignal, the Township of West Hawkesbury, the Township of Longueuil & the Village of Vankleek Hill.
Gary J. Barton, Mayor, 613-678-3101
Paula Knudsen, Chief Administrative Officer-Treasurer

Chapleau
Civic Centre
P.O. Box 129
20 Pine St. West
Chapleau, ON P0M 1K0
Tel: 705-864-1330; *Fax:* 705-864-1824
www.chapleau.ca
Municipal Type: Township
Area: 14.27 sq km
County or District: Sudbury District; *Population in 2011:* 2,116
Provincial Electoral District(s): Algoma-Manitoulin
Federal Electoral District(s): Algoma-Manitoulin-Kapuskasing
Next Election: Oct. 2018 (4 year terms)
Michael J. Levesque, Mayor
Allan D. Pellow, Chief Administrative Officer, 705-864-1330, Fax: 705-864-1824

Chapple
P.O. Box 4
Barwick, ON P0W 1A0
Tel: 807-487-2354; *Fax:* 807-487-2406
info@chapple.on.ca
www.chapple.on.ca
Municipal Type: Township
Area: 529.02 sq km
County or District: Rainy River District; *Population in 2011:* 741
Provincial Electoral District(s): Kenora-Rainy River
Federal Electoral District(s): Thunder Bay-Rainy River
Next Election: Oct. 2018 (4 year terms)
Peter Van Heyst, Reeve
Peggy Johnson, Chief Administrative Officer & Clerk-Treasurer

Charlton & Dack
287237 Sprucegrove Rd. RR#2
Englehart, ON P0J 1H0
Tel: 705-544-7525; *Fax:* 705-544-2369
dack@ntl.sympatico.ca
www.charltonanddack.com
Municipal Type: Municipality
Incorporated: Jan. 1, 2003; *Area:* 92.33 sq km
County or District: Timiskaming District; *Population in 2011:* 671
Provincial Electoral District(s): Timiskaming-Cochrane
Federal Electoral District(s): Timmins-James Bay
Next Election: Oct. 2018 (4 year terms)
Note: Amalgamation of the Town of Charlton & the Township of Dack.
Merril Norman Bond, Reeve
Dan Thibeault, Clerk-Treasurer/Chief Administrative Officer, 705-544-7525, Fax: 705-544-2369

Chatham-Kent
Civic Centre
P.O. Box 640
315 King St. West
Chatham, ON N7M 5K8
Tel: 519-360-1998; *Fax:* 519-436-3204
ckinfo@chatham-kent.ca
www.chatham-kent.ca
Other Information: Toll Free: 1-800-714-7497
Municipal Type: Municipality
Incorporated: Jan. 1, 1998; *Area:* 2,458.06 sq km
Population in 2011: 103,671
Provincial Electoral District(s): Chatham-Kent-Essex; Lambton-Kent-Middlesex
Federal Electoral District(s): Chatham-Kent-Leamington; Lambton-Kent-Middlesex
Next Election: Oct. 2018 (4 year terms)
Note: Formerly the County of Kent.
Randy Hope, Mayor & Chief Executive Officer, 519-436-3219, Fax: 519-436-3236
Bryon Fluker, Councillor, 519-436-3254, Wards: 1., West Kent
Mark Authier, Councillor, Wards: 1., West Kent
Trevor Thompson, Councillor, Wards: 2., South Kent
Karen Herman, Councillor, Wards: 2., South Kent
David Vandamme, Councillor, Wards: 3., East Kent
Steve Pinsonneault, Councillor, 519-436-3253, Fax: 519-692-4203, Wards: 3., East Kent
Joe Faas, Councillor, Councillor, 519-436-3208, Wards: 4., North Kent
Leon Leclair, Councillor, 519-436-3221, Wards: 4., North Kent
Carmen McGregor, Councillor, Wards: 5., Wallaceburg
Jeff Wesley, Councillor, Councillor, 519-436-3229, Wards: 5., Wallaceburg
Darrin Canniff, Councillor, Wards: 6., Chatham
Brock McGregory, Councillor, Wards: 6., Chatham
Michael Bondy, Councillor, Wards: 6., Chatham
Bob Myers, Councillor, 519-436-3216, Wards: 6., Chatham
Derek Robertson, Councillor, 519-350-8709, Wards: 6., Chatham
Douglas Sulman, Councillor, 519-436-3234, Wards: 6., Chatham
Judy Smith, Clerk
Don Shropshire, Chief Administrative Officer
Gord Quinton, Acting Director, Financial Services
April Rietdyk, General Manager, Health & Family Services
Tom Kelly, General Manager, Infrastructure & Engineering Systems
Miguel Pelletier, Director, Public Works
Ken Stuebing, Fire Chief

Chatsworth
316837, Hwy. 6, RR#1
Chatsworth, ON N0H 1G0
Tel: 519-794-3232; *Fax:* 519-794-4499
office@chatsworth.ca
www.chatsworth.ca
Municipal Type: Township
Incorporated: Jan. 1, 2001; *Area:* 595.35 sq km
County or District: Grey; *Population in 2011:* 6,437
Provincial Electoral District(s): Bruce-Grey-Owen Sound
Federal Electoral District(s): Bruce-Grey-Owen Sound
Next Election: Oct. 2018 (4 year terms)
Note: Amalgamation of the Townships of Holland & Sullivan & the Village of Chatsworth.
Bob Pringle, Mayor, 519-794-2579
Will Moore, Chief Administrative Officer & Clerk, 519-794-3232

Chisholm
2847 Chiswick Line, RR#4
Powassan, ON P0H 1Z0
Tel: 705-724-3526; *Fax:* 705-724-5099
info@chisholm.ca; twpchisholm@ontera.ca
www.chisholm.ca
Other Information: Phone, Public Works: 705-724-5530
Municipal Type: Township
Incorporated: 1912; *Area:* 205.26 sq km
County or District: Nipissing District; *Population in 2011:* 1,263
Provincial Electoral District(s): Nipissing
Federal Electoral District(s): Nipissing-Timiskaming
Next Election: Oct. 2018 (4 year terms)
Leo Jobin, Mayor
Alice Lauzon, Acting Clerk-Treasurer

Clarington
40 Temperance St.
Bowmanville, ON L1C 3A6
Tel: 905-623-3379; *Fax:* 905-623-6506
info@clarington.net; communications@clarington.net
www.clarington.net
Other Information: Toll-Free Phone: 1-800-563-1195
Municipal Type: Municipality
Area: 611.1 sq km
County or District: Durham Reg. Mun.; *Population in 2011:* 84,548
Provincial Electoral District(s): Durham
Federal Electoral District(s): Durham
Next Election: Oct. 2018 (4 year terms)
Adrian Foster, Mayor
Joe Neal, Regional Councillor, Wards: 1 & 2
Willie Woo, Regional Councillor, Wards: 3 & 4
Steven Cooke, Local Councillor, Wards: 1
Ron Hooper, Local Councillor, Wards: 2
Corinna Trail, Local Councillor, Wards: 3
Wendy Partner, Local Councillor, Wards: 4
Anne Greentree, Municipal Clerk
Franklin Wu, Chief Administrative Officer
Nancy Taylor, Treasurer & Director, Finance
Tony Cannella, Director, Engineering Services
Joseph Caruana, Director, Community Services
David Crome, Director, Planning Services
Fred Horvath, Director, Operations
Marie Marano, Director, Corporate Services
Gord Weir, Fire Chief

Clearview
P.O. Box 200
217 Gideon St.
Stayner, ON L0M 1S0
Tel: 705-428-6230; *Fax:* 705-428-0288
www.clearview.ca
Municipal Type: Township
Area: 557.32 sq km
County or District: Simcoe; *Population in 2011:* 13,734
Provincial Electoral District(s): Simcoe-Grey
Federal Electoral District(s): Simcoe-Grey
Next Election: Oct. 2018 (4 year terms)
Christopher Vanderkruys, Mayor
Barry Burton, Deputy Mayor & Councillor
Doug Measures, Councillor, Wards: 1
Kevin Elwood, Councillor, Wards: 2
Robert Walker, Councillor, Wards: 3
Shawn Davidson, Councillor, Wards: 4
Thom Paterson, Councillor, Wards: 5
Connie Leishman, Councillor, Wards: 6
Deborah Bronée, Councillor, Wards: 7
Pamela Fettes, Clerk
Steve Sage, Chief Administrative Officer
Edward Henley, Treasurer
Mike Rawn, General Manager, Environmental Services
Mara Burton, Director, Community Services
Colin Shewell, Fire Chief

Cobalt
P.O. Box 70
18 Silver St.
Cobalt, ON P0J 1C0
Tel: 705-679-8877;
www.cobalt.ca
Municipal Type: Town
Area: 2.11 sq km
County or District: Timiskaming District; *Population in 2011:* 1,133
Provincial Electoral District(s): Timiskaming-Cochrane
Federal Electoral District(s): Nipissing-Timiskaming
Next Election: Oct. 2018 (4 year terms)
Tina Sartoretto, Mayor
Candice Bedard, Chief Administrative Officer & Clerk-Treasurer, 705-679-8877

Cochrane
P.O. Box 490
171 - 4 Ave.
Cochrane, ON P0L 1C0
Tel: 705-272-4361; *Fax:* 705-272-6068
townhall@town.cochrane.on.ca
www.town.cochrane.on.ca
Municipal Type: Town
Incorporated: 1910; *Area:* 538.76 sq km
County or District: Cochrane District; *Population in 2011:* 5,340
Provincial Electoral District(s): Timiskaming-Cochrane
Federal Electoral District(s): Timmins-James Bay
Next Election: Oct. 2018 (4 year terms)
Peter Politis, Mayor
Jean-Pierre Ouellette, Chief Administrative Officer & Clerk

Cochrane
c/o CDSSAB
500 Algonquin Blvd. East
Cochrane, ON P4N 1B7
Tel: 705-268-7722; *Fax:* 705-268-8302
www.cdssab.on.ca
Municipal Type: District
Area: 141,247.30 sq km
Population in 2011: 81,122
David Landers, CAO & Director, Ontario Works and Children's Services, Cochrane District Social Services Administration Board, 705-268-7722, Fax: 705-268-8290

Cockburn Island
General Delivery
Walford, ON P0P 2E0
Tel: 705-844-2289; *Fax:* 705-844-1101
Municipal Type: Township
Area: 167.6 sq km
County or District: Manitoulin District;
Provincial Electoral District(s): Algoma-Manitoulin
Federal Electoral District(s): Algoma-Manitoulin-Kapuskasing
Next Election: Oct. 2018 (4 year terms)
Brenda Jones, Reeve
Brent St. Denis, Clerk-Treasurer

Coleman
937907 Marsh Bay Rd.
Coleman, ON P0J 1C0
Tel: 705-679-8833; *Fax:* 705-679-8300
toc@ontera.net
www.colemantownship.ca
Municipal Type: Township
Incorporated: 1906; *Area:* 177.6 sq km
County or District: Timiskaming District; *Population in 2011:* 597
Provincial Electoral District(s): Timiskaming-Cochrane
Federal Electoral District(s): Nipissing-Timiskaming
Next Election: Oct. 2018 (4 year terms)
Dan Cleroux, Mayor, 705-679-5678
Claire Bigelow, Clerk-Treasurer

Conmee
RR#1
Kakabeka Falls, ON P0T 1W0
Tel: 807-475-5229; *Fax:* 807-475-4793
info@conmee.com
www.conmee.com
Municipal Type: Township
Area: 167.53 sq km
County or District: Thunder Bay District; *Population in 2011:* 764
Provincial Electoral District(s): Thunder Bay-Atikokan
Federal Electoral District(s): Thunder Bay-Rainy River
Next Election: Oct. 2018 (4 year terms)
Kevin Holland, Mayor
Patricia Maxwell, Clerk-Treasurer

Cramahe
P.O. Box 357
1 Toronto St.
Colborne, ON K0K 1S0
Tel: 905-355-2821; *Fax:* 905-355-3430
www.visitcramahe.ca
Other Information: Toll-Free Phone: 1-877-272-4263
Municipal Type: Township
Area: 201.56 sq km
County or District: Northumberland; *Population in 2011:* 6,073
Provincial Electoral District(s): Northumberland-Quinte West
Federal Electoral District(s): Northumberland-Peterborough South
Next Election: Oct. 2018 (4 year terms)
Marc Coombs, Mayor
Christie Alexander, Chief Administrative Officer & Clerk

Dawn-Euphemia
4591 Lambton Line, RR#4
Dresden, ON N0P 1M0
Tel: 519-692-5148; *Fax:* 519-692-5511
admin@dawneuphemia.on.ca
www.lambtononline.ca/county_councillors
Municipal Type: Township
Area: 445.05 sq km
County or District: Lambton; *Population in 2011:* 2,049
Provincial Electoral District(s): Lambton-Kent-Middlesex

Federal Electoral District(s): Lambton-Kent-Middlesex
Next Election: Oct. 2018 (4 year terms)
Alan Broad, Mayor
Michael Schnare, Administrator-Clerk

Dawson
P.O. Box 427
211 Fourth St.
Rainy River, ON P0W 1L0
Tel: 807-852-3529; *Fax:* 807-852-3529
dawsontownship.weebly.com
Municipal Type: Township
Area: 338.35 sq km
County or District: Rainy River District; *Population in 2011:* 563
Provincial Electoral District(s): Kenora-Rainy River
Federal Electoral District(s): Thunder Bay-Rainy River
Next Election: Oct. 2018 (4 year terms)
Linda Armstrong, Mayor
Patrick W. Giles, Clerk-Treasurer

Deep River
P.O. Box 400
100 Deep River Rd.
Deep River, ON K0J 1P0
Tel: 613-584-2000; *Fax:* 613-584-3237
townmail@deepriver.ca
www.deepriver.ca
Municipal Type: Town
Area: 50.84 sq km
County or District: Renfrew; *Population in 2011:* 4,193
Provincial Electoral District(s): Renfrew-Nipissing-Pembroke
Federal Electoral District(s): Renfrew-Nipissing-Pembroke
Next Election: Oct. 2018 (4 year terms)
Joan Lougheed, Mayor
Ric McGee, Chief Administrative Officer & Clerk

Deseronto
P.O. Box 310
331 Main St.
Deseronto, ON K0K 1X0
Tel: 613-396-2440; *Fax:* 613-396-3141
jcarter@deseronto.ca (Public Works)
www.deseronto.ca
Other Information: E-mail, Economic Dev.:
mconger@deseronto.ca
Municipal Type: Town
Incorporated: 1889; *Area:* 2.52 sq km
County or District: Hastings; *Population in 2011:* 1,835
Provincial Electoral District(s): Prince Edward-Hastings
Federal Electoral District(s): Hastings-Lennox and Addington
Next Election: Oct. 2018 (4 year terms)
Norm Clark, Mayor
Ellen Hamel, Chief Administrative Officer/Clerk

Dorion
170 Dorion Loop Rd., RR#1
Dorion, ON P0T 1K0
Tel: 807-857-2289; *Fax:* 807-857-2203
office@doriontownship.ca
www.doriontownship.ca
Municipal Type: Township
Area: 212.07 sq km
County or District: Thunder Bay District; *Population in 2011:* 338
Provincial Electoral District(s): Thunder Bay-Superior North
Federal Electoral District(s): Thunder Bay-Superior North
Next Election: Oct. 2018 (4 year terms)
Ed Chambers, Reeve
Helena Tamminen, Clerk-Treasurer

Douro-Dummer
P.O. Box 92
894 South St.
Warsaw, ON K0L 3A0
Tel: 705-652-8392; *Fax:* 705-652-5044
info@dourodummer.on.ca
www.dourodummer.on.ca
Other Information: Toll-Free Phone: 1-800-899-8785
Municipal Type: Township
Area: 458.36 sq km
County or District: Peterborough; *Population in 2011:* 6,805
Provincial Electoral District(s): Peterborough
Federal Electoral District(s): Peterborough-Kawartha
Next Election: Oct. 2018 (4 year terms)
J. Murray Jones, Reeve, 705-652-6325, Fax: 705-652-6325
David Clifford, Chief Administrative Officer

Drummond-North Elmsley
310 Port Elmsley Rd., RR#5
Perth, ON K7H 3L7
Tel: 613-267-6500; *Fax:* 613-267-2083
admin@drummondnorthelmsley.com
www.drummondnorthelmsley.com
Municipal Type: Township
Incorporated: 1998; *Area:* 364.78 sq km
County or District: Lanark; *Population in 2011:* 7,487
Provincial Electoral District(s): Lanark-Frontenac-Lennox & Addington
Federal Electoral District(s): Lanark-Frontenac-Kingston
Next Election: Oct. 2018 (4 year terms)
Note: Amalgamation of the Townships of Drummond and North Elmsley.
Aubrey Churchill, Reeve, 613-264-8404
Cindy Halcrow, Clerk-Administrator

Dryden
30 Van Horne Ave.
Dryden, ON P8N 2A7
Tel: 807-223-1147; *Fax:* 807-223-1126
generalinquiries@dryden.ca
www.dryden.ca
Other Information: Alternative Phone: 807-223-1126
Municipal Type: Town
Area: 65.2 sq km
County or District: Kenora; *Population in 2011:* 7,617
Provincial Electoral District(s): Kenora-Rainy River
Federal Electoral District(s): Kenora
Next Election: Oct. 2018 (4 year terms)
Craig Nuttall, Mayor
André Larabie, Chief Administrative Officer, 807-223-1194

Dubreuilville
P.O. Box 367
23 Pine St.
Dubreuilville, ON P0S 1B0
Tel: 705-884-2340; *Fax:* 705-884-2626
www.dubreuilville.ca
Municipal Type: Township
Incorporated: 1978; *Area:* 89.57 sq km
County or District: Algoma District; *Population in 2011:* 635
Provincial Electoral District(s): Algoma-Manitoulin
Federal Electoral District(s): Algoma-Manitoulin-Kapuskasing
Next Election: Oct. 2018 (4 year terms)
Alain Lacroix, Mayor
Shelley Casey, Chief Administrative Officer & Clerk

Dutton-Dunwich
P.O. Box 329
199 Currie Rd.
Dutton, ON N0L 1J0
Tel: 519-762-2204; *Fax:* 519-762-2278
info@duttondunwich.on.ca
www.duttondunwich.on.ca
Municipal Type: Municipality
Area: 294.63 sq km
County or District: Elgin; *Population in 2011:* 3,876
Provincial Electoral District(s): Elgin-Middlesex-London
Federal Electoral District(s): Elgin-Middlesex-London
Next Election: Oct. 2018 (4 year terms)
Cameron McWilliam, Mayor
Laurie Spence-Bannerman, Chief Administrative Officer

Dysart et al
P.O. Box 389
135 Maple Ave.
Haliburton, ON K0M 1S0
Tel: 705-457-1740; *Fax:* 705-457-1964
info@dysartetal.ca
www.dysartetal.ca
Municipal Type: Township
Incorporated: Jan. 7, 1867; *Area:* 1,474.07 sq km
County or District: Haliburton; *Population in 2011:* 5,966
Provincial Electoral District(s): Haliburton-Kawartha Lakes-Brock
Federal Electoral District(s): Haliburton-Kawartha Lakes-Brock
Next Election: Oct. 2018 (4 year terms)
Murray Fearrey, Reeve
Tamara Wilbee, Chief Administrative Officer

Ear Falls
P.O. Box 309
Ear Falls, ON P0V 1T0
Tel: 807-222-3624; *Fax:* 807-222-2384
eftownship@ear-falls.com
www.ear-falls.com
Other Information: E-mail, Public Services & Ops:
pdyck@ear-falls.com
Municipal Type: Township
Area: 330.99 sq km
County or District: Kenora District; *Population in 2011:* 1,026
Provincial Electoral District(s): Kenora-Rainy River
Federal Electoral District(s): Kenora
Next Election: Oct. 2018 (4 year terms)
Kevin Kahoot, Mayor
Kimberly Ballance, Clerk-Treasurer & Administrator

East Ferris
390 Hwy. 94
Corbeil, ON P0H 1K0
Tel: 705-752-2740;
eastferris.ca
Municipal Type: Township
Area: 149.76 sq km
County or District: Nipissing District; *Population in 2011:* 4,512
Provincial Electoral District(s): Nipissing
Federal Electoral District(s): Nipissing-Timiskaming
Next Election: Oct. 2018 (4 year terms)
William Vrebosch, Mayor
John B. Fior, Clerk

East Garafraxa
374028 6th Line, RR#3
Orton, ON L0N 1N0
Tel: 519-928-5298; *Fax:* 519-941-1802
township@amaranth-eastgary.ca
www.amaranth-eastgary.ca
Other Information: Alternative Phone: 519-941-1007
Municipal Type: Township
Incorporated: Jan. 1, 1869; *Area:* 165.72 sq km
County or District: Dufferin; *Population in 2011:* 2,595
Provincial Electoral District(s): Dufferin-Caledon
Federal Electoral District(s): Dufferin-Caledon
Next Election: Oct. 2018 (4 year terms)
Guy Gardhouse, Mayor
Susan M. Stone, AMCT, Chief Administrative Officer & Clerk-Treasurer

East Hawkesbury
P.O. Box 340
5151 County Rd. 14
St Eugene, ON K0B 1P0
Tel: 613-674-2170; *Fax:* 613-674-2989
www.easthawkesbury.ca
Municipal Type: Township
Incorporated: Jan. 1, 1850; *Area:* 235.09 sq km
County or District: Prescott & Russell; *Population in 2011:* 3,335
Provincial Electoral District(s): Glengarry-Prescott-Russell
Federal Electoral District(s): Glengarry-Prescott-Russell
Next Election: Oct. 2018 (4 year terms)
Robert Kirby, Mayor, 613-632-4841, Fax: 613-632-4841
Linda Rozon, Chief Administrative Officer & Clerk-Treasurer

East Zorra-Tavistock
P.O. Box 100
90 Loveys St.
Hickson, ON N0J 1L0
Tel: 519-462-2697; *Fax:* 519-462-2961
ezt@twp.ezt.on.ca
www.twp.ezt.on.ca
Municipal Type: Township
Area: 247.42 sq km
County or District: Oxford; *Population in 2011:* 6,836
Provincial Electoral District(s): Oxford
Federal Electoral District(s): Oxford
Next Election: Oct. 2018 (4 year terms)
Don McKay, Mayor, 519-532-2500
Jeff Carswell, Chief Administrative Officer

Edwardsburgh/Cardinal
P.O. Box 129
18 Centre St.
Spencerville, ON K0E 1X0
Tel: 613-658-3055; *Fax:* 613-658-3445
www.twpec.ca
Other Information: Toll-Free Phone: 1-866-848-9099
Municipal Type: Township
Area: 311.83 sq km
County or District: Leeds & Grenville; *Population in 2011:* 6,959
Provincial Electoral District(s): Leeds-Grenville
Federal Electoral District(s): Leeds-Grenville-Thousand Islands and Rideau Lakes
Next Election: Oct. 2018 (4 year terms)
Patrick Sayeau, Mayor
Debra McKinstry, CAO/Clerk

Elizabethtown-Kitley
6544 New Dublin Rd., RR#2
Addison, ON K0E 1A0
Tel: 613-345-7480; *Fax:* 613-345-7235
mail@elizabethtown-kitley.on.ca
www.elizabethtown-kitley.on.ca
Other Information: Toll-Free Phone: 1-800-492-3175
Municipal Type: Township
Area: 554.24 sq km
County or District: Leeds & Grenville; *Population in 2011:* 9,724
Provincial Electoral District(s): Leeds-Grenville
Federal Electoral District(s): Leeds-Grenville-Thousand Islands

and Rideau Lakes
Next Election: Oct. 2018 (4 year terms)
Jim Pickard, Mayor, 613-342-5721
Jason Barlow, Councillor
Dan Downey, Councillor, 613-275-1460
Chrsitina Eady, Councillor
Brayton Earl, Councillor
Jim Miller, Councillor
Rob Smith, Councillor, 613-498-0827
Yvonne L. Robert, Administrator-Clerk, 613-345-7480
Dale Kulp, Director, Public Works
Jim Donovan, Fire Chief, 613-498-2460

Emo
P.O. Box 520
39 Roy St.
Emo, ON P0W 1E0
Tel: 807-482-2378; *Fax:* 807-482-2741
township@emo.ca
www.emo.ca
Municipal Type: Township
Incorporated: 1899; *Area:* 203.54 sq km
County or District: Rainy River District; *Population in 2011:* 1,252
Provincial Electoral District(s): Kenora-Rainy River
Federal Electoral District(s): Thunder Bay-Rainy River
Next Election: Oct. 2018 (4 year terms)
Jack Siemens, Mayor
Brenda J. Cooke, Chief Administrative Officer & Clerk-Treasurer

Englehart
P.O. Box 399
61 Fifth Ave.
Englehart, ON P0J 1H0
Tel: 705-544-2244;
englehrt@ntl.sympatico.ca
www.englehart.ca
Municipal Type: Town
Incorporated: 1908; *Area:* 3.04 sq km
County or District: Timiskaming District; *Population in 2011:* 1,519
Provincial Electoral District(s): Timiskaming-Cochrane
Federal Electoral District(s): Timmins-James Bay
Next Election: Oct. 2018 (4 year terms)
Nina Wallace, Mayor
Susan Renaud, Clerk

Enniskillen
4465 Rokeby Line, RR#1
Petrolia, ON N0N 1R0
Tel: 519-882-2490;
www.enniskillen.ca
Municipal Type: Township
Area: 338.18 sq km
County or District: Lambton; *Population in 2011:* 2,930
Provincial Electoral District(s): Sarnia-Lambton
Federal Electoral District(s): Sarnia-Lambton
Next Election: Oct. 2018 (4 year terms)
Kevin Marriot, Mayor
Duncan McTavish, Administrator-Clerk

Espanola
#2, 100 Tudhope St.
Espanola, ON P5E 1S6
Tel: 705-869-1540; *Fax:* 705-869-0083
www.espanola.ca
Municipal Type: Town
Incorporated: March 1, 1958; *Area:* 82.37 sq km
County or District: Sudbury District; *Population in 2011:* 5,364
Provincial Electoral District(s): Algoma-Manitoulin
Federal Electoral District(s): Algoma-Manitoulin-Kapuskasing
Next Election: Oct. 2018 (4 year terms)
Ron Piche, Mayor
Cynthia Townsend, Clerk-Treasurer & Administrator

Essa
5786 County Rd. 21
Utopia, ON L0M 1T0
Tel: 705-424-9770; *Fax:* 705-424-2367
info@essatownship.on.ca
www.essatownship.on.ca
Other Information: TTY: 705-424-5302
Municipal Type: Township
Incorporated: 1850; *Area:* 279.57 sq km
County or District: Simcoe; *Population in 2011:* 18,505
Provincial Electoral District(s): Simcoe-Grey
Federal Electoral District(s): Barrie-Innisfil; Simcoe-Grey
Next Election: Oct. 2018 (4 year terms)
Terry Dowdall, Mayor, 705-423-1154
Sandie Macdonald, Deputy Mayor & Councillor, 705-424-6844
Keith White, Councillor, 705-424-2727, Wards: 1
Michael Smith, Councillor, 705-794-3230, Wards: 2
Ron Henderson, Councillor, 705-424-9752, Wards: 3

Greg Murphy, Chief Administrative Officer
Bonnie Sander, Clerk
Julie Barrett, Treasurer & Deputy Clerk
Colleen Healey, Manager, Planning & Development
Cynthia Ross Tustin, Fire Chief
Heather Rutherford, Chief Building Official

Evanturel
P.O. Box 209
245453 Hwy. 659
Englehart, ON P0J 1H0
Tel: 705-544-8200; *Fax:* 705-544-8206
www.evanturel.com
Other Information: E-mail, Building: cbo@ntl.sympatico.ca
Municipal Type: Township
Incorporated: Jan. 1, 1904; *Area:* 88.99 sq km
County or District: Timiskaming District; *Population in 2011:* 452
Provincial Electoral District(s): Timiskaming-Cochrane
Federal Electoral District(s): Timmins-James Bay
Next Election: Oct. 2018 (4 year terms)
Derek Mundle, Reeve
Amy Vickery-Menard, Clerk-Treasurer

Faraday
P.O. Box 929
29860 Hwy. 28 South
Bancroft, ON K0L 1C0
Tel: 613-332-3638; *Fax:* 613-332-3006
faraday@reztel.net
www.faraday.ca
Municipal Type: Township
Area: 215.23 sq km
County or District: Hastings; *Population in 2011:* 1,468
Provincial Electoral District(s): Prince Edward-Hastings
Federal Electoral District(s): Hastings-Lennox and Addington
Next Election: Oct. 2018 (4 year terms)
Carl A. Tinney, Reeve, 613-332-2050
Brenda Vader, Clerk-Treasurer & Tax Collector

Fauquier-Strickland
P.O. Box 40
25 Grzela Rd.
Fauquier, ON P0L 1G0
Tel: 705-339-2521; *Fax:* 705-339-2421
info@fauquierstrickland.com
fauquierstrickland.com
Municipal Type: Township
Area: 1,013.54 sq km
County or District: Cochrane District; *Population in 2011:* 530
Provincial Electoral District(s): Timmins-James Bay
Federal Electoral District(s): Algoma-Manitoulin-Kapuskasing
Next Election: Oct. 2018 (4 year terms)
Madeleine Tremblay, Reeve
Robert Courchesne, Administrator & Clerk-Treasurer

Fort Frances
320 Portage Ave.
Fort Frances, ON P9A 3P9
Tel: 807-274-5323; *Fax:* 807-274-8479
town@fort-frances.com
www.fort-frances.com
Municipal Type: Town
Incorporated: 1903; *Area:* 26.85 sq km
County or District: Rainy River District; *Population in 2011:* 7,952
Provincial Electoral District(s): Kenora-Rainy River
Federal Electoral District(s): Thunder Bay-Rainy River
Next Election: Oct. 2018 (4 year terms)
Roy Avis, Mayor
Elizabeth Slomke, Clerk

French River, Municipality of / Municipalité de la Rivière des Français
P.O. Box 156
#1, 44 St. Christophe St.
Noëlville, ON P0M 2N0
Tel: 705-898-2294; *Fax:* 705-898-2181
www.frenchriver.ca
Municipal Type: Town
Incorporated: Jan. 1, 1999; *Area:* 734.26 sq km
County or District: Sudbury District; *Population in 2011:* 2,442
Provincial Electoral District(s): Timiskaming-Cochrane; Nickle Belt
Federal Electoral District(s): Nickel Belt
Next Election: Oct. 2018 (4 year terms)
Claude Bouffard, Mayor
Sébastien Goyer, Chief Administrative Officer & Clerk

Front of Yonge
P.O. Box 130
1514 County Rd. 2
Mallorytown, ON K0E 1R0
Tel: 613-923-2251; *Fax:* 613-923-2421
admin@frontofyonge.com
www.frontofyonge.com
Other Information: Phone, Public Works: 613-923-5074
Municipal Type: Township
Area: 127.85 sq km
County or District: Leeds & Grenville; *Population in 2011:* 2,680
Provincial Electoral District(s): Leeds-Grenville
Federal Electoral District(s): Leeds-Grenville-Thousand Islands and Rideau Lakes
Next Election: Oct. 2018 (4 year terms)
Roger Haley, Reeve
Elaine A. Covey, Clerk

Frontenac Islands
P.O. Box 130
Rd. 96
Wolfe Island, ON K0H 2Y0
Tel: 613-385-2216; *Fax:* 613-385-1032
www.municipality.frontenacislands.on.ca
Municipal Type: Township
Incorporated: Jan. 1, 1998; *Area:* 174.99 sq km
County or District: Frontenac; *Population in 2011:* 1,864
Provincial Electoral District(s): Kingston & the Islands
Federal Electoral District(s): Kingston & the Islands
Next Election: Oct. 2018 (4 year terms)
Note: Amalgamation of Howe Island & Wolfe Island.
Dennis Doyle, Mayor, 613-385-2763
Darlene Plumley, AMCT, Chief Administrative Officer & Clerk

Galway-Cavendish & Harvey
P.O. Box 820
701 County Rd. 36, RR#3
Bobcaygeon, ON K0M 1A0
Tel: 705-738-3800; *Fax:* 705-738-3801
www.galwaycavendishharvey.ca
Other Information: Toll-Free Phone: 1-800-374-4009
Municipal Type: Township
Area: 848.26 sq km
County or District: Peterborough; *Population in 2011:* 5,105
Provincial Electoral District(s): Haliburton-Kawartha Lakes-Brock
Federal Electoral District(s): Peterborough-Kawartha
Next Election: Oct. 2018 (4 year terms)
Bev Matthews, Reeve
Lois O'Neill-Jackson, Chief Administrative Officer

Gananoque
Town Hall
P.O. Box 100
30 King St. East
Gananoque, ON K7G 2T6
Tel: 613-382-2149; *Fax:* 613-382-8587
www.townofgananoque.com
Municipal Type: Separated for Municipal Purposes Only
Area: 7.01 sq km
County or District: Leeds & Grenville; *Population in 2011:* 5,194
Provincial Electoral District(s): Leeds-Grenville
Federal Electoral District(s): Leeds-Grenville-Thousand Islands and Rideau Lakes
Next Election: Oct. 2018 (4 year terms)
Erika Demchuk, Mayor
Robert W. Small, Chief Administrative Officer

Gauthier
P.O. Box 65
92 McPherson St.
Dobie, ON P0K 1B0
Tel: 705-568-8951; *Fax:* 705-568-8951
Municipal Type: Township
Area: 88.36 sq km
County or District: Timiskaming District; *Population in 2011:* 123
Provincial Electoral District(s): Timiskaming-Cochrane
Federal Electoral District(s): Timmins-James Bay
Next Election: Oct. 2018 (4 year terms)
William Johnson, Reeve
Dianne Quinn, Clerk-Treasurer

Georgian Bay
99 Lone Pine Rd.
Port Severn, ON L0K 1S0
Tel: 705-538-2337; *Fax:* 705-538-1850
clerks@township.georgianbay.on.ca
www.township.georgianbay.on.ca
Other Information: Toll-Free Phone: 1-800-567-0187
Municipal Type: Township
Area: 535.48 sq km
County or District: Muskoka District Municipality; *Population in 2011:* 2,124

Provincial Electoral District(s): Parry Sound-Muskoka
Federal Electoral District(s): Parry Sound-Muskoka
Next Election: Oct. 2018 (4 year terms)
Larry Braid, Mayor
Laurie Kennard, Chief Administrative Officer

Georgian Bluffs
177964 Grey Rd. 18, RR#3
Owen Sound, ON N4K 5N5
Tel: 519-376-2729; *Fax:* 519-372-1620
office@georgianbluffs.on.ca
www.georgianbluffs.on.ca
Municipal Type: Township
Incorporated: Jan. 1, 2001; *Area:* 603.58 sq km
County or District: Grey; *Population in 2011:* 10,404
Provincial Electoral District(s): Bruce-Grey-Owen Sound
Federal Electoral District(s): Bruce-Grey-Owen Sound
Next Election: Oct. 2018 (4 year terms)
Note: Amalgamation of the Townships of Derby, Keppel & Sarawak.
Alan Barfoot, Mayor
Dwight Burley, Deputy Mayor & Councillor
Carol Barfoot, Councillor
Sue Carleton, Councillor
Paul Sutherland, Councillor
Ryan Thompson, Councillor
Tom Wiley, Councillor
Holly Morrison, CAO/Clerk
Christine Fraser-McDonald, Deputy Clerk
Holly Morrison, Treasurer
Peter Paquette, Director, Operations
Josh Planz, Chief Building Official
Rick Winters, Director, Operations

Gillies
1092 Hwy. 595, RR#1
South Gillies, ON P0T 1W0
Tel: 807-475-3185; *Fax:* 807-473-0767
gillies@tbaytel.net
www.gilliestownship.com
Other Information: E-mail, Building: cmaki@xplornet.com
Municipal Type: Township
Area: 92.67 sq km
County or District: Thunder Bay District; *Population in 2011:* 473
Provincial Electoral District(s): Thunder Bay-Atikokan
Federal Electoral District(s): Thunder Bay-Rainy River
Next Election: Oct. 2018 (4 year terms)
Rick Kieri, Reeve
Rosalie A. Evans, Solicitor-Clerk & Deputy Treasurer

Goderich
Municipal Office, Town Hall
57 West St.
Goderich, ON N7A 2K5
Tel: 519-524-8344; *Fax:* 519-524-7209
townhall@goderich.ca
www.goderich.ca
Municipal Type: Town
Area: 7.91 sq km
County or District: Huron; *Population in 2011:* 7,521
Provincial Electoral District(s): Huron-Bruce
Federal Electoral District(s): Huron-Bruce
Next Election: Oct. 2018 (4 year terms)
Kevin Morrison, Mayor
Larry J. McCabe, Chief Administrative Officer

Gordon / Barrie Island
P.O. Box 680
29 Noble Side Rd.
Gore Bay, ON P0P 1H0
Tel: 705-282-2702; *Fax:* 705-282-2722
adminoffice@gordonbarrieisland.ca
www.gordonbarrieisland.ca
Municipal Type: Municipality
Incorporated: Jan. 1, 2009
County or District: Manitoulin District; *Population in 2011:* 526
Provincial Electoral District(s): Algoma-Manitoulin
Federal Electoral District(s): Algoma-Manitoulin-Kapuskasing
Next Election: Oct. 2018 (4 year terms)
Note: Amalgamation of the former Township of Gordon & Allan West & the Township of Barrie Island.
Lee Hayden, Reeve
Carrie Lewis, Clerk-Treasurer

Gore Bay
P.O. Box 590
15 Water St.
Gore Bay, ON P0P 1H0
Tel: 705-282-2420; *Fax:* 705-282-3076
www.gorebay.ca
Other Information: E-mail, Treasury: pbond@gorebay.ca
Municipal Type: Town
Incorporated: 1890; *Area:* 5.27 sq km
County or District: Manitoulin District; *Population in 2011:* 850
Provincial Electoral District(s): Algoma-Manitoulin
Federal Electoral District(s): Algoma-Manitoulin-Kapuskasing
Next Election: Oct. 2018 (4 year terms)
Ron Lane, Mayor
Annette Clarke, Clerk

Grand Valley
5 Main St. North
Grand Valley, ON L9W 5S6
Tel: 519-928-5652; *Fax:* 519-928-2275
mail@townofgrandvalley.ca
www.eastluthergrandvalley.ca
Municipal Type: Township
Incorporated: Dec. 27, 1880; *Area:* 158.2 sq km
County or District: Dufferin; *Population in 2011:* 2,726
Provincial Electoral District(s): Dufferin-Caledon
Federal Electoral District(s): Dufferin-Caledon
Next Election: Oct. 2018 (4 year terms)
Note: Amalgamation of the Township of East Luther & the Village of Grand Valley on Jan. 1, 1995.
Steve Soloman, Mayor
Jane M. Wilson, Chief Administrative Officer & Clerk-Treasurer

Greater Madawaska
P.O. Box 180
1101 Francis St.
Calabogie, ON K0J 1H0
Tel: 613-752-2222; *Fax:* 613-752-2617
admin@greatermadawaska.com
www.townshipofgreatermadawaska.com
Other Information: Toll Free: 1-800-347-7224
Municipal Type: Township
Incorporated: Jan. 1, 2001; *Area:* 1,011.67 sq km
County or District: Renfrew; *Population in 2011:* 2,485
Provincial Electoral District(s): Renfrew-Nipissing-Pembroke
Federal Electoral District(s): Renfrew-Nipissing-Pembroke
Next Election: Oct. 2018 (4 year terms)
Note: Amalgamation of Bagot, Blythfield & Brougham Township & Griffith & Matawatchan Township.
Glenda McKay, Mayor
Allison Hotzhauer, Chief Administrative Officer/Clerk-Treasurer

Greenstone, Municipality of
P.O. Box 70
301 East St.
Geraldton, ON P0T 1M0
Tel: 807-854-1100; *Fax:* 807-854-1947
www.greenstone.ca
Municipal Type: Town
Area: 2,780.99 sq km
County or District: Thunder Bay; *Population in 2011:* 4,724
Provincial Electoral District(s): Thunder Bay-Superior North
Federal Electoral District(s): Thunder Bay-Superior North
Next Election: Oct. 2018 (4 year terms)
Renald Beaulieu, Mayor
Roy Sinclair, Chief Administrative Officer

Grey Highlands, Municipality of
P.O. Box 409
#1, 206 Toronto St. South
Markdale, ON N0C 1H0
Tel: 519-986-2811; *Fax:* 519-986-3643
info@greyhighlands.ca
www.greyhighlands.ca
Other Information: Toll-Free Phone: 1-888-342-4059
Municipal Type: Township
Incorporated: Jan. 1, 2001; *Area:* 880.6 sq km
County or District: Grey; *Population in 2011:* 9,520
Provincial Electoral District(s): Bruce-Grey-Owen Sound
Federal Electoral District(s): Bruce-Grey-Owen Sound
Next Election: Oct. 2018 (4 year terms)
Note: Amalgamation of Flesherton, Artemesia, Euphrasia, Markdale & Osprey.
Paul McQueen, Mayor
Dan Best, Chief Administrative Officer, 519-986-2811

Guelph/Emarosa
P.O. Box 700
8348 Wellington Rd. 124
Rockwood, ON N0B 2K0
Tel: 519-856-9951; *Fax:* 519-856-2240
general@get.on.ca
www.get.on.ca
Other Information: Toll-Free Phone: 1-800-267-1465
Municipal Type: Township
Incorporated: Jan. 1, 1999; *Area:* 291.73 sq km
County or District: Wellington; *Population in 2011:* 12,380
Provincial Electoral District(s): Wellington-Halton Hills
Federal Electoral District(s): Wellington-Halton Hills
Next Election: Oct. 2018 (4 year terms)
Note: Amalgamation of the Townships of Guelph, Eramosa, Pilkington & Nichol.
Chris White, Mayor
Kim Wingrove, Chief Administrative Officer
Shawn Armstrong, Fire Chief, 519-824-6590
Brad Roelfson, Manager, Property & Leisure Services
Ken Gagnon, Manager, Public Works
Mark Thorpe, Officer, Bylaw Enforcement
Mike Newark, Chief Building Official

Hamilton
P.O. Box 1060
8285 Majestic Hills Dr.
Cobourg, ON K9A 4W5
Tel: 905-342-2810; *Fax:* 905-342-2818
info@hamiltontownship.ca
www.hamiltontownship.ca
Municipal Type: Township
Area: 256.11 sq km
County or District: Northumberland; *Population in 2011:* 10,702
Provincial Electoral District(s): Northumberland-Quinte West
Federal Electoral District(s): Northumberland-Peterborough South
Next Election: Oct. 2018 (4 year terms)
Mark Lovshin, Mayor
Gary Woods, Deputy Mayor & Councillor
Bill Cane, Councillor
Scott Jibb, Councillor
Pat McCourt, Councillor
Kate Surerus, Clerk
Arthur Anderson, Chief Administrative Officer
Fran Aird, Acting Tax Collector & Treasurer
Sandra Stothart, Coordinator, Planning

Hanover
341 - 10th St.
Hanover, ON N4N 1P5
Tel: 519-364-2780; *Fax:* 519-364-6456
civic@hanover.ca
www.hanover.ca
Municipal Type: Town
Incorporated: Jan. 1, 2001; *Area:* 9.81 sq km
County or District: Grey; *Population in 2011:* 7,490
Provincial Electoral District(s): Bruce-Grey-Owen Sound
Federal Electoral District(s): Bruce-Grey-Owen Sound
Next Election: Oct. 2018 (4 year terms)
Sue Paterson, Mayor
Brian Tocheri, Chief Administrative Officer & Clerk

Harley
903303 Hanbury Rd., RR#2
New Liskeard, ON P0J 1P0
Tel: 705-647-5439; *Fax:* 705-647-6373
harleytwp@parolink.net
www.harley.ca
Municipal Type: Township
Incorporated: 1904; *Area:* 91.73 sq km
County or District: Timiskaming District; *Population in 2011:* 539
Provincial Electoral District(s): Timiskaming-Cochrane
Federal Electoral District(s): Timmins-James Bay
Next Election: Oct. 2018 (4 year terms)
Pauline Archambault, Reeve
Michel Lachapelle, Clerk-Treasurer

Harris
Site 4-96, RR#3
New Liskeard, ON P0J 1P0
Tel: 705-647-5094; *Fax:* 705-647-0041
harris@ntl.sympatico.ca
Municipal Type: Township
Area: 50.17 sq km
County or District: Timiskaming District; *Population in 2011:* 523
Provincial Electoral District(s): Timiskaming-Cochrane
Federal Electoral District(s): Timmins-James Bay
Next Election: Oct. 2018 (4 year terms)
Ron Sutton, Mayor

Hastings Highlands
P.O. Box 130
33011 Hwy. 62 North
Maynooth, ON K0L 2S0
Tel: 613-338-2811; *Fax:* 613-338-3292
office@hastingshighlands.ca
www.hastingshighlands.ca
Other Information: Toll-Free Phone: 1-877-338-2818
Municipal Type: Municipality
Area: 967.34 sq km
County or District: Hastings; *Population in 2011:* 4,168
Provincial Electoral District(s): Prince Edward-Hastings
Federal Electoral District(s): Hastings-Lennox and Addington
Next Election: Oct. 2018 (4 year terms)

Vivian Bloom, Mayor
Robyn Rogers, Manager of Corporate Services & Clerk

Havelock-Belmont-Methuen
P.O. Box 10
1 Ottawa St. East
Havelock, ON K0L 1Z0
Tel: 705-778-2308; *Fax:* 705-778-5248
havbelmet@hbmtwp.ca
www.havelockbelmontmethuen.on.ca
Other Information: Toll-Free Phone: 1-877-767-2795
Municipal Type: Township
Area: 526.02 sq km
County or District: Peterborough; *Population in 2011:* 4,523
Provincial Electoral District(s): Peterborough
Federal Electoral District(s): Peterborough-Kawartha
Next Election: Oct. 2018 (4 year terms)
Ronald Gerow, Reeve, 705-778-2092
Pat Kemp, Chief Administrative Officer

Head, Clara & Maria
15 Township Hall Rd.
Stonecliffe, ON K0J 2K0
Tel: 613-586-2526; *Fax:* 613-586-2596
twpshcm@xplornet.com
www.townshipsofheadclaramaria.ca
Other Information: Phone, Building Inspection: 613-586-1950
Municipal Type: Township
Area: 727.96 sq km
County or District: Renfrew; *Population in 2011:* 235
Provincial Electoral District(s): Renfrew-Nipissing-Pembroke
Federal Electoral District(s): Renfrew-Nipissing-Pembroke
Next Election: Oct. 2018 (4 year terms)
Jim Gibson, Reeve
Melinda Reith, Municipal Clerk

Hearst
Town Hall
P.O. Box 5000
925 Alexandra St.
Hearst, ON P0L 1N0
Tel: 705-362-4341; *Fax:* 705-362-5902
townofhearst@hearst.ca
www.hearst.ca
Municipal Type: Town
Incorporated: 1922; *Area:* 98.67 sq km
County or District: Cochrane District; *Population in 2011:* 5,090
Provincial Electoral District(s): Timmins-James Bay
Federal Electoral District(s): Algoma-Manitoulin-Kapuskasing
Next Election: Oct. 2018 (4 year terms)
Roger Sigouin, Mayor
Claude J. Laflamme, Chief Administrative Officer & Clerk, 705-372-2817

Highlands East, Municipality of
P.O. Box 295
County Rd. 648
Wilberforce, ON K0L 3C0
Tel: 705-448-2981; *Fax:* 705-448-2532
www.highlandseast.ca
Municipal Type: Township
Incorporated: Jan. 1, 2001; *Area:* 701.32 sq km
County or District: Haliburton; *Population in 2011:* 3,249
Provincial Electoral District(s): Haliburton-Kawartha Lakes-Brock
Federal Electoral District(s): Haliburton-Kawartha Lakes-Brock
Next Election: Oct. 2018 (4 year terms)
Note: Amalgamation of the Townships of Bicroft, Cardiff, Glamorgan & Monmouth.
Dave Burton, Reeve, 705-448-9355
Sharon Stoughton-Craig, CMO, Chief Administrative Officer, Fax: 705-448-2532

Hilliard
P.O. Box 12
RR#3
Thornloe, ON P0J 1S0
Tel: 705-563-2593; *Fax:* 705-563-2593
twphill@ntl.sympatico.ca
Municipal Type: Township
Area: 91.17 sq km
County or District: Timiskaming District; *Population in 2011:* 204
Provincial Electoral District(s): Timiskaming-Cochrane
Federal Electoral District(s): Timmins-James Bay
Next Election: Oct. 2018 (4 year terms)
Morgan Carson, Reeve
Janet Gore, Clerk-Treasurer

Hilton
P.O. Box 205
2983 Base Line
Hilton Beach, ON P0R 1G0
Tel: 705-246-2472; *Fax:* 705-246-0132
admin@hiltontownship.ca
www.hiltontownship.ca
Other Information: Phone, Roads: 705-246-1781
Municipal Type: Township
Incorporated: 1883; *Area:* 115.78 sq km
County or District: Algoma District; *Population in 2011:* 261
Provincial Electoral District(s): Algoma-Manitoulin
Federal Electoral District(s): Algoma-Manitoulin-Kapuskasing
Next Election: Oct. 2018 (4 year terms)
Rod Wood, Reeve
Valerie Obarymskyj, Clerk-Treasurer

Hilton Beach
P.O. Box 25
3100 Bowker St.
Hilton Beach, ON P0R 1G0
Tel: 705-246-2242; *Fax:* 705-246-2913
info@hiltonbeach.com
www.hiltonbeach.com
Municipal Type: Village
Area: 2.46 sq km
County or District: Algoma District; *Population in 2011:* 145
Provincial Electoral District(s): Algoma-Manitoulin
Federal Electoral District(s): Algoma-Manitoulin-Kapuskasing
Next Election: Oct. 2018 (4 year terms)
Robert Hope, Mayor
Peggy Cramp, Clerk & Treasurer

Hornepayne
P.O. Box 370
68 Front St.
Hornepayne, ON P0M 1Z0
Tel: 807-868-2020; *Fax:* 807-868-2787
www.townshipofhornepayne.ca
Municipal Type: Township
Area: 204.52 sq km
County or District: Algoma District; *Population in 2011:* 1,050
Provincial Electoral District(s): Algoma-Manitoulin
Federal Electoral District(s): Algoma-Manitoulin-Kapuskasing
Next Election: Oct. 2018 (4 year terms)
Morley Forster, Mayor
Julie Roy-Ward, Chief Administration Officer

Horton
2253 Johnston Rd., RR#5
Renfrew, ON K7V 3Z8
Tel: 613-432-6271; *Fax:* 613-432-7298
www.hortontownship.ca
Municipal Type: Township
Area: 158.38 sq km
County or District: Renfrew; *Population in 2011:* 2,719
Provincial Electoral District(s): Renfrew-Nipissing-Pembroke
Federal Electoral District(s): Renfrew-Nipissing-Pembroke
Next Election: Oct. 2018 (4 year terms)
Robert Kingsbury, Mayor
Mackie J. McLaren, Chief Administrative Officer & Clerk

Howick
P.O. Box 89
Hwy 87
Gorrie, ON N0G 1X0
Tel: 519-335-3208; *Fax:* 519-335-6208
office@town.howick.on.ca
www.town.howick.on.ca
Municipal Type: Township
Area: 287.17 sq km
County or District: Huron; *Population in 2011:* 3,856
Provincial Electoral District(s): Huron-Bruce
Federal Electoral District(s): Huron-Bruce
Next Election: Oct. 2018 (4 year terms)
Art Versteeg, Reeve
Carol Watson, Clerk

Hudson
903303 Hanbury Rd., RR#2
New Liskeard, ON P0J 1P0
Tel: 705-647-5439; *Fax:* 705-647-6373
harleytwp@parolink.net
www.hudson.ca
Municipal Type: Township
Area: 90.46 sq km
County or District: Timiskaming District; *Population in 2011:* 476
Provincial Electoral District(s): Timiskaming-Cochrane
Federal Electoral District(s): Timmins-James Bay
Next Election: Oct. 2018 (4 year terms)
Larry Craig, Reeve
Michel Lachapelle, Clerk-Treasurer

Huron East, Municipality of
P.O. Box 610
72 Main St. South
Seaforth, ON N0K 1W0
Tel: 519-527-0160; *Fax:* 519-527-2561
webmaster@huroneast.com
www.huroneast.com
Other Information: Toll-Free Phone: 1-888-868-7513
Municipal Type: Town
Incorporated: Jan. 1, 2001; *Area:* 669.16 sq km
County or District: Huron; *Population in 2011:* 9,264
Provincial Electoral District(s): Huron-Bruce
Federal Electoral District(s): Huron-Bruce
Next Election: Oct. 2018 (4 year terms)
Note: Amalgamation of the Town of Seaforth, the Village of Brussels, & the Townships of Grey, McKillop and Tuckersmith.
Bernie MacLellan, Mayor, 519-233-7489, Fax: 519-233-3405
Brad Knight, Clerk-Administrator

Huron Shores
P.O. Box 460
7 Bridge St.
Iron Bridge, ON P0R 1H0
Tel: 705-843-2033; *Fax:* 705-843-2035
email@huronshores.ca
www.huronshores.ca
Municipal Type: Municipality
Area: 455.33 sq km
County or District: Algoma District; *Population in 2011:* 1,723
Provincial Electoral District(s): Algoma-Manitoulin
Federal Electoral District(s): Algoma-Manitoulin-Kapuskasing
Next Election: Oct. 2018 (4 year terms)
Lionel Reeves, Mayor
Deborah Tonelli, AMCT, Administrator-Clerk

Huron-Kinloss
P.O. Box 130
21 Queen St.
Ripley, ON N0G 2R0
Tel: 519-395-3735; *Fax:* 519-395-4107
info@huronkinloss.com
www.huronkinloss.com
Municipal Type: Township
Incorporated: 1999; *Area:* 440.59 sq km
County or District: Bruce; *Population in 2011:* 6,790
Provincial Electoral District(s): Huron-Bruce
Federal Electoral District(s): Huron-Bruce
Next Election: Oct. 2018 (4 year terms)
Note: Amalgamation of the Village of Lucknow & the Townships of Ripley-Huron & Kinloss.
Mitch Twolan, Mayor, 519-395-0717
Sonya Watson, Clerk

Ignace
P.O. Box 248
34 Hwy. 17 West
Ignace, ON P0T 1T0
Tel: 807-934-2202; *Fax:* 807-934-2864
ecdev@tbaytel.net
www.town.ignace.on.ca
Municipal Type: Township
Incorporated: 1908; *Area:* 72.66 sq km
County or District: Kenora District; *Population in 2011:* 1,202
Provincial Electoral District(s): Kenora-Rainy River
Federal Electoral District(s): Kenora
Next Election: Oct. 2018 (4 year terms)
Lee Kennard, Mayor
Wayne Hanchard, Administrator & Treasurer

Iroquois Falls
P.O. Box 230
253 Main St.
Iroquois Falls, ON P0K 1G0
Tel: 705-232-5700; *Fax:* 705-232-4241
www.iroquoisfalls.com
Municipal Type: Town
Area: 599.43 sq km
County or District: Cochrane District; *Population in 2011:* 4,595
Provincial Electoral District(s): Timiskaming-Cochrane
Federal Electoral District(s): Timmins-James Bay
Next Election: Oct. 2018 (4 year terms)
Michael Shea, Mayor
Michelle Larose, Administrator-Clerk

James
P.O. Box 10
372 Third St.
Elk Lake, ON P0J 1G0
Tel: 705-678-2237; *Fax:* 705-678-2495
elklake@ntl.sympatico.ca
www.elklake.ca

Municipal Type: Township
Incorporated: 1909; *Area:* 86.19 sq km
County or District: Timiskaming District; *Population in 2011:* 424
Provincial Electoral District(s): Timiskaming-Cochrane
Federal Electoral District(s): Timmins-James Bay
Next Election: Oct. 2018 (4 year terms)
Terry Fiset, Reeve
Myrna J. Hayes, Clerk-Treasurer

Jocelyn
RR#1
Richards Landing, ON P0R 1J0
Tel: 705-246-2025; *Fax:* 705-246-3282
jocelynt@soonet.ca
Municipal Type: Township
Area: 131.37 sq km
County or District: Algoma District; *Population in 2011:* 237
Provincial Electoral District(s): Algoma-Manitoulin
Federal Electoral District(s): Algoma-Manitoulin-Kapuskasing
Next Election: Oct. 2018 (4 year terms)
Mark Henderson, Reeve
Janet Boucher, Clerk

Johnson
P.O. Box 160
1 Johnson Dr.
Desbarats, ON P0R 1E0
Tel: 705-782-6601; *Fax:* 705-782-6780
johnsontwp@bellnet.ca
www.johnsontwp.ca
Municipal Type: Township
Area: 119.67 sq km
County or District: Algoma District; *Population in 2011:* 750
Provincial Electoral District(s): Algoma-Manitoulin
Federal Electoral District(s): Algoma-Manitoulin-Kapuskasing
Next Election: Oct. 2018 (4 year terms)
Ted Hicks, Mayor, 705-782-6348
Ruth Kelso, Clerk & Chief Administrative Officer

Joly
P.O. Box 519
871 Forest Lake Rd.
Sundridge, ON P0A 1Z0
Tel: 705-384-5428; *Fax:* 705-384-0845
office@townshipofjoly.com
www.townshipofjoly.com
Municipal Type: Township
Area: 193.82 sq km
County or District: Parry Sound District; *Population in 2011:* 284
Provincial Electoral District(s): Parry Sound-Muskoka
Federal Electoral District(s): Parry Sound-Muskoka
Next Election: Oct. 2018 (4 year terms)
Bruce Baker, Reeve
Linda Maurer, Clerk

Kapuskasing
Civic Centre
88 Riverside Dr.
Kapuskasing, ON P5N 1B3
Tel: 705-335-2341; *Fax:* 705-337-1741
townkap@ntl.sympatico.ca
www.kapuskasing.ca
Municipal Type: Town
Incorporated: 1921; *Area:* 83.98 sq km
County or District: Cochrane District; *Population in 2011:* 8,196
Provincial Electoral District(s): Timmins-James Bay
Federal Electoral District(s): Algoma-Manitoulin-Kapuskasing
Next Election: Oct. 2018 (4 year terms)
Alan Spacek, Mayor
Yves Labelle, Chief Administrative Officer

Kearney
P.O. Box 38
8 Main St.
Kearney, ON P0A 1M0
Tel: 705-636-7752; *Fax:* 705-636-0527
kearney1@vianet.ca
www.townofkearney.com
Municipal Type: Town
Incorporated: 1908; *Area:* 529.5 sq km
County or District: Parry Sound District; *Population in 2011:* 841
Provincial Electoral District(s): Parry Sound-Muskoka
Federal Electoral District(s): Parry Sound-Muskoka
Next Election: Oct. 2018 (4 year terms)
Lance Thrale, Mayor
Brenda Fraser, Clerk Administrator

Kenora
Kenora District Services Board Admin Office
#1, 211 Princess St.
Dryden, ON P8N 3L5
Tel: 807-223-2100; *Fax:* 807-223-6500
kdsb@kdsb.on.ca
www.kdsb.on.ca
Municipal Type: District
Area: 407,192.66 sq km
Population in 2011: 64,419
Barry Baltessen, Chair, Kenora District Services Board of Directors
Henry Wall, Chief Administrative Officer

Kerns
903303 Hanbury Rd., RR#2
New Liskeard, ON P0J 1P0
Tel: 705-647-5439; *Fax:* 705-647-6373
harleytwp@parolink.net
www.kerns.ca
Municipal Type: Township
Incorporated: 1904; *Area:* 90.44 sq km
County or District: Timiskaming District; *Population in 2011:* 359
Provincial Electoral District(s): Timiskaming-Cochrane
Federal Electoral District(s): Timmins-James Bay
Next Election: Oct. 2018 (4 year terms)
Terry Phillips, Reeve
Michel Lachapelle, Clerk-Treasurer

Killaloe, Hagarty & Richards
P.O. Box 39
1 John St.
Killaloe, ON K0J 2A0
Tel: 613-757-2300; *Fax:* 613-757-3634
info@khrtownship.ca
www.killaloe-hagarty-richards.ca
Municipal Type: Township
Incorporated: July 1, 2000; *Area:* 395.91 sq km
County or District: Renfrew; *Population in 2011:* 2,402
Provincial Electoral District(s): Renfrew-Nipissing-Pembroke
Federal Electoral District(s): Renfrew-Nipissing-Pembroke
Next Election: Oct. 2018 (4 year terms)
Note: Amalgamation of the Township of Hagarty & Richards & the former Village of Killaloe.
Janice Visneskie Moore, Mayor
Lorna Hudder, Chief Administrative Officer & Clerk-Treasurer

Killarney, Municipality of
32 Commissioner St.
Killarney, ON P0M 2A0
Tel: 705-287-2424; *Fax:* 705-287-2660
townkill@vianet.on.ca
www.municipality.killarney.on.ca
Other Information: Toll-Free Phone: 1-888-597-2721
Municipal Type: Town
Incorporated: Jan. 1, 1999; *Area:* 1,513.58 sq km
County or District: Sudbury District; *Population in 2011:* 505
Provincial Electoral District(s): Algoma-Manitoulin
Federal Electoral District(s): Nickel Belt
Next Election: Oct. 2018 (4 year terms)
Ginny Rock, Mayor
Candy Beavais, Clerk-Treasurer

Kincardine
1475 Conc. 5, RR#5
Kincardine, ON N2Z 2X6
Tel: 519-396-3468; *Fax:* 519-396-8288
ssmith@kincardine.net
www.kincardine.net
Municipal Type: Municipality
Area: 537.65 sq km
County or District: Bruce; *Population in 2011:* 11,174
Provincial Electoral District(s): Huron-Bruce
Federal Electoral District(s): Huron-Bruce
Next Election: Oct. 2018 (4 year terms)
Anne Eadie, Mayor
Jacqueline Faubert, Councillor at Large
Andrew White, Councillor at Large
Jacqueline Faubert, Councillor at Large
Laura Haight, Councillor at Large
Maureen A. Couture, Councillor, Wards: 1
Mike Leggett, Councillor, 519-396-4529, Wards: 1
Linda McKee, Councillor, Wards: 2
Randy Roppel, Councillor, 519-368-7792, Wards: 3
Murray Clarke, Chief Administrative Officer
Roxana Baumann, Treasurer, 519-396-3468
Michele Barr, Director, Building & Planning
Don Huston, Operations Manager, Public Works
Kent Padfield, Fire Chief
Karen Kieffer, Recreation Director

King
2075 King Rd.
King City, ON L7B 1A1
Tel: 905-833-5321; *Fax:* 905-833-2300
online@king.ca
www.king.ca
Municipal Type: Township
Incorporated: 1850; *Area:* 333.04 sq km
County or District: York Reg. Mun.; *Population in 2011:* 19,899
Provincial Electoral District(s): Oak Ridges-Markham; York-Simcoe
Federal Electoral District(s): King-Vaughan; York-Simcoe
Next Election: Oct. 2018 (4 year terms)
Steve Pellegrini, Mayor
Cleve Mortelliti, Councillor, Wards: 1
David Boyd, Councillor, Wards: 2
Linda Pabst, Councillor, Wards: 3
Bill Cober, Councillor, Wards: 4
Debbie Schaefer, Councillor, Wards: 5
Avia Eek, Councillor, Wards: 6
Kathryn Smyth, Director of Clerks
Susan Plamondon, Chief Administrative Officer
Allan Evelyn, Director, Finance & Treasurer
Mike Cole, Deputy Director, Engineering & Development
Chris Fasciano, Director, Parks, Recreation & Culture
Cara Tuch, Manager, Human Resources
Gaspare Ritacca, Manager, Planning & Development
Jim Wall, Fire Chief

Kirkland Lake
P.O. Box 1757
3 Kirkland St. West
Kirkland Lake, ON P2N 3P4
Tel: 705-567-9361; *Fax:* 705-567-3535
kirklandlake.ca
Municipal Type: Town
Incorporated: 1972; *Area:* 262.24 sq km
County or District: Timiskaming District; *Population in 2011:* 8,133
Provincial Electoral District(s): Timiskaming-Cochrane
Federal Electoral District(s): Timmins-James Bay
Next Election: Oct. 2018 (4 year terms)
Note: Formerly known as the Township of Teck.
Tony Antoniazzi, Mayor
Nancy Allick, Chief Administrative Officer

Laird
3 Pumpkin Point Rd., RR#4
Echo Bay, ON P0S 1C0
Tel: 705-248-2395; *Fax:* 705-248-1138
lairdtwp@soonet.ca
www.lairdtownship.ca
Municipal Type: Township
Incorporated: 1891; *Area:* 101.77 sq km
County or District: Algoma District; *Population in 2011:* 1,057
Provincial Electoral District(s): Algoma-Manitoulin
Federal Electoral District(s): Algoma-Manitoulin-Kapuskasing
Next Election: Oct. 2018 (4 year terms)
Richard (Dick) Beitz, Mayor
Phyllis L. MacKay, Clerk-Treasurer, Tax Collector, & License Issuing Officer

Lake of Bays
1012 Dwight Beach Rd., RR#1
Dwight, ON P0A 1H0
Tel: 705-635-2272; *Fax:* 705-635-2132
contact@lakeofbays.on.ca
www.lakeofbays.on.ca
Other Information: Toll-Free Phone: 1-877-566-0005
Municipal Type: Township
Incorporated: 1971; *Area:* 671.46 sq km
County or District: Muskoka Dist. Mun.; *Population in 2011:* 3,284
Provincial Electoral District(s): Parry Sound-Muskoka
Federal Electoral District(s): Parry Sound-Muskoka
Next Election: Oct. 2018 (4 year terms)
Note: Amalgamation of the former Townships of Franklin, Ridout, McLean & Sinclair/Finlayson.
Bob Young, Mayor, 705-635-1845
Michelle Percival, Chief Administrative Officer

Lake of the Woods
P.O. Box 427
211 Fourth St.
Rainy River, ON P0W 1L0
Tel: 807-852-3529; *Fax:* 807-852-3529
www.lakeofthewoods.ca
Municipal Type: Township
Incorporated: Jan. 1, 1998; *Area:* 751.17 sq km
County or District: Rainy River District; *Population in 2011:* 296
Provincial Electoral District(s): Kenora-Rainy River
Federal Electoral District(s): Thunder Bay-Rainy River

Next Election: Oct. 2018 (4 year terms)
Note: Amalgamation of the Township of Morson & McCrosson-Tovell.
Valerie Pizey, Mayor
Patrick W. Giles, Clerk-Treasurer

Lakeshore
419 Notre Dame Rd.
Belle River, ON N0R 1A0
Tel: 519-728-2700; *Fax:* 519-728-9530
webmaster@lakeshore.ca
www.lakeshore.ca
Municipal Type: Town
Incorporated: 1999; *Area:* 530.32 sq km
County or District: Essex; *Population in 2011:* 34,546
Provincial Electoral District(s): Essex
Federal Electoral District(s): Essex
Next Election: Oct. 2018 (4 year terms)
Note: Amalgamation of the former Town of Belle River & the former Townships of Maidstone, Rochester, Tilbury North & Tilbury West.
Tom Bain, Mayor
Al Fazio, Deputy Mayor & Councillor
Steven Wilder, Councillor, Wards: 1
Len Janisse, Councillor, Wards: 2
Dave Monk, Councillor, Wards: 3
Tracey Bailey, Councillor, Wards: 4
Dan Diemer, Councillor, Wards: 5
Linda McKinlay, Councillor, Wards: 6
Mary Masse, Town Clerk
Kirk Foran, Chief Administrative Officer & Director, Corporate Services
Cheryl Horrobin, Director, Finance & Performance Service
Steven Salmons, Director, Community & Development Services
Tom Touralias, Director, Engineering & Infrastructure Services
Don Williamson, Fire Chief
Chuck Chevalier, Manager, Public Works
Kim Darroch, Manager, Development Services
Tony DiCiocco, Manager, Engineering Services
Tony Francisco, Manager, Environmental Services
Maureen Lesperance, Coordinator, Planning

Lambton Shores
P.O. Box 610
7883 Amtelecom Pkwy.
Forest, ON N0N 1J0
Tel: 519-786-2335; *Fax:* 519-786-2135
administration@lambtonshores.ca
www.lambtonshores.ca
Other Information: Toll Free: 1-877-786-2335
Municipal Type: Municipality
Incorporated: 2001; *Area:* 331.08 sq km
County or District: Lambton; *Population in 2011:* 10,656
Provincial Electoral District(s): Lambton-Kent-Middlesex
Federal Electoral District(s): Lambton-Kent-Middlesex
Next Election: Oct. 2018 (4 year terms)
Note: Amalgamation of the Towns of Bosanquet & Forest, & the Villages of Thedford, Arkona & Grand Bend.
Bill Weber, Mayor, 519-649-6885
Doug Cooke, Deputy Mayor & Councillor
Dave Maguire, Councillor, 519-238-8687, Wards: 1
Doug Bonesteel, Councillor, 519-238-1799, Wards: 2
Gerry Rupke, Councillor, Wards: 3
Ronn E. Dodge, Councillor, Wards: 4
Rick Goodhand, Councillor, Wards: 5
James Finlay, Councillor, Wards: 6
Jeff Wilcox, Councillor, Wards: 7
Carol McKenzie, Clerk, 519-786-2335, Fax: 519-786-2135
Kevin Williams, Chief Administrative Officer, 519-786-2335, Fax: 519-786-2135
Janet Ferguson, Treasurer, 519-238-8461, Fax: 519-238-8577
Stephen McAuley, Director, Community Services, 519-243-1400
Patti Richardson, Senior Planner, 519-786-2335, Fax: 519-786-2135
Randy Lovie, Chief Building Official, 519-786-2335

Lanark Highlands
P.O. Box 340
75 George St.
Lanark, ON K0G 1K0
Tel: 613-259-2398; *Fax:* 613-259-2291
mailbag@lanarkhighlands.ca
www.lanarkhighlands.ca
Other Information: Toll-Free Phone: 1-800-239-4695
Municipal Type: Township
Incorporated: July 1, 1997; *Area:* 1,033.3 sq km
County or District: Lanark; *Population in 2011:* 5,128
Provincial Electoral District(s): Lanark-Frontenac-Lennox & Addington
Federal Electoral District(s): Lanark-Frontenac-Kingston
Next Election: Oct. 2018 (4 year terms)
Note: Amalgamation of North West Lanark Township & Darling Township.
Brian Stewart, Mayor
Rob Wittkie, Chief Administrative Officer & Clerk

Larder Lake
P.O. Box 40
13 Godfrey St.
Larder Lake, ON P0K 1L0
Tel: 705-643-2158; *Fax:* 705-643-2311
www.larderlake.net
Municipal Type: Township
Area: 228.73 sq km
County or District: Timiskaming District; *Population in 2011:* 684
Provincial Electoral District(s): Timiskaming-Cochrane
Federal Electoral District(s): Timmins-James Bay
Next Election: Oct. 2018 (4 year terms)
Gary Cunnington, Mayor
Dwight McTaggart, Clerk-Treasurer/CAO

Latchford
P.O. Box 10
10 Main St.
Latchford, ON P0J 1N0
Tel: 705-676-2416; *Fax:* 705-676-2121
www.latchford.ca
Municipal Type: Town
Incorporated: 1907; *Area:* 153.27 sq km
County or District: Timiskaming District; *Population in 2011:* 387
Provincial Electoral District(s): Timiskaming-Cochrane
Federal Electoral District(s): Nipissing-Timiskaming
Next Election: Oct. 2018 (4 year terms)
George Lefebvre, Mayor
Jaime Allen, Municipal Clerk, 705-676-2416

Laurentian Hills
34465 Hwy. 17, Point Alexander, RR#1
Deep River, ON K0J 1P0
Tel: 613-584-3114; *Fax:* 613-584-3285
info@laurentianhills.ca
www.laurentianhills.ca
Municipal Type: Town
Incorporated: Jan. 1, 2000; *Area:* 640.37 sq km
County or District: Renfrew; *Population in 2011:* 2,811
Provincial Electoral District(s): Renfrew-Nipissing-Pembroke
Federal Electoral District(s): Renfrew-Nipissing-Pembroke
Next Election: Oct. 2018 (4 year terms)
Note: Amalgamation of the United Townships of Rolph, Buchanan, Wylie & McKay & the Village of Chalk River.
John Reinwald, Mayor
Sherry Batten, Chief Administrative Officer & Clerk, 613-584-3114

Laurentian Valley
460 Witt Rd., RR#4
Pembroke, ON K8A 6W5
Tel: 613-735-6291; *Fax:* 613-735-5820
laurentian@laurvall.on.ca
www.laurentianvalleytwsp.on.ca
Municipal Type: Township
Incorporated: Jan. 1, 2000; *Area:* 552.44 sq km
County or District: Renfrew; *Population in 2011:* 9,657
Provincial Electoral District(s): Renfrew-Nipissing-Pembroke
Federal Electoral District(s): Renfrew-Nipissing-Pembroke
Next Election: Oct. 2018 (4 year terms)
Note: Amalgamation of the former Townships of Stafford-Pembroke & Alice & Fraser.
Steve Bennet, Mayor
Dean Sauriol, Chief Administrative Officer & Clerk, 613-735-6291, Fax: 613-735-5820

Leamington
111 Erie St. North
Leamington, ON N8H 2Z3
Tel: 519-326-5761; *Fax:* 519-326-2481
info@leamington.ca
www.leamington.ca
Other Information: E-mail, Public Works: publicworks@leamington.ca
Municipal Type: Municipality
Incorporated: 1874; *Area:* 261.92 sq km
County or District: Essex; *Population in 2011:* 28,403
Provincial Electoral District(s): Chatham-Kent-Essex
Federal Electoral District(s): Chatham-Kent-Leamington
Next Election: Oct. 2018 (4 year terms)
Note: Incorporated as a town in 1890. Restructuring occurred in 1999.
John Paterson, Mayor, 519-326-5761
Hilda MacDonald, Deputy Mayor & Councillor
Larry Verbeke, Councillor
Rick Allen, Councillor
John Jacobs, Councillor
John Hammond, Councillor
Tim Wilkinson, Councillor
Brian R. Sweet, B.A., LL.B, Municipal Clerk, Corporate Counsel & Director, Corporate Services
Peter Neufeld, Chief Administrative Officer
Cheryl L. Horrobin, B.Comm, CA, AMCT, Director, Finance & Business Services
Tracey Pillon-Abbs, Director, Development Services
Robert Sharon, Director, Community Services
Chuck Parsons, Fire Chief
Bechara Daher, Manager, Building Services
Allan Botham, Manager, Engineering
Kit Woods, Manager, Environmental Services

Leeds & Grenville
#100, 25 Central Ave. West
Brockville, ON K6V 4N6
Tel: 613-342-3840; *Fax:* 613-342-2101
www.leedsgrenville.com
Other Information: Toll-Free Phone: 1-800-770-2170
Municipal Type: United County
Area: 3,350.18 sq km
Population in 2011: 99,306
Next Election: Oct. 2018 (4 year terms)
David Gordon, Warden, Wards: North Grenville Municipality
Herb Scott, Councillor, Wards: Athens Township
Doug Malanka, Councillor, Wards: Augusta Township
Patrick Sayeau, Councillor, Wards: Edwardsburgh/Cardinal Township
Jim Pickard, Councillor, Wards: Elizabethtown-Kitley Township
Roger Haley, Councillor, Wards: Front of Yonge Township
Joe Baptista, Councillor, Wards: Leeds & the Thousand Islands
David Nash, Councillor, Wards: Merrickville-Wolford
Ronald E. Holman, Councillor, Wards: Rideau Lakes Township
Robin Patricia Jones, Councillor, Wards: Westport
Lesley Todd, Clerk
Andy Brown, Chief Administrative Officer
Pat Huffman, Treasurer
Leslie Shepherd, Director, Works, Planning Services & Asset Management
James Alexander (Sandy) Hay, Manager, Planning Services
Geoff McVey, Manager, Forest
Kevin Spencer, Manager, Public Safety
Ann Weir, Manager, Economic Development

Leeds & The Thousand Islands
P.O. Box 280
1233 Prince St.
Lansdowne, ON K0E 1L0
Tel: 613-659-2415; *Fax:* 613-659-3619
www.leeds1000islands.ca
Other Information: Toll-Free Phone: 1-866-220-2327
Municipal Type: Township
Incorporated: Jan. 1, 2001; *Area:* 607.18 sq km
County or District: Leeds & Grenville; *Population in 2011:* 9,277
Provincial Electoral District(s): Leeds-Grenville
Federal Electoral District(s): Leeds-Grenville-Thousand Islands and Rideau Lakes
Next Election: Oct. 2018 (4 year terms)
Note: Amalgamation of Front of Leeds & Lansdowne, Rear of Leeds & Lansdowne & Front of Escott.
Joe Baptista, Mayor
Milena Avramovic, Chief Administrative Officer

Limerick
89 Limerick Lake Rd., RR#2
Gilmour, ON K0L 1W0
Tel: 613-474-2863; *Fax:* 613-474-0478
assistant@township.limerick.on.ca
www.township.limerick.on.ca
Municipal Type: Township
Incorporated: 1887; *Area:* 200.59 sq km
County or District: Hastings; *Population in 2011:* 352
Provincial Electoral District(s): Prince Edward-Hastings
Federal Electoral District(s): Hastings-Lennox and Addington
Next Election: Oct. 2018 (4 year terms)
Sharon Carson, Reeve
Jennifer Trumble, Clerk-Treasurer/CAO, 613-474-2863

Loyalist
P.O. Box 70
263 Main St.
Odessa, ON K0H 2H0
Tel: 613-386-7351; *Fax:* 613-386-3833
www.loyalisttownship.ca
Municipal Type: Township
Incorporated: 1998; *Area:* 340.02 sq km
County or District: Lennox & Addington; *Population in 2011:* 16,221
Provincial Electoral District(s): Lanark-Frontenac-Lennox & Addington
Federal Electoral District(s): Hastings-Lennox and Addington

Next Election: Oct. 2018 (4 year terms)
Note: Amalgamation of the Townships of Ernestown, Amherst Island & the Village of Bath.
Bill Lowry, Mayor
Ric Bresee, Deputy Mayor
Duncan Ashley, Councillor, Wards: 1 Amherst Island
Ed Daniliunas, Councillor, Wards: 2 Bath
Jim Hegadorn, Councillor, Wards: 3 Ernestown
Ron Gordon, Councillor, Wards: 3 Ernestown
Penny Porter, Councillor, Wards: 3 Ernestown
Bob Maddocks, Chief Administrative Officer
Alida Moffat, Deputy Chief Administrative Officer
Kate Tindal, Director, Finance
Andree Ferris, Director, Recreation Services
David Thompson, Director, Infrastructure Services
Murray Beckel, Chief Building Official & Director, Planning & Development Services
Fred Stephenson, Fire Chief
Jenna Campbell, Manager, Engineering
Lorie McFarland, Manager, Utilities
David MacPherson, Manager, Public Works

Lucan Biddulph
P.O. Box 190
33351 Richmond St., RR#3
Lucan, ON N0M 2J0
Tel: 519-227-4491; *Fax:* 519-227-4998
www.lucanbiddulph.on.ca
Municipal Type: Township
Incorporated: Jan. 1, 1999; *Area:* 169.15 sq km
County or District: Middlesex; *Population in 2011:* 4,338
Provincial Electoral District(s): Lambton-Kent-Middlesex
Federal Electoral District(s): Lambton-Kent-Middlesex
Next Election: Oct. 2018 (4 year terms)
Note: Amalgamation of the Village of Lucan and the Township of Biddulph.
Cathy Burghardt-Jesson, Mayor
Ron Reymer, Chief Administrative Officer

MacDonald, Meredith & Aberdeen Additional
P.O. Box 10
208 Church St.
Echo Bay, ON P0S 1C0
Tel: 705-248-2441;
twpmacd@onlink.net
www.echobay.ca
Municipal Type: Township
Incorporated: 1899; *Area:* 161.73 sq km
County or District: Algoma District; *Population in 2011:* 1,464
Provincial Electoral District(s): Algoma-Manitoulin
Federal Electoral District(s): Algoma-Manitoulin-Kapuskasing
Next Election: Oct. 2018 (4 year terms)
Lynn Watson, Mayor
Lynne Duguay, Clerk Administrator

Machar
P.O. Box 70
73 Municipal Rd. North
South River, ON P0A 1X0
Tel: 705-386-7741; *Fax:* 705-386-0765
www.machartownship.net
Municipal Type: Township
Area: 184.38 sq km
County or District: Parry Sound District; *Population in 2011:* 923
Provincial Electoral District(s): Parry Sound-Muskoka
Federal Electoral District(s): Parry Sound-Muskoka
Next Election: Oct. 2018 (4 year terms)
Lynda Carleton, Mayor
Brenda Paul, AMCT, Clerk Administrator

Machin
P.O. Box 249
75 Spruce St.
Vermilion Bay, ON P0V 2V0
Tel: 807-227-2633; *Fax:* 807-227-5443
deputyclerk@visitmachin.com
www.visitmachin.com
Municipal Type: Township
Area: 288.85 sq km
County or District: Kenora District; *Population in 2011:* 935
Provincial Electoral District(s): Kenora-Rainy River
Federal Electoral District(s): Kenora
Next Election: Oct. 2018 (4 year terms)
Drew Myers, Mayor
Tammy Rob, Clerk-Treasurer

Madawaska Valley
P.O. Box 1000
85 Bay St.
Barry's Bay, ON K0J 1B0
Tel: 613-756-2747; *Fax:* 613-756-0553
info@madawaskavalley.ca
www.madawaskavalley.on.ca
Other Information: Toll Free: 1-866-222-8699
Municipal Type: Township
Incorporated: Jan. 1, 2001; *Area:* 670.11 sq km
County or District: Renfrew; *Population in 2011:* 4,282
Provincial Electoral District(s): Renfrew-Nipissing-Pembroke
Federal Electoral District(s): Renfrew-Nipissing-Pembroke
Next Election: Oct. 2018 (4 year terms)
Note: Amalgamation of Barry's Bay Village, Radcliffe Township & Sherwood, Jones & Burns Township.
Kim Love, Mayor
Craig Kelley, Chief Administrative Officer/Clerk, 613-756-2747, Fax: 613-756-0553

Madoc
P.O. Box 503
15651 Hwy. 62, RR#2
Madoc, ON K0K 2K0
Tel: 613-473-2677; *Fax:* 613-473-5580
www.madoc.ca
Other Information: E-mail, Building: building@madoc.ca
Municipal Type: Township
Incorporated: 1850; *Area:* 269.98 sq km
County or District: Hastings; *Population in 2011:* 2,197
Provincial Electoral District(s): Prince Edward-Hastings
Federal Electoral District(s): Hastings-Lennox and Addington
Next Election: Oct. 2018 (4 year terms)
Robert Sager, Reeve
W.G. (Bill) Lebow, B.A., AMCT, Clerk Administrator

Magnetawan, Municipality of
P.O. Box 70
4304 Hwy. 520
Magnetawan, ON P0A 1P0
Tel: 705-387-3947; *Fax:* 705-387-4875
admin@magnetawan.com
www.magnetawan.com
Other Information: E-mail, Roads: roads@magnetawan.com
Municipal Type: Township
Incorporated: July 4, 1997; *Area:* 523.07 sq km
County or District: Parry Sound District; *Population in 2011:* 1,454
Provincial Electoral District(s): Parry Sound-Muskoka
Federal Electoral District(s): Parry Sound-Muskoka
Next Election: Oct. 2018 (4 year terms)
Sam Dunnett, Mayor
Roger Labelle, Clerk

Malahide
87 John St. South
Aylmer, ON N5H 2C3
Tel: 519-773-5344; *Fax:* 519-773-5334
malahide.ca
Municipal Type: Township
Incorporated: Jan. 1, 1998; *Area:* 395.07 sq km
County or District: Elgin; *Population in 2011:* 9,146
Provincial Electoral District(s): Elgin-Middlesex-London
Federal Electoral District(s): Elgin-Middlesex-London
Next Election: Oct. 2018 (4 year terms)
Note: Amalgamation of the Township of Malahide, Village of Springfield & Township of South Dorchester.
Dave Mennill, Mayor, 519-773-8850
Michelle M. Casavecchia-Sommers, Chief Administrative Officer & Clerk

Manitoulin
Gore Bay, ON
Municipal Type: District
Area: 4,759.74 sq km
Population in 2011: 13,048
Provincial Electoral District(s): Algoma-Manitoulin
Federal Electoral District(s): Algoma-Manitoulin-Kapuskasing
Note: The District incorporates the towns of Gore Bay, & Northeastern Manitoulin & the Islands; communities in the townships of Assiginack, Barrie Isl., Billing, Burpe & Mills, Central Manitoulin, Cockburn Isl., Gordon, & Tehkummah; & 1st Nations reserves

Manitouwadge
1 Mississauga Rd.
Manitouwadge, ON P0T 2C0
Tel: 807-826-3227; *Fax:* 807-826-4592
www.manitouwadge.ca
Municipal Type: Township
Area: 351.97 sq km
County or District: Thunder Bay District; *Population in 2011:* 2,105
Provincial Electoral District(s): Algoma-Manitoulin
Federal Electoral District(s): Thunder Bay-Superior North
Next Election: Oct. 2018 (4 year terms)
Andy Major, Mayor
Margaret Hartling, Chief Administrative Officer, Clerk & Treasurer, 807-826-3227

Mapleton
P.O. Box 160
7275 Sideroad 3
Drayton, ON N0G 1P0
Tel: 519-638-3313; *Fax:* 519-638-5113
www.mapleton.ca
Other Information: Toll-Free Phone: 1-800-385-7248
Municipal Type: Township
Incorporated: Jan. 1, 1999; *Area:* 534.71 sq km
County or District: Wellington; *Population in 2011:* 9,989
Provincial Electoral District(s): Perth-Wellington
Federal Electoral District(s): Perth-Wellington
Next Election: Oct. 2018 (4 year terms)
Note: Amalgamation of the Townships of Maryborough & Peel & the Village of Drayton.
S. Neil Driscoll, Mayor
Patty Sinnamon, Chief Administrative Officer & Clerk

Marathon
P.O. Box TM
4 Hemlo Dr.
Marathon, ON P0T 2E0
Tel: 807-229-1340; *Fax:* 807-229-1999
info@marathon.ca; clerk@marathon.ca
www.marathon.ca
Municipal Type: Town
Area: 170.48 sq km
County or District: Thunder Bay District; *Population in 2011:* 3,353
Provincial Electoral District(s): Thunder Bay-Superior North
Federal Electoral District(s): Thunder Bay-Superior North
Next Election: Oct. 2018 (4 year terms)
Rick Dumas, Mayor
Brian Tocheri, Chief Administrative Officer & Clerk

Markstay-Warren, Municipality of
P.O. Box 79
21 Main St. South
Markstay, ON P0M 2G0
Tel: 705-853-4536; *Fax:* 705-853-4964
info@markstay-warren.ca
www.markstay-warren.ca
Other Information: Toll-Free Phone: 1-866-710-1065
Municipal Type: Town
Incorporated: Jan. 1, 1999; *Area:* 510.12 sq km
County or District: Sudbury District; *Population in 2011:* 2,297
Provincial Electoral District(s): Timiskaming-Cochrane
Federal Electoral District(s): Nickel Belt
Next Election: Oct. 2018 (4 year terms)
Note: Amalgamation of the Towns of Warren, Markstay & the Townships of Awrey, Street, Hawley, Loughrin & Henry.
Stephen Salonin, Mayor
Denis Turcot, Chief Administrative Officer & Clerk

Marmora & Lake, Municipality of
P.O. Box 459
12 Bursthall St.
Marmora, ON K0K 2M0
Tel: 613-472-2629; *Fax:* 613-472-5330
www.marmoraandlake.ca
Other Information: Toll-Free Phone: 1-866-518-2282
Municipal Type: Township
Area: 533.75 sq km
County or District: Hastings; *Population in 2011:* 4,074
Provincial Electoral District(s): Prince Edward-Hastings
Federal Electoral District(s): Hastings-Lennox and Addington
Next Election: Oct. 2018 (4 year terms)
Terry Clemens, Reeve
Ron Chittick, Chief Adminsitrative Officer

Matachewan
P.O. Box 177
Matachewan, ON P0K 1M0
Tel: 705-565-2274; *Fax:* 705-565-2564
township@ntl.sympatico.ca
www.matachewan.com
Municipal Type: Township
Area: 543.63 sq km
County or District: Timiskaming District; *Population in 2011:* 268
Provincial Electoral District(s): Timiskaming-Cochrane
Federal Electoral District(s): Timmins-James Bay
Next Election: Oct. 2018 (4 year terms)
Cheryl Drummond, Reeve

Andrew Van Oosten, Chief Administrative Officer & Clerk-Treasurer

Mattawa
P.O. Box 390
160 Water St.
Mattawa, ON P0H 1V0
Tel: 705-744-5611; *Fax:* 705-744-0104
info@mattawa.info
www.mattawa.info
Municipal Type: Town
Area: 3.66 sq km
County or District: Nipissing District; *Population in 2011:* 2,023
Provincial Electoral District(s): Nipissing
Federal Electoral District(s): Nipissing-Timiskaming
Next Election: Oct. 2018 (4 year terms)
Dean Backer, Mayor
David Burke, Acting Administrator/Clerk/Treasurer

Mattawan
P.O. Box 610
Mattawa, ON P0H 1V0
Tel: 705-744-5680; *Fax:* 705-744-4141
info@mattawan.info
www.mattawan.info
Municipal Type: Township
Area: 199.52 sq km
County or District: Nipissing District; *Population in 2011:* 162
Provincial Electoral District(s): Nipissing
Federal Electoral District(s): Nipissing-Timiskaming
Next Election: Oct. 2018 (4 year terms)
Peter Murphy, Mayor
Deborah Miller, Clerk

Mattice-Val Côté
P.O. Box 129
500 Hwy. 11
Mattice, ON P0L 1T0
Tel: 705-364-6511; *Fax:* 705-364-6431
matticevalcote.ca
Municipal Type: Township
Area: 414.64 sq km
County or District: Cochrane District; *Population in 2011:* 686
Provincial Electoral District(s): Timmins-James Bay
Federal Electoral District(s): Algoma-Manitoulin-Kapuskasing
Next Election: Oct. 2018 (4 year terms)
Michel Brière, Mayor
Gilbert Brisson, Administrator-Clerk

McDougall
5 Barager Blvd., RR#3
Parry Sound, ON P2A 2W9
Tel: 705-342-5252; *Fax:* 705-342-5573
www.municipalityofmcdougall.com
Municipal Type: Township
Incorporated: May 1, 1872; *Area:* 262.69 sq km
County or District: Parry Sound District; *Population in 2011:* 2,705
Provincial Electoral District(s): Parry Sound-Muskoka
Federal Electoral District(s): Parry Sound-Muskoka
Next Election: Oct. 2018 (4 year terms)
Dale Robinson, Mayor
Dave Rushton, Chief Administrative Officer

McGarry
P.O. Box 99
27 Webster St.
Virginiatown, ON P0K 1X0
Tel: 705-634-2145; *Fax:* 705-634-2700
admin@mcgarry.ca
www.mcgarry.ca
Municipal Type: Township
Area: 86.05 sq km
County or District: Timiskaming District; *Population in 2011:* 595
Provincial Electoral District(s): Timiskaming-Cochrane
Federal Electoral District(s): Timmins-James Bay
Next Election: Oct. 2018 (4 year terms)
Clermont Lapointe, Reeve
Kathleen Thur, Clerk-Treasurer

McKellar
P.O. Box 69
701 Hwy. 124
McKellar, ON P0G 1C0
Tel: 705-389-2842; *Fax:* 705-389-1244
www.township.mckellar.on.ca
Municipal Type: Township
Incorporated: 1873; *Area:* 177.48 sq km
County or District: Parry Sound District; *Population in 2011:* 1,144
Provincial Electoral District(s): Parry Sound-Muskoka
Federal Electoral District(s): Parry Sound-Muskoka
Next Election: Oct. 2018 (4 year terms)
Peter Hopkins, Reeve, 705-389-2842
Shawn Boggs, AMCT, Clerk Administrator

McMurrich/Monteith
P.O. Box 70
31 William St.
Sprucedale, ON P0A 1Y0
Tel: 705-685-7901; *Fax:* 705-685-7393
mcmurric@surenet.net
www.mcmurrichmonteith.com
Municipal Type: Township
Area: 273.33 sq km
County or District: Parry Sound District; *Population in 2011:* 779
Provincial Electoral District(s): Parry Sound-Muskoka
Federal Electoral District(s): Parry Sound-Muskoka
Next Election: Oct. 2018 (4 year terms)
Joanne Griffiths, Reeve
Cheryl Marshall, Clerk

McNab / Braeside
2508 Russett Dr., RR#2
Arnprior, ON K7S 3G8
Tel: 613-623-5756; *Fax:* 613-623-9138
info@mcnabbraeside.com
www.mcnabbraeside.com
Other Information: Toll-Free Phone: 1-800-957-4621
Municipal Type: Township
Incorporated: Jan. 1, 1998; *Area:* 253.87 sq km
County or District: Renfrew; *Population in 2011:* 7,371
Provincial Electoral District(s): Renfrew-Nipissing-Pembroke
Federal Electoral District(s): Renfrew-Nipissing-Pembroke
Next Election: Oct. 2018 (4 year terms)
Note: Amalgamation of Braeside Village & McNab Township.
Tom Peckett, Mayor
Lindsey Parkes, Chief Administrative Officer & Clerk

Meaford
21 Trowbridge St. West
Meaford, ON N4L 1A1
Tel: 519-538-1060; *Fax:* 519-538-5240
www.meaford.ca
Other Information: Alternate Fax: 519-538-1556
Municipal Type: Municipality
Incorporated: Jan. 1, 2001; *Area:* 588.47 sq km
County or District: Grey; *Population in 2011:* 11,100
Provincial Electoral District(s): Bruce-Grey-Owen Sound
Federal Electoral District(s): Bruce-Grey-Owen Sound
Next Election: Oct. 2018 (4 year terms)
Note: Formerly the Town of Georgian Highlands. Amalgamation of Sydenham, St. Vincent & Meaford.
Barb Clumpus, Mayor
Harley Greenfield, Deputy Mayor & Councillor, 519-538-2570
Steven Bartley, Councillor
Tony Bell, Councillor
Jaden Calvert, Councillor
Shirley Keaveney, Councillor
Mike Poetker, Councillor
Robert Tremblay, Clerk
Denyse Morrissey, Chief Administrative Officer
Robert Armstrong, Director, Planning & Building
Darcy Chapman, Director, Financial Services
Stephen Vokes, Director, Operations
Rick Carefoot, Chief Building Official
Chris Collyer, Chief Operator, Environmental Services
Mike Molloy, Fire Chief

Melancthon
157101 Hwy. 10, RR#6
Shelburne, ON L0N 1S9
Tel: 519-925-5525; *Fax:* 519-925-1110
info@melancthontownship.ca
www.melancthontownship.ca
Municipal Type: Township
Incorporated: Jan. 1, 1853; *Area:* 310.88 sq km
County or District: Dufferin; *Population in 2011:* 2,839
Provincial Electoral District(s): Dufferin-Caledon
Federal Electoral District(s): Dufferin-Caledon
Next Election: Oct. 2018 (4 year terms)
Darren White, Mayor
Denise B. Holmes, Chief Administrative Officer & Clerk-Treasurer

Merrickville-Wolford
P.O. Box 340
317 Brock St. West
Merrickville, ON K0G 1N0
Tel: 613-269-4791; *Fax:* 613-269-3095
reception@merrickville-wolford.ca
www.merrickville-wolford.ca
Other Information: E-mail, Admin.: admin@merrickville-wolford.ca
Municipal Type: Village
Area: 213.77 sq km
County or District: Leeds-Grenville; *Population in 2011:* 2,850
Provincial Electoral District(s): Leeds-Grenville
Federal Electoral District(s): Leeds-Grenville-Thousand Islands and Rideau Lakes
Next Election: Oct. 2018 (4 year terms)
David Nash, Mayor
Jill Armstrong, Chief Administrative Officer & Clerk, 613-269-4791

Middlesex Centre
10227 Ilderton Rd., RR#2
Ilderton, ON N0M 2A0
Tel: 519-666-0190; *Fax:* 519-666-0271
cormans@middlesexcentre.on.ca
www.middlesexcentre.on.ca
Other Information: Toll-Free Phone: 1-800-220-8968
Municipal Type: Township
Incorporated: Jan. 1, 1998; *Area:* 588.05 sq km
County or District: Middlesex; *Population in 2011:* 16,487
Provincial Electoral District(s): Lambton-Kent-Middlesex
Federal Electoral District(s): Lambton-Kent-Middlesex
Next Election: Oct. 2018 (4 year terms)
Note: Amalgamation of the former Townships of Delaware, Lobo, & London.
Al Edmondson, Mayor
Clare Bloomfield, Deputy Mayor
Stephen Harvey, Councillor, Wards: 1
John Brennan, Councillor, Wards: 2
Sharon McMillan, Councillor, Wards: 3
Aina DeViet, Councillor, Wards: 4
Frank Berze, Councillor, Wards: 5
Stephanie Troyer-Boyd, Clerk
Michelle Smibert, Chief Administrative Officer
Greg Watterton, Director, Finance
Brian Lima, Director, Public Works & Engineering
Arnie Marsman, Director, Planning & Development Svs., & Chief Building Official
Ken Sheridan, Fire Chief
Jim Reeve, Superintendent, Drainage
Mauro Castrilli, Manager, Transportation
Greg LaForge, Environmental Technologist

Minden Hills
P.O. Box 359
7 Milne St.
Minden, ON K0M 2K0
Tel: 705-286-1260; *Fax:* 705-286-4917
admin@mindenhills.ca
www.mindenhills.ca
Other Information: Treasury/Bldg./By-law/Planning, Fax: 705-286-6005
Municipal Type: Township
Area: 847.76 sq km
County or District: Haliburton; *Population in 2011:* 5,655
Provincial Electoral District(s): Haliburton-Kawartha Lakes-Brock
Federal Electoral District(s): Haliburton-Kawartha Lakes-Brock
Next Election: Oct. 2018 (4 year terms)
Brent Devolin, Reeve
Lorrie Blanchard, CAO/Treasurer, 705-286-1260

Minto
5941 Hwy. 89
Harriston, ON N0G 1Z0
Tel: 519-338-2511; *Fax:* 519-338-2005
peg@town.minto.on.ca (Clerical Assistant)
www.town.minto.on.ca
Other Information: E-mail, Treasury: gordon@town.minto.on.ca
Municipal Type: Town
Area: 300.37 sq km
County or District: Wellington; *Population in 2011:* 8,334
Provincial Electoral District(s): Perth-Wellington
Federal Electoral District(s): Perth-Wellington
Next Election: Oct. 2018 (4 year terms)
George Bridge, Mayor
Bill White, Chief Administrative Officer & Clerk

Mono
347209 MonoCenter Rd., RR#1
Orangeville, ON L9W 2Y8
Tel: 519-941-3599; *Fax:* 519-941-9490
info@townofmono.com
www.townofmono.com
Municipal Type: Town
Incorporated: June 1, 1999; *Area:* 277.67 sq km
County or District: Dufferin; *Population in 2011:* 7,546
Provincial Electoral District(s): Dufferin-Caledon
Federal Electoral District(s): Dufferin-Caledon
Next Election: Oct. 2018 (4 year terms)
Laura Ryan, Mayor
Keith J. McNenly, Chief Administrative Officer & Clerk

Montague
P.O. Box 755
6547 Roger Stevens Dr.
Smiths Falls, ON K7A 4W6
Tel: 613-283-7478; *Fax:* 613-283-3112
info@township.montague.on.ca
www.township.montague.on.ca
Municipal Type: Township
Area: 277.03 sq km
County or District: Lanark; *Population in 2011:* 3,483
Provincial Electoral District(s): Lanark-Frontenac-Lennox & Addington
Federal Electoral District(s): Lanark-Frontenac-Kingston
Next Election: Oct. 2018 (4 year terms)
Bill Dobson, Reeve
Glenn Barnes, Chief Administrative Officer

Moonbeam
P.O. Box 330
53 St. Aubin Ave.
Moonbeam, ON P0L 1V0
Tel: 705-367-2244; *Fax:* 705-367-2610
moonbeam@moonbeam.ca
www.moonbeam.ca
Municipal Type: Township
Area: 235.17 sq km
County or District: Cochrane District; *Population in 2011:* 1,101
Provincial Electoral District(s): Timmins-James Bay
Federal Electoral District(s): Algoma-Manitoulin-Kapuskasing
Next Election: Oct. 2018 (4 year terms)
Gilles Audet, Mayor
Carole Gendron, Clerk-Treasurer

Moosonee
P.O. Box 727
5 First St.
Moosonee, ON P0L 1Y0
Tel: 705-336-2993; *Fax:* 705-336-2426
www.moosonee.ca
Municipal Type: Town
Area: 555.35 sq km
County or District: Cochrane District; *Population in 2011:* 1,725
Provincial Electoral District(s): Timmins-James Bay
Federal Electoral District(s): Timmins-James Bay
Next Election: Oct. 2018 (4 year terms)
Wayne Taipale, Mayor
Shannon MacGillivray, Chief Administrative Officer

Morley
P.O. Box 40
Stratton, ON P0W 1N0
Tel: 807-483-5455; *Fax:* 807-483-5882
morley@nwonet.net
www.townshipofmorley.ca
Municipal Type: Township
Incorporated: 1903; *Area:* 375.61 sq km
County or District: Rainy River District; *Population in 2011:* 474
Provincial Electoral District(s): Kenora-Rainy River
Federal Electoral District(s): Thunder Bay-Rainy River
Next Election: Oct. 2018 (4 year terms)
George Heyens, Reeve
Teresa Desserre, CMO, Clerk-Treasurer

Morris-Turnberry
41342 Morris Rd., RR#4
Brussels, ON N0G 1H0
Tel: 519-887-6137; *Fax:* 519-887-6424
mail@morristurnberry.ca
www.morristurnberry.ca
Municipal Type: Township
Incorporated: Jan. 1, 2001; *Area:* 376.45 sq km
County or District: Huron; *Population in 2011:* 3,413
Provincial Electoral District(s): Huron-Bruce
Federal Electoral District(s): Huron-Bruce
Next Election: Oct. 2018 (4 year terms)
Note: Amalgamation of the Township of Morris & the Township of Turnberry.
Paul Gowing, Mayor
Nancy Michie, Administrator & Clerk-Treasurer

Mulmur
758070 2nd Line East, RR#2
Lisle, ON L0M 1M0
Tel: 705-466-3341; *Fax:* 705-466-2922
info@mulmurtownship.ca
www.mulmurtownship.ca
Other Information: Toll-Free Phone: 1-866-472-0417 (In 519 area code)
Municipal Type: Township
Incorporated: 1851; *Area:* 286.73 sq km
County or District: Dufferin; *Population in 2011:* 3,391
Provincial Electoral District(s): Dufferin-Caledon
Federal Electoral District(s): Dufferin-Caledon
Next Election: Oct. 2018 (4 year terms)
Paul Mills, Mayor
Terry M. Horner, AMCT, Chief Administrative Officer & Clerk

Muskoka Lakes
P.O. Box 129
1 Bailey St.
Port Carling, ON P0B 1J0
Tel: 705-765-3156; *Fax:* 705-765-6755
www.muskokalakes.ca
Municipal Type: Township
Incorporated: Jan. 1971; *Area:* 781.55 sq km
County or District: Muskoka Dist. Mun.; *Population in 2011:* 6,324
Provincial Electoral District(s): Parry Sound-Muskoka
Federal Electoral District(s): Parry Sound-Muskoka
Next Election: Oct. 2018 (4 year terms)
Don Furniss, Mayor
Cheryl Mortimer, AMCT, Clerk

Nairn & Hyman
64 McIntyre St.
Nairn Centre, ON P0M 2L0
Tel: 705-869-4232;
information@nairncentre.ca
www.nairncentre.ca
Municipal Type: Township
Incorporated: 1896; *Area:* 159.03 sq km
County or District: Sudbury District; *Population in 2011:* 477
Provincial Electoral District(s): Algoma-Manitoulin
Federal Electoral District(s): Algoma-Manitoulin-Kapuskasing
Next Election: Oct. 2018 (4 year terms)
Laurier P. Falldien, Mayor
Robert Deschene, Chief Administrative Officer & Clerk-Treasurer

The Nation
958 Rte. 500 West
Casselman, ON K0A 1M0
Tel: 613-764-5444; *Fax:* 613-764-3310
mmccuaig@nationmun.ca
www.nationmun.ca
Other Information: Toll-Free Phone: 1-800-475-2855
Municipal Type: Municipality
Incorporated: Jan. 1, 1998; *Area:* 657.16 sq km
County or District: Prescott & Russell; *Population in 2011:* 11,668
Provincial Electoral District(s): Glengarry-Prescott-Russell
Federal Electoral District(s): Glengarry-Prescott-Russell
Next Election: Oct. 2018 (4 year terms)
Note: Amalgamation of the Townships of Cambridge, South Plantagenet, Caledonia & the Village of St. Isidore.
François St. Amour, Mayor
Marie-Noelle Lanthier, Councillor, Wards: 1
Marcel Legault, Councillor, 613-524-2873, Wards: 2
Marc Laflèche, Councillor, Wards: 3
Francis Biere, Councillor, Wards: 4
Mary J. McCuaig, Chief Administrative Officer & Clerk, 613-764-5444, Fax: 613-764-3310
Cécile Lortie, Treasurer, 613-764-5444, Fax: 613-764-3310
Marc Legault, Director, Public Works, 613-524-2932, Fax: 613-524-1140
Carol Ann Scott, Coordinator, Recreation, 613-524-2529
Todd Bayly, Chief Building Official, 613-764-5444, Fax: 613-764-3310
Yannick Hamel, Network Administrator, 613-764-5444
Guylain Laflèche, Municipal Planner, 613-764-5444, Fax: 613-764-3310
Mario Bertrand, Municipal Law Enforcement Officer, 613-764-5444
Roger Parent, Coordinator, Landfill Sites, 613-524-2932, Fax: 613-524-1140
Josée Leroux, Clerk, Water & Sewers

Neebing, Municipality of
4766 Hwy. 61
Thunder Bay, ON P7L 0B5
Tel: 807-474-5331; *Fax:* 807-474-5332
neebing@neebing.org
www.neebing.org
Other Information: Information Phone Line: 807-474-5338
Municipal Type: Town
Area: 875.51 sq km
County or District: Thunder Bay District; *Population in 2011:* 1,986
Provincial Electoral District(s): Thunder Bay-Atikokan
Federal Electoral District(s): Thunder Bay-Rainy River
Next Election: Oct. 2018 (4 year terms)
Ziggy Polkowski, Mayor
Delma Stajkowski, AMCT, Clerk

Newbury
P.O. Box 130
22910 Hagerty Rd.
Newbury, ON N0L 1Z0
Tel: 519-693-4941; *Fax:* 519-693-4340
office@newbury.ca
www.newbury.ca
Municipal Type: Village
Incorporated: 1873; *Area:* 1.85 sq km
County or District: Middlesex; *Population in 2011:* 447
Provincial Electoral District(s): Lambton-Kent-Middlesex
Federal Electoral District(s): Lambton-Kent-Middlesex
Next Election: Oct. 2018 (4 year terms)
Diane Brewer, Reeve
Betty D. Gordon, Clerk-Treasurer

Nipigon
P.O. Box 160
52 Front St.
Nipigon, ON P0T 2J0
Tel: 807-887-3135; *Fax:* 807-887-3564
info@nipigon.net
www.nipigon.net
Other Information: E-mail, Recreation Inquiries: nipigonrec@shaw.ca
Municipal Type: Township
Area: 109.14 sq km
County or District: Thunder Bay District; *Population in 2011:* 1,631
Provincial Electoral District(s): Thunder Bay-Superior North
Federal Electoral District(s): Thunder Bay-Superior North
Next Election: Oct. 2018 (4 year terms)
Richard Harvey, Mayor
Lindsay Mannila, Chief Administrative Officer

Nipissing
45 Beatty St.
Nipissing, ON P0H 1W0
Tel: 705-724-2144; *Fax:* 705-724-5385
www.nipissingtownship.com
Municipal Type: Township
Area: 387.4 sq km
County or District: Parry Sound District; *Population in 2011:* 1,704
Provincial Electoral District(s): Nipissing; Timiskaming-Cochrane
Federal Electoral District(s): Nipissing-Timiskaming
Next Election: Oct. 2018 (4 year terms)
Pat Haufe, Mayor, 705-729-5343
Charles H. Barton, Chief Administrative Officer & Clerk

Nipissing
District Social Services Administration Bd.
P.O. Box 750
200 McIntyre St. East
North Bay, ON P1B 8J8

info@dnssab.on.ca
www.dnssab.on.ca
Municipal Type: District
Area: 17,065.07 sq km
Population in 2011: 84,736
George Maroosis, Chair, District of Nipissing Social Services Administration Board, 705-474-2151, Fax: 705-474-0136
Joseph Bradbury, CAO, District of Nipissing Social Services Administration Board, 705-474-2151, Fax: 705-474-7155

North Algona Wilberforce
1091 Shaw Woods Rd., RR#1
Eganville, ON K0J 1T0
Tel: 613-628-2080; *Fax:* 613-628-3341
naw@nalgonawil.com
www.nalgonawil.com
Municipal Type: Township
Incorporated: Jan. 1, 1999; *Area:* 378.53 sq km
County or District: Renfrew; *Population in 2011:* 2,873

Provincial Electoral District(s): Renfrew-Nipissing-Pembroke
Federal Electoral District(s): Renfrew-Nipissing-Pembroke
Next Election: Oct. 2018 (4 year terms)
Note: Amalgamation of North Algona Township & Wilberforce Township.
Deborah Farr, Mayor
Marilyn M. Schruder, Clerk-Treasurer

North Dumfries
1171 Greenfield Rd., RR#4
Cambridge, ON N1R 5S5
Tel: 519-621-0340; *Fax:* 519-623-7641
www.northdumfries.ca
Other Information: Toll-Free Phone: 1-800-563-5595
Municipal Type: Township
Area: 187.22 sq km
County or District: Waterloo Regional Municipality; *Population in 2011:* 9,334
Provincial Electoral District(s): Cambridge
Federal Electoral District(s): Cambridge
Next Election: Oct. 2018 (4 year terms)
Sue Foxton, Mayor, 519-574-4001
Roger Mordue, Chief Administrative Officer & Clerk, 519-621-0340

North Dundas
P.O. Box 489
636 St. Lawrence St.
Winchester, ON K0C 2K0
Tel: 613-774-2105; *Fax:* 613-774-5699
info@northdundas.com
www.northdundas.com
Other Information: Toll-Free Phone: 1-800-795-0437
Municipal Type: Township
Incorporated: Jan. 1, 1998; *Area:* 503.18 sq km
County or District: Stormont, Dundas & Glengarry; *Population in 2011:* 11,225
Provincial Electoral District(s): Stormont-Dundas-South Glengarry
Federal Electoral District(s): Stormont-Dundas-South Glengarry
Next Election: Oct. 2018 (4 year terms)
Note: Amalgamation of the former Townships of Winchester & Mountain & the villages of Chesterville & Winchester.
Eric Duncan, Mayor, 613-774-1081
Gerry Boyce, Deputy Mayor, 613-989-2330
Allan Armstrong, Councillor, 613-774-0752
Tony Fraser, Councillor, 613-774-2182
John Thompson, Councillor, 613-448-2963
Jo-Anne McCaslin, Clerk, 613-774-2105
Howard F. Smith, Chief Administrative Officer, 613-774-2105
John J. Gareau, CA, AMCT, Treasurer
Greg Trizisky, Chief Building Official & Officer, Property Standards, 613-774-2105
Arden Carruthers, Director, Public Works, & Fire Chief, Morewood, 613-774-2105
Mark Guy, Director, Recreation & Culture
Calvin Pol, BES, MCIP, RPP, Director, Planning, Building, & Enforcement, 613-774-2105
Rob Hunter, Officer, Economic Development & Communications, 613-774-2105
Doug Froats, Coordinator, Waste Management
Mike Gruich, Fire Chief, Chesterville
Dan Kelly, Fire Chief, Winchester
Scott Patterson, Fire Chief, Mountain

North Frontenac
P.O. Box 97
6648 Rd. 506
Plevna, ON K0H 2M0
Tel: 613-479-2231; *Fax:* 613-479-2352
info@northfrontenac.ca
www.northfrontenac.com
Other Information: Toll-Free Phone: 1-800-234-3953
Municipal Type: Township
Incorporated: Jan. 1, 1998; *Area:* 1,135.75 sq km
County or District: Frontenac; *Population in 2011:* 1,842
Provincial Electoral District(s): Hastings-Frontenac-Lennox & Addington
Federal Electoral District(s): Lanark-Frontenac-Kingston
Next Election: Oct. 2018 (4 year terms)
Ron Higgins, Mayor, 613-966-9222
Cheryl Robson, Chief Administrative Officer, 613-479-2231

North Glengarry
P.O. Box 700
90 Main St. South
Alexandria, ON K0C 1A0
Tel: 613-525-1110; *Fax:* 613-525-1649
www.northglengarry.ca
Municipal Type: Township
Area: 642.4 sq km
County or District: Stormont, Dundas & Glengarry; *Population in 2011:* 10,251
Provincial Electoral District(s): Glengarry-Prescott-Russell
Federal Electoral District(s): Glengarry-Prescott-Russell
Next Election: Oct. 2018 (4 year terms)
Chris McDonell, Mayor, 613-525-1110, Fax: 613-525-1649
Jamie MacDonald, Deputy Mayor & Councillor, 613-525-1110
Jacques Massie, Councillor at Large, 613-525-1110
Michel Depratto, Councillor, 613-525-1110, Wards: Alexandria
Jeff Manley, Councillor, 613-525-1110, Wards: Kenyon
Brian Caddell, Councillor, 613-525-1110, Wards: Lochiel
Carma Williams, Councillor, 613-525-1110, Wards: Maxville
Daniel Gagnon, Chief Administrative Officer, 613-525-1110
Johanna (Annie) Levac, Treasurer, 613-525-1110
André Bachand, Manager, Public Works, 613-525-1110
Dean McDonald, Manager, Water Works, 613-525-1110
Gerry Murphy, Manager, Planning & By-law Enforcement, & Chief Building Official, 613-525-1110
Stephane Ouimet, Director, Recreation, 613-525-0614
Manson Barton, Superintendent, Drainage & Beaver Management, 613-525-1110

North Grenville
P.O. Box 130
285 County Rd. 44
Kemptville, ON K0G 1J0
Tel: 613-258-9569; *Fax:* 613-258-9620
www.northgrenville.ca
Municipal Type: MN
Incorporated: July 14, 2003; *Area:* 350.14 sq km
County or District: Leeds-Grenville; *Population in 2011:* 15,085
Provincial Electoral District(s): Leeds-Grenville
Federal Electoral District(s): Leeds-Grenville-Thousand Islands and Rideau Lakes
Next Election: Oct. 2018 (4 year terms)
David Gordon, Mayor, 613-258-9569
Ken Finnerty, Deputy Mayor, 613-258-9569
Terry Butler, Councillor, 613-258-9569, Fax: 613-258-9620
Tim Sutton, Councillor, 613-258-9569, Fax: 613-258-9620
Barb Tobin, Councillor, 613-258-9569, Fax: 613-258-9620
Cahl Pominville, Clerk & Director, Corporate Services
Brian J. Carre, Chief Administrative Officer
Sheila Kehoe, Treasurer
Karen Dunlop, Director, Public Works
Mark Guy, Director, Parks, Recreation & Culture
Forbes Symon, Director, Planning & Development
Paul Hutt, Fire Chief
Randy Wilkinson, Chief Building Official
Gary Boal, Superintendent, Waste Site, 613-258-9677
Doug Scott, Superintendent, Roads
Mark Tenbult, Engineering Technologist
Gary Simser, Technician, Regulatory Water / Wastewater Compliance

North Huron
P.O. Box 90
274 Josephine St.
Wingham, ON N0G 2W0
Tel: 519-357-3550; *Fax:* 519-357-1110
www.northhuron.ca
Municipal Type: Township
Incorporated: Jan. 1, 2001; *Area:* 178.98 sq km
County or District: Huron; *Population in 2011:* 4,884
Provincial Electoral District(s): Huron-Bruce
Federal Electoral District(s): Huron-Bruce
Next Election: Oct. 2018 (4 year terms)
Note: Amalgamation of the Village of Blyth, the Township of East Wawanosh & the Town of Wingham.
Neil Vincent, Reeve, 519-357-2336
Gary Long, Clerk Administrator, 519-357-3550

North Kawartha
P.O. Box 550
280 Burleigh St.
Apsley, ON K0L 1A0
Tel: 705-656-4445; *Fax:* 705-656-4446
d.page@northkawartha.on.ca (Reception)
www.northkawartha.on.ca
Other Information: Toll-Free Phone: 1-800-755-6931
Municipal Type: Township
Area: 765.02 sq km
County or District: Peterborough; *Population in 2011:* 2,289
Provincial Electoral District(s): Haliburton-Kawartha Lakes-Brock
Federal Electoral District(s): Peterborough-Kawartha
Next Election: Oct. 2018 (4 year terms)
Rick Woodcock, Mayor
Connie Parent, Clerk

North Middlesex
Administrative Centre
P.O. Box 9
229 Parkhill Main St.
Parkhill, ON N0M 2K0
Tel: 519-294-6244; *Fax:* 519-294-0573
clerk@northmiddlesex.on.ca
www.northmiddlesex.on.ca
Other Information: Toll-Free Phone: 1-888-793-9637
Municipal Type: Municipality
Incorporated: Jan. 1, 2001; *Area:* 597.86 sq km
County or District: Middlesex; *Population in 2011:* 6,658
Provincial Electoral District(s): Lambton-Kent-Middlesex
Federal Electoral District(s): Lambton-Kent-Middlesex
Next Election: Oct. 2018 (4 year terms)
Note: Amalgamation of the Townships of East Williams, West Williams & McGillivray, the Town of Parkhill & the Village of Ailsa Craig.
Don F. Shipway, Mayor, 519-293-3219
Marsha Paley, Chief Administrative Officer, 519-294-6244

The North Shore
P.O. Box 108
1385 Hwy. 17 West
Algoma Mills, ON P0R 1A0
Tel: 705-849-2213; *Fax:* 705-849-2428
www.townshipofthenorthshore.ca
Municipal Type: Township
Incorporated: March 1, 1973; *Area:* 230.79 sq km
County or District: Algoma District; *Population in 2011:* 509
Provincial Electoral District(s): Algoma-Manitoulin
Federal Electoral District(s): Algoma-Manitoulin-Kapuskasing
Next Election: Oct. 2018 (4 year terms)
Note: Incorporated as a township on Dec. 1, 1978.
Randi Condie, Mayor, 705-849-2489
Brenda Green, Clerk

North Stormont
P.O. Box 99
15 Union St.
Berwick, ON K0C 1G0
Tel: 613-984-2821; *Fax:* 613-984-2908
www.northstormont.ca
Other Information: Toll-Free Phone: 1-877-984-2821
Municipal Type: Township
Area: 515.55 sq km
County or District: Stormont, Dundas & Glengarry; *Population in 2011:* 6,775
Provincial Electoral District(s): Stormont-Dundas-South Glengarry
Federal Electoral District(s): Stormont-Dundas-South Glengarry
Next Election: Oct. 2018 (4 year terms)
Dennis Fife, Mayor, 613-984-2821, Fax: 613-984-2908
Karen McPherson, Municipal Clerk, 613-984-2821, Fax: 613-984-2908

Northeastern Manitoulin & the Islands
P.O. Box 2000
15 Manitowaning Rd.
Little Current, ON P0P 1K0
Tel: 705-368-3500; *Fax:* 705-368-2245
info@townofnemi.on.ca
www.townofnemi.on.ca
Municipal Type: Town
Area: 495.04 sq km
County or District: Manitoulin District; *Population in 2011:* 2,706
Provincial Electoral District(s): Algoma-Manitoulin
Federal Electoral District(s): Algoma-Manitoulin-Kapuskasing
Next Election: Oct. 2018 (4 year terms)
Alan MacNevin, Mayor
Janet Moore, Clerk, 705-368-3500

Northern Bruce Peninsula
56 Lindsay Rd. 5, RR#2
Lion's Head, ON N0H 1W0
Tel: 519-793-3552; *Fax:* 519-793-3823
northernbrucepen@amtelecom.net
www.northbrucepeninsula.ca
Municipal Type: Municipality
Incorporated: Jan. 1999; *Area:* 781.51 sq km
County or District: Bruce; *Population in 2011:* 3,744
Provincial Electoral District(s): Bruce-Grey-Owen Sound
Federal Electoral District(s): Bruce-Grey-Owen Sound
Next Election: Oct. 2018 (4 year terms)
Note: Amalgamation of of the former Townships of St. Edmunds, Lindsay, Eastnor & the Village of Lion's Head.
Milton McIver, Mayor, 519-592-3076
Bill Jones, Chief Administrative Officer, 519-793-3522

Norwich
P.O. Box 100
210 Main St. East
Otterville, ON N0J 1R0
Tel: 519-863-2709; *Fax:* 519-879-6385
www.twp.norwich.on.ca
Other Information: Alternative Phone: 519-879-6568
Municipal Type: Township
Area: 431.28 sq km
County or District: Oxford; *Population in 2011:* 10,721
Provincial Electoral District(s): Oxford
Federal Electoral District(s): Oxford
Next Election: Oct. 2018 (4 year terms)
Larry Martin, Mayor, 519-468-5609
John Scholten, Councillor, Wards: 1
Jim Palmer, Councillor, Wards: 2
Wayne Robert Buchanan, Councillor, Wards: 3
Kyle Kruger, Chief Administrative Officer & Clerk
Mike Legge, Treasurer & Director, Finance, 519-879-6568
Brad Smale, Chief Building Official
Patrick Hovorka, Director, Community Development Services, 519-863-3733
Ron Smith, Superintendent, Public Works
Monica Bratley, Coordinator, Customer Service & Records Management, 519-879-6568

O'Connor
RR#1
Kakabeka Falls, ON P0T 1W0
Tel: 807-476-1451; *Fax:* 807-473-0891
twpoconn@tbaytel.net
www.oconnortownship.ca
Municipal Type: Township
Incorporated: January 1, 1907; *Area:* 108.58 sq km
County or District: Thunder Bay District; *Population in 2011:* 685
Provincial Electoral District(s): Thunder Bay-Atikokan
Federal Electoral District(s): Thunder Bay-Rainy River
Next Election: Oct. 2018 (4 year terms)
Ron Nelson, Mayor, 807-475-9213
Lorna Buob, Clerk-Treasurer

Oil Springs
P.O. Box 22
4591 Oil Springs Line
Oil Springs, ON N0N 1P0
Tel: 519-834-2939; *Fax:* 519-834-2333
oilsprings@ciaccess.com
www.oilsprings.ca
Municipal Type: Village
Incorporated: 1865; *Area:* 8.18 sq km
County or District: Lambton; *Population in 2011:* 704
Provincial Electoral District(s): Sarnia-Lambton
Federal Electoral District(s): Sarnia-Lambton
Next Election: Oct. 2018 (4 year terms)
Ian Veen, Mayor
Jennifer Turk, Clerk-Treasurer

Oliver Paipoonge, Municipality of
P.O. Box 10
4569 Oliver Rd.
Murillo, ON P0T 2G0
Tel: 807-935-2613; *Fax:* 807-935-2161
sharron.martyn@oliverpaipoonage.on.ca
www.oliverpaipoonge.on.ca
Municipal Type: Township
Incorporated: Jan. 1, 1998; *Area:* 350.27 sq km
County or District: Thunder Bay District; *Population in 2011:* 5,732
Provincial Electoral District(s): Thunder Bay-Atikokan
Federal Electoral District(s): Thunder Bay-Rainy River
Next Election: Oct. 2018 (4 year terms)
Note: Amalgamation of the Township of Oliver & the Township of Paipoonge.
Lucy Kloosterhuis, Mayor, 807-473-5658, Fax: 807-935-2161
Jamie Cressman, Chief Administrative Officer & Clerk, 807-935-2613, Fax: 807-935-2123

Opasatika
P.O. Box 100
50 Government Rd.
Opasatika, ON P0L 1Z0
Tel: 705-369-4531; *Fax:* 705-369-2002
twpopas@persona.ca
www.opasatika.net
Municipal Type: Township
Area: 329.98 sq km
County or District: Cochrane District; *Population in 2011:* 214
Provincial Electoral District(s): Timmins-James Bay
Federal Electoral District(s): Algoma-Manitoulin-Kapuskasing
Next Election: Oct. 2018 (4 year terms)
Donald Nolet, Mayor
Denis Dorval, Clerk-Treasurer, 705-369-4531, Fax: 705-369-2002

Oro-Medonte
148 Line 7 South
Oro, ON L0L 2X0
Tel: 705-487-2171; *Fax:* 705-487-0133
www.oro-medonte.ca
Municipal Type: Township
Area: 586.65 sq km
County or District: Simcoe; *Population in 2011:* 20,078
Provincial Electoral District(s): Simcoe North
Federal Electoral District(s): Barrie-Springwater-Oro-Medonte; Simcoe North
Next Election: Oct. 2018 (4 year terms)
Harry Hughes, Mayor, 705-487-2128
Ralph Hough, Deputy Mayor, 705-835-2770
Barbara Coutanche, Councillor, Wards: 1
Scott Alexander Macpherson, Councillor, Wards: 2
Phil Hall, Councillor, Wards: 3
John Crawford, Councillor, 705-487-3373, Wards: 4
Scott Jermey, Councillor, Wards: 5
Doug Irwin, Clerk & Director, Corporate Services, 705-487-2171
Robin Dunn, Chief Administrative Officer
Paul Gravelle, Treasurer, Deputy CAO, & Director, Finance
Andria Leigh, Director, Development Services, 705-487-2171
Shawn Bunns, Director, Recreation & Community Services, 705-487-2171
Jerry Ball, Director, Transportation & Environmental Services, 705-487-2171
Derek Witlib, Manager, Planning Services, 705-487-2171
Hugh Murray, Fire Chief, 705-487-2171

Otonabee-South Monaghan
Municipal Office
P.O. Box 70
20 Third St.
Keene, ON K0L 2G0
Tel: 705-295-6852; *Fax:* 705-295-6405
info@osmtownship.ca
www.osmtownship.ca
Other Information: Toll-Free Phone: 1-800-999-4861 (In 705 area code)
Municipal Type: Township
Area: 349.22 sq km
County or District: Peterborough; *Population in 2011:* 6,660
Provincial Electoral District(s): Peterborough
Federal Electoral District(s): Northumberland-Peterborough South
Next Election: Oct. 2018 (4 year terms)
David Nelson, Reeve, 705-295-4628
Heather Scott, Clerk, 705-295-6852

Oxford
P.O. Box 1614
21 Reeve St.
Woodstock, ON N4S 7Y3
Tel: 519-539-9800;
www.oxfordcounty.ca
Other Information: Toll-Free Phone: 1-800-755-0394
Municipal Type: Restructured County
Area: 2,039.46 sq km
Population in 2011: 105,719
Next Election: Oct. 2018 (4 year terms)
David Mayberry, Warden, 519-485-3642, Wards: South-West Oxford
Ted J. Comiskey, Deputy Warden, Wards: Ingersoll
Marion Wearn, Councillor, Wards: Blandford-Blenheim
Don McKay, Councillor, 519-532-2500, Wards: East Zorra-Tavistock
Larry Martin, Councillor, 519-468-5609, Wards: Norwich
Stephen Molnar, Councillor, Wards: Tillsonburg
Trevor T. Birtch, Councillor, Wards: Woodstock
Deb A. Tait, Councillor, 519-421-7449, Wards: Woodstock
Sandra J. Talbot, Councillor, 519-788-0639, Wards: Woodstock
Margaret E. Lupton, Councillor, 519-475-4443, Wards: Zorra
Brenda J. Tabor, Clerk, 519-539-0015
Peter M. Crockett, P. Eng., Chief Administrative Officer, 519-539-0015
Lynn Beath, Director, Public Health & Emergency Services, 519-539-9800
Lynn Buchner, Director, Corporate Services
Gordon K. Hough, Director, Community & Strategic Planning, 519-539-9800
Paul Beaton, Director, Human Services, 519-539-9800
Robert Walton, Director, Public Works, 519-539-9800

Papineau-Cameron
P.O. Box 630
4861 Hwy. 17
Mattawa, ON P0H 1V0
Tel: 705-744-5610; *Fax:* 705-744-0434
www.papineaucameron.ca
Municipal Type: Township
Area: 561.37 sq km
County or District: Nipissing District; *Population in 2011:* 978
Provincial Electoral District(s): Nipissing
Federal Electoral District(s): Nipissing-Timiskaming
Next Election: Oct. 2018 (4 year terms)
Robert Corriveau, Mayor
Sandra J. Morin, Clerk-Treasurer

Parry Sound
52 Seguin St.
Parry Sound, ON P2A 1B4
Tel: 705-746-2101; *Fax:* 705-746-7461
middaugh@townofparrysound.com (Economic Dev. & Leisure Svs.)
www.townofparrysound.com
Municipal Type: Town
Area: 13.33 sq km
County or District: Parry Sound District; *Population in 2011:* 6,191
Provincial Electoral District(s): Parry Sound-Muskoka
Federal Electoral District(s): Parry Sound-Muskoka
Next Election: Oct. 2018 (4 year terms)
Jamie McGarvey, Mayor
Rob Mens, Chief Administrative Officer

Parry Sound
District Social Services Administration Bd.
1 Beechwood Dr., 2nd Fl.
Parry Sound, ON P2A 1J2
Tel: 705-746-7777; *Fax:* 705-746-7783
www.psdssab.org
Municipal Type: District
Area: 9,222.04 sq km
Population in 2011: 42,162
Rick Zanussi, Chair, Parry Sound District Social Services Administration Board
Janet Patterson, Chief Administrative Officer, District Social Service Admin Board, 705-746-7777

Pelee
1045 West Shore Rd.
Pelee Island, ON N0R 1M0
Tel: 519-724-2931; *Fax:* 519-724-2470
info@pelee.ca
www.pelee.org
Other Information: Toll-Free Phone: 1-866-889-5203
Municipal Type: Township
Incorporated: 1869; *Area:* 41.79 sq km
County or District: Essex; *Population in 2011:* 171
Provincial Electoral District(s): Essex
Federal Electoral District(s): Chatham-Kent-Leamington
Next Election: Oct. 2018 (4 year terms)
Rick Masse, Mayor
Ann Mitchell, Clerk-Treasurer

Penetanguishene
P.O. Box 5009
10 Robert St. West
Penetanguishene, ON L9M 2G2
Tel: 705-549-7453; *Fax:* 705-549-3743
www.penetanguishene.ca
Other Information: Public Works, Phone: 705-549-7992
Municipal Type: Town
Incorporated: Feb. 22, 1882; *Area:* 25.38 sq km
County or District: Simcoe; *Population in 2011:* 9,111
Provincial Electoral District(s): Simcoe North
Federal Electoral District(s): Simcoe North
Next Election: Oct. 2018 (4 year terms)
Gerry Marshall, Mayor
Holly Bryce, Town Clerk

Perry
P.O. Box 70
1695 Emsdale Rd.
Emsdale, ON P0A 1J0
Tel: 705-636-5941; *Fax:* 705-636-5759
info@townshipofperry.ca; perrylib@ontera.net (library)
www.townshipofperry.ca
Other Information: Public Works Email: publicworks@townshipofperry.ca
Municipal Type: Township
Area: 186.63 sq km
County or District: Parry Sound District; *Population in 2011:* 2,317
Provincial Electoral District(s): Parry Sound-Muskoka

Federal Electoral District(s): Parry Sound-Muskoka
Next Election: Oct. 2018 (4 year terms)
Norm Hofstetter, Mayor, 705-636-5727
Beth Morton, Clerk & Planning Administrator, 705-636-5941

Perth
Town Hall
80 Gore St. East
Perth, ON K7H 1H9
Tel: 613-267-3311; *Fax:* 613-267-5635
www.perthcanada.com
Other Information: After hour water & sewer emergencies: 613-267-1072
Municipal Type: Town
Area: 10.36 sq km
County or District: Lanark; *Population in 2011:* 5,840
Provincial Electoral District(s): Lanark-Frontenac-Lennox & Addington
Federal Electoral District(s): Lanark-Frontenac-Kingston
Next Election: Oct. 2018 (4 year terms)
John Fenik, Mayor, 613-267-3311
Lauren Walton, Clerk, 613-267-3311

Perth East
P.O. Box 455
25 Mill St. East
Milverton, ON N0K 1M0
Tel: 519-595-2800; *Fax:* 519-595-2801
township@pertheast.on.ca
www.pertheast.ca
Municipal Type: Township
Area: 715.07 sq km
County or District: Perth; *Population in 2011:* 12,028
Provincial Electoral District(s): Perth-Wellinton
Federal Electoral District(s): Perth-Wellington
Next Election: Oct. 2018 (4 year terms)
Note: Amalgamation of North Easthope Township, South Easthope Township, Ellice Township, Village of Milverton & Mornington Township.
Bob McMillan, Mayor
Rhonda Ehgoetz, Deputy Mayor
Don Brunk, Councillor, Wards: Ellice
Jerry Smith, Councillor, Wards: Milverton
Helen Dowd, Councillor, Wards: Mornington
Jeff Cressman, Councillor, Wards: North Easthope
Andrew MacAlpine, Councillor, Wards: South Easthope
Theresa Campbell, Municipal Clerk, 519-595-2800
Glenn Schwendinger, Chief Administrative Officer, 519-595-2800
Rhonda Fischer, Municipal Treasurer & Manager, Finance Department, 519-595-2800
Bill Hunter, Fire Chief, 519-595-2800
Grant Schwartzentruber, Chief Building Official, 519-595-2800
Becky Boertien, Manager, Perth East Recreation Complex, 519-595-2244, Fax: 519-595-4067
Wes Kuepfer, Manager, Public Works & Parks, 519-595-2800
Donna Chaffe, Coordinator, Human Resources, 519-595-2800
Martin Feeney, By-law Enforcement Officer & Building & Sewage Inspector, 519-595-2800
Geoff VanderBaaren, Planner, 519-271-0531

Perth South
3191 Rd. 122
St. Pauls, ON N0K 1V0
Tel: 519-271-0619; *Fax:* 519-271-0647
township@perthsouth.ca
www.perthsouth.ca
Other Information: Toll-Free Phone: 1-866-771-0619
Municipal Type: Township
Area: 393.01 sq km
County or District: Perth; *Population in 2011:* 3,993
Provincial Electoral District(s): Perth-Wellington
Federal Electoral District(s): Perth-Wellington
Next Election: Oct. 2018 (4 year terms)
Note: Amalgamation of Blanshard Township & Downie Township.
Robert Wilhelm, Mayor, 519-225-2304
Lizet Scott, Clerk, 519-271-0619

Petrolia
P.O. Box 1270
411 Greenfield St.
Petrolia, ON N0N 1R0
Tel: 519-882-2350; *Fax:* 519-882-3373
petrolia@town.petrolia.on.ca
www.town.petrolia.on.ca
Other Information: After Hours Emergency, Phone: 519-882-2351
Municipal Type: Town
Area: 12.68 sq km
County or District: Lambton; *Population in 2011:* 5,528
Provincial Electoral District(s): Lambton-Kent-Middlesex
Federal Electoral District(s): Sarnia-Lambton
Next Election: Oct. 2018 (4 year terms)
John McCharles, Mayor, 519-882-2455
Dianne Caryn, Chief Administrative Officer & Clerk

Pickle Lake
P.O. Box 340
2 Anne St.
Pickle Lake, ON P0V 3A0
Tel: 807-928-2034; *Fax:* 807-928-2708
reception@picklelake.org
www.picklelake.ca
Other Information: Toll-Free Phone: 1-800-565-9189
Municipal Type: Township
Incorporated: Dec. 1980; *Area:* 255.08 sq km
County or District: Kenora District; *Population in 2011:* 425
Provincial Electoral District(s): Kenora-Rainy River
Federal Electoral District(s): Kenora
Next Election: Oct. 2018 (4 year terms)
Karl Hoph, Mayor
Manuela Batovanja, Clerk-Treasurer

Plummer Additional
38 Railway Cres., RR#2
Bruce Mines, ON P0R 1C0
Tel: 705-785-3479; *Fax:* 705-785-3135
plumtwsp@onlink.net
www.plummertownship.ca
Municipal Type: Township
Area: 221.31 sq km
County or District: Algoma District; *Population in 2011:* 650
Provincial Electoral District(s): Algoma-Manitoulin
Federal Electoral District(s): Algoma-Manitoulin-Kapuskasing
Next Election: Oct. 2018 (4 year terms)
Beth West, Mayor
Vicky Goertzen-Cooke, Clerk-Treasurer

Plympton-Wyoming
P.O. Box 250
546 Niagara St.
Wyoming, ON N0N 1T0
Tel: 519-845-3939; *Fax:* 519-845-0597
feedback@plympton-wyoming.ca
www.plympton-wyoming.com
Other Information: Toll-Free Phone: 1-877-313-3939
Municipal Type: Town
Incorporated: Jan. 1, 2001; *Area:* 318.76 sq km
County or District: Lambton; *Population in 2011:* 7,576
Provincial Electoral District(s): Sarnia-Lambton
Federal Electoral District(s): Sarnia-Lambton
Next Election: Oct. 2018 (4 year terms)
Note: Amalgamation of the Village of Wyoming & the Township of Plympton.
Lonny Napper, Mayor
Caroline DeSchutter, Clerk & Deputy Chief Administrative Officer

Point Edward
Municipal Office
135 Kendall St.
Point Edward, ON N7V 4G6
Tel: 519-337-3021; *Fax:* 519-337-5963
info@villageofpointedward.com
www.villageofpointedward.com
Municipal Type: Village
Incorporated: 1878; *Area:* 3.27 sq km
County or District: Lambton; *Population in 2011:* 2,034
Provincial Electoral District(s): Sarnia-Lambton
Federal Electoral District(s): Sarnia-Lambton
Next Election: Oct. 2018 (4 year terms)
Larry MacKenzie, Mayor, 519-336-9315
Jim Burns, Chief Administrative Officer & Clerk, 519-337-3021

Port Hope
Town Hall
56 Queen St.
Port Hope, ON L1A 3Z9
Tel: 905-885-4544; *Fax:* 905-885-7698
admin@porthope.ca
www.porthope.ca
Municipal Type: Municipality
Incorporated: March 6, 1834; *Area:* 278.97 sq km
County or District: Northumberland; *Population in 2011:* 16,214
Provincial Electoral District(s): Northumberland-Quinte West
Federal Electoral District(s): Northumberland-Peterborough South
Next Election: Oct. 2018 (4 year terms)
Bob Sanderson, Mayor
Terry Hickey, Councillor, Wards: 1
Les Andrews, Councillor, Wards: 1
Greg W. Burns, Councillor, 905-797-9616, Wards: 2
Louse Ferrie-Blecher, Councillor, Wards: 2
Sue Dawe, Clerk & Director, Corporate Services, 905-885-4544
C. Carl Cannon, Chief Administrative Officer, 905-885-4544
David Baxter, Director, Finance, 905-885-4544
Peter Angelo, P.Eng., Director, Works & Engineering, 905-885-2431
Jim Wheeler, Fire Chief, 905-753-2230
Judy Selvig, Director, Economic Development & Tourism, 905-885-2431
Jim McCormack, Director, Parks, Recreation & Culture, 905-885-8760
Gina Jackson, Manager, Human Resources, 905-885-4544
Sandra Weeks, Coordinator, Communications, 905-885-4544

Powassan, Municipality of
P.O. Box 250
466 Main St.
Powassan, ON P0H 1Z0
Tel: 705-724-2813; *Fax:* 705-724-5533
info@powassan.net
www.powassan.net
Municipal Type: Town
Incorporated: Nov. 30, 1904; *Area:* 222.75 sq km
County or District: Parry Sound District; *Population in 2011:* 3,378
Provincial Electoral District(s): Nipissing
Federal Electoral District(s): Nipissing-Timiskaming
Next Election: Oct. 2018 (4 year terms)
Peter McIsaac, Mayor, 705-491-0374
Maureen Lang, Clerk-Treasurer, 795-724-2813, Fax: 705-724-5533

Prescott
P.O. Box 160
360 Dibble St. West
Prescott, ON K0E 1T0
Tel: 613-925-2812; *Fax:* 613-925-4381
info@prescott.ca
www.prescott.ca
Municipal Type: Town
Area: 4.95 sq km
County or District: Leeds & Grenville; *Population in 2011:* 4,284
Provincial Electoral District(s): Leeds-Grenville
Federal Electoral District(s): Leeds-Grenville-Thousand Islands and Rideau Lakes
Next Election: Oct. 2018 (4 year terms)
Brett Todd, Mayor, 613-925-2812
Randy Haller, Chief Administrative Officer & Clerk, 613-925-2812, Fax: 613-925-4381

Prescott & Russell
P.O. Box 303
59 Court St.
L'Orignal, ON K0B 1K0
Tel: 613-675-4661; *Fax:* 613-675-2519
www.prescott-russell.on.ca
Other Information: Toll-Free Phone: 1-800-667-6307
Municipal Type: United County
Incorporated: 1820; *Area:* 2,001.18 sq km
Population in 2011: 85,381
Next Election: Oct. 2018 (4 year terms)
Robert Kirby, Warden, 613-674-2170, Fax: 613-632-4841, Wards: East Hawkesbury
Fernard Dicaire, Councillor, Wards: Alfred & Plantagenet
Gary J. Baron, Councillor, Wards: Champlain
Jeanne Charlebois, Councillor, Wards: Hawkesbury
Guy Desjardins, Councillor, Wards: Clarence-Rockland
Claude Levac, Councillor, 613-764-3139, Fax: 613-764-5709, Wards: Casselman
François St. Amour, Councillor, 613-764-5444, Wards: Nation Municipality
Pierre Leroux, Councillor, Wards: Russell
Stéphane P. Parisien, Chief Administrative Officer & Clerk, 613-675-4661
Louise Lepage-Gareau, Treasurer, 613-675-4661, Fax: 613-675-4547
Michel Chrétien, Director, Emergency Services, 613-673-5139, Fax: 613-673-1401
Marc Clermont, Director, Public Works, 613-675-4661, Fax: 613-675-1007
Louis Prévost, Director, Planning & Forestry, 613-675-4661, Fax: 613-675-1007
Jonathan B. Roy, Director, Human Resources, 613-675-4661, Fax: 613-675-4547
Anne Comtois Lalonde, Administrator, Social Services Management, 613-675-4642, Fax: 613-675-2030

Prince
3042 2nd Line West
Sault Ste Marie, ON P6A 6K4
Tel: 705-779-2992; *Fax:* 705-779-2725
www.princetwp.ca
Municipal Type: Township
Area: 84.28 sq km
County or District: Algoma District; *Population in 2011:* 1,031
Provincial Electoral District(s): Algoma Manitoulin

Federal Electoral District(s): Sault Ste Marie
Next Election: Oct. 2018 (4 year terms)
Ken Lamming, Reeve, 705-779-2875
Peggy Greco, Chief Administrative Officer & Administrator

Puslinch
7404 Wellington Rd. 34, RR#3
Guelph, ON N1H 6H9
Tel: 519-763-1226; *Fax:* 519-763-5846
admin@puslinch.ca
www.puslinch.ca
Municipal Type: Township
Incorporated: Jan. 1, 1850; *Area:* 214.44 sq km
County or District: Wellington; *Population in 2011:* 7,029
Provincial Electoral District(s): Wellington-Halton Hills
Federal Electoral District(s): Wellington-Halton Hills; Guelph
Next Election: Oct. 2018 (4 year terms)
Dennis Lever, Mayor, 226-971-2067
Karen Landry, Chief Administrative Officer & Clerk-Treasurer, 519-763-1226

Rainy River
P.O. Box 488
Rainy River, ON P0W 1L0
Tel: 807-852-3244; *Fax:* 807-852-3553
rainyriver@tbaytel.net
www.rainyriver.ca
Municipal Type: Town
Incorporated: 1904; *Area:* 2.99 sq km
County or District: Rainy River District; *Population in 2011:* 842
Provincial Electoral District(s): Kenora-Rainy River
Federal Electoral District(s): Thunder Bay-Rainy River
Next Election: Oct. 2018 (4 year terms)
Deborah Ewald, Mayor
Veldron Vogan, Chief Administrative Officer

Rainy River
District Social Services Administration Bd.
450 Scott St.
Fort Frances, ON P9A 1H2
Tel: 807-274-5349; *Fax:* 807-274-0678
www.rrdssab.ca
Other Information: Toll-Free Phone: 1-800-265-5349
Municipal Type: District
Area: 15,472.94 sq km
Population in 2011: 20,370
Ross Donaldson, Chair, Rainy River District Social Services Administration Board
Dan McCormick, CAO, Rainy River District Social Services Administration Board

Ramara
Ramara Administration Building
P.O. Box 130
2297 Hwy. 12
Brechin, ON L0K 1B0
Tel: 705-484-5374; *Fax:* 705-484-0441
ramara@ramara.ca
www.ramara.ca
Other Information: Toll-Free Phone: 1-800-663-4054 (for 689 exchange)
Municipal Type: Township
Area: 417.25 sq km
County or District: Simcoe; *Population in 2011:* 9,275
Provincial Electoral District(s): Simcoe North
Federal Electoral District(s): Simcoe North
Next Election: Oct. 2018 (4 year terms)
Basil Clarke, Mayor
Janice McKinnon, Chief Administrative Officer, 705-484-5374

Red Lake
P.O. Box 1000
2 Fifth St.
Balmertown, ON P0V 1C0
Tel: 807-735-2096; *Fax:* 807-735-2286
municipality@red-lake.com
www.red-lake.com
Municipal Type: Municipality
Incorporated: July 1, 1998; *Area:* 610.38 sq km
County or District: Kenora District; *Population in 2011:* 4,366
Provincial Electoral District(s): Kenora-Rainy River
Federal Electoral District(s): Kenora
Next Election: Oct. 2018 (4 year terms)
Note: Amalgamation of the former Unorganized Territory of Madsen, the Township of Red Lake, & the Township of Golden.
Phil T. Vinet, Mayor, 807-735-2096, Fax: 807-735-2286
Shelly Kocis, Clerk, 807-735-2096, Fax: 807-735-2286

Red Rock
P.O. Box 447
Red Rock, ON P0T 2P0
Tel: 807-886-2245; *Fax:* 807-886-2793
info@redrocktownship.com
www.redrocktownship.com
Other Information: Phone, Public Works: 807-886-2524
Municipal Type: Township
Area: 62.93 sq km
County or District: Thunder Bay District; *Population in 2011:* 942
Provincial Electoral District(s): Thunder Bay-Superior North
Federal Electoral District(s): Thunder Bay-Superior North
Next Election: Oct. 2018 (4 year terms)
Gary Nelson, Mayor, 807-886-2503
Kal Pristanski, CAO, Clerk-Treasurer, Tax Collector, & Commissioner of Oaths

Renfrew
127 Raglan St. South
Renfrew, ON K7V 1P8
Tel: 613-432-4848; *Fax:* 613-432-7245
info@town.renfrew.on.ca
www.town.renfrew.on.ca
Municipal Type: Town
Area: 12.77 sq km
County or District: Renfrew; *Population in 2011:* 8,218
Provincial Electoral District(s): Renfrew-Nipissing-Pembroke
Federal Electoral District(s): Renfrew-Nipissing-Pembroke
Next Election: Oct. 2018 (4 year terms)
Don Eady, Mayor, 613-432-4848
Kim R. Bulmer, Town Clerk, 613-432-4848

Rideau Lakes
1439 County Rd. 8
Delta, ON K0E 1G0
Tel: 613-928-2251; *Fax:* 613-928-3097
info@twprideaulakes.on.ca
www.twprideaulakes.on.ca
Other Information: Toll-Free Phone: 1-800-928-2250
Municipal Type: Township
Incorporated: Jan. 1, 1998; *Area:* 710.25 sq km
County or District: Leeds-Grenville; *Population in 2011:* 10,207
Provincial Electoral District(s): Leeds-Grenville
Federal Electoral District(s): Leeds-Grenville-Thousand Islands and Rideau Lakes
Next Election: Oct. 2018 (4 year terms)
Note: Amalgamation of the former Townships of North Crosby, South Crosby, Bastard & South Burgess, South Elmsley & the Village of Newboro.
Ron Holman, Mayor, 613-283-0724, Fax: 613-283-5517
Ron Pollard, Deputy Mayor & Councillor, 613-273-5491, Wards: North Crosby
Doug Good, Councillor, Wards: Bastard & South Burgess
Cathy Livingston, Councillor, Wards: Bastard & South Burgess
Cathy Monck, Councillor, 613-272-3453, Wards: Newboro
Bob Lavoie, Councillor, 613-273-8177, Wards: North Crosby
Linda Carr, Councillor, 613-272-2227, Wards: South Crosby
Claire Gunnewiek, Councillor, Wards: South Crosby
Jeff Banks, Councillor, 613-800-2790, Wards: South Elmsley
Arie Hoogenboom, Councillor, Wards: South Elmsley
Dianna Bresee, Clerk, 613-928-2251
Mike Dwyer, Chief Administrative Officer, 613-928-2251
Joseph Whyte, Treasurer, 613-928-2251
Susan Dunfield, Manager, Community & Leisure Services, 613-928-2251
Sheldon Laidman, Manager, Development Services, 613-928-2251
Dan Chant, Roads Coordinator & Drainage Superintendent, 613-928-2251
Jay DeBernardi, Fire Chief, 613-928-2251

Russell
717 Notre Dame St.
Embrun, ON K0A 1W1
Tel: 613-443-3066; *Fax:* 613-443-1042
info@russell.ca; publicworks.voirie@russell.ca
www.russell.ca
Other Information: Bylaws, E-mail: bylaws.reglements@russell.ca
Municipal Type: Township
Area: 198.96 sq km
County or District: Prescott & Russell; *Population in 2011:* 15,247
Provincial Electoral District(s): Glengarry-Prescott-Russell
Federal Electoral District(s): Glengarry-Prescott-Russell
Next Election: Oct. 2018 (4 year terms)
Pierre Leroux, Mayor
Amanda Simard, Councillor
Andre Brisson, Councillor
Jamie Laurin, Councillor
Joanne Camiré-Laflamme, Municipal Clerk
Christiane B. Brault, Treasurer & Director, Finance
Millie Bourdeau, Director, Public Safety & Enforcement
Cathy Parent, Director, Public Utilities, 613-443-1747
Manon Babin, Director, Public Works, 613-443-5078
Bruce Armstrong, Fire Chief

Ryerson
28 Midlothian Rd., RR#1
Burks Falls, ON P0A 1C0
Tel: 705-382-3232; *Fax:* 705-382-3286
admin@ryersontownship.ca
www.ryersontownship.ca
Municipal Type: Township
Area: 186.79 sq km
County or District: Parry Sound District; *Population in 2011:* 634
Provincial Electoral District(s): Parry Sound-Muskoka
Federal Electoral District(s): Parry Sound-Muskoka
Next Election: Oct. 2018 (4 year terms)
Glenn Miller, Reeve, 705-382-2898
Judy Kosowan, Chief Administrative Officer & Clerk-Treasurer

Sables-Spanish Rivers
PO Box 5, Site 1, 11 Birch Lake Rd. RR#3
Massey, ON P0P 1P0
Tel: 705-865-2646; *Fax:* 705-865-2736
inquiries@sables-spanish.ca
www.sables-spanish.ca
Municipal Type: Township
Incorporated: July 1998; *Area:* 806.27 sq km
County or District: Sudbury District; *Population in 2011:* 3,075
Provincial Electoral District(s): Algoma-Manitoulin
Federal Electoral District(s): Algoma-Manitoulin-Kapuskasing
Next Election: Oct. 2018 (4 year terms)
Leslie Gamble, Mayor, 705-865-2655
Kim Sloss, Clerk-Administrator, 705-865-2646, Fax: 705-865-2736

St.-Charles, Municipality of
P.O. Box 70
2 King St. East
St Charles, ON P0M 2W0
Tel: 705-867-2032; *Fax:* 705-867-5789
cta@stcharlesontario.ca; tourism@stcharlesontario.ca
www.stcharlesontario.ca
Other Information: Toll-Free Phone: 1-877-867-2032
Municipal Type: Town
Area: 318.47 sq km
County or District: Sudbury District; *Population in 2011:* 1,282
Provincial Electoral District(s): Timiskaming-Cochrane
Federal Electoral District(s): Nickel Belt
Next Election: Oct. 2018 (4 year terms)
Paul Schoppman, Mayor
Theresa Niemi, Clerk-Treasurer & Administrator

St. Clair
Civic Centre
1155 Emily St.
Mooretown, ON N0N 1M0
Tel: 519-867-2021; *Fax:* 519-867-5509
webmaster@twp.stclair.on.ca; publicworks@twp.stclair.on.ca
www.twp.stclair.on.ca
Other Information: Toll-Free Phone: 1-800-809-0301 (Sombra & Lambton)
Municipal Type: Township
Area: 619.3 sq km
County or District: Lambton; *Population in 2011:* 14,515
Provincial Electoral District(s): Sarnia-Lambton
Federal Electoral District(s): Sarnia-Lambton
Next Election: Oct. 2018 (4 year terms)
Steve Arnold, Mayor, 519-381-7440
Peter Gilliland, Deputy Mayor, 519-862-3534
Jeff Agar, Councillor, 519-862-5062, Wards: 1
Tracy Kingston, Councillor, Wards: 1
Jim DeGurse, Councillor, 519-862-3060, Wards: 1
Steve Miller, Councillor, 519-677-5676, Wards: 2
Darrell Randell, Councillor, 519-627-3764, Wards: 2
John DeMars, Clerk, Deputy CAO, & Director, Administration, 519-867-2021
John Rodey, MCIP, RPP, Chief Administrative Officer, 519-867-2021, Fax: 519-867-5509
Charles Quenneville, B.Com., CMA, Treasurer, 519-867-2024
Roy Dewhirst, Fire Chief

St. Joseph
P.O. Box 187
1669 Arthur St.
Richards Landing, ON P0R 1J0
Tel: 705-246-2625; *Fax:* 705-246-3142
stjosephtownship@bellnet.ca
www.stjosephtownship.com
Municipal Type: Township
Area: 129.18 sq km

County or District: Algoma District; *Population in 2011:* 1,201
Provincial Electoral District(s): Algoma-Manitoulin
Federal Electoral District(s): Algoma-Manitoulin-Kapuskasing
Next Election: Oct. 2018 (4 year terms)
Jody Wildman, Mayor, 705-246-0616
Carol O. Trainor, A.M.C.T., Clerk Administrator

St. Marys
P.O. Box 998
175 Queen St. East, 2nd Fl.
St. Marys, ON N4X 1B6
Tel: 519-284-2340; *Fax:* 519-284-3881
www.townofstmarys.com
Municipal Type: Town
Area: 12.48 sq km
County or District: Perth; *Population in 2011:* 6,655
Provincial Electoral District(s): Perth-Wellington
Federal Electoral District(s): Perth-Wellington
Next Election: Oct. 2018 (4 year terms)
Al Strathdee, Mayor, 519-284-2340
Robert Brindley, Chief Administrative Officer, 519-284-2340

Schreiber
P.O. Box 40
204 Alberta St.
Schreiber, ON P0T 2S0
Tel: 807-824-2711; *Fax:* 807-824-3231
executiveassistant@schreiber.ca
www.schreiber.ca
Municipal Type: Township
Area: 36.79 sq km
County or District: Thunder Bay District; *Population in 2011:* 1,126
Provincial Electoral District(s): Thunder Bay-Superior North
Federal Electoral District(s): Thunder Bay-Superior North
Next Election: Oct. 2018 (4 year terms)
Mark Figliomeni, Mayor, 807-824-2711
Jon Hall, Clerk & Deputy Treasurer, 807-824-2711

Scugog
P.O. Box 780
181 Perry St.
Port Perry, ON L9L 1A7
Tel: 905-985-7346; *Fax:* 905-985-9914
www.scugog.ca
Municipal Type: Township
Area: 474.63 sq km
County or District: Durham Regional Municipality; *Population in 2011:* 21,569
Provincial Electoral District(s): Durham
Federal Electoral District(s): Durham
Next Election: Oct. 2018 (4 year terms)
Tom Rowett, Mayor, 905-985-7346
Bobbie Drew, Regional Councillor, 905-985-7183
Betty Somerville, Councillor, Wards: 1
Janna Guido, Councillor, Wards: 2
Don Kett, Councillor, Wards: 3
Wilma Wotten, Councillor, 905-986-4975, Wards: 4
Jennifer Back, Councillor, Wards: 5
Don Gordon, Interim Chief Administrative Officer, 905-985-7346, Fax: 905-985-9914
T. DeBruijn, Treasurer & Director, Finance
D. Gordon, Director, Community Services
Richard Miller, Fire Chief, 905-985-2384

Seguin
5 Humphrey Dr., RR#2
Parry Sound, ON P2A 2W8
Tel: 705-732-4300; *Fax:* 705-732-6347
info@seguin.ca
www.seguin.ca
Other Information: Toll-Free Phone: 1-877-473-4846
Municipal Type: Township
Incorporated: May 8, 1997; *Area:* 586.17 sq km
County or District: Parry Sound District; *Population in 2011:* 3,988
Provincial Electoral District(s): Parry Sound-Muskoka
Federal Electoral District(s): Parry Sound-Muskoka
Next Election: Oct. 2018 (4 year terms)
Bruce Gibbon, Mayor, Fax: 705-732-2730
Craig Jeffery, Clerk & Officer, Lottery Licensing

Selwyn
P.O. Box 270
1310 Centre Line, RR#4
Bridgenorth, ON K0L 1H0
Tel: 705-292-9507; *Fax:* 705-292-8964
www.selwyntownship.ca
Other Information: Toll-Free Phone: 1-877-213-7419 (in 705 area code)
Municipal Type: Township
Area: 318.77 sq km
County or District: Peterborough; *Population in 2011:* 16,846
Provincial Electoral District(s): Peterborough
Federal Electoral District(s): Peterborough-Kawartha
Next Election: Oct. 2018 (4 year terms)
Mary Smith, Mayor, 705-652-0784
Sherry Senis, Deputy Mayor, 705-931-4873
Donna Ballantyne, Councillor, 705-292-7174, Wards: Ennismore
Anita Locke, Councillor, 705-652-1086, Wards: Lakefield
Gerry Herron, Councillor, Wards: Smith
Angela Chittick, Clerk, 705-292-9507
Janice Lavalley, Chief Administrative Officer, 705-292-9507
R. Lane Vance, Treasurer & Manager, Financial Services, 705-292-9507
Ed Barber, Manager, Recreation, 705-292-9507
Stephen Crough, Manager, Public Works, 705-292-9507
Robert Lamarre, Manager, Building & Planning, 705-292-9507
Gord Jopling, Fire Chief, 705-292-7282
Kim Berry, Coordinator, Human Resources, 705-292-9507

Severn
P.O. Box 159
1024 Hurlwood Lane
Orillia, ON L3V 6J3
Tel: 705-325-2315; *Fax:* 705-327-5818
severn@encode.com
www.townshipofsevern.com
Municipal Type: Township
Incorporated: Jan. 1, 1994; *Area:* 534.78 sq km
County or District: Simcoe; *Population in 2011:* 12,377
Provincial Electoral District(s): Simcoe North
Federal Electoral District(s): Simcoe North
Next Election: Oct. 2018 (4 year terms)
Mike Burkett, Mayor
Judith Cox, Deputy Mayor
Mark Taylor, Councillor, Wards: 1
Jane Dunlop, Councillor, Wards: 2
Ian Crichton, Councillor, Wards: 3
Ron Stevens, Councillor, Wards: 4
Donald Westcott, Councillor, Wards: 5
W. Henry Sander, Chief Administrative Officer, 705-325-2315, Wards: 5
Henry Sander, Clerk-Treasurer & Director, Corporate Services, 705-325-2315
Andrew Fyfe, Director, Planning, 705-325-2315
Eric Marshall, Supervisor, Public Works, 705-325-2315
Tim Cranney, Fire Chief, 705-325-2315

Shelburne
Town of Shelburne Municipal Office
203 Main St. East
Shelburne, ON L0N 1S0
Tel: 519-925-2600; *Fax:* 519-925-6134
www.townofshelburne.on.ca
Municipal Type: Town
Incorporated: March 22, 1879; *Area:* 6.44 sq km
County or District: Dufferin; *Population in 2011:* 5,846
Provincial Electoral District(s): Dufferin-Caledon
Federal Electoral District(s): Dufferin-Caledon
Next Election: Oct. 2018 (4 year terms)
Note: Incorporated as a town on Dec. 31, 1976.
Kenneth Bennington, Mayor, 519-925-2600, Fax: 519-925-6134
John Telfer, AMCT, Chief Administrative Officer & Town Clerk, 519-925-2600

Shuniah
420 Leslie Ave.
Thunder Bay, ON P7A 1X8
Tel: 807-683-4545;
shuniah@shuniah.org
www.shuniah.org
Municipal Type: Township
Incorporated: 1873; *Area:* 569.18 sq km
County or District: Thunder Bay District; *Population in 2011:* 2,737
Provincial Electoral District(s): Thunder Bay-Superior North
Federal Electoral District(s): Thunder Bay-Superior North
Next Election: Oct. 2018 (4 year terms)
Wendy Landry, Reeve, 807-983-2276
Wendy Hamlin, Clerk

Sioux Lookout, Municipality of
P.O. Box 158
25 Fifth Ave.
Sioux Lookout, ON P8T 1A4
Tel: 807-737-2700;
admin@siouxlookout.ca
www.siouxlookout.ca
Municipal Type: Town
Incorporated: 1912; *Area:* 378.61 sq km
County or District: Kenora District; *Population in 2011:* 5,037
Provincial Electoral District(s): Kenora-Rainy River
Federal Electoral District(s): Kenora
Next Election: Oct. 2018 (4 year terms)
Dennis Leney, Mayor
Mary L. MacKenzie, Municipal Clerk

Sioux Narrows-Nestor Falls
P.O. Box 417
Sioux Narrows, ON P0X 1N0
Tel: 807-226-5241; *Fax:* 807-226-5712
www.snnf.ca
Municipal Type: Township
Area: 1,221.56 sq km
County or District: Kenora District; *Population in 2011:* 720
Provincial Electoral District(s): Kenora-Rainy River
Federal Electoral District(s): Kenora
Next Election: Oct. 2018 (4 year terms)
Jerry O'Leary, Mayor
Wanda Kabel, Chief Administrative Officer

Smiths Falls
77 Beckwith St. North
Smiths Falls, ON K7A 4T6
Tel: 613-283-4124;
info@smithsfalls.ca
www.smithsfalls.ca
Municipal Type: Separated for Municipal Purposes Only
Incorporated: 1854; *Area:* 8.2 sq km
County or District: Lanark; *Population in 2011:* 8,978
Provincial Electoral District(s): Lanark-Frontenac-Lennox & Addington
Federal Electoral District(s): Lanark-Frontenac-Kingston
Next Election: Oct. 2018 (4 year terms)
Note: Incorporated as a town on Jan. 1, 1883. In Dec. 1902, the Town of Smiths Falls became the Separated Town of Smiths Falls.
Shawn James Pankow, Mayor
Kerry Costello, Clerk, 613-283-4124

Smooth Rock Falls
P.O. Box 249
142 First St.
Smooth Rock Falls, ON P0L 2B0
Tel: 705-338-2717; *Fax:* 705-338-2584
comments@townsrf.ca
www.townofsmoothrockfalls.ca
Municipal Type: Town
Incorporated: 1929; *Area:* 199.79 sq km
County or District: Cochrane District; *Population in 2011:* 1,376
Provincial Electoral District(s): Timmins-James Bay
Federal Electoral District(s): Algoma-Manitoulin-Kapuskasing
Next Election: Oct. 2018 (4 year terms)
Michel Arseneault, Mayor
Luc Denault, Chief Administrative Officer

South Algonquin
P.O. Box 217
7 - 3 Ave.
Whitney, ON K0J 2M0
Tel: 613-637-2650; *Fax:* 613-637-5368
southalgonquin@xplornet.com
www.township.southalgonquin.on.ca
Other Information: Toll-Free Phone: 1-888-307-3187
Municipal Type: Township
Area: 871.31 sq km
County or District: Nipissing District; *Population in 2011:* 1,211
Provincial Electoral District(s): Renfrew-Nipissing-Pembroke
Federal Electoral District(s): Renfrew-Nipissing-Pembroke
Next Election: Oct. 2018 (4 year terms)
Jane A.E. Dumas, Mayor, 613-332-8357
Suzanne Klatt, CAO/Clerk-Treasurer, 613-637-2650, Fax: 613-637-5368

South Bruce
P.O. Box 540
21 Gordon St. East
Teeswater, ON N0G 2S0
Tel: 519-392-6623; *Fax:* 519-392-6266
clerk@town.southbruce.on.ca
www.town.southbruce.on.ca
Municipal Type: Municipality
Incorporated: 1999; *Area:* 487.17 sq km
County or District: Bruce; *Population in 2011:* 5,685
Provincial Electoral District(s): Huron-Bruce
Federal Electoral District(s): Huron-Bruce
Next Election: Oct. 2018 (4 year terms)
Note: Amalgamation of the Village of Mildmay, the Township of Carrick, the Village of Teeswater, & the Township of Culross.
Robert Buckle, Mayor
Angie Cathrae, Clerk

South Bruce Peninsula
P.O. Box 310
315 George St.
Wiarton, ON N0H 2T0
Tel: 519-534-1400; *Fax:* 519-534-4862
admin@southbrucepeninsula.com
www.southbrucepeninsula.com
Other Information: Toll-Free Phone: 1-877-534-1400
Municipal Type: Town
Area: 531.9 sq km
County or District: Bruce; *Population in 2011:* 8,413
Provincial Electoral District(s): Bruce-Grey-Owen Sound
Federal Electoral District(s): Bruce-Grey-Owen Sound
Next Election: Oct. 2018 (4 year terms)
Janice Jackson, Mayor, 519-534-1589
Angie Cathrae, Clerk, 519-534-1400

South Dundas
P.O. Box 160
4296 County Rd. 31
Williamsburg, ON K0C 2H0
Tel: 613-535-2673; *Fax:* 613-535-2099
mail@southdundas.com
www.southdundas.com
Other Information: Toll-Free Phone: 1-800-265-0619
Municipal Type: Township
Area: 519.98 sq km
County or District: Stormont, Dundas & Glengarry; *Population in 2011:* 10,794
Provincial Electoral District(s): Stormont-Dundas-South Glengarry
Federal Electoral District(s): Stormont-Dundas-South Glengarry
Next Election: Oct. 2018 (4 year terms)
Evonne Delegarde, Mayor, Fax: 613-535-2746
Jim Locke, Deputy Mayor, Fax: 613-652-2233
Bill Ewing, Councillor
Marc St Pierre, Councillor
Archie L. Mellan, Councillor
Brenda M. Brunt, Clerk
Stephen McDonald, Chief Administrative Officer
Shannon Geraghty, Treasurer
Hugh Garlough, Manager, Public Works
Don J.W. Lewis, Manager, Planning & Enforcement
Don W. Lewis, Manager, Recreation
Chris McDonough, Fire Chief

South Frontenac
P.O. Box 100
4432 George St.
Sydenham, ON K0H 2T0
Tel: 613-376-3027; *Fax:* 613-376-6657
www.southfrontenac.net
Other Information: Toll-Free Phone: 1-800-559-5862
Municipal Type: Township
Incorporated: Jan. 1, 1998; *Area:* 941.28 sq km
County or District: Frontenac; *Population in 2011:* 18,113
Provincial Electoral District(s): Lanark-Frontenac-Lennox & Addington
Federal Electoral District(s): Lanark-Frontenac-Kingston
Next Election: Oct. 2018 (4 year terms)
Ron Vandewal, Mayor
Pat Barr, Councillor, Wards: Bedford
Alan Revill, Councillor, Wards: Bedford
Mark Schjerning, Councillor, Wards: Loughborough
Ross Sutherland, Councillor, Wards: Loughborough
John R. McDougall, Councillor, Wards: Portland
Bill W.L. Robinson, Councillor, Wards: Portland
Norm Roberts, Councillor, Wards: Storrington
Ronald Sleeth, Councillor, Wards: Storrington
Wayne Orr, Chief Administrative Officer, 613-376-3027
Deborah Bracken, Treasurer, 613-376-3027
Mark Segsworth, Manager, Public Works, 613-376-3027
Rick Chesebrough, Fire Chief, 613-376-3027
Alan Revill, Chief Building Inspector, 613-376-3027
Lindsay Mills, Coordinator, Planning, 613-376-3027

South Glengarry
6 Oak St.
Lancaster, ON K0C 1N0
Tel: 613-347-1166;
info@southglengarry.com
www.southglengarry.com
Municipal Type: Township
Incorporated: Jan. 1, 1998; *Area:* 604.91 sq km
County or District: Stormont, Dundas & Glengarry; *Population in 2011:* 13,162
Provincial Electoral District(s): Stormont-Dundas-South Glengarry
Federal Electoral District(s): Stormont-Dundas-South Glengarry
Next Election: Oct. 2018 (4 year terms)
Ian McLeod, Mayor
Frank Prevost, Deputy Mayor
Trevor Bougie, Councillor
Joyce Gravelle, Councillor
Lyle Warden, Councillor
Marilyn Lebrun, Clerk, 613-347-1166, Fax: 613-347-3411
Derik Brandt, Chief Administrative Officer, 613-347-1166, Fax: 613-347-3411
Michel J. Samson, Treasurer & Deputy Clerk, 613-347-1166, Fax: 613-347-3411
Joanne Haley, General Manager, Community Services, 613-347-1166, Fax: 613-347-3411
Ewen MacDonald, General Manager, Infrastructure Services, 613-347-2040, Fax: 613-347-3411
Dwane Crawford, Director, Development, 613-347-1166, Fax: 613-347-3411
Shawn Killoran, Director, Water & Wastewater, 613-931-3036
Roger Lapierre, Director, Roads, 613-930-3445, Fax: 613-347-3411
Gary Poupart, Manager, Property Standards & Enforcement, 613-347-1166, Fax: 613-347-3411

South Huron
P.O. Box 759
322 Main St. South
Exeter, ON N0M 1S6
Tel: 519-235-0310; *Fax:* 519-235-3304
info@southhuron.ca
www.southhuron.ca
Other Information: Toll-Free: 1-877-204-0747
Municipal Type: Municipality
Incorporated: 2001; *Area:* 425.35 sq km
County or District: Huron; *Population in 2011:* 9,945
Provincial Electoral District(s): Huron-Bruce
Federal Electoral District(s): Huron-Bruce
Next Election: Oct. 2018 (4 year terms)
Maureen Cole, Mayor
John Maddox, Acting Chief Administrative Officer, 519-235-0310

South River
P.O. Box 310
63 Marie St.
South River, ON P0A 1X0
Tel: 705-386-2573;
info@southriverontario.com
www.southriverontario.com
Other Information: Public Works, Phone: 705-386-0245
Municipal Type: Village
Incorporated: 1907; *Area:* 4.04 sq km
County or District: Parry Sound District; *Population in 2011:* 1,049
Provincial Electoral District(s): Parry Sound-Muskoka
Federal Electoral District(s): Parry Sound-Muskoka
Next Election: Oct. 2018 (4 year terms)
Jim Coleman, Mayor
Susan Arnold, Administrator & Clerk

South Stormont
P.O. Box 84
2 Mille Roches Rd.
Long Sault, ON K0C 1P0
Tel: 613-534-8889; *Fax:* 613-534-2280
info@southstormont.ca
www.southstormont.ca
Other Information: Toll-Free Phone: 1-800-265-3915
Municipal Type: Township
Area: 447.46 sq km
County or District: Stormont, Dundas & Glengarry; *Population in 2011:* 12,617
Provincial Electoral District(s): Stormont-Dundas-South Glengarry
Federal Electoral District(s): Stormont-Dundas-South Glengarry
Next Election: Oct. 2018 (4 year terms)
Jim Bancroft, Mayor, 613-577-0753
Tammy Hart, Deputy Mayor, 613-984-2543
Donna Primeau, Councillor
Richard F. Waldroff, Councillor, 613-537-8226, Fax: 613-362-7596
David Smith, Councillor
Betty de Haan, Chief Administrative Officer & Clerk, 613-534-8889
Johanna Barkley, Treasurer, 613-534-8889
Hilton Cryderman, Manager, Building & Development, 613-534-8889
Dan Pilon, Manager, Public Works, 613-534-8889
Roger Desjardins, Fire Chief, 613-534-8889
Harry Hutchinson, Deputy Chief Building Official & Superintendent, Drainage, 613-534-8889
Gord Ramsay, Officer, Law Enforcement, 613-534-8889

Southgate
185667 Grey Rd. 9, RR#1
Dundalk, ON N0C 1B0
Tel: 519-923-2110; *Fax:* 519-923-9262
info@southgate.ca
www.southgate.ca
Other Information: Toll-Free Phone: 1-888-560-6607
Municipal Type: Township
Incorporated: Jan. 1, 2001; *Area:* 643.95 sq km
County or District: Grey; *Population in 2011:* 7,190
Provincial Electoral District(s): Bruce-Grey-Owen Sound
Federal Electoral District(s): Bruce-Grey-Owen Sound
Next Election: Oct. 2018 (4 year terms)
Note: Amalgamation of the Village of Dundalk, the Township of Proton & the Township of Egremont.
Anna-Marie Fosbrooke, Mayor
Dave Milliner, Chief Adminstrative Officer, 519-923-9262

Southwest Middlesex, Municipality of
P.O. Box 218
153 McKellar St.
Glencoe, ON N0L 1M0
Tel: 519-287-2015; *Fax:* 519-287-2359
info@southwestmiddlesex.ca
www.southwestmiddlesex.ca
Municipal Type: Township
Incorporated: Jan. 1, 2001; *Area:* 427.92 sq km
County or District: Middlesex; *Population in 2011:* 5,860
Provincial Electoral District(s): Lambton-Kent-Middlesex
Federal Electoral District(s): Lambton-Kent-Middlesex
Next Election: Oct. 2018 (4 year terms)
Note: Amalgamation of the Villages of Glencoe & Wardsville & the Townships of Ekfrid & Mosa.
Vance Blackmore, Mayor
Janneke Newitt, Administrator & Clerk, 519-287-2015

South-West Oxford
312915 Dereham Line
Mount Elgin, ON N0J 1N0
Tel: 519-485-0477; *Fax:* 519-485-2932
dbarnes@swox.org (Office)
www.swox.org
Other Information: Phone, Works Department: 519-877-2702
Municipal Type: Township
Area: 370.63 sq km
County or District: Oxford; *Population in 2011:* 7,544
Provincial Electoral District(s): Oxford
Federal Electoral District(s): Oxford
Next Election: Oct. 2018 (4 year terms)
David Mayberry, Mayor, 519-485-3642
Mary Ellen Greb, Chief Administrative Officer, 519-877-2702

Southwold
General Delivery
35663 Fingal Line
Fingal, ON N0L 1K0
Tel: 519-769-2010; *Fax:* 519-769-2837
southwold@southwold.ca
www.southwold.ca
Municipal Type: Township
Area: 301.71 sq km
County or District: Elgin; *Population in 2011:* 4,494
Provincial Electoral District(s): Elgin-Middlesex-London
Federal Electoral District(s): Elgin-Middlesex-London
Next Election: Oct. 2018 (4 year terms)
Grant Jones, Mayor, 519-764-9764
Donna Ethier, Chief Administrative Officer, Clerk, & Deputy Treasurer

Spanish
P.O. Box 70
8 Trunk Rd.
Spanish, ON P0P 2A0
Tel: 705-844-2300; *Fax:* 705-844-2622
info@townofspanish.com
www.townofspanish.com
Municipal Type: Town
Area: 106.02 sq km
County or District: Algoma District; *Population in 2011:* 696
Provincial Electoral District(s): Algoma-Manitoulin
Federal Electoral District(s): Algoma-Manitoulin-Kapuskasing
Next Election: Oct. 2018 (4 year terms)
Note: Formerly the Township of Shedden. Effective Oct. 1, 2004, the name was changed to the Town of Spanish.
Ted Clague, Mayor
Brent St. Denis, Chief Administrative Officer & Clerk-Treasurer

Springwater
Township of Springwater Administrative Ctr.
2231 Nursery Rd.
Minesing, ON L0L 1Y2
Tel: 705-728-4784; *Fax:* 705-728-6957
info@springwater.ca; council@springwater.ca
www.springwater.ca
Municipal Type: Township
Incorporated: Jan. 1, 1994; *Area:* 536.3 sq km
County or District: Simcoe; *Population in 2011:* 18,223
Provincial Electoral District(s): Simcoe-Grey
Federal Electoral District(s): Barrie-Springwater-Oro-Medonte
Next Election: Oct. 2018 (4 year terms)
Bill French, Mayor
Don Allen, Deputy Mayor
Katy Austin, Councillor, Wards: 1
Perry Ritchie, Councillor, 705-728-4784, Fax: 705-728-6957, Wards: 2
Jennifer Coughlin, Councillor, Wards: 3
Sandy McConkey, Councillor, 705-728-4784, Fax: 705-737-4729, Wards: 4
Jack Hanna, Councillor, 705-728-4784, Fax: 705-728-6957, Wards: 5
John Daly, Clerk & Director, Corporate Services, 705-728-4784, Fax: 705-728-6957
Winanne Grant, Chief Administrative Officer, 705-728-4784, Fax: 705-728-6957
Laurie Kennard, CA, Treasurer & Director, Finance, 705-728-4784
Ron Belcourt, Director, Recreation Services, 705-728-4784
Brad Sokach, Director, Public Works, 705-728-4784
Tony Van Dam, Director, Fire & Emergency Services, 705-728-4784, Fax: 705-726-7223
Nick Ippolito, Chief Building Official, 705-728-4784, Fax: 705-728-2759
Barb Fralick, Manager, Human Resources, 705-728-4784, Fax: 705-728-6957
Jennett Mays, Coordinator, Communications, 705-728-4784, Fax: 705-728-6957
Brent Spagnol, Planner, 705-728-4784, Fax: 705-728-6957

Stirling-Rawdon
P.O. Box 40
14 Demorest Rd.
Stirling, ON K0K 3E0
Tel: 613-395-3380; *Fax:* 613-395-0864
info@stirling-rawdon.com
www.stirling-rawdon.com
Municipal Type: Township
Area: 280.63 sq km
County or District: Hastings; *Population in 2011:* 4,978
Provincial Electoral District(s): Prince Edward-Hastings
Federal Electoral District(s): Hastings-Lennox and Addington
Next Election: Oct. 2018 (4 year terms)
Rodney Cooney, Mayor, 613-395-3947
Charles Croll, Clerk-Administrator

Stone Mills
4504 County Rd. 4
Centreville, ON K0K 1N0
Tel: 613-378-2475; *Fax:* 613-378-0033
caoclerk@stonemills.com
www.stonemills.com
Municipal Type: Township
Incorporated: Jan. 1, 1998; *Area:* 688.28 sq km
County or District: Lennox-Addington; *Population in 2011:* 7,560
Provincial Electoral District(s): Lanark-Frontenac-Lennox & Addington
Federal Electoral District(s): Hastings-Lennox and Addington
Next Election: Oct. 2018 (4 year terms)
Note: Amalgamation of the former Township of Camden East, Township of Sheffield & Village of Newburgh.
Clarence Kennedy, Reeve
Bryan Brooks, Chief Administrative Officer & Municipal Clerk, 613-378-2475

Stormont, Dundas & Glengarry
26 Pitt St.
Cornwall, ON K6J 3P2
Tel: 613-932-1515; *Fax:* 613-936-2913
info@sdgcounties.ca
www.sdgcounties.ca
Other Information: Toll-Free Phone: 1-800-267-7158
Municipal Type: United County
Area: 3,306.86 sq km
Population in 2011: 111,164
Next Election: Oct. 2018 (4 year terms)
Eric Duncan, Warden, Wards: North Dundas
Gerry Boyce, Deputy Mayor, Wards: North Dundas
Chris McDonell, Mayor, Wards: North Glengarry
Jamie MacDonald, Councillor, Wards: North Glengarry
Dennis Fife, Councillor, Wards: North Stormont
Bill McGimpsey, Councillor, Wards: North Stormont
Evonne Delegarde, Councillor, Wards: South Dundas
Jim Locke, Councillor, Wards: South Dundas
Ian McLeod, Councillor, Wards: South Glengarry
Frank Prevost, Councillor, Wards: South Glengarry
Jim Bancroft, Councillor, Wards: South Stormont
Tammy Hart, Councillor, Wards: South Stormont
Helen Thomson, Clerk
Tim J. Simpson, Chief Administrative Officer
Vanessa Bennett, Treasurer
Benjamin deHaan, P.Eng., Director, Transportation & Planning
Michael Otis, County Planner

Strathroy-Caradoc
52 Frank St.
Strathroy, ON N7G 2R4
Tel: 519-245-1070; *Fax:* 519-245-6353
general@strathroy-caradoc.ca
www.strathroy-caradoc.ca
Municipal Type: Township
Incorporated: 2001; *Area:* 274.19 sq km
County or District: Middlesex; *Population in 2011:* 20,978
Provincial Electoral District(s): Lambton-Kent-Middlesex
Federal Electoral District(s): Lambton-Kent-Middlesex
Next Election: Oct. 2018 (4 year terms)
Note: Amalgamation of the Town of Strathroy & the Township of Caradoc.
Joanne Vanderheyden, Mayor, 519-245-1105, Fax: 519-245-6353
Brad Richards, Deputy Mayor, 519-245-1105, Fax: 519-245-6353
Marie Baker, Councillor, 519-245-8696, Fax: 519-245-0076, Wards: 1 - Strathroy
John G. Brennan, Councillor, 519-245-2680, Wards: 1 - Strathroy
Dave Cameron, Councillor, Wards: 1 - Strathroy
Steve Pelkman, Councillor, 519-245-5277, Wards: 1 - Strathroy
Larry Cowan, Councillor, Wards: 2 - Caradoc
Steve Dausett, Councillor, 519-246-1900, Wards: 2 - Caradoc
Neil Flegel, Councillor, Wards: 2 - Caradoc
Angela Toth, Clerk & Director, Corporate Services, 519-245-1105
Jane McPherson, Treasurer & Director, Financial Services, 519-245-1105, Fax: 519-245-2177
Tom Gibson, Director, Fire Services & Fire Chief, 519-245-1990
Tim Hanna, Director, Recreation & Leisure Services, 519-245-1105, Fax: 519-245-9534
Mark Harris, Director, Environmental Services, 519-245-2010
Matthew Stephenson, Director, Building & Waste Services, 519-245-1105
Brad Dausett, Manager, Roads, 519-245-1105, Fax: 519-245-6353
Andrew Meyer, Manager, Community Development, 519-245-0492, Fax: 519-245-1073
Leslie Pommer, Coordinator, Customer Services & Concession, 519-245-7557
Paul Hicks, Planner, 519-245-1105, Fax: 519-245-6353

Strong
P.O. Box 1120
28 Municipal Lane
Sundridge, ON P0A 1Z0
Tel: 705-384-5819; *Fax:* 705-384-5892
www.strongtownship.com
Municipal Type: Township
Area: 158.73 sq km
County or District: Parry Sound District; *Population in 2011:* 1,341
Provincial Electoral District(s): Parry Sound-Muskoka
Federal Electoral District(s): Parry Sound-Muskoka
Next Election: Oct. 2018 (4 year terms)
Christine Ellis, Mayor, 705-384-5243
Linda Maurer, Clerk & Treausurer, 705-384-5819

Sudbury District
c/o Manitoulin-Sudbury District Services Bd
210 Mead Blvd.
Espanola, ON P5E 1R9

www.msdsb.net
Municipal Type: District
Area: 38,504.53 sq km
Population in 2011: 21,196
Provincial Electoral District(s): Algoma-Manitoulin; Nickel Belt
Federal Electoral District(s): Nickel Belt; Algoma-Manitoulin-Kapuskasing
Les Gamble, Board Chair, Manitoulin-Sudbury District Services Board, 705-865-2646
Fern Dominelli, Chief Administrative Officer, Manitoulin-Sudbury District Svs Bd, 705-862-7850, Fax: 705-862-7866

Sundridge
P.O. Box 129
110 Main St.
Sundridge, ON P0A 1Z0
Tel: 705-384-5316; *Fax:* 705-384-7874
villageoffice@sundridge.ca
www.sundridge.ca
Municipal Type: Village
Incorporated: 1889; *Area:* 2.23 sq km
County or District: Parry Sound District; *Population in 2011:* 985
Provincial Electoral District(s): Parry Sound-Muskoka
Federal Electoral District(s): Parry Sound-Muskoka
Next Election: Oct. 2018 (4 year terms)
Lyle Hall, Mayor
Lillian S. Fowler, Chief Administrative Officer & Clerk, 705-384-5316

Tarbutt & Tarbutt Additional
27 Barr Rd. South
Desbarats, ON P0R 1E0
Tel: 705-782-6776; *Fax:* 705-782-4274
tarbutttownship@bellnet.ca
www.tarbutttownship.com
Municipal Type: Township
Incorporated: 1889; *Area:* 52.82 sq km
County or District: Algoma District; *Population in 2011:* 396
Provincial Electoral District(s): Algoma-Manitoulin
Federal Electoral District(s): Algoma-Manitoulin-Kapuskasing
Next Election: Oct. 2018 (4 year terms)
Chris Burton, Mayor, 705-782-4386
Glenn Martin, Clerk-Treasurer

Tay
P.O. Box 100
450 Park St.
Victoria Harbour, ON L0K 2A0
Tel: 705-534-7248; *Fax:* 705-534-4493
taytownship@tay.ca
www.tay.ca
Municipal Type: Township
Area: 138.93 sq km
County or District: Simcoe; *Population in 2011:* 9,736
Provincial Electoral District(s): Simcoe North
Federal Electoral District(s): Simcoe North
Next Election: Oct. 2018 (4 year terms)
Scott Warnock, Mayor
Alison Thomas, Clerk, 795-534-7248

Tay Valley
217 Harper Rd., RR#4
Perth, ON K7H 3C6
Tel: 613-267-5353; *Fax:* 613-264-8516
treasurer@tayvalleytwp.ca
www.tayvalleytwp.ca
Other Information: Toll-Free Phone: 1-800-810-0161
Municipal Type: Township
Area: 527.46 sq km
County or District: Lanark; *Population in 2011:* 5,571
Provincial Electoral District(s): Lanark-Frontenac-Lennox & Addington
Federal Electoral District(s): Lanark-Frontenac-Kingston
Next Election: Oct. 2018 (4 year terms)
Note: Formerly the Township of Bathurst Burgess Sherbrooke.
Keith Kerr, Reeve, 613-267-4025
Amanda Mabo, Clerk & Returning Officer, 613-267-5353

Tehkummah
Municipal Building
456 Hwy. 542A
Tehkummah, ON P0P 2C0
Tel: 705-859-3293; *Fax:* 705-859-2605
www.manitoulin-island.com/tehkummah/
Municipal Type: Township
Incorporated: 1881; *Area:* 132.48 sq km
County or District: Manitoulin District; *Population in 2011:* 406
Provincial Electoral District(s): Algoma-Manitoulin
Federal Electoral District(s): Algoma-Manitoulin-Kapuskasing
Next Election: Oct. 2018 (4 year terms)
Gary Brown, Reeve

Temagami
P.O. Box 220
Temagami, ON P0H 2H0
Tel: 705-569-3421; *Fax:* 705-569-2834
visit@temagami.ca; finance@temagami.ca
www.temagami.ca
Other Information: E-mail, Public Works: publicworks@temagami.ca
Municipal Type: Municipality
Incorporated: Jan. 1, 1998; *Area:* 1,906.42 sq km
County or District: Nipissing District; *Population in 2011:* 820
Provincial Electoral District(s): Timiskaming-Cochrane

Federal Electoral District(s): Nipissing-Timiskaming
Next Election: Oct. 2018 (4 year terms)
Lorie Hunter, Mayor
Patrick Cormier, Chief Administrative Officer, 705-569-3421

Terrace Bay
P.O. Box 40
1 Selkirk Ave.
Terrace Bay, ON P0T 2W0
Tel: 807-825-3315; *Fax:* 807-825-9576
info@terracebay.ca
www.terracebay.ca
Municipal Type: Township
Incorporated: Sept. 1, 1947; *Area:* 151.04 sq km
County or District: Thunder Bay District; *Population in 2011:* 1,471
Provincial Electoral District(s): Thunder Bay-Superior North
Federal Electoral District(s): Thunder Bay-Superior North
Next Election: Oct. 2018 (4 year terms)
Note: Incorporated as a municipality on July 1, 1959.
George (Jody) Davis, Mayor, 807-825-3501
Carmelo Notarbartolo, Chief Administrative Officer, 807-825-3315

Thames Centre
4305 Hamilton Rd.
Dorchester, ON N0L 1G3
Tel: 519-268-7334; *Fax:* 519-268-3928
inquiries@thamescentre.on.ca
www.thamescentre.on.ca
Other Information: Toll-Free Phone: 1-866-425-7306
Municipal Type: Municipality
Incorporated: Jan. 1, 2001; *Area:* 433.8 sq km
County or District: Middlesex; *Population in 2011:* 13,000
Provincial Electoral District(s): Elgin-Middlesex-London
Federal Electoral District(s): Elgin-Middlesex-London
Next Election: Oct. 2018 (4 year terms)
Note: Amalgamation of the former Township of West Nissouri & the Township of North Dorchester.
Jim Maudsley, Mayor
Marcel Meyer, Deputy Mayor
Kelly Elliot, Councillor, Wards: 1
Jennifer Coughlin, Councillor, Wards: 2
Alison Warwick, Councillor, Wards: 3
Margaret Lewis, Clerk & Manager, Cemetery, 519-268-7334, Fax: 519-268-3928
Stewart Findlater, Chief Administrative Officer, 519-268-7334, Fax: 519-268-3928
Mary Ellen Weatherhead, Treasurer & Director, Financial Services, 519-268-7334, Fax: 519-268-3928
Paddy Thomson, Director, Environmental Services, 519-268-7334
Stewart Findlater, Director, Community Services & Development, 519-268-7334, Fax: 519-268-3928
Randy Kalan, Fire Chief
Dave Armstrong, Manager, Information Systems, 519-268-7334, Fax: 519-268-3928
Jarrod Craven, Superintendent, Environmental Services, 519-268-7490

Thessalon
P.O. Box 220
169 Main St.
Thessalon, ON P0R 1L0
Tel: 705-842-2217; *Fax:* 705-842-2572
townthess@bellnet.ca
www.thessalon.ca
Municipal Type: Town
Area: 4.37 sq km
County or District: Algoma District; *Population in 2011:* 1,279
Provincial Electoral District(s): Algoma-Manitoulin
Federal Electoral District(s): Algoma-Manitoulin-Kapuskasing
Next Election: Oct. 2018 (4 year terms)
James Orlando, Mayor
Robert P. MacLean, Clerk-Treasurer

Thornloe
P.O. Box 30
Main St.
Thornloe, ON P0J 1S0
Tel: 705-563-8303; *Fax:* 705-563-8303
thorn@ntl.sympatico.ca
Municipal Type: Village
Area: 6.49 sq km
County or District: Timiskaming District; *Population in 2011:* 123
Provincial Electoral District(s): Timiskaming-Cochrane
Federal Electoral District(s): Timmins-James Bay
Next Election: Oct. 2018 (4 year terms)
Ron Vottero, Reeve
Janet Gore, Clerk-Treasurer

Thunder Bay
District Social Services Administration Bd.
231 May St. South
Thunder Bay, ON P7E 1B5
Tel: 807-766-2111; *Fax:* 807-345-7921
www.tbdssab.ca
Municipal Type: District
Area: 103,706.27 sq km
Population in 2011: 146,057
Iain Angus, Chair, District of Thunder Bay Social Services Administration Bd., 807-474-0926, Fax: 807-474-0881
Melissa Harrison, CAO, District of Thunder Bay Social Services Administration Board, 807-766-2103, Fax: 807-345-6146

Timiskaming
District Social Services Administrative Bd.
P.O. Box 310
29 Duncan Ave. North
Kirkland Lake, ON P2N 3H7
Tel: 705-567-9366;
www.dtssab.com
Other Information: Toll-Free Phone: 1-888-544-5555
Municipal Type: District
Area: 13,279.88 sq km
Population in 2011: 32,634
Jim Whipple, Chair, District of Timiskaming Social Services Administration Bd.
Don Studholme, CAO, District of Timiskaming Social Services Administration Board, 705-567-9366, Fax: 705-567-3908

Tiny
130 Balm Beach Rd. West, RR#1
Perkinsfield, ON L0L 2J0
Tel: 705-526-4204; *Fax:* 705-526-2372
www.tiny.ca
Other Information: Toll-Free Phone: 1-866-939-8469
Municipal Type: Township
Area: 343.19 sq km
County or District: Simcoe; *Population in 2011:* 11,232
Provincial Electoral District(s): Simcoe North
Federal Electoral District(s): Simcoe North
Next Election: Oct. 2018 (4 year terms)
George Cornell, Mayor
Steffen Walma, Deputy Mayor
Gibb Wishart, Councillor
Cindy Hastings, Councillor
Richard Hinton, Councillor
Doug Luker, Chief Administrative Officer-Clerk, 705-526-4204
Doug Taylor, Treasurer & Manager, Administrative Services, 705-526-4204
Henk Blom, Manager, Public Works
Shawn Persaud, Manager, Planning & Development
Tony Mintoff, Fire Chief/Manager of Emergency Services
Steven Harvey, Chief Municipal Law Enforcement Officer, 705-526-4136

Trent Hills
P.O. Box 1030
66 Front St. South
Campbellford, ON K0L 1L0
Tel: 705-653-1900; *Fax:* 705-653-5203
info@trenthills.ca
www.trenthills.ca
Other Information: Public Works Emergency, Phone: 705-653-2610
Municipal Type: Municipality
Area: 510.83 sq km
County or District: Northumberland; *Population in 2011:* 12,604
Provincial Electoral District(s): Northumberland-Quinte West
Federal Electoral District(s): Northumberland-Peterborough South
Next Election: Oct. 2018 (4 year terms)
Hector MacMillan, Mayor, 705-653-1900
Rosemary Kelleher-MacLennan, Councillor, 705-653-3456, Fax: 705-653-5300, Wards: 1 - Campbellford / Seymour
Catherine Redden, Councillor, Wards: 1 - Campbellford / Seymour
William J. Thompson, Councillor, 705-653-3540, Fax: 705-653-5360, Wards: 1 - Campbellford / Seymour
Rick English, Councillor, Wards: 2 - Percy
Ken Tully, Councillor, Wards: 2 - Percy
Robert Crate, Councillor, Wards: 3 - Hastings
Marg Montgomery, Clerk, 705-653-1900
Mike Rutter, Chief Administrative Officer, 705-653-1900
Shelley Eliopoulos, Treasurer & Director, Finance, 705-653-1900
Scott White, General Manager, Public Works, 705-653-1900
Jim Peters, Director, Planning & Development, 705-653-1900
Kevin Fillier, Deputy Chief Building Official, 705-653-1900
Neil Allanson, Manager, Roads & Urban Services
Scott White, Manager, Water & Wastewater Operations
Julie Reid, Officer, Bylaw Enforcement, 705-653-1900
Scott Rose, Officer, Community Services, 705-653-1900
Kari Petherick, Coordinator, Health & Safety & Human Resources, 705-653-1900

Tudor & Cashel
P.O. Box 436
371 Weslemkoon Lake Rd., RR#2
Gilmour, ON K0L 1W0
Tel: 613-474-2583; *Fax:* 613-474-0664
clerk@tudorandcashel.com
www.tudorandcashel.com
Municipal Type: Township
Incorporated: 1869; *Area:* 433.49 sq km
County or District: Hastings; *Population in 2011:* 586
Provincial Electoral District(s): Prince Edward-Hastings
Federal Electoral District(s): Hastings-Lennox and Addington
Next Election: Oct. 2018 (4 year terms)
Wanda Donaldson, Reeve, 613-473-4806
Bernice Crocker, Chief Administrative Officer, 613-474-2583

Tweed
P.O. Box 729
255 Metcalf St.
Tweed, ON K0K 3J0
Tel: 613-478-2535; *Fax:* 613-478-6457
info@twp.tweed.on.ca
www.tweed.ca
Municipal Type: Municipality
Incorporated: 1998; *Area:* 896.98 sq km
County or District: Hastings; *Population in 2011:* 6,057
Provincial Electoral District(s): Prince Edward-Hastings
Federal Electoral District(s): Hastings-Lennox and Addington
Next Election: Oct. 2018 (4 year terms)
Jo-Anne Albert, Reeve
Patricia Bergeron, Chief Administrative Officer & Clerk

Tyendinaga
859 Melrose Rd., RR#1
Shannonville, ON K0K 3A0
Tel: 613-396-1944; *Fax:* 613-396-2080
info@tyendinagatownship.com
www.tyendinagatownship.com
Municipal Type: Township
Area: 311.94 sq km
County or District: Hastings; *Population in 2011:* 4,150
Provincial Electoral District(s): Prince Edward-Hastings
Federal Electoral District(s): Hastings-Lennox and Addington
Next Election: Oct. 2018 (4 year terms)
Rick Phillips, Reeve, 613-477-3129
Steve Mercer, Clerk-Treasurer

Val Rita-Harty
P.O. Box 100
2 Eglise Ave.
Val Rita, ON P0L 2G0
Tel: 705-335-6146; *Fax:* 705-337-6292
www.valharty.ca
Municipal Type: Township
Area: 382.64 sq km
County or District: Cochrane District; *Population in 2011:* 817
Provincial Electoral District(s): Timmins-James Bay
Federal Electoral District(s): Algoma-Manitoulin-Kapuskasing
Next Election: Oct. 2018 (4 year terms)
Johanne Baril, Mayor
Christiane Potvin, Clerk-Treasurer

La Vallée
P.O. Box 99
56 Church Rd.
Devlin, ON P0W 1C0
Tel: 807-486-3452; *Fax:* 807-486-3863
lavalley@nwonet.net
www.lavallee.ca
Municipal Type: Township
Area: 237.26 sq km
County or District: Rainy River District; *Population in 2011:* 988
Provincial Electoral District(s): Kenora-Rainy River
Federal Electoral District(s): Thunder Bay-Rainy River
Next Election: Oct. 2018 (4 year terms)
Ken McKinnon, Reeve
Sylvia Smeeth, Municipal Clerk

Wainfleet
P.O. Box 40
31940 Hwy. 3
Wainfleet, ON L0S 1V0
Tel: 905-899-3463; *Fax:* 905-899-2340
sluey@township.wainfleet.on.ca
www.wainfleet.ca
Municipal Type: Township
Area: 217.29 sq km
County or District: Niagara Reg. Mun.; *Population in 2011:* 6,356

Provincial Electoral District(s): Welland
Federal Electoral District(s): Niagara West
Next Election: Oct. 2018 (4 year terms)
April Jeffs, Mayor, 905-899-3463, *Fax:* 905-899-2340
Tanya Lamb, Township Clerk, 905-899-3463

Warwick
6332 Nauvoo Rd.
Watford, ON N0M 2S0
Tel: 519-849-3926; *Fax:* 519-849-6136
info@warwicktownship.ca
www.warwicktownship.ca
Municipal Type: Township
Incorporated: 1998; *Area:* 290.2 sq km
County or District: Lambton; *Population in 2011:* 3,717
Provincial Electoral District(s): Lambton-Kent-Middlesex
Federal Electoral District(s): Lambton-Kent-Middlesex
Next Election: Oct. 2018 (4 year terms)
Todd Case, Mayor
Don R. Bruder, Administrator-Treasurer

Wawa
P.O. Box 500
40 Broadway Ave.
Wawa, ON P0S 1K0
Tel: 705-856-2244; *Fax:* 705-856-2120
info@wawa.cc
www.wawa.cc
Other Information: Toll-Free Phone: 1-800-367-9292
Municipal Type: Township
Area: 417.78 sq km
County or District: Algoma District; *Population in 2011:* 2,875
Provincial Electoral District(s): Algoma-Manitoulin
Federal Electoral District(s): Algoma-Manitoulin-Kapuskasing
Next Election: Oct. 2018 (4 year terms)
Ron Rody, Mayor
Chris Wray, Chief Administrative Officer & Clerk-Treasurer, 705-856-2244

Wellesley
Administration Office
4639 Lobsinger Line, RR#1
St Clements, ON N0B 2M0
Tel: 519-699-4611; *Fax:* 519-699-4540
www.township.wellesley.on.ca
Municipal Type: Township
Area: 277.84 sq km
County or District: Waterloo Regional Municipality; *Population in 2011:* 10,713
Provincial Electoral District(s): Kitchener-Conestoga
Federal Electoral District(s): Kitchener-Conestoga
Next Election: Oct. 2018 (4 year terms)
Joe Novak, Mayor
Susan Duke, Clerk & Executive Director, Corporate Services

Wellington North
P.O. Box 125
7490 Sideroad 7 West
Kenilworth, ON N0G 2E0
Tel: 519-848-3620;
township@wellington-north.com
www.wellington-north.com
Other Information: Toll-Free Phone: 1-866-848-3620
Municipal Type: Township
Incorporated: Jan. 1, 1999; *Area:* 524.38 sq km
County or District: Wellington; *Population in 2011:* 11,477
Provincial Electoral District(s): Perth-Wellington
Federal Electoral District(s): Perth-Wellington
Next Election: Oct. 2018 (4 year terms)
Note: Amalgamation of the Township of Arthur, Arthur Village, the Township of West Luther & the Town of Mount Forest.
Andy Lennox, Mayor, 519-323-9146
Dan Yake, Councillor, 519-323-2334, Wards: 1
Sherry Burke, Councillor, 519-323-2604, Wards: 2
Mark Goetz, Councillor, 519-848-3380, Wards: 3
Steve McCabe, Councillor, Wards: 4
Lorraine (Lori) Heinbuch, Chief Administrative Officer & Clerk, 519-848-3620
John W. Jeffery, Treasurer, 519-848-3620
Barry Trood, Director, Public Works, 519-848-3620
Darren Jones, Chief Building Official, 519-848-3620
Dale Clark, Superintendent, Roads, 519-848-3620
Mark Van Patter, Senior Planner, 519-837-2600

West Elgin
P.O. Box 490
22413 Hoskins Line
Rodney, ON N0L 2C0
Tel: 519-785-0560; *Fax:* 519-785-0644
westelgin@westelgin.net
www.westelgin.net
Municipal Type: Municipality
Area: 322.52 sq km
County or District: Elgin; *Population in 2011:* 5,157
Provincial Electoral District(s): Elgin-Middlesex-London
Federal Electoral District(s): Elgin-Middlesex-London
Next Election: Oct. 2018 (4 year terms)
Bernie Wiehle, Mayor, 519-785-0405, *Fax:* 519-785-0644
Scott Gawley, CGA, Administrator/Treasurer, 519-785-0560

West Grey
402813 Grey Rd., RR#2
Durham, ON N0G 1R0
Tel: 519-369-2200; *Fax:* 519-369-5962
info@westgrey.com
www.westgrey.com
Other Information: Toll-Free Phone: 1-800-538-9647
Municipal Type: Municipality
Incorporated: Jan 1, 2001; *Area:* 875.37 sq km
County or District: Grey; *Population in 2011:* 12,286
Provincial Electoral District(s): Bruce-Grey-Owen Sound
Federal Electoral District(s): Bruce-Grey-Owen Sound
Next Election: Oct. 2018 (4 year terms)
Note: Amalgamation of Bentinck, Glenelg, Normanby, Neustadt & Durham.
Kevin Eccles, Mayor, 519-799-5476
John A. Bell, Deputy Mayor, 519-369-6894
Bev Cutting, Councillor, 519-986-4635
Doug Hutchinson, Councillor
Carol Lawrence, Councillor, 519-369-3816
Don Marshall, Councillor, 519-369-7221
Robert Thompson, Councillor
Mark Turner, Clerk, 519-369-2200
Larry C. Adams, Chief Administrative Officer, 519-369-2200
Kerri Mighton, Treasurer & Director, Finance, 519-369-2200
Brent Glasier, Director, Infrastructure & Public Works, 519-369-2200
Phil Schwartz, Fire Chief, 519-269-2505

West Lincoln
P.O. Box 400
318 Canborough St.
Smithville, ON L0R 2A0
Tel: 905-957-3346; *Fax:* 905-957-3219
reception@westlincoln.ca
www.westlincoln.ca
Other Information: Toll-Free Phone: 1-800-350-3876; TTY: 905-957-0680
Municipal Type: Township
Incorporated: Jan. 1, 1970; *Area:* 387.72 sq km
County or District: Niagara Reg. Mun.; *Population in 2011:* 13,837
Provincial Electoral District(s): Niagara West-Glanbrook
Federal Electoral District(s): Niagara West
Next Election: Oct. 2018 (4 year terms)
Note: Amalgamation of the former Townships of South Grimsby, Caistor, & Gainsborough.
Douglas Joyner, Mayor, 905-957-4926
Mike Rehner, Alderman, Wards: 1
Jason Trombetta, Alderman, Wards: 1
Dave Bylsma, Alderman, Wards: 2
Joan Chechalk, Alderman, Wards: 2
Terry Bell, Alderman, Wards: 3
Alex Micallef, Alderman, Wards: 3
Carolyn Langley, Clerk, 905-957-3346
Derrick Thomson, Chief Administrative Officer, 905-957-3346
Stephanie Nagel, Treasurer & Director, Finance, 905-957-3346
Brian Treble, Director, Planning & Building, 905-957-3346
Dennis Fisher, Fire Chief, 905-957-3346

West Nipissing
Municipal Office
#101, 225 Holditch St.
Sturgeon Falls, ON P2B 1T1
Tel: 705-753-2250; *Fax:* 705-753-3950
www.westnipissingouest.ca
Municipal Type: Municipality
Area: 1,989.57 sq km
County or District: Nipissing District; *Population in 2011:* 14,149
Provincial Electoral District(s): Timiskaming-Cochrane
Federal Electoral District(s): Nickel Belt
Next Election: Oct. 2018 (4 year terms)
Joanne Savage, Mayor, 705-753-2250, *Fax:* 705-753-3950
Denise Brisson, Councillor, 705-753-3136, Wards: 1
Léo Malette, Councillor, 705-753-3568, Wards: 2
Yvon Duhaime, Councillor, Wards: 3
Jamie Restoule, Councillor, 705-753-9396, Wards: 4
Guilles Tessier, Councillor, 705-753-3559, Wards: 5
Ronald Larabie, Councillor, Wards: 6
Normand Roberge, Councillor, 705-594-9486, Wards: 7
Guy Fortier, Councillor, 705-594-2301, Wards: 8
Mélanie Ducharme, Municipal Clerk & Planner, 705-753-2250
Jean-Pierre (Jay) Barbeau, Chief Administrative Officer, 705-753-2250
Julie Labrosse Landry, Manager, Museum & Marina, 705-753-4716
Marc Gagnon, Director, Operations, 705-753-2250
Stephan Poulin, Director, Economic Development & Community Services, 705-753-2250
Alain Bazinet, Chief Building Official & Officer, Property Maintenance, 705-753-2250
Richard Savage, Fire Chief, 705-753-1171
Denis Lafreniere, Manager, Solid Waste, 705-753-6913
Raymond Lortie, Manager, Power Plant, 705-753-6364
Peter Ming, Manager, Water & Wastewater Operations, 705-753-6454
Brigitte Carrière, Assistant Manager, Ancillary Services, 705-753-2250

West Perth, Municipality of
169 St. David St.
Mitchell, ON N0K 1N0
Tel: 519-348-8429;
info@westperth.com
www.westperth.com
Municipal Type: Township
Area: 579.4 sq km
County or District: Perth; *Population in 2011:* 8,919
Provincial Electoral District(s): Perth-Wellington
Federal Electoral District(s): Perth-Wellington
Next Election: Oct. 2018 (4 year terms)
Note: Amalgamation of Fullarton Township, Hibbert Township, Logan Township & the Town of Mitchell.
Walter McKenzie, Mayor
Susan Cronin, Municipal Clerk, 519-348-8429

Westport
P.O. Box 68
30 Bedford St.
Westport, ON K0G 1X0
Tel: 613-273-2191; *Fax:* 613-273-3460
village2@rideau.net
www.village.westport.on.ca
Municipal Type: Village
Incorporated: 1904; *Area:* 1.71 sq km
County or District: Leeds & Grenville; *Population in 2011:* 628
Provincial Electoral District(s): Leeds-Grenville
Federal Electoral District(s): Leeds-Grenville-Thousand Islands and Rideau Lakes
Next Election: Oct. 2018 (4 year terms)
Robin Patricia Jones, Mayor
Scott Bryce, Clerk-Treasurer

White River
P.O. Box 307
102 Durham St.
White River, ON P0M 3G0
Tel: 807-822-2450; *Fax:* 807-822-2719
info@whiteriver.ca
www.whiteriver.ca
Municipal Type: Township
Area: 96.94 sq km
County or District: Algoma District; *Population in 2011:* 607
Provincial Electoral District(s): Algoma-Manitoulin
Federal Electoral District(s): Algoma-Manitoulin-Kapuskasing
Next Election: Oct. 2018 (4 year terms)
Angelo Bazzoni, Mayor
Marilyn Parent Lethbridge, Clerk Administrator, 807-822-2450, Fax: 807-822-2179

Whitestone
General Delivery
21 Church St.
Dunchurch, ON P0A 1G0
Tel: 705-389-2466; *Fax:* 705-389-1855
info@whitestone.ca
www.whitestone.ca
Municipal Type: Township
Incorporated: 2000; *Area:* 946.56 sq km
County or District: Parry Sound District; *Population in 2011:* 918
Provincial Electoral District(s): Parry Sound-Muskoka
Federal Electoral District(s): Parry Sound-Muskoka
Next Election: Oct. 2018 (4 year terms)
Chris Armstrong, Mayor, 705-389-3721
Liliane Nolan, Chief Administrative Officer & Clerk, 705-389-2466

Whitewater Region
P.O. Box 40
44 Main St.
Cobden, ON K0J 1K0
Tel: 613-646-2282; *Fax:* 613-646-2283
info@whitewaterregion.ca
www.whitewaterregion.ca
Other Information: Toll-Free Phone: 1-877-646-2282
Municipal Type: Township
Incorporated: Jan. 1, 2001; *Area:* 537.96 sq km
County or District: Renfrew; *Population in 2011:* 6,921
Provincial Electoral District(s): Renfrew-Nipissing-Pembroke
Federal Electoral District(s): Renfrew-Nipissing-Pembroke
Next Election: Oct. 2018 (4 year terms)
Note: Amalgamation of Beachburg Village, Cobden Village, Westmeath Township & Ross Township.
Hal Johnson, Mayor
Terry Millar, Reeve
Dean Sauriol, Chief Administrative Officer & Clerk

Wilmot
60 Snyder's Rd. West
Baden, ON N3A 1A1
Tel: 519-634-8444; *Fax:* 519-634-5522
info@wilmot.ca
www.wilmot.ca
Other Information: Toll-Free Phone: 1-800-469-5576
Municipal Type: Township
Area: 263.73 sq km
County or District: Waterloo Regional Municipality; *Population in 2011:* 19,223
Provincial Electoral District(s): Kitchener-Conestoga
Federal Electoral District(s): Kitchener-Conestoga
Next Election: Oct. 2018 (4 year terms)
Les Armstrong, Mayor, Fax: 519-662-2764
Al Junker, Councillor, 519-696-3922, Wards: 1
Peter Roe, Councillor, 519-886-6395, Fax: 519-886-6395, Wards: 2
Barry Fisher, Councillor, 519-634-8916, Wards: 3
Jeff Gerber, Councillor, 519-662-6658, Wards: 4
Mark Murray, Councillor, 519-662-2625, Fax: 519-662-2601, Wards: 4
Barbara McLeod, Director, Clerk's Services, 519-634-8444, Fax: 519-634-5522
Grant Whittington, Chief Administrative Officer, 519-634-8444, Fax: 519-634-5522
Rosita Tse, Treasurer & Director, Finance, 519-634-8444, Fax: 519-634-5522
Gary Charbonneau, Director, Public Works, 519-634-8444, Fax: 519-634-5044
Scott Nancekivell, Director, Facilities & Recreation, 519-634-8444, Fax: 519-634-5044
Harold O'Krafka, Director, Development Services, 519-634-8444, Fax: 519-634-5044
John Ritz, Fire Chief, 519-634-8444, Fax: 519-634-5660
Doug Robertson, Chief Building Official, 519-634-8444, Fax: 519-634-5044
Derek Wallace, Senior Officer, Municipal Law Enforcement, 519-634-8444, Fax: 519-634-5522
Andrew Martin, Planner & Officer, Economic Development, 519-634-8444, Fax: 519-634-5044

Wollaston
P.O. Box 99
90 Wollaston Lake Rd.
Coe Hill, ON K0L 1P0
Tel: 613-337-5731; *Fax:* 613-337-5789
wollaston@bellnet.ca
www.township.wollaston.on.ca
Municipal Type: Township
Incorporated: 1880; *Area:* 215.22 sq km
County or District: Hastings; *Population in 2011:* 708
Provincial Electoral District(s): Prince Edward-Hastings
Federal Electoral District(s): Hastings-Lennox and Addington
Next Election: Oct. 2018 (4 year terms)
Graham Blair, Reeve
Christine FitzSimons, Chief Administrative Officer & Clerk

Woolwich
P.O. Box 158
24 Church St. West
Elmira, ON N3B 2Z6
Tel: 519-669-1647; *Fax:* 519-669-1820
woolwich.mail@woolwich.ca
www.woolwich.ca
Other Information: Toll-Free Phone: 1-877-969-0094
Municipal Type: Township
Incorporated: Jan. 1, 1973; *Area:* 326 sq km
County or District: Waterloo Regional Municipality; *Population in 2011:* 23,145
Provincial Electoral District(s): Kitchener-Conestoga
Federal Electoral District(s): Kitchener-Conestoga
Next Election: Oct. 2018 (4 year terms)
Sandy Shantz, Mayor, 519-669-0591
Scott Hahn, Councillor, Wards: 1
Patrick Merlihan, Councillor, Wards: 1
Mark Bauman, Councillor, 519-664-3318, Wards: 2
Murray Martin, Councillor, Wards: 3
Larry Shantz, Councillor, Wards: 3
Christine Broughton, Clerk & Director, Council & Information Services, 519-669-1647
David Brenneman, Chief Administrative Officer, 519-669-1647
Richard Petherick, Treasurer & Director, Finance, 519-669-1647
Larry Devitt, Director, Recreation & Facilities Services, 519-669-1647
Dan Kennaley, Director, Engineering & Planning Services, 519-669-1647
Rick Pedersen, Township Fire Chief, 519-664-2887
Peter vanderBeek, Chief Building Official, 519-669-1647
Barry Baldasaro, Superintendent, Public Works, 519-669-1647
Laurel Davies-Snyder, Officer, Economic Development & Tourism, 519-669-1647

Zorra
Municipal Office
P.O. Box 306
274620 - 27th Line, RR#3
Ingersoll, ON N5C 3K5
Tel: 519-485-2490; *Fax:* 519-485-2520
admin@zorra.on.ca
www.zorra.on.ca
Other Information: Toll-Free Phone: 1-888-699-3868
Municipal Type: Township
Area: 528.78 sq km
County or District: Oxford; *Population in 2011:* 8,058
Provincial Electoral District(s): Oxford
Federal Electoral District(s): Oxford
Next Election: Oct. 2018 (4 year terms)
Margaret Lupton, Mayor, 519-475-4443, Fax: 519-485-2520
Karen Graham, Clerk, 519-485-2490, Fax: 519-485-2520

PRINCE EDWARD ISLAND

Enabling legislation in P.E.I. includes the Charlottetown Area Municipalities Act, the City of Summerside Act, and the Municipalities Act. The first two provide governance for the cities of Charlottetown and Summerside, while the third provides the framework for 71 municipalities, consisting of 10 towns and 61 communities. There are no population considerations for incorporation of a municipality, but a petition must be made by at least 25 residents of an area indicating their desire to incorporate; stating the boundaries of the area, whether it is to be a town or a community, and the services which are to be provided.

Elections are held every four years on the first Monday of November (2014, 2018, etc.).

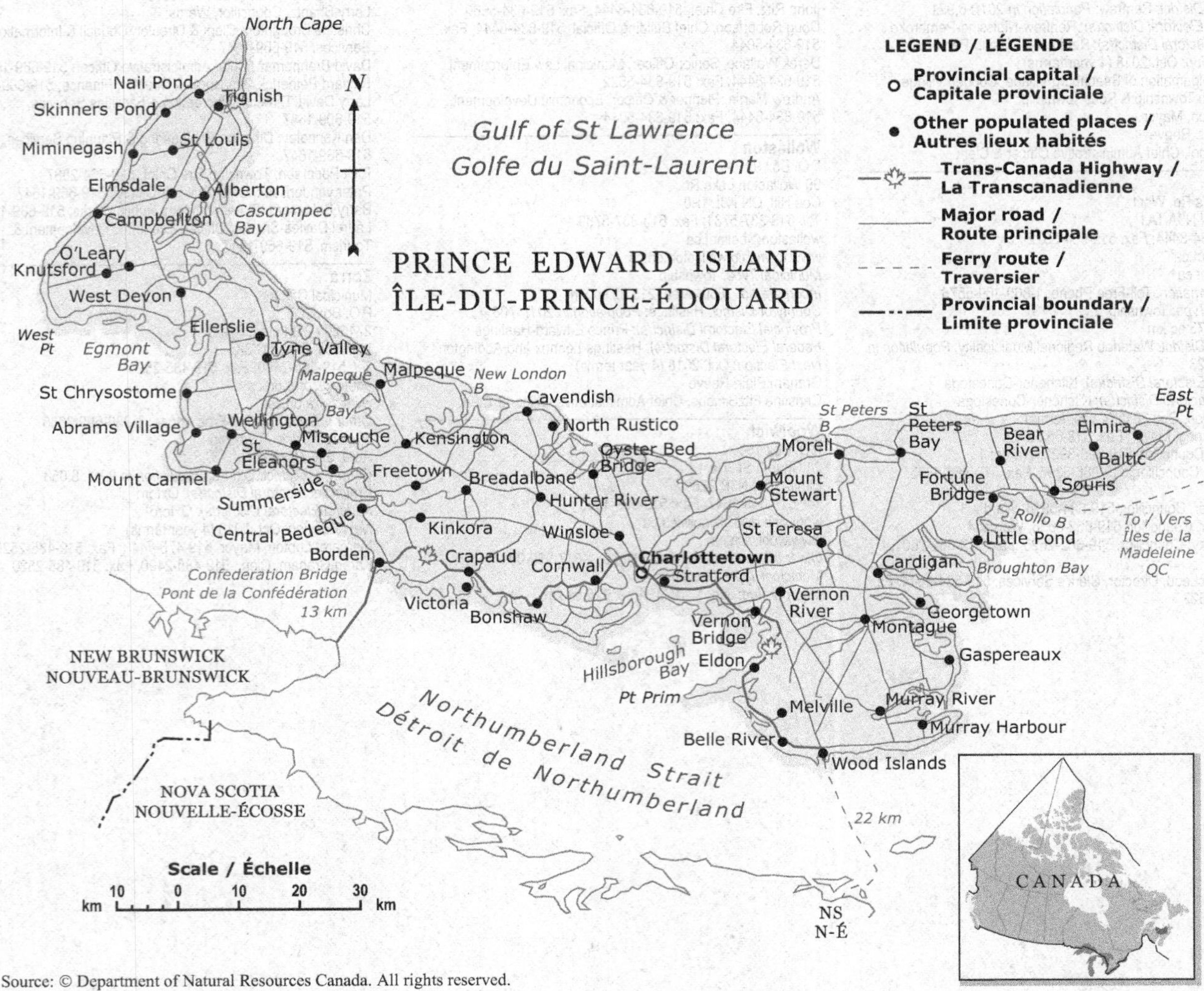

Prince Edward Island

Major Municipalities in Prince Edward Island

Charlottetown
P.O. Box 98
199 Queen St.
Charlottetown, PE C1A 7K2
Tel: 902-566-5548; *Fax:* 902-566-4701
city@city.charlottetown.pe.ca
www.city.charlottetown.pe.ca
Municipal Type: City
Incorporated: 1855; *Area:* 44.33 sq km
County or District: Hillsborough; *Population in 2011:* 34,562
Provincial Electoral District(s): Charlottetown-Sherwood; Charlottetown-Parkdale; Charlottetown-Victoria Park; Charlottetown-Brighton; Charlottetown-Lewis Point
Federal Electoral District(s): Charlottetown
Next Election: Nov. 5, 2018 (4 year terms)
Clifford J. Lee, Mayor, 902-566-5548, Fax: 902-566-4701
Edward Rice, Councillor, 902-626-7732, Wards: 1
Terry MacLeod, Councillor, 902-566-5548, Fax: 902-455-4701, Wards: 2. Belvedere
Mike Duffy, Councillor, 902-566-5548, Fax: 902-566-4701, Wards: 3. Brighton
Mitchell G. Tweel, B.A., Councillor, 902-566-5548, Fax: 902-566-4701, Wards: 4. St. Avard's
Kevin Ramsay, Councillor, 902-566-5548, Fax: 902-566-4701, Wards: 5. Spring Park
Bob Doiron, Councillor, 902-566-5548, Fax: 902-566-4701, Wards: 6. Mount Edward
Greg Rivard, Councillor, 902-566-5548, Fax: 902-566-4701, Wards: 7. Beach Grove
Jason E. Coady, Councillor, 902-566-5548, Fax: 902-566-4701, Wards: 8. Highfield
Melissa Hilton, B.A., Councillor, 902-566-5548, Fax: 902-566-4701, Wards: 9. Stonepark
Terry Bernard, Councillor, 902-566-5548, Fax: 902-566-4701, Wards: 10. Falconwood
Peter Kelly, Chief Administrative Officer, 902-566-5548, Fax: 902-566-4701
Donna Waddell, Director, Corporate Services
Bill Clair, Works Superintendent, Water & Sewer Utility, 902-629-4015
Ron Atkinson, Economic Development Officer, Economic Development, Tourism & Events
Mandy Feuerstack, Manager, Human Resources
Mel Cheverie, Chief Building Inspector, Planning & Development
Vada Fernandez, Purchasing Officer, Finance
Lance Jones, Streets Maintenance Supervisor, Public Works
Nancy McMinn, Parks Superintendent, Parks & Recreation
Scott Ryan, M.B.A., CMA, FCMA, Manager, Finance
Randy MacDonald, Fire Chief, Fire Services
Paul Johnston, Manager, Public Works, 902-894-5208
Frank Quin, Manager, Parks & Recreation
Paul Smith, Chief of Police

Summerside
275 Fitzroy St.
Summerside, PE C1N 1H9
Tel: 902-432-1230; *Fax:* 902-436-9296
contactus@city.summerside.pe.ca
www.city.summerside.pe.ca
Municipal Type: City
Incorporated: 1995; *Area:* 28.36 sq km
County or District: Egmont; *Population in 2011:* 14,751
Provincial Electoral District(s): Wilmot-Summerside; St. Eleanors-Summerside
Federal Electoral District(s): Egmont
Next Election: Nov. 5, 2018 (4 year terms)
Bil Martin, Mayor, 902-432-1244
Bruce MacDougall, Deputy Mayor & Councillor, 902-432-1246, Fax: 902-436-9296, Wards: 1. St. Eleanors-Bayview
Frank Costa, Councillor, 902-432-1246, Fax: 902-436-9296, Wards: 2. St. Eleanors-Slemon Park
Gordie Whitlock, Councillor, 902-432-4268, Wards: 3. Summerside-North
Brent Gallant, Councillor, 902-436-3684, Fax: 902-436-9296, Wards: 4. Clifton/Market
Greg Campbell, Councillor, 902-786-7902, Fax: 902-436-9296, Wards: 5. Hillcrest-Platte River
Norma McColeman, Councillor, 902-786-8476, Fax: 902-436-9296, Wards: 6. Centre East-Downtown
Brian McFeely, Councillor, 902-439-3326, Fax: 902-436-9296, Wards: 7. Greenhouse-Three Oaks
Tyler DesRoches, Councillor, 902-432-2488, Fax: 902-436-9296, Wards: 8. Wilmot
Bob Ashley, Chief Administrative Officer, 902-432-1248, Fax: 902-436-9296
Rob Philpott, Director, Financial Services, 902-432-1250
JP Desrosiers, Director, Community Services
Jim Peters, Director, Fire Services, 902-432-1224
J. David Poirier, Director, Police Services, 902-432-1201
Michael Thususka, Director, Economic Development, 902-432-1255

Other Municipalities in Prince Edward Island

Abrams Village
P.O. Box 3805
Wellington, PE C0B 2E0
Tel: 902-854-2255; *Fax:* 902-854-2266
abvillage@bellaliant.com
Municipal Type: Community
Incorporated: 1974; *Area:* 1.37 sq km
Population in 2011: 267
Provincial Electoral District(s): Evangeline-Miscouche
Federal Electoral District(s): Egmont
Next Election: Nov. 5, 2018
Roger Gallant, Chairperson
Lorraine Gallant, Chief Administrative Officer, 902-854-2255, Fax: 902-854-2266

Afton
P.O. Box 836
1552 Route 19
New Dominion, PE C0A 1H6
Tel: 902-675-2567
afton.cic@gmail.com
Municipal Type: Community
Incorporated: 1974
Population in 2011: 1,222
Provincial Electoral District(s): Tracadie-Fort Augustus
Federal Electoral District(s): Malpeque
Next Election: Nov. 5, 2018
Brian Hughes, Chairperson
Beverley McIsaac, Chief Administrative Officer, 902-675-2567

Alberton
P.O. Box 153
3 Emma Dr.
Alberton, PE C0B 1B0
Tel: 902-853-2720; *Fax:* 902-853-2314
info@townofalberton.ca
www.townofalberton.ca
Municipal Type: Town
Incorporated: May 1913; *Area:* 4.50 sq km
County or District: Egmont; *Population in 2011:* 1,135
Provincial Electoral District(s): Alberton-Miminegash
Federal Electoral District(s): Egmont
Next Election: Nov. 5, 2018
Michael Murphy, Mayor
Susan Wallace-Flynn, Chief Administrative Officer, 902-853-2720, Fax: 902-853-2314

Alexandra
P.O. Box 2683
Charlottetown, PE C1A 8C3
Tel: 902-569-4760
sgw@hotmail.com
Municipal Type: Community
Incorporated: 1972
County or District: Cardigan; *Population in 2011:* 224
Provincial Electoral District(s): Belfast-Pownal Bay
Federal Electoral District(s): Cardigan
Next Election: Nov. 5, 2018
John Brehaut, Chairperson
Sheila Whiteway-McNeill, Chief Administrative Officer, 902-569-4760

Annandale-Little Pond-Howe Bay
RR#4
Souris, PE C0A 2B0
Tel: 902-583-2865
Municipal Type: Community
Incorporated: 1975
County or District: Cardigan; *Population in 2011:* 262
Provincial Electoral District(s): Georgetown-Baldwin's Road
Federal Electoral District(s): Cardigan
Next Election: Nov. 5, 2018
Ben MacDonald, Chairperson
Paul MacDonald, Chief Administrative Officer, 902-388-0648

Bedeque & Area
P.O. Box 3937
34 Reid St.
Bedeque, PE C0B 1G0
Tel: 902-902-8872; *Fax:* 902-887-3226
Municipal Type: Community
Incorporated: 1978; *Area:* 0.68 sq km
County or District: Malpeque; *Population in 2011:* 143
Provincial Electoral District(s): Borden-Kinkora
Federal Electoral District(s): Malpeque
Next Election: Nov. 5, 2018
Rom Rayner, Chairperson
Earle Smith, Chief Administrative Officer, 902-887-2422

Belfast
3278 Route 1
South Pinette, PE C0A 1B0
Tel: 902-659-2989; *Fax:* 902-659-2813
belfast.cap@pei.sympatico.ca
www3.pei.sympatico.ca/belfast.cap/public_html
Municipal Type: Community
Incorporated: 1972
County or District: Cardigan; *Population in 2011:* 1,637
Provincial Electoral District(s): Belfast-Pownal Bay
Federal Electoral District(s): Cardigan
Next Election: Nov. 5, 2018
Paul MacDonald, Chairperson
Janice MacDonald, Chief Administrative Officer, 902-659-2813

Bonshaw
599 Riverdale Rd., RR#3
Bonshaw, PE C0A 1C0
Tel: 902-675-3670; *Fax:* 902-368-1239
Municipal Type: Community
Incorporated: 1977
County or District: Malpeque; *Population in 2011:* 218
Provincial Electoral District(s): Crapaud-Hazel Grove
Federal Electoral District(s): Malpeque
Next Election: Nov. 5, 2018
Art Ortenburger, Chairperson
Dianne Dowling, Chief Administrative Officer, 902-675-3670, Fax: 902-368-1239

Borden-Carleton
P.O. Box 89
167 Industrial Dr.
Borden-Carleton, PE C0B 1X0
Tel: 902-437-2225; *Fax:* 902-437-2610
bcadmin@borden-carleton.ca
www.borden-carleton.ca
Municipal Type: Community
Incorporated: July 1, 1995; *Area:* 13.16 sq km
County or District: Malpeque; *Population in 2011:* 750
Provincial Electoral District(s): Borden-Kinkora
Federal Electoral District(s): Malpeque
Next Election: Nov. 5, 2018
Dean Sexton, Chairperson
Kevin Coady, Chief Administrative Officer, 902-437-2225, Fax: 902-437-2610

Brackley
576 Brackley Point Rd.
Brackley, PE C1E 1Z3
Tel: 902-368-8274
mecbrackley@gmail.com
Municipal Type: Community
Incorporated: 1983; *Area:* 8.92 sq km
County or District: Malpeque; *Population in 2011:* 340
Provincial Electoral District(s): Stanhope-East Royalty
Federal Electoral District(s): Malpeque
Next Election: Nov. 5, 2018
Leonard MacCormack, Chairperson
Maureen Cudmore, Chief Administrative Officer, 902-368-8274

Breadalbane
20 Grafton St.
Breadalbane, PE C0A 1E0
Tel: 902-964-2730
Municipal Type: Community
Incorporated: 1991; *Area:* 12.57 sq km
Population in 2011: 173
Provincial Electoral District(s): Crapaud-Hazel Grove
Federal Electoral District(s): Malpeque
Next Election: Nov. 5, 2018
Margo Dooks, Chairperson
Kim MacLeod, Chief Administrative Officer, 902-964-2730

Brudenell
415 Brudenell Point Rd., RR#5
Montague, PE C0A 1R0
Tel: 902-838-4160; *Fax:* 902-838-3517
www.brudenellpei.com
Municipal Type: Community
Incorporated: 1973
County or District: Cardigan; *Population in 2011:* 362
Provincial Electoral District(s): Montague-Kilmuir
Federal Electoral District(s): Cardigan
Next Election: Nov. 5, 2018
Peggy Coffin, Chairperson

Linda Barry, Chief Administrative Officer, 902-838-4160, Fax: 902-838-3517

Cardigan
P.O. Box 40
Cardigan, PE C0A 1G0
Tel: 902-583-2198; *Fax:* 902-583-3198
villageofcardigan@gmail.com
Municipal Type: Community
Incorporated: 1954; *Area:* 5.28 sq km
County or District: Cardigan; *Population in 2011:* 332
Provincial Electoral District(s): Georgetown-Baldwin's Road
Federal Electoral District(s): Cardigan
Next Election: Nov. 5, 2018
Dalene Stewart, Chairperson
Jimmy Mooney, Chief Administrative Officer, 902-583-3200, Fax: 902-583-3210

Central Kings
P.O. Box 10
Bridgetown, RR#5
Cardigan, PE C0A 1G0
Tel: 902-583-2248
Municipal Type: Community
Incorporated: 1975
Population in 2011: 329
Provincial Electoral District(s): Morell-Fortune Bay
Federal Electoral District(s): Cardigan
Next Election: Nov. 5, 2018
Craig Jackson, Chairperson
Micheline Downe, Chief Administrative Officer, 902-593-2248, Fax: 902-687-3733

Clyde River
P.O. Box 644
Cornwall, PE C0A 1H0
Tel: 902-675-4747
clyderiver.cic@pei.sympatico.ca
clyderiverpei.com
Municipal Type: Community
Incorporated: 1974; *Area:* 16.05 sq km
County or District: Malpeque; *Population in 2011:* 576
Provincial Electoral District(s): Crapaud-Hazel Grove
Federal Electoral District(s): Malpeque
Next Election: Nov. 5, 2018
Douglas Gillespie, Chairperson, 902-675-4318
Bruce Brine, Chief Administrative Officer

Cornwall
P.O. Box 430
39 Lowther Dr.
Cornwall, PE C0A 1H0
Tel: 902-566-2354; *Fax:* 902-566-5228
town@cornwallpe.ca
www.cornwallpe.ca
Municipal Type: Town
Incorporated: 1995; *Area:* 28.2 sq km
County or District: Malpeque; *Population in 2011:* 5,162
Provincial Electoral District(s): North River-Rice Point
Federal Electoral District(s): Malpeque
Next Election: Nov. 5, 2018 (4 year terms)
Minerva McCourt, Mayor, 902-566-2354
Kevin McCarville, Chief Administrative Officer, 902-566-2354

Crapaud
P.O. Box 30
Crapaud, PE C0A 1J0
Tel: 902-658-2558
crapaudadmin@pei.aibn.com
Municipal Type: Community
Incorporated: 1950; *Area:* 2.16 sq km
County or District: Malpeque; *Population in 2011:* 345
Provincial Electoral District(s): Crapaud-Hazel Grove
Federal Electoral District(s): Malpeque
Next Election: Nov. 5, 2018
Joanne Harvey, Chairperson
Susan Williams, Chief Administrative Officer, 902-658-2558

Darlington
30 Darbrook Rd., RR#4
North Wiltshire, PE C0A 1Y0
Tel: 902-964-2438
wandb@pei.sympatico.ca
Municipal Type: Community
Incorporated: 1983
County or District: Malpeque; *Population in 2011:* 109
Provincial Electoral District(s): Crapaud-Hazel Grove
Federal Electoral District(s): Malpeque
Next Election: Nov. 5, 2018
Matthew Sanford, Chairperson
Bonnie MacDonald, Chief Administrative Officer, 902-964-2438

Eastern Kings
85 Munns Rd.
Bothwell, PE C0A 1K0
Tel: 902-357-2894; *Fax:* 902-357-2607
easternkingspe@gmail.com
www.easternkingspei.com
Municipal Type: Community
Incorporated: 1974
County or District: Cardigan; *Population in 2011:* 702
Provincial Electoral District(s): Souris-Elmira
Federal Electoral District(s): Cardigan
Next Election: Nov. 5, 2018
Anne McPhee, Chairperson
Horatio Toledo, Chief Administrative Officer, 902-357-2534

Ellerslie-Bideford
P.O. Box 13
Ellerslie, PE C0B 1J0
Tel: 902-831-3268
ellersliebideford@hotmail.com
Municipal Type: Community
Incorporated: 1977
County or District: Egmont; *Population in 2011:* 357
Provincial Electoral District(s): Cascumpec-Grand River
Federal Electoral District(s): Egmont
Next Election: Nov. 5, 2018
Ron Millar, Chairperson
Myron Hutchinson, Chief Administrative Officer, 902-831-2720

Georgetown
P.O. Box 89
36 Kent St.
Georgetown, PE C0B 1L0
Tel: 902-652-2924; *Fax:* 902-652-2701
georgetown@pei.sympatico.ca
www.georgetown.ca
Municipal Type: Town
Incorporated: 1912; *Area:* 1.65 sq km
County or District: Cardigan; *Population in 2011:* 675
Provincial Electoral District(s): Georgetown-Baldwin's Road
Federal Electoral District(s): Cardigan
Next Election: Nov. 5, 2018
Lewis Lavandier, Mayor
Tonya Cameron, Chief Administrative Officer, 902-652-2924, Fax: 902-652-2701

Grand Tracadie
York, PE C0A 1P0
Tel: 902-672-3429
Municipal Type: Community
Incorporated: 1984
County or District: Cardigan; *Population in 2011:* 293
Provincial Electoral District(s): Tracadie-Fort Augustus
Federal Electoral District(s): Cardigan
Next Election: Nov. 5, 2018
Kim Meunier, Chairperson
Patsy MacKinnon, Chief Administrative Officer, 902-672-3429

Greenmount-Montrose
1981 Union Rd., RR#2
Alberton, PE C0B 1B0
Tel: 902-853-3949; *Fax:* 902-853-2583
Municipal Type: Community
Incorporated: 1977
County or District: Egmont; *Population in 2011:* 258
Provincial Electoral District(s): Tignish-DeBlois
Federal Electoral District(s): Egmont
Next Election: Nov. 5, 2018
David Pizio, Chairperson
Donna Gallant, Chief Administrative Officer, 902-853-3949, Fax: 902-853-2583

Hampshire
RR#2
North Wiltshire, PE C0A 1Y0
Tel: 902-368-1144
Municipal Type: Community
Incorporated: 1974
County or District: Malpeque; *Population in 2011:* 420
Provincial Electoral District(s): North River-Rice Point; Crapaud-Hazel Grove
Federal Electoral District(s): Malpeque
Next Election: Nov. 5, 2018
Gordon Lank, Chairperson
Gail Stewart, Chief Administrative Officer

Hazelbrook
P.O. Box 1023
101 Kent St.
Charlottetown, PE C1A 1M0
Tel: 902-892-5819; *Fax:* 902-892-5760
council@communityofhazelbrook.com
www.communityofhazelbrook.com
Municipal Type: Community
Incorporated: 1974
County or District: Cardigan; *Population in 2011:* 172
Provincial Electoral District(s): Belfast-Pownal Bay; Tracadie-Fort Augustus
Federal Electoral District(s): Cardigan
Next Election: Nov. 5, 2018
Brian Gallant, Chairperson
Ruth Copeland, Chief Administrative Officer, 902-893-5819, Fax: 902-892-5760

Hunter River
P.O. Box 154
Hunter River, PE C0A 1N0
Tel: 902-621-2170; *Fax:* 902-621-0836
admin.hunter.river@gmail.com
Municipal Type: Community
Incorporated: 1974; *Area:* 6.08 sq km
County or District: Malpeque; *Population in 2011:* 294
Provincial Electoral District(s): Crapaud-Hazel Grove; Park Corner-Oyster Bed
Federal Electoral District(s): Malpeque
Next Election: Nov. 5, 2018
Terry McGrath, Chairperson
Sarah McQuaid, Chief Administrative Officer, 902-621-2170

Kensington
P.O. Box 418
55 Victoria St. East
Kensington, PE C0B 1M0
Tel: 902-836-3781; *Fax:* 902-836-3741
townmanager@townofkensington.com
www.kensington.com
Municipal Type: Town
Incorporated: 1914; *Area:* 3.02 sq km
County or District: Malpeque; *Population in 2011:* 1,496
Provincial Electoral District(s): Kensington-Malpeque
Federal Electoral District(s): Malpeque
Next Election: Nov. 5, 2018
Rowan Caseley, Mayor
Geoff Baker, Chief Administrative Officer

Kingston
P.O. Box 648
Cornwall, PE C0A 1H0
Tel: 902-675-3670; *Fax:* 902-368-1239
www.kingstoncc.ca
Municipal Type: Community
Incorporated: 1974
County or District: Malpeque; *Population in 2011:* 794
Provincial Electoral District(s): North River-Rice Point; Crapaud-Hazel Grove
Federal Electoral District(s): Malpeque
Next Election: Nov. 5, 2018
Alan Miller, Chairperson
Dianne Dowling, Chief Administrative Officer, 902-675-3670, Fax: 902-368-1239

Kinkora
P.O. Box 38
45 Anderson St.
Kinkora, PE C0B 1N0
Tel: 902-887-2868; *Fax:* 902-887-3514
communityofkinkora@bellaliant.com
www.kinkorapei.com
Municipal Type: Community
Incorporated: 1955; *Area:* 3.82 sq km
County or District: Malpeque; *Population in 2011:* 339
Provincial Electoral District(s): Borden-Kinkora
Federal Electoral District(s): Malpeque
Next Election: Nov. 5, 2018
Pat Duffy, Chairperson
Aaron Gauthier, Chief Administrative Officer, 902-887-2868, Fax: 902-887-3514

Lady Slipper
11703 Rte. 11, RR#2
Tyne Valley, PE C0B 2C0
Tel: 902-831-3496
Municipal Type: Community
Incorporated: 1983
County or District: Egmont; *Population in 2011:* 805
Provincial Electoral District(s): Casumpec-Grand River
Federal Electoral District(s): Egmont
Next Election: Nov. 5, 2018

Julie Smith, Chairperson
Douglas MacLeod, Chief Administrative Officer, 902-831-3496

Linkletter
211 Glenn Dr.
Linkletter, PE C1N 5N2
Tel: 902-724-0914
communityoflinkletter@gmail.com
www.linklettercommunity.com
Municipal Type: Community
Incorporated: 1972; *Area:* 9.05 sq km
County or District: Egmont; *Population in 2011:* 320
Provincial Electoral District(s): St. Eleanors-Summerside
Federal Electoral District(s): Egmont
Next Election: Nov. 5, 2018
David Linkletter, Chairperson
Brian Morrison, Chief Administrative Officer, 902-724-0914

Lorne Valley
415 Brudenell Point Rd., RR#5
Montague, PE C0A 1R0
Tel: 902-838-4160
Municipal Type: Community
Incorporated: 1978
County or District: Cardigan; *Population in 2011:* 106
Provincial Electoral District(s): Georgetown-Baldwin's Road
Federal Electoral District(s): Cardigan
Next Election: Nov. 5, 2018
Karen MacLeod, Chairperson
Linda Barry, Chief Administrative Officer

Lot 11 & Area
P.O. Box 40
Ellerslie, PE C0B 1J0
Tel: 902-859-3594
www.lot11andarea.org
Municipal Type: Community
Incorporated: 1982
County or District: Egmont; *Population in 2011:* 635
Provincial Electoral District(s): Cascumpec-Grand River
Federal Electoral District(s): Egmont
Next Election: Nov. 5, 2018
Susan Milligan, Chairperson
Shirley Phillips, Chief Administrative Officer, 902-859-3594

Lower Montague
P.O. Box 821
Montague, PE C0A 1R0
Tel: 902-838-5405; *Fax:* 902-838-3617
administrator@lowermontague.ca
www.lowermontague.ca
Municipal Type: Community
Incorporated: 1974
County or District: Cardigan; *Population in 2011:* 665
Provincial Electoral District(s): Montague-Kilmuir
Federal Electoral District(s): Cardigan
Next Election: Nov. 5, 2018
Scott Annear, Chairperson
Elizabeth Nicholson, Chief Administrative Officer, 902-838-3359, Fax: 902-838-3617

Malpeque Bay
P.O. Box 405
Kensington, PE C0B 1M0
Tel: 902-836-5029
communityofmalpequebay@gmail.com
www.malpequebay.ca
Municipal Type: Community
Incorporated: 1973
County or District: Malpeque; *Population in 2011:* 1,029
Provincial Electoral District(s): Kensington-Malpeque
Federal Electoral District(s): Malpeque
Next Election: Nov. 5, 2018
Jamie Crozier, Chairperson
Joanne McCarvill, Chief Administrative Officer, 902-836-5029

Meadowbank
P.O. Box 1162
Cornwall, PE C0A 1H0
Tel: 902-566-3215
communityofmeadowbank@gmail.com
Municipal Type: Community
Incorporated: 1974; *Area:* 9.25 sq km
County or District: Malpeque; *Population in 2011:* 338
Provincial Electoral District(s): North River-Rice Point
Federal Electoral District(s): Malpeque
Next Election: Nov. 5, 2018
Helen Smith-MacPhail, Chairperson
Kathy Daley, Chief Administrative Officer

Miltonvale Park
7B New Glasgow Rd., Rte. 224
North Milton, PE C1E 0S7
Tel: 902-368-3090; *Fax:* 902-368-1152
admin@miltonvalepark.com
www.miltonvalepark.com
Municipal Type: Community
Incorporated: 1974; *Area:* 35.32 sq km
County or District: Malpeque; *Population in 2011:* 1,153
Provincial Electoral District(s): Winsloe-West Royalty
Federal Electoral District(s): Malpeque
Next Election: Nov. 5, 2018
Hal Parker, Chairperson
Shari MacDonald, Chief Administrative Officer, 902-368-3090, Fax: 902-368-1152

Miminegash
11315 Rte. 14
Miminegash, PE C0B 1S0
Tel: 902-882-3223
Municipal Type: Community
Incorporated: 1968; *Area:* 1.85 sq km
County or District: Egmont; *Population in 2011:* 173
Provincial Electoral District(s): Alberton-Miminegash
Federal Electoral District(s): Egmont
Next Election: Nov. 5, 2018
Audrey Callaghan, Chairperson
Lou Ann Gallant, Chief Administrative Officer, 902-882-3223

Miscouche
P.O. Box 70
Miscouche, PE C0B 1T0
Tel: 902-436-4962; *Fax:* 902-436-4963
communityofmiscouche@pei.aibn.com
Municipal Type: Community
Incorporated: 1957; *Area:* 3.34 sq km
County or District: Egmont; *Population in 2011:* 869
Provincial Electoral District(s): Evangeline-Miscouche
Federal Electoral District(s): Egmont
Next Election: Nov. 5, 2018
Peter Mallett, Chairperson
Judy Gallant, Chief Administrative Officer, 902-436-4962

Montague
P.O. Box 546
24 Queens Rd.
Montague, PE C0A 1R0
Tel: 902-838-2528; *Fax:* 902-838-3392
townhall@montaguepei.ca
www.montaguepei.ca
Municipal Type: Town
Incorporated: 1917; *Area:* 3.04 sq km
County or District: Cardigan; *Population in 2011:* 1,895
Provincial Electoral District(s): Montague-Kilmuir
Federal Electoral District(s): Cardigan
Next Election: Nov. 5, 2018
Richard Collins, Mayor
Andrew Daggett, Chief Administrative Officer, 902-838-2528

Morell
P.O. Box 307
25 Sunset Cres.
Morell, PE C0A 1S0
Tel: 902-961-2900; *Fax:* 902-739-2900
morellcommunity@eastlink.ca
www.morellpei.com
Municipal Type: Community
Incorporated: 1953; *Area:* 1.40 sq km
County or District: Cardigan; *Population in 2011:* 313
Provincial Electoral District(s): Morell-Fortune Bay
Federal Electoral District(s): Cardigan
Next Election: Nov. 5, 2018
Jean Eldershaw, Chairperson, 902-961-2066
Donna Sturgess, Chief Administrative Officer, 902-961-2900

Mount Stewart
P.O. Box 143
Mount Stewart, PE C0A 1T0
Tel: 902-676-2881; *Fax:* 902-731-3111
mountstewart@eastlink.ca
Municipal Type: Community
Incorporated: 1953; *Area:* 1.22 sq km
County or District: Cardigan; *Population in 2011:* 225
Provincial Electoral District(s): Tracadie-Fort Augustus
Federal Electoral District(s): Cardigan
Next Election: Nov. 5, 2018
Maxine Doucette, Chairperson
Christine Watts, Chief Administrative Officer, 902-676-2881, Fax: 902-731-3111

Murray Harbour
P.O. Box 72
1311 Main St.
Murray Harbour, PE C0A 1V0
Tel: 902-962-3835
villoffice@eastlink.ca
www.murrayharbourpei.com
Municipal Type: Community
Incorporated: 1953; *Area:* 4.01 sq km
County or District: Cardigan; *Population in 2011:* 320
Provincial Electoral District(s): Murray River-Gaspereaux
Federal Electoral District(s): Cardigan
Next Election: Nov. 5, 2018
Faye Fraser, Chairperson, 908-962-2157
Sylvain Lafontaine, Chief Administrative Officer, 908-962-3835

Murray River
P.O. Box 266
Murray River, PE C0A 1W0
Tel: 902-962-2820; *Fax:* 902-962-3671
mrvillage@isnhighspeed.ca
www.murrayriverpei.com
Municipal Type: Community
Incorporated: 1955; *Area:* 1.43 sq km
County or District: Cardigan; *Population in 2011:* 334
Provincial Electoral District(s): Murray River-Gaspereaux
Federal Electoral District(s): Cardigan
Next Election: Nov. 5, 2018
Patricia Bray, Chairperson, 902-962-3983
Dianne MacDonald, Chief Administrative Officer, 902-962-2820, Fax: 902-962-3671

New Haven-Riverdale
599 Riverdale Rd., RR#3
Bonshaw, PE C0A 1C0
Tel: 902-629-4024; *Fax:* 902-368-1239
newhavenriverdalecc.ca
Municipal Type: Community
Incorporated: 1974
County or District: Malpeque; *Population in 2011:* 485
Provincial Electoral District(s): Crapaud-Hazel Grove
Federal Electoral District(s): Malpeque
Next Election: Nov. 5, 2018
Claus Brodersen, Chairperson
Dianne Dowling, Chief Administrative Officer, 902-629-4024

North Rustico
P.O. Box 38
North Rustico, PE C0A 1X0
Tel: 902-963-3211; *Fax:* 902-963-3321
northrustico@pei.aibn.com
www.northrustico.net
Municipal Type: Community
Incorporated: 1954; *Area:* 2.45 sq km
County or District: Malpeque; *Population in 2011:* 583
Provincial Electoral District(s): Park Corner-Oyster Bed
Federal Electoral District(s): Malpeque
Next Election: Nov. 5, 2018
Anne Kirk, Mayor
Patsy Gamauf, Chief Administrative Officer, 902-963-3211, Fax: 902-963-3321

North Shore
P.O. Box 134 Post Office
York, PE C0A 1P0
Tel: 902-672-1586; *Fax:* 902-672-1766
nscc@pei.aibn.com
www.stanhopecovehead.pe.ca
Municipal Type: Community
Incorporated: 1974
County or District: Malpeque; *Population in 2011:* 1,112
Provincial Electoral District(s): Stanhope-East Royalty
Federal Electoral District(s): Malpeque
Next Election: Nov. 5, 2018
Gordon Ellis, Chairperson
Tracey Allen, Chief Administrative Officer, 902-672-1586

North Wiltshire
1605 Kinkora Rd.
North Wiltshire, PE C0A 1Y0
Tel: 902-621-1908
Municipal Type: Community
Incorporated: 1974
County or District: Egmont; *Population in 2011:* 182
Provincial Electoral District(s): Crapaud-Hazel Grove
Federal Electoral District(s): Malpeque
Next Election: Nov. 5, 2018
Robert Bertram, Chairperson
Charlene Waddell, Chief Administrative Officer

Northport
P.O. Box 466
Alberton, PE C0B 1B0
Tel: 902-853-2551
Municipal Type: Community
Incorporated: 1974
County or District: Egmont; *Population in 2011:* 188
Provincial Electoral District(s): Alberton-Miminegash
Federal Electoral District(s): Egmont
Next Election: Nov. 5, 2018
Wendy McNeil, Chairperson
Paula Foley, Chief Administrative Officer, 902-853-2551

O'Leary
P.O. Box 130
O'Leary, PE C0B 1V0
Tel: 902-859-3311; *Fax:* 902-859-2341
olearyadm@eastlink.ca
www.communityofoleary.com
Municipal Type: Town
Incorporated: 1951; *Area:* 1.60 sq km
County or District: Egmont; *Population in 2011:* 812
Provincial Electoral District(s): West Point-Bloomfield
Federal Electoral District(s): Egmont
Next Election: Nov. 5, 2018
Eric Gavin, Mayor
Beverley Shaw, Chief Administrative Officer, 902-859-3311

Pleasant Grove
P.O. Box 2
1103 Pleasant Grove
York RR#2, PE C0A 1P0
Tel: 902-672-3325
Municipal Type: Community
Incorporated: 1980
County or District: Malpeque; *Population in 2011:* 496
Provincial Electoral District(s): Stanhope-East Royalty
Federal Electoral District(s): Malpeque
Next Election: Nov. 5, 2018
Kim Doyle, Chairperson
Joe Doran, Chief Administrative Officer

Resort Municipality
RR#2
Hunter River, PE C0A 1N0
Tel: 902-963-2698; *Fax:* 902-963-2932
resort@pei.aibn.com
Municipal Type: Community
Incorporated: 1990; *Area:* 37.74 sq km
Population in 2011: 266
Provincial Electoral District(s): Park Corner-Oyster Bed
Federal Electoral District(s): Malpeque
Next Election: Nov. 5, 2018
Matthew Jelley, Chairperson
Brenda MacDonald, Chief Administrative Officer, 902-963-2698, Fax: 902-963-2932

St. Felix
P.O. Box 22
Tignish, PE C0B 2B0
Tel: 902-882-4015
Municipal Type: Community
Incorporated: 1977
County or District: Egmont; *Population in 2011:* 348
Provincial Electoral District(s): Tignish-DeBlois
Federal Electoral District(s): Egmont
Next Election: Nov. 5, 2018
Claude Gaudette, Chairperson
Joanne Gaudette, Chief Administrative Officer, 902-882-4015, Fax: 902-882-3443

St. Louis
P.O. Box 40
St. Louis, PE C0B 1Z0
Tel: 902-882-2447
Municipal Type: Community
Incorporated: 1964; *Area:* 0.62 sq km
County or District: Egmont; *Population in 2011:* 51
Provincial Electoral District(s): Alberton-Miminegash; Tignish-DeBlois
Federal Electoral District(s): Egmont
Next Election: Nov. 5, 2018
Everett (Sonny) Wedge, Chairperson
Linda McCue, Chief Administrative Officer, 902-882-2447

St. Nicholas
3702 St. Nicholas
Miscouche, PE C0B 1T0
Tel: 902-854-2731
Municipal Type: Community
Incorporated: 1991
Population in 2011: 198
Provincial Electoral District(s): Evangeline-Miscouche
Federal Electoral District(s): Egmont
Next Election: Nov. 5, 2018
Pam Dawson, Chairperson
Corina Mundy, Chief Administrative Officer, 902-854-2507

St. Peter's Bay
P.O. Box 51
St. Peter's Bay, PE C0A 2A0
Tel: 902-961-2268; *Fax:* 902-961-3148
stpeters@eastlink.ca
Municipal Type: Community
Incorporated: 1953; *Area:* 4.24 sq km
County or District: Cardigan; *Population in 2011:* 253
Provincial Electoral District(s): Morell-Fortune Bay
Federal Electoral District(s): Cardigan
Next Election: Nov. 5, 2018
Ron MacInnis, Chairperson
Mary Burge, Chief Administrative Officer, 902-961-2268

Sherbrooke
P.O. Box 1344
Summerside, PE C1N 4K2
Tel: 902-436-7005; *Fax:* 902-436-9170
Municipal Type: Community
Incorporated: 1972; *Area:* 8.83 sq km
Population in 2011: 172
Provincial Electoral District(s): Wilmot-Summerside
Federal Electoral District(s): Egmont
Next Election: Nov. 5, 2018
Ron Chappell, Chair
Peggy Kilbride, Chief Administrative Officer, 902-436-7005, Fax: 902-436-9170

Souris
P.O. Box 628
75 Main St.
Souris, PE C0A 2B0
Tel: 902-687-2157; *Fax:* 902-687-4426
town@sourispei.com
www.sourispei.com
Municipal Type: Town
Incorporated: 1910; *Area:* 3.42 sq km
County or District: Cardigan; *Population in 2011:* 1,173
Provincial Electoral District(s): Souris-Elmira
Federal Electoral District(s): Cardigan
Next Election: Nov. 5, 2018
David McDonald, Mayor, 902-969-3361
Shelley LaVie, Chief Administrative Officer, 902-687-2157, Fax: 902-687-4426

Souris West
P.O. Box 680
Souris, PE C0A 2B0
Tel: 902-687-2485
Municipal Type: Community
Incorporated: 1972
County or District: Cardigan; *Population in 2011:* 399
Provincial Electoral District(s): Souris-Elmira
Federal Electoral District(s): Cardigan
Next Election: Nov. 5, 2018
Pat O'Connor, Chairperson
Cathy Williams, Chief Administrative Officer, 902-368-6886

Stratford
234 Shakespeare Dr.
Stratford, PE C1B 2V8
Tel: 902-569-6251; *Fax:* 902-569-5000
info@town.stratford.pe.ca
townofstratford.ca
Municipal Type: Town
Incorporated: April 1, 1995; *Area:* 22.48 sq km
Population in 2011: 8,574
Provincial Electoral District(s): Glen Stewart-Bellevue Cove
Federal Electoral District(s): Cardigan
Next Election: Nov. 5, 2018 (4 year terms)
David Dunphy, CA, Mayor, 902-569-2149
Robert Hughes, P.Eng, Chief Administrative Officer, 902-569-6251

Tignish
P.O. Box 57
209 Phillip St.
Tignish, PE C0B 2B0
Tel: 902-882-2600; *Fax:* 902-882-2414
administrator@tignish.com
www.tignish.com
Municipal Type: Community
Incorporated: 1952; *Area:* 5.86 sq km
County or District: Egmont; *Population in 2011:* 779
Provincial Electoral District(s): Tignish-DeBlois
Federal Electoral District(s): Egmont
Next Election: Nov. 5, 2018
Allan McInnis, Chairperson, 902-853-5228
Karen Gaudet-Gavin, Chief Administrative Officer, 902-882-2600, Fax: 902-882-2414

Tignish Shore
RR#1
Tignish, PE C0B 2B0
Tel: 902-853-3931
Municipal Type: Community
Incorporated: 1975
Population in 2011: 73
Provincial Electoral District(s): Tignish-DeBlois
Federal Electoral District(s): Egmont
Next Election: Nov. 5, 2018
Ronnie McRae, Chairperson
Donna MacKay, Chief Administrative Officer, 902-882-3811

Tyne Valley
P.O. Box 39
Tyne Valley, PE C0B 2C0
Tel: 902-831-2938
Municipal Type: Community
Incorporated: 1966; *Area:* 1.74 sq km
County or District: Egmont; *Population in 2011:* 222
Provincial Electoral District(s): Cascumpec-Grand River
Federal Electoral District(s): Egmont
Next Election: Nov. 5, 2018
Kevin Kadey, Chairperson
Marie Barlow, Chief Administrative Officer, 902-831-2938, Fax: 902-831-3395

Union Road
P.O. Box 20114
161 St. Peters Rd.
Charlottetown, PE C1A 9E3
Tel: 902-566-4097; *Fax:* 902-367-9862
admin@communityofunionroadpei.com
www.communityofunionroadpei.com
Municipal Type: Community
Incorporated: 1977; *Area:* 9.95 sq km
County or District: Malpeque; *Population in 2011:* 235
Provincial Electoral District(s): Georgetown-Baldwin's Road
Federal Electoral District(s): Malpeque; Cardigan
Next Election: Nov. 5, 2018
Fern Yeo, Chairperson, 902-368-8207
Ruth Copeland, Chief Administrative Officer, 902-892-5819

Valleyfield
1783 Queens Rd.
Lyndale, PE C0A 1R0
Tel: 902-838-4447; *Fax:* 902-838-3649
Municipal Type: Community
Incorporated: 1974
County or District: Cardigan; *Population in 2011:* 672
Provincial Electoral District(s): Georgetown-Baldwin's Road; Montague-Kilmuir; Belfast-Pownal Bay
Federal Electoral District(s): Cardigan
Next Election: Nov. 5, 2018
Graham Jones, Chairperson
Margaret Campion, Chief Administrative Officer, 902-838-4447, Fax: 902-838-3649

Victoria
P.O. Box 7
Victoria, PE C0A 2G0
Tel: 902-658-2541
victoriaadmin@eastlink.ca
Municipal Type: Community
Incorporated: 1951; *Area:* 1.40 sq km
County or District: Malpeque; *Population in 2011:* 104
Provincial Electoral District(s): Crapaud-Hazel Grove
Federal Electoral District(s): Malpeque
Next Election: Nov. 5, 2018
Henry Dunsmore, Chairperson
Hilary Price, Chief Administrative Officer, 902-658-2541

Warren Grove
P.O. Box 963
Cornwall, PE C0A 1H0
Tel: 902-675-3558
communityofwarrengrove@gmail.com
Municipal Type: Community
Incorporated: 1985; *Area:* 10.32 sq km
County or District: Malpeque; *Population in 2011:* 367
Provincial Electoral District(s): North River-Rice Point
Federal Electoral District(s): Malpeque
Next Election: Nov. 5, 2018
Amber Tawil, Chairperson
Joanne Smith, Chief Administrative Officer, 902-675-2788

Wellington

P.O. Box 26
Wellington, PE C0B 2E0
Tel: 902-854-2920
vaniercenter@gmail.com
Municipal Type: Community
Incorporated: 1959; *Area:* 1.80 sq km
County or District: Egmont; *Population in 2011:* 409
Provincial Electoral District(s): Cascumpec-Grand River; Evangeline-Miscouche
Federal Electoral District(s): Egmont
Next Election: Nov. 5, 2018
Alcide Bernard, Chairperson
Claudette Gallant, Chief Administrative Officer, 902-854-2920

West River

#322, 140 Heron Drive
Stratford, PE C1A 0L6
Tel: 902-569-1792; *Fax:* 902-367-1147
Municipal Type: Community
Incorporated: 1974
County or District: Malpeque; *Population in 2011:* 741
Provincial Electoral District(s): North River-Rice Point
Federal Electoral District(s): Malpeque
Next Election: Nov. 5, 2018
Eric MacArthur, Chairperson
Bill Grant, Chief Administrative Officer, 902-569-1792, Fax: 902-367-1147

Winsloe South

465 Winsloe Rd., Rte 223
South Winsloe, PE C1E 2Y2
Tel: 902-368-1444
Municipal Type: Community
Incorporated: 1986; *Area:* 9.63 sq km
County or District: Malpeque; *Population in 2011:* 221
Provincial Electoral District(s): Winsloe-West Royalty
Federal Electoral District(s): Malpeque
Next Election: Nov. 5, 2018
Brian Turner, Chairperson
Joanne Turner, Chief Administrative Officer, 902-368-1444

York

P.O. Box 8910
669 Rte. 25, York Rd.
Charlottetown, PE C0A 1P0
Tel: 902-566-5653; *Fax:* 902-569-1132
Municipal Type: Community
Incorporated: 1986
Population in 2011: 284
Provincial Electoral District(s): Stanhope-East Royalty
Federal Electoral District(s): Malpeque
Next Election: Nov. 5, 2018
Irwin Campbell, Chairperson
Carolyn Kellough, Chief Administrative Officer, 902-566-5653

QUÉBEC

Québec legislation recognizes two levels of municipal organization: the local and the regional.

Major municipal reform has reduced the number of local municipalities from nearly 1,400 in 1998 to 1,136 as of 2016. Of this number, 227 fall under the jurisdiction of the Cities and Towns Act (RSQ, chap. C-19). Nine of them have over 100,000 inhabitants and account for 53% of the Québec population. There are also 883 municipalities that are governed by the Municipal Code of Québec, 14 northern villages that fall under the Act Respecting Northern Villages and the Katvik Regional Government, and 9 villages governed by the Cree Villages and the Naskapi Village Act.

The regional level of municipal territorial organization includes the Montréal and Québec City metropolitan communities, the 87 regional county municipalities (RCMs), and the Kativik Regional Government. The metropolitan communities and RCMs are made up of local municipalities. RCMs may also include unorganized territories.

The regional organizations were created to ensure that issues that go beyond local boundaries were handled at the regional or metropolitan level. Although their structures, operation and powers vary, they are based on identical principles. The Montréal and Québec City metropolitan communities are responsible at their level for land use planning, economic development, international economic promotion, artistic and cultural development, regional orientations in public transit, waste management planning, establishing a tax base sharing program, as well as for determining and financing regional facilities, infrastructures, activities, and services. RCMs also meet regional needs, including land use planning and the pooling of services. In addition, they exercise certain powers in the areas of economic development, public security and the environment. The Kativik Regional Government is in charge of local administration, police, transport, communications and labour force training and use, and may also set minimum standards by ordinance for things like house and building construction.

Eight local municipalities belong neither to a metropolitan community nor to one of the regional county municipalities. They do, however, wield some of the same powers as RCMs. This also holds true for six other cities, which although situated within one of the two metropolitan communities, nonetheless exercise certain of the powers of an RCM.

Eight cities are divided into boroughs. The boroughs have consultative and decision-making powers, are responsible for delivering certain neighbourhood services, and are represented by an elected borough council. Elections in the province are held every four years on the first Sunday of November (2017, 2021, etc.)

Source: © Department of Natural Resources Canada. All rights reserved.

Québec

Major Municipalities in Québec

Alma
140, rue St-Joseph
Alma, QC G8B 3R1
Tél: 418-669-5000; *Téléc:* 418-669-5029
info@ville.alma.qc.ca
www.ville.alma.qc.ca
Entité municipal: City
Incorporation: 21 février 2001; *Area:* 202,10 km2
Comté ou district: Lac-Saint-Jean-Est; *Population au 2011:* 30,904
Circonscription(s) électorale(s) provinciale(s): Lac-St-Jean
Circonscription(s) électorale(s) fédérale(s): Lac-Saint-Jean
Prochaines élections: 5e novembre 2017
Marc Asselin, Maire, 418-669-5005, Fax: 418-668-8923
Lucien Boily, Conseiller, 418-669-1070, Wards: 1. Delisle
Jocelyn Fradette, Conseiller, 418-450-1359, Wards: 2. Isle-Maligne Albert-Naud
Gilles Girard, Conseiller, 418-668-6815, Wards: 3. Melançon
Frédéric Tremblay, Conseiller, 418-668-5014, Wards: 4. Damase-Boulanger
Gino Villeneuve, Conseiller, 418-321-3458, Wards: 5. Saint-Pierre
Sylvie Beaumont, Conseillère, 418-668-0919, Wards: 6. Champagnat
Pascal Pilote, Conseiller, 418-480-1417, Wards: 7. Scott
Alain Fortin, Conseiller, 418-669-1083, Wards: 8. Signay-Labarre
Jean Paradis, Greffier, 418-669-5001
Sylvain Duchesne, Directeur général, 418-669-5001
Yves Thériault, Trésorier, 418-669-5001
Pierre Landry, Directeur général adjoint, 418-669-5001
Bernard Dallaire, Directeur, Prévention des incendies, 418-669-5059
Karine Morel, Directrice, Travaux publics, 418-669-5001
Alain Tremblay, Directeur, Service des ressources humaines, 418-669-5001
Denis Verrette, Directeur et urbaniste, Urbanisme, 418-669-5031

Amos
182, 1re Rue est
Amos, QC J9T 2G1
Tél: 819-732-3254; *Téléc:* 819-727-9792
infos@ville.amos.qc.ca
www.ville.amos.qc.ca
Entité municipal: City
Incorporation: 17 janvier 1987; *Area:* 430,84 km2
Comté ou district: Abitibi; *Population au 2011:* 12,671
Circonscription(s) électorale(s) provinciale(s): Abitibi-Ouest
Circonscription(s) électorale(s) fédérale(s): Abitibi-Témiscamingue
Prochaines élections: 5e novembre 2017
Ulrick Chérubin, Maire
Sébastien D'Astous, Conseiller, Infrastructures & services aux citoyens, Wards: 1
Martin Roy, Conseiller, Développement communautaire, social et service à la population, Wards: 2
Donald Blanchet, Conseiller, Développement économique, industriel & commercial, Wards: 3
Denis Chandonnet, Conseiller, Administration & sports, Wards: 4
Mario Brunet, Conseiller, Culture et patrimoine, Wards: 5
Micheline Godbout, Conseillère, Qualité de vie et famille, Wards: 6
Claudyne Maurice, Greffière
Gérald Lavoie, CMA, Trésorier
Guy Nolet, Directeur général
Pierre Gagnon, Directeur, Service sécurité d'incendie

L'Ancienne-Lorette
1575, rue Turmel
L'Ancienne-Lorette, QC G2E 3J5
Tél: 418-872-9811; *Téléc:* 418-641-6019
info@lancienne-lorette.org
www.lancienne-lorette.org
Entité municipal: City
Incorporation: 1er janvier 2006; *Area:* 7,63 km2
Comté ou district: Communauté métropolitaine de Québec; *Population au 2011:* 16,745
Circonscription(s) électorale(s) provinciale(s): La Peltrie
Circonscription(s) électorale(s) fédérale(s): Louis-Saint-Laurent
Prochaines élections: 5e novembre 2017
Émile Loranger, Maire, 418-872-0104
Josée Ossio, Conseiller, 418-871-0758, Wards: 1. Saint-Jacques
André Laliberté, Conseiller, 418-864-7545, Wards: 2. Notre-Dame
Gaétan Pageau, Conseiller, 418-877-4378, Wards: 3. Saint-Paul
Yvon Godin, Conseiller, 418-871-7774, Wards: 4. Saint-Oliver
Sylvie Papillon, Conseillère, 418-977-4028, Wards: 5. Saint-Jean-Baptiste
Sylvie Falardeau, Conseillère, 418-872-6949, Wards: 6. des Pins
Claude Deschênes, Greffier
Donald Tremblay, Directeur général, Administration
André Rousseau, Directeur général, Opérations
Ariane Tremblay, Trésorière

L'Assomption
399, rue Dorval
L'Assomption, QC J5W 1A1
Tél: 450-589-5671; *Téléc:* 450-589-4512
information@ville.lassomption.qc.ca
www.ville.lassomption.qc.ca
Entité municipal: City
Incorporation: 1er juillet 2000; *Area:* 100,09 km2
Comté ou district: L'Assomption; Communauté métropolitaine de Montréal; *Population au 2011:* 20,065
Circonscription(s) électorale(s) provinciale(s): L'Assomption
Circonscription(s) électorale(s) fédérale(s): Repentigny
Prochaines élections: 5e novembre 2017
Claude Rivest, Conseiller, 450-589-5671, Wards: 1. Hector-Charland
Jean Raynault, Conseillère, 450-589-5671, Wards: 2. Wilfrid Laurier
Nicole Martel, Conseillère, 450-589-5671, Wards: 3. Pierre-LeSueur
Maryse Turgeon, Conseillère, 450-589-5671, Wards: 4. Louis Laberge
Michel Gagnon, Conseiller, 450-589-5671, Wards: 5. Albert-Racette
Fernand Gendron, Conseiller, 450-589-5671, Wards: 6. Maurice-Lafortune
Michel Archambault, Directeur général
Dominique Valiquette, Trésorière, 450-589-5671, Fax: 450-589-4512
Christian Demers, Directeur, Travaux publics, 450-589-5671, Fax: 450-589-6125
Jean-Charles Drapeau, Directeur, Urbanisme, 450-589-5671, Fax: 450-587-9213

Baie-Comeau
19, av Marquette
Baie-Comeau, QC G4Z 1K5
Tél: 418-296-4931; *Téléc:* 418-296-3759
www.ville.baie-comeau.qc.ca
Entité municipal: City
Incorporation: 23 juin 1982; *Area:* 371,69 km2
Comté ou district: Manicouagan; *Population au 2011:* 22,113
Circonscription(s) électorale(s) provinciale(s): René-Lévesque
Circonscription(s) électorale(s) fédérale(s): Manicouagan
Prochaines élections: 5e novembre 2017
Claude Martel, Maire, 418-296-8142, Fax: 418-296-4194
Yves Montigny, Conseiller, Wards: La Chasse
Réjean Girard, Conseiller, 418-589-5059, Wards: Mgr-Bélanger
Carole Deschênes, Conseillère, 418-589-8734, Wards: N.-A. Labrie
Reina Savoie-Jourdain, Conseillère, 418-296-5231, Wards: Sainte-Amélie
Yvon Boudreau, Conseiller, 418-296-2672, Wards: Saint-Georges
Léa Thibault, Conseillère, 418-296-4654, Wards: Saint-Nom-de-Marie
Sébastien Langlois, Conseiller, 418-445-1634, Wards: Saint-Sacrement
Alain Charest, Conseiller, 418-589-6893, Wards: Trudel
Annick Tremblay, Greffière et directrice, Affaires juridiques, 418-296-8109, Fax: 418-296-8151
François Corriveau, Directeur général, 418-296-8104, Fax: 418-296-8121
Jeanie Caron, Trésorière et directrice, Finances, 418-296-8128, Fax: 418-296-8349
Ghislain Gauthier, Directeur, Travaux publics, 418-296-4931, Fax: 418-296-3095
François LeBlond, Directeur, Loisirs, sports et vie communautaire, 418-296-8358, Fax: 418-296-8399
Alain Miville, Directeur (par intérim), Sécurité publique - Protection incendie, 418-589-1504, Fax: 418-589-1582
Christine Reis, Chef de division, Gestion de l'eau et développement durable, 418-296-5207

Beaconsfield
303, boul Beaconsfield
Beaconsfield, QC H9W 4A7
Tél: 514-428-4400; *Téléc:* 514-428-4424
www.beaconsfield.ca
Entité municipal: City
Incorporation: 1er janvier 2006; *Area:* 10,64 km2
Comté ou district: Communauté métropolitaine de Montréal; *Population au 2011:* 19,505
Circonscription(s) électorale(s) provinciale(s): Jacques-Cartier
Circonscription(s) électorale(s) fédérale(s): Lac-Saint-Louis
Prochaines élections: 5e novembre 2017
Georges Bourelle, Maire, 514-428-4410
David Pelletier, Conseiller, 514-249-8843, Wards: 1
Karen Messier, Conseillère, 514-428-8975, Wards: 2
Wade Staddon, Conseiller, 514-448-1349, Wards: 3
Pierre Demers, Conseiller, 514-630-4274, Wards: 4
Roger Moss, Conseiller, 514-426-2144, Wards: 5
Peggy Alexopoulos, Conseillère, 514-428-4400, Wards: 6
Nathalie Libersan-Laniel, Greffière
Patrice Boileau, Directeur général
Michel Guy, Trésorier
Denis Chabot, Directeur, Urbanisme et permis, 514-428-4430
Andrew Duffield, Directeur, Travaux publics, 514-428-4500
Bernard Côté, Évaluateur signataire

Beauharnois
#100, 660, rue Ellice
Beauharnois, QC J6N 1Y1
Tél: 450-429-3546; *Téléc:* 450-429-2478
reception@ville.beauharnois.qc.ca
www.ville.beauharnois.qc.ca
Entité municipal: City
Incorporation: 1er janvier 2002; *Area:* 73,05 km2
Comté ou district: Beauharnois-Salaberry; Communauté métropolitaine de Montréal; *Population au 2011:* 12,011
Circonscription(s) électorale(s) provinciale(s): Beauharnois
Circonscription(s) électorale(s) fédérale(s): Salaberry-Suroît
Prochaines élections: 5e novembre 2017
Claude Haineault, Maire
Gaëtan Dagenais, Conseiller, 450-429-3546, Wards: 1
Michel Quevillon, Conseiller, 450-429-3546, Wards: 2
Guillaume Lévesque-Sauvé, Conseiller, 450-429-3546, Wards: 3
Patrick Laniel, Conseiller, 450-429-3546, Wards: 4
Jocelyne Rajotte, Conseillère, 450-429-3546, Wards: 5
Linda Toulouse, Conseillère, 450-429-3546, Wards: 6
Manon Fortier, Greffière, 450-429-3546
Julie Fortin, Directrice générale, 450-429-3546
Guylaine Côte, Trésorière, 450-429-3546
Sylvain Gendron, Directeur, Travaux publics et de l'hygiène du milieu, 450-225-0650
Nathalie Morin, Chef de section, Géomatique et urbanisme et de l'occupation du territoire, 450-429-3546
Jean-Maurice Marleau, Directeur, Service de la sécurité incendie et de la sécurité civile, 450-225-2222

Bécancour
1295, av Nicolas-Perrot
Bécancour, QC G9H 1A1
Tél: 819-294-6500; *Téléc:* 819-294-6535
becancour@ville.becancour.qc.ca
www.becancour.net
Entité municipal: City
Incorporation: 17 octobre 1965; *Area:* 434,28 km2
Comté ou district: Bécancour; *Population au 2011:* 12,438
Circonscription(s) électorale(s) provinciale(s): Nicolet-Bécancour
Circonscription(s) électorale(s) fédérale(s): Bécancour-Nicolet-Saurel
Prochaines élections: 5e novembre 2017
Jean-Guy Dubois, Maire
Fernand Croteau, Conseiller, Wards: Bécancour
Alain Mercier, Conseiller, Wards: Gentilly
Mario Gagné, Conseiller, Wards: Précieux-Sang
René Morrissette, Conseiller, Wards: Saint-Grégoire
Carmen Lampron-Pratte, Conseillère, Wards: Sainte-Angèle-de-Laval
Raymond St-Onge, Conseiller, Wards: Sainte-Gertrude
France Leclerc, Greffière
Jean-Marc Dirouard, Directeur général
Daniel Brunelle, Trésorier et directeur, Finances, 819-294-6500, Fax: 819-294-6535
Émilie Hogue, Responsable, Loisirs

Beloeil
777, rue Laurier
Beloeil, QC J3G 4S9
Tél: 450-467-2835; *Téléc:* 450-464-5445
info@ville.beloeil.qc.ca
www.ville.beloeil.qc.ca
Entité municipal: City
Incorporation: 9e décembre 1903; *Area:* 24 km2
Comté ou district: La Vallée-du-Richelieu; Communauté métropolitaine de Montréal; *Population au 2011:* 20,783
Circonscription(s) électorale(s) provinciale(s): Borduas
Circonscription(s) électorale(s) fédérale(s): Beloeil-Chambly
Prochaines élections: 5e novembre 2017
Diane Lavoie, Mairesse, 450-467-2835
Louise Allie, Conseillère, 450-446-4201, Wards: 1
Renée Trudel, Conseillère, 514-718-2317, Wards: 2
Odette Martin, Conseillère, 450-536-2586, Wards: 3
Denis Corriveau, Conseiller, 450-464-2435, Wards: 4
Guy Bédard, Conseiller, 450-446-7837, Wards: 5

Pierre Verret, Conseiller, 450-467-0630, Wards: 6
Réginald Gagnon, Conseillère, 514-569-4500, Wards: 7
Jean-Yves Labadie, Conseiller, 450-446-0347, Wards: 8
Véronique Landry, Directrice, Services juridiques et Greffe, 450-467-2835
Martine Vallières, CA, MAP, Directrice générale, 450-467-2835
Cathy Goyette, Directrice, Finances et trésorerie, 450-467-2835
Claudia De Courval, ing., Directrice, Génie, 450-467-2835
Sylvain Gagnon, Directeur, Travaux publics, 450-467-2835
Donald Lebrun, Directeur, Sécurité incendie, 450-467-2835
Daniel Marineau, Directeur, Loisirs et vie communautaire, 450-467-2835

Blainville
1000, ch du Plan-Bouchard
Blainville, QC J7C 3S9
Tél: 450-434-5200; *Téléc:* 450-434-8295
accueil@blainville.ca
www.ville.blainville.qc.ca
Entité municipal: City
Incorporation: 1er juillet 1968; *Area:* 54,62 km2
Comté ou district: Thérèse-De Blainville; Communauté métropolitaine de Montréal; *Population au 2011:* 53,510
Circonscription(s) électorale(s) provinciale(s): Blainville; Groulx
Circonscription(s) électorale(s) fédérale(s): Thérèse-De Blainville
Prochaines élections: 5e novembre 2017
Richard Perreault, Maire
Liza Poulin, Conseillère, Wards: 1. Fontainebleau
Alain Portelance, Conseiller, Wards: 2. Côte-Saint-Louis
Serge Paquette, Conseiller, Wards: 3. Saint-Rédempteur
Guy Frigon, Conseiller, Wards: 4. Plan-Bouchard
Normand Dupont, Conseiller, Wards: 5. Notre-Dame-de-l'Assomption
Nicole Ruel, Conseillère, Wards: 6. Chante-Bois
Patrick Marineau, Conseiller, Wards: 7. Hirondelles
Alexandre Poce, Conseiller, Wards: 8. Alençon
François Garand, Conseiller, Wards: 9. Renaissance
Marie-Claude Collin, Conseillère, Wards: 10. Blainvillier
Claude Bertrand, Greffier et directeur, Services juridiques
Éric Lachapelle, Directeur général
Lorraine Barry, Trésorière et directrice, Finances
Michel Chouinard, Directeur, Sécurité incendies
Gaston Courtemanche, Directeur, Génie
Linda Ouimet, Directrice, Police
Jocelyn Tremblay, Directeur, Travaux publics
Annie Lévesque, Contact, Urbanisme et aménagement durable du territoire

Boisbriand
940, boul de la Grande-Allée
Boisbriand, QC J7G 2J7
Tél: 450-435-1954; *Téléc:* 450-435-6398
www.ville.boisbriand.qc.ca
Entité municipal: City
Incorporation: 1er janvier 1946; *Area:* 26,43 km2
Comté ou district: Thérèse-De Blainville; Communauté métropolitaine de Montréal; *Population au 2011:* 26,816
Circonscription(s) électorale(s) provinciale(s): Groulx
Circonscription(s) électorale(s) fédérale(s): Rivière-des-Mille-Iles
Prochaines élections: 5e novembre 2017
Marlene Cordato, Mairesse, 450-435-1954
Lyne Levert, Conseillère, 450-435-8979, Wards: 1. Sanche
Érick Rémy, Conseiller, 514-234-2949, Wards: 2. DuGué
Christine Beaudette, Conseillère, 450-433-9957, Wards: 3. Filion
Jonathan Thibault, Conseiller, 514-758-6538, Wards: 4. Dubois
Daniel Kaeser, Conseiller, 450-434-0004, Wards: 5. Brosseau
Denis Hébert, Conseiller, 514-806-4774, Wards: 6. Labelle
Mario Lavallée, Conseiller, 514-908-7622, Wards: 7. Desjardins
Lori Doucet, Conseiller, 514-971-1188, Wards: 8. Dion
Dianne Grenier, Greffière, 450-435-1954
René Lachance, Directeur général, 450-435-1954
André Drainville, Trésorier, 450-435-1954
André Lapointe, Directeur, Génie, 450-435-1954
Denis LeChasseur, Directeur, Urbanisme, 450-435-1954

Boucherville
500, rue de la Rivière-aux-Pins
Boucherville, QC J4B 2Z7
Tél: 450-449-8100; *Téléc:* 450-655-0086
information@boucherville.ca
www.boucherville.ca
Entité municipal: City
Incorporation: 1er janvier 2006; *Area:* 69,33 km2
Comté ou district: Communauté métropolitaine de Montréal; *Population au 2011:* 40,753
Circonscription(s) électorale(s) provinciale(s): Montarville
Circonscription(s) électorale(s) fédérale(s): Pierre-Boucher-Les Patriotes-Verchères
Prochaines élections: 5e novembre 2017
Jean Martel, Maire
Yan Savaria-Laquerre, Conseiller, Wards: 1. Marie-Victorin
Raouf Absi, Conseiller, Wards: 2. Rivière-aux-Pins
Josée Bissonnette, Conseillère, Wards: 3. Découvreurs
Anne Barabé, Conseillère, Wards: 4. Harmonie
Dominic Lévesque, Conseiller, Wards: 5. Seigneurie
Magalie Queval, Conseillère, Wards: 6. Saint-Louis
Jacqueline Boubane, Conseillère, Wards: 7. Normandie
Lise Roy, Conseillère, Wards: 8. Boisé
Marie-Pier Lamarche, Greffière, 450-449-8605, Fax: 450-655-0086
Claude Caron, Directeur général, 450-449-8125, Fax: 450-449-8370
Gaston Perron, Directeur, Finances, 450-449-8115, Fax: 450-449-1534
Nadia Rousseau, Directrice, Urbanisme et de l'environnement, 450-449-8620, Fax: 450-449-0989
Marie-Josée Salvail, Directrice, Travaux publics et des approvisionnements, 450-449-8630, Fax: 450-449-8344

Brossard
2001, boul Rome
Brossard, QC J4W 3K5
Tél: 450-923-6311
services@brossard.ca
www.ville.brossard.qc.ca
Entité municipal: City
Incorporation: 1er janvier 2006; *Area:* 44,77 km2
Comté ou district: Communauté métropolitaine de Montréal; *Population au 2011:* 79,273
Circonscription(s) électorale(s) provinciale(s): La Pinière
Circonscription(s) électorale(s) fédérale(s): Brossard-Saint Lambert
Prochaines élections: 5e novembre 2017
Paul Leduc, Maire, 450-923-6325
Steve Gagnon, Conseiller, 450-923-6304, Wards: 1
Pierre O'Donoughue, Conseiller, 450-923-6304, Wards: 2
Francine Raymond, Conseillère, 450-923-6304, Wards: 3
Serge Séguin, Conseiller, 450-923-6304, Wards: 4
Claudio Benedetti, Conseiller, 450-923-6304, Wards: 5
Alexandre Plante, Conseiller, 450-923-6304, Wards: 6
Antoine Assaf, Conseiller, 450-923-6304, Wards: 7
Pierre Jetté, Conseiller, 450-923-6304, Wards: 8
Doreen Assaad, Conseillère, 450-923-6304, Wards: 9
Daniel Lucier, Conseiller, 450-923-6304, Wards: 10
Isabelle Grenier, Greffière et directrice, 450-923-6304
Nicolas Bouchard, Directeur général, 450-923-6327
Patrick Quirion, Trésorier et directeur, Finances, 450-923-6304
Luc Duval, Directeur, Travaux publics, 450-923-6304
Marie-Chantal Verrier, Directrice, Génie, 450-923-6304
Mario Verville, Directeur, Urbanisme

Candiac
100, boul Montcalm nord
Candiac, QC J5R 3L8
Tél: 450-444-6000; *Téléc:* 450-444-2480
www.ville.candiac.qc.ca
Entité municipal: City
Incorporation: 31 janvier 1957; *Area:* 16,40 km2
Comté ou district: Roussillon; Communauté métropolitaine de Montréal; *Population au 2011:* 19,876
Circonscription(s) électorale(s) provinciale(s): La Prairie
Circonscription(s) électorale(s) fédérale(s): La Prairie
Prochaines élections: 5e novembre 2017
Normand Dyotte, Maire
Thérèse Gatien, Conseillère, Wards: 1. Promenade
Vincent Chatel, Conseiller, Wards: 2. Saint-Laurent
Kevin Vocino, Conseiller, Wards: 3. Champlain
Anne Scott, Conseillère, Wards: 4. Taschereau
Daniel Grenier, Conseiller, Wards: 5. Montcalm
Marie-Josée Lemieux, Conseiller, Wards: 6. Jean-Leman
Céline Lévesque, Greffière
David C. Johnstone, Directeur général
Diane Dufresne, Trésorière et directrice
Marie Dupont, Directrice et urbaniste, Planification et développement du territoire (urbanisme)
Réjean Vigneault, ing., Directeur, Services techniques, division Génie

Chambly
56, rue Martel
Chambly, QC J3L 1V3
Tél: 450-658-8788; *Téléc:* 450-447-4525
www.ville.chambly.qc.ca
Entité municipal: City
Incorporation: 26 octobre 1848; *Area:* 25,01 km2
Comté ou district: La Vallée-du-Richelieu; Communauté métropolitaine de Montréal; *Population au 2011:* 25,571
Circonscription(s) électorale(s) provinciale(s): Chambly
Circonscription(s) électorale(s) fédérale(s): Beloeil-Chambly
Prochaines élections: 5e novembre 2017
Denis Lavoie, Maire, 450-658-8788
Sandra Bolduc, Conseillère, 514-962-7610, Wards: 1. Canton
Marc Bouthillier, Conseiller, 450-447-8485, Wards: 2. Bassin
Richard Tetreault, Conseiller, 450-658-4282, Wards: 4. Petite Rivière
Serge Gélinas, Conseiller, 514-462-0151, Wards: 5. Antoine-Louis-Fréchette
Luc Ricard, Conseiller, 450-447-1829, Wards: 6. Louis-Franquet
Jean Roy, Conseiller, 450-447-6152, Wards: 7. Ruisseau
Francine Guay, Conseillère, 450-447-5881, Wards: 8. Grandes-Terres
Nancy Poirier, Greffière, 450-658-8788, Fax: 450-658-4214
Jacques Beauregard, Directeur général, 450-658-8788, Fax: 450-447-4525
Annie Nepton, Directrice & trésorière, Service des finances, 450-658-8788, Fax: 450-447-4525
Sébastien Bouchard, Directeur, Technique et environnement, 450-658-2626, Fax: 450-658-3366
Stéphane Dumberry, Directeur, Service d'incendie, 450-658-0662, Fax: 450-658-7976
Michel Potvin, Directeur, Travaux publics, 450-658-2626, Fax: 450-658-3366

Châteauguay
5, boul d'Youville
Châteauguay, QC J6J 2P8
Tél: 450-698-3000; *Téléc:* 450-698-3019
info@ville.chateauguay.qc.ca
www.ville.chateauguay.qc.ca
Entité municipal: City
Incorporation: 3e novembre 1975; *Area:* 35,37 km2
Comté ou district: Roussillon; Communauté métropolitaine de Montréal; *Population au 2011:* 45,904
Circonscription(s) électorale(s) provinciale(s): Châteauguay
Circonscription(s) électorale(s) fédérale(s): Châteauguay-Lacolle
Prochaines élections: 5e novembre 2017
Nathalie Simon, Mairesse
Barry Doyle, Conseiller, 450-699-1984, Wards: 1. La Noue
Pierre Gloutnay, Conseiller, Wards: 2. Filgate
Michel Pinard, Conseiller, 450-698-1485, Wards: 3. Robutel
Lucie Laberge, Conseillère, 450-691-4459, Wards: 4. Bumbray
Marcel Deschamps, Conseiller, 450-699-1120, Wards: 5. Salaberry
Mike Gendron, Conseiller, 514-829-1986, Wards: 6. Lang
Marie-France Reid, Conseillère, 450-692-7029, Wards: 7. Le Moyne
Alain Côté, Conseiller, 450-692-8877, Wards: 8. D'Youville
Vicky Jean, Greffière, 450-698-3246, Fax: 450-698-3259
Daniel Carrier, Directeur général
Manon Tourigny, Trésorière
Stéphane Fleury, Directeur et Chef de police
Michel Lussier, Directeur, Service sécurité d'incendie
Jocelyn Boulanger, Responsable, Urbanisme et émission de permis et de certificats municipaux

Côte-Saint-Luc
5801, boul Cavendish
Côte-Saint-Luc, QC H4W 3C3
Tél: 514-485-6800; *Téléc:* 514-485-8920
info@cotesaintluc.org
www.cotesaintluc.org
Entité municipal: City
Incorporation: 1er janvier 2006; *Area:* 7,35 km2
Comté ou district: Communauté métropolitaine de Montréal; *Population au 2011:* 32,321
Circonscription(s) électorale(s) provinciale(s): D'Arcy-McGee
Circonscription(s) électorale(s) fédérale(s): Mount Royal
Prochaines élections: 5e novembre 2017
Mitchell Brownstein, Maire, 514-485-6945
Sam Goldbloom, Conseiller, Wards: 1
Mike Cohen, Counseiller, Wards: 2
Dida Berku, Conseillère, Wards: 3
Steven Erdelyi, Conseiller, Wards: 4
Allan J. Levine, Conseiller, Wards: 5
Glenn J. Nashen, Conseiller, Wards: 6
Sidney Benizri, Conseiller, Wards: 7
Ruth Kovac, Conseillère, Wards: 8
Jonathan Shecter, Greffier et directeur, Services juridiques, 514-485-6800
Nadia Di Furia, Directrice générale (intérim), 514-485-8645
Ruth Kleinman, Trésorier, 514-485-6800
Beatrice Newman, Directrice, Travaux publics, 514-485-6800
Jordy Reichson, Directeur, Protection civile, 514-485-6800
Charles Senekal, Directeur, Développement urbain, 514-485-6800

Cowansville
220, place Municipale
Cowansville, QC J2K 1T4
Tél: 450-263-0141; *Téléc:* 450-263-9357
hoteldeville@ville.cowansville.qc.ca
www.ville.cowansville.qc.ca
Entité municipal: City
Incorporation: 1er janvier 1876; *Area:* 48,79 km2
Comté ou district: Brome-Missisquoi; *Population au 2011:* 12,489

Circonscription(s) électorale(s) provinciale(s): Brome-Missisquoi
Circonscription(s) électorale(s) fédérale(s): Brome-Missisquoi
Prochaines élections: 5e novembre 2017
Arthur Fauteux, Maire, 450-263-0141
Michel Charbonneau, Conseiller, 450-266-1146, Wards: Bruck
Yvon Pepin, Conseiller, 450-263-1426, Wards: Davignon
Sylvie Beauregard, Conseillère, 450-266-4312, Wards: Fordyce
Corinne Labbé, Conseillère, 450-522-9954, Wards: Ruiter
Lucille Robert, Conseillère, 450-263-3779, Wards: Sweetsburg
Marie-France Beaudry, Conseillère, 450-263-3284, Wards: Vilas
Sandra Ruel, Greffière
Claude Lalonde, Directeur général
Josée Tassé, Trésorier
Gilles Deschamps, Directeur et Chef, Brigade des pompiers
Jean-François Daigle, Directeur, Urbanisme
Claude Lalonde, Responsable, Travaux publics
Manon Moreau, Responsable, Émission de permis et de certificats municipaux

Deux-Montagnes

803, ch d'Oka
Deux-Montagnes, QC J7R 1L8
Tél: 450-473-2796; *Téléc:* 450-473-2417
www.ville.deux-montagnes.qc.ca
Entité municipal: City
Incorporation: 18 août 1921; *Area:* 5,82 km2
Comté ou district: Deux-Montagnes; Communauté métropolitaine de Montréal; *Population au 2011:* 17,552
Circonscription(s) électorale(s) provinciale(s): Deux-Montagnes
Circonscription(s) électorale(s) fédérale(s): Rivière-des-Mille-Îles
Prochaines élections: 5e novembre 2017
Denis Martin, Maire, 450-473-8898
Michel Mendes, Conseiller, 450-473-1145, Wards: Coteau
Frédéric Berithaume, Conseiller, 450-473-1145, Wards: Gare
Margaret Lavallée, Conseillère, 450-473-1145, Wards: Golf
Manon Robitaille, Conseillère, 450-473-1145, Wards: Grand-Moulin
Karine Gauthier, Conseillère, 450-473-1145, Wards: Lac
Micheline Groulx Stabile, Conseillère, 450-473-1145, Wards: Olympia
Jacques Robichaud, Greffier, Fax: 450-473-4434
Jean Langevin, Directeur général
Julie Guindon, Directrice, Finances & Trésorerie, 450-473-2796, Fax: 450-473-3412
Denis Berthelette, Directeur, Gestion du territoire, 450-473-4688, Fax: 450-473-8336

Dolbeau-Mistassini

1100, boul Wallberg
Dolbeau-Mistassini, QC G8L 1G7
Tél: 418-276-0160; *Téléc:* 418-276-8312
hotelville@ville.dolbeau-mistassini.qc.ca
www.ville.dolbeau-mistassini.qc.ca
Entité municipal: City
Incorporation: 17 décembre 1997; *Area:* 296,57 km2
Comté ou district: Maria-Chapdelaine; *Population au 2011:* 14,384
Circonscription(s) électorale(s) provinciale(s): Roberval
Circonscription(s) électorale(s) fédérale(s): Lac-St-Jean
Prochaines élections: 5e novembre 2017
Richard Hébert, Maire
Pascal Cloutier, Conseiller, Wards: 1
Luc Simard, Conseiller, Wards: 2
Daniel Savard, Conseiller, Wards: 3
Rémi Rousseau, Conseiller, Wards: 4
Claire Néron, Conseillère, Wards: 5
Françoise Bergeron, Conseillère, Wards: 6
André Côté, Greffier, 418-276-0160
Frédéric Lemieux, Directeur général, 418-276-0160
Suzie Gagnon, Trésorière et directrice, Finances, 418-276-0160
Denis Boily, Directeur, Travaux publics, 418-276-1534
Daniel Cantin, Directeur, Sécurité incendie, 418-276-0160
Ghislain Néron, Directeur, Ingénierie, 418-276-1534
Thérèse Tremblay, Responsable, Urbanisme, 418-276-0160

Dollard-des-Ormeaux

12001, boul De Salaberry
Dollard-des-Ormeaux, QC H9B 2A7
Tél: 514-684-1010; *Téléc:* 514-684-6894
ville@ddo.qc.ca
www.ville.ddo.qc.ca
Entité municipal: City
Incorporation: 1er janvier 2006; *Area:* 15,20 km2
Comté ou district: Communauté métropolitaine de Montréal; *Population au 2011:* 49,637
Circonscription(s) électorale(s) provinciale(s): Robert-Baldwin
Circonscription(s) électorale(s) fédérale(s): Pierrefonds—Dollard
Prochaines élections: 5e novembre 2017
Ed Janiszewski, Maire
Zoé Bayouk, Conseillère, Wards: 1
Errol Johnson, Conseiller, Wards: 2
Mickey Max Guttman, Conseiller, Wards: 3
Herbert Brownstein, Conseiller, Wards: 4
Morris Vesely, Conseiller, Wards: 5
Peter Prassas, Conseiller, Wards: 6
Alex Bottausci, Conseiller, Wards: 7
Colette Gauthier, Conseillère, Wards: 8
Sophie Valois, Greffière, 514-684-9335
Jack Benzaquen, Directeur général, 514-684-8060
Caroline Thall, Trésorière
Mark Gervais, Directeur, Travaux publics, 514-684-1034
Anna Polito, Directrice, Aménagement, 514-684-1034
Bernard Côté, Évaluateur signataire

Dorval

60, av Martin
Dorval, QC H9S 3R4
Tél: 514-633-4040; *Téléc:* 514-633-4138
dorval@ville.dorval.qc.ca
www.ville.dorval.qc.ca
Entité municipal: City
Incorporation: 1er janvier 2006; *Area:* 20,64 km2
Comté ou district: Communauté métropolitaine de Montréal; *Population au 2011:* 18,208
Circonscription(s) électorale(s) provinciale(s): Marquette
Circonscription(s) électorale(s) fédérale(s): Dorval-Lachine-LaSalle
Prochaines élections: 5e novembre 2017
Edgar Rouleau, Maire
Claude Valiquet, Conseiller, Wards: 1
Michel Hébert, Conseiller, Wards: 2
Daniel da Chao, Conseiller, Wards: 3
Marc Doret, Conseiller, Wards: 4
Heather Allard, Conseillère, Wards: 5
Margo Heron, Conseillère, Wards: 6
Chantale Bilodeau, Greffière et directrice, Service des affaires publiques, 514-633-4142
Robert Bourbeau, Directeur général, 514-633-4044
André Girard, Trésorier et directeur, Services administratifs, 514-633-4040
Carl Minville, Directeur, Travaux publics, 514-633-4046
Gilles Rochette, Directeur, Loisirs et de la culture, 514-633-4000
Mario St-Jean, Directeur, Aménagement urbain, 514-633-4084

Drummondville

CP 398
415, rue Lindsay
Drummondville, QC J2B 6W3
Tél: 819-478-6550; *Téléc:* 819-478-3363
communications@ville.drummondville.qc.ca
www.ville.drummondville.qc.ca
Entité municipal: City
Incorporation: 7e juillet 2004; *Area:* 249,80 km2
Comté ou district: Drummond; *Population au 2011:* 71,852
Circonscription(s) électorale(s) provinciale(s): Johnson; Drummond-Bois-Francs
Circonscription(s) électorale(s) fédérale(s): Drummond
Prochaines élections: 5e novembre 2017
Note: Effective July 7, 2004, the municipalities of St-Charles-de-Drummond & St-Joachim-de-Courval & the cities of St-Nicéphore & Drummondville regrouped to form the new city of Drummondville
Alexandre Cusson, Maire
Cathy Bernier, Conseillère, Wards: 1
Roberto Léveillée, Conseiller, Wards: 2
Catherine Lassonde, Conseillère, Wards: 3
Isabelle Marquis, Conseillère, Wards: 4
John Husk, Conseiller, Wards: 5
William Moreales, Conseiller, Wards: 6
Alain Martel, Conseiller, Wards: 7
Yves Grondin, Conseiller, Wards: 8
Annick Bellavance, Conseillère, Wards: 9
Vincent Chouinard, Conseiller, Wards: 10
Daniel Pelletier, Conseiller, Wards: 11
Pierre Levasseur, Conseiller, Wards: 12
Mélanie Ouellet, Greffière, 819-478-6554, Fax: 819-478-3363
Claude Proulx, Directeur général, 819-478-6557, Fax: 819-478-3363
Benoît Carignan, CPA, CGA, Trésorier et director, Finances, 819-478-6559, Fax: 819-478-3164
Denis Jauron, Directeur, Urbanisme, 819-478-6563, Fax: 819-850-1281
Roger Leblanc, Directeur, Développement durable et de l'environnement, 819-477-5937, Fax: 819-474-6766
Marc Proulx, Director, Travaux publics, 819-478-6572, Fax: 819-478-8531

Gaspé

25, rue de l'Hôtel-de-Ville
Gaspé, QC G4X 2A5
Tél: 418-368-2104; *Téléc:* 418-368-8532
info@ville.gaspe.qc.ca
www.ville.gaspe.qc.ca
Entité municipal: City
Incorporation: 1er janvier 1971; *Area:* 1446,95 km2
Comté ou district: La Côte-de-Gaspé; *Population au 2011:* 15,163
Circonscription(s) électorale(s) provinciale(s): Gaspé
Circonscription(s) électorale(s) fédérale(s): Gaspésie-Les Iles-de-la-Madeleine
Prochaines élections: 5e novembre 2017
Daniel Côté, Maire
Carmelle Mathurin, Conseillère, Wards: 1
Réginald Cotton, Conseiller, Wards: 2
Nelson O'Connor, Conseiller, Wards: 3
Marcel Fournier, Conseiller, Wards: 4
Aline Perry, Conseillère, Wards: 5
Ghislain Smith, Conseiller, Wards: 6
Isabelle Vézina, Directrice, Greffe et services juridiques
Sébastien Fournier, Directeur général
Michel Cotton, Directeur, Travaux publics
Dave Ste-Croix, Directeur, Services administratifs et de l'aéroport
Jocelyn Villeneuve, Directrice, Aménagement du territoire, Urbanisme et Environnement
Alain Dunn, Coordonnateur, Gestion des matières résiduelles

Gatineau

CP 1970 Hull
25, rue Laurier
Gatineau, QC J8X 3Y9
Tél: 819-595-2002
www.ville.gatineau.qc.ca
Other Information: Sans frais: 1-866-299-2002
Entité municipal: City
Incorporation: 1er janvier 2002; *Area:* 344,16 km2
Population au 2011: 265,349
Circonscription(s) électorale(s) provinciale(s): Chapleau; Gatineau; Hull; Papineau; Pontiac
Circonscription(s) électorale(s) fédérale(s): Gatineau; Hull—Aylmer; Pontiac; Argenteuil-La Petite-Nation
Prochaines élections: 5e novembre 2017
Maxime Pedneaud-Jobin, Maire, 819-595-7100
Josée Lacasse, Conseillère, Wards: 1. Aylmer
Mike Duggan, Conseiller, Wards: 2. Lucerne
Richard M. Bégin, Conseiller, Wards: 3. Deschênes
Maxime Tremblay, Conseiller, Wards: 4. Plateau
Jocelyn Blondin, Conseillère, Wards: 5. Man.-des-Trem.-Val-Tétreau
Mireille Apollon, Conseillère, Wards: 6. Orée-du-Parc
Louise Boudrias, Conseillère, Wards: 7. Parc-de-la-Mont.-St-Raymond
Denise Laferrière, Conseillère, Wards: 8. Hull-Wright
Cédric Tessier, Conseiller, Wards: 9. Limbour
Denis Tassé, Conseiller, Wards: 10. Touraine
Myriam Nadeau, Conseillère, Wards: 11. Pointe-Gatineau
Gilles Carpentier, Conseiller, Wards: 12. Carrefour-de-l'Hôpital
Daniel Champagne, Conseiller, Wards: 13. Versant
Sylvie Goneau, Conseillère, Wards: 14. Bellevue
Stéphane Lauzon, Conseiller, Wards: 15. Lac-Beauchamp
Jean Lessard, Conseiller, Wards: 16. Rivière-Blanche
Marc Carrière, Conseiller, Wards: 17. Masson-Angers
Martin Lajeunesse, Conseiller, Wards: 18. Buckingham
Suzanne Ouellet, Greffière
Marie-Hélène Lajoie, Directrice générale
André Barbeau, Trésorier et directeur, Service des finances
Jean Boivin, Directeur, Communications
André Bonneau, Directeur, Sécurité incendie
Mario Harel, Directeur/Chef, Police
Marie-Claude Martel, Directrice, Urbanisme
Marc Pageau, Directeur, Ressources humaines
André Turgeon, Directeur, Environnement

Granby

87, rue Principale
Granby, QC J2G 2T8
Tél: 450-776-8282; *Téléc:* 450-776-8231
communication@ville.granby.qc.ca
www.ville.granby.qc.ca
Entité municipal: City
Incorporation: 1er janvier 2007; *Area:* 156,68 km2
Comté ou district: La Haute-Yamaska; *Population au 2011:* 63,433
Circonscription(s) électorale(s) provinciale(s): Granby
Circonscription(s) électorale(s) fédérale(s): Shefford
Prochaines élections: 5e novembre 2017
Pascal Bonin, Maire, 450-776-8228
Stéphane Giard, Conseiller, 450-521-3250, Wards: 1
Jean-Luc Nappert, Conseiller, 450-994-3945, Wards: 2
Pierre Breton, Conseiller, 450-777-7695, Wards: 3
Jocelyn Dupuis, Conseiller, 450-204-3388, Wards: 4
Joël Desmarais, Conseiller, 450-405-8555, Wards: 5
Serges Ruel, Conseiller, 450-405-4446, Wards: 6
Robert Riel, Conseiller, 450-522-2417, Wards: 7

Éric Duchesneau, Conseiller, 450-991-6585, Wards: 8
Robert Vincent, Conseiller, 450-522-6989, Wards: 9
Michel Mailhot, Conseiller, 450-372-8317, Wards: 10
Catherine Bouchard, Greffière, 450-776-8275, Fax: 450-776-8278
Michel Pineault, Directeur général, 450-776-8232, Fax: 450-776-8279
Jean-Pierre Renaud, Trésorier, 450-776-8287, Fax: 450-776-8384
Dominique Desmet, Directrice, Urbanisme, 450-776-8256, Fax: 450-776-8386
Sylvain Filbotte, Directeur, Travaux publics, 450-776-8366, Fax: 450-776-8370
Pierre Lacombe, Directeur, Incendies, 450-776-8344, Fax: 450-839-0370

L'Île-Perrot
110, boul Perrot
L'Île-Perrot, QC J7V 3G1
Tél: 514-453-1751; *Téléc:* 514-453-2432
ville@ile-perrot.qc.ca
www.ileperrot.qc.ca
Entité municipal: City
Incorporation: 1er juillet 1855; *Area:* 4,86 km2
Comté ou district: Vaudreuil-Soulanges; Communauté métropolitaine de Montréal; *Population au 2011:* 10,503
Circonscription(s) électorale(s) provinciale(s): Vaudreuil
Circonscription(s) électorale(s) fédérale(s): Vaudreuil-Soulanges
Prochaines élections: 5e novembre 2017
Marc Roy, Maire, 514-453-6975
Daniel Taillefer, Conseiller, 514-453-4774, Wards: 2
Marcel Rainville, Conseiller, 514-902-1352, Wards: 3
Michelle L. LeCavalier, Conseillère, 514-453-2599, Wards: 4
Kim Comeau, Conseiller, 514-453-0243, Wards: 5
Daniel Leblanc, Conseiller, 514-425-0403, Wards: 6
Lucie Coallier, Greffière, 514-453-1751
André Morin, Directeur général, 514-453-1751
Danielle Rioux, Trésorière, 514-453-1751
Sébastien Carrière, Directeur, Urbanisme et environnement, 514-453-1751
Roger Forgues, Directeur, Usines, 514-453-1751
Éric Parna, Directeur, Sécurité incendie, 514-453-1751
Luc Prévost, Directeur, Travaux publics, 514-453-1751

Les îles-de-la-Madeleine
460, ch Principal
Cap-aux-Meules, QC G4T 1A1
Tel: 418-986-3100; *Fax:* 418-986-6962
communications@muniles.ca
www.muniles.ca
Municipal Type: City
Incorporated: 1er janvier 2002; *Area:* 166,39 km2
Population in 2011: 12,781
Provincial Electoral District(s): Iles-de-la-Madeleine
Federal Electoral District(s): Gaspésie—Iles-de-la-Madeleine
Next Election: 5e novembre 2017
Jonathan Lapierre, Maire
Germain Leblanc, Conseiller, Wards: 1. L'Ile-du-Havre-Aubert
Léon Deraspe, Conseiller, Wards: 2. L'Étang-du-Nord
Richard Leblanc, Conseiller, Wards: 3. Cap-aux-Meules/Ile-d'Entrée
Roger Chevarie, Conseiller, Wards: 4. Fatima
Jean-Mathieu Poirier, Conseiller, Wards: 5. Havre-aux-Maisons
Gaétan Richard, Conseiller, Wards: 6. Grande-Entrée
Jean-Yves Lebreux, Greffier
Hubert Poirier, Directeur général
Pierre Charron, Directeur, Finances
Jeannot Gagnon, Directrice, Développement du milieu et de l'aménagement du territoire
Jean Richard, Directeur, Hygiène du milieu, des bâtiments et de la sécurité publique

Joliette
614, boul Manseau
Joliette, QC J6E 3E4
Tél: 450-753-8000; *Téléc:* 450-753-8199
www.ville.joliette.qc.ca
Entité municipal: City
Incorporation: 12 novembre 1966; *Area:* 22,36 km2
Comté ou district: Joliette; *Population au 2011:* 19,621
Circonscription(s) électorale(s) provinciale(s): Joliette
Circonscription(s) électorale(s) fédérale(s): Joliette
Prochaines élections: 5e novembre 2017
Alain Beaudry, Maire, 450-753-8020
Luc Beauséjour, Conseiller, Wards: 1
Normand-Guy Lépine, Conseiller, Wards: 2
Patrice Trudel, Conseiller, Wards: 3
Danielle Landreville, Conseillère, Wards: 4
Patrick Lasalle, Conseiller, Wards: 5
Yves Liard, Conseiller, Wards: 6
Richard Leduc, Conseiller, Wards: 7
Mylène Mayer, Directrice, Greffe et affaires juridiques, 450-960-8998
François Pépin, Directeur général, 450-753-8031
France Venne, Directrice, Opérations financières, 450-753-8185
David Beauséjour, Directeur, Travaux publics et services techniques, 450-753-8080
Carl Gauthier, Directeur, Incendies, 450-753-8154

Kirkland
17200, boul Hymus
Kirkland, QC H9J 3Y8
Tél: 514-694-4100; *Téléc:* 514-630-2711
www.ville.kirkland.qc.ca
Entité municipal: City
Incorporation: 1er janvier 2006; *Area:* 9,64 km2
Comté ou district: Communauté métropolitaine de Montréal; *Population au 2011:* 21,253
Circonscription(s) électorale(s) provinciale(s): Nelligan
Circonscription(s) électorale(s) fédérale(s): Lac-Saint-Louis
Prochaines élections: 5e novembre 2017
Michel Gibson, Maire, 514-694-4100
Michael Brown, Conseiller, 514-694-4100, Wards: 1. Timberlea
Luciano Piciacchia, Conseiller, 514-694-4100, Wards: 2. Holleuffer
Tony Di Gennaro, Conseiller, 514-694-4100, Wards: 3. Brunswick
Domenico Zito, Conseiller, 514-694-4100, Wards: 4. Lacey Green Ouest
Brian Swinburne, Conseiller, 514-694-4100, Wards: 5. Lacey Green Est
John Morson, Conseiller, 514-694-4100, Wards: 6. Canvin
Paul Dufort, Conseiller, 514-694-4100, Wards: 7. Saint-Charles
André Allard, Conseiller, 514-694-4100, Wards: 8. Summerhill
Martine Musau, Greffière et directrice, Affaires juridiques, 514-694-4100
Joe Sanalitro, Directeur général, 514-694-4100
Nadine Bassila, Trésorière et directrice, Services administratifs, 514-694-4100
Martin Cuerrier, Directeur, Travaux publics, 514-694-4100
Lise Labrosse, Directrice, Communications et relations publiques, 514-694-4100
Samir Massabni, Directeur, Ingénierie et aménagement urbain, 514-694-4100

Lachute
380, rue Principale
Lachute, QC J8H 1Y2
Tél: 450-562-3781; *Téléc:* 450-562-1431
lachute@ville.lachute.qc.ca
www.ville.lachute.qc.ca
Entité municipal: City
Incorporation: 30 avril 1966; *Area:* 111,20 km2
Comté ou district: Argenteuil; *Population au 2011:* 12,551
Circonscription(s) électorale(s) provinciale(s): Argenteuil
Circonscription(s) électorale(s) fédérale(s): Argenteuil-La Petite-Nation
Prochaines élections: 5e novembre 2017
Carl Péloquin, Maire
Marcelle L. Louis-Seize, Conseillère, Wards: 1
Mario Beaudin, Conseiller, Wards: 2
Denis Richer, Conseiller, Wards: 3
Alain Lanoue, Conseiller, Wards: 4
Guy Desforges, Conseiller, Wards: 5
Hugo Lajoie, Conseiller, Wards: 6
Lynda-Ann Murray, Greffière et directrice, Affaires juridiques
Pierre Gionet, Directeur général
Nathalie Piret, Trésorière
Claude Giguère, Directeur, Sécurité incendie
Pascal Joly, Directeur, Urbanisme
Pascal Larocque, Directeur, Travaux publics
Gilles Neveu, ing., Directeur, Génie

Laval
Hôtel de Ville
CP 422 St-Martin
1, Place du Souvenir
Laval, QC H7V 3Z4
Tél: 450-978-8000; *Téléc:* 450-978-5943
info@ville.laval.qc.ca
www.ville.laval.qc.ca
Other Information: Sans frais: 311
Entité municipal: City
Incorporation: 6e août 1965; *Area:* 245,40 km2
Comté ou district: Communauté métropolitaine de Montréal; *Population au 2011:* 401,553
Circonscription(s) électorale(s) provinciale(s): Chomedey; Fabre; Laval-des-Rapides; Mille-Iles; Sainte-Rose; Vimont
Circonscription(s) électorale(s) fédérale(s): Alfred-Pellan;Bécancour-Nicolet-Saurel; Laval-Les Iles;Marc-Aurèle-Fortin; Vimy
Prochaines élections: 5e novembre 2017
Marc Demers, Maire, 450-662-4140
Jacques St-Jean, Conseiller, 450-666-2509, Wards: 1. Saint-François
Paolo Galati, Conseiller, 438-985-4589, Wards: 2. Saint-Vincent-de-Paul
Christiane Yoakim, Conseillère, 514-245-9878, Wards: 3. Val-des-Arbres
Stéphane Boyer, Conseiller, 438-870-1110, Wards: 4. Duvernay-Pont-Viau
Daniel Hébert, Conseiller, 514-886-8809, Wards: 5. Marigot
Sandra Desmeules, Conseillère, 514-451-0192, Wards: 6. Concorde-Bois-de-Boulogne
Raynald Adams, Conseiller, 514-913-9205, Wards: 7. Renaud
Michel Poissant, Conseiller, 514-867-6717, Wards: 8. Vimont
David De Cotis, Conseiller, 514-467-1712, Wards: 9. Saint-Bruno
Jocelyne Frédéric-Gauthier, Conseillère, 514-515-1293, Wards: 10. Auteuil
Pierre Anthian, Conseiller, 514-973-1717, Wards: 11. Laval-des-Rapides
Jean Coupal, Conseiller, 450-934-4131, Wards: 12. Souvenir-Labelle
Vasilios Karidogiannis, Conseiller, 514-979-2455, Wards: 13. Abord-à-Plouffe
Aglaia Revelakis, Conseillère, 514-242-5761, Wards: 14. Chomedey
Aline Dib, Conseillère, 514-577-6088, Wards: 15. Saint-Martin
Ray Khalil, Conseiller, 514-825-2493, Wards: 16. Sainte-Dorothée
Nicholas Borne, Conseiller, 514-707-6870, Wards: 17. Laval-les-Iles
Alain Lecompte, Conseiller, 514-686-1044, Wards: 18. Orée-des-bois
Gilbert Dumas, Conseiller, 514-629-2059, Wards: 19. Marc-Aurèle-Fortin
Michel Trottier, Conseiller, 438-884-8942, Wards: 20. Fabreville
Virginie Dufour, Conseillère, 514-712-5261, Wards: 21. Sainte-Rose
Guy Collard, Greffier, 450-978-3966
Serge Lamontagne, Directeur général, 450-978-3676
Suzanne Deshaies, Trésorière et directrice, Finances, 450-978-5704
Sylvain Allard, Directeur, Travaux publics, 450-978-8000
Gilles Benoit, Directeur, Environnement, 450-662-7279
Sylvain Dubois, Directeur, Urbanisme, 450-978-8000
Luc Goulet, Directeur, Ingénierie, 450-680-2999
Robert Séguin, Directeur, Sécurité d'incendie, 450-662-4450
Michèle Galipeau, Vérificatrice générale, 450-978-8715

Lavaltrie
1370, rue Notre-Dame
Lavaltrie, QC J0K 1H0
Tél: 450-586-2921; *Téléc:* 450-586-3939
mairie@ville.lavaltrie.qc.ca
www.ville.lavaltrie.qc.ca
Entité municipal: City
Incorporation: 16 mai 2001; *Area:* 68,61 km2
Comté ou district: D'Autray; *Population au 2011:* 13,267
Circonscription(s) électorale(s) provinciale(s): Berthier
Circonscription(s) électorale(s) fédérale(s): Berthier-Maskinongé
Prochaines élections: 5e novembre 2017
Jean-Claude Gravel, Maire, 450-586-2921
Michele Dawe, Conseillère, 450-586-6759, Wards: 1. Terrasses
Pascal Tremblay, Conseiller, 450-586-0573, Wards: 2. Rivière
Isabelle Charette, Conseillère, 450-586-2921, Wards: 3. Chemin du Roy
Lynda Pelletier, Conseillère, 450-586-3593, Wards: 4. Érablière
Christian Goulet, Conseiller, 450-586-0112, Wards: 5. Boisé
Roland Clermont, Conseiller, 450-935-0926, Wards: 6. Golf
Denis Moreau, Conseiller, 450-586-2314, Wards: 7. Chasse-galerie
Gaétan Bérard, Conseiller, 450-586-3780, Wards: 8. Saint-Antoine
Madeleine Barbeau, Greffière, 450-586-2921
Yvon Mousseau, Directeur général, 450-586-2921
Martine Nadeau, Trésorière, 450-586-2921, Fax: 450-586-4060
André Houle, Directeur, Travaux publics, 450-586-2921, Fax: 450-586-3540

Lévis
2175, ch du Fleuve
Lévis, QC G6W 7W9
Tél: 418-839-2002; *Téléc:* 418-839-5548
levis@ville.levis.qc.ca
www.ville.levis.qc.ca
Entité municipal: City
Incorporation: 1er janvier 2002; *Area:* 443,65 km2
Comté ou district: Communauté métropolitaine de Québec; *Population au 2011:* 138,769
Circonscription(s) électorale(s) provinciale(s): Bellechasse; Chutes-de-la-Chaudière; Lévis
Circonscription(s) électorale(s) fédérale(s): Bellechasse-Les

Etchemins-Lévis; Lévis-Lotbinière
Prochaines élections: 5e novembre 2017
Gilles Lehouillier, Maire
Mario Fortier, Conseiller, Wards: 1
Clément Genest, Conseiller, Wards: 2
René Fortin, Conseiller, Wards: 3
Réjean Lamontagne, Conseiller, Wards: 4
Michel Patry, Conseiller, Wards: 5
Michel Turner, Conseiller, Wards: 6
Guy Dumoulin, Conseiller, Wards: 7
Jean-Pierre Bazinet, Conseiller, Wards: 8
Brigitte Duchesneau, Conseillère, Wards: 9
Pierre Lainesse, Conseiller, Wards: 10
Serge Côté, Conseiller, Wards: 11
Janet Jones, Conseillère, Wards: 12
Robert Maranda, Conseiller, Wards: 13
Fleur Paradis, Conseillère, Wards: 14
Ann Jeffrey, Conseillère, Wards: 15
Danielle Bilodeau, Greffière et directrice, Affaires juridiques, 418-839-2002
Simon Rousseau, Directeur général
Marcel Rodrigue, Trésorier et directeur, Finances et services administratifs, 418-839-2002, Fax: 418-835-8522
René Tremblay, Directeur, Vie communautaire
Jean-Claude Belles-Isles, Directeur, Environnement
Sami Doucet, Directeur, Infrastructures
Christian Brière, Directeur, Communications
Yves Després, Directeur, Sécurité incendie
Manon Gauvreau, Directrice, Ressources humaines
Yves Charette, Chef de police
André Matte, Vérificateur général
Gaëtan Drouin, Directeur, Service de la sécurité incendie

Longueuil
4250, ch de la Savane
Longueuil, QC J3Y 9G4
Tél: 450-463-7311; *Téléc:* 450-463-7400
311@ville.longueuil.qc.ca
www.longueuil.ca
Entité municipal: City
Incorporation: 1er janvier 2002; *Area:* 111,50 km2
Comté ou district: Communauté métropolitaine de Montréal; *Population au 2011:* 231,409
Circonscription(s) électorale(s) provinciale(s): Laporte; Marie-Victorin; Taillon; Vachon
Circonscription(s) électorale(s) fédérale(s): Longueuil-Charles-LeMoyne; Longueuil-Saint-Hubert; Montarville
Prochaines élections: 5e novembre 2017
Caroline St-Hilaire, Mairesse
Robert (Bob) Myles, Conseiller, Greenfield Park, Wards: Greenfield Park
Sylvain Joly, Conseiller, Greenfield Park, Wards: 1
Wade Wilson, Conseiller, Greenfield Park, Wards: 2
Éric Beaulieu, Conseiller, Saint-Hubert, Wards: Iberville
Jacques Lemire, Conseiller, Saint-Hubert, Wards: Laflèche
Lorraine Guay Boivin, Conseillère, Saint-Hubert, Wards: Maraîchers
Jacques E. Poitras, Conseiller, Saint-Hubert, Wards: Parc-de-la-Cité
Nathalie Boisclair, Conseillère, Saint-Hubert, Wards: Vieux-Saint-Hubert-la Savane
Michel Lanctôt, Conseiller, Vieux-Longueuil, Wards: Antoinette-Robidoux
Benoît L'Ecuyer, Conseiller, Vieux-Longueuil, Wards: Boisé-Du Tremblay
Monique Bastien, Conseillère, Vieux-Longueuil, Wards: Coteau-Rouge
Stéphane Richer, Conseiller, Vieux-Longueuil, Wards: Explorateurs
Sylvie Parent, Conseillère, Vieux-Longueuil, Wards: Fatima-Parcours-du-Cerf
Xavier Léger, Conseiller, Vieux-Longueuil, Wards: Georges-Dor
Collette Éthier, Conseillère, Vieux-Longueuil, Wards: LeMoyne-Jacques-Cartier
France Dubé, Conseillère, Vieux-Longueuil, Wards: Parc-Michel-Chartrand
Albert Beaudry, Conseiller, Vieux-Longueuil, Wards: Saint-Charles
Annie Bouchard, Greffière et directrice, Greffe
Patrick Savard, Directeur général
Sylvie Toupin, Directrice, Finances
Michel Brousseau, Directeur, Travaux publics
Alain Desgagné, Directeur, Ressources humaines
Denis Desroches, Directeur, Service de police
Michel L. Lesage, Directeur, Grands projets
Martin Lévesque, Directeur, Environnement et du développement durable
Jean Melançon, Directeur, Service de sécurité incendie
Jean-Pierre Richard, Directeur, Génie
Régis Savard, Directeur, Évaluation

Jacques Tétrault, Directeur, Affaires publiques et institutionnelles
Francine Brunette, Vérificatrice générale

Magog
7, rue Principale est
Magog, QC J1X 1Y4
Tél: 819-843-6501; *Téléc:* 819-843-1091
info@ville.magog.qc.ca
www.ville.magog.qc.ca
Entité municipal: City
Incorporation: 9e octobre 2002; *Area:* 145,68 km2
Comté ou district: Memphrémagog; *Population au 2011:* 25,358
Circonscription(s) électorale(s) provinciale(s): Orford
Circonscription(s) électorale(s) fédérale(s): Brome-Missisquoi; Compton-Stanstead
Prochaines élections: 5e novembre 2017
Note: Depuis le 9 oct., le canton de Magog, le village d'Omerville & la ville de Magog sont regroupés pour former la nouvelle ville de Magog.
Vicki May Hamm, Mairesse, 819-843-2880
Steve Robert, Conseiller, 819-868-2086, Wards: 1. La Rivière
Yvon Lamontagne, Conseiller, 819-843-7250, Wards: 2. Omerville
Denise Poulin-Marcotte, Conseillère, 819-843-1146, Wards: 3. Des Sommets
Jean-Guy Gingras, Conseiller, 819-843-3663, Wards: 4. Du Marais
Robert Ranger, Conseiller, 819-620-4134, Wards: 5. Canton Ouest
Jacques Laurendeau, Conseiller, 819-843-3244, Wards: 6. Des Pionniers
Pierre Côté, Conseiller, 819-843-1108, Wards: 7. Centre
Nathalie Bélanger, Conseillère, 819-868-0256, Wards: 8. Monseigneur Vel
Nathalie Pelletier, Conseillère, 819-868-5126, Wards: 9. Des Marinas
Diane Pelletier, Conseillère, 819-570-7597, Wards: 10. Des Deux lacs
Sylviane Lavigne, Greffière, 819-843-6501
Armand Comeau, Directeur général, 819-843-2880
Anne Couturier, Trésorière, 819-843-6501
Luc Paré, Contact, Sécurité incendie, 819-843-3333
Marco Prévost, Contact, Environnement et aménagement du territoire, 819-843-7106
Michel R. Turcotte, Contact, Travaux publics, 819-843-7106

Marieville
682, rue Saint-Charles
Marieville, QC J3M 1P9
Tél: 450-460-4444; *Téléc:* 450-460-2770
administration@ville.marieville.qc.ca
www.ville.marieville.qc.ca
Entité municipal: City
Incorporation: 14 juin 2000; *Area:* 64,25 km2
Comté ou district: Rouville; *Population au 2011:* 10,094
Circonscription(s) électorale(s) provinciale(s): Iberville
Circonscription(s) électorale(s) fédérale(s): Beloeil-Chambly
Prochaines élections: 5e novembre 2017
Gilles Delorme, Maire, 450-460-4444
Caroline Gagnon, Conseillère, Wards: 1
Pierre St-Jean, Conseiller, 450-460-4726, Wards: 2
Marc-André Sévigny, Conseiller, 514-918-4168, Wards: 3
Monic Paquette, Conseillère, 450-460-7324, Wards: 4
Louis Bienvenu, Conseiller, 450-460-2658, Wards: 5
Gilbert Lefort, Conseiller, 450-460-7395, Wards: 6
Nancy Forget, Greffière
Francine Tétreault, Directrice générale
Isabelle Laurin, Trésorière
Jean-François Auclair, Directeur, Urbanisme et environnement
Yves Boulet, Directeur, Travaux publics
Robert Dubuc, Directeur, Protection contre les incendies

Mascouche
3034, ch Ste-Marie
Mascouche, QC J7K 1P1
Tél: 450-474-4133; *Téléc:* 450-474-6401
www.ville.mascouche.qc.ca
Entité municipal: City
Incorporation: 1er juillet 1855; *Area:* 107,95 km2
Comté ou district: Les Moulins; Communauté métropolitaine de Montréal; *Population au 2011:* 42,491
Circonscription(s) électorale(s) provinciale(s): Masson
Circonscription(s) électorale(s) fédérale(s): Montcalm
Prochaines élections: 5e novembre 2017
Guillaume Tremblay, Maire, 450-474-4133
Roger Côté, Conseiller, 450-966-0784, Wards: 1. Louis-Hébert
Eugène Jolicoeur, Conseiller, 514-809-5115, Wards: 2. Laurier
Louise Forest, Conseillère, 450-474-0488, Wards: 3. Le Gardeur
Stéphane Handfield, Conseiller, 514-942-3610, Wards: 4. La Vérendrye

Bertrand Lefebvre, Conseiller, 514-713-1958, Wards: 5. Du Coteau
Don Monahan, Conseiller, 450-474-6435, Wards: 6. Des Hauts-Bois
Anny Mailloux, Conseillère, 514-886-5709, Wards: 7. Du Rucher
Gabriel Michaud, Conseiller, 514-531-7762, Wards: 8. Du Manoir
Denis Villeneuve, Greffier, 450-474-4133
Claude Perrotte, Directeur général, 450-474-4133
Luce Jacques, Trésorier, Finances, 450-474-4133
Jean-Pierre Boudreau, Directeur, Service sécurité d'incendie, 450-474-4133
François Gosselin, Directeur, Travaux publics, 450-474-4133

Matane
230, av St-Jérôme
Matane, QC G4W 3A2
Tél: 418-562-2333; *Téléc:* 418-562-2336
direction@ville.matane.qc.ca
www.ville.matane.qc.ca
Entité municipal: City
Incorporation: 26 septembre 2001; *Area:* 214,63 km2
Comté ou district: La Matanie; *Population au 2011:* 14,462
Circonscription(s) électorale(s) provinciale(s): Matane-Matapédia
Circonscription(s) électorale(s) fédérale(s): Avignon-La Mitis-Matane-Matapédia
Prochaines élections: 5e novembre 2017
Jérôme Landry, Maire
Michel Côté, Conseiller, Wards: 1
Monique Fournier, Conseillère, Wards: 2
Brigitte Michaud, Conseillère, Wards: 3
Mario Hamilton, Conseiller, Wards: 4
Nelson Simard, Conseiller, Wards: 5
Steve Girard, Conseiller, 418-562-4975, Wards: 6
Nicolas Leclerc, Greffier
Gilles Malouin, Directeur général, 418-562-2333
Marie Pelletier, Trésorière, 418-562-2333
Thérèse Des Rochers, Coordonnatrice par intérim, Environnement et au développement durable, 418-562-2333

Mercier
869, boul St-Jean-Baptiste, 2e étage
Mercier, QC J6R 2L3
Tél: 450-691-6090; *Téléc:* 450-691-6529
info@ville.mercier.qc.ca
www.ville.mercier.qc.ca
Entité municipal: City
Incorporation: 1er juillet 1855; *Area:* 45,89 km2
Comté ou district: Roussillon; Communauté métropolitaine de Montréal; *Population au 2011:* 11,584
Circonscription(s) électorale(s) provinciale(s): Châteauguay
Circonscription(s) électorale(s) fédérale(s): Châteauguay-Lacolle
Prochaines élections: 5e novembre 2017
Lise Michaud, Mairesse, 450-691-6090
Stéphane Roy, Conseiller, Wards: 1
Johanne Anderson, Conseillère, Wards: 2
Anik Sauvé, Conseillère, Wards: 3
Philippe Drolet, Conseiller, Wards: 4
Louis Cimon, Conseiller, Wards: 5
Martin Laplaine, Conseiller, Wards: 6
René Chalifoux, Greffier et directeur général, 450-691-6090
Nadia René, Trésorière, 450-691-6090
Jérémie Choquette-Suprenant, Directeur, Urbanisme, 450-691-6090
Stéphane Fleury, Directeur, Police, 450-698-3205
René Larente, Directeur, Incendie, 450-691-6090
Anna Claudia B. Oliveira, Directrice, Travaux publics, 450-691-6090

Mirabel
14111, rue Saint-Jean
Mirabel, QC J7J 1Y3
Tél: 450-475-8653; *Téléc:* 450-475-7195
communications@ville.mirabel.qc.ca
ville.mirabel.qc.ca
Entité municipal: City
Incorporation: 1er janvier 1971; *Area:* 477,86 km2
Comté ou district: Communauté métropolitaine de Montréal; *Population au 2011:* 41,957
Circonscription(s) électorale(s) provinciale(s): Mirabel
Circonscription(s) électorale(s) fédérale(s): Mirabel
Prochaines élections: 5e novembre 2017
Jean Bouchard, Maire
Michel Lauzon, Conseiller, Wards: 1
Guylaine Coursol, Conseillère, Wards: 2
David Marra-Hurtubise, Conseiller, Wards: 3
François Bélanger, Conseiller, Wards: 4
Patrick Charbonneau, Conseiller, Wards: 5
Pierre-Paul Meloche, Conseiller, Wards: 6
Francine Charles, Conseillère, Wards: 7
Guy Laurin, Conseiller, Wards: 8
Suzanne Mireault, Greffière, 450-475-2002

Mario Boily, Directeur général, 450-475-2000, Fax: 450-475-2013
Jeannic D'Aoust, Trésorier, 450-475-2003
Jérôme Duguay, Directeur, Environnement, 450-475-2006
Jean Gaudreault, Directeur, Loisirs, la culture et la vie, 450-475-8656
Mario Lajeunesse, Directeur, Génie, 450-475-2004
Denis Maurice, Directeur, Sécurité incendie, 450-475-2010
Dominic Noiseux, Directeur, Aménagement et de l'urbanisme, 450-475-2007
Bernard Poulin, Directeur, Communications, 450-475-2001
Carl St-Louis, Directeur, Équipement et des travaux publics, 450-475-2005

Mont-Laurier

300, boul Albiny-Paquette
Mont-Laurier, QC J9L 1J9
Tél: 819-623-1221; *Téléc:* 819-623-4840
info@villemontlaurier.qc.ca
www.villemontlaurier.qc.ca
Entité municipal: City
Incorporation: 8e janvier 2003; *Area:* 590,64 km2
Comté ou district: Antoine-Labelle; *Population au 2011:* 13,779
Circonscription(s) électorale(s) provinciale(s): Labelle
Circonscription(s) électorale(s) fédérale(s): Laurentides-Labelle
Prochaines élections: 5e novembre 2017
Note: Dès le 8 janvier 2003, la ville de Mont-Laurier regroupe les municipalités de Des Ruisseaux & Saint-Aimé-du-Lac-des-Iles.
Michel Adrien, Maire
Denis Ethier, Conseiller, Wards: 1
Frank Crépeau, Conseiller, Wards: 2
Jocelyne Cloutier, Conseillère, Wards: 3
Lise Clément, Conseillère, Wards: 4
Daniel Bourdon, Conseiller, Wards: 5
Lise St-Louis, Conseillère, Wards: 6
Blandine Boulianne, Greffière
Jean-Yves Forget, Directeur général
Johanne Nantel, Trésorière, Fax: 819-623-4840
Sébastien Lajoie, Directeur, Service des incendies
Steve Pressé, Directeur, Module qualité du milieu
Julie Richer, Directrice, Aménagement du territoire et urbanisme

Montmagny

143, rue St-Jean-Baptiste est
Montmagny, QC G5V 1K4
Tél: 418-248-3361; *Téléc:* 418-248-0923
info@ville.montmagny.qc.ca
www.ville.montmagny.qc.ca
Entité municipal: City
Incorporation: 2e avril 1966; *Area:* 125,76 km2
Comté ou district: Montmagny; *Population au 2011:* 11,491
Circonscription(s) électorale(s) provinciale(s): Côte-du-Sud
Circonscription(s) électorale(s) fédérale(s): Montmagny-L'Islet-Kamouraska-Rivière-du-Loup
Prochaines élections: 5e novembre 2017
Jean-Guy Desrosiers, Maire
Gaston Morin, Conseiller, Wards: 1
Gaston Caron, Conseiller, Wards: 2
Yves Gendrau, Conseiller, Wards: 3
Michel Mercier, Conseiller, Wards: 4
Marc Laurin, Conseiller, Wards: 5
Rémy Langevin, Conseiller, Wards: 6
Félix Michaud, Greffier, 418-248-3362
Bernard Létourneau, Directeur général, 418-248-3362
André Lévesque, Directeur, Finances et approvisionnement, 418-248-3361, Fax: 418-248-8468
Louise Bhérer, Directrice, Ressources humaines
Pierre Boucher, Directeur/Chef, Brigade des pompiers
Guy Laporte, Directeur, Travaux publics
Jean-François Roy, Directeur, Loisirs

Montréal

275, rue Notre-Dame est
Montréal, QC H2Y 1C6
Tél: 514-872-3142; *Téléc:* 514-872-5655
ville.montreal.qc.ca
Entité municipal: City
Incorporation: 1er janvier 2002; *Area:* 363,52 km2
Comté ou district: Communauté métropolitaine de Montréal; *Population au 2011:* 1,649,519
Circonscription(s) électorale(s) provinciale(s): Acadie;Anjou-Louis-Riel;Bourassa-Sauvé;Bourget;Crémazie;D'Arcy-McGee;Gouin;Hochelaga-Maisonneuve;Jeanne-Mance-Viger;LaFontaine;Laurier-Dorion;Marguerite-Bourgeoys;Mercier;Marquette;Mont-Royal;Nelligan;Notre-Dame-de-Grâce;Outremont;Pointe-aux-Trembles;Robert-Baldwin;Rosemont;St-Henri-Ste-Anne;St-Laurent;Ste-Marie-St-Jacques;Westmount-St-Louis;Verdun;Viau
Circonscription(s) électorale(s) fédérale(s): Ahuntsic-Cartierville; Bourassa; Dorval-Lachine-LaSalle; Hochelaga; Honoré-Mercier; La Pointe-de-l'Ile; LaSalle-Émard-Verdun; Lac-St-Louis; Laurier-Ste-Marie; Mount Royal; Notre-Dame-de-Grâce-Westmount; Outremont; Papineau; Pierrefonds-Dollard; Rosemont-La Petite-Patrie; St-Laurent; St-Léonard-St Michel; Ville-Marie-Le Sud Ouest-Ile-des-Soeurs
Prochaines élections: 5e novembre 2017
Denis Coderre, Maire
Frantz Benjamin, Conseiller de la ville, Saint-Michel, 514-872-7800, Fax: 514-872-2402, Wards: Villeray-St-Michel-Parc-Ext.
Richard Bergeron, Conseiller de la ville, Saint-Jacques, 514-868-5178, Fax: 514-872-8347, Wards: Ville-Marie
Karine Boivin Roy, Conseillère de la ville, Louis-Riel, 514-872-7123, Fax: 514-872-7125, Wards: Mercier-Hochelaga-Maisonneuve
Éric Alan Caldwell, Conseiller de la ville, Hochelaga, 514-872-9899, Fax: 514-872-7125, Wards: Mercier-Hochelaga-Maisonneuve
Richard Celzi, Conseiller de la ville, Tétreaultville, 514-872-7123, Fax: 514-872-7125, Wards: Mercier-Hochelaga-Maisonneuve
Harout Chitilian, Conseiller de la ville, Bordeaux-Cartierville, 514-872-2246, Fax: 514-868-3324, Wards: Ahuntsic-Cartierville
Catherine Clément-Talbot, Conseillère de la ville, Cap-Saint-Jacques, 514-624-1174, Wards: Pierrefonds-Roxboro
Jean-François Cloutier, Conseiller de la ville, Fort-Rolland, 514-634-3471, Fax: 514-634-8164, Wards: Lachine
Suzanne Décarie, Conseillère de la ville, Pointe-aux-Trembles, 514-868-4351, Fax: 514-868-4353, Wards: Riv.-des-Prairies-Pte-aux-Trem
Mary Deros, Conseillère de la ville, Parc-Extension, 514-872-3103, Fax: 514-872-2402, Wards: Villeray-St-Michel-Parc-Ext.
Richard Deschamps, Conseiller de la ville, Sault-St-Louis, 514-367-6000, Fax: 514-367-6600, Wards: LaSalle
Pierre Desrochers, Conseiller de la ville, Saint-Sulpice, 514-872-2246, Fax: 514-868-3324, Wards: Ahuntsic-Cartierville
Sterling Downey, Conseiller de la ville, Desmarchais-Crawford, Wards: Verdun
Érika Duchesne, Conseillère de la ville, Vieux-Rosemont, 514-868-3907, Fax: 514-868-3923, Wards: Rosemont—La Petite-Patrie
Marc-André Gadoury, Conseiller de la ville, Étienne-Desmarteau, 514-872-8390, Fax: 514-868-3932, Wards: Rosemont—La Petite-Patrie
Manon Gauthier, Conseillère de la ville, Champlain-L'Ile-des-Soeurs, Wards: Verdun
Jean-Marc Gibeau, Conseiller de la ville, Ovide-Clermont, 514-328-4000, Fax: 514-328-5577, Wards: Montréal-Nord
Richard Guay, Conseiller de la ville, La Pointe-aux-Prairies, 514-868-4356, Fax: 514-868-4353, Wards: Riv.-des-Prairies-Pte-aux-Trem
Andrée Hénault, Conseillère de la ville, 514-493-8051, Fax: 514-493-8013, Wards: Anjou
Patricia R. Lattanzio, Conseiller de la ville, Saint-Léonard Est, 514-328-8410, Fax: 514-328-8419, Wards: Saint-Léonard
Laurence Lavigne Lalonde, Conseillère de la ville, Maisonneuve-Longue-Pointe, 514-872-9899, Fax: 514-872-7125, Wards: Mercier-Hochelaga-Maisonneuve
Guillaume Lavoie, Conseiller de la ville, Marie-Victorin, 514-868-3931, Fax: 514-868-3932, Wards: Rosemont—La Petite-Patrie
Elsie Lefebvre, Conseillère de la ville, Villeray, 514-872-0755, Fax: 514-872-2196, Wards: Villeray-St-Michel-Parc-Ext.
François Limoges, Conseiller de la ville, Saint-Édouard, 514-872-8234, Fax: 514-868-3932, Wards: Rosemont—La Petite-Patrie
Justine McIntyre, Conseillère de la ville, Bois-de-Liesse, 514-624-1488, Wards: Pierrefonds-Roxboro
Louise Mainville, Conseillère de la ville, De Lorimier, 514-872-8023, Wards: Le Plateau-Mont-Royal
Peter McQueen, Conseiller de la ville, Notre-Dame-de-Grâce, 514-868-4281, Fax: 514-868-3327, Wards: Côte-des-Neiges-N.-D.-de-Grâce
Francesco Miele, Conseiller de la ville, Côte-de-Liesse, 514-855-6000, Fax: 514-855-6049, Wards: Saint-Laurent
Alex Norris, Conseiller de la ville, Jeanne-Mance, 514-872-8023, Wards: Le Plateau-Mont-Royal
Sylvain Ouellet, Conseiller de la ville, François-Perrault, 514-872-7763, Fax: 514-872-2402, Wards: Villeray-St-Michel-Parc-Ext.
Lorraine Pagé, Conseillère de la ville, Sault-au-Récollet, 514-872-2246, Fax: 514-868-3324, Wards: Ahuntsic-Cartierville
Lionel Perez, Conseiller de la ville, Darlington, 514-872-4863, Fax: 514-868-3327, Wards: Côte-des-Neiges-N.-D.-de-Grâce
Dominic Perri, Conseiller de la ville, Saint-Léonard-Ouest, 514-328-8410, Fax: 514-328-8419, Wards: Saint-Léonard
Valérie Plante, Conseillère de la ville, Sainte-Marie, 514-872-8644, Fax: 514-872-8347, Wards: Ville-Marie
Magda Popeanu, Conseillère de la ville, Côte-des-Neiges, 514-872-4863, Fax: 514-868-3327, Wards: Côte-des-Neiges-N.-D.-de-Grâce
Giovanni Rapanà, Conseiller de la ville, Rivière-des-Prairies, 514-868-5558, Fax: 514-868-4353, Wards: Riv.-des-Prairies-Pte-aux-Trem
Marvin Rotrand, Conseiller de la ville, Snowdon, 514-872-4863, Fax: 514-868-3327, Wards: Côte-des-Neiges-N.-D.-de-Grâce
Richard Ryan, Conseiller de la ville, Mile End, 514-872-8023, Wards: Le Plateau-Mont-Royal
Aref Salem, Conseiller de la ville, Norman-McLaren, 514-855-6000, Fax: 514-855-6049, Wards: Saint-Laurent
Craig Sauvé, Conseiller de la ville, St-Henri-Pte-Bourgogne-Pte-St-Charles, 514-872-6814, Wards: Le Sud-Ouest
Jeremy Searle, Conseiller de la ville, Loyola, 514-483-2561, Wards: Côte-des-Neiges-N.-D.-de-Grâce
Steve Shanahan, Conseiller de la ville, Peter McGill, 514-868-5169, Fax: 514-872-8347, Wards: Ville-Marie
Anne-Marie Sigouin, Conseillère de la ville, Saint-Paul-Émard, 514-872-6814, Wards: Le Sud-Ouest
Émilie Thuillier, Conseillère de la ville, Ahuntsic, 514-872-2246, Fax: 514-868-3324, Wards: Ahuntsic-Cartierville
Monique Vallée, Conseillère de la ville, Cecil-P.-Newman, 514-367-6000, Fax: 514-367-6600, Wards: LaSalle
Manon Barbe, Mairesse d'arrondissement/Conseillère de la ville, 514-367-6000, Fax: 514-367-6600, Wards: LaSalle
Dimitrios Jim Beis, Maire d'arrondissement/Conseiller de la ville, 514-624-1400, Wards: Pierrefonds-Roxboro
Michel Bissonnet, Maire d'arrondissement/Conseiller de la ville, 514-328-8410, Fax: 514-328-8413, Wards: Saint-Léonard
Christine Black, Mairesse d'arrondissement/Conseillère de la ville, 514-328-4000, Fax: 514-328-5577, Wards: Montréal-Nord
Marie Cinq-Mars, Mairesse d'arrondissement/Conseillère de la ville, 514-495-6220, Fax: 514-495-6290, Wards: Outremont
Russell Copeman, Maire d'arrondissement/Conseiller de la ville, 514-872-4863, Fax: 514-868-3327, Wards: Côte-des-Neiges-N.-D.-de-Grâce
François W. Croteau, Maire d'arrondissement/Conseiller de la ville, 514-872-6473, Fax: 514-868-3932, Wards: Rosemont—La Petite-Patrie
Claude Dauphin, Maire d'arrondissement/Conseiller de la ville, 514-634-3471, Fax: 514-780-7700, Wards: Lachine
Alan DeSousa, Maire d'arrondissement/Conseiller de la ville, 514-855-6000, Fax: 514-855-6049, Wards: Saint-Laurent
Benoit Dorais, Maire d'arrondissement/Conseiller de la ville, 514-872-6814, Fax: 514-872-3705, Wards: Le Sud-Ouest
Luc Ferrandez, Maire d'arrondissement/Conseiller de la ville, 514-872-8023, Wards: Le Plateau-Mont-Royal
Pierre Gagnier, Maire d'arrondissement/Conseiller de la ville, 514-872-2246, Fax: 514-868-3324, Wards: Ahuntsic-Cartierville
Normand Marinacci, Maire d'arrondissement/Conseiller de la ville, 514-620-6896, Fax: 514-620-8198, Wards: L'Île-Bizard—Ste-Geneviève
Luis Miranda, Maire d'arrondissement/Conseiller de la ville, 514-493-8010, Fax: 514-493-8013, Wards: Anjou
Réal Ménard, Maire d'arrondissement/Conseiller de la ville, 514-872-8759, Fax: 514-868-4551, Wards: Mercier-Hochelaga-Maisonneuve
Jean-François Parenteau, Maire d'arrondissement/Président de commission, Wards: Verdun
Chantal Rouleau, Mairesse d'arrondissement/Conseillère de la ville, 514-868-4050, Fax: 514-868-4353, Wards: Riv.-des-Prairies-Pte-aux-Trem
Anie Samson, Mairesse d'arrondissement/Conseillère de la ville, 514-872-8173, Fax: 514-872-2196, Wards: Villeray-St-Michel-Parc-Ext.
Mario Battista, Conseiller d'arrondissement, Saint-Léonard-Ouest, 514-328-8410, Fax: 514-328-8419, Wards: Saint-Léonard
Gilles Beaudry, Conseiller d'arrondissement, Ouest, 514-493-8019, Fax: 514-493-8013, Wards: Anjou
Michèle D. Biron, Conseillère d'arrondissement, Norman-McLaren, 514-855-6000, Fax: 514-855-6049, Wards: Saint-Laurent
Nancy Blanchet, Conseillère d'arrondissement, Sault-Saint-Louis (1), 514-367-6000, Fax: 514-367-6600, Wards: LaSalle
Marie-Eve Brunet, Conseillère d'arrondissement, Champlain-L'Ile-des-Soeurs (2), Wards: Verdun
Maurice Cohen, Conseiller d'arrondissement, Côte-de-Liesse, 514-855-6000, Fax: 514-855-6049, Wards: Saint-Laurent
Stéphane Côté, Conseiller d'arrondissement, Pierre-Foretier, 514-620-6896, Fax: 514-620-8198, Wards: L'Île-Bizard—Ste-Geneviève
Serge Declos, Conseiller d'arrondissement, Cecil-P.-Newman (1), 514-367-6000, Fax: 514-367-6600, Wards: LaSalle
Michèle Di Genova Zammit, Conseillère d'arrondissement, Centre, 514-493-8085, Fax: 514-493-8013, Wards: Anjou
Éric Dugas, Conseiller d'arrondissement, Ste-Geneviève, 514-620-6896, Fax: 514-620-8198, Wards: L'Île-Bizard—Ste-Geneviève
Gilles Déziel, Conseiller d'arrondissement, Pointe-aux-Trembles, 514-868-4352, Fax: 514-868-4353, Wards: Riv.-des-Prairies-Pte-aux-Trem

Céline Forget, Conseillère d'arrondissement, Joseph-Beaubien, 514-495-7430, Wards: Outremont
Luc Gagnon, Conseiller d'arrondissement, Desmarchais-Crawford (1), Wards: Verdun
Yves Gignac, Conseiller d'arrondissement, Cap-Saint-Jacques, 514-624-1175, Wards: Pierrefonds-Roxboro
Marianne Giguère, Conseillère d'arrondissement, De Lorimer, 514-872-8023, Wards: Le Plateau-Mont-Royal
Christine Gosselin, Conseillère d'arrondissement, Jeanne-Mance, 514-872-8023, Wards: Le Plateau-Mont-Royal
Jacqueline Gremaud, Conseillère d'arrondissement, Jeanne-Sauvé, 514-495-6228, Wards: Outremont
Manuel Guedes, Conseiller d'arrondissement, La Pointe-aux-Prairies, 514-210-9094, Fax: 514-868-4353, Wards: Riv.-des-Prairies-Pte-aux-Trem
Pierre L'Heureux, Conseiller d'arrondissement, Champlain-L'Île-des-Sours (1), Wards: Verdun
Christian Larocque, Conseiller d'arrondissement, Denis-Benjamin-Viger, 514-620-6896, Fax: 514-620-8198, Wards: L'île-Bizard—Ste-Geneviève
Jean-Dominic Lévesque-René, Conseiller d'arrondissement, Jacques-Bizard, 514-620-6896, Fax: 514-620-8198, Wards: L'île-Bizard—Ste-Geneviève
Sylvia Lo Bianco, Conseillère d'arrondissement, Ovide-Clermont, 514-328-4000, Fax: 514-328-5577, Wards: Montréal-Nord
Marie-Andrée Mauger, Conseillère d'arrondissement, Desmarchais-Crawford (2), Wards: Verdun
Laura-Ann Palestini, Conseillère d'arrondissement, Sault-St-Louis (2), 514-367-6000, Fax: 514-367-6600, Wards: LaSalle
Paul-Yvon Perron, Conseiller d'arrondissement, Est, 514-493-8017, Fax: 514-493-8013, Wards: Anjou
Nathalie Pierre-Antoine, Conseillère d'arrondissement, Rivière-des-Prairies, 514-868-4052, Fax: 514-868-4353, Wards: Riv.-des-Prairies-Pte-aux-Trem
Marie Plourde, Conseillère d'arrondissement, Mile End, 514-872-8023, Wards: Le Plateau-Mont-Royal
Mindy Pollak, Conseillère d'arrondissement, Claude-Ryan, 514-495-6230, Wards: Outremont
Marie Potvin, Conseillère d'arrondissement, Robert-Bourassa, 514-495-6248, Wards: Outremont
Daniel Racicot, Conseiller d'arrondissement, J.-Émery-Provost, 514-634-3471, Fax: 514-634-8164, Wards: Lachine
Monica Ricourt, Conseillère d'arrondissement, Marie-Clarac, 514-328-4000, Fax: 514-328-5577, Wards: Montréal-Nord
Kymberley Simonyik, Conseillère d'arrondissement, Fort-Rolland, 514-634-3471, Fax: 514-634-8164, Wards: Lachine
Sophie Thiébaut, Conseil. d'arrondissmnt., St-Henri-Pte-Bourgogne-Pte-St-Charles, 514-872-6814, Fax: 514-872-3705, Wards: Le Sud-Ouest
Lili-Anne Tremblay, Conseillère d'arrondissement, Saint-Léonard-Est, 514-328-8410, Fax: 514-328-8419, Wards: Saint-Léonard
Josée Troilo, Conseillère d'arrondissement, Cecil-P.-Newman (2), 514-367-6000, Fax: 514-367-6600, Wards: LaSalle
Roger Trottier, Conseiller d'arrondissement, Bois-de-Liesse, 514-624-1053, Wards: Pierrefonds-Roxboro
Alain Vaillancourt, Conseiller d'arrondissement, Saint-Paul-Émard, 514-872-6814, Wards: Le Sud-Ouest
Maja Vodanovic, Conseillère d'arrondissement, Canal, 514-634-3471, Fax: 514-634-8164, Wards: Lachine
Yves Saindon, Greffier
Alain Marcoux, Directeur général
Yves Courchesne, Trésorier
Jacques Bergeron, Vérificateur général
Louis Beauchamp, Directeur, Communications
Diane Bouchard, Directrice, Ressources humaines
François Massé, Directeur, Service sécurité d'incendie
Philippe Pichet, Chef de police et directeur, Service de police de la Ville de Montréal
Benoît Dagenais, Directeur général adjointe, Services institutionnels
Chantal Gagnon, Directrice générale adjointe, Qualité de vie
Jacques A. Ulysse, Directeur général adjointe, Développement

Mont-Royal

90, av Roosevelt
Mont-Royal, QC H3R 1Z5
Tél: 514-734-2900; *Téléc:* 514-734-3080
info@ville.mont-royal.qc.ca
www.ville.mont-royal.qc.ca
Entité municipal: City
Incorporation: 1er janvier 2006; *Area:* 7,66 km2
Comté ou district: Communauté métropolitaine de Montréal; *Population au 2011:* 19,503
Circonscription(s) électorale(s) provinciale(s): Mont-Royal
Circonscription(s) électorale(s) fédérale(s): Mount Royal
Prochaines élections: 5e novembre 2017
Philippe Roy, Maire, 514-734-2914, Fax: 514-734-3072
Joseph Daoura, Conseiller, Wards: 1
Minh-Diem Le Thi, Conseillère, Wards: 2
Erin Kennedy, Conseillère, Wards: 3
John Miller, Conseiller, Wards: 4
Michelle Setlakwe, Conseiller, Wards: 5
Daniel Robert, Conseiller, Wards: 6
Alexandre Verdy, Greffier et directeur, Affairs publiques, 514-734-2988
Ava L. Couch, Directrice générale, 514-734-2915
Nathalie Rhéaume, Trésorière et directrice, 514-734-3015
André Maratta, Directreur, Sécurité publique, 514-734-4666, Fax: 514-734-3086
Isabel Tardif, Directrice, Services Techniques, 514-734-3034, Fax: 514-734-3084

Mont-Saint-Hilaire

100, rue du Centre-Civique
Mont-Saint-Hilaire, QC J3H 3M8
Tél: 450-467-2854; *Téléc:* 450-467-6460
information@villemsh.ca
www.villemsh.ca
Entité municipal: City
Incorporation: 12 mars 1966; *Area:* 38,96 km2
Comté ou district: La Vallée-du-Richelieu; Communauté métropolitaine de Montréal; *Population au 2011:* 18,200
Circonscription(s) électorale(s) provinciale(s): Borduas
Circonscription(s) électorale(s) fédérale(s): Beloeil-Chambly
Prochaines élections: 5e novembre 2017
Yves Corriveau, Maire, 450-467-2854
Frédéric Dionne, Conseiller, 450-467-2339, Wards: 1. Déboulis
Emile Gilbert, Conseiller, 450-464-1789, Wards: 2. Patriotes
Sylvain Houle, Conseiller, 450-464-5319, Wards: 3. Piémont
Jean-Pierre Brault, Conseiller, 450-464-5137, Wards: 4. Rouville
Joseph Côté, Conseiller, 450-467-8036, Wards: 5. Montagne
Magalie Joncas, Conseillère, 514-817-4145, Wards: 6. Pommeraie
Anne-Marie Piérard, Greffière, 450-467-2854
Daniel McCraw, Directeur général, 450-467-2854
Sylvie Laplame, Trésorière et directrice, Finances, 450-467-2854
Jean Clément, Directeur, Sécurité incendie, 450-467-2854
Sylvain Gagnon, Directeur, Travaux publics, 450-467-2854
Nathalie Laberge, Directrice, Ingénierie, 450-467-2854
Bernard Morel, Directeur, Aménagement du territoire et de l'environnement, 450-467-2854

Notre-Dame-de-l'Île-Perrot

21, rue de l'Église
Notre-Dame-de-l'Île-Perrot, QC J7V 8P4
Tél: 514-453-4128; *Téléc:* 514-453-8961
info@ndip.org
www.ndip.org
Entité municipal: City
Incorporation: 14 avril 1984; *Area:* 28,14 km2
Comté ou district: Vaudreuil-Soulanges; Communauté métropolitaine de Montréal; *Population au 2011:* 10,620
Circonscription(s) électorale(s) provinciale(s): Vaudreuil
Circonscription(s) électorale(s) fédérale(s): Vaudreuil-Soulanges
Prochaines élections: 5e novembre 2017
Diane Deschênes, Mairesse
Bruno Roy, Conseiller, 514-453-5416, Wards: 1
Sylvain Lemire, Conseiller, 514-453-3625, Wards: 2
Daniel Lauzon, Conseiller, 514-453-5907, Wards: 3
Bernard Groulx, Conseiller, 514-453-8680, Wards: 4
Normand Pigeon, Conseiller, 514-453-9766, Wards: 5
Jean Fournel, Conseiller, 514-453-1396, Wards: 6
Jeanne Briand, Greffière et directrice, Services juridiques, 514-453-4128
Katherine-Erika Vincent, Directrice générale, 514-453-4128
Stéphanie Martin, Trésorière et directrice, Financiers et de l'informatique, 514-453-4128
Mélissa Arbour LaSalle, Directrice, Urbanisme, 514-453-4128
Luc Tessier, Surintendant, Travaux publics, 514-453-4128

Pincourt

919, ch Duhamel
Pincourt, QC J7V 4G8
Tél: 514-453-8981; *Téléc:* 514-453-8401
information@villepincourt.qc.ca
www.villepincourt.qc.ca
Entité municipal: City
Incorporation: 1er janvier 1950; *Area:* 8,36 km2
Comté ou district: Vaudreuil-Soulanges; Communauté métropolitaine de Montréal; *Population au 2011:* 14,305
Circonscription(s) électorale(s) provinciale(s): Vaudreuil
Circonscription(s) électorale(s) fédérale(s): Vaudreuil-Soulanges
Prochaines élections: 5e novembre 2017
Yvan Cardinal, Maire
Alexandre Wolford, Conseiller, Wards: 1
Denise Bergeron, Conseillère, Wards: 2
Sam Ierfino, Conseiller, Wards: 3
Diane Boyer, Conseillère, Wards: 4
Jim Miron, Conseiller, Wards: 5
René Lecavalier, Conseiller, Wards: 6
Etienne Bergevin Byette, Greffier, 514-453-8981
Michel Perrier, Directeur général, 514-453-8981, Fax: 514-453-0934
Nathalie Boisvert, Trésorière, 514-453-8981
Yanick Bernier, Directeur, Urgence et de sécurité publique, 514-453-8981, Fax: 514-453-0934
Richard Dubois, Directeur, Aménagement du territoire, 514-453-8981, Fax: 514-453-0934
Jean-Marc Guy, Directeur, Travaux publics, 514-453-2213, Fax: 514-453-1628

Pointe-Claire

451, boul Saint-Jean
Pointe-Claire, QC H9R 3J3
Tél: 514-630-1200
www.ville.pointe-claire.qc.ca
Entité municipal: City
Incorporation: 1er janvier 2006; *Area:* 18,88 km2
Comté ou district: Communauté métropolitaine de Montréal;
Population au 2011: 30,790
Circonscription(s) électorale(s) provinciale(s): Jacques-Cartier
Circonscription(s) électorale(s) fédérale(s): Lac-Saint-Louis
Prochaines élections: 5e novembre 2017
Morris Trudeau, Maire, 514-630-1207
Claude Cousineau, Conseiller, 514-630-1288, Wards: 1. Cedar/Le Village
Paul Bissonnette, Conseiller, 514-630-1289, Wards: 2. Lakeside
Kelly Thorstad-Cullen, Conseillère, 514-630-1290, Wards: 3. Valois
Aldo Iermieri, Conseiller, 514-630-1291, Wards: 4. Cedar Park Heights
Cynthia Homan, Conseillère, 514-630-1292, Wards: 5. Lakeside Heights
Jean-Pierre Grenier, Conseiller, 514-630-1293, Wards: 6. Seigniory
Dennis Smith, Conseiller, 514-630-1294, Wards: 7. Northview
Jack Beaumont, Conseiller, 514-630-1295, Wards: 8. Oneida
Jean-Denis Jacob, Greffier et directeur général (par intérim), 514-630-1228
Marie-Josée Boissonneault, Trésorière et directrice, Services administratifs
Stéphane Carbonneau, Directeur, Ingénierie, 514-630-1208
Heather C. Leblanc, Directrice, Urbanisme, 514-630-1206
Daniel McDuff, Directeur, Travaux publics, 514-630-1230
Bernard Côté, Évaluateur signataire

La Prairie

#400, 170, boul Taschereau
La Prairie, QC J5R 5H6
Tél: 450-444-6600; *Téléc:* 450-444-6636
info@ville.laprairie.qc.ca
www.ville.laprairie.qc.ca
Entité municipal: City
Incorporation: 30 mars 1846; *Area:* 43,53 km2
Comté ou district: Roussillon; Communauté métropolitaine de Montréal; *Population au 2011:* 23,357
Circonscription(s) électorale(s) provinciale(s): La Prairie
Circonscription(s) électorale(s) fédérale(s): La Prairie
Prochaines élections: 5e novembre 2017
Donat Serres, Maire
Allen Scott, Conseiller, Wards: 1. Milice
Christian Caron, Conseiller, Wards: 2. Christ-Roi
Laurent Blais, Conseiller, Wards: 3. Vieux La Prairie
Marie Eve Plante-Hébert, Conseillère, Wards: 4. Citière
Suzanne Perron, Conseillère, Wards: 5. Clairière
Pierre Vocino, Conseiller, Wards: 6. Magdeleine
Yves Senécal, Conseiller, Wards: 7. Bataille
Eve Barrette-Marchand, Conseillère, Wards: 8. Briqueterie
Danielle Simard, Greffière, 450-444-6625
Jean Bergeron, Directeur général, 450-444-6619
Nathalie Guérin, Trésorière, 450-444-6603
Sylvain Dufresne, Directeur, Sécurité incendie, 450-444-6652
Benoît Fortier, Directeur, Urbanisme, 450-444-6637
Steve Ponton, Directeur, Génie, 450-444-6647
Guy Trahan, Directeur, Travaux publics, 450-444-6684

Prévost

2870, boul du Curé-Labelle
Prévost, QC J0R 1T0
Tél: 450-224-8888; *Téléc:* 450-224-8323
www.ville.prevost.qc.ca
Entité municipal: City
Incorporation: 20 janvier 1973; *Area:* 34,32 km2
Comté ou district: La Rivière-du-Nord; *Population au 2011:* 12,171
Circonscription(s) électorale(s) provinciale(s): Prévost
Circonscription(s) électorale(s) fédérale(s): Rivière-du-Nord
Prochaines élections: 5e novembre 2017
Germain Richer, Maire, 450-224-8888
Gaétan Bordeleau, Conseiller, 450-224-8888, Wards: 1
Danielle Léger, Conseillère, 450-224-8888, Wards: 2
Gilbert Brunet, Conseiller, 450-224-8888, Wards: 3

Claude Leroux, Conseiller, 450-224-8888, Wards: 4
Brigitte Paquette, Conseillère, 450-224-8888, Wards: 5
Joël Badertscher, Conseiller, 450-224-8888, Wards: 6
Laurent Laberge, Greffier, 450-224-8888
Réal Martin, Directeur général, 450-224-8888
Jean-Yves Crispin, Trésorier, 450-224-8888
Éric Gélinas, Directeur, Urbanisme
Réal Martin, Directeur, Travaux publics
Ghislain Patry, Directeur/Chef, Brigade des pompiers
Stéphane Bibeault, Responsable, Émission de permis et de certificats municipaux
Frédérick Marseau, Responsable, Environnement

Québec
Hôtel de Ville
CP 700 Haute-Ville
2, rue des Jardins
Québec, QC G1R 4S9
Tél: 418-641-6010; *Téléc:* 418-641-6357
renseignements@ville.quebec.qc.ca
www.ville.quebec.qc.ca
Entité municipal: City
Incorporation: 1er janvier 2002; *Area:* 451,79 km2
Comté ou district: Communauté métropolitaine de Québec; *Population au 2011:* 516,622
Circonscription(s) électorale(s) provinciale(s): Charlesbourg; Chauveau; Jean-Lesage; Jean-Talon; La Peltrie; Louis-Hébert; Montmorency; Taschereau; Vanier-Les Rivières
Circonscription(s) électorale(s) fédérale(s): Beauport-Limoilou; Beauport-Côte-de-Beaupré-Île d'Orléans-Charlevoix; Charlesbourg-Haute-Saint-Charles; Louis-Hébert; Québec
Prochaines élections: 5e novembre 2017
Régis Labeaume, Maire, 418-641-6434
Julie Lemieux, Conseillère, Beauport, 418-641-6080, Wards: Chute-Montmorency-Seigneurial
Jérémie Ernould, Conseiller, Beauport, 418-641-6501, Wards: Robert-Giffard
Marie France Trudel, Conseillère, Beauport, 418-641-6501, Wards: Sainte-Thérèse-de-Lisieux
Michelle Morin-Doyle, Conseillère, Charlesbourg, 418-641-6080, Wards: Louis-XIV
Patrick Voyer, Conseiller, Charlesbourg, 418-641-6080, Wards: Monts
Vincent Dufresne, Conseiller, Charlesbourg, 418-641-6401, Wards: Saint-Rodrigue
Anne Guérette, Conseillère, La Cité-Limoilou, 418-641-6411, Wards: Cap-aux-Diamants
Suzanne Verreault, Conseillère, La Cité-Limoilou, 418-641-6411, Wards: Limoilou
Geneviève Hamelin, Conseillère, La Cité-Limoilou, 418-641-6411, Wards: Maizerets-Lairet
Yvon Bussières, Conseiller, La Cité-Limoilou, 418-641-6101, Wards: Montcalm-Saint-Sacrement
Chantal Gilbert, Conseillère, La Cité-Limoilou, 418-641-6080, Wards: Saint-Roch-Saint-Sauveur
Steeve Verret, Conseiller, La Haute-Saint-Charles, 418-641-6080, Wards: Lac-Saint-Charles—Saint-Émile
Raymond Dion, Conseiller, La Haute-Saint-Charles, 418-641-6701, Wards: Loretteville-Les Châtels
Sylvain Légaré, Conseiller, La Haute-Saint-Charles, 418-641-6701, Wards: Val-Bélair
Dominique Tanguay, Conseillère, Les Rivières, 418-641-6201, Wards: Duberger-Les Saules
Jonatan Julien, Conseiller, Les Rivières, 418-641-6080, Wards: Neufchâtel-Lebourgneuf
Natacha Jean, Conseillère, Les Rivières, 418-641-6080, Wards: Vanier
Laurent Proulx, Conseiller, Sainte-Foy—Sillery—Cap-Rouge, 418-641-6301, Wards: Cap-Rouge-Laurentien
Rémy Normand, Conseiller, Sainte-Foy—Sillery—Cap-Rouge, 418-641-6080, Wards: Plateau
Anne Corriveau, Conseillère, Sainte-Foy—Sillery—Cap-Rouge, 418-641-6301, Wards: Pointe-de-Sainte-Foy
Paul Shoiry, Conseiller, Sainte-Foy—Sillery—Cap-Rouge, 418-641-6301, Wards: Saint-Louis-Sillery
Sylvain Ouellet, Greffier, 418-641-6212
André Legault, Directeur général, 418-641-6373
Gilles Dufour, Directeur général adjoint, Eau, environnement et équipements d'utilité publique
José Garceau, Directrice générale adjointe, Animation culturelle, sociale et touristique
Chantale Giguère, Directrice générale adjointe, Qualité de vie urbaine
Louis Potvin, Directeur général adjoint, Services de proximité
Pierre St-Michel, Directeur général adjoint, Services de soutien institutionnel
Guy Bélanger, Directeur, Loisirs, sports & vie communautaire, 418-641-6224
Richard Côté, Directeur, Évaluation, 418-641-6193
Michel Desgagné, Directeur, Police
Serge Giasson, Directeur, Affaires juridiques, 418-641-6156
Denis Jean, Directeur, Aménagement du territoire, 418-641-6160
Daniel Lessard, Directeur, Ingénierie, 418-641-6217
Marie-Christine Magnan, Directrice, Communications, 418-641-6651
Daniel Maranda, Directeur, Service des approvisionnements, 418-641-6164
Charles Marceau, Directeur, Développement économique et grands projets, 418-641-6185
Christian Paradis, Directeur, Protection contre l'incendie, 418-641-6231
Chantal Pineault, Directrice, Services des finances, 418-641-6203
Benoit Richer, Directeur, Ressources humaines, 418-641-6234
Rhonda Rioux, Directrice, Culture et relations internationales, 418-641-6181
André Roy, Directeur, Office du tourisme de Québec
Michel Saint-Laurent, Directeur, Technologies de l'information, 418-641-6239
Martin Villeneuve, Directeur, Eau et environnement, 418-641-6189
Michel Samson, Vérificateur général

Rawdon
3647, rue Queen
Rawdon, QC J0K 1S0
Tél: 450-834-2596; *Téléc:* 450-834-3031
www.rawdon.ca
Entité municipal: City
Incorporation: 28 mai 1998; *Area:* 179,73 km2
Comté ou district: Matawinie; *Population au 2011:* 10,416
Circonscription(s) électorale(s) provinciale(s): Rousseau
Circonscription(s) électorale(s) fédérale(s): Joliette
Prochaines élections: 5e novembre 2017
Bruno Guilbault, Maire
Renald Breault, Conseiller
Katy Dupuis, Conseillère
Stéphanie Labelle, Conseillère
Louise Poirier, Conseillère
Raymond Rougeau, Conseiller
Kimberly St Denis, Conseillère
Caroline Gray, Greffière
François Dauphin, Directeur général
Carole Landry, Directrice, Finances
Bruno Jodoin, Directeur, Sécurité d'incendie
Hugo Lebreux, Directeur, Travaux publics
Rémi Racine, Directeur, Planification et du développement

Repentigny
435, boul Iberville
Repentigny, QC J6A 2B6
Tél: 450-470-3000; *Téléc:* 450-470-3082
communication@ville.repentigny.qc.ca
www.ville.repentigny.qc.ca
Entité municipal: City
Incorporation: 1er juin 2002; *Area:* 68,42 km2
Comté ou district: L'Assomption; Communauté métropolitaine de Montréal; *Population au 2011:* 82,000
Circonscription(s) électorale(s) provinciale(s): L'Assomption; Repentigny
Circonscription(s) électorale(s) fédérale(s): Repentigny
Prochaines élections: 5e novembre 2017
Chantal Deschamps, Mairesse, 450-470-3103
André Cyr, Conseiller, 450-585-3410, Wards: 1
Georges Robinson, Conseiller, 450-654-9746, Wards: 2
Denyse Peltier, Conseillère, 450-581-5733, Wards: 3
Cécile Hénault, Conseillère, 450-654-3046, Wards: 4
Eric Chartré, Conseiller, 514-743-9961, Wards: 5
Sylvain Benoit, Conseiller, 514-602-4793, Wards: 6
Raymond Hénault, Conseiller, 450-581-0319, Wards: 7
Normand Venne, Conseiller, 450-585-6497, Wards: 8
Martine Gendron, Conseillère, 450-721-6699, Wards: 9
Bruno Villeneuve, Conseiller, 514-266-2987, Wards: 10
Francine Payer, Conseillère, 450-582-7711, Wards: 11
Normand Urbain, Conseiller, 450-585-3221, Wards: 12
Louis-André Garceau, Greffier, 450-470-3130
David Legault, Directeur général, 450-470-3110
Diane Pelchat, Trésorière, 450-470-3200
Sylvie Bouchard, Directrice, Travaux publics, 450-470-3800
Helen Dion, Directrice, Police (Quartier général), 450-470-3600
Carrol-Ann Forrest, Directrice, Ressources humaines, 450-470-3700
Pierre Fortier, Directeur, Loisirs, culture et vie communautaire, 450-470-3400
Marlène Girard, Directrice, Communications, 470-314-0140
Denis Larose, Directeur, Incendie, 450-470-3620
Julien Lauzon, Directeur, Permis, inspections et urbanisme, 450-470-3840

Rimouski
CP 710
205, av de la Cathédrale
Rimouski, QC G5L 7C7
Tél: 418-723-3313; *Téléc:* 418-724-3183
www.ville.rimouski.qc.ca
Entité municipal: City
Incorporation: 1er janvier 2002; *Area:* 254,16 km2
Comté ou district: Rimouski-Neigette; *Population au 2011:* 46,860
Circonscription(s) électorale(s) provinciale(s): Rimouski
Circonscription(s) électorale(s) fédérale(s): Rimouski-Neigette-Témiscouata-Les Basques
Prochaines élections: 5e novembre 2017
Éric Forest, Maire, 418-724-3126
Serge Dionne, Conseiller, 418-722-7106, Wards: 1. Sacré-Coeur
Rodrigue Joncas, Conseiller, 418-725-4991, Wards: 2. Nazareth
Jennifer Murray, Conseillère, 418-721-7752, Wards: 3. Saint-Germain
Cécilia Michaud, Conseillère, 418-727-5770, Wards: 4. Rimouski-Est
Jacques Lévesque, Conseiller, 418-724-9598, Wards: 5. Pointe-au-Père
Donald Bélanger, Conseiller, 418-723-3467, Wards: 6. Sainte-Odile
Claire Dubé, Conseillère, 418-723-0037, Wards: 7. Saint-Robert
Pierre Chassé, Conseiller, 418-725-5505, Wards: 8. Terrasse Arthur-Buies
Karol Francis, Conseiller, 418-732-2511, Wards: 9. Saint-Pie-X
Dave Dumas, Conseiller, 581-246-5614, Wards: 10. Sainte-Blanche/Mont-Lebel
Marc Parent, Conseiller, 581-246-1824, Wards: 11. (Le Bic)
Monique Sénéchal, Greffière, 418-724-3125, Fax: 418-724-9795
Claude Périnet, Directeur général, 418-724-3171, Fax: 418-724-3183
Rémi Fiola, ing., Directeur, Génie et environnement, 418-724-3135, Fax: 418-724-3284
Sylvain St-Pierre, Directeur, Finances, 418-724-3111, Fax: 418-724-3180

Rivière-du-Loup
CP 37
65, rue de l'Hôtel-de-Ville
Rivière-du-Loup, QC G5R 3Y7
Tél: 418-867-6700; *Téléc:* 418-862-2817
www.ville.riviere-du-loup.qc.ca
Entité municipal: City
Incorporation: 30 décembre 1998; *Area:* 83,39 km2
Comté ou district: Rivière-du-Loup; *Population au 2011:* 19,447
Circonscription(s) électorale(s) provinciale(s): Rivière-du-Loup-Témiscouata
Circonscription(s) électorale(s) fédérale(s): Montmagny-L'Islet-Kamouraska-Rivière-du-Loup
Prochaines élections: 5e novembre 2017
Gaétan Gamache, Maire, 418-867-6625
Steeve Drapeau, Conseiller, 418-862-7358, Wards: Estuaire
Jacques Minville, Conseiller, 418-867-3625, Wards: Fraserville
Sylvie Vignet, Conseillère, 418-862-3222, Wards: Plaine
Gérald Plourde, Conseiller, 418-862-7937, Wards: Pointe
Mario Bastille, Conseiller, 418-867-5495, Wards: Rivière
Jérôme LaViolette-Côté, Conseiller, 418-314-1214, Wards: Saint-Patrice
Georges Deschênes, Greffier, 418-867-6715
Jacques Poulin, Directeur général, 418-867-6707
Marie Lapointe, Directrice, Finances et Trésorerie, 418-867-6711
Éric Côté, Directeur, Environnement et développement durable

Roberval
851, boul St-Joseph
Roberval, QC G8H 2L6
Tél: 418-275-0202; *Téléc:* 418-275-5031
vroberval@ville.roberval.qc.ca
www.ville.roberval.qc.ca
Entité municipal: City
Incorporation: 23 décembre 1976; *Area:* 168,27 km2
Comté ou district: Le Domaine-du-Roy; *Population au 2011:* 10,227
Circonscription(s) électorale(s) provinciale(s): Roberval
Circonscription(s) électorale(s) fédérale(s): Lac-St-Jean
Prochaines élections: 5e novembre 2017
Guy Larouche, Maire
Marcel Lachance, Conseiller, Wards: 1
Nancy Guillemette, Conseillère, Wards: 2
Mélanie Girard, Conseillère, Wards: 3
Michèle Claveau, Conseillère, Wards: 4
Réal Labrecque, Conseiller, Wards: 5
Maurice Gagnon, Conseiller, Wards: 6
Daniel Gauthier, Directeur général
Nancy Boutin, Trésorière
Marc Gagné, Surintendant, Travaux publics
Jean-Luc Gagnon, Directeur, Ingénierie

Régeant Langlois, Directeur, Hygiène du milieu
André Lavoie, Directeur, Approvisionnement
Rémi Parent, Directeur, Service de sécurité incendie
Jacques Valois, Directeur, Urbanisme

Rosemère
100, rue Charbonneau
Rosemère, QC J7A 3W1
Tél: 450-621-3500; *Téléc:* 450-621-7601
info@ville.rosemere.qc.ca
ville.rosemere.qc.ca
Entité municipal: City
Incorporation: 1er janvier 1947; *Area:* 10,35 km2
Comté ou district: Thérèse-De Blainville; Communauté métropolitaine de Montréal; *Population au 2011:* 14,294
Circonscription(s) électorale(s) provinciale(s): Groulx
Circonscription(s) électorale(s) fédérale(s): Rivière-des-Mille-Iles
Prochaines élections: 5e novembre 2017
Medeleine Leduc, Mairesse
Daniel Simoneau, Conseiller, Wards: 1
Guylaine Richer, Conseillère, Wards: 2
Marie-Andrée Bonneau, Conseillère, Wards: 3
Normand Corriveau, Conseiller, Wards: 4
Eric Westram, Conseiller, Wards: 5
Kateri Lesage, Conseillère, Wards: 6
Caroline Asselin, Greffière, 450-621-3500
Mark Rouleau, Directeur général, 450-621-3500
Lison Lefebvre, Directrice, Finances, 450-621-3500
Nathalie Bélanger, Directrice, Hygiène du milieu, 450-621-3500
Denis De Lisio, Directeur, Sécurité incendie, 450-621-3500
Nathalie Legault, Directrice, Urbanisme, permis et inspections, 450-621-3500
Jean-Philippe Lemire, Directreur, Services techniques, travaux publics et environnement, 450-621-3500

Rouyn-Noranda
CP 220
100, rue Taschereau est
Rouyn-Noranda, QC J9X 5C3
Tél: 819-797-7110; *Téléc:* 819-797-7108
www.ville.rouyn-noranda.qc.ca
Entité municipal: City
Incorporation: 1er janvier 2002; *Area:* 6435,64 km2
Population au 2011: 41,012
Circonscription(s) électorale(s) provinciale(s): Rouyn-Noranda—Témiscamingue; Abitibi-Est
Circonscription(s) électorale(s) fédérale(s): Abitibi-Témiscamingue
Prochaines élections: 5e novembre 2017
Mario Provencher, Maire
Marc Bibeau, Conseiller, Wards: 1. Noranda-Nord/Lac-Dufault
Sylvie Turgeon, Conseillère, Wards: 2. Rouyn-Noranda-Ouest
André Philippon, Conseiller, Wards: 3. Rouyn-Sud
Marc Provencher, Conseiller, Wards: 4. Centre-Ville
Robert B. Brière, Conseiller, Wards: 5. Noranda
Philippe Marquis, Conseiller, Wards: 6. Ste-Bernadette
Luc Lacroix, Conseiller, Wards: 7. Granada/Bellecombe
François Cotnoir, Conseiller, Wards: 8. Sud-Est
André Tessier, Conseiller, Wards: 9. Évain
Marcel Maheux, Conseiller, Wards: 10. Kekeko
Jean-Claude Chouinard, Conseiller, Wards: 11. Cadillac
Diane Dallaire, Conseiller, Wards: 12. Nord
Daniel Samson, Greffier, 819-797-7110
Denis Charron, Directeur général, 819-797-7110
Serge Cloutier, Directeur, Environnement et assainissement des eaux, 819-797-7110, Fax: 819-797-7153
Noël Lanouette, Directeur, Travaux publics et services techniques, 819-797-7122, Fax: 819-797-7153
Hélène Piuze, Directrice, Finances et services administratifs, 819-797-7110, Fax: 819-797-7120

Saguenay
CP 129
201, rue Racine est
Chicoutimi, QC G7H 5B8
Tél: 418-698-3000; *Téléc:* 418-541-4524
www.ville.saguenay.qc.ca
Entité municipal: City
Incorporation: 18 février 2002; *Area:* 1,166 km2
Population au 2011: 144,746
Circonscription(s) électorale(s) provinciale(s): Chicoutimi; Dubuc; Jonquière
Circonscription(s) électorale(s) fédérale(s): Chicoutimi-Le Fjord
Prochaines élections: 5e novembre 2017
Jean Tremblay, Maire, 418-698-3330
Christine Boivin, Conseillère, Jonquière, Wards: 1
Jonathan Tremblay, Conseiller, Jonquière, Wards: 2
Sylvie Gaudreault, Conseillère, Jonquière, Wards: 3
Rejean Hudon, Conseiller, Jonquière, Wards: 4
Bernard Noël, Conseiller, Jonquière, Wards: 5
Carl Dufour, Conseiller, Jonquière, Wards: 6
Claude Tremblay, Conseiller, Jonquière, Wards: 7
Julie Dufour, Conseillère, Jonquière, Wards: 8
Jean-Yves Provencher, Conseiller, Chicoutimi, Wards: 9
Marc Pettersen, Conseiller, Chicoutimi, Wards: 10
Simon-Olivier Côté, Conseillère, Chicoutimi, Wards: 11
Michel Tremblay, Conseiller, Chicoutimi, Wards: 12
Jacques Cleary, Conseiller, Chicoutimi, Wards: 13
Josée Néron, Conseillère, Chicoutimi, Wards: 14
Jacques Fortin, Conseiller, Chicoutimi, Wards: 15
Luc Blackburn, Conseiller, Chicoutimi, Wards: 16
Martine Gauthier, Conseillère, La Baie, Wards: 17
Luc Boivin, Conseiller, La Baie, Wards: 18
François Tremblay, Conseiller, La Baie, Wards: 19
Caroline Dion, Greffière, 418-698-3260, Fax: 418-541-5961
Jean-François Boivin, Directeur général, 418-698-3320
Christine Tremblay, Trésorière et directrice, Trésorerie et évaluation, 418-698-3030, Fax: 418-698-3049
Denis Simard, Directeur général, Travaux publics
Jeannot Allard, Directeur, Communications, 418-698-3350, Fax: 418-541-4545
André Barrette, Directeur, Ressources humaines, 418-698-3331, Fax: 418-697-5254
Gaétan Bergeron, Directeur, Arrondissement de La Baie, 418-698-3357, Fax: 418-697-5059
Claude Bouchard, Directeur, Développement industriel
Denis Boucher, Directeur, Sécurité publique, 418-699-6000, Fax: 418-699-8206
Denis Coulombe, Directeur, Aménagement du territoire et urbanisme, 418-698-3130, Fax: 418-698-1158
Guylaine Houde, Directrice, Arts, culture, communautaire et bibliothèque, 418-698-3000, Fax: 418-698-3129
Sylvie Jean, Directrice, Approvisionnements, 418-698-3055, Fax: 418-546-2114
Daniel Larouche, Directeur, Arrondissement de Jonquière, 418-698-3356, Fax: 418-546-2058
André Martin, Directeur, Arrondissement de Chicoutimi, 418-698-3355, Fax: 418-698-3129
Camille Morin, Directrice, Affaires juridiques et du greffe, 418-698-3260, Fax: 418-541-5961
Jean Morneau, Directeur, Immeubles et équipements motorisés, 418-698-3060, Fax: 418-698-3069
Stéphane Poitras, Directeur, Ressources informationnelles, 418-698-3335, Fax: 418-697-5187
Pierre Racine, Directeur, Sports et du plein air, 418-698-3000, Fax: 418-699-6095

Saint-Amable
575, rue Principale
Saint-Amable, QC J0L 1N0
Tél: 450-649-3555; *Téléc:* 450-922-0728
www.st-amable.qc.ca
Entité municipal: City
Incorporation: 13 juin 1921; *Area:* 38,04 km2
Comté ou district: Marguerite-D'Youville; Communauté métropolitaine de Montréal; *Population au 2011:* 10,870
Circonscription(s) électorale(s) provinciale(s): Verchères
Circonscription(s) électorale(s) fédérale(s): Pierre-Boucher-Les Patriotes-Verchères
Prochaines élections: 5e novembre 2017
François Gamache, Maire
Monique Savard, Conseillère, Wards: 1
Dominic Gemmme, Conseiller, Wards: 2
Clairette Gemme McDuff, Conseillère, Wards: 3
Nathalie Poitras, Conseillère, Wards: 4
Mario McDuff, Conseiller, Wards: 5
Pierre Vermette, Conseiller, Wards: 6
Daniel Brazeau, Greffier, 450-649-3555
Carmen McDuff, Directrice générale, 450-649-3555
Josée Desmarais, Directrice, Service de la trésorerie, 450-649-3555
Michel Hugron, Directeur, Techniques, 450-649-3555
Sylvain St-Pierre, Directeur, Services incendies, 450-649-3555

Saint-Augustin-de-Desmaures
200, route de Fossambault
Saint-Augustin-de-Desmaures, QC G3A 2E3
Tél: 418-878-2955; *Téléc:* 418-878-0044
info@ville.st-augustin.qc.ca
www.ville.st-augustin.qc.ca
Entité municipal: City
Incorporation: 1er janvier 2006; *Area:* 85,76 km2
Comté ou district: Communauté métropolitaine de Québec; *Population au 2011:* 18,141
Circonscription(s) électorale(s) provinciale(s): Louis-Hébert
Circonscription(s) électorale(s) fédérale(s): Portneuf—Jacques-Cartier
Prochaines élections: 5e novembre 2017
Sylvain Juneau, Maire
Denis Côté, Conseiller, Wards: 1. Des Coteaux
France Hamel, Conseillère, Wards: 2. Portneuf
Lise Lortie, Conseillère, Wards: 3. Lahaye
Raynald Brulotte, Conseiller, Wards: 4. Du Lac
Guy Marcotte, Conseiller, Wards: 5. Les Bocages
Louis Potvin, Conseiller, Wards: 6. Haut Saint-Laurent
Daniel Martineau, Greffière
Robert Doré, Directeur général
Olivier Trudel, Greffière adjointe
Josée Larocque, Trésorière
François Bélanger, Directeur, Travaux publics
Étienne Pelletier, Directeur, Urbanisme
Éric Talbot, Directeur, Infrastructures

Saint-Basile-le-Grand
204, rue Principale
Saint-Basile-le-Grand, QC J3N 1M1
Tél: 450-461-8000
communciations@ville.saint-basile-le-grand.qc.ca
www.ville.saint-basile-le-grand.qc.ca
Entité municipal: City
Incorporation: 15 juin 1871; *Area:* 34,82 km2
Comté ou district: La Vallée-du-Richelieu; Communauté métropolitaine de Montréal; *Population au 2011:* 16,736
Circonscription(s) électorale(s) provinciale(s): Chambly
Circonscription(s) électorale(s) fédérale(s): Montarville
Prochaines élections: 5e novembre 2017
Bernard Gagnon, Maire, 450-461-8000
Maurice Cantin, Conseiller, Wards: 1
Line Marie Laurin, Conseillère, Wards: 2
Guylaine Yelle, Conseillère, Wards: 3
Jacques Fafard, Conseiller, Wards: 4
Normand Dieumegarde, Conseiller, Wards: 5
Josée Millette, Conseillère, Wards: 6
Sophie Deslauriers, Greffière, 450-461-8000, Fax: 450-461-8029
Jean-Marie Beaupré, Directeur général, 450-461-8000, Fax: 450-461-8039
Normand Lalande, Trésorier, 450-461-8000, Fax: 450-653-4394
François Pelletier, Directeur, Travaux publics, 450-461-8000, Fax: 450-461-8049
Robert Roussel, Directeur, Services techniques (génie et travaux publics), 450-461-8000, Fax: 450-461-8049
Lise Tétreault, Directrice, Urbanisme et de l'environnement, 450-461-8000, Fax: 450-461-8049
Alexandre Tremblay, Directeur, Sécurité incendie, 450-461-8000, Fax: 450-461-8039

Saint-Bruno-de-Montarville
1585, rue Montarville
Saint-Bruno-de-Montarville, QC J3V 3T8
Tél: 450-653-2443; *Téléc:* 450-441-8481
information@stbruno.ca
www.stbruno.ca
Entité municipal: City
Incorporation: 1er janvier 2006; *Area:* 43,28 km2
Comté ou district: Communauté métropolitaine de Montréal; *Population au 2011:* 26,107
Circonscription(s) électorale(s) provinciale(s): Montarville
Circonscription(s) électorale(s) fédérale(s): Montarville
Prochaines élections: 5e novembre 2017
Martin Murray, Maire
Thérèse Hudon, Conseillère, Wards: 1
Michael O'Dowd, Conseiller, Wards: 2
Isabelle Bérubé, Conseillère, Wards: 3
Martin Guevremont, Conseiller, Wards: 4
André Besner, Conseiller, Wards: 5
Marilou Alaire, Conseillère, Wards: 6
Jacques Bédard, Conseiller, Wards: 7
Michèle Archambault, Conseillère, Wards: 8
Lucie Tousignant, Greffière, 450-653-2443
Hélène Hamelin, Directrice générale, 450-645-2904
Roger Robitaille, Directeur, Finances, de la trésorerie et des technologies de l'information, 450-645-2910
Danielle Botella, Directrice, Génie, 450-645-2920
Jean Larose, Directeur, Développement urbain, 450-645-2930
Pierre Morin, Directeur, Travaux publics, 450-645-2960

Saint-Charles-Borromée
370, rue de la Visitation
Saint-Charles-Borromée, QC J6E 4P3
Tél: 450-759-4415; *Téléc:* 450-759-3393
info@st-charles-borromee.org
www.st-charles-borromee.org
Entité municipal: City
Incorporation: 1er juillet 1855; *Area:* 18,60 km2
Comté ou district: Joliette; *Population au 2011:* 13,321
Circonscription(s) électorale(s) provinciale(s): Joliette
Circonscription(s) électorale(s) fédérale(s): Joliette
Prochaines élections: 5e novembre 2017
André Hénault, Maire
Chantal Riopel, Conseillère, Wards: 1
Robert Bibeau, Conseiller, Wards: 2
Claude Bélanger, Conseiller, Wards: 3
Guy Rondeau, Conseiller, Wards: 4
Robert Groulx, Conseiller, Wards: 5
Janie Tremblay, Conseillère, Wards: 6

Claude Crépeau, Directeur général et secrétaire-trésorier
Jacques Fortin, Directeur/Chef, Brigade des pompiers
Johanne Bourdon, Responsable, Émission de permis et de certificats municipaux
Jean-Pierre Hétu, Responsable, Travaux publics
Jonathan Rondeau, Responsable, Urbanisme

Saint-Colomban
330, montée de l'Église
Saint-Colomban, QC J5K 1A1
Tél: 450-436-1453; *Téléc:* 450-436-5955
info@st-colomban.qc.ca
www.st-colomban.qc.ca
Entité municipal: City
Incorporation: 1er juillet 1855; *Area:* 94,24 km2
Comté ou district: La Rivière-du-Nord; *Population au 2011:* 13,080
Circonscription(s) électorale(s) provinciale(s): Argenteuil
Circonscription(s) électorale(s) fédérale(s): Mirabel
Prochaines élections: 5e novembre 2017
Jean Dumais, Maire
Steve Gagnon, Conseiller, Wards: 1
Eric Milot, Conseiller, Wards: 2
Julie Deslauriers, Conseillère, Wards: 3
François Boyer, Conseiller, Wards: 4
Stéphanie Tremblay, Conseillère, Wards: 5
Xavier-Antoine Lalande, Conseiller, Wards: 6
Stéphanie Parent, Greffière
Claude Panneton, Directeur général
Suzanne Rainville, Trésorière
Jacques Desbiens, Directeur, Travaux publics
Simon Harvey, Directeur, Sécurité incendie
Dominic Lirette, Directeur, Aménagement, environnement et urbanisme

Saint-Constant
147, rue St-Pierre
Saint-Constant, QC J5A 2G2
Tél: 450-638-2010; *Téléc:* 450-638-5919
communication@ville.saint-constant.qc.ca
www.ville.saint-constant.qc.ca
Entité municipal: City
Incorporation: 1er juillet 1855; *Area:* 57,04 km2
Comté ou district: Roussillon; Communauté métropolitaine de Montréal; *Population au 2011:* 24,980
Circonscription(s) électorale(s) provinciale(s): Sanguinet
Circonscription(s) électorale(s) fédérale(s): La Prairie
Prochaines élections: 5e novembre 2017
Jean-Claude Boyer, Maire
David Lemelin, Conseiller, Wards: 1
André Camirand, Conseiller, Wards: 2
Gilles Lapierre, Conseiller, Wards: 3
Chantale Boudrias, Conseillère, Wards: 4
Louise Savignac, Conseillère, Wards: 5
Thierry Maheu, Conseiller, Wards: 6
Mario Perron, Conseiller, Wards: 7
Mario Arsenault, Conseiller, Wards: 8
Sophie Laflammme, Greffière, 450-638-2010
Sylvain Boulianne, Directeur général, 450-638-2010
Annie Germain, Trésorière, 450-638-2010, Fax: 450-638-4764
Jean Gariépy, Directeur et chef, Brigade des pompiers, 450-638-2010
Sylvain Boulianne, Coordonnateur, Mesures d'urgence
Monnie Renouf, Responsable, Travaux publics, 450-638-2010, Fax: 450-632-0072
Hugo Sénéchal, Responsable, Urbanisme, 450-638-2010

Sainte-Adèle
1381, boul de Sainte-Adèle
Sainte-Adèle, QC J8B 1A3
Tél: 450-229-2921; *Téléc:* 450-229-4179
info@ville.sainte-adele.qc.ca
www.ville.sainte-adele.qc.ca
Entité municipal: City
Incorporation: 27 août 1997; *Area:* 122,19 km2
Comté ou district: Les Pays-d'en-Haut; *Population au 2011:* 12,137
Circonscription(s) électorale(s) provinciale(s): Bertrand
Circonscription(s) électorale(s) fédérale(s): Laurentides-Labelle
Prochaines élections: 5e novembre 2017
Robert Milot, Maire
Nadine Brière, Conseillère, Wards: 1
Roch Bédard, Conseiller, Wards: 2
Gilles Legault, Conseiller, Wards: 3
John Butler, Conseiller, Wards: 4
Robert Lagacé, Conseiller, Wards: 5
Diane de Passillé, Conseillère, Wards: 6
Simon Filiatreault, Greffier
Pierre Dionne, Directeur général
Brigitte Forget, Trésorière
Jean-Pierre Dontigny, Directeur, Urbanisme et de l'environnement

Patric Lacasse, Directeur, Travaux publics
Stéphane Lavallée, Directeur (part intérim), Sécurité incendie

Sainte-Agathe-des-Monts
50, rue St-Joseph
Sainte-Agathe-des-Monts, QC J8C 1M9
Tél: 819-326-4595; *Téléc:* 819-326-5784
info@ville.sainte-agathe-des-monts.qc.ca
www.ville.sainte-agathe-des-monts.qc.ca
Entité municipal: City
Incorporation: 27 février 2002; *Area:* 129,03 km2
Comté ou district: Les Laurentides; *Population au 2011:* 10,115
Circonscription(s) électorale(s) provinciale(s): Bertrand
Circonscription(s) électorale(s) fédérale(s): Laurentides-Labelle
Prochaines élections: 5e novembre 2017
Denis Chalifoux, Maire
Serge Bossé, Conseiller, Wards: 1
Sylvain Marinier, Conseiller, Wards: 2
Grant MacKenzie, Conseiller, Wards: 3
Yvan Chen, Conseiller, Wards: 4
Lise Gaudreau-Régimbald, Conseillère, Wards: 5
Jean-Léo Legault, Conseiller, Wards: 6
Benoît Fugère, Greffier et directeur général adjoint, 819-326-4595
Denis Savard, Directeur général, 819-326-4595
Roger Arteau, Directeur, Sécurité incendie, 819-326-4595
Marcel Baillargé, Directeur, Hygiène du milieu, 819-326-4595
Gilles Chamberland, Directeur, Services administratifs, 819-326-4595
Yvon Pelletier, Directeur, Travaux publics, 819-326-4595
Michel Thibault, Directeur, Génie et infrastructure, 819-326-4595

Sainte-Anne-des-Plaines
139, boul Ste-Anne
Sainte-Anne-des-Plaines, QC J0N 1H0
Tél: 450-478-0211; *Téléc:* 450-478-5660
info@villesadp.ca
www.villesadp.ca
Entité municipal: City
Incorporation: 1er juillet 1855; *Area:* 92,22 km2
Comté ou district: Thérèse-De Blainville; Communauté métropolitaine de Montréal; *Population au 2011:* 14,535
Circonscription(s) électorale(s) provinciale(s): Blainville
Circonscription(s) électorale(s) fédérale(s): Mirabel
Prochaines élections: 5e novembre 2017
Guy Charbonneau, Mairesse
Sylvie Chaput, Conseillère, Wards: 1
Alain Cassista, Conseiller, Wards: 2
Julie Boivin, Conseillère, Wards: 3
Denys Gagnon, Conseiller, Wards: 4
Mario Gauthier, Conseiller, Wards: 5
Véronique Baril, Conseiller, Wards: 6
Serge Lepage, Greffier et Directeur général
Christiane Joyal, Trésorière
Paul Fournier, Directeur, Travaux publics
Sébastien Laplante, Directeur, Sécurité incendie
Christian Leclair, Directeur, Urbanisme et environnement

Sainte-Catherine
5465, boul Marie-Victorin
Sainte-Catherine, QC J5C 1M1
Tél: 450-632-0590; *Téléc:* 450-632-3298
administration@ville.sainte-catherine.qc.ca
www.ville.sainte-catherine.qc.ca
Entité municipal: City
Incorporation: 30 octobre 1937; *Area:* 9,06 km2
Comté ou district: Roussillon; Communauté métropolitaine de Montréal; *Population au 2011:* 16,762
Circonscription(s) électorale(s) provinciale(s): Sanguinet
Circonscription(s) électorale(s) fédérale(s): La Prairie
Prochaines élections: 5e novembre 2017
Jocelyne Bates, Mairesse
Daniel Lamanque, Conseiller, Wards: 1
Martin Gélinas, Conseiller, Wards: 2
Jocelyne Brossard, Conseillère, Wards: 3
Louise Cormier, Conseillère, Wards: 4
Michel Béland, Conseiller, Wards: 5
Michel Leblanc, Conseiller, Wards: 6
Caroline Thibault, Greffière
Danielle Chevrette, Directrice générale
Serge Courchesne, Trésorier
Jean-Pierre Lacombe, Directeur et Chef, Brigade de pompiers
Pietro De Cubellis, Responsable, Travaux publics
Marie-Josée Halpin, Responsable, Urbanisme

Sainte-Julie
1580, ch du Fer-à-Cheval
Sainte-Julie, QC J3E 2M1
Tél: 450-922-7111; *Téléc:* 450-922-7108
communications@ville.sainte-julie.qc.ca
www.ville.sainte-julie.qc.ca
Entité municipal: City
Incorporation: 1er juillet 1855; *Area:* 47,78 km2
Comté ou district: Marguerite-D'Youville; Communauté métropolitaine de Montréal; *Population au 2011:* 30,104
Circonscription(s) électorale(s) provinciale(s): Verchères
Circonscription(s) électorale(s) fédérale(s): Montarville
Prochaines élections: 5e novembre 2017
Suzanne Roy, Mairesse, 450-922-7053
Isabelle Poulet, Conseillère, Wards: 1. Belle-Rivière/Ringuet
André Lemay, Conseiller, Wards: 2. Moulin
Jocelyn Ducharme, Conseillère, Wards: 3. Vallée
Nicole Marchand, Conseillère, Wards: 4. Rucher
Mario Lemay, Conseiller, Wards: 5. Vieux-Village
Normand Varin, Conseiller, Wards: 6. Grand-Coteau
Henri Corbin, Conseiller, Wards: 7. Arc-en-Ciel
Lucie Bisson, Conseillère, Wards: 8. Montagne
Nathalie Deschesnes, Greffière, 450-922-7050
Pierre Bernardin, Directeur général, 450-922-7102
sylvie Forest, Trésorière, 450-922-7062
Pierre-Luc Blanchard, Directeur, Urbanisme, 450-922-7142
Daniel Chagnon, Directeur, Loisirs, 450-922-7122
Marcel Dallaire, Jr., Directeur, Infrastructures, 450-922-7152

Sainte-Marie
270, av Marguerite-Bourgeoys
Sainte-Marie, QC G6E 3Z3
Tél: 418-387-2301; *Téléc:* 418-387-2454
info@sainte-marie.ca
www.sainte-marie.ca
Entité municipal: City
Incorporation: 15 avril 1978; *Area:* 106,65 km2
Comté ou district: La Nouvelle-Beauce; *Population au 2011:* 12,889
Circonscription(s) électorale(s) provinciale(s): Beauce-Nord
Circonscription(s) électorale(s) fédérale(s): Beauce
Prochaines élections: 5e novembre 2017
Gaétan Vachon, Maire
Luce Lacroix, Conseillère, Wards: 1
Claude Gagnon, Conseiller, Wards: 2
Rosaire Simoneau, Conseiller, Wards: 3
Steve Rouleau, Conseiller, Wards: 4
Nicole Boilard, Conseillère, Wards: 5
Eddy Faucher, Conseiller, Wards: 6
Hélène Gagné, Greffière, 418-387-2301
Jacques Boutin, Directeur général, 418-387-2301
Guy Cliche, Directeur, Police, 418-387-6111
Bruno Gilbert, Directeur, Ingénierie, 418-387-6111
Lucie Gravel, Directrice, Finances et de l'administration, 418-387-2301
Jules Martineau, Directeur, Parcs et des équipements récréatifs, 418-387-2362
Maurice Mercier, Directeur, Travaux publics, 418-387-6111
Claude Morin, Directeur, Sécurité incendie

Sainte-Marthe-sur-le-Lac
3000, ch d'Oka
Sainte-Marthe-sur-le-Lac, QC J0N 1P0
Tél: 450-472-7310; *Téléc:* 450-472-0109
info@ville.sainte-marthe-sur-le-lac.qc.ca
www.ville.sainte-marthe-sur-le-lac.qc.ca
Entité municipal: City
Incorporation: 1er janvier 1960; *Area:* 9,01 km2
Comté ou district: Deux-Montagnes; Communauté métropolitaine de Montréal; *Population au 2011:* 15,689
Circonscription(s) électorale(s) provinciale(s): Mirabel
Circonscription(s) électorale(s) fédérale(s): Mirabel
Prochaines élections: 5e novembre 2017
Sonia Paulus, Mairesse
François Robillard, Conseiller, Wards: 1
Jean-Guy Lajeunesse, Conseiller, Wards: 2
Yves Legault, Conseiller, Wards: 3
André Bessette, Conseiller, Wards: 4
Annie-Claude Lacombe, Conseillère, Wards: 5
François Racine, Conseiller, Wards: 6
Sylvie Brunet, Greffière
André Charron, Directeur général
Cindy Caron, Trésorière
Carl Lavoie, Directeur, Travaux publics
Steven Hall Labonté, Directeur, Services urbains

Sainte-Sophie
2199, boul Sainte-Sophie
Sainte-Sophie, QC J5J 1A1
Tél: 450-438-7784; *Téléc:* 450-438-1080
courrier@stesophie.ca
www.stesophie.ca
Other Information: Sans frais: 1-877-438-7784
Entité municipal: City
Incorporation: 3 mai 2000; *Area:* 108,98 km2
Comté ou district: La Rivière-du-Nord; *Population au 2011:* 13,375
Circonscription(s) électorale(s) provinciale(s): Rousseau

Circonscription(s) électorale(s) fédérale(s): Rivière-du-Nord
Prochaines élections: 5e novembre 2017
Louise Gallant, Mairesse, 450-438-7784
Sophie Astri, Conseillère, 450-438-7784, Wards: 1
Claude Lamontagne, Conseiller, 450-438-7784, Wards: 2
Linda Lalonde, Conseillère, 450-438-7784, Wards: 3
Éric Jutras, Conseiller, 450-438-7784, Wards: 4
Guy Lamothe, Conseiller, 450-438-7784, Wards: 5
Normand Aubin, Conseiller, 450-438-7784, Wards: 6
Matthieu Ledoux, Directeur général, 450-438-7784
Joël Houde, ing., Directeur général adjoint et directeur, Travaux publics, 450-438-7784
Sophie Plouffe, Directrice, Finances et secrétaire-trésorière adjointe, 450-438-7784
Ghislain Grenier, Directeur, Sécurité incendie, 450-438-7784
Alexandre Larouche, Directeur, Urbanisme, 450-438-7784

Sainte-Thérèse
CP 100
6, rue de l'Église
Sainte-Thérèse, QC J7E 4H7
Tél: 450-434-1440; *Téléc:* 450-434-1499
info@sainte-therese.ca
www.ville.sainte-therese.qc.ca
Entité municipal: City
Incorporation: 1er juin 1849; *Area:* 8,62 km2
Comté ou district: Thérèse-De Blainville; Communauté métropolitaine de Montréal; *Population au 2011:* 26,025
Circonscription(s) électorale(s) provinciale(s): Groulx
Circonscription(s) électorale(s) fédérale(s): Thérèse-De Blainville
Prochaines élections: 5e novembre 2017
Sylvie Surprenant, Mairesse
Barbara Morin, Conseillère, Wards: 1. Sève
Patrick Morin, Conseiller, Wards: 2. Verschelden
Patrick Kearney, Conseiller, Wards: 3. Morris
Normand Toupin, Conseiller, Wards: 4. Chapleau
Luc Vézina, Conseiller, Wards: 5. Lonergan
Michel Milette, Conseiller, Wards: 6. Ducharme
Armando Melo, Conseiller, Wards: 7. Blanchard
Johane Michaud, Conseillère, Wards: 8. Marie-Thérèse
Jean-Luc Berthiaume, Greffier
Chantal Gauvreau, Directrice générale
Nathalie Reniers, Trésorière
Éric Boivin, Directeur, Travaux publics
Nicola Cardone, Directeur, Urbanisme et du développement durable
Richard Grenier, Directeur, Sécurité d'incendie

Saint-Eustache
145, rue St-Louis
Saint-Eustache, QC J7R 1X9
Tél: 450-974-5000; *Téléc:* 450-974-5229
sem@ville.saint-eustache.qc.ca
www.ville.saint-eustache.qc.ca
Entité municipal: City
Incorporation: 15 janvier 1972; *Area:* 70,61 km2
Comté ou district: Deux-Montagnes; Communauté métropolitaine de Montréal; *Population au 2011:* 44,154
Circonscription(s) électorale(s) provinciale(s): Deux-Montagnes
Circonscription(s) électorale(s) fédérale(s): Rivière-des-Mille-Îles
Prochaines élections: 5e novembre 2017
Pierre Charron, Maire, Fax: 450-974-5203
Michèle Labelle, Conseillère, 450-623-0809, Wards: 1. Vieux-Saint-Eustache
André Biard, Conseiller, 450-473-2214, Wards: 2. Carrefour
Patrice Paquette, Conseiller, 450-974-1120, Wards: 3. Rivière-Nord
Janique-Aimée Danis, Conseillère, 450-491-2522, Wards: 4. Des Érables
Marc Lamarre, Conseiller, 450-473-4792, Wards: 5. Clair Matin
Julie Desmarais, Conseillère, 450-598-6198, Wards: 6. Seigneurie
Isabelle Lefebvre, Conseillère, 450-473-5400, Wards: 7. Moissons
Raymond Tessier, Conseiller, 450-472-3951, Wards: 8. Îles
Nicole Carignan Lefebvre, Conseillère, 450-623-5730, Wards: 9. Plateau-des-Chênes
Sylvie Cloutier, Conseillère, 450-392-7725, Wards: 10. Jardins
Marc Tourangeau, Greffier
Christian Bellemare, Directeur général, 450-974-5280
Ginette Lacoix, Trésorière, Fax: 450-974-5077
Bastien Morin, Directeur, Services municipaux, 450-974-5001, Fax: 450-974-5229
Stéphanie Bouchard, Directrice, Communications, Fax: 450-974-5223

Saint-Félicien
CP 7000
1209, boul Sacré-Coeur
Saint-Félicien, QC G8K 2R5
Tél: 418-679-2100; *Téléc:* 418-679-1449
info@ville.stfelicien.qc.ca
www.ville.stfelicien.qc.ca
Entité municipal: City
Incorporation: 12 juin 1996; *Area:* 359,69 km2
Comté ou district: Le Domaine-du-Roy; *Population au 2011:* 10,278
Circonscription(s) électorale(s) provinciale(s): Roberval
Circonscription(s) électorale(s) fédérale(s): Lac-St-Jean
Prochaines élections: 5e novembre 2017
Gilles Potvin, Maire, 418-679-2100
Dany Bouchard, Conseiller, Wards: 1
Bernard Boivin, Conseiller, Wards: 2
Michel Gagnon, Conseiller, Wards: 3
Luc Gibbons, Conseiller, Wards: 4
Sonia Boudreault, Conseillère, Wards: 5
Alexandre L. Paradis, Conseiller, Wards: 6
Louise Ménard, Greffière, 418-679-2100
Mario Ménard, Directeur général, 418-679-2100
Dany Coudé, Trésorier, 418-679-2100, Fax: 418-679-2178
Michel Larose, Directeur général adjoint et responsable, Ressources humaines, 418-679-2100, Fax: 418-679-1449
Olivier de Launière, Directeur, Sécurité incendie, 418-679-0313, Fax: 418-679-8217
Denis Simard, Directeur, Services techniques, 418-679-2100, Fax: 418-679-4083
Gilaine Beaudoin, Secrétaire administrative, Travaux publics, 418-679-2100, Fax: 418-679-4083

Saint-Georges
11700, boul Lacroix
Saint-Georges, QC G5Y 1L3
Tél: 418-228-5555; *Téléc:* 418-228-3855
www.ville.saint-georges.qc.ca
Entité municipal: City
Incorporation: 26 septembre 2001; *Area:* 199,51 km2
Comté ou district: Beauce-Sartigan; *Population au 2011:* 31,173
Circonscription(s) électorale(s) provinciale(s): Beauce-Sud
Circonscription(s) électorale(s) fédérale(s): Beauce
Prochaines élections: 5e novembre 2017
Claude Morin, Maire
Serge Thomassin, Conseiller, Wards: 1
Tom Redmond, Conseiller, Wards: 2
Jean Perron, Conseiller, Wards: 3
Irma Quirion, Conseillère, Wards: 4
Manon Bougie, Conseillère, Wards: 5
Jean-Pierre Fortier, Conseiller, Wards: 6
Solange Thibodeau, Conseillère, Wards: 7
Renaud Fortier, Conseiller, Wards: 8
Jean McCollough, Greffier
Marcel Grondin, Directeur général
Isabelle Déchêne, Trésorière
Guy Bilodeau, Directeur, Service des travaux publics
Frances Donovan, Directrice, Service urbanisme
Sylvain Veilleux, Directeur, Service des incendies

Saint-Hyacinthe
CP 10
700, av de l'Hôtel-de-Ville
Saint-Hyacinthe, QC J2S 5B2
Tél: 450-778-8300; *Téléc:* 450-778-8605
communications@ville.st-hyacinthe.qc.ca
www.ville.st-hyacinthe.qc.ca
Entité municipal: City
Incorporation: 27 décembre 2001; *Area:* 189,11 km2
Comté ou district: Les Maskoutains; *Population au 2011:* 53,236
Circonscription(s) électorale(s) provinciale(s): St-Hyacinthe
Circonscription(s) électorale(s) fédérale(s): St-Hyacinthe—Bagot
Prochaines élections: 5e novembre 2017
Claude Corbeil, Maire, 450-778-8302, Fax: 450-778-5800
Donald Côté, Conseiller, Wards: 1. Sainte-Rosalie
Sylvain Savoie, Conseiller, Wards: 2. Yamaska
Johanne Delage, Conseillère, Wards: 3. Saint-Joseph
Bernard Barré, Conseiller, Wards: 4. La Providence
André Beauregard, Conseiller, Wards: 5. Douville
Jacques Denis, Conseiller, Wards: 6. Saint-Thomas-d'Aquin
Annie Pelletier, Conseillère, Wards: 7. Saint-Sacrement
Alain Leclerc, Conseiller, Wards: 8. Bois-Joli
David Bousquet, Conseiller, Wards: 9. Sacré-Coeur
Sylvie Adam, Conseillère, Wards: 10. Cascades
Nicole Dion-Audette, Conseillère, Wards: 11. Hertel-Notre-Dame
Hélène Beauchesne, Greffière, 450-778-8317, Fax: 450-778-2514
Louis Bilodeau, Directeur général, 450-778-8303
Michel Tradif, OMA, Trésorier, 450-778-8306, Fax: 450-778-7749
Chantal Frigon, Directrice générale adjointe
Yvan De Lachevrotière, Directeur, Travaux publics, 450-778-8470, Fax: 450-778-8460
Daniel Dubois, Directeur, Sécurité incendie, 450-778-8550, Fax: 450-778-5853

Saint-Jean-sur-Richelieu
CP 1025
188, rue Jacques-Cartier nord
Saint-Jean-sur-Richelieu, QC J3B 7B2
Tél: 450-357-2100; *Téléc:* 450-357-2285
info@ville.saint-jean-sur-richelieu.qc.ca
www.ville.saint-jean-sur-richelieu.qc.ca
Entité municipal: City
Incorporation: 24 janvier 2001; *Area:* 225,61 km2
Comté ou district: Le Haut-Richelieu; *Population au 2011:* 92,394
Circonscription(s) électorale(s) provinciale(s): Iberville; St-Jean
Circonscription(s) électorale(s) fédérale(s): Saint-Jean
Prochaines élections: 5e novembre 2017
Michel Fecteau, Maire, 450-357-2095, Fax: 450-357-2079
Mélanie Dufresne, Conseillère, 514-714-8410, Wards: 1
Justin Bessette, Conseiller, 514-718-5675, Wards: 2
Hugues Larivière, Conseiller, 450-346-2392, Wards: 3
Jean Fontaine, Conseiller, 450-346-3063, Wards: 4
François Auger, Conseiller, 514-432-3951, Wards: 5
Patricia Poissant, Conseillère, 450-741-1236, Wards: 6
Christiane Marcoux, Conseillère, 450-347-5277, Wards: 7
Marco Savard, Conseiller, 450-349-0473, Wards: 8
Yvan Berthelot, Conseiller, 450-349-0685, Wards: 9
Ian Langlois, Conseiller, 450-515-3259, Wards: 10
Claire Charbonneau, Conseillère, 450-348-0463, Wards: 11
Robert Cantin, Conseiller, 450-349-6661, Wards: 12
François Lapointe, Greffier, 450-357-2077, Fax: 450-357-2362
Daniel Desroches, Directeur général, 450-357-2383, Fax: 450-357-2385
Raymond LeBlanc, Trésorier, 450-357-2392, Fax: 450-357-2286
Roch Arbour, Directeur, Travaux publics, 450-357-2238, Fax: 450-357-2290
Serge Boulerice, Directeur, Police, 450-359-9222, Fax: 450-359-2631
Luc Castonguay, Directeur, Urbanisme, 450-359-2400, Fax: 450-359-2407
Jean-Pierre Laporte, Directeur et chef, Brigade des pompiers

Saint-Jérôme
#301, 10, rue St-Joseph
Saint-Jérôme, QC J7Z 7G7
Tél: 450-436-1511; *Téléc:* 450-436-6626
info@vsj.ca
www.vsj.ca
Entité municipal: City
Incorporation: 1er janvier 2002; *Area:* 89,37 km2
Comté ou district: La Rivière-du-Nord; *Population au 2011:* 68,456
Circonscription(s) électorale(s) provinciale(s): Saint-Jérôme
Circonscription(s) électorale(s) fédérale(s): Rivière-du-Nord
Prochaines élections: 5e novembre 2017
Stéphane Maher, Maire, 450-436-1512
Benoit Beaulieu, Conseiller, 514-234-7226, Wards: 1
Colette Thibault, Conseillère, 450-304-3301, Wards: 2
François Poirier, Conseiller, 450-275-7742, Wards: 3
Marc Bourcier, Conseiller, 450-602-7779, Wards: 4
Bernard Bougie, Conseiller, 450-431-7227, Wards: 5
Benoît Delage, Conseiller, 450-436-6134, Wards: 6
Stéphanie Viens-Proulx, Conseillère, 450-512-2916, Wards: 7
Johanne Dicaire, Conseillère, 450-432-7927, Wards: 8
André Marion, Conseiller, 450-280-9843, Wards: 9
Mario Fauteux, Conseiller, 450-432-7662, Wards: 10
Gilles Robert, Conseiller, 450-512-9391, Wards: 11
Nathalie Lasalle, Conseillère, 450-712-3037, Wards: 12
Luc Savoie, Conseiller, 450-592-3921, Wards: 13
Michèle Céclier, Conseillère, 450-438-1073, Wards: 14
Marie-Josée Larocque, Greffière
Yvan Patenaude, Directeur général et directeur, Communications
Johanne Coursol, Trésorière
Fernand Boudreault, Directeur, Travaux publics
Louis Bruneault, Directeur/Chef, Police
Daniel Hillman, Directeur, Sécurité incendie et des mesures d'urgence
Richard St-Jean, Directeur, Urbanisme

Saint-Lambert
55, avenue Argyle
Saint-Laurent, QC J4P 2H3
Tél: 450-672-4444; *Téléc:* 450-672-3732
info.citoyens@saint-lambert.ca
www.ville.saint-lambert.qc.ca
Entité municipal: City
Incorporation: 1er janvier 2006; *Area:* 6,43 km2
Comté ou district: Communauté métropolitaine de Montréal; *Population au 2011:* 21,555
Circonscription(s) électorale(s) provinciale(s): Laporte

Circonscription(s) électorale(s) fédérale(s): Brossard-Saint-Lambert
Prochaines élections: 5e novembre 2017
Alain Dépatie, Maire, 450-466-3235
Jean Bouchard, Conseiller, 450-671-3532, Wards: 1
Martin Smith, Conseiller, 514-513-8768, Wards: 2
Boris Chassagne, Conseiller, 514-436-5407, Wards: 3
Dominique Lebeau, Conseiller, 438-883-0328, Wards: 4
Jean-Pierre Roy, Conseiller, 450-923-2416, Wards: 5
Hugues Létourneau, Conseiller, 450-465-8712, Wards: 6
David Bowles, Conseiller, 450-812-6237, Wards: 7
Martin Croteau, Conseiller, 450-923-7219, Wards: 8
Mario Gerbeau, Greffier
François Vaillancourt, Directeur général
Jean-Robert Belliveau, Trésorier
Régis Savard, Évaluateur signataire

Saint-Lazare

1960, ch Ste-Angélique
Saint-Lazare, QC J7T 3A3
Tél: 450-424-8000; *Téléc:* 450-455-4712
info@ville.saint-lazare.qc.ca
www.ville.saint-lazare.qc.ca
Entité municipal: City
Incorporation: 29 décembre 1875; *Area:* 67,59 km2
Comté ou district: Vaudreuil-Soulanges; Communauté métropolitaine de Montréal; *Population au 2011:* 19,295
Circonscription(s) électorale(s) provinciale(s): Soulanges
Circonscription(s) électorale(s) fédérale(s): Vaudreuil-Soulanges
Prochaines élections: 5e novembre 2017
Robert Grimaudo, Maire, 450-424-8000
Lise Jolicoeur, Conseillère, 450-424-8000, Wards: 1
Pamela Tremblay, Conseillère, 450-424-8000, Wards: 2
Brigitte Asselin, Conseillère, 450-424-8000, Wards: 3
Denis Briard, Conseiller, 450-424-8000, Wards: 4
Serge David, Conseiller, 450-424-8000, Wards: 5
Richard Nataf, Conseiller, 450-424-8000, Wards: 6
Nathaly Rayneault, Greffière
Serge Tremblay, Directeur général
Brigitte Bonin, Trésorière
Daniel Boyer, Directeur et chef, Brigade des pompiers
Patrick Descheneaux, Responsable, Travaux publics
Francine Parent, Responsable, Émission de permis et de certificats municipaux
Ginette Roy, Responsable, Urbanisme

Saint-Lin-Laurentides

900, 12e av
Saint-Lin-Laurentides, QC J5M 2W2
Tél: 450-439-3130; *Téléc:* 450-439-1525
info@saint-lin-laurentides.com
saint-lin-laurentides.com
Entité municipal: City
Incorporation: 1er mars 2000; *Area:* 117,52 km2
Comté ou district: Montcalm; *Population au 2011:* 17,463
Circonscription(s) électorale(s) provinciale(s): Rousseau
Circonscription(s) électorale(s) fédérale(s): Montcalm
Prochaines élections: 5e novembre 2017
Patrick Massé, Maire, 450-439-3130
Luc Cyr, Conseiller, 450-439-6588, Wards: 1
Mathieu Maisonneuve, Conseiller, 450-772-1849, Wards: 2
Mario Chrétien, Conseiller, 450-439-8055, Wards: 3
Jean-Luc Arène, Conseiller, 450-431-1465, Wards: 4
Benoit Venne, Conseiller, 450-772-0388, Wards: 5
Pierre Lortie, Conseiller, 450-439-8230, Wards: 6
Richard Dufort, Greffier & Directeur général
Sylvain Martel, Trésorier, 450-439-3130
Jean-Pierre Desjardins, Directeur, Incendies, 450-439-3130
André Héroux, Directeur, Travaux publics, 450-439-3130
Robert Marsolais, Directeur, Urbanisme

Salaberry-de-Valleyfield

61, rue Ste-Cécile
Salaberry-de-Valleyfield, QC J6T 1L8
Tél: 450-370-4770; *Téléc:* 450-370-4388
communications@ville.valleyfield.qc.ca
www.ville.valleyfield.qc.ca
Entité municipal: City
Incorporation: 24 avril 2002; *Area:* 100,96 km2
Comté ou district: Beauharnois-Salaberry; *Population au 2011:* 40,077
Circonscription(s) électorale(s) provinciale(s): Beauharnois
Circonscription(s) électorale(s) fédérale(s): Salaberry-Suroît
Prochaines élections: 5e novembre 2017
Denis Lapointe, Maire, 450-370-4819
Denis Laître, Conseiller, 450-373-0954, Wards: 1. Grande-Île
Jean-Marc Rochon, Conseiller, 450-377-2774, Wards: 2. Nitro
Louise Sauvé, Conseillère, 450-377-8597, Wards: 3. Georges-Leduc
Jean-Luc Pomerleau, Conseiller, 450-373-8195, Wards: 4. Champlain
François Labossière, Conseiller, 450-747-3899, Wards: 5. La Baie
Jacques Smith, Conseiller, 450-371-4975, Wards: 6. Robert-Cauchon
Patrick Rancourt, Conseiller, 450-370-1717, Wards: 7. Jules-Léger
Normand Amesse, Conseiller, 450-371-6895, Wards: 8. Saint-Timothée
Alain Gagnon, Greffier, 450-370-4304, Fax: 450-370-4388
Pierre Chevrier, Directeur général, 450-370-4800, Fax: 450-370-4343
Michel Décosse, Trésorier, 450-370-4320, Fax: 450-370-4316
Michel Ménard, Directeur, Sécurité incendie, 450-370-4750, Fax: 450-370-4755
Denis Larochelle, Directeur, Eau, environnement et travaux publics, 450-370-4820, Fax: 450-370-4370
Martin Pharand, Directeur, Urbanisme, 450-370-4310, Fax: 450-370-4772
Danielle Prieur, Coordonnatrice, 450-370-4875, Fax: 450-370-0823

Sept-îles

546, av De Quen
Sept-îles, QC G4R 2R4
Tél: 418-962-2525; *Téléc:* 418-964-3213
communications@ville.sept-iles.qc.ca
www.ville.sept-iles.qc.ca
Entité municipal: City
Incorporation: 12 février 2003; *Area:* 1 969,42 km2
Comté ou district: Sept-Rivières; *Population au 2011:* 25,686
Circonscription(s) électorale(s) provinciale(s): Duplessis
Circonscription(s) électorale(s) fédérale(s): Manicouagan
Prochaines élections: 5e novembre 2017
Note: En 1970, Clarke City est fusionnée à Sept-Iles; le 12 fév., 2003, Moisie & Gallix sont fusionnées à Sept-Iles.
Réjean Porlier, Maire
Élisabeth Chevalier, Conseillère, Wards: 1. Ste-Marguerite
Guylaine Lejeune, Conseillère, Wards: 2. Ferland
Jean Masse, Conseiller, Wards: 3. L'Anse
Denis Miousse, Conseiller, Wards: 4. Marie-Immaculée
Guy Berthe, Conseiller, Wards: 5. Vieux-Quai
Lorraine Dubuc-Johnson, Conseillère, Wards: 6. Mgr-Blanche
Charlotte Audet, Conseillère, Wards: 7. Jacques-Cartier
Michel Bellavance, Conseiller, Wards: 8. Sainte-Famille
Louisette Doiron-Catto, Conseillère, Wards: 9. Moisie-Plages
Valérie Haince, Greffière
Claude Bureau, Directeur général, 418-964-3201
Léna Simard, Présidente, Corporation de protection de l'environnement de Sept-Iles (CPESI)
Serge Gagné, Trésorier et Directeur, Finances, 418-964-3215
Denis Jutras, Directeur, Sécurité incendie, 418-964-3280
Michel Tardiff, Directeur, Ingénierie et des travaux publics, 418-964-3300
Denis Tetreault, Directeur, Urbanisme, 418-964-3233

Shawinigan

CP 400
550, av de l'Hôtel-de-Ville
Shawinigan, QC G9N 6V3
Tél: 819-536-7200; *Téléc:* 819-536-7255
information@shawinigan.ca
www.shawinigan.ca
Entité municipal: City
Incorporation: 1er janvier 2002; *Area:* 781,81 km2
Population au 2011: 50,060
Circonscription(s) électorale(s) provinciale(s): Saint-Maurice; Laviolette
Circonscription(s) électorale(s) fédérale(s): Saint-Maurice-Champlain
Prochaines élections: 5e novembre 2017
Note: 8 nouveaux districts seront en vigueur lors des élections municipal de nov/09.
Michel Angers, Maire, 819-536-7211
Josette Allard-Gignac, Conseillère, 819-537-4727, Wards: Almaville
Martin Asselin, Conseiller, 819-533-5953, Wards: Boisés
Alain Lord, Conseiller, 819-539-8462, Wards: Cité
Jean-Yves Tremblay, Conseiller, 819-536-7211, Wards: Hêtres
Serge Aubry, Conseiller, 819-539-9474, Wards: Montagnes
Nancy Déziel, Conseillère, 819-247-8508, Wards: Rivière
Lucie de Bons, Conseillère, 819-538-7348, Wards: Rocher
Guy Arseneault, Conseiller, 819-536-7010, Wards: Val-Mauricie
Yves Vincent, Greffier, 819-536-7211
Gaétan Béchard, Directeur général, 819-536-7211
Harold Hellefsen, Directeur général adjoint
Sylvie Lavoie, Directrice, Services administratifs, 819-536-7211
Pierre Beaulieu, Directeur, Travaux publics, 819-536-7211
Robert Y. Desjardins, Directeur, Loisirs, culture et vie communautaire, 819-536-5545
François Garceau, Directeur, Ressources humaines, 819-536-7211
Claude Larocque, Directeur, Techniques, 819-536-7211
François Lelièvre, Directeur, Sécurité incendie, 819-538-2248
François St-Onge, Directeur, Communications, 819-536-7211
Robert Taylor, Directeur, Aménagement et de l'environnement, 819-536-7211

Sherbrooke

CP 610
191, rue du Palais
Sherbrooke, QC J1H 5H9
Tél: 819-823-8000; *Téléc:* 819-822-6064
www.ville.sherbrooke.qc.ca
Entité municipal: City
Incorporation: 1er janvier 2002; *Area:* 366,00 km2
Population au 2011: 154,601
Circonscription(s) électorale(s) provinciale(s): St-François; Sherbrooke; Richmond
Circonscription(s) électorale(s) fédérale(s): Sherbrooke
Prochaines élections: 5e novembre 2017
Bernard Sévigny, Maire, 819-821-5969
Benoit Dionne, Conseiller, Brompton, 819-846-4725, Wards: Beauvoir
Nicole Bergeron, Conseillère, Brompton, 819-846-2757, Wards: Brompton
Kathleen Gélinas, Conseillère, Brompton, 819-846-1858, Wards: Moulins
Danielle Berthold, Conseillère, Fleurimont, 819-574-0991, Wards: Desranleau
Louisda Brochu, Conseiller, Fleurimont, 819-565-9954, Wards: Lavigerie
Rémi Demers, Conseiller, Fleurimont, 819-565-1066, Wards: Marie-Rivier
Hélène Dauphinais, Conseillère, Fleurimont, 819-822-3409, Wards: Pin-Solitaire
Vincent Boutin, Conseiller, Fleurimont, 819-345-1029, Wards: Quatre-Saisons
Claude Charron, Conseiller, Lennoxville, 819-563-7525, Wards: Fairview
David W. Price, Conseiller, Lennoxville, 819-569-9388, Wards: Lennoxville
Linda Boulanger, Conseillère, Lennoxville, 819-820-2661, Wards: Uplands
Robert Y. Pouliot, Conseiller, Mont-Bellevue, 819-563-1848, Wards: Ascot
Serge Paquin, Conseiller, Mont-Bellevue, 819-346-9312, Wards: Centre-Sud
Nicole A. Gagnon, Conseillère, Mont-Bellevue, 819-562-3625, Wards: Croix-Lumineuse
Jean-François Rouleau, Conseiller, Mont-Bellevue, 819-569-0208, Wards: Université
Bruno Vachon, Conseiller, Rock Forest-Saint-Élie-Deauville, 819-212-5688, Wards: Châteaux-d'Eau
Diane Délisle, Conseillère, Rock Forest-Saint-Élie-Deauville, 819-864-4656, Wards: Deauville
Annie Godbout, Conseillère, Rock Forest-Saint-Élie-Deauville, 819-432-6537, Wards: Rock Forest
Julien Lachance, Conseiller, Rock Forest-Saint-Élie-Deauville, 819-566-7886, Wards: Saint-Élie
Christine Ouellet, Conseillère, Jacques-Cartier, 819-542-1382, Wards: Beckett
Pierre Tardif, Conseiller, Jacques-Cartier, 819-566-7926, Wards: Carrefour
Chantal L'Espérance, Conseillère, Jacques-Cartier, 819-565-8089, Wards: Domaine Howard
Marc Denault, Conseiller, Jacques-Cartier, 819-565-5555, Wards: Montcalm
Isabelle Sauvé, Greffière, 819-821-5500, Fax: 819-822-6064
Yves Vermette, Directeur général, 819-823-8000, Fax: 819-823-5121
François Poulette, Trésorier, 819-821-5490, Fax: 819-822-6091
René Allaire, Directeur général adjoint et responsable, Travaux publics
Alain Duval, Directeur, Ressources humaines, 819-821-5677, Fax: 819-822-6086
Gaétan Labbé, Directeur et Chef de police, 819-821-5555, Fax: 819-822-6088
Stéphane Simoneau, Directeur, Sécurité d'incendie, 819-822-6098, Fax: 819-821-5516
Colette Ouellet, Responsable, Communications, 819-821-5572, Fax: 819-823-5153

Sorel-Tracy

CP 368
71, rue Charlotte
Sorel-Tracy, QC J3P 7K1
Tél: 450-780-5600; *Téléc:* 450-780-5625
info@ville.sorel-tracy.qc.ca
www.ville.sorel.qc.ca
Entité municipal: City
Incorporation: 15 mars 2000; *Area:* 56,58 km2
Comté ou district: Pierre-De Saurel; *Population au 2011:* 34,600

Circonscription(s) électorale(s) provinciale(s): Richelieu
Circonscription(s) électorale(s) fédérale(s): Bécancour-Nicolet-Saurel
Prochaines élections: 5e novembre 2017
Serge Péloquin, Maire
Sophie Chevalier, Conseillère, 450-780-5600, Wards: 1. Bourgchemin
André Potvin, Conseiller, 450-746-2536, Wards: 2. Richelieu
Yvon Bibeau, Conseiller, 450-746-8987, Wards: 3. Saint-Laurent
Jocelyn Mondou, Conseillère, 450-881-6738, Wards: 4. Vieux-Sorel
Alain Maher, Conseiller, 450-743-8749, Wards: 5. Faubourg
Benoit Guèvremont, Conseiller, 450-780-5600, Wards: 6. Gouverneurs
Patrick Péloquin, Conseiller, 450-780-5600, Wards: 7. Patriotes
Dominique Ouellet, Conseillère, 450-780-1248, Wards: 8. Pierre-De Saurel
René Chevalier, Greffier, 450-780-5600
Mario Lazure, Directeur général, 450-780-5600
Vicky Bussière, Directrice, Finances & Trésorerie, 450-780-5600
Pierre Dauphinias, Directeur, Planification et développement urbain (urbanisme), 450-780-5600
David Gagné, Directeur, Travaux publics, 450-780-5600
Alain Rouleau, Directeur, Sécurité incendie, 450-780-5600

Terrebonne

775, rue St-Jean-Baptiste
Terrebonne, QC J6W 1B5
Tél: 450-961-2001; *Téléc:* 450-471-4482
information@ville.terrebonne.qc.ca
www.ville.terrebonne.qc.ca
Entité municipal: City
Incorporation: 27 juin 2001; *Area:* 155,44 km2
Comté ou district: Les Moulins; Communauté métropolitaine de Montréal; *Population au 2011:* 106,322
Circonscription(s) électorale(s) provinciale(s): L'Assomption; Terrebonne; Masson
Circonscription(s) électorale(s) fédérale(s): Terrebonne
Prochaines élections: 5e novembre 2017
Jean-Marc Robitaille, Maire
Brigitte Villeneuve, Conseillère, 450-478-5929, Wards: 1
Nathalie Bellavance, Conseillère, 450-478-7440, Wards: 2
Marie-Claude Lamarche, Conseillère, 450-477-7565, Wards: 3
Réal Leclerc, Conseiller, 450-433-1310, Wards: 4
Serge Gagnon, Conseiller, 514-647-5266, Wards: 5
Michel Morin, Conseiller, 450-492-1266, Wards: 6
Paul Asselin, Conseiller, 450-964-0467, Wards: 7
Marie-Josée Beaupré, Conseillère, 450-471-0763, Wards: 8
Marc Campagna, Conseiller, 450-704-4972, Wards: 9
Frédéric Asselin, Conseiller, 450-961-0594, Wards: 10
Clermont Lévesque, Conseiller, 450-471-2071, Wards: 11
André Fontaine, Conseiller, 450-492-4212, Wards: 12
Sylvain Tousignant, Conseiller, 450-471-5653, Wards: 13
Claire Messier, Conseillère, 450-964-7269, Wards: 14
Stéphane Berthe, Conseiller, 450-964-5557, Wards: 15
Jean-Guy Sénécal, Conseiller, 450-654-6446, Wards: 16
Denis Bouffard, Greffier
Luc Papillon, Directeur général
Francine Blain, Trésorière
Marc Brisson, Chef de police
Jacques Bérubé, Directeur, Service sécurité d'incendie
Michel Larue, Directeur, Urbanisme durable

Thetford Mines

CP 489
144, rue Notre-Dame sud
Thetford Mines, QC G6G 5T3
Tél: 418-335-2981; *Téléc:* 418-335-7089
infos@ville.thetfordmines.qc.ca
www.ville.thetfordmines.qc.ca
Entité municipal: City
Incorporation: 17 octobre 2001; *Area:* 224,37 km2
Comté ou district: Les Appalaches; *Population au 2011:* 25,709
Circonscription(s) électorale(s) provinciale(s): Lotbinière-Frontenac
Circonscription(s) électorale(s) fédérale(s): Mégantic-L'Érable
Prochaines élections: 5e novembre 2017
Marc-Alexandre Brousseau, Maire
Josée Perreault, Conseillère, 418-423-7387, Wards: 1. Black Lake
Jean-Francois Morissette, Conseiller, 418-332-3600, Wards: 2. Black Lake-Mitchell/Lacs
Michel Verrault, Conseiller, 418-338-1394, Wards: 3. Thetford Mines
Denise P. Bergeron, Conseillère, 418-335-2592, Wards: 4. Thetford Mines
Jean-Francois Delisle, Conseiller, 418-334-0763, Wards: 5. Thetford Mines
Hélène Martin, Conseiller, 418-338-1249, Wards: 6. Thetford Mines
Marco Tanguay, Conseiller, 418-338-8819, Wards: 7. Thetford Mines
Yves Bergeron, Conseiller, 418-338-4770, Wards: 8. Thetford Mines
Francois Madore, Conseiller, 418-338-5313, Wards: 9. Thetford-Sud
Daniel Poudrier, Conseiller, 418-334-0616, Wards: 10. Robertsonville/Pontbriand
Edith Girard, Greffier
René Soucy, Directeur général
Sylvain Tremblay, Trésorier
Jean-Claude Bolduc, Directeur, Sécurité incendie
François Gagnon, Directeur, Sûreté municipale
Olivier Grondin, Directeur et directeur général adjoint, Travaux publics, du génie et de l'environnement

Trois-Rivières

CP 368
1325, place de l'Hôtel-de-Ville
Trois-Rivières, QC G9A 5H3
Tél: 819-374-2002; *Téléc:* 819-372-4636
info@v3r.net
www.v3r.net
Entité municipal: City
Incorporation: 1er janvier 2002; *Area:* 288,50 km2
Population au 2011: 131,338
Circonscription(s) électorale(s) provinciale(s): Trois-Rivières; Maskinongé; Champlain
Circonscription(s) électorale(s) fédérale(s): Trois-Rivières
Prochaines élections: 5e novembre 2017
Yves Lévesque, Maire
André Noël, Conseiller, Wards: Carmel
Jean Perron, Conseiller, Wards: Châteaudun
Marie-Claude Camirand, Conseillère, Wards: Chavigny
Pierre-Luc Fortin, Conseiller, Wards: Estacades
Guy Daigle, Conseiller, Wards: Laviolette
René Goyette, Conseiller, Wards: Madeleine
Jean-François Aubin, Conseiller, Wards: Marie-de-l'Incarnation
Joan Lefebvre, Conseillère, Wards: Plateaux
François Belisle, Conseiller, Wards: Pointe-du-lac
Ginette Bellemare, Conseillère, Wards: Rigaud
Michel Cormier, Conseiller, Wards: St-Louis-de-France
Pierre A. Dupont, Conseiller, Wards: Ste-Marguerite
Daniel Cournoyer, Conseiller, Wards: Ste-Marthe
Sabrina Roy, Conseillère, Wards: Sanctuaire
Yves Landry, Conseiller, Wards: Terrasses
Jeannot Lemieux, Conseiller, Wards: Vieilles-Forges
Gilles Poulin, Directeur, Greffe/Services juridiques, 819-372-4604, Fax: 819-372-4636
France Cinq-Mars, Directrice générale, 819-372-4608, Fax: 819-372-4631
Daniel Thibault, Directeur général adjoint
France Cinq-Mars, Directrice, Finances, 819-374-2002, Fax: 819-372-4630
Sonia Auclair, Directrice, Évaluation, 819-372-4629, Fax: 819-374-2299
Jean-Marc Bergeron, Directeur, Loisirs et communautaires, 819-372-4621, Fax: 819-374-7133
Pierre Desjardins, Directeur, Aménagement, gestion et développement durable du territoire, 819-372-4626, Fax: 819-375-5865
Benoît Gauthier, Directeur, Arts et culture
Francis Gobeil, Directeur, Sécurité publique, 819-370-6700, Fax: 819-374-3506
Jean-François Houde, Directeur, Approvisionnement, 819-379-3735, Fax: 819-379-4057
Ghislain Lachance, ing., Directeur, Travaux publics et du génie, 819-379-3733
Martin Samson, Directeur, Ressources humaines, 819-372-4603, Fax: 819-374-9005

La Tuque

375, rue St-Joseph
La Tuque, QC G9X 1L5
Tél: 819-523-8200; *Téléc:* 819-523-5419
www.ville.latuque.qc.ca
Entité municipal: City
Incorporation: 26 mars 2003; *Area:* 28 421,48 km2
Population au 2011: 11,227
Circonscription(s) électorale(s) provinciale(s): Laviolette
Circonscription(s) électorale(s) fédérale(s): St-Maurice-Champlain
Prochaines élections: 5e novembre 2017
Note: Dès le 26 mars 2003, la nouvelle ville de La Tuque regroupe La Tuque, les municipalités de La Croche, La Bostonnais, & Lac-Édouard, le village de Parent, & 8 autres territoires.
Normand Beaudoin, Maire
Sylvie Lachapelle, Conseillère, 819-667-2323, Fax: 819-667-2542, Wards: 1. Parent
Claude Gagnon, Conseiller, Wards: 2. Croche/Couronee rurale
Luc Martel, Conseiller, Wards: 3. Jacques-Buteux
André Mercier, Conseiller, Wards: 4. Polyvalente
Jean Duchesneau, Conseiller, Wards: 5. Bel-Air/Centre-ville
Julien Boisvert, Conseiller, Wards: 6. Aéroport
Jean-Sébastien Poirier, Greffier
Marco Lethiecq, Directeur général
Pierre Bouchard, Trésorier
Serge Buisson, Directeur, Sécurité d'incendie
Louis Loiselle, Directeur, Travaux publics
Justin Proulx, Directeur, Aménagement

Val-d'Or

CP 400
855, 2e av
Val-d'Or, QC J9P 4P4
Tél: 819-824-9613; *Téléc:* 819-825-6650
info@ville.valdor.qc.ca
www.ville.valdor.qc.ca
Entité municipal: City
Incorporation: 1er janvier 2002; *Area:* 3 958,13 km2
Comté ou district: La Vallée-de-l'Or; *Population au 2011:* 31,862
Circonscription(s) électorale(s) provinciale(s): Abitibi-Est
Circonscription(s) électorale(s) fédérale(s): Abitibi-Baie-James-Nunavik-Eeyou
Prochaines élections: 5e novembre 2017
Pierre Corbeil, Maire
Lorraine Morissette, Conseillère, Wards: 1. Lac Blouin-Centre-ville
Karen Busque, Conseiller, Wards: 2. Paquinville-Fatima
Pierre Potvin, Conseiller, Wards: 3. Belvédère
Céline Brindamour, Conseillère, Wards: 4. Sullivan
Gilles Bérubé, Conseiller, Wards: 5. Val-Senneville-Vassan
Sylvie Hébert, Conseillère, Wards: 6. Bourlamaque-Louvicourt
Bernard Gauthier, Conseiller, Wards: 7. Lemoine-Baie-Carrière
Robert Quesnal, Conseiller, Wards: 8. Dubuisson
Annie Lafond, Greffière, 819-824-9613
Sophie Gareau, Directrice générale, 819-824-9613
Chantale Gilbert, Trésorière, 819-824-9613
Diane Boudoul, Directrice, Ressources humaines, 819-824-9613
Danny Burbridge, ing., Directeur, Infrastructures urbaines, 819-824-9613
Robert Migué, Directeur, Communications, 819-824-9613
Ian Bélanger, Responsable, Division de l'environnement et des parcs, 819-824-9613

Val-des-Monts

1, rte du Carrefour
Val-des-Monts, QC J8N 4E9
Tél: 819-457-9400; *Téléc:* 819-457-4141
administration@val-des-monts.net
www.val-des-monts.net
Entité municipal: City
Incorporation: 1er janvier 1975; *Area:* 457,31 km2
Comté ou district: Les Collines-de-l'Outaouais; *Population au 2011:* 10,420
Circonscription(s) électorale(s) provinciale(s): Papineau
Circonscription(s) électorale(s) fédérale(s): Pontiac
Prochaines élections: 5e novembre 2017
Jacques Laurin, Maire, 819-457-9400
Gaétan Thibault, Conseiller, 819-671-9448, Wards: 1
Pauline Lafrenière, Conseillère, 819-671-2529, Wards: 2
Claude Bergeron, Conseiller, 819-671-0501, Wards: 3
Jules Dagenais, Conseiller, 819-457-9648, Wards: 4
Mireille Brazeau, Conseillère, 819-457-9774, Wards: 5
Roland Tremblay, Conseiller, 819-457-2732, Wards: 6
Patricia Fillet, Directrice générale, 819-457-9400
Stéphanie Giroux, Directrice, Finances, 819-457-9400
Julien Croteau, Directeur général adjoint, Sec.-trés. adjoint et directeur, Ressources humaines et des Communications, 819-457-9400
Charles Éthier, Directeur, Sécurité incendie, 819-457-9400
Jean-Pierre Harvey, Directeur, Travaux publics, 819-457-9400
André Turcotte, Directeur, Environnement et de l'urbanisme, 819-457-9400

Varennes

CP 5000
175, rue Ste-Anne
Varennes, QC J3X 1T5
Tél: 450-652-9888; *Téléc:* 450-652-4349
communication@ville.varennes.qc.ca
ville.varennes.qc.ca
Entité municipal: City
Incorporation: 26 août 1972; *Area:* 93,96 km2
Comté ou district: Marguerite-D'Youville; Communauté métropolitaine de Montréal; *Population au 2011:* 20,994
Circonscription(s) électorale(s) provinciale(s): Verchères
Circonscription(s) électorale(s) fédérale(s): Pierre-Boucher-Les Patriotes-Verchères
Prochaines élections: 5e novembre 2017
Martin Damphousse, Maire
Marc-André Savaria, Conseiller, Wards: 1. Guillaudière

Lyne Beaulieu, Conseillère, Wards: 2. Sitière
Francis Rinfret, Conseiller, Wards: 3. Langloiserie
Denis Le Blanc, Conseiller, Wards: 4. Notre-Dame
Bruno Desjarlais, Conseiller, Wards: 5. Petite Prairie
Natalie Parent, Conseillère, Wards: 6. Seigneuries
Gaétan Marcil, Conseiller, Wards: 7. Saint-Charles
Brigitte Collin, Conseillère, Wards: 8. Martigny
Marc Giard, Greffier
Sébastien Roy, Directeur général
Denise Beauchemin, Trésorière
Denis Guay, Directeur, Travaux publics
Alain Rouette, Directeur, Ingénierie
Dominic Scully, Directeur, Urbanisme

Vaudreuil-Dorion
#200, 2555, rue Dutrisac
Vaudreuil-Dorion, QC J7V 7E6
Tél: 450-455-3371; *Téléc:* 450-424-8540
courriel@ville.vaudreuil-dorion.qc.ca
www.ville.vaudreuil-dorion.qc.ca
Entité municipal: City
Incorporation: 16 mars 1994; *Area:* 73,18 km2
Comté ou district: Vaudreuil-Soulanges; Communauté métropolitaine de Montréal; *Population au 2011:* 33,305
Circonscription(s) électorale(s) provinciale(s): Vaudreuil
Circonscription(s) électorale(s) fédérale(s): Vaudreuil-Soulanges
Prochaines élections: 5e novembre 2017
Guy Pilon, Maire
Claude Beaudoin, Conseiller, Wards: 1. Quinchien
François Séguin, Conseiller, Wards: 2. Harwood
Robert A. Laurence, Conseiller, Wards: 3. Fief-Cavagnal
Céline Chartier, Conseillère, Wards: 4. Seigneurie
Rénald Gabriele, Conseiller, Wards: 5. Chenaux
Gabriel Parent, Conseiller, Wards: 6. Cité-des-Jeunes
Paul M. Normand, Conseiller, Wards: 7. Carrefour
Paul Dumoulin, Conseiller, Wards: 8. Baie
Jean St-Antoine, Greffier
Martin Houde, Directeur général
Marco Pilo, Trésorier
Richard Duhaime, Directeur, Informatique et géomatique
Christian Gendron, Directeur, Eaux
Thierry Rousseau, Directeur, Sécurité incendie
Olivier Van Neste, Directeur, Travaux publics

Victoriaville
CP 370
1, rue Notre-Dame ouest
Victoriaville, QC G6P 6T2
Tél: 819-758-1571; *Téléc:* 819-758-9292
info@ville.victoriaville.qc.ca
www.ville.victoriaville.qc.ca
Entité municipal: City
Incorporation: 23 juin 1993; *Area:* 81,96 km2
Comté ou district: Arthabaska; *Population au 2011:* 43,462
Circonscription(s) électorale(s) provinciale(s): Arthabaska
Circonscription(s) électorale(s) fédérale(s): Richmond-Arthabaska
Prochaines élections: 5e novembre 2017
André Bellavance, Maire, 819-350-7910
Caroline Pilon, Conseillère, 819-758-2096, Wards: 1. Parc-de-l'Amitié
Benoit Gauthier, Conseiller, 819-758-1370, Wards: 2. Parc-de-l'Île
Patrick Paulin, Conseiller, 819-758-8214, Wards: 3. Charles-Édouard-Mailhot
Alexandre Côté, Conseiller, 819-752-1320, Wards: 4. Sainte-Famille
France Auger, Conseillère, 819-758-7330, Wards: 5. Parc-Terre-des-Jeunes
Marc Mortin, Conseiller, 819-758-1864, Wards: 6. Parc-Victoria
Claude Brulotte, Conseiller, 819-752-5454, Wards: 7. Sainte-Victoire
Denis Morin, Conseiller, 819-357-7821, Wards: 8. Arthabaska-Nord
Michael Provencher, Conseiller, 819-357-4025, Wards: 9. Arthabaska-Ouest
Christian Lettre, Conseiller, 819-357-8573, Wards: 10. Arthabaska-Est
Yves Arcand, Greffier
Martin Lessard, Directeur général
Catherine Ouellet, Trésorière, Ressources financières et matérielles
Serge Cyr, Directeur, Service de l'environnement, 819-758-0651
Michel Lachapelle, Directeur, Travaux publics, 819-758-1571
Jean Mercier, Directeur, Ressources humaines
Jean-François Morissette, Directeur, Gestion du territoire

Westmount
4333, rue Sherbrooke ouest
Westmount, QC H3Z 1E2
Tél: 514-989-5200; *Téléc:* 514-989-5200
info@westmount.org
www.westmount.org
Entité municipal: City
Incorporation: 1er janvier 2006; *Area:* 4,02 km2
Comté ou district: Communauté métropolitaine de Montréal; *Population au 2011:* 19,931
Circonscription(s) électorale(s) provinciale(s): Westmount-Saint-Louis
Circonscription(s) électorale(s) fédérale(s): Notre-Dame-de-Grâce-Westmount
Prochaines élections: 5e novembre 2017
Peter F. Trent, Maire
Patrick Martin, Conseiller, Wards: 1
Philip A. Cutler, Conseiller, Wards: 2
Victor M. Drury, Conseiller, Wards: 3
Rosalind Davis, Conseillère, Wards: 4
Christina Smith, Conseillère, Wards: 5
Nicole Forbes, Conseillère, Wards: 6
Cynthia Lulham, Conseillère, Wards: 7
Theodora Samiotis, Conseillère, Wards: 8
Viviana Iturriaga-Espinoza, Greffière et directrice, Services juridiques, 514-989-5318, Fax: 514-989-5270
Duncan E. Campbell, Directeur général, 514-989-5238, Fax: 514-989-5481
Annette Dupré, Trésorière et directrice, Finances, 514-989-5234, Fax: 514-989-5480
Benoit Hurtubise, Directeur, Hydro Westmount, 514-925-1414, Fax: 514-989-5490
Gregory McBain, Directeur, Sécurité publique, 514-989-5222, Fax: 514-989-5487
Joanne Poirier, Directeur, Aménagement urbain, 514-989-5219, Fax: 514-989-5270
Marianne Zalzal, Directrice, Travaux publics, 514-989-5268, Fax: 514-989-5488

Other Municipalities in Québec

Abercorn
10, ch des Églises ouest
Abercorn, QC J0E 1B0
Tél: 450-538-2664; *Téléc:* 450-538-6295
mun.abercorn@vivomail.ca
Entité municipal: Village
Incorporation: 25 juin 1929; *Area:* 27,84 km2
Comté ou district: Brome-Missisquoi; *Population au 2011:* 391
Circonscription(s) électorale(s) provinciale(s): Brome-Missisquoi
Circonscription(s) électorale(s) fédérale(s): Brome-Missisquoi
Prochaines élections: 5e novembre 2017
Robert Nadeau, Maire
Paul McKeogh, Directeur général

Abitibi
CP 214
571, 1re Rue est
Amos, QC J9T 2H3
Tél: 819-732-5356; *Téléc:* 819-732-9607
mrc@mrcabitibi.qc.ca
www.mrcabitibi.qc.ca
Entité municipal: Regional County Municipality
Incorporation: 1er janvier 1983
Population au 2011: 24,354
Note: 17 municipalités & 2 autres territoires.
Martin Roch, Préfet
Alain Halley, Directeur général

Abitibi-Ouest
#105, 6, 8e Av est
La Sarre, QC J9Z 1N6
Tél: 819-339-5671; *Téléc:* 819-339-5400
mrcao@mrcao.qc.ca
www.mrc.ao.ca
Entité municipal: Regional County Municipality
Incorporation: 1er janvier 1982
Population au 2011: 21,003
Note: 21 municipalités & 2 autres territoires.
Jaclin Bégin, Préfète
Nicole Breton, Directrice générale

Acton
CP 99
1037, rue Beaugrand
Acton Vale, QC J0H 1A0
Tél: 450-546-3256; *Téléc:* 450-546-0525
info@mrcacton.qc.ca
www.mrcacton.qc.ca
Entité municipal: Regional County Municipality
Incorporation: 1er janvier 1982
Population au 2011: 15,381
Note: 8 municipalités.
Jean-Marie Laplante, Préfet
Yvan Talbot, Directeur général

Acton Vale
1025, rue Boulay
Acton Vale, QC J0H 1A0
Tél: 450-546-2703; *Téléc:* 450-546-4865
actonvale@ville.actonvale.qc.ca
ville.actonvale.qc.ca
Entité municipal: Town
Incorporation: 26 janvier 2000; *Area:* 90,88 km2
Comté ou district: Acton; *Population au 2011:* 7,664
Circonscription(s) électorale(s) provinciale(s): Johnson
Circonscription(s) électorale(s) fédérale(s): St-Hyacinthe-Bagot
Prochaines élections: 5e novembre 2017
Éric Charbonneau, Maire
Claudine Babineau, Greffière

Adstock
35, rue Principale ouest
Adstock, QC G0N 1S0
Tél: 418-422-2135; *Téléc:* 418-422-2134
www.municipaliteadstock.qc.ca
Entité municipal: Municipality
Incorporation: 24 octobre 2001; *Area:* 289,220 km2
Comté ou district: Les Appalaches; *Population au 2011:* 2,643
Circonscription(s) électorale(s) provinciale(s): Lotbinière-Frontenac
Circonscription(s) électorale(s) fédérale(s): Mégantic-L'Érable
Prochaines élections: 5e novembre 2017
Pascal Binet, Maire
Jean-Rock Turgeon, Directeur général

Aguanish
CP 47
106, rte Jacques-Cartier
Aguanish, QC G0G 1A0
Tél: 418-533-2323; *Téléc:* 418-533-2012
info@mun.aguanish.org
www.aguanish.org
Entité municipal: Municipality
Incorporation: 1er janvier 1957; *Area:* 594,40 km2
Comté ou district: Minganie; *Population au 2011:* 278
Circonscription(s) électorale(s) provinciale(s): Duplessis
Circonscription(s) électorale(s) fédérale(s): Manicouagan
Prochaines élections: 5e novembre 2017
André Leblanc, Maire
Bernard Déraps, Directeur général

Akulivik
CP 50
Akulivik, QC J0M 1V0
Tél: 819-496-2222; *Téléc:* 819-496-2200
www.nvakulivik.ca
Entité municipal: Northern Village
Incorporation: 29 décembre 1979; *Area:* 79,37 km2
Comté ou district: Administration régionale Kativik; *Population au 2011:* 615
Circonscription(s) électorale(s) provinciale(s): Ungava
Circonscription(s) électorale(s) fédérale(s): Abitibi-Baie-James-Nunavik-Eeyou
Mark Qumak, Maire
Eli Aullaluk, Conseiller régional

Albanel
160, rue Principale
Albanel, QC G8M 3J5
Tél: 418-279-5250; *Téléc:* 418-279-3147
info@albanel.ca
www.albanel.ca
Entité municipal: Municipality
Incorporation: 11 avril 1990; *Area:* 195,69 km2
Comté ou district: Maria-Chapdelaine; *Population au 2011:* 2,293
Circonscription(s) électorale(s) provinciale(s): Roberval
Circonscription(s) électorale(s) fédérale(s): Lac-Saint-Jean
Prochaines élections: 5e novembre 2017
Francine Chiasson, Mairesse
Réjean Hudon, Directeur général

Albertville
CP 9
1058, rue Principale
Albertville, QC G0J 1A0
Tél: 418-756-3554; *Téléc:* 418-756-3552
albertville@mrcmatapedia.qc.ca
Entité municipal: Municipality
Incorporation: 29 novembre 1930; *Area:* 104,55 km2
Comté ou district: La Matapédia; *Population au 2011:* 256

Circonscription(s) électorale(s) provinciale(s): Matane-Matapédia
Circonscription(s) électorale(s) fédérale(s): Avignon-La Mitis-Matane-Matapédia
Prochaines élections: 5e novembre 2017
Martin Landry, Maire
Valérie Potvin, Directrice-générale

Alleyn-et-Cawood
10, ch Jondée
Alleyn-et-Cawood, QC J0X 1P0
Tél: 819-467-2941; *Téléc:* 819-467-3133
admin@alleyn-cawood.ca
www.alleyn-cawood.ca
Entité municipal: Municipality
Incorporation: 1er janvier 1877; *Area:* 346,64 km2
Comté ou district: Pontiac; *Population au 2011:* 168
Circonscription(s) électorale(s) provinciale(s): Pontiac
Circonscription(s) électorale(s) fédérale(s): Pontiac
Prochaines élections: 5e novembre 2017
Carl Mayer, Maire
Isabelle Cardinal, Directrice générale

Amherst
CP 30
124, rue St-Louis
Amherst, QC J0T 2L0
Tél: 819-681-3372; *Téléc:* 819-687-8430
amherst@municipalite.amherst.qc.ca
www.municipalite.amherst.qc.ca
Entité municipal: Township
Incorporation: 9e mars 1887; *Area:* 260,82 km2
Comté ou district: Les Laurentides; *Population au 2011:* 1,524
Circonscription(s) électorale(s) provinciale(s): Labelle
Circonscription(s) électorale(s) fédérale(s): Laurentides-Labelle
Prochaines élections: 5e novembre 2017
Bernard Lapointe, Maire
Bernard Davidson, Directeur général

Amqui
20, promenade de l'Hôtel-de-Ville
Amqui, QC G5J 1A1
Tél: 418-629-4242; *Téléc:* 418-629-4090
administration@ville.amqui.qc.ca
www.ville.amqui.qc.ca
Entité municipal: Town
Incorporation: 16 janvier 1991; *Area:* 127,90 km2
Comté ou district: La Matapédia; *Population au 2011:* 6,322
Circonscription(s) électorale(s) provinciale(s): Matane-Matapédia
Circonscription(s) électorale(s) fédérale(s): Avignon-La Mitis-Matane-Matapédia
Prochaines élections: 5e novembre 2017
Gaëtan Ruest, Maire
Marie-Claude Gagnon, Greffière

L'Ange-Gardien
1177, rte 315
L'Ange-Gardien, QC J8L 0L4
Tél: 819-986-7470; *Téléc:* 819-986-8349
info@municipalitedelangegardien.com
www.municipalitedelangegardien.com
Entité municipal: Municipality
Incorporation: 17 mai 1979; *Area:* 224,17 km2
Comté ou district: Les Collines-de-l'Outaouais; Communauté métropolitaine de Québec; *Population au 2011:* 5,051
Circonscription(s) électorale(s) provinciale(s): Papineau
Circonscription(s) électorale(s) fédérale(s): Argenteuil-La Petite-Nation
Prochaines élections: 5e novembre 2017
Robert Goulet, Maire
Alain Descarreaux, Directeur général

L'Ange-Gardien
6355, av Royale
L'Ange-Gardien, QC G0A 2K0
Tél: 418-822-1555; *Téléc:* 418-822-2526
mun-langegardien@bellnet.ca
www.langegardien.qc.ca
Entité municipal: Municipality
Incorporation: 1er juillet 1855; *Area:* 50,67 km2
Comté ou district: La Côte-de-Beaupré; *Population au 2011:* 3,634
Circonscription(s) électorale(s) provinciale(s): Charlevoix-Côte-de-Beaupré
Circonscription(s) électorale(s) fédérale(s): Beauport-Côte-de-Beaupré-Ile d'Orléans-Charlevoix
Prochaines élections: 5e novembre 2017
Pierre Lefrançois, Maire
Lise Drouin, Directrice générale

Ange-Gardien
249, rue St-Joseph
Ange-Gardien, QC J0E 1E0
Tél: 450-293-7575; *Téléc:* 450-293-6635
info@municipalite.ange-gardien.qc.ca
www.municipalite.ange-gardien.qc.ca
Entité municipal: Municipality
Incorporation: 31 décembre 1997; *Area:* 89,07 km2
Comté ou district: Rouville; *Population au 2011:* 2,420
Circonscription(s) électorale(s) provinciale(s): Iberville
Circonscription(s) électorale(s) fédérale(s): Shefford
Prochaines élections: 5e novembre 2017
Yvan Pinsonneault, Maire
Brigitte Vachon, Directrice générale

Angliers
CP 9
14, rue de la Baie Miller
Angliers, QC J0Z 1A0
Tél: 819-949-4351; *Téléc:* 819-949-4321
www.angliers.ca
Entité municipal: Village
Incorporation: 24 mai 1945; *Area:* 378,20 km2
Comté ou district: Témiscamingue; *Population au 2011:* 298
Circonscription(s) électorale(s) provinciale(s): Rouyn-Noranda-Témiscamingue
Circonscription(s) électorale(s) fédérale(s): Abitibi-Témiscamingue
Prochaines élections: 5e novembre 2017
Lyne Pine, Mairesse
Micheline Champoux, Directrice générale

L'Anse-Saint-Jean
3, rue du Couvent
L'Anse-Saint-Jean, QC G0V 1J0
Tél: 418-272-2633; *Téléc:* 418-544-3078
info@lanse-saint-jean.ca
www.lanse-saint-jean.ca
Entité municipal: Municipality
Incorporation: 1er janvier 1859; *Area:* 527,06 km2
Comté ou district: Le Fjord-du-Saguenay; *Population au 2011:* 1,208
Circonscription(s) électorale(s) provinciale(s): Dubuc
Circonscription(s) électorale(s) fédérale(s): Chicoutimi-Le Fjord
Prochaines élections: 5e novembre 2017
Lucien Martel, Maire
Daniel Corbeil, Directeur général

Antoine-Labelle
425, rue du Pont
Mont-Laurier, QC J9L 2R6
Tél: 819-623-3485; *Téléc:* 819-623-5052
administration@mrc-antoine-labelle.qc.ca
www.mrc-antoine-labelle.qc.ca
Entité municipal: Regional County Municipality
Incorporation: 1er janvier 1983
Population au 2011: 35,159
Note: 17 municipalités & 11 autres territoires.
Lyz Beaulieu, Préfète
Jackline Williams, Directrice générale

Les Appalaches
233, boul Frontenac ouest
Thetford Mines, QC G6G 6K2
Tél: 418-423-2757; *Téléc:* 418-423-5122
info@mrcdesappalaches.ca
www.mrcdesappalaches.ca
Entité municipal: Regional County Municipality
Incorporation: 1er janvier 1982
Population au 2011: 43,120
Note: 19 municipalités.
Paul Vachon, Préfet
Marie-Eve Mercier, Directrice générale

Argenteuil
430, rue Grace
Lachute, QC J8H 1M6
Tél: 450-562-2474; *Téléc:* 450-562-1911
mrc@argenteuil.qc.ca
www.argenteuil.qc.ca
Entité municipal: Regional County Municipality
Incorporation: 1er janvier 1983
Population au 2011: 32,117
Note: 9 municipalités.
André Jetté, Préfet
Marc Carrière, Directeur général

Armagh
CP 87
5, rue de la Salle
Armagh, QC G0R 1A0
Tél: 418-466-2916; *Téléc:* 418-466-2409
munarma@globetrotter.net
www.municipalite-armagh.org
Entité municipal: Municipality
Incorporation: 29 décembre 1993; *Area:* 168,15 km2
Comté ou district: Bellechasse; *Population au 2011:* 1,491
Circonscription(s) électorale(s) provinciale(s): Bellechasse
Circonscription(s) électorale(s) fédérale(s): Bellechasse-Les Etchemins-Lévis
Prochaines élections: 5e novembre 2017
Oneil Lemieux, Maire
Sylvie Vachon, Directrice générale

Arthabaska
40, rte de la Grande-Ligne
Victoriaville, QC G6T 0E6
Tél: 819-752-2444; *Téléc:* 819-752-3623
info@mrc-arthabaska.qc.ca
www.mrc-arthabaska.qc.ca
Entité municipal: Regional County Municipality
Incorporation: 1er janvier 1982
Population au 2011: 69,237
Circonscription(s) électorale(s) fédérale(s): Richmond-Arthabaska
Note: 24 municipalités.
Lionel Fréchette, Préfet
Frédérick Michaud, Directeur général

Arundel
2, rue du Village
Arundel, QC J0T 1A0
Tél: 819-687-3991; *Téléc:* 819-687-8760
info@municipalite.arundel.qc.ca
www.municipalite.arundel.qc.ca
Entité municipal: Township
Incorporation: 1er janvier 1878; *Area:* 64,43 km2
Comté ou district: Les Laurentides; *Population au 2011:* 604
Circonscription(s) électorale(s) provinciale(s): Argenteuil
Circonscription(s) électorale(s) fédérale(s): Laurentides-Labelle
Prochaines élections: 5e novembre 2017
Guylaine Berlinguette, Mairesse
France Bellefleur, Directrice générale

Asbestos
345, boul Saint-Luc
Asbestos, QC J1T 2W4
Tél: 819-879-7171; *Téléc:* 819-879-2343
www.ville.asbestos.qc.ca
Entité municipal: Town
Incorporation: 8e décembre 1999; *Area:* 29,55 km2
Comté ou district: Les Sources; *Population au 2011:* 7,096
Circonscription(s) électorale(s) provinciale(s): Richmond
Circonscription(s) électorale(s) fédérale(s): Richmond-Arthabaska
Prochaines élections: 5e novembre 2017
Hugues Grimard, Maire
Georges-André Gagné, Directeur général

L'Ascension
59, rue de l'Hôtel-de-Ville
L'Ascension, QC J0T 1W0
Tél: 819-275-3027; *Téléc:* 819-275-3489
www.municipalite-lascension.qc.ca
Entité municipal: Municipality
Incorporation: 23 septembre 1905; *Area:* 342,83 km2
Comté ou district: Antoine-Labelle; *Population au 2011:* 844
Circonscription(s) électorale(s) provinciale(s): Labelle
Circonscription(s) électorale(s) fédérale(s): Laurentides-Labelle
Prochaines élections: 5e novembre 2017
Yves Meilleur, Maire
Hélène Beauchamp, Directrice générale

L'Ascension-de-Notre-Seigneur
CP 100
1000, 1re rue est
L'Ascension-de-Notre-Seigneur, QC G0W 1Y0
Tél: 418-347-3482; *Téléc:* 418-347-4253
info@ville.ascension.qc.ca
www.ville.ascension.qc.ca
Entité municipal: Parish (Paroisse)
Incorporation: 25 février 1919; *Area:* 131,83 km2
Comté ou district: Lac-Saint-Jean-Est; *Population au 2011:* 1,983
Circonscription(s) électorale(s) provinciale(s): Lac-St-Jean
Circonscription(s) électorale(s) fédérale(s): Lac-St-Jean
Prochaines élections: 5e novembre 2017
Louis Ouellet, Maire
Normand Desgagné, Directeur général

L'Ascension-de-Patapédia
CP 9
70, rue Principale
L'Ascension-de-Patapédia, QC G0J 1R0
Tél: 418-299-2024; *Téléc:* 418-299-2027
munic@globetrotter.net
www.matapedialesplateaux.com
Entité municipal: Municipality
Incorporation: 1er janvier 1968; *Area:* 95,38 km2
Comté ou district: Avignon; *Population au 2011:* 190
Circonscription(s) électorale(s) provinciale(s): Bonaventure
Circonscription(s) électorale(s) fédérale(s): Avignon-La Mitis-Matane-Matapédia
Prochaines élections: 5e novembre 2017
Rémi Gallant, Maire
Josiane Boucher, Directrice générale

Ascot Corner
5655, rte 112
Ascot-Corner, QC J0B 1A0
Tél: 819-560-8560; *Téléc:* 819-560-8561
ascot.corner@hsfqc.ca
www.ascot-corner.com
Entité municipal: Municipality
Incorporation: 28 mars 1901; *Area:* 83,38 km2
Comté ou district: Le Haut-Saint-François; *Population au 2011:* 2,891
Circonscription(s) électorale(s) provinciale(s): Mégantic
Circonscription(s) électorale(s) fédérale(s): Compton-Stanstead
Prochaines élections: 5e novembre 2017
Nathalie Bresse, Mairesse
Daniel St-Onge, Directeur général

L'Assomption
300A, rue Dorval
L'Assomption, QC J5W 3A1
Tél: 450-589-2288; *Téléc:* 450-589-9430
www.mrclassomption.qc.ca
Entité municipal: Regional County Municipality
Incorporation: 1er janvier 1983
Population au 2011: 119,840
Note: 6 municipalités.
Chantal Deschamps, Préfète
Joffrey Bouchard, Directeur général

Aston-Jonction
1300, rue Principale
Aston-Jonction, QC G0Z 1A0
Tél: 819-226-3459; *Téléc:* 819-226-3013
mun.astonjonction@tlb.sympatico.ca
www.municipalite.aston-jonction.qc.ca
Entité municipal: Municipality
Incorporation: 26 mars 1997; *Area:* 26,43 km2
Comté ou district: Nicolet-Yamaska; *Population au 2011:* 410
Circonscription(s) électorale(s) provinciale(s): Nicolet-Bécancour
Circonscription(s) électorale(s) fédérale(s): Bécancour-Nicolet-Saurel
Prochaines élections: 5e novembre 2017
Pierre Gaudet, Maire
Jacqueline Leblanc, Directrice générale

Auclair
773A, rue du Clocher
Auclair, QC G0L 1A0
Tél: 418-899-2834; *Téléc:* 418-899-6958
info@municipaliteauclair.ca
www.municipaliteauclair.ca
Entité municipal: Municipality
Incorporation: 1er janvier 1954; *Area:* 106,66 km2
Comté ou district: Témiscouata; *Population au 2011:* 444
Circonscription(s) électorale(s) provinciale(s): Rivière-du-Loup-Témiscouata
Circonscription(s) électorale(s) fédérale(s): Rimouski-Neigette-Témiscouata-Les Basques
Prochaines élections: 5e novembre 2017
Bruno Bonesso, Maire
Sébastien Bourgault, Directeur général

Audet
CP 27
266, rue Principale
Audet, QC G0Y 1A0
Tél: 819-583-1596; *Téléc:* 819-583-5938
munaudet@axion.ca
munaudet.qc.ca
Entité municipal: Municipality
Incorporation: 26 novembre 1903; *Area:* 132,86 km2
Comté ou district: Le Granit; *Population au 2011:* 724
Circonscription(s) électorale(s) provinciale(s): Mégantic
Circonscription(s) électorale(s) fédérale(s): Mégantic-L'Érable
Prochaines élections: 5e novembre 2017
Guylaine Bilodeau, Mairesse
France Larochelle, Directrice générale

Aumond
664, rue Principale
Aumond, QC J0W 1W0
Tél: 819-449-4006; *Téléc:* 819-449-7448
info@aumond.ca
www.aumond.ca
Entité municipal: Township
Incorporation: 12 décembre 1877; *Area:* 215,12 km2
Comté ou district: La Vallée-de-la-Gatineau; *Population au 2011:* 725
Circonscription(s) électorale(s) provinciale(s): Gatineau
Circonscription(s) électorale(s) fédérale(s): Pontiac
Prochaines élections: 5e novembre 2017
Denis Charron, Maire
Julie Cardinal, Directrice générale

Aupaluk
CP 5
Aupaluk, QC J0M 1X0
Tél: 819-491-7070; *Téléc:* 819-491-7035
www.nvaupaluk.ca
Entité municipal: Northern Village
Incorporation: 2e février 1980; *Area:* 32,93 km2
Comté ou district: Administration régionale Kativik; *Population au 2011:* 195
Circonscription(s) électorale(s) provinciale(s): Ungava
Circonscription(s) électorale(s) fédérale(s): Abitibi-Baie-James-Nunavik-Eeyou
George Eetook, Maire
Eva Grey, Secrétaire-trésorière

Austin
21, ch Millington
Austin, QC J0B 1B0
Tél: 819-843-2388; *Téléc:* 819-843-8211
info@municipalite.austin.qc.ca
www.municipalite.austin.qc.ca
Entité municipal: Municipality
Incorporation: 5 novembre 1938; *Area:* 72,62 km2
Comté ou district: Memphrémagog; *Population au 2011:* 1,880
Circonscription(s) électorale(s) provinciale(s): Orford
Circonscription(s) électorale(s) fédérale(s): Brome-Missisquoi
Prochaines élections: 5e novembre 2017
Lisette Maillé, Mairesse
Anne-Marie Ménard, Directrice générale

Authier
457, rue de la Montée
Authier, QC J0Z 1C0
Tél: 819-782-3093; *Téléc:* 819-782-3203
authier@mrcao.qc.ca
authier.ao.ca
Entité municipal: Municipality
Incorporation: 20 septembre 1918; *Area:* 139,72 km2
Comté ou district: Abitibi-Ouest; *Population au 2011:* 282
Circonscription(s) électorale(s) provinciale(s): Abitibi Ouest
Circonscription(s) électorale(s) fédérale(s): Abitibi-Témiscamingue
Prochaines élections: 5e novembre 2017
Marcel Cloutier, Maire
Édith Coulombe, Directrice générale

Authier-Nord
452, rue Principale
Authier-Nord, QC J0Z 1E0
Tél: 819-782-3914; *Téléc:* 819-782-3916
authier-nord@mrcao.qc.ca
authier-nord.ao.ca
Entité municipal: Municipality
Incorporation: 1er janvier 1983; *Area:* 289,79 km2
Comté ou district: Abitibi-Ouest; *Population au 2011:* 273
Circonscription(s) électorale(s) provinciale(s): Abitibi-Ouest
Circonscription(s) électorale(s) fédérale(s): Abitibi-Témiscamingue
Prochaines élections: 5e novembre 2017
Alain Gagnon, Maire
Élise Gagnon, Directrice générale

L'Avenir
545, rue Principale
L'Avenir, QC J0C 1B0
Tél: 819-394-2422; *Téléc:* 819-394-2222
info@municipalitelavenir.qc.ca
www.municipalitelavenir.qc.ca
Entité municipal: Municipality
Incorporation: 23 décembre 1976; *Area:* 96,47 km2
Comté ou district: Drummond; *Population au 2011:* 1,202
Circonscription(s) électorale(s) provinciale(s): Johnson
Circonscription(s) électorale(s) fédérale(s): Drummond
Prochaines élections: 5e novembre 2017
Jean Parenteau, Maire
Suzie Lemire, Directrice générale

Avignon
CP 128
470, rue Francoeur
Nouvelle, QC G0C 2E0
Tél: 418-794-2221; *Téléc:* 418-794-2076
info@mrcavignon.com
www.mrcavignon.com
Entité municipal: Regional County Municipality
Incorporation: 18 mars 1981
Population au 2011: 15,246
Note: 11 municipalités & 2 autres territoires.
Bertrand Berger, Préfet
Gaétan Bernatchez, Directeur général

Ayer's Cliff
958, rue Main
Ayer's Cliff, QC J0B 1C0
Tél: 819-838-5006; *Téléc:* 819-838-4411
info@ayerscliff.ca
www.ayerscliff.ca
Entité municipal: Village
Incorporation: 24 février 1909; *Area:* 11,15 km2
Comté ou district: Memphrémagog; *Population au 2011:* 1,109
Circonscription(s) électorale(s) provinciale(s): Orford
Circonscription(s) électorale(s) fédérale(s): Compton-Stanstead
Prochaines élections: 5e novembre 2017
Alec Van Zuiden, Maire
Kimball Smith, Directeur général

Baie-D'Urfé
20410, ch Lakeshore
Baie-D'Urfé, QC H9X 1P7
Tél: 514-457-5324; *Téléc:* 514-457-5671
info@baie-durfe.qc.ca
www.baie-durfe.qc.ca
Entité municipal: Town
Incorporation: 1er janvier 2006; *Area:* 6,70 km2
Comté ou district: Communauté métropolitaine de Montréal; *Population au 2011:* 3,850
Circonscription(s) électorale(s) provinciale(s): Jacques-Cartier
Circonscription(s) électorale(s) fédérale(s): Lac-Saint-Louis
Prochaines élections: 5e novembre 2017
Maria Tutino, Mairesse
Nathalie Hadida, Greffière

Baie-des-Sables
CP 39
20, rue du Couvent
Baie-des-Sables, QC G0J 1C0
Tél: 418-772-6218; *Téléc:* 418-772-6455
baiedessables@lamatanie.ca
www.municipalite.baiedessables.ca
Entité municipal: Municipality
Incorporation: 1er janvier 1859; *Area:* 64,54 km2
Comté ou district: La Matanie; *Population au 2011:* 609
Circonscription(s) électorale(s) provinciale(s): Matane-Matapédia
Circonscription(s) électorale(s) fédérale(s): Avignon-La Mitis-Matane-Matapédia
Prochaines élections: 5e novembre 2017
Denis Santerre, Maire
Adam Coulombe, Directeur général

Baie-du-Febvre
CP 10
298, rte Marie-Victorin
Baie-du-Febvre, QC J0G 1A0
Tél: 450-783-6422; *Téléc:* 450-783-6423
municipalite@baie-du-febvre.net
www.baie-du-febvre.net
Entité municipal: Municipality
Incorporation: 26 mars 1983; *Area:* 96,04 km2
Comté ou district: Nicolet-Yamaska; *Population au 2011:* 1,010
Circonscription(s) électorale(s) provinciale(s): Nicolet-Bécancour
Circonscription(s) électorale(s) fédérale(s): Bécancour-Nicolet-Saurel
Prochaines élections: 5e novembre 2017
Claude Lefebvre, Maire
Maryse Baril, Directeur général

Baie-Johan-Beetz
15, rue Johan-Beetz
Baie-Johan-Beetz, QC G0G 1B0
Tél: 418-539-0125; *Téléc:* 418-539-0205
baiejohanbeetz.qc.ca
Entité municipal: Municipality
Incorporation: 1er janvier 1966; *Area:* 425,31 km2
Comté ou district: Minganie; *Population au 2011:* 81
Circonscription(s) électorale(s) provinciale(s): Duplessis

Circonscription(s) électorale(s) fédérale(s): Manicouagan
Prochaines élections: 5e novembre 2017
Frédérick Gagnon, Maire
Myriam Lafleur, Directrice générale

Baie-Saint-Paul
15, rue Forget
Baie-Saint-Paul, QC G3Z 3G1
Tél: 418-435-2205; *Téléc:* 418-435-2688
ville@baiesaintpaul.com
www.baiesaintpaul.com
Entité municipal: Town
Incorporation: 3e janvier 1996; *Area:* 546,73 km2
Comté ou district: Charlevoix; *Population au 2011:* 7,332
Circonscription(s) électorale(s) provinciale(s): Charlevoix-Côte-de-Beaupré
Circonscription(s) électorale(s) fédérale(s): Beauport-Côte-de-Beaupré-Ile d'Orléans-Charlevoix
Prochaines élections: 5e novembre 2017
Jean Fortin, Maire
Émilien Bouchard, Greffier

Baie-Ste-Catherine
CP 10
308, rue Leclerc
Baie-Sainte-Catherine, QC G0T 1A0
Tél: 418-620-5020; *Téléc:* 418-620-5021
municipalite@baiestecatherine.com
www.baiestecatherine.com
Entité municipal: Municipality
Incorporation: 4e novembre 1903; *Area:* 232,16 km2
Comté ou district: Charlevoix-Est; *Population au 2011:* 204
Circonscription(s) électorale(s) provinciale(s): Charlevoix-Côte-de-Beaupré
Circonscription(s) électorale(s) fédérale(s): Beauport-Côte-de-Beaupré-Ile d'Orléans-Charlevoix
Prochaines élections: 5e novembre 2017
Donald Kenny, Maire
Brigitte Boulianne, Directrice générale

Baie-Trinité
CP 100
28, rte 138
Baie-Trinité, QC G0H 1A0
Tél: 418-939-2231; *Téléc:* 418-939-2616
municipalite.baie.trinite@globetrotter.net
www.baietrinite.info
Entité municipal: Village
Incorporation: 1er janvier 1955; *Area:* 536,33 km2
Comté ou district: Manicouagan; *Population au 2011:* 419
Circonscription(s) électorale(s) provinciale(s): René-Lévesque
Circonscription(s) électorale(s) fédérale(s): Manicouagan
Prochaines élections: 5e novembre 2017
Denis Lejeune, Maire
Gérald Jean, Greffier

Barkmere
182, ch de Barkmere
Barkmere, QC J0T 1A0
Tél: 819-687-3373; *Téléc:* 819-681-3375
www.barkmere.ca
Entité municipal: Village
Incorporation: 24 mars 1926; *Area:* 18,07 km2
Comté ou district: Les Laurentides; *Population au 2011:* 58
Circonscription(s) électorale(s) provinciale(s): Argenteuil
Circonscription(s) électorale(s) fédérale(s): Laurentides-Labelle
Prochaines élections: 5e novembre 2017
Luc Trépanier, Maire
Katia Morin, Directrice générale

Barnston-Ouest
741, ch Hunter
Ayer's Cliff, QC J0B 1C0
Tél: 819-838-4334; *Téléc:* 819-838-1717
barnston.ouest@xittel.ca
barnston-ouest.ca
Entité municipal: Municipality
Incorporation: 1er janvier 1946; *Area:* 97,90 km2
Comté ou district: Coaticook; *Population au 2011:* 591
Circonscription(s) électorale(s) provinciale(s): Saint-François
Circonscription(s) électorale(s) fédérale(s): Compton-Stanstead
Prochaines élections: 5e novembre 2017
Johnny Piszar, Maire
Sonia Tremblay, Directrice générale

Barraute
CP 299
481, 8e Av
Barraute, QC J0Y 1A0
Tél: 819-734-6574; *Téléc:* 819-734-5186
mun.barraute@cableamos.com
www.barraute.ca
Entité municipal: Municipality
Incorporation: 5e janvier 1994; *Area:* 495,51 km2
Comté ou district: Abitibi; *Population au 2011:* 1,980
Circonscription(s) électorale(s) provinciale(s): Abitibi-Est
Circonscription(s) électorale(s) fédérale(s): Abitibi-Témiscamingue
Prochaines élections: 5e novembre 2017
Lionel Pelchat, Maire
Richard Nantel, Directeur général

Les Basques
#400, 2, rue Jean-Rioux
Trois-Pistoles, QC G0L 4K0
Tél: 418-851-3206; *Téléc:* 418-851-3171
mrc@mrcdesbasques.com
www.mrcdesbasques.com
Entité municipal: Regional County Municipality
Incorporation: 1er avril 1981
Population au 2011: 9,142
Note: 11 municipalités & 1 autre territoire.
Bertin Denis, Préfet
François Gosselin, Directeur général

Batiscan
395, rue Principale
Batiscan, QC G0X 1A0
Tél: 418-362-2421; *Téléc:* 418-362-3174
municipalite@batiscan.ca
www.batiscan.ca
Entité municipal: Municipality
Incorporation: 1er juillet 1855; *Area:* 44,02 km2
Comté ou district: Les Chenaux; *Population au 2011:* 940
Circonscription(s) électorale(s) provinciale(s): Champlain
Circonscription(s) électorale(s) fédérale(s): St-Maurice-Champlain
Prochaines élections: 5e novembre 2017
Sonya Auclair, Mairesse
Pierre Massicotte, Directeur général

Béarn
CP 369
28, 2e rue nord
Béarn, QC J0Z 1G0
Tél: 819-726-4121; *Téléc:* 819-726-2121
Entité municipal: Municipality
Incorporation: 3e octobre 1912; *Area:* 566,48 km2
Comté ou district: Témiscamingue; *Population au 2011:* 775
Circonscription(s) électorale(s) provinciale(s): Rouyn-Noranda-Témiscamingue
Circonscription(s) électorale(s) fédérale(s): Abitibi-Témiscamingue
Prochaines élections: 5e novembre 2017
Luc Lalonde, Maire
Lynda Gaudet, Directrice générale

Beauce-Sartigan
2727, 6e Av
Saint-Georges, QC G5Y 3Y1
Tél: 418-228-8418; *Téléc:* 418-228-3709
mrcbsart@globetrotter.net
www.mrcbeaucesartigan.com
Entité municipal: Regional County Municipality
Incorporation: 1er janvier 1982
Population au 2011: 50,962
Note: 16 municipalités.
Pierre Bégin, Préfet
Éric Paquet, Directeur général

Beauceville
540, boul Renault
Beauceville, QC G5X 1N1
Tél: 418-774-9137; *Téléc:* 418-774-9141
beauceville@ville.beauceville.qc.ca
www.ville.beauceville.qc.ca
Entité municipal: Town
Incorporation: 25 février 1998; *Area:* 167,76 km2
Comté ou district: Robert-Cliche; *Population au 2011:* 6,354
Circonscription(s) électorale(s) provinciale(s): Beauce-Nord
Circonscription(s) électorale(s) fédérale(s): Beauce
Prochaines élections: 5e novembre 2017
Luc Provençal, Maire
Madeleine Poulin, Greffière

Beauharnois-Salaberry
2, rue Ellice
Beauharnois, QC J6N 1W6
Tél: 450-225-0870; *Téléc:* 450-225-0872
info@mrc-beauharnois-salaberry.com
www.mrc-beauharnois-salaberry.com
Entité municipal: Regional County Municipality
Incorporation: 1er janvier 1982
Population au 2011: 61,950
Note: 7 municipalités.
Yves Daoust, Préfet
Linda Phaneuf, Directrice générale

Beaulac-Garthby
96, rte 112
Beaulac-Garthby, QC G0Y 1B0
Tél: 418-458-2375; *Téléc:* 418-458-1127
municipalitedebeaulac@bellnet.ca
www.beaulac-garthby.com
Entité municipal: Municipality
Incorporation: 15 mars 2000; *Area:* 76,81 km2
Comté ou district: Les Appalaches; *Population au 2011:* 878
Circonscription(s) électorale(s) provinciale(s): Mégantic
Circonscription(s) électorale(s) fédérale(s): Mégantic-L'Érable
Prochaines élections: 5e novembre 2017
Isabelle Gosselin, Mairesse, 418-458-1175
Cynthia Gagné, Directrice générale

Beaumont
48, ch du Domaine
Beaumont, QC G0R 1C0
Tél: 418-833-3369; *Téléc:* 418-833-4788
info@beaumont.qc.com
www.beaumont.qc.com
Entité municipal: Municipality
Incorporation: 1er juillet 1855; *Area:* 45,29 km2
Comté ou district: Bellechasse; *Population au 2011:* 2,420
Circonscription(s) électorale(s) provinciale(s): Bellechasse
Circonscription(s) électorale(s) fédérale(s): Bellechasse-Les Etchemins-Lévis
Prochaines élections: 5e novembre 2017
André Goulet, Maire
Angèle Brochu, Directrice générale

Beaupré
10995, rue des Montagnards
Beaupré, QC G0A 1E0
Tél: 418-827-4541; *Téléc:* 418-827-3818
mairie@villedebeaupre.com
www.villedebeaupre.com
Entité municipal: Town
Incorporation: 23 avril 1928; *Area:* 22,53 km2
Comté ou district: La Côte-de-Beaupré; Communauté métropolitaine de Québec; *Population au 2011:* 3,439
Circonscription(s) électorale(s) provinciale(s): Charlevoix-Côte-de-Beaupré
Circonscription(s) électorale(s) fédérale(s): Beauport-Côte-de-Beaupré-Ile d'Orléans-Charlevoix
Prochaines élections: 5e novembre 2017
Michel Paré, Maire
Johanne Gagnon, Greffière

Bécancour
#1, 3689, boul Bécancour
Bécancour, QC G9H 3W7
Tél: 819-298-2070; *Téléc:* 819-298-2041
info@mrcbecancour.qc.ca
www.mrcbecancour.qc.ca
Other Information: Sans frais: 1-866-441-0404
Entité municipal: Regional County Municipality
Incorporation: 1er janvier 1982
Population au 2011: 20,081
Note: 12 municipalités.
Mario Lyonnais, Préfet
André Roy, Directeur général

Bedford
237, rte 202 est
Canton de Bedford, QC J0J 1A0
Tél: 450-248-7576; *Téléc:* 450-248-0135
municipalite@cantondebedford.ca
www.cantondebedford.ca
Entité municipal: Township
Incorporation: 4e mars 1919; *Area:* 31,06 km2
Comté ou district: Brome-Missisquoi; *Population au 2011:* 699
Circonscription(s) électorale(s) provinciale(s): Brome-Missisquoi
Circonscription(s) électorale(s) fédérale(s): Brome-Missisquoi
Prochaines élections: 5e novembre 2017
Gilles St-Jean, Maire
Manon Blanchet, Directrice générale

Bedford
1, rue Principale
Bedford, QC J0J 1A0
Tél: 450-248-2440; *Téléc:* 450-248-3220
www.ville.bedford.qc.ca
Entité municipal: Town
Incorporation: 21 novembre 1866; *Area:* 4,57 km2
Comté ou district: Brome-Missisquoi; *Population au 2011:* 2,684
Circonscription(s) électorale(s) provinciale(s): Brome-Missisquoi

Circonscription(s) électorale(s) fédérale(s): Brome-Missisquoi
Prochaines élections: 5e novembre 2017
Yves Lévesque, Maire
Yvon Labonté, Directeur général

Bégin
126, rue Brassard
Bégin, QC G0V 1B0
Tél: 418-672-4270; *Téléc:* 418-673-2117
munbegin@hotmail.com
www.begin.ca
Entité municipal: Municipality
Incorporation: 8e février 1922; *Area:* 191,81 km2
Comté ou district: Le Fjord-du-Saguenay; *Population au 2011:* 868
Circonscription(s) électorale(s) provinciale(s): Dubuc
Circonscription(s) électorale(s) fédérale(s): Jonquière
Prochaines élections: 5e novembre 2017
Gérald Savard, Maire
Peggy Lemieux, Directrice générale

Belcourt
CP 22
219, rue Communautaire
Belcourt, QC J0Y 2M0
Tél: 819-737-8894; *Téléc:* 819-737-4084
info@munbelcourt.ca
Entité municipal: Municipality
Incorporation: 24 octobre 1918; *Area:* 411,23 km2
Comté ou district: La Vallée-de-l'Or; *Population au 2011:* 239
Circonscription(s) électorale(s) provinciale(s): Abitibi-Est
Circonscription(s) électorale(s) fédérale(s): Abitibi-Baie-James-Nunavik-Eeyou
Prochaines élections: 5e novembre 2017
Carol Nolet, Maire
Nathalie Lizotte, Directrice générale

Bellechasse
100, rue Monseigneur-Bilodeau
Saint-Lazare-de-Bellechasse, QC G0R 3J0
Tél: 418-883-3347; *Téléc:* 418-883-2555
info@mrcbellechasse.qc.ca
www.mrcbellechasse.qc.ca
Entité municipal: Regional County Municipality
Incorporation: 1er janvier 1982
Population au 2011: 35,318
Note: 20 municipalités.
Hervé Blais, Préfet
Clément Fillion, Directeur général

Belleterre
CP 130
265, 1re av
Belleterre, QC J0Z 1L0
Tél: 819-722-2122; *Téléc:* 819-722-2527
belledg@mrctemiscamingue.qc.ca
Entité municipal: Village
Incorporation: 13 mai 1942; *Area:* 606,33 km2
Comté ou district: Témiscamingue; *Population au 2011:* 298
Circonscription(s) électorale(s) provinciale(s): Rouyn-Noranda-Témiscamingue
Circonscription(s) électorale(s) fédérale(s): Abitibi-Témiscamingue
Prochaines élections: 5e novembre 2017
Bruno Boyer, Maire
Liliane Rochon, Directrice générale

Les Bergeronnes
CP 158
424, rue de la Mer
Les Bergeronnes, QC G0T 1G0
Tél: 418-232-6244; *Téléc:* 418-232-6602
info@bergeronnes.com
www.bergeronnes.net
Entité municipal: Municipality
Incorporation: 29 décembre 1999; *Area:* 291,89 km2
Comté ou district: La Haute-Côte-Nord; *Population au 2011:* 693
Circonscription(s) électorale(s) provinciale(s): René-Lévesque
Circonscription(s) électorale(s) fédérale(s): Manicouagan
Prochaines élections: 5e novembre 2017
Francis Bouchard, Maire
Lynda Tremblay, Directrice générale

Berry
274, rte 399
Berry, QC J0Y 2G0
Tél: 819-732-1815; *Téléc:* 819-732-3289
direction.berry@mrcabitibi.qc.ca
Entité municipal: Municipality
Incorporation: 1er janvier 1982; *Area:* 583,36 km2
Comté ou district: Abitibi; *Population au 2011:* 625
Circonscription(s) électorale(s) provinciale(s): Abitibi-Ouest
Circonscription(s) électorale(s) fédérale(s): Abitibi-Témiscamingue
Prochaines élections: 5e novembre 2017
Raymond Doré, Maire
Sandra Boutin, Directrice générale

Berthier-sur-Mer
5, rue du Couvent
Berthier-sur-Mer, QC G0R 1E0
Tél: 418-259-7343; *Téléc:* 418-259-2038
berthier-sur-mer@montmagny.com
www.berthiersurmer.ca
Entité municipal: Municipality
Incorporation: 1er juillet 1855; *Area:* 26,05 km2
Comté ou district: Montmagny; *Population au 2011:* 1,398
Circonscription(s) électorale(s) provinciale(s): Côte-du-Sud
Circonscription(s) électorale(s) fédérale(s): Montmagny-L'Islet-Kamouraska-Rivière-du-Loup
Prochaines élections: 5e novembre 2017
Richard Galibois, Maire
Suzanne G. Blais, Directrice générale

Berthierville
CP 269
588, rue De Montcalm
Berthierville, QC J0K 1A0
Tél: 450-836-7035; *Téléc:* 450-836-1446
info@ville.berthierville.qc.ca
www.ville.berthierville.qc.ca
Entité municipal: Town
Incorporation: 14 avril 1852; *Area:* 7,20 km2
Comté ou district: D'Autray; *Population au 2011:* 4,091
Circonscription(s) électorale(s) provinciale(s): Berthier
Circonscription(s) électorale(s) fédérale(s): Berthier-Maskinongé
Prochaines élections: 5e novembre 2017
Suzanne Nantel, Maire
Lincoln Le Breton, Directeur général et greffier

Béthanie
1321, ch de Béthanie
Béthanie, QC J0H 1E1
Tél: 450-548-2826; *Téléc:* 450-548-5693
bethanie@cooptel.qc.ca
municipalite.bethanie.qc.ca
Entité municipal: Municipality
Incorporation: 2e mars 1920; *Area:* 47,29 km2
Comté ou district: Acton; *Population au 2011:* 314
Circonscription(s) électorale(s) provinciale(s): Johnson
Circonscription(s) électorale(s) fédérale(s): St-Hyacinthe-Bagot
Prochaines élections: 5e novembre 2017
Boniface Dalle-Vedove, Maire
Jacques Mireault, Directeur général

Biencourt
CP 70
5, rue Berger
Biencourt, QC G0K 1T0
Tél: 418-499-2423; *Téléc:* 418-499-2708
info@biencourt.ca
www.biencourt.ca
Entité municipal: Municipality
Incorporation: 1er janvier 1947; *Area:* 187,80 km2
Comté ou district: Témiscouata; *Population au 2011:* 506
Circonscription(s) électorale(s) provinciale(s): Rivière-du-Loup-Témiscouata
Circonscription(s) électorale(s) fédérale(s): Rimouski-Neigette-Témiscouata-Les Basques
Prochaines élections: 5e novembre 2017
Daniel Boucher, Maire
Julie Vaillancourt, Directrice générale

Blanc-Sablon
CP 400
1149, boul Dr.-Camille-Marcoux
Lourdes-de-Blanc-Sablon, QC G0G 1W0
Tél: 418-461-2707; *Téléc:* 418-461-2529
mbsablon@globetrotter.net
Entité municipal: Municipality
Incorporation: 1er janvier 1990; *Area:* 254,49 km2
Comté ou district: Le Golfe-du-Saint-Laurent; *Population au 2011:* 1,118
Circonscription(s) électorale(s) provinciale(s): Duplessis
Circonscription(s) électorale(s) fédérale(s): Manicouagan
Prochaines élections: 5e novembre 2017
Armand Joncas, Maire
Réjean L. Dumas, Directeur général

Blue Sea
CP 99
10, rue Principale
Blue Sea, QC J0X 1C0
Tél: 819-463-2261; *Téléc:* 819-463-4345
info@bluesea.ca
www.bluesea.ca
Entité municipal: Municipality
Incorporation: 31 janvier 1921; *Area:* 76,89 km2
Comté ou district: La Vallée-de-la-Gatineau; *Population au 2011:* 674
Circonscription(s) électorale(s) provinciale(s): Gatineau
Circonscription(s) électorale(s) fédérale(s): Pontiac
Prochaines élections: 5e novembre 2017
Laurent Fortin, Maire
Sandra Bélisle, Directrice générale

Boileau
702, ch de Boileau
Boileau, QC J0V 1N0
Tél: 819-687-3436; *Téléc:* 819-687-3745
mun.boileau@mrcpapineau.com
www.municipaliteboileau.ca
Entité municipal: Municipality
Incorporation: 8e mars 1882; *Area:* 136,22 km2
Comté ou district: Papineau; *Population au 2011:* 380
Circonscription(s) électorale(s) provinciale(s): Papineau
Circonscription(s) électorale(s) fédérale(s): Argenteuil-La Petite-Nation
Prochaines élections: 5e novembre 2017
Henri Gariépy, Maire
Mathieu Dessureault, Directeur général

Boischatel
45, rue Bédard
Boischatel, QC G0A 1H0
Tél: 418-822-4500; *Téléc:* 418-822-4512
administration@boischatel.net
www.municipalitedeboischatel.ca
Entité municipal: Municipality
Incorporation: 3e avril 1920; *Area:* 19,64
Comté ou district: La Côte-de-Beaupré; Communauté métropolitaine de Québec; *Population au 2011:* 6,465
Circonscription(s) électorale(s) provinciale(s): Charlevoix-Côte-de-Beaupré
Circonscription(s) électorale(s) fédérale(s): Beauport-Côte-de-Beaupré-Ile d'Orléans-Charlevoix
Prochaines élections: 5e novembre 2017
Yves Germain, Maire
Carl Michaud, Directeur général

Bois-des-Filion
375, boul Adophe-Chapleau
Bois-des-Filion, QC J6Z 1H1
Tél: 450-621-1460; *Téléc:* 450-621-8483
ville@ville.bois-des-filion.qc.ca
ville.bois-des-filion.qc.ca
Entité municipal: Town
Incorporation: 1er janvier 1949; *Area:* 4,34 km2
Comté ou district: Thérèse-De Blainville; *Population au 2011:* 9,485
Circonscription(s) électorale(s) provinciale(s): Blainville
Circonscription(s) électorale(s) fédérale(s): Thérèse-De Blainville
Prochaines élections: 5e novembre 2017
Paul Larocque, Maire
Sylvain Rolland, Greffier

Bois-Franc
466, rte 105
Bois-Franc, QC J9E 3A9
Tél: 819-449-2252; *Téléc:* 819-449-4407
info@bois-franc.ca
www.bois-franc.ca
Entité municipal: Municipality
Incorporation: 17 novembre 1920; *Area:* 73,24 km2
Comté ou district: La Vallée-de-la-Gatineau; *Population au 2011:* 447
Circonscription(s) électorale(s) provinciale(s): Gatineau
Circonscription(s) électorale(s) fédérale(s): Pontiac
Prochaines élections: 5e novembre 2017
Julie Jolivette, Mairesse
Annie Pelletier, Directrice générale

Bolton-Est
858, rte Missisquoi
Bolton-Est, QC J0E 1G0
Tél: 450-292-3444; *Téléc:* 450-292-4224
info@boltonest.ca
www.boltonest.ca
Entité municipal: Municipality
Incorporation: 28 décembre 1876; *Area:* 80,78
Comté ou district: Memphrémagog; *Population au 2011:* 910

Circonscription(s) électorale(s) provinciale(s): Orford
Circonscription(s) électorale(s) fédérale(s): Brome-Missisquoi
Prochaines élections: 5e novembre 2017
Joan Westland, Mairesse
Richard Constantineau, Directeur général

Bolton-Ouest
9, ch Town Hall
Bolton-Ouest, QC J0E 2T0
Tél: 450-242-2704; *Téléc:* 450-242-2705
reception@municipalitedeboltonouest.com
www.municipalitedeboltonouest.com
Entité municipal: Municipality
Incorporation: 28 décembre 1876; *Area:* 103,59
Comté ou district: Brome-Missisquoi; *Population au 2011:* 678
Circonscription(s) électorale(s) provinciale(s): Brome-Missisquoi
Circonscription(s) électorale(s) fédérale(s): Brome-Missisquoi
Prochaines élections: 5e novembre 2017
Donald Badger, Maire
Philippe De Courval, Directeur général

Bonaventure
127, av de Louisbourg
Bonaventure, QC G0C 1E0
Tél: 418-534-2313; *Téléc:* 418-534-4336
info@villebonaventure.ca
www.villebonaventure.ca
Entité municipal: Town
Incorporation: 1er janvier 1884; *Area:* 109,20 km2
Comté ou district: Bonaventure; *Population au 2011:* 2,775
Circonscription(s) électorale(s) provinciale(s): Bonaventure
Circonscription(s) électorale(s) fédérale(s): Gaspésie — Les Iles-de-la-Madeleine
Prochaines élections: 5e novembre 2017
Roch Audet, Maire
Rollande Roy, Greffière

Bonaventure
CP 310
51, rue Notre-Dame
New Carlisle, QC G0C 1Z0
Tél: 418-752-6601; *Téléc:* 418-752-6657
mrcbonav@globetrotter.net
www.mrcbonaventure.com
Entité municipal: Regional County Municipality
Incorporation: 8e avril 1981
Population au 2011: 18,000
Note: 13 municipalités & 1 autre territoire.
Jean-Guy Poirier, Préfet
Anne-Marie Flowers, Directrice générale

Bonne-Espérance
CP 40
100, rue Whiteley
Rivière-Saint-Paul, QC G0G 2P0
Tél: 418-379-2911; *Téléc:* 418-379-2959
bonneesperance@xplornet.com
Entité municipal: Municipality
Incorporation: 1er janvier 1990; *Area:* 721,28 km2
Comté ou district: Le Golfe-du-Saint-Laurent; *Population au 2011:* 732
Circonscription(s) électorale(s) provinciale(s): Duplessis
Circonscription(s) électorale(s) fédérale(s): Manicouagan
Prochaines élections: 5e novembre 2017
Lionel Roberts, Maire
René Fequet, Directeur général

Bonsecours
557, rue du Couvent
Bonsecours, QC J0E 1H0
Tél: 450-532-3139; *Téléc:* 450-532-3953
mbonsecours@cooptel.qc.ca
www.municipalite-bonsecours.org
Entité municipal: Municipality
Incorporation: 20 mars 1905; *Area:* 59,92 km2
Comté ou district: Le Val-Saint-François; *Population au 2011:* 577
Circonscription(s) électorale(s) provinciale(s): Orford
Circonscription(s) électorale(s) fédérale(s): Shefford
Prochaines élections: 5e novembre 2017
Cécile Laliberté, Mairesse
Lyne Gaudreau, Directrice générale

La Bostonnais
15, rue de l'Église
La Bostonnais, QC G9X 0A7
Tél: 819-523-5830; *Téléc:* 819-523-5776
info@labostonnais.ca
www.labostonnais.ca
Entité municipal: Municipality
Incorporation: 1er janvier 2006; *Area:* 287,37 km2
Population au 2011: 503
Circonscription(s) électorale(s) provinciale(s): Laviolette
Circonscription(s) électorale(s) fédérale(s): Saint-Maurice-Champlain
Prochaines élections: 5e novembre 2017
Chantal St-Louis, Mairesse
Josée Cloutier, Greffière

Bouchette
CP 59
36, rue Principale
Bouchette, QC J0X 1E0
Tél: 819-465-2555; *Téléc:* 819-465-2318
mun.bouchette@ireseau.com
www.bouchette.ca
Entité municipal: Municipality
Incorporation: 22 mars 1980; *Area:* 131,97 km2
Comté ou district: La Vallée-de-la-Gatineau; *Population au 2011:* 786
Circonscription(s) électorale(s) provinciale(s): Gatineau
Circonscription(s) électorale(s) fédérale(s): Pontiac
Prochaines élections: 5e novembre 2017
Réjean Major, Maire
Claudia Lacroix, Directrice générale

Bowman
214, rte 307
Bowman, QC J0X 3C0
Tél: 819-454-2421; *Téléc:* 819-454-2133
bowman01@mrcpapineau.com
www.bowman.ca
Entité municipal: Municipality
Incorporation: 27 juin 1913; *Area:* 166,99 km2
Comté ou district: Papineau; *Population au 2011:* 677
Circonscription(s) électorale(s) provinciale(s): Papineau
Circonscription(s) électorale(s) fédérale(s): Argenteuil — La Petite-Nation
Prochaines élections: 5e novembre 2017
Michel David, Maire
Mylène Groulx, Directrice générale

Brébeuf
217, rte 323
Brébeuf, QC J0T 1B0
Tél: 819-425-9833; *Téléc:* 819-425-6611
secretariat@brebeuf.ca
www.brebeuf.ca
Entité municipal: Parish (Paroisse)
Incorporation: 4e juin 1910; *Area:* 36,71 km2
Comté ou district: Les Laurentides; *Population au 2011:* 1,012
Circonscription(s) électorale(s) provinciale(s): Labelle
Circonscription(s) électorale(s) fédérale(s): Avignon-La Mitis-Matane-Matapédia; Laurentides-Labelle
Prochaines élections: 5e novembre 2017
Ronald Provost, Maire
Pascal Caron, Directeur général

Brigham
118, av des Cèdres
Brigham, QC J2K 4K4
Tél: 450-263-5942; *Téléc:* 450-263-8380
info@brigham.ca
www.brigham.ca
Entité municipal: Municipality
Incorporation: 1er juillet 1855; *Area:* 84,80 km2
Comté ou district: Brome-Missisquoi; *Population au 2011:* 2,457
Circonscription(s) électorale(s) provinciale(s): Brome-Missisquoi
Circonscription(s) électorale(s) fédérale(s): Brome-Missisquoi
Prochaines élections: 5e novembre 2017
Normand Delisle, Maire
Jean-François Grandmont, Directeur général

Bristol
32, ch d'Aylmer
Bristol, QC J0X 1G0
Tél: 819-647-5555; *Téléc:* 819-647-2424
www.bristolmunicipality.qc.ca
Entité municipal: Municipality
Incorporation: 1er juillet 1855; *Area:* 224,08 km2
Comté ou district: Pontiac; *Population au 2011:* 1,128
Circonscription(s) électorale(s) provinciale(s): Pontiac
Circonscription(s) électorale(s) fédérale(s): Pontiac
Prochaines élections: 5e novembre 2017
Brent Orr, Maire
Christina Peck, Directrice générale

Brome
330, ch Stagecoach
Brome, QC J0E 1K0
Tél: 450-243-0489; *Téléc:* 450-243-1091
bromevillage@axion.ca
Entité municipal: Village
Incorporation: 20 juin 1923; *Area:* 11,75 km2
Comté ou district: Brome-Missisquoi; *Population au 2011:* 271
Circonscription(s) électorale(s) provinciale(s): Brome-Missisquoi
Circonscription(s) électorale(s) fédérale(s): Brome-Missisquoi
Prochaines élections: 5e novembre 2017
Leon Thomas Selby, Maire
Irena Hodorowski, Directrice générale

Brome-Missisquoi
749, rue Principale
Cowansville, QC J2K 1J8
Tél: 450-266-4900; *Téléc:* 450-266-6141
administration@mrcbm.qc.ca
www.brome-missisquoi.ca
Entité municipal: Regional County Municipality
Incorporation: 1er janvier 1983
Population au 2011: 55,621
Note: 21 municipalités.
Arthur Fauteux, Préfet
Robert Desmarais, Directeur général

Bromont
88, boul de Bromont
Bromont, QC J2L 1A1
Tél: 450-534-2021; *Téléc:* 450-534-1025
ville@bromont.com
www.bromont.com
Entité municipal: Town
Incorporation: 27 janvier 1973; *Area:* 108,36 km2
Comté ou district: Brome-Missisquoi; *Population au 2011:* 7,649
Circonscription(s) électorale(s) provinciale(s): Brome-Missisquoi
Circonscription(s) électorale(s) fédérale(s): Brome-Missisquoi
Prochaines élections: 5e novembre 2017
Pauline Quinlan, Mairesse
Joanne Skelling, Greffière

Brownsburg-Chatham
300, rue de l'Hôtel-de-Ville
Brownsburg-Chatham, QC J8G 3B4
Tél: 450-533-6687; *Téléc:* 450-533-5795
secretariat@brownsburgchatham.ca
www.brownsburgchatham.ca
Entité municipal: Town
Incorporation: 6e octobre 1999; *Area:* 249,31 km2
Comté ou district: Argenteuil; *Population au 2011:* 7,209
Circonscription(s) électorale(s) provinciale(s): Argenteuil
Circonscription(s) électorale(s) fédérale(s): Argenteuil-La Petite-Nation
Prochaines élections: 5e novembre 2017
Serge Riendeau, Maire
René Tousignant, Greffière et directeur général

Bryson
CP 190
833, rue Principale
Bryson, QC J0X 1H0
Tél: 819-648-5940; *Téléc:* 819-648-5297
bryson@mrcpontiac.qc.ca
Entité municipal: Municipality
Incorporation: 1er janvier 1873; *Area:* 3,10 km2
Comté ou district: Pontiac; *Population au 2011:* 647
Circonscription(s) électorale(s) provinciale(s): Pontiac
Circonscription(s) électorale(s) fédérale(s): Pontiac; Salaberry-Suroît
Prochaines élections: 5e novembre 2017
Alain Gagnon, Maire
Tracey Hérault, Directrice générale

Bury
569, rue Main
Bury, QC J0B 1J0
Tél: 819-560-8414; *Téléc:* 819-872-3675
information.bury@hsfqc.ca
www.municipalitedebury.qc.ca
Entité municipal: Municipality
Incorporation: 1er juillet 1855; *Area:* 232,52 km2
Comté ou district: Le Haut-Saint-François; *Population au 2011:* 1,159
Circonscription(s) électorale(s) provinciale(s): Mégantic
Circonscription(s) électorale(s) fédérale(s): Compton-Stanstead
Prochaines élections: 5e novembre 2017
Walter Dougherty, Maire
Yvan Fortin, Directeur général

Cacouna
415, rue St-Georges
Cacouna, QC G0L 1G0
Tél: 418-867-1781; *Téléc:* 418-867-5677
municipalite@cacouna.ca
www.cacouna.ca
Entité municipal: Municipality
Incorporation: 22 mars 2006; *Area:* 62,49 km2
Comté ou district: Rivière-du-Loup; *Population au 2011:* 1,939

Circonscription(s) électorale(s) provinciale(s): Rivière-du-Loup-Témiscouata
Circonscription(s) électorale(s) fédérale(s): Montmagny—L'Islet—Kamouraska—Rivière-du-Loup
Prochaines élections: 5e novembre 2017
Ghislaine Daris, Maire
Madeleine Lévesque, Directrice générale

Calixa-Lavallée
771, ch de la Beauce
Calixa-Lavallée, QC J0L 1A0
Tél: 450-583-6470; *Téléc:* 450-583-5508
info@calixa-lavallee.ca
www.calixa-lavallee.ca
Entité municipal: Parish (Paroisse)
Incorporation: 24 juillet 1878; *Area:* 32,42 km2
Comté ou district: Marguerite-D'Youville; Communauté métropolitaine de Montréal; *Population au 2011:* 504
Circonscription(s) électorale(s) provinciale(s): Verchères
Circonscription(s) électorale(s) fédérale(s): Pierre-Boucher-Les Patriotes-Verchères
Prochaines élections: 5e novembre 2017
Daniel Plouffe, Maire
Claude Geoffrion, Directeur général

Campbell's Bay
CP 157
59, rue Leslie
Campbell's Bay, QC J0X 1K0
Tél: 819-648-5811; *Téléc:* 819-648-2045
administration@municipalite.campbellsbay.qc.ca
Entité municipal: Municipality
Incorporation: 23 février 1904; *Area:* 3,08 km2
Comté ou district: Pontiac; *Population au 2011:* 775
Circonscription(s) électorale(s) provinciale(s): Pontiac
Circonscription(s) électorale(s) fédérale(s): Pontiac
Prochaines élections: 5e novembre 2017
William Stewart, Maire
Sarah Bertrand, Directrice générale

Caniapiscau
CP 2025
100, rue le Carrefour
Fermont, QC G0G 1J0
Tél: 418-287-5339; *Téléc:* 418-287-3420
mrc@caniapiscau.net
www.caniapiscau.net
Entité municipal: Regional County Municipality
Incorporation: 1er janvier 1982
Population au : 3,142
Circonscription(s) électorale(s) fédérale(s): Manicouagan
Note: 2 municipalités & 4 autre territoire.
Lise Pelletier, Préfète
Jimmy Morneau, Directeur général

Cantley
8, ch River
Cantley, QC J8V 2Z9
Tél: 819-827-3434; *Téléc:* 819-827-4328
municipalite@cantley.ca
www.cantley.ca
Entité municipal: Municipality
Incorporation: 1er janvier 1989; *Area:* 134,00 km2
Comté ou district: Les Collines-de-l'Outaouais; *Population au 2011:* 9,888
Circonscription(s) électorale(s) provinciale(s): Gatineau
Circonscription(s) électorale(s) fédérale(s): Pontiac
Prochaines élections: 5e novembre 2017
Madeleine Brunette, Mairesse
Sylvie Loublier, Greffière

Cap-Chat
CP 279
53, rue Notre-Dame
Cap-Chat, QC G0J 1E0
Tél: 418-786-5537; *Téléc:* 418-786-5540
ville.capchat@globetrotter.net
www.cap-chat.ca
Entité municipal: Town
Incorporation: 15 mars 2000; *Area:* 183,13 km2
Comté ou district: La Haute-Gaspésie; *Population au 2011:* 2,623
Circonscription(s) électorale(s) provinciale(s): Gaspé
Circonscription(s) électorale(s) fédérale(s): Gaspésie-Les Iles-de-la-Madeleine
Prochaines élections: 5e novembre 2017
Judes Landry, Maire
Jacques Fournier, Greffier

Caplan
CP 360
17, boul Perron est
Caplan, QC G0C 1H0
Tél: 418-388-2075; *Téléc:* 418-388-2429
caplan@globetrotter.net
www.municipalitecaplan.com
Entité municipal: Municipality
Incorporation: 1er janvier 1875; *Area:* 85,05 km2
Comté ou district: Bonaventure; *Population au 2011:* 2,039
Circonscription(s) électorale(s) provinciale(s): Bonaventure
Circonscription(s) électorale(s) fédérale(s): Gaspésie-Les Iles-de-la-Madeleine
Prochaines élections: 5e novembre 2017
Lise Castilloux, Mairesse
Serge Vallée, Directeur général

Cap-Saint-Ignace
850, rte du Souvenir
Cap-Saint-Ignace, QC G0R 1H0
Tél: 418-246-5631; *Téléc:* 418-246-5663
www.capsaintignace.ca
Entité municipal: Municipality
Incorporation: 1er juillet 1855; *Area:* 227,76 km2
Comté ou district: Montmagny; *Population au 2011:* 3,045
Circonscription(s) électorale(s) provinciale(s): Côte-du-Sud
Circonscription(s) électorale(s) fédérale(s): Montmagny-L'Islet-Kamouraska-Rivière-du-Loup
Prochaines élections: 5e novembre 2017
Jocelyne Caron, Mairesse
Sophie Boucher, Directrice générale

Cap-Santé
194, rte 138
Cap-Santé, QC G0A 1L0
Tél: 418-285-1207; *Téléc:* 418-285-0009
villecapsante@globetrotter.net
www.capsante.qc.ca
Entité municipal: Town
Incorporation: 1er juillet 1855; *Area:* 54,38 km2
Comté ou district: Portneuf; *Population au 2011:* 2,996
Circonscription(s) électorale(s) provinciale(s): Portneuf
Circonscription(s) électorale(s) fédérale(s): Portneuf-Jacques-Cartier
Prochaines élections: 5e novembre 2017
Denis Jobin, Maire
Nancy Sirois, Directrice générale

Carignan
2555, ch Bellevue
Carignan, QC J3L 6G8
Tél: 450-658-1066; *Téléc:* 450-658-6079
info@villedecarignan.org
www.villedecarignan.org
Entité municipal: Town
Incorporation: 1er juillet 1855; *Area:* 62,39 km2
Comté ou district: La Vallée-du-Richelieu; Communauté métropolitaine de Montréal; *Population au 2011:* 7,966
Circonscription(s) électorale(s) provinciale(s): Chambly
Circonscription(s) électorale(s) fédérale(s): Beloeil-Chambly; Saint-Maurice-Champlain
Prochaines élections: 5e novembre 2017
René Fournier, Maire
Rémi Raymond, Greffier

Carleton-sur-Mer
629, boul Perron
Carleton, QC G0C 1J0
Tél: 418-364-7073; *Téléc:* 418-364-6011
direction@carletonsurmer.com
www.carletonsurmer.com
Entité municipal: Town
Incorporation: 4e octobre 2000; *Area:* 214,78 km2
Comté ou district: Avignon; *Population au 2011:* 3,991
Circonscription(s) électorale(s) provinciale(s): Bonaventure
Circonscription(s) électorale(s) fédérale(s): Avignon-La Mitis-Matane-Matapédia
Prochaines élections: 5e novembre 2017
Denis Henry, Maire
Danick Boulet, Directeur général et greffière

Cascapédia-Saint-Jules
75, rte Gallagher
Cascapédia-Saint-Jules, QC G0C 1T0
Tél: 418-392-4042; *Téléc:* 418-392-6004
www.cascapediastjules.com
Entité municipal: Municipality
Incorporation: 2e juin 1999; *Area:* 168,00 km2
Comté ou district: Bonaventure; *Population au 2011:* 741
Circonscription(s) électorale(s) provinciale(s): Bonaventure
Circonscription(s) électorale(s) fédérale(s): Gaspésie—Îles-de-la-Madeleine
Prochaines élections: 5e novembre 2017
Pat St. Onge, Maire
Susan Legouffe, Directrice générale

Causapscal
1, rue St-Jacques nord
Causapscal, QC G0J 1J0
Tél: 418-756-3444; *Téléc:* 418-756-3344
causapscal@mrcmatapedia.qc.ca
www.causapscal.net
Entité municipal: Town
Incorporation: 31 décembre 1997; *Area:* 163,88 km2
Comté ou district: La Matapédia; *Population au 2011:* 2,458
Circonscription(s) électorale(s) provinciale(s): Matane-Matapédia
Circonscription(s) électorale(s) fédérale(s): Avignon-La Mitis-Matane-Matapédia
Prochaines élections: 5e novembre 2017
Mario Côté, Maire
Jean-Noël Barriault, Directeur général

Cayamant
6, ch Lachapelle
Lac-Cayamant, QC J0X 1Y0
Tél: 819-463-3587; *Téléc:* 819-463-4020
info@cayamant.ca
www.cayamant.ca
Entité municipal: Municipality
Incorporation: 10 octobre 1906; *Area:* 411,13 km2
Comté ou district: La Vallée-de-la-Gatineau; *Population au 2011:* 875
Circonscription(s) électorale(s) provinciale(s): Gatineau
Circonscription(s) électorale(s) fédérale(s): Pontiac
Prochaines élections: 5e novembre 2017
Chantal Lamarche, Mairesse
Stéphane Hamel, Directeur général

Les Cèdres
1060, ch du Fleuve
Les Cèdres, QC J7T 1A1
Tél: 450-452-4651; *Téléc:* 450-452-4605
info@ville.lescedres.qc.ca
www.ville.lescedres.qc.ca
Entité municipal: Municipality
Incorporation: 9 mars 1985; *Area:* 78,31 km2
Comté ou district: Vaudreuil-Soulanges; Communauté métropolitaine de Montréal; *Population au 2011:* 6,079
Circonscription(s) électorale(s) provinciale(s): Soulanges
Circonscription(s) électorale(s) fédérale(s): Vaudreuil-Soulanges; Hull-Aylmer
Prochaines élections: 5e novembre 2017
Raymond Larouche, Maire
Jimmy Poulin, Directeur général

Chambord
1526, rue Principale
Chambord, QC G0W 1G0
Tél: 418-342-6274; *Téléc:* 418-342-8438
info@chambord.ca
www.chambord.ca
Entité municipal: Municipality
Incorporation: 8e décembre 1973; *Area:* 157,03 km2
Comté ou district: Le Domaine-du-Roy; *Population au 2011:* 1,773
Circonscription(s) électorale(s) provinciale(s): Roberval
Circonscription(s) électorale(s) fédérale(s): Lac-Saint-Jean
Prochaines élections: 5e novembre 2017
Gérard Savard, Maire
Steeve Gagnon, Directeur général

Champlain
CP 250
819, rue Notre-Dame
Champlain, QC G0X 1C0
Tél: 819-295-3979; *Téléc:* 819-295-3032
municipalite.champlain@infoteck.qc.ca
www.municipalite.champlain.qc.ca
Entité municipal: Municipality
Incorporation: 11 décembre 1982; *Area:* 58,59 km2
Comté ou district: Les Chenaux; *Population au 2011:* 1,664
Circonscription(s) électorale(s) provinciale(s): Champlain
Circonscription(s) électorale(s) fédérale(s): Lac-Saint-Jean
Prochaines élections: 5e novembre 2017
Guy Simon, Maire
Jean Houde, Directeur général

Champneuf
12, 6e av nord
Champneuf, QC J0Y 1E0
Tél: 819-754-2053; *Téléc:* 819-754-5749
munichampneuf@cableamos.com
www.champneuf.ca

Entité municipal: Municipality
Incorporation: 1er janvier 1964; *Area:* 241,38 km2
Comté ou district: Abitibi; *Population au 2011:* 127
Circonscription(s) électorale(s) provinciale(s): Abitibi-Ouest
Circonscription(s) électorale(s) fédérale(s):
Abitibi-Témiscamingue
Prochaines élections: 5e novembre 2017
Rosaire Guénette, Maire
Josée Beauregard, Directrice générale

Chandler
CP 459
35, rue Commerciale ouest
Chandler, QC G0C 1K0
Tél: 418-689-2221; *Téléc:* 418-689-3073
hdvchan@globetrotter.net
www.villedechandler.com
Entité municipal: Town
Incorporation: 27 juin 2001; *Area:* 424,90 km2
Comté ou district: Le Rocher-Percé; *Population au 2011:* 7,703
Circonscription(s) électorale(s) provinciale(s): Bonaventure
Circonscription(s) électorale(s) fédérale(s): Gaspésie-Les Iles-de-la-Madeleine
Prochaines élections: 5e novembre 2017
Louisette Langlois, Mairesse
Roch Giroux, Greffier et directeur général

Chapais
CP 380
145, boul Springer
Chapais, QC G0W 1H0
Tél: 418-745-2511; *Téléc:* 418-745-3871
info@villedechapais.com
www.villedechapais.com
Entité municipal: Village
Incorporation: 16 novembre 1955; *Area:* 62,78 km2
Population au 2011: 1,610
Circonscription(s) électorale(s) provinciale(s): Ungava
Circonscription(s) électorale(s) fédérale(s):
Abitibi-Baie-James-Nunavik-Eeyou;
Montmagny-L'Islet-Kamouraska-Rivière-du-Loup
Prochaines élections: 5e novembre 2017
Steve Gamache, Maire
Mariève Bernier, Greffière

Charette
390, rue St-Édouard
Charette, QC G0X 1E0
Tél: 819-221-2095; *Téléc:* 819-221-3493
municipalitecharette@sogetel.net
www.municipalite-charette.ca
Entité municipal: Municipality
Incorporation: 9e février 1918; *Area:* 42,55 km2
Comté ou district: Maskinongé; *Population au 2011:* 993
Circonscription(s) électorale(s) provinciale(s): Maskinongé
Circonscription(s) électorale(s) fédérale(s): Berthier-Maskinongé
Prochaines élections: 5e novembre 2017
Claude Boulanger, Maire
Patricia Adam, Directrice générale

Charlemagne
84, rue du Sacré-Coeur
Charlemagne, QC J5Z 1W8
Tél: 450-581-2541; *Téléc:* 450-581-0597
info@ville.charlemagne.qc.ca
www.ville.charlemagne.qc.ca
Entité municipal: Town
Incorporation: 13 novembre 1906; *Area:* 1,95 km2
Comté ou district: L'Assomption; Communauté métropolitaine de Montréal; *Population au 2011:* 5,853
Circonscription(s) électorale(s) provinciale(s): L'Assomption
Circonscription(s) électorale(s) fédérale(s): Repentigny
Prochaines élections: 5e novembre 2017
Normand Grenier, Maire
Bernard Boudreau, Greffier et Directeur général

Charlevoix
#201, 4, place de l'Église
Baie-Saint-Paul, QC G3Z 1T2
Tél: 418-435-2639; *Téléc:* 418-435-2666
mrc@charlevoix.net
www.mrc-charlevoix.com
Entité municipal: Regional County Municipality
Incorporation: 1er janvier 1982
Population au 2011: 13,338
Note: 6 municipalités & 1 autre territoire.
Dominic Tremblay, Préfet
Karine Horvath, Directrice générale

Charlevoix-Est
172, boul Notre-Dame
Clermont, QC G4A 1G1
Tél: 418-439-3947; *Téléc:* 418-439-2502
direction@mrccharlevoixest.ca
www.mrccharlevoixest.ca
Entité municipal: Regional County Municipality
Incorporation: 1er janvier 1982
Population au 2011: 16,240
Note: 7 municipalités & 2 autres territoires.
Sylvain Tremblay, Préfet
Pierre Girard, Directeur général

Chartierville
27, rue St-Jean-Baptiste
Chartierville, QC J0B 1K0
Tél: 819-560-8522; *Téléc:* 819-560-8523
www.chartierville.ca
Entité municipal: Municipality
Incorporation: 1er janvier 1879; *Area:* 139,13 km2
Comté ou district: Le Haut-Saint-François; *Population au 2011:* 307
Circonscription(s) électorale(s) provinciale(s): Mégantic
Circonscription(s) électorale(s) fédérale(s): Compton-Stanstead
Prochaines élections: 5e novembre 2017
Jean Belhumeur, Maire
Maryse Prud'homme, Directrice générale

Château-Richer
8006, av Royale
Château-Richer, QC G0A 1N0
Tél: 418-824-4294; *Téléc:* 418-824-3277
chateau.richer@videotron.ca
www.chateauricher.qc.ca
Entité municipal: Town
Incorporation: 1er juillet 1855; *Area:* 228,99 km2
Comté ou district: La Côte-de-Beaupré; Communauté métropolitaine de Québec; *Population au 2011:* 3,834
Circonscription(s) électorale(s) provinciale(s):
Charlevoix-Côte-de-Beaupré
Circonscription(s) électorale(s) fédérale(s):
Beauport-Côte-de-Beaupré-Ile d'Orléans-Charlevoix
Prochaines élections: 5e novembre 2017
Frédéric Dancause, Maire
Lucie Gagnon, Greffière

Chazel
752, 1er Avenue ouest
Chazel, QC J0Z 1N0
Tél: 819-333-4758; *Téléc:* 819-333-3818
chazel@mrcao.qc.ca
chazel.ao.ca
Entité municipal: Municipality
Incorporation: 19 février 1938; *Area:* 134,57 km2
Comté ou district: Abitibi-Ouest; *Population au 2011:* 289
Circonscription(s) électorale(s) provinciale(s): Abitibi-Ouest
Circonscription(s) électorale(s) fédérale(s):
Abitibi-Témiscamingue
Prochaines élections: 5e novembre 2017
Daniel Favreau, Maire
Huguette Audet, Directrice générale

Chelsea
100, ch d'Old Chelsea
Chelsea, QC J9B 1C1
Tél: 819-827-1124; *Téléc:* 819-827-2672
info@chelsea.ca
www.chelsea.ca
Entité municipal: Municipality
Incorporation: 1er janvier 1875; *Area:* 111,2 km2
Comté ou district: Les Collines-de-l'Outaouais; *Population au 2011:* 6,977
Circonscription(s) électorale(s) provinciale(s): Gatineau
Circonscription(s) électorale(s) fédérale(s): Pontiac
Prochaines élections: 5e novembre 2017
Caryl Green, Mairesse
Charles Ricard, Directeur général

Les Chenaux
630, rue Principale
Saint-Luc-de-Vincennes, QC G0X 3K0
Tél: 819-840-0704; *Téléc:* 819-295-5117
info@mrcdeschenaux.ca
www.mrcdeschenaux.ca
Entité municipal: Regional County Municipality
Incorporation: 1er janvier 2002
Population au 2011: 17,865
Circonscription(s) électorale(s) fédérale(s): Trois-Rivières
Note: 10 municipalités.
Gérard Bruneau, Préfet
Pierre St-Onge, Directeur général

Chénéville
63, rue de l'Hôtel-de-Ville
Chénéville, QC J0V 1E0
Tél: 819-428-3583; *Téléc:* 819-428-4838
adm.cheneville@mrcpapineau.com
www.ville.cheneville.qc.ca
Entité municipal: Municipality
Incorporation: 21 août 1996; *Area:* 65,22 km2
Comté ou district: Papineau; *Population au 2011:* 792
Circonscription(s) électorale(s) provinciale(s): Papineau
Circonscription(s) électorale(s) fédérale(s): Argenteuil-La Petite-Nation
Prochaines élections: 5e novembre 2017
Gilles Tremblay, Maire
Suzanne Prévost, Directrice générale

Chertsey
333, av de l'Amitié
Chertsey, QC J0K 3K0
Tél: 450-882-2920; *Téléc:* 450-882-3333
general@municipalite.chertsey.qc.ca
www.municipalite.chertsey.qc.ca
Entité municipal: Municipality
Incorporation: 13 novembre 1991; *Area:* 313,22 km2
Comté ou district: Matawinie; *Population au 2011:* 4,836
Circonscription(s) électorale(s) provinciale(s): Bertrand
Circonscription(s) électorale(s) fédérale(s): Joliette
Prochaines élections: 5e novembre 2017
Michel Suprenant, Maire
Pierre Mercier, Directeur général

Chesterville
472, rue de l'Accueil
Chesterville, QC G0P 1J0
Tél: 819-382-2059; *Téléc:* 819-382-2073
info@municipalite.chesterville.qc.ca
www.chesterville.net
Entité municipal: Municipality
Incorporation: 18 décembre 1982; *Area:* 114,89 km2
Comté ou district: Arthabaska; *Population au 2011:* 891
Circonscription(s) électorale(s) provinciale(s):
Drummond-Bois-Francs
Circonscription(s) électorale(s) fédérale(s):
Richmond-Arthabaska
Prochaines élections: 5e novembre 2017
Maryse Beauchesne, Mairesse
René Bougie, Directeur général

Chibougamau
650, 3e rue
Chibougamau, QC G8P 1P1
Tél: 418-748-2688; *Téléc:* 418-748-6562
infogenerale@ville.chibougamau.qc.ca
www.ville.chibougamau.qc.ca
Entité municipal: Town
Incorporation: 8e novembre 1952; *Area:* 1,041,97 km2
Population au 2011: 7,541
Circonscription(s) électorale(s) provinciale(s): Ungava
Circonscription(s) électorale(s) fédérale(s):
Abitibi-Baie-James-Nunavik-Eeyou
Prochaines élections: 5e novembre 2017
Manon Cyr, Mairesse
Mario Asselin, Greffier

Chichester
CP 158
75, rue Notre-Dame
Chapeau, QC J0X 1M0
Tél: 819-689-2266; *Téléc:* 819-689-5619
chichester@mrcpontiac.qc.ca
www.chichestermunicipality.com
Entité municipal: Township
Incorporation: 1er janvier 1857; *Area:* 225,71 km2
Comté ou district: Pontiac; *Population au 2011:* 368
Circonscription(s) électorale(s) provinciale(s): Pontiac
Circonscription(s) électorale(s) fédérale(s): Pontiac
Prochaines élections: 5e novembre 2017
Donald Gagnon, Maire
Richard Vaillancourt, Directeur général

Chisasibi
CP 150
1, rue Riverside
Chisasibi, QC J0M 1E0
Tél: 819-855-2878; *Téléc:* 819-855-2875
www.chisasibi.ca
Entité municipal: Villages Cris
Incorporation: 28 juin 1978; *Area:* 497,80 km2
Circonscription(s) électorale(s) provinciale(s): Ungava
Circonscription(s) électorale(s) fédérale(s):
Abitibi-Baie-James-Nunavik-Eeyou
Davey Bobbish, Maire

Edna Kanatewat, Secrétaire

Chute-aux-Outardes
2, rue de l'École
Chute-aux-Outardes, QC G0H 1C0
Tél: 418-567-2144; *Téléc:* 418-567-4478
administration@municipalitecao.ca
mrcmanicouagan.qc.ca/municipalites/chute-aux-outardes
Entité municipal: Village
Incorporation: 7e mars 1951; *Area:* 8,31 km2
Comté ou district: Manicouagan; *Population au 2011:* 1,644
Circonscription(s) électorale(s) provinciale(s): René-Lévesque
Circonscription(s) électorale(s) fédérale(s): Manicouagan
Prochaines élections: 5e novembre 2017
Yoland Émond, Maire
Rick Tanguay, Directeur général

Chute-Saint-Philippe
21, montée des Chevreuils
Chute-Saint-Philippe, QC J0W 1A0
Tél: 819-585-3397; *Téléc:* 819-585-4949
reception@chute-saint-philippe.ca
www.chute-saint-philippe.ca
Entité municipal: Municipality
Incorporation: 26 octobre 1940; *Area:* 282,28 km2
Comté ou district: Antoine-Labelle; *Population au 2011:* 892
Circonscription(s) électorale(s) provinciale(s): Labelle
Circonscription(s) électorale(s) fédérale(s): Laurentides-Labelle
Prochaines élections: 5e novembre 2017
Normand St-Amour, Maire
Ginette Ippersiel, Directrice générale

Clarendon
CP 777
C427, rte 148
Shawville, QC J0X 2Y0
Tél: 819-647-3862; *Téléc:* 819-647-3822
info@clarendonqc.ca
Entité municipal: Municipality
Incorporation: 1er juillet 1855; *Area:* 327,27 km2
Comté ou district: Pontiac; *Population au 2011:* 1,183
Circonscription(s) électorale(s) provinciale(s): Pontiac
Circonscription(s) électorale(s) fédérale(s): Pontiac
Prochaines élections: 5e novembre 2017
Terry Lloyd Elliott, Maire
Anita Lafleur, Directrice générale

Clermont
722, ch des 4e-et-5e-Rangs est
Saint-Vital-de-Clermont, QC J0Z 3M0
Tél: 819-333-6129; *Téléc:* 819-333-3811
clermont@mrcao.qc.ca
clermont.ao.ca
Entité municipal: Township
Incorporation: 4e mars 1936; *Area:* 155,89 km2
Comté ou district: Abitibi-Ouest; *Population au 2011:* 482
Circonscription(s) électorale(s) provinciale(s): Abitibi-Ouest
Circonscription(s) électorale(s) fédérale(s):
Abitibi-Témiscamingue
Prochaines élections: 5e novembre 2017
Alexandre D. Nickner, Maire
Nancy Duquette, Directrice générale

Clermont
2, rue Maisonneuve
Clermont, QC G4A 1G6
Tél: 418-439-3931; *Téléc:* 418-439-4889
info@ville.clermont.qc.ca
www.ville.clermont.qc.ca
Entité municipal: Town
Incorporation: 16 février 1935; *Area:* 52,99 km2
Comté ou district: Charlevoix-Est; *Population au 2011:* 3,118
Circonscription(s) électorale(s) provinciale(s):
Charlevoix-Côte-de-Beaupré
Circonscription(s) électorale(s) fédérale(s):
Beauport-Côte-de-Beaupré-Ile d'Orléans-Charlevoix
Prochaines élections: 5e novembre 2017
Jean-Pierre Gagnon, Maire
Brigitte Harvey, Directrice générale

Clerval
579, 2e-et-3e rang
Clerval, QC J0Z 1R0
Tél: 819-783-2640; *Téléc:* 819-783-4001
clerval@mrcao.qc.ca
clerval.ao.ca
Entité municipal: Municipality
Incorporation: 12 septembre 1927; *Area:* 101,60 km2
Comté ou district: Abitibi-Ouest; *Population au 2011:* 364
Circonscription(s) électorale(s) provinciale(s): Abitibi-Ouest
Circonscription(s) électorale(s) fédérale(s):
Abitibi-Témiscamingue
Prochaines élections: 5e novembre 2017
Suzanne Théberge, Maire
Marielle Gauthier, Directrice générale

Cleveland
292, ch de la Rivière
Cleveland, QC J0B 2H0
Tél: 819-826-3546; *Téléc:* 819-826-2827
www.cleveland.ca
Entité municipal: Township
Incorporation: 1er juillet 1855; *Area:* 120,82 km2
Comté ou district: Le Val-Saint-François; *Population au 2011:* 1,609
Circonscription(s) électorale(s) provinciale(s): Richmond
Circonscription(s) électorale(s) fédérale(s):
Richmond-Arthabaska
Prochaines élections: 5e novembre 2017
Herman Hebers, Maire
Claudette Lapointe, Directrice générale

Cloridorme
CP 253
472, rte 132
Cloridorme, QC G0E 1G0
Tél: 418-395-2808; *Téléc:* 418-395-2228
dgclori@globetrotter.net
canton-de-cloridorme.com
Entité municipal: Township
Incorporation: 1er janvier 1885; *Area:* 162,10 km2
Comté ou district: La Côte-de-Gaspé; *Population au 2011:* 743
Circonscription(s) électorale(s) provinciale(s): Gaspé
Circonscription(s) électorale(s) fédérale(s): Gaspésie-Les Iles-de-la-Madeleine
Prochaines élections: 5e novembre 2017
Jocelyne Huet, Mairesse
Marie Dufresne, Directrice générale

Coaticook
294, rue St-Jacques nord
Coaticook, QC J1A 2R3
Tél: 819-849-9166; *Téléc:* 819-849-4320
info@mrcdecoaticook.qc.ca
www.mrcdecoaticook.qc.ca
Entité municipal: Regional County Municipality
Incorporation: 1er janvier 1982
Population au 2011: 18,847
Note: 12 municipalités.
Jacques Madore, Préfet
Dominick Faucher, Directeur général

Coaticook
150, rue Child
Coaticook, QC J1A 2B3
Tél: 819-849-2721; *Téléc:* 819-849-9669
www.ville.coaticook.qc.ca
Entité municipal: Town
Incorporation: 30 décembre 1998; *Area:* 218,89 km2
Comté ou district: Coaticook; *Population au 2011:* 9,255
Circonscription(s) électorale(s) provinciale(s): St-François
Circonscription(s) électorale(s) fédérale(s): Compton-Stanstead
Prochaines élections: 5e novembre 2017
Bertrand Lamoureux, Maire
Geneviève Dupras, Greffière

Les Collines-de-l'Outaouais
216, ch Old Chelsea
Chelsea, QC J9B 1J4
Tél: 819-827-0516; *Téléc:* 819-827-9272
gpoulin@mrcdescollines.com
www.mrcdescollinesdeloutaouais.qc.ca
Other Information: Sans frais: 1-800-387-4146
Entité municipal: Regional County Municipality
Incorporation: 4e décembre 1991
Population au 2011: 46,393
Note: 7 municipalités.
Robert Bussière, Préfet
Ghislain Poulin, Directeur général

Colombier
CP 69
568, rue Principale
Colombier, QC G0H 1P0
Tél: 418-565-3343; *Téléc:* 418-565-3289
info@municipalite.colombier.qc.ca
www.municipalite.colombier.qc.ca
Entité municipal: Municipality
Incorporation: 1er janvier 1946; *Area:* 313,20 km2
Comté ou district: La Haute-Côte-Nord; *Population au 2011:* 747
Circonscription(s) électorale(s) provinciale(s): René-Lévesque
Circonscription(s) électorale(s) fédérale(s): Manicouagan
Prochaines élections: 5e novembre 2017
Jean-Roch Barbeau, Maire
Claire Savard, Directrice générale

Compton
3, ch de Hatley
Compton, QC J0B 1L0
Tél: 819-835-5584; *Téléc:* 819-835-5750
info@compton.ca
www.compton.ca
Entité municipal: Municipality
Incorporation: 8e décembre 1999; *Area:* 205,72 km2
Comté ou district: Coaticook; *Population au 2011:* 3,112
Circonscription(s) électorale(s) provinciale(s): St-François
Circonscription(s) électorale(s) fédérale(s): Compton-Stanstead
Prochaines élections: 5e novembre 2017
Bernard Vanasse, Maire
Jacques Leblond, Directeur général

La Conception
1371, rue du Centenaire
La Conception, QC J0T 1M0
Tél: 819-686-3016; *Téléc:* 819-686-5808
info@municipalite.laconception.qc.ca
www.municipalite.laconception.qc.ca
Entité municipal: Municipality
Incorporation: 1er janvier 1882; *Area:* 142,61 km2
Comté ou district: Les Laurentides; *Population au 2011:* 1,287
Circonscription(s) électorale(s) provinciale(s): Labelle
Circonscription(s) électorale(s) fédérale(s): Laurentides-Labelle
Prochaines élections: 5e novembre 2017
Maurice Plouffe, Maire
Marie-France Brisson, Directrice générale

Contrecoeur
5000, rte Marie-Victorin
Contrecoeur, QC J0L 1C0
Tél: 450-587-5901; *Téléc:* 450-587-5855
mairie@ville.contrecoeur.qc.ca
www.ville.contrecoeur.qc.ca
Entité municipal: Town
Incorporation: 1er janvier 1976; *Area:* 61,56 km2
Comté ou district: Marguerite-D'Youville; Communauté métropolitaine de Montréal; *Population au 2011:* 6,252
Circonscription(s) électorale(s) provinciale(s): Verchères
Circonscription(s) électorale(s) fédérale(s): Pierre-Boucher-Les Patriotes-Verchères
Prochaines élections: 5e novembre 2017
Suzanne Dansereau, Mairesse
Yves Beaulieu, Directeur général

Cookshire-Eaton
220, rue Principale est
Cookshire, QC J0B 1M0
Tél: 819-560-8585; *Téléc:* 819-875-5311
www.cookshire-eaton.qc.ca
Entité municipal: Town
Incorporation: 24 juillet 2002; *Area:* 297,60 km2
Comté ou district: Le Haut-Saint-François; *Population au 2011:* 5,171
Circonscription(s) électorale(s) provinciale(s): Mégantic
Circonscription(s) électorale(s) fédérale(s): Compton-Stanstead
Prochaines élections: 5e novembre 2017
Noël Landry, Maire
Martin Tremblay, Directeur général

La Corne
324, rte 111
La Corne, QC J0Y 1R0
Tél: 819-799-3571; *Téléc:* 819-799-3572
mun.lacorne@cableamos.com
lacorne.wordpress.com
Entité municipal: Municipality
Incorporation: 2e août 1975; *Area:* 331,54 km2
Comté ou district: Abitibi; *Population au 2011:* 700
Circonscription(s) électorale(s) provinciale(s): Abitibi-Ouest
Circonscription(s) électorale(s) fédérale(s):
Abitibi-Témiscamingue
Prochaines élections: 5e novembre 2017
Eric Comeau, Maire
Diane St-Pierre, Directrice générale

Coteau-du-Lac
342, ch du Fleuve
Coteau-du-Lac, QC J0P 1B0
Tél: 450-763-5822; *Téléc:* 450-763-0938
info@coteau-du-lac.com
www.coteau-du-lac.com
Entité municipal: Municipality
Incorporation: 6e février 1982; *Area:* 46,57 km2
Comté ou district: Vaudreuil-Soulanges; *Population au 2011:* 6,842
Circonscription(s) électorale(s) provinciale(s): Soulanges

Circonscription(s) électorale(s) fédérale(s): Salaberry-Suroît
Prochaines élections: 5e novembre 2017
Guy Jasmin, Maire
Luc Laberge, Greffier

Les Coteaux
65, rte 338
Les Coteaux, QC J7X 1A2
Tél: 450-267-3531; *Téléc:* 450-267-3532
info@les-coteaux.qc.ca
www.les-coteaux.qc.ca
Entité municipal: Municipality
Incorporation: 18 mai 1994; *Area:* 12,11 km2
Comté ou district: Vaudreuil-Soulanges; *Population au 2011:* 4,568
Circonscription(s) électorale(s) provinciale(s): Soulanges
Circonscription(s) électorale(s) fédérale(s): Salaberry-Suroît
Prochaines élections: 5e novembre 2017
Denise Godin Dostie, Mairesse
Claude Madore, Directeur général

La Côte-de-Beaupré
3, rue de la Seigneurie
Château-Richer, QC G0A 1N0
Tél: 418-824-3444; *Téléc:* 418-824-3917
info@mrccotedebeaupre.qc.ca
www.mrccotedebeaupre.com
Entité municipal: Regional County Municipality
Incorporation: 1er janvier 1982
Population au 2011: 26,172
Note: 9 municipalités & 2 autres territoires.
Jean-Luc Fortin, Préfet
Michel Bélanger, Directeur général

La Côte-de-Gaspé
298A, boul York Sud
Gaspé, QC G4X 2L6
Tél: 418-368-7000; *Téléc:* 418-368-8181
mrc@cotedegaspe.ca
www.cotedegaspe.ca
Entité municipal: Regional County Municipality
Incorporation: 1er janvier 1982
Population au 2011: 17,985
Note: 5 municipalités & 2 autres territoires.
Délisca Ritchie Roussy, Préfète
Bruno Bernatchez, Directeur général

Côte-Nord-du-Golfe-du-Saint-Laurent
Chevery, QC G0G 1G0
Tél: 418-787-2244; *Téléc:* 418-787-2241
mcngsl@xplornet.com
Entité municipal: Municipality
Incorporation: 22 juin 1963; *Area:* 2783,59 km2
Comté ou district: Le Golfe-du-Saint-Laurent; *Population au 2011:* 971
Circonscription(s) électorale(s) provinciale(s): Duplessis
Circonscription(s) électorale(s) fédérale(s): Manicouagan
Prochaines élections: 5e novembre 2017
Darlene Rowsell Roberts, Administratrice

Courcelles
CP 160
116, av du Domaine
Courcelles, QC G0M 1C0
Tél: 418-483-5540; *Téléc:* 418-483-3540
municipal@telcourcelles.net
www.muncourcelles.qc.ca
Entité municipal: Parish (Paroisse)
Incorporation: 6e avril 1904; *Area:* 92,25 km2
Comté ou district: Le Granit; *Population au 2011:* 1,004
Circonscription(s) électorale(s) provinciale(s): Beauce-Sud
Circonscription(s) électorale(s) fédérale(s): Mégantic-L'Érable
Prochaines élections: 5e novembre 2017
Mario Quirion, Maire
Renée Mathieu, Directrice générale

Crabtree
CP 660
111, 4e Av
Crabtree, QC J0K 1B0
Tél: 450-754-3434; *Téléc:* 450-754-2172
info@municipalitecrabtree.qc.ca
www.municipalitecrabtree.qc.ca
Entité municipal: Municipality
Incorporation: 23 octobre 1996; *Area:* 24,71 km2
Comté ou district: Joliette; *Population au 2011:* 3,887
Circonscription(s) électorale(s) provinciale(s): Joliette
Circonscription(s) électorale(s) fédérale(s): Joliette
Prochaines élections: 5e novembre 2017
Denis Laporte, Maire
Pierre Rondeau, Directeur général

D'Autray
CP 1500
550, rue De Montcalm
Berthierville, QC J0K 1A0
Tél: 450-836-7007; *Téléc:* 450-836-1576
mrcautray@mrcautray.com
www.mrcautray.com
Entité municipal: Regional County Municipality
Incorporation: 1er janvier 1982
Population au 2011: 41,650
Note: 15 municipalités.
Gaétan Gravel, Préfet
Danielle Joyal, Directrice générale

Danville
CP 310
150, rue Water
Danville, QC J0A 1A0
Tél: 819-839-2771; *Téléc:* 819-839-2918
info@villededanville.com
www.villededanville.com
Entité municipal: Town
Incorporation: 17 mars 1999; *Area:* 149,51 km2
Comté ou district: Les Sources; *Population au 2011:* 4,070
Circonscription(s) électorale(s) provinciale(s): Richmond
Circonscription(s) électorale(s) fédérale(s): Richmond-Arthabaska
Prochaines élections: 5e novembre 2017
Michel Plourde, Maire
Caroline Lalonde, Directrice générale

Daveluyville
CP 187
337, rue Principale
Daveluyville, QC G0Z 1C0
Tél: 819-367-3395; *Téléc:* 819-367-3550
info@ville.daveluyville.qc.ca
www.ville.daveluyville.qc.ca
Entité municipal: Village
Incorporation: 13 novembre 1901; *Area:* 2,25 km2
Comté ou district: Arthabaska; *Population au 2011:* 96
Circonscription(s) électorale(s) provinciale(s): Nicolet-Bécancour
Circonscription(s) électorale(s) fédérale(s): Richmond-Arthabaska
Prochaines élections: 5e novembre 2017
Antoine Tardif, Maire
Pauline Vrain, Greffière

Dégelis
369, av Principale
Dégelis, QC G5T 2G3
Tél: 418-853-2332; *Téléc:* 418-853-3464
info@ville.degelis.qc.ca
www.ville.degelis.qc.ca
Entité municipal: Town
Incorporation: 13 décembre 1969; *Area:* 562,84 km2
Comté ou district: Témiscouata; *Population au 2011:* 3,051
Circonscription(s) électorale(s) provinciale(s): Rivière-du-Loup-Témiscouata
Circonscription(s) électorale(s) fédérale(s): Rimouski-Neigette-Témiscouata-Les Basques
Prochaines élections: 5e novembre 2017
Normand Morin, Maire
Bernard Caron, Directeur général

Déléage
175, rte 107, RR#1
Déléage, QC J9E 3A8
Tél: 819-449-1979; *Téléc:* 819-449-7441
www.deleage.ca
Entité municipal: Municipality
Incorporation: 1er janvier 1881; *Area:* 249,44 km2
Comté ou district: La Vallée-de-la-Gatineau; *Population au 2011:* 1,856
Circonscription(s) électorale(s) provinciale(s): Gatineau
Circonscription(s) électorale(s) fédérale(s): Pontiac
Prochaines élections: 5e novembre 2017
Bernard Cayen, Maire
Henri-Claude Gagnon, Directeur général

Delson
50, rue Ste-Thérèse
Delson, QC J5B 2B2
Tél: 450-632-1050; *Téléc:* 450-632-1571
communications@ville.delson.qc.ca
www.ville.delson.qc.ca
Entité municipal: Town
Incorporation: 4e janvier 1918; *Area:* 7,76 km2
Comté ou district: Roussillon; Communauté métropolitaine de Montréal; *Population au 2011:* 7,462
Circonscription(s) électorale(s) provinciale(s): La Prairie
Circonscription(s) électorale(s) fédérale(s): La Prairie
Prochaines élections: 5e novembre 2017
Christian Ouellette, Maire
Chantal Bergeron, Greffière

Denholm
419, ch du Poisson-Blanc
Denholm, QC J8N 9C8
Tél: 819-457-2992; *Téléc:* 819-457-9862
info@municipalite.denholm.qc.ca
www.municipalite.denholm.qc.ca
Entité municipal: Municipality
Incorporation: 27 février 1924; *Area:* 191,65 km2
Comté ou district: La Vallée-de-la-Gatineau; *Population au 2011:* 572
Circonscription(s) électorale(s) provinciale(s): Gatineau
Circonscription(s) électorale(s) fédérale(s): Pontiac
Prochaines élections: 5e novembre 2017
Gaétan Guindon, Maire
Sandra Bélisle, Directrice générale

Desbiens
CP 9
925, rue Hébert
Desbiens, QC G0W 1N0
Tél: 418-346-5571; *Téléc:* 418-346-5422
info@ville.desbiens.com
www.ville.desbiens.qc.ca
Entité municipal: Village
Incorporation: 16 août 1926; *Area:* 10,35 km2
Comté ou district: Lac-Saint-Jean-Est; *Population au 2011:* 1,053
Circonscription(s) électorale(s) provinciale(s): Lac-St-Jean
Circonscription(s) électorale(s) fédérale(s): Lac-St-Jean
Prochaines élections: 5e novembre 2017
Nicolas Martel, Maire
Esther Dufour, Directrice générale

Deschaillons-sur-Saint-Laurent
1596, rte Marie-Victorin
Deschaillons-sur-Saint-Laurent, QC G0S 1G0
Tél: 819-292-2085; *Téléc:* 819-292-3194
mun.deschaillons@qc.aira.com
www.deschaillons.ca
Entité municipal: Municipality
Incorporation: 23 mai 1990; *Area:* 37,70 km2
Comté ou district: Bécancour; *Population au 2011:* 954
Circonscription(s) électorale(s) provinciale(s): Nicolet-Bécancour
Circonscription(s) électorale(s) fédérale(s): Bécancour-Nicolet-Saurel
Prochaines élections: 5e novembre 2017
Christian Baril, Maire
France Grimard, Directrice générale

Deschambault-Grondines
CP 220
120, rue St-Joseph
Deschambault, QC G0A 1S0
Tél: 418-286-4511; *Téléc:* 418-286-6511
deschambault-grondines@globetrotter.net
www.deschambault-grondines.com
Entité municipal: Municipality
Incorporation: 27 février 2002; *Area:* 123,60 km2
Comté ou district: Portneuf; *Population au 2011:* 2,131
Circonscription(s) électorale(s) provinciale(s): Portneuf
Circonscription(s) électorale(s) fédérale(s): Portneuf-Jacques-Cartier
Prochaines élections: 5e novembre 2017
Gaston Arcand, Maire
Claire St-Arnaud, Directrice générale

Deux-Montagnes
1, place de la Gare
Saint-Eustache, QC J7R 0B4
Tél: 450-491-1818; *Téléc:* 450-491-3040
info@mrc2m.qc.ca
www.mrc2m.qc.ca
Entité municipal: Regional County Municipality
Incorporation: 1er janvier 1983
Population au 2011: 95,670
Note: 7 municipalités.
Sonia Paulus, Préfète
Nicole Loiselle, Directrice générale

Disraéli
550, av Jacques-Cartier
Disraéli, QC G0N 1E0
Tél: 418-449-2771; *Téléc:* 418-449-4299
dir-gen@villededisraeli.com
www.villededisraeli.com
Entité municipal: Town
Incorporation: 19 novembre 1904; *Area:* 6,470 km2
Comté ou district: Les Appalaches; *Population au 2011:* 2,502

Circonscription(s) électorale(s) provinciale(s): Mégantic
Circonscription(s) électorale(s) fédérale(s): Mégantic-L'Érable
Prochaines élections: 5e novembre 2017
Jacques Lessard, Maire
Guy Laflamme, Directeur général

Disraéli
8306, rte 112
Disraéli, QC G0N 1E0
Tél: 418-449-5329; *Téléc:* 418-449-5459
paroissedisraeli@tlb.sympatico.ca
www.paroissedisraeli.com
Entité municipal: Parish (Paroisse)
Incorporation: 1er janvier 1883; *Area:* 93,880 km2
Comté ou district: Les Appalaches; *Population au 2011:* 1,168
Circonscription(s) électorale(s) provinciale(s): Mégantic
Circonscription(s) électorale(s) fédérale(s): Mégantic-L'Érable
Prochaines élections: 5e novembre 2017
André Gosselin, Maire
Caroline Picard, Directrice générale

Dixville
251, rue Parker
Dixville, QC J0B 1P0
Tél: 819-849-3037; *Téléc:* 819-849-9520
bureaumunicipal@dixville.ca
www.dixville.ca
Entité municipal: Municipality
Incorporation: 27 septembre 1995; *Area:* 76,17 km2
Comté ou district: Coaticook; *Population au 2011:* 710
Circonscription(s) électorale(s) provinciale(s): St-François
Circonscription(s) électorale(s) fédérale(s): Compton-Stanstead
Prochaines élections: 5e novembre 2017
Martin Saindon, Maire
Sylvain Benoit, Directeur général

Le Domaine-du-Roy
901, boul St-Joseph
Roberval, QC G8H 2L8
Tél: 418-275-5044; *Téléc:* 418-275-4049
info@mrcdomaineduroy.ca
www.domaineduroy.ca
Entité municipal: Regional County Municipality
Incorporation: 1er janvier 1983
Population au 2011: 31,870
Note: 9 municipalités & 1 autre territoire.
Gérard Savard, Préfet
Denis Taillon, Directeur général

Donnacona
138, av Pleau
Donnacona, QC G3M 1A1
Tél: 418-285-0110; *Téléc:* 418-285-0020
info@villededonnacona.com
www.villededonnacona.com
Entité municipal: Town
Incorporation: 21 janvier 1967; *Area:* 20,12 km2
Comté ou district: Portneuf; *Population au 2011:* 6,283
Circonscription(s) électorale(s) provinciale(s): Portneuf
Circonscription(s) électorale(s) fédérale(s):
Portneuf-Jacques-Cartier
Prochaines élections: 5e novembre 2017
Jean-Claude Léveillée, Maire
Pierre-Luc Gignac, Greffier

La Doré
5000, rue des Peupliers
La Doré, QC G8J 1E8
Tél: 418-256-3545; *Téléc:* 418-256-3496
info@municipalite.ladore.qc.ca
www.municipalite.ladore.qc.ca
Entité municipal: Parish (Paroisse)
Incorporation: 16 mars 1906; *Area:* 280,83 km2
Comté ou district: Le Domaine-du-Roy; *Population au 2011:* 1,453
Circonscription(s) électorale(s) provinciale(s): Roberval
Circonscription(s) électorale(s) fédérale(s): Lac-St-Jean
Prochaines élections: 5e novembre 2017
Jacques Asselin, Maire
Stéphanie Gagnon, Directrice générale

Dosquet
183, rte St-Joseph
Dosquet, QC G0S 1H0
Tél: 418-728-3653; *Téléc:* 418-728-3338
mundosquet@videotron.ca
www.municipalitededosquet.com
Entité municipal: Municipality
Incorporation: 9e février 1918; *Area:* 67,26 km2
Comté ou district: Lotbinière; *Population au 2011:* 887
Circonscription(s) électorale(s) provinciale(s):
Lotbinière-Frontenac
Circonscription(s) électorale(s) fédérale(s): Lévis-Lotbinière
Prochaines élections: 5e novembre 2017
Yvan Charest, Maire
Jolyane Houle, Directrice générale

Drummond
436, rue Lindsay
Drummondville, QC J2B 1G6
Tél: 819-477-2230; *Téléc:* 819-477-8442
courriel@mrcdrummond.qc.ca
www.mrcdrummond.qc.ca
Entité municipal: Regional County Municipality
Incorporation: 1er janvier 1982
Population au 2011: 98,681
Note: 18 municipalités.
Alexandre Cusson, Préfet
Christine Labelle, Directrice générale

Dudswell
76, rue Main
Bishopton, QC J0B 1G0
Tél: 819-560-8484; *Téléc:* 819-560-8485
helene.leroux@hsfqc.ca
www.ville.dudswell.qc.ca
Entité municipal: Municipality
Incorporation: 11 octobre 1995; *Area:* 214,76 km2
Comté ou district: Le Haut-Saint-François; *Population au 2011:* 1,771
Circonscription(s) électorale(s) provinciale(s): Mégantic
Circonscription(s) électorale(s) fédérale(s): Compton-Stanstead
Prochaines élections: 5e novembre 2017
Jean-Pierre Briand, Maire
Hélène Leroux, Directrice générale

Duhamel
1890, rue Principale
Duhamel, QC J0V 1G0
Tél: 819-428-7100; *Téléc:* 819-428-1941
info.duhamel@mrcpapineau.com
www.municipalite.duhamel.qc.ca
Entité municipal: Municipality
Incorporation: 15 août 1936; *Area:* 449,45 km2
Comté ou district: Papineau; *Population au 2011:* 412
Circonscription(s) électorale(s) provinciale(s): Papineau
Circonscription(s) électorale(s) fédérale(s): Argenteuil-La Petite Nation
Prochaines élections: 5e novembre 2017
David Pharand, Maire
Claire Dinel, Directrice générale

Duhamel-Ouest
361, rte 101 sud
Duhamel-Ouest, QC J9V 1A2
Tél: 819-629-2522; *Téléc:* 819-629-2422
Entité municipal: Municipality
Incorporation: 20 février 1911; *Area:* 127,61 km2
Comté ou district: Témiscamingue; *Population au 2011:* 828
Circonscription(s) électorale(s) provinciale(s):
Rouyn-Noranda-Témiscamingue
Circonscription(s) électorale(s) fédérale(s):
Abitibi-Témiscamingue
Prochaines élections: 5e novembre 2017
Jean-Yves Parent, Maire
Lise Perron, Directrice générale

Dundee
3296, montée Smallman
Dundee, QC J0S 1L0
Tél: 450-264-4674; *Téléc:* 450-264-8044
mun.dundee@sftl.ca
Entité municipal: Township
Incorporation: 1er juillet 1855; *Area:* 94,20 km2
Comté ou district: Le Haut-Saint-Laurent; *Population au 2011:* 408
Circonscription(s) électorale(s) provinciale(s): Huntingdon
Circonscription(s) électorale(s) fédérale(s): Salaberry-Suroît
Prochaines élections: 5e novembre 2017
Jean M. Armstrong, Mairesse
William Daibhib, Directeur général

Dunham
CP 70
3777, rue Principale
Dunham, QC J0E 1M0
Tél: 450-295-2418; *Téléc:* 450-295-2182
www.ville.dunham.qc.ca
Entité municipal: Town
Incorporation: 25 septembre 1971; *Area:* 200,99 km2
Comté ou district: Brome-Missisquoi; *Population au 2011:* 3,471
Circonscription(s) électorale(s) provinciale(s): Brome-Missisquoi
Circonscription(s) électorale(s) fédérale(s): Brome-Missisquoi
Prochaines élections: 5e novembre 2017
Pierre Janecek, Maire
Pierre Loiselle, Greffier

Duparquet
86, rue Principale
Duparquet, QC J0Z 1W0
Tél: 819-948-2266; *Téléc:* 819-948-2466
duparquet@mrcao.qc.ca
duparquet.ao.ca
Entité municipal: Village
Incorporation: 13 avril 1933; *Area:* 157,40 km2
Comté ou district: Abitibi-Ouest; *Population au 2011:* 657
Circonscription(s) électorale(s) provinciale(s): Abitibi-Ouest
Circonscription(s) électorale(s) fédérale(s):
Abitibi-Témiscamingue
Prochaines élections: 5e novembre 2017
Gilbert Rivard, Maire
Jacques Taillefer, Greffier

Dupuy
2, av du Chemin-de-Fer
Dupuy, QC J0Z 1X0
Tél: 819-783-2595; *Téléc:* 819-783-2192
dupuy@mrcao.qc.ca
www.dupuy.ao.ca
Entité municipal: Municipality
Incorporation: 20 septembre 1918; *Area:* 123,48 km2
Comté ou district: Abitibi-Ouest; *Population au 2011:* 930
Circonscription(s) électorale(s) provinciale(s): Abitibi-Ouest
Circonscription(s) électorale(s) fédérale(s):
Abitibi-Témiscamingue
Prochaines élections: 5e novembre 2017
Normand Lagrange, Maire
Pascale Lavigne, Greffière

La Durantaye
539, rue du Piedmont
La Durantaye, QC G0R 1W0
Tél: 418-884-3465; *Téléc:* 418-884-3048
par.ladurantaye@globetrotter.net
www.munladurantaye.qc.ca
Entité municipal: Parish (Paroisse)
Incorporation: 4e août 1910; *Area:* 33,78 km2
Comté ou district: Bellechasse; *Population au 2011:* 722
Circonscription(s) électorale(s) provinciale(s): Bellechasse
Circonscription(s) électorale(s) fédérale(s): Bellechasse-Les Etchemins-Lévis
Prochaines élections: 5e novembre 2017
Yvon Dumont, Maire
Cindy Breton, Directrice générale

Durham-Sud
CP 70
70, rue de l'Hôtel-de-Ville
Durham-Sud, QC J0H 2C0
Tél: 819-858-2044; *Téléc:* 819-858-2044
mun@durham-sud.com
www.durham-sud.com
Entité municipal: Municipality
Incorporation: 1er novembre 1975; *Area:* 92,02 km2
Comté ou district: Drummond; *Population au 2011:* 1,008
Circonscription(s) électorale(s) provinciale(s): Johnson
Circonscription(s) électorale(s) fédérale(s): Drummond
Prochaines élections: 5e novembre 2017
Michel Noël, Maire
Christiane Bastien, Directrice générale

East Broughton
600, 10e av sud
East Broughton, QC G0N 1H0
Tél: 418-427-2608; *Téléc:* 418-427-3414
municipaliteeastbroughton@bellnet.ca
www.municipaliteeastbroughton.com
Entité municipal: Municipality
Incorporation: 5e janvier 1994; *Area:* 9,310 km2
Comté ou district: Les Appalaches; *Population au 2011:* 2,229
Circonscription(s) électorale(s) provinciale(s):
Lotbinière-Frontenac
Circonscription(s) électorale(s) fédérale(s): Mégantic-L'Érable
Prochaines élections: 5e novembre 2017
Kaven Mathieu, Maire
Normand Laplante, Directeur général

East Farnham
228, rue Principale
East Farnham, QC J2K 4T5
Tél: 450-263-4252; *Téléc:* 450-263-6131
eastfarnham@videotron.ca
www.municipalite.eastfarnham.qc.ca
Entité municipal: Village
Incorporation: 27 août 1914; *Area:* 5,29 km2
Comté ou district: Brome-Missisquoi; *Population au 2011:* 553

Circonscription(s) électorale(s) provinciale(s): Brome-Missisquoi
Circonscription(s) électorale(s) fédérale(s): Brome-Missisquoi
Prochaines élections: 5e novembre 2017
Sylvie Dionne-Raymond, Mairesse
Madelyn Marcoux, Directrice générale

East Hereford
15, rue de l'Église
East Hereford, QC J0B 1S0
Tél: 819-844-2463; *Téléc:* 819-844-2463
www.municipalite.easthereford.qc.ca
Entité municipal: Municipality
Incorporation: 1er juillet 1855; *Area:* 71,56 km2
Comté ou district: Coaticook; *Population au 2011:* 306
Circonscription(s) électorale(s) provinciale(s): St-François
Circonscription(s) électorale(s) fédérale(s): Compton-Stanstead
Prochaines élections: 5e novembre 2017
Richard Belleville, Maire
Diane Lauzon-Rioux, Directrice générale

East-Angus
200, rue Saint-Jean Est
East Angus, QC J0B 1R0
Tél: 819-560-8600; *Téléc:* 819-560-8611
info.eastangus@hsfqc.ca
www.ville.east-angus.qc.ca
Entité municipal: Town
Incorporation: 14 mars 1912; *Area:* 8,10 km2
Comté ou district: Le Haut-Saint-François; *Population au 2011:* 3,741
Circonscription(s) électorale(s) provinciale(s): Mégantic
Circonscription(s) électorale(s) fédérale(s): Compton-Stanstead
Prochaines élections: 5e novembre 2017
Robert G. Roy, Maire
Normand Graillon, Directeur général

Eastmain
CP 90
76 Nouchimi
Eastmain, QC J0M 1W0
Tél: 819-977-0211; *Téléc:* 819-977-0281
info@eastmain.ca
www.eastmain.ca
Entité municipal: Villages Cris
Incorporation: 28 juin 1978; *Area:* 334,70 km2
Population au 2011: 767
Circonscription(s) électorale(s) provinciale(s): Ungava
Circonscription(s) électorale(s) fédérale(s):
Abitibi-Baie-James-Nunavik-Eeyou
Edward Gilpin, Maire

Eastman
160, ch George-Bonnallie
Eastman, QC J0E 1P0
Tél: 450-297-3440; *Téléc:* 450-297-3448
info@muneastman.ca
www.muneastman.ca
Entité municipal: Municipality
Incorporation: 30 mai 2001; *Area:* 68,87 km2
Comté ou district: Memphrémagog; *Population au 2011:* 1,740
Circonscription(s) électorale(s) provinciale(s): Orford
Circonscription(s) électorale(s) fédérale(s): Brome-Missisquoi
Prochaines élections: 5e novembre 2017
Yvon Laramée, Maire
Caroline Rioux, Directrice générale

Les Éboulements
2335, route du Fleuve
Les Éboulements, QC G0A 2M0
Tél: 418-489-2988; *Téléc:* 418-489-2989
municipalite@leseboulements.com
www.leseboulements.com
Entité municipal: Municipality
Incorporation: 19 septembre 2001; *Area:* 153,99 km2
Comté ou district: Charlevoix; *Population au 2011:* 1,328
Circonscription(s) électorale(s) provinciale(s):
Charlevoix-Côte-de-Beaupré
Circonscription(s) électorale(s) fédérale(s):
Beauport-Côte-de-Beaupré-Ile d'Orléans-Charlevoix
Prochaines élections: 5e novembre 2017
Pierre Tremblay, Maire
Linda Gauthier, Directrice générale

Egan-Sud
95, rte 105
Egan-Sud, QC J9E 3A9
Tél: 819-449-1702; *Téléc:* 819-449-7423
info@egan-sud.ca
www.egan-sud.ca
Entité municipal: Municipality
Incorporation: 17 novembre 1920; *Area:* 50,67 km2
Comté ou district: La Vallée-de-la-Gatineau; *Population au 2011:* 542
Circonscription(s) électorale(s) provinciale(s): Gatineau
Circonscription(s) électorale(s) fédérale(s): Pontiac
Prochaines élections: 5e novembre 2017
Neil Gagnon, Maire
Mariette Rochon, Directrice générale

Elgin
933,ch de la 2e Concession
Elgin, QC J0S 2E0
Tél: 450-264-2320; *Téléc:* 450-264-6846
www.munelgin.ca
Entité municipal: Township
Incorporation: 1er juillet 1855; *Area:* 69,38 km2
Comté ou district: Le Haut-Saint-Laurent; *Population au 2011:* 401
Circonscription(s) électorale(s) provinciale(s): Huntingdon
Circonscription(s) électorale(s) fédérale(s): Salaberry-Suroît
Prochaines élections: 5e novembre 2017
Deborah Stewart, Mairesse
Danielle Sauvé, Directrice générale

Entrelacs
2351, ch d'Entrelacs
Entrelacs, QC J0T 2E0
Tél: 450-228-2529; *Téléc:* 450-228-4866
www.entrelacs.com
Entité municipal: Municipality
Incorporation: 1er janvier 1860; *Area:* 51,78 km2
Comté ou district: Matawinie; *Population au 2011:* 906
Circonscription(s) électorale(s) provinciale(s): Bertrand
Circonscription(s) électorale(s) fédérale(s): Joliette
Prochaines élections: 5e novembre 2017
Sylvain Breton, Maire
Ginette Brisebois, Directrice générale

L'Épiphanie
331, rang du Bas-de-l'Achigan
L'Épiphanie, QC J5X 1E1
Tél: 450-588-5547; *Téléc:* 450-588-6050
mun@paroisse-lepiphanie.com
www.paroisse-lepiphanie.com
Entité municipal: Parish (Paroisse)
Incorporation: 1er juillet 1855; *Area:* 55,32 km2
Comté ou district: L'Assomption; *Population au 2011:* 3,296
Circonscription(s) électorale(s) provinciale(s): L'Assomption
Circonscription(s) électorale(s) fédérale(s): Montcalm
Prochaines élections: 5e novembre 2017
Denis Lévesque, Maire
Nicole Renaud, Directrice générale

L'Épiphanie
66, rue Notre-Dame
L'Épiphanie, QC J5X 1A1
Tél: 450-588-5515; *Téléc:* 450-588-6171
courrier@ville.lepiphanie.qc.ca
www.ville.lepiphanie.qc.ca
Entité municipal: Town
Incorporation: 30 juin 1967; *Area:* 2,46 km2
Comté ou district: L'Assomption; *Population au 2011:* 5,353
Circonscription(s) électorale(s) provinciale(s): L'Assomption
Circonscription(s) électorale(s) fédérale(s): Montcalm
Prochaines élections: 5e novembre 2017
Steve Plante, Maire
Guylaine Comtois, Directrice générale et greffière

L'Érable
#300, 1783, av St-Édouard
Plessisville, QC G6L 3S7
Tél: 819-362-2333; *Téléc:* 819-362-9150
info@mrc-erable.qc.ca
www.erable.ca/mrc
Entité municipal: Regional County Municipality
Incorporation: 1er janvier 1982
Population au 2011: 23,366
Note: 11 municipalités.
Sylvain Labrecque, Préfet
Rick Lavergne, Directeur général

Les Escoumins
2, rue Sirois
Les Escoumins, QC G0T 1K0
Tél: 418-233-2766; *Téléc:* 418-233-3273
administration.muni@escoumins.ca
www.escoumins.ca
Entité municipal: Municipality
Incorporation: 5 mai 1863; *Area:* 267,33 km2
Comté ou district: La Haute-Côte-Nord; *Population au 2011:* 2,000
Circonscription(s) électorale(s) provinciale(s): René-Lévesque
Circonscription(s) électorale(s) fédérale(s): Manicouagan
Prochaines élections: 5e novembre 2017
André Desrosiers, Maire
Chantale Otis, Directrice générale

Escuminac
13, rue de l'Église
Pointe-à-la-Garde, QC G0C 2M0
Tél: 418-788-5644; *Téléc:* 418-788-2613
munescuminac@globetrotter.net
Entité municipal: Municipality
Incorporation: 10 octobre 1907; *Area:* 109,55 km2
Comté ou district: Avignon; *Population au 2011:* 588
Circonscription(s) électorale(s) provinciale(s): Bonaventure
Circonscription(s) électorale(s) fédérale(s): Avignon-La Mitis-Matane-Matapédia
Prochaines élections: 5e novembre 2017
R. Bruce Wafer, Maire
Sylvie Bossé, Directrice générale

Esprit-Saint
121, rue Principale
Esprit-Saint, QC G0K 1A0
Tél: 418-779-2716; *Téléc:* 418-779-2716
muni.esprit@globetrotter.net
www.municipalite.esprit-saint.qc.ca
Entité municipal: Municipality
Incorporation: 13 mai 1972; *Area:* 169,28 km2
Comté ou district: Rimouski-Neigette; *Population au 2011:* 379
Circonscription(s) électorale(s) provinciale(s): Rimouski
Circonscription(s) électorale(s) fédérale(s):
Rimouski-Neigette-Témiscouata-Les Basques
Prochaines élections: 5e novembre 2017
Réjean Morissette, Maire
Diane Ouellet, Directrice générale

Estérel
115, ch Dupuis
Estérel, QC J0T 1E0
Tél: 450-228-3232; *Téléc:* 450-228-3737
info@villedesterel.com
www.villedesterel.com
Entité municipal: Village
Incorporation: 1er janvier 2006; *Area:* 12,06 km2
Comté ou district: Les Pays-d'en-Haut; *Population au 2011:* 199
Circonscription(s) électorale(s) provinciale(s): Bertrand
Circonscription(s) électorale(s) fédérale(s): Laurentides—Labelle
Prochaines élections: 5e novembre 2017
Jean-Pierre Nepveu, Maire
Luc Lafontaire, Directeur général

Les Etchemins
1137, rte 277
Lac-Etchemin, QC G0R 1S0
Tél: 418-625-9000; *Téléc:* 418-625-9005
mrc@mrcetchemins.qc.ca
www.mrcetchemins.qc.ca
Entité municipal: Regional County Municipality
Incorporation: 1er janvier 1982
Population au 2011: 17,254
Note: 13 muncipalités.
Hector Provençal, Préfet
Luc Leclerc, Directeur général

Farnham
477, rue de l'Hôtel-de-Ville
Farnham, QC J2N 2H3
Tél: 450-293-3178; *Téléc:* 450-293-2989
administration@ville.farnham.qc.ca
www.ville.farnham.qc.ca
Entité municipal: Town
Incorporation: 8e mars 2000; *Area:* 92,53 km2
Comté ou district: Brome-Missisquoi; *Population au 2011:* 8,330
Circonscription(s) électorale(s) provinciale(s): Brome-Missisquoi
Circonscription(s) électorale(s) fédérale(s): Brome-Missisquoi
Prochaines élections: 5e novembre 2017
Josef Hüsler, Maire
Marielle Benoit, Greffière

Fassett
19, rue Gendron
Fassett, QC J0V 1H0
Tél: 819-423-6943; *Téléc:* 819-423-5388
munfassett@mrcpapineau.com
www.village-fassett.com
Entité municipal: Municipality
Incorporation: 1er juillet 1855; *Area:* 13,98 km2
Comté ou district: Papineau; *Population au 2011:* 451
Circonscription(s) électorale(s) provinciale(s): Papineau
Circonscription(s) électorale(s) fédérale(s): Argenteuil-La Petite-Nation
Prochaines élections: 5e novembre 2017
Michel Rioux, Maire
Diane Leduc, Directrice générale

Ferland-et-Boilleau
CP 260
461, rte 381
Ferland-et-Boilleau, QC G0V 1H0
Tél: 418-676-2282; *Téléc:* 418-676-3092
municipalite@ferlandetboilleau.com
www.ferlandetboilleau.com
Entité municipal: Municipality
Incorporation: 1er janvier 1978; *Area:* 418,85 km2
Comté ou district: Le Fjord-du-Saguenay; *Population au 2011:* 583
Circonscription(s) électorale(s) provinciale(s): Dubuc
Circonscription(s) électorale(s) fédérale(s): Chicoutimi-Le Fjord
Prochaines élections: 5e novembre 2017
Hervé Simard, Maire
Sylvie Gagnon, Directrice générale

Ferme-Neuve
125, 12e rue
Ferme-Neuve, QC J0W 1C0
Tél: 819-587-3400; *Téléc:* 819-587-4733
bureau@municipalite.ferme-neuve.qc.ca
www.municipalite.ferme-neuve.qc.ca
Entité municipal: Municipality
Incorporation: 24 décembre 1997; *Area:* 1031,55 km2
Comté ou district: Antoine-Labelle; *Population au 2011:* 2,822
Circonscription(s) électorale(s) provinciale(s): Labelle
Circonscription(s) électorale(s) fédérale(s): Laurentides-Labelle
Prochaines élections: 5e novembre 2017
Gilbert Pilote, Maire
Normand Bélanger, Directeur général

Fermont
CP 2010
100, place Daviault
Fermont, QC G0G 1J0
Tél: 418-287-5411; *Téléc:* 418-287-5413
administration@villedefermont.qc.ca
www.villedefermont.qc.ca
Entité municipal: Town
Incorporation: 15 octobre 1974; *Area:* 497,45 km2
Comté ou district: Caniapiscau; *Population au 2011:* 2,874
Circonscription(s) électorale(s) provinciale(s): Duplessis
Circonscription(s) électorale(s) fédérale(s): Manicouagan
Prochaines élections: 5e novembre 2017
Martin St-Laurent, Maire
Carolle Bourque, Greffière

Le Fjord-du-Saguenay
3110, boul Martel
Saint-Honoré, QC G0V 1L0
Tél: 418-673-1705; *Téléc:* 418-673-7205
reception@mrc-fjord.qc.ca
www.mrc-fjord.qc.ca
Entité municipal: Regional County Municipality
Incorporation: 18e février 2002
Population au 2011: 20,465
Note: 13 municipalités & 3 autres territoires.
Gérald Savard, Préfet
Christine Dufour, Directrice générale

Forestville
1, 2e av
Forestville, QC G0T 1E0
Tél: 418-587-2285; *Téléc:* 418-587-6212
forestville@forestville.ca
www.forestville.ca
Entité municipal: Town
Incorporation: 5e janvier 1980; *Area:* 241,73 km2
Comté ou district: La Haute-Côte-Nord; *Population au 2011:* 3,270
Circonscription(s) électorale(s) provinciale(s): René-Lévesque
Circonscription(s) électorale(s) fédérale(s): Manicouagan
Prochaines élections: 5e novembre 2017
Micheline Anctil, Mairesse
Daniel Brochu, Directeur général

Fort-Coulonge
CP 640
134, rue Principale
Fort-Coulonge, QC J0X 1V0
Tél: 819-683-2259; *Téléc:* 819-683-3627
administration@fortcoulonge.qc.ca
www.fortcoulonge.qc.ca
Entité municipal: Village
Incorporation: 15 décembre 1888; *Area:* 3,44 km2
Comté ou district: Pontiac; *Population au 2011:* 1,377
Circonscription(s) électorale(s) provinciale(s): Pontiac
Circonscription(s) électorale(s) fédérale(s): Pontiac
Prochaines élections: 5e novembre 2017
Raymond Durocher, Maire
Martine Durocher, Directrice générale

Fortierville
198, rue de la Fabrique
Fortierville, QC G0S 1J0
Tél: 819-287-5922; *Téléc:* 819-287-0322
municipalite@fortierville.com
www.fortierville.com
Entité municipal: Municipality
Incorporation: 3e juin 1998; *Area:* 45,53 km2
Comté ou district: Bécancour; *Population au 2011:* 706
Circonscription(s) électorale(s) provinciale(s): Nicolet-Bécancour
Circonscription(s) électorale(s) fédérale(s): Bécancour-Nicolet-Saurel
Prochaines élections: 5e novembre 2017
Normand Gagnon, Maire
Annie Jacques, Directrice générale

Fossambault-sur-le-Lac
145, rue Gingras
Fossambault-sur-le-Lac, QC G0A 3M0
Tél: 418-875-3133; *Téléc:* 418-875-3544
fossam@coopcscf.com
www.fossambault-sur-le-lac.com
Entité municipal: Village
Incorporation: 10 mars 1949; *Area:* 10,96 km2
Comté ou district: La Jacques-Cartier; Communauté métropolitaine de Québec; *Population au 2011:* 1,613
Circonscription(s) électorale(s) provinciale(s): La Peltrie
Circonscription(s) électorale(s) fédérale(s): Portneuf-Jacques-Cartier
Prochaines élections: 5e novembre 2017
Jean Laliberté, Maire
Jacques Arsenault, Greffier

Frampton
107, rue Ste-Anne
Frampton, QC G0R 1M0
Tél: 418-479-5363; *Téléc:* 418-479-5364
munframpton@globetrotter.net
www.nouvellebeauce.com/frampton
Entité municipal: Municipality
Incorporation: 1er juillet 1855; *Area:* 150,76 km2
Comté ou district: La Nouvelle-Beauce; *Population au 2011:* 1,393
Circonscription(s) électorale(s) provinciale(s): Beauce-Nord
Circonscription(s) électorale(s) fédérale(s): Beauce
Prochaines élections: 5e novembre 2017
Jacques Soucy, Maire
Josée Audet, Directrice générale

Franklin
1670, rte 202
Franklin, QC J0S 1E0
Tél: 450-827-2538; *Téléc:* 450-827-2640
franklin@qc.aira.com
Entité municipal: Municipality
Incorporation: 31 mars 1973; *Area:* 112,19 km2
Comté ou district: Le Haut-Saint-Laurent; *Population au 2011:* 1,688
Circonscription(s) électorale(s) provinciale(s): Huntingdon
Circonscription(s) électorale(s) fédérale(s): Salaberry-Suroît
Prochaines élections: 5e novembre 2017
Suzanne Yelle Blair, Mairesse
François Gagnon, Directeur général

Franquelin
CP 10
27, rue des Érables
Franquelin, QC G0H 1E0
Tél: 418-296-1406; *Téléc:* 418-296-6946
munic.franq@globetrotter.net
www.municipalitefranquelin.ca
Entité municipal: Municipality
Incorporation: 1er janvier 1978; *Area:* 529,84 km2
Comté ou district: Manicouagan; *Population au 2011:* 324
Circonscription(s) électorale(s) provinciale(s): René-Lévesque
Circonscription(s) électorale(s) fédérale(s): Manicouagan
Prochaines élections: 5e novembre 2017
Michel Lévesque, Maire
Diane Cyr, Directrice générale

Frelighsburg
2, place de l'Hôtel-de-Ville
Frelighsburg, QC J0J 1C0
Tél: 450-298-5133; *Téléc:* 450-298-5557
municipalite@village.frelighsburg.qc.ca
www.frelighsburg.com
Entité municipal: Municipality
Incorporation: 28 septembre 1985; *Area:* 123,27 km2
Comté ou district: Brome-Missisquoi; *Population au 2011:* 1,094
Circonscription(s) électorale(s) provinciale(s): Brome-Missisquoi
Circonscription(s) électorale(s) fédérale(s): Brome-Missisquoi
Prochaines élections: 5e novembre 2017
Jacques Ducharme, Maire
Anne Pouleur, Directrice générale

Frontenac
2430, rue St-Jean
Frontenac, QC G6B 2S1
Tél: 819-583-3295; *Téléc:* 819-583-0855
adm@municipalitefrontenac.qc.ca
www.municipalitefrontenac.qc.ca
Entité municipal: Municipality
Incorporation: 1er janvier 1882; *Area:* 225,71 km2
Comté ou district: Le Granit; *Population au 2011:* 1,650
Circonscription(s) électorale(s) provinciale(s): Mégantic
Circonscription(s) électorale(s) fédérale(s): Mégantic-L'Érable
Prochaines élections: 5e novembre 2017
Jean-Denis Cloutier, Maire
Bruno Turmel, Directeur général

Fugèreville
33B, rue Principale
Fugèreville, QC J0Z 2A0
Tél: 819-748-3241; *Téléc:* 819-748-2422
Entité municipal: Municipality
Incorporation: 5e février 1904; *Area:* 163,79 km2
Comté ou district: Témiscamingue; *Population au 2011:* 329
Circonscription(s) électorale(s) provinciale(s): Rouyn-Noranda-Témiscamingue
Circonscription(s) électorale(s) fédérale(s): Abitibi-Témiscamingue
Prochaines élections: 5e novembre 2017
André Pâquet, Maire
Claudette Lachance, Directrice générale

Gallichan
207, ch de la Rivière ouest
Gallichan, QC J0Z 2B0
Tél: 819-787-6092; *Téléc:* 819-787-6015
gallichan@mrca.qc.ca
www.gallichan.ao.ca
Entité municipal: Municipality
Incorporation: 1er janvier 1958; *Area:* 73,32 km2
Comté ou district: Abitibi-Ouest; *Population au 2011:* 484
Circonscription(s) électorale(s) provinciale(s): Abitibi-Ouest
Circonscription(s) électorale(s) fédérale(s): Abitibi-Témiscamingue
Prochaines élections: 5e novembre 2017
Henri Bourque, Maire
Johanne Shink, Directrice générale

Girardville
180, rue Principale
Girardville, QC G0W 1R0
Tél: 418-258-3293; *Téléc:* 418-258-3473
admin@ville.girardville.qc.ca
ville.girardville.qc.ca
Entité municipal: Municipality
Incorporation: 11 novembre 1921; *Area:* 125,80 km2
Comté ou district: Maria-Chapdelaine; *Population au 2011:* 1,100
Circonscription(s) électorale(s) provinciale(s): Roberval
Circonscription(s) électorale(s) fédérale(s): Lac-St-Jean
Prochaines élections: 5e novembre 2017
Michel Perreault, Maire
Denis Desmeules, Directeur général

Godbout
CP 248
144, rue Pascal-Comeau
Godbout, QC G0H 1G0
Tél: 418-568-7581; *Téléc:* 418-568-7401
mgodbout144@hotmail.com
Entité municipal: Village
Incorporation: 1er janvier 1955; *Area:* 204,34 km2
Comté ou district: Manicouagan; *Population au 2011:* 298
Circonscription(s) électorale(s) provinciale(s): René-Lévesque
Circonscription(s) électorale(s) fédérale(s): Manicouagan
Prochaines élections: 5e novembre 2017
Nicole Champagne, Mairesse
Martine Morin, Directrice générale

Godmanchester
2282, ch Ridge
Godmanchester, QC J0S 1H0
Tél: 450-264-4116; *Téléc:* 450-264-9749
godmanchester@intermobilex.com
Entité municipal: Township
Incorporation: 1er juillet 1855; *Area:* 138,77 km2
Comté ou district: Le Haut-Saint-Laurent; *Population au 2011:* 1,417
Circonscription(s) électorale(s) provinciale(s): Huntingdon
Circonscription(s) électorale(s) fédérale(s): Salaberry-Suroît
Prochaines élections: 5e novembre 2017
Pierre Poirier, Maire

Élaine Duhème, Directrice générale

Golfe-du-Saint-Laurent
CP 77
Chevery, QC G0G 1G0
Tél: 418-787-2020; *Téléc:* 418-787-0052
info@mrcgsl.ca
www.mrcgsl.ca
Entité municipal: Regional County Municipality
Incorporation: 7er juillet 2010
Population au 2011: 5,126
Note: 5 municipalités & 1 autre territoire.
Bryce Douglas Fequet, Préfet
Karine Monger, Directrice générale

Gore
9, ch Cambria
Lakefield, QC J0V 1K0
Tél: 450-562-2025; *Téléc:* 450-562-5424
info@cantondegore.qc.ca
www.cantondegore.qc.ca
Entité municipal: Township
Incorporation: 1er juillet 1855; *Area:* 93,86 km2
Comté ou district: Argenteuil; *Population au 2011:* 1,775
Circonscription(s) électorale(s) provinciale(s): Argenteuil
Circonscription(s) électorale(s) fédérale(s): Argenteuil-La Petite-Nation; Richmond-Arthabaska
Prochaines élections: 5e novembre 2017
Scott Pearce, Maire
Louise Desjardins, Directrice générale

Gouvernement régional d'Eeyou Istchee Baie-James
CP 500
110, boul de Matagami
Matagami, QC J0Y 2A0
Tél: 819-739-2030; *Téléc:* 819-739-2713
municipalite@villembj.ca
municipalite.baie-james.qc.ca
Entité municipal: Municipality
Incorporation: 14 juillet 1971; *Area:* 333 255,55 km2
Population au 2011: 1,303
Circonscription(s) électorale(s) provinciale(s): Ungava
Circonscription(s) électorale(s) fédérale(s): Abitibi-Baie-James-Nunavik-Eeyou
Note: As of July 24, 2012, the Municipalité de Baie-James was replaced by the Eeyou Istchee James Bay Regional Government, which is comprised of 11 Cree representatives & 11 representatives from surrounding non-aboriginal communities.
Manon Cyr, Présidente
Stéphane Simard, Greffier et directeur général

Gracefield
CP 329
351, rte 105
Gracefield, QC J0X 1W0
Tél: 819-463-3458; *Téléc:* 819-463-4236
infos@gracefield.ca
www.gracefield.ca
Entité municipal: Town
Incorporation: 13 mars 2002; *Area:* 386,95 km2
Comté ou district: La Vallée-de-la-Gatineau; *Population au 2011:* 2,355
Circonscription(s) électorale(s) provinciale(s): Gatineau
Circonscription(s) électorale(s) fédérale(s): Pontiac
Prochaines élections: 5e novembre 2017
Note: Formerly known as Wright-Gracefield-Northfield.
Joanne Poulin, Mairesse
Jean-Marie Gauthier, Greffier et directeur général

Grande-Rivière
CP 188
108, rue de l'Hôtel de Ville
Grande-Rivière, QC G0C 1V0
Tél: 418-385-2282; *Téléc:* 418-385-2290
villegr@globetrotter.net
www.ville.grande-riviere.qc.ca
Entité municipal: Town
Incorporation: 21 septembre 1974; *Area:* 87,15 km2
Comté ou district: Le Rocher-Percé; *Population au 2011:* 3,456
Circonscription(s) électorale(s) provinciale(s): Gaspé
Circonscription(s) électorale(s) fédérale(s): Gaspésie-Les Iles-de-la-Madeleine
Prochaines élections: 5e novembre 2017
Bernard Stevens, Maire
Suzanne Chapados, Greffière

Grandes-Piles
630, 4e av
Grandes-Piles, QC G0X 1H0
Tél: 819-538-9708; *Téléc:* 819-538-6947
info@grandespiles.qc.ca
www.grandespiles.qc.ca
Entité municipal: Village
Incorporation: 10 août 1885; *Area:* 115,38 km2
Comté ou district: Mékinac; *Population au 2011:* 361
Circonscription(s) électorale(s) provinciale(s): Laviolette
Circonscription(s) électorale(s) fédérale(s): St-Maurice-Champlain
Prochaines élections: 5e novembre 2017
Daniel Petit, Maire
Pierre Beauséjour, Directeur général

Grande-Vallée
3, rue St-François-Xavier est
Grande-Vallée, QC G0E 1K0
Tél: 418-393-2161; *Téléc:* 418-393-2274
municipalite@grande-vallee.ca
www.grande-vallee.ca
Entité municipal: Municipality
Incorporation: 15 septembre 1927; *Area:* 154,67 km2
Comté ou district: La Côte-de-Gaspé; *Population au 2011:* 1,137
Circonscription(s) électorale(s) provinciale(s): Gaspé
Circonscription(s) électorale(s) fédérale(s): Gaspésie-Les Iles-de-la-Madeleine
Prochaines élections: 5e novembre 2017
Nathalie Côté, Mairesse
Ghislaine Bouthillette, Directrice générale

Grand-Métis
70, ch Kempt
Grand-Métis, QC G0J 1Z0
Tél: 418-775-6485; *Téléc:* 418-775-3591
grandmetis@mitis.qc.ca
www.municipalite.grand-metis.qc.ca
Entité municipal: Municipality
Incorporation: 13 septembre 1855; *Area:* 25,85 km2
Comté ou district: La Mitis; *Population au 2011:* 237
Circonscription(s) électorale(s) provinciale(s): Matane-Matapédia
Circonscription(s) électorale(s) fédérale(s): Avignon-La Mitis-Matane-Matapédia
Prochaines élections: 5e novembre 2017
Richard Fournier, Maire
Chantal Tremblay, Directrice générale

Grand-Remous
1508, rte Transcanadienne
Grand-Remous, QC J0W 1E0
Tél: 819-438-2877; *Téléc:* 819-438-2364
info@grandremous.ca
www.grandremous.ca
Entité municipal: Municipality
Incorporation: 29 avril 1937; *Area:* 386,55 km2
Comté ou district: La Vallée-de-la-Gatineau; *Population au 2011:* 1,168
Circonscription(s) électorale(s) provinciale(s): Gatineau
Circonscription(s) électorale(s) fédérale(s): Pontiac
Prochaines élections: 5e novembre 2017
Gérard Coulombe, Maire
Julie Rail, Directrice générale

Grand-Saint-Esprit
5410, rte Principale
Grand-Saint-Esprit, QC J0G 1B0
Tél: 819-289-2410; *Téléc:* 819-289-2029
municipalite@grandsaintesprit.qc.ca
www.grandsaintesprit.qc.ca
Entité municipal: Municipality
Incorporation: 14 mai 1938; *Area:* 28,41 km2
Comté ou district: Nicolet-Yamaska; *Population au 2011:* 471
Circonscription(s) électorale(s) provinciale(s): Nicolet-Bécancour
Circonscription(s) électorale(s) fédérale(s): Bécancour-Nicolet-Saurel
Prochaines élections: 5e novembre 2017
Julien Boudreault, Maire
Frederick Marcotte, Directeur général

Le Granit
3502, rue Agnès
Lac-Mégantic, QC G6B 1L3
Tél: 819-583-0181; *Téléc:* 819-583-5327
secretariat@mrcgranit.qc.ca
www.mrcgranit.qc.ca
Entité municipal: Regional County Municipality
Incorporation: 26 mai 1982
Population au 2011: 22,259
Note: 20 municipalités.
Maurice Bernier, Préfet
Serge Bilodeau, Directeur général

Grenville
21, rue Tri-Jean
Grenville, QC J0V 1J0
Tél: 819-242-2146; *Téléc:* 819-242-5891
info@grenville.ca
www.grenville.ca
Entité municipal: Village
Incorporation: 1er janvier 1876; *Area:* 3,05 km2
Comté ou district: Argenteuil; *Population au 2011:* 1,577
Circonscription(s) électorale(s) provinciale(s): Argenteuil
Circonscription(s) électorale(s) fédérale(s): Argenteuil-La Petite-Nation; Jonquière
Prochaines élections: 5e novembre 2017
Ronald Tittlit, Maire
Alain Léveillé, Directeur général

Grenville-sur-la-Rouge
88, rue des Érables
Grenville-sur-la-Rouge, QC J0V 1B0
Tél: 819-242-8762; *Téléc:* 819-242-9341
www.grenvillesurlarouge.ca
Entité municipal: Municipality
Incorporation: 24 avril 2002; *Area:* 321,81 km2
Comté ou district: Argenteuil; *Population au 2011:* 2,746
Circonscription(s) électorale(s) provinciale(s): Argenteuil
Circonscription(s) électorale(s) fédérale(s): Argenteuil-La Petite-Nation
Prochaines élections: 5e novembre 2017
John Saywell, Maire
Jean-François Bertrand, Directeur général

Gros-Mécatina
CP 9
30, rte Mecatina
La Tabatière, QC G0G 1T0
Tél: 418-773-2263; *Téléc:* 418-773-2696
mungrosmecatina@xplornet.com
Entité municipal: Municipality
Incorporation: 1er janvier 1994; *Area:* 961,46 km2
Comté ou district: Le Golfe-du-Saint-Laurent; *Population au 2011:* 499
Circonscription(s) électorale(s) provinciale(s): Duplessis
Circonscription(s) électorale(s) fédérale(s): Manicouagan
Prochaines élections: 5e novembre 2017
Randy Jones, Maire
Rita Collier, Directrice générale

Grosse-île
006, ch Jerry
Grosse-île, QC G4T 6B9
Tél: 418-985-2510; *Téléc:* 418-985-2297
www.mungi.ca
Entité municipal: Municipality
Incorporation: 1er janvier 2006; *Area:* 144,37 km2
Population au 2011: 1,137
Circonscription(s) électorale(s) provinciale(s): îles-de-la-Madeleine
Circonscription(s) électorale(s) fédérale(s): Gaspésie—îles-de-la-Madeleine
Prochaines élections: 5e novembre 2017
Rose Elmonde Clarke, Mairesse
Janice Turnbull, Directrice générale

Grosses-Roches
CP 69
122, rue de la Mer
Grosses-Roches, QC G0J 1K0
Tél: 418-733-4273; *Téléc:* 418-733-4273
grossesroches@lamatanie.ca
www.municipalite.grossesroches.ca
Entité municipal: Municipality
Incorporation: 19 août 1939; *Area:* 63,99 km2
Comté ou district: La Matanie; *Population au 2011:* 411
Circonscription(s) électorale(s) provinciale(s): Matane-Matapédia
Circonscription(s) électorale(s) fédérale(s): Avignon-La Mitis-Matane-Matapédia
Prochaines élections: 5e novembre 2017
André Morin, Maire
Linda Imbeault, Directrice générale

La Guadeloupe
483, 9e rue est
La Guadeloupe, QC G0M 1G0
Tél: 418-459-3342; *Téléc:* 418-459-3507
dglagua@tlb.sympatico.ca
www.munlaguadeloupe.qc.ca
Entité municipal: Village
Incorporation: 6e août 1929; *Area:* 31,67 km2
Comté ou district: Beauce-Sartigan; *Population au 2011:* 1,787
Circonscription(s) électorale(s) provinciale(s): Beauce-Sud
Circonscription(s) électorale(s) fédérale(s): Beauce
Prochaines élections: 5e novembre 2017

Huguette Plante, Mairesse
Marc-André Doyle, Directeur général

Guérin
#101, 516, rue St-Gabriel ouest
Guérin, QC J0Z 2E0
Tél: 819-784-7011; *Téléc:* 819-784-7012
mun.guerin@mrctemiscamingue.qc.ca
Entité municipal: Township
Incorporation: 8e novembre 1911; *Area:* 203,10 km2
Comté ou district: Témiscamingue; *Population au 2011:* 305
Circonscription(s) électorale(s) provinciale(s): Rouyn-Noranda-Témiscamingue
Circonscription(s) électorale(s) fédérale(s): Abitibi-Témiscamingue
Prochaines élections: 5e novembre 2017
Maurice Laverdière, Maire
Doris Gauthier, Directrice générale

Ham-Nord
CP 1271
287, 1ère Av
Ham-Nord, QC G0P 1A0
Tél: 819-344-2424; *Téléc:* 819-344-2806
www.ham-nord.ca
Entité municipal: Township
Incorporation: 1er janvier 1864; *Area:* 101,60 km2
Comté ou district: Arthabaska; *Population au 2011:* 832
Circonscription(s) électorale(s) provinciale(s): Drummond-Bois-Francs
Circonscription(s) électorale(s) fédérale(s): Richmond-Arthabaska
Prochaines élections: 5e novembre 2017
François Marcotte, Maire
Mathieu Couture, Directeur général

Hampden
CP 1055
863, rte 257 nord
Hampden, QC J0B 1Y0
Tél: 819-560-8444; *Téléc:* 819-560-8445
muni.hampden@hsfqc.ca
www.cantonhampden.com
Entité municipal: Township
Incorporation: 1er janvier 1874; *Area:* 110,10 km2
Comté ou district: Le Haut-Saint-François; *Population au 2011:* 214
Circonscription(s) électorale(s) provinciale(s): Mégantic
Circonscription(s) électorale(s) fédérale(s): Compton-Stanstead
Prochaines élections: 5e novembre 2017
Bertrand Prévost, Maire
Diane Carrier, Directrice générale

Hampstead
5569, ch Queen-Mary
Hampstead, QC H3X 1W5
Tél: 514-369-8200; *Téléc:* 514-369-8229
info@hampstead.qc.ca
www.hampstead.qc.ca
Entité municipal: Town
Incorporation: 1er janvier 2006; *Area:* 1,79 km2
Comté ou district: Communauté métropolitaine de Montréal; *Population au 2011:* 7,153
Circonscription(s) électorale(s) provinciale(s): D'Arcy-McGee
Circonscription(s) électorale(s) fédérale(s): Mount Royal
Prochaines élections: 5e novembre 2017
William Steinberg, Maire
Nathalie Lauzière, Greffière

Ham-Sud
9, ch Gosford sud
Saint-Joseph-de-Ham-Sud, QC J0B 3J0
Tél: 819-877-3258; *Téléc:* 819-877-5121
info@ham-sud.ca
www.ham-sud.ca
Entité municipal: Municipality
Incorporation: 1er janvier 1879; *Area:* 150,45 km2
Comté ou district: Les Sources; *Population au 2011:* 225
Circonscription(s) électorale(s) provinciale(s): Richmond
Circonscription(s) électorale(s) fédérale(s): Richmond-Arthabaska
Prochaines élections: 5e novembre 2017
Georges St-Louis, Maire
Caroline Poirier, Directrice générale

Harrington
2811, rte 327
Harrington, QC J8G 2T1
Tél: 819-687-2122; *Téléc:* 819-687-8610
administration@harrington.ca
www.harrington.ca
Entité municipal: Township
Incorporation: 1er juillet 1855; *Area:* 243,87 km2
Comté ou district: Argenteuil; *Population au 2011:* 853
Circonscription(s) électorale(s) provinciale(s): Argenteuil
Circonscription(s) électorale(s) fédérale(s): Argenteuil-La Petite Nation
Prochaines élections: 5e novembre 2017
Jacques Parent, Maire
Sarah Chanell, Directrice générale

Hatley
135, rue Main
North Hatley, QC J0B 2C0
Tél: 819-842-2977; *Téléc:* 819-842-1997
info@cantondehatley.ca
www.cantondehatley.ca
Entité municipal: Township
Incorporation: 1er juillet 1855; *Area:* 65,87 km2
Comté ou district: Memphrémagog; *Population au 2011:* 2,003
Circonscription(s) électorale(s) provinciale(s): Orford
Circonscription(s) électorale(s) fédérale(s): Compton-Stanstead
Prochaines élections: 5e novembre 2017
Martin Primeau, Maire
Liane Breton, Directrice générale

Hatley
2100, rte 143
Hatley, QC J0B 4B0
Tél: 819-838-5877; *Téléc:* 819-838-4646
hatley@xplornet.com
www.municipalitehatley.com
Entité municipal: Municipality
Incorporation: 27 juillet 1995; *Area:* 66,31 km2
Comté ou district: Memphrémagog; *Population au 2011:* 761
Circonscription(s) électorale(s) provinciale(s): Orford
Circonscription(s) électorale(s) fédérale(s): Compton-Stanstead
Prochaines élections: 5e novembre 2017
Denis Ferland, Maire
Roland Gascon, Directeur général

La Haute-Côte-Nord
#101, 26, rue de la Rivière
Les Escoumins, QC G0T 1K0
Tél: 418-233-2102; *Téléc:* 418-233-3010
info@mrchcn.qc.ca
www.mrchcn.qc.ca
Entité municipal: Regional County Municipality
Incorporation: 1er janvier 1982
Population au 2011: 11,546
Note: 8 municipalités & 1 autre territoire.
Micheline Anctil, Préfète
François Gosselin, Directeur général

La Haute-Gaspésie
464, boul Ste-Anne ouest
Sainte-Anne-des-Monts, QC G4V 1T5
Tél: 418-763-7791; *Téléc:* 418-763-7737
mrc.haute-gaspesie@globetrotter.net
www.hautegaspesie.com/accueil.html
Entité municipal: Regional County Municipality
Incorporation: 18 mars 1981
Population au 2011: 12,088
Note: 8 municipalités & 2 autres territoires.
Allen Cormier, Préfet
Sébastien Lévesque, Directeur général

Les Hauteurs
50, rue de l'Église
Les Hauteurs, QC G0K 1C0
Tél: 418-798-8266; *Téléc:* 418-798-4707
leshauteurs@mitis.qc.ca
municipalite.leshauteurs.qc.ca
Entité municipal: Municipality
Incorporation: 7e novembre 1918; *Area:* 105,41 km2
Comté ou district: La Mitis; *Population au 2011:* 524
Circonscription(s) électorale(s) provinciale(s): Matane-Matapédia
Circonscription(s) électorale(s) fédérale(s): Avignon-La Mitis-Matane-Matapédia
Prochaines élections: 5e novembre 2017
Noël Lambert, Maire
Diane Bernier, Directrice générale

La Haute-Yamaska
#100, 142, rue Dufferin
Granby, QC J2G 4X1
Tél: 450-378-9975; *Téléc:* 450-378-2465
mrc@haute-yamaska.ca
www.haute-yamaska.ca
Entité municipal: Regional County Municipality
Incorporation: 3e mars 1982
Population au 2011: 85,042
Note: 8 municipalités.
Pascal Russell, Préfet
Johanne Gaouette, Directrice générale

Le Haut-Richelieu
380, 4e av
Saint-Jean-sur-Richelieu, QC J2X 1W9
Tél: 450-346-3636; *Téléc:* 450-346-8464
info@mrchr.qc.ca
www.mrchr.qc.ca
Entité municipal: Regional County Municipality
Incorporation: 1er janvier 1982
Population au 2011: 114,344
Note: 14 municipalités.
Michel Fecteau, Préfet
Joane Saulnier, Directrice générale

Le Haut-Saint-François
85, rue du Parc
Cookshire, QC J0B 1M0
Tél: 819-560-8400; *Téléc:* 819-560-8479
www.mrchsf.com
Entité municipal: Regional County Municipality
Incorporation: 1er janvier 1982
Population au 2011: 22,065
Note: 14 municipalités.
Nicole Robert, Préfète
Dominique Provost, Directeur général

Le Haut-Saint-Laurent
#400, 10, rue King
Huntingdon, QC J0S 1H0
Tél: 450-264-5411; *Téléc:* 450-264-6885
mrchsl@mrchsl.com
www.mrchsl.com
Entité municipal: Regional County Municipality
Incorporation: 1 janvier 1982
Population au 2011: 21,197
Note: 13 municipalités.
Alain Castagner, Préfet
François Landreville, Directeur général

Havelock
481, rte 203
Havelock, QC J0S 2C0
Tél: 450-826-4741; *Téléc:* 450-826-4800
mun.havelock@xplornet.com
Entité municipal: Township
Incorporation: 1er avril 1863; *Area:* 87,98 km2
Comté ou district: Le Haut-Saint-Laurent; *Population au 2011:* 756
Circonscription(s) électorale(s) provinciale(s): Huntingdon
Circonscription(s) électorale(s) fédérale(s): Salaberry-Suroît
Prochaines élections: 5e novembre 2017
Denis Henderson, Maire
Daniel Pilon, Directeur général

Havre-Saint-Pierre
#01, 1235, rue de la Digue
Hâvre-Saint-Pierre, QC G0G 1P0
Tél: 418-538-2717; *Téléc:* 418-538-3439
info@havresaintpierre.com
www.havresaintpierre.com
Entité municipal: Municipality
Incorporation: 1er janvier 1873; *Area:* 3779,89 km2
Comté ou district: Minganie; *Population au 2011:* 3,418
Circonscription(s) électorale(s) provinciale(s): Duplessis
Circonscription(s) électorale(s) fédérale(s): Manicouagan
Prochaines élections: 5e novembre 2017
Berchmans Boudreau, Maire
Thérèse Coquelin, Directeur général

Hébertville
351, rue Turgeon
Hébertville, QC G8N 1S8
Tél: 418-344-1302; *Téléc:* 418-344-4618
www.ville.hebertville.qc.ca
Entité municipal: Municipality
Incorporation: 16 décembre 1972; *Area:* 263,88 km2
Comté ou district: Lac-Saint-Jean-Est; *Population au 2011:* 2,441
Circonscription(s) électorale(s) provinciale(s): Lac-St-Jean
Circonscription(s) électorale(s) fédérale(s): Lac-St-Jean
Prochaines élections: 5e novembre 2017
Doris Lavoie, Mairesse
René Perron, Directeur général

Hébertville-Station
6, rue Tremblay
Hébertville-Station, QC G0W 1T0
Tél: 418-343-3961; *Téléc:* 418-343-2349
secretariat@hebertville-station.com
hebertville-station.com
Entité municipal: Village
Incorporation: 18 février 1903; *Area:* 33,28 km2

Comté ou district: Lac-Saint-Jean-Est; *Population au 2011:* 1,216
Circonscription(s) électorale(s) provinciale(s): Lac-St-Jean
Circonscription(s) électorale(s) fédérale(s): Lac-St-Jean
Prochaines élections: 5e novembre 2017
Réal Côté, Maire
Dave Corneau, Directeur général

Hemmingford
#3, 505, rue Frontière
Hemmingford, QC J0L 1H0
Tél: 450-247-2050; *Téléc:* 450-247-3283
canton.township@hemmingford.ca
www.hemmingford.ca/canton
Entité municipal: Township
Incorporation: 1er juillet 1855; *Area:* 155,78 km2
Comté ou district: Les Jardins-de-Napierville; *Population au 2011:* 1,747
Circonscription(s) électorale(s) provinciale(s): Huntingdon
Circonscription(s) électorale(s) fédérale(s): Salaberry-Suroît
Prochaines élections: 5e novembre 2017
Paul Viau, Maire
Sara Czyzewski, Directrice générale

Hemmingford
#5, 505, rue Frontière
Hemmingford, QC J0L 1H0
Tél: 450-247-3310; *Téléc:* 450-247-2389
village@hemmingford.ca
www.hemmingford.ca
Entité municipal: Village
Incorporation: 1er janvier 1878; *Area:* 0,85 km2
Comté ou district: Les Jardins-de-Napierville; *Population au 2011:* 808
Circonscription(s) électorale(s) provinciale(s): Huntingdon
Circonscription(s) électorale(s) fédérale(s): Salaberry-Suroît
Prochaines élections: 5e novembre 2017
Drew Somerville, Maire
Diane Lawrence, Directrice générale

Henryville
165, rue de l'Église
Henryville, QC J0J 1E0
Tél: 450-346-4106; *Téléc:* 450-346-4124
henryville@mrchr.qc.ca
www.mrchr.qc.ca/henryville.php
Entité municipal: Municipality
Incorporation: 15 décembre 1999; *Area:* 64,87 km2
Comté ou district: Le Haut-Richelieu; *Population au 2011:* 1,464
Circonscription(s) électorale(s) provinciale(s): Iberville
Circonscription(s) électorale(s) fédérale(s): Brome-Missisquoi
Prochaines élections: 5e novembre 2017
Andrée Clouâtre, Mairesse
Sylvie Larose Asselin, Directrice générale

Hérouxville
1060, rue St-Pierre sud
Hérouxville, QC G0X 1J0
Tél: 418-365-7135; *Téléc:* 418-365-7041
herouxville@regionmekinac.com
www.municipalite.herouxville.qc.ca
Entité municipal: Parish (Paroisse)
Incorporation: 13 avril 1904; *Area:* 54,51 km2
Comté ou district: Mékinac; *Population au 2011:* 1,340
Circonscription(s) électorale(s) provinciale(s): Laviolette
Circonscription(s) électorale(s) fédérale(s): St-Maurice-Champlain
Prochaines élections: 5e novembre 2017
Bernard Thompson, Maire
Denise Cossette, Directrice générale

Hinchinbrooke
1056, ch Brook
Hinchinbrooke, QC J0S 1A0
Tél: 450-264-5353; *Téléc:* 450-264-3787
info@hinchinbrooke.com
Entité municipal: Township
Incorporation: 1er juillet 1855; *Area:* 148,95 km2
Comté ou district: Le Haut-Saint-Laurent; *Population au 2011:* 2,242
Circonscription(s) électorale(s) provinciale(s): Huntingdon
Circonscription(s) électorale(s) fédérale(s): Salaberry-Suroît
Prochaines élections: 5e novembre 2017
Carolyn Cameron, Mairesse
Kevin Neal, Directeur général

Honfleur
320, rue St-Jean
Honfleur, QC G0R 1N0
Tél: 418-885-9195; *Téléc:* 418-885-9195
livro@globetrotter.qc.ca
munhonfleur.net
Entité municipal: Municipality
Incorporation: 5e mars 1915; *Area:* 50,99 km2
Comté ou district: Bellechasse; *Population au 2011:* 765
Circonscription(s) électorale(s) provinciale(s): Bellechasse
Circonscription(s) électorale(s) fédérale(s): Bellechasse-Les Etchemins-Lévis
Prochaines élections: 5e novembre 2017
Marcel Blais, Maire
Jocelyne G. Paré, Directrice générale

Hope
330, rte 132
Hope, QC G0C 2K0
Tél: 418-752-3212; *Téléc:* 418-752-6986
mun.hope@globetrotter.net
www.municipalitedehope.ca
Entité municipal: Township
Incorporation: 1er juillet 1855; *Area:* 71,45 km2
Comté ou district: Bonaventure; *Population au 2011:* 630
Circonscription(s) électorale(s) provinciale(s): Bonaventure
Circonscription(s) électorale(s) fédérale(s): Gaspésie-Les Iles-de-la-Madeleine
Prochaines élections: 5e novembre 2017
Hazen Whittom, Maire
Nancy Castilloux, Directrice générale

Hope Town
CP 146
209, rte 132 ouest
Hope Town, QC G0C 3C0
Tél: 418-752-2137; *Téléc:* 418-752-3789
hopetown@navigue.com
www.municipalitehopetown.ca
Entité municipal: Municipality
Incorporation: 21 novembre 1936; *Area:* 49,80 km2
Comté ou district: Bonaventure; *Population au 2011:* 344
Circonscription(s) électorale(s) provinciale(s): Bonaventure
Circonscription(s) électorale(s) fédérale(s): Gaspésie — Les Iles-de-la-Madeleine
Prochaines élections: 5e novembre 2017
Linda MacWhirter, Mairesse
Hélène Poirier, Directrice générale

Howick
51, rue Colville
Howick, QC J0S 1G0
Tél: 450-825-2032; *Téléc:* 450-825-0026
municipalite@villagehowick.com
www.villagehowick.com
Entité municipal: Village
Incorporation: 29 octobre 1915; *Area:* 0,89 km2
Comté ou district: Le Haut-Saint-Laurent; *Population au 2011:* 630
Circonscription(s) électorale(s) provinciale(s): Huntingdon
Circonscription(s) électorale(s) fédérale(s): Salaberry-Suroît
Prochaines élections: 5e novembre 2017
Richard Raithby, Maire
Claudette Provost, Directrice générale

Huberdeau
101, rue du Pont
Huberdeau, QC J0T 1G0
Tél: 819-687-8321; *Téléc:* 819-687-8808
info@municipalite.huberdeau.qc.ca
www.municipalite.huberdeau.qc.ca
Entité municipal: Municipality
Incorporation: 8e juin 1926; *Area:* 57,18 km2
Comté ou district: Les Laurentides; *Population au 2011:* 894
Circonscription(s) électorale(s) provinciale(s): Labelle
Circonscription(s) électorale(s) fédérale(s): Laurentides-Labelle
Prochaines élections: 5e novembre 2017
Évelyne Charbonneau, Mairesse
Guylaine Maurice, Directrice générale

Hudson
481, rue Principale
Hudson, QC J0P 1H0
Tél: 450-458-5348; *Téléc:* 450-458-4922
www.ville.hudson.qc.ca
Entité municipal: Town
Incorporation: 7e juin 1969; *Area:* 21,62 km2
Comté ou district: Vaudreuil-Soulanges; Communauté métropolitaine de Montréal; *Population au 2011:* 5,135
Circonscription(s) électorale(s) provinciale(s): Vaudreuil
Circonscription(s) électorale(s) fédérale(s): Vaudreuil-Soulanges
Prochaines élections: 5e novembre 2017
Ed Prévost, Maire
Catherine Haulard, Directrice générale

Huntingdon
23, rue King
Huntingdon, QC J0S 1H0
Tél: 450-264-5389; *Téléc:* 450-264-6826
info@villehuntingdon.com
www.villehuntingdon.com
Entité municipal: Town
Incorporation: 9e octobre 1848; *Area:* 2,61 km2
Comté ou district: Le Haut-Saint-Laurent; *Population au 2011:* 2,457
Circonscription(s) électorale(s) provinciale(s): Huntingdon
Circonscription(s) électorale(s) fédérale(s): Salaberry-Suroît
Prochaines élections: 5e novembre 2017
André Brunette, Maire
Denyse Jenneau, Greffière

L'île-Cadieux
50, ch de l'île
L'île-Cadieux, QC J7V 8P3
Tél: 450-424-4273; *Téléc:* 450-424-6327
info.ilecadieux@videotron.ca
www.ilecadieux.ca
Entité municipal: Village
Incorporation: 21 mars 1922; *Area:* 0,62 km2
Comté ou district: Vaudreuil-Soulanges; Communauté métropolitaine de Montréal; *Population au 2011:* 1,105
Circonscription(s) électorale(s) provinciale(s): Vaudreuil
Circonscription(s) électorale(s) fédérale(s): Vaudreuil-Soulanges
Prochaines élections: 5e novembre 2017
Paul Herrbach, Maire
Gisèle Fournier, Directrice générale

L'île-d'Anticosti
CP 160
25B, ch des Forestiers
Port-Menier, QC G0G 2Y0
Tél: 418-535-0311; *Téléc:* 418-535-0381
municipalite@ile-anticosti.com
www.ile-anticosti.com
Entité municipal: Municipality
Incorporation: 1er janvier 1984; *Area:* 7923,16 km2
Comté ou district: Minganie; *Population au 2011:* 240
Circonscription(s) électorale(s) provinciale(s): Duplessis
Circonscription(s) électorale(s) fédérale(s): Manicouagan
Prochaines élections: 5e novembre 2017
Jean-François Boudreault, Maire
Véronique Rodgers, Directrice générale

L'île-d'Orléans
3896, ch Royal
Sainte-Famille, QC G0A 3P0
Tél: 418-829-1011; *Téléc:* 418-829-2513
www.mrcio.qc.ca
Entité municipal: Regional County Municipality
Incorporation: 1er janvier 1982
Population au 2011: 6,711
Note: 6 municipalités.
Jean-Pierre Turcotte, Préfet
Chantale Cormier, Directrice générale

L'île-Dorval
CP 53061
Dorval, QC H9S 5W4
Tél: 514-226-0450
info@liledorvalisland.ca
www.liledorvalisland.ca
Entité municipal: Town
Incorporation: 1er janvier 2006; *Area:* 0,18 km2
Comté ou district: Communauté métropolitaine de Montréal; *Population au 2011:* 5
Circonscription(s) électorale(s) provinciale(s): Marquette
Circonscription(s) électorale(s) fédérale(s): Dorval-Lachine-LaSalle
Prochaines élections: 5e novembre 2017
Gisèle Chapleau, Mairesse
Susan Aubertin, Greffière

L'île-du-Grand-Calumet
CP 130
8, rue Brizard
L'île-du-Grand-Calumet, QC J0X 1J0
Tél: 819-648-5965; *Téléc:* 819-648-2659
ile-du-grand-calumet@mrcpontiac.qc.ca
Entité municipal: Municipality
Incorporation: 1er juillet 1855; *Area:* 130,61 km2
Comté ou district: Pontiac; *Population au 2011:* 731
Circonscription(s) électorale(s) provinciale(s): Pontiac
Circonscription(s) électorale(s) fédérale(s): Pontiac
Prochaines élections: 5e novembre 2017
Jacques Mantha, Directeur général

Inukjuak
CP 234
Inukjuak, QC J0M 1M0
Tél: 819-254-8822; *Téléc:* 819-254-8574
cnaktialuk@nvinukjuak.ca
www.nvinukjuak.ca
Entité municipal: Northern Village
Incorporation: 7e juin 1980; *Area:* 64,45 km2
Comté ou district: Administration régionale Kativik; *Population au 2011:* 1,597
Circonscription(s) électorale(s) provinciale(s): Ungava
Circonscription(s) électorale(s) fédérale(s):
Abitibi-Baie-James-Nunavik-Eeyou
Pauloosie J. Kasudluak, Maire
Caroline Naktialuk, Secrétaire-trésorière

Inverness
CP 129
1799, rte Dublin
Inverness, QC G0S 1K0
Tél: 418-453-2512; *Téléc:* 418-453-2554
info@municipaliteinverness.ca
www.municipaliteinverness.ca
Entité municipal: Municipality
Incorporation: 9e septembre 1998; *Area:* 176,35 km2
Comté ou district: L'Érable; *Population au 2011:* 822
Circonscription(s) électorale(s) provinciale(s): Arthabaska
Circonscription(s) électorale(s) fédérale(s): Mégantic-L'Érable
Prochaines élections: 5e novembre 2017
Michel Berthiaume, Maire
Sonia Tardif, Directrice générale

Irlande
157, ch Gosford
Irlande, QC G6H 2N7
Tél: 418-428-9216; *Téléc:* 418-428-4262
mundirlande@bellnet.ca
www.mundirlande.qc.ca
Entité municipal: Municipality
Incorporation: 1er juillet 1855; *Area:* 110,200 km2
Comté ou district: Les Appalaches; *Population au 2011:* 959
Circonscription(s) électorale(s) provinciale(s):
Lotbinière-Frontenac
Circonscription(s) électorale(s) fédérale(s): Gaspésie-Les Iles-de-la-Madeleine; Mégantic-L'Érable
Prochaines élections: 5e novembre 2017
Bruno Vézina, Maire
Christiane Laroche, Directrice générale

L'Isle-aux-Allumettes
CP 100
75, rue Notre-Dame
L'Isle-aux-Allumettes, QC J0X 1M0
Tél: 819-689-2266; *Téléc:* 819-689-5619
lisle-aux-allumettes@mrcpontiac.qc.ca
www.isle-aux-allumettes.com
Entité municipal: Municipality
Incorporation: 30 décembre 1998; *Area:* 190,19 km2
Comté ou district: Pontiac; *Population au 2011:* 1,345
Circonscription(s) électorale(s) provinciale(s): Pontiac
Circonscription(s) électorale(s) fédérale(s): Pontiac
Prochaines élections: 5e novembre 2017
Winston Sunstrum, Maire
Richard Vaillancourt, Directeur général

L'Isle-aux-Coudres
1026, ch des Coudriers
L'Isle-aux-Coudres, QC G0A 3J0
Tél: 418-760-1060; *Téléc:* 418-760-1061
contact@municipaliteiac.ca
www.municipaliteiac.ca
Entité municipal: Municipality
Incorporation: 23 août 2000; *Area:* 29,54 km2
Comté ou district: Charlevoix; *Population au 2011:* 1,279
Circonscription(s) électorale(s) provinciale(s):
Charlevoix-Côte-de-Beaupré
Circonscription(s) électorale(s) fédérale(s):
Beauport-Côte-de-Beaupré-Ile d'Orléans-Charlevoix
Prochaines élections: 5e novembre 2017
Dominic Tremblay, Maire
Johanne Fortin, Directrice générale

L'Islet
284, boul Nilus-Leclerc
L'Islet, QC G0R 2C0
Tél: 418-247-3060; *Téléc:* 418-247-5085
muni-islet@globetrotter.net
www.lislet.com
Entité municipal: Municipality
Incorporation: 1er janvier 2000; *Area:* 119,44 km2
Comté ou district: L'Islet; *Population au 2011:* 3,999
Circonscription(s) électorale(s) provinciale(s): Côte-du-Sud
Circonscription(s) électorale(s) fédérale(s):
Montmagny-L'Islet-Kamouraska-Rivière-du-Loup
Prochaines élections: 5e novembre 2017
André Caron, Maire
Colette Lord, Directrice générale

L'Islet
34-A, rue Fortin
Saint-Jean-Port-Joli, QC G0R 3G0
Tél: 418-598-3076; *Téléc:* 418-598-6880
administration@mrclislet.com
www.mrclislet.com
Entité municipal: Regional County Municipality
Incorporation: 1er janvier 1982
Population au 2011: 18,517
Note: 14 municipalités.
Jean-Pierre Dubé, Préfet
Harold Leblanc, Directeur général

L'Isle-Verte
CP 159
141, rue St-Jean-Baptiste
L'Isle-Verte, QC G0L 1K0
Tél: 418-898-2812; *Téléc:* 418-898-2788
www.municipalite.lisle-verte.qc.ca
Entité municipal: Municipality
Incorporation: 9 février 2000; *Area:* 112,33 km2
Comté ou district: Rivière-du-Loup; *Population au 2011:* 1,469
Circonscription(s) électorale(s) provinciale(s):
Rivière-du-Loup-Témiscouata
Circonscription(s) électorale(s) fédérale(s):
Montmagny-L'Islet-Kamouraska-Rivière-du-Loup
Prochaines élections: 5e novembre 2017
Ursule Thériault, Mairesse
Guy Bérubé, Directeur général

Ivry-sur-le-Lac
601, ch de la Gare
Ivry-sur-le-Lac, QC J8C 2Z8
Tél: 819-321-2332; *Téléc:* 819-321-3089
info@ivry-sur-le-lac.qc.ca
www.ivry-sur-le-lac.qc.ca
Entité municipal: Municipality
Incorporation: 1er janvier 2006; *Area:* 30,64 km2
Comté ou district: Les Laurentides; *Population au 2011:* 425
Circonscription(s) électorale(s) provinciale(s): Bertrand
Circonscription(s) électorale(s) fédérale(s): Laurentides-Labelle
Prochaines élections: 5e novembre 2017
Kenneth Hague, Maire
Jean-Raymond Dufresne, Directeur général

Ivujivik
CP 20
Ivujivik, QC J0M 1H0
Tél: 819-922-9940; *Téléc:* 819-922-3045
www.nvivujivik.ca
Entité municipal: Northern Village
Incorporation: 27 juin 1981; *Area:* 36,59 km2
Comté ou district: Administration régionale Kativik; *Population au 2011:* 370
Circonscription(s) électorale(s) provinciale(s): Ungava
Circonscription(s) électorale(s) fédérale(s):
Abitibi-Baie-James-Nunavik-Eeyou
Tivi Iyaituk, Maire
Uqittuk Iyaituk, Secrétaire-trésorier

La Jacques-Cartier
60, rue St-Patrick
Shannon, QC G0A 4N0
Tél: 418-844-2160; *Téléc:* 418-844-2664
mrcjc@mrc.lajacquescartier.qc.ca
www.mrc.lajacquescartier.qc.ca
Entité municipal: Regional County Municipality
Incorporation: 1er avril 1981
Population au 2011: 36,883
Note: 9 municipalités & 1 autre territoire.
Robert Miller, Préfet
Francine Breton, Directrice générale

Les Jardins-de-Napierville
1767, rue Principale
Saint-Michel, QC J0L 2J0
Tél: 450-454-0559; *Téléc:* 450-454-0560
info@mrcjardinsdenapierville.ca
www.mrcjardinsdenapierville.ca
Entité municipal: Regional County Municipality
Incorporation: 1er janvier 1982
Population au 2011: 26,234
Circonscription(s) électorale(s) provinciale(s): Huntington
Circonscription(s) électorale(s) fédérale(s):
Beauharnois-Salaberry
Note: 11 municipalités.
Paul Viau, Préfet
Nicole Inkel, Directrice générale

Joliette
632, rue De Lanaudière
Joliette, QC J6E 3M7
Tél: 450-759-2237; *Téléc:* 450-759-2597
information@mrcjoliette.qc.ca
www.mrcjoliette.qc.ca
Entité municipal: Regional County Municipality
Incorporation: 1er janvier 1982
Population au 2011: 63,551
Note: 10 municipalités.
André Hénault, Préfet
Luc Bossé, Directeur général

Kamouraska
67, av Morel
Kamouraska, QC G0L 1M0
Tél: 418-492-6523; *Téléc:* 418-492-9789
mychelle.levesque@kamouraska.ca
www.kamouraska.ca
Entité municipal: Municipality
Incorporation: 25 avril 1987; *Area:* 40,81 km2
Comté ou district: Kamouraska; *Population au 2011:* 589
Circonscription(s) électorale(s) provinciale(s): Côte-du-Sud
Circonscription(s) électorale(s) fédérale(s):
Montmagny-L'Islet-Kamouraska-Rivière-du-Loup
Prochaines élections: 5e novembre 2017
Richard Préfontaine, Maire
Mychelle Lévesque, Directrice générale

Kamouraska
CP 1120
425, av Patry
Saint-Pascal, QC G0L 3Y0
Tél: 418-492-1660; *Téléc:* 418-492-2220
info@mrckamouraska.com
www.mrckamouraska.com
Entité municipal: Regional County Municipality
Incorporation: 1er janvier 1982
Population au 2011: 21,492
Note: 17 municipalités & 2 autres territoires.
Yvon Soucy, Préfet
Yvan Migneault, Directeur général

Kangiqsualujjuaq
CP 120
Kangiqsualujjuaq, QC J0M 1N0
Tél: 819-337-5270; *Téléc:* 819-337-5200
www.nvkangiqsualujjuaq.ca
Entité municipal: Northern Village
Incorporation: 2e février 1980; *Area:* 36,23 km2
Comté ou district: Administration régionale Kativik; *Population au 2011:* 874
Circonscription(s) électorale(s) provinciale(s): Ungava
Circonscription(s) électorale(s) fédérale(s):
Abitibi-Baie-James-Nunavik-Eeyou
Hilda Snowball, Mairesse
Tommy Annanack, Secrétaire-trésorier

Kangiqsujuaq
CP 60
901, ch Sinaitia
Kangiqsujuaq, QC J0M 1K0
Tél: 819-338-3342; *Téléc:* 819-338-3237
www.nvkangiqsujuaq.ca
Entité municipal: Northern Village
Incorporation: 20 septembre 1980; *Area:* 12,47 km2
Comté ou district: Administration régionale Kativik; *Population au 2011:* 696
Circonscription(s) électorale(s) provinciale(s): Ungava
Circonscription(s) électorale(s) fédérale(s):
Abitibi-Baie-James-Nunavik-Eeyou
Charlie Arngak, Maire
Pasa Kiatainaq, Secrétaire-trésorière

Kangirsuk
CP 90
101, ch Kuuvviliariaq
Kangirsuk, QC J0M 1A0
Tél: 819-935-4388; *Téléc:* 819-935-4287
www.nvkangirsuk.ca
Entité municipal: Northern Village
Incorporation: 17 janvier 1981; *Area:* 58,73 km2
Comté ou district: Administration régionale Kativik; *Population au 2011:* 549
Circonscription(s) électorale(s) provinciale(s): Ungava
Circonscription(s) électorale(s) fédérale(s):
Abitibi-Baie-James-Nunavik-Eeyou
Noah Eetook, Maire
Joseph Annahatak, Secrétaire-trésorier

Kawawachikamach
CP 5151
1009, rue Naskapi
Kawawachikamach, QC G0G 2Z0
Tél: 418-585-2686; *Téléc:* 418-585-3130
kawawa@naskapi.ca
www.naskapi.ca
Entité municipal: Villages Naskapi
Incorporation: 10 septembre 1981; *Area:* 284,7 km2
Comté ou district: Administration régionale Kativik
Circonscription(s) électorale(s) provinciale(s): Duplessis
Circonscription(s) électorale(s) fédérale(s): Manicouagan
Noah Swappie, Maire
John Mameamskum, Directeur général

Kazabazua
CP 10
30, ch Begley
Kazabazua, QC J0X 1X0
Tél: 819-467-2852; *Téléc:* 819-467-3872
infos@kazabazua.ca
www.kazabazua.ca
Entité municipal: Municipality
Incorporation: 1er janvier 1862; *Area:* 175,49 km2
Comté ou district: La Vallée-de-la-Gatineau; *Population au 2011:* 847
Circonscription(s) électorale(s) provinciale(s): Gatineau
Circonscription(s) électorale(s) fédérale(s): Pontiac
Prochaines élections: 5e novembre 2017
Ota Hora, Maire
Pierre Vaillancourt, Directeur général

Kiamika
3, ch Valiquette
Kiamika, QC J0W 1G0
Tél: 819-585-3225; *Téléc:* 819-585-3992
info@kiamika.ca
www.kiamika.ca
Entité municipal: Municipality
Incorporation: 3e janvier 1898; *Area:* 348,25 km2
Comté ou district: Antoine-Labelle; *Population au 2011:* 772
Circonscription(s) électorale(s) provinciale(s): Labelle
Circonscription(s) électorale(s) fédérale(s): Laurentides-Labelle
Prochaines élections: 5e novembre 2017
Christian Lacroix, Maire
Josée Lacasse, Directrice générale

Kingsbury
370, rue du Moulin
Kingsbury, QC J0B 1X0
Tél: 819-826-2527; *Téléc:* 819-826-2520
kingsbury@xittel.ca
www.kingsbury.ca
Entité municipal: Village
Incorporation: 7e juillet 1896; *Area:* 6,26 km2
Comté ou district: Le Val-Saint-François; *Population au 2011:* 123
Circonscription(s) électorale(s) provinciale(s): Richmond
Circonscription(s) électorale(s) fédérale(s): Richmond-Arthabaska
Prochaines élections: 5e novembre 2017
Pierre-Luc Gagnon, Maire
Yves Barthe, Directeur général

Kingsey Falls
CP 270
15, rue Caron
Kingsey Falls, QC J0A 1B0
Tél: 819-363-3810; *Téléc:* 819-363-3819
villedekingseyfalls@kingseyfalls.ca
www.kingseyfalls.ca
Entité municipal: Town
Incorporation: 31 décembre 1997; *Area:* 70,14 km2
Comté ou district: Arthabaska; *Population au 2011:* 2,000
Circonscription(s) électorale(s) provinciale(s): Drummond-Bois-Francs
Circonscription(s) électorale(s) fédérale(s): Richmond-Arthabaska
Prochaines élections: 5e novembre 2017
Micheline Pinard-Lampron, Mairesse
Anne Lemieux, Greffière

Kinnear's Mills
120, rue des Églises
Kinnear's Mills, QC G0N 1K0
Tél: 418-424-3377; *Téléc:* 418-424-3015
info@kinnearsmills.com
www.kinnearsmills.com
Entité municipal: Municipality
Incorporation: 1er juillet 1855; *Area:* 93,18 km2
Comté ou district: Les Appalaches; *Population au 2011:* 369
Circonscription(s) électorale(s) provinciale(s): Lotbinière-Frontenac
Circonscription(s) électorale(s) fédérale(s): Mégantic-L'Érable
Prochaines élections: 5e novembre 2017
Paul Vachon, Maire
Claudette Perreault, Directrice générale

Kipawa
15, rue Principale
Kipawa, QC J0Z 2H0
Tél: 819-627-3500; *Téléc:* 819-627-1067
kipawa@mrctemiscamingue.qc.ca
www.kipawa.ca
Entité municipal: Municipality
Incorporation: 1er janvier 1985; *Area:* 47,20 km2
Comté ou district: Témiscamingue; *Population au 2011:* 474
Circonscription(s) électorale(s) provinciale(s): Rouyn-Noranda-Témiscamingue
Circonscription(s) électorale(s) fédérale(s): Abitibi-Témiscamingue
Prochaines élections: 5e novembre 2017
Norman Young, Maire
Danielle Gravelle, Directrice générale

Kuujjuaq
CP 210
400, ch de l'Airport
Kuujjuaq, QC J0M 1C0
Tél: 819-964-2943; *Téléc:* 819-964-2980
www.nvkuujjuaq.ca
Entité municipal: Northern Village
Incorporation: 29 décembre 1979; *Area:* 390,33 km2
Comté ou district: Administration régionale Kativik; *Population au 2011:* 2,375
Circonscription(s) électorale(s) provinciale(s): Ungava
Circonscription(s) électorale(s) fédérale(s): Abitibi-Baie-James-Nunavik-Eeyou
Tunu Napartuk, Maire
Ian D. Robertson, Secrétaire-trésorier

Kuujjuarapik
CP 360
412, av St-Edmund
Kuujjuarapik, QC J0M 1G0
Tél: 819-929-3360; *Téléc:* 819-929-3453
www.nvkuujjuaraapik.ca
Entité municipal: Northern Village
Incorporation: 7e juin 1980; *Area:* 7,46 km2
Comté ou district: Administration régionale Kativik; *Population au 2011:* 657
Circonscription(s) électorale(s) provinciale(s): Ungava
Circonscription(s) électorale(s) fédérale(s): Abitibi-Baie-James-Nunavik-Eeyou
Lucassie Inukpuk, Maire
Pierre Roussel, Secrétaire-trésorier

Labelle
1, rue du Pont
Labelle, QC J0T 1H0
Tél: 819-681-3371; *Téléc:* 819-686-3820
info@municipalite.labelle.qc.ca
www.municipalite.labelle.qc.ca
Entité municipal: Municipality
Incorporation: 27 janvier 1973; *Area:* 217,11 km2
Comté ou district: Les Laurentides; *Population au 2011:* 2,445
Circonscription(s) électorale(s) provinciale(s): Labelle
Circonscription(s) électorale(s) fédérale(s): Laurentides-Labelle
Prochaines élections: 5e novembre 2017
Gilbert Brassard, Maire
Claire Coulombe, Directrice générale

Labrecque
3425, rue Ambroise
Labrecque, QC G0W 2S0
Tél: 418-481-2022; *Téléc:* 418-481-1210
municipalite@ville.labrecque.qc.ca
www.ville.labrecque.qc.ca
Entité municipal: Municipality
Incorporation: 6 octobre 1925; *Area:* 147,37 km2
Comté ou district: Lac-Saint-Jean-Est; *Population au 2011:* 1,215
Circonscription(s) électorale(s) provinciale(s): Lac-St-Jean
Circonscription(s) électorale(s) fédérale(s): Jonquière; Portneuf-Jacques-Cartier
Prochaines élections: 5e novembre 2017
Eric Simard, Maire
Suzanne Couture, Directrice générale

Lac-au-Saumon
CP 98
36, rue Bouillon
Lac-au-Saumon, QC G0J 1M0
Tél: 418-778-3378; *Téléc:* 418-778-3706
lacausaumon@mrcmatapedia.qc.ca
www.lacausaumon.com
Entité municipal: Municipality
Incorporation: 17 décembre 1997; *Area:* 79,74 km2
Comté ou district: La Matapédia; *Population au 2011:* 1,453
Circonscription(s) électorale(s) provinciale(s): Matane-Matapédia
Circonscription(s) électorale(s) fédérale(s): Avignon-La Mitis-Matane-Matapédia
Prochaines élections: 5e novembre 2017
Michel Chevarie, Maire
Karine Dostie, Directrice générale

Lac-aux-Sables
820, rue St-Alphonse
Lac-aux-Sables, QC G0X 1M0
Tél: 418-336-2331; *Téléc:* 418-336-2500
lac-aux-sables@regionmekinac.com
www.lac-aux-sables.qc.ca
Entité municipal: Parish (Paroisse)
Incorporation: 24 avril 1899; *Area:* 285,45 km2
Comté ou district: Mékinac; *Population au 2011:* 1,373
Circonscription(s) électorale(s) provinciale(s): Laviolette
Circonscription(s) électorale(s) fédérale(s): St-Maurice-Champlain
Prochaines élections: 5e novembre 2017
Jean Paul Tessier, Maire
Valérie Cloutier, Directrice générale

Lac-Beauport
65, ch du Tour-du-Lac
Lac-Beauport, QC G3B 0A1
Tél: 418-849-7141; *Téléc:* 418-849-0361
info@lacbeauport.net
www.lac-beauport.ca
Entité municipal: Municipality
Incorporation: 1er juillet 1855; *Area:* 62,72 km2
Comté ou district: La Jacques-Cartier; Communauté métropolitaine de Québec; *Population au 2011:* 7,281
Circonscription(s) électorale(s) provinciale(s): Chauveau
Circonscription(s) électorale(s) fédérale(s): Portneuf-Jacques-Cartier
Prochaines élections: 5e novembre 2017
Michel Beaulieu, Maire
Richard Labrecque, Directeur général

Lac-Bouchette
249, rue Principale
Lac-Bouchette, QC G0W 1V0
Tél: 418-348-6306; *Téléc:* 418-348-9477
munilac@lac-bouchette.com
www.lac-bouchette.com
Entité municipal: Municipality
Incorporation: 25 septembre 1971; *Area:* 919,99 km2
Comté ou district: Le Domaine-du-Roy; *Population au 2011:* 1,174
Circonscription(s) électorale(s) provinciale(s): Roberval
Circonscription(s) électorale(s) fédérale(s): Lac-St-Jean; Argenteuil-La Petite-Nation
Prochaines élections: 5e novembre 2017
Ghislaine M.-Hudon, Mairesse
Jean-Pierre Tremblay, Directeur général

Lac-Brome
122, ch Lakeside
Lac-Brome, QC J0E 1V0
Tél: 450-243-6111; *Téléc:* 450-243-5300
reception@ville.lac-brome.qc.ca
ville.lac-brome.qc.ca
Entité municipal: Town
Incorporation: 2 janvier 1971; *Area:* 209,37 km2
Comté ou district: Brome-Missisquoi; *Population au 2011:* 5,609
Circonscription(s) électorale(s) provinciale(s): Brome-Missisquoi
Circonscription(s) électorale(s) fédérale(s): Brome-Missisquoi
Prochaines élections: 5e novembre 2017
Richard Burcombe, Maire
Edwin John Sullivan, Greffier

Lac-Delage
24, rue du Pied-des-Pentes
Lac-Delage, QC G3C 5A4
Tél: 418-848-2417; *Téléc:* 418-848-1948
ville@lacdelage.qc.ca
www.lacdelage.qc.ca
Entité municipal: Village
Incorporation: 11 février 1959; *Area:* 1,46 km2
Comté ou district: La Jacques-Cartier; Communauté métropolitaine de Québec; *Population au 2011:* 598

Circonscription(s) électorale(s) provinciale(s): Chauveau
Circonscription(s) électorale(s) fédérale(s):
Portneuf-Jacques-Cartier
Prochaines élections: 5e novembre 2017
Dominique Payette, Mairesse
Guylaine Thibault, Directrice générale

Lac-des-Aigles
CP 70
75, rue Principale
Lac-des-Aigles, QC G0K 1V0
Tél: 418-779-2300; *Téléc:* 418-779-3024
info@lacdesaigles.ca
www.lacdesaigles.ca
Entité municipal: Municipality
Incorporation: 1er janvier 1948; *Area:* 85,10 km2
Comté ou district: Témiscouata; *Population au 2011:* 551
Circonscription(s) électorale(s) provinciale(s):
Rivière-du-Loup-Témiscouata
Circonscription(s) électorale(s) fédérale(s):
Rimouski-Neigette-Témiscouata-Les Basques
Prochaines élections: 5e novembre 2017
Claude Breault, Maire
Francine Beaulieu, Directrice générale

Lac-des-Écorces
672, boul St-François
Lac-des-Écorces, QC J0W 1H0
Tél: 819-585-4600; *Téléc:* 819-585-4610
adm@lacdesecorces.ca
www.lacdesecorces.ca
Entité municipal: Municipality
Incorporation: 10 octobre 2002; *Area:* 143,59 km2
Comté ou district: Antoine-Labelle; *Population au 2011:* 2,713
Circonscription(s) électorale(s) provinciale(s): Labelle
Circonscription(s) électorale(s) fédérale(s): Laurentides-Labelle
Prochaines élections: 5e novembre 2017
Note: On October 10, 2002, the Municipality of Beaux-Rivages, the Village of Lac-des-Écorces & the Village of Val-Barrette amalgamated to create the new Municipality of Beaux-Rivages-Lac-des-Écorces-Val-Barrette. The name changed to Lac-des-Écorces in 2003
Pierre Flamand, Maire
Jean Bernier, Directeur général

Lac-des-Plages
2053, ch Tour-du-Lac
Lac-des-Plages, QC J0T 1K0
Tél: 819-426-2391; *Téléc:* 819-426-2085
lacdesplages04@mrcpapineau.com
www.lacdesplages.com
Entité municipal: Municipality
Incorporation: 1er janvier 1950; *Area:* 121,78 km2
Comté ou district: Papineau; *Population au 2011:* 522
Circonscription(s) électorale(s) provinciale(s): Papineau
Circonscription(s) électorale(s) fédérale(s): Argenteuil-La Petite-Nation
Prochaines élections: 5e novembre 2017
Josée Simon, Maire
Denis Dagenais, Directeur général

Lac-des-Seize-îles
47, rue de l'Église
Lac-des-Seize-îles, QC J0T 2M0
Tél: 450-226-3117; *Téléc:* 450-226-1461
adjointe@lac-des-seize-iles.com
www.lac-des-seize-iles.ca
Entité municipal: Municipality
Incorporation: 19 février 1914; *Area:* 8,49 km2
Comté ou district: Les Pays-d'en-Haut; *Population au 2011:* 223
Circonscription(s) électorale(s) provinciale(s): Argenteuil
Circonscription(s) électorale(s) fédérale(s): Argenteuil-La Petite-Nation
Prochaines élections: 5e novembre 2017
Yves Baillargeon, Maire
Diane Taillon, Directrice générale

Lac-Drolet
685, rue Principale
Lac-Drolet, QC G0Y 1C0
Tél: 819-549-2332; *Téléc:* 819-549-2626
www.lacdrolet.ca
Entité municipal: Municipality
Incorporation: 1er janvier 1885; *Area:* 124,94 km2
Comté ou district: Le Granit; *Population au 2011:* 1,071
Circonscription(s) électorale(s) provinciale(s): Mégantic
Circonscription(s) électorale(s) fédérale(s): Mégantic-L'Érable
Prochaines élections: 5e novembre 2017
Rock Couët, Maire
Julie Cloutier, Directrice générale

Lac-du-Cerf
19, ch de l'Église
Lac-du-Cerf, QC J0W 1S0
Tél: 819-597-2424; *Téléc:* 819-597-4036
taxation@lac-du-cerf.ca
www.lac-du-cerf.info
Entité municipal: Municipality
Incorporation: 1er janvier 1955; *Area:* 78,45 km2
Comté ou district: Antoine-Labelle; *Population au 2011:* 415
Circonscription(s) électorale(s) provinciale(s): Labelle
Circonscription(s) électorale(s) fédérale(s): Laurentides-Labelle
Prochaines élections: 5e novembre 2017
Danielle Ouimet, Mairesse
Jacinthe Valiquette, Directrice générale

Lac-Édouard
CP 4049
195, rue Principale
Lac-Édouard, QC G0X 3N0
Tél: 819-653-2238; *Téléc:* 819-653-2338
muni.lacedouard@xplornet.ca
www.lacedouard.ca
Entité municipal: Municipality
Incorporation: 1er janvier 2006; *Area:* 916,22 km2
Population au 2011: 175
Circonscription(s) électorale(s) provinciale(s): Laviolette
Circonscription(s) électorale(s) fédérale(s):
Saint-Maurice-Champlain
Prochaines élections: 5e novembre 2017
Larry Bernier, Maire
Johanne Marchand, Directrice générale

Lac-Etchemin
208, 2e Av
Lac-Etchemin, QC G0R 1S0
Tél: 418-625-4521; *Téléc:* 418-625-3175
munetchemin@sogetel.net
www.municipalite.lac-etchemin.qc.ca
Entité municipal: Municipality
Incorporation: 10 octobre 2001; *Area:* 160,57 km2
Comté ou district: Les Etchemins; *Population au 2011:* 4,061
Circonscription(s) électorale(s) provinciale(s): Bellechasse
Circonscription(s) électorale(s) fédérale(s): Bellechasse-Les Etchemins-Lévis
Prochaines élections: 5e novembre 2017
Harold Gagnon, Maire
Laurent Rheault, Directeur général

Lac-Frontière
22, rue de l'Église
Lac-Frontière, QC G0R 1T0
Tél: 418-245-3553; *Téléc:* 418-245-3552
municipalitelac-frontiere@globetrotter.net
www.lac-frontiere.ca
Entité municipal: Municipality
Incorporation: 7 février 1916; *Area:* 51,33 km2
Comté ou district: Montmagny; *Population au 2011:* 198
Circonscription(s) électorale(s) provinciale(s): Côte-du-Sud
Circonscription(s) électorale(s) fédérale(s):
Montmagny-L'Islet-Kamouraska-Rivière-du-Loup
Prochaines élections: 5e novembre 2017
Guy Garant, Maire
Dany Robert, Directrice générale

Lac-Mégantic
#200, 5527, rue Frontenac
Lac-Mégantic, QC G6B 1H6
Tél: 819-583-2441; *Téléc:* 819-583-5920
info@ville.lac-megantic.qc.ca
www.ville.lac-megantic.qc.ca
Entité municipal: Town
Incorporation: 14 mars 1907; *Area:* 20,33 km2
Comté ou district: Le Granit; *Population au 2011:* 5,932
Circonscription(s) électorale(s) provinciale(s): Mégantic
Circonscription(s) électorale(s) fédérale(s): Mégantic-L'Érable
Prochaines élections: 5e novembre 2017
Colette Roy Laroche, Mairesse
Chantal Dion, Greffière

Lacolle
1, rue de l'Église sud
Lacolle, QC J0J 1J0
Tél: 450-246-3201; *Téléc:* 450-246-4412
www.lacolle.com
Entité municipal: Municipality
Incorporation: 13 septembre 2001; *Area:* 49,17 km2
Comté ou district: Le Haut-Richelieu; *Population au 2011:* 2,680
Circonscription(s) électorale(s) provinciale(s): Huntingdon
Circonscription(s) électorale(s) fédérale(s): Saint-Jean
Prochaines élections: 5e novembre 2017
Roland-Luc Béliveau, Maire
Daniel Prince, Directeur général

Lac-Poulin
CP 1019
208, rte 271
Lac-Poulin, QC G0M 1P0
Tél: 418-228-7585; *Téléc:* 418-222-6931
munlacpoulin@globetrotter.net
www.municipalite.lac-poulin.qc.ca
Entité municipal: Village
Incorporation: 5 mars 1959; *Area:* 1,08 km2
Comté ou district: Beauce-Sartigan; *Population au 2011:* 134
Circonscription(s) électorale(s) provinciale(s): Beauce-Sud
Circonscription(s) électorale(s) fédérale(s): Beauce
Prochaines élections: 5e novembre 2017
Manon Veilleux, Mairesse
Annie Lapointe, Directrice générale

Lac-Saguay
257A, rte 117
Lac-Saguay, QC J0W 1L0
Tél: 819-278-3972; *Téléc:* 819-278-0260
info@lacsaguay.qc.ca
www.lacsaguay.qc.ca
Entité municipal: Village
Incorporation: 1er juillet 1951; *Area:* 176,26 km2
Comté ou district: Antoine-Labelle; *Population au 2011:* 446
Circonscription(s) électorale(s) provinciale(s): Labelle
Circonscription(s) électorale(s) fédérale(s): Laurentides-Labelle
Prochaines élections: 5e novembre 2017
Francine Asselin-Bélisle, Mairesse
Richard Gagnon, Directeur général

Lac-Saint-Jean-Est
625, rue Bergeron ouest
Alma, QC G8B 1V3
Tél: 418-668-3023; *Téléc:* 418-668-5112
info@mrclac.qc.ca
www.mrclacsaintjeanest.qc.ca
Entité municipal: Regional County Municipality
Incorporation: 1er janvier 1982
Population au 2011: 52,520
Note: 14 municipalités & 4 autres territoires.
André Paradis, Préfet
Sabin Larouche, Directeur général

Lac-Saint-Joseph
1048, ch Thomas-Maher
Lac-St-Joseph, QC G3N 0B4
Tél: 418-875-3355; *Téléc:* 418-875-0444
www.villelacstjoseph.com
Entité municipal: Village
Incorporation: 10 juin 1936; *Area:* 32,81 km2
Comté ou district: La Jacques-Cartier; Communauté métropolitaine de Québec; *Population au 2011:* 251
Circonscription(s) électorale(s) provinciale(s): La Peltrie
Circonscription(s) électorale(s) fédérale(s):
Portneuf-Jacques-Cartier
Prochaines élections: 5e novembre 2017
Michael Croteau, Maire
Vivian Viviers, Directrice générale

Lac-Saint-Paul
388, rue Principale
Lac-Saint-Paul, QC J0W 1K0
Tél: 819-587-4283; *Téléc:* 819-587-4892
secretaire@lac-saint-paul.ca
www.lac-saint-paul.ca
Entité municipal: Municipality
Incorporation: 11 septembre 1922; *Area:* 173,06 km2
Comté ou district: Antoine-Labelle; *Population au 2011:* 481
Circonscription(s) électorale(s) provinciale(s): Labelle
Circonscription(s) électorale(s) fédérale(s): Laurentides-Labelle
Prochaines élections: 5e novembre 2017
Louis F. Lanzon, Maire
François St-Amour, Directeur général

Lac-Sergent
1466, ch du Club Nautique
Lac-Sergent, QC G0A 2J0
Tél: 418-875-4854; *Téléc:* 418-875-3805
lac-sergent@derytele.com
www.villelacsergent.com
Entité municipal: Village
Incorporation: 25 février 1921; *Area:* 3,52 km2
Comté ou district: Portneuf; *Population au 2011:* 466
Circonscription(s) électorale(s) provinciale(s): Portneuf
Circonscription(s) électorale(s) fédérale(s):
Portneuf-Jacques-Cartier
Prochaines élections: 5e novembre 2017
Denis Racine, Maire
Josée Brouillette, Directrice générale

Lac-Simon
CP 3550
849, ch du Tour-du-Lac
Chénéville, QC J0V 1E0
Tél: 819-428-3906; *Téléc:* 819-428-3455
mun.lacsimon@mrcpapineau.com
www.lac-simon.net
Entité municipal: Municipality
Incorporation: 1er janvier 1881; *Area:* 96,83 km2
Comté ou district: Papineau; *Population au 2011:* 984
Circonscription(s) électorale(s) provinciale(s): Papineau
Circonscription(s) électorale(s) fédérale(s): Argenteuil-La Petite-Nation
Prochaines élections: 5e novembre 2017
Jacques Maillé, Maire
Benoît Hébert, Directeur général

Lac-Ste-Marie
CP 97
106, ch de Lac-Ste-Marie
Lac-Sainte-Marie, QC J0X 1Z0
Tél: 819-467-5437; *Téléc:* 819-467-3691
municipalite@lac-sainte-marie.com
www.lac-sainte-marie.com
Entité municipal: Municipality
Incorporation: 1er janvier 1872; *Area:* 211,13 km2
Comté ou district: La Vallée-de-la-Gatineau; *Population au 2011:* 611
Circonscription(s) électorale(s) provinciale(s): Gatineau
Circonscription(s) électorale(s) fédérale(s): Pontiac
Prochaines élections: 5e novembre 2017
Gary Lachapelle, Maire
Yvon Blanchard, Directeur général

Lac-Supérieur
1281, ch du Lac-Supérieur
Lac-Supérieur, QC J0T 1J0
Tél: 819-681-3370; *Téléc:* 819-688-3010
info@muni.lacsuperieur.qc.ca
www.muni.lacsuperieur.qc.ca
Entité municipal: Municipality
Incorporation: 1er janvier 1881; *Area:* 380,36 km2
Comté ou district: Les Laurentides; *Population au 2011:* 1,892
Circonscription(s) électorale(s) provinciale(s): Labelle
Circonscription(s) électorale(s) fédérale(s): Laurentides-Labelle
Prochaines élections: 5e novembre 2017
Danielle St-Laurent, Mairesse
David Doughty, Directeur général

Lac-Tremblant-Nord
1984, ch du Village
Mont-Tremblant, QC J8E 1K4
Tél: 819-425-8154; *Téléc:* 819-425-9208
www.lac-tremblant-nord.qc.ca
Entité municipal: Municipality
Incorporation: 1er janvier 2006; *Area:* 20,84 km2
Comté ou district: Les Laurentides; *Population au 2011:* 47
Circonscription(s) électorale(s) provinciale(s): Labelle
Circonscription(s) électorale(s) fédérale(s): Laurentides-Labelle
Prochaines élections: 5e novembre 2017
Hugh Scott, Maire
Martin Paul Gélinas, Directeur général

Laforce
CP 25
703, ch du Village
Laforce, QC J0Z 2J0
Tél: 819-722-2461; *Téléc:* 819-722-2462
www.laforce.ca
Entité municipal: Municipality
Incorporation: 1er janvier 1979; *Area:* 612,65 km2
Comté ou district: Témiscamingue; *Population au 2011:* 147
Circonscription(s) électorale(s) provinciale(s): Rouyn-Noranda-Témiscamingue
Circonscription(s) électorale(s) fédérale(s): Abitibi-Témiscamingue
Prochaines élections: 5e novembre 2017
Isabelle Morin, Maire
Daniel Lizotte, Directeur général

Lamarche
100, rue Principale
Lamarche, QC G0W 1X0
Tél: 418-481-2861; *Téléc:* 418-481-1412
mun.lamarche@ville.lamarche.qc.ca
www.ville.lamarche.qc.ca
Entité municipal: Municipality
Incorporation: 1er janvier 1967; *Area:* 94,79 km2
Comté ou district: Lac-Saint-Jean-Est; *Population au 2011:* 557
Circonscription(s) électorale(s) provinciale(s): Lac-St-Jean
Circonscription(s) électorale(s) fédérale(s): Jonquière
Prochaines élections: 5e novembre 2017
Gilbert Savard, Maire
Fabienne Girard, Directrice générale

Lambton
230, rue du Collège
Lambton, QC G0M 1H0
Tél: 418-486-7438; *Téléc:* 418-486-7440
www.lambton.ca
Entité municipal: Municipality
Incorporation: 23 décembre 1976; *Area:* 106,86 km2
Comté ou district: Le Granit; *Population au 2011:* 1,584
Circonscription(s) électorale(s) provinciale(s): Mégantic
Circonscription(s) électorale(s) fédérale(s): Mégantic-L'Érable
Prochaines élections: 5e novembre 2017
Ghislain Breton, Maire
Marie-Soleil Gilbert, Directrice générale

Landrienne
158, av Principale est
Landrienne, QC J0Y 1V0
Tél: 819-732-4357; *Téléc:* 819-732-3866
www.landrienne.com
Entité municipal: Township
Incorporation: 15 juillet 1918; *Area:* 276,22 km2
Comté ou district: Abitibi; *Population au 2011:* 977
Circonscription(s) électorale(s) provinciale(s): Abitibi-Ouest
Circonscription(s) électorale(s) fédérale(s): Abitibi-Témiscamingue
Prochaines élections: 5e novembre 2017
Guy Baril, Maire
Jacques Perron, Directeur général

Lanoraie
57, rue Laroche
Lanoraie, QC J0K 1E0
Tél: 450-887-1100; *Téléc:* 450-836-5221
info@lanoraie.ca
www.lanoraie.ca
Entité municipal: Municipality
Incorporation: 6 décembre 2000; *Area:* 102,04 km2
Comté ou district: D'Autray; *Population au 2011:* 4,447
Circonscription(s) électorale(s) provinciale(s): Berthier
Circonscription(s) électorale(s) fédérale(s): Berthier-Maskinongé
Prochaines élections: 5e novembre 2017
Gérard Jean, Maire
Michel Dufort, Directeur général

Lantier
CP 39
118, croissant des Trois-Lacs
Lantier, QC J0T 1V0
Tél: 819-326-2674; *Téléc:* 819-326-5204
www.municipalite.lantier.qc.ca
Entité municipal: Municipality
Incorporation: 1er janvier 1948; *Area:* 43,57 km2
Comté ou district: Les Laurentides; *Population au 2011:* 828
Circonscription(s) électorale(s) provinciale(s): Bertrand
Circonscription(s) électorale(s) fédérale(s): Laurentides-Labelle
Prochaines élections: 5e novembre 2017
Richard Forget, Maire
Benoit Charbonneau, Directeur général

Larouche
#205, 610, rue Lévesque
Larouche, QC G0W 1Z0
Tél: 418-695-2201; *Téléc:* 418-693-2119
administration@villedelarouche.qc.ca
www.villedelarouche.qc.ca
Entité municipal: Municipality
Incorporation: 21 mars 1922; *Area:* 88 km2
Comté ou district: Le Fjord-du-Saguenay; *Population au 2011:* 1,277
Circonscription(s) électorale(s) provinciale(s): Lac-St-Jean
Circonscription(s) électorale(s) fédérale(s): Jonquière
Prochaines élections: 5e novembre 2017
Réjean Bédard, Maire
Martin Gagné, Directeur général

Latulipe-et-Gaboury
1B, rue Principale est
Latulipe-et-Gaboury, QC J0Z 2N0
Tél: 819-747-4281; *Téléc:* 819-747-2194
www.latulipeetgaboury.net
Entité municipal: United Township (Cantons)
Incorporation: 18 novembre 1924; *Area:* 298,38 km2
Comté ou district: Témiscamingue; *Population au 2011:* 304
Circonscription(s) électorale(s) provinciale(s): Rouyn-Noranda-Témiscamingue
Circonscription(s) électorale(s) fédérale(s): Abitibi-Témiscamingue
Prochaines élections: 5e novembre 2017
Michel Duval, Maire
Julie Gilbert, Directrice générale

Launay
843, rue des Pionniers
Launay, QC J0Y 1W0
Tél: 819-796-2545; *Téléc:* 819-796-2546
canton.launay@cableamos.com
www.launay.ca
Entité municipal: Township
Incorporation: 18 mai 1921; *Area:* 252,44 km2
Comté ou district: Abitibi; *Population au 2011:* 229
Circonscription(s) électorale(s) provinciale(s): Abitibi-Ouest
Circonscription(s) électorale(s) fédérale(s): Abitibi-Témiscamingue
Prochaines élections: 5e novembre 2017
Rémi Gilbert, Maire
Valérie Normand, Directrice générale

Les Laurentides
1255, ch des Lacs
Saint-Faustin-Lac-Carré, QC J0T 1J2
Tél: 819-425-5555; *Téléc:* 819-688-6590
adm@mrclaurentides.qc.ca
www.mrclaurentides.qc.ca
Entité municipal: Regional County Municipality
Incorporation: 1er janvier 1983
Population au 2011: 45,157
Note: 20 municipalités.
Denis Chalifoux, Préfet
Richard Daveluy, Directeur général

Laurier-Station
121, rue St-André
Laurier-Station, QC G0S 1N0
Tél: 418-728-3852; *Téléc:* 418-728-4801
info@ville.laurier-station.qc.ca
www.ville.laurier-station.qc.ca
Entité municipal: Village
Incorporation: 1er janvier 1951; *Area:* 12,43 km2
Comté ou district: Lotbinière; *Population au 2011:* 2,634
Circonscription(s) électorale(s) provinciale(s): Lotbinière-Frontenac
Circonscription(s) électorale(s) fédérale(s): Lévis-Lotbinière
Prochaines élections: 5e novembre 2017
Pierrette Trépanier, Mairesse
Catherine Fiset, Directrice générale

Laurierville
140, rue Grenier
Laurierville, QC G0S 1P0
Tél: 819-365-4646; *Téléc:* 819-365-4200
www.laurierville.net
Entité municipal: Municipality
Incorporation: 26 novembre 1997; *Area:* 110,62 km2
Comté ou district: L'Érable; *Population au 2011:* 1,454
Circonscription(s) électorale(s) provinciale(s): Arthabaska
Circonscription(s) électorale(s) fédérale(s): Mégantic-L'Érable
Prochaines élections: 5e novembre 2017
Marc Simoneau, Maire
Réjean Gingras, Directeur général

Laverlochère
CP 159
11, rue St-Isidore ouest
Laverlochère, QC J0Z 2P0
Tél: 819-765-5111; *Téléc:* 819-765-2564
laverlochere.net
Entité municipal: Municipality
Incorporation: 3 octobre 1912; *Area:* 107,01 km2
Comté ou district: Témiscamingue; *Population au 2011:* 1,022
Circonscription(s) électorale(s) provinciale(s): Rouyn-Noranda-Témiscamingue
Circonscription(s) électorale(s) fédérale(s): Abitibi-Témiscamingue
Prochaines élections: 5e novembre 2017
Daniel Barrette, Maire
Monique Rivest, Directrice générale

Lawrenceville
2100, rue Dandenault
Lawrenceville, QC J0E 1W0
Tél: 450-535-6398; *Téléc:* 450-535-6537
info@lawrenceville.ca
www.lawrenceville.ca
Entité municipal: Village
Incorporation: 27 avril 1905; *Area:* 17,40 km2
Comté ou district: Le Val-Saint-François; *Population au 2011:* 652
Circonscription(s) électorale(s) provinciale(s): Orford
Circonscription(s) électorale(s) fédérale(s): Shefford
Prochaines élections: 5e novembre 2017
Michel Carbonneau, Maire

François Paquette, Directeur général

Lebel-sur-Quévillon
CP 430
500, place Quévillon
Lebel-sur-Quévillon, QC J0Y 1X0
Tél: 819-755-4826; *Téléc:* 819-755-8124
ville@lebel-sur-quevillon.com
www.lebel-sur-quevillon.com
Entité municipal: Town
Incorporation: 6 août 1965; *Area:* 44,74 km2
Population au 2011: 2,159
Circonscription(s) électorale(s) provinciale(s): Ungava
Circonscription(s) électorale(s) fédérale(s):
Abitibi-Baie-James-Nunavik-Eeyou
Prochaines élections: 5e novembre 2017
Alain Poirier, Maire
Réal Lavigne, Greffier

Leclercville
1014, rue de l'Église
Leclercville, QC G0S 2K0
Tél: 819-292-2331; *Téléc:* 819-292-2639
mun.leclercville@videotron.ca
www.munleclercville.qc.ca
Entité municipal: Municipality
Incorporation: 26 janvier 2000; *Area:* 135,40 km2
Comté ou district: Lotbinière; *Population au 2011:* 477
Circonscription(s) électorale(s) provinciale(s):
Lotbinière-Frontenac
Circonscription(s) électorale(s) fédérale(s): Lévis-Lotbinière
Prochaines élections: 5e novembre 2017
Marcel Richard, Maire
Francine B. Demers, Directrice générale

Lefebvre
186, 10e rang
Lefebvre, QC J0H 2C0
Tél: 819-394-2782; *Téléc:* 819-394-2186
municipalite.lefebvre@xittel.ca
www.mun-lefebvre.ca
Entité municipal: Municipality
Incorporation: 10 octobre 1922; *Area:* 65,75 km2
Comté ou district: Drummond; *Population au 2011:* 867
Circonscription(s) électorale(s) provinciale(s): Johnson
Circonscription(s) électorale(s) fédérale(s): Drummond
Prochaines élections: 5e novembre 2017
Claude Bahl, Maire
Julie Yergeau, Directrice générale

Lejeune
CP 40
69, rue de la Grande-Coulée
Lejeune, QC G0L 1S0
Tél: 418-855-2428; *Téléc:* 418-855-2428
info@municipalitelejeune.ca
www.municipalitelejeune.com
Entité municipal: Municipality
Incorporation: 1er janvier 1964; *Area:* 269,40 km2
Comté ou district: Témiscouata; *Population au 2011:* 286
Circonscription(s) électorale(s) provinciale(s):
Rivière-du-Loup-Témiscouata
Circonscription(s) électorale(s) fédérale(s):
Rimouski-Neigette-Témiscouata-Les Basques
Prochaines élections: 5e novembre 2017
Mélanie Veilleux, Mairesse
Claudine Castonguay, Directrice générale

Lemieux
530, rue de l'Église
Lemieux, QC G0X 1S0
Tél: 819-283-2506; *Téléc:* 819-283-2029
info@municipalitelemieux.ca
www.municipalitelemieux.ca
Entité municipal: Municipality
Incorporation: 14 août 1922; *Area:* 74,79 km2
Comté ou district: Bécancour; *Population au 2011:* 304
Circonscription(s) électorale(s) provinciale(s): Nicolet-Bécancour
Circonscription(s) électorale(s) fédérale(s):
Bécancour-Nicolet-Saurel
Prochaines élections: 5e novembre 2017
Jean-Louis Bélisle, Maire
France Hénault, Directrice générale

Léry
1, rue de l'Hôtel-de-Ville
Léry, QC J6N 1E8
Tél: 450-692-6861; *Téléc:* 450-692-6881
villedelery@videotron.ca
www.lery.ca
Entité municipal: Town
Incorporation: 1er juin 1914; *Area:* 10,98 km2
Comté ou district: Roussillon; Communauté métropolitaine de Montréal; *Population au 2011:* 2,307
Circonscription(s) électorale(s) provinciale(s): Châteauguay
Circonscription(s) électorale(s) fédérale(s): Châteauguay-Lacolle
Prochaines élections: 5e novembre 2017
Walter Letham, Maire
Dale Stewart, Directeur général

Lingwick
72, rte 108
Lingwick, QC J0B 2Z0
Tél: 819-560-8422; *Téléc:* 819-877-3315
canton.lingwick@hsfqc.ca
www.cantondelingwick.com
Entité municipal: Township
Incorporation: 1er juillet 1855; *Area:* 242,83 km2
Comté ou district: Le Haut-Saint-François; *Population au 2011:* 399
Circonscription(s) électorale(s) provinciale(s): Mégantic
Circonscription(s) électorale(s) fédérale(s): Compton-Stanstead
Prochaines élections: 5e novembre 2017
Marcel Langlois, Maire
André Martel, Directeur général

Litchfield
CP 340
1362, rte 148
Campbell's Bay, QC J0X 1K0
Tél: 819-648-5511; *Téléc:* 819-648-5575
litchfield@mrcpontiac.qc.ca
www.litchfield-qc.ca
Entité municipal: Municipality
Incorporation: 1er juillet 1855; *Area:* 178,96 km2
Comté ou district: Pontiac; *Population au 2011:* 456
Circonscription(s) électorale(s) provinciale(s): Pontiac
Circonscription(s) électorale(s) fédérale(s): Pontiac
Prochaines élections: 5e novembre 2017
Colleen Larivière, Mairesse
Julie Bertrand, Directrice générale

Lochaber
326, rue Desaulnac
Thurso, QC J0X 3B0
Tél: 819-985-3291; *Téléc:* 819-985-3487
Entité municipal: Township
Incorporation: 1er juillet 1855; *Area:* 62,17 km2
Comté ou district: Papineau; *Population au 2011:* 409
Circonscription(s) électorale(s) provinciale(s): Papineau
Circonscription(s) électorale(s) fédérale(s): Argenteuil-La Petite-Nation
Prochaines élections: 5e novembre 2017
Alain Gamache, Maire
Marie-Agnès Lacoste, Directrice générale

Lochaber-Partie-Ouest
CP 3442
350, rue Victoria
Thurso, QC J0X 3B0
Tél: 819-985-1553; *Téléc:* 819-985-0790
mun.lochaberouest@mrcpapineau.com
www.lochaber-ouest.ca
Entité municipal: Township
Incorporation: 20 avril 1891; *Area:* 61,22 km2
Comté ou district: Papineau; *Population au 2011:* 646
Circonscription(s) électorale(s) provinciale(s): Papineau
Circonscription(s) électorale(s) fédérale(s): Argenteuil-La Petite-Nation
Prochaines élections: 5e novembre 2017
Jean-Pierre Girard, Maire
Ruth Neveu, Directrice générale

Longue-Pointe-de-Mingan
CP 68
878, ch du Roi
Longue-Pointe-de-Mingan, QC G0G 1V0
Tél: 418-949-2053; *Téléc:* 418-949-2166
munlpm@xplornet.com
longuepointedemingan.ca
Entité municipal: Municipality
Incorporation: 1er janvier 1966; *Area:* 417,60 km2
Comté ou district: Minganie; *Population au 2011:* 479
Circonscription(s) électorale(s) provinciale(s): Duplessis
Circonscription(s) électorale(s) fédérale(s): Manicouagan
Prochaines élections: 5e novembre 2017
Jean-Luc Burgess, Maire
Célyne B.-Loiselle, Directrice générale

Longue-Rive
3, rue de l'Église
Longue-Rive, QC G0T 1Z0
Tél: 418-231-2344; *Téléc:* 418-231-2577
munlonguerive@bellnet.ca
www.municipalite-longue-rive.com
Entité municipal: Municipality
Incorporation: 28 mai 1997; *Area:* 295,35 km2
Comté ou district: La Haute-Côte-Nord; *Population au 2011:* 1,113
Circonscription(s) électorale(s) provinciale(s): René-Lévesque
Circonscription(s) électorale(s) fédérale(s): Manicouagan
Prochaines élections: 5e novembre 2017
Donald Perron, Maire
Hélène Boulianne, Directrice générale

Lorraine
33, boul De Gaulle
Lorraine, QC J6Z 3W9
Tél: 450-621-8550; *Téléc:* 450-621-4763
communication@ville.lorraine.qc.ca
www.ville.lorraine.qc.ca
Entité municipal: Town
Incorporation: 4e février 1960; *Area:* 5,96 km2
Comté ou district: Thérèse-De Blainville; Communauté métropolitaine de Montréal; *Population au 2011:* 9,479
Circonscription(s) électorale(s) provinciale(s): Blainville
Circonscription(s) électorale(s) fédérale(s): Thérèse-De Blainville
Prochaines élections: 5e novembre 2017
Ramez Ayoub, Maire, 450-965-8717
Sylvie Trahan, Greffière, 450-621-8550

Lorrainville
CP 218
2, rue St-Jean-Baptiste est
Lorrainville, QC J0Z 2R0
Tél: 819-625-2167; *Téléc:* 819-625-2380
lorrainville@mrctemiscamingue.qc.ca
www.lorrainville.ca
Entité municipal: Municipality
Incorporation: 16 février 1994; *Area:* 85,12 km2
Comté ou district: Témiscamingue; *Population au 2011:* 1,272
Circonscription(s) électorale(s) provinciale(s):
Rouyn-Noranda-Témiscamingue
Circonscription(s) électorale(s) fédérale(s):
Abitibi-Témiscamingue
Prochaines élections: 5e novembre 2017
Simon Gélinas, Maire
Francyne Bleau, Directrice générale

Lotbinière
7440, rue Marie-Victorin
Lotbinière, QC G0S 1S0
Tél: 418-796-2103; *Téléc:* 418-796-2198
info@municipalite.lotbiniere.qc.ca
www.municipalite.lotbiniere.qc.ca
Entité municipal: Municipality
Incorporation: 1er janvier 1979; *Area:* 78,47 km2
Comté ou district: Lotbinière; *Population au 2011:* 887
Circonscription(s) électorale(s) provinciale(s):
Lotbinière-Frontenac
Circonscription(s) électorale(s) fédérale(s): Lévis-Lotbinière
Prochaines élections: 5e novembre 2017
Maurice Sénécal, Maire
Valérie Le Jeune, Directrice générale

Lotbinière
6375, rue Garneau
Sainte-Croix, QC G0S 2H0
Tél: 418-926-3407; *Téléc:* 418-926-3409
info@mrclotbiniere.org
www.mrclotbiniere.org
Entité municipal: Regional County Municipality
Incorporation: 1 janvier 1982
Population au 2011: 29,617
Note: 18 municipalités.
Maurice Sénécal, Préfet
Daniel Patry, Directeur général

Louiseville
105, av St-Laurent
Louiseville, QC J5V 1J6
Tél: 819-228-9437; *Téléc:* 819-228-2263
hoteldeville@ville.louiseville.qc.ca
www.ville.louiseville.qc.ca
Entité municipal: Town
Incorporation: 31 décembre 1988; *Area:* 62,56 km2
Comté ou district: Maskinongé; *Population au 2011:* 7,517
Circonscription(s) électorale(s) provinciale(s): Maskinongé
Circonscription(s) électorale(s) fédérale(s): Berthier-Maskinongé
Prochaines élections: 5e novembre 2017
Yvon Deshaies, Maire

Maude-Andrée Pelletier, Greffière

Low
4A, ch d'Amour
Low, QC J0X 2C0
Tél: 819-422-3528; *Téléc:* 819-422-3796
info@lowquebec.ca
www.lowquebec.ca
Entité municipal: Township
Incorporation: 1er janvier 1858; *Area:* 259,95 km2
Comté ou district: La Vallée-de-la-Gatineau; *Population au 2011:* 920
Circonscription(s) électorale(s) provinciale(s): Gatineau
Circonscription(s) électorale(s) fédérale(s): Pontiac
Prochaines élections: 5e novembre 2017
Morris O'Connor, Maire
Franceska Gnarowski, Directrice générale

Lyster
2375, rue Bécancour
Lyster, QC G0S 1V0
Tél: 819-389-5787; *Téléc:* 819-389-5981
info@municipalite.lyster.qc.ca
www.municipalite.lyster.qc.ca
Entité municipal: Municipality
Incorporation: 18 septembre 1976; *Area:* 162,35 km2
Comté ou district: L'Érable; *Population au 2011:* 1,628
Circonscription(s) électorale(s) provinciale(s): Arthabaska
Circonscription(s) électorale(s) fédérale(s): Mégantic-L'Érable
Prochaines élections: 5e novembre 2017
Sylvain Labrecque, Maire
Suzie Côté, Directrice générale

Macamic
70, rue Principale
Macamic, QC J0Z 2S0
Tél: 819-782-4604; *Téléc:* 819-782-4283
macamic@mrcao.qc.ca
www.villemacamic.qc.ca
Entité municipal: Town
Incorporation: 6 mars 2002; *Area:* 191,95 km2
Comté ou district: Abitibi-Ouest; *Population au 2011:* 2,734
Circonscription(s) électorale(s) provinciale(s): Abitibi-Ouest
Circonscription(s) électorale(s) fédérale(s): Abitibi-Témiscamingue
Prochaines élections: 5e novembre 2017
Claude Nelson Morin, Maire
Denis Bédard, Directeur général

La Macaza
53, rue des Pionniers
La Macaza, QC J0T 1R0
Tél: 819-275-2077; *Téléc:* 819-275-3429
www.munilamacaza.ca
Entité municipal: Municipality
Incorporation: 1er janvier 2006; *Area:* 162.78 km2
Comté ou district: Antoine-Labelle; *Population au 2011:* 1,053
Circonscription(s) électorale(s) provinciale(s): Labelle
Circonscription(s) électorale(s) fédérale(s): Laurentides-Labelle
Prochaines élections: 5e novembre 2017
Céline Beauregard, Mairesse
Jacques Taillefer, Directeur général

Maddington
86, rte 261 nord
Maddington, QC G0Z 1C0
Tél: 819-367-2577; *Téléc:* 819-367-3137
info@maddington.ca
www.maddington.ca
Entité municipal: Township
Incorporation: 11 janvier 1902; *Area:* 23,38 km2
Comté ou district: Arthabaska; *Population au 2011:* 443
Circonscription(s) électorale(s) provinciale(s): Nicolet-Bécancour
Circonscription(s) électorale(s) fédérale(s): Richmond-Arthabaska
Prochaines élections: 5e novembre 2017
Ghislain Brûlé, Maire
Tammy Voyer, Directrice générale

Malartic
CP 3090
901, rue Royale
Malartic, QC J0Y 1Z0
Tél: 819-757-3611; *Téléc:* 819-757-3084
info@ville.malartic.qc.ca
www.ville.malartic.qc.ca
Entité municipal: Town
Incorporation: 28 avril 1939; *Area:* 159,31 km2
Comté ou district: La Vallée-de-l'Or; *Population au 2011:* 3,449
Circonscription(s) électorale(s) provinciale(s): Abitibi-Est
Circonscription(s) électorale(s) fédérale(s): Abitibi-Baie-James-Nunavik-Eeyou
Prochaines élections: 5e novembre 2017
Martin Ferron, Maire
Alain Halley, Directeur général

La Malbaie
515, boul de Comporté
La Malbaie, QC G5A 1L9
Tél: 418-665-3747; *Téléc:* 418-665-4935
dg@ville.lamalbaie.qc.ca
www.ville.lamalbaie.qc.ca
Entité municipal: Town
Incorporation: 1er décembre 1999; *Area:* 470,57 km2
Comté ou district: Charlevoix-Est; *Population au 2011:* 8,862
Circonscription(s) électorale(s) provinciale(s): Charlevoix-Côte-de-Beaupré
Circonscription(s) électorale(s) fédérale(s): Beauport-Côte-de-Beaupré-Ile d'Orléans-Charlevoix
Prochaines élections: 5e novembre 2017
Michel Couturier, Maire
Caroline Tremblay, Greffière

Mandeville
162, rue Desjardins
Mandeville, QC J0K 1L0
Tél: 450-835-2055; *Téléc:* 450-835-7795
mandeville@intermonde.net
www.mandeville.ca
Entité municipal: Municipality
Incorporation: 20 avril 1904; *Area:* 330,85 km2
Comté ou district: D'Autray; *Population au 2011:* 2,043
Circonscription(s) électorale(s) provinciale(s): Berthier
Circonscription(s) électorale(s) fédérale(s): Berthier-Maskinongé
Prochaines élections: 5e novembre 2017
Francine Bergeron, Mairesse
Hélène Plourde, Directrice générale

Manicouagan
768, rue Bossé
Baie-Comeau, QC G5C 1L6
Tél: 418-589-9594; *Téléc:* 418-589-6383
info@mrcmanicouagan.qc.ca
www.mrcmanicouagan.qc.ca
Entité municipal: Regional County Municipality
Incorporation: 1er avril 1981
Population au 2011: 32,012
Note: 8 municipalités & 1 autre territoire.
Claude Martel, Préfet
Patricia Huet, Directrice générale

Maniwaki
186, rue Principale sud
Maniwaki, QC J9E 1Z9
Tél: 819-449-2800; *Téléc:* 819-449-7078
maniwaki@ville.maniwaki.qc.ca
www.ville.maniwaki.qc.ca
Entité municipal: Town
Incorporation: 15 mars 1904; *Area:* 5,60 km2
Comté ou district: La Vallée-de-la-Gatineau; *Population au 2011:* 3,930
Circonscription(s) électorale(s) provinciale(s): Gatineau
Circonscription(s) électorale(s) fédérale(s): Pontiac
Prochaines élections: 5e novembre 2017
Robert Coulombe, Maire
John-David McFaul, Greffier

Manseau
200, rue Roux
Manseau, QC G0X 1V0
Tél: 819-356-2450; *Téléc:* 819-356-2721
www.manseau.ca
Entité municipal: Municipality
Incorporation: 31 décembre 1997; *Area:* 102,5 km2
Comté ou district: Bécancour; *Population au 2011:* 843
Circonscription(s) électorale(s) provinciale(s): Nicolet-Bécancour
Circonscription(s) électorale(s) fédérale(s): Bécancour-Nicolet-Saurel
Prochaines élections: 5e novembre 2017
Guy St-Pierre, Maire
Nadine Watters, Directrice générale

Mansfield-et-Pontefract
CP 880
300, rue Principale
Mansfield-et-Pontefract, QC J0X 1R0
Tél: 819-683-2944; *Téléc:* 819-683-3590
mansfield@mrcpontiac.qc.ca
www.mansfield-pontefract.com
Entité municipal: Municipality
Incorporation: 1er janvier 1868; *Area:* 420,79 km2
Comté ou district: Pontiac; *Population au 2011:* 2,204
Circonscription(s) électorale(s) provinciale(s): Pontiac
Circonscription(s) électorale(s) fédérale(s): Pontiac
Prochaines élections: 5e novembre 2017
Kathleen Bélec, Mairesse
Éric Rochon, Directeur général

Marguerite-D'Youville
609, rte Marie-Victorin
Verchères, QC J0L 2R0
Tél: 450-583-3301; *Téléc:* 450-583-3592
infomrc@margueritedyouville.ca
www.margueritedyouville.ca
Entité municipal: Regional County Municipality
Incorporation: 1er janvier 1982
Population au 2011: 74,416
Note: 6 municipalités.
Suzanne Dansereau, Préfète
Sylvain Berthiaume, Directeur général

Maria
545, boul Perron
Maria, QC G0C 1Y0
Tél: 418-759-3883; *Téléc:* 418-759-3059
munmaria@globetrotter.net
www.mariaquebec.com
Entité municipal: Municipality
Incorporation: 1er juillet 1855; *Area:* 96,34 km2
Comté ou district: Avignon; *Population au 2011:* 2,536
Circonscription(s) électorale(s) provinciale(s): Bonaventure
Circonscription(s) électorale(s) fédérale(s): Avignon-La Mitis-Matane-Matapédia
Prochaines élections: 5e novembre 2017
Christian Leblanc, Maire
Gilbert Leblanc, Directeur général

Maria-Chapdelaine
173, boul St-Michel
Dolbeau-Mistassini, QC G8L 4N9
Tél: 418-276-2131; *Téléc:* 418-276-7043
portail@mrcmaria.qc.ca
www.mrcdemaria-chapdelaine.ca
Other Information: Sans frais: 1-888-776-2131
Entité municipal: Regional County Municipality
Incorporation: 1er janvier 1983
Population au 2011: 25,279
Note: 12 municipalités & 2 autres territoires.
Jean-Pierre Boivin, Préfet
Christian Bouchard, Directeur général

Maricourt
1195, 3e rang nord
Maricourt, QC J0E 1Y0
Tél: 450-532-2243; *Téléc:* 450-532-2246
munmari@cooptel.qc.ca
www.maricourt.ca
Entité municipal: Municipality
Incorporation: 1er janvier 1864; *Area:* 62,03 km2
Comté ou district: Le Val-Saint-François; *Population au 2011:* 497
Circonscription(s) électorale(s) provinciale(s): Richmond
Circonscription(s) électorale(s) fédérale(s): Shefford
Prochaines élections: 5e novembre 2017
Robert Ledoux, Maire
Valérie Bombardier, Directrice générale

Marsoui
CP 130
8, rte Principale est
Marsoui, QC G0E 1S0
Tél: 418-288-5552; *Téléc:* 418-288-5104
municipalite.marsoui@globetrotter.net
www.marsoui.com
Entité municipal: Village
Incorporation: 1er janvier 1950; *Area:* 182,95 km2
Comté ou district: La Haute-Gaspésie; *Population au 2011:* 309
Circonscription(s) électorale(s) provinciale(s): Gaspé
Circonscription(s) électorale(s) fédérale(s): Gaspésie-Les Iles-de-la-Madeleine
Prochaines élections: 5e novembre 2017
Dario Jean, Maire
Nancy Leclerc, Directrice générale

Marston
175, rte 263 sud
Marston, QC G0Y 1G0
Tél: 819-583-0435; *Téléc:* 819-583-6604
marston@axion.ca
www.munmarston.qc.ca
Entité municipal: Township
Incorporation: 1er janvier 1874; *Area:* 71,77 km2
Comté ou district: Le Granit; *Population au 2011:* 662
Circonscription(s) électorale(s) provinciale(s): Mégantic

Circonscription(s) électorale(s) fédérale(s): Mégantic-L'Érable
Prochaines élections: 5e novembre 2017
Paul Henri Guillemette, Maire
Francine Veilleux, Directrice générale

Martinville
233, rue Principale est
Martinville, QC J0B 2A0
Tél: 819-835-5390; *Téléc:* 819-835-0171
martinville@axion.ca
Entité municipal: Municipality
Incorporation: 21 décembre 1895; *Area:* 48,64 km2
Comté ou district: Coaticook; *Population au 2011:* 469
Circonscription(s) électorale(s) provinciale(s): St-François
Circonscription(s) électorale(s) fédérale(s): Compton-Stanstead
Prochaines élections: 5e novembre 2017
Réjean Masson, Maire
France Veilleux, Directrice générale

La Martre
9, av du Phare
La Martre, QC G0E 2H0
Tél: 418-288-5605; *Téléc:* 418-288-5144
lamartre@globetrotter.net
Entité municipal: Municipality
Incorporation: 18 décembre 1923; *Area:* 185,69 km2
Comté ou district: La Haute-Gaspésie; *Population au 2011:* 245
Circonscription(s) électorale(s) provinciale(s): Gaspé
Circonscription(s) électorale(s) fédérale(s): Gaspésie-Les Îles-de-la-Madeleine
Prochaines élections: 5e novembre 2017
Michel Laperle, Maire
France Bergeron, Directrice générale

Maskinongé
154, boul Ouest, rte 138
Maskinongé, QC J0K 1N0
Tél: 819-227-2243; *Téléc:* 819-227-2097
www.mun-maskinonge.ca
Entité municipal: Municipality
Incorporation: 25 avril 2001; *Area:* 75,98 km2
Comté ou district: Maskinongé; *Population au 2011:* 2,253
Circonscription(s) électorale(s) provinciale(s): Maskinongé
Circonscription(s) électorale(s) fédérale(s): Berthier-Maskinongé
Prochaines élections: 5e novembre 2017
Roger Michaud, Maire
France Gervais, Directrice générale

Maskinongé
651, boul St-Laurent est
Louiseville, QC J5V 1J1
Tél: 819-228-9461; *Téléc:* 819-228-2193
mrcinfo@mrc-maskinonge.qc.ca
www.mrc-maskinonge.qc.ca
Entité municipal: Regional County Municipality
Incorporation: 1er janvier 1982
Population au 2011: 36,286
Note: 17 municipalités.
Robert Lalonde, Préfet
Janyse L. Pichette, Directrice générale

Les Maskoutains
805, av du Palais
Saint-Hyacinthe, QC J2S 5C6
Tél: 450-774-3141; *Téléc:* 450-774-7161
admin@mrcmaskoutains.qc.ca
www.mrcmaskoutains.qc.ca
Entité municipal: Regional County Municipality
Incorporation: 1er janvier 1982
Population au 2011: 84,248
Note: 17 municipalités.
Francine Morin, Préfète
Gabriel Michaud, Directeur général

Massueville
CP 90
881, rue Royale
Massueville, QC J0G 1K0
Tél: 450-788-2957; *Téléc:* 450-788-2050
massueville@pierredesaurel.com
www.massueville.net
Entité municipal: Village
Incorporation: 25 mars 1903; *Area:* 1,29 km2
Comté ou district: Pierre-De Saurel; *Population au 2011:* 516
Circonscription(s) électorale(s) provinciale(s): Richelieu
Circonscription(s) électorale(s) fédérale(s): Bécancour-Nicolet-Saurel
Prochaines élections: 5e novembre 2017
Denis Marion, Maire
France Saint-Pierre, Directrice générale

Matagami
CP 160
195, boul Matagami
Matagami, QC J0Y 2A0
Tél: 819-739-2541; *Téléc:* 819-739-4278
matagami@matagami.com
www.matagami.com
Entité municipal: Village
Incorporation: 1er avril 1963; *Area:* 64,75 km2
Population au 2011: 1,526
Circonscription(s) électorale(s) provinciale(s): Ungava
Circonscription(s) électorale(s) fédérale(s): Abitibi-Baie-James-Nunavik-Eeyou
Prochaines élections: 5e novembre 2017
René Dubé, Maire
Pierre Deslauriers, Greffier, trésorier et directeur général

La Matanie
158, rue Soucy, 2ième étage
Matane, QC G4W 2E3
Tél: 418-562-6734; *Téléc:* 418-562-7265
mrcdelamatanie@lamatanie.ca
www.lamatanie.ca
Entité municipal: Regional County Municipality
Incorporation: 1er janvier 1982
Population au 2011: 21,786
Note: 11 municipalités & 1 autre territoire.
Pierre Thibodeau, Préfet
Line Ross, Directrice générale

Matapédia
CP 207
8, rue Macdonell
Matapédia, QC G0J 1V0
Tél: 418-865-2917; *Téléc:* 418-865-2828
munmata@globetrotter.net
www.matapedialesplateaux.com
Entité municipal: Municipality
Incorporation: 4e novembre 1905; *Area:* 70,75 km2
Comté ou district: Avignon; *Population au 2011:* 664
Circonscription(s) électorale(s) provinciale(s): Bonaventure
Circonscription(s) électorale(s) fédérale(s): Avignon-La Mitis-Matane-Matapédia
Prochaines élections: 5e novembre 2017
Luc Lagacé, Maire
Carole Bélanger, Directrice générale

La Matapédia
#501, 123, rue Desbiens
Amqui, QC G5J 3P9
Tél: 418-629-2053; *Téléc:* 418-629-3195
administration@mrcmatapedia.qc.ca
www.mrcmatapedia.qc.ca
Entité municipal: Regional County Municipality
Incorporation: 1er janvier 1982
Population au 2011: 18,573
Note: 18 municipalités & 7 autres territoires.
Chantale Lavoie, Préfète
Mario Lavoie, Directeur général

Matawinie
3184, 1re Av
Rawdon, QC J0K 1S0
Tél: 450-834-5441; *Téléc:* 450-834-6560
administration@matawinie.org
www.mrcmatawinie.org
Other Information: Sans frais: 1-800-264-5441
Entité municipal: Regional County Municipality
Incorporation: 1er janvier 1982
Population au 2011: 49,516
Note: 15 municipalités & 12 autres territoires.
Gaétan Morin, Préfet
Lyne Arbour, Directrice générale

Mayo
20, ch McAlendin
Gatineau, QC J8L 4J7
Tél: 819-986-3199; *Téléc:* 819-986-8881
mun.mayo@mrcpapineau.com
www.mayo.ca
Entité municipal: Municipality
Incorporation: 1er août 1864; *Area:* 72,67 km2
Comté ou district: Papineau; *Population au 2011:* 572
Circonscription(s) électorale(s) provinciale(s): Papineau
Circonscription(s) électorale(s) fédérale(s): Argenteuil-La Petite-Nation
Prochaines élections: 5e novembre 2017
Normand Vachon, Maire
Martin Cousineau, Directeur général

McMasterville
255, boul Constable
McMasterville, QC J3G 6N9
Tél: 450-467-3580; *Téléc:* 450-467-2493
hoteldeville@municipalitemcmasterville.ca
www.mcmasterville.ca
Entité municipal: Municipality
Incorporation: 31 juillet 1917; *Area:* 3,00 km2
Comté ou district: La Vallée-du-Richelieu; Communauté métropolitaine de Montréal; *Population au 2011:* 5,615
Circonscription(s) électorale(s) provinciale(s): Borduas
Circonscription(s) électorale(s) fédérale(s): Beloeil-Chambly
Prochaines élections: 5e novembre 2017
Gilles Plante, Maire
Lyne Savaria, Directrice générale

Les Méchins
108, rte des Fonds
Les Méchins, QC G0J 1T0
Tél: 418-729-3952; *Téléc:* 418-729-3585
lesmechins@mrcdematane.qc.ca
www.lesmechins.com
Entité municipal: Municipality
Incorporation: 27 novembre 1982; *Area:* 452 km2
Comté ou district: La Matanie; *Population au 2011:* 1,107
Circonscription(s) électorale(s) provinciale(s): Matane-Matapédia
Circonscription(s) électorale(s) fédérale(s): Avignon-La Mitis-Matane-Matapédia
Prochaines élections: 5e novembre 2017
Alain Dugas, Maire
Lyne Fortin, Directrice générale

Mékinac
560, rue Notre-Dame
Saint-Tite, QC G0X 3H0
Tél: 418-365-5151; *Téléc:* 418-365-7377
mrcmekinac@mrcmekinac.com
www.regionmekinac.com
Entité municipal: Regional County Municipality
Incorporation: 1 janvier 1982
Population au 2011: 12,924
Note: 10 municipalités & 4 autres territoires.
Alain Vallée, Préfet
Claude Beaulieu, Directeur général

Melbourne
1257, rte 243
Melbourne, QC J0B 2B0
Tél: 819-826-3555; *Téléc:* 819-826-3981
melcan@qc.aibn.com
www.melbournecanton.ca
Entité municipal: Township
Incorporation: 1er juillet 1855; *Area:* 170,29 km2
Comté ou district: Le Val-Saint-François; *Population au 2011:* 1,004
Circonscription(s) électorale(s) provinciale(s): Richmond
Circonscription(s) électorale(s) fédérale(s): Richmond-Arthabaska
Prochaines élections: 5e novembre 2017
James Johnston, Maire
Cindy Jones, Directrice générale

Memphrémagog
#200, 455, rue MacDonald
Magog, QC J1X 1M2
Tél: 819-843-9292; *Téléc:* 819-843-7295
info@mrcmemphremagog.com
www.mrcmemphremagog.com
Entité municipal: Regional County Municipality
Incorporation: 1er janvier 1982
Population au 2011: 48,551
Note: 17 municipalités.
Jacques Demers, Préfet
Guy Jauron, Directeur général

Messines
70, rue Principale
Messines, QC J0X 2J0
Tél: 819-465-2323; *Téléc:* 819-465-2943
info@messines.ca
www.messines.ca
Entité municipal: Municipality
Incorporation: 19 août 1921; *Area:* 108,46 km2
Comté ou district: La Vallée-de-la-Gatineau; *Population au 2011:* 1,608
Circonscription(s) électorale(s) provinciale(s): Gatineau
Circonscription(s) électorale(s) fédérale(s): Pontiac
Prochaines élections: 5e novembre 2017
Ronald Cross, Maire
Jim Smith, Directeur général

Métabetchouan—Lac-à-la-Croix
87, rue St-André
Métabetchouan—Lac-à-la-Croix, QC G8G 1A1
Tél: 418-349-2060; *Téléc:* 418-349-2395
courrier@ville.metabetchouan.qc.ca
www.ville.metabetchouan.qc.ca
Entité municipal: Town
Incorporation: 6 janvier 1999; *Area:* 185,86 km2
Comté ou district: Lac-Saint-Jean-Est; *Population au 2011:* 4,097
Circonscription(s) électorale(s) provinciale(s): Lac-St-Jean
Circonscription(s) électorale(s) fédérale(s): Lac-St-Jean
Prochaines élections: 5e novembre 2017
Lawrence Potvin, Maire
Mario Bouchard, Greffier

Métis-sur-Mer
138, rue Principale
Métis-sur-Mer, QC G0J 1S0
Tél: 418-936-3255; *Téléc:* 418-936-3117
metissurmer@mitis.qc.ca
www.ville.metis-sur-mer.qc.ca
Entité municipal: Village
Incorporation: 4 juillet 2002; *Area:* 48,01 km2
Comté ou district: La Mitis; *Population au 2011:* 644
Circonscription(s) électorale(s) provinciale(s): Matane-Matapédia
Circonscription(s) électorale(s) fédérale(s): Avignon-La Mitis-Matane-Matapédia
Prochaines élections: 5e novembre 2017
Jean-Pierre Pelletier, Maire
Stéphane Marcheterre, Greffier

Milan
CP 54
403, rang Ste-Marie
Milan, QC G0Y 1E0
Tél: 819-657-4527; *Téléc:* 819-657-2987
munmilan@axion.ca
www.munmilan.qc.ca
Entité municipal: Municipality
Incorporation: 1er juin 1948; *Area:* 130,06 km2
Comté ou district: Le Granit; *Population au 2011:* 270
Circonscription(s) électorale(s) provinciale(s): Mégantic
Circonscription(s) électorale(s) fédérale(s): Mégantic-L'Érable
Prochaines élections: 5e novembre 2017
Yves d'Anjou, Maire
Noëlla Bergeron, Directrice générale

Mille-Isles
1262, ch de Mille-Isles
Mille-Isles, QC J0R 1A0
Tél: 450-438-2958; *Téléc:* 450-438-6157
www.mille-isles.ca
Entité municipal: Municipality
Incorporation: 1er juillet 1855; *Area:* 59,98 km2
Comté ou district: Argenteuil; *Population au 2011:* 1,629
Circonscription(s) électorale(s) provinciale(s): Argenteuil
Circonscription(s) électorale(s) fédérale(s): Argenteuil-La Petite-Nation
Prochaines élections: 5e novembre 2017
Michel Boyer, Maire
Johanne Ringuette, Directrice générale

La Minerve
6, rue Mailloux
La Minerve, QC J0T 1S0
Tél: 819-274-2364; *Téléc:* 819-274-2031
bureau@municipalite.laminerve.qc.ca
www.municipalite.laminerve.qc.ca
Entité municipal: Municipality
Incorporation: 30 décembre 1892; *Area:* 297,78 km2
Comté ou district: Les Laurentides; *Population au 2011:* 1,234
Circonscription(s) électorale(s) provinciale(s): Labelle
Circonscription(s) électorale(s) fédérale(s): Laurentides-Labelle
Prochaines élections: 5e novembre 2017
Jean Pierre Monette, Maire
Pierre Gagnon, Directeur général

Minganie
1303, rue de la Digue
Havre-Saint-Pierre, QC G0G 1P0
Tél: 418-538-2732; *Téléc:* 418-538-3711
info@mrc.minganie.org
www.mrc.minganie.org
Entité municipal: Regional County Municipality
Incorporation: 1er janvier 1982
Population au 2011: 6,582
Note: 8 municipalités & 1 autre territoire.
Luc Noël, Préfet
Nathalie de Grandpré, Directrice générale

Mistissini
187, ch Main
Mistissini, QC G0W 1C0
Tél: 418-923-3461; *Téléc:* 418-923-3115
info@mistissini.ca
www.mistissini.ca
Entité municipal: Villages Cris
Incorporation: 28 juin 1978; *Area:* 841,10 km2
Circonscription(s) électorale(s) provinciale(s): Ungava
Circonscription(s) électorale(s) fédérale(s): Abitibi-Baie-James-Nunavik-Eeyou
Prochaines élections: 1e juillet 2018
Richard Shecapio, Maire
John Longchap, Directeur général

La Mitis
300, av du Sanatorium
Mont-Joli, QC G5H 1V7
Tél: 418-775-8445; *Téléc:* 418-775-9303
mrcmitis@mitis.qc.ca
www.lamitis.ca
Entité municipal: Regional County Municipality
Incorporation: 1er janvier 1982
Population au 2011: 18,942
Note: 16 municipalités & 2 autres territoires.
Noël Lambert, Préfet
Marcel Moreau, Directeur général

Moffet
CP 89
14D, rue Principale
Moffet, QC J0Z 2W0
Tél: 819-747-6116; *Téléc:* 819-747-6117
www.moffet.ca
Entité municipal: Municipality
Incorporation: 1er janvier 1953; *Area:* 431,46 km2
Comté ou district: Témiscamingue; *Population au 2011:* 196
Circonscription(s) électorale(s) provinciale(s): Rouyn-Noranda-Témiscamingue
Circonscription(s) électorale(s) fédérale(s): Abitibi-Témiscamingue
Prochaines élections: 5e novembre 2017
Eric Dubuque, Maire
Linda Roy, Directrice générale

Montcalm
10, rue de l'Hôtel-de-Ville
Montcalm, QC J0T 2V0
Tél: 819-681-3383
www.municipalite.montcalm.qc.ca
Entité municipal: Municipality
Incorporation: 6 mars 1907; *Area:* 119,65 km2
Comté ou district: Les Laurentides; *Population au 2011:* 619
Circonscription(s) électorale(s) provinciale(s): Argenteuil
Circonscription(s) électorale(s) fédérale(s): Laurentides-Labelle
Prochaines élections: 5e novembre 2017
Steven Larose, Maire
Hugues Jacob, Directeur général

Montcalm
1540, rue Albert
Sainte-Julienne, QC J0K 2T0
Tél: 450-831-2182; *Téléc:* 450-831-2647
info@mrcmontcalm.com
www.mrcmontcalm.com
Entité municipal: Regional County Municipality
Incorporation: 1er janvier 1982
Population au 2011: 48,378
Note: 10 municipalités.
Danielle Henri Allard, Préfet
Marc-André Vaillancourt, Directeur général

Mont-Carmel
22, rue de la Fabrique
Mont-Carmel, QC G0L 1W0
Tél: 418-498-2050; *Téléc:* 418-489-2522
direction@mont-carmel.ca
www.mont-carmel.ca
Entité municipal: Municipality
Incorporation: 1er juillet 1855; *Area:* 435,29 km2
Comté ou district: Kamouraska; *Population au 2011:* 1,136
Circonscription(s) électorale(s) provinciale(s): Côte-du-Sud
Circonscription(s) électorale(s) fédérale(s): Montmagny-L'Islet-Kamouraska-Rivière-du-Loup
Prochaines élections: 5e novembre 2017
Denis Lévesque, Maire
France Boucher, Directrice générale

Montcerf-Lytton
18, rue Principale nord
Montcerf-Lytton, QC J0W 1N0
Tél: 819-449-4578; *Téléc:* 819-449-7310
mun.montcerf@ireseau.com
www.montcerf-lytton.com
Entité municipal: Municipality
Incorporation: 19 septembre 2001; *Area:* 358,34 km2
Comté ou district: La Vallée-de-la-Gatineau; *Population au 2011:* 687
Circonscription(s) électorale(s) provinciale(s): Gatineau
Circonscription(s) électorale(s) fédérale(s): Pontiac
Prochaines élections: 5e novembre 2017
Alain Fortin, Maire
Liliane Crytes, Directrice générale

Montebello
550, rue Notre-Dame
Montebello, QC J0V 1L0
Tél: 819-423-5123; *Téléc:* 819-423-5703
reception.montebello@mrcpapineau.com
www.montebello.ca
Entité municipal: Municipality
Incorporation: 29 août 1878; *Area:* 7,85 km2
Comté ou district: Papineau; *Population au 2011:* 978
Circonscription(s) électorale(s) provinciale(s): Papineau
Circonscription(s) électorale(s) fédérale(s): Argenteuil-La Petite Nation
Prochaines élections: 5e novembre 2017
Luc Ménard, Maire
Charles-Guy Beauchamp, Directeur général

Mont-Joli
40, av de l'Hôtel-de-Ville
Mont-Joli, QC G5H 1W8
Tél: 418-775-7285; *Téléc:* 418-775-6320
mont-joli@ville.mont-joli.qc.ca
www.ville.mont-joli.qc.ca
Entité municipal: Town
Incorporation: 13 juin 2001; *Area:* 22,64 km2
Comté ou district: La Mitis; *Population au 2011:* 6,665
Circonscription(s) électorale(s) provinciale(s): Matane-Matapédia
Circonscription(s) électorale(s) fédérale(s): Avignon-La Mitis-Matane-Matapédia
Prochaines élections: 5e novembre 2017
Danielle Doyer, Mairesse
Joël Harrisson, Greffier

Montmagny
#300, 6, rue St-Jean-Baptiste est
Montmagny, QC G5V 1N5
Tél: 418-248-5985; *Téléc:* 418-248-4624
mrc@montmagny.com
www.montmagny.com
Entité municipal: Regional County Municipality
Incorporation: 1er janvier 1982
Population au 2011: 22,877
Note: 14 municipalités.
Jean-Guy Desrosiers, Préfet
Nancy Labrecque, Directrice générale

Montpellier
4, rue du Bosquet
Montpellier, QC J0V 1M0
Tél: 819-428-3663; *Téléc:* 819-428-1221
info.montpellier@mrcpapineau.com
www.montpellier.ca
Entité municipal: Municipality
Incorporation: 11 octobre 1920; *Area:* 249,16 km2
Comté ou district: Papineau; *Population au 2011:* 986
Circonscription(s) électorale(s) provinciale(s): Papineau
Circonscription(s) électorale(s) fédérale(s): Argenteuil-La Petite-Nation
Prochaines élections: 5e novembre 2017
Stéphane Séguin, Maire
Manon Lanthier, Directrice générale

Montréal-Est
11370, rue Notre-Dame, 5e étage
Montréal-Est, QC H1B 2W6
Tél: 514-905-2000
communications@montreal-est.ca
ville.montreal-est.qc.ca
Entité municipal: Town
Incorporation: 1er janvier 2006; *Area:* 12,45 km2
Comté ou district: Communauté métropolitaine de Montréal; *Population au 2011:* 3,728
Circonscription(s) électorale(s) provinciale(s): Pointe-aux-Trembles
Circonscription(s) électorale(s) fédérale(s): La Pointe-de-l'Île
Prochaines élections: 5e novembre 2017
Robert Coutu, Maire

Roch Sergerie, Greffier

Montréal-Ouest
50, av Westminster sud
Montréal-Ouest, QC H4X 1Y7
Tél: 514-481-8125; *Téléc:* 514-481-4554
info@montreal-west.ca
www.montreal-ouest.ca
Entité municipal: Town
Incorporation: 1er janvier 2006; *Area:* 1,41 km2
Comté ou district: Communauté métropolitaine de Montréal; *Population au 2011:* 5,085
Circonscription(s) électorale(s) provinciale(s): Notre-Dame-de-Grâce
Circonscription(s) électorale(s) fédérale(s): Notre-Dame-de-Grâce-Westmount
Prochaines élections: 5e novembre 2017
Beny Masella, Maire
Claude Gilbert, Greffier

Mont-Saint-Grégoire
1, boul du Frère-André
Mont-Saint-Grégoire, QC J0J 1K0
Tél: 450-347-5376; *Téléc:* 450-347-9200
www.mont-saint-gregoire.ca
Entité municipal: Municipality
Incorporation: 21 décembre 1994; *Area:* 79,92 km2
Comté ou district: Le Haut-Richelieu; *Population au 2011:* 3,086
Circonscription(s) électorale(s) provinciale(s): Iberville
Circonscription(s) électorale(s) fédérale(s): Saint-Jean
Prochaines élections: 5e novembre 2017
Suzanne Boulais, Mairesse
Christianne Pouliot, Directrice générale

Mont-Saint-Michel
94, rue de l'Église
Mont-Saint-Michel, QC J0W 1P0
Tél: 819-587-3093; *Téléc:* 819-587-3781
mun.mont-st-michel@tlb.sympatico.ca
www.montsaintmichel.ca
Entité municipal: Municipality
Incorporation: 11 septembre 1928; *Area:* 137,65 km2
Comté ou district: Antoine-Labelle; *Population au 2011:* 633
Circonscription(s) électorale(s) provinciale(s): Labelle
Circonscription(s) électorale(s) fédérale(s): Laurentides-Labelle
Prochaines élections: 5e novembre 2017
André-Marcel Évéquoz, Maire
Manon Lambert, Directrice générale

Mont-Saint-Pierre
CP 9
102, rue Prudent-Cloutier
Mont-Saint-Pierre, QC G0E 1V0
Tél: 418-797-2898; *Téléc:* 418-797-2307
mont-st-pierre@globetrotter.net
www.mont-saint-pierre.ca
Entité municipal: Village
Incorporation: 1er janvier 1947; *Area:* 60,45 km2
Comté ou district: La Haute-Gaspésie; *Population au 2011:* 192
Circonscription(s) électorale(s) provinciale(s): Gaspé
Circonscription(s) électorale(s) fédérale(s): Gaspésie-Les Iles-de-la-Madeleine
Prochaines élections: 5e novembre 2017
Lynda Laflamme, Mairesse

Mont-Tremblant
1145, rue de St-Jovite
Mont-Tremblant, QC J8E 1V1
Tél: 819-425-8614; *Téléc:* 819-425-2528
www.villedemont-tremblant.qc.ca
Entité municipal: Town
Incorporation: 22 novembre 2000; *Area:* 235,97 km2
Comté ou district: Les Laurentides; *Population au 2011:* 9,494
Circonscription(s) électorale(s) provinciale(s): Labelle
Circonscription(s) électorale(s) fédérale(s): Laurentides-Labelle
Prochaines élections: 5e novembre 2017
Luc Brisebois, Maire
Marie Lanthier, Greffière

La Morandière
204, rte 397
La Morandière, QC J0Y 1S0
Tél: 819-734-6143; *Téléc:* 819-734-6143
lamo@cableamos.com
www.lamorandiere.ca
Entité municipal: Municipality
Incorporation: 1er janvier 1983; *Area:* 430 km2
Comté ou district: Abitibi; *Population au 2011:* 233
Circonscription(s) électorale(s) provinciale(s): Abitibi-Ouest
Circonscription(s) électorale(s) fédérale(s): Abitibi-Témiscamingue
Prochaines élections: 5e novembre 2017

Guy Lemire, Maire
Sandra Hardy, Directrice générale

Morin-Heights
567, ch du Village
Morin-Heights, QC J0R 1H0
Tél: 450-226-3232; *Téléc:* 450-226-8786
municipalite@morinheights.com
www.morinheights.com
Entité municipal: Municipality
Incorporation: 1er juillet 1855; *Area:* 55,42 km2
Comté ou district: Les Pays-d'en-Haut; *Population au 2011:* 3,925
Circonscription(s) électorale(s) provinciale(s): Argenteuil
Circonscription(s) électorale(s) fédérale(s): Argenteuil-La Petite-Nation
Prochaines élections: 5e novembre 2017
Timothy Watchorn, Maire
Yves Desmarais, Directeur général

La Motte
CP 644
349, ch St-Luc
La Motte, QC J0Y 1T0
Tél: 819-732-2878; *Téléc:* 819-727-4248
municipalite.lamotte@cableamos.com
www.municipalitedelamotte.ca
Entité municipal: Municipality
Incorporation: 30 mai 1921; *Area:* 224,03 km2
Comté ou district: Abitibi; *Population au 2011:* 457
Circonscription(s) électorale(s) provinciale(s): Abitibi-Ouest
Circonscription(s) électorale(s) fédérale(s): Abitibi-Témiscamingue
Prochaines élections: 5e novembre 2017
René Martineau, Maire
Rachel Cossette, Directrice générale

Les Moulins
CP 204
710, boul des Seigneurs, 2e étage
Terrebonne, QC J6W 1T6
Tél: 450-471-9576; *Téléc:* 450-471-8193
info@mrclesmoulins.ca
www.mrclesmoulins.ca
Entité municipal: Regional County Municipality
Incorporation: 1er janvier 1982
Population au 2011: 148,813
Note: 2 municipalités.
Jean-Marc Robitaille, Préfet
Daniel Pilon, Directeur général

Mulgrave-et-Derry
560, av de Buckingham
Gatineau, QC J8L 2H1
Tél: 819-986-9519; *Téléc:* 819-986-9954
mulgrave-derry@bellnet.ca
Entité municipal: Municipality
Incorporation: 1er janvier 1870; *Area:* 297,74 km2
Comté ou district: Papineau; *Population au 2011:* 246
Circonscription(s) électorale(s) provinciale(s): Papineau
Circonscription(s) électorale(s) fédérale(s): Argenteuil-La Petite-Nation
Prochaines élections: 5e novembre 2017
Michael Kane, Maire
Isabelle Cusson, Directrice générale

Murdochville
CP 1120
635, 5e rue
Murdochville, QC G0E 1W0
Tél: 418-784-2536; *Téléc:* 418-784-2607
www.murdochville.com
Entité municipal: Village
Incorporation: 15 juillet 1953; *Area:* 64,68 km2
Comté ou district: La Côte-de-Gaspé; *Population au 2011:* 764
Circonscription(s) électorale(s) provinciale(s): Gaspé
Circonscription(s) électorale(s) fédérale(s): Gaspésie-Les Iles-de-la-Madeleine
Prochaines élections: 5e novembre 2017
Délisca Ritchie Roussy, Mairesse
Jean-Pierre Cassivi, Greffier

Namur
996, rue du Centenaire
Namur, QC J0V 1N0
Tél: 819-426-2457; *Téléc:* 819-426-3074
www.namur.ca
Entité municipal: Municipality
Incorporation: 1er janvier 1964; *Area:* 57,07 km2
Comté ou district: Papineau; *Population au 2011:* 596
Circonscription(s) électorale(s) provinciale(s): Papineau
Circonscription(s) électorale(s) fédérale(s): Argenteuil-La Petite-Nation
Prochaines élections: 5e novembre 2017
Gilbert Dardel, Maire
Cathy Viens, Directrice générale

Nantes
1244, rue Principale
Nantes, QC G0Y 1G0
Tél: 819-547-3655; *Téléc:* 819-547-3755
munantes@axion.ca
www.munantes.qc.ca
Entité municipal: Municipality
Incorporation: 1er janvier 1874; *Area:* 120,47 km2
Comté ou district: Le Granit; *Population au 2011:* 1,374
Circonscription(s) électorale(s) provinciale(s): Mégantic
Circonscription(s) électorale(s) fédérale(s): Mégantic-L'Érable
Prochaines élections: 5e novembre 2017
Jacques Breton, Maire
Lucie Lortitch, Directrice générale

Napierville
260, rue de l'Église
Napierville, QC J0J 1L0
Tél: 450-245-7210; *Téléc:* 450-245-7691
mun.napierville@qc.aira.com
www.napierville.ca
Entité municipal: Village
Incorporation: 1er janvier 1873; *Area:* 4,53 km2
Comté ou district: Les Jardins-de-Napierville; *Population au 2011:* 3,525
Circonscription(s) électorale(s) provinciale(s): Huntingdon
Circonscription(s) électorale(s) fédérale(s): Châteauguay-Lacolle
Prochaines élections: 5e novembre 2017
Jacques Délisle, Maire
Ginette Leblanc-Pruneau, Directrice générale

Natashquan
CP 99
29, ch d'en-Haut
Natashquan, QC G0G 2E0
Tél: 418-726-3362; *Téléc:* 418-726-3698
muninatashquan@globetrotter.net
www.natashquan.org
Entité municipal: Township
Incorporation: 16 septembre 1907; *Area:* 193,20 km2
Comté ou district: Minganie; *Population au 2011:* 246
Circonscription(s) électorale(s) provinciale(s): Duplessis
Circonscription(s) électorale(s) fédérale(s): Manicouagan
Prochaines élections: 5e novembre 2017
André Barrette, Maire
Léonard Landry, Directeur général

Nédélec
CP 70
33, rue Principale
Nédélec, QC J0Z 2Z0
Tél: 819-784-3311; *Téléc:* 819-784-2126
nedelec@mrctemiscamingue.qc.ca
municipalite.nedelec.qc.ca
Entité municipal: Township
Incorporation: 1er février 1909; *Area:* 369,90 km2
Comté ou district: Témiscamingue; *Population au 2011:* 403
Circonscription(s) électorale(s) provinciale(s): Rouyn-Noranda-Témiscamingue
Circonscription(s) électorale(s) fédérale(s): Abitibi-Témiscamingue
Prochaines élections: 5e novembre 2017
Carmen Rivard, Mairesse
Lorraine McLean, Directrice générale

Nemaska
1, rue Lakeshore
Nemaska, QC J0Y 3B0
Tel: 819-673-2512; *Fax:* 819-673-2542
nation@nemaska.ca
www.nemaska.ca
Municipal Type: Villages Cris
Incorporated: 28 juin 1978; *Area:* 55,40 km2
Provincial Electoral District(s): Ungava
Federal Electoral District(s): Abitibi-Baie-James-Nunavik-Eeyou
Next Election: 5e novembre 2017
Josie Jimiken, Maire
Georges Wapachee, Directeur général

Neuville
230, rue du Père-Rhéaume
Neuville, QC G0A 2R0
Tél: 418-876-2280; *Téléc:* 418-876-3349
mun@ville.neuville.qc.ca
www.ville.neuville.qc.ca
Entité municipal: Town
Incorporation: 2 janvier 1997; *Area:* 72,04 km2

Comté ou district: Portneuf; *Population au 2011:* 3,888
Circonscription(s) électorale(s) provinciale(s): Portneuf
Circonscription(s) électorale(s) fédérale(s):
Portneuf-Jacques-Cartier
Prochaines élections: 5e novembre 2017
Bernard Gaudreau, Maire
Daniel Le Pape, Greffier

New Carlisle
CP 40
138, boul Gérard-D.-Levesque
New Carlisle, QC G0C 1Z0
Tél: 418-752-3141; *Téléc:* 418-752-3140
newcarlisle@globetrotter.net
www.new-carlisle.com
Entité municipal: Municipality
Incorporation: 1er février 1877; *Area:* 66,12 km2
Comté ou district: Bonaventure; *Population au 2011:* 1,358
Circonscription(s) électorale(s) provinciale(s): Bonaventure
Circonscription(s) électorale(s) fédérale(s):
Gaspésie—îles-de-la-Madeleine
Prochaines élections: 5e novembre 2017
Stephen Chatterton, Maire
Denise Dallain, Directrice générale

New Richmond
99, place Suzanne-Guité
New Richmond, QC G0C 2B0
Tél: 418-392-7000; *Téléc:* 418-392-5331
www.villenewrichmond.com
Entité municipal: Town
Incorporation: 1er juillet 1855; *Area:* 168,63 km2
Comté ou district: Bonaventure; *Population au 2011:* 3,810
Circonscription(s) électorale(s) provinciale(s): Bonaventure
Circonscription(s) électorale(s) fédérale(s):
Gaspésie—îles-de-la-Madeleine
Prochaines élections: 5e novembre 2017
Éric Dubé, Maire
Céline Leblanc, Greffiére

Newport
1452, rte 212
Newport, QC J0B 1M0
Tél: 819-560-8565; *Téléc:* 819-560-8566
municipalite.newport@hsfqc.ca
www.municipalitenewport.com
Entité municipal: Municipality
Incorporation: 1er janvier 2006; *Area:* 271,88 km2
Comté ou district: Le Haut-Saint-François; *Population au 2011:* 720
Circonscription(s) électorale(s) provinciale(s): Mégantic
Circonscription(s) électorale(s) fédérale(s): Compton-Stanstead
Prochaines élections: 5e novembre 2017
Lionel Roy, Maire
Lise Houle, Directrice générale

Nicolet
180, rue Monseigneur-Panet
Nicolet, QC J3T 1S6
Tél: 819-293-6901; *Téléc:* 819-293-6767
communication@nicolet.ca
www.nicolet.ca
Entité municipal: Town
Incorporation: 27 décembre 2000; *Area:* 94,50 km2
Comté ou district: Nicolet-Yamaska; *Population au 2011:* 7,828
Circonscription(s) électorale(s) provinciale(s): Nicolet-Bécancour
Circonscription(s) électorale(s) fédérale(s):
Bécancour-Nicolet-Saurel
Prochaines élections: 5e novembre 2017
Alain Drouin, Maire
Monique Corriveau, Greffière

Nicolet-Yamaska
#257, 1, rue de Mgr-Courchesne
Nicolet, QC J3T 2C1
Tél: 819-293-2997; *Téléc:* 819-293-5367
mrcny@mrcny.qc.ca
www.mrcnicolet-yamaska.qc.ca
Entité municipal: Regional County Municipality
Incorporation: 1 janvier 1982
Population au 2011: 22,798
Note: 16 municipalités.
Alain Drouin, Préfet
Jean-François Albert, Directeur général

Nominingue
2110, ch du Tour-du-Lac
Nominingue, QC J0W 1R0
Tél: 819-278-3384; *Téléc:* 819-278-4967
reception@municipalitenominingue.qc.ca
www.municipalitenominingue.qc.ca
Entité municipal: Municipality
Incorporation: 30 octobre 1971; *Area:* 308,34 km2
Comté ou district: Antoine-Labelle; *Population au 2011:* 2,019
Circonscription(s) électorale(s) provinciale(s): Labelle
Circonscription(s) électorale(s) fédérale(s): Laurentides-Labelle
Prochaines élections: 5e novembre 2017
Georges Décarie, Maire
Robert Généreux, Directeur général

Normandin
1048, rue St-Cyrille
Normandin, QC G8M 4R9
Tél: 418-274-2004; *Téléc:* 418-274-7171
lroy@ville.normandin.qc.ca
www.ville.normandin.qc.ca
Entité municipal: Town
Incorporation: 10 mars 1979; *Area:* 211,96 km2
Comté ou district: Maria-Chapdelaine; *Population au 2011:* 3,137
Circonscription(s) électorale(s) provinciale(s): Roberval
Circonscription(s) électorale(s) fédérale(s): Lac-St-Jean
Prochaines élections: 5e novembre 2017
Mario Fortin, Maire
Guy Mailloux, Greffier

Normétal
CP 308
59, 1re rue
Normétal, QC J0Z 3A0
Tél: 819-788-2550; *Téléc:* 819-788-2730
normetal@mrcao.qc.ca
normetal.ao.ca
Entité municipal: Municipality
Incorporation: 1er janvier 1945; *Area:* 55,89 km2
Comté ou district: Abitibi-Ouest; *Population au 2011:* 856
Circonscription(s) électorale(s) provinciale(s): Abitibi-Ouest
Circonscription(s) électorale(s) fédérale(s):
Abitibi-Témiscamingue
Prochaines élections: 5e novembre 2017
Jacques Dickey, Maire
Lyne Blanchet, Directrice générale

North Hatley
3125, ch Capelton
North Hatley, QC J0B 2C0
Tél: 819-842-2754; *Téléc:* 819-842-4501
info@northhatley.org
www.northhatley.org
Entité municipal: Village
Incorporation: 25 octobre 1897; *Area:* 3,23 km2
Comté ou district: Memphrémagog; *Population au 2011:* 654
Circonscription(s) électorale(s) provinciale(s): Orford
Circonscription(s) électorale(s) fédérale(s): Compton-Stanstead
Prochaines élections: 5e novembre 2017
Michael Page, Maire
Léonard Castagner, Directeur général

Notre-Dame-Auxiliatrice-de-Buckland
4340, rue Principale
Buckland, QC G0R 1G0
Tél: 418-789-3119; *Téléc:* 418-789-3535
buckland@globetrotter.net
www.buckland.qc.ca
Entité municipal: Parish (Paroisse)
Incorporation: 1er janvier 1885; *Area:* 96,32 km2
Comté ou district: Bellechasse; *Population au 2011:* 785
Circonscription(s) électorale(s) provinciale(s): Bellechasse
Circonscription(s) électorale(s) fédérale(s): Bellechasse-Les Etchemins-Lévis
Prochaines élections: 5e novembre 2017
Juliette Laflamme, Mairesse
Jocelyne Nadeau, Directrice générale

Notre-Dame-de-Bonsecours
220A, rue Bonsecours
Montebello, QC J0V 1L0
Tél: 819-423-5575; *Téléc:* 819-423-5571
adm.ndbonsecours@mrcpapineau.com
www.ndbonsecours.com
Entité municipal: Municipality
Incorporation: 7 mars 1918; *Area:* 265,75 km2
Comté ou district: Papineau; *Population au 2011:* 261
Circonscription(s) électorale(s) provinciale(s): Papineau
Circonscription(s) électorale(s) fédérale(s): Argenteuil-La Petite-Nation
Prochaines élections: 5e novembre 2017
Carol Fortier, Maire
Suzie Latourelle, Directrice générale

Notre-Dame-de-Ham
25, rue de l'Église
Notre-Dame-de-Ham, QC G0P 1C0
Tél: 819-344-5806; *Téléc:* 819-344-5807
info@notre-dame-de-ham.ca
www.notre-dame-de-ham.ca
Entité municipal: Municipality
Incorporation: 7 octobre 1898; *Area:* 32,34 km2
Comté ou district: Arthabaska; *Population au 2011:* 414
Circonscription(s) électorale(s) provinciale(s):
Drummond-Bois-Francs
Circonscription(s) électorale(s) fédérale(s):
Richmond-Arthabaska
Prochaines élections: 5e novembre 2017
France McSween, Mairesse
Christiane Leblanc, Directrice générale

Notre-Dame-de-la-Merci
1900, montée de la Réserve
Notre-Dame-de-la-Merci, QC J0T 2A0
Tél: 819-424-2113; *Téléc:* 819-424-7347
info@mun-ndm.ca
www.mun-ndm.ca
Entité municipal: Municipality
Incorporation: 1er janvier 1950; *Area:* 251,22 km2
Comté ou district: Matawinie; *Population au 2011:* 978
Circonscription(s) électorale(s) provinciale(s): Bertrand
Circonscription(s) électorale(s) fédérale(s): Joliette
Prochaines élections: 5e novembre 2017
Roxanne Turcotte, Mairesse
Chantal Soucy, Directrice générale

Notre-Dame-de-la-Paix
267, rue Notre-Dame
Notre-Dame-de-la-Paix, QC J0V 1P0
Tél: 819-522-6610; *Téléc:* 819-522-6710
mun.ndlapaix@mrcpapineau.com
www.notredamedelapaix.qc.ca
Entité municipal: Municipality
Incorporation: 3 octobre 1902; *Area:* 105,90 km2
Comté ou district: Papineau; *Population au 2011:* 718
Circonscription(s) électorale(s) provinciale(s): Papineau
Circonscription(s) électorale(s) fédérale(s): Argenteuil-La Petite-Nation
Prochaines élections: 5e novembre 2017
Daniel Bock, Maire
Chantal Delisle, Directrice générale

Notre-Dame-de-la-Salette
CP 59
45, rue des Saules
Notre-Dame-de-la-Salette, QC J0X 2L0
Tél: 819-766-2533; *Téléc:* 819-766-2983
salette@muni-ndsalette.qc.ca
www.muni-ndsalette.qc.ca
Entité municipal: Municipality
Incorporation: 17 mai 1979; *Area:* 117,54 km2
Comté ou district: Les Collines-de-l'Outaouais; *Population au 2011:* 757
Circonscription(s) électorale(s) provinciale(s): Papineau
Circonscription(s) électorale(s) fédérale(s): Argenteuil-La Petite-Nation
Prochaines élections: 5e novembre 2017
Denis Légaré, Maire
Sylvie Gratton, Directrice générale

Notre-Dame-de-Lorette
22, rue Principale
Notre-Dame-de-Lorette, QC G0W 1B0
Tél: 418-276-1934; *Téléc:* 418-276-1934
lorette.muni@hotmail.com
Entité municipal: Municipality
Incorporation: 1er janvier 1966; *Area:* 225,32 km2
Comté ou district: Maria-Chapdelaine; *Population au 2011:* 189
Circonscription(s) électorale(s) provinciale(s): Roberval
Circonscription(s) électorale(s) fédérale(s): Lac-St-Jean
Prochaines élections: 5e novembre 2017
Daniel Tremblay, Maire
Véronique Tremblay, Directrice générale

Notre-Dame-de-Lourdes
837, rue Principale
Lourdes, QC G0S 1T0
Tél: 819-385-4315; *Téléc:* 819-385-4827
info@municipalitelourdes.com
www.municipalitelourdes.com
Entité municipal: Parish (Paroisse)
Incorporation: 7 octobre 1897; *Area:* 83,39 km2
Comté ou district: L'Érable; *Population au 2011:* 700
Circonscription(s) électorale(s) provinciale(s): Arthabaska
Circonscription(s) électorale(s) fédérale(s): Mégantic-L'Érable
Prochaines élections: 5e novembre 2017

Jocelyn Bédard, Maire
Danielle Bédard, Directrice générale

Notre-Dame-de-Lourdes
4050, rue Principale
Notre-Dame-de-Lourdes, QC J0K 1K0
Tél: 450-759-2277; *Téléc:* 450-759-2055
receptionndl@intermonde.net
www.notredamedelourdes.ca
Entité municipal: Municipality
Incorporation: 28 octobre 1925; *Area:* 35,48 km2
Comté ou district: Joliette; *Population au 2011:* 2,595
Circonscription(s) électorale(s) provinciale(s): Joliette
Circonscription(s) électorale(s) fédérale(s): Joliette
Prochaines élections: 5e novembre 2017
Céline Geoffroy, Maire
Nancy Bellerose, Directrice générale

Notre-Dame-de-Montauban
555, av des Loisirs
Notre-Dame-de-Montauban, QC G0X 1W0
Tél: 418-336-2640; *Téléc:* 418-336-2353
www.municipalite.notre-dame-de-montauban.qc.ca
Entité municipal: Municipality
Incorporation: 3 janvier 1976; *Area:* 163,53 km2
Comté ou district: Mékinac; *Population au 2011:* 747
Circonscription(s) électorale(s) provinciale(s): Laviolette
Circonscription(s) électorale(s) fédérale(s):
St-Maurice-Champlain
Prochaines élections: 5e novembre 2017
Jean-Guy Lavoie, Maire
Manon Frenette, Directrice générale

Notre-Dame-de-Pontmain
5, rue de l'Église
Notre-Dame-de-Pontmain, QC J0W 1S0
Tél: 819-597-2382; *Téléc:* 819-597-2231
info@munpontmain.qc.ca
www.munpontmain.qc.ca
Entité municipal: Municipality
Incorporation: 26 janvier 1894; *Area:* 267,92 km2
Comté ou district: Antoine-Labelle; *Population au 2011:* 720
Circonscription(s) électorale(s) provinciale(s): Labelle
Circonscription(s) électorale(s) fédérale(s): Laurentides-Labelle
Prochaines élections: 5e novembre 2017
Lyz Beaulieu, Mairesse
Daisy Constantineau, Directrice générale

Notre-Dame-des-Anges
260, boul Langelier
Québec, QC G1K 5N1
Tél: 418-529-0931; *Téléc:* 418-524-7162
mamj@mediom.com
Entité municipal: Parish (Paroisse)
Incorporation: 1er juillet 1855; *Area:* 0,06 km2
Population au 2011: 394
Circonscription(s) électorale(s) provinciale(s): Taschereau
Circonscription(s) électorale(s) fédérale(s): Québec
Prochaines élections: 5e novembre 2017
Aline Plante, Administratrice
Laurent Charest, Directeur général

Notre-Dame-des-Bois
35, rte de l'Église
Notre-Dame-des-Bois, QC J0B 2E0
Tél: 819-888-2724; *Téléc:* 819-888-2904
www.notredamedesbois.qc.ca
Entité municipal: Municipality
Incorporation: 1er janvier 1877; *Area:* 190,90 km2
Comté ou district: Le Granit; *Population au 2011:* 911
Circonscription(s) électorale(s) provinciale(s): Mégantic
Circonscription(s) électorale(s) fédérale(s): Mégantic-L'Érable
Prochaines élections: 5e novembre 2017
Yvan Goyette, Maire
Guylaine Blais, Directrice générale

Notre-Dame-des-Monts
15, rue Principale
Notre-Dame-des-Monts, QC G0T 1L0
Tél: 418-489-2011; *Téléc:* 418-489-2014
www.notredamedesmonts.com
Entité municipal: Municipality
Incorporation: 11 avril 1935; *Area:* 56,15 km2
Comté ou district: Charlevoix-Est; *Population au 2011:* 815
Circonscription(s) électorale(s) provinciale(s):
Charlevoix-Côte-de-Beaupré
Circonscription(s) électorale(s) fédérale(s):
Beauport-Côte-de-Beaupré-Île d'Orléans-Charlevoix
Prochaines élections: 5e novembre 2017
Mélissa Girard, Mairesse
Marcelle Pedneault, Directrice générale

Notre-Dame-des-Neiges
4, 2e rang Centre
Trois-Pistoles, QC G0L 4K0
Tél: 418-851-3009; *Téléc:* 418-851-3169
admin@notredamedesneiges.qc.ca
www.notredamedesneiges.qc.ca
Entité municipal: Municipality
Incorporation: 1er juillet 1855; *Area:* 92,87 km2
Comté ou district: Les Basques; *Population au 2011:* 1,129
Circonscription(s) électorale(s) provinciale(s):
Rivière-du-Loup-Témiscouata
Circonscription(s) électorale(s) fédérale(s):
Rimouski-Neigette-Témiscouata-Les Basques
Prochaines élections: 5e novembre 2017
André Leblond, Maire
Denis Ouellet, Directeur général

Notre-Dame-des-Pins
CP 40
2790, 1re av
Notre-Dame-des-Pins, QC G0M 1K0
Tél: 418-774-9718; *Téléc:* 418-774-9728
notredamedespins@sogetel.net
www.notredamedespins.qc.ca
Entité municipal: Parish (Paroisse)
Incorporation: 29 juin 1926; *Area:* 24,60 km2
Comté ou district: Beauce-Sartigan; *Population au 2011:* 1,227
Circonscription(s) électorale(s) provinciale(s): Beauce-Sud
Circonscription(s) électorale(s) fédérale(s): Beauce
Prochaines élections: 5e novembre 2017
Pierre Bégin, Maire
Dominique Lamarre, Directrice générale

Notre-Dame-des-Prairies
225, boul Antonio-Barrette
Notre-Dame-des-Prairies, QC J6E 1E7
Tél: 450-759-7741; *Téléc:* 450-759-6255
prairies@notre-dame-des-prairies.org
www.notre-dame-des-prairies.org
Entité municipal: Town
Incorporation: 1er janvier 1957; *Area:* 17,74 km2
Comté ou district: Joliette; *Population au 2011:* 8,868
Circonscription(s) électorale(s) provinciale(s): Joliette
Circonscription(s) électorale(s) fédérale(s): Joliette
Prochaines élections: 5e novembre 2017
Alain Larue, Maire
Sylvie Malo, Greffière

Notre-Dame-des-Sept-Douleurs
6201, ch de l'Île
Notre-Dame-des-Sept-Douleurs, QC G0L 1K0
Tél: 418-898-3451; *Téléc:* 418-898-3492
www.ileverte-municipalite.com
Entité municipal: Parish (Paroisse)
Incorporation: 1er janvier 1874; *Area:* 11,18 km2
Comté ou district: Rivière-du-Loup; *Population au 2011:* 49
Circonscription(s) électorale(s) provinciale(s):
Rivière-du-Loup-Témiscouata
Circonscription(s) électorale(s) fédérale(s):
Montmagny-L'Islet-Kamouraska-Rivière-du-Loup
Prochaines élections: 5e novembre 2017
Léopold Fraser, Maire
Denis Cusson, Directeur général

Notre-Dame-de-Stanbridge
CP 209
900, rue Principale
Notre-Dame-de-Stanbridge, QC J0J 1M0
Tél: 450-296-4710; *Téléc:* 450-296-5001
www.notredamedestanbridge.qc.ca
Entité municipal: Parish (Paroisse)
Incorporation: 21 mars 1889; *Area:* 44,57 km2
Comté ou district: Brome-Missisquoi; *Population au 2011:* 660
Circonscription(s) électorale(s) provinciale(s): Brome-Missisquoi
Circonscription(s) électorale(s) fédérale(s): Brome-Missisquoi
Prochaines élections: 5e novembre 2017
Ginette Simard Gendreault, Mairesse
Béatrice Travers, Directrice générale

Notre-Dame-du-Bon-Conseil
1428, rte 122
Notre-Dame-du-Bon-Conseil, QC J0C 1A0
Tél: 819-336-5374; *Téléc:* 819-336-2389
www.paroissendbc.ca
Entité municipal: Parish (Paroisse)
Incorporation: 15 février 1898; *Area:* 86,42 km2
Comté ou district: Drummond; *Population au 2011:* 979
Circonscription(s) électorale(s) provinciale(s):
Drummond-Bois-Francs
Circonscription(s) électorale(s) fédérale(s): Drummond
Prochaines élections: 5e novembre 2017
Michel Bourgeois, Maire

Valérie Aubin, Directrice générale

Notre-Dame-du-Bon-Conseil
541, rue Notre-Dame
Notre-Dame-du-Bon-Conseil, QC J0C 1A0
Tél: 819-336-2744; *Téléc:* 819-336-2030
nb.bonconseil@cgocable.ca
www.notre-dame-du-bon-conseil-village.qc.ca
Entité municipal: Village
Incorporation: 1er janvier 1957; *Area:* 4,22 km2
Comté ou district: Drummond; *Population au 2011:* 1,404
Circonscription(s) électorale(s) provinciale(s):
Drummond-Bois-Francs
Circonscription(s) électorale(s) fédérale(s): Drummond
Prochaines élections: 5e novembre 2017
Marcel Bergeron, Maire
Isabelle Dumont, Directrice générale

Notre-Dame-du-Laus
CP 10
66, rue Principale
Notre-Dame-du-Laus, QC J0X 2M0
Tél: 819-767-2247; *Téléc:* 819-767-3102
mun.notre-dame-du-laus@tlb.sympatico.ca
www.notre-dame-du-laus.ca
Entité municipal: Municipality
Incorporation: 1er janvier 1876; *Area:* 866,02 km2
Comté ou district: Antoine-Labelle; *Population au 2011:* 1,518
Circonscription(s) électorale(s) provinciale(s): Labelle
Circonscription(s) électorale(s) fédérale(s): Laurentides-Labelle
Prochaines élections: 5e novembre 2017
Stéphane Roy, Maire
Yves Larocque, Directeur général

Notre-Dame-du-Mont-Carmel
3860, rue de l' Hôtel de Ville
Notre-Dame-du-Mont-Carmel, QC G0X 3J0
Tél: 819-375-9856; *Téléc:* 819-373-4045
reception@mont-carmel.org
www.mont-carmel.org
Entité municipal: Parish (Paroisse)
Incorporation: 30 décembre 1858; *Area:* 126,61 km2
Comté ou district: Les Chenaux; *Population au 2011:* 5,467
Circonscription(s) électorale(s) provinciale(s): St-Maurice
Circonscription(s) électorale(s) fédérale(s):
St-Maurice-Champlain
Prochaines élections: 5e novembre 2017
Luc Dostaler, Maire
Danny Roy, Directeur général

Notre-Dame-du-Nord
71, rue Principale nord
Notre-Dame-du-Nord, QC J0Z 3B0
Tél: 819-723-2294; *Téléc:* 819-723-2483
nddn@mrctemiscamingue.qc.ca
municipalite.notre-dame-du-nord.qc.ca
Entité municipal: Municipality
Incorporation: 23 septembre 1919; *Area:* 103,60 km2
Comté ou district: Témiscamingue; *Population au 2011:* 1,075
Circonscription(s) électorale(s) provinciale(s):
Rouyn-Noranda-Témiscamingue
Circonscription(s) électorale(s) fédérale(s):
Abitibi-Témiscamingue
Prochaines élections: 5e novembre 2017
Alain Flageol, Maire
Réjean Pelletier, Directeur général

Notre-Dame-du-Portage
560, rte de la Montagne
Notre-Dame-du-Portage, QC G0L 1Y0
Tél: 418-862-9163; *Téléc:* 418-862-5240
www.municipalite.notre-dame-du-portage.qc.ca
Entité municipal: Municipality
Incorporation: 19 juillet 1856; *Area:* 39,55 km2
Comté ou district: Rivière-du-Loup; *Population au 2011:* 1,193
Circonscription(s) électorale(s) provinciale(s):
Rivière-du-Loup-Témiscouata
Circonscription(s) électorale(s) fédérale(s):
Montmagny-L'Islet-Kamouraska-Rivière-du-Loup
Prochaines élections: 5e novembre 2017
Vincent More, Maire
Louis Breton, Directeur général

Notre-Dame-du-Rosaire
144, rue Principale
Notre-Dame-du-Rosaire, QC G0R 2H0
Tél: 418-469-2802; *Téléc:* 418-469-2802
munndr@globetrotter.net
www.notredamedurosaire.com
Entité municipal: Municipality
Incorporation: 18 décembre 1894; *Area:* 158,53 km2
Comté ou district: Montmagny; *Population au 2011:* 384

Circonscription(s) électorale(s) provinciale(s): Côte-du-Sud
Circonscription(s) électorale(s) fédérale(s):
Montmagny-L'Islet-Kamouraska-Rivière-du-Loup
Prochaines élections: 5e novembre 2017
Danye Anctil, Mairesse
Isabelle Lachance, Directrice générale

Notre-Dame-du-Sacré-Coeur-d'Issoudun
268, rue Principale
Issoudun, QC G0S 1L0
Tél: 418-728-2006; *Téléc:* 418-728-2303
munissoudun@videotron.ca
www.issoudun.qc.ca
Entité municipal: Parish (Paroisse)
Incorporation: 4 janvier 1909; *Area:* 60,81 km2
Comté ou district: Lotbinière; *Population au 2011:* 869
Circonscription(s) électorale(s) provinciale(s):
Lotbinière-Frontenac
Circonscription(s) électorale(s) fédérale(s): Lévis-Lotbinière
Prochaines élections: 5e novembre 2017
Annie Thériault, Mairesse
Chantal Belleau, Directrice générale

Nouvelle
CP 68
470, rue Francoeur
Nouvelle, QC G0C 2E0
Tél: 418-794-2253; *Téléc:* 418-794-2254
nouvellegaspesie.com
Entité municipal: Municipality
Incorporation: 10 octobre 1907; *Area:* 230,63 km2
Comté ou district: Avignon; *Population au 2011:* 1,689
Circonscription(s) électorale(s) provinciale(s): Bonaventure
Circonscription(s) électorale(s) fédérale(s): Avignon-La
Mitis-Matane-Matapédia
Prochaines élections: 5e novembre 2017
Richard St-Laurent, Maire
Simon Gosselin, Directeur général

La Nouvelle-Beauce
#B, 700, rue Notre-Dame nord
Sainte-Marie, QC G6E 2K9
Tél: 418-387-3444; *Téléc:* 418-387-7060
mrc@nouvellebeauce.com
www.nouvellebeauce.com
Entité municipal: Regional County Municipality
Incorporation: 1er janvier 1982
Population au 2011: 35,107
Note: 11 municipalités.
Richard Lehoux, Préfet
Mario Caron, Directeur général

Noyan
1312, ch de la Petite-France
Noyan, QC J0J 1B0
Tél: 450-291-4504; *Téléc:* 450-291-4505
renseignements@ville.noyan.qc.ca
www.ville.noyan.qc.ca
Entité municipal: Municipality
Incorporation: 1er juillet 1855; *Area:* 43,79 km2
Comté ou district: Le Haut-Richelieu; *Population au 2011:* 1,297
Circonscription(s) électorale(s) provinciale(s): Iberville
Circonscription(s) électorale(s) fédérale(s): Brome-Missisquoi
Prochaines élections: 5e novembre 2017
Réal Ryan, Maire
Guy Bérubé, Directeur général

Ogden
70, ch Ogden
Ogden, QC J0B 3E3
Tél: 819-876-7117; *Téléc:* 819-876-2121
info@munogden.ca
www.munogden.ca
Entité municipal: Municipality
Incorporation: 23 janvier 1932; *Area:* 75,49 km2
Comté ou district: Memphrémagog; *Population au 2011:* 770
Circonscription(s) électorale(s) provinciale(s): Orford
Circonscription(s) électorale(s) fédérale(s): Compton-Stanstead
Prochaines élections: 5e novembre 2017
Michael Sudlow, Maire
Vickie Comeau, Directrice générale

Oka
183, rue des Anges
Oka, QC J0N 1E0
Tél: 450-479-8333; *Téléc:* 450-479-1886
info@municipalite.oka.qc.ca
www.municipalite.oka.qc.ca
Entité municipal: Municipality
Incorporation: 8 septembre 1999; *Area:* 67,21 km2
Comté ou district: Deux-Montagnes; Communauté
métropolitaine de Montréal; *Population au 2011:* 3,969
Circonscription(s) électorale(s) provinciale(s): Mirabel
Circonscription(s) électorale(s) fédérale(s): Mirabel
Prochaines élections: 5e novembre 2017
Pascal Quevillon, Maire
Marie Daoust, Directrice générale

Orford
2530, ch du Parc
Orford, QC J1X 8R8
Tél: 819-843-3111; *Téléc:* 819-843-2707
info@canton.orford.qc.ca
www.canton.orford.qc.ca
Entité municipal: Township
Incorporation: 1er juillet 1855; *Area:* 135,25 km2
Comté ou district: Memphrémagog; *Population au 2011:* 3,575
Circonscription(s) électorale(s) provinciale(s): Orford
Circonscription(s) électorale(s) fédérale(s): Brome-Missisquoi
Prochaines élections: 5e novembre 2017
Jean-Pierre Adam, Maire
Brigitte Boisvert, Greffière

Ormstown
81, rue Lambton
Ormstown, QC J0S 1K0
Tél: 450-829-2625; *Téléc:* 450-829-4162
ormstown@ormstown.ca
www.ormstown.ca
Entité municipal: Municipality
Incorporation: 26 janvier 2000; *Area:* 142,39 km2
Comté ou district: Le Haut-Saint-Laurent; *Population au 2011:*
3,595
Circonscription(s) électorale(s) provinciale(s): Huntingdon
Circonscription(s) électorale(s) fédérale(s): Salaberry-Suroît
Prochaines élections: 5e novembre 2017
Chrystian Soucy, Maire
Daniel Théroux, Directeur général

Otter Lake
CP 70
15, av Palmer
Otter Lake, QC J0X 2P0
Tél: 819-453-7049; *Téléc:* 819-453-7311
otter-lake@mrcpontiac.qc.ca
www.otterlakequebec.ca
Entité municipal: Municipality
Incorporation: 1er janvier 1877; *Area:* 496,21 km2
Comté ou district: Pontiac; *Population au 2011:* 1,109
Circonscription(s) électorale(s) provinciale(s): Pontiac
Circonscription(s) électorale(s) fédérale(s): Pontiac
Prochaines élections: 5e novembre 2017
Graham Hawley, Maire
Andrea Lafleur, Directrice générale

Otterburn Park
601, ch Ozias-Leduc
Otterburn Park, QC J3H 2M6
Tél: 450-536-0303; *Téléc:* 450-467-8260
info@ville.otterburnpark.qc.ca
www.ville.otterburnpark.qc.ca
Entité municipal: Town
Incorporation: 1er juillet 1855; *Area:* 5,20 km2
Comté ou district: La Vallée-du-Richelieu; Communauté
métropolitaine de Montréal; *Population au 2011:* 8,450
Circonscription(s) électorale(s) provinciale(s): Borduas
Circonscription(s) électorale(s) fédérale(s): Beloeil-Chambly
Prochaines élections: 5e novembre 2017
Danielle Lavoie, Mairesse
Julie Waite, Greffière

Oujé-Bougoumou
203, Opemiska Meskino
Oujé-Bougoumou, QC G0W 3C0
Tél: 888-745-3905; *Téléc:* 418-745-3544
tourism@ouje.ca
www.ouje.ca
Entité municipal: Villages Cris
Incorporation: 1992; *Area:* 2,54 km2
Population au 2011: 725
Circonscription(s) électorale(s) provinciale(s): Ungava
Circonscription(s) électorale(s) fédérale(s):
Abitibi-Baie-James-Nunavik-Eeyou
Reggie Neeposh, Chief

Packington
35A, rue Principale
Packington, QC G0L 1Z0
Tél: 418-853-2269; *Téléc:* 418-853-6427
info@packington.org
www.packington.org
Entité municipal: Parish (Paroisse)
Incorporation: 6 octobre 1925; *Area:* 117,89 km2
Comté ou district: Témiscouata; *Population au 2011:* 595
Circonscription(s) électorale(s) provinciale(s):
Rivière-du-Loup-Témiscouata
Circonscription(s) électorale(s) fédérale(s):
Rimouski-Neigette-Témiscouata-Les Basques
Prochaines élections: 5e novembre 2017
Émilien Beaulieu, Maire
Denis Moreau, Directeur général

Padoue
CP 15
215, rue Beaulieu
Padoue, QC G0J 1X0
Tél: 418-775-8188; *Téléc:* 418-775-8177
padoue@mitis.qc.ca
www.municipalite.padoue.qc.ca
Entité municipal: Municipality
Incorporation: 31 janvier 1911; *Area:* 67,57 km2
Comté ou district: La Mitis; *Population au 2011:* 411
Circonscription(s) électorale(s) provinciale(s): Matane-Matapédia
Circonscription(s) électorale(s) fédérale(s): Avignon-La
Mitis-Matane-Matapédia
Prochaines élections: 5e novembre 2017
Gilles Laflamme, Maire
Line Fillion, Directrice générale

Palmarolle
CP 309
499, rte 393
Palmarolle, QC J0Z 3C0
Tél: 819-787-2303; *Téléc:* 819-787-2412
palmarolle@mrcao.qc.ca
www.palmarolle.ao.ca
Entité municipal: Municipality
Incorporation: 14 avril 1930; *Area:* 118,36 km2
Comté ou district: Abitibi-Ouest; *Population au 2011:* 1,465
Circonscription(s) électorale(s) provinciale(s): Abitibi-Ouest
Circonscription(s) électorale(s) fédérale(s):
Abitibi-Témiscamingue
Prochaines élections: 5e novembre 2017
Marcel Caron, Maire
Annie Duquette, Directrice générale

Papineau
266, rue Viger
Papineauville, QC J0V 1R0
Tél: 819-427-6243; *Téléc:* 819-427-8318
info@mrcpapineau.com
www.mrcpapineau.com
Entité municipal: Regional County Municipality
Incorporation: 1er janvier 1983
Population au 2011: 22,541
Note: 24 municipalités.
Paulette Lalande, Préfète
Ghislain Ménard, Directeur général

Papineauville
#100, 188, rue Jeanne-D'Arc
Papineauville, QC J0V 1R0
Tél: 819-427-5511; *Téléc:* 819-427-5590
papineauville@mrcpapineau.com
www.papineauville.ca
Entité municipal: Municipality
Incorporation: 29 novembre 2000; *Area:* 48,52 km2
Comté ou district: Papineau; *Population au 2011:* 2,165
Circonscription(s) électorale(s) provinciale(s): Papineau
Circonscription(s) électorale(s) fédérale(s): Argenteuil-La
Petite-Nation
Prochaines élections: 5e novembre 2017
Christian Beauchamp, Maire
Martine Joanisse, Greffière

Parisville
975, rte Principale ouest
Parisville, QC G0S 1X0
Tél: 819-292-2222; *Téléc:* 819-292-1514
info@municipalite.parisville.qc.ca
www.municipalite.parisville.qc.ca
Entité municipal: Parish (Paroisse)
Incorporation: 18 mars 1901; *Area:* 36,85 km2
Comté ou district: Bécancour; *Population au 2011:* 528
Circonscription(s) électorale(s) provinciale(s): Nicolet-Bécancour
Circonscription(s) électorale(s) fédérale(s):
Bécancour-Nicolet-Saurel
Prochaines élections: 5e novembre 2017
Maurice Grimard, Maire
François Gaudreault, Directeur général

Paspébiac
CP 130
5, boul Gérard-D.-Levesque est
Paspébiac, QC G0C 2K0
Tél: 418-752-2277; *Téléc:* 418-752-6566
www.villepaspebiac.ca
Entité municipal: Town
Incorporation: 20 août 1997; *Area:* 94,59 km2
Comté ou district: Bonaventure; *Population au 2011:* 3,198
Circonscription(s) électorale(s) provinciale(s): Bonaventure
Circonscription(s) électorale(s) fédérale(s):
Gaspésie—Îles-de-la-Madeleine
Prochaines élections: 5e novembre 2017
Paul-Arthur Blais, Maire
Paul Langlois, Directeur général

La Patrie
18, rue Chartier
La Patrie, QC J0B 1Y0
Tél: 819-560-8535; *Téléc:* 819-560-8536
www.municipalite.lapatrie.qc.ca
Entité municipal: Municipality
Incorporation: 24 décembre 1997; *Area:* 206,95 km2
Comté ou district: Le Haut-Saint-François; *Population au 2011:* 749
Circonscription(s) électorale(s) provinciale(s): Mégantic
Circonscription(s) électorale(s) fédérale(s): Compton-Stanstead
Prochaines élections: 5e novembre 2017
Bruno Gobeil, Maire
Johanne Latendresse, Directrice générale

Les Pays-d'en-Haut
1014, rue Valiquette
Sainte-Adèle, QC J8B 2M3
Tél: 450-229-6637; *Téléc:* 450-229-5203
info@mrcpdh.org
www.lespaysdenhaut.com
Entité municipal: Regional County Municipality
Incorporation: 1er janvier 1983
Population au 2011: 40,331
Note: 10 municipalités.
Charles Garnier, Préfet
Yvan Genest, Directeur général

La Pêche
1, rue Principale ouest
La Pêche, QC J0X 2W0
Tél: 819-456-2161; *Téléc:* 819-456-4534
reception@villelapeche.qc.ca
www.villelapeche.qc.ca
Entité municipal: Municipality
Incorporation: 1er janvier 1975; *Area:* 597,14 km2
Comté ou district: Les Collines-de-l'Outaouais; *Population au 2011:* 7,619
Circonscription(s) électorale(s) provinciale(s): Gatineau
Circonscription(s) électorale(s) fédérale(s): Pontiac
Prochaines élections: 5e novembre 2017
Robert Bussière, Maire
Annie Racine, Directrice générale

Percé
CP 99
137, rte 132 ouest
Percé, QC G0C 2L0
Tél: 418-782-2933; *Téléc:* 418-782-5487
renseignements@ville.perce.qc.ca
www.ville.perce.qc.ca
Entité municipal: Town
Incorporation: 1er janvier 1971; *Area:* 427,94 km2
Comté ou district: Le Rocher-Percé; *Population au 2011:* 3,312
Circonscription(s) électorale(s) provinciale(s): Gaspé
Circonscription(s) électorale(s) fédérale(s):
Gaspésie—Îles-de-la-Madeleine
Prochaines élections: 5e novembre 2017
André Boudreau, Maire
Gemma Vibert, Greffière

Péribonka
312, rue Édouard-Niquet
Péribonka, QC G0W 2G0
Tél: 418-374-2967; *Téléc:* 418-374-2355
www.peribonka.ca
Entité municipal: Municipality
Incorporation: 19 septembre 1908; *Area:* 113,46 km2
Comté ou district: Maria-Chapdelaine; *Population au 2011:* 464
Circonscription(s) électorale(s) provinciale(s): Roberval
Circonscription(s) électorale(s) fédérale(s): Lac-St-Jean
Prochaines élections: 5e novembre 2017
Ghislain Goulet, Maire
Steve Harvey, Directeur général

Petite-Rivière-Saint-François
CP 10
1067, rue Principale
Petite-Rivière-Saint-François, QC G0A 2L0
Tél: 418-760-1050; *Téléc:* 418-760-1051
info@petiteriviere.com
www.petiteriviere.com
Entité municipal: Municipality
Incorporation: 1er juillet 1855; *Area:* 135,66 km2
Comté ou district: Charlevoix; *Population au 2011:* 744
Circonscription(s) électorale(s) provinciale(s):
Charlevoix-Côte-de-Beaupré
Circonscription(s) électorale(s) fédérale(s):
Beauport-Côte-de-Beaupré-Île d'Orléans-Charlevoix
Prochaines élections: 5e novembre 2017
Gérald Maltais, Maire
Francine Dufour, Directrice générale

Petite-Vallée
CP 1067
45, rue Principale
Petite-Vallée, QC G0E 1Y0
Tél: 418-393-2949; *Téléc:* 418-393-2949
bibliopv@globetrotter.qc.ca
Entité municipal: Municipality
Incorporation: 1er janvier 1957; *Area:* 37,83 km2
Comté ou district: La Côte-de-Gaspé; *Population au 2011:* 178
Circonscription(s) électorale(s) provinciale(s): Gaspé
Circonscription(s) électorale(s) fédérale(s):
Gaspésie—Îles-de-la-Madeleine
Prochaines élections: 5e novembre 2017
Rodrigue Brousseau, Maire
Simon Côté, Directeur général

Petit-Saguenay
35, ch du Quai
Petit-Saguenay, QC G0V 1N0
Tél: 418-272-2323; *Téléc:* 418-544-3077
www.petit-saguenay.com
Entité municipal: Municipality
Incorporation: 12 août 1919; *Area:* 328,72 km2
Comté ou district: Le Fjord-du-Saguenay; *Population au 2011:* 727
Circonscription(s) électorale(s) provinciale(s): Dubuc
Circonscription(s) électorale(s) fédérale(s): Chicoutimi-Le Fjord
Prochaines élections: 5e novembre 2017
Ginette Côté, Mairesse
Alexis Lavoie, Directeur général

Piedmont
670, rue Principale
Piedmont, QC J0R 1K0
Tél: 450-227-1888; *Téléc:* 450-227-6716
info@piedmont.ca
www.piedmont.ca
Entité municipal: Municipality
Incorporation: 22 septembre 1923; *Area:* 23,66 km2
Comté ou district: Les Pays-d'en-Haut; *Population au 2011:* 2,721
Circonscription(s) électorale(s) provinciale(s): Bertrand
Circonscription(s) électorale(s) fédérale(s): Laurentides-Labelle
Prochaines élections: 5e novembre 2017
Clément Cardin, Maire
Gilbert Aubin, Directeur général

Pierre-De Saurel
50, rue du Fort
Sorel-Tracy, QC J3P 7X7
Tél: 450-743-2703; *Téléc:* 450-743-7313
mrc@pierredesaurel.com
www.mrcpierredesaurel.com
Entité municipal: Regional County Municipality
Incorporation: 1er janvier 1982
Population au 2011: 50,900
Note: 12 municipalités.
Claude Pothier, Préfet
Denis Boisvert, Directeur général

Pierreville
CP 300
26, rue Ally
Pierreville, QC J0G 1J0
Tél: 450-568-2139; *Téléc:* 450-568-0689
info@municipalitepierreville.qc.ca
www.pierreville.net
Entité municipal: Municipality
Incorporation: 13 juin 2001; *Area:* 79,54 km2
Comté ou district: Nicolet-Yamaska; *Population au 2011:* 2,176
Circonscription(s) électorale(s) provinciale(s): Nicolet-Bécancour
Circonscription(s) électorale(s) fédérale(s):
Bécancour-Nicolet-Saurel
Prochaines élections: 5e novembre 2017
André Descôteaux, Maire
Lyne Boisvert, Directrice générale

Pike River
CP 93
548, rte 202
St-Pierre-de-Véronne, QC J0J 1P0
Tél: 450-248-2120; *Téléc:* 450-248-4772
pikeriver@axion.ca
www.pikeriver.ca
Entité municipal: Municipality
Incorporation: 3 avril 1912; *Area:* 43,58 km2
Comté ou district: Brome-Missisquoi; *Population au 2011:* 525
Circonscription(s) électorale(s) provinciale(s): Brome-Missisquoi
Circonscription(s) électorale(s) fédérale(s): Brome-Missisquoi
Prochaines élections: 5e novembre 2017
Martin Bellefroid, Maire
Sonia Côté, Directrice générale

Piopolis
403, rue Principale
Piopolis, QC G0Y 1H0
Tél: 819-583-3953; *Téléc:* 819-583-1467
municipalite@piopolis.ca
www.piopolis.ca
Entité municipal: Municipality
Incorporation: 1er janvier 1880; *Area:* 104,14 km2
Comté ou district: Le Granit; *Population au 2011:* 364
Circonscription(s) électorale(s) provinciale(s): Mégantic
Circonscription(s) électorale(s) fédérale(s): Mégantic-L'Érable
Prochaines élections: 5e novembre 2017
Fernand Roy, Maire
Karine Bonneau, Directrice générale

Plaisance
274, rue Desjardins
Plaisance, QC J0V 1S0
Tél: 819-427-5363; *Téléc:* 819-427-5015
ville.plaisance@videotron.ca
www.ville.plaisance.qc.ca
Entité municipal: Municipality
Incorporation: 31 octobre 1900; *Area:* 42,61 km2
Comté ou district: Papineau; *Population au 2011:* 1,103
Circonscription(s) électorale(s) provinciale(s): Papineau
Circonscription(s) électorale(s) fédérale(s): Argenteuil-La Petite-Nation
Prochaines élections: 5e novembre 2017
Paulette Lalande, Mairesse
Paul St-Louis, Directeur général

Plessisville
CP 245
290, rte 165 sud
Plessisville, QC G6L 2Y7
Tél: 819-362-2712; *Téléc:* 819-362-9185
info@paroisseplessisville.com
www.paroisseplessisville.com
Entité municipal: Parish (Paroisse)
Incorporation: 1er juillet 1855; *Area:* 136,29 km2
Comté ou district: L'Érable; *Population au 2011:* 2,678
Circonscription(s) électorale(s) provinciale(s): Arthabaska
Circonscription(s) électorale(s) fédérale(s): Mégantic-L'Érable
Prochaines élections: 5e novembre 2017
Alain Dubois, Maire
Johanne Dubois, Directrice générale

Plessisville
1700, rue St-Calixte
Plessisville, QC G6L 1R3
Tél: 819-362-3284; *Téléc:* 819-362-6421
info@ville.plessisville.qc.ca
www.ville.plessisville.qc.ca
Entité municipal: Town
Incorporation: 27 avril 1855; *Area:* 4,44 km2
Comté ou district: L'Érable; *Population au 2011:* 6,688
Circonscription(s) électorale(s) provinciale(s): Arthabaska
Circonscription(s) électorale(s) fédérale(s): Mégantic-L'Érable
Prochaines élections: 5e novembre 2017
Jean-Noël Bergeron, Maire
Alain Desjardins, Dicecteur général

La Pocatière
412, 9e rue
La Pocatière, QC G0R 1Z0
Tél: 418-856-3394; *Téléc:* 418-856-5465
danielle.caron@lapocatiere.ca
www.lapocatiere.ca
Entité municipal: Town
Incorporation: 1er janvier 1960; *Area:* 22,71 km2
Comté ou district: Kamouraska; *Population au 2011:* 4,266
Circonscription(s) électorale(s) provinciale(s): Côte-du-Sud
Circonscription(s) électorale(s) fédérale(s):

Montmagny-L'Islet-Kamouraska-Rivière-du-Loup
Prochaines élections: 5e novembre 2017
Sylvain Hudon, Maire
Danielle Caron, Greffière

Pohénégamook
1309, rue Principale
Pohénégamook, QC G0L 1J0
Tél: 418-859-2222; *Téléc:* 418-859-3465
www.pohenegamook.net
Entité municipal: Town
Incorporation: 3 novembre 1973; *Area:* 351,97 km2
Comté ou district: Témiscouata; *Population au 2011:* 2,770
Circonscription(s) électorale(s) provinciale(s): Rivière-du-Loup-Témiscouata
Circonscription(s) électorale(s) fédérale(s): Rimouski-Neigette-Témiscouata-Les Basques
Prochaines élections: 5e novembre 2017
Louise Labonté, Mairesse
Charles-Hervé Aka, Greffière

Pointe-à-la-Croix
CP 159
139, boul Inter-Provincial
Pointe-à-la-Croix, QC G0C 1L0
Tél: 418-788-2011; *Téléc:* 418-788-2916
pointe-a-la-croix@globetrotter.net
www.pointe-a-la-croix.com
Entité municipal: Municipality
Incorporation: 7 mai 1983; *Area:* 394,03 km2
Comté ou district: Avignon; *Population au 2011:* 1,472
Circonscription(s) électorale(s) provinciale(s): Bonaventure
Circonscription(s) électorale(s) fédérale(s): Avignon-La Mitis-Matane-Matapédia
Prochaines élections: 5e novembre 2017
Jean-Paul Audy, Maire
Claude Audet, Directeur général

Pointe-aux-Outardes
471, ch Principal
Pointe-aux-Outardes, QC G0H 1M0
Tél: 418-567-2203; *Téléc:* 418-567-4409
municipalite@pointe-aux-outardes.ca
www.pointe-aux-outardes.ca
Entité municipal: Village
Incorporation: 1er janvier 1964; *Area:* 71,56 km2
Comté ou district: Manicouagan; *Population au 2011:* 1,330
Circonscription(s) électorale(s) provinciale(s): René-Lévesque
Circonscription(s) électorale(s) fédérale(s): Manicouagan
Prochaines élections: 5e novembre 2017
André Lepage, Maire
Dania Hovington, Directrice générale

Pointe-Calumet
300, av Basile-Routhier
Pointe-Calumet, QC J0N 1G2
Tél: 450-473-5930; *Téléc:* 450-473-6571
info@municipalite.pointe-calumet.qc.ca
www.municipalite.pointe-calumet.qc.ca
Entité municipal: Municipality
Incorporation: 12 février 1953; *Area:* 4,89 km2
Comté ou district: Deux-Montagnes; Communauté métropolitaine de Montréal; *Population au 2011:* 6,396
Circonscription(s) électorale(s) provinciale(s): Mirabel
Circonscription(s) électorale(s) fédérale(s): Mirabel
Prochaines élections: 5e novembre 2017
Denis Gravel, Maire
Chantal Pilon, Directrice générale

Pointe-des-Cascades
105, ch du Fleuve
Pointe-des-Cascades, QC J0P 1M0
Tél: 450-455-3414; *Téléc:* 450-455-9671
info@pointe-des-cascades.com
www.pointe-des-cascades.com
Entité municipal: Village
Incorporation: 1er mai 1961; *Area:* 2,66 km2
Comté ou district: Vaudreuil-Soulanges; Communauté métropolitaine de Montréal; *Population au 2011:* 1,340
Circonscription(s) électorale(s) provinciale(s): Soulanges
Circonscription(s) électorale(s) fédérale(s): Vaudreuil-Soulanges
Prochaines élections: 5e novembre 2017
Gilles Santerre, Maire
Daniel Leduc, Directeur général

Pointe-Fortune
694, rue du Tisseur
Pointe-Fortune, QC J0P 1N0
Tél: 450-451-5178; *Téléc:* 450-451-4649
mpf@qc.aira.com
pointefortune.ca
Entité municipal: Village
Incorporation: 28 août 1880; *Area:* 9,09 km2
Comté ou district: Vaudreuil-Soulanges; *Population au 2011:* 542
Circonscription(s) électorale(s) provinciale(s): Soulanges
Circonscription(s) électorale(s) fédérale(s): Vaudreuil-Soulanges
Prochaines élections: 5e novembre 2017
Jean-Pierre Daoust, Maire
Andréa Chouinard, Directrice générale

Pointe-Lebel
382, rue Granier
Pointe-Lebel, QC G0H 1N0
Tél: 418-589-8073; *Téléc:* 418-589-6154
www.pointe-lebel.com
Entité municipal: Village
Incorporation: 1er janvier 1964; *Area:* 91,16 km2
Comté ou district: Manicouagan; *Population au 2011:* 1,973
Circonscription(s) électorale(s) provinciale(s): René-Lévesque
Circonscription(s) électorale(s) fédérale(s): Manicouagan
Prochaines élections: 5e novembre 2017
Normand Morin, Maire
Nadia Allard, Directrice générale

Pontiac
2024, rte 148
Pontiac, QC J0X 2G0
Tél: 819-455-2401; *Téléc:* 819-455-9756
info@municipalitepontiac.com
www.municipalitepontiac.com
Other Information: Sans frais: 1-888-455-2401
Entité municipal: Municipality
Incorporation: 1er janvier 1975; *Area:* 446,87 km2
Comté ou district: Les Collines-de-l'Outaouais; *Population au 2011:* 5,681
Circonscription(s) électorale(s) provinciale(s): Pontiac
Circonscription(s) électorale(s) fédérale(s): Pontiac
Prochaines élections: 5e novembre 2017
Roger Larose, Maire
Sylvain Bertrand, Directeur général

Pontiac
602, rte 301
Campbell's Bay, QC J0X 1K0
Tél: 819-648-5689; *Téléc:* 819-648-5810
mrc@mrcpontiac.qc.ca
www.mrcpontiac.qc.ca
Entité municipal: Regional County Municipality
Incorporation: 1er janvier 1983
Population au 2011: 14,358
Note: 18 municipalités & 1 autre territoire.
Raymond Durocher, Préfet
Rémi Bertrand, Directeur général

Pont-Rouge
10, rue de la Fabrique
Pont-Rouge, QC G3H 1A1
Tél: 418-873-4481; *Téléc:* 418-873-3494
info@ville.pontrouge.qc.ca
www.ville.pontrouge.qc.ca
Entité municipal: Town
Incorporation: 3 janvier 1996; *Area:* 121,02 km2
Comté ou district: Portneuf; *Population au 2011:* 8,723
Circonscription(s) électorale(s) provinciale(s): Portneuf
Circonscription(s) électorale(s) fédérale(s): Portneuf-Jacques-Cartier
Prochaines élections: 5e novembre 2017
Ghislain Langlais, Maire
Jocelyne Laliberté, Greffière

Portage-du-Fort
CP 130
24, rue de l'Église
Portage-du-Fort, QC J0X 2T0
Tél: 819-647-2767; *Téléc:* 819-647-1910
therault@hotmail.com
Entité municipal: Village
Incorporation: 1er janvier 1863; *Area:* 4,24 km2
Comté ou district: Pontiac; *Population au 2011:* 266
Circonscription(s) électorale(s) provinciale(s): Pontiac
Circonscription(s) électorale(s) fédérale(s): Pontiac
Prochaines élections: 5e novembre 2017
Lynne Cameron, Mairesse
Tracey Hérault, Directrice générale

Port-Cartier
40, av Parent
Port-Cartier, QC G5B 2G5
Tél: 418-766-2349; *Téléc:* 418-766-3390
www.villeport-cartier.com
Entité municipal: Town
Incorporation: 19 février 2003; *Area:* 1073,70 km2
Comté ou district: Sept-Rivières; *Population au 2011:* 6,651
Circonscription(s) électorale(s) provinciale(s): Duplessis
Circonscription(s) électorale(s) fédérale(s): Manicouagan
Prochaines élections: 5e novembre 2017
Violaine Doyle, Mairesse
Raynald Martel, Greffier

Port-Daniel—Gascons
494, rte 132
Port-Daniel—Gascons, QC G0C 2N0
Tél: 418-396-5225; *Téléc:* 418-396-5588
municipalitedeport-daniel@globetrotter.net
www.port-daniel-gascons.ca
Entité municipal: Municipality
Incorporation: 17 janvier 2001; *Area:* 305,34 km2
Comté ou district: Le Rocher-Percé; *Population au 2011:* 2,453
Circonscription(s) électorale(s) provinciale(s): Bonaventure
Circonscription(s) électorale(s) fédérale(s): Gaspésie—Îles-de-la-Madeleine
Prochaines élections: 5e novembre 2017
Henri Grenier, Maire
Chantal Vignet, Directrice générale

Portneuf
297, 1re Av
Portneuf, QC G0A 2Y0
Tél: 418-286-3844; *Téléc:* 418-286-4304
info@villedeportneuf.com
www.villedeportneuf.com
Entité municipal: Town
Incorporation: 4 juillet 2002; *Area:* 110,43 km2
Comté ou district: Portneuf; *Population au 2011:* 3,107
Circonscription(s) électorale(s) provinciale(s): Portneuf
Circonscription(s) électorale(s) fédérale(s): Portneuf-Jacques-Cartier
Prochaines élections: 5e novembre 2017
Nelson Bédard, Maire
France Marcotte, Greffière

Portneuf
185, rte 138
Cap-Santé, QC G0A 1L0
Tél: 418-285-3744; *Téléc:* 418-285-1703
portneuf@mrc-portneuf.qc.ca
www.portneuf.com
Entité municipal: Regional County Municipality
Incorporation: 1er janvier 1982
Population au 2011: 49,370
Note: 18 municipalités & 3 autres territoires.
Denis Langlois, Préfet
Josée Frenette, Directrice générale

Portneuf-sur-Mer
CP 98
170, rue Principale
Portneuf-sur-Mer, QC G0T 1P0
Tél: 418-238-2642; *Téléc:* 418-238-5319
portneuf-sur-mer@videotron.ca
www.portneuf-sur-mer.ca
Entité municipal: Municipality
Incorporation: 12 septembre 1902; *Area:* 241,23 km2
Comté ou district: La Haute-Côte-Nord; *Population au 2011:* 761
Circonscription(s) électorale(s) provinciale(s): René-Lévesque
Circonscription(s) électorale(s) fédérale(s): Manicouagan
Prochaines élections: 5e novembre 2017
Gontran Tremblay, Maire
Nancy Roussel, Directrice générale

Potton
CP 330
2, rue de Vale Perkins
Mansonville, QC J0E 1X0
Tél: 450-292-3313; *Téléc:* 450-292-5555
info@potton.ca
www.potton.ca
Entité municipal: Township
Incorporation: 1er juillet 1855; *Area:* 264,10 km2
Comté ou district: Memphrémagog; *Population au 2011:* 1,849
Circonscription(s) électorale(s) provinciale(s): Orford
Circonscription(s) électorale(s) fédérale(s): Brome-Missisquoi
Prochaines élections: 5e novembre 2017
Louis Pierre Veillon, Maire
Thierry Gilbert, Directeur général

Poularies
CP 58
990, rue Principale
Poularies, QC J0Z 3E0
Tél: 819-782-5159; *Téléc:* 819-782-5063
poularies@mrcao.qc.ca
poularies.ao.ca
Entité municipal: Municipality
Incorporation: 7 mai 1924; *Area:* 164,95 km2

Comté ou district: Abitibi-Ouest; *Population au 2011:* 679
Circonscription(s) électorale(s) provinciale(s): Abitibi-Ouest
Circonscription(s) électorale(s) fédérale(s):
Abitibi-Témiscamingue
Prochaines élections: 5e novembre 2017
Pierre Godbout, Maire
Katy Rivard, Directrice générale

Preissac
6, rue des Rapides
Preissac, QC J0Y 2E0
Tél: 819-732-4938; *Téléc:* 819-732-4909
info@preissac.com
www.preissac.com
Entité municipal: Municipality
Incorporation: 1er janvier 1979; *Area:* 489,50 km2
Comté ou district: Abitibi; *Population au 2011:* 786
Circonscription(s) électorale(s) provinciale(s): Abitibi-Ouest
Circonscription(s) électorale(s) fédérale(s):
Abitibi-Témiscamingue
Prochaines élections: 5e novembre 2017
Stephan Lavoie, Maire
Gérard Pétrin, Directeur général

La Présentation
772, rue Principale
La Présentation, QC J0H 1B0
Tél: 450-796-2317; *Téléc:* 450-796-1707
lapresentation@mrcmaskoutains.qc.ca
www.municipalitelapresentation.qc.ca
Entité municipal: Parish (Paroisse)
Incorporation: 1er juillet 1855; *Area:* 104,71 km2
Comté ou district: Les Maskoutains; *Population au 2011:* 2,466
Circonscription(s) électorale(s) provinciale(s): Saint-Hyacinthe
Circonscription(s) électorale(s) fédérale(s): St-Hyacinthe-Bagot
Prochaines élections: 5e novembre 2017
Claude Roger, Maire
Lucy Chevrier, Directrice générale

Price
CP 340
18, rue Fournier
Price, QC G0J 1Z0
Tél: 418-775-2144; *Téléc:* 418-775-2459
price@mitis.qc.ca
www.municipaliteprice.com
Entité municipal: Village
Incorporation: 3 mars 1926; *Area:* 2,35 km2
Comté ou district: La Mitis; *Population au 2011:* 1,673
Circonscription(s) électorale(s) provinciale(s): Matane-Matapédia
Circonscription(s) électorale(s) fédérale(s): Avignon-La Mitis-Matane-Matapédia
Prochaines élections: 5e novembre 2017
Fabien Boucher, Maire
Louise Furlong, Greffière

Princeville
50, rue St-Jacques ouest
Princeville, QC G6L 4Y5
Tél: 819-364-3333; *Téléc:* 819-364-5198
info@villedeprinceville.qc.ca
www.villedeprinceville.qc.ca
Entité municipal: Town
Incorporation: 23 février 2000; *Area:* 198,00 km2
Comté ou district: L'Érable; *Population au 2011:* 5,693
Circonscription(s) électorale(s) provinciale(s): Arthabaska
Circonscription(s) électorale(s) fédérale(s): Mégantic-L'Érable
Prochaines élections: 5e novembre 2017
Gilles Fortier, Maire
Mario Juaire, Greffier

Puvirnituq
CP 150
Puvirnituq, QC J0M 1P0
Tél: 819-988-2825; *Téléc:* 819-988-2751
www.nvpuvirnituq.ca
Entité municipal: Northern Village
Incorporation: 2 septembre 1989; *Area:* 111,00 km2
Comté ou district: Administration régionale Kativik; *Population au 2011:* 1,692
Circonscription(s) électorale(s) provinciale(s): Ungava
Circonscription(s) électorale(s) fédérale(s):
Abitibi-Baie-James-Nunavik-Eeyou
Levi Amarualik, Maire
Sarah Beaulne, Secrétaire-trésorière

Quaqtaq
CP 107
Quaqtaq, QC J0M 1J0
Tél: 819-492-9912; *Téléc:* 819-492-9935
www.nvquaqtaq.ca
Entité municipal: Northern Village
Incorporation: 1er novembre 1980; *Area:* 26,49 km2
Comté ou district: Administration régionale Kativik; *Population au 2011:* 376
Circonscription(s) électorale(s) provinciale(s): Ungava
Circonscription(s) électorale(s) fédérale(s):
Abitibi-Baie-James-Nunavik-Eeyou
Robert Deer Sr, Maire
Sammy Tukkiapik, Secrétaire-trésorier

Racine
348, rue de L'Église
Racine, QC J0E 1Y0
Tél: 450-532-2876; *Téléc:* 450-532-2865
www.municipalite.racine.qc.ca
Entité municipal: Municipality
Incorporation: 15 février 1995; *Area:* 107,87 km2
Comté ou district: Le Val-Saint-François; *Population au 2011:* 1,252
Circonscription(s) électorale(s) provinciale(s): Richmond
Circonscription(s) électorale(s) fédérale(s): Jonquière; Shefford
Prochaines élections: 5e novembre 2017
François Boissonneault, Maire
Mélisa Camiré, Directrice générale

Ragueneau
523, rte 138
Ragueneau, QC G0H 1S0
Tél: 418-567-2345; *Téléc:* 418-567-2344
ragueneau@municipalite.ragueneau.qc.ca
www.municipalite.ragueneau.qc.ca
Entité municipal: Parish (Paroisse)
Incorporation: 7 mars 1951; *Area:* 215,92 km2
Comté ou district: Manicouagan; *Population au 2011:* 1,405
Circonscription(s) électorale(s) provinciale(s): René-Lévesque
Circonscription(s) électorale(s) fédérale(s): Manicouagan
Prochaines élections: 5e novembre 2017
Joseph Imbeault, Maire
Audrey Morin, Directrice générale

Rapide-Danseur
535, rue du Village
Rapide-Danseur, QC J0Z 3G0
Tél: 819-948-2152; *Téléc:* 819-948-2265
rapide-danseur@mrcao.qc.ca
rapide-danseur.ao.ca
Entité municipal: Municipality
Incorporation: 1er janvier 1981; *Area:* 185,18 km2
Comté ou district: Abitibi-Ouest; *Population au 2011:* 312
Circonscription(s) électorale(s) provinciale(s): Abitibi-Ouest
Circonscription(s) électorale(s) fédérale(s):
Abitibi-Témiscamingue
Prochaines élections: 5e novembre 2017
Alain Gagnon, Maire
Lucie Gravel, Directrice générale

Rapides-des-Joachims
CP 2-10
48, rue de l'Église
Rapides-des-Joachims, QC J0X 3M0
Tél: 613-586-2532; *Téléc:* 613-586-2720
rapides-des-joachims@mrcpontiac.qc.ca
www.rapidesdesjoachims.ca
Entité municipal: Municipality
Incorporation: 1er janvier 1955; *Area:* 248,92 km2
Comté ou district: Pontiac; *Population au 2011:* 131
Circonscription(s) électorale(s) provinciale(s): Pontiac
Circonscription(s) électorale(s) fédérale(s): Pontiac
Prochaines élections: 5e novembre 2017
James Gibson, Maire
Sylvain Bégin, Directeur général

La Rédemption
CP 39
68, rue Soucy
La Rédemption, QC G0J 1P0
Tél: 418-776-5311; *Téléc:* 418-776-5711
redemption@mitis.qc.ca
www.municipalite.laredemption.qc.ca
Entité municipal: Parish (Paroisse)
Incorporation: 1er janvier 1956; *Area:* 116,29 km2
Comté ou district: La Mitis; *Population au 2011:* 488
Circonscription(s) électorale(s) provinciale(s): Matane-Matapédia
Circonscription(s) électorale(s) fédérale(s): Avignon-La Mitis-Matane-Matapédia
Prochaines élections: 5e novembre 2017
Hervé Lavoie, Maire
Nadine Roussy, Directrice générale

La Reine
1, 3e av ouest
La Reine, QC J0Z 2L0
Tél: 819-947-5271; *Téléc:* 819-947-5271
lareine@mrcao.qc.ca
lareine.ao.ca
Entité municipal: Municipality
Incorporation: 19 septembre 1981; *Area:* 100,01 km2
Comté ou district: Abitibi-Ouest; *Population au 2011:* 340
Circonscription(s) électorale(s) provinciale(s): Abitibi-Ouest
Circonscription(s) électorale(s) fédérale(s):
Abitibi-Témiscamingue
Prochaines élections: 5e novembre 2017
Jean-Guy Boulet, Maire
Sylvie Germain, Directrice générale

Rémigny
1304, ch de l'Église
Rémigny, QC J0Z 3H0
Tél: 819-761-2421; *Téléc:* 819-761-2421
mun.remigny@mrctemiscamingue.qc.ca
www.municipaliteremigny.qc.ca
Entité municipal: Municipality
Incorporation: 1er janvier 1978; *Area:* 985,03 km2
Comté ou district: Témiscamingue; *Population au 2011:* 279
Circonscription(s) électorale(s) provinciale(s):
Rouyn-Noranda-Témiscamingue
Circonscription(s) électorale(s) fédérale(s):
Abitibi-Témiscamingue
Prochaines élections: 5e novembre 2017
Jocelyn Aylwin, Maire
Micheline Champoux, Directrice générale

Richelieu
200, boul Richelieu
Richelieu, QC J3L 3R4
Tél: 450-658-1157; *Téléc:* 450-658-5096
info@ville.richelieu.qc.ca
www.ville.richelieu.qc.ca
Entité municipal: Town
Incorporation: 15 mars 2000; *Area:* 29,75 km2
Comté ou district: Rouville; Communauté métropolitaine de Montréal; *Population au 2011:* 5,467
Circonscription(s) électorale(s) provinciale(s): Chambly
Circonscription(s) électorale(s) fédérale(s): Beloeil-Chambly
Prochaines élections: 5e novembre 2017
Jacques Ladouceur, Maire
Eve-Marie Préfontaine, Greffière

Richmond
745, rue Gouin
Richmond, QC J0B 2H0
Tél: 819-826-3789; *Téléc:* 819-826-2813
commis@ville.richmond.qc.ca
www.ville.richmond.qc.ca
Entité municipal: Town
Incorporation: 29 décembre 1999; *Area:* 7,76 km2
Comté ou district: Le Val-Saint-François; *Population au 2011:* 3,275
Circonscription(s) électorale(s) provinciale(s): Richmond
Circonscription(s) électorale(s) fédérale(s):
Richmond-Arthabaska
Prochaines élections: 5e novembre 2017
Marc-André Martel, Maire
Rémi-Mario Mayette, Directeur général

Rigaud
33, St-Jean-Baptiste ouest
Rigaud, QC J0P 1P0
Tél: 450-451-0869; *Téléc:* 450-451-4227
rigaud@ville.rigaud.qc.ca
www.ville.rigaud.qc.ca
Entité municipal: Municipality
Incorporation: 29 novembre 1995; *Area:* 97,15 km2
Comté ou district: Vaudreuil-Soulanges; *Population au 2011:* 7,346
Circonscription(s) électorale(s) provinciale(s): Soulanges
Circonscription(s) électorale(s) fédérale(s): Vaudreuil-Soulanges
Prochaines élections: 5e novembre 2017
Hans Gruenwald Jr., Maire
Hélène Therrien, Greffière

Rimouski-Neigette
#220, 23, rue de l'Évêché ouest
Rimouski, QC G5L 4H4
Tél: 418-724-5154; *Téléc:* 418-725-4567
administration@mrcrimouskineigette.qc.ca
www.mrcrimouskineigette.qc.ca
Entité municipal: Regional County Municipality
Incorporation: 26 mai 1982
Population au 2011: 55,095
Note: 9 municipalités & 1 autre territoire.

Francis St-Pierre, Préfet
Jean-Maxime Dubé, Directeur général

Ripon
#101, 31, rue Coursol
Ripon, QC J0V 1V0
Tél: 819-983-2000; *Téléc:* 819-983-1327
info.ripon@mrcpapineau.com
www.ville.ripon.qc.ca
Entité municipal: Municipality
Incorporation: 3 mai 2000; *Area:* 140,57 km2
Comté ou district: Papineau; *Population au 2011:* 1,522
Circonscription(s) électorale(s) provinciale(s): Papineau
Circonscription(s) électorale(s) fédérale(s): Argenteuil-La Petite-Nation
Prochaines élections: 5e novembre 2017
Luc Desjardins, Maire
Julie Ricard, Directrice générale

Ristigouche-Partie-Sud-Est
35, ch Kempt, RR#2
Matapédia, QC G0J 1V0
Tél: 418-788-5769; *Téléc:* 418-788-2598
ristigouchesudest@globetrotter.net
www.ristigouchesudest.ca
Entité municipal: Township
Incorporation: 30 juin 1906; *Area:* 48,95 km2
Comté ou district: Avignon; *Population au 2011:* 167
Circonscription(s) électorale(s) provinciale(s): Bonaventure
Circonscription(s) électorale(s) fédérale(s): Avignon-La Mitis-Matane-Matapédia
Prochaines élections: 5e novembre 2017
François Boulay, Maire
Suzanne Bourdages, Directrice générale

Rivière-à-Claude
520, rue Principale est
Rivière-à-Claude, QC G0E 1Z0
Tél: 418-797-2422; *Téléc:* 418-797-2455
munirac@globetrotter.net
Entité municipal: Municipality
Incorporation: 18 décembre 1923; *Area:* 155,39 km2
Comté ou district: La Haute-Gaspésie; *Population au 2011:* 130
Circonscription(s) électorale(s) provinciale(s): Gaspé
Circonscription(s) électorale(s) fédérale(s): Gaspésie-Les Iles-de-la-Madeleine
Prochaines élections: 5e novembre 2017
Réjean Normand, Maire
Claudine Auclair, Directrice générale

Rivière-à-Pierre
CP 648
830, rue Principale
Rivière-à-Pierre, QC G0A 3A0
Tél: 418-323-2112; *Téléc:* 418-323-2111
rivapier@globetrotter.net
www.riviereapierre.com
Entité municipal: Municipality
Incorporation: 11 octobre 1897; *Area:* 521,31 km2
Comté ou district: Portneuf; *Population au 2011:* 671
Circonscription(s) électorale(s) provinciale(s): Portneuf
Circonscription(s) électorale(s) fédérale(s): Portneuf-Jacques-Cartier
Prochaines élections: 5e novembre 2017
Jean Mainguy, Maire
Pascale Bonin, Directrice générale

Rivière-au-Tonnerre
CP 129
473, rue Jacques Cartier
Rivière-au-Tonnerre, QC G0G 2L0
Tél: 418-465-2255; *Téléc:* 418-465-2956
www.riviere-au-tonnerre.ca
Entité municipal: Municipality
Incorporation: 14 décembre 1925; *Area:* 1331,17 km2
Comté ou district: Minganie; *Population au 2011:* 307
Circonscription(s) électorale(s) provinciale(s): Duplessis
Circonscription(s) électorale(s) fédérale(s): Manicouagan
Prochaines élections: 5e novembre 2017
Aline Beaudin, Mairesse
Carmelle Anglehart, Directrice générale

Rivière-Beaudette
663, ch de la Frontière
Rivière-Beaudette, QC J0P 1R0
Tél: 450-269-2931; *Téléc:* 450-269-2815
munrivbeaudette@qc.aira.com
www.riviere-beaudette.com
Entité municipal: Municipality
Incorporation: 17 janvier 1990; *Area:* 19,62 km2
Comté ou district: Vaudreuil-Soulanges; *Population au 2011:* 1,885
Circonscription(s) électorale(s) provinciale(s): Soulanges
Circonscription(s) électorale(s) fédérale(s): Salaberry-Suroît
Prochaines élections: 5e novembre 2017
Patrick Bousez, Maire
Céline Chayer, Directrice générale

Rivière-Bleue
32, rue des Pins est
Rivière-Bleue, QC G0L 2B0
Tél: 418-893-5559; *Téléc:* 418-893-5530
info@riviere-bleue.ca
www.riviere-bleue.ca
Entité municipal: Municipality
Incorporation: 14 juin 1975; *Area:* 179,93 km2
Comté ou district: Témiscouata; *Population au 2011:* 1,299
Circonscription(s) électorale(s) provinciale(s): Rivière-du-Loup-Témiscouata
Circonscription(s) électorale(s) fédérale(s): Rimouski-Neigette-Témiscouata-Les Basques
Prochaines élections: 5e novembre 2017
Claude H. Pelletier, Maire
Claudie Levasseur, Directrice générale

Rivière-du-Loup
310, rue St-Pierre
Rivière-du-Loup, QC G5R 3V3
Tél: 418-867-2485; *Téléc:* 418-867-3100
www.rivieredulou p.ca
Entité municipal: Regional County Municipality
Incorporation: 1 janvier 1982
Population au 2011: 34,375
Note: 13 municipalités.
Michel Lagacé, Préfet
Raymond Duval, Directeur général

La Rivière-du-Nord
#200, 161, rue de la Gare
Saint-Jérôme, QC J7Z 2B9
Tél: 450-436-9321; *Téléc:* 450-436-1977
info@mrcrdn.qc.ca
www.mrcrdn.qc.ca
Entité municipal: Regional County Municipality
Incorporation: 1er janvier 1983
Population au 2011: 115,165
Note: 5 municipalités.
Bruno Laroche, Préfet
Pierre Godin, Directeur général

Rivière-Éternité
418, rte Principale
Rivière-Éternité, QC G0V 1P0
Tél: 418-272-2860; *Téléc:* 418-544-3085
municipalite@riviere-eternite.com
www.riviere-eternite.com
Entité municipal: Municipality
Incorporation: 20 juillet 1974; *Area:* 496,88 km2
Comté ou district: Le Fjord-du-Saguenay; *Population au 2011:* 484
Circonscription(s) électorale(s) provinciale(s): Dubuc
Circonscription(s) électorale(s) fédérale(s): Chicoutimi-Le Fjord
Prochaines élections: 5e novembre 2017
Rémi Gagné, Maire
Denis Houde, Directeur général

Rivière-Héva
CP 60
740, rte St-Paul nord
Rivière-Héva, QC J0Y 2H0
Tél: 819-735-3521; *Téléc:* 819-735-4251
info@mun-r-h.com
www.riviere-heva.com
Entité municipal: Municipality
Incorporation: 1er janvier 1982; *Area:* 166,09 km2
Comté ou district: La Vallée-de-l'Or; *Population au 2011:* 1,433
Circonscription(s) électorale(s) provinciale(s): Abitibi-Est
Circonscription(s) électorale(s) fédérale(s): Abitibi-Baie-James-Nunavik-Eeyou
Prochaines élections: 5e novembre 2017
Réjean Guay, Maire
Nathalie Savard, Directrice générale

Rivière-Ouelle
CP 99
106, rue de l'Église
Rivière-Ouelle, QC G0L 2C0
Tél: 418-856-3829; *Téléc:* 418-856-1790
www.riviereouelle.ca
Entité municipal: Municipality
Incorporation: 1er juillet 1855; *Area:* 54,72 km2
Comté ou district: Kamouraska; *Population au 2011:* 1,058
Circonscription(s) électorale(s) provinciale(s): Côte-du-Sud
Circonscription(s) électorale(s) fédérale(s): Montmagny-L'Islet-Kamouraska-Rivière-du-Loup
Prochaines élections: 5e novembre 2017
Louis-Georges Simard, Maire
Adam Ménard, Directeur général

Rivière-Rouge
25, rue L'Annonciation sud
Rivière-Rouge, QC J0T 1T0
Tél: 819-275-2929; *Téléc:* 819-275-3676
greffe@riviere-rouge.ca
www.riviere-rouge.ca
Entité municipal: Town
Incorporation: 18 décembre 2002; *Area:* 463,18 km2
Comté ou district: Antoine-Labelle; *Population au 2011:* 4,645
Circonscription(s) électorale(s) provinciale(s): Labelle
Circonscription(s) électorale(s) fédérale(s): Laurentides-Labelle
Prochaines élections: 5e novembre 2017
Déborah Bélanger, Mairesse
Lucie Bourque, Greffière

Rivière-Saint-Jean
116, rue du Quai
Rivière-Saint-Jean, QC G0G 2N0
Tél: 418-949-2464; *Téléc:* 418-949-2489
magpiest-jean@globetrotter.net
Entité municipal: Municipality
Incorporation: 1er janvier 1966; *Area:* 652,54 km2
Comté ou district: Minganie; *Population au 2011:* 239
Circonscription(s) électorale(s) provinciale(s): Duplessis
Circonscription(s) électorale(s) fédérale(s): Manicouagan
Prochaines élections: 5e novembre 2017
Josée Brunet, Mairesse
Louise Rodgers, Directrice générale

Robert-Cliche
111A, 107e Rue
Beauceville, QC G5X 2P9
Tél: 418-774-9828; *Téléc:* 418-774-4057
www.beaucerc.com
Entité municipal: Regional County Municipality
Incorporation: 1 janvier 1982
Population au 2011: 19,288
Note: 10 municipalités.
Jean-Roch Veilleux, Préfet
Gilbert Caron, Directeur général

Rochebaucourt
20, rue du Chanoine-Girard
Rochebaucourt, QC J0Y 2J0
Tél: 819-754-2083; *Téléc:* 819-754-5417
muniroche@cableamos.com
www.municipalite-rochebaucourt.org
Entité municipal: Municipality
Incorporation: 1er janvier 1983; *Area:* 185,00 km2
Comté ou district: Abitibi; *Population au 2011:* 161
Circonscription(s) électorale(s) provinciale(s): Abitibi-Ouest
Circonscription(s) électorale(s) fédérale(s): Abitibi-Témiscamingue
Prochaines élections: 5e novembre 2017
Marc Antoine Pelletier, Maire
Nathalie Lyrette, Directrice générale

Rocher-Percé
CP 128
129, boul René-Lévesque ouest
Chandler, QC G0C 1K0
Tél: 418-689-4313; *Téléc:* 418-689-5807
mrc@rocherperce.qc.ca
www.mrcrocherperce.qc.ca
Other Information: Sans frais: 1-888-689-3185
Entité municipal: Regional County Municipality
Incorporation: 1 avril 1981
Population au 2011: 17,979
Circonscription(s) électorale(s) fédérale(s): Lac-Saint-Jean
Note: 5 municipalités & 1 autre territoire.
Nadia Minassian, Préfete
Mario Grenier, Directeur général, 418-689-4017

Roquemaure
15, rue Raymond est
Roquemaure, QC J0Z 3K0
Tél: 819-787-6311; *Téléc:* 819-787-6383
roquemaure@mrcao.qc.ca
roquemaure.ao.ca
Entité municipal: Municipality
Incorporation: 1er janvier 1952; *Area:* 121,67 km2
Comté ou district: Abitibi-Ouest; *Population au 2011:* 414
Circonscription(s) électorale(s) provinciale(s): Abitibi-Ouest
Circonscription(s) électorale(s) fédérale(s): Abitibi-Témiscamingue
Prochaines élections: 5e novembre 2017
Lucie Gravel, Mairesse

Annick Lavoie, Directrice générale

Rougemont
61, ch de Marieville
Rougemont, QC J0L 1M0
Tél: 450-469-3790; *Téléc:* 450-469-0309
reception@rougemont.ca
www.rougemont.ca
Entité municipal: Municipality
Incorporation: 26 janvier 2000; *Area:* 44,48 km2
Comté ou district: Rouville; *Population au 2011:* 2,723
Circonscription(s) électorale(s) provinciale(s): Iberville
Circonscription(s) électorale(s) fédérale(s): Shefford
Prochaines élections: 5e novembre 2017
Alain Brière, Maire
Kathia Joseph, Directrice générale

Roussillon
#200, 260, rue Saint-Pierre
Saint-Constant, QC J5A 2A5
Tél: 450-638-1221; *Téléc:* 450-638-4499
admin@mrcroussillon.qc.ca
www.mrcroussillon.qc.ca
Entité municipal: Regional County Municipality
Incorporation: 1er janvier 1982
Population au 2011: 162,187
Note: 11 municipalités.
Nathalie Simon, Préfète
Pierre Largy, Directeur général

Rouville
#100, 500 rue Desjardins
Marieville, QC J3M 1E1
Tél: 450-460-2127; *Téléc:* 450-460-7169
mrcrouville@on.aira.com
www.mrcrouville.qc.ca
Entité municipal: Regional County Municipality
Incorporation: 1er janvier 1982
Population au 2011: 35,690
Note: 8 municipalités.
Michel Picotte, Préfet
Rosaire Marcil, Directeur général

Roxton
216, rang Ste-Geneviève
Roxton Falls, QC J0H 1E0
Tél: 450-548-2500; *Téléc:* 450-548-2412
www.cantonderoxton.qc.ca
Entité municipal: Township
Incorporation: 1er juillet 1855; *Area:* 149,07 km2
Comté ou district: Acton; *Population au 2011:* 1,093
Circonscription(s) électorale(s) provinciale(s): Johnson
Circonscription(s) électorale(s) fédérale(s): St-Hyacinthe-Bagot
Prochaines élections: 5e novembre 2017
Stéphane Beauregard, Maire
Caroline Choquette, Directrice générale

Roxton Falls
26, rue du Marché
Roxton Falls, QC J0H 1E0
Tél: 450-548-5790; *Téléc:* 450-548-5881
roxton@roxtonfalls.ca
www.roxtonfalls.ca
Entité municipal: Village
Incorporation: 1er janvier 1863; *Area:* 5,25 km2
Comté ou district: Acton; *Population au 2011:* 1,265
Circonscription(s) électorale(s) provinciale(s): Johnson
Circonscription(s) électorale(s) fédérale(s): St-Hyacinthe-Bagot
Prochaines élections: 5e novembre 2017
Jean-Marie Laplante, Maire
Julie Gagné, Directrice générale

Roxton Pond
901, rue St-Jean
Roxton Pond, QC J0E 1Z0
Tél: 450-372-6875; *Téléc:* 450-372-1205
infomun@roxtonpond.ca
www.roxtonpond.ca
Entité municipal: Municipality
Incorporation: 17 décembre 1997; *Area:* 102,11 km2
Comté ou district: La Haute-Yamaska; *Population au 2011:* 3,786
Circonscription(s) électorale(s) provinciale(s): Johnson
Circonscription(s) électorale(s) fédérale(s): Shefford
Prochaines élections: 5e novembre 2017
Raymond Loignon, Maire
Patrice Bissonnette, Directeur général

Sacré-Coeur
88, rue Principale nord
Sacré-Coeur, QC G0T 1Y0
Tél: 418-236-4621; *Téléc:* 418-236-9144
s-c@municipalite.sacre-coeur.qc.ca
www.municipalite.sacre-coeur.qc.ca
Entité municipal: Municipality
Incorporation: 30 juin 1976; *Area:* 341,74 km2
Comté ou district: La Haute-Côte-Nord; *Population au 2011:* 1,881
Circonscription(s) électorale(s) provinciale(s): René-Lévesque
Circonscription(s) électorale(s) fédérale(s): Manicouagan; Rimouski-Neigette-Témiscouata-Les Basques
Prochaines élections: 5e novembre 2017
Marjolaine Gagnon, Mairesse
Nadia Duchesne, Directrice générale

Sacré-Coeur-de-Jésus
4118, rte 112
East Broughton, QC G0N 1G0
Tél: 418-427-3447; *Téléc:* 418-427-4774
info@sacrecoeurdejesus.qc.ca
www.sacrecoeurdejesus.qc.ca
Entité municipal: Parish (Paroisse)
Incorporation: 11 décembre 1889; *Area:* 103,850 km2
Comté ou district: Les Appalaches; *Population au 2011:* 564
Circonscription(s) électorale(s) provinciale(s): Lotbinière-Frontenac
Circonscription(s) électorale(s) fédérale(s): Mégantic-L'Érable
Prochaines élections: 5e novembre 2017
Guy Roy, Maire
Marie-France Létourneau, Directrice générale

Saint-Adalbert
55, rue Principale
Saint-Adalbert, QC G0R 2M0
Tél: 418-356-5271; *Téléc:* 418-356-5317
mstadalb@globetrotter.net
www.saintadalbert.qc.ca
Entité municipal: Municipality
Incorporation: 26 août 1911; *Area:* 213,95 km2
Comté ou district: L'Islet; *Population au 2011:* 536
Circonscription(s) électorale(s) provinciale(s): Côte-du-Sud
Circonscription(s) électorale(s) fédérale(s): Montmagny-L'Islet-Kamouraska-Rivière-du-Loup
Prochaines élections: 5e novembre 2017
René Laverdière, Maire
Magguy Mathault, Directrice générale

Saint-Adelme
CP 39
138, rue Principale
Saint-Adelme, QC G0J 2B0
Tél: 418-733-4044; *Téléc:* 418-733-4111
st-adelme@mrcdematane.qc.ca
www.municipalite.st-adelme.ca
Entité municipal: Parish (Paroisse)
Incorporation: 9 septembre 1933; *Area:* 100,20 km2
Comté ou district: La Matanie; *Population au 2011:* 485
Circonscription(s) électorale(s) provinciale(s): Matane-Matapédia
Circonscription(s) électorale(s) fédérale(s): Avignon-La Mitis-Matane-Matapédia
Prochaines élections: 5e novembre 2017
Jean Roland Lebrun, Maire
Annick Hudon, Directrice générale

Saint-Adelphe
150, rue Baillargeon
Saint-Adelphe-de-Champlain, QC G0X 2G0
Tél: 418-322-5721; *Téléc:* 418-322-5434
st-adelphe@regionmekinac.com
www.st-adelphe.qc.ca
Entité municipal: Parish (Paroisse)
Incorporation: 19 octobre 1891; *Area:* 135,35 km2
Comté ou district: Mékinac; *Population au 2011:* 952
Circonscription(s) électorale(s) provinciale(s): Laviolette
Circonscription(s) électorale(s) fédérale(s): Saint-Maurice-Champlain
Prochaines élections: 5e novembre 2017
Paul Labranche, Maire
Daniel Bacon, Directeur général

Saint-Adolphe-d'Howard
1881, ch du Village
Saint-Adolphe-d'Howard, QC J0T 2B0
Tél: 819-327-2044; *Téléc:* 819-327-2282
info@stadolphedhoward.qc.ca
www.stadolphedhoward.qc.ca
Entité municipal: Municipality
Incorporation: 1er janvier 1883; *Area:* 144,41 km2
Comté ou district: Les Pays-d'en-Haut; *Population au 2011:* 3,702
Circonscription(s) électorale(s) provinciale(s): Argenteuil
Circonscription(s) électorale(s) fédérale(s): Argenteuil-La Petite-Nation
Prochaines élections: 5e novembre 2017
Lisette Lapointe, Mairesse
Mathieu Dessureault, Directeur général

Saint-Adrien
1589, rue Principale
Saint-Adrien, QC J0A 1C0
Tél: 819-828-2872; *Téléc:* 819-828-0442
municipalite@st-adrien.com
st-adrien.com
Entité municipal: Municipality
Incorporation: 1er janvier 1879; *Area:* 97,59 km2
Comté ou district: Les Sources; *Population au 2011:* 490
Circonscription(s) électorale(s) provinciale(s): Richmond
Circonscription(s) électorale(s) fédérale(s): Richmond-Arthabaska
Prochaines élections: 5e novembre 2017
Pierre Therrien, Maire
Maryse Ducharme, Directrice générale

Saint-Adrien-d'Irlande
152, rue Municipale
Saint-Adrien-d'Irlande, QC G0N 1M0
Tél: 418-335-2585; *Téléc:* 418-335-4040
stadriendirlande.ca
Entité municipal: Municipality
Incorporation: 1er janvier 1873; *Area:* 52,780 km2
Comté ou district: Les Appalaches; *Population au 2011:* 389
Circonscription(s) électorale(s) provinciale(s): Lotbinière-Frontenac
Circonscription(s) électorale(s) fédérale(s): Mégantic-L'Érable
Prochaines élections: 5e novembre 2017
Jessika Lacombe, Mairesse
Ghislaine Leblanc, Directrice générale

Saint-Agapit
1080, av Bergeron
Saint-Agapit, QC G0S 1Z0
Tél: 418-888-4620; *Téléc:* 418-888-4791
stagapit@globetrotter.net
st-agapit.qc.ca
Entité municipal: Municipality
Incorporation: 14 avril 1979; *Area:* 65,91 km2
Comté ou district: Lotbinière; *Population au 2011:* 3,567
Circonscription(s) électorale(s) provinciale(s): Lotbinière-Frontenac
Circonscription(s) électorale(s) fédérale(s): Lévis-Lotbinière
Prochaines élections: 5e novembre 2017
Sylvie Fortin Graham, Mairesse
Isabelle Paré, Directrice générale

Saint-Aimé
CP 240
285, rue Bonsecours
Massueville, QC J0G 1K0
Tél: 450-788-2737; *Téléc:* 450-788-3337
staime@pierredesaurel.com
www.saintaime.qc.ca
Entité municipal: Municipality
Incorporation: 1er juillet 1855; *Area:* 61,33 km2
Comté ou district: Pierre-De Saurel; *Population au 2011:* 505
Circonscription(s) électorale(s) provinciale(s): Richelieu
Circonscription(s) électorale(s) fédérale(s): Bécancour-Nicolet-Saurel
Prochaines élections: 5e novembre 2017
Maria Libert, Mairesse
Francine B. Lambert, Directrice générale

Saint-Aimé-des-Lacs
119, rue Principale
Saint-Aimé-des-Lacs, QC G0T 1S0
Tél: 418-439-2229; *Téléc:* 418-439-1475
www.saintaimedeslacs.ca
Entité municipal: Municipality
Incorporation: 1er janvier 1950; *Area:* 101,57 km2
Comté ou district: Charlevoix-Est; *Population au 2011:* 1,073
Circonscription(s) électorale(s) provinciale(s): Charlevoix-Côte-de-Beaupré
Circonscription(s) électorale(s) fédérale(s): Beauport-Côte-de-Beaupré-Ile d'Orléans-Charlevoix
Prochaines élections: 5e novembre 2017
Claire Gagnon, Mairesse
Suzanne Gaudreault, Directrice générale

Saint-Aimé-du-Lac-des-îles
871, ch Diotte
Saint-Aimé-du-Lac-des-îles, QC J0W 1J0
Tél: 819-597-2047; *Téléc:* 819-597-2554
info@saint-aime-du-lac-des-iles.ca
www.saint-aime-du-lac-des-iles.ca
Entité municipal: Municipality
Incorporation: 1er janvier 2006; *Area:* 165,77 km2
Comté ou district: Antoine-Labelle; *Population au 2011:* 778
Circonscription(s) électorale(s) provinciale(s): Labelle
Circonscription(s) électorale(s) fédérale(s): Laurentides-Labelle
Prochaines élections: 5e novembre 2017

Pierre-Paul Goyette, Maire
Gisèle Lépine-Pilotte, Directrice générale

Saint-Alban
204, rue Principale
Saint-Alban, QC G0A 3B0
Tél: 418-268-8026; *Téléc:* 418-268-5073
info@st-alban.qc.ca
www.st-alban.qc.ca
Entité municipal: Municipality
Incorporation: 31 décembre 1991; *Area:* 150,55 km2
Comté ou district: Portneuf; *Population au 2011:* 1,225
Circonscription(s) électorale(s) provinciale(s): Portneuf
Circonscription(s) électorale(s) fédérale(s): Portneuf-Jacques-Cartier
Prochaines élections: 5e novembre 2017
Bernard Naud, Maire
Vincent Lévesque Dostie, Directeur général

Saint-Albert
CP 100
25, rue des Loisirs
Saint-Albert, QC J0A 1E0
Tél: 819-353-3300; *Téléc:* 819-353-3313
stalbert@munstalbert.ca
www.munstalbert.ca
Entité municipal: Municipality
Incorporation: 1er janvier 1864; *Area:* 70,36 km2
Comté ou district: Arthabaska; *Population au 2011:* 1,526
Circonscription(s) électorale(s) provinciale(s): Drummond-Bois-Francs
Circonscription(s) électorale(s) fédérale(s): Richmond-Arthabaska
Prochaines élections: 5e novembre 2017
Alain St-Pierre, Maire
Suzanne Crête, Directrice générale

Saint-Alexandre
453, rue St-Denis
Saint-Alexandre, QC J0J 1S0
Tél: 450-346-6641; *Téléc:* 450-346-0538
www.saint-alexandre.ca
Entité municipal: Municipality
Incorporation: 17 septembre 1988; *Area:* 76,55 km2
Comté ou district: Le Haut-Richelieu; *Population au 2011:* 2,495
Circonscription(s) électorale(s) provinciale(s): Iberville
Circonscription(s) électorale(s) fédérale(s): Saint-Jean
Prochaines élections: 5e novembre 2017
Luc Mercier, Maire
Michèle Bertrand, Directrice générale

Saint-Alexandre-de-Kamouraska
CP 10
629, rte 289
Saint-Alexandre-de-Kamouraska, QC G0L 2G0
Tél: 418-495-2440; *Téléc:* 418-495-2659
www.stalexkamouraska.com
Entité municipal: Municipality
Incorporation: 1er juillet 1855; *Area:* 115,95 km2
Comté ou district: Kamouraska; *Population au 2011:* 2,050
Circonscription(s) électorale(s) provinciale(s): Côte-du-Sud
Circonscription(s) électorale(s) fédérale(s): Montmagny-L'Islet-Kamouraska-Rivière-du-Loup
Prochaines élections: 5e novembre 2017
Anita Ouellet Castonguay, Mairesse
Lyne Dumont, Directrice générale

Saint-Alexandre-des-Lacs
17, rue de l'Église
Saint-Alexandre-des-Lacs, QC G0J 2C0
Tél: 418-778-3532; *Téléc:* 418-778-1315
stalexandre@mrcmatapedia.qc.ca
www.saintalexandredeslacs.com
Entité municipal: Parish (Paroisse)
Incorporation: 1er janvier 1965; *Area:* 92,98 km2
Comté ou district: La Matapédia; *Population au 2011:* 258
Circonscription(s) électorale(s) provinciale(s): Matane-Matapédia
Circonscription(s) électorale(s) fédérale(s): Avignon-La Mitis-Matane-Matapédia
Prochaines élections: 5e novembre 2017
Nelson Pilote, Maire
Caroline Savoie, Directrice générale

Saint-Alexis
232, rue Principale
Saint-Alexis, QC J0K 1T0
Tél: 450-839-7277; *Téléc:* 450-839-6241
info@st-alexis.com
Entité municipal: Municipality
Incorporation: 19 décembre 2012; *Area:* 43,12 km2
Comté ou district: Montcalm; *Population au 2012:* 1,461
Circonscription(s) électorale(s) provinciale(s): Rousseau
Circonscription(s) électorale(s) fédérale(s): Montcalm
Prochaines élections: 5e novembre 2017
Robert Perreault, Maire
Rémy Lanoue, Directeur général

Saint-Alexis-de-Matapédia
CP 99
190, rue Principale
Saint-Alexis-de-Matapédia, QC G0J 2E0
Tél: 418-299-2030; *Téléc:* 418-299-3011
plateau1@globetrotter.qc.ca
www.matapedialesplateaux.com
Entité municipal: Municipality
Incorporation: 1er juillet 1855; *Area:* 83,37 km2
Comté ou district: Avignon; *Population au 2011:* 548
Circonscription(s) électorale(s) provinciale(s): Bonaventure
Circonscription(s) électorale(s) fédérale(s): Avignon-La Mitis-Matane-Matapédia
Prochaines élections: 5e novembre 2017
Guy Gallant, Maire
Lise Pitre, Directrice générale

Saint-Alexis-des-Monts
101, rue de l'Hôtel-de-Ville
Saint-Alexis-des-Monts, QC J0K 1V0
Tél: 819-265-2046; *Téléc:* 819-265-2481
info@saint-alexis-des-monts.ca
www.saint-alexis-des-monts.ca
Entité municipal: Parish (Paroisse)
Incorporation: 21 avril 1984; *Area:* 1153,85 km2
Comté ou district: Maskinongé; *Population au 2011:* 3,046
Circonscription(s) électorale(s) provinciale(s): Maskinongé
Circonscription(s) électorale(s) fédérale(s): Berthier-Maskinongé
Prochaines élections: 5e novembre 2017
Michel Bourassa, Maire
Sylvie Clément, Directrice générale

Saint-Alfred
9, rte du Cap
Saint-Alfred, QC G0M 1L0
Tél: 418-774-2068; *Téléc:* 418-774-2068
municipalitestalfred@sogetel.net
www.st-alfred.qc.ca
Entité municipal: Municipality
Incorporation: 1er janvier 1950; *Area:* 42,42 km2
Comté ou district: Robert-Cliche; *Population au 2011:* 485
Circonscription(s) électorale(s) provinciale(s): Beauce-Nord
Circonscription(s) électorale(s) fédérale(s): Beauce
Prochaines élections: 5e novembre 2017
Jean-Roch Veilleux, Maire
Diane Jacques, Directrice générale

Saint-Alphonse
127, rue Principale est
Saint-Alphonse, QC G0C 2V0
Tél: 418-388-5214; *Téléc:* 418-388-2435
st-alphonsemuni@globetrotter.net
www.st-alphonsegaspesie.com
Entité municipal: Municipality
Incorporation: 9 mai 1902; *Area:* 113,13 km2
Comté ou district: Bonaventure; *Population au 2011:* 691
Circonscription(s) électorale(s) provinciale(s): Bonaventure
Circonscription(s) électorale(s) fédérale(s): Joliette; Shefford
Prochaines élections: 5e novembre 2017
Gérard Porlier, Maire
Reina Goulet, Directrice générale

Saint-Alphonse-de-Granby
360, rue Principale
Saint-Alphonse-de-Granby, QC J0E 2A0
Tél: 450-375-4570; *Téléc:* 450-375-4717
infos@st-alphonse.qc.ca
www.st-alphonse.qc.ca
Entité municipal: Parish (Paroisse)
Incorporation: 30 décembre 1890; *Area:* 50,52 km2
Comté ou district: La Haute-Yamaska; *Population au 2011:* 3,125
Circonscription(s) électorale(s) provinciale(s): Brome-Missisquoi
Circonscription(s) électorale(s) fédérale(s): Shefford
Prochaines élections: 5e novembre 2017
Marcel Gaudreault, Maire
Réal Pitt, Directeur général

Saint-Alphonse-Rodriguez
101, rue de la Plage
Saint-Alphonse-Rodriguez, QC J0K 1W0
Tél: 450-883-2264; *Téléc:* 450-883-0833
info@munsar.ca
www.munsar.ca
Entité municipal: Municipality
Incorporation: 1er juillet 1855; *Area:* 101,37 km2
Comté ou district: Matawinie; *Population au 2011:* 3,134
Circonscription(s) électorale(s) provinciale(s): Berthier
Circonscription(s) électorale(s) fédérale(s): Joliette
Prochaines élections: 5e novembre 2017
Robert W. Desnoyers, Maire
Francine Labelle, Directrice générale

Saint-Ambroise
330, rue Gagnon
Saint-Ambroise, QC G7P 2P9
Tél: 418-672-4765; *Téléc:* 418-672-6126
info@st-ambroise.qc.ca
www.st-ambroise.qc.ca
Entité municipal: Municipality
Incorporation: 25 septembre 1971; *Area:* 148,61 km2
Comté ou district: Le Fjord-du-Saguenay; *Population au 2011:* 3,546
Circonscription(s) électorale(s) provinciale(s): Dubuc
Circonscription(s) électorale(s) fédérale(s): Jonquière
Prochaines élections: 5e novembre 2017
Dino Lapointe, Maire
Michel Perreault, Directeur général

Saint-Ambroise-de-Kildare
CP 57
850, rue Principale
Kildare, QC J0K 1C0
Tél: 450-755-4782; *Téléc:* 450-755-4784
info@saintambroise.ca
www.saintambroise.ca
Entité municipal: Parish (Paroisse)
Incorporation: 1er juillet 1855; *Area:* 66,89 km2
Comté ou district: Joliette; *Population au 2011:* 3,747
Circonscription(s) électorale(s) provinciale(s): Joliette
Circonscription(s) électorale(s) fédérale(s): Joliette
Prochaines élections: 5e novembre 2017
François Desrochers, Maire
Line Laporte, Directrice générale

Saint-Anaclet-de-Lessard
318, rue Principale ouest
Saint-Anaclet, QC G0K 1H0
Tél: 418-723-2816; *Téléc:* 418-723-0436
municipalite@stanaclet.qc.ca
stanaclet.qc.ca
Entité municipal: Parish (Paroisse)
Incorporation: 9 mai 1859; *Area:* 126,26 km2
Comté ou district: Rimouski-Neigette; *Population au 2011:* 3,035
Circonscription(s) électorale(s) provinciale(s): Rimouski
Circonscription(s) électorale(s) fédérale(s): Rimouski-Neigette-Témiscouata-Les Basques
Prochaines élections: 5e novembre 2017
Francis St-Pierre, Maire
Alain Lapierre, Directeur général

Saint-André
122A, rue Principale
Saint-André-de-Kamouraska, QC G0L 2H0
Tél: 418-493-2085; *Téléc:* 418-493-2373
munand@bellnet.ca
www.standredekamouraska.ca
Entité municipal: Municipality
Incorporation: 14 février 1987; *Area:* 68,94 km2
Comté ou district: Kamouraska; *Population au 2011:* 651
Circonscription(s) électorale(s) provinciale(s): Côte-du-Sud
Circonscription(s) électorale(s) fédérale(s): Montmagny-L'Islet-Kamouraska-Rivière-du-Loup
Prochaines élections: 5e novembre 2017
Gervais Darisse, Maire
Claudine Lévesque, Directrice générale

Saint-André-Avellin
119, rue Principale
Saint-André-Avellin, QC J0V 1W0
Tél: 819-983-2318; *Téléc:* 819-983-2344
info@ville.st-andre-avellin.qc.ca
www.ville.st-andre-avellin.qc.ca
Entité municipal: Municipality
Incorporation: 17 décembre 1997; *Area:* 131,05 km2
Comté ou district: Papineau; *Population au 2011:* 3,702
Circonscription(s) électorale(s) provinciale(s): Papineau
Circonscription(s) électorale(s) fédérale(s): Argenteuil-La Petite-Nation
Prochaines élections: 5e novembre 2017
Thérèse Whissell, Mairesse
Claire Tremblay, Directrice générale

Saint-André-d'Argenteuil
10, rue de la Mairie
Saint-André-d'Argenteuil, QC J0V 1X0
Tél: 450-537-3527; *Téléc:* 450-537-3070
info@stada.ca
www.stada.ca

Entité municipal: Municipality
Incorporation: 29 décembre 1999; *Area:* 98,45 km2
Comté ou district: Argenteuil; *Population au 2011:* 3,275
Circonscription(s) électorale(s) provinciale(s): Argenteuil
Circonscription(s) électorale(s) fédérale(s): Argenteuil-La Petite-Nation
Prochaines élections: 5e novembre 2017
André Jetté, Maire
Pascal Surprenant, Directeur général

Saint-André-de-Restigouche
CP 4
163, rue Principale
Saint-André-de-Restigouche, QC G0J 2G0
Tél: 418-865-2234; *Téléc:* 418-865-1393
m.st.and.restigouche@globetrotter.net
www.matapedialesplateaux.com
Entité municipal: Municipality
Incorporation: 1er juillet 1855; *Area:* 146,07 km2
Comté ou district: Avignon; *Population au 2011:* 157
Circonscription(s) électorale(s) provinciale(s): Bonaventure
Circonscription(s) électorale(s) fédérale(s): Avignon-La Mitis-Matane-Matapédia
Prochaines élections: 5e novembre 2017
Doris Deschênes, Mairesse
Blandine Parent, Directrice générale

Saint-André-du-Lac-Saint-Jean
11, rue du Collège
Saint-André-du-Lac-Saint-Jean, QC G0W 2K0
Tél: 418-349-8167; *Téléc:* 418-349-1019
municipalite@standredulac.qc.ca
www.standredulac.qc.ca
Entité municipal: Village
Incorporation: 29 novembre 1969; *Area:* 157,75 km2
Comté ou district: Le Domaine-du-Roy; *Population au 2011:* 488
Circonscription(s) électorale(s) provinciale(s): Roberval
Circonscription(s) électorale(s) fédérale(s): Lac-St-Jean
Prochaines élections: 5e novembre 2017
Gabriel Martel, Maire
Maude Tremblay, Directrice générale

Saint-Anicet
335, av Jules-Léger
Saint-Anicet, QC J0S 1M0
Tél: 450-264-2555; *Téléc:* 450-264-2395
info@stanicet.com
www.stanicet.com
Entité municipal: Parish (Paroisse)
Incorporation: 1er juillet 1855; *Area:* 136,25 km2
Comté ou district: Le Haut-Saint-Laurent; *Population au 2011:* 2,523
Circonscription(s) électorale(s) provinciale(s): Huntingdon
Circonscription(s) électorale(s) fédérale(s): Salaberry-Suroît
Prochaines élections: 5e novembre 2017
Alain Castagner, Maire
Lyne Viau, Directrice générale

Saint-Anselme
134, rue Principale
Saint-Anselme, QC G0R 2N0
Tél: 418-885-4977; *Téléc:* 418-885-9834
municipalite@st-anselme.ca
www.st-anselme.ca
Entité municipal: Municipality
Incorporation: 7 janvier 1998; *Area:* 74,45 km2
Comté ou district: Bellechasse; *Population au 2011:* 3,458
Circonscription(s) électorale(s) provinciale(s): Bellechasse
Circonscription(s) électorale(s) fédérale(s): Bellechasse-Les Etchemins-Lévis
Prochaines élections: 5e novembre 2017
Michel Bonneau, Maire
Louis Felteau, Directeur général

Saint-Antoine de l'Isle-aux-Grues
107, ch de la Volière
L'Isle-aux-Grues, QC G0R 1P0
Tél: 418-248-8060; *Téléc:* 418-248-7955
municipaliteiag@globetrotter.net
www.isle-aux-grues.com
Entité municipal: Parish (Paroisse)
Incorporation: 1er janvier 1860; *Area:* 26,40 km2
Comté ou district: Montmagny; *Population au 2011:* 146
Circonscription(s) électorale(s) provinciale(s): Côte-du-Sud
Circonscription(s) électorale(s) fédérale(s): Montmagny-L'Islet-Kamouraska-Rivière-du-Loup
Prochaines élections: 5e novembre 2017
Frédéric Poulin, Maire
Hélène Painchaud, Directrice générale

Saint-Antoine-de-Tilly
CP 10
3870, ch de Tilly
Saint-Antoine-de-Tilly, QC G0S 2C0
Tél: 418-886-2441; *Téléc:* 418-886-2075
info@saintantoinedetilly.com
www.saintantoinedetilly.com
Entité municipal: Municipality
Incorporation: 1er juillet 1855; *Area:* 60,29 km2
Comté ou district: Lotbinière; *Population au 2011:* 1,604
Circonscription(s) électorale(s) provinciale(s): Lotbinière-Frontenac
Circonscription(s) électorale(s) fédérale(s): Lévis-Lotbinière
Prochaines élections: 5e novembre 2017
Christian Richard, Maire
Jacques Alain, Directeur général (par intérim)

Saint-Antoine-sur-Richelieu
1060, rue des Ormes
Saint-Antoine-sur-Richelieu, QC J0L 1R0
Tél: 450-787-3497; *Téléc:* 450-787-2852
municipalite@sasr.ca
www.saint-antoine-sur-richelieu.ca
Entité municipal: Municipality
Incorporation: 6 novembre 1982; *Area:* 65,26 km2
Comté ou district: La Vallée-du-Richelieu; *Population au 2011:* 1,659
Circonscription(s) électorale(s) provinciale(s): Borduas
Circonscription(s) électorale(s) fédérale(s): Pierre-Boucher-Les Patriotes-Verchères
Prochaines élections: 5e novembre 2017
Denis Campeau, Maire
Élise Guertin, Directrice générale

Saint-Antonin
CP 340
261, rue Principale
Saint-Antonin, QC G0L 2J0
Tél: 418-862-1056; *Téléc:* 418-862-3268
www.municipalitedesaintantonin.qc.ca
Entité municipal: Parish (Paroisse)
Incorporation: 30 août 1856; *Area:* 182,66 km2
Comté ou district: Rivière-du-Loup; *Population au 2011:* 4,027
Circonscription(s) électorale(s) provinciale(s): Rivière-du-Loup-Témiscouata
Circonscription(s) électorale(s) fédérale(s): Montmagny-L'Islet-Kamouraska-Rivière-du-Loup
Prochaines élections: 5e novembre 2017
Michel Nadeau, Maire
Sylvain Tousignant, Directeur général et secrétaire-trésorier

Saint-Apollinaire
11, rue Industrielle
Saint-Apollinaire, QC G0S 2E0
Tél: 418-881-3996; *Téléc:* 418-881-4152
www.st-apollinaire.com
Entité municipal: Municipality
Incorporation: 6 avril 1974; *Area:* 96,63 km2
Comté ou district: Lotbinière; *Population au 2011:* 5,102
Circonscription(s) électorale(s) provinciale(s): Lotbinière-Frontenac
Circonscription(s) électorale(s) fédérale(s): Lévis-Lotbinière
Prochaines élections: 5e novembre 2017
Bernard Ouellet, Maire
Martine Couture, Directrice générale

Saint-Armand
444, ch Bradley
Saint-Armand, QC J0J 1T0
Tél: 450-248-2344; *Téléc:* 450-248-3820
starmand@bellnet.ca
www.municipalite.saint-armand.qc.ca
Entité municipal: Municipality
Incorporation: 3 février 1999; *Area:* 84,26 km2
Comté ou district: Brome-Missisquoi; *Population au 2011:* 1,248
Circonscription(s) électorale(s) provinciale(s): Brome-Missisquoi
Circonscription(s) électorale(s) fédérale(s): Brome-Missisquoi
Prochaines élections: 5e novembre 2017
Réal Pelletier, Maire
Jacqueline Connolly, Directrice générale

Saint-Arsène
#101, 49, rue de l'Église
Saint-Arsène, QC G0L 2K0
Tél: 418-867-2205; *Téléc:* 418-867-2025
www.municipalite.saint-arsene.qc.ca
Entité municipal: Parish (Paroisse)
Incorporation: 1er juillet 1855; *Area:* 71,01 km2
Comté ou district: Rivière-du-Loup; *Population au 2011:* 1,253
Circonscription(s) électorale(s) provinciale(s): Rivière-du-Loup-Témiscouata
Circonscription(s) électorale(s) fédérale(s): Montmagny-L'Islet-Kamouraska-Rivière-du-Loup
Prochaines élections: 5e novembre 2017
Claire Bérubé, Maire
François Michaud, Directeur général

Saint-Athanase
CP 108
6081, ch de l'Église
Saint-Athanase, QC G0L 2L0
Tél: 418-863-7706; *Téléc:* 418-863-7707
info@saint-athanase.com
www.saint-athanase.com
Entité municipal: Municipality
Incorporation: 1er janvier 1955; *Area:* 289,08 km2
Comté ou district: Témiscouata; *Population au 2011:* 301
Circonscription(s) électorale(s) provinciale(s): Rivière-du-Loup-Témiscouata
Circonscription(s) électorale(s) fédérale(s): Rimouski-Neigette-Témiscouata-Les Basques
Prochaines élections: 5e novembre 2017
André St-Pierre, Maire
Francine Morin, Directrice générale

Saint-Aubert
14, rue des Loisirs
Saint-Aubert, QC G0R 2R0
Tél: 418-598-3368; *Téléc:* 418-598-3369
administration@saint-aubert.net
saint-aubert.net
Entité municipal: Municipality
Incorporation: 1er juillet 1857; *Area:* 97,15 km2
Comté ou district: L'Islet; *Population au 2011:* 1,409
Circonscription(s) électorale(s) provinciale(s): Côte-du-Sud
Circonscription(s) électorale(s) fédérale(s): Montmagny-L'Islet-Kamouraska-Rivière-du-Loup
Prochaines élections: 5e novembre 2017
Yvon Fournier, Maire
Serge Roussel, Directeur général

Saint-Augustin
CP 279
Saint-Augustin, QC G0G 2R0
Tél: 418-947-2404; *Téléc:* 418-947-2533
director.msa@globetrotter.net
Entité municipal: Municipality
Incorporation: 1er janvier 1993; *Area:* 1435,82 km2
Comté ou district: Le Golfe-du-Saint-Laurent; *Population au 2011:* 478
Circonscription(s) électorale(s) provinciale(s): Duplessis
Circonscription(s) électorale(s) fédérale(s): Lac-Saint-Jean; Manicouagan; Mirabel
Prochaines élections: 5e novembre 2017
Glen Mckinnon, Maire
Stephanie Kennedy, Directrice générale

Saint-Augustin
686, rue Principale
Saint-Augustin, QC G0W 1K0
Tél: 418-374-2147; *Téléc:* 418-374-2984
info@saint-augustin.net
www.saint-augustin.net
Entité municipal: Parish (Paroisse)
Incorporation: 14 mai 1925; *Area:* 103,96 km2
Comté ou district: Maria-Chapdelaine; *Population au 2011:* 400
Circonscription(s) électorale(s) provinciale(s): Roberval
Circonscription(s) électorale(s) fédérale(s): Lac-St-Jean
Prochaines élections: 5e novembre 2017
Daniel Côté, Maire
Joane Dallaire, Directrice générale

Saint-Augustin-de-Woburn
590, rue St-Augustin
Woburn, QC G0Y 1R0
Tél: 819-544-4211; *Téléc:* 819-544-9236
mun.woburn@axion.ca
www.saintaugustindewoburn.ca
Entité municipal: Parish (Paroisse)
Incorporation: 13 janvier 1900; *Area:* 280,80 km2
Comté ou district: Le Granit; *Population au 2011:* 695
Circonscription(s) électorale(s) provinciale(s): Mégantic
Circonscription(s) électorale(s) fédérale(s): Mégantic-L'Érable
Prochaines élections: 5e novembre 2017
Raoul Proteau, Maire
Gaétane Allard, Directrice générale

Saint-Barnabé
CP 250
70, rue Duguay
Saint-Barnabé, QC G0X 2K0
Tél: 819-264-2085; *Téléc:* 819-264-2079
municipalitest-barnabe@telmilot.net
www.saint-barnabe.ca

Entité municipal: Parish (Paroisse)
Incorporation: 1er juillet 1855; *Area:* 58,81 km2
Comté ou district: Maskinongé; *Population au 2011:* 1,179
Circonscription(s) électorale(s) provinciale(s): Maskinongé
Circonscription(s) électorale(s) fédérale(s): Berthier-Maskinongé
Prochaines élections: 5e novembre 2017
Michel Lemay, Maire
Denis Gélinas, Directeur général

Saint-Barnabé-Sud
251, rang de Michaudville
Saint-Barnabé-Sud, QC J0H 1G0
Tél: 450-792-3030; *Téléc:* 450-792-3759
munstbarnabesud@mrcmaskoutains.qc.ca
www.saintbarnabesud.ca
Entité municipal: Municipality
Incorporation: 1er juillet 1855; *Area:* 57,08 km2
Comté ou district: Les Maskoutains; *Population au 2011:* 859
Circonscription(s) électorale(s) provinciale(s): St-Hyacinthe
Circonscription(s) électorale(s) fédérale(s): St-Hyacinthe-Bagot
Prochaines élections: 5e novembre 2017
Alain Jobin, Maire
Sylvie Gosselin, Directrice générale

Saint-Barthélemy
1980, rue Bonin
Saint-Barthélémy, QC J0K 1X0
Tél: 450-885-3511; *Téléc:* 450-836-5220
municipalite@saint-barthelemy.ca
www.saint-barthelemy.ca
Entité municipal: Parish (Paroisse)
Incorporation: 1er juillet 1855; *Area:* 98,80 km2
Comté ou district: D'Autray; *Population au 2011:* 1,883
Circonscription(s) électorale(s) provinciale(s): Berthier
Circonscription(s) électorale(s) fédérale(s): Berthier-Maskinongé
Prochaines élections: 5e novembre 2017
Jacques Patry, Maire
Julien Bernier, Directeur général

Saint-Basile
20, rue St-Georges
Saint-Basile, QC G0A 3G0
Tél: 418-329-2204; *Téléc:* 418-329-2788
greffe@saintbasile.qc.ca
www.saintbasile.qc.ca
Entité municipal: Town
Incorporation: 1er mars 2000; *Area:* 97,69 km2
Comté ou district: Portneuf; *Population au 2011:* 2,463
Circonscription(s) électorale(s) provinciale(s): Portneuf
Circonscription(s) électorale(s) fédérale(s):
Portneuf-Jacques-Cartier
Prochaines élections: 5e novembre 2017
Jean Poirier, Maire
Paulin Leclerc, Directeur général

Saint-Benjamin
CP 100
440, av du Collège
Saint-Benjamin, QC G0M 1N0
Tél: 418-594-8156; *Téléc:* 418-594-6068
munstbenjamin@aclcable.ca
www.st-benjamin.qc.ca
Entité municipal: Municipality
Incorporation: 9 janvier 1897; *Area:* 110,53 km2
Comté ou district: Les Etchemins; *Population au 2011:* 891
Circonscription(s) électorale(s) provinciale(s): Beauce-Sud
Circonscription(s) électorale(s) fédérale(s): Beauce
Prochaines élections: 5e novembre 2017
Martine Boulet, Maire
France Veilleux, Directrice générale

Saint-Benoît-du-Lac
1, rue Principale
Saint-Benoît-du-Lac, QC J0B 2M0
Tél: 819-843-4080; *Téléc:* 819-843-0256
muni.sbl@axion.ca
www.st-benoit-du-lac.com
Entité municipal: Municipality
Incorporation: 16 mars 1939; *Area:* 2,27 km2
Comté ou district: Memphrémagog; *Population au 2011:* 50
Circonscription(s) électorale(s) provinciale(s): Orford
Circonscription(s) électorale(s) fédérale(s): Brome-Missisquoi
Prochaines élections: 5e novembre 2017
André Laberge, Administrateur

Saint-Benoît-Labre
216, rte 271
Saint-Benoît-Labre, QC G0M 1P0
Tél: 418-228-9250; *Téléc:* 418-228-0518
munstben@globetrotter.net
www.saintbenoitlabre.qc.ca

Entité municipal: Municipality
Incorporation: 4 janvier 1894; *Area:* 83,92 km2
Comté ou district: Beauce-Sartigan; *Population au 2011:* 1,612
Circonscription(s) électorale(s) provinciale(s): Beauce-Sud
Circonscription(s) électorale(s) fédérale(s): Beauce
Prochaines élections: 5e novembre 2017
Carmelle Carrier, Mairesse
Édith Quirion, Directrice générale

Saint-Bernard
CP 70
1512, rue St-Georges
Saint-Bernard, QC G0S 2G0
Tél: 418-475-6060; *Téléc:* 418-475-6069
stbernard@globetrotter.net
www.municipalite-saint-bernard.com
Entité municipal: Municipality
Incorporation: 9 mai 1987; *Area:* 87,56 km2
Comté ou district: La Nouvelle-Beauce; *Population au 2011:* 2,131
Circonscription(s) électorale(s) provinciale(s): Beauce-Nord
Circonscription(s) électorale(s) fédérale(s): Beauce
Prochaines élections: 5e novembre 2017
André Gagnon, Maire
Marie-Eve Parent, Directrice générale

Saint-Bernard-de-Lacolle
116, rang St-Claude
Saint-Bernard-de-Lacolle, QC J0J 1V0
Tél: 450-246-3348; *Téléc:* 450-246-4380
info@municipalite-de-saint-bernard-de-lacolle.ca
www.municipalite-de-saint-bernard-de-lacolle.ca
Entité municipal: Parish (Paroisse)
Incorporation: 1er juillet 1855; *Area:* 112,63 km2
Comté ou district: Les Jardins-de-Napierville; *Population au 2011:* 1,477
Circonscription(s) électorale(s) provinciale(s): Huntingdon
Circonscription(s) électorale(s) fédérale(s): Châteauguay-Lacolle
Prochaines élections: 5e novembre 2017
Robert Duteau, Maire
Daniel Striletsky, Directeur général

Saint-Bernard-de-Michaudville
390, rue Principale
Saint-Bernard-de-Michaudville, QC J0H 1C0
Tél: 450-792-3190; *Téléc:* 450-792-3591
munstbernard@mrcmaskoutains.qc.ca
saintbernarddemichaudville.qc.ca
Entité municipal: Municipality
Incorporation: 31 août 1908; *Area:* 64,80 km2
Comté ou district: Les Maskoutains; *Population au 2011:* 521
Circonscription(s) électorale(s) provinciale(s): Richelieu
Circonscription(s) électorale(s) fédérale(s): St-Hyacinthe-Bagot
Prochaines élections: 5e novembre 2017
Francine Morin, Mairesse
Sylvie Chaput, Directrice générale

Saint-Blaise-sur-Richelieu
795, rue des Loisirs
Saint-Blaise-sur-Richelieu, QC J0J 1W0
Tél: 450-291-5944; *Téléc:* 450-291-3832
info@municipalite.saint-blaise-sur-richelieu.qc.ca
www.municipalite.saint-blaise-sur-richelieu.qc.ca
Entité municipal: Municipality
Incorporation: 20 juin 1892; *Area:* 68,42 km2
Comté ou district: Le Haut-Richelieu; *Population au 2011:* 1,837
Circonscription(s) électorale(s) provinciale(s): St-Jean
Circonscription(s) électorale(s) fédérale(s): Saint-Jean
Prochaines élections: 5e novembre 2017
Jacques Desmarais, Maire
Francine Milot, Directrice générale

Saint-Bonaventure
720, rue Plante
Saint-Bonaventure, QC J0C 1C0
Tél: 819-396-2335; *Téléc:* 819-396-2335
info@saint-bonaventure.ca
www.saint-bonaventure.ca
Entité municipal: Municipality
Incorporation: 1er janvier 1867; *Area:* 78,83 km2
Comté ou district: Drummond; *Population au 2011:* 1,017
Circonscription(s) électorale(s) provinciale(s): Nicolet-Bécancour
Circonscription(s) électorale(s) fédérale(s): Drummond
Prochaines élections: 5e novembre 2017
Félicien Cardin, Maire
Claire Côté, Directrice générale

Saint-Boniface
140, rue Guimont
Saint-Boniface, QC G0X 2L0
Tél: 819-535-3811; *Téléc:* 819-535-1242
www.municipalitesaint-boniface.ca

Entité municipal: Municipality
Incorporation: 1er janvier 1962; *Area:* 112,12 km2
Comté ou district: Maskinongé; *Population au 2011:* 4,511
Circonscription(s) électorale(s) provinciale(s): St-Maurice
Circonscription(s) électorale(s) fédérale(s): Berthier-Maskinongé
Prochaines élections: 5e novembre 2017
Claude Caron, Maire
Jacques Caron, Directeur général

Saint-Bruno
563, av St-Alphonse
Saint-Bruno, QC G0W 2L0
Tél: 418-343-2303; *Téléc:* 418-343-2662
info@ville.saint-bruno.qc.ca
www.ville.saint-bruno.qc.ca
Entité municipal: Municipality
Incorporation: 12 juillet 1975; *Area:* 77,88 km2
Comté ou district: Lac-Saint-Jean-Est; *Population au 2011:* 2,636
Circonscription(s) électorale(s) provinciale(s): Lac-St-Jean
Circonscription(s) électorale(s) fédérale(s): Lac-St-Jean
Prochaines élections: 5e novembre 2017
Réjean Bouchard, Maire
Gilles Boudreault, Directeur général

Saint-Bruno-de-Guigues
CP 130
21, rue Principale nord
Saint-Bruno-de-Guigues, QC J0Z 2G0
Tél: 819-728-2186; *Téléc:* 819-728-2404
www.temiscamingue.net/guigues
Entité municipal: Municipality
Incorporation: 3 octobre 1912; *Area:* 188,99 km2
Comté ou district: Témiscamingue; *Population au 2011:* 1,100
Circonscription(s) électorale(s) provinciale(s):
Rouyn-Noranda-Témiscamingue
Circonscription(s) électorale(s) fédérale(s):
Abitibi-Témiscamingue
Prochaines élections: 5e novembre 2017
Donald Alarie, Maire
Serge Côté, Directeur général

Saint-Bruno-de-Kamouraska
CP 10
4, rue du Couvent
Saint-Bruno-de-Kamouraska, QC G0L 2M0
Tél: 418-492-2612; *Téléc:* 418-492-9076
mun.stbrunokam@globetrotter.net
www.stbrunokam.qc.ca
Entité municipal: Municipality
Incorporation: 1er janvier 1887; *Area:* 186,79 km2
Comté ou district: Kamouraska; *Population au 2011:* 534
Circonscription(s) électorale(s) provinciale(s): Côte-du-Sud
Circonscription(s) électorale(s) fédérale(s):
Montmagny-L'Islet-Kamouraska-Rivière-du-Loup
Prochaines élections: 5e novembre 2017
Roger Lavoie, Maire
Constance Gagné, Directrice générale

Saint-Calixte
6230, rue de l'Hôtel-de-Ville
Saint-Calixte, QC J0K 1Z0
Tél: 450-222-2782; *Téléc:* 450-222-2789
www.mscalixte.qc.ca
Entité municipal: Municipality
Incorporation: 1er juillet 1855; *Area:* 147,68 km2
Comté ou district: Montcalm; *Population au 2011:* 5,934
Circonscription(s) électorale(s) provinciale(s): Rousseau
Circonscription(s) électorale(s) fédérale(s): Montcalm
Prochaines élections: 5e novembre 2017
Louis-Charles Thouin, Maire
Denis Lemay, Directeur général

Saint-Camille
85, rue Desrivières
Saint-Camille, QC J0A 1G0
Tél: 819-828-3222; *Téléc:* 819-828-3723
www.saint-camille.ca
Entité municipal: Township
Incorporation: 1er janvier 1860; *Area:* 81,27 km2
Comté ou district: Les Sources; *Population au 2011:* 511
Circonscription(s) électorale(s) provinciale(s): Richmond
Circonscription(s) électorale(s) fédérale(s):
Richmond-Arthabaska
Prochaines élections: 5e novembre 2017
Benoit Bourassa, Maire
Marie-Claude Couture, Directrice générale

Saint-Camille-de-Lellis
CP 70
217, rue Principale
Saint-Camille-de-Lellis, QC G0R 2S0
Tél: 418-595-2233; *Téléc:* 418-595-2238
mustcam@sogetel.net
www.saint-camille.net
Entité municipal: Parish (Paroisse)
Incorporation: 11 janvier 1904; *Area:* 252,08 km2
Comté ou district: Les Etchemins; *Population au 2011:* 844
Circonscription(s) électorale(s) provinciale(s): Bellechasse
Circonscription(s) électorale(s) fédérale(s): Bellechasse-Les Etchemins-Lévis
Prochaines élections: 5e novembre 2017
Adélard Couture, Maire
Nicole Mathieu, Directrice générale

Saint-Casimir
CP 220
220, boul de la Montagne
Saint-Casimir, QC G0A 3L0
Tél: 418-339-2543; *Téléc:* 418-339-3105
st-casimir@infoteck.qc.ca
www.saint-casimir.com
Entité municipal: Municipality
Incorporation: 21 juin 2000; *Area:* 65,93 km2
Comté ou district: Portneuf; *Population au 2011:* 1,500
Circonscription(s) électorale(s) provinciale(s): Portneuf
Circonscription(s) électorale(s) fédérale(s): Portneuf-Jacques Cartier
Prochaines élections: 5e novembre 2017
Dominic Tessier-Perry, Maire
René Savard, Directeur général

Saint-Célestin
990, rang du Pays-Brûlé
Saint-Célestin, QC J0C 1G0
Tél: 819-229-3745; *Téléc:* 819-229-1386
info@saint-celestin.net
www.saint-celestin.net
Entité municipal: Municipality
Incorporation: 1er juillet 1864; *Area:* 78,72 km2
Comté ou district: Nicolet-Yamaska; *Population au 2011:* 611
Circonscription(s) électorale(s) provinciale(s): Nicolet-Bécancour
Circonscription(s) électorale(s) fédérale(s): Bécancour-Nicolet-Saurel
Prochaines élections: 5e novembre 2017
Maurice Morin, Maire
Gisèle Plourde, Directrice générale

Saint-Célestin
510, rue Marquis
Saint-Célestin, QC J0C 1G0
Tél: 819-229-3642; *Téléc:* 819-229-1149
info@village-st-celestin.net
www.village-st-celestin.net
Entité municipal: Village
Incorporation: 25 novembre 1896; *Area:* 1,61 km22
Comté ou district: Nicolet-Yamaska; *Population au 2011:* 781
Circonscription(s) électorale(s) provinciale(s): Nicolet-Bécancour
Circonscription(s) électorale(s) fédérale(s): Bécancour-Nicolet-Saurel
Prochaines élections: 5e novembre 2017
Raymond Noël, Maire
Pascale Lamoureux, Directrice générale

Saint-Césaire
1111, av St-Paul
Saint-Césaire, QC J0L 1T0
Tél: 450-469-3108; *Téléc:* 450-469-5275
administration@ville.saint-cesaire.qc.ca
www.ville.saint-cesaire.qc.ca
Entité municipal: Town
Incorporation: 26 janvier 2000; *Area:* 84,14 km2
Comté ou district: Rouville; *Population au 2011:* 5,686
Circonscription(s) électorale(s) provinciale(s): Iberville
Circonscription(s) électorale(s) fédérale(s): Shefford
Prochaines élections: 5e novembre 2017
Guy Benjamin, Maire
Isabelle François, Greffière

Saint-Charles-de-Bellechasse
2815, av Royale
Saint-Charles-de-Bellechasse, QC G0R 2T0
Tél: 418-887-6600; *Téléc:* 418-887-6779
info@saint-charles.ca
www.saint-charles.ca
Entité municipal: Municipality
Incorporation: 22 décembre 1993; *Area:* 94,73 km2
Comté ou district: Bellechasse; *Population au 2011:* 2,246
Circonscription(s) électorale(s) provinciale(s): Bellechasse
Circonscription(s) électorale(s) fédérale(s): Bellechasse-Les Etchemins-Lévis
Prochaines élections: 5e novembre 2017
Dominic Roy, Maire
Denis Labbé, Directeur général

Saint-Charles-de-Bourget
357, 2e rang
Saint-Charles-de-Bourget, QC G0V 1G0
Tél: 418-672-2624; *Téléc:* 418-673-2118
info@stcharlesdebourget.ca
www.stcharlesdebourget.ca
Entité municipal: Municipality
Incorporation: 29 septembre 1885; *Area:* 62,31 km2
Comté ou district: Le Fjord-du-Saguenay; *Population au 2011:* 690
Circonscription(s) électorale(s) provinciale(s): Dubuc
Circonscription(s) électorale(s) fédérale(s): Jonquière
Prochaines élections: 5e novembre 2017
Michel Ringuette, Maire
Audrey Thibeault, Directrice générale

Saint-Charles-Garnier
CP 39
38, rue Principale
Saint-Charles-Garnier, QC G0K 1K0
Tél: 418-798-4305; *Téléc:* 418-798-4499
stcharles@mitis.qc.ca
www.municipalite.saint-charles-garnier.qc.ca
Entité municipal: Parish (Paroisse)
Incorporation: 1er janvier 1966; *Area:* 83,73 km2
Comté ou district: La Mitis; *Population au 2011:* 271
Circonscription(s) électorale(s) provinciale(s): Matane-Matapédia
Circonscription(s) électorale(s) fédérale(s): Avignon-La Mitis-Matane-Matapédia
Prochaines élections: 5e novembre 2017
Jean-Pierre Bélanger, Maire
Josette Bouillon, Directrice générale

Saint-Charles-sur-Richelieu
#101, 405, ch des Patriotes
Saint-Charles-sur-Richelieu, QC J0H 2G0
Tél: 450-584-3484; *Téléc:* 450-584-2965
info@saint-charles-sur-richelieu.ca
www.saint-charles-sur-richelieu.ca
Entité municipal: Municipality
Incorporation: 22 mars 1995; *Area:* 63,59 km2
Comté ou district: La Vallée-du-Richelieu; *Population au 2011:* 1,643
Circonscription(s) électorale(s) provinciale(s): Borduas
Circonscription(s) électorale(s) fédérale(s): Pierre-Boucher-Les Patriotes-Verchères
Prochaines élections: 5e novembre 2017
Sébastien Raymond, Maire
Nancy Fortier, Directrice générale

Saint-Christophe-d'Arthabaska
418, av Pie-X
Saint-Christophe-d'Arthabaska, QC G6R 0M9
Tél: 819-357-9031; *Téléc:* 819-357-9087
directiongenerale@saint-christophe-darthabaska.ca
www.saint-christophe-darthabaska.ca
Entité municipal: Parish (Paroisse)
Incorporation: 1er juillet 1855; *Area:* 74,87 km2
Comté ou district: Arthabaska; *Population au 2011:* 2,892
Circonscription(s) électorale(s) provinciale(s): Arthabaska
Circonscription(s) électorale(s) fédérale(s): Richmond-Arthabaska
Prochaines élections: 5e novembre 2017
Michel Larochelle, Maire
Francine Moreau, Directrice générale

Saint-Chrysostome
624, rue Notre-Dame, 2e étage
Saint-Chrysostome, QC J0S 1R0
Tél: 450-826-3911; *Téléc:* 450-826-0568
information@mun-sc.ca
www.mun-sc.ca
Entité municipal: Municipality
Incorporation: 29 septembre 1999; *Area:* 99,54 km2
Comté ou district: Le Haut-Saint-Laurent; *Population au 2011:* 2,522
Circonscription(s) électorale(s) provinciale(s): Huntingdon
Circonscription(s) électorale(s) fédérale(s): Salaberry-Suroît
Prochaines élections: 5e novembre 2017
Gilles Dagenais, Maire
Céline Ouimet, Directrice générale

Saint-Claude
295, rte de l'Église
Saint-Claude, QC J0B 2N0
Tél: 819-845-7795; *Téléc:* 819-845-2479
directrice@st-claude.ca
www.municipalite.st-claude.ca
Entité municipal: Municipality
Incorporation: 15 novembre 1912; *Area:* 120,38 km2
Comté ou district: Le Val-Saint-François; *Population au 2011:* 1,106
Circonscription(s) électorale(s) provinciale(s): Richmond
Circonscription(s) électorale(s) fédérale(s): Richmond-Arthabaska
Prochaines élections: 5e novembre 2017
Hervé Provencher, Maire
France Lavertu, Directrice générale

Saint-Clément
CP 40
25A, rue St-Pierre
Saint-Clément, QC G0L 2N0
Tél: 418-963-2258; *Téléc:* 418-963-2619
postmaster@st-clement.ca
www.st-clement.ca
Entité municipal: Parish (Paroisse)
Incorporation: 1er janvier 1885; *Area:* 80,44 km2
Comté ou district: Les Basques; *Population au 2011:* 499
Circonscription(s) électorale(s) provinciale(s): Rivière-du-Loup-Témiscouata
Circonscription(s) électorale(s) fédérale(s): Rimouski-Neigette-Témiscouata-Les Basques
Prochaines élections: 5e novembre 2017
Éric Blanchard, Maire
Line Caron, Directrice générale

Saint-Cléophas
350, rue Principale
Saint-Cléophas, QC G0J 3N0
Tél: 418-536-3023; *Téléc:* 418-536-1349
stcleophas@mrcmatapedia.qc.ca
www.stcleophas.com
Entité municipal: Parish (Paroisse)
Incorporation: 19 mai 1921; *Area:* 97,46 km2
Comté ou district: La Matapédia; *Population au 2011:* 334
Circonscription(s) électorale(s) provinciale(s): Matane-Matapédia
Circonscription(s) électorale(s) fédérale(s): Avignon-La Mitis-Matane-Matapédia
Prochaines élections: 5e novembre 2017
Jean-Paul Bélanger, Maire
Katie St-Pierre, Directrice générale

Saint-Cléophas-de-Brandon
750, rue Principale
Saint-Cléophas-de-Brandon, QC J0K 2A0
Tél: 450-889-5683; *Téléc:* 450-835-6076
www.st-cleophas.qc.ca
Entité municipal: Municipality
Incorporation: 7 octobre 1897; *Area:* 14,76 km2
Comté ou district: D'Autray; *Population au 2011:* 276
Circonscription(s) électorale(s) provinciale(s): Berthier
Circonscription(s) électorale(s) fédérale(s): Berthier-Maskinongé
Prochaines élections: 5e novembre 2017
Denis Gamelin, Maire
Chantal Piette, Directrice générale

Saint-Clet
4, rue du Moulin
Saint-Clet, QC J0P 1S0
Tél: 450-456-3363; *Téléc:* 450-456-3879
st-clet@videotron.ca
www.st-clet.com
Entité municipal: Municipality
Incorporation: 31 août 1974; *Area:* 38,61 km2
Comté ou district: Vaudreuil-Soulanges; *Population au 2011:* 1,738
Circonscription(s) électorale(s) provinciale(s): Soulanges
Circonscription(s) électorale(s) fédérale(s): Salaberry-Suroît
Prochaines élections: 5e novembre 2017
Daniel Beaupré, Maire
Nathalie Pharand, Directrice générale

Saint-Côme
1673, 55e rue
Saint-Côme, QC J0K 2B0
Tél: 450-883-2726; *Téléc:* 450-883-6431
www.stcomelanaudiere.ca
Entité municipal: Parish (Paroisse)
Incorporation: 1er janvier 1873; *Area:* 167,26 km2
Comté ou district: Matawinie; *Population au 2011:* 2,198
Circonscription(s) électorale(s) provinciale(s): Berthier
Circonscription(s) électorale(s) fédérale(s): Joliette
Prochaines élections: 5e novembre 2017

Martin Bordeleau, Maire
Alice Riopel, Directrice générale

Saint-Côme-Linière
1375, 18e rue
Saint-Côme-Linière, QC G0M 1J0
Tél: 418-685-3825; *Téléc:* 418-685-2566
st-come@globetrotter.net
www.stcomeliniere.com
Entité municipal: Municipality
Incorporation: 13 avril 1994; *Area:* 151,24 km2
Comté ou district: Beauce-Sartigan; *Population au 2011:* 3,274
Circonscription(s) électorale(s) provinciale(s): Beauce-Sud
Circonscription(s) électorale(s) fédérale(s): Beauce
Prochaines élections: 5e novembre 2017
Yvon Paquet, Maire
Yvan Bélanger, Directeur général

Saint-Cuthbert
CP 100
1891, rue Principale
Saint-Cuthbert, QC J0K 2C0
Tél: 450-836-4852; *Téléc:* 450-836-4833
www.st-cuthbert.qc.ca
Entité municipal: Municipality
Incorporation: 7 janvier 1998; *Area:* 133,71 km2
Comté ou district: D'Autray; *Population au 2011:* 1,839
Circonscription(s) électorale(s) provinciale(s): Berthier
Circonscription(s) électorale(s) fédérale(s): Berthier-Maskinongé
Prochaines élections: 5e novembre 2017
Bruno Vadnais, Maire
Richard Lauzon, Directeur général

Saint-Cyprien
CP 9
101B, rue Collin
Saint-Cyprien, QC G0L 2P0
Tél: 418-963-2730; *Téléc:* 418-963-3490
www.municipalite.saint-cyprien.qc.ca
Entité municipal: Municipality
Incorporation: 1er janvier 1883; *Area:* 136,14 km2
Comté ou district: Rivière-du-Loup; *Population au 2011:* 1,163
Circonscription(s) électorale(s) provinciale(s):
Rivière-du-Loup-Témiscouata
Circonscription(s) électorale(s) fédérale(s):
Montmagny-L'Islet-Kamouraska-Rivière-du-Loup
Prochaines élections: 5e novembre 2017
Michel Lagacé, Maire
Sanny Beaulieu, Greffière

Saint-Cyprien
CP 100
399, rue Principale
Saint-Cyprien-des-Etchemins, QC G0R 1B0
Tél: 418-383-5274; *Téléc:* 418-383-5269
corpmun@sogetel.net
www.st-cyprien.qc.ca
Entité municipal: Parish (Paroisse)
Incorporation: 22 février 1918; *Area:* 92,82 km2
Comté ou district: Les Etchemins; *Population au 2011:* 548
Circonscription(s) électorale(s) provinciale(s): Bellechasse
Circonscription(s) électorale(s) fédérale(s): Bellechasse-Les Etchemins-Lévis
Prochaines élections: 5e novembre 2017
Rejean Bédard, Maire
Pauline Fortier, Directrice générale

Saint-Cyprien-de-Napierville
121, rang Cyr
Saint-Cyprien-de-Napierville, QC J0J 1L0
Tél: 450-245-3658; *Téléc:* 450-245-7824
info@st-cypriendenapierville.ca
www.st-cypriendenapierville.ca
Entité municipal: Parish (Paroisse)
Incorporation: 1er juillet 1855; *Area:* 97,62 km2
Comté ou district: Les Jardins-de-Napierville; *Population au 2011:* 1,869
Circonscription(s) électorale(s) provinciale(s): Huntingdon
Circonscription(s) électorale(s) fédérale(s): Châteauguay-Lacolle
Prochaines élections: 5e novembre 2017
Normand Lefebvre, Maire
Nancy Trottier, Directrice générale

Saint-Cyrille-de-Lessard
282, rue Principale
Saint-Cyrille-de-Lessard, QC G0R 2W0
Tél: 418-247-5186; *Téléc:* 418-247-7086
info@st-cyrille-de-lessard.ca
www.st-cyrille-de-lessard.ca
Entité municipal: Parish (Paroisse)
Incorporation: 1er juillet 1855; *Area:* 228,95 km2
Comté ou district: L'Islet; *Population au 2011:* 753
Circonscription(s) électorale(s) provinciale(s): Côte-du-Sud
Circonscription(s) électorale(s) fédérale(s):
Montmagny-L'Islet-Kamouraska-Rivière-du-Loup
Prochaines élections: 5e novembre 2017
Luc Caron, Maire
Josée Godbout, Directrice générale

Saint-Cyrille-de-Wendover
4055, rue Principale
Saint-Cyrille-de-Wendover, QC J1Z 1C8
Tél: 819-397-4226; *Téléc:* 819-397-5505
municipalite@stcyrille.qc.ca
www.stcyrille.qc.ca
Entité municipal: Municipality
Incorporation: 6 septembre 1905; *Area:* 112,24 km2
Comté ou district: Drummond; *Population au 2011:* 4,389
Circonscription(s) électorale(s) provinciale(s):
Drummond-Bois-Francs
Circonscription(s) électorale(s) fédérale(s): Drummond
Prochaines élections: 5e novembre 2017
Daniel Lafond, Maire
Mario Picotin, Directeur général

Saint-Damase
115, rue St-Étienne
Saint-Damase, QC J0H 1J0
Tél: 450-797-3341; *Téléc:* 450-797-3543
info@st-damase.qc.ca
www.st-damase.qc.ca
Entité municipal: Municipality
Incorporation: 5 octobre 2001; *Area:* 79,06 km2
Comté ou district: Les Maskoutains; *Population au 2011:* 2,506
Circonscription(s) électorale(s) provinciale(s): St-Hyacinthe
Circonscription(s) électorale(s) fédérale(s): St-Hyacinthe-Bagot
Prochaines élections: 5e novembre 2017
Note: Effective October 10, 2001, the Village & Parish of St-Damase amalgamated to create the Municipality of St-Damase.
Christian Martin, Maire
Sylvie V. Fréchette, Directrice générale

Saint-Damase
18, av du Centenaire
Sainte-Damase, QC G0J 2J0
Tél: 418-776-2103; *Téléc:* 418-776-2183
stdamase@mrcmatapedia.qc.ca
Entité municipal: Parish (Paroisse)
Incorporation: 31 décembre 1885; *Area:* 117,02 km2
Comté ou district: La Matapédia; *Population au 2011:* 397
Circonscription(s) électorale(s) provinciale(s): Matane-Matapédia
Circonscription(s) électorale(s) fédérale(s): Avignon-La Mitis-Matane-Matapédia
Prochaines élections: 5e novembre 2017
Jean-Marc Durant, Maire
Colette D'Astous, Directrice générale

Saint-Damase-de-L'Islet
26, rue du Village est
Saint-Damase-de-L'Islet, QC G0R 2X0
Tél: 418-598-9370; *Téléc:* 418-598-9396
stdamase3@hotmail.com
Entité municipal: Municipality
Incorporation: 9 novembre 1898; *Area:* 259,72 km2
Comté ou district: L'Islet; *Population au 2011:* 591
Circonscription(s) électorale(s) provinciale(s): Côte-du-Sud
Circonscription(s) électorale(s) fédérale(s):
Montmagny-L'Islet-Kamouraska-Rivière-du-Loup
Prochaines élections: 5e novembre 2017
Paulette Lord, Maire
Dany Marois, Directrice générale

Saint-Damien
6850, ch Montauban
Saint-Damien, QC J0K 2E0
Tél: 888-835-3419; *Téléc:* 450-835-5538
infos@st-damien.com
www.st-damien.com
Entité municipal: Parish (Paroisse)
Incorporation: 6 septembre 1870; *Area:* 260,38 km2
Comté ou district: Matawinie; *Population au 2011:* 2,020
Circonscription(s) électorale(s) provinciale(s): Berthier
Circonscription(s) électorale(s) fédérale(s): Berthier-Maskinongé
Prochaines élections: 5e novembre 2017
André Dutremble, Maire
Diane Desjardins, Directrice générale

Saint-Damien-de-Buckland
75, rte St-Gérard
Saint-Damien-de-Buckland, QC G0R 2Y0
Tél: 418-789-2526; *Téléc:* 418-789-2125
info@saint-damien.com
www.saint-damien.com
Entité municipal: Parish (Paroisse)
Incorporation: 20 décembre 1890; *Area:* 85,17 km2
Comté ou district: Bellechasse; *Population au 2011:* 2,071
Circonscription(s) électorale(s) provinciale(s): Bellechasse
Circonscription(s) électorale(s) fédérale(s): Bellechasse-Les Etchemins-Lévis
Prochaines élections: 5e novembre 2017
Hervé Blais, Maire
Jacques Thibault, Directeur général

Saint-David
16, rue Saint-Charles
Saint-David, QC J0G 1L0
Tél: 450-789-2288; *Téléc:* 450-789-3023
stdavid@pierredesaurel.com
www.stdavid.qc.ca
Entité municipal: Municipality
Incorporation: 1er juillet 1855; *Area:* 91,08 km2
Comté ou district: Pierre-De Saurel; *Population au 2011:* 832
Circonscription(s) électorale(s) provinciale(s): Richelieu
Circonscription(s) électorale(s) fédérale(s):
Bécancour-Nicolet-Saurel
Prochaines élections: 5e novembre 2017
Michel Blanchard, Maire
Sylvie Letendre, Directrice générale

Saint-David-de-Falardeau
CP 130
140, boul St-David
Saint-David-de-Falardeau, QC G0V 1C0
Tél: 418-673-4647; *Téléc:* 418-673-3266
info@villefalardeau.ca
www.villefalardeau.ca
Entité municipal: Municipality
Incorporation: 1er janvier 1948; *Area:* 379,23 km2
Comté ou district: Le Fjord-du-Saguenay; *Population au 2011:* 2,657
Circonscription(s) électorale(s) provinciale(s): Dubuc
Circonscription(s) électorale(s) fédérale(s): Jonquière
Prochaines élections: 5e novembre 2017
Serge Gauthier, Maire
Daniel Hudon, Directeur général

Saint-Denis-De La Bouteillerie
5, rte 287
Saint-Denis, QC G0L 2R0
Tél: 418-498-2968; *Téléc:* 418-498-2948
www.munstdenis.com
Entité municipal: Municipality
Incorporation: 1er juillet 1855; *Area:* 33,84 km2
Comté ou district: Kamouraska; *Population au 2011:* 503
Circonscription(s) électorale(s) provinciale(s): Côte-du-Sud
Circonscription(s) électorale(s) fédérale(s):
Montmagny-L'Islet-Kamouraska-Rivière-du-Loup
Prochaines élections: 5e novembre 2017
Jean Dallaire, Maire
Anne Desjardins, Directrice générale

Saint-Denis-de-Brompton
CP 120
2050, rue Ernest-Camiré
Saint-Denis-de-Brompton, QC J0B 2P0
Tél: 819-846-2744; *Téléc:* 819-846-0915
mstdenis@videotron.ca
www.saintdenisdebrompton.com
Entité municipal: Parish (Paroisse)
Incorporation: 6 mars 1935; *Area:* 70,25 km2
Comté ou district: Le Val-Saint-François; *Population au 2011:* 3,402
Circonscription(s) électorale(s) provinciale(s): Richmond
Circonscription(s) électorale(s) fédérale(s):
Richmond-Arthabaska
Prochaines élections: 5e novembre 2017
Jean-Luc Beauchemin, Maire
Jean-Pierre Boulé, Directeur général

Saint-Denis-sur-Richelieu
599, ch des Patriotes
Saint-Denis-sur-Richelieu, QC J0H 1K0
Tél: 450-787-2244; *Téléc:* 450-787-2635
municipalitedestdenis@bellnet.ca
www.stdenissurrichelieu.ca
Entité municipal: Municipality
Incorporation: 24 décembre 1997; *Area:* 82,20 km2
Comté ou district: La Vallée-du-Richelieu; *Population au 2011:* 2,285
Circonscription(s) électorale(s) provinciale(s): Borduas
Circonscription(s) électorale(s) fédérale(s): Pierre-Boucher-Les Patriotes-Verchères
Prochaines élections: 5e novembre 2017
Jacques Villemaire, Maire
Pascal Smith, Directeur général

Saint-Didace
380, rue Principale
Saint-Didace, QC J0K 2G0
Tél: 450-835-4184; *Téléc:* 450-835-0602
info@saint-didace.com
www.saint-didace.com
Entité municipal: Parish (Paroisse)
Incorporation: 27 août 1863; *Area:* 99,66 km2
Comté ou district: D'Autray; *Population au 2011:* 593
Circonscription(s) électorale(s) provinciale(s): Berthier
Circonscription(s) électorale(s) fédérale(s): Berthier-Maskinongé
Prochaines élections: 5e novembre 2017
Yves Germain, Maire
André Allard, Directeur général

Saint-Dominique
467, rue Deslandes
Saint-Dominique, QC J0H 1L0
Tél: 450-774-9939; *Téléc:* 450-774-1595
admin@municipalite.saint-dominique.qc.ca
www.municipalite.saint-dominique.qc.ca
Entité municipal: Municipality
Incorporation: 1er juillet 1855; *Area:* 70,16 km2
Comté ou district: Les Maskoutains; *Population au 2011:* 2,327
Circonscription(s) électorale(s) provinciale(s): St-Hyacinthe
Circonscription(s) électorale(s) fédérale(s): St-Hyacinthe-Bagot
Prochaines élections: 5e novembre 2017
Robert Houle, Maire
Christine Massé, Directrice générale

Saint-Dominique-du-Rosaire
235, rue Principale
Saint-Dominique-du-Rosaire, QC J0Y 2K0
Tél: 819-727-9544; *Téléc:* 819-727-4344
mun.stdomrosaire@cableamos.com
www.st-dominique-du-rosaire.org
Entité municipal: Municipality
Incorporation: 1er janvier 1978; *Area:* 512,24 km2
Comté ou district: Abitibi; *Population au 2011:* 434
Circonscription(s) électorale(s) provinciale(s): Abitibi-Ouest
Circonscription(s) électorale(s) fédérale(s):
Abitibi-Témiscamingue
Prochaines élections: 5e novembre 2017
Maurice Godbout, Maire
Nathalie Boire, Directrice générale

Saint-Donat
CP 70
194, av du Mont-Comi
Saint-Donat-de-Rimouski, QC G0K 1L0
Tél: 418-739-4634; *Téléc:* 418-739-5003
www.saintdonat.ca
Entité municipal: Parish (Paroisse)
Incorporation: 10 mars 1869; *Area:* 93,23 km2
Comté ou district: La Mitis; *Population au 2011:* 890
Circonscription(s) électorale(s) provinciale(s): Matane-Matapédia
Circonscription(s) électorale(s) fédérale(s): Avignon-La Mitis-Matane-Matapédia
Prochaines élections: 5e novembre 2017
Olivier Gillet, Maire
Gil Bérubé, Directeur général

Saint-Donat
490, rue Principale
Saint-Donat, QC J0T 2C0
Tél: 819-424-2383; *Téléc:* 819-424-5020
www.saint-donat.ca
Entité municipal: Municipality
Incorporation: 19 février 1904; *Area:* 361,42 km2
Comté ou district: Matawinie; *Population au 2011:* 4,130
Circonscription(s) électorale(s) provinciale(s): Bertrand
Circonscription(s) électorale(s) fédérale(s): Joliette
Prochaines élections: 5e novembre 2017
Joé Deslauriers, Maire
Sophie Charpentier, Directrice générale

Sainte-Agathe-de-Lotbinière
CP 159
254, rue St-Pierre
Sainte-Agathe-de-Lotbinière, QC G0S 2A0
Tél: 418-599-2605; *Téléc:* 418-599-2905
administration@coopsteagathe.com
www.ste-agathelotb.qc.ca
Entité municipal: Municipality
Incorporation: 3 février 1999; *Area:* 169,50 km2
Comté ou district: Lotbinière; *Population au 2011:* 1,145
Circonscription(s) électorale(s) provinciale(s):
Lotbinière-Frontenac
Circonscription(s) électorale(s) fédérale(s): Lévis-Lotbinière
Prochaines élections: 5e novembre 2017
Gilbert Breton, Maire
Monique Boilard, Directrice générale

Sainte-Angèle-de-Mérici
CP 129
23, rue de la Fabrique
Sainte-Angèle-de-Mérici, QC G0J 2H0
Tél: 418-775-7733; *Téléc:* 418-775-5722
steangele@mitis.qc.ca
www.municipalite.sainte-angele-de-merici.qc.ca
Entité municipal: Municipality
Incorporation: 26 avril 1989; *Area:* 108,41 km2
Comté ou district: La Mitis; *Population au 2011:* 999
Circonscription(s) électorale(s) provinciale(s): Matane-Matapédia
Circonscription(s) électorale(s) fédérale(s): Avignon-La Mitis-Matane-Matapédia
Prochaines élections: 5e novembre 2017
Alain Carrier, Maire
Bernard Dufour, Directrice générale

Sainte-Angèle-de-Monnoir
5, ch du Vide
Sainte-Angèle-de-Monnoir, QC J0L 1P0
Tél: 450-460-7838; *Téléc:* 450-460-3853
www.municipalite.sainte-angele-de-monnoir.qc.ca
Entité municipal: Parish (Paroisse)
Incorporation: 15 mars 1865; *Area:* 45,49 km2
Comté ou district: Rouville; *Population au 2011:* 1,812
Circonscription(s) électorale(s) provinciale(s): Iberville
Circonscription(s) électorale(s) fédérale(s): Shefford
Prochaines élections: 5e novembre 2017
Michel Picotte, Maire
Jacqueline Houle, Directrice générale

Sainte-Angèle-de-Prémont
2451, rue Camirand
Sainte-Angèle-de-Prémont, QC J0K 1R0
Tél: 819-268-5526; *Téléc:* 819-268-5536
adminmuni@municpremont.ca
www.sainte-angele-de-premont.ca
Entité municipal: Municipality
Incorporation: 28 août 1917; *Area:* 38,51 km2
Comté ou district: Maskinongé; *Population au 2011:* 647
Circonscription(s) électorale(s) provinciale(s): Maskinongé
Circonscription(s) électorale(s) fédérale(s): Berthier-Maskinongé
Prochaines élections: 5e novembre 2017
Barbara Paillé, Mairesse
Jean Charland, Directeur général

Sainte-Anne-de-Beaupré
9336, av Royale
Sainte-Anne-de-Beaupré, QC G0A 3C0
Tél: 418-827-3191; *Téléc:* 418-827-8275
info@sainteannedebeaupre.com
www.sainteannedebeaupre.com
Entité municipal: Town
Incorporation: 27 janvier 1973; *Area:* 64,38 km2
Comté ou district: La Côte-de-Beaupré; Communauté métropolitaine de Québec; *Population au 2011:* 2,854
Circonscription(s) électorale(s) provinciale(s): Charlevoix
Circonscription(s) électorale(s) fédérale(s):
Beauport-Côte-de-Beaupré-Ile d'Orléans-Charlevoix
Prochaines élections: 5e novembre 2017
Jean-Luc Fortin, Maire
Frédéric Drolet-Gervais, Directeur général

Sainte-Anne-de-Bellevue
109, rue Sainte-Anne
Sainte-Anne-de-Bellevue, QC H9X 1M2
Tél: 514-457-5500; *Téléc:* 514-457-6087
info@sadb.qc.ca
www.sadb.qc.ca
Entité municipal: Town
Incorporation: 1er janvier 2006; *Area:* 10,57 km2
Comté ou district: Communauté métropolitaine de Montréal; *Population au 2011:* 5,073
Circonscription(s) électorale(s) provinciale(s): Jacques-Cartier
Circonscription(s) électorale(s) fédérale(s): Lac-Saint-Louis
Prochaines élections: 5e novembre 2017
Paola L. Hawa, Mairesse
Catherine Blais-Adam, Greffière

Sainte-Anne-de-la-Pérade
200, rue Principale
Sainte-Anne-de-la-Pérade, QC G0X 2J0
Tél: 418-325-2841; *Téléc:* 418-325-3070
municipalite@sainteannedelaperade.net
www.sainteannedelaperade.net
Entité municipal: Municipality
Incorporation: 10 mai 1989; *Area:* 107,94 km2
Comté ou district: Les Chenaux; *Population au 2011:* 2,072
Circonscription(s) électorale(s) provinciale(s): Champlain
Circonscription(s) électorale(s) fédérale(s):
St-Maurice-Champlain
Prochaines élections: 5e novembre 2017
Diane Aubut, Mairesse
René Roy, Directeur général

Sainte-Anne-de-la-Pocatière
395, ch des Sables est
Sainte-Anne-de-la-Pocatière, QC G0R 1Z0
Tél: 418-856-3192; *Téléc:* 418-856-9936
paroisse@ste-anne-de-la-pocatiere.com
www.ste-anne-de-la-pocatiere.com
Entité municipal: Parish (Paroisse)
Incorporation: 1er juillet 1855; *Area:* 53,68 km2
Comté ou district: Kamouraska; *Population au 2011:* 1,717
Circonscription(s) électorale(s) provinciale(s): Côte-du-Sud
Circonscription(s) électorale(s) fédérale(s):
Montmagny-L'Islet-Kamouraska-Rivière-du-Loup
Prochaines élections: 5e novembre 2017
Rosaire Ouellet, Maire
Sylvie Dionne, Directrice générale

Sainte-Anne-de-la-Rochelle
145, rue l'Église
Sainte-Anne-de-la-Rochelle, QC J0E 2B0
Tél: 450-539-1654; *Téléc:* 450-539-2317
mun.steannedelarochelle@axion.ca
www.steannedelarochelle.ca
Entité municipal: Municipality
Incorporation: 1er juillet 1855; *Area:* 60,96 km2
Comté ou district: Le Val-Saint-François; *Population au 2011:* 611
Circonscription(s) électorale(s) provinciale(s): Orford
Circonscription(s) électorale(s) fédérale(s): Shefford
Prochaines élections: 5e novembre 2017
Louis Coutu, Maire
Majella René, Directrice générale

Sainte-Anne-de-Sabrevois
CP 60
1218, rte 133
Sabrevois, QC J0J 2G0
Tél: 450-347-0066; *Téléc:* 450-347-4040
info.sabrevois@videotron.ca
Entité municipal: Parish (Paroisse)
Incorporation: 1er mars 1888; *Area:* 45,24 km2
Comté ou district: Le Haut-Richelieu; *Population au 2011:* 2,074
Circonscription(s) électorale(s) provinciale(s): Iberville
Circonscription(s) électorale(s) fédérale(s): Saint-Jean
Prochaines élections: 5e novembre 2017
Denis Rolland, Maire
Fredy Serreyn, Directeur général

Sainte-Anne-des-Lacs
773, ch de Ste-Anne-des-Lacs
Sainte-Anne-des-Lacs, QC J0R 1B0
Tél: 450-224-2675; *Téléc:* 450-224-8672
www.sadl.qc.ca
Entité municipal: Parish (Paroisse)
Incorporation: 28 mars 1946; *Area:* 23,45 km2
Comté ou district: Les Pays-d'en-Haut; *Population au 2011:* 3,363
Circonscription(s) électorale(s) provinciale(s): Bertrand
Circonscription(s) électorale(s) fédérale(s): Laurentides-Labelle
Prochaines élections: 5e novembre 2017
Monique Monette Laroche, Mairesse
Jean-François René, Directeur général

Sainte-Anne-des-Monts
6, 1re av ouest
Sainte-Anne-des-Monts, QC G4V 1A1
Tél: 418-763-5511; *Téléc:* 418-763-3473
sadmonts@globetrotter.net
www.villesainte-anne-des-monts.qc.ca
Entité municipal: Town
Incorporation: février 2000; *Area:* 263,62 km2
Comté ou district: La Haute-Gaspésie; *Population au 2011:* 6,933
Circonscription(s) électorale(s) provinciale(s): Gaspé
Circonscription(s) électorale(s) fédérale(s): Gaspésie-Les Iles-de-la-Madeleine
Prochaines élections: 5e novembre 2017
Micheline Pelletier, Mairesse
Sylvie Lepage, Greffière

Sainte-Anne-de-Sorel
1685, ch du Chenal-du-Moine
Sainte-Anne-de-Sorel, QC J3P 5N3
Tél: 450-742-1616; *Téléc:* 450-742-1118
info@sainteannedesorel.ca
www.sainteannedesorel.ca
Entité municipal: Municipality
Incorporation: 14 mai 1877; *Area:* 36,51 km2
Comté ou district: Pierre-De Saurel; *Population au 2011:* 2,742
Circonscription(s) électorale(s) provinciale(s): Richelieu

Circonscription(s) électorale(s) fédérale(s):
Bécancour-Nicolet-Saurel
Prochaines élections: 5e novembre 2017
Michel Péloquin, Maire
Maxime Dauplaise, Directeur général

Sainte-Anne-du-Lac
1, rue St-François-Xavier
Sainte-Anne-du-Lac, QC J0W 1V0
Tél: 819-586-2110; *Téléc:* 819-586-2203
municipalite@steannedulac.ca
www.municipalite.sainte-anne-du-lac.qc.ca
Entité municipal: Municipality
Incorporation: 30 décembre 1976; *Area:* 345,28 km2
Comté ou district: Antoine-Labelle; *Population au 2011:* 619
Circonscription(s) électorale(s) provinciale(s): Labelle
Circonscription(s) électorale(s) fédérale(s): Laurentides-Labelle
Prochaines élections: 5e novembre 2017
Annick Brault, Mairesse
Denise Bélec, Directrice générale

Sainte-Anne-du-Sault
1025, rte Principale
Sainte-Anne-du-Sault, QC G0Z 1C0
Tél: 819-367-2210; *Téléc:* 819-367-4011
info@municipalite.sainte-anne-du-sault.qc.ca
www.municipalite.sainte-anne-du-sault.qc.ca
Entité municipal: Municipality
Incorporation: 21 mars 1889; *Area:* 56,09 km2
Comté ou district: Arthabaska; *Population au 2011:* 1,268
Circonscription(s) électorale(s) provinciale(s): Nicolet-Bécancour
Circonscription(s) électorale(s) fédérale(s):
Richmond-Arthabaska
Prochaines élections: 5e novembre 2017
Ghyslain Noël, Maire
Tammy Voyer, Directrice générale

Sainte-Apolline-de-Patton
105, rte de l'Église
Sainte-Apolline-de-Patton, QC G0R 2P0
Tél: 418-469-3031; *Téléc:* 418-469-3051
munapoli@globetrotter.net
www.sainteapollinedepatton.ca
Entité municipal: Parish (Paroisse)
Incorporation: 14 décembre 1909; *Area:* 255,70 km2
Comté ou district: Montmagny; *Population au 2011:* 541
Circonscription(s) électorale(s) provinciale(s): Côte-du-Sud
Circonscription(s) électorale(s) fédérale(s):
Montamagny-L'Islet-Kamouraska-Rivière-du-Loup
Prochaines élections: 5e novembre 2017
Karine Nadeau, Mairesse
Doris Godbout, Directrice générale

Sainte-Aurélie
151A, ch des Bois Francs
Sainte-Aurélie, QC G0M 1M0
Tél: 418-593-3021; *Téléc:* 418-593-3961
munsteau@sogetel.net
www.ste-aurelie.qc.ca
Entité municipal: Municipality
Incorporation: 3 avril 1909; *Area:* 78,52 km2
Comté ou district: Les Etchemins; *Population au 2011:* 910
Circonscription(s) électorale(s) provinciale(s): Beauce-Sud
Circonscription(s) électorale(s) fédérale(s): Beauce
Prochaines élections: 5e novembre 2017
Gilles Gaudet, Maire
Andrée-Anne Verreault, Directrice générale

Sainte-Barbe
470, ch de l'Église
Sainte-Barbe, QC J0S 1P0
Tél: 450-371-2504; *Téléc:* 450-371-2575
info@ste-barbe.com
www.ste-barbe.com
Entité municipal: Municipality
Incorporation: 12 juin 1882; *Area:* 39,78 km2
Comté ou district: Le Haut-Saint-Laurent; *Population au 2011:* 1,403
Circonscription(s) électorale(s) provinciale(s): Huntingdon
Circonscription(s) électorale(s) fédérale(s): Salaberry-Suroît
Prochaines élections: 5e novembre 2017
Louise Lebrun, Mairesse
Chantal Girouard, Directrice générale

Sainte-Béatrix
861, rue de l'Église
Sainte-Béatrix, QC J0K 1Y0
Tél: 450-883-2245; *Téléc:* 450-883-1772
www.sainte-beatrix.com
Entité municipal: Municipality
Incorporation: 11 mai 1864; *Area:* 83,52 km2
Comté ou district: Matawinie; *Population au 2011:* 1,849

Circonscription(s) électorale(s) provinciale(s): Berthier
Circonscription(s) électorale(s) fédérale(s): Joliette
Prochaines élections: 5e novembre 2017
Normand Montagne, Maire
Patricia Labby, Directrice générale

Sainte-Brigide-d'Iberville
555, rue Principale
Sainte-Brigide-d'Iberville, QC J0J 1X0
Tél: 450-293-7511; *Téléc:* 450-293-1077
ste_brigide@bellnet.ca
www.sainte-brigide.qc.ca
Entité municipal: Municipality
Incorporation: 1er juillet 1855; *Area:* 68,89 km2
Comté ou district: Le Haut-Richelieu; *Population au 2011:* 1,331
Circonscription(s) électorale(s) provinciale(s): Iberville
Circonscription(s) électorale(s) fédérale(s): Saint-Jean
Prochaines élections: 5e novembre 2017
Mario van Rossum, Maire
Murielle Papineau, Directrice générale

Sainte-Brigitte-de-Laval
414, av Ste-Brigitte
Sainte-Brigitte-de-Laval, QC G0A 3K0
Tél: 418-825-2515; *Téléc:* 418-825-3114
mairie@sbdl.net
www.sbdl.net
Entité municipal: Municipality
Incorporation: 11 février 1875; *Area:* 111,49 km2
Comté ou district: La Jacques-Cartier; Communauté métropolitaine de Québec; *Population au 2011:* 5,696
Circonscription(s) électorale(s) provinciale(s): Montmorency
Circonscription(s) électorale(s) fédérale(s): Portneuf-Jacques Cartier
Prochaines élections: 5e novembre 2017
Wanita Daniele, Mairesse
Marc Proulx, Directeur général

Sainte-Brigitte-des-Saults
319, rue Principale
Sainte-Brigitte-des-Saults, QC J0C 1E0
Tél: 819-336-4460; *Téléc:* 819-336-4410
municipalite@stebrigittedessaults.ca
www.saintebrigittedessaults.ca
Entité municipal: Parish (Paroisse)
Incorporation: 9 mars 1878; *Area:* 69,23
Comté ou district: Drummond; *Population au 2011:* 737
Circonscription(s) électorale(s) provinciale(s): Nicolet-Bécancour
Circonscription(s) électorale(s) fédérale(s): Drummond
Prochaines élections: 5e novembre 2017
Jean-Guy Hébert, Maire
Manon Lemaire, Directrice générale

Sainte-Catherine-de-Hatley
CP 30
35, ch de North Hatley
Sainte-Catherine-de-Hatley, QC J0B 1W0
Tél: 819-843-1935; *Téléc:* 819-843-8527
munstecatherinehatley@qc.aira.com
www.sainte-catherine-de-hatley.ca
Entité municipal: Municipality
Incorporation: 28 mars 1901; *Area:* 81,43 km2
Comté ou district: Memphrémagog; *Population au 2011:* 2,464
Circonscription(s) électorale(s) provinciale(s): Orford
Circonscription(s) électorale(s) fédérale(s): Compton-Stanstead
Prochaines élections: 5e novembre 2017
Jacques Demers, Maire
Serge Caron, Directeur général

Sainte-Catherine-de-la-Jacques-Cartier
CP 250
1, rue Rouleau
Ste-Catherine-de-la-J-Cartier, QC G3N 2S5
Tél: 418-875-2758; *Téléc:* 418-875-2170
info@villescjc.com
www.villescjc.com
Entité municipal: Town
Incorporation: 1er juillet 1855; *Area:* 120,61 km2
Comté ou district: La Jacques-Cartier; Communauté métropolitaine de Québec; *Population au 2011:* 6,319
Circonscription(s) électorale(s) provinciale(s): La Peltrie
Circonscription(s) électorale(s) fédérale(s):
Portneuf-Jacques-Cartier
Prochaines élections: 5e novembre 2017
Pierre Dolbec, Maire
Marcel Grenier, Directeur général

Sainte-Cécile-de-Lévrard
235, rue Principale
Sainte-Cécile-de-Lévrard, QC G0X 2M0
Tél: 819-263-2104; *Téléc:* 819-263-1043
info@munstececilelvrd.ca

Entité municipal: Parish (Paroisse)
Incorporation: 11 septembre 1908; *Area:* 33,35 km2
Comté ou district: Bécancour; *Population au 2011:* 362
Circonscription(s) électorale(s) provinciale(s): Nicolet-Bécancour
Circonscription(s) électorale(s) fédérale(s):
Bécancour-Nicolet-Saurel
Prochaines élections: 5e novembre 2017
Simon Brunelle, Maire
Réjean Poisson, Directeur général

Sainte-Cécile-de-Milton
CP 201
136, rue Principale
Sainte-Cécile-de-Milton, QC J0E 2C0
Tél: 450-378-1942; *Téléc:* 450-378-4621
www.stececiledemilton.qc.ca
Entité municipal: Township
Incorporation: 1er janvier 1864; *Area:* 74,04 km2
Comté ou district: La Haute-Yamaska; *Population au 2011:* 2,128
Circonscription(s) électorale(s) provinciale(s): Johnson
Circonscription(s) électorale(s) fédérale(s): Shefford
Prochaines élections: 5e novembre 2017
Paul Sarrazin, Maire
Francine Rivest, Directrice générale

Sainte-Cécile-de-Whitton
4554, rue Principale
Sainte-Cécile-de-Whitton, QC G0Y 1J0
Tél: 819-583-0770; *Téléc:* 819-583-0518
muncecilewhitton@axion.ca
www.stececiledewhitton.qc.ca
Entité municipal: Municipality
Incorporation: 19 septembre 1889; *Area:* 146,59 km2
Comté ou district: Le Granit; *Population au 2011:* 892
Circonscription(s) électorale(s) provinciale(s): Mégantic
Circonscription(s) électorale(s) fédérale(s): Mégantic-L'Érable
Prochaines élections: 5e novembre 2017
Diane Turgeon, Maire
Françoise Audet, Directrice générale

Sainte-Christine
629, rue des Loisirs
Sainte-Christine, QC J0H 1H0
Tél: 819-858-2828; *Téléc:* 819-858-9911
stechristine@cooptel.qc.ca
www.ste-christine.com
Entité municipal: Parish (Paroisse)
Incorporation: 8 janvier 1894; *Area:* 89,40 km2
Comté ou district: Acton; *Population au 2011:* 673
Circonscription(s) électorale(s) provinciale(s): Johnson
Circonscription(s) électorale(s) fédérale(s): St-Hyacinthe-Bagot
Prochaines élections: 5e novembre 2017
Huguette St-Pierre-Beaulac, Mairesse
Caroline Lamothe, Directrice-générale

Sainte-Christine-d'Auvergne
80, rue Principale
Sainte-Christine-d'Auvergne, QC G0A 1A0
Tél: 418-329-3304; *Téléc:* 418-329-3356
ste-christine@globetrotter.net
www.ste-christine.qc.ca
Entité municipal: Municipality
Incorporation: 10 avril 1896; *Area:* 145,58 km2
Comté ou district: Portneuf; *Population au 2011:* 448
Circonscription(s) électorale(s) provinciale(s): Portneuf
Circonscription(s) électorale(s) fédérale(s): Portneuf-Jacques Cartier
Prochaines élections: 5e novembre 2017
Pierre Tourigny, Maire
Véronique Lille, Directrice générale

Sainte-Claire
135, rue Principale
Sainte-Claire, QC G0R 2V0
Tél: 418-883-3314; *Téléc:* 418-883-3845
msclaire@globetrotter.qc.ca
www.municipalite.sainte-claire.qc.ca
Entité municipal: Municipality
Incorporation: 1er octobre 1977; *Area:* 88,63 km2
Comté ou district: Bellechasse; *Population au 2011:* 3,325
Circonscription(s) électorale(s) provinciale(s): Bellechasse
Circonscription(s) électorale(s) fédérale(s): Bellechasse-Les Etchemins-Lévis
Prochaines élections: 5e novembre 2017
Denise Dulac, Mairesse
Dany Fournier, Directeur général

Sainte-Clotilde
2452, ch de l'Église
Sainte-Clotilde, QC J0L 1W0
Tél: 450-826-3129; *Téléc:* 450-826-3217
www.ste-clotilde.ca

Entité municipal: Parish (Paroisse)
Incorporation: 2 avril 1885; *Area:* 78,96 km2
Comté ou district: Les Jardins-de-Napierville; *Population au 2011:* 1,704
Circonscription(s) électorale(s) provinciale(s): Huntingdon
Circonscription(s) électorale(s) fédérale(s): Châteauguay-Lacolle
Prochaines élections: 5e novembre 2017
Clément Lemieux, Maire
Lucie Riendeau, Directrice générale

Sainte-Clotilde-de-Beauce
307B, rue du Couvent
Sainte-Clotilde-de-Beauce, QC G0N 1C0
Tél: 418-427-2637; *Téléc:* 418-427-4303
info@ste-clotilde.com
www.ste-clotilde.com
Entité municipal: Municipality
Incorporation: 19 novembre 1938; *Area:* 58,680 km2
Comté ou district: Les Appalaches; *Population au 2011:* 650
Circonscription(s) électorale(s) provinciale(s): Beauce-Sud
Circonscription(s) électorale(s) fédérale(s): Mégantic-L'Érable
Prochaines élections: 5e novembre 2017
Gérald Grenier, Maire
Pascale Trépanier, Directrice générale

Sainte-Clotilde-de-Horton
CP 29
17, rte 122
Sainte-Clotilde-de-Horton, QC J0A 1H0
Tél: 819-336-5344; *Téléc:* 819-336-5440
info@steclotildehorton.ca
www.steclotildedehorton.ca
Entité municipal: Municipality
Incorporation: 26 mars 1997; *Area:* 118,44 km2
Comté ou district: Arthabaska; *Population au 2011:* 1,616
Circonscription(s) électorale(s) provinciale(s):
Drummond-Bois-Francs
Circonscription(s) électorale(s) fédérale(s):
Richmond-Arthabaska
Prochaines élections: 5e novembre 2017
Simon Boucher, Maire
Gaby Tessier, Directeur général

Sainte-Croix
6310, rue Principale
Sainte-Croix, QC G0S 2H0
Tél: 418-926-3494; *Téléc:* 418-926-2570
www.ville.sainte-croix.qc.ca
Entité municipal: Municipality
Incorporation: 5 octobre 2001; *Area:* 69,64 km2
Comté ou district: Lotbinière; *Population au 2011:* 2,352
Circonscription(s) électorale(s) provinciale(s):
Lotbinière-Frontenac
Circonscription(s) électorale(s) fédérale(s): Lévis-Lotbinière
Prochaines élections: 5e novembre 2017
Jacques Gauthier, Maire
France Dubuc, Directrice générale

Saint-Edmond-de-Grantham
1393, rue Notre-Dame-de-Lourdes
Saint-Edmond-de-Grantham, QC J0C 1K0
Tél: 819-395-2562; *Téléc:* 819-395-2666
municipalite@st-edmond-de-grantham.qc.ca
www.st-edmond-de-grantham.qc.ca
Entité municipal: Parish (Paroisse)
Incorporation: 9 février 1918; *Area:* 48,79 km2
Comté ou district: Drummond; *Population au 2011:* 673
Circonscription(s) électorale(s) provinciale(s): Johnson
Circonscription(s) électorale(s) fédérale(s): Drummond
Prochaines élections: 5e novembre 2017
Marie-Andrée Auger, Mairesse
Julie Galarneau, Directrice générale

Saint-Edmond-les-Plaines
561, ch Principale
Saint-Edmond-les-Plaines, QC G0W 2M0
Tél: 418-274-3069; *Téléc:* 418-274-5629
stedmond@destination.ca
www.stedmond.ca
Entité municipal: Municipality
Incorporation: 3 septembre 1938; *Area:* 87,15 km2
Comté ou district: Maria-Chapdelaine; *Population au 2011:* 390
Circonscription(s) électorale(s) provinciale(s): Roberval
Circonscription(s) électorale(s) fédérale(s): Lac-Saint-Jean
Prochaines élections: 5e novembre 2017
Rodrigue Cantin, Maire
Danielle Bernard, Directrice générale

Saint-Édouard
CP 230
405C, montée Lussier
Saint-Édouard, QC J0L 1Y0
Tél: 450-454-6333; *Téléc:* 450-454-4921
dgstedouard@derytele.com
Entité municipal: Parish (Paroisse)
Incorporation: 1er juillet 1855; *Area:* 52,91 km2
Comté ou district: Les Jardins-de-Napierville; *Population au 2011:* 1,312
Circonscription(s) électorale(s) provinciale(s): Huntingdon
Circonscription(s) électorale(s) fédérale(s): Châteauguay-Lacolle
Prochaines élections: 5e novembre 2017
Ronald Lécuyer, Maire
Christine Tremblay, Directeur général

Saint-Édouard-de-Fabre
CP 70
620, rue de l'Église
Saint-Édouard-de-Fabre, QC J0Z 1Z0
Tél: 819-634-4441; *Téléc:* 819-634-2646
municipalitefabre@mrctemiscamingue.qc.ca
Entité municipal: Parish (Paroisse)
Incorporation: 3 octobre 1912; *Area:* 216,18 km2
Comté ou district: Témiscamingue; *Population au 2011:* 649
Circonscription(s) électorale(s) provinciale(s):
Rouyn-Noranda-Témiscamingue
Circonscription(s) électorale(s) fédérale(s):
Abitibi-Témiscamingue
Prochaines élections: 5e novembre 2017
Mario Drouin, Maire
Aline Desjardins, Directrice générale

Saint-Édouard-de-Lotbinière
2595, rue Principale
Saint-Edouard-de-Lotbinière, QC G0S 1Y0
Tél: 418-796-2971; *Téléc:* 418-796-2228
info@st-edouard.com
www.municipalite.st-edouard.qc.ca
Entité municipal: Parish (Paroisse)
Incorporation: 1er décembre 1862; *Area:* 98,57 km2
Comté ou district: Lotbinière; *Population au 2011:* 1,248
Circonscription(s) électorale(s) provinciale(s):
Lotbinière-Frontenac
Circonscription(s) électorale(s) fédérale(s): Lévis-Lotbinière
Prochaines élections: 5e novembre 2017
Denise Poulin, Maire
Ghislaine Gravel, Directrice générale

Saint-Édouard-de-Maskinongé
3851, rue Notre-Dame
Saint-Édouard-de-Maskinongé, QC J0K 2H0
Tél: 819-268-2833; *Téléc:* 819-268-2883
municipalitestedouard@telmilot.net
mrc-maskinonge.qc.ca/municipalites/st-edouard-de-maskinonge.html
Entité municipal: Municipality
Incorporation: 1er janvier 1950; *Area:* 55,06 km2
Comté ou district: Maskinongé; *Population au 2011:* 774
Circonscription(s) électorale(s) provinciale(s): Maskinongé
Circonscription(s) électorale(s) fédérale(s): Berthier-Maskinongé
Prochaines élections: 5e novembre 2017
Michel Lemay, Maire
Sylvie Vallières, Directrice générale

Sainte-Edwidge-de-Clifton
1439, chemin Favreau
Sainte-Edwidge-de-Clifton, QC J0B 2R0
Tél: 819-849-7740; *Téléc:* 819-849-4212
info@ste-edwidge.ca
www.ste-edwidge.ca
Entité municipal: Township
Incorporation: 21 décembre 1895; *Area:* 99,35 km2
Comté ou district: Coaticook; *Population au 2011:* 484
Circonscription(s) électorale(s) provinciale(s): St-François
Circonscription(s) électorale(s) fédérale(s): Compton-Stanstead
Prochaines élections: 5e novembre 2017
Bernard Marion, Maire
Réjean Fauteux, Directeur général

Sainte-Élisabeth
2270, rue Principale
Sainte-Élisabeth, QC J0K 2J0
Tél: 450-759-2875; *Téléc:* 450-836-5210
info@ste-elisabeth.qc.ca
www.ste-elisabeth.qc.ca
Entité municipal: Parish (Paroisse)
Incorporation: 1er juillet 1855; *Area:* 81,66 km2
Comté ou district: D'Autray; *Population au 2011:* 1,559
Circonscription(s) électorale(s) provinciale(s): Berthier
Circonscription(s) électorale(s) fédérale(s): Berthier-Maskinongé
Prochaines élections: 5e novembre 2017
Mario Houle, Maire
Lorraine C. Garnelin, Directrice générale

Sainte-Élizabeth-de-Warwick
243, rue Principale
Sainte-Élizabeth-de-Warwick, QC J0A 1M0
Tél: 819-358-5162; *Téléc:* 819-358-9192
info@sainte-elizabeth-de-warwick.ca
www.sainte-elizabeth-de-warwick.ca
Entité municipal: Parish (Paroisse)
Incorporation: 18 mai 1887; *Area:* 50,51 km2
Comté ou district: Arthabaska; *Population au 2011:* 374
Circonscription(s) électorale(s) provinciale(s):
Drummond-Bois-Francs
Circonscription(s) électorale(s) fédérale(s):
Richmond-Arthabaska
Prochaines élections: 5e novembre 2017
Luc Le Blanc, Maire
Josée Leblond, Directrice générale

Sainte-Émélie-de-l'Énergie
241, rue Coutu
Sainte-Émélie-de-l'Énergie, QC J0K 2K0
Tél: 450-886-3823; *Téléc:* 450-886-9175
stemelie@intermonde.net
www.ste-emelie-de-lenergie.qc.ca
Entité municipal: Municipality
Incorporation: 10 juin 1884; *Area:* 170,68 km2
Comté ou district: Matawinie; *Population au 2011:* 1,644
Circonscription(s) électorale(s) provinciale(s): Berthier
Circonscription(s) électorale(s) fédérale(s): Joliette
Prochaines élections: 5e novembre 2017
Atchez Arbour, Maire
Brigitte Belleville, Directrice générale

Sainte-Eulalie
757, rue des Bouleaux
Sainte-Eulalie, QC G0Z 1E0
Tél: 819-225-4345; *Téléc:* 819-225-4078
info@municipalite.sainte-eulalie.qc.ca
www.municipalite.sainte-eulalie.qc.ca
Entité municipal: Municipality
Incorporation: 1er juillet 1864; *Area:* 90,79 km2
Comté ou district: Nicolet-Yamaska; *Population au 2011:* 871
Circonscription(s) électorale(s) provinciale(s): Nicolet-Bécancour
Circonscription(s) électorale(s) fédérale(s):
Bécancour-Nicolet-Saurel
Prochaines élections: 5e novembre 2017
André Demers, Maire
Yvon Douville, Directeur général

Sainte-Euphémie-sur-Rivière-du-Sud
220, rue Principal est
Ste-Euphémie-sur-Rivière-du-Su, QC G0R 2Z0
Tél: 418-469-3427; *Téléc:* 418-469-3427
municipalitesteeuphemie@globetrotter.net
www.sainte-euphemie.qc.ca
Entité municipal: Municipality
Incorporation: 20 juillet 1907; *Area:* 93,21 km2
Comté ou district: Montmagny; *Population au 2011:* 329
Circonscription(s) électorale(s) provinciale(s): Côte-du-Sud
Circonscription(s) électorale(s) fédérale(s):
Montmagny-L'Islet-Kamouraska-Rivière-du-Loup
Prochaines élections: 5e novembre 2017
Denis Giroux, Maire
Liliane Morin, Directrice générale

Sainte-Famille
3894, ch Royal
Sainte-Famille, QC G0A 3P0
Tél: 418-829-3572; *Téléc:* 418-829-2513
info@munstefamille.org
www.ste-famille.iledorleans.com
Entité municipal: Parish (Paroisse)
Incorporation: 1er juillet 1855; *Area:* 46,43 km2
Comté ou district: L'Île-d'Orléans; Communauté métropolitaine de Québec; *Population au 2011:* 851
Circonscription(s) électorale(s) provinciale(s):
Charlevoix-Côte-de-Beaupré
Circonscription(s) électorale(s) fédérale(s):
Beauport-Côte-de-Beaupré-Ile d'Orléans-Charlevoix
Prochaines élections: 5e novembre 2017
Jean-Pierre Turcotte, Maire
Sylvie Beaulieu, Directrice générale

Sainte-Félicité
5, rte de l'Église nord
Sainte-Félicité, QC G0R 4P0
Tél: 418-359-2321; *Téléc:* 418-359-2321
mun.ste-felicite@globetrotter.net
www.ste-felicite.ca

Entité municipal: Municipality
Incorporation: 1er janvier 1950; *Area:* 95,82 km2
Comté ou district: L'Islet; *Population au 2011:* 413
Circonscription(s) électorale(s) provinciale(s): Côte-du-Sud
Circonscription(s) électorale(s) fédérale(s):
Montmagny-l'Islet-Kamouraska-Rivière-du-Loup
Prochaines élections: 5e novembre 2017
Alphé St-Pierre, Maire
Julie Bélanger, Directrice générale

Sainte-Félicité
CP 9
192, rue St-Joseph
Sainte-Félicité, QC G0J 2K0
Tél: 418-733-4628; *Téléc:* 418-733-8377
ste-felicite@mrcdematane.qc.ca
www.sainte-felicite.com
Entité municipal: Municipality
Incorporation: 10 janvier 1996; *Area:* 89,76 km2
Comté ou district: La Matanie; *Population au 2011:* 1,175
Circonscription(s) électorale(s) provinciale(s): Matane-Matapédia
Circonscription(s) électorale(s) fédérale(s): Avignon-La Mitis-Matane-Matapédia
Prochaines élections: 5e novembre 2017
Réginald Desrosiers, Maire
Yves Chassé, Directeur général

Sainte-Flavie
775, rte Flavie-Drapeau
Sainte-Flavie, QC G0J 2L0
Tél: 418-775-7050; *Téléc:* 418-775-5672
info@sainte-flavie.net
www.sainte-flavie.net
Entité municipal: Parish (Paroisse)
Incorporation: 1er juillet 1855; *Area:* 37,62 km2
Comté ou district: La Mitis; *Population au 2011:* 919
Circonscription(s) électorale(s) provinciale(s): Matane-Matapédia
Circonscription(s) électorale(s) fédérale(s): Avignon-La Mitis-Matane-Matapédia
Prochaines élections: 5e novembre 2017
Rose-Marie Gallagher, Mairesse
Francine Roy, Directrice générale

Sainte-Florence
CP 9
29, rue des Loisirs
Sainte-Florence, QC G0J 2M0
Tél: 418-756-3491; *Téléc:* 418-756-5079
steflorence@mrcmatapedia.qc.ca
www.sainte-florence.org
Entité municipal: Municipality
Incorporation: 12 avril 1911; *Area:* 103,00 km2
Comté ou district: La Matapédia; *Population au 2011:* 414
Circonscription(s) électorale(s) provinciale(s): Matane-Matapédia
Circonscription(s) électorale(s) fédérale(s): Avignon-La Mitis-Matane-Matapédia
Prochaines élections: 5e novembre 2017
David Althot, Maire
Natacha Gallant, Directrice générale

Sainte-Françoise
563, 10e-et-11e rang est
Sainte-Françoise-de-Lotbinière, QC G0S 2N0
Tél: 819-287-5755; *Téléc:* 819-287-5838
municipalite@ste-francoise.com
www.visitedefermeeducative.com
Entité municipal: Municipality
Incorporation: 1er janvier 1947; *Area:* 89,12 km2
Comté ou district: Bécancour; *Population au 2011:* 479
Circonscription(s) électorale(s) provinciale(s): Nicolet-Bécancour
Circonscription(s) électorale(s) fédérale(s):
Bécancour-Nicolet-Saurel
Prochaines élections: 5e novembre 2017
Mario Lyonnais, Maire
Isabelle Dubois, Directrice générale

Sainte-Françoise
156, rue Jérémie-Beaulieu
Sainte-Françoise, QC G0L 3B0
Tél: 418-851-1502; *Téléc:* 418-851-0926
municipal@ste-francoise.ca
www.sainte-francoise.org
Entité municipal: Parish (Paroisse)
Incorporation: 6 décembre 1873; *Area:* 88,54 km2
Comté ou district: Les Basques; *Population au 2011:* 399
Circonscription(s) électorale(s) provinciale(s):
Rivière-du-Loup-Témiscouata
Circonscription(s) électorale(s) fédérale(s):
Rimouski-Neigette-Témiscouata-Les Basques
Prochaines élections: 5e novembre 2017
Jean-Yves Belzile, Maire
Véronique Pelletier, Directrice générale

Sainte-Geneviève-de-Batiscan
30, rue St-Charles
Sainte-Geneviève-de-Batiscan, QC G0X 2R0
Tél: 418-362-2078; *Téléc:* 418-362-2111
www.stegenevieve.ca
Entité municipal: Parish (Paroisse)
Incorporation: 1er juillet 1855; *Area:* 97,09 km2
Comté ou district: Les Chenaux; *Population au 2011:* 1,060
Circonscription(s) électorale(s) provinciale(s): Champlain
Circonscription(s) électorale(s) fédérale(s):
St-Maurice-Champlain
Prochaines élections: 5e novembre 2017
Christian Gendron, Maire
Luc Mathon, Directrice générale

Sainte-Geneviève-de-Berthier
400, rang de la Rivière-Bayonne sud
Sainte-Geneviève-de-Berthier, QC J0K 1A0
Tél: 450-836-4333; *Téléc:* 450-836-7260
info@munisgb.ca
www.sainte-genevieve-de-berthier.org
Entité municipal: Parish (Paroisse)
Incorporation: 1er juillet 1855; *Area:* 74,67
Comté ou district: D'Autray; *Population au 2011:* 2,365
Circonscription(s) électorale(s) provinciale(s): Berthier
Circonscription(s) électorale(s) fédérale(s): Berthier-Maskinongé
Prochaines élections: 5e novembre 2017
Richard Giroux, Maire
Martine Beaudoin, Directrice générale

Sainte-Germaine-Boulé
CP 5 Boulé
199, rue Roy
Sainte-Germaine-Boulé, QC J0Z 1M0
Tél: 819-787-6221; *Téléc:* 819-787-2560
direction@saintegermaineboule.com
www.saintegermaineboule.com
Entité municipal: Municipality
Incorporation: 1er janvier 1954; *Area:* 108,46 km2
Comté ou district: Abitibi-Ouest; *Population au 2011:* 895
Circonscription(s) électorale(s) provinciale(s): Abitibi-Ouest
Circonscription(s) électorale(s) fédérale(s):
Abitibi-Témiscamingue
Prochaines élections: 5e novembre 2017
Jaclin Bégin, Maire
Gisèle Bisson-Lapointe, Directrice générale

Sainte-Gertrude-Manneville
2, rue de l'École
Sainte-Gertrude-Manneville, QC J0Y 2L0
Tél: 819-727-2244; *Téléc:* 819-727-3293
stegertman@cableamos.com
Entité municipal: Municipality
Incorporation: 1er janvier 1980; *Area:* 329,84 km2
Comté ou district: Abitibi; *Population au 2011:* 757
Circonscription(s) électorale(s) provinciale(s): Abitibi-Ouest
Circonscription(s) électorale(s) fédérale(s):
Abitibi-Témiscamingue
Prochaines élections: 5e novembre 2017
Pascal Rheault, Maire
Laurence Demers, Directrice générale

Sainte-Hedwidge
1090, rue Principale
Sainte-Hedwidge, QC G0W 2R0
Tél: 418-275-3020; *Téléc:* 418-275-4163
www.ste-hedwidge.qc.ca
Entité municipal: Municipality
Incorporation: 10 mars 1909; *Area:* 469,07 km2
Comté ou district: Le Domaine-du-Roy; *Population au 2011:* 824
Circonscription(s) électorale(s) provinciale(s): Roberval
Circonscription(s) électorale(s) fédérale(s): Lac-St-Jean
Prochaines élections: 5e novembre 2017
Gilles Toulouse, Maire
Sylvain Privé, Directeur général

Sainte-Hélène
CP 216
531, rue de l'Église sud
Sainte-Hélène, QC G0L 3J0
Tél: 418-492-6830; *Téléc:* 418-492-1854
munhel@bellnet.ca
www.sainte-helene.net
Entité municipal: Parish (Paroisse)
Incorporation: 1er juillet 1855; *Area:* 60,34 km2
Comté ou district: Kamouraska; *Population au 2011:* 911
Circonscription(s) électorale(s) provinciale(s): Côte-du-Sud
Circonscription(s) électorale(s) fédérale(s):
Montmagny-L'Islet-Kamourask-Rivière-du-Loup
Prochaines élections: 5e novembre 2017
Louise Hémond, Mairesse
Marie-Eve Bergeron, Directrice générale

Sainte-Hélène-de-Bagot
379, 7e av
Sainte-Hélène-de-Bagot, QC J0H 1M0
Tél: 450-791-2455; *Téléc:* 450-791-2550
mun.ste-helene@mrcmaskoutains.qc.ca
www.saintehelenedebagot.com
Entité municipal: Municipality
Incorporation: 9 juillet 1977; *Area:* 73,53 km2
Comté ou district: Les Maskoutains; *Population au 2011:* 1,637
Circonscription(s) électorale(s) provinciale(s): Johnson
Circonscription(s) électorale(s) fédérale(s): St-Hyacinthe-Bagot
Prochaines élections: 5e novembre 2017
Yves Petit, Maire
Véronique Piché, Directrice générale

Sainte-Hélène-de-Chester
440, rue de l'Église
Sainte-Hélène-de-Chester, QC G0O 1H0
Tél: 819-382-2650; *Téléc:* 819-382-9933
municipalite@sainte-helene-de-chester.ca
www.sainte-helene-de-chester.ca
Entité municipal: Municipality
Incorporation: 1er janvier 1859; *Area:* 83,96 km2
Comté ou district: Arthabaska; *Population au 2011:* 358
Circonscription(s) électorale(s) provinciale(s):
Drummond-Bois-Francs
Circonscription(s) électorale(s) fédérale(s):
Richmond-Arthabaska
Prochaines élections: 5e novembre 2017
Lionel Fréchette, Maire
Isabelle Leclerc, Directrice générale

Sainte-Hélène-de-Mancebourg
451, rang 2e-et-3e
Mancebourg, QC J0Z 2T0
Tél: 819-333-5766; *Téléc:* 819-333-9514
mancebourg@mrcao.qc.ca
ste-helene.ao.ca
Entité municipal: Parish (Paroisse)
Incorporation: 10 mai 1941; *Area:* 68,29 km2
Comté ou district: Abitibi-Ouest; *Population au 2011:* 354
Circonscription(s) électorale(s) provinciale(s): Abitibi-Ouest
Circonscription(s) électorale(s) fédérale(s):
Abitibi-Témiscamingue
Prochaines élections: 5e novembre 2017
Florent Bédard, Maire
Sylvie Boutin-Bergeron, Directrice générale

Sainte-Hénédine
CP 6
111, rue Principale
Sainte-Hénédine, QC G0S 2R0
Tél: 418-935-7125; *Téléc:* 418-935-3113
munisthe@globetrotter.net
www.ste-henedine.com
Entité municipal: Parish (Paroisse)
Incorporation: 1er juillet 1855; *Area:* 53,06
Comté ou district: La Nouvelle-Beauce; *Population au 2011:* 1,212
Circonscription(s) électorale(s) provinciale(s): Beauce-Nord
Circonscription(s) électorale(s) fédérale(s): Beauce
Prochaines élections: 5e novembre 2017
Michel Duval, Maire
Yvon Marcoux, Directeur général

Sainte-Irène
362, rue de la Fabrique
Sainte-Irène, QC G0J 2P0
Tél: 418-629-5705; *Téléc:* 418-629-3220
www.sainteirene.com
Entité municipal: Parish (Paroisse)
Incorporation: 1er janvier 1953; *Area:* 134,03
Comté ou district: La Matapédia; *Population au 2011:* 341
Circonscription(s) électorale(s) provinciale(s): Matane-Matapédia
Circonscription(s) électorale(s) fédérale(s): Avignon-La Mitis-Matane-Matapédia
Prochaines élections: 5e novembre 2017
Alain Duchemin, Maire
Caroline Lapointe, Directrice générale

Sainte-Jeanne-d'Arc
CP 40
205, rue Principale
Sainte-Jeanne-d'Arc, QC G0J 2T0
Tél: 418-776-5660; *Téléc:* 418-776-5660
stejeanne@mitis.qc.ca
www.municipalite.sainte-jeanne-darc.qc.ca
Entité municipal: Parish (Paroisse)
Incorporation: 30 janvier 1922; *Area:* 110,82 km2
Comté ou district: La Mitis; *Population au 2011:* 313
Circonscription(s) électorale(s) provinciale(s): Matane-Matapédia
Circonscription(s) électorale(s) fédérale(s): Avignon-La

Mitis-Matane-Matapédia
Prochaines élections: 5e novembre 2017
Maurice Chrétien, Maire
Louise Boivin, Directrice générale

Sainte-Jeanne-d'Arc
378, rue François-Bilodeau
Sainte-Jeanne-d'Arc, QC G0W 1E0
Tél: 418-276-3166; *Téléc:* 418-276-7648
info@stejeannedarc.qc.ca
www.stejeannedarc.qc.ca
Entité municipal: Village
Incorporation: 24 janvier 1970; *Area:* 270,88 km2
Comté ou district: Maria-Chapdelaine; *Population au 2011:* 1,089
Circonscription(s) électorale(s) provinciale(s): Roberval
Circonscription(s) électorale(s) fédérale(s): Lac-St-Jean
Prochaines élections: 5e novembre 2017
Yvan Pilote, Maire
Régis Martin, Directeur général

Sainte-Julienne
1400, rte 125
Sainte-Julienne, QC J0K 2T0
Tél: 450-831-2688; *Téléc:* 450-831-4433
municipalite@sainte-julienne.com
www.sainte-julienne.com
Entité municipal: Municipality
Incorporation: 1er juillet 1855; *Area:* 102,10 km2
Comté ou district: Montcalm; *Population au 2011:* 9,331
Circonscription(s) électorale(s) provinciale(s): Rousseau
Circonscription(s) électorale(s) fédérale(s): Montcalm
Prochaines élections: 5e novembre 2017
Marcel Jetté, Maire
France Landry, Directrice générale

Sainte-Justine
167, rte 204
Sainte-Justine, QC G0R 1Y0
Tél: 418-383-5397; *Téléc:* 418-383-5398
sjustine@sogetel.net
www.stejustine.net
Entité municipal: Municipality
Incorporation: 1er janvier 1870; *Area:* 124,55 km2
Comté ou district: Les Etchemins; *Population au 2011:* 1,845
Circonscription(s) électorale(s) provinciale(s): Bellechasse
Circonscription(s) électorale(s) fédérale(s): Bellechasse-Les Etchemins-Lévis
Prochaines élections: 5e novembre 2017
Denis Beaulieu, Maire
Gilles Vézina, Directeur général

Sainte-Justine-de-Newton
CP 270
2627, rue Principale
Sainte-Justine-de-Newton, QC J0P 1T0
Tél: 450-764-3573; *Téléc:* 450-764-3180
ste-justine@rocler.qc.ca
www.sainte-justine-de-newton.ca
Entité municipal: Municipality
Incorporation: 1er juillet 1855; *Area:* 84,14 km2
Comté ou district: Vaudreuil-Soulanges; *Population au 2011:* 973
Circonscription(s) électorale(s) provinciale(s): Soulanges
Circonscription(s) électorale(s) fédérale(s): Salaberry-Suroît
Prochaines élections: 5e novembre 2017
Gisèle Fournier, Mairesse
Denis Perrier, Directeur général

Saint-Élie-de-Caxton
52, ch des Loisirs
Saint-Élie, QC G0X 2N0
Tél: 819-221-2839; *Téléc:* 819-221-4039
saintelie@sogetel.com
www.st-elie-de-caxton.com
Entité municipal: Municipality
Incorporation: 12 avril 1865; *Area:* 118,75 km2
Comté ou district: Maskinongé; *Population au 2011:* 1,676
Circonscription(s) électorale(s) provinciale(s): Maskinongé
Circonscription(s) électorale(s) fédérale(s): Berthier-Maskinongé
Prochaines élections: 5e novembre 2017
Réjean Audet, Maire
Isabelle Bournival, Directrice générale

Saint-Éloi
CP 9
183, rue Principale
Saint-Éloi, QC G0L 2V0
Tél: 418-898-2734; *Téléc:* 418-898-2305
st-eloi@st-eloi.qc.ca
www.st-eloi.qc.ca
Entité municipal: Parish (Paroisse)
Incorporation: 1er juillet 1855; *Area:* 67,69 km2
Comté ou district: Les Basques; *Population au 2011:* 311
Circonscription(s) électorale(s) provinciale(s): Rivière-du-Loup-Témiscouata
Circonscription(s) électorale(s) fédérale(s): Rimouski-Neigette-Témiscouata-Les Basques
Prochaines élections: 5e novembre 2017
Mario St-Louis, Maire
Annie Roussel, Directrice générale

Sainte-Louise
CP 2130
80, rte de la Station
Sainte-Louise, QC G0R 3K0
Tél: 418-354-2509; *Téléc:* 418-354-7730
info@saintelouise.qc.ca
www.saintelouise.qc.ca
Entité municipal: Parish (Paroisse)
Incorporation: 11 décembre 1860; *Area:* 73,03 km2
Comté ou district: L'Islet; *Population au 2011:* 704
Circonscription(s) électorale(s) provinciale(s): Côte-du-Sud
Circonscription(s) électorale(s) fédérale(s): Montmagny-L'Islet-Kamouraska-Rivière-du-Loup
Prochaines élections: 5e novembre 2017
Denis Gagnon, Maire
Marie-Hélène Viau, Directrice générale

Saint-Elphège
245, rang St-Antoine
Saint-Elphege, QC J0G 1J0
Tél: 450-568-0288; *Téléc:* 450-568-0288
mun.stelphege@sogetel.net
www.st-elphege.ca
Entité municipal: Parish (Paroisse)
Incorporation: 12 mars 1886; *Area:* 40,32 km2
Comté ou district: Nicolet-Yamaska; *Population au 2011:* 292
Circonscription(s) électorale(s) provinciale(s): Nicolet-Bécancour
Circonscription(s) électorale(s) fédérale(s): Bécancour-Nicolet-Saurel
Prochaines élections: 5e novembre 2017
Mario Lefebvre, Maire
France Dionne, Directrice générale

Sainte-Luce
1, rue Langlois
Sainte-Luce, QC G0K 1P0
Tél: 418-739-4317; *Téléc:* 418-739-4823
sainte-luce@sainteluce.ca
www.sainteluce.ca
Entité municipal: Municipality
Incorporation: 29 octobre 2001; *Area:* 74,88 km2
Comté ou district: La Mitis; *Population au 2011:* 2,851
Circonscription(s) électorale(s) provinciale(s): Matane-Matapédia
Circonscription(s) électorale(s) fédérale(s): Avignon-La Mitis-Matane-Matapédia
Prochaines élections: 5e novembre 2017
Paul-Eugène Gagnon, Maire
Jean Robidoux, Directeur général

Sainte-Lucie-de-Beauregard
21, rte des Chutes
Sainte-Lucie-de-Beauregard, QC G0R 3L0
Tél: 418-223-3122; *Téléc:* 418-223-3121
ste-lucie@globetrotter.net
www.sainteluciedebeauregard.net
Entité municipal: Municipality
Incorporation: 18 novembre 1924; *Area:* 80,18 km2
Comté ou district: Montmagny; *Population au 2011:* 304
Circonscription(s) électorale(s) provinciale(s): Côte-du-Sud
Circonscription(s) électorale(s) fédérale(s): Montmagny-L'Islet-Kamouraska-Rivière-du-Loup
Prochaines élections: 5e novembre 2017
Louis Lachance, Maire
Bianca Deschênes, Directrice générale

Sainte-Lucie-des-Laurentides
2121, ch des Hauteurs
Sainte-Lucie-des-Laurentides, QC J0T 2J0
Tél: 819-326-3198; *Téléc:* 819-326-0592
www.municipalite.sainte-lucie-des-laurentides.qc.ca
Entité municipal: Municipality
Incorporation: 1er janvier 1874; *Area:* 115,15 km2
Comté ou district: Les Laurentides; *Population au 2011:* 1,269
Circonscription(s) électorale(s) provinciale(s): Bertrand
Circonscription(s) électorale(s) fédérale(s): Laurentides-Labelle
Prochaines élections: 5e novembre 2017
Serge Chénier, Maire
Normand Dupont, Directeur général

Saint-Elzéar
CP 40
148, ch Principal
Saint-Elzéar-de-Bonaventure, QC G0C 2W0
Tél: 418-534-2611; *Téléc:* 866-499-8558
muni@saint-elzear.net
www.saintelzear.net
Entité municipal: Municipality
Incorporation: 1er janvier 1965; *Area:* 198,75 km2
Comté ou district: Bonaventure; *Population au 2011:* 467
Circonscription(s) électorale(s) provinciale(s): Bonaventure
Circonscription(s) électorale(s) fédérale(s): Gaspésie—Îles-de-la-Madeleine
Prochaines élections: 5e novembre 2017
Raymond Marcoux, Maire
Marjolaine St-Pierre, Directrice générale

Saint-Elzéar
672, av Principale
Saint-Elzéar, QC G0S 2J0
Tél: 418-387-2534; *Téléc:* 418-387-4378
direction@st-elzear.ca
www.st-elzear.ca
Entité municipal: Municipality
Incorporation: 30 novembre 1994; *Area:* 85,12 km2
Comté ou district: La Nouvelle-Beauce; *Population au 2011:* 2,107
Circonscription(s) électorale(s) provinciale(s): Beauce-Nord
Circonscription(s) électorale(s) fédérale(s): Beauce
Prochaines élections: 5e novembre 2017
Richard Lehoux, Maire
Mathieu Genest, Directrice générale

Saint-Elzér-de-Témiscouata
209, rue de l'Église
Saint-Elzér-de-Témiscouata, QC G0L 2W0
Tél: 418-854-7690; *Téléc:* 418-854-3279
admin@saintelzear.ca
www.saintelzear.ca
Entité municipal: Municipality
Incorporation: 19 novembre 1938; *Area:* 151,54 km2
Comté ou district: Témiscouata; *Population au 2011:* 343
Circonscription(s) électorale(s) provinciale(s): Rivière-du-Loup-Témiscouata
Circonscription(s) électorale(s) fédérale(s): Rimouski-Neigette-Témiscouata-Les Basques
Prochaines élections: 5e novembre 2017
Carmen Massé, Mairesse
Denise Dubé, Directrice générale

Sainte-Madeleine
850, rue St-Simon
Sainte-Madeleine, QC J0H 1S0
Tél: 450-795-3822; *Téléc:* 450-795-3736
administration@villestemadeleine.qc.ca
www.villestemadeleine.qc.ca
Entité municipal: Village
Incorporation: 30 décembre 1919; *Area:* 5,39 km2
Comté ou district: Les Maskoutains; *Population au 2011:* 2,356
Circonscription(s) électorale(s) provinciale(s): Borduas
Circonscription(s) électorale(s) fédérale(s): St-Hyacinthe-Bagot
Prochaines élections: 5e novembre 2017
André Lefebvre, Maire
Carole Dulude, Directrice générale

Sainte-Madeleine-de-la-Rivière-Madeleine
104, rte Principale
Madeleine-Centre, QC G0E 1P0
Tél: 418-393-2428; *Téléc:* 418-393-2869
munste-madeleine@globetrotter.net
www.stemadeleine.ca
Entité municipal: Municipality
Incorporation: 27 février 1915; *Area:* 269,35 km2
Comté ou district: La Haute-Gaspésie; *Population au 2011:* 334
Circonscription(s) électorale(s) provinciale(s): Gaspé
Circonscription(s) électorale(s) fédérale(s): Gaspésie-Les Iles-de-la-Madeleine
Prochaines élections: 5e novembre 2017
Joël Côté, Maire
Vital Côté, Directeur général

Sainte-Marcelline-de-Kildare
500, rue Principale
Sainte-Marcelline-de-Kildare, QC J0K 2Y0
Tél: 450-883-2241; *Téléc:* 450-883-2242
info@ste-marcelline.com
www.ste-marcelline.com
Entité municipal: Municipality
Incorporation: 1er janvier 1956; *Area:* 33,66 km2
Comté ou district: Matawinie; *Population au 2011:* 1,567
Circonscription(s) électorale(s) provinciale(s): Berthier

Circonscription(s) électorale(s) fédérale(s): Joliette
Prochaines élections: 5e novembre 2017
Gaétan Morin, Maire
Richard Gagné, Directeur général

Sainte-Marguerite
235, rue St-Jacques
Sainte-Marguerite, QC G0S 2X0
Tél: 418-935-7103; *Téléc:* 418-935-3709
munste-marguerite@nouvellebeauce.com
Entité municipal: Parish (Paroisse)
Incorporation: 1er juillet 1855; *Area:* 82,56 km2
Comté ou district: La Nouvelle-Beauce; *Population au 2011:* 1,073
Circonscription(s) électorale(s) provinciale(s): Beauce-Nord
Circonscription(s) électorale(s) fédérale(s): Beauce
Prochaines élections: 5e novembre 2017
Adrienne Gagné, Mairesse
Nicole Chabot, Directrice générale

Sainte-Marguerite-du-Lac-Masson
88, ch Masson
Ste-Marguerite-du-Lac-Masson, QC J0T 1L0
Tél: 450-228-2543; *Téléc:* 450-228-4008
comm@lacmasson.com
www.ste-marguerite.qc.ca
Entité municipal: Town
Incorporation: 17 octobre 2001; *Area:* 98,65 km2
Comté ou district: Les Pays-d'en-Haut; *Population au 2011:* 2,740
Circonscription(s) électorale(s) provinciale(s): Bertrand
Circonscription(s) électorale(s) fédérale(s): Laurentides-Labelle
Prochaines élections: 5e novembre 2017
Gilles Boucher, Maire
Denis Leclerc, Greffier et directeur général (par intérim)

Sainte-Marguerite-Marie
15, rte de La Vérendrye
Sainte-Marguerite-Marie, QC G0J 2Y0
Tél: 418-756-3364; *Téléc:* 418-756-3364
stemarguerite@mrcmatapedia.qc.ca
Entité municipal: Municipality
Incorporation: 1er janvier 1957; *Area:* 83,94 km2
Comté ou district: La Matapédia; *Population au 2011:* 203
Circonscription(s) électorale(s) provinciale(s): Matane-Matapédia
Circonscription(s) électorale(s) fédérale(s): Avignon-La Mitis-Matane-Matapédia
Prochaines élections: 5e novembre 2017
Marlène Landry, Mairesse
Odette Corbin, Directrice générale

Sainte-Marie-de-Blandford
492, rte des Bosquets
Sainte-Marie-de-Blandford, QC G0X 2W0
Tél: 819-283-2127; *Téléc:* 819-283-2169
mun@saintemariedeblandford.qc.ca
www.saintemariedeblandford.org
Entité municipal: Municipality
Incorporation: 23 décembre 1976; *Area:* 68,29 km2
Comté ou district: Bécancour; *Population au 2011:* 466
Circonscription(s) électorale(s) provinciale(s): Nicolet-Bécancour
Circonscription(s) électorale(s) fédérale(s): Bécancour-Nicolet-Saurel
Prochaines élections: 5e novembre 2017
Louis Martel, Maire
Galina Papantcheva, Directrice générale

Sainte-Marie-Madeleine
3541, boul Laurier
Sainte-Marie-Madeleine, QC J0H 1S0
Tél: 450-795-6272; *Téléc:* 450-795-3180
info@stemariemadeleine.qc.ca
www.sainte-marie-madeleine.ca
Entité municipal: Parish (Paroisse)
Incorporation: 13 août 1879; *Area:* 49,53 km2
Comté ou district: Les Maskoutains; *Population au 2011:* 2,935
Circonscription(s) électorale(s) provinciale(s): Borduas
Circonscription(s) électorale(s) fédérale(s): St-Hyacinthe-Bagot
Prochaines élections: 5e novembre 2017
Simon Lacombe, Maire
Ginette Daigle, Directrice générale

Sainte-Marie-Salomé
690, ch St-Jean
Sainte-Marie-Salomé, QC J0K 2Z0
Tél: 450-839-6212; *Téléc:* 450-839-6106
smsalome@intermonde.net
Entité municipal: Parish (Paroisse)
Incorporation: 27 décembre 1888; *Area:* 34,44 km2
Comté ou district: Montcalm; *Population au 2011:* 1,164
Circonscription(s) électorale(s) provinciale(s): Joliette
Circonscription(s) électorale(s) fédérale(s): Montcalm
Prochaines élections: 5e novembre 2017
Véronique Venne, Mairesse
Denise Desmarais, Directrice générale

Sainte-Marthe
776, rue des Loisirs
Sainte-Marthe, QC J0P 1W0
Tél: 450-459-4284; *Téléc:* 450-459-4627
www.sainte-marthe.ca
Entité municipal: Municipality
Incorporation: 27 décembre 1980; *Area:* 80,23 km2
Comté ou district: Vaudreuil-Soulanges; *Population au 2011:* 1,075
Circonscription(s) électorale(s) provinciale(s): Soulanges
Circonscription(s) électorale(s) fédérale(s): Salaberry-Suroît
Prochaines élections: 5e novembre 2017
Aline Guillotte, Mairesse
Bernard Charlebois, Directeur général

Sainte-Martine
3, rue des Copains
Sainte-Martine, QC J0S 1V0
Tél: 450-427-3050; *Téléc:* 450-427-7331
info@municipalite.sainte-martine.qc.ca
www.municipalite.sainte-martine.qc.ca
Entité municipal: Municipality
Incorporation: 8 septembre 1999; *Area:* 59,79 km2
Comté ou district: Beauharnois-Salaberry; *Population au 2011:* 4,966
Circonscription(s) électorale(s) provinciale(s): Huntingdon
Circonscription(s) électorale(s) fédérale(s): Châteauguay-Lacolle
Prochaines élections: 5e novembre 2017
Éric Brault, Maire
Lise Bédard, Greffière

Sainte-Mélanie
10, rue Louis-Charles-Panet
Sainte-Mélanie, QC J0K 3A0
Tél: 450-889-5871; *Téléc:* 450-889-4527
info@sainte-melanie.ca
www.sainte-melanie.ca
Entité municipal: Municipality
Incorporation: 1er juillet 1855; *Area:* 77,05 km2
Comté ou district: Joliette; *Population au 2011:* 2,892
Circonscription(s) électorale(s) provinciale(s): Joliette
Circonscription(s) électorale(s) fédérale(s): Joliette
Prochaines élections: 5e novembre 2017
Marcel Loyer, Maire
Claude Gagné, Directrice générale

Saint-Émile-de-Suffolk
299, rte des Cantons
Saint-Émile-de-Suffolk, QC J0V 1Y0
Tél: 819-426-2987; *Téléc:* 819-426-3447
adminis.stemile@mrcpapineau.com
www.st-emile-de-suffolk.com
Entité municipal: Municipality
Incorporation: 1er janvier 1881; *Area:* 54,07 km2
Comté ou district: Papineau; *Population au 2011:* 566
Circonscription(s) électorale(s) provinciale(s): Papineau
Circonscription(s) électorale(s) fédérale(s): Argenteuil-La Petite-Nation
Prochaines élections: 5e novembre 2017
Hugo Desormeaux, Maire
Sylvie Désilets, Directrice générale

Sainte-Monique
101, rue Honfleur
Sainte-Monique-de-Honfleur, QC G0W 2T0
Tél: 418-347-3592; *Téléc:* 418-347-3335
ste.monique@ville.ste-monique.qc.ca
www.ville.ste-monique.qc.ca
Entité municipal: Municipality
Incorporation: 30 octobre 1930; *Area:* 155,15 km2
Comté ou district: Lac-Saint-Jean-Est; *Population au 2011:* 865
Circonscription(s) électorale(s) provinciale(s): Lac-St-Jean
Circonscription(s) électorale(s) fédérale(s): Lac-St-Jean
Prochaines élections: 5e novembre 2017
Dolorès Boily, Mairesse
Jean-Claude Duchesne, Directeur général

Sainte-Monique
247, rue Principale
Sainte-Monique, QC J0G 1N0
Tél: 819-289-2051; *Téléc:* 819-289-2344
info@sainte-monique.ca
www.sainte-monique.ca
Entité municipal: Municipality
Incorporation: 3 janvier 1996; *Area:* 58,79 km2
Comté ou district: Nicolet-Yamaska; *Population au 2011:* 548
Circonscription(s) électorale(s) provinciale(s): Nicolet-Bécancour
Circonscription(s) électorale(s) fédérale(s): Bécancour-Nicolet-Saurel
Prochaines élections: 5e novembre 2017
Marc Descôteaux, Maire
Line Camiré, Directrice générale

Sainte-Paule
102, rue Banville
Sainte-Paule, QC G0J 3C0
Tél: 418-737-4296; *Téléc:* 418-737-9460
ste-paule@lamatanie.ca
www.municipalite.sainte-paule.qc.ca
Entité municipal: Municipality
Incorporation: 1er janvier 1968; *Area:* 86,64 km2
Comté ou district: La Matanie; *Population au 2011:* 201
Circonscription(s) électorale(s) provinciale(s): Matane-Matapédia
Circonscription(s) électorale(s) fédérale(s): Avignon-La Mitis-Matane-Matapédia
Prochaines élections: 5e novembre 2017
Pierre Dugré, Maire
Mélissa Levasseur, Directeur général

Sainte-Perpétue
#201, 366, rue Principale sud
Sainte-Perpétue, QC G0R 3Z0
Tél: 418-359-2966; *Téléc:* 418-359-2707
munistep@globetrotter.net
www.sainteperpetue.com
Entité municipal: Municipality
Incorporation: 21 janvier 1888; *Area:* 284,51 km2
Comté ou district: L'Islet; *Population au 2011:* 1,774
Circonscription(s) électorale(s) provinciale(s): Côte-du-Sud
Circonscription(s) électorale(s) fédérale(s): Montmagny-L'Islet-Kamouraska-Rivière-du-Loup
Prochaines élections: 5e novembre 2017
Céline Avoine, Mairesse
Marie-Claude Chouinard, Directrice générale

Sainte-Perpétue
2197, rang St-Joseph
Sainte-Perpétue, QC J0C 1R0
Tél: 819-336-6740; *Téléc:* 819-336-6770
municipalite@ste-perpetue.qc.ca
www.ste-perpetue.qc.ca
Entité municipal: Parish (Paroisse)
Incorporation: 9 mars 1878; *Area:* 71,14 km2
Comté ou district: Nicolet-Yamaska; *Population au 2011:* 983
Circonscription(s) électorale(s) provinciale(s): Nicolet-Bécancour
Circonscription(s) électorale(s) fédérale(s): Bécancour-Nicolet-Saurel
Prochaines élections: 5e novembre 2017
Line Théroux, Mairesse
Silvie Leclerc, Directrice générale

Sainte-Pétronille
3, ch de l'Église
Sainte-Pétronille, QC G0A 4C0
Tél: 418-828-2270; *Téléc:* 418-828-1364
ste-petronille@qc.aira.com
www.ste-petronille.iledorleans.com
Entité municipal: Village
Incorporation: 1er janvier 1874; *Area:* 4,58 km2
Comté ou district: L'Île-d'Orléans; Communauté métropolitaine de Québec; *Population au 2011:* 1,041
Circonscription(s) électorale(s) provinciale(s): Charlevoix-Côte-de-Beaupré
Circonscription(s) électorale(s) fédérale(s): Beauport-Côte-de-Beaupré-Ile d'Orléans-Charlevoix
Prochaines élections: 5e novembre 2017
Harold Noël, Maire
Jean-François Labbé, Directeur général

Saint-Éphrem-de-Beauce
#101, 34, rte 271 sud
Saint-Éphrem-de-Beauce, QC G0M 1R0
Tél: 418-484-5716; *Téléc:* 418-484-2305
munise@telstep.net
www.saint-ephrem.com
Entité municipal: Municipality
Incorporation: 24 décembre 1997; *Area:* 115,35 km2
Comté ou district: Beauce-Sartigan; *Population au 2011:* 2,567
Circonscription(s) électorale(s) provinciale(s): Beauce-Sud
Circonscription(s) électorale(s) fédérale(s): Beauce
Prochaines élections: 5e novembre 2017
Normand Roy, Maire
Luc Lemieux, Directeur général

Saint-Épiphane
280, rue Bernier
Saint-Épiphane, QC G0L 2X0
Tél: 418-862-0052; *Téléc:* 418-862-7753
www.saint-epiphane.ca

Entité municipal: Municipality
Incorporation: 1er juillet 1855; *Area:* 82,36 km2
Comté ou district: Rivière-du-Loup; *Population au 2011:* 849
Circonscription(s) électorale(s) provinciale(s): Rivière-du-Loup-Témiscouata
Circonscription(s) électorale(s) fédérale(s): Montmagny-L'Islet-Kamouraska-Rivière-du-Loup
Prochaines élections: 5e novembre 2017
Renald Côté, Maire
Nicolas Dionne, Directeur général

Sainte-Praxède
4795, rte 263
Sainte-Praxède, QC G0N 1E0
Tél: 418-449-2250; *Téléc:* 418-449-2251
info@ste-praxede.ca
www.ste-praxede.ca
Entité municipal: Municipality
Incorporation: 1er janvier 1944; *Area:* 135,680 km2
Comté ou district: Les Appalaches; *Population au 2011:* 363
Circonscription(s) électorale(s) provinciale(s): Mégantic
Circonscription(s) électorale(s) fédérale(s): Mégantic-L'Érable
Prochaines élections: 5e novembre 2017
Daniel Talbot, Maire
Josée Vachon, Directrice générale

Sainte-Rita
CP 39
5, rue de l'Église ouest
Sainte-Rita, QC G0L 4G0
Tél: 418-963-2967; *Téléc:* 418-963-6539
www.municipalite.sainte-rita.qc.ca
Entité municipal: Municipality
Incorporation: 1er janvier 1948; *Area:* 142,88 km2
Comté ou district: Les Basques; *Population au 2011:* 313
Circonscription(s) électorale(s) provinciale(s): Rivière-du-Loup-Témiscouata
Circonscription(s) électorale(s) fédérale(s): Rimouski-Neigette-Témiscouata-Les Basques
Prochaines élections: 5e novembre 2017
Michel Colpron, Maire
Marguerite D. Michaud, Directrice générale

Sainte-Rose-de-Watford
CP 39
695, rue Carrier
Sainte-Rose-de-Watford, QC G0R 4G0
Tél: 418-267-5811; *Téléc:* 418-267-5812
municipaliteste-rose@sogetel.net
www.sainterosedewatford.qc.ca
Entité municipal: Municipality
Incorporation: 17 novembre 1897; *Area:* 112,74 km2
Comté ou district: Les Etchemins; *Population au 2011:* 787
Circonscription(s) électorale(s) provinciale(s): Bellechasse
Circonscription(s) électorale(s) fédérale(s): Bellechasse-Les Etchemins-Lévis
Prochaines élections: 5e novembre 2017
Hector Provençal, Maire
Lyse Audet, Directrice générale

Sainte-Rose-du-Nord
126, rue de la Descente-des-Femmes
Sainte-Rose-du-Nord, QC G0V 1T0
Tél: 418-675-2250; *Téléc:* 418-673-2115
admin@ste-rosedunord.qc.ca
www.ste-rosedunord.qc.ca
Entité municipal: Parish (Paroisse)
Incorporation: 1er janvier 1942; *Area:* 119,03 km2
Comté ou district: Le Fjord-du-Saguenay; *Population au 2011:* 413
Circonscription(s) électorale(s) provinciale(s): Dubuc
Circonscription(s) électorale(s) fédérale(s): Jonquière
Prochaines élections: 5e novembre 2017
Laurent Thibeault, Maire
Maryse Girard, Directrice générale

Sainte-Sabine
#201, 4, rue St-Charles
Sainte-Sabine, QC G0R 4H0
Tél: 418-383-5488; *Téléc:* 418-383-5484
munisabine@sogetel.net
www.ste-sabine.qc.ca
Entité municipal: Parish (Paroisse)
Incorporation: 26 août 1908; *Area:* 67,28 km2
Comté ou district: Les Etchemins; *Population au 2011:* 386
Circonscription(s) électorale(s) provinciale(s): Bellechasse
Circonscription(s) électorale(s) fédérale(s): Bellechasse-Les Etchemins-Lévis
Prochaines élections: 5e novembre 2017
Denis Boutin, Maire
Pierre Chabot, Directeur général

Sainte-Sabine
185, rue Principale
Sainte-Sabine, QC J0J 2B0
Tél: 450-293-7686; *Téléc:* 450-293-7604
administration@saintesabine.ca
www.saintesabine.ca
Entité municipal: Municipality
Incorporation: 19 mars 1921; *Area:* 55,42 km2
Comté ou district: Brome-Missisquoi; *Population au 2011:* 1,120
Circonscription(s) électorale(s) provinciale(s): Brome-Missisquoi
Circonscription(s) électorale(s) fédérale(s): Brome-Missisquoi
Prochaines élections: 5e novembre 2017
Laurent Phoenix, Maire
Chantal St-Germain, Directrice générale

Sainte-Séraphine
2660, rue du Centre-Communautaire
Sainte-Séraphine, QC J0A 1E0
Tél: 819-336-3200; *Téléc:* 819-336-3800
info@munsainteseraphine.ca
www.munsainteseraphine.ca
Entité municipal: Parish (Paroisse)
Incorporation: 7 mars 1931; *Area:* 75,73 km2
Comté ou district: Arthabaska; *Population au 2011:* 378
Circonscription(s) électorale(s) provinciale(s): Drummond-Bois-Francs
Circonscription(s) électorale(s) fédérale(s): Richmond-Arthabaska
Prochaines élections: 5e novembre 2017
David Vincent, Maire
Julie Paris, Directrice générale

Sainte-Sophie-d'Halifax
10, rue de l'Église
Sainte-Sophie-d'Halifax, QC G0P 1L0
Tél: 819-362-2225; *Téléc:* 819-362-6749
info@saintesophiedhalifax.com
www.saintesophiedhalifax.com
Entité municipal: Municipality
Incorporation: 17 décembre 1997; *Area:* 91,11 km2
Comté ou district: L'Érable; *Population au 2011:* 666
Circonscription(s) électorale(s) provinciale(s): Arthabaska
Circonscription(s) électorale(s) fédérale(s): Mégantic-L'Érable
Prochaines élections: 5e novembre 2017
Marie-Claude Chouinard, Mairesse
Suzanne Savage, Directrice générale

Sainte-Sophie-de-Lévrard
174A, rang St-Antoine
Sainte-Sophie-de-Lévrard, QC G0X 3C0
Tél: 819-288-5804; *Téléc:* 819-602-8913
municipalite@ste-sophie-de-levrard.com
www.ste-sophie-de-levrard.com
Entité municipal: Parish (Paroisse)
Incorporation: 23 avril 1875; *Area:* 82,38 km2
Comté ou district: Bécancour; *Population au 2011:* 733
Circonscription(s) électorale(s) provinciale(s): Nicolet-Bécancour
Circonscription(s) électorale(s) fédérale(s): Bécancour-Nicolet-Saurel
Prochaines élections: 5e novembre 2017
Jean-Guy Beaudet, Maire
Micheline St-Onge, Directrice générale

Saint-Esprit
21, rue Principale
Saint-Esprit, QC J0K 2L0
Tél: 450-831-2114; *Téléc:* 450-839-6070
info@saint-esprit.ca
www.saint-esprit.ca
Entité municipal: Municipality
Incorporation: 1er juillet 1855; *Area:* 54,36 km2
Comté ou district: Montcalm; *Population au 2011:* 1,963
Circonscription(s) électorale(s) provinciale(s): Rousseau
Circonscription(s) électorale(s) fédérale(s): Montcalm
Prochaines élections: 5e novembre 2017
Michel Brisson, Maire
Caroline Aubertin, Directrice générale

Sainte-Thècle
301, rue St-Jacques
Sainte-Thècle, QC G0X 3G0
Tél: 418-289-2070; *Téléc:* 418-289-3014
ste-thecle@regionmekinac.com
www.ste-thecle.qc.ca
Entité municipal: Municipality
Incorporation: 7 juin 1989; *Area:* 216,64 km2
Comté ou district: Mékinac; *Population au 2011:* 2,478
Circonscription(s) électorale(s) provinciale(s): Laviolette
Circonscription(s) électorale(s) fédérale(s): St-Maurice-Champlain
Prochaines élections: 5e novembre 2017
Alain Vallée, Maire
Louise Paillé, Directeur général

Sainte-Thérèse-de-Gaspé
CP 160
374, rte 132
Sainte-Thérèse-de-Gaspé, QC G0C 3B0
Tél: 418-385-3313; *Téléc:* 418-385-3799
www.saintetheresedegaspe.com
Entité municipal: Municipality
Incorporation: 6 septembre 1930; *Area:* 34,36 km2
Comté ou district: Le Rocher-Percé; *Population au 2011:* 1,055
Circonscription(s) électorale(s) provinciale(s): Gaspé
Circonscription(s) électorale(s) fédérale(s): Gaspésie—Iles-de-la-Madeleine
Prochaines élections: 5e novembre 2017
Léo Lelièvre, Maire
Luc Lambert, Directeur général

Sainte-Thérèse-de-la-Gatineau
CP 155
27, ch Principal
Sainte-Thérèse-de-la-Gatineau, QC J0X 2X0
Tél: 819-449-4134; *Téléc:* 819-449-2194
info@sainte-therese-de-la-gatineau.ca
www.sainte-therese-de-la-gatineau.ca
Entité municipal: Municipality
Incorporation: 1er janvier 1946; *Area:* 67,85 km2
Comté ou district: La Vallée-de-la-Gatineau; *Population au 2011:* 526
Circonscription(s) électorale(s) provinciale(s): Gatineau
Circonscription(s) électorale(s) fédérale(s): Pontiac
Prochaines élections: 5e novembre 2017
André Carle, Maire
Nathalie Lewis, Directrice générale

Saint-Étienne-de-Beauharnois
489, ch St-Louis
Saint-Étienne-de-Beauharnois, QC J0S 1S0
Tél: 450-225-1000; *Téléc:* 450-225-1011
stetienne@videotron.ca
www.st-etiennedebeauharnois.qc.ca
Entité municipal: Municipality
Incorporation: 1er janvier 1867; *Area:* 41,62 km2
Comté ou district: Beauharnois-Salaberry; *Population au 2011:* 806
Circonscription(s) électorale(s) provinciale(s): Beauharnois
Circonscription(s) électorale(s) fédérale(s): Salaberry-Suroît
Prochaines élections: 5e novembre 2017
Gaétan Ménard, Maire
Ginette Prud'Homme, Directrice générale

Saint-Étienne-de-Bolton
9, rang de la Montagne
Saint-Étienne-de-Bolton, QC J0E 2E0
Tél: 450-297-3353; *Téléc:* 450-297-0412
www.sedb.qc.ca
Entité municipal: Municipality
Incorporation: 27 mai 1939; *Area:* 47,99 km2
Comté ou district: Memphrémagog; *Population au 2011:* 534
Circonscription(s) électorale(s) provinciale(s): Orford
Circonscription(s) électorale(s) fédérale(s): Brome-Missisquoi
Prochaines élections: 5e novembre 2017
Michèle Turcotte, Mairesse
Pauline Desautels, Directrice générale

Saint-Étienne-des-Grès
1230, rue Principale
Saint-Étienne-des-Grès, QC G0X 2P0
Tél: 819-299-3832; *Téléc:* 819-535-1246
www.mun-stedg.qc.ca
Entité municipal: Parish (Paroisse)
Incorporation: 14 avril 1859; *Area:* 103,52 km2
Comté ou district: Maskinongé; *Population au 2011:* 4,217
Circonscription(s) électorale(s) provinciale(s): Maskinongé
Circonscription(s) électorale(s) fédérale(s): Berthier-Maskinongé
Prochaines élections: 5e novembre 2017
Robert Landry, Maire
Nathalie Vallée, Directrice générale

Saint-Eugène
CP 120
1065, rang de l'Église
Saint-Eugène, QC J0C 1J0
Tél: 819-396-3000; *Téléc:* 819-396-3576
www.saint-eugene.ca
Entité municipal: Municipality
Incorporation: 31 octobre 1879; *Area:* 76,37 km2
Comté ou district: Drummond; *Population au 2011:* 1,131
Circonscription(s) électorale(s) provinciale(s): Johnson
Circonscription(s) électorale(s) fédérale(s): Drummond
Prochaines élections: 5e novembre 2017
Andre Deslauriers, Maire

Maryse Desbiens, Directrice générale

Saint-Eugène-d'Argentenay
CP 70
439, rue Principale
Saint-Eugène-d'Argentenay, QC G0W 1B0
Tél: 418-276-1787; *Téléc:* 418-276-9356
argentenay@derytele.com
municipalites-du-quebec.org/municipalites/st-eugene-argentenay
Entité municipal: Municipality
Incorporation: 14 novembre 2009; *Area:* 83,37 km2
Comté ou district: Maria-Chapdelaine; *Population au 2011:* 546
Circonscription(s) électorale(s) provinciale(s): Roberval
Circonscription(s) électorale(s) fédérale(s): Lac-St-Jean
Prochaines élections: 5e novembre 2017
Michel Villeneuve, Maire
Karine Ouellet, Directrice générale

Saint-Eugène-de-Guigues
CP 1070
4, rue Notre-Dame ouest
Saint-Eugène-de-Guigues, QC J0Z 3L0
Tél: 819-785-2301; *Téléc:* 819-785-2302
munst-eugene@mrctemiscamingue.qc.ca
Entité municipal: Municipality
Incorporation: 20 novembre 1912; *Area:* 113,02 km2
Comté ou district: Témiscamingue; *Population au 2011:* 454
Circonscription(s) électorale(s) provinciale(s):
Rouyn-Noranda-Témiscamingue
Circonscription(s) électorale(s) fédérale(s):
Abitibi-Témiscamingue
Prochaines élections: 5e novembre 2017
Édith Lafond, Mairesse
Hugo Bellehumeur, Directeur général

Saint-Eugène-de-Ladrière
155, rue Principale
Saint-Eugène-de-Ladrière, QC G0L 1P0
Tél: 418-869-2582; *Téléc:* 418-869-2582
ladriere@globetrotter.net
www.municipalite.saint-eugene-de-ladriere.qc.ca
Entité municipal: Parish (Paroisse)
Incorporation: 1er janvier 1962; *Area:* 355,09 km2
Comté ou district: Rimouski-Neigette; *Population au 2011:* 421
Circonscription(s) électorale(s) provinciale(s): Rimouski
Circonscription(s) électorale(s) fédérale(s):
Rimouski-Neigette-Témiscouata-Les Basques
Prochaines élections: 5e novembre 2017
Gilbert Pigeon, Maire
Christiane Berger, Directrice générale

Sainte-Ursule
CP 60
215, rue Lessard
Sainte-Ursule, QC J0K 3M0
Tél: 819-228-4345; *Téléc:* 819-228-8326
www.ste-ursule.ca
Entité municipal: Parish (Paroisse)
Incorporation: 1er juillet 1855; *Area:* 65,37 km2
Comté ou district: Maskinongé; *Population au 2011:* 1,375
Circonscription(s) électorale(s) provinciale(s): Maskinongé
Circonscription(s) électorale(s) fédérale(s): Berthier-Maskinongé
Prochaines élections: 5e novembre 2017
Réjean Carle, Maire
Diane Faucher, Directrice générale

Saint-Eusèbe
222, rue Principale
Saint-Eusèbe, QC G0L 2Y0
Tél: 418-899-2762; *Téléc:* 418-899-0194
www.sainteusebe.ca
Entité municipal: Parish (Paroisse)
Incorporation: 5 janvier 1911; *Area:* 120,12 km2
Comté ou district: Témiscouata; *Population au 2011:* 614
Circonscription(s) électorale(s) provinciale(s):
Rivière-du-Loup-Témiscouata
Circonscription(s) électorale(s) fédérale(s):
Rimouski-Neigette-Témiscouata-Les Basques
Prochaines élections: 5e novembre 2017
Gaston Chouinard, Maire
Chantal Bouchard, Directrice générale

Saint-Évariste-de-Forsyth
495, rue Principale
Saint-Évariste-de-Forsyth, QC G0M 1S0
Tél: 418-459-6488; *Téléc:* 418-459-6268
munstevar@tlb.sympatico.ca
www.st-evariste.qc.ca
Entité municipal: Municipality
Incorporation: 1er mars 1870; *Area:* 111,36 km2
Comté ou district: Beauce-Sartigan; *Population au 2011:* 525
Circonscription(s) électorale(s) provinciale(s): Beauce-Sud
Circonscription(s) électorale(s) fédérale(s): Beauce
Prochaines élections: 5e novembre 2017
Gaétan Bégin, Maire
Nathalie Poulin, Directrice générale

Sainte-Victoire-de-Sorel
517, ch Ste-Victoire
Sainte-Victoire-de-Sorel, QC J0G 1T0
Tél: 450-782-3111; *Téléc:* 450-782-2687
www.saintevictoiredesorel.qc.ca
Entité municipal: Municipality
Incorporation: 1er juillet 1855; *Area:* 74,90 km2
Comté ou district: Pierre-De Saurel; *Population au 2011:* 2,501
Circonscription(s) électorale(s) provinciale(s): Richelieu
Circonscription(s) électorale(s) fédérale(s):
Bécancour-Nicolet-Saurel
Prochaines élections: 5e novembre 2017
Jean-François Villiard, Maire
Michel Saint-Martin, Directeur général

Saint-Fabien
CP 9
10, 7e av
Saint-Fabien, QC G0L 2Z0
Tél: 418-869-2950; *Téléc:* 418-869-3265
informations@saintfabien.net
www.saintfabien.net
Entité municipal: Parish (Paroisse)
Incorporation: 1er juillet 1855; *Area:* 128,07 km2
Comté ou district: Rimouski-Neigette; *Population au 2011:* 1,906
Circonscription(s) électorale(s) provinciale(s): Rimouski
Circonscription(s) électorale(s) fédérale(s):
Rimouski-Neigette-Témiscouata-Les Basques
Prochaines élections: 5e novembre 2017
Marnie Perreault, Mairesse
Yves Galbrand, Directeur général

Saint-Fabien-de-Panet
195, rue Bilodeau
Saint-Fabien-de-Panet, QC G0R 2J0
Tél: 418-249-4471; *Téléc:* 418-249-4470
munpanet@globetrotter.net
www.stfabiendepanet.com
Entité municipal: Parish (Paroisse)
Incorporation: 26 mars 1907; *Area:* 185,31 km2
Comté ou district: Montmagny; *Population au 2011:* 992
Circonscription(s) électorale(s) provinciale(s): Côte-du-Sud
Circonscription(s) électorale(s) fédérale(s):
Montmagny-L'Islet-Kamouraska-Rivière-du-Loup
Prochaines élections: 5e novembre 2017
Claude Doyon, Maire
Julie Lapointe, Directrice générale

Saint-Faustin-Lac-Carré
100, Place de la Mairie
Saint-Faustin-Lac-Carré, QC J0T 1J2
Tél: 819-688-2161; *Téléc:* 819-688-6791
www.municipalite.stfaustin.qc.ca
Entité municipal: Municipality
Incorporation: 3 janvier 1996; *Area:* 119,86 km2
Comté ou district: Les Laurentides; *Population au 2011:* 3,467
Circonscription(s) électorale(s) provinciale(s): Labelle
Circonscription(s) électorale(s) fédérale(s): Laurentides-Labelle
Prochaines élections: 5e novembre 2017
Pierre Poirier, Maire
Jacques Brisebois, Directeur général

Saint-Félix-d'Otis
455, rue Principale
Saint-Félix-d'Otis, QC G0V 1M0
Tél: 418-544-5543; *Téléc:* 418-544-9122
municipalite@st-felix-dotis.qc.ca
www.st-felix-dotis.qc.ca
Entité municipal: Municipality
Incorporation: 3 octobre 1923; *Area:* 235,94 km2
Comté ou district: Le Fjord-du-Saguenay; *Population au 2011:* 801
Circonscription(s) électorale(s) provinciale(s): Dubuc
Circonscription(s) électorale(s) fédérale(s): Chicoutimi-Le Fjord
Prochaines élections: 5e novembre 2017
Pierre Deslauriers, Maire
Hélène Gagnon, Directrice générale

Saint-Félix-de-Dalquier
CP 219
41, rue de L'Aqueduc
Saint-Felix-de-Dalquier, QC J0Y 1G0
Tél: 819-727-1732; *Téléc:* 819-727-9685
mun.stfelixdedalquier@cableamos.com
www.stfelixdedalquier.ca
Entité municipal: Municipality
Incorporation: 29 octobre 1932; *Area:* 112,12 km2
Comté ou district: Abitibi; *Population au 2011:* 856
Circonscription(s) électorale(s) provinciale(s): Abitibi-Ouest
Circonscription(s) électorale(s) fédérale(s):
Abitibi-Témiscamingue
Prochaines élections: 5e novembre 2017
Raymond Carignan, Maire
Richard Michaud, Directeur général

Saint-Félix-de-Kingsey
CP 30
1205, rue de l'Église
Saint-Félix-de-Kingsey, QC J0B 2T0
Tél: 819-848-2321; *Téléc:* 819-848-2202
direction.generale@saintfelixdekingsey.ca
www.saintfelixdekingsey.ca
Entité municipal: Municipality
Incorporation: 1er juillet 1855; *Area:* 125,38
Comté ou district: Drummond; *Population au 2011:* 1,563
Circonscription(s) électorale(s) provinciale(s):
Drummond-Bois-Francs
Circonscription(s) électorale(s) fédérale(s): Drummond
Prochaines élections: 5e novembre 2017
Thérèse Francoeur, Mairesse
Nancy Lussier, Directrice générale

Saint-Félix-de-Valois
600, ch de Joliette
Saint-Félix-de-Valois, QC J0K 2M0
Tél: 450-889-5589; *Téléc:* 450-889-5259
www.st-felix-de-valois.com
Entité municipal: Municipality
Incorporation: 24 décembre 1997; *Area:* 85,79 km2
Comté ou district: Matawinie; *Population au 2011:* 6,029
Circonscription(s) électorale(s) provinciale(s): Berthier
Circonscription(s) électorale(s) fédérale(s): Berthier-Maskinongé
Prochaines élections: 5e novembre 2017
Gyslain Loyer, Maire
René Charbonneau, Directeur général

Saint-Ferdinand
375, rue Principale
Saint-Ferdinand, QC G0N 1N0
Tél: 418-428-3480; *Téléc:* 418-428-9724
info@municipalite.saint-ferdinand.qc.ca
www.municipalite.saint-ferdinand.qc.ca
Entité municipal: Municipality
Incorporation: 29 novembre 2000; *Area:* 137,07 km2
Comté ou district: L'Érable; *Population au 2011:* 2,067
Circonscription(s) électorale(s) provinciale(s): Arthabaska
Circonscription(s) électorale(s) fédérale(s): Mégantic-L'Érable
Prochaines élections: 5e novembre 2017
Rosaire Croteau, Maire
Sylvie Tardif, Directrice générale

Saint-Ferréol-les-Neiges
33, rue de l'Église
Saint-Ferréol-les-Neiges, QC G0A 3R0
Tél: 418-826-2253; *Téléc:* 418-826-0489
info@saintferreollesneiges.qc.ca
www.saintferreollesneiges.qc.ca
Entité municipal: Municipality
Incorporation: 1er juillet 1855; *Area:* 82,28 km2
Comté ou district: La Côte-de-Beaupré; Communauté métropolitaine de Québec; *Population au 2011:* 2,964
Circonscription(s) électorale(s) provinciale(s):
Charlevoix-Côte-de-Beaupré
Circonscription(s) électorale(s) fédérale(s):
Beauport-Côte-de-Beaupré-Ile d'Orléans-Charlevoix
Prochaines élections: 5e novembre 2017
Parise Cormier, Mairesse
François Drouin, Directeur général

Saint-Flavien
177, rue Prinipale
Saint-Flavien, QC G0S 2M0
Tél: 418-728-4190; *Téléc:* 418-728-3775
municipalite@st-flavien.com
www.st-flavien.com
Entité municipal: Municipality
Incorporation: 29 décembre 1999; *Area:* 67,56 km2
Comté ou district: Lotbinière; *Population au 2011:* 1,578
Circonscription(s) électorale(s) provinciale(s):
Lotbinière-Frontenac
Circonscription(s) électorale(s) fédérale(s): Lévis-Lotbinière
Prochaines élections: 5e novembre 2017
Normand Côté, Maire
Mario Roy, Directeur général

Saint-Fortunat
173, rue Principale
Saint-Fortunat, QC G0P 1G0
Tél: 819-344-5399; *Téléc:* 819-344-5399
mun.st-fortunat@tlb.sympatico.ca
municipalitesaint-fortunat.net
Entité municipal: Municipality
Incorporation: 1er janvier 1873; *Area:* 75,520 km2
Comté ou district: Les Appalaches; *Population au 2011:* 280
Circonscription(s) électorale(s) provinciale(s): Lotbinière-Frontenac
Circonscription(s) électorale(s) fédérale(s): Mégantic-L'Érable
Prochaines élections: 5e novembre 2017
Denis Fortier, Maire
Lise Henri, Directrice générale

Saint-François-d'Assise
399, ch Central
Saint-François-d'Assise, QC G0J 2N0
Tél: 418-299-2066; *Téléc:* 418-299-3037
munstfrs@globetrotter.net
www.matapedialesplateaux.com
Entité municipal: Municipality
Incorporation: 3 septembre 1926; *Area:* 171,97 km2
Comté ou district: Avignon; *Population au 2011:* 706
Circonscription(s) électorale(s) provinciale(s): Bonaventure
Circonscription(s) électorale(s) fédérale(s): Avignon-La Mitis-Matane-Matapédia
Prochaines élections: 5e novembre 2017
Ghislain Michaud, Maire
Pauline Gallant, Directrice générale

Saint-François-de-l'Ile-d'Orléans
337, ch Royal
Saint-François, QC G0A 3S0
Tél: 418-829-3100; *Téléc:* 418-829-1004
info@msfio.ca
www.msfio.ca
Entité municipal: Municipality
Incorporation: 1er juillet 1855; *Area:* 30,76 km2
Comté ou district: L'Île-d'Orléans; Communauté métropolitaine de Québec; *Population au 2011:* 527
Circonscription(s) électorale(s) provinciale(s): Charlevoix-Côte-de-Beaupré
Circonscription(s) électorale(s) fédérale(s): Beauport-Côte-de-Beaupré-Ile d'Orléans-Charlevoix
Prochaines élections: 5e novembre 2017
Lina Labbé, Maire
Marco Langlois, Directeur général

Saint-François-de-la-Rivière-du-Sud
534, ch St-François ouest
St-François-de-la-Riv.-du-Sud, QC G0R 3A0
Tél: 418-259-7228; *Téléc:* 418-259-2056
munistfrancois@videotron.ca
www.stfrancois.ca
Entité municipal: Municipality
Incorporation: 1er juillet 1855; *Area:* 95,49 km2
Comté ou district: Montmagny; *Population au 2011:* 1,596
Circonscription(s) électorale(s) provinciale(s): Côte-du-Sud
Circonscription(s) électorale(s) fédérale(s): Montmagny-L'Islet-Kamouraska-Rivière-du-Loup
Prochaines élections: 5e novembre 2017
Rénald Roy, Maire
Yves Laflamme, Directeur général

Saint-François-de-Sales
541, rue Principale
Saint-François-de-Sales, QC G0W 1M0
Tél: 418-348-6736; *Téléc:* 418-348-9439
municipalite@stfrancoisdesales.qc.ca
stfrancoisdesales.qc.ca
Entité municipal: Municipality
Incorporation: 14 mai 1888; *Area:* 200,56 km2
Comté ou district: Le Domaine-du-Roy; *Population au 2011:* 654
Circonscription(s) électorale(s) provinciale(s): Roberval
Circonscription(s) électorale(s) fédérale(s): Lac-St-Jean
Prochaines élections: 5e novembre 2017
Cindy Plourde, Maire
Renaud Blanchette, Directeur général

Saint-François-du-Lac
CP 60
400, rue Notre-Dame
Saint-François-du-Lac, QC J0G 1M0
Tél: 450-568-2124; *Téléc:* 450-568-7465
municipalite@saint-francois-du-lac.ca
www.saint-francois-du-lac.ca
Entité municipal: Municipality
Incorporation: 31 décembre 1997; *Area:* 63,11 km2
Comté ou district: Nicolet-Yamaska; *Population au 2011:* 1,957
Circonscription(s) électorale(s) provinciale(s): Nicolet-Bécancour
Circonscription(s) électorale(s) fédérale(s): Bécancour-Nicolet-Saurel
Prochaines élections: 5e novembre 2017
Pierre Yelle, Maire
Peggy Péloquin, Directrice générale

Saint-François-Xavier-de-Brompton
CP 10
94, rue Principale
St-François-Xavier-de-Brompton, QC J0B 2V0
Tél: 819-845-3954; *Téléc:* 819-845-7711
info@sfxb.qc.ca
www.municipalite.sfxb.qc.ca
Entité municipal: Parish (Paroisse)
Incorporation: 28 décembre 1887; *Area:* 96,11 km2
Comté ou district: Le Val-Saint-François; *Population au 2011:* 2,101
Circonscription(s) électorale(s) provinciale(s): Richmond
Circonscription(s) électorale(s) fédérale(s): Richmond-Arthabaska
Prochaines élections: 5e novembre 2017
Claude Sylvian, Maire
Sylvie Champagne, Directrice générale

Saint-François-Xavier-de-Viger
123, rue Principale
Saint-François-Xavier-de-Viger, QC G0L 3C0
Tél: 418-497-2302; *Téléc:* 418-497-2302
www.municipalite.saint-francois-xavier-de-viger.qc.ca
Entité municipal: Municipality
Incorporation: 1er janvier 1950; *Area:* 110,19 km2
Comté ou district: Rivière-du-Loup; *Population au 2011:* 256
Circonscription(s) électorale(s) provinciale(s): Rivière-du-Loup-Témiscouata
Circonscription(s) électorale(s) fédérale(s): Montmagny-L'Islet-Kamourask-Rivière-du-Loup
Prochaines élections: 5e novembre 2017
Yvon Caron, Maire
Yvette Beaulieu, Directrice générale

Saint-Frédéric
850, rue de l'Hôtel-de-Ville
Saint-Frédéric, QC G0N 1P0
Tél: 418-426-3357; *Téléc:* 418-426-1259
municipal@saint-frederic.com
www.saint-frederic.com
Entité municipal: Parish (Paroisse)
Incorporation: 1er juillet 1855; *Area:* 71,58 km2
Comté ou district: Robert-Cliche; *Population au 2011:* 1,085
Circonscription(s) électorale(s) provinciale(s): Beauce-Nord
Circonscription(s) électorale(s) fédérale(s): Beauce
Prochaines élections: 5e novembre 2017
Henri Gagné, Maire
Cathy Poulin, Directrice générale

Saint-Fulgence
253, rue du Saguenay
Saint-Fulgence, QC G0V 1S0
Tél: 418-674-2588; *Téléc:* 418-673-2116
www.ville.st-fulgence.qc.ca
Entité municipal: Municipality
Incorporation: 1er mai 1973; *Area:* 354,68 km2
Comté ou district: Le Fjord-du-Saguenay; *Population au 2011:* 1,949
Circonscription(s) électorale(s) provinciale(s): Dubuc
Circonscription(s) électorale(s) fédérale(s): Jonquière
Prochaines élections: 5e novembre 2017
Gilbert Simard, Maire
Jimmy Houde, Directeur général

Saint-Gabriel
45, rue Beausoleil
Saint-Gabriel, QC J0K 2N0
Tél: 450-835-2212; *Téléc:* 450-835-9852
mairie@ville.stgabriel.qc.ca
www.ville.stgabriel.qc.ca
Entité municipal: Town
Incorporation: 17 décembre 1892; *Area:* 2,9 km2
Comté ou district: D'Autray; *Population au 2011:* 2,844
Circonscription(s) électorale(s) provinciale(s): Berthier
Circonscription(s) électorale(s) fédérale(s): Berthier-Maskinongé
Prochaines élections: 5e novembre 2017
Gaétan Gravel, Maire
Michel St-Laurent, Greffier et directeur général

Saint-Gabriel-de-Brandon
5111, ch du Lac
Saint-Gabriel-de-Brandon, QC J0K 2N0
Tél: 450-835-3494; *Téléc:* 450-835-3495
info@munstgab.com
Entité municipal: Parish (Paroisse)
Incorporation: 30 juin 1864; *Area:* 95,87 km2
Comté ou district: D'Autray; *Population au 2011:* 2,679
Circonscription(s) électorale(s) provinciale(s): Berthier
Circonscription(s) électorale(s) fédérale(s): Berthier-Maskinongé
Prochaines élections: 5e novembre 2017
Manon Rainville, Maire
Jeanne Pelland, Directrice générale

Saint-Gabriel-de-Rimouski
248, rue Principale
Saint-Gabriel-de-Rimouski, QC G0K 1M0
Tél: 418-798-4938; *Téléc:* 418-798-4108
stgabriel@mitis.qc.ca
www.municipalite.saint-gabriel-de-rimouski.qc.ca
Entité municipal: Municipality
Incorporation: 7 janvier 1989; *Area:* 132,10 km2
Comté ou district: La Mitis; *Population au 2011:* 1,180
Circonscription(s) électorale(s) provinciale(s): Matane-Matapédia
Circonscription(s) électorale(s) fédérale(s): Avignon-La Mitis-Matane-Matapédia
Prochaines élections: 5e novembre 2017
Georges Deschênes, Maire
Martin Norman, Directeur général

Saint-Gabriel-de-Valcartier
1743, boul Valcartier
Saint-Gabriel-de-Valcartier, QC G0A 4S0
Tél: 418-844-1218; *Téléc:* 418-844-3030
admin@munsgdv.ca
www.saint-gabriel-de-valcartier.ca
Entité municipal: Municipality
Incorporation: 5 octobre 1985; *Area:* 441,17 km2
Comté ou district: La Jacques-Cartier; Communauté métropolitaine de Québec; *Population au 2011:* 2,933
Circonscription(s) électorale(s) provinciale(s): La Peltrie
Circonscription(s) électorale(s) fédérale(s): Portneuf-Jacques-Cartier
Prochaines élections: 5e novembre 2017
Brent Montgomery, Maire
Joan Sheehan, Directrice générale

Saint-Gabriel-Lalemant
12, ave des Érables
Saint-Gabriel-Lalemant, QC G0L 3E0
Tél: 418-852-2801; *Téléc:* 418-852-3390
info@saintgabriellalemant.qc.ca
www.saintgabriellalemant.qc.ca
Entité municipal: Municipality
Incorporation: 27 mai 1939; *Area:* 80,49 km2
Comté ou district: Kamouraska; *Population au 2011:* 799
Circonscription(s) électorale(s) provinciale(s): Côte-du-Sud
Circonscription(s) électorale(s) fédérale(s): Montmagny-L'Islet-Kamouraska-Rivière-du-Loup
Prochaines élections: 5e novembre 2017
Raymond Chouinard, Maire
Marc Morin, Directeur général

Saint-Gédéon
208, rue De Quen
Saint-Gédéon, QC G0W 2P0
Tél: 418-345-8001; *Téléc:* 418-345-2306
mairie@ville.st-gedeon.qc.ca
www.st-gedeon.qc.ca
Entité municipal: Municipality
Incorporation: 6 décembre 1975; *Area:* 64,17 km2
Comté ou district: Lac-Saint-Jean-Est; *Population au 2011:* 2,001
Circonscription(s) électorale(s) provinciale(s): Lac-St-Jean
Circonscription(s) électorale(s) fédérale(s): Lac-St-Jean
Prochaines élections: 5e novembre 2017
Jean-Paul Boucher, Maire
Dany Dallaire, Directeur général

Saint-Gédéon-de-Beauce
102 - 1re av sud
Saint-Gédéon-de-Beauce, QC G0M 1T0
Tél: 418-582-3341; *Téléc:* 418-582-6016
stgedeon@globetrotter.net
www.st-gedeon-de-beauce.qc.ca
Entité municipal: Municipality
Incorporation: 12 février 1003; *Area:* 193,45 km2
Comté ou district: Beauce-Sartigan; *Population au 2011:* 2,277
Circonscription(s) électorale(s) provinciale(s): Beauce-Sud
Circonscription(s) électorale(s) fédérale(s): Beauce
Prochaines élections: 5e novembre 2017
Note: Effective October 12, 2003, the Municipality of St-Gédéon-de-Beauce & the Parish of St-Gédéon amalgamated to create the new Municipality of St-Gédéon-de-Beauce.
Eric Lachance, Maire
Pierre-Alain Pelchat, Directeur général

Saint-Georges-de-Clarenceville
1350, ch Middle
Saint-Georges-de-Clarenceville, QC J0J 1B0
Tél: 450-294-2464; *Téléc:* 450-294-2016
info@clarenceville.qc.ca
www.clarenceville.qc.ca
Entité municipal: Municipality
Incorporation: 27 décembre 1989; *Area:* 63,76 km2
Comté ou district: Le Haut-Richelieu; *Population au 2011:* 1,056
Circonscription(s) électorale(s) provinciale(s): Iberville
Circonscription(s) électorale(s) fédérale(s): Brome-Missisquoi
Prochaines élections: 5e novembre 2017
Renée Rouleau, Mairesse
Thérèse Lacombe, Directrice générale

Saint-Georges-de-Windsor
527, rue Principale
Saint-Georges-de-Windsor, QC J0A 1J0
Tél: 819-828-2716; *Téléc:* 819-828-0213
www.st-georges-de-windsor.org
Entité municipal: Municipality
Incorporation: 30 novembre 2009; *Area:* 126,57 km2
Comté ou district: Les Sources; *Population au 2011:* 911
Circonscription(s) électorale(s) provinciale(s): Richmond
Circonscription(s) électorale(s) fédérale(s):
Richmond-Arthabaska
Prochaines élections: 5e novembre 2017
René Perreault, Maire
Armande Perreault, Directrice générale

Saint-Gérard-Majella
435, rang St-Antoine
Saint-Gérard-Majella, QC J0G 1X0
Tél: 450-789-5777; *Téléc:* 450-789-1188
info@munistgerardmajella.com
www.saintgerardmajella.ca
Entité municipal: Parish (Paroisse)
Incorporation: 18 février 1907; *Area:* 37,81 km2
Comté ou district: Pierre-De Saurel; *Population au 2011:* 246
Circonscription(s) électorale(s) provinciale(s): Richelieu
Circonscription(s) électorale(s) fédérale(s):
Bécancour-Nicolet-Saurel
Prochaines élections: 5e novembre 2017
Luc Cloutier, Maire
Anny Boisjoli, Directeur général

Saint-Germain
146, rang des Côtes
Saint-Germain, QC G0L 3G0
Tél: 418-492-9771; *Téléc:* 418-492-9772
www.munsaintgermain.ca
Entité municipal: Parish (Paroisse)
Incorporation: 29 juin 1893; *Area:* 26,70 km2
Comté ou district: Kamouraska; *Population au 2011:* 280
Circonscription(s) électorale(s) provinciale(s): Côte-du-Sud
Circonscription(s) électorale(s) fédérale(s):
Montmagny-L'Islet-Kamouraska-Rivière-du-Loup
Prochaines élections: 5e novembre 2017
Daniel Laplante, Maire
Hélène B.-Bernier, Directrice générale

Saint-Germain-de-Grantham
233, ch Yamaska
Saint-Germain-de-Grantham, QC J0C 1K0
Tél: 819-395-5496; *Téléc:* 819-395-5200
reception@st-germain.info
www.st-germain.info
Entité municipal: Municipality
Incorporation: 22 février 1995; *Area:* 86,29 km2
Comté ou district: Drummond; *Population au 2011:* 4,551
Circonscription(s) électorale(s) provinciale(s): Johnson
Circonscription(s) électorale(s) fédérale(s): Drummond
Prochaines élections: 5e novembre 2017
Mario Van Doorn, Maire
Nathalie Lemoine, Directrice générale

Saint-Gervais
CP 9
150, rue Principale
Saint-Gervais, QC G0R 3C0
Tél: 418-887-6116; *Téléc:* 418-887-6312
info@saint-gervais.ca
www.saint-gervais.ca
Entité municipal: Municipality
Incorporation: 1er juillet 1855; *Area:* 87,23 km2
Comté ou district: Bellechasse; *Population au 2011:* 2,058
Circonscription(s) électorale(s) provinciale(s): Bellechasse
Circonscription(s) électorale(s) fédérale(s): Bellechasse-Les
Etchemins-Lévis
Prochaines élections: 5e novembre 2017
Gilles Nadeau, Maire
Patrick Côté, Directeur général

Saint-Gilbert
110, rue Principale
Saint-Gilbert, QC G0A 3T0
Tél: 418-268-8194; *Téléc:* 418-268-6466
saint-gilbert@globetrotter.net
www.municipalite.saint-gilbert.qc.ca
Entité municipal: Parish (Paroisse)
Incorporation: 27 avril 1893; *Area:* 36,95 km2
Comté ou district: Portneuf; *Population au 2011:* 282
Circonscription(s) électorale(s) provinciale(s): Portneuf
Circonscription(s) électorale(s) fédérale(s):
Portneuf-Jacques-Cartier
Prochaines élections: 5e novembre 2017
Léo Gignac, Maire
Christian Fontaine, Directeur général

Saint-Gilles
1540, rue Principale
Saint-Gilles, QC G0S 2P0
Tél: 418-888-3198; *Téléc:* 418-888-5145
info@stgilles.net
www.st-gilles.qc.ca
Entité municipal: Parish (Paroisse)
Incorporation: 1er juillet 1855; *Area:* 174,74 km2
Comté ou district: Lotbinière; *Population au 2011:* 2,138
Circonscription(s) électorale(s) provinciale(s):
Lotbinière-Frontenac
Circonscription(s) électorale(s) fédérale(s): Lévis-Lotbinière
Prochaines élections: 5e novembre 2017
Robert Samson, Maire
Sandra Bélanger, Directrice générale

Saint-Godefroi
CP 157
109C, rte 132
Saint-Godefroi, QC G0C 3C0
Tél: 418-752-6316; *Téléc:* 418-752-6396
stgodefroi@navigue.com
www.municipalitestgodefroi.com
Entité municipal: Township
Incorporation: 16 décembre 1913; *Area:* 60,32 km2
Comté ou district: Bonaventure; *Population au 2011:* 405
Circonscription(s) électorale(s) provinciale(s): Bonaventure
Circonscription(s) électorale(s) fédérale(s):
Gaspésie—Îles-de-la-Madeleine
Prochaines élections: 5e novembre 2017
Gérard-Raymond Blais, Maire
Céline Roussy, Directrice générale

Saint-Guillaume
106, rue St-Jean-Baptiste
Saint-Guillaume, QC J0C 1L0
Tél: 819-396-2403; *Téléc:* 819-396-0184
municipalite.st-guillaume@sogetel.net
www.municipalite-st-guillaume.qc.ca
Entité municipal: Municipality
Incorporation: 8 novembre 1995; *Area:* 86,83 km2
Comté ou district: Drummond; *Population au 2011:* 1,547
Circonscription(s) électorale(s) provinciale(s): Nicolet-Bécancour
Circonscription(s) électorale(s) fédérale(s): Drummond
Prochaines élections: 5e novembre 2017
Jean-Pierre Vallée, Maire
Martine Bernier, Directeur général

Saint-Guy
52, rue Principal
Saint-Guy, QC G0K 1W0
Tél: 418-963-2601; *Téléc:* 418-963-2601
admin@st-guy.qc.ca
www.st-guy.qc.ca
Entité municipal: Municipality
Incorporation: 1er janvier 1958; *Area:* 140,09 km2
Comté ou district: Les Basques; *Population au 2011:* 91
Circonscription(s) électorale(s) provinciale(s):
Rivière-du-Loup-Témiscouata
Circonscription(s) électorale(s) fédérale(s):
Rimouski-Neigette-Témiscouata-Les Basques
Prochaines élections: 5e novembre 2017
Jean-Noël Bolduc, Maire
Marie-Eve Chouinard, Directrice générale

Saint-Henri
219, rue Commerciale
Saint-Henri, QC G0R 3E0
Tél: 418-882-2401; *Téléc:* 418-882-0302
munhenri@globetrotter.net
www.municipalite.saint-henri.qc.ca
Entité municipal: Municipality
Incorporation: 9 octobre 1976; *Area:* 121,78 km2
Comté ou district: Bellechasse; *Population au 2011:* 5,023
Circonscription(s) électorale(s) provinciale(s): Bellechasse
Circonscription(s) électorale(s) fédérale(s): Bellechasse-Les
Etchemins-Lévis
Prochaines élections: 5e novembre 2017
Yvon Bruneau, Maire
Jérôme Fortier, Directeur général

Saint-Henri-de-Taillon
401, rue de l'Hôtel-de-Ville
Saint-Henri-de-Taillon, QC G0W 2X0
Tél: 418-347-3243; *Téléc:* 418-347-1138
municipalite@ville.st-henri-de-taillon.qc.ca
www.ville.st-henri-de-taillon.qc.ca
Entité municipal: Municipality
Incorporation: 12 août 1903; *Area:* 62,95 km2
Comté ou district: Lac-Saint-Jean-Est; *Population au 2011:* 760
Circonscription(s) électorale(s) provinciale(s): Lac-St-Jean
Circonscription(s) électorale(s) fédérale(s): Lac-St-Jean
Prochaines élections: 5e novembre 2017
André Paradis, Maire
Rachel Bourget, Directrice générale

Saint-Herménégilde
776, rue Principale
Saint-Herménégilde, QC J0B 2W0
Tél: 819-849-4443; *Téléc:* 819-849-6924
municipalite@st-hermenegilde.qc.ca
www.st-hermenegilde.qc.ca
Entité municipal: Municipality
Incorporation: 12 octobre 1985; *Area:* 169,90 km2
Comté ou district: Coaticook; *Population au 2011:* 702
Circonscription(s) électorale(s) provinciale(s): St-François
Circonscription(s) électorale(s) fédérale(s): Compton-Stanstead
Prochaines élections: 5e novembre 2017
Gérard Duteau, Maire
Nathalie Isabelle, Directrice générale

Saint-Hilaire-de-Dorset
847, rue Principale
Saint-Hilaire-de-Dorset, QC G0M 1G0
Tél: 418-459-6872; *Téléc:* 418-459-6882
munsthilaire@hotmail.com
Entité municipal: Parish (Paroisse)
Incorporation: 12 avril 1916; *Area:* 252,52 km2
Comté ou district: Beauce-Sartigan; *Population au 2011:* 50
Circonscription(s) électorale(s) provinciale(s): Beauce-Sud
Circonscription(s) électorale(s) fédérale(s): Beauce
Prochaines élections: 5e novembre 2017
Céline Bilodeau, Mairesse
Johanne Jacques, Directrice générale

Saint-Hilarion
306, ch Cartier Nord
Saint-Hilarion, QC G0A 3V0
Tél: 418-457-3463; *Téléc:* 418-457-3805
municipalite@sainthilarion.ca
www.sainthilarion.ca
Entité municipal: Parish (Paroisse)
Incorporation: 1er juillet 1855; *Area:* 97,77 km2
Comté ou district: Charlevoix; *Population au 2011:* 1,181
Circonscription(s) électorale(s) provinciale(s):
Charlevoix-Côte-de-Beaupré
Circonscription(s) électorale(s) fédérale(s):
Beauport-Côte-de-Beaupré-Ile d'Orléans-Charlevoix
Prochaines élections: 5e novembre 2017
Rénald Marier, Maire
Madeleine Tremblay, Directrice générale

Saint-Hippolyte
2253, ch des Hauteurs
Saint-Hippolyte, QC J8A 1A1
Tél: 450-563-2505; *Téléc:* 450-563-2362
municipalite@saint-hippolyte.ca
www.saint-hippolyte.ca
Entité municipal: Parish (Paroisse)
Incorporation: 1er juillet 1855; *Area:* 121,19 km2
Comté ou district: La Rivière-du-Nord; *Population au 2011:* 8,083
Circonscription(s) électorale(s) provinciale(s): Bertrand
Circonscription(s) électorale(s) fédérale(s): Rivière-du-Nord
Prochaines élections: 5e novembre 2017
Bruno Laroche, Maire
Christiane Côté, Directrice générale

Saint-Honoré
3611, boul Martel
Saint-Honoré, QC G0V 1L0
Tél: 418-673-3405; *Téléc:* 418-673-3871
admin@ville.sthonore.qc.ca
www.ville.sthonore.qc.ca
Entité municipal: Municipality
Incorporation: 16 décembre 1972; *Area:* 189,82 km2
Comté ou district: Jonquière; *Population au 2011:* 5,257
Circonscription(s) électorale(s) provinciale(s): Dubuc

Circonscription(s) électorale(s) fédérale(s): Chicoutimi-Le Fjord
Prochaines élections: 5e novembre 2017
Bruno Tremblay, Maire
Stéphane Leclerc, Directeur général

Saint-Honoré-de-Shenley
CP 128
499, rue Principale
Saint-Honoré-de-Shenley, QC G0M 1V0
Tél: 418-485-6738; *Téléc:* 418-485-6171
mun.sthonore@telstep.net
www.sthonoredeshenley.com
Entité municipal: Municipality
Incorporation: 19 avril 2000; *Area:* 136,46 km2
Comté ou district: Beauce-Sartigan; *Population au 2011:* 1,610
Circonscription(s) électorale(s) provinciale(s): Beauce-Sud
Circonscription(s) électorale(s) fédérale(s): Beauce
Prochaines élections: 5e novembre 2017
Dany Quirion, Maire
Francine Talbot, Directrice générale

Saint-Honoré-de-Témiscouata
99, rue Principale
Saint-Honoré-de-Témiscouata, QC G0L 3K0
Tél: 418-497-2588; *Téléc:* 418-497-1656
admin@sainthonoredetemiscouata.ca
www.sainthonoredetemiscouata.ca
Entité municipal: Municipality
Incorporation: 1er janvier 1881; *Area:* 251,58 km2
Comté ou district: Témiscouata; *Population au 2011:* 780
Circonscription(s) électorale(s) provinciale(s):
Rivière-du-Loup-Témiscouata
Circonscription(s) électorale(s) fédérale(s):
Rimouski-Neigette-Témiscouata-Les Basques
Prochaines élections: 5e novembre 2017
Richard F. Dubé, Maire
Lucie April, Directrice générale

Saint-Hubert-Rivière-du-Loup
CP 218
10, rue Saint-Rosaire
Saint-Hubert-Rivière-du-Loup, QC G0L 3L0
Tél: 418-497-3394; *Téléc:* 418-497-1187
www.municipalite.saint-hubert-de-riviere-du-loup.qc.ca
Entité municipal: Municipality
Incorporation: 4 janvier 1894; *Area:* 183,99 km2
Comté ou district: Rivière-du-Loup; *Population au 2011:* 1,235
Circonscription(s) électorale(s) provinciale(s):
Rivière-du-Loup-Témiscouata
Circonscription(s) électorale(s) fédérale(s):
Montmagney-L'Islet-Kamouraska-Rivière-du-Loup
Prochaines élections: 5e novembre 2017
Gilles Couture, Maire
Sylvie Samson, Directrice générale

Saint-Hugues
508, rue Notre-Dame
Saint-Hugues, QC J0H 1N0
Tél: 450-794-2030; *Téléc:* 450-794-2474
munst-huguesdirection@mrcmaskoutains.qc.ca
www.saint-hugues.com
Entité municipal: Municipality
Incorporation: 6 novembre 1982; *Area:* 89,39 km2
Comté ou district: Les Maskoutains; *Population au 2011:* 1,292
Circonscription(s) électorale(s) provinciale(s): St-Hyacinthe
Circonscription(s) électorale(s) fédérale(s): St-Hyacinthe-Bagot
Prochaines élections: 5e novembre 2017
Richard Veilleux, Maire
Carole Thibault, Directrice générale

Saint-Ignace-de-Loyola
25, rue Laforest
Saint-Ignace-de-Loyola, QC J0K 2P0
Tél: 450-836-3376; *Téléc:* 450-836-1400
st.ignace.loyola@intermonde.net
www.stignacedeloyola.qc.ca
Entité municipal: Parish (Paroisse)
Incorporation: 11 février 1897; *Area:* 30,76 km2
Comté ou district: D'Autray; *Population au 2011:* 2,086
Circonscription(s) électorale(s) provinciale(s): Berthier
Circonscription(s) électorale(s) fédérale(s): Berthier-Maskinongé
Prochaines élections: 5e novembre 2017
Jean-Luc Barthe, Maire
Fabrice St-Martin, Directeur général

Saint-Ignace-de-Stanbridge
692, rang de l'Église nord
Saint-Ignace-de-Stanbridge, QC J0J 1Y0
Tél: 450-296-4467; *Téléc:* 450-296-4461
stignace@videotron.ca
www.saint-ignace-de-stanbridge.com
Entité municipal: Parish (Paroisse)
Incorporation: 21 mars 1889; *Area:* 69,33 km2
Comté ou district: Brome-Missisquoi; *Population au 2011:* 638
Circonscription(s) électorale(s) provinciale(s): Brome-Missisquoi
Circonscription(s) électorale(s) fédérale(s): Brome-Missisquoi
Prochaines élections: 5e novembre 2017
Albert Santerre, Maire
Mélanie Thibault, Directrice générale

Saint-Irénée
475, rue Principale
Saint-Irénée, QC G0T 1V0
Tél: 418-620-5015; *Téléc:* 418-620-5017
dg@saintirenee.ca
www.saintirenee.ca
Entité municipal: Parish (Paroisse)
Incorporation: 1er juillet 1855; *Area:* 60,29 km2
Comté ou district: Charlevoix-Est; *Population au 2011:* 674
Circonscription(s) électorale(s) provinciale(s):
Charlevoix-Côte-de-Beaupré
Circonscription(s) électorale(s) fédérale(s):
Beauport-Côte-de-Beaupré-Ile d'Orléans-Charlevoix
Prochaines élections: 5e novembre 2017
Pierre Boudreault, Maire
Marie-Claude Lavoie, Directrice générale

Saint-Isidore
671, rue St-Régis
Saint-Isidore, QC J0L 2A0
Tél: 450-454-3919; *Téléc:* 450-454-7485
www.municipalite.saint-isidore.qc.ca
Entité municipal: Parish (Paroisse)
Incorporation: 1er juillet 1855; *Area:* 52,00 km2
Comté ou district: Roussillon; Communauté métropolitaine de Montréal; *Population au 2011:* 2,581
Circonscription(s) électorale(s) provinciale(s): Châteauguay
Circonscription(s) électorale(s) fédérale(s): Châteauguay-Lacolle
Prochaines élections: 5e novembre 2017
Sylvain Payant, Maire
Daniel Vinet, Directeur général

Saint-Isidore
128, route Coulombe
Saint-Isidore, QC G0S 2S0
Tél: 418-882-5670; *Téléc:* 418-882-5902
info@saint-isidore.net
www.saint-isidore.net
Entité municipal: Municipality
Incorporation: 22 septembre 1993; *Area:* 101,18 km2
Comté ou district: La Nouvelle-Beauce; *Population au 2011:* 2,947
Circonscription(s) électorale(s) provinciale(s): Beauce-Nord
Circonscription(s) électorale(s) fédérale(s): Beauce
Prochaines élections: 5e novembre 2017
Réal Turgeon, Maire
Louise Trachy, Directrice générale

Saint-Isidore-de-Clifton
66, ch Auckland
Saint-Isidore-de-Clifton, QC J0B 2X0
Tél: 819-658-3637; *Téléc:* 819-560-8559
Bureau.StIsidoredeclifton@hsfqc.ca
www.st-isidore-clifton.qc.ca
Entité municipal: Municipality
Incorporation: 24 décembre 1997; *Area:* 178,43 km2
Comté ou district: Le Haut-Saint-François; *Population au 2011:* 716
Circonscription(s) électorale(s) provinciale(s): Mégantic
Circonscription(s) électorale(s) fédérale(s): Compton-Stanstead
Prochaines élections: 5e novembre 2017
Yann Vallières, Maire
Gaétan Perron, Directeur général

Saint-Jacques
16, rue Maréchal
Saint-Jacques, QC J0K 2R0
Tél: 450-839-3671; *Téléc:* 450-839-2387
info@st-jacques.org
www.st-jacques.org
Entité municipal: Municipality
Incorporation: 20 mai 1998; *Area:* 64,69 km2
Comté ou district: Montcalm; *Population au 2011:* 4,021
Circonscription(s) électorale(s) provinciale(s): Joliette
Circonscription(s) électorale(s) fédérale(s): Montcalm
Prochaines élections: 5e novembre 2017
Pierre La Salle, Maire
Josée Favreau, Directrice générale

Saint-Jacques-de-Leeds
355, rue Principale
Saint-Jacques-de-Leeds, QC G0N 1J0
Tél: 418-424-3321; *Téléc:* 418-424-0126
mun.leeds@cableeds.com
www.stjacquesdeleeds.com
Entité municipal: Municipality
Incorporation: 23 septembre 1929; *Area:* 81,830 km2
Comté ou district: Les Appalaches; *Population au 2011:* 711
Circonscription(s) électorale(s) provinciale(s):
Lotbinière-Frontenac
Circonscription(s) électorale(s) fédérale(s): Mégantic-L'Érable
Prochaines élections: 5e novembre 2017
Camille David, Maire
Nathalie Laflamme, Directrice générale

Saint-Jacques-le-Majeur-de-Wolfestown
877, rte 263
Saint-Jacques-le-Majeur, QC G0N 1E0
Tél: 418-449-1531; *Téléc:* 418-449-1876
stjacqueslemajeur@hotmail.com
www.st-jacques-le-majeur-de-wolfestown.ca
Entité municipal: Parish (Paroisse)
Incorporation: 30 septembre 1909; *Area:* 59,330 km2
Comté ou district: Les Appalaches; *Population au 2011:* 189
Circonscription(s) électorale(s) provinciale(s):
Lotbinière-Frontenac
Circonscription(s) électorale(s) fédérale(s): Mégantic-L'Érable
Prochaines élections: 5e novembre 2017
Steven Laprise, Maire
France Moisan, Directrice générale

Saint-Jacques-le-Mineur
91, rue Principale
Saint-Jacques-le-Mineur, QC J0J 1Z0
Tél: 450-347-5446; *Téléc:* 450-347-5754
info@sjlm.ca
www.saint-jacques-le-mineur.ca
Entité municipal: Parish (Paroisse)
Incorporation: 1er juillet 1855; *Area:* 65,19 km2
Comté ou district: Les Jardins-de-Napierville; *Population au 2011:* 1,672
Circonscription(s) électorale(s) provinciale(s): Huntingdon
Circonscription(s) électorale(s) fédérale(s): Châteauguay-Lacolle
Prochaines élections: 5e novembre 2017
Lise Trotter, Mairesse
Jean-Pierre Cayer, Directeur général

Saint-Janvier-de-Joly
729, rue des Loisirs
Saint-Janvier-de-Joly, QC G0S 1M0
Tél: 418-728-2984; *Téléc:* 418-728-2997
info@municipalitedejoly.com
www.municipalitedejoly.com
Other Information: Alt. Courriel: joly33065@videotron.ca
Entité municipal: Municipality
Incorporation: 1er janvier 1944; *Area:* 109,86 km2
Comté ou district: Lotbinière; *Population au 2011:* 968
Circonscription(s) électorale(s) provinciale(s):
Lotbinière-Frontenac
Circonscription(s) électorale(s) fédérale(s): Lévis-Lotbinière
Prochaines élections: 5e novembre 2017
Bernard Fortier, Maire
Mélanie Boilard, Directrice générale

Saint-Jean-Baptiste
3041, rue Principale
Saint-Jean-Baptiste, QC J0L 2B0
Tél: 450-467-3456; *Téléc:* 450-467-8813
info@msjb.qc.ca
www.msjb.qc.ca
Entité municipal: Municipality
Incorporation: 1er juillet 1855; *Area:* 75,98 km2
Comté ou district: La Vallée-du-Richelieu; Communauté métropolitaine de Montréal; *Population au 2011:* 3,191
Circonscription(s) électorale(s) provinciale(s): Borduas
Circonscription(s) électorale(s) fédérale(s): Beloeil-Chambly
Prochaines élections: 5e novembre 2017
Marilyn Nadeau, Mairesse
Denis Meunier, Directeur général

Saint-Jean-de-Brébeuf
844, rue de l'Église
Saint-Jean-de-Brébeuf, QC G6G 0A1
Tél: 418-453-7774; *Téléc:* 418-453-2339
stjeandebrebeuf@bellnet.ca
Entité municipal: Municipality
Incorporation: 1er janvier 1946; *Area:* 79,680 km2
Comté ou district: Les Appalaches; *Population au 2011:* 359
Circonscription(s) électorale(s) provinciale(s):
Lotbinière-Frontenac

Circonscription(s) électorale(s) fédérale(s): Mégantic-L'Érable
Prochaines élections: 5e novembre 2017
Ghyslain Hamel, Maire
Paule Bizier, Directrice générale

Saint-Jean-de-Cherbourg
10, 8e rang
Saint-Jean-de-Cherbourg, QC G0J 2R0
Tél: 418-733-8177; *Téléc:* 418-733-8177
www.st-jeandecherbourg.ca
Entité municipal: Parish (Paroisse)
Incorporation: 1er mai 1954; *Area:* 113,23 km2
Comté ou district: La Matanie; *Population au 2011:* 193
Circonscription(s) électorale(s) provinciale(s): Matane-Matapédia
Circonscription(s) électorale(s) fédérale(s): Avignon-La Mitis-Matane-Matapédia
Prochaines élections: 5e novembre 2017
Jocelyn Bergeron, Maire
Jacinthe Imbeault, Directrice générale

Saint-Jean-de-Dieu
32, rue Principale sud
Saint-Jean-de-Dieu, QC G0L 3M0
Tél: 418-963-3529; *Téléc:* 418-963-2903
secretariat1@saintjeandedieu.ca
www.saintjeandedieu.ca
Entité municipal: Municipality
Incorporation: 1er janvier 1865; *Area:* 151,32 km2
Comté ou district: Les Basques; *Population au 2011:* 1,606
Circonscription(s) électorale(s) provinciale(s): Rivière-du-Loup-Témiscouata
Circonscription(s) électorale(s) fédérale(s): Rimouski-Neigette-Témisouata-Les Basques
Prochaines élections: 5e novembre 2017
Alain Bélanger, Maire
Normand Morency, Directeur général

Saint-Jean-de-l'Ile-d'Orléans
8, ch des Côtes
Saint-Jean-de-l'Ile-d'Orléans, QC G0A 3W0
Tél: 418-829-2206; *Téléc:* 418-829-0997
stjeanio@bellnet.ca
www.municipalite.saintjeaniledorleans.ca
Entité municipal: Municipality
Incorporation: 1er juillet 1855; *Area:* 43,64 km2
Comté ou district: L'Ile-d'Orléans; Communauté métropolitaine de Québec; *Population au 2011:* 923
Circonscription(s) électorale(s) provinciale(s): Charlevoix-Côte-de-Beaupré
Circonscription(s) électorale(s) fédérale(s): Beauport-Côte-de-Beaupré-Ile d'Orléans-Charlevoix
Prochaines élections: 5e novembre 2017
Jean-Claude Pouliot, Maire
Lucie Lambert, Directrice générale

Saint-Jean-de-la-Lande
810, rue Principale
Saint-Jean-de-la-Lande, QC G0L 3N0
Tél: 418-853-3703; *Téléc:* 418-853-3475
info@saintjeandelalande.ca
saintjeandelalande.ca
Entité municipal: Municipality
Incorporation: 1er janvier 1965; *Area:* 108,80 km2
Comté ou district: Témiscouata; *Population au 2011:* 310
Circonscription(s) électorale(s) provinciale(s): Rivière-du-Loup-Témiscouata
Circonscription(s) électorale(s) fédérale(s): Rimouski-Neigette-Témiscouata-Les Basques
Prochaines élections: 5e novembre 2017
Jean-Marc Belzile, Maire
Danielle Rousseau, Directrice générale

Saint-Jean-de-Matha
170, rue Ste-Louise
Saint-Jean-de-Matha, QC J0K 2S0
Tél: 450-886-3867; *Téléc:* 450-886-3398
info@matha.ca
www.municipalitestjeandematha.com
Entité municipal: Municipality
Incorporation: 1er juillet 1855; *Area:* 117,01 km2
Comté ou district: Matawinie; *Population au 2011:* 4,335
Circonscription(s) électorale(s) provinciale(s): Berthier
Circonscription(s) électorale(s) fédérale(s): Berthier-Maskinongé
Prochaines élections: 5e novembre 2017
Normand Champagne, Maire
Nicole D. Archambault, Directrice générale

Saint-Jean-Port-Joli
7, place de l'Église
Saint-Jean-Port-Joli, QC G0R 3G0
Tél: 418-598-3084; *Téléc:* 418-598-3085
munisjpj@globetrotter.net
www.saintjeanportjoli.com
Entité municipal: Municipality
Incorporation: 1er juillet 1855; *Area:* 68,55 km2
Comté ou district: L'Islet; *Population au 2011:* 3,304
Circonscription(s) électorale(s) provinciale(s): Côte-du-Sud
Circonscription(s) électorale(s) fédérale(s): Montmagny-L'Islet-Kamouraska-Rivière-du-Loup
Prochaines élections: 5e novembre 2017
Jean-Pierre Dubé, Maire
Stéphen Lord, Directeur général

Saint-Joachim
172, rue de l'Église
Saint-Joachim, QC G0A 3X0
Tél: 418-827-3755; *Téléc:* 418-827-8574
dg@saintjoachim.qc.ca
www.saintjoachim.qc.ca
Entité municipal: Parish (Paroisse)
Incorporation: 1er juillet 1855; *Area:* 40,68 km2
Comté ou district: La Côte-de-Beaupré; Communauté métropolitaine de Québec; *Population au 2011:* 1,458
Circonscription(s) électorale(s) provinciale(s): Charlevoix-Côte-de-Beaupré
Circonscription(s) électorale(s) fédérale(s): Beauport-Côte-de-Beaupré-Ile d'Orléans-Charlevoix
Prochaines élections: 5e novembre 2017
Marc Dubeau, Maire
Roger Carrier, Directeur général

Saint-Joachim-de-Shefford
615, rue Principale
Saint-Joachim-de-Shefford, QC J0E 2G0
Tél: 450-539-3201; *Téléc:* 450-539-3145
mairie@st-joachim.ca
www.st-joachim.ca
Entité municipal: Parish (Paroisse)
Incorporation: 10 juin 1884; *Area:* 126,98 km2
Comté ou district: La Haute-Yamaska; *Population au 2011:* 1,171
Circonscription(s) électorale(s) provinciale(s): Johnson
Circonscription(s) électorale(s) fédérale(s): Shefford
Prochaines élections: 5e novembre 2017
René Beauregard, Maire
France Lagrandneur, Directrice générale

Saint-Joseph-de-Beauce
843, av du Palais
Saint-Joseph-de-Beauce, QC G0S 2V0
Tél: 418-397-4358; *Téléc:* 418-397-5715
info@vsjb.ca
www.vsjb.ca
Entité municipal: Town
Incorporation: 27 janvier 1999; *Area:* 108,54 km2
Comté ou district: Robert-Cliche; *Population au 2011:* 4,722
Circonscription(s) électorale(s) provinciale(s): Beauce-Nord
Circonscription(s) électorale(s) fédérale(s): Beauce
Prochaines élections: 5e novembre 2017
Michel Cliche, Maire
Danielle Maheu, Greffière

Saint-Joseph-de-Coleraine
88, av St-Patrick
Saint-Joseph-de-Coleraine, QC G0N 1B0
Tél: 418-423-4000; *Téléc:* 418-423-4150
coleraine@bellnet.ca
www.coleraine.qc.ca
Entité municipal: Municipality
Incorporation: 11 novembre 1891; *Area:* 125,11 km2
Comté ou district: Les Appalaches; *Population au 2011:* 1,870
Circonscription(s) électorale(s) provinciale(s): Lotbinière-Frontenac
Circonscription(s) électorale(s) fédérale(s): Mégantic-L'Érable
Prochaines élections: 5e novembre 2017
Gilles Gosselin, Maire
Martin Cadorette, Directeur général

Saint-Joseph-de-Kamouraska
300A, rue Principale ouest
Saint-Joseph-de-Kamouraska, QC G0L 3P0
Tél: 418-493-2214; *Téléc:* 418-493-1126
stjosephkam@bellnet.ca
www.stjosephkam.ca
Entité municipal: Parish (Paroisse)
Incorporation: 14 janvier 1924; *Area:* 84,61 km2
Comté ou district: Kamouraska; *Population au 2011:* 418
Circonscription(s) électorale(s) provinciale(s): Côte-du-Sud
Circonscription(s) électorale(s) fédérale(s): Montmagny-L'Islet-Kamouraska-Rivière-du-Loup
Prochaines élections: 5e novembre 2017
Tony Charest, Maire
Nathalie Blais, Directrice générale

Saint-Joseph-de-Lepage
70, rue de la Rivière
Saint-Joseph-de-Lepage, QC G5H 3N8
Tél: 418-775-4171; *Téléc:* 418-775-3004
stjoseph@mitis.qc.ca
www.municipalite.saint-joseph-de-lepage.qc.ca
Entité municipal: Parish (Paroisse)
Incorporation: 29 septembre 1873; *Area:* 30,27 km2
Comté ou district: La Mitis; *Population au 2011:* 527
Circonscription(s) électorale(s) provinciale(s): Matane-Matapédia
Circonscription(s) électorale(s) fédérale(s): Avignon-La Mitis-Matane-Matapédia
Prochaines élections: 5e novembre 2017
Réginald Morissette, Maire
Tammy Caron, Directrice générale

Saint-Joseph-des-Érables
370A, rang des Érables
Saint-Joseph-des-Érables, QC G0S 2V0
Tél: 418-397-4772; *Téléc:* 418-397-1555
municipalite@stjosephdeserables.com
www.stjosephdeserables.com
Entité municipal: Municipality
Incorporation: 26 novembre 2009; *Area:* 50,01 km2
Comté ou district: Robert-Cliche; *Population au 2011:* 420
Circonscription(s) électorale(s) provinciale(s): Beauce-Nord
Circonscription(s) électorale(s) fédérale(s): Beauce
Prochaines élections: 5e novembre 2017
Jeannot Roy, Maire
Mélanie Jacques, Directrice générale

Saint-Joseph-de-Sorel
700, rue Montcalm
Saint-Joseph-de-Sorel, QC J3R 1C9
Tél: 450-742-3744; *Téléc:* 450-742-1315
ville@vsjs.ca
www.vsjs.ca
Entité municipal: Village
Incorporation: 1er mai 1907; *Area:* 1,4 km2
Comté ou district: Pierre-De Saurel; *Population au 2011:* 1,677
Circonscription(s) électorale(s) provinciale(s): Richelieu
Circonscription(s) électorale(s) fédérale(s): Bécancour-Nicolet-Saurel
Prochaines élections: 5e novembre 2017
Olivar Gravel, Maire
Martin Valois, Directeur général

Saint-Joseph-du-Lac
1110, ch Principal
Saint-Joseph-du-Lac, QC J0N 1M0
Tél: 450-623-1072; *Téléc:* 450-623-2889
www.sjdl.qc.ca
Entité municipal: Municipality
Incorporation: 1er juillet 1855; *Area:* 40,81 km2
Comté ou district: Deux-Montagnes; Communauté métropolitaine de Montréal; *Population au 2011:* 6,195
Circonscription(s) électorale(s) provinciale(s): Mirabel
Circonscription(s) électorale(s) fédérale(s): Mirabel
Prochaines élections: 5e novembre 2017
Benoit Proulx, Maire
Guylaine Comtois, Directrice générale

Saint-Jude
940, rue du Centre
Saint-Jude, QC J0H 1P0
Tél: 450-792-3855; *Téléc:* 450-792-3828
munstjude@mrcmaskoutains.qc.ca
www.saint-jude.ca
Entité municipal: Municipality
Incorporation: 1er juillet 1855; *Area:* 77,36 km2
Comté ou district: Les Maskoutains; *Population au 2011:* 1,235
Circonscription(s) électorale(s) provinciale(s): Richelieu
Circonscription(s) électorale(s) fédérale(s): St-Hyacinthe-Bagot
Prochaines élections: 5e novembre 2017
Yves de Bellefeuille, Maire
Nancy Carvalho, Directrice générale

Saint-Jules
390, rte Principale
Saint-Jules, QC G0N 1R0
Tél: 418-397-5444; *Téléc:* 418-397-5007
mun.st-jules@axion.ca
www.st-jules.qc.ca
Entité municipal: Parish (Paroisse)
Incorporation: 28 mai 1919; *Area:* 57,08 km2
Comté ou district: Robert-Cliche; *Population au 2011:* 573
Circonscription(s) électorale(s) provinciale(s): Beauce-Nord

Circonscription(s) électorale(s) fédérale(s): Beauce
Prochaines élections: 5e novembre 2017
Ghislaine Doyon, Mairesse
Claire Roy, Directrice générale

Saint-Julien
787, ch St-Julien
Saint-Julien, QC G0N 1B0
Tél: 418-423-4295; *Téléc:* 418-423-2384
municipalite@st-julien.ca
www.st-julien.ca
Entité municipal: Municipality
Incorporation: 1er juillet 1855; *Area:* 82,300 km2
Comté ou district: Les Appalaches; *Population au 2011:* 406
Circonscription(s) électorale(s) provinciale(s): Lotbinière-Frontenac
Circonscription(s) électorale(s) fédérale(s): Mégantic-L'Érable
Prochaines élections: 5e novembre 2017
Serge Laliberté, Maire
Josée Bournival, Directrice générale

Saint-Just-de-Bretenières
CP 668
250, rue Principale
Saint-Just-de-Bretenières, QC G0R 3H0
Tél: 418-244-3637; *Téléc:* 418-244-3636
st-just-de-bretenieres@globetrotter.net
www.saintjustdebretenieres.com
Entité municipal: Municipality
Incorporation: 27 mai 1918; *Area:* 132,35 km2
Comté ou district: Montmagny; *Population au 2011:* 709
Circonscription(s) électorale(s) provinciale(s): Côte-du-Sud
Circonscription(s) électorale(s) fédérale(s): Montmagny-L'Islet-Kamouraska-Rivière-du-Loup
Prochaines élections: 5e novembre 2017
Réal Bolduc, Maire
Isabelle Simard, Directrice générale

Saint-Juste-du-Lac
CP 38
28, ch Principal
Saint-Juste-du-Lac, QC G0L 3R0
Tél: 418-899-2855; *Téléc:* 418-899-2938
info@saintjustedulac.com
www.saintjustedulac.com
Entité municipal: Municipality
Incorporation: 23 mai 1923; *Area:* 170,11 km2
Comté ou district: Témiscouata; *Population au 2011:* 585
Circonscription(s) électorale(s) provinciale(s): Rivière-du-Loup-Témiscouata
Circonscription(s) électorale(s) fédérale(s): Montmagny-L'Islet-Kamouraska-Rivière-du-Loup
Prochaines élections: 5e novembre 2017
Céline Dubé Ouellet, Mairesse
Nicole Dubé-Chouinard, Directrice générale

Saint-Justin
1281, rue Gérin
Saint-Justin, QC J0K 2V0
Tél: 819-227-2838; *Téléc:* 819-227-4876
info@saint-justin.ca
www.saint-justin.ca
Entité municipal: Parish (Paroisse)
Incorporation: 1er juillet 1855; *Area:* 82,46 km2
Comté ou district: Maskinongé; *Population au 2011:* 1,060
Circonscription(s) électorale(s) provinciale(s): Maskinongé
Circonscription(s) électorale(s) fédérale(s): Berthier-Maskinongé
Prochaines élections: 5e novembre 2017
Jean-Claude Gauthier, Maire
Caroline Gagnon, Directrice générale

Saint-Lambert
CP 86
509, rte 5e-au-8e Rang
Des Méloizes, QC J0Z 1V0
Tél: 819-788-2491; *Téléc:* 819-788-2491
st-lambert@mrcao.qc.ca
st-lambert.ao.ca
Entité municipal: Parish (Paroisse)
Incorporation: 14 mai 1938; *Area:* 101,76 km2
Comté ou district: Abitibi-Ouest; *Population au 2011:* 211
Circonscription(s) électorale(s) provinciale(s): Abitibi-Ouest
Circonscription(s) électorale(s) fédérale(s): Abitibi-Témiscamingue
Prochaines élections: 5e novembre 2017
Diane Provost, Maire
Nataly Morin, Directrice générale

Saint-Lambert-de-Lauzon
1200, rue du Pont
Saint-Lambert-de-Lauzon, QC G0S 2W0
Tél: 418-889-9715; *Téléc:* 418-889-0660
info@mun-sldl.ca
www.mun-sldl.ca
Entité municipal: Parish (Paroisse)
Incorporation: 1er juillet 1855; *Area:* 107,32 km2
Comté ou district: La Nouvelle-Beauce; *Population au 2011:* 6,177
Circonscription(s) électorale(s) provinciale(s): Beauce-Nord
Circonscription(s) électorale(s) fédérale(s): Lévis-Lotbinière
Prochaines élections: 5e novembre 2017
François Barret, Maire
Magdalen Blanchet, Directrice générale

Saint-Laurent-de-l'île-d'Orléans
1430, ch Royal
St-Laurent-de-l'île-d'Orléans, QC G0A 3Z0
Tél: 418-828-2322; *Téléc:* 418-828-2170
info@saintlaurentio.com
www.stlaurentio.com
Entité municipal: Municipality
Incorporation: 1er juillet 1855; *Area:* 35,32 km2
Comté ou district: L'île-d'Orléans; Communauté métropolitaine de Québec; *Population au 2011:* 1,580
Circonscription(s) électorale(s) provinciale(s): Charlevoix-Côte-de-Beaupré
Circonscription(s) électorale(s) fédérale(s): Beauport-Côte-de-Beaupré-Ile d'Orléans-Charlevoix
Prochaines élections: 5e novembre 2017
Yves Coulombe, Maire
Michelle Moisan, Directrice générale

Saint-Lazare-de-Bellechasse
116, rue de la Fabrique
Saint-Lazare-de-Bellechasse, QC G0R 3J0
Tél: 418-883-3841; *Téléc:* 418-883-2551
munstlaz@globetrotter.net
www.st-lazare.qc.com
Entité municipal: Municipality
Incorporation: 1er juillet 1855; *Area:* 85,53 km2
Comté ou district: Bellechasse; *Population au 2011:* 1,172
Circonscription(s) électorale(s) provinciale(s): Bellechasse
Circonscription(s) électorale(s) fédérale(s): Bellechasse-Les Etchemins-Lévis
Prochaines élections: 5e novembre 2017
Martin J. Côté, Maire
Richard Côté, Directeur général

Saint-Léandre
2005, rue de l'Église
Saint-Léandre, QC G0J 2V0
Tél: 418-737-4973; *Téléc:* 418-737-4876
st-leandre@lamatanie.ca
www.mrcdematane.qc.ca/stleandre.html
Entité municipal: Parish (Paroisse)
Incorporation: 20 mars 1912; *Area:* 102,62 km2
Comté ou district: La Matanie; *Population au 2011:* 402
Circonscription(s) électorale(s) provinciale(s): Matane-Matapédia
Circonscription(s) électorale(s) fédérale(s): Avignon-La Mitis-Matane-Matapédia
Prochaines élections: 5e novembre 2017
Jean-Pierre Chouinard, Maire
Josée Simard, Directrice générale

Saint-Léonard-d'Aston
370, rue Principale
Saint-Léonard-d'Aston, QC J0C 1M0
Tél: 819-399-2596; *Téléc:* 819-399-2333
municipalite@saint-leonard-daston.net
www.saint-leonard-daston.net
Entité municipal: Municipality
Incorporation: 13 avril 1994; *Area:* 81,83 km2
Comté ou district: Nicolet-Yamaska; *Population au 2011:* 2,271
Circonscription(s) électorale(s) provinciale(s): Nicolet-Bécancour
Circonscription(s) électorale(s) fédérale(s): Bécancour-Nicolet-Saurel
Prochaines élections: 5e novembre 2017
Daniel Coutu, Maire
Carmelle L. Dupuis, Directrice générale

Saint-Léonard-de-Portneuf
260, rue Pettigrew
Saint-Léonard-de-Portneuf, QC G0A 4A0
Tél: 418-337-6741; *Téléc:* 418-337-6742
saintleonard@derytele.com
www.municipalite.st-leonard.qc.ca
Entité municipal: Municipality
Incorporation: 22 juillet 1899; *Area:* 138,71 km2
Comté ou district: Portneuf; *Population au 2011:* 1,019
Circonscription(s) électorale(s) provinciale(s): Portneuf
Circonscription(s) électorale(s) fédérale(s): Portneuf-Jacques-Cartier
Prochaines élections: 5e novembre 2017
Denis Langlois, Maire
Eddy Alain, Directeur-général

Saint-Léon-de-Standon
CP 130
100A, rue St-Pierre
Saint-Léon-de-Standon, QC G0R 4L0
Tél: 418-642-5034; *Téléc:* 418-642-2570
mun.st-leon@globetrotter.net
www.stleondestandon.qc.ca
Entité municipal: Parish (Paroisse)
Incorporation: 1er janvier 1874; *Area:* 136,90 km2
Comté ou district: Bellechasse; *Population au 2011:* 1,128
Circonscription(s) électorale(s) provinciale(s): Bellechasse
Circonscription(s) électorale(s) fédérale(s): Bellechasse-Les Etchemins-Lévis
Prochaines élections: 5e novembre 2017
Bernard Morin, Maire
Michel Lacasse, Directeur général

Saint-Léon-le-Grand
CP 188
277, rue Plourde
Saint-Léon-le-Grand, QC G0J 2W0
Tél: 418-743-2914; *Téléc:* 418-743-2914
stleonlegrand@mrcmatapedia.qc.ca
www.saintleonlegrand.com
Entité municipal: Parish (Paroisse)
Incorporation: 12 août 1903; *Area:* 127,73 km2
Comté ou district: La Matapédia; *Population au 2011:* 970
Circonscription(s) électorale(s) provinciale(s): Matane-Matapédia
Circonscription(s) électorale(s) fédérale(s): Avignon-La Mitis-Matane-Matapédia
Prochaines élections: 5e novembre 2017
Daniel Dumais, Maire
Philippe Côté, Directeur général

Saint-Léon-le-Grand
49, rue de la Fabrique
Saint-Léon-le-Grand, QC J0K 2W0
Tél: 819-228-3236; *Téléc:* 819-228-8088
www.st-leon.com
Entité municipal: Parish (Paroisse)
Incorporation: 1er juillet 1855; *Area:* 72,57 km2
Comté ou district: Maskinongé; *Population au 2011:* 992
Circonscription(s) électorale(s) provinciale(s): Maskinongé
Circonscription(s) électorale(s) fédérale(s): Berthier-Maskinongé
Prochaines élections: 5e novembre 2017
Robert Lalonde, Maire
Andrée Ricard, Directrice générale

Saint-Liboire
CP 120
21, place Mauriac
Saint-Liboire, QC J0H 1R0
Tél: 450-793-2811; *Téléc:* 450-793-4428
admin@municipalite.st-liboire.qc.ca
Entité municipal: Municipality
Incorporation: 17 août 1994; *Area:* 72,90 km2
Comté ou district: Les Maskoutains; *Population au 2011:* 3,051
Circonscription(s) électorale(s) provinciale(s): St-Hyacinthe
Circonscription(s) électorale(s) fédérale(s): St-Hyacinthe-Bagot
Prochaines élections: 5e novembre 2017
Denis Chabot, Maire
Josée Vendette, Directrice générale

Saint-Liguori
750, rue Principale
Saint-Liguori, QC J0K 2X0
Tél: 450-753-3570; *Téléc:* 450-753-4638
info@saint-liguori.com
www.saint-liguori.com
Entité municipal: Parish (Paroisse)
Incorporation: 1er juillet 1855; *Area:* 50,91 km2
Comté ou district: Montcalm; *Population au 2011:* 1,976
Circonscription(s) électorale(s) provinciale(s): Joliette
Circonscription(s) électorale(s) fédérale(s): Montcalm
Prochaines élections: 5e novembre 2017
Ghislaine Pomerleau, Maire
Édith Gagné, Directrice générale

Saint-Louis
765B, rue St-Joseph
Saint-Louis, QC J0G 1K0
Tél: 450-788-2631; *Téléc:* 450-788-2231
mstlouis@mrcmaskoutains.qc.ca
www.saint-louis.ca
Entité municipal: Parish (Paroisse)
Incorporation: 29 août 1881; *Area:* 45,92 km2

Comté ou district: Les Maskoutains; *Population au 2011:* 775
Circonscription(s) électorale(s) provinciale(s): Richelieu
Circonscription(s) électorale(s) fédérale(s): St-Hyacinthe-Bagot
Prochaines élections: 5e novembre 2017
Stéphane Bernier, Maire
Pascale Dalcourt, Directrice générale

Saint-Louis-de-Blandford
CP 140
80-1, rue Principale
Saint-Louis-de-Blandford, QC G0Z 1B0
Tél: 819-364-7007; *Téléc:* 819-364-2781
info@saint-louis-de-blandford.ca
www.saint-louis-de-blandford.ca
Entité municipal: Parish (Paroisse)
Incorporation: 1er juillet 1855; *Area:* 106,70 km2
Comté ou district: Arthabaska; *Population au 2011:* 903
Circonscription(s) électorale(s) provinciale(s): Arthabaska
Circonscription(s) électorale(s) fédérale(s):
Richmond-Arthabaska
Prochaines élections: 5e novembre 2017
Gilles Marchand, Maire
Marilou Charland, Directrice générale

Saint-Louis-de-Gonzague
108, rue de l'Église
Ravignan, QC G0R 2L0
Tél: 418-267-5931; *Téléc:* 418-267-5930
munstlouis@sogetel.net
www.st-louisdegonzague.qc.ca
Entité municipal: Municipality
Incorporation: 17 mars 1923; *Area:* 116,36 km2
Comté ou district: Les Etchemins; *Population au 2011:* 421
Circonscription(s) électorale(s) provinciale(s): Bellechasse
Circonscription(s) électorale(s) fédérale(s): Bellechasse-Les Etchemins-Lévis
Prochaines élections: 5e novembre 2017
Sylvie Lajoie, Mairesse
Odette Poulin, Directrice générale

Saint-Louis-de-Gonzague
140, rue Principale
Saint-Louis-de-Gonzague, QC J0S 1T0
Tél: 450-371-0523; *Téléc:* 450-371-6229
info@saint-louis-de-gonzague.com
saint-louis-de-gonzague.com
Entité municipal: Parish (Paroisse)
Incorporation: 1er juillet 1855; *Area:* 78,52 km2
Comté ou district: Beauharnois-Salaberry; *Population au 2011:* 1,389
Circonscription(s) électorale(s) provinciale(s): Beauharnois
Circonscription(s) électorale(s) fédérale(s): Salaberry-Suroît
Prochaines élections: 5e novembre 2017
Yves Daoust, Maire
Dany Michaud, Directrice générale et secrétaire-trésorière

Saint-Louis-de-Gonzague-du-Cap-Tourmente
CP 460 Haute-Ville
1, rue des Remparts
Québec, QC G1R 4R7
Tél: 418-692-3981; *Téléc:* 418-692-4345
jroberge@globetrotter.net
Entité municipal: Parish (Paroisse)
Incorporation: 1er janvier 1917
Comté ou district: La Côte-de-Beaupré; Communauté métropolitaine de Québec; *Population au 2011:* 18
Circonscription(s) électorale(s) provinciale(s):
Charlevoix-Côte-de-Beaupré
Circonscription(s) électorale(s) fédérale(s):
Beauport-Côte-de-Beaupré-Ile d'Orléans-Charlevoix
Prochaines élections: 5e novembre 2017
Jacques Roberge, Administrateur

Saint-Louis-du-Ha!-Ha!
95, rue St-Charles
Saint-Louis-du-Ha!-Ha!, QC G0L 3S0
Tél: 418-854-2260; *Téléc:* 418-854-0717
municipalite@saintlouisduhaha.com
www.saintlouisduhaha.com
Entité municipal: Parish (Paroisse)
Incorporation: 14 juillet 1874; *Area:* 114,45 km2
Comté ou district: Témiscouata; *Population au 2011:* 1,318
Circonscription(s) électorale(s) provinciale(s):
Rivière-du-Loup-Témiscouata
Circonscription(s) électorale(s) fédérale(s):
Rimouski-Neigette-Témiscouata-Les Basques
Prochaines élections: 5e novembre 2017
Sonia Larrivée, Mairesse
Gratien Ouellet, Directeur général

Saint-Luc-de-Bellechasse
115, rue de la Fabrique
Saint-Luc-de-Bellechasse, QC G0R 1L0
Tél: 418-636-2176; *Téléc:* 418-636-2175
munstluc@sogetel.net
www.st-luc-bellechasse.qc.ca
Entité municipal: Municipality
Incorporation: 12 août 1921; *Area:* 160,03 km2
Comté ou district: Les Etchemins; *Population au 2011:* 480
Circonscription(s) électorale(s) provinciale(s): Bellechasse
Circonscription(s) électorale(s) fédérale(s): Bellechasse-Les Etchemins-Lévis
Prochaines élections: 5e novembre 2017
Denis Laflamme, Maire
Huguette Lavigne, Directrice générale

Saint-Luc-de-Vincennes
CP 450
600, rue Principale
Saint-Luc-de-Vincennes, QC G0X 3K0
Tél: 819-295-3782; *Téléc:* 819-295-3782
municipalite@stlucdevincennes.com
www.stlucdevincennes.com
Entité municipal: Municipality
Incorporation: 19 janvier 1865; *Area:* 52,73 km2
Comté ou district: Les Chenaux; *Population au 2011:* 591
Circonscription(s) électorale(s) provinciale(s): Champlain
Circonscription(s) électorale(s) fédérale(s):
St-Maurice-Champlain
Prochaines élections: 5e novembre 2017
Jean-Claude Milot, Maire
Manon Shallow, Directrice générale

Saint-Lucien
5350, 7e rang
Saint-Lucien, QC J0C 1N0
Tél: 819-397-4679; *Téléc:* 819-397-2732
Entité municipal: Parish (Paroisse)
Incorporation: 11 novembre 1907; *Area:* 113,61 km2
Comté ou district: Drummond; *Population au 2011:* 1,584
Circonscription(s) électorale(s) provinciale(s):
Drummond-Bois-Francs
Circonscription(s) électorale(s) fédérale(s): Drummond
Prochaines élections: 5e novembre 2017
Suzanne Pinard Lebeau, Mairesse
Lynda Lalancette, Directrice générale

Saint-Ludger
212, rue La Salle
Saint-Ludger, QC G0M 1W0
Tél: 819-548-5408; *Téléc:* 819-548-5743
munstludger@sogetel.net
www.st-ludger.qc.ca
Entité municipal: Municipality
Incorporation: 25 février 1998; *Area:* 124,46 km2
Comté ou district: Le Granit; *Population au 2011:* 1,255
Circonscription(s) électorale(s) provinciale(s): Beauce-Sud
Circonscription(s) électorale(s) fédérale(s): Mégantic-L'Érable
Prochaines élections: 5e novembre 2017
Bernadin Gagnon, Maire
Julie Létourneau, Directrice générale

Saint-Ludger-de-Milot
739, rue Gaudreault
Saint-Ludger-de-Milot, QC G0W 2B0
Tél: 418-373-2266; *Téléc:* 418-373-2554
administration@ville.st-ludger-de-milot.qc.ca
www.ville.st-ludger-de-milot.qc.ca
Entité municipal: Municipality
Incorporation: 1er janvier 1948; *Area:* 106,81 km2
Comté ou district: Lac-Saint-Jean-Est; *Population au 2011:* 678
Circonscription(s) électorale(s) provinciale(s): Lac-St-Jean
Circonscription(s) électorale(s) fédérale(s): Lac-St-Jean
Prochaines élections: 5e novembre 2017
Marc Laliberté, Maire
Rita Ouellet, Directrice générale

Saint-Magloire
130, rue Principale
Saint-Magloire, QC G0R 3M0
Tél: 418-257-4421; *Téléc:* 418-257-4422
stmagloire@sogetel.net
www.saint-magloire.com
Entité municipal: Municipality
Incorporation: 1er janvier 1875; *Area:* 208,64 km2
Comté ou district: Les Etchemins; *Population au 2011:* 725
Circonscription(s) électorale(s) provinciale(s): Bellechasse
Circonscription(s) électorale(s) fédérale(s): Bellechasse-Les Etchemins-Lévis
Prochaines élections: 5e novembre 2017
Émile Lapointe, Maire
Caroline Boutin, Directrice générale

Saint-Majorique-de-Grantham
1966, boul St-Joseph ouest
Saint-Majorique-de-Grantham, QC J2B 8A8
Tél: 819-478-7058; *Téléc:* 819-478-8479
municipalite.st-majorique@reseaualliance.com
www.st-majoriquedegrantham.qc.ca
Entité municipal: Parish (Paroisse)
Incorporation: 13 juillet 1901; *Area:* 57,26 km2
Comté ou district: Drummond; *Population au 2011:* 1,251
Circonscription(s) électorale(s) provinciale(s): Johnson
Circonscription(s) électorale(s) fédérale(s): Drummond
Prochaines élections: 5e novembre 2017
Robert Boucher, Maire
Hélène Ruel, Directrice générale

Saint-Malachie
610, 7e rue
Saint-Malachie, QC G0R 3N0
Tél: 418-642-2102; *Téléc:* 418-642-2231
munimala@globetrotter.net
www.st-malachie.qc.ca
Entité municipal: Parish (Paroisse)
Incorporation: 1er juin 1874; *Area:* 100,59 km2
Comté ou district: Bellechasse; *Population au 2011:* 1,489
Circonscription(s) électorale(s) provinciale(s): Bellechasse
Circonscription(s) électorale(s) fédérale(s): Bellechasse-Les Etchemins-Lévis
Prochaines élections: 5e novembre 2017
Donald Therrien, Maire
Hélène Bissonnette, Directrice générale

Saint-Malo
228, rte 253 sud
Saint-Malo, QC J0B 2Y0
Tél: 819-658-2174; *Téléc:* 819-658-1169
info@saint-malo.ca
www.saint-malo.ca
Entité municipal: Municipality
Incorporation: 1er janvier 1870; *Area:* 129,30 km2
Comté ou district: Coaticook; *Population au 2011:* 483
Circonscription(s) électorale(s) provinciale(s): St-François
Circonscription(s) électorale(s) fédérale(s): Compton-Stanstead
Prochaines élections: 5e novembre 2017
Jacques Madore, Maire
Édith Rouleau, Directrice générale

Saint-Marc-de-Figuery
CP 12
10, av Michaud
Saint-Marc-de-Figuery, QC J0Y 1J0
Tél: 819-732-8501; *Téléc:* 819-732-4324
mun.stmard@cableamos.com
www.saint-marc-de-figuery.org
Entité municipal: Parish (Paroisse)
Incorporation: 10 novembre 1926; *Area:* 91,10 km2
Comté ou district: Abitibi; *Population au 2011:* 771
Circonscription(s) électorale(s) provinciale(s): Abitibi-Ouest
Circonscription(s) électorale(s) fédérale(s):
Abitibi-Témiscamingue
Prochaines élections: 5e novembre 2017
Jacques Riopel, Maire
Céline Dupras, Directrice générale

Saint-Marc-des-Carrières
965, av Bona-Dussault
Saint-Marc-des-Carrières, QC G0A 4B0
Tél: 418-268-3862; *Téléc:* 418-268-8776
info@villestmarc.com
www.villestmarc.com
Entité municipal: Town
Incorporation: 24 octobre 1918; *Area:* 16,73 km2
Comté ou district: Portneuf; *Population au 2011:* 2,862
Circonscription(s) électorale(s) provinciale(s): Portneuf
Circonscription(s) électorale(s) fédérale(s):
Portneuf-Jacques-Cartier
Prochaines élections: 5e novembre 2017
Guy Denis, Maire
Maryon Leclerc, Directeur général

Saint-Marc-du-Lac-Long
18-A, rue de l'Église
Saint-Marc-du-Lac-Long, QC G0L 1T0
Tel: 418-893-2643; *Fax:* 418-893-7228
admin@saintmarcdulaclong.ca
www.saintmarcdulaclong.ca
Municipal Type: Parish (Paroisse)
Incorporated: 11 juin 1938; *Area:* 147,16 km2
County or District: Témiscouata; *Population in 2011:* 440
Provincial Electoral District(s): Rivière-du-Loup-Témiscouata
Federal Electoral District(s):
Rimouski-Neigette-Témiscouata-Les Basques
Next Election: 5e novembre 2017

Martine Lévesque, Mairesse
Sylvie Dumont, Directrice générale

Saint-Marcel
48, ch Taché est
Saint-Marcel, QC G0R 3R0
Tél: 418-356-2691; *Téléc:* 418-356-2820
mun.sm@globetrotter.net
www.saintmarcel.qc.ca
Entité municipal: Municipality
Incorporation: 30 juillet 1904; *Area:* 178,86 km2
Comté ou district: L'Islet; *Population au 2011:* 439
Circonscription(s) électorale(s) provinciale(s): Côte-du-Sud
Circonscription(s) électorale(s) fédérale(s): Montmagny-L'Islet-Kamouraska-Rivière-du-Loup
Prochaines élections: 5e novembre 2017
Eddy Morin, Maire
Zoée Lord, Directrice générale

Saint-Marcel-de-Richelieu
117, rue Saint-Louis
Saint-Marcel-de-Richelieu, QC J0H 1T0
Tél: 450-794-2832; *Téléc:* 450-794-1140
munst-marcel@mrcmaskoutains.qc.ca
www.saintmarcelderichelieu.ca
Entité municipal: Municipality
Incorporation: 1er juillet 1855; *Area:* 50,21 km2
Comté ou district: Les Maskoutains; *Population au 2011:* 543
Circonscription(s) électorale(s) provinciale(s): Richelieu
Circonscription(s) électorale(s) fédérale(s): St-Hyacinthe-Bagot
Prochaines élections: 5e novembre 2017
Réjean Bernier, Maire
Christiane Janelle, Directrice générale

Saint-Marcellin
336, rte 234
Saint-Marcellin, QC G0K 1R0
Tél: 418-798-4382; *Téléc:* 418-798-4383
munstmar@globetrotter.net
www.st-marcellin.qc.ca
Entité municipal: Parish (Paroisse)
Incorporation: 19 novembre 1924; *Area:* 117,01 km2
Comté ou district: Rimouski-Neigette; *Population au 2011:* 323
Circonscription(s) électorale(s) provinciale(s): Rimouski
Circonscription(s) électorale(s) fédérale(s): Rimouski-Neigette-Témiscouata-Les Basques
Prochaines élections: 5e novembre 2017
André-Pierre Vignola, Maire
Brigitte Rouleau, Directrice générale

Saint-Marc-sur-Richelieu
102, rue de la Fabrique
Saint-Marc-sur-Richelieu, QC J0L 2E0
Tél: 450-584-2258; *Téléc:* 450-584-2795
www.ville.saint.marc-sur-richelieu.qc.ca
Entité municipal: Municipality
Incorporation: 1er juillet 1855; *Area:* 59,51 km2
Comté ou district: La Vallée-du-Richelieu; *Population au 2011:* 2,050
Circonscription(s) électorale(s) provinciale(s): Borduas
Circonscription(s) électorale(s) fédérale(s): Pierre-Boucher-Les Patriotes-Verchères
Prochaines élections: 5e novembre 2017
Jean Murray, Maire
Sylvie Burelle, Directrice générale

Saint-Martin
131, 1e av est
Saint-Martin, QC G0M 1B0
Tél: 418-382-5035; *Téléc:* 418-382-5561
postmaster@st-martin.qc.ca
www.st-martin.qc.ca
Entité municipal: Parish (Paroisse)
Incorporation: 12 octobre 1911; *Area:* 119,34 km2
Comté ou district: Beauce-Sartigan; *Population au 2011:* 2,462
Circonscription(s) électorale(s) provinciale(s): Beauce-Sud
Circonscription(s) électorale(s) fédérale(s): Beauce
Prochaines élections: 5e novembre 2017
Jean-Marc Paquet, Maire
Brigitte Quirion, Directrice générale

Saint-Mathias-sur-Richelieu
300, ch des Patriotes
Saint-Mathias-sur-Richelieu, QC J3L 6Z5
Tél: 450-658-2841; *Téléc:* 450-447-1416
info@st-mathias.org
www.saint-mathias-sur-richelieu.org
Entité municipal: Municipality
Incorporation: 1er juillet 1855; *Area:* 48,22 km2
Comté ou district: Rouville; Communauté métropolitaine de Montréal; *Population au 2011:* 4,618
Circonscription(s) électorale(s) provinciale(s): Chambly
Circonscription(s) électorale(s) fédérale(s): Beloeil-Chambly
Prochaines élections: 5e novembre 2017
Jocelyne G. Deswarte, Mairesse
Catherine Chartrand, Greffière

Saint-Mathieu
299, ch St-Édouard
Saint-Mathieu, QC J0L 2H0
Tél: 450-632-9528; *Téléc:* 450-632-9544
info@municipalite.saint-mathieu.qc.ca
www.municipalite.saint-mathieu.qc.ca
Entité municipal: Municipality
Incorporation: 1er août 1917; *Area:* 32,27 km2
Comté ou district: Roussillon; Communauté métropolitaine de Montréal; *Population au 2011:* 1,879
Circonscription(s) électorale(s) provinciale(s): Sanguinet
Circonscription(s) électorale(s) fédérale(s): La Prairie
Prochaines élections: 5e novembre 2017
Lise Poissant, Mairesse
Louise Hébert, Directrice générale

Saint-Mathieu-d'Harricana
203, ch Lanoix
Saint-Mathieu-d'Harricana, QC J0Y 1M0
Tél: 819-727-9557; *Téléc:* 819-727-2052
mun.st-mathieu@cableamos.com
Entité municipal: Municipality
Incorporation: 1er janvier 1943; *Area:* 104,09 km2
Comté ou district: Abitibi; *Population au 2011:* 696
Circonscription(s) électorale(s) provinciale(s): Abitibi-Ouest
Circonscription(s) électorale(s) fédérale(s): Abitibi-Témiscamingue
Prochaines élections: 5e novembre 2017
Martin Roch, Maire
Anne-Renée Jacob, Directrice générale

Saint-Mathieu-de-Beloeil
5000, rue des Loisirs
Saint-Mathieu-de-Beloeil, QC J3G 2C9
Tél: 450-467-7490; *Téléc:* 450-467-2999
reception@munstmathbel.ca
www.saint-mathieu-de-beloeil.com
Entité municipal: Municipality
Incorporation: 1er juillet 1855; *Area:* 39,26 km2
Comté ou district: La Vallée-du-Richelieu; Communauté métropolitaine de Montréal; *Population au 2011:* 2,624
Circonscription(s) électorale(s) provinciale(s): Borduas
Circonscription(s) électorale(s) fédérale(s): Pierre-Boucher-Les Patriotes-Verchères
Prochaines élections: 5e novembre 2017
Michel Aubin, Maire
Doris Parent, Directrice générale

Saint-Mathieu-de-Rioux
41, rue de l'Église
Saint-Mathieu-de-Rioux, QC G0L 3T0
Tél: 418-738-2953; *Téléc:* 418-738-2454
admin@stmathieuderioux.qc.ca
www.st-mathieu-de-rioux.ca
Entité municipal: Parish (Paroisse)
Incorporation: 18 août 1865; *Area:* 102,35 km2
Comté ou district: Les Basques; *Population au 2011:* 678
Circonscription(s) électorale(s) provinciale(s): Rivière-du-Loup-Témiscouata
Circonscription(s) électorale(s) fédérale(s): Rimouski-Neigette-Témiscouata-Les Basques
Prochaines élections: 5e novembre 2017
Yvon Ouellet, Maire
Michelle Lafontaine, Directrice générale

Saint-Mathieu-du-Parc
561, ch Déziel
Saint-Mathieu-du-Parc, QC G0X 1N0
Tél: 819-299-3830; *Téléc:* 819-532-2415
info@saint-mathieu-du-parc.ca
saint-mathieu-du-parc.ca
Entité municipal: Municipality
Incorporation: 30 juin 1886; *Area:* 196,45 km2
Comté ou district: Maskinongé; *Population au 2011:* 1,407
Circonscription(s) électorale(s) provinciale(s): St-Maurice
Circonscription(s) électorale(s) fédérale(s): Berthier-Maskinongé
Prochaines élections: 5e novembre 2017
Claude McManus, Maire
Valérie Bergeron, Directeur général

Saint-Maurice
CP 9
2510, rang St-Jean
Saint-Maurice, QC G0X 2X0
Tél: 819-374-4525; *Téléc:* 819-374-9132
municipalite@st-maurice.ca
www.st-maurice.ca
Entité municipal: Parish (Paroisse)
Incorporation: 1er juillet 1855; *Area:* 90,33 km2
Comté ou district: Les Chenaux; *Population au 2011:* 2,775
Circonscription(s) électorale(s) provinciale(s): Champlain
Circonscription(s) électorale(s) fédérale(s): St-Maurice-Champlain
Prochaines élections: 5e novembre 2017
Gérard Bruneau, Maire
Andrée Neault, Directrice générale

Saint-Maxime-du-Mont-Louis
CP 130
1, 1re av ouest
Saint-Maxime-du-Mont-Louis, QC G0E 1T0
Tél: 418-797-2310; *Téléc:* 418-797-2928
www.st-maxime.qc.ca
Entité municipal: Municipality
Incorporation: 10 juin 1884; *Area:* 220,38 km2
Comté ou district: La Haute-Gaspésie; *Population au 2011:* 1,118
Circonscription(s) électorale(s) provinciale(s): Gaspé
Circonscription(s) électorale(s) fédérale(s): Gaspésie-Les Iles-de-la-Madeleine
Prochaines élections: 5e novembre 2017
Serge Chrétien, Maire
Suzanne Roy, Directrice générale

Saint-Médard
51-A, rue Principale est
Saint-Médard, QC G0L 3V0
Tél: 418-963-6276; *Téléc:* 418-963-6468
admin@st-medard.qc.ca
Entité municipal: Municipality
Incorporation: 1er janvier 1949; *Area:* 67,59 km2
Comté ou district: Les Basques; *Population au 2011:* 222
Circonscription(s) électorale(s) provinciale(s): Rivière-du-Loup-Témiscouata
Circonscription(s) électorale(s) fédérale(s): Rimouski-Neigette-Témiscouata-Les Basques
Prochaines élections: 5e novembre 2017
Louis-Philippe Sirois, Maire
Andrée O. Beaulieu, Directrice générale

Saint-Michel
1700, rue Principale
Saint-Michel, QC J0L 2J0
Tél: 450-454-4502; *Téléc:* 450-454-7508
www.municipalite-saint-michel.ca
Entité municipal: Parish (Paroisse)
Incorporation: 1er juillet 1855; *Area:* 57,36 km2
Comté ou district: Les Jardins-de-Napierville; *Population au 2011:* 2,884
Circonscription(s) électorale(s) provinciale(s): Huntingdon
Circonscription(s) électorale(s) fédérale(s): Châteauguay-Lacolle
Prochaines élections: 5e novembre 2017
Jean-Guy Hamelin, Maire
Gino Dubé, Directeur général

Saint-Michel-de-Bellechasse
129, rte 132 est
Saint-Michel-de-Bellechasse, QC G0R 3S0
Tél: 418-884-2865; *Téléc:* 418-884-2866
munstmic@globetrotter.net
www.saintmicheldebellechasse.com
Entité municipal: Municipality
Incorporation: 1er juillet 1855; *Area:* 53,43 km2
Comté ou district: Bellechasse; *Population au 2011:* 1,816
Circonscription(s) électorale(s) provinciale(s): Bellechasse
Circonscription(s) électorale(s) fédérale(s): Bellechasse-Les Etchemins-Lévis
Prochaines élections: 5e novembre 2017
Gilles Vézina, Maire
Ronald Gonthier, Directeur général

Saint-Michel-des-Saints
441, rue Brassard
Saint-Michel-des-Saints, QC J0K 3B0
Tél: 450-886-4502; *Téléc:* 450-833-6081
info@saintmicheldessaints.com
www.saintmicheldesaints.com
Entité municipal: Municipality
Incorporation: 3 mars 1979; *Area:* 563,72 km2
Comté ou district: Matawinie; *Population au 2011:* 2,201
Circonscription(s) électorale(s) provinciale(s): Berthier
Circonscription(s) électorale(s) fédérale(s): Joliette
Prochaines élections: 5e novembre 2017
Réjean Gouin, Maire
Alain Bellerose, Directeur général

Saint-Michel-du-Squatec
CP 280
150, rue St-Joseph
Saint-Michel-du-Squatec, QC G0L 4H0
Tél: 418-855-2185; *Téléc:* 418-855-2935
info@squatec.qc.ca
www.squatec.qc.ca
Entité municipal: Parish (Paroisse)
Incorporation: 16 avril 1928; *Area:* 363,10 km2
Comté ou district: Témiscouata; *Population au 2011:* 1,171
Circonscription(s) électorale(s) provinciale(s): Rivière-du-Loup-Témiscouata
Circonscription(s) électorale(s) fédérale(s): Rimouski-Neigette-Témiscouata-Les Basques
Prochaines élections: 5e novembre 2017
Jacqueline Caron, Mairesse
Danielle Albert, Directrice générale

Saint-Modeste
312, rue Principale
Saint-Modeste, QC G0L 3W0
Tél: 418-867-2352; *Téléc:* 418-867-5359
municipalite@saint-modeste.ca
www.municipalite.saint-modeste.qc.ca
Entité municipal: Parish (Paroisse)
Incorporation: 1er juillet 1855; *Area:* 107,91 km2
Comté ou district: Rivière-du-Loup; *Population au 2011:* 1,128
Circonscription(s) électorale(s) provinciale(s): Rivière-du-Loup-Témiscouata
Circonscription(s) électorale(s) fédérale(s): Montmagny-L'Islet-Kamouraska-Rivière-du-Loup
Prochaines élections: 5e novembre 2017
Louis-Marie Bastille, Maire
Alain Vila, Directeur général

Saint-Moïse
CP 8
117-B, rue Principale
Saint-Moïse, QC G0J 2Z0
Tél: 418-776-2833; *Téléc:* 418-776-2835
muni.moise@globetrotter.net
www.municipalitestmoise.ca
Entité municipal: Parish (Paroisse)
Incorporation: 1er janvier 1878; *Area:* 106,83 km2
Comté ou district: La Matapédia; *Population au 2011:* 577
Circonscription(s) électorale(s) provinciale(s): Matane-Matapédia
Circonscription(s) électorale(s) fédérale(s): Avignon-La Mitis-Matane-Matapédia
Prochaines élections: 5e novembre 2017
Paul Lepage, Maire
Nadine Beaulieu, Directrice générale

Saint-Narcisse
353, rue Notre-Dame
Saint-Narcisse, QC G0X 2Y0
Tél: 418-328-8645; *Téléc:* 418-328-4348
municipalite@saint-narcisse.com
www.saint-narcisse.com
Entité municipal: Parish (Paroisse)
Incorporation: 1er juillet 1855; *Area:* 103,49 km2
Comté ou district: Les Chenaux; *Population au 2011:* 1,762
Circonscription(s) électorale(s) provinciale(s): Champlain
Circonscription(s) électorale(s) fédérale(s): St-Maurice-Champlain
Prochaines élections: 5e novembre 2017
Guy Veillette, Maire
Stéphane Bourassa, Directeur général

Saint-Narcisse-de-Beaurivage
#1, 508, rue de l'École
Saint-Narcisse-de-Beaurivage, QC G0S 1W0
Tél: 418-475-6842; *Téléc:* 418-475-6880
saintnarcisse@globetrotter.net
www.saintnarcissedebeaurivage.ca
Entité municipal: Parish (Paroisse)
Incorporation: 1er mai 1874; *Area:* 60,83 km2
Comté ou district: Lotbinière; *Population au 2011:* 1,091
Circonscription(s) électorale(s) provinciale(s): Lotbinière-Frontenac
Circonscription(s) électorale(s) fédérale(s): Lévis-Lotbinière
Prochaines élections: 5e novembre 2017
Denis Dion, Maire
Dany Lehoux, Directrice générale

Saint-Narcisse-de-Rimouski
7, rue du Pavillon
Saint-Narcisse-de-Rimouski, QC G0K 1S0
Tél: 418-735-2638; *Téléc:* 418-735-6021
informations@saintnarcisse.net
www.saintnarcisse.net
Entité municipal: Parish (Paroisse)
Incorporation: 13 février 1922; *Area:* 166,83 km2
Comté ou district: Rimouski-Neigette; *Population au 2011:* 1,017
Circonscription(s) électorale(s) provinciale(s): Rimouski
Circonscription(s) électorale(s) fédérale(s): Rimouski-Neigette-Témiscouata-Les Basques
Prochaines élections: 5e novembre 2017
Robert Duchesne, Maire
Gilles Lepage, Directeur général

Saint-Nazaire
199, rue Principale
Saint-Nazaire, QC G0W 2V0
Tél: 418-662-4154; *Téléc:* 418-662-5467
www.ville.saint-nazaire.qc.ca
Entité municipal: Municipality
Incorporation: 23 septembre 1905; *Area:* 147,78 km2
Comté ou district: Lac-Saint-Jean-Est; *Population au 2011:* 2,114
Circonscription(s) électorale(s) provinciale(s): Lac-St-Jean
Circonscription(s) électorale(s) fédérale(s): Jonquière
Prochaines élections: 5e novembre 2017
Martin Sauvé, Maire
Desneiges Simard, Directeur général

Saint-Nazaire-d'Acton
750, rue des Loisirs
Saint-Nazaire-d'Acton, QC J0H 1V0
Tél: 819-392-2347; *Téléc:* 819-392-2039
Entité municipal: Parish (Paroisse)
Incorporation: 8 janvier 1894; *Area:* 57,49 km2
Comté ou district: Acton; *Population au 2011:* 826
Circonscription(s) électorale(s) provinciale(s): Johnson
Circonscription(s) électorale(s) fédérale(s): St-Hyacinthe-Bagot
Prochaines élections: 5e novembre 2017
André Fafard, Maire
Guylaine Bourgoin, Directrice générale

Saint-Nazaire-de-Dorchester
61A, rue Principale
Saint-Nazaire, QC G0R 3T0
Tél: 418-642-1305; *Téléc:* 418-642-2945
mun_st_nazaire@globetrotter.net
www.saint-nazaire-de-dorchester.org
Entité municipal: Parish (Paroisse)
Incorporation: 9 mars 1906; *Area:* 51,43 km2
Comté ou district: Bellechasse; *Population au 2011:* 355
Circonscription(s) électorale(s) provinciale(s): Bellechasse
Circonscription(s) électorale(s) fédérale(s): Bellechasse-Les Etchemins-Lévis
Prochaines élections: 5e novembre 2017
Claude Lachance, Maire
Francine Brochu, Directrice générale

Saint-Nérée-de-Bellechasse
1990, rte Principale
Saint-Nérée, QC G0R 3V0
Tél: 418-243-2735; *Téléc:* 418-243-2136
muneree@globetrotter.net
www.st-neree.qc.ca
Entité municipal: Parish (Paroisse)
Incorporation: 29 mars 1887; *Area:* 75,73 km2
Comté ou district: Bellechasse; *Population au 2011:* 743
Circonscription(s) électorale(s) provinciale(s): Bellechasse
Circonscription(s) électorale(s) fédérale(s): Bellechasse-Les Etchemins-Lévis
Prochaines élections: 5e novembre 2017
Pascal Fournier, Maire
Michaël Couture, Directeur général

Saint-Noël
CP 99
51, rue de l'Église
Saint-Noël, QC G0J 3A0
Tél: 418-776-2936; *Téléc:* 418-776-5521
stnoel@mrcmatapedia.qc.ca
Entité municipal: Village
Incorporation: 2 octobre 1906; *Area:* 45,68 km2
Comté ou district: La Matapédia; *Population au 2011:* 434
Circonscription(s) électorale(s) provinciale(s): Matane-Matapédia
Circonscription(s) électorale(s) fédérale(s): Avignon-La Mitis-Matane-Matapédia
Prochaines élections: 5e novembre 2017
Gilbert Sénéchal, Maire
Manon Caron, Directrice générale

Saint-Norbert
4, rue Laporte
Saint-Norbert, QC J0K 3C0
Tél: 450-836-4700; *Téléc:* 450-836-4004
www.saint-norbert.net
Entité municipal: Parish (Paroisse)
Incorporation: 1er juillet 1855; *Area:* 77,31 km2
Comté ou district: D'Autray; *Population au 2011:* 1,059
Circonscription(s) électorale(s) provinciale(s): Berthier
Circonscription(s) électorale(s) fédérale(s): Berthier-Maskinongé
Prochaines élections: 5e novembre 2017
Guy Paradis, Maire, 450-835-7379
Lucie Poulette, Directrice générale, 450-836-4700

Saint-Norbert-d'Arthabaska
44, rue Landry
Saint-Norbert-d'Arthabaska, QC G0P 1B0
Tél: 819-369-9318; *Téléc:* 819-369-8686
www.saint-norbert-darthabaska.ca
Entité municipal: Municipality
Incorporation: 30 novembre 1994; *Area:* 113,66 km2
Comté ou district: Arthabaska; *Population au 2011:* 1,185
Circonscription(s) électorale(s) provinciale(s): Arthabaska
Circonscription(s) électorale(s) fédérale(s): Richmond-Arthabaska
Prochaines élections: 5e novembre 2017
Alain Tourigny, Maire
Linda Trottier, Directrice générale

Saint-Octave-de-Métis
201A, rue de l'Église
Saint-Octave-de-Métis, QC G0J 3B0
Tél: 418-775-2996; *Téléc:* 418-775-0099
stoctave@mitis.qc.ca
Entité municipal: Parish (Paroisse)
Incorporation: 25 avril 1908; *Area:* 74,63 km2
Comté ou district: La Mitis; *Population au 2011:* 345
Circonscription(s) électorale(s) provinciale(s): Matane-Matapédia
Circonscription(s) électorale(s) fédérale(s): Avignon-La Mitis-Matane-Matapédia
Prochaines élections: 5e novembre 2017
Guillaume Bérubé, Maire
Maxime Richard-Dubé, Directeur général

Saint-Odilon-de-Cranbourne
CP 100
111, rue de l'Hôtel-de-Ville
Saint-Odilon, QC G0S 3A0
Tél: 418-464-4801; *Téléc:* 418-464-4800
info@saint-odilon.qc.ca
www.saint-odilon.qc.ca
Entité municipal: Parish (Paroisse)
Incorporation: 1er juillet 1855; *Area:* 128,77 km2
Comté ou district: Robert-Cliche; *Population au 2011:* 1,459
Circonscription(s) électorale(s) provinciale(s): Beauce-Nord
Circonscription(s) électorale(s) fédérale(s): Beauce
Prochaines élections: 5e novembre 2017
André Labbé, Maire
Dominique Giguère, Directrice générale

Saint-Omer
243, rang des Pelletier
Saint-Omer, QC G0R 4R0
Tél: 418-356-5634; *Téléc:* 418-356-2965
municipalitest-omer@globetrotter.net
www.st-omer.qc.ca
Entité municipal: Municipality
Incorporation: 1er janvier 1954; *Area:* 125,35 km2
Comté ou district: L'Islet; *Population au 2011:* 310
Circonscription(s) électorale(s) provinciale(s): Côte-du-Sud
Circonscription(s) électorale(s) fédérale(s): Montmagny-L'Islet-Kamouraska-Rivière-du-Loup
Prochaines élections: 5e novembre 2017
Clément Fortin, Maire
Tina Godin, Directrice générale

Saint-Onésime-d'Ixworth
12, rue de l'Église
Saint-Onésime-d'Ixworth, QC G0R 3W0
Tél: 418-856-3018; *Téléc:* 418-856-6626
municipalite@stonesime.com
www.st-onesime.ca
Entité municipal: Parish (Paroisse)
Incorporation: 13 mai 1895; *Area:* 103,59 km2
Comté ou district: Kamouraska; *Population au 2011:* 559
Circonscription(s) électorale(s) provinciale(s): Côte-du-Sud
Circonscription(s) électorale(s) fédérale(s): Montmagny-L'Islet-Kamouraska-Rivière-du-Loup
Prochaines élections: 5e novembre 2017
André Hudon, Maire
Geneviève Cloutier, Directrice générale

Saint-Ours
CP 129
2540, rue de l'Immaculée-Conception
Saint-Ours, QC J0G 1P0
Tél: 450-785-2203; *Téléc:* 450-785-2254
villestours@pierredesaurel.com
www.ville.saintours.qc.ca
Entité municipal: Village
Incorporation: 17 avril 1991; *Area:* 58,50 km2

Comté ou district: Pierre-De Saurel; *Population au 2011:* 1,721
Circonscription(s) électorale(s) provinciale(s): Richelieu
Circonscription(s) électorale(s) fédérale(s):
Bécancour-Nicolet-Saurel
Prochaines élections: 5e novembre 2017
Sylvain Dupuis, Maire
Pierre Dion, Directeur général

Saint-Pacôme
CP 370
27, rue St-Louis
Saint-Pacôme, QC G0L 3X0
Tél: 418-852-2356; *Téléc:* 418-852-2977
stpacome@bellnet.ca
www.st-pacome.ca
Entité municipal: Municipality
Incorporation: 5 janvier 1980; *Area:* 29,31 km2
Comté ou district: Kamouraska; *Population au 2011:* 1,658
Circonscription(s) électorale(s) provinciale(s): Côte-du-Sud
Circonscription(s) électorale(s) fédérale(s):
Montmagny-L'Islet-Kamouraska-Rivière-du-Loup
Prochaines élections: 5e novembre 2017
Nathan Lévesque, Maire
Fréderick Lee, Directeur général

Saint-Pamphile
3, rte Elgin sud
Saint-Pamphile, QC G0R 3X0
Tél: 418-356-5501; *Téléc:* 418-356-5502
pamphile@globetrotter.qc.ca
www.saintpamphile.ca
Entité municipal: Town
Incorporation: 21 janvier 1888; *Area:* 136,80 km2
Comté ou district: L'Islet; *Population au 2011:* 2,685
Circonscription(s) électorale(s) provinciale(s): Côte-du-Sud
Circonscription(s) électorale(s) fédérale(s):
Montmagny-L'Islet-Kamouraska-Rivière-du-Loup
Prochaines élections: 5e novembre 2017
Mario Leblanc, Maire
Richard Pelletier, Directeur général

Saint-Pascal
CP 250
405, rue Taché
Saint-Pascal, QC G0L 3Y0
Tél: 418-492-2312; *Téléc:* 418-492-9862
hoteldeville@villestpascal.com
www.villesaintpascal.qc.ca
Entité municipal: Town
Incorporation: 1er mars 2000; *Area:* 57,75 km2
Comté ou district: Kamouraska; *Population au 2011:* 3,490
Circonscription(s) électorale(s) provinciale(s): Côte-du-Sud
Circonscription(s) électorale(s) fédérale(s):
Montmagny-L'Islet-Kamouraska-Rivière-du-Loup
Prochaines élections: 5e novembre 2017
Rénald Bernier, Maire
Louise Saint-Pierre, Greffière

Saint-Patrice-de-Beaurivage
#100, 486, rue Principale
Saint-Patrice-de-Beaurivage, QC G0S 1B0
Tél: 418-596-2362; *Téléc:* 418-596-2430
st.patrice@globetrotter.net
www.ville.saint-patrice-de-beaurivage.qc.ca
Entité municipal: Municipality
Incorporation: 29 septembre 1984; *Area:* 86,18 km2
Comté ou district: Lotbinière; *Population au 2011:* 1,080
Circonscription(s) électorale(s) provinciale(s):
Lotbinière-Frontenac
Circonscription(s) électorale(s) fédérale(s): Lévis-Lotbinière
Prochaines élections: 5e novembre 2017
Claude Fortin, Maire
Frédéric Desjardins, Directrice générale

Saint-Patrice-de-Sherrington
300, rue St-Patrice
Saint-Patrice-de-Sherrington, QC J0L 2N0
Tél: 450-454-4959; *Téléc:* 450-454-5677
info@st-patrice-sherrington.com
www.st-patrice-sherrington.com
Entité municipal: Parish (Paroisse)
Incorporation: 1er juillet 1855; *Area:* 91,47 km2
Comté ou district: Les Jardins-de-Napierville; *Population au 2011:* 1,971
Circonscription(s) électorale(s) provinciale(s): Huntingdon
Circonscription(s) électorale(s) fédérale(s): Châteauguay-Lacolle
Prochaines élections: 5e novembre 2017
Daniel Lussier, Maire
Michel Demers, Directeur général

Saint-Paul
18, boul Brassard
Saint-Paul, QC J0K 3E0
Tél: 450-759-4040; *Téléc:* 450-759-6396
mairie@municipalitestpaul.qc.ca
www.municipalitestpaul.qc.ca
Entité municipal: Municipality
Incorporation: 1er juillet 1855; *Area:* 48,17 km2
Comté ou district: Joliette; *Population au 2011:* 5,122
Circonscription(s) électorale(s) provinciale(s): Joliette
Circonscription(s) électorale(s) fédérale(s): Joliette
Prochaines élections: 5e novembre 2017
Alain Bellemarre, Maire
Richard-B. Morasse, Directeur général

Saint-Paul-d'Abbotsford
926, rue Principale est
Saint-Paul-d'Abbotsford, QC J0E 1A0
Tél: 450-379-5408; *Téléc:* 450-379-9905
info@saintpauldabbotsford.qc.ca
www.saintpauldabbotsford.qc.ca
Entité municipal: Parish (Paroisse)
Incorporation: 1er juillet 1855; *Area:* 79,59 km2
Comté ou district: Rouville; *Population au 2011:* 2,870
Circonscription(s) électorale(s) provinciale(s): Iberville
Circonscription(s) électorale(s) fédérale(s): Shefford
Prochaines élections: 5e novembre 2017
Jacques Viens, Maire
Daniel-Eric St-Onge, Directeur général

Saint-Paul-de-l'Ile-aux-Noix
959, rue Principale
Saint-Paul-de-l'Ile-aux-Noix, QC J0J 1G0
Tél: 450-291-3166; *Téléc:* 450-291-5930
info@ileauxnoix.qc.ca
www.ileauxnoix.com
Entité municipal: Parish (Paroisse)
Incorporation: 18 novembre 1898; *Area:* 29,47 km2
Comté ou district: Le Haut-Richelieu; *Population au 2011:* 1,877
Circonscription(s) électorale(s) provinciale(s): Huntingdon
Circonscription(s) électorale(s) fédérale(s): Saint-Jean
Prochaines élections: 5e novembre 2017
Claude Leroux, Maire
Marie-Lili Lenoir, Directrice générale

Saint-Paul-de-la-Croix
CP 70
1A, rue du Parc
Saint-Paul-de-la-Croix, QC G0L 3Z0
Tél: 418-898-2031; *Téléc:* 418-898-2322
www.municipalite.saint-paul-de-la-croix.qc.ca
Entité municipal: Parish (Paroisse)
Incorporation: 1er janvier 1873; *Area:* 84,25 km2
Comté ou district: Rivière-du-Loup; *Population au 2011:* 367
Circonscription(s) électorale(s) provinciale(s):
Rivière-du-Loup-Témiscouata
Circonscription(s) électorale(s) fédérale(s):
Montmagny-L'Islet-Kamouraska-Rivière-du-Loup
Prochaines élections: 5e novembre 2017
Phillipe Dionne, Maire
Hélène Malenfant, Directrice générale

Saint-Paul-de-Montminy
CP 160
309, 4e av
Saint-Paul-de-Montminy, QC G0R 3Y0
Tél: 418-469-3120; *Téléc:* 418-469-3358
municipalitest-paul@globetrotter.net
www.stpauldemontminy.com
Entité municipal: Municipality
Incorporation: 1er janvier 1862; *Area:* 162,80 km2
Comté ou district: Montmagny; *Population au 2011:* 824
Circonscription(s) électorale(s) provinciale(s): Côte-du-Sud
Circonscription(s) électorale(s) fédérale(s):
Montmagny-L'Islet-Kamouraska-Rivière-du-Loup
Prochaines élections: 5e novembre 2017
Émile Tanguay, Maire
Claudette Aubé, Directrice générale

Saint-Paulin
CP 120
3051, rue Bergeron
Saint-Paulin, QC J0K 3G0
Tél: 819-268-2026; *Téléc:* 819-268-2890
munistpaulindg@telmilot.net
www.st-paulin.qc.ca
Entité municipal: Municipality
Incorporation: 27 février 1988; *Area:* 96,40 km2
Comté ou district: Maskinongé; *Population au 2011:* 1,534
Circonscription(s) électorale(s) provinciale(s): Maskinongé
Circonscription(s) électorale(s) fédérale(s): Berthier-Maskinongé
Prochaines élections: 5e novembre 2017

Serge Dubé, Maire
Ghislain Lemay, Directeur général

Saint-Philémon
1531, rue Principale
Saint-Philémon, QC G0R 4A0
Tél: 418-469-2890; *Téléc:* 418-469-2726
munphile@globetrotter.net
www.saintphilemon.com
Entité municipal: Parish (Paroisse)
Incorporation: 1er janvier 1867; *Area:* 146,51 km2
Comté ou district: Bellechasse; *Population au 2011:* 742
Circonscription(s) électorale(s) provinciale(s): Bellechasse
Circonscription(s) électorale(s) fédérale(s): Bellechasse-Les Etchemins-Lévis
Prochaines élections: 5e novembre 2017
Daniel Pouliot, Maire
Diane Labrecque, Directrice générale

Saint-Philibert
376, rue Principale
Saint-Philibert, QC G0M 1X0
Tél: 418-228-8759; *Téléc:* 418-228-0432
infos@st-philibert.qc.ca
www.st-philibert.qc.ca
Entité municipal: Municipality
Incorporation: 25 février 1921; *Area:* 57,26 km2
Comté ou district: Beauce-Sartigan; *Population au 2011:* 367
Circonscription(s) électorale(s) provinciale(s): Beauce-Sud
Circonscription(s) électorale(s) fédérale(s): Beauce
Prochaines élections: 5e novembre 2017
Jean-Guy Plante, Maire
Chantale Gareau, Directrice générale

Saint-Philippe
#201, 175, ch Sanguinet
Saint-Philippe, QC J0L 2K0
Tél: 450-659-7701; *Téléc:* 450-659-7702
info@ville.saintphilippe.quebec
www.municipalite.saint-philippe.qc.ca
Entité municipal: Municipality
Incorporation: 1er juillet 1855; *Area:* 61,66 km2
Comté ou district: Roussillon; Communauté métropolitaine de Montréal; *Population au 2011:* 5,495
Circonscription(s) électorale(s) provinciale(s): La Prairie
Circonscription(s) électorale(s) fédérale(s): La Prairie
Prochaines élections: 5e novembre 2017
Lise Martin, Mairesse
Martin Lelièvre, Directeur général

Saint-Philippe-de-Néri
CP 130
12, côte de l'Église
Saint-Philippe-de-Néri, QC G0L 4A0
Tél: 418-498-2744; *Téléc:* 418-498-2193
munic.s.phil.neri@qc.aira.com
www.stphilippedeneri.com
Entité municipal: Parish (Paroisse)
Incorporation: 29 décembre 1875; *Area:* 33,08 km2
Comté ou district: Kamouraska; *Population au 2011:* 868
Circonscription(s) électorale(s) provinciale(s): Côte-du-Sud
Circonscription(s) électorale(s) fédérale(s):
Montmagny-L'Islet-Kamouraska-Rivière-du-Loup
Prochaines élections: 5e novembre 2017
Gilles Lévesque, Maire
Pierre Leclerc, Directeur général

Saint-Pie
77, rue St-Pierre
Saint-Pie, QC J0H 1W0
Tél: 450-772-2488; *Téléc:* 450-772-2233
st-pie@villest-pie.ca
www.villest-pie.ca
Entité municipal: Town
Incorporation: 28 février 2003; *Area:* 106,47 km2
Comté ou district: Les Maskoutains; *Population au 2011:* 5,438
Circonscription(s) électorale(s) provinciale(s): St-Hyacinthe
Circonscription(s) électorale(s) fédérale(s): St-Hyacinthe-Bagot
Prochaines élections: 5e novembre 2017
Note: Effective February 28, 2003, the Parish & the Village of St-Pie amalgamated to create the new City of St-Pie.
Mario St-Pierre, Maire
Claude Gratton, Greffier

Saint-Pie-de-Guire
435, rue Principale
Saint-Pie-de-Guire, QC J0G 1R0
Tél: 450-784-2278; *Téléc:* 450-784-0133
stpiedeguire@bellnet.ca
www.stpiedeguire.ca
Entité municipal: Parish (Paroisse)
Incorporation: 14 juin 1866; *Area:* 52,34 km2

Comté ou district: Drummond; *Population au 2011:* 456
Circonscription(s) électorale(s) provinciale(s): Nicolet-Bécancour
Circonscription(s) électorale(s) fédérale(s): Drummond
Prochaines élections: 5e novembre 2017
Benoît Bourque, Maire
Claire Roy, Directrice générale

Saint-Pierre
485, ch du Village-de-St-Pierre nord
Joliette, QC J6E 0H2
Tél: 450-756-2592; *Téléc:* 450-756-2735
villagestpierre@qc.aira.com
Entité municipal: Village
Incorporation: 24 avril 1922; *Area:* 10,60 km2
Comté ou district: Joliette; *Population au 2011:* 305
Circonscription(s) électorale(s) provinciale(s): Joliette
Circonscription(s) électorale(s) fédérale(s): Joliette
Prochaines élections: 5e novembre 2017
Roland Charest, Maire
Édith Gagné, Directrice générale

Saint-Pierre-Baptiste
532, rte de l'Église
Saint-Pierre-Baptiste, QC G0P 1K0
Tél: 418-453-2286; *Téléc:* 418-453-2286
info@saintpierrebaptiste.qc.ca
www.saintpierrebaptiste.qc.ca
Entité municipal: Parish (Paroisse)
Incorporation: 1er janvier 1874; *Area:* 80,72 km2
Comté ou district: L'Érable; *Population au 2011:* 485
Circonscription(s) électorale(s) provinciale(s): Arthabaska
Circonscription(s) électorale(s) fédérale(s): Mégantic-L'Érable
Prochaines élections: 5e novembre 2017
Bertrand Fortier, Maire
Ginette Jasmin, Directrice générale

Saint-Pierre-de-Broughton
CP 90
29, rue de la Fabrique
Saint-Pierre-de-Broughton, QC G0N 1T0
Tél: 418-424-3572; *Téléc:* 418-424-0389
muni.stpierre@ville.st-pierre-de-broughton.qc.ca
www.ville.st-pierre-de-broughton.qc.ca
Entité municipal: Municipality
Incorporation: 12 octobre 1974; *Area:* 147,460 km2
Comté ou district: Les Appalaches; *Population au 2011:* 882
Circonscription(s) électorale(s) provinciale(s):
Lotbinière-Frontenac
Circonscription(s) électorale(s) fédérale(s): Mégantic-L'Érable
Prochaines élections: 5e novembre 2017
France Laroche, Mairesse
Renée Vachon, Directrice générale

Saint-Pierre-de-l'île-d'Orléans
515, rte des Prêtres
Saint-Pierre-Ile-d'Orléans, QC G0A 4E0
Tél: 418-828-2855; *Téléc:* 418-828-0724
www.st-pierre.iledorleans.com
Entité municipal: Municipality
Incorporation: 1er juillet 1855; *Area:* 31,13 km2
Comté ou district: L'île-d'Orléans; Communauté métropolitaine de Québec; *Population au 2011:* 1,789
Circonscription(s) électorale(s) provinciale(s):
Charlevoix-Côte-de-Beaupré
Circonscription(s) électorale(s) fédérale(s):
Beauport-Côte-de-Beaupré-Ile d'Orléans-Charlevoix
Prochaines élections: 5e novembre 2017
Sylvain Bergeron, Maire
Gérard Cossette, Directeur général

Saint-Pierre-de-Lamy
115, rte de l'Église
Saint-Pierre-de-Lamy, QC G0L 4B0
Tél: 418-497-2447; *Téléc:* 418-497-2447
admin@saint-pierre-de-lamy.org
municipalites-du-quebec.org/municipalites/saint-pierre-de-lamy
Entité municipal: Municipality
Incorporation: 4 juin 1977; *Area:* 115,46 km2
Comté ou district: Témiscouata; *Population au 2011:* 112
Circonscription(s) électorale(s) provinciale(s):
Rivière-du-Loup-Témiscouata
Circonscription(s) électorale(s) fédérale(s):
Rimouski-Neigette-Témiscouata-Les Basques
Prochaines élections: 5e novembre 2017
Gaston Caron, Maire
Mireille Plourde, Directrice générale

Saint-Pierre-de-la-Rivière-du-Sud
645, 2e av
St-Pierre-de-la-Rivière-du-Sud, QC G0R 4B0
Tél: 418-248-8277; *Téléc:* 418-248-7068
st-pierre.rivsud@globetrotter.net
www.stpierredelarivieredusud.ca
Entité municipal: Parish (Paroisse)
Incorporation: 1er juillet 1855; *Area:* 92,28 km2
Comté ou district: Montmagny; *Population au 2011:* 920
Circonscription(s) électorale(s) provinciale(s): Côte-du-Sud
Circonscription(s) électorale(s) fédérale(s):
Montmagny-L'Islet-Kamouraska-Rivière-du-Loup
Prochaines élections: 5e novembre 2017
Alain Fortier, Maire
Georges Baillargeon, Directeur général

Saint-Pierre-les-Becquets
110, rue des Loisirs
Saint-Pierre-les-Becquets, QC G0X 2Z0
Tél: 819-263-2622; *Téléc:* 819-263-0798
municipalite@st-pierre-les-becquets.qc.ca
www.st-pierre-les-becquets.qc.ca
Entité municipal: Municipality
Incorporation: 22 février 1986; *Area:* 43,00 km2
Comté ou district: Bécancour; *Population au 2011:* 1,223
Circonscription(s) électorale(s) provinciale(s): Nicolet-Bécancour
Circonscription(s) électorale(s) fédérale(s):
Bécancour-Nicolet-Saurel
Prochaines élections: 5e novembre 2017
Yves Tousignant, Maire
Martine Lafond, Directrice générale

Saint-Placide
281, montée St-Vincent
Saint-Placide, QC J0V 2B0
Tél: 450-258-2305; *Téléc:* 450-258-3059
infosp@municipalite.st-placide.qc.ca
www.municipalite.saint-placide.qc.ca
Entité municipal: Municipality
Incorporation: 3 août 1994; *Area:* 41,95 km2
Comté ou district: Deux-Montagnes; *Population au 2011:* 1,715
Circonscription(s) électorale(s) provinciale(s): Mirabel
Circonscription(s) électorale(s) fédérale(s): Mirabel
Prochaines élections: 5e novembre 2017
Denis Lavigne, Maire
Lise Lavigne, Directrice générale

Saint-Polycarpe
CP 380
1263, ch Élie-Auclair
Saint-Polycarpe, QC J0P 1X0
Tél: 450-265-3777; *Téléc:* 450-265-3010
www.munstpolycarpe.qc.ca
Entité municipal: Municipality
Incorporation: 31 décembre 1988; *Area:* 70,80 km2
Comté ou district: Vaudreuil-Soulanges; *Population au 2011:* 1,969
Circonscription(s) électorale(s) provinciale(s): Soulanges
Circonscription(s) électorale(s) fédérale(s): Salaberry-Suroît
Prochaines élections: 5e novembre 2017
Jean-Yves Poirier, Maire
Jacques Brisson, Directeur général

Saint-Prime
599, rue Principale
Saint-Prime, QC G8J 1T2
Tél: 418-251-2116; *Téléc:* 418-251-2823
administration@saint-prime.ca
www.saint-prime.ca
Entité municipal: Municipality
Incorporation: 29 juin 1968; *Area:* 147,43 km2
Comté ou district: Le Domaine-du-Roy; *Population au 2011:* 2,758
Circonscription(s) électorale(s) provinciale(s): Roberval
Circonscription(s) électorale(s) fédérale(s): Lac-Saint-Jean
Prochaines élections: 5e novembre 2017
Lucien Boivin, Maire
Régis Girard, Directeur général

Saint-Prosper
2025, 29e rue
Saint-Prosper, QC G0M 1Y0
Tél: 418-594-8135; *Téléc:* 418-594-8865
info@saint-prosper.com
www.saint-prosper.com
Entité municipal: Municipality
Incorporation: 26 septembre 1887; *Area:* 136, 95 km2
Comté ou district: Les Etchemins; *Population au 2011:* 3,605
Circonscription(s) électorale(s) provinciale(s): Beauce-Sud
Circonscription(s) électorale(s) fédérale(s): Beauce
Prochaines élections: 5e novembre 2017
Richard Couët, Maire
Johanne Nadeau, Directrice générale

Saint-Prosper-de-Champlain
CP 68
375, rue St-Joseph
Saint-Prosper, QC G0X 3A0
Tél: 418-840-0461; *Téléc:* 418-328-4267
municipalite@st-prosper.ca
www.st-prosper.ca
Entité municipal: Parish (Paroisse)
Incorporation: 1er juillet 1855; *Area:* 92,03 km2
Comté ou district: Les Chenaux; *Population au 2011:* 505
Circonscription(s) électorale(s) provinciale(s): Champlain
Circonscription(s) électorale(s) fédérale(s):
St-Maurice-Champlain
Prochaines élections: 5e novembre 2017
Michel Grosleau, Maire
Francine Masse, Directrice générale

Saint-Raphaël
CP 1091
19, av Chanoine-Audet
Saint-Raphaël, QC G0R 4C0
Tél: 418-243-2853; *Téléc:* 418-243-2605
muraph@globetrotter.net
www.municipalite.saint-raphael.qc.ca
Entité municipal: Municipality
Incorporation: 8 décembre 1993; *Area:* 120,06 km2
Comté ou district: Bellechasse; *Population au 2011:* 2,463
Circonscription(s) électorale(s) provinciale(s): Bellechasse
Circonscription(s) électorale(s) fédérale(s): Bellechasse-Les Etchemins-Lévis
Prochaines élections: 5e novembre 2017
Gilles Breton, Maire
Paul Beaudoin, Directeur général

Saint-Raymond
375, rue St-Joseph
Saint-Raymond, QC G3L 1A1
Tél: 418-337-2202; *Téléc:* 418-337-2203
info@villesaintraymond.com
www.villesaintraymond.coma
Entité municipal: Town
Incorporation: 29 mars 1995; *Area:* 684,65 km2
Comté ou district: Portneuf; *Population au 2011:* 9,615
Circonscription(s) électorale(s) provinciale(s): Portneuf
Circonscription(s) électorale(s) fédérale(s):
Portneuf-Jacques-Cartier
Prochaines élections: 5e novembre 2017
Daniel Dion, Maire
Chantal Plamandon, Greffière

Saint-Rémi
105, rue de la Mairie
Saint-Rémi, QC J0L 2L0
Tél: 450-454-3993; *Téléc:* 450-454-7978
administration@ville.saint-remi.qc.ca
www.ville.saint-remi.qc.ca
Entité municipal: Town
Incorporation: 20 septembre 1975; *Area:* 79,66 km2
Comté ou district: Les Jardins-de-Napierville; *Population au 2011:* 7,265
Circonscription(s) électorale(s) provinciale(s): Sanguinet
Circonscription(s) électorale(s) fédérale(s): Châteauguay-Lacolle
Prochaines élections: 5e novembre 2017
Sylvie Gagnon-Breton, Mairesse
Diane Soucy, Greffière

Saint-Rémi-de-Tingwick
156, rue Principale
Saint-Rémi-de-Tingwick, QC J0A 1K0
Tél: 819-359-2731; *Téléc:* 819-359-3532
info@st-remi-de-tingwick.qc.ca
www.st-remi-de-tingwick.qc.ca
Entité municipal: Parish (Paroisse)
Incorporation: 1er janvier 1882; *Area:* 72,18 km2
Comté ou district: Arthabaska; *Population au 2011:* 474
Circonscription(s) électorale(s) provinciale(s):
Drummond-Bois-Francs
Circonscription(s) électorale(s) fédérale(s):
Richmond-Arthabaska
Prochaines élections: 5e novembre 2017
Estelle Luneau, Mairesse
Chantal Cantin, Directrice générale

Saint-René
778, rte Principale
Saint-René, QC G0M 1Z0
Tél: 418-382-5226; *Téléc:* 418-382-3655
muni.st.rene@globetrotter.net
www.st-rene.ca

Entité municipal: Parish (Paroisse)
Incorporation: 1er janvier 1945; *Area:* 61,53 km3
Comté ou district: Beauce-Sartigan; *Population au 2011:* 658
Circonscription(s) électorale(s) provinciale(s): Beauce-Sud
Circonscription(s) électorale(s) fédérale(s): Beauce
Prochaines élections: 5e novembre 2017
Jean-Guy Deblois, Maire
Michel Gilbert, Directeur général

Saint-René-de-Matane
CP 58
178, av St-René
Saint-René-de-Matane, QC G0J 3E0
Tél: 418-224-3306; *Téléc:* 418-224-3259
www.saintrene.ca
Entité municipal: Municipality
Incorporation: 18 décembre 1982; *Area:* 255,58 km2
Comté ou district: La Matanie; *Population au 2011:* 1,089
Circonscription(s) électorale(s) provinciale(s): Matane-Matapédia
Circonscription(s) électorale(s) fédérale(s): Avignon-La Mitis-Matane-Matapédia
Prochaines élections: 5e novembre 2017
Roger Vaillancourt, Maire
Yvette Boulay, Directrice générale

Saint-Robert
CP 150
666, ch de St-Robert
Saint-Robert, QC J0G 1S0
Tél: 450-782-2844; *Téléc:* 450-782-2733
strobert@pierredesaurel.com
www.saintrobert.qc.ca
Entité municipal: Municipality
Incorporation: 17 octobre 1857; *Area:* 64,93 km2
Comté ou district: Pierre-De Saurel; *Population au 2011:* 1,794
Circonscription(s) électorale(s) provinciale(s): Richelieu
Circonscription(s) électorale(s) fédérale(s): Bécancour-Nicolet-Saurel
Prochaines élections: 5e novembre 2017
Gilles Salvas, Maire
Nathalie Lussier, Directrice générale

Saint-Robert-Bellarmin
10, rue Nadeau
Saint-Robert-Bellarmin, QC G0M 2E0
Tél: 418-582-3420; *Téléc:* 418-582-0052
mun-st-robert@bellarmin.ca
www.st-robertbellarmin.qc.ca
Entité municipal: Municipality
Incorporation: 1er janvier 1949; *Area:* 234,82 km2
Comté ou district: Le Granit; *Population au 2011:* 676
Circonscription(s) électorale(s) provinciale(s): Beauce-Sud
Circonscription(s) électorale(s) fédérale(s): Mégantic-L'Érable
Prochaines élections: 5e novembre 2017
Jeannot Lachance, Maire
Suzanne Lescomb, Directrice générale

Saint-Roch-de-l'Achigan
7, rue du Dr.-Wilfrid-Locat
Saint-Roch-de-l'Achigan, QC J0K 3H0
Tél: 450-588-2326; *Téléc:* 450-588-4478
reception@saint-roch-de-lachigan.ca
www.saint-roch-de-lachigan.ca
Entité municipal: Parish (Paroisse)
Incorporation: 1er juillet 1855; *Area:* 78,83 km2
Comté ou district: Montcalm; *Population au 2011:* 4,892
Circonscription(s) électorale(s) provinciale(s): Rousseau
Circonscription(s) électorale(s) fédérale(s): Montcalm
Prochaines élections: 5e novembre 2017
Georges Locas, Maire
Philippe Riopelle, Directeur général

Saint-Roch-de-Mékinac
1212, rue Principale
Saint-Roch-de-Mékinac, QC G0X 2E0
Tél: 819-646-5635; *Téléc:* 819-646-5010
st-roch@regionmekinac.com
www.strochdemekinac.com
Entité municipal: Parish (Paroisse)
Incorporation: 2 novembre 2009; *Area:* 155,39 km2
Comté ou district: Mékinac; *Population au 2011:* 438
Circonscription(s) électorale(s) provinciale(s): Laviolette
Circonscription(s) électorale(s) fédérale(s): St-Maurice-Champlain
Prochaines élections: 5e novembre 2017
Guy Dessureault, Maire
Sylvie Genois, Directrice générale

Saint-Roch-de-Richelieu
1111, rue du Parc
Saint-Roch-de-Richelieu, QC J0L 2M0
Tél: 450-785-2755; *Téléc:* 450-785-3098
stroch@pierredesaurel.com
www.saintrochderichelieu.qc.ca
Entité municipal: Municipality
Incorporation: 4 juin 1859; *Area:* 34,86 km2
Comté ou district: Pierre-De Saurel; *Population au 2011:* 2,122
Circonscription(s) électorale(s) provinciale(s): Richelieu
Circonscription(s) électorale(s) fédérale(s): Bécancour-Nicolet-Saurel
Prochaines élections: 5e novembre 2017
Claude Pothier, Maire
Reynald Castonguay, Directeur général

Saint-Roch-des-Aulnaies
379, rte de l'Église
Saint-Roch-des-Aulnaies, QC G0R 4E0
Tél: 418-354-2892; *Téléc:* 418-354-2059
munirock@globetrotter.net
www.saintrochdesaulnaies.ca
Entité municipal: Parish (Paroisse)
Incorporation: 1er juillet 1855; *Area:* 48,28 km2
Comté ou district: L'Islet; *Population au 2011:* 967
Circonscription(s) électorale(s) provinciale(s): Côte-du-Sud
Circonscription(s) électorale(s) fédérale(s): Montmagny-L'Islet-Kamouraska-Rivière-du-Loup
Prochaines élections: 5e novembre 2017
Michel Castonguay, Maire
Cécile Morin, Directrice générale

Saint-Roch-Ouest
806, rang de la Rivière sud, RR#2
Saint-Roch-Ouest, QC J0K 3H0
Tél: 450-588-6060; *Téléc:* 450-588-0975
info@saint-roch-ouest.ca
www.saint-roch-ouest.ca
Entité municipal: Municipality
Incorporation: 4 juin 1921; *Area:* 20,90 km2
Comté ou district: Montcalm; *Population au 2011:* 267
Circonscription(s) électorale(s) provinciale(s): Rousseau
Circonscription(s) électorale(s) fédérale(s): Montcalm
Prochaines élections: 5e novembre 2017
Mario Racette, Maire
Sherron Kollar, Directrice générale

Saint-Romain
355, rue Principale
Saint-Romain, QC G0Y 1L0
Tél: 418-486-7374; *Téléc:* 418-486-7875
municipalite-st-romain@tellambton.net
www.st-romain.ca
Entité municipal: Municipality
Incorporation: 1er janvier 1858; *Area:* 112,92 km2
Comté ou district: Le Granit; *Population au 2011:* 707
Circonscription(s) électorale(s) provinciale(s): Mégantic
Circonscription(s) électorale(s) fédérale(s): Mégantic-L'Érable
Prochaines élections: 5e novembre 2017
Jean-Luc Filion, Maire
Nicole P. Roy, Directrice générale

Saint-Rosaire
208, 6e rang
Saint-Rosaire, QC G0Z 1K0
Tél: 819-752-6178; *Téléc:* 819-752-3959
info@municipalitestrosaire.qc.ca
www.municipalitestrosaire.qc.ca
Entité municipal: Parish (Paroisse)
Incorporation: 23 mai 1896; *Area:* 109,84 km2
Comté ou district: Arthabaska; *Population au 2011:* 838
Circonscription(s) électorale(s) provinciale(s): Arthabaska
Circonscription(s) électorale(s) fédérale(s): Richmond-Arthabaska
Prochaines élections: 5e novembre 2017
Harold Poisson, Maire
Céline Raymond, Directrice générale

Saint-Samuel
140, rue de l'Église
Saint-Samuel, QC G0Z 1G0
Tél: 819-353-1242; *Téléc:* 819-353-1499
info@saint-samuel.ca
www.saint-samuel.ca
Entité municipal: Parish (Paroisse)
Incorporation: 9 mars 1878; *Area:* 42,89 km2
Comté ou district: Arthabaska; *Population au 2011:* 743
Circonscription(s) électorale(s) provinciale(s): Drummond-Bois-Francs
Circonscription(s) électorale(s) fédérale(s): Richmond-Arthabaska
Prochaines élections: 5e novembre 2017
Denis Lampron, Maire
Suzie Constant, Directrice générale

Saints-Anges
494, av Principale
Saints-Anges, QC G0S 3E0
Tél: 418-253-5230; *Téléc:* 418-253-5613
munsts-anges@nouvellebeauce.com
www.nouvellebeauce.com
Entité municipal: Parish (Paroisse)
Incorporation: 29 décembre 1880; *Area:* 68,61 km2
Comté ou district: La Nouvelle-Beauce; *Population au 2011:* 1,149
Circonscription(s) électorale(s) provinciale(s): Beauce-Nord
Circonscription(s) électorale(s) fédérale(s): Beauce
Prochaines élections: 5e novembre 2017
Jean-Marie Pouliot, Maire
Louise Turmel, Directrice générale

Saint-Sauveur
1, place de la Mairie
Saint-Sauveur, QC J0R 1R6
Tél: 450-227-4633; *Téléc:* 450-227-3834
directiongenerale@ville.saint-sauveur.qc.ca
www.ville.saint-sauveur.qc.ca
Entité municipal: Town
Incorporation: 11 septembre 2002; *Area:* 47,99 km2
Comté ou district: Les Pays-d'en-Haut; *Population au 2011:* 9,881
Circonscription(s) électorale(s) provinciale(s): Bertrand
Circonscription(s) électorale(s) fédérale(s): Laurentides-Labelle
Prochaines élections: 5e novembre 2017
Note: Effective September 9, 2002, the Parish of St-Sauveur & the Village of St-Sauveur-des-Monts amalgamated to create the City of St-Sauveur.
Jacques Gariépy, Maire
Normand Patrice, Greffier

Saint-Sébastien
582, rue Principale
Saint-Sébastien, QC G0Y 1M0
Tél: 819-652-2727; *Téléc:* 819-652-2584
info@st-sebastien.com
www.st-sebastien.com
Entité municipal: Municipality
Incorporation: 15 mars 1975; *Area:* 91,19 km2
Comté ou district: Le Granit; *Population au 2011:* 697
Circonscription(s) électorale(s) provinciale(s): Mégantic
Circonscription(s) électorale(s) fédérale(s): Mégantic-L'Érable
Prochaines élections: 5e novembre 2017
France Bisson, Mairesse
Martine Rouleau, Directrice générale

Saint-Sébastien
CP 126
176, rue Dussault
Saint-Sébastien, QC J0J 2C0
Tél: 450-346-4205; *Téléc:* 450-346-4207
info@municipalite-saint-sebastien.ca
www.paroisse-saint-sebastien.ca
Entité municipal: Municipality
Incorporation: 17 février 1865; *Area:* 62,56 km2
Comté ou district: Le Haut-Richelieu; *Population au 2011:* 736
Circonscription(s) électorale(s) provinciale(s): Iberville
Circonscription(s) électorale(s) fédérale(s): Brome-Missisquoi
Prochaines élections: 5e novembre 2017
Martin Thibert, Maire
Manon Donais, Directrice générale

Saint-Sévère
59, rue Principale
Saint-Sévère, QC G0X 3B0
Tél: 819-264-5656; *Téléc:* 819-519-9800
www.st-severe.ca
Entité municipal: Parish (Paroisse)
Incorporation: 1er juillet 1855; *Area:* 31,83 km2
Comté ou district: Maskinongé; *Population au 2011:* 318
Circonscription(s) électorale(s) provinciale(s): Maskinongé
Circonscription(s) électorale(s) fédérale(s): Berthier-Maskinongé
Prochaines élections: 5e novembre 2017
Laurent Lavergne, Maire
Marie-Andrée Cadorette, Directeur général

Saint-Séverin
900, rue des Lacs
Saint-Séverin, QC G0N 1V0
Tél: 418-426-2423; *Téléc:* 418-426-1274
munseverin@novicomfusion.com
www.st-severin.qc.ca
Entité municipal: Parish (Paroisse)
Incorporation: 24 décembre 1875; *Area:* 56,22 km2
Comté ou district: Robert-Cliche; *Population au 2011:* 266

Circonscription(s) électorale(s) provinciale(s): Beauce-Nord
Circonscription(s) électorale(s) fédérale(s): Beauce
Prochaines élections: 5e novembre 2017
Jean-Paul Cloutier, Maire
Myriam Taschereau, Directeur général

Saint-Séverin
CP 120
1986, place du Centre
Saint-Séverin, QC G0X 2B0
Tél: 418-365-5844; *Téléc:* 418-365-7544
st-severin@regionmekinac.com
www.st-severin.ca
Entité municipal: Parish (Paroisse)
Incorporation: 11 avril 1890; *Area:* 61,97 km2
Comté ou district: Mékinac; *Population au 2011:* 860
Circonscription(s) électorale(s) provinciale(s): Laviolette
Circonscription(s) électorale(s) fédérale(s):
St-Maurice-Champlain
Prochaines élections: 5e novembre 2017
Julie Trepanier, Mairesse
Jocelyn St-Amant, Directeur général

Saint-Siméon
CP 98
502, rue St-Laurent
Saint-Siméon, QC G0T 1X0
Tél: 418-620-5010; *Téléc:* 418-620-5011
info@saintsimeon.ca
www.saintsimeon.ca
Entité municipal: Municipality
Incorporation: 25 avril 2001; *Area:* 289,73 km2
Comté ou district: Charlevoix-Est; *Population au 2011:* 1,300
Circonscription(s) électorale(s) provinciale(s):
Charlevoix-Côte-de-Beaupré
Circonscription(s) électorale(s) fédérale(s):
Beauport-Côte-de-Beaupré-Île d'Orléans-Charlevoix
Prochaines élections: 5e novembre 2017
Sylvain Tremblay, Maire
Sylvie Foster, Directrice générale

Saint-Siméon
CP 39
111, av de l'Église
Saint-Siméon, QC G0C 3A0
Tél: 418-534-2155; *Téléc:* 418-534-3830
munsseon@globetrotter.net
www.stsimeon.ca
Entité municipal: Parish (Paroisse)
Incorporation: 29 octobre 1914; *Area:* 56,12 km2
Comté ou district: Bonaventure; *Population au 2011:* 1,179
Circonscription(s) électorale(s) provinciale(s): Bonaventure
Circonscription(s) électorale(s) fédérale(s):
Gaspésie—Îles-de-la-Madeleine
Prochaines élections: 5e novembre 2017
Jean-Guy Poirier, Maire
Jean-Pierre Gauthier, Directeur général

Saint-Simon
CP 40
30, rue de l'Église
Saint-Simon, QC G0L 4C0
Tél: 418-738-2896; *Téléc:* 418-738-2934
admin@st-simon.qc.ca
www.st-simon.qc.ca
Entité municipal: Parish (Paroisse)
Incorporation: 1er juillet 1855; *Area:* 75,62 km2
Comté ou district: Les Basques; *Population au 2011:* 438
Circonscription(s) électorale(s) provinciale(s):
Rivière-du-Loup-Témiscouata
Circonscription(s) électorale(s) fédérale(s):
Rimouski-Neigette-Témiscouata-Les Basques
Prochaines élections: 5e novembre 2017
Wilfrid Lepage, Maire
Yolande Théberge, Directrice générale

Saint-Simon
49, rue du Couvent
Saint-Simon-de-Bagot, QC J0H 1Y0
Tél: 450-798-2276; *Téléc:* 450-798-2498
st-simon@mrcmaskoutains.qc.ca
www.saint-simon.ca
Entité municipal: Municipality
Incorporation: 1er juillet 1855; *Area:* 68,66 km2
Comté ou district: Les Maskoutains; *Population au 2011:* 1,231
Circonscription(s) électorale(s) provinciale(s): St-Hyacinthe
Circonscription(s) électorale(s) fédérale(s): St-Hyacinthe-Bagot
Prochaines élections: 5e novembre 2017
Normand Corbeil, Maire
France Desjardins, Directrice générale

Saint-Simon-les-Mines
3338, rue Principale
Saint-Simon-les-Mines, QC G0M 1K0
Tél: 418-774-3317; *Téléc:* 418-774-3362
municipalitestsimonlesmines@sogetel.net
www.stsimonlesmines.qc.ca
Entité municipal: Municipality
Incorporation: 1er juin 1950; *Area:* 44,80 km2
Comté ou district: Beauce-Sartigan; *Population au 2011:* 496
Circonscription(s) électorale(s) provinciale(s): Beauce-Sud
Circonscription(s) électorale(s) fédérale(s): Beauce
Prochaines élections: 5e novembre 2017
Christine Caron, Mairesse
Francine Poulin, Directrice générale

Saint-Sixte
19-B, rue Principale
Saint-Sixte, QC J0X 3B0
Tél: 819-983-3155; *Téléc:* 819-983-3409
Entité municipal: Municipality
Incorporation: 7 février 1893; *Area:* 83,44 km2
Comté ou district: Papineau; *Population au 2011:* 460
Circonscription(s) électorale(s) provinciale(s): Papineau
Circonscription(s) électorale(s) fédérale(s): Argenteuil-La Petite-Nation
Prochaines élections: 5e novembre 2017
André Bélisle, Maire
Michel Tardif, Directeur général

Saints-Martyrs-Canadiens
13, ch du Village
Saints-Martyrs-Canadiens, QC G0Y 1A1
Tél: 819-344-5171; *Téléc:* 819-344-2298
info@saints-martyrs-canadiens.ca
www.saints-martyrs-canadiens.ca
Entité municipal: Parish (Paroisse)
Incorporation: 1er janvier 1943; *Area:* 109,37 km2
Comté ou district: Arthabaska; *Population au 2011:* 227
Circonscription(s) électorale(s) provinciale(s):
Drummond-Bois-Francs
Circonscription(s) électorale(s) fédérale(s):
Richmond-Arthabaska
Prochaines élections: 5e novembre 2017
André Henri, Maire
Thérèse Lemay, Directrice générale

Saint-Stanislas
33, rue du Pont
Saint-Stanislas, QC G0X 3E0
Tél: 819-840-0703; *Téléc:* 418-328-4121
municipalite@saint-stanislas.ca
www.saint-stanislas.ca
Entité municipal: Municipality
Incorporation: 17 avril 1976; *Area:* 86,37 km2
Comté ou district: Les Chenaux; *Population au 2011:* 1,029
Circonscription(s) électorale(s) provinciale(s): Champlain
Circonscription(s) électorale(s) fédérale(s):
St-Maurice-Champlain
Prochaines élections: 5e novembre 2017
Alain Guillemette, Maire
Marie-Claude Jean, Directrice générale

Saint-Stanislas
953, rue Principale
Saint-Stanislas, QC G8L 7B4
Tél: 418-276-4476; *Téléc:* 418-276-4476
admin@st-stanislas.qc.ca
www.st-stanislas.com
Entité municipal: Municipality
Incorporation: 24 octobre 1931; *Area:* 159,45 km2
Comté ou district: Maria-Chapdelaine; *Population au 2011:* 353
Circonscription(s) électorale(s) provinciale(s): Roberval
Circonscription(s) électorale(s) fédérale(s): Lac-Saint-Jean
Prochaines élections: 5e novembre 2017
Mario Biron, Maire
Caroline Gagnon, Directrice générale

Saint-Stanislas-de-Kostka
CP 120
221, rue Centrale
Saint-Stanislas-de-Kostka, QC J0S 1W0
Tél: 450-373-8944; *Téléc:* 450-373-8949
info@st-stanislas-de-kostka.ca
www.st-stanislas-de-kostka.ca
Entité municipal: Municipality
Incorporation: 1er juillet 1855; *Area:* 62,16 km2
Comté ou district: Beauharnois-Salaberry; *Population au 2011:* 1,553
Circonscription(s) électorale(s) provinciale(s): Beauharnois
Circonscription(s) électorale(s) fédérale(s): Salaberry-Suroît
Prochaines élections: 5e novembre 2017
Caroline Huot, Mairesse

Louise Maheu Denis, Directrice générale

Saint-Sulpice
1089, rue Notre-Dame
Saint-Sulpice, QC J5W 1G1
Tél: 450-589-4450; *Téléc:* 450-589-9647
www.municipalitesaintsulpice.com
Entité municipal: Parish (Paroisse)
Incorporation: 1er juillet 1855; *Area:* 37 km2
Comté ou district: L'Assomption; Communauté métropolitaine de Montréal; *Population au 2011:* 3,273
Circonscription(s) électorale(s) provinciale(s): Repentigny
Circonscription(s) électorale(s) fédérale(s): Repentigny
Prochaines élections: 5e novembre 2017
Michel Champagne, Maire
Marie-Josée Masson, Directrice générale

Saint-Sylvère
837, 8e rang
Saint-Sylvère, QC G0Z 1H0
Tél: 819-285-2075; *Téléc:* 819-285-2040
mun.st.sylvere@infoteck.qc.ca
www.saint-sylvere.ca
Entité municipal: Municipality
Incorporation: 18 septembre 1976; *Area:* 85,02 km2
Comté ou district: Bécancour; *Population au 2011:* 865
Circonscription(s) électorale(s) provinciale(s): Nicolet-Bécancour
Circonscription(s) électorale(s) fédérale(s):
Bécancour-Nicolet-Saurel
Prochaines élections: 5e novembre 2017
Adrien Pellerin, Maire
Ginette Richard, Directrice générale

Saint-Sylvestre
CP 70
423B, rue Principale
Saint-Sylvestre, QC G0S 3C0
Tél: 418-596-2384; *Téléc:* 418-596-2375
munisylvestre@altanet.ca
www.ville.saint-sylvestre.qc.ca
Entité municipal: Municipality
Incorporation: 4 décembre 1996; *Area:* 143,34 km2
Comté ou district: Lotbinière; *Population au 2011:* 1,035
Circonscription(s) électorale(s) provinciale(s):
Lotbinière-Frontenac
Circonscription(s) électorale(s) fédérale(s): Lévis-Lotbinière
Prochaines élections: 5e novembre 2017
Mario Grenier, Maire
Ginette Roger, Directrice générale

Saint-Télesphore
1425, rte 340
Saint-Télesphore, QC J0P 1Y0
Tél: 450-269-2999; *Téléc:* 450-269-2257
st-telesphore@xittel.ca
www.saint-telesphore.com
Entité municipal: Municipality
Incorporation: 10 avril 1877; *Area:* 59,62 km2
Comté ou district: Vaudreuil-Soulanges; *Population au 2011:* 762
Circonscription(s) électorale(s) provinciale(s): Soulanges
Circonscription(s) électorale(s) fédérale(s): Salaberry-Suroît
Prochaines élections: 5e novembre 2017
Yvon Bériault, Maire
Nicole St-Pierre, Directrice générale

Saint-Tharcisius
CP 10
55, rue Principale
Saint-Tharcisius, QC G0J 3G0
Tél: 418-629-4727; *Téléc:* 418-629-4727
sttharcisius@mrcmatapedia.qc.ca
www.sainttharcisius.com
Entité municipal: Parish (Paroisse)
Incorporation: 4 décembre 2009; *Area:* 79,61 km2
Comté ou district: La Matapédia; *Population au 2011:* 464
Circonscription(s) électorale(s) provinciale(s): Matapédia
Circonscription(s) électorale(s) fédérale(s): Avignon-La Mitis-Matane-Matapédia
Prochaines élections: 5e novembre 2017
Jocelyn Jean, Maire
Joyce Kathie Collin, Directrice générale

Saint-Théodore-d'Acton
1661, rue Principale
Saint-Théodore-d-Acton, QC J0H 1Z0
Tél: 450-546-2634; *Téléc:* 450-546-2526
www.st-theodore.com
Entité municipal: Municipality
Incorporation: 1er janvier 1864; *Area:* 83,60 km2
Comté ou district: Acton; *Population au 2011:* 1,471
Circonscription(s) électorale(s) provinciale(s): Johnson

Circonscription(s) électorale(s) fédérale(s): St-Hyacinthe-Bagot
Prochaines élections: 5e novembre 2017
Guy Bond, Maire
Marc Lévesque, Directrice générale

Saint-Théophile
CP 10
644, rue du Collège
Saint-Théophile, QC G0M 2A0
Tél: 418-597-3998; *Téléc:* 418-597-3015
muntheo@globetrotter.net
www.sainttheophile.qc.ca
Entité municipal: Municipality
Incorporation: 28 juin 1975; *Area:* 429,58 km2
Comté ou district: Beauce-Sartigan; *Population au 2011:* 743
Circonscription(s) électorale(s) provinciale(s): Beauce-Sud
Circonscription(s) électorale(s) fédérale(s): Beauce
Prochaines élections: 5e novembre 2017
Gaston Létourneau, Maire
Paula Lacoursière, Directrice générale

Saint-Thomas
1240, rte 158
Saint-Thomas, QC J0K 3L0
Tél: 450-759-3405; *Téléc:* 450-759-0059
municipalite@saintthomas.qc.ca
www.saintthomas.qc.ca
Entité municipal: Municipality
Incorporation: 1er juillet 1855; *Area:* 97,26 km2
Comté ou district: Joliette; *Population au 2011:* 3,193
Circonscription(s) électorale(s) provinciale(s): Joliette
Circonscription(s) électorale(s) fédérale(s): Joliette
Prochaines élections: 5e novembre 2017
Marc Corriveau, Maire
Danielle Lambert, Directrice générale

Saint-Thomas-Didyme
9, av du Moulin
Saint-Thomas-Didyme, QC G0W 1P0
Tél: 418-274-3638; *Téléc:* 418-274-4176
www.stthomasdidyme.qc.ca
Entité municipal: Municipality
Incorporation: 11 mai 1923; *Area:* 325,36 km2
Comté ou district: Maria-Chapdelaine; *Population au 2011:* 677
Circonscription(s) électorale(s) provinciale(s): Roberval
Circonscription(s) électorale(s) fédérale(s): Lac-Saint-Jean
Prochaines élections: 5e novembre 2017
Denis Tremblay, Maire
Jean-Marc Paradis, Directeur général

Saint-Thuribe
CP 69
385, rue Principale
Saint-Thuribe, QC G0A 4H0
Tél: 418-339-2171; *Téléc:* 418-339-3435
municipalitestthuribe@globetrotter.net
www.st-thuribe.net
Entité municipal: Parish (Paroisse)
Incorporation: 14 février 1898; *Area:* 50,81 km2
Comté ou district: Portneuf; *Population au 2011:* 288
Circonscription(s) électorale(s) provinciale(s): Portneuf
Circonscription(s) électorale(s) fédérale(s):
Portneuf-Jacques-Cartier
Prochaines élections: 5e novembre 2017
Alain Fréchette, Maire
Lise Chalifour, Directrice générale

Saint-Tite
540, rue Notre-Dame
Saint-Tite, QC G0X 3H0
Tél: 418-365-5143; *Téléc:* 418-365-4020
hoteldeville@villest-tite.com
www.villest-tite.com
Entité municipal: Town
Incorporation: 23 décembre 1998; *Area:* 91,01 km2
Comté ou district: Mékinac; *Population au 2011:* 3,880
Circonscription(s) électorale(s) provinciale(s): Laviolette
Circonscription(s) électorale(s) fédérale(s):
St-Maurice-Champlain
Prochaines élections: 5e novembre 2017
André Léveillé, Maire
Alyne Trépanier, Directrice générale

Saint-Tite-des-Caps
1, rue Leclerc
Saint-Tite-des-Caps, QC G0A 4J0
Tél: 418-823-2239; *Téléc:* 418-823-2527
info@sainttitedescaps.com
www.sainttitedescaps.com
Entité municipal: Municipality
Incorporation: 24 décembre 1872; *Area:* 130,01 km2
Comté ou district: La Côte-de-Beaupré; Communauté métropolitaine de Québec; *Population au 2011:* 1,506
Circonscription(s) électorale(s) provinciale(s):
Charlevoix-Côte-de-Beaupré
Circonscription(s) électorale(s) fédérale(s):
Beauport-Côte-de-Beaupré-Ile d'Orléans-Charlevoix
Prochaines élections: 5e novembre 2017
Majella Pichette, Maire
Marc Lachance, Directeur général

Saint-Ubalde
427B, boul Chabot
Saint-Ubalde, QC G0A 4L0
Tél: 418-277-2124; *Téléc:* 418-277-2055
saintubalde.com
Entité municipal: Municipality
Incorporation: 3 mars 1973; *Area:* 141,28 km2
Comté ou district: Portneuf; *Population au 2011:* 1,403
Circonscription(s) électorale(s) provinciale(s): Portneuf
Circonscription(s) électorale(s) fédérale(s):
Portneuf-Jacques-Cartier
Prochaines élections: 5e novembre 2017
Pierre Saint-Germain, Maire
Serge Deraspe, Directeur général

Saint-Ulric
128, av Ulric-Tessier
Saint-Ulric, QC G0J 3H0
Tél: 418-737-4341; *Téléc:* 418-737-9242
st-ulric@lamatanie.ca
www.st-ulric.ca
Entité municipal: Municipality
Incorporation: 12 janvier 2000; *Area:* 118,68 km2
Comté ou district: La Matanie; *Population au 2011:* 1,642
Circonscription(s) électorale(s) provinciale(s): Matane-Matapédia
Circonscription(s) électorale(s) fédérale(s): Avignon-La Mitis-Matane-Matapédia
Prochaines élections: 5e novembre 2017
Pierre Thibodeau, Maire
Louise Coll, Directrice générale

Saint-Urbain
CP 100
917, rue St-Édouard
Saint-Urbain, QC G0A 4K0
Tél: 418-639-2467; *Téléc:* 418-639-1056
munsturb@sainturbain.qc.ca
www.sainturbain.qc.ca
Entité municipal: Parish (Paroisse)
Incorporation: 1er juillet 1855; *Area:* 327,68 km2
Comté ou district: Charlevoix; *Population au 2011:* 1,474
Circonscription(s) électorale(s) provinciale(s):
Charlevoix-Côte-de-Beaupré
Circonscription(s) électorale(s) fédérale(s):
Beauport-Côte-de-Beaupré-Ile d'Orléans-Charlevoix
Prochaines élections: 5e novembre 2017
Claudette Simard, Mairesse
Josée Desmeules, Directrice générale

Saint-Urbain-Premier
204, rue Principale
Saint-Urbain-Premier, QC J0S 1Y0
Tél: 450-427-3987; *Téléc:* 450-427-2056
sainturbainpremier@videotron.ca
www.saint-urbain-premier.com
Entité municipal: Municipality
Incorporation: 1er juillet 1855; *Area:* 52,24
Comté ou district: Beauharnois-Salaberry; *Population au 2011:* 1,148
Circonscription(s) électorale(s) provinciale(s): Huntingdon
Circonscription(s) électorale(s) fédérale(s): Châteauguay-Lacolle
Prochaines élections: 5e novembre 2017
Francine Daigle, Mairesse
Michael Morneau, Directeur général

Saint-Valentin
790, ch de la Quatrième-Ligne
Saint-Valentin, QC J0J 2E0
Tél: 450-291-5422; *Téléc:* 450-291-5327
administration@municipalite.saint-valentin.qc.ca
www.municipalite.saint-valentin.qc.ca
Entité municipal: Municipality
Incorporation: 1er juillet 1855; *Area:* 40,09 km2
Comté ou district: Le Haut-Richelieu; *Population au 2011:* 470
Circonscription(s) électorale(s) provinciale(s): Huntingdon
Circonscription(s) électorale(s) fédérale(s): Saint-Jean
Prochaines élections: 5e novembre 2017
Pierre Chamberland, Maire
Serge Gibeau, Directeur général

Saint-Valère
2, rue du Parc
Saint-Valère, QC G0P 1M0
Tél: 819-353-3450; *Téléc:* 819-353-3459
stvalere@msvalere.qc.ca
www.msvalere.qc.ca
Entité municipal: Municipality
Incorporation: 1er janvier 1862; *Area:* 108,13 km2
Comté ou district: Arthabaska; *Population au 2011:* 1,286
Circonscription(s) électorale(s) provinciale(s): Arthabaska
Circonscription(s) électorale(s) fédérale(s):
Richmond-Arthabaska
Prochaines élections: 5e novembre 2017
Louis Hébert, Maire
Jocelyn Jutras, Directeur général

Saint-Valérien
CP 9
181, rte Centrale
Saint-Valérien-de-Rimouski, QC G0L 4E0
Tél: 418-736-5047; *Téléc:* 418-736-5922
direction@municipalite.saint-valerien.qc.ca
municipalite.saint-valerien.qc.ca
Entité municipal: Parish (Paroisse)
Incorporation: 19 juin 1885; *Area:* 149,69 km2
Comté ou district: Rimouski-Neigette; *Population au 2011:* 893
Circonscription(s) électorale(s) provinciale(s): Rimouski
Circonscription(s) électorale(s) fédérale(s):
Rimouski-Neigette-Témiscouata-Les Basques
Prochaines élections: 5e novembre 2017
Robert Savoie, Maire
Marie-Paule Cimon, Directrice générale

Saint-Valérien-de-Milton
960, ch de Milton
Saint-Valérien-de-Milton, QC J0H 2B0
Tél: 450-549-2463; *Téléc:* 450-549-2993
administration.st-valerien@mrcmaskoutains.qc.ca
www.st-valerien-de-milton.qc.ca
Entité municipal: Municipality
Incorporation: 1er janvier 1864; *Area:* 106,44 km2
Comté ou district: Les Maskoutains; *Population au 2011:* 1,840
Circonscription(s) électorale(s) provinciale(s): Johnson
Circonscription(s) électorale(s) fédérale(s): St-Hyacinthe-Bagot
Prochaines élections: 5e novembre 2017
Raymonde Plamondon, Mairesse
Robert Leclerc, Directeur général

Saint-Vallier
375, montée de la Station
Saint-Vallier, QC G0R 4J0
Tél: 418-884-2559; *Téléc:* 418-884-2454
svallier@globetrotter.net
www.stvallierbellechasse.qc.ca
Entité municipal: Municipality
Incorporation: 10 mars 1993; *Area:* 42,24 km2
Comté ou district: Bellechasse; *Population au 2011:* 1,046
Circonscription(s) électorale(s) provinciale(s): Bellechasse
Circonscription(s) électorale(s) fédérale(s): Bellechasse-Les Etchemins-Lévis
Prochaines élections: 5e novembre 2017
Benoît Tanguay, Maire
Claire St-Laurent, Directrice générale

Saint-Venant-de-Paquette
5, ch du Village
Saint-Venant-de-Paquette, QC J0B 1S0
Tél: 819-658-3660; *Téléc:* 819-658-0985
stvenant@axion.ca
Entité municipal: Municipality
Incorporation: 11 juin 1917; *Area:* 58,17 km2
Comté ou district: Coaticook; *Population au 2011:* 104
Circonscription(s) électorale(s) provinciale(s): St-François
Circonscription(s) électorale(s) fédérale(s): Compton-Stanstead
Prochaines élections: 5e novembre 2017
Henri Pariseau, Maire
Manon Jacques, Directeur général

Saint-Vianney
CP 39
170, av Centrale
Saint-Vianney, QC G0J 3J0
Tél: 418-629-4082; *Téléc:* 418-629-4821
www.saint-vianney.net
Entité municipal: Municipality
Incorporation: 27 août 1926; *Area:* 145,24 km2
Comté ou district: La Matapédia; *Population au 2011:* 477
Circonscription(s) électorale(s) provinciale(s): Matane-Matapédia
Circonscription(s) électorale(s) fédérale(s): Avignon-La Mitis-Matane-Matapédia
Prochaines élections: 5e novembre 2017
Georges Guénard, Maire

Roselle Caron, Directrice générale

Saint-Victor
CP 40
287, rue Marchand
Saint-Victor, QC G0M 2B0
Tél: 418-588-6854; *Téléc:* 418-588-6855
www.st-victor.qc.ca
Entité municipal: Municipality
Incorporation: 31 décembre 1996; *Area:* 120,94 km2
Comté ou district: Robert-Cliche; *Population au 2011:* 2,451
Circonscription(s) électorale(s) provinciale(s): Beauce-Nord
Circonscription(s) électorale(s) fédérale(s): Beauce
Prochaines élections: 5e novembre 2017
Jonathan V. Bolduc, Maire
Marc Bélanger, Directeur général

Saint-Wenceslas
1065, rue Richard
Saint-Wenceslas, QC G0Z 1J0
Tél: 819-224-7784; *Téléc:* 819-224-4036
mun.stwen@sogetel.net
www.municipalitestwenceslas.com
Entité municipal: Municipality
Incorporation: 11 octobre 1995; *Area:* 78,42 km2
Comté ou district: Nicolet-Yamaska; *Population au 2011:* 1,064
Circonscription(s) électorale(s) provinciale(s): Nicolet-Bécancour
Circonscription(s) électorale(s) fédérale(s):
Bécancour-Nicolet-Saurel
Prochaines élections: 5e novembre 2017
Réal Deschênes, Maire
Carole Hélie, Directrice générale

Saint-Zacharie
735, 15e rue
Saint-Zacharie, QC G0M 2C0
Tél: 418-593-3185; *Téléc:* 418-593-3085
munzac@cablezach.com
www.st-zacharie.qc.ca
Entité municipal: Municipality
Incorporation: 18 avril 1990; *Area:* 189,70 km2
Comté ou district: Les Etchemins; *Population au 2011:* 1,751
Circonscription(s) électorale(s) provinciale(s): Beauce-Sud
Circonscription(s) électorale(s) fédérale(s): Beauce
Prochaines élections: 5e novembre 2017
Jean Paradis, Maire
Brigitte Larivière, Dirctrice générale

Saint-Zénon
6101, rue Principale
Saint-Zénon, QC J0K 3N0
Tél: 450-884-5987; *Téléc:* 450-884-5285
municipalite@st-zenon.net
www.st-zenon.org
Entité municipal: Municipality
Incorporation: 7 octobre 1895; *Area:* 488,69 km2
Comté ou district: Matawinie; *Population au 2011:* 1,115
Circonscription(s) électorale(s) provinciale(s): Berthier
Circonscription(s) électorale(s) fédérale(s): Joliette
Prochaines élections: 5e novembre 2017
Richard Rondeau, Maire
Julie Martin, Directrice générale

Saint-Zénon-du-Lac-Humqui
CP 39
156, rte 195
Lac-Humqui, QC G0J 1N0
Tél: 418-743-2177; *Téléc:* 418-743-2177
info@lachumqui.com
www.lachumqui.com
Entité municipal: Parish (Paroisse)
Incorporation: 28 avril 1920; *Area:* 112,97 km2
Comté ou district: La Matapédia; *Population au 2011:* 366
Circonscription(s) électorale(s) provinciale(s): Matane-Matapédia
Circonscription(s) électorale(s) fédérale(s): Avignon-La
Mitis-Matane-Matapédia
Prochaines élections: 5e novembre 2017
Réginald Duguay, Maire
Maryline Pronovost, Directrice générale

Saint-Zéphirin-de-Courval
CP 40
1471, rue St-Pierre
Saint-Zéphirin-de-Courval, QC J0G 1V0
Tél: 450-564-2188; *Téléc:* 450-564-2339
municipalite@saint-zephirin.ca
www.saint-zephirin.ca
Entité municipal: Parish (Paroisse)
Incorporation: 1er juillet 1855; *Area:* 71,01 km2
Comté ou district: Nicolet-Yamaska; *Population au 2011:* 737
Circonscription(s) électorale(s) provinciale(s): Nicolet-Bécancour
Circonscription(s) électorale(s) fédérale(s): Avignon-La
Mitis-Matane-Matapédia
Prochaines élections: 5e novembre 2017
Mathieu Lemire, Maire
Hélène Chassé, Directrice générale

Saint-Zotique
1250, rue Principale
Saint-Zotique, QC J0P 1Z0
Tél: 450-267-9335; *Téléc:* 450-267-0907
www.st-zotique.com
Entité municipal: Municipality
Incorporation: 27 mai 1967; *Area:* 24,24 km2
Comté ou district: Vaudreuil-Soulanges; *Population au 2011:* 6,773
Circonscription(s) électorale(s) provinciale(s): Soulanges
Circonscription(s) électorale(s) fédérale(s): Salaberry-Suroît
Prochaines élections: 5e novembre 2017
Yvon Chiasson, Maire
Jean-François Messier, Directeur général

Salluit
CP 240
74, rue Aqqutituqaq
Salluit, QC J0M 1S0
Tél: 819-255-8953; *Téléc:* 819-255-8802
www.nvsalluit.ca
Entité municipal: Northern Village
Incorporation: 29 décembre 1979; *Area:* 14,33 km2
Comté ou district: Administration régionale Kativik; *Population au 2011:* 1,347
Circonscription(s) électorale(s) provinciale(s): Ungava
Circonscription(s) électorale(s) fédérale(s):
Abitibi-Baie-James-Nunavik-Eeyou
Paulusie Saviadjuk, Maire
Susie P. Alaku, Secrétaire-trésorière

La Sarre
6, 4e av est
La Sarre, QC J9Z 1J9
Tél: 819-333-2282; *Téléc:* 819-333-3090
info@ville.lasarre.qc.ca
www.ville.lasarre.qc.ca
Entité municipal: Town
Incorporation: 19 avril 1980; *Area:* 148,21 km2
Comté ou district: Abitibi-Ouest; *Population au 2011:* 7,719
Circonscription(s) électorale(s) provinciale(s): Abitibi-Ouest
Circonscription(s) électorale(s) fédérale(s):
Abitibi-Témiscamingue
Prochaines élections: 5e novembre 2017
Normand Houde, Maire
François Casaubon, Greffier

Sayabec
3, rue Keable
Sayabec, QC G0J 3K0
Tél: 418-536-5440; *Téléc:* 418-536-5572
sayabec@mrcmatapedia.qc.ca
www.municipalitesayabec.com
Entité municipal: Municipality
Incorporation: 24 décembre 1982; *Area:* 130,29 km2
Comté ou district: La Matapédia; *Population au 2011:* 1,864
Circonscription(s) électorale(s) provinciale(s): Matane-Matapédia
Circonscription(s) électorale(s) fédérale(s): Avignon-La
Mitis-Matane-Matapédia
Prochaines élections: 5e novembre 2017
Danielle Marcoux, Mairesse
Francis Ouellet, Directeur général

Schefferville
505, rue Fleming
Schefferville, QC G0G 2T0
Tél: 418-585-2471; *Téléc:* 418-585-2256
municipalite_schefferville@xplornet.ca
www.ville-schefferville.ca
Entité municipal: Village
Incorporation: 1er août 1955; *Area:* 39,02 km2
Comté ou district: Caniapiscau; *Population au 2011:* 213
Circonscription(s) électorale(s) provinciale(s): Duplessis
Circonscription(s) électorale(s) fédérale(s): Manicouagan
Prochaines élections: 5e novembre 2017
Paul Joncas, Administrateur

Scotstown
101, ch Victoria ouest
Scotstown, QC J0B 3B0
Tél: 819-560-8433; *Téléc:* 819-560-8434
ville.scotstown@hsfgc.ca
www.scotstown-hsf.com
Entité municipal: Village
Incorporation: 24 juin 1892; *Area:* 12,40 km2
Comté ou district: Le Haut-Saint-François; *Population au 2011:* 547
Circonscription(s) électorale(s) provinciale(s): Mégantic
Circonscription(s) électorale(s) fédérale(s): Compton-Stanstead
Prochaines élections: 5e novembre 2017
Chantal Ouellet, Mairesse
Monique Polard, Directrice générale

Scott
1070, rte du Président-Kennedy
Scott, QC G0S 3G0
Tél: 418-387-2037; *Téléc:* 418-387-1837
info@municipalitescott.com
www.municipalitescott.com
Entité municipal: Municipality
Incorporation: 29 mars 1995; *Area:* 32,91 km2
Comté ou district: La Nouvelle-Beauce; *Population au 2011:* 2,089
Circonscription(s) électorale(s) provinciale(s): Beauce-Nord
Circonscription(s) électorale(s) fédérale(s): Beauce
Prochaines élections: 5e novembre 2017
Clément Marcoux, Maire
Nicole Thibodeau, Directrice générale

Senneterre
CP 700
100, rue le Portage
Senneterre, QC J0Y 2M0
Tél: 819-737-2842; *Téléc:* 819-737-4668
info@paroissesenneterre.qc.ca
www.paroissesenneterre.qc.ca
Entité municipal: Parish (Paroisse)
Incorporation: 23 mars 1923; *Area:* 432,98 km2
Comté ou district: La Vallée-de-l'Or; *Population au 2011:* 1,218
Circonscription(s) électorale(s) provinciale(s): Abitibi-Est
Circonscription(s) électorale(s) fédérale(s):
Abitibi-Baie-James-Nunavik-Eeyou
Prochaines élections: 5e novembre 2017
Jacline Rouleau, Mairesse
Louise Leroux, Directrice générale

Senneterre
CP 789
551, 10e av
Senneterre, QC J0Y 2M0
Tél: 819-737-2296; *Téléc:* 819-737-4215
info@ville.senneterre.qc.ca
www.ville.senneterre.qc.ca
Entité municipal: Town
Incorporation: 13 juin 1919; *Area:* 16 524,89 km2
Comté ou district: La Vallée-de-l'Or; *Population au 2011:* 2,953
Circonscription(s) électorale(s) provinciale(s): Abitibi-Est
Circonscription(s) électorale(s) fédérale(s):
Abitibi-Baie-James-Nunavik-Eeyou
Prochaines élections: 5e novembre 2017
Jean-Maurice Matte, Maire
Hélène Veillette, Greffière

Senneville
35, ch de Senneville
Senneville, QC H9X 1B8
Tél: 514-457-6020; *Téléc:* 514-457-0447
info@villagesenneville.qc.ca
www.villagesenneville.qc.ca
Entité municipal: Town
Incorporation: 1er janvier 2006; *Area:* 7,49 km2
Comté ou district: Communauté métropolitaine de Montréal;
Population au 2011: 920
Circonscription(s) électorale(s) provinciale(s): Jacques-Cartier
Circonscription(s) électorale(s) fédérale(s): Lac-Saint-Louis
Prochaines élections: 5e novembre 2017
Jane Guest, Mairesse
Joanne Bouclin, Greffière

Sept-Rivières
#400, 106, rue Napoléon
Sept-Îles, QC G4R 3L7
Tél: 418-962-1900; *Téléc:* 418-962-3365
info@mrc.septrivieres.qc.ca
www.mrc.septrivieres.qc.ca
Entité municipal: Regional County Municipality
Incorporation: 18 mars 1981; *Area:* 32 153,95 km2
Population au 2011: 39,500
Note: 2 municipalités & 2 autres territoires.
Violaine Doyle, Préfète
Alain Lapierre, Directeur général

Shannon
50, rue St-Patrick
Shannon, QC G0A 4N0
Tél: 418-844-3778; *Téléc:* 418-844-2111
municipalite@shannon.ca
www.shannon.ca

Entité municipal: Municipality
Incorporation: 1er janvier 1947; *Area:* 61,79 km2
Comté ou district: La Jacques-Cartier; Communauté métropolitaine de Québec; *Population au 2011:* 5,086
Circonscription(s) électorale(s) provinciale(s): La Peltrie
Circonscription(s) électorale(s) fédérale(s): Portneuf-Jacques-Cartier
Prochaines élections: 5e novembre 2017
Clive Kiley, Maire
Me Hugo Lépine, Directeur général

Shawville
CP 339
350, rue Main
Shawville, QC J0X 2Y0
Tél: 819-647-2979; *Téléc:* 819-647-6895
info@town.shawville.qc.ca
www.town.shawville.qc.ca
Entité municipal: Municipality
Incorporation: 1er janvier 1874; *Area:* 5,25 km2
Comté ou district: Pontiac; *Population au 2011:* 1,664
Circonscription(s) électorale(s) provinciale(s): Pontiac
Circonscription(s) électorale(s) fédérale(s): Pontiac
Prochaines élections: 5e novembre 2017
Sandra A. Murray, Mairesse
Crystal Webb, Directrice générale

Sheenboro
59, ch de Sheenboro
Sheenboro, QC J0X 2Z0
Tél: 819-683-3027; *Téléc:* 819-683-1815
sheenboro.municipalite@yahoo.ca
www.sheenboro.ca
Entité municipal: Municipality
Incorporation: 1er janvier 1860; *Area:* 571,01 km2
Comté ou district: Pontiac; *Population au 2011:* 130
Circonscription(s) électorale(s) provinciale(s): Pontiac
Circonscription(s) électorale(s) fédérale(s): Pontiac
Prochaines élections: 5e novembre 2017
Doris Ranger, Mairesse
Fernand Roy, Directeur général

Shefford
245, ch Picard
Shefford, QC J2M 1J2
Tél: 450-539-2258; *Téléc:* 450-539-4951
info@cantonshefford.qc.ca
www.cantonshefford.qc.ca
Entité municipal: Township
Incorporation: 1er juillet 1855; *Area:* 116,62 km2
Comté ou district: La Haute-Yamaska; *Population au 2011:* 6,711
Circonscription(s) électorale(s) provinciale(s): Brome-Missisquoi
Circonscription(s) électorale(s) fédérale(s): Shefford
Prochaines élections: 5e novembre 2017
André Pontbriand, Maire
Sylvie Gougeon, Directrice générale

Shigawake
180, rte 132
Shigawake, QC G0C 3E0
Tél: 418-752-2474; *Téléc:* 418-752-7474
shigawake@navigue.com
www.municipalityshigawake.com
Entité municipal: Municipality
Incorporation: 15 décembre 1924; *Area:* 77,36 km2
Comté ou district: Bonaventure; *Population au 2011:* 338
Circonscription(s) électorale(s) provinciale(s): Bonaventure
Circonscription(s) électorale(s) fédérale(s): Gaspésie—Îles-de-la-Madeleine
Prochaines élections: 5e novembre 2017
Denzil Ross, Maire
Joann Ross, Directrice général

Les Sources
309, rue Chassé
Asbestos, QC J1T 2B4
Tél: 819-879-6661; *Téléc:* 819-879-5188
mrcdessources@mrcdessources.com
www.mrcdessources.com
Entité municipal: Regional County Municipality
Incorporation: 1er janvier 1982
Population au 2011: 14,756
Note: 7 municipalités.
Hughes Grimard, Préfet
Rachid El Idrissi, Directeur général

Stanbridge East
12, rue Maple
Stanbridge East, QC J0J 2H0
Tél: 450-248-3188; *Téléc:* 450-248-7744
stanbridge@axion.ca
www.stanbridgeeast.ca
Entité municipal: Municipality
Incorporation: 1er juillet 1855; *Area:* 49,05 km2
Comté ou district: Brome-Missisquoi; *Population au 2011:* 873
Circonscription(s) électorale(s) provinciale(s): Brome-Missisquoi
Circonscription(s) électorale(s) fédérale(s): Brome-Missisquoi
Prochaines élections: 5e novembre 2017
Gregory Vaughan, Maire
Nicole Blinn, Directrice générale

Stanbridge Station
229, ch Principal
Stanbridge Station, QC J0J 2J0
Tél: 450-248-2125; *Téléc:* 450-248-1132
munistanbridge-station@bellnet.ca
www.stanbridge-station.ca
Entité municipal: Municipality
Incorporation: 21 mars 1889; *Area:* 18,11 km2
Comté ou district: Brome-Missisquoi; *Population au 2011:* 276
Circonscription(s) électorale(s) provinciale(s): Brome-Missisquoi
Circonscription(s) électorale(s) fédérale(s): Brome-Missisquoi
Prochaines élections: 5e novembre 2017
Gilles Rioux, Maire
Carole Pigeon, Directrice générale

Stanstead
425, rue Dufferin
Stanstead, QC J0B 3E2
Tél: 819-876-7181; *Téléc:* 819-876-5560
info@stanstead.ca
www.stanstead.ca
Entité municipal: Town
Incorporation: 15 février 1995; *Area:* 21,93 km2
Comté ou district: Memphrémagog; *Population au 2011:* 2,857
Circonscription(s) électorale(s) provinciale(s): Orford
Circonscription(s) électorale(s) fédérale(s): Compton-Stanstead
Prochaines élections: 5e novembre 2017
Philippe Dutil, Maire
Caroline Gaulin, Greffière

Stanstead
778, ch Sheldon
Stanstead, QC J1X 3W4
Tél: 819-876-2948; *Téléc:* 819-876-7007
info@cantonstanstead.ca
www.cantonstanstead.ca
Entité municipal: Township
Incorporation: 1er juillet 1855; *Area:* 113,93 km2
Comté ou district: Memphrémagog; *Population au 2011:* 1,038
Circonscription(s) électorale(s) provinciale(s): Orford
Circonscription(s) électorale(s) fédérale(s): Compton-Stanstead
Prochaines élections: 5e novembre 2017
Francine Caron Markwell, Mairesse
Josiane Hudon, Directrice générale

Stanstead-Est
7015, route 143
Stanstead-Est, QC J0B 3E0
Tél: 819-876-7292; *Téléc:* 819-876-7170
stansteadest@xittel.ca
Entité municipal: Municipality
Incorporation: 16 juillet 1932; *Area:* 111,70 km2
Comté ou district: Coaticook; *Population au 2011:* 603
Circonscription(s) électorale(s) provinciale(s): St-François
Circonscription(s) électorale(s) fédérale(s): Compton-Stanstead
Prochaines élections: 5e novembre 2017
Gilbert Ferland, Maire
Claudine Tremblay, Directrice générale

Stoke
403, rue Principale
Stoke, QC J0B 3G0
Tél: 819-878-3790; *Téléc:* 819-878-3804
www.stoke.ca
Entité municipal: Municipality
Incorporation: 1er janvier 1864; *Area:* 239,89 km2
Comté ou district: Le Val-Saint-François; *Population au 2011:* 2,765
Circonscription(s) électorale(s) provinciale(s): Mégantic
Circonscription(s) électorale(s) fédérale(s): Compton-Stanstead
Prochaines élections: 5e novembre 2017
Luc Cayer, Maire
Julie Plamondon, Directrice générale

Stoneham-et-Tewkesbury
325, ch du Hibou
Stoneham-et-Tewkesbury, QC G3C 1R8
Tél: 418-848-2381; *Téléc:* 418-848-1748
mairie@villestoneham.com
www.villestoneham.com
Entité municipal: United Township (Cantons)
Incorporation: 1er juillet 1855; *Area:* 684,75 km2
Comté ou district: La Jacques-Cartier; Communauté métropolitaine de Québec; *Population au 2011:* 7,106
Circonscription(s) électorale(s) provinciale(s): Chauveau
Circonscription(s) électorale(s) fédérale(s): Portneuf-Jacques-Cartier
Prochaines élections: 5e novembre 2017
Robert Miller, Maire
Lisa Kennedy, Directeur général

Stornoway
CP 98
507, rte 108 ouest
Stornoway, QC G0Y 1N0
Tél: 819-652-2800; *Téléc:* 819-652-2105
administration@munstornoway.qc.ca
www.munstornoway.qc.ca
Entité municipal: Municipality
Incorporation: 1er janvier 1858; *Area:* 178,32 km2
Comté ou district: Le Granit; *Population au 2011:* 559
Circonscription(s) électorale(s) provinciale(s): Mégantic
Circonscription(s) électorale(s) fédérale(s): Mégantic-L'Érable
Prochaines élections: 5e novembre 2017
Mario Lachance, Maire
Simone Grenier, Directrice générale

Stratford
165, av Centrale nord
Stratford, QC G0Y 1P0
Tél: 418-443-2307; *Téléc:* 418-443-2603
mun.stratford@ccdstratford.com
www.munstratford.qc.ca
Entité municipal: Township
Incorporation: 1er janvier 1874; *Area:* 125,61 km2
Comté ou district: Le Granit; *Population au 2011:* 1,062
Circonscription(s) électorale(s) provinciale(s): Mégantic
Circonscription(s) électorale(s) fédérale(s): Mégantic-L'Érable
Prochaines élections: 5e novembre 2017
André Gamache, Maire
Manon Goulet, Directrice générale

Stukely-Sud
101, place de la Mairie
Stukely-Sud, QC J0E 2J0
Tél: 450-297-3407; *Téléc:* 450-297-3759
info@stukely-sud.com
www.stukely-sud.com
Entité municipal: Village
Incorporation: 19 septembre 1934; *Area:* 66,31 km2
Comté ou district: Memphrémagog; *Population au 2011:* 999
Circonscription(s) électorale(s) provinciale(s): Orford
Circonscription(s) électorale(s) fédérale(s): Brome-Missisquoi
Prochaines élections: 5e novembre 2017
Gérald Allaire, Maire
Louisette Tremblay, Directrice générale

Sutton
11, rue Principale sud
Sutton, QC J0E 2K0
Tél: 450-538-2290; *Téléc:* 450-538-0930
ville@sutton.ca
www.sutton.ca
Entité municipal: Town
Incorporation: 4 juillet 2002; *Area:* 243,51 km2
Comté ou district: Brome-Missisquoi; *Population au 2011:* 3,906
Circonscription(s) électorale(s) provinciale(s): Brome-Missisquoi
Circonscription(s) électorale(s) fédérale(s): Brome-Missisquoi
Prochaines élections: 5e novembre 2017
Louis Dandenault, Maire
Jean-François D'Amour, Directeur général

Tadoussac
162, rue des Jésuites
Tadoussac, QC G0T 2A0
Tél: 418-235-4446; *Téléc:* 418-235-4433
ville@tadoussac.com
www.tadoussac.com
Entité municipal: Village
Incorporation: 10 octobre 1899; *Area:* 74,59 km2
Comté ou district: La Haute-Côte-Nord; *Population au 2011:* 813
Circonscription(s) électorale(s) provinciale(s): René-Lévesque
Circonscription(s) électorale(s) fédérale(s): Manicouagan
Prochaines élections: 5e novembre 2017
Hugues Tremblay, Maire
Marie-Claude Guérin, Directrice générale

Taschereau
CP 150
52, rue Morin
Taschereau, QC J0Z 3N0
Tél: 819-796-2219; *Téléc:* 819-796-2220
taschereau@mrcao.qc.ca
www.taschereau.ao.ca

Entité municipal: Municipality
Incorporation: 27 décembre 2001; *Area:* 265,62 km2
Comté ou district: Abitibi-Ouest; *Population au 2011:* 986
Circonscription(s) électorale(s) provinciale(s): Abitibi-Ouest
Circonscription(s) électorale(s) fédérale(s):
Abitibi-Témiscamingue
Prochaines élections: 5e novembre 2017
Manon Luneau, Maire
Yves Aubut, Directeur général

Tasiujaq
CP 54
Tasiujaq, QC J0M 1T0
Tél: 819-633-9924; *Téléc:* 819-633-5026
www.nvtasiujaq.ca
Entité municipal: Northern Village
Incorporation: 2 février 1980; *Area:* 68,08 km2
Comté ou district: Administration régionale Kativik; *Population au 2011:* 303
Circonscription(s) électorale(s) provinciale(s): Ungava
Circonscription(s) électorale(s) fédérale(s):
Abitibi-Baie-James-Nunavik-Eeyou
Billy Cain, Maire
Chelsey Mesher, Secrétaire-trésorière

Témiscaming
CP 730
20, rue Humphrey
Témiscaming, QC J0Z 3R0
Tél: 819-627-3273; *Téléc:* 819-627-3019
ville.temiscaming@temiscaming.net
www.temiscaming.net
Entité municipal: Town
Incorporation: 26 mars 1988; *Area:* 861,77 km2
Comté ou district: Témiscamingue; *Population au 2011:* 2,385
Circonscription(s) électorale(s) provinciale(s):
Rouyn-Noranda-Témiscamingue
Circonscription(s) électorale(s) fédérale(s):
Abitibi-Témiscamingue
Prochaines élections: 5e novembre 2017
Nicole Rochon, Maire
Maurice Paquin, Directeur général

Témiscamingue
#209, 21, rue Notre-Dame-de-Lourdes
Ville-Marie, QC J9V 1X8
Tél: 819-629-2829; *Téléc:* 819-629-3472
mrc@mrctemiscamingue.qc.ca
www.temiscamingue.net
Other Information: Sans frais: 1-855-622-6728
Entité municipal: Regional County Municipality
Incorporation: 15 avril 1981; *Area:* 19 243,88 km2
Population au 2011: 16,425
Note: 20 municipalités & 2 autres territoires.
Arnaud Warolin, Préfet
Lyne Gironne, Directrice générale

Témiscouata
#101, 5, rue de l'Hôtel de Ville
Notre-Dame-du-Lac, QC G0L 1X0
Tél: 418-899-6725; *Téléc:* 418-899-2000
admin@mrctemis.ca
www.mrctemiscouata.qc.ca
Other Information: Sans frais: 1-877-303-6725
Entité municipal: Regional County Municipality
Incorporation: 1 janvier 1982; *Area:* 3 920,90 km2
Population au 2011: 20,572
Note: 19 municipalités.
Guylaine Sirois, Préfète
Jacky Ouellet, Directeur général

Témiscouata-sur-le-Lac
861, rue Commerciale nord
Témiscouata-sur-le-Lac, QC G0L 1E0
Tél: 418-854-2116; *Téléc:* 418-854-0118
info@temiscouatasurlelac.ca
temiscouatasurlelac.ca
Entité municipal: Town
Incorporation: 5e mai 2010; *Area:* 227,91 km2
Comté ou district: Témiscouata; *Population au 2011:* 5,096
Circonscription(s) électorale(s) provinciale(s):
Rivière-du-Loup-Témiscouata
Circonscription(s) électorale(s) fédérale(s):
Rimouski-Neigette—Témiscouata—Les Basques
Prochaines élections: 5e novembre 2017
Note: Le 5e mai 2010, les villes de Cabano et Notre-Dame-du-Lac ont été amalgamé sous le nom de Témiscouata-sur-le-Lac.
Gilles Garon, Maire
Chantal-Karen Caron, Directeur général

Terrasse-Vaudreuil
74, 7e av
Terrasse-Vaudreuil, QC J7V 3M9
Tél: 514-453-8120; *Téléc:* 514-453-1180
info@terrasse-vaudreuil.ca
www.terrasse-vaudreuil.ca
Entité municipal: Municipality
Incorporation: 1er janvier 1952; *Area:* 1,08 km2
Comté ou district: Vaudreuil-Soulanges; Communauté métropolitaine de Montréal; *Population au 2011:* 1,971
Circonscription(s) électorale(s) provinciale(s): Vaudreuil
Circonscription(s) électorale(s) fédérale(s): Vaudreuil-Soulanges
Prochaines élections: 5e novembre 2017
Michel Bourdeau, Jr., Maire
Ronald Kelley, Directeur général

Thérèse-de-Blainville
479, boul Adolphe-Chapleau
Bois-des-Filion, QC J6Z 1J9
Tél: 450-621-5546; *Téléc:* 450-621-2628
reception@mrc-tdb.org
www.mrctheresedeblainville.qc.ca
Entité municipal: Regional County Municipality
Incorporation: 26 mai 1982
Population au 2011: 154,144
Note: 7 municipalités.
Paul Larocque, Préfet
Kamal El-Batal, Directeur général

Thorne
775, rte 366
Ladysmith, QC J0X 2A0
Tél: 819-647-3206; *Téléc:* 819-647-2086
thorne@mrcpontiac.qc.ca
www.thornequebec.ca
Entité municipal: Municipality
Incorporation: 1er janvier 1860; *Area:* 177,33 km2
Comté ou district: Pontiac; *Population au 2011:* 292
Circonscription(s) électorale(s) provinciale(s): Pontiac
Circonscription(s) électorale(s) fédérale(s): Pontiac
Prochaines élections: 5e novembre 2017
Terence Murdock, Maire
Stacy Lafleur, Directrice générale

Thurso
161, rue Galipeau
Thurso, QC J0X 3B0
Tél: 819-985-2000; *Téléc:* 819-985-0134
ville.thurso@mrcpapineau.com
www.ville.thurso.qc.ca
Entité municipal: Town
Incorporation: 16 janvier 1886; *Area:* 6,77 km2
Comté ou district: Papineau; *Population au 2011:* 2,455
Circonscription(s) électorale(s) provinciale(s): Papineau
Circonscription(s) électorale(s) fédérale(s): Argenteuil-La Petite-Nation
Prochaines élections: 5e novembre 2017
Benoit Lauzon, Maire
Mario Boyer, Greffier et directeur général

Tingwick
CP 150
12, rue de l'Hôtel-de-Ville
Tingwick, QC J0A 1L0
Tél: 819-359-2454; *Téléc:* 819-359-2233
www.tingwick.ca
Entité municipal: Municipality
Incorporation: 12 décembre 1981; *Area:* 168,93 km2
Comté ou district: Arthabaska; *Population au 2011:* 1,395
Circonscription(s) électorale(s) provinciale(s):
Drummond-Bois-Francs
Circonscription(s) électorale(s) fédérale(s):
Richmond-Arthabaska
Prochaines élections: 5e novembre 2017
Réal Fortin, Maire
Chantale Ramsay, Directrice générale

Tourville
#100, 962, rue des Trembles
Tourville, QC G0R 4M0
Tél: 418-359-2106; *Téléc:* 418-359-3671
municipal.tourville@globetrotter.net
www.muntourville.qc.ca
Entité municipal: Municipality
Incorporation: 14 novembre 1918; *Area:* 161,51 km2
Comté ou district: L'Islet; *Population au 2011:* 633
Circonscription(s) électorale(s) provinciale(s): Côte-du-Sud
Circonscription(s) électorale(s) fédérale(s):
Montmagny-L'Islet-Kamouraska-Rivière-du-Loup
Prochaines élections: 5e novembre 2017
Benoit Dubé, Maire
Normand Blier, Directeur général

Trécesson
314, rue Sauvé
Trécesson, QC J0Y 2S0
Tél: 819-732-8524; *Téléc:* 819-732-8322
mun.trecesson@cableamos.com
www.trecesson.ca
Entité municipal: Township
Incorporation: 15 juillet 1918; *Area:* 198,38 km2
Comté ou district: Abitibi; *Population au 2011:* 1,138
Circonscription(s) électorale(s) provinciale(s): Abitibi-Ouest
Circonscription(s) électorale(s) fédérale(s):
Abitibi-Témiscamingue
Prochaines élections: 5e novembre 2017
Anita Bédard-Larochelle, Maire
Katy Fortier, Directrice générale

Très-Saint-Rédempteur
769, rte Principale
Très-Saint-Rédempteur, QC J0P 1P0
Tél: 450-451-5203; *Téléc:* 450-451-8894
mun.tsr@tressaintredempteur.ca
www.tressaintredempteur.ca
Entité municipal: Municipality
Incorporation: 30 décembre 1880; *Area:* 25,40 km2
Comté ou district: Vaudreuil-Soulanges; *Population au 2011:* 863
Circonscription(s) électorale(s) provinciale(s): Soulanges
Circonscription(s) électorale(s) fédérale(s): Salaberry-Suroît
Prochaines élections: 5e novembre 2017
Jean Lalonde, Maire
Louise Sisla Héroux, Directrice générale

Très-Saint-Sacrement
CP 160
1180, rte 203
Howick, QC J0S 1G0
Tél: 450-825-0192; *Téléc:* 450-825-0193
mun-trst@videotron.ca
Entité municipal: Parish (Paroisse)
Incorporation: 2 avril 1885; *Area:* 97,30 km2
Comté ou district: Le Haut-Saint-Laurent; *Population au 2011:* 1,155
Circonscription(s) électorale(s) provinciale(s): Huntingdon
Circonscription(s) électorale(s) fédérale(s): Salaberry-Suroît
Prochaines élections: 5e novembre 2017
François Rochefort, Maire
Suzanne Côté, Directrice générale

Tring-Jonction
247, rue Notre-Dame
Tring-Jonction, QC G0N 1X0
Tél: 418-426-2497; *Téléc:* 418-426-2498
tring@cgocable.ca
www.tringjonction.qc.ca
Entité municipal: Village
Incorporation: 21 novembre 1918; *Area:* 25,71 km2
Comté ou district: Robert-Cliche; *Population au 2011:* 1,473
Circonscription(s) électorale(s) provinciale(s): Beauce-Nord
Circonscription(s) électorale(s) fédérale(s): Beauce
Prochaines élections: 5e novembre 2017
Mario Groleau, Maire
Julie Lemelin, Directrice générale

La Trinité-des-Monts
CP 9
12, rue Principale ouest
La Trinité-des-Monts, QC G0K 1B0
Tél: 418-779-2421; *Téléc:* 418-779-2454
muntrinite@globetrotter.net
Entité municipal: Parish (Paroisse)
Incorporation: 1er janvier 1965; *Area:* 233,09 km2
Comté ou district: Rimouski-Neigette; *Population au 2011:* 256
Circonscription(s) électorale(s) provinciale(s): Rimouski
Circonscription(s) électorale(s) fédérale(s):
Rimouski-Neigette-Témiscouata-Les Basques
Prochaines élections: 5e novembre 2017
Charles Sirois, Maire
Nadia Lavoie, Directrice générale

Trois-Pistoles
5, rue Notre-Dame est
Trois-Pistoles, QC G0L 4K0
Tél: 418-851-1995; *Téléc:* 418-851-3567
administration@ville-trois-pistoles.ca
www.ville-trois-pistoles.ca
Entité municipal: Town
Incorporation: 9 mars 1916; *Area:* 7,74 km2
Comté ou district: Les Basques; *Population au 2011:* 3,456
Circonscription(s) électorale(s) provinciale(s):
Rivière-du-Loup-Témiscouata
Circonscription(s) électorale(s) fédérale(s):
Rimouski-Neigette-Témiscouata-Les Basques
Prochaines élections: 5e novembre 2017

Jean-Pierre Rioux, Maire
Pascale Rioux, Directrice générale

Trois-Rives
258, ch St-Joseph
Trois-Rives, QC G0X 2C0
Tél: 819-646-5686; *Téléc:* 819-646-5688
trois-rives@regionmekinac.com
www.trois-rives.com
Entité municipal: Municipality
Incorporation: 2 septembre 1972; *Area:* 675,09 km2
Comté ou district: Mékinac; *Population au 2011:* 490
Circonscription(s) électorale(s) provinciale(s): Laviolette
Circonscription(s) électorale(s) fédérale(s):
St-Maurice-Champlain
Prochaines élections: 5e novembre 2017
Lucien Mongrain, Maire
Nicole Léveillé, Directrice générale

Ulverton
151, rte 143
Ulverton, QC J0B 2B0
Tél: 819-826-5049; *Téléc:* 819-826-5181
municipalite.ulverton@bellnet.ca
www.municipaliteulverton.ca
Entité municipal: Municipality
Incorporation: 1er juillet 1855; *Area:* 51,28 km2
Comté ou district: Le Val-Saint-François; *Population au 2011:* 416
Circonscription(s) électorale(s) provinciale(s): Richmond
Circonscription(s) électorale(s) fédérale(s):
Richmond-Arthabaska
Prochaines élections: 5e novembre 2017
Claude Mercier, Maire
Louise Saint-Pierre, Directrice générale

Umiujaq
CP 108
Umiujaq, QC J0M 1Y0
Tél: 819-331-7000; *Téléc:* 819-331-7057
www.nvumiujaq.ca
Entité municipal: Northern Village
Incorporation: 20 décembre 1986; *Area:* 25,50 km2
Comté ou district: Administration régionale Kativik; *Population au 2011:* 444
Circonscription(s) électorale(s) provinciale(s): Ungava
Circonscription(s) électorale(s) fédérale(s):
Abitibi-Baie-James-Nunavik-Eeyou
Louisa Tookalook, Maire
Sam Nuktie, Secrétaire-trésorier

Upton
863, rue Lanoie
Upton, QC J0H 2E0
Tél: 450-549-5611; *Téléc:* 450-549-5045
secretariat@upton.ca
www.upton.ca
Entité municipal: Municipality
Incorporation: 25 février 1998; *Area:* 51,02 km2
Comté ou district: Acton; *Population au 2011:* 2,075
Circonscription(s) électorale(s) provinciale(s): Johnson
Circonscription(s) électorale(s) fédérale(s): St-Hyacinthe-Bagot
Prochaines élections: 5e novembre 2017
Yves Croteau, Maire
Cynthia Bossé, Directrice générale

Val-Alain
CP 10
1245, 2e rang
Val-Alain, QC G0S 3H0
Tél: 819-744-3222; *Téléc:* 819-744-1330
municipalitevalalain@globetrotter.net
www.val-alain.com
Entité municipal: Municipality
Incorporation: 1er janvier 1950; *Area:* 103,80 km2
Comté ou district: Lotbinière; *Population au 2011:* 955
Circonscription(s) électorale(s) provinciale(s):
Lotbinière-Frontenac
Circonscription(s) électorale(s) fédérale(s): Lévis-Lotbinière
Prochaines élections: 5e novembre 2017
Rénald Grondin, Maire
Caroline Fortin, Directrice générale

Val-Brillant
CP 220
11, rue St-Pierre ouest
Val-Brillant, QC G0J 3L0
Tél: 418-742-3212; *Téléc:* 418-742-3624
administration@valbrillant.ca
www.valbrillant.ca
Entité municipal: Municipality
Incorporation: 20 décembre 1986; *Area:* 80,00 km2
Comté ou district: La Matapédia; *Population au 2011:* 955
Circonscription(s) électorale(s) provinciale(s): Matane-Matapédia
Circonscription(s) électorale(s) fédérale(s): Avignon-La Mitis-Matane-Matapédia
Prochaines élections: 5e novembre 2017
Jacques Pelletier, Maire
Lise Tremblay, Directrice générale

Valcourt
9040B, rue de la Montagne
Valcourt, QC J0E 2L0
Tél: 450-532-2688; *Téléc:* 450-532-5570
info@cantonvalcourt.qc.ca
www.cantonvalcourt.qc.ca
Entité municipal: Township
Incorporation: 1er juillet 1855; *Area:* 79,64 km2
Comté ou district: Le Val-Saint-François; *Population au 2011:* 1,047
Circonscription(s) électorale(s) provinciale(s): Richmond
Circonscription(s) électorale(s) fédérale(s): Shefford
Prochaines élections: 5e novembre 2017
Patrice Desmarais, Maire
Sylvie Courtemanche, Directrice générale

Valcourt
1155, rue St-Joseph
Valcourt, QC J0E 2L0
Tél: 450-532-3313; *Téléc:* 450-532-3424
ville.valcourt@valcourt.ca
www.valcourt.ca
Entité municipal: Town
Incorporation: 19 octobre 1929; *Area:* 5,17 km2
Comté ou district: Le Val-Saint-François; *Population au 2011:* 2,349
Circonscription(s) électorale(s) provinciale(s): Richmond
Circonscription(s) électorale(s) fédérale(s): Shefford
Prochaines élections: 5e novembre 2017
Renald Chênevert, Maire
Manon Beauchemin, Greffière

Val-David
2579, rue de l'Église
Val-David, QC J0T 2N0
Tél: 819-324-5678; *Téléc:* 819-322-6327
info@valdavid.com
www.valdavid.com
Entité municipal: Village
Incorporation: 10 mai 1921; *Area:* 43,17 km2
Comté ou district: Les Laurentides; *Population au 2011:* 4,450
Circonscription(s) électorale(s) provinciale(s): Bertrand
Circonscription(s) électorale(s) fédérale(s): Laurentides-Labelle
Prochaines élections: 5e novembre 2017
Nicole Davidson, Mairesse
Hafida Daoudi, Greffière

Val-des-Bois
CP 69
595, rte 309
Val-des-Bois, QC J0X 3C0
Tél: 819-454-2280; *Téléc:* 819-454-2211
mun.valdesbois@mrcpapineau.com
www.val-des-bois.ca
Entité municipal: Municipality
Incorporation: 1er janvier 1885; *Area:* 224,34 km2
Comté ou district: Papineau; *Population au 2011:* 938
Circonscription(s) électorale(s) provinciale(s): Papineau
Circonscription(s) électorale(s) fédérale(s): Argenteuil-La Petite-Nation
Prochaines élections: 5e novembre 2017
Daniel Rochon, Maire
Anick Morin, Directrice générale

Val-des-Lacs
349, ch de Val-des-Lacs
Val-des-Lacs, QC J0T 2P0
Tél: 819-326-5624; *Téléc:* 819-326-7065
municipalite.val-des-lacs.qc.ca
Entité municipal: Municipality
Incorporation: 6 février 1932; *Area:* 121,82 km2
Comté ou district: Les Laurentides; *Population au 2011:* 721
Circonscription(s) électorale(s) provinciale(s): Bertrand
Circonscription(s) électorale(s) fédérale(s): Laurentides-Labelle
Prochaines élections: 5e novembre 2017
Jean François Delisle, Maire
Sylvain Michaudville, Directeur général

Val-Joli
500, rte 249
Val-Joli, QC J1S 2L5
Tél: 819-845-7663; *Téléc:* 819-845-4399
val-jolidg@axion.ca
www.municipalite.val-joli.qc.ca
Entité municipal: Municipality
Incorporation: 1er juillet 1855; *Area:* 90,61 km2
Comté ou district: Le Val-Saint-François; *Population au 2011:* 1,501
Circonscription(s) électorale(s) provinciale(s): Richmond
Circonscription(s) électorale(s) fédérale(s):
Richmond-Arthabaska
Prochaines élections: 5e novembre 2017
Rolland Camiré, Maire
Julie Brousseau, Directrice générale

La Vallée-de-l'Or
42, place Hammond
Val-d'Or, QC J9P 3A9
Tél: 819-825-7733; *Téléc:* 819-825-4137
info@mrcvo.qc.ca
www.mrcvo.qc.ca
Entité municipal: Regional County Municipality
Incorporation: 8e avril 1981
Population au 2011: 42,896
Note: 6 municipalités & 4 autres territoires.
Jean-Maurice Matte, Préfet
Louis Bourget, Directeur général

La Vallée-de-la-Gatineau
7, rue de la Polyvalente
Gracefield, QC J0X 1W0
Tél: 819-463-3241; *Téléc:* 819-463-3632
info@mrcvg.qc.ca
www.mrcvg.qc.ca
Entité municipal: Regional County Municipality
Incorporation: 1er janvier 1983
Population au 2011: 20,530
Note: 17 municipalités & 5 autres territoires.
Michel Merleau, Préfet
Lynn Kearney, Directeur général

La Vallée-du-Richelieu
#100, 255, boul Laurier
McMasterville, QC J3G 0B7
Tél: 450-464-0339; *Téléc:* 450-464-3827
info@mrcvr.ca
www.mrcvr.ca
Entité municipal: Regional County Municipality
Incorporation: 1er janvier 1982
Population au 2011: 116,773
Note: 13 municipalités.
Gilles Plante, Préfet
Bernard Roy, Directeur général

Vallée-Jonction
259, boul Jean-Marie Rousseau
Vallée-Jonction, QC G0S 3J0
Tél: 418-253-5515; *Téléc:* 418-253-6731
admin@valleejonction.qc.ca
www.valleejonction.qc.ca
Entité municipal: Municipality
Incorporation: 22 mars 1989; *Area:* 24,41 km2
Comté ou district: La Nouvelle-Beauce; *Population au 2011:* 1,940
Circonscription(s) électorale(s) provinciale(s): Beauce-Nord
Circonscription(s) électorale(s) fédérale(s): Beauce
Prochaines élections: 5e novembre 2017
Réal Bisson, Maire
Julie Cliche, Directrice générale

Val-Morin
6120, rue Morin
Val-Morin, QC J0T 2R0
Tél: 819-322-5670; *Téléc:* 819-322-3923
municipalite@val-morin.ca
www.val-morin.ca
Entité municipal: Municipality
Incorporation: 27 juin 1922; *Area:* 39,00 km2
Comté ou district: Les Laurentides; *Population au 2011:* 2,772
Circonscription(s) électorale(s) provinciale(s): Bertrand
Circonscription(s) électorale(s) fédérale(s): Laurentides-Labelle
Prochaines élections: 5e novembre 2017
Guy Drouin, Maire
Pierre Delage, Directeur général

Val-Racine
CP 1
2991, ch St-Léon
Val-Racine, QC G0Y 1E0
Tél: 819-657-4790; *Téléc:* 819-657-4790
vracine@xplornet.com
www.municipalite.val-racine.qc.ca
Entité municipal: Parish (Paroisse)
Incorporation: 26 avril 1907; *Area:* 116,80 km2
Comté ou district: Le Granit; *Population au 2011:* 170
Circonscription(s) électorale(s) provinciale(s): Mégantic

Circonscription(s) électorale(s) fédérale(s): Mégantic-L'Érable
Prochaines élections: 5e novembre 2017
Sonia Cloutier, Mairesse
Chantal Grégoire, Directrice générale

Le Val-Saint-François
CP 3160
810, montée du Parc
Richmond, QC J0B 2H0
Tél: 819-826-6505; *Téléc:* 819-826-3484
mrc@val-saint-francois.qc.ca
www.val-saint-francois.qc.ca
Entité municipal: Regional County Municipality
Incorporation: 26 mai 1982
Population au 2011: 29,654
Note: 18 municipalités.
Luc Cayer, Préfet
Manon Fortin, Directrice générale

Val-Saint-Gilles
801, rue Principale
Val-Saint-Gilles, QC J0Z 3T0
Tél: 819-333-2158; *Téléc:* 819-333-3116
valstgilles@mrcao.qc.ca
valst-gilles.ao.ca
Entité municipal: Municipality
Incorporation: 1er avril 1939; *Area:* 110,54 km2
Comté ou district: Abitibi-Ouest; *Population au 2011:* 178
Circonscription(s) électorale(s) provinciale(s): Abitibi-Ouest
Circonscription(s) électorale(s) fédérale(s):
Abitibi-Témiscamingue
Prochaines élections: 5e novembre 2017
Réjean Lambert, Maire
Sylvie Lambert, Directrice générale

Vaudreuil-Soulanges
420, av Saint-Charles
Vaudreuil-Dorion, QC J7V 2N1
Tél: 450-455-5753; *Téléc:* 450-455-0145
info@mrcvs.ca
www.mrcvs.ca
Entité municipal: Regional County Municipality
Incorporation: 14 avril 1982
Population au 2011: 139,353
Note: 23 municipalités.
Jean A. Lalonde, Préfet
Guy-Lin Beaudoin, Directeur général

Vaudreuil-sur-le-Lac
44, rue de l'Église
Vaudreuil-sur-le-Lac, QC J7V 8P3
Tél: 450-455-1133; *Téléc:* 450-455-8614
vsll@videotron.ca
www.vsll.ca
Entité municipal: Village
Incorporation: 29 mai 1920; *Area:* 1,73 km2
Comté ou district: Vaudreuil-Soulanges; Communauté métropolitaine de Montréal; *Population au 2011:* 1,359
Circonscription(s) électorale(s) provinciale(s): Vaudreuil
Circonscription(s) électorale(s) fédérale(s): Vaudreuil-Soulanges
Prochaines élections: 5e novembre 2017
Claude Pilon, Maire
Carolyn Ayoub, Directrice générale

Venise-en-Québec
CP 270
237, 16e av ouest
Venise-en-Québec, QC J0J 2K0
Tél: 450-244-5838; *Téléc:* 450-346-4266
information@venise-en-quebec.ca
www.municipalite.venise-en-quebec.qc.ca
Entité municipal: Municipality
Incorporation: 1er janvier 1950; *Area:* 13,57 km2
Comté ou district: Le Haut-Richelieu; *Population au 2011:* 1,547
Circonscription(s) électorale(s) provinciale(s): Iberville
Circonscription(s) électorale(s) fédérale(s): Brome-Missisquoi
Prochaines élections: 5e novembre 2017
Jacques Landry, Maire
Diane Bégin, Directrice générale

Verchères
581, rte Marie-Victorin
Verchères, QC J0L 2R0
Tél: 450-583-3307; *Téléc:* 450-583-3637
mairie@ville.vercheres.qc.ca
www.ville.vercheres.qc.ca
Entité municipal: Municipality
Incorporation: 18 septembre 1971; *Area:* 7,277 km2
Comté ou district: Marguerite-D'Youville; Communauté métropolitaine de Montréal; *Population au 2011:* 5,692
Circonscription(s) électorale(s) provinciale(s): Verchères
Circonscription(s) électorale(s) fédérale(s): Pierre-Boucher-Les Patriotes-Verchères
Prochaines élections: 5e novembre 2017
Alexandre Bélisle, Maire
Luc Forcier, Directeur général

Ville-Marie
Édifice Gérard-Caron
21, rue St-Gabriel sud
Ville-Marie, QC J9V 1A1
Tél: 819-629-2881; *Téléc:* 819-629-3215
vvm.info@mrctemiscamingue.qc.ca
www.ville-marie.ca
Entité municipal: Town
Incorporation: 13 octobre 1897; *Area:* 11,94 km2
Comté ou district: Témiscamingue; *Population au 2011:* 2,595
Circonscription(s) électorale(s) provinciale(s):
Rouyn-Noranda-Témiscamingue
Circonscription(s) électorale(s) fédérale(s):
Abitibi-Témiscamingue
Prochaines élections: 5e novembre 2017
Bernard Flébus, Maire
Martin Lecomte, Directeur général

Villeroy
378, rue Principale
Villeroy, QC G0S 3K0
Tél: 819-385-4605; *Téléc:* 819-385-4754
info@municipalite-villeroy.ca
www.municipalite-villeroy.ca
Entité municipal: Municipality
Incorporation: 22 septembre 1924; *Area:* 100,41 km2
Comté ou district: L'Érable; *Population au 2011:* 485
Circonscription(s) électorale(s) provinciale(s): Arthabaska
Circonscription(s) électorale(s) fédérale(s): Mégantic-L'Érable
Prochaines élections: 5e novembre 2017
Michel Poisson, Maire
Sylvie Côté, Directrice générale

La Visitation-de-l'Île-Dupas
113, rue de l'Église
La Visitation-de-l'Île-Dupas, QC J0K 2P0
Tél: 450-836-6019; *Téléc:* 450-836-8266
admin@ile-dupas.ca
Entité municipal: Municipality
Incorporation: 1er juillet 1855; *Area:* 24,86 km2
Comté ou district: D'Autray; *Population au 2011:* 619
Circonscription(s) électorale(s) provinciale(s): Berthier
Circonscription(s) électorale(s) fédérale(s): Berthier-Maskinongé
Prochaines élections: 5e novembre 2017
François Drainville, Maire
Sylive Toupin, Directrice générale

La Visitation-de-Yamaska
21, rue Principale
La Visitation, QC J0G 1C0
Tél: 450-564-2818; *Téléc:* 450-564-9923
info@lavisitationdeyamaska.net
www.lavisitationdeyamaska.net
Entité municipal: Municipality
Incorporation: 2 février 1899; *Area:* 41,86 km2
Comté ou district: Nicolet-Yamaska; *Population au 2011:* 331
Circonscription(s) électorale(s) provinciale(s): Nicolet-Bécancour
Circonscription(s) électorale(s) fédérale(s):
Bécancour-Nicolet-Saurel
Prochaines élections: 5e novembre 2017
Sylvain Laplante, Maire
Suzanne Bibeau, Directrice générale

Waltham
CP 160
69, rue de l'Hôtel-de-Ville
Waltham, QC J0X 3H0
Tél: 819-683-3027; *Téléc:* 819-683-1815
Entité municipal: Municipality
Incorporation: 1er janvier 1859; *Area:* 451,43 km2
Comté ou district: Pontiac; *Population au 2011:* 384
Circonscription(s) électorale(s) provinciale(s): Pontiac
Circonscription(s) électorale(s) fédérale(s): Pontiac
Prochaines élections: 5e novembre 2017
Garry Marchand, Maire
Fernand Roy, Directeur général

Warden
172, rue Principale
Warden, QC J0E 2M0
Tél: 450-539-1349; *Téléc:* 450-539-0096
info@village.warden.gc.ca
Entité municipal: Village
Incorporation: 31 mars 1916; *Area:* 5,28 km2
Comté ou district: La Haute-Yamaska; *Population au 2011:* 358
Circonscription(s) électorale(s) provinciale(s): Brome-Missisquoi
Circonscription(s) électorale(s) fédérale(s): Shefford
Prochaines élections: 5e novembre 2017
Philip Tétrault, Maire
Jacques Mireault, Directeur général

Warwick
8, rue de l'Hôtel-de-Ville
Warwick, QC J0A 1M0
Tél: 819-358-4300; *Téléc:* 819-358-4319
ville@ville.warwick.qc.ca
www.ville.warwick.qc.ca
Entité municipal: Town
Incorporation: 15 mars 2000; *Area:* 114,01 km2
Comté ou district: Arthabaska; *Population au 2011:* 4,766
Circonscription(s) électorale(s) provinciale(s):
Drummond-Bois-Francs
Circonscription(s) électorale(s) fédérale(s):
Richmond-Arthabaska
Prochaines élections: 5e novembre 2017
Diego Scalzo, Maire
Lise Lemieux, Directrice générale

Waskaganish
CP 60
70, rue Waskaganish
Waskaganish, QC J0M 1R0
Tél: 819-895-8650; *Téléc:* 819-895-8901
www.waskaganish.ca
Entité municipal: Villages Cris
Population au 2011: 2,206
Circonscription(s) électorale(s) provinciale(s): Ungava
Circonscription(s) électorale(s) fédérale(s):
Abitibi-Baie-James-Nunavik-Eeyou
Gordon J. Blackned, Maire
Susan Esau, Secrétaire-Trésorière

Waswanipi
Édifice Diom-Blacksmith
CP 8
Waswanipi, QC J0Y 3C0
Tél: 819-753-2587; *Téléc:* 819-753-2555
communications.officer@waswanipi.com
www.waswanipi.com
Entité municipal: Villages Cris
Population au 2011: 1,777
Circonscription(s) électorale(s) provinciale(s): Ungava
Circonscription(s) électorale(s) fédérale(s):
Abitibi-Baie-James-Nunavik-Eeyou
Paul Gull, Maire
Samuel Gull, Directeur général

Waterloo
CP 50
417, rue de la Cour
Waterloo, QC J0E 2N0
Tél: 450-539-2282; *Téléc:* 450-539-3257
administration@ville.waterloo.gc.ca
www.ville.waterloo.qc.ca
Entité municipal: Town
Incorporation: 1er janvier 1867; *Area:* 11,52 km2
Comté ou district: La Haute-Yamaska; *Population au 2011:* 4,330
Circonscription(s) électorale(s) provinciale(s): Brome-Missisquoi
Circonscription(s) électorale(s) fédérale(s): Shefford
Prochaines élections: 5e novembre 2017
Pascal Russell, Maire
Éric Sévigny, Greffier

Waterville
170, rue Principale sud
Waterville, QC J0B 3H0
Tél: 819-837-2456; *Téléc:* 819-837-0786
adm@waterville.ca
www.waterville.ca
Entité municipal: Village
Incorporation: 1er janvier 1876; *Area:* 44,53 km2
Comté ou district: Coaticook; *Population au 2011:* 2,028
Circonscription(s) électorale(s) provinciale(s): St-François
Circonscription(s) électorale(s) fédérale(s): Compton-Stanstead
Prochaines élections: 5e novembre 2017
Nathalie Dupuis, Mairesse
François Fréchette, Directeur général

Weedon
520, 2e av
Weedon, QC J0B 3J0
Tél: 819-560-8550; *Téléc:* 819-560-8551
adm.weedon@hsfgc.ca
www.weedon.ca
Entité municipal: Municipality
Incorporation: 9 février 2000; *Area:* 215,02 km2
Comté ou district: Le Haut-Saint-François; *Population au 2011:* 2,683

Circonscription(s) électorale(s) provinciale(s): Mégantic
Circonscription(s) électorale(s) fédérale(s): Compton-Stanstead
Prochaines élections: 5e novembre 2017
Richard Tanguay, Maire
Émile Royer, Directeur général

Wemindji
CP 60
21, Hilltop Dr.
Wemindji, QC J0M 1L0
Tél: 819-978-0264; *Téléc:* 819-978-0258
www.wemindji.ca
Entité municipal: Villages Cris
Incorporation: 28 juin 1978; *Area:* 186,22 km2
Population au 2011: 1,378
Circonscription(s) électorale(s) provinciale(s): Ungava
Circonscription(s) électorale(s) fédérale(s):
Abitibi-Baie-James-Nunavik-Eeyou
Prochaines élections: 6e septembre 2017
Dennis Georgekish, Maire
Tony Gull, Directeur général

Wentworth
114, ch Louisa
Wentworth, QC J8H 0C7
Tél: 450-562-0701; *Téléc:* 450-562-0703
info@wentworth.ca
www.wentworth.ca
Entité municipal: Township
Incorporation: 1er juillet 1855; *Area:* 88,99 km2
Comté ou district: Argenteuil; *Population au 2011:* 502
Circonscription(s) électorale(s) provinciale(s): Argenteuil
Circonscription(s) électorale(s) fédérale(s): Argenteuil-La Petite-Nation
Prochaines élections: 5e novembre 2017
Marcel Harvey, Maire
Natalie Black, Directrice générale

Wentworth-Nord
3488, rte Principale
Wentworth-Nord, QC J0T 1Y0
Tél: 450-226-2416; *Téléc:* 450-226-2109
www.wentworth-nord.ca
Other Information: Sans frais: 1-800-770-2416
Entité municipal: Municipality
Incorporation: 1er janvier 1958; *Area:* 155,71 km2
Comté ou district: Les Pays-d'en-Haut; *Population au 2011:* 1,440
Circonscription(s) électorale(s) provinciale(s): Argenteuil
Circonscription(s) électorale(s) fédérale(s): Argenteuil-La Petite-Nation
Prochaines élections: 5e novembre 2017
André Genest, Maire
Sophie Bélanger, Directrice générale

Westbury
168, rte 112
Westbury, QC J0B 1R0
Tél: 819-560-8450; *Téléc:* 819-560-8451
info@cantonwestbury.com
www.cantonwestbury.com
Entité municipal: Township
Incorporation: 16 août 1858; *Area:* 65,78 km2
Comté ou district: Le Haut-Saint-François; *Population au 2011:* 997
Circonscription(s) électorale(s) provinciale(s): Mégantic
Circonscription(s) électorale(s) fédérale(s): Compton-Stanstead
Prochaines élections: 5e novembre 2017
Kenneth Coates, Maire
Adèle Madore, Directrice générale

Whapmagoostui
CP 390
Whapmagoostui, QC J0M 1G0
Tél: 819-929-3384; *Téléc:* 819-929-3203
chief@whapmagoostuifn.ca
www.whapmagoostuifn.ca
Entité municipal: Villages Cris
Incorporation: 28 juillet 1978; *Area:* 113,70 km2
Population au 2011: 874
Circonscription(s) électorale(s) provinciale(s): Ungava
Circonscription(s) électorale(s) fédérale(s):
Abitibi-Baie-James-Nunavik-Eeyou
Stanley George, Maire
Patricia-George Kawapit, Secrétaire

Wickham
893, rue Moreau
Wickham, QC J0C 1S0
Tél: 819-398-6878; *Téléc:* 819-398-7166
wickham@bellnet.ca
www.wickham.ca
Entité municipal: Municipality
Incorporation: 23 décembre 1972; *Area:* 97,72 km2
Comté ou district: Drummond; *Population au 2011:* 2,470
Circonscription(s) électorale(s) provinciale(s): Johnson
Circonscription(s) électorale(s) fédérale(s): Drummond
Prochaines élections: 5e novembre 2017
Carole Côté, Mairesse
Réal Dulmaine, Directeur général

Windsor
CP 90
22, rue St-Georges
Windsor, QC J1S 2L7
Tél: 819-845-7888; *Téléc:* 819-845-7606
info@villedewindsor.qc.ca
www.villedewindsor.qc.ca
Entité municipal: Town
Incorporation: 29 décembre 1999; *Area:* 13,78 km2
Comté ou district: Le Val-Saint-François; *Population au 2011:* 5,367

Circonscription(s) électorale(s) provinciale(s): Richmond
Circonscription(s) électorale(s) fédérale(s):
Richmond-Arthabaska
Prochaines élections: 5e novembre 2017
Sylvie Bureau, Mairesse
Sylvain Saint-Cyr, Directeur général & Greffier

Wotton
CP 60
396, rue Monseigneur-L'Heureux
Wotton, QC J0A 1N0
Tél: 819-828-2112; *Téléc:* 819-828-3594
direction@wotton.ca
www.wotton.ca
Entité municipal: Municipality
Incorporation: 10 mars 1993; *Area:* 142,41 km2
Comté ou district: Les Sources; *Population au 2011:* 1,453
Circonscription(s) électorale(s) provinciale(s): Richmond
Circonscription(s) électorale(s) fédérale(s):
Richmond-Arthabaska
Prochaines élections: 5e novembre 2017
Katy St-Cyr, Mairesse
Carole Vaillancourt, Directrice générale

Yamachiche
366, rue Ste-Anne
Yamachiche, QC G0X 3L0
Tél: 819-296-3795; *Téléc:* 819-296-3542
hoteldeville@yamachiche.ca
www.yamachiche.ca
Entité municipal: Municipality
Incorporation: 26 décembre 1987; *Area:* 106,30 km2
Comté ou district: Maskinongé; *Population au 2011:* 2,787
Circonscription(s) électorale(s) provinciale(s): Maskinongé
Circonscription(s) électorale(s) fédérale(s): Berthier-Maskinongé
Prochaines élections: 5e novembre 2017
Michel Isabelle, Maire
Linda Lafrenière, Directrice générale

Yamaska
CP 120
100, rue Guilbault
Yamaska, QC J0G 1X0
Tél: 450-789-2489; *Téléc:* 450-789-2970
yamaska@pierredesaurel.com
www.yamaska.ca
Entité municipal: Municipality
Incorporation: 19 décembre 2001; *Area:* 74,44 km2
Comté ou district: Pierre-De Saurel; *Population au 2011:* 1,644
Circonscription(s) électorale(s) provinciale(s): Richelieu
Circonscription(s) électorale(s) fédérale(s):
Bécancour-Nicolet-Saurel
Prochaines élections: 5e novembre 2017
Louis R. Joyal, Maire
Karine Lussier, Directrice générale

SASKATCHEWAN

Acts governing the municipal system in Saskatchewan are The Urban Municipality Act, 1984; The Rural Municipality Act, 1989; and The Northern Municipalities Act, 2010. In southern Saskatchewan there are 755 incorporated municipalities; 459 are urban municipalities, which include 16 cities; 146 towns; 257 villages and 40 resort villages. Of the 755, 296 are rural municipalities. In northern Saskatchewan, there are 24 incorporated municipalities: 2 northern towns; 11 northern villages and 11 northern hamlets. Unincorporated areas of the province include hamlets and organized hamlets within rural municipalities. There are 147 organized hamlets as defined by The Municipalities Act. Unicorporated areas of northern Saskatchewan are part of the Northern Saskatchewan Administration District (NSAD); there are 11 northern settlements within the NSAD.

Elections in Saskatchewan occur every four years. For cities, (southern) towns and villages, elections occur on the fourth Wednesday of October. For resort villages, elections occur on the last Saturday of July, and for northern municipalities, elections occur on either the second last Wednesday in September, the last Wednesday in September or the first Wednesday in October (as decided upon by Council).

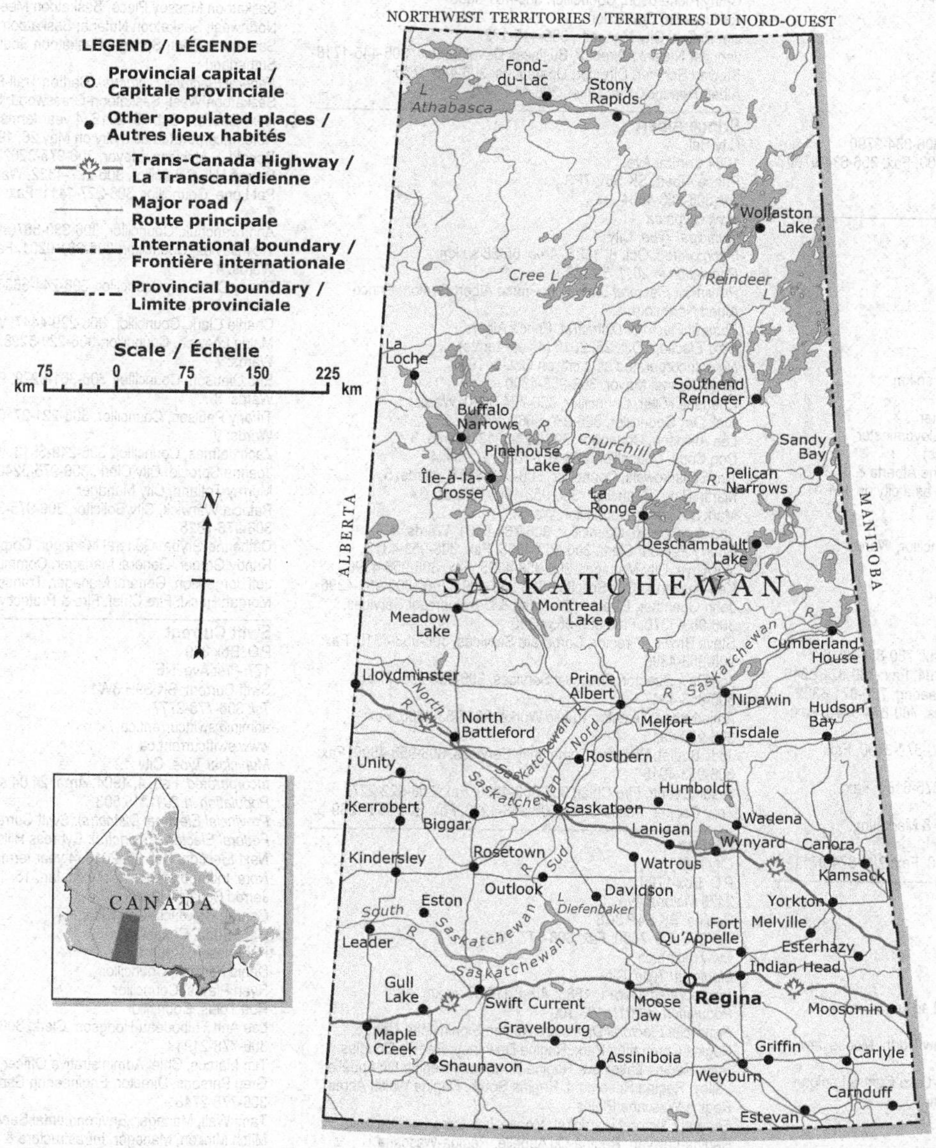

Saskatchewan

Major Municipalities in Saskatchewan

Estevan
1102 - 4th St.
Estevan, SK S4A 0W7
Tel: 306-634-1800; *Fax:* 306-634-9790
a.smale@estevan.ca
www.estevan.ca
Municipal Type: City
Incorporated: Nov. 2, 1899; *Area:* 17.56 sq km
Population in 2011: 11,054
Provincial Electoral District(s): Estevan
Federal Electoral District(s): Souris-Moose Mountain
Next Election: Oct. 26, 2016 (4 year terms)
Note: Incorporated as city on March 1, 1957.
Roy Ludwig, Mayor, 306-634-3050
Greg Hoffort, Councillor
Kevin Smith, Councillor, 306-634-5429
Trevor Knibbs, Councillor
Lori Carr, Councillor
Brian Johnson, Councillor
Dennis Moore, Councillor
Judy Pilloud, Clerk, 306-634-1852, Fax: 306-634-9790
Amber Smale, City Manager, 306-634-1800, Fax: 306-634-9790
Tim Leson, Treasurer
Trina Sieben, Assessor

Lloydminster
City Hall
4420 - 50 Ave.
Lloydminster, SK T9V 0W2
Tel: 780-875-6184; *Fax:* 780-871-8345
info@lloydminster.ca
www.lloydminster.ca
Municipal Type: City
Incorporated: Nov. 25, 1903; *Area:* 17.34 sq km
Population in 2011: 27,804
Provincial Electoral District(s): Lloydminster
Federal Electoral District(s): Battlefords-Lloydminster
Next Election: Oct. 26, 2016 (4 year terms)
Note: Population figure represents both the Alberta & Saskatchewan populations. Incorporated as a city on Jan. 1, 1958.
Rob Saunders, Mayor
Linnea Goodhand, Deputy Mayor & Councillor, Wards: 5
Jason Whiting, Councillor, Wards: 1
Lachlan Cummine, Councillor, Wards: 2
Chris McQuid, Councillor, Wards: 3
Larry Sauer, Councillor, Wards: 4
Ken Baker, Councillor, Wards: 6
Amy Smart, City Clerk, 780-871-8329, Fax: 780-871-8346
Glenn Carroll, City Manager, 780-875-6184, Fax: 780-871-8346
Terry Burton, Director, Planning & Engineering, 780-871-8332
Don Stang, Director, Community Services, 780-874-3710, Fax: 780-874-3711
Alan Cayford, Director, Public Works, 780-874-3700, Fax: 780-874-3701
Nicole Reiniger, Director, Finance, 780-875-6184, Fax: 780-871-8345
Leo Pare, Coordinator, Communications & Marketing, 780-875-6184, Fax: 780-871-8345
Jordan Newton, Fire Chief, 780-874-3710, Fax: 780-874-3711

Moose Jaw
228 Main St. North
Moose Jaw, SK S6H 3J8
Tel: 306-694-4400; *Fax:* 306-694-4480
www.moosejaw.ca
Municipal Type: City
Incorporated: Jan. 19, 1884; *Area:* 46.82 sq km
Population in 2011: 33,274
Provincial Electoral District(s): Moose Jaw North; Moose Jaw Wakamow
Federal Electoral District(s): Moose Jaw-Lake Centre-Lanigan
Next Election: Oct. 26, 2016 (4 year terms)
Note: Incorporated as a city on Nov. 20, 1903.
Deb Higgins, Mayor
Brian Swanson, Councillor, 306-692-6263
Candis Kirkpatrick, Councillor, 306-692-7035
Dawn Luhning, Councillor
Don Mitchell, Councillor
Heather Eby, Councillor
Patrick Boyle, Councillor
Myron Gulka-Tiechco, City Clerk
Matt Noble, City Manager
Brenda Hendrickson, Treasurer & Assessor
Sandy Campbell, Comptroller
Rod Montgomery, Fire Chief

North Battleford
P.O. Box 460
1291 - 101st St.
North Battleford, SK S9A 2Y6
Tel: 306-445-1700; *Fax:* 306-445-0411
www.cityofnb.ca
Municipal Type: City
Incorporated: March 21, 1906; *Area:* 33.55 sq km
Population in 2011: 13,888
Provincial Electoral District(s): The Battlefords
Federal Electoral District(s): Battlefords-Lloydminster
Next Election: Oct. 26, 2016 (4 year terms)
Note: Proclaimed as a city on May 1, 1913.
Ian Hamilton, Mayor
Ryan Bater, Councillor, 306-445-1968
Don Buglas, Councillor
Ray Fox, Councillor, 306-937-6898
Greg Lightfoot, Councillor
Cathy Richardson, Councillor, 306-481-6583
Kelli Hawtin, Councillor
Jim Puffalt, City Manager, 306-445-1727
Jennifer Niesink, Director, Business Development, 306-445-1718
Stewart Schafer, Director, Operations, 306-445-1735
Albert Headrick, Fire Chief, 306-445-1779

Prince Albert
City Hall
1084 Central Ave.
Prince Albert, SK S6V 7P3
Tel: 306-953-4884
www.citypa.ca
Municipal Type: City
Incorporated: Oct. 8, 1885; *Area:* 65.68 sq km
Population in 2011: 35,129
Provincial Electoral District(s): Prince Albert Carlton; Prince Albert Northcote
Federal Electoral District(s): Prince Albert
Next Election: Oct. 26, 2016 (4 year terms)
Note: Incorporated as a city on Oct. 8, 1904.
Greg Dionne, Mayor, 306-953-4300
Charlene Miller, Councillor, 306-764-3690, Wards: 1
Rick Orr, Councillor, 306-960-3663, Wards: 2
Lee Atkinson, Councillor, 306-922-5313, Wards: 3
Don Cody, Councillor, 306-961-7870, Wards: 4
Tim Scharkowski, Councillor, 306-922-6181, Wards: 5
Martin Ring, Councillor, 306-953-1900, Wards: 6
Mark D. Tweidt, Councillor, Wards: 7
Ted Zurakowski, Councillor, 306-764-6461, Wards: 8
Sherry Person, Clerk, 306-953-4305, Fax: 306-953-4313
Jim Toye, City Manager, 306-953-4395, Fax: 306-953-4396
Ken Paskaruk, City Solicitor, 306-953-4395, Fax: 306-953-4396
John Guenther, Director, Planning & Development Services, 306-953-4370, Fax: 306-953-4380
Steve Brown, Director, Corporate Services, 306-953-4310, Fax: 306-953-4396
Joe Day, Director, Financial Services, 306-953-4350, Fax: 306-953-4347
Amjad Khan, Director, Public Works, 306-953-4900, Fax: 306-953-4915
Jody Boulet, Director, Community Services, 306-953-4800, Fax: 306-953-4915
Jason Everitt, Fire Chief, 306-953-4200, Fax: 306-922-2272
Troy Cooper, Police Chief, 306-953-4222, Fax: 306-953-4239

Regina
City Hall
P.O. Box 1790
2476 Victoria Ave.
Regina, SK S4P 3C8
Tel: 306-777-7000; *Fax:* 306-777-7609
www.regina.ca
Municipal Type: City
Incorporated: Dec. 1, 1883; *Area:* 118.87 sq km
Population in 2011: 193,100
Provincial Electoral District(s): Regina Elphinstone-Centre; Regina Coronation Park; Regina Dewdney; Regina Douglas Park; Regina Lakeview; Regina Northeast; Regina Qu'Appelle Valley; Regina Rosemont; Regina South; Regina Walsh Acres; Regina Wascana Plains
Federal Electoral District(s): Moose Jaw-Lake Centre-Lanigan; Regina-Lewvan; Regina-Qu'Appelle; Regina-Wascana
Next Election: Oct. 26, 2016 (4 year terms)
Note: Incorporated as a city on June 19, 1903.
Michael Fougere, Mayor
Barbara Young, Councillor, 306-539-4081, Wards: 1
Bob Hawkins, Councillor, 306-789-2888, Wards: 2
Shawn Fraser, Councillor, 306-551-5030, Wards: 3
Bryon Burnett, Councillor, 306-737-3347, Wards: 4
John Findura, Councillor, 306-536-4250, Wards: 5
Wade Murray, Councillor, 306-596-1035, Wards: 6
Sharron Bryce, R.N., Councillor, 306-949-5025, Wards: 7
Mike O'Donnell, Councillor, 306-545-7300, Wards: 8
Terry Hincks, Councillor, 306-949-9690, Wards: 9
Jerry Flegel, Councillor, 306-537-9888, Wards: 10
Jim Nicol, City Clerk, 306-777-7262
Chris Holden, City Manager
Ernie Polsom, Fire Chief
Dean Rae, Acting Police Chief

Saskatoon
City Hall
222 - 3rd Ave. North
Saskatoon, SK S7K 0J5
Tel: 306-975-3200
www.saskatoon.ca
Municipal Type: City
Incorporated: Nov. 16, 1901; *Area:* 170.83 sq km
Population in 2011: 222,189
Provincial Electoral District(s): Saskatoon Centre; Saskatoon Eastview; Saskatoon Fairview; Saskatoon Greystone; Saskatoon Massey Place; Saskatoon Meewasin; Saskatoon Northwest; Saskatoon Nutana; Saskatoon Riversdale; Saskatoon Silver Springs; Saskatoon Southeast; Saskatoon Sutherland
Federal Electoral District(s): Carlton Trail-Eagle Creek; Saskatoon West; Saskatoon-Grasswood; Saskatoon-University
Next Election: Oct. 26, 2016 (4 year terms)
Note: Incorporated as a city on May 26, 1906.
Donald J. Atchison, Mayor, 306-975-3202, Fax: 306-975-3144
Darren Hill, Councillor, 306-227-4322, Wards: 1
Pat Lorje, Councillor, 306-227-1411, Fax: 306-384-4783, Wards: 2
Ann Iwanchuk, Councillor, 306-380-6870, Wards: 3
Troy Davies, Councillor, 306-361-0201, Fax: 306-664-2112, Wards: 4
Randy Donauer, Councillor, 306-244-6634, Fax: 306-244-6637, Wards: 5
Charlie Clark, Councillor, 306-229-4447, Wards: 6
Mairin Loewen, Councillor, 306-229-5298, Fax: 306-975-2784, Wards: 7
Eric Olauson, Councillor, 306-361-0229, Fax: 306-975-2784, Wards: 8
Tiffany Paulsen, Councillor, 306-221-2716, Fax: 306-955-0567, Wards: 9
Zach Jeffries, Councillor, 306-249-5513, Wards: 10
Joanne Sproule, City Clerk, 306-975-3240, Fax: 306-975-2784
Murray Totland, City Manager
Patricia Warwick, City Solicitor, 306-975-3270, Fax: 306-975-7828
Catherine Gryba, General Manager, Corporate Performance
Randy Grauer, General Manager, Community Services
Jeff Jorgenson, General Manager, Transportation & Utilities
Morgan Hackl, Fire Chief, Fire & Protective Services

Swift Current
P.O. Box 340
177 - 1st Ave. NE
Swift Current, SK S9H 3W1
Tel: 306-778-2777
admin@swiftcurrent.ca
www.swiftcurrent.ca
Municipal Type: City
Incorporated: Feb. 4, 1904; *Area:* 24.04 sq km
Population in 2011: 15,503
Provincial Electoral District(s): Swift Current
Federal Electoral District(s): Cypress Hills-Grasslands
Next Election: Oct. 26, 2016 (4 year terms)
Note: Incorporated as a city on Jan. 15, 1914.
Jerrod Schafer, Mayor
George Bowditch, Councillor
Gord Budd, Councillor
Pat Friesen, Councillor
Denis Perrault, Councillor
Ryan Plewis, Councillor
Ron Toles, Councillor
Lee Ann Thibodeau-Hodgson, Clerk, 306-778-2768, Fax: 306-778-2194
Tim Marcus, Chief Administrative Officer, 306-778-2723
Greg Parsons, Director, Engineering Services & Operations, 306-778-2748
Tami Wall, Manager, Environmental Services
Mitch Minken, Manager, Infrastructure & Operations
Denis Pilon, Fire Chief, 306-778-2760

Warman
P.O. Box 340
107 Central St. West
Warman, SK S0K 4S0
Tel: 306-933-2133; *Fax:* 306-933-1987
town.warman@sasktel.net
www.warman.ca
Municipal Type: City
Incorporated: Aug. 3, 1906; *Area:* 5.34 sq km

Population in 2011: 7,084
Provincial Electoral District(s): Martensville
Federal Electoral District(s): Carlton Trail-Eagle Creek
Next Election: Oct. 26, 2016 (4 year terms)
Note: Incorporated as a city on October 27th, 2012.
Sheryl Spence, Mayor, 306-933-0011
Stanley Westby, City Manager

Weyburn
P.O. Box 370
157 - 3rd St. NE
Weyburn, SK S4H 2K6
Tel: 306-848-3200; *Fax:* 306-842-2001
questions@weyburn.ca
www.weyburn.ca
Municipal Type: City
Incorporated: Oct. 22, 1900; *Area:* 15.78 sq km
Population in 2011: 10,484
Provincial Electoral District(s): Weyburn-Big Muddy
Federal Electoral District(s): Souris-Moose Mountain
Next Election: Oct. 26, 2016 (4 year terms)
Note: Incorporated as a city on Sept. 1, 1913.
Debra Button, Mayor
Winston Bailey, Councillor, 306-842-1614
Dick Michel, Councillor, 306-842-6479
Laura Morrissette, Councillor, 306-842-7894
Rob Stephanson, Councillor, 306-842-1305
Nancy Styles, Councillor, 306-842-3897
Mel Van Betuw, Councillor, 306-861-1855
Donette Ritcher, City Clerk, 306-848-3209
Robert (Bob) Smith, City Manager
Laura Missal, Director, Finance, 306-848-3214
Mathew Warren, Director, Leisure Services, 306-848-3217
Greg Button, Manager, Facilities, 306-848-3270
Drew Bakken, Officer, Planning & Development, 306-848-3211
Claude Morin, Superintendent, Public Works, 306-848-3294, Fax: 306-842-1766
Sean Abram, Director, Engineering, 306-848-3232
Simon Almond, Fire Chief
Marlo Pritchard, Police Chief

Yorkton
P.O. Box 400
37 - 3rd Ave. North
Yorkton, SK S3N 2W3
Tel: 306-786-1700; *Fax:* 306-786-6880
www.yorkton.ca
Municipal Type: City
Incorporated: July 11, 1894; *Area:* 24.57 sq km
Population in 2011: 15,669
Provincial Electoral District(s): Yorkton
Federal Electoral District(s): Yorkton-Melville
Next Election: Oct. 26, 2016 (4 year terms)
Note: Incorporated as a city on Feb. 1, 1928.
Bob Maloney, Mayor, 306-786-1701
Les Arnelien, Councillor, 306-786-4800
Ross Fisher, Councillor, 306-786-0506
Randy Goulden, Councillor, 306-783-8707
Larry Pearen, Councillor, 306-782-4182
James Wilson, Councillor, 306-621-1401
Chris Wyatt, Councillor, 306-782-0686
Kathy Ritchie, City Clerk, 306-786-1717
Lonnie Kaal, City Manager, 306-786-1703
Michael Buchholzer, Director, Environmental Services, 306-828-2470
Shannon Bell, Director, Finance, 306-786-1721
Trent Mandzuk, Director, Public Works, 306-786-1760
Darcy McLeod, Director, Community Development, Parks & Recreation, 306-786-1750
Michael Eger, Director, Planning, Building & Development, 306-786-1758
Samuel Twumasi, Officer, Economic Development, 306-786-1747
Trevor Morrissey, Fire Chief, Fire Protective Services, 306-786-1798

Other Municipalities in Saskatchewan

Abbey
P.O. Box 210
Abbey, SK S0N 0A0
Tel: 306-689-2412; *Fax:* 306-689-2901
rm229@sasktel.net
Municipal Type: Village
Incorporated: Sept. 2, 1913; *Area:* 0.77 sq km
Population in 2011: 115
Provincial Electoral District(s): Cypress Hills
Federal Electoral District(s): Cypress Hills-Grasslands
Next Election: Oct. 26, 2016 (4 year terms)
Bruce Walker, Mayor
Dianne Scriven, Administrator

Aberdeen
401C Main St.
Aberdeen, SK S0K 0A0
Tel: 306-253-4311; *Fax:* 306-253-4201
townaberdeen@sasktel.net
www.aberdeen.ca
Municipal Type: Town
Incorporated: March 13, 1907; *Area:* 1.95 sq km
Population in 2011: 599
Provincial Electoral District(s): Humboldt
Federal Electoral District(s): Carlton Trail-Eagle Creek
Next Election: Oct. 26, 2016 (4 year terms)
Note: Proclaimed as town on Nov. 1, 1988.
Bruce Voldeng, Mayor
Susan Thompson, Chief Administrative Officer

Abernethy
P.O. Box 189
Abernethy, SK S0A 0A0
Tel: 306-333-2271; *Fax:* 306-333-2276
village@abernethy.ca
www.abernethy.ca
Municipal Type: Village
Incorporated: July 26, 1904; *Area:* 1.03 sq km
Population in 2011: 196
Provincial Electoral District(s): Last Mountain-Touchwood
Federal Electoral District(s): Regina-Qu'Appelle
Next Election: Oct. 26, 2016 (4 year terms)
Janet Englot, Mayor
Sheree Emmerson, Administrator

Air Ronge
123 Cessna St. West
Air Ronge, SK S0J 3G0
Tel: 306-425-2107; *Fax:* 306-425-3108
nvoar@sasktel.net
www.airronge.ca
Municipal Type: Northern Village
Incorporated: Oct. 1, 1983; *Area:* 6.00 sq km
Population in 2011: 1,043
Provincial Electoral District(s): Cumberland
Federal Electoral District(s): Desnethé-Missinippi-Churchill River
Next Election: Autumn 2016 (4 year terms)
Gordon Stomp, Mayor
Charmayne Szatkowski, Administrator

Alameda
P.O. Box 36
Alameda, SK S0C 0A0
Tel: 306-489-2077; *Fax:* 306-489-4602
townofalameda@sasktel.net
www.townofalameda.ca
Municipal Type: Town
Incorporated: Dec. 29, 1898; *Area:* 2.55 sq km
Population in 2011: 342
Provincial Electoral District(s): Cannington
Federal Electoral District(s): Souris-Moose Mountain
Next Election: Oct. 26, 2016 (4 year terms)
Note: Proclaimed as town on April 15, 1907.
Mike Warner, Mayor
Lynne Hewitt, Administrator

Albertville
P.O. Box 83
212 St. James Ave South
Albertville, SK S0J 0A0
Tel: 306-929-2110; *Fax:* 306-929-4744
albertville@inet2000.com
Municipal Type: Village
Incorporated: Jan. 1, 1986; *Area:* 1.11 sq km
Population in 2011: 140
Provincial Electoral District(s): Saskatchewan Rivers
Federal Electoral District(s): Prince Albert
Next Election: Oct. 26, 2016 (4 year terms)
Louis Hradecki, Mayor
Audrey Veer, Administrator

Alice Beach
P.O. Box 70
Dilke, SK S0G 1C0
Tel: 306-519-3939
rvab@sasktel.net
Municipal Type: Resort Village
Area: 0.71 sq km
Population in 2011: 45
Provincial Electoral District(s): Thunder Creek
Federal Electoral District(s): Moose Jaw-Lake Centre-Lanigan
Next Election: July 2020 (4 year terms)
Ronald Ziegler, Mayor
Rhonda Woelk, Administrator

Alida
P.O. Box 6
Alida, SK S0C 0B0
Tel: 306-443-2228; *Fax:* 306-443-2568
villageofalida@sasktel.net
Municipal Type: Village
Incorporated: Feb. 19, 1926; *Area:* 0.35 sq km
Population in 2011: 131
Provincial Electoral District(s): Cannington
Federal Electoral District(s): Souris-Moose Mountain
Next Election: Oct. 26, 2016 (4 year terms)
James Boettcher, Mayor
Kathy Anthony, Administrator

Allan
P.O. Box 159
224 Main St.
Allan, SK S0K 0C0
Tel: 306-257-3272; *Fax:* 306-257-3337
townofallan@sasktel.net
www.allan.ca
Municipal Type: Town
Incorporated: June 9, 1910; *Area:* 1.78 sq km
Population in 2011: 648
Provincial Electoral District(s): Humboldt
Federal Electoral District(s): Moose Jaw-Lake Centre-Lanigan
Next Election: Oct. 26, 2016 (4 year terms)
Note: Proclaimed as town on Dec. 1, 1965.
Rob Vogelgesang, Mayor
Christine Dyck, Administrator

Alvena
P.O. Box 8
Alvena, SK S0K 0E0
Tel: 306-943-2101; *Fax:* 306-943-2139
villageofalvena@yahoo.ca
Municipal Type: Village
Incorporated: July 1, 1936; *Area:* 0.43 sq km
Population in 2011: 55
Provincial Electoral District(s): Batoche
Federal Electoral District(s): Carlton Trail-Eagle Creek
Next Election: Oct. 26, 2016 (4 year terms)
Ernie Sawitsky, Mayor
Pamela Hilkewich, Clerk

Annaheim
P.O. Box 130
Annaheim, SK S0K 0G0
Tel: 306-598-2006; *Fax:* 306-598-2008
villageofannaheim@sasktel.net
Municipal Type: Village
Incorporated: April 1, 1977; *Area:* 0.78 sq km
Population in 2011: 219
Provincial Electoral District(s): Melfort
Federal Electoral District(s): Carlton Trail-Eagle Creek
Next Election: Oct. 26, 2016 (4 year terms)
Donald Willenborg, Mayor
Debra Parry, Administrator

Antler
P.O. Box 70
Redvers, SK S0C 2HO
Tel: 306-452-3263; *Fax:* 306-452-3518
rm61@sasktel.net
Municipal Type: Village
Incorporated: March 15, 1905; *Area:* 0.72 sq km
Population in 2011: 41
Provincial Electoral District(s): Cannington
Federal Electoral District(s): Souris-Moose Mountain
Next Election: Oct. 26, 2016 (4 year terms)
Ron Henderson, Reeve
Melissa Roberts, Administrator

Aquadeo
P.O. Box 501
1006 Hwy. 4 North
Cochin, SK S0M 0L0
Tel: 306-386-2942; *Fax:* 306-386-2544
aquadeoadmin@gmail.com
www.aquadeo.net
Municipal Type: Resort Village
Area: 0.74 sq km
Population in 2011: 84
Provincial Electoral District(s): Cut Knife-Turtleford
Federal Electoral District(s): Battlefords-Lloydminster
Next Election: July 2020 (4 year terms)
Cameron Duncan, Mayor, 306-386-3112
Darlene Moline, Administrator

Arborfield
P.O. Box 95
Arborfield, SK S0E 0A0
Tel: 306-769-0101; *Fax:* 306-769-8301
townarborfield@sasktel.net
www.arborfieldsk.ca
Municipal Type: Town
Incorporated: June 16, 1933; *Area:* 0.88 sq km
Population in 2011: 326
Provincial Electoral District(s): Carrot River Valley
Federal Electoral District(s): Prince Albert
Next Election: Oct. 26, 2016 (4 year terms)
Note: Proclaimed as town on June 1, 1950.
Alvin Alyea, Mayor
Lisa Hamelin, Administrator

Archerwill
P.O. Box 130
Archerwill, SK S0E 0B0
Tel: 306-323-2161; *Fax:* 306-323-2106
villageofarcherwill@sasktel.net
www.newsaskcfdc.ca/archerwill.html
Municipal Type: Village
Incorporated: Jan. 1, 1947; *Area:* 0.83 sq km
Population in 2011: 200
Provincial Electoral District(s): Kelvington-Wadena
Federal Electoral District(s): Yorkton-Melville
Next Election: Oct. 26, 2016 (4 year terms)
Geraldine Fountain, Administrator

Arcola
P.O. Box 359
127 Main St.
Arcola, SK S0C 0G0
Tel: 306-455-2212; *Fax:* 306-455-2445
admin@townofarcola.ca
www.townofarcola.ca
Municipal Type: Town
Incorporated: April 11, 1901; *Area:* 2.59 sq km
Population in 2011: 649
Provincial Electoral District(s): Cannington
Federal Electoral District(s): Souris-Moose Mountain
Next Election: Oct. 26, 2016 (4 year terms)
Note: Proclaimed as town on Nov. 20, 1903.
Harry Laurent, Mayor
Christie Hislop, Administrator

Arran
P.O. Box 40
Arran, SK S0A 0B0
Tel: 306-595-4521; *Fax:* 306-595-4531
rm331@sasktel.net
Municipal Type: Village
Incorporated: Sept. 21, 1916; *Area:* 0.69 sq km
Population in 2011: 40
Provincial Electoral District(s): Canora-Pelly
Federal Electoral District(s): Yorkton-Melville
Next Election: Oct. 26, 2016 (4 year terms)
Rick Nahnybida, Mayor
Yvonne Bilsky, Administrator

Asquith
P.O. Box 160
535 Main St.
Asquith, SK S0K 0J0
Tel: 306-329-4341; *Fax:* 306-329-4969
town.asquith@sasktel.net
www.townofasquith.com
Municipal Type: Town
Incorporated: Dec. 10, 1907; *Area:* 1.23 sq km
Population in 2011: 603
Provincial Electoral District(s): Biggar
Federal Electoral District(s): Carlton Trail-Eagle Creek
Next Election: Oct. 26, 2016 (4 year terms)
Note: Proclaimed as a town on Aug. 15, 1908.
Gail Erhart, Mayor
Holly Cross, Chief Administrative Officer

Assiniboia
P.O. Box 1470
131 Third Ave. West
Assiniboia, SK S0H 0B0
Tel: 306-642-3382; *Fax:* 306-642-5622
townoffice@assiniboia.net
www.assiniboia.net
Municipal Type: Town
Incorporated: Dec. 19, 1912; *Area:* 3.78 sq km
Population in 2011: 2,418
Provincial Electoral District(s): Wood River
Federal Electoral District(s): Cypress Hills-Grasslands
Next Election: Oct. 26, 2016 (4 year terms)
Note: Proclaimed as a town on Oct. 1, 1913.
Bob Himbeault, Mayor
Carol White, Chief Administrative Officer

Atwater
P.O. Box 17
Atwater, SK S0A 0C0
Tel: 306-793-2193
villageofatwater@gmail.com
Municipal Type: Village
Incorporated: Aug. 12, 1910; *Area:* 1.79 sq km
Population in 2011: 31
Provincial Electoral District(s): Melville-Saltcoats
Federal Electoral District(s): Yorkton-Melville
Next Election: Oct. 26, 2016 (4 year terms)
James Ferguson, Mayor
Sheila Shivak, Clerk

Avonlea
P.O. Box 209
203 Main St.
Avonlea, SK S0H 0C0
Tel: 306-868-2221; *Fax:* 306-868-2040
avonlea@sasktel.net
www.villageofavonlea.com
Municipal Type: Village
Incorporated: Feb. 10, 1912; *Area:* 0.96 sq km
Population in 2011: 398
Provincial Electoral District(s): Indian Head-Milestone
Federal Electoral District(s): Moose Jaw-Lake Centre-Lanigan
Next Election: Oct. 26, 2016 (4 year terms)
Joel Miller, Mayor
Jaimie Paranuik, Administrator

Aylesbury
P.O. Box 151
316 Main St.
Aylesbury, SK S0G 0B0
Tel: 306-734-2250; *Fax:* 306-734-2257
rm222@sasktel.net
Municipal Type: Village
Incorporated: March 31, 1910; *Area:* 1.28 sq km
Population in 2011: 10
Provincial Electoral District(s): Thunder Creek
Federal Electoral District(s): Moose Jaw-Lake Centre-Lanigan
Next Election: Oct. 26, 2016 (4 year terms)
Douglas Watt, Mayor
Sarah Wells, Administrator

Aylsham
P.O. Box 64
Aylsham, SK S0E 0C0
Tel: 306-862-9415
villageofaylsham@sasktel.net
Municipal Type: Village
Incorporated: Aug. 4, 1947; *Area:* 0.48 sq km
Population in 2011: 71
Provincial Electoral District(s): Carrot River Valley
Federal Electoral District(s): Prince Albert
Next Election: Oct. 26, 2016 (4 year terms)
Elizabeth F. Archer, Mayor
Tammy Gray, Clerk

Balcarres
P.O. Box 130
209 Main St.
Balcarres, SK S0G 0C0
Tel: 306-334-2566; *Fax:* 306-334-2907
balcarrestown@sasktel.net
www.townofbalcarres.ca
Municipal Type: Town
Incorporated: Nov. 21, 1904; *Area:* 1.57 sq km
Population in 2011: 617
Provincial Electoral District(s): Last Mountain-Touchwood
Federal Electoral District(s): Regina-Qu'Appelle
Next Election: Oct. 26, 2016 (4 year terms)
Note: Proclaimed as a town on Jan. 1, 1951.
Dwight Dixon, Mayor
Bev Gelech, Administrator

Balgonie
P.O. Box 310
129 South Railway St. East
Balgonie, SK S0G 0E0
Tel: 306-771-2284; *Fax:* 306-771-2899
townofbalgonie@sasktel.net
www.townofbalgonie.ca
Municipal Type: Town
Incorporated: April 20, 1903; *Area:* 3.15 sq km
Population in 2011: 1,625
Provincial Electoral District(s): Indian Head-Milestone
Federal Electoral District(s): Regina-Qu'Appelle
Next Election: Oct. 26, 2016 (4 year terms)
Note: Proclaimed as a town on Jan. 1, 1951.
Frank Thauberger, Mayor
Valerie Hubbard, Administrator

Bangor
P.O. Box 35
Bangor, SK S0A 0E0
Tel: 306-728-4084
Municipal Type: Village
Incorporated: June 8, 1911; *Area:* 1.65 sq km
Population in 2011: 46
Provincial Electoral District(s): Melville-Saltcoats
Federal Electoral District(s): Yorkton-Melville
Next Election: Oct. 26, 2016 (4 year terms)
Jerome Bomberak, Mayor
Joan C. Bomberak, Clerk

Battleford
P.O. Box 40
Battleford, SK S0M 0E0
Tel: 306-937-6200; *Fax:* 306-937-2450
admin@battleford.ca
www.battleford.ca
Municipal Type: Town
Incorporated: Jan. 6, 1899; *Area:* 23.33 sq km
Population in 2011: 4,065
Provincial Electoral District(s): The Battlefords
Federal Electoral District(s): Battlefords-Lloydminster
Next Election: Oct. 26, 2016 (4 year terms)
Note: Proclaimed as a town on June 15, 1904.
Derek Mahon, Mayor
Sheryl Ballendine, Administrator

Bear Creek
P.O. Box 69
Buffalo Narrows, SK S0M 0J0
Tel: 306-235-1726; *Fax:* 306-235-1727
Municipal Type: NS
Population in 2010: 47
Provincial Electoral District(s): Athabasca
Federal Electoral District(s): Desnethé-Missinippi-Churchill River
Next Election: Autumn 2016 (4 year terms)
Dean Herman, Chair
Bruce Leier, Advisor

Beatty
P.O. Box 60
Beatty, SK S0J 0C0
Tel: 306-752-2028; *Fax:* 306-752-5687
villageofbeatty@sasktel.net
Municipal Type: Village
Incorporated: March 31, 1921; *Area:* 0.82 sq km
Population in 2011: 63
Provincial Electoral District(s): Melfort
Federal Electoral District(s): Prince Albert
Next Election: Oct. 26, 2016 (4 year terms)
Harvey Rainville, Mayor
Linda Logan, Clerk

Beauval
P.O. Box 19
Lavoie St.
Beauval, SK S0M 0G0
Tel: 306-288-2110; *Fax:* 306-288-2348
admin.beauval@sasktel.net
Municipal Type: Northern Village
Incorporated: Oct. 1, 1983; *Area:* 6.71 sq km
Population in 2011: 756
Provincial Electoral District(s): Athabasca
Federal Electoral District(s): Desnethé-Missinippi-Churchill River
Next Election: Autumn 2016 (4 year terms)
Fred Roy, Mayor
Lydia Gauthier, Clerk

Beaver Flat
P.O. Box 991
Swift Current, SK S9H 3X1
Tel: 306-778-7638
rvbeaverflat@gmail.com
www.beaverflatsk.ca
Municipal Type: Resort Village
Area: 0.92 sq km
Population in 2011: 40
Provincial Electoral District(s): Thunder Creek
Federal Electoral District(s): Cypress Hills-Grasslands
Next Election: July 2020 (4 year terms)
Bill Bresett, Mayor
Dianne Hahn, Clerk

Beechy
P.O. Box 153
Beechy, SK S0L 0C0
Tel: 306-859-2205; *Fax:* 306-859-2290
beechy@sasktel.net
www.beechysask.ca
Municipal Type: Village
Incorporated: May 11, 1925; *Area:* 1.06 sq km
Population in 2011: 239
Provincial Electoral District(s): Rosetown-Elrose
Federal Electoral District(s): Cypress Hills-Grasslands
Next Election: Oct. 26, 2016 (4 year terms)
Francis Fleuter, Mayor
Mel Hanke, Administrator

Belle Plaine
P.O. Box 63
Belle Plaine, SK S0G 0G0
Tel: 306-345-1200
Municipal Type: Village
Incorporated: Aug. 12, 1910; *Area:* 1.34 sq km
Population in 2011: 66
Provincial Electoral District(s): Thunder Creek
Federal Electoral District(s): Moose Jaw-Lake Centre-Lanigan
Next Election: Oct. 26, 2016 (4 year terms)
Edwin Siemens, Mayor
Leane Johnston, Administrator

Bengough
P.O. Box 188
181 Main St.
Bengough, SK S0C 0K0
Tel: 306-268-2927; *Fax:* 306-268-2988
town.bengough@sasktel.net
www.bengough.com
Municipal Type: Town
Incorporated: March 15, 1912; *Area:* 1.07 sq km
Population in 2011: 313
Provincial Electoral District(s): Weyburn-Big Muddy
Federal Electoral District(s): Souris-Moose Mountain
Next Election: Oct. 26, 2016 (4 year terms)
Note: Proclaimed as a town on April 1, 1958.
Dennis Mazenc, Mayor
Penny Nergard, Administrator

Bethune
P.O. Box 209
507 Main St.
Bethune, SK S0G 0H0
Tel: 306-638-3188; *Fax:* 306-638-3102
villageofbethune@sasktel.net
www.villageofbethune.com
Municipal Type: Village
Incorporated: Aug. 2, 1912; *Area:* 1.04 sq km
Population in 2011: 400
Provincial Electoral District(s): Thunder Creek
Federal Electoral District(s): Moose Jaw-Lake Centre-Lanigan
Next Election: Oct. 26, 2016 (4 year terms)
Doug Patience, Mayor
Rodney Audette, Administrator

Bienfait
P.O. Box 220
Bienfait, SK S0C 0M0
Tel: 306-388-2969; *Fax:* 306-388-2449
bienfait@sasktel.net
www.bienfait.ca
Municipal Type: Town
Incorporated: April 16, 1912; *Area:* 3.09 sq km
Population in 2011: 780
Provincial Electoral District(s): Estevan
Federal Electoral District(s): Souris-Moose Mountain
Next Election: Oct. 26, 2016 (4 year terms)
Note: Proclaimed as a town on March 1, 1957.
Jamie Bonokoski, Mayor
Laurel Gilroy, Administrator

Big River
P.O. Box 220
Big River, SK S0J 0E0
Tel: 306-469-2112; *Fax:* 306-469-4856
bigriver@sasktel.net
www.bigriver.ca
Municipal Type: Town
Incorporated: Aug. 18, 1923; *Area:* 2.11 sq km
Population in 2011: 639
Provincial Electoral District(s): Saskatchewan Rivers
Federal Electoral District(s): Desnethé-Missinippi-Churchill River
Next Election: Oct. 26, 2016 (4 year terms)
Note: Proclaimed as a town on Oct. 1, 1966.
Rob Buckingham, Mayor
Noreen Olsen, Administrator

Big Shell
P.O. Box 130
Shell Lake, SK S0J 2G0
Tel: 306-427-2188; *Fax:* 306-427-1203
villagebigshell@gmail.com
Municipal Type: Resort Village
Area: 1.02 sq km
Population in 2011: 45
Provincial Electoral District(s): Rosthern-Shellbrook
Federal Electoral District(s): Desnethé-Missinippi-Churchill River
Next Election: July 2020 (4 year terms)
Jim Wilkie, Mayor
Tara Bueckert, Administrator

Biggar
P.O. Box 489
202 - 3rd Ave. West
Biggar, SK S0K 0M0
Tel: 306-948-3317; *Fax:* 306-948-5134
townoffice@townofbiggar.com
www.townofbiggar.com
Municipal Type: Town
Incorporated: May 18, 1909; *Area:* 15.75
Population in 2011: 2,161
Provincial Electoral District(s): Biggar
Federal Electoral District(s): Carlton-Eagle Creek
Next Election: Oct. 26, 2016 (4 year terms)
Note: Proclaimed as a town on Nov. 1, 1911.
Raymond Sadler, Mayor
Barb Barteski, Administrator

Birch Hills
P.O. Box 206
Birch Hills, SK S0J 0G0
Tel: 306-749-2232; *Fax:* 306-749-2545
birchhills@town.sasktel.net
www.birchhills.ca
Municipal Type: Town
Incorporated: July 19, 1907; *Area:* 1.82 sq km
Population in 2011: 1,064
Provincial Electoral District(s): Batoche
Federal Electoral District(s): Prince Albert
Next Election: Oct. 26, 2016 (4 year terms)
Note: Proclaimed as a town on Aug. 1, 1960.
Shirley Ulvild, Mayor
Tara Gariepy, Administrator

Bird's Point
P.O. Box 1019
169 Currie Ave.
Whitewood, SK S0G 5C0
Tel: 306-793-4552; *Fax:* 306-793-2017
rvbirdspoint@sasktel.net
Municipal Type: Resort Village
Area: 0.58 sq km
Population in 2011: 103
Provincial Electoral District(s): Melville-Saltcoats
Federal Electoral District(s): Yorkton-Melville
Next Election: July 2020 (4 year terms)
Kelly Bear, Mayor
Lila Sippola, Administrator

Bjorkdale
P.O. Box 27
213B Forest View
Bjorkdale, SK S0E 0E0
Tel: 306-886-2167; *Fax:* 306-886-2181
villageofbjorkdale@live.com
www.villageofbjorkdale.ca
Municipal Type: Village
Incorporated: April 1, 1968; *Area:* 1.39 sq km
Population in 2011: 199
Provincial Electoral District(s): Kelvington-Wadena
Federal Electoral District(s): Yorkton-Melville
Next Election: Oct. 26, 2016 (4 year terms)
James Majewski, Mayor, 306-886-2181
Kate Clarke, Administrator, 306-886-2167, Fax: 306-886-2181

Black Point
P.O. Box 640
La Loche, SK S0M 1G0
Tel: 306-822-2727; *Fax:* 306-822-2268
Municipal Type: Northern Hamlet
Population in 2010: 47
Provincial Electoral District(s): Athabasca
Federal Electoral District(s): Desnethé-Missinippi-Churchill River
Next Election: Autumn 2016 (4 year terms)
Annette Petit, Mayor
Dale Petit, Clerk

Bladworth
P.O. Box 90
Bladworth, SK S0G 0J0
Tel: 306-567-5564; *Fax:* 306-567-4730
davidsoncd@sasktel.net
Municipal Type: Village
Incorporated: July 27, 1906; *Area:* 0.84 sq km
Population in 2011: 60
Provincial Electoral District(s): Arm River-Watrous
Federal Electoral District(s): Moose Jaw-Lake Centre-Lanigan
Next Election: Oct. 26, 2016 (4 year terms)
Ron Bessey, Mayor
Donna Bessey, Clerk

Blaine Lake
P.O. Box 10
Blaine Lake, SK S0J 0J0
Tel: 306-497-2531; *Fax:* 306-497-2511
blainelake@sasktel.net
www.blainelake.ca
Municipal Type: Town
Incorporated: March 15, 1912; *Area:* 1.75 sq km
Population in 2011: 510
Provincial Electoral District(s): Rosthern-Shellbrook
Federal Electoral District(s): Carlton Trail-Eagle Creek
Next Election: Oct. 26, 2016 (4 year terms)
Note: Proclaimed as a town on March 1, 1954.
Andy Ciona, Mayor
Anna Brad, Administrator

Borden
P.O. Box 210
200 Shepard St.
Borden, SK S0K 0N0
Tel: 306-997-2134; *Fax:* 306-997-2201
office@bordensask.ca
www.bordensask.ca
Municipal Type: Village
Incorporated: July 19, 1907; *Area:* 0.76 sq km
Population in 2011: 245
Provincial Electoral District(s): Biggar
Federal Electoral District(s): Carlton Trail-Eagle Creek
Next Election: Oct. 26, 2016 (4 year terms)
Tom Redhead, Mayor
Jennifer King, Administrator

Brabant Lake
c/o Government Relations
P.O. Box 5000
La Ronge, SK S0J 1L0
Tel: 306-758-4888; *Fax:* 306-758-4888
Other Information: Toll-Free Phone: 1-800-663-1555
Municipal Type: NS
Population in 2010: 102
Provincial Electoral District(s): Athabasca
Federal Electoral District(s): Desnethé-Missinippi-Churchill River
Next Election: Autumn 2016 (4 year terms)
Rebecca Shirley Bueckert, Chair
Valerie Antoniuk, Advisor, 306-425-4323

Bracken
P.O. Box 41
Bracken, SK S0N 0G0
Tel: 306-293-2119
Municipal Type: Village
Incorporated: Jan. 4, 1926; *Area:* 0.60 sq km
Population in 2011: 30
Provincial Electoral District(s): Wood River
Federal Electoral District(s): Cypress Hills-Grasslands
Next Election: Oct. 26, 2016 (4 year terms)
Michael Mitchell, Mayor
Monique Fehr, Administrator

Bradwell
P.O. Box 100
Bradwell, SK S0K 0P0
Tel: 306-257-4141; *Fax:* 306-257-3303
rm343@sasktel.net
Municipal Type: Village
Incorporated: July 13, 1910; *Area:* 0.42 sq km
Population in 2011: 230
Provincial Electoral District(s): Humboldt
Federal Electoral District(s): Moose Jaw-Lake Centre-Lanigan
Next Election: Oct. 26, 2016 (4 year terms)
Ken Hartz, Mayor
R. Doran Scott, Administrator

Bredenbury
P.O. Box 87
Bredenbury, SK S0A 0H0
Tel: 306-898-2055; *Fax:* 306-898-2333
bredenbury@sasktel.net
www.townofbredenbury.ca
Municipal Type: Town
Incorporated: May 3, 1911; *Area:* 4.80 sq km
Population in 2011: 364
Provincial Electoral District(s): Melville-Saltcoats
Federal Electoral District(s): Yorkton-Melville
Next Election: Oct. 26, 2016 (4 year terms)
Note: Proclaimed as a town on May 1, 1913.
Russell Slowski, Mayor
Kim Varga, Administrator

Briercrest
P.O. Box 25
Briercrest, SK S0H 0K0
Tel: 306-799-2066; *Fax:* 306-799-2067
villageofbriercrest@sasktel.net
villageofbriercrest.ca
Municipal Type: Village
Incorporated: April 17, 1912; *Area:* 0.62 sq km
Population in 2011: 111
Provincial Electoral District(s): Indian Head-Milestone
Federal Electoral District(s): Moose Jaw-Lake Centre-Lanigan
Next Election: Oct. 26, 2016 (4 year terms)
Ray Briggs, Mayor
Linda Senchuk, Administrator

Broadview
P.O. Box 430
524 Main St.
Broadview, SK S0G 0K0
Tel: 306-696-2533; *Fax:* 306-696-3573
town.of.broadview@sasktel.net
www.broadview.ca
Municipal Type: Town
Incorporated: Dec. 29, 1898; *Area:* 2.45 sq km
Population in 2011: 574
Provincial Electoral District(s): Moosomin
Federal Electoral District(s): Souris-Moose Mountain
Next Election: Oct. 26, 2016 (4 year terms)
Note: Proclaimed as a town on May 15, 1907.
Sidney Criddle, Mayor
Mervin J. Schmidt, Administrator

Brock
P.O. Box 70
Brock, SK S0L 0H0
Tel: 306-379-2116
brockadmin@sasktel.net
www.brocksk.com
Municipal Type: Village
Incorporated: July 7, 1910; *Area:* 0.74 sq km
Population in 2011: 127
Provincial Electoral District(s): Rosetown-Elrose
Federal Electoral District(s): Cypress Hills-Grasslands
Next Election: Oct. 26, 2016 (4 year terms)
David Wicks, Mayor
Shannon Beheil, Administrator

Broderick
P.O. Box 29
Broderick, SK S0H 0L0
Tel: 306-867-8578
villageofbroderick@yourlink.ca
Municipal Type: Village
Incorporated: Sept. 13, 1909; *Area:* 0.91 sq km
Population in 2011: 71
Provincial Electoral District(s): Rosetown-Elrose
Federal Electoral District(s): Moose Jaw-Lake Centre-Lanigan
Next Election: Oct. 26, 2016 (4 year terms)
Randy Downton, Mayor
Shannon Pederson, Clerk

Brownlee
P.O. Box 89
Brownlee, SK S0H 0M0
Tel: 306-759-2302
Municipal Type: Village
Incorporated: Dec. 29, 1908; *Area:* 2.42 sq km
Population in 2011: 50
Provincial Electoral District(s): Thunder Creek
Federal Electoral District(s): Moose Jaw-Lake Centre-Lanigan
Next Election: Oct. 26, 2016 (4 year terms)
Lyle Swanson, Mayor
Jackie Leggott, Clerk

Bruno
P.O. Box 370
Bruno, SK S0K 0S0
Tel: 306-369-2514; *Fax:* 306-369-2878
bruno@sasktel.net
www.townofbruno.wordpress.com
Municipal Type: Town
Incorporated: March 9, 1909; *Area:* 0.95 sq km
Population in 2011: 574
Provincial Electoral District(s): Humboldt
Federal Electoral District(s): Carlton Trail-Eagle Creek
Next Election: Oct. 26, 2016 (4 year terms)
Note: Proclaimed as a town on Jan. 1, 1962.
Audrey Ludwig, Mayor
Lorna Beaton, Administrator

B-Say-Tah
P.O. Box 908
842 Broadway St.
Fort Qu'Appelle, SK S0G 1S0
Tel: 306-332-6449; *Fax:* 306-332-2923
bsaytah@sasktel.net
www.bsaytah.ca
Municipal Type: Resort Village
Area: 1.33 sq km
Population in 2011: 187
Provincial Electoral District(s): Indian Head-Milestone
Federal Electoral District(s): Regina-Qu'Appelle
Next Election: July 2020 (4 year terms)
Isaac Sneath, Mayor
Richelle Haanstra, Administrator

Buchanan
P.O. Box 479
300 Central Ave.
Buchanan, SK S0A 0J0
Tel: 306-592-2144; *Fax:* 306-592-4471
buchananvillage@sasktel.net
Municipal Type: Village
Incorporated: June 11, 1907; *Area:* 1.29 sq km
Population in 2011: 225
Provincial Electoral District(s): Canora-Pelly
Federal Electoral District(s): Yorkton-Melville
Next Election: Oct. 26, 2016 (4 year terms)
Garry Kupchinski, Mayor
Sheila Ottmann, Administrator

Buena Vista
1050 Grand Ave.
Buena Vista, SK S2V 1A2
Tel: 306-729-4385; *Fax:* 306-729-4518
buenavista@sasktel.net
www.buenavista.ca
Other Information: After Hours Emergency: 306-729-3239
Municipal Type: Village
Incorporated: Nov. 18, 1983; *Area:* 3.61 sq km
Population in 2011: 524
Provincial Electoral District(s): Thunder Creek
Federal Electoral District(s): Moose Jaw-Lake Centre-Lanigan
Next Election: Oct. 26, 2016 (4 year terms)
Bill Dinsu, Mayor, 306-729-3201
Lorna Davies, Administrator

Buffalo Narrows
P.O. Box 98
1 - 1491 Pedersen Ave.
Buffalo Narrows, SK S0M 0J0
Tel: 306-235-4225; *Fax:* 306-235-4699
villageofbuffalo@sasktel.net
Municipal Type: Northern Village
Incorporated: Oct. 1, 1983; *Area:* 34.10 sq km
Population in 2011: 1,153
Provincial Electoral District(s): Athabasca
Federal Electoral District(s): Desnethé-Missinippi-Churchill River
Next Election: Autumn 2016 (4 year terms)
Estelle Laliberte, Mayor
Therese Chartier, Administrator

Bulyea
P.O. Box 37
Bulyea, SK S0G 0L0
Tel: 306-725-4936
info@bulyea.com
www.bulyea.com
Municipal Type: Village
Incorporated: March 9, 1909; *Area:* 1.28 sq km
Population in 2011: 102
Provincial Electoral District(s): Last Mountain-Touchwood
Federal Electoral District(s): Moose Jaw-Lake Centre-Lanigan
Next Election: Oct. 26, 2016 (4 year terms)
Terry Myers, Mayor
Jenna Johnson, Administrator, 306-725-4936

Burstall
P.O. Box 250
428 Martin St.
Burstall, SK S0N 0H0
Tel: 306-679-2000; *Fax:* 306-679-2275
burstall@sasktel.net
www.burstall.ca
Municipal Type: Town
Incorporated: May 31, 1921; *Area:* 1.11 sq km
Population in 2011: 301
Provincial Electoral District(s): Cypress Hills
Federal Electoral District(s): Cypress Hills-Grasslands
Next Election: Oct. 26, 2016 (4 year terms)
Note: Proclaimed as a town on Nov. 1, 1976.
Terry Volk, Mayor
Lucein Stuebing, Administrator

Cabri
P.O. Box 200
202 Centre St.
Cabri, SK S0N 0J0
Tel: 306-587-2500; *Fax:* 306-587-2392
townofcabri@sasktel.net
www.cabri.ca
Municipal Type: Town
Incorporated: May 13, 1912; *Area:* 1.33 sq km
Population in 2011: 399
Provincial Electoral District(s): Cypress Hills
Federal Electoral District(s): Cypress Hills-Grasslands
Next Election: Oct. 26, 2016 (4 year terms)
Note: Proclaimed as a town on April 16, 1917.
David Gossard, Mayor
Janelle Anderson, Chief Administrative Officer

Cadillac
P.O. Box 189
Cadillac, SK S0N 0K0
Tel: 306-785-2100; *Fax:* 306-785-2101
v.cadillac@sasktel.net
Municipal Type: Village
Incorporated: July 2, 1914; *Area:* 1.05 sq km
Population in 2011: 78
Provincial Electoral District(s): Wood River
Federal Electoral District(s): Cypress Hills-Grasslands
Next Election: Oct. 26, 2016 (4 year terms)
Darren Rutt, Mayor
Betty Moller, Clerk

Calder
P.O. Box 47
Calder, SK S0A 0K0
Tel: 306-742-2158; *Fax:* 306-742-2158
caldervillage@sasktel.net
Municipal Type: Village
Incorporated: Jan. 18, 1911; *Area:* 0.75 sq km
Population in 2011: 97
Provincial Electoral District(s): Melville-Saltcoats
Federal Electoral District(s): Yorkton-Melville
Next Election: Oct. 26, 2016 (4 year terms)
Vaughan Shipp, Mayor
Melba Wiens, Clerk

Camsell Portage
c/o Government Relations
P.O. Box 5000
La Ronge, SK S0J 1L0
Tel: 306-425-4321; *Fax:* 306-425-2401
Other Information: Toll-Free Phone: 1-800-663-1555
Municipal Type: NS
Population in 2010: 37
Provincial Electoral District(s): Athabasca
Federal Electoral District(s): Desnethé-Missinippi-Churchill River
Next Election: Autumn 2016 (4 year terms)
Claire Larocque, Chair
Sandra Galambos, Advisor

Candle Lake
P.O. Box 114
20 Hwy. 265
Candle Lake, SK S0J 3E0
Tel: 306-929-2236; *Fax:* 306-929-2201
rvcandlelakeoffice@sasktel.net
www.candlelakeresort.ca
Municipal Type: Resort Village
Area: 63.32 sq km
Population in 2011: 765
Provincial Electoral District(s): Saskatchewan Rivers
Federal Electoral District(s): Desnethé-Missinippi-Churchill River
Next Election: July 2020 (4 year terms)
John G. Quinn, Mayor
Joan Corneil, Administrator

Canora
P.O. Box 717
418 Main St.
Canora, SK S0A 0L0
Tel: 306-563-5773; *Fax:* 306-563-4336
townofcanora@sasktel.net
www.canora.com
Municipal Type: Town
Incorporated: April 8, 1905; *Area:* 7.31 sq km
Population in 2011: 2,219
Provincial Electoral District(s): Canora-Pelly
Federal Electoral District(s): Yorkton-Melville
Next Election: Oct. 26, 2016 (4 year terms)
Note: Proclaimed as a town on Nov. 1, 1910.
Gina Rakochy, Mayor, 303-563-4314
Michael Mykytyshyn, Chief Administrative Officer, 306-563-6466

Canwood
P.O. Box 172
651 Main St.
Canwood, SK S0J 0K0
Tel: 306-468-2016; *Fax:* 306-468-2805
canwood.town@sasktel.net
www.canwood.ca
Municipal Type: Village
Incorporated: July 18, 1916; *Area:* 2.56 sq km
Population in 2011: 308
Provincial Electoral District(s): Rosthern-Shellbrook
Federal Electoral District(s): Desnethé-Missinippi-Churchill River
Next Election: Oct. 26, 2016 (4 year terms)
Robert Thompson, Mayor, 306-468-2266
Lisa Quessy, Administrator, 303-468-2016

Carievale
P.O. Box 88
128 Broadway St.
Carievale, SK S0C 0P0
Tel: 306-928-2033; *Fax:* 306-928-2021
village.carievale@sasktel.net
Municipal Type: Village
Incorporated: March 14, 1903; *Area:* 0.88 sq km
Population in 2011: 236
Provincial Electoral District(s): Cannington
Federal Electoral District(s): Souris-Moose Mountain
Next Election: Oct. 26, 2016 (4 year terms)
Michael Wolf, Mayor
Elaine Lowdon, Administrator

Carlyle
P.O. Box 10
Carlyle, SK S0C 0R0
Tel: 306-453-2363; *Fax:* 306-453-6380
towncarlyle@sasktel.net
www.townofcarlyle.com
Municipal Type: Town
Incorporated: March 13, 1902; *Area:* 3.03 sq km
Population in 2011: 1,441
Provincial Electoral District(s): Cannington
Federal Electoral District(s): Souris-Moose Mountain
Next Election: Oct. 26, 2016 (4 year terms)
Note: Proclaimed as a town on Jan. 1, 1906.
Wayne Orsted, Mayor
Huguette Lutz, Chief Administrative Officer

Carmichael
P.O. Box 420
Gull Lake, SK S0N 1A0
Tel: 306-672-3501; *Fax:* 306-672-3879
rm109@sasktel.net
Municipal Type: Village
Incorporated: May 25, 1917; *Area:* 0.67 sq km
Population in 2011: 30
Provincial Electoral District(s): Cypress Hills
Federal Electoral District(s): Cypress Hills-Grasslands
Next Election: Oct. 26, 2016 (4 year terms)
Miles C. Wells, Mayor
Collette Jones, Clerk

Carnduff
P.O. Box 100
1312 Railway Ave.
Carnduff, SK S0C 0S0
Tel: 306-482-3300; *Fax:* 306-482-3422
info@carnduff.ca
www.carnduff.ca
Municipal Type: Town
Incorporated: March 29, 1899; *Area:* 2.05 sq km
Population in 2011: 1,126
Provincial Electoral District(s): Cannington
Federal Electoral District(s): Souris-Moose Mountain
Next Election: Oct. 26, 2016 (4 year terms)
Note: Proclaimed as a town on Aug. 12, 1905.
Ross Apperley, Mayor, 306-482-7775
Annette Brown, Administrator

Caronport
P.O. Box 550
Caronport, SK S0H 0S0
Tel: 306-756-2225; *Fax:* 306-756-5007
vcoffice@sasktel.net
Municipal Type: Village
Incorporated: Jan. 1, 1988; *Area:* 1.90 sq km
Population in 2011: 1,068
Provincial Electoral District(s): Thunder Creek
Federal Electoral District(s): Cypress Hills-Grasslands
Next Election: Oct. 26, 2016 (4 year terms)
Darryl Tunall, Mayor
Pat Peecock, Administrator

Carrot River
P.O. Box 147
Carrot River, SK S0E 0L0
Tel: 306-768-2515; *Fax:* 306-768-2930
t.carrotriver@sasktel.net
www.carrotriver.ca
Municipal Type: Town
Incorporated: Nov. 6, 1941; *Area:* 1.46 sq km
Population in 2011: 1,000
Provincial Electoral District(s): Carrot River Valley
Federal Electoral District(s): Prince Albert
Next Election: Oct. 26, 2016 (4 year terms)
Note: Proclaimed as a town on April 1, 1948.
Robert Gagne, Mayor
Kevin Trew, Administrator

Central Butte
P.O. Box 10
Central Butte, SK S0H 0T0
Tel: 306-796-2288; *Fax:* 306-796-4627
townofcentralbutte@sasktel.net
www.centralbutte.ca
Municipal Type: Town
Incorporated: April 9, 1915; *Area:* 2.24 sq km
Population in 2011: 365
Provincial Electoral District(s): Thunder Creek
Federal Electoral District(s): Cypress Hills-Grasslands
Next Election: Oct. 26, 2016 (4 year terms)
Note: Proclaimed as a town on July 1, 1967.
Alvin Klassen, Mayor
Kyle Van Den Bosch, Administrator

Ceylon
P.O. Box 188
Ceylon, SK S0C 0T0
Tel: 306-454-2202; *Fax:* 306-454-2627
rmgap39@sasktel.net
Municipal Type: Village
Incorporated: Sept. 26, 1911; *Area:* 0.75 sq km
Population in 2011: 99
Provincial Electoral District(s): Weyburn-Big Muddy
Federal Electoral District(s): Souris-Moose Mountain
Next Election: Oct. 26, 2016 (4 year terms)
Kurt McCurry, Mayor
Yvonne Johnston, Administrator

Chamberlain
P.O. Box 8
Chamberlain, SK S0G 0R0
Tel: 306-638-4680; *Fax:* 306-638-3108
chamberlain@canwan.com
Municipal Type: Village
Incorporated: Jan. 31, 1911; *Area:* 0.70 sq km
Population in 2011: 88
Provincial Electoral District(s): Thunder Creek
Federal Electoral District(s): Moose Jaw-Lake Centre-Lanigan
Next Election: Oct. 26, 2016 (4 year terms)
Shaun Ackerman, Mayor
Wanda Erlandson, Administrator

Chaplin
P.O. Box 210
Chaplin, SK S0H 0V0
Tel: 306-395-2221; *Fax:* 306-395-2555
village.chaplin@sasktel.net
www.chaplin.ca
Municipal Type: Village
Incorporated: Oct. 8, 1912; *Area:* 1.26 sq km
Population in 2011: 218
Provincial Electoral District(s): Thunder Creek
Federal Electoral District(s): Cypress Hills-Grasslands
Next Election: Oct. 26, 2016 (4 year terms)
John (Jack) Doell, Mayor
Sandra Crowther, Administrator

Chitek Lake
P.O. Box 70
219 Pine St.
Chitek Lake, SK S0J 0L0
Tel: 306-984-2353; *Fax:* 306-984-1178
rvchitek@sasktel.net
www.rvchiteklake.com
Municipal Type: Resort Village
Area: 2.54 sq km
Population in 2011: 167
Provincial Electoral District(s): Meadow Lake
Federal Electoral District(s): Desnethé-Missinippi-Churchill River
Next Election: July 2020 (4 year terms)
Douglas Struhar, Mayor
Cindy Larson, Administrator

Choiceland
P.O. Box 279
100 Railway Ave. East
Choiceland, SK S0J 0M0
Tel: 306-428-2070; *Fax:* 306-428-2071
choiceland.town@sasktel.net
choiceland.ca
Municipal Type: Town
Incorporated: Sept. 8, 1944; *Area:* 1.12 sq km
Population in 2011: 381
Provincial Electoral District(s): Saskatchewan Rivers
Federal Electoral District(s): Prince Albert
Next Election: Oct. 26, 2016 (4 year terms)
Note: Proclaimed as a town on Jan. 1, 1979.
Robert Mardell, Mayor
Holly Toews, Administrator

Chorney Beach
P.O. Box 328
Foam Lake, SK S0A 1A0
Tel: 306-272-3359; *Fax:* 306-272-3738
chorneybeach@gmail.com
Municipal Type: Resort Village
Area: 0.17 sq km
Population in 2011: 15
Provincial Electoral District(s): Kelvington-Wadena
Federal Electoral District(s): Yorkton-Melville
Next Election: July 2020 (4 year terms)
Peter Olson, Mayor
Bethalyn Rusch, Clerk

Christopher Lake
P.O. Box 163
Christopher Lake, SK S0J 0N0
Tel: 306-982-4242; *Fax:* 306-982-4242
vilchris@sasktel.net
www.villageofchristopherlake.com
Municipal Type: Village
Incorporated: March 1, 1985; *Area:* 3.47 sq km
Population in 2011: 266
Provincial Electoral District(s): Saskatchewan Rivers
Federal Electoral District(s): Desnethé-Missinippi-Churchill River
Next Election: Oct. 26, 2016 (4 year terms)
Denis Daughton, Mayor, 306-982-4686
Jeannie Rip, Administrator, 306-982-4242

Churchbridge
P.O. Box 256
116 Vincent Ave.
Churchbridge, SK S0A 0M0
Tel: 306-896-2240; *Fax:* 306-896-2910
churchbridge@sasktel.net
www.churchbridge.com
Municipal Type: Town
Incorporated: Sept. 17, 1903; *Area:* 2.76 sq km
Population in 2011: 743
Provincial Electoral District(s): Melville-Saltcoats
Federal Electoral District(s): Yorkton-Melville
Next Election: Oct. 26, 2016 (4 year terms)
Note: Proclaimed as a town on March 1, 1964.
Jim Gallant, Mayor
Carla Kaeding, Administrator

Clavet
P.O. Box 68
9 Main St.
Clavet, SK S0K 0Y0
Tel: 306-933-2425; *Fax:* 306-933-1995
clavetvillage@sasktel.net
www.villageofclavet.com
Municipal Type: Village
Incorporated: Dec. 21, 1908; *Area:* 0.61 sq km
Population in 2011: 386
Provincial Electoral District(s): Humboldt
Federal Electoral District(s): Moose Jaw-Lake Centre-Lanigan
Next Election: Oct. 26, 2016 (4 year terms)

Blair Bentley, Mayor
Janet E. Patry, Administrator

Climax
P.O. Box 30
Climax, SK S0N 0N0
Tel: 306-293-2128; *Fax:* 306-293-2702
villageofclimax@sasktel.net
Municipal Type: Village
Incorporated: Dec. 11, 1923; *Area:* 1.00 sq km
Population in 2011: 182
Provincial Electoral District(s): Cypress Hills
Federal Electoral District(s): Cypress Hills-Grasslands
Next Election: Oct. 26, 2016 (4 year terms)
Nancy Kirk, Mayor
Shawna Bertram, Administrator

Cochin
P.O. Box 160
Cochin, SK S0M 0L0
Tel: 306-386-2333; *Fax:* 306-386-2305
cochinadmin@sasktel.net
www.cochin.ca
Municipal Type: Resort Village
Incorporated: 1915; *Area:* 1.35 sq km
Population in 2011: 122
Provincial Electoral District(s): Cut Knife-Turtleford
Federal Electoral District(s): Battlefords-Lloydminster
Next Election: July 2020 (4 year terms)
Brad Pattinson, Mayor
Theres Harty, Administrator

Coderre
P.O. Box 9
Coderre, SK S0H 0X0
Tel: 306-394-2070
vil.of.coderre@sasktel.net
Municipal Type: Village
Incorporated: Aug. 26, 1925; *Area:* 0.85 sq km
Population in 2011: 30
Provincial Electoral District(s): Wood River
Federal Electoral District(s): Cypress Hills-Grasslands
Next Election: Oct. 26, 2016 (4 year terms)
Leonard Lepine, Mayor
Dara Cowan, Administrator

Codette
P.O. Box 100
Codette, SK S0E 0P0
Tel: 306-862-9551; *Fax:* 306-862-2432
villageofcodette@sasktel.net
www.codette.ca
Municipal Type: Village
Incorporated: March 9, 1929; *Area:* 0.37 sq km
Population in 2011: 205
Provincial Electoral District(s): Carrot River Valley
Federal Electoral District(s): Prince Albert
Next Election: Oct. 26, 2016 (4 year terms)
Kevin Hess, Mayor, 306-862-8781
Eunice Rudy, Administrator, 306-862-9551

Cole Bay
P.O. Box 80
Canoe Rd.
Cole Bay, SK S0M 0M0
Tel: 306-829-4232; *Fax:* 306-829-4312
Municipal Type: Northern Village
Incorporated: Jan. 1, 1990; *Area:* 4.95 sq km
Population in 2011: 230
Provincial Electoral District(s): Athabasca
Federal Electoral District(s): Desnethé-Missinippi-Churchill River
Next Election: Autumn 2016 (4 year terms)
Harold Aubichon, Mayor
Delphine Bouvier, Clerk

Coleville
P.O. Box 249
Coleville, SK S0L 0K0
Tel: 306-965-2281; *Fax:* 306-965-2466
rm320@sasktel.net
www.colevillesk.ca
Other Information: Alt. E-mail: rmoakassist@sasktel.net
Municipal Type: Village
Incorporated: July 1, 1953; *Area:* 1.27 sq km
Population in 2011: 311
Provincial Electoral District(s): Kindersley
Federal Electoral District(s): Battlefords-Lloydminster
Next Election: Oct. 26, 2016 (4 year terms)
Mike Smith, Mayor
Gillian Lund, Administrator

Colonsay
P.O. Box 190
100 Jura St.
Colonsay, SK S0K 0Z0
Tel: 306-255-2313; *Fax:* 306-255-2291
town.colonsay@sasktel.net
www.townofcolonsay.ca
Municipal Type: Town
Incorporated: Oct. 6, 1910; *Area:* 2.46 sq km
Population in 2011: 475
Provincial Electoral District(s): Humboldt
Federal Electoral District(s): Moose Jaw-Lake Centre-Lanigan
Next Election: Oct. 26, 2016 (4 year terms)
Note: Proclaimed as a town on Jan. 1, 1977.
James Gray, Mayor
Deborah Prosper, Administrator

Conquest
P.O. Box 250
202 Coulthard St.
Conquest, SK S0L 0L0
Tel: 306-856-2114; *Fax:* 306-856-2114
conquest@sasktel.net
www.villageofconquest.ca
Municipal Type: Village
Incorporated: Oct. 24, 1911; *Area:* 1 sq km
Population in 2011: 176
Provincial Electoral District(s): Rosetown-Elrose
Federal Electoral District(s): Carlton Trail-Eagle Creek
Next Election: Oct. 26, 2016 (4 year terms)
Marc Norris, Mayor
Bobbi Jones, Administrator

Consul
P.O. Box 185
Consul, SK S0N 0P0
Tel: 306-299-2030; *Fax:* 306-299-2031
consul@sasktel.net
Municipal Type: Village
Incorporated: June 12, 1917; *Area:* 0.65 sq km
Population in 2011: 84
Provincial Electoral District(s): Cypress Hills
Federal Electoral District(s): Cypress Hills-Grasslands
Next Election: Oct. 26, 2016 (4 year terms)
Linda Brown, Mayor
Yvonne Leismeister, Administrator

Coronach
P.O. Box 90
Coronach, SK S0H 0Z0
Tel: 306-267-2150; *Fax:* 306-267-2296
townoffice@coronach.ca
www.coronach.ca
Municipal Type: Town
Incorporated: Feb. 3, 1928; *Area:* 2.33 sq km
Population in 2011: 711
Provincial Electoral District(s): Weyburn-Big Muddy
Federal Electoral District(s): Souris-Moose Mountain
Next Election: Oct. 26, 2016 (4 year terms)
Note: Proclaimed as a town on Jan. 1, 1977.
George Peacock, Mayor
Leanne Totton, Administrator

Coteau Beach
219 Greaves Ct.
Saskatoon, SK S7W 1A8
Tel: 306-649-2440
coteaubeach@sasktel.net
www.resortvillageofcoteau.ca
Municipal Type: Resort Village
Incorporated: 1969; *Area:* 0.54 sq km
Population in 2011: 40
Provincial Electoral District(s): Rosetown-Elrose
Federal Electoral District(s): Cypress Hills-Grasslands
Next Election: July 2020 (4 year terms)
Jeff Sopczak, Mayor
Trudy Eggleston, Clerk, 306-649-2440

Craik
P.O. Box 60
Craik, SK S0G 0V0
Tel: 306-734-2250; *Fax:* 306-734-2688
townofcraik@craik.ca
www.craik.ca
Municipal Type: Town
Incorporated: Oct. 22, 1903; *Area:* 5.41 sq km
Population in 2011: 453
Provincial Electoral District(s): Thunder Creek
Federal Electoral District(s): Moose Jaw-Lake Centre-Lanigan
Next Election: Oct. 26, 2016 (4 year terms)
Note: Proclaimed as a town on Aug. 1, 1907.
Rick Rogers, Mayor

Sarah Wells, Administrator

Craven
P.O. Box 30
Craven, SK S0G 0W0
Tel: 306-731-3452; *Fax:* 306-731-3162
villageofcraven@canwan.com
www.villageofcraven.com
Municipal Type: Village
Incorporated: April 11, 1905; *Area:* 1.16 sq km
Population in 2011: 234
Provincial Electoral District(s): Last Mountain-Touchwood
Federal Electoral District(s): Moose Jaw-Lake Centre-Lanigan
Next Election: Oct. 26, 2016 (4 year terms)
Adri Vandeven, Mayor
Wendy Dunn, Administrator

Creelman
P.O. Box 177
Creelman, SK S0G 0X0
Tel: 306-433-2011; *Fax:* 306-433-2011
creelmanvillage@sasktel.net
Municipal Type: Village
Incorporated: April 6, 1906; *Area:* 1.14 sq km
Population in 2011: 115
Provincial Electoral District(s): Cannington
Federal Electoral District(s): Souris-Moose Mountain
Next Election: Oct. 26, 2016 (4 year terms)
Pat Hume, Mayor
Diana Hume, Administrator

Creighton
P.O. Box 100
300 - 1st Street East
Creighton, SK S0P 0A0
Tel: 306-688-8253; *Fax:* 306-688-4764
townofcreighton@sasktel.net
www.townofcreighton.ca
Municipal Type: Northern Town
Incorporated: Oct. 1, 1983; *Area:* 14.39 sq km
Population in 2011: 1,498
Provincial Electoral District(s): Cumberland
Federal Electoral District(s): Desnethé-Missinippi-Churchill River
Next Election: Autumn 2016 (4 year terms)
Bruce Fidler, Mayor
Paula Muench, Administrator

Cudworth
P.O. Box 69
223 Main St.
Cudworth, SK S0K 1B0
Tel: 306-256-3492; *Fax:* 306-256-3515
town.cudworth@sasktel.net
www.townofcudworth.com
Municipal Type: Town
Incorporated: Oct. 23, 1911; *Area:* 2.21 sq km
Population in 2011: 770
Provincial Electoral District(s): Batoche
Federal Electoral District(s): Carlton Trail-Eagle Creek
Next Election: Oct. 26, 2016 (4 year terms)
Note: Proclaimed as a town on Oct. 1, 1961.
Harold Mueller, Mayor
Yvonne Gobolos, Administrator

Cumberland House
P.O. Box 190
Cumberland St.
Cumberland House, SK S0E 0S0
Tel: 306-888-2066; *Fax:* 306-888-2103
northernvillageofchouse@sasktel.net
Municipal Type: Northern Village
Incorporated: Oct. 1, 1983; *Area:* 15.69 sq km
Population in 2011: 772
Provincial Electoral District(s): Cumberland
Federal Electoral District(s): Desnethé-Missinippi-Churchill River
Next Election: Autumn 2016 (4 year terms)
Valerie Deschambeault, Mayor
Marcie Fiddler, Clerk
Jacqueline Fleury, Administrator

Cupar
P.O. Box 397
Cupar, SK S0G 0Y0
Tel: 306-723-4324; *Fax:* 306-723-4644
townofcupar1@sasktel.net
www.townofcupar.com
Municipal Type: Town
Incorporated: March 21, 1906; *Area:* 0.80 sq km
Population in 2011: 579
Provincial Electoral District(s): Last Mountain-Touchwood
Federal Electoral District(s): Regina-Qu'Appelle

Next Election: Oct. 26, 2016 (4 year terms)
Note: Proclaimed as a town on Jan. 1, 1961.
Len Kallichuk, Mayor, 306-723-4514
Karen Herman, Administrator

Cut Knife
P.O. Box 70
Cut Knife, SK S0M 0N0
Tel: 306-398-2363; *Fax:* 306-398-2839
rm439@sasktel.net
www.townofcutknife.ca
Municipal Type: Town
Incorporated: May 17, 1912; *Area:* 1.99 sq km
Population in 2011: 517
Provincial Electoral District(s): Cut Knife-Turtleford
Federal Electoral District(s): Battlefords-Lloydminster
Next Election: Oct. 26, 2016 (4 year terms)
Note: Proclaimed as a town on Aug. 1, 1968.
Gwenn Kaye, Mayor
Don McCallum, Administrator

Dafoe
P.O. Box 142
Dafoe, SK S0K 1C0
Tel: 306-554-3250
Municipal Type: Village
Incorporated: May 28, 1920; *Area:* 0.80 sq km
Population in 2011: 15
Provincial Electoral District(s): Rosetown-Elrose
Federal Electoral District(s): Regina-Qu'Appelle
Next Election: Oct. 26, 2016 (4 year terms)
Bob Pilkey, Mayor
Lana M. Bolt, Clerk

Dalmeny
P.O. Box 400
301 Railway Ave.
Dalmeny, SK S0K 1E0
Tel: 306-254-2133; *Fax:* 306-254-2142
dalmenytownoffice@sasktel.net
www.dalmeny.ca
Municipal Type: Town
Incorporated: June 17, 1912; *Area:* 2.27 sq km
Population in 2011: 1,702
Provincial Electoral District(s): Weyburn-Big Muddy
Federal Electoral District(s): Carlton Trail-Eagle Creek
Next Election: Oct. 26, 2016 (4 year terms)
Note: Proclaimed as a town on April 1, 1983.
Nick Bakker, Mayor
Jim Weninger, Administrator

Davidson
P.O. Box 340
206 Washington Ave.
Davidson, SK S0G 1A0
Tel: 306-567-2040; *Fax:* 306-567-4730
townofdavidson@sasktel.net
www.townofdavidson.com
Municipal Type: Town
Incorporated: March 7, 1904; *Area:* 4.49 sq km
Population in 2011: 1,025
Provincial Electoral District(s): Arm River-Watrous
Federal Electoral District(s): Moose Jaw-Lake Centre-Lanigan
Next Election: Oct. 26, 2016 (4 year terms)
Note: Proclaimed as a town on Nov. 15, 1906.
Clayton Schneider, Mayor
Gary Edom, Administrator

Debden
P.O. Box 400
204 - 2nd Ave. East
Debden, SK S0J 0S0
Tel: 306-724-2040; *Fax:* 306-724-4458
villagedebden@sasktel.net
www.debden.net
Municipal Type: Village
Incorporated: June 7, 1922; *Area:* 1.39 sq km
Population in 2011: 358
Provincial Electoral District(s): Saskatchewan Rivers
Federal Electoral District(s): Desnethé-Missinippi-Churchill River
Next Election: Oct. 26, 2016 (4 year terms)
Aline Hannon, Mayor
Carmen Jean, Administrator

Delisle
P.O. Box 40
201 - 1st St. West
Delisle, SK S0L 0P0
Tel: 306-493-2242; *Fax:* 306-493-2263
delisle@sasktel.net
www.townofdelisle.com
Municipal Type: Town
Incorporated: Dec. 29, 1908; *Area:* 2.35 sq km
Population in 2011: 975
Provincial Electoral District(s): Biggar
Federal Electoral District(s): Carlton Trail-Eagle Creek
Next Election: Oct. 26, 2016 (4 year terms)
Note: Proclaimed as a town on Nov. 1, 1913.
Dave Anderchek, Mayor, 306-493-2258
Mark Dubkowski, Administrator

Denare Beach
P.O. Box 70
512 - 7th Ave.
Denare Beach, SK S0P 0B0
Tel: 306-362-2054; *Fax:* 306-362-2257
denarebeach@aski.ca
www.denarebeach.net
Municipal Type: Northern Village
Incorporated: April 1, 1984; *Area:* 5.84 sq km
Population in 2011: 669
Provincial Electoral District(s): Cumberland
Federal Electoral District(s): Desnethé-Missinippi-Churchill River
Next Election: Autumn 2016 (4 year terms)
Carl Lentowicz, Mayor
Meredith Norman, Administrator

Denholm
P.O. Box 71
Denholm, SK S0M 0R0
Tel: 306-446-0478
Municipal Type: Village
Incorporated: June 25, 1912; *Area:* 0.33 sq km
Population in 2011: 76
Provincial Electoral District(s): Biggar
Federal Electoral District(s): Battlefords-Lloydminster
Next Election: Oct. 26, 2016 (4 year terms)
Donna Oborowsky, Mayor
Lila Yuhasz, Clerk

Denzil
P.O. Box 100
Denzil, SK S0L 0S0
Tel: 306-358-2118; *Fax:* 306-358-4828
villageofdenzil@sasktel.net
www.villageofdenzil.com
Municipal Type: Village
Incorporated: May 3, 1911; *Area:* 0.55 sq km
Population in 2011: 135
Provincial Electoral District(s): Kindersley
Federal Electoral District(s): Battlefords-Lloydminster
Next Election: Oct. 26, 2016 (4 year terms)
Murray Sieben, Mayor
Kathy Reschny, Administrator

Descharme Lake
c/o Government Relations
P.O. Box 69
Buffalo Narrows, SK S0M 0J0
Tel: 306-235-1726; *Fax:* 306-235-1727
Municipal Type: NS
Population in 2010: 42
Provincial Electoral District(s): Athabasca
Federal Electoral District(s): Desnethé-Missinippi-Churchill River
Next Election: Autumn 2016 (4 year terms)
John Frank Sylvestre, Chair
Bruce Leier, Advisor

Dilke
P.O. Box 100
Devon St.
Dilke, SK S0G 1C0
Tel: 306-488-4866; *Fax:* 306-488-4866
dilke@canwan.com
Municipal Type: Village
Incorporated: Dec. 30, 1912; *Area:* 1.28 sq km
Population in 2011: 77
Provincial Electoral District(s): Thunder Creek
Federal Electoral District(s): Moose Jaw-Lake Centre-Lanigan
Next Election: Oct. 26, 2016 (4 year terms)
Arnold Ball, Mayor
Colleen R. Duesing, Clerk

Dinsmore
P.O. Box 278
100 Main St.
Dinsmore, SK S0L 0T0
Tel: 306-846-2220; *Fax:* 306-846-2999
dinsmore@sasktel.net
www.dinsmore.ca
Municipal Type: Village
Incorporated: Nov. 3, 1913; *Area:* 2.59 sq km
Population in 2011: 318
Provincial Electoral District(s): Rosetown-Elrose
Federal Electoral District(s): Carlton Trail-Eagle Creek
Next Election: Oct. 26, 2016 (4 year terms)
Jim Main, Mayor, 306-846-2248
Kirsten Raffos, Administrator

Disley
R.R.#1
Lumsden, SK S0G 3C0
Tel: 306-731-3355
villageofdisley@gmail.com
Municipal Type: Village
Incorporated: June 24, 1907; *Area:* 0.65 sq km
Population in 2011: 111
Provincial Electoral District(s): Thunder Creek
Federal Electoral District(s): Moose Jaw-Lake Centre-Lanigan
Next Election: Oct. 26, 2016 (4 year terms)
Gord Wilson, Mayor
Rhonda Woelk, Administrator

Dodsland
P.O. Box 400
Dodsland, SK S0L 0V0
Tel: 306-356-0011; *Fax:* 306-356-0012
villageofdodsland@yourlink.ca
Municipal Type: Village
Incorporated: Aug. 23, 1913; *Area:* 2.93 sq km
Population in 2011: 212
Provincial Electoral District(s): Rosetown-Elrose
Federal Electoral District(s): Battlefords-Lloydminster
Next Election: Oct. 26, 2016 (4 year terms)
Joey Straza, Mayor
Amy Sittler, Administrator

Dore Lake
P.O. Box 608
Dore Ave.
Big River, SK S0J 0E0
Tel: 306-832-4528; *Fax:* 306-832-4525
northern.dore@sasktel.net
Municipal Type: Northern Hamlet
Incorporated: Jan. 11, 1985; *Area:* 8.03 sq km
Population in 2011: 28
Provincial Electoral District(s): Athabasca
Federal Electoral District(s): Desnethé-Missinippi-Churchill River
Next Election: Autumn 2016 (4 year terms)
Bobby Buffin, Mayor
Hilda McKay, Administrator

Dorintosh
P.O. Box 40
301 1st St. East
Dorintosh, SK S0M 0T0
Tel: 306-236-5166
vill.dor@sasktel.net
www.villageofdorintosh.sasktelwebsite.net
Municipal Type: Village
Incorporated: Jan. 1, 1989; *Area:* 0.88 sq km
Population in 2011: 147
Provincial Electoral District(s): Meadow Lake
Federal Electoral District(s): Desnethé-Missinippi-Churchill River
Next Election: Oct. 26, 2016 (4 year terms)
John Osborne, Mayor
Pam Dallyn, Administrator

Drake
P.O. Box 18
125 Francis St.
Drake, SK S0K 1H0
Tel: 306-363-2109; *Fax:* 306-363-2102
villageofdrake@sasktel.net
www.drake.ca
Municipal Type: Village
Incorporated: Sept. 19, 1910; *Area:* 0.72 sq km
Population in 2011: 202
Provincial Electoral District(s): Arm River-Watrous
Federal Electoral District(s): Moose Jaw-Lake Centre-Lanigan
Next Election: Oct. 26, 2016 (4 year terms)
Peter Nicholson, Mayor, 306-363-2021
Stuart Jantz, Administrator, 306-363-2109

Drinkwater
P.O. Box 66
Drinkwater, SK S0H 1G0
Tel: 306-693-5093; *Fax:* 306-693-4410
villageofdrinkwater@sasktel.net
Municipal Type: Village
Incorporated: June 7, 1904; *Area:* 2.64 sq km
Population in 2011: 65
Provincial Electoral District(s): Indian Head-Milestone
Federal Electoral District(s): Moose Jaw-Lake Centre-Lanigan
Next Election: Oct. 26, 2016 (4 year terms)

Ryan Briggs, Mayor
Colleen Loos, Clerk

Dubuc
P.O. Box 126
Dubuc, SK S0A 0R0
Tel: 306-877-2172; *Fax:* 306-877-0044
villageofdubuc@sasktel.net
Municipal Type: Village
Incorporated: May 29, 1905; *Area:* 0.63 sq km
Population in 2011: 70
Provincial Electoral District(s): Melville-Saltcoats
Federal Electoral District(s): Yorkton-Melville
Next Election: Oct. 26, 2016 (4 year terms)
Peter Nielsen, Mayor
Janet Siever, Clerk

Duck Lake
P.O. Box 430
Duck Lake, SK S0K 1J0
Tel: 306-467-2277; *Fax:* 306-467-4434
town.ducklake@sasktel.net
www.ducklake.ca
Municipal Type: Town
Incorporated: Dec. 29, 1898; *Area:* 2.86 sq km
Population in 2011: 577
Provincial Electoral District(s): Batoche
Federal Electoral District(s): Carlton Trail-Eagle Creek
Next Election: Oct. 26, 2016 (4 year terms)
Note: Proclaimed as a town on Nov. 1, 1911.
Denis Poirier, Mayor
Janet Patry, Administrator

Duff
P.O. Box 57
Duff, SK S0A 0S0
Tel: 306-728-3570
tlynn@yourlink.ca
Municipal Type: Village
Incorporated: May 28, 1920; *Area:* 0.22 sq km
Population in 2011: 30
Provincial Electoral District(s): Last Mountain-Touchwood
Federal Electoral District(s): Yorkton-Melville
Next Election: Oct. 26, 2016 (4 year terms)
David Hollinger, Mayor
Tracey Schuman, Clerk

Dundurn
P.O. Box 185
300 - Third Avenue
Dundurn, SK S0K 1K0
Tel: 306-492-2202; *Fax:* 306-492-2360
town.dundurn@sasktel.net
www.townofdundurn.ca
Municipal Type: Town
Incorporated: July 7, 1905; *Area:* 0.88 sq km
Population in 2011: 693
Provincial Electoral District(s): Arm River-Watrous
Federal Electoral District(s): Moose Jaw-Lake Centre-Lanigan
Next Election: Oct. 26, 2016 (4 year terms)
Note: Proclaimed as a town on Nov. 1, 1980.
Doug Narraway, Mayor
Eileen Prosser, Administrator

Duval
P.O. Box 70
Duval, SK S0G 1G0
Tel: 306-725-3767; *Fax:* 306-725-4339
Municipal Type: Village
Incorporated: Dec. 21, 1910; *Area:* 0.75 sq km
Population in 2011: 97
Provincial Electoral District(s): Arm River-Watrous
Federal Electoral District(s): Moose Jaw-Lake Centre-Lanigan
Next Election: Oct. 26, 2016 (4 year terms)
Dale Campbell, Mayor
Jeff Jones, Clerk

Dysart
P.O. Box 70
Dysart, SK S0G 1H0
Tel: 306-432-2100; *Fax:* 306-432-2265
dysartsk@sasktel.net
www.dysartsk.ca
Municipal Type: Village
Incorporated: April 6, 1909; *Area:* 1.19 sq km
Population in 2011: 218
Provincial Electoral District(s): Last Mountain-Touchwood
Federal Electoral District(s): Regina-Qu'Appelle
Next Election: Oct. 26, 2016 (4 year terms)
Brenda Macknak, Mayor
Bonnie Moleski, Administrator

Earl Grey
P.O. Box 100
Earl Grey, SK S0G 1J0
Tel: 306-939-2062; *Fax:* 306-939-2036
earlgreyvillage@sasktel.net
Municipal Type: Village
Incorporated: July 27, 1906; *Area:* 1.31 sq km
Population in 2011: 239
Provincial Electoral District(s): Last Mountain-Touchwood
Federal Electoral District(s): Moose Jaw-Lake Centre-Lanigan
Next Election: Oct. 26, 2016 (4 year terms)
Malcolm Manz, Mayor
Loretta Young, Administrator

Eastend
P.O. Box 520
Eastend, SK S0N 0T0
Tel: 306-295-3322; *Fax:* 306-295-3571
eastend@sasktel.net
www.dinocountry.com
Municipal Type: Town
Incorporated: Feb. 26, 1914; *Area:* 2.71 sq km
Population in 2011: 527
Provincial Electoral District(s): Cypress Hills
Federal Electoral District(s): Cypress Hills-Grasslands
Next Election: Oct. 26, 2016 (4 year terms)
Note: Proclaimed as a town on March 15, 1920.
Alan Howard, Mayor
Edna Laturnus, Administrator

Eatonia
P.O. Box 237
Eatonia, SK S0L 0Y0
Tel: 306-967-2251; *Fax:* 306-967-2267
eatonia@sasktel.net
www.eatonia.ca
Municipal Type: Town
Incorporated: Jan. 28, 1920; *Area:* 1.68 sq km
Population in 2011: 508
Provincial Electoral District(s): Kindersley
Federal Electoral District(s): Cypress Hills-Grasslands
Next Election: Oct. 26, 2016 (4 year terms)
Note: Proclaimed as a town on Jan. 1, 1954.
R.W. (Bob) Peters, Mayor
Cheryl Bailey, Administrator

Ebenezer
P.O. Box 97
Ebenezer, SK S0A 0T0
Tel: 306-783-1217; *Fax:* 306-793-1218
village.ebenezer@sasktel.net
Municipal Type: Village
Incorporated: July 1, 1948; *Area:* 0.62 sq km
Population in 2011: 175
Provincial Electoral District(s): Canora-Pelly
Federal Electoral District(s): Yorkton-Melville
Next Election: Oct. 26, 2016 (4 year terms)
Braden Ferris, Mayor
Joyce Palagian, Administrator

Echo Bay
P.O. Box 130
Shell Lake, SK S0J 2G0
Tel: 306-427-2188; *Fax:* 306-427-1203
resortechobay@gmail.com
Municipal Type: Resort Village
Area: 0.80 sq km
Population in 2011: 38
Provincial Electoral District(s): Rosthern-Shellbrook
Federal Electoral District(s): Desnethé-Missinippi-Churchill River
Next Election: July 2020 (4 year terms)
Brian McCaig, Mayor, 306-229-1606
Tara Bueckert, Administrator

Edam
P.O. Box 203
Edam, SK S0M 0V0
Tel: 306-397-2223; *Fax:* 306-397-2626
edamvill@sasktel.net
villageofedam.ca
Municipal Type: Village
Incorporated: Oct. 12, 1911; *Area:* 1.13 sq km
Population in 2011: 444
Provincial Electoral District(s): Cut Knife-Turtleford
Federal Electoral District(s): Battlefords-Lloydminster
Next Election: Oct. 26, 2016 (4 year terms)
Larry McDaid, Mayor
Trudy McMurphy, Administrator

Edenwold
P.O. Box 130
Edenwold, SK S0G 1K0
Tel: 306-771-4121; *Fax:* 306-771-2518
office@villageofedenwold.ca
www.villageofedenwold.ca
Municipal Type: Village
Incorporated: Oct. 3, 1912; *Area:* 0.68 sq km
Population in 2011: 238
Provincial Electoral District(s): Indian Head-Milestone
Federal Electoral District(s): Regina-Qu'Appelle
Next Election: Oct. 26, 2016 (4 year terms)
Dean Josephson, Mayor
Christine Galbraith, Administrator

Elbow
P.O. Box 8
201 Saskatchewan St.
Elbow, SK S0H 1J0
Tel: 306-854-2277; *Fax:* 306-854-2229
info@elbowsask.com
www.elbowsask.com
Municipal Type: Village
Incorporated: April 6, 1909; *Area:* 3.92 sq km
Population in 2011: 314
Provincial Electoral District(s): Thunder Creek
Federal Electoral District(s): Moose Jaw-Lake Centre-Lanigan
Next Election: Oct. 26, 2016 (4 year terms)
Robert (Rob) Hundeby, Mayor
Yvonne Jess, Administrator

Elfros
P.O. Box 40
Elfros, SK S0A 0V0
Tel: 306-328-2011; *Fax:* 306-328-4490
rm307@sasktel.net
Municipal Type: Village
Incorporated: Dec. 1, 1909; *Area:* 2.52 sq km
Population in 2011: 96
Provincial Electoral District(s): Kelvington-Wadena
Federal Electoral District(s): Regina-Qu'Appelle
Next Election: Oct. 26, 2016 (4 year terms)
Karilee Zemlak, Mayor
Glenn Thompson, Administrator

Elrose
P.O. Box 458
101 Main St.
Elrose, SK S0L 0Z0
Tel: 306-378-2202; *Fax:* 306-378-2966
townofelrose@sasktel.net
www.elrose.ca
Municipal Type: Town
Incorporated: Oct. 24, 1913; *Area:* 2.76 sq km
Population in 2011: 477
Provincial Electoral District(s): Rosetown-Elrose
Federal Electoral District(s): Cypress Hills-Grasslands
Next Election: Oct. 26, 2016 (4 year terms)
Note: Proclaimed as a town on Feb. 1, 1951.
June Harsch, Mayor
Desiree Bouvier, Administrator

Elstow
P.O. Box 29
Elstow, SK S0K 1M0
Tel: 306-257-3889; *Fax:* 306-257-3709
villageofelstow@gmail.com
Municipal Type: Village
Incorporated: Dec. 17, 1908; *Area:* 0.58 sq km
Population in 2011: 89
Provincial Electoral District(s): Humboldt
Federal Electoral District(s): Moose Jaw-Lake Centre-Lanigan
Next Election: Oct. 26, 2016 (4 year terms)
Mark Wylie, Mayor
Zelma McAdam, Administrator

Endeavour
P.O. Box 307
Endeavour, SK S0A 0W0
Tel: 306-547-3484; *Fax:* 306-547-3484
endeavour@sasktel.net
Municipal Type: Village
Incorporated: April 29, 1953; *Area:* 0.99 sq km
Population in 2011: 94
Provincial Electoral District(s): Canora-Pelly
Federal Electoral District(s): Yorkton-Melville
Next Election: Oct. 26, 2016 (4 year terms)
James German, Mayor
Kathleen Ambrose, Administrator

Englefeld
P.O. Box 44
135 Main St.
Englefeld, SK S0K 1N0
Tel: 306-287-3151; *Fax:* 306-287-9902
villageadmin@englefeld.ca
www.englefeld.ca
Municipal Type: Village
Incorporated: June 13, 1916; *Area:* 0.65 sq km
Population in 2011: 247
Provincial Electoral District(s): Melfort
Federal Electoral District(s): Carlton Trail-Eagle Creek
Next Election: Oct. 26, 2016 (4 year terms)
Darrell Athmer, Mayor
Lani Best, Administrator

Ernfold
P.O. Box 340
401 Main Street
Morse, SK S0H 3C0
Tel: 306-629-3282; *Fax:* 306-629-3212
rm165@sasktel.net
Municipal Type: Village
Incorporated: Dec. 4, 1912; *Area:* 1.19 sq km
Population in 2011: 30
Provincial Electoral District(s): Thunder Creek
Federal Electoral District(s): Cypress Hills-Grasslands
Next Election: Oct. 26, 2016 (4 year terms)
Christine Bauck, Mayor
Mark Wilson, Administrator

Esterhazy
P.O. Box 490
600 Sumner St.
Esterhazy, SK S0A 0X0
Tel: 306-745-3942; *Fax:* 306-745-6797
town.esterhazy@sasktel.net
www.townofesterhazy.wordpress.com
Municipal Type: Town
Incorporated: Dec. 3, 1903; *Area:* 4.75 sq km
Population in 2011: 2,472
Provincial Electoral District(s): Melville-Saltcoats
Federal Electoral District(s): Yorkton-Melville
Next Election: Oct. 26, 2016 (4 year terms)
Note: Proclaimed as a town on March 1, 1957.
Pauline Chewka, Mayor
Donna Rollie, Chief Administrative Officer

Eston
P.O. Box 757
217 Main St. South
Eston, SK S0L 1A0
Tel: 306-962-4444; *Fax:* 306-962-4224
contact@eston.ca
www.eston.ca
Municipal Type: Town
Incorporated: March 28, 1916; *Area:* 2.72 sq km
Population in 2011: 1,031
Provincial Electoral District(s): Rosetown-Elrose
Federal Electoral District(s): Cypress Hills-Grasslands
Next Election: Oct. 26, 2016 (4 year terms)
Note: Proclaimed as a town on Dec. 1, 1928.
Al Heron, Mayor, 306-962-4171
Michelle MacDonald, Chief Administrative Officer, 306-962-4444

Etters Beach
P.O. Box 40
Stalwart, SK S0G 4R0
Tel: 306-963-2532
rvettersbeach@sasktel.net
www.ettersbeach.ca
Municipal Type: Resort Village
Area: 0.12 sq km
Population in 2011: 30
Provincial Electoral District(s): Arm River-Watrous
Federal Electoral District(s): Moose Jaw-Lake Centre-Lanigan
Next Election: July 2020 (4 year terms)
Erin Leier, Mayor, 306-931-7396
Gord Murray, Administrator

Eyebrow
P.O. Box 159
Eyebrow, SK S0H 1L0
Tel: 306-759-2167; *Fax:* 306-759-2168
eyebrowvillage@yourlink.ca
www.villageofeyebrow.ca
Municipal Type: Village
Incorporated: Jan. 8, 1909; *Area:* 2.70 sq km
Population in 2011: 139
Provincial Electoral District(s): Thunder Creek
Federal Electoral District(s): Moose Jaw-Lake Centre-Lanigan
Next Election: Oct. 26, 2016 (4 year terms)
Don Linton, Mayor
Deanne Hartell, Administrator

Fairlight
P.O. Box 55
Fairlight, SK S0G 1M0
Tel: 306-646-2006; *Fax:* 306-646-2009
village_of_fairlight@rfnow.com
Municipal Type: Village
Incorporated: Oct. 5, 1909; *Area:* 2.71 sq km
Population in 2011: 40
Provincial Electoral District(s): Cannington
Federal Electoral District(s): Souris-Moose Mountain
Next Election: Oct. 26, 2016 (4 year terms)
Barry Metz, Mayor
Nadia Metz, Administrator

Fenwood
P.O. Box 66
Fenwood, SK S0A 0Y0
Tel: 306-728-2185
villageoffenwood@sasktel.net
Municipal Type: Village
Incorporated: June 30, 1909; *Area:* 1.74 sq km
Population in 2011: 40
Provincial Electoral District(s): Last Mountain-Touchwood
Federal Electoral District(s): Yorkton-Melville
Next Election: Oct. 26, 2016 (4 year terms)
Byron Dohms, Mayor
Doreen Dohms, Clerk

Fillmore
P.O. Box 185
Fillmore, SK S0G 1N0
Tel: 306-722-3330; *Fax:* 306-722-3340
v.fillmore@sasktel.net
Municipal Type: Village
Incorporated: June 10, 1905; *Area:* 1.33 sq km
Population in 2011: 255
Provincial Electoral District(s): Cannington
Federal Electoral District(s): Souris-Moose Mountain
Next Election: Oct. 26, 2016 (4 year terms)
K. Dean Hanson, Mayor
Angela Lubiens, Administrator

Findlater
P.O. Box 10
Findlater, SK S0G 1P0
Tel: 306-638-4630
villageoffindlater@live.ca
Municipal Type: Village
Incorporated: Sept. 27, 1911; *Area:* 1.20 sq km
Population in 2011: 50
Provincial Electoral District(s): Thunder Creek
Federal Electoral District(s): Moose Jaw-Lake Centre-Lanigan
Next Election: Oct. 26, 2016 (4 year terms)
Bob Lesperance, Mayor
Lorraine Taylor, Administrator

Flaxcombe
P.O. Box 136
Flaxcombe, SK S0L 1E0
Tel: 306-463-2004
flaxcombe@sasktel.net
Municipal Type: Village
Incorporated: June 4, 1913; *Area:* 1.49 sq km
Population in 2011: 117
Provincial Electoral District(s): Kindersley
Federal Electoral District(s): Cypress Hills-Grasslands
Next Election: Oct. 26, 2016 (4 year terms)
Blaine Sautner, Mayor
Charlotte Helfrich, Administrator

Fleming
P.O. Box 129
Fleming, SK S0G 1R0
Tel: 306-435-4244; *Fax:* 306-435-3508
thetownoffleming@sasktel.net
Municipal Type: Town
Incorporated: July 2, 1896; *Area:* 2.17 sq km
Population in 2011: 83
Provincial Electoral District(s): Moosomin
Federal Electoral District(s): Souris-Moose Mountain
Next Election: Oct. 26, 2016 (4 year terms)
Note: Proclaimed as a town on June 15, 1907.
Philip Hamm, Mayor
Helen Gurski, Administrator

Foam Lake
P.O. Box 57
Foam Lake, SK S0A 1A0
Tel: 306-272-3359; *Fax:* 306-272-3738
foamlaketown@sasktel.net
www.foamlake.com
Municipal Type: Town
Incorporated: Oct. 12, 1908; *Area:* 6.06 sq km
Population in 2011: 1,148
Provincial Electoral District(s): Kelvington-Wadena
Federal Electoral District(s): Yorkton-Melville
Next Election: Oct. 26, 2016 (4 year terms)
Note: Proclaimed as a town on March 1, 1924.
Bob Johnson, Mayor
Gloria Leader, Administrator

Forget
P.O. Box 522
Stoughton, SK S0G 4T0
Tel: 306-457-2707; *Fax:* 306-457-2888
forget@sasktel.net
Municipal Type: Village
Incorporated: Nov. 21, 1904; *Area:* 1.39 sq km
Population in 2011: 35
Provincial Electoral District(s): Cannington
Federal Electoral District(s): Souris-Moose Mountain
Next Election: Oct. 26, 2016 (4 year terms)
Yvan Huriet, Mayor
Zandra Slater, Administrator

Fort Qu'Appelle
P.O. Box 309
160 Company Ave. South
Fort Qu'appelle, SK S0G 1S0
Tel: 306-332-5266; *Fax:* 306-332-5087
forttownoffice@sasktel.net
www.fortquappelle.com
Other Information: Alt. Email: forttown@sasktel.net
Municipal Type: Town
Incorporated: June 25, 1898; *Area:* 5.28 sq km
Population in 2011: 2,034
Provincial Electoral District(s): Indian Head-Milestone
Federal Electoral District(s): Regina-Qu'Appelle
Next Election: Oct. 26, 2016 (4 year terms)
Note: Proclaimed as a town on Jan. 1, 1951.
Ron Osika, Mayor
Brandi Morissette, Chief Administrative Officer

Fort San
P.O. Box 99
136 Company Ave.
Fort Qu'Appelle, SK S0G 1S0
Tel: 306-332-5979; *Fax:* 306-332-6028
rm187@sasktel.net
www.4callinglakes.ca/regional/our-communities/fort-san
Municipal Type: Resort Village
Area: 2.90 sq km
Population in 2011: 187
Provincial Electoral District(s): Last Mountain-Touchwood
Federal Electoral District(s): Regina-Qu'Appelle
Next Election: July 2020 (4 year terms)
Blair Walkington, Mayor
Marcy Johnson, Clerk

Fosston
P.O. Box 160
Fosston, SK S0E 0V0
Tel: 306-322-4521
vilfos@sasktel.net
Municipal Type: Village
Incorporated: Jan. 1, 1965; *Area:* 0.59 sq km
Population in 2011: 55
Provincial Electoral District(s): Kelvington-Wadena
Federal Electoral District(s): Yorkton-Melville
Next Election: Oct. 26, 2016 (4 year terms)
William Dyck, Mayor
Valerie Bjerland, Administrator

Fox Valley
P.O. Box 207
Fox Valley, SK S0N 0V0
Tel: 306-666-3020
villoffoxvalley@sasktel.net
Municipal Type: Village
Incorporated: Aug. 30, 1928; *Area:* 0.60 sq km
Population in 2011: 260
Provincial Electoral District(s): Cypress Hills
Federal Electoral District(s): Cypress Hills-Grasslands
Next Election: Oct. 26, 2016 (4 year terms)
Sean Checkley, Mayor
Michelle Sehn, Administrator

Francis
P.O. Box 128
Francis, SK S0G 1V0
Tel: 306-245-3624; *Fax:* 306-245-3326
town.francis@sasktel.net
Municipal Type: Town
Incorporated: Oct. 24, 1904; *Area:* 0.59 sq km
Population in 2011: 176
Provincial Electoral District(s): Indian Head-Milestone
Federal Electoral District(s): Souris-Moose Mountain
Next Election: Oct. 26, 2016 (4 year terms)
Note: Proclaimed as a town on Sept. 24, 1906.
Reg Helfrick, Mayor
Ila Connery, Administrator

Frobisher
P.O. Box 235
423 Main St.
Bienfait, SK S0C 0M0
Tel: 306-388-2742; *Fax:* 306-388-2330
vilfrob@sdcwireless.com
Municipal Type: Village
Incorporated: July 4, 1904; *Area:* 1.35 sq km
Population in 2011: 166
Provincial Electoral District(s): Cannington
Federal Electoral District(s): Souris-Moose Mountain
Next Election: Oct. 26, 2016 (4 year terms)
Keith Newsham, Mayor
Valerie Crossman, Administrator

Frontier
P.O. Box 270
108 1st Ave. West
Frontier, SK S0N 0W0
Tel: 306-296-2250; *Fax:* 306-296-4586
village.frontier@sasktel.net
www.villageoffrontier.com
Municipal Type: Village
Incorporated: July 10, 1930; *Area:* 0.93 sq km
Population in 2011: 351
Provincial Electoral District(s): Cypress Hills
Federal Electoral District(s): Cypress Hills-Grasslands
Next Election: Oct. 26, 2016 (4 year terms)
Connie Korsberg, Mayor
Barb Webber, Administrator

Gainsborough
P.O. Box 120
Gainsborough, SK S0C 0Z0
Tel: 306-685-2010; *Fax:* 306-685-2161
rm.1@sasktel.net
Municipal Type: Village
Incorporated: May 25, 1894; *Area:* 0.87 sq km
Population in 2011: 291
Provincial Electoral District(s): Cannington
Federal Electoral District(s): Souris-Moose Mountain
Next Election: Oct. 26, 2016 (4 year terms)
Victor Huish, Mayor
Erin McMillen, Administrator

Garson Lake
c/o Government Relations
P.O. Box 69
Buffalo Narrows, SK S0M 0J0
Tel: 403-799-8556; *Fax:* 306-235-1727
Municipal Type: NS
Population in 2010: 34
Provincial Electoral District(s): Athabasca
Federal Electoral District(s): Desnethé-Missinippi-Churchill River
Next Election: Autumn 2016 (4 year terms)
Donald Laprise, Chair
Bruce Leier, Advisor

Gerald
P.O. Box 155
Gerald, SK S0A 1B0
Tel: 306-745-6786; *Fax:* 306-745-6590
vofger@sasktel.net
Municipal Type: Village
Incorporated: March 25, 1953; *Area:* 0.80 sq km
Population in 2011: 114
Provincial Electoral District(s): Melville-Saltcoats
Federal Electoral District(s): Yorkton-Melville
Next Election: Oct. 26, 2016 (4 year terms)
Trevor Rieger, Mayor
Susan Gawryluk, Administrator

Gladmar
P.O. Box 8
Gladmar, SK S0C 1A0
Tel: 306-869-2212
Municipal Type: Village
Incorporated: Feb. 15, 1968; *Area:* 0.55 sq km
Population in 2011: 58
Provincial Electoral District(s): Weyburn-Big Muddy
Federal Electoral District(s): Souris-Moose Mountain
Next Election: Oct. 26, 2016 (4 year terms)
Lynlee Labatte, Mayor
Loran Tessier, Administrator

Glaslyn
P.O. Box 279
172 Main St.
Glaslyn, SK S0M 0Y0
Tel: 306-342-2144; *Fax:* 306-342-2135
villageofglaslyn@sasktel.net
glaslyn.ca
Municipal Type: Village
Incorporated: April 16, 1929; *Area:* 1.97 sq km
Population in 2011: 397
Provincial Electoral District(s): Cut Knife-Turtleford
Federal Electoral District(s): Battlefords-Lloydminster
Next Election: Oct. 26, 2016 (4 year terms)
Ken Morrison, Mayor
Kate Clark, Administrator

Glen Ewen
P.O. Box 99
Glen Ewen, SK S0C 1C0
Tel: 306-925-2211; *Fax:* 306-925-2210
office@villageofglenewen.com
www.villageofglenewen.com
Municipal Type: Village
Incorporated: March 24, 1904; *Area:* 2.77 sq km
Population in 2011: 144
Provincial Electoral District(s): Cannington
Federal Electoral District(s): Souris-Moose Mountain
Next Election: Oct. 26, 2016 (4 year terms)
Glen Lewis, Mayor
Myrna-Jean Babbings, Administrator

Glen Harbour
P.O. Box 280
212 Main St.
Nokomis, SK S0G 3R0
Tel: 306-545-5170; *Fax:* 306-528-2083
rvglenharbour@sasktel.net
www.resortvillageofglenharbour.ca
Municipal Type: Resort Village
Area: 0.35 sq km
Population in 2011: 65
Provincial Electoral District(s): Last Mountain-Touchwood
Federal Electoral District(s): Moose Jaw-Lake Centre-Lanigan
Next Election: July 2020 (4 year terms)
Tim Selinger, Mayor
Kevin Kleckner, Administrator

Glenavon
104 Main St.
Glenavon, SK S0G 1Y0
Tel: 306-429-2110; *Fax:* 306-429-2260
rmchester125@sasktel.net
www.glenavonsk.ca
Municipal Type: Village
Incorporated: April 13, 1910; *Area:* 1.32 sq km
Population in 2011: 176
Provincial Electoral District(s): Moosomin
Federal Electoral District(s): Souris-Moose Mountain
Next Election: Oct. 26, 2016 (4 year terms)
Blair Arnott, Mayor
James Hoff, Administrator

Glenside
P.O. Box 99
Glenside, SK S0H 1T0
Tel: 306-867-8932
villageofglenside@xplornet.com
Municipal Type: Village
Incorporated: March 30, 1911; *Area:* 0.77 sq km
Population in 2011: 59
Provincial Electoral District(s): Rosetown-Elrose
Federal Electoral District(s): Moose Jaw-Lake Centre-Lanigan
Next Election: Oct. 26, 2016 (4 year terms)
Rod Simonson, Mayor
Shannon Pederson, Clerk

Golden Prairie
P.O. Box 9
Golden Prairie, SK S0N 0Y0
Tel: 306-662-2883; *Fax:* 306-662-3954
rm141@sasktel.net
Municipal Type: Village
Incorporated: April 15, 1942; *Area:* 0.41 sq km
Population in 2011: 35
Provincial Electoral District(s): Cypress Hills
Federal Electoral District(s): Cypress Hills-Grasslands
Next Election: Oct. 26, 2016 (4 year terms)
Delmar Beck, Mayor
Joanne Yates, Administrator

Goodeve
P.O. Box 160
Main Street
Goodeve, SK S0A 1C0
Tel: 306-876-4633
villageofgoodeve@sasktel.net
Municipal Type: Village
Incorporated: Aug. 18, 1910; *Area:* 2.62 sq km
Population in 2011: 45
Provincial Electoral District(s): Last Mountain-Touchwood
Federal Electoral District(s): Yorkton-Melville
Next Election: Oct. 26, 2016 (4 year terms)
Craig Sawchuk, Mayor
Angela Romanson, Administrator

Goodsoil
P.O. Box 176
Goodsoil, SK S0M 1A0
Tel: 306-238-2094; *Fax:* 306-238-2098
villageofgoodsoil@sasktel.net
www.villageofgoodsoil.com
Municipal Type: Village
Incorporated: Jan. 1, 1960; *Area:* 1.76 sq km
Population in 2011: 281
Provincial Electoral District(s): Meadow Lake
Federal Electoral District(s): Desnethé-Missinippi-Churchill River
Next Election: Oct. 26, 2016 (4 year terms)
John Purves, Mayor
Fred Puffer, Administrator

Goodwater
P.O. Box 280
Weyburn, SK S4H 2K1
Tel: 306-456-2566; *Fax:* 306-456-2440
rm37@sasktel.net
Municipal Type: Village
Incorporated: May 8, 1911; *Area:* 0.59 sq km
Population in 2011: 35
Provincial Electoral District(s): Estevan
Federal Electoral District(s): Souris-Moose Mountain
Next Election: Oct. 26, 2016 (4 year terms)
Elsie Tilley, Mayor
Kevin Melle, Administrator

Govan
P.O. Box 160
Main St.
Govan, SK S0G 1Z0
Tel: 306-484-2011
govan@sasktel.net
www.govansk.com
Municipal Type: Town
Incorporated: Aug. 21, 1907; *Area:* 1.35 sq km
Population in 2011: 216
Provincial Electoral District(s): Arm River-Watrous
Federal Electoral District(s): Moose Jaw-Lake Centre-Lanigan
Next Election: Oct. 26, 2016 (4 year terms)
Note: Proclaimed as a town on Nov. 1, 1911.
Wesley Pearce, Mayor
Kelly Holbrook, Administrator

Grand Coulee
P.O. Box 72
GBS 200, RR#2
Regina, SK S4P 2Z2
Tel: 306-352-8694; *Fax:* 306-352-6659
grandcoulee.cap@sasktel.net
www.grandcoulee.ca
Municipal Type: Village
Incorporated: April 10, 1908; *Area:* 0.30 sq km
Population in 2011: 571
Provincial Electoral District(s): Regina Qu'Appelle Valley
Federal Electoral District(s): Moose Jaw-Lake Centre-Lanigan
Next Election: Oct. 26, 2016 (4 year terms)
Irv Brunas, Mayor
Tobi Duck, Administrator

Grandview Beach
3111 Kanuka Pl.
Regina, SK S4V 2C6
Tel: 306-789-6040
grandview@sasktel.net
Municipal Type: Resort Village
Area: 0.25 sq km
Population in 2011: 25

Provincial Electoral District(s): Thunder Creek
Federal Electoral District(s): Moose Jaw-Lake Centre-Lanigan
Next Election: July 2020 (4 year terms)
Jake Hutton, Mayor
Gail Meyer, Administrator

Gravelbourg
P.O. Box 359
209 Main St.
Gravelbourg, SK S0H 1X0
Tel: 306-648-3301; *Fax:* 306-648-3400
gravelbourg.adm@sasktel.net
www.gravelbourg.ca
Municipal Type: Town
Incorporated: Dec. 30, 1912; *Area:* 3.23 sq km
Population in 2011: 1,116
Provincial Electoral District(s): Wood River
Federal Electoral District(s): Cypress Hills-Grasslands
Next Election: Oct. 26, 2016 (4 year terms)
Note: Proclaimed as a town on Nov. 1, 1916.
Edward Lagassé, Mayor
Chris Costley, Administrator

Grayson
P.O. Box 9
Grayson, SK S0A 1E0
Tel: 306-794-2011
villageofgrayson@sasktel.net
Municipal Type: Village
Incorporated: April 19, 1906; *Area:* 1.47 sq km
Population in 2011: 184
Provincial Electoral District(s): Melville-Saltcoats
Federal Electoral District(s): Yorkton-Melville
Next Election: Oct. 26, 2016 (4 year terms)
Neil Ottenbreit, Mayor
Colleen Stinson, Administrator

Green Lake
P.O. Box 128
Green Lake, SK S0M 1B0
Tel: 306-832-2131; *Fax:* 306-832-2124
green.lake@sasktel.net
www.nvgreenlake.ca
Municipal Type: Northern Village
Incorporated: Oct. 1, 1983; *Area:* 121.92 sq km
Population in 2011: 418
Provincial Electoral District(s): Athabasca
Federal Electoral District(s): Desnethé-Missinippi-Churchill River
Next Election: Autumn 2016 (4 year terms)
Ric Richardson, Mayor, 306-832-2224
Tina Rasmussen, Administrator

Greig Lake
P.O. Box 334
Elrose, SK S0L 0Z0
Tel: 306-378-2351; *Fax:* 306-378-2338
Municipal Type: Resort Village
Area: 0.14 sq km
Population in 2011: 23
Provincial Electoral District(s): Meadow Lake
Federal Electoral District(s): Desnethé-Missinippi-Churchill River
Next Election: July 2020 (4 year terms)
Dale Brander, Mayor
Joan Tatomir, Administrator

Grenfell
P.O. Box 1120
800 Desmond St.
Grenfell, SK S0G 2B0
Tel: 306-697-2815; *Fax:* 306-697-2484
townofgrenfell@sasktel.net
www.grenfell.ca
Municipal Type: Town
Incorporated: April 12, 1894; *Area:* 3.17 sq km
Population in 2011: 1,049
Provincial Electoral District(s): Moosomin
Federal Electoral District(s): Souris-Moose Mountain
Next Election: Oct. 26, 2016 (4 year terms)
Note: Proclaimed as a town on Nov. 1, 1911.
Lloyd Gwilliam, Mayor
Nicole Monchamp, Administrator

Gull Lake
P.O. Box 150
2378 Proton Ave.
Gull Lake, SK S0N 1A0
Tel: 306-672-3361; *Fax:* 306-672-3777
gulllaketown@sasktel.net
www.gulllakesk.ca
Municipal Type: Town
Incorporated: Jan. 12, 1909; *Area:* 2.5 sq km
Population in 2011: 989

Provincial Electoral District(s): Cypress Hills
Federal Electoral District(s): Cypress Hills-Grasslands
Next Election: Oct. 26, 2016 (4 year terms)
Note: Proclaimed as a town on Nov. 1, 1911.
Blake Campbell, Mayor
Dawnette Peterson, Administrator

Hafford
P.O. Box 220
Hafford, SK S0J 1A0
Tel: 306-549-2331; *Fax:* 306-549-2338
town.administrator@hafford.ca
www.hafford.ca
Municipal Type: Town
Incorporated: Dec. 16, 1913; *Area:* 0.80 sq km
Population in 2011: 397
Provincial Electoral District(s): Rosthern-Shellbrook
Federal Electoral District(s): Carlton Trail-Eagle Creek
Next Election: Oct. 26, 2016 (4 year terms)
Note: Proclaimed as a town on Jan. 1, 1981.
Ron Kowalchuk, Mayor
John Sawyshyn, Administrator

Hague
P.O. Box 180
206 Main St.
Hague, SK S0K 1X0
Tel: 306-225-2155; *Fax:* 306-225-4410
town.hague@sasktel.net
www.townofhague.com
Municipal Type: Town
Incorporated: Aug. 25, 1903; *Area:* 1.03 sq km
Population in 2011: 878
Provincial Electoral District(s): Martensville
Federal Electoral District(s): Carlton Trail-Eagle Creek
Next Election: Oct. 26, 2016 (4 year terms)
Note: Proclaimed as a town on Nov. 1, 1991.
Patricia Wagner, Mayor
Deanna Braun, Chief Administrative Officer

Halbrite
P.O. Box 10
Halbrite, SK S0C 1H0
Tel: 306-891-9990; *Fax:* 306-458-2657
halbrite@sasktel.net
Municipal Type: Village
Incorporated: Feb. 26, 1904; *Area:* 1.20 sq km
Population in 2011: 108
Provincial Electoral District(s): Estevan
Federal Electoral District(s): Souris-Moose Mountain
Next Election: Oct. 26, 2016 (4 year terms)
Dwayne Carlson, Mayor
Jan Hoffart, Administrator

Hanley
P.O. Box 270
Hanley, SK S0G 2E0
Tel: 306-544-2223; *Fax:* 306-544-2261
townoffice@townofhanley.ca
www.townofhanley.ca
Municipal Type: Town
Incorporated: April 27, 1905; *Area:* 2.65 sq km
Population in 2011: 522
Provincial Electoral District(s): Arm River-Watrous
Federal Electoral District(s): Moose Jaw-Lake Centre-Lanigan
Next Election: Oct. 26, 2016 (4 year terms)
Note: Proclaimed as a town on Dec. 1, 1906.
Marvin Gerbrandt, Mayor, 306-544-2802
Darice Carlson, Administrator

Harris
P.O. Box 124
Harris, SK S0L 1K0
Tel: 306-656-2122; *Fax:* 306-656-2123
villageofharris@sasktel.net
Municipal Type: Village
Incorporated: Aug. 10, 1909; *Area:* 0.72 sq km
Population in 2011: 213
Provincial Electoral District(s): Rosetown-Elrose
Federal Electoral District(s): Carlton Trail-Eagle Creek
Next Election: Oct. 26, 2016 (4 year terms)
Ron Genest, Mayor
Rhonda Leonard, Clerk

Hawarden
P.O. Box 7
Hawarden, SK S0H 1Y0
Tel: 306-855-2020
villageofhawarden@xplornet.com
Municipal Type: Village
Incorporated: July 16, 1909; *Area:* 1.24 sq km
Population in 2011: 50

Provincial Electoral District(s): Arm River-Watrous
Federal Electoral District(s): Moose Jaw-Lake Centre-Lanigan
Next Election: Oct. 26, 2016 (4 year terms)
Richard Stewart, Mayor
Barabara J. Martin, Clerk

Hazenmore
P.O. Box 36
Hazenmore, SK S0N 1C0
Tel: 306-264-3218
villageofhazenmore@hotmail.ca
Municipal Type: Village
Incorporated: Aug. 20, 1913; *Area:* 0.80 sq km
Population in 2011: 50
Provincial Electoral District(s): Wood River
Federal Electoral District(s): Cypress Hills-Grasslands
Next Election: Oct. 26, 2016 (4 year terms)
Gary Loverin, Mayor
Barb Cutler, Administrator

Hazlet
P.O. Box 150
Hazlet, SK S0N 1E0
Tel: 306-678-2131; *Fax:* 306-678-2132
hazlet@sasktel.net
hazletsk.com
Municipal Type: Village
Incorporated: Jan. 1, 1963; *Area:* 0.55 sq km
Population in 2011: 95
Provincial Electoral District(s): Cypress Hills
Federal Electoral District(s): Cypress Hills-Grasslands
Next Election: Oct. 26, 2016 (4 year terms)
Terry Bailey, Mayor
Terry Erdelyan, Administrator

Hepburn
P.O. Box 217
311 Main St.
Hepburn, SK S0K 1Z0
Tel: 306-947-2170; *Fax:* 306-947-4202
hepburnvillage@sasktel.net
hepburn.ca
Municipal Type: Village
Incorporated: July 5, 1919; *Area:* 1.02 sq km
Population in 2011: 562
Provincial Electoral District(s): Martensville
Federal Electoral District(s): Carlton Trail-Eagle Creek
Next Election: Oct. 26, 2016 (4 year terms)
Barbara Adams-Eichendorf, Mayor
Wendy Davis, Administrator

Herbert
P.O. Box 370
503 Herbert Ave.
Herbert, SK S0H 2A0
Tel: 306-784-2400; *Fax:* 306-784-2402
t.o.herbert@sasktel.net
www.townofherbert.com
Municipal Type: Town
Incorporated: June 11, 1907; *Area:* 3.78 sq km
Population in 2011: 759
Provincial Electoral District(s): Thunder Creek
Federal Electoral District(s): Cypress Hills-Grasslands
Next Election: Oct. 26, 2016 (4 year terms)
Note: Proclaimed as a town on Nov. 1, 1912.
Doreen Schroeder, Mayor
Raegan Funk, Administrator

Heward
P.O. Box 10
Heward, SK S0G 2G0
Tel: 306-457-2707; *Fax:* 306-457-2888
heward@sasktel.net
Municipal Type: Village
Incorporated: Nov. 21, 1904; *Area:* 0.99 sq km
Population in 2011: 40
Provincial Electoral District(s): Cannington
Federal Electoral District(s): Souris-Moose Mountain
Next Election: Oct. 26, 2016 (4 year terms)
Doug Trowell, Mayor
Zandra Slater, Clerk

Hodgeville
P.O. Box 307
Hodgeville, SK S0H 2B0
Tel: 306-677-2223; *Fax:* 306-677-2466
villageofhodgeville@sasktel.net
Municipal Type: Village
Incorporated: June 22, 1921; *Area:* 1.35 sq km
Population in 2011: 172
Provincial Electoral District(s): Wood River

Federal Electoral District(s): Cypress Hills-Grasslands
Next Election: Oct. 26, 2016 (4 year terms)
Garry Wilson, Mayor
Theresa Mokry, Clerk

Holdfast
P.O. Box 160
Roberts St.
Holdfast, SK S0G 2H0
Tel: 306-488-2000; *Fax:* 306-488-4609
rm.sarnia@sasktel.net
Municipal Type: Village
Incorporated: Oct. 5, 1911; *Area:* 1.29 sq km
Population in 2011: 169
Provincial Electoral District(s): Thunder Creek
Federal Electoral District(s): Moose Jaw-Lake Centre-Lanigan
Next Election: Oct. 26, 2016 (4 year terms)
Todd Thauberger, Mayor
Patti Vance, Administrator

Hubbard
P.O. Box 190
Ituna, SK S0A 1N0
Tel: 306-795-2272; *Fax:* 306-795-3330
townofituna@sasktel.net
Municipal Type: Village
Incorporated: June 11, 1910; *Area:* 1.25 sq km
Population in 2011: 46
Provincial Electoral District(s): Last Mountain-Touchwood
Federal Electoral District(s): Regina-Qu'Appelle
Next Election: Oct. 26, 2016 (4 year terms)
Alvin (Joe) Garchinski, Mayor
Geri Kreway, Acting Administrator

Hudson Bay
P.O. Box 730
304 Main St.
Hudson Bay, SK S0E 0Y0
Tel: 306-865-2261; *Fax:* 306-865-2800
hudson.bay@sasktel.net
www.townofhudsonbay.com
Municipal Type: Town
Incorporated: Sept. 25, 1907; *Area:* 17.35 sq km
Population in 2011: 1,477
Provincial Electoral District(s): Carrot River Valley
Federal Electoral District(s): Yorkton-Melville
Next Election: Oct. 26, 2016 (4 year terms)
Note: Proclaimed as a town on Nov. 30, 1946.
Elvina Rumak, Mayor
Richard Dolezsar, Administrator

Humboldt
P.O. Box 640
715 Main St.
Humboldt, SK S0K 2A0
Tel: 306-682-2525; *Fax:* 306-682-3144
info@humboldt.ca
www.cityofhumboldt.ca
Municipal Type: Town
Incorporated: June 30, 1905; *Area:* 11.72 sq km
Population in 2011: 5,678
Provincial Electoral District(s): Humboldt
Federal Electoral District(s): Carlton Trail-Eagle Creek
Next Election: Oct. 26, 2016 (4 year terms)
Note: Incorporated as a city on Nov. 7, 2000.
Malcolm Eaton, Mayor, 303-682-2525
Roy Hardy, City Manager, 306-682-2525

Hyas
P.O. Box 40
Hyas, SK S0A 1K0
Tel: 306-594-2817; *Fax:* 306-594-2944
hyas@sasktel.net
villageofhyas.com
Municipal Type: Village
Incorporated: May 23, 1919; *Area:* 1.17 sq km
Population in 2011: 114
Provincial Electoral District(s): Canora-Pelly
Federal Electoral District(s): Yorkton-Melville
Next Election: Oct. 26, 2016 (4 year terms)
Barry Bogucky, Mayor
Sabrina Chernyk, Administrator

Ile à la Crosse
P.O. Box 280
Lajeunesse Ave.
Ile-a-la-Crosse, SK S0M 1C0
Tel: 306-833-2122; *Fax:* 306-833-2132
village.of.ilealacrosse@sasktel.net
www.sakitawak.ca
Municipal Type: Northern Village
Incorporated: Oct. 1, 1983; *Area:* 23.84 sq km
Population in 2011: 1,365
Provincial Electoral District(s): Athabasca
Federal Electoral District(s): Desnethé-Missinippi-Churchill River
Next Election: Autumn 2016 (4 year terms)
Duane Favel, Mayor
Dianne McCallum, Administrator

Imperial
P.O. Box 90
Imperial, SK S0G 2J0
Tel: 306-963-2220; *Fax:* 306-963-2445
town.imperial@sasktel.net
www.imperial.ca
Municipal Type: Town
Incorporated: July 4, 1911; *Area:* 1.23 sq km
Population in 2011: 349
Provincial Electoral District(s): Arm River-Watrous
Federal Electoral District(s): Moose Jaw-Lake Centre-Lanigan
Next Election: Oct. 26, 2016 (4 year terms)
Note: Proclaimed as a town on April 1, 1962.
Ronald Klenk, Mayor
Sheila Newlove, Administrator

Indian Head
P.O. Box 460
421 Grand Ave.
Indian Head, SK S0G 2K0
Tel: 306-695-3344
townofindianhead@sasktel.net
www.townofindianhead.com
Municipal Type: Town
Incorporated: April 19, 1902; *Area:* 3.17 sq km
Population in 2011: 1,815
Provincial Electoral District(s): Indian Head-Milestone
Federal Electoral District(s): Regina-Qu'Appelle
Next Election: Oct. 26, 2016 (4 year terms)
Sherry Karpa, Mayor
Cam Thauberger, Administrator

Invermay
P.O. Box 234
Invermay, SK S0A 1M0
Tel: 306-593-2242; *Fax:* 306-593-0004
villageofinvermay@sasktel.net
Municipal Type: Village
Incorporated: Sept. 1, 1908; *Area:* 1.22 sq km
Population in 2011: 247
Provincial Electoral District(s): Kelvington-Wadena
Federal Electoral District(s): Yorkton-Melville
Next Election: Oct. 26, 2016 (4 year terms)
Michael J. Kaminski, Mayor
Joyce M. Palagian, Clerk

Island View
Comp. 3, RR#1
Bulyea, SK S0G 0L0
Tel: 306-725-4521; *Fax:* 306-725-4863
islandview@canwan.com
www.resortvillageofislandview.ca
Municipal Type: Resort Village
Incorporated: 1959; *Area:* 0.43 sq km
Population in 2011: 65
Provincial Electoral District(s): Last Mountain-Touchwood
Federal Electoral District(s): Moose Jaw-Lake Centre-Lanigan
Next Election: July 2020 (4 year terms)
Alan Schafer, Mayor
Sharon Moreau, Administrator

Ituna
P.O. Box 580
7 - 1st Ave. NE
Ituna, SK S0A 1N0
Tel: 306-795-2272; *Fax:* 306-795-3330
townofituna@sasktel.net
www.ituna.ca
Municipal Type: Town
Incorporated: May 30, 1910; *Area:* 1.56 sq km
Population in 2011: 711
Provincial Electoral District(s): Last Mountain-Touchwood
Federal Electoral District(s): Regina-Qu'Appelle
Next Election: Oct. 26, 2016 (4 year terms)
Note: Proclaimed as a town on Oct. 1, 1961.
Joe Garchinski, Mayor
Diane Smith, Administrator

Jans Bay
Maurice Ave., General Delivery
Canoe Narrows, SK S0M 0K0
Tel: 306-829-4320; *Fax:* 306-829-4424
jansbay@sasktel.net
Municipal Type: Northern Village
Incorporated: Oct. 1, 1983; *Area:* 5.94 sq km
Population in 2011: 187
Provincial Electoral District(s): Athabasca
Federal Electoral District(s): Desnethé-Missinippi-Churchill River
Next Election: Autumn 2016 (4 year terms)
Tony Maurice, Mayor
Roxanne Gamble, Clerk

Jansen
P.O. Box 116
Jansen, SK S0K 2B0
Tel: 306-364-2013; *Fax:* 306-364-2088
jansen@jansen.ca
www.jansen.ca
Municipal Type: Village
Incorporated: Oct. 19, 1908; *Area:* 0.85 sq km
Population in 2011: 126
Provincial Electoral District(s): Arm River-Watrous
Federal Electoral District(s): Moose Jaw-Lake Centre-Lanigan
Next Election: Oct. 26, 2016 (4 year terms)
Albert Cardinal, Mayor, 306-364-2028
Joni Mack, Administrator, 306-364-2013

Kamsack
P.O. Box 729
161 Queen Elizabeth Blvd. West
Kamsack, SK S0A 1S0
Tel: 306-542-2155; *Fax:* 306-542-2975
www.kamsack.ca
Municipal Type: Town
Incorporated: March 14, 1905; *Area:* 5.85 sq km
Population in 2011: 1,825
Provincial Electoral District(s): Canora-Pelly
Federal Electoral District(s): Yorkton-Melville
Next Election: Oct. 26, 2016 (4 year terms)
Note: Proclaimed as a town on Nov. 1, 1911.
Rod Gardner, Mayor
Laura Lomenda, Administrator, 306-542-3806, Fax: 306-542-2975

Kannata Valley
P.O. Box 166
101 Cowen Rd.
Silton, SK S0G 4L0
Tel: 306-731-2447; *Fax:* 306-731-2415
office@kannatavalley.com
www.kannatavalley.com
Other Information: Toll-Free Phone: 1-877-731-2447
Municipal Type: Resort Village
Incorporated: 1966; *Area:* 0.63 sq km
Population in 2011: 101
Provincial Electoral District(s): Last Mountain-Touchwood
Federal Electoral District(s): Moose Jaw-Lake Centre-Lanigan
Next Election: July 2020 (4 year terms)
Ken MacDonald, Mayor, 306-533-3936
Jack McHardy, Administrator

Katepwa
P.O. Box 250
41 Elm St.
Lebret, SK S0G 2Y0
Tel: 306-332-6645; *Fax:* 306-332-5808
katepwabeach@sasktel.net
www.katepwabeach.com
Municipal Type: Resort Village
Incorporated: 1914; *Area:* 5.78 sq km
Population in 2011: 403
Provincial Electoral District(s): Last Mountain-Touchwood
Federal Electoral District(s): Regina-Qu'Appelle
Next Election: July 2020 (4 year terms)
Don Jewitt, Mayor
Laurie Rudolph, Chief Administrative Officer

Keeler
P.O. Box 33
Keeler, SK S0H 2E0
Tel: 306-759-2302
Municipal Type: Village
Incorporated: July 5, 1910; *Area:* 1.02 sq km
Provincial Electoral District(s): Thunder Creek
Federal Electoral District(s): Moose Jaw-Lake Centre-Lanigan
Next Election: Oct. 26, 2016 (4 year terms)
Duncan Keeler, Mayor
Rhonda Purdy, Clerk

Kelliher
P.O. Box 190
406 - 2nd Ave.
Kelliher, SK S0A 1V0
Tel: 306-675-2226; *Fax:* 306-675-2240
villageofkelliher@sasktel.net
www.kelliher.ca

Municipal Type: Village
Incorporated: April 27, 1909; *Area:* 2.81 sq km
Population in 2011: 216
Provincial Electoral District(s): Last Mountain-Touchwood
Federal Electoral District(s): Regina-Qu'Appelle
Next Election: Oct. 26, 2016 (4 year terms)
Darcy King, Mayor
Gerry Burym, Administrator

Kelvington
P.O. Box 10
201 Main St.
Kelvington, SK S0A 1W0
Tel: 306-327-4482; *Fax:* 306-327-4946
info@townofkelvington.com
www.townofkelvington.com
Municipal Type: Town
Incorporated: Nov. 18, 1921; *Area:* 3.89 sq km
Population in 2011: 864
Provincial Electoral District(s): Kelvington-Wadena
Federal Electoral District(s): Yorkton-Melville
Next Election: Oct. 26, 2016 (4 year terms)
Note: Proclaimed as a town on May 1, 1944.
Ed Tetelowski, Mayor
Kelsey Robinson, Administrator

Kenaston
P.O. Box 129
Kenaston, SK S0G 2N0
Tel: 306-252-2211; *Fax:* 306-252-2248
kenaston@sasktel.net
www.kenaston.ca
Municipal Type: Village
Incorporated: July 18, 1910; *Area:* 1.17 sq km
Population in 2011: 285
Provincial Electoral District(s): Arm River-Watrous
Federal Electoral District(s): Moose Jaw-Lake Centre-Lanigan
Next Election: Oct. 26, 2016 (4 year terms)
M.L. Whittles, Mayor
Carman Fowler, Administrator

Kendal
P.O. Box 97
115 Main St.
Kendal, SK S0G 2P0
Tel: 306-424-2722; *Fax:* 306-424-2722
villageofkendal@sasktel.net
Municipal Type: Village
Incorporated: Feb. 17, 1919; *Area:* 0.65 sq km
Population in 2011: 77
Provincial Electoral District(s): Indian Head-Milestone
Federal Electoral District(s): Souris-Moose Mountain
Next Election: Oct. 26, 2016 (4 year terms)
Lea Zhoner, Mayor
Coleen Hoffman, Administrator

Kennedy
P.O. Box 93
Kennedy, SK S0G 2R0
Tel: 306-538-2194; *Fax:* 306-538-4522
village.kennedy@sasktel.net
www.angelfire.com/ca/kennedysk
Municipal Type: Village
Incorporated: Nov. 5, 1907; *Area:* 1.60 sq km
Population in 2011: 241
Provincial Electoral District(s): Moosomin
Federal Electoral District(s): Souris-Moose Mountain
Next Election: Oct. 26, 2016 (4 year terms)
Linc Brickley, Mayor
Ward Frazer, Administrator

Kenosee Lake
P.O. Box 30
Kenosee Lake, SK S0C 2S0
Tel: 306-577-2139; *Fax:* 306-577-2261
village.kenosee@sasktel.net
Municipal Type: Village
Incorporated: Oct. 1, 1987; *Area:* 0.35 sq km
Population in 2011: 258
Provincial Electoral District(s): Cannington
Federal Electoral District(s): Souris-Moose Mountain
Next Election: Oct. 26, 2016 (4 year terms)
Stuart Balfour, Mayor
Andrea Kosior, Administrator

Kerrobert
P.O. Box 558
433 Manitoba Ave.
Kerrobert, SK S0L 1R0
Tel: 306-834-2361; *Fax:* 306-834-2633
kerrobert@sasktel.net
www.kerrobertsk.com

Municipal Type: Town
Incorporated: Nov. 9, 1910; *Area:* 7.49 sq km
Population in 2011: 1,061
Provincial Electoral District(s): Kindersley
Federal Electoral District(s): Battlefords-Lloydminster
Next Election: Oct. 26, 2016 (4 year terms)
Note: Proclaimed as a town on Nov. 1, 1911.
Erhard Poggemiller, Mayor
Cheryl Fedirko, Administrator

Killaly
P.O. Box 69
Railway Ave.
Killaly, SK S0A 1X0
Tel: 306-748-2540
rm185@sasktel.net
www.villageofkillaly.ca
Municipal Type: Village
Incorporated: April 28, 1909; *Area:* 2.59 sq km
Population in 2011: 74
Provincial Electoral District(s): Melville-Saltcoats
Federal Electoral District(s): Yorkton-Melville
Next Election: Oct. 26, 2016 (4 year terms)
Angie Rogalski, Mayor
Linda Hanowski, Administrator

Kincaid
P.O. Box 177
20 Dominion Ave. West
Kincaid, SK S0H 2J0
Tel: 306-264-3910; *Fax:* 306-264-3903
villageofkincaid@hotmail.com
www.villageofkincaid.ca
Municipal Type: Village
Incorporated: July 19, 1913; *Area:* 0.82 sq km
Population in 2011: 114
Provincial Electoral District(s): Wood River
Federal Electoral District(s): Cypress Hills-Grasslands
Next Election: Oct. 26, 2016 (4 year terms)
Cynthia Gross, Mayor
Melanie Huyghebaert, Administrator

Kindersley
P.O. Box 1269
106 - 5th Ave. East
Kindersley, SK S0L 1S0
Tel: 306-463-2675; *Fax:* 306-463-4577
office@kindersley.ca
www.kindersley.ca
Municipal Type: Town
Incorporated: Jan. 10, 1910; *Area:* 12.55 sq km
Population in 2011: 4,678
Provincial Electoral District(s): Kindersley
Federal Electoral District(s): Cypress Hills-Grasslands
Next Election: Oct. 26, 2016 (4 year terms)
Note: Proclaimed as a town on Nov. 1, 1910.
John Enns-Wind, Mayor
Bernie Morton, Chief Administrative Officer

Kinistino
P.O. Box 10
212 Main St.
Kinistino, SK S0J 1H0
Tel: 306-864-2461; *Fax:* 306-864-2880
townofkinistino@sasktel.net
www.townofkinistino.ca
Municipal Type: Town
Incorporated: July 30, 1905; *Area:* 0.89 sq km
Population in 2011: 743
Provincial Electoral District(s): Batoche
Federal Electoral District(s): Prince Albert
Next Election: Oct. 26, 2016 (4 year terms)
Note: Proclaimed as a town on Feb. 7, 1952.
Leonard Margolis, Mayor
Rhonda Bacon, Administrator

Kinley
P.O. Box 51
Kinley, SK S0K 2E0
Tel: 306-237-4601; *Fax:* 306-237-4605
villageofkinley@sasktel.net
Municipal Type: Village
Incorporated: Jan. 7, 1909; *Area:* 1.18 sq km
Population in 2011: 45
Provincial Electoral District(s): Biggar
Federal Electoral District(s): Carlton Trail-Eagle Creek
Next Election: Oct. 26, 2016 (4 year terms)
Cindy Latta, Mayor
Lynne Tolley, Administrator

Kipling
P.O. Box 299
301 - 6th Ave.
Kipling, SK S0G 2S0
Tel: 306-736-2515; *Fax:* 306-736-8448
kiptown@sasktel.net
www.townofkipling.ca
Other Information: Alt. E-mail: kiplingadmin@sasktel.net
Municipal Type: Town
Incorporated: Sept. 13, 1909; *Area:* 2.15 sq km
Population in 2011: 1,051
Provincial Electoral District(s): Moosomin
Federal Electoral District(s): Souris-Moose Mountain
Next Election: Oct. 26, 2016 (4 year terms)
Note: Proclaimed as a town on Jan. 1, 1954.
Duane Leicht, Mayor
Gail Dakue, Administrator

Kisbey
P.O. Box 249
Kisbey, SK S0C 1L0
Tel: 306-462-2212; *Fax:* 306-462-2279
vill.kisbey@signaldirect.ca
Municipal Type: Village
Incorporated: May 8, 1907; *Area:* 2.77 sq km
Population in 2011: 139
Provincial Electoral District(s): Cannington
Federal Electoral District(s): Souris-Moose Mountain
Next Election: Oct. 26, 2016 (4 year terms)
John Houston, Mayor
Judy Graham, Administrator

Kivimaa-Moonlight Bay
P.O. Box 120
Livelong, SK S0M 1J0
Tel: 306-845-3336; *Fax:* 306-845-3686
rvkmb@littleloon.ca
www.rvkmb.com
Municipal Type: Resort Village
Area: 0.55 sq km
Population in 2011: 84
Provincial Electoral District(s): Meadow Lake
Federal Electoral District(s): Battlefords-Lloydminster
Next Election: July 2020 (4 year terms)
Steven Nasby, Mayor
Jackie Helgeton, Administrator

Krydor
P.O. Box 160
Hafford, SK S0J 1A0
Tel: 306-549-2333; *Fax:* 306-549-2435
rm435@littleloon.ca
Municipal Type: Village
Incorporated: Aug. 25, 1914; *Area:* 0.82 sq km
Population in 2011: 15
Provincial Electoral District(s): Rosthern-Shellbrook
Federal Electoral District(s): Carlton Trail-Eagle Creek
Next Election: Oct. 26, 2016 (4 year terms)
Stan Lucko, Mayor
Alan J. Tanchak, Clerk

Kyle
P.O. Box 520
Kyle, SK S0L 1T0
Tel: 306-375-2525; *Fax:* 306-375-2534
townofkyle@sasktel.net
www.townofkyle.ca
Municipal Type: Town
Incorporated: April 13, 1926; *Area:* 1.01 sq km
Population in 2011: 437
Provincial Electoral District(s): Rosetown-Elrose
Federal Electoral District(s): Cypress Hills-Grasslands
Next Election: Oct. 26, 2016 (4 year terms)
Note: Proclaimed as a town on Jan. 1, 1959.
Doug Barker, Mayor
Audrey Blohm, Administrator

Lafleche
P.O. Box 250
35 - 2nd Ave. East
Lafleche, SK S0H 2K0
Tel: 306-472-5292; *Fax:* 306-472-3706
town.of.lafleche@sasktel.net
www.town.lafleche.sk.ca
Municipal Type: Town
Incorporated: Sept. 3, 1913; *Area:* 1.51 sq km
Population in 2011: 406
Provincial Electoral District(s): Wood River
Federal Electoral District(s): Cypress Hills-Grasslands
Next Election: Oct. 26, 2016 (4 year terms)
Note: Proclaimed as a town on June 1, 1953.
Rhys Frostad, Mayor

Brekke Masse, Administrator

Laird
P.O. Box 189
220A Main St.
Laird, SK S0K 2H0
Tel: 306-223-4343; *Fax:* 306-223-4349
lairdvillage@sasktel.net
www.lairdvillage.ca
Municipal Type: Village
Incorporated: May 4, 1911; *Area:* 1.29 sq km
Population in 2011: 287
Provincial Electoral District(s): Rosthern-Shellbrook
Federal Electoral District(s): Carlton Trail-Eagle Creek
Next Election: Oct. 26, 2016 (4 year terms)
Dave Loewen, Mayor
Michelle Zurakowski, Administrator

Lake Alma
P.O. Box 163
Lake Alma, SK S0C 1M0
Tel: 306-447-2002; *Fax:* 306-447-2023
rmalma@sasktel.net
Municipal Type: Village
Incorporated: Jan. 1, 1949; *Area:* 0.47 sq km
Population in 2011: 30
Provincial Electoral District(s): Estevan
Federal Electoral District(s): Souris-Moose Mountain
Next Election: Oct. 26, 2016 (4 year terms)
Wilfred Jacobson, Mayor
Myrna Lohse, Administrator

Lake Lenore
P.O. Box 148
Lake Lenore, SK S0K 2J0
Tel: 306-368-2344; *Fax:* 306-368-2226
lakelenorevil@sasktel.net
www.lakelenore.ca
Municipal Type: Village
Incorporated: April 28, 1921; *Area:* 0.97 sq km
Population in 2011: 297
Provincial Electoral District(s): Batoche
Federal Electoral District(s): Carlton Trail-Eagle Creek
Next Election: Oct. 26, 2016 (4 year terms)
Scott Lessmeister, Mayor
Barb Politeski, Administrator

Lampman
P.O. Box 70
Lampman, SK S0C 1N0
Tel: 306-487-2462; *Fax:* 306-487-2285
browning.lampman@sasktel.net
Municipal Type: Town
Incorporated: Aug. 16, 1910; *Area:* 2.23 sq km
Population in 2011: 713
Provincial Electoral District(s): Cannington
Federal Electoral District(s): Souris-Moose Mountain
Next Election: Oct. 26, 2016 (4 year terms)
Note: Proclaimed as a town on June 1, 1963.
Sean Paxman, Mayor
Greg Wallin, Administrator

Lancer
P.O. Box 3
Lancer, SK S0N 1G0
Tel: 306-689-2925; *Fax:* 306-689-2890
Municipal Type: Village
Incorporated: Sept. 11, 1913; *Area:* 1.33 sq km
Population in 2011: 61
Provincial Electoral District(s): Cypress Hills
Federal Electoral District(s): Cypress Hills-Grasslands
Next Election: Oct. 26, 2016 (4 year terms)
Ernest Wagner, Mayor
Karen Hartman, Clerk

Landis
P.O. Box 153
100 Princess St.
Landis, SK S0K 2K0
Tel: 306-658-2155; *Fax:* 306-658-2156
villageoflandis@sasktel.net
www.villageoflandis.com
Municipal Type: Village
Incorporated: May 17, 1909; *Area:* 0.80 sq km
Population in 2011: 139
Provincial Electoral District(s): Biggar
Federal Electoral District(s): Battlefords-Lloydminster
Next Election: Oct. 26, 2016 (4 year terms)
Joe Sarrasin, Mayor
Alicia Leclercq, Administrator

Lang
P.O. Box 97
223 Main St.
Lang, SK S0G 2W0
Tel: 306-464-2024; *Fax:* 306-464-2050
voflang@sasktel.net
www.langsk.com
Municipal Type: Village
Incorporated: July 27, 1906; *Area:* 0.64 sq km
Population in 2011: 200
Provincial Electoral District(s): Indian Head-Milestone
Federal Electoral District(s): Souris-Moose Mountain
Next Election: Oct. 26, 2016 (4 year terms)
Al Broderick, Mayor
Darlene Wingert, Administrator

Langenburg
P.O. Box 400
Langenburg, SK S0A 2A0
Tel: 306-743-2432; *Fax:* 306-743-2723
langenburgt@sasktel.net
www.langenburg.ca
Municipal Type: Town
Incorporated: March 30, 1903; *Area:* 3.46 sq km
Population in 2011: 1,148
Provincial Electoral District(s): Melville-Saltcoats
Federal Electoral District(s): Yorkton-Melville
Next Election: Oct. 26, 2016 (4 year terms)
Note: Proclaimed as a town on Sept. 15, 1959.
Don Fogg, Mayor
Glenda Hodson, Chief Administrative Officer

Langham
P.O. Box 289
230 Main St. East
Langham, SK S0K 2L0
Tel: 306-283-4842; *Fax:* 306-283-4772
admin@langham.ca
www.langham.ca
Municipal Type: Town
Incorporated: June 8, 1906; *Area:* 3.98 sq km
Population in 2011: 1,290
Provincial Electoral District(s): Biggar
Federal Electoral District(s): Carlton Trail-Eagle Creek
Next Election: Oct. 26, 2016 (4 year terms)
Note: Proclaimed as a town on Aug. 1, 1907.
Beverly Panas, Mayor
Jamie Nagy, Administrator

Lanigan
P.O. Box 280
110 Main St.
Lanigan, SK S0K 2M0
Tel: 306-365-2809; *Fax:* 306-365-2960
town.lanigan@sasktel.net
www.town.lanigan.sk.ca
Municipal Type: Town
Incorporated: Aug. 21, 1907; *Area:* 8.34 sq km
Population in 2011: 1,390
Provincial Electoral District(s): Humboldt
Federal Electoral District(s): Moose Jaw-Lake Centre-Lanigan
Next Election: Oct. 26, 2016 (4 year terms)
Note: Proclaimed as a town on April 15, 1908.
Andrew Cebryk, Mayor
Jennifer Thompson, Administrator

Lashburn
P.O. Box 328
78 Main St.
Lashburn, SK S0M 1H0
Tel: 306-285-3533; *Fax:* 306-285-3358
townoflashburn@sasktel.net
www.lashburn.ca
Municipal Type: Town
Incorporated: Dec. 8, 1906; *Area:* 3.11 sq km
Population in 2011: 967
Provincial Electoral District(s): Cut Knife-Turtleford
Federal Electoral District(s): Battlefords-Lloydminster
Next Election: Oct. 26, 2016 (4 year terms)
Note: Proclaimed as a town on March 1, 1979.
Steven Turnbull, Mayor
Vicki Seabrook, Administrator

Leader
P.O. Box 39
151 - 1st St. West
Leader, SK S0N 1H0
Tel: 306-628-3868; *Fax:* 306-628-4337
town.leader@sasktel.net
www.leader.ca
Other Information: Toll Free Phone: 1-800-424-8335
Municipal Type: Town
Incorporated: Sept. 13, 1913; *Area:* 1.70 sq km
Population in 2011: 821
Provincial Electoral District(s): Cypress Hills
Federal Electoral District(s): Cypress Hills-Grasslands
Next Election: Oct. 26, 2016 (4 year terms)
Note: Proclaimed as a town on May 1, 1947.
Craig Tondevold, Mayor
Rochelle Francis, Administrator

Leask
P.O. Box 40
15 Main St.
Leask, SK S0J 1M0
Tel: 306-466-2229; *Fax:* 306-466-2239
village.leask@sasktel.net
www.leask.ca
Municipal Type: Village
Incorporated: Sept. 3, 1912; *Area:* 0.75 sq km
Population in 2011: 413
Provincial Electoral District(s): Rosthern-Shellbrook
Federal Electoral District(s): Carlton Trail-Eagle Creek
Next Election: Oct. 26, 2016 (4 year terms)
Maurice Stieb, Mayor
Brenda Lockhart, Administrator

Lebret
P.O. Box 40
Lebret, SK S0G 2Y0
Tel: 306-332-6545; *Fax:* 306-332-5338
villageoflebret@sasktel.net
Municipal Type: Village
Incorporated: Oct. 14, 1912; *Area:* 1.32 sq km
Population in 2011: 218
Provincial Electoral District(s): Last Mountain-Touchwood
Federal Electoral District(s): Regina-Qu'Appelle
Next Election: Oct. 26, 2016 (4 year terms)
Ralph Blondeau, Mayor
Caroline MacMurphy, Administrator

Lemberg
P.O. Box 399
Lemberg, SK S0A 2B0
Tel: 306-335-2244; *Fax:* 306-335-2257
townoffice.lemberg@sasktel.net
www.lemberg-sk-ca.weebly.com
Municipal Type: Town
Incorporated: July 12, 1904; *Area:* 2.67 sq km
Population in 2011: 274
Provincial Electoral District(s): Last Mountain-Touchwood
Federal Electoral District(s): Yorkton-Melville
Next Election: Oct. 26, 2016 (4 year terms)
Note: Proclaimed as a town on Sept. 1, 1907.
John Kittler, Mayor
Joyce Hauck, Secretary

Leoville
P.O. Box 280
Leoville, SK S0J 1N0
Tel: 306-984-2140; *Fax:* 306-984-2337
leoville@sasktel.net
Municipal Type: Village
Incorporated: June 26, 1944; *Area:* 1.11 sq km
Population in 2011: 366
Provincial Electoral District(s): Meadow Lake
Federal Electoral District(s): Desnethé-Missinippi-Churchill River
Next Election: Oct. 26, 2016 (4 year terms)
Ron Craswell, Mayor
Mona Chalifour, Clerk

Leross
P.O. Box 68
Leross, SK S0A 2C0
Tel: 306-675-4429; *Fax:* 306-675-0024
villageofleross@sasktel.net
Municipal Type: Village
Incorporated: Dec. 1, 1909; *Area:* 1.21 sq km
Population in 2011: 37
Provincial Electoral District(s): Last Mountain-Touchwood
Federal Electoral District(s): Regina-Qu'Appelle
Next Election: Oct. 26, 2016 (4 year terms)
Francis Klyne, Mayor
Elaine Klyne, Clerk

Leroy
P.O. Box 40
Leroy, SK S0K 2P0
Tel: 306-286-3288; *Fax:* 306-286-3400
leroy@leroy.ca
www.leroy.ca
Municipal Type: Town
Incorporated: Dec. 5, 1922; *Area:* 1.06 sq km

Population in 2011: 427
Provincial Electoral District(s): Melfort
Federal Electoral District(s): Moose Jaw-Lake Centre-Lanigan
Next Election: Oct. 26, 2016 (4 year terms)
Note: Proclaimed as a town on March 1, 1963.
Brian Thoen, Mayor
Connie Porten, Administrator

Leslie Beach
P.O. Box 478
Foam Lake, SK S0A 1A0
Tel: 306-272-4579; *Fax:* 306-272-3960
Municipal Type: Resort Village
Area: 0.56 sq km
Population in 2011: 23
Provincial Electoral District(s): Kelvington-Wadena
Federal Electoral District(s): Yorkton-Melville
Next Election: July 2020 (4 year terms)
Roger Nupdal, Mayor
Brenda Kipling, Clerk

Lestock
P.O. Box 209
320 Touchwood Hills Ave.
Lestock, SK S0A 2G0
Tel: 306-274-2277; *Fax:* 306-274-2275
lestockv@sasktel.net
www.lestock.ca
Municipal Type: Village
Incorporated: April 17, 1912; *Area:* 0.87 sq km
Population in 2011: 125
Provincial Electoral District(s): Last Mountain-Touchwood
Federal Electoral District(s): Regina-Qu'Appelle
Next Election: Oct. 26, 2016 (4 year terms)
Shawn Bellrose, Mayor
Lesle Lajoure, Administrator

Liberty
P.O. Box 59
Stalwart, SK S0G 4R0
Tel: 306-963-2402; *Fax:* 306-963-2405
villageofliberty@sasktel.net
Municipal Type: Village
Incorporated: Jan. 23, 1912; *Area:* 1.37 sq km
Population in 2011: 88
Provincial Electoral District(s): Arm River-Watrous
Federal Electoral District(s): Moose Jaw-Lake Centre-Lanigan
Next Election: Oct. 26, 2016 (4 year terms)
Jennifer Langlois, Mayor
Yvonne (Bonny) Goodsman, Administrator

Limerick
P.O. Box 129
Limerick, SK S0H 2P0
Tel: 306-263-2020; *Fax:* 306-263-2013
rm73@sasktel.net
Municipal Type: Village
Incorporated: July 10, 1913; *Area:* 0.79 sq km
Population in 2011: 115
Provincial Electoral District(s): Wood River
Federal Electoral District(s): Cypress Hills-Grasslands
Next Election: Oct. 26, 2016 (4 year terms)
Robert Smith, Mayor
Tammy Franks, Administrator

Lintlaw
P.O. Box 10
Lintlaw, SK S0A 2H0
Tel: 306-325-2006; *Fax:* 306-325-2006
villageoflintlaw@sasktel.net
Municipal Type: Village
Incorporated: Dec. 14, 1921; *Area:* 1.23 sq km
Population in 2011: 162
Provincial Electoral District(s): Kelvington-Wadena
Federal Electoral District(s): Yorkton-Melville
Next Election: Oct. 26, 2016 (4 year terms)
Ervin Lindholm, Mayor
Kathleen Ambrose, Administrator

Lipton
P.O. Box 219
201 Main St.
Lipton, SK S0G 3B0
Tel: 306-336-2505; *Fax:* 306-336-2505
lipton@sasktel.net
www.villageoflipton.com
Municipal Type: Village
Incorporated: May 15, 1905; *Area:* 0.75 sq km
Population in 2011: 372
Provincial Electoral District(s): Last Mountain-Touchwood
Federal Electoral District(s): Regina-Qu'Appelle
Next Election: Oct. 26, 2016 (4 year terms)
Ron Tomolak, Mayor
Marlene Bausmer, Administrator

La Loche
P.O. Box 310
La Loche Ave.
La Loche, SK S0M 1G0
Tel: 306-822-2032; *Fax:* 306-822-2078
nor.vill.laloche@sasktel.net
Municipal Type: Northern Village
Incorporated: Oct. 1, 1983; *Area:* 15.59 sq km
Population in 2011: 2,611
Provincial Electoral District(s): Athabasca
Federal Electoral District(s): Desnethé-Missinippi-Churchill River
Next Election: Autumn 2016 (4 year terms)
Georgina Jolibois, Mayor
Doug Gailey, Clerk

Loon Lake
P.O. Box 40
Loon Lake, SK S0M 1L0
Tel: 306-837-2090; *Fax:* 306-837-2282
rm561@sasktel.net
www.loonlakesask.com
Municipal Type: Village
Incorporated: Jan. 1, 1950; *Area:* 0.66 sq km
Population in 2011: 314
Provincial Electoral District(s): Meadow Lake
Federal Electoral District(s): Desnethé-Missinippi-Churchill River
Next Election: Oct. 26, 2016 (4 year terms)
Larry Heon, Mayor, 306-837-7605
Laurie Lehoux, Administrator

Loreburn
P.O. Box 177
Loreburn, SK S0H 2S0
Tel: 306-644-2097; *Fax:* 306-644-4847
villageofloreburn@sasktel.net
www.villageofloreburn.ca
Municipal Type: Village
Incorporated: May 20, 1909; *Area:* 0.62 sq km
Population in 2011: 107
Provincial Electoral District(s): Arm River-Watrous
Federal Electoral District(s): Moose Jaw-Lake Centre-Lanigan
Next Election: Oct. 26, 2016 (4 year terms)
Steven South, Mayor
Brandy Losie, Clerk

Love
P.O. Box 94
Love, SK S0J 1P0
Tel: 306-276-2525
villageoflove@sasktel.net
www.villageoflove.ca
Municipal Type: Village
Incorporated: June 2, 1945; *Area:* 0.46 sq km
Population in 2011: 65
Provincial Electoral District(s): Saskatchewan Rivers
Federal Electoral District(s): Prince Albert
Next Election: Oct. 26, 2016 (4 year terms)
Jackie Hazelwood, Mayor, 306-276-2321
Yvonne Moore, Administrator, 306-276-5750

Lucky Lake
P.O. Box 99
Lucky Lake, SK S0L 1Z0
Tel: 306-858-2234; *Fax:* 306-858-9134
rm225.vll@sasktel.net
www.luckylake.ca
Municipal Type: Village
Incorporated: Nov. 23, 1920; *Area:* 0.66 sq km
Population in 2011: 287
Provincial Electoral District(s): Rosetown-Elrose
Federal Electoral District(s): Cypress Hills-Grasslands
Next Election: Oct. 26, 2016 (4 year terms)
Note: Formerly known as Devil's Lake.
David Jessiman, Mayor
D.B. (Blair) Cleaveley, Administrator

Lumsden
P.O. Box 160
300 James St. North
Lumsden, SK S0G 3C0
Tel: 306-731-2404; *Fax:* 306-731-3572
town.lumsden@sasktel.net
www.lumsden.ca
Municipal Type: Town
Incorporated: Dec. 29, 1898; *Area:* 3.82 sq km
Population in 2011: 1,631
Provincial Electoral District(s): Thunder Creek
Federal Electoral District(s): Moose Jaw-Lake Centre-Lanigan
Next Election: Oct. 26, 2016 (4 year terms)
Note: Proclaimed as a town on March 15, 1905.
Bryan Matheson, Mayor, 306-731-3603
Darcie Cooper, Chief Administrative Officer

Lumsden Beach
P.O. Box 704
Regina Beach, SK S0G 4C0
Tel: 306-222-0087
lumsdenbeach@sasktel.net
www.lumsdenbeach.com
Municipal Type: Resort Village
Incorporated: 1918; *Area:* 0.47 sq km
Population in 2011: 35
Provincial Electoral District(s): Thunder Creek
Federal Electoral District(s): Moose Jaw-Lake Centre-Lanigan
Next Election: July 2020 (4 year terms)
Ross Wilson, Mayor
Myron Becker, Administrator, 306-729-4441

Luseland
P.O. Box 130
Luseland, SK S0L 2A0
Tel: 306-372-4218; *Fax:* 306-347-4700
luseland@sasktel.net
www.townofluseland.com
Municipal Type: Town
Incorporated: Dec. 10, 1910; *Area:* 1.53 sq km
Population in 2011: 566
Provincial Electoral District(s): Kindersley
Federal Electoral District(s): Battlefords-Lloydminster
Next Election: Oct. 26, 2016 (4 year terms)
Note: Proclaimed as a town on Jan. 1, 1954.
Len Schlosser, Mayor
Karyl Richardson, Administrator

Macklin
P.O. Box 69
Macklin, SK S0L 2C0
Tel: 306-753-2256; *Fax:* 306-753-3234
town.macklin@sasktel.net
www.macklin.ca
Municipal Type: Town
Incorporated: Nov. 8, 1909; *Area:* 2.85 sq km
Population in 2011: 1,415
Provincial Electoral District(s): Kindersley
Federal Electoral District(s): Battlefords-Lloydminster
Next Election: Oct. 26, 2016 (4 year terms)
Note: Proclaimed as a town on Nov. 1, 1912.
Patrick Doetzel, Mayor
Kim G. Gartner, Administrator

MacNutt
P.O. Box 10
MacNutt, SK S0A 2K0
Tel: 306-742-4391; *Fax:* 306-742-4391
macnuttvillage@iewireless.ca
www.macnuttsaskatchewan.com
Municipal Type: Village
Incorporated: Feb. 22, 1913; *Area:* 0.81 sq km
Population in 2011: 65
Provincial Electoral District(s): Melville-Saltcoats
Federal Electoral District(s): Yorkton-Melville
Next Election: Oct. 26, 2016 (4 year terms)
Shayne Wagner, Mayor
Kendra Busch, Clerk

Macoun
P.O. Box 58
Macoun, SK S0C 1P0
Tel: 306-634-9352; *Fax:* 306-634-9377
macoun.sask@gmail.com
Municipal Type: Village
Incorporated: Oct. 16, 1903; *Area:* 1.68 sq km
Population in 2011: 246
Provincial Electoral District(s): Estevan
Federal Electoral District(s): Souris-Moose Mountain
Next Election: Oct. 26, 2016 (4 year terms)
Stuart Sovdi, Mayor
Carmen Dodd-Vicary, Administrator

Macrorie
P.O. Box 37
Main St.
Macrorie, SK S0L 2E0
Tel: 306-243-2010; *Fax:* 306-243-2010
vmacro@sasktel.net
Municipal Type: Village
Incorporated: Feb. 8, 1912; *Area:* 0.77 sq km
Population in 2011: 65
Provincial Electoral District(s): Rosetown-Elrose

Federal Electoral District(s): Carlton Trail-Eagle Creek
Next Election: Oct. 26, 2016 (4 year terms)
Cliff Kvale, Mayor
Ilona Naab, Administrator

Maidstone
P.O. Box 208
112 - 1st Ave. West
Maidstone, SK S0M 1M0
Tel: 306-893-2373; *Fax:* 306-893-4378
townofmaidstone@sasktel.net
www.townofmaidstone.com
Municipal Type: Town
Incorporated: July 19, 1907; *Area:* 4.56 sq km
Population in 2011: 1,156
Provincial Electoral District(s): Cut Knife-Turtleford
Federal Electoral District(s): Battlefords-Lloydminster
Next Election: Oct. 26, 2016 (4 year terms)
Note: Proclaimed as a town on March 1, 1955.
Connie McCulloch, Mayor
Lorne Kachur, Administrator, 306-903-7099

Major
P.O. Box 179
Major, SK S0L 2H0
Tel: 306-834-5493
www.villageofmajor.ca
Municipal Type: Village
Incorporated: Sept. 29, 1914; *Area:* 2.78 sq km
Population in 2011: 61
Provincial Electoral District(s): Kindersley
Federal Electoral District(s): Battlefords-Lloydminster
Next Election: Oct. 26, 2016 (4 year terms)
Terry Zunti, Mayor
Margaret Ostrowski, Clerk, 306-834-5508

Makwa
P.O. Box 159
Makwa, SK S0M 1N0
Tel: 306-236-3919; *Fax:* 306-236-3913
villageofmakwa@sasktel.net
Municipal Type: Village
Incorporated: June 1, 1965; *Area:* 0.66 sq km
Population in 2011: 97
Provincial Electoral District(s): Meadow Lake
Federal Electoral District(s): Desnethé-Missinippi-Churchill River
Next Election: Oct. 26, 2016 (4 year terms)
Maurice Jeannotte, Mayor
Raylene Barthel, Clerk

Manitou Beach
701 Lakeview Ave.
Manitou Beach, SK S0K 4T1
Tel: 306-946-2831; *Fax:* 306-946-2017
manbe@sasktel.net
www.manitoubeach.ca
Municipal Type: Resort Village
Incorporated: 1919; *Area:* 3.09 sq km
Population in 2011: 257
Provincial Electoral District(s): Arm River-Watrous
Federal Electoral District(s): Moose Jaw-Lake Centre-Lanigan
Next Election: July 2020 (4 year terms)
Eric Upshall, Mayor
Beverley Laird, Administrator

Mankota
P.O. Box 336
Mankota, SK S0H 2W0
Tel: 306-478-2331; *Fax:* 306-478-2525
village.mankota@sasktel.net
Municipal Type: Village
Incorporated: Feb. 3, 1941; *Area:* 1.55 sq km
Population in 2011: 211
Provincial Electoral District(s): Wood River
Federal Electoral District(s): Cypress Hills-Grasslands
Next Election: Oct. 26, 2016 (4 year terms)
Grant Martin, Mayor
April Williamson, Administrator

Manor
P.O. Box 295
45 Main St.
Manor, SK S0C 1R0
Tel: 306-448-2273; *Fax:* 306-448-2274
admin.manor@sasktel.net
Municipal Type: Village
Incorporated: April 15, 1902; *Area:* 2.79 sq km
Population in 2011: 322
Provincial Electoral District(s): Cannington
Federal Electoral District(s): Souris-Moose Mountain
Next Election: Oct. 26, 2016 (4 year terms)
Vickie Akins, Mayor
Lisa Ironside, Administrator

Maple Creek
P.O. Box 428
205 Jasper St.
Maple Creek, SK S0N 1N0
Tel: 306-662-2244; *Fax:* 306-662-4131
townofmaplecreek@sasktel.net
www.maplecreek.ca
Other Information: After Hours Phone: 306-662-7333
Municipal Type: Town
Incorporated: April 28, 1896; *Area:* 4.42 sq km
Population in 2011: 2,176
Provincial Electoral District(s): Cypress Hills
Federal Electoral District(s): Cypress Hills-Grasslands
Next Election: Oct. 26, 2016 (4 year terms)
Note: Proclaimed as a town on April 30, 1903.
Barry Rudd, Mayor
Michele Schmidt, Administrator

Marcelin
P.O. Box 39
100 - 1st Ave. North
Marcelin, SK S0J 1R0
Tel: 306-226-2168; *Fax:* 306-226-2171
vmarcelin@sasktel.net
www.marcelin.ca
Municipal Type: Village
Incorporated: Sept. 25, 1911; *Area:* 1.32 sq km
Population in 2011: 158
Provincial Electoral District(s): Rosthern-Shellbrook
Federal Electoral District(s): Carlton Trail-Eagle Creek
Next Election: Oct. 26, 2016 (4 year terms)
Norman Desjardins, Mayor
Leanne McCormick, Administrator

Marengo
P.O. Box 70
Marengo, SK S0L 2K0
Tel: 306-968-2922; *Fax:* 306-968-2278
rm292.rm322@sasktel.net
Municipal Type: Village
Incorporated: Nov. 5, 1910; *Area:* 0.87 sq km
Population in 2011: 47
Provincial Electoral District(s): Kindersley
Federal Electoral District(s): Cypress Hills-Grasslands
Next Election: Oct. 26, 2016 (4 year terms)
Travis McKillop, Mayor
Robin Busby, Administrator

Margo
P.O. Box 28
Margo, SK S0A 2M0
Tel: 306-324-2134; *Fax:* 306-324-4563
villagemargo@sasktel.net
Municipal Type: Village
Incorporated: April 24, 1911; *Area:* 0.80 sq km
Population in 2011: 100
Provincial Electoral District(s): Kelvington-Wadena
Federal Electoral District(s): Yorkton-Melville
Next Election: Oct. 26, 2016 (4 year terms)
George Dawe, Mayor
Gail Selch, Administrator

Markinch
P.O. Box 29
Markinch, SK S0G 3J0
Tel: 306-726-4355; *Fax:* 306-726-4355
vofmarkinch@canwan.com
Municipal Type: Village
Incorporated: Feb. 16, 1911; *Area:* 0.68 sq km
Population in 2011: 72
Provincial Electoral District(s): Last Mountain-Touchwood
Federal Electoral District(s): Regina-Qu'Appelle
Next Election: Oct. 26, 2016 (4 year terms)
Wendell Langford, Mayor
Rita T. Orb, Clerk

Marquis
P.O. Box 40
Marquis, SK S0H 2X0
Tel: 306-788-2022; *Fax:* 306-788-2168
rm191@sasktel.net
Municipal Type: Village
Incorporated: March 21, 1910; *Area:* 0.63 sq km
Population in 2011: 92
Provincial Electoral District(s): Thunder Creek
Federal Electoral District(s): Moose Jaw-Lake Centre-Lanigan
Next Election: Oct. 26, 2016 (4 year terms)
Ken Marcyniuk, Mayor
Ronald Gasper, Administrator

Marsden
P.O. Box 69
Marsden, SK S0M 1P0
Tel: 306-826-5215; *Fax:* 306-826-5512
rm442@sasktel.net
Municipal Type: Village
Incorporated: April 24, 1931; *Area:* 0.94 sq km
Population in 2011: 284
Provincial Electoral District(s): Cut Knife-Turtleford
Federal Electoral District(s): Battlefords-Lloydminster
Next Election: Oct. 26, 2016 (4 year terms)
Craig Watson, Mayor
Joanne Loy, Administrator

Marshall
P.O. Box 125
17 Main St.
Marshall, SK S0M 1R0
Tel: 306-387-6340; *Fax:* 306-387-6161
townofmarshallcao@outlook.com
www.townofmarshall.ca
Municipal Type: Town
Incorporated: Jan. 21, 1914; *Area:* 1.01 sq km
Population in 2011: 533
Provincial Electoral District(s): Lloydminster
Federal Electoral District(s): Battlefords-Lloydminster
Next Election: Oct. 26, 2016 (4 year terms)
Note: Proclaimed as a town on Oct. 26, 2006.
Cory Tavener, Mayor
Colleen Digness, Administrator

Martensville
P.O. Box 970
37 Centennial Dr. South
Martensville, SK S0K 2T0
Tel: 306-931-2166; *Fax:* 306-933-2468
inquiry@martensville.ca
www.martensville.ca
Municipal Type: Town
Incorporated: Sept. 1, 1966; *Area:* 4.78 sq km
Population in 2011: 7,716
Provincial Electoral District(s): Martensville
Federal Electoral District(s): Carlton Trail-Eagle Creek
Next Election: Oct. 26, 2016 (4 year terms)
Note: Proclaimed as a town on Jan. 1, 1969.
Kent Muench, Mayor
Carla Budnick, Clerk

Maryfield
P.O. Box 58
Maryfield, SK S0G 3K0
Tel: 306-646-2143; *Fax:* 306-646-2193
villageofmaryfield@sasktel.net
www.maryfieldsaskatchewan.com
Municipal Type: Village
Incorporated: Aug. 21, 1907; *Area:* 2.69 sq km
Population in 2011: 365
Provincial Electoral District(s): Cannington
Federal Electoral District(s): Souris-Moose Mountain
Next Election: Oct. 26, 2016 (4 year terms)
David Hill, Mayor
Denine Neufeld, Administrator

Maymont
P.O. Box 160
Maymont, SK S0M 1T0
Tel: 306-389-2077; *Fax:* 306-389-2078
villageofmaymont@sasktel.net
Municipal Type: Village
Incorporated: June 24, 1907; *Area:* 0.66 sq km
Population in 2011: 146
Provincial Electoral District(s): Biggar
Federal Electoral District(s): Carlton Trail-Eagle Creek
Next Election: Oct. 26, 2016 (4 year terms)
Denise Bernier, Administrator

McLean
P.O. Box 56
McLean, SK S0G 3E0
Tel: 306-699-7279; *Fax:* 306-699-2347
villageofmclean@sasktel.net
www.mcleansask.com
Municipal Type: Village
Incorporated: Jan. 24, 1913; *Area:* 1.33 sq km
Population in 2011: 304
Provincial Electoral District(s): Indian Head-Milestone
Federal Electoral District(s): Regina-Qu'Appelle
Next Election: Oct. 26, 2016 (4 year terms)
Mark Towers, Mayor, 306-699-2303
Nadine Jensen, Administrator

McTaggart
P.O. Box 134
McTaggart, SK S0G 3G0
Tel: 306-861-1886; *Fax:* 306-842-1661
Municipal Type: Village
Incorporated: Oct. 5, 1909; *Area:* 0.69 sq km
Population in 2011: 125
Provincial Electoral District(s): Weyburn-Big Muddy
Federal Electoral District(s): Souris-Moose Mountain
Next Election: Oct. 26, 2016 (4 year terms)
Kevin Donald, Mayor
Wendy Wood, Administrator

Meacham
P.O. Box 9
Meacham, SK S0K 2V0
Tel: 306-376-2003; *Fax:* 306-376-2006
villageofmeacham@baudoux.ca
www.meacham.ca
Municipal Type: Village
Incorporated: June 19, 1912; *Area:* 1.27 sq km
Population in 2011: 84
Provincial Electoral District(s): Humboldt
Federal Electoral District(s): Moose Jaw-Lake Centre-Lanigan
Next Election: Oct. 26, 2016 (4 year terms)
Flo Frank, Mayor
Juaneta Bendig, Administrator

Meadow Lake
120 - 1st St. East
Meadow Lake, SK S9X 1Y5
Tel: 306-236-3622; *Fax:* 306-236-4299
cityhall@meadowlake.ca
www.meadowlake.ca
Municipal Type: Town
Incorporated: Aug. 24, 1931; *Area:* 7.95 sq km
Population in 2011: 5,045
Provincial Electoral District(s): Meadow Lake
Federal Electoral District(s): Desnethé-Missinippi-Churchill River
Next Election: Oct. 26, 2016 (4 year terms)
Note: Proclaimed as a town on Feb. 1, 1936.
Gary Vidal, Mayor
Jessica Walters, City Clerk

Meath Park
P.O. Box 255
Meath Park, SK S0J 1T0
Tel: 306-929-2112; *Fax:* 306-929-2281
villpark@sasktel.net
Municipal Type: Village
Incorporated: May 23, 1938; *Area:* 0.77 sq km
Population in 2011: 205
Provincial Electoral District(s): Saskatchewan Rivers
Federal Electoral District(s): Prince Albert
Next Election: Oct. 26, 2016 (4 year terms)
Tristen Wood, Mayor
Elaine Esopenko, Administrator

Medstead
P.O. Box 148
209 - 2nd Ave.
Medstead, SK S0M 1W0
Tel: 306-342-4898; *Fax:* 306-342-4422
villageofmedstead@sasktel.net
Municipal Type: Village
Incorporated: April 23, 1931; *Area:* 0.67 sq km
Population in 2011: 120
Provincial Electoral District(s): Rosthern-Shellbrook
Federal Electoral District(s): Battlefords-Lloydminster
Next Election: Oct. 26, 2016 (4 year terms)
Trevor Short, Mayor
Coleen Kitching, Administrator

Melfort
City Hall
P.O. Box 2230
202 Burrows Ave. West
Melfort, SK S0E 1A0
Tel: 306-752-5911; *Fax:* 306-752-5556
city@cityofmelfort.ca
www.cityofmelfort.ca
Municipal Type: Town
Incorporated: Nov. 4, 1903; *Area:* 14.78 sq km
Population in 2011: 5,576
Provincial Electoral District(s): Melfort
Federal Electoral District(s): Prince Albert
Next Election: Oct. 26, 2016 (4 year terms)
Note: Incorporated as a city on Sept. 2, 1980.
Rick Lang, Mayor, 306-752-3374
Heather Audette, Clerk

Melville
P.O. Box 1240
430 Main St.
Melville, SK S0A 2P0
Tel: 306-728-6840; *Fax:* 306-728-5911
cityhall@melville.ca
www.melville.ca
Municipal Type: Town
Incorporated: Dec. 21, 1908; *Area:* 14.82 sq km
Population in 2011: 4,517
Provincial Electoral District(s): Melville-Saltcoats
Federal Electoral District(s): Yorkton-Melville
Next Election: Oct. 26, 2016 (4 year terms)
Note: Incorporated as a city on Aug. 1, 1960.
Walter Streelasky, Mayor
Audrey Ulmer, City Manager, 306-728-6844

Melville Beach
P.O. Box 3250
Melville, SK S0A 2P0
Tel: 306-728-7697; *Fax:* 306-728-3180
rvmelvillebeach@gmail.com
Municipal Type: Resort Village
Area: 48.0 sq km
Population in 2011: 10
Provincial Electoral District(s): Melville-Saltcoats
Federal Electoral District(s): Yorkton-Melville
Next Election: July 2020 (4 year terms)
David Boulding, Mayor
Diane Smith, Administrator

Mendham
P.O. Box 69
Mendham, SK S0N 1P0
Tel: 306-679-2000; *Fax:* 306-679-2275
burstall@sasktel.net
Municipal Type: Village
Incorporated: April 1, 1930; *Area:* 0.5 sq km
Population in 2011: 35
Provincial Electoral District(s): Cypress Hills
Federal Electoral District(s): Cypress Hills-Grasslands
Next Election: Oct. 26, 2016 (4 year terms)
Kevin Angerman, Mayor
Lucein Stuebing, Clerk

Meota
P.O. Box 123
Meota, SK S0M 1X0
Tel: 306-892-2277; *Fax:* 306-892-2275
vmeota@sasktel.net
www.meota.ca
Municipal Type: Village
Incorporated: July 6, 1911; *Area:* 1.55 sq km
Population in 2011: 307
Provincial Electoral District(s): Cut Knife-Turtleford
Federal Electoral District(s): Battlefords-Lloydminster
Next Election: Oct. 26, 2016 (4 year terms)
John R. MacDonald, Mayor, 306-892-2452
Jennifer Fisher, Administrator

Mervin
P.O. Box 35
9 Main St.
Mervin, SK S0M 1Y0
Tel: 306-845-2784; *Fax:* 306-845-3563
villageofmervin@littleloon.ca
www.villageofmervin.com
Municipal Type: Village
Incorporated: March 17, 1920; *Area:* 0.73 sq km
Population in 2011: 160
Provincial Electoral District(s): Cut Knife-Turtleford
Federal Electoral District(s): Battlefords-Lloydminster
Next Election: Oct. 26, 2016 (4 year terms)
George Smith, Mayor
Lora Hundt, Administrator

Metinota
P.O. Box 47
Meota, SK S0M 1X0
Tel: 306-892-2557; *Fax:* 306-892-2250
rvmetinota@sasktel.net
Municipal Type: Resort Village
Area: 170.0 sq km
Population in 2011: 89
Provincial Electoral District(s): Cut Knife-Turtleford
Federal Electoral District(s): Battlefords-Lloydminster
Next Election: July 2020 (4 year terms)
Glen Wouters, Mayor
Carmen Menssa, Administrator

Michel Village
Sylvestre Place
P.O. Box 250
Dillon, SK S0M 0S0
Tel: 306-282-4401; *Fax:* 306-282-2155
michelvillage@sasktel.net
Municipal Type: Northern Hamlet
Incorporated: Nov. 1, 1983; *Area:* 3.73 sq km
Population in 2011: 66
Provincial Electoral District(s): Athabasca
Federal Electoral District(s): Desnethé-Missinippi-Churchill River
Next Election: Autumn 2016 (4 year terms)
Brent Janvier, Mayor
Allison Janvier, Clerk

Midale
P.O. Box 128
233 Main St.
Midale, SK S0C 1S0
Tel: 306-458-2400; *Fax:* 306-458-2209
lindugan@sasktel.net
www.townofmidale.com
Municipal Type: Town
Incorporated: Aug. 10, 1907; *Area:* 1.53 sq km
Population in 2011: 562
Provincial Electoral District(s): Estevan
Federal Electoral District(s): Souris-Moose Mountain
Next Election: Oct. 26, 2016 (4 year terms)
Note: Proclaimed as a town on March 1, 1962.
Allan Hauglum, Mayor, 306-458-2807
Linda M. Dugan, Administrator

Middle Lake
P.O. Box 119
Middle Lake, SK S0K 2X0
Tel: 306-367-2149; *Fax:* 306-367-4963
middlelake@sasktel.net
www.middlelake.ca
Municipal Type: Village
Incorporated: Jan. 1, 1963; *Area:* 1.26 sq km
Population in 2011: 242
Provincial Electoral District(s): Batoche
Federal Electoral District(s): Carlton Trail-Eagle Creek
Next Election: Oct. 26, 2016 (4 year terms)
Ken Herman, Mayor
Colette Hauser, Clerk

Milden
P.O. Box 70
202 Centre St.
Milden, SK S0L 2L0
Tel: 306-935-2131; *Fax:* 306-935-2020
vmilden@sasktel.net
www.villageofmilden.com
Municipal Type: Village
Incorporated: July 20, 1911; *Area:* 1.18 sq km
Population in 2011: 181
Provincial Electoral District(s): Rosetown-Elrose
Federal Electoral District(s): Carlton Trail-Eagle Creek
Next Election: Oct. 26, 2016 (4 year terms)
Lester Wall, Mayor
Heather Maxemniuk, Administrator

Milestone
P.O. Box 74
105 Main St.
Milestone, SK S0G 3L0
Tel: 306-436-2130; *Fax:* 306-436-2051
milcal@sasktel.net
www.milestonesk.ca
Municipal Type: Town
Incorporated: March 14, 1903; *Area:* 2.17 sq km
Population in 2011: 618
Provincial Electoral District(s): Indian Head-Milestone
Federal Electoral District(s): Moose Jaw-Lake Centre-Lanigan
Next Election: Oct. 26, 2016 (4 year terms)
Note: Proclaimed as a town on Aug. 15, 1906.
Jeff Brown, Mayor
Stephen Schury, Administrator

Minton
P.O. Box 52
Minton, SK S0C 1T0
Tel: 306-969-2144; *Fax:* 306-969-2127
rmnine@sasktel.net
Municipal Type: Village
Incorporated: Jan. 1, 1951; *Area:* 0.3 sq km
Population in 2011: 60
Provincial Electoral District(s): Weyburn-Big Muddy
Federal Electoral District(s): Souris-Moose Mountain
Next Election: Oct. 26, 2016 (4 year terms)
Dennis Simpart, Mayor

Loran Tessier, Clerk

Missinipe
c/o Government Relations
P.O. Box 5000
La Ronge, SK S0J 1L0
Tel: 306-425-4321; *Fax:* 306-425-2401
Municipal Type: Northern Hamlet
Incorporated: Feb. 1, 1984; *Area:* 1.87 sq km
Population in 2011: 39
Provincial Electoral District(s): Cumberland
Federal Electoral District(s): Desnethé-Missinippe-Churchill River
Next Election: Autumn 2016 (4 year terms)
Sandra Galambos, Advisor

Mistatim
P.O. Box 145
Mistatim, SK S0E 1B0
Tel: 306-889-2008; *Fax:* 306-889-4439
villageofmistatim@yourlink.ca
Municipal Type: Village
Incorporated: July 1, 1952; *Area:* 0.47 sq km
Population in 2011: 73
Provincial Electoral District(s): Carrot River Valley
Federal Electoral District(s): Yorkton-Melville
Next Election: Oct. 26, 2016 (4 year terms)
Gene Legare, Mayor
Cathy Murray, Administrator

Mistusinne
P.O. Box 160
Elbow, SK S0H 1J0
Tel: 306-854-4637; *Fax:* 306-854-4668
mistusinne@sasktel.net
www.mistusinne.com
Other Information: Maintenance Phone: 306-854-2068
Municipal Type: Resort Village
Area: 1.49 sq km
Population in 2011: 66
Provincial Electoral District(s): Thunder Creek
Federal Electoral District(s): Cypress Hills-Grasslands
Next Election: July 2020 (4 year terms)
Lynne Saas, Mayor, 306-854-4658
Yvonne Jess, Administrator
Leanne Hurlburt, Clerk

Montmartre
P.O. Box 146
Montmartre, SK S0G 3M0
Tel: 306-424-2040; *Fax:* 306-424-2065
rm126@sasktel.net
www.montmartre-sk.com
Municipal Type: Village
Incorporated: Oct. 19, 1908; *Area:* 1.63 sq km
Population in 2011: 476
Provincial Electoral District(s): Moosomin
Federal Electoral District(s): Souris-Moose Mountain
Next Election: Oct. 26, 2016 (4 year terms)
Robert Chittenden, Mayor
Dale Brenner, Administrator

Moosomin
P.O. Box 730
701 Main St.
Moosomin, SK S0G 3N0
Tel: 306-435-2988; *Fax:* 306-435-3343
twn.moosomin@sasktel.net
www.moosomin.com
Municipal Type: Town
Incorporated: March 20, 1889; *Area:* 5.97 sq km
Population in 2011: 2,485
Provincial Electoral District(s): Moosomin
Federal Electoral District(s): Souris-Moose Mountain
Next Election: Oct. 26, 2016 (4 year terms)
Larry Tomlinson, Mayor
Paul Listrom, Administrator

Morse
P.O. Box 270
400 Main St.
Morse, SK S0H 3C0
Tel: 306-629-3300; *Fax:* 306-629-3235
morse@sasktel.net
morsesask.com
Municipal Type: Town
Incorporated: March 11, 1910; *Area:* 1.45 sq km
Population in 2011: 240
Provincial Electoral District(s): Thunder Creek
Federal Electoral District(s): Cypress Hills-Grasslands
Next Election: Oct. 26, 2016 (4 year terms)
Note: Proclaimed as a town on Nov. 1, 1912.
George Byklum, Mayor
Tamara Knight, Administrator

Mortlach
P.O. Box 10
116 Rose St.
Mortlach, SK S0H 3E0
Tel: 306-355-2554; *Fax:* 306-355-2557
village.mortlach@sasktel.net
www.mortlach.ca
Municipal Type: Village
Incorporated: April 19, 1906; *Area:* 2.76 sq km
Population in 2011: 289
Provincial Electoral District(s): Thunder Creek
Federal Electoral District(s): Cypress Hills-Grasslands
Next Election: Oct. 26, 2016 (4 year terms)
Dale Domeij, Mayor, 306-355-2370
Faye Campbell, Administrator

Mossbank
P.O. Box 370
311 Main St.
Mossbank, SK S0H 3G0
Tel: 306-354-2294; *Fax:* 306-354-7725
townofmossbank@sasktel.net
www.mossbank.ca
Municipal Type: Town
Incorporated: Dec. 14, 1915; *Area:* 1.75 sq km
Population in 2011: 327
Provincial Electoral District(s): Wood River
Federal Electoral District(s): Cypress Hills-Grasslands
Next Election: Oct. 26, 2016 (4 year terms)
Note: Proclaimed as a town on May 15, 1959.
Gregg Nagel, Mayor
Chris Costley, Chief Administrative Officer

Muenster
P.O. Box 98
Muenster, SK S0K 2Y0
Tel: 306-682-2794; *Fax:* 306-682-4179
muenster@sasktel.net
Municipal Type: Village
Incorporated: Aug. 18, 1908; *Area:* 1.24 sq km
Population in 2011: 422
Provincial Electoral District(s): Humboldt
Federal Electoral District(s): Carlton Trail-Eagle Creek
Next Election: Oct. 26, 2016 (4 year terms)
Reva Bauer, Mayor
Rose M. Haeusler, Administrator

Naicam
P.O. Box 238
Naicam, SK S0K 2Z0
Tel: 306-874-2280; *Fax:* 306-874-5444
naicam@sasktel.net
www.townofnaicam.ca
Municipal Type: Town
Incorporated: April 28, 1921; *Area:* 1.69 sq km
Population in 2011: 686
Provincial Electoral District(s): Melfort
Federal Electoral District(s): Yorkton-Melville
Next Election: Oct. 26, 2016 (4 year terms)
Note: Proclaimed as a town on Sept. 1, 1954.
Rodger Hayward, Mayor
Lowell Prefontaine, Administrator

Neilburg
P.O. Box 280
39 L.E. Gibbons Centre St.
Neilburg, SK S0M 2C0
Tel: 306-823-4321; *Fax:* 306-823-4477
neilburg@sasktel.net
www.neilburg.ca
Municipal Type: Village
Incorporated: Jan. 1, 1947; *Area:* 1.16 sq km
Population in 2011: 448
Provincial Electoral District(s): Cut Knife-Turtleford
Federal Electoral District(s): Battlefords-Lloydminster
Next Election: Oct. 26, 2016 (4 year terms)
Brent Wiens, Mayor
Janet L. Black, Administrator

Netherhill
P.O. Box 4
Netherhill, SK S0L 2M0
Tel: 306-463-2905; *Fax:* 306-463-2905
hendersonl@sasktel.net
Municipal Type: Village
Incorporated: April 28, 1910; *Area:* 0.73 sq km
Population in 2011: 25
Provincial Electoral District(s): Rosetown-Elrose
Federal Electoral District(s): Cypress Hills-Grasslands
Next Election: Oct. 26, 2016 (4 year terms)
Lorne Gerwing, Mayor
Leona Henderson, Clerk

Neudorf
P.O. Box 187
Neudorf, SK S0A 2T0
Tel: 306-748-2551; *Fax:* 306-748-2647
vneudorf@sasktel.net
www.neudorf1.sasktelwebhosting.com
Municipal Type: Village
Incorporated: April 25, 1905; *Area:* 2.05 sq km
Population in 2011: 272
Provincial Electoral District(s): Last Mountain-Touchwood
Federal Electoral District(s): Yorkton-Melville
Next Election: Oct. 26, 2016 (4 year terms)
Murray J. Hanowski, Mayor
Anne Redding, Administrator

Neville
P.O. Box 88
Neville, SK S0N 1T0
Tel: 306-627-3255; *Fax:* 306-627-3546
village.neville@sasktel.net
Municipal Type: Village
Incorporated: July 5, 1912; *Area:* 1.10 sq km
Population in 2011: 83
Provincial Electoral District(s): Wood River
Federal Electoral District(s): Cypress Hills-Grasslands
Next Election: Oct. 26, 2016 (4 year terms)
Donald Forness, Mayor
Cindy Berry, Clerk

Nipawin
P.O. Box 2134
210 Second Ave. East
Nipawin, SK S0E 1E0
Tel: 306-862-9866; *Fax:* 306-862-3076
info@nipawin.com
www.nipawin.com
Municipal Type: Town
Incorporated: May 7, 1925; *Area:* 8.03 sq km
Population in 2011: 4,265
Provincial Electoral District(s): Carrot River Valley
Federal Electoral District(s): Prince Albert
Next Election: Oct. 26, 2016 (4 year terms)
Note: Proclaimed as a town on May 1, 1937.
David Trann, Mayor, 306-862-3320
Lesley Richer, Administrator

Nokomis
P.O. Box 189
101 - 3rd Ave. West
Nokomis, SK S0G 3R0
Tel: 306-528-2010; *Fax:* 306-528-2024
townofnokomis@sasktel.net
www.nokomisweb.com
Municipal Type: Town
Incorporated: March 5, 1908; *Area:* 2.61 sq km
Population in 2011: 397
Provincial Electoral District(s): Arm River-Watrous
Federal Electoral District(s): Moose Jaw-Lake Centre-Lanigan
Next Election: Oct. 26, 2016 (4 year terms)
Note: Proclaimed as a town on Aug. 15, 1908.
David Mark, Mayor
Tanya Zdunich, Assistant Administrator

Norquay
P.O. Box 327
25 Main St.
Norquay, SK S0A 2V0
Tel: 306-594-2101; *Fax:* 306-594-2347
norquay@sasktel.net
www.norquay.ca
Municipal Type: Town
Incorporated: June 4, 1913; *Area:* 1.69 sq km
Population in 2011: 435
Provincial Electoral District(s): Canora-Pelly
Federal Electoral District(s): Yorkton-Melville
Next Election: Oct. 26, 2016 (4 year terms)
Note: Proclaimed as a town on March 1, 1963.
Don Tower, Acting Mayor
Rona Seidle, Administrator

North Grove
P.O. Box 473
#5, 1410 Caribou St. W
Moose Jaw, SK S6H 4P1
Tel: 306-694-8300; *Fax:* 306-395-2767
rvnorthgrove@shaw.ca
www.northgrovesk.wordpress.com

Municipal Type: Resort Village
Area: 1.03 sq km
Population in 2011: 49
Provincial Electoral District(s): Thunder Creek
Federal Electoral District(s): Moose Jaw-Lake Centre-Lanigan
Next Election: July 2020 (4 year terms)
Sherry Hetherington, Mayor
Tracy Edwards, Administrator

North Portal
P.O. Box 119
204 Park Ave.
North Portal, SK S0C 1W0
Tel: 306-927-5050; *Fax:* 306-927-2033
villagen@sasktel.net
Municipal Type: Village
Incorporated: Nov. 16, 1903; *Area:* 2.49 sq km
Population in 2011: 143
Provincial Electoral District(s): Estevan
Federal Electoral District(s): Souris-Moose Mountain
Next Election: Oct. 26, 2016 (4 year terms)
Murray Arnold, Mayor
Lindsay Davis, Administrator

Odessa
P.O. Box 91
Odessa, SK S0G 3S0
Tel: 306-957-2020; *Fax:* 306-957-4502
villageofodessa@sasktel.net
www.odessask.com
Municipal Type: Village
Incorporated: March 14, 1911; *Area:* 1.18 sq km
Population in 2011: 239
Provincial Electoral District(s): Indian Head-Milestone
Federal Electoral District(s): Souris-Moose Mountain
Next Election: Oct. 26, 2016 (4 year terms)
Larry Lockert, Mayor, 306-957-2047
Leticia Gould, Administrator

Ogema
P.O. Box 159
112 Main St.
Ogema, SK S0C 1Y0
Tel: 306-459-2262; *Fax:* 306-459-2762
townofogema@sasktel.net
www.ogema.ca
Other Information: Community Development E-mail: ogemaedo@gmail.com
Municipal Type: Town
Incorporated: Jan. 18, 1911; *Area:* 1.43 sq km
Population in 2011: 368
Provincial Electoral District(s): Weyburn-Big Muddy
Federal Electoral District(s): Souris-Moose Mountain
Next Election: Oct. 26, 2016 (4 year terms)
Note: Proclaimed as a town on Jan. 7, 1913.
Wayne Myren, Mayor
Peggy Tuchscherer, Administrator

Osage
P.O. Box 96
Osage, SK S0G 3T0
Tel: 306-722-3747
Municipal Type: Village
Incorporated: May 8, 1906; *Area:* 0.59 sq km
Population in 2011: 20
Provincial Electoral District(s): Indian Head-Milestone
Federal Electoral District(s): Souris-Moose Mountain
Next Election: Oct. 26, 2016 (4 year terms)
Garry Kreutzer, Mayor
Linda R. Kreutzer, Clerk

Osler
P.O. Box 190
228 Willow Dr.
Osler, SK S0K 3A0
Tel: 306-239-2155; *Fax:* 306-239-2194
info@townofosler.com
www.osler-sk.ca
Municipal Type: Town
Incorporated: April 9, 1904; *Area:* 0.98 sq km
Population in 2011: 1,088
Provincial Electoral District(s): Martensville
Federal Electoral District(s): Carlton Trail-Eagle Creek
Next Election: Oct. 26, 2016 (4 year terms)
Note: Proclaimed as a town on Nov. 1, 1985.
Ben Buhler, Mayor
Sandra MacArthur, Chief Administrative Officer

Outlook
P.O. Box 518
400 Saskatchewan Ave. West
Outlook, SK S0L 2N0
Tel: 306-867-8663; *Fax:* 306-867-9898
town@town.outlook.sk.ca
www.town.outlook.sk.ca
Municipal Type: Town
Incorporated: Dec. 19, 1908; *Area:* 7.83 sq km
Population in 2011: 2,204
Provincial Electoral District(s): Rosetown-Elrose
Federal Electoral District(s): Moose Jaw-Lake Centre-Lanigan; Carlton Trail-Eagle Creek
Next Election: Oct. 26, 2016 (4 year terms)
Note: Proclaimed as a town on Nov. 1, 1909.
Bob Stephenson, Mayor
Trent Michelman, Municipal Manager

Oxbow
P.O. Box 149
307 Main St.
Oxbow, SK S0C 2B0
Tel: 306-483-2300; *Fax:* 306-483-5277
www.oxbow.ca
Municipal Type: Town
Incorporated: March 7, 1899; *Area:* 3.1 sq km
Population in 2011: 1,285
Provincial Electoral District(s): Cannington
Federal Electoral District(s): Souris-Moose Mountain
Next Election: Oct. 26, 2016 (4 year terms)
Note: Proclaimed as a town on May 30, 1904.
Dale Ching, Mayor
Dickson Bailey, Administrator

Paddockwood
P.O. Box 188
Paddockwood, SK S0J 1Z0
Tel: 306-989-2033; *Fax:* 306-989-1212
vpaddockwood@inet2000.com
Municipal Type: Village
Incorporated: Jan. 1, 1949; *Area:* 0.65 sq km
Population in 2011: 163
Provincial Electoral District(s): Saskatchewan Rivers
Federal Electoral District(s): Prince Albert
Next Election: Oct. 26, 2016 (4 year terms)
Rick Nolan, Mayor
Joan Carriere, Clerk

Pangman
P.O. Box 189
Pangman, SK S0C 2C0
Tel: 306-442-2131; *Fax:* 306-442-2144
rm.69@sasktel.net
www.pangman.ca
Municipal Type: Village
Incorporated: May 17, 1911; *Area:* 0.73 sq km
Population in 2011: 214
Provincial Electoral District(s): Weyburn-Big Muddy
Federal Electoral District(s): Souris-Moose Mountain
Next Election: Oct. 26, 2016 (4 year terms)
Rod Rowland, Mayor
Tina Douglas, Administrator

Paradise Hill
P.O. Box 270
Paradise Hill, SK S0M 2G0
Tel: 306-344-2206; *Fax:* 306-344-4941
paradisehill@sasktel.net
www.paradisehill.ca
Municipal Type: Village
Incorporated: Jan. 1, 1947; *Area:* 1.99 sq km
Population in 2011: 515
Provincial Electoral District(s): Lloydminster
Federal Electoral District(s): Battlefords-Lloydminster
Next Election: Oct. 26, 2016 (4 year terms)
Bernard Ecker, Mayor
Marion Hougham, Administrator

Parkside
P.O. Box 48
Parkside, SK S0J 2A0
Tel: 306-747-2235; *Fax:* 306-747-3395
villageofparkside@yourlink.ca
Municipal Type: Village
Incorporated: Feb. 21, 1913; *Area:* 0.92 sq km
Population in 2011: 125
Provincial Electoral District(s): Rosthern-Shellbrook
Federal Electoral District(s): Carlton Trail-Eagle Creek
Next Election: Oct. 26, 2016 (4 year terms)
David K. Moe, Mayor
Gwen Olson, Clerk

Patuanak
P.O. Box 180
Shagwenaw Dr.
Patuanak, SK S0M 2H0
Tel: 306-396-2020; *Fax:* 306-396-2092
hamofpat@outlook.com
Municipal Type: Northern Hamlet
Incorporated: Dec. 1, 1983; *Area:* 1.34 sq km
Population in 2011: 64
Provincial Electoral District(s): Athabasca
Federal Electoral District(s): Desnethé-Missinippi-Churchill River
Next Election: Autumn 2016 (4 year terms)
Hazel Maurice, Mayor
Sarah Dawatsare, Clerk

Paynton
P.O. Box 100
Paynton, SK S0M 2J0
Tel: 306-895-2023; *Fax:* 306-895-2053
village470@sasktel.net
Municipal Type: Village
Incorporated: May 2, 1907; *Area:* 0.85 sq km
Population in 2011: 151
Provincial Electoral District(s): Cut Knife-Turtleford
Federal Electoral District(s): Battlefords-Lloydminster
Next Election: Oct. 26, 2016 (4 year terms)
John Penner, Mayor
Harold Trew, Administrator

Pebble Baye
P.O. Box 449
Canwood, SK S0J 0K0
Tel: 306-468-3104
resortpebblebaye@gmail.com
www.pebblebaye.com
Municipal Type: Resort Village
Incorporated: 1983; *Area:* 0.74 sq km
Population in 2011: 33
Provincial Electoral District(s): Rosthern-Shellbrook
Federal Electoral District(s): Desnethé-Missinippi-Churchill River; Carlton Trail-Eagle Creek
Next Election: July 2020 (4 year terms)
Bonnie Kraus, Mayor
Terry Lofstrom, Administrator

Pelican Narrows
P.O. Box 10
Bear St.
Pelican Narrows, SK S0P 0E0
Tel: 306-632-2225; *Fax:* 306-632-2006
Municipal Type: Northern Village
Incorporated: Jan. 1, 1989; *Area:* 3.70 sq km
Population in 2011: 790
Provincial Electoral District(s): Cumberland
Federal Electoral District(s): Desnethé-Missinippi-Churchill River
Next Election: Autumn 2016 (4 year terms)
Horace Morin, Mayor
Robn Merasty, Clerk

Pelican Pointe
P.O. Box 187
Silton, SK S0G 4L0
Tel: 306-729-4614
pelicanpointe-rv.sk.ca
Municipal Type: Resort Village
Area: 0.12 sq km
Population in 2011: 15
Provincial Electoral District(s): Last Mountain-Touchwood
Federal Electoral District(s): Moose Jaw-Lake Centre-Lanigan
Next Election: July 2020 (4 year terms)
Robert Phillips, Mayor
Lynda Stack, Clerk

Pelly
P.O. Box 220
Pelly, SK S0A 2Z0
Tel: 306-595-2124; *Fax:* 306-595-2050
town.pelly@sasktel.net
www.pelly.ca
Municipal Type: Village
Incorporated: May 4, 1911; *Area:* 0.96 sq km
Population in 2011: 283
Provincial Electoral District(s): Canora-Pelly
Federal Electoral District(s): Yorkton-Melville
Next Election: Oct. 26, 2016 (4 year terms)
Sharon Nelson, Mayor
Sheri Kosar, Administrator

Pennant
P.O. Box 57
Pennant, SK S0N 1X0
Tel: 306-626-3255; *Fax:* 306-626-3661
villageofpennant@sasktel.net
Municipal Type: Village
Incorporated: July 29, 1912; *Area:* 0.65 sq km
Population in 2011: 120
Provincial Electoral District(s): Swift Current
Federal Electoral District(s): Cypress Hills-Grasslands
Next Election: Oct. 26, 2016 (4 year terms)
Keaton Dowdeswell, Mayor
Brandi Prentice, Administrator

Pense
P.O. Box 125
243 Brunswick St.
Pense, SK S0G 3W0
Tel: 306-345-2332; *Fax:* 306-345-2340
townofpense@sasktel.net
www.pense.ca
Municipal Type: Village
Incorporated: March 7, 1904; *Area:* 1.32 sq km
Population in 2011: 532
Provincial Electoral District(s): Thunder Creek
Federal Electoral District(s): Moose Jaw-Lake Centre-Lanigan
Next Election: Oct. 26, 2016 (4 year terms)
Michele LeBlanc, Mayor
Jennifer Lendvay, Administrator

Perdue
P.O. Box 190
Perdue, SK S0K 3C0
Tel: 306-237-4337; *Fax:* 306-237-4874
villageofperdue@sasktel.net
www.villageofperdue.com
Municipal Type: Village
Incorporated: July 15, 1909; *Area:* 1.10 sq km
Population in 2011: 362
Provincial Electoral District(s): Biggar
Federal Electoral District(s): Carlton Trail-Eagle Creek
Next Election: Oct. 26, 2016 (4 year terms)
Dave Miller, Mayor
Andrea Ball, Administrator

Pierceland
P.O. Box 39
177 Main St.
Pierceland, SK S0M 2K0
Tel: 306-839-2015; *Fax:* 306-839-2057
plandvillage@sasktel.net
www.villageofpierceland.sasktelwebhosting.com
Municipal Type: Village
Incorporated: Jan. 1, 1973; *Area:* 2.69 sq km
Population in 2011: 551
Provincial Electoral District(s): Lloydminster
Federal Electoral District(s): Desnethé-Missinippi-Churchill River
Next Election: Oct. 26, 2016 (4 year terms)
Jim Krushelnitzky, Mayor
Tammy Landry, Administrator

Pilger
P.O. Box 24
Pilger, SK S0K 3G0
Tel: 306-367-4631; *Fax:* 306-367-4621
Municipal Type: Village
Incorporated: Jan. 1, 1969; *Area:* 0.52 sq km
Population in 2011: 65
Provincial Electoral District(s): Batoche
Federal Electoral District(s): Carlton Trail-Eagle Creek
Next Election: Oct. 26, 2016 (4 year terms)
Joyce Bauer, Mayor
Rhonda Hemm, Clerk

Pilot Butte
Pilot Butte Recreation Complex
P.O. Box 253
222 Diamond Pl.
Pilot Butte, SK S0G 3Z0
Tel: 306-781-4547; *Fax:* 306-781-4477
townofpilotbutte@sasktel.net
www.pilotbutte.ca
Municipal Type: Town
Incorporated: Nov. 8, 1913; *Area:* 4.69 sq km
Population in 2011: 1,848
Provincial Electoral District(s): Regina Wascana Plains
Federal Electoral District(s): Regina-Qu'Appelle
Next Election: Oct. 26, 2016 (4 year terms)
Note: Proclaimed as a town on Nov. 1, 1980.
Nat Ross, Mayor
Laurie Rudolph, Administrator

Pinehouse
P.O. Box 298
Pinehouse Ave.
Pinehouse, SK S0J 2B0
Tel: 306-884-2030; *Fax:* 306-884-2021
nvp@sasktel.net
www.pinehouselake.com
Municipal Type: Northern Village
Incorporated: Oct. 1, 1983; *Area:* 6.84 sq km
Population in 2011: 978
Provincial Electoral District(s): Athabasca
Federal Electoral District(s): Desnethé-Missinippi-Churchill River
Next Election: Autumn 2016 (4 year terms)
Mike Natomagan, Mayor
Martine Smith, Clerk

Pleasantdale
P.O. Box 147
Pleasantdale, SK S0K 3H0
Tel: 306-874-5743; *Fax:* 306-874-5743
villageofpleasantdale@gmail.com
Municipal Type: Village
Incorporated: Jan. 1, 1987; *Area:* 0.56 sq km
Population in 2011: 76
Provincial Electoral District(s): Melfort
Federal Electoral District(s): Yorkton-Melville
Next Election: Oct. 26, 2016 (4 year terms)
Barry Jordan, Mayor
Angela Jordan, Administrator

Plenty
P.O. Box 177
Plenty, SK S0L 2R0
Tel: 306-932-2045; *Fax:* 306-932-2044
vop@sasktel.net
www.villageofplenty.ca
Municipal Type: Village
Incorporated: March 25, 1911; *Area:* 0.65 sq km
Population in 2011: 131
Provincial Electoral District(s): Rosetown-Elrose
Federal Electoral District(s): Battlefords-Lloydminster
Next Election: Oct. 26, 2016 (4 year terms)
Larry Horysh, Mayor
Karen Peters, Administrator

Plunkett
P.O. Box 149
Plunkett, SK S0K 3J0
Tel: 306-944-4514; *Fax:* 306-944-4512
Municipal Type: Village
Incorporated: Dec. 28, 1921; *Area:* 0.64 sq km
Population in 2011: 75
Provincial Electoral District(s): Humboldt
Federal Electoral District(s): Moose Jaw-Lake Centre-Lanigan
Next Election: Oct. 26, 2016 (4 year terms)
Richard Hayes, Mayor
Helen Miller, Clerk

Ponteix
P.O. Box 330
213 Centre St.
Ponteix, SK S0N 1Z0
Tel: 306-625-3222; *Fax:* 306-625-3204
town.ponteix@sasktel.net
www.ponteix.ca
Municipal Type: Town
Incorporated: June 24, 1914; *Area:* 1.09 sq km
Population in 2011: 605
Provincial Electoral District(s): Wood River
Federal Electoral District(s): Cypress Hills-Grasslands
Next Election: Oct. 26, 2016 (4 year terms)
Note: Proclaimed as a town on April 1, 1957.
Shawn Larochelle, Mayor
Lynne Lemieux, Administrator

Porcupine Plain
P.O. Box 310
151 McAllister Ave.
Porcupine Plain, SK S0E 1H0
Tel: 306-278-2262; *Fax:* 306-278-3378
porcupineplain@sasktel.net
www.porcupineplain.com
Municipal Type: Town
Incorporated: April 9, 1942; *Area:* 2.27 sq km
Population in 2011: 855
Provincial Electoral District(s): Kelvington-Wadena
Federal Electoral District(s): Yorkton-Melville
Next Election: Oct. 26, 2016 (4 year terms)
Note: Proclaimed as a town on Jan. 1, 1968.
Carol Belchamber, Mayor, 306-278-2798
Lynne Lemieux, Administrator

Preeceville
P.O. Box 560
239 Highway Ave. East
Preeceville, SK S0A 3B0
Tel: 306-547-2810; *Fax:* 306-547-3116
preeceville@sasktel.net
www.townofpreeceville.ca
Other Information: Toll Free Phone: 1-877-706-3196
Municipal Type: Town
Incorporated: Feb. 6, 1912; *Area:* 2.79 sq km
Population in 2011: 1,070
Provincial Electoral District(s): Canora-Pelly
Federal Electoral District(s): Yorkton-Melville
Next Election: Oct. 26, 2016 (4 year terms)
Note: Incorporated as a town on Nov. 30, 1946.
Garth Harris, Mayor
Lorelei Karcha, Administrator

Prelate
P.O. Box 40
203 Main St.
Prelate, SK S0N 2B0
Tel: 306-673-2340; *Fax:* 306-673-2340
villageofprelate@sasktel.net
www.prelate.ca/node/8
Municipal Type: Village
Incorporated: Oct. 25, 1913; *Area:* 0.87 sq km
Population in 2011: 124
Provincial Electoral District(s): Cypress Hills
Federal Electoral District(s): Cypress Hills-Grasslands
Next Election: Oct. 26, 2016 (4 year terms)
Darrah Duchscherer, Mayor
Darlene Wagner, Administrator

Primate
P.O. Box 6
Primate, SK S0L 2S0
Tel: 306-753-2429
villageofprimate@gmail.com
Municipal Type: Village
Incorporated: April 5, 1922; *Area:* 0.94 sq km
Population in 2011: 45
Provincial Electoral District(s): Kindersley
Federal Electoral District(s): Battlefords-Lloydminster
Next Election: Oct. 26, 2016 (4 year terms)
Connie Henning, Mayor
Kim Gartner, Administrator

Prud'homme
P.O. Box 38
Railway Ave.
Prud'Homme, SK S0K 3K0
Tel: 306-654-2001; *Fax:* 306-654-2007
voprud@sasktel.net
www.prudhommevillage.ca
Municipal Type: Village
Incorporated: Nov. 15, 1922; *Area:* 0.84 sq km
Population in 2011: 172
Provincial Electoral District(s): Humboldt
Federal Electoral District(s): Carlton Trail-Eagle Creek
Next Election: Oct. 26, 2016 (4 year terms)
Margret Asmuss, Mayor
Holly Maas, Administrator

Punnichy
P.O. Box 250
Punnichy, SK S0A 3C0
Tel: 306-835-2135; *Fax:* 306-835-2401
punnichy@aski.ca
Municipal Type: Village
Incorporated: Oct. 22, 1909; *Area:* 0.68 sq km
Population in 2011: 246
Provincial Electoral District(s): Last Mountain-Touchwood
Federal Electoral District(s): Regina-Qu'Appelle
Next Election: Oct. 26, 2016 (4 year terms)
Lawrence Beyer, Mayor
Wanda Lloyd, Administrator

Qu'Appelle
P.O. Box 60
Qu'Appelle, SK S0G 4A0
Tel: 306-699-2279; *Fax:* 306-699-2306
townquappelle@sasktel.net
www.townofquappelle.ca
Municipal Type: Town
Incorporated: Feb. 20, 1904; *Area:* 4.22 sq km
Population in 2011: 668
Provincial Electoral District(s): Indian Head-Milestone
Federal Electoral District(s): Regina-Qu'Appelle
Next Election: Oct. 26, 2016 (4 year terms)
Linda Andrew, Mayor
Brenna Ackerman, Administrator

Quill Lake
P.O. Box 9
60 Main St.
Quill Lake, SK S0A 3E0
Tel: 306-383-2592; *Fax:* 306-383-2255
quilllake@sasktel.net
Municipal Type: Village
Incorporated: Dec. 8, 1906; *Area:* 1.30 sq km
Population in 2011: 409
Provincial Electoral District(s): Melfort
Federal Electoral District(s): Yorkton-Melville
Next Election: Oct. 26, 2016 (4 year terms)
Robert Benjamin, Mayor
Judy L. Kanak, Administrator

Quinton
P.O. Box 128
Quinton, SK S0A 3G0
Tel: 306-835-2515; *Fax:* 306-835-2515
quintonvillage@aski.ca
Municipal Type: Village
Incorporated: March 1, 1910; *Area:* 0.96 sq km
Population in 2011: 111
Provincial Electoral District(s): Arm River-Watrous
Federal Electoral District(s): Regina-Qu'Appelle
Next Election: Oct. 26, 2016 (4 year terms)
Colette Brockman, Mayor
Elaine Perry, Administrator

Rabbit Lake
P.O. Box 9
Rabbit Lake, SK S0M 2L0
Tel: 306-824-2125; *Fax:* 306-824-2150
rabbitlake@yourlink.ca
Municipal Type: Village
Incorporated: April 13, 1928; *Area:* 0.92 sq km
Population in 2011: 127
Provincial Electoral District(s): Rosthern-Shellbrook
Federal Electoral District(s): Battlefords-Lloydminster; Carlton Trail-Eagle Creek
Next Election: Oct. 26, 2016 (4 year terms)
Dave Plummer, Mayor
Cindy Miller, Administrator

Radisson
P.O. Box 69
Radisson, SK S0K 3L0
Tel: 306-827-2218; *Fax:* 306-827-4747
tradisson@sasktel.net
www.radisson.ca
Municipal Type: Town
Incorporated: Feb. 3, 1906; *Area:* 2.07 sq km
Population in 2011: 505
Provincial Electoral District(s): Biggar
Federal Electoral District(s): Carlton Trail-Eagle Creek
Next Election: Oct. 26, 2016 (4 year terms)
Note: Proclaimed as a town on July 1, 1913.
Dave Summers, Mayor
Darrin Beaudoin, Administrator

Radville
P.O. Box 339
522 Healy Ave.
Radville, SK S0C 2G0
Tel: 306-869-2477; *Fax:* 306-869-3100
town.radville@sasktel.net
www.radville.ca
Municipal Type: Town
Incorporated: Jan. 3, 1911; *Area:* 1.86 sq km
Population in 2011: 860
Provincial Electoral District(s): Estevan
Federal Electoral District(s): Souris-Moose Mountain
Next Election: Oct. 26, 2016 (4 year terms)
Note: Proclaimed as a town on May 1, 1913.
Rene Bourassa, Mayor
Shauna Bourassa, Administrator

Rama
P.O. Box 205
Rama, SK S0A 3H0
Tel: 306-593-6065; *Fax:* 306-593-2273
villagerama@yourlink.ca
Municipal Type: Village
Incorporated: Dec. 18, 1919; *Area:* 0.67 sq km
Population in 2011: 75
Provincial Electoral District(s): Kelvington-Wadena
Federal Electoral District(s): Yorkton-Melville
Next Election: Oct. 26, 2016 (4 year terms)
Darrell Dutchak, Mayor
Tammy Loerzel, Administrator

Raymore
P.O. Box 10
107 Main St.
Raymore, SK S0A 3J0
Tel: 306-746-2100; *Fax:* 306-746-4314
raymoretown@aski.ca
www.raymore.ca
Municipal Type: Town
Incorporated: Aug. 11, 1909; *Area:* 2.75 sq km
Population in 2011: 568
Provincial Electoral District(s): Arm River-Watrous
Federal Electoral District(s): Regina-Qu'Appelle
Next Election: Oct. 26, 2016 (4 year terms)
Note: Proclaimed as a town on Aug. 1, 1963.
Malcolm Koncz, Mayor
Joanne Hamilton, Administrator

Redvers
P.O. Box 249
25 Railway Ave.
Redvers, SK S0C 2H0
Tel: 306-452-3533; *Fax:* 306-452-3701
town.of.redvers@sasktel.net
www.redvers.ca
Municipal Type: Town
Incorporated: July 9, 1904; *Area:* 2.83 sq km
Population in 2011: 975
Provincial Electoral District(s): Cannington
Federal Electoral District(s): Souris-Moose Mountain
Next Election: Oct. 26, 2016 (4 year terms)
Note: Proclaimed as a town on July 6, 1960.
Brian Dangstorp, Mayor
Bonnie Rutten, Administrator

Regina Beach
P.O. Box 10
218 Centre St.
Regina Beach, SK S0G 4C0
Tel: 306-729-2202; *Fax:* 306-729-3411
townofreginabeach@sasktel.net
www.reginabeach.ca
Municipal Type: Town
Incorporated: Sept. 30, 1920; *Area:* 2.58 sq km
Population in 2011: 1,081
Provincial Electoral District(s): Thunder Creek
Federal Electoral District(s): Moose Jaw-Lake Centre-Lanigan
Next Election: Oct. 26, 2016 (4 year terms)
Note: Proclaimed as a town on Nov. 1, 1980.
Cameron Hart, Mayor
Lynette Gaetz, Chief Administrative Officer

Rhein
P.O. Box 40
Rhein, SK S0A 3K0
Tel: 306-273-2155; *Fax:* 306-273-9993
villageofrhein@yourlink.ca
Municipal Type: Village
Incorporated: March 10, 1913; *Area:* 1.09 sq km
Population in 2011: 158
Provincial Electoral District(s): Canora-Pelly
Federal Electoral District(s): Yorkton-Melville
Next Election: Oct. 26, 2016 (4 year terms)
James Herman, Mayor
Valerie Stricker, Administrator

Richard
P.O. Box 6
Richard, SK S0M 2P0
Tel: 306-549-2331
vrichard@sasktel.net
Municipal Type: Village
Incorporated: Oct. 11, 1916; *Area:* 0.73 sq km
Population in 2011: 30
Provincial Electoral District(s): Rosthern-Shellbrook
Federal Electoral District(s): Carlton Trail-Eagle Creek
Next Election: Oct. 26, 2016 (4 year terms)
Merilyn Wawryk, Mayor
Valerie Fendelet, Administrator

Richmound
P.O. Box 29
Richmound, SK S0N 2E0
Tel: 306-669-4415; *Fax:* 306-669-2044
admin@richmound.ca
www.richmound.ca
Municipal Type: Village
Incorporated: May 5, 1947; *Area:* 0.47 sq km
Population in 2011: 154
Provincial Electoral District(s): Cypress Hills
Federal Electoral District(s): Cypress Hills-Grasslands
Next Election: Oct. 26, 2016 (4 year terms)
Barry Manz, Mayor
Nadine Munro, Administrator

Ridgedale
P.O. Box 25
Tisdale, SK S0E 1T0
Tel: 306-873-2657; *Fax:* 306-873-4442
rm457@sasktel.net
Municipal Type: Village
Incorporated: Dec. 15, 1921; *Area:* 0.72 sq km
Population in 2011: 80
Provincial Electoral District(s): Carrot River Valley
Federal Electoral District(s): Prince Albert
Next Election: Oct. 26, 2016 (4 year terms)
Harvey Reimer, Mayor
Tamie McLean, Administrator

Riverhurst
P.O. Box 116
Riverhurst, SK S0H 3P0
Tel: 306-353-2220; *Fax:* 306-353-2221
riverhurst@outlook.com
www.riverhurst.ca
Municipal Type: Village
Incorporated: June 22, 1916; *Area:* 0.91 sq km
Population in 2011: 114
Provincial Electoral District(s): Thunder Creek
Federal Electoral District(s): Cypress Hills-Grasslands
Next Election: Oct. 26, 2016 (4 year terms)
Lawny Gustafson, Mayor
Kyle Van Den Bosch, Administrator

Rocanville
P.O. Box 265
103 Ellice St.
Rocanville, SK S0A 3L0
Tel: 306-645-2022; *Fax:* 306-645-4492
rocanville.town@sasktel.net
www.rocanville.ca
Municipal Type: Town
Incorporated: March 24, 1904; *Area:* 2.43 sq km
Population in 2011: 857
Provincial Electoral District(s): Moosomin
Federal Electoral District(s): Souris-Moose Mountain
Next Election: Oct. 26, 2016 (4 year terms)
Note: Incorporated as a town on Aug. 1, 1967.
Daryl Fingas, Mayor
Monica Merkosky, Administrator

Roche Percée
P.O. Box 237
Bienfait, SK S0C 0M0
Tel: 306-634-4661; *Fax:* 306-634-4693
villageofrochepercee@sasktel.net
Municipal Type: Village
Incorporated: Jan. 12, 1909; *Area:* 2.59 sq km
Population in 2011: 153
Provincial Electoral District(s): Estevan
Federal Electoral District(s): Souris-Moose Mountain
Next Election: Oct. 26, 2016 (4 year terms)
Jim Bragg, Mayor
Lynne Hewitt, Administrator

Rockglen
P.O. Box 267
Rockglen, SK S0H 3R0
Tel: 306-476-2144; *Fax:* 306-476-2339
rockglen1@sasktel.net
Municipal Type: Town
Incorporated: July 12, 1927; *Area:* 2.85 sq km
Population in 2011: 400
Provincial Electoral District(s): Wood River
Federal Electoral District(s): Cypress Hills-Grasslands
Next Election: Oct. 26, 2016 (4 year terms)
Note: Proclaimed as a town on Sept. 1, 1957.
Richard Prefontaine, Mayor
Sherri Foley, Administrator

La Ronge
P.O. Box 5680
1212 Hildebrandt Dr.
La Ronge, SK S0J 1L0
Tel: 306-425-2066; *Fax:* 306-425-3883
www.laronge.ca
Municipal Type: Northern Town
Incorporated: May 3, 1905; *Area:* 11.86 sq km
Population in 2011: 2,304
Provincial Electoral District(s): Cumberland
Federal Electoral District(s): Desnethé-Missinippi-Churchill River
Next Election: Autumn 2016 (4 year terms)
Note: Proclaimed as a northern town on Oct. 1, 1983.
Thomas Sierzycki, Mayor
Victoria MacDonald, Administrator

Rose Valley
P.O. Box 460
Rose Valley, SK S0E 1M0
Tel: 306-322-2232; *Fax:* 306-322-4461
rosevalley@sasktel.net
www.townofrosevalley.com
Municipal Type: Town
Incorporated: Sept. 24, 1940; *Area:* 1.12 sq km
Population in 2011: 296
Provincial Electoral District(s): Kelvington-Wadena
Federal Electoral District(s): Yorkton-Melville
Next Election: Oct. 26, 2016 (4 year terms)
Note: Proclaimed as a town on Jan. 1, 1962.
Daniel Veilleux, Mayor
Marjorie A. Zarowny, Clerk

Rosetown
P.O. Box 398
417 Main St.
Rosetown, SK S0L 2V0
Tel: 306-882-2214; *Fax:* 306-882-3166
townofrosetown@sasktel.net
www.rosetown.ca
Municipal Type: Town
Incorporated: Aug. 24, 1909; *Area:* 10.59 sq km
Population in 2011: 2,317
Provincial Electoral District(s): Rosetown-Elrose
Federal Electoral District(s): Carlton Trail-Eagle Creek
Next Election: Oct. 26, 2016 (4 year terms)
Note: Proclaimed as a town on Nov. 1, 1911.
Brian Gerow, Mayor
Steven Piermantier, Administrator

Rosthern
P.O. Box 416
710 Railway Ave.
Rosthern, SK S0K 3R0
Tel: 306-232-4826; *Fax:* 306-232-5638
townoffice@rosthern.com
www.rosthern.com
Municipal Type: Town
Incorporated: Dec. 29, 1898; *Area:* 4.01 sq km
Population in 2011: 1,572
Provincial Electoral District(s): Rosthern-Shellbrook
Federal Electoral District(s): Carlton Trail-Eagle Creek
Next Election: Oct. 26, 2016 (4 year terms)
Note: Proclaimed as a town on Nov. 20, 1903.
Dennis Helmuth, Mayor
Nicole J. Lerat, Administrator

Rouleau
P.O. Box 250
Rouleau, SK S0G 4H0
Tel: 306-776-2270; *Fax:* 306-776-2482
info@townofrouleau.com
www.townofrouleau.com
Municipal Type: Town
Incorporated: July 23, 1903; *Area:* 1.65 sq km
Population in 2011: 453
Provincial Electoral District(s): Indian Head-Milestone
Federal Electoral District(s): Moose Jaw-Lake Centre-Lanigan
Next Election: Oct. 26, 2016 (4 year terms)
Note: Proclaimed as a town on March 1, 1907.
Grant Clarke, Mayor
Guy Lagrandeur, Administrator

Ruddell
P.O. Box 7
Ruddell, SK S0M 2S0
Tel: 306-441-4108
Municipal Type: Village
Incorporated: March 18, 1914; *Area:* 0.47 sq km
Population in 2011: 20
Provincial Electoral District(s): Biggar
Federal Electoral District(s): Carlton Trail-Eagle Creek
Next Election: Oct. 26, 2016 (4 year terms)
Geordie Smith, Mayor
Les Klippentein, Administrator

Rush Lake
P.O. Box 126
Rush Lake, SK S0H 3S0
Tel: 306-784-3504
vilrushlake@sasktel.net
Municipal Type: Village
Incorporated: Oct. 16, 1911; *Area:* 0.74 sq km
Population in 2011: 65
Provincial Electoral District(s): Thunder Creek
Federal Electoral District(s): Cypress Hills-Grasslands
Next Election: Oct. 26, 2016 (4 year terms)
Stacey Beisel, Mayor
Terrie Unger, Clerk

St. Benedict
P.O. Box 99
St Benedict, SK S0K 3T0
Tel: 306-289-2072; *Fax:* 306-289-2077
benedictvillage@gmail.com
Municipal Type: Village
Incorporated: Jan. 1, 1964; *Area:* 0.54 sq km
Population in 2011: 82
Provincial Electoral District(s): Batoche
Federal Electoral District(s): Carlton Trail-Eagle Creek
Next Election: Oct. 26, 2016 (4 year terms)
Blake Peters, Mayor
Amanda Peacock, Administrator

St. Brieux
P.O. Box 249
105 Main St.
St. Brieux, SK S0K 3V0
Tel: 306-275-2257; *Fax:* 306-275-4949
brieux@sasktel.net
www.townofstbrieux.com
Municipal Type: Town
Incorporated: Nov. 11, 1913; *Area:* 2.02 sq km
Population in 2011: 590
Provincial Electoral District(s): Batoche
Federal Electoral District(s): Yorkton-Melville
Next Election: Oct. 26, 2016 (4 year terms)
Note: Proclaimed as a town on Nov. 8, 2006.
Leon Rheaume, Mayor
Dawn Lugrin, Administrator

St. George's Hill
P.O. Box 160
Desjarlais St.
Dillon, SK S0M 0S0
Tel: 306-282-4408; *Fax:* 306-282-2002
sgh123@sasktel.net
Municipal Type: Northern Hamlet
Incorporated: Dec. 1, 1983; *Area:* 1.46 sq km
Population in 2011: 100
Provincial Electoral District(s): Athabasca
Federal Electoral District(s): Desnethé-Missinippi-Churchill River
Next Election: Autumn 2016 (4 year terms)
Donna Janvier, Mayor
Diana Janvier, Clerk

St. Gregor
P.O. Box 19
St Gregor, SK S0K 3X0
Tel: 306-366-2129; *Fax:* 306-366-2128
stgregorsk@sasktel.net
Municipal Type: Village
Incorporated: March 26, 1920; *Area:* 0.91 sq km
Population in 2011: 98
Provincial Electoral District(s): Melfort
Federal Electoral District(s): Carlton Trail-Eagle Creek
Next Election: Oct. 26, 2016 (4 year terms)
Doug Hogemann, Mayor
Darlene Kuz, Administrator

St. Louis
P.O. Box 40
172 Riverside Dr.
St Louis, SK S0J 2C0
Tel: 306-422-8471; *Fax:* 306-422-8450
villageofstlouis@sasktel.net
www.villageofstlouis.com
Municipal Type: Village
Incorporated: May 19, 1959; *Area:* 1.08 sq km
Population in 2011: 449
Provincial Electoral District(s): Batoche
Federal Electoral District(s): Prince Albert
Next Election: Oct. 26, 2016 (4 year terms)
Les Rancourt, Mayor
Robin Boyer, Administrator

St. Walburg
P.O. Box 368
134 Main St.
St Walburg, SK S0M 2T0
Tel: 306-248-3232; *Fax:* 306-248-3484
info@st.walburg.com
www.stwalburg.ca
Municipal Type: Town
Incorporated: Jan. 18, 1922; *Area:* 2.12 sq km
Population in 2011: 716
Provincial Electoral District(s): Meadow Lake
Federal Electoral District(s): Battlefords-Lloydminster
Next Election: Oct. 26, 2016 (4 year terms)
Note: Proclaimed as a town on Feb. 1, 1953.
A.V. "Tony" Leeson, Mayor
Muriel Rosser-Swift, Administrator

Saltcoats
P.O. Box 120
Saltcoats, SK S0A 3R0
Tel: 306-744-2212; *Fax:* 306-744-2239
saltcoats.town@sasktel.net
townofsaltcoats.ca
Municipal Type: Town
Incorporated: April 4, 1894; *Area:* 1.35 sq km
Population in 2011: 474
Provincial Electoral District(s): Melville-Saltcoats
Federal Electoral District(s): Yorkton-Melville
Next Election: Oct. 26, 2016 (4 year terms)
Note: Proclaimed as a town on Nov. 1, 1910.
Grant McCallum, Mayor
Diane Jamieson, Administrator

Sandy Bay
P.O. Box 130
Hill St. & Sandy Bay Ave.
Sandy Bay, SK S0P 0G0
Tel: 306-754-2165; *Fax:* 306-754-2157
nvsb@sasktel.net
Municipal Type: Northern Village
Incorporated: Oct. 1, 1983; *Area:* 14.85 sq km
Population in 2011: 1,233
Provincial Electoral District(s): Cumberland
Federal Electoral District(s): Desnethé-Missinippi-Churchill River
Next Election: Autumn 2016 (4 year terms)
Daniel Bear, Mayor
Henrietta Ray, Administrator

Saskatchewan Beach
249 Lakeview Ave.
Saskatchewan Beach, SK S0G 4L0
Tel: 306-729-4410; *Fax:* 306-729-2017
www.saskatchewanbeach.ca
Municipal Type: Resort Village
Area: 1.57 sq km
Population in 2011: 213
Provincial Electoral District(s): Last Mountain-Touchwood
Federal Electoral District(s): Moose Jaw-Lake Centre-Lanigan
Next Election: July 2020 (4 year terms)
Harvey McEwen, Mayor
Sharie Hall, Administrator

Sceptre
P.O. Box 128
Sceptre, SK S0N 2H0
Tel: 306-623-4244; *Fax:* 306-623-4244
sceptrevillage@hotmail.com
Municipal Type: Village
Incorporated: April 30, 1913; *Area:* 1.23 sq km
Population in 2011: 97
Provincial Electoral District(s): Cypress Hills
Federal Electoral District(s): Cypress Hills-Grasslands
Next Election: Oct. 26, 2016 (4 year terms)
Clarence Hegg, Mayor
Sherry Egeland, Clerk

Scott
P.O. Box 96
104 Main St.
Scott, SK S0K 4A0
Tel: 306-228-2621; *Fax:* 306-228-2303
unity.admin@sasktel.net
Municipal Type: Town
Incorporated: Nov. 17, 1908; *Area:* 4.39 sq km
Population in 2011: 75
Provincial Electoral District(s): Kindersley
Federal Electoral District(s): Battlefords-Lloydminster
Next Election: Oct. 26, 2016 (4 year terms)
Note: Proclaimed as a town on Nov. 1, 1910.
Eric Schell, Mayor
Aileen Garrett, Administrator

Sedley
P.O. Box 130
117 Broadway St.
Sedley, SK S0G 4K0
Tel: 306-885-2133; *Fax:* 306-885-2132
villageofsedley@sasktel.net
www.villageofsedley.com
Municipal Type: Village
Incorporated: Aug. 3, 1907; *Area:* 1.31 sq km
Population in 2011: 337
Provincial Electoral District(s): Indian Head-Milestone
Federal Electoral District(s): Souris-Moose Mountain
Next Election: Oct. 26, 2016 (4 year terms)
Bryan Leier, Mayor
Samantha Gillies, Clerk

Semans
P.O. Box 113
Semans, SK S0A 3S0
Tel: 306-524-2144; *Fax:* 306-524-2145
semans@aski.ca
www.semans-sask.com
Municipal Type: Village
Incorporated: Dec. 14, 1908; *Area:* 1.18 sq km
Population in 2011: 204
Provincial Electoral District(s): Arm River-Watrous
Federal Electoral District(s): Moose Jaw-Lake Centre-Lanigan
Next Election: Oct. 26, 2016 (4 year terms)
Duane Linford, Mayor
Ashley Greenshields, Clerk

Senlac
P.O. Box 93
Senlac, SK S0L 2Y0
Tel: 306-228-4330
Municipal Type: Village
Incorporated: Oct. 11, 1916; *Area:* 0.60 sq km
Population in 2011: 46
Provincial Electoral District(s): Cut Knife-Turtleford
Federal Electoral District(s): Battlefords-Lloydminster
Next Election: Oct. 26, 2016 (4 year terms)
Corinne McWatters, Mayor
Maureen Forbes, Clerk

Shamrock
P.O. Box 119
Shamrock, SK S0H 3W0
Tel: 306-394-4311; *Fax:* 306-394-4309
Municipal Type: Village
Incorporated: April 30, 1924; *Area:* 0.79 sq km
Population in 2011: 20
Provincial Electoral District(s): Wood River
Federal Electoral District(s): Cypress Hills-Grasslands
Next Election: Oct. 26, 2016 (4 year terms)
Rene Fortin, Mayor
Cathy Marchessault, Clerk

Shaunavon
P.O. Box 820
401 - 3rd St. West
Shaunavon, SK S0N 2M0
Tel: 306-297-2605; *Fax:* 306-297-2608
shaunavon@sasktel.net
www.shaunavon.com
Municipal Type: Town
Incorporated: Nov. 27, 1913; *Area:* 5.10 sq km
Population in 2011: 1,756
Provincial Electoral District(s): Cypress Hills
Federal Electoral District(s): Cypress Hills-Grasslands
Next Election: Oct. 26, 2016 (4 year terms)
Note: Proclaimed as a town on Nov. 1, 1914.
Sharon J. Dickie, Mayor
Rhonda Bellefeuille, Acting Chief Administrative Officer

Sheho
P.O. Box 130
Sheho, SK S0A 3T0
Tel: 306-849-2044
shehovillage@sasktel.net
Municipal Type: Village
Incorporated: June 30, 1905; *Area:* 1.95 sq km
Population in 2011: 130
Provincial Electoral District(s): Kelvington-Wadena
Federal Electoral District(s): Yorkton-Melville
Next Election: Oct. 26, 2016 (4 year terms)
Lorn Korpatniski, Mayor
Pamela Hawreluik, Clerk

Shell Lake
P.O. Box 280
Shell Lake, SK S0J 2G0
Tel: 306-427-2272; *Fax:* 306-427-4800
village.sl@sasktel.net
www.villageofshelllake.ca
Municipal Type: Village
Incorporated: Oct. 18, 1940; *Area:* 1.09 sq km
Population in 2011: 99
Provincial Electoral District(s): Rosthern-Shellbrook
Federal Electoral District(s): Desnethé-Missinippi-Churchill River
Next Election: Oct. 26, 2016 (4 year terms)
Anita Weiers, Mayor
Tara Bueckert, Administrator

Shellbrook
P.O. Box 40
71 Main St.
Shellbrook, SK S0J 2E0
Tel: 306-747-4900; *Fax:* 306-747-3111
shellbrook@sasktel.net
www.shellbrook.net
Municipal Type: Town
Incorporated: Nov. 18, 1909; *Area:* 2.13 sq km
Population in 2011: 1,433
Provincial Electoral District(s): Rosthern-Shellbrook
Federal Electoral District(s): Prince Albert
Next Election: Oct. 26, 2016 (4 year terms)
Note: Proclaimed as a town on April 1, 1948.
George Tomporowski, Mayor
Kelly Hoare, Administrator

Shields
P.O. Box 81
Dundurn, SK S0K 1K0
Tel: 306-492-2259; *Fax:* 306-492-2068
shields@xplornet.ca
www.shields.ca
Municipal Type: Resort Village
Area: 0.72 sq km
Population in 2011: 220
Provincial Electoral District(s): Arm River-Watrous
Federal Electoral District(s): Moose Jaw-Lake Centre-Lanigan
Next Election: July 2020 (4 year terms)
Eldon MacKay, Mayor, 306-492-4639
Jessie Williams, Administrator

Silton
P.O. Box 1
Silton, SK S0G 4L0
Tel: 306-731-3222
villageofsilton@xplornet.ca
Municipal Type: Village
Incorporated: July 2, 1914; *Area:* 1.07 sq km
Population in 2011: 95
Provincial Electoral District(s): Last Mountain-Touchwood
Federal Electoral District(s): Moose Jaw-Lake Centre-Lanigan
Next Election: Oct. 26, 2016 (4 year terms)
Warren Wild, Mayor
Brenda Small, Clerk

Simpson
P.O. Box 10
303 George St.
Simpson, SK S0G 4M0
Tel: 306-836-2020; *Fax:* 306-836-4460
rm281@aski.ca
www.simpsonsask.ca
Municipal Type: Village
Incorporated: July 11, 1911; *Area:* 1.41 sq km
Population in 2011: 131
Provincial Electoral District(s): Arm River-Watrous
Federal Electoral District(s): Moose Jaw-Lake Centre-Lanigan
Next Election: Oct. 26, 2016 (4 year terms)
Jeremy Nimchuk, Mayor
Darlene Mann, Administrator

Sintaluta
P.O. Box 150
Sintaluta, SK S0G 4N0
Tel: 306-727-2100; *Fax:* 306-727-2100
sintaluta@yourlink.ca
Municipal Type: Town
Incorporated: Oct. 27, 1898; *Area:* 2.70 sq km
Population in 2011: 120
Provincial Electoral District(s): Indian Head-Milestone
Federal Electoral District(s): Regina-Qu'Appelle
Next Election: Oct. 26, 2016 (4 year terms)
Note: Proclaimed as a town on June 1, 1907.
Anita Ryder, Mayor
Donna Pitre, Administrator

Sled Lake
P.O. Box 850
Big River, SK S0J 0E0
Tel: 306-832-4442; *Fax:* 306-832-2269
Municipal Type: NS
Population in 2010: 35
Provincial Electoral District(s): Athabasca
Federal Electoral District(s): Desnethé-Missinippi-Churchill River
Next Election: Autumn 2016 (4 year terms)
Ralph D. Michayluk, Chair
Bruce Leier, Advisor

Smeaton
P.O. Box 70
Smeaton, SK S0J 2J0
Tel: 306-426-2044; *Fax:* 306-426-2291
smeaton@sasktel.net
Municipal Type: Village
Incorporated: March 7, 1944; *Area:* 1.38 sq km
Population in 2011: 181
Provincial Electoral District(s): Saskatchewan Rivers
Federal Electoral District(s): Prince Albert
Next Election: Oct. 26, 2016 (4 year terms)
Sonia Fidyk, Mayor
Michelle Grunerud, Administrator

Smiley
P.O. Box 90
Smiley, SK S0L 2Z0
Tel: 306-838-2020; *Fax:* 306-838-4343
rm321@sasktel.net
Municipal Type: Village
Incorporated: Nov. 26, 1913; *Area:* 0.64 sq km
Population in 2011: 60
Provincial Electoral District(s): Kindersley
Federal Electoral District(s): Battlefords-Lloydminster
Next Election: Oct. 26, 2016 (4 year terms)
Chris Ward, Mayor
Charlotte Helfrich, Administrator

South Lake
#6, 1410 Caribou St. W
Moose Jaw, SK S6H 7S9
Tel: 306-692-7399; *Fax:* 306-692-7380
southlake@sasktel.net
www.southlakeresort.ca
Municipal Type: Resort Village
Area: 1.15 sq km
Population in 2011: 48
Provincial Electoral District(s): Thunder Creek
Federal Electoral District(s): Moose Jaw-Lake Centre-Lanigan
Next Election: July 2020 (4 year terms)
Art Schick, Mayor
Judy Szuch, Clerk

Southend
c/o Government Relations
P.O. Box 5000
La Ronge, SK S0J 2L0
Tel: 306-425-4323; *Fax:* 306-425-2401
Other Information: Toll-Free Phone: 1-800-663-1555
Municipal Type: Northern Hamlet
Population in 2010: 35
Provincial Electoral District(s): Cumberland
Federal Electoral District(s): Desnethé-Missinippi-Churchill River
Next Election: Autumn 2016 (4 year terms)
Valerie Antoniuk, Advisor, 306-425-4323

Southey
P.O. Box 248
260 Keats St.
Southey, SK S0G 4P0
Tel: 306-726-2202; *Fax:* 306-726-2916
townofsouthey@sasktel.net
www.southey.ca
Municipal Type: Town
Incorporated: Nov. 9, 1907; *Area:* 1 sq km
Population in 2011: 778
Provincial Electoral District(s): Last Mountain-Touchwood
Federal Electoral District(s): Regina-Qu'Appelle
Next Election: Oct. 26, 2016 (4 year terms)
Note: Proclaimed as a town on Nov. 1, 1980.
Leigh Bishop, Mayor
Ferne Senft, Administrator

Spalding
P.O. Box 280
Spalding, SK S0K 4C0
Tel: 306-872-2276; *Fax:* 306-872-2275
spalding.village@sasktel.net
www.villageofspalding.ca
Municipal Type: Village
Incorporated: March 11, 1924; *Area:* 1.18 sq km
Population in 2011: 242
Provincial Electoral District(s): Melfort
Federal Electoral District(s): Yorkton-Melville
Next Election: Oct. 26, 2016 (4 year terms)
Richelle Beaudry, Mayor
Cathy Holt, Administrator

Speers
P.O. Box 974
Speers, SK S0M 2V0
Tel: 306-246-2114; *Fax:* 306-246-2173
rm436@littleloon.ca
Municipal Type: Village
Incorporated: Dec. 24, 1915; *Area:* 0.69 sq km
Population in 2011: 65
Provincial Electoral District(s): Rosthern-Shellbrook
Federal Electoral District(s): Carlton Trail-Eagle Creek
Next Election: Oct. 26, 2016 (4 year terms)
Kenneth Rebeyka, Mayor
Dean Nicholson, Clerk

Spiritwood
P.O. Box 460
Spiritwood, SK S0J 2M0
Tel: 306-883-2161; *Fax:* 306-883-3212
tos@sasktel.net
www.townofspiritwood.ca
Municipal Type: Town
Incorporated: Oct. 1, 1935; *Area:* 2.95 sq km
Population in 2011: 916
Provincial Electoral District(s): Rosthern-Shellbrook
Federal Electoral District(s): Desnethé-Missinippi-Churchill River
Next Election: Oct. 26, 2016 (4 year terms)
Note: Proclaimed as a town on Sept. 1, 1965.
Gary Von Holwede, Mayor
Rhonda Saam, Chief Administrative Officer

Springside
P.O. Box 414
Springside, SK S0A 3V0
Tel: 306-792-2022; *Fax:* 306-792-2210
springside.town@sasktel.net
www.townofspringside.com
Municipal Type: Town
Incorporated: Nov. 11, 1909; *Area:* 0.64 sq km
Population in 2011: 534
Provincial Electoral District(s): Canora-Pelly
Federal Electoral District(s): Yorkton-Melville
Next Election: Oct. 26, 2016 (4 year terms)
Note: Proclaimed as a town on Nov. 1, 1985.
Al Langley, Mayor
Nancy Duns, Administrator

Spy Hill
P.O. Box 69
Spy Hill, SK S0A 3W0
Tel: 306-534-2255; *Fax:* 306-534-4520
spyhillvillage@sasktel.net
www.villageofspyhill.ca
Municipal Type: Village
Incorporated: April 22, 1910; *Area:* 1.19 sq km
Population in 2011: 204
Provincial Electoral District(s): Melville-Saltcoats
Federal Electoral District(s): Yorkton-Melville
Next Election: Oct. 26, 2016 (4 year terms)
Elgin Clark, Mayor
Susan Gawryluk, Administrator

Stanley Mission
c/o Government Relations
P.O. Box 5000
La Ronge, SK S0J 2P0
Tel: 306-425-4321; *Fax:* 306-425-2401
Other Information: Toll-Free Phone: 1-800-663-1555
Municipal Type: NS
Population in 2010: 124
Provincial Electoral District(s): Cumberland
Federal Electoral District(s): Desnethé-Missinippi-Churchill River
Next Election: Autumn 2016 (4 year terms)
Annie McLeod, Chair
Sandra Galambos, Advisor, 306-425-4321

Star City
P.O. Box 250
145 - 4th St.
Star City, SK S0E 1P0
Tel: 306-863-2282; *Fax:* 306-863-2277
town.starcity@sasktel.net
www.townofstarcity.com
Municipal Type: Town
Incorporated: April 6, 1906; *Area:* 0.7 sq km
Population in 2011: 460
Provincial Electoral District(s): Melfort
Federal Electoral District(s): Prince Albert
Next Election: Oct. 26, 2016 (4 year terms)
Note: Proclaimed as a town on Nov. 1, 1921.
Herb Reid, Mayor
Anita Tkachuk, Administrator

Stenen
P.O. Box 160
Stenen, SK S0A 3X0
Tel: 306-548-4334; *Fax:* 306-548-4334
villageofstenen@sasktel.net
www.stenensask.com
Municipal Type: Village
Incorporated: Aug. 14, 1912; *Area:* 0.58 sq km
Population in 2011: 79
Provincial Electoral District(s): Canora-Pelly
Federal Electoral District(s): Yorkton-Melville
Next Election: Oct. 26, 2016 (4 year terms)
Jason Anaka, Mayor
Sabrina Chernyk, Administrator

Stewart Valley
P.O. Box 10
Stewart Valley, SK S0N 2P0
Tel: 306-778-2105; *Fax:* 306-778-2152
vlg.stvalley@sasktel.net
Municipal Type: Village
Incorporated: Jan. 1, 1958; *Area:* 0.86 sq km
Population in 2011: 76
Provincial Electoral District(s): Swift Current
Federal Electoral District(s): Cypress Hills-Grasslands
Next Election: Oct. 26, 2016 (4 year terms)
Mike Moen, Mayor
Corie Lanceleve, Clerk

Stockholm
P.O. Box 265
Stockholm, SK S0A 3Y0
Tel: 306-793-2151; *Fax:* 306-793-4597
stockholm@sasktel.net
www.stockholmsask.com
Municipal Type: Village
Incorporated: June 30, 1905; *Area:* 1.64 sq km
Population in 2011: 341
Provincial Electoral District(s): Melville-Saltcoats
Federal Electoral District(s): Yorkton-Melville
Next Election: Oct. 26, 2016 (4 year terms)
Fran Herperger, Mayor
Lorie Jackson, Administrator

Stony Rapids
P.O. Box 120
Johnson St.
Stony Rapids, SK S0J 2R0
Tel: 306-439-2173; *Fax:* 306-439-2098
nhstonyrap@sasktel.net
Municipal Type: Northern Hamlet
Incorporated: April 1, 1992; *Area:* 3.96 sq km
Population in 2011: 243
Provincial Electoral District(s): Athabasca
Federal Electoral District(s): Desnethé-Missinippi-Churchill River
Next Election: Autumn 2016 (4 year terms)
Daniel Powder, Mayor
Shauna Sayazie, Clerk

Storthoaks
P.O. Box 40
Storthoaks, SK S0C 2K0
Tel: 306-449-2262; *Fax:* 306-449-2210
rm31@sasktel.net
Municipal Type: Village
Incorporated: June 5, 1940; *Area:* 0.49 sq km
Population in 2011: 93
Provincial Electoral District(s): Cannington
Federal Electoral District(s): Souris-Moose Mountain
Next Election: Oct. 26, 2016 (4 year terms)
Sydney Chicoine, Mayor
Gisele Bouchard, Administrator

Stoughton
P.O. Box 397
232 Main St.
Stoughton, SK S0G 4T0
Tel: 306-457-2413; *Fax:* 306-457-3162
stoughtontown@sasktel.net
stoughtonsk.ca
Other Information: Alt. E-mail: office@stoughtonsk.ca
Municipal Type: Town
Incorporated: Feb. 26, 1904; *Area:* 2.13 sq km
Population in 2011: 694
Provincial Electoral District(s): Cannington
Federal Electoral District(s): Souris-Moose Mountain
Next Election: Oct. 26, 2016 (4 year terms)
Note: Proclaimed as a town on June 1, 1960.
Bill Knous, Mayor
Chris Miskolczi, Administrator

Strasbourg
P.O. Box 369
1 - 200 Mountain St.
Strasbourg, SK S0G 4V0
Tel: 306-725-3707; *Fax:* 306-725-3613
strasbourg@sasktel.net
www.townofstrasbourg.ca
Municipal Type: Town
Incorporated: April 19, 1906; *Area:* 5.70 sq km
Population in 2011: 752
Provincial Electoral District(s): Last Mountain-Touchwood
Federal Electoral District(s): Moose Jaw-Lake Centre-Lanigan
Next Election: Oct. 26, 2016 (4 year terms)
Note: Proclaimed as a town on July 1, 1907.
Ken Swanston, Mayor, 306-725-3007
Jennifer Josephson, Administrator

Strongfield
P.O. Box 87
Strongfield, SK S0H 3Z0
Tel: 306-857-2200; *Fax:* 306-857-2201
villageofstrongfield@yourlink.ca
Municipal Type: Village
Incorporated: May 3, 1912; *Area:* 0.8 sq km
Population in 2011: 40
Provincial Electoral District(s): Arm River-Watrous
Federal Electoral District(s): Moose Jaw-Lake Centre-Lanigan
Next Election: Oct. 26, 2016 (4 year terms)
Carol Wick, Mayor
Brandy Losie, Clerk

Sturgis
P.O. Box 520
209 - 1st Ave. SE
Sturgis, SK S0A 4A0
Tel: 306-548-2108; *Fax:* 306-548-2948
townofsturgis@sasktel.net
www.townofsturgis.com
Municipal Type: Town
Incorporated: Sept. 3, 1912; *Area:* 3.39 sq km
Population in 2011: 620
Provincial Electoral District(s): Canora-Pelly
Federal Electoral District(s): Yorkton-Melville
Next Election: Oct. 26, 2016 (4 year terms)
Note: Proclaimed as a town on March 1, 1951.
Don Olson, Mayor
Olivia (Bim) Bartch, Administrator

Success
P.O. Box 40
Success, SK S0N 2R0
Tel: 306-773-7934
success1@yourlink.ca
Municipal Type: Village
Incorporated: Oct. 25, 1912; *Area:* 1.38 sq km
Population in 2011: 40
Provincial Electoral District(s): Swift Current
Federal Electoral District(s): Cypress Hills-Grasslands
Next Election: Oct. 26, 2016 (4 year terms)
Doodnath Gajadhar, Mayor
Donna Butler, Clerk

Sun Valley
P.O. Box 2260
Moose Jaw, SK S6H 7W6
Tel: 306-694-0055
rvsunvalley@yahoo.com
Municipal Type: Resort Village
Area: 2.33 sq km
Population in 2011: 46
Provincial Electoral District(s): Thunder Creek
Federal Electoral District(s): Moose Jaw-Lake Centre-Lanigan
Next Election: July 2020 (4 year terms)
Barry Gunther, Mayor
Kathy Mealing, Administrator

Sunset Cove
P.O. Box 68
Strasbourg, SK S0G 4V0
Tel: 306-725-3485
rvsunsetcove@sasktel.net
www.rvsunsetcove.ca
Municipal Type: Resort Village
Incorporated: 1959; *Area:* 0.17 sq km
Population in 2011: 25
Provincial Electoral District(s): Last Mountain-Touchwood
Federal Electoral District(s): Moose Jaw-Lake Centre-Lanigan
Next Election: July 2020 (4 year terms)
Tom Fulcher, Mayor
Barbara Griffin, Administrator

Tantallon
P.O. Box 70
Tantallon, SK S0A 4B0
Tel: 306-643-2112; *Fax:* 306-643-2113
tantallon@sasktel.net
Municipal Type: Village
Incorporated: June 17, 1904; *Area:* 0.84 sq km
Population in 2011: 105
Provincial Electoral District(s): Melville-Saltcoats
Federal Electoral District(s): Yorkton-Melville
Next Election: Oct. 26, 2016 (4 year terms)
Jim Johnson, Mayor
Susan Gawryluk, Administrator

Tessier
P.O. Box 34
Tessier, SK S0L 3G0
Tel: 306-656-4580
Municipal Type: Village
Incorporated: Aug. 24, 1909; *Area:* 1 sq km
Population in 2011: 25
Provincial Electoral District(s): Rosetown-Elrose
Federal Electoral District(s): Carlton Trail-Eagle Creek
Next Election: Oct. 26, 2016 (4 year terms)
L.B. Johnson, Mayor
Barbara Shaw, Clerk

Theodore
P.O. Box 417
102 Main St.
Theodore, SK S0A 4C0
Tel: 306-647-2315; *Fax:* 306-647-2476
theodore.village@sasktel.net
Municipal Type: Village
Incorporated: July 5, 1907; *Area:* 1.73 sq km
Population in 2011: 345
Provincial Electoral District(s): Kelvington-Wadena
Federal Electoral District(s): Yorkton-Melville
Next Election: Oct. 26, 2016 (4 year terms)
Kevin Kotzer, Mayor
Cheryl Linden, Administrator

Thode
P.O. Box 202
Dundurn, SK S0K 1K0
Tel: 306-492-2259; *Fax:* 306-492-2068
admin@resortvillageofthode.ca
www.resortvillageofthode.ca
Municipal Type: Resort Village
Area: 0.73 sq km
Population in 2011: 157
Provincial Electoral District(s): Arm River-Watrous
Federal Electoral District(s): Moose Jaw-Lake Centre-Lanigan
Next Election: July 2020 (4 year terms)
Alan Thomarat, Mayor
Jessie Williams, Administrator

Timber Bay
General Delivery
Timber Bay, SK S0J 2T0
Tel: 306-663-5885; *Fax:* 306-663-5052
northerntimberbay@sasktel.net
Municipal Type: Northern Hamlet
Incorporated: Oct. 1, 1983; *Area:* 4.44 sq km
Population in 2011: 93
Provincial Electoral District(s): Cumberland
Federal Electoral District(s): Desnethé-Missinippi-Churchill River
Next Election: Autumn 2016 (4 year terms)
Peggy Hennie, Mayor
Celinda Lavallee, Administrator

Tisdale
P.O. Box 1090
901 - 100 St.
Tisdale, SK S0E 1T0
Tel: 306-873-2681; *Fax:* 306-873-5700
thetownoffice@townoftisdale.com
www.townoftisdale.com
Municipal Type: Town
Incorporated: May 15, 1905; *Area:* 4.62 sq km
Population in 2011: 3,180
Provincial Electoral District(s): Carrot River Valley
Federal Electoral District(s): Prince Albert
Next Election: Oct. 26, 2016 (4 year terms)
Note: Proclaimed as a town on Nov. 1, 1920.
Al Jellicoe, Mayor
Brad Hvidston, Administrator

Tobin Lake
P.O. Box 1479
Nipawin, SK S0E 1E0
Tel: 306-862-2895; *Fax:* 306-862-9320
rvtobinlake@sasktel.net
www.resortvillageoftobinlake.com
Municipal Type: Resort Village
Area: 1.81 sq km
Population in 2011: 90
Provincial Electoral District(s): Carrot River Valley
Federal Electoral District(s): Prince Albert
Next Election: July 2020 (4 year terms)
Robert Taylor, Mayor
Karalee Davis, Administrator

Togo
P.O. Box 100
Togo, SK S0A 4E0
Tel: 306-597-2114; *Fax:* 306-597-4766
villageoftogo@sasktel.net
villageoftogo.com
Municipal Type: Village
Incorporated: Sept. 4, 1906; *Area:* 1.5 sq km
Population in 2011: 87
Provincial Electoral District(s): Canora-Pelly
Federal Electoral District(s): Yorkton-Melville
Next Election: Oct. 26, 2016 (4 year terms)
Loretta Erhardt, Mayor
Trudy Lockhart, Administrator

Tompkins
P.O. Box 247
#5, 2nd St.
Tompkins, SK S0N 2S0
Tel: 306-622-2020; *Fax:* 306-622-2025
villageoftompkins@sasktel.net
www.villageoftompkins.ca
Municipal Type: Village
Incorporated: June 2, 1910; *Area:* 2.65 sq km
Population in 2011: 170
Provincial Electoral District(s): Cypress Hills
Federal Electoral District(s): Cypress Hills-Grasslands
Next Election: Oct. 26, 2016 (4 year terms)
John Woodward, Mayor
Tammy Sloan, Clerk

Torquay
P.O. Box 6
Torquay, SK S0C 2L0
Tel: 306-923-2172; *Fax:* 306-923-2172
villageoftorquay@sasktel.net
www.villageoftorquay.com
Municipal Type: Village
Incorporated: Dec. 11, 1923; *Area:* 1.35 sq km
Population in 2011: 236
Provincial Electoral District(s): Estevan
Federal Electoral District(s): Souris-Moose Mountain
Next Election: Oct. 26, 2016 (4 year terms)
Michael Strachan, Mayor, 306-421-7827
Thera-Lee Deschner, Administrator

Tramping Lake
P.O. Box 157
Tramping Lake, SK S0K 4H0
Tel: 306-755-2002; *Fax:* 306-755-2002
Municipal Type: Village
Incorporated: April 10, 1917; *Area:* 1.39 sq km
Population in 2011: 55
Provincial Electoral District(s): Kindersley
Federal Electoral District(s): Battlefords-Lloydminster
Next Election: Oct. 26, 2016 (4 year terms)
Joe Fruhstuk, Mayor
Rose Simon, Clerk

Tribune
P.O. Box 61
Tribune, SK S0C 2M0
Tel: 306-456-2213; *Fax:* 306-456-2213
Municipal Type: Village
Incorporated: Feb. 18, 1914; *Area:* 1.61 sq km
Population in 2011: 25
Provincial Electoral District(s): Estevan
Federal Electoral District(s): Souris-Moose Mountain
Next Election: Oct. 26, 2016 (4 year terms)
Glenn Walkeden, Mayor
Dallas Locken, Clerk

Tugaske
P.O. Box 159
Tugaske, SK S0H 4B0
Tel: 306-759-2211; *Fax:* 306-759-2249
info@tugaske.com
www.tugaske.com
Municipal Type: Village
Incorporated: May 7, 1909; *Area:* 0.76 sq km
Population in 2011: 92
Provincial Electoral District(s): Thunder Creek
Federal Electoral District(s): Moose Jaw-Lake Centre-Lanigan
Next Election: Oct. 26, 2016 (4 year terms)
Kevin Wilson, Mayor
Daryl Dean, Administrator

Turnor Lake
P.O. Box 130
Turnor Street
Turnor Lake, SK S0M 3E0
Tel: 306-894-2080; *Fax:* 306-894-2138
turnorlakehamlet@sasktel.net
Municipal Type: Northern Hamlet
Incorporated: Oct. 1, 1984; *Area:* 4.62 sq km
Provincial Electoral District(s): Athabasca
Federal Electoral District(s): Desnethé-Missinippi-Churchill River
Next Election: Autumn 2016 (4 year terms)
Jeannie Daigneault, Mayor
Doreen Morin, Clerk

Turtleford
P.O. Box 38
Turtleford, SK S0M 2Y0
Tel: 306-845-2156; *Fax:* 306-845-3320
info@townofturtleford.ca
Municipal Type: Town
Incorporated: Oct. 9, 1914; *Area:* 1.64 sq km
Population in 2011: 525
Provincial Electoral District(s): Cut Knife-Turtleford
Federal Electoral District(s): Battlefords-Lloydminster
Next Election: Oct. 26, 2016 (4 year terms)
Note: Proclaimed as a town on July 1, 1983.
Roland Olson, Mayor
Deanna M. Kahl Lundberg, Administrator

Tuxford
#5, 1410 Caribou St. West
Moose Jaw, SK S0H 4C0
Tel: 306-972-9987
www.villageoftuxford.ca
Municipal Type: Village
Incorporated: July 19, 1907; *Area:* 0.62 sq km
Population in 2011: 91
Provincial Electoral District(s): Thunder Creek
Federal Electoral District(s): Moose Jaw-Lake Centre-Lanigan
Next Election: Oct. 26, 2016 (4 year terms)
Chad Johnson, Mayor
Tracy Edwards, Administrator

Unity
P.O. Box 1030
#2, 100 First Ave. West
Unity, SK S0K 4L0
Tel: 306-228-2621; *Fax:* 306-228-4221
www.townofunity.com
Municipal Type: Town
Incorporated: May 18, 1909; *Area:* 9.77 sq km
Population in 2011: 2,389
Provincial Electoral District(s): Kindersley
Federal Electoral District(s): Battlefords-Lloydminster
Next Election: Oct. 26, 2016 (4 year terms)
Note: Proclaimed as a town on Nov. 1, 1919.
Sylvia Maljan, Mayor
Aileen Garrett, Administrator

Uranium City
c/o Government Relations
P.O. Box 5000
La Ronge, SK S0J 1L0
Fax: 306-425-2401
Other Information: Toll-Free Phone: 1-800-663-1555
Municipal Type: NS
Population in 2010: 201
Provincial Electoral District(s): Athabasca
Federal Electoral District(s): Desnethé-Missinippi-Churchill River
Next Election: Autumn 2016 (4 year terms)
Dean Classen, Chair
Sandra Galambos, Advisor, 306-425-4321

Val Marie
P.O. Box 178
103 - 1st Ave. East
Val Marie, SK S0N 2T0
Tel: 306-298-2022; *Fax:* 306-298-2224
vovm@sasktel.net
www.valmarie.ca
Municipal Type: Village
Incorporated: Sept. 13, 1926; *Area:* 0.42 sq km
Population in 2011: 98
Provincial Electoral District(s): Wood River
Federal Electoral District(s): Cypress Hills-Grasslands
Next Election: Oct. 26, 2016 (4 year terms)
Roland Facette, Mayor
Cathy Legault, Administrator

Valparaiso
P.O. Box 473
Star City, SK S0E 1P0
Tel: 306-863-2522; *Fax:* 306-863-2255
r.m.starcity@sasktel.net
Municipal Type: Village
Incorporated: July 18, 1924; *Area:* 0.69 sq km
Population in 2011: 15
Provincial Electoral District(s): Melfort
Federal Electoral District(s): Prince Albert
Next Election: Oct. 26, 2016 (4 year terms)
Margaret Emro, Mayor
Ann Campbell, Clerk

Vanguard
P.O. Box 187
601 Dominion St.
Vanguard, SK S0N 2V0
Tel: 306-582-2295; *Fax:* 306-582-2296
vill.vanguard@sasktel.net
www.vanguardsk.ca
Municipal Type: Village
Incorporated: July 8, 1912; *Area:* 1.86 sq km
Population in 2011: 152
Provincial Electoral District(s): Wood River
Federal Electoral District(s): Cypress Hills-Grasslands
Next Election: Oct. 26, 2016 (4 year terms)
Allen Kuhlmann, Mayor
Sandra Krushelniski, Administrator

Vanscoy
P.O. Box 480
109 Main St.
Vanscoy, SK S0L 3J0
Tel: 306-668-2008; *Fax:* 306-978-0237
vanscoy@sasktel.net
www.vanscoyvillage.com
Municipal Type: Village
Incorporated: June 17, 1919; *Area:* 1.49 sq km
Population in 2011: 377
Provincial Electoral District(s): Biggar
Federal Electoral District(s): Carlton Trail-Eagle Creek
Next Election: Oct. 26, 2016 (4 year terms)
Robin Odnokon, Mayor
Dawn Steeves, Administrator

Vibank
Vibank Heritage Centre
P.O. Box 204
101 - 2nd Ave.
Vibank, SK S0G 4Y0
Tel: 306-762-2130; *Fax:* 306-762-4722
administrator@vibank.ca
www.vibank.ca
Municipal Type: Village
Incorporated: June 23, 1911; *Area:* 0.73 sq km
Population in 2011: 374
Provincial Electoral District(s): Indian Head-Milestone
Federal Electoral District(s): Souris-Moose Mountain
Next Election: Oct. 26, 2016 (4 year terms)
Tracey Schaffer, Mayor, 306-762-2249
Ronda Heisler, Chief Administrative Officer

Viscount
P.O. Box 99
Viscount, SK S0K 4M0
Tel: 306-944-2199; *Fax:* 306-944-2198
viscount.office@sasktel.net
www.viscount.ca
Municipal Type: Village
Incorporated: Dec. 17, 1908; *Area:* 1.18 sq km
Population in 2011: 252
Provincial Electoral District(s): Humboldt
Federal Electoral District(s): Moose Jaw-Lake Centre-Lanigan
Next Election: Oct. 26, 2016 (4 year terms)
Moe Kirzinger, Mayor
Valerie Schlosser, Administrator

Vonda
P.O. Box 308
204 Main St.
Vonda, SK S0K 4N0
Tel: 306-258-2035; *Fax:* 306-258-4420
vonda.to@baudoux.ca
www.townofvonda.ca
Municipal Type: Town
Incorporated: Aug. 29, 1905; *Area:* 2.86 sq km
Population in 2011: 353
Provincial Electoral District(s): Humboldt
Federal Electoral District(s): Carlton Trail-Eagle Creek
Next Election: Oct. 26, 2016 (4 year terms)
Note: Proclaimed as a town on May 6, 1907.
Daniel Sembalerus, Mayor
Linda Denis, Clerk

Wadena
P.O. Box 730
102 Main St. North
Wadena, SK S0A 4J0
Tel: 306-338-2145; *Fax:* 306-338-3804
townofwadena.com
Municipal Type: Town
Incorporated: Oct. 6, 1906; *Area:* 2.91 sq km
Population in 2011: 1,306
Provincial Electoral District(s): Kelvington-Wadena
Federal Electoral District(s): Yorkton-Melville
Next Election: Oct. 26, 2016 (4 year terms)
Note: Proclaimed as a town on April 1, 1912.
Greg Linnen, Mayor
Kelly Dodd, Chief Administrative Officer

Wakaw
P.O. Box 669
121 Main St.
Wakaw, SK S0K 4P0
Tel: 306-233-4223; *Fax:* 306-233-5234
town.wakaw@sasktel.net
www.wakaw.ca
Municipal Type: Town
Incorporated: Dec. 26, 1911; *Area:* 3.12 sq km
Population in 2011: 985
Provincial Electoral District(s): Batoche
Federal Electoral District(s): Carlton Trail-Eagle Creek
Next Election: Oct. 26, 2016 (4 year terms)
Note: Proclaimed as a town on Aug. 1, 1953.
Ed Kidd, Mayor
Lois Gartner, Chief Administrative Officer

Wakaw Lake
P.O. Box 58
126 - 1st St. South
Wakaw, SK S0K 4P0
Tel: 306-233-5671; *Fax:* 306-233-5672
rvwakawlake@gmail.com
www.wakawresortvillage.com
Municipal Type: Resort Village
Area: 0.59 sq km
Population in 2011: 30
Provincial Electoral District(s): Batoche
Federal Electoral District(s): Carlton Trail-Eagle Creek
Next Election: July 2020 (4 year terms)
Maurice Rivard, Mayor, 306-222-5753
Helen Martinka, Administrator

Waldeck
P.O. Box 97
Waldeck, SK S0H 4J0
Tel: 306-773-6275; *Fax:* 306-773-6275
villageofwaldeck@sasktel.net
Municipal Type: Village
Incorporated: Dec. 23, 1913; *Area:* 2 sq km
Population in 2011: 297
Provincial Electoral District(s): Thunder Creek
Federal Electoral District(s): Cypress Hills-Grasslands
Next Election: Oct. 26, 2016 (4 year terms)
Mark Cornelson, Mayor
Barb Cornelson, Administrator

Waldheim
P.O. Box 460
3027 Central Ave.
Waldheim, SK S0K 4R0
Tel: 306-945-2161; *Fax:* 306-945-2360
town.waldheim@sasktel.net
www.waldheim.ca
Municipal Type: Town
Incorporated: June 10, 1912; *Area:* 1.97 sq km
Population in 2011: 1,035
Provincial Electoral District(s): Martensville
Federal Electoral District(s): Carlton Trail-Eagle Creek
Next Election: Oct. 26, 2016 (4 year terms)
Note: Proclaimed as a town on March 1, 1967.
John N. Bollinger, Mayor, 306-945-2356
D. Chris Adams, Chief Administrative Officer

Waldron
P.O. Box 87
Waldron, SK S0A 4K0
Tel: 306-728-2371
Municipal Type: Village
Incorporated: July 17, 1909; *Area:* 1.45 sq km
Population in 2011: 20
Provincial Electoral District(s): Melville-Saltcoats
Federal Electoral District(s): Yorkton-Melville
Next Election: Oct. 26, 2016 (4 year terms)
Raymond Kitch, Mayor
Arlene Maguire, Clerk

Wapella
P.O. Box 189
Wapella, SK S0G 4Z0
Tel: 306-532-4343; *Fax:* 306-532-4342
townofwapella@sasktel.net
www.townofwapella.com
Municipal Type: Town
Incorporated: Dec. 29, 1898; *Area:* 2.56 sq km
Population in 2011: 333
Provincial Electoral District(s): Moosomin
Federal Electoral District(s): Souris-Moose Mountain
Next Election: Oct. 26, 2016 (4 year terms)
Note: Proclaimed as a town on Nov. 20, 1903.
Sandy Hintz, Mayor
Heidi Berlin, Administrator

Waseca
P.O. Box 88
102 - First St. East
Waseca, SK S0M 3A0
Tel: 306-893-2211; *Fax:* 306-893-4193
villageofwaseca@sasktel.net
Municipal Type: Village
Incorporated: March 15, 1911; *Area:* 0.68 sq km
Population in 2011: 154
Provincial Electoral District(s): Cut Knife-Turtleford
Federal Electoral District(s): Battlefords-Lloydminster
Next Election: Oct. 26, 2016 (4 year terms)
Curtis Sutherland, Mayor
Sandra Sutherland, Administrator

Watrous
P.O. Box 730
404 Main St.
Watrous, SK S0K 4T0
Tel: 306-946-3369; *Fax:* 306-946-2974
townofwatrous@sasktel.net
www.townofwatrous.com
Municipal Type: Town
Incorporated: Oct. 15, 1908; *Area:* 11.17 sq km
Population in 2011: 1,857
Provincial Electoral District(s): Arm River-Watrous
Federal Electoral District(s): Moose Jaw-Lake Centre-Lanigan
Next Election: Oct. 26, 2016 (4 year terms)
Note: Proclaimed as a town on Dec. 30, 1909.
Ed Collins, Mayor
Orrin Redden, Administrator

Watson
P.O. Box 276
300 Main St. NE
Watson, SK S0K 4V0
Tel: 306-287-3224; *Fax:* 306-287-3442
info@townofwatson.ca
www.townofwatson.ca
Municipal Type: Town
Incorporated: Oct. 6, 1906; *Area:* 2.83 sq km
Population in 2011: 777
Provincial Electoral District(s): Melfort
Federal Electoral District(s): Yorkton-Melville
Next Election: Oct. 26, 2016 (4 year terms)
Note: Proclaimed as a town on Aug. 1, 1908.
Norma Weber, Mayor
Cathy Coleman-Kavalench, Administrator

Wawota
P.O. Box 58
308 Railway Ave.
Wawota, SK S0G 5A0
Tel: 306-739-2216; *Fax:* 306-739-2216
wawota.town@sasktel.net
www.wawota.com

Municipal Type: Town
Incorporated: Dec. 10, 1907; *Area:* 1.24 sq km
Population in 2011: 560
Provincial Electoral District(s): Cannington
Federal Electoral District(s): Souris-Moose Mountain
Next Election: Oct. 26, 2016 (4 year terms)
Note: Proclaimed as a town on Feb. 1, 1975.
Neil Birnie, Mayor
Cheryl De Roo, Administrator

Webb
P.O. Box 100
Webb, SK S0N 2X0
Tel: 306-674-2230; *Fax:* 306-674-2324
rm138@xplornet.com
Municipal Type: Village
Incorporated: June 18, 1910; *Area:* 1.41 sq km
Population in 2011: 58
Provincial Electoral District(s): Cypress Hills
Federal Electoral District(s): Cypress Hills-Grasslands
Next Election: Oct. 26, 2016 (4 year terms)
Robert Jamieson, Mayor
Raylene Packet, Administrator

Wee Too Beach
3111 Kanuka Pl.
Regina, SK S4V 2C6
Tel: 306-789-6040
weetoo@sasktel.net
Municipal Type: Resort Village
Area: 0.17 sq km
Population in 2011: 35
Provincial Electoral District(s): Thunder Creek
Federal Electoral District(s): Moose Jaw-Lake Centre-Lanigan
Next Election: July 2020 (4 year terms)
Kevin Peachey, Mayor
Gail Meyer, Administrator

Weekes
P.O. Box 159
Weekes, SK S0E 1V0
Tel: 306-278-2800; *Fax:* 306-278-2395
weekes123@xplornet.ca
Municipal Type: Village
Incorporated: Jan. 13, 1947; *Area:* 0.59 sq km
Population in 2011: 42
Provincial Electoral District(s): Kelvington-Wadena
Federal Electoral District(s): Yorkton-Melville
Next Election: Oct. 26, 2016 (4 year terms)
Kenneth Harris, Mayor
Betty Gagnon, Clerk

Weirdale
P.O. Box 57
204 - 2nd St. East
Weirdale, SK S0J 2Z0
Tel: 306-929-2625; *Fax:* 306-929-2631
weirdale@hotmail.com
www.weirdalesk.ca
Municipal Type: Village
Incorporated: April 1, 1948; *Area:* 1.36 sq km
Population in 2011: 75
Provincial Electoral District(s): Saskatchewan Rivers
Federal Electoral District(s): Prince Albert
Next Election: Oct. 26, 2016 (4 year terms)
Rolena Krawec, Mayor
Sherry Dearing, Administrator

Weldon
P.O. Box 190
Weldon, SK S0J 3A0
Tel: 306-887-2070; *Fax:* 306-752-3882
villageofweldon@sasktel.net
Municipal Type: Village
Incorporated: Jan. 24, 1914; *Area:* 1.1 sq km
Population in 2011: 196
Provincial Electoral District(s): Batoche
Federal Electoral District(s): Prince Albert
Next Election: Oct. 26, 2016 (4 year terms)
Howard Tarry, Mayor
Jacquelynne Mann, Administrator

Welwyn
P.O. Box 118
Welwyn, SK S0A 4L0
Tel: 306-733-2077; *Fax:* 306-733-2078
welwynvillage@hotmail.com
Municipal Type: Village
Incorporated: June 11, 1907; *Area:* 0.64 sq km
Population in 2011: 135
Provincial Electoral District(s): Moosomin
Federal Electoral District(s): Souris-Moose Mountain
Next Election: Oct. 26, 2016 (4 year terms)
Joe Santer, Mayor
Monica Pethick, Clerk

West End
P.O. Box 1765
Esterhazy, SK S0A 0X0
Tel: 306-745-2060
resortwestend@sasktel.net
Municipal Type: Resort Village
Area: 0.34 sq km
Population in 2011: 17
Provincial Electoral District(s): Melville-Saltcoats
Federal Electoral District(s): Yorkton-Melville
Next Election: July 2020 (4 year terms)
Darcey Niemi, Mayor
Lorrayne Smith, Administrator

Weyakwin
P.O. Box 295
Weyakwin Rd.
Weyakwin, SK S0J 1W0
Tel: 306-663-5820; *Fax:* 306-663-5112
weyakwin@sasktel.net
Municipal Type: Northern Hamlet
Incorporated: Dec. 1, 1983; *Area:* 8.2 sq km
Population in 2011: 135
Provincial Electoral District(s): Cumberland
Federal Electoral District(s): Desnethé-Missinippi-Churchill River
Next Election: Autumn 2016 (4 year terms)
Stella Brown, Mayor
Flora Kraus, Clerk

White City
P.O. Box 220 Main
14 Ramm Ave. East
White City, SK S4L 5B1
Tel: 306-781-2355; *Fax:* 306-781-2194
townoffice@whitecity.ca
www.whitecity.ca
Municipal Type: Town
Incorporated: March 1, 1967; *Area:* 4.64 sq km
Population in 2011: 1,894
Provincial Electoral District(s): Regina Wascana Plains
Federal Electoral District(s): Regina-Qu'Appelle
Next Election: Oct. 26, 2016 (4 year terms)
Note: Proclaimed as a town on Nov. 1, 2000.
Bruce Evans, Mayor
Shauna Bzdel, Office Manager, 306-781-2355

White Fox
P.O. Box 38
116 Main St.
White Fox, SK S0J 3B0
Tel: 306-276-2106; *Fax:* 306-276-2131
villageofwhitefox@sasktel.net
www.whitefox.ca
Municipal Type: Village
Incorporated: July 21, 1941; *Area:* 0.85 sq km
Population in 2011: 364
Provincial Electoral District(s): Saskatchewan Rivers
Federal Electoral District(s): Prince Albert
Next Election: Oct. 26, 2016 (4 year terms)
Brian Lane, Mayor
Kimberley Issacson, Administrator

Whitewood
P.O. Box 129
731 Lalonde St.
Whitewood, SK S0G 5C0
Tel: 306-735-2210; *Fax:* 306-735-2262
general@townofwhitewood.ca
www.townofwhitewood.ca
Municipal Type: Town
Incorporated: Dec. 31, 1892; *Area:* 3.04 sq km
Population in 2011: 950
Provincial Electoral District(s): Moosomin
Federal Electoral District(s): Souris-Moose Mountain
Next Election: Oct. 26, 2016 (4 year terms)
Doug Armstrong, Mayor
Sharon Rodgers, Chief Administrative Officer

Wilcox
P.O. Box 130
33 Main St.
Wilcox, SK S0G 5E0
Tel: 306-732-0011; *Fax:* 306-732-9002
villagewilcox@sasktel.net
www.wilcox.ca
Municipal Type: Village
Incorporated: April 20, 1907; *Area:* 1.48 sq km
Population in 2011: 339
Provincial Electoral District(s): Indian Head-Milestone
Federal Electoral District(s): Moose Jaw-Lake Centre-Lanigan
Next Election: Oct. 26, 2016 (4 year terms)
Donald Strickland, Mayor
Tammy Ritchie, Administrator

Wilkie
P.O. Box 580
206 - 2nd Ave. West
Wilkie, SK S0K 4W0
Tel: 306-843-2692; *Fax:* 306-843-3151
wilkieoffice@sasktel.net
www.townofwilkie.com
Municipal Type: Town
Incorporated: July 18, 1908; *Area:* 9.48 sq km
Population in 2011: 1,301
Provincial Electoral District(s): Biggar
Federal Electoral District(s): Battlefords-Lloydminster
Next Election: Oct. 26, 2016 (4 year terms)
Note: Proclaimed as a town on Nov. 1, 1910.
David Ziegler, Mayor
Lana Gerein, Administrator

Willow Bunch
P.O. Box 189
16 Edouard Beaupré St.
Willow Bunch, SK S0H 4K0
Tel: 306-473-2450; *Fax:* 306-473-2312
www.willowbunch.ca
Municipal Type: Town
Incorporated: Nov. 15, 1929; *Area:* 0.84 sq km
Population in 2011: 286
Provincial Electoral District(s): Weyburn-Big Muddy
Federal Electoral District(s): Cypress Hills-Grasslands
Next Election: Oct. 26, 2016 (4 year terms)
Note: Proclaimed as a town on Oct. 1, 1960.
Wayne Joyal, Mayor
Margaret L. Brown, Administrator

Windthorst
P.O. Box 98
202 Angus St.
Windthorst, SK S0G 5G0
Tel: 306-224-2033; *Fax:* 306-224-4610
village.windthorst@sasktel.net
www.windthorstvillage.ca
Municipal Type: Village
Incorporated: Aug. 21, 1907; *Area:* 1.43 sq km
Population in 2011: 215
Provincial Electoral District(s): Moosomin
Federal Electoral District(s): Souris-Moose Mountain
Next Election: Oct. 26, 2016 (4 year terms)
Norm Jones, Mayor
Shelley Krecsy, Administrator

Wiseton
P.O. Box 160
Wiseton, SK S0L 3M0
Tel: 306-357-2022; *Fax:* 306-357-2027
villageofwiseton@sasktel.net
Municipal Type: Village
Incorporated: Sept. 23, 1913; *Area:* 0.77 sq km
Population in 2011: 88
Provincial Electoral District(s): Rosetown-Elrose
Federal Electoral District(s): Carlton Trail-Eagle Creek
Next Election: Oct. 26, 2016 (4 year terms)
Les Meyers, Mayor
Cheryl Joel, Administrator

Wollaston Lake
c/o Government Relations
P.O. Box 5000
Wollaston Lake, SK S0J 3C0
Tel: 306-633-2255; *Fax:* 306-633-2254
Municipal Type: NS
Population in 2010: 129
Provincial Electoral District(s): Cumberland
Federal Electoral District(s): Desnethé-Missinippi-Churchill River
Next Election: Autumn 2016 (4 year terms)
Terri Daniels, Chair
Valerie Antoniuk, Advisor

Wolseley
P.O. Box 310
Wolseley, SK S0G 5H0
Tel: 306-698-2477; *Fax:* 306-698-2953
townofwolseley@sasktel.net
www.wolseley.ca
Municipal Type: Town
Incorporated: Oct. 20, 1898; *Area:* 5.93 sq km
Population in 2011: 864

Provincial Electoral District(s): Moosomin
Federal Electoral District(s): Regina-Qu'Appelle
Next Election: Oct. 26, 2016 (4 year terms)
Dennis Fjestad, Mayor
Candice Quintyn, Administrator

Wood Mountain
P.O. Box 89
Wood Mountain, SK S0H 4L0
Tel: 306-266-4810; *Fax:* 306-266-2020
Municipal Type: Village
Incorporated: March 4, 1930; *Area:* 0.61 sq km
Population in 2011: 25
Provincial Electoral District(s): Wood River
Federal Electoral District(s): Cypress Hills-Grasslands
Next Election: Oct. 26, 2016 (4 year terms)
Michael Klein, Mayor
Vanessa Fogal, Administrator

Wynyard
P.O. Box 220
435 Bosworth St.
Wynyard, SK S0A 4T0
Tel: 306-554-2123; *Fax:* 306-554-3224
town.office.wynyard@sasktel.net
www.townofwynyard.com
Municipal Type: Town
Incorporated: Oct. 9, 1908; *Area:* 5.29 sq km
Population in 2011: 1,767
Provincial Electoral District(s): Arm River-Watrous
Federal Electoral District(s): Regina-Qu'Appelle
Next Election: Oct. 26, 2016 (4 year terms)
Note: Proclaimed as a town on Nov. 1, 1911.
Ted Czarnecki, Mayor
Jason Chorneyko, Administrator

Yarbo
P.O. Box 96
Yarbo, SK S0A 4V0
Tel: 306-745-3532; *Fax:* 306-745-3366
villageofyarbo@sasktel.net
Municipal Type: Village
Incorporated: July 1, 1964; *Area:* 0.83 sq km
Population in 2011: 53
Provincial Electoral District(s): Melville-Saltcoats
Federal Electoral District(s): Yorkton-Melville
Next Election: Oct. 26, 2016 (4 year terms)
Terry Haas, Mayor
Rowland Maggie, Clerk

Yellow Grass
209 Railway Ave. West
Yellow Grass, SK S0G 5J0
Tel: 306-465-2400; *Fax:* 306-465-2802
yellowgrass@signaldirect.ca
www.yellowgrass.ca
Municipal Type: Town
Incorporated: July 22, 1903; *Area:* 2.68 sq km
Population in 2011: 440
Provincial Electoral District(s): Weyburn-Big Muddy
Federal Electoral District(s): Souris-Moose Mountain
Next Election: Oct. 26, 2016 (4 year terms)
Note: Proclaimed as a town on Feb. 15, 1906.
Dave Byrns, Mayor, 306-465-2872
Wendy Carver, Administrator

Young
P.O. Box 359
116 Main St.
Young, SK S0K 4Y0
Tel: 306-259-2242; *Fax:* 306-259-2247
villageoffice@young.ca
www.young.ca
Municipal Type: Village
Incorporated: June 7, 1910; *Area:* 2.51 sq km
Population in 2011: 239
Provincial Electoral District(s): Arm River-Watrous
Federal Electoral District(s): Moose Jaw-Lake Centre-Lanigan
Next Election: Oct. 26, 2016 (4 year terms)
Brian Rowan, Mayor
Belinda Rowan, Administrator

Zealandia
P.O. Box 52
Zealandia, SK S0L 3N0
Tel: 306-882-3825; *Fax:* 306-882-4178
townofzealandia@yahoo.com
Municipal Type: Town
Incorporated: May 22, 1909; *Area:* 1.38 sq km
Population in 2011: 80
Provincial Electoral District(s): Rosetown-Elrose
Federal Electoral District(s): Carlton Trail-Eagle Creek
Next Election: Oct. 26, 2016 (4 year terms)
Note: Proclaimed as a town on Nov. 1, 1911.
Darren Haugen, Mayor
Amanda Bors, Clerk

Zelma
Zelma GMB #14
Allan, SK S0K 0C0
Tel: 306-257-3927; *Fax:* 306-257-4125
Municipal Type: Village
Incorporated: Aug. 10, 1910; *Area:* 0.72 sq km
Population in 2011: 35
Provincial Electoral District(s): Humboldt
Federal Electoral District(s): Moose Jaw-Lake Centre-Lanigan
Next Election: Oct. 26, 2016 (4 year terms)
R. Glen Crockett, Mayor
Maxine A. Fischer, Clerk

Zenon Park
P.O. Box 278
Zenon Park, SK S0E 1W0
Tel: 306-767-2233; *Fax:* 306-767-2226
vofzenon@sasktel.net
www.zenonpark.com
Municipal Type: Village
Incorporated: July 28, 1941; *Area:* 0.56 sq km
Population in 2011: 187
Provincial Electoral District(s): Carrot River Valley
Federal Electoral District(s): Prince Albert
Next Election: Oct. 26, 2016 (4 year terms)
Gilbert Ferre, Mayor
Lisa LeBlanc, Administrator

Rural Municipalities in Saskatchewan

Aberdeen No. 373
P.O. Box 40
101 Industrial Dr.
Aberdeen, SK S0K 0A0
Tel: 306-253-4312; *Fax:* 306-253-4445
rm373@sasktel.net
www.rmofaberdeen.ca
Municipal Type: Rural Municipalities
Incorporated: Dec. 13, 1909; *Area:* 673.43 sq km
Population in 2011: 1,016
Federal Electoral District(s): Carlton Trail-Eagle Creek
Next Election: Oct. 26, 2016 (4 year terms)
Martin Bettker, Reeve
Gary Dziadyk, Administrator

Abernethy No. 186
P.O. Box 249
Abernethy, SK S0A 0A0
Tel: 306-333-2044; *Fax:* 306-333-2285
rm186@sasktel.net
www.abernethy.ca/rm186.html
Municipal Type: Rural Municipalities
Incorporated: Dec. 11, 1911; *Area:* 779.42 sq km
Population in 2011: 387
Federal Electoral District(s): Regina-Qu'Appelle
Next Election: Oct. 26, 2016 (4 year terms)
John Fishley, Reeve
Karissa Lingelbach, Administrator

Antelope Park No. 322
P.O. Box 70
Marengo, SK S0L 2K0
Tel: 306-968-2922; *Fax:* 306-968-2278
rm292.rm322@sasktel.net
Municipal Type: Rural Municipalities
Incorporated: Dec. 11, 1911; *Area:* 612.66 sq km
Population in 2011: 150
Federal Electoral District(s): Battlefords-Lloydminster
Next Election: Oct. 26, 2016 (4 year terms)
Gordon Dommett, Reeve
Robin Busby, Administrator

Antler No. 61
P.O. Box 70
Redvers, SK S0C 2H0
Tel: 306-452-3263; *Fax:* 306-452-3518
rm61@sasktel.net
Municipal Type: Rural Municipalities
Incorporated: Dec. 13, 1909; *Area:* 832.23 sq km
Population in 2011: 536
Federal Electoral District(s): Souris-Moose Mountain
Next Election: Oct. 26, 2016 (4 year terms)
Ron Henderson, Reeve
Melissa Roberts, Administrator

Arborfield No. 456
P.O. Box 280
Arborfield, SK S0E 0A0
Tel: 306-769-8533; *Fax:* 306-769-8301
arborfieldrm456@sasktel.net
Municipal Type: Rural Municipalities
Incorporated: Jan. 1, 1913; *Area:* 1,416.01 sq km
Population in 2011: 453
Federal Electoral District(s): Prince Albert
Next Election: Oct. 26, 2016 (4 year terms)
Donald Underhill, Reeve
Allan Frisky, Administrator

Argyle No. 1
P.O. Box 120
Gainsborough, SK S0C 0Z0
Tel: 306-685-2010; *Fax:* 306-685-2161
rm.1@sasktel.net
Municipal Type: Rural Municipalities
Incorporated: Dec. 19, 1912; *Area:* 579.99 sq km
Population in 2011: 270
Federal Electoral District(s): Souris-Moose Mountain
Next Election: Oct. 26, 2016 (4 year terms)
Robert Meredith, Reeve
Erin McMillen, Administrator

Arlington No. 79
P.O. Box 1115
264 Centre St.
Shaunavon, SK S0N 2M0
Tel: 306-297-2108; *Fax:* 306-297-2144
rm79@sasktel.net
Municipal Type: Rural Municipalities
Incorporated: Jan. 1, 1913; *Area:* 846.79 sq km
Population in 2011: 345
Federal Electoral District(s): Cypress Hills-Grasslands
Next Election: Oct. 26, 2016 (4 year terms)
Donald Lundberg, Reeve
Richard Goulet, Administrator

Arm River No. 252
P.O. Box 250
Lincoln St.
Davidson, SK S0G 1A0
Tel: 306-567-3103; *Fax:* 306-567-3266
rm253@sasktel.net
www.rmarmriver.com
Municipal Type: Rural Municipalities
Incorporated: Dec. 13, 1909; *Area:* 725.26 sq km
Population in 2011: 249
Federal Electoral District(s): Moose Jaw-Lake Centre-Lanigan
Next Election: Oct. 26, 2016 (4 year terms)
Lorne Willner, Reeve
Yvonne (Bonny) Goodsman, Administrator

Auvergne No. 76
P.O. Box 60
Ponteix, SK S0N 1Z0
Tel: 306-625-3210; *Fax:* 306-625-3681
rm76@sasktel.net
www.rm76.weebly.com
Municipal Type: Rural Municipalities
Incorporated: Jan. 1, 1913; *Area:* 853.40 sq km
Population in 2011: 354
Federal Electoral District(s): Cypress-Hills-Grasslands
Next Election: Oct. 26, 2016 (4 year terms)
Allan R. Oliver, Reeve, 306-588-2520
Roxanne Empey, Administrator

Baildon No. 131
P.O. Box 1902
#1, 1410 Caribou St. West
Moose Jaw, SK S6H 7S9
Tel: 306-693-2166; *Fax:* 306-693-2170
rm131@sasktel.net
myrm.ca/131
Municipal Type: Rural Municipalities
Incorporated: Dec. 9, 1912; *Area:* 846.21 sq km
Population in 2011: 594
Federal Electoral District(s): Moose Jaw-Lake Centre-Lanigan
Next Election: Oct. 26, 2016 (4 year terms)
Wilfred Yuke, Reeve
Brenda Thiessen, Administrator

Barrier Valley No. 397
P.O. Box 246
Archerwill, SK S0E 0B0
Tel: 306-323-2101; *Fax:* 306-323-2106
rm397@sasktel.net
Municipal Type: Rural Municipalities
Incorporated: Oct. 29, 1917; *Area:* 819.99 sq km
Population in 2011: 498

Federal Electoral District(s): Yorkton-Melville
Next Election: Oct. 26, 2016 (4 year terms)
Wayne Black, Reeve
Glenda Smith, Administrator

Battle River No. 438
P.O. Box 159
Battleford, SK S0M 0E0
Tel: 306-937-2235; *Fax:* 306-937-2235
rm438@sasktel.net
Municipal Type: Rural Municipalities
Incorporated: Dec. 12, 1910; *Area:* 1,061.40 sq km
Population in 2011: 1,099
Federal Electoral District(s): Battlefords-Lloydminster
Next Election: Oct. 26, 2016 (4 year terms)
Joseph Beckman, Reeve
Betty Johnson, Administrator

Bayne No. 371
P.O. Box 130
Bruno, SK S0K 0S0
Tel: 306-369-2511; *Fax:* 306-369-2528
rm371@sasktel.net
Municipal Type: Rural Municipalities
Incorporated: Dec. 12, 1910; *Area:* 802.93 sq km
Population in 2011: 493
Federal Electoral District(s): Carlton Trail-Eagle Creek
Next Election: Oct. 26, 2016 (4 year terms)
David Leuschen, Reeve
Lonnie Sowa, Administrator

Beaver River No. 622
P.O. Box 129
159 Main St.
Pierceland, SK S0M 2K0
Tel: 306-839-2060; *Fax:* 306-839-2178
rm622@sasktel.net
www.rmofbeaverriver622.ca
Municipal Type: Rural Municipalities
Incorporated: Jan. 1, 1978; *Area:* 2,370.25 sq km
Population in 2011: 1,017
Federal Electoral District(s): Desnethé-Missinippi-Churchill River
Next Election: Oct. 26, 2016 (4 year terms)
Jim Peno, Reeve, 780-812-8204
Morgan Kennedy, Administrator

Bengough No. 40
P.O. Box 429
Bengough, SK S0C 0K0
Tel: 306-268-2055; *Fax:* 306-268-2054
rm40@sasktel.net
Municipal Type: Rural Municipalities
Incorporated: Jan. 1, 1913; *Area:* 1,036.91 sq km
Population in 2011: 329
Federal Electoral District(s): Souris-Moose Mountain
Next Election: Oct. 26, 2016 (4 year terms)
Eugene Hoffart, Reeve
Lara Hazen, Administrator

Benson No. 35
P.O. Box 69
Benson, SK S0C 0L0
Tel: 306-634-9410; *Fax:* 306-634-8804
rm35@sasktel.net
Municipal Type: Rural Municipalities
Incorporated: Dec. 13, 1909; *Area:* 836.39 sq km
Population in 2011: 490
Federal Electoral District(s): Souris-Moose Mountain
Next Election: Oct. 26, 2016 (4 year terms)
David Hoffort, Reeve
Laureen Keating, Administrator

Big Arm No. 251
P.O. Box 10
Stalwart, SK S0G 4R0
Tel: 306-963-2402; *Fax:* 306-963-2405
rm251@sasktel.net
www.rmbigarm.com
Municipal Type: Rural Municipalities
Incorporated: Dec. 11, 1911; *Area:* 699.47 sq km
Population in 2011: 200
Federal Electoral District(s): Moose Jaw-Lake Centre-Lanigan
Next Election: Oct. 26, 2016 (4 year terms)
Eugene Lucas, Reeve
Nicole Heck, Clerk

Big Quill No. 308
P.O. Box 898
Wynyard, SK S0A 4T0
Tel: 306-554-2533; *Fax:* 306-554-3935
rm308@sasktel.net
Municipal Type: Rural Municipalities
Incorporated: Dec. 13, 1909; *Area:* 739.86 sq km

Population in 2011: 587
Federal Electoral District(s): Regina-Qu'Appelle
Next Election: Oct. 26, 2016 (4 year terms)
Eugene McSymytz, Reeve
Gail Wolfe, Administrator

Big River No. 555
P.O. Box 219
606 First St. North
Big River, SK S0J 0E0
Tel: 306-469-2323; *Fax:* 306-469-2428
rm555@sasktel.net
www.bigriver.ca/about-big-river/rm-of-big-river
Municipal Type: Rural Municipalities
Incorporated: Oct. 1, 1977; *Area:* 2,488.22 sq km
Population in 2011: 855
Federal Electoral District(s): Desnethé-Missinippi-Churchill River
Next Election: Oct. 26, 2016 (4 year terms)
John Teer, Reeve, 306-469-5671
Donna Tymiak, Administrator

Big Stick No. 141
P.O. Box 9
Golden Prairie, SK S0N 0Y0
Tel: 306-662-2883; *Fax:* 306-662-3954
rm141@sasktel.net
Municipal Type: Rural Municipalities
Incorporated: Dec. 11, 1911; *Area:* 821.40 sq km
Population in 2011: 148
Federal Electoral District(s): Cypress Hills-Grasslands
Next Election: Oct. 26, 2016 (4 year terms)
Edward Feil, Reeve
Joanne Yates, Administrator

Biggar No. 347
P.O. Box 280
Biggar, SK S0K 0M0
Tel: 306-948-2422; *Fax:* 306-948-2250
rm347@sasktel.net
Municipal Type: Rural Municipalities
Incorporated: Dec. 11, 1911; *Area:* 1,597.87 sq km
Population in 2011: 820
Federal Electoral District(s): Carlton Trail-Eagle Creek
Next Election: Oct. 26, 2016 (4 year terms)
Kent Dubreuil, Reeve
Cheryl Martens (Forbes), Administrator

Birch Hills No. 460
P.O. Box 369
126 McCallum Ave.
Birch Hills, SK S0J 0G0
Tel: 306-749-2233; *Fax:* 306-749-2220
rm460@sasktel.net
www.rmbirchhills460.ca
Municipal Type: Rural Municipalities
Incorporated: Dec. 11, 1911; *Area:* 554.52 sq km
Population in 2011: 663
Federal Electoral District(s): Prince Albert
Next Election: Oct. 26, 2016 (4 year terms)
Alan Evans, Reeve
Shirley Pratchler, Administrator

Bjorkdale No. 426
P.O. Box 10
Crooked River, SK S0E 0R0
Tel: 306-873-2470; *Fax:* 306-873-2365
rm.426.bjork@xplornet.com
Municipal Type: Rural Municipalities
Incorporated: Jan. 1, 1913; *Area:* 1,458.79 sq km
Population in 2011: 900
Federal Electoral District(s): Yorkton-Melville
Next Election: Oct. 26, 2016 (4 year terms)
Wayne Dmytriw, Reeve
Lise Carpentier, Administrator

Blaine Lake No. 434
P.O. Box 38
Blaine Lake, SK S0J 0J0
Tel: 306-497-2282; *Fax:* 306-497-2511
rm434@sasktel.net
www.blainelake.ca/RM/rm434.html
Municipal Type: Rural Municipalities
Incorporated: Dec. 9, 1912; *Area:* 799.89 sq km
Population in 2011: 288
Federal Electoral District(s): Carlton Trail-Eagle Creek
Next Election: Oct. 26, 2016 (4 year terms)
Eugene Chudskov, Reeve, 306-497-3133
Tony Obrigewitch, Administrator

Blucher No. 343
P.O. Box 100
Bradwell, SK S0K 0P0
Tel: 306-257-3344; *Fax:* 306-257-3303
rm343@sasktel.net
Municipal Type: Rural Municipalities
Incorporated: Dec. 13, 1909; *Area:* 789.28 sq km
Population in 2011: 1,787
Federal Electoral District(s): Moose Jaw-Lake Centre-Lanigan
Next Election: Oct. 26, 2016 (4 year terms)
Daniel Greschuk, Reeve
R. Doran Scott, Administrator

Bone Creek No. 108
P.O. Box 459
Shaunavon, SK S0N 2M0
Tel: 306-297-2570; *Fax:* 306-297-6270
rmbc@sasktel.net
Municipal Type: Rural Municipalities
Incorporated: Dec. 11, 1911; *Area:* 847.16 sq km
Population in 2011: 340
Federal Electoral District(s): Cypress Hills-Grasslands
Next Election: Oct. 26, 2016 (4 year terms)
Mel Larson, Reeve
Lana Bavle, Administrator

Bratt's Lake No. 129
P.O. Box 130
Wilcox, SK S0G 5E0
Tel: 306-732-2030; *Fax:* 306-732-4495
rm129@sasktel.net
Municipal Type: Rural Municipalities
Incorporated: Jan. 1, 1913; *Area:* 844.94 sq km
Population in 2011: 350
Federal Electoral District(s): Moose Jaw-Lake Centre-Lanigan
Next Election: Oct. 26, 2016 (4 year terms)
J. Barry Hamdorf, Reeve
Kevin S. Ritchie, Administrator

Britannia No. 502
P.O. Box 661
4824 - 47th St.
Lloydminster, SK S9V 0Y7
Tel: 306-825-2610; *Fax:* 306-825-8894
rm502@sasktel.net
www.rmbritannia.com
Municipal Type: Rural Municipalities
Incorporated: Dec. 13, 1909; *Area:* 950.87 sq km
Population in 2011: 1,734
Federal Electoral District(s): Battlefords-Lloydminster
Next Election: Oct. 26, 2016 (4 year terms)
John Light, Reeve
Wanda Boon, Administrator

Brock No. 64
P.O. Box 247
Kisbey, SK S0C 1L0
Tel: 306-462-2010; *Fax:* 306-462-2016
rm64@signaldirect.ca
Municipal Type: Rural Municipalities
Incorporated: Dec. 12, 1910; *Area:* 827.53 sq km
Population in 2011: 238
Federal Electoral District(s): Souris-Moose Mountain
Next Election: Oct. 26, 2016 (4 year terms)
Paul Cameron, Reeve
Treena Heshka, Administrator

Brokenshell No. 68
23 - 6th St. NE
Weyburn, SK S4H 1A7
Tel: 306-842-2314; *Fax:* 306-842-1002
rm.68@sasktel.net
Municipal Type: Rural Municipalities
Incorporated: Dec. 13, 1909; *Area:* 850.01 sq km
Population in 2011: 308
Federal Electoral District(s): Souris-Moose Mountain
Next Election: Oct. 26, 2016 (4 year terms)
Garry Christopherson, Reeve
Pamela Scott, Administrator

Browning No. 34
P.O. Box 40
Lampman, SK S0C 1N0
Tel: 306-487-2444; *Fax:* 306-487-2496
browning.lampman@sasktel.net
www.rmofbrowning.ca
Municipal Type: Rural Municipalities
Incorporated: Dec. 11, 1911; *Area:* 823.39 sq km
Population in 2011: 399
Federal Electoral District(s): Souris-Moose Mountain
Next Election: Oct. 26, 2016 (4 year terms)
Pius Loustel, Reeve, 306-421-0141

Greg Wallin, Administrator

Buchanan No. 304
P.O. Box 10
Buchanan, SK S0A 0J0
Tel: 306-592-2055; *Fax:* 306-592-4436
rm304@sasktel.net
Municipal Type: Rural Municipalities
Incorporated: Jan. 1, 1913; *Area:* 738.80 sq km
Population in 2011: 406
Federal Electoral District(s): Yorkton-Melville
Next Election: Oct. 26, 2016 (4 year terms)
Thomas Dutchak, Reeve
Twila Hadubiak, Administrator

Buckland No. 491
99 River St. East
Prince Albert, SK S6V 0A1
Tel: 306-763-2585; *Fax:* 306-763-6369
rm491@sasktel.net
www.rmbuckland.ca
Municipal Type: Rural Municipalities
Incorporated: Dec. 11, 1911; *Area:* 791.55 sq km
Population in 2011: 3,658
Federal Electoral District(s): Prince Albert
Next Election: Oct. 26, 2016 (4 year terms)
Don Fyrk, Reeve, 306-922-9174
Tara Kerber, Administrator

Buffalo No. 409
P.O. Box 100
214 - 2nd Ave. East
Wilkie, SK S0K 4W0
Tel: 306-843-2342; *Fax:* 306-843-2455
rm409@sasktel.net
Municipal Type: Rural Municipalities
Incorporated: Dec. 13, 1909; *Area:* 1,222.08 sq km
Population in 2011: 506
Federal Electoral District(s): Battlefords-Lloydminster
Next Election: Oct. 26, 2016 (4 year terms)
Leslie Krochinski, Reeve
Sherry Huber, Administrator

Calder No. 241
P.O. Box 10
Wroxton, SK S0A 4S0
Tel: 306-742-4233; *Fax:* 306-742-4559
calderrm@sasktel.net
Municipal Type: Rural Municipalities
Incorporated: Jan. 1, 1913; *Area:* 807.15 sq km
Population in 2011: 322
Federal Electoral District(s): Yorkton-Melville
Next Election: Oct. 26, 2016 (4 year terms)
Melvin Woloschuk, Reeve
Linda Napady, Administrator

Caledonia No. 99
P.O. Box 328
Milestone, SK S0G 3L0
Tel: 306-436-2050; *Fax:* 306-436-2051
milcal@sasktel.net
Municipal Type: Rural Municipalities
Incorporated: Dec. 13, 1909; *Area:* 845.68 sq km
Population in 2011: 257
Federal Electoral District(s): Moose Jaw-Lake Centre-Lanigan
Next Election: Oct. 26, 2016 (4 year terms)
Richard Linton, Reeve
Stephen Schury, Administrator

Cambria No. 6
P.O. Box 210
Torquay, SK S0C 2L0
Tel: 306-923-2000; *Fax:* 306-923-2099
rm.cambria@sasktel.net
Municipal Type: Rural Municipalities
Incorporated: Dec. 13, 1909; *Area:* 814.14 sq km
Population in 2011: 304
Federal Electoral District(s): Souris-Moose Mountain
Next Election: Oct. 26, 2016 (4 year terms)
Darwin Daae, Reeve
Monica Wheeler, Administrator

Cana No. 214
P.O. Box 550
Melville, SK S0A 2P0
Tel: 306-728-5645; *Fax:* 306-728-3807
rmcana@sasktel.net
Municipal Type: Rural Municipalities
Incorporated: Dec. 13, 1909; *Area:* 820.81 sq km
Population in 2011: 858
Federal Electoral District(s): Yorkton-Melville
Next Election: Oct. 26, 2016 (4 year terms)
Robert Almasi, Reeve

Donna Westerhaug, Administrator

Canaan No. 225
P.O. Box 99
Lucky Lake, SK S0L 1Z0
Tel: 306-858-2234; *Fax:* 306-858-9134
rm225.vll@sasktel.net
Municipal Type: Rural Municipalities
Incorporated: Jan. 1, 1913; *Area:* 549.09 sq km
Population in 2011: 149
Federal Electoral District(s): Cypress Hills-Grasslands
Next Election: Oct. 26, 2016 (4 year terms)
Lars Bjorgan, Reeve
D.B. (Blair) Cleaveley, Administrator

Canwood No. 494
P.O. Box 10
Canwood, SK S0J 0K0
Tel: 306-468-2014; *Fax:* 306-468-2666
rm494@sasktel.net
Municipal Type: Rural Municipalities
Incorporated: Jan. 1, 1913; *Area:* 1,945.20 sq km
Population in 2011: 1,424
Federal Electoral District(s): Desnethé-Missinippi-Churchill River
Next Election: Oct. 26, 2016 (4 year terms)
Colin Hughes, Reeve
Lorna Benson, Administrator

Carmichael No. 109
P.O. Box 420
Gull Lake, SK S0N 1A0
Tel: 306-672-3501; *Fax:* 306-672-3295
rm109@sasktel.net
Municipal Type: Rural Municipalities
Incorporated: Dec. 9, 1912; *Area:* 846.40 sq km
Population in 2011: 440
Federal Electoral District(s): Cypress Hills-Grasslands
Next Election: Oct. 26, 2016 (4 year terms)
Jim Bradley, Reeve
Collette Jones, Administrator

Caron No. 162
2 - 1410 Caribou St. West
Moose Jaw, SK S6H 7S9
Tel: 306-692-2293; *Fax:* 306-692-2193
rm162@sasktel.net
Municipal Type: Rural Municipalities
Incorporated: Dec. 9, 1912; *Area:* 569.87 sq km
Population in 2011: 516
Federal Electoral District(s): Cypress Hills-Grasslands
Next Election: Oct. 26, 2016 (4 year terms)
Gregory McKeown, Reeve
John Morris, Administrator

Chaplin No. 164
P.O. Box 60
Chaplin, SK S0H 0V0
Tel: 306-395-2244; *Fax:* 306-395-2767
rm164@sasktel.net
Municipal Type: Rural Municipalities
Incorporated: Jan. 1, 1913; *Area:* 802.74 sq km
Population in 2011: 147
Federal Electoral District(s): Cypress Hills-Grasslands
Next Election: Oct. 26, 2016 (4 year terms)
Duane Doell, Reeve
Tammy Knight, Administrator

Chester No. 125
P.O. Box 180
Glenavon, SK S0G 1Y0
Tel: 306-429-2110; *Fax:* 306-429-2260
rmchester125@sasktel.net
5
Municipal Type: Rural Municipalities
Incorporated: Dec. 13, 1909; *Area:* 837.08 sq km
Population in 2011: 373
Federal Electoral District(s): Souris-Moose Mountain
Next Election: Oct. 26, 2016 (4 year terms)
Merril Wozniak, Reeve
James Hoff, Administrator

Chesterfield No. 261
P.O. Box 70
Eatonia, SK S0L 0Y0
Tel: 306-967-2222; *Fax:* 306-967-2424
rm261@sasktel.net
www.eatonia.ca/rmoffice
Municipal Type: Rural Municipalities
Incorporated: Dec. 9, 1912; *Area:* 1,942.72 sq km
Population in 2011: 480
Federal Electoral District(s): Cypress Hills-Grasslands
Next Election: Oct. 26, 2016 (4 year terms)
Karrie Derouin, Reeve, 306-967-0000

Beverly Dahl, Administrator

Churchbridge No. 211
P.O. Box 211
Churchbridge, SK S0A 0M0
Tel: 306-896-2522; *Fax:* 306-896-2743
rmchurchbridge@sasktel.net
Municipal Type: Rural Municipalities
Incorporated: Jan. 1, 1913; *Area:* 958.98 sq km
Population in 2011: 673
Federal Electoral District(s): Yorkton-Melville
Next Election: Oct. 26, 2016 (4 year terms)
Neil Mehrer, Reeve
Brenda Goulden, Administrator

Clayton No. 333
P.O. Box 220
Hyas, SK S0A 1K0
Tel: 306-594-2832; *Fax:* 306-594-2944
rm333@sasktel.net
Municipal Type: Rural Municipalities
Incorporated: Jan. 1, 1913; *Area:* 1,401.69 sq km
Population in 2011: 669
Federal Electoral District(s): Yorkton-Melville
Next Election: Oct. 26, 2016 (4 year terms)
Hal Griffith, Reeve
Kelly Kim Rea, Administrator

Clinworth No. 230
P.O. Box 120
Sceptre, SK S0N 2H0
Tel: 306-623-4229; *Fax:* 306-623-4229
rm230@yourlink.ca
Municipal Type: Rural Municipalities
Incorporated: Dec. 9, 1912; *Area:* 1,432.75 sq km
Population in 2011: 211
Federal Electoral District(s): Cypress Hills-Grasslands
Next Election: Oct. 26, 2016 (4 year terms)
Ken Dietz, Reeve
Sherry Egeland, Administrator

Coalfields No. 4
P.O. Box 190
Bienfait, SK S0C 0M0
Tel: 306-388-2323; *Fax:* 306-388-2330
rm.04@sasktel.net
Municipal Type: Rural Municipalities
Incorporated: Jan. 1, 1913; *Area:* 819.76 sq km
Population in 2011: 382
Federal Electoral District(s): Souris-Moose Mountain
Next Election: Oct. 26, 2016 (4 year terms)
Stanley Lainton, Reeve
Valerie Crossman, Administrator

Colonsay No. 342
P.O. Box 130
100 Jura St.
Colonsay, SK S0K 0Z0
Tel: 306-255-2233; *Fax:* 306-255-2291
rm342@sasktel.net
www.townofcolonsay.ca/rural-municipality
Municipal Type: Rural Municipalities
Incorporated: Dec. 13, 1909; *Area:* 549.99 sq km
Population in 2011: 240
Federal Electoral District(s): Moose Jaw-Lake Centre-Lanigan
Next Election: Oct. 26, 2016 (4 year terms)
Gerald Yausie, Reeve
Deborah Prosper, Administrator

Connaught No. 457
P.O. Box 25
Tisdale, SK S0E 1T0
Tel: 306-873-2657; *Fax:* 306-873-4442
rm457@sasktel.net
Municipal Type: Rural Municipalities
Incorporated: Dec. 11, 1911; *Area:* 853.11 sq km
Population in 2011: 629
Federal Electoral District(s): Prince Albert
Next Election: Oct. 26, 2016 (4 year terms)
Francis Chabot, Reeve
Tamie McLean, Administrator

Corman Park No. 344
111 Pinehouse Dr.
Saskatoon, SK S7K 5W1
Tel: 306-242-9303; *Fax:* 306-242-6965
rm344@rmcormanpark.ca
www.rmcormanpark.ca
Municipal Type: Rural Municipalities
Incorporated: Jan. 1, 1970; *Area:* 1,978.14 sq km
Population in 2011: 8,354
Federal Electoral District(s): Carlton Trail-Eagle Creek;

Saskatoon West; Saskatoon-Grasswood
Next Election: Oct. 26, 2016 (4 year terms)
Judy Harwood, Reeve
Adam Tittemore, Administrator

Cote No. 271
P.O. Box 669
Kamsack, SK S0A 1S0
Tel: 306-542-2121; *Fax:* 306-542-2428
rm271@sasktel.net
www.rmofcote271.com
Municipal Type: Rural Municipalities
Incorporated: Dec. 12, 1910; *Area:* 880.23 sq km
Population in 2011: 580
Federal Electoral District(s): Yorkton-Melville
Next Election: Oct. 26, 2016 (4 year terms)
Jim Tomochko, Reeve, 306-590-7111
Sherry Guenther, Administrator

Coteau No. 255
P.O. Box 30
Birsay, SK S0L 0G0
Tel: 306-573-2047; *Fax:* 306-573-2111
rm255@sasktel.net
Municipal Type: Rural Municipalities
Incorporated: Dec. 12, 1910; *Area:* 899.27 sq km
Population in 2011: 420
Federal Electoral District(s): Cypress Hills-Grasslands
Next Election: Oct. 26, 2016 (4 year terms)
Clayton Ylioja, Reeve
Lindsay Hargrave, Administrator

Coulee No. 136
1680 Chaplin St. East
Swift Current, SK S9H 1K8
Tel: 306-773-5420; *Fax:* 306-773-1859
rm136@sasktel.net
Municipal Type: Rural Municipalities
Incorporated: Dec. 12, 1910; *Area:* 842.95 sq km
Population in 2011: 582
Federal Electoral District(s): Cypress Hills-Grasslands
Next Election: Oct. 26, 2016 (4 year terms)
Greg Targerson, Reeve
Laurel Dyck, Administrator

Craik No. 222
P.O. Box 420
Craik, SK S0G 0V0
Tel: 306-734-2242; *Fax:* 306-734-2257
rmofcraik222@craik.ca
www.craik.ca/rmofcraik.html
Municipal Type: Rural Municipalities
Incorporated: Dec. 9, 1912; *Area:* 883.02 sq km
Population in 2011: 299
Federal Electoral District(s): Moose Jaw-Lake Centre-Lanigan
Next Election: Oct. 26, 2016 (4 year terms)
Hilton Spencer, Reeve
Shawn McCauley, Administrator

Cupar No. 218
P.O. Box 400
Cupar, SK S0G 0Y0
Tel: 306-723-4726; *Fax:* 306-723-4726
rm218@sasktel.net
www.rmofcupar.ca
Municipal Type: Rural Municipalities
Incorporated: Dec. 13, 1909; *Area:* 919.01 sq km
Population in 2011: 554
Federal Electoral District(s): Regina-Qu'Appelle
Next Election: Oct. 26, 2016 (4 year terms)
Raymond Orb, Reeve
Nicole Czemeres, Administrator

Cut Knife No. 439
P.O. Box 70
Cut Knife, SK S0M 0N0
Tel: 306-398-2353; *Fax:* 306-398-2839
rm439@sasktel.net
Municipal Type: Rural Municipalities
Incorporated: Dec. 13, 1909; *Area:* 651.43 sq km
Population in 2011: 359
Federal Electoral District(s): Battlefords-Lloydminster
Next Election: Oct. 26, 2016 (4 year terms)
Lorne Veikle, Reeve
Don McCallum, Administrator

Cymri No. 36
P.O. Box 238
Midale, SK S0C 1S0
Tel: 306-458-2244; *Fax:* 306-458-2699
rmcymri@sasktel.net
Municipal Type: Rural Municipalities
Incorporated: Dec. 13, 1909; *Area:* 832.36 sq km

Population in 2011: 524
Federal Electoral District(s): Souris-Moose Mountain
Next Election: Oct. 26, 2016 (4 year terms)
Joe Vilcu, Reeve
Gwen Johnston, Administrator

Deer Forks No. 232
P.O. Box 250
Burstall, SK S0N 0H0
Tel: 306-679-2000; *Fax:* 306-679-2275
rm232@sasktel.net
Municipal Type: Rural Municipalities
Incorporated: Jan. 1, 1913; *Area:* 735.49 sq km
Population in 2011: 223
Federal Electoral District(s): Cypress Hills-Grasslands
Next Election: Oct. 26, 2016 (4 year terms)
Doug Smith, Reeve
Tim C. Lozinsky, Administrator

Douglas No. 436
P.O. Box 964
Speers, SK S0M 2V0
Tel: 306-246-2171; *Fax:* 306-246-2173
rm436@littleloon.ca
Municipal Type: Rural Municipalities
Incorporated: Dec. 13, 1909; *Area:* 820.37 sq km
Population in 2011: 331
Federal Electoral District(s): Carlton Trail-Eagle Creek
Next Election: Oct. 26, 2016 (4 year terms)
Nick Partyka, Reeve
Charles W. Linnell, Administrator

Duck Lake No. 463
P.O. Box 250
Duck Lake, SK S0K 1J0
Tel: 306-467-2011; *Fax:* 306-476-4423
rm463@sasktel.net
www.rmducklake.com
Municipal Type: Rural Municipalities
Incorporated: Jan. 1, 1913; *Area:* 1,046.57 sq km
Population in 2011: 867
Federal Electoral District(s): Carlton Trail-Eagle Creek
Next Election: Oct. 26, 2016 (4 year terms)
Marcel Perrin, Reeve
Marnee Gehon, Administrator

Dufferin No. 190
P.O. Box 67
507 Main St.
Bethune, SK S0G 0H0
Tel: 306-638-3112; *Fax:* 306-638-3102
190@sasktel.net
www.rmofdufferin190.com
Municipal Type: Rural Municipalities
Incorporated: Dec. 9, 1912; *Area:* 961.44 sq km
Population in 2011: 512
Federal Electoral District(s): Moose Jaw-Lake Centre-Lanigan
Next Election: Oct. 26, 2016 (4 year terms)
Terry Neugebauer, Reeve
Rodney Audette, Administrator

Dundurn No. 314
P.O. Box 159
314 - 2nd St.
Dundurn, SK S0K 1K0
Tel: 306-492-2132; *Fax:* 306-492-4758
admin.314@sasktel.net
www.myrm.ca/314
Municipal Type: Rural Municipalities
Incorporated: Dec. 13, 1909; *Area:* 800.91 sq km
Population in 2011: 1,148
Federal Electoral District(s): Moose Jaw-Lake Centre-Lanigan
Next Election: Oct. 26, 2016 (4 year terms)
R. Fred Wilson, Reeve
Judy Douglas, Administrator

Eagle Creek No. 376
P.O. Box 278
First St.
Arelee, SK S0K 0H0
Tel: 306-237-4424; *Fax:* 306-237-4294
rm376eaglecreek@xplornet.ca
Municipal Type: Rural Municipalities
Incorporated: Dec. 13, 1909; *Area:* 833.08 sq km
Population in 2011: 580
Federal Electoral District(s): Carlton Trail-Eagle Creek
Next Election: Oct. 26, 2016 (4 year terms)
Faith Struhan, Reeve
Lloyd Cross, Administrator

Edenwold No. 158
P.O. Box 10
100 Queen St.
Balgonie, SK S0G 0E0
Tel: 306-771-2522; *Fax:* 306-771-2631
rm158@sasktel.net
www.rmedenwold.ca
Municipal Type: Rural Municipalities
Incorporated: Dec. 9, 1912; *Area:* 882.67 sq km
Population in 2011: 4,167
Federal Electoral District(s): Regina-Qu'Appelle
Next Election: Oct. 26, 2016 (4 year terms)
Mitchell Huber, Reeve
Kim McIvor, Administrator & Chief Administrative Officer

Elcapo No. 154
P.O. Box 668
Broadview, SK S0G 0K0
Tel: 306-696-2474; *Fax:* 306-696-3573
rm154@sasktel.net
Municipal Type: Rural Municipalities
Incorporated: Dec. 12, 1910; *Area:* 846.54 sq km
Population in 2011: 481
Federal Electoral District(s): Souris-Moose Mountain
Next Election: Oct. 26, 2016 (4 year terms)
Richard Schoepp, Reeve
Mervin Schmidt, Administrator

Eldon No. 471
P.O. Box 130
212 Main St.
Maidstone, SK S0M 1M0
Tel: 306-893-2391; *Fax:* 306-893-4644
rm471@sasktel.net
www.rmeldon.ca
Municipal Type: Rural Municipalities
Incorporated: Dec. 13, 1909; *Area:* 1,007.59 sq km
Population in 2011: 751
Federal Electoral District(s): Battlefords-Lloydminster
Next Election: Oct. 26, 2016 (4 year terms)
Garry Taylor, Reeve
Ken E. Reiter, Administrator

Elfros No. 307
P.O. Box 40
Elfros, SK S0A 0V0
Tel: 306-328-2011; *Fax:* 306-328-4490
rm307@sasktel.net
Municipal Type: Rural Municipalities
Incorporated: Dec. 13, 1909; *Area:* 696.71 sq km
Population in 2011: 432
Federal Electoral District(s): Regina-Qu'Appelle
Next Election: Oct. 26, 2016 (4 year terms)
Michael Yaskowich, Reeve
Liz Parker, Administrator

Elmsthorpe No. 100
P.O. Box 240
Avonlea, SK S0H 0C0
Tel: 306-868-2221; *Fax:* 306-868-2040
rm.100@sasktel.net
Municipal Type: Rural Municipalities
Incorporated: Dec. 12, 1910; *Area:* 843.12 sq km
Population in 2011: 210
Federal Electoral District(s): Moose Jaw-Lake Centre-Lanigan
Next Election: Oct. 26, 2016 (4 year terms)
Ken Miller, Reeve
Jaimie Paranuik, Administrator

Emerald No. 277
P.O. Box 160
Wishart, SK S0A 4R0
Tel: 306-576-2002; *Fax:* 306-576-2132
rm277@sasktel.net
www.rm277emerald.ca
Municipal Type: Rural Municipalities
Incorporated: Dec. 12, 1910; *Area:* 854.44 sq km
Population in 2011: 447
Federal Electoral District(s): Regina-Qu'Appelle
Next Election: Oct. 26, 2016 (4 year terms)
Morris Karakochuk, Reeve
Sharolyn Prisiak, Administrator

Enfield No. 194
P.O. Box 70
2nd Ave. West
Central Butte, SK S0H 0T0
Tel: 306-796-2025; *Fax:* 306-796-2025
rm194@sasktel.net
Municipal Type: Rural Municipalities
Incorporated: Dec. 13, 1909; *Area:* 1,014.10 sq km
Population in 2011: 270

Federal Electoral District(s): Cypress Hills-Grasslands
Next Election: Oct. 26, 2016 (4 year terms)
Jim Campbell, Reeve
Joe Van Leuken, Administrator

Enniskillen No. 3
P.O. Box 179
307 Main St.
Oxbow, SK S0C 2B0
Tel: 306-483-2277; *Fax:* 306-483-2598
rm3@sasktel.net
Municipal Type: Rural Municipalities
Incorporated: Dec. 13, 1909; *Area:* 834.78 sq km
Population in 2011: 452
Federal Electoral District(s): Souris-Moose Mountain
Next Election: Oct. 26, 2016 (4 year terms)
Brian Northeast, Reeve
Myrna-Jean Babbings, Administrator

Enterprise No. 142
P.O. Box 150
Richmound, SK S0N 2E0
Tel: 306-669-2000; *Fax:* 306-669-2052
rm142@sasktel.net
Municipal Type: Rural Municipalities
Incorporated: April 18, 1913; *Area:* 988.80 sq km
Population in 2011: 140
Federal Electoral District(s): Cypress Hills-Grasslands
Next Election: Oct. 26, 2016 (4 year terms)
Wayne Freitag, Reeve
Rolande Davis, Administrator

Estevan No. 5
#1, 322 - 4th St.
Estevan, SK S4A 0T8
Tel: 306-634-2222; *Fax:* 306-634-2223
rm5@sasktel.net
rmestevan.ca
Municipal Type: Rural Municipalities
Incorporated: Dec. 12, 1910; *Area:* 774.67 sq km
Population in 2011: 1,139
Federal Electoral District(s): Souris-Moose Mountain
Next Election: Oct. 26, 2016 (4 year terms)
Kelly Lafrentz, Reeve
Grace Potter, Administrator

Excel No. 71
P.O. Box 100
Viceroy, SK S0H 4H0
Tel: 306-268-4555; *Fax:* 306-268-4547
rm71.excel@gmail.com
Municipal Type: Rural Municipalities
Incorporated: Jan. 1, 1913; *Area:* 1,122.02 sq km
Population in 2011: 427
Federal Electoral District(s): Souris-Moose Mountain
Next Election: Oct. 26, 2016 (4 year terms)
Glenn Roszell, Reeve
Sheri-Lyn Simpson, Administrator

Excelsior No. 166
P.O. Box 180
Rush Lake, SK S0H 3S0
Tel: 306-784-3121; *Fax:* 306-784-3479
rm166@sasktel.net
Municipal Type: Rural Municipalities
Incorporated: Dec. 13, 1909; *Area:* 1,198.35 sq km
Population in 2011: 959
Federal Electoral District(s): Cypress Hills-Grasslands
Next Election: Oct. 26, 2016 (4 year terms)
Harold Martens, Reeve
Dianne Hahn, Administrator

Eye Hill No. 382
P.O. Box 39
Macklin, SK S0L 2C0
Tel: 306-753-2075; *Fax:* 306-753-2304
rm382@sasktel.net
Municipal Type: Rural Municipalities
Incorporated: Dec. 12, 1910; *Area:* 797.96 sq km
Population in 2011: 614
Federal Electoral District(s): Battlefords-Lloydminster
Next Election: Oct. 26, 2016 (4 year terms)
Robert Brost, Reeve
Jason Pilat, Administrator

Eyebrow No. 193
P.O. Box 99
Eyebrow, SK S0H 1L0
Tel: 306-759-2101; *Fax:* 306-759-2026
rm193@yourlink.ca
Municipal Type: Rural Municipalities
Incorporated: Dec. 13, 1909; *Area:* 835.04 sq km
Population in 2011: 230
Federal Electoral District(s): Moose Jaw-Lake Centre-Lanigan
Next Election: Oct. 26, 2016 (4 year terms)
Michael Cavan, Reeve
Chris Bueckert, Administrator

Fertile Belt No. 183
P.O. Box 190
100 Ohlen St.
Stockholm, SK S0A 3Y0
Tel: 306-793-2061; *Fax:* 306-793-2063
rm183@sasktel.net
www.yellowheadreda.com/rmfertilebelt.htm
Municipal Type: Rural Municipalities
Incorporated: January 1, 1913; *Area:* 1,006.68 sq km
Population in 2011: 785
Federal Electoral District(s): Yorkton-Melville
Next Election: Oct. 26, 2016 (4 year terms)
Arlynn Kurtz, Reeve
Lorie Jackson, Administrator

Fertile Valley No. 285
P.O. Box 70
Conquest, SK S0L 0L0
Tel: 306-856-2037; *Fax:* 306-856-2211
rmfv285@yourlink.ca
Municipal Type: Rural Municipalities
Incorporated: Dec. 13, 1909; *Area:* 1,016.37 sq km
Population in 2011: 511
Federal Electoral District(s): Carlton Trail-Eagle Creek
Next Election: Oct. 26, 2016 (4 year terms)
Alvin Barrington, Reeve
L. Jean Jones, Administrator

Fillmore No. 96
P.O. Box 130
Fillmore, SK S0G 1N0
Tel: 306-722-3251; *Fax:* 306-722-3775
rm96@sasktel.net
Municipal Type: Rural Municipalities
Incorporated: Dec. 13, 1909; *Area:* 828.33 sq km
Population in 2011: 255
Federal Electoral District(s): Souris-Moose Mountain
Next Election: Oct. 26, 2016 (4 year terms)
Gerald Nixon, Reeve
Vernna Wiggins, Administrator

Fish Creek No. 402
P.O. Box 160
Wakaw, SK S0K 4P0
Tel: 306-233-4412; *Fax:* 306-233-5234
rm402@sasktel.net
Municipal Type: Rural Municipalities
Incorporated: Jan. 1, 1913; *Area:* 597.90 sq km
Population in 2011: 304
Federal Electoral District(s): Carlton Trail-Eagle Creek
Next Election: Oct. 26, 2016 (4 year terms)
Dennis Sawitsky, Reeve
Gartner Lois, Administrator

Flett's Springs No. 429
P.O. Box 160
Melfort, SK S0E 1A0
Tel: 306-752-3606; *Fax:* 306-752-3882
rm429@sasktel.net
Municipal Type: Rural Municipalities
Incorporated: Dec. 13, 1909; *Area:* 844.61 sq km
Population in 2011: 751
Federal Electoral District(s): Prince Albert
Next Election: Oct. 26, 2016 (4 year terms)
Blaine Forsyth, Reeve
Shelley L. Holmes, Administrator

Foam Lake No. 276
P.O. Box 490
Foam Lake, SK S0A 1A0
Tel: 306-272-3334; *Fax:* 306-272-4722
rm276@sasktel.net
Municipal Type: Rural Municipalities
Incorporated: Dec. 12, 1910; *Area:* 1,345.91 sq km
Population in 2011: 587
Federal Electoral District(s): Yorkton-Melville
Next Election: Oct. 26, 2016 (4 year terms)
Chris Gislason, Reeve
Shanna Loeppky, Administrator

Fox Valley No. 171
P.O. Box 190
100 Centre St.
Fox Valley, SK S0N 0V0
Tel: 306-666-2055; *Fax:* 306-666-2074
rm171@sasktel.net
www.rm171fv.com
Municipal Type: Rural Municipalities
Incorporated: Oct. 29, 1913; *Area:* 1,253.79 sq km
Population in 2011: 345
Federal Electoral District(s): Cypress Hills-Grasslands
Next Election: Oct. 26, 2016 (4 year terms)
Anthony Hoffart, Reeve
Stephanie MacPhail, Administrator

Francis No. 127
P.O. Box 36
Francis, SK S0G 1V0
Tel: 306-245-3256; *Fax:* 306-245-3203
rm127@sasktel.net
www.myrm.ca/127
Municipal Type: Rural Municipalities
Incorporated: Dec. 13, 1909; *Area:* 1,106.80 sq km
Population in 2011: 676
Federal Electoral District(s): Souris-Moose Mountain
Next Election: Oct. 26, 2016 (4 year terms)
Schmidt Clayton, Reeve
Megan Macomber, Administrator

Frenchman Butte No. 501
P.O. Box 180
Paradise Hill, SK S0M 2G0
Tel: 306-344-2034; *Fax:* 306-344-4434
rm501@sasktel.net
www.rmfrenchmanbutte.ca
Municipal Type: Rural Municipalities
Incorporated: Jan. 1, 1954; *Area:* 1,928.32 sq km
Population in 2011: 1,438
Federal Electoral District(s): Battlefords-Lloydminster
Next Election: Oct. 26, 2016 (4 year terms)
B. Bonnie Mills-Midgley, Reeve
Bryson Leganchuk, Administrator

Frontier No. 19
P.O. Box 30
Frontier, SK S0N 0W0
Tel: 306-296-2030; *Fax:* 306-296-2175
rm19@sasktel.net
Municipal Type: Rural Municipalities
Incorporated: Jan. 1, 1913; *Area:* 1,675.02 sq km
Population in 2011: 371
Federal Electoral District(s): Cypress Hills-Grasslands
Next Election: Oct. 26, 2016 (4 year terms)
Troy Heggestad, Reeve
Barb Webber, Administrator

The Gap No. 39
P.O. Box 188
Ceylon, SK S0C 0T0
Tel: 306-454-2202; *Fax:* 306-454-2627
rmgap39@sasktel.net
Municipal Type: Rural Municipalities
Incorporated: Dec. 12, 1903; *Area:* 830.92 sq km
Population in 2011: 230
Federal Electoral District(s): Souris-Moose Mountain
Next Election: Oct. 26, 2016 (4 year terms)
Keith Kaufmann, Reeve
Yvonne Johnston, Administrator

Garden River No. 490
P.O. Box 70
Meath Park, SK S0J 1T0
Tel: 306-929-2020; *Fax:* 306-929-2281
rm490@sasktel.net
Municipal Type: Rural Municipalities
Incorporated: Jan. 1, 1913; *Area:* 662.90 sq km
Population in 2011: 641
Federal Electoral District(s): Prince Albert
Next Election: Oct. 26, 2016 (4 year terms)
Kent Buckler, Reeve
Elaine Esopenko, Administrator

Garry No. 245
P.O. Box 10
Jedburgh, SK S0A 1R0
Tel: 306-647-2450; *Fax:* 306-647-2452
rm245@yourlink.ca
Municipal Type: Rural Municipalities
Incorporated: Jan. 1, 1913; *Area:* 853.59 sq km
Population in 2011: 412
Federal Electoral District(s): Yorkton-Melville
Next Election: Oct. 26, 2016 (4 year terms)
Garry Dubiel, Reeve
Tanis Ferguson, Administrator

Glen Bain No. 105
P.O. Box 39
Glen Bain, SK S0N 0X0
Tel: 306-264-3607; *Fax:* 306-264-3956
rm105@sasktel.net

Municipal Type: Rural Municipalities
Incorporated: Dec. 11, 1911; *Area:* 843.40 sq km
Population in 2011: 205
Federal Electoral District(s): Cypress Hills-Grasslands
Next Election: Oct. 26, 2016 (4 year terms)
Ivan Braun, Reeve
Marilyn Scheller, Administrator

Glen McPherson No. 46
P.O. Box 277
Mankota, SK S0H 2W0
Tel: 306-478-2323; *Fax:* 306-478-2606
rm45.46@sasktel.net
Municipal Type: Rural Municipalities
Incorporated: Jan. 1, 1913; *Area:* 848.29 sq km
Population in 2011: 73
Federal Electoral District(s): Cypress Hills-Grasslands
Next Election: Oct. 26, 2016 (4 year terms)
Gordon Kruger, Reeve
Michael Sherven, Administrator

Glenside No. 377
P.O. Box 1084
Biggar, SK S0K 0M0
Tel: 306-948-3681; *Fax:* 306-948-3684
rm377@sasktel.net
Municipal Type: Rural Municipalities
Incorporated: Dec. 13, 1909; *Area:* 905.74 sq km
Population in 2011: 267
Federal Electoral District(s): Carlton Trail-Eagle Creek; Battlefords-Lloydminster
Next Election: Oct. 26, 2016 (4 year terms)
Elmer Dove, Reeve
Joanne Fullerton, Administrator

Golden West No. 95
P.O. Box 70
Corning, SK S0G 0T0
Tel: 306-224-4456; *Fax:* 306-224-2196
goldwest@sasktel.net
Municipal Type: Rural Municipalities
Incorporated: Dec. 13, 1909; *Area:* 790.13 sq km
Population in 2011: 315
Federal Electoral District(s): Souris-Moose Mountain
Next Election: Oct. 26, 2016 (4 year terms)
Richard Stajniak, Reeve
Edward Mish, Administrator

Good Lake No. 274
P.O. Box 896
401 Main St.
Canora, SK S0A 0L0
Tel: 306-563-5244; *Fax:* 306-563-5005
rm274@sasktel.net
www.goodlakerm.com
Municipal Type: Rural Municipalities
Incorporated: Jan. 1, 1913; *Area:* 800.06 sq km
Population in 2011: 684
Federal Electoral District(s): Yorkton-Melville
Next Election: Oct. 26, 2016 (4 year terms)
David Popowich, Reeve
Joan Popoff, Administrator

Grandview No. 349
P.O. Box 39
Kelfield, SK S0K 2C0
Tel: 306-932-4911; *Fax:* 306-932-4923
rm349@xplornet.com
Municipal Type: Rural Municipalities
Incorporated: Dec. 11, 1911; *Area:* 712.05 sq km
Population in 2011: 340
Federal Electoral District(s): Battlefords-Lloydminster
Next Election: Oct. 26, 2016 (4 year terms)
Note: On Dec. 31st 2013, the village of Ruthilda dissolved into the Rural Municipality of Grandview No. 349.
Iain Keller, Reeve
Shonda Toner, Administrator

Grant No. 372
P.O. Box 190
Vonda, SK S0K 4N0
Tel: 306-258-2022; *Fax:* 306-258-2011
rm372@baudoux.ca
Municipal Type: Rural Municipalities
Incorporated: Dec. 13, 1909; *Area:* 666.16 sq km
Population in 2011: 425
Federal Electoral District(s): Carlton Trail-Eagle Creek
Next Election: Oct. 26, 2016 (4 year terms)
Francois Denis, Reeve
Brenda Skakun, Administrator

Grass Lake No. 381
P.O. Box 40
101 Main St.
Reward, SK S0K 3N0
Tel: 306-228-2988; *Fax:* 306-228-4188
rm381@sasktel.net
Municipal Type: Rural Municipalities
Incorporated: Dec. 13, 1909; *Area:* 801.29 sq km
Population in 2011: 369
Federal Electoral District(s): Battlefords-Lloydminster
Next Election: Oct. 26, 2016 (4 year terms)
Scott Vetter, Reeve
Brenda M. Kasas, Administrator

Grassy Creek No. 78
P.O. Box 400
Shaunavon, SK S0N 2M0
Tel: 306-297-2520; *Fax:* 306-297-3162
rm77.78@sasktel.net
Municipal Type: Rural Municipalities
Incorporated: Jan. 1, 1913; *Area:* 837.40 sq km
Population in 2011: 284
Federal Electoral District(s): Cypress Hills-Grasslands
Next Election: Oct. 26, 2016 (4 year terms)
Kerry Kronberg, Reeve
Rhonda Bellefeuille, Administrator

Gravelbourg No. 104
P.O. Box 510
Gravelbourg, SK S0H 1X0
Tel: 306-648-2412
rm104@sasktel.net
www.rmofgravelbourg.com
Municipal Type: Rural Municipalities
Incorporated: Dec. 9, 1912; *Area:* 842.08 sq km
Population in 2011: 306
Federal Electoral District(s): Cypress Hills-Grasslands
Next Election: Oct. 26, 2016 (4 year terms)
Donald Green, Reeve
Dara Cowan, Administrator

Grayson No. 184
P.O. Box 69
131 Taylor St.
Grayson, SK S0A 1E0
Tel: 306-794-2044; *Fax:* 306-794-4655
grayson184@sasktel.net
www.rmofgrayson.ca
Municipal Type: Rural Municipalities
Incorporated: Jan. 1, 1913; *Area:* 875.22 sq km
Population in 2011: 495
Federal Electoral District(s): Yorkton-Melville
Next Election: Oct. 26, 2016 (4 year terms)
Ray Bernhardt, Reeve
Darlene Paquin, Administrator

Great Bend No. 405
P.O. Box 150
200 Shepard St.
Borden, SK S0K 0N0
Tel: 306-997-2101; *Fax:* 306-997-2201
rm405@sasktel.net
Municipal Type: Rural Municipalities
Incorporated: Dec. 12, 1910; *Area:* 830.57 sq km
Population in 2011: 499
Federal Electoral District(s): Carlton Trail-Eagle Creek
Next Election: Oct. 26, 2016 (4 year terms)
Ron Saunders, Reeve
Valerie Fendelet, Administrator

Griffin No. 66
P.O. Box 70
Griffin, SK S0C 1G0
Tel: 306-842-6298; *Fax:* 306-842-6400
rm66@sasktel.net
Municipal Type: Rural Municipalities
Incorporated: Dec. 13, 1909; *Area:* 816.59 sq km
Population in 2011: 398
Federal Electoral District(s): Souris-Moose Mountain
Next Election: Oct. 26, 2016 (4 year terms)
Stacey Lund, Reeve
Tawnya Moore, Administrator

Gull Lake No. 139
P.O. Box 180
Gull Lake, SK S0N 1A0
Tel: 306-672-4430; *Fax:* 306-672-3879
rm139@sasktel.net
www.rmgulllake.ca
Municipal Type: Rural Municipalities
Incorporated: Jan. 1, 1913; *Area:* 836.41 sq km
Population in 2011: 201

Federal Electoral District(s): Cypress Hills-Grasslands
Next Election: Oct. 26, 2016 (4 year terms)
Doug Steele, Reeve
Jeanette Kerr, Administrator

Happy Valley No. 10
P.O. Box 39
Big Beaver, SK S0H 0G0
Tel: 306-267-4540; *Fax:* 306-267-4540
rm10@sasktel.net
Municipal Type: Rural Municipalities
Incorporated: Jan. 1, 1913; *Area:* 812.74 sq km
Population in 2011: 148
Federal Electoral District(s): Souris-Moose Mountain
Next Election: Oct. 26, 2016 (4 year terms)
David Schwab, Reeve
Michael Rattray, Administrator

Happyland No. 231
P.O. Box 339
106 - 3rd St. West
Leader, SK S0N 1H0
Tel: 306-628-3800; *Fax:* 306-628-4228
rm231@sasktel.net
www.rmofhappyland.ca
Municipal Type: Rural Municipalities
Incorporated: Jan. 1, 1913; *Area:* 1,259 sq km
Population in 2011: 284
Federal Electoral District(s): Cypress Hills-Grasslands
Next Election: Oct. 26, 2016 (4 year terms)
Timothy Geiger, Reeve, 306-628-4335
Tim Lozinsky, Administrator

Harris No. 316
P.O. Box 146
Harris, SK S0L 1K0
Tel: 306-656-2072; *Fax:* 306-656-2151
rm316@sasktel.net
Municipal Type: Rural Municipalities
Incorporated: Dec. 12, 1910; *Area:* 805.42 sq km
Population in 2011: 224
Federal Electoral District(s): Carlton Trail-Eagle Creek
Next Election: Oct. 26, 2016 (4 year terms)
David Husband, Reeve
Adrienne Urban, Administrator

Hart Butte No. 11
P.O. Box 210
Coronach, SK S0H 0Z0
Tel: 306-267-2005; *Fax:* 306-267-2391
rm11@sasktel.net
Municipal Type: Rural Municipalities
Incorporated: Jan. 1, 1913; *Area:* 841.98 sq km
Population in 2011: 264
Federal Electoral District(s): Souris-Moose Mountain
Next Election: Oct. 26, 2016 (4 year terms)
Donald Kirby, Reeve
Michael Rattray, Administrator

Hazel Dell No. 335
P.O. Box 87
Okla, SK S0A 2X0
Tel: 306-325-4315; *Fax:* 306-352-4314
rm335@sasktel.net
Municipal Type: Rural Municipalities
Incorporated: Jan. 1, 1913; *Area:* 1,394.02 sq km
Population in 2011: 511
Federal Electoral District(s): Yorkton-Melville
Next Election: Oct. 26, 2016 (4 year terms)
Jerry Klassen, Reeve
Miranda Serhan, Administrator

Hazelwood No. 94
P.O. Box 270
Kipling, SK S0G 2S0
Tel: 306-736-8121; *Fax:* 306-736-2496
rm94@sasktel.net
Municipal Type: Rural Municipalities
Incorporated: Jan. 1, 1913; *Area:* 780.68 sq km
Population in 2011: 246
Federal Electoral District(s): Souris-Moose Mountain
Next Election: Oct. 26, 2016 (4 year terms)
Allan LaRose, Reeve
Gary Vargo, Administrator

Heart's Hill No. 352
P.O. Box 458
Luseland, SK S0L 2A0
Tel: 306-372-4224; *Fax:* 306-372-4770
Municipal Type: Rural Municipalities
Incorporated: Nov. 15, 1910; *Area:* 838.20 sq km
Population in 2011: 260

Federal Electoral District(s): Battlefords-Lloydminster
Next Election: Oct. 26, 2016 (4 year terms)
Gordon Stang, Reeve, 306-834-5041
Janet Fisher, Administrator

Hillsborough No. 132
#4, 1410 Caribou St. West
Moose Jaw, SK S6H 7S9
Tel: 306-693-1329; *Fax:* 306-693-2810
rm.132@sasktel.net
Municipal Type: Rural Municipalities
Incorporated: Jan. 1, 1913; *Area:* 445.25 sq km
Population in 2011: 114
Federal Electoral District(s): Cypress Hills-Grasslands
Next Election: Oct. 26, 2016 (4 year terms)
Blaine Barnett, Reeve
Charlene Loos, Administrator

Hillsdale No. 440
P.O. Box 280
39 Centre St.
Neilburg, SK S0M 2C0
Tel: 306-823-4321; *Fax:* 306-823-4477
rm440@sasktel.net
www.rmofhillsdale.com
Municipal Type: Rural Municipalities
Incorporated: Jan. 1, 1913; *Area:* 1,028.75 sq km
Population in 2011: 563
Federal Electoral District(s): Battlefords-Lloydminster
Next Election: Oct. 26, 2016 (4 year terms)
Glenn Goodfellow, Reeve, 306-823-4560
Janet L. Black, Administrator

Hoodoo No. 401
Cudworth, SK S0K 1B0
Tel: 306-256-3281; *Fax:* 306-256-7147
rm401@sasktel.net
Municipal Type: Rural Municipalities
Incorporated: Jan. 1, 1913; *Area:* 810.61 sq km
Population in 2011: 706
Federal Electoral District(s): Carlton Trail-Eagle Creek
Next Election: Oct. 26, 2016 (4 year terms)
Linus Hackl, Reeve
David Yorke, Administrator

Hudson Bay No. 394
P.O. Box 520
Hudson Bay, SK S0E 0Y0
Tel: 306-865-2691; *Fax:* 306-865-2857
rm394@sasktel.net
Municipal Type: Rural Municipalities
Incorporated: May 1, 1977; *Area:* 12,460.90 sq km
Population in 2011: 1,122
Federal Electoral District(s): Yorkton-Melville
Next Election: Oct. 26, 2016 (4 year terms)
Neal Hardy, Reeve
Tracy Smith, Administrator

Humboldt No. 370
P.O. Box 420
Humboldt, SK S0K 2A0
Tel: 306-682-2242; *Fax:* 306-682-3239
r.m.humboldt@sasktel.net
Municipal Type: Rural Municipalities
Incorporated: Jan. 1, 1913; *Area:* 798.51 sq km
Population in 2011: 885
Federal Electoral District(s): Carlton Trail-Eagle Creek
Next Election: Oct. 26, 2016 (4 year terms)
Jordan Bergermann, Reeve
Corinne Richardson, Administrator

Huron No. 223
P.O. Box 159
Tugaske, SK S0H 4B0
Tel: 306-759-2211; *Fax:* 306-759-2249
rm223@sasktel.net
Municipal Type: Rural Municipalities
Incorporated: Dec. 12, 1910; *Area:* 842.11 sq km
Population in 2011: 196
Federal Electoral District(s): Moose Jaw-Lake Centre-Lanigan
Next Election: Oct. 26, 2016 (4 year terms)
Corey Doerksen, Reeve
Daryl Dean, Administrator

Indian Head No. 156
P.O. Box 39
Indian Head, SK S0G 2K0
Tel: 306-695-3464; *Fax:* 306-695-3462
rm156@sasktel.net
Municipal Type: Rural Municipalities
Incorporated: Aug. 6, 1884; *Area:* 759.98 sq km
Population in 2011: 380

Federal Electoral District(s): Regina-Qu'Appelle
Next Election: Oct. 26, 2016 (4 year terms)
Lorne Scott, Reeve
Lorelei Theaker, Administrator

Insinger No. 275
P.O. Box 179
Insinger, SK S0A 1L0
Tel: 306-647-2422; *Fax:* 306-647-2740
rm275@yourlink.ca
Municipal Type: Rural Municipalities
Incorporated: Jan. 1, 1913; *Area:* 849.38 sq km
Population in 2011: 325
Federal Electoral District(s): Yorkton-Melville
Next Election: Oct. 26, 2016 (4 year terms)
Terry Eritz, Reeve
Sonya Butuk, Administrator

Invergordon No. 430
P.O. Box 40
Crystal Springs, SK S0K 1A0
Tel: 306-749-2852; *Fax:* 306-749-2499
rm430@sasktel.net
Municipal Type: Rural Municipalities
Incorporated: Dec. 11, 1911; *Area:* 853.55 sq km
Population in 2011: 651
Federal Electoral District(s): Prince Albert
Next Election: Oct. 26, 2016 (4 year terms)
Bruce Hunter, Reeve
Trent Smith, Administrator

Invermay No. 305
P.O. Box 130
Invermay, SK S0A 1M0
Tel: 306-593-2152; *Fax:* 306-593-2132
rm.inv.305@sasktel.net
Municipal Type: Rural Municipalities
Incorporated: Dec. 11, 1911; *Area:* 728.23 sq km
Population in 2011: 334
Federal Electoral District(s): Yorkton-Melville
Next Election: Oct. 26, 2016 (4 year terms)
Jack Prychak, Reeve
Dana Jack, Administrator

Ituna Bon Accord No. 246
P.O. Box 190
Ituna, SK S0A 1N0
Tel: 306-795-2202; *Fax:* 306-795-2202
rmofituna@sasktel.net
Municipal Type: Rural Municipalities
Incorporated: Jan. 1, 1913; *Area:* 837.23 sq km
Population in 2011: 435
Federal Electoral District(s): Regina-Qu'Appelle
Next Election: Oct. 26, 2016 (4 year terms)
Terry Berezny, Reeve
Wilma Hrenyk, Administrator

Kellross No. 247
P.O. Box 10
222 Main St.
Leross, SK S0A 2C0
Tel: 306-675-4423; *Fax:* 306-675-2097
rm247@sasktel.net
www.kellross.ca
Municipal Type: Rural Municipalities
Incorporated: Dec. 13, 1909; *Area:* 834.09 sq km
Population in 2011: 362
Federal Electoral District(s): Regina-Qu'Appelle
Next Election: Oct. 26, 2016 (4 year terms)
John Olinik, Reeve, 306-675-4970
Edith Goddard, Administrator

Kelvington No. 366
P.O. Box 519
201 Main St.
Kelvington, SK S0A 1W0
Tel: 306-327-4222; *Fax:* 306-327-4222
rm366@sasktel.net
Municipal Type: Rural Municipalities
Incorporated: Jan. 1, 1913; *Area:* 907.37 sq km
Population in 2011: 499
Federal Electoral District(s): Yorkton-Melville
Next Election: Oct. 26, 2016 (4 year terms)
Stanley Elmy, Reeve
Tim G. Leurer, Administrator

Key West No. 70
P.O. Box 159
Ogema, SK S0C 1Y0
Tel: 306-459-2262; *Fax:* 306-459-2762
rm.70@sasktel.net
Municipal Type: Rural Municipalities
Incorporated: Dec. 12, 1910; *Area:* 825.26 sq km

Population in 2011: 287
Federal Electoral District(s): Souris-Moose Mountain
Next Election: Oct. 26, 2016 (4 year terms)
Rick Dunn, Reeve
Peggy Tuchscherer, Administrator

Keys No. 303
P.O. Box 899
203 Main St.
Canora, SK S0A 0L0
Tel: 306-563-5331; *Fax:* 306-563-6759
rm303@sasktel.net
Municipal Type: Rural Municipalities
Incorporated: Jan. 1, 1913; *Area:* 661.61 sq km
Population in 2011: 417
Federal Electoral District(s): Yorkton-Melville
Next Election: Oct. 26, 2016 (4 year terms)
Vivian Morgan, Reeve
Barry Hvidston, Administrator

Kindersley No. 290
P.O. Box 1210
417 Main St.
Kindersley, SK S0L 1S0
Tel: 306-463-2524; *Fax:* 306-463-4197
rm290@sasktel.net
www.rmofkindersley.ca
Other Information: Alt. URL: www.rm290.blogspot.ca
Municipal Type: Rural Municipalities
Incorporated: Dec. 12, 1910; *Area:* 2,113.36 sq km
Population in 2011: 987
Federal Electoral District(s): Cypress Hills-Grasslands
Next Election: Oct. 26, 2016 (4 year terms)
Glen Harrison, Reeve, 306-463-3189
Glenda M. Giles, Administrator

King George No. 256
P.O. Box 100
Dinsmore, SK S0L 0T0
Tel: 306-846-2022; *Fax:* 306-846-2032
rm256@sasktel.net
Municipal Type: Rural Municipalities
Incorporated: Dec. 11, 1911; *Area:* 831.97 sq km
Population in 2011: 217
Federal Electoral District(s): Cypress Hills-Grasslands
Next Election: Oct. 26, 2016 (4 year terms)
Norm McIntyre, Reeve
Cheryl Joel, Administrator

Kingsley No. 124
P.O. Box 239
Kipling, SK S0G 2S0
Tel: 306-736-2272; *Fax:* 306-736-2798
rm124@sasktel.net
Municipal Type: Rural Municipalities
Incorporated: Dec. 12, 1910; *Area:* 844.61 sq km
Population in 2011: 421
Federal Electoral District(s): Souris-Moose Mountain
Next Election: Oct. 26, 2016 (4 year terms)
Gordon Sproat, Reeve
Holly Kemp, Administrator

Kinistino No. 459
P.O. Box 310
Kinistino, SK S0J 1H0
Tel: 306-864-2474; *Fax:* 306-864-2880
rm459@sasktel.net
Municipal Type: Rural Municipalities
Incorporated: Dec. 11, 1911; *Area:* 949.13 sq km
Population in 2011: 531
Federal Electoral District(s): Prince Albert
Next Election: Oct. 26, 2016 (4 year terms)
Vance Shmyr, Reeve
Shelley L. Holmes, Administrator

Lac Pelletier No. 107
P.O. Box 70
Neville, SK S0N 1T0
Tel: 306-627-3226; *Fax:* 306-627-3641
rm107@sasktel.net
Municipal Type: Rural Municipalities
Incorporated: Jan. 1, 1913; *Area:* 849.27 sq km
Population in 2011: 607
Federal Electoral District(s): Cypress Hills-Grasslands
Next Election: Oct. 26, 2016 (4 year terms)
Cornie Martens, Reeve
Rose Lawrence, Administrator

Lacadena No. 228
P.O. Box 39
Lacadena, SK S0L 1V0
Tel: 306-574-4753; *Fax:* 306-574-4705
rm228@yourlink.ca

Municipal Type: Rural Municipalities
Incorporated: Dec. 12, 1910; *Area:* 1,890.08 sq km
Population in 2011: 572
Federal Electoral District(s): Cypress Hills-Grasslands
Next Election: Oct. 26, 2016 (4 year terms)
Bradley Sander, Reeve
Wilma Moen, Administrator

Laird No. 404
P.O. Box 160
3025 Central Ave.
Waldheim, SK S0K 4R0
Tel: 306-945-2133; *Fax:* 306-945-4824
rmlaird@sasktel.net
www.rmoflaird.ca
Municipal Type: Rural Municipalities
Incorporated: Dec. 12, 1910; *Area:* 729.98 sq km
Population in 2011: 1,240
Federal Electoral District(s): Carlton Trail-Eagle Creek
Next Election: Oct. 26, 2016 (4 year terms)
Terry Knippel, Reeve
Paulette Wolkowski, Administrator

Lajord No. 128
P.O. Box 36
Lajord, SK S0G 2V0
Tel: 306-781-2744; *Fax:* 306-781-1023
rm128@yourlink.ca
www.myrm.ca/128
Municipal Type: Rural Municipalities
Incorporated: Dec. 13, 1909; *Area:* 943.87 sq km
Population in 2011: 993
Federal Electoral District(s): Souris-Moose Mountain
Next Election: Oct. 26, 2016 (4 year terms)
Erwin Beitel, Reeve
Rod Heise, Administrator

Lake Alma No. 8
P.O. Box 100
Lake Alma, SK S0C 1M0
Tel: 306-447-2022; *Fax:* 306-447-2023
rmalma@sasktel.net
Municipal Type: Rural Municipalities
Incorporated: May 5, 1913; *Area:* 822.47 sq km
Population in 2011: 250
Federal Electoral District(s): Souris-Moose Mountain
Next Election: Oct. 26, 2016 (4 year terms)
Robert Thue, Reeve
Myrna Lohse, Administrator

Lake Johnston No. 102
P.O. Box 160
Mossbank, SK S0H 3G0
Tel: 306-354-2414; *Fax:* 306-354-7725
rm102.103@sasktel.net
Municipal Type: Rural Municipalities
Incorporated: Dec. 9, 1912; *Area:* 567.24 sq km
Population in 2011: 160
Federal Electoral District(s): Cypress Hills-Grasslands
Next Election: Oct. 26, 2016 (4 year terms)
Kevin Stark, Reeve
Sherry Green, Administrator

Lake Lenore No. 399
P.O. Box 280
200 Main St.
St Brieux, SK S0K 3V0
Tel: 306-275-2066; *Fax:* 306-275-4667
rmll@sasktel.net
www.townofstbrieux.com/r-m-of-lake-lenore-399
Municipal Type: Rural Municipalities
Incorporated: Jan. 1, 1913; *Area:* 724.06 sq km
Population in 2011: 536
Federal Electoral District(s): Yorkton-Melville
Next Election: Oct. 26, 2016 (4 year terms)
Jean Kernaleguen, Reeve
Jennifer Thompson, Administrator

Lake of the Rivers No. 72
P.O. Box 610
Assiniboia, SK S0H 0B0
Tel: 306-642-3533; *Fax:* 306-642-4382
rm72@sasktel.net
Municipal Type: Rural Municipalities
Incorporated: Dec. 11, 1911; *Area:* 677.51 sq km
Population in 2011: 302
Federal Electoral District(s): Cypress Hills-Grasslands
Next Election: Oct. 26, 2016 (4 year terms)
Norm Nordgulen, Reeve
Ellen Klein, Administrator

Lakeland No. 521
P.O. Box 27
Christopher Lake, SK S0J 0N0
Tel: 306-982-2010; *Fax:* 306-982-2589
office@lakeland521.ca
www.lakeland521.ca
Municipal Type: Rural Municipalities
Incorporated: Aug. 1, 1977; *Area:* 494.06 sq km
Population in 2011: 884
Federal Electoral District(s): Desnethé-Missinippi-Churchill River
Next Election: Oct. 26, 2016 (4 year terms)
E.E. Christensen, Reeve, 306-982-4599
Dave Dmytruk, Administrator

Lakeside No. 338
P.O. Box 9
Quill Lake, SK S0A 3E0
Tel: 306-383-2261; *Fax:* 306-383-2255
rm338@sasktel.net
Municipal Type: Rural Municipalities
Incorporated: Dec. 12, 1910; *Area:* 636.80 sq km
Population in 2011: 387
Federal Electoral District(s): Yorkton-Melville
Next Election: Oct. 26, 2016 (4 year terms)
Arnold Boyko, Reeve
Judy Kanak, Administrator

Lakeview No. 337
P.O. Box 220
Wadena, SK S0A 4J0
Tel: 306-338-2341; *Fax:* 306-338-2595
rm337@sasktel.net
www.myrm.ca/337
Municipal Type: Rural Municipalities
Incorporated: Dec. 13, 1909; *Area:* 724.89 sq km
Population in 2011: 336
Federal Electoral District(s): Yorkton-Melville
Next Election: Oct. 26, 2016 (4 year terms)
Mervin Kryzanowski, Reeve
Carrie Turnbull, Administrator

Langenburg No. 181
P.O. Box 489
120 Carl Ave. West
Langenburg, SK S0A 2A0
Tel: 306-743-2341; *Fax:* 306-743-5282
rm181@sasktel.net
www.langenburg.ca/town_office/rm_of_langenburg.html
Municipal Type: Rural Municipalities
Incorporated: Jan. 1, 1913; *Area:* 675.66 sq km
Population in 2011: 572
Federal Electoral District(s): Yorkton-Melville
Next Election: Oct. 26, 2016 (4 year terms)
Ken Apland, Reeve
Krystal Johnston, Administrator

Last Mountain Valley No. 250
P.O. Box 160
Govan, SK S0G 1Z0
Tel: 306-484-2011; *Fax:* 306-484-2113
rm250@sasktel.net
Municipal Type: Rural Municipalities
Incorporated: Dec. 13, 1909; *Area:* 871.17 sq km
Population in 2011: 267
Federal Electoral District(s): Moose Jaw-Lake Centre-Lanigan
Next Election: Oct. 26, 2016 (4 year terms)
Allan Magel, Reeve
Kelly Holbrook, Administrator

Laurier No. 38
P.O. Box 219
505 Healy Ave.
Radville, SK S0C 2G0
Tel: 306-869-2255; *Fax:* 306-869-2524
rm.38@sasktel.net
www.radville.ca
Municipal Type: Rural Municipalities
Incorporated: Dec. 13, 1909; *Area:* 840.86 sq km
Population in 2011: 321
Federal Electoral District(s): Souris-Moose Mountain
Next Election: Oct. 26, 2016 (4 year terms)
Todd Labbie, Reeve
Ursula Scott, Administrator

Lawtonia No. 135
P.O. Box 10
Hodgeville, SK S0H 2B0
Tel: 306-677-2266; *Fax:* 306-677-2446
rm135@sasktel.net
myrm.ca/135
Municipal Type: Rural Municipalities
Incorporated: Dec. 12, 1910; *Area:* 845.28 sq km

Population in 2011: 434
Federal Electoral District(s): Cypress Hills-Grasslands
Next Election: Oct. 26, 2016 (4 year terms)
Barry Leisle, Reeve
Art Thompson, Administrator

Leask No. 464
P.O. Box 190
Leask, SK S0J 1M0
Tel: 306-466-2000; *Fax:* 306-466-2091
admin.464@sasktel.net
www.leask.ca/rmoffice.html
Municipal Type: Rural Municipalities
Incorporated: Dec. 9, 1912; *Area:* 1,257.36 sq km
Population in 2011: 775
Federal Electoral District(s): Carlton Trail-Eagle Creek
Next Election: Oct. 26, 2016 (4 year terms)
Jim Joanette, Reeve
Judy Lychak, Administrator

Leroy No. 339
P.O. Box 100
Leroy, SK S0K 2P0
Tel: 306-286-3261; *Fax:* 306-286-3400
rm339@sasktel.net
Municipal Type: Rural Municipalities
Incorporated: Jan. 1, 1913; *Area:* 840.40 sq km
Population in 2011: 490
Federal Electoral District(s): Moose Jaw-Lake Centre-Lanigan
Next Election: Oct. 26, 2016 (4 year terms)
Jerry McGrath, Reeve
Wendy Gowda, Administrator

Lipton No. 217
P.O. Box 40
Lipton, SK S0G 3B0
Tel: 306-336-2244; *Fax:* 306-336-2322
rm.217@sasktel.net
Municipal Type: Rural Municipalities
Incorporated: Dec. 11, 1911; *Area:* 813.69 sq km
Population in 2011: 424
Federal Electoral District(s): Regina-Qu'Appelle
Next Election: Oct. 26, 2016 (4 year terms)
Corey Senft, Reeve
Frank Kosa, Administrator

Livingston No. 331
P.O. Box 40
Arran, SK S0A 0B0
Tel: 306-595-4521; *Fax:* 306-595-4531
rm331@sasktel.net
Municipal Type: Rural Municipalities
Incorporated: Jan. 1, 1913; *Area:* 1,338.64 sq km
Population in 2011: 311
Federal Electoral District(s): Yorkton-Melville
Next Election: Oct. 26, 2016 (4 year terms)
Don Hrycenko, Reeve
Yvonne Bilsky, Administrator

Lomond No. 37
P.O. Box 280
Weyburn, SK S4H 2K1
Tel: 306-456-2566; *Fax:* 306-456-2440
rm37@sasktel.net
Municipal Type: Rural Municipalities
Incorporated: Dec. 11, 1911; *Area:* 833.95 sq km
Population in 2011: 304
Federal Electoral District(s): Souris-Moose Mountain
Next Election: Oct. 26, 2016 (4 year terms)
Desmond McKenzie, Reeve
Kevin Melle, Administrator

Lone Tree No. 18
P.O. Box 30
Climax, SK S0N 0N0
Tel: 306-293-2124; *Fax:* 306-293-2702
rmltno.18@sasktel.net
Municipal Type: Rural Municipalities
Incorporated: Dec. 8, 1913; *Area:* 838 sq km
Population in 2011: 145
Federal Electoral District(s): Cypress Hills-Grasslands
Next Election: Oct. 26, 2016 (4 year terms)
Larry Jarman, Reeve
Shawna Bertram, Administrator

Longlaketon No. 219
P.O. Box 100
Earl Grey, SK S0G 1J0
Tel: 306-939-2144; *Fax:* 306-939-2036
rm219@sasktel.net
Municipal Type: Rural Municipalities
Incorporated: Dec. 12, 1910; *Area:* 1,024.61 sq km
Population in 2011: 962

Federal Electoral District(s): Moose Jaw-Lake Centre-Lanigan; Regina-Qu'Appelle
Next Election: Oct. 26, 2016 (4 year terms)
Mark Ritter, Reeve
Loretta Young, Administrator

Loon Lake No. 561
P.O. Box 40
Loon Lake, SK S0M 1L0
Tel: 306-837-2076; *Fax:* 306-837-2282
rm561@sasktel.net
www.rmloonlake.com
Municipal Type: Rural Municipalities
Incorporated: Jan. 1, 1978; *Area:* 2,802.51 sq km
Population in 2011: 725
Federal Electoral District(s): Desnethé-Missinippi-Churchill River
Next Election: Oct. 26, 2016 (4 year terms)
Greg Cardinal, Reeve, 306-236-3637
Laurie Lehoux, Administrator

Loreburn No. 254
P.O. Box 40
Loreburn, SK S0H 2S0
Tel: 306-644-2022; *Fax:* 306-644-2064
rm254@sasktel.net
www.rmloreburn.ca
Municipal Type: Rural Municipalities
Incorporated: Dec. 12, 1910; *Area:* 966.78 sq km
Population in 2011: 346
Federal Electoral District(s): Moose Jaw-Lake Centre-Lanigan
Next Election: Oct. 26, 2016 (4 year terms)
Kevin Vollmer, Reeve
Vanessa Tastad, Administrator

Lost River No. 313
P.O. Box 159
Allan, SK S0K 0C0
Tel: 306-257-3272; *Fax:* 306-257-3337
rm313@sasktel.net
Municipal Type: Rural Municipalities
Incorporated: Dec. 11, 1911; *Area:* 549.90 sq km
Population in 2011: 209
Federal Electoral District(s): Moose Jaw-Lake Centre-Lanigan
Next Election: Oct. 26, 2016 (4 year terms)
Charles E. Smith, Reeve
Christine Dyck, Administrator

Lumsden No. 189
P.O. Box 160
300 James St. North
Lumsden, SK S0G 3C0
Tel: 306-731-2404; *Fax:* 306-731-3572
rm189@sasktel.net
www.lumsden.ca
Municipal Type: Rural Municipalities
Incorporated: Dec. 9, 1912; *Area:* 818.66 sq km
Population in 2011: 1,733
Federal Electoral District(s): Moose Jaw-Lake Centre-Lanigan; Regina-Qu'Appelle
Next Election: Oct. 26, 2016 (4 year terms)
Jim Hipkin, Reeve, 306-731-3255
Darcie Cooper, Chief Administrative Officer

Manitou Lake No. 442
P.O. Box 69
Marsden, SK S0M 1P0
Tel: 306-826-5215; *Fax:* 306-826-5512
rm442@sasktel.net
www.rmmanitou.ca
Municipal Type: Rural Municipalities
Incorporated: Dec. 12, 1910; *Area:* 850.32 sq km
Population in 2011: 547
Federal Electoral District(s): Battlefords-Lloydminster
Next Election: Oct. 26, 2016 (4 year terms)
Ian Lamb, Reeve
Joanne Loy, Administrator

Mankota No. 45
P.O. Box 148
Mankota, SK S0H 2W0
Tel: 306-478-2323; *Fax:* 306-478-2606
rm45.46@sasktel.net
Municipal Type: Rural Municipalities
Incorporated: Jan. 1, 1913; *Area:* 1,696.22 sq km
Population in 2011: 322
Federal Electoral District(s): Cypress Hills-Grasslands
Next Election: Oct. 26, 2016 (4 year terms)
Gary Munford, Reeve
Michael E. Sherven, Administrator

Maple Bush No. 224
P.O. Box 160
Riverhurst, SK S0H 3P0
Tel: 306-353-2292; *Fax:* 306-353-2293
rm224@xplornet.com
Municipal Type: Rural Municipalities
Incorporated: Dec. 13, 1909; *Area:* 811.95 sq km
Population in 2011: 167
Federal Electoral District(s): Cypress Hills-Grasslands
Next Election: Oct. 26, 2016 (4 year terms)
Maurice Bartzen, Reeve
JoAnne Wandler, Administrator

Maple Creek No. 111
P.O. Box 188
Maple Creek, SK S0N 1N0
Tel: 306-662-2300; *Fax:* 306-662-3566
rm111@sasktel.net
Municipal Type: Rural Municipalities
Incorporated: Dec. 10, 1917; *Area:* 3,242.96 sq km
Population in 2011: 1,154
Federal Electoral District(s): Cypress Hills-Grasslands
Next Election: Oct. 26, 2016 (4 year terms)
Howard Eiserman, Reeve
Barbi-Rose Weisgerber, Administrator

Mariposa No. 350
P.O. Box 228
603 Atlantic Ave.
Kerrobert, SK S0L 1R0
Tel: 306-834-5037; *Fax:* 306-834-5047
rm350@sasktel.net
Municipal Type: Rural Municipalities
Incorporated: Dec. 12, 1910; *Area:* 636.73 sq km
Population in 2011: 220
Federal Electoral District(s): Battlefords-Lloydminster
Next Election: Oct. 26, 2016 (4 year terms)
Robert Grobb, Reeve
Kathy Wurz, Administrator

Marquis No. 191
P.O. Box 40
Marquis, SK S0H 2X0
Tel: 306-788-2022; *Fax:* 306-788-2168
rm191@sasktel.net
myrm.ca/191
Municipal Type: Rural Municipalities
Incorporated: Dec. 11, 1911; *Area:* 805.48 sq km
Population in 2011: 252
Federal Electoral District(s): Moose Jaw-Lake Centre-Lanigan
Next Election: Oct. 26, 2016 (4 year terms)
Kenneth Waldenberger, Reeve
Ronald Gasper, Administrator

Marriott No. 317
P.O. Box 366
Rosetown, SK S0L 2V0
Tel: 306-882-4030; *Fax:* 306-882-4401
rm317@sasktel.net
Municipal Type: Rural Municipalities
Incorporated: Dec. 12, 1910; *Area:* 843.29 sq km
Population in 2011: 372
Federal Electoral District(s): Carlton Trail-Eagle Creek
Next Election: Oct. 26, 2016 (4 year terms)
Colin Ahrens, Reeve
Jill Omiecinski, Administrator

Martin No. 122
P.O. Box 1109
Moosomin, SK S0G 3N0
Tel: 306-435-3113; *Fax:* 306-435-4313
rm121@sasktel.net
www.myrm.ca/122
Municipal Type: Rural Municipalities
Incorporated: Jan. 1, 1913; *Area:* 556.50 sq km
Population in 2011: 333
Federal Electoral District(s): Souris-Moose Mountain
Next Election: Oct. 26, 2016 (4 year terms)
Gerald Flaman, Reeve
Cheryl Barrett, Administrator

Maryfield No. 91
P.O. Box 70
Maryfield, SK S0G 3K0
Tel: 306-646-2033; *Fax:* 306-646-2033
rm91@sasktel.net
Municipal Type: Rural Municipalities
Incorporated: Dec. 9, 1912; *Area:* 759.63 sq km
Population in 2011: 319
Federal Electoral District(s): Souris-Moose Mountain
Next Election: Oct. 26, 2016 (4 year terms)
Cameron Thompson, Reeve
Anna Macksymchuk, Administrator

Mayfield No. 406
P.O. Box 100
Maymont, SK S0M 1T0
Tel: 306-389-2112; *Fax:* 306-389-2162
rm406@sasktel.net
Municipal Type: Rural Municipalities
Incorporated: Dec. 13, 1909; *Area:* 782.50 sq km
Population in 2011: 389
Federal Electoral District(s): Battlefords-Lloydminster; Carlton Trail-Eagle Creek
Next Election: Oct. 26, 2016 (4 year terms)
Craig Hamilton, Reeve
Laurie DuBois, Administrator

McCraney No. 282
P.O. Box 129
Kenaston, SK S0G 2N0
Tel: 306-252-2240; *Fax:* 306-252-2248
rm282@sasktel.net
Municipal Type: Rural Municipalities
Incorporated: Dec. 13, 1909; *Area:* 948.36 sq km
Population in 2011: 307
Federal Electoral District(s): Moose Jaw-Lake Centre-Lanigan
Next Election: Oct. 26, 2016 (4 year terms)
Murray Kadlec, Reeve
Mark Zdunich, Administrator

McKillop No. 220
P.O. Box 369
2 - 200 Mountain St.
Strasbourg, SK S0G 4V0
Tel: 306-725-3230; *Fax:* 306-725-3206
rm220@sasktel.net
www.rmofmckillop220.com
Municipal Type: Rural Municipalities
Incorporated: Dec. 13, 1909; *Area:* 668.45 sq km
Population in 2011: 575
Federal Electoral District(s): Moose Jaw-Lake Centre-Lanigan
Next Election: Oct. 26, 2016 (4 year terms)
Gary Gilbert, Reeve, 306-725-3062
Michele Cruise-Pratchler, Administrator

McLeod No. 185
P.O. Box 130
Neudorf, SK S0A 2T0
Tel: 306-748-2233; *Fax:* 306-748-2647
rm185@sasktel.net
Municipal Type: Rural Municipalities
Incorporated: Jan. 1, 1913; *Area:* 886.6 sq km
Population in 2011: 446
Federal Electoral District(s): Regina-Qu'Appelle; Souris-Moose Mountain; Yorkton-Melville
Next Election: Oct. 26, 2016 (4 year terms)
Wilfred G. Goebel, Reeve
Murray J. Hanowski, Administrator

Meadow Lake No. 588
P.O. Box 668
#1, 225 Centre St.
Meadow Lake, SK S9X 1L5
Tel: 306-236-5651; *Fax:* 306-236-3115
rm588@sasktel.net
rmmeadowlake.com
Municipal Type: Rural Municipalities
Incorporated: Feb. 1, 1976; *Area:* 6,303.31 sq km
Population in 2011: 2,677
Federal Electoral District(s): Desnethé-Missinippi-Churchill River
Next Election: Oct. 26, 2016 (4 year terms)
Roger Zuchotzki, Reeve
Gina Bernier, Administrator

Medstead No. 497
P.O. Box 12
209 - 2nd Avenue
Medstead, SK S0M 1W0
Tel: 306-342-4609; *Fax:* 306-342-2067
rm497@sasktel.net
Municipal Type: Rural Municipalities
Incorporated: Jan. 1, 1913; *Area:* 1,203.22 sq km
Population in 2011: 513
Federal Electoral District(s): Battlefords-Lloydminster; Desnethé-Missinippi-Churchill River
Next Election: Oct. 26, 2016 (4 year terms)
Albert Schmirler, Reeve
Christin Egeland, Administrator

Meeting Lake No. 466
P.O. Box 26
Mayfair, SK S0M 1S0
Tel: 306-246-4228; *Fax:* 306-246-4974
rm466@sasktel.net
www.myrm.ca/466
Municipal Type: Rural Municipalities
Incorporated: Jan. 1, 1913; *Area:* 1,066.74 sq km
Population in 2011: 376
Federal Electoral District(s): Carlton Trail-Eagle Creek
Next Election: Oct. 26, 2016 (4 year terms)
Randy Aumack, Reeve
Janelle Lavallee, Administrator

Meota No. 468
P.O. Box 80
300 - 1st St. East
Meota, SK S0M 1X0
Tel: 306-892-2061; *Fax:* 306-892-2449
rm.468@sasktel.net
www.rmmeota468.ca
Municipal Type: Rural Municipalities
Incorporated: Dec. 13, 1909; *Area:* 651.09 sq km
Population in 2011: 936
Federal Electoral District(s): Battlefords-Lloydminster
Next Election: Oct. 26, 2016 (4 year terms)
Wilbert Fennig, Reeve
Nicolle Griffith, Administrator

Mervin No. 499
P.O. Box 130
211 Main St.
Turtleford, SK S0M 2Y0
Tel: 306-845-2045; *Fax:* 306-845-2950
rm499@sasktel.net
www.rmofmervin.com
Municipal Type: Rural Municipalities
Incorporated: Jan. 1, 1913; *Area:* 1,594.64 sq km
Population in 2011: 1,224
Federal Electoral District(s): Battlefords-Lloydminster
Next Election: Oct. 26, 2016 (4 year terms)
Tom Brown, Reeve, 306-845-2325
L. Ryan Domotor, Administrator

Milden No. 286
P.O. Box 160
113 Centre St.
Milden, SK S0L 2L0
Tel: 306-935-2181; *Fax:* 306-935-2046
rm286@sasktel.net
Municipal Type: Rural Municipalities
Incorporated: Dec. 12, 1910; *Area:* 735.31 sq km
Population in 2011: 283
Federal Electoral District(s): Carlton Trail-Eagle Creek
Next Election: Oct. 26, 2016 (4 year terms)
Arnold Somerville, Reeve
Melody Nieman, Administrator

Milton No. 292
P.O. Box 70
Marengo, SK S0L 2K0
Tel: 306-968-2922; *Fax:* 306-968-2278
rm292.rm322@sasktel.net
www.myrm.ca/292
Municipal Type: Rural Municipalities
Incorporated: Dec. 11, 1911; *Area:* 655.76 sq km
Population in 2011: 312
Federal Electoral District(s): Cypress Hills-Grasslands
Next Election: Oct. 26, 2016 (4 year terms)
David Bond, Reeve
Robin Busby, Administrator

Miry Creek No. 229
P.O. Box 210
Abbey, SK S0N 0A0
Tel: 306-689-2281; *Fax:* 306-689-2901
rm229@sasktel.net
www.rm229.com
Municipal Type: Rural Municipalities
Incorporated: Jan. 1, 1913; *Area:* 1,220.38 sq km
Population in 2011: 374
Federal Electoral District(s): Cypress Hills-Grasslands
Next Election: Oct. 26, 2016 (4 year terms)
Note: On December 31st 2013, the village of Shackleton dissolved into the Rural Municipality of Miry Creek No. 229.
Morgan Powell, Reeve, 306-689-2643
Jan Stern, Administrator

Monet No. 257
P.O. Box 370
210 Railway Ave. East
Elrose, SK S0L 0Z0
Tel: 306-378-2212; *Fax:* 306-378-2212
rm257@sasktel.net
www.elrose.ca/r-m-of-monet-257
Municipal Type: Rural Municipalities
Incorporated: Dec. 13, 1909; *Area:* 1,591.75 sq km
Population in 2011: 495
Federal Electoral District(s): Cypress Hills-Grasslands
Next Election: Oct. 26, 2016 (4 year terms)
Duncan Campbell, Reeve
Lori McDonald, Administrator

Montmartre No. 126
P.O. Box 120
136 Central Ave.
Montmartre, SK S0G 3M0
Tel: 306-424-2040; *Fax:* 306-424-2065
rm126@sasktel.net
www.myrm.ca/126
Municipal Type: Rural Municipalities
Incorporated: Dec. 13, 1909; *Area:* 853.91 sq km
Population in 2011: 488
Federal Electoral District(s): Souris-Moose Mountain
Next Election: Oct. 26, 2016 (4 year terms)
Kenneth W. Weichel, Reeve
Dale Brenner, Administrator

Montrose No. 315
P.O. Box 129
First Ave. North
Delisle, SK S0L 0P0
Tel: 306-493-2694; *Fax:* 306-493-3057
rm315@sasktel.net
www.rmmontrose.ca
Municipal Type: Rural Municipalities
Incorporated: Dec. 13, 1909; *Area:* 898.38 sq km
Population in 2011: 712
Federal Electoral District(s): Carlton Trail-Eagle Creek
Next Election: Oct. 26, 2016 (4 year terms)
Murray Purcell, Reeve
Donna Goertzen, Administrator

Moose Creek No. 33
P.O. Box 10
118 - 5th St.
Alameda, SK S0C 0A0
Tel: 306-489-2044; *Fax:* 306-489-2112
rm33@sasktel.net
www.rmofmoosecreek.ca
Municipal Type: Rural Municipalities
Incorporated: Dec. 12, 1910; *Area:* 842.03 sq km
Population in 2011: 372
Federal Electoral District(s): Souris-Moose Mountain
Next Election: Oct. 26, 2016 (4 year terms)
Murray Rossow, Reeve, 306-483-7454
Sentura Freitag, Administrator

Moose Jaw No. 161
#3, 1410 Caribou St. West
Moose Jaw, SK S6H 7S9
Tel: 306-692-3446; *Fax:* 306-691-0015
rm161@sasktel.net
www.moosejawrm161.ca
Municipal Type: Rural Municipalities
Incorporated: Dec. 11, 1911; *Area:* 797.60 sq km
Population in 2011: 1,147
Federal Electoral District(s): Moose Jaw-Lake Centre-Lanigan
Next Election: Oct. 26, 2016 (4 year terms)
Ron Brumwell, Reeve, 306-694-1956
Mike Wirges, Administrator

Moose Mountain No. 63
P.O. Box 445
105 - 100 Main St.
Carlyle, SK S0C 0R0
Tel: 306-453-6175; *Fax:* 306-453-2430
rm63@sasktel.net
Municipal Type: Rural Municipalities
Incorporated: Dec. 11, 1911; *Area:* 740.91 sq km
Population in 2011: 480
Federal Electoral District(s): Souris-Moose Mountain
Next Election: Oct. 26, 2016 (4 year terms)
Lyle Brown, Reeve
Sandra McClement, Administrator

Moose Range No. 486
P.O. Box 699
40 Railway Dr.
Carrot River, SK S0E 0L0
Tel: 306-768-2212; *Fax:* 306-768-2211
rm486@sasktel.net
www.myrm.ca/486
Municipal Type: Rural Municipalities
Incorporated: Dec. 11, 1916; *Area:* 2,419.06 sq km
Population in 2011: 1,131
Federal Electoral District(s): Prince Albert
Next Election: Oct. 26, 2016 (4 year terms)
Bud Charko, Reeve, 306-768-2297
Richard C. Colborn, Administrator

Moosomin No. 121
P.O. Box 1109
602 Main St.
Moosomin, SK S0G 3N0
Tel: 306-435-3113; *Fax:* 306-435-4313
rm121@sasktel.net
www.rm121.com
Municipal Type: Rural Municipalities
Incorporated: Jan. 1, 1913; *Area:* 566.39 sq km
Population in 2011: 504
Federal Electoral District(s): Souris-Moose Mountain
Next Election: Oct. 26, 2016 (4 year terms)
David Moffatt, Reeve
Kendra Lawrence, Administrator

Morris No. 312
P.O. Box 130
121 Main St.
Young, SK S0K 4Y0
Tel: 306-259-2211; *Fax:* 306-259-2225
rm312@sasktel.net
www.young.ca/rm-morris.htm
Municipal Type: Rural Municipalities
Incorporated: Dec. 13, 1909; *Area:* 847.16 sq km
Population in 2011: 316
Federal Electoral District(s): Moose Jaw-Lake Centre-Lanigan
Next Election: Oct. 26, 2016 (4 year terms)
Dengler Gordon, Reeve
Pamela Garner, Administrator

Morse No. 165
P.O. Box 340
401 Main St.
Morse, SK S0H 3C0
Tel: 306-629-3282; *Fax:* 306-629-3212
rm165@sasktel.net
Municipal Type: Rural Municipalities
Incorporated: Dec. 11, 1911; *Area:* 1,244.38 sq km
Population in 2011: 401
Federal Electoral District(s): Cypress Hills-Grasslands
Next Election: Oct. 26, 2016 (4 year terms)
Bruce Gall, Reeve
Mark Wilson, Administrator

Mount Hope No. 279
P.O. Box 190
Semans, SK S0A 3S0
Tel: 306-524-2055; *Fax:* 306-524-4526
rm279@sasktel.net
www.myrm.ca/279
Municipal Type: Rural Municipalities
Incorporated: Dec. 11, 1911; *Area:* 1,669.29 sq km
Population in 2011: 567
Federal Electoral District(s): Moose Jaw-Lake Centre-Lanigan; Regina-Qu'Appelle
Next Election: Oct. 26, 2016 (4 year terms)
Len Kelln, Reeve
Cal Shaw, Administrator

Mount Pleasant No. 2
P.O. Box 278
1312 Railway Ave.
Carnduff, SK S0C 0S0
Tel: 306-482-3313; *Fax:* 306-482-3422
rm.2@sasktel.net
Municipal Type: Rural Municipalities
Incorporated: Dec. 11, 1911; *Area:* 781.48 sq km
Population in 2011: 383
Federal Electoral District(s): Souris-Moose Mountain
Next Election: Oct. 26, 2016 (4 year terms)
Slade Boyes, Reeve
Valerie A. Olney, Administrator

Mountain View No. 318
P.O. Box 130
Herschel, SK S0L 1L0
Tel: 306-377-2144; *Fax:* 306-377-2023
rm318@sasktel.net
Municipal Type: Rural Municipalities
Incorporated: Dec. 13, 1909; *Area:* 838.67 sq km
Population in 2011: 333
Federal Electoral District(s): Carlton Trail-Eagle Creek
Next Election: Oct. 26, 2016 (4 year terms)
Rodney G. Wiens, Reeve
Rachel Deobald, Administrator

Newcombe No. 260
P.O. Box 40
Glidden, SK S0L 1H0
Tel: 306-463-3338; *Fax:* 306-463-4748
rm260@yourlink.ca
Municipal Type: Rural Municipalities
Incorporated: Dec. 11, 1911; *Area:* 1,075.6 sq km
Population in 2011: 400
Federal Electoral District(s): Cypress Hills-Grasslands
Next Election: Oct. 26, 2016 (4 year terms)
Ken McBride, Reeve
Monica Buddecke, Administrator

Nipawin No. 487
P.O. Box 250
Codette, SK S0E 0P0
Tel: 306-862-9551; *Fax:* 306-862-2432
rm487@sasktel.net
www.myrm.ca/487
Municipal Type: Rural Municipalities
Incorporated: Dec. 9, 1912; *Area:* 886.73 sq km
Population in 2011: 1,030
Federal Electoral District(s): Prince Albert
Next Election: Oct. 26, 2016 (4 year terms)
Mark Knox, Reeve
Eunice Rudy, Administrator

North Battleford No. 437
#4, 1462 - 100th St.
North Battleford, SK S9A 0W2
Tel: 306-445-3604; *Fax:* 306-445-3694
rm437@sasktel.net
Municipal Type: Rural Municipalities
Incorporated: Dec. 12, 1910; *Area:* 797.20 sq km
Population in 2011: 733
Federal Electoral District(s): Battlefords-Lloydminster
Next Election: Oct. 26, 2016 (4 year terms)
Dan Bartko, Reeve
Debbie Arsenault, Administrator

North Qu'Appelle No. 187
P.O. Box 99
Fort Qu'Appelle, SK S0G 1S0
Tel: 306-332-5202; *Fax:* 306-332-6028
rm187@sasktel.net
Municipal Type: Rural Municipalities
Incorporated: Dec. 12, 1910; *Area:* 494.98 sq km
Population in 2011: 728
Federal Electoral District(s): Regina-Qu'Appelle
Next Election: Oct. 26, 2016 (4 year terms)
Harry McDonald, Reeve
Marcy Johnson, Administrator

Norton No. 69
P.O. Box 189
410 Mergens St.
Pangman, SK S0C 2C0
Tel: 306-442-2131; *Fax:* 306-442-2144
rm.69@sasktel.net
www.myrm.ca/069
Municipal Type: Rural Municipalities
Incorporated: Dec. 13, 1909; *Area:* 844.8 sq km
Population in 2011: 259
Federal Electoral District(s): Souris-Moose Mountain
Next Election: Oct. 26, 2016 (4 year terms)
Leon Van de Walle, Reeve
Tina Douglas, Administrator

Oakdale No. 320
P.O. Box 249
200 Main St.
Coleville, SK S0L 0K0
Tel: 306-965-2281; *Fax:* 306-965-2466
rm320@sasktel.net
www.colevillesk.ca
Other Information: Alt. E-mail: rmoakassist@sasktel.net
Municipal Type: Rural Municipalities
Incorporated: Dec. 13, 1909; *Area:* 806.52 sq km
Population in 2011: 258
Federal Electoral District(s): Battlefords-Lloydminster
Next Election: Oct. 26, 2016 (4 year terms)
Darwin Whitfield, Reeve
Gillain Lund, Administrator

Old Post No. 43
P.O. Box 70
Wood Mountain, SK S0H 4L0
Tel: 306-266-2002; *Fax:* 306-266-2020
rm43@sasktel.net
Municipal Type: Rural Municipalities
Incorporated: Jan. 1, 1967; *Area:* 1,757 sq km
Population in 2011: 395
Federal Electoral District(s): Cypress Hills-Grasslands
Next Election: Oct. 26, 2016 (4 year terms)
Vickie Greffard, Administrator

Orkney No. 244
26 - 5th Ave. North
Yorkton, SK S3N 0Y8
Tel: 306-782-2333; *Fax:* 306-782-5177
orkney@sasktel.net
Municipal Type: Rural Municipalities
Incorporated: Jan. 1, 1913; *Area:* 815.87 sq km
Population in 2011: 1,860
Federal Electoral District(s): Yorkton-Melville
Next Election: Oct. 26, 2016 (4 year terms)
Dale Rhinas, Reeve
Clint Mauthe, Administrator

Paddockwood No. 520
P.O. Box 187
Paddockwood, SK S0J 1Z0
Tel: 306-989-2124; *Fax:* 306-989-4625
rm520@sasktel.net
www.rmofpaddockwood.com
Municipal Type: Rural Municipalities
Incorporated: Jan. 1, 1978; *Area:* 2,456.51 sq km
Population in 2011: 966
Federal Electoral District(s): Desnethé-Missinippi-Churchill River; Prince Albert
Next Election: Oct. 26, 2016 (4 year terms)
Leander (Lance) Fehr, Reeve, 306-982-4805
Naomi Hrischuk, Administrator

Parkdale No. 498
P.O. Box 310
Glaslyn, SK S0M 0Y0
Tel: 306-342-2015; *Fax:* 306-342-4442
rm498@sasktel.ca
www.rmofparkdale498.com
Municipal Type: Rural Municipalities
Incorporated: Jan. 1, 1913; *Area:* 1,388.91 sq km
Population in 2011: 631
Federal Electoral District(s): Battlefords-Lloydminster
Next Election: Oct. 26, 2016 (4 year terms)
Robert Pylypow, Reeve, 306-342-7325
Jennifer Ernst, Administrator, 306-845-8129, *Fax:* 306-845-3481

Paynton No. 470
P.O. Box 10
Paynton, SK S0M 2J0
Tel: 306-895-2020; *Fax:* 306-895-4800
rm470@sasktel.net
Municipal Type: Rural Municipalities
Incorporated: Jan. 1, 1913; *Area:* 593.95 sq km
Population in 2011: 268
Federal Electoral District(s): Battlefords-Lloydminster
Next Election: Oct. 26, 2016 (4 year terms)
Kevin Garrett, Reeve
Jade Johnson, Administrator

Pense No. 160
P.O. Box 190
324 Elder St.
Pense, SK S0G 3W0
Tel: 306-345-2303; *Fax:* 306-345-2583
rm160@sasktel.net
www.pense160.ca
Municipal Type: Rural Municipalities
Incorporated: Jan. 1, 1913; *Area:* 841.48 sq km
Population in 2011: 471
Federal Electoral District(s): Moose Jaw-Lake Centre-Lanigan
Next Election: Oct. 26, 2016 (4 year terms)
Tom Lemon, Reeve
Cathy Ripplinger, Administrator

Perdue No. 346
P.O. Box 208
Perdue, SK S0K 3C0
Tel: 306-237-4202; *Fax:* 306-237-4202
rm346@sasktel.net
www.myrm.ca/346
Municipal Type: Rural Municipalities
Incorporated: Dec. 13, 1909; *Area:* 826.14 sq km
Population in 2011: 463
Federal Electoral District(s): Carlton Trail-Eagle Creek
Next Election: Oct. 26, 2016 (4 year terms)
Bill Peters, Reeve
Allan Kirzinger, Administrator

Piapot No. 110
P.O. Box 100
Piapot, SK S0N 1Y0
Tel: 306-558-2011; *Fax:* 306-558-2125
rm110@sasktel.net
www.myrm.ca/110
Municipal Type: Rural Municipalities
Incorporated: Dec. 8, 1913; *Area:* 1,912.81 sq km
Population in 2011: 324
Federal Electoral District(s): Cypress Hills-Grasslands
Next Election: Oct. 26, 2016 (4 year terms)
John Wagner, Reeve
Jenny Robinson, Administrator

Pinto Creek No. 75
P.O. Box 239
Kincaid, SK S0H 2J0
Tel: 306-264-3277; *Fax:* 306-264-3254
rm75@sasktel.net
Municipal Type: Rural Municipalities
Incorporated: Jan. 1, 1913; *Area:* 845.01 sq km
Population in 2011: 239
Federal Electoral District(s): Cypress Hills-Grasslands
Next Election: Oct. 26, 2016 (4 year terms)
Brian Corcoran, Reeve
Roxanne Empey, Administrator

Pittville No. 169
P.O. Box 150
Hazlet, SK S0N 1E0
Tel: 306-678-2131; *Fax:* 306-678-2132
rm169@sasktel.net
Municipal Type: Rural Municipalities
Incorporated: Jan. 1, 1913; *Area:* 1,258.06 sq km
Population in 2011: 204
Federal Electoral District(s): Cypress Hills-Grasslands
Next Election: Oct. 26, 2016 (4 year terms)
Larry Sletten, Reeve
Terry Erdelyan, Administrator

Pleasant Valley No. 288
P.O. Box 2080
Rosetown, SK S0L 2V0
Tel: 306-882-4030; *Fax:* 306-882-4401
rm317@sasktel.net
Municipal Type: Rural Municipalities
Incorporated: Dec. 11, 1911; *Area:* 830.53 sq km
Population in 2011: 345
Federal Electoral District(s): Carlton Trail-Eagle Creek
Next Election: Oct. 26, 2016 (4 year terms)
Blake Jeffries, Reeve
Jill Omiecinski, Administrator

Pleasantdale No. 398
P.O. Box 70
Naicam, SK S0K 2Z0
Tel: 306-874-5732; *Fax:* 306-874-2225
rm398@sasktel.net
Municipal Type: Rural Municipalities
Incorporated: Dec. 11, 1911; *Area:* 757.91 sq km
Population in 2011: 611
Federal Electoral District(s): Yorkton-Melville
Next Election: Oct. 26, 2016 (4 year terms)
Forrest Pederson, Reeve
Lowell Prefontaine, Administrator

Ponass Lake No. 367
P.O. Box 98
Rose Valley, SK S0E 1M0
Tel: 306-322-2162; *Fax:* 306-322-2168
rm367@sasktel.net
Municipal Type: Rural Municipalities
Incorporated: Jan. 1, 1913; *Area:* 770.21 sq km
Population in 2011: 527
Federal Electoral District(s): Yorkton-Melville
Next Election: Oct. 26, 2016 (4 year terms)
Allan Nelson, Reeve
Loretta Prevost, Administrator

Poplar Valley No. 12
P.O. Box 190
Rockglen, SK S0H 3R0
Tel: 306-476-2062; *Fax:* 306-476-2175
rm12@sasktel.net

Municipal Type: Rural Municipalities
Incorporated: Jan. 1, 1913; *Area:* 769.37 sq km
Population in 2011: 200
Federal Electoral District(s): Cypress Hills-Grasslands
Next Election: Oct. 26, 2016 (4 year terms)
Nairn Nielsen, Reeve
Lynn Fisher, Administrator

Porcupine No. 395
P.O. Box 190
440 McAllister Ave.
Porcupine Plain, SK S0E 1H0
Tel: 306-278-2368; *Fax:* 306-278-3473
rm395@sasktel.net
www.porcupineplain.com/residents/rm-of-porcupine-no-395
Municipal Type: Rural Municipalities
Incorporated: Feb. 28, 1944; *Area:* 2,339.96 sq km
Population in 2011: 820
Federal Electoral District(s): Yorkton-Melville
Next Election: Oct. 26, 2016 (4 year terms)
Dean Lanning, Reeve, 306-278-2037
Nicole Smith, Administrator

Prairie Rose No. 309
P.O. Box 89
Main St.
Jansen, SK S0K 2B0
Tel: 306-364-2013; *Fax:* 306-364-2088
rm309@sasktel.net
www.myrm.ca/309
Municipal Type: Rural Municipalities
Incorporated: Dec. 12, 1910; *Area:* 839.08 sq km
Population in 2011: 259
Federal Electoral District(s): Moose Jaw-Lake Centre-Lanigan; Regina-Qu'Appelle
Next Election: Oct. 26, 2016 (4 year terms)
Bruce Elke, Reeve
Joni Mack, Administrator

Prairiedale No. 321
P.O. Box 90
Main St.
Smiley, SK S0L 2Z0
Tel: 306-838-2020; *Fax:* 306-838-4343
rm321@sasktel.net
www.rmofprairiedale.ca
Municipal Type: Rural Municipalities
Incorporated: Dec. 13, 1909; *Area:* 546.74 sq km
Population in 2011: 253
Federal Electoral District(s): Battlefords-Lloydminster
Next Election: Oct. 26, 2016 (4 year terms)
Tim Richelhoff, Reeve, 306-384-5590
Charlotte Helfrich, Administrator

Preeceville No. 334
P.O. Box 439
33 - 1st Ave. NW
Preeceville, SK S0A 3B0
Tel: 306-547-2029; *Fax:* 306-547-2081
rm334@sasktel.net
www.townofpreeceville.ca
Municipal Type: Rural Municipalities
Incorporated: Jan. 1, 1913; *Area:* 1,394.80 sq km
Population in 2011: 859
Federal Electoral District(s): Yorkton-Melville
Next Election: Oct. 26, 2016 (4 year terms)
Richard Pristie, Reeve
Lisa Peterson, Administrator

Prince Albert No. 461
99 River St. East
Prince Albert, SK S6V 0A1
Tel: 306-763-2469; *Fax:* 306-763-6369
rm461@sasktel.net
www.rmprincealbert.ca
Municipal Type: Rural Municipalities
Incorporated: Dec. 9, 1912; *Area:* 1,019.01 sq km
Population in 2011: 3,580
Federal Electoral District(s): Prince Albert
Next Election: Oct. 26, 2016 (4 year terms)
Norma Sheldon, Reeve, 306-922-3453
Terrence Schneider, Administrator

Progress No. 351
P.O. Box 460
Luseland, SK S0L 2A0
Tel: 306-372-4322; *Fax:* 306-372-4146
rm351@sasktel.net
Municipal Type: Rural Municipalities
Incorporated: Dec. 12, 1910; *Area:* 803.09 sq km
Population in 2011: 260

Federal Electoral District(s): Battlefords-Lloydminster
Next Election: Oct. 26, 2016 (4 year terms)
Dennis Gintaut, Reeve
Kim Adams, Administrator

Reciprocity No. 32
P.O. Box 70
302 Highway 361
Alida, SK S0C 0B0
Tel: 306-443-2212; *Fax:* 306-443-2287
rm.of.reciprocity@sasktel.net
www.rmofreciprocity.ca
Municipal Type: Rural Municipalities
Incorporated: Dec. 11, 1911; *Area:* 733.06 sq km
Population in 2011: 386
Federal Electoral District(s): Souris-Moose Mountain
Next Election: Oct. 26, 2016 (4 year terms)
Alan Arthur, Reeve
Marilyn Larsen, Administrator

Redberry No. 435
P.O. Box 160
Hafford, SK S0J 1A0
Tel: 306-549-2333; *Fax:* 306-549-2435
rm435@littleloon.ca
Municipal Type: Rural Municipalities
Incorporated: Jan. 1, 1913; *Area:* 1,015.53 sq km
Population in 2011: 372
Federal Electoral District(s): Carlton Trail-Eagle Creek
Next Election: Oct. 26, 2016 (4 year terms)
Douglas Herring, Reeve
Alan Tanchak, Administrator

Redburn No. 130
P.O. Box 250
Rouleau, SK S0G 4H0
Tel: 306-776-2270; *Fax:* 306-776-2482
redrou@sasktel.net
Municipal Type: Rural Municipalities
Incorporated: Jan. 1, 1913; *Area:* 847.91 sq km
Population in 2011: 250
Federal Electoral District(s): Moose Jaw-Lake Centre-Lanigan
Next Election: Oct. 26, 2016 (4 year terms)
Ronald Hughes, Reeve
Guy Lagrandeur, Administrator

Reford No. 379
P.O. Box 100
214 - 2nd Ave. East
Wilkie, SK S0K 4W0
Tel: 306-843-2342; *Fax:* 306-843-2455
rm409@sasktel.net
Municipal Type: Rural Municipalities
Incorporated: Dec. 12, 1910; *Area:* 707.06 sq km
Population in 2011: 235
Federal Electoral District(s): Battlefords-Lloydminster
Next Election: Oct. 26, 2016 (4 year terms)
Gerald Gerlinsky, Reeve
Sherry Huber, Administrator

Reno No. 51
P.O. Box 90
Consul, SK S0N 0P0
Tel: 306-299-2133; *Fax:* 306-299-4433
rm51@sasktel.net
Municipal Type: Rural Municipalities
Incorporated: Dec. 11, 1911; *Area:* 3,460.66 sq km
Population in 2011: 399
Federal Electoral District(s): Cypress Hills-Grasslands
Next Election: Oct. 26, 2016 (4 year terms)
Brian McMillan, Reeve
Kim Lacelle, Administrator

Riverside No. 168
P.O. Box 129
211 Standard St.
Pennant, SK S0N 1X0
Tel: 306-626-3255; *Fax:* 306-626-3661
rm168@sasktel.net
www.rm168.ca
Municipal Type: Rural Municipalities
Incorporated: Jan. 1, 1913; *Area:* 1,295.21 sq km
Population in 2011: 490
Federal Electoral District(s): Cypress Hills-Grasslands
Next Election: Oct. 26, 2016 (4 year terms)
Richard Bye, Reeve
Brandi Prentice, Administrator

Rocanville No. 151
P.O. Box 298
Rocanville, SK S0A 3L0
Tel: 306-645-2055; *Fax:* 306-645-2697
rm151@sasktel.net
www.myrm.ca/151
Municipal Type: Rural Municipalities
Incorporated: Dec. 9, 1912; *Area:* 758.64 sq km
Population in 2011: 533
Federal Electoral District(s): Souris-Moose Mountain
Next Election: Oct. 26, 2016 (4 year terms)
Murray Reid, Reeve
Sylvia Anderson, Administrator

Rodgers No. 133
#4, 1410 Caribou St. West
Moose Jaw, SK S6H 7S9
Tel: 306-693-1329; *Fax:* 306-693-2810
rm133@sasktel.net
Municipal Type: Rural Municipalities
Incorporated: Dec. 9, 1912; *Area:* 719.80 sq km
Population in 2011: 101
Federal Electoral District(s): Cypress Hills-Grasslands
Next Election: Oct. 26, 2016 (4 year terms)
Lawrence Johnstone, Reeve
Charlene Loos, Administrator

Rosedale No. 283
P.O. Box 150
Hanley, SK S0G 2E0
Tel: 306-544-2202; *Fax:* 306-544-2252
rm283@sasktel.net
Municipal Type: Rural Municipalities
Incorporated: Dec. 13, 1909; *Area:* 921.50 sq km
Population in 2011: 515
Federal Electoral District(s): Moose Jaw-Lake Centre-Lanigan
Next Election: Oct. 26, 2016 (4 year terms)
Garry Dubyk, Reeve
Samantha Millard, Administrator

Rosemount No. 378
P.O. Box 184
Landis, SK S0K 2K0
Tel: 306-658-2034; *Fax:* 306-658-2028
rm378@sasktel.net
Municipal Type: Rural Municipalities
Incorporated: Dec. 12, 1910; *Area:* 571.35 sq km
Population in 2011: 198
Federal Electoral District(s): Battlefords-Lloydminster
Next Election: Oct. 26, 2016 (4 year terms)
A. Ed Egert, Reeve
Kara Kirilenko, Administrator

Rosthern No. 403
P.O. Box 126
2022 - 6th St.
Rosthern, SK S0K 3R0
Tel: 306-232-4393; *Fax:* 306-232-5321
rm403@sasktel.net
www.rmofrosthern.ca
Municipal Type: Rural Municipalities
Incorporated: Dec. 9, 1912; *Area:* 954.66 sq km
Population in 2011: 2,015
Federal Electoral District(s): Carlton Trail-Eagle Creek
Next Election: Oct. 26, 2016 (4 year terms)
Martin Penner, Reeve
Rochelle Neff, Administrator

Round Hill No. 467
P.O. Box 9
Rabbit Lake, SK S0M 2L0
Tel: 306-824-2044; *Fax:* 306-824-2044
rm467@yourlink.ca
www.myrm.ca/467
Municipal Type: Rural Municipalities
Incorporated: Dec. 11, 1911; *Area:* 815.21 sq km
Population in 2011: 319
Federal Electoral District(s): Battlefords-Lloydminster
Next Election: Oct. 26, 2016 (4 year terms)
Alvin Wiebe, Reeve
Cindy Miller, Administrator

Round Valley No. 410
P.O. Box 538
Unity, SK S0K 4L0
Tel: 306-228-2248; *Fax:* 306-228-3483
rm410@sasktel.net
www.myrm.ca/410
Municipal Type: Rural Municipalities
Incorporated: Dec. 13, 1909; *Area:* 810.57 sq km
Population in 2011: 361

Federal Electoral District(s): Battlefords-Lloydminster
Next Election: Oct. 26, 2016 (4 year terms)
Francis Boskill, Reeve
Mervin Bosch, Administrator

Rudy No. 284
P.O. Box 1010
400 Saskatchewan Ave. West
Outlook, SK S0L 2N0
Tel: 306-867-9349; *Fax:* 306-867-9898
rmrudy@sasktel.net
www.rmrudy.ca
Municipal Type: Rural Municipalities
Incorporated: Dec. 13, 1909; *Area:* 813.86 sq km
Population in 2011: 496
Federal Electoral District(s): Moose Jaw-Lake Centre-Lanigan
Next Election: Oct. 26, 2016 (4 year terms)
Dennis Fuglerud, Reeve, 306-867-8903
Trent Michelman, Administrator

St. Andrews No. 287
P.O. Box 488
Rosetown, SK S0L 2V0
Tel: 306-882-2314; *Fax:* 306-882-3287
rm.287@sasktel.net
www.myrm.ca/287
Municipal Type: Rural Municipalities
Incorporated: Dec. 12, 1910; *Area:* 805.30 sq km
Population in 2011: 532
Federal Electoral District(s): Carlton Trail-Eagle Creek
Next Election: Oct. 26, 2016 (4 year terms)
Garry Nisbet, Reeve
Joan Babecy, Administrator

St. Louis No. 431
P.O. Box 28
Hoey, SK S0J 1E0
Tel: 306-422-6170; *Fax:* 306-422-8520
rm431@sasktel.net
Municipal Type: Rural Municipalities
Incorporated: Jan. 1, 1913; *Area:* 790.18 sq km
Population in 2011: 969
Federal Electoral District(s): Prince Albert
Next Election: Oct. 26, 2016 (4 year terms)
Henry Gareau, Reeve
Louise Hodgson, Administrator

St. Peter No. 369
P.O. Box 70
Annaheim, SK S0K 0G0
Tel: 306-598-2122; *Fax:* 306-598-4526
rm369@sasktel.net
www.myrm.ca/369
Municipal Type: Rural Municipalities
Incorporated: Dec. 11, 1911; *Area:* 823.22 sq km
Population in 2011: 790
Federal Electoral District(s): Carlton Trail-Eagle Creek
Next Election: Oct. 26, 2016 (4 year terms)
Danny Breker, Reeve
Angie Peake, Administrator

St. Philips No. 301
P.O. Box 220
Pelly, SK S0A 2Z0
Tel: 306-595-2050; *Fax:* 306-595-4941
rm301@sasktel.net
Municipal Type: Rural Municipalities
Incorporated: Jan. 1, 1913; *Area:* 655.79 sq km
Population in 2011: 235
Federal Electoral District(s): Yorkton-Melville
Next Election: Oct. 26, 2016 (4 year terms)
Gilles Comeault, Reeve
Sheri Kosar, Administrator

Saltcoats No. 213
P.O. Box 150
Saltcoats, SK S0A 3R0
Tel: 306-744-2202; *Fax:* 306-744-2455
rm.saltcoats@sasktel.net
www.rmsaltcoats.ca
Municipal Type: Rural Municipalities
Incorporated: Dec. 9, 1912; *Area:* 830.58 sq km
Population in 2011: 673
Federal Electoral District(s): Yorkton-Melville
Next Election: Oct. 26, 2016 (4 year terms)
Don Taylor, Reeve, 306-898-2065
Ronald R. Risling, Administrator, 306-744-2202

Sarnia No. 221
P.O. Box 160
125 Roberts St.
Holdfast, SK S0G 2H0
Tel: 306-488-2033; *Fax:* 306-488-4609
rm.sarnia@sasktel.net
Municipal Type: Rural Municipalities
Incorporated: Dec. 13, 1909; *Area:* 870.11 sq km
Population in 2011: 266
Federal Electoral District(s): Moose Jaw-Lake Centre-Lanigan
Next Election: Oct. 26, 2016 (4 year terms)
Brian Gottselig, Reeve
Patti Vance, Administrator

Saskatchewan Landing No. 167
P.O. Box 40
Stewart Valley, SK S0N 2P0
Tel: 306-778-2105; *Fax:* 306-778-2152
rm167@sasktel.net
www.myrm.ca/167
Municipal Type: Rural Municipalities
Incorporated: Jan. 1, 1913; *Area:* 797.52 sq km
Population in 2011: 462
Federal Electoral District(s): Cypress Hills-Grasslands
Next Election: Oct. 26, 2016 (4 year terms)
Darwin Johnsgaard, Reeve
Corrie Lanceleve, Administrator

Sasman No. 336
P.O. Box 130
Kuroki, SK S0A 1Y0
Tel: 306-338-2263; *Fax:* 306-338-2048
rm336@yourlink.ca
Municipal Type: Rural Municipalities
Incorporated: Jan. 1, 1913; *Area:* 1,006.49 sq km
Population in 2011: 818
Federal Electoral District(s): Yorkton-Melville
Next Election: Oct. 26, 2016 (4 year terms)
Dwayne Nakrayko, Reeve
Shandy Wegwitz, Administrator

Scott No. 98
P.O. Box 210
Yellow Grass, SK S0G 5J0
Tel: 306-465-2512; *Fax:* 306-465-2802
rm98@sasktel.net
Municipal Type: Rural Municipalities
Incorporated: Dec. 13, 1909; *Area:* 850.08 sq km
Population in 2011: 176
Federal Electoral District(s): Souris-Moose Mountain
Next Election: Oct. 26, 2016 (4 year terms)
Douglas Watson, Reeve
Shelly Robertson, Administrator

Senlac No. 411
P.O. Box 130
Senlac, SK S0L 2Y0
Tel: 306-228-3339; *Fax:* 306-228-2264
rm411@sasktel.net
Municipal Type: Rural Municipalities
Incorporated: Jan. 1, 1913; *Area:* 1,026.25 sq km
Population in 2011: 195
Federal Electoral District(s): Battlefords-Lloydminster
Next Election: Oct. 26, 2016 (4 year terms)
Owen Mawbey, Reeve
Pauline Herle, Administrator

Shamrock No. 134
P.O. Box 40
Shamrock, SK S0H 3W0
Tel: 306-648-3594; *Fax:* 306-648-3687
rm134@sasktel.net
www.shamrockpark.ca
Municipal Type: Rural Municipalities
Incorporated: Dec. 9, 1912; *Area:* 757.52 sq km
Population in 2011: 227
Federal Electoral District(s): Cypress Hills-Grasslands
Next Election: Oct. 26, 2016 (4 year terms)
Wayne Rudd, Reeve
Jody Kennedy, Administrator

Shellbrook No. 493
P.O. Box 250
71 Main St.
Shellbrook, SK S0J 2E0
Tel: 306-747-2178; *Fax:* 306-747-4315
rm493@sasktel.net
www.rmofshellbrook.com
Municipal Type: Rural Municipalities
Incorporated: Jan. 1, 1913; *Area:* 1,237.29 sq km
Population in 2011: 1,533
Federal Electoral District(s): Prince Albert;
Desnethé-Missinippi-Churchill River
Next Election: Oct. 26, 2016 (4 year terms)
Robert Ernst, Reeve
Karen Beauchesne, Administrator

Sherwood No. 159
4400 Campbell St.
Regina, SK S4W 0L3
Tel: 306-525-5237; *Fax:* 306-352-1760
info@rmofsherwood.ca
www.rmofsherwood.ca
Municipal Type: Rural Municipalities
Incorporated: Dec. 11, 1911; *Area:* 719.32 sq km
Population in 2011: 929
Federal Electoral District(s): Regina-Qu'Appelle
Next Election: Oct. 26, 2016 (4 year terms)
Jeff Poissant, Reeve
Ron McCullough, Chief Administrative Officer

Silverwood No. 123
P.O. Box 700
Whitewood, SK S0G 5C0
Tel: 306-735-2500; *Fax:* 306-735-2524
rm123@sasktel.net
www.myrm.ca/123
Municipal Type: Rural Municipalities
Incorporated: Oct. 31, 1911; *Area:* 844.61 sq km
Population in 2011: 466
Federal Electoral District(s): Souris-Moose Mountain
Next Election: Oct. 26, 2016 (4 year terms)
William MacPherson, Reeve
Jennalee Beutler, Administrator

Sliding Hills No. 273
P.O. Box 70
Mikado, SK S0A 2R0
Tel: 306-563-5285; *Fax:* 306-563-4447
slidinghills_rm273@sasktel.net
Municipal Type: Rural Municipalities
Incorporated: Jan. 1, 1913; *Area:* 853.76 sq km
Population in 2011: 520
Federal Electoral District(s): Yorkton-Melville
Next Election: Oct. 26, 2016 (4 year terms)
Harvey Malanowich, Reeve
Todd Steele, Administrator

Snipe Lake No. 259
P.O. Box 786
213 Main St.
Eston, SK S0L 1A0
Tel: 306-962-3214; *Fax:* 306-962-4330
rm259@sasktel.net
Municipal Type: Rural Municipalities
Incorporated: Dec. 11, 1911; *Area:* 1,573.80 sq km
Population in 2011: 452
Federal Electoral District(s): Cypress Hills-Grasslands
Next Election: Oct. 26, 2016 (4 year terms)
Ted Koester, Reeve
Debbie Shaw, Administrator

Souris Valley No. 7
P.O. Box 40
Oungre, SK S0C 1Z0
Tel: 306-456-2676; *Fax:* 306-456-2480
rm07@sasktel.net
www.rmsv7.sasktelwebhosting.com
Municipal Type: Rural Municipalities
Incorporated: Dec. 13, 1909; *Area:* 817.52 sq km
Population in 2011: 240
Federal Electoral District(s): Souris-Moose Mountain
Next Election: Oct. 26, 2016 (4 year terms)
Steven Berg, Reeve
Erica Pederson, Administrator

South Qu'Appelle No. 157
P.O. Box 66
Qu'Appelle, SK S0G 4A0
Tel: 306-699-2257; *Fax:* 306-699-2671
rm157@sasktel.net
www.rm157.ca
Municipal Type: Rural Municipalities
Incorporated: Aug. 6, 1884; *Area:* 889.73 sq km
Population in 2011: 1,271
Federal Electoral District(s): Regina Qu'Appelle
Next Election: Oct. 26, 2016 (4 year terms)
Jeannie DesRochers, Reeve, 306-699-2814
Lynette Herauf, Administrator

Spalding No. 368
P.O. Box 10
Spalding, SK S0K 4C0
Tel: 306-872-2166; *Fax:* 306-872-2275
bob368@sasktel.net

Municipal Type: Rural Municipalities
Incorporated: Dec. 11, 1911; *Area:* 811.47 sq km
Population in 2011: 447
Federal Electoral District(s): Yorkton-Melville
Next Election: Oct. 26, 2016 (4 year terms)
Eugene Eggerman, Reeve
Cathy Holt, Administrator

Spiritwood No. 496
P.O. Box 340
Spiritwood, SK S0J 2M0
Tel: 306-883-2034; *Fax:* 306-883-2557
rm496@sasktel.net
www.rmofspiritwood.ca
Municipal Type: Rural Municipalities
Incorporated: Dec. 9, 1929; *Area:* 2,410.62 sq km
Population in 2011: 1,382
Federal Electoral District(s): Desnethé-Missinippi-Churchill River; Carlton Trail-Eagle Creek; Battlefords-Lloydminster
Next Election: Oct. 26, 2016 (4 year terms)
Shirley Dauvin, Reeve
Colette Bussiere, Administrator

Spy Hill No. 152
P.O. Box 129
Spy Hill, SK S0A 3W0
Tel: 306-534-2022; *Fax:* 306-534-2230
rm152@sasktel.net
www.myrm.ca/152
Municipal Type: Rural Municipalities
Incorporated: Dec. 11, 1911; *Area:* 679.28 sq km
Population in 2011: 366
Federal Electoral District(s): Yorkton-Melville
Next Election: Oct. 26, 2016 (4 year terms)
Bob Bruce, Reeve, 306-745-2551
Carey Nicholauson, Administrator

Stanley No. 215
P.O. Box 70
238 - 3rd Ave. West
Melville, SK S0A 2P0
Tel: 306-728-2818; *Fax:* 306-728-2818
rm.ofstanley@sasktel.net
Municipal Type: Rural Municipalities
Incorporated: Jan. 1, 1913; *Area:* 855.40 sq km
Population in 2011: 516
Federal Electoral District(s): Regina-Qu'Appelle; Yorkton-Melville
Next Election: Oct. 26, 2016 (4 year terms)
Kenneth Petlock, Reeve
Marie Steiner, Administrator

Star City No. 428
P.O. Box 370
Star City, SK S0E 1P0
Tel: 306-863-2522; *Fax:* 306-863-2255
r.m.starcity@sasktel.ca
www.myrm.ca/428
Municipal Type: Rural Municipalities
Incorporated: Jan. 1, 1913; *Area:* 824.85 sq km
Population in 2011: 911
Federal Electoral District(s): Prince Albert
Next Election: Oct. 26, 2016 (4 year terms)
Kenneth Naber, Reeve
Levina Cronk, Administrator

Stonehenge No. 73
P.O. Box 129
Limerick, SK S0H 2P0
Tel: 306-263-2020; *Fax:* 306-263-2013
rm73@sasktel.net
www.myrm.ca/073
Municipal Type: Rural Municipalities
Incorporated: Dec. 11, 1911; *Area:* 985.74 sq km
Population in 2011: 403
Federal Electoral District(s): Cypress Hills-Grasslands
Next Election: Oct. 26, 2016 (4 year terms)
Larry Lethbridge, Reeve
Tammy Franks, Administrator

Storthoaks No. 31
P.O. Box 40
Storthoaks, SK S0C 2K0
Tel: 306-449-2262; *Fax:* 306-449-2210
rm31@sasktel.net
Municipal Type: Rural Municipalities
Incorporated: Dec. 11, 1911; *Area:* 582.57 sq km
Population in 2011: 304
Federal Electoral District(s): Souris-Moose Mountain
Next Election: Oct. 26, 2016 (4 year terms)
Brian Chicoine, Reeve
Elissa Henrion, Administrator

Surprise Valley No. 9
P.O. Box 52
Minton, SK S0C 1T0
Tel: 306-969-2144; *Fax:* 306-969-2127
rmnine@sasktel.net
Municipal Type: Rural Municipalities
Incorporated: Jan. 1, 1913; *Area:* 813.38 sq km
Population in 2011: 193
Federal Electoral District(s): Souris-Moose Mountain
Next Election: Oct. 26, 2016 (4 year terms)
Herb Axten, Reeve
Loran Tessier, Administrator

Sutton No. 103
P.O. Box 100
Mossbank, SK S0H 3G0
Tel: 306-354-2414; *Fax:* 306-354-7725
rm102.103@sasktel.net
www.myrm.ca/103
Municipal Type: Rural Municipalities
Incorporated: Dec. 11, 1911; *Area:* 822.40 sq km
Population in 2011: 240
Federal Electoral District(s): Cypress Hills-Grasslands
Next Election: Oct. 26, 2016 (4 year terms)
Richard Nagel, Reeve
Sherry Green, Administrator

Swift Current No. 137
2024 South Service Rd. West
Swift Current, SK S9H 5J5
Tel: 306-773-7314; *Fax:* 306-773-9538
rmsc137@sasktel.net
www.rmswiftcurrent.ca
Municipal Type: Rural Municipalities
Incorporated: Dec. 12, 1910; *Area:* 1,107.7 sq km
Population in 2011: 2,032
Federal Electoral District(s): Cypress Hills-Grasslands
Next Election: Oct. 26, 2016 (4 year terms)
Robert Neufeld, Reeve, 306-773-4167
Linda Boser, Administrator

Tecumseh No. 65
P.O. Box 300
Stoughton, SK S0G 4T0
Tel: 306-457-2277; *Fax:* 306-457-3149
rm65@sasktel.net
www.myrm.ca/65
Municipal Type: Rural Municipalities
Incorporated: Dec. 13, 1909; *Area:* 826.11 sq km
Population in 2011: 270
Federal Electoral District(s): Souris-Moose Mountain
Next Election: Oct. 26, 2016 (4 year terms)
Zandra Slater, Reeve
Lloyd Muma, Administrator

Terrell No. 101
P.O. Box 60
Spring Valley, SK S0H 3X0
Tel: 306-475-2803; *Fax:* 306-475-2805
street101@sasktel.net
www.rmofterrell.ca
Municipal Type: Rural Municipalities
Incorporated: Jan. 1, 1913; *Area:* 864.06 sq km
Population in 2011: 224
Federal Electoral District(s): Moose Jaw-Lake Centre-Lanigan
Next Election: Oct. 26, 2016 (4 year terms)
Darrell Howe, Reeve, 306-354-2698
Kimberly Sippola, Administrator

Three Lakes No. 400
P.O. Box 100
Middle Lake, SK S0K 2X0
Tel: 306-367-2172; *Fax:* 306-367-2011
rm400@sasktel.net
Municipal Type: Rural Municipalities
Incorporated: Jan. 1, 1913; *Area:* 772.49 sq km
Population in 2011: 620
Federal Electoral District(s): Carlton Trail-Eagle Creek
Next Election: Oct. 26, 2016 (4 year terms)
Allen Baumann, Reeve
Tim Schmidt, Administrator

Tisdale No. 427
P.O. Box 128
Tisdale, SK S0E 1T0
Tel: 306-873-2334; *Fax:* 306-873-4442
rm427@sasktel.net
www.myrm.ca/427
Municipal Type: Rural Municipalities
Incorporated: Dec. 9, 1912; *Area:* 849.24 sq km
Population in 2011: 916
Federal Electoral District(s): Prince Albert
Next Election: Oct. 26, 2016 (4 year terms)
Ian Allan, Reeve
Fern Lucas, Administrator

Torch River No. 488
P.O. Box 40
White Fox, SK S0J 3B0
Tel: 306-276-2066; *Fax:* 306-276-2099
rm488@sasktel.net
www.rmtorchriver.ca
Municipal Type: Rural Municipalities
Incorporated: Jan. 1, 1950; *Area:* 5,179 sq km
Population in 2011: 1,468
Federal Electoral District(s): Prince Albert; Desnethé-Missinippi-Churchill River
Next Election: Oct. 26, 2016 (4 year terms)
Dave Smith, Reeve, 306-428-2807
Nathalie Hipkins, Administrator

Touchwood No. 248
P.O. Box 160
Punnichy, SK S0A 3C0
Tel: 306-835-2110; *Fax:* 306-835-2100
rm248@aski.ca
Municipal Type: Rural Municipalities
Incorporated: Dec. 12, 1910; *Area:* 706.72 sq km
Population in 2011: 267
Federal Electoral District(s): Regina-Qu'Appelle
Next Election: Oct. 26, 2016 (4 year terms)
Ernest Matai, Reeve
Lorelei Paulsen, Administrator

Tramping Lake No. 380
P.O. Box 129
104 Main St.
Scott, SK S0K 4A0
Tel: 306-247-2033; *Fax:* 306-247-2055
rmtrampinglake@xplornet.com
Municipal Type: Rural Municipalities
Incorporated: Dec. 12, 1910; *Area:* 615.56 sq km
Population in 2011: 410
Federal Electoral District(s): Battlefords-Lloydminster
Next Election: Oct. 26, 2016 (4 year terms)
Peter Volk, Reeve
Stacy Hawkins, Administrator

Tullymet No. 216
P.O. Box 190
Balcarres, SK S0G 0C0
Tel: 306-334-2366; *Fax:* 306-334-2930
rm216@sasktel.net
www.townofbalcarres.ca
Municipal Type: Rural Municipalities
Incorporated: Jan. 1, 1913; *Area:* 562.99 sq km
Population in 2011: 220
Federal Electoral District(s): Regina-Qu'Appelle
Next Election: Oct. 26, 2016 (4 year terms)
Larry Jankoski, Reeve
Sheila Keisig, Administrator

Turtle River No. 469
P.O. Box 128
Edam, SK S0M 0V0
Tel: 306-397-2311; *Fax:* 306-397-2346
rm469@sasktel.net
Municipal Type: Rural Municipalities
Incorporated: Dec. 9, 1912; *Area:* 664.49 sq km
Population in 2011: 360
Federal Electoral District(s): Battlefords-Lloydminster
Next Election: Oct. 26, 2016 (4 year terms)
Louis McCaffrey, Reeve
Nicole Collins, Administrator

Usborne No. 310
P.O. Box 310
220 St Samson St.
Guernsey, SK S0K 2M0
Tel: 306-365-2924; *Fax:* 306-365-2129
rm310@sasktel.net
Municipal Type: Rural Municipalities
Incorporated: Dec. 13, 1909; *Area:* 810.38 sq km
Population in 2011: 547
Federal Electoral District(s): Moose Jaw-Lake Centre-Lanigan
Next Election: Oct. 26, 2016 (4 year terms)
Ken Bartel, Reeve
Keith Schulze, Administrator

Val Marie No. 17
P.O. Box 59
Val Marie, SK S0N 2T0
Tel: 306-298-2009; *Fax:* 306-298-2224
rm17@sasktel.net

Municipal Type: Rural Municipalities
Incorporated: Jan. 1, 1969; *Area:* 3,105.26 sq km
Population in 2011: 405
Federal Electoral District(s): Cypress Hills-Grasslands
Next Election: Oct. 26, 2016 (4 year terms)
Larry Grant, Reeve
Cathy Legault, Administrator

Vanscoy No. 345
P.O. Box 187
Vanscoy, SK S0L 3J0
Tel: 306-668-2060; *Fax:* 306-668-1338
rm345@sasktel.net
www.rmvanscoy.ca
Municipal Type: Rural Municipalities
Incorporated: Dec. 13, 1909; *Area:* 866.68 sq km
Population in 2011: 2,714
Federal Electoral District(s): Carlton Trail-Eagle Creek
Next Election: Oct. 26, 2016 (4 year terms)
Floyd Chapple, Reeve, 306-329-4697
Tony Obrigewitch, Administrator

Victory No. 226
P.O. Box 100
Beechy, SK S0L 0C0
Tel: 306-859-2270; *Fax:* 306-859-2271
rm226@sasktel.net
Municipal Type: Rural Municipalities
Incorporated: Dec. 8, 1919; *Area:* 1,375.44 sq km
Population in 2011: 443
Federal Electoral District(s): Cypress Hills-Grasslands
Next Election: Oct. 26, 2016 (4 year terms)
Leah Ringrose, Reeve
Diane Watt, Administrator

Viscount No. 341
P.O. Box 100
215 Bangor Ave.
Viscount, SK S0K 4M0
Tel: 306-944-2044; *Fax:* 306-944-2016
patrm341@sasktel.net
www.myrm.ca/341
Municipal Type: Rural Municipalities
Incorporated: Dec. 13, 1909; *Area:* 831.23 sq km
Population in 2011: 371
Federal Electoral District(s): Moose Jaw-Lake Centre-Lanigan
Next Election: Oct. 26, 2016 (4 year terms)
Gordon Gusikoski, Reeve
Patrick T. Clavelle, Administrator

Wallace No. 243
26 - 5th Ave. North
Yorkton, SK S3N 0Y8
Tel: 306-782-2455; *Fax:* 306-782-5177
wallace@sasktel.net
www.rmwallace.ca
Municipal Type: Rural Municipalities
Incorporated: Dec. 11, 1911; *Area:* 832.01 sq km
Population in 2011: 879
Federal Electoral District(s): Yorkton-Melville
Next Election: Oct. 26, 2016 (4 year terms)
Garry Liebrecht, Reeve, 306-621-1776
Bridgette Rushkewich, Administrator

Walpole No. 92
P.O. Box 117
Wawota, SK S0G 5A0
Tel: 306-739-2545; *Fax:* 306-739-2777
rm92@sasktel.net
Municipal Type: Rural Municipalities
Incorporated: Dec. 12, 1910; *Area:* 844.66 sq km
Population in 2011: 338
Federal Electoral District(s): Souris-Moose Mountain
Next Election: Oct. 26, 2016 (4 year terms)
Hugh Smyth, Reeve
Deborah C. Saville, Administrator

Waverley No. 44
P.O. Box 70
Glentworth, SK S0H 1V0
Tel: 306-266-4920; *Fax:* 306-266-2077
rm44@yourlink.ca
Municipal Type: Rural Municipalities
Incorporated: Feb. 1, 1913; *Area:* 1,429.30 sq km
Population in 2011: 359
Federal Electoral District(s): Cypress Hills-Grasslands
Next Election: Oct. 26, 2016 (4 year terms)
Lloyd Anderson, Reeve
Deidre Nelson, Administrator

Wawken No. 93
P.O. Box 90
Wawota, SK S0G 5A0
Tel: 306-739-2332; *Fax:* 306-739-2222
rm93@sasktel.net
www.myrm.ca/093
Municipal Type: Rural Municipalities
Incorporated: Jan. 1, 1913; *Area:* 766.53 sq km
Population in 2011: 559
Federal Electoral District(s): Souris-Moose Mountain
Next Election: Oct. 26, 2016 (4 year terms)
Hector Lamontagne, Reeve
Linda Klimm, Administrator

Webb No. 138
P.O. Box 100
Webb, SK S0N 2X0
Tel: 306-674-2230; *Fax:* 306-674-2324
rm138@xplornet.com
www.myrm.ca/138
Municipal Type: Rural Municipalities
Incorporated: Dec. 13, 1909; *Area:* 1,098.78 sq km
Population in 2011: 533
Federal Electoral District(s): Cypress Hills-Grasslands
Next Election: Oct. 26, 2016 (4 year terms)
Dennis Fiddler, Reeve
Raylene Packet, Administrator

Wellington No. 97
P.O. Box 1390
2nd Ave.
Weyburn, SK S4H 3J9
Tel: 306-842-5606; *Fax:* 306-842-5601
rm97@sasktel.net
Municipal Type: Rural Municipalities
Incorporated: Dec. 13, 1909; *Area:* 838.68 sq km
Population in 2011: 356
Federal Electoral District(s): Souris-Moose Mountain
Next Election: Oct. 26, 2016 (4 year terms)
Kelly Schneider, Reeve
Heather Wawro, Administrator

Weyburn No. 67
23 - 6th St. NE
Weyburn, SK S4H 1A7
Tel: 306-842-2314; *Fax:* 306-842-1002
rm.67@sasktel.net
www.rmweyburn.ca
Municipal Type: Rural Municipalities
Incorporated: Dec. 13, 1909; *Area:* 811.70 sq km
Population in 2011: 1,048
Federal Electoral District(s): Souris-Moose Mountain
Next Election: Oct. 26, 2016 (4 year terms)
Carmen Sterling, Reeve, 306-842-5409
Pam Scott, Administrator

Wheatlands No. 163
P.O. Box 129
Mortlach, SK S0H 3E0
Tel: 306-355-2233; *Fax:* 306-355-2351
rm163@sasktel.net
Municipal Type: Rural Municipalities
Incorporated: Dec. 13, 1909; *Area:* 827.4 sq km
Population in 2011: 149
Federal Electoral District(s): Cypress Hills-Grasslands
Next Election: Oct. 26, 2016 (4 year terms)
Ryan Nilson, Reeve
Julie Gerbrandt, Administrator

Whiska Creek No. 106
P.O. Box 10
Vanguard, SK S0N 2V0
Tel: 306-582-2133; *Fax:* 306-582-4950
rm106@sasktel.net
Municipal Type: Rural Municipalities
Incorporated: Jan. 1, 1913; *Area:* 851.89 sq km
Population in 2011: 499
Federal Electoral District(s): Cypress Hills-Grasslands
Next Election: Oct. 26, 2016 (4 year terms)
Keith Carleton, Reeve
Teresa Richards, Administrator

White Valley No. 49
P.O. Box 520
Eastend, SK S0N 0T0
Tel: 306-295-3553; *Fax:* 306-295-3571
rm49@sasktel.net
Municipal Type: Rural Municipalities
Incorporated: Jan. 1, 1913; *Area:* 2,026.88 sq km
Population in 2011: 478
Federal Electoral District(s): Cypress Hills-Grasslands
Next Election: Oct. 26, 2016 (4 year terms)
James Leroy, Reeve
Edna Laturnus, Administrator

Willner No. 253
P.O. Box 250
101 Lincoln St.
Davidson, SK S0G 1A0
Tel: 306-567-3103; *Fax:* 306-567-3266
rm253@sasktel.net
www.rmwillner.com
Municipal Type: Rural Municipalities
Incorporated: Jan. 1, 1913; *Area:* 834.97 sq km
Population in 2011: 245
Federal Electoral District(s): Moose Jaw-Lake Centre-Lanigan
Next Election: Oct. 26, 2016 (4 year terms)
Len Palmer, Reeve, 306-567-7034
Yvonne (Bonny) Goodsman, Administrator

Willow Bunch No. 42
P.O. Box 220
16 Edouard Beaupré St.
Willow Bunch, SK S0H 4K0
Tel: 306-473-2450; *Fax:* 306-473-2312
rm.42@sasktel.net
www.willowbunch.ca
Municipal Type: Rural Municipalities
Incorporated: Nov. 21, 1912; *Area:* 1,047.8 sq km
Population in 2011: 361
Federal Electoral District(s): Cypress Hills-Grasslands
Next Election: Oct. 26, 2016 (4 year terms)
David Kirby, Reeve
Margaret L. Brown, Administrator

Willow Creek No. 458
P.O. Box 5
Brooksby, SK S0E 0H0
Tel: 306-863-4143; *Fax:* 306-863-2366
rm458@staffcomm.com
www.myrm.ca/458
Municipal Type: Rural Municipalities
Incorporated: Dec. 9, 1912; *Area:* 845.18 sq km
Population in 2011: 693
Federal Electoral District(s): Prince Albert
Next Election: Oct. 26, 2016 (4 year terms)
James Arsenie, Reeve
Vicki Baptist, Administrator

Willowdale No. 153
P.O. Box 58
Whitewood, SK S0G 5C0
Tel: 306-735-2344; *Fax:* 306-735-4495
rm153@sasktel.net
www.myrm.ca/153
Municipal Type: Rural Municipalities
Incorporated: Jan. 1, 1913; *Area:* 605.06 sq km
Population in 2011: 297
Federal Electoral District(s): Souris-Moose Mountain
Next Election: Oct. 26, 2016 (4 year terms)
Kenneth Aldous, Reeve, 306-735-7634
Robert (Bob) Lang, Administrator

Wilton No. 472
P.O. Box 40
Marshall, SK S0M 1R0
Tel: 306-387-6244; *Fax:* 306-387-6598
info@rmwilton.ca
www.rmwilton.ca
Municipal Type: Rural Municipalities
Incorporated: Dec. 13, 1909; *Area:* 1,042.72 sq km
Population in 2011: 1,494
Federal Electoral District(s): Battlefords-Lloydminster
Next Election: Oct. 26, 2016 (4 year terms)
Glen Dow, Reeve
Darren Elder, Chief Administrative Officer

Winslow No. 319
P.O. Box 310
Dodsland, SK S0L 0V0
Tel: 306-356-2106; *Fax:* 306-356-2085
rm319@sasktel.net
www.myrm.ca/319
Municipal Type: Rural Municipalities
Incorporated: Dec. 13, 1909; *Area:* 798.07 sq km
Population in 2011: 324
Federal Electoral District(s): Battlefords-Lloydminster
Next Election: Oct. 26, 2016 (4 year terms)
Martin McGrath, Reeve
Regan MacDonald, Administrator

Wise Creek No. 77
P.O. Box 400
Shaunavon, SK S0N 2M0
Tel: 306-297-2520; *Fax:* 306-297-3162
rm77.78@sasktel.net
Municipal Type: Rural Municipalities
Incorporated: Jan. 1, 1913; *Area:* 843.85 sq km
Population in 2011: 157
Federal Electoral District(s): Cypress Hills-Grasslands
Next Election: Oct. 26, 2016 (4 year terms)
Denis Chenard, Reeve
Kathy Collins, Administrator

Wolseley No. 155
P.O. Box 370
Wolseley, SK S0G 5H0
Tel: 306-698-2522; *Fax:* 306-698-2664
rm155@sasktel.net
myrm.ca/155
Municipal Type: Rural Municipalities
Incorporated: Dec. 13, 1909; *Area:* 774.26 sq km
Population in 2011: 405
Federal Electoral District(s): Regina-Qu'Appelle; Souris-Moose Mountain
Next Election: Oct. 26, 2016 (4 year terms)
Bev Kenny, Reeve
Rose Zimmer, Administrator

Wolverine No. 340
P.O. Box 28
Burr, SK S0K 0T0
Tel: 306-682-3640; *Fax:* 306-682-3614
rm340@sasktel.net
www.myrm.ca/340
Municipal Type: Rural Municipalities
Incorporated: Dec. 13, 1909; *Area:* 834.78 sq km
Population in 2011: 464
Federal Electoral District(s): Moose Jaw-Lake Centre-Lanigan
Next Election: Oct. 26, 2016 (4 year terms)
Bryan Gibney, Reeve
Sandi Dunne, Administrator

Wood Creek No. 281
P.O. Box 10
303 George St.
Simpson, SK S0G 4M0
Tel: 306-836-2020; *Fax:* 306-836-4460
rm281@sasktel.net
www.myrm.ca/281
Municipal Type: Rural Municipalities
Incorporated: Dec. 13, 1909; *Area:* 832.34 sq km
Population in 2011: 205
Federal Electoral District(s): Moose Jaw-Lake Centre-Lanigan
Next Election: Oct. 26, 2016 (4 year terms)
John McArthur, Reeve
Darlene Mann, Administrator

Wood River No. 74
P.O. Box 250
35 - 2nd Ave. East
Lafleche, SK S0H 2K0
Tel: 306-472-5235; *Fax:* 306-472-3706
rm74@sasktel.net
www.myrm.ca/074
Municipal Type: Rural Municipalities
Incorporated: Dec. 9, 1912; *Area:* 838.45 sq km
Population in 2011: 324
Federal Electoral District(s): Cypress Hills-Grasslands
Next Election: Oct. 26, 2016 (4 year terms)
Duane Filson, Reeve
Brekke Massé, Administrator

Wreford No. 280
P.O. Box 99
Nokomis, SK S0G 3R0
Tel: 306-528-2202; *Fax:* 306-528-4411
rm280@sasktel.net
www.myrm.ca/280
Municipal Type: Rural Municipalities
Incorporated: Dec. 12, 1910; *Area:* 798.55 sq km
Population in 2011: 150
Federal Electoral District(s): Moose Jaw-Lake Centre-Lanigan
Next Election: Oct. 26, 2016 (4 year terms)
Dean Hobman, Reeve
Melanie Rich, Administrator

YUKON TERRITORY

The Department of Community Services administers the following key legislation regarding municipalities in the territory. Some of these Acts include: Municipal Act, Municipal Finance and Community Grants Act and Assessment and Taxation Act.

Requirements for municipal incorporation in the Yukon are based on population: town 300–2,500, city over 2,500. Any community may become a Local Advisory Area, an advisory body to the minister, as a first step in local governance. A community may also incorporate as a Rural Government with limited powers, as a developmental step in becoming a full municipality. The Yukon Municipal Act does not include provisions for unorganized settlements or First Nation communities.

Municipal elections are held every three years and polling day is the third Thursday of October in each election year. Mayors and councillors are elected for a three-year period (2018, 2021, etc.).

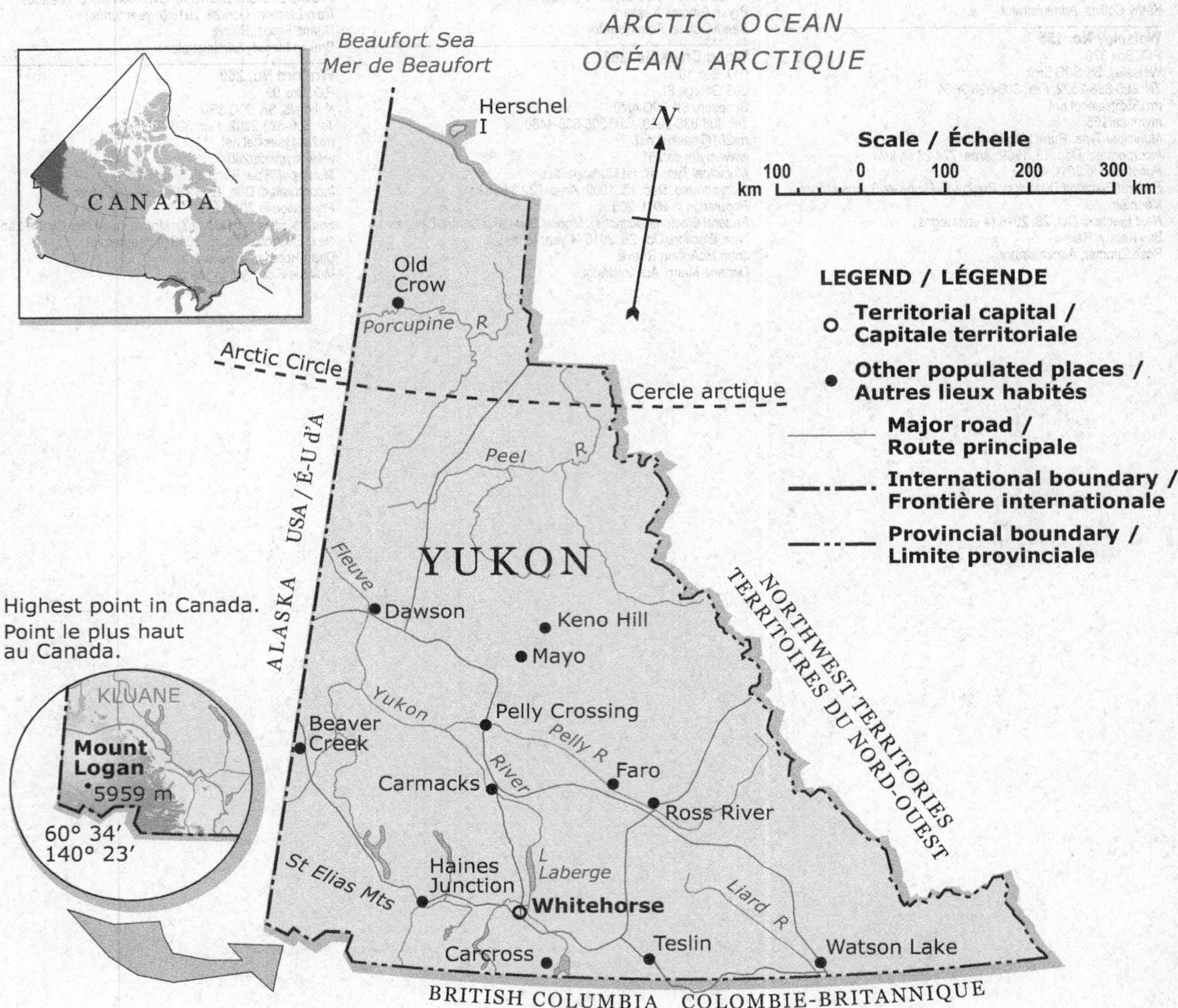

www.atlas.gc.ca

Yukon Territory

Major Municipalities in Yukon Territory

Whitehorse
2121 Second Ave.
Whitehorse, YT Y1A 1C2
Tel: 867-667-6401
mayorandcouncil@whitehorse.ca
city.whitehorse.yk.ca
Municipal Type: City
Incorporated: June 1, 1950; *Area:* 416.43 sq km
Population in 2011: 23,276
Provincial Electoral District(s): Whitehorse Centre; Whitehorse West; Copperbelt North; Copperbelt South; McIntyre-Takhini; Mountainview; Porter Creek Centre; Porter Creek North; Porter Creek South; Riverdale North; Riverdale South
Federal Electoral District(s): Yukon
Next Election: Oct. 2018 (3 year terms)
Dan Curtis, Mayor, 867-668-8626
Jocelyn Curteanu, Councillor, 897-336-3867
Rob Fendrick, Councillor
Betty Irwin, Councillor, 867-633-5499
Roslyn Woodcock, Councillor
Dan Boyd, Councillor
Samson Hartland, Councillor
Christine Smith, City Manager, 867-668-8626
Mike Gau, Director, Development Services, 867-335-4455
Linda Rapp, Director, Community & Recreation Services, 867-668-8329
Shannon Clohosey, Manager, Environmental Sustainability, 867-334-2111
Cheri Malo, Manager, Transit, 867-668-8391
Dave Pruden, Manager, Bylaw Services, 867-334-1082
Mike Stevely, Manager, Business & Information Technology, 867-334-2100
Wayne Tuck, Manager, Engineering Services, 867-668-8306
Kevin Lyslo, Fire Chief, 867-668-8383

Other Municipalities in Yukon Territory

Carmacks
P.O. Box 113
Carmacks, YT Y0B 1C0
Tel: 867-863-6271; *Fax:* 867-863-6606
carmacks@northwestel.net
carmacks.ca
Other Information: Public Works, Phone: 867-863-5503
Municipal Type: Village
Incorporated: Nov. 1, 1984; *Area:* 36.90 sq km
Population in 2011: 503
Provincial Electoral District(s): Mayo-Tatchun
Federal Electoral District(s): Yukon
Next Election: Oct. 2018 (3 year terms)
Lee Bodie, Mayor, 867-863-5656
Cory Bellmore, Chief Administrative Officer

Dawson City
P.O. Box 308
1336 Front St.
Dawson City, YT Y0B 1G0
Tel: 867-993-7400; *Fax:* 867-993-7434
cityofdawson.ca
Municipal Type: Town
Incorporated: Jan. 9, 1902; *Area:* 32.45 sq km
Population in 2011: 1,319
Provincial Electoral District(s): Klondike
Federal Electoral District(s): Yukon
Next Election: Oct. 2018 (3 year terms)
Wayne Potoroka, Mayor, 867-993-7400
André Larabie, Chief Administrative Officer, 867-993-7400

Deep Creek Development Area
Whitehorse, YT
Other Information: Yukon Land Planning Office Phone: 867-456-3827
Municipal Type: Local Advisory Area
Incorporated: 2001; *Area:* 1.39 sq km
Population in 2011: 20
Provincial Electoral District(s): Lake LaBerge
Federal Electoral District(s): Yukon

Faro
P.O. Box 580
200 Campbell St.
Faro, YT Y0B 1K0
Tel: 867-994-2728; *Fax:* 867-994-3154
cao-faro@faroyukon.ca
faroyukon.ca
Municipal Type: Town
Incorporated: June 13, 1969; *Area:* 203.57 sq km
Population in 2011: 344
Provincial Electoral District(s): Pelly-Nisutlin
Federal Electoral District(s): Yukon
Next Election: Oct. 2018 (3 year terms)
Jack Bowers, Mayor
Ian Dunlop, Chief Administrative Officer

Haines Junction
P.O. Box 5339
Haines Junction, YT Y0B 1L0
Tel: 867-634-7100; *Fax:* 867-634-2008
vhj@yknet.ca
hainesjunctionyukon.com
Municipal Type: Village
Incorporated: Oct. 1, 1984; *Area:* 34.08 sq km
Population in 2011: 593
Provincial Electoral District(s): Kluane
Federal Electoral District(s): Yukon
Next Election: Oct. 2018 (3 year terms)
Michael Riseborough, Mayor
Monika Schittek, Chief Administrative Officer, 867-634-7100

Ibex Valley
P.O. Box 20624
Whitehorse, YT Y1A 7A2
Tel: 867-667-7844; *Fax:* 867-393-1966
ibexvalleycommunity@gmail.com
ibexvalley.com
Municipal Type: Local Advisory Area
Area: 209.06 sq km
Population in 2011: 346
Provincial Electoral District(s): Kluane-Lake LaBerge
Federal Electoral District(s): Yukon
Martin Loos, Chair

Marsh Lake
P.O. Box 1325
Marsh Lake, YT Y0B 1Y1
Tel: 867-660-5347
marshlakelac@mail.com
Municipal Type: Local Advisory Area
Population in 2011: 619
Provincial Electoral District(s): Mount Lorne-Southern Lakes
Federal Electoral District(s): Yukon
Jo-Anne Smith, Co-Chair & Councillor, 867-660-4510, Wards: 4. Army Beach
Perry Savoie, Co-Chair & Councillor, 867-660-5116, Wards: 4. Army Beach
Helen Smith, Secretary/Treasurer & Councillor, 867-660-4402, Wards: 1. Judas Creek

Mayo
P.O. Box 160
Mayo, YT Y0B 1M0
Tel: 867-996-2317; *Fax:* 867-996-2907
mayo@northwestel.net
villageofmayo.ca
Municipal Type: Village
Incorporated: June 1, 1984; *Area:* 0.87 sq km
Population in 2011: 226
Provincial Electoral District(s): Mayo/Tatchun
Federal Electoral District(s): Yukon
Next Election: Oct. 2018 (3 year terms)
Scott Bolton, Mayor
Margrit Wozniak, Chief Administrative Officer, 867-996-4300

Mount Lorne
P.O. Box 10009
Whitehorse, YT Y1A 7A1
Tel: 867-667-7083; *Fax:* 867-667-7083
mtlorne@northwestel.net
mountlorne.yk.net
Municipal Type: Local Advisory Area
Area: 160.15 sq km
Population in 2011: 408
Provincial Electoral District(s): Mount Lorne-Southern Lakes
Federal Electoral District(s): Yukon
Al Foster, Chair & Councillor, 867-667-7083, Wards: Cowley Lake

South Klondike
P.O. Box 4
Carcross, YT Y0B 1B0
Tel: 867-821-3461
southklondikelac@gmail.com
Municipal Type: Local Advisory Area
Incorporated: Aug. 15, 2006; *Area:* 15.96 sq km
Population in 2011: 289
Provincial Electoral District(s): Mount Lorne-Southern Lakes
Federal Electoral District(s): Yukon
Daniel Kemble, Chair & Councillor, Wards: 3

Tagish
P.O. Box 92
Tagish, YT Y0B 1T0
Tel: 867-399-4002; *Fax:* 867-399-3006
tacadmin@tagishyukon.org
www.tagishyukon.org
Municipal Type: Local Advisory Area
Incorporated: 2005; *Area:* 43.38 sq km
Population in 2011: 391
Provincial Electoral District(s): Mount Lorne-Southern Lakes
Federal Electoral District(s): Yukon
Paul Dabbs, Chair & Treasurer, 867-399-2047
Randy Taylor, Administrator

Teslin
P.O. Box 32
Teslin, YT Y0A 1B0
Tel: 867-390-2530; *Fax:* 867-390-2104
info@teslin.ca
teslin.ca
Municipal Type: Village
Incorporated: Aug. 1, 1984; *Area:* 2.22 sq km
Population in 2011: 122
Provincial Electoral District(s): Pelly-Nisutlin
Federal Electoral District(s): Yukon
Next Election: Oct. 2018 (3 year terms)
Clara Jules, Mayor
Shelley Hassard, Chief Administrative Officer, 867-390-2530, Fax: 867-390-2104

Watson Lake
P.O. Box 590
710 Adela Trail
Watson Lake, YT Y0A 1C0
Tel: 867-536-8000; *Fax:* 867-536-7522
twl@northwestel.net
watsonlake.ca
Municipal Type: Town
Incorporated: April 1, 1984; *Area:* 5.16 sq km
Population in 2011: 802
Provincial Electoral District(s): Watson Lake
Federal Electoral District(s): Yukon
Next Election: Oct. 2018 (3 year terms)
Justin Brown, Mayor
Stephen Conway, Chief Administrative Officer, 867-536-8000

SECTION 9

GOVERNMENT: JUDICIAL

Following the federal listings, this section is arranged by province. Within each province, listings are by type of court, then by city.

Federal

Supreme Court of Canada
301 Wellington St., Ottawa, ON K1A 0J1
Tel: 613-995-4330; *Fax:* 613-996-3063
Toll-Free: 888-551-1185
reception@scc-csc.gc.ca
www.scc-csc.gc.ca
Other information: TTY: 613-944-7895; Registry, E-mail: registry-greffe@scc-csc.gc.ca; Court Library, E-mail: library-bibliotheque@scc-csc.gc.ca; Tours, E-mail: tour-visite@scc-csc.gc.ca

In 1875, the Supreme Court of Canada was created by an Act of Parliament. The Court is a general court of appeal, which consists of nine judges. The Governor in Council appoints the judges, who remain in the position until the age of 75. There is a Chief Justice of Canada, plus seven puisne judges. A Registrar is also appointed by the Governor in Council. The Registrar is responsible for all the administrative work in the Court, & answers directly to the Chief Justice. There are approximately 200 employees of the Supreme Court. The Supreme Court sits in Ottawa where, each year, three sessions are held. Approximately 80 appeals are heard by the Court every year. The hearings are open to the public. Cases for review come from the provincial & territorial appellate courts & the Federal Court of Appeal, in criminal, civil, constitutional & administrative law matters. Decisions of the Supreme Court of Canada may be unanimous, or a majority may decide. In July of 2016, The Right Hon. Justin Trudeau announced a new selection process for Supreme Court Justices. A seven-member, independent, non-partisan advisory board will identify suitable candidates. Any qualified Canadian lawyer or judge will be able to put forward their name for consideration by the board.

Chief Justice of Canada: The Rt. Hon. Madam Chief Justice Beverley McLachlin
Puisne Judges (The Honourable Mr. / Madam Justice)
Suzanne Côté
Rosalie Silberman Abella
Russell Brown
Michael J. Moldaver
Andromache Karakatsanis
Robert Wagner
Clément Gascon
Administration:
Registrar: Roger Bilodeau, 613-996-9277, Fax: 613-996-9138
Deputy Registrar: David Power, 613-996-7521, Fax: 613-941-5817
Director General: Corporate Services Sector, Catherine Laforce, 613-947-0682, Fax: 613-947-2860
Director: Library & Information Management Branch, Rosalie Fox, 613-996-9971, Fax: 613-991-0258
Director: Financial & Strategic Planning & Reporting, Tommy Pham, 613-992-1765, Fax: 613-947-2860
Director: Information Technology, Philippe Authier, 613-944-7722
Director: Human Resources, Anne-Marie Larivière, 613-995-4224, Fax: 613-996-7266

Federal Court of Appeal
Cour d'appel fédérale
Courts Administration Service, Thomas D'Arcy McGee Bldg., 90 Sparks St., Ottawa, ON K1A 0H9
Tel: 613-996-6795 *Toll-Free:* 800-565-0541
information@fca-caf.gc.ca
www.fca-caf.gc.ca
Other information: TTY: 613-995-4640

The Federal Court of Appeal was established by Parliament in accordance with provision of section 101 of the Constitution Act, 1867. The Court is a bilingual tribunal, which sits & hears cases anywhere in Canada. Both common law & civil law are administered by the Federal Court of Appeal. Decisions of the Federal Court of Appeal impact all Canadians. Responsibilities of the Court include enforcing rights & obligations between Canadians & the federal government, & interpreting & implementing Canada's international obligations.

Chief Justice of the Federal Court of Appeal: The Hon. Marc Noël, 613-995-5106
Judges (The Hon. Mr. / Madam Justice):
Yves de Montigny
Donald J. Rennie
Marc Nadon (Supernumerary)
C. Michael Ryer
613-995-2459
J.D. Denis Pelletier (Supernumerary)
613-947-0185
Eleanor R. Dawson
Johanne Gauthier
Johanne Trudel (Supernumerary)
613-944-2203
David W. Stratas
Mary Gleason
Wyman W. Webb
David G. Near
André F.J. Scott
Richard Boivin
Administration:
Judicial Administrator: Suzelle Bazinet, 613-995-5117, Fax: 613-952-6439

Court Martial Appeal Court of Canada
Cour d'Appel de la Cour Martiale
Courts Administration Service, Thomas D'Arcy McGee Bldg., 90 Sparks St., Ottawa, ON K1A 0H9
Tel: 613-996-6795; *Fax:* 613-952-7226
Media Enquiries: media-fca@fca-caf.gc.ca
www.cmac-cacm.ca
Other information: TTY: 613-947-0407

The Court Martial Appeal Court of Canada was established by the Parliament of Canada, pursuant to its authority under section 101 of the Constitution Act,1867. The Court administers the National Defence Act & the Criminal Code. The Court Martial Appeal Court of Canada hears appeals from military courts. Military courts, known as courts martial, try members of the Canadian Forces, as well as civilians accompanying military personnel abroad, for crimes & offences against the Code of Service Discipline. The Code of Service Discipline is found in Part III & Part VII of the National Defence Act. Military personnel are subjected to military law, except when the offence has little to do with their military role. Offences, such as murder & manslaughter, are tried in civilian courts. There is a right of appeal to the Supreme Court of Canada from the Court Martial Appeal Court of Canada on questions of law.

Chief Justice: The Hon. Mr. Justice B. Richard Bell, 613-995-7886
Designated Judges (The Hon. Mr. / Madam Justice):
René LeBlanc
Yvan Roy
Joanne B. Veit
Marc Noël
Sandra J. Simpson
Marc Nadon
Danièle Tremblay-Lamer
Karen M. Weiler
Cecily Y. Strickland
Douglas R. Campbell
Peter Annis
Elizabeth A. Bennett
Eleanor R. Dawson
Elizabeth Heneghan
Luc Martineau
Simon Noël
Johanne Gauthier
James O'Reilly
James Russell
J. David Watt
Glennys L. McVeigh
Deborah J. McCawley
Sean J. Harrington
Richard G. Mosley
Michel M.J. Shore
Michael L. Phelan
Anne L. Mactavish
Yves de Montigny
Roger T. Hughes
Robert L. Barnes
Johanne Trudel
Leonard S. Mandamin
Russel W. Zinn
Guy Cournoyer
Douglas N. Abra
Richard Boivin
David Near
Robert Mainville
Jamie W.S. Saunders
David W. Stratas
Paul S. Crampton
Marie-Josée Bédard
André J.F. Scott
Donald J. Rennie
François Doyon
André Vincent
Wyman W. Webb
Mary J.L. Gleason
Jocelyne Gagné
Catherine M. Kane
Michael D. Manson
Martine St-Louis
George R. Locke
Keith M. Boswell
Alan Diner
Henry S. Brown
Patrick K. Gleeson
J. Edward Scanlan
Vital Ouellette
Kathleen Quigg
Bradley V. Green
Administration:
Chief Administrator of the Court: Daniel Gosselin, 613-996-4778
Judicial Administrator: Diane Cyr, 613-995-7886

Tax Court of Canada
200 Kent St., Ottawa, ON K1A 0M1
Tel: 613-992-0901 *Toll-Free:* 800-927-5499
web@tcc-cci.gc.ca
www.tcc-cci.gc.ca
Other information: TTY: 613-943-0946

In 1983, the Tax Court of Canada was established, pursuant to the Tax Court of Canada Act. The Court operates independently of the Canada Revenue Agency & other departments of the Government of Canada. Many of the appeals to the Tax Court of Canada are related to income tax, the goods & services tax, & employment insurance. References are also heard from the Canada Revenue Agency to provide interpretations of the legislation within its jurisdiction.

Chief Justice: The Honourable Mr. Justice Eugene P. Rossiter, 613-992-1994
Associate Chief Justice: The Honourable Mr. Justice Lucie Lamarre, 613-992-2159
Pierre Archambault (Supernumerary Judge)
613-992-6743
Alain Tardif (Supernumerary Judge)
Diane Campbell (Supernumerary Judge)
Joe E. Hershfield (Supernumerary Judge)
Campbell J. Miller (Supernumerary Judge)
613-992-0739
Brent Paris
613-992-8477
Judith Woods
613-992-2368
Réal Favreau
613-992-0672
Gaston Jorré
613-947-0945
Patrick J. Boyle
613-947-5332
Valerie Miller
613-943-2915
Robert James Hogan
613-944-6300
Steven K. D'Arcy
613-947-0523
Frank J. Pizzitelli
613-947-2128
Johanne D'Auray
Randall S. Bocock
David E. Graham
Kathleen T. Lyons
John R. Owen
Dominique Lafleur
Sylvain Ouimet
Don R. Sommerfeldt
Henry A. Visser
Guy R. Smith
Administration:
Registrar of the Court: Donald MacNeil, 613-944-7758

Federal Court
Cour fédérale
Courts Administration Service, Thomas D'Arcy McGee Bldg., 90 Sparks St., Ottawa, ON K1A 0H9
Tel: 613-992-4238; *Fax:* 613-952-3653
Toll-Free: 800-663-2096
Media Enquiries: media-fct@fct-cf.gc.ca
www.fct-cf.gc.ca
Other information: TTY: 613-995-4640

The Federal Court is a trial court. The jurisdiction of the Federal Court is conferred by the Federal Courts Act, as well as close to one hundred other applicable federal statutes. Its broad federal jurisdiction includes the following: Crown litigation, access to information, admiralty & maritime disputes, citizenship, communications, customs, immigration & refugee matters, intellectual property rights, labour relations, national security, parole & penitentiary proceedings, tax, transportation & aeronautics, war veterans & limited criminal jurisdiction. The Court conducts hearings & renders decisions in disputes anywhere in Canada.

Chief Justice of the Federal Court: The Hon. Mr. Justice Paul S. Crampton, 613-996-5901
Judges (The Hon. Mr. / Madam Justice):
Sandra J. Simpson (Supernumerary)
613-943-2345
Danièle Tremblay-Lamer (Supernumerary)
613-947-1995
Douglas R. Campbell (Supernumerary)
613-947-7871

Elizabeth Heneghan
613-947-4654
Luc Martineau
613-995-1235
Simon Noël
613-944-4062
James Russell
613-947-2516
James W. O'Reilly
613-947-2491
Sean J. Harrington (Supernumerary)
613-947-4672
Richard Mosley
613-995-1276
Michel M.J. Shore
613-944-4090
Michael L. Phelan
613-943-1450
Anne L. Mactavish
613-943-1041
Roger T. Hughes
613-943-1913
Robert L. Barnes
613-947-4668
Leonard S. Mandamin
613-947-4785
Russel W. Zinn
613-947-9136
Jocelyne Gagné
Catherine M. Kane
Michael D. Manson
Yvan Roy
Cecily Y. Strickland
Peter B. Annis
Glennys L. McVeigh
René LeBlanc
Martine St-Louis
George R. Locke
Henry S. Brown
Alan Diner
Keith Boswell
Simon Fothergill
B. Richard Bell
Denis Gascon
Richard F. Southcottt
Patrick Gleeson
Robin Camp
E. Susan Elliot
Sylvie Roussel
Ann Marie McDonald

Prothonotaries:
Richard Morneau, 514-496-7840
Roger Lafrenière, 604-666-7435
Mireille Tabib, 613-947-2453
Martha Milczynski, 416-954-9006
Kevin R. Aalto, 416-954-9009
Mandy Aylen

Administration:
Registrar of the Federal Court: Manon Pitre
Judicial Administrator: Giovanna Calamo, 613-995-0108

Courts Administration Service
Service administratif des tribunaux judiciaires

Thomas D'Arcy McGee Bldg., 90 Sparks St., Ottawa, ON K1A 0H9
Tel: 613-943-4355
Media Enquiries: reception@cas-satj.gc.ca
www.cas-satj.gc.ca

In 2003, the Courts Administration Service was established by the Courts Administration Service Act, S.C. 2002, c. 8. The Courts Administration Service provides administrative services to the following courts of law: the Federal Court, the Federal Court of Appeal, the Tax Court of Canada, & the Court Martial Appeal Court of Canada. Examples of the duties of the Courts Administration Service are as follows: providing support services, such as library services, to judges, prothonotaries, & staff; maintaining courts records; providing facilities & security for judges, prothonotaries, & staff; & informing litigants on rules of practice & procedures.

Administration:
Chief Administrator: Daniel Gosselin, 613-996-4778
Deputy Chief Administrator, Judicial & Registry Services: Richard Tardiff, 613-943-3458
Deputy Chief Administrator & Chief Financial Officer: Corporate Services, Francine Côté, 613-996-1611
Director General: Information Management & Information Technology, Shane Brunas, 613-992-9393
Director General, Human Resources: Margarida Janeiro, 613-995-4453
Director General, Finance & Contracting Services: Paul Waksberg, 613-992-1745, Fax: 613-941-4915
Acting Director, Corporate Secretariat: Lucia Fevrier-President, 613-943-4782
Director, Library Services: Paul Sawa, 613-995-1382
Coordinator & Advisor: Communications, Adam Wilkinson, 613-943-4356

Registry of the Courts Administration Service
Principal Office, Ottawa, ON K1A 0H9

Local Offices:

Calgary
Canadian Occidental Tower, 635 - 8th Ave. SW, Calgary, AB T2P 3M3
Tel: 403-492-5555; *Fax:* 403-292-5329
Other information: TTY: 403-292-5329
Director: Patricia Esposito, 403-292-5328

Charlottetown
Sir Louis Henry Davies Law Courts Bldg., 42 Water St., P.O. Box 2000, Charlottetown, PE C1A 8B9
Tel: 800-565-0541
Registry Officer: Marjorie MacDonald

Edmonton
Tower 1, Scotia Place, #530, 10060 Jasper Ave., P.O. Box 51, Edmonton, AB T5J 3R8
Tel: 780-495-4651; *Fax:* 780-495-4681
Other information: TTY: 780-495-2428
Director: Kathy Dobransky, 780-495-2216

Fredericton
#100, 82 Westmorland St., Fredericton, NB E3B 3L3
Tel: 506-452-2036; *Fax:* 506-452-3584
Other information: TTY: 506-452-3036
Director: Willa Doyle, 506-452-3016
Registry Officer: Michel Morneault, 506-452-3016

Halifax
#1720, 1801 Hollis St., 17th Fl., Halifax, NS B3J 3N4
Tel: 902-426-5326; *Fax:* 902-426-5514
Other information: TTY: 902-426-9776
Director: Elizabeth Caverly, 902-426-3282
Registry Officer: Michael Kowalchuk, 902-426-3282

Québec
Palais de Justice, #500A, #500E, boul Jean Lesage, Québec, QC G1K 8K6
Tel: 418-648-4964; *Fax:* 418-648-4051
Other information: TTY: 418-648-4644
Director: Claire Drolet, 418-648-7778

Regina
Court House, 2425 Victoria Ave., Regina, SK S4P 3V7
Toll-Free: 800-565-0541
Acting Director: Gordon C Dauncey, 306-787-5380
Registry Officer: Margaret Pelletier, 306-787-5421

Saint John
Law Courts, 10 Peel Plaza, P.O. Box 5001, Saint John, NB E2L 3G6
Toll-Free: 800-565-0541
Registry Officer: Edward Joas, 506-636-4990

St. John's
#209, 354 Water St., St. John's, NL A1C 1C4
Tel: 709-772-5862; *Fax:* 709-772-5600
Deputy District Administrator: Darlene Wells, 709-772-2811
Registry Officer: Daphne Lewis, 709-772-2884

Saskatoon
The Court House, 520 Spadina Cres. East, Saskatoon, SK S7K 2H6
Tel: 800-565-0541
District Administrator: Dennis Berezowsky, 306-933-5139

Whitehorse
Andrew A. Phillipsen Law Centre, 2134 - 2nd Ave., Whitehorse, YT Y1A 5H6
Tel: 867-667-5441; *Fax:* 867-393-6212
District Administrator: Shauna Curtin, 867-667-5441
Registry Officer: Sue Bergren, 867-667-5441

Winnipeg
#400, 363 Broadway St., Winnipeg, MB R3C 3N9
Tel: 204-983-2232; *Fax:* 204-983-7636
Other information: TTY: 204-984-4440
Director: Jennifer MacGillivray, 204-983-2509
Registry Officer: Robert M'vondo, 204-983-2509
Registry Officer: Renée Taillefer, 204-983-2509

Yellowknife
Court House, 4905 - 49th St., P.O. Box 1320, Yellowknife, NT X1A 2L9
Tel: 800-565-0541
District Administrator: Robin Anne Mould, 867-873-2044
Registry Officer: Bernice Dillman, 867-873-2044

Alberta

Alberta Court of Appeal

Law Courts, 1A Sir Winston Churchill Sq., Edmonton, AB T5J 0R2
Tel: 780-422-2416; *Fax:* 780-422-4127
albertacourts.ca/court-of-appeal

The Alberta Court of Appeal hears appeals from the following courts: the Provincial Court; the Court of Queen's Bench; & administrative tribunals. The Court of Appeal also provides opinions on questions referred from the Lieutenant Governor under the Judicature Act. Court of Appeal justices are appointed by the federal government. Sittings are held in Edmonton & Calgary.

Chief Justice of Alberta: The Honourable Catherine A. Fraser

Justices of the Court of Appeal (The Hon. Mr. / Madam Justice):
R.L. Berger
Peter T. Costigan
J. Watson Paperny
F.F. Slatter
M.B. Bielby
B.L. Veldhuis
T.W. Wakeling
F.L. Schutz
S.J. Greckol

Administration:
Registrar: Mary MacDonald, 780-422-7710, Fax: 780-427-5507
mary.macdonald@gov.ab.ca
Deputy Registrar: Danielle Umrysh, 780-422-7714, Fax: 780-422-4127
danielle.umrysh@gov.ab.ca

Courts:

Calgary: Court of Appeal
TransCanada Pipelines Tower, #2600, 450 - 1st St. SW, Calgary, AB T2P 5H1
Tel: 403-297-2206; *Fax:* 403-297-5294
albertacourts.ca

Justices of the Court of Appeal (The Hon. Mr. / Madam Justice):
Marina S. Paperny
Peter W.L. Martin
S.L. Martin
Patricia A. Rowbotham
J.D. Bruce McDonald
B.K. O'Ferrall

Administration:
Registrar: Mary MacDonald
Deputy Registrar: Ileen Moore
Director, Operations: Donna Beaton

Alberta Court of Queen's Bench

Calgary Courts Centre, #705N, 601 - 5th St. SW, Calgary, AB T2P 5P7
Tel: 403-297-7538; *Fax:* 403-297-8617
www.albertacourts.ab.ca

In Alberta, the Court of Queen's Bench is the Superior Trial Court. The Court hears trials in both civil & criminal matters, as well as appeals from decisions of the Provincial Court. The Chief Justice & other Justices are also judges of Surrogate Matters. Sittings of the Court of Queen's Bench are held in various areas throughout Alberta.

Chief Justice: The Honourable Neil C. Wittmann
Associate Chief Justice: The Honourable J.D. Rooke

Justices (The Honourable Mr. / Madam Justice):
B.L. Rawlins
S.M. Bensler
C.A. Kent
P.J. McIntyre
C.S. Phillips
P.M. Clark
S.J. LoVecchio
W.P. Sullivan
C.L. Kenny
G.C. Hawco
C.S. Brooker
B.E.C. Romaine
R.E. Nation
A.G. Park
B.E. Mahoney
Elizabeth A. Hughes
Marshsa C. Erb
Karen M. Horner
Sheilah L. Martin
Alan D. Macleod
K.M. Eidsvik
E.C. Wilson
J. Strekaf
K.D. Yamauchi
P.R. Jeffrey
S.L. Hunt McDonald

J.T. McCarthy
W.A. Tilleman
R.J. Hall
G.H. Poelman
B.A. Millar
K.D. Nixon
C.S. Anderson
G.A. Campbell
C. Dario
D.B. Nixon
R.A. Nuefeld
M.D. Gates
C.M. Jones

Courts:

Drumheller: Court of Queen's Bench
Court House, 511 - 3 Ave. West, P.O. Box 759, Drumheller, AB T0J 0Y0
Tel: 403-820-7300; *Fax:* 403-823-6073
www.albertacourts.ab.ca
Manager: C. Parkinson

Edmonton: Court of Queen's Bench
Law Courts, 1A Sir Winston Churchill Sq., Edmonton, AB T5J 0R2
Tel: 780-422-2492; *Fax:* 780-422-9742
www.albertacourts.ab.ca
Associate Chief Justice: The Hon. J.D. Rooke
Justices (The Honourable Mr. / Madam Justice):
Donald Lee
Mary T. Moreau
Richard P. Marceau
R. Paul Belzil
Sterling M. Sanderman
Doreen A. Sulyma
Brian R. Burrows
Gerald A. Verville
L. Darlene Acton
Terrance D. Clackson
Andrea B. Moen
S.J. Greckol
Joanne B. Veit
Eric F. Macklin
Vital O. Ouellette
Donna C. Read
Stephen D. Hillier
Juliana E. Topolniski
Adam W. Germain
June M. Ross
John J. Gill
Dennis R.G. Thomas
R.A. Graesser
D.L. Shelley
K.G. Nielsen
M.G. Crighton
D.J. Manderscheid
Beverley A. Browne
J.H. Goss
P.B. Michalyshyn
E.J. Simpson
D. Pentelechuk
D.A. Yungwirth
L.R.A. Ackerl
W.N. Renke
Administration:
Senior Manager: Maria Lavorato, 780-422-2492, Fax: 780-427-0629
maria.lavorato@gov.ab.ca
Manager: Susan Logan, 780-422-9475, Fax: 780-427-0629
susan.logan@gov.ab.ca

Fort McMurray: Court of Queen's Bench
Court House, 9700 Franklin Ave., Fort McMurray, AB T9H 4W3
Tel: 780-743-7136; *Fax:* 780-743-7135
www.albertacourts.ab.ca
Manager: M. Reagen

Grande Prairie: Court of Queen's Bench
Court House, 10260 - 99 St., Grande Prairie, AB T8V 2H4
Fax: 780-538-5493
Toll-Free: 855-738-4747
www.albertacourts.ab.ca
Manager: Rogena Hunt

High Level: Court of Queen's Bench
Court House, 10106 - 100 Ave., P.O. Box 1560, High Level, AB T0H 1Z0
Fax: 780-926-4068
Toll-Free: 855-738-4747
www.albertacourts.ab.ca
Criminal sittings are held as required.
Manager: S. Rendle

Hinton: Court of Queen's Bench
Court House, 237 Jasper St. West, P.O. Box 6450, Hinton, AB T7V 1X7
Fax: 780-865-8253
Toll-Free: 855-738-4747
www.albertacourts.ab.ca
Manager: K. Hanington

Lethbridge: Court of Queen's Bench
Court House, 320 - 4 St. South, Lethbridge, AB T1J 1Z8
Fax: 403-381-5128
Toll-Free: 855-738-4747
www.albertacourts.ca
Justices (The Honourable Mr. / Madam Justice):
J.H. Langston
D.K. Miller
R.A. Jerke
Administration:
D. Hartigan (Manager)

Medicine Hat: Court of Queen's Bench
Law Courts, 460 - 1st St. SE, Medicine Hat, AB T1A 0A8
Fax: 403-529-8607
Toll-Free: 855-738-4747
www.albertacourts.ab.ca
Acting Manager: D. Hartigan

Peace River: Court of Queen's Bench
Court House, 9905 - 97 Ave., P.O. Box 900-34, Peace River, AB T8S 1T4
Fax: 780-624-7101
Toll-Free: 855-738-4747
www.albertacourts.ab.ca
Manager: S. Rendle

Red Deer: Court of Queen's Bench
Court House, 4909 - 48 Ave., Red Deer, AB T4N 3T5
Fax: 403-340-7984
Toll-Free: 855-738-4747
albertacourts.ca
Justices (The Honourable Mr. / Madam Justice):
K.L. Sisson
Monica R. Bast
J.W. Hopkins
T. Kintzel (Manager)

St. Paul: Court of Queen's Bench
Court House, 4704 - 50 St., P.O. Box 1900, St. Paul, AB T0A 3A0
Fax: 780-645-6273
Toll-Free: 855-738-4747
www.albertacourts.ab.ca
Manager: R. Westman

Wetaskiwin: Court of Queen's Bench
Law Courts, 4605 - 51 St., Wetaskiwin, AB T9A 1K7
Fax: 780-361-1319
Toll-Free: 855-738-4747
www.albertacourts.ab.ca
Manager: C. Walker

Alberta Provincial Court

Law Courts, 1A Sir Winston Churchill Sq., Edmonton, AB T5J 0R2
Tel: 780-427-8713; *Fax:* 780-422-9736
albertacourts.ca

The Provincial Court of Alberta serves as the point of entry to the justice system in the following areas of law: civil matters (Small Claims Court), related to damages & debt & pretrial conferences; criminal law; family law, such as Parenting & Contact Orders; traffic offences, under federal statutes, provincial statutes, & municipal bylaws; & Criminal Code offences committed by youth from ages 12 to 17. Circuit point courts are situated throughout the province.
Judges:
T.J. Matchett (Chief Judge)
L.K. McLellan (Deputy Chief Judge)
L.G. Anderson (Assistant Chief Judge (Family & Youth))

Courts:

Calgary - Civil, Criminal, Family, Regional, Traffic, & Youth
Calgary Courts Centre, 601 - 5th St. SW, Calgary, AB T2P 5P7
Tel: 403-297-3122; *Fax:* 403-297-3179
albertacourts.ca
Judges:
T.J. Matchett (Chief Judge)
L.K. McLellan (Deputy Chief Judge)
Administration:
Senior Manager: Basem Hage

Calgary - Civil
Calgary Courts Centre, #606S, 601 - 5th St. SW, Calgary, AB T2P 5P7
Tel: 403-297-7217; *Fax:* 403-297-7374
albertacourts.ca
Judges:
L.D. Young (Assistant Chief Judge)
L.L. Burt
N.R. Hess
D.B. Higa
M.A. McCorquodale
Administration:
Administrator: Marilyn Clisdell

Calgary - Criminal
Calgary Courts Centre, #402S, 601 - 5th St. SW, Calgary, AB T2P 5P7
Tel: 403-297-3122; *Fax:* 403-297-3179
albertacourts.ca
Judges:
L.K. McLellan (Deputy Chief Judge)
J.J. Ogle (Assistant Chief Judge (Calgary & Calgary Region))
J.D. Bascom
A.J. Brown
D.R. Pahl
M.D. Slawinsky
W.J. Cummings
C.L. Daniel
M.C. Dinkel
G.S. Dunnigan
M.J. Durant
A.A. Fradsham
B.R. Fraser
M.L. Graham
K.Z. Jivraj
H.A. Lamoureux
F.L. Maloney
P.J. Mason
K.R. McLeod
G.M. Meagher
T.C. Semenuk
C.M. Skene
M.T.C. Tyndale
S.L. Van de Veen
H.M. Van Harten
R.J. Wilkins
G.K. Wong
L.W. Robertson
Administration:
Manager: C. Robitaille

Calgary - Family & Youth
Calgary Courts Centre, #704N, 601 - 5 St. SW, Calgary, AB T2P 5P7
Tel: 403-297-3471; *Fax:* 403-297-3461
albertacourts.ca
Youth Ste: 201-N
Judges:
R.J. O'Gorman (Assistant Chief Judge)
G.J. Burrell
D. Mah
L.T.L. Cook-Stanhope
G.H. Cornfield
N.W. D'Souza
K.J. Jordan
T. LaRochelle
S.E. Lipton
J.R. Shaw
V.T. Tousignant
Administration:
Acting Manager: S. Hage

Calgary - Regional
Calgary Courts Centre, #607S, 601 - 5th St. SW, Calgary, AB T2P 5P7
Tel: 403-297-3010; *Fax:* 403-297-3237
albertacourts.ca
Circuit point courts are located in the following places: Airdrie (#113, 104 - 1 Ave. NW), Canmore (#101, 800 Railway Ave.), Cochrane (213 - 1 St., West), Didsbury (1611 - 15 Ave.), Okotoks (98 McRae St.), & Tsuu T'ina Nation (9911 Chula Blvd., Sarcee).
Judges:
J.J. Ogle (Assistant Chief Judge, Calgary & Calgary Regional)
P.B. Barley
E.J. Creighton
G.J. Gaschler
L.R. Grieve
P.M. McIlhargey
J. Shriar
Administration:
Manager: L. Blair-Kaye

Calgary - Traffic & Civil
Calgary Courts Centre, #203S, 601 - 5th St. SW, Calgary, AB T2P 5P7
Tel: 403-297-2283; *Fax:* 403-297-2220
albertacourts.ca
Acting Manager: L. Quinton

Camrose
Court House, 5210 - 49 Ave., Camrose, AB T4V 3Y2
Tel: 780-679-1240; *Fax:* 780-679-1253
albertacourts.ca

A circuit point court is located in Killam (4903 - 50 St.).
Judges:
W.A. Andreassen
Administration:
Manager: Debbie Tkachuk

Drumheller
Court House, 511 - 3 Ave. West, P.O. Box 759, Drumheller, AB T0J 0Y0
Tel: 403-820-7300; *Fax:* 403-823-6073
albertacourts.ca

Circuit point courts are situated in the following places: Hanna (401 Centre St.), Siksika Nation (Junction of Highways 901 & 547), & Strathmore (226 - 2 Ave.).
Administration:
Manager: Janice McGuckin

Edmonton - Civil, Criminal, Family & Youth, & Traffic
Law Courts, 1A Sir Winston Churchill Sq., Edmonton, AB T5J 0R2
Tel: 780-427-8713; *Fax:* 780-422-9736
albertacourts.ca

Judges:
K.A. Holmstrom (Assistant Chief Judge (Family & Youth))
L.G. Anderson (Assistant Chief Judge (Edmonton Region))
L.D. Young (Assistant Chief Judge (Civil))
Administration:
Director: B. Haynes

Edmonton - Civil
Law Courts, 1A Sir Winston Churchill Sq., Edmonton, AB T5J 0R2
Tel: 780-422-2508; *Fax:* 780-427-4348
albertacourts.ca

Judges:
L.D. Young (Assistant Chief Judge)
K. Haymour
G.W. Sharek
J.L. Skitsko
Administration:
Administrator: E. Cruz

Edmonton - Criminal
Law Courts, 1A Sir Winston Churchill Sq., Edmonton, AB T5J 0R2
Tel: 780-427-7868; *Fax:* 780-422-9736
albertacourts.ca

Judges:
T.J. Matchett (Chief Judge)
L.K. McLellan (Deputy Chief Judge)
J.L. Lester
L.G. Anderson (Assistant Chief Judge)
M.G. Allen
S.M.L. Bilodeau
L.K. Stevens
Raymond Bodnarek
H.A. Bridges
M.M. Carminati
S.R. Creagh
R.R.M. Crochard
J.L. Dixon
D.M. Groves
E.A. Johnson
J.B. Kerby
G.B. Lepp
F.E. LeReverend
F.K. MacDonald
L.E. Malin
J.J. Moher
S.E. Richardson
D.R. Valgardson
E.J.M. Walter
C.J. Sharpe
Administration:
Manager: K. Lucas

Edmonton - Family & Youth
Law Courts, 1A Sir Winston Churchill Sq., Edmonton, AB T5J 0R2
Tel: 780-427-2743; *Fax:* 780-427-5797
albertacourts.ca

Judges:
K.A. Holmstrom (Assistant Chief Judge)
W.S. Andrew
M.J. Burch
D. Dalton
J.G. Easton
J.M. Filice
G.B.N. Ho
P.E. Kvill
S.C. Miller
M.J. Savaryn
A. Veylan
D. Zalmanowitz
Administration:
Acting Manager: A. Cappellano

Edmonton - Regional
Law Courts, 1A Sir Winston Churchill Sq., Edmonton, AB T5J 0R2
Tel: 780-422-2691; *Fax:* 780-422-2971
albertacourts.ca

Judges:
C.D. Gardner (Assistant Chief Judge)

Edmonton - Traffic & Civil
Law Courts, 1A Sir Winston Churchill Sq., Edmonton, AB T5J 0R2
Tel: 780-427-5913; *Fax:* 780-427-5791
www.albertacourts.ab.ca

Administration:
Manager: L. Malcolm

Fort McMurray
Court House, 9700 Franklin Ave., Fort McMurray, AB T9H 4W3
Tel: 780-743-7195; *Fax:* 780-743-7395
albertacourts.ca

A circuit point court is located in Fort Chipewyan (Multi-Plex, Flett St.).
Judges:
S.A. Cleary
J.R. Jacques
Administration:
Acting Manager: M. Reagen

Fort Saskatchewan
Court House, 10504 - 100 Ave., Fort Saskatchewan, AB T8L 3S9
Tel: 780-998-1200; *Fax:* 780-998-7222
albertacourts.ca

A circuit point court is located in Boyle (5006 - 3 St.).
Judges:
P. Ayotte
D.G. Rae
Administration:
Manager: Bonnie Matvichuk

Grande Prairie
Court House, 10260 - 99 St., Grande Prairie, AB T8V 2H4
Tel: 780-538-5340; *Fax:* 780-538-5454
albertacourts.ca

Circuit point courts are located in the following places: Fox Creek (100 - 4 Ave.) & Valleyview (5102 - 50 Ave.).
Judges:
M.B. Golden (Assistant Chief Judge)
B.R. Hougestol
Administration:
Manager: Rogena Hunt

High Level
Court House, 10106 - 100 Ave., P.O. Box 1560, High Level, AB T0H 1Z0
Tel: 780-926-3715; *Fax:* 780-926-4068
albertacourts.ca

Circuit point courts are located in the following places: Assumption (Court House, Chateh) & Fort Vermilion (4607 River Rd.).
Manager: S. Rendle

High Prairie
Court House, 4911 - 53 Ave., P.O. Box 1470, High Prairie, AB T0G 1E0
Tel: 780-523-6600; *Fax:* 780-523-6643
albertacourts.ca

Circuit point courts are located in the following places: Red Earth Creek (122 Forestry Rd.), Slave Lake (101 - 3 St., SW), & Wabasca-Desmarais (867 Stony Point Rd.).
Judges:
D.R. Shynkar
G.W. Paul
Administration:
Manager: Mae Fjeld

Hinton
Court House, 237 Jasper St. West, P.O. Box 6450, Hinton, AB T7V 1X7
Tel: 780-865-8280; *Fax:* 780-865-8253
albertacourts.ca

Circuit point courts are located in the following places: Edson (111 - 54 St.), Grande Cache (Provincial Building, Hoppe Ave.), & Jasper (629 Patricia St.).
Judges:
J.P. Higgerty
D.C. Norheim
Administration:
Manager: Karen Hanington

Leduc
Court House, 4612 - 50 St., Leduc, AB T9E 6L1
Tel: 780-986-6911; *Fax:* 780-986-0345
albertacourts.ca

Circuit point courts are located in the following places: Breton (4911 - 50 Ave.) & Drayton Valley (5136 - 51 Ave.).
Judges:
C.G. Purvis
J. Schaffter
M.M. White
Administration:
Manager: Marilea McMullen, 780-986-6911, Fax: 780-986-0345
marilea.mcmullen@gov.ab.ca

Lethbridge
Court House, 320 - 4th St. South, Lethbridge, AB T1J 1Z8
Tel: 403-381-5223; *Fax:* 403-381-5763
albertacourts.ca

Circuit point courts are located in the following places: Cardston (576 Main St.), Pincher Creek (782 Main St.), & Taber (5126 - 49 Ave.).
Judges:
J.N. LeGrandeur (Assistant Chief Judge, Southern Region)
T.G. Hironaka
G.S. Maxwell
S.L. Oishi
E.W. Peterson
P.G. Pharo
D.G. Redman
Administration:
Manager: Maria McCulloch

Medicine Hat
Law Courts, 460 - 1 St. SE, Medicine Hat, AB T1A 0A8
Tel: 403-529-8644; *Fax:* 403-529-8606
albertacourts.ca

Judges:
E.D. Brooks
F.C. Fisher
D.J. Greaves
G.K. Krinke
Administration:
Acting Manager: N. Slauenwhite

Peace River
Court House, 9905 - 97 Ave., P.O. Box 900-34, Peace River, AB T8S 1T4
Tel: 780-624-6256; *Fax:* 780-624-6175
albertacourts.ca

Circuit point courts are located in the following places: Fairview (10209 - 109 St.) & Falher (028 Main St., SE).
Judges:
G.R. Ambrose
J.R. McIntosh
C.K.W. Thietke
Administration:
Acting Manager: L. McFaddin

Red Deer
Court House, 4909 - 48 Ave., Red Deer, AB T4N 3T5
Tel: 403-340-5250; *Fax:* 403-340-7985
albertacourts.ca

Circuit point courts are located in the following places: Coronation (4909 Royal St.), Rimbey (5025 - 55 St.), Rocky Mountain House (4919 - 51 St.), & Stettler (4705 - 49 Ave.).
Judges:
J.A. Hunter (Assistant Chief Judge, Central Region)
G.E. Deck
J.A. Glass
G.A.G. Yake
J.D. Holmes
J.B. Mitchell
W.A. Skinner
E.D. Riemer
Administration:
Acting Manager: C. Smith
Acting Senior Manager: C. Reynolds

St Albert
Court House, 3 St. Anne St., St Albert, AB T8N 2E8
Tel: 780-458-7300; *Fax:* 780-460-2963
www.albertacourts.ca

Circuit point courts are located in the following places: Athabasca (4903 - 50 St.), Barrhead (6203 - 49 St.), Morinville (10008 - 107 St.), & Westlock (10003 - 100 St.).
Judges:
B.H. Fraser
B.R. Garriock
V.H. Myers
Administration:
Manager: J. Fraser, 780-458-7300, Fax: 780-460-2963

St Paul
Court House, 4704 - 50 St., P.O. Box 1900, St Paul, AB T0A 3A0
Tel: 780-645-6324; *Fax:* 780-645-6273
albertacourts.ca
Circuit point courts are located in the following places: Bonnyville (4902 - 50 Ave.) & Lac La Biche (9503 Beaver Hill Rd.).
Judges:
R.M. Saccomani
K.D. Williams
Administration:
Acting Manager: B. Longpre

Sherwood Park
Court House, 190 Chippewa Rd., Sherwood Park, AB T8A 4H5
Tel: 780-464-0114; *Fax:* 780-449-1490
albertacourts.ca
Judges:
J. Maher
Administration:
Manager: B. Longpre

Stony Plain
Court House, 4711 - 44 Ave., Stony Plain, AB T7Z 1N5
Tel: 780-963-6205; *Fax:* 780-963-6402
albertacourts.ca
Circuit point courts are located in the following places: Evansburg (4921 - 50 St.), Glenevis (Administration Office, Alexis Reserve), Mayerthorpe (5013 - 50 St.), & Whitecourt (5020 - 52 Ave.).
Judges:
K.E. Tjosvold
K.R. Wilberg
Administration:
Manager: J. Fraser

Vermilion
Provincial Building, 4701 - 52nd St., P.O. Box 30, Vermilion, AB T9X 1J9
Tel: 780-853-8130; *Fax:* 780-853-8200
albertacourts.ca
Circuit point courts are located in the following places: Lloydminster (5124 - 50 St.), Vegreville (4809 - 50 St.), & Wainwright (738 - 2 Ave.).
Judges:
P.T. Johnston
Administration:
Manager: Ruth Westman

Wetaskiwin
Law Courts, 4605 - 51 St., Wetaskiwin, AB T9A 1K7
Tel: 780-361-1204; *Fax:* 780-361-1338
albertacourts.ca
A circuit point court is located in Ponoka (5110 - 49 Ave.).
Judges:
B.D. Rosborough
Administration:
Manager: Edwina Segboer

British Columbia

British Columbia Court of Appeal
The Law Courts, #400, 800 Hornby St., Vancouver, BC V6Z 2C5
Tel: 604-660-2468; *Fax:* 604-660-1951
www.courts.gov.bc.ca/Court_of_Appeal
The Court of Appeal is the highest court in the province. It hears appeals from the Supreme Court, & from the Provincial Court on some criminal matters. It also hears reviews and appeals from some administrative boards and tribunals.
Chief Justice *June 16, 2013*: The Hon. Robert James Bauman
Justices of Appeal (The Hon. Mr./Madam Justice):
Elizabeth A. Bennett *May 14, 2009*
Ian T. Donald *January 27, 1994*
Gail M. Dickson *July 29, 2015*
Lauri Ann Fenlon *June 15, 2015*
Gregory J. Fitch *September 1, 2015*
S. David Frankel *May 10, 2007*
Nicole J. Garson *May 14, 2009*
Richard Goepel *November 7, 2013*
Harvey M. Groberman *May 8, 2008*
David C. Harris *April 10, 2012*
Pamela A. Kirkpatrick *June 2, 2005*
P.D. Lowry *June 30, 2003*
Anne W. MacKenzie *December 31, 2011*
Mary V. Newbury *September 26, 1995*
John E.D. Savage *December 11, 2014*
Mary E. Saunders *July 1, 1999*
Daphne M. Smith *May 8, 2008*
Sunni Stromberg-Stein *June 7, 2013*
David Franklin Tysoe *May 22, 2007*
Peter M. Willcock *May 7, 2013*
Administration:
Registrar: Timothy Outerbridge, 604-660-2729

British Columbia Supreme Court
The Law Courts, 800 Smithe St., Vancouver, BC V6Z 2E1
Tel: 604-660-2847; *Fax:* 604-660-2420
www.courts.gov.bc.ca/supreme_court
The Supreme Court is a trial court of original jurisdiction for all civil & criminal matters arising in B.C., save & except matters expressly excluded by statute. It hears most appeals from the Provincial Court.
Chief Justice *November 7, 2013*: The Hon. Christopher E. Hinkson
Assoc. Chief Justice *December 31, 2011*: The Hon. Austin F. Cullen
Judges (The Hon. Mr./Madam Justice):
Patrice Abrioux *September 30, 2011*
Elaine J. Adair *November 28, 2008*
Kenneth N. Affleck *June 24, 2011*
David M. Masuhara *October 11, 2002*
Maria Morellato *June 17, 2016*
Elliott M. Myers *November 22, 2005*
Paul J. Pearlman *January 31, 2008*
Sandra K. Ballance *December 11, 2002*
Carol J. Ross *March 12, 2001*
Loryl D. Russell *April 14, 2005*
Terence A. Schultes *August 14, 2009*
Gregory T.W. Bowden *October 2, 2009*
Robert J. Sewell *January 22, 2009*
Neena Sharma *December 19, 2013*
Brenda Brown *April 18, 2002*
Jon S. Sigurdson *January 27, 1994*
Catherine J. Bruce *September 14, 2006*
Emily M. Burke *May 13, 2014*
Grant D. Burnyeat *December 19, 1996*
G. Bruce Butler *March 30, 2007*
Arne H. Silverman *November 26, 2004*
Grace Choi *May 29, 2015*
Ronald A. Skolrood *June 6, 2013*
Frank W. Cole *March 19, 1996*
Harry A. Slade *March 27, 2001*
D. Jane Dardi *June 18, 2008*
Barry M. Davies *January 10, 1996*
Nathan H. Smith *May 19, 2005*
Janice R. Dillon *April 25, 1995*
John J. Steeves *October 5, 2012*
Peter G. Voith *January 22, 2009*
Paul W. Walker *June 18, 2008*
Jennifer M.I. Duncan *December 19, 2013*
Lisa A. Warren *June 6, 2013*
William Ehrcke *October 28, 2003*
Barbara Fisher *November 26, 2004*
Jeanne E. Watchuk *October 28, 2010*
Gordon C. Weatherill *May 31, 2012*
Catherine A. Wedge *April 4, 2001*
James W. Williams *October 10, 2002*
Shelley C. Fitzpatrick *June 18, 2010*
Barbara M. Young *June 19, 2015*
Margot L. Fleming *June 6, 2013*
Gordon S. Funt *October 5, 2012*
Laura B. Gerow *October 10, 2002*
J. Christopher Grauer *April 11, 2008*
Victoria Gray *September 27, 2001*
Bruce M. Greyell *May 14, 2009*
Susan A. Griffin *February 20, 2008*
J. Miriam Gropper *April 14, 2005*
Joel R. Groves *May 19, 2005*
Wendy J. Harris *June 6, 2013*
Heather J. Holmes *March 21, 2001*
Mary A. Humphries *January 27, 1994*
Hope Hyslop *May 14, 2009*
Stephen F. Kelleher *July 24, 2003*
Nigel P. Kent *December 19, 2013*
Peter D. Leask *November 22, 2005*
Linda A. Loo *September 24, 1996*
George Macintosh *December 19, 2013*
Miriam A. Maisonville *March 19, 2010*

Courts:

Campbell River
500 - 13 Ave., Campbell River, BC V9W 6P1
Tel: 250-286-7510; *Fax:* 250-286-7512
Toll-Free: 877-741-3820
Registry (County): Vancouver Island

Chilliwack
Court House, 46085 Yale Rd., Chilliwack, BC V2P 2L8
Tel: 604-795-8350; *Fax:* 604-795-8393
Registry (County): Westminster
Judges (The Hon.):
Neill Brown *July 30, 2008*
William G.E. Grist *June 20, 1996*

Courtenay
Court House, #100, 420 Cumberland Rd., Courtenay, BC V9N 2C4
Tel: 250-334-1115; *Fax:* 250-334-1191
Toll-Free: 877-741-3820
Registry (County): Vancouver Island

Cranbrook
Court House, #147, 102 - 11 Ave. South, Cranbrook, BC V1C 2P3
Tel: 250-426-1234; *Fax:* 250-426-1352
Registry (County): Kootenay

Dawson Creek
Court House, 1201 - 103 Ave., Dawson Creek, BC V1G 4J2
Tel: 250-784-2278; *Fax:* 250-784-2339
Toll-Free: 866-614-2750
Registry (County): Kootenay

Duncan
Court House, 238 Government St., Duncan, BC V9L 1A5
Tel: 250-746-1258; *Fax:* 250-746-1244
Toll-Free: 877-288-0828
Registry (County): Vancouver Island

Fort Nelson
4604 Sunset Dr., P.O. Box 1000, Fort Nelson, BC V0C 1R0
Tel: 250-774-5999; *Fax:* 250-774-6904
Toll-Free: 866-614-2750
Registry (County): Cariboo

Fort St. John
Court House, 10600 - 100 St., Fort St. John, BC V1J 4L6
Tel: 250-787-3231; *Fax:* 250-787-3518
Toll-Free: 866-614-2750
Registry (County): Cariboo

Golden
837 Park Dr., P.O. Box 1500, Golden, BC V0A 1H0
Tel: 250-344-7581; *Fax:* 250-344-7715
Registry (County): Kootenay

Kamloops
Court House, #223, 455 Columbia St., Kamloops, BC V2C 6K4
Tel: 250-828-4344; *Fax:* 250-828-4332
Registry (County): Yale
Judges (The Hon. Mr./Madam Justice):
S.Dev Dley *March 19, 2010*
Sheri Ann Donegan *June 6, 2013*
Hope Hyslop *May 14, 2009*
Ian C. Meiklem *October 11, 1991*

Kelowna
Court House, 1355 Water St., Kelowna, BC V1Y 9R3
Tel: 250-470-6900; *Fax:* 250-470-6939
Registry (County): Yale
Alison J. Beames *August 7, 1996*
D. Allan Betton *June 24, 2011*
Peter J. Rogers *December 14, 2001*

Nanaimo
Court House, 35 Front St., Nanaimo, BC V9R 5J1
Tel: 250-716-5908; *Fax:* 250-716-5911
Registry (County): Vancouver Island
Judges (The Hon.):
Robin A.M. Baird *October 5, 2012*
Douglas W. Thompson *December 13, 2012*

Nelson
Court House, 320 Ward St., Nelson, BC V1L 1S6
Tel: 250-354-6165; *Fax:* 250-354-6139
Toll-Free: 888-526-8555
Registry (County): Kootenay
Judges (The Hon.):
T. Mark McEwan *August 7, 1996*

New Westminster
Court House, Begbie Sq., 651 Carnarvon St., New Westminster, BC V3M 1C9
Tel: 604-660-8551; *Fax:* 604-660-2072
Registry (County): Vancouver
Judges (The Hon.):
Trevor C. Armstrong *October 1, 2010*
Elizabeth A. Arnold-Bailey *April 14, 2005*
Kenneth W. Ball *November 2, 2012*
Lance W. Bernard *July 24, 2003*
Murray B. Blok *March 30, 2007*
Martha M. Devlin *December 12, 2014*
R. Crawford *September 27, 2001*
John S. Harvey *January 22, 2009*
Robert W. Jenkins *December 31, 2011*
Ian B. Josephson *July 1, 1990*
Kathleen M. Ker *June 18, 2008*
Anthony Saunders *November 26, 2009*
John D. Truscott *October 10, 2002*
Frits E. Verhoeven *January 22, 2009*

Gary P. Weatherill *October 2, 2013*

Penticton
Court House, 100 Main St., Penticton, BC V2A 5A5
Tel: 250-492-1231; *Fax:* 250-492-1378
Toll-Free: 888-526-8555
Registry (County): Yale

Port Alberni
2999 - 4 Ave., Port Alberni, BC V9Y 8A5
Tel: 250-720-2424; *Fax:* 250-720-2426
Toll-Free: 877-741-3820
Registry (County): Vancouver Island

Powell River
#103, 6953 Alberni St., Powell River, BC V8A 2B8
Tel: 604-485-3630; *Fax:* 604-485-3637
Toll-Free: 877-741-3820
Registry (County): Vancouver Island

Prince George
Court House
J.O. Wilson Sq., 250 George St., Prince George, BC V2L 5S2
Tel: 250-614-2700; *Fax:* 250-614-2737
Registry (County): Cariboo
Judges (The Hon.):
Marguerite H. Church *June 17, 2016*
Judges (The Hon.):
Ronald S. Tindale *October 20, 2011*

Prince Rupert
Court House, 100 Market Pl., Prince Rupert, BC V8J 1B8
Tel: 250-624-7525; *Fax:* 250-624-7538
Registry (County): Prince Rupert
Judges (The Hon.):
Robert D. Punnett *June 19, 2009*

Quesnel
Court House, #305, 350 Barlow Ave., Quesnel, BC V2J 2C1
Tel: 250-992-4256; *Fax:* 250-992-4171
Toll-Free: 866-614-2750
Registry (County): Cariboo

Rossland
Court House, 2288 Columbia Ave., P.O. Box 639, Rossland, BC V0G 1Y0
Tel: 250-362-7368; *Fax:* 250-362-9632
Toll-Free: 888-526-8555
Registry (County): Kootenay

Salmon Arm
Court House, 550 - 2 Ave. NE, P.O. Box 100 Main, Salmon Arm, BC V1E 4S4
Tel: 250-832-1610; *Fax:* 250-832-1749
Toll-Free: 888-828-4351
Registry (County): Yale

Smithers
3793 Alfred Ave., P.O. Box 5000, Smithers, BC V0J 2N0
Tel: 250-847-7376; *Fax:* 250-847-7710
Registry (County): Prince Rupert
Judges (The Hon.):
M. Marvyn Koenigsberg *November 27, 1992*

Terrace
Court House, 3408 Kalum St., Terrace, BC V8G 2N6
Tel: 250-638-2111; *Fax:* 250-638-2123
Registry (County): Prince Rupert

Vernon
Court House, 3001 - 27 St., Vernon, BC V1T 4W5
Tel: 250-549-5422; *Fax:* 205-549-5621
Toll-Free: 888-526-8555
Registry (County): Yale

Victoria
Court House, 850 Burdett Ave., P.O. Box 9248 Prov Govt, Victoria, BC V8W 9J2
Tel: 250-356-1478; *Fax:* 250-356-6669
Registry (County): Vancouver Island
Judges (The Hon.):
J. Keith Bracken *March 30, 2007*
Jacqueline L. Dorgan *October 11, 1991*
Geoffrey R.J. Gaul *February 1, 2008*
Robert Johnston *November 26, 2004*
Brian D. MacKenzie *October 23, 2009*
Jennifer A. Power *August 6, 2010*

Williams Lake
Court House, 540 Borland St., Williams Lake, BC V2G 1R8
Tel: 250-398-4301; *Fax:* 250-398-4459
Toll-Free: 866-614-2750
Registry (County): Cariboo

British Columbia Provincial Court
#337, 800 Hornby St., Vancouver, BC V6Z 2C5
Tel: 604-660-2864; *Fax:* 604-660-1108
info@provincialcourt.bc.ca
www.provincialcourt.bc.ca

The Provincial Court is a statutory, trial court. It hears cases in criminal, family, youth, small claims & traffic matters.
Chief Judge: The Hon. Thomas Crabtree
Assoc. Chief Judge: Melissa Gillespie
Assoc. Chief Judge: Susan Wishart
Judges (The Hon.):
Margaret Rae
Administration:
G. Hayes (Acting Administrative Judicial Justice)
P. Schwartz (Acting Administrative Judicial Justice)

Courts:

Abbotsford
32203 South Fraser Way, Abbotsford, BC V2T 1W6
Tel: 604-855-3200; *Fax:* 604-855-7057
Judges (The Hon.):
Gregory J. Brown
Brent G. Hoy
William G. MacDonald
Steven Point
Edna Ritchie
Jill Rounthwaite
K.D. Skilnick
Jay Solomon

Atlin
3 St., Atlin, BC V0W 1A0
Tel: 250-651-7595

Burns Lake
508 Yellowhead Highway, Burns Lake, BC V0J 1E0
Tel: 250-692-7711

Campbell River
500 - 13 Ave., Campbell River, BC V9W 6P1
Tel: 250-286-7510
Judges (The Hon.):
Barbara Flewelling

Chilliwack
46085 Yale Rd., Chilliwack, BC V2P 2L8
Tel: 604-795-8350
Chief Judge: The Hon. Thomas J. Crabtree
Judges (The Hon.):
Richard Browning
Wendy A. Young

Clearwater
209 Dutch Lake Rd., Clearwater, BC V0E 1N2
Tel: 250-674-2113

Courtenay
#100, 420 Cumberland Rd., Courtenay, BC V9N 2C4
Tel: 250-334-1115
Judges (The Hon.):
Peter M. Doherty

Cranbrook
#147, 102 - 11 Ave. South, Cranbrook, BC V1C 2P3
Tel: 250-426-1234
Judges (The Hon.):
W. Grant Sheard
Ronald J. Webb
Administration:
Judicial Case Manager: Arlene McCormack

Dawson Creek
#205, 1201 - 103 Ave., Dawson Creek, BC V1G 4J2
Tel: 250-784-2278
Judges (The Hon.):
Richard R. Blaskovits
Administration:
Judicial Case manager: Faye Campbell

Duncan
238 Government St., Duncan, BC V9L 1A5
Tel: 250-746-1528
Judges (The Hon.):
Roger Cutler
Administration:
Judicial Case Manager: Shannon L. Cole

Fort Nelson
4604 Sunset Dr., Fort Nelson, BC V0C 1R0
Tel: 250-774-5999; *Fax:* 250-774-6904

Fort St John
10600 - 100 St., Fort St John, BC V1J 4L6
Tel: 250-787-3231
Judges (The Hon.):
Rita S. Bowry
Brian A. Daley
Administration:
Judicial Case Manager: Faye Campbell

Golden
837 Park Dr., P.O. Box 1500, Golden, BC V0A 1H0
Tel: 250-344-7581; *Fax:* 250-344-7715
Registry Administrator: Loriann Roseberry

Kamloops
#223, 455 Columbia St., Kamloops, BC V2C 6K4
Tel: 250-828-4344
Judges (The Hon.):
Christopher D. Cleaveley
Roy C. Dickey
Stella Frame
Stephen R. Harrison
Leonard Marchand
Administration:
Judicial Case Manager: Sheila D. Paul

Kelowna
#1, 1355 Water St., Kelowna, BC V1Y 9R3
Tel: 250-470-6900; *Fax:* 250-470-6810
Judges (The Hon.):
Robin R. Smith (Interior Regional Administrative Judge)
E.M. Burdett
J.P. Cartwright
B.J. Chapman
P.V. Hogan
W.W. Klinger
J.J. Threlfall
Administration:
Judicial Case Manager: Kathy Bullach

Mackenzie
64 Centennial Dr., P.O. Box 2050, Mackenzie, BC V0J 2C0
Tel: 250-997-3377; *Fax:* 250-997-5617

Masset
1666 Orr St., P.O. Box 230, Masset, BC V0T 1M0
Tel: 250-626-5512

Nanaimo
Court House, 35 Front St., Nanaimo, BC V9R 5J1
Tel: 250-716-5908
Judges (The Hon.):
J. Douglas Cowling
Ted E. Gouge
Brian R. Klaver
Ronald G. Lamperson
Parker MacCarthy
Administration:
Judicial Case Manager: Veronica Mitchell

Nelson
320 Ward St., Nelson, BC V1L 1S6
Tel: 250-354-6165
Judges (The Hon.):
C. Richard Hewson
Administration:
Judicial Case Manager: Sandra Hadikin

New Westminster
Law Courts, 651 Carnarvon St., New Westminster, BC V3M 1C9
Tel: 604-660-8522; *Fax:* 604-775-1052
Judges (The Hon.):
Therese Alexander
D.M.B. Steinberg
Rory Walters
Administration:
Judicial Case Manager: Suzanne Steele

North Vancouver
200 - East 23 St., North Vancouver, BC V7L 4R4
Tel: 604-981-0200; *Fax:* 604-981-0268
Judges (The Hon.):
Joanne Challenger
Bryce A. Dyer
John R. Milne
Douglas E. Moss
W.J. Rodgers
Administration:
Judicial Case Manager: Suzanne McLarty

Penticton
100 Main St., Penticton, BC V2A 5A5
Tel: 250-492-1231; *Fax:* 250-492-1297
Judges (The Hon.):
Gregory W. Koturbash
Marguerite Shaw
G.G. Sinclair
Administration:
Judicial Case Manager: Marj Warwick

Port Alberni
2999 - 4 Ave., Port Alberni, BC V9Y 8A5
Tel: 250-720-2424; *Fax:* 250-720-2426

Judges (The Hon.):
Justine E. Saunders
Administration:
Veronica Mitchell (Judicial Case Manager)

Port Coquitlam
2620 Mary Hill Rd., #A, Port Coquitlam, BC V3C 3B2
Tel: 604-927-2100; *Fax:* 604-927-2233
Judges (The Hon.):
Marion Buller
P.L.J. de Couto
Shehni Dossa
Patricia L. Janzen
Deirdre D. Pothecary
Garth N. Smith
Thomas S. Woods
Administration:
Judicial Case Manager: Marylynn deKeruzec

Port Hardy
9300 Trustee Rd., P.O. Box 279, Port Hardy, BC V0N 2P0
Tel: 604-949-6122
Administration:
Verna Carlson (Registry Administrator, Justice of the Peace)

Powell River
#103, 6953 Alberni St., Powell River, BC V8A 2B8
Tel: 604-485-3630; *Fax:* 604-485-3637

Prince George
J.O. Wilson Square, 250 George St., Prince George, BC V2L 5S2
Tel: 250-614-2700; *Fax:* 250-614-2790
Judges (The Hon.):
Michael J. Brecknell (Northern Regional Administrative Judge)
Randall W. Callan
M.A. Gray
Shannon Keyes
D.H. Weatherly
Administration:
Judicial Case Manager: Donna Bigras

Prince Rupert
#200, 100 Market Pl., Prince Rupert, BC V8J 1B8
Tel: 250-624-7525; *Fax:* 250-627-7538
Judges (The Hon.):
Herman J. Seidemann III
Dwight Stewart
Administration:
Judicial Case Manager: Crystal M. Foerster

Quesnel
#115, 350 Barlow Ave., Quesnel, BC V2J 2C1
Tel: 250-992-4256; *Fax:* 250-992-4171
Judges (The Hon.):
R. Dennis Morgan
Administration:
Judicial Case Manager: Rhonda Hykawy

Richmond
7577 Elmridge Way, Richmond, BC V6X 4J2
Tel: 604-660-6900; *Fax:* 604-660-7736
Judges (The Hon.):
R. Patrick Chen
Bonnie Craig
Lyndsay Smith
Administration:
Judicial Case Manager: Barbara Brown-Sayson

Rossland
Court House, 2288 Columbia Ave., P.O. Box 639, Rossland, BC V0G 1Y0
Tel: 250-362-7368

Salmon Arm
550 - 2nd Ave. NE, P.O. Box 100 Main, Salmon Arm, BC V1E 4S4
Tel: 250-832-1610; *Fax:* 250-832-1749
Judges (The Hon.):
Edmond F. de Walle

Sechelt
5480 Shorncliffe Ave., Sechelt, BC V0N 3A0
Tel: 604-740-8929
Judges (The Hon.):
Steven Merrick

Smithers
3793 Alfred Ave., P.O. Box 5000, Smithers, BC V0J 2N0
Tel: 250-847-7376; *Fax:* 250-847-7710
Judges (The Hon.):
Christine Birnie
William F.M. Jackson
Administration:
Judicial Case Manager: Sharon MacGregor

Surrey
14340 - 57 Ave., Surrey, BC V3X 1B2
Tel: 604-572-2200; *Fax:* 604-572-6917
Judges (The Hon.):
Gurmail S. Gill
Robert Hamilton (Fraser Regional Administrative Judge)
Kimberley A. Arthur-Leung
Patricia M. Bond
Andrea Brownstone
Valli Chettiar
J.G. Cohen
Melissa Gillespie (Associate Chief Judge)
P.M. Dohm
Kathryn Ferriss
Donald R. Gardner
Ellen Gordon
Peder Gilbransen
J.F. Lenaghan
R.D. Miller
Jennifer A. Oulton
Jill Rounthwaite
James I.S. Sutherland
Administration:
Judicial Case Manager: Heather Holt
Judicial Case Manager: Sandra Thorne
Judicial Case Manager: Bianca L. West

Terrace
3408 Kalum St., Terrace, BC V8G 2N6
Tel: 250-638-2111
Judicial Case Manager: Lyne Leonardes

Valemount
38 Dogwood St., Valemount, BC V0E 2Z0
Tel: 250-566-4652

Vancouver - Civil Division
Robson Sq., 800 Hornby St., P.O. Box 21, Vancouver, BC V6Z 2C5
Tel: 604-660-8989; *Fax:* 604-660-8405
Judges (The Hon.):
Laura Bakan
Kathryn Denhoff
Paul R. Meyers
Valmond Romilly
Jodie F. Werier
James O. Wingham
Judicial Case Manager: Judith Norton

Vancouver - Criminal Division
222 Main St., Vancouver, BC V6A 2S8
Tel: 604-660-4200; *Fax:* 604-660-4322
Judges (The Hon.):
Raymond R. Low (Vancouver Regional Administrative Judge)
James D. Bahen
Elisabeth Burgess
Harbans Dhillon
Joseph Galati
Maria Giardini
Thomas Gove
Reginald P. Harris
Frances Howard
Malcolm MacLean
Gregory M. Rideout
Donna Senniw
David A. St. Pierre
Karen Walker
Administration:
Judicial Case Manager: Kelly Butler
Judicial Case Manager: Laura Caporale
Judicial Case Manager: Teresa L. Hill
Judicial Case Manager: Jovanka Mihic
Judicial Case Manager: Lori Stokes

Vernon
3001 - 27 St., Vernon, BC V1T 4W5
Tel: 250-549-5422; *Fax:* 250-549-5621
Judges (The Hon.):
D. Mayland McKimm
M.G. Takahashi
Administration:
Judicial Case Manager: Lisa Wyatt
Judicial Case Manager: Dalene Krenz

Victoria
#2, 850 Burdett Ave., Victoria, BC V8W 1B4
Tel: 250-356-1478; *Fax:* 250-256-6779
Regional Administrative Judge: The Hon. Robert A. Higinbotham
Judges (The Hon.):
Adrian F. Brooks
L.F.E. Chaperon
L.J.M. Harvey
Christine Lowe
Lisa Mrozinski
Brian Neal
E.J. Quantz (Admin. Judge)
L.W. Smith
S.E. Wishart
Administration:
Judicial Case Manager: A. Bruce
Judicial Case Manager: Deborah Henry
Judicial Case Manager: Yvonne Locke

Victoria - Western Communities
1756 Island Hwy., Victoria, BC V9B 1H8
Tel: 250-391-2888; *Fax:* 250-474-9704
Judges (The Hon.):
Evan Blake
Administration:
Judicial Case Manager: Shannon Cole

Williams Lake
540 Borland St., Williams Lake, BC V2G 1R8
Tel: 250-398-4301; *Fax:* 250-398-4415
Judges (The Hon.):
Elizabeth L. Bayliff
Marguerite H. Church
Victor Galbraith
Administration:
Judicial Case Manager: Rhonda Hykawy

Manitoba

Manitoba Court of Appeal
Law Courts Bldg., #100E, 408 York Ave., Winnipeg, MB R3C 0P9
Tel: 204-945-2647; *Fax:* 204-948-2072
www.manitobacourts.mb.ca

The Court is the senior & final court in the province & has appellate jurisdiction in all civil & criminal cases adjudicated by the Court of Queen's Bench & indictable offences adjudicated by the Provincial Court. The Court hears, in limited circumstances & as mandated by statute, appeals from professional bodies & some government boards & tribunals.

Chief Justice: The Hon. Mr. Richard J.F Chartier
Justices of Appeal (The Hon. Mr./Madam Justice):
Diana M. Cameron *November 2, 2012*
Barbara M. Hamilton (Supernumerary) *July 16, 2002*
Marc M. Monnin (Supernumerary) *February 3, 2011*
Alan D. MacInnes (Supernumerary) *June 22, 2007*
Jennifer A. Pfuetzner *June 19, 2015*
Freda M. Steel (Supernumerary) *February 28, 2000*
Holly C. Beard *September 9, 2009*
Michel A. Monnin (Supernumerary) *July 26, 1995*
William J. Burnett *March 7, 2013*
Christopher J. Mainella *October 1, 2013*
Janice leMaistre *June 19, 2015*

Manitoba Court of Queen's Bench
Law Courts Bldg., 408 York Ave., Winnipeg, MB R3C 0P9
Tel: 204-945-0344; *Fax:* 204-948-2369
www.manitobacourts.mb.ca

The highest trial court for the province, The Court of Queen's Bench is a court of original jurisdiction & hears all civil & criminal cases arising in Manitoba, except matters expressly excluded by statute. The Court is comprised of the General Division, and the Family Division; it also has appellate jurisdiction & hears appeals from decisions of the Provincial Court in less serious criminal & quasi-criminal matters, decisions of the Hearing Officers in small claims matters, & decisions made by Masters of the court.

Chief Justice *February 3, 2011*: The Hon. Mr. Glenn D. Joyal
Assoc. Chief Justice *March 7, 2013*: General Division, The Hon. Mr. Shane I. Perlmutter
Assoc. Chief Justice *May 22, 2015*: Family Division, The Hon. Madam Marianne Rivoalen
Judges, General Division (The Hon. Mr./Madam Justice):
Kaye E. Dunlop *June 19, 2015*
Shawn D. Greenberg *October 28, 2003*
Kenneth R. Hanssen (Supernumerary) *March 23, 1984*
Karen I. Simonsen *December 9, 2004*
Brenda L. Keyser (Supernumerary) *October 3, 1995*
Deborah J. McCawley *September 16, 1997*
Gwen B. Hatch *June 7, 2013*
Sheldon W. Lanchbery *June 7, 2013*
Lori T. Spivak *May 19, 2005*
Colleen Suche *July 16, 2002*
Laurie P. Allen *October 6, 1998*
Frank Aquila (Supernumerary) *December 21, 1994*
Douglas N. Abra *June 22, 2007*
Robert A. Dewar *September 9, 2009*
Robyn M. Diamond (Supernumerary) *September 15, 1989*
Robert B. Doyle *February 28, 2000*
A. Catherine Everett *November 22, 2006*
Marilyn E. Goldberg *July 16, 2002*
William Johnston *July 30, 2009*
Donald M. Little *February 10, 1998*

Joan G. McKelvey *September 27, 2001*
Joan A. MacPhail *January 22, 2009*
Chris W. Martin *January 22, 2009*
Regan Thatcher *June 19, 2015*
Richard A. Saull *February 10, 2010*
James G. Edmond
Victor E. Toews
Sadie Bond
Allan D. Dueck *May 9, 2014*
Michael A. Thomson *June 1, 2007*
Donald P. Bryk (Supernumerary) *February 16, 1999*
Gerald L. Chartier
Herbert Rempel

Courts:

Brandon
Court of Queen's Bench, #100, 1104 Princess Ave., Brandon, MB R7A 0P9
Tel: 204-726-6240; *Fax:* 204-726-6547
Judges (The Hon. Mr./Madam Justice):
Robert G. Cummings *July 31, 2008*
John A. Menzies *October 6, 1998*

Dauphin
Court of Queen's Bench, 114 River Ave. West, Dauphin, MB R7N 0J7
Tel: 204-622-2087; *Fax:* 204-622-2099
Judges (The Hon. Mr./Madam Justice):
Sandra Zinchuk *February 26, 2015*

Flin Flon
Court of Queen's Bench, #104, 143 Main St., Flin Flon, MB R8A 1K2
Tel: 204-687-1670; *Fax:* 204-687-1673

Minnedosa
Court of Queen's Bench, 70 - 3rd Ave. SW, P.O. Box 414, Minnedosa, MB R0J 1E0
Tel: 204-867-4722; *Fax:* 204-867-4720

Morden
Court of Queen's Bench, 301 Wardrop St., Morden, MB R6M 1X6
Tel: 204-822-2882; *Fax:* 204-822-2883

Portage la Prairie
Court of Queen's Bench, 20 - 3rd St. SE, Portage la Prairie, MB R1N 1M9
Tel: 204-239-3383; *Fax:* 204-239-3402

St. Boniface
Court of Queen's Bench, #100, 614 Desmeurons St., St. Boniface, MB R2H 2P9
Tel: 204-945-8010; *Fax:* 204-945-5562
Justices (The Hon. Mr./Madam Justice):
Donald H. Layh
J.L. Pritchard (Supernumerary)
Administration:
Local Registrar/Sheriff: Yvonne Rohatynsky

Selkirk
Court of Queen's Bench, #101, 235 Eaton Ave., Selkirk, MB R1A 0W7
Tel: 204-785-5122; *Fax:* 204-785-5125

Swan River
Court of Queen's Bench, 201 - 4th Ave. South, P.O. Box 206, Swan River, MB R0L 1Z0
Tel: 204-734-2252; *Fax:* 204-734-9544

Virden
Court of Queen's Bench, 232 Wellington St. West, P.O. Box 1478, Virden, MB R0M 2C0
Tel: 204-748-4288; *Fax:* 204-748-2980

The Pas
Court of Queen's Bench, 300 - 3rd St. East, P.O. Box 1259, The Pas, MB R9A 1L2
Tel: 204-627-8420; *Fax:* 204-623-6528

Thompson
Court of Queen's Bench, 59 Elizabeth Dr., P.O. Box 34, Thompson, MB R8N 1X4
Tel: 204-677-6757; *Fax:* 204-677-6686

Manitoba Provincial Court
Law Courts Bldg., 408 York Ave., Main Fl., Winnipeg, MB R3C 0P9
Tel: 204-945-3454; *Fax:* 204-945-7130
www.manitobacourts.mb.ca
The Provincial Court has jurisdiction in youth & select family & criminal matters, including summary conviction offences.
Chief Judge *December 12, 2012*: The Hon. Margaret I. Wiebe
Assoc. Chief Judge *January 29, 2009*: The Hon. Shauna Hewitt-Michta
Assoc. Chief Judge *August 15, 1989*: The Hon. John P. Guy
Murray Thompson
Ryan Rolston
Lindy Choy
Catherine Carlson *November 22, 2006*
Sandra L. Chapman *August 4, 2009*
Brian M. Corrin *March 4, 1988*
Kathlyn Mary A. Curtis (Senior Judge) *February 28, 2001*
Judith A. Elliott (Senior Judge) *July 26, 2000*
Robin A. Finlayson *January 31, 2006*
Marvin F. Garfinkel (Senior Judge) *December 5, 1979*
Wanda M. Garreck *November 19, 2008*
Mary Kate Harvie *July 26, 2000*
Robert M. Heinrichs *September 1, 2009*
Sidney B. Lerner *August 4, 1999*
Theodore J. Lismer *January 17, 1977*
Tracey M. Lord *November 19, 2008*
Lee Ann M. Martin *September 17, 2007*
Kelly Moar *April 13, 2005*
Timothy Preston *April 30, 2003*
Heather R. Pullan *December 21, 1994*
Fred H. Sandhu (Senior Judge) *April 30, 2003*
Dale C. Schille *May 19, 2010*
Marva J. Smith (Senior Judge) *October 27, 1999*
Lynn A. Stannard *August 4, 1999*
Brent D. Stewart *April 15, 1998*
Raymond E. Wyant (Senior Judge) *May 20, 1998*
R.L. (Rocky) Pollack *December 14, 2006*
Carena Roller *September 17, 2007*
Cynthia A. Devine *July 23, 2012*
Timothy J.P. Killeen *July 23, 2012*
Anne Krahn *June 5, 2013*
Dale Harvey *July 10, 2013*

Courts:

Brandon
Provincial Court, #100, 1104 Princess Ave., Brandon, MB R7A 0P9
Tel: 204-726-7114; *Fax:* 204-726-6995
Shauna Hewitt-Michta (Associate Chief Judge) *January 29, 2009*
Donovan Dvorak *February 27, 2013*
Judges (His/Her Hon.):
John Combs *March 26, 2003*

Dauphin
Provincial Court, 114 River Ave. West, Dauphin, MB R7N 0J7
Tel: 204-622-2192; *Fax:* 204-622-2099
Judges (His/Her Hon.):
Christine Harapiak *April 13, 2005*
Donald R. Slough *July 28, 2010*

Portage la Prairie
Provincial Court, 25 Tupper St. North, Portage la Prairie, MB R1N 3K1
Tel: 204-239-3337; *Fax:* 204-239-3402
Judges (His/Her Hon.):
Jean McBride *June 18, 2008*

The Pas
300 - 3 St. East, P.O. Box 1259, The Pas, MB R9A 1L2
Tel: 204-627-8420; *Fax:* 204-623-6528
Judges (His/Her Hon.):
Herbert Lawrence Allen *January 29, 2009*
Malcolm W. McDonald *February 3, 2010*

Thompson
Provincial Court, 59 Elizabeth Rd., P.O. Box 34, Thompson, MB R8N 1X4
Tel: 204-677-6761; *Fax:* 204-677-6584
Judges (His/Her Hon.):
Brian G. Colli (Senior Judge) *September 21, 1994*
Doreen Redhead *April 4, 2007*
Catherine Hembroff *July 16, 2014*
Alain Huberdeau *September 24, 2014*

New Brunswick

New Brunswick Court of Appeal
Justice Bldg., #202, 427 Queen St., P.O. Box 6000, Fredericton, NB E3B 5H1
Tel: 506-453-4230; *Fax:* 506-453-7921
www.gnb.ca/cour
The Court of Appeal has appellate jurisdiction in civil & criminal matters.
Chief Justice: The Hon. J. Ernest Drapeau
Justices of Appeal (The Hon. Mr./Madam Justice):
Alexandre Deschênes (Supernumerary)
Margaret E.L. Larlee (Supernumerary)
Barbara Baird
Raymond French
Bradley V. Green
Kathleen A. Quigg
J.C. Marc Richard

New Brunswick Court of Queen's Bench
Justice Bldg., 427 Queen St., P.O. Box 6000, Fredericton, NB E3B 5H1
Tel: 506-453-2015; *Fax:* 506-444-5675
www.gnb.ca/cour
The Court of Queen's Bench is a court of original jurisdiction, having jurisdiction in all civil & criminal matters arising in New Brunswick, except those expressly excluded by statute. The Court is comprised of two divisions: Trial & Family.
***Moncton:* Chief Justice:** The Hon. David D. Smith

Courts:

Bathurst
Court House, 254 St. Patrick St., P.O. Box 5001, Bathurst, NB E2A 3Z9
Tel: 506-547-2150; *Fax:* 506-547-2966
Judges (His/Her Hon.):
Réginald Léger
Michel A. Robichaud

Campbellton
City Centre Mall, #202, 157 Water St., P.O. Box 5001, Campbellton, NB E3N 3H5
Tel: 506-789-2364; *Fax:* 506-789-2062
Judges (His/Her Hon.)
Larry Landry

Edmundston
Carrefour Assomption, 121, rue de l'Église, P.O. Box 5001, Edmundston, NB E3V 1J9
Tel: 506-735-2029; *Fax:* 506-737-4419
Judges (His/Her Hon.):
Lucie A. LaVigne
Thomas E. Cyr

Fredericton
Justice Bldg., 427 Queen St., P.O. Box 6000, Fredericton, NB E3B 5H1
Tel: 506-453-2015; *Fax:* 506-444-5675
Judges (His/Her Hon.):
Myrna F. Athey (Supernumerary Judge)
Judy L. Clendening
Paulette C. Garnett
Terrence Morrison
Bruce Noble
Anne D. Wooder

Moncton
Moncton Law Courts, 145 Assumption Blvd., P.O. Box 5001, Moncton, NB E1C 8R3
Tel: 506-856-2304; *Fax:* 506-856-2951
Judges (His/Her Hon.):
George Rideout (Supernumerary Judge)
Zoël Dionne
Colette d'Entremont
Stephen McNally
Jean-Paul Ouellette
Brigitte Robichaud
Robert L. Tuck

Miramichi
Court House, 673 King George Hwy., Miramichi, NB E1V 1N6
Tel: 506-627-4023; *Fax:* 506-627-4069
Judges (His/Her Hon.):
Frederick P. Ferguson
John Walsh

Saint John
10 Peel Plaza, P.O. Box 5001, Saint John, NB E2L 3G6
Tel: 506-658-2560; *Fax:* 506-658-2400
Judges (His/Her Hon.):
Hugh H. McLellan (Supernumerary Judge)
Peter S. Glennie (Supernumerary Judge)
Marie-Claude Blais
Thonmas Christie
William T. Grant
Deobrah Hackett
Darrell Stephenson

Woodstock
Court House, 689 Main St., P.O. Box 5001, Woodstock, NB E7M 5C6
Tel: 506-325-4414; *Fax:* 506-325-4484
Judges (His/Her Hon.):
Richard Petrie

New Brunswick Provincial Court
Justice Bldg., #105, 427 Queen St., P.O. Box 6000, Fredericton, NB E3B 5H1
Tel: 506-453-2120
www.gnb.ca/cour
The Provincial Court has jurisdiction in select criminal matters as well as youth matters.
Chief Judge: His Hon. Pierre W. Arseneault
Assoc. Chief Judge: The Hon. Mary Jane Richards

Courts:
Bathurst
#223, 254 St. Patrick St., P.O. Box 5001, Bathurst, NB E2A 3Z9
Tel: 506-547-2155

Judges (His/Her Hon.):
Camille A. Dumas (Supernumerary Judge)
Ronald LeBlanc
Brigitte Sivret

Burton
23 Route #102, Burton, NB E2V 2Y6
Tel: 506-357-4020

Judges (His/Her Hon.):
Pierre F. Dubé
Kenneth Oliver

Campbellton
#202, 157 Water St., P.O. Box 5001, Campbellton, NB E3N 3H5
Tel: 506-789-2337

Judges (His/Her Hon.):
Suzanne C. Bernard

Caraquet
P.O. Box 5559, Caraquet, NB E1W 1B7
Tel: 506-726-2502

The courthouse is located at 23 Route 102 Highway, River Road, in Burton, NB.
Judges (His/Her Hon.):
Yvette Finn

Edmundston
Carrefour Assomption, #235, 121, rue de l'Église, P.O. Box 5001, Edmundston, NB E3V 3L3
Tel: 506-735-2026

Judges (His/Her Hon.):
Brigitte Volpé

Fredericton
Justice Building, #105, 427 Queen St., P.O. Box 6000, Fredericton, NB E3B 5H1
Tel: 506-453-2120

Mary Jane Richards (Associate Chief Judge)
Judges (His/Her Hon.):
Julian Dickson

Miramichi
673 King George Hwy., Miramichi, NB E1V 1N6
Tel: 506-627-4018

Judges (His/Her Hon.):
Denis T. Lordon (Supernumerary)
Geri A. Mahoney

Moncton
Moncton Law Courts, 145 Assumption Blvd., P.O. Box 5001, Moncton, NB E1C 8R3
Tel: 506-856-2307

Chief Judge: The Hon. Pierre W. Arseneault
Judges (His/Her Hon.):
Anne Dugas-Horsman (Supernumerary)
Irwin E. Lampert
Paul E. Duffie
Joseph C. Michaud (Supernumerary)
Jolène Richard
D. Troy Sweet
J. Camille Vautour (Supernumerary)
Denise A. LeBlanc

Saint John
10 Peel Plaza, P.O. Box 5001, Saint John, NB E2L 3G6
Tel: 506-658-2568

Judges (His/Her Hon.):
Alfred H. Brien (Supernumerary)
William McCarroll (Supernumerary)
Anne Jeffries (Per Diem)
James G. McNamee (Per Diem)
Marco Robert Cloutier
W. Andrew LeMesurier
Richard Andrew Palmer
David C. Walker (Supernumerary)
Henrik G. Tonning

Tracadie-Sheila
Place Tracadie, 3514 Main St., 1st Fl., Tracadie-Sheila, NB E1X 1C9
Tel: 506-394-3700

Judges (His/Her Hon.):
Donald J. LeBlanc (Supernumerary)
Judges (His/Her Hon.):
Éric P. Sonier

Woodstock
689 Main St., P.O. Box 5001, Woodstock, NB E7M 5C6
Tél: 506-325-4415

Judges (His/Her Hon.):
R. Leslie Jackson (Supernumerary Judge)

Brian McLean

New Brunswick Probate Court
Justice Bldg., 423 Queen St., P.O. Box 6000, Fredericton, NB E3B 5H1
Tel: 506-453-2015
www.gnb.ca/cour

The Probate Court has jurisdiction in estate matters. Clerks of the Court of Queen's Bench are, ex officio, Clerks of Probate Court. Court locations throughout New Brunswick; contact: Clerk of Probate, Court Services Office (Queen's Bench).

Newfoundland & Labrador

Supreme Court of Newfoundland & Labrador: Judicial Centres
Courthouse, 309 Duckworth St., P.O. Box 937, St. John's, NL A1C 5M3
Tel: 709-729-1137; *Fax:* 709-729-6623
inquiries@supreme.court.nl.ca
www.court.nl.ca/supreme/general

The Supreme Court also has jurisdiction in Bankruptcy.
Judges (The Hon.)
Raymond P. Whalen (Chief Justice) *December 11, 2014*
David B. Orsborn (Supernumerary) *February 10, 1993*
Seamus B. O'Regan (Supernumerary) *August 27, 1986*
Raymond J. Halley (Supernumerary) *November 17, 1986*
Maureen Dunn (Supernumerary) *April 10, 1994*
James P. Adams (Supernumerary) *August 7, 1996*
Robert M. Hall (Supernumerary) *June 10, 1998*
Wayne G. Dymond (Supernumerary) *March 9, 1999*
Robert A. Fowler (Supernumerary) *June 20, 2000*
Richard D. LeBlanc *June 20, 2000*
Carl R. Thompson *April 12, 2001*
Alphonsus E. Faour *May 11, 2003*
Gillian D. Butler *March 2, 2007*
William H. N. Goodridge *February 3, 2007*
Deborah E. Fry *March 30, 2007*
Valerie L. Marshall *April 29, 2009*
Robert P. Stack *September 22, 2013*
Deborah J. Paquette *June 18, 2010*
Rosalie McGrath *May 31, 2012*
Donald H. Burrage *April 10, 2012*
Jane M. Fitzpatrick *March 27, 2015*
Cillian Sheahan *June 20, 2015*

Courts:
Corner Brook
Courthouse, 82 Mt. Bernard Ave., P.O. Box 2006, Corner Brook, NL A2H 6J8
Tel: 709-637-2633; *Fax:* 709-637-2569

Judges (The Hon.):
Brian F. Furey *March 2, 2007*
Laura A. Mennie *December 12, 2008*
David F. Hurley *March 27, 2001*

Gander
Law Court Bldg., 98 Airport Blvd., P.O. Box 2222, Gander, NL A1V 2N9
Tel: 709-256-1115; *Fax:* 709-256-1120

Judges (The Hon.):
David A. Peddle *June 19, 2008*

Grand Bank
T. Alex Hickman Courthouse, P.O. Box 910, Grand Bank, NL A0E 1W0
Tel: 709-832-1720; *Fax:* 709-832-2755

Judges (The Hon.):
Garrett A. Handrigan *March 27, 2001*

Grand Falls—Windsor
The Law Courts, 3 Cromer Ave., Grand Falls, NL A2A 1W9
Tel: 709-292-4260; *Fax:* 709-292-4224

Judges (The Hon.):
Kendra J. Goulding *February 21, 1989*

Happy Valley—Goose Bay
Courthouse, 214 Hamilton River Rd., P.O. Box 3014 B, Happy Valley-Goose Bay, NL A0P 1E0
Tel: 709-896-7892; *Fax:* 709-896-9212

Judges (The Hon.):
George L. Murphy *November 27, 2009*

Supreme Court of Newfoundland & Labrador: Court of Appeal
287 Duckworth St., P.O. Box 937, St. John's, NL A1C 5M3
Tel: 709-729-0066; *Fax:* 709-729-7909
coaregistry@supreme.court.nl.ca
www.court.nl.ca/supreme/appeal

The Court of Appeal has appellate jurisdiction in criminal & civil matters from decisions of the lower courts & designated administrative boards & tribunals.
Chief Justice ***March 27, 2009***: The Hon. J.D. Green
Justices of Appeal (The Hon. Mr./Madam Justice):
Leo Barry *September 1, 2009*
Michael F. Harrington *March 2, 2007*
Lois R. Hoegg *June 1, 2007*
Malcolm Rowe
Gale Welsh
Charles W. White *April 29, 2009*

Supreme Court of Newfoundland & Labrador: Family Court
21 King's Bridge Rd., St. John's, NL A1C 3K4
Tel: 709-729-2258; *Fax:* 709-729-0784
familyinquiries@supreme.court.nl.ca
www.court.nl.ca/supreme/family

Judicial matters regarding families are shared/divided between the Supreme & Provincial Courts along geographical boundaries. The Family Court, a division of the Supreme Court, has exclusive jurisdiction for all family matters on the Avalon Peninsula (including Bell Is.). In the "expanded service area" of the United Family Court (from Holyrood to Port Blandford & Bonavista Peninsula), however, there is concurrent jurisdiction.There is a second location at 82 Mt. Bernard Ave., Corner Brook, NL, P.O. Box 2006, A2H 6J8.

Provincial Court of Newfoundland & Labrador
Atlantic Place, 215 Water St., P.O. Box 68, St. John's, NL A1C 6C9
Tel: 709-729-1004; *Fax:* 709-729-4319
inquiries@provincial.court.nl.ca
www.court.nl.ca/provincial

The Provincial Court has jurisdiction in select criminal & family (outside the judicial area of St. John's) matters as well as small claims & youth matters.
Chief Judge: The Hon. Pamela Goulding
Michael Madden (Associate Chief Judge)
Jacqueline Brazil
Judges (The Hon.):
Colin J. Flynn
Lori A. Marshall
David Orr
D. Mark Pike
Lois Skanes
James G. Walsh
Lynn Spracklin (Per Diem)
Joseph A. Woodrow (Per Diem)
Gregory O. Brown (Per Diem)
William English (Per Diem)
Robert B. Hyslop (Per Diem)
Patrick J.B. Kennedy (Per Diem)
Joseph A. Woodrow (Per Diem)
Lynn Spracklin (Per Diem)

Courts:
Clarenville
47 Marine Dr., Clarenville, NL A5A 1M5
Tel: 709-466-2635; *Fax:* 709-466-3147

Corner Brook
82 Mt. Bernard Ave., P.O. Box 2006, Corner Brook, NL A2H 6J8
Tel: 709-637-2323; *Fax:* 709-637-2656

Judges (The Hon.):
Catherine Allen-Westby *October 28, 2002*
Wayne Gorman *November 9, 2000*
Kymil Howe *March 11, 1993*

Gander
100 Airport Rd., P.O. Box 2222, Gander, NL A1V 2N9
Tel: 709-256-1100; *Fax:* 709-256-1097

Judges (The Hon.):
Jacqueline Jenkins *September 24, 2008*
Mark T. Linehan *November 1, 2003*

Grand Bank
Grand Bank-Fortune Hwy., P.O. Box 339, Grand Bank, NL A0E 1W0
Tel: 709-832-1450; *Fax:* 709-832-1758

Judges (The Hon.):
Harold Porter *October 12, 2001*

Grand Falls—Windsor
Law Courts Bldg., Grand Falls—Windsor, NL A2A 1W9
Tel: 709-292-4212; *Fax:* 709-292-4388

Judges (The Hon.):
Timothy Chalker *April 26, 2002*

Happy Valley-Goose Bay
P.O. Box 3014 B, Happy Valley-Goose Bay, NL A0P 1E0
Tel: 709-896-7870; *Fax:* 709-896-8767

Judges (The Hon.):
Phyllis Harris *June 10, 2014*
John Joy *September 1, 2006*

Harbour Grace
2 Harvey St., P.O. Box 519, Harbour Grace, NL A0A 2M0
Tel: 709-596-6141; *Fax:* 709-596-4304

Judges (The Hon.):
Bruce Short *February 3, 2010*

Stephenville
35 Alabama Dr., Stephenville, NL A2N 3K9
Tel: 709-643-2966; *Fax:* 709-643-4022
Judges (The Hon.):
Lynn E. Cole *March 4, 2014*

Wabush
Whiteway Dr., P.O. Box 1060, Wabush, NL A0R 1B0
Tel: 709-282-6617; *Fax:* 709-282-6905
Judges (The Hon.):
Wynne Anne Trahey *June 8, 2007*

Northwest Territories

Northwest Territories: Court of Appeal
4903 - 49th St., P.O. Box 550, Yellowknife, NT X1A 2N4
Tel: 867-873-7643; *Fax:* 867-873-0291
www.nwtcourts.ca/courts/ca.htm
The Court of Appeal has appellate jurisdiction in criminal & civil matters from the Supreme Court & Territorial Court.
Chief Justice: The Hon. C.A. Fraser
Justices of Appeal (The Hon. Mr./Madam Justice):
Ronald L. Berger
M.B. Bielby
L.A.M. Charbonneau
S. Cooper
Peter T. Costigan
L.F. Gower
E.D. Johnson
Robert G. Kilpatrick
A. Mahar
P.W.L. Martin
J.D.B. McDonald
T.W. Wakeling
B.K. O'Ferrall
M.S. Paperny
P.A. Rowbotham
K. Shaner
N.A. Sharkey
F.F. Slatter
S.H. Smallwood
B. Tulloch
Ronald S. Veale
B. Veldhuis
J. Watson

Northwest Territories: Supreme Court
4903 - 49th St., P.O. Box 550, Yellowknife, NT X1A 2N4
Tel: 867-920-8760; *Fax:* 867-873-0291
www.nwtcourts.ca/Courts/sc.htm
The Supreme Court is a court of original jurisdiction & has jurisdiction in all civil & criminal matters arising in the Northwest Territories, except those expressly excluded by statute.
Senior Judge: The Hon. L.A. Charbonneau
Judges (The Hon. Mr./Madam Justice):
A.M. Mahar
K. Shaner
S. Smallwood

Northwest Territories: Territorial Court
4903 - 49th St., P.O. Box 550, Yellowknife, NT X1A 2N4
Tel: 867-873-7602; *Fax:* 867-873-0291
www.nwtcourts.ca/Courts/tc.htm
The Territorial Court has jurisdiction in small claims, youth, family & select criminal matters.
Chief Judge: The Hon. Christine Gagnon
Judges (His/Her Hon.):
Bernadette E. Schmaltz
Robert D. Gorin
Garth Malakoe

Northwest Territories: Justice of the Peace Court
4903 - 49th St., P.O. Box 550, Yellowknife, NT X1A 2N4
Tel: 867-920-8020; *Fax:* 867-873-0203
Toll-Free: 844-300-7015
www.nwtcourts.ca/Courts/jp.htm
The Justices of the Peace have jurisdiction in summary conviction matters arising out of territorial statute, municipal by-law & select criminal matters.

Nova Scotia

Nova Scotia Court of Appeal
The Law Courts Bldg., 1815 Upper Water St., Halifax, NS B3J 1S7
Tel: 902-424-4900; *Fax:* 902-424-0524
www.courts.ns.ca/Appeal_Court/NSCA_home.htm
Other information: twitter.com/CourtsNS_NSCA
The Nova Scotia Court of Appeal is the province's highest court and has appellate jurisdiction in civil & criminal matters. It sits only in Halifax and hears appeals from both the Supreme and Provincial Courts.
Chief Justice: The Hon. Michael MacDonald
Justices of Appeal (The Hon. Justice):
Duncan R. Beveridge
Elizabeth Van den Eynden
Cindy A. Bourgeois
Peter M.S. Bryson
David P.S. Farrar
Joel E. Fichaud
J. Edward (Ted) Scanlan
M. Jill Hamilton (Supernumerary)
Linda L. Oland (Supernumerary)
Jamie W.S. Saunders (Supernumerary)

Nova Scotia Supreme Court
The Law Courts Bldg., 1815 Upper Water St., Halifax, NS B3J 1S7
Tel: 902-424-4900; *Fax:* 902-424-0524
www.courts.ns.ca/Supreme_Court/NSSC_home.htm
The Supreme Court is the highest trial court in the province with jurisdiction in all civil & criminal matters, except those expressly excluded by statute. It hears appeals on Provincial Court, Small Claims Court and Residential Tenancies Board matters.
Chief Justice: The Hon. Joseph P. Kennedy
Assoc. Chief Justice: The Hon. Deborah K. Smith
Judges (The Hon. Mr./Madam Justice):
Joshua M. Arnold
Allan Boudreau (Supernumerary)
Denise Boudreau
Felix A. Cacchione (Supernumerary)
Jamie S. Campbell
James L. Chipman
C. Richard Coughlan (Supernumerary)
Kevin Coady
Patrick J. Duncan
Suzanne M. Hood (Supernumerary)
Arthur J. LeBlanc (Supernumerary)
Glen G. McDougall
Gerald R.P. Moir
John D. Murphy
Arthur W. D. Pickup
M. Heather Robertson (Supernumerary)
Peter Rosinski
Michael J. Wood
Robert Wright (Supernumerary)
Judges, Family Division (The Hon. Mr./Madam Justice):
Associate Chief Justice: Lawrence I. O'Neil
Carole A. Beaton
Lou Ann Chiasson
Cindy G. Cormier
Leslie J. Dellapinna
Deborah Gass (Supernumerary)
R. Lester Jesudason
Elizabeth Jollimore
Beryl A. MacDonald
R. James Williams (Supernumerary)
Administration:
Registrar in Bankruptcy: Richard W. Cregan, 902-424-0259

Courts:

Amherst
54 Victoria St. East, Amherst, NS B4H 3G5
Tel: 902-667-2256; *Fax:* 902-667-1108

Annapolis Royal
119 Queen St., P.O. Box 1089, Annapolis Royal, NS B0V 1A0
Tel: 902-245-7134; *Fax:* 902-245-6722
Judges (The Hon.):
Pierre Muise

Antigonish
Justice Centre, 11 James St., Antigonish, NS B2G 1R6
Tel: 902-863-7300; *Fax:* 902-863-7479
Judges (The Hon.):
Nick M. Scaravelli

Bridgewater
Justice Centre, 141 High St., Bridgewater, NS B4V 1W2
Tel: 902-543-4679; *Fax:* 902-543-0678
Justices (The Hon.):
Margaret Stewart (Supernumerary)
Mona Lynch

Digby
Justice Centre, 119 Queen St., P.O. Box 1089, Digby, NS B0V 1A0
Tel: 902-245-7134; *Fax:* 902-245-6722
Judges (The Hon.):
Pierre L. Muise

Kentville
Justice Centre, 87 Cornwallis St., Kentville, NS B4N 2E5
Tel: 902-679-5540; *Fax:* 902-679-6178
Judges (The Hon.):
Gregory M. Warner

Pictou/New Glasgow
Court House, 69 Water St., P.O. Box 1750, Pictou, NS B0K 1H0
Tel: 902-485-7350; *Fax:* 902-485-6737
Judges (The Hon.):
Nick M. Scaravelli

Port Hawkesbury
Justice Centre, 15 Kennedy St., Port Hawkesbury, NS B9A 2Y1
Tel: 902-625-2665; *Fax:* 902-625-4084

Sydney
Justice Centre, #1 & 2, 136 Charlotte St., Sydney, NS B1P 1C3
Tel: 902-563-3550; *Fax:* 902-563-2224
Judges (The Hon.):
Frank C. Edwards (Supernumerary)
Robin C. M. Gogan
Simon J. MacDonald (Supernumerary)
Patrick J. Murray
Theresa M. Forgeron
Kenneth Haley
M. Clare MacLellan
Robert M. Gregan
Lee Anne MacLeod-Archer
Darryl W. Wilson (Supernumerary)

Truro
Justice Centre, 1 Church St., Truro, NS B2N 3Z5
Tel: 902-893-3953; *Fax:* 902-893-6114
Judges (The Hon.):
Jeffrey R. Hunt

Yarmouth
Justice Centre, 164 Main St., Yarmouth, NS B5A 1C2
Tel: 902-742-4142; *Fax:* 902-742-0678
Judges (The Hon.):
Pierre L. Muise

Nova Scotia Probate Court
Law Courts Bldg, 1815 Upper Water St., Halifax, NS B3J 1S7
Tel: 902-424-7422; *Fax:* 902-424-0524
www.courts.ns.ca/Probate_Court/NSPBC_home.htm
The Probate Court has jurisdiction in respect of estate matters.

Courts:

Amherst
Justice Centre, 16 Church St., 3rd Fl., Amherst, NS B4H 3A6
Tel: 902-667-2256; *Fax:* 902-667-1108

Annapolis Royal
Justice Centre, 377 St. George St., P.O. Box 129, Annapolis Royal, NS B0S 1A0
Tel: 902-532-5462; *Fax:* 902-532-7225

Antigonish
Justice Centre, 11 James St., Antigonish, NS B2G 1R6
Tel: 902-863-7396; *Fax:* 902-863-7479

Bridgewater
Justice Centre, 141 High St., Bridgewater, NS B4V 1W2
Tel: 902-543-4679; *Fax:* 902-543-0678

Digby
Court House, 119 Queen St., P.O. Box 1089, Digby, NS B0V 1A0
Tel: 902-245-4567; *Fax:* 902-245-6722

Halifax
Law Courts Bldg., 1815 Upper Water St., Halifax, NS B3J 1S7
Tel: 902-424-7422; *Fax:* 902-424-0524

Kentville
Justice Centre, 87 Cornwallis St., Kentville, NS B4N 2E5
Tel: 902-679-5540; *Fax:* 902-679-6178

Pictou/New Glasgow
69 Water St., P.O. Box 1750, Pictou, NS B0K 1H0
Tel: 902-485-7350; *Fax:* 902-485-6737

Port Hawkesbury
Justice Centre, 15 Kennedy St., Port Hawkesbury, NS B9A 2Y1
Tel: 902-625-2665; *Fax:* 902-625-4084

Sydney
Justice Centre, #6, 136 Charlotte St., Sydney, NS B1P 1C3
Tel: 902-563-3545; *Fax:* 902-563-5701

Truro
Justice Centre, 1 Church St., Truro, NS B2N 3Z5
Tel: 902-893-5870; *Fax:* 902-893-6114

Yarmouth
Justice Centre, 164 Main St., Yarmouth, NS B5A 1C2
Tel: 902-742-5469; *Fax:* 902-742-0678

Nova Scotia Provincial Court
5250 Spring Garden Rd., Halifax, NS B3J 1E7
Tel: 902-424-8718; *Fax:* 902-424-0551
www.courts.ns.ca/Provincial_Court/NSPC_home.htm
The Provincial Court has jurisdiction over almost all indictable charges under provincial & federal statutes and regulations. When judges are not available, presiding Justices of the Peace deal with release or detention of those arrested.
Chief Judge: The Hon. Pamela S. Williams
Judges (The Hon.):
Alan T. Tufts (Associate Chief Judge)
Barbara Beach
M.C. Chisholm
Patrick Curran
Anne S. Derrick
W.B. Digby
Gregory E. Lenehan
Daniel MacRury
Michael B. Sherar

Courts:
Amherst
16 Church St., 3rd Fl., Amherst, NS B4H 3A6
Tel: 902-667-2256; *Fax:* 902-667-1108
S. Raymond Morse
Judges (The Hon.):
Elizabeth A. Buckle

Annapolis Royal
Satellite Court, 377 St. George St., Annapolis Royal, NS B0S 1A0
Tel: 902-245-4567

Antigonish
11 James St., Antigonish, NS B2G 1R6
Tel: 902-863-3676; *Fax:* 902-863-7479
Judges (The Hon.):
Richard J. MacKinnon

Bridgewater
Justice Centre, 141 High St., Bridgewater, NS B4V 1W2
Tel: 902-543-4679; *Fax:* 902-543-0678
Judges (The Hon.):
James H. Burrill
Paul B. Scovil
William Dyer

Dartmouth
277 Pleasant St., Dartmouth, NS B2Y 4B7
Tel: 902-424-2390; *Fax:* 902-424-0677
Judges (The Hon.):
Pamela S. Williams (Chief Judge of the Provincial/Family Courts)
Flora I. Buchan
D. Timothy Gabriel
Frank P. Hoskins
Alanna Murphy
Corrine Sparks
Theodore K. Tax

Digby
119 Queen St., P.O. Box 1089, Digby, NS B0V 1A0
Tel: 902-245-4567; *Fax:* 902-245-6722
Judges (The Hon.):
Timothy D. Landry

Kentville
Justice Centre, 87 Cornwallis St., Kentville, NS B4N 2E5
Tel: 902-679-6070; *Fax:* 902-679-6190
Judges (The Hon.):
Alan T. Tufts (Associate Chief Judge)
Marci Lin Melvin

Pictou
Justice Centre, 69 Water St., P.O. Box 1750, Pictou, NS B0K 1H0
Tel: 902-485-7350; *Fax:* 902-485-3552
Also serving New Glasgow
Jim Wilson
Judges (The Hon.):
Del W. Atwood
Timothy Daley

Port Hawkesbury
Justice Centre, 15 Kennedy St., Port Hawkesbury, NS B9A 2Y1
Tel: 902-625-2665; *Fax:* 902-625-4084
Judges (The Hon.):
Laurel J. Halfpenny-MacQuarrie

Sydney
Justice Centre, #4 & 5, 136 Charlotte St., Sydney, NS B1P 1C3
Tel: 902-563-3510; *Fax:* 902-563-3421
Judges (The Hon.):
E. Ann Marie MacInnes
Peter Ross
Brian D. Williston
David J. Ryan
Jean M. Whalen

Truro
Justice Centre, 540 Prince St., Truro, NS B2N 1G1
Tel: 902-893-5840; *Fax:* 902-893-6261
Judges (The Hon.):
Jean M. Dewolfe
Alain Bégin
David R. Hubley
S. Raymond Morse
Warren Zimmer

Yarmouth
Justice Centre, 164 Main St., Yarmouth, NS B5A 1C2
Tel: 902-742-0500; *Fax:* 902-742-0678
Judges (The Hon.):
Michelle Christenson
Timothy Landry
Robert M. Prince
John D. Comeau

Nova Scotia Supreme Court: Family Division
3380 Devonshire Ave., P.O. Box 8988 A, Halifax, NS B3K 5M6
Tel: 902-424-3990; *Fax:* 902-424-0562
www.courts.ns.ca/Supreme_Court_Family/NSSCFD_home.htm
The Family Court has jurisdiction in family matters & also functions as a Youth Court for cases involving youths aged 12 to 15 years.
Lawrence I. O'Neil (Associate Chief Justice)
Carole A. Beaton
Lou Ann Chiasson
Cindy G. Cormier
Leslie J. Dellapinna
Deborah Gass (Supernumerary)
R. Lester Jesudason
Elizabeth Jollimore
Beryl A. MacDonald
R. James Williams

Courts:
Amherst
Justice Centre, 16 Church St., 3rd Fl., Amherst, NS B4H 3A6
Tel: 902-667-2256; *Fax:* 902-667-1108

Antigonish
Justice Centre, 11 James St., Antigonish, NS B2G 1R6
Tel: 902-863-7312; *Fax:* 902-863-7479

Bridgewater
Justice Centre, 141 High St., Bridgewater, NS B4V 1W2
Tel: 902-543-4679; *Fax:* 902-543-0678

Digby/Annapolis
Justice Centre, 119 Queen St., P.O. Box 1089, Digby, NS B0V 1A0
Tel: 902-245-4567; *Fax:* 902-245-6722

Kentville
87 Cornwallis St., Kentville, NS B4N 4E5
Tel: 902-679-5540; *Fax:* 902-679-6178

Port Hawkesbury
15 Kennedy St., Port Hawkesbury, NS B9A 2Y1
Tel: 902-625-2665; *Fax:* 902-625-4084
Judges (The Hon.):
Moira C. Legere Sers

Sydney
#1 & #2, 136 Charlotte St., Sydney, NS B1P 1C3
Tel: 902-563-3550; *Fax:* 902-563-2224
Judges (The Hon.):
Theresa M. Forgeron
Robert M. Gregan
Kenneth Haley
Clare MacLellan
Lee Anne MacLeod-Archer
Darryl W. Wilson

Truro
1 Church St., Truro, NS B2N 3Z5
Tel: 902-893-3953; *Fax:* 902-893-6114

Yarmouth
Justice Centre, 164 Main St., Yarmouth, NS B5A 1C2
Tel: 902-742-0550; *Fax:* 902-742-0678

Nunavut

Nunavut Court of Appeal
#224, Arnakallak Bldg., P.O. Box 297, Iqaluit, NU X0A 0H0
Tel: 867-975-6100; *Fax:* 867-975-6168
Toll-Free: 866-286-0546
www.nunavutcourts.ca/nunavut-court-of-appeal
Chief Justice: The Hon. Catherine Fraser
Justices (The Hon. Mr./Madam Justice):
E. Picard
T. Wakeling
R.S. Brown
Ronald Berger
P. Bychok
S. Greckol
Peter Costigan
S. Martin
Louise Charbonneau
Frans Slatter
Marina Paperny
Leigh Gower
Peter Martin
Jack Watson
Patricia Rowbotham
Neil Sharkey
John McDonald
Susan Cooper
Myra Bielby
Brian O'Ferrall
Karan Shaner
Shannon Smallwood
Andrew Mahar
Bonnie Tulloch
Barbara Veldhuis

Nunavut Court of Justice
#224, Arnakallak Bldg., P.O. Box 297, Iqaluit, NU X0A 0H0
Tel: 867-975-6100; *Fax:* 867-975-6168
Toll-Free: 866-286-0546
www.nunavutcourts.ca/nunavut-court-of-justice
Justices (The Hon. Mr./Madam Justice):
R. Kilpatrick (Senior Judge)
Neil Sharkey
S. Cooper
Paul Bychok
B. Tulloch

Ontario

Court of Appeal for Ontario
Osgoode Hall, 130 Queen St. West, Toronto, ON M5H 2N5
Tel: 416-327-5020; *Fax:* 416-327-5032
Toll-Free: 855-718-1756
www.ontariocourts.ca/coa/en
The Court of Appeal is the final court of appeal for Ontario. Appeals from the Court of Appeal may be pursued in the Supreme Court of Canada.
Chief Justice: The Hon. Mr. George R. Strathy
Assoc. Chief Justice: The Hon. Mr. Alexandra Hoy
Justices (The Hon. Mr./Madam Justice):
Mary Lou Benotto
Robert A. Blair
David M. Brown
Eleanore A. Cronk
David H. Doherty
Gloria J. Epstein
Kathryn N. Feldman
Eileen E. Gillese
C. William Hourigan
Grant Huscroft
Russell G. Juriansz
Harry S. LaForme
John I. Laskin
Peter D. Lauwers
Jean L. MacFarland
James MacPherson
Sarah E. Pepall
Bradley Miller
Paul S. Rouleau
Robert J. Sharpe
Janet M. Simmons
Gladys Pardu
Michael H Tulloch
David Watt
Karen M. Weiler
Katherine van Rensburg
Administration:
Senior Legal Officer: Alison Warner, 416-327-1179
Registrar & Manager: Court Operations, Daniel Marentic
Deputy Registrar & Manager of Court Operations: Sandra Theroulde

Deputy Registrar & Manager of Judicial Support: Adam Langley

Ontario Superior Court of Justice

Osgoode Hall, 130 Queen St. West, Toronto, ON M5H 2N5
Tel: 416-327-5036; *Fax:* 416-327-5417
www.ontariocourts.ca/scj/en

In addition to its regular trial court functions, the Superior Court of Justice has two branches: the Divisional Court which generally hears appeals from a final order of a Judge of the Superior Court involving disputes of up to $25,000, & the Small Claims Court which generally hears cases involving claims up to $10,000. The Governor General appoints the Judges to all but the Ontario Court of Justice.

Chief Justice: The Hon. Heather Forster Smith
Assoc. Chief Justice: The Hon. Frank N. Marrocco, 416-327-5000
Senior Judge of the Family Court: The Hon. George Czutrin

Central East Region

50 Eagle St. West, 4th Fl., Newmarket, ON L3Y 6B1
Tel: 905-853-4827; *Fax:* 905-853-4826

Regional Senior Justice: Michelle Fuerst
Justices (The Hon. Mr./Madam Justice):

Stephen T. Bale
R. Cary Boswell
J. Christopher Corkery
Guy P. DiTomaso
Peter A. Douglas
Margaret Eberhard
Mark L. Edwards
Jane Ferguson
Richard T. Bennett
Laura A. Bird
Robert Charney
Laura E. Fryer
Cory A. Gilmore
Bruce A. Glass
Fred Graham
Drew S. Gunsolus
Mary J. Hatton
Susan E. Healey
Jayne E. Hughes
David Jarvis
Alan P. Ingram
Ronald P. Kaufman
Myrna L. Lack
Barry G. A. MacDougall
J. Robert MacKinnon
Peter Z. Magda
John R. McCarthy
John P.L. McDermot
Heather A. McGee
Michael K. McKelvey
Edwin B. Minden
J. Scott McLeod
Gregory M. Mulligan
Anne Mullins
Clifford S. Nelson
Paul W. Nicholson
Hugh K. O'Connell
Lydia M. Olah
Elizabeth Quinlan
Sherrill M. Rogers
Allan R. Rowsell
David Salmers
Margaret A. C. Scott
J. Bryan Shaughnessy
Alexander Sosna
Phillip Sutherland
D. Roger Timms
Mary E. Vallee
Ramona A. Wildman
Thomas M. Wood
Susan Woodley

Central South Region

45 Main St. East, Hamilton, ON L8N 2B7
Tel: 905-645-5323; *Fax:* 905-645-5374

Regional Senior Justice: James R.H. Turnbull
Justices (The Hon. Mr./Madam Justice):

Catrina Braid
Andrew J. Goodman
Harrison S. Arrell
David L. Edwards
David A. Broad
Antonio Skarica
Caroline E. Brown
Grant A. Campbell
Kim A. Carpenter-Gunn
Deborah L. Chappel
Patrick J. Flynn
C. Stephen Glithero
Donald J. Gordon
P.B. Hambly
R. John Harper
Joseph R. Henderson
Cheryl Lafrenière
Richard A. Lococo
Thomas R. Lofchik
Wendy L. MacPherson
Theresa Maddalena
Randolph Mazza
Mary Jo McLaren
Jane A. Milanetti
Robert J. Nightingale
Dale Parayeski
Alex Pazaratz
Joseph W. Quinn
James A Ramsay
Robert B. Reid
Robert D. Reilly
J. Wilma Scott
James W. Sloan
Gerald E. Taylor
Paul R. Sweeney
Linda M. Walters
Alan C. R. Whitten

Central West Region

#100, 7755 Hurontario St., Brampton, ON L6W 4T6
Tel: 905-456-4837; *Fax:* 905-456-4836

Regional Senior Justice: Peter A. Daley
Justices (The Hon. Mr./Madam Justice):

Irving W. André
Deena F. Baltman
Kofi N. Barnes
Thomas A. Bielby
Ivan S. Bloom
Kendra D. Coats
Clayton Conlan
Steve A. Coroza
J. Michal Fairburn
Fletcher Dawson
Meredith Donohue
Bruce Durno
Michael G. Emery
Dale F. Fitzpatrick
Joseph M. Fragomeni
Michael R. Gibson
Douglas K. Gray
Casimir N. Herold
S. Casey Hill
William Le May
Gordon D. Lemon
Lucy K. McSweeney
Gisele M. Miller
Nancy M. Mossip
David Price
Leonard Ricchetti
Silja S. Seppi
Lorna-Lee Snowie
John R. Sproat
Robert M. Thompson
Jamie K. Trimble
E. Ria Tzimas
Francine Van Melle
Bonnie J. Wein
Jennifer Woollcombe

East Region

161 Elgin St., Ottawa, ON K2P 2K1
Tel: 613-239-1527; *Fax:* 613-239-1067

Regional Senior Justice: James E. McNamara
Justices (The Hon. Mr./Madam Justice):

Brian W. Abrams
Catherine D. Aitken
Calum U.C. MacLeod
Graeme Mew
Robert N. Beaudoin
Jennifer A. Blishen
Richard G. Byers
Michel Z. Charbonneau
Sylvia Corthorn
Charles T. Hackland
Adriana Doyle
Martin S. James
John M. Johnston
Paul B. Kane
Stanley J. Kershman
Marc R. Labrosse
Johanne Lafrance-Cardinal
Laurie Lacelle
Ronald M. Laliberté
Rick Leroy
Maria T. Linhares de Sousa
V. Jennifer MacKinnon
Helen K. MacLeod-Beliveau
Robert L. Maranger
Colin D. A. McKinnon
Hugh R. McLean
Timothy Minnema
Julianne A. Parfett
Kenneth E. Pedlar
Robert Pelletier
Kevin B. Phillips
Michael Quigley
Lynn D. Ratushny
Timothy D. Ray
Cheryl Robertson
Pierre E. Roger
Douglas J. A. Rutherford
Mark P. Shelston
Robert F. Scott
Elizabeth Sheard
Alan D. Sheffield
G. Patrick Smith
Robert J. Smith
Wolfram Tausendfreund
Giovanna Toscano Roccamo
Gary W. Trammer
Anne C. Trousdale
Bonnie Warkentin

Toronto Region

361 University Ave., Toronto, ON M5G 1T3
Tel: 416-327-5000; *Fax:* 416-327-9931

Regional Senior Justice: The Hon. Geoffrey B. Morawetz
Justices (The Hon. Mr./Madam Justice):

Suhail A.Q. Akhtar
Freya Kristjanson
Beth A. Allen
Todd L. Archibald
Nancy L. Backhouse
Edward P. Belobaba
Carole J. Brown
Michael F. Brown
Kenneth L. Campbell
Victoria R. Chiappetta
Robert A. Clark
Michael Code
Barbara A. Conway
David L. Corbett
Katherine B. Corrick
Bonnie L. Croll
Michael R. Dambrot
James F. Diamond
Grant R. Dow
Todd Ducharme
Tamarin M. Dunnet
Sean F. Dunphy
Mario D. Faieta
Stephen E. Firestone
Maureen D. Forestell
E. Eva Frank
Arthur M. Gans
Nola E. Garton
Benjamin T. Glustein
Robert F. Goldstein
Susanne R. Goodman
Glenn A. Hainey
Alison Harvison Young
Susan G. Himel
Kenneth G. Hood
Carolyn J. Horkins
Jane E. Kelly
Frances P. Kiteley
Emile R. Kruzick
Thomas R. Lederer
Sidney N. Lederman
Wailan Low
Ian A. MacDonnell
Wendy M. Matheson
J. David McCombs
Thomas J. McEwen
John B. McMahon
Faye E. McWatt
Ruth E. Mesbur
Anne M. Molloy
J. Patrick Moore
Edward W. Morgan
Frederick L. Myers
Frank J. C. Newbould
Ian V. B. Nordheimer
Alfred J. O'Marra
Brian P. O'Marra
Victor Paisley
Laurence A. Pattillo
Michael A. Penny

Paul M. Perell
Craig Perkins
Andra Pollack
Michael G. Quigley
Harriet E. Sachs
Mary A. Sanderson
Gertrude F. Siegel
Christopher Speyer
Nancy J. Spies
Suzanne M. Stevenson
Elizabeth M. Stewart
David G. Stinson
Katherine E. Swinton
Edward F. Then
Julie A. Thornburn
W. Brian Trafford
Gary T. Trotter
Kevin W. Whitaker
Darla A. Wilson
Janet Wilson
Herman J. Wilton-Siegel
Kelly P. Wright

Northeast Region
155 Elm St., Sudbury, ON P3C 1T9
Tel: 705-564-7814; *Fax:* 705-564-7902
Regional Senior Justice: Robbie D. Gordon
Justices (The Hon. Mr./Madam Justice):
R. Dan Cornell
Robert G. S. Del Frate
M. Gregory Ellies
Edward E. Gareau
Louise L. Gauthier
Patricia C. Hennessy
Norman M. Karam
Edward J. Koke
Alexander Kurke
Cindy A. M. MacDonald
Ian S. McMillan
David J. Nadeau
John S. Poupore
Annalisa Rasaiah
Robert A. Riopelle
Paul U. Rivard
Robin Tremblay
George T. Valin
Michael N. Varpio
W. Larry Whalen
James A. S. Wilcox

Northwest Region
125 Brodie St. North, Thunder Bay, ON P7C 0A3
Tel: 807-626-7083; *Fax:* 807-626-7090
Regional Senior Justice: Douglas C. Shaw
Justices (The Hon. Mr./Madam Justice):
F. Bruce Fitzpatrick
John S. Fregeau
W. Danial Newton
Helen Pierce
Terrence A. Platana

Southwest Region
80 Dundas St., London, ON N6A 6A2
Tel: 519-660-2291; *Fax:* 519-660-2294
Regional Senior Justice: Thomas A. Heeney
Justices (The Hon. Mr./Madam Justice):
David Aston
Christopher Bondy
Scott K. Campbell
Thomas J. Carey
John Desotti
Joseph M. W. Donohue
Marc A. Garson
Jonathon C. George
Kelly A. Gorman
A. Duncan Grace
Roland J. Haines
Pamela L. Hebner
Paul J. Henderson
Peter B. Hockin
Paul R. Howard
George W. King
Denise M Korpan
Ian F. Leach
Lynne Leitch
Magaret A. McSorley
Alissa K. Mitchell
Victor Mitrow
Johanne N. Morissette
Kirk W. Munroe
Terrence L. J. Patterson
Renee M. Pomerance
Helen A. Rady
Russell M. Raikes
Steven Rogin
Lynda Templeton
Bruce G. Thomas
Gregory J. Verbeem
Henry Vogelsang

Ontario Court of Justice
#2300, 1 Queen St. East, P.O. Box 91, Toronto, ON M5C 2W5
Tel: 416-327-5660; *Fax:* 416-326-4782
www.ontariocourts.on.ca/ocj

The Ontario Court of Justice generally performs functions assigned to it by Acts such as the *Criminal Code* the *Provincial Offences Act* the *Family Law Act* the *Children's Law Reform Act* & the *Child & Family Services Act* & is a youth court. The Lieutenant Governor in Council, on the recommendation of the Attorney General, appoints the justices.
Chief Justice: The Hon. Lise Maisonneuve
Assoc. Chief Justice: The Hon. Peter DeFreitas
Assoc. Chief Justice: The Hon. Faith M. Finnestad

Central East Region
50 Eagle St. West, 2nd Fl., Newmarket, ON L3Y 6B1
Tel: 905-853-4890; *Fax:* 902-853-4891
Regional Senior Justice: Simon C. Armstrong
Justices (The Hon.):
John F. Adamson
Amit A. Ghosh
George Beatty
Robert W. Beninger
Michael Block
Peter N. Bourque
Lisa Cameron
Howard I. Chisvin
Nancy A. Dawson
Joseph A. De Filippis
Marquis S. V. Felix
Mary Teresa E. Devlin
Jon-Jo Douglas
John D. D. Evans
Robert Graydon
Michael Harpur
C. Roland Harris
Ferhan Javed
Cynthia Johnston
Joseph F. Kenkel
Stuart Konyer
Glenn D. Krelove
Susan C. MacLean
Enno J. Meijers
Nyron Dwyer
Mary E. Misener
John A. Payne
John N. Olver
David S. Rose
Esther Rosenberg
David M. Stone
Peter Tetley
Graham Wakefield
Peter C. West
Timothy C. Whetung
Cecile Applegate
Jonathan Bliss

Central West Region
#762, 45 Main St. East, Hamilton, ON L8N 2B7
Tel: 905-645-5344; *Fax:* 905-645-5375
Regional Senior Justice: The Hon. Sharon M. Nicklas
Justices (The Hon.):
P.H. Marjoh Agro
Kathleen A. Baker
Lesley M. Baldwin
Patrice F. Band
W. James Blacklock
Louise Botham
Joseph W. Bovard
Stephen D. Brown
Frederic M. Campling
Steven R. Clark
Philip J. Clay
Tory Colvin
Jill M. Copeland
Alan D. Cooper
Ian B. Cowan
Timothy A. Culver
Paul R. Currie
Bruce W. Duncan
Patrick W. Dunn
Gethin B. Edward
George S. Gage
Robert Gee
Nathalie Gregson
David Harris
Kathryn L. Hawke
Nancy S. Kastner
James J. Keaney
Sonia V. Khemani
Richard J. LeDressay
June Maresca
Eileen Martin
Douglas B. Maund
Donald McLeod
Katherine L. McLeod
Paul F. Monahan
Joseph Nadel
C. Ann Nelson
Alison R. MacKay
Lise S. Parent
Manjusha Pawagi
Bruce E. Pugsley
Elinore A. Ready
P. Andras Schreck
Richard H. K. Schwarzl
Kevin Sherwood
Colette D. Good
Victoria A Starr
James Stribopoulos
Anthony Sullivan
Marvin Kurz
D. Terry Vyse
Ann Watson
Peter H. Wilkie
Bernd E. Zabel
Roselyn Zisman
Martha Zivolak

East Region
161 Elgin St., Ottawa, ON K2P 2L1
Tel: 613-239-1520; *Fax:* 613-239-1572
Regional Senior Justice: The Hon. Jean G. Legault
Justices (The Hon.):
Julie Bourgeois
Ann Alder
Peter K. Doody
Jonathan Brunet
Elaine Deluzio
Célynne S. Dorval
Franco Giamberardino
Geoffrey Griffin
Mitch Hoffman
Stephen J. Hunter
Catherine A Kehoe
Richard T. Knott
Diane M. Lahaie
Allan G. Letourneau
Jacqueline Loignon
Wendy Malcolm
Michael G. March
Kimberly Moore
Larry B. O'Brien
David Paciocco
Heather E. Perkins-McVey
Hugh L. Fraser
Gilles Renaud
Robert G. Selkirk
Robert Wadden
Matthew C Webber
Jane N. Wilson
J. Peter Wright

Northeast Region
#201, 159 Cedar St., Sudbury, ON P3E 6A5
Tel: 705-564-7624; *Fax:* 705-564-7620
Regional Senior Justice: The Hon. Patrick J. Boucher
Justices (The Hon.):
Andrew Buttazzoni
John P. Condon
Melanie D. Dunn
G. Normand Glaude
André L. Guay
John D. Keast
Lawrence Klein
Romuald F. Kwolek
Randall W. Lalande
Martin P. Lambert
Karen L. Lische
Joseph G. R. Maille
Catherine Mathias McDonald
Malcolm McLeod
Alain H. Perron
Michelle Rocheleau
Gregory P. Rodgers
Louise Serré
Robert P. Villeneuve

Northwest Region
#6, 125 Brodie St. North, Thunder Bay, ON P7C 0A3
Tel: 807-626-7048; *Fax:* 807-626-7091
Regional Senior Justice: The Hon. Joyce Elder
Justices (The Hon.):
Peter T. Bishop
Marc Bode
Sarah S. Cleghorn
Dino DiGiuseppe
David M. Gibson
Jennifer R. Hoshizaki
Joyce L. Pelletier
Francesco Valente

Toronto Region
Old City Hall, #257, 60 Queen St. West, Toronto, ON M5H 2M4
Tel: 416-327-5659; *Fax:* 416-326-4788
Regional Senior Justice: The Hon. Timothy R. Lipson
Kimberley A. Crosbie
Sheilagh O'Connell
Melanie Sager
Maria Speyer
Justices (The Hon.):
Sandra Bacchus
Feroza Bhabha
Robert G. Bigelow
Miriam Bloomenfeld
Richard Blouin
Ronald D. Boivin
Howard Borenstein
Carol Brewer
Beverly A. Brown
Harvey P. Brownstone
Lloyd M. Budzinski
Kathleen J. Caldwell
James R. Chaffe
Leslie A. P. Chapin
Thomas P Cleary
Marion L. Cohen
David P. Cole
Frank D. Crewe
Carole Curtis
Antonio Di Zio
Kate Doorly
Philip Anthony Downes
Lucia Favret
Lawrence T. Feldman
Paul French
Melvyn Green
Mara B. Greene
Jack M. Grossman
Aston Joseph Hall
Peter A. J. Harris
Mary L. Hogan
William B. Horkins
Carolyn J. Jones
Penny J. Jones
Edward J. Kelly
Robert Kelly
Ramez Khawly
Brent Knazan
Neil L. Kozloff
Gerald S. Lapkin (Senior Judge)
Eric (Rick) N. Libman
Sally E. Marin
Heather Adair McArthur
Salvatore Merenda
Cathy Mocha
John C. Moore
Katrina Mulligan
Ellen B. Murray
Shaun S. Nakatsuru
Petra E. Newton
Fergus C. O'Donnell
Diane I. Oleskiw
Russell J. Otter
Debra A. W. Paulseth
Leslie C. Pringle
Sheila Ray
John M. Ritchie
Paul Robertson
Rebecca Rutherford
Richard D. Schneider
Brian M. Scully
S. Rebecca Shamai
Riun Shandler
Stanley B. Sherr
Geraldine N. Sparrow
Robert J. Spence
Andrea Tuck-Jackson
Charles H. Vaillancourt
Brian Weagant
Fern M. Weinper
William R. Wolski
Mavin Wong
Bruce J. Young
Marvin A. Zuker

West Region
80 Dundas St. East, 1st Fl., #L, London, ON N6A 6A8
Tel: 519-660-2292; *Fax:* 519-660-3138
Regional Senior Justice: The Hon. Stephen J. Fuerth
Justices (The Hon.):
J. Elliott Allen
Deborah J. Austin
Sharman S. Bondy
Pamela Borghesan
George J. Brophy
Stephen E.J. Paull
Gregory A. Campbell
Jane E. Caspers
Lloyd C. Dean
Norman S. Douglas
Michael J. Epstein
Lucy C. Glenn
M. Edward Graham
Steven P. Harrison
Gary F. Hearn
G. Mark Hornblower
Paul J. S. Kowalyshyn
Jeanine Elisabeth LeRoy
John T. Lynch
Allan Maclure
Ronald A. Marion
Anne E. E. McFadyen
Kevin G. McHugh
A. Thomas McKay
Kathryn L. McKerlie
Julia A. Morneau
Katherine S. Neill
Michael P. O'Dea
Craig A. Parry
Douglas W. Phillips
Wayne G. Rabley
Micheline A. Rawlins
Lynda J. Rogers
Robert W. Rogerson
Lynda S. Ross
Eleanor M. Schnall
John S. Skowronski
Melanie A. Sopinka
Barry Tobin
Colin R. Westman
Gerry Lynn Wong

Court Services Division

McMurtry-Scott Bldg., #204, 720 Bay St., Toronto, ON M7A 2S9
Tel: 416-326-4263; *Fax:* 416-326-2652
www.attorneygeneral.jus.gov.on.ca/english/courts

Court Services Division manages the court offices in communities across Ontario: scheduling court cases, maintaining records & files, collecting fines & fees, enforcing civil orders, and providing information to the public. It also provides administration support to judicial offices in the Superior Court of Justice & the Ontario Court of Justice: providing clerks, court reporters, registrars and interpreters for court proceedings.

Barrie
45 Cedar Pointe Dr., Barrie, ON L4N 5R7
Tel: 705-739-4291; *Fax:* 705-739-4292

Belleville
235 Pinnacle St., 3rd Fl., Belleville, ON K8N 3A9
Tel: 613-966-0331; *Fax:* 613-966-7045

Bracebridge - Muskoka
76 Pine St., Bracebridge, ON P1L 0C4
Tel: 705-645-1231; *Fax:* 705-645-5319
poa@muskoka.on.ca
www.muskoka.on.ca

Brampton
5 Ray Lawson Blvd., Brampton, ON L6Y 5L7
Tel: 905-450-4770; *Fax:* 905-450-4794
provincialoffencescourt@brampton.ca
Other information: TTY: 905-874-2130

Brantford
102 Wellington Sq., P.O. Box 760, Brantford, ON N3T 5R7
Tel: 519-751-9100; *Fax:* 519-751-0404
brantfordpoa@brantford.ca

Brockville
#100, 32 Wall St., Brockville, ON K6V 4R9
Tel: 613-342-2357; *Fax:* 613-342-8891
Toll-Free: 800-539-8685
poacourt@uclg.on.ca
www.leedsgrenville.com/en/live/provincialoffences/provincialoffences.asp
Other information: TTY: 613-341-3854

Caledon East
6311 Old Church Rd., Caledon East, ON L7C 1J6
Tel: 905-584-2273; *Fax:* 905-584-2861
www.caledon.ca/en/townhall/provincialoffencescourt.asp

Cayuga
45 Munsee St. North, P.O. Box 220, Cayuga, ON N0A 1E0
Tel: 905-772-3327; *Fax:* 905-772-5810
www.haldimandcounty.on.ca/residents.aspx?id=178

Chatham-Kent
21633 Communication Rd., RR#5, Bleheim, ON N0P 1A0
Tel: 519-352-8484; *Fax:* 519-352-7979
CKpoc@chatham-kent.ca
www.chatham-kent.ca/ProvincialOffencesCourt/Pages/ProvincialOffencesCourt.aspx

Cobourg-Northumberland
860 William St., Cobourg, ON K9A 3A9
Tel: 905-372-3329; *Fax:* 905-372-6529
www.northumberlandcounty.ca

Cochrane
171 - 4 Ave, P.O. Box 1867, Cochrane, ON P0L 1C0
Tel: 705-272-2538; *Fax:* 705-272-3593

Cornwall - Stormont, Dundas & Glengarry
#308, 26 Pitt St., Cornwall, ON K6J 3P2
Tel: 613-933-4301; *Fax:* 613-933-4161
courtservices@sdgcounties.ca
www.sdgcounties.ca

Dryden
116 Queen St., P.O. Box 105, Dryden, ON P8N 2Y7
Tel: 807-223-1429; *Fax:* 807-223-5839
www.dryden.ca

Elliott Lake & Espanola
#4, 100 Tudhope St., Espanola, ON P5E 1S6
Tel: 705-862-7875; *Fax:* 705-862-7876
www.espanola.ca/index.php/poa

Fort Frances
320 Portage Ave., Fort Frances, ON P9A 3P9
Tel: 807-274-1676; *Fax:* 807-274-0446
www.fort-frances.com

Goderich-Huron
1 Court House Sq., Goderich, ON N7A 1M2
Tel: 519-524-8394; *Fax:* 519-524-2044
poa@huroncounty.ca
www.huroncounty.ca

Gore Bay
15 Water St., P.O. Box 500, Gore Bay, ON P0P 1H0
Tel: 705-282-2837; *Fax:* 705-282-3076
gorebaypoa@gorebay.ca

Guelph
59 Carden St., Guelph, ON N1H 2Z9
Tel: 519-826-0762; *Fax:* 519-826-6814
courtservices@guelph.ca
guelph.ca/court
Other information: TTY: 519-826-9771

Haileybury - Temiskaming Shores
325 Farr Dr., P.O. Box 2050, Haileybury, ON P0J 1K0
Tel: 705-672-3221; *Fax:* 705-672-2911
www.temiskamingshores.ca

Halton Region
2051 Plains Rd. East, Burlington, ON L7R 5A5
Tel: 905-637-1274; *Fax:* 905-637-5919
poaenquires@burlington.ca
www.burlington.ca/en/halton-court-services/Halton-Home.asp

Hamilton
#408, 45 Main St. East, Hamilton, ON L8N 2B7
Tel: 905-540-5592; *Fax:* 905-540-5730
www.hamilton.ca

Lindsay - Kawartha Lakes
440 Kent St. West, Lindsay, ON K9V 5P2
Tel: 705-324-3962; *Fax:* 705-324-7991
www.city.kawarthalakes.on.ca

Kenora
1 Main St. South, Kenora, ON P9N 3X2
Tel: 807-467-2984; *Fax:* 807-467-8530
poa@kenora.ca
www.kenora.ca/cityhall/city-services/provincial-offences.aspx

Kingston
362 Montreal St., Kingston, ON K7K 3H5
Tel: 613-547-8557; *Fax:* 613-547-8558
contactus@cityofkingston.ca
www.cityofkingston.ca
Other information: TTY: 613-546-4889

Kitchener - Cambridge - Waterloo
77 Queen St. North, Kitchener, ON N2H 2H1
Tel: 519-745-9446; *Fax:* 519-742-1112
www.regionofwaterloo.ca/en/regionalgovernment/provincialoffencescourt.asp
Other information: TTY: 519-575-4607

L'Orignal - Prescott Russell
28 Court St., P.O. Box 347, L'Orignal, ON K0B 1K0
Tel: 613-675-4661; *Fax:* 613-675-4940
Toll-Free: 800-667-6307
lip-poa@prescott-russell.on.ca
www.prescott-russell.on.ca

London
824 Dundas St. East, London, ON N5W 5R1
Tel: 519-661-1882; *Fax:* 519-661-1944
POAAdmin@london.ca
www.london.ca/Provincial_Offences/provincialoffencesact.htm

Mississauga
950 Burnhamthorpe Rd. West, Mississauga, ON L5C 3B4
Tel: 905-615-4500; *Fax:* 905-615-4038
www.mississauga.ca/portal/cityhall/courtadministration

Napanee - Lennox & Addington
97 Thomas St. East, Napanee, ON K7R 4B9
Tel: 613-354-4883; *Fax:* 613-354-3112
www.lennox-addington.on.ca

Niagara Falls - Niagara Region
4635 Queen St., Niagara Falls, ON L2E 2L7
Tel: 905-687-6590; *Fax:* 905-687-6614
www.niagararegion.ca/business/poa/default.aspx

North Bay
200 McIntyre St. East, P.O. Box 360, North Bay, ON P1B 8H8
Tel: 705-474-0626; *Fax:* 705-474-8302

Orangeville
55 Zina St., Orangeville, ON L9W 1E5
Tel: 519-941-5808; *Fax:* 519-940-3685
www.caledon.ca/en/townhall/provincialoffencescourt.asp

Orillia
#10, 575 West St. South, Orillia, ON L3V 7N6
Tel: 705-326-2960; *Fax:* 705-326-3613

Ottawa
100 Constellation Cres., Ottawa, ON K2G 6J8
Tel: 613-580-2665; *Fax:* 613-580-2664

Owen Sound/Walkerton - Grey Bruce
595 - 9 Ave. East, Owen Sound, ON N4K 3E3
Tel: 519-376-3470; *Fax:* 519-376-0638
poa@grey.ca
www.grey.ca/poa

Parry Sound
52 Seguin St., Parry Sound, ON P2A 1B4
Tel: 705-746-2553; *Fax:* 705-746-7461

Pembroke - Renfrew
141 Lake St., Pembroke, ON K8A 5L8
Tel: 613-735-3482; *Fax:* 613-735-8484
poaoffice@countyofrenfrew.on.ca
www.countyofrenfrew.on.ca

Perth - Lanark
80 Gore St. East, Perth, ON K7H 1H9
Tel: 613-267-3311; *Fax:* 613-267-5635
www.perth.ca

Peterborough
99 Simcoe St., Peterborough, ON K9H 2H3
Tel: 705-742-7777; *Fax:* 705-743-9292
poacourt@peterborough.ca
www.peterborough.ca/poa

Picton - Prince Edward County
332 Main St., Picton, ON K0K 2T0
Tel: 613-476-2148; *Fax:* 613-476-8356

Sarnia - Lambton
150 North Christina St., P.O. Box 1060, Sarnia, ON N7T 7K2
Tel: 519-344-8880; *Fax:* 519-344-9379
poa@lambton-county.on.ca
www.lambtononline.com

Sault Ste Marie
99 Foster Dr., 1st Fl., P.O. Box 580, Sault Ste Marie, ON P6A 5N1
Tel: 705-541-7334; *Fax:* 705-759-5395
www.city.sault-ste-marie.on.ca

Simcoe - Norfolk
#100, 185 Robinson St., Simcoe, ON N3Y 5L6
Tel: 519-426-5870; *Fax:* 519-427-5900
poa@norfolkcounty.ca
www.norfolkcounty.ca/government/provincial-offences-office

St Catharines - Niagara
71 King St., St Catharines, ON L2R 3H7
Tel: 905-687-6590; *Fax:* 905-687-6614
poaenquiries@niagararegion.ca
www.niagararegion.ca

St Thomas - Elgin
450 Sunset Dr., St Thomas, ON N5R 5V1
Tel: 519-631-1460; *Fax:* 519-631-4549
poa@elgin-county.on.ca
www.elgincounty.ca/main-menu/living-elgin/provincial-offences

Stratford - Perth
1 Huron St., Stratford, ON N5A 5S4
Tel: 519-271-0531; *Fax:* 519-271-7993
poa@perthcounty.ca
www.perthcounty.ca

Sudbury
#102, 199 Larch St., Sudbury, ON P3A 5P3
Tel: 705-674-4455; *Fax:* 705-673-9505
poacourt@greatersudbury.ca
www.greatersudbury.ca

Thunder Bay
Victoriaville Mall, 125 South Syndicate Ave., P.O. Box 1600, Thunder Bay, ON P7C 6A9
Tel: 807-625-2999; *Fax:* 807-623-7751

Timmins
220 Algonquin Blvd. East, Timmins, ON P4N 1B3
Tel: 705-360-2620; *Fax:* 705-360-2694
poa@timmins.ca
www.timmins.ca

Toronto East
1530 Markham Rd., Main Fl., Toronto, ON M1B 3M4
Tel: 416-338-7320; *Fax:* 416-338-7700
courtaccesseast@toronto.ca
www.toronto.ca/court_services
Other information: TTY: 416-338-7394

Toronto South
137 Edward St., Toronto, ON M5G 2P8
Tel: 416-338-7320; *Fax:* 416-338-2762
poacourt@toronto.ca
www.toronto.ca/court_services
Other information: TTY: 416-338-7394

Toronto West
York Civic Centre, 2700 Eglinton Ave. West, Toronto, ON M6M 1V1
Tel: 416-338-7320; *Fax:* 416-338-6892
poacourt@toronto.ca
www.toronto.ca/court_services
Other information: TTY: 416-338-7394

Windsor
Westcourt Pl., #300, 251 Goyeau St., Windsor, ON N9A 6V2
Tel: 519-255-6555; *Fax:* 519-255-6556
www.citywindsor.ca/cityhall/Legal-Services-/Pages/Legal-Services.aspx

Woodstock
P.O. Box 1614, Woodstock, ON N4S 7Y3
Tel: 519-537-4890; *Fax:* 519-537-3024
poa@oxfordcounty.ca
www.oxfordcounty.ca

York Region-Newmarket
#200, 465 Davis Dr., Newmarket, ON L3Y 7T9
Tel: 905-898-0425; *Fax:* 905-898-5218
www.york.ca

York Region-Richmond Hill
50 High Tech Rd., 1st Fl., Richmond Hill, ON L4B 4N7
Tel: 905-762-2105; *Fax:* 905-762-2106
www.york.ca

Prince Edward Island

Prince Edward Island Supreme Court
Sir Louis Henry Davies Law Courts Bldg., 42 Water St., P.O. Box 2000, Charlottetown, PE C1A 7N8
Tel: 902-368-6000; *Fax:* 902-368-6123
www.courts.pe.ca/supreme

The Supreme Court is a Court of original jurisdiction & has jurisdiction in all civil (including family, estate & small claims) & criminal matters arising in Prince Edward Island.
Chief Justice: The Hon. Madam Jacqueline Matheson
Justices (The Hon. Mr./Madam Justice):
Gordon Campbell
Wayne Cheverie
Nancy L. Key
Benjamin Taylor
Administration:
Acting Protonothary & Registrar in Bankruptcy: Terri MacPherson, 902-368-6067
Deputy Registrar: Estates Section, Kerrilee MacConnell
Deputy Registrar: General Section, Elizabeth Murray, 902-368-6001
Deputy Registrar: Small Claims Section, Marguerite Atchison, 902-368-6002
Deputy Registrar: Family Section, Roxanne Smith, 902-368-6003
Deputy Registrar: Family Section, Wilhelmina Stevenson, 902-368-6003
Court Services Manager: Judy Turpin, 902-368-6005

Courts:
Summerside
108 Central St., Summerside, PE C1N 3L4
Tel: 902-888-8190; *Fax:* 902-888-8222

Georgetown
Kings County Courthouse, 60 Kent St., P.O. Box 70, Georgetown, PE C0A 1L0
Tel: 902-652-8990; *Fax:* 902-652-8992

Prince Edward Island Supreme Court: Court of Appeal
Sir Louis Henry Davies Law Courts Bldg., 42 Water St., P.O. Box 2000, Charlottetown, PE C1A 7N8
Tel: 902-368-6004; *Fax:* 902-368-6774
www.courts.pe.ca/appeal/

The Court of Appeal has appellate jurisdiction in criminal & civil matters.
Chief Justice: The Hon. Mr. David H. Jenkins
Justices (The Hon. Mr./Madam Justice):
John K. Mitchell
Michele M. Murphy
Administration:
Registrar: Charles Thompson

Prince Edward Island Provincial Court
Kelly Bldg., 3 Harbourside Access Rd., P.O. Box 2000, Charlottetown, PE C1N 7N8
Tel: 902-368-6040
www.courts.pe.ca

The Provincial Court has jurisdiction in select criminal matters as well as youth matters.
Chief Judge: The Hon. John R. Douglas, 902-368-6011, Fax: 902-368-6743
Judges (The Hon.):
Nancy K. Orr
Jeffrey E. Lantz

Québec

Cour Supérieure du Québec
Québec Superior Court
300, boul Jean-Lesage, Québec, QC G1K 8K6
Tél: 418-649-3400; *Téléc:* 418-528-0932
www.tribunaux.qc.ca/c-superieure/index-cs.html

Affaires civiles et commerciales dont l'enjeu est de 70 000$ ou plus; litiges en matières administratives et familiale, faillite, procès devant jury en matière pénale, et appels en matière de poursuites sommaires
Juge en chef *October 1, 2002*: L'hon. Jacques R. Fournier
Juge en chef associé *May 2, 1989*: L'hon. Robert Pidgeon
Juge en chef adjoint *December 15, 2006*: L'hon. Eva Petras
Juges (Les honorables)
Jacques Babin (Juge surnuméraire) *November 28, 1995*
Johanne April *May 18, 2010*
Jocelyn Rancourt *June 20, 2015*
France Bergeron *October 1, 2009*
Lise Bergeron *October 4, 2012*
Jacques Blanchard *November 2, 2012*
Danielle Blondin (Juge surnuméraire) *December 23, 1991*
Claude Bouchard *October 22, 2004*
Jacques G. Bouchard *November 2, 2012*
Michel Caron (Juge surnuméraire) *June 20, 2000*
Louis Dionne *February 7, 2013*
Michel Beaupré *May 9, 2014*
Guy De Blois *April 10, 2014*
Bernard Godbout *March 1, 2001*
Pierre C. Bellavance (Juge surnuméraire) *November 7, 2013*
Richard Grenier *June 23, 1998*
Suzanne Hardy-Lemieux *July 15, 1998*
François Huot *July 29, 2009*
Denis Jacques *April 1, 2004*
Michèle Lacroix *June 6, 2000*
Catherine La Rosa *November 22, 2006*
Jean Lemelin (Juge surnuméraire) *November 8, 1996*

Marc Lesage (Juge surnuméraire) *December 1, 1998*
Manon Lavoie *December 17, 2013*
Alain Michaud *May 18, 2010*
Daniel Dumais *April 10, 2014*
Benoit Moulin *March 19, 2002*
Pierre Ouellet *May 14, 2009*
Suzanne Ouellet *September 29, 2005*
Marc Paradis *November 2, 2012*
Suzanne Gagné *June 19, 2015*
Simon Hébert *May 28, 2015*
Clement Samson *December 15, 2011*
Alicia Soldevila *September 14, 2006*
Georges Taschereau (Juge surnuméraire) *November 4, 1997*
Claudette Tessier Couture (Juge surnuméraire) *July 24, 2003*
Simon Ruel *October 10, 2014*
Bernard Tremblay *June 30, 2015*

Abitibi—Rouyn-Noranda—Témiscamingue
QC
Juges (Les honorables):
Robert Dufresne *December 23, 2006*
Jocelyn Geoffroy *February 20, 2008*
Michel Girouard *September 30, 2010*

Alma
QC
Juges (Les honorables):
Sandra Bouchard *November 2, 2012*
Gratien Duchesne (Juge surnuméraire) *October 3, 1995*

Arthabaska
QC
Juges (Les honorables):
Jules Allard (Juge surnuméraire) *April 16, 1986*

Baie-Comeau—Mingan
QC
Juges (Les honorables):
Paul Corriveau (Juge surnuméraire) *July 5, 1985*
Serge Francoeur

Beauharnois
QC
Juges (Les honorables):
Nicole-M. Gibeau *June 30, 1989*

Bonaventure
QC
Juges (Les honorables):
Jean-Roch Landry (Juge surnuméraire) *July 5, 1994*

Chicoutimi
QC
Juges (Les honorables):
Nicole Tremblay *December 11, 2014*
Roger Banford (Juge surnuméraire) *May 6, 1992*
Martin Dallaire *July 29, 2009*
Carl Lachance *October 22, 2004*

Drummond
QC
Juges (Les honorables)
Lise Matteau *February 26, 2002*

Gatineau—Pontiac—Labelle
QC
Juges (Les honorables):
Martin Bédard (Juge surnuméraire) *June 20, 2000*
Pierre Dallaire *July 30, 2008*
Dominique Goulet *April 27, 2007*
Pierre Isabelle (Juge surnuméraire) *February 16, 1999*
Marie-Josée Bédard *June 20, 2015*
Carole Therrien *December 2, 2011*
Suzanne Tessier *June 5, 2007*

Joliette
QC
Juges (Les honorables)
Claude Auclair *September 24, 2004*

Laval
QC
Juges (Les honorables):
Christiane Alary *November 5, 2003*
Pierre Journet (Juges surnuméraire) *May 9, 1995*

Longueuil
QC
Juges (Les honorables):
Jean-Jude Chabot (Juge surnuméraire) *September 1, 1987*
Carole Julien *November 1, 1994*
Chantal Masse *November 29, 2006*
Sophie Picard *April 27, 2007*

Montréal
QC
Juges (Les honorables):
Louisa Arcand *June 19, 2009*
Guylène Beaugé *March 2, 2007*
Pierre Béliveau (Juge surnuméraire) *November 1, 1994*
Nicole Bénard (Juge surnuméraire) *December 23, 1991*
Marc-André Blanchard *March 2, 2007*
Sylviane W. Borenstein (Juge surnuméraire) *September 20, 1994*
Sophie Bourque *February 25, 2005*
Christian J. Brossard *October 4, 2012*
James L. Brunton *February 27, 2003*
Jean-François Buffoni *February 26, 2002*
Pepita G. Capriolo *September 15, 1999*
Kirkland Casgrain *May 29, 2003*
Robert Castiglio *December 11, 2008*
Martin Castonguay *June 22, 2007*
Claude Champagne *June 20, 2000*
France Charbonneau *February 26, 2004*
Jean-Pierre Chrétien *July 5, 2000*
Carol Cohen *November 4, 1997*
David R. Collier *October 20, 2011*
Chantal Corriveau *February 25, 2005*
Guy Cournoyer *May 11, 2007*
Babak Barin *July 10, 2015*
Marie-France Courville (Juge surnuméraire) *October 20, 1998*
Louis Crête (Juge surnuméraire) *September 20, 1994*
Alexandre Boucher *June 29, 2015*
Claude Dallaire *September 9, 2009*
Marc David *November 23, 2005*
Thomas M. Davis *September 29, 2011*
Wilbrod Claude Décarie (Juge surnuméraire) *November 1, 1994*
Chantal Chatelain *July 1, 2015*
Sylvie Devito *July 3, 2005*
Marc De Wever *November 7, 2001*
Hélène Di Salvo *December 13, 2012*
Silvana Conte *July 5, 2015*
Jean-Guy Dubois (Juge surnuméraire) *January 29, 1997*
Gérard Dugré (Juge surnuméraire) *January 22, 2009*
France Dulude *October 4, 2012*
François P. Duprat *April 5, 2012*
Benoît Emery *December 12, 2002*
Lucie Fournier *May 14, 2009*
William Fraiberg (Juge surnuméraire) *February 10, 1999*
Pierre-C. Gagnon *December 12, 2002*
Suzanne Couchesne *October 9, 2014*
Marie Gaudreau *September 16, 2003*
Serge Gaudet *May 29, 2015*
Louis J. Gouin *February 3, 2011*
Lukasz Granosik *December 11, 2014*
Carole Hallée *November 7, 2001*
Karen Kear Jodoin *March 7, 2013*
Hélène Langlois *February 10, 1999*
Pierre Labrie *February 7, 2013*
Louis Lacoursière *December 12, 2002*
Marie-Claude Lalande *April 5, 2012*
Jean-Yves Lalonde *November 5, 2003*
Julien Lanctôt *June 23, 1998*
Hélène Le Bel (Juge surnuméraire) *November 3, 1987*
Luc Lefebvre *October 20, 1998*
Louise Lemelin (Juge surnuméraire) *November 1, 1994*
Johanne Maynville *November 22, 2006*
Catherine Mandeville *May 14, 2009*
Marie-Claude Armstrong *April 10, 2014*
Florence Lucas *June 19, 2015*
Michel Pennou *February 27, 2015*
Paul Mayer *June 18, 2008*
Danièle Mayrand *March 1, 2001*
Jean-François Michaud *February 7, 2013*
Michèle Monast *February 28, 2000*
Élise Poisson *October 9, 2014*
Robert Mongeon *June 6, 2001*
Gary D.D. Morrison *April 5, 2012*
Richard Nadeau (Juge surnuméraire) *February 10, 1999*
Francine Nantel *March 2, 2007*
Pierre Nollet *April 23, 2010*
Maire-Anne Paquette *August 6, 2010*
Daniel W. Payette *July 3, 2008*
Mark G. Peacock *March 2, 2007*
Micheline Perrault *June 18, 2010*
Eliane Perreault *December 17, 2013*
Claudette Picard (Juge surnuméraire) *September 23, 1997*
Yves Poirier *June 19, 2009*
Chantal Tremblay *May 29, 2015*
André Prévost *December 9, 2004*
Steve J. Reimnitz *December 13, 2007*
Brian J. Riordan *December 9, 2004*
André Roy *November 5, 2003*
Claudine Roy *March 3, 2011*
Stéphane Sansfaçon *March 3, 2011*
André Wery *November 4, 1997*
Joel Avery Silcoff (Juge surnuméraire) *June 6, 2000*
Johanne St-Gelais *September 30, 2010*
Chantal Lamarche *April 10, 2014*
Donald Bisson *April 10, 2014*
Clément Trudel (Juge surnuméraire) *June 17, 1987*
Danielle Turcotte *September 9, 2009*
Stephen W. Hamilton *October 4, 2013*
Michael Stober *February 3, 2011*
André Vincent *May 10, 2007*
Michel Yergeau *May 31, 2012*
Jerry Zigman (Juge surnuméraire) *September 1, 1987*
Pierre Labelle *May 9, 2014*
Michel A. Pinsonnault *December 7, 2013*
Élise Poisson *October 9, 2014*
Eva Petras *December 15, 2006*
Michel Déziel *November 5, 2003*
Anne Jacob *July 20, 2015*
Karen Kear Jodoin *March 7, 2013*

Richelieu—St-Hyacinthe
QC
Juges (Les honorables):
Louis-Paul Cullen *November 22, 2006*

Rimouski
QC
Juges (Les honorables):
Daniel Beaulieu *November 2, 2012*
Gilles Blanchet (Juge surnuméraire) *November 28, 1995*
Claude-Henri Gendreau (Juge surnuméraire) *October 7, 1997*

St-François—Bedford—Mégantic
QC
Juges (Les honorables):
P.-Marcel Bellavance (Juge surnuméraire) *July 11, 1991*
Sylvain Provencher *June 19, 2015*
Claude Villeneuve *June 19, 2015*
Suzanne Mireault *December 28, 1995*

St-Maurice
QC
Juges (Les honorables):
Raymond W. Pronovost *January 29, 1997*

Terrebonne
QC
Juges (Les honorables)
Michel A. Caron *March 14, 2005*

Trois-Rivières
Juges (Les honorables):
Alain Bolduc *September 6, 2010*
Robert Legris (Juge surnuméraire) *June 17, 1987*
Danye Daigle *June 19, 2015*
Marc St-Pierre *June 18, 2008*

Cour du Québec
Court of Québec

300, boul Jean-Lesage, Québec, QC G1K 8K6
Tél: 418-649-3400; *Téléc:* 418-528-0932
www.tribunaux.qc.ca/c-quebec/index-cq.html

Composée d'au plus 290 juges dont la juge en chef, le juge en chef associé, 4 juges en chef adjoints, et 18 juges coordonnateurs et coordonnateurs adjoints; matières civile, criminelle et pénale; matière de jeunesse; matière administrative ou en appel dans les cas prévus par la loi; cour d'archives.

Juge en chef: L'honorable Élizabeth Corte
Juge en chef associé: L'honorable Mario Tremblay
Hélène Bourassa
Juge en chef adjointe: Chambre criminelle et pénale, L'honorable Jean-Louis Lemay
Juge en chef adjoint: Chambre de la jeunesse, L'honorable Claude C. Boulanger
Juges (Les honorables)
Lucille Chabot (Juge coordonnatrice)
Richard Côté (Juge coordonnateur)
Conrad Chapdelaine (Juge coordonnateur)
Robert Proulx (Juge coordonnateur)
Richard Laflamme (Juge coordonnateur)
Denis Saulnier (Juge coordonnateur)
Charles G. Grenier (Juge coordonnateur)
Jean-Pierre Archambault (Juge coordonnateur)
Pierre E. Labelle (Juge coordonnateur adjoint)
Marc Bisson (Juge coordonnateur adjoint)
François Boisjoli (Juge coordonnateur adjoint)
Claude Boulanger (Juge en chef adjoint)
Jean Asselin
Hélène Carrier
Andrée Bergeron
Réna Émond
Hélène Bouillon
Christian Boulet
Hélène Bourassa
Geneviève Cotnam
R. Peter Bradley
André-J. Brochet
Pierre Coderre
René de la Sablonnière
Pierre A. Gagnon

Paule Gaumond
Marie-Claude Gilbert
Chantal Gosselin
Christine Gosselin
Dominique Langis
Daniel Lavoie
Jean Lebel
Bernard Lemieux
Alain Morand
Dominic Pagé
Chantale Pelletier
Lucie Rondeau
Pierre-L. Rousseau
Johanne Roy
Carol St-Cyr
Claude Tremblay
Jacques Tremblay
Steve Magnan
Nathalie DuPerron Roy (Juge de paix magistrat)
Sylvie Marcotte (Juge de paix magistrat)
Nicole Martin (Juge de paix magistrat)
Administration:
Anne Bélanger (Directrice déléguée à l'administration)

Abitibi-Témiscamingue - Amos
891, 3e rue ouest, Amos, QC J9T 2T4
Tél: 819-444-5577; *Téléc:* 819-444-5204
Juges (Les honorables):
Claude P. Bigué
Marc Ouimette
Lucille Chabot

Abitibi-Témiscamingue - Rouyn-Noranda
2, av du Palais, Rouyn-Noranda, QC J9X 2N9
Tél: 819-763-3058; *Téléc:* 819-763-3389
Juges (Les honorables):
Marc E. Grimard
Josée Bélanger
Nancy McKenna
Marie-Claude Bélanger (Juge de paix magistrat)

Abitibi-Témiscamingue - Val d'Or
900, 7e Rue, Val d'Or, QC J9P 3P8
Tél: 819-354-4462; *Téléc:* 819-354-4447
Juges (Les honorables):
Jean-Pierre Gervais
Denise Descôteaux
Renée Lemoine
Administration:
Juge de paix magistrat: Jacques Barbès
Jacques Ladouceur

Baie-Comeau
71, av Mance, Baie-Comeau, QC G4Z 1N2
Tél: 418-296-5534; *Téléc:* 418-294-8717
Ligne sans frais: 866-854-4075
Juges (Les honorables):
François Boisjoli (Juge coordonnateur adjoint)
Michel Dionne
Sonia Bérubé

Matane
382, av Saint-Jérôme, Matane, QC G4W 3B3
Tél: 418-562-2497; *Téléc:* 418-560-8746
Juges (Les honorables):
Jules Berthelot

New Carlisle
87, boul Gérard-D.-Lévesque, P.O. Box 517, New Carlisle, QC G0C 1Z0
Tél: 418-752-3376; *Téléc:* 418-752-6979
Juges (Les honorables):
Janick Poirier
Celestina Almeida
Luc Marchildon (Juge de paix magistrat)

Percé
124, rte 132, Percé, QC G0C 2L0
Tél: 418-782-2055; *Téléc:* 418-782-2906
Juges (Les honorables):
Denis Paradis

Rimouski
183, av de la Cathédrale, Rimouski, QC G5L 5J1
Tél: 418-727-3852; *Téléc:* 418-727-3635
Juges (Les honorables)
Richard Côté (Juge Coordonnateur)
Andrée St-Pierre
James Rondeau
Lucie Morissette
Anne-Marie Sincennes (Juge de paix magistrat)

Rivière-du-Loup
33, rue de la Cour, Rivière-du-Loup, QC G5R 1J1
Tél: 418-862-3579; *Téléc:* 418-867-8794
Ligne sans frais: 800-463-8009

Juges (Les honorables):
Martin Gagnon
Luce Kennedy
Hermina Popescu
Julie Dionne (Juge de paix magistrat)

Sept-Iles
425, boul Laure, Sept-×les, QC G4R 1X6
Tél: 418-962-3044; *Téléc:* 418-964-8714
Ligne sans frais: 866-405-7951
Juges (Les honorables):
Nathalie Aubry
François Paré (Juge de paix magistrat)
Michel Parent
Louise Gallant

Estrie - Drummondville
1680, boul Saint-Joseph, Drummondville, QC J2C 2G3
Tél: 819-478-2513; *Téléc:* 819-475-8459
Juges (Les honorables):
Gilles Lafrenière
Marie-Josée Ménard

Estrie - Granby
Édifice Roger-Paré, #1.32, 77, rue Principale, Granby, QC J2G 9B3
Tél: 450-776-7110; *Téléc:* 450-776-4080
Juges (Les honorables):
Julie Beauchesne
Serge Champoux
Johanne Denis
François Marchand
Monique Perron (Juge de paix magistrat)

Estrie - Sherbrooke
375, rue King ouest, Sherbrooke, QC J1H 6B9
Tél: 819-822-6910; *Téléc:* 819-820-3134
Juges (Les honorables):
Madeleine Aubé
Conrad Chapdelaine (Juge Coordonnateur)
Claire Desgens
Alain Désy
Marie-Pierre Jutras
Paul Dunnigan
Monique Lavallée
Hélène Fabi
Lise Gagnon
Patrick Théroux
Erick Vanchestein
Sylvie Desmeules (Juge de paix magistrat)
Danielle Côté (Juge en chef adjointe)

Laval—Lanaudière—Laurentides—Labelle - Joliette
200, rue Saint-Marc, Joliette, QC J6E 8C2
Tél: 450-753-4807
Juges (Les honorables):
Normand Bonin
François Landry (Juge coordonnateur adjoint)
Richard Landry
Denis Le Reste
Claude Lachapelle
Jean Roy
Sophie Gravel
Luc Joly
Bruno Leclerc
Danielle Michaud (Juge de paix magistrat)

Laval—Lanaudière—Laurentides—Labelle - Laval
2800, boul Saint-Martin ouest, Laval, QC H7T 2S9
Tél: 450-686-5006
Juges (Les honorables):
Jean-Pierre Archambault (Juge coordonnateur adjoint)
Lise Gaboury
Françoise Garneau-Fournier
Dominique Larochelle
Marie-Suzanne Lauzon
Julie Messier
Gilles Garneau
Yvan Nolet
Benoit Sabourin
Pierre Hamel
Gaby Dumas (Juge de paix magistrat)
Caroline Roy (Juge de paix magistrat)

Laval—Lanaudière—Laurentides—Labelle - Saint-Jérôme
25, rue de Martigny ouest, Saint-Jérôme, QC J7Y 4Z1
Tél: 450-431-4407
Juges (Les honorables):
Pierre E. Audet (Juge en chef adjoint)
Michel Bellehumeur
Élaine Bolduc (Juge coordonnatrice adjointe)
Annie Breault
Paul Chevalier
Antoine Cloutier
Pierre Cliche

Sandra Blanchard
Denis Lapierre
Lyne Foucault
Sylvain Lépine
Jean La Rue
Ginette Maillet
Georges Massol
Diane Roux
Carol Richer
Jimmy Vallée
Michèle Toupin (Juge coordonnatrice)
Lucie Marier (Juge de paix magistrat)
Jean-Georges Laliberté (Juge de paix magistrat)
Marie-Pierre Bellemare

Mauricie—Bois-Francs—Centre-du-Québec - Shawinigan
212, 6e rue de la Pointe, Shawinigan, QC G9N 8B6
Tél: 819-536-2571; *Téléc:* 819-536-2992
Juges (Les honorables):
David Bouchard

Mauricie—Bois-Francs—Centre-du-Québec - Trois-Rivières
850, rue Hart, Trois-Rivières, QC G9A 1T9
Tél: 819-372-4153; *Téléc:* 819-371-6096
Juges (Les honorables):
Pierre Allen
Jacques Lacoursière
Guy Lambert
Maryse Brouillette
Daniel Perreault
Jacques Rioux
Dominique Slater (Juge coordinatrice)
Guylaine Tremblay
Alain Trudel
Jacques Trudel
Annie Vanasse (Juge de paix magistrat)

Mauricie—Bois-Francs—Centre-du-Québec - Victoriaville
800, boul Bois-Francs sud, Victoriaville, QC G6P 5W5
Tél: 819-357-2054; *Téléc:* 819-357-5517
Juges (Les honorables):
Pierre Labbé
Bruno Langelier
Gaétan Ratté (Juge de paix magistrat)

Montérégie - Longueuil
1111, boul Jacques-Cartier est, Longueuil, QC J4M 2J6
Tél: 450-646-4010; *Téléc:* 450-928-7982
Juges (Les honorables):
Mireille Allaire
Ann-Mary Beauchemin
Pierre Bélisle
Marc Bisson (Juge coordonnateur adjoint (criminelle et pénale))
Virgile Buffoni (Juge coordonnatrice adjoint (civile))
Monique Dupuis
Maurice Galarneau
Francine Gendron
Mario Gervais
Stéphane Godri
Anne-Marie Jacques
Marco LaBrie
Julie-Maude Greffe
Claude Laporte
Louise Leduc
Richard Marleau
Nancy Moreau
Lyne Morin
Jean-Pierre Authier
Robert Proulx (Juge coordonnateur)
Mélanie Roy
Chantal Sirois
Marie-Josée Hénault (Juge de paix magistrat)
Josée Fontaine (Juge de paix magistrat)
Jacques Roullier (Juge de paix magistrat)

Montérégie - Saint-Hyacinthe
1550, rue Dessaulles, Saint-Hyacinthe, QC J2S 2S8
Tél: 450-778-6569
Juges (Les honorables):
Gilles Charpentier
Marc-Nicolas Foucault
Suzanne Paradis
Viviane Primeau
Robert Lanctôt (Juge de paix magistrat)

Montérégie - Saint-Jean-sur-Richelieu
109, rue Saint-Charles, Saint-Jean-sur-Richelieu, QC J3B 2C2
Tél: 450-347-3716
Juges (Les honorables):
Michel Bédard
Éric Simard

Montérégie - Salaberry-de-Valleyfield
74, rue Académie, Salaberry-de-Valleyfield, QC J6T 0B8
Tél: 450-370-4006; *Téléc:* 450-370-3022
Ligne sans frais: 866-455-1585

Juges (Les honorables):
Béatrice Clément
Marie-Chantal Doucet
Céline Gervais
Éric Hamel
Gilbert Lanthier
Michel Mercier
Claude Montpetit
Bernard St-Arnaud
Patricia Compagnone (Juge de paix magistrat)
Nancy Lecompte (Juge de paix magistrat)

Montérégie - Sorel-Tracy
46, rue Charlotte, Sorel-Tracy, QC J3P 6N5
Juges (Les Honorables):
Denys Noël

Montréal
1, rue Notre-Dame est, Montréal, QC H2Y 1B6
Tél: 514-393-2721; *Téléc:* 514-873-4760

Juges (Les honorables):
Martine L. Tremblay
Daniel Bédard
François Bousquet
Joëlle Roy
Jean-Paul Braun
Alain Breault
David L. Cameron
Nathalie Chalifour
Brigitte Charron
Louise Comeau (Juge coordonnatrice adjointe)
Sylvain Coutlée
Serge Délisle
Antonio de Michele
Linda Despots
Marie-Josée Di Lallo
Daniel Dortélus
Sylvie Durand (Juge responsable, Perfectionnement)
Jeffrey Edwards
Nathalie Fafard
Gatien Fournier
Dominique Gibbens
Brigette Gouin
Geneviève Graton
Yves Hamel
Patrick Healy
Martin Hébert (Président, Tribunal des professions)
Scott Hughes
Dominique B. Joly
Ann-Marie Jones (Présidente, Tribunal des droits de la personne)
Silvie Kovacevich
Pierre E. Labelle (Juge coordonnatrice adjointe, Chambre criminelle et pénale)
Myriam Lachance
Sylvie Lachapelle
Gilles Lareau
André Perreault (Juge responsable, cours municipales)
Marie Michelle Lavigne
Claude Leblond
Magali Lewis
Robert Marchi
Eliana Marengo
Salvatore Mascia
Denis Mondor
Hélène V. Morin
Thierry Nadon
Manon Ouimet
Jacques Paquet
Yves Paradis
Claude Parent
Vincenzo Piazza
Yvan Poulin
Diane Quenneville
Isabelle Rheault
Henri Richard
Julie Riendeau
Emmanuelle Saucier
Denis Saulnier (Juge coordonateur, Montréal)
Mark Shamie
Christian M. Tremblay
Martine L. Tremblay
Suzanne Vadboncoeur
Julie Veilleux (Vice-présidente, Tribunal des professions)
Louise Villemure
Dominique Vézina
Lori Renée Weitzman
Marie Archambault
Line Bachand
Alain Brillon
Carole Brosseau
Taya di Pietro
Odette Fafard
Lucie Godin
Louis Grégoire
Partice Hurtubise
Pauline Reinhardt Laforce
Claude Lamoureux
Daniel Lavery
Louis Grégoire
Jacques A. Nadeau
Karen Ohayon
Anne-Marie Otis
Jacky Roy
Dominique Wilhelmy
Annie Savard
Martine Nolin
François Ste-Marie
Suzanne Bousquet (Juge responsable, juges de paix magistrats)
Serge Cimon
Josée De Carufel
Louis Duguay
Pierre Fortin
François Kouri
Julie Laliberté
Johanne White
Guylaine Rivest
Juges de paix magistra:
Dominique Benoit

Outaouais - Gatineau
17, rue Laurier, Gatineau, QC J8X 4C1
Tél: 819-776-8100

Juges (Les honorables):
Valmont Beaulieu
Patsy Bouthillette
Anouk Desaulniers
Jean Faullem
Jean-François Gosselin
Line Gosselin
Richard Laflamme (Juge coordonateur)
Lynne Landry
Gaston Paul Langevin
Réal R. Lapointe
Serge Laurin
Rosemarie Millar
Marie Pratte
Sylvain Meunier
Christine Auger (Juge de paix magistrat)
Christine Lafrance (Juge de paix magistrat)

Québec—Chaudière-Appalaches - Montmagny
110, av Jacques-Cartier, Montmagny, QC G5V 0G5
Tél: 418-248-0909; *Téléc:* 418-248-2437
Juges (Les honorables):
Sébastien Proulx

Québec—Chaudière-Appalaches - Saint-Joseph-de-Beauce
795, av du Palais, Saint-Joseph-de-Beauce, QC G0S 2V0
Tél: 418-397-7187; *Téléc:* 418-397-7968
Juges (Les honorables):
Hubert Couture
Yannick Couture (Juge de paix magistrat)

Saguenay—Lac-Saint-Jean - Alma
725, rue Harvey ouest, Alma, QC G8B 1P5
Tél: 418-668-3334; *Téléc:* 418-662-3697
Juges (Les honorables):
Jean Hudon

Saguenay—Lac-Saint-Jean - Saguenay (Chicoutimi)
227, rue Racine est, 1er étage, Chicoutimi, QC G7H 7B4
Tél: 418-696-9926; *Téléc:* 418-698-3558
Juges (Les honorables):
Michel Boudreault
Richard P. Daoust (Juge coordonnateur)
Paul Guimond
Pierre Lortie
Kathy Beaumont
Sonia Rouleau
Pierre Simard
Doris Thibault
Réjean Bédard (Juge de paix magistrat)

Saguenay—Lac-Saint-Jean - Roberval
750, boul Saint-Joseph, Roberval, QC G8H 2L5
Tél: 418-275-3666; *Téléc:* 418-275-6169
Juges (Les honorables):
Isabelle Boillat
Michel Boissonneault (Juge de paix magistrat)

Points de service de justice
Judicial Service Centres
QC

Points de service:
Amqui
29, boul Saint-Benoît ouest, Amqui, QC G5J 2E4
Tél: 418-629-4488; *Téléc:* 418-629-6450

Carleton
17, rue Lacroix, Carleton, QC G0C 1J0
Tél: 418-364-3442; *Téléc:* 418-364-6028

Dolbeau-Mistassini
1420, boul Walberg, 1er étage, Dolbeau-Mistassini, QC G8L 1H4
Tél: 418-276-0683; *Téléc:* 418-276-6110

Forestville
134, rte 138 est, P.O. Box 400, Forestville, QC G0T 1E0
Tél: 418-587-4471; *Téléc:* 418-587-6639
Ligne sans frais: 866-854-4075

Gaspé
#101, 11, rue de la Cathédrale, Gaspé, QC G4X 2V9
Tél: 418-368-5756; *Téléc:* 416-360-8030

Jonquière
Édifice Marguerite-Belley, 3950, boul Harvey, Rez-de-chaussée, Jonquière, QC G7X 8L6
Tél: 418-695-7991; *Téléc:* 418-698-3558

Lachute
#216, 505, av Béthany, Lachute, QC J8H 4A6
Tél: 450-562-3711; *Téléc:* 450-569-7645

Magog
Hôtel de Ville, #127, 7, rue Principale est, Magog, QC J1X 1Y4
Tél: 819-843-7323; *Téléc:* 819-843-4533

Matane
382, av Saint-Jérôme, Matane, QC G4W 3B3
Tél: 418-562-2497; *Téléc:* 418-560-8746

Mont-Joli
40, rue de l'Hôtel-de-Ville, Mont-Joli, QC G5H 1W8
Tél: 418-775-8811; *Téléc:* 418-775-7517

Sainte-Agathe-des-Monts
85, rue Saint-Vincent, Sainte-Agathe-des-Monts, QC J8C 2A8
Tél: 819-326-6462; *Téléc:* 450-569-7645

Sainte-Anne-des-Monts
10-B, boul Sainte-Anne ouest, Sainte-Anne-des-Monts, QC G4V 1P3
Tél: 418-763-2791; *Téléc:* 418-763-3107

Cour d'Appel du Québec
Québec Court of Appeal
Édifice Ernest-Cormier, 100, rue Notre-Dame est, Montréal, QC H2Y 4B6
Tél: 514-393-2022; *Téléc:* 514-864-7270
courdappelmtl@justice.gouv.qc.ca
courdappelduquebec.ca
Other information: twitter.com/cour_d_appel

Le plus haut tribunal du Québec; la cour est la gardienne de l'intégrité du droit civil de la province; en matière civile, la cour entend les appels des jugements finals de la Cour supérieure et de la Cour du Québec lorsque la valeur de l'objet du litige en appel est à 50 000$ ou plus; outrage, adoption, évaluation psychiatrique, garde en établissement, faillite et divorce.

Juge en chef ***November 22, 2006***: L'hon. Nicole Duval Hesler
Juges (Les honorables):
Étienne Parent *June 30, 2015*
Marie-France Bich *September 24, 2004*
Marie-Josée Hogue *June 19, 2015*
Jean Bouchard *October 1, 2009*
Jacques Chamberland (Juge surnuméraire) *June 10, 1993*
Jean-François Émond *June 13, 2014*
François Doyon *May 7, 2004*
Jacques Dufresne (Juge surnuméraire) *May 13, 2005*
Julie Dutil *September 24, 2004*
Jacques J. Levesque (Juge surnuméraire) *November 2, 2012*
Guy Gagnon *September 27, 2009*
Mark Schrager *June 13, 2014*
Dominique Bélanger *November 2, 2012*
Lorne Giroux (Juge surnuméraire) *February 25, 2005*
Manon Savard *April 25, 2013*
Allan Ross Hilton (Juge surnuméraire) *September 26, 2003*
Claude C. Gagnon *November 8, 2013*
Nicholas Kasirer *July 29, 2009*
Martin Vauclair *December 17, 2013*
Geneviève Marcotte *April 10, 2014*
Benoît Morin (Juge surnuméraire) *December 4, 2001*
Yves-Marie Morissette *November 7, 2002*
François Pelletier (Juge surnuméraire) *June 6, 2000*

Louis Rochette (Juge surnuméraire) *February 1, 2000*
Robert Mainville *July 1, 2014*
Marie St-Pierre *April 5, 2012*
France Thibault (Juge surnuméraire) *December 1, 1998*
Paul Vézina (Juge surnuméraire) *February 25, 2005*

Montréal
Édifice Ernest-Cormier, 100, rue Notre-Dame est, Montréal, QC H2Y 4B6
Tél: 514-393-2022; *Téléc:* 514-864-7270
courdappel@justice.gouv.qc.ca

Québec
Palais de justice de Québec, #4.27, 300, boul Jean-Lesage, Québec, QC G1K 8K6
Tél: 418-649-3401; *Téléc:* 418-646-6961
courdappelqc@justice.gouv.qc.ca

Cours municipales du Québec
Québec Municipal Courts

Édifice Louis-Philippe-Pigeon, 1200, route de l'Église, 6e étage, Québec, QC G1V 4M1
Tél: 418-643-5140*Ligne sans frais:* 866-536-5140
informations@justice.gouv.qc.ca
www.justice.gouv.qc.ca

Les cours municipales ont une compétence limitée en matière civile, notamment dans le domaine des réclamations de taxes; en matière pénale en ce qui concerne les infractions aux règlements municipaux et les infractions aux lois québécoises; et pour entendre et juger les infractions visées par la partie XXVII du Code criminel.

Judges (The Hon.):
Juge responsable: André Perreault

Courts:

Acton Vale
1025, rue Boulay, P.O. Box 640, Acton Vale, QC J0H 1A0
Tél: 450-546-2703

Alma
140, rue St-Joseph sud, Alma, QC G8B 3R1
Tél: 418-669-5001
courmunicipale@ville.alma.qc.ca

Asbestos
341, boul Saint-Luc, Asbestos, QC J1T 2W4
Tél: 819-879-7171; *Téléc:* 819-879-2343
cour@ville.asbestos.qc.ca
ville.asbestos.qc.ca/cour-municipale

Autray MRC
550, rue Montcalm, Berthierville, QC J0K 1A0
Tél: 450-836-7007

Baie-Comeau
9, av Marquette, Baie-Comeau, QC G4Z 1K4
Tél: 418-296-8172

Bellechasse MRC
100, Monseigneur Bilodeau, P.O. Box 130, St-Lazare-de-Bellechasse, QC G0R 3J0
Tél: 418-883-3347
www.mrcbellechasse.qc.ca

Beloeil
Hôtel de ville, 777, boul Laurier, Beloeil, QC J3G 4S9
Tél: 450-467-2835; *Téléc:* 450-464-5445
cour-mun@ville.beloeil.qc.ca
ville.beloeil.qc.ca

Blainville
Hôtel de ville, 1000, ch du Plan-Bouchard, Blainville, QC J7C 3S9
Tél: 450-434-5225
www.ville.blainville.qc.ca

Boisbriand
#120, 940, boul de la Grande-Allée, Boisbriand, QC J7G 2J7
Tél: 450-435-1954; *Téléc:* 450-435-6398

Candiac
100, boul Montcalm nord, Candiac, QC J5R 3L8
Tél: 450-444-6060; *Téléc:* 450-444-0789
cour@ville.candiac.qc.ca

Chambly
1, Place de la Mairie, Chambly, QC J3L 4X1
Tél: 450-658-0613; *Téléc:* 450-658-4214
cour@ville.chambly.qc.ca

Juge municipal désigné:
Pierre-Armand Tremblay

Châteauguay
#101, 265, boul d'Anjou, Châteauguay, QC J6J 5J9
Tél: 450-698-3246; *Téléc:* 450-698-3259
cour.municipale@ville.chateauguay.qc.ca
www.ville.chateauguay.qc.ca

La cour a le mandat de veiller à l'application des lois et des règlements municipaux, provinciaux et fédéraux pour Châteauguay, Mercier, Léry et Beauharnois.

Chibougamau
650, 3e rue, Chibougamau, QC G8P 1P1
Tél: 418-748-3132
courmunicipale@ville.chibougamau.qc.ca
Greffière et perceptrice d'amendes: Nathalie Vallières
nathaliev@ville.chibougamau.qc.ca

Coaticook
150, rue Child, Coaticook, QC J1A 2B3
Tél: 819-849-2721

Colline-de-L'Outaouais
216, ch Old Chelsea, Chelsea, QC J9B 1J4
Tél: 819-827-0516

Côte-de-Beaupré MRC
3, rue de la Seigneurie, Château-Richer, QC G0A 1N0
Tél: 418-824-3444; *Téléc:* 418-824-3917
courmunicipale@mrccotedebeaupre.qc.ca

Cowansville
220, Place Municipale, Cowansville, QC J2K 1T4
Tél: 450-263-5434; *Téléc:* 450-263-4332

Deux-Montagnes
1502, ch d'Oka, Deux-Montagnes, QC J7R 1M8
Tél: 450-473-8688; *Téléc:* 450-473-0094

Dolbeau-Mistassini
1420, boul Walberg, Dolbeau, QC G8L 1G7
Tél: 418-276-0683; *Téléc:* 418-276-6110

Donnacona
138, av Pleau, Donnacona, QC G3M 1A1
Tél: 418-285-3163; *Téléc:* 418-285-0020

Drummondville
415, rue Lindsay, P.O. Box 398, Drummondville, QC J2B 6W3
Tél: 819-478-6556; *Téléc:* 819-478-0920
courmunicipale@ville.drummondville.qc.ca
www.ville.drummondville.qc.ca/cour-municipale-mission

Gatineau
25, rue Laurier, Gatineau, QC J8X 4C8
Tél: 819-595-7272

Granby
735, rue Dufferin, Granby, QC J2H 2H5
Tél: 450-776-8340; *Téléc:* 450-776-8342
cour.municipale@ville.granby.qc.ca

Haut-Saint Laurent MRC
#400, 10, rue King, Huntingdon, QC J0S 1H0
Tél: 450-264-5411; *Téléc:* 450-264-6885
courmunicipale@mrchsl.com

Joliette
614, Manseau, Joliette, QC J6E 3E4
Tél: 450-753-8123

L'Assomption
399, rue Dorval, L'Assomption, QC J5W 1A1
Tél: 450-589-5671; *Téléc:* 450-589-4512
courmunicipale@ville.lassomption.qc.ca
www.ville.lassomption.qc.ca

La Pocatière
412, 9e rue, La Pocatière, QC G0R 1Z0
Tél: 418-856-3394; *Téléc:* 418-856-5465

La Prairie
#400, 170, boul Taschereau, La Prairie, QC J5R 5H6
Tél: 450-444-6626; *Téléc:* 450-444-6636
cour@ville.laprairie.qc.ca

La Tuque
375, rue St-Joseph, La Tuque, QC G9X 1L5
Tél: 819-523-8200; *Téléc:* 819-523-5419

Lac-Mégantic
#201, 5527, rue Frontenac, Lac-Mégantic, QC G6B 1H6
Tél: 819-583-2815; *Téléc:* 819-583-2841
cour.municipale@ville.lac-megantic.qc.ca
www.ville.lac-megantic.qc.ca

Lachute
380, rue Principale, Lachute, QC J8H 1Y2
Tél: 450-562-3781

Laval
55, boul des Laurentides, Laval, QC H7G 2T1
Tél: 450-662-4466; *Téléc:* 450-662-8501

Lévis
5333, rue de la Symphonie, Charny, QC G6X 3B6
Tél: 418-832-4695; *Téléc:* 418-832-0247
csaccourmunicipale@ville.levis.qc.ca
www.ville.levis.qc.ca

L'Islet MRC
34A, rue Fortin, Saint-Jean-Port-Joli, QC G0R 3G0
Tél: 418-598-3076; *Téléc:* 418-598-6880

Longueuil
#290, 100, Place Charles-Lemoyne, P.O. Box 1000, Longueuil, QC J4K 5H3
Tél: 450-463-7006; *Téléc:* 450-646-8897
www.longueuil.ca

Lotbinière MRC
#4, 372, rue St-Joseph, P.O. Box 40, Laurier-Station, QC G0S 1N0
Tél: 418-728-2787; *Téléc:* 418-728-2501
cour.municipale@mrclotbiniere.org

Magog
7, rue Principale est, Magog, QC J1X 1Y4
Tél: 819-843-6501; *Téléc:* 819-843-3599

Mascouche
3038, ch Ste-Marie, Mascouche, QC J7K 1P1
Tél: 450-474-4133
ville.mascouche.qc.ca

Maskinongé MRC
651, av St-Laurent est, Louiseville, QC J5V 1J1
Tél: 819-228-9461

Matawinie MRC
3184, 1e av, P.O. Box 1239, Rawdon, QC J0K 1S0
Tél: 450-834-5441; *Téléc:* 450-834-6560
cour@mrcmatawinie.qc.ca

Mirabel
17690, boul du Val d'Espoir, Mirabel, QC J7J 1A1
Tél: 450-475-2009

Mont-Saint-Hilaire
Hôtel de Ville, 100, rue du Centre-Civique, Mont-Saint-Hilaire, QC J3H 3M8
Tél: 450-467-2854; *Téléc:* 450-467-7459
cour.municipale@villemsh.ca
www.ville.mont-saint-hilaire.qc.ca

Montcalm
1530, rue Albert, P.O. Box 308, Sainte-Julienne, QC J0K 2T0
Tél: 450-831-2182; *Téléc:* 450-831-4712
courmunicipale@mrcmontcalm.com

Montmagny
143, rue St-Jean-Baptiste est, Montmagny, QC G5V 1K4
Tél: 418-248-3361

Montréal
775, rue Gosford, Montréal, QC H2Y 3B9
Tél: 514-872-2964; *Téléc:* 514-872-8271
cour-municipale@ville.montreal.qc.ca
www.ville.montreal.qc.ca

Nicolet
180, Mgr. Panet, Nicolet, QC J3T 1S6
Tél: 819-293-6901; *Téléc:* 819-293-6767

Plessisville
1700, rue St-Calixte, Plessisville, QC G6L 1R3
Tél: 819-362-3284

Princeville
50, St-Jacques ouest, Princeville, QC G6L 4Y5
Tél: 819-364-3333; *Téléc:* 819-364-5198

Québec
285, rue de la Maréchaussée, Québec, QC G1K 8W5
Tél: 418-641-6179
greffecourmunicipale@ville.quebec.qc.ca
www.ville.quebec.qc.ca

Repentigny
1, Montée des Arsenaux, Repentigny, QC J5Z 2C1
Tél: 450-470-3500

Rimouski
205, av de la Cathédrale, P.O. Box 710, Rimouski, QC G5L 7C7
Tél: 418-724-3181; *Téléc:* 418-724-9795
cour.municipale@ville.rimouski.qc.ca

Roberval
851, boul Saint-Joseph, Roberval, QC G8H 2L6
Tél: 418-275-0202; *Téléc:* 418-275-5031

Rosemère
100, rue Charbonneau, Rosemère, QC J7A 3W1
Tél: 450-621-3500; *Téléc:* 450-621-1022
www.ville.rosemere.qc.ca/cour-municipale

Saguenay
201, rue Racine est, P.O. Box 129, Chicoutimi, QC G7H 5B8
Tél: 418-698-3160

Ste-Adèle
1381, boul Sainte-Adele, Sainte-Adèle, QC J8B 1A3
Tél: 450-229-2921; *Téléc:* 450-229-5300
cour@ville.sainte-adele.qc.ca

Ste-Agathe-des-Monts
50, rue St-Joseph, Sainte-Agathe-des-Monts, QC J8C 1M9
Tél: 819-326-4595
cour@ville.sainte-agathe-des-monts.qc.ca

St-Césaire
1111, av St-Paul, Saint-Césaire, QC J0L 1T0
Tél: 450-469-3108; *Téléc:* 450-469-5275

St-Constant
Quartier de la Gare, #100, 121, rue Saint-Pierre, Saint-Constant, QC J5A 2G9
Tél: 450-638-2010; *Téléc:* 450-632-0788

St-Félicien
1209, boul. Sacré-Coeur, P.O. Box 7000, Saint-Félicien, QC G8K 2R5
Tél: 418-679-0251

St-Georges
11700, boul. Lacroix, St-Georges, QC G5Y 1L3
Tél: 418-228-5555; *Téléc:* 418-226-2282
cour.municipale@saint-georges.ca

Saint-Hyacinthe
700, de l'Hôtel-de-Ville, Saint-Hyacinthe, QC J2S 5B2
Tél: 450-778-8319; *Téléc:* 450-778-8393
cour-municipale@ville.st-hyacinthe.qc.ca

Saint-Jean-sur-Richelieu
855, 1re rue, Saint-Jean-sur-Richelieu, QC J2X 3C7
Tél: 450-357-2087; *Téléc:* 450-357-2750
cour.municipale@ville.saint-jean-sur-richelieu.qc.ca

St-Jérôme MRC
280, rue Labelle, Saint-Jérome, QC J7Z 5L1
Tél: 450-436-1511; *Téléc:* 450-436-4506
cour@vsj.ca

Ste-Marie
270, av Marguerite Bourgeoys, P.O. Box 1750, Sainte-Marie, QC G6E 3Z3
Tél: 418-387-2301

St-Rémi
105, rue de la Mairie, Saint-Rémi, QC J0L 2L0
Tél: 450-454-3994; *Téléc:* 450-454-6898

Ste-Thérèse
6, rue de l'Église, P.O. Box 100, Sainte-Thérèse, QC J7E 3L1
Tél: 450-434-1440
cour@sainte-therese.ca

Salaberry-de-Valleyfield
29, rue Fabre, Salaberry-de-Valleyfield, QC J6S 4K5
Tél: 450-370-4810; *Téléc:* 450-370-4868

Sept-Iles
546, av de Quen, Sept-Iles, QC G4R 2R4
Tél: 418-964-3250
greffe@ville.sept-iles.qc.ca

Shawinigan
550, av de l'Hôtel-de-Ville, P.O. Box 400, Shawinigan, QC G9N 6V3
Tél: 819-536-7211

Sherbrooke
191, rue Palais, P.O. Box 1614, Sherbrooke, QC J1H 5M4
Tél: 819-821-5600; *Téléc:* 819-821-5599

Sorel-Tracy
3025, boul de Tracy, Sorel-Tracy, QC J3P 7K1
Tél: 450-742-7775
courmunicipale@ville.sorel-tracy.qc.ca

Terrebonne
3630, Émile-Roy, Terrebonne, QC J7M 1A1
Tél: 450-961-2001; *Téléc:* 450-471-9322

Thetford-Mines
144, rue Notre-Dame ouest, P.O. Box 489, Thetford Mines, QC G6G 5T3
Tél: 418-335-2981; *Téléc:* 418-335-7089
info@ville.thetfordmines.qc.ca

Trois-Rivières
#100, 80, rue Paré, Trois-Rivières, QC G8T 9W2
Tél: 819-372-4628; *Téléc:* 819-371-9777
courmunicipale@v3r.net

Val-d'Or
855, 2e av, P.O. Box 400, Val-d'Or, QC J9P 4P4
Tél: 819-824-9613; *Téléc:* 819-825-6650
info@ville.valdor.qc.ca

Val-St-François MRC
#101, 3, Greenlay sud, Windsor, QC J1S 2J1
Tél: 819-845-2016; *Téléc:* 819-845-3209
cour.municipale@val-saint-francois.qc.ca

Vaudreuil-Soulanges MRC
#27, 2555, rue Dutrisac, Vaudreuil-Dorion, QC J7V 7E6
Tél: 450-455-9480; *Téléc:* 450-455-8856
cmrvs@mrcvs.ca
mrcvs.ca/fr/cour-municipale-regionale

Victoriaville
1, Notre-Dame ouest, P.O. Box 370, Victoriaville, QC G6P 6T2
Tél: 819-758-1571
greffe@victoriaville.ca

Waterloo
#210, 417, rue de la Cour, Waterloo, QC J0E 2N0
Tél: 450-539-2282

Saskatchewan

Saskatchewan Court of Appeal
2425 Victoria Ave., Regina, SK S4P 3W6
Tel: 306-787-5382; *Fax:* 306-787-5815
www.sasklawcourts.ca

The Court of Appeal has appellate jurisdiction with respect to any judgement, order or decree made by the Court of Queen's Bench & any matter granted to it by statute.

Chief Justice of Saskatchewan: The Hon. Robert Richards
Justices of Appeal (The Hon. Mr./Madam Justice):
Neal Caldwell
Maurice Herauf
Georgina Jackson
Gary Lane (Supernumerary)
Ralph Ottenbreit
Jacelyn Ryan-Froslie
Peter Whitmore
Administration:
Registrar: Melanie Baldwin, 306-787-5382
caregistrar@sasklawcourts.ca

Saskatchewan Court of Queen's Bench
2425 Victoria Ave., Regina, SK S4P 4W6
Tel: 306-787-5377; *Fax:* 306-787-7217
www.sasklawcourts.ca

The Court of Queen's Bench is a court of original jurisdiction having jurisdiction in civil & criminal matters arising in Saskatchewan, except those matters expressly excluded by statute.

Chief Justice: The Hon. M.D. Popescul
Justices (The Hon. Mr./Madam Justice):
D.P. Ball (Supernumerary)
B.A. Barrington-Foote
C.L. Dawson
R.W. Elson
E.J. Gunn (Supernumerary)
J.D. Kalmakoff
F.J. Kovach (Supernumerary)
L.L. Krogan
J.E. McMurtry
L.M. Schwann
T.C. Zarzeczny (Supernumerary)
Judges, Family Division (The Hon. Mr./Madam Justice):
D.J. Brown
G.M. Kraus (Supernumerary)
D.E.W. McIntyre (Supernumerary)
M.T. Megaw
J.A. Tholl
Administration:
Registrar: Jennifer Fabian
jfabian@judicom.ca

Courts:

Battleford
Court House, 291 - 23 St. West, P.O. Box 340, Battleford, SK S0M 0E0
Tel: 306-446-7675; *Fax:* 306-446-7737
Judges (His/Her Hon.):
D.B. Konkin
Judges (His/Her Hon.):
Debbie Zayac-Sheppard

Estevan
Court House, 1016 - 4 St., Estevan, SK S4A 0W5
Tel: 306-637-4527; *Fax:* 306-637-4536
Justices (The Hon. Mr./Madam Justice):
G.A.J. Chicoine
Administration:
Amy Stapleton (Sheriff & Local Registrar)

Melfort
Court House, 409 Main St., P.O. Box 6500, Melfort, SK S0E 1A0
Tel: 306-752-6265; *Fax:* 306-752-6264
Administration:
Sheriff & Local Registrar: Leanna Pickering

Moose Jaw
Court House, 64 Ominica St. West, Moose Jaw, SK S6H 6V2
Tel: 306-694-3602; *Fax:* 306-694-3056
Judges (His/Her Hon.):
D.C. Chow
Administration:
Carol Meier (Acting Local Registrar/Sheriff)

Prince Albert
Court House, 1800 Central Ave., Prince Albert, SK S6V 4W7
Tel: 306-953-3200; *Fax:* 306-953-3210
Justices (The Hon. Mr./Madam Justice):
G.A. Meschishnick
Judges, Family Division (The Hon. Mr./Madam Justice):
R.D. Maher (Supernumerary)
L.W. Zuk
Administration:
Sheriff & Local Registrar: Ann Courtney

Saskatoon
520 Spadina Cres. East, Saskatoon, SK S7K 3G7
Tel: 306-933-5135; *Fax:* 306-975-4818
Justices (The Hon. Mr./Madam Justice):
M.D. Acton
G.N. Allbright
G.M. Currie
R.W. Danyliuk
M.L. Dovell
D.E. Labach
N.G. Gabrielson
G.D. Dufour
R.C. Mills
B.J. Scherman
R.S. Smith
Judges, Family Division (The Hon. Mr./Madam Justice):
G.D. Dufour
G.V. Goebel
F.N. Turcotte
Y.G.K Wilkinson
D.L. Wilson
Administration:
Local Registrar: Glen Metivier
Sheriff: Gord Laing

Swift Current
Court House, 121 Lorne St. West, Swift Current, SK S9H 0J4
Tel: 306-778-8400; *Fax:* 306-778-8581
Justices (The Hon. Mr./Madam Justice):
T.J. Keene
Administration:
Sheriff & Local Registrar: Nikki Barlow

Weyburn
Court House, 301 Prairie Ave., Weyburn, SK S4H 0L4
Tel: 306-848-2361; *Fax:* 306-848-2540
Sheriff & Local Registrar: Amy Stapleton

Yorkton
Court House, 29 Darlington St. East, Yorkton, SK S3N 0C2
Tel: 306-786-1515; *Fax:* 306-786-1521

Saskatchewan Provincial Court
1815 Smith St., Regina, SK S4P 2N5
Tel: 306-787-5250; *Fax:* 306-787-7037
www.sasklawcourts.ca

The Provincial Court has jurisdiction in both civil (including small claims & family) & select criminal (including young offender) matters.

Chief Judge: The Hon. J.A. Plemel

Courts:

Estevan
Court House, 1016 - 4th St., Estevan, SK S4A 0W5
Tel: 306-637-4528; *Fax:* 306-637-4536
Judges (The Hon.):
L. Wiegers

La Ronge
1320 La Ronge Ave., La Ronge, SK S0J 1L0
Tel: 306-425-4505; *Fax:* 306-425-4269
Judges (The Hon.):
R. Lane
Sid Robinson

Lloydminster
4815 - 50 St., Lloydminster, SK S9V 0M8
Tel: 306-825-6420; *Fax:* 306-825-6497
Judges (The Hon.):

K.J. Young

Meadow Lake
207 - 3 Ave. East, Meadow Lake, SK S9X 1E7
Tel: 306-236-7575; *Fax:* 306-236-7598
Judges (The Hon.):
D.J. Bird
Miguel Martinez
Janet McIvor

Melfort
107 Crawford Ave. East, Melfort, SK S0E 1A0
Tel: 306-752-6230; *Fax:* 306-752-6126
Judges (The Hon.):
I.J. Cardinal
J. Rybchuk

Moose Jaw
#211, 110 Ominica St. West, Moose Jaw, SK S6H 6V2
Tel: 306-694-3612; *Fax:* 306-694-3043
Judges (The Hon.):
D.J. Kovatch
M. Gordon

North Battleford
3 Railway Ave. East, North Battleford, SK S9A 2P9
Tel: 306-446-7400; *Fax:* 306-446-7432
Judges (The Hon.):
B. Bauer
L.D. Dyck
D. O'Hanlon

Prince Albert
188 - 11th St. West, P.O. Box 3003, Prince Albert, SK S6V 6G1
Tel: 306-953-2640; *Fax:* 306-953-2819
Judges (The Hon.):
S. Schiefner
F.M.A.L. Daunt
H.W. Harradence (Administrative Judge)
E. Kalenith
S.D. Loewen
G.M. Morin

Regina
1815 Smith St., Regina, SK S4P 2N5
Tel: 306-787-5250; *Fax:* 306-787-7037
Judges (The Hon.):
C.C. Toth
M.T. Beaton
A. Crugnole-Reid
P. Demong
L. Halliday
B.D. Henning (Administrative Judge for Facilities and Security)
M. J. Hinds (Associate Chief Judge)
C.A. Snell
K.A. Lang
B.J. Tomkins

Saskatoon
220 - 19 St. East, Saskatoon, SK S7K 0A2
Tel: 306-933-7052; *Fax:* 306-933-7043
Judges (The Hon.):
S. Anand (Administrative Judge)
Q.D. Agnew
M. Gray
V.M. Enweani
R.D. Jackson
B.M. Klause
M.M. Baniak
S. Metivier
B.G. Morgan
D.C. Scott
B. Singer
B. Wright

Swift Current
Court House, 121 Lorne St. West, Swift Current, SK S9H 0J4
Tel: 306-778-8390; *Fax:* 306-778-8581
Judges (The Hon.):
K.P. Bazin

Wynyard
Court House, 410 Ave. C East, P.O. Box 1449, Wynyard, SK S0A 4T0
Tel: 306-554-5521; *Fax:* 306-554-5531
Judges (The Hon.):
M. Marquette

Yorkton
Court House, 120 Smith St. East, Yorkton, SK S3N 3V3
Tel: 306-786-1400; *Fax:* 306-786-1422
Judges (The Hon.):
R. Green
P.R. Koskie
P.A. Reis

Yukon Territory

Yukon Territory: Court of Appeal
Court Registry, 2134 - 2nd Ave., Ground Fl., Whitehorse, YT Y1A 5H6
Tel: 867-456-3821; *Fax:* 867-393-6212
Toll-Free: 800-661-0408
courtservices@gov.yk.ca
www.yukoncourts.ca/courts/appeal.html

The Court of Appeal has appellate jurisdiction in all civil & criminal matters from decisions by the Territorial Court & Supreme Court.

Justices of Appeal (The Hon. Mr./Madam Justice):
Robert J. Bauman
Elizabeth A. Bennett
Gail M. Dickson
Ian T. Donald
Lauri Ann Fenlon
S. David Frankel
Nicole J. Garson
Richard Goepel
Harvey M. Groberman
David C. Harris
Pamela A. Kirkpatrick
P.D. Lowry
Anne W. Mackenzie
Mary Newbury
M.E. Saunders
John Savage
Daphne M. Smith
Sunni Stromberg-Stein
David Franklin Tysoe
Peter M. Willcock
Administration:
Registrar: Timothy Outerbridge

Yukon Territory: Supreme Court
Court Services J-3, 2134 - 2nd Ave., P.O. Box 2703, Whitehorse, YT Y1A 2C6
Tel: 867-667-5937; *Fax:* 867-393-6212
courtservices@gov.yk.ca
www.yukoncourts.ca/courts/supreme.html

The Supreme Court is a superior court of record having original jurisdiction in all civil & criminal matters arising in the Yukon, unless excluded by statute.

Ronald S. Veale (Senior Judge)
Earl Johnson
Robert G. Kilpatrick
Virginia A. Schuler
John Z. Vertes
Deputy Judges (The Hon. Mr./Madam Justice):
Mary Lou Benotto
J. Keith Bracken
C. Scott Brooker
Beverley Browne
Louise Charbonneau
Francis W. Cole
Susan Cooper
Wallace M. Darichuk
Barry Davies
Todd Ducharme
Marsha Erb
René P. Foisy
Geoffrey Gaul
Adam Germain
John Gill
Ross Goodwin
Stephen Goudge
Harvey Groberman
Joel Groves
R.J. Haines
Gerard C. Hawco
Thomas Heeney
Stephen D. Hillier
Elizabeth A. Hughes
Mary Humphries
Stephen Kelleher
Colleen Kenny
Adele Kent
Brenda Keyser
Sal Joseph LoVecchio
Miriam A. Maisonville
Richard P. Marceau
Sheilah Martin
Peter McIntyre
John Menzies
Andrea Moen
Mary Moreau
Rosemary Nation
Dennis O'Connor
Jeffrey J. Oliphant
Vital Ouellette
Jacelyn Ryan-Froslie
Karan M. Shaner
Neil Sharkey
Shannon Smallwood
Erwin Stach
Sunni Stromberg-Stein
Bonnie Tulloch
David Watt
Alan Whitten
Peter Willcock
James W. Williams
Randall Wong

Yukon Territory: Territorial Court
Court Services J-3E, 2134 - 2nd Ave., P.O. Box 2703, Whitehorse, YT Y1A 2C6
Tel: 867-667-5438; *Fax:* 867-393-6400
Toll-Free: 800-661-0408
courtservices@gov.yk.ca
www.yukoncourts.ca/courts/territorial.html

The Territorial Court has jurisdiction in family, youth & select criminal matters.

Chief Judge: The Hon. Karen Ruddy
Judges (The Hon. Mr./Madam Justice):
Michael Cozens
Peter Chisholm
Richard D. Schneider
Herman J. Seidemann III
Pamela Williams
David C. Walker
Thomas Crabtree
Michael S. Block
Joseph De Filippis
William Digby
John Faulkner
Timothy W. White
Christine V. Harapiak
Murray J. Hinds
Heino Lilles
Deborah Livingstone
Donald S. Luther
Brian M. Neal
Nancy K. Orr
James Plemel
E. Dennis Schmidt
Richard W. Thompson
Raymond E. Wyant

SECTION 10
HOSPITALS & HEALTH CARE FACILITIES

Listings in this section are arranged by province, and then by city. Each provincial section includes the following six categories.

Government Department

Regional Health Authorities

Hospitals

Community Health Centres

Long Term/Retirement Care

Mental Health Facilities

Alberta

Government Departments in Charge

Edmonton: Alberta Health
PO Box 1360 Stn. Main, Edmonton, AB T5J 2N3
Tel: 780-427-7164
TTY: 780-427-9999
www.health.alberta.ca
Note: Alberta Health is the ministry that sets policy, legislation and standards for the health system in Alberta. The ministry allocates health funding and administers provincial programs such as the Alberta Health Care Insurance Plan and provides expertise on communicable disease control.
Hon. Sarah Hoffman, Minister of Health
Dr. Karen Grimsrud, Chief Medical Officer of Health

Regional Health Authorities

Edmonton: Alberta Health Services (AHS)
Seventh Street Plaza, 14th Fl., North Tower, 10030 - 107 St. NW, Edmonton, AB T5J 3E4
Tel: 780-342-2000; *Fax:* 780-342-2060
Toll-Free: 888-342-2471
ahsinfo@albertahealthservices.ca
www.albertahealthservices.ca
Info Line: 811
Social Media: www.facebook.com/179579998746821; twitter.com/AHS_media; www.youtube.com/ahschannel
Year Founded: 2009
Number of Beds: 23,742 continuing care beds; 8,471 acute care beds; 208 palliative & hospice beds; 2,439 mental health beds
Population Served: 4000000
Note: Provincial governance board, overseeing hospitals, other health facilities, & ground ambulance service in Alberta. The agency employes over 108,000 employees.
Vernab Yiu, President & CEO
Dr. David Mador, Vice-President & Medical Director, Northern Alberta
Deb Gordon, Vice-President & Chief Health Operations Officer, Northern Alberta
Brenda Huband, Vice-President & Chief Health Operations Officer, Central & Southern Alberta

Hospitals - General

Athabasca: Athabasca Healthcare Centre
Affiliated with: Alberta Health Services
3100 - 48 Ave., Athabasca, AB T9S 1M9
Tel: 780-675-6000; *Fax:* 780-675-7050
www.albertahealthservices.ca
Social Media: www.facebook.com/179579998746821; twitter.com/AHS_media; www.youtube.com/ahschannel
Number of Beds: 26 acute care beds; 1 palliative care bed; 23 continuing care beds
Note: Programs & services include: emergency services; diagnostic imaging; laboratory services; acute care; obstetrics; pediatrics; continuing care; rehabilitation; recreation services; palliative care; & x-ray.
Dr. Adrian Mol, Contact
Dr. Brian Oldale, Contact

Banff: Banff - Mineral Springs Hospital
Covenant Health
Affiliated with: Alberta Health Services
PO Box 1050, 305 Lynx St., Banff, AB T1L 1H7
Tel: 403-762-2222; *Fax:* 403-762-4193
info@banffmineralspringshospital.com
banffmineralspringshospital.com
Social Media: www.facebook.com/Banff.MSH
Year Founded: 1930
Note: Programs & services include: emergency services; surgery; acute care; maternal & child care; physiotherapy; occupational therapy; recreation therapy; music therapy; mental health services; P.A.R.T.Y. program, to Prevent Alcohol & Risk-Related Trauma in Youth; continuing care; outpatient clinics; & palliative care.
Shelley Buchan, Site Administrator

Barrhead: Barrhead Healthcare Centre
Affiliated with: Alberta Health Services
4815 - 51 Ave., Barrhead, AB T7N 1M1
Tel: 780-674-2221; *Fax:* 780-674-3541
www.albertahealthservices.ca
Social Media: www.facebook.com/179579998746821; twitter.com/AHS_media; www.youtube.com/ahschannel
Number of Beds: 34 beds
Note: Programs & services include: emergency services; diagnostic imaging; laboratory services; obstetrics; community cancer centre; rehabilitation services; social work; diet counselling; education programs; outpatient clinics; & palliative care.

Bassano: Bassano Health Centre
Affiliated with: Alberta Health Services
608 - 5 Ave., Bassano, AB T0J 0B0
Tel: 403-641-6100; *Fax:* 403-641-2157
www.albertahealthservices.ca
Social Media: www.facebook.com/179579998746821; twitter.com/AHS_media; www.youtube.com/ahschannel
Year Founded: 1914
Number of Beds: 4 acute care beds; 8 continuing care beds; 1 palliative care bed; 1 respite care bed
Note: Programs & services include: emergency services; diagnostic imaging; acute care; physiotherapy; occupational therapy; physiotherapy; mental health services; nutrition services; social work; continuing care; respite care; & palliative care.

Beaverlodge: Beaverlodge Municipal Hospital
Affiliated with: Alberta Health Services
PO Box 480, 422 - 10A St., Beaverlodge, AB T0H 0C0
Tel: 780-354-2136; *Fax:* 780-354-8355
www.albertahealthservices.ca
Social Media: www.facebook.com/179579998746821; twitter.com/AHS_media; www.youtube.com/ahschannel
Number of Beds: 18 acute care beds
Note: Programs & services include: emergency services; general radiography; medical laboratory; acute care; obstetrics; physiotherapy; occupational therapy; & palliative care.
Janet Wallace, Site Manager

Black Diamond: Oilfields General Hospital
Affiliated with: Alberta Health Services
717 Government Rd., Black Diamond, AB T0L 0H0
Tel: 403-933-2222; *Fax:* 403-933-2031
www.albertahealthservices.ca
Social Media: www.facebook.com/179579998746821; twitter.com/AHS_media; www.youtube.com/ahschannel
Note: Programs & services include: adult Aboriginal mental health services; Healthy Moms, Health Babies Program; diagnostic imaging; laboratory services; occupational therapy; physical therapy; & speech language pathology.

Blairmore: Crowsnest Pass Health Centre
Affiliated with: Alberta Health Services
2001 - 107 St., Blairmore, AB T0K 0E0
Tel: 403-562-5011; *Fax:* 403-562-8992
www.albertahealthservices.ca
Social Media: www.facebook.com/179579998746821; twitter.com/AHS_media; www.youtube.com/AHSChannel
Note: Programs & services include: emergency services; diagnostic imaging services; laboratory services; surgery; obstetrics; neonatal intensive care nursery; pediatrics; critical care services; acute care; rehabilitation services, including occupational therapy & therapeutic recreation; Southern Alberta Renal Program; continuing care; & palliative care.

Bonnyville: Bonnyville Healthcare Centre
Covenant Health
Affiliated with: Alberta Health Services
5001 Lakeshore Dr., Bonnyville, AB T9N 2J7
Tel: 780-826-3311; *Fax:* 780-826-6527
www.covenanthealth.ca/hospitals-care-centres/bonnyville-health-centre
Social Media: www.facebook.com/179579998746821; twitter.com/AHS_media; www.youtube.com/ahschannel
Year Founded: 1986
Number of Beds: 63 beds
Number of Employees: 317
Note: Programs & services include: emergency services; regional laboratory services; diagnostic imaging; pathology; surgery; acute care; community cancer centre; cardiac stress testing; obstetrics; rehabilitation; medical accupunture; occupational therapy; respiratory therapy; continuing care; & palliative care.

Bow Island: Bow Island Health Centre
Affiliated with: Alberta Health Services
938 Centre St., Bow Island, AB T0K 0G0
Tel: 403-545-3200; *Fax:* 403-545-2281
www.albertahealthservices.ca
Social Media: www.facebook.com/179579998746821; twitter.com/AHS_media; www.youtube.com/ahschannel
Number of Beds: 10 acute care beds; 20 continuing care beds
Note: Programs & services include: emergency services; diagnostic imaging & laboratory services; acute care; physiotherapy; occupational therapy; continuing care; & respite services.

Boyle: Boyle Healthcare Centre
Affiliated with: Alberta Health Services
5004 Lakeview Rd., Boyle, AB T0A 0M0
Tel: 780-689-3731; *Fax:* 780-689-3951
www.albertahealthservices.ca
Social Media: www.facebook.com/179579998746821; twitter.com/AHS_media; www.youtube.com/ahschannel
Year Founded: 1966
Number of Beds: 19 acute care beds; 1 palliative care bed
Note: Programs & services include: emergency services; diagnostic imaging; laboratory services; acute care services; nutrition services; community health; social work; & palliative care.

Brooks: Brooks Health Centre
Affiliated with: Alberta Health Services
440 - 3rd St. East, Brooks, AB T1R 0G5
Tel: 403-501-3232; *Fax:* 403-362-6039
www.albertahealthservices.ca
Social Media: www.facebook.com/179579998746821; twitter.com/AHS_media; www.youtube.com/ahschannel
Number of Beds: 40 acute care beds; 75 long term care beds
Note: Programs & services include: emergency services; ambulatory care; acute care; obstetrics; pediatrics; physiotherapy; occupational therapy; recreational therapy; Living Healthy Program / cardiac rehabilitation; diabetes education; community health; continuing care; & palliative care.

Calgary: Alberta Children's Hospital
Affiliated with: Alberta Health Services
Former Name: Alberta Crippled Children's Hospital; Junior Red Cross Hospital
West Campus, University of Calgary, 2888 Shaganappi Trail NW, Calgary, AB T3B 6A8
Tel: 403-955-7211
www.calgaryhealthregion.ca/ACH
Social Media: www.facebook.com/179579998746821; twitter.com/AHS_media; www.youtube.com/AHSChannel
Year Founded: 2006
Note: Programs & services include: Aboriginal services; angiography; pediatrics (birth to age 18); emergency services; surgery; complex pain service; diagnostic imaging; burn treatment; eating disorder program - day treatment; sexual assault response team; child abuse service; child & adolescent mental health inpatient services; community education service; & Infant Headshape Program.

Calgary: Foothills Medical Centre
Affiliated with: Alberta Health Services
1403 - 29 St. NW, Calgary, AB T2N 2T9
Tel: 403-944-1110
www.albertahealthservices.ca
Social Media: www.facebook.com/179579998746821; twitter.com/AHS_media; www.youtube.com/ahschannel
Year Founded: 1966
Note: Programs & services include: emergency services; trauma services; diagnostic imaging; acute care; gynecology; newborn care; cardiology; gastrointestinal services; hematology; adult neuropsychology service; neurology; psychiatry; renal services; Movement Disorders Program; respiratory services; social work; & addiction services.

Calgary: Peter Lougheed Centre
Affiliated with: Alberta Health Services
3500 - 26 Ave. NE, Calgary, AB T1Y 6J4
Tel: 403-943-4555
www.albertahealthservices.ca
Social Media: www.facebook.com/179579998746821; twitter.com/AHS_media; www.youtube.com/AHSChannel
Year Founded: 1988
Number of Beds: 600 beds
Note: Programs & services include: Aboriginal services; abortion; angiography; anticoagulation management; bronchoscopy; cardiology; clinics; CT imaging; mental health services; surgery; diabetes, hypertension & cholesterol; diagnostic imaging; electroencephalography; emergency; enterostomal therapy; fluoroscopy; gastrointestinal; general medicine; general radiography; hematology; hemodialysis; intensive care; laboratory; magnetic resonance imaging; neurology; nuclear medicine; nutrition; occupational therapy; oncology; palliative care; pharmacy; psychiatry; speech language pathology; social work; & ultrasound.

Calgary: Rockyview General Hospital
Affiliated with: Alberta Health Services
7007 - 14 St. SW, Calgary, AB T2V 1P9
Tel: 403-943-3000
www.albertahealthservices.ca
Social Media: www.facebook.com/179579998746821; twitter.com/AHS_media; www.youtube.com/AHSChannel
Number of Beds: 650 beds
Note: Programs & services include: emergency; acute care; CT

imaging; cardiac intensive care/coronary care units; colorectal surgery; cystoscopy; diagnostic imaging; electroencephalography; endoscopy; geriatric assessment & rehabilitation; & obstetrics/gynecology outpatient.
Nancy Guebert, Vice-President

Calgary: South Health Campus (SHC)
Affiliated with: Alberta Health Services
4448 Front St. SE, Calgary, AB T3M 1M4
Tel: 403-956-1111
www.albertahealthservices.ca/facilities/shc
Social Media: www.facebook.com/179579998746821; twitter.com/ahs_media; www.youtube.com/user/AHSChannel
Year Founded: 2012
Note: Programs & services include: clinics; angiography; bronchoscopy; cardiology; child & adolescent addiction & mental health; CT services; surgery; diabetes; diagnostic imaging; electroencephalography; electromyography; emergency; endocrinology; gastrointestinal; general medicine; radiography; hematology; infectious diseases; intensive care; magnetic resonance; neurology; nuclear medicine; nutrition; obstetrics; orthopedics; pediatric; pharmacy; psychiatric; respiratory/pulmonary; rheumatology; speech language pathology; & ultrasound.

Camrose: St. Mary's Hospital
Covenant Health
Affiliated with: Alberta Health Services
4607 - 53 St., Camrose, AB T4V 1Y5
Tel: 780-679-6100; *Fax:* 780-679-6196
www.stmaryscamrose.com
Social Media: www.facebook.com/179579998746821; twitter.com/AHS_media; www.youtube.com/ahschannel
Year Founded: 1924
Number of Beds: 76 beds
Population Served: 15000
Note: Programs & services include: emergency; cardiology; diabetic education; diagnostic imaging (CT scans, fluoroscopy, radiology, mammography, ultrasound); community cancer clinic; women's health; pediatrics; palliative care; respiratory therapy; occupational therapy; mental health; & urology.

Canmore: Canmore General Hospital
Affiliated with: Alberta Health Services
1100 Hospital Pl., Canmore, AB T1W 1N2
Tel: 403-678-5536; *Fax:* 403-678-9874
www.albertahealthservices.ca
Social Media: www.facebook.com/179579998746821; twitter.com/AHS_media; www.youtube.com/ahschannel
Year Founded: 1984
Number of Employees: 350
Note: Programs & services include: emergency services; diagnostic imaging; laboratory services; surgical services; obstetrics; newborn care; acute care; cardiology; audiology; chemotherapy treatments; wound centre; occupational therapy; physical therapy; recreation therapy; speech language pathology; mental health; aboriginal hospital Liaison; diabetes prevention; adult day support program; respite care; long term care; & palliative care.

Castor: Our Lady of the Rosary Hospital
Covenant Health
Affiliated with: Alberta Health Services
5402 - 47 St., Castor, AB T0C 0X0
Tel: 403-882-3434; *Fax:* 403-882-2751
www.covenanthealth.ca/hospitals-care-centres/our-lady-of-the-rosary-hospital
Social Media: www.facebook.com/179579998746821; twitter.com/AHS_media; www.youtube.com/ahschannel
Number of Beds: 26 beds
Number of Employees: 85
Note: One of the provincial heritage sites in Castor. Programs & services include: addiction services; emergency; occupational therapy (acute & continuing care); speech language pathology; diagnostic imaging; laboratory; long-term care; palliative care; & pharmacy.
Marilyn Weber, Site Lead
Barry Straub, Supervisor, Facilities Management
barry.straub@covenanthealth.ca

Claresholm: Claresholm General Hospital
Affiliated with: Alberta Health Services
221 - 43 Ave., Claresholm, AB T0L 0T0
Tel: 403-682-3700; *Fax:* 403-682-3789
www.albertahealthservices.ca
Social Media: www.facebook.com/179579998746821; twitter.com/AHS_media; www.youtube.com/AHSChannel
Year Founded: 1972
Number of Beds: 16 beds
Note: Programs & services include: emergency services; diagnostic imaging; cardiology electrocardiogram services; Holter monitoring; acute care; physiotherapy; respite care; & palliative care.

Coaldale: Coaldale Health Centre
Affiliated with: Alberta Health Services
Former Name: Coaldale Community Health
2100 - 11 St., Coaldale, AB T1M 1L2
Tel: 403-345-3075; *Fax:* 403-345-2681
www.albertahealthservices.ca
Social Media: www.facebook.com/179579998746821; twitter.com/AHS_media; www.youtube.com/ahschannel
Note: Programs & services include: continuing care; diagnostic imaging; general radiography; laboratory; occupational & physical therapy; primary care; speech language pathology; & therapeutic recreation.

Cold Lake: Cold Lake Healthcare Centre
Affiliated with: Alberta Health Services
314 - 25 St., Cold Lake, AB T9M 1G6
Tel: 780-639-3322; *Fax:* 780-639-2255
www.albertahealthservices.ca
Social Media: www.facebook.com/179579998746821; twitter.com/AHS_media; www.youtube.com/ahschannel
Number of Beds: 30 continuing care beds; 24 acute care beds
Note: Programs & services include: emergency services; diagnostic imaging services; laboratory services; surgical services; acute care; ambulatory care; obstetrics; pediatrics; eating disorder services; rehabilitation services, including physiotherapy, occupational therapy, recreation therapy, & respiratory therapy; continuing care; dementia care; respite services; & palliative care.
Dr. Siegfried Heydenrych, Chief, Medical Staff
James Murray, Manager

Consort: Consort Hospital & Care Centre
Affiliated with: Alberta Health Services
5402 - 52 Ave., Consort, AB T0C 1B0
Tel: 403-577-3555; *Fax:* 403-577-3950
www.albertahealthservices.ca
Social Media: www.facebook.com/179579998746821; twitter.com/AHS_media; www.youtube.com/ahschannel
Note: Programs & services include: emergency services; diagnostic imaging; laboratory services; acute care; occupational therapy; physiotherapy; continuing care; & palliative care.

Coronation: Coronation Hospital & Care Centre
Affiliated with: Alberta Health Services
Also Known As: Coronation Hospital
5000 Municipal Rd., Coronation, AB T0C 1C0
Tel: 403-577-3803; *Fax:* 403-578-3474
www.albertahealthservices.ca
Social Media: www.facebook.com/179579998746821; twitter.com/AHS_media; www.youtube.com/ahschannel
Number of Beds: 10 acute beds; 19 assisted living beds
Note: Programs & services include: emergency services; diagnostic imaging; laboratory services; acute care; occupational therapy; physical therapy; speech language pathology; continuing care; supportive living; Seniors Mental Health Program; & palliative care.

Daysland: Daysland Health Centre
Affiliated with: Alberta Health Services
5920 - 51st Ave., Daysland, AB T0B 1A0
Tel: 780-374-3746; *Fax:* 780-374-2111
www.albertahealthservices.ca
Social Media: www.facebook.com/179579998746821; twitter.com/AHS_media; www.youtube.com/ahschannel
Number of Beds: 16 acute care beds; 10 rehabilitation beds
Note: Programs & services include: emergency services; laboratory services; surgery; acute care; obstetrics; rehabilitation services, including occupational therapy, physiotherapy, & respiratory therapy; pediatric speech language services; respite care; & palliative care.
Mariann Wolbeck, Health Centre Coordinator

Devon: Devon General Hospital
Affiliated with: Alberta Health Services
101 Erie St. South, Devon, AB T9G 1A6
Tel: 780-342-7000
www.albertahealthservices.ca
Social Media: www.facebook.com/179579998746821; twitter.com/AHS_media; www.youtube.com/ahschannel
Number of Beds: 9 acute care beds; 10 continuing care beds; 2 respite beds
Note: Programs & services include: emergency services; laboratory services; radiology services; acute care; rehabilitation services; mental health therapy; public health; tuberculosis testing & immunization; diabetes education; nutrition information; social work; adult day program; home care; & continuing care.

Didsbury: Didsbury District Health Services
Affiliated with: Alberta Health Services
1210 - 20 Ave., Didsbury, AB T0M 0W0
Tel: 403-335-9393; *Fax:* 403-335-4816
www.albertahealthservices.ca
Social Media: www.facebook.com/179579998746821; twitter.com/AHS_media; www.youtube.com/ahschannel
Note: Programs & services include: emergency services; laboratory services; diagnostic imaging; acute care; rehabilitation, including occupational therapy & physiotherapy; speech language pathology; clinical nutrition services; public health services; respite care; long term care; & palliative care.

Drayton Valley: Drayton Valley Hospital & Care Centre
Affiliated with: Alberta Health Services
4550 Madsen Ave., Drayton Valley, AB T7A 1N8
Tel: 780-542-5321; *Fax:* 780-621-4966
www.albertahealthservices.ca
Social Media: www.facebook.com/179579998746821; twitter.com/AHS_media; www.youtube.com/ahschannel
Number of Beds: 34 acute care beds; 50 long term care beds
Population Served: 23000
Note: Programs & services include: emergency services; diagnostic imaging; laboratory services; acute care; obstetrics; Northern Alberta Renal Program; occupational therapy, physiotherapy, & recreation therapy; diabetes education; nutrition services; long-term care; & palliative care.

Drumheller: Drumheller Health Centre
Affiliated with: Alberta Health Services
351 - 9 St. NW, Drumheller, AB T0J 0Y1
Tel: 403-823-6500; *Fax:* 403-823-5076
www.albertahealthservices.ca
Social Media: www.facebook.com/179579998746821; twitter.com/AHS_media; www.youtube.com/ahschannel
Note: Programs & services include: emergency services; diagnostic imaging; acute care; obstetrics; cardiac rehabilitation program; occupational therapy, physical therapy, & recreation therapy; mental health services; nutrition services; public health; asthma education; continuing care; respite care; home care; & palliative care.

Edmonton: Grey Nuns Community Hospital
Covenant Health
Affiliated with: Alberta Health Services
Former Name: Grey Nuns Community Hospital & Health Centre
1100 Youville Dr. West, Edmonton, AB T6L 5X8
Tel: 780-735-7000
www.covenanthealth.ca/hospitals-care-centres/grey-nuns-community-hospital
Social Media: www.facebook.com/179579998746821; twitter.com/AHS_media; www.youtube.com/ahschannel
Number of Beds: 351 beds
Note: Programs & services include: emergency; general & vascular surgery; intensive & cardiac care; children's health; women's health; diagnostics; & mental health.

Edmonton: Misericordia Community Hospital
Covanent Health
Affiliated with: Alberta Health Services
Former Name: Misericordia Community Hospital & Health Centre
16940 - 87 Ave., Edmonton, AB T5R 4H5
Tel: 780-735-2000
www.albertahealthservices.ca
Social Media: www.facebook.com/179579998746821; twitter.com/AHS_media; www.youtube.com/ahschannel
Number of Beds: 259 beds
Note: Programs & services include: emergency care; surgery; orthopedics; urology; plastic surgery; intensive & coronary care; pediatrics; geriatrics; mental health; women's health; diagnostics; & ambulatory care. The hospital is also home to the Institute for Reconstructive Sciences in Medicine (iRSM) & the Mother Rosalie Health Services Centre.

Edmonton: Royal Alexandra Hospital
Affiliated with: Alberta Health Services
10240 Kingsway Ave., Edmonton, AB T5H 3V9
Tel: 780-735-4111
www.albertahealthservices.ca
Social Media: www.facebook.com/179579998746821; twitter.com/AHS_media; www.youtube.com/ahschannel
Number of Beds: 678 beds
Note: Programs & services include: emergency; acute care of the elderly; clinics; otolaryngology; angiography; child & adolescent psychiatry; colonoscopy; diagnostic imaging; electroencephalography; gastroscopy; radiology; intensive care; mental health; nutrition counselling; ophthalmology; plastics surgery; rehabilitation services; sexual assault response team;

ultrasound; & urology. Located in this hospital is the Lois Hole Hospital for Women.

Edmonton: Stollery Children's Hospital University of Alberta Hospital
Affiliated with: Alberta Health Services
8440 - 112 St., Edmonton, AB T6G 2B7
Tel: 780-407-8822
www.albertahealthservices.ca
Area Served: Northern & Central Alberta; parts of Manitoba
Specialties: Organ transplantation
Note: Western Canada's referral centre for pediatric cardiac surgery. Programs & services include: clinics; audiology; Child & Adolescent Protection Centre; chronic pain service; Diabetes Education Centre; diagnostic imaging; endocrinology; gastroenterology & nutrition; hematology; home nutrition support/dietician; infectious diseases; medicine; Neonatal Intensive Care Unit; Northern Alberta Children's Cancer Program; Northern Alberta Pediatric Sleep Program; occupational & physical therapy; otolaryngology; palliative care; Pediatric Comprehensive Epilepsy Program; feeding & swallowing service; hemophilia; intensive care; Medicine/Surgical Ambulatory Unit; neurology; social work; speech language pathology; & surgery.

Edmonton: University of Alberta Hospital
Affiliated with: Alberta Health Services
8440 - 112 St. NW, Edmonton, AB T6G 2B7
Tel: 780-407-8822
www.albertahealthservices.ca
Social Media: www.facebook.com/17957998746821; twitter.com/AHS_media; www.youtube.com/ahschannel
Number of Beds: 687 beds
Specialties: Organ & Tissue Transplant Program
Note: A clinical, research & teaching facility, its specialized services include cardiac sciences, neurosciences, surgery, medicine, renal, critical & trauma care, & a burn unit. Other areas of focus include: anaesthesiology; angiography; audiology; bronchoscopy; cardiology; CT scans; dental clinic; ENT; ears nose & throat surgery; eating disorders; endoscopy; fluoroscopy; gastroenterology & hepatology; general surgery; general systems intensive care unit; geriatric assessment; hemodialysis; laboratory; MRI; nuclear medicine; nutrition counselling; occupational therapy; palliative care; physical therapy; plastic surgery; psychiatry; pulmonary medicine; respiratory therapy; rheumatology; sexual assault response; social work; speech language pathology; spiritual care; stroke; surgery; transplantation; tuberculosis; ultrasound; & vascular interventional neuro radiology. Also located within the facility are the Mazankowski Alberta Heart Institute & the Stollery Children's Hospital, specializing in pediatric cardiac surgery & organ transplantation.
Dr. Verna Yiu, President/CEO, AHS
Dr. Francois Belanger, Interim CMO & Vice-President, Quality

Edson: Edson Healthcare Centre
Affiliated with: Alberta Health Services
4716 - 5 Ave., Edson, AB T7E 1S8
Tel: 780-723-3331; *Fax:* 780-723-7787
www.albertahealthservices.ca
Social Media: www.facebook.com/17957998746821; twitter.com/AHS_media; www.youtube.com/AHSChannel
Note: Programs & services include: emergency services; diagnostic imaging; laboratory services; surgical services & recovery; acute care; ambulatory care; obstetrics; pediatrics; rehabilitation services; social work; respite care; continuing care; & palliative care.

Elk Point: Elk Point Healthcare Centre
Affiliated with: Alberta Health Services
5310 - 50th Ave., Elk Point, AB T0A 1A0
Tel: 780-724-3847; *Fax:* 780-724-3085
www.albertahealthservices.ca
Social Media: www.facebook.com/17957998746821; twitter.com/AHS_media; www.youtube.com/ahschannel
Number of Beds: 12 beds
Note: Programs & services include: diagnostic imaging; laboratory services; acute care; ambulatory care; rehabilitation services, including physical therapy & recreation therapy; community health services; social work; continuing care; respite care; & palliative care.
Bev Belland, Manager
Dr. Drew Ramful, Contact

Fairview: Fairview Health Complex
Affiliated with: Alberta Health Services
10628 - 110 St., Fairview, AB T0H 1L0
Tel: 780-835-6100; *Fax:* 780-835-5789
www.albertahealthservices.ca
Social Media: www.facebook.com/17957998746821; twitter.com/AHS_media; www.youtube.com/ahschannel
Number of Beds: 22 beds
Note: Programs & services include: Early Intervention Program; emergency services; intensive care unit; acute care; obstetrics; pediatrics; rehabilitation services, including occupational therapy, physiotherapy, & therapeutic recreation; mental health services; prenatal education & counselling; Environmental Public Health Program; Newborn Hearing Screening Program; Respiratory Health Program; social work; nutrition services; continuing care; & palliative care.

Fort McMurray: Northern Lights Regional Health Centre
Affiliated with: Alberta Health Services
7 Hospital St., Fort McMurray, AB T9H 1P2
Tel: 780-791-6161; *Fax:* 780-791-6167
www.albertahealthservices.ca
Social Media: www.facebook.com/17957998746821; twitter.com/AHS_media; www.youtube.com/ahschannel
Note: Programs & services include: emergency; laboratory; x-ray; mental health; general surgery; ambulatory care; rehabilitation; home care; speech language; & community health.

Fort Saskatchewan: Fort Saskatchewan Community Hospital
Affiliated with: Alberta Health Services
Former Name: Fort Saskatchewan Health Centre
9401 - 86 Ave., Fort Saskatchewan, AB T8L 0C6
Tel: 780-998-2256
www.albertahealthservices.ca
Social Media: www.facebook.com/17957998746821; twitter.com/AHS_media; www.youtube.com/ahschannel
Number of Beds: 32 beds
Note: Programs & services include: emergency; surgery; public health; home care addiction & mental health; audiology; respiratory therapy; occupational therapy; & nutritional counseling.

Fort Vermilion: St. Theresa General Hospital
Affiliated with: Alberta Health Services
4506 - 46 Ave., Fort Vermilion, AB T0H 1N0
Tel: 780-927-3761; *Fax:* 780-927-6207
www.albertahealthservices.ca
Social Media: www.facebook.com/17957998746821; twitter.com/AHS_media; www.youtube.com/ahschannel
Number of Beds: 36 acute care beds; 10 long-term care beds
Note: Programs & services include: emergency; clinical nutrition; continuing care; diagnostic imaging; interpretive services; laboratory; maternity; mental health; occupational therapy; palliative care; pediatrics; physical therapy; & spiritual care.

Fox Creek: Fox Creek Healthcare Centre
Affiliated with: Alberta Health Services
600 - 3rd St., Fox Creek, AB T0H 1P0
Tel: 780-622-3545; *Fax:* 780-622-3474
www.albertahealthservices.ca
Social Media: www.facebook.com/17957998746821; twitter.com/AHS_media; www.youtube.com/ahschannel
Number of Beds: 4 acute care beds
Note: Programs & services include: clinics; community health; diagnostic imaging; emergency services; environmental services; general radiography; laboratory services; acute care; pediatrics; diabetes education; mental health; nutrition; oral health; home care; palliative care; Parenting Preschoolers; pharmacy; speech language pathology; travel health services; & tuberculosis testing.

Grande Cache: Grande Cache Community Health Complex
Affiliated with: Alberta Health Services
PO Box 629, 10200 Shand Ave., Grande Cache, AB T0E 0Y0
Tel: 780-827-3701; *Fax:* 780-827-2859
www.albertahealthservices.ca
Social Media: www.facebook.com/17957998746821; twitter.com/AHS_media; www.youtube.com/ahschannel
Number of Beds: 10 acute care beds; 4 continuing care beds
Note: Programs & services include: cardiology; continuing care; diagnostic imaging; emergency; environmental; general radiography; laboratory services; nutrition; occupational & physical therapy; palliative care; pediatrics; & respiratory health.

Grande Prairie: Queen Elizabeth II Hospital
Affiliated with: Alberta Health Services
10409 - 98 St., Grande Prairie, AB T8V 2E8
Tel: 780-538-7100; *Fax:* 780-538-7665
www.albertahealthservices.ca
Social Media: www.facebook.com/17957998746821; twitter.com/AHS_media; www.youtube.com/ahschannel
Year Founded: 1978
Number of Beds: 167 beds
Population Served: 250000
Note: Programs & services include: Aboriginal health; acute care; hip & knee clinics; angiography; cardiology; computed tomography; continuing care; day surgery; diagnostic imaging; EEG; echocardiography; emergency; fluroscopy; general radiography; hemodialysis; intensive care; laboratory; obstetrics; magnetic resonance imaging; mammography; medicine; nuclear medicine; occupational therapy; orthopedics; pediatrics; pharmacy; respiratory; social work; ultrasound; & urology.

Grimshaw: Grimshaw/Berwyn & District Community Health Centre
Affiliated with: Alberta Health Services
5621 - 50 Ave., Grimshaw, AB T0H 1W0
Tel: 780-332-6500; *Fax:* 780-332-1177
www.albertahealthservices.ca
Social Media: www.facebook.com/17957998746821; twitter.com/AHS_media; www.youtube.com/AHSChannel
Note: Programs & services include: clinics; community health; continuing care; diagnostic imaging; emergency; environmental; general radiography; home care; laboratory; oral health; palliative care; physical therapy; social work; travel health services; & tuberculosis testing.

Hanna: Hanna Health Centre
Affiliated with: Alberta Health Services
PO Box 730, 904 Centre St. North, Hanna, AB T0J 1P0
Tel: 403-854-3331; *Fax:* 403-854-3253
www.albertahealthservices.ca
Social Media: www.facebook.com/17957998746821; twitter.com/AHS_media; www.youtube.com/ahschannel
Number of Beds: 17 acute care beds; 61 continuing care beds
Note: Programs & services include: acute care; continuing care; emergency; minor surgery; obstetrics; mental health; & palliative care.

Hardisty: Hardisty Health Centre
Affiliated with: Alberta Health Services
PO Box 269, 4531 - 47 Ave., Hardisty, AB T0B 1V0
Tel: 780-888-3742; *Fax:* 780-888-2427
www.albertahealthservices.ca
Social Media: www.facebook.com/17957998746821; twitter.com/AHS_media; www.youtube.com/ahschannel
Number of Beds: 5 acute care beds; 14 continuing care beds; 1 respite bed
Note: Programs & services include: acute care; clinics; child & adolescent services; diagnostic imaging; emergency; general radiography; laboratory services; long-term care; mental health; nutrition; occupational & physical therapy; palliative care; pulmonary/respiratory; respite care; speech language services; & Vital Heart Response/STEMI Program.

High Level: Northwest Health Centre
Affiliated with: Alberta Health Services
11202 - 100 St., High Level, AB T0H 1Z0
Tel: 780-841-3200; *Fax:* 780-926-7378
www.albertahealthservices.ca
Social Media: www.facebook.com/17957998746821; twitter.com/AHS_media; www.youtube.com/ahschannel
Note: Programs & services include: acute care; community health; community nutrition; continuing care; emergency; mental health; laboratory; public health; palliative care; & x-ray.

High Prairie: High Prairie Health Complex
Affiliated with: Alberta Health Services
4620 - 53 Ave, High Prairie, AB T0G 1E0
Tel: 780-523-6440; *Fax:* 780-523-6642
www.albertahealthservices.ca
Social Media: www.facebook.com/17957998746821; twitter.com/AHS_media; www.youtube.com/ahschannel
Number of Beds: 30 acute care beds; 67 continuing care beds
Note: Programs & services include: acute care; continuing care; emergency; rehabilitation; palliative care; pediatrics; radiology; recreational therapy; & speech-language pathology.
Roxanne Stuckless, Site Manager

High River: High River General Hospital
Affiliated with: Alberta Health Services
560 - 9 Ave. SW, High River, AB T1V 1B3
Tel: 403-652-2200; *Fax:* 403-652-0199
www.albertahealthservices.ca
Social Media: www.facebook.com/17957998746821; twitter.com/AHS_media; www.youtube.com/ahschannel
Year Founded: 1982
Number of Beds: 32 active treatment beds; 75 long-term care beds
Note: Programs & services include: cancer treatment & care; cardiology; CT imaging; continuing care; diagnostic imaging; emergency services; gynecological surgery; holter monitoring; laboratory; nutrition; & physical therapy.

Hinton: **Hinton Healthcare Centre**
Affiliated with: Alberta Health Services
1280 Switzer Dr., Hinton, AB T7V 1V2
Tel: 780-865-3333; *Fax:* 780-865-1099
www.albertahealthservices.ca
Social Media: www.facebook.com/179579998746821; twitter.com/AHS_media; www.youtube.com/ahschannel
Number of Beds: 23 beds; 1 palliative bed
Note: Programs & services include: acute care; community cancer centre; diabetic nephropathy; pharmacy; rehabilitation; ultrasound; x-ray, CT scan; & MRI.
Fiona Murray-Galbraith, Site Manager

Innisfail: **Innisfail Health Centre**
Affiliated with: Alberta Health Services
5023 - 42 St., Innisfail, AB T4G 1A9
Tel: 403-227-7800; *Fax:* 403-227-8781
www.albertahealthservices.ca
Social Media: www.facebook.com/179579998746821; twitter.com/AHS_media; www.youtube.com/ahschannel
Note: Programs & services include: addiction & mental health services; child & adolescent services; community health; continuing care; diagnostic imaging; emergency; general radiography; laboratory services; long-term care; nutrition; occupational & physical therapy; oral health program; palliative care; pharmacy; public health; pulmonary function testing; rehabilitation; respite care; speech language pathology; spiritual care; & tuberculosis testing.
Suzanne Telford, Site Leader

Jasper: **Seton - Jasper Healthcare Centre**
Affiliated with: Alberta Health Services
PO Box 310, 518 Robson St., Jasper, AB T0E 1E0
Tel: 780-852-3344; *Fax:* 780-852-3413
www.albertahealthservices.ca
Social Media: www.facebook.com/179579998746821; twitter.com/AHS_media; www.youtube.com/ahschannel
Number of Beds: 12 active treatment beds; 16 long-term care beds
Note: Programs & services include: emergency; acute care services; diagnostic imaging; eating disorder services; mental health services; occupational therapy; palliative care; physiotherapy; & social work.
Lorna Chisholm, Site Manager

Killam: **Killam Health Care Centre**
Covenant Health
Affiliated with: Alberta Health Services
5203 - 49 Ave., Killam, AB T0B 2L0
Tel: 780-385-3741; *Fax:* 780-385-3904
www.covenanthealth.ca/hospitals-care-centres/killam-health-centre
Social Media: www.facebook.com/179579998746821; twitter.com/AHS_media; www.youtube.com/AHSChannel
Year Founded: 1930
Number of Beds: 50 beds
Number of Employees: 103
Note: Programs & services include: adult day support; diagnostic imaging; emergency; general radiography; laboratory; long-term care; palliative care; respiratory/pulmonary; respite; & Vital Heart Response/STEMI Program.
Geri Clark, Chief Executive Officer

Lac La Biche: **William J. Cadzow - Lac La Biche Healthcare Centre**
Affiliated with: Alberta Health Services
9110 - 93 St., Lac La Biche, AB T0A 2C0
Tel: 780-623-4404; *Fax:* 780-623-5904
www.albertahealthservices.ca
Social Media: www.facebook.com/179579998746821; twitter.com/AHS_media; www.youtube.com/ahschannel
Number of Beds: 23 acute care beds; 42 long-term care beds; 1 palliative bed; 1 respite bed
Note: Programs & services include: ambulatory services; clinics; continuing care; day surgery; diagnostic imaging; emergency; environmental; general medicine; general radiography; hemodialysis; laboratory; nutrition; obstetrics; occupational & physical therapy; palliative care; pastoral care; pediatrics; pharmacy; respiratory; respite care; social work; special care unit; stress testing; & therapeutic recreation.

Lacombe: **Lacombe Hospital & Care Centre**
Affiliated with: Alberta Health Services
5430 - 47 Ave., Lacombe, AB T4L 1G8
Tel: 403-782-3336; *Fax:* 403-782-2818
www.albertahealthservices.ca
Social Media: www.facebook.com/179579998746821; twitter.com/AHS_media; www.youtube.com/ahschannel
Number of Beds: 24 beds; 75 long-term care beds; 2 palliative care suites; 5 transition beds
Note: Programs & services include: acute care; continuing care; crisis response team (rural); diagnostic imaging; emergency; general radiography; laboratory; long-term care; nutrition; obstetrics; occupational & physical therapy; palliative care; pharmacy; pulmonary; speech language pathology; spiritual care; surgery; & ultrasound.

Lamont: **Lamont Health Care Centre**
Affiliated with: Alberta Health Services
PO Box 479, 5216 - 53 St., Lamont, AB T0B 2R0
Tel: 780-895-2211; *Fax:* 780-895-7305
www.lamonthealthcarecentre.com
Year Founded: 1912
Number of Beds: 14 acute beds; 101 continuing care beds; 2 palliative care beds; 2 respite beds; 6 day surgery beds; 2 surgical suites
Population Served: 10000
Note: Programs & services include: acute & continuing care; emergency; surgery; ophthalmology; radiology; rehabilitation; & palliative care. Affiliated with the United Church of Canada.
Harold James, Executive Director

Leduc: **Leduc Community Hospital**
Affiliated with: Alberta Health Services
Former Name: Leduc Community Hospital & Health Centre
4210 - 48 St., Leduc, AB T9E 5Z3
Tel: 780-986-7711
www.albertahealthservices.ca
Social Media: www.facebook.com/179579998746821; twitter.com/AHS_media; www.youtube.com/ahschannel
Number of Beds: 34 acute beds; 22 subacute beds; 14 transition beds
Note: Programs & services include: inpatient medical & surgical care; general & specialized day surgery; rehabilitation programs; laboratory services; diagnostic imaging; outpatient clinics; emergency; audiology; echocardiography; endoscopy; fluoroscopy; radiography; infectious diseases; nutrition; pediatrics; Pulmonary Rehabilitation Program; Sexual Assault Response Team; social work; & ultrasound.

Lethbridge: **Chinook Regional Hospital**
Affiliated with: Alberta Health Services
Former Name: Lethbridge Regional Hospital
960 - 19 St. South, Lethbridge, AB T1J 1W5
Tel: 403-382-6111; *Fax:* 403-388-6011
www.albertahealthservices.ca
Social Media: www.facebook.com/179579998746821; twitter.com/AHS_media; www.youtube.com/AHSChannel
Year Founded: 1988
Number of Beds: 232 acute care beds
Population Served: 150000
Note: Programs & services include: acute geriatrics; angiography; breast health program; cardiology; CT imaging; surgery; diagnostic imaging; echocardiography; emergency; fluoroscopy; clinics; general radiography; hemodialysis; laboratory; children & adolescent mental health program; labour delivery & maternal child services; magnetic resonance imaging; occupational therapy; palliative care; post partum & gynecology; pediatrics; social work; speech language pathology; therapeutic recreation; & ultrasound.
Dr. Peter Kwan, Chief of Emergency

Manning: **Manning Community Health Centre**
Affiliated with: Alberta Health Services
Bag 1260, 600 - 2 St. NE, Manning, AB T0H 2M0
Tel: 780-836-3391; *Fax:* 780-836-7352
www.albertahealthservices.ca
Social Media: www.facebook.com/179579998746821; twitter.com/AHS_media; www.youtube.com/ahschannel
Number of Beds: 10 acute care beds; 16 long-term care beds
Note: Programs & services include: acute care; clinics; cardiology; community health services; continuing care; diabetes prevention & wellness program; diagnostic imaging; early childhood development; eating disorder services; emergency; environmental; general radiography; home care; laboratory; mental health; newborn hearing screening program; nutrition; occupational & physical therapy; oral health; palliative care; pediatrics; pharmacy; prenatal education; P.A.R.T.Y. (Prevent Alcohol & Risk Related Trauma in Youth); respiratory; social work; therapeutic recreation; travel health; tuberculosis testing; & ultrasound.
Jo Kelemen, Director, Health Services

Mayerthorpe: **Mayerthorpe Healthcare Centre**
Affiliated with: Alberta Health Services
4417 - 45 St., Mayerthorpe, AB T0E 1N0
Tel: 780-786-2261; *Fax:* 780-786-2023
www.albertahealthservices.ca
Social Media: www.facebook.com/179579998746821; twitter.com/AHS_media; www.youtube.com/ahschannel
Number of Beds: 25 active beds; 30 auxiliary beds
Note: Programs & services include: acute care; continuing care; community health; emergency; pharmacy; rehabilitation; x-ray; & laboratory.

McLennan: **Sacred Heart Community Health Centre**
Affiliated with: Alberta Health Services
Former Name: McLennan Sacred Heart Community Health Centre
350 - 3 Ave. NW, McLennan, AB T0H 2L0
Tel: 780-324-3730; *Fax:* 780-324-4206
www.albertahealthservices.ca
Social Media: www.facebook.com/179579998746821; twitter.com/AHS_media; www.youtube.com/ahschannel
Number of Beds: 120 beds
Note: Programs & services include: acute care; emergency; French & Aboriginal services; intensive care; obstetrics; rehabilitation; palliative care; & pediatrics.
Barbara Mader, Director, Health Services
Dr. Pieter De Wet, Chief of Staff

Medicine Hat: **Medicine Hat Regional Hospital**
Affiliated with: Alberta Health Services
666 - 5 St. SW, Medicine Hat, AB T1A 4H6
Tel: 403-529-8000; *Fax:* 403-529-8950
www.albertahealthservices.ca
Social Media: www.facebook.com/179579998746821; twitter.com/AHS_media; www.youtube.com/ahschannel
Number of Beds: 190 acute care beds; 135 long-term care beds
Note: Programs & services include: acute care; supportive rehab; laboratory; surgery; mental health; critical care; pediatrics; emergency; ambulatory care; obstetrics; neonatal intensive care; geriatric services; community health; home care; & x-ray.
Linda Iwasiw, Senior Operating Officer, Acute Care

Olds: **Olds Hospital & Care Centre**
Affiliated with: Alberta Health Services
3901 - 57 Ave., Olds, AB T4H 1T4
Tel: 403-556-3381; *Fax:* 403-556-2199
www.albertahealthservices.ca
Social Media: www.facebook.com/179579998746821; twitter.com/AHS_media; www.youtube.com/ahschannel
Number of Beds: 30 acute care beds; 3 palliative care beds; 50 LTC beds; 4 surgical beds; 2 coronary care beds; 2 labour & delivery beds; 4 day surgery beds
Note: Programs & services include: clinics; continuing care; crisis response team (rural); diagnostic imaging; emergency; general radiography; hemodialysis; laboratory services; long-term care; nutrition; obstetrics; occupational & physical therapy; palliative care; pharmacy; pulmonary/respiratory; seniors mental health program; speech language pathology; spiritual care; surgical; & Vital Heart Response/STEMI Program.
Colleen Simon, Site Manager

Oyen: **Big Country Hospital**
Affiliated with: Alberta Health Services
312 - 3 Ave. East, Oyen, AB T0J 2J0
Tel: 403-664-4300; *Fax:* 403-664-4325
www.albertahealthservices.ca
Social Media: www.facebook.com/179579998746821; twitter.com/AHS_media; www.youtube.com/ahschannel
Number of Beds: 10 acute care beds; 30 continuing care beds; 1 palliative care suite
Note: Programs & services include: acute care; continuing care; diagnostic imaging; emergency; general radiography; laboratory; labour delivery & maternal child services; occupational & physical therapy; respiratory services; respite services; & therapeutic recreation.

Peace River: **Peace River Community Health Centre**
Affiliated with: Alberta Health Services
10101 - 68 St., Peace River, AB T8S 1T6
Tel: 780-624-7500; *Fax:* 780-618-3472
www.albertahealthservices.ca
Social Media: www.facebook.com/179579998746821; twitter.com/AHS_media; www.youtube.com/AHSChannel
Number of Beds: 30 acute care beds; 40 long-term care beds
Note: Programs & services include: acute care; emergency care; intensive care; rehabilitation; palliative care; pediatrics; respiratory therapy; x-ray & laboratory.

Pincher Creek: **Pincher Creek Health Centre**
Affiliated with: Alberta Health Services
Former Name: Pincher Creek Hospital
1222 Bev McLachlin Dr., Pincher Creek, AB T0K 1W0
Tel: 403-627-1234; *Fax:* 403-627-5275
www.albertahealthservices.ca
Social Media: www.facebook.com/179579998746821; twitter.com/AHS_media; www.youtube.com/ahschannel
Number of Beds: 16 acute care beds; 3 long-term beds
Note: Programs & services include: audiology; diagnostic imaging; emergency; general radiography; laboratory; nutrition; & pediatrics.

***Ponoka:* Ponoka Hospital & Healthcare Centre**
Affiliated with: Alberta Health Services
5800 - 57 Ave., Ponoka, AB T4J 1P1
Tel: 403-783-3341; *Fax:* 403-783-6907
www.albertahealthservices.ca
Social Media: www.facebook.com/179579998746821; twitter.com/AHS_media; www.youtube.com/ahschannel
Number of Beds: 75 beds (34 acute care beds)
Note: Programs & services include: acute care; continuing care; emergency; general medicine; laboratory; obstetrics; surgery; pediatrics; & radiology.

***Provost:* Provost Health Centre**
Affiliated with: Alberta Health Services
5002 - 54 Ave., Provost, AB T0B 3S0
Tel: 780-753-2291; *Fax:* 780-753-6132
www.albertahealthservices.ca
Social Media: www.facebook.com/179579998746821; twitter.com/AHS_media; www.youtube.com/ahschannel
Number of Beds: 15 acute care; 36 continuing care beds; 15 surgical beds; 4 day surgery beds; 2 labour & delivery beds; 1 coronary care beds
Note: Programs & services include: acute care; continuing care; day support; emergency; respite & palliative care; surgery; obstetrics; & x-ray.
Lana Clark, Manager

***Raymond:* Prairie Ridge Good Samaritan Society**
Affiliated with: Alberta Health Services
Former Name: Prairie Ridge Hospital
PO Box 630, 328 Broadway South, Raymond, AB T0K 2S0
Tel: 403-752-3441; *Fax:* 403-752-3250
goodsaminfo@gss.org
www.gss.org
Number of Beds: 50 supportive living suites; 30 geriatric mental health care beds; 5 community support beds
Shawn Terlson, President & CEO, Good Samaritan Society
sterlson@gss.org

***Raymond:* Raymond Health Centre**
Affiliated with: Alberta Health Services
Former Name: Raymond Hospital
150 North 4th St. East, Raymond, AB T0K 2S0
Tel: 403-752-5411; *Fax:* 403-752-3554
www.albertahealthservices.ca
Social Media: www.facebook.com/179579998746821; twitter.com/AHS_media; www.youtube.com/ahschannel
Note: Programs & services include: continuing care; diagnostic imaging; emergency; general radiography; laboratory; nutrition; occupational & physical therapy; & therapeutic recreation.

***Red Deer:* Red Deer Regional Hospital Centre**
Affiliated with: Alberta Health Services
3942 - 50A Ave., Red Deer, AB T4N 4E7
Tel: 403-343-4422
www.albertahealthservices.ca
Social Media: www.facebook.com/179579998746821; twitter.com/AHS_media; www.youtube.com/ahschannel
Number of Beds: 336 acute care beds; 40 mental health beds
Note: Programs & services include: Aboriginal health; mental health (adult & child); angiography; laboratories; bronchoscopy; cardiology; clinics; CT scan; crisis response team; diagnostic imaging; echocardiography; electroencephalography; electromyography; emergency; Fibromyalgia group; fluoroscopy; general radiography; hemodialysis; MRI; neonatal intensive care; nuclear medicine; nuclear stress testing; nutrition; obstetrics; palliative care; pediatrics; perinatal bereavement program; pharmacy; physical therapy; pulmonary/respiratory; rehabilitation; specialized geriatric services; speech language pathology; spiritual care; stress echocardiography; surgery; & ultrasound.

***Redwater:* Redwater Health Centre**
Affiliated with: Alberta Health Services
4812 - 58 St., Redwater, AB T0A 2W0
Tel: 780-942-3932; *Fax:* 780-942-2373
www.albertahealthservices.ca
Social Media: www.facebook.com/179579998746821; twitter.com/AHS_media; www.youtube.com/AHSChannel
Year Founded: 1973
Number of Beds: 14 acute care beds; 7 long-term care beds; 1 palliative care bed
Note: Programs & services include: emergency; palliative care; laboratory; respiratory services; radiology; nutritional counselling; & visiting optometrist.

***Rimbey:* Rimbey Hospital & Care Centre**
Affiliated with: Alberta Health Services
PO Box 440, 5228 - 50 St., Rimbey, AB T0C 2J0
Tel: 403-843-2271; *Fax:* 403-843-2506
www.albertahealthservices.ca
Social Media: www.facebook.com/179579998746821; twitter.com/AHS_media; www.youtube.com/AHSChannel
Note: Programs & services include: addiction & mental health; child & adolescent services; continuing care counselling; crisis response team (rural); diagnostic imaging; emergency; general radiography; laboratory; long-term care; nutrition; obstetrics; occupational & physical therapy; palliative care; pharmacy; respite care; speech language pathology; & spiritual care.

***Rocky Mountain House:* Rocky Mountain House Health Centre**
Affiliated with: Alberta Health Services
5016 - 52 Ave., Rocky Mountain House, AB T4T 1T2
Tel: 403-845-3347; *Fax:* 403-845-7030
www.albertahealthservices.ca
Social Media: www.facebook.com/179579998746821; twitter.com/AHS_media; www.youtube.com/ahschannel
Number of Beds: 30 continuing care beds
Note: Programs & services include: Aboriginal health; addiction & mental health; child & adolescent services; community health centres; continuing care counselling; crisis response team (rural); diagnostic imaging; emergency; environmental public health; general radiography; hemodialysis; home care; laboratory; long-term care; nutrition; obstetrics; occupational & physical therapy; oral health; palliative care; pharmacy; prenatal education; public health; respiratory; speech language pathology; spiritual care; surgery; tuberculosis testing; ultrasound; & Vital Heart Response/STEMI Program.

***Sherwood Park:* Strathcona Community Hospital**
Affiliated with: Alberta Health Services
Former Name: Health First Strathcona
9000 Emerald Dr., Sherwood Park, AB T8H 0J3
Tel: 780-449-5380
www.albertahealthservices.ca/Facilities/strathcona
Social Media: www.facebook.com/179579998746821; twitter.com/AHS_media; www.youtube.com/ahschannel
Year Founded: 2014
Note: Programs & services include: addiction/mental health; CT scans; diabetes program; diagnostic imaging; emergency; laboratory; IV therapy; ambulatory clinics; rehabilitation; radiography; chronic disease management; & ultrasound.

***Slave Lake:* Slave Lake Healthcare Centre**
Affiliated with: Alberta Health Services
309 - 6 St. NE, Slave Lake, AB T0G 2A2
Tel: 780-805-3500; *Fax:* 780-805-3577
www.albertahealthservices.ca
Social Media: www.facebook.com/179579998746821; twitter.com/AHS_media; www.youtube.com/ahschannel
Number of Beds: 24 inpatient beds; 20 long-term care beds; 9 emergency beds; 2 special care beds; 1 palliative care bed
Note: Programs & services include: emergency; acute care; continuing care; mental health; pharmacy; renal dialysis; rehabilitation; obstetrics; occupational therapy; pediatrics; respiratory therapy; social work; ultrasound; & X-Ray.
Steve Marcotte, Site Manager

***Smoky Lake:* George McDougall - Smoky Lake Healthcare Centre**
Affiliated with: Alberta Health Services
PO Box 340, 4212 - 55 Ave., Smoky Lake, AB T0A 3C0
Tel: 780-656-3034; *Fax:* 780-656-5010
www.albertahealthservices.ca
Social Media: www.facebook.com/179579998746821; twitter.com/AHS_media; www.youtube.com/ahschannel
Number of Beds: 12 active beds; 23 auxiliary beds
Note: Programs & services include: emergency services; diagnostic imaging; laboratory services; ambulatory services; acute care; rehabilitation; occupational therapy; physical therapy services; therapeutic recreation; community health services; nutrition services; social work; continuing care; & palliative care.

***Spirit River:* Central Peace Health Complex**
Affiliated with: Alberta Health Services
5010 - 45th Ave., Spirit River, AB T0H 3G0
Tel: 780-864-3993; *Fax:* 780-864-3495
www.albertahealthservices.ca
Social Media: www.facebook.com/179579998746821; twitter.com/AHS_media; www.youtube.com/ahschannel
Year Founded: 1972
Number of Beds: 10 acute care beds; 16 continuing care beds
Note: Programs & services include: emergency care; laboratory services; acute care; newborn hearing screening program; pediatrics; rehabilitation; physical therapy; nutrition counselling; continuing care; & palliative care

***St Albert:* Sturgeon Community Hospital**
Affiliated with: Alberta Health Services
Former Name: Sturgeon Community Hospital & Health Centre
201 Boudreau Rd., St Albert, AB T8N 6C4
Tel: 780-418-8200
www.albertahealthservices.ca
Social Media: www.facebook.com/179579998746821; twitter.com/AHS_media; www.youtube.com/ahschannel
Year Founded: 1992
Number of Beds: 167 beds
Note: Programs & services include: emergency; cardiac rehabilitation; diagnostic imaging (CT scans, radiology, fluoroscopy); intensive care unit; mental health emergency; nutrition counselling; obstetrics; physical therapy/occupational therapy; prenatal program; sexual assault response team; spiritual care; & surgery.
Wendy Tanaka Collins, Site Director

***St. Paul:* St. Therese - St. Paul Healthcare Centre**
Affiliated with: Alberta Health Services
4713 - 48 Ave., St. Paul, AB T0A 3A3
Tel: 780-645-3331; *Fax:* 780-645-1702
www.albertahealthservices.ca
Social Media: www.facebook.com/179579998746821; twitter.com/AHS_media; www.youtube.com/ahschannel
Note: Programs & services include: emergency; diagnostic imaging (ultrasound, x-ray); eating disorder services; obstetrics; pharmacy; rehabilitation; renal dialysis; & laboratory.
Bev Belland, Manager
Dr. Albert Harmse, Contact

***Stettler:* Stettler Hospital & Care Centre**
Affiliated with: Alberta Health Services
5912 - 47 Ave., Stettler, AB T0C 2L0
Tel: 403-742-7400; *Fax:* 403-742-1244
www.albertahealthservices.ca
Social Media: www.facebook.com/179579998746821; twitter.com/AHS_media; www.youtube.com/ahschannel
Note: Programs & services include: emergency; continuing care; diagnostic imaging; mental health; obstetrics; occupational therapy (for acute & continuing care); palliative care; pharmacy; physical therapy; renal dialysis; respiratory therapy; sleep program; & speech language pathology.

***Stony Plain:* WestView Health Centre**
Affiliated with: Alberta Health Services
4405 South Park Dr., Stony Plain, AB T7Z 2M7
Tel: 780-968-3600
www.albertahealthservices.ca
Social Media: www.facebook.com/179579998746821; twitter.com/AHS_media; www.youtube.com/AHSChannel
Number of Beds: 16 inpatient beds; 50 continuing care beds
Note: Programs & services include: acute care; continuing care; emergency; diagnostic imaging; laboratory; day surgery; public health; environmental health; community care; rehabilitation services; dental; & mental health.
Ellen Billay, Site Director

***Strathmore:* Strathmore District Health Services**
Affiliated with: Alberta Health Services
200 Brent Blvd., Strathmore, AB T1P 1J9
Tel: 403-361-7000; *Fax:* 403-361-7048
www.albertahealthservices.ca
Social Media: www.facebook.com/179579998746821; twitter.com/AHS_media; www.youtube.com/ahschannel
Number of Beds: 25 acute care beds; 23 long-term care beds
Note: Programs & services include: cardiology; continuing care; diabetes education; diagnostic imaging; cardiology; laboratory; occupational therapy; palliative care; pharmacy; physical therapy; respiratory services; respite care; & speech language pathology.

***Sundre:* Sundre Hospital & Care Centre**
Affiliated with: Alberta Health Services
709 - 1 St. NE, Sundre, AB T0M 1X0
Tel: 403-638-3033; *Fax:* 403-636-6284
www.albertahealthservices.ca
Social Media: www.facebook.com/179579998746821; twitter.com/AHS_media; www.youtube.com/ahschannel
Number of Beds: 13 acute care beds; 15 continuing care beds
Note: Programs & services include: emergency; nutrition; continuing care counseling; diagnostic imaging; laboratory; obstetrics; occupational therapy; palliative care; pharmacy; physical therapy; & speech language pathology.
Larry Gratton, Site Manager

***Swan Hills:* Swan Hills Healthcare Centre**
Affiliated with: Alberta Health Services
PO Box 261, 29 Freeman Dr., Swan Hills, AB T0G 2C0
Tel: 780-333-7000; *Fax:* 780-333-7009
www.albertahealthservices.ca
Social Media: www.facebook.com/179579998746821; twitter.com/AHS_media; www.youtube.com/AHSChannel
Year Founded: 1985
Number of Beds: 24 hospital beds
Note: Programs & services include: ambulatory services; clinics; community health; diagnostic imaging; early childhood development; eating disorder services; emergency; environmental; general medicine; general radiography; home care; laboratory; mental health; nutrition; oral health; palliative care; pharmacy; P.A.R.T.Y. (Prevent Alcohol & Risk Related Trauma in Youth); sexual health; & social work.
Lois Burletoff, Site Manager

***Taber:* Taber Health Centre**
Affiliated with: Alberta Health Services
Former Name: Taber Hospital
4326 - 50 Ave., Taber, AB T0K 2G0
Tel: 403-223-4461; *Fax:* 403-223-1703
www.albertahealthservices.ca
Social Media: www.facebook.com/179579998746821; twitter.com/AHS_media; www.youtube.com/AHSChannel
Note: Programs & services include: continuing care; emergency; diagnostic imaging; laboratory; nutrition; occupational therapy; pediatrics; radiography & therapeutic recreation.

***Three Hills:* Three Hills Health Centre**
Affiliated with: Alberta Health Services
1504 - 2nd St. North, Three Hills, AB T0M 2A0
Tel: 403-443-2444; *Fax:* 403-443-5565
www.albertahealthservices.ca
Social Media: www.facebook.com/179579998746821; twitter.com/AHS_media; www.youtube.com/ahschannel
Note: Programs & services include: community health; continuing care; diagnostic imaging; early intervention program; emergency; fluoride protection for toddlers; general radiography; home care & Alberta Aids to Daily Living; laboratory; long-term care; nutrition; obstetrics; occupational & physical therapy; oral health; palliative care; pharmacy; prenatal education; public health; pulmonary; rehabilitation; respite care; speech language pathology; surgery; travel health services; tuberculosis testing; & ultrasound.

***Tofield:* Tofield Health Centre**
Affiliated with: Alberta Health Services
5543 - 44 St., Tofield, AB T0B 4J0
Tel: 780-662-3263; *Fax:* 780-662-3835
www.albertahealthservices.ca
Social Media: www.facebook.com/179579998746821; twitter.com/AHS_media; www.youtube.com/AHSChannel
Number of Beds: 50 beds
Note: Programs & services include: emergency; acute care; communicable disease control; continuing care; home care; laboratory; occupational therapy; palliative care; physiotherapy; postnatal services; radiography; respiratory therapy; respite care; speech language services; & surgery.

***Two Hills:* Two Hills Health Centre**
Affiliated with: Alberta Health Services
4401 - 53 Ave., Two Hills, AB T0B 4K0
Tel: 780-657-3344; *Fax:* 780-657-2508
www.albertahealthservices.ca
Social Media: www.facebook.com/179579998746821; twitter.com/AHS_media; www.youtube.com/AHSChannel
Year Founded: 1986
Number of Beds: 6 acute care beds; 60 continuing care beds; 9 stroke rehabilitation beds
Note: Programs & services include: emergency; acute care; community health; nutrition; continuing care; home care; general radiography; laboratory; occupational therapy; oral health; palliative care; pharmacy; prenatal education; respiratory therapy; respite care; & stroke & geriatric empowerment unit.
Valerie Thompson, Site Manager

***Valleyview:* Valleyview Health Centre**
Affiliated with: Alberta Health Services
Former Name: Valleyview Health Complex
4802 Highway St., Valleyview, AB T0H 3N0
Tel: 780-524-3356; *Fax:* 780-524-2107
www.albertahealthservices.ca
Social Media: www.facebook.com/179579998746821; twitter.com/AHS_media; www.youtube.com/AHSChannel
Number of Beds: 35 acute care beds; 25 extended care beds
Note: Programs & services include: Aboriginal health; cardiology; continuing care; diagnostic imaging; early intervention; emergency; environmental; general radiology; laboratory; newborn hearing screening program; nutrition; occupational & physical therapy; palliative care; pediatrics; pharmacy; respiratory; social work; therapeutic recreation; & tuberculosis testing.
Tracy Brown, Site Manager

***Vegreville:* St. Joseph's General Hospital Covenant Health**
Affiliated with: Alberta Health Services
5241 - 43 St., Vegreville, AB T9C 1R5
Tel: 780-632-2811; *Fax:* 780-603-4401
www.covenanthealth.ca/hospitals-care-centres/st-josephs-general-hospital
Social Media: www.facebook.com/179579998746821; twitter.com/AHS_media; www.youtube.com/AHSChannel
Year Founded: 1910
Number of Beds: 25 beds
Number of Employees: 169
Note: Programs & services include: emergency; medicine; laboratory; diagnostic imaging (x-ray, ultrasound); dialysis; diabetic education; occupational & physical therapy; respiratory therapy; palliative care & day support.

***Vermilion:* Vermilion Health Centre**
Affiliated with: Alberta Health Services
5720 - 50 Ave., Vermilion, AB T9X 1K7
Tel: 780-853-5305; *Fax:* 780-853-4786
www.albertahealthservices.ca
Social Media: www.facebook.com/179579998746821; twitter.com/AHS_media; www.youtube.com/AHSChannel
Number of Beds: 25 acute care beds; 48 continuing care beds; 4 day surgery beds
Note: Programs & services include: acute care; clinics; diagnostic imaging; emergency; general radiography; laboratory; long-term care; nutrition; occupational & physical therapy; palliative care; pharmacy; pulmonary/respiratory; surgery; ultrasound; & Vital Heart Response/STEMI Program.
Debora Okrainetz, Area Director

***Viking:* Viking Health Centre**
Affiliated with: Alberta Health Services
PO Box 60, 5110 - 57 Ave., Viking, AB T0B 4N0
Tel: 780-336-4786; *Fax:* 780-336-4983
www.albertahealthservices.ca
Social Media: www.facebook.com/179579998746821; twitter.com/AHS_media; www.youtube.com/AHSChannel
Number of Beds: 16 acute care beds
Note: Programs & services include: emergency; acute; continuing & palliative care; surgery; obstetrics; rehabilitation, respiratory therapy, x-ray; & mammography.

***Vulcan:* Vulcan Community Health Centre**
Affiliated with: Alberta Health Services
610 Elizabeth St. South, Vulcan, AB T0L 2B0
Tel: 403-485-3333; *Fax:* 403-485-2336
www.albertahealthservices.ca
Social Media: www.facebook.com/179579998746821; twitter.com/AHS_media; www.youtube.com/AHSChannel
Number of Beds: 8 acute care beds; 15 long-term care beds
Note: Programs & services include: adult day program; Holter monitoring; electrocardiogram; continuing care; diabetes education; diagnostic imaging; emergency; general medicine; general radiography; surgery; Healthy Moms, Healthy Babies Program; Home Parenteral Therapy Program; laboratory; mental health; nutrition; palliative care; pharmacy; & respiratory.

***Wabasca:* Wabasca/Desmarais Healthcare Centre**
Affiliated with: Alberta Health Services
Former Name: Wabasca/Desmarais General Hospital
881 Mistassiniy Rd., Wabasca, AB T0G 2K0
Tel: 780-891-3007; *Fax:* 780-891-3784
www.albertahealthservices.ca
Social Media: www.facebook.com/179579998746821; twitter.com/AHS_media; www.youtube.com/ahschannel
Number of Beds: 10 beds
Note: Serves the Wabasca, Desmarais, Sandy Lake, Chipewyan Lake & Bigstone Cree Nation area. Programs & services include: emergency; laboratory; rehabilitation; & x-ray.

***Wainwright:* Wainwright Health Centre**
Affiliated with: Alberta Health Services
530 - 6 Ave., Wainwright, AB T9W 1R6
Tel: 780-842-3324; *Fax:* 780-842-4290
www.albertahealthservices.ca
Social Media: www.facebook.com/179579998746821; twitter.com/AHS_media; www.youtube.com/AHSChannel
Number of Beds: 25 acute care beds; 69 continuing care beds; 2 intensive care beds; 3 labour & delivery beds; 5 day surgery beds
Note: Programs & services include: acute care; day support; emergency; continuing care; respite & palliative care; surgery; obstetrics; cardiac education; stress testing; rehabilitation; psychiatry; & x-ray.
Cheryl Huxley, Site Manager

***Westlock:* Westlock Healthcare Centre**
Affiliated with: Alberta Health Services
10220 - 93 St., Westlock, AB T7P 2G4
Tel: 780-349-3301; *Fax:* 780-349-6973
www.albertahealthservices.ca
Social Media: www.facebook.com/179579998746821; twitter.com/AHS_media; www.youtube.com/AHSChannel
Number of Beds: 62 beds
Note: Programs & services include: ambulatory services; day surgery; diagnostic imaging; emergency; environmental; fluoroscopy; general medicine; general radiography; laboratory; MRI; obstetrics; occupational therapy; orthopedic; palliative care; pastoral care; pediatrics; respiratory; special care; & ultrasound.
Karen Bouman, Site Manager

***Wetaskiwin:* Wetaskiwin Hospital & Care Centre**
Affiliated with: Alberta Health Services
Former Name: Crossroads Hospital & Health Centre - Wetaskiwin
6910 - 47 St., Wetaskiwin, AB T9A 3N3
Tel: 780-361-7100; *Fax:* 780-361-4107
Toll-Free: 866-361-7101
www.albertahealthservices.ca
Social Media: www.facebook.com/179579998746821; twitter.com/AHS_media; www.youtube.com/AHSChannel
Number of Beds: 83 acute care beds; 105 long-term care beds
Note: Programs & services include: Aboriginal Health Program; bronchoscopy; cardiology; CT imaging; continuing care; Northern Alberta Renal Program; diagnostic imaging; emergency; fluoroscopy; general radiography; hemodialysis; laboratory; mammography; nutrition; obstetrics; occupational therapy/physical therapy; palliative care; pharmacy; respiratory/pulmonary; respite care; sleep program; speech language pathology; surgery; & ultrasound.
Cheryl Deckert, Site Manager

***Whitecourt:* Whitecourt Healthcare Centre**
Affiliated with: Alberta Health Services
20 Sunset Blvd., Whitecourt, AB T7S 1M8
Tel: 780-778-2285; *Fax:* 780-778-5161
www.albertahealthservices.ca
Social Media: www.facebook.com/179579998746821; twitter.com/AHS_media; www.youtube.com/AHSChannel
Number of Beds: 24 beds; 2 special care beds; 1 palliative care bed
Note: Services provided include: acute care; special care; palliative care; emergency; pharmacy; rehabilitation; ultrasound; x-ray; ambulatory; audiology; clinics; community health services; day surgery; diagnostic imaging; early childhood development; Early Intervention Program; eating disorder services; environmental services; general medicine; general radiography; home care; laboratory; mental health; nutrition; obstetrics; occupational & physical therapy; pastoral care; pediatrics; prenatal education; P.A.R.T.Y. (Prevent Alcohol & Risk Related Trauma in Youth); respiratory; sexual health; social work; stress testing; travel health; tuberculosis testing; & ultrasound.
Marj Stockwell, Facility Supervisor

Auxiliary Hospitals

***Breton:* Breton Health Centre**
Affiliated with: Alberta Health Services
4919 - 49th Ave., Breton, AB T0C 0P0
Tel: 780-696-4713; *Fax:* 780-696-4747
www.albertahealthservices.ca
Year Founded: 1994
Number of Beds: 23 long term care beds
Note: Programs & services include: laboratory services; occupational therapy; physical therapy; speech language pathology; nutrition; continuing care; & palliative care.

***Cardston:* Cardston Health Centre**
Affiliated with: Alberta Health Services
PO Box 1440, 144 - 2nd St. West, Cardston, AB T0K 0K0
Tel: 403-653-5234; *Fax:* 403-653-4399
www.albertahealthservices.ca
Social Media: www.facebook.com/179579998746821; twitter.com/AHS_media; www.youtube.com/AHSChannel
Note: Programs & services include: emergency services; diagnostic imaging; surgery; obstetrics: acute care; rehabilitation; therapeutic recreation; speech language pathology; continuing care; & palliative care.

***Claresholm:* Willow Creek Continuing Care Centre**
Affiliated with: Alberta Health Services
4221 - 8 St., Claresholm, AB T0L 0T0
Tel: 403-625-3361; *Fax:* 403-625-3822
www.albertahealthservices.ca
Number of Beds: 100 beds
Note: Continuing care facility

***Edmonton:* St. Joseph's Auxiliary Hospital**
Covenant Health
Affiliated with: Alberta Health Services
10707 - 29 Ave. NW, Edmonton, AB T6J 6W1
Tel: 780-430-9110; *Fax:* 780-430-9777
www.stjosephs.ab.ca
Year Founded: 1927
Number of Beds: 202 beds
Note: Continuing care hospital

***Lacombe:* Lacombe Community Health Centre**
Affiliated with: Alberta Health Services
5010 - 51 St., Lacombe, AB T4L 1W2
Tel: 403-782-3218; *Fax:* 403-782-2866
www.albertahealthservices.ca
Note: Programs & services include: community health; continuing care; home care; clinics; oral health; prenatal education; public health; rehabilitation; travel health; & tuberculosis testing.

***Lethbridge:* St. Michael's Health Centre**
Covenant Health
Affiliated with: Alberta Health Services
1400 - 9 Ave. South, Lethbridge, AB T1J 4V5
Tel: 403-382-6400; *Fax:* 403-382-6433
www.covenanthealth.ca/hospitals-care-centres/st-michaels-health-centre
Year Founded: 1929
Number of Beds: 210 beds
Note: A long-term care (continuing care) facility focusing on assisted living, palliative care, & post-acute rehabilitative program; offers the Bridges program (care for the elderly in their own home).

***Mundare:* Mary Immaculate Hospital**
Covenant Health
Affiliated with: Alberta Health Services
PO Box 349, Mundare, AB T0B 3H0
Tel: 780-764-3730; *Fax:* 780-764-2112
www.covenanthealth.ca/hospitals-care-centres/mary-immaculate-hospital
Social Media: www.facebook.com/179579998746821; twitter.com/AHS_media; www.youtube.com/ahschannel
Year Founded: 1929
Number of Beds: 30 continuing care
Number of Employees: 67
Note: Programs & services include: adult day program; ambulatory care; continuing care; palliative care; & spiritual care.
Anthony Brannen, Executive Director

***Trochu:* St. Mary's Health Care Centre**
Covenant Health
Affiliated with: Alberta Health Services
451 de Chauney Ave., Trochu, AB T0M 2C0
Tel: 403-442-3955
www.covenanthealth.ca/hospitals-care-centres/st-marys-health-care-centre
Number of Beds: 56 beds
Number of Employees: 72
Note: Programs & services include: continuing care counselling; diagnostic imaging; general radiography; interpretive services; laboratory; long-term care; occupational therapy; & palliative care.

Community Health Care Centres

***Airdrie:* Airdrie Regional Health Centre**
Affiliated with: Alberta Health Services
604 Main St. South, Airdrie, AB T4B 1C9
Tel: 403-912-8400; *Fax:* 403-948-6284
www.albertahealthservices.ca

***Anzac:* Anzac Community Health Services**
Affiliated with: Alberta Health Services
240 Christina Dr., Anzac, AB T0P 1J0
Tel: 780-334-2023; *Fax:* 780-791-6288
www.albertahealthservices.ca

***Athabasca:* Athabasca Community Health Services**
Affiliated with: Alberta Health Services
3401 - 48 Ave., Athabasca, AB T9S 1M7
Tel: 780-675-2231; *Fax:* 780-675-3111
www.albertahealthservices.ca

***Banff:* Banff Community Health Centre**
Affiliated with: Alberta Health Services
Former Name: Banff National Park Health Unit Office
301 Lynx St., Banff, AB T1L 1B3
Tel: 403-762-2990; *Fax:* 403-762-5570
www.albertahealthservices.ca

***Barrhead:* Barrhead Community Health Services**
Affiliated with: Alberta Health Services
6203 - 49 St., Barrhead, AB T7N 1A1
Tel: 780-674-3408; *Fax:* 780-674-3941
www.albertahealthservices.ca

***Bashaw:* Bashaw Community Health Centre**
Affiliated with: Alberta Health Services
5308 - 53 St., Bashaw, AB T0B 0H0
Tel: 780-372-3731; *Fax:* 780-372-4050
www.albertahealthservices.ca

***Beaumont:* Beaumont Public Health Centre**
Affiliated with: Alberta Health Services
4918 - 50 Ave., Beaumont, AB T4X 1J9
Tel: 780-929-4822
www.albertahealthservices.ca

***Beaverlodge:* Beaverlodge Community Health Services**
Affiliated with: Alberta Health Services
Former Name: Beaverlodge Public Health Centre
412 - 10A St., Beaverlodge, AB T0H 0C0
Tel: 780-354-2647; *Fax:* 780-354-8410
www.albertahealthservices.ca

***Black Diamond:* Black Diamond Public Health Unit at Oilfields General Hospital**
Affiliated with: Alberta Health Services
717 Government Rd. S, Black Diamond, AB T0L 0H0
Tel: 403-933-6505; *Fax:* 403-933-2031
www.albertahealthservices.ca
Note: Community health services

***Blairmore:* Crowsnest Pass Provincial Building**
Affiliated with: Alberta Health Services
12501 - 20 Ave., Blairmore, AB T0K 0E0
Tel: 403-562-5030; *Fax:* 403-562-7379
www.albertahealthservices.ca
Note: Environmental public health

***Bonnyville:* Bonnyville Community Health Services**
Affiliated with: Alberta Health Services
4904 - 50 Ave., Bonnyville, AB T9N 2G4
Tel: 780-826-3381; *Fax:* 780-826-6470
www.albertahealthservices.ca

***Bow Island:* Bow Island Provincial Building**
Affiliated with: Alberta Health Services
Former Name: Bow Island Public Health/Home Care
802 - 6 St. East, Bow Island, AB T0K 0G0
Tel: 403-525-2296; *Fax:* 403-525-6357
www.albertahealthservices.ca

***Boyle:* Boyle Healthcare Centre**
Affiliated with: Alberta Health Services
5004 Lakeview Rd., Boyle, AB T0A 0M0
Tel: 780-689-2677; *Fax:* 780-689-3951
www.albertahealthservices.ca
Note: Home care office

***Brooks:* Brooks Community Health Care**
Affiliated with: Alberta Health Services
440 - 3rd St. East, Brooks, AB T1R 0X8
Tel: 403-501-3300; *Fax:* 403-501-3323
www.albertahealthservices.ca

***Brooks:* Brooks Home Care**
Affiliated with: Alberta Health Services
311 - 9 St. SE, Brooks, AB T1R 1B7
Tel: 403-362-7766; *Fax:* 403-362-7778
www.albertahealthservices.ca

***Buffalo Lake Settlement:* Buffalo Lake Settlement Community Health Services**
Affiliated with: Alberta Health Services
Buffalo Lake Dr., Buffalo Lake Settlement, AB T0A 0R0
Tel: 780-689-4771; *Fax:* 780-623-2615
www.albertahealthservices.ca

***Cadotte Lake:* Woodland Cree Health Centre**
Affiliated with: Alberta Health Services
General Delivery, Cadotte Lake, AB T0H 0N0
Tel: 780-629-8963
www.albertahealthservices.ca

***Calgary:* Acadia Community Health Centre**
Affiliated with: Alberta Health Services
151 - 86 Ave. SE, Calgary, AB T2H 3A5
Tel: 403-944-7200; *Fax:* 403-253-5129
www.albertahealthservices.ca

***Calgary:* East Calgary Health Centre**
Affiliated with: Alberta Health Services
4715 - 8 Ave. SE, Calgary, AB T2A 3N4
Tel: 403-955-1000; *Fax:* 403-955-1011
www.albertahealthservices.ca

***Calgary:* North Hill Community Health Centre**
Affiliated with: Alberta Health Services
1527 - 19 St. NW, Calgary, AB T2N 2K2
Tel: 403-944-7400; *Fax:* 403-944-7447
www.albertahealthservices.ca

***Calgary:* Ranchlands Village Mall**
Affiliated with: Alberta Health Services
Former Name: High Level General Hospital; Northwest Community Health Centre
Northwest Community Health Centre, #109, 1829 Ranchlands Blvd. NW, Calgary, AB T3G 2A7
Tel: 403-943-9700; *Fax:* 403-943-9735
www.albertahealthservices.ca

***Calgary:* Shaganappi Complex**
Affiliated with: Alberta Health Services
3415 - 8th Ave. SW, Calgary, AB T3C 0E8
Tel: 403-944-7373; *Fax:* 403-246-0326
www.albertahealthservices.ca

***Calgary:* Sheldon M. Chumir Health Centre**
Affiliated with: Alberta Health Services
1213 - 4 St. SW, Calgary, AB T2R 0X7
Tel: 403-955-6200
www.albertahealthservices.ca

***Calgary:* South Calgary Health Centre**
Affiliated with: Alberta Health Services
31 Sunpark Plaza SE, Calgary, AB T2X 3W5
Tel: 403-943-9300
www.albertahealthservices.ca
Note: Open 365 days a year

***Calgary:* Thornhill Library / Community Health Centre**
Affiliated with: Alberta Health Services
Former Name: Thornhill District Office
6617 Centre St. N, Calgary, AB T2K 4Y5
Tel: 403-944-7500; *Fax:* 403-275-9064
www.albertahealthservices.ca

***Calgary:* Village Square Community Health Centre**
Affiliated with: Alberta Health Services
2623 - 56 St. NE, Calgary, AB T1Y 6E7
Tel: 403-944-7000; *Fax:* 403-285-6304
www.albertahealthservices.ca

***Calling Lake:* Calling Lake Community Health Services**
Affiliated with: Alberta Health Services
General Delivery, Calling Lake, AB T0G 0K0
Tel: 780-331-3760; *Fax:* 780-331-2200
www.albertahealthservices.ca

***Camrose:* Camrose Public Health / Rehab**
Affiliated with: Alberta Health Services
5510 - 46 Ave., Camrose, AB T4V 4P8
Tel: 780-679-2980; *Fax:* 780-679-2999
www.albertahealthservices.ca

***Canmore:* Canmore Provincial Building**
Affiliated with: Alberta Health Services
Former Name: Canmore Public Health Office
800 Railway Ave., Canmore, AB T1W 1P1
Tel: 403-678-5656; *Fax:* 403-678-5068
www.albertahealthservices.ca
Note: Public health programs

***Cardston:* Cardston Health Unit**
Affiliated with: Alberta Health Services
Former Name: Cardston Community Health Centre
576 Main St., Cardston, AB T0K 0K0
Tel: 403-653-5230; *Fax:* 403-653-2926
www.albertahealthservices.ca

***Castor:* Castor Community Health Centre**
Affiliated with: Alberta Health Services
4909 - 50 Ave., Castor, AB T0C 0X0
Tel: 403-882-3404; *Fax:* 403-882-2387
www.albertahealthservices.ca

***Claresholm:* Claresholm Community Health Centre**
Affiliated with: Alberta Health Services
PO Box 1391, 5221 - 2nd St. West, Claresholm, AB T0L 0T0
Tel: 403-625-4061; *Fax:* 403-625-4062
www.albertahealthservices.ca

Cochrane: **Cochrane Community Health Centre**
Affiliated with: Alberta Health Services
60 Grande Blvd., Cochrane, AB T4C 0S4
Tel: 403-851-6000
www.albertahealthservices.ca

Cold Lake: **Cold Lake Community Health Services**
Affiliated with: Alberta Health Services
4720 - 55 St., Cold Lake, AB T9M 1V9
Tel: 780-594-4404; *Fax:* 780-594-2404
www.albertahealthservices.ca

Consort: **Consort Community Health Centre**
Affiliated with: Alberta Health Services
5410 - 52 Ave., Consort, AB T0C 1B0
Tel: 403-577-3770; *Fax:* 403-577-2235
www.albertahealthservices.ca

Coronation: **Coronation Community Health Centre**
Affiliated with: Alberta Health Services
4909 Royal St., Coronation, AB T0C 1C0
Tel: 403-578-3200; *Fax:* 403-578-2702
www.albertahealthservices.ca

Drayton Valley: **Drayton Valley Community Health Centre**
Affiliated with: Alberta Health Services
4110 - 50 Ave., Drayton Valley, AB T7A 0B3
Tel: 780-542-4415; *Fax:* 780-621-4998
www.albertahealthservices.ca

Drumheller: **Drumheller Environmental Health & Support Services**
Affiliated with: Alberta Health Services
601 - 7 St. East, Drumheller, AB T0J 0Y5
Tel: 403-823-3341; *Fax:* 403-823-5076
www.albertahealthservices.ca

East Prairie Metis Settle: **East Prairie Metis Settlement**
Affiliated with: Alberta Health Services
East Prairie Metis Settle, AB T0G 1E0
Tel: 780-523-2594
www.albertahealthservices.ca

Eckville: **Eckville Community Health Centre**
Affiliated with: Alberta Health Services
PO Box 150, 5120 - 51 Ave., Eckville, AB T0M 0X0
Tel: 403-746-2201; *Fax:* 403-746-2185
www.albertahealthservices.ca

Edmonton: **Belvedere Medical Clinic Medigroup Inc.**
Affiliated with: Alberta Health Services
12720 - 66 St., Edmonton, AB T5C 0A3
Tel: 780-761-8529
medigroup.ca

Edmonton: **Bonnie Doon Public Health Centre**
Affiliated with: Alberta Health Services
8314 - 88 Ave. NW, Edmonton, AB T6C 1L1
Tel: 780-342-1520
www.albertahealthservices.ca

Edmonton: **Boyle McCauley Health Centre**
Affiliated with: Alberta Health Services
10628 - 96 St., Edmonton, AB T5H 2J2
Tel: 780-422-7333; *Fax:* 780-422-7343
www.bmhc.net
Social Media:
www.facebook.com/BoyleMcCauleyHealthCentre.BMHC; twitter.com/BMHC_HealthCare
Cecilia Blasetti, Executive Director
cecilia.blasetti@albertahealthservic

Edmonton: **Capilano Medical Centre Medigroup Inc.**
Affiliated with: Alberta Health Services
5818 Terrace Rd., Edmonton, AB T6A 3Y8
Tel: 780-761-3330
medigroup.ca

Edmonton: **East Edmonton Health Centre**
Affiliated with: Alberta Health Services
7910 - 112 Ave. NW, Edmonton, AB T5B 0C2
Tel: 780-342-4700
www.albertahealthservices.ca

Edmonton: **Eastwood Medical Clinic Medigroup Inc.**
Affiliated with: Alberta Health Services
7919 - 118 Ave. NW, Edmonton, AB T5B 0R5
Tel: 780-756-3666
medigroup.ca

Edmonton: **Kensington Medical Clinic Medigroup Inc.**
Affiliated with: Alberta Health Services
12620A - 132 Ave., Edmonton, AB T5L 3P9
Tel: 780-990-1820
medigroup.ca

Edmonton: **Millwoods Public Health Centre**
Affiliated with: Alberta Health Services
7525 - 38 Ave. NW, Edmonton, AB T6K 3X9
Tel: 780-342-1660
www.albertahealthservices.ca

Edmonton: **Mother Rosalie Health Services Centre Misericordia Community Hospital**
Affiliated with: Alberta Health Services
16930 - 87 Ave., Edmonton, AB T5R 4H5
Tel: 780-735-2413
www.albertahealthservices.ca
Note: Programs & services include: diabetes education; urodynamics; child health; outpatient psychiatry; & physiotherapy.

Edmonton: **Northeast Community Health Centre**
Affiliated with: Alberta Health Services
14007 - 50 St., Edmonton, AB T5A 5E4
Tel: 780-342-4000
www.albertahealthservices.ca

Edmonton: **Northgate Centre**
Affiliated with: Alberta Health Services
9499 - 137 Ave., Edmonton, AB T5E 5R8
Tel: 780-342-2800; *Fax:* 780-457-5638
www.albertahealthservices.ca

Edmonton: **Rutherford Health Centre**
Affiliated with: Alberta Health Services
11153 Ellerslie Rd., Edmonton, AB T6W 0E9
Tel: 780-342-6800
www.albertahealthservices.ca

Edmonton: **Seniors' Clinic Good Samaritan Society**
Affiliated with: Alberta Health Services
9534 - 87 St., Edmonton, AB T6C 3J1
Tel: 780-440-8274; *Fax:* 780-469-6495
goodsaminfo@gss.org
www.gss.org
Note: Physician's office for seniors
Shawn Terlson, President & CEO, Good Samaritan Society
sterlson@gss.org

Edmonton: **Seventh Street Plaza**
Affiliated with: Alberta Health Services
10030 - 107 St., Edmonton, AB T5J 3E4
Tel: 780-735-0010
www.albertahealthservices.ca

Edmonton: **Tipaskan Medical Clinic Medigroup Inc.**
Affiliated with: Alberta Health Services
#3236, 3206 - 82 St., Edmonton, AB T6K 3Y3
Tel: 780-761-3335
medigroup.ca

Edmonton: **Twin Brooks Public Health Centre**
Affiliated with: Alberta Health Services
1110 - 113 St. NW, Edmonton, AB T6J 7J4
Tel: 780-342-1560
www.albertahealthservices.ca

Edmonton: **West Jasper Place Public Health Centre**
Affiliated with: Alberta Health Services
9720 - 182 St. NW, Edmonton, AB T5T 3T9
Tel: 780-342-1234; *Fax:* 780-484-9516
www.albertahealthservices.ca

Edmonton: **Westmount Medical Clinic Medigroup Inc.**
Affiliated with: Alberta Health Services
11035 Groat Rd., Edmonton, AB T5M 3J9
Tel: 780-705-4090
medigroup.ca

Edmonton: **Woodcroft Public Health Centre**
Affiliated with: Alberta Health Services
Westmount Shopping Centre, 111 Ave. & Groat Rd., Edmonton, AB T5M 4B7
Tel: 780-342-1600; *Fax:* 780-451-5886
www.albertahealthservices.ca

Edson: **Edson Community Health Services**
Affiliated with: Alberta Health Services
5028 - 3 Ave., Edson, AB T7E 1X4
Tel: 780-723-4421; *Fax:* 780-723-6299
www.albertahealthservices.ca

Elizabeth Metis Settlemen: **Elizabeth Settlement Community Health Services**
Affiliated with: Alberta Health Services
Elizabeth Metis Settlemen, AB T9M 1V8
Tel: 780-594-3383; *Fax:* 780-594-3384
www.albertahealthservices.ca

Elk Point: **Elk Point Community Health Services**
Affiliated with: Alberta Health Services
5310 - 50th Ave., Elk Point, AB T0A 1A0
Tel: 780-724-3532; *Fax:* 780-724-2867
www.albertahealthservices.ca

Elnora: **Elnora Community Health Centre**
Affiliated with: Alberta Health Services
PO Box 659, 425 - 8 Ave., Elnora, AB T0M 0Y0
Tel: 403-773-3636; *Fax:* 403-773-3949
www.albertahealthservices.ca

Fishing Lake Metis Settle: **Fishing Lake Metis Settlement Community Health Services**
Affiliated with: Alberta Health Services
Fishing Lake Metis Settle, AB T0A 1A0
Tel: 780-943-3058; *Fax:* 780-943-2575
www.albertahealthservices.ca

Fort MacLeod: **Fort Macleod Community Health**
Affiliated with: Alberta Health Services
744 - 26 St. South, Fort MacLeod, AB T0L 0Z0
Tel: 403-553-5351; *Fax:* 403-553-4567
www.albertahealthservices.ca

Fort MacLeod: **Fort Macleod Health Centre**
Affiliated with: Alberta Health Services
744 - 26 St. South, Fort MacLeod, AB T0L 0Z0
Tel: 403-553-5311; *Fax:* 403-553-4567
www.albertahealthservices.ca

Fort McMurray: **Fort McMurray Community Health Services**
Affiliated with: Alberta Health Services
113 Thickwood Blvd., Fort McMurray, AB T9H 5E5
Tel: 780-791-6247; *Fax:* 780-791-6282
www.albertahealthservices.ca

Fort Saskatchewan: **Sherrit Health Centre**
Affiliated with: Alberta Health Services
Former Name: Fort Saskatchewan Health
9401 - 86 Ave., Fort Saskatchewan, AB T8L 0C6
Tel: 780-342-2366; *Fax:* 780-342-3342
www.albertahealthservices.ca

Fort Vermilion: **Fort Vermilion Community Health Centre**
Affiliated with: Alberta Health Services
4804 - 50 St., Fort Vermilion, AB T0H 1N0
Tel: 780-927-3391
www.albertahealthservices.ca

Fox Creek: **Fox Creek Public Health Centre**
Affiliated with: Alberta Health Services
Former Name: Aspen Health Services
600 - 3rd St., Fox Creek, AB T0H 1P0
Tel: 780-622-3730; *Fax:* 780-622-3474
www.albertahealthservices.ca

Gibbons: **Gibbons Health Unit**
Affiliated with: Alberta Health Services
4720 - 50 Ave., Gibbons, AB T0A 1N0
Tel: 780-342-2660
www.albertahealthservices.ca

Gift Lake: **Gift Lake Community Health Services**
Affiliated with: Alberta Health Services
Main St., Gift Lake, AB T0G 1B0
Tel: 780-767-2101; *Fax:* 780-767-2490
www.albertahealthservices.ca

Glendon: **Glendon Community Health Services**
Affiliated with: Alberta Health Services
Former Name: Glendon Community Health Clinic
2nd St. Railway Ave., Glendon, AB T0A 1P0
Tel: 780-635-3861; *Fax:* 780-635-4213
www.albertahealthservices.ca

Grande Cache: **Grande Cache Provincial Building**
Affiliated with: Alberta Health Services
Public Health Centre, 10001 Hoppe Ave., Grande Cache, AB T0E 0Y0
Tel: 780-827-3504; *Fax:* 780-827-2728
www.albertahealthservices.ca

Grande Prairie: **Community Village**
Affiliated with: Alberta Health Services
10116 - 102 Ave., Grande Prairie, AB T8V 1A1
Tel: 780-513-7500
www.albertahealthservices.ca

Grande Prairie: **Grande Prairie College & Community Health Centre**
Affiliated with: Alberta Health Services
10620 - 104 Ave., Grande Prairie, AB T8V 8J8
Tel: 780-814-5800
www.albertahealthservices.ca

Grande Prairie: **Grande Prairie Provincial Building**
Affiliated with: Alberta Health Services
Former Name: Public Health Centre
10320 - 99 St., Grande Prairie, AB T8V 6J4
Tel: 780-513-7500
www.albertahealthservices.ca

Grande Prairie: **Grande Prairie Virene Building (Home Care)**
Affiliated with: Alberta Health Services
10121 - 97 Ave., Grande Prairie, AB T8V 0N5
Tel: 780-532-4447; *Fax:* 780-532-2477
Toll-Free: 855-371-4122
www.albertahealthservices.ca

Hanna: **Hanna Health Centre**
Affiliated with: Alberta Health Services
Former Name: Hanna Health Unit
PO Box 730, 904 Centre St. North, Hanna, AB T0J 1P0
Tel: 403-854-5236; *Fax:* 403-854-3253
www.albertahealthservices.ca

High Prairie: **High Prairie Public Health Centre**
Affiliated with: Alberta Health Services
4620 - 53 Ave., High Prairie, AB T0G 1E0
Tel: 780-523-6450; *Fax:* 780-523-6458
www.albertahealthservices.ca

High River: **High River Public Health Centre**
Affiliated with: Alberta Health Services
310 Macleod Trail, High River, AB T1V 1M7
Tel: 403-652-2200
www.albertahealthservices.ca

Hobbema: **Maskwacis Health Services**
PO Box 100, Hobbema, AB T0C 1N0
Tel: 780-585-3830; *Fax:* 780-585-2203
maskwacishealth.ca
Note: Programs & services include: community health; environmental health; HIV/AIDS education; medical clinic; optical; dental; pharmacy; home care; diabetes; counselling & support services; National Native Alcohol & Drug Awareness Program; & Indian Residential School Support Program.

Jasper: **Seton - Jasper Healthcare Centre**
Affiliated with: Alberta Health Services
Former Name: Jasper Community Health Services
Public Health Centre, PO Box 310, 518 Robson St., Jasper, AB T0E 1E0
Tel: 780-852-4759
www.albertahealthservices.ca

Kikino: **Kikino Metis Settlement Community Health Services**
Affiliated with: Alberta Health Services
Kikino, AB T0A 2B0
Tel: 780-623-7797; *Fax:* 780-623-4212
www.albertahealthservices.ca

Kinuso: **Kinuso Community Health Services**
Affiliated with: Alberta Health Services
230 Centre St., Kinuso, AB T0G 1K0
Tel: 780-775-3501; *Fax:* 780-775-3944
www.albertahealthservices.ca

Kitscoty: **Kitscoty Public Health / Rehab**
Affiliated with: Alberta Health Services
4922 - 49 Ave., Kitscoty, AB T0B 2P0
Tel: 780-846-2824; *Fax:* 780-846-2731
www.albertahealthservices.ca

La Crete: **La Crete Continuing Care Centre**
Affiliated with: Alberta Health Services
Former Name: La Crete Health Centre
10601 - 100 Ave., La Crete, AB T0H 2H0
Tel: 780-928-4215; *Fax:* 780-928-4237
www.albertahealthservices.ca
Note: Offers community health services as well as continuing care

Lac La Biche: **Lac La Biche Provincial Building**
Affiliated with: Alberta Health Services
Former Name: Lac La Biche Community Health Services
PO Box 297, 9503 Beaver Hill Rd., Lac La Biche, AB T0A 2C0
Tel: 780-623-4471; *Fax:* 780-623-4212
www.albertahealthservices.ca

Lamont: **Lamont Health Care Centre**
Affiliated with: Alberta Health Services
PO Box 479, 5216 - 53 St., Lamont, AB T0B 2R0
Tel: 780-895-2211; *Fax:* 780-895-7305
www.lamonthealthcarecentre.com
Note: Affiliated with the United Church of Canada.

Leduc: **Leduc Public Health Centre**
Affiliated with: Alberta Health Services
4219 - 50 St., Leduc, AB T9E 8C9
Tel: 780-980-4644; *Fax:* 780-980-4666
www.albertahealthservices.ca

Lethbridge: **Lethbridge Community Health Centre**
Affiliated with: Alberta Health Services
801 - 1 Ave. South, Lethbridge, AB T1J 4L5
Tel: 403-388-6666; *Fax:* 403-328-5934
www.albertahealthservices.ca
Note: Includes prenatal education

Magrath: **Magrath Community Health Centre**
Affiliated with: Alberta Health Services
Former Name: Magrath Hospital
PO Box 550, 37E - 2 Ave. North, Magrath, AB T0K 1J0
Tel: 403-758-4422; *Fax:* 403-758-3332
www.albertahealthservices.ca

Manning: **Manning Community Health Centre**
Affiliated with: Alberta Health Services
Former Name: Peace Country Health Unit
Bag 1260, 600 - 2 St. NE, Manning, AB T0H 2M0
Tel: 780-836-7361
www.albertahealthservices.ca

Mayerthorpe: **Mayerthorpe Healthcare Centre**
Affiliated with: Alberta Health Services
4417 - 45 St., Mayerthorpe, AB T0E 1N0
Tel: 780-786-2488; *Fax:* 780-786-2023
www.albertahealthservices.ca

McLennan: **Public Health Centre**
Affiliated with: Alberta Health Services
Former Name: Peace Country Health Unit - McLennan
c/o Sacred Heart Community Health Centre, 350 - 3 Ave., McLennan, AB T0H 2L0
Tel: 780-324-3750
www.albertahealthservices.ca

Medicine Hat: **Medicine Hat Community Health Services**
Affiliated with: Alberta Health Services
2948 Dunmore Rd. SE, Medicine Hat, AB T1A 8E3
Tel: 403-502-8200; *Fax:* 403-528-2250
www.albertahealthservices.ca

Milk River: **Milk River Health Centre**
Affiliated with: Alberta Health Services
Former Name: Milk River Hospital
PO Box 90, 517 Centre Ave. East, Milk River, AB T0K 1M0
Tel: 403-647-3500; *Fax:* 403-647-2337
www.albertahealthservices.ca

Morinville: **Morinville Provincial Building**
Affiliated with: Alberta Health Services
Former Name: Morinville Public Health Centre; Morinville Health Services
10008 - 107 St., Morinville, AB T8R 1L3
Tel: 780-342-2600; *Fax:* 780-939-7126
www.albertahealthservices.ca

Note: Public health services

Myrnam: **Myrnam Home Care**
Affiliated with: Alberta Health Services
PO Box 220, 4802 - 49 Ave., Myrnam, AB T0B 3K0
Tel: 780-366-3870; *Fax:* 780-366-3919
www.albertahealthservices.ca

Nanton: **Nanton Community Health Centre**
Affiliated with: Alberta Health Services
2214 - 20th St., Nanton, AB T0L 1R0
Tel: 403-646-2218; *Fax:* 403-646-3046
www.albertahealthservices.ca

Okotoks: **Okotoks Health & Wellness Centre**
Affiliated with: Alberta Health Services
11 Cimarron Common, Okotoks, AB T1S 2E9
Tel: 403-995-2600; *Fax:* 403-995-2663
www.albertahealthservices.ca

Olds: **Olds Campus Community Health Centre**
Affiliated with: Alberta Health Services
Ralph Klein Centre, #2029, 4500 - 50th St., Olds, AB T4H 1R6
Tel: 403-559-2150; *Fax:* 403-559-2151
www.albertahealthservices.ca

Olds: **Olds Provincial Building**
Affiliated with: Alberta Health Services
Former Name: Olds Community Health Centre
5030 - 50th St., Olds, AB T4H 1S1
Tel: 403-556-8441; *Fax:* 403-556-6842
www.albertahealthservices.ca
Note: Public health programs

Onoway: **Onoway Community Health Services**
Affiliated with: Alberta Health Services
4919 Lac St. Anne Trail, Onoway, AB T0E 1V0
Tel: 780-967-6200; *Fax:* 780-967-4433
www.albertahealthservices.ca

Oyen: **Oyen Community Health Services**
Affiliated with: Alberta Health Services
PO Box 296, 315 - 3 St. East, Oyen, AB T0J 2J0
Tel: 403-664-3651; *Fax:* 403-664-2934
www.albertahealthservices.ca

Paddle Prairie: **Paddle Prairie Health Centre**
Affiliated with: Alberta Health Services
PO Box 46, Paddle Prairie, AB T0H 2W0
Tel: 780-841-3342; *Fax:* 780-926-7394
Toll-Free: 855-371-4122
www.albertahealthservices.ca

Peerless Lake: **Peerless Lake Community Health Services**
Affiliated with: Alberta Health Services
Peerless Lake, AB T0G 2W0
Tel: 780-869-3930; *Fax:* 780-869-2053
www.albertahealthservices.ca

Picture Butte: **Piyami Health Centre**
Affiliated with: Alberta Health Services
Former Name: Picture Butte Hospital
300-A Rogers Ave., Picture Butte, AB T0K 1V0
Tel: 403-732-4762
www.albertahealthservices.ca

Pincher Creek: **Pincher Creek Community Health Centre**
Affiliated with: Alberta Health Services
1222 Bev McLachlin Dr., Pincher Creek, AB T0K 1W0
Tel: 403-627-3266; *Fax:* 403-627-2771
www.albertahealthservices.ca

Ponoka: **Ponoka Community Health Centre**
Affiliated with: Alberta Health Services
5900 Hwy. 2A, Ponoka, AB T4J 1P6
Tel: 403-783-4491; *Fax:* 403-783-3825
www.albertahealthservices.ca

Provost: **Provost Provincial Building**
Affiliated with: Alberta Health Services
Former Name: Hughenden Public Health: Home Care
5419 - 44 St., Provost, AB T0B 3S0
Tel: 780-753-6180; *Fax:* 780-753-2064
www.albertahealthservices.ca

Rainbow Lake: **Rainbow Lake Community Health Services**
Affiliated with: Alberta Health Services
Former Name: Rainbow Lake Health Centre
PO Box 177, 6A Commercial Rd., Rainbow Lake, AB T0H 2Y0
Tel: 780-956-3646
www.albertahealthservices.ca

Raymond: **Raymond Community Health**
Affiliated with: Alberta Health Services
200N - 2nd St. West, Raymond, AB T0K 2S0
Tel: 403-752-5430; *Fax:* 403-752-4655
www.albertahealthservices.ca

Red Deer: **Red Deer - 49th Street Community Health Centre**
Affiliated with: Alberta Health Services
4755 - 49th St., Red Deer, AB T4N 1T6
Tel: 403-314-5225; *Fax:* 403-314-5230
www.albertahealthservices.ca

Red Deer: **Red Deer - Bremner Ave. Community Health Centre**
Affiliated with: Alberta Health Services
2845 Bremner Ave., Red Deer, AB T4R 1S2
Tel: 403-341-2100; *Fax:* 403-341-2196
www.albertahealthservices.ca

Red Deer: **Red Deer - Johnstone Crossing Community Health Centre**
Affiliated with: Alberta Health Services
300 Jordan Pkwy., Red Deer, AB T4P 0G8
Tel: 403-356-6300; *Fax:* 403-356-6440
www.albertahealthservices.ca

Red Earth Creek: **Red Earth Creek Community Health Services**
Affiliated with: Alberta Health Services
Red Earth Creek, AB T0G 1X0
Tel: 780-649-2242; *Fax:* 780-649-2029
www.albertahealthservices.ca

Redwater: **Redwater Health Centre**
Affiliated with: Alberta Health Services
4812 - 58 St., Redwater, AB T0A 2W0
Tel: 780-942-3932; *Fax:* 780-942-2373
www.albertahealthservices.ca

Rimbey: **Rimbey Community Health Centre**
Affiliated with: Alberta Health Services
4709 - 51 Ave., Rimbey, AB T0C 2J0
Tel: 403-843-2288; *Fax:* 403-843-3050
www.albertahealthservices.ca

Rocky Mountain House: **Rocky Mountain House Health Centre**
Affiliated with: Alberta Health Services
5016 - 52 Ave., Rocky Mountain House, AB T4T 1T2
Tel: 403-845-3030; *Fax:* 403-845-4975
www.albertahealthservices.ca

Sedgewick: **Sedgewick Home Care / Public Health / Rehab**
Affiliated with: Alberta Health Services
4822 - 50 St., Sedgewick, AB T0B 4C0
Tel: 780-384-3652; *Fax:* 780-384-3699
www.albertahealthservices.ca

Sherwood Park: **Strathcona County Health Centre**
Affiliated with: Alberta Health Services
2 Brower Dr., Sherwood Park, AB T8H 1V4
Tel: 780-342-4600; *Fax:* 780-449-1338
www.albertahealthservices.ca

Slave Lake: **Slave Lake Healthcare Centre**
Affiliated with: Alberta Health Services
Public Health Centre, 309 - 6 St. NE, Slave Lake, AB T0G 2A4
Tel: 780-849-3947; *Fax:* 780-805-3550
www.albertahealthservices.ca

Smoky Lake: **George McDougall - Smoky Lake Healthcare Centre**
Affiliated with: Alberta Health Services
4212 - 55 Ave., Smoky Lake, AB T0A 3C0
Tel: 780-656-3595; *Fax:* 780-943-2242
www.albertahealthservices.ca

Spirit River: **Spirit River Community Health Services**
Affiliated with: Alberta Health Services
Former Name: Mistahia Health Unit - Spirit River
5003 - 45 Ave., Spirit River, AB T0H 3G0
Tel: 780-864-3063; *Fax:* 780-864-4187
www.albertahealthservices.ca

Spruce Grove: **Spruce Grove Health Unit**
Affiliated with: Alberta Health Services
505 Queen St., Spruce Grove, AB T7X 2V2
Tel: 780-342-1301; *Fax:* 780-342-1328
www.albertahealthservices.ca

Spruce Grove: **Stan Woloshyn Building**
Affiliated with: Alberta Health Services
205 Diamond Ave., Spruce Grove, AB T7X 3A8
Tel: 780-342-1380; *Fax:* 780-960-0369
www.albertahealthservices.ca
Note: Primarily provides environmental health services

St Paul: **St. Paul Community Health Services**
Affiliated with: Alberta Health Services
5610 - 50 Ave., St Paul, AB T0A 3A1
Tel: 780-645-3396; *Fax:* 780-645-6609
www.albertahealthservices.ca

St. Albert: **St. Albert Public Health Centre**
Affiliated with: Alberta Health Services
23 Sir Winston Churchill Ave., St. Albert, AB T8N 2S7
Tel: 780-459-6671; *Fax:* 780-460-7062
www.albertahealthservices.ca

Stettler: **Stettler Community Health Centre**
Affiliated with: Alberta Health Services
5911 - 50 Ave., Stettler, AB T0C 2L0
Tel: 403-742-3326; *Fax:* 403-742-1353
www.albertahealthservices.ca

Strathmore: **Strathmore Public Health Office**
Affiliated with: Alberta Health Services
650 Westchester Rd., Strathmore, AB T1P 1H8
Tel: 403-361-7200; *Fax:* 403-361-7244
www.albertahealthservices.ca

Sundre: **Sundre Community Health Centre**
Affiliated with: Alberta Health Services
212 - 6 Ave. NE, Sundre, AB T0M 1X0
Tel: 403-638-4063; *Fax:* 403-638-4460
www.albertahealthservices.ca

Swan Hills: **Swan Hills Healthcare Centre**
Affiliated with: Alberta Health Services
Public Health Centre, PO Box 261, 29 Freeman Dr., Swan Hills, AB T0G 2C0
Tel: 780-333-7077; *Fax:* 780-333-7009
www.albertahealthservices.ca

Sylvan Lake: **Sylvan Lake Community Health Centre**
Affiliated with: Alberta Health Services
4602 - 49 Ave., Sylvan Lake, AB T4S 1M7
Tel: 403-887-2241; *Fax:* 403-887-2610
www.albertahealthservices.ca

Taber: **Taber Community Health Centre**
Affiliated with: Alberta Health Services
5009 - 56th St., Taber, AB T1G 1M8
Tel: 403-223-7230; *Fax:* 403-223-8733
www.albertahealthservices.ca

Thorhild: **Thorhild Community Health Services**
Affiliated with: Alberta Health Services
302 - 2 Ave., Thorhild, AB T0A 3J0
Tel: 780-398-3879; *Fax:* 780-398-2671
www.albertahealthservices.ca

Thorsby: **Thorsby Public Health Centre**
Affiliated with: Alberta Health Services
4825 Hankin St., Thorsby, AB T0C 2P0
Tel: 780-789-4800; *Fax:* 780-789-4811
www.albertahealthservices.ca

Trout Lake: **Trout Lake Community Health Services**
Affiliated with: Alberta Health Services
Former Name: Trout Lake Health Station
General Delivery, Trout Lake, AB T0G 2N0
Tel: 780-869-3922; *Fax:* 780-869-2054
www.albertahealthservices.ca

Two Hills: **Two Hills Health Centre**
Affiliated with: Alberta Health Services
4401 - 53 Ave., Two Hills, AB T0B 4K0
Tel: 780-657-3361; *Fax:* 780-657-2508
www.albertahealthservices.ca

Valleyview: **Valleyview Community Health Services**
Affiliated with: Alberta Health Services
Former Name: Mistahia Health Unit, Valleyview; Valleyview District Home Care Office
5112 - 50 Ave., Valleyview, AB T0H 3N0
Tel: 780-524-3338
www.albertahealthservices.ca

Vauxhall: **Vauxhall Community Health**
Affiliated with: Alberta Health Services
406 - 1 Ave. North, Vauxhall, AB T0K 2K0
Tel: 403-223-7229; *Fax:* 403-654-2134
www.albertahealthservices.ca

Vegreville: **Vegreville Community Health Centre**
Affiliated with: Alberta Health Services
5318 - 50 St., Vegreville, AB T9C 1R1
Tel: 780-632-3331; *Fax:* 780-632-4334
www.albertahealthservices.ca

Vermilion: **Vermilion Provincial Building**
Affiliated with: Alberta Health Services
Former Name: Vermilion Public Health, Home Care, Rehab
4701 - 52 St., Vermilion, AB T9X 1J9
Tel: 780-853-5270; *Fax:* 780-853-7362
www.albertahealthservices.ca

Viking: **Viking 5224 - 50 Street**
Affiliated with: Alberta Health Services
Former Name: Viking Health Centre
5224 - 50 St., Viking, AB T0B 4N0
Tel: 780-336-4780
www.albertahealthservices.ca

Vilna: **Vilna Community Health Services**
Affiliated with: Alberta Health Services
Former Name: Our Lady's Health Centre
5103 - 48 St., Vilna, AB T0A 3L0
Tel: 780-636-3533; *Fax:* 780-656-2242
www.albertahealthservices.ca

Vulcan: **Vulcan Health Unit**
Affiliated with: Alberta Health Services
Vulcan Community Health Centre, PO Box 214, 610 Elizabeth St., Vulcan, AB T0L 2B0
Tel: 403-485-2285; *Fax:* 403-485-2639
www.albertahealthservices.ca

Wabasca: **Wabasca/Desmarais Community Health Services**
Affiliated with: Alberta Health Services
867 Stoney Point Rd., Wabasca, AB T0G 2K0
Tel: 780-891-3931; *Fax:* 780-891-3011
www.albertahealthservices.ca

Wainwright: **Wainwright Provincial Building**
Affiliated with: Alberta Health Services
810 - 14 Ave., Wainwright, AB T9W 1R2
Tel: 780-842-4077; *Fax:* 780-842-3151
www.albertahealthservices.ca

Westlock: **Westlock Community Health Services**
Affiliated with: Alberta Health Services
10024 - 107 St., Westlock, AB T7P 1H7
Tel: 780-349-3316; *Fax:* 780-349-5725
www.albertahealthservices.ca

Wetaskiwin: **Wetaskiwin Community Health Centre**
Affiliated with: Alberta Health Services
5610 - 40 Ave., Wetaskiwin, AB T9A 3E4
Tel: 780-361-4333; *Fax:* 780-361-4335
www.albertahealthservices.ca

Whitecourt: **Whitecourt Community Health Services**
Affiliated with: Alberta Health Services
4707 - 50 Ave., Whitecourt, AB T7S 1P1
Tel: 780-706-3173; *Fax:* 780-706-7154
www.albertahealthservices.ca

Winfield: **Winfield Community Health Centre**
Affiliated with: Alberta Health Services
Former Name: Crossroads Health Unit - Winfield
PO Box 114, 10 - 2 Ave. West, Winfield, AB T0C 2X0
Tel: 780-682-4755; *Fax:* 780-682-4750
www.albertahealthservices.ca

Worsley: **Worsley Community Health Services**
Affiliated with: Alberta Health Services
General Delivery, Worsley, AB T0H 3W0
Tel: 780-685-3752
www.albertahealthservices.ca

Zama City: Zama City Community Health Services
Affiliated with: Alberta Health Services
General Delivery, Zama City, AB T0H 4E0
Tel: 780-683-2220
www.albertahealthservices.ca

Nursing Stations

Chateh: Hay Lake Assumption Nursing Station
PO Box 90, Chateh, AB T0H 0S0
Tel: 780-321-3971; *Fax:* 780-321-3820

Rocky Mountain House: Big Horn Health Station
PO Box 1617, Rocky Mountain House, AB T4T 1B2
Tel: 403-845-3660

Special Treatment Centres

Banff: Cascade Plaza
Affiliated with: Alberta Health Services
#320, 317 Banff Ave., Banff, AB T1L 1B4
Tel: 403-678-3133; *Fax:* 403-678-3138
www.albertahealthservices.ca
Note: Addiction prevention & adult & youth counselling

Barrhead: Barrhead - 5143-50 Street
Affiliated with: Alberta Health Services
PO Box 4504, 5143 - 50 St., Barrhead, AB T7N 1A4
Tel: 780-674-8239; *Fax:* 780-674-8294
Toll-Free: 866-332-2322
barrhead@albertahealthservices.ca
www.albertahealthservices.ca
Note: Addiction prevention & adult & youth counselling

Barrhead: Barrhead Community Cancer Centre
Affiliated with: Alberta Health Services
Barrhead Healthcare Centre, 4815 - 51 Ave., Barrhead, AB T7N 1M1
Tel: 780-674-2231
albertacancer.ca

Blackfoot: Thorpe Recovery Centre (TRC)
Affiliated with: Alberta Health Services
Also Known As: Walter A. "Slim" Thorpe Recovery Centre
PO Box 291, Blackfoot, AB T0B 0L0
Tel: 780-875-8890; *Fax:* 780-875-2161
Toll-Free: 877-875-8890
info@thorperecoverycentre.org
www.thorperecoverycentre.org
Year Founded: 1975
Note: Detox, residential & transitional services
Teressa Krueckl, Executive Director

Bonnyville: Bonnyville Community Cancer Centre
Affiliated with: Alberta Health Services
Bonnyville Healthcare Centre, 5001 Lakeshore Dr., Bonnyville, AB T9N 2J7
Tel: 780-826-3346
albertacancer.ca

Bonnyville: Bonnyville Provincial Building
Affiliated with: Alberta Health Services
PO Box 7085, #201, 4904 - 50 Ave., Bonnyville, AB T9N 2J6
Tel: 780-826-8054; *Fax:* 780-826-8057
Toll-Free: 866-332-2322
www.albertahealthservices.ca
Note: Addiction prevention & adult & youth counselling

Brooks: Brooks - 403-2 Avenue West
Affiliated with: Alberta Health Services
403 - 2nd Ave. West, Brooks, AB T1R 0S3
Tel: 403-362-1265; *Fax:* 403-362-1248
Toll-Free: 866-332-2322
brooks@albertahealthservices.ca
www.albertahealthservices.ca
Note: Addiction prevention & adult & youth counselling

Calgary: Alpha House
Affiliated with: Alberta Health Services
203 - 15 Ave. SE, Calgary, AB T2G 1G4
Tel: 403-237-8341; *Fax:* 403-237-8361
alphahousecalgary.com
Social Media: twitter.com/alphahouseyyc
Note: Programs & services include: outreach; shelter; detox; & housing
Kathy Christiansen, Executive Director
kathy@alphahousecalgary.com

Calgary: Aventa Addiction Treatment For Women
Affiliated with: Alberta Health Services
610 - 25 Ave. SW, Calgary, AB T2S 0L6
Tel: 403-245-9050; *Fax:* 403-245-9485
info@aventa.org
www.aventa.org
Social Media: www.facebook.com/AventaAddictionTreatmentForWomen
Kim Turgeon, Executive Director
kturgeon@Aventa.org

Calgary: Calgary - 1177-11 Avenue SW
Affiliated with: Alberta Health Services
Stephenson Bldg., 1177 - 11th Ave. SW, Calgary, AB T2R 1K9
Tel: 403-297-3071; *Fax:* 403-297-3036
Toll-Free: 866-332-2322
www.albertahealthservices.ca
Note: Addiction prevention & adult counselling

Calgary: Calgary Youth Addiction Services Centre
Affiliated with: Alberta Health Services
1005 - 17 St. NW, Calgary, AB T2N 2E5
Tel: 403-297-4664; *Fax:* 403-297-4668
Toll-Free: 866-332-2322
www.albertahealthservices.ca

Calgary: Fresh Start Recovery Centre
Affiliated with: Alberta Health Services
411 - 41 Ave. NE, Calgary, AB T2E 2N4
Tel: 403-387-6266; *Fax:* 403-235-1532
info@freshstartrecovery.ca
www.freshstartrecovery.ca
Social Media: www.facebook.com/FreshStartRecovery; twitter.com/FreshStartRC
Year Founded: 1992
Number of Beds: 50 beds
Note: Residential alcohol & drug addiction treatment centre for men

Calgary: Renfrew Recovery Detoxification Centre
Affiliated with: Alberta Health Services
1611 Remington Rd. NE, Calgary, AB T2E 5K6
Tel: 403-297-3337; *Fax:* 403-297-4592
Toll-Free: 866-332-2322
www.albertahealthservices.ca

Calgary: Sunrise Native Addictions Services Society
Affiliated with: Alberta Health Services
Also Known As: SUNRISE
1231 - 34 Ave. NE, Calgary, AB T2E 6N4
Tel: 403-261-7921; *Fax:* 403-261-7945
nasgeneral@nass.ca
www.nass.ca
Year Founded: 1974
Note: Aboriginal-based addiction programming
Eve MacMillan, Executive Director

Calgary: Tom Baker Cancer Centre (TBCC)
Affiliated with: Alberta Health Services
1331 - 29 St. NW, Calgary, AB T2N 4N2
Tel: 403-521-3723; *Fax:* 403-355-3206
Toll-Free: 866-238-3735
calgarypsychosocial@albertahealthservices.ca
www.albertahealthservices.ca
Year Founded: 1958
Note: Programs & services include: medical oncology; surgery (E-mail, Alberta Radiosurgery Centre: arcinfo@cancerboard.ab.ca); radiation oncology; radiology; chemotherapy treatments; psychosocial resources; pathology; genetics; & research.
Teresa Davidson, Executive Director

Calgary: Women's Health Resources (WHR)
Affiliated with: Alberta Health Services
Former Name: Grace Women's Health Centre
Foothills Medical Centre, #185, 1403 - 29 St. NW, Calgary, AB T2N 2T9
Tel: 403-944-2270; *Fax:* 403-944-2271
whr@albertahealthservices.ca
calgarywomenshealth.ca

Calgary: Youville Recovery Residence for Women
Affiliated with: Alberta Health Services
3210 - 29th St., Calgary, AB T3E 2L1
Tel: 403-242-0722; *Fax:* 403-242-3915
www.youville.net
Social Media: www.facebook.com/130590742166
Year Founded: 1977
Cheryll Nandee, Executive Director
ed@youville.net

Canmore: Bow Valley Community Cancer Centre
Affiliated with: Alberta Health Services
Canmore General Hospital, 1100 Hospital Pl., Canmore, AB T1W 1N2
Tel: 403-678-7226
albertacancer.ca

Canmore: Camrose Community Cancer Centre
Affiliated with: Alberta Health Services
St. Mary's Hospital, 4607 - 53 St., Canmore, AB T4V 1Y5
Tel: 780-679-6100
albertacancer.ca

Canmore: Canmore Boardwalk Building
Affiliated with: Alberta Health Services
743 Railway Ave., Canmore, AB T1W 1P2
Tel: 403-678-3133; *Fax:* 403-678-3138
Toll-Free: 866-332-2322
www.albertahealthservices.ca
Note: Addiction prevention & adult & youth counselling

Claresholm: Lander Treatment Centre
Affiliated with: Alberta Health Services
221 - 42 Ave. West, Claresholm, AB T0L 0T0
Tel: 403-625-1395
www.albertahealthservices.ca
Note: Adult residential addiction services

Cold Lake: Cold Lake - 5013-51 Street
Affiliated with: Alberta Health Services
5013 - 51 St., Cold Lake, AB T9M 1P3
Tel: 780-594-7556; *Fax:* 780-594-2144
Toll-Free: 866-332-2322
www.albertahealthservices.ca
Note: Addiction prevention & adult & youth counselling

Drayton Valley: Drayton Valley Community Cancer Centre
Affiliated with: Alberta Health Services
Drayton Valley Hospital & Health Centre, 4550 Madsen Ave., Drayton Valley, AB T7A 1N8
Tel: 780-542-5321
albertacancer.ca

Drumheller: Drumheller Community Cancer Centre
Affiliated with: Alberta Health Services
Drumheller District Health Services, 351 - 9th St. NW, Drumheller, AB T0J 0Y1
Tel: 780-542-5321
albertacancer.ca

Edmonton: Addiction Recovery Centre
Affiliated with: Alberta Health Services
10302 - 107 St. NW, Edmonton, AB T5J 1K2
Tel: 780-427-4291; *Fax:* 780-638-3074
www.albertahealthservices.ca
Note: Adult detoxification

Edmonton: Cross Cancer Institute
Affiliated with: Alberta Health Services
11560 University Ave. NW, Edmonton, AB T6G 1Z2
Tel: 780-432-8771; *Fax:* 780-432-8411
www.albertahealthservices.ca
Social Media: www.facebook.com/179579998746821; twitter.com/AHS_media; www.youtube.com/AHSChannel
Number of Beds: 56 beds
Note: Cancer prevention, research & treatment program in northern Alberta.
Dr. Carol Cass, Contact
carol.cass@ualberta.ca

Edmonton: Edmonton Addiction Youth Services
Affiliated with: Alberta Health Services
12325 - 140 St. NW, Edmonton, AB T5L 2C9
Tel: 780-422-7383; *Fax:* 780-427-0213
Toll-Free: 866-332-2322
www.albertahealthservices.ca

Edmonton: Flagstaff Family & Community Services
Affiliated with: Alberta Health Services
4809 - 49 Ave., Edmonton, AB T0B 2L0
Tel: 780-672-1181; *Fax:* 780-679-1737
www.albertahealthservices.ca
Note: Adult & youth addiction counselling services

Edmonton: Glenrose Rehabilitation Hospital
Affiliated with: Alberta Health Services
10230 - 111 Ave., Edmonton, AB T5G 0B7
Tel: 780-735-7999
www.albertahealthservices.ca/facilities/grh
Social Media: www.facebook.com/179579998746821; twitter.com/AHS_media; www.youtube.com/AHSChannel

Year Founded: 1964
Number of Beds: 244 beds
Note: Rehabilitation centre for both adults & children; research & training centre for rehabilitation fields.
Lisa Froese, Site Director
Dr. Charles Harley, Facility Medical Director

Edmonton: Henwood Treatment Centre
Affiliated with: Alberta Health Services
RR 6, LCD 1, 18750 - 18th St. NW, Edmonton, AB T5K 4B3
Tel: 780-422-9069; *Fax:* 780-422-2223
www.albertahealthservices.ca
Note: Adult residential addiction services

Edmonton: Lois Hole Hospital for Women
Royal Alexandra Hospital
Affiliated with: Alberta Health Services
10240 Kingsway Ave., Edmonton, AB T5H 3V9
Tel: 780-735-4111
www.royalalex.org/loisholehospital
Social Media: www.facebook.com/132603820123065
Note: Programs & services include: clinical care (high-risk obstetrics, gynecological services & surgery); & innovation, research, education & prevention in women's health issues. Located within the Royal Alexandra Hospital.
Elise Cerny, Director, Communications
780-735-5458, ecerny@royalalex.org

Edmonton: Mazankowski Alberta Heart Institute
University of Alberta Hospital
Affiliated with: Alberta Health Services
11220 - 83 Ave., Edmonton, AB T6G 2B7
Tel: 780-407-8407
MazResourceCentres@albertahealthservices.ca
www.albertahealthservices.ca/facilities/home1024455.asp
Year Founded: 2001
Note: Programs & services include: cardiac surgery, cardiology services & patient education.
Mishaela Houle, Executive Director, Cardiac Services, Edmonton Zone

Edmonton: McConnell Place North
CapitalCare
Affiliated with: Alberta Health Services
9113 - 144 Ave., Edmonton, AB T5E 6K2
Tel: 780-496-2575; *Fax:* 780-472-6699
www.capitalcare.net/centres/mcconnell_north.html
Social Media: www.facebook.com/capitalcare.edmonton; twitter.com/CapitalCareYEG
Year Founded: 1995
Number of Beds: 36 beds
Note: Residential care for persons with Alzheimer disease; Reminiscence therapy
Iris Neumann, Chief Operating Officer, CapitalCare

Edmonton: Our House Addiction Recovery Centre
Affiliated with: Alberta Health Services
22210 Stony Plain Rd. NW, Edmonton, AB T5S 2C3
Tel: 780-474-8945; *Fax:* 780-479-2271
house@ourhouseedmonton.com
www.ourhouseedmonton.com
Social Media: www.facebook.com/107496326001549
Note: Offers a residential program for men over 18 years; addiction recovery programs for men & women; & education initiatives.
Patricia Bencz, Executive Director

Edmonton: Poundmaker's Lodge Treatment Centres
Affiliated with: Alberta Health Services
PO Box 34007, Edmonton, AB T5G 3G4
Tel: 780-458-1884; *Fax:* 780-459-1876
Toll-Free: 866-458-1884
info@poundmaker.org
www.poundmakerslodge.com
Note: Aboriginal addiction treatment centre; located at 25108 Poundmaker Rd., Sturgeon County, AB T8T 2A2

Edmonton: Santa Rosa
Affiliated with: Alberta Health Services
6705 - 120 Ave., Edmonton, AB T5B 0C7
Tel: 780-644-3627; *Fax:* 780-643-6804
www.albertahealthservices.ca
Note: Youth detoxification & stabilization

Edmonton: Woman's Health Options
Former Name: Morgentaler Clinic of Edmonton
12409 - 109A Ave., Edmonton, AB T5M 4A7
Tel: 780-484-1124; *Fax:* 780-489-3379
info@whol.ca
www.womanshealthoptions.com
Note: Provides reproductive health services, primarily abortion

Fort McMurray: Fort McMurray Community Cancer Centre
Affiliated with: Alberta Health Services
Northern Lights Regional Health Centre, 7 Hospital St., Fort McMurray, AB T9H 1P2
Tel: 780-791-6161
albertacancer.ca

Fort McMurray: Fort McMurray Provincial Building
Affiliated with: Alberta Health Services
#410, 9915 Franklin Ave., Fort McMurray, AB T9H 2K4
Tel: 780-743-7187; *Fax:* 780-743-7112
Toll-Free: 866-332-2322
fortmcmurray@albertahealthservices.ca
www.albertahealthservices.ca
Note: Addiction prevention, day treatment & adult & youth counselling

Grande Prairie: Grande Praire Mountain Plains Youth Residential Detox Program
Affiliated with: Alberta Health Services
Grande Prairie Aberdeen Centre, #300, 9728 Montrose Ave., Grande Prairie, AB T8V 5B6
Tel: 780-538-6330; *Fax:* 780-538-5256
Toll-Free: 866-332-2322
www.albertahealthservices.ca

Grande Prairie: Grande Prairie Cancer Centre
Affiliated with: Alberta Health Services
Queen Elizabeth II Hospital, 10409 - 98 St., Grande Prairie, AB T8V 2E8
Tel: 780-538-7588; *Fax:* 780-532-9120
albertacancer.ca
Note: Programs & services include: cancer treatment & care; chemotherapy; laboratory; nuclear medicine; pastoral care; pharmacy; social work; & symptom control & palliative care.

Grande Prairie: Northern Addictions Centre
Affiliated with: Alberta Health Services
11333 - 106 St., Grande Prairie, AB T8V 6T7
Tel: 780-538-5210; *Fax:* 780-538-6359
www.albertahealthservices.ca

Hanna: Hanna Provincial Building
Affiliated with: Alberta Health Services
401 Centre St., Hanna, AB T0J 1P0
Tel: 403-823-1660; *Fax:* 403-823-1762
Toll-Free: 866-332-2322
www.albertahealthservices.ca
Note: Addiction prevention & adult & youth counselling

High Level: Action North Recovery Centre
Affiliated with: Alberta Health Services
PO Box 872, High Level, AB T0H 1Z0
Tel: 780-926-3113; *Fax:* 780-926-2060
intake@actionnorth.org
www.actionnorth.org
Note: Residential addictions treatment facility

High River: High River Community Cancer Centre
Affiliated with: Alberta Health Services
High River General Auxiliary Hospital, 560 - 9th Ave. West, High River, AB T1V 1B3
Tel: 403-652-2200
albertacancer.ca

Hinton: Hinton Civic Centre Building
Affiliated with: Alberta Health Services
#102, 131 Civic Centre Rd., Hinton, AB T7V 2E8
Tel: 780-865-8263; *Fax:* 780-865-8314
Toll-Free: 866-332-2322
www.albertahealthservices.ca
Note: Addiction prevention & adult & youth counselling

Hinton: Hinton Community Cancer Centre
Affiliated with: Alberta Health Services
Hinton General Hospital, 1280 Switzer Dr., Hinton, AB T7V 1V2
Tel: 780-865-3333
albertacancer.ca

Jasper: Jasper - 612 Connaught Drive
Affiliated with: Alberta Health Services
612 Connaught Dr., Jasper, AB T0E 1E0
Tel: 780-852-2100; *Fax:* 780-852-2147
Toll-Free: 866-332-2322
www.albertahealthservices.ca
Note: Addiction prevention & adult & youth counselling

Lake Louise: Lake Louise - 200 Hector Street
Affiliated with: Alberta Health Services
200 Hector St., Lake Louise, AB T0L 1E0
Tel: 403-678-3133; *Fax:* 403-678-3138
www.albertahealthservices.ca
Note: Addiction prevention & adult & youth counselling; ambulatory community physiotherapy

Lethbridge: Jack Ady Cancer Centre
Affiliated with: Alberta Health Services
960 - 19th St. South, Lethbridge, AB T1J 1W5
Tel: 403-388-6200
albertacancer.ca
Note: Programs & services include: cancer treatment & care; chemotherapy; diagnostic imaging; laboratory; palliative care; radiation therapy; & social work.

Lethbridge: Lethbridge Youth Treatment Centre
Affiliated with: Alberta Health Services
402 - 6th Ave. North, Lethbridge, AB T1H 6J9
Tel: 403-388-7600; *Fax:* 403-388-7619
www.albertahealthservices.ca
Note: Addictions counselling & treatment

Lethbridge: Sifton Family & Youth Services
528 Stafford Dr. North, Lethbridge, AB T1H 2B2
Tel: 403-381-5411; *Fax:* 403-382-4565
Note: Provides a treatment program for young people with behavioural &/or emotional problems

Lloydminster: Lloydminster Community Cancer Centre
Affiliated with: Alberta Health Services
Lloydminster Hospital, 3820 - 43 Ave., Lloydminster, AB S9V 1Y5
Tel: 306-820-6130
albertacancer.ca

Medicine Hat: Margery E. Yuill Cancer Centre
Affiliated with: Alberta Health Services
Medicine Hat Regional Hospital, 666 - 5th St. SW, Medicine Hat, AB T1A 4H6
Tel: 403-529-8817
albertacancer.ca
Year Founded: 1989
Number of Beds: 4 treatment beds
Note: Programs & services include: cancer treatment & care; chemotherapy; colposcopy; diagnostic imaging; laboratory; nuclear medicine; & social work.

Medicine Hat: Medicine Hat Community Detox Centre
Affiliated with: Alberta Health Services
Co-Op Mall Medicine Hat, #105, 3030 - 13th Ave. SE, Medicine Hat, AB T1B 1E3
Tel: 403-529-1222; *Fax:* 403-529-1216
www.albertahealthservices.ca
Note: Adult detoxification; General Phone: 403-527-8998

Oyen: Oyen Provincial Building
Affiliated with: Alberta Health Services
201 Main St., Oyen, AB T0J 2J0
Tel: 403-529-3582; *Fax:* 403-529-3130
www.albertahealthservices.ca
Note: Adult addiction counselling

Peace River: Peace River Community Cancer Centre
Affiliated with: Alberta Health Services
Peace River Community Health Centre, 10101 - 68 St., Peace River, AB T8S 1T6
Tel: 780-624-7593
albertacancer.ca

Peace River: Peace River Provincial Building
Affiliated with: Alberta Health Services
Bag 900-1, 9621 - 96 Ave., Peace River, AB T8S 1T4
Tel: 780-624-6193; *Fax:* 780-624-6579
Toll-Free: 866-332-2322
www.albertahealthservices.ca
Note: Addictions prevention & adult & youth counselling

Red Deer: Central Alberta Cancer Centre
Affiliated with: Alberta Health Services
PO Box 5030, 3942 - 50A Ave., Red Deer, AB T4N 4E7
Tel: 403-343-4526; *Fax:* 403-346-1160
albertacancer.ca
Note: Programs & services include: cancer treatment & care; chemotherapy; clinical breast health program; nutrition; laboratory; palliative care; pharmacy; radiation therapy; & spiritual care.

***Red Deer:* Red Deer Provincial Building**
Affiliated with: Alberta Health Services
4920 - 51 St., Red Deer, AB T4N 6K8
Tel: 403-340-5274; *Fax:* 403-340-4804
Toll-Free: 866-332-2322
www.albertahealthservices.ca
Note: Addictions prevention; adult & youth counselling & treatment

***Red Deer:* Safe Harbour Society for Health & Housing**
Affiliated with: Alberta Health Services
5246 - 53 Ave., Red Deer, AB T4N 5K2
Tel: 403-347-0181; *Fax:* 403-347-7275
www.albertahealthservices.ca
Year Founded: 2007
Number of Employees: 60
Note: Adult detox & shelter
Kath Hoffman, Executive Director
kath@safeharboursociety.org

***Slave Lake:* Slave Lake - 101-3 Street SW**
Affiliated with: Alberta Health Services
#104, 101 - 3rd St. SW, Slave Lake, AB T0G 2A2
Tel: 780-849-7127; *Fax:* 780-849-7394
www.albertahealthservices.ca
Note: Addiction prevention & adult & youth counselling

***St. Paul:* St. Paul Provincial Building**
Affiliated with: Alberta Health Services
#116, 5025 - 49 Ave., St. Paul, AB T0A 3A4
Tel: 780-645-6346; *Fax:* 780-645-6249
Toll-Free: 866-332-2322
www.albertahealthservices.ca
Note: Addiction prevention & adult & youth counselling

***Stettler:* Stettler - 4837-50 Main Street**
Affiliated with: Alberta Health Services
4837 - 50 Main St., Stettler, AB T0C 2L0
Tel: 403-742-7523; *Fax:* 403-742-7596
Toll-Free: 866-332-2322
www.albertahealthservices.ca
Note: Addiction prevention & adult & youth counselling

***Strathmore:* Hilton Plaza**
Affiliated with: Alberta Health Services
209 - 3 St., Strathmore, AB T1P 1K2
Tel: 403-361-7277 *Toll-Free:* 877-652-4700
www.albertahealthservices.ca
Note: Addiction prevention & adult & youth counselling

***Vegreville:* Vegreville Provincial Building**
Affiliated with: Alberta Health Services
4809 - 50 St., Vegreville, AB T9C 1R1
Tel: 780-632-6617; *Fax:* 780-632-6618
vegaldrug@digitalweb.net
www.albertahealthservices.ca
Note: Addiction prevention & adult & youth counselling

***Whitecourt:* Whitecourt Provincial Building**
Affiliated with: Alberta Health Services
5020 - 52 Ave., Whitecourt, AB T7S 1N2
Tel: 780-778-7123; *Fax:* 780-778-7220
Toll-Free: 866-332-2322
www.albertahealthservices.ca
Note: Addiction prevention & adult & youth counselling

Long Term Care Facilities

***Airdrie:* Bethany Airdrie**
Bethany Care Society
Affiliated with: Alberta Health Services
1736 - 1st Ave. NW, Airdrie, AB T4B 2C4
Tel: 403-948-6022; *Fax:* 403-948-3897
info@bethanyseniors.com
www.bethanyseniors.com
Social Media: www.facebook.com/bethanyseniors; twitter.com/BethanyCare; www.youtube.com/user/BethanyCareSociety; www.linkedin.com/company/88398
Jennifer McCue, President & CEO, Bethany Care Society

***Athabasca:* Athabasca Healthcare Centre**
Affiliated with: Alberta Health Services
3100 - 48 Ave., Athabasca, AB T9S 1M9
Tel: 780-675-6030; *Fax:* 780-675-7050
Toll-Free: 855-371-4122
www.albertahealthservices.ca
Number of Beds: 23 beds

***Barrhead:* Barrhead Continuing Care Centre**
Affiliated with: Alberta Health Services
Former Name: Keir Care Centre
5336 - 59 Ave., Barrhead, AB T7N 1L2
Tel: 780-674-4506; *Fax:* 780-674-3003
www.albertahealthservices.ca
Number of Beds: 115 beds

***Bentley:* Bentley Care Centre**
Affiliated with: Alberta Health Services
4834 - 52 Ave., Bentley, AB T0C 0J0
Tel: 403-748-4115; *Fax:* 403-748-2727
www.albertahealthservices.ca
Note: Programs & services include: continuing care services; physiotherapy; occupational therapy; recreational therapy; & palliative care.

***Calagry:* Newport Harbour Park Place Seniors Living**
Affiliated with: Alberta Health Services
10 Country Village Cove, Calagry, AB T3K 5T9
Tel: 403-567-5100; *Fax:* 403-567-5105
nhccadmin@parkplaceseniorsliving.com
www.parkplaceseniorsliving.com
Number of Beds: 131 beds

***Calgary:* Bethany Calgary**
Bethany Care Society
Affiliated with: Alberta Health Services
916 - 18A St. NW, Calgary, AB T2N 1C6
Tel: 403-284-6000; *Fax:* 403-284-6085
info@bethanyseniors.com
www.bethanyseniors.com
Social Media: www.facebook.com/bethanyseniors; twitter.com/BethanyCare; www.youtube.com/user/BethanyCareSociety; www.linkedin.com/company/88398
Number of Beds: 400 residents
Note: Specialized care, including for younger adults with disabilities & individuals with complex dementia
Jennifer McCue, President & CEO, Bethany Care Society

***Calgary:* Bethany Harvest Hills**
Bethany Care Society
Affiliated with: Alberta Health Services
19 Harvest Gold Manor NE, Calgary, AB T3K 4Y1
Tel: 403-226-8200; *Fax:* 403-226-7265
info@bethanyseniors.com
www.bethanyseniors.com
Social Media: www.facebook.com/bethanyseniors; twitter.com/BethanyCare; www.youtube.com/user/BethanyCareSociety; www.linkedin.com/company/88398
Number of Beds: 60 long-term care beds
Note: Care centre for persons with Alzheimer disease & other forms of dementia
Jennifer McCue, President & CEO, Bethany Care Society

***Calgary:* Beverly Centre - Glenmore**
AgeCare
Affiliated with: Alberta Health Services
1729 - 90 Ave. SW, Calgary, AB T2V 4S1
Tel: 403-253-8806; *Fax:* 403-212-3530
receptionbcg@agecare.ca
www.agecare.ca/glenmore
Year Founded: 1971
Number of Beds: 200 beds
Population Served: 200; *Number of Employees:* 400

***Calgary:* Beverly Centre - Lake Midnapore**
AgeCare
Affiliated with: Alberta Health Services
500 Midpark Way SE, Calgary, AB T2X 3S3
Tel: 403-873-2600
bclm@agecare.ca
www.agecare.ca/beverly-centre-lake-midnapore
Number of Beds: 270 residents

***Calgary:* Bow-Crest**
Revera Inc.
Affiliated with: Alberta Health Services
5927 Bowness Rd. NW, Calgary, AB T3B 0C7
Tel: 403-288-2373; *Fax:* 403-288-2403
www.reveraliving.com/bowcrest
Number of Beds: 150 beds
Thomas G. Wellner, President & CEO, Revera Inc.

***Calgary:* Carewest Dr. Vernon Fanning Centre**
Affiliated with: Alberta Health Services
722 - 16 Ave. NE, Calgary, AB T2E 6V7
Tel: 403-230-6900; *Fax:* 403-230-6902
www.carewest.ca
Number of Beds: 294 beds

***Calgary:* Carewest Garrison Green**
Affiliated with: Alberta Health Services
3108 Don Ethell Blvd. SW, Calgary, AB T3E 6Z5
Tel: 403-944-0100; *Fax:* 403-944-0180
www.carewest.ca

***Calgary:* Carewest Glenmore Park**
Affiliated with: Alberta Health Services
6909 - 14 St. SW, Calgary, AB T2V 1P8
Tel: 403-258-7650; *Fax:* 403-258-7676
www.carewest.ca
Number of Beds: 147 beds

***Calgary:* Carewest Rouleau Manor**
Affiliated with: Alberta Health Services
2208 - 2nd St. SW, Calgary, AB T2S 3C1
Tel: 403-943-9850
www.carewest.ca
Number of Beds: 77 beds

***Calgary:* Carewest Royal Park**
Affiliated with: Alberta Health Services
4222 Sarcee Rd. SW, Calgary, AB T3E 7J8
Tel: 403-240-7475; *Fax:* 403-240-7476
www.carewest.ca
Number of Beds: 50 beds

***Calgary:* Carewest Signal Pointe**
Affiliated with: Alberta Health Services
6363 Simcoe Rd. SW, Calgary, AB T3H 4M3
Tel: 403-240-7950; *Fax:* 403-240-7958
www.carewest.ca

***Calgary:* Carewest**
Affiliated with: Alberta Health Services
10101 Southport Rd. SW, Calgary, AB T2W 3N2
Tel: 403-943-8140; *Fax:* 403-943-8188
www.carewest.ca
Year Founded: 1961
Note: Adminstration location for Carewest
Dale R. Forbes, Executive Director

***Calgary:* Intercare - Brentwood Care Centre**
Intercare Corporate Group Inc.
Affiliated with: Alberta Health Services
2727 - 16 Ave. NW, Calgary, AB T2N 3Y6
Tel: 403-289-2576; *Fax:* 403-282-7027
www.intercarealberta.com/brentwood-care-centre.html
Number of Beds: 235 private & semi-private rooms
Christopher Kane, Facility Leader

***Calgary:* Intercare - Chinook Care Centre**
Intercare Corporate Group Inc.
Affiliated with: Alberta Health Services
1261 Glenmore Trail SW, Calgary, AB T2V 4Y8
Tel: 403-252-0141; *Fax:* 403-253-0292
www.intercarealberta.com/chinook-care-centre.html
Number of Beds: Long-term care: 203 private & semi-private; Hospice: 14 private
Lorraine Nygard, Facility Leader

***Calgary:* Intercare @ Millrise**
Intercare Corporate Group Inc.
Affiliated with: Alberta Health Services
14911 - 5th St. SW, Calgary, AB T2Y 3E2
Tel: 403-451-4211; *Fax:* 403-451-4223
www.intercarealberta.com/intercare-millrise.html
Number of Beds: 51 private & semi-private rooms
Ali Bezuidenhout, Clinical Team Leader

***Calgary:* Mayfair Care Centre**
Affiliated with: Alberta Health Services
Former Name: Mayfair Nursing Home
8240 Collucutt St. SW, Calgary, AB T2V 1X1
Tel: 403-252-4445; *Fax:* 403-253-6216
admin@mayfaircarecentre.com
www.mayfaircarecentre.com
Number of Beds: 142 beds
Joel Bond, Administrator

***Calgary:* McKenzie Towne Care Centre**
Revera Inc.
Affiliated with: Alberta Health Services
80 Promenade Way SE, Calgary, AB T2Z 4G4
Tel: 403-508-9808; *Fax:* 403-257-9268
www.reveraliving.com/mckenzie-ccc
Thomas G. Wellner, President & CEO, Revera Inc.

***Calgary:* Mount Royal Care Centre**
Revera Inc.
Affiliated with: Alberta Health Services
1813 - 9 St. SW, Calgary, AB T2T 3C2
Tel: 403-244-8994
www.reveraliving.com/mountroyal

Number of Beds: 107 beds
Thomas G. Wellner, President & CEO, Revera Inc.

***Calgary:* The Salvation Army Agapé Hospice**
1302 - 8 Ave. NW, Calgary, AB T2N 1B8
Tel: 403-282-6588; *Fax:* 403-284-1778
information@agapehospice.ca
www.agapehospice.ca
Social Media:
www.facebook.com/thesalvationarmyagapehospice

Year Founded: 1992
Number of Beds: 18 beds
Note: Hospice for terminally ill

***Camrose:* The Bethany Group**
Affiliated with: Alberta Health Services
Also Known As: Rosehaven Care Centre
4612 - 53 St., Camrose, AB T4V 1Y6
Tel: 780-679-2000; *Fax:* 780-679-2001
www.thebethanygroup.ca

Number of Beds: 270 beds
Note: Faith-based organization that operates homes & services for older, disabled & vulnerable people in the Central Alberta area, serving over 2300 residents through over 900 staff members.
Denis Beesley, President & CEO
780-679-2010, denis.beesley@bethanygrp.ca

***Camrose:* Louise Jensen Care Centre**
The Bethany Group
Affiliated with: Alberta Health Services
5400 - 46 Ave., Camrose, AB T4V 4P8
Tel: 780-679-3097; *Fax:* 780-679-2001
www.thebethanygroup.ca

***Camrose:* Rosehaven Care Centre**
The Bethany Group
Affiliated with: Alberta Health Services
4612 - 53 St., Camrose, AB T4V 1Y6
Tel: 780-679-3000; *Fax:* 780-679-2001
www.thebethanygroup.ca

***Cochrane:* Bethany Cochrane**
Bethany Care Society
Affiliated with: Alberta Health Services
302 Quigley Dr., Cochrane, AB T4C 1M2
Tel: 403-932-6422; *Fax:* 403-932-4617
info@bethanyseniors.com
www.bethanyseniors.com
Social Media: www.facebook.com/bethanyseniors;
twitter.com/BethanyCare;
www.youtube.com/user/BethanyCareSociety;
www.linkedin.com/company/88398
Jennifer McCue, President & CEO, Bethany Care Society

***Cold Lake:* Cold Lake Healthcare Centre**
Affiliated with: Alberta Health Services
314 - 25 St., Cold Lake, AB T9M 1G6
Tel: 780-639-6515; *Fax:* 780-639-2255
Toll-Free: 855-371-4122
www.albertahealthservices.ca

***Didsbury:* Bethany Didsbury**
Bethany Care Society
Affiliated with: Alberta Health Services
1201 - 15th Ave., Didsbury, AB T0M 0W0
Tel: 403-335-4775; *Fax:* 403-335-4233
info@bethanyseniors.com
www.bethanyseniors.com
Social Media: www.facebook.com/bethanyseniors;
twitter.com/BethanyCare;
www.youtube.com/user/BethanyCareSociety;
www.linkedin.com/company/88398

Number of Beds: 100 suites
Jennifer McCue, President & CEO, Bethany Care Society

***Edmonton:* Allen Gray Continuing Care Centre**
Affiliated with: Alberta Health Services
5005 - 28 Ave. NW, Edmonton, AB T6L 7G1
Tel: 780-469-2371; *Fax:* 780-465-2073
www.albertahealthservices.ca

***Edmonton:* CapitalCare Dickinsfield**
Affiliated with: Alberta Health Services
14225 - 94 St. NW, Edmonton, AB T5E 6C6
Tel: 780-371-6500; *Fax:* 780-371-6583
www.capitalcare.net/centres/dickinsfield.html
Social Media: www.facebook.com/capitalcare.edmonton;
twitter.com/CapitalCareYEG

Year Founded: 1979
Number of Beds: 275 beds
Note: Programs & services include: continuing care; secure units for residents with dementia; supportive & comfort units for residents in middle to later stages of dementia; care for young adults who are disabled; & young adult day support program.

***Edmonton:* CapitalCare Grandview**
Affiliated with: Alberta Health Services
6215 - 124 St. NW, Edmonton, AB T6H 3V1
Tel: 780-496-7100; *Fax:* 780-496-7150
www.capitalcare.net/centres/grandview.html
Social Media: www.facebook.com/capitalcare.edmonton;
twitter.com/CapitalCareYEG

Year Founded: 1973
Number of Beds: 179 beds
Note: Programs & services include: continuing care for persons with dementia & who are chronically disabled; secure unit for residents with dementia who are at risk of leaving the building; supportive & comfort units for residents in middle to later stages of dementia; & orthopedic sub-acute program.

***Edmonton:* CapitalCare Lynnwood**
Affiliated with: Alberta Health Services
8740 - 165 St., Edmonton, AB T5R 2R8
Tel: 780-341-2500; *Fax:* 780-341-2363
www.capitalcare.net/centres/lynnwood.html
Social Media: www.facebook.com/capitalcare.edmonton;
twitter.com/CapitalCareYEG

Year Founded: 1966
Number of Beds: 300 beds
Note: Programs & services include: continuing care; behavioural assessment & stabilization suit; secure unit for residents with dementia; supportive & comfore care units for rsidents in middle to later stages of dementia; & mental health services.

***Edmonton:* CapitalCare Norwood**
Affiliated with: Alberta Health Services
10410 - 111 Ave., Edmonton, AB T5G 3A2
Tel: 780-496-3200; *Fax:* 780-474-9806
www.capitalcare.net/centres/norwood.html
Social Media: www.facebook.com/capitalcare.edmonton;
twitter.com/CapitalCareYEG

Year Founded: 1964
Number of Beds: 205 beds
Note: Programs & services include: continuing care; brian injury unit; chronic ventilator unit; medical sub-acute program; transition program; & palliative care.

***Edmonton:* Devonshire Care Centre**
Park Place Seniors Living
Affiliated with: Alberta Health Services
1808 Rabbit Hill Rd., Edmonton, AB T6R 3H2
Tel: 780-665-8050; *Fax:* 780-665-8051
devonshire@parkplaceseniorsliving.com
devonshirecarecentre.com

***Edmonton:* Dianne & Irving Kipnes Centre for Veterans**
CapitalCare
Affiliated with: Alberta Health Services
4470 McCrae Ave., Edmonton, AB T5E 6M8
Tel: 780-442-5700; *Fax:* 780-442-5711
www.capitalcare.net/centres/kipnes.html
Social Media: www.facebook.com/capitalcare.edmonton;
twitter.com/CapitalCareYEG

Year Founded: 2005
Number of Beds: 120 residents
Iris Neumann, Chief Operating Officer, CapitalCare

***Edmonton:* Dr. Gerald Zetter Care Centre**
Good Samaritan Society
Affiliated with: Alberta Health Services
9649 - 71 Ave., Edmonton, AB T6E 5J2
Tel: 780-431-3600; *Fax:* 780-431-3699
goodsaminfo@gss.org
www.gss.org
Number of Beds: 190 long-term care suites; 10 sub-acute beds
Shawn Terlson, President & CEO, Good Samaritan Society
sterlson@gss.org

***Edmonton:* Edmonton Chinatown Care Centre**
Affiliated with: Alberta Health Services
9539 - 102A Ave., Edmonton, AB T5H 0G2
Tel: 780-429-0888; *Fax:* 780-429-0803
info@edmccc.net
www.edmccc.net
Anthony Lam, Chief Executive Officer

***Edmonton:* Edmonton General Continuing Care Centre**
Covenant Health
Affiliated with: Alberta Health Services
11111 Jasper Ave., Edmonton, AB T5K 0L4
Tel: 780-735-7000
www.covenanthealth.ca/hospitals-care-centres/edmonton-general-continuing-care-centre

Year Founded: 1895
Number of Beds: 14 long-term care units
Note: Houses a continuing care program for seniors

***Edmonton:* Extendicare - Eaux Claires**
Extendicare Canada
Affiliated with: Alberta Health Services
Former Name: Extendicare - Somerset
16503 - 95th St., Edmonton, AB T5Z 0G7
Tel: 780-472-1106
cnh_eauxclaires@extendicare.com
www.extendicarecanada.com/eaux_claires
Number of Beds: 180 bed

***Edmonton:* Hardisty Care Centre**
Park Place Seniors Living
Affiliated with: Alberta Health Services
Former Name: Hardisty Nursing Home
6420 - 101 Ave. NW, Edmonton, AB T6A 0H5
Tel: 780-466-9267; *Fax:* 780-450-8046
hardisty@parkplaceseniorsliving.com
www.parkplaceseniorsliving.com

Year Founded: 1958
Number of Beds: 180 beds

***Edmonton:* Jasper Place**
Revera Inc.
Affiliated with: Alberta Health Services
8903 - 168th St., Edmonton, AB T5R 2V6
Tel: 780-489-4931
www.reveraliving.com/jasper
Thomas G. Wellner, President & CEO, Revera Inc.

***Edmonton:* McConnell Place West**
CapitalCare
Affiliated with: Alberta Health Services
8720 - 165 St., Edmonton, AB T5R 5Y8
Tel: 780-413-4770; *Fax:* 780-413-4773
www.capitalcare.net/centres/mcconnell_west.html
Social Media: www.facebook.com/capitalcare.edmonton;
twitter.com/CapitalCareYEG

Number of Beds: 36 beds
Iris Neumann, Chief Operating Officer, CapitalCare

***Edmonton:* Mill Woods Centre**
Good Samaritan Society
Affiliated with: Alberta Health Services
101 Youville Dr. East, Edmonton, AB T6L 7A4
Tel: 780-413-3501; *Fax:* 780-462-8850
goodsaminfo@gss.org
www.gss.org

Number of Beds: 60 beds
Shawn Terlson, President & CEO, Good Samaritan Society
sterlson@gss.org

***Edmonton:* Miller Crossing Long Term Care**
Revera Inc.
Affiliated with: Alberta Health Services
145251 - 50 St., Edmonton, AB T5A 5J4
Tel: 780-478-9212; *Fax:* 780-478-2894
www.reveraliving.com/miller
Thomas G. Wellner, President & CEO, Revera Inc.

***Edmonton:* St. Michael's Long Term Care Centre**
St. Michael's Health Group
Affiliated with: Alberta Health Services
7404 - 139 Ave., Edmonton, AB T5C 3H7
Tel: 780-473-5621; *Fax:* 780-472-4506
Toll-Free: 800-472-6169
smeccs@smhg.ca
www.smhg.ca
Social Media: www.facebook.com/www.smhg.ca
Number of Beds: 153 beds
Stan C. Fisher, President & CEO

Edmonton: The Salvation Army Edmonton Grace Manor
Former Name: Sunset Lodge
12510 - 140 Ave., Edmonton, AB T5X 6C4
Tel: 780-454-5484; *Fax:* 780-455-7196
www.edmontongracemanor.ca
Year Founded: 2002
Number of Beds: 100 beds
Note: Intermediate care

Edmonton: Shepherd's Care - Kensington Campus
Shepherd's Care Foundation
Affiliated with: Alberta Health Services
12603 - 135 Ave., Edmonton, AB T5L 5B1
Tel: 780-447-3840; *Fax:* 780-452-3794
www.shepherdscare.org/kensington-campus.php
Year Founded: 1998
Number of Beds: 600 residents

Edmonton: Shepherd's Care - Millwoods Campus
Shepherd's Care Foundation
Affiliated with: Alberta Health Services
6620 - 28 Ave., Edmonton, AB T6K 2R1
Tel: 780-463-9810; *Fax:* 780-462-1643
www.shepherdscare.org/millwoods-campus.php

Edmonton: South Terrace Long Term Care
Revera Living
5905 - 112 St. NW, Edmonton, AB T6H 3J4
Tel: 780-434-1451; *Fax:* 780-436-4300
www.reveraliving.com/southterrace
Year Founded: 1961

Edmonton: Southgate Care Centre
Good Samaritan Society
Affiliated with: Alberta Health Services
4225 - 107 St. NW, Edmonton, AB T6J 2P1
Tel: 780-431-3854; *Fax:* 780-431-3898
goodsaminfo@gss.org
www.gss.org
Year Founded: 1973
Number of Beds: 226 beds
Shawn Terlson, President & CEO, Good Samaritan Society
sterlson@gss.org

Edmonton: Touchmark at Wedgewood
Touchmark, LLC
Affiliated with: Alberta Health Services
18333 Lessard Rd. NW, Edmonton, AB T6M 0A1
Tel: 780-800-7189
www.touchmarkedmonton.com
Social Media: www.facebook.com/TouchmarkAtWedgewood; www.youtube.com/user/TouchmarkRetirement
Year Founded: 1980
Number of Beds: 66 bungalows; 115-suite complex
Note: Retirement community with long-term care options
Leanne Gugenheimer, Executive Director

Edmonton: Venta Care Centre
Affiliated with: Alberta Health Services
Former Name: Venta Nursing Home
13525 - 102 St. NW, Edmonton, AB T5E 4K3
Tel: 780-476-6633; *Fax:* 780-476-6943
www.ventacarecentre.com
Year Founded: 1953
Dr. Peter Birzgalis, CEO/Administrator

Edson: Edson Healthcare Centre
Affiliated with: Alberta Health Services
4716 - 5 Ave., Edson, AB T7E 1S8
Tel: 780-723-2229; *Fax:* 780-723-2135
Toll-Free: 855-371-4122
www.albertahealthservices.ca

Evansburg: Pembina Village
Good Samaritan Society
Affiliated with: Alberta Health Services
5225 - 50 St., Evansburg, AB T0E 0T0
Tel: 780-727-2288
goodsaminfo@gss.org
www.gss.org
Number of Beds: 30 supportive living suites; 30 long-term care suites; 10 bed dementia care cottage
Shawn Terlson, President & CEO, Good Samaritan Society
sterlson@gss.org

Fairview: Fairview Health Complex
Affiliated with: Alberta Health Services
10628 - 110 St., Fairview, AB T0H 1L0
Tel: 780-835-6180; *Fax:* 855-776-3805
Toll-Free: 855-371-4122
www.albertahealthservices.ca

Number of Beds: 51 continuing care beds (11 dementia beds); 1 respite bed

Fort McMurray: Northern Lights Regional Health Centre
Affiliated with: Alberta Health Services
7 Hospital St., 4th Fl., Fort McMurray, AB T9H 1P2
Tel: 780-791-6066; *Fax:* 855-776-3805
Toll-Free: 855-371-4122
www.albertahealthservices.ca
Number of Beds: 30 beds

Fort Saskatchewan: Rivercrest Care Centre
Qualicare Corporation
Affiliated with: Alberta Health Services
Former Name: Rivercrest Lodge Nursing Home
10104 - 101 Ave., Fort Saskatchewan, AB T8L 2A5
Tel: 780-998-2425; *Fax:* 780-992-9432
reception@rivercrestlodge.com
www.qualicarehealthservices.com/rivercrest
Number of Beds: 85 beds

Fort Vermilion: St. Theresa General Hospital
Affiliated with: Alberta Health Services
4506 - 46 Ave., Fort Vermilion, AB T0H 1N0
Tel: 780-841-3207; *Fax:* 855-776-3805
Toll-Free: 855-371-4122
www.albertahealthservices.ca
Number of Beds: 8 beds

Grande Prairie: Mackenzie Place Continuing Care
Affiliated with: Alberta Health Services
Queen Elizabeth II Hospital, 10409 - 98 St., Grande Prairie, AB T8V 2E8
Tel: 780-538-7100; *Fax:* 855-776-3805
Toll-Free: 855-371-4122
www.albertahealthservices.ca
Number of Beds: 3 respite beds

Grande Prairie: Points West Living Grande Prairie
Affiliated with: Alberta Health Services
11460 - 104 Ave., Grande Prairie, AB T8V 3G9
Tel: 780-357-5700; *Fax:* 780-357-5710
info.grandeprairie@pointswestliving.com
pointswestliving.com/gp_pwl_home.php
Year Founded: 2011
Number of Beds: 155 units
Note: Long-term care; hospice; supportive living; & independent living

High Level: Northwest Health Centre
Affiliated with: Alberta Health Services
11202 - 100 St., High Level, AB T0H 1Z0
Tel: 780-841-3207; *Fax:* 855-776-3805
Toll-Free: 855-371-4122
www.albertahealthservices.ca

High Prairie: High Prairie J.B. Wood Continuing Care
Affiliated with: Alberta Health Services
High Prairie Health Complex, 4620 - 53 Ave., High Prairie, AB T0G 1E0
Tel: 780-523-6470; *Fax:* 780-523-6642
Toll-Free: 855-371-4122
www.albertahealthservices.ca
Number of Beds: 35 beds; 2 respite beds

Hythe: Hythe Continuing Care Centre
Affiliated with: Alberta Health Services
10307 - 100 St., Hythe, AB T0H 2C0
Tel: 780-356-3818; *Fax:* 780-356-3633
Toll-Free: 855-371-4122
www.albertahealthservices.ca
Number of Beds: 30 long-term care beds; 1 respite bed

Islay: Islay Assisted Living
Affiliated with: Alberta Health Services
5016 - 53 St., Islay, AB T0B 2J0
Tel: 780-744-3795; *Fax:* 780-744-3922
www.albertahealthservices.ca

La Crete: La Crete Continuing Care Centre
Affiliated with: Alberta Health Services
10601 - 100 Ave., La Crete, AB T0H 2H0
Tel: 780-841-3207; *Fax:* 855-776-3508
Toll-Free: 855-371-4122
www.albertahealthservices.ca

Lac La Biche: William J. Cadzow - Lac La Biche Healthcare Centre
Affiliated with: Alberta Health Services
9110 - 93 St., Lac La Biche, AB T0A 2C0
Tel: 780-623-5911; *Fax:* 855-776-3805
Toll-Free: 855-371-4122
www.albertahealthservices.ca
Number of Beds: 42 long-term care beds; 1 palliative bed; 1 respite bed

Leduc: Extendicare - Leduc
Extendicare Canada
Affiliated with: Alberta Health Services
4309 - 50 St., Leduc, AB T9E 6K6
Tel: 780-986-2245; *Fax:* 780-986-0669
cnh_leduc@extendicare.com
www.extendicarecanada.com/leduc

Lethbridge: Edith Cavell Care Centre
Chantelle Management Ltd.
Affiliated with: Alberta Health Services
1255 - 5 Ave. South, Lethbridge, AB T1J 0V6
Tel: 403-328-6631; *Fax:* 403-320-9061
edithcavell@chantellegroup.com
www.chantellegroup.com/edith_cavell.htm
Year Founded: 2000
Number of Beds: 120 rooms; 30 special care rooms

Mannville: Mannville Care Centre
Affiliated with: Alberta Health Services
5007 - 46 St., Mannville, AB T0B 2W0
Tel: 780-763-3621; *Fax:* 780-763-3678
Toll-Free: 855-371-4122
www.albertahealthservices.ca
Number of Beds: 23 beds

McLennan: Manoir du Lac
Integrated Life Care Inc.
Affiliated with: Alberta Health Services
164 - 3rd Ave., McLennan, AB T0H 2L0
Tel: 780-324-2513; *Fax:* 780-324-2060
www.integratedlifecare.ca
Lloyd Del Rosario, Manager & Director, Care
mdlnm@integratedlifecare.ca

Medicine Hat: Riverview Long Term Care
Revera Inc.
Affiliated with: Alberta Health Services
603 Prospect Dr. SW, Medicine Hat, AB T1A 4C2
Tel: 403-527-5531; *Fax:* 403-527-5175
www.reveraliving.com
Thomas G. Wellner, President & CEO, Revera Inc.

Medicine Hat: South Ridge Village
Good Samaritan Society
Affiliated with: Alberta Health Services
550 Spruce Way SE, Medicine Hat, AB T1B 4P1
Tel: 403-528-5050; *Fax:* 403-504-2520
goodsaminfo@gss.org
www.gss.org
Number of Beds: 70 continuing care suites; 42 supportive living suites; three 10-bed dementia care cottages
Shawn Terlson, President & CEO, Good Samaritan Society
sterlson@gss.org

Morinville: Aspen House
Affiliated with: Alberta Health Services
9706 - 100 Ave., Morinville, AB T8R 1T2
Tel: 780-939-1416; *Fax:* 780-939-6144
www.albertahealthservices.ca
Note: Supportive living

Olds: Olds Hospital & Care Centre
Affiliated with: Alberta Health Services
3901 - 57 Ave., Olds, AB T4H 1T4
Tel: 403-507-8110
www.albertahealthservices.ca

Peace River: Sutherland Place Continuing Care Centre
Affiliated with: Alberta Health Services
Peace River Community Health Centre, 10101 - 68 St., Peace River, AB T8S 1T6
Tel: 780-624-7538; *Fax:* 855-776-3805
Toll-Free: 855-371-4122
www.albertahealthservices.ca
Number of Beds: 27 continuing care beds; 12 dementia beds; 1 respite bed

Ponoka: **Northcott Care Centre**
Qualicare Corporation
Affiliated with: Alberta Health Services
4209 - 48 Ave., Ponoka, AB T4J 1P4
Tel: 403-783-4764; *Fax:* 403-783-6420
tserle@northcottcarecentre.com
www.qualicarehealthservices.com/northcott
Number of Beds: 73 beds

Radway: **Radway Continuing Care Centre**
Affiliated with: Alberta Health Services
5002 - 52 St., Radway, AB T0A 2V0
Tel: 780-736-3740; *Fax:* 780-736-2353
Toll-Free: 855-371-4122
www.albertahealthservices.ca

Red Deer: **Bethany CollegeSide**
Bethany Care Society
Affiliated with: Alberta Health Services
99 College Circle, Red Deer, AB T0M 1R0
Tel: 403-357-3700; *Fax:* 403-341-5613
info@bethanyseniors.com
www.bethanyseniors.com
Social Media: www.facebook.com/bethanyseniors; twitter.com/BethanyCare; www.youtube.com/user/BethanyCareSociety; www.linkedin.com/company/88398
Jennifer McCue, President & CEO, Bethany Care Society

Rimbey: **Rimbey Hospital & Care Centre**
Affiliated with: Alberta Health Services
5228 - 50 St., Rimbey, AB T0C 2J0
Tel: 403-843-7807
www.albertahealthservices.ca

Rocky Mountain House: **Clearwater Centre**
Good Samaritan Society
Affiliated with: Alberta Health Services
5615 - 60 St., Rocky Mountain House, AB T4T 1W2
Tel: 403-845-6033; *Fax:* 403-845-6420
goodsaminfo@gss.org
www.gss.org
Number of Beds: 30 long-term care suites; 29 supportive living suites; 2 dementia care cottages
Shawn Terlson, President & CEO, Good Samaritan Society
sterlson@gss.org

Sherwood Park: **CapitalCare Strathcona**
Affiliated with: Alberta Health Services
12 Brower Dr., Sherwood Park, AB T8H 1V3
Tel: 780-467-3366; *Fax:* 780-467-4095
www.capitalcare.net/centres/strathcona.html
Social Media: www.facebook.com/capitalcare.edmonton; twitter.com/CapitalCareYEG
Year Founded: 1994
Number of Beds: 111 beds
Note: Programs & services include: continuing care; secure dementia unit; Eden Alternative philosophy of care; recreational programs; occupational therapy; respite program; & adult community day support program.

Sherwood Park: **Sherwood Care**
Affiliated with: Alberta Health Services
Former Name: Sherwood Park Care Center
2020 Brentwood Blvd., Sherwood Park, AB T8A 0X1
Tel: 780-467-2281; *Fax:* 780-449-1529
sherwoodcare.com
Year Founded: 1969

Smoky Lake: **George McDougall - Smoky Lake Healthcare Centre**
Affiliated with: Alberta Health Services
4607 - 52 Ave., Smoky Lake, AB T0A 3C0
Tel: 780-656-3818; *Fax:* 855-776-3805
Toll-Free: 855-371-4122
www.albertahealthservices.ca
Number of Beds: 32 beds

St Albert: **Citadel Care Centre**
Qualicare Corporation
Affiliated with: Alberta Health Services
25 Erin Ridge Rd., St Albert, AB T8N 7K8
Tel: 780-458-3044; *Fax:* 780-458-8563
chowatt@citadelcarecentre.com
www.qualicarehealthservices.com/citadel
Number of Beds: 115 continuing care rooms; 7 semi-private rooms

St. Albert: **Youville Home**
Covenant Health
Affiliated with: Alberta Health Services
9A St. Vital Ave., St. Albert, AB T8N 1K1
Tel: 780-460-6900; *Fax:* 780-459-4139
www.covenanthealth.ca/hospitals-care-centres/youville-home
Year Founded: 1963
Number of Beds: 227 beds
Number of Employees: 420

Standoff: **Kainai Continuing Care Centre**
Blood Tribe Department of Health Inc.
PO Box 380, Standoff, AB T0L 1Y0
Tel: 403-737-3652
btdh.ca/staff/kainai-continuing-care-centre
Number of Beds: 21 extended care beds; 2 respite care beds; 2 palliative care beds
Crystal Day Chief, Director

Stony Plain: **Stony Plain Care Centre**
Good Samaritan Society
Affiliated with: Alberta Health Services
4800 - 55 Ave., Stony Plain, AB T7Z 1P9
Tel: 780-963-2261; *Fax:* 780-963-5156
goodsaminfo@gss.org
www.gss.org
Number of Beds: 120 long-term care beds; 30-bed dementia care cottage
Shawn Terlson, President & CEO, Good Samaritan Society
sterlson@gss.org

Stony Plain: **WestView Continuing Care Centre**
Affiliated with: Alberta Health Services
4405 South Park Dr., Stony Plain, AB T7Z 2M7
Tel: 780-968-3656; *Fax:* 780-968-3657
www.albertahealthservices.ca

Sylvan Lake: **Bethany Sylvan Lake**
Bethany Care Society
Affiliated with: Alberta Health Services
4700 - 47 Ave., Sylvan Lake, AB T4S 2M3
Tel: 403-887-7741; *Fax:* 403-887-8447
info@bethanyseniors.com
www.bethanyseniors.com
Social Media: www.facebook.com/bethanyseniors; twitter.com/BethanyCare; www.youtube.com/user/BethanyCareSociety; www.linkedin.com/company/88398
Jennifer McCue, President & CEO, Bethany Care Society

Three Hills: **Three Hills Health Centre**
Affiliated with: Alberta Health Services
1504 - 2nd St. North, Three Hills, AB T0M 2A0
Tel: 403-443-8006
www.albertahealthservices.ca

Vegreville: **Vegreville Care Centre**
Affiliated with: Alberta Health Services
4525 - 50 St., Vegreville, AB T9C 0A1
Tel: 780-632-2871; *Fax:* 780-632-6680
www.albertahealthservices.ca

Westlock: **Westlock Continuing Care Centre**
Affiliated with: Alberta Health Services
Former Name: Westlock Long Term Care Centre
10203 - 96 St., Westlock, AB T7P 2R3
Tel: 780-349-3306; *Fax:* 780-349-5647
Toll-Free: 855-371-4122
www.albertahealthservices.ca
Number of Beds: 120 beds

Wetaskiwin: **Wetaskiwin Hospital & Care Centre**
Affiliated with: Alberta Health Services
Former Name: Crossroads Hospital & Health Centre - Wetaskiwin
6910 - 47 St., Wetaskiwin, AB T9A 3N3
Tel: 780-312-3628; *Fax:* 780-312-3727
www.albertahealthservices.ca
Number of Beds: 105 long-term care beds

Nursing Homes

Athabasca: **Extendicare - Athabasca**
Extendicare Canada
Affiliated with: Alberta Health Services
4517 - 53 St., Athabasca, AB T9S 1K4
Tel: 780-675-2291; *Fax:* 780-675-3833
cnh_athabasca@extendicare.com
www.extendicarecanada.com/athabasca
Number of Beds: 50 beds

Blairmore: **York Creek Lodge**
Crowsnest Pass Senior Housing
Affiliated with: Alberta Health Services
PO Box 1050, 1810 - 112 St., Blairmore, AB T0K 0E0
Tel: 403-562-2102
www.crowsnestpass-seniorhousing.com
Social Media: www.facebook.com/YorkCreekLodge
Year Founded: 1980
Number of Beds: 20 beds

Bonnyville: **Extendicare - Bonnyville**
Extendicare Canada
Affiliated with: Alberta Health Services
PO Box 1080, 4602 - 47 Ave., Bonnyville, AB T9N 2E8
Tel: 780-826-3341; *Fax:* 780-826-4890
cnh_bonnyville@extendicare.com
www.extendicarecanada.com/bonnyville
Number of Beds: 50 beds

Calgary: **Bow View Manor**
Brenda Strafford Foundation Ltd.
Affiliated with: Alberta Health Services
4628 Montgomery Blvd. NW, Calgary, AB T3B 0K7
Tel: 403-288-4446; *Fax:* 403-288-8522
www.straffordfoundation.org
Year Founded: 1961
Number of Beds: 193 beds
Lynda Poissant, Administrator
Lynda.Poissant@straffordfoundation.o

Calgary: **Carewest George Boyack**
Affiliated with: Alberta Health Services
1203 Centre Ave. NE, Calgary, AB T2E 0A5
Tel: 403-267-2750; *Fax:* 403-267-2757
www.carewest.ca
Number of Beds: 221 beds

Calgary: **Carewest Sarcee**
Affiliated with: Alberta Health Services
3504 Scarcee Rd. SW, Calgary, AB T3E 4T4
Tel: 403-686-8100; *Fax:* 403-686-8104
www.carewest.ca

Calgary: **Clifton Manor**
Brenda Strafford Foundation Ltd.
Affiliated with: Alberta Health Services
Former Name: Forest Grove Care Centre
4726 - 8 Ave. SE, Calgary, AB T2A 0A8
Tel: 403-272-9831; *Fax:* 403-248-5788
www.straffordfoundation.org
Number of Beds: 258 beds
Brenda Hannah, Administrator
Brenda.Hannah@straffordfoundation.or

Calgary: **Extendicare - Cedars Villa**
Extendicare Canada
Affiliated with: Alberta Health Services
3330 - 8 Ave. SW, Calgary, AB T3C 0E7
Tel: 403-249-8915; *Fax:* 403-246-7561
cnh_cedarsvilla@extendicare.com
www.extendicarecanada.com/calgarycedarsvilla
Number of Beds: 248 beds
Lori Young, Administrator

Calgary: **Extendicare - Hillcrest**
Extendicare Canada
Affiliated with: Alberta Health Services
1512 - 8 Ave. NW, Calgary, AB T2N 1C1
Tel: 403-289-0236; *Fax:* 403-289-2350
cnh_hillcrest@extendicare.com
www.extendicarecanada.com/calgaryhillcrest
Number of Beds: 112 beds

Calgary: **Father Lacombe Care Centre**
Affiliated with: Alberta Health Services
270 Providence Blvd. SE, Calgary, AB T2X 0V6
Tel: 403-256-4641; *Fax:* 403-254-6297
info@flnh.net
www.flnh.net
Number of Beds: 110 beds
Raymond Cormie, Chief Executive Officer

Calgary: **Glamorgan Care Centre**
Affiliated with: Alberta Health Services
105 Galbraith Dr. S, Calgary, AB T3E 4Z5
Tel: 403-242-5911; *Fax:* 403-242-7613
www.albertahealthservices.ca
Number of Beds: 52 beds

Calgary: **Intercare - Southwood Care Centre**
Intercare Corporate Group Inc.
Affiliated with: Alberta Health Services
211 Heritage Dr. SE, Calgary, AB T2H 1M9
Tel: 403-252-1194; *Fax:* 403-253-0393
www.intercarealberta.com/southwood-care-centre.html
Number of Beds: Long term care: 183 private & semi-private rooms; Hospice: 24 private; Specialty Unit (Brain Injury): 23 private
Lydia Wright, Facility Leader

Calgary: **Wentworth Manor**
Brenda Strafford Foundation Ltd.
Affiliated with: Alberta Health Services
5717 - 14 Ave. SW, Calgary, AB T3H 3M2
Tel: 403-242-5005; *Fax:* 403-686-8702
www.straffordfoundation.org
Jenny Robinson, Administrator
Jenny.Robinson@straffordfoundation.o

Calgary: **Wing Kei Care Centre**
Chinese Christian Wing Kei Nursing Home Association
Affiliated with: Alberta Health Services
1212 Centre St. NE, Calgary, AB T2E 2R4
Tel: 403-277-7433; *Fax:* 403-230-3857
admin@wingkei.org
www.wingkeicarecentre.org
Year Founded: 2005
Number of Beds: 135 beds

Calgary: **Wing Kei Greenview**
Chinese Christian Wing Kei Nursing Home Association
Affiliated with: Alberta Health Services
307 - 35 Ave. NE, Calgary, AB T2E 2K6
Tel: 403-520-0400; *Fax:* 403-520-0418
admin@wingkei.org
www.wingkeicarecentre.org
Year Founded: 2014
Number of Beds: 95 beds

Camrose: **Bethany Meadows**
The Bethany Group
Affiliated with: Alberta Health Services
4209 - 55 St., Camrose, AB T4V 1Y6
Tel: 780-679-1001; *Fax:* 780-679-1020
www.thebethanygroup.ca
Number of Beds: 130 beds; 78 supportive housing

Derwent: **Northern Lights Manor**
Eagle Hill Foundation
102 - 1 St. West, Derwent, AB T0B 1C0
Tel: 780-657-2061; *Fax:* 780-657-0044
admin@eaglehillfoundation.com
www.eaglehillfoundation.ca/dervent_northern_lights.php
Adrienne Kuzio, Foundation Administrator

Drumheller: **Hillview Lodge**
Drumheller & District Seniors Foundation
Affiliated with: Alberta Health Services
696 - 6th Ave. East, Drumheller, AB T0J 0Y5
Tel: 403-823-3290; *Fax:* 403-823-3777
reception@ddsf.ca
www.ddsf.ca
Note: Supportive living
Janet Senior, Chief Administrative Officer

Drumheller: **Sunshine Lodge**
Drumheller & District Seniors Foundation
Affiliated with: Alberta Health Services
698 - 6th Ave. East, Drumheller, AB T0J 0Y5
Tel: 403-823-3290; *Fax:* 403-823-3777
reception@ddsf.ca
www.ddsf.ca
Note: Supportive living
Janet Senior, Chief Administrative Officer

Edmonton: **Extendicare - Holyrood**
Extendicare Canada
Affiliated with: Alberta Health Services
8008 - 95 Ave., Edmonton, AB T6C 2T1
Tel: 780-469-1307; *Fax:* 780-469-5196
cnh_holyrood@extendicare.com
www.extendicarecanada.com/edmontonholyrood

Edmonton: **Jubilee Lodge Nursing Home**
Qualicare Corporation
Affiliated with: Alberta Health Services
10333 - 76 St., Edmonton, AB T6A 3A8
Tel: 780-469-4456; *Fax:* 780-450-3297
officemanager@jubileelodgenursinghome.com
www.qualicarehealthservices.com/jubilee
Number of Beds: 156 beds

Fort MacLeod: **Extendicare - Fort Macleod**
Extendicare Canada
Affiliated with: Alberta Health Services
PO Box 189, 654 - 29 St., Fort MacLeod, AB T0L 0Z0
Tel: 403-553-3955; *Fax:* 403-553-2812
cnh_fortmacleod@extendicare.com
www.extendicare.com/fortmacleod
Number of Beds: 50 beds

Galahad: **Galahad Care Centre**
Affiliated with: Alberta Health Services
102 Lady Helen Ave., Galahad, AB T0B 1R0
Tel: 780-583-3788; *Fax:* 780-583-2105
www.albertahealthservices.ca
Note: Programs & services include: continuing care; respite care; & palliative care.

Grande Prairie: **Grande Prairie Care Centre**
Chantelle Management Ltd.
Affiliated with: Alberta Health Services
9705 - 94 Ave., Grande Prairie, AB T8V 3A2
Tel: 780-532-3525; *Fax:* 780-532-6504
grandeprairie@chantellegroup.com
www.chantellegroup.com/grande_prairie.htm
Number of Beds: 120 suites

Leduc: **Salem Manor Nursing Home**
Affiliated with: Alberta Health Services
4419 - 46 St., Leduc, AB T9E 6L2
Tel: 780-986-8654; *Fax:* 780-986-4130
www.albertahealthservices.ca

Lethbridge: **Alberta Rose Lodge**
Green Acres Foundation
2251 - 32 St. South, Lethbridge, AB T1K 4J9
Tel: 403-327-5745
www.greenacres.ab.ca/residence/alberta-rose
Number of Beds: 47 rooms
Note: Independent living; rooms for patients undergoing treatment at the Lethbridge Regional Hospital & the Jack Ady Cancer Treatment Centre.
Adrian Boe, Manager

Lethbridge: **Black Rock Terrace**
Green Acres Foundation
105 - 5th Ave. South, Lethbridge, AB T1J 0Z7
Tel: 403-328-3194
www.greenacres.ab.ca/residence/black-rock-terrace
Number of Beds: 121 rooms
Note: Independent living

Lethbridge: **Blue Sky Lodge**
Green Acres Foundation
1431 - 16 Ave. North, Lethbridge, AB T1H 4B9
Tel: 403-328-9422
www.greenacres.ab.ca/residence/blue-sky
Number of Beds: 81 rooms
Note: Independent living
Yamura Coteron, Manager

Lethbridge: **Columbia**
AgeCare
Affiliated with: Alberta Health Services
785 Columbia Blvd. West, Lethbridge, AB T1K 4T8
Tel: 403-320-9363; *Fax:* 403-327-9676
calreception@agecare.ca
www.agecare.ca/columbia
Number of Beds: 50 beds

Lethbridge: **Extendicare - Fairmont Park**
Extendicare Canada
Affiliated with: Alberta Health Services
115 Fairmont Blvd. South, Lethbridge, AB T1K 5V2
Tel: 403-320-0102; *Fax:* 403-327-0083
cnhfairmontpark@extendicare.com
www.extendicarecanada.com/fairmont_park
Number of Beds: 140 beds

Lethbridge: **Garden View Lodge**
Green Acres Foundation
751 - 1st Ave. South, Lethbridge, AB T1J 4N7
Tel: 403-327-3387
www.greenacres.ab.ca/residence/garden-view
Note: Independent living
Jackie Gray, Manager

Lethbridge: **Heritage Lodge**
Green Acres Foundation
601 - 6th St. South, Lethbridge, AB T1H 2E4
Tel: 403-327-1116
www.greenacres.ab.ca/residence/heritage-lodge
Number of Beds: 74 rooms
Note: Independent living
Pauline McCran, Manager

Lethbridge: **Martha's House**
Covenant Health
Affiliated with: Alberta Health Services
950 - 14th St. South, Lethbridge, AB T1J 2Y8
Tel: 403-327-7564; *Fax:* 403-327-3020
www.covenanthealth.ca/hospitals-care-centres/marthas-house

Lethbridge: **Pemmican Lodge West**
Green Acres Foundation
102 - 5th Ave. South, Lethbridge, AB T1J 0S9
Tel: 403-328-4127
www.greenacres.ab.ca/residence/pemmican-west-lodge
Number of Beds: 60 rooms
Note: Independent living
Roger Hacior, Manager

Mayerthorpe: **Extendicare - Mayerthorpe**
Extendicare Canada
Affiliated with: Alberta Health Services
PO Box 569, 4706 - 54 St., Mayerthorpe, AB T0E 1N0
Tel: 780-786-2211; *Fax:* 780-786-4710
cnh_mayerthorpe@extendicare.com
www.extendicarecanada.com/mayerthorpe
Number of Beds: 50 beds

Okotoks: **Tudor Manor**
Brenda Strafford Foundation Ltd.
Affiliated with: Alberta Health Services
200 Sandstone Dr., Okotoks, AB T1S 1R1
Tel: 403-995-9540
www.straffordfoundation.org
Year Founded: 2012
Number of Beds: 150 beds
Lesia Mullings, Administrator
Lesia.Mullings@straffordfoundation.o

Pincher Creek: **Vista Village**
Good Samaritan Society
Affiliated with: Alberta Health Services
1240 Ken Thornton Blvd., Pincher Creek, AB T0K 1W0
Tel: 403-627-1900; *Fax:* 403-627-3939
goodsaminfo@gss.org
www.gss.org
Number of Beds: 45 supportive living suites; 20 independent living suites; two 10-bed dementia care cottages; 10 enhanced care; 5 community support beds
Shawn Terlson, President & CEO, Good Samaritan Society
sterlson@gss.org

Red Deer: **Extendicare - Michener Hill**
Extendicare Canada
Affiliated with: Alberta Health Services
12 Michener Blvd., Red Deer, AB T4P 0M1
Tel: 403-348-0340; *Fax:* 403-348-5970
cnh_michenerhill@extendicare.com
www.extendicarecanada.com/michener
Number of Beds: 220 continuing care beds; 60 supportive living beds

Spruce Grove: **Spruce Grove Centre**
Good Samaritan Society
Affiliated with: Alberta Health Services
415 King St., Spruce Grove, AB T7X 3Y8
Tel: 780-962-3415; *Fax:* 780-962-3416
goodsaminfo@gss.org
www.gss.org
Number of Beds: 30 supportive living suites
Shawn Terlson, President & CEO, Good Samaritan Society
sterlson@gss.org

St Paul: **Extendicare - St. Paul**
Extendicare Canada
Affiliated with: Alberta Health Services
4614 - 47 Ave., St Paul, AB T0A 3A0
Tel: 780-645-3375; *Fax:* 780-645-4290
cnh_st.paul@extendicare.com
www.extendicarecanada.com/saintpaul
Number of Beds: 76 beds

Stony Plain: George Hennig Place
Good Samaritan Society
Affiliated with: Alberta Health Services
4808 - 57 Ave., Stony Plain, AB T7Z 2J9
Tel: 780-963-3403; *Fax:* 780-963-9808
goodsaminfo@gss.org
www.gss.org
Number of Beds: 30 supportive living suites
Shawn Terlson, President & CEO, Good Samaritan Society
sterlson@gss.org

Taber: Clearview Lodge
Taber & District Housing Foundation
4730 - 50th Ave., Taber, AB T1G 1N6
Tel: 780-223-2822; *Fax:* 866-283-1812
www.taberhsg.ca
Number of Beds: 20 beds
Joan Hart, Lodge Manager
JoanH@taberhsg.ca

Three Hills: Chateau Three Hills
inSite Housing, Hospitality & Health Services
Affiliated with: Alberta Health Services
920 Main St. East, Three Hills, AB T0M 2A0
Tel: 403-443-2121; *Fax:* 403-443-2151
c3hadmin@insiteseniorcare.com
www.insiteseniorcare.com
Angela Senneker, Community Manager
asenneker@insiteseniorcare.com

Two Hills: Eventide Homes
Eagle Hill Foundation
PO Box 279, 4801 - 53 Ave., Two Hills, AB T0B 4K0
Tel: 780-657-2061; *Fax:* 780-657-0044
admin@eaglehillfoundation.com
www.eaglehillfoundation.ca/two_hills_eventide.php
Adrienne Kuzio, Foundation Administrator

Viking: Extendicare - Viking
Extendicare Canada
Affiliated with: Alberta Health Services
PO Box 430, 5020 - 57 Ave., Viking, AB T0B 4N0
Tel: 780-336-4790; *Fax:* 780-336-4004
cnh_viking@extendicare.com
extendicarecanada.com/viking
Number of Beds: 60 beds

Vulcan: Extendicare - Vulcan
Extendicare Canada
Affiliated with: Alberta Health Services
PO Box 810, 715 - 2nd Ave. South, Vulcan, AB T0L 2B0
Tel: 403-485-2022; *Fax:* 403-485-2879
cnh_vulcan@extendicare.com
www.extendicarecanada.com/vulcan
Number of Beds: 46 beds

Retirement Residences

Airdrie: Luxstone Manor Seniors' Residence
Integrated Life Care Inc.
Affiliated with: Alberta Health Services
2014 Luxstone Blvd., Airdrie, AB T4B 0L6
Tel: 403-945-4700; *Fax:* 403-945-4701
Toll-Free: 888-948-0544
info@luxstonemanor.ca
www.luxstonemanor.ca
Social Media: twitter.com/luxstonemanor
Year Founded: 2009

Calgary: Carewest Colonel Belcher
Affiliated with: Alberta Health Services
1939 Veterans Way NW, Calgary, AB T3B 5Y8
Tel: 403-944-7800; *Fax:* 403-944-7870
www.carewest.ca
Year Founded: 2003
Number of Beds: 175 residents in seniors' residence, most of whom are veterans

Devon: Discovery Place
Integrated Life Care Inc.
Affiliated with: Alberta Health Services
2 Highwood Blvd., Devon, AB T9G 2G2
Tel: 780-987-6500; *Fax:* 780-987-6502
info@discoveryplace.ca
www.discoveryplace.ca
Note: Assisted living

Drayton Valley: Sunrise Village Drayton Valley
Continuum Health Care Holdings Ltd.
Affiliated with: Alberta Health Services
3902 - 47 St., Drayton Valley, AB T7A 0A2
Tel: 780-542-5572; *Fax:* 780-542-5548
www.sunrisevillages.com
Number of Beds: 68 suites
Shirley Block, Site Administrator
pmahan@sunrisevillages.com

Edmonton: Good Samaritan Place
Good Samaritan Society
Affiliated with: Alberta Health Services
8425 - 83 St., Edmonton, AB T6C 2Z2
Tel: 780-413-3500; *Fax:* 780-989-3290
goodsaminfo@gss.org
www.gss.org
Number of Beds: 40 apartments
Shawn Terlson, President & CEO, Good Samaritan Society
sterlson@gss.org

Lethbridge: Sunrise Village Lethbridge
Continuum Health Care Holdings Ltd.
Affiliated with: Alberta Health Services
1730 - 10th Ave. South, Lethbridge, AB T1K 0B5
Tel: 403-320-2270; *Fax:* 403-331-2402
sunrisevillageleth@telus.net
www.sunrisevillages.com
Number of Beds: 58 suites
Sharon Annas, Site Administrator

Red Deer: Parkvale Lodge
Piper Creek Foundation
Affiliated with: Alberta Health Services
4277 - 46A Ave., Red Deer, AB T4N 6T6
Tel: 403-343-0688
www.pipercreek.ca
Number of Beds: 61 rooms; 4 couples' suites
Lisa Manning-Eaton, Manager

Red Deer: Piper Creek Lodge
Piper Creek Foundation
Affiliated with: Alberta Health Services
4820 - 33 St., Red Deer, AB T4N 0N5
Tel: 403-343-1066
www.pipercreek.ca
Number of Beds: 65 rooms

Wetaskiwin: Northtown Village
Good Samaritan Society
Affiliated with: Alberta Health Services
4710 Northmount Dr., Wetaskiwin, AB T9A 3P6
Tel: 780-352-6671
goodsaminfo@gss.org
www.gss.org
Note: Life lease retirement community
Shawn Terlson, President & CEO, Good Samaritan Society
sterlson@gss.org

Personal Care Homes

Airdrie: Arbor Manor
Bethany Care Society
Affiliated with: Alberta Health Services
1736 - 1st Ave. NW, Airdrie, AB T4B 2C4
Tel: 403-948-6022; *Fax:* 403-948-3897
info@bethanyseniors.com
www.bethanyseniors.com
Social Media: www.facebook.com/bethanyseniors; twitter.com/BethanyCare; www.youtube.com/user/BethanyCareSociety; www.linkedin.com/company/88398
Number of Beds: 52 supportive living suites
Note: Located inside Bethany Airdrie
Jennifer McCue, President & CEO, Bethany Care Society

Barrhead: Shepherd's Care - Barrhead
Shepherd's Care Foundation
Affiliated with: Alberta Health Services
5236 - 59 Ave., Barrhead, AB T7N 0A3
Tel: 780-674-4249; *Fax:* 780-674-4204
www.shepherdscare.org/barrhead.php
Year Founded: 2007
Number of Beds: 43 units

Brooks: Sunrise Gardens
AgeCare
Affiliated with: Alberta Health Services
1235 - 3rd St. West, Brooks, AB T1R 0P7
Tel: 403-794-2105
sgreception@agecare.ca
www.agecare.ca/sunrise-gardens

Calgary: Evanston Grand Village
Golden Life Management
40 Evanston Way NW, Calgary, AB T3P 0B1
Tel: 403-274-6416
goldenlifemanagement.ca
Number of Beds: 1300 residents
Note: Independent & assisted living

Calgary: Hillside Manor
Bethany Care Society
Affiliated with: Alberta Health Services
916 - 18A St. NW, Calgary, AB T2N 1C6
Tel: 403-284-6000; *Fax:* 403-284-6085
info@bethanyseniors.com
www.bethanyseniors.com
Social Media: www.facebook.com/bethanyseniors; twitter.com/BethanyCare; www.youtube.com/user/BethanyCareSociety; www.linkedin.com/company/88398
Number of Beds: 19 supportive living suites
Note: Located inside Bethany Calgary
Jennifer McCue, President & CEO, Bethany Care Society

Calgary: Walden Heights
AgeCare
Affiliated with: Alberta Health Services
250 Walden Heights Dr. SE, Calgary, AB T2X 0M7
Tel: 403-873-4700
walden@agecare.ca
www.agecare.ca/walden-heights

Camrose: Faith House
The Bethany Group
Affiliated with: Alberta Health Services
4832 - 54 St., Camrose, AB T4V 2A4
Tel: 780-679-5427
www.thebethanygroup.ca

Camrose: Sunrise Village Camrose
Continuum Health Care Holdings Ltd.
Affiliated with: Alberta Health Services
6821 - 50 Ave., Camrose, AB T4V 5G5
Tel: 780-672-2746; *Fax:* 780-672-2985
www.sunrisevillages.com
Number of Beds: 59 private suites; 82 supportive living suites
Nicole Almost, Site Administrator
nalmost@sunrisevillages.com

Cardston: Lee Crest
Good Samaritan Society
Affiliated with: Alberta Health Services
989 - 1st St. East, Cardston, AB T0K 0K0
Tel: 403-653-2034; *Fax:* 403-653-1103
goodsaminfo@gss.org
www.gss.org
Number of Beds: 95 supportive living suites; 5 community support beds
Shawn Terlson, President & CEO, Good Samaritan Society
sterlson@gss.org

Coaldale: Sunny South Lodge
Green Acres Foundation
1122 - 20 Ave., Coaldale, AB T1M 1L4
Tel: 403-345-5955
www.greenacres.ab.ca/residence/sunny-south
Number of Beds: 88 rooms (13 supportive living)
Note: Independent living & enhanced care options
Glen Herbst, Manager

Cochrane: Quigley Manor
Bethany Care Society
Affiliated with: Alberta Health Services
302 Quigley Dr., Cochrane, AB T4C 1M2
Tel: 403-932-6422; *Fax:* 403-932-4617
info@bethanyseniors.com
www.bethanyseniors.com
Social Media: www.facebook.com/bethanyseniors; twitter.com/BethanyCare; www.youtube.com/user/BethanyCareSociety; www.linkedin.com/company/88398
Jennifer McCue, President & CEO, Bethany Care Society

Cold Lake: Points West Living Cold Lake
Affiliated with: Alberta Health Services
512 - 25 St., Cold Lake, AB T9M 1G6
Tel: 780-639-1260; *Fax:* 780-639-0834
reception.coldlake@pointswestliving.com
pointswestliving.com/cold_lake_home.php
Number of Beds: 52 supportive living units

Daysland: **Providence Place**
Affiliated with: Alberta Health Services
6120 - 51 Ave., Daysland, AB T0B 1A0
Tel: 780-374-2527; *Fax:* 780-374-2529
www.albertahealthservices.ca

Drayton Valley: **Serenity House**
Affiliated with: Alberta Health Services
4552 Madsen Ave., Drayton Valley, AB T7A 1T2
Tel: 780-542-3610
www.albertahealthservices.ca

Eckville: **Eckville Manor House**
Lacombe Foundation
Affiliated with: Alberta Health Services
5111 - 51 Ave., Eckville, AB T0M 0X0
Tel: 403-746-2661; *Fax:* 403-746-3903
lacombe.foundation@bethanygrp.ca
www.lacombefoundation.ca

Edmonton: **Laurier House Lynnwood**
CapitalCare
Affiliated with: Alberta Health Services
16815 - 88 Ave., Edmonton, AB T5R 5Y7
Tel: 780-413-4712; *Fax:* 780-413-4736
www.capitalcare.net/centres/lh_lynnwood.html
Social Media: www.facebook.com/capitalcare.edmonton; twitter.com/CapitalCareYEG
Year Founded: 1997
Number of Beds: 80 beds
Note: Life-lease supportive care living
Iris Neumann, Chief Operating Officer, CapitalCare

Edmonton: **Shepherd's Care - Greenfield**
Shepherd's Care Foundation
Affiliated with: Alberta Health Services
3820 - 114 St., Edmonton, AB T6J 1M5
Tel: 780-430-3613; *Fax:* 780-430-0833
www.shepherdscare.org/greenfield.php
Number of Beds: 30 beds

Edmonton: **Shepherd's Care - Southside Manor**
Shepherd's Care Foundation
Affiliated with: Alberta Health Services
10745 - 29 Ave., Edmonton, AB T6J 5H6
Tel: 780-435-3169; *Fax:* 780-435-3169
www.shepherdscare.org/southside-manor.php

Edmonton: **Shepherd's Care - Vanguard**
Shepherd's Care Foundation
Affiliated with: Alberta Health Services
10311 - 122 Ave., Edmonton, AB T5G 0K8
Tel: 780-474-1798
www.shepherdscare.org/vanguard.php
Year Founded: 2011
Number of Beds: 115 units

Edmonton: **The Waterford of Summerlea**
Chantelle Management Ltd.
Affiliated with: Alberta Health Services
9395 - 172 St., Edmonton, AB T5T 5S6
Tel: 780-444-4545; *Fax:* 780-487-8443
waterford@chantellegroup.com
www.thewaterford.ca

Edmonton: **Wedman House & Village**
Good Samaritan Society
Affiliated with: Alberta Health Services
10525 - 19 Ave. NW, Edmonton, AB T6J 6X9
Tel: 780-413-3520; *Fax:* 780-435-8435
goodsaminfo@gss.org
www.gss.org
Number of Beds: 30 supportive living suites; 3 dementia care cottages
Shawn Terlson, President & CEO, Good Samaritan Society
sterlson@gss.org

High River: **Sunrise Village High River**
Continuum Health Care Holdings Ltd.
Affiliated with: Alberta Health Services
660 - 7th St., High River, AB T1V 1S7
Tel: 403-652-1581; *Fax:* 403-652-2287
www.sunrisevillages.com
Number of Beds: 68 private suites; 108 supportive living suites
Trisha Prosser, Site Administrator
tprosser@sunrisevillages.com

Hinton: **Mountain View Centre**
Good Samaritan Society
Affiliated with: Alberta Health Services
1290 Switzer Dr., Hinton, AB T7V 2E9
Tel: 780-865-5926; *Fax:* 780-865-4098
goodsaminfo@gss.org
www.gss.org
Number of Beds: 37 supportive living suites; 10 bed dementia care cottage
Shawn Terlson, President & CEO, Good Samaritan Society
sterlson@gss.org

Innisfail: **Sunset Manor**
Chantelle Management Ltd.
Affiliated with: Alberta Health Services
3312 - 52 Ave., Innisfail, AB T4G 0C3
Tel: 403-227-8200; *Fax:* 403-227-8201
innisfail@chantellegroup.com
www.chantellegroup.com/sunset_manor.htm
Number of Beds: 102 supportive living suites

Lacombe: **Royal Oak Manor**
Good Samaritan Society
Affiliated with: Alberta Health Services
4501 College Ave., Lacombe, AB T4L 2M8
Tel: 403-782-4435; *Fax:* 403-782-9735
goodsaminfo@gss.org
www.gss.org
Number of Beds: 23 supportive living suites; 50 life lease apartments
Shawn Terlson, President & CEO, Good Samaritan Society
sterlson@gss.org

Lethbridge: **Golden Acres Lodge**
Green Acres Foundation
1615 - 13th St. North, Lethbridge, AB T1H 2V2
Tel: 403-328-5111
www.greenacres.ab.ca/residence/golden-acres
Number of Beds: 45 beds
Note: Independent living & enhanced care options
Yumara Coteron, Manager

Lethbridge: **Park Meadows**
Good Samaritan Society
Affiliated with: Alberta Health Services
1511 - 15 Ave. North, Lethbridge, AB T1H 1W2
Tel: 403-328-9404; *Fax:* 403-328-8208
goodsaminfo@gss.org
www.gss.org
Number of Beds: 40 supportive living suites; four 10-bed dementia care cottages; three 12-bed dementia care cottages; 5 community support beds
Shawn Terlson, President & CEO, Good Samaritan Society
sterlson@gss.org

Lethbridge: **St. Therese Villa**
Covenant Health
Affiliated with: Alberta Health Services
253 Southgate Blvd. South, Lethbridge, AB T1K 2S1
Tel: 403-332-5300
www.covenanthealth.ca/hospitals-care-centres/st-therese-villa
Number of Beds: 124 private studio suites; 16 couple suites; 60 secure dementia suites
Note: Supportive living facility

Lethbridge: **West Highland Centre & Estates**
Good Samaritan Society
Affiliated with: Alberta Health Services
2867 Gary Dr. West, Lethbridge, AB T1J 5A3
Tel: 403-380-6275; *Fax:* 403-380-6732
goodsaminfo@gss.org
www.gss.org
Number of Beds: 90 supportive living suites; 49 independent living apartments; 10 bed dementia care cottage
Shawn Terlson, President & CEO, Good Samaritan Society
sterlson@gss.org

Linden: **Westview Care Community**
Affiliated with: Alberta Health Services
Former Name: Linden Nursing Home
PO Box 220, 700 Nursing Home Rd., Linden, AB T0M 1J0
Tel: 403-546-3966; *Fax:* 403-546-4061
lindennursinghome.ca
Number of Beds: 37 beds; 18 supportive living suites

Lloydminster: **Points West Living Lloydminster**
Affiliated with: Alberta Health Services
4025 - 56 Ave., Lloydminster, AB T9V 1N9
Tel: 780-874-4300; *Fax:* 780-874-9199
reception.lloydminster@pointswestliving.com
pointswestliving.com/lloydminster_home.php

Number of Beds: 55 studios; 5 couples suites; 5 cottages with 12 one-bedroom suites

Magrath: **Garden Vista**
Good Samaritan Society
Affiliated with: Alberta Health Services
37 East & 2nd Ave. North, Magrath, AB T0K 1J0
Tel: 403-758-6149; *Fax:* 403-758-6053
goodsaminfo@gss.org
www.gss.org
Number of Beds: 22 supportive living suites; 10-bed dementia care cottage; 3 community support beds
Shawn Terlson, President & CEO, Good Samaritan Society
sterlson@gss.org

Medicine Hat: **St. Joseph's Home**
Covenant Health
Affiliated with: Alberta Health Services
156 - 3rd St. NE, Medicine Hat, AB T1A 5M1
Tel: 403-526-3818; *Fax:* 403-528-8942
www.covenanthealth.ca/hospitals-care-centres/st-therese-villa
Year Founded: 1951
Note: Assisted living program

Medicine Hat: **Valleyview**
AgeCare
Affiliated with: Alberta Health Services
65 Valleyview Dr., Medicine Hat, AB T1A 7K5
Tel: 403-526-7000
valleyview@agecare.ca
www.agecare.ca/valleyview

Medicine Hat: **The Wellington**
Park Place Seniors Living
Affiliated with: Alberta Health Services
1595 Southview Dr. SE, Medicine Hat, AB T1B 0A1
Tel: 403-526-5762; *Fax:* 403-526-9479
mlmccrodan@parkplaceseniorsliving.com
www.thewellingtonmh.com
Year Founded: 2005

Myrname: **Eagle View Lodge**
Eagle Hill Foundation
Affiliated with: Alberta Health Services
PO Box 280, 4802 - 49 Ave., Myrname, AB T0B 3K0
Tel: 780-366-3750; *Fax:* 780-366-2297
info.eagleview@eaglehillfoundation.com
www.eaglehillfoundation.ca/myrnam_eagle_view.php
Sandra Charchun, Lodge Supervisor

Olds: **Sunrise Encore Olds**
Continuum Health Care Holdings Ltd.
Affiliated with: Alberta Health Services
3300 - 57 Ave., Olds, AB T4H 1C4
Tel: 403-556-2232
www.sunrisevillages.com
Number of Beds: 47 private suites; 60 supportive living suites
Angela Arp, Site Administrator
aarp@sunrisevillages.com

Olds: **Sunrise Village Olds**
Continuum Health Care Holdings Ltd.
Affiliated with: Alberta Health Services
5600 Sunrise Cres., Olds, AB T4H 1W4
Tel: 403-556-3446; *Fax:* 403-556-3475
www.sunrisevillages.com
Number of Beds: 40 supportive living suites
Lisa Woodworth, Site Administrator
lisa.woodworth@airenet.com

Peace River: **Points West Living Peace River**
Affiliated with: Alberta Health Services
11011 - 99 St., Peace River, AB T8S 1B3
Tel: 780-624-0700; *Fax:* 780-624-0701
reception.peaceriver@pointswestliving.com
pointswestliving.com/peaceriver_home.php
Number of Beds: 53 supportive living units

Picture Butte: **Piyami Lodge**
Green Acres Foundation
301 Rogers Ave., Picture Butte, AB T0K 1V0
Tel: 403-732-4811; *Fax:* 403-732-4580
www.greenacres.ab.ca/residence/piyami-lodge
Number of Beds: 32 rooms
Note: Independent living & enhanced care options
Brenda McDonald, Manager

Pincher Creek: **Whispering Winds Village**
Golden Life Management
PO Box 579, 941 Elizabeth St., Pincher Creek, AB T0K 1W0
Tel: 403-627-1997
wwvmanager@glm.ca
goldenlifemanagement.ca

Note: Independent & assisted living
Eileen Woolf, Community Manager
ewoolf@glm.ca

Ponoka: Sunrise Village Ponoka
Continuum Health Care Holdings Ltd.
Affiliated with: Alberta Health Services
4004 - 40 St., Ponoka, AB T4J 0A3
Tel: 403-783-3373; *Fax:* 403-783-3324
www.sunrisevillages.com
Number of Beds: 68 suites (20 designated supportive living)
Loretta Nickerson, Site Administrator
lnickerson@sunrisevillages.com

Red Deer: Pines Lodge
Piper Creek Foundation
Affiliated with: Alberta Health Services
52 Pipe Dr., Red Deer, AB T4P 1H8
Tel: 403-343-0656; *Fax:* 403-343-7789
www.pipercreek.ca
Number of Beds: 64 rooms; 20 supportive living suites; 1 couples' suite
Thea Mawbey, Manager

Red Deer: West Park Lodge
Affiliated with: Alberta Health Services
5715 - 41 St. Crescent, Red Deer, AB T4N 1B3
Tel: 403-343-7471; *Fax:* 403-343-3424
info@westparklodge.com
www.westparklodge.com
Year Founded: 1996
Number of Beds: 36 suites

Sherwood Park: Laurier House Strathcona
CapitalCare
Affiliated with: Alberta Health Services
12 Brower Dr., Sherwood Park, AB T8V 1V3
Tel: 780-467-3366; *Fax:* 780-417-4350
www.capitalcare.net/centres/lh_strathcona.html
Social Media: www.facebook.com/capitalcare.edmonton; twitter.com/CapitalCareYEG
Year Founded: 2001
Number of Beds: 42 beds
Note: Life-lease supportive care living
Iris Neumann, Chief Operating Officer, CapitalCare

Stettler: Points West Living Stettler
Affiliated with: Alberta Health Services
4501 - 70 St., Stettler, AB T0C 2L3
Tel: 403-740-7700; *Fax:* 403-742-1514
reception.stettler@pointswestliving.com
pointswestliving.com/stettler_home.php
Number of Beds: 104 supportive living units

Strathmore: Sagewood
AgeCare
Affiliated with: Alberta Health Services
140 Cambridge Glen Dr., Strathmore, AB T1P 0E2
Tel: 403-361-8000
swreception@agecare.ca
www.agecare.ca/sagewood

Taber: Linden View
Good Samaritan Society
Affiliated with: Alberta Health Services
4700 - 64 Ave., Taber, AB T1G 0C6
Tel: 403-223-3341; *Fax:* 403-223-2360
goodsaminfo@gss.org
www.gss.org
Number of Beds: 64 supportive living suites; three 12-bed dementia care cottages; 5 community support beds
Shawn Terlson, President & CEO, Good Samaritan Society
sterlson@gss.org

Two Hills: Hillside Lodge
Eagle Hill Foundation
PO Box 279, 4801 - 53 Ave., Two Hills, AB T0B 4K0
Tel: 780-657-2061; *Fax:* 780-657-0044
info.hillside@eaglehillfoundation.com
www.eaglehillfoundation.ca/two_hills_hillside.php
Nancy Lawrence, Site Supervisor

Vegreville: Points West Heritage House
Affiliated with: Alberta Health Services
4570 Maple St., Vegreville, AB T9C 1X2
Tel: 780-603-0853; *Fax:* 780-603-2237
reception.heritagehouse@pointswestliving.com
pointswestliving.com/heritage_house_home.php

Vegreville: Points West Living Century Park
Affiliated with: Alberta Health Services
4613 - 50 St., Vegreville, AB T9C 1L7
Tel: 780-632-3042; *Fax:* 780-632-2732
reception.centurypark@pointswestliving.com
pointswestliving.com/vegreville_home.php
Number of Beds: 40 supportive living spaces; 40 apartments

Vermilion: Vermilion - Valley Lodge
Affiliated with: Alberta Health Services
4610 - 53 Ave., Vermilion, AB T9X 1G6
Tel: 780-853-5706; *Fax:* 780-853-1951
www.albertahealthservices.ca

Vilna: Vilna Lodge
Affiliated with: Alberta Health Services
5404 - 50 St., Vilna, AB T0A 3L0
Tel: 780-636-3545; *Fax:* 780-636-3555
www.albertahealthservices.ca

Wainwright: Points West Living Wainwright
Affiliated with: Alberta Health Services
2710 - 11th Ave., Wainwright, AB T9W 0B1
Tel: 780-845-2080; *Fax:* 780-845-2090
reception.wainwright@pointswestliving.com
pointswestliving.com/wainwright_home.php
Number of Beds: 59 supportive living spaces; 16 rental suites; 16 life lease apartments

Wetaskiwin: Good Shepherd Home
Good Samaritan Society
Affiliated with: Alberta Health Services
4702 Northmount Dr., Wetaskiwin, AB T9A 3T3
Tel: 403-353-3628; *Fax:* 403-352-3379
goodsaminfo@gss.org
www.gss.org
Number of Beds: 68 supportive living suites; 1 community support bed
Shawn Terlson, President & CEO, Good Samaritan Society
sterlson@gss.org

Wetaskiwin: Sunrise Village Wetaskiwin
Continuum Health Care Holdings Ltd.
Affiliated with: Alberta Health Services
5430 - 37A Ave., Wetaskiwin, AB T9A 3A8
Tel: 780-352-4725; *Fax:* 780-361-1970
www.sunrisevillages.com
Number of Beds: 92 suites (20 designated supportive living)
Nicole Almost, Site Administrator
svwetadm@telus.net

Willingdon: Eagle Hill Lodge
Eagle Hill Foundation
Affiliated with: Alberta Health Services
PO Box 387, 5303 - 49 St., Willingdon, AB T0B 4R0
Tel: 780-367-2717; *Fax:* 780-367-2717
info.eaglehill@eaglehillfoundation.com
www.eaglehillfoundation.ca/willingdon_eagle_hill.php
Delores Wiward, Supervisor

Mental Health Hospitals/Facilities

Airdrie: Airdrie - 209 Centre Avenue West
Affiliated with: Alberta Health Services
#100, 209 Centre Ave. West, Airdrie, AB T4B 3L8
Tel: 403-948-8553; *Fax:* 403-912-3307
Toll-Free: 866-332-2322
www.albertahealthservices.ca

Airdrie: Airdrie Provincial Building
Affiliated with: Alberta Health Services
Former Name: Airdrie Mental Health Clinic
104 - 1 Ave. NW, Airdrie, AB T4B 0R2
Tel: 403-948-3878; *Fax:* 403-948-7926
Toll-Free: 877-652-4700
www.albertahealthservices.ca

Athabasca: Athabasca Community Health Services
Affiliated with: Alberta Health Services
3401 - 48 Ave., Athabasca, AB T9S 1M7
Tel: 780-675-5404; *Fax:* 780-675-3994
www.albertahealthservices.ca

Banff: Banff - Mineral Springs Hospital
Affiliated with: Banff Community Health Centre
305 Lynx St., Banff, AB T1L 1B3
Tel: 403-762-4451; *Fax:* 403-762-5570
www.albertahealthservices.ca
Note: Mental health urgent care

Barrhead: Barrhead Healthcare Centre
Affiliated with: Alberta Health Services
PO Box 4504, 4815 - 51 Ave., Barrhead, AB T7N 1M1
Tel: 780-674-8243; *Fax:* 780-674-8352
www.albertahealthservices.ca

Black Diamond: Black Diamond Public Health Unit at Oilfields General Hospital
Affiliated with: Alberta Health Services
717 Government Road, Black Diamond, AB T0L 0H0
Tel: 403-933-3800; *Fax:* 403-933-4353
Toll-Free: 877-652-4700
www.albertahealthservices.ca

Blairmore: Crowsnest Pass Provincial Building
Affiliated with: Alberta Health Services
12501 - 20 Ave., Blairmore, AB T0K 0E0
Tel: 403-562-3222
www.albertahealthservices.ca

Bon Accord: Oak Hills Boys Ranch
PO Box 97, Bon Accord, AB T0A 0K0
Tel: 403-921-2121; *Fax:* 403-921-2379
www.oakhillboysranch.ca
Number of Beds: 32 beds
Note: Residential treatment facility for young males (11-16) suffering from issues such as mental health & substance abuse.

Bonnyville: Bonnyville New Park Place
Affiliated with: Alberta Health Services
Bonnyville Remax Building, 5201 - 44 St., Bonnyville, AB T9N 2H4
Tel: 780-826-2404; *Fax:* 780-826-6114
www.albertahealthservices.ca

Bow Island: Bow Island Provincial Building
Affiliated with: Alberta Health Services
Former Name: Bow Island Mental Health Clinic
802 - 6 St., Bow Island, AB T0K 0G0
Tel: 403-529-3500; *Fax:* 403-529-3562
www.albertahealthservices.ca

Brooks: Brooks Community Mental Health Clinic
Affiliated with: Alberta Health Services
440 - 3rd St. East, Brooks, AB T1R 1C5
Tel: 403-793-6655; *Fax:* 403-795-6656
www.albertahealthservices.ca

Calgary: Arnika Centre
Affiliated with: Alberta Health Services
3465 - 26 Ave. NE, Calgary, AB T1Y 6L4
Tel: 403-943-8301; *Fax:* 403-943-8367
www.albertahealthservices.ca
Note: Psychiatric assessment for people 16 years & older

Calgary: Bridgeland Seniors Health Centre
Affiliated with: Alberta Health Services
1070 Mcdougall Rd. NE, Calgary, AB T2E 7Z2
Tel: 403-955-1500; *Fax:* 403-955-1564
www.albertahealthservices.ca

Calgary: Calgary - 316-7 Avenue SE
Affiliated with: Alberta Health Services
316 - 7 Ave. SE, Calgary, AB T2G 0J2
www.albertahealthservices.ca

Calgary: Carewest Operational Stress Injury Clinic
Affiliated with: Alberta Health Services
Also Known As: Carewest OSI Clinic
Market Mall, 3625 Shaganappi Trail NW, Calgary, AB T3A 0E2
Tel: 403-216-9860; *Fax:* 403-216-9861
www.carewest.ca
Note: Provides programs & services to deal with mental health problems caused by shock or stress for veterans, Canadian Forces members, RCMP members & their families.

Calgary: Distress Centre Calgary (DCC)
Affiliated with: Alberta Health Services
#300, 1010 - 8th Ave. SW, Calgary, AB T2P 1J2
Tel: 403-266-1601
info@distresscentre.com
www.distresscentre.com
Info Line: 403-266-4357
Social Media: www.facebook.com/distresscentre; twitter.com/Distress_Centre; www.youtube.com/user/DistressCentreYYC
Joan Roy, Executive Director

Calgary: East Calgary Health Centre
Affiliated with: Alberta Health Services
4715 - 8 Ave. SE, Calgary, AB T2A 3N4
Tel: 403-955-1161; *Fax:* 403-955-1013
www.albertahealthservices.ca
Note: Perinatal mental health; child & adolescent addiction & mental health

Calgary: Northeast Calgary Mental Health Clinic
Affiliated with: Alberta Health Services
Sunridge Mall, 2580 - 32 St. NE, Calgary, AB T1Y 7M8
Tel: 403-944-9700
www.albertahealthservices.ca

Calgary: Northwest Community Mental Health Centre
Affiliated with: Alberta Health Services
Former Name: Foothills Professional Building
#280, 1620 - 29th St. NW, Calgary, AB T2N 4L7
Tel: 403-297-7345; *Fax:* 403-297-4543
www.albertahealthservices.ca

Calgary: Society for Treatment of Autism (STA)
404 - 94 Ave. SE, Calgary, AB T2J 0E8
Tel: 403-253-2291; *Fax:* 403-253-6974
Toll-Free: 888-301-2872
autismtreatment@sta-ab.com
www.autism.ca
Number of Beds: 20 beds
Note: Programs & services for people with Autism & other Pervasive Developmental Disorders
Dave Mikkelsen, Executive Director

Calgary: South Calgary Health Centre
Affiliated with: Alberta Health Services
31 Sunpark Plaza SE, 2nd Fl., Calgary, AB T2X 3W5
Tel: 403-943-9374
www.albertahealthservices.ca

Calgary: Sunridge Professional Building
Affiliated with: Alberta Health Services
#5, 2675 - 36 St. NE, Calgary, AB T1Y 6H6
Tel: 403-297-7701
www.albertahealthservices.ca
Note: Mental health forensic adolescent program

Calgary: Wood's Homes - Bowness Campus
Affiliated with: Alberta Health Services
9400 - 48 Ave. NW, Calgary, AB T3B 2B2
Tel: 403-247-6751; *Fax:* 403-268-0878
askus@woodshomes.ca
www.woodshomes.ca
Social Media: www.facebook.com/woodshomesnfp; twitter.com/ChildMntlHealth; www.youtube.com/user/WoodsHomes1; www.linkedin.com/company/wood%27s-homes
Number of Beds: 110 beds

Calgary: Wood's Homes - Parkdale Campus
Affiliated with: Alberta Health Services
805 - 37 St. NW, Calgary, AB T2N 4N8
Tel: 403-270-4102; *Fax:* 403-283-9735
askus@woodshomes.ca
www.woodshomes.ca
Social Media: www.facebook.com/woodshomesnfp; twitter.com/ChildMntlHealth; www.youtube.com/user/WoodsHomes1; www.linkedin.com/company/wood%27s-homes
Number of Beds: 150 beds
Population Served: 20,000; *Number of Employees:* 350
Note: Day treatment, educational, outreach services; longterm care: permanent care (child welfare services) residential; treatment centre for adolescents & families; services for street youth; educational/day treatment services; & caregiver services.
Dr. Jane Matheson, CEO

Camrose: Camrose Addiction & Mental Health Clinic
Affiliated with: Alberta Health Services
4911 - 47 St., Camrose, AB T4V 1J9
Tel: 780-679-1241; *Fax:* 780-679-1740
www.albertahealthservices.ca

Canmore: Canmore Provincial Building
Affiliated with: Alberta Health Services
800 Railway Ave., Canmore, AB T1W 1P1
Tel: 403-678-4696; *Fax:* 403-678-1951
www.albertahealthservices.ca

Cardston: Cardston Community Mental Health Clinic
Affiliated with: Alberta Health Services
576 Main St., Cardston, AB T0K 0K0
Tel: 403-653-5115; *Fax:* 403-653-2926
www.albertahealthservices.ca

Chestermere: Chestermere Health Centre
Affiliated with: Alberta Health Services
124 East Chestermere Dr., Chestermere, AB T1X 1M1
Tel: 403-207-8773; *Fax:* 403-944-2224
www.albertahealthservices.ca

Claresholm: Claresholm Centre for Mental Health & Addictions
Affiliated with: Alberta Health Services
PO Box 490, 139 - 43 Ave. West, Claresholm, AB T0L 0T0
Tel: 403-682-3500; *Fax:* 403-625-4318
claresholmcentre@albertahealthservices.ca
claresholmcentre.com
Year Founded: 1933
Number of Beds: 120 beds

Claresholm: Claresholm Mental Health Clinic
Affiliated with: Alberta Health Services
4901 - 2nd St. West, Claresholm, AB T0L 0T0
Tel: 403-625-4068; *Fax:* 403-625-4177
www.albertahealthservices.ca

Cochrane: Cochrane Addiction & Mental Health Clinic
Affiliated with: Alberta Health Services
60 Grande Blvd., Cochrane, AB T4C 0S4
Tel: 403-851-6100; *Fax:* 403-851-6101
www.albertahealthservices.ca

Cold Lake: Cold Lake Healthcare Centre
Affiliated with: Alberta Health Services
#208, 314 - 25 St., Cold Lake, AB T9M 1G6
Tel: 780-639-4922; *Fax:* 780-639-4990
www.albertahealthservices.ca

Consort: Consort Community Health Centre
Affiliated with: Alberta Health Services
5410 - 52 Ave., Consort, AB T0C 1B0
Tel: 403-577-3770; *Fax:* 403-577-2235
www.albertahealthservices.ca

Didsbury: Didsbury District Health Services
Affiliated with: Alberta Health Services
1210 - 20 Ave., Didsbury, AB T0M 0W0
Tel: 403-335-7285
www.albertahealthservices.ca

Drayton Valley: Drayton Valley Mental Health Clinic
Affiliated with: Alberta Health Services
4110 - 50 Ave., Drayton Valley, AB T7A 0B3
Tel: 780-542-3140; *Fax:* 780-542-4461
www.albertahealthservices.ca

Drumheller: Drumheller Health Centre
Affiliated with: Alberta Health Services
351 - 9 St. NW, Drumheller, AB T0J 0Y1
Tel: 403-820-7863; *Fax:* 403-820-7865
www.albertahealthservices.ca

Edmonton: 108 Street Building
Affiliated with: Alberta Health Services
9942 - 108th St. NW, Edmonton, AB T5K 2J5
Tel: 780-342-7700; *Fax:* 780-342-7602
www.albertahealthservices.ca

Edmonton: Addiction Services Edmonton
Affiliated with: Alberta Health Services
10010 - 102A Ave. NW, Edmonton, AB T5J 0G5
Tel: 780-427-2736; *Fax:* 780-427-4180
Toll-Free: 866-332-2322
www.albertahealthservices.ca
Note: Addiction prevention & mental health promotion

Edmonton: Alberta Hospital Edmonton
Affiliated with: Alberta Health Services
17480 Fort Rd., Edmonton, AB T5J 2J7
Tel: 780-342-5555
www.albertahealthservices.ca
Year Founded: 1923
Number of Beds: 410 beds
Note: Provides assessment, diagnosis, treatment, education & consultation. Conducts research. Programs include: Adult Psychiatry, Geriatric Psychiatry, & the Northern Alberta Forensic Psychiatry Program.

Edmonton: Forensic & Community Services
Affiliated with: Alberta Health Services
10225 - 106 St., Edmonton, AB T5J 1H5
Tel: 780-342-6400; *Fax:* 780-342-6249
www.albertahealthservices.ca
Note: Assessments of young offenders with mental health or behaviour problems; corrections transition program; treatment & education programs also available.

Edmonton: Hys Medical Centre
Affiliated with: Alberta Health Services
#215, 11010 - 101 St., Edmonton, AB T5H 4B9
Tel: 780-342-9100; *Fax:* 780-424-4964
www.albertahealthservices.ca
Note: Geriatric psychiatry & laboratory services

Edmonton: Northeast Community Health Centre
Affiliated with: Alberta Health Services
14007 - 50 St., Edmonton, AB T5A 5E4
Tel: 780-342-4027; *Fax:* 780-342-4195
www.albertahealthservices.ca
Note: Addictions & mental health services

Edmonton: Villa Caritas
Covenant Health
Affiliated with: Alberta Health Services
16515 - 88 Ave. NW, Edmonton, AB T5R 0A4
Tel: 780-342-6500; *Fax:* 780-735-2701
www.covenanthealth.ca/hospitals-care-centres/villa-caritas
Number of Beds: 120 acute geriatric psychiatry beds; 30 geriatric psychiatry transitional beds
Note: Acute mental health facility for seniors, located on the Misericordia Community Hospital campus.

Edson: Edson Provincial Building
Affiliated with: Alberta Health Services
Former Name: Edson Mental Health Centre
#100, 111 - 54 St., Edson, AB T7E 1T2
Tel: 780-723-8294; *Fax:* 780-723-8297
www.albertahealthservices.ca

Fairview: Fairview Health Complex
Affiliated with: Alberta Health Services
PO Box 2201, 10628 - 110 St., Fairview, AB T0H 1L0
Tel: 780-835-6149; *Fax:* 780-835-6185
Toll-Free: 877-823-6433
www.albertahealthservices.ca

Fort MacLeod: Fort Macleod Community Health
Affiliated with: Alberta Health Services
744 - 26 St. South, Fort MacLeod, AB T0L 0Z0
Tel: 403-553-5340; *Fax:* 403-553-4940
www.albertahealthservices.ca

Fort McMurray: Northern Lights Regional Health Centre
Affiliated with: Alberta Health Services
7 Hospital St., Fort McMurray, AB T9H 1P2
Tel: 780-791-6194; *Fax:* 780-791-6219
www.albertahealthservices.ca

Fort Saskatchewan: Fort Saskatchewan Community Hospital
Affiliated with: Alberta Health Services
Former Name: Fort Saskatchewan Health Centre
9401 - 86 Ave., Fort Saskatchewan, AB T8L 0C6
Tel: 780-342-2388; *Fax:* 780-342-3348
www.albertahealthservices.ca

Fort Vermilion: St. Theresa General Hospital
Affiliated with: Alberta Health Services
4506 - 46 Ave., Fort Vermilion, AB T0H 1N0
Tel: 780-841-3229; *Fax:* 780-926-3738
Toll-Free: 877-823-6433
www.albertahealthservices.ca

Fox Creek: Fox Creek Healthcare Centre
Affiliated with: Alberta Health Services
600 - 3rd St., Fox Creek, AB T0H 1P0
Tel: 780-706-3281; *Fax:* 780-622-3474
www.albertahealthservices.ca

Grande Cache: Pine Plaza Building
Affiliated with: Alberta Health Services
702 Pine Plaza, Grande Cache, AB T0E 0Y0
Tel: 780-827-4998; *Fax:* 780-827-7313
www.albertahealthservices.ca
Info Line: 877-303-2642
Note: Addictions & mental health services

Grande Prairie: Grande Prairie Nordic Court
Affiliated with: Alberta Health Services
Former Name: Nordic Court Mental Health Clinic
#600, 10014 - 99th St., Grande Prairie, AB T8V 3N4
Tel: 780-538-5160; *Fax:* 780-538-6279
www.albertahealthservices.ca

Hanna: Hanna Health Centre
Affiliated with: Alberta Health Services
PO Box 730, 904 Centre St. North, Hanna, AB T0J 1P0
Tel: 403-854-5276; *Fax:* 403-854-3253
www.albertahealthservices.ca

High Level: **Northwest Health Centre**
Affiliated with: Alberta Health Services
11202 - 100 St., High Level, AB T0H 1Z0
Tel: 780-841-3229; *Fax:* 780-926-3738
Toll-Free: 877-823-6433
www.albertahealthservices.ca

High Prairie: **High Prairie Health Complex**
Affiliated with: Alberta Health Services
4620 - 53 Ave., High Prairie, AB T0G 1E0
Tel: 780-523-6490; *Fax:* 780-523-6491
Toll-Free: 877-823-6433
www.albertahealthservices.ca

High River: **High River Addiction & Mental Health Clinic**
Affiliated with: Alberta Health Services
#200, 617 - 1 St. West, High River, AB T1V 1M5
Tel: 403-652-8340; *Fax:* 403-652-5455
Toll-Free: 877-652-4700
www.albertahealthservices.ca

Hinton: **Hinton Community Health Services**
Affiliated with: Alberta Health Services
Former Name: Hinton Mental Health Centre
1280A Switzer Dr., Hinton, AB T7V 1T5
Tel: 780-865-2277; *Fax:* 780-865-3727
www.albertahealthservices.ca

Innisfail: **Innisfail Health Centre**
Affiliated with: Alberta Health Services
5023 - 42 St., Innisfail, AB T4G 1A9
Tel: 403-227-4601; *Fax:* 403-227-5683
www.albertahealthservices.ca

Jasper: **Seton - Jasper Healthcare Centre**
Affiliated with: Alberta Health Services
PO Box 310, 518 Robson St., Jasper, AB T0E 1E0
Tel: 780-852-6616; *Fax:* 780-852-3413
Toll-Free: 877-303-2642
www.albertahealthservices.ca

Killam: **Killam 4811 - 49 Avenue**
Affiliated with: Alberta Health Services
4811 - 49 Ave., Killam, AB T0B 2L0
Tel: 780-385-7161; *Fax:* 780-385-3329
www.albertahealthservices.ca

La Crete: **La Crete Continuing Care Centre**
Affiliated with: Alberta Health Services
10601 - 100 Ave., La Crete, AB T0H 2H0
Tel: 780-928-2410; *Fax:* 877-853-5380
Toll-Free: 877-823-6433
www.albertahealthservices.ca

Lac La Biche: **Lac La Biche Provincial Building**
Affiliated with: Alberta Health Services
Former Name: Lac La Biche Community Health Services
PO Box 297, 9503 Beaver Hill Rd., Lac La Biche, AB T0A 2C0
Tel: 780-623-5230; *Fax:* 780-623-5232
www.albertahealthservices.ca

Lacombe: **Lacombe Mental Health Centre**
Affiliated with: Alberta Health Services
5033 - 52 St., Lacombe, AB T4L 2A6
Tel: 403-782-3413; *Fax:* 403-782-3878
www.albertahealthservices.ca

Lamont: **Lamont Health Care Centre**
Affiliated with: Alberta Health Services
PO Box 479, 5216 - 53 St., Lamont, AB T0B 2R0
Tel: 780-895-5817
www.lamonthealthcarecentre.com
Note: Affiliated with the United Church of Canada.

Leduc: **Leduc Community Hospital**
Affiliated with: Alberta Health Services
4210 - 48 St., Leduc, AB T9E 5Z3
Tel: 780-986-2660; *Fax:* 780-986-9292
www.albertahealthservices.ca

Leduc: **Leduc Neighbourhood Centre**
Affiliated with: Alberta Health Services
4901 - 50 Ave., Leduc, AB T9E 6W7
Tel: 780-980-7580; *Fax:* 780-980-7581
Toll-Free: 866-332-2322
www.albertahealthservices.ca
Note: Addiction & mental health services

Lethbridge: **Chinook Regional Hospital**
Affiliated with: Alberta Health Services
Former Name: Lethbridge Regional Hospital
960 - 19 St. South, Lethbridge, AB T1J 1W5
Tel: 403-388-6244; *Fax:* 403-388-6250
www.albertahealthservices.ca
Note: Child & adolescent mental health; day treatment centre

Lethbridge: **Lethbridge Provincial Building**
Affiliated with: Alberta Health Services
200 - 5th Ave. South, Lethbridge, AB T1K 4L1
Tel: 403-381-5260; *Fax:* 403-382-4518
www.albertahealthservices.ca
Note: Addictions & mental health services

Mayerthorpe: **Mayerthorpe Healthcare Centre**
Affiliated with: Alberta Health Services
4417 - 45 St., Mayerthorpe, AB T0E 1N0
Tel: 780-786-2279; *Fax:* 780-786-2023
www.albertahealthservices.ca

Medicine Hat: **Medicine Hat Provincial Building**
Affiliated with: Alberta Health Services
Former Name: Medicine Hat Community Mental Health
346 - 3 St. SE, Medicine Hat, AB T1A 0G7
Tel: 403-529-3500; *Fax:* 403-529-3562
www.albertahealthservices.ca

Medicine Hat: **Regional Resource Centre**
Affiliated with: Alberta Health Services
631 Prospect Dr. SW, Medicine Hat, AB T1A 4C2
Tel: 403-529-8030; *Fax:* 403-502-8618
www.albertahealthservices.ca
Note: Child & adolescent mental health program

Morinville: **Morinville Provincial Building**
Affiliated with: Alberta Health Services
10008 - 107 St., Morinville, AB T8R 1L3
Tel: 780-342-2620; *Fax:* 780-939-1216
www.albertahealthservices.ca
Note: Addiction & mental health community clinics

Okotoks: **Okotoks Mental Health Centre**
Affiliated with: Alberta Health Services
11 Cimarron Common, Okotoks, AB T1S 2E9
Tel: 403-995-2712 *Toll-Free:* 877-652-4700
www.albertahealthservices.ca

Olds: **Olds Provincial Building**
Affiliated with: Alberta Health Services
#212, 5025 - 50th St., Olds, AB T4H 1R9
Tel: 403-507-8174; *Fax:* 403-556-1584
www.albertahealthservices.ca
Note: Addictions & mental health services

Onoway: **Onoway Community Health Services**
Affiliated with: Alberta Health Services
5115 Lac St. Anne Trail, Onoway, AB T0E 1V0
Tel: 780-967-9117; *Fax:* 780-967-2547
www.albertahealthservices.ca

Peace River: **Peace River Mental Health Clinic**
Affiliated with: Alberta Health Services
Bag 900-8, 10015 - 98 St., Peace River, AB T8S 1T4
Tel: 780-624-6151; *Fax:* 780-624-6565
www.albertahealthservices.ca

Pincher Creek: **Pincher Creek Community Mental Health Clinic**
Affiliated with: Alberta Health Services
782 Main St., Pincher Creek, AB T0K 1W0
Tel: 403-627-1121; *Fax:* 403-627-1145
www.albertahealthservices.ca

Ponoka: **Centennial Centre for Mental Health & Brain Injury**
Affiliated with: Alberta Health Services
PO Box 1000, Ponoka, AB T4J 1R8
Tel: 403-783-7600
mentalhealthexcellence.ca
Note: Specialized mental health & brain injury treatment & care

Ponoka: **Ponoka Provincial Building**
Affiliated with: Alberta Health Services
#223, 5110 - 49th Ave., Ponoka, AB T4J 1R6
Tel: 403-783-7903; *Fax:* 403-783-7926
www.albertahealthservices.ca
Note: Addictions & mental health services

Provost: **Provost Provincial Building**
Affiliated with: Alberta Health Services
5419 - 44 St., Provost, AB T0B 3S0
Tel: 780-753-2575; *Fax:* 780-753-8096
www.albertahealthservices.ca

Raymond: **Raymond Community Mental Health Clinic**
Affiliated with: Alberta Health Services
150N - 400 St. East, Raymond, AB T0K 2S0
Tel: 403-752-5440; *Fax:* 403-752-4147
www.albertahealthservices.ca

Red Deer: **Red Deer - 49th Street Community Health Centre**
Affiliated with: Alberta Health Services
4733 - 49 St., Red Deer, AB T4N 1T6
Tel: 403-340-5466; *Fax:* 403-340-4874
www.albertahealthservices.ca

Rocky Mountain House: **Rocky Mountain House Health Centre**
Affiliated with: Alberta Health Services
5016 - 52 Ave., Rocky Mountain House, AB T4T 1T2
Tel: 403-844-5235; *Fax:* 403-844-5236
www.albertahealthservices.ca

Sherwood Park: **Strathcona County Health Centre**
Affiliated with: Alberta Health Services
2 Brower Dr., Sherwood Park, AB T8H 1V4
Tel: 780-342-4675; *Fax:* 780-464-3705
www.albertahealthservices.ca

Slave Lake: **Slave Lake Mental Health Services**
Affiliated with: Alberta Health Services
Slave Lake Health Complex, 309 - 6 St. NE, Slave Lake, AB T0G 2A2
Tel: 780-805-3502; *Fax:* 780-805-3550
www.albertahealthservices.ca

Smoky Lake: **George McDougall - Smoky Lake Healthcare Centre**
Affiliated with: Alberta Health Services
Smoky Lake Health Unit, 4212 - 55 Ave., Smoky Lake, AB T0A 3C0
Tel: 780-656-3595; *Fax:* 780-656-2242
www.albertahealthservices.ca

Spirit River: **Spirit River Community Health Services**
Affiliated with: Alberta Health Services
Former Name: Mistahia Health Unit - Spirit River
5003 - 45 Ave., Spirit River, AB T0H 3G0
Tel: 780-538-5160; *Fax:* 780-538-6279
Toll-Free: 877-823-6433
www.albertahealthservices.ca

Spruce Grove: **Stan Woloshyn Building**
Affiliated with: Alberta Health Services
#140, 205 Diamond Ave., Spruce Grove, AB T7X 3A8
Tel: 780-342-1370; *Fax:* 780-962-7566
www.albertahealthservices.ca
Note: Addiction & mental health services for children & youth

St Albert: **St. Albert Provincial Building**
Affiliated with: Alberta Health Services
30 Sir Winston Churchill Ave., St Albert, AB T8N 3A3
Tel: 780-460-4971; *Fax:* 780-460-4979
Toll-Free: 866-332-2322
www.albertahealthservices.ca

St. Paul: **St. Therese - St. Paul Healthcare Centre**
Affiliated with: Alberta Health Services
4713 - 48 Ave., St. Paul, AB T0A 3A3
Tel: 780-645-1850; *Fax:* 780-645-2788
www.albertahealthservices.ca

Standoff: **Kainai Continuing Care Centre**
Blood Tribe Department of Health Inc.
PO Box 229, Standoff, AB T0L 1Y0
Tel: 403-737-3883; *Fax:* 403-737-2036
btdh.ca/staff/kainai-wellness-centre
Year Founded: 1985
Note: Counselling services for the Blood Tribe Community
Sandy Many Chief, Director
sandi.mc@btdh.ca

Stettler: **Stettler Hospital & Care Centre**
Affiliated with: Alberta Health Services
5912 - 47 Ave., Stettler, AB T0C 2L0
Tel: 403-743-2000; *Fax:* 403-740-8880
www.albertahealthservices.ca

Stony Plain: **WestView Health Centre**
Affiliated with: Alberta Health Services
4405 South Park Dr., Stony Plain, AB T7Z 2M7
Tel: 780-963-8098; *Fax:* 780-963-7186
Toll-Free: 866-332-2322
www.albertahealthservices.ca
Note: Addiction prevention & mental health promotion services; community clinics for adults (780-963-6151)

Swan Hills: **Swan Hills Healthcare Centre**
Affiliated with: Alberta Health Services
PO Box 261, 29 Freeman Dr., Swan Hills, AB T0G 2C0
Tel: 780-333-4241; *Fax:* 780-333-7009
www.albertahealthservices.ca

Sylvan Lake: **Sylvan Lake Community Health Centre**
Affiliated with: Alberta Health Services
4602 - 49 Ave., Sylvan Lake, AB T4S 1M7
Tel: 403-887-6777; *Fax:* 403-887-6721
www.albertahealthservices.ca

Taber: **Taber Provincial Building**
Affiliated with: Alberta Health Services
5011 - 49 Ave., Taber, AB T1G 1V9
Tel: 403-223-7932
www.albertahealthservices.ca
Note: Addictions (403-223-7953) & mental health services

Three Hills: **Three Hills Provincial Building**
Affiliated with: Alberta Health Services
Former Name: Three Hills Mental Health Centre
160 - 3 Ave. South, Three Hills, AB T0M 2A0
Tel: 403-443-8532; *Fax:* 403-443-8541
www.albertahealthservices.ca
Note: Addictions (403-823-1660) & mental health services

Tofield: **Tofield - 5024-51 Avenue**
Affiliated with: Alberta Health Services
5024 - 51 Ave., Tofield, AB T0B 4J0
Tel: 780-662-7061; *Fax:* 780-662-3854
www.albertahealthservices.ca
Note: Child & adolescent mental health services

Vegreville: **Vegreville Community Health Centre**
Affiliated with: Alberta Health Services
5318 - 50 St., Vegreville, AB T9C 1R1
Tel: 780-632-2714; *Fax:* 780-632-4954
www.albertahealthservices.ca

Vermilion: **Vermilion Provincial Building**
Affiliated with: Alberta Health Services
4701 - 52 St., Vermilion, AB T9X 1J9
Tel: 780-581-8000; *Fax:* 780-851-8001
www.albertahealthservices.ca

Vulcan: **Vulcan Community Health Centre**
Affiliated with: Alberta Health Services
610 Elizabeth St. South, Vulcan, AB T0L 2B0
Tel: 403-485-3356 *Toll-Free:* 877-652-4700
www.albertahealthservices.ca

Wainwright: **Wainwright Provincial Building**
Affiliated with: Alberta Health Services
810 - 14 Ave., Wainwright, AB T9W 1R2
Tel: 780-842-7522; *Fax:* 780-842-7520
www.albertahealthservices.ca

Westlock: **Westlock Community Health Services**
Affiliated with: Alberta Health Services
10024 - 107 St., Westlock, AB T7P 1H7
Tel: 780-349-5246; *Fax:* 780-349-5846
www.albertahealthservices.ca

Wetaskiwin: **Wetaskiwin Provincial Building**
Affiliated with: Alberta Health Services
#101, 5201 - 50 Ave., Wetaskiwin, AB T9A 0S7
Tel: 780-361-1245; *Fax:* 780-361-1387
www.albertahealthservices.ca

Whitecourt: **Whitecourt Healthcare Centre**
Affiliated with: Alberta Health Services
20 Sunset Blvd., Whitecourt, AB T7S 1M8
Tel: 780-706-3281; *Fax:* 780-706-7154
www.albertahealthservices.ca

Special Care Homes

Lloydminster: **Dr. Cooke Extended Care Centre**
Affiliated with: Prairie North Health Region
3915 - 56 Ave., Lloydminster, AB T9V 1N9
Tel: 780-871-7900; *Fax:* 780-875-3505
www.albertahealthservices.ca
Info Line: 306-820-5970
Number of Beds: 105 beds
Joan Zimmer, Director, Continuing Care

British Columbia

Government Departments in Charge

Victoria: **British Columbia Ministry of Health Services**
PO Box 9644 Stn. Prov Govt, Victoria, BC V9W 9P1
Tel: 250-952-1887; *Fax:* 250-952-1883
EnquiryBC@gov.bc.ca
www.gov.bc.ca/health
Hon. Terry Lake, Minister of Health
250-953-3547, hlth.minister@gov.bc.ca

Regional Health Authorities

Kelowna: **Interior Health Authority**
Corporate Office, #220, 1815 Kirschner Rd., Kelowna, BC V1Y 4N7
Tel: 250-862-4200; *Fax:* 250-862-4201
www.interiorhealth.ca
Info Line: 811
Social Media: www.facebook.com/InteriorHealth; twitter.com/Interior_Health; www.youtube.com/user/InteriorHealthAuth; www.linkedin.com/company/interior-health-authority
Year Founded: 2001
Number of Beds: 6,584 residential care & assisted living beds; 1,391 hospital beds
Area Served: 215,000 sq km; *Population Served:* 750000; *Number of Employees:* 19000
Note: Serves cities such as Kelowna, Kamloops, Cranbrook, Trail, Penticton & Vernon, as well as rural & remote communities. Services include: Acute care, health promotion & prevention, community care, residential care, mental health & substance use, & public health.
Erwin Malzer, Board Chair
Chris Mazurkewich, President & CEO
Dr. Trevor Corneil, Chief Medical Health Officer & Vice-Presient, Population Health
Donna Lommer, Chief Financial Officer & Vice-President, Support Services
Susan Brown, COO & Vice-President, Hospitals & Communities
Dr. Alan Stewart, Vice-President, Medicine & Quality
Mal Griffin, Vice-President, Human Resources & Organizational Development
Martin McMahon, Vice-President, Integration & Strategic Services
Jamie Braman, Vice-President, Communications & Public Engagement
Norma Malanowich, Vice-President & Chief Information Officer

Prince George: **Northern Health Authority**
Former Name: Northern Interior Health Board
Corporate Office, #600, 299 Victoria St., Prince George, BC V2L 5B8
Tel: 250-565-2649; *Fax:* 250-565-2640
hello@northernhealth.ca
www.northernhealth.ca
Info Line: 811
Social Media: www.facebook.com/NorthernHealth; twitter.com/northern_health; www.youtube.com/northernhealthbc; www.linkedin.com/company/northern-health-authority
Number of Beds: 1,015 HCC residential care beds; 560 hospital beds
Area Served: 600,000 sq km in northern British Columbia; *Population Served:* 300000; *Number of Employees:* 7000
Note: Services administered through 3 service delivery areas: Northwest, Northeast, Northern Interior.
Charles Jago, Board Chair
Cathy Ulrich, President & CEO
Penny Anguish, Chief Operating Officer & Chief Nursing Executive, Northwest
Michael McMillan, Chief Operating Officer, Northern Interior
Angela De Smit, Chief Operating Officer, Northeast

Surrey: **Fraser Health Authority**
Central City Tower, #400, 13450 - 102nd Ave., Surrey, BC V3T 0H1
Tel: 604-587-4600; *Fax:* 604-587-4666
Toll-Free: 877-935-5669
feedback@fraserhealth.ca
www.fraserhealth.ca
Info Line: 811
Social Media: www.facebook.com/FraserHealthAuthority; twitter.com/Fraserhealth; www.youtube.com/fraserhealth; www.linkedin.com/company/fraser-health-authority
Number of Beds: 12 acute care hospitals; 7760 residental care beds; mental health care, public health, home & community care services
Area Served: Burnaby to Hope to Boston Bar in British Columbia; *Population Served:* 1600000; *Number of Employees:* 25000
Note: Communities served include around 38,100 First Nations people, associated with 32 bands.
Karen Matty, Board Chair
Michael Marchbank, President & CEO
Dr. Victoria Lee, Chief Medical Health Officer & Vice-President, Population Health
Brenda Liggett, Chief Financial Officer
Philip Barker, Vice-President, Planning, Informatics & Analytics
Linda Dempster, Vice-President, Patient Experience
Vivian Giglio, Vice-President, Regional Hospitals & Communities
Dr. Shallen Letwin, Vice-President, Community Hospitals & Programs
Naseem Nuraney, Vice-President, Communications & Public Affairs
Wendy Strugnell, Vice-President, People & Organization Development
Dr. Roy Morton, Vice-President, Medicine

Vancouver: **Provincial Health Services Authority (PHSA)**
#700, 1380 Burrard St., Vancouver, BC V6Z 2H3
Tel: 604-675-7400; *Fax:* 604-708-2700
phsacomm@phsa.ca
www.phsa.ca
Info Line: 811
Social Media: twitter.com/PHSAofBC; www.youtube.com/ProvHealthServAuth; www.linkedin.com/company/provincial-health-services-authority
Note: PHSA operates provincial agencies including BC Children's Hospital, BC Transplant, & BC Cancer Agency. It is also responsible for specialized provincial health services like chest surgery & trauma services.
Wynne Powell, Board Chair
Carl Roy, President & CEO
Arden Krystal, Executive Vice-President, Patient & Employee Experience
Thomas Chan, Chief Financial Officer
Nick Foster, Vice-President, Consolidated Services, Clinical & Systems Transformation & Spec. Projects
Dave Cunningham, Chief Communications Officer
Sandra MacKay, Chief Freedom of Information & Privacy Officer, & General Counsel
Linda Lupini, Executive Vice-President, PHSA & BCEHS
Carla Gregor, Vice-President, Acute Specialty Services
Oliver Grüter-Andrew, Chief Information Officer
Colleen Hart, Vice-President, Provincial Population Health, Chronic Conditions & Specialized Populations

Vancouver: **Vancouver Coastal Health**
Corporate Office, 601 West Broadway, 11th Fl., Vancouver, BC V5Z 4C2
Tel: 604-736-2033 *Toll-Free:* 866-884-0888
feedback@vch.ca
www.vch.ca
Info Line: 811
Social Media: www.facebook.com/VCHhealthcare; twitter.com/vchhealthcare; www.youtube.com/user/VCHhealthcare
Population Served: 1000000; *Number of Employees:* 13080
Note: Area Served: Vancouver; Richmond; the North Shore; Coast Garibaldi; Sea-to-Sky; Sunshine Coast; Powell River; Bella Bella; & Bella Coola. OPerates 13 hospitals, & provides the following services: primary care; community-based residential & home health care; mental health; addiction services; public health; hospital care; & research.
Kip Woodward, Board Chair
Mary Ackenhusen, President & CEO
Laura Case, Chief Operating Officer, Vancouver Community
Vivian Eliopoulos, Chief Operating Officer, Vancouver Acute
Jennifer MacKenzie, Chief Operating Officer, Richmond
Mike Nader, Chief Operating Officer, Coastal
Dr. Patricia Daly, Chief Medical Health Officer & Vice-President, Public Health
Glen Copping, Chief Financial Officer & Vice-President, Systems Development & Performance
Barb Lawrie, Chief Clinical Information Officer & Vice-President, Professional Practice

Victoria: **Vancouver Island Health Authority**
Former Name: Capital Health Region
Also Known As: Island Health
1952 Bay St., Victoria, BC V8R 1J8
Tel: 250-370-8699 *Toll-Free:* 877-370-8699
info@viha.ca
www.viha.ca
Info Line: 811
Social Media: www.facebook.com/135150073228437; twitter.com/vanislandhealth

Area Served: Vancouver Island & the islands of the George Strait; *Population Served:* 765000; *Number of Employees:* 18000
Don Hubbard, Board Chair
Dr. Brendan Carr, President & CEO
Dr. Richard Stanwick, Chief Medical Health Officer
Jeremy Etherington, Chief Medical Officer & Executive Vice-President
Catherine Mackay, Chief Operating Officer & Executive Vice-President
Kim Kerrone, Chief Financial Officer & Vice-President, Corporate Services
Dawn Nedzelski, Chief Nursing Officer & Chief, Professional Practice
Catherine Claiter-Larsen, Chief Information Officer & Vice-President
Kathy MacNeil, Executive Vice-President, Quality, Safety & Experience
Joe Murphy, Vice-President, Planning & Operations Support
Toni O'Keeffe, Vice-President & Chief, Communications & Public Relations

***West Vancouver:* First Nations Health Authority (FNHA)**
#501, 100 Park Royal South, West Vancouver, BC V7T 1A2
Tel: 604-693-6500; *Fax:* 604-913-2081
Toll-Free: 866-913-0033
info@fnha.ca
www.fnha.ca
Info Line: 855-550-5454
Social Media: www.facebook.com/firstnationshealthauthority; twitter.com/FNHA; www.youtube.com/user/fnhealthcouncil; www.linkedin.com/company/first-nations-health-authority
Year Founded: 2013
Area Served: 5 regions; 955,186 sq km
Note: Assumed the following responsibilities, formerly handled by Health Canada's First Nations Inuit Health Branch - Pacific Region: to plan, design, manage, & fund the delivery of First Nations health programs & services in BC. Health services include: primary care services; children, youth & maternal health; mental health & addictions programming; health & wellness planning; health infrastructure & human resources; environmental health & research; First Nations health benefits; & eHealth technology.
Areas served include the following regions: Fraser Salish; Interior; North; Vancouver Coastal; & Vancouver Island.
Lydia Hwitsum, Board Chair
Joe Gallagher, Chief Executive Officer
Tally Bains, Chief Financial Officer
Joseph Mendez, Chief Information Officer & Vice-President, Innovation & Information Management Services
Dr. Evan Adams, Chief Medical Officer
Richard Jock, Chief Operating Officer
John Mah, Vice-President, First Nations Health Benefits
Greg Shea, Executive Director

Hospitals - General

***Abbotsford:* Abbotsford Regional Hospital & Cancer Centre**
Affiliated with: Fraser Health Authority
32900 Marshall Rd., Abbotsford, BC V2S 0C2
Tel: 604-851-4700
feedback@fraserhealth.ca
www.fraserhealth.ca
Social Media: www.facebook.com/FraserHealthAuthority; twitter.com/Fraserhealth; www.youtube.com/fraserhealth; www.linkedin.com/company/fraser-health-authority
Number of Beds: 300 beds
Note: Programs & services include: acute care; ambulatory care; angiography; antepartum care; audiology; bone densitometry; cardiac; clinics; CT scans; echocardiography; emergency; enterostomal therapy; fluoroscopy; forensic nursing; general medicine, radiography & surgery; geriatric; haemodialysis; inpatient psychiatric unit; intensive care; interventional radiography; MRI; mammography; maternity; medical oncology; nuclear medicine; outpatient services; pediatrics; pharmacy; postpartum; pulmonary function lab; sleep lab; spiritual care; & ultrasound.
Dr. Shallen Letwin, Executive Director

***Alert Bay:* Cormorant Island Health Centre**
Affiliated with: Vancouver Island Health Authority
49 School Rd., Alert Bay, BC V0N 1A0
Tel: 250-974-5585
info@viha.ca
www.viha.ca
Social Media: www.facebook.com/135150073228437; twitter.com/vanislandhealth
Note: Programs & services include: emergency; acute care; residential care; ambulatory outpatient services; laboratory; medical imaging; palliative care; emergency obstetrics; visiting specialists; & medical detox.
Sarah Kowalenko, Communications & Public Relations Assistant, VIHA
250-740-6951, Sarah.Kowalenko@viha.ca

***Ashcroft:* Ashcroft & District General Hospital**
Affiliated with: Interior Health Authority
700 Ash-Cache Creek Hwy., Ashcroft, BC V0K 1A0
Tel: 250-453-2211; *Fax:* 250-453-9685
Toll-Free: 877-499-6599
www.interiorhealth.ca
Social Media: www.facebook.com/InteriorHealth; twitter.com/Interior_Health; www.interiorHealthAuth; www.linkedin.com/company/interior-health-authority
Year Founded: 1970
Number of Beds: 24 extended care beds; 4 emergency beds; 1 respite bed
Note: Programs & services include: diabetes education program; laboratory & radiology; urgent care; ambulatory care; community services; long-term residential care; & on-site doctors' offices.

***Bella Coola:* Bella Coola General Hospital (BCGH)**
Affiliated with: Vancouver Coastal Health
1025 Elcho St., Bella Coola, BC V0T 1C0
Tel: 250-799-5311; *Fax:* 250-799-5635
feedback@vch.ca
www.vch.ca
Social Media: www.facebook.com/VCHhealthcare; twitter.com/VCHhealthcare; www.youtube.com/VCHhealthcare
Number of Beds: 15 beds
Note: Programs & services include: adult day program; community bath program; diabetes & foot care; emergency; long-term care; meals on wheels; pharmacy; residential care; wound care; & x-ray/radiology.
Michel Bazille, Chief Operating Officer
michel.bazille@vch.ca

***Burnaby:* Burnaby Hospital**
Affiliated with: Fraser Health Authority
3935 Kincaid St., Burnaby, BC V5G 2X6
Tel: 604-412-6131; *Fax:* 604-412-6190
feedback@fraserhealth.ca
www.fraserhealth.ca
Social Media: www.facebook.com/FraserHealthAuthority; twitter.com/Fraserhealth; www.youtube.com/fraserhealth; www.linkedin.com/company/fraser-health-authority
Number of Beds: 295 beds
Note: Programs & services include: acute care; ambulatory care; antepartum care; cardiac; CT scan; concurrent disorders; echocardiography; emergency; fluoroscopy; general medicine, radiography & surgery; geriatric; inpatient psychiatry unit; intensive care; interventional radiography; MRI; mammography; maternity; medical oncology; neonatal intensive care; nuclear medicine; opthalmology services; orthopaedic surgery; outpatient services; pharmacy; postpartum care; pulmonary function lab; & ultrasound.
Sheila Finamore, Interim Executive Director

***Burns Lake:* Lakes District Hospital & Health Centre**
Affiliated with: Northern Health Authority
PO Box 7500, 741 Centre St., Burns Lake, BC V0J 1E0
Tel: 250-692-2400; *Fax:* 250-692-2403
www.northernhealth.ca
Number of Beds: 16 beds
Note: Programs & services include: acute care; emergency; diagnostic imaging; laboratory; public health; mental health & addictions; home & community care; pharmacy; & rehabilitation.

***Campbell River:* Campbell River & District Regional Hospital**
Affiliated with: Vancouver Island Health Authority
Also Known As: Campbell River Hospital
375 - 2nd Ave., Campbell River, BC V9W 3V1
Tel: 250-850-2141; *Fax:* 250-286-9675
info@viha.ca
www.viha.ca
Social Media: www.facebook.com/135150073228437; twitter.com/vanislandhealth
Note: Programs & services include: Aboriginal health nurse; diabetes education; heart function clinic; heart health services; laboratory; medical imaging; nutrition; pacemaker clinic; rehabilitation; & surgery.
Sheri Drover, Acting Site Director
Sandy Miller, Nurse, Aboriginal Health
250-830-6961, Sandy.P.Miller@viha.ca

***Chetwynd:* Chetwynd Hospital & Health Centre**
Affiliated with: Northern Health Authority
PO Box 507, 5500 Hospital Rd., Chetwynd, BC V0C 1J0
Tel: 250-788-2236; *Fax:* 250-788-7247
www.northernhealth.ca
Social Media: www.facebook.com/NorthernHealth; twitter.com/northern_health; www.youtube.com/northernhealthbc; www.linkedin.com/company/northern-health-authroity
Number of Beds: 12 beds (7 long-term care & 5 acute care)
Note: Programs & services include: aboriginal liaison; emergency; medical inpatient; palliative; public health nursing; home & community nursing; home support; & respiratory therapy.

***Chilliwack:* Chilliwack General Hospital**
Affiliated with: Fraser Health Authority
45600 Menholm Rd., Chilliwack, BC V2P 1P7
Tel: 604-795-4141; *Fax:* 604-795-4110
feedback@fraserhealth.ca
www.fraserhealth.ca
Social Media: www.facebook.com/FraserHealthAuthority; twitter.com/Fraserhealth; www.youtube.com/fraserhealth; www.linkedin.com/company/fraser-health-authority
Number of Beds: 135 beds
Note: Programs & services include: acute care; ambulatory care; angiography; antepartum care; cardiac; CT scan; emergency; enterostomal therapy; fluoroscopy; general medicine, radiography & surgery; geriatric; home detox; inpatient psychiatry unit; intensive care; interventional radiography; mammography; maternity; medical oncology; ophthalmology; orthopaedic surgery; outpatient services; pantomography; pharmacy; postpartum; pulmonary function lab; spiritual care; substance use; & ultrasound.
Tracy Irwin, Executive Director
Carol Peters, Aboriginal Patient Liaison
carol.peters@fraserhealth.ca

***Clearwater:* Dr. Helmcken Memorial Hospital (DHM)**
Affiliated with: Interior Health Authority
640 Park Dr., RR#1, Clearwater, BC V0E 1N0
Tel: 250-674-2244; *Fax:* 250-674-2477
www.interiorhealth.ca
Social Media: www.facebook.com/InteriorHealth; twitter.com/Interior_Health; www.youtube.com/InteriorHealthAuth; www.linkedin.com/interior-health-authority
Number of Beds: 6 beds
Note: Programs & services include: community care; emergency; end of life/palliative care; extended care; general medicine; general rehabilitation; geriatric medicine; hematology; hospice; laboratory; nutrition; orthotics; physiotherapy; radiology; telehealth; & wound care.

***Comox:* St. Joseph's General Hospital**
Affiliated with: Vancouver Island Health Authority
2137 Comox Ave., Comox, BC V9M 1P2
Tel: 250-339-2242; *Fax:* 250-339-1432
administration@sjghcomox.ca
www.sjghcomox.ca
Year Founded: 1913
Number of Beds: 241 beds
Note: Programs & services include: colposcopy; daycare; diabetes; diagnostic imaging (mammography, radiology, ultrasound); emergency; extended care; intensive care; laboratory; maternity; nursing; nutritional; oncology; paediatrics; physical medicine; psychiatry; social work; & surgery.
Jane Murphy, President & CEO
Dr. Robert Angus, Medical Director
Cathie Sturam, Site Director, Acute Care

***Cranbrook:* East Kootenay Regional Hospital (EKRH)**
Affiliated with: Interior Health Authority
13 - 24th Ave. North, Cranbrook, BC V1C 3H9
Tel: 250-426-5281; *Fax:* 250-426-5285
Toll-Free: 866-288-8082
www.interiorhealth.ca
Social Media: www.facebook.com/InteriorHealth; twitter.com/Interior_Health; www.youtube.com/InteriorHealthAuth; www.linkedin.com/company/interior-health-authority
Note: Programs & services include: antepartum care; bone density; cardioversion; chemotherapy; chronic obstructive pulmonary disease services; community care; convalescent care; CT scan; dental surgery; diagnostic bronchoscopy; diagnostic cardiology; ear, nose & throat; echocardiogram, ECG/EKG; emergency; end of life/palliative care; endoscopy; enterostomal therapy; fluoroscopy; general medicine; general rehabilitation; general surgery; hematology; holter monitor; intensive care; intrapartum care; laboratory; mammography; maternity; mental health & substance abuse; microbiology; MRI;

nuclear medicine; nutrition; oncology; opthalmology; orthotics; pediatrics; pharmacy; physiotherapy; postpartum care; pulmonary diagnostics; radiology; respiratory therapy; speech-language pathology; spiritual care; telehealth; transfusion; ultrasound; urology; vasectomy; & wound care. Also hosts the Mary Pack Arthritis Program, a service of Vancouver Coastal Health.
Erica Phillips, Administrator, Acute Health Service

Creston: Creston Valley Hospital & Health Care (CVH)
Affiliated with: Interior Health Authority
312 - 15th Ave. North, Creston, BC V0B 1G0
Tel: 250-428-2286; *Fax:* 250-428-4860
www.interiorhealth.ca
Social Media: www.facebook.com/InteriorHealth; twitter.com/Interior_Health; www.youtube.com/InteriorHealthAuth; www.linkedin.com/company/interior-health-authority
Number of Beds: 16 beds
Note: Programs & services include: adult day services; antepartum care; community care; community nursing; community nutrition; community respiratory therapy; convalescent care; diabetes education program; dental surgery; ear, nose & throat; ECG/EKG; emergency; end of life/palliative care; endoscopy; enterostomal therapy; general medicine; general rehabilitation; general surgery; hematology; holter monitor; home support; hospice; intrapartum care; laboratory; maternity; pharmacy; physiotherapy; postpartum care; psychiatry; radiology; social work; telehealth; transfusion; ultrasound; vasectomy; vision; & wound care.
Cindy Kozak-Campbell, Interior Health Authority Health Services Administrator, Creston

Dawson Creek: Dawson Creek & District Hospital
Affiliated with: Northern Health Authority
11100 - 13th St., Dawson Creek, BC V1G 3W8
Tel: 250-782-8501; *Fax:* 250-783-7301
www.northernhealth.ca
Social Media: www.facebook.com/NorthernHealth; twitter.com/northern_health; www.youtube.com/northernhealthbc; www.linkedin.com/company/northern-health-authority
Number of Beds: 31 acute care beds; 15 adult psychiatric beds
Note: Programs & services include: emergency; ICU; medical & surgical inpatient care; day surgery; maternity; respiratory therapy; rehab therapy; diabetic education; primary care; general surgery; diagnostics (laboratory & medical imaging); cancer care; & visiting specialists in urology, dermatology & pediatrics.

Delta: Delta Hospital
Affiliated with: Fraser Health Authority
5800 Mountain View Blvd., Delta, BC V4K 3V6
Tel: 604-946-1121
feedback@fraserhealth.ca
www.fraserhealth.ca
Social Media: www.facebook.com/FraserHealthAuthority; twitter.com/Fraserhealth; www.youtube.com/fraserhealth; www.linkedin.com/company/fraser-health-authority
Number of Beds: 80 beds
Note: Programs & services include: acute care; ambulatory care; cardiac; CT scan; emergency; fluoroscopy; general medicine, radiography & surgery; mammography; outpatient services; pharmacy; pulmonary function lab; spiritual care; & ultrasound.
Catherine Butler, Executive Director

Duncan: Cowichan District Hospital (CDH)
Affiliated with: Vancouver Island Health Authority
3045 Gibbins Rd., Duncan, BC V9L 1E5
Tel: 250-709-3000
info@viha.ca
www.viha.ca
Social Media: www.facebook.com/135150073228437; twitter.com/vanisalandhealth
Number of Beds: 95 beds
Note: Programs & services include: Aboriginal health nurse; acute inpatient psychiatric services; diabetes education; eye health; heart health; laboratory; medical imaging; mental health; nutrition; rehabilitation; spiritual care; & surgery.
Sarah Kowalenko, Communications & Public Relations Assistant, VIHA
250-740-6951, Sarah.Kowalenko@viha.ca
Helen Dunlop, Aboriginal Liaison Nurse, Cowichan & Surrounding Area
250-746-6184, Helen.Dunlop@cowichantribes.com
Jim Potts, Manager, CDH Pharmacy

Fernie: Elk Valley Hospital
Affiliated with: Interior Health Authority
PO Box 670, 1501 - 5th Ave., Fernie, BC V0B 1M0
Tel: 250-423-4453; *Fax:* 250-423-3732
www.interiorhealth.ca
Social Media: www.facebook.com/InteriorHealth; twitter.com/Interior_Health; www.youtube.com/InteriorHealthAuth; www.linkedin.com/interior-health-authority
Number of Beds: 20 beds
Note: Programs & services include: antepartum care; community care; convalescent care; dental surgery; ear, nose & throat; ECG/EKG; emergency; end of life/palliative care; endoscopy; enterostomal therapy; gastroenterology; general medicine; general rehabilitation; general surgery; hematology; holter monitor; hospice; intrapartum care; laboratory; maternity; mental health & substance abuse; nutrition; pharmacy; physiotherapy; postpartum care; radiology; telehealth; transfusion; urology; vasectomy; & wound care.

Fort Nelson: Fort Nelson Hospital
Affiliated with: Northern Health Authority
PO Box 60, 5315 Liard Street, Fort Nelson, BC V0C 1R0
Tel: 250-774-8100; *Fax:* 250-774-8110
www.northernhealth.ca
Social Media: www.facebook.com/NorthernHealth; twitter.com/northern_health; www.youtube.com/northernhealthbc; www.linkedin.com/company/northern-health-authority
Number of Beds: 25 acute care beds; 8 long-term care beds
Note: Programs & services include: acute care; child & youth programs; counselling services; dental clinic; drug & alcohol programs; health unit; laboratory & x-ray; obstetrics; surgeries; specialists (pediatricians & OB-GYN); & complementary massage therapy, acupuncture & physiotherapy.

Fort St James: Stuart Lake Hospital
Affiliated with: Northern Health Authority
PO Box 1060, 600 Stuart Dr. East, Fort St James, BC V0J 1P0
Tel: 250-996-8201; *Fax:* 250-996-8777
www.northernhealth.ca
Social Media: www.facebook.com/NorthernHealth; twitter.com/northern_health; www.youtube.com/northernhealthbc; www.linkedin.com/company/northern-health-authority
Number of Beds: 12 beds
Note: Programs & services include: acute care; emergency; maternity; medicine; laboratory; & pharmacy.

Fort St John: Fort St. John Hospital & Peace Villa
Affiliated with: Northern Health Authority
Former Name: Fort St. John Hospital & Health Centre
8407 - 112 Ave., Fort St John, BC V1J 0J5
Tel: 250-262-5200; *Fax:* 250-262-5294
www.northernhealth.ca
Social Media: www.facebook.com/NorthernHealth; twitter.com/northern_health; www.youtube.com/northernhealthbc; www.linkedin.com/company/northern-health-authority
Number of Beds: 55 beds; 123 residential care beds
Population Served: 21000
Note: Programs & services include: aboriginal liaison; acute care; diagnostics; surgery; medicine; ICU; maternity; mental health & addictions; palliative care; community cancer centre; community hemodialysis; social work; & visiting specialists. Also connected to the Fort St. John Health Unit, North Peace Villa & Heritage Manor II.

Golden: Golden & District General Hospital
Affiliated with: Interior Health Authority
835 - 9th Ave. South, Golden, BC V0A 1H0
Tel: 250-344-5271; *Fax:* 250-344-2511
www.interiorhealth.ca
Social Media: www.facebook.com/InteriorHealth; twitter.com/Interior_Health; www.youtube.com/InteriorHealthAuth; www.linkedin.com/company/interior-health-authority
Number of Beds: 8 beds
Note: Programs & services include: antepartum care; community care; community respiratory therapy; convalescent care; diabetes education program; ear, nose & throat; ECG/EKG; emergency; end of life/palliative care; endoscopy; general medicine; general rehabilitation; general surgery; hematology; holter monitor; hospice; intrapartum care; laboratory; maternity; nutrition; orthopedics; postpartum care; psychiatry; pulmonary diagnostics; radiology; telehealth; transfusion; ultrasound; vasectomy; & wound care.

Grand Forks: Boundary Hospital
Affiliated with: Interior Health Authority
7649 - 22nd St., Grand Forks, BC V0H 1H2
Tel: 250-443-2100; *Fax:* 250-442-8331
www.interiorhealth.ca
Social Media: www.facebook.com/InteriorHealth; twitter.com/Interior_Health; www.youtube.com/InteriorHealthAuth; www.linkedin.com/company/interior-health-authority
Number of Beds: 12 acute care beds
Note: Programs & services include: chemotherapy; community care; community respiratory therapy; diabetes education program; ECG/EKG; emergency; end of life/palliative; extended care; general medicine; holter monitor; hospice; laboratory; mental health & substance abuse; nutrition; oncology; physiotherapy; pulomary diagnostics; radiology; telehealth; transfusion; ultrasound; & wound care.
Louise Fitzgerald, Hospice Contact
250-443-2162, Louise.Fitzgerald@interiorhealth.ca

Hazelton: Wrinch Memorial Hospital
Affiliated with: Northern Health Authority
Bag 999, 2510 Hwy 62, Hazelton, BC V0J 1Y0
Tel: 250-842-5211; *Fax:* 250-842-5865
www.northernhealth.ca
Number of Beds: 10 acute care beds; 9 complex care beds; 1 respite bed; 1 psychiatric observation room
Population Served: 7000; *Number of Employees:* 70
Note: Affliated with Northern Health, but is owned & operated by United Church Health Services. Programs & services include: acute care; complex care; diabetes education; doctors clinic; emergency room; home & community care; laboratory (ultrasound & x-ray); pharmacy; physiotherapy & occupational therapy; & visiting specialists.

Hope: Fraser Canyon Hospital
Affiliated with: Fraser Health Authority
1275 - 7th Ave., Hope, BC V0X 1L4
Tel: 604-869-5656; *Fax:* 604-860-7732
feedback@fraserhealth.ca
www.fraserhealth.ca
Social Media: www.facebook.com/FraserHealthAuthority; twitter.com/Fraserhealth; www.youtube.com/fraserhealth; www.linkedin.com/company/fraser-health-authority
Number of Beds: 10 beds
Note: Programs & services include: acute care; ambulatory care; emergency; general medicine & radiography; hospice residence; outpatient services; & spiritual care.
Keith McBain, Executive Director

Invermere: Invermere & District Hospital
Affiliated with: Interior Health Authority
850 - 10th Ave., Invermere, BC V0A 1K0
Tel: 250-342-9201; *Fax:* 250-342-6303
www.interiorhealth.ca
Social Media: www.facebook.com/InteriorHealth; twitter.com/Interior_Health; www.twitter.com/InteriorHealthAuth; www.linkedin.com/company/interior-health-authority
Number of Beds: 8 acute care, 30 residential beds
Note: Programs & services include: antepartum care; community care; community respiratory therapy; convalescent care; diabetes education program; ear, nose & throat; ECG/EKG; end of life/palliative care; general medicine; general rehabilitation; hematology; holter monitor; hospice; intrapartum care; laboratory; maternity; nutrition; postpartum care; psychiatry; pulmonary diagnostics; radiology; transfusion; & wound care.

Kamloops: Royal Inland Hospital
Affiliated with: Interior Health Authority
311 Columbia St., Kamloops, BC V2C 2T1
Tel: 250-374-5111; *Fax:* 250-314-2333
Toll-Free: 877-288-5688
www.interiorhealth.ca
Social Media: www.facebook.com/InteriorHealth; twitter.com/Interior_Health; www.youtube.com/InteriorHealthAuth; www.linkedin.com/company/interior-health-authority
Number of Beds: 224 beds
Note: Programs & services include: acute neurology; antepartum care; cardioversion; chemotherapy; chronic obstructive pulmonary disease services; community care; community respiratory therapy; convalescent care; CT scan; dental surgery; diabetes education program; diagnostic bronchoscopy; ear, nose & throat; echocardiogram; ECG/EKG; emergency; end of life/palliative; endoscopy; enterostomal therapy; fluoroscopy; gastroenterology; general medicine, rehabilitation & surgery; geriatric medicine; hematology; holter monitor; hospice; intensive care; intrapartum care; laboratory; mammography; maternity; mental health & substance abuse; microbiology; MRI; neonatal intensive care; nutrition; oncology; opthalmology; orthotics; otolaryngology surgery; pediatrics; pharmacy; physiotherapy; plastic surgery; postpartum care; pulmonary diagnostics;

radiology; respiratory therapy; sleep disorders; speech-language pathology; spiritual care; telehealth; transfusion; ultrasound; urology; vascular & thoracic; vasectomy; & wound care.
Marg Brown, Administrator
Gloria Big Sorrel Horse, Aboriginal Patient Navigator
gloria.bigsorrelhorse@interiorhealth

Kelowna: Kelowna General Hospital
Affiliated with: Interior Health Authority
2268 Pandosy St., Kelowna, BC V1Y 1T2
Tel: 250-862-4000; *Fax:* 250-862-4201
Toll-Free: 888-877-4442
www.interiorhealth.ca
Social Media: www.facebook.com/InteriorHealth; twitter.com/Interior_Health; www.youtube.com/InteriorHealthAuth; www.linkedin.com/company/interior-health-authority
Number of Beds: 300+ beds
Note: Programs & services include: acute neurology; acute psychiatry; angioplasty; antepartum care; arthritis rehabilitation; cardiac angiogram; cardioversion; chemotherapy; chronic obstructive pulmonary disease services; community care; community respiratory therapy; convalescent care; CT scan; dental surgery; diabetes education program; diagnostic bronchoscopy; diagnostic cardiology; ear, nose & throat; echocardiogram; ECG/EKG; emergency; end of life/palliative; endocrinology; endoscopy; enterostomal therapy; fluoroscopy; gastroenterology; general medicine, rehabilitation & surgery; geriatric medicine; hematology; holter monitor; hospice; intensive care; intrapartum care; laboratory; mammorgaphy; maternity; mental health & substance abuse; microbiology; MRI; nuclear medicine; nutrition; oncology; ophthalmology; orthotics; otolaryngology surgery; pediatrics; pharmacy; physiotherapy; plastic surgery; postpartum care; psoriasis & phototherapy; radiology; respiratory therapy; sleep disorders; speech-language pathology; spiritual care; telehealth; transfusion; ultrasound; urology; vascular & thoracic surgery; vasectomy; vision; & wound care
Tracy McDonald, Administrator, Health Services

Kitimat: Kitimat General Hospital & Health Centre
Affiliated with: Northern Health Authority
920 Lahakas Blvd. South, Kitimat, BC V8C 2S3
Tel: 250-632-2121; *Fax:* 250-632-8726
www.northernhealth.ca
Social Media: www.facebook.com/NorthernHealth; twitter.com/northern_health; www.youtube.com/northernhealthbc; www.linkedin.com/company/northern-health-authority
Number of Beds: 31 acute care beds; 36 residential care beds
Note: Programs & services include: acute care; medicine; pediatrics; surgery; obstetrics; emergency; physiotherapy; radiology; laboratory; home support/home nursing; long-term care case management; orthopedics; & visiting specialists in urology, ENT surgery, dermatology, neurology, ophthalmology, & radiology.

Langley: Langley Memorial Hospital
Affiliated with: Fraser Health Authority
Former Name: Langley Health Services
22051 Fraser Hwy., Langley, BC V3A 4H4
Tel: 604-514-6000; *Fax:* 604-534-8283
feedback@fraserhealth.ca
www.fraserhealth.ca
Social Media: www.facebook.com/FraserHealthAuthority; twitter.com/Fraserhealth; www.youtube.com/fraserhealth; www.linkedin.com/company/fraser-health-authority
Number of Beds: 166 acute care beds; 224 extended care beds
Note: Programs & services include: acute care; ambulatory care; antepartum care; CT scan; echocardiography; emergency; fluoroscopy; general medicine, radiography & surgery; hospice residence; inpatient psychiatry unit; intensive care; interventional radiography; maternity; outpatient services; pediatrics; pharmacy; postpartum care; spiritual care; & ultrasound.
Andy Libbiter, Executive Director

Lillooet: Lillooet Hospital & Health Centre
Affiliated with: Interior Health Authority
Former Name: Lillooet District Hospital & Community Health Programs
951 Murray St., Lillooet, BC V0K 1V0
Tel: 250-256-4233; *Fax:* 250-256-1336
Toll-Free: 855-656-4233
www.interiorhealth.ca
Social Media: www.facebook.com/InteriorHealth; twitter.com/Interior_Health; www.youtube.com/InteriorHealthAuth; www.linkedin.com/company/interior-health-authority
Number of Beds: 6 beds
Note: Programs & services include: antepartum care; community care; dental surgery; diabetes education program; ECG/EKG; emergency; end of life/palliative care; endoscopy; general medicine; general surgery; holter monitor; home support; hospice; intrapartum care; laboratory; maternity; mental health & substance issues; nutrition; physiotherapy; postpartum care; prenatal; radiology; rehabilitation; social work; telehealth; vasectomy; & wound care.
Jennifer Thur, Administrator

MacKenzie: MacKenzie & District Hospital & Health Centre
Affiliated with: Northern Health Authority
Former Name: Mackenzie & District Hospital
PO Box 249, 45 Centennial Dr., MacKenzie, BC V0J 2C0
Tel: 250-997-3263; *Fax:* 250-997-3940
www.northernhealth.ca
Social Media: www.facebook.com/NorthernHealth; twitter.com/northern_health; www.youtube.com/northernhealthbc; www.linkedin.com/company/northern-health-authority
Number of Beds: 5 beds
Population Served: 3900
Note: Programs & services include: emergency; medicine; medical imaging; laboratory; home care nursing; public health; & mental health & addictions.

Maple Ridge: Ridge Meadows Hospital
Affiliated with: Fraser Health Authority
Former Name: Ridge Meadows Hospice Society
PO Box 5000, 11666 Laity St., Maple Ridge, BC V2X 7G5
Tel: 604-463-4111; *Fax:* 604-463-1888
feedback@fraserhealth.ca
www.fraserhealth.ca
Social Media: www.facebook.com/FraserHealthAuthority; twitter.com/Fraserhealth; www.youtube.com/fraserhealth; www.linkedin.com/company/fraser-health-authority
Number of Beds: 125 acute care beds; 148 residential care beds; 20 psychiatric beds; 10 convalescent beds; 10 hospice beds
Note: Programs & services include: acute care; ambulatory care; antepartum care; cardiac; CT scan; emergency; fluoroscopy; general medicine, radiography, rehabilitation & surgery; inpatient psychiatry; intensive care; interventional radiography; mammography; maternity; medical daycare; medical oncology; outpatient services; pediatrics; pharmacy; postpartum, pulmonary; spiritual care; & ultrasound.
Valerie Spurrell, Executive Director

Masset: Northern Haida Gwaii Hospital & Health Centre
Affiliated with: Northern Health Authority
PO Box 319, 2520 Harrison Ave., Masset, BC V0T 1M0
Tel: 250-626-4700; *Fax:* 250-626-4709
www.northernhealth.ca
Number of Beds: 4 acute care beds; 4 long-term care beds
Note: Programs & services include: acute care; emergency; general medicine; surgery; community health; public health; & mental health.

McBride: McBride & District Hospital
Affiliated with: Northern Health Authority
1136 - 5th Ave., McBride, BC V0J 2E0
Tel: 250-569-2251; *Fax:* 250-569-2230
www.northernhealth.ca
Social Media: www.facebook.com/NorthernHealth; twitter.com/northern_health; www.youtube.com/northernhealthbc; www.linkedin.com/company/northern-health-authority
Number of Beds: 3 acute care beds; 8 long-term care beds

Merritt: Nicola Valley Hospital & Health Centre
Affiliated with: Interior Health Authority
Former Name: Nicola Valley General Hospital
3451 Voght St., Merritt, BC V1K 1C6
Tel: 250-378-2242; *Fax:* 250-378-3287
www.interiorhelath.ca
Social Media: www.facebook.com/InteriorHealth; www.twitter.com/interior_health; www.youtube.com/InteriorHealthAuth; www.linkedin.com/company/interior-health-authority
Number of Beds: 8 beds
Note: Programs & services include: diabetes education program; emergency; rehabilitation & physiotherapy; public health; mental health; home & community care nursing; home support; laboratory; & x-ray.

Mission: Mission Memorial Hospital
Affiliated with: Fraser Health Authority
7324 Hurd St., Mission, BC V2V 3H5
Tel: 604-826-6261; *Fax:* 604-826-9513
feedback@fraserhealth.ca
www.fraserhealth.ca
Social Media: www.facebook.com/FraserHealthAuthority; twitter.com/Fraserhealth; www.youtube.com/fraserhealth; www.linkedin.com/company/fraser-health-authority
Number of Beds: 20 beds; 2 palliative care beds
Note: Programs & services include: acute care; ambulatory care; emergency; general medicine & radiography; hospice residence; orthopaedic surgery; outpatient laboratory; residential care; spiritual care; & ultrasound.
Dr. Shallen Letwin, Executive Director

Nakusp: Arrow Lakes Hospital
Affiliated with: Interior Health Authority
97 East 1st Ave., Nakusp, BC V0G 1R0
Tel: 250-265-3622; *Fax:* 250-265-4435
www.interiorhealth.ca
Social Media: www.facebook.com/InteriorHealth; twitter.com/Interior_Health; www.youtube.com/InteriorHealthAuth; www.linkedin.com/company/interior-health-authority
Number of Beds: 14 beds
Note: Programs & services include: community care; community respiratory therapy; diabetes education program; emergency; end of life/palliative care; extended care; general medicine; hospice; laboratory; mental health & substance abuse; nutrition/dietitian; physiotherapy; pulmonary diagnostics; radiology; telehealth; transfusion; & wound care.

Nanaimo: Nanaimo Regional General Hospital
Affiliated with: Vancouver Island Health Authority
1200 Dufferin Cres., Nanaimo, BC V9S 2B7
Tel: 250-755-7691 *Toll-Free:* 250-947-8214
www.viha.ca
Social Media: www.facebook.com/135150073228437; twitter.com/vanislandhealth
Number of Beds: 220+ beds
Note: Programs & services include: Aboriginal health nurse; acute inpatient psychiatric services; cardiac risk reduction; diabetes education; eye health; heart function; heart health; laboratory; medical imaging; neurophysiology; nutrition; pacemaker; pain program; rehabilitation; spiritual care; & surgery.
Allison Cutler, Executive Director, Population & Community Health
Melina Simonian, Aboriginal Patient Liaison
Melina.simonian@viha.ca

Nelson: Kootenay Lake Hospital
Affiliated with: Interior Health Authority
3 View St., Nelson, BC V1L 2V1
Tel: 250-352-3111; *Fax:* 250-354-2320
Toll-Free: 866-352-3111
www.interiorhealth.ca
Social Media: www.facebook.com/InteriorHealth; twitter.com/Interior_Health; www.youtube.com/InteriorHealthAuth; www.linkedin.com/company/interior-health-authority
Number of Beds: 30 beds
Note: Services offered include: antepartum care; chemotherapy; chronic obstructive pulmonary disease services; community care; community respiratory therapy; convalescent care; CT scan; dental surgery; diabetes education program; echocardiogram; ECG/EKG; emergency; end of life/palliative care; endoscopy; general medicine & rehabilitation; geriatric medicine; hematology; holter monitor; hospice; intrapartum care; laboratory; mammography; maternity; microbiology; nutrition; oncology; opthalmology; pediatrics; pharmacy; physiotherapy; postpartum care; pulmonary diagnostics & rehabilitation; radiology; telehealth; transfusion; & ultrasound.
Dorothy Wayling, Contact

New Westminster: Royal Columbian Hospital
Affiliated with: Fraser Health Authority
330 East Columbia St., New Westminster, BC V3L 3W7
Tel: 604-520-4253
feedback@fraserhealth.ca
www.fraserhealth.ca
Social Media: www.facebook.com/FraserHealthAuthority; twitter.com/Fraserhealth; www.youtube.com/fraserhealth; www.linkedin.com/company/fraser-health-institute
Year Founded: 1862
Number of Beds: 402 acute care beds
Note: Programs & services include: emergency; acute care; care for the elderly, angiography; antepartum care; bone densitometry; cardiac; bronchoscopy services; ultrasound; fluoroscopy; radiography; surgery unit; haemodialysis; psychiatry; intensive care unit; MRI; mammography; oncology;

neonatal intensive care; neurological services; orthopaedic surgery; paediatrics; pantomography; physiotherapy; plastic surgery; & vascular & thoracic surgery.
Judith Hockney, Executive Director

***North Vancouver:* North Vancouver: Lions Gate Hospital**
Affiliated with: Vancouver Coastal Health
231 - 15 St. East, North Vancouver, BC V7L 2L7
Tel: 604-988-3131; *Fax:* 604-984-5838
feedback@vch.ca
www.vch.ca
Social Media: www.facebook.com/VCHhealthcare; twitter.com/VCHhealthcare; www.youtube.com/VCHhealthcare
Number of Beds: 268 beds
Note: Programs & services include: acute care; angiography; antepartum services; bone densitometry; cardiac; chemotherapy; COPD clinic; CT scan; emergency; fluoroscopy; interventional radiology; joint replacement; MRI; mammography; maternity; neonatal intensive care; neurological rehabilitation; nuclear medicine; Osteoarthritis Service Integration System (OASIS); pediatrics; palliative care; psychiatrics; pulmonary/respiratory; speech-language pathology; spirometry testing; ultrasound; & x-ray/radiology.
Wendy Hansson, Chief Operating Officer

***Oliver:* South Okanagan General Hospital**
Affiliated with: Interior Health Authority
911 McKinney Rd., Oliver, BC V0H 1T0
Tel: 250-498-5000; *Fax:* 250-498-5004
www.interiorhealth.ca
Social Media: www.facebook.com/InteriorHealth; twitter.com/Interior_Health; www.youtube.com/InteriorHealthAuth; www.linkedin.com/company/interior-health-authority
Number of Beds: 18 beds
Note: Programs & services include: chronic obstructive pulmonary disease services; community care; diabetes education program; ECG/EKG; emergency; end of life/palliative care; extended care; fluoroscopy; general medicine; hematology; holter monitor; hospice; laboratory; nutrition; pharmacy; physiotherapy; radiology; telehealth; & wound care.
Sherry Uribe, Administrator
Jayne Taylor, Aboriginal Patient Liaison
jayne.taylor@interiorhealth.ca

***Penticton:* Penticton Regional Hospital (PRH)**
Affiliated with: Interior Health Authority
550B Carmi Ave., Penticton, BC V2A 3G6
Tel: 250-492-4000; *Fax:* 250-492-9068
www.interiorhealth.ca
Social Media: www.facebook.com/InteriorHealth; twitter.com/Interior_Health; www.youtube.com/InteriorHealthAuth; www.linkedin.com/interior-health-authority
Number of Beds: 137 beds
Note: Programs & services include: acute neurology & psychiatric services; antepartum care; cardioversion; chemotherapy; chronic obstructive pulmonary disease services; community care; community respiratory therapy; CT scan; diabetes education program; diagnostic bronchoscopy; diagnostic cardiology; ear, nose & throat; echocardiogram; ECG/EKG; emergency; endoscopy; enterostomal therapy; extended care; fluoroscopy; gastroenterology; general medicine, rehabilitation & surgery; hematology; holter monitor; hospice; intensive care; intrapartum care; laboratory; mammography; maternity; mental health & substance abuse; microbiology; MRI; nutrition; oncology; opthalmology; orthotics; otolaryngology surgery; pediatrics; pharmacy; physiotherapy; postpartum care; pulmonary diagnostics; radiology; respiratory therapy; speech-language pathology; spiritual care; telehealth; transesophageal echocardiogram (TEE); transfusion; ultrasound; urology; vasectomy; & wound care. Also offers the Mary Pack Arthritis Program, a service of Vancouver Coastal Health.
Lori Motluk, Senior Administrator

***Port Alberni:* West Coast General Hospital**
Affiliated with: Vancouver Island Health Authority
3949 Port Alberni Hwy., Port Alberni, BC V9Y 4S1
Tel: 250-723-1370
info@viha.ca
www.viha.ca
Social Media: www.facebook.com/135150073228437; twitter.com/vanislandhealth
Number of Beds: 52 acute care beds; 32 extended care beds
Note: Programs & services include: Aboriginal health; diabetes education; laboratory; nutrition; rehabilitation; & surgery.
Sarah Kowalenko, Communications & Public Relations Assistant, VIHA
250-740-6951, Sarah.Kowalenko@viha.ca
Ina Seitcher, First Nations Advocate Nurse
inaseitcher@viha.ca

***Port Hardy:* Port Hardy Hospital**
Affiliated with: Vancouver Island Health Authority
9120 Granville, Port Hardy, BC V0N 2P0
Tel: 250-949-6011
info@viha.ca
www.viha.ca
Social Media: www.facebook.com/135150073228437; twitter.com/vanislandhealth
Number of Beds: 17 beds
Note: Programs & services include: Aboriginal health; acute care; emergency; residential care; ambulatory outpatient services; laboratory; medical detox; palliative care; emergency obstetrics; visiting specialists; & x-ray.
Dr. Ron Hiebert, Medical Director, Rural Health Services
Caroline Kennard, Aboriginal Patient Liaison
250-370-8847, caroline.kennard@viha.ca

***Port McNeill:* Port McNeill & District Hospital**
Affiliated with: Vancouver Island Health Authority
Also Known As: Port McNeill Hospital
2750 Kingcome Place, Port McNeill, BC V0N 2R0
Tel: 250-956-4461
info@viha.ca
www.viha.ca
Social Media: www.facebook.com/135150073228437; twitter.com/vanislandhealth
Number of Beds: 11 acute care beds
Note: Services include: acute care; ambulatory outpatient services; diabetes education; emergency; laboratory; medical detox; medical imaging; nutrition; palliative care; regional obstetrics; & visiting specialists.
Sarah Kowalenko, Communications & Public Relations Assistant, VIHA
250-740-6951, Sarah.Kowalenko@viha.ca

***Port Moody:* Eagle Ridge Hospital (ERH)**
Affiliated with: Fraser Health Authority
475 Guildford Way, Port Moody, BC V3H 3W9
Tel: 604-461-2022; *Fax:* 604-461-9972
feedback@fraserhealth.ca
www.fraserhealth.ca
Social Media: www.facebook.com/FraserHealthAuthority; twitter.com/Fraserhealth; www.youtube.com/fraserhealth; www.linkedin.com/company/fraser-health-authority
Year Founded: 1984
Number of Beds: 90 beds
Note: Programs & services include: acute care; ambulatory care; cardiac; CT scan; emergency; fluoroscopy; general medicine, radiography & surgery; high intensity rehabilitation unit; outpatient services; pharmacy; spiritual care; & ultrasound.
Lakh Bagri, Executive Director

***Powell River:* Powell River General Hospital**
Affiliated with: Vancouver Coastal Health
5000 Joyce Ave., Powell River, BC V8A 5R3
Tel: 604-485-3211; *Fax:* 604-485-3243
feedback@vhc.ca
www.vha.ca
Social Media: www.facebook.com/VCHhealthcare; twitter.com/VCHhealthcare; www.youtube.com/VCHhealthcare
Number of Beds: 33 beds
Note: Programs & services include: community outreach for the elderly; CT scan; diabetes education; emergency; fluoroscopy; intensive care; laboratory medicine; mammography; maternity; nutrition; pharmacy; ultrasound; & x-ray/radiology.

***Prince George:* University Hospital of Northern British Columbia (UHNBC)**
Affiliated with: Northern Health Authority
Former Name: Prince George Regional Hospital
1475 Edmonton St., Prince George, BC V2M 1S2
Tel: 250-565-2000; *Fax:* 250-565-2343
www.northernhealth.ca
Social Media: www.facebook.com/NorthernHealth; twitter.com/Northern_Health; www.youtube.com/nothernhealthBC; www.linkedin.com/company/northern-health-authority
Number of Beds: 338 beds
Note: Hospital & clinical academic campus run by the University of British Columbia & University of Northern British Columbia.

***Prince Rupert:* Prince Rupert Regional Hospital**
Affiliated with: Northern Health Authority
1305 Summit Ave., Prince Rupert, BC V8J 2A6
Tel: 250-624-2171; *Fax:* 250-624-2195
www.northernhealth.ca
Social Media: www.facebook.com/NorthernHealth; twitter.com/northern_health; www.youtube.com/northernhealthBC; www.linkedin.com/company/northern-health-authority
Number of Beds: 25 beds
Note: Programs & services include: acute care; diagnostics; ultrasound; CAT scan; surgery; emergency; day care; extended care; diabetes education; healthy heart; rehabilitation; & specialists in pediatrics, radiology, obstetrics, gynecology, surgery, internal medicine, podiatry & orthopedics.

***Princeton:* Princeton General Hospital**
Affiliated with: Interior Health Authority
98 Ridgewood Ave., Princeton, BC V0X 1W0
Tel: 250-295-3233
www.interiorhealth.ca
Social Media: www.facebook.com/InteriorHealth; twitter.com/Interior_Health; www.youtube.com/InteriorHealthAuth; www.linkedin.com/company/interior-health-authority
Number of Beds: 6 acute care beds
Note: Programs & services include: community care; convalescent care; diabetes education program; drug & alcohol resources; ECG/EKG; emergency; end of life/palliative care; general medicine; holter monitor; hospice; laboratory; psychiatry; radiology; telehealth; transfusion; & wound care.

***Queen Charlotte:* Queen Charlotte Islands General Hospital**
Affiliated with: Northern Health Authority
PO Box 9, 3200 Oceanview Dr., Queen Charlotte, BC V0T 1S0
Tel: 250-559-4300; *Fax:* 250-559-4312
www.northernhealth.ca
Social Media: www.facebook.com/NorthernHealth; twitter.com/northern_health; www.youtube.com/northernhealthBC; www.linkedin.com/company/northern-health-authority
Number of Beds: 16 beds
Population Served: 3000
Note: Programs & services include: acute care; long-term care; general medicine; obstetrics; emergency; minor surgery; & affiliations with alcohol & drug counsellors, public health nurses, social workers & Native community health workers.

***Quesnel:* GR Baker Memorial Hospital**
Affiliated with: Northern Health Authority
543 Front St., Quesnel, BC V2J 2K7
Tel: 250-985-5600; *Fax:* 250-992-5652
www.northernhealth.ca
Social Media: www.facebook.com/NorthernHealth; twitter.com/northern_health; www.youtube.com/northernhealthBC; www.linkedin.com/company/northern-health-authority
Year Founded: 1955
Number of Beds: 38 acute care beds; 40 extended care beds; 5 crisis stabilization beds; 4 ICU beds
Note: Programs & services include: cardiology; urology; & surgery (ENT & general). Facilities include the Dunrovin Park Lodge Care Facility & Maple House.

***Revelstoke:* Queen Victoria Hospital & Health Centre**
Affiliated with: Interior Health Authority
1200 Newlands Rd., Revelstoke, BC V0E 2S0
Tel: 250-837-2131; *Fax:* 250-837-4788
www.interiorhealth.ca
Social Media: www.facebook.com/InteriorHealth; twitter.com/Interior_Health; www.youtube.com/InteriorHealthAuth; www.linkedin.com/company/interior-health-authority
Number of Beds: 48 residential beds; 10 acute beds
Note: Programs & services include: antepartum care; chemotherapy; dental surgery; diabetes education program; ECG/EKG; emergency; end of life/palliative care; endoscopy; flouroscopy; general medicine, rehabilitation & surgery; hematology; holter monitor; hospice; intrapartum care; laboratory; maternity; mental health & substance abuse; nutrition; physiotherapy services; postpartum care; radiology; spiritual care; telehealth; transfusion; & ultrasound.
Julie Lowes, Manager

***Richmond:* Richmond Hospital**
Affiliated with: Vancouver Coastal Health
Former Name: The Richmond Hospital
7000 Westminster Hwy., Richmond, BC V6X 1A2
Tel: 604-278-9711; *Fax:* 604-244-5552
feedback@vch.ca
www.vch.ca
Social Media: www.facebook.com/VCHhealthcare; twitter.com/VCHhealthcare; www.youtube.com/VCHhealthcare
Number of Beds: 200 beds
Note: Programs & services include: acute care; ambulatory care; angiography; CT scan; continuing health services case management; diabetes education; drug & alcohol resource team; emergency; fluoroscopy; geriatrics; integrated transition team; intensive care; interventional radiology; laboratory medicine; mammography; maternity; mental health; nuclear medicine; palliative access lines; psychiatrics; rehabilitation;

speech-language pathology; spirometry testing; ultrasound; & x-ray/radiology.

Saanichton: Saanich Peninsula Hospital
Affiliated with: Vancouver Island Health Authority
2166 Mount Newton Cross Rd., Saanichton, BC V8M 2B2
Tel: 250-544-7676 *Toll-Free:* 877-370-8699
www.viha.ca
Social Media: www.facebook.com/135150073228437; twitter.com/vanislandhealth
Number of Beds: 48 acute care beds; 144 extended care beds
Note: Programs & services include: eye health; heart health; laboratory; medical imaging; nutrition; rehabilitation; residential; spiritual care; & surgery.
Sarahd Kowalenko, Communications & Public Relations Assistant, VIHA
250-740-6951, Sarah.Kowalenko@viha.ca

Salmon Arm: Shuswap Lake General Hospital
Affiliated with: Interior Health Authority
PO Box 520, 601 - 10th St. NE, Salmon Arm, BC V1E 4N6
Tel: 250-833-3600; *Fax:* 250-833-3611
Toll-Free: 877-299-1599
www.interiorhealth.ca
Social Media: www.facebook.com/InteriorHealth; twitter.com/Interior_Health; www.youtube.com/InteriorHealthAuth; www.linkedin.com/company/interior-health-authority
Number of Beds: 40 beds
Note: Programs & services include: antepartum care; cardioversion; chemotherapy; CT scan; dental surgery; diabetes education program; echocardiogram; ECG/EKG; emergency; end of life/palliative; endoscopy; gastroenterology; general medicine, rehabilitation & surgery; hematology; holter monitor; hospice; intensive care; intrapartum care; laboratory; maternity; nutrition; oncology; pharmacy; physiotherapy; postpartum care; pulmonary diagnostics & rehabilitation; radiology; speech-language pathology; spiritual care; telehealth; transfusion; ultrasound; urology; vascular & thoracic; & vasectomy.
Mark Pugh, Manager

Salt Spring Island: The Lady Minto Gulf Islands Hospital
Affiliated with: Vancouver Island Health Authority
Former Name: Lady Minto Hospital
135 Crofton Rd., Salt Spring Island, BC V8K 1T1
Tel: 250-538-4800; *Fax:* 250-538-4870
info@viha.ca
www.viha.ca
Social Media: www.facebook.com/135150073228437; twitter.com/vanislandhealth
Number of Beds: 19 acute care beds; 31 extended care beds
Note: Programs & services include: emergency; acute care; heart health; residential care; obstetrics; psychiatry; laboratory; medical imaging; spiritual care; endoscopy; pharmacy; physiotherapy; & internal medicine.
Bill Relph, Manager, Rural Services

Sechelt: St. Mary's Hospital
Affiliated with: Vancouver Coastal Health
5544 Sunshine Coast Highway, Sechelt, BC V0N 3A0
Tel: 604-885-2224; *Fax:* 604-885-8628
feedback@vch.ca
www.vch.ca
Social Media: www.facebook.com/VCHhealthcare; twitter.com/VCHhealthcare; www.youtube.com/VCHhealthcare
Number of Beds: 38 beds
Note: Programs & services include: CT scan; crisis response; emergency; fluoroscopy; laboratory medicine; mammography; pharmacy; psychiatric inpatient unit; ultrasound; & x-ray/radiology.
Dr. Eddie Berinstein, Medical Director

Smithers: Bulkley Valley District Hospital
Affiliated with: Northern Health Authority
PO Box 370, 3950 - 8th Ave., Smithers, BC V0J 2N0
Tel: 250-847-2611; *Fax:* 250-847-2446
www.northernhealth.ca
Social Media: www.facebook.com/NorthernHealth; twitter.com/northern_health; www.youtube.com/northernhealthBC; www.linkedin.com/company/northern-health-authority
Number of Beds: 25 beds
Area Served: Communities from Houston in the east to Hazelton in the west
Note: Programs & services include: acute care; emergency; medical; surgical; maternity; & palliative care.

Squamish: Squamish General Hospital
Affiliated with: Vancouver Coastal Health
38140 Behrner Dr., Squamish, BC V0N 3G0
Tel: 604-892-5211; *Fax:* 604-892-9417
feedback@vch.ca
www.vch.ca
Social Media: www.facebook.com/VCHhealthcare; twitter.com/VCHhealthcare; www.youtube.com/VCHhealthcare
Number of Beds: 21 beds
Note: Programs & services include: emergency; general medicine & surgery; obstetrics; palliative care; physiotherapy; pharmacy; diagnostic imaging; laboratory; ambulatory care; chemotherapy; fluoroscopy; diabetic day clinic; & x-ray/radiology.
Jane McQuinn, Manager, Pharmacy

Stewart: Stewart Health Centre
Affiliated with: Northern Health Authority
PO Box 8, 904 Brightwell St., Stewart, BC V0T 1W0
Tel: 250-636-2221; *Fax:* 250-636-2715
www.northernhealth.ca
Note: Programs & services include: public health; infant & child care; walk-in emergency; & doctor's clinic.

Surrey: Surrey Memorial Hospital
Affiliated with: Fraser Health Authority
13750 - 96 Ave., Surrey, BC V3V 1Z2
Tel: 604-581-2211; *Fax:* 604-588-3320
feedback@fraserhealth.ca
www.fraserhealth.ca
Social Media: www.facebook.com/FraserHealthAuthority; twitter.com/Fraserhealth; www.youtube.com/fraserhealth; www.linkedin.com/company/fraser-health-authority
Number of Beds: 499 beds
Note: Programs & services include: emergency; adolescent psychiatry; angiography; antepartum care; diagnostic imaging (CT scans, bone densitometry, fluoroscopy, mammography, MRI, radiology, ultrasound); cardiology; outpatient services; dental surgery; acute tertiary palliative care; intensive care; neonatal intensive care; ophthalmology; otolaryngology; paediatrics; pharmacy; plastic surgery; postpartum care; psychiatry; sleep lab; speech language pathology; spiritual care; urological surgery; & vascular & thoracic surgery.
Cathy Heritage, Executive Director
Dr. Urbain Ip, Medical Coordinator

Terrace: Mills Memorial Hospital
Affiliated with: Northern Health Authority
4720 Haugland Ave., Terrace, BC V8G 2W7
Tel: 250-635-2211; *Fax:* 250-638-4017
www.northernhealth.ca
Social Media: www.facebook.com/northernhealth; twitter.com/northern_health; www.youtube.com/northernhealthBC; www.linkedin.com/company/northern-health-authority
Number of Beds: 39 acute care beds
Note: Programs & services include: acute care; community based programs; CT & nuclear medicine; obstetrics/gynecology; psychiatry; surgery; urology; ophthalmology; otolaryngology; anaesthetics; radiology; nuclear medicine; pathology; ENT; podiatrists; pediatrics; & internal medicine.

Tofino: Tofino General Hospital
Affiliated with: Vancouver Island Health Authority
PO Box 190, 261 Neill St., Tofino, BC V0R 2Z0
Tel: 250-725-4010
info@viha.ca
www.viha.ca
Social Media: www.facebook.com/135150073228437; twitter.com/vanislandhelath
Year Founded: 1954
Number of Beds: 10 acute care beds
Note: Programs & services include: acute care; emergency; emergency obstetrics; outpatient ambulatory care; telehealth; medical imaging; laboratory services; outpatient blood collection; & rehabilitation.
Kathryn Kilpatrick, Site Manager
250-725-4005, Kathryn.Kilpatrick@viha.ca

Trail: Kootenay Boundary Regional Hospital
Affiliated with: Interior Health Authority
Former Name: Trail Regional Hospital
1200 Hospital Bench, Trail, BC V1R 4M1
Tel: 250-368-3311; *Fax:* 250-364-3422
Toll-Free: 866-368-3314
info@kbrh.ca
www.kbrh.ca
Number of Beds: 75 beds
Note: Programs & services include: antepartum care; arthritis rehabilitation; cardioversion; chemotherapy; chronic obstructive pulmonary disease services; community care; convalescent care; CT scan; dental surgery; diabetes education program; ear, nose & throat; echocardiogram; ECG/EKG; emergency; end of life/palliative; endoscopy; enterostomal therapy; extended care; fluoroscopy; general medicine, rehabilitation & surgery; geriatric medicine; hematology; holter monitor; hospice; intensive care; intrapartum care; laboratory; mammography; maternity; mental health & substance abuse; microbiology; MRI; nuclear medicine; nutrition; oncology; opthalmology; orthotics; otolaryngology surgery; pediatrics; physiotherapy; plastic surgery; postpartum care; psoriasis & phototherapy; psychiatry; pulmonary diagnostics; radiology; respiratory therapy; speech-language pathology; spiritual care; telehealth; transfusion; ultrasound; urology; vasectomy; & wound care.

Vancouver: Mount Saint Joseph Hospital
Providence Health Care
Affiliated with: Vancouver Coastal Health
Also Known As: MSJ
3080 Prince Edward St., Vancouver, BC V5T 3N4
Tel: 604-874-1141
www.providencehealthcare.org
Social Media: www.facebook.com/ProvidenceHealthCare.BC; twitter.com/Providence_Hlth; www.youtube.com/ProvidenceVancouver; www.linkedin.com/company/8151
Number of Beds: 240 acute care beds; 100 extended care beds
Note: Programs & services include: cardiac care; chronic disease management; dermatology; ear, nose & throat; emergency; end of life; eye care; geriatrics; infectious diseases; intensive care; lung care; mental health; neurology; organ transplants; pathology & lab; plastic surgery; primary health care; prostate; radiology; rehabilitation; residential care; & surgery.
Dianne Doyle, President & CEO, Providence Health Care

Vancouver: St. Paul's Hospital
Providence Health Care
Affiliated with: Vancouver Coastal Health
1081 Burrard St., Vancouver, BC V6Z 1Y6
Tel: 604-682-2344
www.providencehealthcare.org
Social Media: www.facebook.com/ProvidenceHealthCare.BC; twitter.com/Providence_Hlth; www.youtube.com/ProvidenceVancouver; www.linkedin.com/company/8151
Number of Beds: 440 acute care beds
Note: Programs & services include: addiction; allergy/immunology; arthritis; blood; bones, muscles & joints; cardiac; chronic disease management; dermatology; diabetes, hormones & metabolism; digestive system; ear, nose & throat; emergency; end of life; eye care; female reproductive health; geriatrics; infectious diseases; intensive care; kidney; lung; maternity & obstetrics; mental health; neurology; organ transplants; pathology & lab; plastic surgery; primary health care; prostate; radiology; rehabilitation; & surgery.
Dianne Doyle, President & CEO, Providence Health Care

Vancouver: UBC Hospital
Affiliated with: Vancouver Coastal Health
Also Known As: UBC Health Sciences Centre Hospital
2211 Westbrook Mall, Vancouver, BC V6T 2B5
Tel: 604-822-7121
www.vch.ca
Social Media: www.facebook.com/VCHhealthcare; twitter.com/VCHhealthcare; www.youtube.com/VCHhealthcare
Year Founded: 1968
Number of Beds: 332 beds
Note: Divided into 3 buildings: the Detwiller Pavilion is known for its psychiatric unit; the Purdy Pavilion offers the BC Centre for Sexual Medicine, MRI, movement disorder clinic, & residential care; & the Koerner Pavilion offers angiography, bladder care, breast reconstruction program, Alzeimer's clinic, CT scan, fluoroscopy, interventional radiology, laboratory medicine, medical daycare, nuclear medicine, nutrition, sleep disorders program, speech-language pathology, spirometry testing, surgical clinic, swallowing clinic, ultrasound, urgent care & x-ray/radiology.
Vivian Eliopoulos, Chief Operating Officer, Vancouver Acute, VCH

Vancouver: Vancouver General Hospital - Centennial Pavilion
Affiliated with: Vancouver Coastal Health
855 West 12th Ave., Vancouver, BC V5Z 1M9
Tel: 604-875-4111
feedback@vch.ca
www.vch.ca
Social Media: www.facebook.com/VCHhealthcare; twitter.com/VCHhealthcare; www.youtube.com/VCHhealthcare
Number of Beds: 1,000+ beds
Note: Programs & services include: angiography; BC Leukemia Bone Marrow Transplant Program; bone densitometry; bronchoscopy; cardiac; CT scan; dialysis services; ECG;

endoscopy clinic; epilepsy program; Eye Bank of British Columbia; fluoroscopy; hyperbaric chamber; intensive care; interventional radiology; mental health; MRI; nuclear medicine; palliative care; perioperative care; psychiatric assessment; sexual assault service; speech-language pathology; spiritual care; spirometry testing; Short Term Assessment & Treatment (STAT) Centre; ultrasound; vascular access clinic; & wound, ostomy & continence nurse clinic.
Vivian Eliopoulos, Chief Operating Officer, Vancouver Acute, VCH

Vanderhoof: St. John Hospital
Affiliated with: Northern Health Authority
3255 Hospital Rd., Vanderhoof, BC V0J 3A0
Tel: 250-567-2211; *Fax:* 250-567-9713
www.northernhealth.ca
Social Media: www.facebook.com/NorthernHealth; twitter.com/Northern_Health; www.youtube.com/northernhealthBC; www.linkedin.com/company/northern-health-authority
Year Founded: 1941
Number of Beds: 24 acute care; 8 bassinets
Population Served: 5000; *Number of Employees:* 180
Note: Programs & services include: emergency; labor & delivery; diagnostic imaging (X-ray, ultrasound); orthopedic surgery; general surgeries; physiotherapy; & visiting specialists.

Vernon: Vernon Jubilee Hospital (VJH)
Affiliated with: Interior Health Authority
2101 - 32 St. South, Vernon, BC V1T 5L2
Tel: 250-558-2211; *Fax:* 250-545-0369
www.interiorhealth.ca
Social Media: www.facebook.com/InteriorHealth; twitter.com/Interior_Health; www.youtube.com/InteriorHealthAuth; www.linkedin.com/company/interior-health-authority
Number of Beds: 148 beds
Note: Programs & services include: acute neurology; antepartum care; arthritis rehabilitation; cardioversion; chemotherapy; chronic obstructive pulmonary disease services; community care; CT scan; dental surgery; diabetes education program; ear, nose & throat; echocardiogram; ECG/EKG; emergency; end of life/palliative care; endoscopy; enterostomal therapy; extended care; fluoroscopy; general medicine, rehabilitation & surgery; hematology; holter monitor; intensive care; intrapartum care; laboratory; mammography; maternity; mental health & substance abuse; microbiology; nuclear medicine; nutrition; oncology; ophthalmology; orthopaedic surgery; otolaryngology surgery; pediatrics; pharmacy; physiotherapy; postpartum care; pulmonary diagnostics & rehabilitation; radiology; respiratory therapy; social work; speech-language pathology; spiritual care; telehealth; transesophageal echocardiogram (TEE); transfusion; ultrasound; urology; vasectomy; & wound care.
Nancy Serwo, Administrator, Health Services

Victoria: Queen Alexandra Centre for Children's Health
Affiliated with: Vancouver Island Health Authority
2400 Arbutus Rd., Victoria, BC V8N 1V7
Tel: 250-519-5390
www.viha.ca
Social Media: www.facebook.com/135150073228437; twitter.com/vanislandhealth
Note: Acute & extended care
Dr. Brendan Carr, President & CEO, VIHA

Victoria: Royal Jubilee Hospital
Affiliated with: Vancouver Island Health Authority
1952 Bay St., Victoria, BC V8R 1J8
Tel: 250-370-8000 *Toll-Free:* 877-370-8699
info@viha.ca
www.viha.ca
Social Media: www.facebook.com/135150073228437; twitter.com/vanislandhealth
Note: Acute care, cystic fibrosis clinic, rehabilitation services, breast physiotherapy, breast surgical oncology. Located in Memorial Pavilion.
Dr. Brendan Carr, President & CEO, VIHA

Victoria: Victoria General Hospital
Affiliated with: Vancouver Island Health Authority
1 Hospital Way, Victoria, BC V8Z 6R5
Tel: 250-727-4212 *Toll-Free:* 877-370-8699
www.viha.ca
Social Media: www.facebook.com/135150073228437; twitter.com/vanislandhealth
Note: Programs & services include: Aboriginal health nurses; breast health; diabetes education; eye health; heart health; Jeneece Place; laboratory; medical imaging; neurosciences; nutrition; rehabiliation; spiritual care; stroke rapid assessment; & surgery.
Dr. Brendan Carr, President & CEO, VIHA

White Rock: Peace Arch Hospital
Affiliated with: Fraser Health Authority
15521 Russell Ave., White Rock, BC V4B 2R4
Tel: 604-531-5512
feedback@fraserhealth.ca
www.fraserhealth.ca
Social Media: www.facebook.com/FraserHealthAuthority; twitter.com/Fraserhealth; www.youtube.com/fraserhealth; www.linkedin.com/company/fraser-health-authority
Number of Beds: 475 acute care beds; 300 residential care beds
Note: Programs & services include: acute care; adult community support; ambulatory care; angiography; antepartum care; cardiac; CT scan; diagnostic bronchoscopy; echocardiography; emergency; fluoroscopy; general medicine, radiography, rehabilitation & surgery; geriatrics; hospice residence; inpatient psychiatry unit; intensive care; MRI; mammography; maternity; nuclear medicine; outpatient services; pharmacy; postpartum care; pulmonary function lab; spiritual care; & ultrasound.
Loraine Jenkins, Executive Director

Williams Lake: Cariboo Memorial Hospital
Affiliated with: Interior Health Authority
517 North 6th Ave., Williams Lake, BC V2G 2G8
Tel: 250-392-4411; *Fax:* 250-392-2157
www.interiorhealth.ca
Social Media: www.facebook.com/InteriorHealth; twitter.com/Interior_Health; www.youtube.com/InteriorHealthAuth; www.linkedin.com/company/interior-health-authority
Number of Beds: 31 beds
Note: Programs & services include: antepartum care; chemotherapy; dietitian; community care; community respiratory therapy; CT scan; dental surgery; diabetes education program; diagnostic bronchoscopy; echocardiogram; ECG/EKG; emergency; end of life/palliative care; endoscopy; general medicine; general rehabilitation; general surgery; hematology; holter monitor; intensive care; intrapartum care; laboratory; mammography; maternity services; mental health & substance abuse; nutrition; oncology; pediatrics; physiotherapy; postpartum care; pulmonary diagnostics/rehabilitation; radiology; spiritual care; telehealth; transfusion; ultrasound; & vasectomy.
Deb Runge, Director, Acute Care
Barbara Mack, Aboriginal Health Liaison
250-392-8266, Barbara.Mack@interiorhealth.ca

Federal Hospitals

Abbotsford: Pacific Institution / Regional Treatment Centre
Correctional Services Canada, Dept. of the Solicitor General
Former Name: Regional Health Centre (Pacific)
Also Known As: Pacific Institution
PO Box 3000, 33344 King Rd., Abbotsford, BC V2S 4P4
Tel: 604-870-7700; *Fax:* 604-870-7746
www.csc-scc.gc.ca/text/facilit/institutprofiles/pacific-eng.shtml
Year Founded: 1972
Number of Beds: 122 beds
Note: Psychiatric care unit, health centre, rehabilitation unit, regional reception/assessment centre and intensive program unit; a mens' facility

Private Hospitals

Abbotsford: Menno Hospital
32945 Marshall Rd., Abbotsford, BC V2S 1K1
Tel: 604-859-7631; *Fax:* 604-859-6931
www.mennoplace.ca
Number of Beds: 150 beds
Karen Baillie, CEO
Kathrin McMath, Executive Director, Finance & Operations

Burnaby: Willingdon Care Centre
Affiliated with: Fraser Health Authority
Former Name: Willingdon Private Hospital
4435 Grange St., Burnaby, BC V5H 1P4
Tel: 604-433-2455; *Fax:* 604-433-5804

Coquitlam: Lakeshore Care Centre
Affiliated with: The Care Group
657 Gatensbury St., Coquitlam, BC V3J 5G9
Tel: 604-939-9277; *Fax:* 604-939-6518
tcgcare.com
Number of Beds: 95 beds
Lynn Aarvold, Administrator
lynnaarvold@tcgcare.com

Hope: Fraser Hope Lodge
Affiliated with: Fraser Health Authority
1275A - 7th Ave., Hope, BC V0X 1L4
Tel: 604-860-7706; *Fax:* 604-860-7708

Maple Ridge: Holyrood Manor
Revera Living
22710 Holyrood Ave., Maple Ridge, BC V2X 3E6
Tel: 604-467-8831; *Fax:* 604-467-8262
holyrood@reveraliving.com
www.reveraliving.com
Social Media: www.facebook.com/400950748267; twitter.com/Revera_Inc; www.youtube.com/user/ReveraInc; www.linkedin.com/company/revera-inc
Number of Beds: 123 beds
Jeffrey C. Lozon, President & CEO, Revera Living

North Vancouver: Lynn Valley Care Centre
Affiliated with: North Shore Private Hospital
1070 Lynn Valley Rd., North Vancouver, BC V7J 1Z8
Tel: 604-417-5477
www.lynnvalleycare.com
Leslie Cymet, Director, Care
604-982-3700, lesliecymet@nsph.ca

Vancouver: Amherst Private Hospital & Nursing Home
Affiliated with: Vancouver Coastal Health
375 West 59 Ave., Vancouver, BC V5X 1X3
Tel: 604-321-6777; *Fax:* 604-322-0123
Year Founded: 1964
Number of Beds: 74 beds
Note: Hospital Specialties: Complex care

Vancouver: Point Grey Private Hospital
The Care Group
Affiliated with: Vancouver Coastal Health
2423 Cornwall Ave., Vancouver, BC V6K 1B9
Tel: 604-733-7133; *Fax:* 604-731-6056
www.tcgcare.com
Number of Beds: 75 beds
Maureen McIntosh, Owner
mcintosh.mo@gmail.com

Victoria: Wayside House
550 Foul Bay Rd., Victoria, BC V8S 4H1
Tel: 250-598-4521; *Fax:* 250-598-4547
inquiries@waysidehousevictoria.org
www.waysidehousevictoria.org
Number of Beds: 9 beds

Auxiliary Hospitals

100 Mile House: 100 Mile District General Hospital
Affiliated with: Interior Health Authority
South Cariboo Health Centre, 555 Cedar Ave. South, 100 Mile House, BC V0K 2E0
Tel: 250-395-7600; *Fax:* 250-395-7578
www.interiorhealth.ca
Social Media: www.facebook.com/InteriorHealth; twitter.com/Interior_Health; www.youtube.com/InteriorHealthAuth; www.linkedin.com/company/interior-health-authority
Note: Programs & services include: antepartum care; brain injury; chemotherapy; dietitian; dental surgery; ECG/EKG; emergency; end of life/palliative care; endoscopy; gastroenterology; general medicine; general rehabilitation; general surgery; hematology; holter monitor; hospice; intrapartum care; laboratory; maternity; mental health & substance abuse; oncology; physiotherapy; postpartum care; psychiatry; radiology; spiritual care; telehealth; & vasectomy.
Gayle Dunsmuir, Contact, Hospice
gayle.hospice@shawbiz.ca
Wendy Reilly, Contact, Residential Care
Wendy.Reilly@interiorhealth.ca

Bella Bella: R.W. Large Memorial Hospital
Affiliated with: Vancouver Coastal Health
88 Waglisla St., Bella Bella, BC V0T 1Z0
Tel: 250-957-2314; *Fax:* 250-957-2612
feedback@vch.ca
www.vch.ca
Social Media: www.facebook.com/VCHhealthcare; twitter.com/VCHhealthcare; www.youtube.com/VCHhealthcare
Number of Beds: 6 acute care beds; 7 continuing care beds; 3 emergency beds
Note: Residential care, including laboratory, diagnostic imaging, telehealth, medical clinic, pharmacy & ambulance services.

Vancouver: BC Children's Hospital
Affiliated with: Provincial Health Services Authority
Former Name: Crippled Children's Hospital; Children's Hospital
4480 Oak St., Vancouver, BC V6H 3V4
Tel: 604-875-2345 *Toll-Free:* 888-300-3088
comm@cw.bc.ca
www.bcchildrens.ca

Year Founded: 1928
Note: Programs & services include: Children's Heart Centre; child & youth mental health; clinical, diagnostic & family services; critical care; endocrinology & diabetes; emergency; family support; pain service; medical genetics; neurosciences; oncology, hematology & BMT; specialized pediatrics; Sunny Hill Health Centre; surgery; & trauma service.
Leslie Arnold, President

Vancouver: BC Women's Hospital & Health Centre
Affiliated with: Provincial Health Services Authority
4500 Oak St., Vancouver, BC V6H 3N1
Tel: 604-875-2424 *Toll-Free:* 888-300-3088
comm@cw.bc.ca (Communications)
www.bcwomens.ca
Info Line: 604-875-2929
Note: Hospital Specialties: Health care for women, newborn, & families; Gynecological & reproductive health services; Sexual assault service; HIV care of women & children; Birth control & abortion support & counselling; Substance dependency; Psychology; Social work; Aboriginal Health Program; Osteoporosis
Dr. Jan Christilaw, President

Vancouver: Holy Family Hospital
Providence Health Care
Affiliated with: Vancouver Coastal Health
7801 Argyle St., Vancouver, BC V5P 3L6
Tel: 604-321-2661; *Fax:* 604-321-6886
www.providencehealthcare.org
Social Media: www.facebook.com/ProvidenceHealthCare.BC; twitter.com/Providence_Hlth; www.youtube.com/ProvidenceVancouver; www.linkedin.com/company/8151
Number of Beds: 142 extended care beds
Note: Rehabilitation & residential services
Dianne Doyle, President & CEO, Providence Health Care

Victoria: Aberdeen Hospital
Affiliated with: Vancouver Island Health Authority
1450 Hillside Ave., Victoria, BC V8T 2B7
Tel: 250-370-5626 *Toll-Free:* 866-995-3299
info@viha.ca
www.viha.ca/hcc/residential/locations/aberdeen.htm
Note: Extended care hospital
Sarah Kowalenko, Communications & Public Relations Assistant, VIHA
250-740-6951, Sarah.Kowalenko@viha.ca

Victoria: Glengarry Hospital
Affiliated with: Vancouver Island Health Authority
Former Name: Glengarry Extended Care Hospital
1780 Fairfield Rd., Victoria, BC V8S 1G7
Tel: 250-370-5626 *Toll-Free:* 866-995-3299
info@viha.ca
www.viha.ca/hcc/residential/locations/glengarry.htm
Year Founded: 1963
Number of Beds: 165 units
Note: Extended care hospital

Victoria: Mount Tolmie Extended Care Hospital
Affiliated with: Vancouver Island Health Authority
3690 Richmond Rd., Victoria, BC V8P 4R6
Tel: 250-370-5626 *Toll-Free:* 866-995-3299
info@viha.ca
www.viha.ca/hcc/residential/locations/mount_tolmie.htm
Number of Beds: 73 units
Note: Extended care hospital

Victoria: Priory Hospital
Affiliated with: Vancouver Island Health Authority
567 Goldstream Ave., Victoria, BC V9B 2W4
Tel: 250-370-5626 *Toll-Free:* 866-995-3299
info@viha.ca
www.viha.ca/hcc/residential/locations/priory_hiscock_heritage_woods.htm
Social Media: www.facebook.com/135150073228437; twitter.com/vanislandhealth
Number of Beds: 140 units
Note: Extended care hospital

Community Health Care Centres

100 Mile House: South Cariboo Health Centre
Affiliated with: Interior Health Authority
555 Cedar Ave. South, 100 Mile House, BC V0K 2E0
Tel: 250-395-7676
www.interiorhealth.ca

Abbotsford: Abbotsford Health Protection Office
Affiliated with: Fraser Health Authority
2776 Bourquin Cres. West, Abbotsford, BC V2S 6A4
Tel: 604-870-7900; *Fax:* 604-870-7901

Abbotsford: Abbotsford Home Health Office
Affiliated with: Fraser Health Authority
34194 Marshall Rd., Abbotsford, BC V2S 5E4
Tel: 604-556-5000; *Fax:* 604-556-5010

Abbotsford: Abbotsford Public Health Unit
Affiliated with: Fraser Health Authority
34194 Marshall Rd., Abbotsford, BC V2S 5E4
Tel: 604-864-3400; *Fax:* 604-864-3410

Agassiz: Agassiz Health Protection Office
Affiliated with: Fraser Health Authority
7243 Pioneer Ave., Agassiz, BC V0M 1A0
Tel: 604-793-7160

Agassiz: Agassiz Home Health Office
Affiliated with: Fraser Health Authority
7243 Pioneer Ave., Agassiz, BC V0M 1A0
Tel: 604-793-7160; *Fax:* 604-796-8587

Agassiz: Agassiz Public Health Unit
Affiliated with: Fraser Health Authority
7243 Pioneer Ave., Agassiz, BC V0M 1A0
Tel: 604-793-7160; *Fax:* 604-796-8587

Alexis Creek: Alexis Creek Health Centre
Affiliated with: Interior Health Authority
2592 Morton Rd., Alexis Creek, BC V0L 1A0
Tel: 250-394-4313; *Fax:* 250-964-5179
www.interiorhealth.ca

Armstrong: Armstrong Community Services
Affiliated with: Interior Health Authority
3800 Patten Dr., Armstrong, BC V0E 1B2
Tel: 250-546-4752
www.interiorhealth.ca

Armstrong: Pleasant Valley Health Centre
Affiliated with: Interior Health Authority
3800 Patten Dr., Armstrong, BC V0E 1B2
Tel: 250-546-4700; *Fax:* 250-546-8834
www.interiorhealth.ca

Bamfield: Bamfield Health Centre
Affiliated with: Vancouver Island Health Authority
PO Box 40, 353 Bamfield Rd., Bamfield, BC V0R 1B0
Tel: 250-728-3312
Kathryn Kilpatrick, Manager
Kathryn.Kilpatrick@viha.ca

Barriere: Barriere Adult Day Program
Affiliated with: Interior Health Authority
4431 Barriere Town Rd., Barriere, BC V0E 1E1
Tel: 250-672-0025
www.interiorhealth.ca

Barriere: Barriere Health Centre
Affiliated with: Interior Health Authority
4251 Barriere Town Rd., Barriere, BC V0E 1M0
Tel: 250-672-9731; *Fax:* 250-672-5144
www.interiorhealth.ca

Blue River: Blue River Health Centre
Affiliated with: Interior Health Authority
Former Name: Red Cross Outpost Hospital
858 Main St., Blue River, BC V0E 1J0
Tel: 250-673-8311
www.interiorhealth.ca

Burnaby: Burnaby Health Protection Office
Affiliated with: Fraser Health Authority
#300, 4946 Canada Way, Burnaby, BC V5G 4H7
Tel: 604-918-7683; *Fax:* 604-918-7520

Burnaby: Burnaby Home Health Office
Affiliated with: Fraser Health Authority
4946 Canada Way, Burnaby, BC V5G 4H7
Tel: 604-918-7447; *Fax:* 604-918-7631

Burnaby: Burnaby Public Health Unit
Affiliated with: Fraser Health Authority
4946 Canada Way, Burnaby, BC V5G 4H7
Tel: 604-918-7605; *Fax:* 604-918-7630

Castlegar: Castlegar & District Community Health Centre
Castlegar & District Hospital Foundation
Affiliated with: Interior Health Authority
709 - 10th St., Castlegar, BC V1N 2H7
Tel: 250-365-7711; *Fax:* 250-365-1236
www.interiorhealth.ca

Celista: Scotch Creek Medical Clinic
Affiliated with: Interior Health Authority
#2, 3874 Squilax-Anglemont Rd., Celista, BC V2C 2T1
Tel: 250-955-0660
www.interiorhealth.ca

Chase: Chase Health Centre
Affiliated with: Interior Health Authority
825 Thompson Ave., Chase, BC V0E 1M0
Tel: 250-679-3312; *Fax:* 250-679-5329
www.interiorhealth.ca

Chase: Chase Primary Health Care Clinic
Affiliated with: Interior Health Authority
826 Thompson Ave., Chase, BC V0E 1M0
Tel: 250-679-1400
www.interiorhealth.ca

Chemainus: Chemainus Health Authority
Affiliated with: Vancouver Island Health Authority
PO Box 499, 9909 Esplanade St., Chemainus, BC V0R 1K0
Tel: 250-737-2040; *Fax:* 250-246-3844
Number of Beds: 75 beds
Note: diagnostic & treatment centre, multilevel care facility

Chetwynd: Chetwynd Health Unit
Affiliated with: Northern Health Authority
PO Box 507, 5500 Hospital Rd., Chetwynd, BC V0C 1J0
Tel: 250-788-7200; *Fax:* 250-788-7247
www.northernhealth.ca

Chilliwack: Chilliwack Health Protection Office
Affiliated with: Fraser Health Authority
45470 Menholm Rd., Chilliwack, BC V2P 1M2
Tel: 604-702-4950

Chilliwack: Chilliwack Home Health Office
Affiliated with: Fraser Health Authority
45470 Menholm Rd., Chilliwack, BC V2P 1M2
Tel: 604-702-4800; *Fax:* 604-702-4801

Chilliwack: Chilliwack Mental Health Office
Affiliated with: Fraser Health Authority
45470 Menholm Rd., Chilliwack, BC V2P 1M2
Tel: 604-702-4860; *Fax:* 604-702-4861

Chilliwack: Chilliwack Public Health Unit
Affiliated with: Fraser Health Authority
45470 Menholm Rd., Chilliwack, BC V2P 1M2
Tel: 604-702-4900; *Fax:* 604-702-4901

Clearwater: Clearwater Community Health
Affiliated with: Interior Health Authority
640 Park Dr., Clearwater, BC V0E 1N0
Tel: 250-674-3141
www.interiorhealth.ca

Clearwater: Clearwater Home Support Program
Affiliated with: Interior Health Authority
144 Evergreen Place, Clearwater, BC V0E 1N0
www.interiorhealth.ca
Note: Provides home-based services such as: assessment & case management; nursing; rehabilitation; home support; & palliative care.

Clinton: Clinton Health & Wellness Centre
Affiliated with: Interior Health Authority
1510 Cariboo Hwy., Clinton, BC V0K 1K0
Tel: 250-459-2080 *Toll-Free:* 855-459-2080
www.interiorhealth.ca

Cranbrook: Associated Medical Clinic
Affiliated with: Interior Health Authority
123 - 10th Ave. South, Cranbrook, BC V1C 2N1
Tel: 250-426-4231
www.interiorhealth.ca

Cranbrook: Cranbrook Better Babies
Affiliated with: Interior Health Authority
209 - 16th Ave. North, Cranbrook, BC V1V 5S8
Tel: 250-489-5011
www.interiorhealth.ca

Cranbrook: Cranbrook Community Dialysis Clinic
Affiliated with: Interior Health Authority
13 - 24th Ave. North, Cranbrook, BC V1C 3H9
Tel: 250-417-3588 *Toll-Free:* 866-288-8082
www.interiorhealth.ca

Cranbrook: Cranbrook Health Centre
Affiliated with: Interior Health Authority
20 - 24th Ave. South, Cranbrook, BC V1C 5V1
Tel: 250-420-2200
www.interiorhealth.ca

***Cranbrook:* Cranbrook Home Support Services**
Affiliated with: Interior Health Authority
20 - 23rd Ave. South, Cranbrook, BC V1C 5V1
Tel: 250-417-6161
www.interiorhealth.ca
Note: Provides home-based services such as: assessment & case management; nursing; rehabilitation; home support; & palliative care.

***Cranbrook:* Cranbrook Wellness Centre**
Affiliated with: Interior Health Authority
20 - 23rd Ave. South, Cranbrook, BC V1C 5V1
Tel: 250-489-6414
www.interiorhealth.ca

***Cranbrook:* East Kootenay Area Heart Function Clinic**
Affiliated with: Interior Health Authority
20 - 23rd Ave. South, Cranbrook, BC V1C 5V1
Tel: 250-489-6414
www.interiorhealth.ca
Note: Support for patients with chronic heart failure

***Cranbrook:* East Kootenay CKD Clinic**
Affiliated with: Interior Health Authority
20 - 23rd Ave. South, Cranbrook, BC V1C 5V1
Tel: 250-489-6414
www.interiorhealth.ca
Note: Hemodialysis clinic

***Crawford Bay:* East Shore Community Health Centre**
Affiliated with: Interior Health Authority
15985 Hwy. 3A, Crawford Bay, BC V0B 1E0
www.interiorhealth.ca

***Creston:* Creston Community Dialysis Clinic**
Affiliated with: Interior Health Authority
312 - 15th Ave. North, Creston, BC V0B 1G0
Tel: 250-428-3830
www.interiorhealth.ca

***Creston:* Creston Health Unit**
Affiliated with: Interior Health Authority
312 - 15th Ave. North, Creston, BC V0B 1G0
Tel: 250-428-3873
www.interiorhealth.ca

***Cumberland:* Cumberland Health Care Centre**
Affiliated with: Vancouver Island Health Authority
PO Box 400, 2696 Windermere Ave., Cumberland, BC V0R 1S0
Tel: 250-331-8505; *Fax:* 250-336-2100
Number of Beds: 75 beds

***Dawson Creek:* Dawson Creek Health Unit**
Affiliated with: Northern Health Authority
1001 - 11th Ave., Dawson Creek, BC V1G 4X3
Tel: 250-719-6500; *Fax:* 250-719-6513
www.northernhealth.ca

***Delta:* Delta Health Protection Office**
Affiliated with: Fraser Health Authority
11245 - 84 Ave., Delta, BC V4C 2L9
Tel: 604-507-5478; *Fax:* 604-507-5492

***Delta:* Delta-South Home Health Office**
Affiliated with: Fraser Health Authority
4470 Clarence Taylor Cres., Delta, BC V4K 3W3
Tel: 604-952-3552; *Fax:* 604-946-6953

***Edgewood:* Edgewood Health Centre**
Affiliated with: Interior Health Authority
Former Name: Red Cross Outpost Nursing Station
322 Monashee Ave., Edgewood, BC V0G 1J0
Tel: 250-269-7313; *Fax:* 250-269-7520
www.interiorhealth.ca

***Elkford:* Elkford Health Centre**
Affiliated with: Interior Health Authority
212 Alpine Way, Elkford, BC V0B 1H0
Tel: 250-865-2247
www.interiorhealth.ca

***Enderby:* Enderby Community Health Centre**
Affiliated with: Interior Health Authority
707 - 3rd Ave., Enderby, BC V0E 1V0
Tel: 250-838-2450
www.interiorhealth.ca
Note: Primary health care centre

***Enderby:* Granville Building - Adult Day Program**
Affiliated with: Interior Health Authority
712 Granville St., Enderby, BC V0E 1V0
Tel: 250-838-2480
www.interiorhealth.ca

***Fernie:* Fernie Health Centre**
Affiliated with: Interior Health Authority
1501 - 5th Ave., Fernie, BC V0B 1M0
Tel: 250-423-8288
www.interiorhealth.ca

***Fort Nelson:* Fort Nelson Health Unit**
Affiliated with: Northern Health Authority
Bag 1000, 5217 Airport Dr., Fort Nelson, BC V0C 1R0
Tel: 250-774-7092; *Fax:* 250-774-7096
www.northernhealth.ca

***Fort Smith:* Fort Smith Public Health Unit**
Affiliated with: Fort Smith Health & Social Services Authority
PO Box 1080, Fort Smith, BC Z0E 0P0
Tel: 867-872-6203; *Fax:* 867-872-6260

***Fort St James:* Fort St. James Health Unit**
Affiliated with: Northern Health Authority
#121, 250 Stuart Dr. NE, Fort St James, BC V0J 1P0
Tel: 250-996-7178; *Fax:* 250-996-2216
www.northernhealth.ca

***Fort St John:* Fort St. John Health Unit**
Affiliated with: Northern Health Authority
10115 - 110 Ave., Fort St John, BC V1J 6M9
Tel: 250-263-6000; *Fax:* 250-263-6086
www.northernhealth.ca

***Fort St John:* Fort St. John Unattached Patient Clinic**
Affiliated with: Northern Health Authority
10011 - 96th St., Fort St John, BC V1J 3P3
Tel: 250-262-5210
www.northernhealth.ca

***Fraser Lake:* Fraser Lake Community Health Centre**
Affiliated with: Northern Health Authority
130 Chowsunket St., Fraser Lake, BC V0J 1S0
Tel: 250-699-7742; *Fax:* 250-699-6987
www.northernhealth.ca

***Gibsons:* Gibsons Health Unit**
Affiliated with: Vancouver Coastal Health
494 Fletcher Rd. South, Gibsons, BC V0N 1V0
Tel: 604-886-5600; *Fax:* 604-886-2250

***Gold River:* Gold River Health Centre**
Affiliated with: Vancouver Island Health Authority
601 Trumpeter Dr., Gold River, BC V0P 1G0
Tel: 250-283-2626; *Fax:* 250-283-7561
Note: Urgent care centre; laboratory; addiction services; child health care.

***Golden:* Golden & District Home Support**
Affiliated with: Interior Health Authority
835 - 9th Ave. South, Golden, BC V0A 1H0
Tel: 250-344-3005
www.interiorhealth.ca
Note: Provides home-based services such as: assessment & case management; nursing; rehabilitation; home support; & palliative care.

***Golden:* Golden Health Centre**
Affiliated with: Interior Health Authority
835 - 9th Ave. South, Golden, BC V0A 1H0
Tel: 250-344-3001
www.interiorhealth.ca

***Grand Forks:* Boundary Community Health Centre**
Affiliated with: Interior Health Authority
7649 - 22nd St., Grand Forks, BC V0H 1H2
www.interiorhealth.ca

***Grand Forks:* Glanville Family Centre**
Boundary Family & Individual Services Society
Affiliated with: Interior Health Authority
PO Box 2498, 1200 Central Ave., Grand Forks, BC V0H 1H0
Tel: 250-442-2267 *Toll-Free:* 877-442-5355
info@bfiss.org
www.boundaryfamily.org
Note: Programs for children, youth, women & families

***Grand Forks:* Grand Forks Community Dialysis Clinic**
Affiliated with: Interior Health Authority
7649 - 22nd St., Grand Forks, BC V0H 1H0
Tel: 250-443-2119
www.interiorhealth.ca

***Grand Forks:* Grand Forks Public Health**
Affiliated with: Interior Health Authority
1200 Central Ave., Grand Forks, BC V0H 1H0
Tel: 250-443-3150
www.interiorhealth.ca

***Granisle:* Granisle Community Health Centre**
Affiliated with: Northern Health Authority
PO Box 219, 1 Hagen St., Granisle, BC V0J 1W0
Tel: 250-697-2251; *Fax:* 250-697-6221
www.northernhealth.ca

***Hazelton:* Hazelton Community Health**
Affiliated with: Northern Health Authority
Bag 999, 2510 Hwy. 62, Hazelton, BC V0J 1Y0
Tel: 250-842-4640; *Fax:* 250-842-4642
www.northernhealth.ca

***Houston:* Houston Health Centre**
Affiliated with: Northern Health Authority
PO Box 538, 3202 - 14 St., Houston, BC V0J 1Z0
Tel: 250-845-2294; *Fax:* 250-845-7884
www.northernhealth.ca

***Hudson's Hope:* Hudson's Hope Health Centre**
Affiliated with: Northern Health Authority
Former Name: Hudson's Hope Gething Diagnostic & Treatment Centre
PO Box 599, 10309 Kyllo St., Hudson's Hope, BC V0C 1V0
Tel: 250-783-9991; *Fax:* 250-783-9125
www.northernhealth.ca
Number of Beds: 2 emergency beds
Population Served: 1000

***Invermere:* Invermere Health Centre**
Affiliated with: Interior Health Authority
PO Box 2069, 850 - 10th Ave., Invermere, BC V0A 1K0
Tel: 250-342-2360
www.interiorhealth.ca

***Kamloops:* Kamloops Community Dialysis Clinic**
Affiliated with: Interior Health Authority
795 Tranquille Rd., Kamloops, BC V2B 3J3
Tel: 250-314-2100
www.interiorhealth.ca

***Kamloops:* Kamloops Downtown Health Centre**
Affiliated with: Interior Health Authority
#36, 450 Lansdowne St., Kamloops, BC V2C 1Y3
Tel: 250-851-7954
www.interiorhealth.ca

***Kamloops:* Kamloops Home & Community Care**
Affiliated with: Interior Health Authority
#37, 450 Lansdowne St., Kamloops, BC V2C 1Y2
Tel: 250-851-7900
www.interiorhealth.ca

***Kamloops:* Kamloops Pacemaker Clinic**
Affiliated with: Interior Health Authority
311 Columbia St., 2nd Fl., Kamloops, BC V2C 2T1
Tel: 250-314-2100
www.interiorhealth.ca

***Kamloops:* Kamloops Public Health Unit**
Affiliated with: Interior Health Authority
519 Columbia St., Kamloops, BC V2C 2T8
Tel: 250-851-7300 *Toll-Free:* 866-847-4372
www.interiorhealth.ca

***Kamloops:* North Shore X-Ray Clinic**
Affiliated with: Interior Health Authority
789 Fortune Dr., #B3, Kamloops, BC V2B 2L3
Tel: 250-314-2420
www.interiorhealth.ca

***Kamloops:* TCS Heart Function Clinic**
Affiliated with: Interior Health Authority
311 Columbia St., Kamloops, BC V2C 2T1
Tel: 250-314-2727
www.interiorhealth.ca
Note: Support for patients with chronic heart failure. Also includes the Vascular Improvement Clinic.

***Kamloops:* Thompson Cariboo Shuswap Chronic Kidney Disease Clinic**
Affiliated with: Interior Health Authority
Royal Inland Hospital, 311 Columbia St., Kamloops, BC V2C 2T1
Tel: 250-314-2849
www.interiorhealth.ca
Note: Also the Thompson Cariboo Shuswap Peritoneal Hemodialysis Clinic (250-314-2100, ext. 3259), Thompson Cariboo Shuswap Home Hemodialysis Clinic, Thompson Cariboo Shuswap In-Center Hemodialysis Clinic & Thompson Cariboo Shuswap Transplant Clinic (250-314-2260).

***Kaslo:* Kaslo Physiotherapy**
Affiliated with: Interior Health Authority
673 A Ave., Kaslo, BC V0G 1M0
Tel: 250-353-2742
www.interiorhealth.ca

***Kaslo:* Kaslo Primary Health Centre**
Affiliated with: Interior Health Authority
673 A Ave., Lower Level, Kaslo, BC V0G 1M0
Tel: 250-353-2291
www.interiorhealth.ca

***Kaslo:* Victorian Community Health Centre of Kaslo**
Affiliated with: Interior Health Authority
Former Name: Victoria Hospital of Kaslo
673 A Ave., Kaslo, BC V0G 1M0
Tel: 250-353-2211; *Fax:* 250-353-2738

***Kelowna:* Capri Community Health Centre**
Affiliated with: Interior Health Authority
Capri Centre Mall, #200, 1835 Gordon Dr., Kelowna, BC V1Y 3H4
Tel: 250-980-1400
www.interiorhealth.ca

***Kelowna:* Central Okanagan Heart Function Clinic**
Affiliated with: Interior Health Authority
#118, 1835 Gordon Dr., Kelowna, BC V1Y 3H4
Tel: 250-980-1456
www.interiorhealth.ca
Note: Support for patients with chronic heart failure

***Kelowna:* Kelowna Chronic Kidney Disease Clinic**
Affiliated with: Interior Health Authority
2268 Pandosy St., Kelowna, BC V1Y 1T2
Tel: 250-862-4156
www.interiorhealth.ca
Note: Also the Kelowna Peritoneal Dialysis Clinic, Kelowna Home Hemodialysis Clinic & the Kelowna In-Centre Hemodialysis Clinic (250-862-4345).

***Kelowna:* Kelowna Health Centre**
Affiliated with: Interior Health Authority
1340 Ellis St., Kelowna, BC V1Y 9N1
Tel: 250-868-7700
www.interiorhealth.ca

***Kelowna:* Kelowna Pacemaker Clinic**
Affiliated with: Interior Health Authority
2268 Pandosy St., Kelowna, BC V2Y 1T2
Tel: 250-862-4450
www.interiorhealth.ca

***Kelowna:* Kelowna Research Centre**
Affiliated with: Interior Health Authority
2309 Abbott St., Kelowna, BC V1Y 1T2
Tel: 250-862-9777
www.interiorhealth.ca

***Kelowna:* Kelowna TIA Clinic**
Affiliated with: Interior Health Authority
2251 Pandosy St., Kelowna, BC V1Y 1T1
Tel: 250-980-1392
www.interiorhealth.ca
Note: Services for identifying & treating transient ischemic attack (TIA)

***Kelowna:* Kelowna Transplant Clinic**
Affiliated with: Interior Health Authority
2268 Pandosy St., Kelowna, BC V1Y 1T2
Tel: 250-862-4156
www.interiorhealth.ca
Note: Follow-up care for organ transplant recipients, primarily renal transplant.

***Kelowna:* May Bennett Wellness Centre**
Affiliated with: Interior Health Authority
Former Name: May Bennett Home
135 Davie Rd., Kelowna, BC V1X 1Y8
Tel: 250-980-1400
www.interiorhealth.ca

***Kelowna:* Outreach Urban Health Centre**
Affiliated with: Interior Health Authority
455 Leon Ave., Kelowna, BC V1V 6J3
Tel: 250-868-2230
www.interiorhealth.ca
Note: Primary health centre

***Kelowna:* Rutland Aurora Health Centre**
Affiliated with: Interior Health Authority
#102, 285 Aurora Cres., Kelowna, BC V1X 7N6
Tel: 250-491-1100
www.interiorhealth.ca

***Kelowna:* Rutland Community Dialysis**
Affiliated with: Interior Health Authority
125 Park Rd., Kelowna, BC V1X 3E3
Tel: 250-491-7613
www.interiorhealth.ca

***Kelowna:* Rutland Health Centre**
Affiliated with: Interior Health Authority
155 Gray Rd., Kelowna, BC V1X 1W6
Tel: 250-980-4825
www.interiorhealth.ca

***Kelowna:* Surgical Optimization Clinic (Hip & Knee)**
Affiliated with: Interior Health Authority
#115A, 1835 Gordon Dr., Kelowna, BC V1Y 3H5
Tel: 250-980-1515
www.interiorhealth.ca

***Keremeos:* South Similkameen Health Centre**
Affiliated with: Interior Health Authority
700 - 3rd St., Keremeos, BC V0X 1N3
Tel: 250-499-3000
www.interiorhealth.ca
Note: Community services (250-499-3029)

***Kimberley:* Kidney Care Clinic**
Affiliated with: Interior Health Authority
260 - 4th Ave., Kimberley, BC V1A 2R6
www.interiorhealth.ca

***Kimberley:* Kimberley Health Centre & Home Support**
Affiliated with: Interior Health Authority
260 - 4th Ave., Kimberley, BC V1A 2R6
Tel: 250-427-2215
www.interiorhealth.ca
Note: A primary health care centre also providing home-based services such as: assessment & case management; nursing; rehabilitation; home support; & palliative care.

***Kincolith:* Kincolith Nursing Station**
1303 Fireman St., Kincolith, BC V0V 1B0
Tel: 250-326-4242

***Ladysmith:* Ladysmith Community Health Centre**
Affiliated with: Vancouver Island Health Authority
Former Name: Ladysmith & District General Hospital
PO Box 10, 1111 - 4 Ave., Ladysmith, BC V9G 1A1
Tel: 250-739-5777; *Fax:* 250-740-2689
info@viha.ca
www.viha.ca
Social Media: www.facebook.com/135150073228437; twitter.com/vanislandhealth

Heather Dunne, Site Manager
Heather.Dunne@viha.ca

***Lake Country:* Public Health Satellite Office**
Affiliated with: Interior Health Authority
10080 Main St., Lake Country, BC V4V 1T8
www.interiorhealth.ca

***Lillooet:* Lillooet Home & Community Centre**
Affiliated with: Interior Health Authority
951 Murray St., Lillooet, BC V0K 1V0
Tel: 250-256-4233
www.interiorhealth.ca

***Logan Lake:* Logan Lake Adult Day Care**
Affiliated with: Interior Health Authority
311 Opal Dr., Logan Lake, BC V0K 1W0
Tel: 250-523-6935
www.interiorhealth.ca

***Logan Lake:* Logan Lake Primary Health Care**
Affiliated with: Interior Health Authority
Former Name: Logan Lake Health Centre
5 Beryl Ave., Logan Lake, BC V0K 1W0
Tel: 250-523-9414; *Fax:* 250-523-6869
www.interiorhealth.ca

***Lumby:* Lumby Health Unit**
Affiliated with: Interior Health Authority
2135 Norris Ave., Lumby, BC V0E 2G0
Tel: 250-547-9741
www.interiorhealth.ca

***Lumby:* Whitevalley Community Resource Centre**
Affiliated with: Interior Health Authority
2114 Shuswap Ave., Lumby, BC V0E 2G0
Tel: 250-547-8866
www.interiorhealth.ca

***Lytton:* St. Bartholomew's Health Centre**
Affiliated with: Interior Health Authority
531 Main St., Lytton, BC V0K 1Z0
Tel: 250-455-2221; *Fax:* 250-455-6621
Toll-Free: 855-955-2221
www.interiorhealth.ca

***Madeira Park:* Pender Harbour & District Health Centre**
Affiliated with: Vancouver Coastal Health
5066 Francis Peninsula Rd., Madeira Park, BC V0N 2H0
Tel: 604-883-2764; *Fax:* 604-883-2780

***Masset:* Masset Community Health**
Affiliated with: Northern Health Authority
PO Box 215, 2520 Harrison Ave., Masset, BC V0T 1M0
Tel: 250-626-4727; *Fax:* 250-626-5279
www.northernhealth.ca

***McBride:* McBride Health Unit**
Affiliated with: Northern Health Authority
1126 - 5th Ave., McBride, BC V0J 2E0
Tel: 250-569-2251; *Fax:* 250-569-2232
www.northernhealth.ca
Info Line: 888-562-1214

***Merritt:* Merritt Adult Day Centre**
Affiliated with: Interior Health Authority
2201 Jackson Ave., Merritt, BC V1K 1C6
www.interiorhealth.ca

***Merritt:* Merritt Public Health**
Affiliated with: Interior Health Authority
3451 Voght St., Merritt, BC V1K 1C6
Tel: 250-378-3400
www.interiorhealth.ca

***Midway:* Midway Health Unit**
Affiliated with: Interior Health Authority
540 - 7th Ave., Midway, BC V0H 1M0
Tel: 250-449-2887
www.interiorhealth.ca

***Nakusp:* Arrow & Slocan Lakes Community Services**
Affiliated with: Interior Health Authority
205 - 6th Ave., Nakusp, BC V0G 1R0
Tel: 250-265-3674
www.interiorhealth.ca

***Nakusp:* Nakusp Health Unit**
Affiliated with: Interior Health Authority
97 - 1st Ave. NE, Nakusp, BC V0G 1R0
Tel: 250-265-3608
www.interiorhealth.ca

***Nelson:* Chronic Disease Management Clinic**
Affiliated with: Interior Health Authority
#443, 3 View St., Nelson, BC V1L 2V1
Tel: 250-354-2397
www.interiorhealth.ca
Note: Heart function clinic with cardiac rehab

***Nelson:* Gordon Road Wellness Centre**
Affiliated with: Interior Health Authority
905 Gordon Rd., Nelson, BC V1L 3L8
Tel: 250-352-1401
www.interiorhealth.ca
Note: Provides an adult day program

***Nelson:* Nelson Health Centre**
Affiliated with: Interior Health Authority
333 Victoria St., Nelson, BC V1L 4K3
Tel: 250-505-7200
www.interiorhealth.ca

New Denver: **Slocan Community Health Centre**
Affiliated with: Interior Health Authority
401 Galena Ave., New Denver, BC V0G 1S0
Tel: 250-358-7911; *Fax:* 250-358-7117
www.interiorhealth.ca
Number of Beds: 30 beds
Note: Primary health care centre

North Vancouver: **Central Community Health Centre**
Affiliated with: Vancouver Coastal Health
132 Esplanade West, North Vancouver, BC V7M 1A2
Tel: 604-983-6700; *Fax:* 604-983-6839

North Vancouver: **Parkgate Community Health Centre**
Affiliated with: Vancouver Coastal Health
3625 Banff Ct., North Vancouver, BC V7H 2Z8
Tel: 604-904-6450; *Fax:* 604-904-6470
Year Founded: 1999

Oliver: **Oliver Cardiac Rehab Clinic**
Affiliated with: Interior Health Authority
36003 - 79th St., Oliver, BC V0H 1T0
Tel: 250-770-5507
www.interiorhealth.ca
Note: Offers a 5-week supervised exercise program to improve lung & heart health

Oliver: **Oliver Health Centre**
Affiliated with: Interior Health Authority
930 Spillway Rd., Oliver, BC V0H 1T0
Tel: 250-498-5080
www.interiorhealth.ca
Note: Speech-language services available at this location (250-498-0351)

Osoyoos: **Osoyoos Cardiac Rehab Clinic**
Affiliated with: Interior Health Authority
4816 - 89 St., Osoyoos, BC V0H 1V1
Tel: 250-495-4633
www.interiorhealth.ca
Note: Offers a 5-week supervised exercise program to improve lung & heart health

Osoyoos: **Osoyoos Health Centre**
Affiliated with: Interior Health Authority
4816 - 89 St., Osoyoos, BC V0H 1V1
Tel: 250-495-4633
www.interiorhealth.ca

Parksville: **Oceanside Health Centre**
Affiliated with: Vancouver Island Health Authority
489 Albemi Hwy., Parksville, BC V9P 1M9
Tel: 250-951-9550
oceanside_health_centre@viha.ca
www.viha.ca/locations/oceanside
Note: The Centre is able to care for approximately 75% of patients who might typically visit an Emergency Department and not need to be admitted.

Pemberton: **Pemberton Health Centre**
Affiliated with: Vancouver Coastal Health
Former Name: Pemberton Diagnostic & Treatment Centre
1403 Portage Rd., Pemberton, BC V0N 2L0
Tel: 604-894-6939; *Fax:* 604-894-6918
Note: Services include emergency health, family health, laboratory and addiction.

Penticton: **IHC Heart Function Clinic (HFC)**
Affiliated with: Interior Health Authority
Also Known As: Cardiopulmonary Wellness Clinic
740 Carmi Ave., Penticton, BC V2A 8P9
Tel: 250-770-3530
www.interiorhealth.ca
Note: For patients with a diagnosis of heart failure

Penticton: **Penticton Chronic Kidney Disease Clinic**
Affiliated with: Interior Health Authority
Penticton Health Centre, 740 Carmi Ave., Penticton, BC V2A 8P9
Tel: 250-770-5507
www.interiorhealth.ca

Penticton: **Penticton Health Centre**
Affiliated with: Interior Health Authority
740 Carmi Ave., Penticton, BC V2A 8P9
Tel: 250-770-3434
www.interiorhealth.ca

Penticton: **Penticton Home Hemodialysis Clinic**
Affiliated with: Interior Health Authority
550 Carmi Ave., Penticton, BC V2A 3G6
Tel: 250-492-4000
www.interiorhealth.ca
Note: Also the Penticton In-Centre Hemodialysis Clinic (250-492-9059), Penticton Peritoneal Dialysis Clinic (250-492-4000, ext. 2650) & Penticton Transplant Clinic (250-492-4000, ext. 2603).

Penticton: **Penticton Pacemaker Clinic**
Affiliated with: Interior Health Authority
550 Carmi Ave., Penticton, BC V2A 3G6
Tel: 250-492-4000
www.interiorhealth.ca

Port Alice: **Port Alice Health Centre**
Affiliated with: Vancouver Island Health Authority
Former Name: Port Alice Hospital
1090 Marine Dr., Port Alice, BC V0N 2N0
Tel: 250-284-3555
info@viha.ca
www.viha.ca

Prince George: **Centre for Healthy Living**
Affiliated with: Northern Health Authority
1788 Diefenbaker Dr., Prince George, BC V2N 4V7
Tel: 250-649-7011
www.northernhealth.ca

Prince George: **Highland Community Centre**
Affiliated with: Northern Health Authority
#101, 155 McDermid Dr., Prince George, BC V2M 4T8
Tel: 250-565-7317; *Fax:* 250-565-7410
www.northernhealth.ca

Prince George: **Northern Interior Health Unit - Prince George**
Affiliated with: Northern Health Authority
1444 Edmonton St., Prince George, BC V2M 6W5
Tel: 250-565-7311; *Fax:* 250-565-5702
www.northernhealth.ca

Prince George: **Prince George Family Resource Centre**
Affiliated with: Northern Health Authority
1200 Lasalle Ave., Prince George, BC V2L 4J8
Tel: 250-614-9449; *Fax:* 250-614-9448
www.northernhealth.ca

Prince Rupert: **Prince Rupert Community Health**
Affiliated with: Northern Health Authority
300 - 3rd Ave. West, Prince Rupert, BC V8J 1L4
Tel: 250-622-6380; *Fax:* 250-622-6391
www.northernhealth.ca

Princeton: **Princeton Health Centre**
Affiliated with: Interior Health Authority
98 Ridgewood Dr., Princeton, BC V0X 1W0
Tel: 250-295-4442
www.interiorhealth.ca

Queen Charlotte: **Queen Charlotte Islands Community Health**
Affiliated with: Northern Health Authority
3211 - 3rd Ave., Queen Charlotte, BC V0T 1S0
Tel: 250-559-2350
www.northernhealth.ca

Quesnel: **Quesnel Health Unit - Nursing**
Affiliated with: Northern Health Authority
511 Reid St., Quesnel, BC V2J 2M8
Tel: 250-991-7571; *Fax:* 250-991-7577
www.northernhealth.ca

Quesnel: **Quesnel Health Unit - Preventative**
Affiliated with: Northern Health Authority
523 Front St., Quesnel, BC V2J 2K7
Tel: 250-983-6810; *Fax:* 250-992-1031
www.northernhealth.ca

Revelstoke: **Queen Victoria Health Centre**
Affiliated with: Interior Health Authority
1200 Newlands Rd., Revelstoke, BC V0E 2S0
Tel: 250-837-2131
www.interiorhealth.ca

Revelstoke: **Revelstoke Adult Day Care**
Affiliated with: Interior Health Authority
711 West First St., Revelstoke, BC V0E 2S0
www.interiorhealth.ca

Revelstoke: **Revelstoke Public Health**
Affiliated with: Interior Health Authority
1200 Newlands Rd., Revelstoke, BC V0E 2S0
Tel: 250-814-2244
www.interiorhealth.ca

Revelstoke: **Revelstoke Speech & Language Clinic**
Affiliated with: Interior Health Authority
1001 Mackenzie Ave., Revelstoke, BC V0E 2S0
Tel: 250-837-4285
www.interiorhealth.ca

Richmond: **Richmond Health Services**
Affiliated with: Vancouver Coastal Health
8100 Granville Ave., Richmond, BC V6Y 3T6
Tel: 604-233-3150; *Fax:* 604-233-3198
feedback@vch.ca
www.vch.ca

Rock Creek: **Rock Creek Health Centre**
Affiliated with: Interior Health Authority
Hwy. 3, Rock Creek, BC V0H 1Y0
Tel: 250-446-2223
www.interiorhealth.ca

Salmo: **Salmo Health & Wellness Centre**
Affiliated with: Interior Health Authority
413 Baker Ave., Salmo, BC V0G 1Z0
Tel: 250-357-0104
www.interiorhealth.ca

Salmon Arm: **Salmon Arm Health Centre**
Affiliated with: Interior Health Authority
851 - 16th St. NE, Salmon Arm, BC V1E 4N7
Tel: 250-833-4100
www.interiorhealth.ca

Salmon Arm: **Salmon Arm Pacemaker Clinic**
Affiliated with: Interior Health Authority
601 - 10th St. NE, Salmon Arm, BC V1E 4N6
Tel: 250-833-3636
www.interiorhealth.ca

Salmon Arm: **Salmon Arm Physiotherapy**
Affiliated with: Interior Health Authority
#1, 2770 - 10th Ave., Salmon Arm, BC V1E 2E8
www.interiorhealth.ca

Salmon Arm: **Shuswap Home & Community Care**
Affiliated with: Interior Health Authority
2770 - 10th Ave. North, #B, Salmon Arm, BC V1E 4N6
Tel: 250-832-6643
www.interiorhealth.ca

Sechelt: **Sechelt Health Unit**
Affiliated with: Vancouver Coastal Health
5571 Inlet Ave., Sechelt, BC V0N 3A0
Tel: 604-885-5164; *Fax:* 604-885-9725
feedback@vch.ca
www.vch.ca

Sicamous: **Sicamous Health Centre**
Affiliated with: Interior Health Authority
1133 Hwy. 97A, Sicamous, BC V0E 2V0
Tel: 250-836-4835
www.interiorhealth.ca

Skidgate: **Skidegate Seniors Centre**
Affiliated with: Northern Health Authority
149 Front St., Skidgate, BC V0T 1S0
Tel: 250-559-4781
www.northernhealth.ca
Note: Supportive group programs & health services for seniors.

Smithers: **Smithers Community Health**
Affiliated with: Northern Health Authority
Bag 5000, 3783 Alfred Ave., Smithers, BC V0J 2N0
Tel: 250-847-6400; *Fax:* 250-847-5908
www.northernhealth.ca

Smithers: **Smithers Home & Community Care**
Affiliated with: Northern Health Authority
PO Box 370, 3950 - 8th Ave., Smithers, BC V0J 2N0
Tel: 250-847-6234; *Fax:* 250-847-6239
www.northernhealth.ca

Sorrento: **Sorrento & Area Community Health Centre**
Affiliated with: Interior Health Authority
1250 TransCanada Hwy., Sorrento, BC V0E 2W1
Tel: 250-803-5251
www.interiorhealth.ca

***Sparwood:* Sparwood Community Dialysis Clinic**
Affiliated with: Interior Health Authority
570 Pine Ave., Sparwood, BC V0B 2G0
Tel: 250-425-4527
www.interiorhealth.ca

***Sparwood:* Sparwood Mental Health**
Affiliated with: Interior Health Authority
570 Pine Ave., Sparwood, BC V0B 2G0
Tel: 250-425-2064
www.interiorhealth.ca

***Sparwood:* Sparwood Primary Health Care**
Affiliated with: Interior Health Authority
570 Pine Ave., Sparwood, BC V0B 2G0
Tel: 250-425-6212; *Fax:* 250-425-2313
www.interiorhealth.ca

***Squamish:* Squamish Community Health Centre**
Affiliated with: Vancouver Coastal Health
1140 Hunter Pl., Squamish, BC V8B 0A2
Tel: 604-892-2293; *Fax:* 604-892-2327
Toll-Free: 877-892-2231

***Stikine:* Stikine Health Centre**
Affiliated with: Northern Health Authority
PO Box 386, 7171 Hwy. 37, Stikine, BC V0C 1L0
Tel: 250-771-4444; *Fax:* 250-771-3911
www.northernhealth.ca

***Summerland:* Summerland Health Centre**
Affiliated with: Interior Health Authority
12815 Atkinson Rd., Summerland, BC V0H 1Z0
Tel: 250-404-8000
www.interiorhealth.ca

***Surrey:* Guildford Public Health Unit**
Affiliated with: Fraser Health Authority
10233 - 153 St., Surrey, BC V3R 0Z7
Tel: 604-587-4750; *Fax:* 604-587-4777

***Tahsis:* Tahsis Health Centre**
Affiliated with: Vancouver Island Health Authority
PO Box 399, 1085 Maquinna Dr., Tahsis, BC V0P 1X0
Tel: 250-934-6322; *Fax:* 250-934-6404
info@viha.ca
www.viha.ca
Enid O'Hara, Manager, Rural Services
250-283-2626, *Fax:* 250-283-7561, enid.o'hara@viha.ca

***Tatla Lake:* West Chilcotin Health Centre**
Affiliated with: Interior Health Authority
16452 Hwy. 20, Tatla Lake, BC V0L 1V0
Tel: 250-476-1114; *Fax:* 250-476-1266
www.interiorhealth.ca

***Terrace:* Terrace Adult Sunshine Centre**
Affiliated with: Northern Health Authority
4707 Kerby Ave., Terrace, BC V8G 2W2
Tel: 250-631-4198
www.northernhealth.ca
Note: Group programs & health services for seniors

***Terrace:* Terrace Health Unit**
Affiliated with: Northern Health Authority
3412 Kalum St., Terrace, BC V8G 4T2
Tel: 250-631-4200; *Fax:* 250-638-2264
www.northernhealth.ca

***Trail:* Kiro Wellness Centre**
Affiliated with: Interior Health Authority
1500 Columbia Ave., Trail, BC V1R 1J9
Tel: 250-364-6219
www.interiorhealth.ca

***Trail:* Kootenay Boundary Chronic Kidney Disease Clinic**
Affiliated with: Interior Health Authority
1200 Hospital Bench, Trail, BC V1R 4M1
Tel: 250-364-6270
www.interiorhealth.ca
Note: Also the Kootenay Boundary Home Hemodialysis Clinic, Kootenay Boundary In-Center Hemodialysis Clinic, & Kootenay Boundary Peritoneal Dialysis Clinic (250-364-3450).

***Trail:* Kootenay Boundary Transplant Clinic**
Affiliated with: Interior Health Authority
1200 Hospital Bench, Trail, BC V1R 4M1
Tel: 250-364-3494
www.interiorhealth.ca
Note: Follow-up care for organ transplant recipients, primarily renal transplant.

***Trail:* Trail Heart Function Clinic**
Affiliated with: Interior Health Authority
1500 Columbia Ave., Trail, BC V1R 1J9
Tel: 250-364-6297
www.interiorhealth.ca

***Trail:* Trail Pacemaker Clinic**
Affiliated with: Interior Health Authority
1200 Hospital Bench, Trail, BC V1R 4M1
Tel: 250-368-3311
www.interiorhealth.ca

***Tumbler Ridge:* Tumbler Ridge Community Health Unit**
Affiliated with: Northern Health Authority
PO Box 1090, 220 Front St., Tumbler Ridge, BC V0C 2W0
Tel: 250-242-4262; *Fax:* 250-242-4009
www.northernhealth.ca

***Tumbler Ridge:* Tumbler Ridge Health Care Centre**
Affiliated with: Northern Health Authority
PO Box 80, 220 Front St., Tumbler Ridge, BC V0C 2W0
Tel: 250-242-5271; *Fax:* 250-242-3889
www.northernhealth.ca
Gail Neumann, Site Manager
gail.neumann@northernhealth.ca

***Valemount:* Valemount Community Health Centre**
Affiliated with: Northern Health Authority
1445 - 5 Ave., Valemount, BC V0E 2Z0
Tel: 250-566-9138; *Fax:* 250-566-4319
www.northernhealth.ca

***Vancouver:* Evergreen Community Health Centre**
Affiliated with: Vancouver Coastal Health
3425 Crowley Dr., Vancouver, BC V5R 6G3
Tel: 604-872-2511

***Vancouver:* Mid-Main Community Health Centre**
Affiliated with: Vancouver Coastal Health
3998 Main St., Vancouver, BC V5V 3P2
Tel: 604-873-3666; *Fax:* 604-875-8790
midmain.info@gmail.com
www.midmain.net
Social Media: twitter.com/Mid_MainCHC
Irene Clarence, Executive Director

***Vancouver:* Orbit Wilson Dental Imaging Centre**
Affiliated with: Vancouver Coastal Health
#500, 805, Weest Broadway, Vancouver, BC V5Z 1K1
Tel: 604-879-9449; *Fax:* 604-879-9442
www.wilsonradiographic.ca

***Vancouver:* Pacific Spirit Community Health Centre**
Affiliated with: Vancouver Coastal Health
2110 West 43rd Ave., Vancouver, BC V6M 2E1
Tel: 604-261-6366; *Fax:* 604-261-7220
feedback@vch.ca
www.vch.ca

***Vancouver:* Pender Community Health Centre**
Affiliated with: Vancouver Coastal Health
59 West Pender St., Vancouver, BC V6B 1R3
Tel: 604-669-9181; *Fax:* 604-688-9775
Year Founded: 1999

***Vancouver:* Raven Song Community Health Centre**
Affiliated with: Vancouver Coastal Health
2450 Ontario St., Vancouver, BC V5T 4T7
Tel: 604-709-6400; *Fax:* 604-879-9173
feedback@vch.ca
www.vch.ca

***Vancouver:* Robert & Lily Lee Family Community Health Centre**
Affiliated with: Vancouver Coastal Health
1669 Broadway East, Vancouver, BC V5N 1V9
Tel: 604-675-3980

***Vancouver:* South Community Health Centre**
Affiliated with: Vancouver Coastal Health
6405 Knight St., Vancouver, BC V5P 2V9
Tel: 604-321-6151; *Fax:* 604-321-2947

***Vancouver:* Three Bridges Community Health Centre**
Affiliated with: Vancouver Coastal Health
1292 Hornby St., Vancouver, BC V6Z 1W2
Tel: 604-736-9844; *Fax:* 604-844-2223

***Vanderhoof:* Vanderhoof Health Unit**
Affiliated with: Northern Health Authority
3299 Hospital Rd., Vanderhoof, BC V0J 3A2
Tel: 250-567-6900; *Fax:* 250-567-6170
www.northernhealth.ca

***Vernon:* Day-Break Adult Day Centre**
Affiliated with: Interior Health Authority
Gateby Care Facility, 3000 Gateby Pl., Vernon, BC V1T 1P4
Tel: 250-545-4456
www.interiorhealth.ca

***Vernon:* North Okanagan Heart Function Clinic**
Affiliated with: Interior Health Authority
2101 - 32nd St., Vernon, BC V1T 5L2
Tel: 250-558-1200
www.interiorhealth.ca
Note: Support for patients with chronic heart failure. Secondary phones: 250-306-9700 & 250-503-8805.

***Vernon:* Vernon - Ortho Clinic**
Affiliated with: Interior Health Authority
3210 - 25th Ave., Vernon, BC V1T 2T1
www.interiorhealth.ca

***Vernon:* Vernon Cardiac Rehab Clinic**
Affiliated with: Interior Health Authority
2101 - 32nd St., Vernon, BC V1T 5L2
Tel: 250-503-3712
www.interiorhealth.ca
Note: Also includes the Vernon Pacemaker Clinic (250-558-1200)

***Vernon:* Vernon Community Care Health Services**
Affiliated with: Interior Health Authority
4505 - 25th St., Vernon, BC V1T 4S8
Tel: 250-541-2200
www.interiorhealth.ca

***Vernon:* Vernon Downtown Primary Care Centre**
Affiliated with: Interior Health Authority
3306A - 32nd St., Vernon, BC V1T 2M6
Tel: 250-541-1097
www.interiorhealth.ca

***Vernon:* Vernon Health Unit**
Affiliated with: Interior Health Authority
1440 - 14th Ave., Vernon, BC V1B 2T1
Tel: 250-549-5700
www.interiorhealth.ca

***Vernon:* Vernon Renal Clinic**
Affiliated with: Interior Health Authority
#700, 3115 - 48th Ave., Vernon, BC V1T 3R5
Tel: 250-503-3320
www.interiorhealth.ca

***West Kelowna:* West Kelowna Health Centre**
Affiliated with: Interior Health Authority
#160, 2300 Carrington Rd., West Kelowna, BC V4T 2N6
Tel: 250-980-5150
www.interiorhealth.ca

***West Vancouver:* West Vancouver Community Health Centre**
Affiliated with: Vancouver Coastal Health
2121 Marine Dr., West Vancouver, BC V7V 4Y2
Tel: 604-904-6200; *Fax:* 604-904-6262

***Williams Lake:* Cariboo Memorial Health Centre**
Affiliated with: Interior Health Authority
517 North 6th Ave., Williams Lake, BC V2G 2G8
Tel: 250-392-4411
www.interiorhealth.ca

***Williams Lake:* Williams Lake Community Dialysis**
Affiliated with: Interior Health Authority
517 - 6th Ave. North, Williams Lake, BC V2G 2G8
Tel: 250-302-3209
www.interiorhealth.ca

Nursing Stations

***Alexis Creek:* Red Cross Outpost Nursing Station**
2591 Morton Rd., Alexis Creek, BC V0L 1A0
Tel: 250-394-4313; *Fax:* 250-394-5179
Note: Red Cross Outpost Nursing Stations correspondence should be sent to Manager of Outpost Hospital Program, Canadian Red Cross Society, 4750 Oak St., 3rd Fl., Vancouver BC V6H 2N9

***Anahim Lake:* Anahim Lake Nursing Station**
Affiliated with: Interior Health Authority
PO Box 207, 6674 Clinic Lane, Anahim Lake, BC V0L 1C0
Tel: 250-742-3305
www.interiorhealth.ca

Atlin: Atlin Health Centre
Affiliated with: Northern Health Authority
Former Name: Red Cross Outpost Hospital
PO Box 330, 164 - 3rd St., Atlin, BC V0W 1A0
Tel: 250-651-7677; *Fax:* 250-651-7687
www.northernhealth.ca
Note: Non-emergency services on a walk-in basis; two nurses

Fort James: Takla Landing Nursing Station
117 Bah'Lats Rd., Fort James, BC V0J 1P0
Tel: 250-996-7780

Hartley Bay: Hartley Bay Nursing Station
341 Wee Xaa Avenue, Hartley Bay, BC V0V 1A0
Tel: 250-841-2556; *Fax:* 250-841-2554
hbnshd@citytel.net
Angela Clifton, Health Director

Iskut: Iskut Nursing Station
Affiliated with: Northern Health Authority
PO Box 9, Iskut, BC V0J 1K0
Tel: 250-234-3511; *Fax:* 250-234-3512
www.ivhs.ca

Kitkatla: Kitkatla Nursing Station
PO Box 150, Kitkatla, BC V0V 1C0
Tel: 250-848-2254; *Fax:* 250-848-2263
dmoody@gitxaala.com

Klemtu: Klemtu Nursing Station
General Delivery, Klemtu, BC V0T 1L0
Tel: 250-839-1221; *Fax:* 250-839-1184

Kyuquot: Red Cross Outpost Nursing Station
100 Okime St., Kyuquot, BC V0P 1J0
Tel: 250-332-5289; *Fax:* 250-332-5215
Pat Kermeen, Manager, Outpost Hospital Program

Telegraph Creek: Telegraph Creek Nursing Station
PO Box 112, Telegraph Creek, BC V0J 2W0
Tel: 250-235-3211; *Fax:* 250-235-3213
theresa.quock@thssa.ca

Special Treatment Centres

Burnaby: The Burnaby Centre for Mental Health & Addiction (BCMHA)
Affiliated with: Interior Health Authority
3405 Willingdon Ave., Burnaby, BC V5G 3H4
burnabycentreinfo@interiorhealth.ca
www.interiorhealth.ca
Number of Beds: 100 beds
Note: Six to nine-month residential treatment program for BC residents with concurrent disorders

Chilliwack: Cedar Ridge
Affiliated with: Fraser Health Authority
9090 Newman Rd., Chilliwack, BC V2P 3Z8
Tel: 604-701-3671; *Fax:* 604-701-3672

Kamloops: Phoenix Centre
922 - 3 Ave., Kamloops, BC V2C 6W5
Tel: 250-374-4634; *Fax:* 250-374-4621
Toll-Free: 877-318-1177
www.phoenixcentre.org
Number of Beds: 20 beds
Note: detox centre

Kelowna: BC Cancer Agency Sindi Ahluwalia Hawkins Centre for the Southern Interior
Affiliated with: Interior Health Authority
Also Known As: Cancer Centre for the Southern Interior
399 Royal Ave., Kelowna, BC V1Y 5L3
Tel: 250-712-3900 *Toll-Free:* 888-563-7773
www.bccancer.bc.ca/rs/centreforthesouthterninterior
Number of Employees: 220

Kelowna: Central Okanagan Hospice House
Central Okanagan Hospice Association (COHA)
Affiliated with: Interior Health Authority
2035 Ethel St., Kelowna, BC V1Y 2Z6
Tel: 250-862-4126; *Fax:* 250-862-4129
www.hospicecoha.org
Social Media: www.facebook.com/155973737764339; twitter.com/COHospiceAssoc; pinterest.com/cohospiceassoc; www.linkedin.com/company/2759641
Note: Provides palliative/end of life care
Susan Steen, Executive Director

Penticton: Moog & Friends Hospice House
Penticton & District Hospice Society
Affiliated with: Interior Health Authority
PO Box 1105, 1701 Government St., Penticton, BC V2A 6J9
Tel: 250-492-9071; *Fax:* 250-492-9097
www.pentictonhospice.com
Year Founded: 1998
Note: Palliative/end of life care
Tania Linning, Coordinator, Palliative Care Services
tania.linning@interiorhealth.ca

Port Coquitlam: Community Integration Services Society
2175 Mary Hill Rd., Port Coquitlam, BC V3C 3A2
Tel: 604-461-2131; *Fax:* 778-285-5520
www.gociss.org
Year Founded: 1990
Note: Helps adults with disabilities gain training and skill that they use to become more active members of society.
Shari Mahar, Executive Director
604-568-4753, smahar@gociss.org

Richmond: Back in Motion, Richmond
Affiliated with: Vancouver Coastal Health
#140, 6651 Elmbridge Way, Richmond, BC V7C 5C2
Tel: 604-273-7600; *Fax:* 604-273-7662
Toll-Free: 800-350-4225
info@backinmotion.com
www.backinmotion.com
Note: rehabilitation treatment centre
Debbie Samsom, President

Vancouver: Arthritis Society
Affiliated with: Vancouver Coastal Health
Former Name: The Arthris Centre
895 West 10 Ave., Vancouver, BC V5Z 1L7
Tel: 604-714-5550; *Fax:* 604-714-5555
Toll-Free: 866-414-7766
info@bc.arthritis.ca
www.arthritis.ca
Social Media: www.facebook.com/ArthritisSociety; twitter.com/arthritissoc
Janet Yale, President & CEO

Vancouver: Blusson Spinal Cord Centre
Affiliated with: Vancouver Coastal Health
818 West 10th Ave., Vancouver, BC V5Z 1M9
Tel: 604-675-8810
icord.org/our-facility
Note: Specialties: spinal cord injuries; spinal cord research
Wolfram Tetzlaff, Director
tetzlaff@icord.org

Vancouver: British Columbia Cancer Agency Vancouver
Affiliated with: Provincial Health Services Authority
600 - 10 Ave. West, Vancouver, BC V5Z 4E6
Tel: 604-877-6000; *Fax:* 604-872-4596
Toll-Free: 800-663-3333
www.bccancer.bc.ca
Note: cancer treatment
Dr. Max Coppes, President
Nick Foster, CEO

Vancouver: Elizabeth Bagshaw Women's Clinic
Affiliated with: Vancouver Coastal Health
#200, 1177 West Broadway, Vancouver, BC V6H 1G3
Tel: 604-736-7878; *Fax:* 604-736-8081
Toll-Free: 877-736-7171
ebwc.ca
Note: abortion clinic

Vancouver: Everywoman's Health Centre Abortion Control Clinic
Affiliated with: Vancouver Coastal Health
#210, 2525 Commercial Dr., Vancouver, BC V5N 4C1
Tel: 604-322-6576; *Fax:* 604-322-6632
www.everywomanshealthcentre.ca
Note: abortion clinic

Vancouver: G.F. Strong Rehabilitation Centre
Affiliated with: Vancouver Coastal Health
4255 Laurel St., Vancouver, BC V5Z 2G9
Tel: 604-734-1313; *Fax:* 604-737-6359
Note: rehabilitation treatment centre

Vancouver: The Skin Care Centre
Affiliated with: Vancouver Coastal Health
835 West 10th Ave., Vancouver, BC V5Z 4E8
Tel: 604-875-5151
www.skincarecentre.ca

Vancouver: Sunny Hill Health Centre for Children
Affiliated with: Provincial Health Services Authority
3644 Slocan St., Vancouver, BC V5M 3E8
Tel: 604-453-8300; *Fax:* 604-453-8301
TTY: 604-453-8315
www.bcchildrens.ca
Number of Beds: 18 beds
Note: Provincial rehabilitation & assessment centre for children with disabilities

Vancouver: Vancouver Community Audiology Centre
Affiliated with: Vancouver Coastal Health
999 Broadway West, Vancouver, BC V5Z 1K5
Tel: 604-659-1100; *Fax:* 604-659-1109

Victoria: British Columbia Cancer Agency - Vancouver Island Centre
Affiliated with: Vancouver Coastal Health
2410 Lee Ave., Victoria, BC V8R 6V5
Tel: 250-519-5500 *Toll-Free:* 800-670-3322
www.bccancer.bc.ca
Note: comprehensive cancer centre
Dr. Max Coppes, President

Whistler: Whistler Health Care Centre
Affiliated with: Vancouver Coastal Health
Former Name: Whistler Diagnostic & Treatment Centre
4380 Lorimer Rd., Whistler, BC V0N 1B4
Tel: 604-932-4911; *Fax:* 604-932-4992
feedback@vch.ca
www.vch.ca

Long Term Care Facilities

100 Mile House: Mill Site Lodge & Fischer Place
Affiliated with: Interior Health Authority
555 Cedar Ave. South, 100 Mile House, BC V0K 2E0
Tel: 250-395-7690
www.interiorhealth.ca
Number of Beds: 79 beds

Abbotsford: Bevan Lodge
Trillium Care
Affiliated with: Fraser Health Authority
33386 Bevan Ave., Abbotsford, BC V2S 5G6
Tel: 604-850-5416; *Fax:* 604-850-5418
info@bevanvillage.ca
bevanvillage.ca
Social Media: www.facebook.com/TrilliumCare; twitter.com/TrilliumCare; www.youtube.com/user/TrilliumCare
Number of Beds: 15 beds
Angelo Boholst, Executive Director

Abbotsford: M.S.A. Manor
Maplewood Seniors Care Society
Affiliated with: Fraser Health Authority
2510 Gladwin Rd., Abbotsford, BC V2T 3N9
Tel: 604-853-5831; *Fax:* 604-853-1647
admin@maplewood.bc.ca
www.maplewood.bc.ca
Heidi Mannis, Interim CEO

Abbotsford: Maplewood House
Affiliated with: Fraser Health Authority
1919 Jackson St., Abbotsford, BC V2S 2Z8
Tel: 604-853-5585; *Fax:* 604-853-5590
admin@maplewood.bc.ca
www.maplewood.bc.ca
Number of Beds: 77 beds
Heidi Mannis, Interim CEO

Abbotsford: Sherwood Crescent Manor Ltd.
Affiliated with: Fraser Health Authority
32073 Sherwood Cres., Abbotsford, BC V2T 1C1
Tel: 604-853-7854; *Fax:* 604-853-9910
sherwoodcrescentmanor@telus.net
tcgcare.com/sherwood.html
Number of Beds: 41 permanent, 10 transitional care, 3 respite beds
Note: intermediate/residential care

Abbotsford: Tabor Home
Affiliated with: Fraser Health Authority
31944 Sunrise Cres., Abbotsford, BC V2T 1N5
Tel: 604-859-8715; *Fax:* 604-859-6695
info.home@taborhome.org.
www.taborhome.org
Year Founded: 1960
Dan Levitt, Executive Director

***Abbotsford:* Valhaven Rest Home**
Affiliated with: Fraser Health Authority
4212 Balmoral St., Abbotsford, BC V4X 1Y5
Tel: 604-856-2812; *Fax:* 604-856-3243
office@communitascare.com

***Agassiz:* Glenwood Care Centre**
Affiliated with: Fraser Health Authority
1458 Glenwood Dr., Agassiz, BC V0M 1A2
Tel: 604-796-9202; *Fax:* 604-796-9186
Note: Glenwood Care Centre provide residential care & day programs for the elderly.

***Aldergrove:* La Rosa de Matsqui**
28711 Huntington Rd., Aldergrove, BC V0X 1A0
Tel: 604-856-1555; *Fax:* 604-856-3252
Number of Beds: 15 beds

***Armstrong:* Pioneer Square**
Kaigo Retirement Communities Ltd.
Affiliated with: Interior Health Authority
2865 Willowdale Dr., Armstrong, BC V0E 1B1
Tel: 250-546-3396; *Fax:* 250-546-9033
www.kaigo.ca
Number of Beds: 17 suites

***Armstrong:* Pleasant Valley Manor**
Affiliated with: Interior Health Authority
3800 Patten Dr., Armstrong, BC V0E 1B2
Tel: 250-546-4707
www.interiorhealth.ca
Number of Beds: 81 permanent beds; 1 respite bed
Note: Complex care facility

***Ashcroft:* Jackson House**
Affiliated with: Interior Health Authority
700 Ash-Cache Creek Hwy., Ashcroft, BC V0K 1A0
Tel: 250-453-1913 *Toll-Free:* 877-499-6599
www.interiorhealth.ca
Number of Beds: 25 beds
Note: Residential care facility

***Burnaby:* Carlton Gardens Long Term Care**
Affiliated with: Chartwell Retirement Residences
4108 Norfolk St., Burnaby, BC V5G 0B4
Tel: 604-419-3000
www.chartwell.com
Number of Beds: 128 beds
W. Brent Binions, President & CEO, Chartwell Retirement Residences

***Burnaby:* Dania Home Society**
Affiliated with: Fraser Health Authority
4279 Norland Ave., Burnaby, BC V5G 3Z6
Tel: 604-299-2414; *Fax:* 604-299-7775
info@dania.bc.ca
www.dania.bc.ca
Number of Beds: 67 beds
Margaret Douglas-Matthews, Executive Director

***Burnaby:* Fair Haven United Church Homes**
Affiliated with: Fraser Health Authority
7557 Sussex Ave., Burnaby, BC V5J 3V6
Tel: 604-435-0525; *Fax:* 604-435-7031
info@fairhaven.bc.ca
www.fairhaven.bc.ca
Year Founded: 1978
Carol Mathersill, CEO
604-433-2939

***Burnaby:* Fellburn Care Centre**
Affiliated with: Fraser Health Authority
6050 Hastings St. East, Burnaby, BC V5B 1R6
Tel: 604-412-6510; *Fax:* 604-299-1015
Number of Beds: 110 beds
Note: extended care facility

***Burnaby:* Finnish Manor**
Finnish Canadian Rest Home Association
Affiliated with: Fraser Health Authority
3460 Kalyk Ave., Burnaby, BC V5G 3B2
Tel: 604-434-2666; *Fax:* 604-439-7448
info@finncare.ca
finncare.ca
Year Founded: 1975
Number of Beds: 60 beds
Tanya Rautava, Administrator
604-325-8241

***Burnaby:* George Derby Centre**
Affiliated with: Fraser Health Authority
7550 Cumberland St., Burnaby, BC V3N 3X5
Tel: 604-521-2676; *Fax:* 604-521-0220
info@georgederby.ca
www.georgederbycentre.ca
Social Media: www.facebook.com/georgederbycentre; twitter.com/gderbycentre; www.youtube.com/channel/UCm5d_BAVtyYhU7qJZ_G8zgg
Year Founded: 1988
Note: Care facility for veterans
Ricky Kwan, Executive Director
rkwan@georgederby.ca

***Burnaby:* New Vista Society**
Affiliated with: Fraser Health Authority
Former Name: New Vista Care Home
7550 Rosewood St., Burnaby, BC V5E 3Z3
Tel: 604-521-7764; *Fax:* 604-527-6001
info@newvista.bc.ca
www.newvista.bc.ca
Number of Beds: 236 beds
Number of Employees: 25
Note: The Society operates a complex care home and provides housing for low-income families and seniors.
Carol Finnie, CEO

***Burnaby:* Normanna Rest Home**
Affiliated with: Fraser Health Authority
7725 - 4 St., Burnaby, BC V3N 5B6
Tel: 604-522-5812; *Fax:* 604-522-5803
info@normanna.ca
www.normanna.ca
Number of Beds: 100 beds
Note: multi level care
Margaret Douglas-Matthews, Executive Director

***Burns Lake:* The Pines**
Affiliated with: Northern Health Authority
PO Box 7500, 800 Center St., Burns Lake, BC V0J 1E0
Tel: 250-692-2490; *Fax:* 250-692-2492
www.northernhealth.ca
Number of Beds: 30 beds

***Campbell River:* Yucalta Lodge**
Affiliated with: Vancouver Island Health Authority
555 - 2 Ave., Campbell River, BC V9W 3V1
Tel: 250-850-2900
Year Founded: 2001
Number of Beds: 100 beds
Note: multi-level care

***Castlegar:* Castleview Care Centre (CVCC)**
Chantelle Management Ltd.
Affiliated with: Interior Health Authority
2300 - 14 Ave., Castlegar, BC V1N 4A6
Tel: 250-365-7277; *Fax:* 250-365-3291
castleview@chantellegroup.com
www.chantellegroup.com
Year Founded: 1991
Number of Beds: 61 beds

***Castlegar:* Talarico Place**
Affiliated with: Interior Health Authority
Castlegar & District Community Health Centre, 709 - 10 St., Castlegar, BC V1N 1A1
Tel: 250-365-7221; *Fax:* 250-304-1238
www.interiorhealth.ca
Number of Beds: 49 rooms

***Chilliwack:* Bradley Centre**
Affiliated with: Fraser Health Authority
45600 Menholm Rd., Chilliwack, BC V2P 1P7
Tel: 604-795-4103; *Fax:* 604-795-4150

***Chilliwack:* The Cascades**
Baltic Properties Group
Affiliated with: Fraser Health Authority
44586 McIntosh Dr., Chilliwack, BC V2P 7W8
Tel: 604-795-2500; *Fax:* 604-795-5693
www.balticproperties.ca
Cheryl Dawes, General Manager
cheryl.dawes@balticproperties.ca

***Chilliwack:* Heritage Village**
Affiliated with: Fraser Health Authority
7525 Topaz Dr., Chilliwack, BC V2R 3C9
Tel: 604-858-1833; *Fax:* 604-793-7130

***Chilliwack:* Valleyhaven Guest Home**
Affiliated with: Fraser Health Authority
45450 Menholm Rd., Chilliwack, BC V2P 1M2
Tel: 604-792-0037; *Fax:* 604-792-6766

***Chilliwack:* Waverly Seniors Village**
Retirement Concepts
8445 Young Rd., Chilliwack, BC V2P 4P2
Tel: 604-792-6340; *Fax:* 604-792-5611
www.retirementconcepts.com
Number of Beds: 119 beds
Debbie Davidson, Administrator
604-792-6340, ddavidson@retirementconcepts.com

***Clearwater:* Forest View Place**
Affiliated with: Interior Health Authority
Dr. Helmcken Memorial Hospital, 640 Park Dr., Clearwater, BC V0E 1N1
Tel: 250-674-2244
www.interiorhealth.ca
Number of Beds: 19 permanent residential beds; 2 palliative & respite beds

***Coquitlam:* Cartier House**
Park Place Seniors Living
Affiliated with: Fraser Health Authority
1419 Cartier Ave., Coquitlam, BC V3K 2C6
Tel: 604-939-4654; *Fax:* 604-939-6442
cartierhouse@parkplaceseniorsliving.com
www.parkplaceseniorsliving.com
Number of Beds: 78 beds
Al Jina, Owner

***Coquitlam:* Dufferin Care Centre**
Affiliated with: Fraser Health Authority
1131 Dufferin St., Coquitlam, BC V3B 7X5
Tel: 604-552-1166; *Fax:* 604-552-3116

***Coquitlam:* Foyer Maillard**
Affiliated with: Fraser Health Authority
1010 Alderson Ave., Coquitlam, BC V3K 1W1
Tel: 604-937-5578; *Fax:* 604-937-7133
www.foyermaillard.com
Year Founded: 1969

***Courtenay:* Glacier View Lodge**
2450 Back Rd., Courtenay, BC V9N 9G8
Tel: 250-338-1451; *Fax:* 250-338-1115
www.glacierviewlodge.ca
Number of Beds: 100 beds
Michael Aikins, CEO

***Cranbrook:* F.W. Green Memorial Home**
Affiliated with: Interior Health Authority
1700 - 4th St. South, Cranbrook, BC V1C 6E1
Tel: 250-426-3710; *Fax:* 250-426-3622
www.interiorhealth.ca
Number of Beds: 60 beds (2 tertiary geriatric, 1 rehabilitative)

***Cranbrook:* Rocky Mountain Lodge**
20 - 23rd Ave. South, Cranbrook, BC V1C 5V1
Tel: 250-489-3361; *Fax:* 250-489-3545
Number of Beds: 63 beds

***Creston:* Swan Valley Lodge**
Affiliated with: Interior Health Authority
818 Vancouver St., Creston, BC V0B 1G0
Tel: 250-428-2283; *Fax:* 250-428-9318
www.interiorhealth.ca
Number of Beds: 90 beds; 23-bed dementia unit; 6 respite beds
Note: Residential care

***Dawson Creek:* Rotary Manor**
Affiliated with: Northern Health Authority
1121 - 90 Ave., Dawson Creek, BC V1G 5A3
Tel: 250-719-3480; *Fax:* 250-719-3781
www.northernhealth.ca

***Delta:* Delta Lodge**
4501 Arthur Dr., Delta, BC V4K 2X3
Tel: 604-946-6221; *Fax:* 604-946-6542
Number of Beds: 21 beds

***Delta:* Delta View Habilitation Centre**
Affiliated with: Fraser Health Authority
9341 Burns Dr., Delta, BC V4K 3N3
Tel: 604-596-8842; *Fax:* 604-596-8858
info@deltaview.ca
www.deltaview.ca
Social Media: twitter.com/deltaviewcentre
Number of Beds: 80 beds
Note: cares for peoples with Alzheimer's disease; specializing in caring for people with difficult behaviour

***Delta:* KinVillage West Court**
Affiliated with: Fraser Health Authority
5410 - 10 Ave., Delta, BC V4M 3X8
Tel: 604-943-0155; *Fax:* 604-943-0947
kinsmen.vcn.bc.ca

Number of Beds: 100 beds
Donna Ellis, Chief Executive Officer
dellis@kinvillage.org

Delta: Northcrest Care Centre
Affiliated with: Fraser Health Authority
6771 - 120 St., Delta, BC V4E 2A7
Tel: 604-597-7878; *Fax:* 604-597-7805
general@northcrestcare.ca

Delta: West Shore Laylum
Affiliated with: Fraser Health Authority
4900 Central Ave., Delta, BC V4K 2G7
Tel: 604-946-2822; *Fax:* 604-946-2217
laylumrh@telus.net

Duncan: Cairnsmore Place
Affiliated with: Vancouver Island Health Authority
250 Cairnsmore St., Duncan, BC V9L 4H2
Tel: 250-709-3080; *Fax:* 250-746-0351
Number of Beds: 100 beds

Enderby: Parkview Place
Affiliated with: Interior Health Authority
707 - 3 Ave., Enderby, BC V0E 1V0
Tel: 250-838-2470
www.interiorhealth.ca
Number of Beds: 31 beds
Note: Complex care facility

Enderby: Schaffer Residence at Oakside
Schaffer Residences
Affiliated with: Interior Health Authority
Former Name: Oakside Manor
9455 Firehall Frontage Rd., Enderby, BC V0E 1V3
Tel: 250-832-6767; *Fax:* 250-832-6779
oakside@schafferresidences.com
www.schafferresidences.com
Year Founded: 1965
Number of Beds: 42 beds
Note: Provides complex care, extended care, palliative care & respite care.
Julianna Cook, Director of Care

Fort Langley: Simpson Manor
Affiliated with: Fraser Health Authority
PO Box 40, Fort Langley, BC V1M 2R4
Tel: 604-888-0711; *Fax:* 604-888-1218
inquiries@simpsonManor.ca
www.simpsonmanor.ca
Note: intermediate & extended care

Fort St. John: North Peace Care Centre
9907 - 110 Ave., Fort St. John, BC V1J 2S9
Tel: 250-785-8941; *Fax:* 250-785-2296
Number of Beds: 47 beds
Note: Complex care special care unit

Grand Forks: Hardy View Lodge
Affiliated with: Interior Health Authority
7649 - 22 St., RR#2, Grand Forks, BC V0H 1H0
Tel: 250-443-2100
www.interiorhealth.ca
Number of Beds: 80 beds

Invermere: Columbia House
Affiliated with: Interior Health Authority
1030 - 10th St., Invermere, BC V0A 1K0
Tel: 250-342-2329
www.interiorhealth.ca
Number of Beds: 20 beds

Kamloops: The Hamlets at Westsyde
H&H Total Care Services Inc.
Affiliated with: Interior Health Authority
3255 Overlander Dr., Kamloops, BC V2B 0A5
Tel: 250-579-9061; *Fax:* 250-579-9069
info@thehamletsatwestsyde.com
www.thehamletsatwestsyde.com
Note: Residential care & assisted living

Kamloops: Hilltop House
Affiliated with: Interior Health Authority
470 Hilltop Ave., Kamloops, BC V2B 2S3
Tel: 250-376-3788; *Fax:* 250-376-9141
www.interiorhealth.ca
Number of Beds: 6 adult tertiary specialized residential beds

Kamloops: Ridgeview Lodge
Baltic Properties Group
Affiliated with: Interior Health Authority
920 Desmond St., Kamloops, BC V2B 5K6
Tel: 250-376-3131; *Fax:* 250-376-3151
www.balticproperties.ca
Number of Beds: 129 units
Note: Complex & respite care
Dana Levere, General Manager
dana.levere@balticproperties.ca

Kaslo: Victorian Community Residential Care
Affiliated with: Interior Health Authority
673 A Ave., Kaslo, BC V0G 1M0
Tel: 250-353-2211
www.interiorhealth.ca

Kelowna: Avonlea House
1658 Blondeaux Cres., Kelowna, BC V1Y 4J7
Tel: 250-762-4378; *Fax:* 250-762-0167
avonleahouse@avonleacare.com
www.avonleacare.com
Number of Beds: 14 beds
Note: specialized care home for severely brain-injured
Lynda Asselstine, Senior Manager & Director of Care
lyndacaringforpeople@shaw.ca

Kelowna: Brandt's Creek Mews
inSite Housing, Hospitality & Health Services
Affiliated with: Interior Health Authority
2081 Cross Rd., Kelowna, BC V1V 2G2
Tel: 778-478-8800; *Fax:* 778-478-8801
www.insiteseniorcare.com
Number of Beds: 102 complex care beds
Todd Mallen, Community Administrator
tmallen@insiteseniorcare.com

Kelowna: Cottonwoods Care Centre
Affiliated with: Interior Health Authority
2255 Ethel St., Kelowna, BC V1Y 2Z9
Tel: 250-862-4100
www.interiorhealth.ca
Number of Beds: 153 residential beds; 60 short-stay beds; 2 respite beds

Kelowna: David Lloyd Jones Home
Affiliated with: Interior Health Authority
934 Bernard Ave., Kelowna, BC V1Y 6P8
Tel: 250-762-2706; *Fax:* 250-762-5961
www.interiorhealth.ca
Number of Beds: 64 permanent beds; 3 respite residential beds

Kelowna: Mountainview Village
Good Samaritan Society
Affiliated with: Interior Health Authority
1540 KLO Rd., Kelowna, BC V1W 3P6
Tel: 250-717-3918
goodsaminfo@gss.org
www.gss.org
Number of Beds: 89 assisted living suites; 90 complex care suites; 83 life lease apartments
Shawn Terlson, President & CEO, Good Samaritan Society
sterlson@gss.org

Kelowna: Parkside Residence Ltd.
265 Gray Rd., Kelowna, BC V1X 1W8
Tel: 250-765-8482; *Fax:* 250-765-8213
Number of Beds: 23 beds

Kelowna: Spring Valley Care Centre
Park Place Seniors Living
Affiliated with: Interior Health Authority
Former Name: Windsor Manor
355 Terai Ct., Kelowna, BC V1X 5X6
Tel: 250-979-6000; *Fax:* 250-979-6002
springvalley@parkplaceseniorsliving.com
www.parkplaceseniorsliving.com
Number of Beds: 150 beds

Kelowna: Sun Pointe Village
Baptist Housing
Affiliated with: Interior Health Authority
700 Rutland Rd. North, Kelowna, BC V1X 7W8
Tel: 250-491-1400
sunpointe@baptisthousing.org
www.baptisthousing.org
Social Media: www.facebook.com/130827606961613; twitter.com/BaptistHousing; www.youtube.com/user/BaptistHousing
Number of Beds: 100 residential care suites; 20 assisted living suites

Kelowna: Sutherland Hills
Affiliated with: Interior Health Authority
3081 Hall Rd., Kelowna, BC V1W 2R5
Tel: 250-860-2330; *Fax:* 250-860-2399
www.interiorhealth.ca
Year Founded: 1972
Number of Beds: 99 rooms

Kelowna: Three Links Manor
Affiliated with: Interior Health Authority
1449 Kelglen Cres., Kelowna, BC V1Y 8P4
Tel: 250-763-2585; *Fax:* 250-763-6773
www.interiorhealth.ca
Number of Beds: 80 beds

Kelowna: Village at Mill Creek
Baptist Housing
Affiliated with: Interior Health Authority
Former Name: Still Waters Private Hospital
1450 Sutherland Ave., Kelowna, BC V1Y 5Y5
Tel: 250-860-2216
millcreek@baptisthousing.org
www.baptisthousing.org
Social Media: www.facebook.com/130827606961613; twitter.com/BaptistHousing; www.youtube.com/user/BaptistHousing
Number of Beds: 96 residential care suites; 38 assisted living suites
Howard Johnson, President & CEO, Baptist Housing

Keremeos: Orchard Heaven
Affiliated with: Interior Health Authority
700 - 3rd St., Keremeos, BC V0X 1N0
Tel: 250-499-3030
www.interiorhealth.ca
Number of Beds: 35 rooms; 10-bed dementia care unit

Ladysmith: Lodge on 4th
Affiliated with: Vancouver Island Health Authority
PO Box 820, 1127 - 4 Ave., Ladysmith, BC V9G 1A6
Tel: 250-245-3318
info@lodgeon4th.ca
4allseasonscare.com
Number of Beds: 22 beds
Spencer Atkinson, Manager

Lake Country: Lake Country Lodge & Manor
Baltic Properties Group
Affiliated with: Interior Health Authority
10163 Konschuh Rd., Lake Country, BC V4V 2M2
Tel: 250-766-3007; *Fax:* 250-766-3316
www.lakecountrylodge.ca
Number of Beds: 45 residential beds
Note: Supportive housing, complex care, & respite care
Moises Castro, General Manager & Director of Care
manager@lakecountrylodge.ca

Langley: Highland Lodge
20619 Eastleigh Cres., Langley, BC V3A 4C3
Tel: 604-534-7186
Number of Beds: 60 beds

Langley: Jackman Manor
Affiliated with: Fraser Health Authority
27447 - 28 Ave., Langley, BC V4W 3L9
Tel: 604-856-4161; *Fax:* 604-856-2562

Langley: Langley Lodge
Affiliated with: Fraser Health Authority
5451 - 204 St., Langley, BC V3A 5M9
Tel: 604-530-2305
www.langleylodge.org
Social Media: www.facebook.com/LangleyLodge; twitter.com/langleylodge
Number of Beds: 139 beds
Note: seniors
Debra Haupman, Chief Executive Officer

Lillooet: Mountain View Lodge
Affiliated with: Interior Health Authority
951 Murray St., Lillooet, BC V0K 1V0
Tel: 250-256-1312
www.interiorhealth.ca
Number of Beds: 22 beds

Lytton: Spintlum Lodge
Affiliated with: Interior Health Authority
533 Main St., Lytton, BC V0K 1Z0
Tel: 250-455-2221
www.interiorhealth.ca
Number of Beds: 6 suites

***Merritt:* Gillis House**
Affiliated with: Interior Health Authority
Former Name: Coquihalla Gillis House
1699 Tutill Crt., Merritt, BC V1K 1B8
Tel: 250-378-3271
www.interiorhealth.ca
Number of Beds: 74 residential care beds
Note: Complex care facility

***Midway:* Parkview Manor**
Affiliated with: Interior Health Authority
PO Box 427, 670 - 9th Ave., Midway, BC V0H 1M0
Tel: 250-449-2842
www.interiorhealth.ca
Number of Beds: 15 supportive/independent units; 5 assisted living units

***Mission:* Pleasant View Care Home**
Affiliated with: Fraser Health Authority
7380 Hurd St., Mission, BC V2V 3H9
Tel: 604-826-2154; *Fax:* 604-826-8672
pleasantview@pvhs.ca
www.missionseniors.ca

***Nakusp:* Halcyon House**
Affiliated with: Interior Health Authority
PO Box 910, 83 - 8th Ave. NW, Nakusp, BC V0G 1R0
Tel: 250-265-3692; *Fax:* 250-265-4141
halcyonhouse@telus.net
www.interiorhealth.ca
Number of Beds: 10 suites
Karolina Moskal, Site Manager

***Nakusp:* Minto House**
Affiliated with: Interior Health Authority
Arrow Lakes Hospital, 97 - 1st Ave. NE, Nakusp, BC V0G 1R0
Tel: 250-265-3622
www.interiorhealth.ca
Number of Beds: 14 residential beds

***Nanaimo:* Kiwanis Village Lodge**
Affiliated with: Vancouver Island Health Authority
1221 Kiwanis Cres., Nanaimo, BC V9S 5Y1
Tel: 250-753-6471; *Fax:* 250-740-2816
info@kiwanisvillage.ca
www.kiwanisvillage.ca
Number of Beds: 102 beds
Sue Abermann, Interim CEO

***Nanaimo:* Malaspina Gardens Inc.**
Affiliated with: Chartwell Retirement Residences
388 Machleary St., Nanaimo, BC V9R 2G9
Tel: 250-754-7711; *Fax:* 250-754-2175
www.chartwell.com
Number of Beds: 135 beds
W. Brent Binions, President & CEO, Chartwell Retirement Residences

***Nanaimo:* Nanaimo Travellers Lodge**
Affiliated with: Vancouver Island Health Authority
1298 Nelson St., Nanaimo, BC V9S 2K5
Tel: 250-758-4676; *Fax:* 250-758-4698
office@nantralodge.bc.ca
www.nanaimotravellerslodge.com
Year Founded: 2004
Number of Beds: 90 beds
Carolyn Kavanagh, Director, Care
250-760-2630, carolyn.kavanagh@nantralodge.bc.ca

***Nelson:* Mountain Lake Seniors Community**
Park Place Seniors Living
Affiliated with: Interior Health Authority
908 - 11th St., Nelson, BC V1L 7A6
Tel: 250-352-2600; *Fax:* 250-352-2665
mountainlake@parkplaceseniorsliving.com
www.parkplaceseniorsliving.com
Year Founded: 2005
Number of Beds: 135 beds
Note: Complex care & assisted living

***Nelson:* Nelson Jubilee Manor**
Affiliated with: Interior Health Authority
500 West Beasley St. West, Nelson, BC V1L 6G9
Tel: 250-352-7011; *Fax:* 250-352-7044
www.interiorhealth.ca
Number of Beds: 39 beds

***New Denver:* Slocan Community Health Centre**
Affiliated with: Interior Health Authority
401 Galena Ave., New Denver, BC V0G 1S0
Tel: 250-358-7911; *Fax:* 250-358-7117
www.interiorhealth.ca
Number of Beds: 10 rooms

***New Westminster:* Buchanan Lodge**
Affiliated with: Fraser Health Authority
409 Blair Ave., New Westminster, BC V3L 4A4
Tel: 604-522-7033; *Fax:* 604-522-3689
admin@buchanan-lodge.com

***New Westminster:* Honour House**
Former Name: Blue Spruce Cottage
509 St. George St., New Westminster, BC V3L 1L1
Tel: 778-397-4399; *Fax:* 778-397-4396
admin@honourhouse.ca
www.honourhouse.ca
Number of Beds: 15 beds
Craig Longstaff, General & House Manager

***New Westminster:* Kiwanis Intermediate Care Centre**
Affiliated with: Fraser Health Authority
35 Clute St., New Westminster, BC V3L 1Z5
Tel: 604-525-6471; *Fax:* 604-525-8522
reception@kiwaniscarecentre.com
kiwaniscarecentre.com
Year Founded: 1982
Number of Beds: 75 beds
Note: intermediate care
Lorrie Gerrard, Executive Director
lgerrard@kiwaniscarecentre.com

***New Westminster:* Queen's Park Care Centre**
Affiliated with: Fraser Health Authority
315 McBride Blvd., New Westminster, BC V3L 5E8
Tel: 604-520-0911; *Fax:* 604-517-8651
Note: extended care facility

***New Westminster:* Royal City Manor Long Term Care**
Revera Living
77 Jamieson Ct., New Westminster, BC V3L 5P8
Tel: 604-522-6699; *Fax:* 604-522-1022
royalcitymanor@reveraliving.com
www.reveraliving.com
Jeffrey C. Lozon, President & CEO, Revera Living

***New Westminster:* Salvation Army Buchanan Lodge**
Affiliated with: Fraser Health Authority
409 Blair Ave., New Westminster, BC V3L 4A4
Tel: 604-522-7033; *Fax:* 604-522-3689
admin@buchanan-lodge.com
www.buchanan-lodge.com
Number of Beds: 112 beds
Famella Altejos, Executive Director

***North Vancouver:* Cedar Garden**
Affiliated with: Vancouver Coastal Health
1250 Cedar Village Close, North Vancouver, BC V7J 3P3
Tel: 604-904-6409; *Fax:* 604-904-6440
feedback@vch.ca
www.vch.ca
Number of Beds: 30 beds

***North Vancouver:* Cedarview Lodge**
Affiliated with: Vancouver Coastal Health
1200 Cedar Village Close, North Vancouver, BC V7J 3P3
Tel: 604-904-6400; *Fax:* 604-904-6411
Note: intermediate care

***North Vancouver:* Evergreen House**
Affiliated with: Vancouver Coastal Health
231 - 15 St. East, North Vancouver, BC V7L 2L7
Tel: 604-988-3131; *Fax:* 604-984-3784
feedback@vch.ca
www.vch.ca
Year Founded: 1971
Number of Beds: 292 beds

***North Vancouver:* N.S. Kiwanis Care Centre**
Affiliated with: Vancouver Coastal Health
2444 Burr Pl., North Vancouver, BC V7H 3A5
Tel: 604-924-8300; *Fax:* 604-924-8325
feedback@vch.ca
www.vch.ca
Number of Beds: 192 beds

***Oliver:* McKinney Place Extended Care**
Affiliated with: Interior Health Authority
911 McKinney Rd., Oliver, BC V0H 1T0
Tel: 250-498-5040
www.interiorhealth.ca
Number of Beds: 75 rooms

***Oliver:* Sunnybank Retirement Centre**
Affiliated with: Interior Health Authority
6553 Park Dr., Oliver, BC V0H 1T0
Tel: 250-498-4951; *Fax:* 250-498-2287
www.interiorhealth.ca
Number of Beds: 51 beds; 13-bed dementia unit

***Osoyoos:* Country Squire Retirement Villa**
Affiliated with: Interior Health Authority
9707 North 87 St., Osoyoos, BC V0H 1V0
Tel: 250-495-6568; *Fax:* 250-495-7466
www.interiorhealth.ca
Note: Provides tertiary psychiatric services
Deb McCartney, Contact
deb.mccartney@thecountrysquire.ca

***Osoyoos:* Mariposa Gardens**
Baltic Properties Group
Affiliated with: Interior Health Authority
8816 - 97th St., Osoyoos, BC V0H 1V5
Tel: 250-495-8124; *Fax:* 250-495-8134
www.balticproperties.ca
Number of Beds: 10 units
Note: Assisted living & residential care
Marlese Hutter, General Manager
marlese.hutter@balticproperties.ca

***Parksville:* Arrowsmith Lodge**
266A Moilliet St., Parksville, BC V9P 1M9
Tel: 250-248-4331; *Fax:* 250-248-4813
arrowsmithlodge.ca
Year Founded: 1971
Number of Beds: 75 beds
David McDowell, Secretary/Treasurer

***Parksville:* Halliday House**
PO Box 518, 188 McCarter St., Parksville, BC V9P 1A1
Tel: 250-248-2835; *Fax:* 250-248-2403
Number of Beds: 20 beds

***Penticton:* The Hamlets at Penticton**
H&H Total Care Services Inc.
Affiliated with: Interior Health Authority
103 Duncan Ave., Penticton, BC V2A 2Y3
Tel: 250-490-8503; *Fax:* 250-490-8523
info@thehamletsatpenticton.com
www.thehamletsatpenticton.com
Year Founded: 2008
Number of Beds: 98 beds
Note: Services include: complex care; dementia care; brain injured/young adult care; & respite care.

***Penticton:* Haven Hill Retirement Centre**
Affiliated with: Interior Health Authority
415 Haven Hill Rd., Penticton, BC V2A 4E9
Tel: 250-492-2600
www.havenhill.ca
Number of Beds: 152 beds

***Penticton:* Penticton & District Society for Community Living (PSDCL)**
180 Industrial Ave. West, Penticton, BC V2A 6X9
Tel: 250-493-0312; *Fax:* 250-493-9113
admin@pdscl.org
www.pdscl.org
Year Founded: 1958
Note: Offers a number of community services including assisted living and activities for seniors

***Penticton:* Trinity Care Centre**
Affiliated with: Interior Health Authority
75 West Green Ave., Penticton, BC V2A 7N6
Tel: 250-493-6601
www.interiorhealth.ca
Number of Beds: 75 rooms

***Penticton:* Village by the Station**
Good Samaritan Society
Affiliated with: Interior Health Authority
270 Hastings Ave., Penticton, BC V2A 2V6
Tel: 250-490-4949; *Fax:* 250-490-9733
goodsaminfo@gss.org
www.gss.org
Number of Beds: 35 assisted living suites; four 10-bed dementia care cottages; 60 residential care suites
Shawn Terlson, President & CEO, Good Samaritan Society
sterlson@gss.org

***Penticton:* Westview Place**
Affiliated with: Interior Health Authority
550 Carmi Ave., Penticton, BC V2A 3G6
Tel: 250-492-7174
www.interiorhealth.ca

Number of Beds: 102 rooms

Port Alberni: Echo Village
Affiliated with: Vancouver Island Health Authority
4200 - 10 Ave., Port Alberni, BC V9Y 4X3
Tel: 250-724-1090; *Fax:* 250-724-2115
Number of Beds: 68 beds

Port Alberni: Fir Park Village
Affiliated with: Vancouver Island Health Authority
4411 Wallace St., Port Alberni, BC V9Y 7Y5
Tel: 250-724-6541
www.viha.ca
Number of Beds: 65 beds

Port Alberni: Tsawaayuus-Rainbow Gardens
Affiliated with: Vancouver Island Health Authority
6151 Russell Pl., Port Alberni, BC V9Y 7W3
Tel: 250-724-5655; *Fax:* 250-724-5666
info@rainbowgardens.bc.ca
rainbowgardens.bc.ca
Year Founded: 1992
Shaunee Casavant, Manager

Port Coquitlam: Hawthorne Seniors Care Community
Affiliated with: Fraser Health Authority
2111 Hawthorne Ave., Port Coquitlam, BC V3C 1W3
Tel: 604-941-4051; *Fax:* 604-941-5829
hawthornecare.com
Year Founded: 1970
Number of Beds: 271 beds
Lenore Pickering, Executive Director
607-468-5003, lpickering@hawthornecare.com

Port Moody: Eagle Ridge Manor
Affiliated with: Fraser Health Authority
475 Guildford Way, Port Moody, BC V3H 3W9
Tel: 604-469-3211; *Fax:* 604-949-8212

Pouce Coupe: Peace River Haven
PO Box 188, 5213 - 50th Ave., Pouce Coupe, BC V0C 2C0
Tel: 250-786-6100; *Fax:* 250-786-6107
Number of Beds: 60 beds
Note: Residential care facility for seniors.

Powell River: Evergreen Extended Care
Affiliated with: Vancouver Coastal Health
4970 Joyce Ave., Powell River, BC V8A 5P2
Tel: 604-485-2208; *Fax:* 604-485-3271
feedback@vch.ca
www.vch.ca
Number of Beds: 75 beds

Prince George: AiMHi - Prince George Association for Community Living
950 Kerry St., Prince George, BC V2M 5A3
Tel: 250-564-6408; *Fax:* 250-564-6801
aimhi@aimhi.ca
www.aimhi.ca
Social Media: www.facebook.com/AiMHibc; twitter.com/AiMHiBC
Note: Non-profit, supports individuals with developmental disabilities & children with special needs
Melinda Heidsma, Executive Director

Prince George: Hazelton Street Residence
Affiliated with: Northern Health Authority
2554 Hazelton St., Prince George, BC V2L 1H1
Tel: 250-960-1499
www.northernhealth.ca
Number of Beds: 6 long-term beds
Note: Programs & services include: assistance with daily activities; medication management; & support & education for clients, families & caregivers. Managed by Western Human Resource Corporation.

Prince George: Jubilee Lodge
Affiliated with: Northern Health Authority
1475 Edmonton St., Prince George, BC V2M 1S2
Tel: 250-565-2286; *Fax:* 250-565-2778
www.northernhealth.ca
Note: Local seniors' programs & care services: 250-565-7317 & 250-565-7325.

Prince George: Parkside Care Facility
Affiliated with: Northern Health Authority
788 Ospika Blvd., Prince George, BC V2M 6Y2
Tel: 250-563-1916; *Fax:* 250-563-9424
www.northernhealth.ca
Note: Local seniors' programs & care services: 250-565-7317 & 250-565-7325.

Prince George: Simon Fraser Lodge
2410 Laurier Cres., Prince George, BC V2M 2B3
Tel: 250-563-3413; *Fax:* 250-563-7209
Number of Beds: 124 beds
Ceceilia Parent, Contact
250-563-3413

Princeton: Ridgewood Lodge
Affiliated with: Interior Health Authority
95A Ridgewood Dr., Princeton, BC V0X 1W0
Tel: 250-295-3211
www.interiorhealth.ca
Number of Beds: 37 rooms

Qualicum Beach: Arranglen Gardens
2300 Fowler Rd., Qualicum Beach, BC V9K 2A5
Tel: 250-752-9277; *Fax:* 250-752-5525
Number of Beds: 85 beds

Qualicum Beach: Eagle Park Health Care Facility
Affiliated with: Vancouver Island Health Authority
777 Jones St., Qualicum Beach, BC V9K 2L1
Tel: 250-947-8220
Number of Beds: 10 beds

Revelstoke: Mt. Cartier Court
Affiliated with: Interior Health Authority
1200 Newlands Rd., Revelstoke, BC V0E 2S1
Tel: 250-814-2232
www.interiorhealth.ca
Number of Beds: 44 rooms
Note: Residential living for individuals with complex health needs

Richmond: Austin Harris Residence
Affiliated with: Vancouver Coastal Health
5411 Moncton St., Richmond, BC V7E 0A8
Tel: 604-277-9819; *Fax:* 604-277-8834
feedback@vch.ca
www.vch.com
Year Founded: 2007
Number of Beds: 50 beds
Note: Assisted housing; health services

Richmond: Courtyard Gardens
Affiliated with: Vancouver Coastal Health
7051 Moffatt Rd., Richmond, BC V6Y 3W2
Tel: 604-273-1225; *Fax:* 604-273-9253
off.mgr.cyg@diversicare.ca
courtyardgardens.ca

Richmond: Fraserview Intermediate Care Lodge
Affiliated with: Vancouver Coastal Health
9580 Williams Rd., Richmond, BC V7A 1H2
Tel: 604-274-3510; *Fax:* 604-277-1844
fraserview@qwik.net
www.vch.ca
Year Founded: 1970
Number of Beds: 105 beds

Richmond: Pinegrove Place
Affiliated with: Vancouver Coastal Health
11331 Mellis Dr., Richmond, BC V6X 1L8
Tel: 604-278-1296; *Fax:* 604-273-0050
Number of Beds: 93 beds

Richmond: Richmond Lions Manor
Affiliated with: Vancouver Coastal Health
11771 Fentiman Pl., Richmond, BC V7E 3M4
Tel: 604-675-2590; *Fax:* 604-274-2543
Year Founded: 1972

Richmond: Rosewood Manor
Affiliated with: Vancouver Coastal Health
6260 Blundell Rd., Richmond, BC V7C 5C4
Tel: 604-271-3590; *Fax:* 604-271-3551
www.rosewoodmanor.org
Number of Beds: 155 beds
Note: intermediate & complex care
Deborah Goegan, Administrator
604-271-3590, dgoegan@rosewoodmanor.org

Salmon Arm: Hillside Village Good Samaritan Society
Affiliated with: Interior Health Authority
2891 - 15 Ave. NE, Salmon Arm, BC V1E 2B6
Tel: 250-833-5877; *Fax:* 250-833-5890
goodsaminfo@gss.org
www.gss.org
Number of Beds: 112 residential care suites (including six 12-bed dementia care cottages)
Shawn Terlson, President & CEO, Good Samaritan Society
sterlson@gss.org

Salmon Arm: Piccadilly Care Home Park Place Seniors Living
Affiliated with: Interior Health Authority
821 - 10th Ave. SW, Salmon Arm, BC V1E 1T2
Tel: 250-804-1676; *Fax:* 250-804-0672
piccadilly@parkplaceseniorsliving.com
www.parkplaceseniorsliving.com
Number of Beds: 56 rooms
Note: Complex care

Salt Spring Island: Greenwoods Care Facility
Affiliated with: Greenwoods Elder Care Society
133 Blain Rd., Salt Spring Island, BC V8K 1Z9
Tel: 250-537-5561; *Fax:* 250-537-1124
Toll-Free: 888-533-2273
www.greenwoodseldercare.com
Year Founded: 1979
Number of Beds: 50 beds
Andrew Brown, Executive Director
250-537-5561, director@greenwoodseldercare.com

Sechelt: Shorncliffe Intermediate Care
Affiliated with: Vancouver Coastal Health
Former Name: Shorncliffe
5847 Medusa St., Sechelt, BC V0N 3A0
Tel: 604-885-5126; *Fax:* 604-885-5140
Number of Beds: 60 beds

Shawnigan Lake: Acacia Ty Mawr Lodge
PO Box 100, 2655 Shawnigan Lake Rd., Shawnigan Lake, BC V0R 2W0
Tel: 250-743-2124; *Fax:* 250-743-2130
www.acaciatymawr.ca
Number of Beds: 35 beds
Jerri Maw, Director, Care

Sidney: Sidney Intermediate Care Home Ltd.
9888 - 5 St., Sidney, BC V8L 2X3
Tel: 250-656-0121; *Fax:* 250-656-0189
Number of Beds: 52 beds

Smithers: Bulkley Lodge
Affiliated with: Northern Health Authority
PO Box 3640, 3668 - 11th Ave., Smithers, BC V0J 2N0
Tel: 250-847-4443; *Fax:* 250-847-3895
www.northernhealth.ca

Squamish: Hilltop House
Affiliated with: Vancouver Coastal Health
38146 Behrner Dr., Squamish, BC V8B 0J3
Tel: 604-892-9337; *Fax:* 604-892-6091
Year Founded: 1984
Number of Beds: 10 beds for dementia care, 31 intermediate care, 20 extended
Note: long term care

Summerland: Kelly Care Centre
12801 Kelly Ave., Summerland, BC V0H 1Z0
Tel: 250-494-7911; *Fax:* 250-494-4027
Number of Beds: 79 beds

Summerland: Summerland Extended Care
Affiliated with: Interior Health Authority
Dr. Andrew Pavillion, 12815 Atkinson Rd., Summerland, BC V0H 1Z0
Tel: 250-404-8020
www.interiorhealth.ca
Number of Beds: 50 rooms

Surrey: Amenida Seniors' Community
Affiliated with: Fraser Health Authority
Former Name: Newton Regency Care Home
13855 - 68th Ave., Surrey, BC V3W 2G9
Tel: 604-235-1933; *Fax:* 604-597-8032
www.homecareliving.ca
Social Media: www.facebook.com/150449131720398
Year Founded: 2010
Note: Independent, assisted living
Teena Love, General Manager
604-597-9333, teena.love@homecareliving.ca
Sandra Prance, Administrative Coordinator
604-597-9333, sandra.prance@homecareliving.ca

Surrey: Carelife/Fleetwood
Affiliated with: Fraser Health Authority
8265 - 159 St., Surrey, BC V4N 5T5
Tel: 604-598-7200; *Fax:* 604-598-7229

Surrey: Crescent Gardens Retirement Community
Affiliated with: Chartwell Retirement Residences
1222 King George Blvd., Surrey, BC V4A 9W6
Tel: 604-541-8861; *Fax:* 604-541-8871
www.chartwell.com

W. Brent Binions, President & CEO, Chartwell Retirement Residences

Surrey: Evergreen Hamlets
Affiliated with: Fraser Health Authority
15660 - 84 Ave., Surrey, BC V4N 0W3
Tel: 604-597-7906; *Fax:* 604-597-9025
info@evergreenhamlets.com

Surrey: Fleetwood Place
Affiliated with: Fraser Health Authority
16011 - 83rd Ave., Surrey, BC V3S 8M2
Tel: 604-590-6860
info@fleetwoodplace.ca
www.fleetwoodplace.ca

Surrey: Guildford Seniors Village
Retirement Concepts
Affiliated with: Fraser Health Authority
14568 - 104A Ave., Surrey, BC V3R 1R3
Tel: 604-582-0808; *Fax:* 604-582-7011
www.retirementconcepts.com

Year Founded: 2001
Number of Beds: 69 beds
Bianca Goldberg, Contact
604-582-0808, bgoldberg@retirementconcepts.com

Surrey: H & H Total Care Services
8382 - 156 St., Surrey, BC V3S 3R7
Tel: 604-597-7931; *Fax:* 604-596-3641
info@hhtotalcare.com
www.hhtotalcare.com

Year Founded: 1989
Note: Parent company operating residential care facilities that focus on helping people with brain injuries and mental health issues.
Hank Van Ryk, CEO

Surrey: Hilton Villa Care Centre
Park Place Seniors Living
Affiliated with: Alberta Health Services
13525 Hilton Rd., Surrey, BC V3R 5J3
Tel: 604-588-3424; *Fax:* 604-588-3433
hiltonvilla@parkplaceseniorsliving.com
www.parkplaceseniorsliving.com

Number of Beds: 124 beds
Al Jina, President
604-266-1436, Fax: 604-266-8557,
ajina@parkplaceseniorsliving.com

Surrey: Kinsmen Place Lodge
Affiliated with: Fraser Health Authority
9650 - 137A St., Surrey, BC V3T 5A2
Tel: 604-588-0445; *Fax:* 604-588-7211
info@kinsmenplace.org
www.kinsmenplace.org
Social Media: www.facebook.com/127417500669218
Note: intermediate care
Kathleen Strath, CEO

Surrey: Morgan Place
Affiliated with: Fraser Health Authority
3288 - 156A St., Surrey, BC V3S 9T1
Tel: 604-535-7328
admin@morganplace.ca
www.morganplace.ca

Surrey: Zion Park Manor
Affiliated with: Fraser Health Authority
5939 - 180th St., Surrey, BC V3S 4L2
Tel: 604-576-2891
www.zionparkmanor.com
Social Media: www.facebook.com/zionparkmanor
Number of Beds: 99 beds
Erroll Hastings, Executive Director
ehastings@zionparkmanor.com

Terrace: Terraceview Lodge
Affiliated with: Northern Health Authority
4707 Kerby St., Terrace, BC V8G 5G9
Tel: 250-638-0223; *Fax:* 250-635-9775
www.northernhealth.ca

Number of Beds: 95 beds
Doris Mitchell, Administrator

Trail: Columbia View Lodge
Affiliated with: Interior Health Authority
2920 Laburnum Dr., Trail, BC V1R 4N2
Tel: 250-364-1271; *Fax:* 250-364-0911
www.interiorhealth.ca
Number of Beds: 76 beds
Note: Complex care facility

Trail: Kiro Manor
1500 Columbia Ave., Trail, BC V1R 1J9
Tel: 250-364-1214; *Fax:* 250-364-1261
Number of Beds: 9 beds

Trail: Poplar Ridge Pavillion
Affiliated with: Interior Health Authority
1200 Hospital Bench, Trail, BC V1R 4M1
Tel: 250-368-3311; *Fax:* 250-364-3422
www.interiorhealth.ca
Number of Beds: 15 double rooms; 4 single rooms; four 4-bed rooms

Vancouver: Adanac Park Lodge
Affiliated with: Vancouver Coastal Health
851 Boundary Rd., Vancouver, BC V5K 4T2
Tel: 604-299-7567; *Fax:* 604-299-7424
apl-reception@littlemountaincare.org
www.littlemountaincare.org

Year Founded: 2000
Number of Beds: 64 beds
Janice Howes, Executive Director
jhowes@littlemountaincare.org

Vancouver: Amica at Arbutus Manor
2125 Eddington Dr., Vancouver, BC V6L 3A9
Tel: 604-736-8936; *Fax:* 604-731-8933
arbutus@amica.ca
www.amica.ca

Number of Beds: 125 beds

Vancouver: Arbutus Care Centre
Revera Living
Affiliated with: Vancouver Coastal Health
4505 Valley Dr., Vancouver, BC V6L 2L1
Tel: 604-261-4292; *Fax:* 604-261-7849
www.reveraliving.com

Year Founded: 1961
Note: Specialty: Complex residential care; Nursing care; Foot care; Social work; Recreational therapy; Music therapy

Vancouver: Blenheim Lodge
Affiliated with: Vancouver Coastal Health
3263 Blenheim St., Vancouver, BC V6L 2X7
Tel: 604-732-8717; *Fax:* 604-732-7316

Year Founded: 1969
Number of Beds: 97 beds

Vancouver: Braddan Private Hospital
Affiliated with: Vancouver Coastal Health
2450 West 2 Ave., Vancouver, BC V6K 1J6
Tel: 604-731-2127; *Fax:* 604-731-0283

Number of Beds: 51 beds
Maureen McIntosh, Administrator
mcintosh@axion.net

Vancouver: Broadway Pentecostal Lodge
Affiliated with: Vancouver Coastal Health
1377 Lamey's Mill Rd., Vancouver, BC V6H 3S9
Tel: 604-733-1441

Number of Beds: 116 beds

Vancouver: Chalmers Lodge Personal Care Home
Affiliated with: Vancouver Coastal Health
1450 West 12th Ave., Vancouver, BC V6H 1M9
Tel: 604-731-3178; *Fax:* 604-731-3140
info@chalmerslodge.ca
www.chalmerslodge.ca

Year Founded: 1970
Number of Beds: 115 units
Note: Personal care home

Vancouver: City Centre Care Society - Central City Lodge
Affiliated with: Vancouver Coastal Health
415 West Pender St., Vancouver, BC V6B 1V2
Tel: 604-681-9111; *Fax:* 604-681-5546
info@cccares.org
www.cccares.org

Year Founded: 1993
Number of Beds: 122 beds
Note: multilevel care; supportive housing - addictions recovery
Seamus O'Melinn, Executive Director

Vancouver: City Centre Care Society - Cooper Place
Affiliated with: Vancouver Coastal Health
306 East Cordova St., Vancouver, BC V6A 1L5
Tel: 604-684-2545; *Fax:* 604-684-2575
www.cccares.org

Year Founded: 1983
Seamus O'Melinn, Executive Director

Vancouver: Columbus Residence
Affiliated with: Vancouver Coastal Health
704 West 69th Ave., Vancouver, BC V6P 2W3
Tel: 604-321-4405; *Fax:* 604-321-4543
www.columbusresidence.ca

Number of Beds: 76 beds
Dale Clements, Administrator
dclements@columbusresidence.ca

Vancouver: Crofton Manor
Revera Living
2803 West 41 Ave., Vancouver, BC V6N 4B4
Tel: 604-263-0921; *Fax:* 604-263-7719
www.reveraliving.com/crofton
Social Media: www.facebook.com/400950748267;
twitter.com/Revera_Inc

Year Founded: 1961
Number of Beds: 194 suites
Jeffrey C. Lozon, President & CEO, Revera Living

Vancouver: Dogwood Lodge
Affiliated with: Vancouver Coastal Health
500 West 57th Ave., Vancouver, BC V6P 6E8
Tel: 604-324-6882; *Fax:* 604-324-7226

Susan Fong, Administrator
susan.fong@vch.ca

Vancouver: Fair Haven United Church Home
Affiliated with: Vancouver Coastal Health
2720 East 48th St., Vancouver, BC V5S 1G7
Tel: 604-433-2939; *Fax:* 604-433-4547

Year Founded: 2002
Number of Beds: 100 beds

Vancouver: False Creek Residence
Affiliated with: Vancouver Coastal Health
1167 Forge Walk, Vancouver, BC V6H 3R1
Tel: 604-731-0401; *Fax:* 604-731-9546
info@rils.ca
www.rils.ca

Number of Beds: 24 beds

Vancouver: German-Canadian Care Home
German-Canadian Benevolent Society of BC
Affiliated with: Vancouver Coastal Health
2010 Harrison Dr., Vancouver, BC V5P 2P6
Tel: 604-713-6500; *Fax:* 604-713-6548
info@gcch.ca
www.gcch.ca

Number of Beds: 137 beds
Jutta Purchase, CEO

Vancouver: Haro Park Centre
Affiliated with: Vancouver Coastal Health
1233 Haro St., Vancouver, BC V6E 3Y5
Tel: 604-687-5584; *Fax:* 604-687-0645
info@haropark.org
www.haropark.org
Social Media: www.facebook.com/206023427599
Year Founded: 1980

Vancouver: Icelandic Care Home
Affiliated with: Vancouver Coastal Health
2020 Harrison Dr., Vancouver, BC V5P 0A1
Tel: 604-321-3812
feedback@vch.ca
www.vch.ca

Number of Beds: 77 beds

Vancouver: Kopernik Lodge
Kopernik Nicolaus Foundation
Affiliated with: Vancouver Coastal Health
3150 Rosemont Dr., Vancouver, BC V5S 2C9
Tel: 604-438-2474; *Fax:* 604-438-5344
admin@kopernik-lodge.bc.ca
www.kopernik-foundation.org

Year Founded: 1972
Number of Beds: 87 beds
Note: intermediate care facility

Vancouver: Lakeview Care Centre
Affiliated with: Vancouver Coastal Health
3490 Porter St., Vancouver, BC V5N 5W4
Tel: 604-874-2803; *Fax:* 604-874-2806

Number of Beds: 165 beds

Vancouver: Little Mountain Place
Affiliated with: Vancouver Coastal Health
330 East 36th Ave., Vancouver, BC V5W 3Z4
Tel: 604-325-2298; *Fax:* 604-325-3655
reception@littlemountaincare.org
www.littlemountaincare.org

Year Founded: 1987
Number of Beds: 117 beds
Angie Martinez, Senior Operations Leader
a.martinez@littlemountaincare.org

Vancouver: Renfrew Care Centre
Retirement Concepts
1880 Renfrew St., Vancouver, BC V5M 3H9
Tel: 604-255-7723; *Fax:* 604-255-2045
www.retirementconcepts.com
Number of Beds: 88 beds
Loraine Coffin, General Manager
lcoffin@retirementconcepts.com

Vancouver: Royal Arch Masonic Home
Affiliated with: Vancouver Coastal Health
7850 Champlain Cres., Vancouver, BC V5S 4C7
Tel: 604-437-7343; *Fax:* 604-437-7373
www.royalarchmasonichome.bc.ca
Number of Beds: 151 beds
Gregory Runzer, Administrator
604-437-7343, grunzer@ramh.ca

Vancouver: Royal Ascot Care Centre
Affiliated with: Vancouver Coastal Health
2455 East Broadway, Vancouver, BC V5M 1Y7
Tel: 604-254-5559; *Fax:* 604-254-5523
Year Founded: 1996
Number of Beds: 82 beds

Vancouver: St. Bernard House
547 - 12th Ave. East, Vancouver, BC V5T 2H6
Tel: 604-874-8657; *Fax:* 604-984-7933
Number of Beds: 12 beds

Vancouver: St. Vincent's Hospital
Brock Fahrni Pavilion
Affiliated with: Vancouver Coastal Health
4650 Oak St., Vancouver, BC V6H 4J4
Tel: 604-806-9710; *Fax:* 604-806-9706
www.providencehealthcare.org
Number of Beds: 148 beds
Note: extended care facility
Dianne Doyle, President & CEO

Vancouver: St. Vincent's Hospital Langara
Affiliated with: Vancouver Coastal Health
255 West 62nd Ave., Vancouver, BC V5X 4V4
Tel: 604-325-4116; *Fax:* 604-806-9756
www.providencehealthcare.org
Year Founded: 1991
Note: long-term care facility
Dianne Doyle, President & CEO

Vancouver: Salvation Army Southview Terrace
Affiliated with: Vancouver Coastal Health
7252 Kerr St., Vancouver, BC V3S 3V2
Tel: 604-438-3367; *Fax:* 604-438-0262
www.salvationarmy.ca
Year Founded: 2007
Number of Beds: 57 unites
Note: personal care facility
Barbara Brown, Contact

Vancouver: South Granville Park Lodge
Affiliated with: Vancouver Coastal Health
1645 West 14th Ave., Vancouver, BC V6J 2J4
Tel: 604-732-8633; *Fax:* 604-732-9833
sgplodge@telus.net
www.sgplodge.com
Year Founded: 1969
Deborah Tobias, Director, Admissions

Vancouver: Three Links Care Centre
Three Links Care Society
Affiliated with: Vancouver Coastal Health
2934 East 22 Ave., Vancouver, BC V5M 2Y4
Tel: 604-434-7211; *Fax:* 604-438-7563
info@threelinks.com
www.threelinks.com
Year Founded: 1982
Number of Beds: 90 beds
Note: complex care facility
Tom Novak, CEO

Vancouver: Villa Cathay Care Home
Affiliated with: Vancouver Coastal Health
970 Union St., Vancouver, BC V6A 3V1
Tel: 604-254-5621; *Fax:* 604-254-5230
info@villacathay.ca
www.villacathay.ca
Year Founded: 1978
Number of Beds: 188 beds

Hudson Chong, COO

Vancouver: Windermere Care Centre
Affiliated with: Vancouver Coastal Health
900 West 12 Ave., Vancouver, BC V5Z 1N3
Tel: 604-736-8676; *Fax:* 604-736-8682
infor@windermerecare.ca
www.windermerecare.ca
Number of Beds: 197 beds
Note: complex care
Ross Sugimoto, Administrator
rsugimoto@windermerecare.ca

Vancouver: Yaletown House Society
Affiliated with: Vancouver Coastal Health
1099 Cambie St., Vancouver, BC V6B 5A8
Tel: 604-689-0022; *Fax:* 604-662-7954
info@yaletown.org
www.yaletown.org
Number of Beds: 130 beds
Carol Crichton, Executive Director
604-806-4202, cacrichton@yaletown.org

Vancouver: Youville Residence
Affiliated with: Vancouver Coastal Health
4950 Heather St., Vancouver, BC V5Z 3L9
Tel: 604-261-9371; *Fax:* 604-261-9047
www.providencehealthcare.org
Number of Beds: 42 beds
Note: intermediate care facility with Alzheimer ward
Dianne Doyle, President & CEO

Vanderhoof: Stuart Nechako Manor
Affiliated with: Northern Health Authority
3277 Hospital Rd., Vanderhoof, BC V0J 3A2
Tel: 250-567-2013; *Fax:* 250-567-2018
www.northernhealth.ca

Vernon: Creekside Landing Assisted Living
Kaigo Retirement Communities Ltd.
Affiliated with: Interior Health Authority
6190 Okanagan Landing Rd., Vernon, BC V1H 1M3
Tel: 250-549-9550
www.kaigo.ca
Number of Beds: 24 suites
Note: Complex care facility

Vernon: Heritage Square
Kaigo Retirement Communities Ltd.
Affiliated with: Interior Health Authority
3904 - 27 St., Vernon, BC V1T 4X7
Tel: 250-545-2060; *Fax:* 250-545-4060
www.kaigo.ca
Number of Beds: 50 private care suites; 26 assisted living suites
Note: Combined health care services & assisted living for adults who are not able to live alone.

Vernon: Heron Grove
Good Samaritan Society
Affiliated with: Interior Health Authority
4900 - 20th St., Vernon, BC V1T 9W3
Tel: 250-542-6101; *Fax:* 250-542-6227
goodsaminfo@gss.org
www.gss.org
Number of Beds: 40 assisted living suites; six 12-bed complex care cottages for dementia; two 14-bed complex care cottages; 15 life lease apartments
Shawn Terlson, President & CEO, Good Samaritan Society
sterlson@gss.org

Vernon: Noric House
Affiliated with: Interior Health Authority
1400 Mission Rd., Vernon, BC V1T 9C3
Tel: 250-545-9167; *Fax:* 250-545-4980
www.interiorhealth.ca
Number of Beds: 85 beds

Victoria: Beacon Hill Villa
Retirement Concepts
635 Superior St., Victoria, BC V8V 1V1
Tel: 250-383-5447; *Fax:* 753-546-2231
www.retirementconcepts.com
Number of Beds: 80 beds
Dr. Azim Jamal, President & CEO

Victoria: Beckley Farm Lodge
Affiliated with: Vancouver Island Health Authority
530 Simcoe St., Victoria, BC V8V 1V1
Tel: 250-381-4421; *Fax:* 250-381-0112
www.viha.ca
Number of Beds: 65 beds
Note: complex care & adult day centre

Victoria: Central Care Home
Baptist Housing
844 Johnston St., Victoria, BC V8W 1N3
Tel: 250-384-1313; *Fax:* 250-384-9760
inquiry@baptisthousing.org
www.baptisthousing.org
Social Media: www.facebook.com/130827606961613; twitter.com/BaptistHousing; www.youtube.com/user/BaptistHousing
Number of Beds: 147 beds
Note: intermediate care
Howard Johnson, President & CEO, Baptist Housing

Victoria: Chinatown Care Centre
555 Herald St., Victoria, BC V8W 1S5
Tel: 250-381-4322; *Fax:* 250-920-0318
Year Founded: 1982
Number of Beds: 31 beds

Victoria: Craigdarroch Care Home
Affiliated with: Vancouver Island Health Authority
1048 Craigdarroch Rd., Victoria, BC V8S 2A4
Tel: 250-595-3813; *Fax:* 250-595-3836
info@craigdarrochcarehome.ca
www.craigdarrochcarehome.ca
Number of Beds: 18 beds

Victoria: Hart Home Seniors Residence
1961 Fairfield Rd., Victoria, BC V8S 1H5
Tel: 250-598-3542; *Fax:* 250-598-2594
harthouse@shaw.ca
www.harthousevictoria.com
Number of Beds: 20 beds
Note: intermediate care home

Victoria: James Bay Long Term Care
Revera Living
336 Simcoe St., Victoria, BC V8V 1L2
Tel: 250-388-6457; *Fax:* 250-381-2969
www.reveraliving.com
Social Media: www.facebook.com/400950748267; twitter.com/Revera_Inc; www.youtube.com/user/ReveraInc; www.linkedin.com/company/revera-inc
Number of Beds: 208 beds
Note: intermediate care
Stan Dubas, Administrator

Victoria: The Kensington Retirement Living
3965 Shelbourne St., Victoria, BC V8N 6J4
Tel: 250-477-1232; *Fax:* 250-472-1271
www.reveraliving.com/kensington-victoria
Number of Beds: 116 suites
Alaine Reimer, General Manager

Victoria: Kiwanis Pavilion
Affiliated with: Vancouver Island Health Authority
Former Name: Oak Bay Kiwanis Pavilion
3034 Cedar Hill Rd., Victoria, BC V8T 3J3
Tel: 250-598-2022; *Fax:* 250-598-0023
admin@obkp.org
www.kiwanispavilion.ca
Number of Beds: 117 beds
Note: multi level care facility
Barb Ruegg, Director, Administration and Hospitality Services
250-598-2022

Victoria: Lodge at Broadmead
Affiliated with: Broadmead Care
4579 Chatterton Way, Victoria, BC V8X 4Y7
Tel: 250-658-0311; *Fax:* 250-658-0948
info@broadmeadcare.com
www.broadmeadcare.com
Number of Beds: 229 beds
David Cheperdak, CEO

Victoria: Luther Court
Affiliated with: Luther Court Society
1525 Cedar Hill Cross Rd., Victoria, BC V8P 5M1
Tel: 250-477-7241; *Fax:* 250-477-5740
www.luthercourt.org
Number of Beds: 66 beds
Karen Johnson-Lefsrud, Executive Director

Victoria: Mount Edwards Court Care Home
Baptist Housing
1002 Vancouver St., Victoria, BC V8V 3V8
Tel: 250-385-2241; *Fax:* 250-385-4842
mtedwardsinquiry@baptisthousing.org
Social Media: www.facebook.com/130827606961613; twitter.com/BaptistHousing; www.youtube.com/user/BaptistHousing
Number of Beds: 83 beds
Howard Johnson, President & CEO, Baptist Housing

***Victoria:* Mount St. Mary Hospital**
Affiliated with: Vancouver Island Health Authority
861 Fairfield Rd., Victoria, BC V8V 5A9
Tel: 250-480-3100; *Fax:* 250-480-3110
msm@mtstmary.victoria.bc.ca
www.mtstmary.victoria.bc.ca
Social Media: twitter.com/Marythoners
Number of Beds: 200 beds
Note: extended care
Sarah John Fowler, CEO
250-480-3101, sfowler@mtstmary.victoria.bc.ca

***Victoria:* Oak Bay Lodge**
Affiliated with: Vancouver Island Health Authority
2251 Cadboro Bay Rd., Victoria, BC V8R 5H3
Tel: 250-370-6600; *Fax:* 250-370-6601
Year Founded: 1970
Number of Beds: 245 beds

***Victoria:* Rose Manor**
857 Rupert Terrace, Victoria, BC V8V 3E5
Tel: 250-383-0414; *Fax:* 250-360-2039
www.rosemanor.ca
Year Founded: 1898
Number of Beds: 128 beds

***Victoria:* Sandringham Long Term Care**
Revera Living
1650 Fort St., Victoria, BC V8R 1H9
Tel: 250-595-2313; *Fax:* 250-595-4137
www.reveraliving.com
Number of Beds: 85 beds
Jeffrey C. Lozon, President & CEO

***Victoria:* Victoria Sunset Lodge**
Affiliated with: Salvation Army
752 Arm Street, Victoria, BC V9A 4G7
Tel: 250-385-3422; *Fax:* 250-995-3858
www1.salvationarmy.org
Number of Beds: 41 beds
Note: seniors' lodge with residential mental health program
Blake Mooney, Executive Director

***West Kelowna:* Village at Smith Creek**
Baptist Housing
Affiliated with: Interior Health Authority
2425 Orlin Rd., West Kelowna, BC V4T 3C7
Tel: 250-768-0488
smithcreek@baptisthousing.org
www.baptisthousing.org
Social Media: www.facebook.com/130827606961613;
twitter.com/BaptistHousing;
www.youtube.com/user/BaptistHousing
Year Founded: 1992
Number of Beds: 130 residential care rooms; 22 assisted living suites
Howard Johnson, President & CEO, Baptist Housing

***West Vancouver:* Capilano Long Term Care**
Revera Living
525 Clyde Ave., West Vancouver, BC V7T 1C4
Tel: 604-926-6856; *Fax:* 604-926-0245
www.reveraliving.com
Social Media: www.facebook.com/400950748267;
twitter.com/Revera_Inc; www.youtube.com/user/ReveraInc;
www.linkedin.com/company/revera-inc
Number of Beds: 217 beds
Jeffrey C. Lozon, President & CEO, Revera Living

***West Vancouver:* Hollyburn House**
Revera Living
2095 Marine Dr., West Vancouver, BC V7V 4V5
Tel: 604-922-7616; *Fax:* 604-922-9163
www.reveraliving.com
Social Media: www.facebook.com/400950748267;
twitter.com/Revera_Inc; www.youtube.com/user/ReveraInc;
www.linkedin.com/company/revera-inc
Number of Beds: 102 suites
Jeffrey C. Lozon, President & CEO, Revera Living

***West Vancouver:* Inglewood Care Centre**
Affiliated with: Vancouver Coastal Health
725 Inglewood Ave., West Vancouver, BC V7T 1X5
Tel: 604-922-9394; *Fax:* 604-922-2709
www.inglewoodcarecentre.com
Year Founded: 1964
Number of Beds: 235 beds
Note: multi-level care
Susan Gooding, Administrator

***Westbank:* Brookhaven Care Centre**
Affiliated with: Interior Health Authority
1775 Shannon Lake Rd., Westbank, BC V4T 2N7
Tel: 250-862-4040; *Fax:* 250-862-4048
www.interiorhealth.ca
Number of Beds: 83 residential beds; 20 specialized geriatric CBDU beds; 1 respite bed

***Westbank:* Pine Acres Home**
Affiliated with: Interior Health Authority
1902 Pheasant Lane, Westbank, BC V4T 2H4
Tel: 250-768-7676; *Fax:* 250-768-3234
www.wfn.ca/salmon/pineacreshome.htm
Year Founded: 1983
Number of Beds: 63 complex care beds; 53 private rooms; 5 semi-private rooms; 40 Interior Health beds; 23 Indian Affairs beds; 1 respite room
Note: Intermediate care
Steve Gardner, Administrator
250-768-7676

***White Rock:* Evergreen Baptist Home**
Affiliated with: Fraser Health Authority
1550 Oxford St., White Rock, BC V4B 3R5
Tel: 604-536-3344
info@evergreen-home.com
www.evergreen-home.com
Social Media: www.facebook.com/158535384275255;
twitter.com/EvergreenCare1
Year Founded: 1959
Number of Beds: 157 beds
Stephen Bennett, Executive Director
s.bennett@evergreen-home.com

***White Rock:* Ocean View Care Home**
Affiliated with: Fraser Health Authority
15628 Buena Vista Ave., White Rock, BC V4B 1Z4
Tel: 604-531-2273; *Fax:* 604-531-8782
Number of Beds: 71 beds
Note: Specialty: Residential care for seniors; Secure unit for persons with dementia

***White Rock:* Peace Portal Lodge**
15441 - 16 Ave., White Rock, BC V4A 8T8
Tel: 604-535-2273; *Fax:* 604-535-3051
www.retirementconcepts.com
Number of Beds: 27 beds
Diane Miller, General Manager
dmiller@retirementconcepts.com

***Williams Lake:* Deni House**
Affiliated with: Interior Health Authority
517 North 6th Ave., Williams Lake, BC V2G 2G8
Tel: 250-392-4411
www.interiorhealth.ca
Note: Complex care facility

***Williams Lake:* Jubilee Care Home**
Affiliated with: Canadian Mental Health Association
196 - 2 Ave. North, Williams Lake, BC V2G 1Z6
Tel: 250-398-7736; *Fax:* 250-398-7736
jubilee.house@cmhawl.org
Number of Beds: 7 beds
Note: Mental health group home
Doris Foote, Administrator

***Williams Lake:* Williams Lake Seniors Village**
Retirement Concepts
Affiliated with: Interior Health Authority
1455 Western Ave., Williams Lake, BC V2G 5N1
Tel: 250-305-1131; *Fax:* 250-305-3333
www.williamslakeseniorsvillage.com
Number of Beds: 113 residential care rooms; 101 assisted living suites; 17 independent living suites
Nancy Fenner, General Manager
nfenner@retirementconcepts.com

Nursing Homes

***Abbotsford:* Hallmark on the Park**
Affiliated with: Fraser Health Authority
3055 Princess St., Abbotsford, BC V2T 4A8
Tel: 604-859-0053 *Toll-Free:* 866-399-0053
info@hallmarkretirement.ca
hallmarkretirement.ca

***Abbotsford:* Menno Home**
Affiliated with: Fraser Health Authority
32945 Marshall Rd., Abbotsford, BC V2S 1K1
Tel: 604-859-7631
info@mennoplace.ca
www.mennoplace.ca
Social Media: www.facebook.com/mennoplacelife;
twitter.com/MennoPlace; www.youtube.com/mennoplace
Karen L. Baillie, Chief Executive Officer

***Abbotsford:* Sunrise Special Care Facility**
2411 Railway St., Abbotsford, BC V2S 2E3
Tel: 604-853-3078

***Agassiz:* Cheam Village**
Cheam Village Holdings Ltd.
Affiliated with: Fraser Health Authority
1525 MacKay Cres., Agassiz, BC V0M 1A2
Tel: 604-796-3886; *Fax:* 604-796-3844
inquiries@valleycare.info
www.valleycare.info/cheam.php
Year Founded: 2008
Number of Beds: 68 beds

***Burnaby:* Carlton Gardens Care Centre**
Chartwell Retirement Residences
Affiliated with: Fraser Health Authority
4108 Norfolk St., Burnaby, BC V5G 0B4
Tel: 604-229-1385
chartwell.com

***Burnaby:* Dania Manor**
Dania Home Society
Affiliated with: Fraser Health Authority
4155 Norland Ave., Burnaby, BC V5G 3S7
Tel: 604-299-1379; *Fax:* 604-299-7775
www.dania.bc.ca

***Burnaby:* St. Michael's Centre**
Affiliated with: Fraser Health Authority
7451 Sussex Ave., Burnaby, BC V5J 5C2
Tel: 604-434-1323; *Fax:* 604-434-6469
info@stmichaels.bc.ca
www.stmichaels.bc.ca
Number of Beds: 128 extended care beds
Dianne Doyle, Executive Director
ddoyle@stmichaels.bc.ca
David Thompson, Executive Director
dthompson@stmichaels.bc.ca

***Chilliwack:* Eden Care Centre**
Affiliated with: Fraser Health Authority
Former Name: Eden Rest Home
9100 Charles St., Chilliwack, BC V2P 5K6
Tel: 604-792-8166; *Fax:* 604-792-1111

***Coquitlam:* Belvedere Care Centre**
Affiliated with: Fraser Health Authority
Also Known As: Belvedere Care Centre & Residences at Belvedere
739 Alderson Ave., Coquitlam, BC V3K 7B3
Tel: 604-939-5991; *Fax:* 604-939-5910
belvederecare@telus.net
www.belvederecare.com
Number of Beds: 148 complex care beds at care centre; 114 units for seniors at assisted living centre, including a secure unit for 11 residents
Note: Specialties: Complex care for seniors; Assisted living for residents with mild cognitive impairment; Wellness programs; Diabetes management; Therapy; Rehabilitation; Dementia care; Chronic care; Palliative care
Berton B. Evertt, Chair; Chief Executive Officer
Annamae Clarke, Vice-President

***Coquitlam:* Burquitlam Lions Care Centre**
Affiliated with: Fraser Health Authority
560 Sydney Ave., Coquitlam, BC V3K 6A4
Tel: 604-939-6485; *Fax:* 604-939-4728
info@burquitlamlionscare.com
www.burquitlamlionscare.com
Year Founded: 1981
Number of Beds: 76 beds

***Coquitlam:* Dufferin Care Centre**
Retirement Concepts
1131 Dufferin St., Coquitlam, BC V3B 7X5
Tel: 604-552-1166; *Fax:* 604-552-3116
www.retirementconcepts.com
Number of Beds: 153 beds
Note: Specialties: Continuing care; Nursing care; Physiotherapy; Recreation therapy; Music therapy
Joyce Halliday, General Manager
jhalliday@retirementconcepts.com

Melissa Palana, Director, Care
mpalana@retirementconcepts.com
Ken Thomson, Coordinator, Administration
kthomson@retirementconcepts.com

***Coquitlam:* Dufferin Care Centre**
Retirement Concepts
Affiliated with: Fraser Health Authority
1131 Dufferin St., Coquitlam, BC V3B 7X5
Tel: 604-552-1166; *Fax:* 604-552-3116
www.retirementconcepts.com
Number of Beds: 153 beds
Melissa Palana, Contact
mpalana@retirementconcepts.com

***Delta:* Delta View Life Enrichment Centre**
Affiliated with: Fraser Health Authority
9321 Burns Dr., Delta, BC V4K 3N3
Tel: 604-501-6700; *Fax:* 604-596-7613
info@deltaview.ca
deltaview.ca
Number of Beds: 212 beds

***Duncan:* Cowichan Lodge**
Affiliated with: Vancouver Island Health Authority
2041 Tzouhalem Rd., Duncan, BC V9L 4H2
Tel: 250-709-3098; *Fax:* 250-709-3335
www.viha.ca
Number of Beds: 51 beds
Laurie Chisholm

***Gibsons:* Christenson Village**
Good Samaritan Society
Affiliated with: Vancouver Coastal Health
585 Shaw Rd., Gibsons, BC V0N 1V8
Tel: 604-886-8747; *Fax:* 604-886-8790
feedback@vch.ca
www.gss.org
Number of Beds: 60 beds
Shawn Terlson, President & CEO, The Good Samaritan Society

***Golden:* Henry Durand Manor**
Affiliated with: Interior Health Authority
803 - 9th Ave. South, Golden, BC V0A 1H0
Tel: 250-344-5271; *Fax:* 250-344-2511
www.interiorhealth.ca
Number of Beds: 26 beds
Note: Group home for the elderly mainly who are no longer able to live in the community

***Kamloops:* Kamloops Personal Care Home Ltd. - Garden Manor**
63 Nicola St. West, Kamloops, BC V2C 1J5
Tel: 250-374-7612
Number of Beds: 24 beds
John H. Stewart, Administrator

***Kamloops:* Overlander Residential Care**
Affiliated with: Interior Health Authority
Former Name: Overlander Extended Care Hospital
953 Southill St., Kamloops, BC V2B 7Z9
Tel: 250-554-2323
www.interiorhealth.ca
Number of Beds: 183 beds

***Kamloops:* Pine Grove Care Centre**
Park Place Seniors Living
Affiliated with: Interior Health Authority
313 McGowan Ave., Kamloops, BC V2B 2N8
Tel: 250-376-5701; *Fax:* 250-376-2453
pinegrove@parkplaceseniorsliving.com
www.parkplaceseniorsliving.com
Number of Beds: 75 beds

***Kitimat:* Mountainview Lodge Residential Care Kitimat**
Affiliated with: Northern Health Authority
920 Lahakas Blvd. South, Kitimat, BC V8C 2S3
Tel: 250-632-2121
www.northernhealth.ca
Number of Beds: 36 beds

***Langley:* Cedar Hill**
Affiliated with: Fraser Health Authority
22051 Fraser Hwy., Langley, BC V3A 4H4
Tel: 604-533-6413; *Fax:* 604-533-6468

***Langley:* Murrayville Manor Ltd.**
21616 - 46 Ave., Langley, BC V3A 3J4
Tel: 604-530-9033; *Fax:* 604-530-9023
Number of Beds: 39 beds
Wayne Mills, Administrator

***Maple Ridge:* Baillie House**
Affiliated with: Fraser Health Authority
11666 Laity St., Maple Ridge, BC V2X 7G5
Tel: 604-476-7888; *Fax:* 604-463-1894
Number of Beds: 148 beds

***Nanaimo:* Columbian Centre Society**
2356 Rosstown Rd., Nanaimo, BC V9T 3R7
Tel: 250-758-8711; *Fax:* 250-751-1128
info@columbiancentre.org
www.columbiancentre.org
Number of Beds: 10 beds
Tom Grauman, Administrator

***Nanaimo:* Kiwanis Village Care Home**
1233 Kiwanis Cres., Nanaimo, BC V9S 5Y1
Tel: 250-753-6471; *Fax:* 250-740-2816
info@kiwanisvillage.ca
www.kiwanisvillage.ca
Number of Beds: 75 rooms
Dennis Regnier, Site Manager

***Parksville:* Trillium Lodge**
Affiliated with: Vancouver Island Health Authority
PO Box 940, 401 Moilliet St., Parksville, BC V9P 2G9
Tel: 250-947-8230
Number of Beds: 75 beds

***Port Coquitlam:* Hawthorne Care Centre**
Affiliated with: Fraser Health Authority
2111 Hawthorne Ave., Port Coquitlam, BC V3C 1W3
Tel: 604-941-4051; *Fax:* 604-941-5829

***Powell River:* Kiwanis Garden Manor**
Affiliated with: Vancouver Coastal Health
4923 Kiwanis Ave., Powell River, BC V8A 5H5
Tel: 604-485-5210; *Fax:* 604-485-5250
feedback@vch.ca
www.kiwanishousing.com
Number of Beds: 40 units
Karen Anne Martin, Executive Director
karenanne.martin@kiwanishousing.com

***Powell River:* Olive Devaud Residence**
Affiliated with: Vancouver Coastal Health
7105 Kemano St., Powell River, BC V8A 1L8
Tel: 604-485-9868; *Fax:* 604-485-4994
Number of Beds: 72 beds

***Prince George:* Gateway Residential Care Facility**
Affiliated with: Northern Health Authority
1462 - 20th Ave., Prince George, BC V2L 0B3
Tel: 250-645-6100
www.northernhealth.ca
Note: Local seniors' programs & care services: 250-565-7317 & 250-565-7325.

***Prince George:* Legion Wing, Seniors Housing**
Affiliated with: Northern Health Authority
2175 - 9th Ave., Prince George, BC V2M 5E3
Tel: 250-561-1499
www.northernhealth.ca
Note: Semi-independent housing for seniors experiencing dementia, or mental health/substance issues.

***Richmond:* Minoru Residence**
Affiliated with: Vancouver Coastal Health
6111 Minoru Blvd., Richmond, BC V6Y 1Y4
Tel: 604-244-5300; *Fax:* 604-244-5305
Year Founded: 1993

***Salmon Arm:* Bastion Place**
Affiliated with: Interior Health Authority
700 - 11 St. NE, Salmon Arm, BC V1E 4P9
Tel: 250-833-3616; *Fax:* 250-833-3605
www.interiorhealth.ca
Number of Beds: 101 beds

***Sechelt:* Totem Lodge**
Affiliated with: Vancouver Coastal Health
5544 Sunshine Coast Hwy., Sechelt, BC V0N 3A0
Tel: 604-885-8602; *Fax:* 604-885-8651

***Sidney:* Rest Haven Lodge**
2281 Mills Rd., Sidney, BC V8L 2C3
Tel: 250-656-0717; *Fax:* 250-656-4745
Year Founded: 1982
Number of Beds: 73 beds

***Surrey:* Argyll Lodge**
14590 - 106A Ave., Surrey, BC V3R 1T4
Tel: 604-581-4174
Number of Beds: 25 beds
Baljit Kandola, Administrator

***Surrey:* Cherington Place**
Belvedere Seniors Living
Affiliated with: Fraser Health Authority
13453 - 111A Ave., Surrey, BC V3R 2C5
Tel: 604-581-2885; *Fax:* 604-582-9028
belvederecare@telus.net
www.belvederebc.com
Number of Beds: 75 beds
Berton B. Evertt, Chairman & CEO

***Surrey:* K & C Care Ltd.**
1504 - 160 St., Surrey, BC V4A 4N9
Tel: 604-531-7900
Number of Beds: 10 beds
Kwan-Ying Jen, President

***Vancouver:* Ananda**
1249 - 8 Ave. East, Vancouver, BC V5T 1V3
Tel: 604-872-7134
Number of Beds: 20 beds
Darrell Burnham, Executive Director

***Vancouver:* Britannia Lodge**
1090 Victoria Dr., Vancouver, BC V5L 4G2
Tel: 604-255-3711

***Vancouver:* George Pearson Centre (GPC)**
Affiliated with: Vancouver Coastal Health
700 West 57 Ave., Vancouver, BC V6P 1S1
Tel: 604-321-3231; *Fax:* 604-321-7833
Year Founded: 1952
Number of Beds: 120 beds; 1 respite bed
Note: Specialties: Residential & complex medical care for adults with severe disabilities, such as cerebral palsy, multiple sclerosis, & spinal cord & traumatic brain injury; Special care units for ventilator dependent residents & persons with tracheostomies; Occupational therapy, physical therapy, pool therapy, music therapy, & respiratory therapy; Speech language pathology; Social work

***Vancouver:* Gordon Neighbourhood House**
1019 Broughton St., Vancouver, BC VGG 2A7
Tel: 604-683-2554; *Fax:* 604-683-4486
welcome@gordonhouse.org
gordonhouse.org
Social Media: www.facebook.com/GordonNeighbourhoodHouse
Number of Beds: 8 beds
Valerie Bosch, Administrator

***Vancouver:* Harmony House**
Affiliated with: Vancouver Coastal Health
580 Shanghai Alley, Vancouver, BC V6B 1N8
Tel: 604-648-0012; *Fax:* 604-648-0056
feedback@vch.ca
www.vch.ca
Number of Beds: 33 units

***Vancouver:* Honoria Conway at St. Vincent's Heather**
Affiliated with: Vancouver Coastal Health
4875 Heather St., Vancouver, BC V5Z 0A7
Tel: 604-876-7191
feedback@vch.ca
www.vch.ca
Number of Beds: 60 units

***Vancouver:* Louis Brier Home & Hospital**
Affiliated with: Vancouver Coastal Health
1055 West 41st Ave., Vancouver, BC V6M 1W9
Tel: 604-261-9376; *Fax:* 604-266-8712
info@louisbrier.com
www.louisbrier.com
Number of Beds: 107 intermediate care; 91 beds extended care; 17 special care
Robert Breen, CEO
604-267-4777, rbreen@louisbrier.com

***Vancouver:* St. Jude's Anglican Home**
Affiliated with: Vancouver Coastal Health
810 West 27 Ave., Vancouver, BC V5Z 2G7
Tel: 604-874-3200; *Fax:* 604-874-3459
info@stjudes.bc.ca
www.stjudes.ca
Number of Beds: 55 beds
Chris Norman, Administrator

***Vancouver:* Simon KY Lee Seniors Home**
Affiliated with: Vancouver Coastal Health
555 Carrall St., Vancouver, BC V6B 2J8
Tel: 604-608-8800; *Fax:* 604-408-6728
Number of Beds: 23 beds

***Vancouver:* Villa Carital**
Affiliated with: Vancouver Coastal Health
3050 Penticton St., Vancouver, BC V5M 4W2
Tel: 604-434-0995; *Fax:* 604-434-0985
www.villacarital.com
Maria Favero, Administrator

***Vancouver:* Weinberg Residence**
Affiliated with: Vancouver Coastal Health
5650 Osler St., Vancouver, BC V6M 2W9
Tel: 604-261-9622; *Fax:* 604-261-9644
www.weinbergresidence.com
Year Founded: 1945
Number of Beds: 60 units
Vanssa Trester, Manager

***Vernon:* Polson Residential Care**
Affiliated with: Interior Health Authority
2101 - 32nd St., Vernon, BC V1T 5L2
Tel: 250-558-1200
www.interiorhealth.ca
Number of Beds: 97 beds

***Vernon:* Twin Cedars Rest Home**
3201 - 37 Ave., Vernon, BC V1T 2Y4
Tel: 250-542-4983; *Fax:* 250-542-4924
kay.ramsey.twincedars@shawbiz.ca
Number of Beds: 29 beds
Charlene Fair, Administrator

***Victoria:* Glenwarren Lodge**
1230 Balmoral Rd., Victoria, BC V8T 1B3
Tel: 250-383-2323
www.reveraliving.com/glenwarren
Number of Beds: 131 beds
Note: intermediate & extended care
Norman Carelius, Administrator

***West Vancouver:* Capilano Long Term Care Centre**
Revera Living
Affiliated with: Vancouver Coastal Health
525 Clyde Ave., West Vancouver, BC V7T 1C4
Tel: 604-926-6856; *Fax:* 604-926-9169
capilano@reveraliving.com
www.reveraliving.com
Social Media: www.facebook.com/400950748267; twitter.com/Revera_Inc; www.youtube.com/user/ReveraInc; www.linkedin.com/company/revera-inc
Year Founded: 1961
Number of Beds: 215 beds
Thomas G. Wellner, President & CEO, Revera Living

***West Vancouver:* Kiwanis Manor**
Affiliated with: Vancouver Coastal Health
959 - 21st St., West Vancouver, BC V7J 1P2
Tel: 604-913-9083; *Fax:* 604-913-9830
Number of Beds: 35 units
Anne Fraser, Community Manager
afraser@insiteseniorcare.com

***West Vancouver:* West Vancouver Care Centre**
Affiliated with: Vancouver Coastal Health
1675 - 27 St., West Vancouver, BC V7V 4K9
Tel: 604-925-1247; *Fax:* 604-925-3507

***White Rock:* Buena Vista Rest Home**
15628 Buena Vista Ave., White Rock, BC V4B 1Z4
Tel: 604-536-6752; *Fax:* 604-531-8782
Number of Beds: 12 beds
Elaine Lasoto, Administrator

Retirement Residences

***Agassiz:* Glenwood Care Centre**
Affiliated with: Fraser Health Authority
1458 Glenwood Dr., Agassiz, BC V0M 1A2
Tel: 604-796-9202; *Fax:* 604-796-9186
Number of Beds: 37 beds

***Burnaby:* Carlton Gardens Long Term Care Residence**
Affiliated with: Chartwell Retirement Residences
4108 Norfolk St., Burnaby, BC V5G 0B4
Tel: 604-419-3000
www.chartwell.com
Number of Beds: 128 beds
Note: Specialty: Care for the elderly

***Coquitlam:* Parkwood Manor**
1142 Dufferin St., Coquitlam, BC V3B 6V4
Tel: 604-941-7651
www.reveraliving.com/parkwoodmanor
Number of Beds: 139 suites
Note: Independent living, convalescent & respite options
Wilma Mitchell, General Manager

***Delta:* Augustine House**
Affiliated with: Fraser Health Authority
3820 Arthur Dr., Delta, BC V4K 5E6
Tel: 604-940-6005; *Fax:* 604-940-6015
Toll-Free: 866-940-6005
info@augustinehouse.ca
augustinehouse.ca
Social Media: twitter.com/AugustineHouse
Year Founded: 2003
Tanya Snow, Executive Director
tsnow@augustinehouse.ca

***Fruitvale:* Mountain Side Village**
Golden Life Management
Affiliated with: Interior Health Authority
135 Mountain Side Village, Fruitvale, BC V0G 1L0
Tel: 250-367-9870
mountainside@glm.ca
goldenlifemanagement.ca
Note: Independent living community
John Turco, Community Manager
Sue Turco, Community Manager

***Grand Forks:* Silver Kettle Village**
Golden Life Management
Affiliated with: Interior Health Authority
2350 - 72nd Ave., Grand Forks, BC V0H 1H0
Tel: 250-442-0667
goldenlifemanagement.ca
Note: Independent living community

***Langley:* Langley Gardens**
Affiliated with: Chartwell Retirement Residences
8888 - 202 St., Langley, BC V1M 4A7
Tel: 604-888-0228
ww.chartwell.com
Number of Beds: 208 beds
W. Brent Binions, President & CEO

***North Vancouver:* Churchill House Retirement Residence**
Chartwell
Affiliated with: Vancouver Coastal Health
150 West 29th St., North Vancouver, BC V7N 0A1
Tel: 604-904-1199; *Fax:* 604-904-1191
feedback@vch.ca
chartwell.com
Year Founded: 2006
Number of Beds: 37 beds
Brent Binions, President & CEO, Chartwell

***Squamish:* Shannon Falls Retirement Residence**
Affiliated with: Vancouver Coastal Health
#114, 38225 - 3rd Ave., Squamish, BC V8B 0S2
Tel: 604-848-2000 *Toll-Free:* 877-345-6788
www.shannonfalls.ca
Number of Beds: 20 beds

***Surrey:* Fleetwood Villa**
Revera Inc.
Affiliated with: Fraser Health Authority
16028 - 83rd Ave., Surrey, BC V4N 0N2
Tel: 604-590-2889; *Fax:* 604-590-2887
www.reveraliving.com
Thomas G. Wellner, President & CEO

***Surrey:* Freedom Place**
Affiliated with: Fraser Health Authority
10342 - 148 St., Surrey, BC V3R 3X3
Tel: 604-936-9944

***Surrey:* Gateway Independent Living for Seniors**
Affiliated with: Fraser Health Authority
13787 - 100 Ave., Surrey, BC V3T 5X7
Tel: 604-585-2906; *Fax:* 604-495-4560
thegateway@shawlink.ca
gatewayassistedliving.ca
Number of Beds: 60 suites
Daljit Gill, Owner/Operator

***Surrey:* Guru Nanak Niwas**
Affiliated with: Fraser Health Authority
12075 - 75A Ave., Surrey, BC V3W 1S8
Tel: 604-596-0052; *Fax:* 604-596-7721

***Surrey:* Whitecliff**
15501 - 16th Ave., Surrey, BC V4A 9M5
Tel: 604-538-7227
www.reveraliving.com/whitecliff
Year Founded: 1961
Number of Beds: 133 suites; 18 beds
Note: Independent living, convalescent & respite options
Sherry Fossum, General Manager

***Vancouver:* Cedars at Beulah Gardens**
Affiliated with: Vancouver Coastal Health
3350 East 5th Ave., Vancouver, BC V5M 1P4
Tel: 604-251-4114; *Fax:* 604-251-4116
off.mgr.thecedars@diversicare.ca
www.beulahgardenhomes.com
Number of Beds: 89 units

***Vancouver:* Clarendon Court**
Affiliated with: Vancouver Coastal Health
6404 Clarendon St., Vancouver, BC V5S 4X9
Tel: 604-324-6230
feedback@vch.ca
www.vch.ca
Year Founded: 2006
Number of Beds: 56 beds

***Vancouver:* Millennium Tower**
Affiliated with: Vancouver Coastal Health
1175 Broughton St., Vancouver, BC V6G 3K9
Tel: 604-408-9897; *Fax:* 604-408-9868
feedback@vch.ca

***Vancouver:* Terraces on 7th**
Affiliated with: Vancouver Coastal Health
1570 West 7th Ave., Vancouver, BC V6J 5M1
Tel: 604-738-8380; *Fax:* 604-738-8386
Number of Beds: 85 units

***Victoria:* Parkwood Court**
3000 Shelbourne St., Victoria, BC V8R 4M8
Tel: 250-598-1575
www.reveraliving.com/parkwoodcourt
Number of Beds: 83 suites
Note: Assisted living, respite & convalescent options
Jan Bard, General Manager

***Victoria:* Parkwood Place**
3051 Shelbourne St., Victoria, BC V8R 6T2
Tel: 250-598-1565
www.reveraliving.com/parkwoodplace
Linda Bartel, Director, Marketing

***White Rock:* Evergreen Heights**
Affiliated with: Fraser Health Authority
1501 Everall St., White Rock, BC V4B 3S8
Tel: 604-541-3832; *Fax:* 604-541-3803

Personal Care Homes

***100 Mile House:* Carefree Manor**
Affiliated with: Interior Health Authority
812 Cariboo Trail, 100 Mile House, BC V0K 2E0
Tel: 250-395-4807; *Fax:* 250-395-4847
www.carefreemanor.ca
Number of Beds: 36 assisted & supportive living units
Mel Torgerson, General Manager
mel.carefree@shawcable.com

***Ashcroft:* Thompson View Lodge**
Affiliated with: Interior Health Authority
710 Elm St., Ashcroft, BC V0K 1A0
Tel: 250-453-9223
tvms@telus.net
www.interiorhealth.ca
Number of Beds: 10 suites
Note: Assisted living for seniors & persons with disabilities

***Barriere:* Yellowhead Pioneer Residence**
Affiliated with: Interior Health Authority
PO Box 212, 4557 Barriere Town Rd., Barriere, BC V0E 1E0
Tel: 250-672-0019
www.interiorhealth.ca
Number of Beds: 10 suites

***Burnaby:* Harmony Court Centre**
AgeCare
Affiliated with: Fraser Health Authority
Former Name: Canada Way Care Centre & Lodge
7195 Canada Way, Burnaby, BC V5E 3R7
Tel: 604-527-3300
hcreception@agecare.ca
www.agecare.ca/harmony-court
Year Founded: 1976
Dr. Kabir Jivraj, Managing Director

Burns Lake: **Tweedsmuir House**
Affiliated with: Northern Health Authority
53 - 9th Ave., Burns Lake, BC V0J 1E0
Tel: 250-692-3781
www.northernhealth.ca
Note: Assisted living

Castlegar: **Castle Wood Village**
Golden Life Management
Affiliated with: Interior Health Authority
525 Columbia Ave., Castlegar, BC V1N 1G8
Tel: 250-365-6686
castlewood@glm.ca
goldenlifemanagement.ca
Number of Beds: 110 suites
Linda Frew, Community Manager
Jane Phillips, Community Manager

Chase: **Parkside Community**
Affiliated with: Interior Health Authority
743 Okanagan Ave., Chase, BC V0E 1M0
Fax: 250-679-4496
Toll-Free: 866-930-3572
parksidecommunity.ca
Number of Beds: 20 units
Note: Assisted & independent living
Juergen Mueller, General Manager

Cranbrook: **Joseph Creek Village**
Golden Life Management
Affiliated with: Interior Health Authority
1901 Willowbrook Dr., Cranbrook, BC V1C 6S4
Tel: 250-417-0666
goldenlifemanagement.ca
Number of Beds: 102 residential care suites; 28 assisted living suites
Allan Brander, Community Manager

Creston: **Crest View Care Village**
Golden Life Management
Affiliated with: Interior Health Authority
800 Cavell St., Creston, BC V0B 1G0
Tel: 250-428-9986
goldenlifemanagement.ca
Number of Beds: 31 residential care suites; 23 assisted living suites; 51 independent living suites
Kathy Castellarin, Community Manager
kcastellarin@glm.ca

Fernie: **Rocky Mountain Village**
Golden Life Management
Affiliated with: Interior Health Authority
55 Cokato Rd., Fernie, BC V0B 1M4
Tel: 250-423-4214
goldenlifemanagement.ca
Number of Beds: 12 assisted living suites; 12 independent living suites
Sandra Peterson, Community Manager
speterson@glm.ca

Fort St James: **Pioneer Lodge**
Affiliated with: Northern Health Authority
200 School Rd., Fort St James, BC V0J 1P0
Tel: 250-804-4814; *Fax:* 250-804-4815
www.northernhealth.ca
Number of Beds: 30 assisted living suites

Fort St. John: **Heritage Manor II**
Affiliated with: Northern Health Authority
9824 - 106 Ave., Fort St. John, BC V1J 2N9
Tel: 250-263-6000; *Fax:* 250-263-6086
www.northernhealth.ca
Number of Beds: 24 assisted living units

Golden: **Mountain View**
Affiliated with: Interior Health Authority
#120, 750 - 8th Ave. South, Golden, BC V0A 1H0
Tel: 250-344-7924
www.interiorhealth.ca
Note: Assisted living

Grand Forks: **Boundary Lodge**
Affiliated with: Interior Health Authority
7130 - 9 St., Grand Forks, BC V0H 1H4
Tel: 250-443-0006; *Fax:* 250-443-0015
www.interiorhealth.ca
Number of Beds: 10 living suites

Hazelton: **Skeena Place**
Affiliated with: Northern Health Authority
4780 Janze Way, Hazelton, BC V0J 1Y0
Tel: 250-842-5217
www.northernhealth.ca

Number of Beds: 6 assisted living units
Note: Independent & assisted living

Houston: **Cottonwood Manor**
Affiliated with: Northern Health Authority
3322 - 13th St., Houston, BC V0J 1Z0
Tel: 250-845-3770
www.northernhealth.ca
Note: Assisted living

Invermere: **Columbia Garden Village**
Golden Life Management
Affiliated with: Interior Health Authority
800 - 10th Ave., Invermere, BC V0A 1K0
Tel: 250-341-3350
columbiagarden@glm.ca
goldenlifemanagement.ca
Number of Beds: 63 independent & assisted living suites
Adrienne Turner, Community Manager

Kamloops: **Bedford Manor**
The John Howard Society of the Thompson Region
Affiliated with: Interior Health Authority
529 Seymour St., Kamloops, BC V2C 0A1
Tel: 250-434-1702; *Fax:* 250-434-1704
info@jhstr.ca
www.jhstr.ca/housing/bedford-manor
Number of Beds: 76 units

Kamloops: **Kamloops Seniors Village**
Retirement Concepts
Affiliated with: Interior Health Authority
1220 Hugh Allan Dr., Kamloops, BC V1S 2B3
Tel: 250-571-1800; *Fax:* 250-571-1799
www.kamloopsseniorsvillage.com
Number of Beds: 101 independent/assisted living suites; 100 funded rooms; 14 private pay residential care rooms
Sean Adams, General Manager
sadams@retirementconcepts.com

Keremeos: **Kyalami Place**
Lower Similkameen Community Services Society
Affiliated with: Interior Health Authority
700 - 3rd St., Keremeos, BC V0X 1N3
Tel: 250-499-2352
admin@lscss.com
ttpwebhost.com/lscss/kyalamiplace.html
Number of Beds: 13 one-bedroom apartments; 1 two-bedroom apartment
Note: Assisted living

Kimberley: **Garden View Village**
Golden Life Management
Affiliated with: Interior Health Authority
280 - 4th Ave., Kimberley, BC V1A 2R6
Tel: 250-427-4014
goldenlifemanagement.ca
Number of Beds: 74 independent apartments; 13 assisted living suites
LeeAnn McDonald, Community Manager
lmcdonald@glm.ca

Lake Country: **Blue Heron Villa**
Affiliated with: Interior Health Authority
#100, 9509 Main St., Lake Country, BC V4V 2N3
Tel: 250-766-1660
info@blueheronvilla.com
blueheronvilla.com
Number of Beds: 25 suites

Langley: **Evergreen Timbers**
Affiliated with: Fraser Health Authority
5464 - 203 St., Langley, BC V3A 0A4
Tel: 604-530-7171; *Fax:* 604-530-7104
Note: Evergreen Timbers is an assisted living residence that is owned & operated by the Langley Lions Senior Citizens Housing Society.

Merritt: **Nicola Meadows**
Affiliated with: Interior Health Authority
PO Box 39, 2670 Garcia St., Merritt, BC V1K 1B8
Tel: 250-378-4254; *Fax:* 250-378-4264
nmeadows@telus.net
www.nicolameadows.com
Note: Assisted living

Nelson: **Lake View Village**
Golden Life Management
Affiliated with: Interior Health Authority
1020 - 7th St., Nelson, BC V1L 3A3
Tel: 250-352-0051
goldenlifemanagement.ca
Note: Independent & assisted living

Janet Boisvert, Community Manager
jboisvert@glm.ca

Oliver: **Heritage House**
Benchmark Lifestyles Inc.
Affiliated with: Interior Health Authority
#100, 409 Salamander Ave., Oliver, BC V0H 1T3
Tel: 250-498-0622; *Fax:* 250-498-8842
heritagehouse@benchlife.com
www.benchlife.com
Social Media: www.facebook.com/100008183678517; twitter.com/benchlife
Number of Beds: 33 units
Note: Assisted living

Penticton: **Chestnut Place**
Affiliated with: Interior Health Authority
453 Winnipeg St., Penticton, BC V2A 5M7
Tel: 250-490-0200
www.interiorhealth.ca

Penticton: **The Concorde**
Diversicare Canada Management Services Inc
Affiliated with: Interior Health Authority
3235 Skaha Lake Rd., Penticton, BC V2A 6G5
Tel: 250-490-8800; *Fax:* 250-490-8810
www.diversicare.ca
Number of Beds: 77 units
Note: Assisted living

Prince George: **Alward Place**
Affiliated with: Northern Health Authority
2121 - 6th Ave., Prince George, BC V2M 1L9
Tel: 250-646-6100
www.northernhealth.ca
Number of Beds: 120 apartments

Prince George: **Gateway Lodge Assisted Living**
Affiliated with: Northern Health Authority
1462 - 20th Ave., Prince George, BC V2L 0B3
Tel: 250-645-6100
www.northernhealth.ca
Note: Local seniors' programs & care services: 250-565-7317 & 250-565-7325.

Prince George: **Laurier Manor**
Affiliated with: Northern Health Authority
2175 - 9th Ave., Prince George, BC V2M 5E3
Tel: 250-561-1499
www.northernhealth.ca
Note: Assisted living

Prince George: **Rainbow Adult Day Centre**
Affiliated with: Northern Health Authority
1000 Laird Dr., Prince George, BC V2M 3Z3
Tel: 250-649-7290; *Fax:* 250-563-4376
www.northernhealth.ca
Number of Beds: 36 beds
Note: Local seniors' programs & care services: 250-565-7317 & 250-565-7325.

Prince Rupert: **Acropolis Manor**
Affiliated with: Northern Health Authority
1325 Summit Ave., Prince Rupert, BC V8J 4C1
Tel: 250-622-6400; *Fax:* 250-627-1490
www.northernhealth.ca
Year Founded: 2009
Number of Beds: 15 apartments
Karen Inkpen, Clinical Coordinator

Queen Charlotte: **Martin Manor**
Affiliated with: Northern Health Authority
306 - 2nd Ave., Queen Charlotte, BC V0T 1S0
Tel: 250-555-1234
www.northernhealth.ca
Note: Assisted living

Quesnel: **Dunrovin Park Lodge Care Facility**
Affiliated with: Northern Health Authority
900 St. Laurent Ave., Quesnel, BC V2J 3S3
Tel: 250-985-5800
www.northernhealth.ca
Note: Located at the GR Baker Memorial Hospital site. Personal care residential facilities; programs & services to allow seniors & adults with disabilities to continue to live in their own homes.

Revelstoke: **Moberly Manor**
Arrow & Slocan Lakes Community Services
Affiliated with: Interior Health Authority
PO Box 1570, 712 - 2nd St. East, Revelstoke, BC V0E 2S0
Tel: 250-265-3674; *Fax:* 250-837-5720
moberly@rctvonline.net
www.aslcs.com

Number of Beds: 11 units
Note: Assisted living
Tim Payne, Executive Director
tim.payne@aslcs.com
Agata Lofts, Site Manager

***Richmond:* Kinsmen Adult Day Centre**
Affiliated with: Vancouver Coastal Health
6100 Bowling Green Rd., Richmond, BC V6Y 4G2
Tel: 604-272-3237; *Fax:* 604-272-1328
Note: Assist seniors & disabled adults to continue living independently

***Salmon Arm:* Pioneer Lodge**
Good Samaritan Society
Affiliated with: Interior Health Authority
1051 - 6th Ave. NE, Salmon Arm, BC V1E 0A6
Tel: 250-804-4814; *Fax:* 250-804-4815
goodsaminfo@gss.org
www.gss.org
Number of Beds: 30 assisted living suites
Shawn Terlson, President & CEO, Good Samaritan Society
sterlson@gss.org

***Sicamous:* Eagle Valley Manor**
Eagle Valley Senior Citizen's Housing Society
Affiliated with: Interior Health Authority
319 Gordon Mackie Lane, Sicamous, BC V0E 2V1
Tel: 250-836-2310
www.interiorhealth.ca
Number of Beds: 12 units
Note: Assisted living complex

***Summerland:* Summerland Seniors Village**
Retirement Concepts
Affiliated with: Interior Health Authority
12803 Atkinson Rd., Summerland, BC V0H 1Z4
Tel: 250-404-4400; *Fax:* 250-404-4399
www.retirementconcepts.com
Number of Beds: 120 independent/assisted living suites
Scott Shearer, General Manager
sshearer@retirementconcepts.com

***Trail:* Rose Wood Village**
Golden Life Management
Affiliated with: Interior Health Authority
8125 Devito Dr., Trail, BC V1R 4X9
Tel: 250-364-3150
rosewood@glm.ca
goldenlifemanagement.ca
Number of Beds: 40 independent & assisted living suites
Jane Power, Community Manager
jpower@glm.ca

***Vanderhoof:* Omineca Lodge**
Affiliated with: Northern Health Authority
3255 Hospital Rd., Vanderhoof, BC V0J 3A2
Tel: 250-567-2216
www.northernhealth.ca
Note: Assisted living

***Vernon:* Gateby Care Facility**
Affiliated with: Interior Health Authority
3000 Gateby Pl., Vernon, BC V1T 1P4
Tel: 250-545-4456; *Fax:* 250-545-4439
www.interiorhealth.ca
Number of Beds: 75 beds

***West Vancouver:* West Vancouver Adult Day Center**
Affiliated with: Vancouver Coastal Health
990 - 22nd St., West Vancouver, BC V7V 4C2

Mental Health Hospitals/Facilities

***100 Mile House:* 100 Mile Mental Health**
Affiliated with: Interior Health Authority
555 Cedar Ave. South, 100 Mile House, BC V0K 2E0
Tel: 250-395-7676
www.interiorhealth.ca

***Abbotsford:* Abbotsford Mental Health Office**
Affiliated with: Fraser Health Authority
32700 George Ferguson Way, Abbotsford, BC V2T 4V6
Tel: 604-870-7800; *Fax:* 604-870-7801

***Agassiz:* Agassiz Mental Health Office**
Affiliated with: Fraser Health Authority
7243 Pioneer Ave., Agassiz, BC V0M 1A0
Tel: 604-793-7160; *Fax:* 604-796-8587

***Ashcroft:* Ashcroft Mental Health**
Affiliated with: Interior Health Authority
700 Ash-Cache Creek Hwy, Ashcroft, BC V0K 1A0
Tel: 250-453-2211 *Toll-Free:* 877-499-6599
www.interiorhealth.ca

***Barriere:* Barriere Mental Health**
Affiliated with: Interior Health Authority
4251 Barriere Town Rd., Barriere, BC V0E 1M0
Tel: 250-672-9731
www.interiorhealth.ca

***Burnaby:* Burnaby Mental Health Office**
Affiliated with: Fraser Health Authority
3935 Kincaid St., Burnaby, BC V5G 2X6
Tel: 604-453-1930; *Fax:* 604-453-1929

***Burnaby:* Craigend Rest Home**
5488 Patterson Ave., Burnaby, BC V5H 2M5
Tel: 604-433-8600
Number of Beds: 10 beds

***Castlegar:* Castlegar Mental Health**
Affiliated with: Interior Health Authority
707 - 10th St., Castlegar, BC V1N 2H7
Tel: 250-304-1846
www.interiorhealth.ca

***Chase:* Chase Mental Health**
Affiliated with: Interior Health Authority
825 Thompson Ave., Chase, BC V0E 1M0
Tel: 250-679-3312
www.interiorhealth.ca

***Clearwater:* Clearwater Mental Health**
Affiliated with: Interior Health Authority
612 Park Dr., Clearwater, BC V0E 1N0
Tel: 250-674-2600
www.interiorhealth.ca

***Cranbrook:* Clover Club House**
Affiliated with: Interior Health Authority
400 Victoria Ave. North, Cranbrook, BC V1C 3Y3
www.interiorhealth.ca

***Cranbrook:* Cranbrook Development Disability Mental Health Services**
Affiliated with: Interior Health Authority
1212 - 2nd St. North, Cranbrook, BC V1C 4T6
www.interiorhealth.ca

***Cranbrook:* Cranbrook Mental Health**
Affiliated with: Interior Health Authority
20 - 23rd Ave. South, Cranbrook, BC V1C 5V1
Tel: 250-420-2210
www.interiorhealth.ca

***Cranbrook:* Tamarack Cottage**
Affiliated with: Interior Health Authority
2005 - 5th St. North, Cranbrook, BC V1C 4Y2
Tel: 250-417-0103
www.interiorhealth.ca
Number of Beds: 5 tertiary specialized residential beds; 2 tertiary rehabilitative beds

***Creston:* Creston Mental Health Centre**
Affiliated with: Interior Health Authority
243 - 16th Ave. North, Creston, BC V0B 1G0
Tel: 250-428-8734
www.interiorhealth.ca

***Delta:* Delta-North Mental Health Office**
Affiliated with: Fraser Health Authority
6345 - 120th St., Delta, BC V4E 2A6
Tel: 604-592-3700; *Fax:* 604-591-2302

***Delta:* Delta-South Mental Health Office**
Affiliated with: Fraser Health Authority
1835 - 56 St., Delta, BC V4L 2L8
Tel: 604-948-7010; *Fax:* 604-943-0872

***Gibsons:* Sumac Place**
Affiliated with: Vancouver Coastal Health
841 Kiwanis Way, Gibsons, BC V0N 1V9
Tel: 604-606-0327

***Golden:* Golden Mental Health**
Affiliated with: Interior Health Authority
835 - 9th Ave. South, Golden, BC V0A 1H0
Tel: 250-344-3015
www.interiorhealth.ca

***Grand Forks:* Boundary Mental Health & Substance Use Services**
Affiliated with: Interior Health Authority
7474 - 3rd St., Grand Forks, BC V0H 1H0
Tel: 250-442-0330
www.interiorhealth.ca

***Grand Forks:* Granby Clubhouse**
Affiliated with: Interior Health Authority
8443 Riverside Dr., Grand Forks, BC V0H 1H0
Tel: 250-442-2465
www.interiorhealth.ca

***Hazelton:* Hazelton Mental Health & Addictions**
Affiliated with: Northern Health Authority
Wrinch Memorial Hospital, #70, 2510 Hwy. 62, Hazelton, BC V0J 1Y0
Tel: 250-842-5144; *Fax:* 250-842-2179
www.northernhealth.ca
Info Line: 888-562-1214
Note: Programs & services include: assessment & treatment; life skills training; recreational therapy; observation unit; perinatal depression; supportive recovery; & community response unit.

***Invermere:* Invermere Mental Health**
Affiliated with: Interior Health Authority
850 - 10th Ave., Invermere, BC V0A 1K0
Tel: 250-342-9201
www.interiorhealth.ca

***Kamloops:* Apple Lane Tertiary Mental Health Geriatric Unit**
Affiliated with: Interior Health Authority
#200, 945 Southill St., Kamloops, BC V2B 7Z9
Tel: 250-554-5590
www.interiorhealth.ca
Number of Beds: 6 beds

***Kamloops:* Development Disability Mental Health Child, Youth & Children's Assessment Network**
Affiliated with: Interior Health Authority
624 Tranquille Rd., Kamloops, BC V2B 3H6
Tel: 250-554-0085
www.interiorhealth.ca

***Kamloops:* Forensic Psychiatric Services Commission (B.C.)**
Kamloops Clinic
#5, 1315 Summit Dr., Kamloops, BC V2C 5R9
Tel: 250-377-2660; *Fax:* 250-371-3894
www.bcmhas.ca/ForensicService/ForensicRegionalServices.htm
Dr. Deirdre Ryan, Medical Director

***Kamloops:* Hillside Centre**
Affiliated with: Interior Health Authority
Royal Inland Hospital, 311 Columbia St., Kamloops, BC V2C 2T1
Tel: 250-314-2700
www.interiorhealth.ca
Year Founded: 2006
Number of Beds: 44 beds
Note: Services for adults & elderly individuals with acute illness &/or severely dysfunctional behaviours

***Kamloops:* Kamloops Development Disability Mental Health Services**
Affiliated with: Interior Health Authority
#202, 300 Columbia St., Kamloops, BC V2C 6L1
www.interiorhealth.ca

***Kamloops:* Kamloops Mental Health & Substance Use**
Affiliated with: Interior Health Authority
126 King St., Kamloops, BC V2C 4N6
Tel: 250-376-7855
www.interiorhealth.ca

***Kamloops:* Lansdowne Centre**
Affiliated with: Interior Health Authority
#200, 235 Lansdowne St., Kamloops, BC V2C 1X8
Tel: 250-377-6500
www.interiorhealth.ca

***Kamloops:* South Hills Tertiary Psychiatric Rehabilitation Centre**
Affiliated with: Interior Health Authority
#200, 945 Southill St., Kamloops, BC V2B 7Z9
Tel: 250-554-5590
www.interiorhealth.ca
Number of Beds: 40 beds

Kamloops: **Youth Forensic Psychiatric Services Kamloops Outpatient Clinic**
#8 Tudor Village, 1315 Summit Dr., Kamloops, BC V2C 5R9
Tel: 250-828-4940; *Fax:* 250-828-4946
Note: for young offenders directed by court/probation to assessment/treatment

Kaslo: **Kaslo Mental Health**
Affiliated with: Interior Health Authority
673 A Ave., Kaslo, BC V0G 1M0
Tel: 250-353-2291
www.interiorhealth.ca

Kelowna: **Cara Centre**
Affiliated with: Interior Health Authority
160 Nickel Rd., Kelowna, BC V1X 4E6
Tel: 250-763-4144
www.interiorhealth.ca

Year Founded: 2011
Number of Beds: 11 beds
Note: For individuals who have a mental illness or psychiatric concerns

Kelowna: **Central Okanagan Brain Injury Society**
Affiliated with: Interior Health Authority
#11, 368 Industrial Ave., Kelowna, BC V1Y 4N7
Tel: 250-762-3233
www.interiorhealth.ca
Note: Services for people with brain injury & their families

Kelowna: **Kelowna Development Disability Mental Health Services**
Affiliated with: Interior Health Authority
#309, 1664 Richter St., Kelowna, BC V1Y 8N3
Tel: 250-868-7791
www.interiorhealth.ca

Kelowna: **Kelowna Mental Health & Substance Use**
Affiliated with: Interior Health Authority
1340 Ellis St., Kelowna, BC V1Y 1Z8
Tel: 250-868-7788
www.interiorhealth.ca

Kelowna: **Seniors Mental Health & Eating Disorders Program**
Affiliated with: Interior Health Authority
#100, 540 Groves Ave., Kelowna, BC V1Y 4Y7
Tel: 250-870-5777
www.interiorhealth.ca

Kelowna: **White Heather Manor**
3728 Casorso Rd., Kelowna, BC V1W 4M8
Tel: 250-763-6554; *Fax:* 250-763-6754
Number of Beds: 44 beds

Keremeos: **Princeton/Keremeos Mental Health Centre**
Affiliated with: Interior Health Authority
700 - 3rd St., Keremeos, BC V0X 1N3
Tel: 250-499-3029 *Toll-Free:* 800-663-7867
www.interiorhealth.ca

Kimberley: **Kimberley Mental Health**
Affiliated with: Interior Health Authority
260 - 4th Ave., Kimberley, BC V1A 2R6
Tel: 250-427-2215
www.interiorhealth.ca

Lillooet: **Lillooet Mental Health**
Affiliated with: Interior Health Authority
951 Murray St., Lillooet, BC V0K 1V0
Tel: 250-256-1343
www.interiorhealth.ca
Note: Also includes Lillooet Substance Use Services

Logan Lake: **Logan Lake Mental Health**
Affiliated with: Interior Health Authority
5 Beryl Ave., Logan Lake, BC V0K 1W0
Tel: 250-523-9414
www.interiorhealth.ca

Lytton: **Lytton Mental Health**
Affiliated with: Interior Health Authority
533 Main St., Lytton, BC V0K 1Z0
Tel: 250-455-2216
www.interiorhealth.ca

Maple Ridge: **Trejan Lodge Ltd.**
25402 Hilland Ave., Maple Ridge, BC V4R 1G3
Tel: 604-467-3377; *Fax:* 604-467-0705
Note: Specialty: Long-term care

Merritt: **Merritt Mental Health**
Affiliated with: Interior Health Authority
3451 Voght St., Merritt, BC V1K 1C6
Tel: 250-378-3401
www.interiorhealth.ca

Midway: **Boundary Access Centre**
Affiliated with: Interior Health Authority
7th Ave., Midway, BC V0H 1M0
Tel: 250-449-2887
www.interiorhealth.ca

Nakusp: **Nakusp Mental Health**
Affiliated with: Interior Health Authority
97 - 1st Ave. NE, Nakusp, BC V0G 1R0
Tel: 250-265-5253
www.interiorhealth.ca

Nakusp: **Terra Pondera Clubhouse**
Affiliated with: Interior Health Authority
97 - 2nd Ave. NW, Nakusp, BC V0G 1R0
Tel: 250-265-0064
www.interiorhealth.ca

Nanaimo: **Forensic Psychiatric Services Commission (B.C.) Regional**
Former Name: Nanaimo Adult Forensic Psychiatric Community Services
#101, 190 Wallace St., Nanaimo, BC V9R 5B1
Tel: 250-739-5000; *Fax:* 250-739-5001
www.bcmhas.ca/ForensicService/ForensicRegionalServices.htm

Nanaimo: **Youth Forensic Psychiatric Services Nanaimo Outpatient Clinic**
1 - 1925 Bowenr Rd., Nanaimo, BC V9S 1H1
Tel: 250-760-0409
www.mcf.gov.bc.ca/yfps/index.htm
Note: youth forensic psychiatric outpatient clinic
André Picard, Coordinator

Nelson: **McKim Cottage**
Affiliated with: Interior Health Authority
916 - 11th St., Nelson, BC V1L 3V3
Tel: 250-352-2022
www.interiorhealth.ca

Nelson: **Nelson Friendship Outreach Clubhouse**
Affiliated with: Interior Health Authority
818 Vernon Rd., Nelson, BC V1L 4G4
Tel: 250-352-7730
www.interiorhealth.ca

Nelson: **Nelson Mental Health**
Affiliated with: Interior Health Authority
333 Victoria St., Nelson, BC V1L 4K3
Tel: 250-505-7248
www.interiorhealth.ca

New Westminster: **Westminster House**
Affiliated with: Vancouver Coastal Health
228 - 7 St., New Westminster, BC V3M 3K3
Tel: 604-524-5633; *Fax:* 604-524-4634
Toll-Free: 866-524-5633
info@westminsterhouse.ca
www.westminsterhouse.ca
Social Media: www.facebook.com/WomenDoRecover; twitter.com/WomenDoRecover; www.youtube.com/user/WomenDoRecover; www.linkedin.com/company/westminster-house
Sarah Franklen, Executive Director
sarah@westminsterhouse.ca

Old Masset: **Old Masset Adult Day Program**
Affiliated with: Northern Health Authority
510 Naanii Rd., Old Masset, BC V0T 1M0
Tel: 250-565-2649; *Fax:* 250-565-2640
Toll-Free: 866-565-2999
www.northernhealth.ca
Note: Programs & services to assist seniors & adults with disabilities to continue to live in their own homes.

Oliver: **Desert Sun Counselling & Resource Centre**
Affiliated with: Interior Health Authority
762 Fairview Rd., Oliver, BC V0X 1C0
Tel: 250-498-2538
desert_suncounselling@telus.net
www.desertsuncounselling.ca
Social Media: www.facebook.com/desertsuncounselling

Oliver: **Robert Bateman House**
Affiliated with: Interior Health Authority
538 Fairview Rd., Oliver, BC V0H 1T0
Tel: 250-485-0043
www.interiorhealth.ca

Osoyoos: **Osoyoos Health Centre**
Affiliated with: Interior Health Authority
4816 - 89 St., Osoyoos, BC V0H 1V1
Tel: 250-495-6433
www.interiorhealth.ca

Penticton: **Braemore Lodge**
Affiliated with: Interior Health Authority
2402 South Main St., Penticton, BC V2A 5H9
Tel: 250-492-2969
www.interiorhealth.ca
Number of Beds: 16 beds (4 tertiary specialized residential beds)

Penticton: **Penticton Mental Health**
Affiliated with: Interior Health Authority
740 Carmi Ave., Penticton, BC V2A 8P9
Tel: 250-770-3555
www.interiorhealth.ca

Port Coquitlam: **BC Mental Health & Addiction Services**
Forensic Psychiatric Hospital
70 Colony Farm Rd., Port Coquitlam, BC V3C 5X9
Tel: 604-524-7700; *Fax:* 604-524-7905
www.bcmhas.ca/ForensicService/ForensicHospital/default.htm
Number of Beds: 190 beds
Note: State-of-the-art facility which provides specialized clinical services & comprehensive rehabilitative & vocational programs.

Prince George: **Forensic Psychiatric Services Commission (B.C.)**
Prince George Clinic
1594 - 7 Ave., 2nd Fl., Prince George, BC V2L 3P4
Tel: 250-561-8060; *Fax:* 250-561-8075
www.bcmhas.ca/ForensicService/ForensicRegionalServices.htm

Prince George: **Iris House**
Affiliated with: Northern Health Authority
1111 Lethbridge St., Prince George, BC V2M 7E9
Tel: 250-649-7245; *Fax:* 250-563-2706
www.northernhealth.ca
Note: Tertiary rehabilitation & residential facility for adults with severe or persistent mental illness. Affiliated with Seven Sisters in Terrace, BC.

Prince George: **Urquhart House**
Affiliated with: Northern Health Authority
4418 Urquhart Cres., Prince George, BC V2M 5H1
Tel: 250-564-0987; *Fax:* 250-564-2847
www.northernhealth.ca
Note: Community residential services for adults

Princeton: **Anchorage Drop-In Centre**
Affiliated with: Interior Health Authority
136 Vermillion Ave., Princeton, BC V0X 1W0
Tel: 250-295-6936
www.interiorhealth.ca

Queen Charlotte: **Queen Charlotte City Health Centre**
Affiliated with: Northern Health Authority
302 - 2nd Ave., Queen Charlotte, BC V0T 1S0
Tel: 250-559-8765; *Fax:* 250-559-8765
www.northernhealth.ca
Note: Programs & services include: mental health & addictions; home care nursing; & home support.

Quesnel: **Quesnel Mental Health Team & QUESST Unit**
Affiliated with: Northern Health Authority
627 Walkem St., Quesnel, BC V2J 2J6
Tel: 250-983-6828; *Fax:* 250-983-6825
Toll-Free: 866-565-2999
www.northernhealth.ca
Note: Programs & services for mental health & addictions issues include: intake; outreach; crisis response; short-term counselling; & long-term case management. QUESST stands for Quesnel Unit for Emergency Short Stay Treatment.

Revelstoke: **Revelstoke Mental Health**
Affiliated with: Interior Health Authority
1200 Newlands Rd., Revelstoke, BC V0E 2S0
Tel: 250-814-2241
www.interiorhealth.ca

***Salmo:* Salmo Mental Health**
Affiliated with: Interior Health Authority
311 Railway Ave., Salmo, BC V0G 1Z0
Tel: 250-357-2277
www.interiorhealth.ca

***Salmon Arm:* Mental Health/Addictions & Public Health**
Affiliated with: Interior Health Authority
433 Hudson Rd., 2nd Fl., Salmon Arm, BC V1E 4S1
www.interiorhealth.ca

***Salmon Arm:* Salmon Arm Mental Health**
Affiliated with: Interior Health Authority
851 - 16th St. NE, Salmon Arm, BC V1E 4N7
Tel: 250-833-4100
www.interiorhealth.ca

***Surrey:* Timber Creek Tertiary Care Facility**
Affiliated with: Fraser Health Authority
13646 - 94A Ave., Surrey, BC V3V 1N1
Tel: 604-580-6500; *Fax:* 604-580-6516
Note: Specializes in psychological rehabilitation

***Terrace:* Birchwood Place**
Affiliated with: Northern Health Authority
3183 Kofoed Dr., Terrace, BC V8G 3P8
Tel: 250-635-2171; *Fax:* 250-635-7057
www.northernhealth.ca
Note: Supported living residential care

***Terrace:* Seven Sisters Residence**
Affiliated with: Northern Health Authority
2815 Tetrault St., Terrace, BC V8G 2W6
Tel: 250-631-4121; *Fax:* 250-631-4129
www.northernhealth.ca
Note: Tertiary rehabilitation & residential facility for adults with severe or persistent mental illness. Affiliated with Iris House in Prince George, BC.

***Terrace:* Terrace Community Mental Health Services**
Affiliated with: Northern Health Authority
#34, 3412 Kalum St., Terrace, BC V8G 0G5
Tel: 250-631-4202; *Fax:* 250-631-4282
www.northernhealth.ca
Info Line: 250-638-4082

***Trail:* Friend of Friends Clubhouse**
Affiliated with: Interior Health Authority
1454 - 2nd Ave., Trail, BC V1R 1M2
Tel: 250-368-6343
www.interiorhealth.ca

***Trail:* Harbour House**
Affiliated with: Interior Health Authority
1100 Hospital Bench, Trail, BC V1R 4M1
Tel: 250-364-9995
www.interiorhealth.ca
Number of Beds: 6 tertiary specialized residential beds; 3 tertiary rehabilitative beds
Note: Intended for longer-term residential psychosocial rehabilitation

***Trail:* Trail Mental Health**
Affiliated with: Interior Health Authority
#3, 1500 Columbia Ave., Trail, BC V1R 1J9
Tel: 250-364-6262
www.interiorhealth.ca

***Tumbler Ridge:* Tumbler Ridge Mental Health & Addictions**
Affiliated with: Northern Health Authority
PO Box 1205 Stn. Front St., Tumbler Ridge, BC V0C 2W0
Tel: 250-242-5505; *Fax:* 250-242-3595
www.northernhealth.ca

***Vancouver:* British Columbia Operational Stress Injury Clininc**
Affiliated with: Vancouver Coastal Health
175 West Broadway, Vancouver, BC V5Y 1P4
Tel: 604-331-8990; *Fax:* 604-874-1750
Toll-Free: 855-331-8990
bcosi@vch.ca
www.bcosi.ca
Year Founded: 2009
Note: Specialties: operational stress injury; post traumatic stress disorder; anixety disorders; depressive disorders; substance use
Sian Hoe Cheong, Manager

***Vancouver:* Djavad Mowafaghian Centre for Brain Health**
Affiliated with: Vancouver Coastal Health
2215 Wesbrook Mall, Vancouver, BC V6T 1Z3
Tel: 604-822-7246; *Fax:* 604-822-0361
info@brain.ubc.ca
www.centreforbrainhealth.ca
Brian A. MacVicar, Co-Director
A. Jon Stoessl, Co-Director

***Vancouver:* Downtown Community Health Centre**
Affiliated with: Vancouver Coastal Health
569 Powell St., Vancouver, BC V6A 1G8
Tel: 604-255-3151; *Fax:* 604-255-0314
feedback@vch.ca
www.vch.ca

***Vanderhoof:* Vanderhoof Health Unit**
Affiliated with: Northern Health Authority
3299 Hospital Rd., Vanderhoof, BC V0J 3A2
Tel: 250-567-5994; *Fax:* 250-567-6171
www.northernhealth.ca

***Vernon:* Aberdeen House**
Affiliated with: Interior Health Authority
9604 Shamanski Dr., Vernon, BC V1B 2L7
Tel: 250-542-9350
aberdeenhouse@shawbiz.ca
www.interiorhealth.ca
Number of Beds: 14 beds (7 tertiary specialized residential)

***Vernon:* Okanagan House**
Affiliated with: Interior Health Authority
4007 - 24th Ave., Vernon, BC V1T 4N7
Tel: 250-549-5737
www.interiorhealth.ca

***Vernon:* Vernon Mental Health**
Affiliated with: Interior Health Authority
1440 - 14th Ave., Vernon, BC V1B 2T1
Tel: 250-549-5737
www.interiorhealth.ca

***Vernon:* Willowview**
Affiliated with: Interior Health Authority
1808 - 30th St., Vernon, BC V1T 5C5
Tel: 250-542-4890
www.interiorhealth.ca

***Victoria:* Pacific Operational Trauma & Stress Support Centre (OTSSC)**
Canadian Forces Health Services
1200 Colville Rd., Victoria, BC V9A 7N2
Tel: 250-363-4411
Year Founded: 1999
Note: Specialties: Assistance to serving members of the Canadian Forces & their families, who are dealing with psychological, emotional, spiritual, & social problems stemming from military operations, especially deployments abroad; Psychiatry; Psychology; Social work; Community health nursing; Educational programs; Chaplain services

***Victoria:* Youth Forensic Psychiatric Services Victoria Outpatient Clinic**
1515 Quadra St., Victoria, BC V8V 3P3
Tel: 250-387-2830; *Fax:* 250-387-3217
www.mcf.gov.bc.ca/yfps/index.htm

***Williams Lake:* Gateway Crisis Stabilization Unit**
Affiliated with: Interior Health Authority
Cariboo Memorial Hospital, 517 North 6th Ave., 3rd Fl., Williams Lake, BC V2G 2P3
Tel: 250-392-8261
www.interiorhealth.ca

***Williams Lake:* Williams Lake Mental Health Centre**
Affiliated with: Interior Health Authority
487 Borland St., Williams Lake, BC V2G 1R9
Tel: 250-392-1483
www.interiorhealth.ca

Special Care Homes

***Kamloops:* Ponderosa Lodge**
Affiliated with: Interior Health Authority
425 Columbia St., Kamloops, BC V2C 2T4
Tel: 250-374-5671; *Fax:* 250-374-8873
www.interiorhealth.ca
Number of Beds: 68 First Appropriate beds; 68 Pathway to Home beds
Note: Short-term beds for residents waiting for a permanent bed in a residential care facility; convalescent care & respite care beds.

***Kimberley:* Kimberley Special Care Home**
Affiliated with: Interior Health Authority
386 - 2nd Ave., Kimberley, BC V1A 2Z8
Tel: 250-427-4807; *Fax:* 250-427-5377
www.interiorhealth.ca
Number of Beds: 53 residential beds; 2 flexible short-stay beds

***Langley:* Arbutus Place**
Affiliated with: Fraser Health Authority
20619 Eastleigh Cres., Langley, BC V3A 4C3
Tel: 604-539-7800; *Fax:* 604-539-7805
Note: Specialties: geriatric psychiatrics

***Vancouver:* St. James Cottage Hospice**
Affiliated with: Vancouver Coastal Health
650 North Penticton St., Vancouver, BC V6A 1G5
Tel: 604-606-0327
Year Founded: 1999
Number of Beds: 10 beds
Cielo Nacpil, Care Coordinator

***Vernon:* Polson Special Care**
Affiliated with: Interior Health Authority
2101 - 32nd St., Vernon, BC V1T 5L2
Tel: 250-558-1318
www.interiorhealth.ca
Number of Beds: 5 tertiary specialized residential beds
Note: For geriatric patients

Manitoba

Government Departments in Charge

***Winnipeg:* Manitoba Health, Seniors & Active Living**
300 Carlton St., Winnipeg, MB R3B 3M9
Tel: 204-786-7303; *Fax:* 204-783-2171
Toll-Free: 800-392-1207
TTY: 204-774-8618
www.gov.mb.ca/health
Hon. Kelvin Goertzen, Minister

Regional Health Authorities

***Flin Flon:* Northern Regional Health Authority**
Also Known As: Northern Health Region
84 Church St., Flin Flon, MB R8A 1L8
Tel: 204-687-1300; *Fax:* 204-687-6405
Toll-Free: 888-340-6742
www.northernhealthregion.ca
Year Founded: 2012
Area Served: 396,000 sq km; *Population Served:* 74175
Note: Northern Regional Health Authority is an amalgamation of NOR-MAN Regional Health Authority & Burntwood Regional Health Authority.
Doug Lauvstad, Board Chair
Helga Bryant, Chief Executive Officer & Chief Nursing Officer
Vacant, Chief Medical Officer & Vice-President, Medical Services
Shawn Hnidy, Chief Financial Officer & Vice-President, Corporate Services
Rusty Beardy, Chief Allied Health Officer & Vice-President, Aboriginal Health Services
Wanda Reader, Chief Human Resources Officer & Vice-President, Human Resources
Joy Tetlock, Vice-President, Planning & Innovation

***La Broquerie:* Southern Health-Santé Sud**
PO Box 470, 94 Principle St., La Broquerie, MB R0A 0W0
Tel: 204-424-5880; *Fax:* 204-424-5888
Toll-Free: 800-742-6509
info@southernhealth.ca
www.southernhealth.ca
Year Founded: 2012
Area Served: 27,025 sq km; *Population Served:* 194000;
Number of Employees: 5600
Note: Southern RHA is an amalgamation of South Eastman Regional Health Authority & Regional Health Authority Central Manitoba.
Guy Lévesque, Board Chair
Kathy McPhail, Chief Executive Officer

***Norway House:* Norway House Health Services Inc. (NHHS)**
PO Box 250, Norway House, MB R0B 1B0
Tel: 204-359-6704; *Fax:* 204-359-6161
www.nhcn.ca/health_division
Year Founded: 2003
Area Served: 19,435 acre reserve
Note: Provides health services to the community of the Norway House Cree Nation. Oversees Pinaow Wachi Personal Care Home, Kinosao Sipi Dental Centre, Norway House Community

Clinic & Norway House Hospital/Norway House Nursing Station (with Northern Regional Health Authority).

Selkirk: Interlake-Eastern Regional Health Authority
Former Name: Interlake Regional Health Authority, North Eastman Regional Health Authority
Corporate Office, 233A Main St., Selkirk, MB R1A 1S1
Tel: 204-785-4700; *Fax:* 204-482-4300
Toll-Free: 855-347-8500
www.ierha.ca
Social Media: twitter.com/baldguyceo
Area Served: 61,000 sq km; *Population Served:* 124000;
Number of Employees: 3100
Note: Interlake-Eastern RHA is an amalgamation of Interlake Regional Health Authority & North Eastman Regional Health Authority.
Oral Johnston, Board Chair
Ron Van Denakker, Chief Executive Officer
Dr. Tim Hilderman, Medical Officer of Health
204-467-4410
Dr. Karen Robinson, Medical Officer of Health
204-467-4410
Dr. Myron Thiessen, Chief Medical Officer & Vice-President, Primary Health Care
204-642-4524
Cynthia Ostapyk, Vice-President, Finance
204-785-7431
Karen Stevens-Chambers, Chief Allied Health Officer & Vice-President, Community Services
204-785-4706
Marion Ellis, Chief Nursing Officer & Vice-President, Acute Care
204-785-4707

Souris: Prairie Mountain Health/Santé Prairie Mountain
PO Box 579, 192 - 1st Ave. West, Souris, MB R0K 2C0
Tel: 204-483-5000; *Fax:* 204-483-5005
Toll-Free: 888-682-2253
www.prairiemountainhealth.ca
Year Founded: 2012
Number of Employees: 8700
Note: Prairie Mountain Health is an amalgamation of Brandon Regional Health Authority, Assiniboine Regional Health Authority & Parkland Regional Health Authority. Services include: public health, home care, long term care, mental health services, comprehensive health services (cancer care, cardiac, birthing & neonatal, rehabilitation, & surgery). Note that websites for the former RHAs are still active until the transition to Prairie Mountain Health has been fully completed.
Harry Showdra, Board Chair
Penny Gilson, Chief Executive Officer

Winnipeg: Winnipeg Regional Health Authority (WRHA)
650 Main St., 4th Fl., Winnipeg, MB R3B 1E2
Tel: 204-926-7000; *Fax:* 204-926-7007
www.wrha.mb.ca
Social Media: www.facebook.com/winnipeghealthregion; twitter.com/wpghealthregion; www.youtube.com/user/WinnipegHealthRegion
Population Served: 700000; *Number of Employees:* 28000
Note: The WRHA provides services to residents of the City of Winnipeg as well as the surrounding Rural Municipalities of East & West St. Paul, & the Town of Churchill in northern Manitoba. The authority also provides support & referral services to Manitobans who live outside its boundaries, as well as to residents of northwestern Ontario & Nunavut.
Robert Brennan, Board Chair
Milton Sussman, President & CEO
Dr. Brock Wright, Chief Medical Officer & Senior Vice-President, Clinical Services
Réal Cloutier, Chief Operating Officer & Vice-President, Long Term Care & Community Area Services
Glenn McLennan, Chief Financial Officer & Vice-President
Dave Leschasin, Chief Human Resources Officer & Vice-President
Dr. Catherine Cook, Vice-President, Population & Aboriginal Health

Hospitals - General

Altona: Altona Community Memorial Health Centre/Eastview Place
Affiliated with: Southern Health-Santé Sud
PO Box 660, 240 - 5 Ave. NE, Altona, MB R0G 0B0
Tel: 204-324-6411; *Fax:* 204-324-8482
info@southernhealth.ca
www.southernhealth.ca
Number of Beds: 22 acute care beds; 65 personal care beds
Number of Employees: 210
Brad Street, Director, Health Services - Altona & Area
bstreet@southernhealth.ca

Arborg: Arborg & District Hospital
Affiliated with: Interlake-Eastern Regional Health Authority
Former Name: Arborg & District Health Centre
PO Box 10, 234 Gislason Dr., Arborg, MB R0C 0A0
Tel: 204-376-5247; *Fax:* 204-376-5669
info@ierha.ca
www.ierha.ca
Number of Beds: 13 acute care beds
Note: Services offered include: acute care; diagnositic imaging; laboratory; occupational therapy; physiotherapy; medical clinic

Ashern: Lakeshore General Hospital
Affiliated with: Interlake-Eastern Regional Health Authority
PO Box 110, 1 Steenson Dr., Ashern, MB R0C 0E0
Tel: 204-768-2461; *Fax:* 204-768-2337
info@ierha.ca
www.ierha.ca
Number of Beds: 16 acute care beds
Note: Programs & services include: acute care; dental clinic; diagnostic imaging; laboratory; hemodialysis; emergency/out patient; EMS/ambulance; palliative care; rehab; spiritual care; dietician; First Nations liaison worker

Beausejour: Beausejour Hospital in Beausejour Health Centre
Affiliated with: Interlake-Eastern Regional Health Authority
PO Box 1178, 151 First St. South, Beausejour, MB
Tel: 204-268-1076; *Fax:* 204-268-1207
info@ierha.ca
www.ierha.ca
Number of Beds: 30 acute care beds
Note: Programs & services include: acute care; regional staff educator; regional pharmacist; lab & imaging; physiotherapy/occupational therapy

Boissevain: Boissevain Health Centre
Affiliated with: Prairie Mountain Health
PO Box 899, Boissevain, MB R0K 0E0
Tel: 204-534-2451; *Fax:* 204-534-6487
www.assiniboine-rha.ca
Number of Beds: 20 beds
Note: Programs & services include: acute care; diagnostic; emergency; public health; mental health; home care; physicians clinic; palliative care; occupational & physiotherapy; dietitian; meals on wheels; respite care; & community bath.
D. Graham, Area Manager
dgraham@arha.ca

Brandon: Brandon Regional Health Centre
Affiliated with: Prairie Mountain Health
Former Name: Brandon General Hospital
150 McTavish Ave. East, Brandon, MB R7A 2B3
Tel: 204-578-2300; *Fax:* 204-578-4969
www.brandonrha.mb.ca
Info Line: 204-578-4000
Number of Beds: 300+ beds
Number of Employees: 2500+
Note: A regional referral acute care & teaching facility. Services include in- & out-patient care; rehabilitation; diagnostics; & clinics.
Penny Gilson, CEO
Dr. Shaun Gauthier, Chief Medical Officer
Pat Cockburn, Senior Advisor, Acute Care & Nursing

Carman: Carman Memorial Hospital
Affiliated with: Southern Health-Santé Sud
PO Box 610, 350 - 4 St. SW, Carman, MB R0G 0J0
Tel: 204-745-2021; *Fax:* 204-745-2756
info@southernhealth.ca
www.southernhealth.ca
Number of Beds: 25 beds
Number of Employees: 190
Note: Progams & services include: family medicine; surgery; diabetic education; physiotherapy; dental surgery; palliative care; dietitian; & pharmacy.
Mary Heard, Director, Health Services - Carman
mheard@southernhealth.ca

Crystal City: Rock Lake Health District Hospital
Affiliated with: Southern Health-Santé Sud
PO Box 130, 135 Machray Ave., Crystal City, MB R0K 0N0
Tel: 204-873-2132; *Fax:* 204-873-2185
www.rocklakehealthdistrict.ca
Number of Beds: 16 acute care beds
Note: An affiliate health corporation within Southern Health-Santé Sud.
Ginger Collins, CEO & Director, Health Services - Rock Lake Health District
vcollins@southernhealth.ca

Dauphin: Dauphin Regional Health Centre (DRHC)
Affiliated with: Prairie Mountain Health
625 - 3rd St. SW, Dauphin, MB R7N 1R7
Tel: 204-638-3010
www.prha.mb.ca
Number of Beds: 90 beds
Note: Programs & services include: acute medicine; acute in-patient; psychiatry; cardiac stress testing; chemotherapy; Computer Tomography (CT); EKG; hemodialysis; inpatient day surgery; inpatient rehabilitation; laboratory testing; major/minor surgical services; obstetrical/newborn care; outpatient services; palliative care; respiratory therapy; special care unit; telehealth; ultrasound; x-ray; & 24-hour emergency services.

Deloraine: Deloraine Health Centre
Affiliated with: Prairie Mountain Health
PO Box 447, Deloraine, MB R0M 0M0
Tel: 204-747-2745; *Fax:* 204-747-2160
www.assiniboine-rha.ca
Number of Beds: 16 personal care beds (Delwynda Court PCH); 30 personal care beds (Bren-del-Win Lodge)
Note: Programs & services include: acute care; diagnostic; emergency; public health; mental health; home care; Manitoba Telehealth; community bath program; adult day program; meals on wheels; physicians clinic; palliative care; occupational & physiotherapy; dietitian; & community cancer program.
D. Graham, Area Manager
dgraham@arha.ca

Eriksdale: Eriksdale - E.M. Crowe Memorial Hospital
Affiliated with: Interlake-Eastern Regional Health Authority
PO Box 130, 40 Railway Ave., Eriksdale, MB R0C 0W0
Tel: 204-739-2611; *Fax:* 204-739-2065
info@ierha.ca
www.ierha.ca
Number of Beds: 13 acute care
Note: Programs & services include: acute care; diagnostic imaging; laboratory; emergency/out patient; palliative care; & physiotherapy

Flin Flon: Flin Flon General Hospital Inc.
Affiliated with: Northern Regional Health Authority
PO Box 340, Flin Flon, MB R8A 1N2
Tel: 204-687-7591; *Fax:* 204-687-8494
www.northernhealthregion.ca
Number of Beds: 42 acute care beds
Note: Hospital Specialty: Acute care

Gillam: Gillam Hospital Inc.
Affiliated with: Northern Regional Health Authority
PO Box 2000, 115 Gillam Dr., Gillam, MB R0B 0L0
Tel: 204-652-2600; *Fax:* 204-652-2536
www.northernhealthregion.ca
Number of Beds: 7 acute care beds
Note: Programs & services include: emergency services; laboratory services; acute care; public health; long term care; x-ray; medical clinic; visiting specialists (optometry, chiropractic & pediatrics); full-time Public Health Nurse; Mental Health Worker; Probation Officer; Employment & Income Assistance Counsellor; & Addictions Foundation Rehabilitation Counsellor.

Gimli: Gimli Community Health Centre (GCHC)
Affiliated with: Interlake-Eastern Regional Health Authority
PO Box 250, 120 - 6th Ave., Gimli, MB R0C 1B0
Tel: 204-642-5116; *Fax:* 204-642-5860
info@ierha.ca
www.ierha.ca
Year Founded: 2004
Number of Beds: 26 acute care beds
Note: The centre contains the following: Johnson Memorial Hospital; Community Health Office; & Gimli Clinic.
Programs & services include: acute care; adult day program; chemotherapy; community cancer; diagnostic imaging; laboratory; emergency/out patient; EMS/ambulance; hemodialysis; occupational therapy; palliative care; physiotherapy; medical clinic

Gladstone: Seven Regions Health Centre
Affiliated with: Southern Health-Santé Sud
PO Box 1000, 24 Mill St., Gladstone, MB R0J 0T0
Tel: 204-385-2968; *Fax:* 204-385-3053
info@southernhealth.ca
www.southernhealth.ca
Number of Beds: 14 transitional care beds
Note: Offers community health services such as home care, public health & mental health.
JoAnn Egilson, Director, Health Services - Gladstone
jegilson@southernhealth.ca

***Grandview:* Grandview District Hospital**
Affiliated with: Prairie Mountain Health
PO Box 339, 644 Mill St., Grandview, MB R0L 0Y0
Tel: 204-546-2425
www.prha.mb.ca
Number of Beds: 18 beds
Note: Programs & services include: acute medicine; EKG; laboratory testing; outpatient services; palliative care; telehealth; x-ray; & 24-hour emergency services.

***Hodgson:* Percy E. Moore Hospital**
Affiliated with: Interlake-Eastern Regional Health Authority
PO Box 190, Hodgson, MB R0C 1N0
Tel: 204-372-8444; *Fax:* 204-372-6991
info@ierha.ca
www.ierha.ca
Year Founded: 1973
Area Served: RM of Fisher, Peguis, Fisher River, & Kinonjeoshtegon; *Population Served:* 10,000
Note: The hospital is operated by First Nations & Inuit Health of Health Canada.

***Lynn Lake:* Lynn Lake District Hospital**
Affiliated with: Northern Regional Health Authority
PO Box 2030, 2040 Camp St., Lynn Lake, MB R0B 0W0
Tel: 204-356-2474; *Fax:* 204-356-8023
www.northernhealthregion.ca
Number of Beds: 11 acute care beds
Marianne Jantz-Olson, Contact
llafontaine@brha.mb.ca

***McCreary:* McCreary/Alonsa Health Centre**
Affiliated with: Prairie Mountain Health
PO Box 250, 613 PTH 50, McCreary, MB R0J 1B0
Tel: 204-835-2482
www.prha.mb.ca
Number of Beds: 13 beds
Note: Programs & services include: blood drawing; EKG; medicine; palliative care; & telehealth.

***Melita:* Melita Health Centre**
Affiliated with: Prairie Mountain Health
PO Box 459, Melita, MB R0M 1L0
Tel: 204-522-3403; *Fax:* 204-522-3161
www.assiniboine-rha.ca
Number of Beds: 20 personal care home beds
Note: Programs & services include: acute care; EMS/ambulance; diagnostic; emergency; public health; mental health; home care; physicians clinic; palliative care; occupational & physiotherapy; dietitian; & meals on wheels.
K. Oberlin, Area Manager
koberlin@arha.ca

***Morris:* Morris General Hospital**
Affiliated with: Southern Health-Santé Sud
PO Box 519, 215 Railroad Ave. East, Morris, MB R0G 1K0
Tel: 204-746-2301; *Fax:* 204-746-2197
info@southernhealth.ca
www.southernhealth.ca
Number of Beds: 23 acute care beds
Note: Programs & services include: medical clinic (4 physicians); emergency; diagnostic; minor out-patient surgery; home care; mental health; public health; physiotherapy; dietitian; & palliative care.
Ronald Morrice, Director, Health Services - Morris & Area
rmorrice@southernhealth.ca

***Neepawa:* Neepawa Health Centre**
Affiliated with: Prairie Mountain Health
Former Name: Neepawa District Memorial Hospital
PO Box 1240, Neepawa, MB R0J 1H0
Tel: 204-476-2394; *Fax:* 204-476-5007
www.assiniboine-rha.ca
Number of Beds: 38 beds
Note: Programs & services include: acute care; general surgery; obstetrics; community cancer program; diagnostic; ultrasound; EMS/ambulance; public health; mental health; home care; physicians clinics; palliative care; occupational & physiotherapy; dietitian; pharmacy services; & meals on wheels.
J. Gabler, Area Manager
jgabler@arha.ca

***Notre Dame de Lourdes:* Notre Dame Hospital**
Affiliated with: Southern Health-Santé Sud
Former Name: Notre Dame Medical Nursing Inc.
PO Box 130, 283 Notre Dame Ave. West, Notre Dame de Lourdes, MB R0G 1M0
Tel: 204-248-2112; *Fax:* 204-248-2499
info@southernhealth.ca
www.southernhealth.ca
Number of Beds: 9 acute care beds
Number of Employees: 170
Note: Staff include physicians, registered & licensed nurses & allied health professionals. Provides obstetrical services to surrounding communities.
Mona Spencer, Director, Health Services - Notre Dame & St. Claude
mspencer@southernhealth.ca

***Pinawa:* Pinawa Hospital**
Affiliated with: Interlake-Eastern Regional Health Authority
PO Box 220, 30 Vanier Dr., Pinawa, MB R0E 1L0
Tel: 204-753-2334; *Fax:* 204-753-2219
info@ierha.ca
www.ierha.ca
Year Founded: 1964
Number of Beds: 17 beds
Note: Programs & services include: acute care; community cancer care; dietitians; diagnostics; EMS/ambulance; medical clinic; occupational therapy; physiotherapy

***Pine Falls:* Pine Falls Hospital in Pine Falls Health Complex**
Affiliated with: Interlake-Eastern Regional Health Authority
PO Box 2000, 37 Maple St., Pine Falls, MB R0E 1M0
Tel: 204-367-4441; *Fax:* 204-367-8981
info@ierha.ca
www.ierha.ca
Number of Beds: 23 beds
Note: Programs & services include: dieticians; diagnostic imaging; laboratory; hemodialysis; occupational therapy; physiotherapy

***Portage la Prairie:* Portage District General Hospital**
Affiliated with: Southern Health-Santé Sud
524 - 5 St. SE, Portage la Prairie, MB R1N 3A8
Tel: 204 239-2211; *Fax:* 204-239-1941
info@southernhealth.ca
www.southernhealth.ca
Number of Beds: 88 acute care beds
Population Served: 50000; *Number of Employees:* 660
Kristy Radke, Director, Support Services - Portage
kradke@southernhealth.ca
Noreen Shirtliff, Director, Health Services - Portage
nshirtliff@southernhealth.ca

***Roblin:* Roblin Health Centre**
Affiliated with: Prairie Mountain Health
PO Box 940, 15 Hospital St., Roblin, MB R0L 1P0
Tel: 204-937-2142; *Fax:* 204-629-3453
www.prha.mb.ca
Number of Beds: 25 beds
Note: Programs & services include: acute medicine; EKG; laboratory testing; outpatient service; palliative care; telehealth; x-ray; & 24-hour emergency service.

***Russell:* Russell Health Centre**
Affiliated with: Prairie Mountain Health
Bag Service 2, Russell, MB R0J 1W0
Tel: 204-773-2125; *Fax:* 204-773-2142
www.assiniboine-rha.ca
Note: Programs & services include: acute care; community cancer program; diagnostic; EMS/ambulance; public health; mental health; home care; Manitoba Telehealth; physicians clinic; palliative care; occupational & physiotherapy; dietitian; meals on wheels; & pharmacy.
D. Ciprick, Area Manager
dciprick@arha.ca

***Selkirk:* Selkirk & District General Hospital**
Affiliated with: Interlake-Eastern Regional Health Authority
PO Box 5000, 100 Easton Dr., Selkirk, MB R1A 2M2
Tel: 204-482-5800; *Fax:* 204-785-9113
info@ierha.ca
www.ierha.ca
Year Founded: 1907
Number of Beds: 51 beds
Note: Programs & services include: acute care; chemotherapy; community cancer care; diagnostic imaging & ultrasound; dialysis; emergency/out patient; EMS/ambulance; obstetrical program; occupational therapy; palliative care; physiotherapy; regional surgical services

***Shoal Lake:* Shoal Lake/Strathclair Health Centre**
Affiliated with: Prairie Mountain Health
PO Box 490, Shoal Lake, MB R0J 1Z0
Tel: 204-759-2336; *Fax:* 204-759-2230
www.assiniboine-rha.ca
Number of Beds: 40 personal care beds
Note: Programs & services include: acute care; diagnostic; EMS/ambulance; public health; mental health; home care; physicians clinic; palliative care; occupational & physiotherapy; dietitian; meals on wheels; & Elderly Person's Housing (Lakeshore Lodge & Morley House).
R. Yaremchuk, Area Manager
ryaremchuk@arha.ca

***Souris:* Souris Health Centre**
Affiliated with: Prairie Mountain Health
PO Box 10, Souris, MB R0K 2C0
Tel: 204-483-2121; *Fax:* 204-483-2310
www.assiniboine-rha.ca
Number of Beds: 42 long-term care beds; 1 respite care bed
Note: Programs & services include: acute care; EMS; general surgery; diagnostic; public health; mental health; home care; physicians clinic; palliative care; occupational & physiotherapy; dietitian; & meals on wheels.
G. Paddock, Area Manager
gpaddock@arha.ca

***St Claude:* St. Claude Health Centre**
Affiliated with: Southern Health-Santé Sud
PO Box 400, 33 Roy St., St Claude, MB R0G 1Z0
Tel: 204-379-2211; *Fax:* 204-379-2655
info@southernhealth.ca
www.southernhealth.ca
Year Founded: 1957
Number of Beds: 10 transitional care beds; 18 personal care beds
Note: Programs & services include: family physicians; clinic nurse; home care; public health; palliative care; & healthy living.
Mona Spencer, Director, Health Services - Notre-Dame & St. Claude
mspencer@southernhealth.ca

***St Pierre Jolys:* Centre Médico-Social De Salaberry District Health Centre**
Affiliated with: Southern Health-Santé Sud
PO Box 320, 354 Prefontaine Ave., St Pierre Jolys, MB R0A 1V0
Tel: 204-433-7611; *Fax:* 204-433-7455
info@southernhealth.ca
www.southernhealth.ca
Number of Beds: 14 hospital beds; 22 personal care home beds
Note: Programs & services include: emergency; lab & diagnostics; long-term care; medicine; nurse-managed care; occupational therapy; palliative care; physiotherapy; spiritual care; & Health Corner (health education).
Norm Vigier, Director, Health Services - St-Pierre-Jolys & Area
nvigier@southernhealth.ca

***Ste Anne:* Hôpital Ste-Anne Hospital**
Affiliated with: Southern Health-Santé Sud
52 St Gérard St., Ste Anne, MB R5H 1C4
Tel: 204-422-8837; *Fax:* 204-422-9929
info@southernhealth.ca
www.southernhealth.ca
Number of Beds: 21 beds
Note: Programs & services include: emergency; lab & diagnostics; medicine; nurse-managed care; obstetrics; occupational therapy; palliative care; physiotherapy; spiritual care; & surgical care.
Jo-Anne Marion, Director, Health Services
jmarion2@southernhealth.ca

***Ste Rose du Lac:* Ste Rose General Hospital**
Affiliated with: Prairie Mountain Health
Also Known As: Ste Rose Health Centre
PO Box 60, 480 - 3rd Ave. East, Ste Rose du Lac, MB R0L 1S0
Tel: 204-447-2131; *Fax:* 204-629-3460
www.prha.mb.ca
Number of Beds: 26 beds
Note: Programs & services include: acute medical service; EKG; laboratory testing; outpatient service; palliative care; ultrasound (mobile); telehealth; x-ray; & 24-hour emergency service.

***Steinbach:* Bethesda Regional Health Centre**
Affiliated with: Southern Health-Santé Sud
Former Name: Bethesda Hospital
316 Henry St., Steinbach, MB R5G 0P9
Tel: 204-326-6411
info@southernhealth.ca
www.southernhealth.ca
Year Founded: 1929
Number of Beds: 84 acute care beds
Population Served: 35000; *Number of Employees:* 400
Note: Provides primary, secondary & community health care.
Jan Gunness, Chief Nursing Officer & Vice-President, Clinical Standards
jgunness@southernhealth.ca

***Stonewall:* Stonewall & District Health Centre**
Affiliated with: Interlake-Eastern Regional Health Authority
589 - 3rd Ave. South, Stonewall, MB R0C 2Z0
Tel: 204-467-5514; *Fax:* 204-467-4431
info@ierha.ca
www.ierha.ca
Number of Beds: 14 acute care beds; 1 palliative care bed; 3 observation beds
Note: Centre contains: hospital; community health office; & clinic.
Programs & services include: diagnostic imaging; laboratory; emergency/out patient; EMS/ambulance; occupational therapy; palliative care; physiotherapy.

***Swan Lake:* Lorne Memorial Hospital**
Affiliated with: Southern Health-Santé Sud
PO Box 40, 9 - 2nd St. North, Swan Lake, MB R0G 2S0
Tel: 204-836-2132; *Fax:* 204-836-2044
info@southernhealth.ca
www.southernhealth.ca
Number of Beds: 18 acute care beds
Number of Employees: 60
Note: Staff includes 2 physicians, registered & licensed practical nurses & allied health professionals. Programs include advanced palliative care.
Kristal McKitrick-Bazin, Director, Health Services - Swan Lake
kbazin@southernhealth.ca

***Swan River:* Swan Valley Health Centre**
Affiliated with: Prairie Mountain Health
PO Box 448, 1011 Main St., Swan River, MB R0L 1Z0
Tel: 204-734-3441; *Fax:* 204-629-3484
www.prha.mb.ca
Year Founded: 2005
Number of Beds: 52 acute-care beds
Note: Programs & services include: public health; home care; diagnostics; dialysis; physiotherapy; speech therapy; pharmacy; maintenance; surgery; administration; mental health; emergency; chemotherapy; medical records; telehealth; occupational therapy; respiratory therapy; housekeeping; materials management; & special care auxiliary.

***Teulon:* Teulon - Hunter Memorial Hospital**
Affiliated with: Interlake-Eastern Regional Health Authority
PO Box 89, 162 - 3rd Ave. SE, Teulon, MB R0C 3B0
Tel: 204-886-2433; *Fax:* 204-886-2653
info@ierha.ca
www.ierha.ca
Number of Beds: 20 acute care beds
Note: Programs & services include: acute care; diagnostic imaging; laboratory; emergency/out patient; EMS/ambulance; physiotherapy/occupational therapy; dietary

***The Pas:* St. Anthony's General Hospital**
Affiliated with: Northern Regional Health Authority
Also Known As: The Pas Health Complex
PO Box 240, 67 - 1 St. West, The Pas, MB R9A 1K4
Tel: 204-623-6431; *Fax:* 204-623-9263
www.northernhealthregion.ca
Year Founded: 1969
Number of Beds: 40 acute care; 8 in-patient acute care adult psychiatric beds

***Thompson:* Thompson General Hospital**
Affiliated with: Northern Regional Health Authority
867 Thompson Dr. South, Thompson, MB R8N 0C8
Tel: 204-677-2381; *Fax:* 204-778-1413
Toll-Free: 877-677-5353
www.northernhealthregion.ca
Number of Beds: 74 beds; 10 in-patient acute care adult psychiatric beds
Note: Programs & services include: emergency; community mental health; cancer services/chemotherapy; consultation clinic; diagnostic (lab & radiology); general medicine; Northern Patient Transportation Program (NPTP); nutritional services; obstetrics; pediatrics; physiotherapy; surgery & telehealth.

***Winkler:* Boundary Trails Health Centre**
Affiliated with: Southern Health-Santé Sud
PO Box 2000 Stn. Main, Winkler, MB R6W 1H8
Tel: 204-331-8800; *Fax:* 204-331-8804
info@southernhealth.ca
www.southernhealth.ca
Number of Beds: 94 beds
Population Served: 40,000; *Number of Employees:* 450
Note: Programs & services include: home care; public health; mental health; emergency; ambulatory care clinics; intensive care; observation; diagnostics; laboratory; medical; surgery/day surgery; obstetrics; chemotherapy; dialysis; rehab/assess & rehab services OT/PT; & speech & audiology.

Maureen Gamache, Director, Health Services
mgamache@southernhealth.ca

***Winnipeg:* Concordia Hospital**
Affiliated with: Winnipeg Regional Health Authority
1095 Concordia Ave., Winnipeg, MB R2K 3S8
Tel: 204-667-1560; *Fax:* 204-667-1049
www.concordiahospital.mb.ca
Year Founded: 1928
Number of Beds: Includes the 140-bed Concordia Place Personal Care Home
Number of Employees: 1100
Specialties: Orthopaedics - lower & upper joint replacement
Note: Programs & services include: emergency services; diagnostic imaging; laboratory services (204-661-7174); surgery (a major centre for hip & knee replacements); intensive care; A.M.I. (Acute Myocardial Infarcation) Program; occupational therapy (204-661-7216); physiotherapy (204-661-7354); respiratory therapy (204-661-7346); oncology haematology service; social work (204-661-7185); cardiac teaching program (nurse home visit); & lifeline personal response & support services
Valerie Wiebe, President & COO

***Winnipeg:* Grace Hospital**
Affiliated with: Winnipeg Regional Health Authority
Former Name: The Salvation Army Grace General Hospital
300 Booth Dr., Winnipeg, MB R3J 3M7
Tel: 204-837-0111
pr@ggh.mb.ca
www.gracehospital.ca
Year Founded: 1904
Number of Beds: 251 beds
Note: Programs & services include: emergency & critical care; surgery; mental health; Aboriginal health services; & hospice care.

***Winnipeg:* Health Sciences Centre (HSC)**
Affiliated with: Winnipeg Regional Health Authority
820 Sherbrook St., Winnipeg, MB R3A 1R9
Tel: 204-787-3661; *Fax:* 204-787-1233
Toll-Free: 877-499-8774
info@hsc.mb.ca
www.hsc.mb.ca
Social Media: www.facebook.com/184583582309; www.twitter.com/hsc_winnipeg
Year Founded: 1973
Area Served: Manitoba, northwestern Ontario & Nunavut;
Number of Employees: 8000
Specialties: Transplants, burns, neurosciences & pediatric care
Note: A teaching hospital & the designated Trauma Centre for Manitoba. Programs & services include: Aboriginal health services; adult emergency; adult mental health; anesthesia; child & adolescent mental health; child health; clinical health psychology; critical care; diagnostic imaging; dialysis; medicine; oncology; rehab; geriatrics; surgery; & women's health.
Dana Erickson, Chief Operating Officer
Kathy Doerksen, Chief Nursing Officer
Dr. Perry Gray, Vice-President & Chief Medical Officer

***Winnipeg:* Hôpital St-Boniface Hospital**
Affiliated with: Winnipeg Regional Health Authority
Former Name: St. Boniface General Hospital
409 Taché Ave., Winnipeg, MB R2H 2A6
Tel: 204-233-8563
sbghweb@sbgh.mb.ca
www.sbgh.mb.ca
Social Media: twitter.com/sbh_winnipeg; www.youtube.com/stbonifacehosp
Year Founded: 1871
Number of Employees: 4000
Note: Catholic tertiary care facility & teaching hospital affiliated with the University of Manitoba & dedicated to the values of care of the Sisters of Charity of Montreal (Grey Nuns). Programs & services include: Aboriginal health services; emergency services; family medicine; mental health; geriatrics & rehabilitation; surgery; women's health; & paediatrics.
Dr. Bruce Roe, Chief Medical Officer & Executive Director, Clinical Programs
204-237-2317

***Winnipeg:* Seven Oaks General Hospital**
Affiliated with: Winnipeg Regional Health Authority
2300 McPhillips St., Winnipeg, MB R2V 3M3
Tel: 204-632-7133
www.sogh.ca
Social Media: www.facebook.com/SevenOaksGeneralHospital; twitter.com/sevenoakswpg
Year Founded: 1981
Number of Beds: 304 beds
Note: Programs & services include: Aboriginal health; core rehabilitation; day hospital; diagnostic; emergency; family medicine; geriatric mental health; geriatric rehabilitation; health library; intensive care; kidney health; Koldonan Medical Centre; laboratory; mental health; oncology clinic; orthopedic clinic; pharmacy; Prairie Trail at the Oaks; respiratory therapy; surgery; Surgery Centre; Urology Centre; & Wellness Institute.
Carrie Solmundson, President & COO
Dr. Ricardo Lobato de Faria, Chief Medical Officer

***Winnipeg:* Victoria General Hospital (VGH)**
Affiliated with: Winnipeg Regional Health Authority
2340 Pembina Hwy., Winnipeg, MB R3T 2E8
Tel: 204-269-3570
info@vgh.mb.ca
www.vgh.mb.ca
Social Media: www.facebook.com/135150073228437; twitter.com/Vanislandhealth
Year Founded: 1971
Number of Beds: 203 beds
Note: Programs & services include: allied health services; audiology; mental health; emergency; surgery; Mature Womens Centre; critical care; oncology; & medicine/family medicine.

***Winnipegosis:* Winnipegosis Health Centre**
Affiliated with: Prairie Mountain Health
Former Name: Winnipegosis General Hospital
Also Known As: Winnipegosis & District Health Centre
PO Box 280, 230 Bridge St., Winnipegosis, MB R0L 2G0
Tel: 204-656-4881; *Fax:* 204-629-3489
www.prha.mb.ca
Number of Beds: 15 acute care beds
Note: Programs & services include: acute medicine; outpatient; palliative care; & 24-hour emergency services.

Community Health Care Centres

***Alonsa:* Alonsa Community Health**
Affiliated with: Prairie Mountain Health
General Delivery, 27 Railway Ave. South, Alonsa, MB R0H 0A0
Tel: 204-767-3000
www.prha.mb.ca

***Arborg:* Arborg & District Health Centre**
Affiliated with: Interlake-Eastern Regional Health Authority
234 Gislason Dr., Arborg, MB R0C 0A0
Tel: 204-376-2781

***Baldur:* Baldur Health Centre**
Affiliated with: Prairie Mountain Health
PO Box 128, Baldur, MB R0K 0B0
Tel: 204-535-2373; *Fax:* 204-535-2116
www.assiniboine-rha.ca
Number of Beds: 20 personal care beds
Note: Programs & services include: transitional care; laboratory; public health; mental health; home care; physicians clinic; adult day program; palliative care; occupational & physiotherapy; dietitian; & meals on wheels.
D. Rea, Area Manager
drea@arha.ca

***Beausejour:* Beausejour HEW Primary Health Care Centre**
Affiliated with: Interlake-Eastern Regional Health Authority
31 - 1st St., Beausejour, MB R0E 0C0
Tel: 204-268-2288

***Beausejour:* Beausejour Primary Health Care Centre**
Affiliated with: Interlake-Eastern Regional Health Authority
151 - 1st St. South, Beausejour, MB R0E 0C0
Tel: 204-268-4966

***Benito:* Benito Health Centre**
Affiliated with: Prairie Mountain Health
PO Box 290, 200 - 1st St. East, Benito, MB R0L 0C0
Tel: 204-539-2815
www.prha.mb.ca
Note: Includes home care services (204-539-2075)

***Birtle:* Birtle Health Centre**
Affiliated with: Prairie Mountain Health
PO Box 2000, Birtle, MB R0M 0C0
Tel: 204-842-3317; *Fax:* 204-842-3375
www.assiniboine-rha.ca
Number of Beds: 20 personal care beds
Note: Programs & services include: transitional care; diagnostic; EMS/ambulance; public health; mental health; home care; physicians clinic; palliative care; occupational & physiotherapy;

dietitian; elderly persons housing unit (30 suites); & congregate meal program
D. Ciprick, Area Manager
dciprick@arha.ca

***Brandon:* 7th Street Health Access Centre**
Affiliated with: Prairie Mountain Health
Also Known As: ACCESS Brandon
20 - 7th St., Brandon, MB R7A 6M8
Tel: 204-578-4800; *Fax:* 204-578-4950
www.brandonrha.mb.ca
Note: ACCESS Centres offer health & social services. Programs & services at this location include: Nurse Practitioner; Community Health Nurse; Adult Community Mental Health Worker; Community Social Worker; Addictions Services; Housing Resource Worker; Cultural Facilitators; Consumer Peer Support Educator; & Community Volunteer Income Tax Program.

***Camperville:* Camperville Health Centre**
Affiliated with: Prairie Mountain Health
PO Box 177, Camperville, MB R0L 0J0
Tel: 204-524-2169
www.prha.mb.ca
Note: Includes home care services (204-539-2075)

***Carberry:* Carberry Plains Health Centre**
Affiliated with: Prairie Mountain Health
PO Box 2000, Carberry, MB R0K 0H0
Tel: 204-834-2144; *Fax:* 204-834-3333
www.assiniboine-rha.ca
Note: Programs & service include: acute care; diagnostic; emergency; EMS/ambulance; public health; mental health; home care; physicians clinic; primary care nurse; dietitian; meals on wheels; palliative care; & occupational & physiotherapy. Also has a Personal Care Home on site.
J. Gabler, Area Manager
jgabler@arha.ca

***Cartwright:* Davidson Memorial Health Centre**
Affiliated with: Prairie Mountain Health
Former Name: Cartwright & District Hospital
PO Box 118, Cartwright, MB R0K 0L0
Tel: 204-529-2483; *Fax:* 204-529-2562
www.assiniboine-rha.ca
Note: Programs & services include: personal care; community bath program; occupational & physiotherapy; dietitian; meals on wheels; public health; mental health; & home care.
D. Obach, Area Manager
dobach@arha.ca

***Churchill:* Churchill Health Centre**
Affiliated with: Winnipeg Regional Health Authority
General Delivery, Churchill, MB R0B 0E0
Tel: 204-675-8881; *Fax:* 204-675-2243
www.churchillrha.com
Area Served: Churchill; Kivalliq Region of Nunavut
Note: Health & social services include: emergency; acute care; primary care clinic; diagnostic; dental clinic/oral surgery; clinical & retail pharmacy; optometry; physiotherapy; chiropractic; massage therapy; mental health; public health; probation; addictions; children & family; child & youth receiving home; home care; Children's Centre; & telehealth.
Services provided through the J.A. Hildes Northern Medical Unit, Department of Community Medicine, University of Manitoba, include: anaesthesia; orthopedics; surgery; geriatrics; internal medicine; gynaecology; ophthalmology; otolaryngology; paediatrics; colposcopy; psychiatry; pediatric dental surgery; & urology.
Patti Macewan, Chief Operating Officer, Churchill Regional Health Authority Inc.
pmacewan@wrha-ch.ca

***Cormorant:* Cormorant Health Care Centre**
Affiliated with: Northern Regional Health Authority
PO Box 42, Cormorant, MB R0B 0G0
Tel: 204-357-2161; *Fax:* 204-357-2259
www.northernhealthregion.ca

***Cranberry Portage:* Cranberry Portage Wellness Centre**
Affiliated with: Northern Regional Health Authority
PO Box 186, Cranberry Portage, MB R0B 0H0
Tel: 204-472-3338; *Fax:* 204-472-3389
www.northernhealthregion.ca

***Crane River:* Crane River Health Services**
Affiliated with: Prairie Mountain Health
PO Box 156, Crane River, MB R0L 0M0
Tel: 204-732-2286
www.prha.mb.ca

***Dauphin:* Dauphin Community Health Services**
Affiliated with: Prairie Mountain Health
625 - 3rd St. SW, Dauphin, MB R7N 1R7
Tel: 204-638-2118
www.prha.mb.ca
Note: Includes home care services (204-638-2105)

***Duck Bay:* Duck Bay Community Health**
Affiliated with: Prairie Mountain Health
PO Box 133, Duck Bay, MB R0L 0N0
Tel: 204-524-2176
www.prha.mb.ca
Note: Includes home care services (204-539-2075)

***Ebb & Flow:* Bacon Ridge Community Health**
Affiliated with: Prairie Mountain Health
General Delivery, Post Office Bldg., Ebb & Flow, MB R0L 0R0
Tel: 204-448-2229
www.prha.mb.ca

***Emerson:* Emerson Health Centre**
Affiliated with: Southern Health-Santé Sud
Former Name: Emerson Hospital
PO Box 428, 26 Main St., Emerson, MB R0A 0L0
Tel: 204-373-2109; *Fax:* 204-373-2748
info@southernhealth.ca
www.southernhealth.ca
Number of Beds: 4 transitional care beds; 20 personal home care beds
Note: Provides community health services such as home care, public health & mental health.
Ronald Morrice, Director, Health Services - Morris, Emerson & Area
rmorrice@southernhealth.ca

***Erickson:* Erickson Health Centre**
Affiliated with: Prairie Mountain Health
PO Box 250, Erickson, MB R0J 0P0
Tel: 204-636-7777; *Fax:* 204-636-2471
www.assiniboine-rha.ca
Number of Beds: 16 personal care beds
Note: Programs & services include: transitional care; diagnostic; EMS/ambulance; public health; mental health; home care; physicians; primary care nurse; palliative care; occupational & physiotherapy; dietitian; meals on wheels; & community bath program.
M. Koroscil, Area Manager
mkoroscil@arha.ca

***Ethelbert:* Ethelbert Health Centre**
Affiliated with: Prairie Mountain Health
PO Box 156, 31 Railway Ave., Ethelbert, MB R0L 0T0
Tel: 204-742-4400
www.prha.mb.ca
Note: Includes home care services (204-656-4721)

***Fort Garry:* Fort Garry Community Office**
Affiliated with: Winnipeg Regional Health Authority
2735 Pembina Hwy., Fort Garry, MB R3T 2H5
Tel: 204-940-2015
www.wrha.mb.ca
Note: Provides services related to: healthy parenting & early childhood development; healthy children & youth; nutrition promotion; communicable disease prevention & management; immunization; & more.

***Gilbert Plains:* Gilbert Plains Health Centre**
Affiliated with: Prairie Mountain Health
PO Box 368, 100 Cutforth St. North, Gilbert Plains, MB R0L 0X0
Tel: 204-548-2161
www.prha.mb.ca
Note: Physician clinic attached to Gilbert Plains Personal Care Home. Includes home care services (204-548-2765).

***Glenboro:* Glenboro Health Centre**
Affiliated with: Prairie Mountain Health
Former Name: Glenboro Health District Hospital
PO Box 310, Glenboro, MB R0K 0X0
Tel: 204-827-2438; *Fax:* 204-827-2199
www.assiniboine-rha.ca
Number of Beds: 20 personal care beds
Note: Programs & services include: acute care; diagnostic; EMS/ambulance; public health; mental health; home care; physicians clinic; palliative care; occupational & physiotherapy; dietitian; & meals on wheels. Also includes a Personal Care Home on site.
D. Rea, Area Manager
drea@arha.ca

***Grandview:* Grandview Community Health**
Affiliated with: Prairie Mountain Health
PO Box 339, Grandview, MB R0L 0Y0
Tel: 204-546-5150
www.prha.mb.ca
Note: Includes home care services (204-548-2765)

***Hamiota:* Hamiota Health Centre**
Affiliated with: Prairie Mountain Health
177 Birch Ave., Hamiota, MB R0M 0T0
Tel: 204-764-2412; *Fax:* 204-764-2049
www.assiniboine-rha.ca
Number of Beds: 30 personal care home beds
Note: Programs & services include: acute care; community cancer program; diagnostic; EMS/ambulance; public health; mental health; home care; Manitoba Telehealth; physicians clinic; primary care nurse; palliative care; occupational & physiotherapy; dietitian; meals on wheels; Lilac Elderly Person Housing (30 units); & congregate meal program.
R. Yaremchuk, Area Manager
ryaremchuk@arha.ca

***Hartney:* Hartney Health Centre**
Affiliated with: Prairie Mountain Health
Former Name: Hartney Medical Nursing Unit
PO Box 280, Hartney, MB R0M 0X0
Tel: 204-858-2054; *Fax:* 204-858-2303
www.assiniboine-rha.ca
Number of Beds: 20 personal care beds
Note: Programs & services include: palliative care; occupational & physiotherapy; dietitian; public health; mental health; home care; & meals on wheels. Also includes a Personal Care Home on site.
K. Oberlin, Area Manager
koberlin@arha.ca

***Ilford:* Ilford Community Health Centre**
Affiliated with: Northern Regional Health Authority
53 First St., Ilford, MB R0B 0S0
Tel: 204-288-4348; *Fax:* 204-288-4248
www.northernhealthregion.ca

***Killarney:* Tri-Lake Health Centre**
Affiliated with: Prairie Mountain Health
PO Box 5000, Killarney, MB R0K 1G0
Tel: 204-523-4661; *Fax:* 204-523-8948
www.assiniboine-rha.ca
Number of Beds: 60 personal care beds
Note: Programs & services include: acute care; diagnostic; EMS/ambulance; public health; mental health; home care; Manitoba Telehealth; physicians clinic; palliative care; occupational & physiotherapy; dietitian; & meals on wheels.
D. Obach, Area Manager
dobach@arha.ca

***La Broquerie:* Centre de bien-être communautaire - La Broquerie**
Affiliée à: Southern Health-Santé Sud
CP 519, 94, rue Principale, La Broquerie, MB R0A 0W0
Tél: 204-424-5575; *Téléc:* 204-424-5662
cmoquin@southernhealth.ca
www.southernhealth.ca

***Lac du Bonnet:* Lac du Bonnet District Health Centre**
Affiliated with: Interlake-Eastern Regional Health Authority
89 McIntosh Ave., Lac du Bonnet, MB R0E 1A0
Tel: 204-345-8647; *Fax:* 204-268-8609
Note: Diagnostics; physiotherapy; counseling; clinic.

***Leaf Rapids:* Leaf Rapids Health Centre**
Affiliated with: Northern Regional Health Authority
PO Box 370, Leaf Rapids, MB R0B 1W0
Tel: 204-473-2441; *Fax:* 204-473-8273
www.northernhealthregion.ca
Year Founded: 1973

***Lorette:* South Eastman Health Centre - Lorette**
Affiliated with: Southern Health-Santé Sud
PO Box 628, #9, 1321 Dawson Rd., Lorette, MB R0A 0Y0
Tel: 204-424-5575; *Fax:* 204-878-9775
cgagne@southernhealth.ca
www.southernhealth.ca

***Lundar:* Lundar Health Centre**
Affiliated with: Interlake-Eastern Regional Health Authority
97 - 1st St. South, Lundar, MB R0C 1Y0
Tel: 204-762-6076
Note: Nurse Practitioner Clinic (one day a week)

***Lundar:* Lundar Medical Clinic**
38 Main St., Lundar, MB R0C 1Y0
Tel: 204-762-5609
Note: Private clinic

***MacGregor:* MacGregor Health Centre**
Affiliated with: Southern Health-Santé Sud
PO Box 250, 87 Grafton St. South, MacGregor, MB R0H 0R0
Tel: 204-685-2850; *Fax:* 204-685-2529
info@southernhealth.ca
www.southernhealth.ca
Number of Beds: 6 transitional care beds; 20 personal care home beds
Note: Provides community health services such as home care, public health & mental health.
Margaret Warner, Director, Health Services/Seniors - Portage & Area
mwarner@southernhealth.ca

***Manitou:* Pembina-Manitou Health Centre**
Affiliated with: Southern Health-Santé Sud
PO Box 129, 232 Carrie St., Manitou, MB R0G 1G0
Tel: 204-242-2744; *Fax:* 204-242-3062
info@southernhealth.ca
www.southernhealth.ca
Number of Beds: 8 transitional care beds; 18 long-term care beds
Note: Provides community health services such as home care, public health & mental health.
Kristal McKitrick-Bazin, Director, Health Services - Manitou
kbazin@southernhealth.ca

***McCreary:* McCreary Community Health**
Affiliated with: Prairie Mountain Health
PO Box 208, McCreary, MB R0J 1B0
Tel: 204-835-5010
www.prha.mb.ca
Note: Includes home care services (204-835-5010)

***Minnedosa:* Minnedosa Health Centre**
Affiliated with: Prairie Mountain Health
PO Box 960, Minnedosa, MB R0J 1E0
Tel: 204-867-2701; *Fax:* 204-867-2239
www.assiniboine-rha.ca
Note: Programs & services include: acute care; general surgery; diagnostic; EMS/ambulance; public health; mental health; home care; physicians clinic; palliative care; occupational & physiotherapy; dietitian; & meals on wheels.
M. Koroscil, Area Manager
mkoroscil@arha.ca

***Morden:* Agassiz Medical Centre (AMC)**
Affiliated with: Southern Health-Santé Sud
#130, 30 Stephen St., Morden, MB R6M 2G3
Tel: 204-822-4474; *Fax:* 204-822-6886
www.agassizmedicalcentre.com
Note: Community-owned clinic located within Boundary Trails Place
Karen Chezick, Clinic Manager
kchezick@agassizmedicalcentre.com

***Niverville:* Niverville Medical Clinic**
Affiliated with: Southern Health-Santé Sud
PO Box 538, 111 - 2nd Ave. South, Niverville, MB R0A 1E0
Tel: 204-388-6626; *Fax:* 204-388-5091
www.nivmedical.ca
Year Founded: 2005
Note: Includes 3 family physicians; services include travel health, walk-in appointments & prenatal care. Part of the Niverville Primary Health Care Centre, which is located within the Niverville Heritage Centre.

***Niverville:* Niverville Primary Health Care Centre**
Affiliated with: Southern Health-Santé Sud
PO Box 538, 111 - 2nd Ave. South, Niverville, MB R0A 1E0
Tel: 204-388-2030
heritagecentre.ca/services
Year Founded: 2003
Note: Programs & services include: clinical services (nurse practitioner, primary health care nurse & lab services); healthy lifestyle programs; & community health programs. Located within the Niverville Heritage Centre.

***Notre Dame de Lourdes:* Clinique Notre-Dame Clinic**
Affiliated with: Southern Health-Santé Sud
PO Box 130, 44 Rogers Rd., Notre Dame de Lourdes, MB R0G 1M0
Tel: 204-248-2252; *Fax:* 204-248-2087
info@southernhealth.ca
www.southernhealth.ca
Note: Programs & services include: medical (family physicians & a clinic nurse); community services; & telehealth. Located in the Centre Albert-Galliot Wellness Centre.

***Opaskwayak:* Beatrice Wilson Health Centre**
Affiliated with: Northern Regional Health Authority
245 Waller Rd., Opaskwayak, MB R0B 1E0
Tel: 204-627-7410; *Fax:* 204-623-1491
www.northernhealthregion.ca

***Pelican Rapids:* Pelican Rapids Community Health**
Affiliated with: Prairie Mountain Health
General Delivery, Council Office, Lakeview Dr., Pelican Rapids, MB R0L 0L0
Tel: 204-587-2191
www.prha.mb.ca

***Pikwitonei:* Pikwitonei Health Centre**
Affiliated with: Northern Regional Health Authority
General Delivery, Pikwitonei, MB R0B 1E0
Tel: 204-458-2402; *Fax:* 204-458-2468
www.northernhealthregion.ca

***Pinawa:* Pinawa Primary Health Care Centre**
Affiliated with: Interlake-Eastern Regional Health Authority
30 Vanier Dr., Pinawa, MB R0E 1L0
Tel: 204-753-2351

***Pine Falls:* Pine Falls Primary Health Care Centre**
Affiliated with: Interlake-Eastern Regional Health Authority
37 Maple St., Pine Falls, MB R0E 1M0
Tel: 204-367-2278

***Reston:* Reston Health Centre**
Affiliated with: Prairie Mountain Health
PO Box 250, Reston, MB R0M 1X0
Tel: 204-877-3925; *Fax:* 204-877-3998
www.assiniboine-rha.ca
Number of Beds: 20 personal care beds
Note: Programs & services include: transition beds; laboratory; EMS/ambulance; public health; mental health; home care; palliative care; occupational & physiotherapy; dietitian; & meals on wheels.
K. Oberlin, Area Manager
koberlin@arha.ca

***Rivers:* Rivers Health Centre**
Affiliated with: Prairie Mountain Health
PO Box 428, 512 Quebec St., Rivers, MB R0K 1X0
Tel: 204-328-5321; *Fax:* 204-328-7130
www.assiniboine-rha.ca
Number of Beds: 20 personal care beds
Note: Programs & services include: rehabilitation unit; diagnostic; EMS/ambulance; public health; mental health; home care; physicians clinics; palliative care; occupational & physiotherapy; dietitian; meals on wheels & elderly persons housing (12 units).
G. Paddock, Area Manager
gpaddock@arha.ca

***Riverton:* Riverton Clinic**
Affiliated with: Interlake-Eastern Regional Health Authority
Riverton, MB R0C 2R0
Tel: 204-378-2460

***Roblin:* Roblin Community Health Service**
Affiliated with: Prairie Mountain Health
PO Box 880, 15 Hospital St., Roblin, MB R0L 1P0
Tel: 204-937-2151
www.prha.mb.ca
Note: Includes home care services (204-937-2151)

***Rossburn:* Rossburn District Health Centre**
Affiliated with: Prairie Mountain Health
PO Box 40, Rossburn, MB R0J 1V0
Tel: 204-859-2413; *Fax:* 204-859-2526
www.assiniboine-rha.ca
Number of Beds: 20 personal care beds
Note: Programs & services include: transitional care; diagnostic; EMS/ambulance; public health; mental health; home care; physician clinic; primary care nurse; palliative care; occupational & physiotherapy; & dietitian.
D. Ciprick, Area Manager
dciprick@arha.ca

***Selkirk:* Clandeboye Medical Clinic & Interlake Surgical Associates**
210 Clandeboye Ave., Selkirk, MB R1A 2J7
Tel: 204-785-2555; *Fax:* 204-482-4525
Note: Interlake Surgical Associates Phone: 204-785-5507. Clandeboye Medical Clinic specializes in general & family practice.
Interlake Surgical Associates specialize in general, endoscopic & laparoscopic surgery.

***Selkirk:* Eveline Street Clinic**
Affiliated with: Interlake-Eastern Regional Health Authority
66 Eveline St., Selkirk, MB R1A 1K6
Tel: 204-785-5550
Note: Alternate phone: 204-785-5552

***Selkirk:* Red River Walk-In Clinic**
Affiliated with: Interlake-Eastern Regional Health Authority
366 Main St., Selkirk, MB R1A 2J7
Tel: 204-482-8953

***Selkirk:* Selkirk Medical Centre**
Affiliated with: Interlake-Eastern Regional Health Authority
353 Eveline St., Selkirk, MB R1A 1N1
Note: Physicians at this location should be contacted directly

***Selkirk:* Selkirk QuickCare Clinic**
Affiliated with: Interlake-Eastern Regional Health Authority
#3, 1020 Manitoba Ave., Selkirk, MB R1A 4M2
Tel: 204-482-4399
Note: Part of Manitoba's QuickCare Clinic initiative; for diagnosing & treating minor health issues

***Selkirk:* Selkirk Travel Health Clinic**
Affiliated with: Interlake-Eastern Regional Health Authority
#202, 237 Manitoba Ave., Selkirk, MB R1A 0Y4
Tel: 204-785-4891
Note: Appointments available only on Wednesdays

***Sherridon:* Sherridon Health Centre**
Affiliated with: Northern Regional Health Authority
General Delivery, Sherridon, MB R0B 1L0
Tel: 204-468-2012; *Fax:* 204-468-2167
www.northernhealthregion.ca

***Snow Lake:* Snow Lake Health Centre**
Affiliated with: Northern Regional Health Authority
100 Lakeshore Dr., Snow Lake, MB R0B 1M0
Tel: 204-358-2300; *Fax:* 204-358-7095
www.northernhealthregion.ca

***Sprague:* East Borderland Primary Health Care Centre**
Affiliated with: Southern Health-Santé Sud
PO Box 11, 80147 Hwy 12, Sprague, MB R0A 1Z0
Tel: 204-437-3015
www.southernhealth.ca
Year Founded: 1999
Area Served: Piney, Buffalo Point & Moose Lake
Note: Programs & services include: clinical services; healthy lifestyle programs; community health programs; & community partnerships.

***Sprague:* East Borderland Primary Health Care Local Health Promotion**
Affiliated with: Southern Health-Santé Sud
PO Box 40, 80147 Hwy 12, Sprague, MB R0A 1Z0
Tel: 204-425-5118; *Fax:* 204-425-2884
sbarrow@southernhealth.ca
www.southernhealth.ca

***St Pierre Jolys:* Promotion locale de santé St. Pierre Local Health Promotion**
Affiliated with: Southern Health-Santé Sud
PO Box 320, 354 Prefontaine Ave., St Pierre Jolys, MB R0A 1V0
Tel: 204-433-7611; *Fax:* 204-433-7455
adesharnais@southernhealth.ca
www.southernhealth.ca

***St. Laurent:* St. Laurent Health Centre**
Affiliated with: Interlake-Eastern Regional Health Authority
1 Parish Lane, St. Laurent, MB R0C 0E7
Tel: 204-762-6076
Note: Nurse Practitioner Clinic (one day a week)

***Ste Agathe:* Centre de bien-être communautaire francophone - Sainte-Agathe**
Affiliated with: Southern Health-Santé Sud
PO Box 282, 310 Pembina Trail Rd., Ste Agathe, MB R0G 1Y0
Tel: 204-882-2827; *Fax:* 204-882-2790
lrobert@southernhealth.ca
www.southernhealth.ca

***Ste Rose:* Ste Rose Community Health Services**
Affiliated with: Prairie Mountain Health
PO Box 149, 603 - 1st Ave. East, Ste Rose, MB R0L 1S0
Tel: 204-447-4080
www.prha.mb.ca
Note: Includes home care services (204-447-4080)

***Steinbach:* South Eastman Health Centre - Clearspring**
Affiliated with: Southern Health-Santé Sud
#8, 178 Hwy 12 North, Steinbach, MB R5G 1T7
Tel: 204-326-7569; *Fax:* 204-326-7665
www.southernhealth.ca
Note: Programs & services include: physician; chronic disease & health management team; mental health; midwifery; & public health.

***Steinbach:* Steinbach Family Medical Clinic**
Affiliated with: Southern Health-Santé Sud
#10, 333 Loewen Blvd., Steinbach, MB R5G 0C3
Tel: 204-326-3401; *Fax:* 204-326-3899
www.steinbachfamilymedical.com
Note: Same-day care clinic with lab services on-site; houses 19 family physicians & 3 general surgeons.
Fred Pauls, Clinic Manager
204-326-8859, Fax: 204-326-8885,
fred@steinbachfamilymedical.com

***Steinbach:* Steinbach Local Health Promotion**
Affiliated with: Southern Health-Santé Sud
Steinbach, MB R5G 0R9
Tel: 204-346-6694; *Fax:* 204-346-6693
leslieb@southernhealth.ca
www.southernhealth.ca
Note: Several locations across Steinbach

***Steinbach:* Steinbach QuickCare Clinic**
Affiliated with: Southern Health-Santé Sud
Clearspring Centre, #8, 178 Hwy 12 North, Steinbach, MB R5G 1T7
Tel: 204-326-7569
info@southernhealth.ca
www.southernhealth.ca
Year Founded: 2012
Note: Part of Manitoba's QuickCare Clinic initiative; for diagnosing & treating minor health issues.

***Stonewall:* Hope Medical Clinic**
Affiliated with: Interlake-Eastern Regional Health Authority
#4B, 408 Main St., Stonewall, MB R0C 2Z0
Tel: 204-467-7595

***Stonewall:* Interlake Medical Clinic**
Affiliated with: Interlake-Eastern Regional Health Authority
#2, 330 - 3rd Ave. South, Stonewall, MB R0C 2Z0
Tel: 204-467-5717

***Stonewall:* Rockwood Medical Clinic**
Affiliated with: Interlake-Eastern Regional Health Authority
#5, 403 - 3rd Ave. South, Stonewall, MB R0C 2Z0
Tel: 204-467-9707

***Swan River:* Swan River Community Health Services**
Affiliated with: Prairie Mountain Health
PO Box 1028, 1011 Main St., Swan River, MB R0L 1Z0
Tel: 204-734-6603
www.prha.mb.ca
Note: Includes home care services (204-734-6602)

***Teulon:* Teulon - Private Clinic**
34 Main St., Teulon, MB R0C 3B0
Tel: 204-886-3039

***Thompson:* Burntwood Community Health Resource Centre**
Affiliated with: Northern Regional Health Authority
50 Selkirk Ave., Thompson, MB R8N 0M7
Tel: 204-677-1777; *Fax:* 204-677-1755
Note: Family doctor.

***Treherne:* Tiger Hills Health Centre**
Affiliated with: Prairie Mountain Health
PO Box 130, Treherne, MB R0G 2V0
Tel: 204-723-2133; *Fax:* 204-723-2869
www.assiniboine-rha.ca
Number of Beds: 22 personal care beds
Note: Programs & services include: acute; diagnostic; emergency; public health; mental health; home care; physician clinic; palliative care; occupation & physiotherapy; dietitian; meals on wheels; & Elderly Person's Housing (21 units).
D. Rea, Area Manager
drea@arha.ca

***Virden:* Virden Health Centre**
Affiliated with: Prairie Mountain Health
PO Box 400, Virden, MB R0M 2C0
Tel: 204-748-1230; *Fax:* 204-748-2053
www.assiniboine-rha.ca
Note: Programs & services include: acute care; diagnostic; EMS/ambulance; public health; mental health; home care; Manitoba Telehealth; physician clinic; palliative care; occupational & physiotherapy; & dietitian.
G. Henuset, Area Manager
ghenuset@arha.ca

***Vita:* Vita & District Health Centre**
Affiliated with: Southern Health-Santé Sud
PO Box 160, 217 - 1st Ave. West, Vita, MB R0A 2K0
Tel: 204-425-3804
info@southernhealth.ca
www.southernhealth.ca
Number of Beds: 10 acute care beds; 44 long-term care beds
Note: Programs & services include: emergency; lab & diagnostics; long-term care; medicine; nurse-managed care; occupational therapy; palliative care; physiotherapy; & spiritual care.
Janet Chobotar, Director, Health Services
jchobotar@southernhealth.ca

***Vita:* Vita & District Personal Care Home**
Vita & District Health Centre
Affiliated with: Southern Health-Santé Sud
Also Known As: Whispering Pines Lodge
PO Box 160, 217 - 1st Ave. West, Vita, MB R0A 2K0
Tel: 204-425-3325
info@southernhealth.ca
www.southernhealth.ca
Year Founded: 1976
Number of Beds: 44 beds
Janet Chobotar, Director, Health Services
jchobotar@southernhealth.ca

***Wabowden:* Wabowden Community Health Centre**
Affiliated with: Northern Regional Health Authority
88 Lakeside Dr., Wabowden, MB R0B 1S0
Tel: 204-689-2600; *Fax:* 204-689-2180
www.northernhealthregion.ca

***Waterhen:* Waterhen Health Centre**
Affiliated with: Prairie Mountain Health
PO Box 10, 104 North Mallard Rd., Waterhen, MB R0L 2C0
Tel: 204-628-3019
www.prha.mb.ca

***Wawanesa:* Wawanesa Health Centre**
Affiliated with: Prairie Mountain Health
Former Name: Wawanesa & District Memorial Health Centre
PO Box 309, 506 George St., Wawanesa, MB R0K 2G0
Tel: 204-824-2335; *Fax:* 204-824-2148
www.assiniboine-rha.ca
Number of Beds: 20 personal care beds
Note: Programs & services include: transition care; diagnostic; EMS/ambulance; public health; mental health; home care; physician clinic; primary care nurse; palliative care; occupational & physiotherapy; dietitian; & meals on wheels.
D. Obach, Area Manager
dobach@arha.ca

***Whitemouth:* Whitemouth Primary Health Care Centre**
Affiliated with: Interlake-Eastern Regional Health Authority
75 Hospital St., Whitemouth, MB R0E 2G0
Tel: 204-348-2291

***Winkler:* Dr. C.W. Wiebe Medical Centre**
Affiliated with: Southern Health-Santé Sud
ALG Professional Bldg., 385 Main St., Winkler, MB R6W 1J2
Tel: 204-325-4312; *Fax:* 204-325-4594
info@cwwiebemedical.ca
www.cwwiebemedical.ca
Note: Programs & services include: physician assistants; on-site lab; x-ray; dietian; mental health; & employer services (audiograms, drug/alcohol testing & physicals).
Jim Neufeld, Administrative Contact
jim@cwwiebemedical.ca

***Winnipeg:* Aboriginal Health & Wellness Centre**
Affiliated with: Winnipeg Regional Health Authority
#215, 181 Higgins Ave., Winnipeg, MB R3B 3G1
Tel: 204-925-3700; *Fax:* 204-925-3709
www.abcentre.org
Note: Programs & services include: traditional medicine; children's health; & health promotion.

***Winnipeg:* ACCESS Downtown**
Affiliated with: Winnipeg Regional Health Authority
640 Main St., Winnipeg, MB R3B 0L8
Tel: 204-940-3638
www.gov.mb.ca/health/primarycare/public/access/access.html
Note: ACCESS Centres offer health & social services; programs & services vary by community

***Winnipeg:* ACCESS NorWest**
Affiliated with: Winnipeg Regional Health Authority
785 Keewatin St., Winnipeg, MB R2X 3B9
Tel: 204-938-5900
www.gov.mb.ca/health/primarycare/public/access/access.html
Note: ACCESS Centres offer health & social services; programs & services vary by community. This branch is in the same location as NorWest Co-op Community Health.

***Winnipeg:* ACCESS River East**
Affiliated with: Winnipeg Regional Health Authority
975 Henderson Hwy, Winnipeg, MB R2K 4L7
Tel: 204-938-5000
www.gov.mb.ca/health/primarycare/public/access/access.html
Note: ACCESS Centres offer health & social services; programs & services vary by community

***Winnipeg:* ACCESS Transcona**
Affiliated with: Winnipeg Regional Health Authority
845 Regent Ave. West, Winnipeg, MB R2C 3A9
Tel: 204-938-5555
www.gov.mb.ca/health/primarycare/public/access/access.html
Note: ACCESS Centres offer health & social services; programs & services vary by community

***Winnipeg:* ACCESS Winnipeg West**
Affiliated with: Winnipeg Regional Health Authority
280 Booth Dr., Winnipeg, MB R3J 3R5
Tel: 204-940-2040
www.gov.mb.ca/health/primarycare/public/access/access.html
Note: ACCESS Centres offer health & social services; programs & services vary by community. St. James clients (204-940-2397); Assiniboia South clients (204-940-2453).

***Winnipeg:* Centre de santé Saint-Boniface/St. Boniface Health Centre**
Hôpital St-Boniface Hospital
Affiliated with: Winnipeg Regional Health Authority
#D-1048, 409, av Taché, Winnipeg, MB R2H 2A6
Tel: 204-235-3910; *Fax:* 204-237-9057
access@centredesante.mb.ca
www.centredesante.mb.ca
Note: Bilingual primary health centre. Programs & services include: medical; nutrition; mental health; community support; & Health Links - Info Santé.
Susan Stratford, Executive Director

***Winnipeg:* Downtown East Community Office**
Affiliated with: Winnipeg Regional Health Authority
#2, 640 Main St., Winnipeg, MB R3B 0L8
Tel: 204-940-3638
www.wrha.mb.ca
Note: Provides services related to: healthy parenting & early childhood development; healthy children & youth; nutrition promotion; communicable disease prevention & management; immunization; & more. This office is in the same location as ACCESS Downtown.

***Winnipeg:* Downtown West Community Office**
Affiliated with: Winnipeg Regional Health Authority
755 Portage Ave., Winnipeg, MB R3G 0N2
Tel: 204-940-2236
www.wrha.mb.ca

***Winnipeg:* Health Action Centre**
Affiliated with: Winnipeg Regional Health Authority
425 Elgin Ave., Winnipeg, MB R3A 1P2
Tel: 204-940-3160
www.wrha.mb.ca

***Winnipeg:* Hope Centre Health Care Inc.**
Affiliated with: Winnipeg Regional Health Authority
240 Powers St., Winnipeg, MB R2W 5L1
Tel: 204-589-8354; *Fax:* 204-586-4260
www.wrha.mb.ca
Year Founded: 1982

***Winnipeg:* Klinic Community Health Centre**
Affiliated with: Winnipeg Regional Health Authority
870 Portage Ave., Winnipeg, MB R3G 0P1
Tel: 204-784-4090; *Fax:* 204-784-4013
klinic@klinic.mb.ca
www.klinic.mb.ca
Nicole Chammartin, Executive Director

***Winnipeg:* MFL Occupational Health Centre, Inc.**
Affiliated with: Winnipeg Regional Health Authority
#102, 275 Broadway, Winnipeg, MB R3C 4M6
Tel: 204-949-0811; *Fax:* 204-956-0848
Toll-Free: 888-843-1229
mflohc@mflohc.mb.ca
www.mflohc.mb.ca
Year Founded: 1983
Note: Specializes in occupational health (health issues related to work experiences), improvement of workplace health & safety conditions & elimination of hazards.
Sonia Kowalewich, Executive Director
204-926-7900, sonia.kowalewich@mflohc.mb.ca

***Winnipeg:* Misericordia Health Centre (MHC)**
Affiliated with: Winnipeg Regional Health Authority
99 Cornish Ave., Winnipeg, MB R3C 1A2
Tel: 204-774-6581; *Fax:* 204-783-6052
info@misericordia.mb.ca
www.misericordia.mb.ca
Social Media: www.facebook.com/263816864499; twitter.com/MisericordiaMB; instagram.com/misericordiamb
Year Founded: 1898
Number of Beds: 250 beds; 100 personal care home beds
Note: Research & teaching health centre, with programs & services including: ambulatory care; Buhler Eye Care Centre; Community IV Program; diagnostics; Easy Street rehabilitation program; eye bank; interim care; laboratory; long-term care (through Misericordia Place); Health Care for Lungs; occupational therapy; ophthalmology; pediatric dental surgery; Provincial Health Contact Centre; physiotherapy; recreation therapy; rehabilitation services; respiratory therapy; Sleep Disorder Centre; social work; spiritual & religious care; support services; & Urgent Care Centre.
Rosie Jacuzzi, President & CEO

***Winnipeg:* Mount Carmel Clinic**
Affiliated with: Winnipeg Regional Health Authority
886 Main St., Winnipeg, MB R2W 5L4
Tel: 204-582-2311; *Fax:* 204-582-6006
info@mountcarmel.ca
www.mountcarmel.ca
Year Founded: 1926
Note: Health services include: aboriginal health & wellness; child; dental; general health; Hepatitis C clinic; homeless/harm reduction; immigrant/refugee; LGBT; mental health; pregnancy/parenting; reproductive/sexual health; & youth.
Bobbette Shoffner, Executive Director
204-582-0311, bshoffner@mountcarmel.ca

***Winnipeg:* Nine Circles Community Health Centre**
Affiliated with: Winnipeg Regional Health Authority
705 Broadway, Winnipeg, MB R3G 0X2
Tel: 204-940-6000; *Fax:* 204-940-6003
Toll-Free: 888-305-8647
ninecircles@ninecircles.ca
www.ninecircles.ca
Social Media: www.facebook.com/NineCirclesCommunityHealthCentre; twitter.com/ninecircleschc
Note: Non-profit centre specializing in STI/HIV prevention & care services
Michael Payne, Executive Director

***Winnipeg:* NorWest Co-op Community Health**
Affiliated with: Winnipeg Regional Health Authority
Also Known As: Inkster/Nor'west Co-op Community Health Centre
785 Keewatin St., Winnipeg, MB R2X 3B9
Tel: 204-938-5900; *Fax:* 204-938-5994
www.norwestcoop.ca
Social Media: www.facebook.com/193978229794; twitter.com/NorWestCoop; www.youtube.com/user/NorwestCoop
Note: Programs & services include: primary health care; community development; counselling & support services; & early learning & childcare. This health centre is in the same location as ACCESS NorWest.
Ivan Sabesky, President & Board Chair

***Winnipeg:* Point Douglas Community Health Centre**
Affiliated with: Winnipeg Regional Health Authority
601 Aikins St., Winnipeg, MB R2W 4J5
Tel: 204-940-2025
www.wrha.mb.ca
Note: Provides services related to: healthy parenting & early childhood development; healthy children & youth; nutrition promotion; communicable disease prevention & management; immunization; & more.

***Winnipeg:* River Heights Community Health Service Centre**
Affiliated with: Winnipeg Regional Health Authority
1001 Corydon Ave., Winnipeg, MB R3M 0B6
Tel: 204-940-2005
www.wrha.mb.ca

***Winnipeg:* River Heights Health & Social Services Centre**
Affiliated with: Winnipeg Regional Health Authority
#6, 677 Stafford St., Winnipeg, MB R3M 2X7
Tel: 204-938-5500
www.wrha.mb.ca
Note: Provides services related to: healthy parenting & early childhood development; healthy children & youth; nutrition promotion; communicable disease prevention & management; immunization; & more.

***Winnipeg:* St. Boniface Community Office**
Affiliated with: Winnipeg Regional Health Authority
#240, 614 Des Meurons St., Winnipeg, MB R2H 2P9
Tel: 204-940-2035
www.wrha.mb.ca
Note: Provides services related to: healthy parenting & early childhood development; healthy children & youth; nutrition promotion; communicable disease prevention & management; immunization; & more.

***Winnipeg:* St. Vital Community Office**
Affiliated with: Winnipeg Regional Health Authority
St. Vital Square, #6, 845 Dakota St., Winnipeg, MB R2M 5M3
Tel: 204-940-2045
www.wrha.mb.ca
Note: Provides services related to: healthy parenting & early childhood development; healthy children & youth; nutrition promotion; communicable disease prevention & management; immunization; & more. This office is in the same location as the Youville Community Health Centre.

***Winnipeg:* Seven Oaks Health & Social Services Centre**
Affiliated with: Winnipeg Regional Health Authority
#3, 1050 Leila Ave., Winnipeg, MB R2P 1W6
Tel: 204-938-5600
www.wrha.mb.ca
Note: Provides services related to: healthy parenting & early childhood development; healthy children & youth; nutrition promotion; communicable disease prevention & management; immunization; & more.

***Winnipeg:* Street Connections**
Affiliated with: Winnipeg Regional Health Authority
496 Hargrave St., Winnipeg, MB R3A 0X7
Tel: 204-981-0742
www.streetconnections.ca
Note: Mobile health clinic specializing in harm reduction & free services to those in need. Programs & services include: general assistance (housing, addictions, food, legal, & more); counselling; nursing services; prenatal services; clean drug use supplies; needle exchange; safe sex supplies; & home visits.

***Winnipeg:* Win Gardner Place**
Affiliated with: Winnipeg Regional Health Authority
Former Name: North End Wellness Centre
363 McGregor St., Winnipeg, MB R2W 4X4
Tel: 204-925-4486
www.wingardnerplace.ca
Social Media: www.facebook.com/WinGardnerPlace; twitter.com/WinGardnerPlace
Note: A collaborative effort between the following organizations: Ma Mawi Wi Chi Itata Centre, the YMCA-YWCA of Winnipeg, SPLASH Child Enrichment Centre & the Winnipeg Regional Health Authority.

***Winnipeg:* Winnipeg West Integrated Health & Social Services**
Affiliated with: Winnipeg Regional Health Authority
280 Booth Dr., Winnipeg, MB R3J 3R5
Tel: 204-940-2040
www.wrha.mb.ca
Note: This office is in the same location as ACCESS Winnipeg West.

***Winnipeg:* Women's Health Clinic Inc. (WHC)**
Affiliated with: Winnipeg Regional Health Authority
419 Graham Ave., Unit A, Winnipeg, MB R3C 0M3
Tel: 204-947-1517; *Fax:* 204-943-3844
Toll-Free: 866-947-1517
TTY: 204-956-0385
whc@womenshealthclinic.org
www.womenshealthclinic.org
Social Media: facebook.com/WHCwpg; twitter.com/whcwpg
Year Founded: 1981

***Winnipeg:* Youville Centre - Community Health Resource Centre**
Affiliated with: Winnipeg Regional Health Authority
Also Known As: Youville Community Health Centre
St. Vital Square, #6, 845 Dakota St., Winnipeg, MB R2M 5M3
Tel: 204-255-4840; *Fax:* 204-255-4903
www.youville.ca
Year Founded: 1984
Note: Programs & services include: health care & wellness education; counselling; & support. This Centre is in the same location as the WRHA St. Vital Community Office.
Patrick Griffith, Executive Director

***Winnipegosis:* Winnipegosis Community Health**
Affiliated with: Prairie Mountain Health
PO Box 340, 230 Bridge St., Winnipegosis, MB R0L 1C0
Tel: 204-656-4721
www.prha.mb.ca
Note: Includes home care services (204-656-4721)

Nursing Stations

***Berens River:* Berens River Nursing Station**
First Nations Health Group
Affiliated with: Interlake-Eastern Regional Health Authority
General Delivery, Berens River, MB R0B 0A0
Tel: 204-382-2265; *Fax:* 204-382-2005
info@ierha.ca
www.ierha.ca
Population Served: 1800; *Number of Employees:* 5

***Bloodvein:* Bloodvein Nursing Station**
First Nations Health Group
Affiliated with: Interlake-Eastern Regional Health Authority
General Delivery, Bloodvein, MB R0C 0J0
Tel: 204-395-2161; *Fax:* 204-395-2087
info@ierha.ca
www.ierha.ca
Population Served: 950; *Number of Employees:* 2

***Brochet:* Brochet/Barren Lands Nursing Station**
Affiliated with: Northern Regional Health Authority
General Delivery, Brochet, MB R0B 0B0
Tel: 204-323-2120; *Fax:* 204-323-2650
www.northernhealthregion.ca
Number of Beds: 6 beds
Number of Employees: 3

***Cross Lake:* Cross Lake Nursing Station**
First Nations Health Group
Affiliated with: Northern Regional Health Authority
PO Box 160, Cross Lake, MB R0B 0J0
Tel: 204-676-2011; *Fax:* 204-676-3179
www.northernhealthregion.ca
Population Served: 5000; *Number of Employees:* 15

***Easterville:* Easterville/Chemawawin Nursing Station**
Affiliated with: Northern Regional Health Authority
PO Box 122, Easterville, MB R0C 0V0
Tel: 204-329-2212; *Fax:* 204-329-2337
www.northernhealthregion.ca
Number of Employees: 6

***Garden Hill:* Garden Hill Nursing Station**
First Nations Health Group
Affiliated with: Northern Regional Health Authority
PO Box 264, Garden Hill, MB R0B 0T0
Tel: 204-456-2615; *Fax:* 204-456-2866
www.northernhealthregion.ca
Population Served: 3200; *Number of Employees:* 4

***God's Lake:* God's Lake Nursing Station**
First Nations Health Group
Affiliated with: Northern Regional Health Authority
Former Name: God's Lake Narrows Nursing Station
General Delivery, God's Lake, MB R0B 0M0
Tel: 204-335-2557; *Fax:* 204-335-2043
www.northernhealthregion.ca
Population Served: 2170; *Number of Employees:* 3

God's River: **God's River/Manto Sipi Nursing Station**
First Nations Health Group
Affiliated with: Northern Regional Health Authority
Also Known As: God's River Health Station
PO Box 100, God's River, MB R0B 0N0
Tel: 204-366-2355; *Fax:* 204-366-2474
www.northernhealthregion.ca
Population Served: 620; *Number of Employees:* 2

Grand Rapids: **Grand Rapids/Misipawistik Nursing Station**
Affiliated with: Northern Regional Health Authority
PO Box 53, Grand Rapids, MB R0C 1E0
Tel: 204-639-2215; *Fax:* 204-639-2448
www.northernhealthregion.ca

Ilford: **Ilford Nursing Station**
Affiliated with: Northern Regional Health Authority
General Delivery, Ilford, MB R0B 0S0
Tel: 204-288-4348; *Fax:* 204-288-4360
www.northernhealthregion.ca

Lac Brochet: **Lac Brochet/Northlands Nursing Station**
First Nations Health Group
Affiliated with: Northern Regional Health Authority
PO Box 90, Lac Brochet, MB R0B 2E0
Tel: 204-337-2161; *Fax:* 204-337-2143
www.northernhealthregion.ca
Population Served: 630; *Number of Employees:* 2

Little Grand Rapids: **Little Grand Rapids Nursing Station**
First Nations Health Group
Affiliated with: Interlake-Eastern Regional Health Authority
General Delivery, Little Grand Rapids, MB R0B 0V0
Tel: 204-397-2115; *Fax:* 204-397-2016
info@ierha.ca
www.ierha.ca
Population Served: 990; *Number of Employees:* 2

Moose Lake: **Moose Lake/Mosakahiken Nursing Station**
Affiliated with: Northern Regional Health Authority
General Delivery, Moose Lake, MB R0B 0Y0
Tel: 204-678-2252; *Fax:* 204-678-2343
www.northernhealthregion.ca

Negginan: **Poplar River Nursing Station**
First Nations Health Group
Affiliated with: Interlake-Eastern Regional Health Authority
General Delivery, Negginan, MB R0B 0Z0
Tel: 204-244-2102; *Fax:* 204-244-2001
info@ierha.ca
www.ierha.ca
Population Served: 1200; *Number of Employees:* 2

Nelson House: **Nelson House/Nisichawayasihk Nursing Station**
First Nations Health Group
Affiliated with: Northern Regional Health Authority
General Delivery, Nelson House, MB R0B 1A0
Tel: 204-484-2031; *Fax:* 204-484-2284
www.northernhealthregion.ca
Population Served: 2500; *Number of Employees:* 5

Norway House: **Norway House Nursing Station**
Norway House Health Services Inc.
Affiliated with: Northern Regional Health Authority
Also Known As: Norway House Hospital
PO Box 730, Norway House, MB R0B 1B0
Tel: 204-359-8230; *Fax:* 204-359-6599
www.nhhsinc.ca
Number of Employees: 20
Note: Programs & services include: dialysis; laboratory; x-ray; & dietary.

Oxford House: **Oxford House/Bunibonibee Nursing Station**
First Nations Health Group
Affiliated with: Northern Regional Health Authority
General Delivery, Oxford House, MB R0B 1C0
Tel: 204-538-2347; *Fax:* 204-538-2445
www.northernhealthregion.ca
Year Founded: 2011
Population Served: 2250; *Number of Employees:* 4

Pauingassi: **Pauingassi Nursing Station**
First Nations Health Group
Affiliated with: Interlake-Eastern Regional Health Authority
PO Box 32, Pauingassi, MB R0B 2G0
Tel: 204-397-2395; *Fax:* 204-397-2104
info@ierha.ca
www.ierha.ca
Population Served: 535; *Number of Employees:* 2

Pikwitonei: **Pikwitonei Nursing Station**
Affiliated with: Northern Regional Health Authority
307 Cordell Rd., Pikwitonei, MB R0B 1E0
Tel: 204-458-2402; *Fax:* 204-458-2468
www.northernhealthregion.ca
Number of Employees: 2

Pukatawagan: **Pukatawagan/Mathias Colomb Nursing Station**
First Nations Health Group
Affiliated with: Northern Regional Health Authority
Also Known As: Nikawiy Nursing Station
General Delivery, Pukatawagan, MB R0B 1G0
Tel: 204-553-2271; *Fax:* 204-553-2241
www.northernhealthregion.ca
Population Served: 1464; *Number of Employees:* 5

Red Sucker Lake: **Red Sucker Lake Nursing Station**
First Nations Health Group
Affiliated with: Northern Regional Health Authority
General Delivery, Red Sucker Lake, MB R0B 1H0
Tel: 204-469-5351; *Fax:* 204-469-5769
www.northernhealthregion.ca
Population Served: 814; *Number of Employees:* 3

Shamattawa: **Shamattawa Nursing Station**
First Nations Health Group
Affiliated with: Northern Regional Health Authority
General Delivery, Shamattawa, MB R0B 1K0
Tel: 204-565-2370; *Fax:* 204-565-2519
www.northernhealthregion.ca
Population Served: 920; *Number of Employees:* 4

South Indian Lake: **South Indian Lake/O-Pipon-Na-Piwin Nursing Station**
First Nations Health Group
Affiliated with: Northern Regional Health Authority
PO Box 22, South Indian Lake, MB R0B 1N0
Tel: 204-374-2013; *Fax:* 204-374-2039
www.northernhealthregion.ca
Number of Beds: 5 beds
Population Served: 1100; *Number of Employees:* 3

Split Lake: **Split Lake/Tataskweyak Nursing Station**
First Nations Health Group
Affiliated with: Northern Regional Health Authority
General Delivery, Split Lake, MB R0B 1P0
Tel: 204-342-2033; *Fax:* 204-342-2319
www.northernhealthregion.ca
Year Founded: 2009
Population Served: 1500; *Number of Employees:* 5

St Theresa Point: **St Theresa Point Nursing Station**
First Nations Health Group
Affiliated with: Northern Regional Health Authority
General Delivery, St Theresa Point, MB R0B 1J0
Tel: 204-462-2264; *Fax:* 204-462-2642
www.northernhealthregion.ca
Year Founded: 2010
Population Served: 2630; *Number of Employees:* 5

Tadoule Lake: **Tadoule Lake/Sayisi Nursing Station**
First Nations Health Group
Affiliated with: Northern Regional Health Authority
General Delivery, Tadoule Lake, MB R0B 2C0
Tel: 204-684-2031; *Fax:* 204-684-2049
www.northernhealthregion.ca
Population Served: 330; *Number of Employees:* 2

Thicket Portage: **Thicket Portage Nursing Station**
Affiliated with: Northern Regional Health Authority
Former Name: Thicket Portage Health Centre
398 Evans Ave., Thicket Portage, MB R0B 1R0
Tel: 204-286-3254; *Fax:* 204-286-3216
www.northernhealthregion.ca
Number of Employees: 1

Waasagamach: **Waasagamach Nursing Station**
Affiliated with: Northern Regional Health Authority
General Delivery, Waasagamach, MB R0B 1Z0
Tel: 204-457-2189; *Fax:* 204-457-2348
www.northernhealthregion.ca

Wasagamack Bay: **Wasagamack Nursing Station**
First Nations Health Group
Affiliated with: Northern Regional Health Authority
General Delivery, Wasagamack Bay, MB R0B 1Z0
Tel: 204-457-2024; *Fax:* 204-457-2348
www.northernhealthregion.ca
Population Served: 1400; *Number of Employees:* 4

Winnipeg: **First North Health Group**
#1, 1700 Ness Ave., Winnipeg, MB R3J 3Y1
Tel: 204-943-5160; *Fax:* 866-985-4060
Toll-Free: 885-559-6649
www.firstnorthhealthgroup.ca
Year Founded: 1997
Number of Employees: 100
Specialties: Helping 22 First Nations communities
Garry Archer, President

York Landing: **York Landing Nursing Station**
First Nations Health Group
Affiliated with: Northern Regional Health Authority
General Delivery, York Landing, MB R0B 2B0
Tel: 204-341-2325; *Fax:* 204-341-2179
www.northernhealthregion.ca
Year Founded: 2010
Population Served: 464; *Number of Employees:* 2

Special Treatment Centres

Brandon: **Western Manitoba Cancer Centre (WMCC)**
Brandon Regional Health Centre
Affiliated with: Prairie Mountain Health
300 McTavish Ave. East, Brandon, MB R7A 2B3
Tel: 204-578-2222; *Fax:* 204-578-4991
www.brandonrha.mb.ca
Year Founded: 2011

St Norbert: **The Behavioural Health Foundation, Inc. (BHF)**
Affiliated with: Winnipeg Regional Health Authority
PO Box 250, 35, av de la Digue, St Norbert, MB R3V 1L6
info@bhf.ca
www.bhf.ca
Note: Long-term residential addictions treatment for men, women, teens & families
Molly Hochbaum, Coordinator/Student Advisor, kellib@bhf.ca
204-261-3312, St. Norbert Adult Education Centre

Winnipeg: **Addictions Recovery Inc. (ARI)**
Affiliated with: Winnipeg Regional Health Authority
93 Cathedral Ave., Winnipeg, MB R2W 0W7
Tel: 204-586-2550
ari@mts.net
www.addictionsrecovery.ca
Year Founded: 1979
Note: Provides an alcohol & drug addiction treatment program; runs two recovery homes in Winnipeg.

Winnipeg: **CancerCare Manitoba**
Affiliated with: Winnipeg Regional Health Authority
675 McDermot Ave., Winnipeg, MB R3E 0V9
Tel: 204-787-2197; *Fax:* 204-787-1184
Toll-Free: 866-561-1026
www.cancercare.mb.ca
Social Media: twitter.com/cancercaremb; www.youtube.com/user/CancerCareMB/videos
Number of Employees: 800
Note: Provides cancer treatment in all areas: prevention, early detection, diagnosis, treatment & care, & end of life care.
Dr. Sri Navaratnam, President & CEO
Valerie Wiebe, Vice-President & Chief Officer, Patient Services
Bill Funk, Interim Chief Operating Officer

Winnipeg: **Esther House**
Affiliated with: Winnipeg Regional Health Authority
PO Box 68022 Stn. Osborne Vill., Winnipeg, MB R3L 2V9
estherhs@mymts.net
www.estherhousewinnipeg.ca
Year Founded: 1997
Number of Beds: 6 beds
Note: Provides second-stage addiction recovery treatment for women. Works in cooperation with the Addictions Foundation of Manitoba.

Winnipeg: **The Laurel Centre**
Affiliated with: Winnipeg Regional Health Authority
104 Roslyn Rd., Winnipeg, MB R3L 0G6
Tel: 204-783-5460; *Fax:* 204-774-2912
info@thelaurelcentre.com
thelaurelcentre.com

Note: Provides dual treatment for women with substance addictions & who are experiencing the traumatic effects of childhood/adolescent sexual abuse.

Winnipeg: Main Street Project (MSP)
Affiliated with: Winnipeg Regional Health Authority
75 Martha St., Winnipeg, MB R3B 1A4
Tel: 204-982-8245; *Fax:* 204-943-9474
admin@mainstreetproject.ca
www.mainstreetproject.ca
Year Founded: 1972
Note: Programs & services include: emergency shelter & food; drug & alcohol detoxification unit; on-site counseling; transitional housing; & other critical services.
Lisa Goss, Executive Director

Winnipeg: Native Addictions Council of Manitoba (NACM)
Affiliated with: Winnipeg Regional Health Authority
160 Salter St., Winnipeg, MB R2W 4K1
Tel: 204-586-8395; *Fax:* 204-589-3921
info@nacm.ca
www.mts.net/~nacm
Year Founded: 1971
Note: Provides holistic treatment of addictions

Winnipeg: New Directions for Children, Youth, Adults & Families
Former Name: Children's Home of Winnipeg
#400, 491 Portage Ave., Winnipeg, MB R3B 2E4
Tel: 204-786-7051; *Fax:* 204-774-6468
TTY: 204-774-8541
www.newdirections.mb.ca
Year Founded: 1885
Note: Programs & services in the following categories: Counselling, Assessment, Support & Prevention Programs; Training & Education Programs; & Residential & Support Programs.
Dr. Jennifer Frain, Chief Executive Officer

Winnipeg: Rehabilitation Centre for Children (RCC)
Affiliated with: Winnipeg Regional Health Authority
633 Wellington Cres., Winnipeg, MB R3M 0A8
Tel: 204-452-4311; *Fax:* 204-477-5547
www.rccinc.ca.php53-10.ord1-1.websitetestlink.com
Note: Provides services to children with physical & developmental challenges.

Winnipeg: Reh-Fit Centre
Affiliated with: Winnipeg Regional Health Authority
Former Name: Manitoba Cardiac Institute
1390 Taylor Ave., Winnipeg, MB R3M 3V8
Tel: 204-488-8023; *Fax:* 204-488-4819
reh-fit@reh-fit.com
www.reh-fit.com
Social Media: www.facebook.com/RehFit; twitter.com/RehFit
Year Founded: 1979
Note: A certified medical fitness facility specializing in cardiac rehabilitation.
David Thompson, Board Chair
Sue Boreskie, Chief Executive Officer
204-488-5850
Patrick Harrington, Director, Finance
204-488-5858, patrick.harrington@reh-fit.com
Janet Cranston, Director, Support Services
204-488-5855, janet.cranston@reh-fit.com

Winnipeg: Tamarack Recovery Centre Inc.
Affiliated with: Winnipeg Regional Health Authority
Former Name: Kia Zan Inc.
60 Balmoral St., Winnipeg, MB R3C 1X4
Tel: 204-772-9836; *Fax:* 204-772-9908
info@tamarackrecovery.org
www.tamarackrehab.org
Year Founded: 1974
Note: Provides abstinence-based addictions treatment & recovery services.
Lisa Cowan, Executive Director
204-772-9836

Long Term Care Facilities

Arborg: Riverdale Place Homes Inc.
PO Box 968, 332 Ingolfs St., Arborg, MB R0C 0A0
Tel: 204-376-2940; *Fax:* 204-376-5051
riverdale@mts.net
Year Founded: 1977
Number of Beds: 19 beds
Note: Provides residential services to adults with intellectual disabilities.

St-Malo: Chalet Malouin Inc.
PO Box 1010, 14 St. Hilaire St., St-Malo, MB R0A 1T0
Tel: 204-347-5753; *Fax:* 204-347-5107
chaletmalouin@mts.net
www.chaletmalouin.com
Social Media: www.facebook.com/chaletmalouin
Year Founded: 1971
Number of Beds: 47 independent living apartments; 38 assisted living / supportive housing suites
Note: Chalet Malouin is a bilingual housing complex for seniors.
Louise Maynard, Administrator

Winnipeg: Deer Lodge Centre
Affiliated with: Winnipeg Regional Health Authority
2109 Portage Ave., Winnipeg, MB R3J 0L3
Tel: 204-837-1301; *Fax:* 204-889-0430
info@deerlodge.mb.ca
www.deerlodge.mb.ca
Year Founded: 1916
Number of Beds: 431 beds, including 155 personal care beds for veterans
Note: Provides rehabilitation services, including physiotherapy, occupational therapy, respiratory therapy, & therapeutic recreation services. Inpatient programs include: assessment & rehabilitation; chronic care; personal care; peritoneal dialysis; & respite care. Outpatient programs include: PRIME health care for seniors program; day hospital; diagnostics; geriatric mental health team; speech & language pathology for personal care home; physiotherapy; & Get-Away Club adult day programming. Services for advanced care & communications devices are also available.
Gina Trinidad, Chief Operating Officer/Chief Nursing Officer
Dr. David Strang, Chief Medical Officer

Winnipeg: Riverview Health Centre
Affiliated with: Winnipeg Regional Health Authority
1 Morley Ave., Winnipeg, MB R3L 2P4
Tel: 204-478-6203; *Fax:* 204-284-9446
rhcinfo@rhc.mb.ca
www.riverviewhealthcentre.com
Number of Beds: 387 beds
Note: Provides long-term care, catering to the needs of the elderly & rehabilitation patients
Norman Kasian, President & CEO
Dr. Daryl Perry, Chief Medical Officer

Winnipeg: St. Amant Inc.
Affiliated with: Winnipeg Regional Health Authority
440 River Rd., Winnipeg, MB R2M 3Z9
Tel: 204-256-4301; *Fax:* 204-257-4349
inquiries@stamant.mb.ca
www.stamant.ca
Social Media: www.facebook.com/StAmantMB; twitter.com/StAmantMB; www.youtube.com/user/StAmantMB; www.linkedin.com/company/st-amant
Year Founded: 1931
Number of Beds: 212 beds
Note: Developmental disability resource centre
John Leggat, President & CEO

Nursing Homes

Steinbach: Rest Haven Nursing Home
Affiliated with: Southern Health-Santé Sud
Former Name: Rest Haven Care Services
185 Woodhaven Ave., Steinbach, MB R5G 1K7
Tel: 204-326-2206; *Fax:* 204-326-3521
hginfo@southernhealth.ca
www.havengroup.ca
Year Founded: 1946
Number of Beds: 60 long-term care beds
Note: An affiliate health corporation within Southern Health-Santé Sud. Owned & operated by seven area Evangelical Mennonite Conference churches. Attached to Woodhaven Manor (66 life lease suites & 20 rent-geared-to-income suites).
David Driedger, Chief Executive Officer
204-346-5004

Virden: Sherwood Nursing Home
Affiliated with: Prairie Mountain Health
PO Box 2000, Virden, MB R0M 2C0
Tel: 204-748-1546; *Fax:* 204-748-2053
www.assiniboine-rha.ca
Number of Beds: 46 long-term care beds; 1 respite care bed
Note: Programs & services include: adult day program; meals on wheels; palliative care; & congregate meal program.
G. Henuset, Area Manager
ghenuset@arha.ca

Virden: West-Man Nursing Home
Affiliated with: Prairie Mountain Health
PO Box 1630, Virden, MB R0M 2C0
Tel: 204-748-4335; *Fax:* 204-748-3432
www.assiniboine-rha.ca
Number of Beds: 49 personal care beds; 1 respite care bed
Note: Programs & services include: meals on wheels; palliative care; & occupational & physiotherapy.
G. Henuset, Area Manager
ghenuset@arha.ca

Retirement Residences

Selkirk: Cambridge House
Affiliated with: Interlake-Eastern Regional Health Authority
c/o Woodland Courts, 387 Annie St., Selkirk, MB R1A 3Y8
Tel: 204-785-1066; *Fax:* 204-482-4369
www.geriatricare.ca/cambridgehouse
Number of Beds: 34 rental & assisted living suites
Joyce Lloyd, Residence Manager
204-785-1066, jloyd@geriatricare.ca

Selkirk: Woodland Courts
Affiliated with: Interlake-Eastern Regional Health Authority
387 Annie St., Selkirk, MB R1A 3Y8
Tel: 204-785-1066; *Fax:* 204-482-4369
www.geriatricare.ca/woodlandcourts
Number of Beds: 53 one- & two-bedroom suites
Note: An assisted-living retirement community.
Joyce Lloyd, Residence Manager
204-785-1066, jloyd@geriatricare.ca

Shoal Lake: Lakeshore Lodge
Shoal Lake/Strathclair Health Centre
Affiliated with: Prairie Mountain Health
c/o Shoal Lake/Strathclair Health Centre, PO Box 490, Shoal Lake, MB 0J 1Z0
Tel: 204-759-2118
www.assiniboine-rha.ca
Number of Beds: 9 units
Note: Elderly Person's Housing
Kim Manuliak, Contact

Shoal Lake: Morley House
Shoal Lake/Strathclair Health Centre
Affiliated with: Prairie Mountain Health
PO Box 459, Shoal Lake, MB R0J 1Z0
Tel: 204-759-2118
www.assiniboine-rha.ca
Number of Beds: 18 units
Note: Elderly Person's Housing with on-call medical services
Susan Richardson, Contact

Winnipeg: Portsmouth
Revera Inc.
125 Portsmouth Blvd., Winnipeg, MB R3P 2M3
Tel: 204-284-5432
www.reveraliving.com/portsmouth
Thomas G. Wellner, President & CEO, Revera Inc.

Winnipeg: Rosewood
Revera Inc.
857 Wilkes Ave., Winnipeg, MB R3P 2M2
Tel: 204-487-9600
www.reveraliving.com/rosewood
Thomas G. Wellner, President & CEO, Revera Inc.

Winnipeg: St. James Kiwanis Village
Kiwanis Club of St. James
109 Sinawik Bay, Winnipeg, MB R3J 2Z4
Tel: 204-837-2305; *Fax:* 204-889-6476
stjameskiwanisvillage.ca
Year Founded: 1958
Note: Five separate seniors' housing projects surrounding a central recreation centre

Winnipeg: The Waverley
Revera Inc.
857 Wilkes Ave., Winnipeg, MB R3P 2M2
Tel: 204-487-9600
www.reveraliving.com/waverley
Thomas G. Wellner, President & CEO, Revera Inc.

Winnipeg: The Wellington
Revera Inc.
3161 Grant Ave., Winnipeg, MB R3R 3R1
Tel: 204-831-0788
www.reveraliving.com/wellington
Thomas G. Wellner, President & CEO, Revera Inc.

Personal Care Homes

Arborg: Arborg Personal Care Home
Affiliated with: Interlake-Eastern Regional Health Authority
Former Name: Pioneer Health Services Inc
PO Box 10, 233 St. Phillips Dr., Arborg, MB R0C 0A0
Tel: 204-376-5226; *Fax:* 204-376-3691
info@ierha.ca
www.ierha.ca

Number of Beds: 40 beds

Ashern: Ashern Personal Care Home
Affiliated with: Interlake-Eastern Regional Health Authority
PO Box 110, 1 Steenson Dr., Ashern, MB R0C 0E0
Tel: 204-768-5216; *Fax:* 204-768-2337
info@ierha.ca
www.ierha.ca

Number of Beds: 20 beds

Baldur: Baldur Personal Care Home
Baldur Health Centre
Affiliated with: Prairie Mountain Health
PO Box 128, Baldur, MB R0K 0B0
Tel: 204-535-2373; *Fax:* 204-535-2116
www.assiniboine-rha.ca

Number of Beds: 20 beds
D. Rea, Area Manager
drea@arha.ca

Beausejour: East-Gate Lodge
Affiliated with: Interlake-Eastern Regional Health Authority
PO Box 1690, 646 James Ave., Beausejour, MB R0E 0C0
Tel: 204-268-1029; *Fax:* 204-268-3525
info@ierha.ca
www.ierha.ca

Number of Beds: 60 beds

Benito: Benito Health Centre Personal Care Home
Affiliated with: Prairie Mountain Health
PO Box 490, 200 - 1st St. SE, Benito, MB R0L 0C0
Tel: 204-539-2815
prha@prh.mb.ca
www.prha.mb.ca

Number of Beds: 20 beds
Note: Includes home care services (204-539-2075)

Birtle: Birtle Personal Care Home
Birtle Health Centre
Affiliated with: Prairie Mountain Health
PO Box 2000, Birtle, MB R0M 0C0
Tel: 204-842-3317; *Fax:* 204-842-3375
www.assiniboine-rha.ca

Number of Beds: 20 beds
Note: Programs & services include: community bath program; palliative care; occupational & physiotherapy; dietitian; congregate meal program; & Elderly Persons Housing Unit (30 suites).
D. Ciprick, Area Manager
dciprick@arha.ca

Boissevain: Evergreen Place
Affiliated with: Prairie Mountain Health
PO Box 899, Boissevain, MB R0K 0E0
Tel: 204-534-6389; *Fax:* 204-534-6487
Number of Beds: 20 beds
D. Graham, Area Manager
dgraham@arha.ca

Boissevain: Westview Lodge
Boissevain Health Centre
Affiliated with: Prairie Mountain Health
PO Box 819, Boissevain, MB R0K 0E0
Tel: 204-534-2455; *Fax:* 204-534-6633
www.assiniboine-rha.ca

Number of Beds: 42 beds

Brandon: Dinsdale Personal Care Home
Affiliated with: Prairie Mountain Health
510 - 6th St., Brandon, MB R7A 3N9
Tel: 204-727-3636; *Fax:* 204-727-2103
dinsdalepch@dinsdalepch.ca
dinsdalepch.ca

Number of Beds: 60 private rooms
Wayne McDonough, Executive Director
wayne_mcdonough@can.salvationarmy.or

Brandon: Fairview Home
Affiliated with: Prairie Mountain Health
1351 - 13th St., Brandon, MB R7A 4S5
Tel: 204-578-2600; *Fax:* 204-578-2842
www.brandonrha.mb.ca

Number of Beds: 248 beds
Note: Programs & services include: long-term care & adult day program.
Shannon Webber, Director, PCH Programs - Brandon

Brandon: Hillcrest Place Inc.
Extendicare Canada
Affiliated with: Prairie Mountain Health
930 - 26th St., Brandon, MB R7B 2B8
Tel: 204-728-6690; *Fax:* 204-726-0089
cnh_hillcrestplace@extendicare.com
www.extendicarecanada.com

Number of Beds: 100 beds

Brandon: Rideau Park Personal Care Home
Affiliated with: Prairie Mountain Health
525 Victoria Ave. East, Brandon, MB R7A 6S9
Tel: 204-578-2670; *Fax:* 204-578-2848
www.brandonrha.mb.ca

Number of Beds: 100 beds
Shannon Webber, Director, PCH Programs - Brandon

Brandon: Valleyview Care Centre
Revera Inc.
Affiliated with: Prairie Mountain Health
3015 Victoria Ave., Brandon, MB R7B 2K2
Tel: 204-728-2030; *Fax:* 204-729-8351
www.reveraliving.com/valleyview

Thomas G. Wellner, President & CEO, Revera Inc.

Carberry: Carberry Plains Personal Care Home
Carberry Plains Health Centre
Affiliated with: Prairie Mountain Health
PO Box 2000, Carberry, MB R0K 0H0
Tel: 204-834-2144; *Fax:* 204-834-3333
www.assiniboine-rha.ca

Number of Beds: 36 beds
Note: Programs & services include: adult day program; community bath program; dietitian; meals on wheels; palliative care; & occupational & physiotherapy.
J. Gabler, Area Manager
jgabler@arha.ca

Carman: Boyne Lodge
Affiliated with: Southern Health-Santé Sud
PO Box 910, 120 - 4th Ave. SW, Carman, MB R0G 0J0
Tel: 204-745-6715; *Fax:* 204-745-6152
www.southernhealth.ca

Number of Beds: 70 long-term care beds; 11 alternative care beds
Number of Employees: 190
Note: Attached to Boyne Towers seniors' apartment complex (36 studios; 4 single suites).
Mary Heard, Director, Health Services - Carman
mheard@southernhealth.ca

Dauphin: Dauphin Personal Care Home
Affiliated with: Prairie Mountain Health
625 - 3 St. SW, Dauphin, MB R7N 1R7
Tel: 204-638-3010
www.prha.mb.ca

Number of Beds: 90 beds; 5 respite beds
Note: Includes home care services (204-638-2105)

Dauphin: St. Paul's Home
Affiliated with: Prairie Mountain Health
703 Jackson St., Dauphin, MB R7N 2N2
Tel: 204-638-3129
www.prha.mb.ca

Number of Beds: 70 beds
Note: Offers an adult day program.

Deloraine: Bren-Del-Win Lodge
Deloraine Health Centre
Affiliated with: Prairie Mountain Health
PO Box 447, Deloraine, MB R0M 0M0
Tel: 204-747-1826; *Fax:* 204-747-2284
www.assiniboine-rha.ca

Number of Beds: 30 beds
Note: Includes a meals on wheels program
D. Graham, Area Manager
dgraham@arha.ca

Deloraine: Delwynda Court
Deloraine Health Centre
Affiliated with: Prairie Mountain Health
PO Box 447, Deloraine, MB R0M 0M0
Tel: 204-747-1816; *Fax:* 204-747-3845
www.assiniboine-rha.ca

Number of Beds: 16 beds
Note: Programs & services include: adult day program & community bath program.
D. Graham, Area Manager
dgraham@arha.ca

Elkhorn: Elkwood Manor Personal Care Home
Affiliated with: Prairie Mountain Health
PO Box 70, Elkhorn, MB R0M 0N0
Tel: 204-845-2575; *Fax:* 204-845-2371
www.assiniboine-rha.ca

Number of Beds: 24 beds
Note: Programs & services include: community bath program; itinerant physician clinic; palliative care; occupational & physiotherapy; dietitian; meals on wheels; public health; mental health; & home care.
G. Henuset, Area Manager
ghenuset@arha.ca

Emerson: Emerson Personal Care Home
Affiliated with: Southern Health-Santé Sud
PO Box 428, 26 Main St., Emerson, MB R0A 0L0
Tel: 204-373-2109; *Fax:* 204-373-2748
info@southernhealth.ca
www.southernhealth.ca

Number of Beds: 20 beds
Ronald Morrice, Director, Health Services - Morris, Emerson & Area
rmorrice@southernhealth.ca

Erickson: Erickson Personal Care Home
Erickson Health Centre
Affiliated with: Prairie Mountain Health
PO Box 250, Erickson, MB R0J 0P0
Tel: 204-636-7777; *Fax:* 204-636-2471
Number of Beds: 16 beds
Note: Programs & services include: community bath program; palliative care; occupational & physiotherapy; dietitian; & meals on wheels.
M. Koroscil, Area Manager
mkoroscil@arha.ca

Eriksdale: Eriksdale Personal Care Home
Affiliated with: Interlake-Eastern Regional Health Authority
PO Box 130, 40 Railway Ave., Eriksdale, MB R0C 0W0
Tel: 204-739-4416; *Fax:* 204-739-5593
info@ierha.ca
www.ierha.ca

Number of Beds: 20 beds

Fisher Branch: Fisher Branch Personal Care Home
Affiliated with: Interlake-Eastern Regional Health Authority
PO Box 119, 7 Chalet Dr., Fisher Branch, MB R0C 0Z0
Tel: 204-372-8703; *Fax:* 204-372-8710
info@ierha.ca
www.ierha.ca

Number of Beds: 30 beds

Flin Flon: Flin Flon Personal Care Home
Affiliated with: Northern Regional Health Authority
PO Box 340, 50 Church St., Flin Flon, MB R8A 1N2
Tel: 204-687-9630; *Fax:* 204-687-9613
www.northernhealthregion.ca

Number of Beds: 30 beds

Flin Flon: Northern Lights Manor
Affiliated with: Northern Regional Health Authority
274 Bracken St., Flin Flon, MB R8A 1P4
Tel: 204-687-7325; *Fax:* 204-687-4573
www.norman-rha.mb.ca

Number of Beds: 36 beds

Gilbert Plains: Gilbert Plains Personal Care Home
Affiliated with: Prairie Mountain Health
PO Box 368, 100 Cutforth St. North, Gilbert Plains, MB R0L 0X0
Tel: 204-548-2161
www.prha.mb.ca

Number of Beds: 30 beds; 1 respite bed
Note: Attached to Gilbert Plains Health Centre physician clinic. Includes home care services (204-548-2765).

Gillam: **Gillam Hospital**
Affiliated with: Northern Regional Health Authority
PO Box 2000, 115 Gillam Dr., Gillam, MB R0B 0L0
Tel: 204-652-2600; *Fax:* 204-652-2536
www.northernhealthregion.ca
Number of Beds: 3 long-term care beds

Gimli: **Gimli - Betel Personal Care Home**
Betel Home Foundation
Affiliated with: Interlake-Eastern Regional Health Authority
PO Box 10, Gimli, MB R0C 1B0
Tel: 204-642-5556; *Fax:* 204-642-7243
www.betelhomefoundation.ca/gimli.html
Number of Beds: 80 beds
Angela Eyjolfson, Chief Executive Officer
aeyjolfson@ierha.ca

Gladstone: **Third Crossing Manor**
Affiliated with: Southern Health-Santé Sud
PO Box 1000, 175 Dennis St. West, Gladstone, MB R0J 0T0
Tel: 204-385-2474; *Fax:* 204-385-2163
www.southernhealth.ca
Year Founded: 1974
Number of Beds: 50 residential capacity
JoAnn Egilson, Director, Health Services - Gladstone
jegilson@southernhealth.ca

Glenboro: **Glenboro Personal Care Home**
Glenboro Health Centre
Affiliated with: Prairie Mountain Health
PO Box 310, Glenboro, MB R0K 0X0
Tel: 204-827-5304; *Fax:* 204-827-2199
www.assiniboine-rha.ca
Number of Beds: 20 beds
Note: Programs & services include: adult day program; community bath program; palliative care; occupational & physiotherapy; dietitian; & meals on wheels.
D. Rea, Area Manager
drea@arha.ca

Grandview: **Grandview Personal Care Home**
Affiliated with: Prairie Mountain Health
PO Box 130, 308 Jackson St., Grandview, MB R0L 0Y0
Tel: 204-546-2769
www.prha.mb.ca
Number of Beds: 39 beds; 1 respite bed
Note: Includes home care services (204-548-2765). Offers an adult day program for residents.

Grunthal: **Menno Home for the Aged**
Affiliated with: Southern Health-Santé Sud
PO Box 280, 235 Park St., Grunthal, MB R0A 0R0
Tel: 204-434-6496; *Fax:* 204-434-9131
mennohome@pli.mb.ca
mhfta.mennonite.net
Year Founded: 1960
Number of Beds: 40 beds
Note: An affiliate health corporation within Southern Health-Santé Sud. A faith-based care provider. Attached to Greendale Estate, a supportive housing & assisted living apartment complex built in 2010.

Hamiota: **Hamiota Personal Care Home**
Hamiota Health Centre
Affiliated with: Prairie Mountain Health
177 Birch Ave., Hamiota, MB R0M 0T0
Tel: 204-764-2412; *Fax:* 204-764-2049
www.assiniboine-rha.ca
Number of Beds: 30 beds
Note: Programs & services include: adult day program; community bath program; palliative care; occupational & physiotherapy; dietitian; meals on wheels; congregate meal program; & Lilac Elderly Person Housing (30 units).
R. Yaremchuk, Area Manager
ryaremchuk@arha.ca

Hartney: **Hartney Personal Care Home**
Hartney Health Centre
Affiliated with: Prairie Mountain Health
PO Box 280, Hartney, MB R0M 0X0
Tel: 204-858-2054; *Fax:* 204-858-2303
www.assiniboine-rha.ca
Number of Beds: 20 beds
Note: Programs & services include: adult day program; community bath program; palliative care; occupational & physiotherapy; dietitian; & meals on wheels.
K. Oberlin, Area Manager
koberlin@arha.ca

Killarney: **Tri-Lake Personal Care Home**
Tri-Lake Health Centre
Affiliated with: Prairie Mountain Health
Former Name: Bayside Personal Care Home Inc.
PO Box 5000, Killarney, MB R0K 1G0
Tel: 204-523-4661; *Fax:* 204-523-8948
www.assiniboine-rha.ca
Number of Beds: 60 beds
Note: Programs & services include: adult day program; community bath program; palliative care; occupational & physiotherapy; dietitian; & meals on wheels.
D. Obach, Area Manager
dobach@arha.ca

Lac du Bonnet: **Lac du Bonnet Personal Care Home**
Affiliated with: Interlake-Eastern Regional Health Authority
PO Box 1030, 75 McIntosh Ave., Lac du Bonnet, MB R0E 1A0
Tel: 204-345-1222; *Fax:* 204-345-9245
info@ierha.ca
www.ierha.ca
Number of Beds: 20 beds

Lundar: **Lundar Personal Care Home**
Affiliated with: Interlake-Eastern Regional Health Authority
97 - 1st St. South, Lundar, MB R0C 1Y0
Tel: 204-762-5663; *Fax:* 204-762-5164
Number of Beds: 20 beds

Lynn Lake: **Lynn Lake Hospital**
Affiliated with: Northern Regional Health Authority
PO Box 2030, 2040 Camp St., Lynn Lake, MB R0B 0W0
Tel: 204-356-2474; *Fax:* 204-356-8023
www.northernhealthregion.ca
Number of Beds: 8 long-term care beds

MacGregor: **MacGregor Personal Care Home**
Affiliated with: Southern Health-Santé Sud
PO Box 250, 87 Grafton St. South, MacGregor, MB R0H 0R0
Tel: 204-685-2850; *Fax:* 204-685-2529
info@southernhealth.ca
www.southernhealth.ca
Number of Beds: 20 beds
Margaret Warner, Director, Health Services/Seniors - Portage & Area
mwarner@southernhealth.ca

Manitou: **Pembina-Manitou Personal Care Home**
Affiliated with: Southern Health-Santé Sud
PO Box 129, 232 Carrie St., Manitou, MB R0G 1G0
Tel: 204-242-2744; *Fax:* 204-242-3062
info@southernhealth.ca
www.southernhealth.ca
Number of Beds: 18 beds
Kristal McKitrick-Bazin, Director, Health Services - Manitou
kbazin@southernhealth.ca

McCreary: **McCreary/Alonsa Personal Care Home**
Affiliated with: Prairie Mountain Health
PO Box 250, 613 PTH 50, McCreary, MB R0J 1B0
Tel: 204-835-2482
www.prha.mb.ca
Number of Beds: 20 beds
Note: Offers an adult day program.

Melita: **Melita Personal Care Home**
Melita Health Centre
Affiliated with: Prairie Mountain Health
PO Box 459, 147 Summit St., Melita, MB R0M 1L0
Tel: 204-522-3403; *Fax:* 204-522-3161
www.assiniboine-rha.ca
Year Founded: 1967
Number of Beds: 20 beds
Note: Programs & services include: adult day program; community bath program; palliative care; occupational & physiotherapy; dietitian; & meals on wheels.
K. Oberlin, Area Manager
koberlin@arha.ca

Minnedosa: **Minnedosa Personal Care Home**
Minnedosa Health Centre
Affiliated with: Prairie Mountain Health
PO Box 960, Minnedosa, MB R0J 1E0
Tel: 204-867-2569; *Fax:* 204-867-2239
www.assiniboine-rha.ca
Number of Beds: 50 personal care beds
Note: Programs & services include: adult day program & community bath program.
M. Koroscil, Area Manager
mkoroscil@arha.ca

Morden: **Tabor Home Inc.**
Affiliated with: Southern Health-Santé Sud
230 - 9th St. South, Morden, MB R6M 1Y3
Tel: 204-822-4848; *Fax:* 204-822-5289
info@taborhome.ca
www.taborhome.ca
Year Founded: 1951
Number of Beds: 60 beds; 12 alternative need beds
Note: An affiliate health corporation within Southern Health-Santé Sud. A faith-based facility. Programs & services include: nursing; activities; social work; & adult day program. Elderly Person's Housing available in Tabor Units & Tabor Apartments.
Sherry Hildebrand, Chief Executive Officer
shildebrand@taborhome.ca

Morris: **Red River Valley Lodge Inc. (RRVL)**
Affiliated with: Southern Health-Santé Sud
PO Box 507, 136 Ottawa St. West, Morris, MB R0G 1K0
Tel: 204-746-2394; *Fax:* 204-746-2123
info@southernhealth.ca
www.southernhealth.ca
Year Founded: 1974
Number of Beds: 40 beds
Note: Provides nursing care & medical supervision.
Ronald Morrice, Director, Health Services - Morris & Area
rmorrice@southernhealth.ca

Neepawa: **Neepawa Personal Care Home**
Affiliated with: Prairie Mountain Health
Also Known As: Country Meadows
Neepawa, MB R0J 1H0
Tel: 204-476-2383; *Fax:* 204-476-3645
www.assiniboine-rha.ca
Number of Beds: 100 personal care beds
Note: Programs & services include: adult day program; community bath program; & respite program.
J. Gabler, Area Manager
jgabler@arha.ca

Nelson House: **Nisichawaysihk Personal Care Home**
Also Known As: NCN Personal Care Home
General Delivery, Nelson House, MB R0B 1A0
Tel: 204-484-2350; *Fax:* 204-484-2392
ncninfo@ncncree.com
www.ncncree.com/ncn/pch.html
Number of Beds: 24 beds

Niverville: **Heritage Life Personal Care Home**
Niverville Heritage Holdings Inc. (NHHI)
Affiliated with: Southern Health-Santé Sud
Also Known As: Heritage Life - Retirement Living
#SS40, 100 Heritage Trail, Niverville, MB R0A 1E0
Tel: 204-388-5000
heritagecentre.ca/life-lease
Social Media: www.facebook.com/nivervilleheritagecentre
Note: An affiliate health corporation within Southern Health-Santé Sud. Located within the Niverville Heritage Centre, along with the Niverville Primary Health Care Centre, Niverville Medical Clinic, Niverville Heritage Dental Centre, Growing Minds Child Care Centre, Niverville Pharmacy & Niverville Service to Seniors.
Steve Neufeld, Chief Operating Officer, Niverville Heritage Centre
steve.neufeld@heritagecentre.ca

Norway House: **Pinaow Wachi Inc. Personal Care Home**
Affiliated with: Norway House Health Services Inc.
PO Box 98, Norway House, MB R0B 1B0
Tel: 204-359-6606; *Fax:* 204-359-6949
www.nhhsinc.ca
Note: Offers adult day care

Notre Dame de Lourdes: **Foyer Notre Dame**
Affiliated with: Southern Health-Santé Sud
PO Box 190, 40 Rogers St., Notre Dame de Lourdes, MB R0G 1M0
Tel: 204-248-2092; *Fax:* 204-248-2499
info@southernhealth.ca
www.southernhealth.ca
Number of Beds: 60 beds
Number of Employees: 170
Note: Staff include physicians, nurses, a social worker, a registered psychiatric nurse, an occupational therapist, a recreation worker, a dietitian & support staff. The home includes an Alzheimer Unit.
Mona Spencer, Director, Health Services - Notre Dame & St. Claude
mspencer@southernhealth.ca

Oakbank: Kin Place Personal Care Home
Affiliated with: Interlake-Eastern Regional Health Authority
PO Box 28, 680 Pine Dr., Oakbank, MB R0E 1J0
Tel: 204-444-2004; *Fax:* 204-444-7868
info@ierha.ca
www.ierha.ca
Number of Beds: 40 beds

Pilot Mound: Prairie View Lodge
Affiliated with: Southern Health-Santé Sud
#26, 424 Broadway Ave. West, Pilot Mound, MB R0G 1P0
Tel: 204-825-2717; *Fax:* 204-873-2185
www.rocklakehealthdistrict.ca/prairieviewlodge.shtml
Number of Beds: 30 beds (21 EPH units)
Number of Employees: 125
Note: An affiliate health corporation within Southern Health-Santé Sud.
Ginger Collins, CEO & Director, Health Services - Rock Lake Health District
vcollins@southernhealth.ca

Pilot Mound: Rock Lake Personal Care Home Inc.
Affiliated with: Southern Health-Santé Sud
#27, 115 Brown St. South, Pilot Mound, MB R0G 1P0
Tel: 204-825-2246; *Fax:* 204-873-2185
www.rocklakehealthdistrict.ca/personalcarehome.shtml
Number of Beds: 24 beds
Number of Employees: 125
Note: An affiliate health corporation within Southern Health-Santé Sud.
Ginger Collins, CEO & Director, Health Services - Rock Lake Health District
vcollins@southernhealth.ca

Pine Falls: Sunnywood Personal Care Home
Affiliated with: Interlake-Eastern Regional Health Authority
PO Box 2000, 37 Maple St., Pine Falls, MB R0E 1M0
Tel: 204-367-8201; *Fax:* 204-367-4583
info@ierha.ca
www.ierha.ca
Number of Beds: 20 beds

Portage la Prairie: Douglas Campbell Lodge
Affiliated with: Southern Health-Santé Sud
160 - 9 St. SE, Portage la Prairie, MB R1N 3T6
Tel: 204-239-6006; *Fax:* 204-239-0055
www.southernhealth.ca
Number of Beds: 60 beds
Margaret Warner, Director, Health Services/Seniors - Portage & Area
mwarner@southernhealth.ca

Portage la Prairie: Lions Prairie Manor
Affiliated with: Southern Health-Santé Sud
24 - 9th St. SE, Portage la Prairie, MB R1N 3V4
Tel: 204-857-7864; *Fax:* 204-857-8207
info@southernhealth.ca
www.southernhealth.ca
Number of Beds: 136 beds
Margaret Warner, Director, Health Services/Seniors - Portage & Area
mwarner@southernhealth.ca

Reston: Reston Personal Care Home
Reston Health Centre
Affiliated with: Prairie Mountain Health
PO Box 250, Reston, MB R0M 1X0
Tel: 204-877-3925; *Fax:* 204-877-3998
www.assiniboine-rha.ca
Number of Beds: 20 beds
Note: Programs & services include: community bath program; palliative care; occupational & physiotherapy; dietitian; & meals on wheels.
K. Oberlin, Area Manager
koberlin@arha.ca

Rivers: Rivers Personal Care Home
Rivers Health Centre
Affiliated with: Prairie Mountain Health
PO Box 428, Rivers, MB R0K 1X0
Tel: 204-328-5321; *Fax:* 204-328-7130
www.assiniboine-rha.ca
Number of Beds: 20 beds
Note: Programs & services include: adult day program; palliative care; occupational & physiotherapy; dietitian; meals on wheels; & Elderly Person's Housing (12 units).
G. Paddock, Area Manager
gpaddock@arha.ca

Roblin: Crocus Court Personal Care Home
Affiliated with: Prairie Mountain Health
PO Box 940, 15 Hospital St., Roblin, MB R0L 1P0
Tel: 204-937-2149
www.prha.mb.ca
Number of Beds: 60 beds; 1 respite bed
Note: Offers an adult day program for residents.

Rossburn: Rossburn Personal Care Home
Rossburn Health Centre
Affiliated with: Prairie Mountain Health
PO Box 40, Rossburn, MB R0J 1V0
Tel: 204-859-2413; *Fax:* 204-859-2526
www.assiniboine-rha.ca
Number of Beds: 20 beds
Note: Programs & services include: community bath program; palliative care; occupational & physiotherapy; & dietitian.
D. Ciprick, Area Manager
dciprick@arha.ca

Russell: Russell Personal Care Home
Russell Health Centre
Affiliated with: Prairie Mountain Health
PO Box 2, Russell, MB R0J 1W0
Tel: 204-773-3117; *Fax:* 204-773-2142
Number of Beds: 40 long-term care beds
Note: Programs & services include: adult day program & community bath program.
D. Ciprick, Area Manager
dciprick@arha.ca

Sandy Lake: Sandy Lake Personal Care Home
Affiliated with: Prairie Mountain Health
Former Name: Sandy Lake Medical Nursing Home
PO Box 7, Sandy Lake, MB R0J 1X0
Tel: 204-585-2107; *Fax:* 204-585-5352
www.assiniboine-rha.ca
Number of Beds: 35 beds
Note: Programs & services include: palliative care; occupational & physiotherapy; dietitian; & pharmacy.
M. Koroscil, Area Manager
mkoroscil@arha.ca

Selkirk: Red River Place
Extendicare Canada
Affiliated with: Interlake-Eastern Regional Health Authority
133 Manchester Ave., Selkirk, MB R1A 0B5
Tel: 204-482-3036; *Fax:* 204-482-9499
lpalmer@extendicare.com
www.extendicarecanada.com/selkirk
Number of Beds: 104 beds
Note: Personal care facility, member of the Long Term Care Association of Manitoba

Selkirk: Selkirk - Betel Personal Care Home
Betel Home Foundation
Affiliated with: Interlake-Eastern Regional Health Authority
212 Manchester Ave., Selkirk, MB R1A 0B6
Tel: 204-482-5469; *Fax:* 204-482-4651
www.betelhomefoundation.ca/selkirk.html
Number of Beds: 62 single rooms; 15 double rooms
Angela Eyjolfson, Chief Executive Officer
aeyjolfson@ierha.ca

Selkirk: Tudor House
Affiliated with: Interlake-Eastern Regional Health Authority
800 Manitoba Ave., Selkirk, MB R3C 2C9
Tel: 204-482-6601; *Fax:* 204-482-4369
tudor@geriatricare.ca
www.geriatricare.ca/tudorhouse
Year Founded: 1971
Number of Beds: 76 beds
Note: Specialties: Care for seniors, physically & mentally handicapped adults, & persons with dementia; Hospice-type care for the dying
John Ashley Martyniw, CEO/Administrator

Shoal Lake: Shoal Lake/Strathclair Personal Care Home
Shoal Lake/Strathclair Health Centre
Affiliated with: Prairie Mountain Health
PO Box 490, Shoal Lake, MB R0J 1Z0
Tel: 204-759-2336; *Fax:* 204-759-2230
www.assiniboine-rha.ca
Number of Beds: 40 beds
Note: Programs & services include: community bath program; palliative care; occupational & physiotherapy; dietitian; & meals on wheels.
R. Yaremchuk, Area Manager
ryaremchuk@arha.ca

Snow Lake: Snow Lake Health Centre
Affiliated with: Northern Regional Health Authority
PO Box 453, 100 Lakeshore Dr. East, Snow Lake, MB R0B 1M0
Tel: 204-358-2597; *Fax:* 204-358-7310
www.northernhealthregion.ca
Number of Beds: 3 long-term care beds

Souris: Souris Personal Care Home
Souris Health Centre
Affiliated with: Prairie Mountain Health
PO Box 10, Souris, MB R0K 2C0
Tel: 204-483-2121; *Fax:* 204-483-2310
www.assiniboine-rha.ca
Number of Beds: 42 long-term care beds; 1 respite care bed
Note: Programs & services include: adult day program; community bath program; palliative care; occupational & physiotherapy; dietitian; & meals on wheels.
G. Paddock, Area Manager
gpaddock@arha.ca

St Pierre Jolys: Repos Jolys
Affiliated with: Southern Health-Santé Sud
PO Box 320, 354 Prefontaine Ave., St Pierre Jolys, MB R0A 1V0
Tel: 204-433-7443
info@southernhealth.ca
www.southernhealth.ca
Year Founded: 1995
Number of Beds: 22 beds
Note: Part of the Centre Médico-Social De Salaberry District Health Centre
Norm Vigier, Director, Health Services - St-Pierre-Jolys & Area
nvigier@southernhealth.ca

Ste Anne: Villa Youville Inc.
Affiliated with: Southern Health-Santé Sud
15 Charrière Rd., Ste Anne, MB R5H 1C9
Tel: 204-422-5624; *Fax:* 204-422-5842
info@southernhealth.ca
www.southernhealth.ca
Year Founded: 2002
Number of Beds: 85 suites; 24 supportive housing; 5 assisted-living units
Note: An affiliate health corporation within Southern Health-Santé Sud.

Ste Rose: Dr. Gendreau Personal Care Home
Affiliated with: Prairie Mountain Health
PO Box 420, 515 Mission St., Ste Rose, MB R0L 1S0
Tel: 204-447-2019
www.prha.mb.ca
Number of Beds: 65 beds; 1 respite bed
Note: Offers an adult day program.

Steinbach: Bethesda Place
Affiliated with: Southern Health-Santé Sud
399 Hospital St., Steinbach, MB R5G 0E6
Tel: 204-326-6411
info@southernhealth.ca
www.southernhealth.ca
Year Founded: 2002
Note: Can house up to 60 residents in four community groupings; located adjacent to Bethesda Regional Health Centre.
Debbie Rigaux, Clinical Manager
drigaux@southernhealth.ca

Stonewall: Rosewood Lodge Personal Care Home
Affiliated with: Interlake-Eastern Regional Health Authority
513 - 1 Ave. North, Stonewall, MB R0C 2Z0
Tel: 204-467-5257; *Fax:* 204-467-4750
info@ierha.ca
www.ierha.ca
Number of Beds: 50 beds

Swan River: Swan River Valley Personal Care Home Inc.
Affiliated with: Prairie Mountain Health
PO Box 1390, 334 - 8 Ave. South, Swan River, MB R0L 1Z0
Tel: 204-734-4521
www.prha.mb.ca
Number of Beds: 45 beds; 2 respite beds
Note: Includes home care services (204-734-6602)

Swan River: Swan Valley Lodge (1991) Inc.
Affiliated with: Prairie Mountain Health
PO Box 1450, 1013 Main St., Swan River, MB R0L 1Z0
Tel: 204-734-3441
www.prha.mb.ca
Number of Beds: 70 beds
Note: Offers an adult day program.

Teulon: Goodwin Lodge Personal Care Home
Affiliated with: Interlake-Eastern Regional Health Authority
PO Box 89, 162 - 3rd Ave. SE, Teulon, MB R0C 3B0
Tel: 204-886-2108; *Fax:* 204-886-2653
info@ierha.ca
www.ierha.ca
Number of Beds: 20 beds

The Pas: St. Paul's Personal Care Home
Affiliated with: Northern Regional Health Authority
PO Box 240, 34 - 2nd St., The Pas, MB R9A 1K4
Tel: 204-623-9226; *Fax:* 204-623-9605
www.northernhealthregion.ca
Number of Beds: 60 beds

Thompson: Northern Spirit Manor
Affiliated with: Northern Regional Health Authority
879 Thompson Dr., Thompson, MB R8N 0A9
Tel: 204-778-3805; *Fax:* 204-778-1563
www.northernhealthregion.ca
Number of Beds: 35 beds

Treherne: Tiger Hills Personal Care Home
Affiliated with: Prairie Mountain Health
Former Name: Tiger Hills Manor Inc.
PO Box 130, Treherne, MB R0G 2V0
Tel: 204-723-2133; *Fax:* 204-723-2869
www.assiniboine-rha.ca
Number of Beds: 22 beds
Note: Programs & services include: adult day program; community bath program; palliative care; occupational & physiotherapy; dietitian; meals on wheels; Elderly Person's Housing (21 units).
D. Rea, Area Manager
drea@arha.ca

Wawanesa: Wawanesa Personal Care Home
Wawanesa Health Centre
Affiliated with: Prairie Mountain Health
PO Box 309, 506 George St., Wawanesa, MB R0K 2G0
Tel: 204-824-2335; *Fax:* 204-824-2148
www.assiniboine-rha.ca
Number of Beds: 20 beds
Note: Programs & services include: community bath program; palliative care; occupational & physiotherapy; dietitian; & meals on wheels.
D. Obach, Area Manager
dobach@arha.ca

Whitemouth: Whitemouth District Health Centre PCH
Affiliated with: Interlake-Eastern Regional Health Authority
PO Box 160, 75 Hospital St., Whitemouth, MB R0E 2G0
Tel: 204-348-7191; *Fax:* 204-348-7911
info@ierha.ca
www.ierha.ca
Number of Beds: 26 beds

Winkler: Salem Home Inc.
Affiliated with: Southern Health-Santé Sud
165 - 15 St., Winkler, MB R6W 1T8
Tel: 204-325-4316; *Fax:* 204-325-5442
salemhome.ca
Number of Beds: 145 beds
Number of Employees: 290
Note: An affiliate health corporation within Southern Health-Santé Sud. Owned & operated by 13 Mennonite churches.
Sherry Janzen, Contact
sjanzen@salemhome.net

Winnipeg: 285 Pembina Inc.
Bethania Group
Affiliated with: Winnipeg Regional Health Authority
Also Known As: Deaf Centre
285 Pembina Hwy., Winnipeg, MB R3L 2E1
Tel: 204-478-7954
www.bethania.ca
Note: Independent living residence for adults who are deaf or hard of hearing, & students enrolled in the Deaf Studies Program.

Winnipeg: Actionmarguerite (Saint-Boniface)
Affiliated with: Winnipeg Regional Health Authority
Former Name: Taché Centre
Also Known As: Actionmarguerite - Taché
185 Despins St., Winnipeg, MB R2H 2B3
Tel: 204-233-3692; *Fax:* 204-233-6803
www.actionmarguerite.ca
Year Founded: 1935
Number of Beds: 309 beds
Number of Employees: 470
Note: Programs & service include: personal care; dementia care; adults with complex health needs; & day program.
Charles Gagné, Chief Executive Officer, Actionmarguerite

Winnipeg: Actionmarguerite (Saint-Vital)
Affiliated with: Winnipeg Regional Health Authority
Former Name: Foyer Valade
Also Known As: Actionmarguerite - Valade
450 River Rd., Winnipeg, MB R2M 5M4
Tel: 204-254-3332; *Fax:* 204-254-0329
www.actionmarguerite.ca
Year Founded: 1988
Number of Beds: 154 beds; 39-bed dementia care unit
Number of Employees: 220
Note: Owned by the Catholic Health Corporation of Manitoba
Charles Gagné, Chief Executive Officer, Actionmarguerite

Winnipeg: Beacon Hill Lodge
Revera Inc.
Affiliated with: Winnipeg Regional Health Authority
190 Fort St., Winnipeg, MB R3C 1C9
Tel: 204-942-7541; *Fax:* 204-944-0135
www.reveraliving.com/beaconhill
Number of Beds: 175 beds
Thomas G. Wellnershek, President & CEO, Revera Inc.
Tara-Lee Yakielashek, Administrator

Winnipeg: Bethania Mennonite Personal Care Home Inc.
Bethania Group
Affiliated with: Winnipeg Regional Health Authority
1045 Concordia Ave., Winnipeg, MB R2K 3S7
Tel: 204-667-0795; *Fax:* 204-667-7078
general.inquiries@bethania.ca
www.bethania.ca/bethania-pch
Number of Beds: 148 beds; 2 respite care beds
Gary Ledoux, Chief Executive Officer, Bethania Group
Jack Friesen, Acting Manager, Resident Care

Winnipeg: Calvary Place Personal Care Home
Affiliated with: Winnipeg Regional Health Authority
1325 Erin St., Winnipeg, MB R3E 3R6
Tel: 204-943-4424; *Fax:* 204-783-7524
calvaryplacepch.ca
Number of Beds: 100 beds
Note: Sponsored by the Heritage Benevolent Association of Manitoba, Inc.
Kevin Friesen, CEO/DOC
kfriesen@calvaryplace.mb.ca

Winnipeg: Charleswood Care Centre
Revera Inc.
Affiliated with: Winnipeg Regional Health Authority
5501 Roblin Blvd., Winnipeg, MB R3R 0G8
Tel: 204-888-3363; *Fax:* 204-896-4763
www.reveraliving.com/charleswood
Number of Beds: 155 beds
Thomas G. Wellnerc, President & CEO, Revera Inc.
Linda Sundevic, Administrator

Winnipeg: Concordia Place Personal Care Home
Concordia Hospital
Affiliated with: Winnipeg Regional Health Authority
1000 Molson St., Winnipeg, MB R2K 4L5
Tel: 204-661-7372; *Fax:* 204-661-7297
www.concordiahospital.mb.ca/cp.html
Year Founded: 2000
Number of Beds: 140 beds
Les W. Janzen, Chief Operating Officer

Winnipeg: Convalescent Home of Winnipeg
Affiliated with: Winnipeg Regional Health Authority
276 Hugo St. North, Winnipeg, MB R3M 2N6
Tel: 204-453-4663; *Fax:* 204-453-7149
www.wrha.mb.ca
Number of Beds: 84 residents
Sharon Wilms, Administrator

Winnipeg: Donwood Manor Personal Care Home
Affiliated with: Winnipeg Regional Health Authority
171 Donwood Dr., Winnipeg, MB R2G 0V9
Tel: 204-668-4410; *Fax:* 204-663-5429
info@donwoodmanor.org
www.donwoodmanor.org
Year Founded: 1970
Number of Beds: 121 beds
Note: Faith-based facility supported by eight Winnipeg-based Mennonite Brethren Churches.
James Heinrichs, Chief Executive Officer

Winnipeg: Extendicare - Oakview Place
Extendicare Canada
Affiliated with: Winnipeg Regional Health Authority
2395 Ness Ave., Winnipeg, MB R3J 1A5
Tel: 204-888-3005; *Fax:* 204-831-8101
cnh_oakviewplace@extendicare.com
www.extendicarecanada.com/winnipegoakviewplace
Number of Beds: 245 beds; 1 respite bed
Note: Programs & services include: nursing & supportive care; rehabilitation & rehabilitative services; optometry services; dental services; social & therapeutic programs; adult day program; care for persons with alzheimer's disease & related dementias; & palliative care.
Loree Simcox, Administrator

Winnipeg: Extendicare - Tuxedo Villa
Extendicare Canada
Affiliated with: Winnipeg Regional Health Authority
2060 Corydon Ave., Winnipeg, MB R3P 0N3
Tel: 204-889-2650; *Fax:* 204-896-0258
cnh_tuxedovilla@extendicare.com
www.extendicarecanada.com/winnipegtuxedovilla
Number of Beds: 213 beds
Note: Programs & services include: professional nursing & supportive care; rehabilitation services; care for persons with Alzheimer's disease & related dementias; optometry services; & social & therapeutic programs.
Sandra Goers, Administrator

Winnipeg: Extendicare - Vista Park Lodge
Extendicare Canada
Affiliated with: Winnipeg Regional Health Authority
144 Nova Vista Dr., Winnipeg, MB R2N 1P8
Tel: 204-257-6688; *Fax:* 204-257-0446
www.extendicarecanada.com/winnipegvistapark
Number of Beds: 100 beds
Gwen Johnston, Administrator

Winnipeg: Fred Douglas Lodge
Fred Douglas Society Inc.
Affiliated with: Winnipeg Regional Health Authority
1275 Burrows Ave., Winnipeg, MB R2X 0B8
Tel: 204-586-8541; *Fax:* 204-586-5510
admin@fdl.mb.ca
www.freddouglassociety.com
Number of Beds: 136 beds; 11 beds for behaviorally challenged
Note: Owned by the United Church of Canada. Programs & services include: life-lease housing; independent living apartments; supportive housing suites; respite; & an adult day program.
Roslyn Garofalo, Chief Executive Officer
204-586-8541, rgarofalo@freddouglassociety.com
Glen Didyk, Director of Care
204-586-8541, gdidyk@freddouglassociety.com

Winnipeg: Golden Door Geriatric Centre
Affiliated with: Winnipeg Regional Health Authority
1679 Pembina Hwy., Winnipeg, MB R3T 2G6
Tel: 204-269-6308; *Fax:* 204-269-5626
info@goldendoor.ca
www.goldendoor.ca
Number of Beds: 78 beds
Scarlet Pollock, Administrator

Winnipeg: Golden Links Lodge
Affiliated with: Winnipeg Regional Health Authority
2280 St. Mary's Rd., Winnipeg, MB R2N 3Z6
Tel: 204-257-9947; *Fax:* 204-257-2405
info@goldenlinks.mb.ca
www.goldenlinks.mb.ca
Number of Beds: 88 beds; 2 respite beds; 17-bed unit for dementia care
Note: Owned by the Oddfellows & Rebekahs

Winnipeg: Heritage Lodge Personal Care Home
Revera Inc.
Affiliated with: Winnipeg Regional Health Authority
3555 Portage Ave., Winnipeg, MB R3K 0X2
Tel: 204-888-7940; *Fax:* 204-832-6544
www.reveraliving.com/heritage-pch

Number of Beds: 86 beds
Thomas G. Wellneron, President & CEO, Revera Inc.
Joanne Sigfusson, Administrator

Winnipeg: Holy Family Home
Affiliated with: Winnipeg Regional Health Authority
165 Aberdeen Ave., Winnipeg, MB R2W 1T9
Tel: 204-589-7381; *Fax:* 204-589-8605
info@holyfamilyhome.mb.ca
www.holyfamilyhome.mb.ca
Number of Beds: 276 beds
Note: Personal care home for the elderly within the Ukrainian & Slavic communities. Includes programs such as respite care & an adult day program.
Jean R. Piché, Chief Executive Officer

Winnipeg: Kildonan Personal Care Centre
Revera Inc.
Affiliated with: Winnipeg Regional Health Authority
Former Name: Kildonan Long Term Care
1970 Henderson Hwy., Winnipeg, MB R2G 1P2
Tel: 204-334-4633; *Fax:* 204-334-4632
www.reveraliving.com/kildonan
Number of Beds: 120 beds
Thomas G. Wellner, President & CEO, Revera Inc.
Nina Labun, Administrator

Winnipeg: Lions Personal Care Centre
Affiliated with: Winnipeg Regional Health Authority
320 Sherbrook St., Winnipeg, MB R3B 2W6
Tel: 204-784-1240; *Fax:* 204-784-2723
www.wrha.mb.ca
Number of Beds: 116 rooms
Note: Programs & services include a supportive housing program & an adult day program.
Laurel Ann Kalupar, Administrator

Winnipeg: Luther Home
Affiliated with: Winnipeg Regional Health Authority
1081 Andrews St., Winnipeg, MB R2V 2G9
Tel: 204-338-4641; *Fax:* 204-338-4643
www.lutherhome.com
Year Founded: 1969
Number of Beds: 63 single rooms; 4 double roomes; 2 quadrouples; 1 respite
Note: Sponsored by the Christ Lutheran Church
Keith Bytheway, Administrator

Winnipeg: Maples Care Centre
Revera Inc.
Affiliated with: Winnipeg Regional Health Authority
Also Known As: Maples Personal Care Home
500 Mandalay Dr., Winnipeg, MB R2P 1V4
Tel: 204-632-8570; *Fax:* 204-697-0249
maples@reveraliving.com
www.reveraliving.com/maples
Year Founded: 1982
Number of Beds: 200 beds
Thomas G. Wellner, President & CEO, Revera Inc.
Jason Chester, Administrator

Winnipeg: Meadowood Manor
Affiliated with: Winnipeg Regional Health Authority
577 St. Anne's Rd., Winnipeg, MB R2M 5B2
Tel: 204-257-2394; *Fax:* 204-254-5402
info@meadowood.ca
www.meadowood.ca
Number of Beds: 88 beds; 1 respite care bed; 90 suite apartment complex
Note: Faith-based facilitiy affiliated with the North American Baptist Conference. Programs & services include: long-term care; rehabilitation services; foot care services; social work; recreation programs; respite care; & palliative care.
Laurie Cerqueti, Administrator

Winnipeg: Middlechurch Home of Winnipeg Inc.
Affiliated with: Winnipeg Regional Health Authority
280 Balderstone Ave., Winnipeg, MB R4A 4A6
Tel: 204-339-1947; *Fax:* 204-334-2503
www.middlechurchhome.mb.ca
Year Founded: 1884
Number of Beds: 197 beds
Number of Employees: 320
Note: Programs & services include: activity centre; physiotherapy; occupational therapy; speech therapy; pet therapy; dentist; foot care; adult day program; physicians; & respite care.
Lynda Braccio, Director, Operations
laurie@middlechurchhome.mb.ca

Winnipeg: Misericordia Place
Misericordia Health Centre
Affiliated with: Winnipeg Regional Health Authority
99 Cornish Ave., Winnipeg, MB R3C 1A2
Tel: 204-774-6581; *Fax:* 204-783-6052
info@misericordia.mb.ca
www.misericordia.mb.ca/Programs/LTCare.html
Social Media: www.facebook.com/263816864499; twitter.com/MisericordiaMB; instagram.com/misericordiamb
Number of Beds: 100 beds
Note: Misericordia Health Centre also provides interim care for up to 145 residents waiting for placement in the personal care home of their choice.
Rosie Jacuzzi, President & CEO
Patty Johnson, Director, Long-Term Care Program
204-788-8451, pjohnson@misericordia.mb.ca

Winnipeg: Park Manor Personal Care Home Inc.
Affiliated with: Winnipeg Regional Health Authority
301 Redonda St., Winnipeg, MB R2C 1L7
Tel: 204-222-3251; *Fax:* 204-222-3237
www.parkmanor.ca
Number of Beds: 44 private rooms + 20 semi-private rooms + 4 four-bed rooms
Note: Owned by the Seventh-day Adventist Church. Specialties: Therapeutic recreation; Education sessions for residents & families; Adult day program; Palliative care
Collin Akre, Chief Executive Officer & Chief Financial Officer
cakre@parkmanor.ca

Winnipeg: Parkview Place Long Term Care
Revera Inc.
Affiliated with: Winnipeg Regional Health Authority
440 Edmonton St., Winnipeg, MB R3B 2M4
Tel: 204-942-5291; *Fax:* 204-947-1969
parkviewplace@reveraliving.com
www.reveraliving.com/parkviewplace
Number of Beds: 277 beds
Thomas G. Wellner, President & CEO, Revera Inc.
Donald Solar, Administrator

Winnipeg: Pembina Place Mennonite Personal Care Home
Bethania Group
Affiliated with: Winnipeg Regional Health Authority
1045 Concordia Ave., Winnipeg, MB R2K 3S7
Tel: 204-667-0795; *Fax:* 204-667-7078
general.inquiries@bethania.ca
www.bethania.ca/pembina-place-pch
Year Founded: 1998
Number of Beds: 57 beds
Specialties: Accommodating language & cultural needs of Deaf persons
Gary Ledoux, Chief Executive Officer
Andrea Grozli, Manager, Resident Care

Winnipeg: Poseidon Care Centre
Rivera Inc.
Affiliated with: Winnipeg Regional Health Authority
70 Poseidon Bay, Winnipeg, MB R3M 3E5
Tel: 204-452-6204; *Fax:* 204-474-2173
poseidon@reveraliving.com
www.reveraliving.com/poseidon
Number of Beds: 218 beds
Thomas G. Wellner, President & CEO, Revera Inc.
Wendy Gilmour, Senior Vice-President, Long Term Care
Wanda Metro, Administrator

Winnipeg: River East Personal Care Home Ltd.
Affiliated with: Winnipeg Regional Health Authority
1375 Molson St., Winnipeg, MB R2K 4K8
Tel: 204-668-7460; *Fax:* 204-668-7459
dsaunders@extendicare.com
www.rivereast.ca
Year Founded: 1993
Number of Beds: 120 beds

Winnipeg: River Park Gardens
Affiliated with: Winnipeg Regional Health Authority
735 St. Annes Rd., Winnipeg, MB R2N 0C4
Tel: 204-255-9073; *Fax:* 204-257-6467
www.wrha.mb.ca
Number of Beds: 80 beds
Mary Baranski, Administrator

Winnipeg: St. Joseph's Residence Inc.
Affiliated with: Winnipeg Regional Health Authority
1149 Leila Ave., Winnipeg, MB R2P 1S6
Tel: 204-697-8031; *Fax:* 204-697-8075
admin@sjri.ca
sjri.ca
Number of Beds: 100 beds
Note: Owned by The Catholic Health Corporation of Manitoba
Charles Gagné, Chief Executive Officer
cgagne@sjri.ca

Winnipeg: St. Norbert Personal Care Home
Affiliated with: Winnipeg Regional Health Authority
50 St. Pierre St., Winnipeg, MB R3V 1J6
Tel: 204-269-4538; *Fax:* 204-269-6374
www.wrha.mb.ca
Year Founded: 1971
Number of Beds: 91 beds

Winnipeg: The Salvation Army Golden West Centennial Lodge
Affiliated with: Winnipeg Regional Health Authority
811 School Rd., Winnipeg, MB R2Y 0S8
Tel: 204-888-3311; *Fax:* 204-831-0544
goldenwest.ca
Number of Beds: 116 beds
Note: Programs & services include: outings; recreation; rehabilitation; music therapy; & an adult day program.
Joyce Kristjansson, Administrator

Winnipeg: The Saul & Claribel Simkin Centre
The Sharon Home Inc.
Affiliated with: Winnipeg Regional Health Authority
Also Known As: The Simkin Centre
1 Falconridge Dr., Winnipeg, MB R3Y 1V9
Tel: 204-586-9781; *Fax:* 204-589-9760
info@simkincentre.ca
www.simkincentre.ca
Year Founded: 2002
Number of Beds: 200 beds
Note: Provides care for elders of Jewish community; therapeutic recreation; walking track for residents recovering from hip surgery or a stroke; tracking program for resident safety; & an adult day program.
Alanna Kull, Director of Care
Alanna.Kull@sharonhome.mb.ca

Winnipeg: Southeast Personal Care Home Inc. (SEPCH)
Southeast Resource Development Council Corp.
Affiliated with: Winnipeg Regional Health Authority
1265 Lee Blvd., Winnipeg, MB R3T 2M3
Tel: 204-269-7111; *Fax:* 204-269-8819
www.serdc.mb.ca/programs-and-services/sepersonalcarehome
Year Founded: 2011
Number of Beds: 80 beds
Note: Personal care home for Aboriginal elders
Jean Foster, Executive Director

Winnipeg: West Park Manor Personal Care Home Inc.
Affiliated with: Winnipeg Regional Health Authority
3199 Grant Ave., Winnipeg, MB R3R 1X2
Tel: 204-889-3330; *Fax:* 204-832-9555
www.wrha.mb.ca
Number of Beds: 150 beds; 1 respite care bed
Note: Faith-based facility sponsored by the Seventh-day Adventist Church.
Ruben Wollmann, Administrator

Winnipegosis: Winnipegosis & District Personal Care Home
Affiliated with: Prairie Mountain Health
PO Box 280, 230 Bridge St., Winnipegosis, MB R0L 2G0
Tel: 204-656-4881
www.prha.mb.ca
Number of Beds: 20 beds
Note: Includes home care services (204-656-4721)

Mental Health Hospitals/Facilities

Altona: Blue Sky Opportunities Inc.
PO Box 330, 122 - 10th Ave. NW, Altona, MB R0G 0B0
Tel: 204-324-5401; *Fax:* 204-324-5094
bsoinc@mts.net
www.blueskyop.com
Note: Employment & training opportunities for adults with intellectual disabilities, as well as non-vocational services.
Richard Neufeld, General Manager
204-324-5401, bsogm@mts.net

Boissevain: Prairie Partners Inc.
PO Box 1116, Boissevain, MB R0K 0E0
Tel: 204-534-2956; *Fax:* 204-534-7093
execassist@prairiepartners.ca
prairiepartners.ca
Note: Residential & employment services for adults with intellectual disabilities.

Jason L. Dyck, Executive Director & CEO

Brandon: Brandon Community Options Inc.
136 - 11th St., Brandon, MB R7A 4J4
Tel: 204-571-5770; *Fax:* 204-571-5780
bdnco@mymts.net
www.brandoncommunityoptionsinc.com
Note: Residential & day programs for adults living with mental disabilities.

Brandon: Brandon Support Services
1540 Rosser Ave., Brandon, MB R7A 0M6
Tel: 204-728-2025; *Fax:* 204-728-2052
admin@bssmb.ca
www.bssmb.ca
Area Served: Brandon, Portage La Prairie, MacGregor & Carberry
Note: Community-based agency providing supportive services to individuals with intellectual &/or physical disabilities

Brandon: Centre for Adult Psychiatry (CAP)
Affiliated with: Prairie Mountain Health
Brandon Regional Health Centre, #AP1, 150 McTavish Ave. East, Brandon, MB R7A 2B3
Tel: 204-578-4555; *Fax:* 204-578-4940
cap@brandonrha.mb.ca
www.brandonrha.mb.ca
Number of Beds: 25 beds
Note: Acute services for adults 18-64 experiencing a psychiatric illness (DSM IV diagnosis) &/or severe psychosocial crisis.
Tasha Colbourne, Program Manager

Brandon: Centre for Geriatric Psychiatry
Affiliated with: Prairie Mountain Health
Assiniboine Centre, 150 McTavish Ave. East, Brandon, MB R7A 2B3
Tel: 204-578-5460; *Fax:* 204-578-4948
cgpcommon@brandonrha.mb.ca
www.brandonrha.mb.ca
Number of Beds: 22 beds
Area Served: Parkland, Assiniboine, Brandon
Note: Provides assessment & short-term treatment for adults 65 years & over experiencing difficulties with day to day functioning due to mental health issues.
Pamela Gulay, Manager

Brandon: Child & Adolescent Treatment Centre (CATC)
Affiliated with: Prairie Mountain Health
1240 - 10 St., Brandon, MB R7A 7L6
Tel: 204-578-2700; *Fax:* 204-578-2850
Toll-Free: 844-403-5459
www.brandonrha.mb.ca
Note: Programs & services include: mental health assessments & treatment; crisis stabilization; individualized treatment plans; individual, group & family therapy; & mental health education/promotion.
Elizabeth McLeod, Manager

Brandon: Community Mental Health Services
Affiliated with: Prairie Mountain Health
The Town Centre, #B13, 800 Rosser Ave., Brandon, MB R7A 6N5
Tel: 204-578-2400; *Fax:* 204-578-2822
mhpc@brandonrha.mb.ca
www.brandonrha.mb.ca
Lynda Stiles, Director
Wendy Dryburgh, Manager, Adult Community Mental Health
204-578-2415
Darlene Henry, Manager, Mental Health Services for the Elderly
204-578-2458
Brent White, Manager, Residential & Support Services
204-578-2445
Sharon Young, Manager, Psychosocial Rehabilitation
204-578-2439

Brandon: Family Visions Inc.
2705 Victoria Ave., Brandon, MB R7B 0N1
Tel: 204-726-5602; *Fax:* 204-571-0907
reception@familyvisions.ca
www.familyvisions.ca
Year Founded: 2000
Note: Residential & day services for adults with intellectual disabilities.
Kim Longstreet, Interim Executive Director
executive.director@familyvisions.ca

Brandon: Westman Crisis Centre
Affiliated with: Prairie Mountain Health
Also Known As: Westman Crisis Services
The Town Centre, #B13, 800 Rosser Ave., Brandon, MB R7A 6N5
Toll-Free: 888-379-7699
www.brandonrha.mb.ca
Area Served: Brandon & Assiniboine regions
Note: Services for individuals in a mental health or psychosocial crisis.
Crisis Stabilization Unit (CSU): 204-727-2555; Mobile Crisis Unit (MCU): 204-725-4411.
Allison Done, Program Manager
204-725-3107

Ninette: Southwest Community Options Inc. (SWCO)
PO Box 46, 210 Queen St. North, Ninette, MB R0K 1R0
Tel: 204-528-5060; *Fax:* 204-528-5065
www.swco.ca
Year Founded: 2000
Note: Residential & day services for adults with intellectual disabilities.
Kim Steele, Executive Director

Notre Dame de Lourdes: Mountain Industries
Also Known As: Atelier la Montagne
65 Notre-Dame Ave., Notre Dame de Lourdes, MB R0G 1M0
www.mountainindustries.ca
Year Founded: 1978
Note: Provides a day program for over 25 individuals with special needs

Pine Falls: Wings of Power Inc.
PO Box 66, 39 Pine St., Pine Falls, MB R0E 1M0
Tel: 204-367-9641; *Fax:* 204-367-9784
www.wingsofpower.org
Note: Community & family resource centre. Programs & services include: prenatal/postnatal; children's; summer; school; & programs for adults with disabilities.
Kathy Oakes, Executive Director
wingsdirector@mymts.net

Portage la Prairie: Manitoba Developmental Centre
3rd St. NE, Portage la Prairie, MB R1N 3C6
Tel: 204-856-4200; *Fax:* 204-856-4258
csd@gov.mb.ca
www.gov.mb.ca/fs/pwd/mdc.html
Number of Beds: 200 resident capacity
Note: Developmental centre for residents with an intellectual disability. Programs & services include: Extended Care Program & Habilitation/Specialty Program.

Portage la Prairie: Portage ARC Industries Inc.
1675 Saskatchewan Ave. West, Portage la Prairie, MB R1N 0R4
Tel: 204-857-7752; *Fax:* 204-239-0968
portagearc@mts.net
Note: Activities for individuals with special needs

Selkirk: Hearthstone Community Group
209 Superior Ave., Selkirk, MB R1A 0Z7
Tel: 204-817-1996; *Fax:* 204-817-1997
www.hearthstone-community-group.ca
Note: Community living homes & day programs.
Lori Zdebiak, General Manager

Selkirk: Selkirk Mental Health Centre
Affiliated with: Interlake-Eastern Regional Health Authority
PO Box 9600, 825 Manitoba Ave., Selkirk, MB R1A 2B5
Tel: 204-482-3810; *Fax:* 204-785-8936
Toll-Free: 800-881-3073
smhc@gov.mb.ca
www.gov.mb.ca/health/smhc
Number of Beds: 252 beds
Note: Long-term mental health inpatient care & rehabilitation; also provides mental health services to people from the Territory of Nunavut
D. Bellehumeur, Chief Executive Officer
Dr. P. Barchet, Medical Director
R. Cromarty, Director, Programs
J. Klainchar, Director, Operations

St Malo: Smile of St. Malo Inc./Epic de St. Malo Inc.
112 St. Malo Ave., St Malo, MB R0A 1T0
Tel: 204-347-5418
info@epicsmile.ca
www.epicsmile.ca
Note: Provides residential & day programs for adults with intellectual disabilities.

Steinbach: enVision Community Living
84 Brandt St., Steinbach, MB R5G 0E1
Tel: 204-326-7539; *Fax:* 204-346-3639
info@envisioncl.com
www.envisioncl.com
Social Media: www.facebook.com/128477617196963; twitter.com/enVisioncl
Note: Provides residential & daytime support services to adults living with intellectual disabilities.
Jeannette Delong, Executive Director
Jdelong@envisioncl.com

Winkler: Eden Mental Health Centre
Eden Health Care Services
Affiliated with: Southern Health-Santé Sud
1500 Pembina Ave., Winkler, MB R6W 1T4
Tel: 204-325-4325; *Fax:* 204-325-8429
Toll-Free: 866-559-2555
ehcs@edenhealthcare.ca
www.edenhealth.mb.ca
Social Media: www.facebook.com/edenhealthcareservices
Year Founded: 1967
Number of Beds: 30 beds
Note: An affiliate health corporation within Southern Health-Santé Sud.

Winkler: Gateway Resources Inc.
PO Box 1448, 1582 Pembina Ave., Winkler, MB R6W 4B4
Tel: 204-325-7304; *Fax:* 204-325-1958
gradmin@gatewayresourcesinc.com
www.gatewayresourcesinc.com
Area Served: Winkler/Morden area of South Central Manitoba
Note: Operates 13 group homes that provide services & programs for individuals living with an intellectual disability.
Kim Nelson, Chief Executive Officer
204-331-2652, kim@gatewayresourcesinc.com

Winnipeg: Arcane Horizon Inc. (AHI)
#62, 1313 Border St., Winnipeg, MB R3H 0X4
Tel: 204-897-5482
www.arcanehorizon.org
Social Media: www.facebook.com/arcanehorizon
Note: Support services for adults living with developmental disabilities.

Winnipeg: L'Avenir Cooperative Inc.
80 Sherbrook St., Winnipeg, MB R3C 2B3
Tel: 204-789-9777; *Fax:* 204-837-8614
www.lavenircoop.ca
Year Founded: 1983
Note: Provides supports to people with intellectual &/or physical disabilities.
Marc Piché, Executive Director
mpiche@lavenircoop.ca

Winnipeg: Changes
959 Portage Ave., Winnipeg, MB R3G 0R2
Tel: 204-953-5075; *Fax:* 204-953-5305
info@changeswinnipeg.ca
changeswinnipeg.ca
Note: Services for adults requiring support in their homes & communities.

Winnipeg: Clubhouse of Winnipeg, Inc.
Affiliated with: Winnipeg Regional Health Authority
172 Sherbrook St., Winnipeg, MB R3C 2B6
Tel: 204-783-9400; *Fax:* 204-783-9890
Note: Employment & educational opportunities to people coping with mental illness.

Winnipeg: Community Respite Service Inc.
825 Sherbrook St., Winnipeg, MB R3A 1M5
Tel: 204-953-2400; *Fax:* 204-775-6214
comresp@mts.net
www.communityrespiteservice.ca
Year Founded: 1984
Note: Respite care for families & individuals with intellectual & physical disabilities.

Winnipeg: Crisis Response Centre (CRC)
Affiliated with: Winnipeg Regional Health Authority
Also Known As: Adult Mental Health Crisis Response Centre
817 Bannatyne Ave., Winnipeg, MB R3E 0Y1
Tel: 204-940-1781
TTY: 204-779-8902
www.wrha.mb.ca/facilities/crisis-response-centre.php
Year Founded: 2013
Note: Provides 24/7 walk-in & schedules urgent care services; acts as a base for a Mobile Crisis Team.
Carolyn Strutt, Regional Director, Adult Mental Health, WRHA
Heather Forrest, Manager

Winnipeg: DASCH Inc.
Also Known As: Direct Action in Support of Community Homes
#1, 117 Victor Lewis Dr., Winnipeg, MB R3P 1J6
Tel: 204-987-1550; *Fax:* 204-987-1552
www.dasch.mb.ca
Social Media: www.facebook.com/DASCHInc; twitter.com/dasch_inc
Year Founded: 1974
Note: Provides residential, day program, respite & foster care programs & services.
Karen Fonseth-Schlossbe, Chief Executive Officer

Winnipeg: Friends Housing Inc.
Affiliated with: Winnipeg Regional Health Authority
#100, 890 Sturgeon Rd., Winnipeg, MB R2Y 0L2
Tel: 204-953-1160; *Fax:* 204-953-1162
fhousing@mymts.net
www.friendshousinginc.ca
Note: Provides housing & daily living support for people with mental illnesses, or people in need of subsidized housing.

Winnipeg: Innovative LIFE Options Inc. (LIFE)
Also Known As: Living in Friendship Everyday
#4, 120 Maryland St., Winnipeg, MB R3G 1L1
Tel: 204-772-3557; *Fax:* 204-784-4816
Toll-Free: 866-516-5445
info@icof-life.ca
www.icof-life.ca
Social Media: www.facebook.com/LifeIsGoodInTheCompanyOfFriendsicof; twitter.com/lifeisgoodicof
Year Founded: 2000
Note: Provides guidance, resources, training, & information to individuals receiving funding through Manitoba Family Service's program In the Company of Friends (ICOF).
Patti Chiappetta, Executive Director
204-784-4814, patti@icof-life.ca

Winnipeg: Manitoba Adolescent Treatment Centre Inc. (MATC)
Affiliated with: Winnipeg Regional Health Authority
120 Tecumseh St., Winnipeg, MB R3E 2A9
Tel: 204-477-6391; *Fax:* 204-783-8948
info@matc.ca
www.matc.ca
Number of Beds: 25 beds
Note: Mental health services for children, youth, & families

Winnipeg: Norshel Inc.
Also Known As: Norshel Centre
890 Nairn Ave., Winnipeg, MB R2L 0X8
Tel: 204-654-6117
www.norshel.mb.ca
Social Media: www.facebook.com/309500839098006
Note: Provides supports for adults with physical & developmental disabilities.
Colin Rivers, Executive Director
colinrivers@norshel.mb.ca

Winnipeg: Opportunities For Independence, Inc.
1070 Portage Ave., Winnipeg, MB R3G 0S3
Tel: 204-786-0100; *Fax:* 204-786-0109
www.ofii.ca
Year Founded: 1983
Number of Employees: 100
Note: Programs & services for adults with intellectual disabilities, who engage in high-risk behavior, include: residential; alternative vocational programming; living skills training; & therapeutic programs.
Donald Welch, Staff Representative

Winnipeg: Pulford Community Living Services Inc. (PCLS)
#5, 1146 Waverley St., Winnipeg, MB R3T 0P4
Tel: 204-284-2255; *Fax:* 204-453-5657
www.pulford.ca
Year Founded: 1986
Note: Provides housing & support services for people with developmental disabilities.
John Pollard, President & Treasurer

Winnipeg: The Salvation Army Community Venture
1100 Fife St., Winnipeg, MB R2X 3A5
Tel: 204-946-9418; *Fax:* 204-946-5347
director@communityventure.mb.ca
www.communityventure.mb.ca
Note: Programs & services for adults living with developmental disabilities include: day programs; residential services; transportation; & outreach & respite.

Winnipeg: Sara Riel Inc.
Affiliated with: Winnipeg Regional Health Authority
66 Moore Ave., Winnipeg, MB R2M 2C4
Tel: 204-237-9263; *Fax:* 204-233-2564
www.sararielinc.com
Social Media: www.facebook.com/126140684102302
Year Founded: 1977
Note: Provides housing support, rehabilitation & employment counselling to individuals with mental health issues.
Lucy Warman, President
lwarman@sararielinc.com

Winnipeg: Shalom Residences Inc.
1033 McGregor St., Winnipeg, MB R2V 3H4
Tel: 204-582-7064; *Fax:* 204-582-7162
shalom@mts.net
www.shalomresidences.com
Note: Community based care homes for adults with intellectual disabilities; Judaic-oriented programs.
Nancy Hughes, Executive Director

Winnipeg: Special People in Kildonan East Inc. (SPIKE)
Also Known As: SPIKE House
1303 Dugald Rd., #B, Winnipeg, MB R2J 0H3
Tel: 204-338-0773; *Fax:* 204-338-1129
www.spikeinc.org
Year Founded: 1978
Note: Permanent & respite care for the mentally &/or physically handicapped.
Peter Court, Executive Director
204-339-2990, pcourt@mymts.net

Winnipeg: Turning Leaf Community Support Services Inc.
Also Known As: Turning Leaf Inc.
2585 Portage Ave., 2nd Fl., Winnipeg, MB R3J 0P5
Tel: 204-221-5594; *Fax:* 204-219-1821
www.turningleafservices.com
Social Media: www.facebook.com/TurningLeafCommunitySupportServicesIncorporated; twitter.com/TLServicesInc; linkedin.com/company/turning-leaf-community-support-services-inc-
Note: Provides treatment & support for youth & adults with intellectual challenges & mental illnesses.
Barkley Engel, Founder & CEO
204-221-5594, bjengel@turningleafservices.com

Winnipeg: Visions of Independence Inc.
#211, 530 Century St., Winnipeg, MB R3H 0Y4
Tel: 204-453-5982; *Fax:* 204-452-0714
visionsofindependence.org
Social Media: www.facebook.com/302198003189392
Note: Provides housing & programs to people with intellectual disabilities. Programs & services include: residential; day programs; & supported independent living/respite.
Jennifer Hagedorn, Executive Director
jhagedorn@visionsofindependence.org

New Brunswick

Government Departments in Charge

Fredericton: New Brunswick Department of Health
Former Name: Dept. of Health & Community Services
HSBC Place, PO Box 5100, Fredericton, NB E3B 5G8
Tel: 506-457-4800; *Fax:* 506-453-5243
www.gnb.ca/0051
Hon. Victor Boudreau, Minister

Regional Health Authorities

Bathurst: Vitalité Health Network/Réseau de santé Vitalité
Former Name: Restigouche Health Authority/Régie de la santé du Restigouche
#600, 275 Main St., Bathurst, NB E2A 1A9
Tel: 506-544-2133; *Fax:* 506-544-2145
Toll-Free: 888-472-2220
info@vitalitenb.ca
www.vitalitenb.ca
Year Founded: 2008
Number of Beds: 965 beds; 60 veterans' beds; 172 Restigouche Hospital Centre beds
Population Served: 239600; *Number of Employees:* 7390
Note: The Vitalité Health Network amalgamates Regional Health Authority 4, the Restigouche Health Authority, the Acadie-Bathurst Health Authority, & the Beauséjour Health Authority. The network is comprised of 11 hospitals, 9 health centres, 5 clinics, 10 community mental health centres, 4 addiction service centres, 2 veterans' centres, 11 public & sexual health offices & 12 extra-mural program offices.
Michelyne Paulin, Board Chair
Gilles Lanteigne, President & CEO
Dr. France Desrosiers, Vice-President, Medical Services, Training & Research
Gisèle Beaulieu, Vice-President, Performance, Quality & Corporate Services
Jacques Duclos, Vice-President, Community Services & Mental Health
Stéphane Legacy, Vice-President, Outpatient & Professional Services
Johanne Roy, Vice-President, Clinical Services

Fredericton: Horizon Health Network/Réseau de santé Horizon
Former Name: Regional Health Authority B
180 Woodbridge St., Fredericton, NB E3B 4R3
Tel: 506-623-5500; *Fax:* 506-623-5533
horizon@horizonnb.ca
www.horizonnb.ca
Social Media: www.facebook.com/HorizonNB; twitter.com/HorizonHealthNB; www.linkedin.com/company/horizon-health-network
Year Founded: 2008
Number of Beds: 1,650 beds
Area Served: Provinces of New Brunswick, PEI, & northern Nova Scotia; *Number of Employees:* 12400
Note: Along with the Vitalité Health Network, the Horizon Health Network amalgamates the 8 former regional health authorities in New Brunswick. Horizon Health Network servies the Moncton, Saint John, Fredericton & Miramichi areas, as well as communities in Nova Scotia & Prince Edward Island.
Grace Losier, Board Chair
John McGarry, President & CEO
Andrea Seymour, Chief Operating Officer & Vice-President, Corporate
Jean Daigle, Vice-President, Community
Gary Foley, Vice-President, Professional Services
Geri Geldart, Vice-President, Clinical
Dr. Édouard Hendriks, Vice-President, Medical, Academic & Research
Margaret Melanson, Vice-President, Quality & Patient Centred Care

Hospitals - General

Bathurst: Hôpital régional Chaleur
Affiliée à: Vitalité Health Network
Ancien nom: Centre hospitalier régional
1750, promenade Sunset, Bathurst, NB E2A 4L7
Tél: 506-544-3000; *Téléc:* 506-544-2533
info@vitalitenb.ca
www.vitalitenb.ca
Nombre de lits: 215 beds
Note: Services: diagnostiques; chirurgie; cliniques de soins ambulatoires; mère et à l'enfant; specialises; spécialisés de réadaptation; thérapeutiques; programme de suivi des porteurs d'implants cochléaires du Nouveau-Brunswick; et Pavillon UCT.

Campbellton: Campbellton Regional Hospital/Hôpital régional de Campbellton
Affiliated with: Vitalité Health Network
PO Box 880, 189 Lily Lake Rd., Campbellton, NB E3N 3H3
Tel: 506-789-5000
info@vitalitenb.ca
www.vitalitenb.ca
Year Founded: 1991
Number of Beds: 163 beds/lits
Number of Employees: 900
Note: Programs & services include: acute psychiatry; ambulatory care; audiology; care for veterans; clinical nutrition; diagnostic imaging & laboratory; emergency; ENT (ears, nose & throat); geriatrics; general surgery; intensive care; medical; obstetrics/gynecology; occupational therapy; orthopedics; palliative care; pediatrics; psychology; recreology; rehabilitation; social work; speech-language pathology; & urology.
Dan Arseneau, Executive Director

Caraquet: Hôpital de l'Enfant-Jésus (RHSJT)
Affiliated with: Vitalité Health Network
Former Name: Hôpital de l'Enfant-Jésus RHSJ
1, boul St-Pierre ouest, Caraquet, NB E1W 1B6
Tel: 506-726-2100; *Fax:* 506-726-2188
info@vitalitenb.ca
www.vitalitenb.ca
Note: Services: clinique avec un infirmier praticien; clinique de phénylcétonurie (PCU); clinique de tests de Pap; clinique mère-enfant; cliniques et programmes multidisciplinaires; Lifeline; médecine / soins palliatifs; programme de réadaptation cardiaque; services diagnostiques; services thérapeutiques;

soins ambulatoires; soins spirituels et religieux; télésanté; unité de formation médicale; et urgence.

Edmundston: Hôpital régional d'Edmundston/Edmundston Regional Hospital
Affiliée à: Vitalité Health Network
275, boul Hébert, Edmundston, NB E3V 4E4
Tél: 506-739-2200; *Téléc:* 506-739-2231
info@vitalitenb.ca
www.vitalitenb.ca
Nombre de lits: 169 lits
Personnel: 1000
Note: Services: audiologie; bénévoles et soins spirituels et religieux; clinique de réadaptation cardiaque; clinique sur les maladies pulmonaires; dialyse rénale; électrodiagnostic; ergothérapie; imagerie médicale; médecine; nutrition clinique; obstétrique; oncologie; orthophonie; pédiatrie; pharmacie; psychiatrie; psychologie; services diagnostiques; soins ambulatoires; soins intensifs; soins prolongés et soins palliatifs; thérapie respiratoire; travailleurs sociaux en milieu hospitalier; unités de chirurgie; et urgence.

Fredericton: Dr. Everett Chalmers Regional Hospital
Affiliated with: Horizon Health Network
PO Box 9000, 700 Priestman St., Fredericton, NB E3B 5N5
Tel: 506-452-5400; *Fax:* 506-452-5670
www.horizonnb.ca
Social Media: www.facebook.com/120963024660628; twitter.com/HorizonHealthNB; www.linkedin.com/company/horizon-health-network
Year Founded: 1976
Number of Beds: 315 beds
Note: Programs & services include: Addictions & Mental Health (community forensics, children & youth treatment programs); Clinical Services (day surgery, dermatology, dialysis, ear, nose & throat, emergency, family medicine, gastroenterology, general surgery, geriatrics, gynecology surgery, intensive care, internal medicine, minor surgery, neonatal intensive care, opthalmology surgery, orthopedic surgery, pediatrics, palliative care, plastic surgery, physiatry, psychiatry, obstetrics, thoracic surgery, urology surgery, vascular surgery & oncology); Diagnostics & Testing (blood & specimen, bone marrow, breathing function, bronchoscopy, CT scan, cystoscopy, endoscopy, ECG, fluoroscopy, holter monitoring, EEG, pathology, MRI, mammography, nuclear medicine, spirometry, ultrasound & x-ray); Public Health Programs (health emergency, health promotion, healthy learners, children & adolescents, immunization, communicable disease prevention, HIV testing & sexual health program); & Support & Therapy (audiology, clinical nutrition, occupational, physiotherapy, psychology, recreational, respiratory, speech-language pathology, spiritual care, social work & telehealth).
Nicole Tupper, Executive Director

Grand Manan: Grand Manan Hospital
Affiliated with: Horizon Health Network
196 Rte. 776, Grand Manan, NB E5G 1A3
Tel: 506-662-4060
horizon@horizonnb.ca
www.horizonnb.ca
Social Media: www.facebook.com/120963024660628; twitter.com/HorizonHealthNB; www.linkedin.com/company/horizon-health-network
Number of Beds: 10 beds
Population Served: 5000
Specialties: Chronic diseases and women's health issues
Note: Programs & services include: Clinical Services (emergency, family medicine & palliative care); Diagnostics & Testing (blood & specimen collection, ECG & x-ray); & Support & Therapy (physiotherapy & telehealth).
Courtney Budgell, Hospital Manager

Grand-Sault: Hôpital général de Grand-Sault inc./Grand Falls General Hospital Inc.
Affiliée à: Vitalité Health Network
CP 7061, 625, boul Evérard H. Daigle, Grand-Sault, NB E3Z 2R9
Tél: 506-473-7555; *Téléc:* 506-473-7530
info@vitalitenb.ca
www.vitalitenb.ca
Fondée en: 1962
Nombre de lits: 20 lits
Population desservi: 15000
Note: Services: chirurgie mineure; clinique du diabète; clinique sur l'hypertension; dermatologie; électrocardiographie; endocrinologie; gastro-entérologie; gynécologie/obstétrique; imagerie médicale; inhalothérapie; laboratoire; médecine interne; nutrition; oncologie; ophtalmologie; orthopédie; oto-rhino-laryngologie; pédiatrie; physiothérapie; programme mère/enfant; réadaptation cardiaque; rhumatologie; services de traitement des dépendances; soins préanesthésiques; soins médicaux d'un jour; traitement anticoagulant; traitements mineurs; et urologie.
Nicole Labrie, Directrice d'établissement

Lamèque: Hôpital de Lamèque/Centre de santé communautaire de Lamèque
Affiliée à: Vitalité Health Network
Également connu sous le nom de: Hôpital et CSC de Lamèque
29, rue de l'Hôpital, Lamèque, NB E8T 1C5
Tél: 506-344-2261; *Téléc:* 506-344-3403
info@vitalitenb.ca
www.vitalitenb.ca
Nombre de lits: 12 lits
Note: Services: clinique de dépistage du cancer du col de l'utérus (test Pap); clinique de gériatrie; clinique de vaccination contre la grippe; clinique pour femmes enceintes; clinique pour les patients sans médecin de famille (suivi par les infirmières praticiennes); développement communautaire; électrodiagnostic cardiaque; ergothérapie; imagerie médicale; laboratoire; médecine; nutrition clinique; pharmacie; physiothérapie; programme d'abandon du tabac; programme Santé active; programme Mes choix, Ma santé; programme pour les endeuillés; soins des problèmes de santé chroniques; soutien à l'allaitement; télésanté; thérapie respiratoire (inhalothérapie); travail social; et unité de médecine familiale.

Miramichi: Miramichi Regional Hospital
Affiliated with: Horizon Health Network
500 Water St., Miramichi, NB E1V 3G5
Tel: 506-623-3000; *Fax:* 506-623-3465
horizon@horizonnb.ca
www.horizonnb.ca
Social Media: www.facebook.com/120963024660628; twitter.com/HorizonHealthNB; www.linkedin.com/company/horizon-health-network
Number of Beds: 150 beds
Note: Programs & services include: Addictions & Mental Health (children & youth, gambling, inpatient acute care psychiatric unit, inpatient addictions, individual family & group counseling, community care, methadone treatment, substance abuse, smoking cessation program & youth outpatient); Clinical Services (day surgery, dermatology, ear, nose & throat, emergency, family medicine, general surgery, gynecology surgery, geriatrics, intensive care, internal medicine, minor surgery, obstetrics, pediatrics, palliative care, psychiatry, oncology, ophthalmology surgery, orthopedic surgery, rehabilitation & urology surgery); Diagnostics & Testing (blood & specimen collection, breathing function lab, CT scan, cystoscopy, endoscopy, ECG, fluoroscopy, holter monitoring, pathology, MRI, mammography, ultrasound, x-rays & spirometry); Public Health Programs (early childhood, health emergency & promotion, healthy learners, immunization, communicable disease, HIV testing & sexual health); & Support & Therapy (audiology, clinical nutrition, occupational, physiotherapy, recreational, respiratory, speech-language pathology, spiritual care, social work & telehealth).
Marilyn Underhill, Executive Director

Moncton: Le Centre hospitalier universitaire Dr-Georges-L.-Dumont (CHUDGLD)
Affiliated with: Vitalité Health Network
330, av Université, Moncton, NB E1C 2Z3
Tel: 506-862-4000
info@vitalitenb.ca
www.vitalitenb.ca
Number of Beds: 302 lits
Note: Services: Appel Dumont Response; Auberge Mgr-Henri-Cormier; audiologie; chirurgie; clinique d'obstétrique; clinique de gynéco-oncologie; clinique de santé du sein; clinique de traitement; clinique d'oncologie médicale et clinique de radio-oncologie; clinique d'oncologie palliative; curiethérapie de la prostate; imagerie médicale; laboratoire et prises de sang; médecine générale et médecine interne; néphrologie; nutrition clinique; physiothérapie; physique médicale; programme provincial de PCU et centre de coordination du dépistage des troubles métaboliques; psychologie; service de travail social; service d'ergothérapie; service d'orthophonie; soins ambulatoires; soins spirituels et religieux; thérapie respiratoire; travail social; urgence; service de radiothérapie; soins palliatifs; thérapie systémique communautaire; unité 4D (unité d'oncologie); unité des naissances (3B); et unité de pédiatrie (3D).
Richard Losier, Chef des opérations de la zone Beauséjour

Moncton: The Moncton Hospital/L'Hôpital de Moncton
Affiliated with: Horizon Health Network
135 MacBeath Ave., Moncton, NB E1C 6Z8
Tel: 506-857-5511; *Fax:* 506-857-5545
horizon@horizonnb.ca
www.horizonnb.ca
Social Media: www.facebook.com/120963024660628; twitter.com/HorizonHealthNB; www.linkedin.com/company/horizon-health-network
Number of Beds: 381 beds
Specialties: Critical care & trauma cases
Note: Programs & services include: Addictions & Mental Health (inpatient acute care psychiatric unit, inpatient addictions, individual family & group counseling, community care, methadone treatment & smoking cessation program); Clinical Services (day surgery, dermatology, ear, nose & throat, emergency, family medicine, general surgery, gynecology surgery, gastroenterology, geriatrics, intensive care, internal medicine, neurology, neurosurgery, neonatal intensive care, minor surgery, obstetrics, oncology, ophthalmology surgery, orthopedic surgery, palliative care, plastic surgery, rehabilitation, rheumatology, thoracic surgery, urology surgery & vascular surgery); Diagnostics & Testing (blood & specimen, bone marrow, breathing function, bronchoscopy, CT scan, cystoscopy, endoscopy, ECG, fluoroscopy, holter monitoring, neuro electrodiagnostics, pathology, MRI, mammography, nuclear medicine, spirometry, ultrasound & x-ray); & Support & Therapy (audiology, clinical nutrition, occupational, physiotherapy, psychology, recreational, respiratory, speech-language pathology, spiritual care, social work & telehealth).
Nancy Parker, Executive Director

Oromocto: Oromocto Public Hospital
Affiliated with: Horizon Health Network
103 Winnebago St., Oromocto, NB E2V 1C6
Tel: 506-357-4700
horizon@horizonnb.ca
www.horizonnb.ca
Social Media: www.facebook.com/120963024660628; twitter.com/HorizonHealthNB; www.linkedin.com/company/horizon-health-network
Number of Beds: 45 beds
Note: Programs & services include: Clinical Services (day surgery, ear, nose & throat, emergency, family medicine, general surgery, gynecology surgery, gastroenterology, geriatrics, minor surgery, opthalmology surgery, plastic surgery, palliative care, rehabilitation & urology surgery); Diagnostics & Testing (blood & specimen collection, bronchoscopy, cystoscopy, endoscopy, ECG, fluoroscopy, holter monitoring, mammography, spirometry, ultrasound & x-ray); & Support & Therapy (audiology, clinical nutrition, occupational, physiotherapy, recreational, respiratory, speech-language pathology, spiritual care & social work).
Robyn Dean, Assistant to Facility Manager

Perth-Andover: Hotel-Dieu of St. Joseph/Hôtel-Dieu Saint-Joseph
Affiliated with: Horizon Health Network
10 Woodland Hill, Perth-Andover, NB E7H 5H5
Tel: 506-273-7100; *Fax:* 506-273-7200
horizon@horizonnb.ca
www.horizonnb.ca
Social Media: www.facebook.com/120963024660628; twitter.com/HorizonHealthNB; www.linkedin.com/company/horizon-health-network
Number of Beds: 27 beds
Population Served: 6000
Note: Programs & services include: Addictions & Mental Health (smoking cessation program); Clinical Services (day surgery, emergency, general surgery, family medicine, minor surgery, pediatrics, palliative care, oncology, rehabilitation); Diagnostics & Testing (blood & specimen collection, endoscopy, ECG, fluoroscopy, holter monitoring, mammography, spirometry, x-rays & ultrasound); & Support & Therapy (clinical nutrition, occupational therapy, physiotherapy, respiratory therapy, speech-language pathology, spiritual care, social work & telehealth).

Plaster Rock: Tobique Valley Community Health Centre (TVCHC)
Affiliated with: Horizon Health Network
Former Name: Tobique Valley Hospital Inc.
120 Main St., Plaster Rock, NB E7G 2E5
Tel: 506-356-6600; *Fax:* 506-356-6618
horizon@horizonnb.ca
www.horizonnb.ca
Year Founded: 1957

***Sackville:* Sackville Memorial Hospital/L'Hôpital mémorial de Sackville**
Affiliated with: Horizon Health Network
8 Main St., Sackville, NB E4L 4A3
Tel: 506-364-4100; *Fax:* 506-536-1983
generalinquiries@serha.ca
www.horizonnb.ca
Social Media: www.facebook.com/120963024660628; twitter.com/HorizonHealthNB; www.linkedin.com/company/horizon-health-network
Number of Beds: 21 beds
Number of Employees: 105
Note: Programs & services include: Addictions & Mental Health (geriatrics, smoking cessation program); Clinical Services (day surgery, emergency, family medicine & geriatrics); Diagnostics & Testing (ECG & x-ray); & Support & Therapy (clinical nutrition, occupational, physiotherapy, respiratory, speech-language pathology, spiritual care, social work & telehealth).

***Saint John:* Saint John Regional Hospital**
Affiliated with: Horizon Health Network
PO Box 5200, 400 University Ave., Saint John, NB E2L 4L4
Tel: 506-648-6000; *Fax:* 506-648-6364
horizon@horizonnb.ca
www.horizonnb.ca
Social Media: www.facebook.com/120963024660628; twitter.com/HorizonHealthNB; www.linkedin.com/company/horizon-health-network
Number of Beds: 445 beds
Note: Teaching hospital affiliated with Dalhousie University, New Brunswick Community College, University of New Brunswick & Memorial University in St. John's Newfoundland.
Programs & services include: Addictions & Mental Health (emergency & inpatient acute care psychiatry); Clinical Services (cardiac surgery, day surgery, dermatology, dialysis, ear, nose & throat, emergency, family medicine, general surgery, gynecology surgery, gastroenterology, geriatrics, intensive care, internal medicine, neonatal intensive care, minor surgery, pediatrics, palliative care, physiatry, plastic & burns, psychiatry, neurology, neurosurgery, obstetrics, oncology, ophthalmology surgery, orthopedic surgery, plastic surgery, rehabilitation, rheumatology, sleep centre, thoracic surgery, urology surgery, & vascular surgery); Diagnostics & Testing (blood & specimen, bone marrow, breathing function, bronchoscopy, CT scan, cystoscopy, endoscopy, ECG, fluoroscopy, holter monitoring, neuro electrodiagnostics, pathology, MRI, mammography, positron emissions tomography, nuclear medicine, spirometry, ultrasound & x-ray); & Support & Therapy (audiology, clinical nutrition, occupational, physiotherapy, psychology, recreational, respiratory, speech-language pathology, spiritual care, social work & telehealth).

***Saint John:* St. Joseph's Hospital**
Affiliated with: Horizon Health Network
130 Bayard Dr., Saint John, NB E2L 3L6
Tel: 506-632-5555; *Fax:* 506-632-5551
horizon@horizonnb.ca
www.horizonnb.ca
Social Media: www.facebook.com/120963024660628; twitter.com/HorizonHealthNB; www.linkedin.com/company/horizon-health-network
Number of Beds: 103 beds
Note: Programs & services include: Addictions & Mental Health (methadone treatment program); Clinical Services (day surgery, ear, nose & throat, emergency, general surgery, gynecology surgery, gastroenterology, geriatrics, minor surgery, oncology, ophthalmology surgery, orthopedic surgery, palliative care, plastic surgery & urology surgery); Diagnostics & Testing (blood & specimen collection, CT scan, cystoscopy, endoscopy, ECG, fluoroscopy, holter monitoring, neuro electrodiagnostics, mammography, spirometry, ultrasound & x-ray); & Support & Therapy (clinical nutrition, occupational, physiotherapy, recreational, respiratory, speech-language pathology, spiritual care, social work & telehealth).
Heather Oakley, Facility Administrator

***Saint-Quentin:* Hôtel-Dieu St-Joseph de Saint-Quentin**
Affiliée à: Vitalité Health Network
21, rue Canada, Saint-Quentin, NB E8A 2P6
Tél: 506-235-2300; *Téléc:* 506-235-7201
info@vitalitenb.ca
www.vitalitenb.ca
Nombre de lits: 6 lits
Population desservi: 6000; *Personnel:* 80
Note: Services: anticoagulant; clinique du prédiabète; clinique pulmonaire; diabète; gastroentérologie; hypertension artérielle; imagerie médicale; laboratoire; médecine interne; mère-enfant; nutrition; obstétrique; oncologie; ophtalmologie; pédiatrie; physiothérapie; préanesthésie; santé mentale; soins médicaux d'un jour; traitement des dépendances; traitements mineurs; urologie; et urgence.
Nicole Labrie, Directrice d'établissement

***St Stephen:* Charlotte County Hospital**
Affiliated with: Horizon Health Network
4 Garden St., St Stephen, NB E3L 2L9
Tel: 506-465-4444; *Fax:* 506-465-4418
horizon@horizonnb.ca
www.horizonnb.ca
Social Media: www.facebook.com/120963024660628; twitter.com/HorizonHealthNB; www.linkedin.com/company/horizon-health-network
Number of Beds: 44 beds
Note: Programs & services include: Addictions & Mental Health (methadone treatment program); Clinical Services (day surgery, dialysis, emergency, family medicine, geriatrics, intensive care, minor surgery & palliative care); Diagnostics & Testing (blood & specimen, endoscopy, ECG, holter monitoring, mammography, ultrasound, spirometry & x-ray); & Support & Therapy (clinical nutrition, occupational therapy, physiotherapy, respiratory therapy & speech-language pathology).
Sharon Tucker, Facility Administrator

***Ste-Anne-de-Kent:* Hôpital Stella-Maris-de-Kent**
Affiliée à: Vitalité Health Network
7714, rte 134, Ste-Anne-de-Kent, NB E4S 1H5
Tél: 506-743-7800
info@vitalitenb.ca
www.vitalitenb.ca
Nombre de lits: 20 lits
Note: Services: alimentation et nutrition / clinique de nutrition; clinique de santé; clinique de soins de la femme; clinique du diabète; cliniques externes avec spécialistes; électrocardiogramme; ergothérapie; imagerie diagnostique; laboratoire; liaison autochtone; orthophonie; pharmacie; physiothérapie; service de l'environnement; services spirituels et religieux; thérapie respiratoire; unité de médecine; et urgence.

***Sussex:* Sussex Health Centre**
Affiliated with: Horizon Health Network
75 Leonard Dr., Sussex, NB E4E 2P7
Tel: 506-432-3100; *Fax:* 506-432-3106
horizon@horizonnb.ca
www.horizonnb.ca
Social Media: www.facebook.com/120963024660628; twitter.com/HorizonHealthNB; www.linkedin.com/company/horizon-health-network
Number of Beds: 25 beds
Population Served: 30000
Note: Programs & services include: Clinical Services (day surgery, emergency, family medicine, general surgery, palliative care & rehabilitation); Diagnostics & Testing (blood & specimen collection, ECG, holter monitoring, mammography, spirometry, ultrasound & x-ray); & Support & Therapy (audiology, clinical nutrition, occupational, physiotherapy, respiratory, speech-language pathology & spiritual care).

***Tracadie-Sheila:* Hôpital de Tracadie-Sheila**
Affiliée à: Vitalité Health Network
CP 3180, 400, rue des Hospitalières, Tracadie-Sheila, NB E1X 1G5
Tél: 506-394-3000; *Téléc:* 506-394-3034
info@vitalitenb.ca
www.vitalitenb.ca
Fondée en: 1991
Note: Services: 2e nord et soins concentres; diététique; électrodiagnostic; ergothérapie; imagerie médicale; laboratoire; médecine et pédiatrie; orthophonie; physiothérapie; service alimentaire; service de psychologie; soins ambulatoires; travail social; services spirituels et religieux; thérapie respiratoire; traitement des dépendances; unité satellite de dialyse; et urgence.

***Waterville:* Upper River Valley Hospital**
Affiliated with: Horizon Health Network
11300 Rte. 130, Waterville, NB E7P 0A4
Tel: 506-375-5900
horizon@horizonnb.ca
www.horizonnb.ca
Social Media: www.facebook.com/120963024660628; twitter.com/HorizonHealthNB; www.linkedin.com/company/horizon-health-network
Number of Beds: 45 beds
Population Served: 45000; *Number of Employees:* 800
Note: Programs & services include: Addictions & Mental Health (smoking cessation program); Clinical Services (day surgery, dialysis, emergency, family medicine, general surgery, gastroenterology, geriatrics, intensive care, internal medicine, minor surgery, pediatrics, palliative care, obstetrics, oncology, ophthalmology surgery, rehabilitation & urology surgery); Diagnostics & Testing (blood & specimen collection, bone marrow biopsies, breathing function lab, CT scan, endoscopy, ECG, fluoroscopy, holter monitoring, MRI, mammography, spirometry, ultrasound & x-ray); Public Health Programs (health emergency & promotion, healthy learners program, children & adolescents, immunization, communicable disease prevention, HIV testing & sexual health); & Support & Therapy (audiology, clinical nutrition, occupational, physiotherapy, psychology, respiratory, speech-language pathology, spiritual care, social work & telehealth).
Dean Cummings, Executive Director

Auxiliary Hospitals

***Saint John:* Saint John Regional Hospital - Ridgewood Veterans Wing (RVW)**
Affiliated with: Horizon Health Network
PO Box 2100, 422 Bay St., Saint John, NB E2L 4L2
Tel: 506-635-2420; *Fax:* 506-635-2425
horizon@horizonnb.ca
www.horizonnb.ca
Social Media: www.facebook.com/120963024660628; twitter.com/HorizonHealthNB; www.linkedin.com/company/horizon-health-network
Year Founded: 1976
Number of Beds: 80 beds
Note: A facility for veterans who require long-term care; maintains a close relationship with Veteran Affairs Canada & the Royal Canadian Legion.

Community Health Care Centres

***Baie-Sainte-Anne:* Baie-Ste-Anne Health Centre/Centre de santé Baie-Ste-Anne**
Affiliated with: Horizon Health Network
13, rue de l'Église, Baie-Sainte-Anne, NB E9A 1A9
Tel: 506-228-2004; *Fax:* 506-228-2008
www.horizonnb.ca
Note: Patients may access the services of a physician who works 3 days per week, & a full time nurse on site; monthly public health & diabetic clinics; weekly lab.

***Bathurst:* NB Extra Mural Program Bathurst Unit**
1745 Vallée-Lourdes Dr., Bathurst, NB E2A 4P8
Tel: 506-455-3030; *Fax:* 506-544-3029

***Belledune:* Centre de santé de Jacquet River Health Centre**
Affiliated with: Vitalité Health Network
41 Mack St., Belledune, NB E8G 2R3
Tel: 506-237-3222; *Fax:* 506-237-3224
www.santerestigouchehealth.com
Lynn DeGroot, Administratrice d'établissement

***Blacks Harbour:* Fundy Health Centre**
Affiliated with: Horizon Health Network
34 Hospital St., Blacks Harbour, NB E5H 1K2
Tel: 506-456-4200; *Fax:* 506-456-4259
horizon@horizonnb.ca
www.horizonnb.ca

***Blackville:* Blackville Health Centre**
Affiliated with: Horizon Health Network
2 Shaffer Lane, Blackville, NB E9B 1P4
Tel: 506-843-2910; *Fax:* 506-843-2911
horizonnb.ca

***Boiestown:* Boiestown Health Centre**
Affiliated with: Horizon Health Network
#2, 6154 rte 8, Boiestown, NB E6A 1M4
Tel: 506-369-2700; *Fax:* 506-369-2702
horizonnb.ca

***Campobello:* NB Extra Mural Program St Stephen Unit - Campobello Office**
Affiliated with: Horizon Health Network
640, rte 774, Campobello, NB E5E 1A5
Tel: 506-752-4100; *Fax:* 506-752-4106

***Caraquet:* NB Extra Mural Program - Caraquet Unit**
Affiliated with: Vitalité Health Network
442 St. Pierre Blvd. West, Caraquet, NB E1W 1A3
Tel: 506-726-2800; *Fax:* 506-726-2808

***Chipman:* Chipman Health Centre**
Affiliated with: Horizon Health Network
9 Civic Ct., Chipman, NB E4A 2H8
Tel: 506-339-7650; *Fax:* 506-339-7652
horizonnb.ca

Dalhousie: **Centre de santé communautaire St. Joseph/St. Joseph Community Health Centre**
Affiliated with: Vitalité Health Network
#1, 280, rue Victoria, Dalhousie, NB E8C 2R6
Tel: 506-684-7000; *Fax:* 506-684-4751
www.santerestigouchehealth.com; www.santevitalitehealth.ca
Note: Le Réseau de santé Vitalité regroupe les huit anciennes régies régionales dans la province. Le Centre a pour mission d'améliorer l'accès aux soins de santé primaires, et l'état de santé des collectivités; promotion de la santé, prévention des maladies et blessures, et traitement des maladies chroniques; services diagnostiques; soins ambulatoires.

Dalhousie: **NB Extra Mural Program - Restigouche Unit**
Affiliated with: Vitalité Health Network
#2, 280 Victoria St., Dalhousie, NB E8C 2R6
Tel: 506-684-7060; *Fax:* 506-684-7334

Doaktown: **Central Miramichi Community Health Centre (CMCHC)**
Affiliated with: Horizon Health Network
Former Name: Upper Miramichi Health Services Centre - Doaktown
11 Prospect St., Doaktown, NB E9C 1C8
Tel: 506-365-6100; *Fax:* 506-365-6104
horizonnb.ca
Lorri Amos, Nurse Manager

Edmundston: **NB Extra Mural Program Edmundston Unit**
4th Fl., 275 Hebert blvd., Edmundston, NB E3V 4N4
Tel: 506-739-2160; *Fax:* 506-739-2163

Fairhaven: **Deer Island Health Centre**
Affiliated with: Horizon Health Network
999 Rte. 772, Fairhaven, NB E5V 1P2
Tel: 506-747-4150; *Fax:* 506-747-4151
horizonnb.ca

Fredericton: **NB Extra Mural Program Fredericton Unit**
Affiliated with: Horizon Health Network
PO Box 9000, 700 Priestman St., Fredericton, NB E3B 5N5
Tel: 506-452-5800; *Fax:* 506-452-5858
horizonnb.ca
Christine DeJong, Manager
christine.dejong@horizonnb.ca

Fredericton: **NB Extra Mural Program Sussex Unit**
Affiliated with: Horizon Health Network
Health Services Complex, #4, 20 Kennedy Dr., Fredericton, NB E4E 2P1
Tel: 506-432-3280; *Fax:* 506-432-3250

Fredericton: **NB Extra Mural Program Fredericton Unit - Boiestown Office**
Affiliated with: Horizon Health Network
PO Box 9000, 700 Priestman St., Fredericton, NB E3B 5N5
Tel: 506-452-5800; *Fax:* 506-452-5858

Fredericton Junction: **Fredericton Junction Health Centre**
Affiliated with: Horizon Health Network
233 Sunbury Dr., Fredericton Junction, NB E5L 1S1
Tel: 506-368-6501; *Fax:* 506-368-6502
horizonnb.ca

Grand Manan: **NB Extra Mural Program**
Affiliated with: Horizon Health Network
Grand Manan Hospital, 196 Rte. 776, Grand Manan, NB E5G 1A3
Tel: 506-662-4055; *Fax:* 506-662-4054

Grand-Sault: **Programme extra mural du NB - Unite de Grand-Sault**
Affiliée à: Vitalité Health Network
CP 7812, 532, ch Madawaska, Grand-Sault, NB E3Z 3E8
Tél: 506-473-7492; *Téléc:* 506-473-7476
Carlene Pelletier, Manager

Harvey Station: **Harvey Health Centre**
Affiliated with: Horizon Health Network
Former Name: Harvey Community Hospital Ltd.
2019 Rte. 3, Harvey Station, NB E6K 3E9
Tel: 506-366-6400; *Fax:* 506-366-6403
horizon@horizonnb.ca
www.horizonnb.ca

Kedgwick: **NB Extra Mural Program Kedgwick Unit**
PO Box 10012, 7970 rte 17, Kedgwick, NB E8B 1Z7
Tel: 506-284-3444; *Fax:* 506-284-3446

Lamèque: **NB Extra Mural Program - Lamèque Unit**
Affiliated with: Vitalité Health Network
29 Hospital St., Lamèque, NB E8T 1C5
Tel: 506-344-3000; *Fax:* 506-344-3001
Norma McGraw, Manager

McAdam: **MacLean Memorial Hospital**
Affiliated with: Vitalité Health Network
PO Box 311, 15 Saunders Rd., McAdam, NB E6J 1K9
Tel: 506-784-6300; *Fax:* 506-784-6306

Minto: **Queens North Community Health Centre**
Affiliated with: Horizon Health Network
PO Box 1004, 1100 Pleasant Dr., Minto, NB E4B 3Y6
Tel: 506-327-7800; *Fax:* 506-327-7850
horizonnb.ca

Miramichi: **NB Extra Mural Program Miramichi Unit**
Affiliated with: Horizon Health Network
500 Water St., Miramichi, NB E1V 3G5
Tel: 506-623-6350; *Fax:* 506-623-6370

Miramichi: **NB Extra Mural Program Miramichi Unit - Blackville Office**
Affiliated with: Horizon Health Network
500 Water St., Miramichi, NB E1V 3G5
Tel: 506-623-6312; *Fax:* 506-623-6370

Miramichi: **NB Extra Mural Program Miramichi Unit - Neguac Office**
Affiliated with: Horizon Health Network
500 Water St., Miramichi, NB E1V 3G5
Tel: 506-623-6312; *Fax:* 506-623-6370

Moncton: **NB Extra Mural Program Blanche-Bourgeois Unit**
Affiliated with: Beausejour Regional Health Authority
35 Providence St., Moncton, NB E1A 8X3
Tel: 506-862-4400

Moncton: **NB Extra Mural Program/Programme extra-mural - unité Driscoll Driscoll Unit**
Affiliated with: Horizon Health Network
#107, 1600 Main St., Moncton, NB E1E 1G5
Tel: 506-867-6500; *Fax:* 506-867-6509
horizonnb.ca
Note: Home healthcare program for eligible residents

Nackawic: **Nackawic Community Health Centre**
Affiliated with: Horizon Health Network
Nackawic Shopping Centre, Upper Floor, #201, 135 Otis Dr., Nackawic, NB E6G 1H1
Tel: 506-575-6600; *Fax:* 506-575-6603

Néguac: **Neguac Health Centre**
Affiliated with: Horizon Health Network
38 Otho St., Néguac, NB E9C 4H3
Tel: 506-776-3876; *Fax:* 506-776-3877
horizonnb.ca

Oromocto: **NB Extra Mural Program Oromocto Unit**
Affiliated with: Horizon Health Network
275A Restigouche Rd., Oromocto, NB E2V 2H1
Tel: 506-357-4900; *Fax:* 506-357-4904

Oromocto: **NB Extra Mural Program Oromocto Unit - Minto Office**
Affiliated with: Horizon Health Network
275A Restigouche Rd., Oromocto, NB E2V 2H1
Tel: 506-327-4900; *Fax:* 506-327-4904

Paquetville: **Centre de santé de Paquetville**
Affiliée à: Vitalité Health Network
1096, rue du Parc, Paquetville, NB E8R 1J4
Tél: 506-764-2424; *Téléc:* 506-764-2425

Perth-Andover: **NB Extra Mural Program Perth Unit**
Affiliated with: Horizon Health Network
35F Tribe Rd., Perth-Andover, NB E7H 0A8
Tel: 506-273-7222; *Fax:* 506-273-7220
horizonnb.ca

Petitcodiac: **Petitcodiac Health Centre/Centre de santé de Petitcodiac**
Affiliated with: Horizon Health Network
2501, 32 Railway Ave., Petitcodiac, NB E4Z 6H4
Tel: 506-756-3400; *Fax:* 506-756-3406
generalinquiries@serha.ca
www.serha.ca/petitcodiac
Note: Number of staff: 3 physicians, 1 dentist. Foot care & diabetes clinics by appointment, drop-in services, visiting dietician

Pointe-Verte: **Centre de santé de Chaleur Health Centre**
Affiliée à: Vitalité Health Network
Ancien nom: Centre de santé Pointe Verte
382, rue Principale, Pointe-Verte, NB E8J 2X6
Tél: 506-542-2434; *Téléc:* 506-783-8623

Quispamsis: **NB Extra Mural Program Kennebecasis Valley Unit**
Affiliated with: Horizon Health Network
Quispmsis Village Centre, PO Box 21025, 175 Old Hampton Rd., Quispamsis, NB E2E 4Z4
Tel: 506-848-4600; *Fax:* 506-848-4620
horizonnb.ca

Rexton: **Health Services Centre Rexton/Le Centre de santé de Rexton**
Affiliated with: Horizon Health Network
33 Main St., Rexton, NB E4W 5N4
Tel: 506-523-7940; *Fax:* 506-523-7949
horizonnb.ca
Year Founded: 1974
Note: Drop-in services, clinics, immunization, nutrition & diabetes education

Riverside-Albert: **Albert County Health & Wellness Centre/Le Centre de santé & de mieux-être du comté d'Albert**
Affiliated with: Horizon Health Network
8 Forestdale Rd., Riverside-Albert, NB E4H 3Y7
Tel: 506-882-3100; *Fax:* 506-882-3101
horizonnb.ca
Year Founded: 1961
Note: Multidisciplinary, primary health care services

Rogersville: **Rogersville Health Centre**
Affiliated with: Horizon Health Network
9, rue des Ormes, Rogersville, NB E4Y 1S6
Tel: 506-775-2030; *Fax:* 506-775-2025

Sackville: **NB Extra Mural Program/Programme extra-mural - unité Tantramar Tantramar Unit**
Affiliated with: Horizon Health Network
8 Main St., Sackville, NB E4L 4A3
Tel: 506-364-4400; *Fax:* 506-364-4405
horizonnb.ca
Year Founded: 1979
Note: Home healthcare program for eligible residents

Saint John: **Hospice Greater Saint John**
Affiliated with: Horizon Health Network
Former Name: Hospice Saint John & Sussex
385 Dufferin Row, Saint John, NB E2M 2J9
Tel: 506-632-5593; *Fax:* 506-632-5592
info@hospicesj.ca
www.hospicesj.ca
Year Founded: 1983
Number of Beds: 10 beds
Note: Number of employees: 4
Sandy Johnson, CEO
506-632-5723, sjohnson@hospicesj.ca

Saint John: **NB Extra Mural Program Saint John Unit**
Affiliated with: Horizon Health Network
Meditrust Pharmacy Building, 1490 Manawagonish Rd., Saint John, NB E2M 3Y4
Tel: 506-649-2626; *Fax:* 506-649-2540
horizonnb.ca
Note: in-home support
Sue Ness, Manager

Saint John: **St. Joseph's Community Health Centre**
Affiliated with: Horizon Health Network
116 Coburg St., Saint John, NB E2L 3K1
Tel: 506-632-5537; *Fax:* 506-632-5539
en.horizonnb.ca
Dawn Marie Buck, Contact

***Saint John:* Senior Watch Inc.**
Affiliated with: Horizon Health Network
33 Hanover St., Saint John, NB E2L 3G1
Tel: 506-634-8906; *Fax:* 506-633-2992
Toll-Free: 800-561-2463
services@seniorwatch.com
www.seniorwatch.com
Year Founded: 1987
Note: New Brunswick-based firm specializing in developing and managing new programs for Seniors
Jean E. Porter Mowatt, President & CEO

***Sainte-Anne-de-Madawaska:* Centre de santé Ste-Anne**
Affiliated with: Vitalité Health Network
1, rue de la Clinique, Sainte-Anne-de-Madawaska, NB E7E 1B9
Tel: 506-445-6200; *Fax:* 506-445-6201
Dr. Édouard Hendriks, Administrateur d'établissement (par intérim)

***Shediac:* Centre médical régional de Shédiac**
Affiliated with: Vitalité Health Network
PO Box 1477, 419, rue Main, Shediac, NB E4P 2B8
Tel: 506-533-2700
www.beausejour-nb.ca
Lise Guerrette-Daigle, Administrateur d'établissement

***Shediac:* NB Extra Mural Program Shediac Unit**
Affiliated with: Beausejour Regional Health Authority
423 Main St., Shediac, NB E1C 2B6
Tel: 506-533-2800

***St Stephen:* NB Extra Mural Program St Stephen Unit**
Affiliated with: Horizon Health Network
#100, 73 Milltown Blvd., St Stephen, NB E3L 1G5
Tel: 506-465-4520; *Fax:* 506-465-4523
horizonnb.ca

***St. George:* NB Extra Mural Program Eastern Charlotte Unit**
Affiliated with: Horizon Health Network
122 Main St., St. George, NB E5C 3S3
Tel: 506-755-4660; *Fax:* 506-755-4665
horizonnb.ca

***Stanley:* Stanley Health Services Centre**
Affiliated with: Horizon Health Network
PO Box 340, Stanley, NB E6B 2K5
Tel: 506-367-7730; *Fax:* 506-367-7738
horizonnb.ca

***Ste-Anne de Kent:* Programme extra mural du NB - Kent Unit**
Affiliée à: Vitalité Health Network
Stella-Maris-de-Kent Hospital, 7717 route 134, Ste-Anne de Kent, NB E4S 1H5
Tél: 506-743-2000

***Tracadie-Sheila:* NB Extra Mural Program - Tracadie Unit**
Affiliated with: Vitalité Health Network
PO Box 3180 Stn. Bureau-Chef, 400 Hospitalières St., Tracadie-Sheila, NB E1X 1V5
Tel: 506-394-4100; *Fax:* 506-394-4117

***Waterville:* NB Extra Mural Program - Woodstock Unit**
Affiliated with: Horizon Health Network
11300 rte 130, Waterville, NB E7P 0A4
Tel: 506-375-2539; *Fax:* 506-375-2675

Special Treatment Centres

***Campbellton:* Notre-Dame House Inc./Maison Notre-Dame**
PO Box 158, Campbellton, NB E3N 3G4
Tel: 506-789-0390; *Fax:* 506-753-3718
maisonnotredame@nb.aibn.com
Note: Maison Notre-Dame is a shelter for women who have experienced violence or abuse.
Stefanie Savoie, Executive Director

***Edmundston:* Services de toxicomanie**
Affiliée à: Vitalité Health Network
62, rue Queen, Edmundston, NB E3V 1A1
Tél: 506-735-2092; *Téléc:* 506-835-2700
www.rrs4-rha4.nb.ca
Nombre de lits: 10 lits
Note: Service de désintoxification interne
Johanne Lavoie, Directeur
johanne.lavoie@vitalitenb.ca

***Fredericton:* Fredericton Addiction Services**
Affiliated with: Horizon Health Network
c/o Victoria Health Centre, 65 Brunswick St., Fredericton, NB E3B 1G5
Tel: 506-452-5558; *Fax:* 506-452-5533
Gordon Skead, Regional Director

***Fredericton:* Fredericton Site of The Morgentaler Clinic**
The Morgentaler Clinic
Affiliated with: Horizon Health Network
554 Brunswick St., Fredericton, NB E3B 1H5
Tel: 506-451-9060; *Fax:* 506-451-9062
nbclinic@nb.aibn.com
www.morgentalernb.ca
Note: Specialties: Abortion care services; Abortion aftercare

***Fredericton:* Stan Cassidy Centre for Rehabilitation**
Affiliated with: Horizon Health Network
800 Priestman St., Fredericton, NB E3B 0C7
Tel: 506-452-5225; *Fax:* 506-452-5190
Number of Beds: 20 beds

***Moncton:* Moncton Addiction Services/Services de traitement des dépendances**
Affiliated with: Horizon Health Network
125 Mapleton Rd., Moncton, NB E1C 9G8
Tel: 506-856-2333; *Fax:* 506-856-2796
horizonnb.ca
Number of Beds: 20 beds
Note: Detoxification unit, methadone maintenance treatment program, addiction prevention & education, counseling, assessments

***Petit-Rocher:* Services Résidentiels Nepisiguit Inc.**
#312, 702, rue Principale, Petit-Rocher, NB E8J 1V1
Tél: 506-542-2404; *Téléc:* 506-542-2406
sminc@nb.aibn.com
www.gnb.ca
Nombre de lits: 22 lits
Note: Service résidentiel à toutes les personnes ayant des handicaps de la région Nepisiguit
Luc DeRoche, Directeur général

***Saint John:* WorkSafeNB Rehabilitation Centre**
Affiliated with: Horizon Health Network
PO Box 160, 1 Portland St., Saint John, NB E2L 3X9
Tel: 506-738-8411; *Fax:* 888-629-4722
Toll-Free: 800-222-9775
worksafenb.ca
Year Founded: 1965
Note: Occupational rehabilitation
Gerard M. Adams, President & CEO
Shelly Dauphinee, Vice-President, WorkSafe Services

***Saint John West:* Ridgewood Addiction Services**
Affiliated with: Horizon Health Network
416 Bay St., Saint John West, NB E2M 4Y1
Tel: 506-674-4300; *Fax:* 506-658-3774
Number of Beds: 90 beds
Note: Comprehensive addiction treatment programs, detoxification, outpatient & short term residential services, addiction prevention & education, community reintegration

Long Term Care Facilities

***Acadieville:* Villa Acadie Ltée**
4057, rte. 480, Acadieville, NB E4Y 1Z3
Tél: 506-775-6088
Nombre de lits: 13 lits

***Baker Brook:* Résidence Notre Dame**
CP 38, 3741, rue Principale, Baker Brook, NB E7A 2A5
Tél: 506-258-3322
Nombre de lits: 18 lits

***Fredericton:* Women's Institute Home**
681 Union St., Fredericton, NB E3A 3N8
Tel: 506-454-0798
nbwi@nb.aibn.com
www.nbwi.ca
Social Media:
www.facebook.com/pages/Womens-Institute-Home/2842958017 81170
Year Founded: 1911
Number of Beds: 21 rooms

***Miramichi:* Howard Henderson House Inc.**
Affiliated with: Horizon Health Network
225 Wellington St., Miramichi, NB E1N 1N1
Tel: 506-773-6522
Note: Residential care is provided for adults who are mentally or physically challenged.

***Moncton:* Alternative Residences Alternatives (ARA)**
Affiliated with: Horizon Health Network
100 Botsford St., Moncton, NB E1C 4W9
Tel: 506-854-7229; *Fax:* 506-853-6051
altres@rogers.com
www.alternativeresidences.org
Year Founded: 1984
Note: Alternative Residences provides supervision & support to persons with a mental illness. Services include assistance with medication intake, the development of social & personal skills, dietary guidance, assistance with budgets, & searches for housing.
Alternative Residences' subidized shared housing complexes accommodate 28, with minimal staff support. The organization's affordable community apartments house 16 clients.
Chantal Ricker, General Manager & Human Resources Officer
Susan McLure, Accounting Officer

***Moncton:* Birchmount Lodge**
Affiliated with: Horizon Health Network
144 Birchmount Dr., Moncton, NB E1C 8E7
Tel: 506-384-7573
Number of Beds: 32 beds
Donald Vossburgh, Administrator

***Moncton:* Moncton Community Residences Inc.**
Affiliated with: Horizon Health Network
Former Name: Reade House
357 Collishaw St., Moncton, NB E1C 9R2
Tel: 506-858-0550; *Fax:* 506-858-0271
mcri@nb.aibn.com
www.monctoncommunityresidences.com
Number of Beds: 5 beds
Note: Provides residential services to people with developmental challenges, ranging from group homes to assistance with independent living

***Pennfield:* Collingwood Special Care Home**
249 Rte. 176, Pennfield, NB E5H 1R9
Tel: 506-456-3533
Number of Beds: 20 beds
Nancy Drost, Administrator

***Riverview:* Grass Home**
Former Name: N-Joy Homes Ltd.
774 Coverdale Rd., Riverview, NB E1B 3L5
Tel: 506-386-1740; *Fax:* 506-386-7040
Number of Beds: 24 beds
John Grass, Proprietor/Administrator

***Robertville:* La Villa Sormany Inc.**
1730, route 322, Robertville, NB E8K 2V8
Tél: 506-542-2731; *Téléc:* 506-542-2733
Nombre de lits: 40 lits

***Sackville:* Drew Nursing Home**
165 Main St., Sackville, NB E4L 4S2
Tel: 506-364-4900; *Fax:* 506-364-4921
office@drewnursinghome.ca
www.drewnursinghome.ca
Number of Beds: 130 beds
Note: senior apartments

***Saint John:* New Direction Inc.**
Affiliated with: Horizon Health Network
PO Box 549, 44 Peters St., Saint John, NB E2L 3Z8
Tel: 506-643-6207; *Fax:* 506-643-6209
newdir3@nb.aibn.com
Number of Beds: 43 beds
Note: Provides housing and support services to persons suffering from mental illness
Gayle Capson, Executive Director

***Saint John:* Westport Residential Facility**
Affiliated with: Horizon Health Network
427 Prince St., Saint John, NB E2M 1R2
Tel: 506-674-2069; *Fax:* 506-832-0808
Number of Beds: 15 beds

***Sainte-Anne-de-Madawaska:* Foyer Mont St-Joseph**
8, rue St-Joseph, Sainte-Anne-de-Madawaska, NB E7E 1L1
Tél: 506-445-2755

***Tabusintac:* Foyer Prime Breau**
14 Covedell Rd., Tabusintac, NB E9H 1E6
Tél: 506-779-4445
Nombre de lits: 2 lits

Roséanna Breau, Propriétrice

Nursing Homes

Bath: River View Manor Inc.
Affiliated with: Vitalité Health Network
96 Hospital St., Bath, NB E7J 1B9
Tel: 506-278-6030; *Fax:* 506-278-5962
rvmadministrator@nb.aibn.com
www.riverviewmanor.ca

Year Founded: 1981
Number of Beds: 40 beds
Note: Nursing home
Kay Simonds, Administrator
Randy Giberson, Supervisor, Plant Maintenance

Bathurst: Le Foyer Notre-Dame de Lourdes Inc.
Affiliée à: Vitalité Health Network
2055, Vallée-Lourdes Dr., Bathurst, NB E2A 4P8
Tél: 506-549-5085; *Téléc:* 506-548-5052
fndl.org

Nombre de lits: 100 lits
Claire Savoie, Directrice générale
506-549-5085, dg.fndl@nb.aibn.com

Bathurst: Robert L. Knowles Veterans Unit, Villa Chaleur
795, rue Champlain, Bathurst, NB E2A 4M8
Tel: 506-549-5582; *Fax:* 506-545-6424

Number of Beds: 13 beds
Lucie Fournier, Administrator

Blacks Harbour: Fundy Nursing Home
34 Hospital St., Blacks Harbour, NB E5H 1C2
Tel: 506-456-4218; *Fax:* 506-456-4259

Number of Beds: 26 beds
Debbie Harris, Administrator

Boiestown: Central New Brunswick Nursing Home Inc.
Affiliated with: Vitalité Health Network
3458 Rte. 625, Boiestown, NB E6A 1C8
Tel: 506-369-7262; *Fax:* 506-369-2331

Number of Beds: 30 beds

Bouctouche: Manoir Saint-Jean Baptiste
Affiliée à: Vitalité Health Network
5, av Richard, Bouctouche, NB E4S 3T2
Tél: 506-743-7344; *Téléc:* 506-743-7343

Nombre de lits: 50 lits
Ian Drapeau, Directeur Général

Campbellton: Campbellton Nursing Home Inc.
Affiliated with: Vitalité Health Network
PO Box 850, 101 Dover St., Campbellton, NB E3N 3K6
Tel: 506-789-7350; *Fax:* 506-789-7360

Number of Beds: 100 beds

Caraquet: Villa Beauséjour Inc.
Affiliée à: Vitalité Health Network
CP 5608, 253, boul St-Pierre ouest, Caraquet, NB E1W 1B7
Tél: 506-726-2744

Nombre de lits: 62 lits
Roger Landry, Directeur général
506-726-2741
Annette Chiasson, Director, Nursing
Dennis Power, Maintenance Supervisor

Dalhousie: Dalhousie Nursing Home Inc.
Affiliated with: Vitalité Health Network
#1, 296 Victoria St., Dalhousie, NB E8C 2R8
Tel: 506-684-7800; *Fax:* 506-684-7832

Number of Beds: 105 beds

Edmundston: Villa des Jardins Inc.
Affiliée à: Vitalité Health Network
50, rue Queen, Edmundston, NB E3V 3N4
Tél: 506-735-2112; *Téléc:* 506-735-2462

Nombre de lits: 30 lits
Carole Ouellette, Administrateur
506-735-2115

Fredericton: Pine Grove
Affiliated with: Horizon Health Network
521 Woodstock Rd., Fredericton, NB E3B 2J2
Tel: 506-444-3400; *Fax:* 506-444-3407
adminclerk@pinegrovenh.com
www.pinegrovenh.com

Cheryl Wiggins, Administrator

Fredericton: York Care Centre
Affiliated with: Horizon Health Network
Former Name: York Manor Inc.
100 Sunset Dr., Fredericton, NB E3A 1A3
Tel: 506-444-3880; *Fax:* 506-444-3544
info@yorkmanor.nb.ca
www.yorkmanor.nb.ca

Number of Beds: 198 beds
Kevin Harter, President & CEO
506-444-3880, kharter@yorkcarecentre.ca

Fredericton Junction: White Rapids Manor Inc.
Affiliated with: Horizon Health Network
233 Sunbury Dr., Fredericton Junction, NB E5L 1S1
Tel: 613-368-6508; *Fax:* 613-368-6512
brees@whiterapidsmanor.nb.ca

Number of Beds: 36 beds
Kathy Jenkins, Administrator

Gagetown: Orchard View Long Term Care Facility
Affiliated with: Vitalité Health Network
Former Name: Gagetown Nursing Home Ltd.
2230 Rte 102, Gagetown, NB E5M 1J6
Tel: 506-488-3544; *Fax:* 506-488-3551
www.orchardviewcare.ca

Year Founded: 1972
Number of Beds: 40 beds
Betty Daniels, Administrator
506-488-3586, bdaniels@orchardviewltc.ca
Charlotte Hiscock, Director of Care
506-488-3585, chiscock@orchardviewltc.ca

Grand Falls: Villa Des Chutes
Affiliated with: Vitalité Health Network
433, rue Evangeline, Grand Falls, NB E3Y 0A9
Tel: 506-473-7726; *Fax:* 506-473-7849

Number of Beds: 69 lits
Maurice Richard, Administrateur
506-473-7726

Grand Manan: Grand Manan Nursing Home Inc.
Affiliated with: Horizon Health Network
266, Rte. 776, Grand Manan, NB E5G 1A5
Tel: 506-662-7111; *Fax:* 506-662-7117

Number of Beds: 30 beds
Joanne Ingalls, Administrator
506-662-7111

Hampton: Dr. V.A. Snow Centre Inc.
54 Demille Ct., Hampton, NB E5N 5S7
Tel: 506-832-6210; *Fax:* 506-832-7674
info@snownursing.com
snownursing.com

Number of Beds: 50 beds
Terry MacNeill, Administrator
506-832-6210

Hartland: Central Carleton Nursing Home Inc.
139 Rockland Rd., Hartland, NB E7P 1E9
Tel: 506-375-3033; *Fax:* 506-375-3035

Number of Beds: 30 beds
Malcolm Clendenning, Administrator

Inkerman: Résidences Inkerman Inc.
1171, ch Pallot, Inkerman, NB E8P 1C2
Tel: 506-336-3909; *Fax:* 506-336-3912

Number of Beds: 30 lits

Lamèque: Les Résidences Lucien Saindon Inc.
26, rue de l'Hôpital, Lamèque, NB E8T 1C3
Tél: 506-344-3232; *Téléc:* 506-344-3240

Nombre de lits: 54 lits

Memramcook: Foyer St. Thomas de la Vallée de Memramcook Inc.
100, rue Notre-Dame, Memramcook, NB E3K 3W3
Tél: 506-758-2110; *Téléc:* 506-758-9489
www.memramcook.com

Nombre de lits: 30 lits
Pierre Landry, Directeur général
pierrela@nb.aibn.com

Mill Cove: Mill Cove Nursing Home Inc.
5647 Rte 105, Mill Cove, NB E4C 3A5
Tel: 506-488-3033

Note: Specialties: Nursing care for persons with special needs; Podiatry; Psychology; Rehabilitation; Snoezelen rooms
G. Paul Mills, Administrator
506-488-3033, ext. 2

Minto: W.G. Bishop Nursing Home
PO Box 1004, 1100 Pleasant Dr., Minto, NB E4B 3Y6
Tel: 506-327-7853; *Fax:* 506-327-7812
www.wgbishopnursinghome.org

Number of Beds: 30 beds
Kathy Donaldson, Administrator
506-327-7809

Miramichi: Miramichi Senior Citizens Home Inc.
Affiliated with: Horizon Health Network
1400 Water St., Miramichi, NB E1N 1A4
Tel: 506-778-6810; *Fax:* 506-778-6860

Number of Beds: 81 beds
Margaret Manderson, Administrator
Macrena Jardine, Director, Plant Maintenance

Miramichi: Mount Saint Joseph Nursing Home
Affiliated with: Horizon Health Network
51 Lobban Ave., Miramichi, NB E1N 2W8
Tel: 506-778-6550; *Fax:* 506-778-0193
www.mountsj.ca

Number of Beds: 133 beds
Robert B. Stewart, Executive Director
506-778-6555,
Jan Flieger, Director, Support Services

Moncton: Kenneth E. Spencer Memorial Home Inc.
Affiliated with: Horizon Health Network
35 Atlantic Baptist Ave., Moncton, NB E1E 4N3
Tel: 506-858-7870; *Fax:* 506-858-9674
info@abschi.com

Year Founded: 1973
Number of Beds: 200 beds

Moncton: Villa du Repos Inc.
Affiliée à: Horizon Health Network
125 Ave. Murphy, Moncton, NB E1A 8V2
Tél: 506-857-3560; *Téléc:* 506-859-1619
villadurepos.ca

Nombre de lits: 126 lits
Paul Williams, Directeur général
Louis Audet, Directeur, Installations matériels

Paquetville: Manoir Édith B. Pinet Inc.
1189, rue des Fondateurs, Paquetville, NB E8R 1A9
Tél: 506-764-2444

Nombre de lits: 30 lits
Léonard Légère, Administrateur
506-764-2445
Guy Thériault, Directeur, Installations phys.

Perth-Andover: Victoria Glen Manor Inc.
30 Beech Glen Rd., Perth-Andover, NB E7H 1J9
Tel: 506-273-4885
activity@vgm.ca
www.vgm.ca

Number of Beds: 65 beds
Note: Long-term care home
Eric Haddad, Administrator
506-273-4824

Port Elgin: Westford Nursing Home
57 West Main St., Port Elgin, NB E4M 1L7
Tel: 506-538-2307; *Fax:* 506-538-7293
www.westfordnursinghome.com

Year Founded: 1986
Number of Beds: 30 beds
Note: Home for seniors and physically and mentally challenged adults
Judith White, Executive Director
Ian Hurley, Manager, Environmental Support Services

Rexton: Rexton Lions Nursing Home Inc.
84 Main St., Rexton, NB E4W 2B3
Tel: 506-523-7720; *Fax:* 506-523-7703
rex_general@nb.aibn.com

Number of Beds: 30 beds
Number of Employees: 43
Dianne Robichaud, Administrator
506-523-7778

Riverview: The Salvation Army Lakeview Manor
50 Suffolk St., Riverview, NB E1B 4K6
Tel: 506-387-2012; *Fax:* 506-387-7200
www.salvationarmy.ca

Number of Beds: 50 beds
Note: Specialties: Geriatric care; Care for persons with dementia
Maj. Shirley King, Executive Director

Rogersville: Foyer Assomption
62, rue Assomption, Rogersville, NB E4Y 1S5
Tél: 506-775-2040; *Téléc:* 506-775-2053
dg.fa@nb.aibn.com

Fondée en: 1981
Nombre de lits: 50 lits
Anne Cormier, Directrice générale

***Saint John:* Carleton-Kirk Lodge**
Affiliated with: Horizon Health Network
2 Carleton Kirk Pl., Saint John, NB E2M 5B8
Tel: 506-635-7040; *Fax:* 506-635-7038
www.carletonkirklodge.com

Number of Beds: 70 beds
Tim Stevens, Administrator
506-643-7043, tstev1@nb.aibn.com

***Saint John:* Church of St. John & St. Stephen Home Inc.**
Affiliated with: Horizon Health Network
130 University Ave., Saint John, NB E2K 4K3
Tel: 506-634-6001

Note: Specialty: Long-term care
Darlene Cannell, Administrator

***Saint John:* Kennebec Manor Inc.**
Affiliated with: Horizon Health Network
475 Woodward Ave., Saint John, NB E2K 4N1
Tel: 506-632-9628; *Fax:* 506-658-9376

Number of Beds: 70 beds

***Saint John:* Loch Lomond Villa, Inc.**
Affiliated with: Horizon Health Network
185 Loch Lomond Rd., Saint John, NB E2J 3S3
Tel: 506-643-7175; *Fax:* 506-643-7198
www.lochlomondvilla.com

Year Founded: 1973
Number of Beds: 196 beds
Note: Specialties: Specialized units for Alzheimers & Psychogeriatric needs
Cindy Donovan, Administrator
506-643-7130
Valerie O'Leary, Director, Nursing
Paul Mills, Director, Operations

***Saint John:* Rocmaura Inc.**
Affiliated with: Horizon Health Network
10 Park St., Saint John, NB E2K 4P1
Tel: 506-643-7050; *Fax:* 506-643-7053
reception@rocmaura.com
www.rocmaura.com

Year Founded: 1972
Number of Beds: 150 beds
Note: Christian nursing home; affiliated with the Sisters of Charity of the Immaculate Conception (SCIC)
Sr. Susan Quinn, Administrator
506-643-7060
Harry Seele, Maintenance Supervisor

***Saint John:* Turnbull Nursing Home Inc.**
Affiliated with: Horizon Health Network
Former Name: Turnbull Home
231 Britain St., Saint John, NB E2L 0A4
Tel: 506-643-7200

Number of Beds: 50 beds
Note: Specialty: Long-term care
Elizabeth Crouchman, Administrator
506-643-7211
Brian Worden, Director, Physical Plant

***Saint-Antoine:* Foyer Saint-Antoine**
7, av de l'Église, Saint-Antoine, NB E4V 1L6
Tél: 506-525-4040; *Téléc:* 506-525-4090
www3.nbnet.nb.ca/fsa

Nombre de lits: 30 lits
Gilles C. Ouellette, Administrateur
506-525-4042, dgfsa@nb.aibn.com

***Saint-Basile:* Foyer Saint-Joseph de Saint-Basile Inc.**
475, rue Principale, Saint-Basile, NB E7C 1J2
Tél: 506-263-3462; *Téléc:* 506-263-3467

Nombre de lits: 126 lits

***Saint-Léonard:* Foyer Notre-Dame de Saint-Léonard Inc.**
604, rue Principale, Saint-Léonard, NB E7E 2H5
Tél: 506-423-3100; *Téléc:* 506-423-3152

Nombre de lits: 45 lits
Denis J. Michaud, Administrateur
506-423-3150

***Saint-Louis-de-Kent:* Villa Maria Inc.**
19, rue du College, Saint-Louis-de-Kent, NB E4X 1C2
Tél: 506-876-3488

Nombre de lits: 73 lits
Jean Paul Mazerolle, Administrateur
Sylvio Gigou, Directeur, Installations matériels

***Saint-Quentin:* Résidence Mgr. Melanson Inc.**
11, rue Levesque, Saint-Quentin, NB E8A 1T1
Tél: 506-235-6030

Nombre de lits: 42 lits
Susie Roy, Directrice générale
Rejeanne Chouinere, Superviseur
Claude Paquet, Chef, Installations

***Shediac:* Villa Providence Shédiac Inc.**
403, rue Main, Shediac, NB E4P 2B9
Tél: 506-532-4484
roger.hebert@vp-vr.ca

Nombre de lits: 190 lits
Roger T. Hébert, Directeur général
Regin LeBlanc, Chef, Entretien ménager

***Shippagan:* Les Résidences Mgr. Chiasson Inc.**
130, boul. J.D.-Gauthier, Shippagan, NB E8S 1X7
Tél: 506-336-3266; *Téléc:* 506-336-3097
recreologue.rmc@nb.aibn.com

Nombre de lits: 100 lits
Anselme Albert

***St Andrews:* Passamaquoddy Lodge Inc.**
230 Sophia St., St Andrews, NB E5B 2C2
Tel: 506-529-5240; *Fax:* 506-529-5258
lezlie.leblanc@nb.aibn.com
www.passamaquoddylodge.ca

Number of Beds: 60 beds
Note: Nursing home
Catherine Smith, Administrator
506-529-5242
F. Meredith, Supervisor, Plant Maintenance

***St Stephen:* Lincourt Manor Inc.**
PO Box 116, 1 Chipman St., St Stephen, NB E3L 2W9
Tel: 506-466-7855; *Fax:* 506-466-7853
www.lincourtmanor.ca

Note: Specialty: Long term care
Jane Lyons, Administrator
Ron Hall, Maintenance Supervisor

***St Stephen:* Maria F. Ganong Seniors Residence**
Former Name: Maria F. Ganong Old Folks Home
Also Known As: Lonicera Hall
28 Union St., St Stephen, NB E3L 1T1
Tel: 506-466-1471
lonicerahall@nb.aibn.com
www.lonicerahall.com

Number of Beds: 19 rooms
Pat Steves, Administrator

***Stanley:* Nashwaak Villa Inc.**
67 Limeklin Rd., Stanley, NB E6B 1E9
Tel: 506-367-7731
info@nashwaakvilla.ca
www.nashwaakvilla.ca

Number of Beds: 30 beds
Bonnie MacNeil, Administrator
506-367-7734

***Sussex:* Kiwanis Nursing Home Inc.**
11 Bryant Dr., Sussex, NB E4E 2P3
Tel: 506-432-3118; *Fax:* 506-432-3104
knhi@nb.aibn.com
www.kiwanisnursinghome.com

Number of Beds: 70 beds
Keri Marr, CA, Administrator
506-432-3118

***Tabusintac:* Tabusintac Nursing Home**
14 Old Manse Rd., Tabusintac, NB E9H 1Z5
Tel: 506-779-8228; *Fax:* 506-779-8149

Betty Blake, Administrator

***Tracadie-Sheila:* Villa Saint-Joseph Inc.**
3400, rue Albert, Tracadie-Sheila, NB E1X 1C8
Tél: 506-394-4800

Nombre de lits: 64 lits
Paul Arseneau, Directeur général
506-394-4820

***Welshpool:* Campobello Lodge**
Affiliated with: Horizon Health Network
#2, 640 Rte. 774, Welshpool, NB E5E 1A5
Tel: 506-752-7101; *Fax:* 506-752-7105

Number of Beds: 30 beds
Sherry Johnston, Administrator
506-752-7101, admin_cmplodge@nb.aibn.com

Mental Health Hospitals/Facilities

***Campbellton:* Centre Hospitalier Restigouche/Restigouche Hospital Centre**
Affiliée à: Vitalité Health Network
CP 10, 63, ch Gallant, Campbellton, NB E3N 3G2
Tél: 506-789-7000; *Téléc:* 506-789-7065
info@vitalitenb.ca
www.vitalitenb.ca

Nombre de lits: 172 lits

***Saint John:* Centracare Saint John Inc.**
Affiliated with: Horizon Health Network
PO Box 3220 Stn. B, 414 Bay St., Saint John, NB E2M 4H7
Tel: 506-649-2550; *Fax:* 506-649-2520
horizonnb.ca

Number of Beds: 50 beds

***Shippagan:* Pavillon St-Jérôme Inc.**
150, 17e rue, Shippagan, NB E8S 1G4
Tel: 506-336-8609; *Fax:* 506-336-8652
pavillon.stj@nb.aibn.com

Number of Beds: 12 lits
Note: résidence pour adultes handicapés intellectuels
Marie-Reine Hébert, Directrice

Special Care Homes

***Campbellton:* Duguay's Special Care Home**
20 Dover St., Campbellton, NB E3N 1P3
Tel: 506-789-1208

Note: Duguay's is a licensed special care home in New Brunswick.
Susan Duguay, Administrator

***Harvey Station:* Swanhaven Adult Residential Facility**
1915, Rte. 3, Harvey Station, NB E6K 3K1
Tel: 506-366-1113

Number of Beds: 25 units
Note: Specialty: Long-term care
Frances P. Ward, Owner

***Moncton:* Ritchie V Manor II**
Affiliated with: Horizon Health Network
2031 Mountain Rd., Moncton, NB E1G 1B1
Tel: 506-384-7658; *Fax:* 506-855-8994

Number of Beds: 20 beds
Debbie Teakles, Proprietor

***Moncton:* Smith Special Care Home Ltd.**
Affiliated with: Horizon Health Network
56 Dorchester St., Moncton, NB E1E 3A7
Tel: 506-874-0757

Number of Beds: 10 beds
Connie Whitman, Contact

***Ratters Corner:* Wilson Special Care Home**
510 Drury's Cove Rd., Ratters Corner, NB E4E 3L4
Tel: 506-433-5532

Number of Beds: 2 beds
Sharon Wilson, Proprietor

***Saint John:* Forest Hills Special Care Home**
Affiliated with: Horizon Health Network
Former Name: Burnside Special Care Home
30 Mountain Rd., Saint John, NB E2J 2W8
Tel: 506-633-0743

Number of Beds: 10 beds
Janet Hebert, Proprietor

***Titusville:* Yvonne's Special Care Home**
1773 Rte. 860, Titusville, NB E5N 3W2
Tel: 506-832-7186

Number of Beds: 18 units
Note: Yvonne's is a special care home for the elderly.
Yvonne Clark, Proprietor

Newfoundland & Labrador

Government Departments in Charge

***St. John's:* Newfoundland & Labrador Department of Health & Community Services**
1st Floor West Block, Confederation Bldg., PO Box 8700, St. John's, NL A1B 4J6
Tel: 709-729-4984
healthinfo@gov.nl.ca
www.gov.nl.ca/health

Hon. John Haggie, Minister
709-729-3124, hcsminister@gov.nl.ca

Regional Health Authorities

Corner Brook: Western Regional Health Authority
Former Name: Western Regional Integrated Health Authority
Also Known As: Western Health
Western Memorial Hospital, PO Box 2005, 1 Brookfield Ave., Corner Brook, NL A2H 6C7
Tel: 709-637-5245; *Fax:* 709-637-5159
www.westernhealth.nl.ca
Social Media: twitter.com/WesternHealthNL; www.youtube.com/WesternHealthNL
Number of Beds: 293 acute care beds; 464 long-term care beds; 40 enhanced assisted living beds
Population Served: 78000; *Number of Employees:* 3100
Note: Health facilities include two hospitals: Sir Thomas Roddick Hospital (Stephenville) & Western Memorial Regional Hospital (Corner Brook); four health centres: Dr. Charles L. LeGrow Health Centre (Port aux Basques), Bonne Bay Health Centre (Norris Point), Calder Health Centre (Burgeo) & Rufus Guinchard Health Centre (Port Saunders); & two long-term care centres: Corner Brook Long Term Care Centre (Corner Brook) & Bay St. George Long Term Care Centre (Stephenville Crossing).
Tom O'Brien, Acting Board Chair
Dr. Susan Gillam, President & CEO
Catherine McDonald, Acting Chief Nursing Officer & Vice-President, Professional Practice & Health Protection
Cynthia Davis, Vice-President, Patient Services
Devon Goulding, CFO & Vice-President, Financial & Decision Support
Donna Hicks, Acting Vice-President, Information & Quality
Michelle House, Vice-President, Population Health & Human Resources
Kelli O'Brien, Vice-President, Long Term Care & Rural Health
Dr. Dennis Rashleigh, Vice-President, Medical Services
Tara Pye, Acting Regional Director, Communications

Grand Falls-Windsor: Central Regional Health Authority
Also Known As: Central Health
Regional Office, 21 Carmelite Rd., Grand Falls-Windsor, NL A2A 1Y4
Tel: 709-292-2138; *Fax:* 709-292-2249
www.centralhealth.nl.ca
Number of Beds: 510 long-term care; 247 acute care; 13 palliative care; 9 respite; 5 restorative; 3 residential; & 24 bassinets
Area Served: 177 communities; half the landmass of the island; *Population Served:* 94000; *Number of Employees:* 3184
John George, Board Chair
Rosemary Goodyear, Chief Executive Officer
Sherry Freake, Chief Operating Officer & Vice-President, Acute Care (Gander)
Sean Tulk, Chief Operating Officer & Vice-President, Diagnostics & IM (Grand Falls-Windsor)
Trudy Stuckless, Chief Nursing Officer & Vice-President, Population Health
Heather Brown, Vice-President, Long Term Care, Community Supports & Rural Health
Dr. Jeff Cole, Vice-President, Medical Services
Terry Ings, Vice-President, Human Resources & Support Services
John Kattenbusch, Vice-President, Finance & Infrastructure
Stephanie Power, Director, Corporate Communications
709-256-5660, stephanie.power@centralhealth.nl.ca

Happy Valley-Goose Bay: Labrador-Grenfell Regional Health Authority
Former Name: Grenfell Regional Health Services; Health Labrador Corporation
Also Known As: Labrador-Grenfell Health
Administration Bldg., Labrador-Grenfell Health, PO Box 7000 Stn. C, Happy Valley-Goose Bay, NL A0P 1C0
Fax: 709-896-4032
Toll-Free: 855-897-2267
www.lghealth.ca
Year Founded: 2005
Area Served: North of Bartlett's Harbour on the Northern Peninsula, Labrador; *Population Served:* 37000; *Number of Employees:* 1505
Note: Labrador-Grenfell Health partners with the following to deliver services to aboriginal communities: Nunatsiavut Department of Health & Social Development; 2 Innu Band Councils; NunatuKavut (formerly the Labrador Métis Nation); Health Canada; & private practitioners.
Ray Norman, Board Chair
Tony Wakeham, Chief Executive Officer
Roger Snow, Chief Financial Officer
Barbara Blake, COO (South) & Vice-President, People & Information
Della Connell, COO (Labrador East) & Vice-President, Community & Aboriginal Affairs
Ozette Simpson, COO, Labrador West & Quality Management
Donnie Sampson, Chief Nurse & Vice-President, Nursing
Dr. Michael Jong, Vice-President, Medical Services

St. John's: Eastern Regional Health Authority
Also Known As: Eastern Health
Health Sciences Centre, Prince Philip Dr., St. John's, NL A1B 3V6
Tel: 709-777-6500 *Toll-Free:* 877-444-1399
client.relations@easternhealth.ca
www.easternhealth.ca
Info Line: 811
Social Media: www.facebook.com/EasternHealthNL; twitter.com/EasternHealthNL
Number of Beds: 1,696 long term care beds; 987 acute care beds; 9 observation beds
Area Served: Avalon, Burin & Bonavista Peninsulas; 21,000 sq km; *Population Served:* 300000; *Number of Employees:* 13000
Note: Area served includes 111 incorporated municipalities, 69 local service districts, & 66 unincorporated municipal units.
Michael J. O'Keefe, Board Chair
David S. Diamond, President & CEO
Collette Smith, Vice-President
Katherine Chubbs, Chief Nursing Officer & Vice-President
George Butt, Vice-President & Chief Financial Officer
Ron Johnson, Interim Chief Information Officer
Oscar Howell, Vice-President, Healthcare Technology & Data Management
Alice Kennedy, Vice-President, Long Term Care
Debbie Molloy, Interim Vice-President, Human Resources
Lynette Oates, Chief Communications Officer

Hospitals - General

Carbonear: Carbonear General Hospital
Affiliated with: Eastern Regional Health Authority
86 Highroad South, Carbonear, NL A1Y 1A4
Tel: 709-945-5111; *Fax:* 709-945-5511
client.relations@easternhealth.ca
www.easternhealth.ca
Social Media: www.facebook.com/EasternHealthNL; twitter.com/EasternHealthNL
Number of Beds: 80 beds
Note: Programs & services include: blood collection; diagnostic imaging; dialysis; emergency; inpatient services; laboratory; outpatient services; radiography; & surgery.
Tonya Somerton, Acute Care Nursing Manager, Surgical Services & Children's & Women's Health

Clarenville: Dr. G.B. Cross Memorial Hospital
Affiliated with: Eastern Regional Health Authority
67 Manitoba Dr., Clarenville, NL A5A 1K3
Tel: 709-466-3411
client.relations@easternhealth.ca
www.easternhealth.ca
Social Media: www.facebook.com/EasternHealthNL; twitter.com/EasternHealthNL
Number of Beds: 56 beds (including basinets)
Note: Programs & services include: blood collection; diagnostic imaging; emergency; inpatient services; outpatient services; surgery; & x-ray.

Corner Brook: Western Memorial Regional Hospital
Affiliated with: Western Regional Health Authority
PO Box 2005, 1 Brookfield Avenue, Corner Brook, NL A2H 6J7
Tel: 709-637-5000; *Fax:* 709-637-5410
www.westernhealth.nl.ca
Social Media: twitter.com/WesternHealthNL; www.youtube.com/WesternHealthNL
Number of Beds: 192 acute care beds
Population Served: 82000
Note: Programs & services include: cardiology; emergency; geriatrics; internal medicine & surgery; intensive care; laboratory; medical imaging; medical; nephrology; neurology; nursing; obstetrics/gynecology; opthamology; orthopedics; pediatrics; pharmacy; psychiatry; renal care; surgical services; & urology.
M. Wasmeier

Fogo: Fogo Island Health Centre
Affiliated with: Central Regional Health Authority
PO Box 9, Fogo, NL A0G 2B0
Tel: 709-266-2221
www.centralhealth.nl.ca
Year Founded: 2004
Note: Programs & services include: acute care; long-term care; emergency; laboratory; community health services; & x-ray.
Natasha Decker, Client Care Manager
natasha.decker@centralhealth.nl.ca

Gander: James Paton Memorial Regional Health Centre
Affiliated with: Central Regional Health Authority
125 TransCanada Hwy., Gander, NL A1V 1P7
Tel: 709-256-2500; *Fax:* 709-256-7800
www.centralhealth.nl.ca
Number of Beds: 92 acute care beds
Note: Programs & services include: acute care; emergency; & specialized medical services.
Lori Hillyard, Chief Operating Officer
lori.hillyard@centralhealth.nl.ca

Grand Falls-Windsor: Central Newfoundland Regional Health Centre (CNRHC)
Affiliated with: Central Regional Health Authority
50 Union St., Grand Falls-Windsor, NL A2A 2E1
Tel: 709-292-2500; *Fax:* 709-292-2249
www.centralhealth.nl.ca
Number of Beds: 130 acute care beds
Note: Programs & services include: anesthesia; general internal medicine; general surgery; neurology; obstetrics/gynecology; ophthalmology; pediatrics; pathology; psychiatry; urology; radiology; otolaryngology; dermatology; emergency; diagnostic imaging; & laboratory.
Kelly Adams, Chief Operating Officer
kelly.adams@centralhealth.nl.ca

Happy Valley-Goose Bay: Labrador Health Centre
Affiliated with: Labrador-Grenfell Regional Health Authority
Former Name: Melville Hospital
PO Box 7000 Stn. C, Happy Valley-Goose Bay, NL A0P 1C0
Tel: 709-897-2000
www.lghealth.ca
Number of Beds: 25 beds
Note: Programs & services include: emergency; satellite dialysis; laboratory & diagnostic imaging; physiotherapy; occupational therapy; speech-language pathology; oncology/chemotherapy; respiratory therapy; dietitian; community health & home care nursing; mental health & addictions; & obstetrics/gynecology

Labrador City: Labrador West Health Centre
Affiliated with: Labrador-Grenfell Regional Health Authority
Former Name: Captain William Jackman Memorial Hospital
1700 Nichols-Adam Hwy., Labrador City, NL A2V 0B2
Tel: 709-285-8100
www.lghealth.ca
Number of Beds: 28 beds (including 14 long-term care beds)
Note: Programs & services include: emergency; outpatient; surgery; satellite dialysis; maternity care; obstetrics/gynecology; laboratory & diagnostic imaging; physiotherapy; occupational therapy; speech-language pathology; audiology; respiratory therapy; EEG; EKG; oncology/chemotherapy; dietary; diabetes education; mental health & addictions; & population health.

St. Anthony: Charles S. Curtis Memorial Hospital
Affiliated with: Labrador-Grenfell Regional Health Authority
Also Known As: Curtis Hospital
#178, 200 West St., St. Anthony, NL A0K 4S0
Tel: 709-454-3333
www.lghealth.ca
Number of Beds: 50 hospital beds; 47 long term care beds at the John M. Gray Centre, which is attached to Charles S. Curtis Memorial Hospital
Note: Programs & services include: acute care; anaesthesia; dentistry; family practice; general surgery; internal medicine; obstetrics/gynecology; ophthalmology; orthopedics; pathology; pediatrics; emergency; intensive care; oncology/chemotherapy; day surgery; satellite dialysis; laboratory & diagnostic imaging; physiotherapy; occupational therapy; speech-language pathology; respiratory therapy; EEG/ECG; pharmacy; audiology; clinical nutrition; diabetes education; social work; mental health & addictions; & psychology.

St. John's: Health Sciences Centre - General Hospital
Affiliated with: Eastern Regional Health Authority
300 Prince Phillip Dr., St. John's, NL A1B 3V6
Tel: 709-777-6300
client.relations@easternhealth.ca
www.easternhealth.ca
Social Media: www.facebook.com/EasternHealthNL; twitter.com/EasternHealthNL
Note: A tertiary acute care facility & teaching hospital affiliated with Memorial University Schools of Medicine, Nursing, & Pharmacy. Programs & services include: blood collection; diagnostic imaging; dialysis; emergency; inpatient services; laboratory; outpatient services; radiography; & surgery.

St. John's: Janeway Children's Health & Rehabilitation Centre
Affiliated with: Eastern Regional Health Authority
300 Prince Philip Dr., St. John's, NL A1B 3V6
Tel: 709-777-6300
client.relations@easternhealth.ca
www.easternhealth.ca
Social Media: www.facebook.com/EasternHealthNL; twitter.com/EasternHealthNL
Number of Beds: 83 beds
Note: Teaching hospital for the Memorial University of Newfoundland Faculty of Medicine. Programs & services include: children & women's health; diagnostic services; dialysis; emergency services; inpatient services; laboratory; outpatient services; radiography; & surgery.

St. John's: St. Clare's Mercy Hospital
Affiliated with: Eastern Regional Health Authority
154 LeMarchant Rd., St. John's, NL A1C 5B8
Tel: 709-777-5000
client.relations@easternhealth.ca
www.easternhealth.ca
Social Media: www.facebook.com/EasternHealthNL; twitter.com/EasternHealthNL
Year Founded: 1922
Note: Tertiary hospital. Programs & services include: blood collection; diagnostic imaging; dialysis; emergency; inpatient services; laboratory; outpatient services; radiography; & surgery.

Stephenville: Sir Thomas Roddick Hospital
Affiliated with: Western Regional Health Authority
142 Minnesota Dr., Stephenville, NL A2N 1H0
Tel: 709-643-5111
www.westernhealth.nl.ca
Social Media: twitter.com/WesternHealthNL; www.youtube.com/WesternHealthNL
Year Founded: 2003
Number of Beds: 44 acute care beds
Population Served: 24000
Note: Programs & services include: emergency; medical; nursing; obstetric/gynecaelogical; outpatient; pharmacy; renal care; speciality clinics; & surgical.
Karen Alexander, Site Manager

Community Health Care Centres

Baie Verte: Baie Verte Peninsula Health Centre
Affiliated with: Central Regional Health Authority
1 Columbus Dr., Baie Verte, NL A0K 1B0
Tel: 709-532-4281; *Fax:* 709-532-4939
Number of Beds: 26 acute care, 18 long-term care beds, 1 respite bed, 6 acute care beds, 1 palliative care bed
Note: Acute & long term care; dental clinic; addiction treatment.
Tracey Comeau, Director, Health Services
tracey.comeau@centralhealth.nl.ca

Bell Island: Dr. Walter Templeman Community Health Centre
Affiliated with: Eastern Regional Health Authority
PO Box 580, Wabana, Bell Island, NL A0A 4H0
Tel: 709-488-2821; *Fax:* 709-488-2600
Number of Beds: 20 Beds

Bonavista: Bonavista Peninsula Health Centre
Affiliated with: Eastern Regional Health Authority
Former Name: Bonavista Community Health Centre
PO Box 1510, 123 Confederation Dr., Bonavista, NL A0C 1B0
Tel: 709-468-7881; *Fax:* 709-468-7223
Number of Beds: 10 beds

Brookfield: Brookfield/Bonnews Health Care Centre
Affiliated with: Central Regional Health Authority
#57, 61 Main St., Brookfield, NL A0G 1B0
Tel: 709-536-2405; *Fax:* 709-536-3334
www.cehcib.nf.ca
Year Founded: 1944
Number of Beds: 12 beds
Roma Norris, Manager, Client Care
roma.norris@centralhealth.nl.ca
Winston Perry, Director, Maintenance Services

Burgeo: Calder Health Care Centre
Affiliated with: Western Regional Health Authority
PO Box 190, Burgeo, NL A0M 1A0
Tel: 709-886-3350; *Fax:* 709-886-3382
westernhealth.nl.ca
Number of Beds: 3 acute care, 18 continuing care beds
Population Served: 2000
Note: Services include: diagnostic and laboratory services; recreational therapy; occupational and physiotherapy; telehealth; chemotherapy
Laurie Porter, Director of Nursing/Site Coordinator

Burin: Burin Peninsula Health Care Centre
Affiliated with: Eastern Regional Health Authority
PO Box 340, #51, 85 Main St., Burin, NL A0E 1E0
Tel: 709-891-1040
www.easternhealth.ca
Note: Features an interim clinic staffed with three hospital physicians

Churchill Falls: Churchill Falls Community Health Centre
Affiliated with: Labrador-Grenfell Regional Health Authority
General Delivery, Churchill Falls, NL A0R 1A0
Tel: 709-925-3381; *Fax:* 709-925-3246
www.lghealth.ca
Tony Wakeham, Chief Executive Officer

Flowers Cove: Strait of Belle Isle Health Centre
Affiliated with: Labrador-Grenfell Regional Health Authority
PO Box 59, Flowers Cove, NL A0K 2N0
Tel: 709-456-2401; *Fax:* 709-456-2562
Number of Beds: 3 beds
Note: Specialties: Ambulatory care; Family medicine; Public health services; Pre-natal classes; Post-natal visiting; Preschool & baby assessments; Dental services; Rehabilitation services; Home care

Grand Bank: Grand Bank Community Health Centre
Affiliated with: Eastern Regional Health Authority
PO Box 310, 3 Grandview Blvd., Grand Bank, NL A0E 1W0
Tel: 709-832-2500; *Fax:* 709-832-1164

Harbour Breton: Connaigre Peninsula Health Centre
Affiliated with: Central Regional Health Authority
Former Name: Harbour Breton Health Centre
PO Box 70, 1 Alexander Ave., Harbour Breton, NL A0H 1P0
Tel: 709-885-2043; *Fax:* 709-885-2358
Number of Beds: 20 beds: 6 acute, 12 continuing , 1 palliative, 1 respite
Trena Snook, Director, Health Services
trena.snook@centralhealth.nl.ca

Hopedale: Hopedale Community Clinic
Affiliated with: Labrador-Grenfell Regional Health Authority
General Delivery, Hopedale, NL A0P 1G0
Tel: 709-933-3857; *Fax:* 709-933-3744
Number of Beds: 3 beds

Nain: Nain Community Clinic
Affiliated with: Labrador-Grenfell Regional Health Authority
General Delivery, Nain, NL A0P 1L0
Tel: 709-922-2912; *Fax:* 709-922-2103

Norris Point: Bonne Bay Health Centre
Affiliated with: Western Regional Health Authority
PO Box 70, Norris Point, NL A0K 3V0
Tel: 709-458-2211; *Fax:* 709-458-2074
Number of Beds: 8 acute care, 14 continuing care beds

Northwest River: Mani Ashini Health Clinic
Affiliated with: Labrador-Grenfell Regional Health Authority
PO Box 450, 289 Shenum St., Northwest River, NL A0P 1M0
Tel: 709-497-8351; *Fax:* 709-497-8521

Old Perlican: Dr. A.A. Wilkinson Memorial Health Centre
Affiliated with: Eastern Regional Health Authority
PO Box 70, Old Perlican, NL A0A 3G0
Tel: 709-587-2200; *Fax:* 709-587-2275
Number of Beds: 4 beds

Port Saunders: Rufus Guinchard Health Care Centre
Affiliated with: Western Regional Health Authority
PO Box 40, Port Saunders, NL A0K 4H0
Tel: 709-861-3139; *Fax:* 709-861-3772
Number of Beds: 1 palliative care, 6 acute care, 22 continuing care beds
Note: Laboratory; diagnostics; therapy; pharmacy; dietician.

Port aux Basques: Dr. Charles L. LeGrow Health Centre
Affiliated with: Western Regional Health Authority
PO Box 250, Port aux Basques, NL A0M 1C0
Tel: 709-695-2175; *Fax:* 709-695-3118
westernhealth.nl.ca
Number of Beds: 14 acute care, 30 continuing care beds
Note: Pharmacy; dietician; physiotherapy; labratory; diagnostics.

Springdale: Green Bay Community Health Centre
Affiliated with: Central Regional Health Authority
PO Box 280, Springdale, NL A0J 1T0
Tel: 709-673-3911; *Fax:* 709-673-3186
Number of Beds: 8 beds; 1 special care, 2 convalescent, 1 palliative
Melinda Noel, Director, Health Services
melinda.noel@centralhealth.nl.ca

Twillingate: Notre Dame Bay Memorial Health Centre
Affiliated with: Central Regional Health Authority
General Delivery, Twillingate, NL A0G 4M0
Tel: 709-884-2131; *Fax:* 709-884-2586
Number of Beds: 31 long-term care beds + 18 acute care beds
Note: Specialties: Outpatient services; Social work; Physiotherapy; Recreation therapy; Dietetics; Diabetes education; Health promotion & protection; Respite care, for children with special needs
Victor Shea, Director, Health Services
victor.shea@centralhealth.nl.ca
B. Hamlyn, Supervisor, Plant Maintenance

Whitbourne: Dr. W. H. Newhook Community Health Centre
Affiliated with: Eastern Regional Health Authority
PO Box 449, 7 Whitbourne Ave, Whitbourne, NL A0B 3K0
Tel: 709-759-2300; *Fax:* 709-759-2387
Note: Emergency centre; family physicians; laboratory.
L. English

Nursing Stations

Black Tickle: Black Tickle Nursing Station
Affiliated with: Labrador-Grenfell Regional Health Authority
General Delivery, Black Tickle, NL A0K 1N0
Tel: 709-471-8872; *Fax:* 709-471-8893

Cartwright: Cartwright Community Clinic
Affiliated with: Labrador-Grenfell Regional Health Authority
General Delivery, Cartwright, NL A0K 1V0
Tel: 709-938-7285
Number of Beds: 1 bed
Number of Employees: 9

Charlottetown: Charlottetown Community Clinic
Affiliated with: Labrador-Grenfell Regional Health Authority
Former Name: Charlottetown Nursing Station
General Delivery, Charlottetown, NL A0K 5Y0
Tel: 709-949-0259
Number of Beds: 3 beds
Number of Employees: 4

Forteau: Labrador South Health Centre
Affiliated with: Labrador-Grenfell Regional Health Authority
Forteau, NL A0K 2P0
Tel: 709-931-2450; *Fax:* 709-931-2000
Number of Beds: 15 long-term care beds; 5 in-patient beds

Makkovik: Makkovik Community Health Clinic
Affiliated with: Labrador-Grenfell Regional Health Authority
General Delivery, Makkovik, NL A0P 1J0
Tel: 709-923-2229; *Fax:* 709-923-2428
Note: Specialties: Pharmaceutical services; Social work. Number of Employees: 2 nurses + 1 part time physician

Mary's Harbour: Mary's Harbour Community Clinic
Affiliated with: Labrador-Grenfell Regional Health Authority
Mary's Harbour, NL A0K 3P0
Tel: 709-921-6228; *Fax:* 709-921-6975
Number of Beds: 1 holding bed + 1 crib
Note: Number of Employees: 3 nurses + 1 social worker + 1 personal care attendant + 1 maintenance person

Natuashish: Natuashish Nursing Station
Affiliated with: Labrador-Grenfell Regional Health Authority
Former Name: Davis Inlet Nursing Station
General Delivery, Natuashish, NL A0P 1A0
Tel: 709-478-8842; *Fax:* 709-478-8817

***Port Hope Simpson:* Port Hope Simpson Community Clinic**
Affiliated with: Labrador-Grenfell Regional Health Authority
General Delivery, Port Hope Simpson, NL A0K 4E0
Tel: 709-960-0271; *Fax:* 709-960-0392
www.lghealth.ca
Year Founded: 1975
Note: Specialties: Emergency room, basic trauma, cardiac monitoring & resuscitation, dental suite. Number of staff: 9

***Postville:* Postville Community Clinic**
Affiliated with: Labrador-Grenfell Regional Health Authority
General Delivery, Postville, NL A0P 1N0
Tel: 709-479-9851
www.lghealth.ca
Number of Beds: 1 bed, 1 crib
Number of Employees: 3

***Rigolet:* Rigolet Nursing Station**
Affiliated with: Labrador-Grenfell Regional Health Authority
General Delivery, Rigolet, NL A0P 1P0
Tel: 709-947-3386; *Fax:* 709-947-3401
Note: Number of staff: 2 Registered Nurses; visiting physician, dentist & specialists

***Roddickton:* White Bay Central Health Centre**
Affiliated with: Labrador-Grenfell Regional Health Authority
General Delivery, Roddickton, NL A0K 4P0
Tel: 709-457-2215

***St Lewis:* St. Lewis Nursing Station**
Affiliated with: Labrador-Grenfell Regional Health Authority
General Delivery, St Lewis, NL A0K 4W0
Tel: 709-939-2230; *Fax:* 709-939-2342

Special Treatment Centres

***St. John's:* Dr. H. Bliss Murphy Cancer Centre**
Newfoundland Cancer Treatment & Research Foundatio, 300 Prince Philip Dr., St. John's, NL A1B 3V6
Tel: 709-777-6555

***St. John's:* St. John's Site of The Morgentaler Clinic**
The Morgentaler Clinic
#408, unit 50 Hamlyn Rd. Plaza, St. John's, NL A1E 5X7
Tel: 709-754-3572; *Fax:* 709-754-6626
Toll-Free: 800-755-2044
sjmc@nf.aibn.com
Year Founded: 1990
Note: Specialties: Abortion services; Counselling

Long Term Care Facilities

***Bonavista:* Golden Heights Manor**
Affiliated with: Eastern Regional Health Authority
27 - 43 Campbell St., Bonavista, NL A0C 1B0
Tel: 709-468-2043
www.easternhealth.ca
Year Founded: 1986
Number of Beds: 70 beds
Pauline Pardy

***Placentia:* Placentia Health Centre**
Affiliated with: Eastern Regional Health Authority
PO Box 480, 1 Corrigan Pl., Placentia, NL A0B 2Y0
Tel: 709-227-2061; *Fax:* 709-227-5476
www.easternhealth.ca
Number of Beds: 10 acute care, 75 long term care beds
Note: Acute care, long term care (Lions Manor Nursing Home), on an in-patient & out-patient basis

***St Lawrence:* U.S. Memorial Health Centre**
Affiliated with: Eastern Regional Health Authority
PO Box 398, 1 Memorial Dr., St Lawrence, NL A0E 2V0
Tel: 709-873-2330; *Fax:* 709-873-2390
www.easternhealth.ca
Number of Beds: 40 beds
Note: Long term & protective care units, ambulatory care clinic, nutritional services, pharmacy, visiting specialty clinics

***St. John's:* Dr. Leonard A. Miller Centre**
Affiliated with: Eastern Regional Health Authority
Former Name: Quidi Vidi Hospital
Also Known As: The Miller Centre
100 Forest Rd., St. John's, NL A1A 1E5
Tel: 709-777-6555
www.easternhealth.ca
Year Founded: 1851
Note: Provides continuing care, rehabilitation, residential care for veterans of Newfoundland & Labrador, & includes a centre for Nursing Studies.

Nursing Homes

***Botwood:* Dr. Hugh Twomey Health Care Centre**
Affiliated with: Central Regional Health Authority
PO Box 250, Botwood, NL A0H 1E0
Tel: 709-257-2874; *Fax:* 709-257-4613
doug.prince@centralhealth.nl.ca
www.centralhealth.nl.ca/dr-hugh-twomey-health-centre
Number of Beds: 77 long-term care, 2 respite, 1 palliative care beds
Doug Prince, Director, Health Services
doug.prince@centralhealth.nl.ca

***Buchans:* A.M. Guy Memorial Health Centre**
Affiliated with: Central Regional Health Authority
PO Box 39, Buchans, NL A0H 1G0
Tel: 709-672-3304
Number of Beds: 22 beds: 18 long-term, 2 acute care, 1 holding, 1 palliative
Pamela Brace, Manager, Client Care
pamela.brace@centralhealth.nl.ca

***Carbonear:* Harbour Lodge Nursing Home**
Affiliated with: Eastern Regional Health Authority
86 Highroad South, Carbonear, NL A1Y 1A4
Tel: 709-945-5400
www.easternhealth.ca
Number of Beds: 127 beds
Debbie Farrell, Facility Manager
Harry Meados, Director, Environmental Services

***Carbonear:* Inter Faith Citizens Home**
Affiliated with: Eastern Regional Health Authority
41 Water St., Carbonear, NL A1Y 1B1
Tel: 709-945-5300; *Fax:* 709-945-5323
Number of Beds: 53 beds
Deborah Farrell, Facility Manager

***Clarke's Beach:* Pentecostal Senior Citizen's Home**
Affiliated with: Eastern Regional Health Authority
PO Box 130, Clarke's Beach, NL A0A 1W0
Tel: 709-786-2993
www.easternhealth.ca
Number of Beds: 75 beds
Note: Specialties: Nursing care for persons who require Level I, II, & III type care; Social work; Physiotherapy; Occupational therapy; Podiatry; Hearing & vision care
Beverley Bellefleur, Facility Manager

***Corner Brook:* Corner Brook Long Term Care Home (CBLTC)**
Affiliated with: Western Regional Health Authority
40 University Dr., Corner Brook, NL A2H 5G4
Tel: 709-637-3999
Year Founded: 2010
Number of Beds: 250 long-term care beds

***Corner Brook:* J.I. O'Connell Centre**
Affiliated with: Western Regional Health Authority
PO Box 2005, 1 Hospital Hill, Corner Brook, NL A2H 6J7
Tel: 709-637-5000; *Fax:* 709-634-3047
Number of Beds: 104 beds

***Gander:* Lakeside Homes**
Affiliated with: Central Regional Health Authority
95 Airport Blvd., Gander, NL A1V 2L7
Tel: 709-256-8850; *Fax:* 709-256-4259
centralhealth.nl.ca/gander-health-services-area
Number of Beds: 102 beds; 1 respite
Marlyce Greene, Facility Manager
Sam Butt, Maintenance Supervisor

***Gander Bay South:* Riverview Retirement Home Ltd.**
Also Known As: Gander Bay Retirement Home
9 Main St., Gander Bay South, NL A0G 2H0
Tel: 709-676-2773

***Grand Bank:* Blue Crest Inter Faith Home**
Affiliated with: Eastern Regional Health Authority
PO Box 160, Grand Bank, NL A0E 1W0
Tel: 709-832-1660
Number of Beds: 70 long-term care beds
Joan Penney, Director, Patient/Resident Care
Cyril Parsons, Maintenance Manager

***Grand Falls-Windsor:* Carmelite House**
Affiliated with: Central Regional Health Authority
21 Carmelite Rd., Grand Falls-Windsor, NL A2A 1Y4
Tel: 709-292-2528; *Fax:* 709-292-2593
Number of Beds: 60 longterm care beds
Michelle Hatt, Facility Director
mhatt@cwhc.nl.ca

***Happy Valley-Goose Bay:* Harry L. Paddon Memorial Home**
Affiliated with: Labrador-Grenfell Regional Health Authority
PO Box 766 Stn. B, Happy Valley-Goose Bay, NL A0P 1E0
Tel: 709-896-2469
www.lghealth.ca
Number of Beds: 50 beds
K. White
Ronald Lyall, Supervisor, Maintenance

***Lewisporte:* North Haven Manor Senior Citizens' Home**
Affiliated with: Central Regional Health Authority
PO Box 880, 21 Centennial Dr., Lewisporte, NL A0G 3A0
Tel: 709-535-6767
Number of Beds: 62 long-term care, 1 palliative, 2 respite beds
Debbie Colbourne, Facility Director

***Mount Pearl:* Masonic Park Nursing Home**
Affiliated with: Eastern Regional Health Authority
Former Name: Masonic Park Senior Citizen's Home
Mount Carson Ave., Mount Pearl, NL A1N 3K5
Tel: 709-368-6081
www.masonicpark.ca; www.easternhealth.ca
Year Founded: 1982
Number of Beds: 40 long term beds + 200 self-contained cottage & apt. units
Note: Specialties: Long-term care for seniors
Rolanda Ryan, Resident Care Manager

***Springdale:* Valley Vista Senior Citizens' Home**
Affiliated with: Central Regional Health Authority
PO Box 130, Springdale, NL A0J 1T0
Tel: 709-673-3936; *Fax:* 709-673-2832

***St Anthony:* John M. Gray Centre**
Affiliated with: Labrador-Grenfell Regional Health Authority
Former Name: St. Anthony Interfaith Home
PO Box 69, St Anthony, NL A0K 4S0
Tel: 709-454-0371
Year Founded: 1998
Number of Beds: 47 long-term care beds
Dr. Michael Jong, Vice President Medical Affairs
Boyd Rowe, Chief Executive Officer

***St. John's:* Agnes Pratt Nursing Home**
Affiliated with: Eastern Regional Health Authority
239 Topsail Rd., St. John's, NL A1E 2B4
Tel: 709-579-0185
www.easternhealth.ca
Year Founded: 1972
Number of Beds: 134 long-term care beds
Linda Colllingwood, Administrator

***St. John's:* Hoyles-Escasoni Complex**
Affiliated with: Eastern Regional Health Authority
10 Escasoni Pl., St. John's, NL A1A 3R6
Tel: 709-753-7590; *Fax:* 709-753-9620
Number of Beds: 377 beds

***St. John's:* Saint Luke's Home**
Affiliated with: Eastern Regional Health Authority
24 Road Deluxe, St. John's, NL A1E 5Z3
Tel: 709-579-0052; *Fax:* 709-579-7317
www.easternhealth.ca
Year Founded: 1965
Number of Beds: 124 beds
Note: Nursing homel also owns and operates 54 independent living cottages and the 76-unit Bishop John Meaden Manor Complex
Barbara Ivany, Administrator

***St. John's:* St. Patrick's Mercy Home**
Affiliated with: Eastern Regional Health Authority
146 Elizabeth Ave., St. John's, NL A1B 1S5
Tel: 709-726-2687
www.easternhealth.ca
Number of Beds: 214 beds
Note: Long-term care facility affiliated with the Roman Catholic Diocese of St. John's
Sr. Phyllis Corbett, Administrator

Stephenville Crossing: Bay St. George Long Term Care Centre
Affiliated with: Western Regional Health Authority
Former Name: Bay St. George Senior Citizens Home
PO Box 250, Stephenville Crossing, NL A0N 2C0
Tel: 709-646-5800; *Fax:* 709-646-2375

Number of Beds: 114 beds
Anne Doyle, Nursing

Personal Care Homes

Arnolds Cove: Hilltop Manor
PO Box 430, 96 Spencers Cove Rd., Arnolds Cove, NL A1A 4Y6
Tel: 709-463-5000
hollismetcalge@hotmail.com

Number of Beds: 32 beds
Trey Metcalfe

Baie Verte: Baie Verte Manor Ltd.
PO Box 561, 20 High St., Baie Verte, NL A0K 1B0
Tel: 709-532-4615; *Fax:* 709-532-4643

Number of Beds: 30 beds
Donna Rideout, Owner/Administrator

Baie Verte: H. Pardy Manor
PO Box 1, Baie Verte, NL A0K 1B0
Tel: 709-532-4603

Number of Beds: 22 beds
Kim Sacrey, Manager

Bay Bulls: Walsh's Personal Care Home
PO Box 42, Rte. 10, Bay Bulls, NL A0A 1C0
Tel: 709-334-2619

Number of Beds: 10 beds
Delores Walsh, Proprietor

Bell Island: Island Manor
PO Box 728, Bell Island, NL A0A 4H0
Tel: 709-488-2966

Number of Beds: 10 beds
Jocelyn Russell

Bishops Falls: Exploits Manor
26 Exploits Lane, Bishops Falls, NL A0H 1C0
Tel: 709-258-6446

Cape Anguille: Hilliard's Personal Care Home
PO Box 18, Cape Anguille, NL A0N 1H0
Tel: 709-955-2339

Number of Beds: 14 beds
Minnie Hilliard, Owner/Administrator

Carmanville: Carmanville Manor
PO Box 42, Carmanville, NL A0G 1N0
Tel: 709-534-2244
www.centralhealth.nl.ca/carmanville-manor

Number of Beds: 21 beds
Jeanne Clarke

Catalina: Shirley's Haven
PO Box 29, Catalina, NL A0C 1J0
Tel: 709-469-3160; *Fax:* 709-469-3161
Social Media:
facebook.com/pages/Shirleys-Haven-Personal-Care-Home/7799 4615307

Number of Beds: 50 beds
Shirley Barney

Clarenville: Cozy Quarters Personal Care Home
13 Whiteway Pl., Clarenville, NL A5A 2B5
Tel: 709-466-2447; *Fax:* 709-466-4447
cozyquarters@nf.aibn.com
www.cozyquartersnl.ca

Number of Beds: 34 beds

Conception Bay South: Woodford's Golden Care Home
Con Bay Hwy., Conception Bay South, NL A0A 2R0
Tel: 709-229-3343

Number of Beds: 10 beds
Josephine Woodford, Contact

Corner Brook: Brake's Personal Care Home
292 Curling St., Corner Brook, NL A2H 3J7
Tel: 709-785-5092

Number of Beds: 6 beds
Vera Brake
Vivian Brake

Corner Brook: Mountain View House
PO Box 3850, RR#2, Corner Brook, NL A2H 6B9
Tel: 709-783-2019

Number of Beds: 30 beds
Note: Nursing home
Byron Brake

Corner Brook: Mountain View Retirement Centre
161 Premier Dr., Corner Brook, NL A2H 7M6
Tel: 709-637-7960; *Fax:* 709-634-0235
www.mountainviewretirementcentre.com

Note: Nursing home
Barbara Baker, Contact

Corner Brook: Xavier House Inc.
19 Mount Bernard Ave., Corner Brook, NL A2H 6K7
Tel: 709-634-2787

Number of Beds: 20 beds
Sr. Rosalie Carey, Administrator

Deer Lake: Deer Lake Manor
#119, 123 Nicholsville Rd., Deer Lake, NL A8A 1W6
Tel: 709-635-2868

Number of Beds: 31 Beds
Dwight Ball, Contact

Embree: Twilight Manor
19 Main St., Embree, NL A0G 2A0
Tel: 709-535-6094

Flowers Cove: Ivey Durley Place
Former Name: Straits-St Barbe Chronic Care
PO Box 157, Flowers Cove, NL A0K 2N0
Tel: 709-456-9104

Number of Beds: 20 beds
Judy Way, Contact
709-456-2022
Dennis Coates, Contact
704-456-2022

Fogo: Riverhead Manor
PO Box 375, Fogo, NL A0G 2B0
Tel: 709-266-2336

Gander: Nightingale Manor
11 Hadfield Pl., Gander, NL A1V 2V6
Tel: 709-256-3711; *Fax:* 709-256-3712
info@nightingalemanor.com
nightingalemanor.com

Number of Beds: 60 beds
Lawrence Guy

Glovertown: Baywatch Manor
PO Box 120, Glovertown, NL A0G 2M0
Tel: 709-533-6999; *Fax:* 709-533-6994
baywatchmanor@nf.aibn.com
www.baywatchmanor.ca

Number of Beds: 38 beds
Denise Button

Glovertown: Oram's Birchview Manor
PO Box 10, Glovertown, NL A0G 2L0
Tel: 709-266-2336
www.centralhealth.nl.ca

Number of Beds: 50 beds
Note: Specialty: Personal care
Paul Oram

Goulds: Kelly's Personal Care Home
Former Name: Kelly Boarding Home
478 Main Road, Goulds, NL A1S 1G3
Tel: 709-745-5343

Number of Beds: 19 beds
Linda Spurrell, Proprietor
709-745-5343

Goulds: Lawlor's Personal Care Home
PO Box 419, Goulds, NL A1S 1G5
Tel: 709-745-1956

Number of Beds: 14 beds
Albert Lawlor

Goulds: Maloney's Personal Care Home
PO Box 568, Barton's Rd., Goulds, NL A1S 1G3
Tel: 709-745-4986

Number of Beds: 10 beds
Note: Nursing Home
Mary Maloney, Contact

Grand Falls-Windsor: Golden Years Estate
348 Grenfell Heights, Grand Falls-Windsor, NL A2A 2J2
Tel: 709-489-7363; *Fax:* 709-489-7306
tgyestate.com
Info Line: 709-489-7263

Number of Beds: 67 beds
Zetta Lane, Owner

Grand Falls-Windsor: Islandside Manor
PO Box 814, Grand Falls-Windsor, NL A2A 2P7
Tel: 709-483-2121

Number of Beds: 24 beds
Max Arnold

Grand Falls-Windsor: Twin Town Manor
15 King St., Grand Falls-Windsor, NL A1B 1J6
Tel: 709-489-0988

Number of Beds: 96 beds
Guy Bailey, Contact

Happy Valley-Goose Bay: Pine Lodge Personal Care Home
PO Box 264 Stn. C, 3 Spruce Ave., Happy Valley-Goose Bay, NL A0P 1C0
Tel: 709-896-5512; *Fax:* 709-896-5465

Note: Specialties: Personal care for seniors & person with an intellectual disability
Diane Oliver-Scales

Holyrood: Kennedy's Riverside Boarding Home Ltd.
PO Box 114, Holyrood, NL A0A 2R0
Tel: 709-229-6886

Number of Beds: 33 beds
Geneviève Kennedy

Holyrood: Tobin's Guest Home Inc.
PO Box 95, Holyrood, NL A0A 2R0
Tel: 709-229-7464

Number of Beds: 30 beds
Betty Tobin
Walter Tobin

Holyrood: Woodford's Golden Care
PO Box 158, Holyrood, NL A0A 2R0
Tel: 709-229-3343

Kelligrews: Gully Pond Manor
39 Gully Pond Rd., Kelligrews, NL A1X 6Z2
Tel: 709-834-8083

Kilbride: Hennessey's Personal Care Home
222 Old Bay Bulls Rd., Kilbride, NL A1G 1E1
Tel: 709-368-5558; *Fax:* 709-368-4910

Lark Harbour: Guardian Angel Seniors Home
PO Box 91, Lark Harbour, NL A0L 1L0
Tel: 709-681-2288

Number of Beds: 20 beds
Brian Park

Lewisporte: Pleasantville Manor
PO Box 207, Lewisporte, NL A0G 3A0
Tel: 709-535-0941
www.centralhealth.nl.ca

Number of Beds: 60 beds
Rhonda Simms, Owner, Operator

Long Pond: Allison's Manor
PO Box 14099, 332 Ancorage Rd., Long Pond, NL A0A 2Y0
Tel: 709-834-8541; *Fax:* 709-834-6336

Number of Beds: 42 beds
Sharon Stone, Administrator

Manuels: Greenslade's Personal Care Home
Former Name: Greenslade Special Care Home
PO Box 84, Manuels, NL A1W 2K1
Tel: 709-834-3047

Mary's Harbour: Harbourview Manor
186 Main St., Mary's Harbour, NL A0K 3P0
Tel: 709-921-6440

Mount Carmel: Riverside Country Manor
PO Box 86, Mount Carmel, NL A0B 2M0
Tel: 709-521-2377

Number of Beds: 25 beds
Angela DeCaria

Mount Pearl: Pearl House
163 Park Ave., Mount Pearl, NL A1N 1K6
Tel: 709-368-3850

Number of Beds: 44 beds
Lawrence Guy

Musgrave Harbour: Hillcrest Manor
PO Box 100, Musgrave Harbour, NL A0G 3J0
Tel: 709-655-2777

Musgravetown: Greenwood Rest Home Ltd.
PO Box 9, Bunyan's Cove Rd., Musgravetown, NL A0C 1Z0
Tel: 709-467-5243

***New Harbour:* Jackson's Country Manor**
New Harbour Barrens, New Harbour, NL A0B 2P0
Tel: 709-588-2382
Number of Beds: 39 Beds
Wallace Jackson, Contact
709-582-2888,

***Norris Point:* Crockers Retirement Home**
PO Box 1, Norris Point, NL A0K 3V0
Tel: 709-458-2429
Number of Beds: 20 beds
Gerald Crocker

***Pollards Point:* Main River Manor Ltd.**
Former Name: Golden Crest Haven
General Delivery, Pollards Point, NL A0K 4B0
Tel: 709-482-2334
Number of Beds: 20 beds
Dale Gillingham, Contact

***Port aux Basques:* Mountain Hope Manor**
PO Box 957, Port aux Basques, NL A0M 1C0
Tel: 709-695-3458
Number of Beds: 32 beds
Ida Lawrence

***Porterville:* Bayside Manor**
PO Box 134, RR#1, Porterville, NL A0G 3A0
Tel: 709-654-3171; *Fax:* 709-654-2176
Number of Beds: 50 beds
Ron Sheppard, Proprietor

***Roddickton:* Roddickton House**
Former Name: Claudelle Manor
PO Box 40, Roddickton, NL A0K 4P0
Tel: 709-457-2166; *Fax:* 709-457-2079
Number of Beds: 22 beds
Note: Nursing home
Chris Decker

***Shearstown:* Pondview Manor**
100 Shearstown Rd., Shearstown, NL A0A 3V0
Tel: 709-786-7051
Note: Nursing home

***St Albans:* K.M. Homes Limited**
8 Meadow Pl, St Albans, NL A0H 2E0
Tel: 709-538-3162
www.centralhealth.nl.ca/k-m-homes-ltd
Number of Beds: 30 beds
Shirley Ingram

***St Lawrence:* Mount Margaret Manor**
PO Box 278, St Lawrence, NL A0E 2V0
Tel: 709-873-3199
Number of Beds: 31 beds
Mildred Marsden

***St Marys:* Lewis' Personal Care Home, Inc.**
PO Box 219, St Marys, NL A0B 3B0
Tel: 709-525-2244
Number of Beds: 20 beds
Carolann Lewis, Proprietor

***St Marys:* Neville's Special Care Home**
General Delivery, St Marys, NL A0B 3B0
Tel: 709-525-2098
Number of Beds: 21 beds
Paul Neville

***St. Anthony:* Shirley's Haven Personal Care Home**
PO Box 74, St. Anthony, NL A0K 4S0
Tel: 709-454-1070
Social Media: www.facebook.com/144461468186
Note: Personal care home

***St. John's:* Katherine House**
90 Lemarchant Rd., St. John's, NL A1C 2H1
Tel: 709-754-3864

***St. John's:* Margaret's Manor**
57 Bonaventure Ave., St. John's, NL A1C 3Z3
Tel: 709-722-4040
Note: Nursing home

***St. John's:* North Pond Home**
34 Virginia Place, St. John's, NL A1A 3G6
Tel: 709-437-1415
Number of Beds: 35 beds
Maxine Isaacs
Barry Isaacs

***Stephenville:* Silverwood Manor**
42 Kippens Rd., Stephenville, NL A2N 1A7
Tel: 709-643-6550
westernhealth.nl.ca
Number of Beds: 30 beds
Judy Gallant

***Trepassey:* Ocean View Rest Home**
PO Box 5, Trepassey, NL A0A 4B0
Tel: 709-438-2227

***Twillingate:* Sunset Manor**
PO Box 638, Twillingate, NL A0G 4M0
Tel: 709-884-5301
Number of Beds: 23 beds
Note: Rest home
Margaret Woods

***Wesleyville:* Otterbury Manor**
PO Box 42, 428 Main St., Wesleyville, NL A0G 4R0
Tel: 709-536-3383
Number of Beds: 30 beds
Elsie Carter

***Witless Bay:* Alderwood Estates Encore Living**
Former Name: Dunn's Personal Care Home
PO Box 10, 112 Harbour Rd., Witless Bay, NL A0A 4K0
Tel: 709-334-2183
Info@EncoreLiving.ca
encoreliving.ca
Number of Beds: 35 suites
Debbie Dunne, Manager

Mental Health Hospitals/Facilities

***St. John's:* Waterford Hospital**
Affiliated with: Eastern Regional Health Authority
306 Waterford Bridge Rd., St. John's, NL A1E 4J8
Tel: 709-777-3300; *Fax:* 709-777-3993
www.easternhealth.ca
Note: Programs & services include: mental health program; acute & outpatient care; dialysis services; blood collection; & x-ray.

Northwest Territories

Government Departments in Charge

***Yellowknife:* Department of Health & Social Services**
PO Box 1320, 5015 - 49 St., Yellowknife, NT X1A 2L9
Tel: 867-669-2388 *Toll-Free:* 800-661-0830
www.hss.gov.nt.ca
Glen Abernathy, Minister of Health & Social Services, Executive
867-669-2388
Nick Saturnino, Director, Health Services Administration
867-777-7400

Regional Health Authorities

***Behchoko:* Tlicho Community Services Agency**
PO Box 5, Behchoko, NT X0E 0Y0
Tel: 867-392-3000; *Fax:* 867-392-3001
tcsa@tlicho.net
www.tlicho.ca
Note: A person can contact a member of the primary community care team in their home community & receive access to healthcare services in their own community, in the region &, as necessary, outside the NWT.
Kevin Armstrong, Chief Executive Officer

***Fort Simpson:* Dehcho Health & Social Services Authority (DHSSA)**
Former Name: Deh Cho Health & Social Services Board
9706 - 100 St., Fort Simpson, NT X0E 0N0
Tel: 867-695-3815
www.dhssa.hss.gov.nt.ca
Social Media: www.youtube.com/user/HSSCommunications
Year Founded: 1997
Population Served: 3400; *Number of Employees:* 90
Note: Area Served: Fort Liard; Fort Providence; Fort Simpson; Hay River Reserve; Jean Marie River; Kakisa; Nahanni Butte; Trout Lake; Wrigley, Dehcho Region, NWT. This authority, as well as 5 others, merged in Aug. 2016.
Jim Antoine, Public Administrator
Georgina Veldhorst, Chief Executive Officer
Carsen Hardisty, Director, Quality & Risk Management
Carsen_Hardisty@gov.nt.ca

***Fort Smith:* Fort Smith Health & Social Services Authority (FSHSSA)**
Fort Smith Health Centre, 41 Breynat St., Fort Smith, NT X0E 0P0
Tel: 867-872-6200
www.fshssa.hss.gov.nt.ca
Social Media: www.youtube.com/user/HSSCommunications
Population Served: 2400; *Number of Employees:* 100
Note: Facilities: Fort Smith Health & Social Services Centre; Northern Lights Special Care Home; Polar Crescent Group Home; Sutherland House; Tapwe House; Trailcross Treatment Centre; Fort Smith Wellness Centre. Area Covered: Southern Northwest Territories, including the Town of Fort Smith, Salt River First Nations, & Métis Nation Local 50. This authority, as well as 5 others, merged in Aug. 2016.

***Hay River:* Hay River Health & Social Services Authority (HRHSSA)**
37911 MacKenzie Hwy., Hay River, NT X0E 0R6
Tel: 867-874-8140
www.hrhssa.org
Social Media: www.youtube.com/user/HSSCommunications
Number of Beds: 29 hospital beds; 15 long-term care beds
Area Served: Southern shore of Great Slave Lake, NWT, Enterprise & Hay River; *Population Served:* 3800; *Number of Employees:* 185
Note: Facilities: Hay River Emergency Group Home; Hay River Public Health Unit; Hay River Social Services Office; H.H. Williams Memorial Hospital; Hay River Medical Clinic; Woodland Manor; Hay River Reserve Health Station; Hay River Reserve Social Services; Enterprise Social Services. Area served includes six outlying communities with a total population of more than 6,000 people.
Erin Griffiths, Chief Executive Officer
867-874-8160, erin_griffiths@gov.nt.ca
Merle Engel, Director, Finance
867-874-7119, merle_engel@gov.nt.ca
Sheryl Courtoreille, Director, Client Services
867-874-7162, sheryl_courtoreille@gov.nt.ca
Bonnie Kimble, Contact, Quality Improvement
867-874-8150, hrhssa_clientrelations@gov.nt.ca

***Inuvik:* Beaufort-Delta Health & Social Services Authority (BDHSSA)**
Former Name: Inuvik Regional Health & Social Services Authority
PO Box Bag 2, #285, 289 Mackenzie Rd., Inuvik, NT X0E 0T0
Tel: 867-777-8000
bdhssa_info@gov.nt.ca
www.bdhssa.hss.gov.nt.ca
Social Media: www.youtube.com/user/HSSCommunications
Year Founded: 1988
Number of Beds: 51 beds
Population Served: 6700; *Number of Employees:* 300
Note: Serves the communities of Aklavik, Fort McPherson, Inuvik, Paulatuk, Sachs Harbour, Tsiigehtchic, Tuktoyaktuk, & Ulukhaktok. Services provided through the Inuvik Regional Hospital & community clinics, & include continuing care, health promotion, counselling, social programs, nutrition, telehealth, rehabilitation & diabetes education. This authority, as well as 5 others, merged in Aug. 2016.
Arlene Jorgensen, Chief Executive Officer & Director, Social Programs
867-777-8146
Nadia Salvaterra, Medical Director
867-777-8108
Joanne Engram, Director, Client Services
867-777-8182
Roger Israel, Director, Finance & Operations
867-777-8055

***Norman Wells:* Sahtu Health & Social Services Authority (SHSSA)**
PO Box 340, 227 MacKenzie Dr., Norman Wells, NT X0E 0V0
Tel: 867-587-3650; *Fax:* 867-587-3436
www.shssa.org
Social Media: www.youtube.com/user/HSSCommunications
Year Founded: 2003
Area Served: Communities along the Mackenzie Valley; *Population Served:* 2600; *Number of Employees:* 70
Note: This authority, as well as 5 others, merged in Aug. 2016.
Art Bungay, Director, Finance & Administration
Mireille (Mimi) Hamlyn, Acting CEO & Director, Health & Social Programs
Vacant, Director, Quality & Risk Management

***Yellowknife:* Stanton Territorial Health Authority (STHA)**
Former Name: Stanton Regional Health Board
PO Box 10, 550 Byrne Rd., Yellowknife, NT X1A 2N1
Tel: 867-669-4111
sthainfo@gov.nt.ca
www.stha.hss.gov.nt.ca
Social Media: www.youtube.com/user/HSSCommunications
Area Served: Yellowknife; all regions of NWT; Kitikmeot Region of NU; *Population Served:* 48959; *Number of Employees:* 520
Note: Provides acute inpatient & ambulatory care through Stanton Territorial Hospital, Stanton Eye Clinic, Stanton Medical Clinic, Stanton Medical Centre, & travelling clinics throughout NWT & Nunavut. Also responsible for health programs such as Medical Travel & Med-Response. This authority, as well as 5 others, merged in Aug. 2016.
Brenda Fitzgerald, Chief Executive Officer
Gloria Badari, Chief Financial Officer & Director, Corporate Services
Dr. Bing Guthrie, Medical Director
David Keselman, Director, Ambulatory Care & Medical Affairs

***Yellowknife:* Yellowknife Health & Social Services Authority (YHSSA)**
Former Name: Yellowknife Health & Social Services Board
Goga Cho Bldg., PO Box 608, 4916 - 47th St., 2nd Fl., Yellowknife, NT X1A 2N5
Tel: 867-873-7224; *Fax:* 867-873-0161
yhssa@gov.nt.ca
www.yhssa.org
Social Media: www.youtube.com/user/HSSCommunications
Area Served: Dettah, Fort Resolution, Lutsel K'e, NDilo & Yellowknife; *Population Served:* 20000
Note: Provides community health & social services programs. This authority, as well as 5 others, merged in Aug. 2016.
Elizabeth Wyman, Board Chair
Les Harrison, Chief Executive Officer
Dr. Sarah Cook, Medical Director, Family Medicine
Jo-Anne Hubert, Director, Primary Health Care
Eddie Vasblom, Director, Finance & Administration
Nathalie Nadeau, Director, Social Programs
Leanne Towgood, Director, Community Health

Hospitals - General

***Hay River:* H.H. Williams Memorial Hospital**
Affiliated with: Hay River Health & Social Service Authority
3 Gaetz Dr., Hay River, NT X0E 0R8
Tel: 867-874-7169; *Fax:* 867-874-2926
Number of Beds: 10 beds
Note: Provides physician & emergency services; also includes a long-term care facility.

***Inuvik:* Inuvik Regional Hospital**
Affiliated with: Beaufort-Delta Health & Social Services Authority
Bag 2, Inuvik, NT X0E 0T0
Tel: 867-777-8000; *Fax:* 867-777-8054
www.bdhssa.hss.gov.nt.ca
Social Media: www.youtube.com/HSSCommunications
Number of Beds: 51 beds
Note: Location: #285, 289 Mackenzie Rd., Inuvik. Programs & services include: acute care; dermatology; diagnostic imaging; ear, nose & throat (ENT); emergency; gynecology; health promotion; internal medicine; laboratory; long term care; medical social work; neurology; nutrition; obstetrical care; ophthalmology; orthopedics; pediatrics; pharmacy; physician family clinics; psychiatry; regional mental health & addictions program; regional; social services; rehabilitation; surgery; telehealth; & visiting specialist clinics.

***Yellowknife:* Stanton Territorial Hospital**
Affiliated with: Stanton Territorial Health Authority
PO Box 10, 550 Byrne Rd., Yellowknife, NT X1A 2N1
Tel: 867-669-4111
www.stha.hss.gov.nt.ca
Social Media: www.youtube.com/user/HSSCommunications
Note: Programs & services include: diagnostic imaging; emergency; intensive care; medical day care; medicine; obstetrics; pediatrics; psychiatry; surgery; & surgical day care.
Brenda Fitzgerald, Chief Executive Officer, Stanton Territorial Health Authority
Dr. Bing Guthrie, Medical Director, Stanton Territorial Health Authority
David Keselman, Director, Patient Care Services, Stanton Territorial Health Authority

Community Health Care Centres

***Aklavik:* Susie Husky Health & Social Services Centre**
Affiliated with: Beaufort-Delta Health & Social Services Authority
Former Name: Susie Husky Health Centre
PO Box 114, Aklavik, NT X0E 0A0
Tel: 867-978-2516; *Fax:* 867-978-2160
www.bdhssa.nt.ca
Note: Specialties: Clinics, such as chronic disease & well child, woman, & man clinics; School health program; Health promotion; Dental therapy; Home care; Immunization programs; Rehabilitative services; Child protection; Child & family services; Palliative care. Number of Employees: 1 nurse in charge + 3 community health nurses + 2 community social service workers; 1 dental therapist + 1 community health representative + 1 home support worker + 1 clerk + 1 caretaker

***Behchoko:* Behchoko Health Centre**
Affiliated with: Tlicho Community Services Agency
Former Name: Rae Health Centre
Bag 5, Behchoko, NT X0E 0Y0
Tel: 867-392-6351; *Fax:* 867-392-6612
www.tlicho.ca

***Deline:* Deline Health Centre**
Affiliated with: Sahtu Health & Social Services Authority
PO Box 199, Deline, NT X0E 0G0
Tel: 867-589-3111; *Fax:* 867-589-5570

***Fort Good Hope:* Fort Good Hope Health Centre**
Affiliated with: Sahtu Health & Social Services Authority
PO Box 9, Fort Good Hope, NT X0E 0H0
Tel: 867-598-2211; *Fax:* 867-598-2605
Population Served: 585

***Fort Liard:* Fort Liard Health Centre**
Affiliated with: Dehcho Health & Social Services Authority
General Delivery, Fort Liard, NT X0G 0A0
Tel: 867-770-4301; *Fax:* 867-770-3235

***Fort McPherson:* William Firth Health Centre**
Affiliated with: Beaufort-Delta Health & Social Services Authority
PO Box 56, Fort McPherson, NT X0E 0J0
Tel: 867-952-2586; *Fax:* 867-952-2620

***Fort Providence:* Fort Providence Health Centre**
Affiliated with: Dehcho Health & Social Services Authority
PO Box 229, Fort Providence, NT X0E 0L0
Tel: 867-699-4311

***Fort Simpson:* Fort Simpson Health Centre**
Affiliated with: Dehcho Health & Social Services Authority
PO Box 246, Fort Simpson, NT X0E 0N0
Tel: 867-695-7000; *Fax:* 867-695-7017

***Fort Smith:* Fort Smith Health Centre**
Affiliated with: Fort Smith Health & Social Services Authority
c/o Fort Smith Health & Social Services, PO Box 1080, Fort Smith, NT X0E 0P0
Tel: 867-872-6203; *Fax:* 867-872-6275
www.pws.gov.nt.ca/projects/FortSmithHealthCentre
Number of Beds: 25 beds

***Gameti:* Gamèti Health Centre**
Affiliated with: Tlicho Community Services Agency
General Delivery, Gameti, NT X0E 1R0
Tel: 867-997-3141; *Fax:* 867-997-3045
www.tlicho.ca

***Hay River:* Hay River Public Health Unit**
Affiliated with: Hay River Health & Social Service Authority
3 Gaetz Dr., Hay River, NT X0E 0R8
Tel: 867-874-7100; *Fax:* 867-874-7109
www.hrhssa.org
Erin Griffiths, Executive Assistant
867-874-7115, erin_griffiths@gov.nt.ca

***Inuvik:* Inuvik Public Health Unit**
Affiliated with: Beaufort-Delta Health & Social Services Authority
Bag 2, Inuvik, NT X0E 0T0
Tel: 867-777-7246; *Fax:* 867-777-3255
Barb Lennie, Nurse-in-Charge

***Jean Marie River:* Jean Marie River Health Cabin**
Affiliated with: Dehcho Health & Social Services Authority
General Delivery, Jean Marie River, NT X0E 0N0
Tel: 867-809-2900; *Fax:* 867-809-2902

***Lutselk'e:* Lutselk'e Health Centre**
Affiliated with: Yellowknife Health & Social Services Authority
PO Box 56, Lutselk'e, NT X0E 1A0
Tel: 867-370-3111; *Fax:* 867-370-3022
Note: Specialties: Public health programs; Counselling & crisis intervention & referrals

***Nahanni Butte:* Nahanni Butte Health Cabin**
Affiliated with: Dehcho Health & Social Services Authority
General Delivery, Nahanni Butte, NT X0E 0N0
Tel: 867-602-2203; *Fax:* 867-602-2021

***Norman Wells:* Norman Wells Health Centre**
Affiliated with: Sahtu Health & Social Services Authority
PO Box 8, Norman Wells, NT X0E 0V0
Tel: 867-587-3675; *Fax:* 867-587-2934

***Paulatuk:* Paulatuk Health Centre**
Affiliated with: Beaufort-Delta Health & Social Services Authority
PO Box 114, Paulatuk, NT X0E 1N0
Tel: 867-580-3231; *Fax:* 867-580-3300
Number of Beds: 1 bed

***Sachs Harbour:* Sachs Harbour Health Centre**
Affiliated with: Beaufort-Delta Health & Social Services Authority
PO Box 14, Sachs Harbour, NT X0E 0Z0
Tel: 867-690-4181; *Fax:* 867-690-3802

***Tuktoyaktuk:* Rosie Ovayouk Health Centre**
Affiliated with: Beaufort-Delta Health & Social Services Authority
PO Box 1000, Tuktoyaktuk, NT X0E 1C0
Tel: 867-977-2321; *Fax:* 867-977-2535
Note: Diagnosis; rehabilitation; home care.

***Tulita:* Tulita Health Centre**
Affiliated with: Sahtu Health & Social Services Authority
PO Box 145, Tulita, NT X0E 0K0
Tel: 867-588-4251; *Fax:* 867-588-3000
www.shssa.org
Note: Specialties: Primary care; Health promotion & prevention. Number of Employees: 3 nurses + 2 prevention & health promotion workers + 1 community social service worker + 1 mental health & addictions worker + 1 home support worker + support staff

***Ulukhaktok:* Emegak Health Centre**
Affiliated with: Beaufort-Delta Health & Social Services Authority
PO Box 160, Ulukhaktok, NT X0E 0S0
Tel: 867-396-3111; *Fax:* 867-396-3221

***Ulukhaktok:* Ulukhaktok Health Services**
Affiliated with: Beaufort-Delta Health & Social Services Authority
c/o Emegak Health & Social Services Centre, PO Box 160, Ulukhaktok, NT X0E 0S0
Tel: 867-396-3111; *Fax:* 867-396-3221
Note: Specialties: Assessments; Crisis intervention; Therapeutic counselling; Education & awareness. Number of Employees: 1 mental health & addictions counsellor + 1 community wellness worker

***Wekweti:* Wekweèti Health Centre**
Affiliated with: Tlicho Community Services Agency
General Delivery, Wekweti, NT X0E 1W0
Tel: 867-713-2904; *Fax:* 867-713-2903

***Wha Ti:* Whati Health Centre**
Affiliated with: Tlicho Community Services Agency
General Delivery, Wha Ti, NT X0E 1P0
Tel: 867-573-3261; *Fax:* 867-573-3701
www.tlicho.ca

***Wrigley:* Wrigley Health Centre**
Affiliated with: Dehcho Health & Social Services Authority
PO Box 58, General Delivery, Wrigley, NT X0E 1E0
Tel: 867-581-3441

***Yellowknife:* Yellowknife Public Health Centre**
Affiliated with: Yellowknife Health & Social Services Authority
PO Box 608, Yellowknife, NT X1A 2N5
Tel: 867-920-6570; *Fax:* 867-873-0158

Nursing Stations

***Colville Lake:* Colville Lake Health Station**
Affiliated with: Sahtu Health & Social Services Authority
PO Box 50, Colville Lake, NT X0E 1L0
Tel: 867-709-2409; *Fax:* 867-709-2504

***Fort Resolution:* Fort Resolution Health Centre**
Affiliated with: Yellowknife Health & Social Services Authority
General Delivery, Fort Resolution, NT X0E 0M0
Tel: 867-394-4511; *Fax:* 867-394-3117
www.yhssa.org

***Inuvik:* Beaufort-Delta Health & Social Services**
Affiliated with: Beaufort-Delta Health & Social Services Authority
285 Mackenzie Rd., Inuvik, NT X0E 0T0
Tel: 867-777-8000
bdhssa.nt.ca

***Trout Lake:* Trout Lake Health Station**
Affiliated with: Dehcho Health & Social Services Authority
Trout Lake Health Cabin, PO Box 39, Trout Lake, NT X0E 1Z0
Tel: 867-206-2838; *Fax:* 867-206-2024
Versa Vendron

Special Treatment Centres

***Fort Liard:* Fort Liard Mental Health & Addictions Program**
Affiliated with: Dehcho Health & Social Services Authority
General Delivery, Fort Liard, NT X0G 0A0
Tel: 867-770-4770; *Fax:* 867-770-4813

***Fort Simpson:* Fort Simpson Mental Health & Addictions Program**
Affiliated with: Dehcho Health & Social Services Authority
PO Box 246, Fort Simpson, NT X0E 0N0
Tel: 867-695-3815; *Fax:* 867-695-2920
Elsie Gresl, Coordinator

***Hay River:* Hay River Reserve Wellness Centre**
Affiliated with: Dehcho Health & Social Services Authority
#3 Gaetz Dr., Hay River, NT X0E 0R8
Tel: 867-874-2838; *Fax:* 867-874-6305
www.hrhssa.org
Anne Firth-Jones, Community Wellness Worker

Long Term Care Facilities

***Behchoko:* Jimmy Erasmus Seniors Home**
Affiliated with: Tlicho Community Services Agency
General Delivery, Behchoko, NT X0E 0Y0
Tel: 867-392-3018; *Fax:* 867-392-3001
www.tlicho.ca
Number of Beds: 7 beds; 1 respite bed

***Fort Simpson:* Fort Simpson Long Term Care Home**
Affiliated with: Dehcho Health & Social Services Authority
PO Box 246, Fort Simpson, NT X0E 0N0
Tel: 867-695-7080; *Fax:* 867-695-7083

***Fort Simpson:* Stanley Isaiah Supportive Independent Living Home**
Affiliated with: Dehcho Health & Social Services Authority
PO Box 240, Fort Simpson, NT X0E 0N0
Tel: 867-695-2365; *Fax:* 867-695-2364
Note: independent living adult

***Hay River:* Woodland Manor**
Affiliated with: Hay River Health & Social Service Authority
52A Woodland Dr., Hay River, NT X0E 0R8
Tel: 867-874-7226; *Fax:* 867-874-7234
www.hlthss.gov.nt.ca
Number of Beds: 15 beds

***Inuvik:* Billy Moore Home**
Affiliated with: Beaufort-Delta Health & Social Services Authority
PO Box 1078, Inuvik, NT X0E 0T0
Tel: 867-777-3204; *Fax:* 867-777-2472

***Inuvik:* Charlotte Vehus Home**
Affiliated with: Beaufort-Delta Health & Social Services Authority
PO Box 1800, Inuvik, NT X0E 0T0
Tel: 867-777-4780; *Fax:* 867-777-4687

Nursing Homes

***Fort Smith:* Northern Lights Special Care Home**
Affiliated with: Fort Smith Health & Social Services Authority
PO Box 1319, Fort Smith, NT X0E 0P0
Tel: 867-872-5403; *Fax:* 867-872-5404
www.hss.gov.nt.ca
Number of Beds: 28 beds
Suzanne Sihikal, Administrator

***Yellowknife:* Aven Manor**
Affiliated with: AVENS - A Community for Seniors
Also Known As: Aven Cottage
#1, 5710 - 50th Ave., Yellowknife, NT X1A 1E9
Tel: 867-920-2443; *Fax:* 867-873-9915
avensseniors.com
Year Founded: 1987
Number of Beds: 29 beds
Jeff Renaud, CEO

Mental Health Hospitals/Facilities

***Yellowknife:* Yellowknife Mental Health Clinic**
Affiliated with: Yellowknife Health & Social Services Authority
PO Box 10, Yellowknife, NT X1A 2N5
Tel: 867-873-7042; *Fax:* 867-873-0487
Corliss McCloskey, Manager, Psychiatric Services

Nova Scotia

Government Departments in Charge

***Halifax:* Nova Scotia Department of Health & Wellness**
PO Box 488, Halifax, NS B3J 2R8
Tel: 902-424-5818 *Toll-Free:* 800-387-6665
TTY: 800-670-8888
novascotia.ca/dhw
Hon. Leo A. Glavine, Minister
902-424-3377, Health.Minister@novascotia.ca

Regional Health Authorities

***Halifax:* Halifax, Eastern Shore & West Hants Regional Office**
Affiliated with: Nova Scotia Health Authority
#5, 7 Mellor Ave., Halifax, NS B3B 0E6
Tel: 902-481-5800; *Fax:* 902-481-5803
Toll-Free: 1-844-491-5894
Dr. Gaynor Watson-Creed, Medical Officer of Health
Dr. Robin Taylor, Medical Officer of Health

***Halifax:* Nova Scotia Health Authority**
#201, 90 Lovett Lake Ct., Halifax, NS B3S 0H6
Toll-Free: 1-844-491-5890
wearelistening@nshealth.ca
www.nshealth.ca
Info Line: 811
Social Media: www.facebook.com/NovaScotiaHealthAuthority; twitter.com/healthns
Year Founded: 2015
Number of Beds: 3,198
Area Served: Province of Nova Scotia; *Number of Employees:* 23400
Note: All former Nova Scotia health districts mergerd in 2015, forming the Nova Scotia Health Authority. The new organization will oversee 10 hospitals, 35 community health centres, 33 auxiliaries & 37 community health boards.
Janet Knox, President & CEO
Steven Parker, Chair
Allan Horsburgh, CFO & Vice-President, Stewardship & Accountability
Lindsay Peach, Vice-President, Integrated Health Services Community Support
Tricia Cochrane, Vice-President, Population Health
Tim Guest, Chief Nursing Officer & Vice-President, Integrated Health Services Program Care 2
Paula Bond, Vice-President, Integrated Health Services Program Care 1
Catherine Gaulton, Chief Legal Officer & Vice-President, Quality & System Performance
Dr. Lynne Harrigan, Vice-President, Medicine & Integrated Health Services
Carmelle d'Entremont, Vice-President, People & Organizational Development
Patrick McGrath, Vice-President, Research, Innovation & Knowledge Translation

***Kentville:* Nova Scotia Health Authority - Annapolis Valley, South Shore & South West Nova Scotia Regional Office**
Affiliated with: Nova Scotia Health Authority
5 Chipman Dr., Kentville, NS B4N 3V7
Tel: 902-678-7381 *Toll-Free:* 1-844-491-5891
www.avdha.nshealth.ca
Info Line: 811

***Sydney:* Nova Scotia Health Authority - Cape Breton, Guysborough & Antigonish Regional Office**
Affiliated with: Nova Scotia Health Authority
1482 George St., Sydney, NS B1P 1P3
Tel: 902-567-8000; *Fax:* 902-564-9305
Toll-Free: 1-844-491-5892
www.cbdha.nshealth.ca

***Truro:* Nova Scotia Health Authority - Colchester-East Hants, Cumberland & Pictou Regional Office**
Affiliated with: Nova Scotia Health Authority
600 Abenaki Dr., Truro, NS B2N 5A1
Tel: 902-893-5554 *Toll-Free:* 1-844-491-5893
www.cehha.nshealth.ca

Hospitals - General

***Amherst:* Cumberland Regional Health Care Centre (CRHCC)**
Affiliated with: Nova Scotia Health Authority
19428 Hwy 2, RR #6, Amherst, NS B4H 1N6
Tel: 902-667-3361; *Fax:* 902-667-6306
www.cha.nshealth.ca
Year Founded: 2002
Note: Programs & services include: level 2 emergency; ICU; surgery; maternal/child services; laboratory; diagnostic imaging; pharmacy; respiratory therapy; & physiotherapy & occupational therapy.

***Antigonish:* St. Martha's Regional Hospital**
Affiliated with: Nova Scotia Health Authority
25 Bay St., Antigonish, NS B2G 2G5
Tel: 902-867-4500; *Fax:* 902-863-1176
www.gasha.nshealth.ca
Year Founded: 1906
Number of Beds: 89 beds
Note: Programs & services include: anesthesia; bone densitometry; cancer & supportive care; cardio-respiratory; chemotherapy; chronic pain clinic; clinical nutrition; colposcopy clinic; cystometry clinic; diabetes education; diagnostic imaging; emergency; foot clinic; general medical/surgical; geriatric assessment & rehabilitation/clinic; gynecology/obstetrics/midwifery; heart health clinic; hospice & palliative care; internal medicine; laboratory services; mental health inpatient/outpatient; obstetrics; occupational therapy; Open Arms Clinic; ophthalmology; orthoptics clinic; ostomy clinic; otolaryngology; pediatrics; physiotherapy; plastic surgery; pre-surgical assessment clinic; social work; spiritual & religious care; & wound care clinic.
Andrea Boyd-White, Co-manager
Andrea.Boyd-White@gasha.nshealth.ca
David MacKenzie, Co-manager
David.MacKenzie@gasha.nshealth.ca

***Baddeck:* Victoria County Memorial Hospital**
Affiliated with: Nova Scotia Health Authority
PO Box 220, 30 Old Margaree Rd., Baddeck, NS B0E 1B0
Tel: 902-295-2112
www.cbdha.nshealth.ca
Social Media: www.facebook.com/300633586615252
Year Founded: 1949
Number of Beds: 12 beds
Patricia MacDonald, Facility Manager

***Bridgewater:* South Shore Regional Hospital**
Affiliated with: Nova Scotia Health Authority
Former Name: Health Services Association of the South Shore
90 Glen Allan Dr., Bridgewater, NS B4V 3S6
Tel: 902-543-4603; *Fax:* 902-543-4719
www.southshorehealth.ca

Number of Beds: 80 beds
Specialties: Trauma care
Note: Programs & services include: ambulatory care; anesthesiology; breast feeding clinic; cardiology; chemotherapy; colposcopy; diagnostic imaging; dietary counselling; EKG; emergency; family medicine; gastroenterology; heart function; internal medicine; laboratory; mental health; obstetrics/gynecology; ophthalmology; palliative care; pathology; pediatrics; pharmacy; plastic surgery; prenatal; psychiatry; radiology; rehabilitation; respiratory; rheumatology; sleep disorder; surgery; & walk-in clinic.

Canso: Eastern Memorial Hospital
Affiliated with: Nova Scotia Health Authority
PO Box 10, 1746 Union St., Canso, NS B0H 1H0
Tel: 902-366-2794; *Fax:* 902-366-2740
www.gasha.nshealth.ca

Year Founded: 1948
Number of Beds: 6 beds
Note: Programs & services include: diabetes education; diagnostic imaging; EKG; emergency; cancer & supportive care; laboratory; mental health outpatient services; physiotherapy; social work; TEAM (Teaching Eating & Activity Management); & Well Women's Clinics.
Elaine MacMaster, Facility Manager
Elaine.MacMaster@gasha.nshealth.ca

Cheticamp: Sacred Heart Community Health Centre
Affiliated with: Nova Scotia Health Authority
Former Name: Sacred Heart Hospital
PO Box 129, 15102 Cabot Trail, Cheticamp, NS B0E 1H0
Tel: 902-224-1500; *Fax:* 902-224-2903
www.cbdha.nshealth.ca
Social Media: www.facebook.com/300633586615252

Year Founded: 1999
Number of Beds: 10 beds
Note: Programs & services include: chemotherapy preparation; diabetic education; diagnostic imaging; emergency/outpatient; eye clinics; foot clinics; laboratory; medical social work; nutritional counseling; occupational therapy; palliative care; & physiotherapy.

Dartmouth: Dartmouth General Hospital (DGH)
Affiliated with: Nova Scotia Health Authority
325 Pleasant St., Dartmouth, NS B2Y 4G8
Tel: 902-465-8300
healthcareexperience@cdha.nshealth.ca
www.cdha.nshealth.ca
Social Media: www.facebook.com/CapitalHealth; twitter.com/capital_health; www.linkedin.com/company/capital-district-health-authority
Year Founded: 1976
Population Served: 120000
Note: Programs & services include: CT scanning; dentistry; ear, nose & throat surgery; general radiography; general surgery; gynaecology; inpatient medical, surgical care & critical care; laboratory services; mammography; oral maxillofacial surgery; ophthalmology; orthopaedic surgery; outpatient services; outreach programs; plastic surgery; renal dialysis; urology; & vascular surgery.
Dr. Ravi Parkash, Site Chief
Heather Francis, Director, Health Services

Digby: Digby General Hospital
Affiliated with: Nova Scotia Health Authority
75 Warwick St., Digby, NS B0V 1A0
Tel: 902-245-2502; *Fax:* 902-245-2803
www.swndha.nshealth.ca
Number of Beds: 11 acute beds; 13 restorative care beds; 9 transition beds
Population Served: 18992
Note: Programs & services include: addiction; cardiac/respiratory; continuing care; day surgery; diabetes education; diagnostic imaging; dietitian (outpatient); emergency; health records; hearing & speech; laboratory; mental health; Nova Scotia Hearing & Speech Centres; nursing; occupational health nurse & infection control practitioner; palliative & supportive care; plant operations/maintenance; public health rehabilitation services; restorative care; telehealth; volunteer opportunities; & Victorian Order of Nurses.
Hubert d'Entremont, Site Manager
902-245-2502, hubertdentremont@swndha.nshealth.ca

Evanston: Strait Richmond Hospital
Affiliated with: Nova Scotia Health Authority
138 Hospital Rd., Evanston, NS B0E 1J0
Tel: 902-625-3100; *Fax:* 902-625-3804
www.gasha.nshealth.ca
Year Founded: 1980
Number of Beds: 15 beds; 5 restorative care beds
Note: Programs & services include: chemotherapy; diabetes education; diagnostic imaging; dialysis (QEII Satellite Clinic); EKG; emergency; EN pap screening program; foot care; hospice & palliative care; internal medicine; laboratory; mental health outpatient; nutrition & dietetic counseling; occupational therapy; pediatrics; physiotherapy; rheumatology; Seniors Advisory Committee; social work services; & Well Men's Clinic (Urology).
Rose Richardson, Facility Manager
Rose.Richardson@gasha.nshealth.ca

Guysborough: Guysborough Memorial Hospital
Affiliated with: Nova Scotia Health Authority
PO Box 170, 10560 Rte. 16, Guysborough, NS B0H 1N0
Tel: 902-533-3702; *Fax:* 902-533-4066
www.gasha.nshealth.ca

Number of Beds: 10 beds
Note: Programs & services include: diabetes education; diagnostic imaging; EKG; emergency; foot care clinic; laboratory; mental health outpatient; nutrition & diet counseling; physiotherapy; social work; & Well Men's Clinic (urology).
Elaine MacMaster, Facility Manager
emacmaster@gasha.nshealth.ca

Halifax: IWK Health Centre
PO Box 9700, 5850/5980 University Ave., Halifax, NS B3K 6R8
Tel: 902-470-8888
feedback@iwk.nshealth.ca
www.iwk.nshealth.ca
Social Media: www.facebook.com/iwkhealthcentre; twitter.com/iwkhealthcentre; www.youtube.com/iwkhealthcentre
Number of Employees: 3600
Note: The IWK Health Centre provides care to women, children, youth and families in the Maritime provinces and beyond. In addition to providing highly specialized (tertiary) care, the IWK also provides primary care services.
Tracy Kitch, President/CEO
Jocelyn Vince, Chief Nurse Executive & Vice-President, Patient Care

Halifax: Queen Elizabeth II Health Sciences Centre (QEII)
Affiliated with: Nova Scotia Health Authority
1796 Summer St., Halifax, NS B3H 2A7
Tel: 902-473-2700
www.cdha.nshealth.ca
Social Media: www.facebook.com/CapitalHealth; twitter.com/capital_health; www.linkedin.com/company/capital-district-health-authority
Note: The largest teaching hospital in Atlantic Canada, made up of 10 buildings on 2 sites (the Halifax Infirmary site & the Victoria General site). The QEII provides general & specialized medical care, including mental health programs; cancer care; long-term care; geriatric assessment & restorative care.

Inverness: Inverness Consolidated Memorial Hospital
Affiliated with: Nova Scotia Health Authority
Former Name: Inverness Consolidated Hospital
PO Box 610, 39 James St., Inverness, NS B0E 1N0
Tel: 902-258-2100
www.cbdha.nshealth.ca
Social Media: www.facebook.com/300633586615252
Number of Beds: 48 beds
Note: Acute & continuing care

Kentville: Valley Regional Hospital
Affiliated with: Nova Scotia Health Authority
150 Exhibition St., Kentville, NS B4N 5E3
Tel: 902-678-7381; *Fax:* 902-679-1904
www.avdha.nshealth.ca

Year Founded: 1992
Number of Employees: 700
Note: Programs & services include: addiction services; anaesthesia; asthma care; chronic pain; diabetes; diagnostic imaging; emergency; laboratory; mental health; Nova Scotia Hearing & Speech Centre; organ & tissue donation; palliative care; pastoral care; pharmacy; residential mental health; seniors mental health; & surgery.

Liverpool: Queens General Hospital
Affiliated with: Nova Scotia Health Authority
PO Box 370, 175 School St., Liverpool, NS B0T 1K0
Tel: 902-354-3436
www.southshorehealth.ca

Number of Beds: 22 beds
Note: Programs & services include: addiction; day surgery/ambulatory care; diagnostic imaging; EKG; emergency; endoscopy; family practice; laboratory; mental health; palliative care; pharmacy; rehabilitation; renal dialysis (operated by QEII); & respiratory therapy.

Lunenburg: Fishermen's Memorial Hospital
Affiliated with: Nova Scotia Health Authority
PO Box 1180, 14 High St., Lunenburg, NS B0J 2C0
Tel: 902-634-8801
www.southshorehealth.ca
Number of Beds: 23 veterans' care beds; 10 addiction services beds; 12 restorative care beds; 12 alternate level of care beds; 6 acute care beds; 2 observation beds
Note: Hospital Specialties: Laboratory services; Diagnostic imaging; Acute care; Ambulatory care; Addiction services; Rehabilitation services; Restorative care; Respiratory therapy; Asthma Care Centre; Palliative care

Middle Musquodoboit: Musquodoboit Valley Memorial Hospital
Affiliated with: Nova Scotia Health Authority
492 Archibald Brook Rd., Middle Musquodoboit, NS B0N 1X0
Tel: 902-384-2220; *Fax:* 902-384-3310
healthcareexperience@cdha.nshealth.ca
www.cdha.nshealth.ca
Social Media: www.facebook.com/CapitalHealth; twitter.com/capital_health; www.linkedin.com/company/capital-district-health-authority
Number of Beds: 6 inpatient beds; palliative care room
Note: Programs & services include: acute home nursing care; clinical nutrition; diabetic clinic & meals-on-wheels; diagnostic services (including laboratory, EKG & radiology); emergency services; occupational therapy; outpatient services; palliative services; physiotherapy; public health; shared care mental health; social work; & The Musquodoboit Valley Family Practice.

Middleton: Soldiers Memorial Hospital
Affiliated with: Nova Scotia Health Authority
PO Box 730, 462 Main St., Middleton, NS B0S 1P0
Tel: 902-825-3411; *Fax:* 902-825-0599
www.avdha.nshealth.ca

Population Served: 40000
Note: Programs & services include: acute care; addictions care; cardiac; diabetes; diagnostic imaging; emergency; enterostomal therapy; laboratory; long-term care; mental health; Nova Scotia Hearing & Speech Centre; occupational therapy; organ & tissue donation; palliative care; pharmacy; physiotherapy; public health; seniors mental health; speech language; surgery; & transitional care.

Musquodoboit Harbour: Twin Oaks Memorial Hospital
Affiliated with: Nova Scotia Health Authority
7704 - 7 Hwy., Musquodoboit Harbour, NS B0J 2L0
Tel: 902-889-2200
healthcareexperience@cdha.nshealth.ca
www.cdha.nshealth.ca
Social Media: www.facebook.com/CapitalHealth; twitter.com/capital_health; www.linkedin.com/company/capital-district-health-authority
Year Founded: 1976
Number of Beds: 14 beds
Note: Programs & services include: acupuncture clinic; acute care; addiction; Beltone Hearing Centre; diabetic & foot clinics; diagnostic imaging; emergency; Home Care Nova Scotia; laboratory; meals on wheels; Nova Scotia Hearing & Speech Clinic; nutrition counseling; occupational therapy; outpatient care; palliative & respite services; physiotherapy; & social services.
Marilyn Cipak, Manager, Health Services
902-889-4106, marilyn.cipak@cdha.nshealth.ca

Neils Harbour: Buchanan Memorial Community Health Centre
Affiliated with: Nova Scotia Health Authority
32610 Cabot Trail, Neils Harbour, NS B0C 1N0
Tel: 902-336-2200
www.cbdha.nshealth.ca
Social Media: www.facebook.com/300633586615252
Year Founded: 1943
Population Served: 4200
Note: Programs & services include: Addiction services; Cardiac clinics; Chemotherapy preparation; Diabetic clinics; Dietitian; Emergency; Foot clinics; Home Care Nova Scotia; Male wellness clinics; Medical social worker; Orthopedics; Palliative care; Pediatrics; Public health; & RN pap clinic.

New Glasgow: Aberdeen Hospital
Affiliated with: Nova Scotia Health Authority
835 East River Rd., New Glasgow, NS B2H 3S6
Tel: 902-752-8311
www.pcha.nshealth.ca

Number of Beds: 104 beds
Population Served: 48000
Note: Provides inpatient, outpatient & community-based services such as: anesthesia; cardiology; diagnostic imaging; emergency;

general surgery; internal medicine; obstetrics & gynecology; ophthalmology; orthopedics; pathology; pediatrics; psychiatry; & urology.

North Sydney: **Northside General Hospital**
Affiliated with: Nova Scotia Health Authority
PO Box 399, 520 Purves St., North Sydney, NS B2A 3M4
Tel: 902-794-8521
www.cbdha.nshealth.ca
Social Media: www.facebook.com/300633586615252
Note: Programs & services include: acute care; ambulatory care; day surgery; diabetic education; diagnostic imaging; emergency medicine; laboratory; medical/CCA unit; medical social work; mental health clinic; orthoptics; pastoral care; physiotherapy; surgical unit; ultrasound; & Well Women's Clinic.

Parrsboro: **South Cumberland Community Care Centre**
Affiliated with: Nova Scotia Health Authority
PO Box 489, 50 Jenks Ave., Parrsboro, NS B0M 1S0
Tel: 902-254-2540; *Fax:* 902-254-2504
www.cha.nshealth.ca
Year Founded: 1975
Number of Beds: 16 beds (14 long-term care; 2 swing/palliative care beds)
Note: Programs & services include: emergency; primary health care; long-term care; laboratory & diagnostic imaging; diabetes education; physiotherapy & occupational therapy; social work; dietary; & mental health.

Pictou: **Sutherland Harris Memorial Hospital**
Affiliated with: Nova Scotia Health Authority
PO Box 1059, 222 Haliburton Rd., Pictou, NS B0K 1H0
Tel: 902-485-4324; *Fax:* 902-485-8835
www.pcha.nshealth.ca
Year Founded: 1966
Number of Beds: 20 long-term beds for veterans; 12 restorative care beds
Note: Programs & services include: Northumberland Veterans Unit; Restorative Care Unit; blood collection; geriatric consultation; occupational therapy; palliative care; pastoral care; physiotherapy; recreation; satellite hemodialysis clinic; social work; speech-language therapy; special clinics (for walk-ins, diabetes education, & women's health).

Pugwash: **North Cumberland Memorial Hospital**
Affiliated with: Nova Scotia Health Authority
260 Church St., Pugwash, NS B0K 1L0
Tel: 902-243-2521; *Fax:* 902-243-2941
www.cha.nshealth.ca
Year Founded: 1966
Note: Short-term stay facility; provides emergency, inpatient, outpatient, ambulatory care, palliative care & health promotion services.

Sheet Harbour: **Eastern Shore Memorial Hospital**
Affiliated with: Nova Scotia Health Authority
22737 Hwy. #7, Sheet Harbour, NS B0J 3B0
Tel: 902-885-2554; *Fax:* 902-885-3200
healthcareexperience@cdha.nshealth.ca
www.cdha.nshealth.ca
Social Media: www.facebook.com/CapitalHealth; twitter.com/capital_health; www.linkedin.com/company/capital-district-health-authority
Year Founded: 1976
Number of Beds: 16 beds
Note: Programs & services include: acute care; addiction prevention & treatment services; adult day clinic; ambulatory care; clinical nutrition; diabetic clinic; diagnostic imaging; Home Care Nova Scotia; IWK Health Centre - mental health & family services; laboratory services; meals-on-wheels; Nova Scotia hospital outreach; occupational therapy; outpatient/emergency; palliative & respite care; physiotherapy; public health; & social services.
Margaret Merlin-Wilson, Director, Health Services
902-869-6107, margaret.merlin@cdha.nshealth.ca
Tracy Manuge, Facility Secretary
902-885-3678, tracy.manuge@cdha.nshealth.ca

Shelburne: **Roseway Hospital**
Affiliated with: Nova Scotia Health Authority
PO Box 610, 1606 Sandy Point Rd., Shelburne, NS B0T 1W0
Tel: 902-875-3011; *Fax:* 902-875-1580
www.swndha.nshealth.ca
Number of Beds: 19 beds
Population Served: 15000
Note: Programs & services include: addiction; audiology; cardiac stress testing; continuing care; diagnostic services (radiology, laboratory & EKG); emergency; gastroscopy; internal medicine; mental health centre; nutrition counseling & diabetes education; obstetrics & gynecology; otolaryngology; palliative care; physiotherapy & occupational therapy; plastic surgery; speech therapy; surgery; Victorian Order of Nurses; & Well Woman clinics.
Jodi Ybarra, Site Manager
jybarra@swndha.nshealth.ca

Sherbrooke: **St. Mary's Memorial Hospital**
Affiliated with: Nova Scotia Health Authority
PO Box 299, 91 Hospital Rd., Sherbrooke, NS B0J 3C0
Tel: 902-522-2882; *Fax:* 902-522-2556
www.gasha.nshealth.ca
Year Founded: 1949
Number of Beds: 6 beds
Note: Programs & services include: diabetes education; diagnositc imaging; EKG; emergency; foot care clinic; hospice & palliative care; laboratory; nutrition & dietetic counseling; physiotherapy; social work; telehealth/telederm; & Well Men's Clinic (urology).
Teresa MacInnis, Facility Manager
Teresa.MacInnic@gasha.nshealth.ca

Springhill: **All Saints Springhill Hospital (ASSH)**
Affiliated with: Nova Scotia Health Authority
Also Known As: All Saints Hospital
PO Box 700, 10 Princess St., Springhill, NS B0M 1X0
Tel: 902-597-3773; *Fax:* 902-597-3440
www.cha.nshealth.ca
Year Founded: 1963
Number of Beds: 10 restorative care beds; 10 inpatient addictions treatment beds; 8 transitional beds; 2 palliative care beds
Note: Programs & services include: rehabilitation; addictions treatment; palliative care; emergency; primary health services; ambulatory care; outpatient restorative care; health promotion; & diagnostic services.

Sydney: **Cape Breton Regional Hospital**
Affiliated with: Nova Scotia Health Authority
1482 George St., Sydney, NS B1P 1P3
Tel: 902-567-8000
www.cbdha.nshealth.ca
Social Media: www.facebook.com/300633586615252
Year Founded: 1995
Note: Programs & services include: acute care; ambulatory care; anatomical & histology; angiography; cardiac diagnostic testing; CT Scan; coronary care unit; diabetic education; diagnostic imaging; ECHO; EEG; emergency; EMG; endocrinology; general & specialty surgery; geriatric medicine; intensive care unit; mammography; medical & radiation oncology; medical social work; mental health program & clinics; Mi'kmaq interpreter/liaison; neonatal intensive care unit; non invasive vascular laboratory; nuclear medicine; obstetrics; occupational therapy; palliative care services; pastoral care; physiotherapy; renal dialysis unit; respiratory therapy; speech therapy; & ultrasound.

Tatamagouche: **Lillian Fraser Memorial Hospital**
Affiliated with: Nova Scotia Health Authority
PO Box 40, 110 Blair Ave., Tatamagouche, NS B0K 1V0
Tel: 902-657-2382; *Fax:* 902-657-3745
www.cehha.nshealth.ca
Number of Beds: 10 beds
Note: Programs & services include: diabetes clinic; diagnostic imaging; emergency; food services; inpatient medical unit; laboratory; medical day unit; nutrition counseling; outpatient; palliative care; perinatal & gynecology; physiotherapy/rehabilitation; telehealth; & surgical clinic.

Truro: **Colchester East Hants Health Centre**
Affiliated with: Nova Scotia Health Authority
Former Name: Colchester Regional Hospital
600 Abenaki Rd., Truro, NS B2N 5A1
Tel: 902-893-5554; *Fax:* 902-893-5559
Toll-Free: 800-460-2110
www.cehha.nshealth.ca
Number of Beds: 98 beds
Note: Programs & services include: asthma care; blood/specimen collection; breast screening; cardiovascular; colpolscopy; coronary care; CT scan; dermatology; diabetes; diagnostic imaging; dialysis; dietary/nutrition; ECG; emergency; enterostomal therapy; general medicine; hearing & speech; intensive care; laboratory; medical day unit; mental health & addiction; occupational therapy; oncology; opthalmology; ostomy clinic; outpatients; palliative care; pastoral care; perinatal; pharmacy; physiotherapy; pre-operative clinic; rehabilitation; respiratory; seniors' clinic; social work; surgery; telehealth; water testing; women & children's health; & wound management.

Windsor: **Hants Community Hospital**
Affiliated with: Nova Scotia Health Authority
89 Payzant Dr., Windsor, NS B0N 2T0
Tel: 902-792-2000; *Fax:* 902-798-6002
healthcareexperience@cdha.nshealth.ca
www.cdha.nshealth.ca
Social Media: www.facebook.com/CapitalHealth; twitter.com/capital_health; www.linkedin.com/company/capital-district-health-authority
Number of Beds: 24 general beds; 14 transitional beds
Note: Programs & services include: acute medical; diagnostic imaging; general surgical care; Home Care Nova Scotia; Home Support Central; laboratory; Nova Scotia Hearing & Speech Clinic; physiotherapy; public health services; respiratory; social work; & Victorian Order of Nurses.
Dr. Mike Clory, Site Chief
Sherri Parker, Director, Health Services

Yarmouth: **Yarmouth Regional Hospital**
Affiliated with: Nova Scotia Health Authority
60 Vancouver St., Yarmouth, NS B5A 2P5
Tel: 902-742-3541; *Fax:* 902-742-0369
www.swndha.nshealth.ca
Number of Beds: 124 beds
Population Served: 64000
Note: Programs & services include: addiction & drug dependency; alternate level of care unit; ambulatory care/visiting clinic; anesthesiology; cancer clinic; day surgery; diabetes education; diagnostic imaging; EKG; emergency; intensive care; internal medicine; laboratory; maternal/child; medical inpatient; mental health services inpatient & outpatient; obstetrics/gynecology; ophthalmology; otolaryngology; palliative care; pathology; pediatrics; psychiatry; rehabilitation; renal dialysis; respiratory therapy; pharmacy services; radiology; speech & language therapy; surgery; & veteran's unit.
Cathy Blades, Vice President, Clinical Care

Auxiliary Hospitals

Advocate Harbor: **Bayview Memorial Health Centre**
Affiliated with: Nova Scotia Health Authority
Advocate Harbor, NS B0M 1A0
Tel: 902-392-2859; *Fax:* 902-392-2625
www.cha.nshealth.ca
Year Founded: 1989
Number of Beds: 10 beds (including 8 long-term-care beds)
Note: Provides community health services & long-term care.

Community Health Care Centres

Annapolis Royal: **Annapolis Community Health Centre**
Affiliated with: Nova Scotia Health Authority
PO Box 426, 821 St. George St., Annapolis Royal, NS B0S 1A0
Tel: 902-532-2381; *Fax:* 902-532-2113

Berwick: **Western Kings Memorial Health Centre**
Affiliated with: Nova Scotia Health Authority
PO Box 490, 121 Orchard St., Berwick, NS B0P 1E0
Tel: 902-538-3111; *Fax:* 902-538-9590
www.avdha.nshealth.ca
Note: Outpatient department, lab, diagnostic imaging, physiotherapy, nutritional counseling, dialysis, mental health clinic, Victorian Order of Nurses Adult Day Care

Lower Sackville: **Cobequid Community Health Centre (CCHC)**
Affiliated with: Nova Scotia Health Authority
40 Freer Lane, Lower Sackville, NS B4C 0A2
Tel: 902-869-6100; *Fax:* 902-869-6148
www.capitalhealth.ca
Note: Ambulatory care facility
Dr. Mike Clory, Site Chief
Margaret Merlin-Wilson, Director, Health Services

Sydney: **Public Health Services**
Affiliated with: Nova Scotia Health Authority
2nd Fl., 235 Townsend St., Sydney, NS B1P 5E7
Tel: 902-563-2400; *Fax:* 902-563-0508

Wolfville: **Eastern Kings Memorial Community Health Centre**
Affiliated with: Nova Scotia Health Authority
Former Name: Eastern Kings Community Health Centre
PO Box 1180, 23 Earnscliffe Ave., Wolfville, NS B4P 1X0
Tel: 902-542-2266; *Fax:* 902-542-4619
www.avdha.nshealth.ca

Special Treatment Centres

***Halifax:* IWK Health Centre**
Halifax Community Mental Health and Central Referral Service
Former Name: Atlantic Child Guidance Center
#1001, 6080 Young St., Halifax, NS B3K 5L2
Tel: 902-464-4110; *Fax:* 902-464-3008
www.iwk.nshealth.ca
Anne McGuire, President & CEO

***Halifax:* Nova Scotia Hearing & Speech Centres**
Provincial Centre, Park Lane Terraces, PO Box 120, #401, 5657 Spring Garden Rd., Halifax, NS B3J 3R4
Tel: 902-492-8289; *Fax:* 902-423-0532
Toll-Free: 888-780-3330
info@nshsc.nshealth.ca
www.nshsc.ns.ca
Note: Specialties: Speech-language pathology services; Audiology services Augmentative communication program; Cochlear implant program; Industrial & community audiology; Newborn hearing screening program
D. Lynn Fraser, President & CEO

***Waterville:* Kings Regional Rehabilitation Centre**
PO Box 128, 1349 County Home Rd., Waterville, NS B0P 1V0
Tel: 902-538-3103; *Fax:* 902-538-7022
krrc.nsnet.org
Number of Beds: 199 beds
Note: residential rehab
Judy Heffern, Chief Executive Officer

***Yarmouth:* Addiction Services**
District Health Authorities 1, 2, & 3
Former Name: Western Drug Dependency Program
c/o Yarmouth Regional Hospital, 60 Vancouver St., Yarmouth, NS B5A 2P5
Tel: 902-742-2406; *Fax:* 902-742-0684
addictions-yrh@swndha.nshealth.ca
www.swndha.nshealth.ca

Long Term Care Facilities

***Advocate Harbour:* Chignecto Manor Co-op Ltd.**
24 Bayview Manor Rd., Advocate Harbour, NS B0M 1A0
Tel: 902-392-2028

***Antigonish:* Highland Crest Home**
Affiliated with: Nova Scotia Health Authority
44 Hillcrest St., Antigonish, NS B2G 1Z3
Tel: 902-863-3855; *Fax:* 902-863-1833
www.high-crest.com
Number of Beds: 40 beds
Note: residential care facility
Mary Beaver, Administrator
mbeaver@high-crest.com

***Barrington:* Bayside Home Adult Residential Centre**
96 Bayside Dr., Barrington, NS
Tel: 902-637-2098
www.baysidehome.ca
Number of Beds: 62 beds
Note: Adult residential centre
Paula Hatfield, Administrator

***Berwick:* New Visions Home for Seniors**
PO Box 566, 4507 Hwy. 1, Berwick, NS B0P 1E0
Tel: 902-538-9579; *Fax:* 902-538-0390
newvision2@ns.sympatico.ca
www.newvision2.ca
Year Founded: 1993
Number of Beds: 25 beds + 1 respite
Helen B. Walsh, Administrator

***Bridgetown:* Grace Haven Enterprises Ltd.**
9791 Hwy 1, Bridgetown, NS B0S 1C0
Tel: 902-665-4224
Note: residential care facility

***Bridgetown:* Meadow Adult Residential Centre**
Annapolis County Municipal Housing Corporation
200 Church St., Bridgetown, NS B0S 1C0
Tel: 902-665-4566; *Fax:* 902-665-5265
homesforcare.com
Year Founded: 1987
Note: Adult residential centre

***Bridgetown:* Saunders Rest Home**
PO Box 114, 9 Freeman St., Bridgetown, NS B0S 1C0
Tel: 902-665-4331; *Fax:* 902-665-4768
Number of Beds: 8 beds
Shaun Saunders, Administrator

***Bridgewater:* La Have Manor Corp. Adult Residential Centre**
PO Box 270, Bridgewater, NS B4V 2W9
Tel: 902-543-7851; *Fax:* 902-543-8332
info@lahavemanor.ca
www.lahavemanor.ca
Note: Adult residential centre
Joanne Wentzell, CEO

***Bridgewater:* LaHave Manor Corp. Group Home**
PO Box 270, Bridgewater, NS B4V 2W8
Tel: 902-543-7851; *Fax:* 902-543-8332
info@lahavemanor.ca
www.lahavemanor.ca
Number of Beds: 9 beds
Note: group home for mentally challenged adults
Joanne Wentzell, CEO

***Chelsea:* Hillsview Acres**
PO Box 4, 14 Middlefield Rd., RR#1, Chelsea, NS B0T 1E0
Tel: 902-685-2966; *Fax:* 902-685-2446
Number of Beds: 28 beds + 1 respite

***Chester:* Bonny Lea Farm**
PO Box 560, Chester, NS B0J 1J0
Tel: 902-275-5622; *Fax:* 902-275-2567
www.bonnyleafarm.ca
Year Founded: 1973
Number of Beds: 35 beds
Note: Adult residential centre; small option units & apartments
David Outhouse, Managing Director
davidouthouse@sswap.ca

***Dartmouth:* Harbour Glen Manor Ltd.**
229 Pleasant St., Dartmouth, NS B2Y 3R5
Tel: 902-465-5770
Note: Residential care facility

***Dartmouth:* Hilltop Villa**
Affiliated with: Nova Scotia Health Authority
200 Main St., Dartmouth, NS B2X 1S3
Tel: 902-435-6186; *Fax:* 902-435-9354
Number of Beds: 24 beds

***Dartmouth:* Regional Residential Services Society (RRSS)**
#LKD1, 202 Brownlow Ave., Dartmouth, NS B3B 1T5
Tel: 902-465-4022; *Fax:* 902-465-3124
www.rrss.ns.ca
Number of Beds: 185 beds
Note: Developmental residences & group homes, supported apartments, short & long term respite services, personal support planning, counseling, assessment. Number of staff: 400+
Carol Ann Brennan, Executive Director
902-465-2702, carolann.brennan@rrss.ns.ca

***Enfield:* Corridor Community Options Society**
Former Name: Lantz Residential Programs
21 Convent Rd., Enfield, NS B2T 1C9
Tel: 902-883-9404; *Fax:* 902-883-1251
Number of Beds: 11 beds
Note: Group home/small options home; vocational training/social enterprise; runs the Lantz Residential Programs & Corridor Community Options for Adults
Robin C. Strickland, Executive Director
ccosdirector@gmail.com

***Glace Bay:* Terrace Manor**
208 South St., Glace Bay, NS B1A 1W1
Tel: 902-849-2849; *Fax:* 902-842-0359

***Halifax:* Basinview Drive Developmental Residence**
3838 Basinview Dr., Halifax, NS B3K 5A2
Tel: 902-455-7421
Number of Beds: 8 beds
Ruth McIver, Supervisor

***Halifax:* Haven Manor**
6411 Cobourg Rd., Halifax, NS B3H 2A6
Tel: 902-421-1167
Number of Beds: 17 beds
Hilda Stevens, Administrator

***Halifax:* Homes for Independent Living**
2505 Oxford St., Halifax, NS B3L 2T5
Tel: 902-422-9591; *Fax:* 902-425-3151
hil@hfx.eastlink.ca
www.nsnet.org/hil/
Year Founded: 1980
Number of Beds: 6 group home beds, with 1 respite bed
Note: Specialty: Programs & accommodation for young adults with physical disabilities; Community outreach programs
Lee-Anne Penny, Executive Director

***Halifax:* Lynden Rest Home**
1019 Lucknow St., Halifax, NS B3H 2T2
Tel: 902-420-0697; *Fax:* 902-492-3936

***Halifax:* Melville Gardens Residential & Level 2 Nursing Care Facility**
11 Ramsgate Lane, Halifax, NS B3P 2S9
Tel: 902-477-3135; *Fax:* 902-477-2718
www.gemhealth.com
Year Founded: 1991
Number of Beds: 91 beds
Cecile Adair, Administrator
cecile.adair@gemhealth.com

***Halifax:* Point Pleasant Lodge**
1121 South Park St., Halifax, NS B3H 2W6
Tel: 902-421-1599; *Fax:* 902-429-9722
guestservices@pointpleasantlodge.com
www.pointpleasantlodge.com
Number of Beds: 100 guest rooms
Note: A specialty hotel, with guest rooms for people directly or indirectly associated with medical attention in the Halifax area

***Halifax:* Robert Allen Drive Development Residence**
31 Robert Allen Dr., Halifax, NS B3M 3G9
Tel: 902-443-6804
Number of Beds: 7 beds
Note: developmental residence

***Halifax:* Vernon St. Group Home**
1648 Vernon St., Halifax, NS B3H 3N1
Tel: 902-422-6742
Number of Beds: 7 beds
Note: group home

***Kentville:* Wedgewood House**
19 Leverett Ave., Kentville, NS B4N 2K5
Tel: 902-678-1242; *Fax:* 902-679-2808
info@thewedgewood.ca
www.thewedgewood.ca
Number of Beds: 15 beds
Note: Residential care facility

***Lower West Pubnico:* Pont du Marais Home Ltd.**
Affiliated with: Nova Scotia Health Authority
PO Box 236, Lower West Pubnico, NS B0W 2C0
Tel: 902-762-3099; *Fax:* 902-762-2072
pdm@auracom.com
Number of Beds: 23 beds + 2 respite
Note: Residential care facility

***Margaree Valley:* Brookside Residential Care Facility**
843 East Big Intervale Rd., Margaree Valley, NS B0E 2C0
Tel: 902-248-2181
Note: Residential care facility

***Meteghan:* Au Logis Meteghan Ltd.**
Affiliated with: Nova Scotia Health Authority
PO Box 128, Meteghan, NS B0W 2J0
Tel: 902-645-3594; *Fax:* 902-645-2429
Number of Beds: 20 beds, 2 respite
Note: residential care

***Meteghan:* Cottage Celeste**
Affiliated with: Nova Scotia Health Authority
PO Box 314, 8064 Hwy. 1, Meteghan, NS B0W 2J0
Tel: 902-645-2248
foyerceleste@bellaliant.net
Number of Beds: 19 beds
Kathy MacDonald, Administrator

***Musquodoboit Harbour:* Braeside Nursing Home**
Archibald Rd., Musquodoboit Harbour, NS B0N 1X0
Tel: 902-384-3007; *Fax:* 902-384-3310

***New Glasgow:* High-Crest Home New Glasgow**
Affiliated with: Nova Scotia Health Authority
Former Name: Sunset Haven Home
253 Forbes St., New Glasgow, NS B2H 4P5
Tel: 902-752-3461; *Fax:* 902-752-2672
www.high-crest.com
Number of Beds: 29 beds
Note: Specialties: Medication monitoring; Recreational program
Michelle Gammon, Administrator
mgammon@high-crest.com

***Oxford:* Four Seasons Manor Special Care**
63 Water St., Oxford, NS B0M 1P0
Tel: 902-447-2819
Note: Residential care facility

***Oxford:* Shady Rest Ltd.**
237 Water St., Oxford, NS B0M 1P0
Tel: 902-447-2786

Note: residential care facility

Pugwash: Sunset Residential & Rehabilitation Services Inc.
140 Sunset Ln., Pugwash, NS B0K 1L0
Tel: 902-243-2571; *Fax:* 902-243-3222
sunsetcommunity.ca
Note: Specialties: Residential care & support services for persons who are mentally challenged & disabled; Day programs; Life & vocational skills programs; Social development programs; Advocacy services
Mary Ellen Pittoello, CEO
mepittoello@sunsetcommunity.ca

Saulnierville: La Maison au Coucher du Soleil Ltd.
RR#1, Saulnierville, NS B0W 2Z0
Tél: 902-769-2270
info@maisonaucoucher.com
www.maisonaucoucher.com
Fondée en: 1972
Nombre de lits: 25 lits
Note: Residential care facility

Shelburne: Mary's Abide-A-While Home Ltd.
Affiliated with: Nova Scotia Health Authority
PO Box 609, 188 Water St., Shelburne, NS B0T 1W0
Tel: 902-875-4384; *Fax:* 902-875-4384
Number of Beds: 14 beds
Mary Davis, Administrator

Stellarton: Highland Community Residential Services (HCRS)
PO Box 2140, 276 Foord St., Stellarton, NS B0K 1S0
Tel: 902-752-1755; *Fax:* 902-752-4256
info@hcrsweb.ca
hcrsweb.ca
Year Founded: 1977
Note: Residential care facility

Stellarton: Riverview Home Corp.
6105 Trafalgar Rd., RR#1, Stellarton, NS B0K 1S0
Tel: 902-755-4884; *Fax:* 902-755-3207
info@riverviewhome.ca
riverviewhome.ca
Number of Beds: 106 beds + 3 community homes & supervised depts.
Note: Residential care facility for mentally and/or physically challenged adults, group homes, & developmental residence.
Number of staff: 150
Patricia Bland, CEO

Stewiacke: Elmwood Manor Limited
98 Riverside Ave., Stewiacke, NS B0N 2J0
Tel: 902-639-9003
Note: Residential care facility

Sydney: Cape Breton Community Housing Association
PO Box 1292, 50 Dorchester St., 2nd Fl., Sydney, NS B1P 6K3
Tel: 902-539-0025; *Fax:* 902-562-5476
communityhousing@cbcha.ca
www.cbcha.ca
Year Founded: 1977
Note: The organization helps clients develop skills so they may live independently in the community. Information sessions are held on a regular basis.

Sydney: Mayfair Guest Home
1038 Upper Prince St., Sydney, NS B1P 5P6
Tel: 902-539-5611

Sydney: My Cape Breton Home for Seniors
Affiliated with: Nova Scotia Health Authority
137 ROverdale Dr., Sydney, NS B1R 0A9
Tel: 902-564-4461; *Fax:* 902-564-4247
www.mycbhome.ca
Number of Beds: 16 beds
Sherry MacNeil, Owner/Operator
sherry@mycbhome.ca

Sydney: Resi-Care (Cape Breton) Association
146 Vulcan Ave., Sydney, NS B1P 5W5
Tel: 902-539-0935; *Fax:* 902-562-0717
rescare2@ns.sympatico.ca
Number of Beds: 60 beds
Note: group home
Michael Walsh, Executive Director

Sydney River: Breton Ability Centre
Former Name: Braemore Home
1300 Kings Rd., Sydney River, NS B1S 0H3
Tel: 902-539-7640; *Fax:* 902-539-5340
www.bretonabilitycentre.ca

Number of Beds: 124 beds
Note: adult residential & rehabilitation
Millie Colbourne, CEO
mcolbourne@cb-bac.ca

Tatamagouche: Maplewood Manor
Affiliated with: Nova Scotia Health Authority
150 Blair Ave., Tatamagouche, NS B0K 1V0
Tel: 902-657-2876; *Fax:* 902-657-1022
maplewood.manor@ns.aliantzinc.ca
Social Media: www.linkedin.com/in/jeffersonwilliams
Number of Beds: 6 beds
Jeff Williams, Owner & Administrator

Truro: Karlaine Place Ltd.
Affiliated with: Nova Scotia Health Authority
PO Box 691, 104 Pictou Rd., Truro, NS B2N 5E5
Tel: 902-895-5111; *Fax:* 902-893-1513
Number of Beds: 8 beds
Note: residential care facility

Truro: Townsview Estates
Affiliated with: Nova Scotia Health Authority
PO Box 1825, 310 Abenaki Rd., Truro, NS B2N 5Z5
Tel: 902-895-9559; *Fax:* 902-893-8094
Number of Beds: 85 beds
Note: Residential care facility

Truro: Wynn Park Villa
32 Windsor Way, Truro, NS B2N 0B4
Tel: 902-893-3939; *Fax:* 902-893-3936
contact@wynnparkvilla.ca
wynnparkvilla.ca
Year Founded: 2008
Number of Beds: 60 beds
Sheila Peck, Administrator
speck@wynnparkvilla.ca

Windsor: Kendall Lane Housing Society
PO Box 556, Windsor, NS B0N 2T0
Tel: 902-798-4375; *Fax:* 902-798-4378
vpghinc@gmail.com
www.vpgh.ca
Year Founded: 1993
Number of Beds: 6 beds
Note: small option home

Windsor: Kings Meadows Residence
RR#1, Windsor, NS B0N 2T0
Tel: 902-798-4657
www.nsnet.org/meadow
Year Founded: 1969
Number of Beds: 10 beds
Barbara Campbell, Administrator

Windsor: Victoria Park Guest House
Affiliated with: Nova Scotia Health Authority
PO Box 556, 350 King St., Windsor, NS B0N 2T0
Tel: 902-798-4375; *Fax:* 902-798-4378
vpghinc@@gmail.com
www.vpgh.ca
Year Founded: 1989
Number of Beds: 12 beds
Note: Adult residential care facility
Dorothy Blakely, Administrator
Sue Sheehy, Administrator

Wolfville: Wolfville Elms (The Elms Rest Home)
701 Main St., Wolfville, NS B4P 2N4
Tel: 902-542-2420; *Fax:* 902-542-1048
Number of Beds: 23 beds
Paul MacDonald, Administrator

Yarmouth: Sunset Terrace
8 James St., Yarmouth, NS B5A 2V1
Tel: 902-742-3322

Nursing Homes

Annapolis Royal: Annapolis Royal Nursing Home
9745 Hwy. 8, RR#2, Annapolis Royal, NS B0S 1A0
Tel: 902-532-2240; *Fax:* 902-532-7151
annapolisroyalnursinghome.ca
Number of Beds: 51 beds; 2 respite
Linda R. Bailey, Administrator

Annapolis Royal: Northhills Nursing Home Ltd.
PO Box 220, 5038 Granville Rd., Annapolis Royal, NS B0S 1A0
Tel: 902-532-5555
Number of Beds: 50 beds
Note: adult residential centre
Leonard S. Tedds, Administrator

Antigonish: R.K. MacDonald Nursing Home
Affiliated with: Nova Scotia Health Authority
64 Pleasant St., Antigonish, NS B2G 1W7
Tel: 902-863-2578
www.rkmacdonald.ca
Number of Beds: 137 beds

Arichat: St. Anne Community & Nursing Care Centre
Affiliated with: Nova Scotia Health Authority
PO Box 30, 2313 Hwy. 206, Arichat, NS B0E 1A0
Tel: 902-226-2826; *Fax:* 902-226-1529
stannecentre.ca
Number of Beds: 24 beds
Annette Fougere, Administrator
annette.fougere@sacentre.nshealth.ca

Beaverbank: Scotia Nursing Homes Ltd.
Affiliated with: Nova Scotia Health Authority
Former Name: Scotia Nursing Homes Ltd.
125 Knowles Cres., Beaverbank, NS B4G 1E7
Tel: 902-865-6364; *Fax:* 902-865-3582
Number of Beds: 49 beds + 1 respite
Patricia Bland, Administrator

Berwick: Grand View Manor
110A Commercial St., Berwick, NS B0P 1E0
Tel: 902-538-3118; *Fax:* 902-538-3998
jorge.vanslyke@grandviewmanor.org
www.grandviewmanor.org
Number of Beds: 142 beds
Graham E. Hardy, Administrator

Bridgetown: Mountain Lea Lodge
170 Church St., RR#1, Bridgetown, NS B0S 1C0
Tel: 902-665-4489; *Fax:* 902-665-2900
homesforcare.com
Social Media: www.facebook.com/acmhc
Number of Beds: 106 beds + 1 respite
Larry Marsters, Administrator

Bridgewater: Hillside Pines
77 Exhibition Dr., Bridgewater, NS B4V 3K6
Tel: 902-543-1525; *Fax:* 902-543-8083
info@hillsidepines.com
www.hillsidepines.com
Number of Beds: 50 beds
Sheila MacKinnon, Administrator

Caledonia: North Queens Nursing Home
9565 Highway #8, Caledonia, NS B0T 1B0
Tel: 902-682-2553
www.nqnh.ca
Number of Beds: 42 beds + 2 respite
Note: adult residential centre
Norma Lenco, Administrator

Canso: Canso Seaside Manor
PO Box 70, 1748 Union St., Canso, NS B0H 1H0
Tel: 902-366-3030; *Fax:* 902-366-2154
Number of Beds: 15 beds

Cheticamp: Foyer Père Fiset
Affiliée à: Nova Scotia Health Authority
CP 219, 15092 Cabot Trail, Cheticamp, NS B0E 1H0
Tél: 902-224-2087; *Téléc:* 902-224-1188
foyer.fiset@ns.sympatico.ca
www.cbdha.nshealth.ca
Nombre de lits: 60 lits
Betty Ann Aucoin, Administrator

Conway: Tideview Terrace
Affiliated with: Nova Scotia Health Authority
PO Box 1120, 74 Pleasant St., Conway, NS B0V 1A0
Tel: 902-245-4718; *Fax:* 902-245-6674
mnelson@swndha.nshealth.ca
www.tideviewterrace.ca
Social Media: www.facebook.com/435053349912023
Year Founded: 1973
Number of Beds: 89 beds
Note: Specialties: Long-term care (level II); Dementia care; Adult day programs; Respite care; Palliative care
Lynda Casey, Administrator

Dartmouth: Oakwood Terrace
Affiliated with: Nova Scotia Health Authority
10 Mount Hope Ave., Dartmouth, NS B2Y 4K1
Tel: 902-469-3702; *Fax:* 902-469-3824
www.oakwoodterrace.ns.ca
Year Founded: 1982
Number of Beds: 111 beds
Number of Employees: 160
Note: Specialties: Physiotherapy; Adult Day Program; Medical services; Palliative care

Leonard Tedds, Administrator
Pat Nightingale, Nurse Manager
Gary Comeau, Coordinator, Recreation Therapy & Volunteer Services

Dartmouth: Woodside Manor
351 Pleasant St., Dartmouth, NS B2Y 3S4
Tel: 902-463-5845
Number of Beds: 29 beds
Cathy Prothro, Site Manager

Eastern Passage: Ocean View Manor
Affiliated with: Nova Scotia Health Authority
PO Box 130, 1909 Caldwell Rd., Eastern Passage, NS B3G 1M4
Tel: 902-465-6020; *Fax:* 902-465-4929
admin@OVCCC.ca
www.ovm.ca
Year Founded: 1967
Number of Beds: 176 residents
Note: Specialties: Physiotherapy; Occupational therapy; Recreation therapy; Social work; Respite care; Palliative care
Dion Mouland, Administrator

Falmouth: Windsor Elms Village for Continuing Care Society
Affiliated with: Nova Scotia Health Authority
174 Dyke Rd., Falmouth, NS B0P 1L0
Tel: 902-798-2251; *Fax:* 902-798-3302
Number of Beds: 107 beds + 1 respite
Sherry Keen, Administrator
sherry.keen@winelms.ca

Glace Bay: Seaview Manor
Affiliated with: Nova Scotia Health Authority
275 South St., Glace Bay, NS B1A 1W6
Tel: 902-849-7300; *Fax:* 902-849-7401
cathypower@seaside.ns.ca
www.seaviewmanor.ca
Number of Beds: 101 beds, 2 respite
Catherine Power, Administrator

Glace Bay: Taigh Na Mara
Affiliated with: Nova Scotia Health Authority
974 Main St., Glace Bay, NS B1A 4L8
Tel: 902-842-3900; *Fax:* 902-842-3926
Number of Beds: 67 beds
Note: Continuing care for residents & veterans
Sharon Sheppard, Administrator

Glace Bay: Victoria Haven Nursing Home
PO Box 219, 5 Third St., Glace Bay, NS B1A 5V2
Tel: 902-849-4127; *Fax:* 902-849-8826
www.victoriahaven.ca
Number of Beds: 50 beds, 4 respite
Marie McPhee, Administrator

Glenwood: Nakile Home for Special Care
Affiliated with: Nova Scotia Health Authority
Former Name: Nakile Home for the Aged
35 Nakile Dr., RR#1, Glenwood, NS B0W 1W0
Tel: 902-643-2707; *Fax:* 902-643-2862
www.nakilehome.ca
Number of Beds: 35 beds + 1 respite
Bertha Brannen, Administrator

Halifax: Harbourstone Enhanced Care
Affiliated with: Nova Scotia Health Authority
48 Lovett Lake Crt., Halifax, NS B3S 1B8
Tel: 902-454-7499; *Fax:* 902-453-5412
Toll-Free: 877-742-6639
info@shannex.com
www.shannex.com
Year Founded: 2002
Number of Beds: 268 beds + 4 respite
Ellen Stoddard, Administrator

Halifax: Maplestone Enhanced Care
Affiliated with: Nova Scotia Health Authority
245 Main Ave., Halifax, NS B3M 1B7
Tel: 902-443-1971; *Fax:* 902-443-9037
maplestoneinfo@shannex.com
shannex.com
Number of Beds: 87 beds
Note: Nursing home
Renee Donovan-Grey, Administrator
Debbie Thompson, Environmental Services

Halifax: Melville Lodge Long Term Care Centre
50 Shoreham Lane, Halifax, NS B3P 2R3
Tel: 902-479-1030; *Fax:* 902-477-1663
melvillelodge@gemhealth.com
www.gemhealth.com

Year Founded: 1984
Number of Beds: 122 beds
Bernice Clake-Dibblee, Administrator

Halifax: Northwoodcare Inc.
Affiliated with: Nova Scotia Health Authority
2615 Northwood Terrace, Halifax, NS B3K 3S5
Tel: 902-454-8311
information@nwood.ns.ca
www.nwood.ns.ca
Number of Beds: 406 beds
Note: Adult residental centre
Lloyd O. Brown, Administrator

Halifax: Parkstone Enhanced Care
Affiliated with: Nova Scotia Health Authority
156 Parkland Dr., Halifax, NS B3S 1N9
Tel: 902-446-8501; *Fax:* 902-446-4044
parkstoneinfo@shannex.com
shannex.com
Number of Beds: 185 beds, 5 respite beds
Note: Nursing home
Carol Ann Gallant, Administrator

Halifax: Saint Vincent's Nursing Home
Affiliated with: Nova Scotia Health Authority
Former Name: Saint Vincent Guest Home
2080 Windsor St., Halifax, NS B3K 5B2
Tel: 902-429-0550; *Fax:* 902-492-3703
info@svnh.ca
www.svnh.ca
Number of Beds: 149 beds
Note: Nursing home affiliated with the Roman Catholic Archdiocese of Halifax
Kristin Schmitz, Administrator

Inverness: Aite Curam
Affiliated with: Nova Scotia Health Authority
PO Box 610, 39 James St., Inverness, NS B0E 1N0
Tel: 902-258-2100
Note: Part of Inverness Consolidated Memorial Hospital

Kentville: Evergreen Home for Special Care
655 Park St., Kentville, NS B4N 3V7
Tel: 902-678-7355; *Fax:* 902-678-5292
evergreen@evergreenhome.ns.ca
evergreenhome.ns.ca
Number of Beds: 97 beds; 20 children's beds; 2 respite beds
Note: adult residential centre
Fred Houghton, Administrator

Liverpool: Queens Manor
PO Box 1283, 20 Hollands Dr., Liverpool, NS B0T 1K0
Tel: 902-354-3451; *Fax:* 902-354-5383
www.queensmanor.ca
Number of Beds: 60 beds + 1 respite

Lockeport: Surf Lodge Nursing Home
Affiliated with: Nova Scotia Health Authority
PO Box 160, 73 Howe St., Lockeport, NS B0T 1L0
Tel: 902-656-2014; *Fax:* 902-656-2026
www.surflodge.ca
Note: Specialties: Long-term care; Massage therapy; Activity program; Physiotherapy
Doug Stephens, Administrator
doug@macleodgroup.ca

Lunenburg: Harbour View Haven
PO Box 1480, 25 Blockhouse Hill Rd., Lunenburg, NS B0J 2C0
Tel: 902-634-8836; *Fax:* 902-634-8792
mcauley@hvh.ca
www.hvh.ca
Number of Beds: 129 beds + 1 respite
Barry Granter, Administrator

Mahone Bay: Mahone Nursing Home
PO Box 320, 640 Main St., Mahone Bay, NS B0J 2E0
Tel: 902-624-8341; *Fax:* 902-624-6338
www.mahonenursinghome.com
Year Founded: 1965
Number of Beds: 22
Note: Specialties: Long-term care Physiotherapy & occupational therapy; Palliative care
Anne Kennedy, Administrator

Meteghan: Villa Acadienne
Affiliée à: Nova Scotia Health Authority
CP 248, 8403 Hwy. 1, Meteghan, NS B0W 2K0
Tél: 902-645-2065; *Téléc:* 902-645-3899
lucillemaillet@villaacadienne.ca
www.villaacadienne.com
Média social: www.facebook.com/VillaAcadienne

Fondée en: 1975
Nombre de lits: 84 beds + 2 respite
Lucille Maillet, Administrator

Middle Musquodoboit: Musquodoboit Valley Home for Special Care (Braeside)
Affiliated with: Nova Scotia Health Authority
126 Higginsville Rd., Middle Musquodoboit, NS B0N 1X0
Tel: 902-384-3007; *Fax:* 902-384-3310
Number of Beds: 28 beds + 1 respite
Diana Graham-Lentz, Site Manager

Musquodoboit Harbour: Twin Oaks/Birches
Health Care Charitable Foundation, PO Box 186, Musquodoboit Harbour, NS B0J 2L0
Tel: 902-889-3474
www.twinoaksbirches.ca
Number of Beds: 42 residents
Note: Specialties: Long-term care for older adults; Community outreach adult day programs
Sheila Martin, Manager, Health Care Facility

New Germany: Rosedale Home for Special Care
Former Name: Rosedale Home
Hwy. 10, New Germany, NS B0R 1E0
Tel: 902-644-2008; *Fax:* 902-644-3260
Year Founded: 1984
Number of Beds: 39 beds
Maureen Wade, Administrator

New Glasgow: Glen Haven Manor
Affiliated with: Nova Scotia Health Authority
739 East River Rd., New Glasgow, NS B2H 5E9
Tel: 902-752-2588; *Fax:* 902-752-0053
info@glenhavenmanor.ca
www.glenhavenmanor.ca
Number of Beds: 202 beds
Note: adult residential centre
Lisa M. Smith, Administrator
902-752-2588

New Waterford: Maple Hill Manor
Affiliated with: Nova Scotia Health Authority
700 King St., New Waterford, NS B1H 3Z5
Tel: 902-862-6495
www.maplehillmanor.ca
Number of Beds: 50 beds
Note: Long term & secured care
Cathy MacPhee, Administrator

New Waterford: Waterford Heights
Affiliated with: Nova Scotia Health Authority
716 King St., New Waterford, NS B1H 3Z5
Tel: 902-862-6411
Number of Beds: 24 beds
Sharon Sheppard, Administrator

North Sydney: Northside Community Guest Home
Affiliated with: Nova Scotia Health Authority
11 Queen St., North Sydney, NS B2A 1A2
Tel: 902-794-4733
www.northsideguesthome.com
Number of Beds: 144 beds
Joanne MacNeil, Administrator

Pictou: Maritime Odd Fellows Home
Affiliated with: Nova Scotia Health Authority
143 Norway Point Rd., Pictou, NS B0K 1H0
Tel: 902-485-5492; *Fax:* 902-485-9233
adminioof@eastlink.ca
maritimeoddfellowshome.ca
Number of Beds: 47 beds
Note: Specialty: Long-term care; Therapeutic recreation
Janet Johnston, Administrator

Pictou: Shiretown Nursing Home
Affiliated with: Nova Scotia Health Authority
PO Box 250, 270 Haliburton Rd., Pictou, NS B0K 1H0
Tel: 902-485-4341; *Fax:* 902-485-9203
bonniel@shiretown.ca
www.shiretown.ca
Number of Beds: 89 beds
Note: Nursing & residential care
Bonnie Linkletter, Administrator
Tammy MacKenzie, Director of Care

Port Hawkesbury: Port Hawkesbury Nursing Home
Affiliated with: Nova Scotia Health Authority
2 MacQuarrie Dr. Extension, Port Hawkesbury, NS B9A 3A2
Tel: 902-625-1460; *Fax:* 902-625-3232
www.porthawkesburynursinghome.ca
Number of Beds: 50 beds + 4 respite
Note: Adult residential centre

Leona Wilneff, Administrator

***Sheet Harbour:* Duncan MacMillan Nursing Home**
Affiliated with: Nova Scotia Health Authority
Former Name: Duncan MacMillan Home for the Aged
PO Box 68, 22639 7 Hwy., Sheet Harbour, NS B0J 3B0
Tel: 902-885-2545; *Fax:* 902-885-3289
Year Founded: 1948
Number of Beds: 25 beds + 1 respite
Sheila Martin, Health Care Facility Manager

***Shelburne:* Roseway Manor Inc.**
Affiliated with: Nova Scotia Health Authority
PO Box 518, 1604 Lake Rd., Shelburne, NS B0T 1W0
Tel: 902-875-4707; *Fax:* 902-875-4105
admin@rosewaymanor.ca
www.rosewaymanor.com
Number of Beds: 65 beds + 1 respite
Jerry Fraser, Administrator

***Sherbrooke:* High-Crest Sherbrooke Home for Special Care**
Affiliated with: Nova Scotia Health Authority
PO Box 284, 53 Court St., Sherbrooke, NS B0J 3C0
Tel: 902-522-2147; *Fax:* 902-522-2628
GGrant@high-crest.com
www.high-crest.com
Number of Beds: 39 beds
Marion Carroll, Administrator

***St Peters:* Richmond Villa**
Affiliated with: Nova Scotia Health Authority
PO Box 250, 9361 Pepperell St., St Peters, NS B0E 3B0
Tel: 902-535-3030; *Fax:* 902-535-2256
carson.samson@richmondvilla.ca
www.richmondvilla.ca
Number of Beds: 59 nursing home beds, 8 resident care beds
Note: Nursing & residential care centre
Margaret Morrison, Administrator
Heather MacQueen, Director of Care

***Stellarton:* Valley View Villa**
Affiliated with: Nova Scotia Health Authority
6125 Trafalgar Rd., RR#1, Stellarton, NS B0K 1S0
Tel: 902-755-5780; *Fax:* 902-755-3104
emaceachern@vvvilla.ca
www.valleyviewvilla.com
Year Founded: 1978
Number of Beds: 109 beds + 4 respite
Note: Home for special care
Norman Ferguson, Administrator

***Sydney:* Celtic Court**
16 St. Anthony Dr., Sydney, NS B1S 2R5
Tel: 902-270-4700; *Fax:* 902-270-4701
celticcourtinfo@shannex.com
shannex.com
Number of Beds: 36 beds

***Sydney:* Cove Guest Home**
Affiliated with: Nova Scotia Health Authority
320 Alexander St., Sydney, NS B1S 2G1
Tel: 902-539-5267; *Fax:* 902-539-7565
cdeveaux@coveguesthome.com
www.coveguesthome.com
Year Founded: 1944
Archie MacKeigan, CEO

***Sydney:* New Dawn Guest Home**
75 Prince St., Sydney, NS B1P 5J9
Tel: 902-539-9560; *Fax:* 902-539-7210
newdawn@newdawn.ca
newdawn.ca
Number of Beds: 30 beds + 1 respite
Note: Residential care facility
Janet Gillis-Hussey, Administrator

***Sydney:* R.C. MacGillivray Guest Home Society**
Affiliated with: Nova Scotia Health Authority
25 Xavier Dr., Sydney, NS B1S 2R9
Tel: 902-539-6110; *Fax:* 902-567-0437
michelle.huntington@mggh.org
www.mggh.org
Number of Beds: 78 beds, 2 respite, 1 adult protection
John W. Coffey, Administrator

***Sydney Mines:* Miner's Memorial Manor**
Affiliated with: Nova Scotia Health Authority
15 Lorne St., Sydney Mines, NS B1V 3B9
Tel: 902-736-1992
Number of Beds: 35 beds + 2 respite
Harry Blinkhorn, Administrator

***Tatamagouche:* Willow Lodge**
Affiliated with: Nova Scotia Health Authority
PO Box 249, 100 Blair Ave., Tatamagouche, NS B0K 1V0
Tel: 902-657-3101; *Fax:* 902-657-3859
Number of Beds: 61 beds

***Truro:* Cedarstone Enhanced Care**
Affiliated with: Nova Scotia Health Authority
378 Young St., Truro, NS B2N 7H2
Tel: 902-895-2891; *Fax:* 902-893-2361
cedarstoneinfo@shannex.com
shannex.com/cedarstone_enhanced_care.html
Number of Beds: 124 beds + 2 respite
Population Served: 126

***Truro:* The Mira Long Term Care Centre**
426 Young St., Truro, NS B2N 7B1
Tel: 902-895-8715; *Fax:* 902-897-1903
themira@gemhealth.com
www.gemhealth.com
Year Founded: 1999
Number of Beds: 90 beds
Note: Specialty: Long-term care for seniors; Medication administration; Peritoneal dialysis unit; Seniors' dental clinic; Palliative care
Lynn Smith, Administrator

***Windsor:* Haliburton Place**
Affiliated with: Nova Scotia Health Authority
89 Payzant Dr., Windsor, NS B0N 2T0
Tel: 902-792-2026; *Fax:* 902-798-6002
Number of Beds: 30 beds + 2 respite
Theresa Fillatre, Healthcare Facility Manager

***Windsor:* Hants County Residence for Senior Citizens**
Affiliated with: Nova Scotia Health Authority
Former Name: Dykeland Lodge
124 Cottage St., Windsor, NS B0N 2T0
Tel: 902-798-8346; *Fax:* 902-798-8312
info@dykelandlodge.ca
www.dykelandlodge.ca
Year Founded: 1974
Number of Beds: 111 beds
Emily Samson, Administrator
administrator@dykelandlodge.ca

***Windsor:* Windsor House**
PO Box 938, 16 Wentworth St., Windsor, NS B0N 2T0
Tel: 902-798-2115
Number of Beds: 16 beds
Gordon Armsworthy, Proprietor

***Wolfville:* Wolfville Nursing Home**
601 Main St., Wolfville, NS B4P 1E9
Tel: 902-542-2429
Number of Beds: 66 beds + 1 respite bed
Paul MacDonald, Administrator

***Yarmouth:* Harbourside Lodge**
62 Vancouver St., Yarmouth, NS B5A 2P5
Tel: 902-742-3542; *Fax:* 902-749-0622
pthibodeau@swndha.nshealth.ca
harboursidelodge.ca
Number of Beds: 32 beds
Sandra M. Boudreau, Executive Director

***Yarmouth:* Villa Saint Joseph-du-Lac**
Affiliated with: Nova Scotia Health Authority
PO Box 810, RR1, Yarmouth, NS B5A 4A5
Tel: 902-742-7128; *Fax:* 902-742-4230
rickatkinson@villasaintjoseph.com
www.villasaintjoseph.com
Number of Beds: 79 beds
Barry Granter, Administrator

Mental Health Hospitals/Facilities

***Dartmouth:* East Coast Forensic Psychiatric Hospital**
Affiliated with: Nova Scotia Health Authority
88 Gloria McClusky Ave., Dartmouth, NS B3B 2B8
Tel: 902-460-7300; *Fax:* 902-460-7337
Number of Beds: 30 rehabilitation beds; 24 mentally ill offender beds

***Dartmouth:* The Nova Scotia Hospital**
Affiliated with: Nova Scotia Health Authority
PO Box 1004, 300 Pleasant St., Dartmouth, NS B2Y 3Z9
Tel: 902-464-3111; *Fax:* 902-464-6032
www.cdha.nshealth.ca
Note: Specialties: Mental health programs
John McCarthy, Board Development Officer
902-473-1143, Fax: 902-473-3368,
john.mccarthy@cdha.nshealth.ca

***Halifax:* Metro Community Housing Association**
Tower 1, #215, 7001 Mumford Rd., Halifax, NS B3L 4N9
Tel: 902-453-6444; *Fax:* 902-453-1188
info@mcha.ns.ca
www.mcha.ns.ca
Number of Beds: 86 residential capacity & 79 supported apartments
Note: Specialties: Support & residential services to persons who have experienced mental health difficulties

Special Care Homes

***Canning:* Tibbetts Home Wilmot**
PO Box 70, 9711 Main St., Canning, NS B0P 1H0
Tel: 902-582-7157; *Fax:* 902-582-7157
tibbco2001@yahoo.com
annapolisvalleychamber.ca
Number of Beds: 25 beds
Wanda Tibbetts, Administrator

***Glace Bay:* Jones Manor**
Affiliated with: Nova Scotia Health Authority
1 Minto St., Glace Bay, NS B1Z 5B2
Tel: 902-849-1605
Number of Beds: 7 beds
Calvin Jones, Administrator

Nunavut

Government Departments in Charge

***Iqaluit:* Nunavut Department of Health**
PO Box 1000 Stn. 1000, Iqaluit, NU X0A 0H0
Tel: 867-975-5700; *Fax:* 867-975-5705
www.hss.gov.nu.ca
Hon. Monica Ell-Kanayuk, Minister
Dr. Maureen Blaikie, Chief Medical Officer of Health
mbaikie@gov.nu.ca

Hospitals - General

***Iqaluit:* Qikiqtani General Hospital**
1 Ring Rd., Iqaluit, NU X0A 0H0
Tel: 867-975-8600
www.gov.nu.ca/health/information/qikiqtani-general-hospital
Number of Beds: 35 beds
Population Served: 16000
Note: Programs & services include: allergist; cardiology; dermatology; ENT (ear, nose & throat specialist); internal medicine; gynaecology; neurology; ophthalmology; orthopaedics; paediatric cardiology, orthopedics, neurology; respirology; rheumatology; & urology.

Community Health Care Centres

***Arctic Bay:* Arctic Bay Health Centre**
PO Box 60, Arctic Bay, NU X0A 0A0
Tel: 867-439-8816; *Fax:* 867-439-8315

***Arviat:* Arviat Health Centre**
PO Box 510, Arviat, NU X0C 0E0
Tel: 867-857-3100; *Fax:* 867-857-3149
Sandy Ranahan, Nurse Manager

***Baker Lake:* Baker Lake Health Centre**
PO Box 120, Baker Lake, NU X0C 0A0
Tel: 867-793-2816; *Fax:* 867-793-2812

***Cambridge Bay:* Cambridge Bay Health Centre**
PO Box 83, Cambridge Bay, NU X0E 0C0
Tel: 867-983-2531; *Fax:* 867-983-2262
www.cambridgebay.ca/services/health.htm
Number of Beds: 2 beds

***Cape Dorset:* Cape Dorset Health Centre**
PO Box 180, Cape Dorset, NU X0A 0C0
Tel: 867-897-8820; *Fax:* 867-897-8914

***Chesterfield Inlet:* Chesterfield Inlet Health Centre**
PO Box 9, Chesterfield Inlet, NU X0C 0B0
Tel: 867-898-9968

***Clyde River:* Clyde River Health Centre**
PO Box 40, Clyde River, NU X0A 0E0
Tel: 867-924-6377; *Fax:* 867-924-6244

***Coral Harbour:* Coral Harbour Health Centre**
PO Box 120, Coral Harbour, NU X0C 0C0
Tel: 867-925-9916; *Fax:* 867-925-8380

Gjoa Haven: **Gjoa Haven Haputtit Health Centre**
General Delivery, Gjoa Haven, NU X0E 1J0
Tel: 867-360-7441; *Fax:* 867-360-6110

Grise Fjord: **Grise Fjord Health Centre**
PO Box 81, Grise Fjord, NU X0A 0J0
Tel: 867-980-9923; *Fax:* 867-980-9067

Hall Beach: **Hall Beach Health Centre**
General Delivery, Hall Beach, NU X0A 0K0
Tel: 867-928-8827; *Fax:* 867-928-8847

Igloolik: **Igloolik Health Centre**
PO Box 240, Igloolik, NU X0A 0L0
Tel: 867-934-8837; *Fax:* 867-934-8901

Iqaluit: **Iqaluit Public Health Clinic**
PO Box 200, Iqaluit, NU X0A 0H0
Tel: 867-979-5306; *Fax:* 867-979-4830

Kimmirut: **Kimmirut Health Centre**
PO Box 30, Kimmirut, NU X0A 0N0
Tel: 867-939-2217; *Fax:* 867-939-2068

Kugaaruk: **St. Theresa Kugaaruk Health Centre**
General Delivery, Kugaaruk, NU X0E 1K0
Tel: 867-769-6441; *Fax:* 867-769-6059

Kugluktuk: **Kugluktuk Health Centre**
PO Box 288, Kugluktuk, NU X0E 0E0
Tel: 867-982-4531; *Fax:* 867-982-3115

Pangnirtung: **Pangnirtung Health Centre**
PO Box 454, Pangnirtung, NU X0A 0R0
Tel: 867-473-8977; *Fax:* 867-473-8519
www.pangnirtung.ca/home
Note: Specialty: General health care by registered nurses; Individual counseling & referral; Massage therapy; Workshops for stress relief

Pond Inlet: **Pond Inlet Health Centre**
General Delivery, Pond Inlet, NU X0A 0S0
Tel: 867-899-7500
Year Founded: 2004
Population Served: 1290
Note: Comprehensive health care. Number of employees: 20
Di Schulze, Supervisor, Health & Community Programs

Qikiqtarjuaq: **Qikiqtarjuaq Health Centre**
PO Box 911, Qikiqtarjuaq, NU X0A 0B0
Tel: 867-927-8916; *Fax:* 867-927-8217

Rankin Inlet: **Rankin Inlet Health Centre**
PO Box 008, Rankin Inlet, NU X0C 0G0
Tel: 867-645-2816; *Fax:* 867-645-2688

Repulse Bay: **Repulse Bay Health Centre**
General Delivery, Repulse Bay, NU X0C 0H0
Tel: 867-462-9916; *Fax:* 867-462-4212
Number of Beds: 2 beds
Population Served: 612

Resolute: **Resolute Health Centre**
PO Box 180, Resolute, NU X0A 0V0
Tel: 867-252-3844; *Fax:* 867-252-3601

Sanikiluaq: **Sanikiluaq Health Centre**
PO Box 145, Sanikiluaq, NU X0A 0W0
Tel: 867-266-8965; *Fax:* 867-266-8802
Note: Provides general health care, counseling & referral. Services in Inuktitut & English

Taloyoak: **Taloyoak Judy Hill Memorial Health Centre**
General Delivery, Taloyoak, NU X0E 1B0
Tel: 867-561-5111; *Fax:* 867-561-6906
Number of Employees: 5

Whale Cove: **Whale Cove Health Centre**
PO Box 3, Whale Cove, NU X0A 0K0
Tel: 867-896-9916; *Fax:* 867-896-9115
hbhamlet@nunanet.com

Nursing Stations

Broughton Island: **Qikiqtarjuaq Health Centre**
PO Box 911, Broughton Island, NU X0A 0B0
Tel: 867-927-8916; *Fax:* 867-927-8217

Long Term Care Facilities

Arviat: **Andy Aulatjut Elders' Centre**
PO Box 147, Arviat, NU X0C 0E0
Tel: 867-857-4351

Chesterfield Inlet: **Naja Isabelle Home**
PO Box 1, Chesterfield Inlet, NU X0C 0B0
Tel: 867-898-5600; *Fax:* 867-898-9288
Note: Homecare facility

Iqaluit: **Iqaluit Elders' Facility**
Pairijait Tigumivik Society, PO Box 640, Iqaluit, NU X0A 0H0
Tel: 867-979-2733; *Fax:* 867-979-3413

Mental Health Hospitals/Facilities

Iqaluit: **Akausisarvik Mental Health Facilty**
Baffin Hospital, PO Box 1000 Stn. 1048, Iqaluit, NU X0A 0H0
Tel: 867-979-7631
Number of Beds: 13 beds

Ontario

Government Departments in Charge

Toronto: **Ministry of Health & Long-Term Care**
Hepburn Block, Queen's Park, 80 Grosvenor St., 10th Fl., Toronto, ON M7A 2C4
Tel: 416-327-4327 *Toll-Free:* 800-268-1153
TTY: 800-387-5559
www.health.gov.on.ca
Social Media: www.facebook.com/217753654940869; twitter.com/ONThealth; www.youtube.com/user/ontariomohltc
Dr. Eric Hoskins, Minister

Regional Health Authorities

Ajax: **Central East Local Health Integration Network/RLISS du Centre-Est**
Also Known As: Central East LHIN
Harwood Plaza, #204A, 314 Harwood Ave. South, Ajax, ON L1S 2J1
Tel: 905-427-5497; *Fax:* 905-427-9659
Toll-Free: 866-804-5446
centraleast@lhins.on.ca
www.centraleastlhin.on.ca
Social Media: twitter.com/CentralEastLHIN
Year Founded: 2005
Area Served: From Victoria Park to Algonquin Park; 16,673 sq km; *Population Served:* 1400000
Margaret Risk, Acting Board Chair
Deborah Hammons, Chief Executive Officer
Stewart Sutley, Senior Director, System Finance & Performance Management
Brian Laundry, Senior Director, System Design & Implementation

Arnprior: **Arnprior Regional Health (ARH)**
350 John St. North, Arnprior, ON K7S 2P6
Tel: 613-623-3166
www.arnpriorregionalhealth.ca
Year Founded: 2005
Note: Acute, long-term & other healthcare services
Barbara Darlow, Board Chair
Eric Hanna, President & CEO
Dr. Christine Schriver, Chief of Staff
Susan Leach, Chief Nursing Executive & Vice-President, Patient/Resident Services
Gail Atwill, Vice-President, Finance & Support
Ron Marcotte, Vice-President, Human Resources
Wendy Knechtel, Manager, Communications

Belleville: **South East Local Health Integration Network/RLISS du Sud-Est**
Also Known As: South East LHIN
71 Adam St., Belleville, ON K8N 5K3
Tel: 613-967-0196; *Fax:* 613-967-1341
Toll-Free: 866-831-5446
southeast@lhins.on.ca
www.southeastlhin.on.ca
Social Media: www.facebook.com/227389740864; twitter.com/SouthEastLHIN; www.youtube.com/user/SouthEastLHIN
Year Founded: 2005
Population Served: 10000
Note: The South East region extends from Brighton on the west to Prescott & Cardinal on the east, north to Perth & Smith Falls, & back to Bancroft. Includes 7 hospitals, 37 long-term care homes, 1 Community Care Access Centre, 5 Community Health Centres, 12 Family Health Teams, 19 Addictions & Mental Health Services, & 27 Community Support Services
Donna Segal, Board Chair
Paul Huras, Chief Executive Officer
Sherry Kennedy, Chief Operating Officer
Andrei Tchouvelev, Senior Director, Enabling Technologies
Steve Goetz, Director, Performance Optimization
Paula Heinemann, Controller & Director, Corporate Service
Larry Hofmeister, Director, HSP Funding & Allocations
Michael Spinks, Chief Knowledge Officer

Brampton: **Central West Local Health Integration Network/RLISS du Centre-Ouest**
Also Known As: Central West LHIN
#300, 8 Nelson St. West, Brampton, ON L6X 4J2
Tel: 905-455-1281; *Fax:* 905-455-0427
Toll-Free: 866-370-5446
centralwest@lhins.on.ca
www.centralwestlhin.on.ca
Year Founded: 2005
Area Served: From northern Dufferin County to northern Peel Region; *Population Served:* 840000
Note: 50 health service providers in central west Ontario including a community care access centre, 2 community health centres, 14 community support services, 2 hospitals (three sites), 23 long-term care homes, & 8 mental health & addiction agencies.
Maria Britto, Board Chair
Scott McLeod, Chief Executive Officer
scott.mcleod@lhins.on.ca
Mark Edmonds, Acting Senior Director, Health System Integration
mark.edmonds@lhins.on.ca
Brock Hovey, Senior Director, Health System Performance
brock.hovey@lhins.on.ca
Neil McIntosh, Director, Performance & Accountability
neil.mcintosh@lhins.on.ca
Tom Miller, Director, Communications & Community Engagement
tom.miller@lhins.on.ca
Elizabeth Salvaterra, Director, ER/ALC & Decision Support
elizabeth.salvaterra@lhins.on.ca

Chatham: **Erie St. Clair Local Health Integration Network (ESC LHIN)/RLISS d'Érié St. Clair**
Also Known As: Erie St. Clair LHIN
180 Riverview Dr., Chatham, ON N7M 5Z8
Tel: 519-351-5677; *Fax:* 519-351-9672
Toll-Free: 866-231-5446
www.eriestclairlhin.on.ca
Social Media: www.facebook.com/111002926463; twitter.com/ESCLHIN; www.youtube.com/user/esclhin
Year Founded: 2006
Area Served: 7234 sq km; *Population Served:* 636020
Note: Serves the counties of Chatham-Kent, Sarnia/Lambton & Windsor/Essex
Martin Girash, Board Chair
Ralph Ganter, Acting Chief Executive Officer
ralph.ganter@lhins.on.ca
Ralph Ganter, Senior Director, Health System Design & Implementation
ralph.ganter@lhins.on.ca
Pete Crvenkovski, Director, Performance Quality & Knowledge Management
pete.crvenkovski@lhins.on.ca
Shannon Sasseville, Director, Communications, Public Affairs & Organizational Development
shannon.sasseville@lhins.on.ca
Jacquie Séguin, Coordinator, Performance & Finance
jacquelin.seguin@lhins.on.ca
Julie Franchuk, Communications Coordinator
julie.goodison@lhins.on.ca

Grimsby: **Hamilton Niagara Haldimand Brant Local Health Integration Network (HNHB LHI)/RLISS de Hamilton Niagara Haldimand Brant**
Also Known As: Hamilton Niagara Haldimand Brant LHIN
264 Main St. East, Grimsby, ON L3M 1P8
Tel: 905-945-4930; *Fax:* 905-945-1992
Toll-Free: 866-363-5446
hamiltonniagarahaldimandbrant@lhins.on.ca
www.hnhblhin.on.ca
Social Media: twitter.com/HNHB_LHINgage; www.youtube.com/user/hnhblhin
Year Founded: 2005
Area Served: Brant, Burlington, Haldimand, Hamilton, Niagara, Norfolk; *Population Served:* 1400000
Note: Facilities: 87 long term care homes; 9 hospitals (22 hospital sites); 7 community health centres (10 sites); 1 community care access centre. Programs: 80 community support services; 45 community mental health & addictions programs.
Michael Shea, Board Chair
Donna Cripps, Chief Executive Officer
donna.cripps@lhins.on.ca
Derek Bodden, Director, Finance
derek.bodden@lhins.on.ca
Emily Christoffersen, Director, Quality & Risk Management
emily.christoffersen@lhins.on.ca

Linda Hunter, Director, Health Links & Strategic Initiatives
linda.hunter@lhins.on.ca
Steve Isaak, Director, Health System Transformation
steven.isaak@lhins.on.ca
Trish Nelson, Director, Communications, Community Engagement, & Corporate Services
trish.nelson@lhins.on.ca
Rosalind Tarrant, Director, Access to Care
rosalind.tarrant@lhins.on.ca
Jennifer Everson, Physician Lead, Clinical Health System Transformation
jennifer.everson@lhins.on.ca

Kitchener: Waterloo Wellington Local Health Integration Network (WWLHIN)/RLISS de Waterloo Wellington
Also Known As: Waterloo Wellington LHIN

East Bldg., #220, 50 Sportsworld Crossing Rd., Kitchener, ON N2P 0A4
Tel: 519-650-4472; *Fax:* 519-650-3155
Toll-Free: 866-306-5446
waterloowellington@lhins.on.ca
www.waterloowellingtonlhin.on.ca
Social Media: www.facebook.com/1419574922543419; twitter.com/WW_LHIN; www.youtube.com/user/TheWWLHIN
Year Founded: 2005
Area Served: Waterloo, Wellington, Guelph & southern Grey County; 4,800 sq km; *Population Served:* 775000
Note: A crown agency of Ontario that works to plan, integrate, & fund local health services
Joan Fisk, Board Chair
Bruce Lauckner, Chief Executive Officer
Toni Lemon, Chief Strategy Officer
Zeynep Danis, Senior Director, Finance & Corporate Support
Stacey Rous, Director, Performance & Accountability
Gloria Cardoso, Senior Director, Health System Integration

London: South West Local Health Integration Network/RLISS du Sud-Ouest
Also Known As: South West LHIN

#700, 201 Queens Ave., London, ON N6A 1J1
Tel: 519-672-0445 *Toll-Free:* 866-294-5446
southwest@lhins.on.ca
www.southwestlhin.on.ca
Social Media: www.facebook.com/SouthWestLHIN; twitter.com/SouthWestLHIN; www.youtube.com/user/SouthWestLHIN; linkedin.com/company/south-west-local-health-integration-network
Year Founded: 2005
Area Served: Area from Lake Erie to the Bruce Peninsula; 21,639 sq km; *Number of Employees:* 200
Note: The South West Local Health Integration Network (LHIN) is a crown agency responsible for the planning, integration & funding of nearly 200 health service providers including hospitals, long-term care homes, mental health & addictions agencies, community support services, community health centres, & the South West Community Care Access Centre.
Jeff Low, Board Chair
Michael Barrett, Chief Executive Officer
Mark Brintnell, Senior Director, Performance & Accountability
Kelly Gillis, Senior Director, System Design & Integration
Lorri Lowe, Controller & Manager, Corporate Services

Markham: Central Local Health Integration Network/RLISS du Centre
Also Known As: Central LHIN

#300, 60 Renfrew Dr., Markham, ON L3R 0E1
Tel: 905-948-1872; *Fax:* 905-948-8011
Toll-Free: 866-392-5446
central@lhins.on.ca
www.centrallhin.on.ca
Social Media: www.youtube.com/user/TheCentralLHIN
Year Founded: 2005
Area Served: 2,730 sq km; *Population Served:* 1800000
Note: Areas served include parts of northern Toronto & Etobicoke, most of York Region, & South Simcoe County.
Warren Jestin, Board Chair
Andrea Gates, Director, Program Implementation & Improvement
andrea.gates@lhins.on.ca
Kim Baker, Chief Executive Officer
Kim.Baker@lhins.on.ca
Karin Dschankilic, Chief Financial Officer & Senior Director, Performance & Contracts
karin.dschankilic@lhins.on.ca
Chantell Tunney, Senior Director, Planning, Integration & Community Engagement
Chantell.Tunney@lhins.on.ca
Nancy Lum-Wilson, Director, Health System Planning & Design
Nancy.LumWilson@lhins.on.ca

Jennifer Scott, Director, Performance, Contract & Allocation
Jennifer.Scott@lhins.on.ca
Vacant, Director, Finance & Risk Management

North Bay: North East Local Health Integration Network
Also Known As: North East LHIN

555 Oak St. East, 3rd Fl., North Bay, ON P1B 8E3
Tel: 705-840-2872; *Fax:* 705-840-0142
Toll-Free: 866-906-5446
northeast@lhins.on.ca
www.nelhin.on.ca
Social Media: www.facebook.com/NorthEastLHIN; twitter.com/NorthEastLHIN; www.youtube.com/user/LHIN101; linkedin.com/company/north-east-local-health-integration-network
Year Founded: 2005
Area Served: 400,000 sq km; *Population Served:* 565000
Note: The North East LHIN brings 150 of the region's health care partners together - hospitals, community support services, mental health & addictions, community health centres, long-term care homes, & the Community Care Access Centre.
Danielle Bélanger-Corbin, Board Chair
Louise Paquette, Chief Executive Officer
Tamara Shewciw, Chief Information Officer, eHealth & Project Management Office
Catherine Matheson, Senior Director, Health System Transformation & Implementation
Kate Fyfe, Senior Director, System Performance
Terry Tilleczek, Senior Director, Policy & Health System Planning
Cynthia Stables, Director, Community Engagement, Community, & Cultural Diversity

Oakville: Mississauga Halton Local Health Integration Network (MH LHIN)/RLISS Mississauga Halton
Also Known As: Mississauga Halton LHIN

#500, 700 Dorval Dr., Oakville, ON L6K 3V3
Tel: 905-337-7131; *Fax:* 905-337-8330
Toll-Free: 866-371-5446
mississaugahalton@lhins.on.ca
www.mississaugahaltonlhin.on.ca
Social Media: www.youtube.com/user/mhlhin
Year Founded: 2005
Area Served: 900 sq km
Note: Includes the south-west portion of the City of Toronto, the south part of Peel Region, & all of Halton Region except for Burlington, which is part of the Hamilton Niagara Haldimand Brant LHIN; includes the municipalities of South Etobicoke, Mississauga, Halton Hills, Oakville, & Milton
Graeme Goebelle, Board Chair
Bill MacLeod, Chief Executive Officer
Andrew Hussain, Regional CIO
Judy Bowyer, Senior Director, Health System Performance
Liane Fernandes, Senior Director, Health System Development & Community Engagement
Dale McGregor, CFO & Senior Director, Finance

Orillia: North Simcoe Muskoka Local Health Integration Network/RLISS de Simcoe Nord Muskoka
Also Known As: North Simcoe Muskoka LHIN

#128, 210 Memorial Ave., Orillia, ON L3V 7V1
Tel: 705-326-7750; *Fax:* 705-326-1392
Toll-Free: 866-903-5446
northsimcoemuskoka@lhins.on.ca
www.nsmlhin.on.ca
Social Media: twitter.com/NSMLHIN
Year Founded: 2005
Population Served: 453710; *Number of Employees:* 35
Note: Encompasses the District of Muskoka, most of the County of Simcoe and a portion of Grey County. North Simcoe Muskoka is home to four First Nations. Health service providers include: 7 hospitals, 26 long-term care homes, 1 community care access centre, 3 community health centre, 29 community support services & 9 community mental health providers.
Robert Morton, Board Chair
Jill Tettmann, Chief Executive Officer
jill.tettmann@lhins.on.ca
Neil Walker, Chief Operating Officer
neil.walker@lhins.on.ca
Archie Outar, Senior Manager, Finance
archie.outar@lhins.on.ca
Jessica Dolan, Associate, Communications & New Media
jessica.dolan@lhins.on.ca

Ottawa: Champlain Local Health Integration Network/RLISS de Champlain
Also Known As: Champlain LHIN

#204, 1900 City Park Dr., Ottawa, ON K1J 1A3
Tel: 613-747-6784; *Fax:* 613-747-6519
Toll-Free: 866-902-5446
champlain@lhins.on.ca
www.champlainlhin.on.ca
Social Media: twitter.com/champlainlhin; www.youtube.com/user/ChamplainLHIN
Year Founded: 2005
Population Served: 1200000
Note: Area Served: Renfrew County; City of Ottawa; Prescott & Russell; Stormont; Dundas & Glengarry; North Grenville; four parts of North Lanark
Jean-Pierre Boisclair, Board Chair
Chantale LeClerc, Chief Executive Officer
Glenn Alexander, Chief Information Officer
Cal Martell, Senior Director, Health System Performance
Eric Partington, Senior Director, Health System Performance
Elaine Medline, Director, Communications

Thunder Bay: North West Local Health Integration Network
Also Known As: North West LHIN

#201, 975 Alloy Dr., Thunder Bay, ON P7B 5Z8
Tel: 807-684-9425; *Fax:* 807-684-9533
Toll-Free: 866-907-5446
northwest@lhins.on.ca.
www.northwestlhin.on.ca
Year Founded: 2005
Population Served: 231000
Note: The North West LHIN is responsible for planning, integrating & funding local health services, including hospitals, the Community Care Access Centre, community health centres, long-term care homes, community support service agencies & community mental health & addiction services. The North West LHIN extends from just west of White River to the Manitoba border & from Hudson Bay in the north down to the United States border.
Dan Levesque, Interim Board Chair
Laura Kokocinski, Chief Executive Officer
Brian Ktytor, Senior Director, Health System Performance
Susan Pilatzke, Senior Director, Health System Transformation
Chris Wcislo, Manager, Corporate Services/Controller

Toronto: Toronto Central Local Health Integration Network (TC LHIN)/RLISS du Centre-Toronto
Also Known As: Toronto Central LHIN

#201, 425 Bloor St. East, Toronto, ON M4W 3R4
Tel: 416-921-7453; *Fax:* 416-921-0117
Toll-Free: 866-383-5446
torontocentral@lhins.on.ca
www.torontocentrallhin.on.ca
Social Media: twitter.com/tc_lhin; www.youtube.com/user/TorontoCentralLHIN
Year Founded: 2005
Area Served: City of Toronto, Scarborough, North York & Etobicoke; *Population Served:* 1200000
Note: 170 health service providers including hospitals, the Toronto Central Community Care Access Centre, community support services, community health centres, mental health & addictions agencies & long-term care homes are funded through the TC LHIN.
John Fraser, Acting Board Chair
Susan Fitzpatrick, Chief Executive Officer
Sophia Ikura, Senior Director, Strategy, Community Engagement & Corporate Affairs
Raj Krishnapillai, Senior Director, Finance & Corporate & Shared Services
William B. Manson, Senior Director, Performance Management

Hospitals - General

Ajax: Rouge Valley Ajax & Pickering
Rouge Valley Health System
Affiliated with: Central East Local Health Integration Network

580 Harwood Ave. South, Ajax, ON L1S 2J4
Tel: 905-683-2320
patientrelations@rougevalley.ca
www.rougevalley.ca
Social Media: www.facebook.com/rougevalleyhealthsystem; twitter.com/RougeValley; www.youtube.com/user/RougeValleyHealthSys
Number of Beds: 172 beds
Note: Programs & services include: clinical nutrition; diabetes education; emergency; mental health; obstetrics; Ontario Breast Screening Program; paediatrics; physiotherapy; regional cardiac care; speech-language pathology; & surgery.
Andrée Robichaud, President & CEO, RVHS

Dr. Naresh Mohan, Chief of Staff, RVHS
Amelia McCutcheon, Chief Nursing Executive & Vice-President, Patient Services, RHVS
Leigh Duncan, Director, Government Relations & Communications, RHVS
647-294-8885, leduncan@rougevalley.ca

Alexandria: Glengarry Memorial Hospital (HGMH)/Hôpital Glengarry Memorial
Affiliated with: Champlain Local Health Integration Network
20260 County Road 43, Alexandria, ON K0C 1A0
Tel: 613-525-2222
www.hgmh.on.ca
Year Founded: 1965
Note: Programs & services include: chronic care; dermatology; diabetes; dietary; foot care; gastroenterology; internal medicine; laboratory; neurology; obstetrics/gynecology; orthopedic medicine/surgery; orthotics; physiotherapy; psychiatry; pulmonary function; radiology; rehabilitation; surgery; & urology.
Linda Morrow, Chief Executive Officer
Dr. N. Kucherepa, Chief of Staff
Shelley Coleman, Chief Nursing Officer & Vice-President, Clinical Services

Alliston: Stevenson Memorial Hospital (SMH)
Affiliated with: Central Local Health Integration Network
PO Box 4000, 200 Fletcher Cres., Alliston, ON L9R 1W7
Tel: 705-435-3377
www.smhosp.on.ca
Social Media: twitter.com/Stevenson_News; www.youtube.com/channel/UC9yZ4YnEocvc48T35ptQPCw
Year Founded: 1928
Number of Beds: 32 acute beds
Note: Programs & services include: acute care; day surgery; diagnostic imaging; dialysis; emergency; laboratory; mental health; obstetrics & gynecology; outpatient clinics; pharmacy; & physiotherapy/occupational therapy.
Jody Levac, President & CEO
Dr. Oswaldo C. Ramirez, Chief of Staff

Almonte: Almonte General Hospital (AGH)
Affiliated with: Champlain Local Health Integration Network
75 Spring St., Almonte, ON K0A 1A0
Tel: 613-256-2500; *Fax:* 613-256-8549
tmclelland@agh-fvm.com
www.almontegeneral.com
Number of Beds: 52 beds (21 medical & surgical, 5 obstetrical, & 26 chronic care)
Population Served: 11000
Note: Programs & services include: acute care; cardiology; complex continuing care; day hospital; dental surgery; diabetic education; emergency; geriatric assessment; long-term care program; obstetrics; occupational therapy; outpatient service clinics; physiotherapy; rehabilitation; respite care/convalescent care; & sexual assault support/treatment.
Mary Wilson Trider, President & CEO
613-256-2514, mwilsontrider@agh-fvm.com
Dr. Melissa Forbes, Chief of Staff
613-256-2514, mforbes@agh-fvm.com
Heather Garnett, Chief Nursing Officer & Vice-President, Patient & Resident Services
613-256-2514, hgarnett@agh-fvm.com

Arnprior: Arnprior & District Memorial Hospital
Affiliated with: Arnprior Regional Health
350 John St. North, Arnprior, ON K7S 2P6
Tel: 613-623-3166; *Fax:* 613-623-4844
www.arnpriorhospital.com
Number of Beds: 105 beds
Population Served: 30000; *Number of Employees:* 300
Note: Hospital Specialties: Emergency services; Diagnostic imaging; Acute care; Ontario Breast Screening Program; Diabetes clinic; Physiotherapy; Speech therapy; Urotherapy; Palliative care
Eric Hanna, President & CEO
eric.hanna@arnpriorhealth.com

Atikokan: Atikokan General Hospital (AGH)
Affiliated with: North West Local Health Integration Network
PO Box 2490, 120 Dorothy St., Atikokan, ON P0T 1C0
Tel: 807-597-4215; *Fax:* 807-597-4305
www.aghospital.on.ca
Social Media: www.facebook.com/AtikokanGeneralHospital; www.twitter.com/AtikokanHosp; www.linkedin.com/company/atikokan-general-hospital
Number of Beds: 41 beds
Number of Employees: 100
Note: Programs & services include: emergency services; diagnostic services; acute care; cardiac care; rehabilitation services; counselling & addictions program; diabetic counselling; complex continuing care; long-term care
Doug Moynihan, Chief Executive Officer
moynihand@aghospital.on.ca
Kim Cross, CFO & Vice-President, Corporate Services
crossk@aghospital.on.ca
Esther Richards, Chief Nursing Officer
richardse@aghospital.on.ca

Bancroft: QHC North Hastings Hospital
Quinte Health Care
Affiliated with: South East Local Health Integration Network
Former Name: North Hastings District Hospital
PO Box 157, 1-H Manor Lane, Bancroft, ON K0L 1C0
Tel: 613-332-2825; *Fax:* 613-332-3847
www.qhc.on.ca
Social Media: www.facebook.com/173689537296; twitter.com/QuinteHealth; www.youtube.com/QuinteHealthCare
Year Founded: 1927
Note: Part of the North Hastings Health Centre Campus, which includes: six-chair dialysis unit; 110-bed long-term care facility; Family Health Team; public health; Community Care Access Centre; & Community Care North Hastings.
Mary Clare Egberts, President & CEO, Quinte Health Care
Dr. Dick Zoutman, Chief of Staff, Quinte Health Care
Katherine Stansfield, Chief Nursing Officer & Vice-President, Quinte Health Care

Barrie: Royal Victoria Regional Health Centre (RVH)
Affiliated with: North Simcoe Muskoka Local Health Integration Network
Former Name: Royal Victoria Hospital
201 Georgian Dr., Barrie, ON L4M 6M2
Tel: 705-728-9802; *Fax:* 705-792-3324
TTY: 705-739-5618
www.rvh.on.ca
Year Founded: 1897
Number of Beds: 299 beds
Number of Employees: 2554
Note: Programs & services include: cardiac; cardio-respiratory; intensive care; chronic disease management; renal services; education; emergency; Home First; imaging; laboratory; medicine; mental health & addictions; internal medicine; pharmacy; rehabilitation & acute geriatrics; stroke program; surgery; telemedicine; & women's & children's program. Has 350 physicians on staff.
Janice Skot, President & CEO
SkotJ@rvh.on.ca
Nancy Savage, Executive Vice-President, Patient & Family Experience
savagen@rvh.on.ca
Dr. Chris Tebbutt, Vice-President, Academic & Medical Affairs
tebbuttc@rvh.on.ca
Treva McCumber, Chief Nursing Officer & Vice-President, Transitions & Diagnostics
mccumbert@rvh.on.ca

Barry's Bay: St. Francis Memorial Hospital (SFMH)
Affiliated with: Champlain Local Health Integration Network
PO Box 129, 7 St. Francis Memorial Dr., Barry's Bay, ON K0J 1B0
Tel: 613-756-3044; *Fax:* 613-756-0168
www.sfmhosp.com
Year Founded: 1960
Number of Beds: 20 beds
Population Served: 10000
Note: Programs & services include: active care unit; addictions treatment; bone density; complex continuing care; diabetic clinic; diagnostic imaging; discharge planning; ear, nose & throat; emergency; foot care clinic; general surgery; hemodialysis & nephrology; holter monitor; internal medicine; meals on wheels; medical laboratories; OBSP/mammography; Ontario Breast Screening Program; orthotist; palliative Care; pastoral care; physiotherapy; pre-op clinics; recreation; respiratory therapy; St. Francis Health Centre; Telemedicine; x-ray; & ultrasound.
Jeremy Stevenson, Chief Operating Officer
613-756-3044
Joan Kuiack, Director, Patient Care Services
613-756-3044

Belleville: QHC Belleville General Hospital
Quinte Health Care
Affiliated with: South East Local Health Integration Network
265 Dundas St. East, Belleville, ON K8N 5A9
Tel: 613-969-7400; *Fax:* 613-968-8234
Toll-Free: 800-483-2811
www.qhc.on.ca
Social Media: www.facebook.com/173689537296; twitter.com/QuinteHealth; www.youtube.com/QuinteHealthCare
Year Founded: 1886
Number of Beds: 206 beds
Note: Programs & services include: cardiology; complex continuing care; children's treatment centre; clinical nutrition; diabetes education; emergency; intensive care; laboratory; maternal/child service; medical day clinic; medical service; oncology; outpatient clinics; orthopaedics; pharmacy; psychiatry/mental health; radiology/diagnostic services; rehabilitation; stroke (District Stroke Centre & stroke prevention clinic); surgery; & symptom management/palliative care.
Mary Clare Egberts, President & CEO, Quinte Health Care
Dr. Dick Zoutman, Chief of Staff, Quinte Health Care
Katherine Standfield, Chief Nursing Officer & Vice-President, Quinte Health Care

Blind River: Blind River District Health Centre (BRDHC)/Pavillion Santé du District de Blind River
Affiliated with: North East Local Health Integration Network
Former Name: Robb Hospital; St. Joseph's General Hospital
PO Box 970, 525 Causley St., Blind River, ON P0R 1B0
Tel: 705-356-2265; *Fax:* 705-356-1220
webinfo@brdhc.on.ca
www.brdhc.on.ca
Year Founded: 1928
Number of Beds: 16 acute care beds
Number of Employees: 185
Note: Programs & services include: acute care; cardiac care; community support services; diabetes; diagnostic imaging; dietician; emergency & ambulatory care; exercise & falls prevention; laboratory; long-term care; oncology; & pharmacy. Has 50 physicians on staff.
Gaston Lavigne, Chief Executive Officer
Dr. Marc Bradford, Chief of Staff
Mary Ellen Luukkonen, Chief Nursing Officer & Director, Clinical Services

Bowmanville: Lakeridge Health - Bowmanville Site
Affiliated with: Central East Local Health Integration Network
47 Liberty St. South, Bowmanville, ON L1C 2N4
Tel: 905-623-3331
patientrelations@lakeridgehealth.on.ca
www.lakeridgehealth.on.ca
Social Media: www.facebook.com/LakeridgeHealth; twitter.com/lakeridgehealth; www.youtube.com/lakeridgehealth
Note: Programs & services include: cancer care; diagnostic centre; emergency; mental health; & senior's health.
Kevin Empey, President & CEO, Lakeridge Health
905-576-8711
Dr. Tony Stone, Chief of Staff, Lakeridge Health
905-576-8711
Lisa Shiozaki, Chief Operating Officer & Chief Nursing Executive, Lakeridge Health
905-576-8711

Bracebridge: South Muskoka Memorial Hospital Site
Muskoka Algonquin Healthcare (MAHC)
Affiliated with: North Simcoe Muskoka Local Health Integration Network
75 Ann St., Bracebridge, ON P1L 2E4
Tel: 705-645-4400; *Fax:* 705-645-4594
www.mahc.ca
Year Founded: 1949
Number of Beds: 43 acute care beds; 24 complex continuing care beds
Number of Employees: 645
Note: Programs & services include: cardio-respiratory; cancer supportive care & infusion clinic; clinical nutrition; complex continuing care; diabetes education; diagnostic imaging; discharge planning; emergency; fracture clinic; general surgery/endoscopy; gynaecological surgery; intensive care; laboratory; obstetrics; palliative care; paediatric clinic; pharmacy; rehabilitation; seniors assessment; speech-language pathology; spiritual care; telemedicine; & urology. Muskoka Algonquin Healthcare employs around 85 physicians.
Natalie Bubela, Chief Executive Officer, MAHC
705-789-0022
Dr. Jan Goossens, Chief of Medical Staff, MAHC
705-789-0022

Karen Fleming, Chief Quality & Nursing Executive, MAHC
705-645-4400

Brampton: Brampton Civic Hospital
William Osler Health System
Affiliated with: Central West Local Health Integration Network
Also Known As: William Osler Health Centre
2100 Bovaird Dr. East, Brampton, ON L6R 3J7
Tel: 905-494-2120
www.williamoslerhs.ca
Social Media: www.facebook.com/WilliamOslerHealth; twitter.com/OslerHealth; www.youtube.com/WilliamOslerTV; www.linkedin.com/company/william-osler-health-system
Year Founded: 2007
Number of Beds: 608 beds
Note: Programs & services include: cancer care; cardiac care; complex continuing care; critical care; diabetes care; diagnostic imaging; emergency; general & internal medicine; joint assessment centre; kidney care; laboratories; mental health & addictions; naturopathic care; palliative care; rehabilitation services; respirology; seniors' care; surgical services; & women's & children's services.
Matthew Anderson, President & CEO, William Osler Health System

Brantford: Brantford General Hospital
Brant Community Healthcare System
Affiliated with: Hamilton Niagara Haldimand Brant Local Health Integration Network
Also Known As: The Brantford General
200 Terrace Hill St., Brantford, ON N3R 1G9
Tel: 519-752-7871
www.bchsys.org
Social Media: www.facebook.com/245452318811922; twitter.com/BCHSYS; www.youtube.com/user/bchsys2011; www.linkedin.com/company/brantford-general-hospital
Year Founded: 1885
Number of Beds: 265 beds
Number of Employees: 1200
Note: Programs & services include: acute care; ambulatory care; Brant Community Cancer Clinic; critical care; CT scan; emergency; gynaecology; mental health; obstetrics; paediatrics; S.C. Johnson Dialysis Clinic; & surgery. Has 175 physicians on staff. Brant Community Healthcare System is affiliated with the Michael G. DeGroote School of Medicine, McMaster University.
James Hornell, President & CEO, Brant Community Healthcare System
Dr. Christopher O'brien, President, Medical Staff
Lina Rinaldi, Chief Operating Officer & Chief Nurse Executive
Dr. David Cameron, Chief of Staff & Vice-President

Brockville: Brockville General Hospital (BGH)
Affiliated with: South East Local Health Integration Network
75 Charles St., Brockville, ON K6V 1S8
Tel: 613-345-5649; *Fax:* 613-345-3529
www.bgh-on.ca
Social Media: www.facebook.com/brockvillegeneralhospital; twitter.com/BrockvilleGener; www.linkedin.com/company/5091498
Year Founded: 1885
Number of Beds: 140+ beds
Population Served: 99000; *Number of Employees:* 830
Note: Programs & services include: cardiology diagnostics; children's speech & language therapy; diagnostic imaging; early language; emergency; gynecology; inpatient rehabilition; infant & child development program; mental health; Ontario Breast Screening Program; Ontario Telehealth Network; outpatient paediatric physiotherapy; pain management; & stroke prevention. BGH's Garden Street Site provides palliative care services.
Tony Weeks, President & CEO
weeto@bgh-on.ca
Cathy Cassidy-Gifford, Chief Nursing Executive & Vice-President
gifca@bgh-on.ca

Burlington: Joseph Brant Hospital
Affiliated with: Hamilton Niagara Haldimand Brant Local Health Integration Network
Former Name: Joseph Brant Memorial Hospital
1230 North Shore Blvd., Burlington, ON L7S 1W7
Tel: 905-632-3737; *Fax:* 905-336-6480
www.jbmh.com
Social Media: www.facebook.com/JosephBrantHospital; twitter.com/Jo_Brant; www.linkedin.com/company/joseph-brant-hospital
Number of Beds: 245 beds
Number of Employees: 1500
Note: Programs & services include: community mental health; emergency; maternal & child; outpatient clinics; paediatric & gestational diabetes clinic; palliative care (outpatient); & Wellness House. Has 175+ physicians on staff.
Eric J. Vandewall, President & CEO
ceo@josephbranthospital.ca
Dr. Wes Stephen, Chief of Staff

Cambridge: Cambridge Memorial Hospital
Affiliated with: Waterloo Wellington Local Health Integration Network
Former Name: South Waterloo Memorial Hospital
700 Coronation Blvd., Cambridge, ON N1R 3G2
Tel: 519-621-2330; *Fax:* 519-740-4938
TTY: 519-621-9180
information@cmh.org
www.cmh.org
Year Founded: 1953
Note: Programs & services include: clinical nutrition & diabetes education; diagnostic imaging; emergency; infection control; information management; inpatient surgery & ambulatory surgical services; laboratory & CRU; medicine/medical day care; mental health (inpatient & outpatient); pastoral care; perioperative; pharmacy; rehabilitation, Allied Health, seniors & COPD; & women's & children's health.
Patrick Gaskin, Chief Executive Officer
519-621-2330
Dr. Kunuk Rhee, Chief of Staff
519-621-2330
Mike Prociw, Chief Financial Officer
519-621-2330
Heather Quesnelle, Chief Nursing Executive & Vice-President, Clinical Programs
519-621-2330
Susan Harris-Howe, Interim Director, Patient Services
519-621-2330

Campbellford: Campbellford Memorial Hospital (CMH)
Affiliated with: Central East Local Health Integration Network
146 Oliver Rd., Campbellford, ON K0L 1L0
Tel: 705-653-1140; *Fax:* 705-653-4371
info@cmh.ca
www.cmh.ca
Social Media: www.facebook.com/69366296602; twitter.com/cmhfoundation; www.youtube.com/cmhfoundation
Number of Beds: 34 beds
Population Served: 30000
Note: Programs & services include: cardiac/diabetes education; emergency; laboratory; long-term care; mammography; mental health; nursing care; palliative care; physiotherapy (inpatient); surgery; & x-ray, bone mineral density & ultrasound.
Brad Hilker, President & CEO
706-653-4371, bhilker@cmh.ca
Jan Raine, Chief Nursing Officer
706-653-4371, jraine@cmh.ca

Carleton Place: Carleton Place & District Memorial Hospital (CPDMH)
Affiliated with: Champlain Local Health Integration Network
211 Lake Ave. East, Carleton Place, ON K7C 1J4
Tel: 613-257-2200; *Fax:* 613-257-3026
info@carletonplacehosp.com
www.carletonplacehospital.ca
Year Founded: 1955
Population Served: 25000
Note: Programs & services include: allergy clinics; audiology services; clinical nutritional services; diabetes education; diagnostic imaging; emergency; general rehabilitation; pharmacy; physiotherapy; sexual assault/domestic violence program; & special care.
Toni Surko, Chief Executive Officer
Dr. Martin White, President, Medical Staff

Chapleau: Chapleau Health Services (SSCHS)/Services de sante de Chapleau
Affiliated with: North East Local Health Integration Network
6 Broomhead Rd., Chapleau, ON P0M 1K0
Tel: 705-864-1520; *Fax:* 705-864-0449
chapleauhr@sschs.ca
www.sschs.ca
Number of Beds: 14 acute care beds at Chapleau General Hospital; 19 long term care beds, 4 chronic care beds, & 2 respite beds at the Bignucolo Residence
Note: Programs & services inclusde: emergency services; acute care; occupational therapy; rehabilitation services; adult mental health services; counselling; services for the for the developmentally disabled; diabetes education; community services, such as meals on wheels, home support services & lifeline; operation of a nursing station in Foleyet; long term care; chronic care; respite care
Gail Bignucolo, Chief Executive Officer
705-864-3050
Dr. Kendra Saari, Chief of Staff

Chatham: Chatham-Kent Health Alliance (CKHA)
Affiliated with: Erie St. Clair Local Health Integration Network
PO Box 2030, 80 Grand Ave. West, Chatham, ON N7M 5L9
Tel: 519-352-6400
www.ckha.on.ca
Social Media: www.facebook.com/ckhamedia; twitter.com/ckhamedia; www.youtube.com/ckhamedia
Year Founded: 1998
Number of Beds: 200+ beds (total for both CKHA sites)
Number of Employees: 1350
Note: Programs & services include: adult & pediatric day surgery; ambulatory care; arthritis & stroke aquatic program; bone mineral densitometry; cardiac; chemotherapy/oncology; chiropody clinic; chronic disease management; continence clinic; coronary artery disease clinic; CT scan; diabetes education; dialysis; district stroke centre; echocardiography; emergency; EMG; endoscopy; fluoroscopy; general radiography; general surgery; gynaecology; health education; inpatient family medicine; inpatient surgical unit; integrated acute stroke unit; intensive care; mammography; mental health & addictions; MRI; nuclear medicine; nurse practitioner clinic; occupational therapy; Ontario Breast Screening Program; ophthalmology; oral surgery/dentistry; orthopedic surgery; orthotist/prosthetist; otolaryngology; outpatient hand clinic; parkinson's class; physiatry consultations/clinic; physiotherapy; progressive care; rehabilitation/complex continuing care; respiratory health; secondary stroke prevention clinic; sexual assault treatment centre; social work; speech-language pathology; supportive care & palliative care; therapeutic recreation; transitional stroke program; ultrasound; urology; women & children's health; & wound, skin & ostomy consultations. Affiliated with the Schulich School of Medicine - University of Western Ontario.
Colin Patey, President & CEO
cpatey@ckha.on.ca
Sarah Padfield, Chief Operating Officer
spadfield@ckha.on.ca
Willi Kirenko, Vice-President & Chief Nursing Executive
wkirenko@ckha.on.ca

Chesley: South Bruce Grey Health Centre - Chesley Site
Affiliated with: South West Local Health Integration Network
Former Name: Chesley & District Memorial Hospital
39 - 2nd St. SE, Chesley, ON N0G 1L0
Tel: 519-363-2340; *Fax:* 519-363-9871
info@sbghc.on.ca
www.sbghc.on.ca
Social Media: www.facebook.com/sbghc; twitter.com/SBG_HC
Year Founded: 1944
Number of Beds: 19 beds (9 acute care beds, 10 restorative care beds)
Note: Programs & services include: cardio-respiratory; diagnostic imaging; emergency department; emergency response system; inpatient medical beds; laboratory; nutrition services; outpatient clinics; palliative care; pastoral care; & restorative care.
Paul Rosebush, President & CEO, SBGHC
prosebush@sbghc.on.ca
Maureen Rydall, Director, Patient Care
mrydall@sbghc.on.ca

Clinton: Clinton Public Hospital
Huron Perth Healthcare Alliance
Affiliated with: South West Local Health Integration Network
98 Shipley St., Clinton, ON N0M 1L0
Tel: 519-482-3440; *Fax:* 519-482-5960
administration@hpha.ca
www.hpha.ca
Number of Beds: 20 acute care beds
Note: Programs & services include: ambulatory clinics & surgical services; emergency; imaging; laboratory; medicine; physiotherapy; social work; & spiritual care.
Andrew Williams, CEO, HPHA
519-272-8202, andrew.williams@hpha.ca
Dr. Laurel Moore, Chief of Staff, HPHA
519-272-8210, dr.laurel.moore@hpha.ca
Mary Cardinal, Site Administrator
519-272-8206, mary.cardinal@hpha.ca

***Cobourg:* Northumberland Hills Hospital**
Affiliated with: Central East Local Health Integration Network
Former Name: Northumberland Health Care Corp.
1000 DePalma Dr., Cobourg, ON K9A 5W6
Tel: 905-372-6811; *Fax:* 905-372-4243
info@nhh.ca
www.nhh.ca
Social Media: twitter.com/NorHillsHosp
Number of Beds: 137 beds
Population Served: 60000; *Number of Employees:* 600
Note: Programs & services include: ambulatory care; cancer & supportive care; community mental health; diagnostic imaging; dialysis (satellite); emergency; inpatient rehabilitation; intensive care; maternal child care; medical/surgical; Ontario Telemedicine Network (OTN); palliative care; restorative care; & women's health.
Linda Davis, President & CEO
905-377-7755
Helen Brenner, Chief Nursing Executive & Vice-President, Patient Services
905-377-7756

***Cochrane:* The Lady Minto Hospital**
MICs Group of Health Services
Affiliated with: North East Local Health Integration Network
PO Box 4000, 241 - 8 St., Cochrane, ON P0L 1C0
Tel: 705-272-7200; *Fax:* 705-258-2624
www.micsgroup.com
Year Founded: 1915
Number of Beds: 25 acute care beds; 8 complex continuing care beds; 33 long-term care beds
Note: Programs & services include: clinical nutrition; complex continuing care; diabetes; diagnostic imaging; emergency; general surgery; laboratory; oncology; physiotherapy; respiratory therapy; telemedicine; & visiting specialty clinics. The Villa Minto chronic care wing houses a long-term care unit.
Paul Chatelain, Chief Executive Officer, MICs Group of Health Services
Dr. George Freundlich, Chief of Staff, MICs Group of Health Services
Karen Hill, Chief Nursing Officer, MICs Group of Health Services

***Collingwood:* Collingwood G&M Hospital**
Affiliated with: North Simcoe Muskoka Local Health Integration Network
Former Name: Collingwood General & Marine Hospital
459 Hume St., Collingwood, ON L9Y 1W9
Tel: 705-445-2550
cgmh.on.ca
Social Media: www.facebook.com/CollingwoodGMHospital; twitter.com/CollingwoodHosp; www.youtube.com/user/CollingwoodGMHosp; www.linkedin.com/company/collingwood-general-and-marine-hospital
Year Founded: 1887
Number of Beds: 72 beds
Note: Programs & services include: ambulatory care; cardio-respiratory; community mental health; diagnostic imaging; dialysis; emergency; general medicine; general surgery; intensive care; laboratory services; obstetrics/gynaecology; orthopaedic surgery; rehabilitation; & telemedicine.
Guy Chartrand, President & CEO
705-445-2550
Norah Holder, Chief Nursing Officer & Vice-President, Patient Services
705-445-2550

***Cornwall:* Cornwall Community Hospital/Hôpital communautaire de Cornwall**
Second Street Site
510 Second St. East, Cornwall, ON K6H 1Z6
Tel: 613-932-3300
communications@cornwallhospital.ca
www.cornwallhospital.ca
Note: Hospital Specialties: Assault & Sexual Abuse Program (Phone: 613-932-3300, ext. 4202; Toll-Free Phone: 1-866-263-1560; TTY: 613-936-4643; E-mail: asap@cornwallhospital.ca); Psychiatric care (613-932-3300, ext. 4204); Outpatient Mental Health Program (613-932-3300, ext. 4278); Withdrawal management services (613-938-8506)
Jeanette Despatie, CEO

***Cornwall:* Cornwall Community Hospital - McConnell Avenue Site/Hôpital communautaire de Cornwall**
Affiliated with: Champlain Local Health Integration Network
840 McConnell Ave., Cornwall, ON K6H 5S5
Tel: 613-938-4240; *Fax:* 613-930-4502
communications@cornwallhospital.ca
www.cornwallhospital.ca
Note: Programs & services include: addiction services; adult counselling & treatment; Arterial Blood Gas (ABG); assault & sexual abuse program; Assertive Community Treatment Team (ACTT); cardiac stress test; cardio-respiratory therapy; children's mental health; critical care; CT scan; day hospital; dentistry; diabetes education; dialysis; ECG/EEG; emergency; geriatrics; gynecology/obstetrics; inpatient psychiatric care unit; internal medicine; laboratory; MRI; mammography; mental health & addictions; neurology; nuclear medicine; ophthalmology; orthopedics; palliative care; pediatrics; psychiatry; psychogeriatric service; radiology; regional hip & knee replacement program; rehabilition; sleep clinic; spiritual care; spirometry; stroke prevention; surgery; thrombosis; ultrasound; urology; women & children's health; & x-ray.
Jeanette Despatie, Chief Executive Officer
Dr. Lorne Scharf, Chief of Staff
Heather Arthur, Chief Nursing Officer & Vice-President, Patient Services

***Deep River:* Deep River & District Hospital (DRDH)**
Affiliated with: Champlain Local Health Integration Network
117 Banting Dr., Deep River, ON K0J 1P0
Tel: 613-584-3333; *Fax:* 613-584-4920
Toll-Free: 866-571-8168
www.drdh.org
Year Founded: 1974
Note: Programs & services include: acute inpatient care; children's speech-language program; diabetes; diagnostic imaging; DRDH physiotherapy centre; emergency; laboratory; mental health; nutritional counselling; & Ontario Telemedicine.
Gary Sims, Chief Executive Officer
Kate Kobbes, Chief Nursing Officer

***Dryden:* Dryden Regional Health Centre (DRHC)**
Affiliated with: North West Local Health Integration Network
PO Box 3003, 58 Goodall St., Dryden, ON P8N 2Z6
Tel: 807-223-8201; *Fax:* 807-223-2370
TTY: 807-223-8295
www.drhc.on.ca
Year Founded: 1952
Number of Beds: 41 beds (31 acute beds & 10 chronic/rehab beds)
Note: Programs & services include: emergency services; diagnostic imaging (807-223-8253); acute care; obstetrics; critical care; mental health & addiction services (807-223-6678); occupational therapy (807-223-8214); physiotherapy (807-223-8259); sexual assault & domestic violence services (807-223-7427); diabetes education (807-223-8208); counselling; chronic care
Dr. Stephen Viherjoki, Chief of Staff
Darlene Furlong, Chief Nursing Executive

***Dunnville:* Haldimand War Memorial Hospital**
Affiliated with: Hamilton Niagara Haldimand Brant Local Health Integration Network
206 John St., Dunnville, ON N1A 2P7
Tel: 905-774-7431; *Fax:* 905-774-6776
kanger@hwmh.ca
www.hwmh.ca
Number of Beds: 22 acute care beds; 2 transitional beds; 1 palliative care bed; 4 day surgery beds; 4 assess & restore beds; 13 chronic care beds
Note: Specializes in diagnostic imaging for acute life-threatening injuries or severe illnesses, as well as treatment for non-life-threatening injuries or illnesses such as broken bones, cuts, earaches, eye injuries, fever, infections, minor burns, nose & throat issues & sprains & strains.

***Durham:* South Bruce Grey Health Centre - Durham Site**
Affiliated with: South West Local Health Integration Network
Former Name: Durham Memorial Hospital
PO Box 638, 320 College St., Durham, ON N0G 1R0
Tel: 519-369-2340; *Fax:* 519-369-6180
info@sbghc.on.ca
www.sbghc.on.ca
Social Media: www.facebook.com/sbghc; twitter.com/SBG_HC
Year Founded: 1946
Number of Beds: 10 beds
Note: Programs & services include: cardio-respiratory; diagnostic imaging; emergency department; emergency response system; inpatient medical beds; laboratory; nutrition services; outpatient clinics; palliative care; & pastoral care.
Paul Rosebush, President & CEO, SBGHC
prosebush@sbghc.on.ca
Jill Machan, Director, Patient Care
jmachan@sbghc.on.ca

***Elliot Lake:* St. Joseph's General Hospital**
Affiliated with: North East Local Health Integration Network
70 Spine Rd., Elliot Lake, ON P5A 1X2
Tel: 705-848-7182; *Fax:* 705-848-6239
www.sjgh.ca
Year Founded: 1958
Number of Beds: 58 beds
Note: Programs & services include: emergency, bone density, cardiology, chemotherapy, chiropody, clinical nutrition, diabetes education, ears, nose, & throat, electrocardiogram, endoscopy, gastroenterology, gerontology, intensive care, mental health, nephrology, obstetrics, ophthalmology, orthopedics, paediatrics, palliative care, pastoral care, physiotherapy, radiology, renal dialysis (as a satellite of Sudbury Regional Hospital), speech therapy, social work, surgery, urology, ultrasound. The hospital corporation also manages St. Joseph's Manor long term care facility, & the Oaks Substance Abuse Treatment Centre.
Michael Hukezalie, Chief Executive Officer
mhukezalie@sjgh.ca

***Englehart:* Englehart & District Hospital Inc.**
Affiliated with: North East Local Health Integration Network
PO Box 69, 61 - 5th St., Englehart, ON P0J 1H0
Tel: 705-544-2301; *Fax:* 705-544-5222
www.edhospital.on.ca
Note: Programs & services include: acute care; cancer care; complex continuing care; diabetes; diagnostic imaging; emergency; foot care; laboratory; occupational therapy; palliative care; physiotherapy; respiratory therapy; & telemedicine.
Lois Kozak, Chief Executive Officer
705-554-2301
Mark Montminy, Senior Director, Operations
705-554-2301
An Weiler, Director, Clinical Services
705-554-2301

***Espanola:* Espanola Regional Hospital & Health Centre (ERHHC)/Hôpital régional et centre de santé d'espanola**
Affiliated with: North East Local Health Integration Network
Former Name: Espanola General Hospital
825 McKinnon Dr., Espanola, ON P5E 1R4
Tel: 705-869-1420; *Fax:* 705-869-2608
info@esphosp.on.ca
www.erhhc.on.ca
Year Founded: 1949
Note: Programs & services include: diagnostic imaging; emergency/acute care; Espanola Nursing Home; family health team; laboratory; pharmacy; physiotherapy; Queensway Place; & sleep lab.
Ray Hunt, Chief Executive Officer
Nicole Haley, Chief Nursing Officer & Director, Clinical Services

***Exeter:* South Huron Hospital Association (SHHA)**
Affiliated with: South West Local Health Integration Network
24 Huron St. West, Exeter, ON N0M 1S2
Tel: 519-235-2700; *Fax:* 519-235-3405
shha.administration@shha.on.ca
www.shha.on.ca
Year Founded: 1953
Number of Beds: 19 beds
Note: Programs & services include: complex continuing care; diagnostic imaging; emergency; Huron Perth Diabetes Education Program; inpatient unit; inpatient rehabilitation; laboratory; outpatient services; physiotherapy; social work; & speech-language pathology.
Heather Klopp, Interim President & CEO

***Fergus:* Groves Memorial Community Hospital (GMCH)**
Affiliated with: Waterloo Wellington Local Health Integration Network
235 Union St. East, Fergus, ON N1M 1W3
Tel: 519-843-2010; *Fax:* 519-843-5331
info@gmch.fergus.net
www.gmch.ca
Number of Beds: 44 beds
Population Served: 34500; *Number of Employees:* 277
Note: Programs & services include: ambulatory care; chiropody; diabetes education; diagnostic imaging; emergency; geriatric emergency management; Hospital Elder Life Care Program;

inpatient medicine; infection prevention & control; laboratory; nutritional services; obstetrics; Ontario Breast Screening Program; outpatient oncology unit; pastoral services; pharmacy; physiotherapy; respiratory therapy; speech-language pathology; & surgery.
Jerome Quenneville, President & CEO
Dr. Patrick Otto, Chief of Staff
Diane Wilkinson, Chief Nursing Executive & Vice-President, Patient Services

***Fort Albany:* James Bay General Hospital Fort Albany Wing**
General Delivery, Fort Albany, ON P0L 1H0
Tel: 705-278-3330; *Fax:* 705-278-1121
www.jbgh.org
Number of Beds: 17 beds

***Fort Erie:* Douglas Memorial Hospital Site Niagara Health System / Système de santé de Niagara**
Affiliated with: Hamilton Niagara Haldimand Brant Local Health Integration Network
230 Bertie St., Fort Erie, ON L2A 1Z2
Tel: 905-378-4647
patientrelations@niagarahealth.on.ca
www.niagarahealth.on.ca
Social Media: www.facebook.com/NiagaraHealthSystem; twitter.com/niagarahealth; www.youtube.com/niagarahealthsystem
Year Founded: 1931
Number of Beds: 55 beds
Note: Programs & services include: complex care; diagnostic imaging; Hepatitis C care; laboratory; Ontario Breast Screening Clinic; outpatient mental health; & urgent care.
Dr. Suzanne Johnston, President, Niagara Health System
Suzanne.Johnston@niagarahealth.on.ca
Dr. Kevin Smith, Chief Executive Officer, Niagara Health System
Kevin.Smith@niagarahealth.on.ca
Patty Welychka, Chief Nursing Officer, Director, Surgical Services, & Executive Lead, Fort Erie
Patty.Welychka@niagarahealth.on.ca

***Fort Frances:* Riverside Health Care Facilities Inc.**
Affiliated with: North West Local Health Integration Network
110 Victoria Ave., Fort Frances, ON P9A 2B7
Tel: 807-274-3266; *Fax:* 807-274-2898
riverside@rhcf.on.ca
www.riversidehealthcare.ca
Year Founded: 1989
Number of Beds: 55 beds (Fort Frances), 12 beds (Emo), 24 beds (Rainy River)
Note: Operates the La Verendrye General Hospital (Fort Frances- acute care, continuing care, obstetrics & surgery); the Emo Health Centre (Emo- acute care, urgent care, long term care, diagnostic imaging, physiotherapy, dental clinic); & Rainy River Health Centre (Rainy River- acute care, long term care, diagnostic imaging, dental clinic)
Allan Katz, President & CEO
Dr. Phillip Whatley, Chief of Staff
Lori Maki, Chief Nursing Executive

***Fort Frances:* La Verendrye General Hospital Riverside Health Care Facilities Inc.**
Affiliated with: North West Local Health Integration Network
110 Victoria Ave., Fort Frances, ON P9A 2B7
Tel: 807-274-3261; *Fax:* 807-274-2898
Number of Beds: 30 acute care beds; 25 medical & surgical beds
Note: Programs & services include: acute care; intermediate care. The hospital hosts visiting specialists each year.

***Georgetown:* Georgetown Hospital Halton Healthcare Services**
Affiliated with: Mississauga Halton Local Health Integration Network
Former Name: Georgetown & District Memorial Hospital
1 Princess Anne Dr., Georgetown, ON L7G 2B8
Tel: 905-873-0111; *Fax:* 905-873-9653
pr@haltonhealthcare.on.ca
www.haltonhealthcare.on.ca
Social Media: www.facebook.com/HaltonHealthcare; twitter.com/haltonhlthcare; www.youtube.com/channel/UC7xEU3Gq9890M-1Y0pz-Aog; www.linkedin.com/company/3186579
Year Founded: 1961
Number of Beds: 33 acute care beds; 20 continuing care beds
Population Served: 59000; *Number of Employees:* 326
Note: Programs & services include: Butt Out Smoking Cessation program; complex continuing care; diagnostic imaging; emergency; general medicine; mammography; medical & surgical services; obstetrics; outpatient clinics & community programs; rehabilitation & geriatrics; & supportive housing program.
Denise Hardenne, President & CEO, Halton Healthcare
Dr. Lorne Martin, Chief of Staff, Halton Healthcare
Cindy McDonell, COO & Family Practice Program Leader, Georgetown Hospital

***Geraldton:* Geraldton District Hospital/L'Hopital du District de Geraldton**
Affiliated with: North West Local Health Integration Network
500 Hogarth Ave. West, Geraldton, ON P0T 1M0
Tel: 807-854-1862; *Fax:* 807-854-1568
www.geraldtondh.com
Year Founded: 1963
Number of Beds: 23 acute care beds; 26 long term care beds
Note: Programs & services include: emergency services; diagnostic imaging; laboratory services; acute care; physiotherapy; occupational therapy; social work; diabetes education; long term care
Kurt Pristanski, Chief Executive Officer
807-854-1862, kpristanski@geraldtondh.com
Dr. Roy Laine, Chief of Staff
Laurie Heerema, Chief Nursing Officer

***Goderich:* Alexandra Marine & General Hospital (AMGH)**
Affiliated with: South West Local Health Integration Network
120 Napier St., Goderich, ON N7A 1W5
Tel: 519-524-8323; *Fax:* 519-524-5579
amgh.administration@amgh.ca
www.amgh.on.ca
Year Founded: 1901
Number of Beds: 46 beds
Note: Programs & services include: ambulatory clinics; cardiology; critical care; Diabetes Education Centre; diagnostics; dialysis; emergency; general medicine; Huron Perth District Stroke Centre - Telestroke Site; maternal/newborn program; nutrition; obstetrics (nursery); occupational therapy; palliative; physiotherapy; psychiatry; social work; speech-language pathology; & surgery.
Karen Davis, President & CEO
karen.davis@amgh.ca
Dr. Sam Appavoo, Chief of Staff
Dr. Hilary Watson, President, Medical Staff

***Grimsby:* West Lincoln Memorial Hospital Hamilton Health Sciences**
Affiliated with: Hamilton Niagara Haldimand Brant Local Health Integration Network
169 Main St. East, Grimsby, ON L3M 1P3
Tel: 905-945-2253; *Fax:* 905-945-0504
www.wlmh.on.ca
Social Media: www.facebook.com/140084176009847; twitter.com/hamhealthsc; www.vimeo.com/hamiltonhealthsciences
Number of Beds: 60 beds
Population Served: 65000; *Number of Employees:* 391
Note: Programs & services include: complex continuing care; diagnostic imaging; emergency; general medical; geriatric assessment (inpatient & outpatient); intensive care; mental health; obstetrics; outpatient diagnostic & treatment services; palliative care; & surgery. Has 124 medical staff. Affiliated with Michael G. DeGroote School of Medicine, McMaster University.
Rob MacIsaac, President & CEO, Hamilton Health Sciences

***Guelph:* Guelph General Hospital**
Affiliated with: Waterloo Wellington Local Health Integration Network
115 Delhi St., Guelph, ON N1E 4J4
Tel: 519-822-5350; *Fax:* 519 837-6773
TTY: 519 837-6437
info@gghorg.ca
www.gghorg.ca
Social Media: www.facebook.com/162349190488511; twitter.com/FdnofGGH
Year Founded: 1875
Number of Beds: 169 beds (including 22 critical care & step down, 65 surgery, 8 paediatric, 60 medicine & 14 obstetric)
Number of Employees: 1300
Note: Programs & services include: ambulatory care; bariatric surgery; bariatric medical program; cardio respiratory; critical care unit; diagnostic imaging; dietetics/nutritional counselling; emergency; family birthing unit; laboratory; medical unit; paediatric care; pharmacy; rehabilitation therapies; sexual assault & domestic violence; sleep lab; support services; & surgical suite. Employs 300 professional staff.
Marianne Walker, President & CEO

***Guelph:* St. Joseph's Health Centre Guelph St. Joseph's Health System**
Affiliated with: Waterloo Wellington Local Health Integration Network
100 Westmount Road, Guelph, ON N1H 5H8
Tel: 519-824-6000; *Fax:* 519-763-0264
info@sjhcg.ca
www.sjhcg.ca
Year Founded: 1861
Number of Beds: 240 long-term care beds; 91 specialty beds
Note: Programs & services include: clinics & medical services; community outreach; complex care; long-term care; nutrition; palliative care; recreation therapy; rehabilitation; social work; speech-language pathology; spiritual & religious care; & telemedicine.
Jennifer O'Brien, Interim President & CEO
519-824-6000, president@sjhcg.ca

***Hagersville:* West Haldimand General Hospital**
Affiliated with: Hamilton Niagara Haldimand Brant Local Health Integration Network
75 Parkview Rd., Hagersville, ON N0A 1H0
Tel: 905-768-3311; *Fax:* 905-768-1820
webmaster@whgh.ca
www.whgh.ca
Year Founded: 1964
Number of Beds: 23 beds
Note: Programs & services include: acute care; day surgery; diagnostic imaging; emergency; Haldimand Norfolk diabetes services; laboratory; nutrition; outpatient clinics & laboratory services; pastoral care; & physiotherapy.
David Bird, President & CEO
905-768-3311, David.Bird@whgh.ca
Richard Rossman, Chief of Staff
905-768-3311, R.Rossman@whgh.ca
Ingrid Fell, Chief Nursing Executive, Chief Privacy Officer, & Vice-President
905-768-3311, Ingrid.Fell@whgh.ca

***Haliburton:* Haliburton Highlands Health Services - Haliburton Site (HHHS)**
Affiliated with: Central East Local Health Integration Network
PO Box 115, 7199 Gellert Rd., Haliburton, ON K0M 1S0
Tel: 705-457-1392; *Fax:* 705-457-2398
info@hhhs.on.ca
www.hhhs.on.ca
Year Founded: 2000
Number of Beds: 14 acute care beds; 30 long-term care beds
Note: Programs & services include: community programs; diabetes education; long-term care; mental health; physiotherapy; primary care; & ultrasound.
Varouj Eskedjian, President & CEO; Administrator, Long-Term Care
705-457-2527, veskedjian@hhhs.on.ca
Celia OBrien, Chief Nursing Officer & Director, Care & Long-Term Care
705-286-2140, cobrien@hhhs.on.ca

***Hamilton:* Hamilton General Hospital Hamilton Health Sciences**
Affiliated with: Hamilton Niagara Haldimand Brant Local Health Integration Network
237 Barton St. East, Hamilton, ON L8L 2X2
Tel: 905-521-2100
www.hamiltonhealthsciences.ca
Social Media: www.facebook.com/140084176009847; twitter.com/hamhealthsc; www.vimeo.com/hamiltonhealthsciences
Year Founded: 1848
Number of Beds: 304 beds (91 inpatient beds)
Specialties: Cardiovascular care, neurosciences, trauma & burn treatment
Note: Major programs & services include: cardiac & vascular; neurosciences & trauma; & Population Health Institute. Others include: addictions & mental health; emergency; Hospital Elder Life Program; pain management centre; palliative care consultation; Regional Rehabilitation Centre; rehabilitation & seniors health program; seniors health; sexual assault & domestic violence care; & STD clinic.
Rob MacIsaac, President & CEO, Hamilton Health Sciences
Teresa Smith, Vice-President, Adult Regional Care

Hamilton: Juravinski Hospital
Hamilton Health Sciences
Affiliated with: Hamilton Niagara Haldimand Brant Local Health Integration Network
Former Name: Mount Hamilton Hospital
711 Concession St., Hamilton, ON L8V 1C3
Tel: 905-521-2100
www.hamiltonhealthsciences.ca
Social Media: www.facebook.com/140084176009847; twitter.com/hamhealthsc; www.vimeo.com/hamiltonhealthsciences
Year Founded: 1917
Note: Programs & services include: diagnostic services & medical diagnostic unit; emergency hematology oncology medicine & JCC Ambulance Care; perioperative services; rehabilitation; & surgical oncology, orthopedics & critical care program.
Rob MacIsaac, President & CEO, Hamilton Health Services

Hamilton: McMaster Children's Hospital
Hamilton Health Sciences
Affiliated with: Hamilton Niagara Haldimand Brant Local Health Integration Network
1200 Main St. West, Hamilton, ON L8N 3Z5
Tel: 905-521-2100
www.mcmasterchildrenshospital.ca
Social Media: www.facebook.com/140084176009847; twitter.com/hamhealthsc; www.vimeo.com/hamiltonhealthsciences
Year Founded: 1988
Number of Beds: 165 acute care beds; 6 mental health day beds; 4 eating disorder day beds
Specialties: Acute pediatrics
Note: Provides tertiary health care services for children in Hamilton & the surrounding region. Programs & services include: 2G, 2Q & 3E child & youth clinic; audiology; Child Advocacy & Assessment Program (CAAP); child & youth mental health program; children's exercise & nutrition centre; emergency; outpatient clinical services for children with diabetes; pediatric eating disorders program; pharmacy; & sexual assault & domestic violence care centre.
Rob MacIsaac, President & CEO, Hamilton Health Sciences
Dr. Peter Fitzgerald, President, McMaster Children's Hospital

Hamilton: McMaster Children's Hospital - Chedoke Site
Hamilton Health Sciences
Affiliated with: Hamilton Niagara Haldimand Brant Local Health Integration Network
PO Box 2000 Stn. A, Sanitorium Road, MPO, Hamilton, ON LC9 1C4
Tel: 905-521-2100
www.hamiltonhealthsciences.ca
Social Media: www.facebook.com/140084176009847; twitter.com/hamhealthsc; www.vimeo.com/hamiltonhealthsciences
Year Founded: 1906
Note: Programs & services include: autism spectrum disorder service (Hamilton Autism Intervention Program); child & youth mental health programs; cleft lip & palate program; developmental pediatrics & rehabilitation; family resource centre; pediatric lipid clinic; specialized developmental & behavioural services; & technology access clinic.
Rob MacIsaac, President & CEO, Hamilton Health Sciences
president@hhsc.ca
Dr. Peter Fitzgerald, President & CEO, McMaster Children's Hospital

Hamilton: St. Joseph's Healthcare Hamilton - Charlton Campus
St. Joseph's Health System
Affiliated with: Hamilton Niagara Haldimand Brant Local Health Integration Network
50 Charlton Ave. East, Hamilton, ON L8N 4A6
Tel: 905-522-1155
www.stjosham.on.ca
Social Media: www.facebook.com/stjosehshealthcarefoundation; twitter.com/STJOESHAMILTON; www.youtube.com/Stjoesfoundation; www.linkedin.com/company/st-joseph's-healthcare-hamilton
Number of Beds: 786 across the system
Note: Programs & services include: Best Foot Forward; Brant seniors mental health outreach program; audiology; Brant Assertive Community Treatment Team (ACTT); continence care clinic; cleghorn early psychosis intervention program; community schizophrenia service; east region mental health services; geriatric assessment clinic; Niagara seniors mental health outreach program; relaxation group; & spiritual care. Affiliated with the Faculty of Health Sciences at McMaster University & Mohawk College.
Dr. David Higgins, President
Winnie Doyle, Chief Nursing Executive & Vice-President, Clinical Programs

Hamilton: St. Joseph's Healthcare Hamilton - King Campus
St. Joseph's Health System
Affiliated with: Hamilton Niagara Haldimand Brant Local Health Integration Network
2757 King St. East, Hamilton, ON L8G 5E4
Tel: 905-522-1155
www.stjosham.on.ca
Social Media: www.facebook.com/stjosehshealthcarefoundation; twitter.com/STJOESHAMILTON; www.youtube.com/Stjoesfoundation; www.linkedin.com/company/st-joseph's-healthcare-hamilton
Note: Programs & services include: diabetes; east region mental health services; family practice; chiropody clinic; Health for Older Adults; women's health centre; continence care; family asthma education; & urgent care. Affiliated with the Faculty of Health Sciences at McMaster University & Mohawk College.
Dr. David Higgins, President
Winnie Doylens, Chief Nursing Executive & Vice-President, Clinical Programs

Hamilton: St. Peter's Hospital
Hamilton Health Sciences
Affiliated with: Hamilton Niagara Haldimand Brant Local Health Integration Network
88 Maplewood Ave., Hamilton, ON L8M 1W9
Tel: 905-777-3837
www.hamiltonhealthsciences.ca
Social Media: www.facebook.com/140084176009847; twitter.com/hamhealthsc; www.vimeo.com/hamiltonhealthsciences
Year Founded: 1890
Specialties: Care for seniors, aged 65 & over
Note: Programs & services include: behavioural health; Centre for Healthy Aging; complex continuing care; palliative care; & rehabilitation. Affiliated with McMaster University & Mohawk College.
Rob MacIsaac, President & CEO, Hamilton Health Sciences

Hanover: Hanover & District Hospital (HDH)
Affiliated with: South West Local Health Integration Network
90 - 7 Ave., Hanover, ON N4N 1N1
Tel: 519-364-2340; *Fax:* 519-364-6602
info@hdhospital.ca
www.hdhospital.ca
Social Media: www.facebook.com/1496343557318797; twitter.com/HDHospital; www.youtube.com/channel/UCaZOjwJGY-MsD3hRQ7S3L2A; www.linkedin.com/company/hanover-&-district-hospital
Year Founded: 1923
Number of Beds: 80 beds
Note: Programs & services include: day surgery; Diabetic Education & Community Care access Center (CCAC); diagnostic imaging; emergency department; Family Health Team (FHT); hemodialysis unit; Home & Community Support Services (HCSS); laboratory; medical/surgical inpatient unit; obstetrics; palliative care; psychiatry/psychology; rehabilitation; special care unit; specialist clinics; spiritual care; surgery; & Victorian Order of Nurses (VON).
Katrina Wilson, President & CEO
519-364-2341
Dr. Susan Boron, Chief of Staff
Esther Miller, Chief Nursing Officer & Vice-President, Patient Care Services
519-364-2341
Marnie Ferguson, Vice-President, Finance & Operations
519-364-2341

Hawkesbury: Hôpital Général de Hawkesbury & District General Hospital Inc.
Affiliated with: Champlain Local Health Integration Network
1111 Ghislain St., Hawkesbury, ON K6A 3G5
Tel: 613-632-1111; *Fax:* 613-636-6183
Toll-Free: 800-790-8870
info@hgh.ca
www.hgh.ca
Year Founded: 1984
Number of Beds: 69 beds
Note: Programs & services include: diabetes education; emergency; Ontario Breast Screening Program; & sexual assault counselling.
Marc LeBoutillier, Chief Executive Officer
Dr. J. Maranda, Chief of Staff
M. Heuvelmans, Chief Nursing Executive & Vice-President, Acute Care

Hearst: Hôpital Nôtre-Dame Hospital
CP 8000, 1405 Edward St., Hearst, ON P0L 1N0
Tél: 705-362-4291; *Téléc:* 705-372-2923
www.ndh.on.ca
Nombre de lits: 44 lits
France Dallaire, CEO

Hornepayne: Hornepayne Community Hospital
PO Box 190, 278 Front St., Hornepayne, ON P0M 1Z0
Tel: 807-868-2442; *Fax:* 807-868-2697
www.hornepayne.com
Number of Beds: 20 beds; 12 Long-term care, 8 Acute care
Lisa Verrino, CEO
Lisa.Verrino@hornepaynehospital.ca

Huntsville: Huntsville District Memorial Hospital Site
Muskoka Algonquin Healthcare (MAHC)
Affiliated with: North Simcoe Muskoka Local Health Integration Network
100 Frank Miller Dr., Huntsville, ON P1H 1H7
Tel: 705-789-2311; *Fax:* 705-789-0557
www.mahc.ca
Number of Beds: 37 acute care beds
Number of Employees: 645
Note: Programs & services include: cardio-respiratory; chemotherapy, supportive care & infusion clinics; clinical nutrition; dialysis clinic; diabetes education; diagnostic imaging; discharge planning; district stroke centre; emergency; ENT surgery; fracture clinic; general surgery/endoscopy; intensive care; laboratory; obstetrics; ophthalmology; pacemaker clinic; palliative care; paediatric clinic; pharmacy; rehabilitation; speech-language pathology; spiritual care; & telemedicine. Muskoka Algonquin Healthcare employs around 85 physicians.
Natalie Bubela, Chief Executive Officer, MAHC
705-789-0022
Dr. Jan Goossens, Chief of Medical Staff, MAHC
705-789-0022
Karen Fleming, Chief Quality & Nursing Executive, MAHC
705-789-0022

Ingersoll: Alexandra Hospital
Affiliated with: South West Local Health Integration Network
29 Noxon St., Ingersoll, ON N5C 3V6
Tel: 519-485-1700; *Fax:* 519-485-9606
feedback@ah.tvh.ca
www.alexandrahospital.on.ca
Year Founded: 1909
Number of Beds: 35 beds
Note: Programs & services include: ambulatory clinics; complex continuing care; day surgery; Diabetes Education Centre; diagnostics; emergency department; inpatient unit; intensive care; nutrition; occupational therapy; Oxford County Cardiac Rehabilitation & Secondary Prevention Program; palliative care program; & physiotherapy.
Crystal Houzeh, Integrated President & CEO
519-485-1700, Crystal.Houze@ah.tvh.ca
Frank Deutsch, Integrated Vice President/Chief Financial Officer
519-485-1700, Frank.Deutsch@ah.tvh.ca
Tim Rice, Integrated Vice President/Chief Nursing Executive
519-485-1700, Tim.Rice@ah.tvh.ca

Iroquois Falls: Anson General Hospital
MICs Group of Health Services
Affiliated with: North East Local Health Integration Network
58 Anson Dr., Iroquois Falls, ON P0K 1E0
Tel: 705-258-3911; *Fax:* 705-258-2618
www.micsgroup.com
Year Founded: 1955
Number of Beds: 19 acute care beds; 15 complex continuing care beds; 69 long-term care beds
Note: Programs & services include: clinical nutrition; complex continuing care; diabetes; diagnostic imaging; emergency; laboratory; physiotherapy; respiratory therapy; visiting specialty clinics; telemedicine.
Paul Chatelain, Chief Executive Officer, MICs Group of Health Services
Dr. Stephen Chiang, Chief of Staff, MICs Group of Health Services
Karen Hill, Chief Nursing Officer, MICs Group of Health Services

Kapuskasing: Sensenbrenner Hospital
Affiliated with: North East Local Health Integration Network
101 Progress Cres., Kapuskasing, ON P5N 3H5
Tel: 705-337-6111; *Fax:* 705-337-4021
info@sensenbrennerhospital.on.ca
www.senhosp.ca
Number of Beds: 53 beds
Note: Programs & services include: comprehensive primary &

selected secondary care; long term care; palliative care; health promotion services
Allan Yarush, CEO
Keith Landriault, Assistant Administrator, Finance & Hospital Services

Kemptville: Kemptville District Hospital
Affiliated with: Champlain Local Health Integration Network
PO Box 2007, 2675 Concession Rd., Kemptville, ON K0G 1J0
Tel: 613-258-6133; *Fax:* 613-258-4997
info@kdh.on.ca
www.kdh.on.ca
Social Media: www.facebook.com/KemptvilleDistrictHospital; twitter.com/KDHonline; www.youtube.com/user/KemptvilleHospital
Number of Beds: 21 inpatient beds; 4 interim long-term care beds; 8 convalescent care ebds; 8 surgical beds
Note: Programs & services include: convalescent care; diagnostic imaging; education & wellness; emergency; in-hospital care; interim long-term care; outpatient care; & surgery.
Colin Goodfellow, Chief Executive Officer
613-258-6133
Dr. Greg Leonard, Chief of Staff
613-258-6133

Kenora: Lake of the Woods District Hospital (LWDH)
Affiliated with: North West Local Health Integration Network
21 Sylvan St., Kenora, ON P9N 3W7
Tel: 807-468-9861; *Fax:* 807-468-3939
admin@lwdh.on.ca
www.lwdh.on.ca
Year Founded: 1897
Note: Programs & services include: emergency and ambulatory care; mental health programs; acute care; intesive and surgical care services; diagnostic imaging; mammography; sexual assult centre; physiotherapy; pallaitve care
Mark Balcaen, President & CEO

Kincardine: South Bruce Grey Health Centre - Kincardine Site
Affiliated with: South West Local Health Integration Network
Former Name: Kincardine & District General Hospital
43 Queen St., Kincardine, ON N2Z 1G6
Tel: 519-396-3331; *Fax:* 519-881-0452
info@sbghc.on.ca
www.sbghc.on.ca
Social Media: www.facebook.com/sbghc; twitter.com/SBG_HC
Year Founded: 1908
Number of Beds: 25 beds
Note: Programs & services include: cardio-respiratory; family birthing centre; diagnostic imaging; emergency department; emergency response system; inpatient medical beds; laboratory; nutrition services; palliative care; & pastoral care.
Paul Rosebush, President & CEO, SBGHC
prosebush@sbghc.on.ca
Kate Kincaid, Director, Patient Care
kkincaid@sbghc.on.ca

Kingston: Kingston General Hospital (KGH)
Affiliated with: South East Local Health Integration Network
76 Stuart St., Kingston, ON K7L 2V7
Tel: 613-548-3232 *Toll-Free:* 800-567-5722
www.kgh.on.ca
Info Line: 613-549-6666
Year Founded: 1838
Number of Beds: 456 beds
Population Served: 500000
Note: Teaching & research hospital affiliated with Queen's University. Programs & services include: cancer; cardiac; critical care; emergency; endocrinology & metabolism; gastroenterology; imaging; infectious diseases; internal medicine; medical genetics; mental health; nephrology & dialysis; neurology; obstetrics & gynecology; pathology & molecular medicine; pediatrics; pharmacy; respirology; rheumatology; sexual assault & domestic violence; & surgical, perioperative & anesthesiology.
Leslee Thompson, President & CEO
thompsonl@kgh.kari.net
Dr. David Zelt, Chief of Staff & Executive Vice-President
zeltd@kgh.kari.net

Kingston: The Religious Hospitaliers of Saint-Joseph of the Hotel Dieu of Kingston (HDH)
Affiliated with: South East Local Health Integration Network
Also Known As: Hotel Dieu Hospital
166 Brock St., Kingston, ON K7L 5G2
Tel: 613-544-3310; *Fax:* 613-544-4498
Toll-Free: 855-554-3400
www.hoteldieu.com
Social Media: www.facebook.com/HotelDieuHospital; www.youtube.com/user/HDHKingston
Year Founded: 1845
Note: An ambulatory care teaching facility with programs & services including: audiology; cardiac rehabilitation; child development; Children's Outpatient Centre (COPC); day surgery; detox centre; diabetes education; ENT; eating disorders; eye clinic; Geaganano Residence; infant development; infection & immunology; mental health; & urgent care. It is affiliated with Queen's University & is partnered with Kingston's university hospitals.
Dr. David Pichora, CEO
613-544-3400, hdhceo@hdh.kari.net
Dr. Michael Fitzpatrick, Chief of Staff & Chief, Medical & Academic Affairs
Mike McDonald, Chief Nursing Officer & Chief, Patient Care

Kirkland Lake: Kirkland & District Hospital
145 Government Rd. East, Kirkland Lake, ON P2N 3P4
Tel: 705-567-5251; *Fax:* 705-568-2102
administration@kdhospital.com
www.kdhospital.com
Year Founded: 1976
Number of Beds: 62 beds (6 intensive care, 41 medical/surgical, 15 continuing complex care)
Number of Employees: 260
Note: Services include diagnostic imaging; respiratory therapy; diabetic clinic; physiotherapy; pastoral care; telemedicine; renal diaylsis
Gleen Scanlan, CEO
Dr. Mark Spiller, Chief of Staff

Kitchener: Grand River Hospital - Freeport Health Centre
Affiliated with: Waterloo Wellington Local Health Integration Network
PO Box 9056, 3570 King St. East, Kitchener, ON N2A 2W1
Tel: 519-742-3611
info@grhosp.on.ca
www.grhosp.on.ca
Number of Beds: 500 beds (including Kitchener-Waterloo Site)
Note: Programs & services offered across both hospital sites include: cancer care; childbirth; children (including neonatal intensive care); complex continuing care; critical care; emergency; laboratory; medical imaging; medical program & stroke centre; mental health & addictions; renal care; pharmacy; rehabilitation; & surgery.
Malcolm Maxwell, President & CEO
malcolm.maxwell@grhosp.on.ca
Dr. Ashok Sharma, Joint Chief of Staff

Kitchener: Grand River Hospital - Kitchener-Waterloo Site
Affiliated with: Waterloo Wellington Local Health Integration Network
PO Box 9056, 835 King St. West, Kitchener, ON N2G 1G3
Tel: 519-742-3611
info@grhosp.on.ca
www.grhosp.on.ca
Number of Beds: 500 beds (including Freeport Health Centre site)
Note: Programs & services offered across both hospital sites include: cancer care; childbirth; children (including neonatal intensive care); complex continuing care; critical care; emergency; laboratory; medical imaging; medical program & stroke centre; mental health & addictions; renal care; pharmacy; rehabilitation; & surgery.
Malcolm Maxwell, President & CEO
malcolm.maxwell@grhosp.on.ca
Dr. Ashok Sharmal, Joint Chief of Staff

Kitchener: St. Mary's General Hospital
St. Joseph's Health System
Affiliated with: Waterloo Wellington Local Health Integration Network
911 Queen's Blvd., Kitchener, ON N2M 1B2
Tel: 519-744-3311; *Fax:* 519-749-6426
info@smgh.ca
www.smgh.ca
Year Founded: 1924
Number of Beds: 150 acute care beds
Number of Employees: 2000
Note: Catholic hospital, home to the Regional Cardiac Care Centre. Other programs & services include respiratory care, day surgery, general medicine & emergency care.
Don Shilton, President
519-749-6544, dshilton@smgh.ca
Dr. Ashok Sharma, Chief of Staff
Barbara Guidolin, Chief Nursing Executive & Vice-President, Patient Services
519-749-6544, bguidolin@smgh.ca

Leamington: Leamington District Memorial Hospital (LDMH)
Affiliated with: Erie St. Clair Local Health Integration Network
194 Talbot St. West, Leamington, ON N8H 1N9
Tel: 519-322-2373
www.leamingtonhospital.com
Number of Beds: 88 beds
Note: Programs & services include: cardiopulmonary; dialysis; diagnostic imaging; digital mammography/women's centre; emergency; maternal/newborn; inpatient services; surgical program; outpatient services; pharmacy; & pastoral/spiritual care.
Terry Shields, CEO & Privacy Officer
S. Gibson, Chief Financial Officer
C. Deter, Chief Nursing Executive & Interim Vice-President, Patient Services

Lindsay: Ross Memorial Hospital (RMH)
Affiliated with: Central East Local Health Integration Network
10 Angeline St. North, Lindsay, ON K9V 4M8
Tel: 705-324-6111; *Fax:* 705-328-6087
Toll-Free: 800-510-7365
publicrelations@rmh.org
www.rmh.org
Social Media: twitter.com/RossMemorial
Year Founded: 1902
Number of Beds: 175 beds
Population Served: 80000; *Number of Employees:* 820
Note: Programs & services include: continuing care; critical care; diagnostic imaging; dialysis; Health First (disease management); infection prevention & control; laboratory; medical program; mental health; radiation oncology consulation; spiritual; Ontario Telemedicine Network (OTN); pharmacy; surgery; therapy; & woman & child.

Lions Head: Lion's Head Hospital
Grey Bruce Health Services
Affiliated with: South West Local Health Integration Network
22 Moore St., Lions Head, ON N0H 1W0
Tel: 519-793-3424; *Fax:* 519-793-4407
web@gbhs.on.ca
www.gbhs.on.ca
Social Media: twitter.com/greybrucehealth
Number of Beds: 4 acute care beds
Note: Programs & services include: acute care; ambulatory care; diagnostic imaging (general radiography); emergency; laboratory; physiotherapy; spiritual care; & surgery.
Lance Thurston, President & CEO, Grey Bruce Health Services
519-376-2121

Listowel: Listowel Memorial Hospital
Listowel Wingham Hospitals Alliance
Affiliated with: South West Local Health Integration Network
255 Elizabeth St. East, Listowel, ON N4W 2P5
Tel: 519-291-3120; *Fax:* 519-291-5440
www.lwha.ca
Year Founded: 1919
Number of Beds: 50 beds
Note: Programs & services include: breast health centre; complex continuing care; diabetes education; diagnostic imaging; emergency; laboratory; maternal/newborn; medical unit; occupational therapy; outpatient clinics; palliative care; pastoral care; physiotherapy; speech-language pathology; & surgery.
Karl Ellis, President & CEO
519-291-3125, karl.ellis@lwha.ca

Little Current: Manitoulin Health Centre
PO Box 640, 11 Meredith St. West, Little Current, ON P0P 1K0
Tel: 705-368-2300; *Fax:* 705-368-3566
www.manitoulinhealthcentre.com
Number of Beds: 16 beds
Derek Graham, CEO

***London:* London Health Sciences Centre - Children's Hospital**
Affiliated with: South West Local Health Integration Network
PO Box 5010, 800 Commissioners Rd. East, London, ON N6A 5W9
Tel: 519-685-8500
patient_experience@lhsc.on.ca
www.lhsc.on.ca
Info Line: 519-685-8380
Social Media: www.facebook.com/LHSCCanada; twitter.com/LHSCCanada; www.youtube.com/LHSCCanada
Year Founded: 1917
Note: Provides specialized paediatric inpatient & outpatient services, including liver & bowel transplants; oncology; infectious disease programs; trauma; & intensive care.
Murray Glendining, President & CEO
Dr. Paul Atkinson, Senior Director, Women & Children Services

***London:* London Health Sciences Centre - University Hospital Site**
Affiliated with: South West Local Health Integration Network
339 Windermere Rd., London, ON N6A 5A5
Tel: 519-685-8500
patient_experience@lhsc.on.ca
www.lhsc.on.ca
Info Line: 519-685-8380
Social Media: www.facebook.com/LHSCCanada; twitter.com/LHSCCanada; www.youtube.com/LHSCCanada
Note: Programs & services include: carpal tunnel syndrome & mononeuropathy clinic; Clinical Neurological Sciences (CNS); cochlear implant program; Critical Care Outreach Team (CCOT); dentistry; diagnostic imaging; EEG; emergency; family medicine & palliative care; general surgery; general cardiology & cardiovascular surgery; intensive care; motor neuron disease clinic; movement disorder clinic; multi-organ transplant; multiple sclerosis clinic; occupational therapy; orthopaedics; pathology & laboratory medicine; physiotherapy; prescription centre pharmacy; psychological; renal care; social work; speech-language pathology; & surgery.
Murray Glendining, President & CEO

***London:* London Health Sciences Centre - Victoria Hospital Site**
Affiliated with: South West Local Health Integration Network
PO Box 5010, 800 Commissioners Rd. East, London, ON N6A 5W9
Tel: 519-685-8500
patient_experience@lhsc.on.ca
www.lhsc.on.ca
Info Line: 519-685-8380
Social Media: www.facebook.com/LHSCCanada; twitter.com/LHSCCanada; www.youtube.com/LHSCCanada
Year Founded: 1995
Note: Programs & services include: adult mental health care; bleeding disorders; blood conservation; cardiac care; Cardiac Fitness Institute of Southwestern Ontario; Critical Care Trauma Centre (CCTC); emergency; family medicine & palliative care; fertility clinic; maternal newborn care; medical genetics program of Southwestern Ontario; occupational therapy; pathology & laboratory medicine; pharmacy services; physiotherapy; renal care; sleep & apnea assessment unit; sleep medicine clinic; social work; speech-language pathology; surgical services; trauma program; urology; & women's health care.
Murray Glendining, President & CEO

***London:* Parkwood Hospital**
Affiliated with: St. Joseph's Health Care, London
801 Commissioners Rd. East, London, ON N6C 5J1
Tel: 519-685-4000; *Fax:* 519-685-4052
www.sjhc.london.on.ca
Number of Beds: 530 beds

***London:* St. Joseph's Health Care, London**
Affiliated with: South West Local Health Integration Network
268 Grosvenor St., London, ON N6A 4V2
Tel: 519-646-6100
comdept@sjhc.london.on.ca
www.sjhc.london.on.ca
Social Media: www.facebook.com/stjosephslondon; twitter.com/stjosephslondon; www.youtube.com/stjosephslondon
Number of Beds: 1,141 beds
Note: Includes St. Joseph's Hospital; Parkwood Hospital; Regional Mental Health Care London; Southwest Centre for Forensic Mental Health Care; & Mount Hope Centre for Long Term Care. Affiliated with Western University & Fanshawe College.
Dr. Gillian Kernaghan, President & CEO, St. Joseph's Health Care London

***London:* St. Joseph's Hospital**
Affiliated with: St. Joseph's Health Care, London
PO Box 5777, 268 Grosvenor St., London, ON N6A 4V2
Tel: 519-646-6100
www.sjhc.london.on.ca
Number of Beds: 177 beds

***Manitouwadge:* Manitouwadge General Hospital**
Affiliated with: North West Local Health Integration Network
1 Health Care Cres., Manitouwadge, ON P0T 2C0
Tel: 807-826-3251; *Fax:* 807-826-4216
infoserv@mh.on.ca
www.mh.on.ca
Number of Beds: 18 beds
Note: Programs & services include: diabetes education program; physiotherapy; diagnostic imaging & MDSD
Jocelyn Bourgoin, Chief Executive Officer
Dr. J. MacTavish, Chief of Staff

***Marathon:* Wilson Memorial General Hospital**
Affiliated with: North West Local Health Integration Network
PO Box 780, 26 Peninsula Rd., Marathon, ON P0T 2E0
Tel: 807-229-1740; *Fax:* 807-229-1721
wilson@nosh.ca
www.wmgh.net
Year Founded: 1971
Number of Beds: 21 beds
Population Served: 7,500
Note: Programs & services include: chemotherapy; rehabilitation; diabetes education; eye & foot specialty treatment
Adam Brown, CEO
807-229-1740
Janet Gobeil, Chief Nursing Officer
807-229-1740

***Markdale:* Markdale Hospital**
Grey Bruce Health Services
Affiliated with: South West Local Health Integration Network
Also Known As: Centre Grey Hospital
PO Box 406, 55 Isla St., Markdale, ON N0C 1H0
Tel: 519-986-3040
web@gbhs.on.ca
www.gbhs.on.ca
Social Media: twitter.com/greybrucehealth
Number of Beds: 14 acute care beds
Note: Programs & services include: acute care; ambulatory care; Diabetes Grey Bruce; diagnostic imaging; emergency; laboratory; physiotherapy; spiritual care; & surgery.
Lance Thurston, President & CEO, Grey Bruce Health Services
519-376-2121

***Markham:* Markham Stouffville Hospital - Markham Site (MSH)**
Affiliated with: Central Local Health Integration Network
PO Box 1800, 381 Church St., Markham, ON L3P 7P3
Tel: 905-472-7000
TTY: 905-472-7585
myhospital@msh.on.ca
www.msh.on.ca
Info Line: 905-472-7100
Social Media: www.facebook.com/MarkhamStouffvilleHospital; twitter.com/MSHospital; www.youtube.com/MSHospital
Year Founded: 1990
Number of Beds: 224 beds
Note: Programs & services include: ambulatory care; antenatal; asthma; audiology; breastfeeding; cardio-respiratory; chemotherapy; child & adolescent mental health; day surgery; diabetes; diagnostic imaging; emergency; emergency fast track clinics; fractures; genetics counseling; geriatrics; ICU/CCU; medical day unit; mental health (BRIDGE program); obstetrics; occupational/physical therapy; outpatient laboratory; paediatrics; palliative care; plastics; post anaesthetic care unit; pre-natal tours; rehabilitation; sleep disorders; special care nursery; speech-language pathology; spiritual care; surgery; & The Childbirth Centre.
Janet M. Beed, President & CEO
Dr. David Austin, Chief of Staff

***Matheson:* Bingham Memorial Hospital**
MICs Group of Health Services
Affiliated with: North East Local Health Integration Network
PO Box 70, 507 - 8th Ave., Matheson, ON P0K 1N0
Tel: 705-273-2424; *Fax:* 705-273-2515
www.micsgroup.com
Year Founded: 1955
Number of Beds: 11 acute care beds; 6 complex continuing care beds; 20 long-term care beds
Note: Programs & services include: clinical nutrition; diabetes; diagnostic imaging; emergency; laboratory; respiratory therapy; telemedicine; & visiting specialty clinics.
Paul Chatelain, Chief Executive Officer, MICs Group of Health Services
Dr. George Freundlich, Chief of Staff, MICs Group of Health Services
Karen Hill, Chief Nursing Officer, MICs Group of Health Services

***Mattawa:* Mattawa Hospital/Hôpital de Mattawa**
PO Box 70, 217 Turcotte Park Rd., Mattawa, ON P0H 1V0
Tel: 705-744-5511; *Fax:* 705-744-6020
admin@mattawahospital.ca
www.mattawahospital.ca
Year Founded: 1878
Number of Beds: 19 beds
Note: Specialties; Primary care; Acute care; Ambulatory programs; Diabetic resource centre; Adult & children's mental health services; Paediatric, urology, psychiatry, & women's clinic; Physiotherapy services; Palliative care

***Meaford:* Meaford Hospital**
Grey Bruce Health Services
Affiliated with: South West Local Health Integration Network
229 Nelson St. West, Meaford, ON N4L 1A3
Tel: 519-538-1311; *Fax:* 519-538-5500
web@gbhs.on.ca
www.gbhs.on.ca
Social Media: twitter.com/greybrucehealth
Number of Beds: 15 acute care beds
Note: Programs & services include: acute care; ambulatory care; Diabetes Grey Bruce; diagnostic imaging; emergency; laboratory; physiotherapy; spiritual care; & surgery.
Lance Thurston, President & CEO, Grey Bruce Health Services
519-376-2121

***Midland:* Georgian Bay General Hospital - Midland Site/Hôpital général de la baie Georgienne**
Affiliated with: North Simcoe Muskoka Local Health Integration Network
PO Box 760, 1112 St. Andrews Dr., Midland, ON L4R 4P4
Tel: 705-526-1300; *Fax:* 705-526-4491
www.gbgh.on.ca
Number of Beds: 69 acute care beds; 21 complex care beds; 15 rehabilitation beds; 6 ICU beds
Note: Programs & services include: acute & intensive care; emergency; inpatient & ambulatory care; obstetrics; regional complex continuing care; regional rehabilitation; & surgery.
Karen McGrath, President & CEO
Dr. Martin Veall, Chief of Medical Staff
Dianne Sofarelli, Chief Nursing Executive & Interim Vice-President, Patient Services

***Milton:* Milton District Hospital**
Halton Healthcare Services
Affiliated with: Mississauga Halton Local Health Integration Network
7030 Derry Rd., Milton, ON L9T 7H6
Tel: 905-878-2383; *Fax:* 905-878-7047
TTY: 905-878-7202
pr@haltonhealthcare.on.ca
www.haltonhealthcare.on.ca
Social Media: www.facebook.com/HaltonHealthcare; twitter.com/haltonhlthcare; www.youtube.com/channel/UC7xEU3Gq9890M-1Y0pz-Aog; www.linkedin.com/company/3186579
Year Founded: 1959
Number of Beds: 43 acute care beds; 20 complex continuing care beds
Population Served: 100000; *Number of Employees:* 379
Note: Programs & services include: acute hand program; asthma education; audiology & hearing aid services; breastfeeding clinics, drop-ins & prenatal classes; Butt Out Smoking Cessation program; cardiac rehabilitation program; complex continuing care; ConnectCARE; diagnostic imaging; emergency; Falls Intervention Clinic; Halton Diabetes Centre; inpatient rehabilitation; mammography; medical & surgical services; mental health urgent care clinic; obstetrics; outpatient rehabilitation; QuitCare; respiratory rehabilitation program; speech-language pathology; & Work-Fit Total Therapy Centre.
Denise Hardenne, President & CEO, Halton Healthcare
Dr. Lorne Martin, Chief of Staff, Halton Healthcare

***Mindemoya:* Manitoulin Health Centre**
Mindemoya Medical Clinic
PO Box 156, Mindemoya, ON P0P 1S0
Tel: 705-377-5371; *Fax:* 705-377-5372
www.manitoulinhealthcentre.com
Number of Beds: 14 beds
Derek Graham, CEO, Executive Director
1-705-368-2300, Fax: 705-368-3603, dgraham@mhc.on.ca

Minden: Haliburton Highlands Health Services - Minden Site (HHHS)
Affiliated with: Central East Local Health Integration Network
PO Box 30, 6 McPherson St, Minden, ON K0M 2K0
Tel: 705-286-2140; *Fax:* 705-286-6384
info@hhhs.on.ca
www.hhhs.on.ca
Note: Programs & services include: community programs; diabetes education; long-term care; mental health; physiotherapy; primary care; & ultrasound.
Varouj Eskedjian, President & CEO
705-457-2527, veskedjian@hhhs.on.ca
Celia OBrien, Chief Nursing Officer & Director, Care & Long-Term Care
705-286-2140, cobrien@hhhs.on.ca

Mississauga: The Credit Valley Hospital Trillium Health Partners
Affiliated with: Mississauga Halton Local Health Integration Network
2200 Eglinton Ave. West, Mississauga, ON L5M 2N1
Tel: 905-813-2200; *Fax:* 905-813-4444
Toll-Free: 877-292-4284
cvhpr@cvh.on.ca
trilliumhealthpartners.ca
Social Media: twitter.com/Trillium_Health; www.youtube.com/user/TrilliumHealth; www.linkedin.com/company/2949012
Year Founded: 1985
Number of Beds: 421 beds
Number of Employees: 3125
Note: Programs & services include: ambulatory care; asthma education; cardiac; diabetes education; diagnostic imaging; emergency; geriatric emergency; gynaecology; maternity; mental health; obstetrics; oncology; paediatrics; & renal services.
Michelle E. DiEmanuele, President & CEO, Trillium Health Partners
Dr. Dante Morra, Chief of Staff, Trillium Health Partners
Kathryn Haywood-Murray, Chief Nursing Executive & Senior Vice-President, Patient Care Services, Trillium Health Partners

Mississauga: Mississauga Hospital Trillium Health Partners
Affiliated with: Mississauga Halton Local Health Integration Network
Former Name: Queensway General Hospital
100 Queensway West, Mississauga, ON L5B 1B8
Tel: 905-848-7100; *Fax:* 905-848-7140
internetwebmaster@thc.on.ca
trilliumhealthpartners.ca
Social Media: twitter.com/Trillium_Health; www.youtube.com/user/TrilliumHealth; www.linkedin.com/company/2949012
Number of Beds: 751 beds
Note: Programs & services include: emergency care centre; birthing centre; critical care; intensive care; neurosurgery; stroke & cardiac care; sexual assault & domestic violence services; & women's & children's health (Colonel Harland Sanders Family Care Centre).
Michelle E. DiEmanuele, President & CEO, Trillium Health Partners
Dr. Dante Morra, Chief of Staff, Trillium Health Partners
Kathryn Haywood-Murray, Chief Nursing Executive & Senior Vice-President, Patient Care Services, Trillium Health Partners

Moose Factory: Weeneebayko Area Health Authority/Weeneebayko General Hospital (WAHA)
Affiliated with: North East Local Health Integration Network
PO Box 664, 19 Hospital Dr., Moose Factory, ON P0L 1W0
Tel: 705-658-4544; *Fax:* 705-658-4917
www.weeneebaykohealth.ca
Note: Programs & services include: emergency room; operating room; In-Patient; Out-Patient.
Bernie D. Schmidt, President & CEO
Dr. Gordon Green, Chief of Staff

Mount Forest: Louise Marshall Hospital North Wellington Health Care Corporation
Affiliated with: Waterloo Wellington Local Health Integration Network
630 Dublin St., Mount Forest, ON N0G 2L3
Tel: 519-323-2210; *Fax:* 519-323-3741
www.nwhealthcare.ca
Year Founded: 1923
Number of Beds: 15 inpatient beds
Population Served: 15000
Note: Programs & services include: anesthesiology; emergency; ENT; general surgery; gynecology; inpatient & outpatient care; internal medicine; neurology; obstetrics; pathology; pediatrics; radiology; specialist clinics; supportive diagnostic services; & urology.
Jerome Quenneville, President & CEO, North Wellington Health Care
jquenneville@nwhealthcare.ca
Dr. Simon Goodall, Chief of Staff, North Wellington Health Care

Napanee: Lennox & Addington County General Hospital
Affiliated with: South East Local Health Integration Network
8 Richmond Park Dr., Napanee, ON K7R 2Z4
Tel: 613-354-3301; *Fax:* 613-354-7157
www.lacgh.com
Number of Beds: 52 beds (24 active care, 2 surgical, 4 special care, 22 complex continuing care)
Number of Employees: 270
Note: Programs & services include: bone mineral densitometry; cardiopulmonary; chemotherapy; day surgery; diabetes education; diagnostic imaging; emergency; inpatient; laboratory; mammography; nutrition; occupational therapy; pharmacy; physiotherapy; & respiratory therapy.
Wayne Coveyduck, President & CEO
Dr. Kim Morrison, Chief of Staff

New Liskeard: Temiskaming Hospital
Affiliated with: North East Local Health Integration Network
421 Shepherdson Rd., New Liskeard, ON P0J 1P0
Tel: 705-647-8121; *Fax:* 705-647-5800
www.temiskaming-hospital.com
Year Founded: 1980
Number of Beds: 59 beds (40 acute, 11 chronic, 5 obstetric & 3 special care unit beds)
Population Served: 25,000; *Number of Employees:* 219
Note: Programs & services include: emergency; cardiac rehabilitation; diagnostic imaging (CT scans); laboratory; nutrition services; occupational therapy; pastoral care; pharmacy; physiotherapy; respiratory therapy; speech language pathology; telestroke program. Visiting specialists conduct services in neurology, nephrology, obstetrics and gynecology, orthotics, rehab/physical medicine, psychiatry, ophthalmology and pediatrics.
Margaret Beatty, President & CEO
705-647-1088, Fax: 705-647-5800, mbeatty@temiskaming-hospital.com
Dr. Khaled Elgadi, Chief of Staff
705-647-8121

Newbury: Four Counties Health Services (FCHS) Middlesex Hospital Alliance
Affiliated with: South West Local Health Integration Network
1824 Concession Dr., RR#3, Newbury, ON N0L 1Z0
Tel: 519-693-4441
admin@mha.tvh.ca
www.mhalliance.on.ca
Population Served: 23000
Note: Programs & services include: ambulatory care; community support; diabetes education; diagnostic imaging; emergency; medical surgical day services; & physiotherapy.
Todd Stepanuik, President & CEO, Middlesex Hospital Alliance
Dr. Gary Perkin, Chief of Staff, Middlesex Hospital Alliance

Newmarket: Southlake Regional Health Centre
Affiliated with: Central Local Health Integration Network
Former Name: York County Hospital
596 Davis Dr., Newmarket, ON L3Y 2P9
Tel: 905-895-4521; *Fax:* 905-830-5972
communications@southlakeregional.org
www.southlakeregional.org
Social Media: www.facebook.com/southlakeregionalhealthcentre; twitter.com/southlake_news; www.youtube.com/SouthlakeRHC
Year Founded: 1922
Number of Beds: 400 beds
Note: Programs & services include: chronic diseases clinics & programs; emergency; ethics; health information; maternal child; medicine; mental health; muscloskelatal; regional cancer program; regional cardiac care program; rehabilitation; surgery; & spiritual care.
Dr. Dave Williams, President & CEO
Dr. Steven Beatty, Chief of Staff
Paul Clarry, Vice-President, Clinical Support & Facilities
Anette Jones, Chief Nursing Officer & Vice-President, Clinical Experiences

Niagara Falls: Greater Niagara General Site Niagara Health System / Système de santé de Niagara
Affiliated with: Hamilton Niagara Haldimand Brant Local Health Integration Network
5546 Portage Rd., Niagara Falls, ON L2E 6X2
Tel: 905-378-4647
patientrelations@niagarahealth.on.ca
www.niagarahealth.on.ca
Social Media: www.facebook.com/NiagaraHealthSystem; twitter.com/niagarahealth; www.youtube.com/niagarahealthsystem
Year Founded: 1907
Number of Beds: 180+ beds
Note: Programs & services include: cardiology; complex care; critical care; diagnostic imaging; emergency; laboratory; medicine; off-site dialysis centre; Ontario Breast Screening Clinic; outpatient clinics; outpatient mental health; regional geriatric assessment; regional stroke services; surgery; & pharmacy.
Dr. Suzanne Johnston, President, Niagara Health System
Suzanne.Johnston@niagarahealth.on.ca
Dr. Kevin Smith, Chief Executive Officer, Niagara Health System
Kevin.Smith@niagarahealth.on.ca
Derek McNally, Chief Nursing Executive, Executive Vice-President, Clinical Services & Executive Lead, Greater Niagara
Derek.McNally@niagarahealth.on.ca
Linda Boich, Vice-President, Patient Services & Strategy, Niagara Health System
Linda.Boich@niagarahealth.on.ca

Niagara on the Lake: Niagara-on-the-Lake Site Niagara Health System / Système de santé de Niagara
Affiliated with: Hamilton Niagara Haldimand Brant Local Health Integration Network
176 Wellington St., Niagara on the Lake, ON L0S 1J0
Tel: 905-378-4647; *Fax:* 905-468-7690
patientrelations@niagarahealth.on.ca
www.niagarahealth.on.ca
Social Media: www.facebook.com/NiagaraHealthSystem; twitter.com/niagarahealth; www.youtube.com/niagarahealthsystem
Year Founded: 1921
Note: Programs & services include: complex care; diagnostic imaging; & laboratory.
Dr. Suzanne Johnston, President, Niagara Health System
Suzanne.Johnston@niagarahealth.on.ca
Dr. Kevin Smith, Chief Executive Officer, Niagara Health System
Kevin.Smith@niagarahealth.on.ca

Nipigon: Nipigon District Memorial Hospital
Affiliated with: North West Local Health Integration Network
PO Box 37, 125 Hogan Rd., Nipigon, ON P0T 2J0
Tel: 807-887-3026; *Fax:* 807-887-2800
lenders@ndmh.ca
www.ndmh.ca
Number of Beds: 37 beds
Note: Services include acute and complex continuing care; emergency services; diagnostic imaging; physiotherapy; respite care; telehealth
Carl White, Chief Executive Officer
807-887-3026
Dr. John Jackson Hughes, Chief of Staff
Sonja Stephenson, Chief Nursing Officer

North Bay: North Bay Regional Health Centre (NBRHC)/Centre régional de santé de North Bay
Former Name: North Bay General Hospital; Northeast Mental Health Centre
PO Box 2500, 50 College Dr., North Bay, ON P1B 5A4
Tel: 705-474-8600; *Fax:* 705-495-7956
pr@nbrhc.on.ca
www.nbrhc.on.ca
Social Media: www.facebook.com/nbrhc; twitter.com/nbrhc; www.youtube.com/thenbrhc
Number of Beds: 420 beds
Note: The North Bay Regional Health Centre is the result of an amalgamation of the North Bay General Hospital & the Northeast Mental Health Centre, which occurred in 2010. The facility now offers acute, specialist & mental health services to North Bay & the surrounding communities.
Paul Heinrich, President & CEO

Oakville: Oakville-Trafalgar Memorial Hospital
Halton Healthcare Services
Affiliated with: Mississauga Halton Local Health Integration Network
327 Reynolds St., Oakville, ON L6J 3L7
Tel: 905-845-2571; *Fax:* 905-338-4636
TTY: 905-815-5111
pr@haltonhealthcare.on.ca
www.haltonhealthcare.on.ca
Social Media: www.facebook.com/HaltonHealthcare; twitter.com/haltonhlthcare; www.youtube.com/channel/UC7xEU3Gq9890M-1Y0pz-Aog; www.linkedin.com/company/3186579
Number of Beds: 233 acute care beds; 39 rehab beds; 39 complex continuing care beds
Population Served: 183000; *Number of Employees:* 2127
Note: The renovated new Oakville Hospital will be opening in December 2016.
Denise Hardenne, President & CEO, Halton Healthcare
Dr. Lorne Martin, Chief of Staff, Halton Healthcare
Susan Bisaillon, Interim COO, Oakville-Trafalgar Memorial Hospital
Dale Clement, COO, New Oakville Hospital & Clinical Integration

Orangeville: Headwaters Health Care Centre
Affiliated with: Central West Local Health Integration Network
Former Name: Headwaters Orangeville
100 Rolling Hills Dr., Orangeville, ON L9W 4X9
Tel: 519-941-2410; *Fax:* 519-942-0483
www.headwatershealth.ca
Year Founded: 1997
Number of Beds: 87 beds
Note: Programs & services include: ambulatory care; cardiac wellness; complex continuing care; critical care; CT scan; diabetes education; dialysis; digital mammography; emergency; endoscopy; laboratory; medicine; nuclear medicine; occupational therapy; oncology; palliative; physiotherapy; sexual assault/domestic violence; speech-language pathology; surgical; ultrasound; women & children's health; & x-ray.
Liz Ruegg, President & CEO
519-941-2702, lruegg@headwatershealth.ca
Dr. Somaiah Ahmed, Chief of Staff & Vice-President, Medical Affairs
519-941-2702, sahmed@headwatershealth.ca

Orillia: Orillia Soldiers' Memorial Hospital (OSMH)
Affiliated with: North Simcoe Muskoka Local Health Integration Network
170 Colborne St. West, Orillia, ON L3V 2Z3
Tel: 705-325-2201; *Fax:* 705-325-7394
TTY: 705-325-1231
info@osmh.on.ca
www.osmh.on.ca
Social Media: www.facebook.com/TheOrilliaSoldiersMemorialHospital; twitter.com/OSMH_News; www.youtube.com/OSMHVideos; www.linkedin.com/company/orillia-soldiers-memorial-hospital
Number of Beds: 230 inpatient beds
Number of Employees: 1200
Note: Programs & services include: cancer care; chronic disease management; clinical nutrition services; complex continuing care; critical care; diagnostic imaging; emergency; geriatric day hospital; infection prevention & control; laboratory; maternal, child & youth; mental health services; rehabilitation; regional kidney care program; surgical services; & telemedicine. Has 300 physicians on staff.
Pat Campbell, President & CEO
ceo@osmh.on.ca
Dr. Nancy Merrow, Chief of Medical Staff & Vice-President, Medical Affairs
Cheryl Harrison, Chief Nursing Executive & Vice-President, Patient Services

Oshawa: Lakeridge Health - Oshawa Site
Affiliated with: Central East Local Health Integration Network
Former Name: Oshawa General Hospital
1 Hospital Ct., Oshawa, ON L1G 2B9
Tel: 905-576-8711
www.lakeridgehealth.on.ca
Social Media: www.facebook.com/LakeridgeHealth; twitter.com/lakeridgehealth; www.youtube.com/lakeridgehealth
Number of Beds: 363 beds
Note: Programs & services include: ambulatory & rehabilitation centre; Central East Regional Cardiac Care Program; child, youth & family program; community respiratory services; dialysis unit; eating disorders program; emergency department; GAIN geriatric clinic; interact treatment program; mental health day treatment program; Ontario Breast Screening Program; paediatric feeding/swallowing clinic; pain clinic; palliative care; Pinewood Centre (alcohol & addictions); & positive care clinic.
Kevin Empey, President & CEO, Lakeridge Health
905-576-8711
Dr. Tony Stone, Chief of Staff, Lakeridge Health
905-576-8711
Lisa Shiozaki, Chief Operating Officer & Chief Nursing Executive, Lakeridge Health
905-576-8711

Ottawa: Children's Hospital of Eastern Ontario (CHEO)
Affiliated with: Champlain Local Health Integration Network
401 Smyth Rd., Ottawa, ON K1H 8L1
Tel: 613-737-7600 *Toll-Free:* 866-736-2436
webmaster@cheo.on.ca
www.cheo.on.ca
Social Media: www.facebook.com/CHEOkids; twitter.com/cheohospital; www.youtube.com/user/CHEOvideos
Year Founded: 1974
Number of Beds: 112 pediatric, oncology, adolescent medicine, & surgery beds; 25 psychiatry beds; 20 neonatal intensive care unit beds; 10 intensive care unit beds
Number of Employees: 1796
Note: Programs & services include: Autism Program of Eastern Ontario; Centre for Healthy Active Living; child & youth protection service; cleft lip & palate craniofacial clinic; diabetes clinic; Eastern Ontario Regional Genetics Program; inpatient psychiatric units; Kaitlin Atkinson Family Resource Library; mental health outpatient' regional eating disorders program; regional psychiatric emergency service for children & youth; sexually assaulted youth counselling; social work; teen health centre; & Youth Net / Réseau Ado. Has 271 physicians on staff.
Alex Munter, President & CEO
Dr. Lindy Samson, Chief of Staff
Susan Richardson, Vice-President, Patient Care

Ottawa: Hôpital Montfort
Affiliée à: Champlain Local Health Integration Network
713, ch Montréal, Ottawa, ON K1K 0T2
Tél: 613-746-4621 *Ligne sans frais:* 866-670-4621
montfort@montfort.on.ca
www.hopitalmontfort.com
Média social: www.facebook.com/hopital.montfort; twitter.com/hopitalmontfort; www.youtube.com/user/telehopitalmontfort; www.linkedin.com/company/hopital-montfort
Nombre de lits: 289 lits
Note: Services: centre familiale de naissance; medicine; programme de cancérologie; programme de santé mentale; services diagnostiques incluant imagerie diagnostique et laboratoire du sommeil; services de santé cardiovasculaire et pulmonaire; services thérapeutiques y inclus la physiothérapie et clinique pour les troubles de la communication; soins ambulatoires; soins aux malades en phase critique y inclus les soins intensive et soins d'urgence; et soins palliatifs.
Dr. Bernard Leduc, Président-directeur général
Dr. Guy Moreau, Médecin-chef
Suzanne Robichaud, Chef de la pratique infirmière et vice-présidente, Services cliniques

Ottawa: The Ottawa Hospital - Civic Campus/L'Hôpital d'Ottawa
Affiliated with: Champlain Local Health Integration Network
1053 Carling Ave., Ottawa, ON K1Y 4E9
Tel: 613-722-7000
TTY: 613-761-4024
www.ottawahospital.on.ca
Social Media: www.facebook.com/OttawaHospital; twitter.com/OttawaHospital; www.youtube.com/user/TheOttawaHospital
Year Founded: 1845
Number of Beds: 1,122 beds across the system
Note: Programs & services include: cardiology; emergency; family health team; Mohs Surgery Clinic; neurosciences; Regional Geriatric Program for Eastern Ontario; spinal surgery; trauma services; University of Ottawa Skills & Simulation Centre (uOSSC); vascular surgery; weight management clinic - Bariatric Centre of Excellence; & women's breast health centre. Total physicians across hospital system: 1,300.
Dr. Jack Kitts, President & CEO
613-761-4800, jbkitts@toh.ca
Dr. Jeffrey Turnbull, Chief of Staff
613-737-8459, jeturnbull@toh.ca
Dr. Debra A. Bournes, Chief Nursing Executive & Vice-President, Clinical Programs
613-737-8899, dbournes@toh.ca

Ottawa: The Ottawa Hospital - General Campus/L'Hôpital d'Ottawa
Affiliated with: Champlain Local Health Integration Network
501 Smyth Rd., Ottawa, ON K1H 8L6
Tel: 613-722-7000
TTY: 613-761-4024
www.ottawahospital.on.ca
Social Media: www.facebook.com/OttawaHospital; twitter.com/OttawaHospital; www.youtube.com/user/TheOttawaHospital
Year Founded: 1845
Number of Beds: 1,122 beds across the system
Specialties: Cardiovascular
Note: Programs & services include: bone marrow transplant; chest diseases centre; emergency; regional cancer program; rehabilitation centre; robotic surgery; thoracic surgery; total joint replacement; & the University of Ottawa Eye Institute. Total physicians across hospital system: 1,300.
Dr. Jack Kitts, President & CEO
613-761-4800, jbkitts@toh.ca
Dr. Jeffrey Turnbull, Chief of Staff
613-737-8459, jeturnbull@toh.ca
Dr. Debra A. Bournes, Chief Nursing Executive & Vice-President, Clinical Programs
613-737-8899, dbournes@toh.ca

Ottawa: The Ottawa Hospital - Riverside Campus/L'Hôpital d'Ottawa
Affiliated with: Champlain Local Health Integration Network
1967 Riverside Dr., Ottawa, ON K1H 7W9
Tel: 613-722-7000
TTY: 613-761-4024
www.ottawahospital.on.ca
Social Media: www.facebook.com/OttawaHospital; twitter.com/OttawaHospital; www.youtube.com/user/TheOttawaHospital
Year Founded: 1845
Number of Beds: 1,122 beds across the system
Note: Programs & services include: arthritis centre; eye care centre; family health team; Foustanellas Endocrine & Diabetes Centre; nephrology; & Shirley E. Greenberg Women's Health Centre. Total physicians across hospital system: 1,300. Affiliated with the University of Ottawa.
Dr. Jack Kitts, President & CEO
613-761-4800, jbkitts@toh.ca
Dr. Jeffrey Turnbull, Chief of Staff
613-737-8459, jeturnbull@toh.ca
Dr. Debra A. Bournes, Chief Nursing Executive & Vice-President, Clinical Programs
613-737-8899, dbournes@toh.ca

Ottawa: Queensway Carleton Hospital (QCH)
Affiliated with: Champlain Local Health Integration Network
3045 Baseline Rd., Ottawa, ON K2H 8P4
Tel: 613-721-2000 *Toll-Free:* 888-824-9111
www.qch.on.ca
Social Media: www.facebook.com/caregrowswest
Year Founded: 1976
Number of Beds: 264 beds
Population Served: 400000; *Number of Employees:* 1955
Note: Programs & services include: childbirth centre; emergency; geriatric services; medical & surgical services; mental health; & rehabilitation. Has 276 physicians & 8 midwives on staff.
Tom Schonberg, President & CEO
Dr. Andrew Falconer, Chief of Staff
Leah Levesque, Chief Nursing Officer & Vice-President, Patient Care

Owen Sound: Owen Sound Hospital
Grey Bruce Health Services
Affiliated with: South West Local Health Integration Network
PO Box 1800, 1800 - 8th St. East, Owen Sound, ON N4K 6M9
Tel: 519-376-2121
web@gbhs.on.ca
www.gbhs.on.ca
Social Media: twitter.com/greybrucehealth
Number of Beds: 244 beds
Note: Regional referral centre for Grey & Bruce counties. Programs & services include: acute care; acute inpatient rehabilitation; ambulatory care department; cardiac rehabilitation program; critical care; Diabetes Grey Bruce; diagnostic imaging department; dialysis; electro diagnostics; emergency; Grey Bruce District Stroke Centre; health centre pharmacy; mental health; occupational therapy; physiotherapy; respiratory therapy; restorative care unit; sleep lab; social work; spiritual care; surgery; & women & child care.

Lance Thurston, President & CEO, Grey Bruce Health Services
519-376-2121
Dr. Brendan Mulroy, Chief of Staff, Grey Bruce Health Services
519-376-2121

***Palmerston:* Palmerston & District Hospital**
North Wellington Health Care Corporation
Affiliated with: Waterloo Wellington Local Health Integration Network
500 Whites Rd., Palmerston, ON N0G 2P0
Tel: 519-343-2030; *Fax:* 519-343-3821
www.nwhealthcare.ca
Year Founded: 1908
Number of Beds: 15 inpatient beds
Population Served: 15000
Note: Programs & services include: anesthesiology; emergency; ENT; general surgery; gynecology; inpatient & outpatient care; internal medicine; obstetrics; pathology; radiology; specialist clinics; & supportive diagnostic services.
Jerome Quenneville, President & CEO, North Wellington Health Care
jquenneville@nwhealthcare.ca
Dr. Simone Goodallille, Chief of Staff, North Wellington Health Care

***Paris:* Willett Hospital**
Brant Community Healthcare System
Affiliated with: Hamilton Niagara Haldimand Brant Local Health Integration Network
Also Known As: The Willett
238 Grand River St. North, Paris, ON N3L 2N7
Tel: 519-442-2251
www.bchsys.org
Social Media: www.facebook.com/245452318811922; twitter.com/BCHSYS; www.youtube.com/user/bchsys2011; www.linkedin.com/company/brantford-general-hospital
Year Founded: 1922
Number of Beds: A total of 350 beds are part of The Brant Community Healthcare System, which consists of the Willett Hospital & the Brantford General Hospital
Specialties: Urgent care
Note: Programs & services include: diagnostic imaging; fitness centres & programs; rehabilitation (outpatient); walk-in medical clinics & urgent care. Brant Community Healthcare System is affiliated with the Michael G. DeGroote School of Medicine, McMaster University.
James Hornell, President & CEO, Brant Community Healthcare System
Dr. Christopher O'brien, President, Medical Staff
Lina Rinaldi, Chief Operating Officer & Chief Nurse Executive
Dr. David Cameron, Chief of Staff & Vice-President

***Pembroke:* Pembroke Regional Hospital**
Affiliated with: Champlain Local Health Integration Network
Former Name: Pembroke General Hospital
705 MacKay St., Pembroke, ON K8A 1G8
Tel: 613-732-2811; *Fax:* 613-732-9986
pr@pemreghos.org
www.pemgenhos.org
Info Line: 866-996-0991
Social Media: www.youtube.com/user/pembrokeregionalhosp
Number of Beds: 203 beds
Note: Programs & services include: acute mental health; ambulatory clinics; clinical ethics; community mental health; diabetes education & nutrition; diagnostic imaging; dialysis; emergency/ICU; infection prevention & control; laboratory; maternal & child care; medical; rehabiliation (inpatient & outpatient); respiratory therapy; social work; spiritual care; & surgery.
Pierre Noel, President & CEO
pierre.noel@pemreghos.org
Dr. Michael Ferri, Chief of Staff & Vice-President, Medical Affairs
michael.ferri@pemreghos.org
Francois Lemaire, Chief Nursing Executive & Vice-President, Patient Services - Acute Care
francois.lemaire@pemreghos.org

***Penetanguishene:* Georgian Bay General Hospital - Penetanguishene Site/Hôpital général de la baie Georgienne**
Affiliated with: North Simcoe Muskoka Local Health Integration Network
25 Jeffery St., Penetanguishene, ON L9M 1K6
Tel: 705-549-7431; *Fax:* 705-549-4031
www.nsha.on.ca
Note: Programs & services include: dialysis unit; Georgian Bay Cancer Support Centre; & Hospice Huronia. There is no emergency service at this location.
Karen McGrath, President & CEO
Dr. Martin Veall, Chief of Medical Staff

Dianne Sofarelli, Chief Nursing Officer & Interim Vice-President, Patient Services

***Perth:* Perth & Smiths Falls District Hospital - Perth Site**
Also Known As: Great War Memorial Site
33 Drummond St. West, Perth, ON K7H 2K1
Tel: 613-267-1500; *Fax:* 613-264-0365
webinquiry@psfdh.on.ca
www.psfdh.on.ca
Number of Beds: 85 beds
Note: Programs & services include: assistive devices program; breast screening centre; clinics (obstetrical, pain, pediatric, respirology, orthopedics, general surgery & internal medicine); day hospital; diagnostic imaging; early language; emergency; general medicine; health education; internal medicine; laboratory; sexual assault support & domestic violence program; oncology/palliative care; orthopedics; pharmacy; rehabilitation program; stroke prevention; & urology.

***Peterborough:* Peterborough Regional Health Centre (PRHC)**
Affiliated with: Central East Local Health Integration Network
1 Hospital Dr., Peterborough, ON K9J 7C6
Tel: 705-743-2121; *Fax:* 705-876-5120
TTY: 705-876-5141
info@prhc.on.ca
www.prhc.on.ca
Social Media: twitter.com/PRHC1; www.youtube.com/user/PRHChospital; www.linkedin.com/company/1357436
Number of Beds: 494 beds
Population Served: 150000
Note: Programs & services include: diagnostic imaging; emergency; laboratory; medicine; mental health; nutrition; outpatient; rehabilitation; pharmacy; social work; surgery; & woman & child.
Dr. Peter McLaughlin, Interim President/CEO & Chief Medical Officer
Dr. Nancy Martin-Ronson, CNE, CIO & Vice-President, Professional & Diagnostic Services

***Petrolia:* Charlotte Eleanor Englehart Hospital (CEEH)**
Bluewater Health
Affiliated with: Erie St. Clair Local Health Integration Network
Former Name: Charlotte Eleanor Englehart Hospital
450 Blanche St., Petrolia, ON N0N 1R0
Tel: 519-882-4325; *Fax:* 519-882-3711
www.bluewaterhealth.ca
Social Media: www.facebook.com/bluewaterhealth; www.youtube.com/bluewaterhealth
Year Founded: 1911
Number of Beds: 326 beds (total for both Bluewater sites)
Note: Programs & services include: acute care; ambulatory care; continuing care; diagnostic imaging; emergency; internal medicine; laboratory services; & primary care.
Sue Denomy, President & CEO, Bluewater Health
519-464-4400, sdenomy@bluewaterhealth.ca

***Picton:* QHC Prince Edward County Memorial Hospital**
Quinte Health Care
Affiliated with: South East Local Health Integration Network
PO Box 1900, 403 Main St. East, Picton, ON K0K 2T0
Tel: 613-476-1008; *Fax:* 613-476-8600
www.qhc.on.ca
Social Media: www.facebook.com/173689537296; twitter.com/QuinteHealth; www.youtube.com/QuinteHealthCare
Year Founded: 1959
Number of Beds: 15 beds
Note: Programs & services include: adult & geriatric psychiatry; CCAC; emergency; hospice; laboratory; outpatient clinics; pharmacy; physiotherapy; primary care medical inpatients; Prince Edward Family Health Team (PEFHT); radiology; & surgery.
Mary Clare Egberts, President & CEO, Quinte Health Care
Dr. Dick Zoutman, Chief of Staff, Quinte Health Care
Katherine Stansfield, Chief Nursing Officer & Vice-President

***Port Colborne:* Port Colborne Site**
Niagara Health System / Système de santé de Niagara
Affiliated with: Hamilton Niagara Haldimand Brant Local Health Integration Network
260 Sugarloaf St., Port Colborne, ON L3K 2N7
Tel: 905-378-4647
patientrelations@niagarahealth.on.ca
www.niagarahealth.on.ca
Social Media: www.facebook.com/NiagaraHealthSystem; twitter.com/niagarahealth; www.youtube.com/niagarahealthsystem
Year Founded: 1951
Number of Beds: 46 beds inpatient beds for complex continuing care; 35 beds at the New Port Centre for addiction recovery
Note: Programs & services include: addictions services; complex care; diagnostic imaging; laboratory; Ontario Breast Screening Clinic; outpatient clinics; & urgent care.
Dr. Suzanne Johnston, President, Niagara Health System
Suzanne.Johnston@niagarahealth.on.ca
Dr. Kevin Smith, Chief Executive Officer, Niagara Health System
Kevin.Smith@niagarahealth.on.ca
Patty Welychka, Chief Nursing Officer, Director, Surgical Services, & Executive Lead, Port Colborne
Patty.Welychka@niagarahealth.on.ca

***Port Perry:* Lakeridge Health - Port Perry Site**
Affiliated with: Central East Local Health Integration Network
451 Paxton St., Port Perry, ON L9L 1A8
Tel: 905-985-7321; *Fax:* 905-985-5827
www.lakeridgehealth.on.ca
Social Media: www.facebook.com/LakeridgeHealth; twitter.com/lakeridgehealth; www.youtube.com/lakeridgehealth
Note: Programs & services include: ambulatory rehabilitation centres/musculoskeletal physiotherapy clinics; diabetes education; & emergency.
Kevin Empey, President & CEO, Lakeridge Health
905-576-8711
Dr. Tony Stone, Chief of Staff, Lakeridge Health
905-576-8711
Lisa Shiozaki, Chief Operating Officer & Chief Nursing Executive, Lakeridge Health
905-576-8711

***Rainy River:* Rainy River Health Centre**
Riverside Health Care Facilities Inc.
Affiliated with: North West Local Health Integration Network
115 - 4th St., Rainy River, ON P0W 1L0
Tel: 807-274-3261; *Fax:* 807-852-3565
www.riversidehealthcare.ca
Number of Beds: 24 beds
Note: Programs & services include: emergency; diagnostic imaging; acute and long term care facility

***Red Lake:* Red Lake Margaret Cochenour Memorial Hospital**
Affiliated with: North West Local Health Integration Network
Also Known As: Red Lake Hospital
PO Box 5005, 51 Hwy. 105, Red Lake, ON P0V 2M0
Tel: 807-727-2066; *Fax:* 807-727-2923
www.redlakehospital.ca
Year Founded: 1973
Number of Beds: 14 acute care beds, 4 long term care beds
Note: Emergency services; lab; radiology & ultrasound; rehabilitation; sugery; endoscopy; nutritional services; chemotherapy; telehealth.
Angela Bishop, President & CEO
807-727-3800, ceo@redlakehospital.ca
Dr. Wojciech Anoil, Chief of Staff
Rebecca Ross, Chief Nursing Officer

***Renfrew:* Renfrew Victoria Hospital**
Affiliated with: Champlain Local Health Integration Network
Also Known As: RVH
499 Raglan St. North, Renfrew, ON K7V 1P6
Tel: 613-432-4851; *Fax:* 613-432-8649
www.renfrewhosp.com
Social Media: www.facebook.com/renfrewvictoriahospital
Year Founded: 1897
Number of Beds: 101 beds
Number of Employees: 450
Note: Programs & services include: ambulatory; counselling; diagnostic; emergency; inpatient; outreach programs; & rehabilitation. Affiliated with Algonquin College & Cambrian College.
Randy Penney, President & CEO
613-432-4851

Christine Ferguson, Vice-President, Patient Care Services
613-432-4851

Richards Landing: Blind River District Health Centre - Matthews Memorial Hospital Site/Pavillion Santé du District de Blind River
Affiliated with: North East Local Health Integration Network
PO Box 188, 1180 Richards St., Richards Landing, ON P0R 1J0
Tel: 705-356-2265; *Fax:* 705-356-1220
webinfo@brdhc.on.ca
www.brdhc.on.ca
Note: Programs & services include: chemotherapy; diagnostic imaging; emergency; laboratory; & surgery.
Gaston Lavigne, Chief Executive Officer
Dr. Marc Bradford, Chief of Staff
Mary Ellen Luukkonen, Chief Nursing Officer & Director, Clinical Services

Richmond Hill: Mackenzie Richmond Hill Hospital
Mackenzie Health
Affiliated with: Central Local Health Integration Network
Former Name: York Central Hospital
10 Trench St., Richmond Hill, ON L4C 4Z3
Tel: 905-883-1212; *Fax:* 905-883-2455
mackenziehealth.ca
Social Media: www.facebook.com/MackenzieHealth; twitter.com/mackenziehealth; www.youtube.com/user/MackenzieHealthVideo; www.linkedin.com/company/mackenzie-health
Number of Beds: 248 acute care beds; 168 long-term care beds; 84 complex continuing care beds; 22 integrated stroke beds (all Mackenzie Health sites)
Number of Employees: 2403
Note: Has 415 physicians on staff.
Altaf Stationwala, President & CEO, Mackenzie Health
Dr. Steven Jackson, Chief of Staff, Mackenzie Health

Sarnia: Bluewater Health
Affiliated with: Erie St. Clair Local Health Integration Network
Former Name: Charlotte Eleanor Englehart Hospital; Sarnia General Hospital; St. Joseph's Health
Norman Site, 89 Norman St., Sarnia, ON N7T 6S3
Tel: 519-464-4400; *Fax:* 519-336-4407
www.bluewaterhealth.ca
Social Media: www.facebook.com/bluewaterhealth; www.youtube.com/bluewaterhealth
Year Founded: 2002
Number of Beds: 326 beds (total for both Bluewater sites)
Number of Employees: 2500
Note: Programs & services include: ambulatory care; bone density; Cancer Care Assessment & Treatment Centre; cancer clinic; chronic disease transition clinic; communication disorders; complex continuing care; coronary care; CT scan; day hospital; day surgery; diabetes & clinical nutrition; diagnostic imaging; dialysis; district stroke centre; eating disorders; ECG/EKG; emergency; EMG/EEG; endoscopy; infection prevention; inpatient medicine; inpatient rehabilitation; surgery; intensive care; laboratory; mammography/Ontario Breast Screening Program; maternal/infant/child; mental health & addictions; MRI; nuclear medicine; nutrition; occupational therapy; outpatient rehabilitation; palliative care; Pat Mailloux Eye Centre; physiotherapy; pre-admission surgical clinic; recreation therapy; respiratory therapy; rural health; Sarnia-Lambton District Stroke Centre & Secondary Stroke Prevention Clinic; sexual/domestic assault treatment; social work; spiritual care; surgery; telemedicine; ultrasound; & x-ray.
Sue Denomy, President & CEO
519-464-4400, sdenomy@bluewaterhealth.ca
Dr. Mark Taylor, Chief, Professional Staff; Vice-President, Medical Affairs; & Chief, Quality
519-464-4400, marktaylor@bluewaterhealth.ca
Michael Lapaine, Chief Operating Officer & Vice-President, Operations
519-464-4400, mlapaine@bluewaterhealth.ca
Barb O'Neil, Chief Nursing Executive & Chief, Interprofessional Practice & Organizational Dev.
519-464-4400, boneil@bluewaterhealth.ca
Kim Bossy, Chief, Communications & Public Affairs
519-464-4400, kbossy@bluewaterhealth.ca
Lynda Robinson, Vice-President, Operations
519-464-4400, lrobinson@bluewaterhealth.ca

Sault Ste Marie: Sault Area Hospital (SAH)
Affiliated with: North East Local Health Integration Network
750 Great Northern Rd., Sault Ste Marie, ON P6B 0A8
Tel: 705-759-3434; *Fax:* 705-541-7810
publicaffairs@sah.on.ca
www.sah.on.ca
Number of Beds: 293 beds
Population Served: 115,000; *Number of Employees:* 1850
Note: Programs & services include: emergency & critical care; medicine; surgery; obstetrics, maternity & pediatrics; mental health & addiction; complex continuing care; rehabilitation
Ron Gagnon, President & CEO
Dr. Heather O'Brien, Chief of Staff & Medical Affairs
Lori Bertrand, Chief Nursing Officer

Seaforth: Seaforth Community Hospital
Huron Perth Healthcare Alliance
Affiliated with: South West Local Health Integration Network
PO Box 99, 24 Centennial Dr., Seaforth, ON N0K 1W0
Tel: 519-527-1650; *Fax:* 519-527-8414
administration@hpha.ca
www.hpha.ca
Year Founded: 1965
Number of Beds: 20 beds
Note: Programs & services include: adult speech therapy services; ambulatory clinics; community stroke rehabilitation team; complex continuing care; emergency; imaging; Huron Perth Diabetes Education Program; laboratory; medicine; occupational therapy; physiotherapy; & social work.
Andrew Williams, CEO, HPHA
519-272-8202, andrew.williams@hpha.ca
Dr. Laurel Moore, Chief of Staff, HPHA
519-272-8210, dr.laurel.moore@hpha.ca
Anne Campbell, Site Administrator
519-272-8210, anne.campbell@hpha.ca

Simcoe: Norfolk General Hospital
Affiliated with: Hamilton Niagara Haldimand Brant Local Health Integration Network
365 West St., Simcoe, ON N3Y 1T7
Tel: 519-426-0130; *Fax:* 519-429-6998
www.ngh.on.ca
Social Media: www.facebook.com/NGHSimcoe; twitter.com/NorfolkGeneralH
Number of Beds: 106 beds (including 45 chronic beds)
Note: Programs & services include: breast screening; complex care; continence care; detox (Holmes House); diabetes; diagnostic imaging; emergency; ICU; infection control; laboratory; obesity & metabolic surgery; obstetrics; palliative care; rehabilitation; respiratory; social work; stroke clinic; surgery; & surgical day care & endoscopy.
Kelly Isfan, President & CEO
519-426-0130, Fax: 519-429-6998
Gail Johnson, Vice-President, Patient Care
519-426-0130

Sioux Lookout: Sioux Lookout Meno Ya Win Health Centre (SLMHC)
Affiliated with: North West Local Health Integration Network
PO Box 909, 1 Meno Ya Win Way, Sioux Lookout, ON P8T 1B4
Tel: 807-737-3030
info@slmhc.on.ca
www.slmhc.on.ca
Number of Beds: 60 beds
Note: Primary health care services including a broad range of basic and some specialist hospital services, specialized community based programs and services responding to population health needs (withdrawal management, suicide, TB, etc.), long term care and integrated traditional and modern medicine. Serves Nishnawbe-Aski communities north of Sioux Lookout, the Treaty # 3 community of Lac Seul First Nation, as well as to residents of Pickle Lake and Savant Lake.
David Murray, President & CEO
dmurray@slmhc.on.ca
Dr. Teresa O'Driscoll, Chief of Staff
Heather Shepherd, Chief Nursing Executive

Smiths Falls: Perth & Smiths Falls District Hospital - Smiths Falls Site
Affiliated with: South East Local Health Integration Network
60 Cornelia St. West, Smiths Falls, ON K7A 2H9
Tel: 613-283-2330; *Fax:* 613-283-8990
webinquiry@psfdh.on.ca
www.psfdh.on.ca
Year Founded: 1995
Number of Beds: 97 beds
Population Served: 44000
Note: Programs & services include: assistive devices program; clinics; dialysis; diagnostic imaging; emergency; general medicine; general surgery; internal medicine; laboratory; obstetrics/gynaecology; oncology/palliative care; orthopedics; pharmacy; sexual assault support & domestic violence program; & urology.
Beverley McFarlane, President & CEO
613-283-2330, bmcfarlane@psfdh.on.ca
Dr. Peter Roney, Chief of Staff

Smooth Rock Falls: Hôpital de Smooth Rock Falls Hospital (HSRFH)
Affiliated with: North East Local Health Integration Network
Also Known As: SRF Hospital
PO Box 219, 107 Kelly Road, Smooth Rock Falls, ON P0L 2B0
Tel: 705-338-2781; *Fax:* 705-338-4410
info@srfhosp.ca
www.srfhosp.ca
Number of Beds: 14 acute care beds, 23 long term care beds
Number of Employees: 85
Note: Programs & services include: acute care; long term care; emergency services; laboratory; physiotheraphy; diagnostic imaging
Fabien L. Hébert, CEO
705-338-3212, fhebert@srfhosp.ca

Southampton: Southampton Hospital
Grey Bruce Health Services
Affiliated with: South West Local Health Integration Network
340 High St., Southampton, ON N0H 2L0
Tel: 519-797-3230
web@gbhs.on.ca
www.gbhs.on.ca
Social Media: twitter.com/greybrucehealth
Number of Beds: 16 acute care beds
Note: Programs & services include: acute care; ambulatory care; Diabetes Grey Bruce; diagnostic imaging; emergency; laboratory; physiotherapy; spiritual care; & surgery.
Lance Thurston, President & CEO, Grey Bruce Health Services
519-376-2121

St Catharines: St. Catharines General Site
Niagara Health System / Système de santé de Niagara
Affiliated with: Hamilton Niagara Haldimand Brant Local Health Integration Network
1200 Fourth Ave., St Catharines, ON L2S 0A9
Tel: 905-378-4647
patientrelations@niagarahealth.on.ca
www.niagarahealth.on.ca
Social Media: www.facebook.com/NiagaraHealthSystem; twitter.com/niagarahealth; www.youtube.com/niagarahealthsystem
Year Founded: 1865
Number of Beds: 375 beds
Note: Programs & services include: cardiology; children's health; critical care; diagnostic imaging; emergency & urgent care; kidney care; laboratory; medicine; mental health & addictions; Ontario Breast Screening Clinic; outpatient services; pharmacy; surgery; Walker Family Cancer Centre; women's & babies health.
Dr. Suzanne Johnston, President, Niagara Health System
Suzanne.Johnston@niagarahealth.on.ca
Dr. Kevin Smith, Chief Executive Officer, Niagara Health System
Kevin.Smith@niagarahealth.on.ca
Derek McNally, Chief Nursing Executive, Executive Vice-President, Clinical Services & Executive Lead, St. Catharines
Derek.McNally@niagarahealth.on.ca

St Marys: St. Marys Memorial Hospital
Huron Perth Healthcare Alliance
Affiliated with: South West Local Health Integration Network
PO Box 940, 267 Queen St. West, St Marys, ON N4X 1B6
Tel: 519-284-1332; *Fax:* 519-284-8324
administration@hpha.ca
www.hpha.ca
Year Founded: 1950
Number of Beds: 20 beds
Note: Programs & services include: ambulatory clinics; complex continuing care; emergency; Huron Perth Diabetes Education Program; laboratory; medicine unit; occupational therapy; physiotherapy; social work; & spiritual care.
Andrew Williams, CEO, HPHA
519-272-8202, andrew.williams@hpha.ca
Dr. Laurel Moore, Chief Of Staff, HPHA
519-272-8210, dr.laurel.moore@hpha.ca

Marie Ormerod, Site Administrator
519-272-8210, marie.ormerod@hpha.ca

St Thomas: St. Thomas-Elgin General Hospital
Affiliated with: South West Local Health Integration Network
189 Elm St., St Thomas, ON N5R 5C4
Tel: 519-631-2020; *Fax:* 519-631-1825
TTY: 519-631-7789
publicrelations@stegh.on.ca
www.stegh.on.ca
Social Media: www.facebook.com/804890622863889; twitter.com/stegh_cares

Year Founded: 1954
Number of Beds: 156 beds
Number of Employees: 800
Note: Programs & services include: acute medical unit; cardiac intensive care; clinical nutrition; continuing care; diagnostic imaging; education programs; emergency; laboratory; mental health care; pastoral care; surgery; & women & children's program.
Paul Collins, President & CEO
pcollins@stegh.on.ca
Dr. Nancy Whitmore, Vice-President & Chief of Staff
Karen Davies, Vice-President & Chief Nursing Officer

Stratford: Stratford General Hospital
Huron Perth Healthcare Alliance
Affiliated with: South West Local Health Integration Network
46 General Hospital Dr., Stratford, ON N5A 2Y6
Tel: 519-272-8210; *Fax:* 519-271-7137
administration@hpha.ca
www.hpha.ca

Year Founded: 1896
Number of Beds: 135 beds
Note: Programs & services include: ambulatory clinics; cardio respiratory; chemotherapy; complex continuing care & rehabilitation; critical care (ICU & telemetry); dialysis; emergency; Huron Perth Diabetes Education Program; Huron Perth District Stroke Centre; imaging; inpatient mental health services; laboratory services; maternal child unit; medicine; social work; spiritual care; & surgery.
Andrew Williams, CEO, HPHA
519-272-8202, andrew.williams@hpha.ca
Dr. Laurel Moore, Chief of Staff, HPHA
519-272-8210, dr.laurel.moore@hpha.ca
Ken Haworth, Site Administrator
519-272-8210, ken.haworth@hpha.ca

Strathroy: Strathroy Middlesex General Hospital
Middlesex Hospital Alliance
Affiliated with: South West Local Health Integration Network
395 Carrie St., Strathroy, ON N7G 3J4
Tel: 519-245-5295; *Fax:* 519-245-0366
admin@mha.tvh.ca
www.mhalliance.on.ca

Year Founded: 1914
Number of Beds: 54 beds
Population Served: 35000; *Number of Employees:* 300
Note: Programs & services include: ambulatory care clinics; diabetes education program; diagnostic imaging; emergency; intensive care; medical inpatient unit; medical surgical inpatient unit; obstetrics inpatient unit; occupational therapy; physiotherapy; speech-language pathology; & surgery.
Todd Stepanuik, President & CEO, Middlesex Hospital Alliance
Dr. Gary Perkind, Chief of Staff, Middlesex Hospital Alliance

Sturgeon Falls: The West Nipissing General Hospital (WNGH)/L'Hôpital général de Nipissing Ouest
Affiliated with: North East Local Health Integration Network
725 Coursol Rd., Sturgeon Falls, ON P2B 2Y6
Tel: 705-753-3110; *Fax:* 705-753-0210
administration@wngh.ca
www.wngh.ca

Year Founded: 1977
Number of Beds: 98 beds
Note: Programs & services include: diagnostic and screening which includes picture archiving and communication system (PACS); infection prevention and control; physiotherapy; occupational therapy; respiratory therapy.
Cynthia Désormiers, Chief Executive Officer
Dr. Klère Bourgault, Chief of Staff
Jo-Ann Lennon-Murphy, Chief Nursing Officer

Sudbury: Health Sciences North (HSN)
Affiliated with: North East Local Health Integration Network
41 Ramsey Lake Rd., Sudbury, ON P3E 5J1
Tel: 705-523-7100; *Fax:* 705-523-7112
Toll-Free: 866-469-0822
communications@hsnsudbury.ca
www.hsnsudbury.ca
Social Media: www.facebook.com/HSNSudbury; twitter.com/HSN_Sudbury; www.youtube.com/user/healthsciencesnorth; www.linkedin.com/company/health-sciences-north
Number of Beds: 454 beds
Number of Employees: 3900
Note: Programs & services include: cancer care; domestic violence & sexual assault treatment; mental health & addiction services; transitional & rehabilitative care
Dr. Denis-Richard Roy, President & CEO
Dr. Chris Bourdon, Chief of Staff
David McNeil, Chief Nursing Officer

Sudbury: Sudbury Outpatient Centre
Affiliated with: Health Sciences North
865 Regent St. South, Sudbury, ON P3E 3Y9
Tel: 705-523-7100 *Toll-Free:* 866-469-0822
www.hsnsudbury.ca
Number of Beds: 189 beds
Dr. Denis-Richard Roy, President & CEO, Health Sciences North

Sudbury: Sudbury Regional Hospital - Laurentian Site (HRSRH-LS)/Hôpital régional de Sudbury - Emplacement Laurentien
41 Ramsey Lake Rd., Sudbury, ON P3E 5J1
Tel: 705-523-7100; *Fax:* 705-523-7112
Toll-Free: 866-469-0822
Number of Beds: 530 acute care beds
Population Served: 53,000
Note: Complex continuing care, assistive communication clinic, chiropody clinic, eating disorders clinic, HIV/AIDS clinic, intensive rehabilitation, physiotherapy, occupational therapy
Vickie Kaminski, President/CEO

Terrace Bay: The McCausland Hospital
Affiliated with: North West Local Health Integration Network
20B Cartier Rd., Terrace Bay, ON P0T 2W0
Tel: 807-825-3273; *Fax:* 807-825-9623
www.mccauslandhospital.com

Year Founded: 1980
Number of Beds: 45 beds (23 community beds, 22 long-term beds)
Population Served: 4,000
Note: Services include emergency; cancer care; diabetes program; diagnostic imaging (ECG, Holter monitors, radiology, ultrasound); laboratory; obstetrics & gynecology; physiotherapy; seniors drop-in program; surgery.
Adam Brown, CEO
807-825-3273, Fax: 807-825-9623
Dr. Ian Thompson, Chief of Staff
Teresa Roberts, Chief Nursing Officer

Thessalon: Blind River District Health Centre - Thessalon Hospital Site/Pavillion Santé du District de Blind River
Affiliated with: North East Local Health Integration Network
PO Box 60, 135 Dawson St., Thessalon, ON P0R 1L0
Tel: 705-842-2014; *Fax:* 705-842-3214
webinfo@brdhc.on.ca
www.brdhc.on.ca
Note: Programs & services include: diagnostic imaging; emergency; & surgery.
Gaston Lavigne, Chief Executive Officer
Dr. Marc Bradford, Chief of Staff
Mary Ellen Luukkonen, Chief Nursing Officer & Director, Clinical Services

Thunder Bay: St. Joseph's Hospital
St. Joseph's Care Group
Affiliated with: North West Local Health Integration Network
PO Box 3251, 35 Algoma St. North, Thunder Bay, ON P7B 5G7
Tel: 807-343-2431; *Fax:* 807-345-4994
contact.sjcg@tbh.net
www.sjcg.net
Note: Programs & services include: chiropody; foot care; rehabilitation; Multiple Sclerosis clinic; pain management program; palliative care; transition; wound/ostomy/continence clinic.
Tracy Buckler, President & CEO, St. Joseph's Care Group

Thunder Bay: Thunder Bay Regional Health Sciences Centre
Affiliated with: North West Local Health Integration Network
980 Oliver Rd., Thunder Bay, ON P7B 6V4
Tel: 807-684-6000
tbrhsc@tbh.net
www.tbrhsc.net
Year Founded: 2004
Number of Beds: 375 acute care beds (28 beds for anesthetic recovery, 40 beds for day surgery recovery)
Note: A comprehensive, multi-disciplinary, acute care facility with services incuding emergency, ambulatory care, asthma education, cardiology, critical care unit, dentistry, diagnostic imaging (breast MRI, CT scans, radiology), dietitians, forensics, Holter monitoring, Hospice Northwest, ICU, laboratory, maternity, oncology (brachytherapy), paediatrics, renal program, respiratory therapy, surgery, trauma rooms.
The TBRHSC amalgamates the former Port Arthur & McKellar sites of the Thunder Bay Regional Hospital.
Andrée Robichaud, President & CEO
Dr. Mark Henderson, Acting Chief of Staff
Dr. Rhonda Crocker Ellacott, Chief Nursing Executive

Tillsonburg: Tillsonburg District Memorial Hospital (TDMH)
Affiliated with: South West Local Health Integration Network
167 Rolph St., Tillsonburg, ON N4G 3Y9
Tel: 519-842-3611; *Fax:* 519-688-1031
mail@tdmh.on.ca
www.tillsonburghospital.on.ca

Number of Beds: 51 beds
Note: Programs & services include: ambulatory care; complex continuing care; diabetes education; diagnostic & treatment; dialysis; emergency; intensive coronary care; medical/surgical unit; palliative care; rehabilitation; & surgery.
Crystal Houze, President & CEO
Dr. Barry Roth, Chief of Staff
Frank Deutsch, Vice-President & Chief Financial Officer

Timmins: Timmins & District Hospital (TADH)/L'Hôpital de Timmins et du district
Affiliated with: North East Local Health Integration Network
700 Ross Ave. East, Timmins, ON P4N 8P2
Tel: 705-267-2131; *Fax:* 705-267-6311
generalinquiries@tadh.com
www.tadh.com
Year Founded: 1993
Number of Beds: 161 beds
Number of Employees: 920
Note: Programs & services include: mental health services; medical, surgical, obstetrics & pediatrics; intensive care; complex continuing care & interim long term care
Bryan Bennetts, CFO & Interim CEO
Dr. Harry Voogjarv, Chief of Staff
Joan Ludwig, Chief Nursing Officer

Toronto: Etobicoke General Hospital (EGH)
William Osler Health System
Affiliated with: Central West Local Health Integration Network
Also Known As: William Osler Health Centre
101 Humber College Blvd., Toronto, ON M9V 1R8
Tel: 416-747-2120
www.williamoslerhs.ca
Social Media: www.facebook.com/WilliamOslerHealth; twitter.com/OslerHealth; www.youtube.com/WilliamOslerTV; www.linkedin.com/company/william-osler-health-system
Number of Beds: 262 beds
Note: Programs & services include: cancer care; cardiac care; complex continuing care; critical care; diabetes care; diagnostic imaging; emergency; general & internal medicine; joint assessment centre; kidney care; laboratories; mental health & addictions; naturopathic care; palliative care; rehabilition services; respirology; seniors' care; surgical services; & women's & children's services.
Matthew Anderson, President & CEO, William Osler Health System

***Toronto:* The Hospital for Sick Children**
Affiliated with: Toronto Central Local Health Integration Network
Also Known As: SickKids
555 University Ave., Toronto, ON M5G 1X8
Tel: 416-813-1500
www.sickkids.ca
Info Line: 416-813-6621
Social Media: www.facebook.com/sickkidsfoundation; twitter.com/SickKidsNews; www.youtube.com/SickKidsInteractive; www.linkedin.com/company/the-hospital-for-sick-children
Year Founded: 1875
Number of Beds: 370 beds
Note: Paediatric acute care hospital, with programs & services including: adolescent medicine; allergy; anxiety disorders; audiology; blood & marrow transplant; burns; cancer detection & treatment; cardiology; cleft lip & palate; dental clinic; diabetes clinic; dialysis; eating disorders; emergency; genetic counselling; gynecology; hand clinic; hematology; infectious diseases (including HIV); International Patient Office; Motherisk program; ophthalmology; otolaryngology; pain clinic; psychiatry; psychiatric emergency crisis service; respiratory illnesses; SCAN (Suspected Child Abuse & Neglect) program; sleep disorders; social work; speech language clinic; substance abuse outreach & day treatment; Tay Sachs testing; trauma unit; & Young Families Program (Tots of Teens).
Dr. Michael Apkon, President & CEO
Jeff Mainland, Executive Vice-President, Strategy, Quality, Performance & Communications
Marilyn Monk, Executive Vice-President, Clinical
Dr. Denis Daneman, Chief, Paediatrics

***Toronto:* Humber River Regional Hospital - Finch St. Site**
2111 Finch Ave. West, Toronto, ON M3N 1N1
Tel: 416-744-2500
www.hrrh.on.ca
Note: Affiliated with the University of Toronto & Queen's University.

***Toronto:* Humber River Regional Hospital - Wilson Ave. Site**
Affiliated with: Toronto Central Local Health Integration Network
1235 Wilson Ave., Toronto, ON M3M 0B2
Tel: 416-242-1000
www.hrh.ca
Social Media: www.youtube.com/humberriverhospital
Year Founded: 2015
Number of Beds: 656 beds (all sites)
Number of Employees: 3300
Note: Programs & services include: acute care; adult day treatment; assessment program; child & adolescent mental health inpatient unit; child & adolescent outpatient services; community treatment program; early intervention in psychosis program; elective inpatient withdrawal management program; general psychiatry unit; geriatric psychiatry outpatient clinic services; geriatric psychiatry outreach team; Humber River Hospital funded clinic; Humber River Rehabilitation Centre; intensive day treatment; internal geriatric psychiatry consultation teams; outpatient services; psychogeriatric outreach & consultation team; & transition child & adolescent program. Affiliated with the University of Toronto & Queen's University.
Barb Collins, President & CEO
Dr. Narenda Singh, Chief of Staff
Marg Czaus, Chief Nursing Officer

***Toronto:* Michael Garron Hospital - Toronto East Health Network**
Affiliated with: Toronto Central Local Health Integration Network
Former Name: Toronto East General Hospital
825 Coxwell Ave., Toronto, ON M4C 3E7
Tel: 416-461-8272; *Fax:* 416-469-6106
community@tegh.on.ca
www.tegh.on.ca
Info Line: 416-469-6487
Social Media: www.facebook.com/TorontoEastGeneral; twitter.com/EastGeneral; www.youtube.com/user/TorontoEastGeneral; www.linkedin.com/company/toronto-east-general-hospital
Year Founded: 1929
Population Served: 400000; *Number of Employees:* 2500
Note: Affiliated with the University of Toronto. Programs & services include: acute care; breastfeeding centre for families; complex continuing care; inpatient rehabilitation; alternate level of care; cancer care; cardiology; child development centre; DEC NET (Diabetes Education Community Network of East Toronto); diabetes care; diagnostic imaging; East Toronto postpartum adjustment program; emergency; family health centre; geriatric assessment; hematology; mental health outpatient programs; neonatal care; nephrology; obstetrics; palliative care; pediatrics; prolonged-ventilation weaning centre; psychiatry; respiratory diseases; & surgery.
Sarah Downey, President & CEO
Dr. Ian Fraser, Chief of Staff
Irene Andress, Chief Nursing Executive & Program Director, ER/Medicine/Nursing Resource Team

***Toronto:* Mount Sinai Hospital**
Affiliated with: Toronto Central Local Health Integration Network
600 University Ave., Toronto, ON M5G 1X5
Tel: 416-596-4200
TTY: 416-586-8275
communicationsandmarketing@mtsinai.on.ca
www.mountsinai.on.ca
Social Media: www.facebook.com/MountSinaiHospital; twitter.com/MountSinai; www.youtube.com/user/MountSinaiHospital; www.linkedin.com/company/mount-sinai-hospital-toronto
Year Founded: 1923
Number of Beds: 442 beds
Number of Employees: 4528
Note: Teaching & research Hospital, affiliated with the University of Toronto. Home to six Centres of Excellence: Frances Bloomberg Centre for Women's & Infants' Health; Christopher Sharp Centre for Surgical Oncology; The Daryl A. Katz Centre for Urgent & Critical Care; The Centre for Inflammatory Bowel Disease; Centre for Musculoskeletal Disease; & The Lunenfeld-Tanenbaum Research Institute.
Hospital programs & services include: acute care; Alzheimer's support & training centre; arthritis & autoimmune diseases; asthma; audiology; cancer (breast, colon & sarcoma); cardiology; Chinese outreach program; clinic for HIV related concerns; day surgery; dental clinic; diabetes education; digestive diseases; eye clinic; family medicine centre; geriatric psychiatry; nutrition counselling; Ontario Breast Screening Program; orthopedics; pain management; palliative care; psychiatric unit; rehabilitation; speech disorders; sports medicine; urology; & women's & infants' health programs.
Carey Lucki, Interim President & Vice-President, Client Services
Samir Sinha, Chief Clinical Advisor

***Toronto:* North York General Hospital - Branson Ambulatory Care Centre**
Affiliated with: Toronto Central Local Health Integration Network
555 Finch Ave. West, Toronto, ON M2R 1N5
Tel: 416-633-9420
www.nygh.on.ca
Social Media: www.facebook.com/NorthYorkGeneralHospital; twitter.com/NYGH_News; www.youtube.com/user/NYGHNews
Number of Beds: 419 acute beds (all sites); 192 long-term care beds (all sites)
Note: Programs & services include: adolescent eating disorder program; cataract high volume centre; diabetes education centre; Gale & Graham Wright Prostate Centre; laboratory medicine; medical imaging; mental health; pharmacy; Total Joint Assessment Centre (TJAC); & Urgent Care Centre (UCC).
Dr. Tim Rutledge, President & CEO
Dr. Everton Gooden, Chief of Staff
Karyn Popovich, Chief Nursing Executive & Vice-President, Clinical Programs, Quality & Risk

***Toronto:* North York General Hospital - General Site**
Affiliated with: Toronto Central Local Health Integration Network
4001 Leslie St., Toronto, ON M2K 1E1
Tel: 416-756-6000
www.nygh.on.ca
Social Media: www.facebook.com/NorthYorkGeneralHospital; twitter.com/NYGH_News; www.youtube.com/user/NYGHNews
Number of Beds: 419 acute beds (all sites); 192 long-term care beds (all sites)
Note: Community teaching hospital affiliated with the University of Toronto. Programs & services include: cancer care; child & teen; diagnostic imaging; emergency & urgent care; genetics; family & community medicine; laboratory; maternal newborn care; medicine & elder care; mental health; pharmacy; & surgery.
Dr. Tim Rutledge, President & CEO
Everton Gooden, Chief of Staff
Karyn Popovich, Chief Nursing Executive & Vice-President, Clinical Programs, Quality & Risk

***Toronto:* Princess Margaret Hospital**
University Health Network
Affiliated with: Toronto Central Local Health Integration Network
Also Known As: Princess Margaret Cancer Centre
610 University Ave., Toronto, ON M5G 2M9
Tel: 416-946-2000
www.theprincessmargaret.ca
Social Media: www.facebook.com/UniversityHealthNetwork; twitter.com/UHN_News; www.youtube.com/UHNToronto; www.linkedin.com/company/university-health-network
Year Founded: 1952
Number of Beds: 202 beds
Number of Employees: 3000
Note: A teaching hospital of the University of Toronto, & a top cancer treatment & research centre. Programs & services include: allied health; dental oncology, ocular & maxillofacial prosthetics; laboratory medicine; medical imaging; medical oncology & hematology; oncology nursing; patient education & survivorship; pharmacy; psychosocial oncology & palliative care; radiation medicine; & surgical oncology. The Ontario Cancer Institute comprises the research wing of the hospital.

***Toronto:* Queensway Health Centre**
Trillium Health Partners
Affiliated with: Mississauga Halton Local Health Integration Network
150 Sherway Dr., Toronto, ON M9C 1A5
Tel: 416-259-6671
Patient.RelationsMH@trilliumhealthpartners.ca
trilliumhealthpartners.ca
Social Media: twitter.com/Trillium_Health; www.youtube.com/user/TrilliumHealth; www.linkedin.com/company/2949012
Note: An ambulatory care facility with services including urgent care centre, day surgery, diabetes management centre, cardiac wellness & rehabilitation, Kingsway Financial Spine Centre, & The Betty Wallace Women's Health Centre (focusing on osteoporosis & breast disease). There is no emergency centre here; it is located at the Mississauga branch.
Michelle E. DiEmanuele, President & CEO, Trillium Health Partners
Dr. Dante Morra, Chief of Staff, Trillium Health Partners
Kathryn Haywood-Murray, Chief Nursing Executive & Senior Vice-President, Patient Care Services, Trillium Health Partners

***Toronto:* Rouge Valley Centenary**
Rouge Valley Health System
Affiliated with: Central East Local Health Integration Network
2867 Ellesmere Rd., Toronto, ON M1E 4B9
Tel: 416-284-8131
patientrelations@rougevalley.ca
www.rougevalley.ca
Social Media: www.facebook.com/rougevalleyhealthsystem; twitter.com/RougeValley; www.youtube.com/RougeValleyHealthSys
Year Founded: 1967
Number of Beds: 328 beds
Note: Programs & services include: acute care; audiology testing; breastfeeding clinic; cancer care; cardiac care & rehabilitation; complex continuing care; Diabetes Education Centre; digestive diseases; genetic counselling; geriatric care; mental health; obstetrics; Ontario Breast Screening Program; ophthalmology; orthopedics; pediatrics; prenatal & postnatal services; rehabilitation; respiratory care; & surgery.
Rik Ganderton, Interim President/CEO, RVHS
Dr. Naresh Mohan, Chief of Staff, RVHS
Amelia McCutcheon, Chief Nursing Executive & Vice-President, Cardiac, Cancer & Critical Care, RHVS
David Brazeau, Director, Public Affairs & Community Relations, RHVS
647-294-8885, dbrazeau@rougevalley.ca

***Toronto:* St. Joseph's Health Centre Toronto**
Affiliated with: Toronto Central Local Health Integration Network
30 The Queensway, Toronto, ON M6R 1B5
Tel: 416-530-6000
TTY: 416-530-6820
www.stjoe.on.ca
Social Media: www.facebook.com/MySt.Joes; twitter.com/mystjoes; www.youtube.com/user/StJoesHealthCentre; www.linkedin.com/company/st.-joseph's-health-centre-toronto
Year Founded: 1921
Number of Beds: 381 beds
Number of Employees: 2550
Note: Programs & services include: acute care; cardiology; cancer care; diabetes; diagnostic imaging; dialysis; ear, nose & throat (ENT); elderly community health services; family medicine

centre; geriatric emergency & outpatient services; gynecology; Lifeline; mental health programs; obstetrics; ophthalmology; orthopedics; pediatrics; pre & postnatal care; psychiatric unit; respiratory care; sleep lab; speech disorders; surgery; & urology. This teaching hospital was founded by the Sisters of St. Joseph. Has 400 physicians on staff.
Elizabeth Buller, President & CEO
Dr. Ted Rogovein, Chief of Staff
Jenni Glad-Timmons, Chief Nursing Executive & Director, Interprofessional Practice

Toronto: St. Michael's Hospital
Affiliated with: Toronto Central Local Health Integration Network
30 Bond St., Toronto, ON M5B 1W8
Tel: 416-360-4000
www.stmichaelshospital.com
Social Media: www.facebook.com/116986731666237; twitter.com/StMikesHospital; www.youtube.com/user/StMichaelsHospital; www.linkedin.com/company/st.-michael's-hospital
Number of Beds: 463 inpatient beds
Number of Employees: 6066
Note: Catholic hospital with a focus on teaching & research, affiliated with the University of Toronto. Programs & services include: acute care; addiction; arthritis; breast centre; cancer care; cardiology; chiropody; critical care; diabetes clinic; dialysis; fracture clinic; general internal medicine; geriatrics; gynecology; hemophilia; HIV/AIDS; inner city health program; inpatient oncology; mental health; mobility; multiple sclerosis; neo-natal intensive care; neurosurgery; obstetrics; Ontario Breast Screening Program; ophthalmology; osteoporosis; outpatient services; palliative care; pediatrics; services for seniors; stroke centre; respirology; sleep laboratory; specialized complex care; trauma centre; urology; & vascular disease.
Robert Howard, President & CEO
Dr. Douglas Sinclair, Executive Vice-President & Chief Medical Officer
Sonya Canzian, Chief Nursing Executive, Chief Health Disciplines Exec., & Executive Vice-President, Programs

Toronto: The Scarborough Hospital - Birchmount Campus
Affiliated with: Toronto Central Local Health Integration Network
Former Name: The Scarborough Hospital - Grace Campus
3030 Birchmount Rd., Toronto, ON M1W 3W3
Tel: 416-495-2400
www.tsh.to
Social Media: www.facebook.com/ScarboroughHospital; twitter.com/ScarboroughHosp; www.youtube.com/user/TSHCommunications; www.linkedin.com/company/the-scarborough-hospital
Number of Beds: 215 beds
Number of Employees: 3105
Note: A health facility with emphasis on emergency outpatient psychiatric concerns, notably its Regional Crisis Program, an emergency response team to acute psychiatric crises. Affiliated with the University of Toronto.
Robert Biron, President & CEO
Dr. Tom Chan, Chief of Medical Staff
Linda Calhoun, Chief Nursing Executive & Vice-President, Integrated Care & Patient Experience

Toronto: The Scarborough Hospital - General Campus
Affiliated with: Toronto Central Local Health Integration Network
3050 Lawrence Ave. East, Toronto, ON M1P 2V5
Tel: 416-438-2911
www.tsh.to
Social Media: www.facebook.com/ScarboroughHospital; twitter.com/ScarboroughHosp; www.youtube.com/user/TSHCommunications; www.linkedin.com/company/the-scarborough-hospital
Year Founded: 1956
Number of Beds: 277 beds
Number of Employees: 3105
Note: Programs & services include: adult mental health; diabetes education; Dorif Lawrence Breast Clinic; emergency; family & community medicine; maternal/newborn; medical; Ontario Breast Screening Program; outpatient services; paediatrics; prenatal classes; & surgery. Affiliated with the University of Toronto.
Robert Biron, President & CEO
Dr. Tom Chan, Chief of Medical Staff
Linda Calhoun, Chief Nursing Executive & Vice-President, Integrated Care & Patient Experience

Toronto: Sunnybrook Health Sciences Centre - Bayview Campus
Affiliated with: Toronto Central Local Health Integration Network
2075 Bayview Ave., Toronto, ON M4N 3M5
Tel: 416-480-6100
www.sunnybrook.ca
Social Media: www.facebook.com/SunnybrookHSC; twitter.com/Sunnybrook; www.youtube.com/SunnybrookMedia
Year Founded: 1948
Number of Beds: 1,325 beds (including bassinet beds)
Note: A comprehensive health facility with a focus on cancer care (Odette Cancer Centre), cardiac care (Schulich Heart Centre), musculoskeletal care (Holland Musculoskeletal Program), brain science program (stroke, dementias, mood disorders), women's health, infertility, perinatal care, pediatrics, emergency services, trauma & critical care, veterans' care & residence, research & education.
Barry McLellan, President & CEO
Malcolm Moffat, Executive Vice-President, Programs
Andy Smith, Chief Medical Executive & Executive Vice-President, Programs
Michael Young, Chief Admin. Executive & Executive Vice-President

Toronto: Toronto General Hospital (TGH)
University Health Network
Affiliated with: Toronto Central Local Health Integration Network
200 Elizabeth St., Toronto, ON M5G 2C4
Tel: 416-340-3111
www.uhn.ca/corporate/AboutUHN/OurHospitals/TGH
Social Media: www.facebook.com/UniversityHealthNetwork; twitter.com/UHN_News; www.youtube.com/UHNToronto; www.linkedin.com/company/university-health-network
Year Founded: 1829
Number of Beds: 457 beds
Note: A comprehensive health care & teaching facility, its specialties include cardiac care (Peter Munk Cardiac Centre), transplantation, kidney diseases & care, tropical disease, eating disorders, nephrology, psychiatry, HIV/AIDS care, & telemedicine. It is home to the MaRS Discovery District, a not-for-profit research corporation with funding from both private & public sectors. Affiliated with the University of Toronto.

Toronto: Toronto Western Hospital
University Health Network
Affiliated with: Toronto Central Local Health Integration Network
399 Bathurst St., Toronto, ON M5T 2S8
Tel: 416-603-2581
www.uhn.ca/corporate/AboutUHN/OurHospitals/TWH
Social Media: www.facebook.com/UniversityHealthNetwork; twitter.com/UHN_News; www.youtube.com/UHNToronto; www.linkedin.com/company/university-health-network
Year Founded: 1905
Number of Beds: 280 beds
Note: Primary areas of focus are neural & sensory sciences, community & population health & musculoskeletal health & arthritis. Programs & services include: acquired brain injury clinic; aneurysm clinic; artists health centre; asthma; cardiac & pulmonary rehab; diabetes education; eye clinic; memory clinic; mental health & addictions; movement disorders clinic; sleep clinic; stroke clinic; Tourette's Clinic; & tuberculosis clinic. Affiliated with the University of Toronto.

Toronto: University Health Network (UHN)
Affiliated with: Toronto Central Local Health Integration Network
R. Fraser Elliot Building, 1st Fl., 190 Elizabeth St., Toronto, ON M5G 2C4
Tel: 416-340-4800
www.uhn.ca
Social Media: www.facebook.com/UniversityHealthNetwork; twitter.com/UHN_News; www.youtube.com/UHNToronto; www.linkedin.com/company/university-health-network
Number of Beds: 1,295 beds (total, all sites)
Number of Employees: 14318
Note: Comprised of Princess Margaret Hospital, Toronto General Hospital, Toronto Western Hospital & Toronto Rehab, UHN is a comprehensive health care, research & teaching facility with fields of focus including cancer care, cardiac care, musculoskeletal health & arthritis, neuroscience, ophthalmology, surgical & critical care, transplantation. The network is affiliated with the University of Toronto, Faculty of Medicine.
Dr. Peter Pisters, President & CEO
Michael Nader, Executive Vice-President, Clinical Operations
Dr. Charles Chan, Executive Vice-President, Clinical Programs Quality & Safety

Toronto: Women's College Hospital (WCH)
Affiliated with: Toronto Central Local Health Integration Network
76 Grenville St., Toronto, ON M5S 1B2
Tel: 416-323-6400
info@wchospital.ca
www.womenscollegehospital.ca
Social Media: www.facebook.com/wchospital; twitter.com/wchospital; www.youtube.com/wchospital
Year Founded: 1928
Note: Programs & services include: asthma; breastfeeding support; breast screening; cardiac rehabilitation for women; child & family psychiatry; chronic pain; complex care; Crossroads Refugee Health Clinic; day surgery; diabetes education (TRIDEC); environmental health; gynecology; headache clinic; infertility; mental health programs; osteoporosis; prenatal & postnatal support; Ricky Kanee Schacter Dermatology Centre; sexual assault & domestic violence care centre; WISE program; & Women's Health Matters (online resource). The hospital was renovated in 2016, offering updated access to diagnostic imaging services & additional operating rooms.
Marilyn Emery, President & CEO
Dr. Danielle Martin, Vice-President, Medical Affairs & Health System Solutions

Trenton: QHC Trenton Memorial Hospital
Quinte Health Care
Affiliated with: South East Local Health Integration Network
242 King St., Trenton, ON K8V 5S6
Tel: 613-392-2540; *Fax:* 613-392-3749
www.qhc.on.ca
Social Media: www.facebook.com/173689537296; twitter.com/QuinteHealth; www.youtube.com/QuinteHealthCare
Year Founded: 1951
Number of Beds: 31 beds
Note: Programs & services include: cardiology; clinical nutrition; diabetes education; emergency services; laboratory; medical services; Nursing Home Ready Unit; outpatient clinics; pharmacy; psychiatry/mental health crisis clinic; radiology/diagnostic services; surgery; & symptom management/palliative care.
Mary Clare Egberts, President & CEO, Quinte Health Care
Dr. Dick Zoutman, Chief of Staff, Quinte Health Care
Katherine Stansfield, Chief Nursing Officer & Vice-President, Quinte Health Care

Uxbridge: Markham Stouffville Hospital - Uxbridge Site (MSH)
Affiliated with: Central Local Health Integration Network
Also Known As: Uxbridge Cottage Hospital
PO Box 5003, 4 Campbell Dr., Uxbridge, ON L9P 1S4
Tel: 905-852-9771
myhospital@msh.on.ca
www.msh.on.ca
Social Media: www.facebook.com/MarkhamStouffvilleHospital; twitter.com/MSHospital; www.youtube.com/MSHospital
Year Founded: 1959
Number of Beds: 20 beds
Note: Programs & services include: day surgery; diagnostic imaging; emergency; laboratory; & physiotherapy.
Janet Beed, President & CEO
Dr. David Austin, Chief of Staff

Walkerton: South Bruce Grey Health Centre - Walkerton Site
Affiliated with: South West Local Health Integration Network
Former Name: County of Bruce General Hospital
PO Box 1300, 21 McGivern St. West, Walkerton, ON N0G 2V0
Tel: 519-881-1220; *Fax:* 519-881-0452
info@sbghc.on.ca
www.sbghc.on.ca
Social Media: www.facebook.com/sbghc; twitter.com/SBG_HC
Year Founded: 1900
Number of Beds: 31 beds (25 acute care beds, 6 obstetric beds)
Note: Programs & services include: cardio-respiratory; family birthing centre; diagnostic imaging; emergency department; emergency response system; inpatient medical beds; laboratory; nutrition services; outpatient clinics; palliative care; & pastoral care.
Paul Rosebush, President & CEO, SBGHC
prosebush@sbghc.on.ca
Rhonda Ridgeway, Director, Patient Care
rridgeway@sbghc.on.ca

***Wallaceburg:* Chatham-Kent Health Alliance - Sydenham Campus (CKHA)**
Affiliated with: Erie St. Clair Local Health Integration Network
PO Box 2030, 325 Margaret Ave., Wallaceburg, ON N8A 2A7
Tel: 519-352-6400
www.ckha.on.ca
Social Media: www.facebook.com/ckhamedia; twitter.com/ckhamedia; www.youtube.com/ckhamedia
Year Founded: 1952
Number of Beds: 200+ beds (total for both CKHA sites)
Note: Programs & services include: ambulatory care; diabetes education; diagnostic imaging; dietician; emergency; inpatient medicine unit; laboratory; nurse practitioner clinic; pharmacy; rehabilitation/physiotherapy; respiratory services; & social work.
Colin Patey, President & CEO
cpatey@ckha.on.ca

***Wawa:* Lady Dunn Health Centre**
PO Box 179, 17 Government Rd., Wawa, ON P0S 1K0
Tel: 705-856-2335; *Fax:* 705-856-7533
Toll-Free: 866-832-3321
www.ldhc.com
Number of Beds: 26 beds

***Welland:* Welland Hospital Site**
Niagara Health System / Système de santé de Niagara
Affiliated with: Hamilton Niagara Haldimand Brant Local Health Integration Network
65 - 3rd St., Welland, ON L3B 4W6
Tel: 905-378-4647
patientrelations@niagarahealth.on.ca
www.niagarahealth.on.ca
Social Media: www.facebook.com/NiagaraHealthSystem; twitter.com/niagarahealth; www.youtube.com/niagarahealthsystem
Year Founded: 1908
Number of Beds: 155 beds (including 15 nephrology beds)
Note: Programs & services include: ambulatory clinics; complex care; critical care; diabetes education; diagnostic imaging; emergency; laboratory; long-term care; medicine; Ontario Breast Screening Clinic; ophthalmology; outpatient mental health; pharmacy; satellite dialysis centre; & surgery.
Dr. Suzanne Johnston, President, Niagara Health System
Suzanne.Johnston@niagarahealth.on.ca
Dr. Kevin Smith, Chief Executive Officer, Niagara Health System
Kevin.Smith@niagarahealth.on.ca
Patty Welychka, Chief Nursing Officer, Director, Surgical Services, & Executive Lead, Welland
Patty.Welychka@niagarahealth.on.ca

***Whitby:* Lakeridge Health - Whitby Site**
Affiliated with: Central East Local Health Integration Network
300 Gordon St., Whitby, ON L1N 5T2
Tel: 905-668-6831
www.lakeridgehealth.on.ca
Social Media: www.facebook.com/LakeridgeHealth; twitter.com/lakeridgehealth; www.youtube.com/lakeridgehealth
Number of Beds: 42+ beds
Note: Programs & services include: ambulatory rehabilitation centres/musculoskeletal physiotherapy clinics; diabetes education; & respiratory rehabilitation.
Kevin Empey, President & CEO, Lakeridge Health
905-576-8711
Dr. Tony Stone, Chief of Staff, Lakeridge Health
905-576-8711
Lisa Shiozaki, Chief Operating Officer & Chief Nursing Executive, Lakeridge Health
905-576-8711

***Wiarton:* Wiarton Hospital**
Grey Bruce Health Services
Affiliated with: South West Local Health Integration Network
369 Mary St., Wiarton, ON N0H 2T0
Tel: 519-534-1260; *Fax:* 519-534-5159
web@gbhs.on.ca
www.gbhs.on.ca
Social Media: twitter.com/greybrucehealth
Number of Beds: 14 acute care beds
Note: Programs & services include: acute care; ambulatory care; complex continuing care; Diabetes Grey Bruce; diagnostic imaging; emergency; laboratory; North Bruce Community Mental Health Team; physiotherapy; spiritual care; & surgery.
Lance Thurston, President & CEO, Grey Bruce Health Services
519-376-2121

***Winchester:* Winchester District Memorial Hospital (WDMH)**
Affiliated with: Champlain Local Health Integration Network
566 Louise St., Winchester, ON K0C 2K0
Tel: 613-774-2422; *Fax:* 613-774-0453
www.wdmh.on.ca
Number of Beds: 70 beds
Number of Employees: 320
Note: Programs & services include: clinics; complex continuing care; diabetes education; diagnostic imaging; emergency; enhanced care; inpatient laboratory; maternity; medical day care; medical/surgical; occupational therapy; ontario breast screening program; physiotherapy; Robillard Hearing Centre; sleep lab; & surgical day care. Has 135 physicians, dentists & midwives on staff. Affiliated with approximately 20 college & university programs.
Cholly Boland, Chief Executive Officer
cboland@wdmh.on.ca
Lynn Hall, Chief Nursing Executive & Senior Vice-President, Clinical Services & Professional Practice Leader
lhall@wdmh.on.ca

***Windsor:* Hôtel-Dieu Grace Healthcare**
Affiliated with: Erie St. Clair Local Health Integration Network
1453 Prince Rd., Windsor, ON N9C 3Z4
Tel: 519-257-5111
www.hdgh.org
Note: Programs & services include: acquired brain injury; addiction & mental health; adult day program; bariatric assessment & treatment; cardiac; chiropody; clinical psychiatric liaison; community crisis centre; complex continuing care; concurrent disorder program; dual diagnosis; stabilization; geriatrics; mood & anxiety treatment; pharmacy; Positive Parenting Program; Regional Children's Centre; rehabilitation; remedial measures; residential rehabilitation; wellness program for extended psychosis; & withdrawal management services.
Janice Kaffer, President & CEO
Marie Campagna, Chief Financial Officer & Executive Vice-President, Operations
Marg Campigotto, Interim Chief Nursing Officer & Executive Director, Patient Experience & Transition
Dr. Andrea Steen, Vice-President, Medical

***Windsor:* Windsor Regional Hospital - Metropolitan Campus**
Affiliated with: Erie St. Clair Local Health Integration Network
1995 Lens Ave., Windsor, ON N8W 1L9
Tel: 519-254-5577; *Fax:* 519-254-2317
www.wrh.on.ca
Social Media: www.facebook.com/WindsorRegionalHospital; twitter.com/WRHospital; www.youtube.com/user/WRHWeCare
Year Founded: 1928
Number of Beds: 650+ beds (total of all WRH sites)
Population Served: 400000
Note: Programs & services on both campuses include: cardiac care; complex trauma; emergency services; family birthing centre; intensive care; medicine; neonatal intensive care; paediatric services; regional cancer services; renal dialysis; stroke & neurosurgery; & surgery.
David Musyj, President & CEO

***Windsor:* Windsor Regional Hospital - Ouellette Campus**
Affiliated with: Erie St. Clair Local Health Integration Network
1030 Ouellette Ave., Windsor, ON N9A 1E1
Tel: 519-973-4411
www.wrh.on.ca
Social Media: www.facebook.com/WindsorRegionalHospital; twitter.com/WRHospital; www.youtube.com/user/WRHWeCare
Year Founded: 1888
Number of Beds: 650+ beds (total of all WRH sites)
Population Served: 400000
Note: Acquired by Windsor Regional Hospital in 2013; renovations in 2008 expanded emergency services, operating rooms & diagnostic imaging departments. Programs & services on both campuses include: cardiac care; complex trauma; emergency services; family birthing centre; intensive care; medicine; neonatal intensive care; paediatric services; regional cancer services; renal dialysis; stroke & neurosurgery; & surgery.
David Musyj, President & CEO

***Wingham:* Wingham & District Hospital**
Listowel Wingham Hospitals Alliance
Affiliated with: South West Local Health Integration Network
270 Carling Terrace, Wingham, ON N0G 2W0
Tel: 519-357-3210; *Fax:* 519-357-3522
www.lwha.ca
Number of Beds: 36 beds
Note: Programs & services include: chemotherapy; complex continuing care; diabetes education; diagnostic imaging; emergency; inpatient rehabilitation; laboratory; medical; occupational therapy; palliative care; physiotherapy; speech-language pathology; & surgery.
Karl Ellis, President & CEO
519-291-3125, karl.ellis@lwha.ca

***Woodstock:* Woodstock General Hospital**
Affiliated with: South West Local Health Integration Network
310 Juliana Dr., Woodstock, ON N4V 0A4
Tel: 519-421-4211; *Fax:* 519-421-4247
info@wgh.on.ca
www.wgh.on.ca
Number of Beds: 153 beds
Note: Programs & services include: ambulatory care; complex continuing care; critical care; diagnostic imaging; emergency; inpatient rehabilitation; intensive rehabilitation outpatient program; laboratory; Lifeline; maternal child unit; medical/surgical unit; Mental Health Services of Oxford County; pastoral care; social work; & surgery.
Natasa Veljovic, President & CEO
Dr. Malcolm MacLeod, Chief of Staff
Jayne Menard, Chief Nursing Officer & Vice-President, Patient Care

Federal Hospitals

***Ottawa:* Canadian Forces Health Care Centre Ottawa**
Affiliated with: Champlain Local Health Integration Network
713 Montreal Rd., Ottawa, ON K1K 0T2
Tel: 613-945-1140
www.forces.gc.ca/en/caf-community-bases-wings-cfsu-ottawa/dental-medical.page
Note: Hospital Specialties: Primary health care services to the military community in the National Capital Region (613-945-1502); Laboratory services; Surgery; Cardio Pulmonary Unit; Operational Trauma & Stress Support Centre (613-945-1060); Mental health (613-945-1060); Addiction counselling (613-945-1060); Ophthalmology (613-945-1550); & Physiotherapy (613-945-1585).
BGen Jean-Robert Bernier, Commander, Canadian Forces Health Services Group
613-945-6827, Fax: 613-990-1345

Private Hospitals

***Penetanguishene:* Hôpital Privé Beechwood Private Hospital**
58 Church St., Penetanguishene, ON L9M 1B3
Tel: 705-549-7473; *Fax:* 705-549-7194
bph@bellnet.ca
Number of Beds: 20 beds
Larry Bellisle, CEO

***Thornhill:* Shouldice Hospital Ltd.**
Affiliated with: Central Local Health Integration Network
7750 Bayview Ave., Thornhill, ON L3T 4A3
Tel: 905-889-1125; *Fax:* 905-889-4216
Toll-Free: 800-291-7750
postoffice@shouldice.com
www.shouldice.com
Year Founded: 1945
Number of Beds: 89 beds
Specialties: Hernia repair
Note: Has 10 surgeons on staff.

***Toronto:* Don Mills Surgical Unit Inc. (DMSU)**
Centric Health Sergical
Affiliated with: Central Local Health Integration Network
#208, 20 Wynford Dr., Toronto, ON M3C 1J4
Tel: 416-441-2111; *Fax:* 416-441-2114
Toll-Free: 888-857-6069
www.centrichealthepcn.ca/facilities/don-mills-surgical-unit
Year Founded: 1960
Note: Surgical services & procedures offered include: general, orthopaedic, ophthalmology, plastic surgery, upper & lower extremity, cosmetics, dental & ENT. Has 20 surgeons on staff.

***Woodbridge:* Cosmetic Surgery Hospital (CSH)**
The Manor, 4650 Hwy. 7, Woodbridge, ON L4L 1S7
Tel: 905-851-7701; *Fax:* 905-856-4406
info@cosmeticsurgeryhospital.com
www.cosmeticsurgeryhospital.com
Year Founded: 1970
Note: Hospital Specialties: Plastic & cosmetic surgery; Clinical obesity
Dr. Lloyd N. Carlsen, Director

***Woodstock:* Woodstock Private Hospital**
Affiliated with: South West Local Health Integration Network
369 Huron St., Woodstock, ON N4S 7A5
Tel: 519-537-8162; *Fax:* 519-537-7204
www.southwesthealthline.ca
Number of Beds: 16 beds
Note: Chronic care hospital
Lisa Figg, Administrator

Auxiliary Hospitals

***Ottawa:* Bruyère Continuing Care/Soins continus Bruyère**
Affiliated with: Champlain Local Health Integration Network
Former Name: Sisters of Charity of Ottawa Health Service, Élisabeth Bruyère Pavilion
43 Bruyère St., Ottawa, ON K1N 5C8
Tel: 613-562-6262; *Fax:* 613-562-6367
webmestre@bruyere.org
www.bruyere.org
Social Media: www.facebook.com/bruyerecare; twitter.com/bruyere_care
Year Founded: 1993
Number of Beds: 731 beds
Note: Specializes in complex continuing care, rehabilitation, palliative care & long-term care services; includes Bruyère Family Medicine Centre, Élisabeth Bruyère Hospital, Élisabeth Bruyère Residence, Primrose Family Medicine Centre, Saint-Louis Residence, & Saint-Vincent Hospital.
Bernie Blais, President & CEO
Dr. Shaun McGuire, Chief of Staff
Debbie Gravelle, Chief Nursing Executive & Senior Vice-President, Hospital Programs

***Toronto:* Baycrest Hospital**
Affiliated with: Toronto Central Local Health Integration Network
3560 Bathurst St., Toronto, ON M6A 2E1
Tel: 416-785-2500; *Fax:* 416-785-2378
webmaster@baycrest.org
www.baycrest.org
Social Media: www.facebook.com/baycrestcentre; twitter.com/baycrest; www.youtube.com/thebaycrestchannel; www.linkedin.com/company/baycrest
Year Founded: 1986
Number of Beds: 300 hospital beds
Note: Programs & services include: acute geriatric care; rehabilitation; psychiatry; behavioural neurology; complex continuing care for the elderly; & palliative care.
William Reichman, President & CEO
Dr. Paul Katz, Chief of Staff & Vice-President, Medical Services
Carol Anderson, Chief Nursing Executive & Vice-President, Clinical Programs

***Toronto:* Bridgepoint Active Healthcare**
Affiliated with: Toronto Central Local Health Integration Network
Former Name: The Riverdale Hospital
Also Known As: Bridgepoint Hospital
14 St. Matthews Rd., Toronto, ON M4M 2B5
Tel: 416-461-8252; *Fax:* 416-461-5696
info@bridgepointhealth.ca
www.bridgepointhealth.ca
Social Media: www.facebook.com/BridgepointHealth; twitter.com/BridgepointTO; www.youtube.com/bridgepointhospital; www.linkedin.com/company/bridgepoint-health
Number of Beds: 404 beds
Specialties: Complex continuing care & rehabilitation
Marian Walsh, President & CEO
Dr. Reva Adler, Vice-President, Medical Affairs
Danielle Donadio, Chief, Communications & Public Affairs

***Toronto:* Providence Healthcare**
Affiliated with: Toronto Central Local Health Integration Network
Former Name: Providence Centre Home for the Aged, Chronic Care & Rehabilitation Hospital
3276 St. Clair Ave. East, Toronto, ON M1L 1W1
Tel: 416-285-3666; *Fax:* 416-285-3758
info@providence.on.ca
www.providence.on.ca
Social Media: www.facebook.com/ProvidenceHealthcareTO; twitter.com/Providence3276; www.youtube.com/ProvHealthcare
Number of Beds: 288 long-term care; 347 hospital beds
Note: Comprised of Providence Hospital, the Cardinal Ambrozic Houses of Providence, & Providence Community Centre; long-term care, rehabilitation & complex continuing care, community clinics, Alzheimer Day Program, caregiver support services, Tamil Caregiver Project. Focus is on the mission & values of the founding Sisters of St. Joseph.
Josie Walsh, President & CEO
Dr. Peter Nord, Chief of Staff, Chief Medical Officer & Vice-President
Maggie Bruneau, Chief Nurse Executive & Vice-President, Partnerships

***Toronto:* Runnymede Healthcare Centre**
Affiliated with: Toronto Central Local Health Integration Network
625 Runnymede Rd., Toronto, ON M6P 3A3
Tel: 416-762-7316; *Fax:* 416-762-3836
communications@runnymedehc.ca
www.runnymedehc.ca
Social Media: www.facebook.com/RunnymedeHC; twitter.com/RunnymedeHC; www.youtube.com/RunnymedeHC; www.linkedin.com/company/runnymedehc
Year Founded: 1945
Note: Complex continuing care hospital with rehabilitation, speech therapy, dental care & foot care services.
Connie Dejak, President & CEO
Corinne Wong, Chief Operating Officer
Raj Sewda, Chief Nursing Executive & Chief Privacy Officer

***Toronto:* The Salvation Army Toronto Grace Health Centre (TGHC)**
Affiliated with: Toronto Central Local Health Integration Network
Also Known As: Toronto Grace Hospital
47 Austin Terrace, Toronto, ON M5R 1Y8
Tel: 416-925-2251; *Fax:* 416-925-3211
www.torontograce.org
Social Media: www.facebook.com/torontogracehealthcentre; twitter.com/torontogracehc
Year Founded: 1905
Number of Beds: 119 beds
Note: Complex continuing care facility providing services such as foot clinic/chiropody, palliative care & slow-paced rehabilitation.
Marilyn Rook, President & CEO
Dr. John Ruth, Medical Director
Marilyn Wharton, Chief Nursing Executive & Executive Director, Patient Care

Community Health Care Centres

***Ajax:* The Youth Centre**
Former Name: Barbara Black Centre for Youth Resources
#5, 360 Bayly St. West, Ajax, ON L1S 1P1
Tel: 905-428-1212; *Fax:* 905-428-9151
www.theyouthcentre.ca
Social Media: www.facebook.com/pages/The-Youth-Centre/10821991386
Susan Bland, Executive Director

***Armstrong:* NorWest Community Health Centre - Armstrong Site**
Affiliated with: North West Local Health Integration Network
PO Box 104, Armstrong, ON P0T 1A0
Tel: 807-583-1145; *Fax:* 807-583-1147
www.norwestchc.org/armstrong.htm
Social Media: www.facebook.com/NorWestCHC
Wendy Talbot, CEO

***Barrie:* Barrie Community Health Centre**
490 Huronia Rd., Barrie, ON L4N 6M2
Tel: 705-734-9690; *Fax:* 705-734-0239
www.bchc.ca
Note: Community-focused health promotion, illness prevention, & primary care services. Services provided by physicians, registered nurses, social workers, physiotherapists, & dietitians. North Innisfil office located at: 902 Lockhart Rd., 705-431-9245.
Christine Colcy, Executive Director
705-734-9690, Fax: 705-734-0239

***Barrie:* CCAC North Simcoe Muskoka**
#100, 15 Sperling Dr., Barrie, ON L4M 6K9
Tel: 705-721-8010 *Toll-Free:* 888-721-2222 ex
healthcareathome.ca/nsm
Social Media: twitter.com/NSMCCAC; www.youtube.com/ccacnsm
Note: With offices in Barrie & Huntsville, provides health & personal support services for individuals living independently at home or making the transition to alternative care settings; information & referral, advocacy.

***Belleville:* CCAC South East - Belleville Branch Office**
Bayview Mall, 470 Dundas St. East, Belleville, ON K8N 1G1
Tel: 613-966-3530; *Fax:* 613-966-0996
Toll-Free: 800-668-0901
www.ccac-ont.ca
David Vigar, Board Chair

***Brampton:* CCAC Central West**
199 County Court Blvd., 3rd Fl., Brampton, ON L6W 4P3
Tel: 905-796-0040; *Fax:* 905-796-5620
Toll-Free: 800-733-1177
info@cw.ccac-ont.ca
www.ccac-ont.ca
Carmine Domanico, Board Chair

***Brantford:* CCAC Hamilton Niagara Haldimand Brant - Brant Branch Office**
Building 4, #4, 195 Henry St., Brantford, ON N3S 5C9
Tel: 519-759-7752; *Fax:* 519-759-7130
Toll-Free: 866-759-7752
www.ccac-ont.ca
Note: Head office for the region
Melody Miles, CEO

***Burlington:* CCAC Hamilton Niagara Haldimand Brant - Burlington Branch Office**
440 Elizabeth St., 4th Fl., Burlington, ON L7R 2M1
Tel: 905-639-5228; *Fax:* 905-639-5320
Toll-Free: 800-810-0000
www.ccac-ont.ca
Melody Miles, CEO

***Cambridge:* Langs Farm Village Association**
1145 Concession Rd., Cambridge, ON N3H 4L5
Tel: 519-653-1470; *Fax:* 519-653-6277
info@langs.org
William Davidson, Executive Director
519-653-1470 ext 236, billd@langs.org
Kerry-Lynn Wilkie, Director Programs, Partnerships, & Evaluation
519-653-1470 ext 234, kerrylynnw@langs.org

***Chatham:* CCAC Erie St. Clair**
PO Box 306, 712 Richmond St., Chatham, ON N7M 5K4
Tel: 519-436-2222 *Toll-Free:* 888-447-4468
www.ccac-ont.ca
Note: Head Office located at the Chatham-Kent branch, with other branch offices located in Sarnia & Windsor. Provides access to in-home health & personal support services to help individuals live independently at home, & assists with the transition to long term care when living at home is no longer possible
James Greenway, Board Chair

***Cornwall:* CCAC North East - Cornwall Branch Office**
709 Cotton Mill St., Cornwall, ON K6H 7K7
Tel: 310-2222 *Toll-Free:* 800-267-0852
healthcareathome.ca/champlain

***Cornwall:* Centre de santé communautaire de l'Estrie**
#6, 841, rue Sydney, Cornwall, ON K6H 3J7
Tél: 613-937-2683; *Téléc:* 613-937-2698
info@cscestrie.on.ca
www.cscestrie.on.ca
Média social: www.facebook.com/pages/CSCE/179209222111118; twitter.com/CSCE
Marc Bisson

***Ear Falls:* Ear Falls Community Health Centre**
Affiliated with: North West Local Health Integration Network
PO Box 250, 25 Spruce St., Ear Falls, ON P0V 1T0
Tel: 807-222-3728; *Fax:* 807-222-2053
earfallsfht@live.com
Note: Programs & services include: blood & lab work; Ministry of Transportation medical reviews; Northern Ontario Travel Grant Application.

***Emo:* Emo Health Centre**
Riverside Health Care Facilities Inc.
Affiliated with: North West Local Health Integration Network
PO Box 390, 170 Front St., Emo, ON P0W 1E0
Tel: 807-274-3261; *Fax:* 807-482-2493
www.riversidehealthcare.ca
Number of Beds: 12 long-term, 3 acute care beds
Note: Programs & services include: physiotherapy; dietician; diagnostics; urgent care.
Wayne Woods

***Forest:* North Lambton Community Health Centre**
Affiliated with: Erie St. Clair Local Health Integration Network
PO Box 1120, 3 - 59 King St. West, Forest, ON N0N 1J0
Tel: 519-786-4545; *Fax:* 519-786-6318
nlinfo@nlchc.com
www.nlchc.com
Social Media: www.facebook.com/NorthLambtonCHC
Note: Programs for children, seniors, healthy living, excercise & diabetes education.
Kathy Bresett, Executive Director
519-786-4545, kbresett@nlchc.com

***Fort Frances:* Fort Frances Tribal Area Health Services**
Affiliated with: North West Local Health Integration Network
PO Box 608, Fort Frances, ON P9A 3M9
Tel: 807-274-2042; *Fax:* 807-274-2050
www.fftahs.com
Note: Programs & services include: behavioural health services; chiropody & foot care services; diabetes education; home & community care.
Calvin Morrisseau, Executive Director

***Fort Frances:* Gizhewaadiziwin Health Access Centre**
Affiliated with: North West Local Health Integration Network
PO Box 686, Fort Frances, ON P9A 3M9
Tel: 807-274-3131; *Fax:* 807-274-6280
www.gizhac.com
Note: Programs & services include: primary care; nutrition; traditional healing; mental health; diabetes education.

***Grand Bend:* Grand Bend Area Community Health Centre**
PO Box 1269, 29 Gill Rd., Grand Bend, ON N0M 1T0
Tel: 519-238-2362; *Fax:* 519-238-6478
www.gbachc.ca
Dr. Glenn Bartlett, Executive Director

***Guelph:* Waterloo Wellington CCAC - Guelph Branch**
Also Known As: WWCCAC
#201, 450 Speedvale Ave. West, Guelph, ON N1H 7G7
Tel: 519-823-2550
healthcareathome.ca/ww
Note: Long-term care placement services; information & referral to other community services; in-home health services; school health support services; access to long-term care facilities; access to adult day programs; mental health & palliative care services

***Hamilton:* CCAC Hamilton Niagara Haldimand Brant - Hamilton Branch Office**
310 Limeridge Rd. West, Hamilton, ON L9C 2V2
Tel: 905-523-8600; *Fax:* 905-528-1883
Toll-Free: 800-450-8002
www.ccac-ont.ca
Melody Miles, CEO

***Hamilton:* Centre de santé communautaire Hamilton/Niagara**
460, rue Main est, 2e étage, Hamilton, ON L8N 1K4
Tél: 905-528-0163; *Téléc:* 905-528-9196
cschn@cschn.ca
www.centredesantecommunautaire.com
Robert Bisson, Directeur général

***Hamilton:* Hamilton Urban Core Community Health Centre**
71 Rebecca St., Hamilton, ON L8R 1B6
Tel: 905-522-3233; *Fax:* 905-522-3433
www.hucchc.com
Social Media:
www.facebook.com/HamiltonUrbanCoreCommunityHealthCentre; twitter.com/hucchc
Denise Brooks, Executive Director
dbrooks@hucchc.com

***Hamilton:* North Hamilton Community Health Centre**
438 Hughson St. North, Hamilton, ON L8L 4S1
Tel: 905-523-6611; *Fax:* 905-523-5173
www.northhamiltonchc.org
Year Founded: 1987
Note: Offers a variety of services and programs, including programs for men and women living with HIV/AIDS and programs for new immigrants/refugees
Elizabeth Beader, CEO
beader@nhchc.ca

***Huntsville:* Muskoka Algonquin Healthcare**
Huntsville District Memorial Hospital, 100 Frank Miller Dr., Huntsville, ON P1H 1H7
Tel: 705-789-2311; *Fax:* 705-789-0557
www.mahc.ca
Number of Beds: 99 beds
Number of Employees: 645
Note: Provides emergency health services & acute care.
Natalie Bubela, CEO
Dr. Jan Goossens, Chief of Medical Staff
Karen Fleming, Cheif Quality & Nursing Executive

***Ignace:* Mary Berglund Community Health Centre (MBCHC)**
PO Box 450, Ignace, ON P0T 1T0
Tel: 807-934-6719; *Fax:* 807-934-6552
mbchced@bellnet.ca
www.maryberglundchc.com
Note: Specialties: Primary care; Public health nursing; Physiotherapy; Chronic disease follow-up; Health promotion; Men's & women's wellness clinics; Blood sugar & blood pressure screening programs; Chiropractic services; Massage therapy

***Kenora:* CCAC North West - Kenora Branch Office**
#3, 35 Wolsley St., Kenora, ON P9N 3W7
Tel: 807-467-4757; *Fax:* 807-468-1437
Toll-Free: 877-661-6621
www.ccac-ont.ca
Tuija Puiras, CEO
807-346-3273, Fax: 807-345-8868, tuija.puiras@nw.ccac-ont.ca

***Kingston:* CCAC South East - Kingston Head Office**
#200, 1471 John Counter Blvd., Kingston, ON K7M 8S8
Tel: 613-544-7090; *Fax:* 613-544-1494
www.ccac-ont.ca
David Vigar, Board Chair

***Kingston:* Kingston Community Health Centres (KCHC)**
263 Weller Ave., Kingston, ON K7K 2V4
Tel: 613-542-2949; *Fax:* 613-542-3872
info@kchc.ca
www.kchc.ca
Social Media: www.facebook.com/KingstonCHC; twitter.com/kingstonchc
Year Founded: 1988
Hersh Sehdev, Executive Director

***Kirkland Lake:* CCAC North East - Kirkland Lake Branch Office**
53 Government Rd. West, Kirkland Lake, ON P2N 2E5
Tel: 705-567-2222; *Fax:* 705-567-9407
Toll-Free: 888-602-2222
healthcareathome.ca/northeast

***Kitchener:* Kitchener Downtown Community Health Centre**
44 Francis St. South, Kitchener, ON N2G 2A2
Tel: 519-745-4404; *Fax:* 519-745-3709
mail@kdchc.org
www.kdchc.org
Eric Goldberg, Executive Director
519-745-4404, egoldberg@kdchc.org

***Lanark:* North Lanark County Community Health Centre**
207 Robertson Dr., Lanark, ON K0G 1K0
Tel: 613-259-2182; *Fax:* 613-259-5235
Toll-Free: 866-762-0496
lmahon@lanarkcounty.ca
northlanarkchc.on.ca
Wanda MacDonald

***Lindsay:* CCAC Central East - Lindsay Branch Office**
370 Kent St. W, Lindsay, ON K9V 6G8
Tel: 705-324-9165; *Fax:* 705-324-0884
Toll-Free: 800-347-0285
www.cacc-ont.ca
Beverley Dew-Tezak, Board Chair

***London:* CCAC Southwest - London Branch Office**
356 Oxford St. West, London, ON N6H 1T3
Tel: 519-473-2222; *Fax:* 519-472-4045
Toll-Free: 800-811-5146
info-london@sw.ccac-ont.ca
www.ccac-ont.ca
Note: Head office for the South West CCAC & regional office for London & E. Middlesex
Sandra Coleman, CEO, South West CCAC

***London:* London InterCommunity Health Centre**
659 Dundas St., London, ON N5W 2Z1
Tel: 519-660-0874; *Fax:* 519-642-1532
mail@lihc.on.ca (General); orders@lihc.on.ca (Resources)
www.lihc.on.ca
Social Media:
www.facebook.com/LondonInterCommunityHealthCentre; twitter.com/HealthCentre
Year Founded: 1989
Note: Specialties: Inclusive & equitable health & social services to persons who experience barriers to care; Mental health care; Diabetes program; Options clinic HIV anonymous testing; Health & youth outreach services. Number of employees: 70
Ian Peer, Interim Executive Director
execdir@lihc.on.ca

***Longlac:* NorWest Community Health Centre - Longlac Site**
Affiliated with: North West Local Health Integration Network
PO Box 910, 99 Skinner Ave., Longlac, ON P0T 1T0
Tel: 807-876-2271; *Fax:* 807-876-2473
www.norwestchc.org/longlac.htm
Social Media: www.facebook.com/NorWestCHC
Note: Primary care services; programs for children & seniors.
Wendy Talbot, CEO

***Merrickville:* Merrickville District Community Health Centre**
PO Box 550, 354 Read St., Merrickville, ON K0G 1N0
Tel: 613-269-3400; *Fax:* 613-269-4958
info@RideauCHS.ca
www.rvds.ca
Note: Specialties: Social work; Dietitian services; Health education; Individual & family counselling; Case management, such as asthma; Foot care services; Flu clinics; Immunizations
Peter McKenna, Executive Director
613-269-3400, pmckenna@rideauchs.ca

***Mount Brydges:* Southwest Middlesex Health Centre**
22262 Mill Rd., RR#5, Mount Brydges, ON N0L 1W0
Tel: 519-264-2800; *Fax:* 519-264-2742
www.smhc.net
Year Founded: 1974
Area Served: Mount Brydges & the surrounding area
Note: Appointments are necessary.
Gary Wood, Centre Administrator

***New Liskeard:* Centre de santé communautaire du Témiskaming**
CP 38, 20 May St. South, New Liskeard, ON P0J 1P0
Tél: 705-647-5775; *Téléc:* 705-647-6011
Ligne sans frais: 800-835-2728
Jocelyne Maxwell, Directrice générale

***Newmarket:* CCAC Central - Newmarket Head Office**
Former Name: Etobicoke & York CCAC
#1, 1100 Gorham St., Newmarket, ON L3Y 8Y8
Tel: 905-895-1240; *Fax:* 905-952-2404
info@central.ccac-ont.ca
www.ccac-ont.ca
Nevzat Gurmen, Board Chair

***North Bay:* Near North CCAC**
1164 Devonshire Ave., North Bay, ON P1B 6X5
Tel: 705-476-2222; *Fax:* 705-474-0080
Toll-Free: 888-533-2222
www.nearnorth.ccac-ont.ca
Richard Joly, CEO

***Oshawa:* Oshawa Community Health Centre**
Dr. Bryce A. Brown Wellness Centre, 115 Grassmere Ave., Oshawa, ON L1H 3X7
Tel: 905-723-0036; *Fax:* 905-432-3902
info@ochc.ca
www.ochc.ca
Note: Specialties: Child development; Youth recreation; Women's wellness; Health promotion; Fmaily community outreach; Education services, such as the diabetes education program; Counselling; Parenting groups; Regular check-ups; Rehabilitation
Lee Kierstead, Executive Director
905-723-0036

Ottawa: Carlington Community & Health Services
900 Merivale Rd., Ottawa, ON K1Z 5Z8
Tel: 613-722-4000; *Fax:* 613-761-1805
TTY: 613-761-2161
info@carlington.ochc.org
www.carlington.ochc.org
Michael Birmingham, Executive Director

Ottawa: Centretown Community Health Centre
420 Cooper St., Ottawa, ON K2P 2N6
Tel: 613-233-4443
TTY: 613-233-0651
info@centretownchc.org
www.centretownchc.org
Social Media:
www.facebook.com/CentretownCHC.CSCduCentreville;
twitter.com/centretownchc

Ottawa: Ottawa Community Care Access Centre (CCAC)/Centre d'accès aux soins communautaires
#100, 4200 Labelle St., Ottawa, ON K1J 1J8
Tel: 613-745-5525; *Fax:* 613-745-6984
Toll-Free: 800-538-0520
TTY: 613-745-0049
information@champlain.ccac-ont.ca
www.ccac-ont.ca
Note: Specialties: Home care; Coordination of community care; Information about long-term care options
Gilles Lanteigne, CEO

Ottawa: Pinecrest-Queensway Health & Community Services (PQCHC)
1365 Richmond Rd., 2nd Fl., Ottawa, ON K2B 6R7
Tel: 613-820-4922; *Fax:* 613-820-2006
general@pqhcs.com
www.pqchc.com
Social Media: www.facebook.com/PQCHC; twitter.com/PQCHC
Year Founded: 1979
Wanda MacDonald, Executive Director

Ottawa: Sandy Hill Community Health Centre
211 Nelson St., Ottawa, ON K1N 1C7
Tel: 613-789-1500; *Fax:* 613-789-7962
info@sandyhillchc.on.ca
www.sandyhillchc.on.ca
Year Founded: 1973
Note: Provides a variety of Health and Social Services in the Eastern Ottawa region
David Gibson, Executive Director

Ottawa: Somerset West Community Health Centre
55 Eccles St., Ottawa, ON K1R 6S3
Tel: 613-238-8210; *Fax:* 613-238-7595
info@swchc.on.ca
www.swchc.on.ca
Jack McCarthy, Executive Director

Ottawa: South-East Ottawa Centre for a Healthy Community
#600, 1355 Bank St., Ottawa, ON K1H 8K7
Tel: 613-737-5115; *Fax:* 613-739-8199
office@seochc.on.ca
www.seochc.on.ca
Info Line: 613-737-4809

Owen Sound: CCAC North Bruce & Grey Counties
#3009, 1415 - 1 Ave. West, Owen Sound, ON N4K 4K8
Fax: 519-371-5612
www.ccac-ont.ca
Sandra Coleman, CEO, South West CCAC

Parry Sound: West Parry Sound Health Centre (WPSHC)
Affiliated with: North East Local Health Integration Network
6 Albert St., Parry Sound, ON P2A 3A4
Tel: 705-746-9321; *Fax:* 705-746-7364
www.wpshc.com
Year Founded: 1995
Number of Beds: 90 beds
Note: Programs & services include: acute & complex continuing care; rehabilitation; on-site Lakeland Long Term Care Facility; Community Care Access Centre; emergency services; surgery; diagnostic imaging; chemotherapy; sleep disorder clinic; lab; telehealth; Base Hospital Program & nursing stations in Britt, Pointe au Baril, Rosseau, Whitestone, Argyle & Moosedeer; specialist clinics
Donald Sanderson, CEO

Peterborough: CCAC Central East - Peterborough Branch Office
#202, 700 Clonsilla Ave., Peterborough, ON K9J 5Y3
Tel: 705-743-2212; *Fax:* 705-743-9559
Toll-Free: 888-235-7222
www.ccac-ont.ca
Beverley Dew-Tezak, Board Chair

Pickle Lake: Pickle Lake Health Centre
Affiliated with: North West Local Health Integration Network
PO Box 302, Pickle Lake, ON P0V 3A0
Tel: 807-928-2047; *Fax:* 807-928-2584
picklelake.healthclinic@picklelake.org
Note: Programs & services include: chronic disease management; disease prevention; nutritional counselling.

Portland: Country Roads Community Health Centre
PO Box 58, 4319 Cove Rd., Portland, ON K0G 1V0
Tel: 613-272-3302; *Fax:* 613-272-3463
Toll-Free: 888-998-9927
info@crchc.on.ca
www.crchc.on.ca
Sandra Chant, Executive Director

Richmond Hill: CCAC Central - Richmond Hill Site
Former Name: York Region CCAC
#400, 9050 Yonge St., Richmond Hill, ON L4C 9S6
Tel: 905-763-9928; *Fax:* 905-952-2404
info@central.ccac-ont.ca
www.ccac-ont.ca
Nevzat Gurmen, Board Chair

Sault Ste Marie: Community Care Access Centre
390 Bay St. Main Fl., Sault Ste Marie, ON P6A 1X2
Tel: 705-949-1650; *Fax:* 705-949-1663
Toll-Free: 800-668-7705
www.ccac-ont.ca
Note: Provides long term care in home.
Richard Joly, CEO

Sault Ste Marie: Group Health Centre Sault Ste. Marie
240 McNabb St., Sault Ste Marie, ON P6B 1Y5
Tel: 705-759-1234; *Fax:* 705-759-7469
Toll-Free: 800-461-2407
inquiries@ghc.on.ca
www.ghc.on.ca
Note: GHC is a progressive, multidisciplinary, consumer-sponsored health care facility, built by private funds donated by local union members. A partnership of the Sault Ste. Marie & District Group Health Association & the Algoma District Medical Group. Number of staff: 300+
Grant Walsh, President & CEO
705-759-5503, walsh_g@ghc.on.ca

Seaforth: CCAC South West - Seaforth Branch
PO Box 580, 32 Centennial Dr., Seaforth, ON N0K 1W0
Tel: 519-527-0000; *Fax:* 519-527-1255
Toll-Free: 800-267-0535
www.ccac-ont.ca
Sandra Coleman, CEO, South West CCAC

Simcoe: CCAC Hamilton Niagara Haldimand Brant - Haldimand-Norfolk Branch Office
76 Victoria St., Simcoe, ON N3Y 1L5
Tel: 519-426-7400; *Fax:* 519-426-4384
Toll-Free: 800-265-8068
www.ccac-ont.ca
Melody Miles, CEO

Smiths Falls: CCAC South East - Smith Falls Branch Office
#1, 52 Abbott St. North, Smiths Falls, ON K7A 1W3
Tel: 613-283-8012; *Fax:* 613-283-0308
Toll-Free: 800-267-6041
www.ccac-ont.ca
David Vigar, Board Chair

St Catharines: CCAC Hamilton Niagara Haldimand Brant - Niagara Branch Office
149 Hartzel Rd., St Catharines, ON L2P 1N6
Tel: 905-684-9441; *Fax:* 905-684-8463
Toll-Free: 800-263-5480
www.ccac-ont.ca
Melody Miles, CEO

St Jacobs: Woolwich Community Health Centre
10 Parkside Dr., St Jacobs, ON N0B 2N0
Tel: 519-664-3794; *Fax:* 519-664-2182
genmail@wchc.on.ca
www.wchc.on.ca

Year Founded: 1985
Note: Focuses on primary health care services.
Denise Squire, Executive Director

St Thomas: CCAC St. Thomas
#70, 1063 Talbot St., St Thomas, ON N5P 1G4
Fax: 519-631-2236
info-stthomas@sw.ccac-ont.ca
www.ccac-ont.ca
Sandra Coleman, CEO, South West CCAC

Stratford: CCAC South West - Stratford Branch Office
Former Name: Perth County Community Care Access Centre
65 Lorne Ave. East, Stratford, ON N5A 6S4
Tel: 519-273-2222; *Fax:* 519-273-2139
Toll-Free: 800-269-3683
www.ccac-ont.ca
Sandra Coleman, CEO, South West CCAC

Sudbury: CCAC North-East - Sudbury Branch Office
Rainbow Centre, #41-C, 40 Elm St., Sudbury, ON P3C 1S8
Tel: 705-522-3461; *Fax:* 705-522-3855
Toll-Free: 800-461-2919
info@ms.ccac-ont.ca
www.ms.ccac-ont.ca
Nancy Mongeon, Executive Director

Sudbury: Centre de santé communautaire de Sudbury
19, rue de Frood, Sudbury, ON P3C 4Y9
Tél: 705-670-2274; *Téléc:* 705-670-2277
www.santesudbury.ca
Yves Doyon, Président

Sudbury: Sudbury & District Health Unit (SDHU)
1300 Paris St., Sudbury, ON P3E 3A3
Tel: 705-522-9200; *Fax:* 705-522-5182
Toll-Free: 866-522-9200
www.sdhu.com
Social Media: twitter.com/SD_PublicHealth
Number of Employees: 250+
Penny Sutcliffe, Medical Officer of Health & CEO

Thunder Bay: Anishnawbe Mushkiki Thunder Bay Aboriginal Health Centre
Affiliated with: North West Local Health Integration Network
29 Royston Ct., Thunder Bay, ON P7A 4Y7
Tel: 807-343-4843; *Fax:* 807-343-4728
info@mushkiki.com
mushkiki.com
Note: Programs & services include: clinic care; culture; education; intervention; prevention.

Thunder Bay: NorWest Community Health Centre - Thunder Bay Site
Affiliated with: North West Local Health Integration Network
525 Simpson St., Thunder Bay, ON P7C 3J6
Tel: 807-622-8235; *Fax:* 807-622-7637
Toll-Free: 866-357-5454
www.norwestchc.org/thunder_bay.htm
Social Media: www.facebook.com/NorWestCHC
Wendy Talbot, CEO

Timmins: Misiway Milopemahtesewin Community Health Centre
130 Wilson Ave., Timmins, ON P4N 2S9
Tel: 705-264-2200; *Fax:* 705-264-2243
misiwayoa@vianet.ca
www.misiway.ca
Note: Clinic services; traditional healing services.
Pat Chilton, Executive Director

Timmins: North East Community Care Access Centre - Timmins Branch Office
#101, 330 - 2nd Ave., Timmins, ON P4N 8A4
Tel: 705-267-7766; *Fax:* 705-267-7795
Toll-Free: 888-668-2222
healthcareathome.ca/northeast
Richard Joly, CEO

Tobermory: Tobermory Clinic
PO Box 220, 7275 Hwy. 6, Tobermory, ON N0H 2T0
Tel: 519-596-2305; *Fax:* 519-596-2979
Note: Specialties: Family health; Community care; Minor day surgery; Mental health counselling. Number of Employees: 4 physicians + 1 nurse practitioner + 1 social worker + several clinic nurses
Ron Columbus, President, Tobermory Health Services Auxiliary
519-596-2150, roncolumbus@amtelecom.net

***Toronto:* Access Alliance Multicultural Community Health Centre**
#500, 340 College St., Toronto, ON M5T 3A9
Tel: 416-324-8677; *Fax:* 416-324-9074
mail@accessalliance.ca
www.accessalliance.ca
Social Media: www.facebook.com/AccessAlliance; twitter.com/accessalliance
Note: Provides community health services to refugees & immigrants
Brendan Wong, Board Chair

***Toronto:* Anishnawbe Health Toronto**
225 Queen St. East, Toronto, ON M5A 1S4
Tel: 416-360-0486; *Fax:* 416-365-1083
cshah@aht.ca
www.aht.ca
Year Founded: 1984
Note: An accredited community health centre, utilizing traditional healing approaches. A range of services is available, including fetal alcohol spectrum disorder services, diabetic care, HIV testing, mental health services & psychiatry, counselling, naturopathy, chiropody, women's services, massage therapy, & dental services. Other centres located at: 179 Gerrard St. E., 416-920-2605; and 22 Vaughan Rd., 416-657-0379. Mental Health Crisis Management Service: 416-891-8606.
Dr. Chandrakant Shah, Program Director, Cultural Safety Initiative
416-360-0486

***Toronto:* Anne Johnston Health Station**
2398 Yonge St., Toronto, ON M4P 2H4
Tel: 416-486-8666; *Fax:* 416-486-8660
info@ajhs.ca
www.ajhs.ca

***Toronto:* Bernard Betel Centre for Creative Living**
1003 Steeles Ave. West, Toronto, ON M2R 3T6
Tel: 416-225-2112; *Fax:* 416-225-2097
reception@betelcentre.org
www.betelcentre.org
Note: Provides education, recreation, arts, fitness & health services
Adam Silver, Acting Executive Director
416-225-2112 ext 135, adams@betelcentre.org

***Toronto:* Black Creek Community Health Centre**
#5, 2202 Jane St., Toronto, ON M3M 1A4
Tel: 416-249-8000; *Fax:* 416-249-4594
www.bcchc.com
Cary Milner, Executive Director

***Toronto:* CCAC Central - Sheppard Site**
#700, 45 Sheppard Ave. East, Toronto, ON M2N 5W9
Tel: 416-222-2241; *Fax:* 416-222-6517
info@central.ccac-ont.ca
www.ccac-ont.ca
Nevzat Gurmen, Board Chair

***Toronto:* CCAC Central East - Scarborough Branch Office**
#801, 100 Consilium Pl., Toronto, ON M1H 3E3
Tel: 416-750-2444; *Fax:* 416-750-8234
Toll-Free: 866-779-1931
www.ccac-ont.ca
Beverly Dew-Tezak, Board Chair

***Toronto:* CCAC Toronto Central**
#305, 250 Dundas St. West, Toronto, ON M5T 2Z5
Tel: 416-506-9888; *Fax:* 416-506-0374
Toll-Free: 866-243-0061
toronto_ccac@toronto.ccac-ont.ca
www.ccac-ont.ca
Stacey Daub, CEO

***Toronto:* CCAC Toronto Central - Leaside Park Drive Site-East York**
Former Name: East York Access Centre
#1, 1 Leaside Park Dr., Toronto, ON M4H 1R1
Tel: 416-423-3559; *Fax:* 416-423-9800
mail@eastyork.ccac-ont.ca
www.ccac-ont.ca

***Toronto:* Central Toronto Community Health Centres Queen West Community Health Centre**
168 Bathurst St., Toronto, ON M5V 2R4
Tel: 416-703-8482; *Fax:* 416-703-8479
www.ctchc.com
Note: Medical services (with specialized services for the homeless), psychiatric & mental health services, individual & group counselling, harm reduction program (safer sex, safer drug use, Hepatitis C & HIV prevention), needle exchange, diabetes education program, chiropody, perinatal nursing, dental clinic.

***Toronto:* Central Toronto Community Health Centres Shout Clinic**
168 Bathurst St., Toronto, ON M5V 2R4
Tel: 416-703-8482
info@ctchc.com
www.ctchc.com
Year Founded: 1992
Note: Walk-in medical clinic providing comprehensive health care services to homeless & street involved youth, 16-24 years of age.

***Toronto:* Centre francophone de Toronto**
Ancien nom: Centre médico-social communautaire
22, rue College, Toronto, ON M5G 1K3
Tél: 416-922-2672; *Téléc:* 416-922-6624
www.centrefranco.org
Lisa Marie Baudry, Directrice générale

***Toronto:* Davenport Perth Neighbourhood Centre (DPNCHC)**
1900 Davenport Rd., Toronto, ON M6N 1B7
Tel: 416-658-6812; *Fax:* 416-656-1264
info@dpnchc.ca
dpnchc.ca
Keith McNair, Executive Director

***Toronto:* East End Community Health Centre**
1619 Queen St. East, Toronto, ON M4L 3B5
Tel: 416-778-5858; *Fax:* 416-778-5855
Note: Services include counselling, physiotherapy, nutrition & medical.
Joyce Kalsen, Executive Director

***Toronto:* Family Health Centre Toronto East General Hospital**
#105, 840 Coxwell Ave., Toronto, ON M4C 5T2
Tel: 416-469-6464; *Fax:* 416-469-6164
ptrep@tegh.on.ca (Patients); community@tegh.on.ca (Community)
www.tegh.on.ca
Year Founded: 2002
Note: Specialties: Low-risk obstetrics; Psychotherapy; Telephone health advisory service

***Toronto:* Flemingdon Health Centre**
10 Gateway Blvd., Toronto, ON M3C 3A1
Tel: 416-429-4991
fhcinfo@fhc-chc.com
www.fhc-chc.com
Peter Yue, Executive Director

***Toronto:* Four Villages Community Health Centre**
1700 Bloor St. West, Toronto, ON M6P 4C3
Tel: 416-604-0640
www.4villageschc.ca
Almerinda Rebelo, Executive Director

***Toronto:* Lawrence Heights Community Health Centre**
12 Flemington Rd., Toronto, ON M6A 2N4
Tel: 416-787-1661; *Fax:* 416-787-3761
unisonhcs.org
Andrea Cohen, Executive Director

***Toronto:* Parkdale Community Health Centre**
1229 Queen St. West, Toronto, ON M6K 1L2
Tel: 416-537-2455; *Fax:* 416-537-5133
Social Media: twitter.com/ParkdaleCHC
Year Founded: 1984
Note: Specialties: Service in several languages; Primary care; Educational programs, such as pre- and post-natal classes; Support groups; Counselling; Mental health support; HIV testing

***Toronto:* Regent Park Community Health Centre**
465 Dundas St. East, Toronto, ON M5A 2B2
Tel: 416-364-2261; *Fax:* 416-364-0822
rpchc@regentparkchc.org
www.regentparkchc.org
Year Founded: 1973
Note: Emphasis on an integrated approach: health promotion, disease prevention, social services. A community-founded & operated facility, with a focus on comprehensive, accessible care. Services in English, Cantonese, Mandarin, Vietnames, Somali & Spanish. The Pathways to Education Program for youth at risk, created & first implemented in Regent Park, has been adopted by communities across Canada
Greg Webster, Board President

***Toronto:* Scarborough Centre for Healthy Communities**
Former Name: West Hill Community Services
2660 Eglinton Ave. East, Toronto, ON M1K 2S3
Tel: 416-642-9445
www.schcontario.ca
Info Line: 416-847-4173
Year Founded: 1977
Number of Employees: 130
Note: 38 distinct and integrated services across 9 sites. They provide medical assistance through their clinics, are involved in a youth program and have other social support programs including a food bank.
Jeanie Joaquin, CEO
416-847-4093

***Toronto:* South Riverdale Community Health Centre**
955 Queen St. East, Toronto, ON M4M 3P3
Tel: 416-461-1925
www.srchc.ca
Lynne Raskin, Executive Director

***Toronto:* Stonegate Community Health Centre**
150 Berry Rd., Toronto, ON M8Y 1W3
Tel: 416-231-7070; *Fax:* 416-231-2663
info@stonegatechc.org
www.stonegatechc.org
Social Media: www.facebook.com/318730301566322; twitter.com/StonegateCHC
Note: Specialties: Asthma care program research; Pre & post natal programs; Early years programs; Women's programs; Seniors' programs; Housing support & case management

***Toronto:* Women's Health in Women's Hands**
#500, 2 Carlton St., Toronto, ON M5B 1J3
Tel: 416-593-7655; *Fax:* 416-593-5867
info@whiwh.com
www.whiwh.com
Year Founded: 1993
Number of Employees: 33
Note: Provides mental and physical health services for women ages 16 and above.
Notisha Massaquoi, Executive Director

***Tweed:* Gateway Community Health Centre**
PO Box 99, 41 McClellan St., Tweed, ON K0K 3J0
Tel: 613-478-1211; *Fax:* 613-478-6692
info@gatewaychc.org
www.gatewaychc.org
Year Founded: 1991
Jeanne Goodhand, Executive Director

***Waterloo:* CCAC Waterloo Wellington**
141 Weber St. South, Waterloo, ON N2J 2A9
Tel: 519-748-2222; *Fax:* 519-883-5555
Toll-Free: 888-883-3313
information@ww.ccac-ont.ca
www.ccac-ont.ca
Note: Head office for the region
Inta Bregzis, Senior Director, Planning and Performance Management

***West Lorne:* West Elgin Community Health Centre**
153 Main St., West Lorne, ON N0L 2P0
Tel: 519-768-1715; *Fax:* 519-768-2548
info@wechc.on.ca
www.wechc.on.ca
Note: Provides health services and community programs to residents of the western Elgin area
David James, Board Chair

***Whitby:* CCAC Central East - Whitby Head Office**
Former Name: Durham Access to Care
920 Champlain Ct., Whitby, ON L1N 7H8
Tel: 905-430-3308; *Fax:* 905-430-3297
Toll-Free: 800-263-3877
www.ccac-ont.ca
Beverley Dew-Tezak, Board Chair

***Windsor:* CCAC Erie St. Clair - Windsor Branch**
5415 Tecumseh Rd. East, 2nd Fl., Windsor, ON N8T 1C5
Tel: 519-258-8211; *Fax:* 519-351-5842
Toll-Free: 888-447-4468
healthcareathome.ca/eriestclair

***Windsor:* Sandwich Community Health Centre Affiliated with: Windsor Essex Community Health Centre**
749 Felix Ave., Windsor, ON N9C 4E9
Tel: 519-258-6002; *Fax:* 519-528-3693
www.wechc.org
Year Founded: 1982
Note: Focus on providing primary health care & councelling.

Windsor: **Teen Health Centre**
Affiliated with: Windsor Essex Community Health Centre
Head Office, 1585 Ouellette Ave., Windsor, ON N8X 1K5
Tel: 519-253-8481; *Fax:* 519-253-4362
www.wechc.org
Note: Specialties: Counselling; Primary care; Special Additions, a prenatal program; Diabetes In Action, a community based diabetes program; Street Health Homeless Initiative Program, a program to serve homeless or at-risk persons in Windsor & Essex County

Woodstock: **CCAC South West - Woodstock Branch Office**
1147 Dundas St., Woodstock, ON N4S 8W3
Tel: 519-539-1284; *Fax:* 519-539-0065
Toll-Free: 800-561-5490
info-woodstock@sw.ccac-ont.ca
www.ccac-ont.ca
Sandra Coleman, Executive Director, South West CCAC

Nursing Stations

Bearskin Lake: **Bearskin Lake Nursing Station**
Affiliated with: North West Local Health Integration Network
PO Box 56, Bearskin Lake, ON P0V 1E0
Tel: 807-363-2582; *Fax:* 807-363-1021
Note: Programs & services include: diabetes clinic; health awareness workshop; alcohol/drug abuse workshop; communicable diseases clinic.

Special Treatment Centres

Barrie: **Royal Victoria Hospital of Barrie Community Care Centre for Substance Abuse**
70 Wellington St. West, Barrie, ON L4N 1K4
Tel: 705-728-9090; *Fax:* 705-728-7308
www.rvh.on.ca
Number of Beds: 41 beds
Note: Intoxification management, withdrawal management, assessments, family education, discharge planning

Brantford: **Lansdowne Children's Centre**
39 Mount Pleasant St., Brantford, ON N3T 1S7
Tel: 519-753-3153; *Fax:* 519-753-5927
info@lansdownecc.com
www.lansdownecentre.ca
Note: The centre provides services for children and youth with physical, communication and developmental needs.
Rita-Marie Hadley, Executive Director

Cambridge: **KidsAbility Centre for Child Development Cambridge**
Former Name: Rotary Children's Centre
c/o Chaplin Family YMCA, 250 Hespeler Rd., Cambridge, ON N1R 3H3
Fax: 519-886-7292
Toll-Free: 888-372-2259
www.kidsability.ca
Year Founded: 1957
Note: Specialty: Services for children & young adults with physical, developmental, & communication disabilities

Chatham: **Children's Treatment Centre of Chatham-Kent**
Former Name: Prism Centre for Audiology & Children's Rehabilitation
355 Lark St., Chatham, ON N7L 5B2
Tel: 519-354-0520; *Fax:* 519-354-7355
Toll-Free: 877-352-0089
www.childrenstreatment-ck.com
Year Founded: 1948
Note: Services include: music therapy; occupational therapy; physiotherapy; respite service; speech therapy
Donna Litwin-Makey, Executive Director
519-354-0520 ext.228

Cornwall: **Cornwall Withdrawal Management Services**
Cornwall Community Hospital
840 McConnell Ave., Cornwall, ON K6H 5S5
Tel: 613-938-8506; *Fax:* 613-938-2867
www.cornwallhospital.ca/en/WithdrawalManagement
Note: Cornwall's Withdrawal Management Services hosts AA & NA meetings & group therapy for men & women sixteen years of age & over. Strategies & information are provided to prevent substance misuse. The organization is bilingual.

Fergus: **KidsAbility Centre for Child Development Fergus**
Former Name: Rotary Children's Centre
c/o Community Resource Centre, 160 St. David St. South, Fergus, ON N1M 2L3
Fax: 519-843-7597
Toll-Free: 888-372-2259
www.kidsability.ca
Year Founded: 1957
Note: Specialty: Services for children & young adults with physical, developmental, & communication disabilities

Guelph: **KidsAbility Centre for Child Development Guelph**
Former Name: Rotary Children's Centre
c/o West End Community Centre, 21 Imperial Rd. South, Guelph, ON N1K 1X3
Fax: 519-780-0470
Toll-Free: 888-372-2259
info@growinggreatkidsguelph-wellington.com
www.kidsability.ca
Year Founded: 1957
Note: Specialty: Services for children & young adults with physical, developmental, & communication disabilities

Hamilton: **Hamilton Regional Cancer Centre**
699 Concession St., Hamilton, ON L8V 5C2
Tel: 905-387-9495; *Fax:* 905-575-6323
www.jcc.hhsc.ca
Dr. George Browman, CEO

Kingston: **Cancer Centre of Southeastern Ontario**
25 King St. West, Kingston, ON K7L 5P9
Tel: 613-544-2630; *Fax:* 613-544-9708
Toll-Free: 800-567-5722
www.krcc.on.ca

Kingston: **Child Development Centre (CDC)/Le Centre de développement de l'enfant**
Hotel Dieu Hospital
c/o Hotel Dieu Hospital, 166 Brock St., Kingston, ON K7L 5G2
Tel: 613-544-3400; *Fax:* 613-545-3557
www.kingstoncdc.ca
Area Served: Kingston & the surrounding area
Note: Most services at the Child Development Centre require physician referral. The Infant Develpment Program accepts children directly from parents.

Kingston: **Kingston Detoxification Centre**
Hotel Dieu Hospital
240 Brock St., Kingston, ON K7L 5G2
Tel: 613-549-6461
www.hoteldieu.com
Note: The Detoxification Centre provides counselling, self-help groups, & referral to community services

Kitchener: **Waterloo Regional Withdrawal Management Centre**
52 Glasgow St., Kitchener, ON N2G 1N6
Tel: 519-749-4318; *Fax:* 519-749-4328
info@grhosp.on.ca
www.grhosp.on.ca
Number of Beds: 21 beds
Note: Facility that helps addicts recover and rehabilitate

London: **London Regional Cancer Program**
London Health Sciences Centre
PO Box 5165, 790 Commissioners Rd. East, London, ON N6A 4L6
Tel: 519-685-8600
LRCPEducation@lhsc.on.ca (Patient education)
www.lhsc.on.ca
Note: Specialties: Inpatient & outpatient cancer care; Radiation therapy; Chemotherapy; Syooirt services, such as social work & diet & nutrition counselling

London: **Thames Valley Children's Centre**
779 Baseline Rd. East, London, ON N6C 5Y6
Tel: 519-685-8700
tvcc@tvcc.on.ca; innovations@tvcc.on.ca (Innovative products/books)
www.tvcc.on.ca
Year Founded: 1949
Note: Specialties: Rehabilitation services for children with physical disabilities, developmental delays, & communication disorders; Assessment & diagnosis services; Autism intervention program; Intensive behavioural intervention; Physiotherapy; Occupational therapy; Research; School support program.
Number of Employees: 350+ + 500 volunteers + 55 students
John A. LaPorta, CEO

Mississauga: **Erinoak Kids**
2277 South Millway, Mississauga, ON L5L 2M5
Tel: 905-855-2690 *Toll-Free:* 877-374-6625
www.erinoakkids.ca
Social Media: www.facebook.com/ErinoakKids; twitter.com/ErinoakKids; www.youtube.com/ErinoakKidsCentre
Year Founded: 1978
Note: Outpatient services only
Bridget Fewtrell, President & CEO

Oshawa: **Grandview Children's Centre**
Former Name: Grandview Rehabilitation & Treatment Centre of Durham Region
600 Townline Rd. South, Oshawa, ON L1H 7K6
Tel: 905-728-1673; *Fax:* 905-728-2961
Toll-Free: 800-304-6180
www.grandviewcc.ca
Social Media: www.facebook.com/GrandviewChildrensCentre; twitter.com/grandviewcc
Note: A treatment centre for children with physical, developmental and communication disabilities.
Lorraine Sunstrum-Mann, Executive Director
905-728-1673, lorraine.sunstrum-mann@grtc.ca

Ottawa: **The Ottawa Children's Treatment Centre (OCTC)/Le Centre de traitement pour enfants d'Ottawa**
395 Smyth Rd., Ottawa, ON K1H 8L2
Tel: 613-737-0871; *Fax:* 613-523-5167
Toll-Free: 800-565-4839
www.octc.ca
Year Founded: 1951
Note: From several locations in Ottawa & area, The Centre provides specialized care for children with multiple physical, developmental & behavioural needs. Services in English & French
Kathleen Stokely, CEO

Ottawa: **Ottawa Hospital Cancer Program**
General Campus, 501 Smyth Rd., Ottawa, ON K1H 8L6
Tel: 613-247-3525 *Toll-Free:* 888-627-5082
www.ottawahospital.on.ca/sc/cancer/index-e.asp
Note: Specialties: Screening; Early Detection; Diagnosis; Treatment; Supportive Care; Palliative Care; Research
Dr. Jack Kitts, CEO

Ottawa: **The Ottawa Morgentaler Clinic**
65 Bank St., Ottawa, ON K1P 5N2
Tel: 613-567-8300; *Fax:* 613-567-9128
info@yenott.com
www.morgentaler.ca
Note: Specialty: Abortion services; Counselling

Ottawa: **Rehabilitation Centre (TRC)**
The Ottawa Hospital
505 Smyth Rd., Ottawa, ON K1H 8M2
Tel: 613-737-7350
TTY: 613-526-1132
webmaster@ottawahospital.on.ca
www.ottawahospital.on.ca
Note: Specialties: Rehabilitation of persons with a disabling physical illness or injury; Prosthetics & orthotics; Physiotherapy; Occupational therapy; Respiratory therapy; Speech-language pathology; Psychological services; Vocational rehabilitation counselling; Social work; Research
Dr. Jack Kitts, President & CEO

Peterborough: **Five Counties Children's Centre**
872 Dutton Rd., Peterborough, ON K9H 7G1
Tel: 705-748-2221; *Fax:* 705-748-3526
Toll-Free: 888-779-9916
info@fivecounties.on.ca
www.fivecounties.on.ca
Note: Children with special needs 0-19 years of age. Services include: speech and language therapy; occupational therapy; physiotherapy; therapautic recreation; augmentative communication
Diane Pick, CEO

Sarnia: **Pathways Health Centre for Children**
1240 Murphy Rd., Sarnia, ON N7S 2Y6
Tel: 519-542-3471; *Fax:* 519-542-4115
info@pathwayscentre.org
www.pathwayscentre.org
Social Media: www.facebook.com/205417719507560
Year Founded: 1975
Note: Children's treatment centre
Jenny Greensmith, Executive Director

Sault Ste Marie: Children's Rehabiliation Centre Algoma
74 Johnson Ave., Sault Ste Marie, ON P6C 2V5
Tel: 705-759-1131; *Fax:* 705-759-0783
Toll-Free: 855-759-1131
info@crcalgoma.ca
www.crcalgoma.ca
Year Founded: 1952
Note: Outpatient health services centre

Sault Ste Marie: Sault Ste. Marie Detoxification Unit
911 Queen St. East, Sault Ste Marie, ON P6A 2B6
Tel: 705-942-1872; *Fax:* 705-759-6369
Number of Beds: 15 beds
Note: detox centre

St Agatha: kidsLINK (NDSA)
PO Box 190, 1855 Notre Dame Dr., St Agatha, ON N0B 2L0
Tel: 519-746-5437; *Fax:* 519-746-3055
Social Media: twitter.com/kidsLINK; ca.linkedin.com/pub/kidslink-st-agatha
Year Founded: 1966
Number of Beds: 26 beds
Note: Children's mental health residential & day treatment services; outpatient services, respite, prevention & early intervention for children & families
Richard Steinmann, President

St Catharines: Niagara Peninsula Children's Centre
567 Glenridge Ave., St Catharines, ON L2T 4C2
Tel: 905-688-3550; *Fax:* 905-688-1055
Toll-Free: 800-896-5496
info@niagarachildrenscentre.com
niagarachildrenscentre.com
Note: Children's rehabilitation centre
Oksana Fisher, CEO
905-688-1890

St Catharines: Niagara Regional Men's Withdrawal Management Service
Niagara Health System / Système de santé de Niagara
Affiliated with: Hamilton Niagara Haldimand Brant Local Health Integration Network
10 Adams St., St Catharines, ON L2R 2V8
Tel: 905-682-7211
Number of Beds: 18 beds
Note: The withdrawal management service offers crisis intervention, assessments, counselling, self-help groups, & treatment referrals for inpatients & outpatients.

St Catharines: St Catharines Detoxification (Women's) Unit
6 Adams St., St Catharines, ON L2R 2V8
Tel: 905-687-9721; *Fax:* 905-687-9768
Number of Beds: 14 beds
Norma Medulun, Director

St. Catharines: Hôtel Dieu Shaver Health & Rehabilitation Centre
Affiliated with: Hamilton Niagara Haldimand Brant Local Health Integration Network
Former Name: Hôtel-Dieu Health Sciences Hospital - Niagara
541 Glenridge Ave., St. Catharines, ON L2T 4C2
Tel: 905-685-1381; *Fax:* 905-687-4871
info@hoteldieushaver.org
www.hoteldieushaver.org
Number of Beds: 134 beds
Number of Employees: 400
Note: Complex continuing care, rehabilitation & palliative care.
Jane Rufrano, CEO & CFO
Dr. Jack Luce, Chief of Staff

Sudbury: Children's Treatment Centre
Affiliated with: Health Sciences North
41 Ramsey Lake Rd., Sudbury, ON P3E 5J1
Tel: 705-523-7337; *Fax:* 705-560-4273
www.hsnsudbury.ca
Social Media: www.facebook.com/HSNSudbury; twitter.com/HSN_Sudbury; www.youtube.com/user/healthsciencesnorth; www.linkedin.com/company/health-sciences-north
Note: outpatient, community-based rehabilitation centre

Sudbury: Pinegate Men's & Women's Withdrawal Management Centre
336 Pine St., Sudbury, ON P3C 1X8
Tel: 705-671-7167
Number of Beds: 13 beds
Note: non-medical withdrawal management service
Amanda Conrad, Principal

Thunder Bay: George Jeffrey Children's Centre (GJCC)
Former Name: George Jeffrey Children's Treatment Centre
200 Brock St. East, Thunder Bay, ON P7E 0A2
Tel: 807-623-4381; *Fax:* 807-623-7161
Toll-Free: 888-818-7330
www.georgejeffrey.com
Social Media: www.facebook.com/132052553534644
Year Founded: 1948
Note: Services include: occupational therapy; physiotherapy; speech-language pathology
Juliana Jason, Chief Executive Officer

Timmins: Cochrane Temiskaming Children's Treatment Centre/Centre de traitement pour enfants Cochrane Temiskaming
#1, 733 Ross Ave. East, Timmins, ON P4N 8S8
Tel: 705-264-4700; *Fax:* 705-268-3585
Toll-Free: 800-575-3210
Year Founded: 1980
Area Served: Districts of Cochrane and Temiskaming
Note: Services include consultation, assessment, treatment and education.
Mary MacKay, Executive Director

Toronto: Bob Rumball Centre for the Deaf
2395 Bayview Ave., Toronto, ON M2L 1A2
Tel: 416-449-9651; *Fax:* 416-449-8881
TTY: 416-449-2728
info@bobrumball.org
www.bobrumball.org
Number of Beds: 56 beds
Note: long-term care facility for the deaf

Toronto: Cabbagetown Women's Clinic
302 Gerrard St. East, Toronto, ON M5A 2G7
Tel: 416-323-0642; *Fax:* 416-323-3099
Toll-Free: 800-399-1592
www.cabbagetownwomensclinic.com
Year Founded: 1989
Note: Licensed as and Independent Health facility funded by the Ontario Min. of Health & Long Term Care, the clinic provides medical services to women seeking a legal & safe abortion.

Toronto: Casey House Hospice
9 Huntley St., Toronto, ON M4Y 2K8
Tel: 416-962-7600; *Fax:* 416-962-5147
heart@caseyhouse.on.ca
www.caseyhouse.com
Social Media: www.facebook.com/pages/Casey-House-Toronto/111871308199; twitter.com/caseyhouseTO; www.youtube.com/caseyhousetv; www.linkedin.com/company/casey-house-foundation
Year Founded: 1988
Number of Beds: 13 beds
Note: Hospice; home care office
Stephanie Karapita, CEO
Dr. Ann Stewart, MD, MSc, CCFP, Medical Director
416-962-7660

Toronto: Centre for Addiction & Mental Health ARF Site
Former Name: Addiction Research Foundation
33 Russell St., Toronto, ON M5S 2S1
Tel: 416-595-6000; *Fax:* 416-595-9997
Toll-Free: 800-463-6273
webmaster@camh.net
www.camh.net
Social Media: www.facebook.com/CentreforAddictionandMentalHealth; www.twitter.com/CAMHnews; www.youtube.com/camhtv; www.linkedin.com/company/camh
Number of Beds: 614 beds
Note: drug rehabilitation centre
Dr. Catherine Zahn, President and CEO; CAMH

Toronto: Centre for Addiction & Mental Health (Corporate Office)
33 Russell St., Toronto, ON M5S 2S1
Tel: 416-535-8501
webmaster@camh.net
www.camh.ca
Social Media: www.facebook.com/CentreforAddictionandMentalHealth; twitter.com/CAMHnews; www.youtube.com/user/CAMHTV; www.linkedin.com/company/camh
Number of Beds: 614 beds
Note: addiction treatment
Dr. Catherine Zahn, President/CEO

Toronto: Child Development Institute
Former Name: West End Creche Child & Family Clinic
197 Euclid Ave., Toronto, ON M6J 2J8
Tel: 416-868-1827; *Fax:* 416-868-1827
Year Founded: 1909
Tony Diniz, CEO
tdiniz@childdevelop.ca

Toronto: Choice in Health Clinic
#301, 1678 Bloor St. West, Toronto, ON M4X 1W3
Tel: 416-975-9300; *Fax:* 416-975-0314
Toll-Free: 866-565-9300
www.choiceinhealth.ca
Note: abortion clinic

Toronto: Eye Bank of Canada Ontario Division
c/o Dept. of Ophthalmology, University of Toronto, 1929 Bayview Ave., Toronto, ON M5S 2J5
Tel: 416-978-7355; *Fax:* 416-978-1522
eye.bank@utoronto.ca
www.eyebank.utoronto.ca
Year Founded: 1955
Dr. David Rootman, Medical Director
Dr. William Dixon, Medical Co-director

Toronto: Holland Bloorview Kids Rehabilitation Hospital
Affiliated with: Toronto Central Local Health Integration Network
Former Name: Bloorview Children's Hospital
150 Kilgour Road, Toronto, ON M4G 1R8
Tel: 416-425-6220; *Fax:* 416-425-6591
Toll-Free: 800-363-2440
www.hollandbloorview.ca
Social Media: www.facebook.com/HBKRH; twitter.com/bloorviewpr; www.youtube.com/user/PRBloorview
Year Founded: 1899
Number of Beds: 75 beds
Note: Pediatric rehabilitation & continuing care complex
Julia Hanigsberg, President & CEO

Toronto: Marvelle Koffler Breast Centre
J. & W. Lebovic Health Complex, Mount Sinai Hospit, 600 University Ave., 12th Fl., Toronto, ON M5G 1X5
Tel: 416-586-8799
www.mountsinai.on.ca/care/mkbc
Year Founded: 1995
Note: Specialties: Outpatient facility for breast health & disease; Mammography / Breast imaging; Pathology; Surgery; Psychiatry; Nutrition; Boutique addressing the needs of women who have experienced breast cancer; Palliative medicine
Dr. Christine Elser, Head, Familial Breast Cancer Clinic

Toronto: The Morgentaler Clinic
727 Hillsdale Ave. East, Toronto, ON M4S 1V4
Tel: 416-932-0446; *Fax:* 416-932-0837
Toll-Free: 800-556-6835
mclinic@passport.ca
www.morgentaler.ca
Note: Specialties: Abortion services; Counselling; Contraceptive education; Testing for sexually transmitted infections

Toronto: St. Michael's Hospital Detoxification Centre
30 Bond St., Toronto, ON M5B 1W8
Tel: 416-864-6060; *Fax:* 416-864-5996
detox@smh.toronto.on.ca
Number of Beds: 22 beds
Note: detoxification clinic

Toronto: Sunnybrook Health Sciences Centre - Holland Orthopaedic & Arthritic Centre
Affiliated with: Toronto Central Local Health Integration Network
43 Wellesley St. East, Toronto, ON M4Y 1H1
Tel: 416-967-8500; *Fax:* 416-967-8521
www.sunnybrook.ca
Note: Care for complex injuries of the musculoskeletal system, with a focus on traumatic injury management, joint reconstruction & replacement, surgery, sports & activity-related injury management, rehabilitation, rheumatology. The Clinic has a second location at the main Sunnybrook site, 2075 Bayview Ave., Toronto
Dr. Barry A. McLellan, President & CEO

Toronto: Sunnybrook Health Sciences Centre - St. John's Rehab
Affiliated with: Toronto Central Local Health Integration Network
285 Cummer Ave., Toronto, ON M2M 2G1
Tel: 416-226-6780; *Fax:* 416-226-6265
info@stjohnsrehab.com
sunnybrook.ca
Number of Beds: 160 beds
Note: Ontario's only hospital dedicated to specialized rehabilitation services & care: burn injuries, organ transplant rehabilitation, cancer, cardiovascular surgery, strokes & other neurological conditions, traumatic injuries & complex medical conditions. Teaching site for the University of Toronto & a leading research facility. A multicultural & multifaith environment dedicated to the values of care of the Sisters of St. John the Divine
Barry A. McLellan, President & CEO

Toronto: Sunnybrook Health Sciences Centre - The Odette Cancer Centre
Affiliated with: Toronto Central Local Health Integration Network
2075 Bayview Ave., Toronto, ON M4N 3M5
Tel: 416-480-5000; *Fax:* 416-217-1338
www.sunnybrook.ca
Note: Comprehensive cancer care, multidisciplinary, evidence-based approach; research, education & community outreach
Dr. Barry A. McLellan, President & CEO

Toronto: Toronto Rehabilitation Institute University Health Network
Affiliated with: Toronto Central Local Health Integration Network
Also Known As: Toronto Rehab
550 University Ave., Toronto, ON M5G 2A2
Tel: 416-597-3422; *Fax:* 416-597-1977
www.uhn.ca/torontorehab
Social Media: www.facebook.com/UniversityHealthNetwork; twitter.com/UHN_News; www.youtube.com/UHNToronto; www.linkedin.com/company/university-health-network
Note: Rehabilitation & complex continuing care; includes Hillcrest Centre; Lakeside Long-Term Care Centre; Lyndhurst Centre; E.W. Bickle Centre; Rumsey Centre, & University Centre
Robert Bell, President & CEO

Toronto: Toronto Western Hospital - Addiction Outpatient/Aftercare Clinic University Health Network
Affiliated with: Toronto Central Local Health Integration Network
399 Bathurst St., Toronto, ON M5T 2S8
Tel: 416-603-5800; *Fax:* 416-603-5490
www.uhn.ca
Note: Assessment & referral, individual & group therapy, counseling, psychiatric consultation, education. Services in English, French, Portuguese, Polish

Toronto: West Park Healthcare Centre
Affiliated with: Toronto Central Local Health Integration Network
Former Name: West Park Hospital
82 Buttonwood Ave., Toronto, ON M6M 2J5
Tel: 416-243-3600; *Fax:* 416-243-8947
feedback@westpark.org
www.westpark.org
Social Media: www.facebook.com/WestParkHealthcareCentre; twitter.com/westparkhcc; www.youtube.com/WestParkhealthcare; www.linkedin.com/company/218953
Year Founded: 1904
Number of Beds: 200 long-term care beds; 140 complex continung care beds; 130 rehab beds
Number of Employees: 885
Note: Rehabilitation & chronic care facility
Anne-Marie Malek, President & CEO
Dr. Nora Cullen, Chief of Staff

Toronto: Withdrawal Management Centre Toronto East General Hospital
985 Danforth Ave., Toronto, ON M4J 1M1
Tel: 416-461-2010; *Fax:* 416-461-1164
ptrep@tegh.on.ca (Patients); community@tegh.on.ca (Community)
www.tegh.on.ca
Number of Beds: 22 beds
Note: Specialties: Crisis intervention for adult males; Physical care for males in acute states of intoxication; Withdrawal from alcohol & other addictive substances; Addictions assessments; Counselling; Rehabilitation services; Education on substance abuse to family members

Waterloo: KidsAbility - Centre for Child Development
Former Name: Rotary Children's Centre
500 Hallmark Dr., Waterloo, ON N2K 3P5
Tel: 519-886-8886; *Fax:* 519-886-7292
Toll-Free: 888-372-2259
www.kidsability.ca
Social Media: www.facebook.com/184568644892738; twitter.com/KidsAbility
Year Founded: 1957
Note: Specialties: Services for children & young adults with physical, developmental, & communication disabilities; Autism intervention; Occupational therapy; Physiotherapy; Speech-language therapy; Augmentative communication; Therapeutic recreation; Social work. Number of Employees: 200 + 300 volunteers
Linda Kenny, CEO

Windsor: The John McGivney Children's Centre
Former Name: Children's Rehabilitation Centre of Essex County
3945 Matchette Rd., Windsor, ON N9C 4C2
Tel: 519-252-7281; *Fax:* 519-252-5873
info@jmccentre.ca
www.jmccentre.ca
Social Media: www.facebook.com/243715438993933
Note: Services include: augmentative communication; autism services; speech, occupational, & physiotherapy
Carolyn Tavolieri, President

Windsor: Windsor Withdrawal Management Residential Service Windsor Regional Hospital
1453 Prince Rd., Windsor, ON N9C 3Z4
Tel: 519-257-5225; *Fax:* 519-253-1752
www.wrh.on.ca
Number of Beds: 20 beds
Area Served: Counties of Essex, Kent, & Lambton, Ontario
Note: The agency assists men & women who are 16 years of age or older to access treatment for addiction. The service is funded by the Ministry of Health & Long-term Care.
Bill Marcotte, Service Director
bill_marcotte@wrh.on.ca

Long Term Care Facilities

Alliston: Good Samaritan Seniors Complex
481 Victoria St. East, Alliston, ON L9R 1J8
Tel: 705-435-5722; *Fax:* 705-435-0235
www.goodsamseniors.com
Number of Beds: 64 beds

Amherstburg: Richmond Terrace
89 Rankin Ave., Amherstburg, ON N9V 1E7
Tel: 519-736-5571; *Fax:* 519-736-2995
www.richmondterrace.ca
Number of Beds: 115 beds
Laura Scott, Administrator
lscott@richmondterrace.ca

Ancaster: The Willowgrove Long Term Care Residence
Affiliated with: Chartwell Retirement Residences
1217 Old Mohawk Rd., Ancaster, ON L9K 1P6
Tel: 905-304-6781
www.chartwell.com
Number of Beds: 169 units
W. Brent Binions, President & CEO, Chartwell Retirement Residences

Aurora: Aurora Resthaven
Affiliated with: Chartwell Retirement Residences
32 Mill St., Aurora, ON L4G 2R9
Tel: 905-727-1939; *Fax:* 905-727-6299
www.chartwell.com
Number of Beds: 176 beds
W. Brent Binions, President & CEO

Aurora: Blue Hills Child & Family Service
402 Bloomington Rd., Aurora, ON L4G 3G8
Tel: 905-773-4323; *Fax:* 905-773-8133
Toll-Free: 866-536-7608
www.bluehillscentre.ca
Number of Beds: 9 beds
Note: children's mental health centre; special care home; outpatient services; family therapy
Sylvia Pivko, Executive Director
spivko@bluehillschildandfamily.ca

Aylmer: Chateau Gardens Aylmer
Affiliated with: Chartwell Retirement Residences
465 Talbot St. West, Aylmer, ON N5H 1K8
Tel: 519-773-3423
www.chartwell.com
Number of Beds: 60 beds

Barrie: Heritage Place
Affiliated with: IOOF Seniors Homes Inc.
20 Brooks St., Barrie, ON L4N 7X2
Tel: 705-728-2389; *Fax:* 705-728-8149
www.ioof.com
Number of Beds: 90 beds
Doreen M. Saunders, CEO
dsaunders@ioof.com

Barrie: Roberta Place Long-Term Care
503 Essa Rd., Barrie, ON L4N 9E4
Tel: 705-733-3232; *Fax:* 705-733-2592
www.jarlette.com/robertaplace_ltc.html
Number of Beds: 139 long term care beds
Carolyn McLeod, Administrator
cmcleod@jarlette.com

Barrie: Victoria Village Manor
Affiliated with: Specialty Care
78 Ross St., Barrie, ON L4N 1G3
Tel: 705-728-3456; *Fax:* 705-728-4057
suggestions@specialty-care.com
www.specialty-care.com
Number of Beds: 128 long-term care beds, 57 life-lease housing units
Wendy Massarotto, Director, Resident & Family Services
wendy.massarotto@specialty-care.com

Beaverton: Lakeview Manor
133 Main St., Beaverton, ON L0K 1A0
Tel: 705-426-7388; *Fax:* 705-426-4218
Number of Beds: 149 beds
Note: home for the aged
Pearle Perez, Administrator
Barb Surge, Director of Care

Belleville: Welcome to Community Living Belleville & Area
Former Name: Plainfield Community Homes; Plainfield Children's Home
91 Millennium Pkwy., Belleville, ON K8N 4Z5
Tel: 613-969-7407; *Fax:* 613-969-7775
www.communitylivingbelleville.org
Social Media: www.facebook.com/communitylivingbellevilleandarea; twitter.com/CLBelleville
Year Founded: 1951
Note: Community Living Belleville & Area works toward the full inclusion in community life of persons with intellectual disabilities.
John B. Klassen, Executive Director
Stephen Ollerenshaw, Director, Finance
Katherine Potts, Director, Human Resources
Christine Semark, Director, Services
Jim Burgess, Manager, Buildings & Property
Sharon Wright, Manager, Community Development & Volunteer Services

Blind River: Golden Birches Terrace
525 Causley St., Blind River, ON P0R 1B0
Tel: 705-356-2265; *Fax:* 705-356-1220
webinfo@brdhc.on.ca
www.brdhc.on.ca
Number of Beds: 42 beds
Gaston Lavigne, CEO
705-356-2265

Bracebridge: The Pines Long Term Care Home
Also Known As: The Pines
98 Pine St., Bracebridge, ON P1L 1N5
Tel: 705-645-4488; *Fax:* 705-645-6857
mlodge@muskoka.on.ca
www.muskoka.on.ca
Year Founded: 1961
Number of Beds: 160 beds
Note: Long term care residence
Katherine Rannie, Administrator
705-645-4488, krannie@muskoka.on.ca
Charmaine Kaye, Director of Care
705-645-4488, ckaye@muskoka.on.ca

***Bradford:* Bradford Valley**
Affiliated with: Specialty Care
2656 - 6 Line, Bradford, ON L3Z 3H5
Tel: 905-952-2270; *Fax:* 905-775-0263
suggestions@specialty-care.com
www.specialty-care.com

Luanne Campeau, Administrator
luanne.campeau@specialty-care.com

***Brampton:* Leisureworld Caregiving Centre Tullamore**
133 Kennedy Rd. South, Brampton, ON L6W 3G3
Tel: 905-459-2324
adm.tullamore@leisureworld.ca
www.leisureworld.ca

Year Founded: 1965
Number of Beds: 159 beds
Note: Specialties: Long-term care; Restorative care; Occupational therapy; Physiotherapy; Care for persons with Alzheimer's disease; Respite care; Pet therapy; Palliative care
Lois Cormack, CEO, Leisureworld Senior Care Corporation

***Brampton:* Rosedale Retirement Residence**
12 William St., Brampton, ON L6V 1L2
Tel: 905-454-3788; *Fax:* 905-846-0447
www.rosedaleretirement.ca

Number of Beds: 12 beds

***Brampton:* Woodhall Park**
Affiliated with: Specialty Care
10260 Kennedy Rd. North, Brampton, ON L6T 3S1
Tel: 905-495-4695; *Fax:* 905-495-4693
suggestions@specialty-care.com
www.specialty-care.com

Number of Beds: 147 beds
Jennifer Van Klink, Interim Administrator
jennifer.vanklink@specialty-care.com

***Brantford:* Brantwood Residential Development Centre**
Former Name: Brant Sanatorium
Also Known As: Brantwood Centre
25 Bell Lane, Brantford, ON N3T 1E1
Tel: 519-753-2658
www.brantwood.ca

Year Founded: 1913
Number of Employees: 220
Note: Brantwood provides services to persons who live in twelve group homes located in the city of Brantford & Brant County. A community day program is available for individuals who live in the community.
Jo-Anne Link, Executive Director
Ellen Brocklebank, Director, Support Services
Lori Broughton, Director, Support Services
Steve Wood, Director, Finance
Audrey Casey, Nurse Manager

***Brantford:* John Noble Home**
97 Mount Pleasant Rd., Brantford, ON N3T 1T5
Tel: 519-756-2920; *Fax:* 519-754-1521
info@jnh.ca
www.jnh.ca

Number of Beds: 156 beds

***Brantford:* St. Joseph's Lifecare Centre**
Former Name: St. Joseph's Hospital
99 Wayne Gretzky Pkwy., Brantford, ON N3S 6T6
Tel: 519-751-7096; *Fax:* 519-753-7996
www.sjlc.ca

Derrick Bernardo, President
905-522-1155, dbernardo@sjltc.ca

***Brighton:* Maplewood**
PO Box 249, 12 Maplewood Ave., Brighton, ON K0K 1H0
Tel: 613-475-2442; *Fax:* 613-475-4445
www.omniway.ca

Number of Beds: 49 beds
Note: Long-term care residence
Carolyn Adams, Office Manager
cadams@omniway.ca
Nancy McNairn, Administrator
nmcnairn@omniway.ca

***Burlington:* Abeliving Services Thrive Group**
Former Name: Participation House - Hamilton & District
1022 Waterdown Rd., Burlington, ON L7T 1N3
Tel: 905-527-7949; *Fax:* 905-333-8711
info@ableliving.org
www.ableliving.org

Number of Beds: 39 beds
Note: Provides services designed to enhance the quality of life of adults with disabilities
Steve Sherrer, CEO

***Burlington:* Billings Court Manor**
Affiliated with: Conmed Health Care Group
3700 Billings Crt, Burlington, ON L7N 3N6
Tel: 905-333-4006; *Fax:* 905-333-4416
Toll-Free: 888-274-6445
www.conmedhealth.com

Number of Beds: 160 units

***Burlington:* Mount Nemo Christian Nursing Home**
4486 Guelph Line, Burlington, ON L7P 0N2
Tel: 905-335-3636; *Fax:* 905-335-3699
mountnemonursinghome@cogeco.net
www.mountnemochristiannh.on.ca

Number of Beds: 60 beds
Note: long term care home

***Chatham:* Copper Terrace Long Term Care Facility**
91 Tecumseh Rd., Chatham, ON N7M 1B3
Tel: 519-354-5442; *Fax:* 519-354-0362
www.copperterrace.ca

Number of Beds: 151 beds

***Chatham:* Meadow Park Care Centre**
Affiliated with: Jarlette Health Services
110 Sandys St., Chatham, ON N7L 4X3
Tel: 519-351-1330; *Fax:* 519-351-7933
www.jarlette.com

Number of Beds: 97 beds
Anne Marie Rumble, Administrator
amrumble@jarlette.com
Susan Vanek, Director of Care
svanek@jarlette.com

***Chatham:* Riverview Gardens**
Former Name: Thamesview Lodge
519 King St. West, Chatham, ON N7M 1G8
Tel: 519-352-4823; *Fax:* 519-352-2891
CKseniors@chatham-kent.ca
www.chatham-kent.ca

Number of Beds: 320 beds

***Chatsworth:* Country Lane Long Term Care Residence**
RR#3, 317079 Hwy 6 & 10, Chatsworth, ON N0H 1G0
Tel: 519-794-2244; *Fax:* 519-794-2597
country-lane.ca

Number of Beds: 34 beds
Mary Lynne Kennedy-McGregor, Administrator & Director of Care
mkennedy-mcgregor@extendicare.com

***Chesley:* Parkview Manor Extendicare Assist**
98 - 3rd St. SE, Chesley, ON N0G 1L0
Tel: 519-363-2416; *Fax:* 519-363-2171
parkview-manor.ca

Number of Beds: 34 beds
Carole Woods, Administrator
cwoods2@extendicare.com

***Clarence Creek:* Centre d'accueil Roger-Séguin**
435 Lemay St., Clarence Creek, ON K0A 1N0
Tel: 613-488-2053; *Fax:* 613-488-2274
www.centrerogerseguin.org

Number of Beds: 115 beds
Note: charitable
Charles Lefebvre, Administrator
clefebvre@centrerogerseguin.org

***Cobourg:* Golden Plough Lodge**
983 Burnham St., Cobourg, ON K9A 5J6
Tel: 905-372-8759; *Fax:* 905-372-8525
www.northumberlandcounty.ca

Number of Beds: 162 beds
Clare Briggs, Administrator
briggsc@northumberlandcounty.ca

***Cochrane:* Villa Minto**
PO Box 280, 241 - 8 St., Cochrane, ON P0L 1C0
Tel: 705-272-7200; *Fax:* 705-272-4155
www.micsgroup.com

Number of Beds: 33 beds
Note: Villa Minto is an independent LTC facility housed in the chronic care wing of The Lady Minto Hospital

***Cornwall:* Sandfield Place**
Also Known As: 458422 Ontario Limited
220 Emma St., Cornwall, ON K6J 5V8
Tel: 613-933-6972; *Fax:* 613-938-2261
sandfield@bellnet.ca
www.sandfieldplace.ca

Number of Beds: 53 long term care beds, 34 retirement beds
Note: Long term care & retirement living

***Delaware:* Middlesex Terrace**
2094 Gideon Dr., R.R.#1, Delaware, ON N0L 1E0
Tel: 519-652-3483; *Fax:* 519-652-6915
www.middlesexterrace.ca

Number of Beds: 105 beds (103 long term care beds, 2 respite beds)
Note: Services offered include rehabilitation programs; palliative care; footcare
Tanya Pol, Administrator
tpol@middlesexterrace.ca
Jan Shkilnyk, RN, Director of Nursing
jshkilnyk@middlesexterrace.ca

***Dundas:* St. Joseph's Villa (Dundas)**
Affiliated with: Hamilton Niagara Haldimand Brant Local Health Integration Network
56 Governor's Rd., Dundas, ON L9H 5G7
Tel: 905-627-3541; *Fax:* 905-628-0825
www.sjv.on.ca

Year Founded: 1879
Number of Beds: 378 beds
Note: A variety of services are offered including dermatology; dental care; foot care; chiropody; ear, nose and throat services; audiology; mobility and seating clinic. Personal services are also offered, this includes housekeeping; hair salon and a cafe.
Shawn Gadsby, President

***Dundas:* Wentworth Lodge**
41 South St. West, Dundas, ON L9H 4C4
Tel: 905-546-2618; *Fax:* 905-546-2854
wentworthlodge@hamilton.ca
www.hamilton.ca/phcs/wentworth

Number of Beds: 160 beds
Note: home for the aged

***Dunnville:* Grandview Lodge**
657 Lock St. West, Dunnville, ON N1A 1V9
Tel: 905-774-7547; *Fax:* 905-774-1440
www.haldimandcounty.on.ca

Number of Beds: 128 beds
Joanne Jackson, Administrator
905-774-7547 ext 224, jjackson@haldimandcounty.on.ca

***Durham:* Rockwood Terrace**
PO Box 660, 575 Sadler St. East, Durham, ON N0G 1R0
Tel: 519-369-6035; *Fax:* 519-369-6736
www.grey.ca

Number of Beds: 100 beds
Note: Long term care
Karen Kraus, Administrator
kkraus@greycounty.ca

***Elmira:* Chateau Gardens Elmira Long Term Care Residence**
Affiliated with: Chartwell Retirement Residences
11 Herbert St., Elmira, ON N3B 2B8
Tel: 519-669-2921; *Fax:* 519-669-3027
www.chartwell.com

Number of Beds: 48 beds
W. Brent Binoins, President & CEO, Chartwell Retirement Residences

***Elmvale:* Sara-Vista Long Term Care Facility**
27 Simcoe St., Elmvale, ON L0L 1P0
Tel: 705-322-2182
www.reveraliving.com
Social Media: www.facebook.com/400950748267; www.twitter.com/Revera_Inc; www.youtube.com/ReveraInc; www.linkedin.com/company/revera-inc

Year Founded: 1961
Number of Beds: 60 beds
Note: Programs include music therapy; art and creative classes; garden and horticulture activities; Montessori-based dementia program; rehabilitation programs
Karen Jones, Administrator

***Etobicoke:* The Westbury Long Term Care Centre**
Affiliated with: Chartwell Retirement Residences
495 The West Mall, Etobicoke, ON M9C 5S3
Tel: 416-622-7094
www.chartwell.com

Note: Specialties: Nursing & personal care; Restorative care; Social, recreational, & physical activity programs; Specialized neighbourhood for persons with dementia; Palliative care
W. Brent Binions, Chartwell Retirement Residences

Etobicoke: Westside Long-Term Care
Former Name: Central Park Lodge West Side
1145 Albion Rd., Etobicoke, ON M9V 4J7
Tel: 416-745-4800; *Fax:* 416-745-0445
www.reveraliving.com/westside
Social Media: www.facebook.com/400950748267; www.twitter.com/Revera_Inc; www.youtube.com/ReveraInc; www.linkedin.com/company/Revera-Inc
Number of Beds: 218 beds
Area Served: Etobicoke North; Greater Toronto Area; Peel Region
Note: Programs include art and creative classes; 3M skin and wound care; gardening and horicultural activties; snoezelen multi-sensory therapy
Vaishali Thorat, Resident Services Coordinator
416-745-4800 ext 238

Fort Erie: Gilmore Lodge
50 Gilmore Rd., Fort Erie, ON L2A 2M1
Tel: 905-871-6160; *Fax:* 905-871-0435
www.niagararegion.ca
Number of Beds: 79 beds

Fort Erie: Maple Park Lodge
Affiliated with: Conmed Health Care Group
6 Hagey Ave., Fort Erie, ON L2A 5M5
Tel: 905-994-0224; *Fax:* 905-994-8628
www.conmedhealth.com
Year Founded: 2003
Number of Beds: 96 units
Note: Nursing home
Carole Jukosky, Administrator
carolej@conmedhealth.com

Fort Frances: Rainycrest Long Term Care
Riverside Health Care Facilities Inc.
Affiliated with: North West Local Health Integration Network
550 Osborne St., Fort Frances, ON P9A 3T2
Tel: 807-274-3261; *Fax:* 807-274-7368
Note: Home for the aged

Glenburnie: Fairmount Home
2069 Battersea Rd., Glenburnie, ON K0H 1S0
Tel: 613-546-4264; *Fax:* 613-546-0489
www.frontenaccounty.ca
Number of Beds: 128 beds
Note: home for the aged

Gore Bay: Manitoulin Lodge
Affiliated with: Jarlette Health Services
3 Main St., Gore Bay, ON P0P 1H0
Tel: 705-282-2007; *Fax:* 705-282-3422
www.jarlette.com
Number of Beds: 61 beds
Debbie Wright, Administrator
dwright@jarlette.com

Grimsby: Deer Park Villa
150 Central Ave., Grimsby, ON L3M 4Z3
Tel: 905-945-4164
www.niagararegion.ca
Number of Beds: 39 beds

Guelph: The Elliott Community
170 Metcalfe St., Guelph, ON N1E 4Y3
Tel: 519-822-0491; *Fax:* 519-822-5658
info@elliottcommunity.org
www.elliottcommunity.org
Number of Beds: 270 beds
Note: Retirement suites & long term care
Trevor Lee, CEO

Haileybury: Temiskaming Lodge
Affiliated with: Jarlette Health Services
100 Bruce St., Haileybury, ON P0J 1K0
Tel: 705-672-2123; *Fax:* 705-672-5734
www.jarlette.com
Number of Beds: 82 beds
Francine Gosselin, Administrator
fgosselin@jarlette.com

Hamilton: Baywoods Place
Revera Inc.
330 Main St. East, Hamilton, ON L8N 3T9
Tel: 905-523-7134
www.reveraliving.com/baywoods
Note: Programs provided at Baywoods Place include the following: rehabilitation, recreation, music therapy, skin & wound care, Snoezelen multi-sensory therapy, pet therapy, & safety programs.

Hamilton: Grace Villa Long Term Care Home
45 Lockton Cres., Hamilton, ON L8V 4V5
Tel: 905-387-4812; *Fax:* 905-387-4814
www.gracevilla.ca
Number of Beds: 184 beds
Wendy Hall, Administrator
whall@gracevilla.ca

Hamilton: Idlewyld Manor
449 Sanatorium Rd., Hamilton, ON L9C 2A7
Tel: 905-574-2000; *Fax:* 905-574-0482
office@idlewyldmanor.com
www.idlewyldmanor.com
Number of Beds: 101 beds
Maureen Goodram, Executive Director

Hamilton: St. Elizabeth Villa
Affiliated with: St. Elizabeth Home Society
391 Rymal Rd. West, Hamilton, ON L9B 1V2
Tel: 905-388-9691; *Fax:* 905-388-9953
Toll-Free: 855-388-9691
stelizabeth.villa@bellnet.ca
www.stelizabethhomesociety.org
Note: assisted living

Hamilton: St. Peter's Residence at Chedoke
Affiliated with: Thrive Group
125 Redfern Ave., Hamilton, ON L9C 7W9
Tel: 905-383-0448; *Fax:* 905-383-1099
reception@stpeterscc.ca
www.stpeterscc.ca
Number of Beds: 210 beds
Donna Cripps, President/CEO

Hamilton: Shalom Village
70 Macklin St. North, Hamilton, ON L8S 3S1
Tel: 905-529-1613; *Fax:* 905-529-7542
info@shalomvillage.on.ca
www.shalomvillage.on.ca
Number of Beds: 60 beds
Note: Long term care & assisted living, day program; kosher meals provided; Jewish & ecumenical services. Shalom Village Too with 64 beds & 30 apartments is located adjacent
Jeanette O'Leary, CEO
jeanette@shalomvillage.on.ca

Hamilton: Townsview Lifecare Centre
39 Mary St., Hamilton, ON L8R 3L8
Tel: 905-523-6427; *Fax:* 905-528-0610
Number of Beds: 219 beds

Hamilton: The Wellington Retirement Community
1430 Upper Wellington St., Hamilton, ON L9A 5H3
Tel: 905-385-2111; *Fax:* 905-385-2110
Toll-Free: 866-385-2111
www.thewellington.ca
Social Media: www.facebook.com/271440946270671; twitter.com/TheWellingtonCa; www.youtube.com/user/thewellingtonca
Number of Beds: 102 long term care beds, 80 retirement beds
Note: Long term care & retirement community
Doretta DeRosa, Residence Contact
dderosa@thewellington.ca

Huntsville: Muskoka Landing
Affiliated with: Jarlette Health Services
65 Rogers Cove Dr., Huntsville, ON P1H 2L9
Tel: 705-788-7713; *Fax:* 705-788-1424
www.jarlette.com
Number of Beds: 94 long-term care beds
David Jarlette, President
705-549-4889, Fax: 705-549-2494, djarlette@jarlette.com

Jacksons Point: Cedar Lane Lodge
895 Lake Dr., RR#1, Jacksons Point, ON L0E 1L0
Tel: 905-722-8928
Note: Housing is provided for adults who require support for daily living.

Jasper: Rosebridge Manor
131 Roses Bridge Rd., RR#2, Jasper, ON K0G 1G0
Tel: 613-283-5471; *Fax:* 613-283-9012
www.omniway.com
Number of Beds: 78 beds
Dorothy Broeders-Morin, Administrator
613-283-5471, dmorin@omniway.ca
Krikit Craig, Office Manager
613-283-5471, kcraig@omniway.ca

Kincardine: Trillium Court Retirement Living
Revera Living
550 Phillip Pl., Kincardine, ON N2Z 3A6
Tel: 519-396-4400; *Fax:* 519-366-9092
trillium@reveraliving.com
www.reveraliving.com
Number of Beds: 40 beds, 60 retirement suites
Note: Independent & assisted living, retirement lodge, long-term care, respite & convalescent options
Jeffrey C. Lozon, President & CEO
M. Furnvale, Supervisor, Environmental Services

Kingston: Providence Manor
Affiliated with: Providence Care
275 Sydenham St., Kingston, ON K7K 1G7
Tel: 613-549-4164; *Fax:* 613-549-7472
www.providencecare.ca
Number of Beds: 243 beds
Note: Long-term care
Shelagh Nowlan, Vice-President, Long-Term Care
613-548-7222, nowlans@providencecare.ca

Kingston: St. Mary's of the Lake Hospital
Affiliated with: Providence Care
340 Union St., Kingston, ON K7L 5A2
Tel: 613-544-5220; *Fax:* 613-544-8558
bonuttim@providencecare.ca
www.pccchealth.org
Year Founded: 1946
Number of Beds: 144 beds
Note: Acute care, complex continuing care, geriatric medicine, rehabilitation, palliative care, respite care. Serves a teaching hospital with Queen's University.
Michele Bonutti, Site Administrator/CFO

Kingston: Specialty Care Trillium Centre
800 Edgar St., Kingston, ON K7M 8S4
Tel: 613-547-0040; *Fax:* 613-547-3734
suggestions@specialty-care.com
www.specialty-care.com
Number of Beds: 234 units
Note: Comprehensive long-term care services. Trillium Ridge Retirement Community located adjacent
Dawn Black, Administrator
dawn.black@specialty-care.com

Kitchener: Lanark Heights Long-Term Care
Affiliated with: S & R Nursing Homes Ltd.
46 Lanark Cres., Kitchener, ON N2N 2Z8
Tel: 519-743-4200; *Fax:* 519-743-4225
lanarkheights@srgroup.ca
srgroup.ca
Number of Beds: 160 units

Kitchener: Sunnyside Home
247 Franklin St. North, Kitchener, ON N2A 1Y5
Tel: 519-893-8482; *Fax:* 519-893-4450
www.region.waterloo.on.ca
Number of Beds: 251 residential capacity
Note: Specialty: Long-term care
Gail Carlin, Director
519-893-8494, cgail@region.waterloo.on.ca

Kitchener: The Westmount Long Term Care Residence
Affiliated with: Chartwell Retirement Residences
200 David Bergey Dr., Kitchener, ON N2E 3Y4
Tel: 519-570-2115; *Fax:* 519-579-9770
www.chartwell.com
Number of Beds: 160 units
Note: Westmount Long Term Care Residence for seniors offers services to help maintain independence & wellness.
W. Brent Binions, President & CEO, Chartwell Retirement Residences

Komoka: Country Terrace Long Term Care Home
Affiliated with: Omni Health Care
Former Name: Country Terrace Nursing Home
10072 Oxbow Dr., Komoka, ON N0L 1R0
Tel: 519-657-2955; *Fax:* 519-657-8516
www.omniway.ca
Number of Beds: 120 beds
Cheri Armitage, Resident Services Coordinator
carmitage@omniway.ca

L'Orignal: Résidence Champlain
Affiliated with: Chartwell Retirement Residences
428 Front Rd. West, L'Orignal, ON K0B 1K0
Tel: 613-675-4617
www.chartwell.com
Number of Beds: 60 beds
W. Brent Binions, President & CEO, Chartwell Retirement Residences

Lancaster: Chateau Gardens Lancaster
Affiliated with: Chartwell Retirement Residences
PO Box 429, 105 Military Rd. North, Lancaster, ON K0C 1N0
Tel: 613-347-3016; *Fax:* 613-347-1680
www.chartwell.com
Number of Beds: 60 beds
W. Brent Binions, President & CEO, Chartwell Retirement Residences

Limoges: Résidence Limoges
131-133 Ottawa St., Limoges, ON K0A 2M0
Tél: 613-443-5303; *Téléc:* 613-443-1943
Nombre de lits: 25 lits

Limoges: St. Viateur Nursing Home
Affiliated with: Genesis Gardens
1003 Limoges Rd. South, Limoges, ON K0A 2M0
Tel: 613-443-5751; *Fax:* 613-443-9940
info@genesisgardens.ca
www.genesisgardens.ca
Number of Beds: 64 beds
Richard R. Marleau, CEO
613-443-5751, Fax: 613-443-9940, richardmarleau@rogers.com

Lindsay: Frost Manor
225 Mary St. West, Lindsay, ON K9V 5K3
Tel: 705-324-8333; *Fax:* 705-878-5840
www.omniway.com
Number of Beds: 62 beds
Connie Daly, Administrator
cdaly@omniway.ca

London: Anago Resources Inc.
371 Princess Ave., London, ON N6B 2A7
Tel: 519-435-1099; *Fax:* 519-435-0062
info@anago.on.ca
www.anago.on.ca
Social Media: www.facebook.com/245620512245125
Number of Beds: 63 beds
Note: young offenders; developmental handicap group home; child & family intervention treatment
Mandy L. Bennett, Executive Director

London: Chateau Gardens London
2000 Blackwater Rd., London, ON N5X 4K6
Tel: 519-434-2727
www.chartwell.com
Number of Beds: 95 beds

London: Chelsey Park Retirement Community
310 Oxford St. West, London, ON N6H 4N6
Tel: 519-432-1855; *Fax:* 516-432-7548
adm.cpo@diversicare.ca
www.chelseypark.com
Number of Beds: 247 beds
Diane Pope, Customer Relations Manager
519-432-1845, info.cprc@diversicare.ca
Suzi Holster, Administrator
519-432-1855

London: Dearness Long-Term Care Services
710 Southdale Rd. East, London, ON N6E 1R8
Tel: 519-661-0400; *Fax:* 519-661-0446
Number of Beds: 348 beds

London: Longworth Retirement Residence
600 Longworth Rd., London, ON N6K 4X9
Tel: 519-472-1115; *Fax:* 519-472-1132
info@longworth.sifton.com
www.sifton.com
Number of Beds: 160 beds
Note: Specialties: Long term care; Restorative care program; Massage therapy; Physiotherapy; Family & personal counseling services

London: Meadow Park Care Centre & Retirement Lodge London
Affiliated with: Jarlette Health Services
1210 Southdale Rd. East, London, ON N6E 1B4
Tel: 519-686-0484; *Fax:* 519-686-9932
www.jarlette.com
Social Media: twitter.com/Jarlette
Note: Long term care facility & retirement lodge
David Jarlette, President
705-549-4889, djarlette@jarlette.com
Julia King, Director, Long Term Care
705-549-4889, jking@jarlette.com

London: Mount Hope Centre for Long Term Care
Affiliated with: St. Joseph's Health Care, London
21 Grosvenor St., London, ON N6A 1Y1
Tel: 519-646-6100; *Fax:* 519-646-6054
www.sjhc.london.on.ca
Year Founded: 1869
Number of Beds: 390 beds

Markham: The Woodhaven Long Term Care Residence
Affiliated with: Chartwell Retirement Residences
380 Church St., Markham, ON L6B 1E1
Tel: 905-472-3320
www.chartwell.com
Number of Beds: 192 units
W. Brent Binions, President & CEO, Chartwell Retirement Residences

Maxville: Maxville Manor
80 Mechanic St. West, Maxville, ON K0C 1T0
Tel: 613-527-2170; *Fax:* 613-527-3103
www.maxvillemanor.ca
Year Founded: 1968
Number of Beds: 120 beds + 2 respite beds
Note: Specialties: Long-term care services; Therapy services; The Seniors' Centre, providing outreach services to persons in the community with physical disabilities & special needs; Adult day program; Seniors' clinics, such as hearing, optometry, & foot care. Number of Employees: 130
Ivan Coleman, Board Chair

Midland: Hillcrest Village Care Centre
Former Name: St. Andrew's Centennial Manor
255 Russell St., Midland, ON L4R 5L6
Tel: 705-526-3781; *Fax:* 705-526-5656
www.hillcrestvillage.com
Year Founded: 1978
Number of Beds: 164 beds

Milton: Allendale
185 Ontario St. South, Milton, ON L9T 2M4
Tel: 905-825-6000; *Fax:* 905-825-9833
Toll-Free: 866-442-5866
TTY: 905-827-9833
accesshalton@halton.ca
www.halton.ca
Year Founded: 1993
Number of Beds: 200 beds

Mississauga: Cawthra Gardens
590 Lolita Gardens, Mississauga, ON L5A 4N8
Tel: 905-306-9984
www.delcare.com
Number of Beds: 192 beds

Mississauga: Chelsey Park Mississauga Long-Term Care Facility
2250 Hurontario St., Mississauga, ON L5B 1M8
Tel: 905-270-0411
Number of Beds: 237 beds

Mississauga: Chelsey Park Streetsville Long-Term Care Facility
1742 Bristol Rd. West, Mississauga, ON L5M 1X9
Tel: 905-826-3045

Mississauga: Heritage House Retirement Home
73 King St. West, Mississauga, ON L5B 1H1
Tel: 905-279-4800; *Fax:* 905-615-8141
theheritagehouse@rogers.com
www.heritagehouseonline.com
Note: Specialties: Physiotherapy; Occupational therapy; Specialized rehabilitative care; Recovery from surgery; Cardiac care program; Orthopedic care; Acitvity program; Respite or short stays

Mississauga: Specialty Care Mississauga Road
4350 Mississauga Rd., Mississauga, ON L5M 7C8
Tel: 905-812-1175; *Fax:* 905-812-1173
suggestions@specialty-care.com
www.specialty-care.com
Number of Beds: 160 beds
Justine Welburn, Administrator
justine.welburn@specialty-care.com

Mississauga: Villa Forum
Affiliated with: Chartwell Retirement Residences
175 Forum Dr., Mississauga, ON L4Z 4E5
Tel: 905-501-1443; *Fax:* 905-501-0094
www.chartwell.com
Number of Beds: 160 units
Note: Long-term care facility
W. Brent Binions, President & CEO, Chartwell Retirement Residences

Mississauga: The Wenleigh Long Term Care Residence
Affiliated with: Chartwell Retirement Residences
2065 Leanne Blvd., Mississauga, ON L5K 2L6
Tel: 905-822-4663
www.chartwell.com
Number of Beds: 161 units
W. Brent Binions, President & CEO, Chartwell Retirement Residences

Mitchell: Ritz Lutheran Villa
Rd. 164 - 4118A, RR#5, Mitchell, ON N0K 1N0
Tel: 519-348-8612; *Fax:* 519-348-4420
info@ritzlutheranvilla.com
www.ritzlutheranvilla.com
Year Founded: 1974
Number of Beds: 83 beds
Note: charitable home for the aged, retirement community with rental apartments & life lease town homes

Napanee: The John M. Parrott Centre
Former Name: Lenadco Home
309 Bridge St. West, Napanee, ON K7R 2G4
Tel: 613-354-3306; *Fax:* 613-354-7387
www.lennox-addington.on.ca
Number of Beds: 168 beds
Note: Long term care
Brian Smith, Director
613-354-3306, bsmith@lennox-addington.on.ca

Newmarket: Southlake Residential Care Village
Affiliated with: Extendicare Canada
640 Grace St., Newmarket, ON L3Y 2L1
Tel: 905-895-7661; *Fax:* 905-895-9806
extendicaresouthlake.ca
Year Founded: 2004
Number of Beds: 192 beds
Note: Number of staff: 200

Niagara Falls: Bella Senior Care Residence
8720 Willoughby Dr., Niagara Falls, ON L2G 7X3
Tel: 905-295-2727
info@bellaseniorcare.com
www.bellaseniorcare.com
Number of Beds: 160 units

Niagara on the Lake: Chateau Gardens Niagara
Affiliated with: Chartwell Retirement Residences
PO Box 985, 120 Wellington St., Niagara on the Lake, ON L0S 1J0
Tel: 905-468-2111; *Fax:* 905-468-4463
www.chartwell.com
Number of Beds: 124 beds
W. Brent Binions, President & CEO, Chartwell Retirement Residences

Niagara on the Lake: Upper Canada Lodge
272 Wellington St., Niagara on the Lake, ON L0S 1J0
Tel: 905-468-4208; *Fax:* 905-468-0520
uppercanada@niagararegion.ca
Year Founded: 1988
Number of Beds: 80 beds

North Bay: Cassellholme
400 Olive St., North Bay, ON P1B 6J4
Tel: 705-474-4250; *Fax:* 705-474-6129
www.cassellholme.on.ca
Number of Beds: 240 beds
Note: home for the aged
Brenda Loubert, CEO
705-474-4250, loubertb@cassellholme.on.ca

Oakville: The Waterford Long Term Care Residence
Affiliated with: Chartwell Retirement Residences
2140 Baronwood Dr., Oakville, ON L6M 4V6
Tel: 905-827-2405
www.chartwell.com
Year Founded: 2003
Number of Beds: 168 units
W. Brent Binions, President & CEO, Chartwell Retirement Residences

Oakville: Wyndham Manor
291 Reynolds St., Oakville, ON L6J 3L5
Tel: 905-849-7766
Number of Beds: 128 beds

Orillia: The Leacock Care Centre
Affiliated with: Jarlette Health Services
25 Museum Dr., Orillia, ON L3V 7T9
Tel: 705-325-9181; *Fax:* 705-325-5179
www.jarlette.com
Number of Beds: 145 long-term care beds
Carrie Acton, Administrator
705-325-9181, cacton@jarlette.com

Orleans: Kingsway Arms at St. Joseph Manor
1510 St. Joseph Blvd., Orleans, ON K1C 7L1
Tel: 613-830-4000; *Fax:* 613-830-7607
edstjosephmanor@kingswayarms.com
www.kingswayarms.com
Social Media:
www.facebook.com/KingswayArmsStJosephManor
Number of Beds: 80 beds
Diane Pelletier, Executive Director

Orleans: Madonna Long Term Care Facility
1541 St. Joseph Blvd., Orleans, ON K1C 1S9
Tel: 613-824-2040
www.leisureworld.ca
Note: Specialties: Restorative care; Palliative care

Orleans: Résidence Saint-Louis
879, ch Hiawatha Park, Orleans, ON K1C 2Z6
Tél: 613-562-6262
www.bruyere.org
Nombre de lits: 198 lits
Note: Établissement francophone de soins de longue durée

Oshawa: Hillsdale Estates
590 Oshawa Blvd. North, Oshawa, ON L1G 5T9
Tel: 905-579-1777; *Fax:* 905-579-3911
Year Founded: 2003
Number of Beds: 435 beds
Marcey Wilson, Administrator
Jenny Little, Director, Care

Oshawa: Thorntonview
Revera Living
186 Thornton Rd. South, Oshawa, ON L1J 5Y2
Tel: 905-576-5181; *Fax:* 905-576-0078
thorntonview@reveraliving.com
www.reveraliving.com
Social Media: www.facebook.com/400950748267; twitter.com/Revera_Inc; www.youtube.com/user/ReveraInc; www.linkedin.com/company/revera-inc
Number of Beds: 154 beds
Note: Long-term care, palliative care, services for physically challenged adults
Jeffrey C. Lozon, President & CEO, Revera Living

Oshawa: The Wynfield Long Term Care Residence
Affiliated with: Chartwell Retirement Residences
451 Woodmount Dr., Oshawa, ON L1G 8E3
Tel: 905-571-0065; *Fax:* 905-579-4902
www.chartwell.com
Number of Beds: 172 beds
W. Brent Binions, President & CEO, Chartwell Retirement Residences
Stephen Suske, CEO, Chartwell Seniors Housing REIT

Ottawa: Carleton Lodge
55 Lodge Rd., Ottawa, ON K2C 3H1
Tel: 613-825-3763; *Fax:* 613-825-0245
ottawa.ca
Number of Beds: 160 beds

Ottawa: Carlingview Manor
Revera Living
2330 Carling Ave., Ottawa, ON K2B 7H1
Tel: 613-820-9328; *Fax:* 613-820-9774
www.reveraliving.com/carlingview
Social Media: www.facebook.com/400950748267; twitter.com/Revera_Inc; www.youtube.com/user/ReveraInc; www.linkedin.com/company/revera-inc
Year Founded: 1961
Number of Beds: 320 beds
Jeffrey C. Lozon, President & CEO, Revera Living

Ottawa: Hillel Lodge
Also Known As: The Bess & Moe Greenberg Family Hillel Lodge
10 Nadolny Sachs Private, Ottawa, ON K2A 4G7
Tel: 613-728-3900; *Fax:* 613-728-6550
hillel@hillel-ltc.com
www.hillel-ltc.com
Number of Beds: 100 beds
Stephen Schneiderman, Executive Director
613-728-3900, sss@hillel-ltc.com

Ottawa: Manoir Wymering Manor
845 Kirkwood Ave., Ottawa, ON K1Z 5Y1
Tel: 613-722-8811; *Fax:* 613-722-0795
manoirwymeringmanor@gmail.com
Year Founded: 1974
Number of Beds: 30 beds
Note: A residence for women with mental illnesses. Wymering Manor is a member of the Ontario Homes for Special Needs Association.
Linda Lafrance, Administrator

Ottawa: St. Patrick's Home of Ottawa Inc.
2865 Riverside Dr., Ottawa, ON K1V 8N5
Tel: 613-731-4660; *Fax:* 613-731-4056
www.stpats.ca
Number of Beds: 202 beds
Note: Home for the aged
Linda Chaplin, President & CEO
613-731-4660, lindachaplin@stpats.ca

Ottawa: The Salvation Army Ottawa Booth Centre
Former Name: Metropole & Salvage Depot
171 George St., Ottawa, ON K1N 5W5
Tel: 613-241-1573; *Fax:* 613-241-2818
www.ottawaboothcentre.org
Year Founded: 1908
Note: Specialties: Anchorage Program, an addiction treatment program; Street outreach

Owen Sound: Georgian Heights Health Care Centre
1115 - 10 St. East, Owen Sound, ON N4K 6B1
Tel: 519-371-1441; *Fax:* 519-371-1092
Carole Woods, Administrator
cwoods2@extendicare.com

Owen Sound: Maple View Long Term Care
Revera Living
1029 - 4th Ave. West, Owen Sound, ON N4K 4W1
Tel: 519-376-2522; *Fax:* 519-376-3110
mapleview@reveraliving.com
www.reveraliving.com
Number of Beds: 29 beds
Jeffrey C. Lozon, President & CEO, Revera Living

Owen Sound: Summit Place Long Term Care
Revera Living
850 - 4th St. East, Owen Sound, ON N4K 6A3
Tel: 519-376-3212; *Fax:* 519-371-0923
summitplace@reveraliving.com
www.reveraliving.com
Number of Beds: 159 beds
Jeffrey C. Lozon, PResident & CEO, Revera Living

Palmerston: Royal Terrace
600 Whites Rd., Palmerston, ON N0G 2P0
Tel: 519-343-2611; *Fax:* 519-343-2860
royalter@wightman.ca
www.royalterracepalmerston.ca
Number of Beds: 121 beds
Note: Long-term & residential care
Kash Ramchandani, Owner & Administrator
519-343-2611

Paris: Park Lane Terrace
295 Grand River St. North, Paris, ON N3L 2N9
Tel: 519-442-2753; *Fax:* 519-442-6176
www.parklaneterrace.ca
Number of Beds: 132 beds
Joe Anne Holloway, Administrator
jholloway@parklaneterrace.ca

Parry Sound: Lakeland Long Term Care Facility
6 Albert St., Parry Sound, ON P2A 3A4
Tel: 705-746-9667 *Toll-Free:* 866-959-9005
www.lakelandltc.com
Note: Located within the West Parry Sound Health Centre complex
Bob Mitchell, Board Chair

Pembroke: Marianhill
600 Cecelia St., Pembroke, ON K8A 7Z3
Tel: 613-735-6838; *Fax:* 613-732-3934
www.marianhill.ca
Number of Beds: 200 beds
Note: Catholic long-term and chronic care facility
Linda M. Tracey, CEO
613-735-6839

Penetanguishene: Georgian Manor
7 Harriett St., Penetanguishene, ON L9M 1K8
Tel: 705-549-3166; *Fax:* 705-549-6062
www.simcoe.ca
Number of Beds: 107 beds
Note: home for the aged
Lynne Blake, Administrator
lynne.blake@simcoe.ca

Penetanguishene: Ruth Haarer Home for Special Care
Former Name: Ruth Haarer Residence
2 Water St., Penetanguishene, ON L9M 1V6
Tel: 705-549-7296

Peterborough: Fairhaven Home
881 Dutton Rd., Peterborough, ON K9H 7S4
Tel: 705-743-4265; *Fax:* 705-743-6292
info@fairhavenltc.com
fairhavenltc.com
Year Founded: 1960
Number of Beds: 253 beds
Note: home for the aged

Peterborough: Riverview Manor
Affiliated with: Omni Health Care
1155 Water St., Peterborough, ON K9H 3P8
Tel: 705-748-6706; *Fax:* 705-748-5407
www.omniway.ca
Number of Beds: 124 beds
Mary Anne Greco, Administrator
magreco@omniway.ca

Peterborough: Springdale Country Manor
Affiliated with: Omni Health Care
2698 Clifford Line, Peterborough, ON K9J 6X6
Tel: 705-742-8811; *Fax:* 705-742-8812
www.omniway.ca
Number of Beds: 65 beds
Maureen King, Administrator/Director of Care
mking@omniway.ca

Petrolia: Lambton Meadowview Villa
3958 Petrolia Line, Petrolia, ON N0N 1R0
Tel: 519-882-1470; *Fax:* 519-882-1633
www.lambtononline.ca
Number of Beds: 123 beds, 2 short stay beds
Note: home for the aged
Jeff Harvey, Resident Manager
519-882-1470, jeff.harvey@county-lambton.on.ca

Port Colborne: Northland Point
Northland Pointe, 2 Fielden Ave., Port Colborne, ON L3K 6G4
Tel: 905-835-9335; *Fax:* 905-835-6518
northland@niagararegion.ca
www.niagararegion.ca
Number of Beds: 150 beds
Note: Long-term care facility

Port Stanley: Extendicare - Port Stanley
Extendicare Canada
4551 East Rd., Port Stanley, ON N5L 1J6
Tel: 519-782-3339; *Fax:* 519-782-4756
cnh_portstanley@extendicare.com
www.extendicarecanada.com
Number of Beds: 60 beds
Note: Services include denturist; chiropody; respiratory care; physiotherapy; rehabilitation and restorative care

Ridgetown: The Village on the Ridge
Revera Inc.
Former Name: The Village Retirement Residence
9 Myrtle St., Ridgetown, ON N0P 2C0
Tel: 519-674-5427
www.reveraliving.com

Rockland: St. Joseph Long-Term Care Facility
1615 Laurier St., Rockland, ON K4K 1C8
Tel: 613-446-5126
Number of Beds: 64 units

Sarnia: Sumac Lodge Long Term Care
Revera Living
1464 Blackwell Rd., Sarnia, ON N7S 5M4
Tel: 519-542-3421; *Fax:* 519-542-3604
sumaclodge@reveraliving.com
www.reveraliving.com
Number of Beds: 100 beds
Jeffrey C. Lozon, President & CEO, Revera Living

Sarnia: Twin Lakes Terrace
Affiliated with: S & R Nursing Homes Ltd.
1310 Murphy Rd., Sarnia, ON N7S 6K5
Tel: 519-542-2939; *Fax:* 519-542-0879
twinlakesterrace@srgroup.ca
www.srgroup.ca
Number of Beds: 60 beds
Note: Independent & assisted living, convalescent & respite options

Cathy McIntosh, Administrator
cathy_mcintosh@srgroup.ca

Sarsfield: Sarsfield Colonial Home
PO Box 130, 2861 Colonial Rd., Sarsfield, ON K0A 3E0
Tel: 613-835-2977; *Fax:* 613-835-2982

Number of Beds: 46 beds
Chantal Crispin, Owner/Administrator
613-835-2977, chantalcrispin@rogers.com

Scarborough: Ina Grafton Gage Home
40 Bell Estate Rd., Scarborough, ON M1L 0E2
Tel: 416-422-4890; *Fax:* 416-422-1613
info@iggh.org
www.iggh.org

Number of Beds: 128 beds
Denise Bedard-Eldridge, CEO
Dr. Bharat Kalra, Medical Director

Scarborough: McCowan Retirement Residence
2881 Eglinton Ave. East, Scarborough, ON M1J 0A2
Tel: 416-266-4445; *Fax:* 416-264-8377
info@mccowanRR.com
www.mccowanrr.com
Social Media: www.facebook.com/132492233505515
Year Founded: 2004
Gina Cook, Executive Director
Tim Valyear, Director, Marketing
marketingoffice.kams@rogers.com

Shelburne: Dufferin Oaks Long Term Care Home
151 Centre St., Shelburne, ON L0N 1S4
Tel: 519-925-2140; *Fax:* 519-925-5067
dufferinoaks@dufferincounty.ca
www.dufferincounty.on.ca

Number of Beds: 160 beds
Note: non-profit municipal long-term care facility

Simcoe: Norview Lodge
PO Box 604, 44 Rob Blake Way, Simcoe, ON N3Y 4L8
Tel: 519-426-0902; *Fax:* 519-426-9867
www.norfolkcounty.on.ca

Number of Beds: 179 beds
Note: home for the aged

St Catharines: Linhaven
403 Ontario St., St Catharines, ON L2N 1L5
Tel: 905-934-3364; *Fax:* 905-934-6975
www.niagararegion.ca

Number of Beds: 248 beds
Note: Specialties: Long term care; Alzheimer's disease, memory loss, & related dementias; Respite services; Adult day service

St Catharines: Niagara Ina Grafton Gage Home
413 Linwell Rd., St Catharines, ON L2M 7Y2
Tel: 905-935-6822; *Fax:* 905-935-6847
www.niggv.on.ca

Number of Beds: 40 beds
Note: supportive housing for seniors
Patrick O'Neill, CEO
poneill@niggv.on.ca

St Thomas: Kettle Creek Residence
58 St. George St., St Thomas, ON N5P 2L1
Tel: 519-633-7647; *Fax:* 519-633-9312
Helmut Beh, Owner

St. Catharines: Henley House
Affiliated with: Primacare Living Solutions
20 Earnest St., St. Catharines, ON L2N 7T2
Tel: 905-937-9703; *Fax:* 905-937-9723
henley@primacareliving.com
www.primacareliving.com

Number of Beds: 160 beds
Note: Specialties: Long-term nursing & personal care; Therapeutic programs; Physiotherapy; Restorative care; Palliative care
Matthew Melchior, President, Primacare Living Solutions

St. Thomas: Elgin Manor Home for the Aged
Affiliated with: County of Elgin Homes and Seniors Services
39232 Fingal Line RR #1, St. Thomas, ON N5P 3S5
Tel: 519-631-0620; *Fax:* 519-631-2307
www.elgincounty.ca

Number of Beds: 90 beds
Rhonda Duffy, Director, Senior Services
519-773-9205, rduffy@elgin-county.on.ca

St. Thomas: Valleyview Home for the Aged
350 Burwell Rd., St. Thomas, ON N5P 0A3
Tel: 519-631-1030; *Fax:* 519-631-3462
www.city.st-thomas.on.ca

Year Founded: 1969
Number of Beds: 136 beds
Note: home for the aged
Michael Carroll, Administrator
519-631-1030, mcarroll@valleyview.st-thomas.on.ca

Stittsville: Specialty Care Granite Ridge
5501 Abbott St. East, Stittsville, ON K2S 2C5
Tel: 613-836-0331; *Fax:* 613-836-0643
suggestions@specialty-care.com
www.specialty-care.com

Number of Beds: 224 beds
Norm Slatter, Administrator
norm.slatter@specialty-care.com

Stoney Creek: Clarion Nursing Home
337 Hwy. 8, Stoney Creek, ON L8G 1E7
Tel: 905-664-2281; *Fax:* 905-664-2966
info@clarionnursinghome.on.ca
www.clarionnursinghome.on.ca

Number of Beds: 100 beds

Stoney Creek: Heritage Green Long Term Care Centre
353 Isaac Brock Dr., Stoney Creek, ON L8J 2J3
Tel: 905-573-7177; *Fax:* 905-573-7151
hgseniorcare.com

Number of Beds: 167 beds

Stoney Creek: Orchard Terrace Care Centre
Former Name: Stoney Creek Lifecare Centre
199 Glover Rd., Stoney Creek, ON L8E 5J2
Tel: 905-643-1795
info@orchardterracecarecentre.ca
www.responsivegroup.ca

Number of Beds: 45 beds

Stouffville: Specialty Care Bloomington Cove
13621 - 9 Line, Stouffville, ON L4A 7X3
Tel: 905-640-1310; *Fax:* 905-640-0995
suggestions@specialty-care.com
www.specialty-care.com

Number of Beds: 112 beds
Janet Iwaszczenko, Administrator
janet.iwaszczenko@specialty-care.com

Stratford: Greenwood Court
90 Greenwood Dr., Stratford, ON N5A 7W5
Tel: 519-273-4662; *Fax:* 519-273-1458
www.tcmhomes.com

Number of Beds: 45 beds
Joyce Penney, Executive Director
jpenney@greenwoodcourt.com

Thunder Bay: Hogarth Riverview Manor
Affiliated with: St. Joseph's Care Group
300 Lillie St., Thunder Bay, ON P7C 4Y7
Tel: 807-625-1110; *Fax:* 807-623-4520
www.sjcg.net

Number of Beds: 96 beds
Tracy Buckler, President & CEO, St. Joseph's Care Group

Thunder Bay: OPTIONS Northwest Personal Support Services
95 Cumberland St. North, Thunder Bay, ON P7A 4M1
Tel: 807-344-4994; *Fax:* 807-346-5811
www.optionsnorthwest.com

Year Founded: 1965
Note: Specialty: Personal & residential support for persons with developmental challenges, physical disabilities, chronic behaviour problems, & mental health challenges; Counselling; Support groups

Thunder Bay: Roseview Manor
Former Name: Central Park Lodge
99 Shuniah St., Thunder Bay, ON P7A 2Z2
Tel: 807-344-6929; *Fax:* 807-344-7132
roseviewmanor@reveraliving.com
www.reveraliving.com

Number of Beds: 157 beds
Jeffrey C. Lozon, President & CEO, Revera Living

Tilbury: Tilbury Manor Long-Term Care Home
Diversicare Canada Management Services Inc
PO Box 160, 16 Fort St., Tilbury, ON N0P 2L0
Tel: 519-682-0243; *Fax:* 519-682-2358
adm.tilbury@diversicare.ca
www.diversicare.ca

Number of Beds: 75 beds
John Carnella, President & CEO, Diversicare

Toronto: Baycrest Centre for Geriatric Care
3560 Bathurst St., Toronto, ON M6A 2E1
Tel: 416-785-2500; *Fax:* 416-785-2378
www.baycrest.org
Social Media: www.facebook.com/baycrestcentre; twitter.com/baycrest; www.youtube.com/thebaycrestchannel; www.linkedin.com/company/baycrest
Year Founded: 1918
Number of Beds: 300 beds
Note: A research facility as well as a care centre for seniors.
William E. Reichman, President & CEO
Dr. Paul Katz, Vice-President, Medical Services & Chief of Staff
Carol Anderson, Vice-President, Programs & Chief Nursing Executive

Toronto: Cheltenham Long-Term Care Facility
5935 Bathurst St., Toronto, ON M2R 1Y8
Tel: 416-223-4050
adm.cheltenham@leisureworld.ca
www.leisureworld.ca/cheltenham.html

Number of Beds: 170 beds

Toronto: Copernicus Lodge
66 Roncesvalles Ave., Toronto, ON M6R 3A7
Tel: 416-536-7122; *Fax:* 416-536-8242
www.copernicuslodge.com

Number of Beds: 108 beds
Note: home for the aged
Tracy Kamino, CEO

Toronto: Dom Lipa Nursing Home & Seniors Centre
52 Neilson Dr., Toronto, ON M9C 1V7
Tel: 416-621-3820; *Fax:* 416-621-9773
info@domlipa.ca
www.domlipa.ca

Number of Beds: 66 nursing home, 30 retirement beds
Theresa MacDermid, Administrator
t.macdermid@domlipa.ca

Toronto: The Gibson Long Term Care Centre
Affiliated with: Chartwell Retirement Residences
Former Name: Extendicare - North York
1925 Steeles Ave. East, Toronto, ON M2H 2H3
Tel: 416-493-4666; *Fax:* 416-493-4886
gibsonltc@chartwellreit.ca
www.chartwellreit.ca

Number of Beds: 202 beds
W. Brent Binions, President & CEO, Chartwell Retirement Residences

Toronto: Lakeside Long-Term Care Centre
Affiliated with: Extendicare
150 Dunn Ave., Toronto, ON M6K 2R6
Tel: 416-533-2828; *Fax:* 406-533-1984
extendicarelakeside.ca

Number of Beds: 128 Beds

Toronto: Maynard Nursing Home
28 Halton St., Toronto, ON M6J 1R3
Tel: 416-533-5198; *Fax:* 416-533-3492
administrator@maynardnursinghome.com
www.maynardnursinghome.com

Year Founded: 1961
Number of Beds: 77 beds
Note: Specialties: Service to residents of Portuguese origin; Recreational & social activities

Toronto: Nisbet Lodge
740 Pape Ave., Toronto, ON M4K 3S7
Tel: 416-469-1105; *Fax:* 416-469-2996
info@nisbetlodge.com
www.nisbetlodge.com

Number of Beds: 103 beds
Note: Christian long-term care home
Glen Moorhouse, CEO
416-469-1105, g.moorhouse@nisbetlodge.com

Toronto: North York General Hospital - Seniors' Health Centre
Affiliated with: Toronto Central Local Health Integration Network
2 Buchan Ct., Toronto, ON M2J 5A3
Tel: 416-756-6050; *Fax:* 416-756-3144
www.nygh.on.ca

Number of Beds: 192 long-term care beds
Note: Long term care facility, ambulatory geriatric services
Dr. Tim Rutledge, President & CEO, North York General Hospital

Toronto: The O'Neill Centre
33 Christie St., Toronto, ON M6G 3B1
Tel: 416-536-1116; *Fax:* 416-536-6941
www.oneillcentre.ca

Number of Beds: 162 beds
Note: Resident care & retirement living
Cathy Fiore, Administrator

Toronto: Oakdale Child & Family Service Ltd.
291 Chisholm Ave., Toronto, ON M4C 4W5
Tel: 416-699-5600; *Fax:* 416-699-6547
tor-oakdale@bellnet.ca
www.oakdaleservices.com
Note: Specialties: Long & short term care for children with special needs; Teaching independence in life skills, social & community awareness, & appropriate communication methods

Toronto: La Salle Manor
61 Fairfax Cres., Toronto, ON M1L 1Z7
Tel: 416-752-3932
Note: The manor is a private retirement home for De La Salle Brothers & Sisters of Service.

Toronto: Shepherd Lodge
3760 Sheppard Ave. East, Toronto, ON M1T 3K9
Tel: 416-609-5700; *Fax:* 416-609-8329
info@shepherdvillage.org
www.shepherdvillage.org
Year Founded: 1961
Number of Beds: 252 beds

Toronto: Suomi-Koti Toronto
Also Known As: Toronto Finnish Cdn Srs Centre & Nursing Home
795 Eglinton Ave. East, Toronto, ON M4G 4E4
Tel: 416-425-4134; *Fax:* 416-425-6319
seniorscentre@suomikoti.ca
www.suomikoti.ca
Number of Beds: 88 apartment units, 34 nursing beds
Juha Mynttinen, Administrator
416-425-4134, mynttinen@suomikoti.ca
Leila Carnegie, Director of Care
416-421-6719, carnegie@suomikoti.ca

Toronto: Villa Colombo Homes for the Aged Inc.
Affiliated with: Villa Charities
40 Playfair Ave., Toronto, ON M6B 2P9
Tel: 416-789-2113; *Fax:* 416-789-5435
www.villacharities.com
Social Media: www.facebook.com/villa.charities; ww.youtube.com/VillaChannel; www.linkedin.com/company/villa-charities-foundation
Year Founded: 1976
Number of Beds: 391 beds
Carmen Di Mauro, CEO
416-789-2113, dimauro@villacolombo.on.ca
Cinzia Scacchi, Admissions Office
416-789-2113

Toronto: West Park Healthcare Centre
82 Buttonwood Ave., Toronto, ON M6M 2J5
Tel: 416-243-3600; *Fax:* 416-243-8947
feedback@westpark.org
www.westpark.org
Social Media: www.facebook.com/WestParkHealthcareCentre; twitter.com/westparkhcc; www.youtube.com/WestParkhealthcare; www.linkedin.com/company/218953
Year Founded: 1904
Number of Beds: 130 rehab beds; 140 complex continuing care beds; 200 long term care beds
Number of Employees: 885
Note: Rehabilitation, complex continuing care, and long-term care facility
Anne-Marie Malek, President & CEO
Nora Cullen, Chief of Staff
Barbara Bell, Chief Nurse

Trenton: Crown Ridge Place Nursing Home
106 Crown St., Trenton, ON K8V 6R3
Tel: 613-392-1289; *Fax:* 613-394-8672
admin@crownridgeplace.ca
www.crownridgeplace.ca
Number of Beds: 84 beds

Unionville: Union Villa
Affiliated with: Unionville Home Society
Unionville Home Society, 4300 Hwy. #7 East, Unionville, ON L3R 1L8
Tel: 905-477-2822
customerservice@uhs.on.ca
www.uhs.on.ca/uhs_unionvilla.php
Year Founded: 1970
Number of Beds: 160 residential capacity
Note: Specialties: Long-term nursing care; Activation program; Therapeutic mental & physical stimulation; Respite care; Day guest program
Debra Cooper Burger, President & CEO
905-477-2839,

Val Caron: Elizabeth Centre/Centre Elizabeth
Affiliated with: Jarlette Health Services
2100 Main St., Val Caron, ON P3N 1S7
Tel: 705-897-7695; *Fax:* 705-897-0181
www.jarlette.com
Number of Beds: 128 beds
Shelly Murphy, Administrator
smurphy@jarlette.com

Vanier: Centre d'accueil Champlain
275 Perrier Ave., Vanier, ON K1L 5C6
Tel: 613-746-3543; *Fax:* 613-746-5572
ottawa.ca
Year Founded: 1969
Number of Beds: 160 beds
Note: home for the aged

Wallaceburg: Fairfield Park
1934 Dufferin Ave., Wallaceburg, ON N8A 4M2
Tel: 519-627-1663; *Fax:* 519-627-9920
www.fairfieldpark.ca
Year Founded: 2000
Number of Beds: 99 beds

Watford: Watford Quality Care Centre
PO Box 400, 344 Victoria St., Watford, ON N0M 2S0
Tel: 519-876-2520; *Fax:* 519-876-3930
www.watfordqualitycare.ca
Number of Beds: 62 beds
Lynne-Anne Gallaway, Administrator
lgallaway@watfordqualitycare.ca

West Hill: Leisureworld Caregiving Centre Altamont
92 Island Rd., West Hill, ON M1C 2P5
Tel: 416-284-4781; *Fax:* 416-284-3634
adm.altamont@leisureworld.ca
www.leisureworld.ca/Altamont.html
Year Founded: 1968
Number of Beds: 159 beds
Lois Cormack, CEO, Leisureworld Senior Care Corporation

Willowdale: Carefree Lodge
306 Finch Ave. East, Willowdale, ON M2N 4S5
Tel: 416-397-1500; *Fax:* 416-397-1501
ltc-cfl@toronto.ca
Number of Beds: 127 beds
Note: home for the aged

Windsor: Huron Lodge
1881 Cabana Rd. West, Windsor, ON N9G 1C7
Tel: 519-253-6060; *Fax:* 519-977-8027
www.citywindsor.ca
Number of Beds: 256 beds
Note: Number of Employees: 160
Mary Bateman, Acting Administrator & Executive Director
519-253-6060, mbateman@city.windsor.on.ca

Windsor: Regency Park Nursing Home
Affiliated with: Meritas Care Corporation
567 Victoria Ave., Windsor, ON N9A 4N1
Tel: 519-254-1141; *Fax:* 519-254-3759
regency@meritascare.ca
www.meritascare.ca
Number of Beds: 72 beds
Norbert Warnke, President & CEO, Meritas Care Corporation

Woodbridge: Kristus Darzs Latvian Home
11290 Pine Valley Dr., Woodbridge, ON L4L 1A6
Tel: 905-832-3300; *Fax:* 905-832-2029
kristusdarzs@kdlatvianhome.com
www.ccac-ont.ca
Number of Beds: 100 beds

Woodstock: Woodingford Lodge
300 Juliana Dr., Woodstock, ON N4V 0A1
Tel: 519-421-5556; *Fax:* 519-533-0781
www.county.oxford.on.ca
Number of Beds: 160 beds
Corrie Fransen, Administrator

Nursing Homes

Ailsa Craig: Craigwiel Gardens
221 Main St. East, RR#1, Ailsa Craig, ON N0M 1A0
Tel: 519-293-3215; *Fax:* 519-293-3941
info@craigwielgardens.on.ca
www.craigwielgardens.on.ca
Number of Beds: 83 beds

Ajax: Ballycliffe Lodge Ltd.
70 Station Rd., Ajax, ON L1S 1R9
Tel: 905-683-7321; *Fax:* 905-427-5846
ballycliffelodge@chartwellreit.ca
www.chartwellreit.ca
Number of Beds: 100 beds; 65 retirement lodge beds
Note: Retirement centre
W. Brent Binions, President, CEO

Akwesasne: Tsi ion kwa nonh so:te
Former Name: Akwesasne Adult Care Facility
70 Kawehnoke Apartment Rd., Akwesasne, ON K6H 5R7
Tel: 613-932-1409; *Fax:* 613-932-8845
Number of Beds: 30 beds
Note: Specialties: Geriatric residential health care; Water therapy; Palliative care

Alexandria: Community Nursing Home Alexandria
PO Box 300, 92 Centre St., Alexandria, ON K0C 1A0
Tel: 613-525-2022; *Fax:* 613-525-2023
www.cnhalexandria.ca
Number of Beds: 70 beds
Terry A. Dubé
tdube@clmi.ca

Almonte: Almonte Country Haven
Affiliated with: Omni Health Care
333 Country St., Almonte, ON K0A 1A0
Tel: 613-256-3095; *Fax:* 613-256-3096
www.omniway.ca/ourhomes/almonte.htm
Number of Beds: 82 beds
Marilyn Colton, Administrator
613-256-3095, mcolton@omniway.ca

Almonte: Fairview Manor
PO Box 1360, 75 Spring St., Almonte, ON K0A 1A0
Tel: 613-256-3113; *Fax:* 613-256-5780
www.almontegeneral.com
Number of Beds: 100 beds
Mary Wilson Trider, President, CEO
613-256-2514

Amherstview: Helen Henderson Care Centre
343 Amherst Dr., Amherstview, ON K7N 1X3
Tel: 613-384-4585; *Fax:* 613-384-9407
www.gibsonfamilyhealthcare.com
Number of Beds: 70 retirement home beds; 102 nursing home beds
Lisa Gibson, Administrator
613-384-4585, lisagibson@gibsonfamilyhealthcare.co

Arnprior: The Grove Nursing Home
Affiliated with: Arnprior Regional Health
275 Ida St. North, Arnprior, ON K7S 3M7
Tel: 613-623-6547; *Fax:* 613-623-4554
Joan Hughes, Director of Care

Arthur: Caressant Care Arthur
Affiliated with: Caressant Care Nursing and Retirement Homes Limited
PO Box 700, 215 Eliza St., Arthur, ON N0G 1A0
Tel: 519-848-3795; *Fax:* 519-848-2273
www.caressantcare.com
Number of Beds: 80 beds
James Lavelle, President

Aurora: Willows Estate
13837 Yonge St., Aurora, ON L4G 3G8
Tel: 905-727-0128; *Fax:* 905-841-0454
www.omniway.ca
Number of Beds: 84 beds
Note: Specialties: Long-term care; Care for persons with Alzheimer's disease & dementia; Life enrichment program
Alison Duva, Office Manager
aduva@omniway.ca
Linda Burr, Administrator
lburr@omniway.ca

Aylmer: Chateau Gardens Nursing Home
Affiliated with: Chartwell Retirement Homes
465 Talbot St. West, Aylmer, ON N5H 1K8
Tel: 519-773-3423; *Fax:* 519-765-2573
www.chartwell.com
Number of Beds: 59 beds
W. Brent Binoins, President & CEO

Aylmer: Terrace Lodge
475 Talbot St. East, Aylmer, ON N5H 3A5
Tel: 519-773-9205; *Fax:* 519-765-2627
www.elgincounty.ca
Number of Beds: 100 beds
Note: Specialties: Long-term care; Secure unit; Physiotherapy;

Activity program; Adult day program, including a specialized program for Alzheimer's patients; Respite care; Palliative care
Rhonda Duffy, Administrator
519-756-2627 ext 222, rduffy@elgin-county.on.ca

Bancroft: Hastings Centennial Manor
PO Box 758, 1 Manor Lane, Bancroft, ON K0L 1C0
Tel: 613-332-2070; *Fax:* 613-332-2837
www.hastingscounty.com

Number of Beds: 110 beds
Claudette Dignard-Remillard, Director of Long Term Care Service
613-332-2070
Kathy Plunkett, Site Manager
613-332-2070

Barrie: Coleman Care Centre
Affiliated with: Schlegel Villages
140 Cundles Rd. West, Barrie, ON L4M 4S4
Tel: 705-726-8691; *Fax:* 705-726-5085
schlegelvillages.com

Number of Beds: 112 beds
Pam Wiebe, General Manager
pam.wiebe@schlegelvillages.com

Barrie: Grove Park Home for Senior Citizens
234 Cook St., Barrie, ON L4M 4H5
Tel: 705-726-1003; *Fax:* 705-726-1076
business.office@groveparkhome.on.ca
www.groveparkhome.on.ca
Social Media: twitter.com/GroveParkHome

Number of Beds: 143 beds

Barrie: Leisureworld Caregiving Centre - Barrie
130 Owen St., Barrie, ON L4M 3H7
Tel: 705-726-8621; *Fax:* 705-726-0821
www.leisureworld.ca/barrie.html

Number of Beds: 57 beds
Lois Cormack, CEO

Barry's Bay: Valley Manor Nursing Home
PO Box 880, 88 Mintha St., Barry's Bay, ON K0J 1B0
Tel: 613-756-2643; *Fax:* 613-756-7601
www.valleymanor.org

Number of Beds: 90 beds
Note: Adult Day Program

Beamsville: Albright Manor
5050 Hillside Dr., Beamsville, ON L0R 1B2
Tel: 905-563-8252; *Fax:* 905-563-5223
info@albrightcentre.ca

Number of Beds: 231 beds
John E. Buma, CEO

Beeton: Simcoe Manor Home for the Aged
5988 Main St. East, Beeton, ON L0G 1A0
Tel: 905-729-2267; *Fax:* 905-729-4350

Number of Beds: 126 beds

Belleville: Bellmont Long-Term Care Facility
Former Name: Montgomery Lodge Nursing Home.
250 Bridge St. West, Belleville, ON K8P 5N3
Tel: 613-968-4434; *Fax:* 613-968-5443
belmont@cogeco.net

Number of Beds: 128 beds
Denise Mackey, Administrator/Primary Executive
dmackey.belmont@cogeco.net

Belleville: Hastings Manor
PO Box 458, 476 Dundas St. West, Belleville, ON K8N 5B2
Tel: 613-968-6467; *Fax:* 613-967-0128
info@hastingsmanorfoundation.ca
www.hastingsmanorfoundation.ca

Year Founded: 1908
Number of Beds: 253 beds
Jim Pine, Chief Administrative Officer
613-966-1319, Fax: 613-966-2574, pinej@hastingscounty.com

Belleville: Westgate Lodge
37 Wilkie St., Belleville, ON K8P 4E4
Tel: 613-966-1323; *Fax:* 613-968-5644
admin@westgatelodge.ca
www.westgatelodge.ca

Number of Beds: 88 beds

Blenheim: Blenheim Community Village
Revera Living
PO Box 220, 10 Mary Ave., Blenheim, ON N0P 1A0
Tel: 519-676-8119; *Fax:* 519-676-0610
www.reveraliving.com/blenheim
Social Media: www.facebook.com/400950748267; twitter.com/Revera_Inc; www.youtube.com/user/ReveraInc; www.linkedin.com/company/revera-inc

Number of Beds: 101 beds
Note: nursing home & retirement lodge
Jeffrey C. Lozon, President & CEO, Revera Living

Bobcaygeon: Pinecrest Nursing Home
3418 County Rd. 36, RR#2, Bobcaygeon, ON K0M 1A0
Tel: 705-738-2366; *Fax:* 705-738-9414

Number of Beds: 65 beds
Note: Specialties: Activation program
Mary Carr, Administrator
mcarr@pinecrestnh.ca

Bobcaygeon: Specialty Care Case Manor
Former Name: Case Manor Nursing Home
28 Boyd St., Bobcaygeon, ON K0M 1A0
Tel: 705-738-2374; *Fax:* 705-738-3821
suggestions@specialty-care.com
www.specialty-care.com

Number of Beds: 96 beds
Cindy McGregor, Interim Administrator
cindy.mcgregor@specialty-care.com

Bolton: King Nursing Home
49 Sterne St., Bolton, ON L7E 5T1
Tel: 905-857-4117; *Fax:* 905-857-5181

Year Founded: 1966
Number of Beds: 86 beds
Janice L. King, Administrator
janice.king@kingnursinghome.com

Bolton: Vera M. Davis Community Care Centre
80 Allan Dr., Bolton, ON L7E 1P7
Tel: 905-857-0975; *Fax:* 905-857-7872
www.peelregion.ca/ltc/davis

Number of Beds: 64 beds
Wendy Beattie, Administrator

Bourget: Caressant Care Bourget
Affiliated with: Caressant Care Nursing and Retirement Homes Limited
PO Box 99, 2279 Laval St., Bourget, ON K0A 1E0
Tel: 613-487-2331; *Fax:* 613-487-3464
www.caressantcare.com

Number of Beds: 50 beds
James Lavelle, President, Caressant Care Nursing and Retirement Homes Ltd.

Bowmanville: Glen Hill Marnwood
Affiliated with: Durham Christian Homes
26 Elgin St., Bowmanville, ON L1C 3C8
Tel: 905-623-5731; *Fax:* 905-623-4497
www.dchomes.ca

Year Founded: 1983
Number of Beds: 60 beds
Note: Specialties: Social work; Physiotherapy

Bowmanville: Glen Hill Strathaven
264 King St. East, Bowmanville, ON L1C 1P9
Tel: 905-623-2553; *Fax:* 905-623-1374
dchomes.ca

Number of Beds: 199 beds
Shelley Fazackerley, Administrator
sfazackerley@dchomes.ca

Bradford: Specialty Care Bradford Valley
Former Name: Bradford Place Nursing Home
2656 - 6 Line, Bradford, ON L3Z 2A4
Tel: 905-952-2270; *Fax:* 905-775-0263
suggestions@specialty-care.com
www.specialty-care.com

Number of Beds: 246 beds
Luanne Campeau, Administrator
luanne.campeau@specialty-care.com

Brampton: Extendicare - Brampton
Extendicare Canada
7891 McLaughlin Rd., Brampton, ON L6Y 5H8
Tel: 905-459-4904; *Fax:* 905-459-5625
cnh_brampton@extendicare.com
www.extendicarecanada.com/brampton/

Number of Beds: 150 beds

Brampton: Holland Christian Homes Inc.
Former Name: Faith Manor Nursing Home
7900 McLaughlin Rd. South, Brampton, ON L6Y 5A7
Tel: 905-459-3333; *Fax:* 905-459-8667
www.hch.ca

Number of Beds: 120 beds
Note: Dutch Heritage
John Kalverda, Executive Director
johnka@hch.ca
Peter Dykstra, Administrator, Grace Manor
petedy@hch.ca
Anthony Faul, Human Resources
anthfa@hch.ca

Brampton: Leisureworld Caregiving Centre - Brampton Meadows
215 Sunny Meadows Blvd., Brampton, ON L6R 3B5
Tel: 905-458-7604
www.leisureworld.ca

Number of Beds: 160 beds
Angie Heinze, Administrator

Brampton: Leisureworld Caregiving Centre - Brampton Woods
9257 Goreway Dr., Brampton, ON L6T 3Y7
Tel: 905-799-7502
www.leisureworld.ca

Number of Beds: 160 beds
Susan Wendt, Administrator

Brampton: Peel Manor
525 Main St. North, Brampton, ON L6X 1N9
Tel: 905-453-4140; *Fax:* 905-453-9140
www.peelregion.ca/ltc/peel

Number of Beds: 177 beds
Note: Long-term care centre
Jim Egan, Administrator

Brantford: Brierwood Gardens Long Term Care
Revera Living
425 Park Rd. North, Brantford, ON N3R 7G5
Tel: 519-759-1040; *Fax:* 519-759-5343
www.reveraliving.com
Social Media: www.facebook.com/400950748267; twitter.com/Revera_Inc; www.youtube.com/user/ReveraInc; www.linkedin.com/company/revera-inc

Number of Beds: 167 beds
Jeffrey C. Lozon, President & CEO, Revera Living

Brantford: Hardy Terrace Long Term Care
612 Mount Pleasant Rd., RR#2, Brantford, ON N3T 5L5
Tel: 519-484-2431; *Fax:* 519-484-2590
www.diversicare.ca

Number of Beds: 69 beds
Lloyd Smith, Administrator

Brantford: Leisureworld Caregiving Centre - Brantford
389 West St., Brantford, ON N3R 3V9
Tel: 519-759-4666; *Fax:* 519-759-0200
adm.brantford@leisureworld.ca
www.leisureworld.ca

Number of Beds: 120 permanent, 2 short stay beds
Lois Cormack, CEO, Leisureworld Senior Care Corporation

Brockville: St. Lawrence Lodge
PO Box 1130, 1803 Country Rd. East, Brockville, ON K6V 5W2
Tel: 613-345-0255; *Fax:* 613-345-1029
info@stll.org
www.stll.org

Number of Beds: 240 beds
Note: Long-term care home
Tom Harrington, Aministraor
tharrington@stll.org

Brockville: Sherwood Park Manor
1814 County Rd. 2 East, Brockville, ON K6V 5T1
Tel: 613-342-5531; *Fax:* 613-342-3767
www.sherwoodparkmanor.com

Number of Beds: 107 beds
Alfred O'Rourke, Administrator
AOrourke@sherwoodparkmanor.com

Brunner: Country Meadows Retirement Residence
6124 Ana St., Brunner, ON N0K 1C0
Tel: 519-595-8903; *Fax:* 519-595-8272
lb@countrymeadowsrr.com
countrymeadowsrr.ca
Social Media: www.facebook.com/455549397831324

Number of Beds: 43 beds

Brussels: Huronlea Home for the Aged
820 Turnberry St. South, Brussels, ON N0G 1H0
Tel: 519-887-9267; *Fax:* 519-887-9143
inquiries@huroncounty.ca
www.huroncounty.ca/homesaged/

Number of Beds: 64 beds; 2 respite beds
Barb Springhall, Administrator

***Burlington:* The Brant Centre Long Term Care Residence**
Affiliated with: Chartwell Seniors Housing REIT
1182 Northshore Blvd. East, Burlington, ON L7S 1C5
Tel: 905-639-2848
www.chartwellreit.ca/locations/brant-centre-ltc-residence
Year Founded: 2003
Number of Beds: 175 beds
Adam Banks, Administrator
Barbara Murphy, Director of Care
Stephen Suske, CEO, Chartwell Seniors Housing REIT

***Burlington:* Cama Woodlands Nursing Home**
159 Panin Rd., Burlington, ON L7P 5A6
Tel: 905-681-6441; *Fax:* 905-681-2678
www.camawoodlands.com
Number of Beds: 64 beds

***Burlington:* Maple Villa Long Term Care Centre**
441 Maple Ave., Burlington, ON L7S 1L8
Tel: 905-639-2264; *Fax:* 905-639-3034
maplevilla@maplevilla.ca
www.maplevilla.ca
Year Founded: 1971
Number of Beds: 93 beds

***Cambridge:* Caressant Care Nursing and Retirement Homes Limited**
Cambridge Country Manor
3680 Speedsville Rd., Cambridge, ON N3H 4R6
Tel: 519-650-0100
www.caressantcare.com
Number of Beds: 79 beds
Brenda Nadeau, Administrator

***Cambridge:* Fairview Mennonite Home**
515 Langs Dr., Cambridge, ON N3H 5E4
Tel: 519-653-5719; *Fax:* 519-650-1242
info@fairviewmh.com
www.fairviewmh.com
Number of Beds: 84 beds
Jim Williams, Administrator
Marlene Goerz, Director of Care

***Cambridge:* Golden Years Nursing Home**
PO Box 3277, 704 Eagle St., Cambridge, ON N3H 4T3
Tel: 519-653-5493; *Fax:* 519-650-1495
www.goldenyearscambridge.com
Number of Beds: 88 beds
Nancy Kauffman-Lambert, Administrator

***Cambridge:* Riverbend Place Retirement Community**
650 Coronation Blvd., Cambridge, ON N1R 7S6
Tel: 519-740-3820; *Fax:* 519-740-0961
www.reveraliving.com
Number of Beds: 146 beds
Note: Assisted living & independent living programs; short term, respite & convalescent options; community includes nursing home, retirement lodge, apartments
Jeffrey C. Lozon, President & CEO, Revera Living

***Cambridge:* Saint Luke's Place**
1624 Franklin Blvd., Cambridge, ON N3C 3P4
Tel: 519-658-5183; *Fax:* 519-658-2991
www.saintlukesplace.ca
Number of Beds: 150 beds
Note: home for the aged; provides long term care, retirement home & apartments
Rita Soluk, CEO

***Campbellford:* Burnbrae Gardens**
Affiliated with: Omni Health Care
320 - 6 Line East, Campbellford, ON K0L 1L0
Tel: 705-653-4100; *Fax:* 705-653-2598
www.omniway.ca
Number of Beds: 43 beds
Rosie Coppens, Office Manager
rcoppens@omniway.com
April Faux, Administrator
afaux@omniway.ca

***Cannifton:* E.J. McQuigge Lodge**
PO Box 68, 38 Black Diamond Rd., Cannifton, ON K0K 1K0
Tel: 613-966-7717; *Fax:* 613-966-7646
www.mcquiggelodge.com
Number of Beds: 56 beds
Anita Garland, Administrator
agarland@mcquiggelodge.com

***Cannington:* Bon-Air Residence**
Affiliated with: Chartwell Retirement Residences
PO Box 400, 131 Laidlaw St. South, Cannington, ON L0E 1E0
Tel: 705-432-2385; *Fax:* 705-432-3331
www.chartwell.com
Number of Beds: 55 units
W. Brent Binoins, President & CEO, Chartwell Retirement Residences

***Carleton Place:* Stoneridge Manor**
Revera Living
256 High St., Carleton Place, ON K7C 1X1
Tel: 613-257-4355; *Fax:* 613-253-2190
www.reveraliving.com/stoneridge
Social Media: www.facebook.com/400950748267; twitter.com/Revera_Inc; www.youtube.com/user/ReveraInc; www.linkedin.com/company/revera-inc
Number of Beds: 60 beds
Jeffrey C. Lozon, President & CEO, Revera Living

***Chapleau:* Bignucolo Residence**
Chapleau Health Services
PO Box 757, 6 Broomhead Rd., Chapleau, ON P0M 1K0
Tel: 705-864-1520; *Fax:* 705-864-0449
Year Founded: 1998
Number of Beds: 25 beds
Note: Specialties: Long-term care; Chronic care; Respite care; Pet therapy

***Chatham:* St. Andrew's Residence**
99 Park St., Chatham, ON N7M 3R5
Tel: 519-354-8103; *Fax:* 519-351-2407
info@standrewsresidence.com
www.standrewsresidence.com
Number of Beds: 95 beds
Carolynn Barko, CEO
519-354-8103, cbarko@standrewsresidence.com

***Chesley:* Elgin Abbey Nursing & Retirement Home**
PO Box 7, 380 First Ave. North, Chesley, ON N0G 1L0
Tel: 519-363-3195; *Fax:* 519-363-0375
elginabbey@xplornet.ca
Number of Beds: 41 beds; 27 long-term-care, 14 retirement home
Tracee Givens, Administrator

***Clinton:* Huronview Home for the Aged**
77722A London Rd. Hwy 4 South, RR#5, Clinton, ON N0M 1L0
Tel: 519-482-3451; *Fax:* 519-482-5263
www.huroncounty.ca/homesaged
Number of Beds: 119 beds
Barb Springall, Administrator

***Cobden:* Caressant Care Cobden**
Affiliated with: Caressant Care Nursing and Retirement Homes Limited
12 Wren Dr., Cobden, ON K0J 1K0
Tel: 613-646-2109
www.caressantcare.com
Year Founded: 2000
Number of Beds: 60 beds
James Lavelle, President & CEO, Caressant Care Nursing and Retirement Homes Ltd.

***Cobourg:* Extendicare - Cobourg**
Extendicare Canada
130 Densmore Rd., Cobourg, ON K9A 5W2
Tel: 905-372-0377; *Fax:* 905-372-0477
cnh_cobourg@extendicare.com
www.extendicarecanada.com/cobourg
Number of Beds: 69 beds

***Cobourg:* Streamway Villa Nursing Home**
Affiliated with: Omni Health Care
19 James St. West, Cobourg, ON K9A 2J8
Tel: 905-372-0163; *Fax:* 905-372-0581
www.omniway.ca
Number of Beds: 59 beds
Kylie Szczebonski, Administrator, Director of Care
kszczebonski@omniway.ca

***Collingwood:* Bay Haven Senior Care Community**
Former Name: Bay Haven Nursing Home Inc.
499 Hume St., Collingwood, ON L9Y 4H8
Tel: 705-445-6501; *Fax:* 705-445-6506
info@bayhaven.com
www.bayhaven.com
Number of Beds: 60 beds

***Collingwood:* Collingwood Nursing Home Limited**
250 Campbell St., Collingwood, ON L9Y 4J9
Tel: 705-445-3991; *Fax:* 705-445-5060
cnh@collingwoodnursinghome.com
www.collingwoodnursinghome.com
Number of Beds: 60 beds
Peter Zober, President, Owner
peter@collingwoodnursinghome.com

***Collingwood:* Sunset Manor Home & Village**
49 Raglan St., Collingwood, ON L9Y 4X1
Tel: 705-445-4499; *Fax:* 705-445-9742
www.simcoe.ca
Year Founded: 1968
Number of Beds: 148 beds
Note: Sunset Manor Home for the Aged is a municipal, Long-Term Care facility.

***Corbeil:* Nipissing Manor Nursing Care Centre**
PO Box 40, 1202 Hwy. 94, Corbeil, ON P0H 1K0
Tel: 705-752-1100; *Fax:* 705-752-2570
nipissingmanor@bellnet.ca
Number of Beds: 143 beds
Wentworth E. Graham, Administrator

***Cornwall:* Glen-Stor-Dun Lodge**
1900 Montréal Rd., Cornwall, ON K6H 7L1
Tel: 613-933-3384; *Fax:* 613-933-7214
www.cornwall.ca
Year Founded: 1912
Number of Beds: 132 beds
Note: Serves as a municipal home for the older people. Provides a variety of esstential services including dietary, house cleaning, recreation and leisure activities & many more.
Norm Quenneville, Administrator
Donna Derouchie, Administrator

***Cornwall:* Heartwood Long Term Care**
Revera Living
201 - 11 St. East, Cornwall, ON K6H 2Y6
Tel: 613-933-7420
www.reveraliving.com
Number of Beds: 118 beds
Jeffrey C. Lozon, President & CEO, Revera Living

***Cornwall:* Parisien Manor**
439 Second St. East, Cornwall, ON K6H 1Z2
Tel: 613-933-2592; *Fax:* 613-933-3839
www.parisienmanor.ca
Year Founded: 1982
Note: Specialties: Long-term care; Activation programs; Counselling; Social services; Dental services; Music therapy; Physiotherapy; Occupational therapy; Foot care
Terry Dube, Administrator
tadube@clmi.ca

***Cornwall:* St. Joseph's Continuing Care Centre**
14 York St., Cornwall, ON K6J 5T2
Tel: 613-933-6040; *Fax:* 613-933-0163
executiveoffices@stjosephscentre.ca
www.stjosephscentre.ca
Number of Beds: 150 beds
Bonnie Ruest, Executive Director

***Courtland:* Caressant Care Nursing and Retirement Homes Limited**
Caressant Care Courtland
Former Name: Sacred Heart Villa
PO Box 279, 4850 County Rd. 59, Courtland, ON N0J 1E0
Tel: 519-688-0710; *Fax:* 519-688-0052
www.caressantcare.com
Number of Beds: 54 beds
Note: Retirement home
Linda Hare, Administrator
Gilbert Dooms, Supervisor, Maintenance

***Creemore:* Creedan Valley Nursing Home**
Affiliated with: Leisureworld Senior Care Corporation
PO Box 309, 143 Mary St., Creemore, ON L0M 1G0
Tel: 705-466-3437; *Fax:* 705-466-3063
www.leisureworld.ca
Number of Beds: 96 beds
Lois Cormack, CEO, Leisureworld Senior Care Corporation

***Creemore:* Leisureworld Caregiving Centre - Creedan Valley**
143 Mary St., Creemore, ON L0M 1G0
Tel: 705-466-3437
www.leisureworld.ca
Number of Beds: 95 beds
Paula Rentner, Administrator

***Deep River:* North Renfrew Long-Term Care Centre**
PO Box 1988, 47 Ridge Rd., Deep River, ON K0J 1P0
Tel: 613-584-1900; *Fax:* 613-584-9183
nrltc@nrltc.ca
Year Founded: 1994
Number of Beds: 20 long-term care; 9 supportive care; 1 respite
Kim Rodgers, Administrator
kim.rodgers@nrltc.ca

***Delhi:* Delhi Long Term Care Centre**
Affiliated with: peopleCare
750 Gibraltar St., Delhi, ON N4B 3B3
Tel: 519-582-3400; *Fax:* 519-582-0300
peoplecare.ca
Year Founded: 1972
Number of Beds: 60 beds
Tanya King, Executive Director

***Embrun:* St. Jacques Nursing Home/Foyer St-Jacques**
PO Box 870, 915 Notre Dame St., Embrun, ON K0A 1W0
Tel: 613-443-3442; *Fax:* 613-443-1716
info@stjacques.ca
www.stjacques.ca
Number of Beds: 60 beds
Note: Medical services include: phyisotherapy; occupational therapy; podiarty; visits from an optometrist and dentist
Yvon Brisson, President

***Englehart:* Northview Nursing Home**
Affiliated with: Conmed Health Care Group
PO Box 1139, 77 River Rd., Englehart, ON P0J 1H0
Tel: 705-544-8191; *Fax:* 705-544-8255
northview@ntl.sympatico.ca
www.conmedhealth.com
Number of Beds: 48 beds
Tracey Gemmill, Administrator/DOC
tgemmill@conmedhealth.com

***Espanola:* Espanola Nursing Home**
825 McKinnon Dr., Espanola, ON P5E 1R4
Tel: 705-869-1420; *Fax:* 705-869-1420
www.erhhc.on.ca
Number of Beds: 62 beds
Paul L. Davies, Administrator
Diane Mokohonuk, Environmental Manager

***Essex:* Iler Lodge**
Former Name: Essex Health Care Centre
111 Iler Ave., Essex, ON N8M 1T6
Tel: 519-776-9482
www.reveraliving.com
Social Media: www.facebook.com/400950748267; www.twitter.com/Revera_Inc; www.youtube.com/ReveraInc; www.linkedin.com/company/revera-inc
Number of Beds: 104 beds
Note: Programs include physiotherapy; 3M skin and wound care; ALIVE program
Cheryl Labute, Administrator

***Etobicoke:* Eatonville Care Centre**
420 The East Mall, Etobicoke, ON M9B 3Z9
Tel: 416-621-8000; *Fax:* 416-621-8003
eatonvillecarecentre.ca
Number of Beds: 250 beds
Evelyn McDonald, Administrator

***Exeter:* Exeter Villa Nursing & Retirement Home**
Affiliated with: ATK Care Inc.
155 John St. East, Exeter, ON N0M 1S1
Tel: 519-235-1581; *Fax:* 519-235-3219
exevilla@cabletv.on.ca
www.atkcareinc.ca/exeterservices
Number of Beds: 57 nursing care beds, 66 retirement beds
Nancy Tweddle, Administrator

***Fergus:* Caressant Care Fergus**
Affiliated with: Caressant Care Nursing and Retirement Homes Limited
450 Queen St. East, Fergus, ON N1M 2Y7
Tel: 519-843-2400
www.caressantcare.com
Year Founded: 1986
Number of Beds: 87 beds
James Lavelle, President, Caressant Care Nursing and Retirement Homes Ltd.

***Fergus:* Wellington County Terrace Home for the Aged**
474 Wellington Rd. 18, Fergus, ON N1M 0A1
Tel: 519-846-5359; *Fax:* 519-846-9192
www.wellington.ca
Number of Beds: 176 beds
Number of Employees: 242

***Fordwich:* Fordwich Village Nursing Home**
Affiliated with: ATK Care Inc.
3063 Adelaide St., Fordwich, ON N0G 1V0
Tel: 519-335-3168; *Fax:* 519-335-3825
fordwichadmin@tnt21.com
www.atkcareinc.ca/fordwich.htm
Number of Beds: 33 beds
Note: Long term care facility
Susan Jaunzemis, Administrator, Director of Care

***Forest:* North Lambton Rest Home**
PO Box 640, 39 Morris St., Forest, ON N0N 1J0
Tel: 519-786-2151; *Fax:* 519-786-2156
www.lambtononline.ca
Number of Beds: 88 beds
Jane Joris, Manager

***Fort Erie:* Crescent Park Lodge**
Affiliated with: Conmed Health Care Group
4 Hagey Ave., Fort Erie, ON L2A 5M5
Tel: 905-871-8330; *Fax:* 905-991-1456
crescentparklodge@cogeco.net
www.conmedhealth.com
Number of Beds: 68 beds
Lisa Hussman, Director of Nursing
Rose Turner, Administrator

***Gananoque:* Carveth Care Centre**
375 James St., Gananoque, ON K7G 2Z1
Tel: 613-382-4752; *Fax:* 613-382-8514
www.gibsonfamilyhealthcare.com
Number of Beds: 94 beds
Brett Gibson, Administrator
613-382-4752

***Georgetown:* Bennett Health Care Centre**
1 Princess Anne Dr., Georgetown, ON L7G 2B8
Tel: 905-873-0115; *Fax:* 905-873-1403
info@bennetthealthcarecentre.ca
www.bennetthealthcarecentre.ca
Number of Beds: 66 beds
Mark Ewer, Administrator

***Gloucester:* Extendicare - Laurier Manor**
Extendicare Canada
1715 Montréal Rd., Gloucester, ON K1J 6N4
Tel: 613-741-5122; *Fax:* 613-741-8432
cnh_lauriermanor@extendicare.com
www.extendicarecanada.com
Number of Beds: 240 beds

***Goderich:* Maitland Manor**
290 South St., Goderich, ON N7A 4G6
Tel: 519-524-7324; *Fax:* 519-524-8739
maitlandmanor.ca
Number of Beds: 91 beds
Note: Specialties: Long-term care; Restorative care programs; Foot care; Specialized skin & wound care program; Physiotherapy; Music therapy; Respite care
Kyla MacDonald, Administrator
kymacdonald@extendicare.com

***Gravenhurst:* Leisureworld Caregiving Centre - Muskoka**
200 Kelly Dr., Gravenhurst, ON P1P 1P3
Tel: 705-687-3444; *Fax:* 705-687-9094
admin.muskoka@leisureworld.ca
www.leisureworld.ca/muskoka.html
Year Founded: 1999
Number of Beds: 180 long-term care, 2 short term beds, 28 retirement suites
Lois Cormack, CEO

***Grimsby:* Kilean Lodge**
Revera Living
83 Main St. East, Grimsby, ON L3M 1N6
Tel: 905-945-9243; *Fax:* 905-945-1126
Kilean@reveraliving.com
www.reveraliving.com
Social Media: www.facebook.com/400950748267; twitter.com/Revera_Inc; www.youtube.com/user/ReveraInc; www.linkedin.com/company/revera-inc
Number of Beds: 50 beds
Jeffrey C. Lozon, President & CEO, Revera Living

***Grimsby:* Shalom Manor**
12 Bartlett Ave., Grimsby, ON L3M 4N5
Tel: 905-945-9631; *Fax:* 905-945-1211
info@shalommanor.ca
www.shalommanor.ca
Year Founded: 1966
Number of Beds: 144 beds
Note: Home for the aged affiliated with the Christian Reformed Church
Peet Konnie, CEO

***Guelph:* Eden House Nursing Home**
Affiliated with: Waterloo Wellington Local Health Integration Network
5016 Wellington Rd. 29, Guelph, ON N1H 6H8
Tel: 519-856-4622; *Fax:* 519-856-1274
admin@edenhousecarehome.ca
www.edenhousecarehome.ca
Number of Beds: 58 nursing home, 21 retirement home

***Guelph:* Lapointe-Fisher Nursing Home**
271 Metcalfe St., Guelph, ON N1E 4Y8
Tel: 519-821-9030; *Fax:* 519-821-6021
guelph@lapointefisher.ca
www.lapointefisher.ca
Number of Beds: 92 beds

***Hagersville:* Norcliffe LifeCare Centre**
85 Main St. North, Hagersville, ON N0A 1H0
Tel: 905-768-1641; *Fax:* 905-768-1685
Number of Beds: 60 units
Note: Retirement home

***Haileybury:* Extendicare - Tri-Town**
Extendicare Canada
PO Box 999, 143 Bruce St., Haileybury, ON P0J 1K0
Tel: 705-672-2151; *Fax:* 705-672-5348
cnh_tritown@extendicare.com
www.extendicarecanada.com
Number of Beds: 60 beds

***Haliburton:* Extendicare - Haliburton**
Extendicare Canada
PO Box 780, 167 Park St., Haliburton, ON K0M 1S0
Tel: 705-457-1722; *Fax:* 705-457-3914
cnh_haliburton@extendicare.com
www.extendicarecanada.com/haliburton
Number of Beds: 60 beds

***Halton Hills:* Extendicare - Halton Hills**
Extendicare Canada
9 Lindsay Court, Halton Hills, ON L7G 6G9
Tel: 905-702-8760; *Fax:* 905-702-7430
cnh_haltonhills@extendicare.com
www.extendicarecanada.com/georgetown
Number of Beds: 130 beds

***Hamilton:* Arbour Creek Long Term Care Centre**
2717 King St. East, Hamilton, ON L8G 1J3
Tel: 905-573-4900; *Fax:* 905-573-4340
thomashealthcare.com
Number of Beds: 128 beds
Shirley Thomas Weir
sthomasweir@thomashealthcare.com

***Hamilton:* Baywoods Place**
Revera Living
Former Name: Versa-Care Centre - Hamilton
330 Main St. East, Hamilton, ON L8N 3T9
Tel: 905-523-7134
www.reveraliving.com/baywoods
Social Media: www.facebook.com/400950748267; twitter.com/Revera_Inc; www.youtube.com/user/ReveraInc; www.linkedin.com/company/revera-inc
Number of Beds: 128 beds
Jeffrey C. Lozon, President & CEO, Revera Living

***Hamilton:* Extendicare - Hamilton**
Extendicare Canada
90 Chedmac Dr., Hamilton, ON L9C 7S6
Tel: 905-318-4472; *Fax:* 905-318-1162
cnh_hamilton@extendicare.com
www.extendicarecanada.com/hamilton/
Number of Beds: 160 beds

***Hamilton:* Hamilton Continuing Care**
125 Wentworth St. South, Hamilton, ON L8N 2Z1
Tel: 905-527-1482; *Fax:* 905-527-0679
www.hamiltonltc.com
Number of Beds: 64 beds

***Hamilton:* Macassa Lodge**
701 Upper Sherman Ave., Hamilton, ON L8V 3M7
Tel: 905-546-2800; *Fax:* 905-546-4989
MacassaLodge@hamilton.ca
www.hamilton.ca
Number of Beds: 270 beds
Note: Specialties: Long term care; Adult day program; Social work

***Hamilton:* Parkview Nursing Centre**
545 King St. West, Hamilton, ON L8P 1C1
Tel: 905-525-5903; *Fax:* 905-525-8717
www.parkviewnursingcentre.com
Number of Beds: 126 beds

***Hamilton:* St. Olga's Lifecare Centre**
Affiliated with: Central Canadian District of The Christian & Missionary Alliance
570 King St. West, Hamilton, ON L8P 1C2
Tel: 905-522-8572; *Fax:* 905-522-1553
stolgas.com
Number of Beds: 93 beds

***Hamilton:* Victoria Nursing Home**
176 Victoria Ave. North, Hamilton, ON L8L 5G1
Tel: 905-527-9111; *Fax:* 905-526-1871
www.victoriagardens.ca
Number of Beds: 76 beds
Ranka Stipancic, Administrator
ranka@victoriagardens.ca

***Hanover:* Hanover Care Centre**
700 - 19 Ave., Hanover, ON N4N 3S6
Tel: 519-364-3700; *Fax:* 519-364-7194
cancarecentres.ca
Number of Beds: 41 beds
Bill Garcia, Owner
wg@bmts.com

***Harriston:* Caressant Care Harriston**
Affiliated with: Caressant Care Nursing And Retirement Homes Limited
PO Box 520, 24 Louise St., Harriston, ON N0G 1Z0
Tel: 519-338-3700; *Fax:* 519-338-2744
www.caressantcare.com
Number of Beds: 89 beds
Note: Long term care facility, with secure unit for residents with dementia, & adjacent retirement home.
James Lavelle, President, Caressant Care Nursing and Retirement Homes

***Hawkesbury:* Résidence Prescott et Russell/Prescott & Russell Residence**
1020, boul Cartier, Hawkesbury, ON K6A 1W7
Tél: 613-632-2755; *Téléc:* 613-632-4056
www.prescott-russell.on.ca
Fondée en: 1906
Nombre de lits: 146 lits
Note: Maison de soins de longue durée. Employés: 171

***Hearst:* Foyer des Pionniers**
PO Box 1538, 67 - 15 St., Hearst, ON P0L 1N0
Tel: 705-372-2978; *Fax:* 705-372-2996
Number of Beds: 61 beds
Joëlle Lacroix, Director of Care, Administrator
jlacroix@hearst.ca

***Huntsville:* Fairvern Nursing Home Inc.**
Affiliated with: Huntsville District Nursing Home Inc.
14 Mill St., Huntsville, ON P1H 2A4
Tel: 705-789-6011; *Fax:* 705-789-1371
info@fairvern.ca
www.fairvernnursinghome.ca
Number of Beds: 76 beds
Bev MacWilliams, Chair

***Ingersoll:* Leisureworld Caregiving Centre - Oxford**
263 Wonham St. South, Ingersoll, ON N5C 3P6
Tel: 519-485-3920
adm.oxford@leisureworld.ca
www.leisureworld.ca
Year Founded: 1975
Number of Beds: 80 long-term care beds
Note: Specialties: Restorative care; Physiotherapy program; Pet therapy; Palliative care
Lois Cormack, CEO, Leisureworld Senior Care Corporation

***Iroquois Falls:* South Centennial Manor**
240 Fyfe St., Iroquois Falls, ON P0K 1E0
Tel: 705-258-3836; *Fax:* 705-258-3694
www.micsgroup.com
Number of Beds: 69 beds
Note: Services include pastoral care; foot care; nursing and personal care services; assisting with activities of daily living.
Dan O'Mara, CEO
Richard Hadley, Director, Physical Plant

***Kapuskasing:* Extendicare - Kapuskasing**
Extendicare Canada
PO Box 460, 45 Ontario St., Kapuskasing, ON P5N 2Y5
Tel: 705-335-8337; *Fax:* 705-337-6051
cnh_kapuskasing@extendicare.com
www.extendicarecanada.com/kapuskasing/
Number of Beds: 60 beds

***Kapuskasing:* North Centennial Manor**
2 Kimberley Dr., Kapuskasing, ON P5N 1L5
Tel: 705-335-6125; *Fax:* 705-337-1091
Number of Beds: 71 beds
Note: non-profit charitable home for the aged
Andre Filion, Administrator
afilion@NCManor.com

***Kemptville:* Bayfield Manor Nursing & Retirement Home**
PO Box 300, 100 Elvira St., Kemptville, ON K0G 1J0
Tel: 613-258-7484; *Fax:* 613-258-3838
bayfield@bayfieldmanor.on.ca
www.bayfieldmanor.on.ca
Number of Beds: 66 bed nursing home & 46 suite retirement home

***Kenora:* Birchwood Terrace Nursing Home**
237 Lakeview Drive, Kenora, ON P9N 4J7
Tel: 807-468-8625; *Fax:* 807-468-4060
birchwoodterrace@reveraliving.com
birchwoodterrace.ca
Number of Beds: 94 beds
Wendy Sarfi, Administrator
wsarfi@extendicare.com

***Kenora:* Pinecrest Home for the Aged**
1220 Valley Dr., Kenora, ON P9N 2W7
Tel: 807-468-3165; *Fax:* 807-468-6346
www.kenoradistricthomes.ca
Marilyn Fortier
marilyn.fortier@kenoradistricthomes.

***Keswick:* Specialty Care Cedarvale Lodge**
121 Morton Dr., Keswick, ON L4P 2M5
Tel: 905-476-2656; *Fax:* 905-476-5689
suggestions@specialty-care.com
www.specialty-care.com
Number of Beds: 100 beds
Note: Nursing home with 40-bed retirement home attached
Donna Taylor, Administrator
donna.taylor@specialty-care.com

***King City:* King City Lodge Nursing Home**
146 Fog Rd., King City, ON L7B 1A3
Tel: 905-833-5037; *Fax:* 905-833-5925
www.kingcitylodge.com
Number of Beds: 36 beds

***Kingston:* Extendicare - Kingston**
Extendicare Canada
309 Queen Mary Rd., Kingston, ON K7M 6P4
Tel: 613-549-5010; *Fax:* 613-549-7347
cnh_kingston@extendicare.com
extendicarekingston.ca
Number of Beds: 150 beds

***Kingston:* Rideaucrest Home**
175 Rideau St., Kingston, ON K7K 3H6
Tel: 613-530-2818; *Fax:* 613-531-9107
Number of Beds: 170 beds
Note: municipal home for the aged

***Kirkland Lake:* Extendicare - Kirkland Lake**
Extendicare Canada
PO Box 3900, 155 Government Rd. East, Kirkland Lake, ON P2N 3P4
Tel: 705-567-3268; *Fax:* 705-567-4638
cnh_kirklandlake@extendicare.com
www.extendicarecanada.com/kirklandlake/
Number of Beds: 100 beds

***Kirkland Lake:* Teck Pioneer Residence**
PO Box 1757, 145A Government Rd. East, Kirkland Lake, ON P2N 3P4
Tel: 705-567-3257; *Fax:* 705-567-3737
Year Founded: 1965
Note: Specialties: Nursing services for long-term care residents; Dementia care; Activity program; Restorative care
Nancy Theriault, Administrator

***Kitchener:* A.R. Goudie Eventide Home (Salvation Army)**
369 Frederick St., Kitchener, ON N2H 2P1
Tel: 519-744-5182; *Fax:* 519-744-3887
info@argoudieeventide.ca
www.argoudieeventide.ca
Number of Beds: 80 beds

***Kitchener:* Forest Heights Long Term Care Centre**
Revera Living
60 Westheights Dr., Kitchener, ON N2N 2A8
Tel: 519-576-3320; *Fax:* 519-745-3227
generalforestheights@reveraliving.com
www.reveraliving.com
Social Media: www.facebook.com/400950748267; twitter.com/Revera_Inc; www.youtube.com/user/ReveraInc; www.linkedin.com/company/revera-inc
Number of Beds: 240 beds
Jeffrey C. Lozon, President & CEO, Revera Living

***Kitchener:* Trinity Village Care Centre (TVCC)**
2727 Kingsway Dr., Kitchener, ON N2C 1A7
Tel: 519-893-6320; *Fax:* 519-893-3432
www.trinityvillage.com
Number of Beds: 150 residential capacity
Note: Specialties: Eden Alternative Philosophy of Care; Long-term care; Therapeutic services; Recreation programming; Palliative care
Jeanne Jackson, Administrator
519-893-6320

***Kitchener:* Village of Winston Park**
695 Blockline Rd., Kitchener, ON N2E 3K1
Tel: 519-576-2430; *Fax:* 519-576-8990
schlegelvillages.com
Number of Beds: 271 beds
Brad Lawrence, General Manager

***Lakefield:* Extendicare - Lakefield**
Extendicare Canada
24 Fraser St., Lakefield, ON K0L 2H0
Tel: 705-652-7112; *Fax:* 705-652-7733
cnh_lakefield@extendicare.com
www.extendicarecanada.com/lakefield/
Number of Beds: 100 beds

***Leamington:* Franklin Gardens**
Affiliated with: Meritas Care Corporation
24 Franklin Rd., Leamington, ON N8H 4B7
Tel: 519-326-3289; *Fax:* 519-326-0102
franklin@meritascare.ca
www.meritascare.ca
Number of Beds: 120 beds

***Leamington:* Leamington United Mennonite Home**
22 Garrison Ave., Leamington, ON N8H 2P2
Tel: 519-326-6109; *Fax:* 519-326-3595
leamingtonunited.mennonite.net
Number of Beds: 82 beds

***Leamington:* Sun Parlor Home for Senior Citizens**
175 Talbot St. East, Leamington, ON N8H 1L9
Tel: 519-326-5731; *Fax:* 519-326-8952
TTY: 877-624-4832
www.countyofessex.on.ca/countyservices/sunparlor_home.asp
Year Founded: 1900
Number of Beds: 206 beds
Note: Specialties: Long-term care; Mental health services; Physiotherapy; Restorative care programs; Speech therapy; Occupational therapy; Audiology screening; Life enrichment services
Brian Gregg, Acting Administrator
519-776-6441

***Lindsay:* Extendicare - Kawartha Lakes**
Extendicare Canada
125 Colborne St. East, Lindsay, ON K9V 4R3
Tel: 705-878-5392; *Fax:* 705-878-7910
cnh_kawarthalakes@extendicare.com
www.extendicarecanada.com/lindsaykawartha/
Number of Beds: 64 beds

***Lions Head:* Golden Dawn Senior Citizen Home**
PO Box 129, 80 Main St., Lions Head, ON N0H 1W0
Tel: 519-793-3433; *Fax:* 519-793-4503
office@goldendawn.ca
www.goldendawn.ca
Number of Beds: 45 beds
Kevin Jones, Administrator
Deborah Shaw, R.N., Director of Residence Care

***Listowel:* Caressant Care Listowel**
Affiliated with: Caressant Care Nursing and Retirement Homes Limited
710 Reserve Ave., Listowel, ON N4W 2L1
Tel: 519-291-1041; *Fax:* 519-291-5420
www.caressantcare.com
Number of Beds: 52 beds
James Lavelle, President, Caressant Care Nursing and Retirement Homes Ltd.

***Little Current:* Manitoulin Centennial Manor**
PO Box 460, 70 Robinson St. West, Little Current, ON P0P 1K0
Tel: 705-368-3671; *Fax:* 705-368-2694
manitoulincentennial.ca
Number of Beds: 60 beds
Carol McIlveen, Administrator
cmcilveen@extendicare.com

***London:* Chelsey Park Long Term Care**
310 Oxford St. West, London, ON N6H 4N6
Tel: 519-432-1855; *Fax:* 519-679-7324
www.chelseypark.com
Number of Beds: 243 beds
Note: retirement community
Suzi Holster, Administrator
519-432-1855, adm.cpo@diversicare.ca

***London:* Elmwood Place Long Term Care**
Revera Living
Former Name: Elmwood Place
46 Elmwood Pl. West, London, ON N6J 1J2
Tel: 519-433-7259; *Fax:* 519-660-0158
www.reveraliving.com
Social Media: www.facebook.com/400950748267; twitter.com/Revera_Inc; www.youtube.com/user/ReveraInc; www.linkedin.com/company/revera-inc
Number of Beds: 97 beds
Jeffrey C. Lozon, President & CEO, Revera Living

***London:* Extendicare - London**
Extendicare Canada
860 Waterloo St., London, ON N6A 3W6
Tel: 519-433-6658; *Fax:* 519-642-1711
cnh_london@extendicare.com
www.extendicarecanada.com/london/index.aspx
Number of Beds: 170 beds

***London:* McCormick Home**
2022 Kains Rd., London, ON N6K 0A8
Tel: 519-432-2648; *Fax:* 519-645-6982
www.mccormickhome.on.ca
Number of Beds: 160 beds
Note: Specialties: Long-term care; Ddementia care; Alzheimer outreach services day program; Social work

***Long Sault:* Woodland Villa**
30 Mille Roches Rd., Long Sault, ON K0C 1P0
Tel: 613-534-2276; *Fax:* 613-534-8559
www.omniway.ca
Number of Beds: 112 beds
Michael Rasenberg, Administrator
mrasenberg@omniway.ca

***Markdale:* Grey Gables Home for the Aged**
Former Name: Grey Owen Lodge
PO Box 380, 206 Toronto St. South, Markdale, ON N0C 1H0
Tel: 519-986-3010; *Fax:* 519-986-4644
greygablesresident@grey.ca
www.grey.ca
Number of Beds: 66 beds
Jennifer Cornell, Administrator
jennifer.cornell@grey.ca

***Markham:* Leisureworld Caregiving Centre - Elmira**
#200, 302 Town Centre Blvd., Markham, ON L3R 0E8
Tel: 905-477-4006; *Fax:* 905-415-7623
Toll-Free: 855-895-3801
info@leisureworld.ca
www.leisureworld.ca
Number of Beds: 92 permanent, 2 short stay beds
Cathy Holland, Administrator

***Markham:* Markhaven, Home for Seniors**
54 Parkway Ave., Markham, ON L3P 2G4
Tel: 905-294-2233; *Fax:* 905-294-6521
markhaven@markhaven.ca
www.markhaven.ca
Number of Beds: 96 beds
Note: Specialties: Medical care; Nursing care; Physiotherapy; Special needs activities. Number of Employees: 149
Laura Burns, Executive Director
905-294-2233, laura.burns@markhaven.ca

***Marmora:* Caressant Care Marmora**
Affiliated with: Caressant Care Nursing and Retirement Homes Limited
58 Bursthall St., Marmora, ON K0K 2M0
Tel: 613-472-3130; *Fax:* 613-472-5388
www.caressantcare.com
Number of Beds: 84 beds
James Lavelle, President, Caressant Care Nursing and Retirement Homes Ltd.

***Maryhill:* Twin Oaks of Maryhill Inc.**
1360 Maryhill Rd., Maryhill, ON N0B 2B0
Tel: 519-648-2117
www.twinoaksmaryhill.com
Number of Beds: 31 beds
Note: Specialties: Secured area
Ralph Link, Administrator

***Matheson:* Rosedale Centre**
Affiliated with: Bingham Memorial Hospital
507 - 8th Ave., Matheson, ON P0K 1N0
Tel: 705-273-2424; *Fax:* 705-273-2515
www.micsgroup.com
Year Founded: 1989
Number of Beds: 20 beds
Note: Specialty: Long term nursing & supportive care; Foot care; Therapy
Bruce Peterkin, CEO

***Mattawa:* Algonquin Nursing Home**
PO Box 270, 231 - 10 St., Mattawa, ON P0H 1V0
Tel: 705-744-2202; *Fax:* 705-744-2787
Toll-Free: 800-579-4284
anh-admin@anh.ca
www.anh.ca
Number of Beds: 72 beds

***Meaford:* Meaford Long Term Care Centre**
135 William St., Meaford, ON N4L 1T4
Tel: 519-538-1010; *Fax:* 519-538-5699
businessoffice@meafordlongtermcare.com
www.meafordlongtermcare.com
Number of Beds: 77 beds
Note: Specialties; Restorative care program; Psychogeriatric outreach; Life enrichment programs; Services of a wound care specialist; Services of a pain specialist; Palliative care

***Merrickville:* Hilltop Manor Nursing Home Ltd.**
PO Box 430, 1005 St. Lawrence St., Merrickville, ON K0G 1N0
Tel: 613-269-4707; *Fax:* 613-269-3534
www.hilltopmanor.ca
Number of Beds: 89 beds

***Metcalfe:* Township of Osgoode Care Centre**
7650 Snake Island Rd., Metcalfe, ON K0A 2P0
Tel: 613-821-1034; *Fax:* 613-821-0070
www.osgoodecare.ca
Number of Beds: 100 beds
Note: Specialties: Long-term nursing care; Organized leisure activities

***Milverton:* Knollcrest Lodge**
50 William St., Milverton, ON N0K 1M0
Tel: 519-595-8121; *Fax:* 519-595-8199
www.knollcrestlodge.com
Social Media: www.facebook.com/knollcrest.lodge
Number of Beds: 77 beds
Susan Rae, CEO
srae@knollcrestlodge.com

***Minden:* Hyland Crest Senior Citizens' Home**
PO Box 30, 6 McPherson St., Minden, ON K0M 2K0
Tel: 705-286-2140; *Fax:* 705-286-6123
hhhs@halhinet.on.ca
www.hhhs.on.ca
Year Founded: 2000
Number of Beds: 62 beds

***Mississauga:* Carmel Heights Seniors' Residence**
Former Name: Carmel Heights Home for the Aged
1720 Sherwood Forest Circle, Mississauga, ON L5K 1R1
Tel: 905-822-5298
carmelheights@rogers.com
www.carmelheights.ca
Note: Home for the aged residential care
Sr. M. Veronica, Administrator

***Mississauga:* Cooksville Care Centre**
Former Name: Mississauga Lifecare Centre
55 Queensway West, Mississauga, ON L5B 1B5
Tel: 905-270-0170; *Fax:* 905-270-8465
www.cooksvillecarecentre.ca
Number of Beds: 26 respite; 166 long-term care
Nicole Fisher, Administrator
Jennifer Castaneda, Director, Nursing & Personal Care

***Mississauga:* Extendicare - Mississauga**
Extendicare Canada
855 John Watt Blvd., Mississauga, ON L5W 1G2
Tel: 905-696-0719; *Fax:* 905-696-8875
cnh_mississauga@extendicare.com
www.extendicarecanada.com/mississauga
Number of Beds: 140 beds

***Mississauga:* Leisureworld Caregiving Centre Mississauga**
Affiliated with: Leisureworld Senior Care Corporation
2250 Hurontario St., Mississauga, ON L5B 1M8
Tel: 905-270-0411; *Fax:* 905-270-1749
www.leisureworld.ca
Number of Beds: 237 beds
Lois Cormack, CEO, Leisureworld Senior Care Corporation

***Mississauga:* Leisureworld Caregiving Centre Streetsville**
Affiliated with: Leisureworld Senior Care Corporation
1742 Bristol Rd. West, Mississauga, ON L5M 1X9
Tel: 905-826-3045; *Fax:* 905-826-9978
www.leisureworld.ca
Number of Beds: 118 beds
Lois Cormack, CEO, Leisureworld Senior Care Corporation

***Mississauga:* Mississauga Long Term Care Facility**
Former Name: Mississauga Nursing Home Inc.
26 Peter St. North, Mississauga, ON L5H 2G7
Tel: 905-278-2213
www.mltcfacility.com
Number of Beds: 55 beds
Novak Bajin, Administrator
novak@mltcfacility.com

***Mississauga:* Pine Grove Lodge**
#700, 100 Milverton Dr., Mississauga, ON L5R 4H1
Tel: 905-501-9219; *Fax:* 905-501-0813
Toll-Free: 888-584-2386
info@chartwellreit.ca
www.chartwellreit.ca
Year Founded: 1959
Number of Beds: 40 suites
Note: Specialties; Long-term care; Medication administration; Wellness monitoring; Cultural & activity program, catering to Italian & Canadian cultures; Recreation therapy; Occupational therapy; Physiotherapy; Podiatry; Respite care

***Mississauga:* Sheridan Villa**
2460 Truscott Dr., Mississauga, ON L5J 3Z8
Tel: 905-791-7800; *Fax:* 905-823-7971
www.peelregion.ca/ltc/sheridan
Number of Beds: 142 beds
Inga Mazuryk, Administrator

***Mississauga:* Tyndall Nursing Home Ltd.**
1060 Eglinton Ave. East, Mississauga, ON L4W 1K3
Tel: 905-624-1511; *Fax:* 905-629-9346
info@tyndallnursinghome.com
tyndallnursinghome.com
Number of Beds: 151 residents
Note: Specialties: Long-term care; Restorative feeding program
Patricia Bedford, Director, Care
905-624-1511, pbedford@tyndallnursinghome.com

***Mitchell:* Mitchell Nursing Home Ltd.**
Affiliated with: Ritz Lutheran Villa
184 Napier St., Mitchell, ON N0K 1N0
Tel: 519-348-8861; *Fax:* 519-348-8300
www.ritzlutheranvilla.com
Year Founded: 1969
Number of Beds: 48 beds
Ruthanne Lobb, Administrator
rlobb@ritzlutheranvilla.com

***Mount Forest:* Saugeen Valley Nursing Centre Ltd.**
465 Dublin St., Mount Forest, ON N0G 2L3
Tel: 519-323-2140; *Fax:* 519-323-3540
www.svnc.ca
Number of Beds: 87 beds
Note: Nursing & respite care
Cate MacLean, Administrator
519-323-2140, administrator@svnc.ca

New Hamburg: Nithview Community
Affiliated with: Tri-County Mennonite Homes
200 Boullee St., New Hamburg, ON N0B 2G0
Tel: 519-662-2280; *Fax:* 519-662-1090
www.tcmhomes.com
Year Founded: 1972
Number of Beds: 96 beds
Note: Mennonite nursing home
Tracy Richardson, Executive Director
trichardson@nithview.com

Newcastle: Fosterbrooke Long Term Care Facility
Revera Living
330 King St. West, Newcastle, ON L1B 1G9
Tel: 905-987-4703; *Fax:* 905-987-3621
www.reveraliving.com/fosterbrooke
Social Media: www.facebook.com/400950748267; twitter.com/Revera_Inc; www.youtube.com/user/ReveraInc; www.linkedin.com/company/revera-inc
Number of Beds: 88 beds
Jeffrey C. Lozon, President & CEO, Revera Living

Newmarket: Central Care Corporation - Mackenzie Place
52 George St., Newmarket, ON L3Y 4V3
Tel: 905-853-3242
www.reveraliving.com/mackenzieplace
Number of Beds: 93 beds

Newmarket: Eagle Terrace
Revera Living
329 Eagle St., Newmarket, ON L3Y 1K3
Tel: 905-895-5187; *Fax:* 905-895-2645
EagleTerrace@reveraliving.com
www.reveraliving.com
Social Media: www.facebook.com/400950748267; twitter.com/Revera_Inc; www.youtube.com/user/ReveraInc; www.linkedin.com/company/revera-inc
Number of Beds: 70 beds
Jeffrey C. Lozon, President & CEO, Revera Living

Newmarket: Maple Health Centre - York Region Long-Term Care & Seniors Branch
194 Eagle St., Newmarket, ON L3Y 1J6
Tel: 905-895-3628; *Fax:* 905-895-5843
Toll-Free: 866-967-5582
www.york.ca
Number of Beds: 100 beds
Lynn Parsons, Assistant Administrator; Director, Care

Newmarket: Newmarket Health Centre-York Region Long-Term Care & Seniors Branch
194 Eagle St., Newmarket, ON L3Y 1J6
Toll-Free: 866-967-5582
www.york.ca
Marlene Parsons, Assistant Administrator; Director, Care

Niagara Falls: Oakwood Park Lodge
Affiliated with: Conmed Health Care Group
6747 Oakwood Dr., Niagara Falls, ON L2E 7E3
Tel: 905-356-8732; *Fax:* 905-356-2122
oakwoodparklodge@cogeco.net
www.conmedhealth.com
Year Founded: 1975
Number of Beds: 153 beds
Gail Knight, Director, Care

Niagara Falls: The Salvation Army Honorable Ray & Helen Lawson Eventide Home
5050 Jepson St., Niagara Falls, ON L2E 1K5
Tel: 905-356-1221; *Fax:* 905-356-9609
info@niagaraeventide.ca
www.niagaraeventide.ca
Note: Specialties: Long-term care for senior; Activity program

Niagara Falls: Valley Park Lodge
6400 Valley Way, Niagara Falls, ON L2E 7E3
Tel: 905-358-3277; *Fax:* 905-358-3012
info@conmedhealth.com
www.conmedhealth.com
Year Founded: 1985
Number of Beds: 65 beds
Jennifer Kennedy, Administrator

North Bay: Leisureworld Caregiving Centre - North Bay
401 William St., North Bay, ON P1A 1X5
Tel: 705-476-2602; *Fax:* 705-476-1624
www.leisureworld.ca
Number of Beds: 147 suites, 1 short stay bed; 6 convalescent care

North York: Thompson House
1 Overland Dr., North York, ON M3C 2C3
Tel: 416-447-7244; *Fax:* 416-447-6364
info@betterlivinghealth.org
www.betterlivinghealth.org
Number of Beds: 136 beds
Note: Specialties: Long-term care; Nursing care; Physiotherapy; Rehabilitative services; Recreation program; Restorative care; Social work; Palliative care
William Krever, President & CEO, Better Living Health and Community Services

Northbrook: Pine Meadow Nursing Home
PO Box 100, 124 Lloyd St., Northbrook, ON K0H 2G0
Tel: 613-336-9120; *Fax:* 613-336-9144
extendicarepinemeadow.ca
Year Founded: 1993
Number of Beds: 60 beds
Note: Specialties: Residential nursing care for seniors

Norwich: Norvilla Nursing Home
11 Elgin St. East, Norwich, ON N0J 1P0
Tel: 519-863-2717
Number of Beds: 40 beds

Norwood: Pleasant Meadow Manor
Affiliated with: OMNI Health Care
99 Alma St., Norwood, ON K0L 2V0
Tel: 705-639-5308; *Fax:* 705-639-5309
www.omniway.ca
Number of Beds: 61 beds
Note: Long term care
Sandra Tucker, Administrator
sbrow@omniway.ca
Sylvia Sanders, Officer Manager
705-639-5308, ssanders@omniway.ca

Ohsweken: Iroquois Lodge
PO Box 309, 1755 Chiefswood Rd, Ohsweken, ON N0A 1M0
Tel: 519-445-2224; *Fax:* 519-445-4180
Number of Beds: 50 beds
Susanne Mt. Pleasant, Manager
smtpleasant@sixnations.ca

Orangeville: Avalon Care Centre & Retirement Lodge
355 Broadway Ave., Orangeville, ON L9W 3Y3
Tel: 519-941-3351; *Fax:* 519-941-2445
www.jarlette.com
Number of Beds: 137 long term care beds, 77 retirement lodge beds
Note: Long term care centre & retirement residence
Jodi Napper-Campbell, General Manager
519-941-3351, jnapcamp@jarlette.com
Janine Mournahan, Wellness Manager
519-941-3351, jmournahan@jarlette.com

Orillia: Oak Terrace Long Term Care
Revera Living
291 Mississauga St. West, Orillia, ON L3V 3B9
Tel: 705-325-2289; *Fax:* 705-325-7178
oakterrace@reveraliving.com
www.reveraliving.com
Social Media: www.facebook.com/400950748267; twitter.com/Revera_Inc; www.youtube.com/user/ReveraInc; www.linkedin.com/company/revera-inc
Note: Specialties: Foot care; Physiotherapy programs; Restorative care programs; Dental services; Music therapy; Pet therapy
Jeffrey C. Lozon, President & CEO, Revera Living

Orillia: Trillium Manor Home for the Aged
12 Grace Ave., Orillia, ON L3V 2K2
Tel: 705-325-1504; *Fax:* 705-325-7661
www.simcoe.ca
Year Founded: 1969
Number of Beds: 122 beds

Oshawa: Extendicare - Oshawa
Extendicare Canada
82 Park Rd. North, Oshawa, ON L1J 4L1
Tel: 905-579-0011; *Fax:* 905-579-1733
cnh_oshawa@extendicare.com
www.extendicarecanada.com/oshawa/index.aspx
Number of Beds: 175 beds

Ottawa: Elisabeth Bruyère Residence
75 Bruyère St., Ottawa, ON K1N 5C8
Tel: 613-562-6262; *Fax:* 613-562-4223
elisabethbruyereresidence@bruyere.org
www.bruyere.org
Number of Beds: 71 beds
Note: Long-term care

Ottawa: Extendicare - Medex
Extendicare Canada
1865 Baseline Rd., Ottawa, ON K2C 3K6
Tel: 613-225-5650; *Fax:* 613-225-0960
cnh_medex@extendicare.com
www.extendicarecanada.com/ottawamedex
Number of Beds: 193 beds

Ottawa: Extendicare - New Orchard Lodge
Extendicare Canada
99 New Orchard Ave., Ottawa, ON K2B 5E6
Tel: 613-820-2110; *Fax:* 613-820-6380
cnh_neworchardlodge@extendicare.com
www.extendicarecanada.com/ottawaneworchard
Number of Beds: 111 beds

Ottawa: Extendicare - Starwood
Extendicare Canada
114 Starwood Rd., Ottawa, ON K2G 3N5
Tel: 613-224-3960; *Fax:* 613-224-9309
cnh_starwood@extendicare.com
www.extendicarecanada.com/nepean
Number of Beds: 192 beds

Ottawa: Extendicare - West End Villa
Extendicare Canada
2179 Elmira Dr., Ottawa, ON K2C 3S1
Tel: 613-829-3501; *Fax:* 613-829-3504
cnh_westendvilla@extendicare.com
www.extendicarecanada.com/ottawawestendvilla
Number of Beds: 240 beds
Note: nursing home

Ottawa: Garry J Armstrong House
200 Island Lodge Rd., Ottawa, ON K1N 5M2
Tel: 613-789-5100; *Fax:* 613-789-3704
Number of Beds: 180 beds

Ottawa: The Glebe Centre
77 Monk St., Ottawa, ON K1S 5A7
Tel: 613-238-2727; *Fax:* 613-238-4759
www.glebecentre.ca
Janice Bridgewater, Senior Centre Director
jbridgewater@glebecentre.ca

Ottawa: Perley & Rideau Veterans' Health Centre
1750 Russell Rd., Ottawa, ON K1G 5Z6
Tel: 613-526-7170; *Fax:* 613-526-7172
www.perleyrideau.ca
Social Media: www.facebook.com/419832558064505
Year Founded: 1995
Number of Beds: 450 residential capacity
Note: Specialties: Geriatric care; Recreation services; Dementia programming; Respite care for people in the mid-stages of dementia; Convalescent care
Greg Fougère, Executive Director
Bob Paré, Manager, Plant Services
Kerry Kelly, Manager, Housekeeping Linen Svs. & Materials Management

Ottawa: Villa Marconi
1026 Baseline Rd., Ottawa, ON K2C 0A6
Tel: 613-727-6201; *Fax:* 613-727-9352
administrator@villamarconi.com
www.villamarconi.com
Number of Beds: 125 beds
Walter Cibischino, President

Owen Sound: Lee Manor
875 - 6 St. East, Owen Sound, ON N4K 5W5
Tel: 519-376-4420; *Fax:* 519-371-5406
www.greycounty.on.ca
Number of Beds: 150 beds
Note: Municipal home for aged
Renate Cowan, Administrator
renate.cowan@grey.ca

Paris: Telfer Place Retirement Residence
Revera Living
245 Grand River St. North, Paris, ON N3L 3V8
Tel: 519-442-4411; *Fax:* 519-442-6724
telferplaceretirementresidence@reveraliving.com
www.reveraliving.com
Number of Beds: 45 beds
Note: Independent living program; retirement lodge, apartments; long-term care; convalescent & respite options
Jeffrey C. Lozon, President & CEO, Revera Living

Parkhill: Chateau Gardens Parkhill
Affiliated with: Chartwell Retirement Residences
250 Tain St., Parkhill, ON N0M 2K0
Tel: 519-294-6342; *Fax:* 519-294-0107
www.chartwell.com

Number of Beds: 59 beds
W. Brent Binions, President & CEO, Chartwell Retirement Residences

Parry Sound: Belvedere Heights
21 Belvedere Ave., Parry Sound, ON P2A 2A2
Tel: 705-746-5871; *Fax:* 705-774-7300
bh@zeuter.com
www.belvedereheights.com
Year Founded: 1965
Number of Beds: 101 beds

Pembroke: Miramichi Lodge
725 Pembrooke St. West, Pembroke, ON K8A 8S9
Tel: 613-735-0175; *Fax:* 613-735-8061
Year Founded: 1969
Number of Beds: 166 beds

Perth: Lanark Lodge
115 Christie Lake Rd., Perth, ON K7H 3C6
Tel: 613-267-4225; *Fax:* 613-264-2668
lanarklodge@lanarkcounty.ca
www.lanarkcounty.ca
Year Founded: 1967
Number of Beds: 163 beds

Perth: Perth Community Care Centre
101 Christie Lake Rd., RR#4, Perth, ON K7H 3C6
Tel: 613-267-2506; *Fax:* 613-267-7060
www.diversicare.ca
Number of Beds: 121 residential capacity
Note: Specialties: Long-term care; Activity program; Restorative care program; Physiotherapy

Peterborough: Extendicare - Peterborough
Extendicare Canada
860 Alexander Ave., Peterborough, ON K9J 6B4
Tel: 705-743-7552; *Fax:* 705-742-9664
cnh_peterborough@extendicare.com
extendicarepeterborough.com
Number of Beds: 172 beds

Peterborough: St. Joseph's at Fleming
Former Name: Marycrest Home of the Aged; Anson House
659 Brealey Dr., Peterborough, ON K9K 2R8
Tel: 705-743-4744; *Fax:* 705-743-7532
www.stjosephsatfleming.com
Year Founded: 2004
Paul O'Krafka, CEO

Petrolia: Fiddick's Nursing Home
PO Box 340, 437 First Ave., Petrolia, ON N0N 1R0
Tel: 519-882-0370; *Fax:* 519-882-0375
www.fiddicksnursinghome.com
Number of Beds: 128 beds
Michael Fiddick, Administrator

Picton: H.J. MacFarland Memorial Home
603 Hwy 49, RR#2, Picton, ON K0K 2T0
Tel: 613-476-2138; *Fax:* 613-476-6952
hjm.info@pecounty.on.ca
Number of Beds: 84 beds
Beth Piper, Administrator
bpiper@pecounty.on.ca

Picton: Hallowell House Long Term Care
Revera Living
PO Box 800, 13628 Loyalist Pkwy., Picton, ON K0K 2T0
Tel: 613-476-4444; *Fax:* 613-476-1566
www.reveraliving.com
Social Media: www.facebook.com/400950748267; twitter.com/Revera_Inc; www.youtube.com/user/ReveraInc; www.linkedin.com/company/revera-inc
Number of Beds: 97 beds
Area Served: Prince Edward County, South East
Jeffrey C. Lozon, President & CEO, Revera Living

Picton: Kentwood Park
PO Box 1298, 2 Ontario St., Picton, ON K0K 2T0
Tel: 613-476-5671; *Fax:* 613-476-3986
www.omniway.ca
Number of Beds: 48 beds
Tina Cole, Administrator
tcole@omniway.ca

Picton: Picton Manor Nursing Home
9 Hill St. West, Picton, ON K0K 2T0
Tel: 613-476-6140; *Fax:* 613-476-5240
www.pictonmanor.com
Number of Beds: 78 beds
Note: Specialties: Nursing care; Restorative care; Activity program; Life enrichment progran; Palliative care

Picton: West Lake Terrace
PO Box 2229, R.R. #1, 1673 County Rd. #12, Picton, ON K0K 2T0
Tel: 613-393-2055; *Fax:* 613-393-2592
www.omniway.ca
Number of Beds: 47 beds
Mary Lynn Lester, Administrator
mllester@omniway.ca

Plantagenet: Pinecrest Nursing Home Ltd.
PO Box 250, 101 Parent St., RR#1, Plantagenet, ON K0B 1L0
Tel: 613-673-4835; *Fax:* 613-673-2675
Note: Specialties: Long-term care; Activity program
Joanne Neveu, Administrator

Port Dover: Dover Cliffs Long Term Care
Revera Living
Former Name: Versa-Care Centre, Port Dover
PO Box 430, 501 St. George St., Port Dover, ON N0A 1N0
Tel: 519-583-1422; *Fax:* 519-583-3197
www.reveraliving.com
Social Media: www.facebook.com/400950748267; twitter.com/Revera_Inc; www.youtube.com/user/ReveraInc; www.linkedin.com/company/revera-inc
Number of Beds: 70 beds
Jeffrey C. Lozon, President & CEO, Revera Living

Port Hope: Community Nursing Home
20 Hope St. South, Port Hope, ON L1A 2M8
Tel: 905-885-6367; *Fax:* 905-885-6368
www.cnhporthope.ca
Number of Beds: 97 beds
Nancy Jordan, Administrator
njordan@clmi.ca

Port Hope: Extendicare - Port Hope
Extendicare Canada
360 Croft St., Port Hope, ON L1A 4K8
Tel: 905-885-1266; *Fax:* 905-885-5328
cnh_porthope@extendicare.com
www.extendicarecanada.com/porthope
Number of Beds: 128 beds

Port Hope: Regency Manor
Affiliated with: Provincial Long Term Care Inc.
66 Dorset St. East, Port Hope, ON L1A 1E3
Tel: 905-885-4558; *Fax:* 905-885-0238
regency.info@pltchomes.com
pltchomes.com
Social Media: www.facebook.com/158791967489513
Number of Beds: 101 beds

Port Perry: Community Nursing Home
PO Box 660, 15941 Simcoe St., Port Perry, ON L9L 1A6
Tel: 905-985-3205; *Fax:* 905-985-3721
www.cnhportperry.ca
Number of Beds: 107 beds
Carolyn Zacharuk, Administrator
czacharuk@clmi.ca

Powassan: Eastholme Home for the Aged
PO Box 400, 62 Big Bend Ave., Powassan, ON P0H 1Z0
Tel: 705-724-2005; *Fax:* 705-724-5429
easthome@onlink.net
www.eastholme.ca
Number of Beds: 104 beds

Prescott: Wellington House
PO Box 401, 990 Edward St. North, Prescott, ON K0E 1T0
Tel: 613-925-2834; *Fax:* 613-925-5425
www.prescott.ca
Number of Beds: 60 beds
Note: Long-term care facility

Puslinch: Morriston Park Nursing Home Inc.
7363 Calfass Rd., RR#2, Puslinch, ON N0B 2J0
Tel: 519-822-9179; *Fax:* 519-822-4459
www.morristonpark.com
Number of Beds: 28 beds

Red Lake: Northwood Lodge
Affiliated with: District of Kenora Home for the Aged
PO Box 1335, Hwy 105, Red Lake, ON P0V 2M0
Tel: 807-727-2323; *Fax:* 807-727-3546
northwood.lodge@kenoradistricthomes.ca
www.kenoradistricthomes.ca
Number of Beds: 32 beds
Note: home for the aged

Renfrew: Bonnechere Manor
470 Albert St., Renfrew, ON K7V 4L5
Tel: 613-432-4873; *Fax:* 613-432-7138
bonnecheremanor@countyofrenfrew.on.ca
www.countyofrenfrew.on.ca

Year Founded: 1958
Number of Beds: 177 beds

Renfrew: Groves Park Lodge Long Term Care Facility
Former Name: Groves Park Lodge Nursing Home
470 Raglan St. North, Renfrew, ON K7V 1P5
Tel: 613-432-5823; *Fax:* 613-432-5287
grovesparklodge@gemhealth.com
www.gemhealth.com
Number of Beds: 75 beds
Carrol Haywood, Administrator

Richmond Hill: Leisureworld Caregiving Centre - Richmond Hill
170 Red Maple Rd., Richmond Hill, ON L4B 4T8
Tel: 905-731-2273
www.leisureworld.ca
Number of Beds: 160 beds
Jodi MacIsaac, Administrator

Richmond Hill: Mariann Home
9915 Yonge St., Richmond Hill, ON L4C 1V1
Tel: 905-884-9276; *Fax:* 905-884-1800
www.mariannhome.com
Year Founded: 1979
Number of Beds: 64 beds
Note: Specialties: Peritoneal dialysis; Care for seniors with cognitive or psychiatric impairment; Palliative care. Number of employees: 80
Sr. Mary William Verhoeven, Administrator

Rockland: St. Joseph Nursing Home
1615 Laurier St., Rockland, ON K4K 1C8
Tel: 613-446-5126
Number of Beds: 64 beds

Sarnia: Trillium Villa
Affiliated with: S & R Nursing Homes Ltd.
1221 Michigan Ave., Sarnia, ON N7S 3Y3
Tel: 519-542-5529; *Fax:* 519-542-5953
trilliumvilla@srgroup.ca
ltc.srgroup.ca
Year Founded: 1970
Number of Beds: 152 beds
Jennifer Allison, Administrator
jennifer_allison@srgroup.ca

Sarnia: Vision Nursing Home
229 Wellington St., Sarnia, ON N7T 1G9
Tel: 519-336-6551; *Fax:* 519-336-5878
vision74.webs.com
Number of Beds: 108 permanent beds, 2 respite
Note: Christian-based nursing home

Sault Ste Marie: Extendicare - Tendercare
Extendicare Canada
770 Great Northern Rd., Sault Ste Marie, ON P6A 5K7
Tel: 705-949-3611; *Fax:* 705-945-6303
cnh_tendercare@extendicare.com
www.extendicarecanada.com
Number of Beds: 120 beds
Note: Services include denturist; pharmacy; foot care service; respiratory care; education centres; rehabilitation and restorative care

Sault Ste Marie: F.J. Davey Home
733 Third Line East, Sault Ste Marie, ON P6A 5K7
Tel: 705-942-2204; *Fax:* 705-942-2234
www.fjdaveyhome.org
Number of Beds: 184 beds
Specialties: Provides services for people with dementia
Peter J. MacLean, Administrator
705-945-2204 ext 217, pmaclean@fjdaveyhome.org

Sault Ste Marie: Great Northern Retirement Home
760 Great Northern Rd., Sault Ste Marie, ON P6A 5K7
Tel: 705-945-9405; *Fax:* 705-942-2063
greatnorthernn.longo@shaw.ca
www.greatnorthernretirement.com
Number of Beds: 120 retirement, 34 interim nursing home beds
Nadia Longo, Administrator

Sault Ste Marie: Mauno Kaihla Koti
Affiliated with: Ontario Finnish Rest Home Association
723 North St., Sault Ste Marie, ON P6B 6G8
Tel: 705-945-5262; *Fax:* 705-945-1217
info@ontariofinnishresthome.ca
www.ontariofinnishresthome.ca
Number of Beds: 63 beds

***Sault Ste Marie:* Van Daele Manor**
Affiliated with: Extendicare Canada
39 Van Daele St., Sault Ste Marie, ON P6B 4V3
Tel: 705-949-7934; *Fax:* 705-945-0968
cnh_vandaele@extendicare.com
www.extendicarecanada.com/saultsaintmarievandaele
Number of Beds: 150 beds

***Scarborough:* Kennedy Lodge Long Term Care**
Revera Living
1400 Kennedy Rd., Scarborough, ON M1P 4V6
Tel: 416-752-8282; *Fax:* 416-752-0645
kennedylodge@reveraliving.com
www.reveraliving.com
Social Media: www.facebook.com/400950748267;
twitter.com/Revera_Inc; www.youtube.com/user/ReveraInc;
www.linkedin.com/company/revera-inc
Number of Beds: 289 beds
Note: long term care facility
Jeffrey C. Lozon, President & CEO

***Scarborough:* Leisureworld Caregiving Centre - Rockcliffe**
Former Name: Rockcliffe Long Term Care Facility
3015 Lawrence Ave. East, Scarborough, ON M1P 2V7
Tel: 416-264-3201; *Fax:* 416-264-2914
www.leisureworld.ca
Year Founded: 1972
Number of Beds: 204 beds
Lois Cormack, CEO

***Scarborough:* Leisureworld Caregiving Centre - Scarborough**
130 Midland Ave., Scarborough, ON M1N 4B2
Tel: 416-264-2301; *Fax:* 416-264-3704
www.leisureworld.ca
Number of Beds: 299 long-term care, 53 retirement beds
Note: Retirement beds in adjoining Midland Gardens
Lois Cormack, CEO, Leisureworld Senior Care Corporation

***Scarborough:* Seven Oaks**
9 Neilson Rd., Scarborough, ON M1E 5E1
Tel: 416-392-3500; *Fax:* 416-392-3579
www.toronto.ca/ltc/sevenoaks.htm/
Year Founded: 1989
Number of Beds: 249 beds
Note: Services for long term care, including adult day programs, services to the Armenian & Tamil communities, & an on-site child care centre

***Scarborough:* Tendercare Living Centre**
1020 McNicoll Ave., Scarborough, ON M1W 2J6
Tel: 416-499-2020; *Fax:* 416-499-3379
www.tendercare.ca
Number of Beds: 254 beds
Note: Nursing home & retirement community

***Scarborough:* The Wexford Residence Inc.**
1860 Lawrence Ave. East, Scarborough, ON M1R 5B1
Tel: 416-752-8877; *Fax:* 416-752-8414
Toll-Free: 877-807-0810
information@thewexford.org
www.thewexford.org
Year Founded: 1978
Number of Beds: 166 long-term care residents
Note: Specialties: Long-term care & apartment accommodation for seniors; Secure units for persons with cognitive impairments; Physiotherapy; Podiatry; Life enrichment therapy
Sandy Bassett, Executive Director
416-752-8879
Esther Spencer, Director, Care
416-752-4477

***Scarborough:* Yee Hong Centre for Geriatric Care**
2311 McNicoll Ave., Scarborough, ON M1V 5L3
Tel: 416-321-6333; *Fax:* 416-321-6313
centre@yeehong.com
www.yeehong.com
Number of Beds: 250 beds
Kaiyan Fu, CEO

***Schumacher:* Extendicare - Timmins**
Extendicare Canada
PO Box 817, 15 Hollinger Lane, Schumacher, ON P0N 1G0
Tel: 705-360-1913; *Fax:* 705-268-3975
cnh_timmins@extendicare.com
www.extendicarecanada.com/schumacher
Number of Beds: 119 beds
Kelly Roy, Administrator

***Seaforth:* Seaforth Manor Nursing Home**
Affiliated with: Provincial Long Term Care Inc.
100 James St., Seaforth, ON N0K 1W0
Tel: 519-527-0030; *Fax:* 1-855-226-9214
seaforth.info@pltchomes.com
www.pltchomes.com
Social Media: www.facebook.com/184905644858215;
twitter.com/PLTC_Homes
Number of Beds: 118 beds
Note: Nursing & retirement home
Erika King, General Manager
519-527-0030, erika.king@pltchomes.com

***Selby:* Village Green Long Term Care Facility**
Affiliated with: Omni Health Care
160 Pleasant Dr., Selby, ON K0K 2Z0
Tel: 613-388-2693; *Fax:* 613-388-2694
www.omniway.ca
Number of Beds: 66 beds
Linda Pierce, Administrator
lpierce@omniway.ca

***Shelburne:* Shelburne Residence**
200 Robert St., Shelburne, ON L0N 1S1
Tel: 519-925-3746; *Fax:* 519-925-1476
shelburne,info@pltchomes.com
pltchomes.com
Number of Beds: 60 nursing beds, 28 retirement rooms
Note: Combined nursing home & retirement facility
Heidi Vanderhost, General Manager
heidi.vanderhorst@pltchomes.com

***Simcoe:* Cedarwood Village Retirement Apartments**
500 Queensway West, Simcoe, ON N3Y 4R4
Tel: 519-426-8305; *Fax:* 519-426-2511
Number of Beds: 91 beds

***Simcoe:* Norfolk Hospital Nursing Home (NHNH)**
365 West St., Simcoe, ON N3Y 1T7
Tel: 519-426-0130; *Fax:* 519-429-6988
residents@ngh.on.ca (Residents' e-mail)
www.ngh.on.ca
Year Founded: 1975
Number of Beds: 80 beds
Note: Specialties: Long-term nursing care; Activation program; Wound care; Physiotherapy; Occupational therapy; Speech Therapy; Restorative care; Pet therapy; Social work; Psychogeriatics; Palliative care
Vicky Florio, Director, Care
519-429-6973

***Sioux Lookout:* William A. (Bill) George Extended Care Facility**
75 - 5 Ave., Sioux Lookout, ON P8T 1K9
Tel: 807-737-1364; *Fax:* 807-737-2449
www.slmhc.on.ca
Number of Beds: 20 beds

***Smiths Falls:* Broadview Nursing Centre**
210 Brockville St., Smiths Falls, ON K7A 3Z4
Tel: 613-283-1845; *Fax:* 613-283-7073
bnc@on.aibn.com
www.broadviewnc.ca
Number of Beds: 75 beds
Jim Parsons, Administrator
jparsons@on.aibn.com

***St Catharines:* Tufford Manor Retirement Home**
Affiliated with: Hampton Trufford
312 Queenston St., St Catharines, ON L2P 2X4
Tel: 905-682-0503; *Fax:* 905-682-2770
www.hamptontufford.com
Info Line: 905-682-0411
Year Founded: 1960
Number of Beds: 64 residential capacity
Note: Specialties: Long-term nursing care; Social work; Physiotherapy; Podiatry; Activation program; Palliative care

***St Catharines:* West Park Health Centre**
103 Pelham Rd., St Catharines, ON L2S 1S9
Tel: 905-688-1031; *Fax:* 905-688-4495
westparkhealthcentre.ca
Number of Beds: 93 beds
Marjorie Mossman, Administrator
mmossman@extendicare.com

***St Jacobs:* Derbecker's Heritage House Ltd.**
54 Eby St., St Jacobs, ON N0B 2N0
Tel: 519-664-2921; *Fax:* 519-664-2380
Year Founded: 1964
Number of Beds: 72 beds

***St Marys:* Kingsway Lodge**
310 Queen St. East, St Marys, ON N4X 1C8
Tel: 519-284-2921; *Fax:* 519-284-4468
info@kingswaylodge.com
www.kingswaylodge.com
Social Media: twitter.com/Kingsway_Lodge
Number of Beds: 89 beds, 52 units

***St Thomas:* Caressant Care Nursing and Retirement Homes Limited**
Caressant Care St. Thomas - Mary Bucke St. Facility
4 Mary Bucke St., St Thomas, ON N5R 5J6
Tel: 519-633-3164
www.caressantcare.com
Number of Beds: 60 beds
Ann Starswell, Administrator

***St. Catharines:* Extendicare - St. Catharines**
Extendicare Canada
283 Pelham Rd., St. Catharines, ON L2S 1X7
Tel: 905-688-3311; *Fax:* 905-688-5774
cnh_stcatharines@extendicare.com
www.extendicarecanada.com/saintcatherines
Number of Beds: 152 beds

***St. Catharines:* Garden City Manor Long Term Care**
Revera Living
168 Scott St., St. Catharines, ON L2N 1H2
Tel: 905-934-3321; *Fax:* 905-934-9011
www.reveraliving.com
Social Media: www.facebook.com/400950748267;
twitter.com/Revera_Inc; www.youtube.com/user/ReveraInc;
www.linkedin.com/company/revera-inc
Number of Beds: 200 beds
Jeffrey C. Lozon, President & CEO

***St. Catharines:* Heidehof Home for the Aged**
600 Lake St., St. Catharines, ON L2N 4J4
Tel: 905-935-3344; *Fax:* 905-935-0081
www.heidehof.com
Number of Beds: 106 beds
Elena Caddis, Administrator
ecaddis@heidehof.com
Erika Ledwez, Manager, Resident & Community Relations
eledwez@heidehof.com

***St. Catharines:* Tabor Manor**
1 Tabor Dr., St. Catharines, ON L2N 1V9
Tel: 905-934-2548
office@tabormanor.net
www.tabormanor.net/site
Number of Beds: 82 residential capacity
Note: Specialties: Accommodation & nursing care to senior citizens, especially those of the Mennonite constituency in Niagara; Activity program; Foot care
Tim Siemens, Executive Director
905-934-2548, tims@tabormanor.net

***St. Marys:* Wildwood Care Centre Inc.**
PO Box 2200, 100 Ann St., St. Marys, ON N4X 1A1
Tel: 519-284-3628; *Fax:* 519-284-0575
information@wildwoodcarecentre.com
www.wildwoodcarecentre.com
Social Media: www.facebook.com/261059940770;
twitter.com/WildwoodCC
Number of Beds: 82 beds

***St. Thomas:* Caressant Care on Bonnie Place**
Affiliated with: Caressant Care Nursing and Retirement Homes Ltd
15 Bonnie Pl., St. Thomas, ON N5R 5T8
Tel: 519-633-6493; *Fax:* 519-633-9329
www.caressantcare.com
Number of Beds: 182 beds
Note: Long term care facility, with secure unit for residents with dementia.
James Lavelle, President, Caressant Care Nursing and Retirement Homes Ltd.

***Stayner:* Stayner Nursing Home**
PO Box 350, 244 Main St. East, Stayner, ON L0M 1S0
Tel: 705-428-3614; *Fax:* 705-428-0537
Toll-Free: 888-803-8208
staynernursinghome@rogers.com
Year Founded: 1984
Number of Beds: 49 beds
Lorraine Baker, Administrator

***Stirling:* Stirling Manor Nursing Home**
PO Box 220, 218 Edward St., Stirling, ON K0K 3E0
Tel: 613-395-2596; *Fax:* 613-395-0930
www.stirlingmanor.com
Number of Beds: 75 beds

***Stoney Creek:* Pine Villa Nursing Home**
490 Hwy. #8, Stoney Creek, ON L8G 1G6
Tel: 905-573-4900; *Fax:* 905-662-0833
info.pinevilla@thomashealthcare.com
www.thomashealthcare.com
Year Founded: 1967
Number of Beds: 38 beds
Note: Specialties: Nursing care; Enhanced restorative care program; Physiotherapy; Foot care; Massage therapy; Activity program

***Stouffville:* Parkview Home for the Aged**
123 Weldon Rd., Stouffville, ON L4A 0G8
Tel: 905-640-1911; *Fax:* 905-640-4051
admin@parkviewhome.ca
www.parkviewhome.ca
Number of Beds: 109 beds
Note: Long-term care facility
Solange Taylor, Executive Director
905-640-1911, staylor@parkviewhome.ca

***Stratford:* Hillside Manor**
5066 Perth East Line 34, RR#5, Stratford, ON N5A 6S6
Tel: 519-393-5132
www.reveraliving.com/hillside
Number of Beds: 90 beds
Sylvie Ledermueller, Administrator
Mary Anne Weller, Director of Care

***Stratford:* PeopleCare Stratford**
198 Mornington St., Stratford, ON N5A 5G3
Tel: 519-271-4440; *Fax:* 519-271-4446
www.peoplecare.ca
Year Founded: 1980
Number of Beds: 60 residents
Note: Specialties: Long-term care; Activity program; Restorative care
Patricia Kelly, Administrator

***Stratford:* Spruce Lodge Senior Citizens Residence**
643 West Gore St., Stratford, ON N5A 1L4
Tel: 519-271-4090; *Fax:* 519-271-5862
www.sprucelodge.on.ca
Number of Beds: 128 beds
Peter Bolland, Administrator
peterb@sprucelodge.on.ca

***Strathroy:* Sprucedale Care Centre Inc.**
96 Kittridge Ave. East, Strathroy, ON N7G 2A8
Tel: 519-245-2808; *Fax:* 519-245-1767
info@sprucedale.ca
www.sprucedale.ca
Number of Beds: 62 beds
Darren Micallef, Director, Operations
darren@sprucedale.ca

***Strathroy:* Strathmere Lodge**
PO Box 5000, 599 Albert St., Strathroy, ON N7G 3J3
Tel: 519-245-2520; *Fax:* 519-245-5711
www.middlesex.ca
Year Founded: 1880
Note: Specialties: Special care area for Alzheimer residents; Respite care & short stays
Tony Orvidas, Administrator
519-245-2520

***Sturgeon Falls:* Au Château Home for the Aged**
100 Michaud St., Sturgeon Falls, ON P2B 2Z4
Tel: 705-753-1550; *Fax:* 705-753-3135
Number of Beds: 325 beds
Wayne M. Foisey, Administrator
Simone Brazeau, Coordinator, Environmental Services

***Sudbury:* Extendicare - Falconbridge**
Extendicare Canada
281 Falconbridge Rd., Sudbury, ON P3A 5K4
Tel: 705-566-7980; *Fax:* 705-566-2997
cnh_falconbridge@extendicare.com
www.extendicarecanada.com/sudburyfalconbridge/
Number of Beds: 234 beds

***Sudbury:* Extendicare - York**
Extendicare Canada
333 York St., Sudbury, ON P3E 5J3
Tel: 705-674-4221; *Fax:* 705-674-4281
cnh_york@extendicare.com
www.extendicarecanada.com/sudburyyork
Number of Beds: 288 beds

***Sudbury:* St. Joseph's Continuing Care Centre of Sudbury**
Affiliated with: North East Local Health Integration Network
1140 South Bay Rd., Sudbury, ON P3E 0B6
Tel: 705-674-2846; *Fax:* 705-673-1009
info@sjsudbury.com
www.stjosephccc.ca
Note: A long term care facility whose staff works to care for people with disabilities or long term illnesses
Jo-Anne Palkovits, President & CEO
Jacqueline Squarzolo, Director of Care

***Sutton:* River Glen Haven Nursing Home**
Affiliated with: ATK Care Inc.
160 High St., Sutton, ON L0E 1R0
Tel: 905-722-3631; *Fax:* 905-722-8638
rghadmin@bellnet.ca
www.atkcareinc.ca/suttonservices.htm
Number of Beds: 109 beds
Note: Long term & secured care
Karen Ryan, Administrator

***Tavistock:* Bonnie Brae Health Care Centre**
PO Box 489, 55 Woodstock St. North, Tavistock, ON N0B 2R0
Tel: 519-655-2420; *Fax:* 519-655-3432
Number of Beds: 80 beds
Paula Thomson, Administrator
paula.thomson@bonniebrae.ca

***Tavistock:* The Maples Home for Seniors**
Affiliated with: Caressant Care Nursing and Retirement Homes Ltd
94 William St., Tavistock, ON N0B 2R0
Tel: 519-655-2344; *Fax:* 519-655-2162
www.caressantcare.com
Number of Beds: 43 beds
James Lavelle, President, Caressant Care Nursing and Retirement Homes Ltd.

***Tecumseh:* Brouillette Manor**
11900 Brouillette Ct., Tecumseh, ON N8N 4X8
Tel: 519-735-9810; *Fax:* 519-735-8569
Number of Beds: 60 beds
Nancy Comiskey, Administrator

***Tecumseh:* Extendicare - Tecumseh**
Extendicare Canada
2475 St. Alphonse St., Tecumseh, ON N8N 2X2
Tel: 519-739-2998; *Fax:* 519-739-2815
cnh_tecumseh@extendicare.com
www.extendicarecanada.com/tecumseh
Number of Beds: 128 beds

***Thessalon:* Algoma Manor Nursing Home**
135 Dawson St., Thessalon, ON P0R 1L0
Tel: 705-842-6886
algomamanornursinghome.com
Number of Beds: 106 beds
Barbara Harten, Administrator
705-842-2840, barbara.harten@specialty-care.com

***Thornbury:* Errinrung Residence**
Affiliated with: Provincial Long Term Care Inc.
Former Name: Errinrung Nursing & Retirement Home
PO Box 69, 67 Bruce St. South, Thornbury, ON N0H 2P0
Tel: 519-599-2737; *Fax:* 1-855-226-9213
errinrung.info@pltchomes.com
www.pltchomes.com
Social Media: www.facebook.com/128706680509942; twitter.com/PLTC_Homes
Number of Beds: 74 beds
Note: Total Employees: 38 f-t; 30 p-t
Yvonne Taylor, Director of Retirement Home
Deb Hughson, Director of Care

***Thunder Bay:* Bethammi Nursing Home**
Affiliated with: St. Joseph's Care Group
63 Carrie St., Thunder Bay, ON P7A 4J2
Tel: 807-768-4430; *Fax:* 807-768-7793
www.sjcg.net
Number of Beds: 110 beds
Tracy Buckler, President & CEO, St. Joseph's Care Gropu

***Thunder Bay:* Dawson Court Home for the Aged**
523 North Algoma St., Thunder Bay, ON P7A 5C2
Tel: 807-684-2926; *Fax:* 807-345-8854
www.thunderbay.ca
Year Founded: 1957
Number of Beds: 150 beds
Tom Gash, Administrator
807-684-2849, Fax: 807-345-8854, tgash@thunderbay.ca

***Thunder Bay:* Grandview Lodge**
200 North Lillie St., Thunder Bay, ON P7C 5Y2
Tel: 807-625-2923; *Fax:* 807-623-4075
www.thunderbay.ca
Year Founded: 1959
Number of Beds: 150 beds
Wendy Kirkpatrick, Administrator
807-625-2923, Fax: 807-623-4075, wkirkpatrick@thunderbay.ca

***Thunder Bay:* Lakehead Manor Long Term Care**
Revera Living
135 South Vickers St., Thunder Bay, ON P7E 1J2
Tel: 807-623-9511; *Fax:* 807-623-6992
www.reveraliving.com
Social Media: www.facebook.com/400950748267; twitter.com/Revera_Inc; www.youtube.com/user/ReveraInc; www.linkedin.com/company/revera-inc
Number of Beds: 161 beds
Jeffrey C. Lozon, President & CEO, Revera Living

***Thunder Bay:* Pinewood Court Long Term Care**
Revera Living
2625 East Walsh St., Thunder Bay, ON P7E 2E5
Tel: 807-577-1127
pinewoodcourt@reveraliving.com
www.reveraliving.com
Social Media: www.facebook.com/400950748267; twitter.com/Revera_Inc; www.youtube.com/user/ReveraInc; www.linkedin.com/company/revera-inc
Number of Beds: 75 beds
Note: Long term care
Jeffrey C. Lozon, President & CEO, Revera Living

***Thunder Bay:* Pioneer Ridge**
750 Tungsten St., Thunder Bay, ON P7B 6R1
Tel: 807-684-3910; *Fax:* 807-684-3916
www.thunderbay.ca
Number of Beds: 150 beds
Note: Specialties: Long-term nursing care for older persons; Restorative care; Rehabilitation; Units for persons with cognitive challenges, Alzheimer's disease, & other dementias; Secure therapeutic parks; Life enrichment program
Lee Mesic, Administrator
807-684-3917, lmesic@thunderbay.ca

***Tillsonburg:* Maple Manor Nursing Home**
73 Bidwell St., Tillsonburg, ON N4G 3T8
Tel: 519-842-3563; *Fax:* 519-842-3038
Number of Beds: 102 beds
George Kaniuk, Administrator

***Timmins:* Golden Manor Home for the Aged**
481 Melrose Blvd., Timmins, ON P4N 5H3
Tel: 705-360-2664; *Fax:* 705-360-2683
golden_manor@timmins.ca
www.timmins.ca
Number of Beds: 174 beds
Heather Bozzer, Administrator
heather.bozzer@timmins.ca

***Toronto:* Apotex Centre, Jewish Home for the Aged & The Louis & Leah Posluns Centre for Stroke & Cognition**
3560 Bathurst St., Toronto, ON M6A 2E1
Tel: 416-785-2500
www.baycrest.org
Number of Beds: 472 beds
Note: Care is offered to adults 65 years of age & older within the context of orthodox Jewish traditions.

***Toronto:* Bendale Acres**
2920 Lawrence Ave. East, Toronto, ON M1P 2T8
Tel: 416-397-7000; *Fax:* 416-397-7067
Number of Beds: 302 beds
Nicole McGouran
416-397-7000, nmcgour@toronto.ca

***Toronto:* Casa Verde Health Centre**
3595 Keele St., Toronto, ON M3J 1M7
Tel: 416-633-3431; *Fax:* 416-633-6736
recpt.cv@diversacare.ca
www.diversicare.ca
Number of Beds: 252 beds

***Toronto:* Castleview Wychwood Towers**
351 Christie St., Toronto, ON M6G 3C3
Tel: 416-392-5700; *Fax:* 416-392-4157
Number of Beds: 490 beds

***Toronto:* Cedarvale Terrace Long Term Care Home**
429 Walmer Rd., Toronto, ON M5P 2X9
Tel: 416-967-6949; *Fax:* 416-928-1965
www.cedarvaleterrace.ca
Number of Beds: 248 beds
Adele Lopes, Administrator

***Toronto:* Cheltenham Nursing Home**
Affiliated with: Leisureworld Senior Care Corporation
5935 Bathurst St., Toronto, ON M2R 1Y8
Tel: 416-223-4050; *Fax:* 416-223-4159
admin.cheltenham@leisureworld.ca
www.leisureworld.ca/cheltenham.html
Number of Beds: 170 beds
Lois Cormack, CEO, Leisureworld Senior Care Corporation

***Toronto:* Christie Gardens**
600 Melita Cres., Toronto, ON M6G 3Z4
Tel: 416-530-1330; *Fax:* 416-530-1686
www.christiegardens.org
Social Media: www.facebook.com/ChristieGardens; twitter.com/christiegardens
Number of Beds: 88 beds
Grace Sweatman, CEO

***Toronto:* Craiglee Nursing Home**
102 Craiglee Dr., Toronto, ON M1N 2M7
Tel: 416-264-2000; *Fax:* 416-267-8176
craigleenursinghome.ca
Number of Beds: 94 beds
Patrick Brown, Administrator
pjbrown@extendicare.com

***Toronto:* Cummer Lodge Home for the Aged**
205 Cummer Ave., Toronto, ON M2M 2E8
Tel: 416-392-9500; *Fax:* 416-392-9499
Number of Beds: 391 beds
Joanne Meade
416-392-9486, jmeade@toronto.ca

***Toronto:* Ehatare Nursing Home**
40 Old Kingston Rd., Toronto, ON M1E 3J5
Tel: 416-284-0828; *Fax:* 416-284-5595
ehatare@on.aibn.com
www.ehatare.ca
Number of Beds: 32 beds
Ruth McFarlane, Executive Director

***Toronto:* Extendicare - Bayview**
Extendicare Canada
550 Cummer Ave., Toronto, ON M2K 2M2
Tel: 416-226-1331; *Fax:* 416-226-2745
cnh_bayview@extendicare.com
www.extendicarecanada.com/willowdale/
Number of Beds: 203 beds
Niklas Chandrabalan, Administrator
nchandrabalan@extendicare.com

***Toronto:* Extendicare - Guildwood**
Extendicare Canada
60 Guildwood Pkwy., Toronto, ON M1E 1N9
Tel: 416-266-7711; *Fax:* 416-269-5123
cnh_guildwood@extendicare.com
www.extendicarecanada.com/westhill/
Number of Beds: 169 beds

***Toronto:* Extendicare - Rouge Valley**
Extendicare Canada
551 Conlins Rd., Toronto, ON M1B 5S1
Tel: 416-282-6768; *Fax:* 416-282-6766
cnh_rougevalley@extendicare.com
www.extendicarecanada.com/torontorougevalley
Number of Beds: 192 beds

***Toronto:* Extendicare - Scarborough**
Extendicare Canada
3830 Lawrence Ave. East, Toronto, ON M1G 1R6
Tel: 416-439-1243; *Fax:* 416-439-4818
cnh_scarborough@extendicare.com
www.extendicarecanada.com/scarborough/index.aspx
Specialties: Nursing care for seniors; Care for persons with Alzheimer's or other dementias; Physiotherapy; Optometry services; Social & therapeutic programs

***Toronto:* Fairview Nursing Home**
14 Cross St., Toronto, ON M6J 1S8
Tel: 416-534-8829; *Fax:* 416-538-1658
info@fairviewnursinghome.com
ww.fairviewnursinghome.com
Number of Beds: 108 beds

***Toronto:* Fudger House**
439 Sherbourne St., Toronto, ON M4X 1K6
Tel: 416-392-5252; *Fax:* 416-392-4174
Number of Beds: 249 beds

***Toronto:* Garden Court Nursing Home**
1 Sand Beach Rd., Toronto, ON M8V 2W2
Tel: 416-259-6172; *Fax:* 416-259-7925
Number of Beds: 45 beds
Deana Bennett, Administrator
deanab@sympatico.ca

***Toronto:* Hawthorne Place Care Centre**
2045 Finch Ave. West, Toronto, ON M3N 1M9
Tel: 416-745-0811; *Fax:* 416-745-0568
www.hawthorneplacecarecentre.ca
Year Founded: 1973
Number of Beds: 225 beds
Christine Murad, Administrator

***Toronto:* Hellenic Care for Seniors**
33 Winona Dr., Toronto, ON M6G 3Z7
Tel: 416-654-7700; *Fax:* 416-654-1080
hcare@hellenichome.org
www.hellenichome.org
Number of Beds: 81 beds

***Toronto:* Heritage Nursing Home**
1195 Queen St. East, Toronto, ON M4M 1L6
Tel: 416-461-8185; *Fax:* 416-461-5472
administrator@heritagenursinghome.com
www.heritagenursinghome.com
Number of Beds: 201 beds
Note: Specialties: Long-term nursing care; Supervision & security for residents with Alzheimer's Disease or dementia; Restorative care, including physiotherapy; Activation & recreation program; Chinese programs
J. Glick, Administrator
jglick@heritagenursinghome.com

***Toronto:* Humber Valley Terrace Long Term Care Revera Living**
95 Humber College Blvd., Toronto, ON M9V 5B5
Tel: 416-746-7466; *Fax:* 416-740-5812
www.reveraliving.com
Social Media: www.facebook.com/400950748267; twitter.com/Revera_Inc; www.youtube.com/user/ReveraInc; www.linkedin.com/company/revera-inc
Number of Beds: 158 beds
Jeffrey C. Lozon, President & CEO, Revera Living
Glen Elliott, Director, Physical Plant

***Toronto:* Ivan Franko Ukrainian Home (Etobicoke)**
767 Royal York Rd., Toronto, ON M8Y 2T3
Tel: 416-239-7364; *Fax:* 416-239-5102
Number of Beds: 85 beds

***Toronto:* Kipling Acres**
2233 Kipling Ave., Toronto, ON M9W 4L3
Tel: 416-392-2300
Year Founded: 1959
Number of Beds: 337 beds
Gina Filice, Administrator
gfilice@toronto.ca

***Toronto:* Lakeshore Lodge**
3197 Lakeshore Blvd. West, Toronto, ON M8V 3X5
Tel: 416-392-9400; *Fax:* 416-392-9401
www.toronto.ca/ltc/lakeshore.htm
Number of Beds: 150 beds

***Toronto:* Leisureworld Caregiving Centre - Ellesmere**
1000 Ellesmere Rd., Toronto, ON M1P 5G2
Tel: 416-291-0222
www.leisureworld.ca
Number of Beds: 224 beds
Michael Aikins, Administrator

***Toronto:* Leisureworld Caregiving Centre - Etobicoke**
70 Humberline Dr., Toronto, ON M9W 7H3
Tel: 416-213-7300
www.leisureworld.ca
Number of Beds: 160 beds
Lora Palmer, Administrator
Caterina Ierino, Director of Care

***Toronto:* Leisureworld Caregiving Centre - Lawrence**
2005 Lawrence Ave. West, Toronto, ON M9N 3V4
Tel: 416-243-8879
www.leisureworld.ca
Year Founded: 2002
Number of Beds: 224 beds; 2 respite
Gary Bowers, Administrator
Amo Nandlall, Director of Care

***Toronto:* Leisureworld Caregiving Centre - Norfinch**
22 Norfinch Dr., Toronto, ON M3N 1X1
Tel: 416-623-1120; *Fax:* 416-623-1121
www.leisureworld.ca
Year Founded: 2003
Number of Beds: 160 beds
Anne Deelstra McNamara, Administrator
Jane Pristach, Director of Nursing

***Toronto:* Leisureworld Caregiving Centre - O'Connor**
1800 O'Connor Dr., Toronto, ON M4A 1W7
Tel: 416-285-2000
www.leisureworld.ca
Year Founded: 2001
Number of Beds: 318 beds
Jeanette Sanichar, Administrator
Stacey Gamble, Assistant Director of Nursing

***Toronto:* Leisureworld Caregiving Centre - St. George**
225 St. George St., Toronto, ON M5R 2M2
Tel: 416-967-3985
www.leisureworld.ca/stgeorge.html
Number of Beds: 238 beds
Barbara Beecroft, Director of Nursing
Jane Noble, Administrator

***Toronto:* Mon Sheong Home for the Aged**
36 D'Arcy St., Toronto, ON M5T 1J7
Tel: 416-977-3762; *Fax:* 416-977-3231
msf@monsheong.org
www.monsheong.org
Number of Beds: 105 beds
Grace Lo, Administrator
gracelo@monsheong.org

***Toronto:* North Park Nursing Home**
450 Rustic Rd., Toronto, ON M6L 1W9
Tel: 416-247-0531; *Fax:* 416-247-6159
northparknursinghome@rogers.com
Number of Beds: 75 beds

***Toronto:* Norwood Nursing Home Ltd.**
122 Tyndall Ave., Toronto, ON M6K 2E2
Tel: 416-535-3011; *Fax:* 416-535-6439
info@norwoodcare.ca
www.norwoodcare.ca
Year Founded: 1957
Number of Beds: 60 beds
Note: Specialties: Long-term care; Rehabilitative care; Palliative care room
Mike Bakewell, Administrator
416-535-3011, Fax: 416-535-6439, mbakewell@norwoodcare.ca

***Toronto:* The Rekai Centre**
345 Sherbourne St., Toronto, ON M5A 2S3
Tel: 416-964-1599; *Fax:* 416-969-3907
rekaireception@rekaicentre.com
www.rekaicentre.com
Number of Beds: 129 beds
Linda Joyal, Director of Resident Programs

***Toronto:* St. Clair O'Connor Community Nursing Home**
2701 St. Clair Ave. East, Toronto, ON M4B 3M3
Tel: 416-757-8757; *Fax:* 416-751-7315
Number of Beds: 25 beds

***Toronto:* Tony Stacey Centre for Veterans Care**
59 Lawson Rd., Toronto, ON M1C 2J1
Tel: 416-284-9235; *Fax:* 416-284-7169
info@tonystaceycentre.ca
www.tonystaceycentre.ca
Year Founded: 1977
Number of Beds: 100 beds

***Toronto:* True Davidson Acres**
200 Dawes Rd., Toronto, ON M4C 5M8
Tel: 416-397-0400
Year Founded: 1973
Number of Beds: 187 beds
Note: Specialties: Nursing care; Rehabilitation; Recreation program; Music & art therapy
Sylvia Moreland, Administrator

***Toronto:* Ukrainian Canadian Care Centre**
60 Richview Rd., Toronto, ON M9A 5E4
Tel: 416-243-7653; *Fax:* 416-243-7452
uccc@stdemetrius.ca
www.stdemetrius.ca

Number of Beds: 152 beds
Note: Specialties: Long-term care; Therapeutic recreation; Social work
Sandy Lomaszewycz, Executive Director

Toronto: Vermont Square Long Term Care Home
914 Bathurst St., Toronto, ON M5R 3G5
Tel: 416-533-9473; *Fax:* 416-538-2685
www.vermontsquare.ca

Number of Beds: 130 beds
Christine Maragh, Administrator

Toronto: Wesburn Manor
400 The West Mall, Toronto, ON M9C 5S1
Tel: 416-394-3600; *Fax:* 416-394-3606
Year Founded: 2003
Number of Beds: 192 beds

Toronto: White Eagle Long Term Care Residence
Affiliated with: Chartwell Retirement Residences
138 Dowling Ave., Toronto, ON M6K 3A6
Tel: 416-533-7935; *Fax:* 416-533-5154
www.chartwell.com

Number of Beds: 56 beds
W. Brent Binions, President & CEO, Chartwell Retirement Residences

Trenton: Trent Valley Lodge
195 Bay St., Trenton, ON K8V 1H9
Tel: 613-392-9235; *Fax:* 613-392-0688
info@tvlodge.ca
www.tvlodge.ca

Year Founded: 1970
Number of Beds: 102 beds
Note: Specialties: Restorative care; Activation services; Long-term stroke care

Trout Creek: Lady Isabelle Nursing Home
PO Box 10, 102 Corkery St., Trout Creek, ON P0H 2L0
Tel: 705-723-5232; *Fax:* 705-723-5794
main@ladyisabelle.ca
www.ladyisabelle.ca

Number of Beds: 66 beds

Unionville: Bethany Lodge
23 Second St., Unionville, ON L3R 2C2
Tel: 905-477-3838; *Fax:* 905-477-2888
www.bethanylodge.org
Number of Beds: 128 beds

Uxbridge: ReachView Village
Revera Living
Former Name: Versa-Care Centre, Uxbridge
130 Reach St., Uxbridge, ON L9P 1L3
Tel: 905-852-5281; *Fax:* 905-852-0117
reachviewvillage@reveraliving.com
www.reveraliving.com
Social Media: www.facebook.com/400950748267;
twitter.com/Revera_Inc; www.youtube.com/user/ReveraInc;
www.linkedin.com/company/revera-inc
Number of Beds: 100 beds
Jeffrey C. Lozon, President & CEO, Revera Living

Vaughan: Bloomington Cove
400 Applewood Cres., Vaughan, ON L4K 0C3
Tel: 905-695-2930 *Toll-Free:* 888-448-4411
info@specialty-care.com
www.specialty-care.com

Number of Beds: 69 beds
Gerald Harquail, President

Vineland: United Mennonite Home (UMH)
Former Name: United Mennonite Home for the Aged
4024 - 23 St., Vineland, ON L0R 2C0
Tel: 905-562-7385; *Fax:* 905-562-3711
thehome@umh.ca
www.umh.ca

Year Founded: 1955
Number of Beds: 128 beds
Note: Specialties: Activity program; Physiotherapy; Pet therapy
Ron Wiens, Administrator
rwiens@umh.ca

Virgil: Heritage Place
1743 Four Mile Creek Rd., Virgil, ON L0S 1T0
Tel: 905-468-1111
www.pleasantmanor.net

Number of Beds: 36 beds
Tim Siemens, Executive Director, Pleasant Manor Retirement Village
905-934-2548, tims@pleasantmanor.net

Walkerton: Brucelea Haven
PO Box 1600, 41 McGivern St. West, Walkerton, ON N0G 2V0
Tel: 519-881-1570; *Fax:* 519-881-0231
www.brucecounty.on.ca

Year Founded: 1898
Number of Beds: 144 beds
Eleanor MacEwen, Administrator
519-881-1570, emacewen@brucecounty.on.ca

Wardsville: Babcock Community Care Centre
Former Name: Babcock Nursing Home
196 Wellington St., Wardsville, ON N0L 2N0
Tel: 519-693-4415; *Fax:* 519-693-4876
admin@babcockonline.com
www.babcockonline.com
Social Media:
www.facebook.com/BabcockCommunityCareCentre
Number of Beds: 60 beds
Area Served: Elgin, Kent, Lambton, Middlesex

Warkworth: Community Nursing Home
PO Box 68, 97 Mill St., Warkworth, ON K0K 3K0
Tel: 705-924-2311; *Fax:* 705-924-1711
www.cnhwarkworth.ca

Number of Beds: 60 beds
Lisa Allanson, Administrator
lallanson@clmi.ca

Waterdown: Alexander Place
329 Parkside Dr., Waterdown, ON L0K 2H0
Tel: 905-689-2662; *Fax:* 905-689-2625
www.jarlette.com

Number of Beds: 128 beds

Waterloo: Parkwood Mennonite Home Inc.
726 New Hampshire St., Waterloo, ON N2K 4M1
Tel: 519-885-4810; *Fax:* 519-885-6720
info@parkwoodmh.com
parkwoodmh.com

Number of Beds: 96 beds
Elisabeth Piccinin, Administrator
519-747-2151

Waterloo: Pinehaven Nursing Home
229 Lexington Rd., Waterloo, ON N2K 2E1
Tel: 519-885-0255; *Fax:* 519-885-4216
www.pinehaven.ca
Number of Beds: 85 beds
Note: Specialty: long term care

Welland: Foyer Richelieu Welland Inc.
655, av Tanguay, Welland, ON L3B 6A1
Tél: 905-734-1400; *Téléc:* 905-734-1386
www.foyerrichelieu.com

Fondée en: 1989
Nombre de lits: 61 beds
Sean Keays, Directeur général

Welland: Woodlands of Sunset
Affiliated with: Hamilton Niagara Haldimand Brant Local Health Integration Network
920 Pelham St., Welland, ON L3C 1Y5
Tel: 905-892-3845; *Fax:* 905-892-5882
www.niagararegion.ca

Number of Beds: 120 beds
Brent Kerwin, Administrator

Whitby: Fairview Lodge
PO Box 300, 632 Dundas St. West, Whitby, ON L1N 5S3
Tel: 905-668-5851; *Fax:* 905-668-8934
www.durham.ca
Number of Beds: 198 beds
Jennifer Bishop, Acting Administrator

Whitby: Sunnycrest Nursing Home
1635 Dundas St. East, Whitby, ON L1N 2K9
Tel: 905-576-0111; *Fax:* 905-576-4712
info@sunnycrest.ca
www.sunnycrest.ca

Number of Beds: 136 beds

Wiarton: Gateway Haven
PO Box 10, 671 Frank St., Wiarton, ON N0H 2T0
Tel: 519-534-1113; *Fax:* 519-534-4733
bcgwh@brucecounty.on.ca
www.brucecounty.on.ca

Number of Beds: 100 beds
Charles Young, Administrator
cyoung@brucecounty.on.ca

Wikwemikong: Wikwemikong Nursing Home
281 Wikwemikong Way, Wikwemikong, ON P0P 2J0
Tel: 705-859-3107; *Fax:* 705-859-2446
www.wikynursinghome.com

Number of Beds: 60 beds
Elie Maiangowi, Office Manager
Kevin Kay, Head of IT

Winchester: Dundas Manor Nursing Home
PO Box 970, 533 Clarence St., Winchester, ON K0C 2K0
Tel: 613-774-2293; *Fax:* 613-774-4015

Number of Beds: 98 beds
Note: seniors home
Cholly Boland, President
cboland@dundasmanor.ca
Karl Samuelson, Administrator

Windsor: Banwell Gardens
Revera Living
3000 Banwell Rd., Windsor, ON N8N 2M4
Tel: 519-735-3204; *Fax:* 519-735-1836
www.reveraliving.com/banwell
Social Media: www.facebook.com/400950748267;
twitter.com/Revera_Inc; www.youtube.com/user/ReveraInc;
www.linkedin.com/company/revera-inc
Number of Beds: 142 beds
Jeffrey C. Lozon, President & CEO, Revera Living

Windsor: Chateau Park Nursing Home
Affiliated with: Meritas Care Corporation
2990B Riverside Dr. West, Windsor, ON N9C 1A2
Tel: 519-254-4341; *Fax:* 519-254-7931
chateau@meritascare.ca
www.meritascare.ca
Number of Beds: 59 beds

Windsor: Extendicare - Southwood Lakes
Extendicare Canada
1255 North Talbot Rd., Windsor, ON N9G 3A4
Tel: 519-945-7249; *Fax:* 519-945-7816
cnh_southwoodlakes@extendicare.com
www.extendicarecanada.com/windsor
Number of Beds: 150 beds

Windsor: Riverside Place
Revera Living
3181 Meadowbrook Lane, Windsor, ON N8T 0A4
Tel: 519-974-0148; *Fax:* 519-974-7305
riversideplace@reveraliving.com
www.reveraliving.com
Social Media: www.facebook.com/400950748267;
twitter.com/Revera_Inc; www.youtube.com/user/ReveraInc;
www.linkedin.com/company/revera-inc
Jeffrey C. Lozon, President & CEO, Revera Living

Windsor: Rose Garden Villa Long Term Care
Revera Living
350 Dougall Ave., Windsor, ON N9A 4P4
Tel: 519-256-7868; *Fax:* 519-256-1991
vcwindsorplace@reveraliving.com
www.reveraliving
Social Media: www.facebook.com/400950748267;
twitter.com/Revera_Inc; www.youtube.com/user/ReveraInc;
www.linkedin.com/company/revera-inc
Number of Beds: 244 beds
Bonnie Spry, Administrator

Windsor: Villa Maria Home for the Aged
2856 Riverside Dr. West, Windsor, ON N9C 1A2
Tel: 519-254-3763; *Fax:* 519-254-7657
Note: Home for the aged

Woodbridge: Pine Grove Long Term Care & Retirement Resident
Affiliated with: Chartwell Retirement Residences
Former Name: Devonshire Pine Grove Inc.
8403 Islington Ave. North, Woodbridge, ON L4L 1X3
Tel: 905-850-3605
www.chartwellreit.ca

Woodslee: Country Village Health Care Centre
County Rd. 8, RR#2, Woodslee, ON N0R 1V0
Tel: 519-839-4812; *Fax:* 519-839-4813
www.kanataliving.ca
Number of Beds: 104 beds
Mary Butler, Executive Director
519-839-4812, mary.butler@countryvillage.ca

Woodstock: Caressant Care Woodstock
Affiliated with: Caressant Care Nursing and Retirement Homes Ltd
81 Fyfe Ave., Woodstock, ON N4S 8Y3
Tel: 519-539-6461; *Fax:* 519-539-7467
www.caressantcare.com
Number of Beds: 240 beds
James Lavelle, President, Caressant Care Nursing and Retirement Homes Ltd.

Zurich: Blue Water Rest Home
37792 Zurich-Hensall Road, RR 3, Zurich, ON N0M 2T0
Tel: 519-236-4373; *Fax:* 519-236-7685
bwrh.info@bluewaterresthome.com
www.bwrh.ca
Number of Beds: 65 beds
Angie Dunn, Administrator

Retirement Residences

Amherstburg: Victoria Street Manor
184 Victoria St., Amherstburg, ON N9V 2K5
Tel: 519-736-2525; *Fax:* 519-736-8587
www.countyofessex.on.ca
Number of Beds: 14 beds
Note: Specialties: Residential care for seniors; Medication administration
Linda Desjardins, Supervisor
519-736-2525

Amherstview: Briargate Retirement Living Centre
4567 Bath Rd., Amherstview, ON K7N 1A8
Tel: 613-384-9333; *Fax:* 613-384-4443
briargate@reveraliving.com
www.reveraliving.com/briargate
Number of Beds: 95 beds
Leanne Weir, Executive Director

Ancaster: Carrington Place Retirement Home
75 Dunham Dr., Ancaster, ON L9G 1X7
Tel: 905-648-0343
www.carringtonplaceretirement.ca
Note: Services include respite care for seniors, physiotherapy, an exercise program, & social activities.
Elyse Latimer, Administrator
e.latimer@carringtonplaceretirement.
Lynn Gledhill, Director, Activity
Jeanine Lavallee, Director, Community Resources

Ancaster: Highgate Retirement Residence
325 Fiddlers Green Rd., Ancaster, ON L9G 1W9
Tel: 905-648-8399
www.highgateresidence.ca
Year Founded: 1989
Number of Beds: 40 beds
Clare Aiken, Administrator

Arnprior: Arnprior Villa Retirement Residence
15 Arthur St., Arnprior, ON K7S 1A1
Tel: 613-623-0414
www.reveraliving.com/arnprior
Number of Beds: 81 beds
Becky Hollingsworth, Executive Director

Aurora: Aurora Retirement Centre
145 Murray Dr., Aurora, ON L4G 2C7
Tel: 905-841-2777; *Fax:* 905-841-1562
www.kingswayarms.com
Number of Beds: 54 units
Maret Cox, Executive Director

Aurora: Park Place Manor
15055 Yonge St., Aurora, ON L4G 6T4
Tel: 905-727-2952
www.chartwell.com/locations/park-place-manor
Number of Beds: 93 suites
Note: Specialties: Recreational activities; Wellness monitoring; Foot care; Respite, trial, seasonal, & convalescent stay
John Jeffs, Administrator

Barrie: Barrie Manor Retirement Residence
340 Blake St., Barrie, ON L4M 1L3
Tel: 705-722-3611; *Fax:* 705-722-4530
www.barriemanor.ca
Social Media: www.facebook.com/barriemanor
Note: Services include nursing care, senior's day away program, overnight post-op, respite care, physiotherapy, massage therapy, foot care, & recreation.

Barrie: Mulcaster Mews
130 Mulcaster St., Barrie, ON L4M 3M9
Tel: 705-725-9119; *Fax:* 705-725-8848
maggierae@mulcastermews.ca
www.mulcastermews.ca
Number of Beds: 44 rooms
Maggie Rae, Administrator

Barrie: Roberta Place Retirement Lodge
489 Essa Rd., Barrie, ON L4N 9E4
Tel: 705-728-2900; *Fax:* 705-728-8535
www.jarlette.com/roberta_rh.html
Number of Beds: 138 bed retirement lodge
Pam Story, General Manager, Retirement Lodge
pstory@jarlette.com

Barrie: Simcoe Terrace Retirement Community
Affiliated with: Specialty Care Retirement Communities
44 Donald St., Barrie, ON L4N 1E3
Tel: 705-722-5750; *Fax:* 705-722-7041
info@simcoeterrace.com
www.simcoeterrace.com
Note: Simcoe Terrace offers nursing services, physiotherapy, rest & recuperation stays, leisure activities, & spa services.

Barrie: Woods Park Care Centre
110 Lillian Cres., Barrie, ON L4N 5H7
Tel: 705-739-6881; *Fax:* 705-739-0638
suggestions@specialty-care.com
www.specialty-care.com/index.php/woods-park
Number of Beds: 123
Note: nursing home/retirement home
Cathy Cotton, Administrator
ccotton@woodspark.on.ca

Beachburg: Country Haven Retirement Home
1387 Beachburg Rd., RR#1, Beachburg, ON K0J 1C0
Tel: 613-582-7021; *Fax:* 613-582-7075
chrh@nrtco.net
www.countryhavenretirementhome.com
Number of Beds: 75 beds
Anil Verma, M.A., M.B.A., General Manager

Belleville: Bayview Retirement Home
435 Dundas St. West, Belleville, ON K8P 1B6
Tel: 613-966-6268; *Fax:* 613-966-6675
www.chartwellreit.ca
Number of Beds: 60 beds
Patricia Tooze, Administrator

Belleville: The Richmond Retirement Residence
175 North Front St., Belleville, ON K8P 4Y8
Tel: 613-966-4407
www.richmondretirement.ca
Note: Specialties: Medication management; Wellness program; Social & therapeutic programs; Respite stays
Andrea E. McLister, Administrator

Bracebridge: James Street Place
148 James St., Bracebridge, ON P1L 1S7
Tel: 705-645-1431
www.chartwell.com/locations/james-street-place
Number of Beds: 73 suites
Rosalid Taylor, Administrator

Bracebridge: Muskoka Hills Retirement Villa
690 Hwy. 118 West, Bracebridge, ON P1L 1W8
Tel: 705-645-6364
www.bracebridgevilla.ca

Brampton: Woodhall Park Retirement Village
10250 Kennedy Rd., RR#4, Brampton, ON L6T 3S1
Tel: 905-846-1441; *Fax:* 905-846-1451
postmaster@woodhallpark.ca
www.woodhallpark.ca
Number of Beds: 80 suites
Andrew Post, Administrator

Brantford: Amber Lea Place
Affiliated with: Mundi Holdings Ltd.
384 St. Paul Ave., Brantford, ON N3R 4N4
Tel: 519-754-0000; *Fax:* 519-759-1401
info@amberleaplace.com
www.amberleaplace.com
Number of Beds: 50 beds
Dev Mundi, Administrator

Brantford: Charlotte Villa Retirement Residence
120 Darling St., Brantford, ON N3T 5W6
Tel: 519-759-5250
www.reveraliving.com/charlotte
Number of Beds: 80 beds
Note: Independent & assisted living, secured living for dementia care
Carol Sterkenburg, Administrator/Care Coordinator

Brantford: Tranquility Place
PO Box 3000, 436 Powerline Rd., Brantford, ON N3T 6G5
Tel: 519-759-2222
www.chartwell.com/locations/tranquility-place
Year Founded: 1988
Note: Specialties: Physiotherapy; Foot care clinic; Physical activities
Paul Rade, General Manager

Brighton: Applefest Lodge
120 Elizabeth St., Brighton, ON K0K 1H0
Tel: 613-475-3510
applefestlodge@bellnet.ca
www.applefestlodge.ca
Number of Beds: 50 beds
Marilyn McLeod, Manager
interest@applefestlodge.com

Brockville: Bridlewood Manor
1026 Bridlewood Dr., Brockville, ON K6V 7J8
Tel: 613-345-2477
www.reveraliving.com/bridlewood
Number of Beds: 67 units
Dennis Daoust, Executive Director

Brockville: Rosedale Retirement Centre
Affiliated with: Chartwell Seniors Housing REIT
1813 County Rd. 2E, RR#1, Brockville, ON K6V 5T1
Tel: 613-342-0200
www.chartwell.com/locations/rosedale-retirement-centre
Number of Beds: 69 suites
Stephen Suske, CEO, Chartwell Seniors Housing REIT

Burlington: Appleby Place
500 Appleby Line, Burlington, ON L7L 5Z6
Tel: 905-333-1611
www.reveraliving.com/appleby
Number of Beds: 90 units
Mary Turnbull, General Manager

Burlington: Bethany Residence
2387 Industrial St., Burlington, ON L7P 3A1
Tel: 905-335-3463; *Fax:* 905-335-1202
info@bethanyresidence.ca
www.bethanyresidence.ca
Number of Beds: 121 beds
Sheri Levy-Abraham, Manager

Burlington: Christopher Terrace Retirement Home
3131 New St., Burlington, ON L7N 3P8
Tel: 905-632-5072; *Fax:* 905-632-5074
www.chartwell.com
Number of Beds: 80 beds
Laurie Johnston, Manager

Burlington: Lakeshore Place Retirement Residence
5314 Lakeshore Rd., Burlington, ON L7L 6L8
Tel: 905-333-0009; *Fax:* 905-333-3103
info@caregard.ca
www.caregard.ca/lakeshore
Number of Beds: 156 beds (residential care, assisted & daily living)
Note: assisted living retirement residence
Nancy Fischer, Administrator

Burlington: Park Avenue Manor
924 Park Ave. West, Burlington, ON L7T 1N7
Tel: 905-333-3323
www.chartwell.com/locations/park-avenue-manor
Number of Beds: 69 suites
Note: Specialties: Recreational activities; Medication administration; Wellness monitoring; Respite care; Convalescent, seasonal, & trial stays
Carrie T. Campbell, General Manager

Burlington: Wellington Park Care Centre
802 Hager Ave., Burlington, ON L7S 1X2
Tel: 905-637-3481; *Fax:* 905-637-7514
www.wellingtonparkcarecentre.ca
Number of Beds: 178 beds
Charlotte Nevills, Administrator

Cambridge: Avonlea Place
611 Dunbar Rd., Cambridge, ON N3H 2T4
Tel: 519-650-1102

Cambridge: Queen's Square Terrace
Affiliated with: Chartwell Seniors Housing REIT
10 Melville St. North, Cambridge, ON N1S 1H5
Tel: 519-621-2777
www.chartwell.com/locations/chartwell-select-queens-square-terrace
Number of Beds: 80 suites
Stephen Suske, CEO, Chartwell Seniors Housing REIT

Carleton Place: Carleton Place Manor
6 Arthur St., Carleton Place, ON K7C 4S4
Tel: 613-253-7360; *Fax:* 613-253-5048
edcarleton@kingswayarms.com
www.kingswayarms.com/wp/carleton-place
Social Media: www.facebook.com/KingswayArmsCarletonPlace
Number of Beds: 115 rooms
Corrie Berryman, Executive Director

Chatham: Maple City Retirement Residence
97 McFarlane Ave., Chatham, ON N7L 4V6
Tel: 519-354-7111; Fax: 519-351-5780
www.diversicare.ca
Number of Beds: 75 beds
Hilda Michielsen, Administrator

Chatham: Residence on The Thames
Affiliated with: Steeves & Rozema Group
850 Grand Ave. West, Chatham, ON N7L 5H5
Tel: 519-351-7220; Fax: 519-436-0360
residenceonthethames@srgroup.ca
chatham.ontarioretirementcommunity.com
Note: Independent living
Ian Murray, Executive Director
Crystal Houle, Office Manager

Codrington: Golden Pond House Retirement Residence
387 Goodrich Rd., Codrington, ON K0K 1R0
Tel: 613-475-4846; Fax: 613-475-4961
Toll-Free: 866-575-4846
gandrmgt@sympatico.ca
www.goldenpondretirement.ca
Number of Beds: 28 beds
Joan Dorland, Administrator

Cornwall: Chateau Cornwall
41 Amelia St., Cornwall, ON K6H 7E5
Tel: 613-937-4700; Fax: 613-932-6407
www.chartwellreit.ca
Number of Beds: 105 suites
Denis Carr, Manager

Delhi: Delrose Retirement Residence
725 Gibraltar St., Delhi, ON N4B 3C7
Tel: 519-582-4072; Fax: 519-582-0005
delrose@nor-del.com
www.delroseretirement.ca
Bonnie Guthrie, Administrator
bonnieguthrie@nor-del.com

Dresden: Park Street Place Retirement Residence
60 Park St., Dresden, ON N0P 1M0
Tel: 519-683-4474; Fax: 519-683-4555
www.diversicare.ca/home/ind_comm.php?cid=88
Year Founded: 1987
Note: Specialties: Foot care; Physiotherapy; Medication management; Recreational activities; Respite & convalescent stays
Hilda Michielsen, Administrator

Dundas: The Georgian Retirement Residence
Affiliated with: Chartwell Seniors Housing REIT
255 Governor's Rd., Dundas, ON L9H 3K4
Tel: 905-627-8444
www.chartwellreit.ca/locations/georgian-retirement-residence
Number of Beds: 64 suites
Stephen Suske, CEO, Chartwell Seniors Housing REIT

Elliot Lake: Huron Lodge
100 Manitoba Rd., Elliot Lake, ON P5A 3T1
Tel: 705-848-2019; Fax: 705-848-1306
www.huronlodge.ca
Note: Huron Lodge is a residence for 36 older adults. Respite service is available.
Gilbert A. Contant, Chief Executive Officer
gil@huronlodge.ca

Fort Erie: Garrison Place Retirement Residence
Revera Inc.
373 Garrison Rd., Fort Erie, ON L2A 1N1
Tel: 905-871-6410
reveraliving.com/Retirement-Living/Locations/Garrison-Place
Number of Beds: 74 suites
Note: Secured living for dementia care residents; respite & convalescent options

Georgetown: Mountainview Residence
222 Mountainview Rd. North, Georgetown, ON L7G 3R2
Tel: 905-877-1800
info@mountainviewterrace.ca
www.mountainviewterrace.ca
Number of Beds: 82 suites
Christopher Summer, Manager

Gloucester: Blackburn Lodge Seniors Residence
2412 Cléroux Cres., Gloucester, ON K1W 1A3
Tel: 613-837-7467; Fax: 613-837-0250
info@blackburnlodge.com
www.blackburnlodge.com
Note: Health services are provided, as well as personal services & activities.
David Porter, BA, BComm, CA, Executive Director & President
porterd@blackburnlodge.com
Sanjee Mendis, Director, Care
smendis@blackburnlodge.com
Shawna Melanson, Manager, Dining Room
smelanson@blackburnlodge.com
Jude Sheppard, Activity Coordinator
jsheppard@blackburnlodge.com

Gloucester: Camilla Gardens Retirement Residence
1119 Bathgate Dr., Gloucester, ON K1J 9N4
Tel: 613-747-7000; Fax: 613-747-1804
info@camillagardensretirementhome.com
www.camillagardensretirementhome.com
Note: Nursing supervision & assistance with person needs are available. Camilla Gardens also offers short term convalescent, respite, or trial stays.

Gloucester: Elmsmere Retirement Residence
889 Elmsmere St., Gloucester, ON K1J 8G4
Tel: 613-745-2409
www.reveraliving.com/elmsmere
Number of Beds: 57 units
Pierre Lefebvre, Manager

Gloucester: Ogilvie Villa
1345 Ogilvie Rd., Gloucester, ON K1J 7P5
Tel: 613-742-6524
www.reveraliving.com/ogilvie
Year Founded: 1995
Number of Beds: 64 residential capacity
Note: Specialties: Recreation program; Short term stays
Bob Lemay, Manager

Goderich: Goderich Place Retirement Residence
30 Balvina Dr. East, Goderich, ON N7A 4L5
Tel: 519-524-4243
www.goderichplace.com
Social Media: www.facebook.com/GoderichPlace; twitter.com/GoderichPlace; www.youtube.com/user/TheRetirementLife
Note: Goderich Place is a residence for seniors that offers bachelor, one, & two bedroom suites.
Sue Lebeau, Contact
salesgp@hurontel.on.ca

Goderich: Maple Grove Lodge
45 Nelson St. East, Goderich, ON N7A 1R7
Tel: 519-524-8610; Fax: 519-524-5039
Number of Beds: 25 beds
Note: Nursing home

Gravenhurst: Gravenhurst Manor
300 Muskoka Rd. North, Gravenhurst, ON P1P 1N8
Tel: 705-687-3356
www.chartwell.com
Number of Beds: 50 suites
Gay Pengilly, Administrator

Grimsby: Maplecrest Village Retirement Residence
85 Main St., Grimsby, ON L3M 1N6
Tel: 905-945-7044
www.reveraliving.com/maplecrest
Number of Beds: 80 beds
Leanne Dabbs, Administrator

Guelph: College Place Retirement Residence
Former Name: Meadowcroft Place Retirement Centre
166 College Ave. West, Guelph, ON N1G 1S4
Tel: 519-822-0090; Fax: 519-822-2310
www.collegeplace.ca
Note: Specialties: Assisted living program; Podiatry services; Recreation program; Short term stays
Colleen Brosseau, Manager

Guelph: Norfolk Manor
128 Norfolk St., Guelph, ON N1H 4J8
Tel: 519-837-1100; Fax: 519-836-4003
david@norfolkmanor.ca
www.norfolkmanor.ca
Number of Beds: 67 beds
David Ing, Manager

Guelph: Stone Lodge Retirement Residence
165 Cole Rd., Guelph, ON N1G 4N9
Tel: 519-767-0880
www.reveraliving.com/stonelodge
Number of Beds: 130 units
Note: Independent & assisted living; convalescent & respite options
E. Lyn Fisher, Administrator

Guelph: Village of Riverside Glen
60 Woodlawn Rd. East, Guelph, ON N1H 8M8
Tel: 519-822-5272
jane.coronado@schlegelvillages.com
www.schlegelvillages.com/guelph1
Number of Beds: 196 beds
Michell Vermeeren, Manager

Hamilton: Atrium Villa
467 Main St. East, Hamilton, ON L8M 1K1
Tel: 905-521-4442
www.chartwell.com/locations/atrium-villa
Number of Beds: 67 units
Margaret Coulter, Manager

Hamilton: Proctor Manor Retirement Home
Former Name: Proctor Manor Nursing Home
81 Proctor Blvd., Hamilton, ON L8M 2M5
Tel: 905-545-2427

Hamilton: Stinson Manor
112 Stinson St., Hamilton, ON L8N 1S5
Tel: 905-521-9112; Fax: 905-521-9106

Hamilton: Townsview Retirement Residence
52 Catherine St. North, Hamilton, ON L8R 1J1
Tel: 905-527-1200
Number of Beds: 57 residential capacity
Note: Specialties: Personal nursing care; Catheter care; Colostomy care; Diabetes care; Oxygen care; Wellness program; Medication administration; Activity program
Derrick Bernardo, Administrator

Hanover: The Village Seniors Community
101 Tenth St., Hanover, ON N4N 1M9
Tel: 519-364-4320
www.reveraliving.com/Long-Term-Care/Locations/The-Village-Hanover
Year Founded: 1961
Karen Kraus, Administrator

Harrow: Harrowood Seniors Community
Former Name: Harrowood Rest Home
1 Pollard Dr., Harrow, ON N0R 1G0
Tel: 519-738-2286; Fax: 519-738-2700
harrowoodseniorscommunity@bellnet.ca
www.harrowood.ca
Note: Seniors community
Carol Chisholm, Administrator

Hawkesbury: Place Mont Roc
100 Industrial Blvd., Hawkesbury, ON K6A 3M8
Tel: 613-632-2900; Fax: 613-632-9790
Frank Zambito, President

Hensall: Queensway Retirement Living and Long Term Care
PO Box 369, 100 Queen St. East, Hensall, ON N0M 1X0
Tel: 519-262-2830; Fax: 519-262-3403
queensway.info@pltchomes.com
www.pltchomes.com
Social Media: www.facebook.com/147704828612916; www.pltchomes.com
Number of Beds: 60 beds nursing home & 57 beds retirement home
Note: retirement home

Huntsville: Rogers Cove Retirement Residence
Affiliated with: Chartwell Seniors Housing REIT
4 Coveside Dr., Huntsville, ON P1H 2J9
Tel: 705-789-1600
www.chartwellreit.ca/locations/rogers-cove-retirement-residence
Number of Beds: 55 suites
Stephen Suske, CEO, Chartwell Seniors Housing REIT

Ingersoll: Oxford Manor Retirement Home
276 Oxford St., Ingersoll, ON N5G 2W1
Tel: 519-485-0350
www.chartwellreit.ca/locations/oxford-manor
Number of Beds: 46 units
Note: Specialties: Activity program; Medication administration; Wellness monitoring; Respite care; Trial stays
Diance Nant, Administrator

Kanata: Fairfield Manor Retirement Home
17 Lombardo Dr., Kanata, ON K2L 4E8
Tel: 613-592-5772; Fax: 613-592-8928
info@fairfieldmanor.ca
www.fairfieldmanor.ca

Kanata: **Kanata Retirement Residence**
Affiliated with: Chartwell Retirement Residence
20 Shirley's Brook Dr., Kanata, ON K2K 2W8
Tel: 613-591-8939; *Fax:* 613-591-1933
www.chartwell.com
Number of Beds: 81 beds
Johanne Laframboise, General Manager
jlaframboise@chartwellreit.ca
Lisa Giles, Community Relations Manager
lgiles@chartwellreit.ca

Kanata: **Walden Village**
Affiliated with: Kingsway Arms
27 Weaver Cres., Kanata, ON K2K 2Z8
Tel: 613-591-3991; *Fax:* 613-591-9647
edwalden@kingswayarms.com
www.kingswayarms.com/wp/walden-village
Social Media: www.facebook.com/KingswayArmsWaldenVillage
Number of Beds: 1,200
Heidi Eichenberger, General Manager

Kincardine: **Malcolm Place**
PO Box 100, 255 Durham St., Kincardine, ON N2Z 2Y6
Tel: 519-396-5800; *Fax:* 866-615-7760
Toll-Free: 877-669-7760
info@malcolmplace.ca
www.malcolmplace.ca
Number of Beds: 41 beds
Note: Retirement Residence
Dorinda Bowers, Administrator

Kingston: **The Rosewood**
833 Sutton Mills Ct., Kingston, ON K7P 2N9
Tel: 613-384-7131; *Fax:* 613-634-3247
www.specialty-care.com
Number of Beds: 66 units
Note: Independent living
Rhonda Jarvis, Sales & Marketing Manager
rhonda.jarvis@specialty-care.com

Kingston: **St. Lawrence Place**
181 Ontario St., Kingston, ON K7L 5M1
Tel: 613-544-5900
www.reveraliving.com
Year Founded: 1983
Number of Beds: 71 units

Kingston: **Trillium Ridge Retirement Community**
Affiliated with: Specialty Living
800 Edgar St., Kingston, ON K7M 8S4
Tel: 613-547-0040; *Fax:* 613-547-3734
suggestions@specialty-care.com
www.specialty-care.com
Note: Independent living. Specialty Care Trillium Centre long-term care residence located adjacent
Jane Bray, Manager, Resident Services
jane.bray@specialty-care.com

Kingsville: **Kings Manor Residence**
54 Spruce St. North, Kingsville, ON N9Y 3J1
Tel: 519-733-8376
augustinevillas@yahoo.ca
www.kingsmanorresidence.com

Kitchener: **Bankside Terrace**
71 Bankside Dr., Kitchener, ON N2N 3L1
Tel: 519-749-9999; *Fax:* 519-749-1947
www.chartwell.com/locations/chartwell-select-bankside-terrace/index.php
Number of Beds: 89 units
Brad Lawrence, Manager

Kitchener: **Conestoga Lodge Retirement Residence**
55 Hugo Cres., Kitchener, ON N2M 5J1
Tel: 226-214-3287
Number of Beds: 88 beds
Betty Cushing, Manager

Kitchener: **Fergus Place Retirement Residence**
Former Name: Meadowcroft Place
164 Fergus Ave., Kitchener, ON N2A 2H2
Tel: 519-894-9600
www.reveraliving.com/fergus
Number of Beds: 76 residential capacity
Note: Specialty: Short term stays
Jane Hagelberg, Administrator

Kitchener: **Lafontaine Terrace**
169 Borden Ave. North, Kitchener, ON N2H 3J5
Tel: 519-576-2800
info@lafontaineterrace.com
www.lafontaineterrace.com
Jeff Edwards, Administrator

Kitchener: **Lanark Place Retirement Residence**
44 Lanark Cres., Kitchener, ON N2N 2Z8
Tel: 519-743-0121; *Fax:* 519-743-8901
info@lanarkcare.com
www.lanarkcare.com
Number of Beds: 107 units
Nancy Douglas, Manager

Kitchener: **Victoria Place Retirement Residence**
290 Queen St. South, Kitchener, ON N2G 1W3
Tel: 519-576-1300
www.reveraliving.com/victoria
Number of Beds: 73 beds
Note: Independent & assisted living
Deb Gemmell, Executive Director

Leamington: **Erie Glen Manor Retirement Residence**
119 Robson Rd., RR#1, Leamington, ON N8H 3V4
Tel: 519-322-2384; *Fax:* 519-322-1411
Number of Beds: 81 beds
Shelley Gould, Administrator

Leamington: **Leamington Lodge Residential Care Centre Ltd.**
PO Box 353, 24 Russell St., Leamington, ON N8H 3W3
Tel: 519-326-3591; *Fax:* 519-326-8787
Number of Beds: 43 beds

London: **Ashwood Manor Ltd.**
79 David St., London, ON N6P 1B4
Tel: 519-652-9006; *Fax:* 519-652-2592
ashwood.manor.ltd@gmail.com
www.ashwoodmanor.com
Number of Beds: 72 units
Kathleen Hobden, Administrator

London: **Horizon Place Retirement Residence**
760 Horizon Dr., London, ON N6H 5G3
Tel: 519-641-6330; *Fax:* 519-641-0570
www.reveraliving.com/horizon
Number of Beds: 84 residential capacity
Note: Specialties: Assisted living program; Recreation therapy; Podiatry; Short term stays
Marilyn Weekley, Manager

London: **Kensington Village**
1340 Huron St., London, ON N5V 3R3
Tel: 519-455-3910; *Fax:* 519-455-1570
www.kensingtonvillage.org
Year Founded: 1984
Number of Beds: 139 suites
Sharron Brooks, Client Relations Coordinator
519-455-3910, sbrooks@kensingtonvillage.org

London: **Longworth Retirement Residence**
PO Box 5099, London, ON N6A 4M8
Tel: 519-434-1000; *Fax:* 519-434-1009
care@sifton.com
www.sifton.com
Number of Beds: 126 suites
Note: Specialty: Retirement / assisted living; Physiotherapy; Massage therapy; Reiki; Reflexology

London: **Maple View Terrace**
Revera Inc.
279 Horton St., London, ON N6B 1L3
Tel: 519-434-4544
www.reveraliving.com
Number of Beds: 90 units
Note: Assisted living
Robin Cassidy, Executive Director

London: **The Waverley**
Diversicare Canada Management Services Inc
10 Grand Ave., London, ON N5C 1K9
Tel: 519-667-1381; *Fax:* 519-667-9601
www.diversicare.ca/home/ind_comm.php?cid=68
Year Founded: 1987
Number of Beds: 65 beds
Note: Specialties: Supported care services for older adults; Medication administration & supervision; Physiotherapy; Foot care; Recreational program; Respite care; Convalescent stays
Suzi McArthur, Administrator

Midland: **King Place Retirement Residence**
750 King St., Midland, ON L4R 4K5
Tel: 705-526-0514
www.reveraliving.com/kingsplace
Number of Beds: 80 beds
Note: Independent & assisted living; secured living for dementia care residents; respite & convalescent options
Sharon Penrose, Manager

Midland: **The Villa Care Centre & Retirement Lodge**
689 Young St., Midland, ON L4R 2E1
Tel: 705-526-4238; *Fax:* 705-526-5080
www.jarlette.com
Number of Beds: 158 beds
Stephanie Walpole, Administrator
705-526-4238, swalpole@jarlette.com
Christina Bath, Director, Care
705-526-4238, cbath@jarlette.com

Mississauga: **Beechwood Place**
1500 Rathburn Rd. East, Mississauga, ON L4W 4L7
Tel: 905-238-0800; *Fax:* 905-238-4926
beechwoodplace@lrc.ca
Number of Beds: 137 suites
Deborah Rushton, Executive Director
Julie Shuster, Director of Marketing

Mississauga: **Bough Beeches Place Retirement Residence**
Former Name: Meadowcroft Place
1130 Bough Beeches Blvd., Mississauga, ON L4W 4G3
Tel: 905-625-2022
reveraliving.com/Retirement-Living/Locations/Bough-Beeches
Year Founded: 1984
Number of Beds: 98 suites
Note: Specialties: Assisted living program; Secured living program, for persons with dementia & Alzheimers disease; Short term stays; Fitness program; Podiatry services

Mississauga: **Erin Mills Lodge**
2132 Dundas St. West, Mississauga, ON L5K 2K7
Tel: 905-823-6700; *Fax:* 905-823-2410
info@erinmillscare.com
www.sifton.com
Number of Beds: 141 retirement units, 86 long-term care beds

Mississauga: **King Gardens Retirement Residence**
Revera Inc.
85 King St. East, Mississauga, ON L5A 4G6
Tel: 905-566-4545
reveraliving.com/Retirement-Living/Locations/King-Gardens
Year Founded: 1989
Number of Beds: 79 Independent Living suites; 47 Assisted Living suites; 15 Memory Care suites

Morrisburg: **Chartwell Hartford Retirement Residence**
Former Name: Hartford Retirement Centre
3 - 5th St. West, Morrisburg, ON K0C 1X0
Tel: 613-937-7273
chartwell.com/retirement-homes/chartwell-hartford-retirement-residence

Mount Forest: **Birmingham Retirement Community**
356A Birmingham St. East, Mount Forest, ON N0G 2L2
Tel: 519-323-4019; *Fax:* 519-323-3005
adm.birmingham@wightman.ca
birminghamretirement.ca
Number of Beds: 95 units

Napanee: **The Riverine Independent & Retirement Living**
328 Dundas St. West, Napanee, ON K7R 4B5
Tel: 613-354-8188; *Fax:* 613-354-8186
Toll-Free: 866-387-2217
admin@riverine.ca
www.riverine.ca
Number of Beds: 42 beds
Note: Specialties: Medication administration; Social & recreational program
Greg Freeman, Manager

Nepean: **Riverpark Place Retirement Residence**
1 Corkstown Rd., Nepean, ON K2H 1B6
Tel: 613-828-8882; *Fax:* 613-828-8908
info@caregard.ca
www.riverparkplace.ca
Number of Beds: 173 beds (residential care, assisted & daily living)
Cathy Arthurs-Hall, Administrator

Nepean: **Stillwater Creek Retirement Community**
2018 Robertson Rd., Nepean, ON K2H 1C6
Tel: 613-828-7575; *Fax:* 613-828-7524
info@caregard.ca
www.stillwatercreek.ca
Year Founded: 2001
Number of Beds: 204 units
Note: Specialties: Independent living; Assisted living; Recreation programs
Mike Traub, Administrator

***Newmarket:* Alexander Muir Retirement Residence**
Chartwell Retirement Residences
197 Prospect St., Newmarket, ON L3Y 3T7
Tel: 289-366-3690
chartwell.com/retirement-homes/chartwell-alexander-muir-retirement-residence

***Niagara Falls:* Cavendish Manor Retirement Living**
5781 Dunn St., Niagara Falls, ON L2G 2N9
Tel: 905-354-2733; *Fax:* 905-354-4164
www.comfortlife.ca
Number of Beds: 69 units
Janice Amos, Manager

***Niagara Falls:* Chippawa Place Supportive Living**
4118 Main St., Niagara Falls, ON L2G 6C2
Tel: 905-714-9517; *Fax:* 905-714-4558
admin@supportiveliving.ca
www.chippawaplace.com
Year Founded: 1994
Number of Beds: 25 beds

***Niagara Falls:* Lundy Manor Retirement Residence**
7860 Lundy's Lane, Niagara Falls, ON L2H 1H1
Tel: 905-356-1511
www.reveraliving.com/lundy
Number of Beds: 95 capacity
Note: Specialties: Assisted living program; Short term stays; Podiatry services
Art Derbernardi, Manager

***Niagara Falls:* Willoughby Manor**
Affiliated with: Chartwell Seniors Housing REIT
3584 Bridgewater St., Niagara Falls, ON L2G 6H1
Tel: 905-295-6288
www.chartwell.com
Number of Beds: 52 suites
Note: Retirement residence, with convalescent, respite & seasonal stay options
Stephen Suske, CEO, Chartwell Seniors Housing REIT

***North Bay:* Barclay House Retirement Residence**
Affiliated with: Chartwell Seniors Housing REIT
600 Chippewa St. West, North Bay, ON P1B 9E7
Tel: 705-476-6585
www.chartwell.com
Number of Beds: 64 suites
Stephen Suske, CEO, Chartwell Seniors Housing REIT

***Norwood:* Maple View Retirement Centre**
2281 County Rd., RR#2, Norwood, ON K0L 2V0
Tel: 705-639-5374; *Fax:* 705-639-1793
info@mapleviewretirement.com
www.mapleviewretirement.com
Number of Beds: 60 beds
Kim Ward, Administrator

***Oakville:* Churchill Place**
345 Church St., Oakville, ON L6J 7G4
Tel: 905-338-3311
www.reveraliving.com/churchillplace
Number of Beds: 69 suites
Note: Independent living, convalescent & respite options
Carole Huppenthal, General Manager

***Oakville:* The Kensington**
25 Lakeshore Rd. West, Oakville, ON L6K 3X8
Tel: 905-844-4000; *Fax:* 905-842-9229
www.reveraliving.com/kensington-oakville
Number of Beds: 120 suites
Note: Independent living
Judy Martin, General Manager

***Oakville:* Oakville Senior Citizens Residence**
#2220, 2222 Lakeshore Rd. West, Oakville, ON L6L 5G5
Tel: 905-827-4139; *Fax:* 905-827-8047
oscr@oakvilleseniors.com
www.oakvilleseniors.com
Number of Beds: 164 apartment tower units + 172 residential tower rooms

***Oakville:* Trafalgar Lodge Retirement Residence**
299 Randall St., Oakville, ON L6J 6B4
Tel: 905-842-8408; *Fax:* 905-842-8410
www.reveraliving.com/trafalgar
Number of Beds: 75 units
Note: Independent & assisted living; convalescent & respite options
Eileen Brajovic, Executive Director

***Orangeville:* Lord Dufferin Centre**
32 First St., Orangeville, ON L9W 2E1
Tel: 519-941-8433; *Fax:* 519-941-2615
dkholwell@lorddufferincentre.ca
www.lorddufferincentre.ca
Number of Beds: 78 private suites
Note: Specialties: Physiotherapy; Foot care
Donna Holwell, Manager

***Orillia:* Atrium Retirement Residence**
Affiliated with: Chartwell Retirement Residences
230 Coldwater Rd. West, Orillia, ON L3V 3M2
Tel: 705-325-7300
chartwellreit.ca/home_locations/atrium.htm
Number of Beds: 50
Miriam Leduc, Manager

***Orillia:* Birchmere Retirement Residence**
234 Bay St., Orillia, ON L3V 3W8
Tel: 705-326-8520; *Fax:* 705-326-5273
birchmere@on.aibn.com
www.retireorillia.com
Year Founded: 1981
Number of Beds: 77 beds
Jackie Payne, Administrator

***Orillia:* Champlain Manor**
65 Fittons Rd. West, Orillia, ON L3V 3V2
Tel: 705-326-8597; *Fax:* 705-326-9831
champlainmanor@on.aibn.com
www.retireorillia.com
Number of Beds: 65 beds
Jackie Payne, Administrator

***Orillia:* Spencer House**
Affiliated with: Leisureworld Senior Care Corporation
835 West Ridge Blvd., Orillia, ON L3V 8B3
Tel: 705-326-6609
admin.orillia@leisureworld.ca
www.leisureworld.ca
Number of Beds: 120 long-term care; 58 retirement beds
Lois Cormack, CEO

***Oshawa:* Cedarcroft Place (Oshawa)**
649 King St. East, Oshawa, ON L1H 8P9
Tel: 905-723-9490
www.reveraliving.com/cedarcroft
Year Founded: 1990
Number of Beds: 76 units
Brad Meekin, Executive Director

***Ottawa:* Amica at Bearbrook Court**
2645 Innes Rd., Ottawa, ON K1B 3J7
Tel: 613-837-8720
bearbrook@amica.ca
www.amica.ca/bearbrook
Number of Beds: 122 suites
Luke Goulette, General Manager

***Ottawa:* Billings Lodge**
1180 Bélanger Ave., Ottawa, ON K1H 8A2
Tel: 613-737-7877
www.billingslodge.ca
Year Founded: 1984

***Ottawa:* Colonel By Retirement Residence**
43 Aylmer St., Ottawa, ON K1S 4R5
Tel: 613-730-2002
www.reveraliving.com/colonelby
Number of Beds: 135 units

***Ottawa:* The Edinburgh Retirement Residence**
10 Vaughan St., Ottawa, ON K1M 2H6
Tel: 613-747-2233; *Fax:* 613-747-6741
www.reveraliving.com/edinburgh
Number of Beds: 66 beds
Note: Independent & assisted living programs
Mary Albota, Administrator

***Ottawa:* Hunt Club Manor**
1351 Hunt Club Rd., Ottawa, ON K1V 1A6
Tel: 613-733-4776
www.reveraliving.com/huntclub
Number of Beds: 78 beds
Tracy Fowers, General Manager

***Ottawa:* Manoir Gallien**
162 Murray St., Ottawa, ON K1N 5M8
Tel: 613-241-1331; *Fax:* 613-241-2693
info@manoirgalleon.com
Number of Beds: 75 units
Note: Senior's residence
Sandra Sullivan, Administrator

***Ottawa:* New Edinburgh Square**
420 Mackay St., Ottawa, ON K1M 2C4
Tel: 613-744-0901
www.chartwellreit.ca
Number of Beds: 111 suites
Jacqueline Brown, General Manager

***Ottawa:* Parklane Residence**
1095 Merivale Rd., Ottawa, ON K1Z 6A9
Tel: 613-725-1064; *Fax:* 613-728-3533
info@parklaneresidence.com
www.parklaneresidence.com
Number of Beds: 107 beds
Note: Retirement residence
Claude Desforges, Manager

***Ottawa:* Presland Residence**
198 Presland Rd., Ottawa, ON K1K 2B8
Tel: 613-745-0089; *Fax:* 613-745-6060
Number of Beds: 78 beds
Nathalie Grégoire, Administrator
613-745-0089

***Ottawa:* Rideau Place On-The-River**
Affiliated with: Chartwell Seniors Housing REIT
550 Wilbrod St., Ottawa, ON K1N 9M3
Tel: 613-234-6003; *Fax:* 613-234-9498
www.rideauplace.com
Number of Beds: 98 suites
Note: Retirement residence; short-term respite & convalescent care
Stephen Suske, CEO, Chartwell Seniors Housing REIT
Brian Kimberley, Marketing Manager

***Ottawa:* Rothwell Heights Retirement Residence**
1735 Montréal Rd., Ottawa, ON K1J 6N4
Tel: 613-744-2322; *Fax:* 613-745-2320
rothwellheights@bellnet.ca
Number of Beds: 114 units
Anita Hurtubise, Administrator

***Ottawa:* Stittsville Retirement Community**
1354 Stittsville Main St., Ottawa, ON K2S 1V4
Tel: 613-836-2216
www.reveraliving.com/stittsville
Number of Beds: 75 beds
Note: Independent living
Pat Leishman, Manager

***Ottawa:* Thorncliffe Place Retirement Home**
1 Thorncliffe Pl., Ottawa, ON K2H 9N9
Tel: 613-596-3853; *Fax:* 613-596-6225
info@thorncliffeplace.com
www.thorncliffeplace.com
Year Founded: 1989
Number of Beds: 81 suites
Note: Specialties: Activity program; Supervision of medications; Memory support; Elderobics; Convalescent stays
Don Francis, Administrator

***Ottawa:* Watford House Residence**
75 Powell Ave., Ottawa, ON K1S 1Z9
Tel: 613-230-9194
eli.marshall@watfordhouse.ca
www.watfordhouse.ca
Info Line: 613-230-7423
Number of Beds: 22 beds
Anatoli Brouchkov, Administrator

***Ottawa:* The Westwood**
Revera Inc.
Former Name: Central Park Lodges - Ottawa 1
2374 Carling Ave., Ottawa, ON K2B 7G5
Tel: 613-820-7333
reveraliving.com/Retirement-Living/Locations/the-westwood
Year Founded: 1969
Number of Beds: 93 Independent Living suites; 134 Assisted Living suites; 19 Memory Care suites
Note: Independent & assisted living, respite & convalescent options.
Ray Hould, General Manager

***Ottawa:* Windsor Park Manor Retirement Living**
990 Hunt Club Rd., Ottawa, ON K1V 8S8
Tel: 613-249-0722; *Fax:* 613-249-0575
windsorpark@regallc.com
www.windsorparkmanor.com
Note: Convalescence, respite, & short term stays are available.

***Owen Sound:* Central Place**
855 - 3 Ave. East, Owen Sound, ON N4K 2K6
Tel: 519-371-1968; *Fax:* 519-371-5357
info@cpretirement.ca
www.cpretirement.ca

Year Founded: 1998

***Owen Sound:* Hannah Walker Place**
832 - 2 Ave. West, Owen Sound, ON N4K 4M5
Tel: 519-371-1664; *Fax:* 519-371-5286
www.owensoundretirement.com

***Owen Sound:* John Joseph Place**
854 - 2 Ave. West, Owen Sound, ON N4K 4M5
Tel: 519-371-1664; *Fax:* 519-371-5286
www.owensoundretirement.com

***Pakenham:* Country View Lodge**
4676 Darks Side Rd., Pakenham, ON K0A 2X0
Tel: 613-518-6642; *Fax:* 888-960-0247
Toll-Free: 855-932-2729
info@countryviewlodge.ca
www.countryviewlodge.ca
Social Media: www.facebook.com/countryviewlodge; twitter.com/countryviewlodg; www.youtube.com/channel/UCrt0bYf3wv7t4z29nznDepw
Note: Retirement home with assisted living/nursing service
Ali Abbas, General Manager

***Paris:* Penmarvian Retirement Home**
185 Grand River St. North, Paris, ON N3L 2N2
Tel: 519-442-7140; *Fax:* 519-442-7156
info@penmarvian.com
www.penmarvian.com
Year Founded: 1980
Number of Beds: 38 beds
Note: Specialties: Nursing care; Activity program
Maria Toncic, Administrator

***Perth:* Rideau Ferry Country Home**
1333, Rideau Ferry Rd., Perth, ON K7H 3C7
Tel: 613-267-6213; *Fax:* 613-267-6261
ken.mccartney@sympatico.ca
www.rideauferrycountryhome.com
Number of Beds: 45 units
Note: Offers both retirement residences and assisted daily living services
Mary Ross, Administrator

***Peterborough:* Empress Gardens Retirement Residence**
131 Charlotte St., Peterborough, ON K9J 2T6
Tel: 705-876-1314; *Fax:* 705-876-1908
www.empressgardens.ca

***Peterborough:* Peterborough Manor**
1039 Water St., Peterborough, ON K9H 3P5
Tel: 705-748-5343
www.chartwellreit.ca
Number of Beds: 101 suites
Note: Specialties: Medication administration; Wellness monitoring; Assistance to persons with oxygen, catheters, & ostomies; Activity program; Podiatry; Respite care; Convalescent stays
Martha Crealiy, Administrator

***Peterborough:* Princess Gardens Retirement Residence**
100 Charlotte St., Peterborough, ON L9J 7L4
Tel: 705-750-1234; *Fax:* 705-750-0711
Toll-Free: 877-742-9779
www.princessgardens.ca
Number of Beds: 132 beds
Note: Independent retirement amenities; assisted living/enriched care options; respite & convalescent care
Juris Taurins, Manager

***Pickering:* Community Nursing Home**
1955 Valley Farm Rd., Pickering, ON L1V 1X6
Tel: 905-831-2522; *Fax:* 905-420-5030
mlacroxi@clmi.ca
www.cnhpickering.ca
Number of Beds: 233 long-term care beds, 61 retirement suites
Gary Hopkins, Administrator
ghopkins@clmi.ca

***Port Hope:* The Tower of Port Hope Retirement Residence**
Affiliated with: Chartwell Seniors Housing REIT
164 Peter St., Port Hope, ON L1A 1C6
Tel: 905-885-7261
www.chartwellreit.ca
Number of Beds: 44 suites
Stephen Suske, CEO, Chartwell Seniors Housing REIT
Julie Inglis, Administrator

***Port Perry:* West Shore Village**
293 Perry St., Port Perry, ON L9L 1S6
Tel: 905-985-8660 *Toll-Free:* 800-248-0848
info@westshorevillage.ca
www.westshorevillage.ca
Number of Beds: 71 suites
Note: Specialties: Supported living for seniors; Foot care; Reflexology; Massage therapy; Recreational program; Respite care
Karen Arbuckle, Manager

***Renfrew:* Quail Creek Retirement Centre**
450 Albert St., Renfrew, ON K7V 4K4
Tel: 613-432-9502
www.chartwellreit.ca
Number of Beds: 90 suites
Bev Powell, Administrator

***Richmond:* Richmond Lodge Ltd.**
PO Box 1030, 6197 Perth St., Richmond, ON K0A 2Z0
Tel: 613-838-5016; *Fax:* 613-838-5017
activities.richmondlodge@yahoo.ca
richmondlodge.ca
Number of Beds: 42 beds
Note: Retirement residence
Claudette Richel, Administrator

***Richmond Hill:* Brookside/Hilltop Retirement Residence**
980 Elgin Mills Rd. East, Richmond Hill, ON L4S 1M4
Tel: 905-884-9248; *Fax:* 905-884-9745
www.reveraliving.com/brookside
Year Founded: 1961
Number of Beds: 140 units
Sandra Fernandez, Executive Director

***Rockland:* Résidence Jardins Bellerive**
2950 rue Laurier, Rockland, ON K4K 1T3
Tel: 613-446-7122; *Fax:* 613-446-7343
info@jardinsbellerive.com
www.jardinsbellerive.com
Number of Beds: 80 Units
Youri Brouchkov, Administrator

***Rockland:* Résidence Simon Inc.**
CP 400, 845, rue St-Jean, Rockland, ON K4K 1K5
Tél: 613-446-7023; *Téléc:* 613-446-4867
info@residencesimon.ca
www.residencesimon.ca
Fondée en: 1989
Nombre de lits: 46 lits
Albert Bourdeau, Propriétaire

***Sarnia:* Marshall Gowland Manor**
749 Devine St., Sarnia, ON N7T 1X3
Tel: 519-336-3720; *Fax:* 519-336-3734
www.lambtononline.com
Year Founded: 2004
Number of Beds: 126 beds
Note: Specialties: Long-term care; Day programs
Joyce Haneca, Resident Manager
519-336-3720, joyce.haneca@county-lambton.on.ca

***Sarnia:* Residence on the St. Clair**
Affiliated with: Steeves & Rozema Group
#22 - 265 North Front St., Sarnia, ON N7T 7X1
Tel: 519-344-8829; *Fax:* 519-344-8518
general_inquiries@srgroup.ca
www.srgroup.ca
Number of Beds: 73 beds
Note: Independent living, convalescent & respite options
Cathy McIntosh, Managing Director

***Sarnia:* Rosewood Manor**
Affiliated with: Steeves & Rozema Group
711 Indian Rd. North, Sarnia, ON N7T 7Z5
Tel: 519-332-8877; *Fax:* 519-332-5047
rosewoodmanor@srgroup.ca
sarnia.ontarioretirementcommunity.com
Note: Independent & assisted living
Janice Horley, Executive Director

***Sault Ste Marie:* Pathways Retirement Residence**
Former Name: Pathways Seniors Residence
375 Trunk Rd., Sault Ste Marie, ON P6A 6T5
Tel: 705-759-1079; *Fax:* 705-759-1211
info@pathwaysret.com
www.pathwaysretirement.com
Number of Beds: 133 beds

***Seaforth:* Maplewood Manor Comfort of Living**
13 Church St., Seaforth, ON N0K 1W0
Tel: 519-441-2722
info@comfortofliving.com
www.comfortofliving.com

***Simcoe:* Simcoe Heritage Retirement Home**
182 Norfolk St. South, Simcoe, ON N3Y 2W4
Tel: 519-428-0930
www.simcoeheritage.ca
Number of Beds: 31 rooms

***Smiths Falls:* Willowdale Retirement Centre**
Affiliated with: Chartwell Seniors Housing REIT
9 Armstrong Dr., Smiths Falls, ON K7A 5H7
Tel: 613-283-0691
Number of Beds: 59 suites
Stephen Suske, CEO, Chartwell Seniors Housing REIT

***St Catharines:* The Loyalist Retirement Residence**
190 King St., St Catharines, ON L2R 3J7
Tel: 905-641-4422; *Fax:* 905-641-4989
Toll-Free: 800-337-9137
info@loyalist-retirement.com
www.loyalist-retirement.com
Number of Beds: 118 residential capacity
Note: Specialties: Assisted living; Nursing supervision; Medication administration; Podiatry services; Recreation & fitness program; Respite care; Convalescent stays
Lydia Tarasiuk, Administrator

***St Thomas:* Metcalfe Gardens Retirement Residence**
45 Metcalfe St., St Thomas, ON N5R 5Y1
Tel: 519-631-9393; *Fax:* 519-631-2563
Year Founded: 1988
Number of Beds: 97 suites
Note: Specialties: Foot care; Physiotherapy; Recreation programs; Respite care
Deborah Geerlinks, Administrator

***St. Catharines:* Mount Carmel Home**
78 Yates St., St. Catharines, ON L2R 5R9
Tel: 905-685-9155; *Fax:* 905-682-3922
carmel@vaxxine.com
mountcarmelretirement.ca
Year Founded: 1920
Number of Beds: 69 beds
Note: seniors residence
Sr. M. Rosario, Administrator

***St. Catharines:* Tufford Manor Retirement Home**
312 Queenston Rd., St. Catharines, ON L2P 2X4
Tel: 905-682-0411; *Fax:* 905-682-2770
help@hamptontufford.com
www.hamptontufford.com
Number of Beds: 53 beds
Note: Offers long & short-term stays; on-site physiotherapy; medication administration; & maintenance, laundry, & housekeeping

***St. Joachim:* St. Joachim Manor**
2718 County Rd. 42, St. Joachim, ON N0R 1S0
Tel: 519-728-1215; *Fax:* 519-728-0113
Number of Beds: 23 beds
Zlatko Horvat, Owner
Nada Horvat, Owner

***Stoney Creek:* Orchard Terrace Care Centre**
199 Glover Rd., Stoney Creek, ON L8E 5J2
Tel: 905-643-1795; *Fax:* 905-643-1085
www.orchardterracecarecentre.ca
Year Founded: 1994
Number of Beds: 39 units
Note: Specialties: Activity program; Catheter care; Colostomy care; Oxygen care; Diabetes care; Medication administration; Wellness program
Leslie Watson, Administrator

***Stratford:* Anne Hathaway Residence**
480 Downie St., Stratford, ON N5A 7Y5
Tel: 519-275-2125; *Fax:* 519-275-2126
www.chartwellreit.ca
Number of Beds: 67 beds
Dianne Roth, Administrator

***Stratford:* Cedarcroft Place Retirement Residence**
Affiliated with: All Seniors Care Living Centres
260 Church St., Stratford, ON N5A 2R6
Tel: 519-275-0030; *Fax:* 519-273-0373
www.allseniorscare.com/en/residences/on/cedarcroft-place
Number of Beds: 100 beds
Note: Covalescent & respite care are available.

Dan Vito, Director
danvito@allseniorscare.com

Sudbury: Westmount Retirement Residence
Affiliated with: Chartwell Seniors Housing REIT
599 William Ave., Sudbury, ON P3A 5W3
Tel: 705-566-6221
www.chartwellreit.ca
Number of Beds: 84 suites
Stephen Suske, CEO, Chartwell Seniors Housing REIT

Surrey: Brookside Lodge
Affiliated with: Fraser Health Authority
19550 Fraser Hwy., Surrey, ON V3S 6K5
Tel: 604-530-6595; *Fax:* 604-530-6596
www.balticproperties.ca
Number of Beds: 89 beds
Dave Sedore, Proprietor

Temiskaming Shores: Northdale Manor
142-130 Lakeshore Rd., Temiskaming Shores, ON P0J 1P0
Tel: 705-647-6541; *Fax:* 705-647-8284
nordale@ntl.sympatico.ca
www.northdalemanor.ca
Number of Beds: 70 suites
Note: Retirement home
Jan Edwards, Administrator

Thornhill: Glynnwood Retirement Living
Revera Living
7700 Bayview Ave., Thornhill, ON L3T 5W1
Tel: 905-881-9475 *Toll-Free:* 877-929-9222
www.reveraliving.com/glynnwood
Note: Customized care plans are available.
Paul Mitchell, Administrator

Thorold: Cobblestone Gardens Retirement Residence
Affiliated with: Mundi Holdings Ltd.
Former Name: Chestnut Court
10 Ormond St. North, Thorold, ON L2V 1Y7
Tel: 905-227-5550; *Fax:* 905-227-5575
info@cobblestonegardens.ca
www.cobblestonegardens.ca
Year Founded: 1984
Note: Nursing assessments & care plans are available.
Elizabeth Dumoulin, Administrator
Jeannie Redekop, Director, Care

Tilbury: Hudson Manor
PO Box 1150, 36 Lawson St., Tilbury, ON N0P 2L0
Tel: 519-682-3366; *Fax:* 519-682-0688
Number of Beds: 50 beds
Debbie Ouellette, Administrator

Tillsonburg: Tillsonburg Retirement Centre
Affiliated with: Chartwell Seniors Housing REIT
183 Rolph St., Tillsonburg, ON N4G 3Y9
Tel: 519-688-0347; *Fax:* 519-688-2471
www.chartwellreit.ca
Number of Beds: 51 suites
Stephen Suske, CEO, Chartwell Seniors Housing REIT

Timmins: Chateau Georgian Retirement Residence
455 Cedar St. North, Timmins, ON P4N 8K4
Tel: 705-267-7935
www.chartwellreit.ca
Number of Beds: 63 suites
Note: Specialties: Wellness monitoring; Physical therapy; Recreation therapy; Podiatry; Respite care; Convalescent stays
Lynn Budd, Manager

Toronto: The Annex Retirement Residence
123 Spadina Rd., Toronto, ON M5R 2T1
Tel: 416-961-6446; *Fax:* 416-961-3299
www.reveraliving.com/annex
Year Founded: 1961
Number of Beds: 102 beds
Note: Independent & assisted living, secured living for dementia care
Maria Silva, General Manager

Toronto: The Balmoral Club
155 Balmoral Ave., Toronto, ON M4V 1J5
Tel: 416-927-0055; *Fax:* 416-927-0925
balmoralclub@amica.ca
www.amica.ca
Number of Beds: 66 beds
Monica Byrne, Administrator

Toronto: Baycrest Centre for Geriatric Care - Terraces of Baycrest
55 Ameer Ave., Toronto, ON M6A 2Z1
Tel: 416-785-2500; *Fax:* 416-785-2496
mjacobson@baycrest.org
www.baycrest.org
Info Line: 416-785-2379
Social Media: www.facebook.com/baycrestcentre; twitter.com/baycrest; www.youtube.com/thebaycrestchannel; www.linkedin.com/company/baycrest
Number of Beds: 199 Apartments
Note: supportive living
Sheila Smyth, Director

Toronto: Beach Arms Retirement Residence
505 Kingston Rd., Toronto, ON M4L 1V5
Tel: 416-698-0414; *Fax:* 416-698-9839
info@beacharms.com
www.beacharms.com
Number of Beds: 80 beds
Susan Turner, Administrator

Toronto: Belmont House
55 Belmont St., Toronto, ON M5R 1R1
Tel: 416-964-9231; *Fax:* 416-964-1448
information@belmonthouse.com
www.belmonthouse.com
Number of Beds: 55 apartments, 26 retirement suites; 140 long-term care beds
Note: Total employees: 28
Maria Elias, CEO
melias@belmonthouse.com

Toronto: Centennial Park Place Retirement Residence
Former Name: Meadowcroft Place Retirement Residence
25 Centennial Park Rd., Toronto, ON M9C 5H1
Tel: 416-621-2139
www.reveraliving.com/cemtennial
Number of Beds: 48 residential capacity
Note: Specialty: Podiatry services; Fitness program
Naida McKechnie, Manager

Toronto: Central Park Lodges - Queens Drive 2
303 Queens Dr., Toronto, ON M6L 3C1
Tel: 416-241-1113; *Fax:* 416-241-1801
www.reveraliving.com/westongardens
Number of Beds: 156 units
Note: Independent & assisted living. Central Park Lodge Queens Drive 1 located at 265 Queens Drive
L. Kabot, Administrator

Toronto: Chartwell Guildwood Retirement Residence
65 Livingston Rd., Toronto, ON M1E 1L1
Tel: 647-846-7004
chartwell.com/retirement-homes/chartwell-guildwood-retirement-residence
Note: Specialities: Physiotherapy; Foot care

Toronto: Don Mills Seniors' Apartments
Revera Inc.
1055-1057 Don Mills Rd., Toronto, ON M3C 1W9
Tel: 416-445-5532
www.reveraliving.com/donmills
Number of Beds: 143 suites

Toronto: Donway Place
Revera Inc.
8 The Donway East, Toronto, ON M3C 3R7
Tel: 416-445-7555
www.reveraliving.com/Retirement-Living/Locations/Donway-Place.aspx
Number of Beds: 145 independant living suites; 90 assisted living suites

Toronto: Eden Manor
251 St George St., Toronto, ON M5R 2M2
Tel: 416-515-1136; *Fax:* 416-515-1137
edenmanor@bellnet.ca
www.edenmanor.ca
Year Founded: 1910
Number of Beds: 25 beds
W. Boggs, Administrator

Toronto: Fellowship Towers
877 Yonge St., Toronto, ON M4W 3M2
Tel: 416-923-8887; *Fax:* 416-923-1343
inquiries@fellowshiptowers.com
www.fellowshiptowers.com
Number of Beds: 284 beds
Marilyn Burton, Administrator
mburton@fellowshiptowers.com

Toronto: Forest Hill Place
645 Castlefield Ave., Toronto, ON M5N 3A5
Tel: 416-785-1511; *Fax:* 416-785-6228
www.reveraliving.com/foresthill
Number of Beds: 125 suites

Toronto: Glebe Manor Retirement Residence
17 Glebe Rd. West, Toronto, ON M5P 1C8
Tel: 416-485-1150; *Fax:* 416-485-6378
J.T. Whitebread, Administrator

Toronto: Grenadier Retirement Residence
2100 Bloor St. West, Toronto, ON M6S 1M7
Tel: 416-769-2885; *Fax:* 416-769-7238
www.diversicare.ca
Note: Specialties: Physiotherapy; Wellness program; Activity program; Medication administration; Short-term stays
Dwight Mountney, Administrator

Toronto: Harold & Grace Baker Centre
Revera Living
1 Northwestern Ave., Toronto, ON M6M 2J7
Tel: 416-654-2889; *Fax:* 416-654-0217
www.bakercentre.com
Social Media: www.facebook.com/400950748267; twitter.com/Revera_Inc; www.youtube.com/user/ReveraInc; www.linkedin.com/company/revera-inc
Number of Beds: 233 beds
Milena Sujer, Executive Director
milena.sujer@reveraliving.com

Toronto: Hazelton Place
111 Avenue Rd., Toronto, ON M5R 3J8
Tel: 416-928-0111
info.hazelton@diversicare.ca
www.hazeltonplace.ca
Number of Beds: 130 units
Lillian Russell, General Manager

Toronto: Lansing Retirement Residence
10 Senlac Rd., Toronto, ON M2N 6P8
Tel: 416-250-7029; *Fax:* 416-250-7853
www.chartwell.com
Number of Beds: 110 beds
Jill Estioko, Manager

Toronto: Leaside Retirement Residence
10 William Morgan Dr., Toronto, ON M4H 1E7
Tel: 416-425-3722; *Fax:* 416-425-3946
www.reveraliving.com/leaside
Year Founded: 1961
Number of Beds: 211 beds
Note: Secured living for dementia care
P. Lemdal, General Manager

Toronto: McNicoll Manor
Affiliated with: Tendercare
1020 McNicoll Ave., Toronto, ON M1W 2J6
Tel: 416-499-3313
www.tendercare.ca/mcnicoll
Note: Specialties: Physiotherapy
Maureen McAlaster, Coordinator

Toronto: New Horizons Tower
1140 Bloor St. West, Toronto, ON M6H 4E6
Tel: 416-536-6111; *Fax:* 416-536-6748
info@newhorizonstower.com
www.newhorizonstower.com
Number of Beds: 197 beds
Note: Christian nursing home
Ian C. Logan, Administrator

Toronto: Pine Villa Retirement Residence
1035 Eglinton Ave. West, Toronto, ON M6C 2C8
Tel: 416-787-5626
www.reveraliving.com/pinevilla
Year Founded: 1961
Number of Beds: 71 units
Note: Specialties: Medication administration; Assistance for residents who require oxygen, catheters, & ostomies; Physiotherapy; Podiatry; Recreation therapy
Sharon Rosenblum, Executive Director

Toronto: Rayoak Place Retirement Residence
1340 York Mills Rd., Toronto, ON M3A 3R1
Tel: 416-391-0633
www.reveraliving.com/rayoak
Number of Beds: 66 beds
Note: Independent & assisted living
Linda Mullins, Manager

***Toronto:* Shepherd Terrace Retirement Suites**
3758 Sheppard Ave. East, Toronto, ON M1T 3K9
Tel: 416-609-5700; *Fax:* 416-293-6229
www.shepherdvillage.org
Number of Beds: 144 units, including 112 assisted living suites

***Toronto:* Terrace Gardens Retirement Residence**
3705 Bathurst St., Toronto, ON M6A 2E8
Tel: 416-789-7670
www.reveraliving.com/terracegardens
Note: Jewish retirement residence; independent & assisted living, secured living for dementia care, convalescent & respite options; COR supervised, mashgiach on site

***Toronto:* Weston Gardens Retirement Residence**
303 Queens Dr., Toronto, ON M6L 3C1
Tel: 416-241-1113
www.westongardens.ca
Note: Independent & assisted living, respite & convalescent options.

***Trenton:* The Carrington, A Retirement Residence**
114 Whites Rd., RR#2, Trenton, ON K8V 5P5
Tel: 613-392-1615; *Fax:* 613-392-3879
Toll-Free: 877-392-1615
info@thecarringtonretirement.ca
www.thecarringtonretirement.com
Number of Beds: 37 units
Note: The Carrington is an approved member of the Ontario Retirement Communities Association. Services include the availability of nuses & health care aides, assistance with daily living activities & outside agency services, plus social, cultural, & recreational programming.

***Utterson:* Rowanwood Retirement Residence**
81 Rowanwood Rd., RR#3, Utterson, ON P0B 1M0
Tel: 705-789-6424; *Fax:* 705-789-1821
Number of Beds: 86 beds
Gail Sargeant, Manager

***Vankleek Hill:* Heritage Lodge Retirement Residence**
Former Name: Vankleek Residence
48 Wall St., Vankleek Hill, ON K0B 1R0
Tel: 613-678-2690 *Toll-Free:* 877-929-9222
www.reveraliving.com/heritage
Number of Beds: 72 beds
Sandra McCormick, Executive Director

***Varry's Bay:* Water Tower Lodge**
9 Stafford St., Varry's Bay, ON K0J 1B0
Tel: 613-756-9086; *Fax:* 613-756-9369
info@watertowerlodge.com
www.watertowerlodge.com
Number of Beds: 44 units

***Vineland:* The Orchards Retirement Residence**
Heritage Village, 3421 Frederick Ave., Vineland, ON L0R 2C0
Tel: 905-562-7357
info@theorchardsresidence.ca
theorchardsresidence.ca
Year Founded: 1999
Note: Specialties: Medication management; Personal care assistance; Activities program; Physiotherapy; Respite & convalescence care
Dustin Gibson, General Manager

***Walkerton:* Maple Court Villa**
Affiliated with: Chartwell Retirement Residences
PO Box 879, 5 Fourth St., Walkerton, ON N0G 2V0
Tel: 519-881-2233; *Fax:* 519-881-0336
www.chartwell.com/locations/maple-court-villa
Number of Beds: 47 Suites
Note: Nursing home
JoAnn Todd, Administrator

***Waterloo:* Luther Village on the Park**
Luthewood
139 Father David Bauer Dr., Waterloo, ON N2L 6L1
Tel: 519-747-4413
www.luthervillage.org
Note: Specialties: Assisted living

***Waterloo:* Oak Park Terrace**
Affiliated with: Chartwell Seniors Housing REIT
1750 North Service Rd., Waterloo, ON N8E 1Y3
Tel: 519-972-3330
www.chartwell.com/locations/chartwell-classic-oak-park-terrace
Number of Beds: 112
Stephen Suske, CEO, Chartwell Seniors Housing REIT

***Windsor:* Devonshire Seniors' Residence**
901 Riverside Dr. West, Windsor, ON N9A 7J6
Tel: 519-252-2273; *Fax:* 519-252-2324
Toll-Free: 877-521-5686
www.chartwell.com/locations/devonshire-seniors-residence
Number of Beds: 195 beds
Sharon Woodward, General Manager

***Windsor:* The Grandview Retirement Living Revera Living**
3387 Riverside Dr. East, Windsor, ON N8Y 1A8
Tel: 519-948-5293; *Fax:* 519-948-7513
www.reveraliving.com
Social Media: www.facebook.com/400950748267; twitter.com/Revera_Inc; www.youtube.com/user/ReveraInc; www.linkedin.com/company/revera-inc
Number of Beds: 141 units
Note: Independent & assisted living, secured living for dementia care, respite & convalescent options
Jeffrey C. Lozon, President & CEO
Marc St. Pierre, Manager, Physical Plant

***Wingham:* Braemar Retirement Centre**
719 Josephine St., Wingham, ON N0G 2W0
Tel: 519-357-3430; *Fax:* 519-357-2303
Toll-Free: 888-817-5828
info@braemar-rc.com
www.braemar-rc.com
Number of Beds: 25 beds
Archie Macgowan, Administrator
519-357-3430, macgowana@hurontel.on.ca

Personal Care Homes

***Ottawa:* Governor's Walk AgeCare**
150 Stanley Ave., Ottawa, ON K1M 2J7
Tel: 613-564-9255
www.governorswalkresidence.com
Social Media: www.facebook.com/GovernorsWalk
Note: Services include personal care, dementia care & temporary care

Mental Health Hospitals/Facilities

***Aurora:* Southdown Institute**
1335 St. John's Rd. East, Aurora, ON L4G 3G8
Tel: 905-727-4214; *Fax:* 905-727-4214
www.southdown.on.ca
Number of Beds: 44 beds
Note: Specialties: Residential & outpatient psychological treatment to clergy & religious; Psychodynamic group therapy; Individual & group addiction counselling; 12-step groups; Specialized group treatment for persons who have violated sexual boundaries; Art therapy; Health education
Miriam Ukeritis, CEO

***Brockville:* Brockville Mental Health Centre**
Former Name: Brockville Psychiatric Hospital
PO Box 1050, 1804 Hwy. 2 East, Brockville, ON K6V 5W7
Tel: 613-345-1461; *Fax:* 613-342-6194
mharc@theroyal.ca
www.theroyal.ca
Number of Beds: 200 beds
George Weber, President/CEO
613-722-6521, george.weber@rohcg.on.ca

***Fergus:* Trellis Mental Health & Developmental Services**
Fergus Community Mental Health Clinic
234 St. Patrick St. East, Upper Level, Fergus, ON N1M 1M6
Tel: 519-843-6191; *Fax:* 519-843-7608
Toll-Free: 800-265-7723
www.trellis.on.ca
Note: Services include mental health assessments, medication monitoring, individual & group therapy, & education.
Fred Wagner, Executive Director
519-821-2060

***Guelph:* Homewood Health Centre**
150 Delhi St., Guelph, ON N1E 6K9
Tel: 519-824-1010; *Fax:* 519-824-8751
www.homewood.org/healthcentre/main.php
Social Media: www.facebook.com/403805842986024; twitter.com/homewoodhc; plus.google.com/104148724373320858058/; www.linkedin.com/company/homewood-health-centre
Year Founded: 1883
Number of Beds: 312 beds
Number of Employees: 650
Specialties: Mental Health
Note: Number of Employees: 650; Specialty: Behavioural, addiction & psychiatric services
Jagoda Pike, President & CEO
Colin Ferguson, Vice-President, Hotel Services & Human Resources
Al Van Leeuwen, Vice-President, Planning & Development
Dr. Wilson Lit, Chief Medical Officer
Charlotte Burkhardt, Vice-President, Quality & Patient Experience
Ric Ament, Vice-President, Marketing & Communications
Kimberly Mirotta, Vice-President, Finance
Dan Land, Chief Nursing Officer

***Hamilton:* St. Joseph's Centre for Mountain Health Services**
Affiliated with: St. Joseph's Healthcare Hamilton
PO Box 585, 100 - 5 St. West, Hamilton, ON L8N 3K7
Tel: 905-388-2511; *Fax:* 905-575-6038
www.stjosham.on.ca
Social Media: www.facebook.com/stjosephshealthcarefoundation; twitter.com/STJOESHAMILTON; www.youtube.com/Stjoesfoundation; www.linkedin.com/company/st.-joseph's-healthcare-hamilton
Number of Beds: 650 beds
Specialties: Mental Health
Dr. David Higgins, President
905-522-1155, president@stjoes.ca

***Hamilton:* St. Joseph's Healthcare Hamilton - West 5th Campus**
St. Joseph's Health System
Affiliated with: Hamilton Niagara Haldimand Brant Local Health Integration Network
100 West 5th St., Hamilton, ON L9C 0E3
Tel: 905-522-1155
www.stjosham.on.ca
Info Line: 905-522-4941
Social Media: www.facebook.com/stjosehshealthcarefoundation; twitter.com/STJOESHAMILTON; www.youtube.com/Stjoesfoundation; www.linkedin.com/company/st-joseph's-healthcare-hamilton
Note: Offers mental health & medical services, as well as teaching & research facilities. Affiliated with the Faculty of Health Sciences at McMaster University & Mohawk College.
Dr. David Higgins, President
Romeo Cercone, Vice-President, Quality & Strategic Planning, & Mental Health & Addiction Programs

***Kingston:* Ongwanada Hospital**
191 Portsmouth Ave., Kingston, ON K7M 8A6
Tel: 613-548-4417; *Fax:* 613-548-8135
www.ongwanada.com
Social Media: www.facebook.com/Ongwanada1
Year Founded: 1948
Number of Beds: 227 beds
Note: Specialties: Support for persons with developmental disabilities; Day support; Medical services; Vocational & life skills training; Occupational therapy; Physiotherapy; Hydrotherapy; Snoezelen Room; Community behavioural services; Respite care; Research. Number of employees: 494
Dr. Robert W. Seaby, Executive Director

***Kingston:* Providence Care - Mental Health Services**
Affiliated with: Providence Care
Former Name: Kingston Psychiatric Hospital
PO Box 603, 752 King St., Kingston, ON K7L 4X3
Tel: 613-546-1101; *Fax:* 613-548-5588
prowsea@providencecare.ca
www.pccchealth.org
Number of Beds: 198 beds
Note: Adult Treatment & Rehabilitation, Geriatric Psychiatry, Forensic Psychiatry. Affilated with Queen's University.
Allen Prowse, Vice President, Mental Health; Administrator

***Lindsay:* Chimo Youth & Family Services**
227 Kent St. West, Lindsay, ON K9V 2Z1
Tel: 705-324-3300; *Fax:* 705-324-3304
Toll-Free: 888-454-6275
www.chimoyouth.ca
Note: Chimo Youth & Family Services is accredited under Children's Mental Health Ontario. Programs include clinical & crisis care, group meetings, day treatment, & residential & respite care.

***London:* Child & Parent Resource Institute (CPRI)**
600 Sanatorium Rd., London, ON N6H 3W7
Tel: 519-858-2774; *Fax:* 519-858-3913
Toll-Free: 877-494-2774
www.cpri.ca/content/home/home.aspx
Number of Beds: 75 beds
Dr. Shannon Stewart, Program Manager

***London:* Regional Mental Healthcare, London**
Affiliated with: St. Joseph's Health Care, London
PO Box 5532 Stn. B, 850 Highbury Ave., London, ON N6A 4H1
Tel: 519-455-5110; *Fax:* 519-455-9986
Communications.Department@sjhc.london.on.ca
www.sjhc.london.on.ca

Number of Beds: 385 beds

***North Bay:* North Bay Regional Health Centre - Mental Health Clinic**
Former Name: North Bay Psychiatric Hospital
120 King St. West, North Bay, ON P1B 5Z7
Tel: 705-494-3050; *Fax:* 705-494-3092
www.nbrhc.on.ca

***Oakville:* Central West Specialized Developmental Services**
Former Name: Oaklands Regional Centre
53 Bond St., Oakville, ON L6K 1L8
Tel: 905-844-7864; *Fax:* 905-844-3545
Year Founded: 1975
Note: Specialties: Care & support to persons with multiple developmental disabilities; Basic life skill development; Psychiatry; Behaviour therapy; Occupational therapy; Speech therapy; Respite care

***Ottawa:* Royal Ottawa Mental Health Centre**
1145 Carling Ave., Ottawa, ON K1Z 7K4
Tel: 613-722-6521 *Toll-Free:* 800-987-6424
www.theroyal.ca
Social Media: www.facebook.com/YouKnowWhoIAmROHCG; twitter.com/TheRoyalMHC
Year Founded: 1910
Number of Beds: 188
George Weber, President & CEO
Dr. Raj Bhatla, Psychiatrist-in-Chief
Alison Freeland, Associate Chief, Psychiatry
Dr. A.G. Ahmed, Associate Chief, Integrated Forensic Program
Cal Crocker, Chief Financial Officer
Jim Allin, Vice-President, Patient Care Services
Nicole Loreto, Chief Communications Officer

***Penetanguishene:* Waypoint Centre for Mental Health Care**
Former Name: Penetanguishene Mental Health Centre
500 Church St., Penetanguishene, ON L9M 1G3
Tel: 705-549-3181; *Fax:* 705-549-3778
Toll-Free: 877-341-4729
info@waypointcentre.ca
www.mhcva.on.ca
Year Founded: 1859
Number of Beds: 312
Number of Employees: 1100
Specialties: Mental Health
Carol Lambie, President & CEO
Janet Harris, Vice-President, Clinical Services
Howard Barbaree, Vice-President, Research & Academics
Lorraine Smith, Vice-President, Corporate Services
Angie Bowman, Vice-President, Human Resources & Organizational Development
Bob Savage, Vice-President, Redevelopment
Deborah Duncan, Vice-President, Regional Programs
Dr. Brian Jones, Vice-President, Provincial Forensic Programs
Robert Desroches, Director, Patient/Client Flow
Dr. Jamie Karagianis, Psychiatrist-in-Chief

***St. Thomas:* Southwest Centre for Foresnsic Mental Health Care**
Affiliated with: St. Joseph's Health Care, London
401 Sunset Dr., St. Thomas, ON N5R 3C6
Tel: 519-664-6000
www.sjhc.london.on.ca
Dr. Gillian Kernaghan, President & CEO

***Sudbury:* North Bay Regional Health Centre (NBRHC)/Centre régional de santé de North Bay Kirkwood Place**
Former Name: Northeast Mental Health Centre, Sudbury Campus
680 Kirkwood Dr., Sudbury, ON P3E 1X3
Tel: 705-675-9193; *Fax:* 705-675-6817
pr@nbrhc.on.ca
www.nbrhc.on.ca
Social Media: www.facebook.com/nbrhc; twitter.com/nbrhc; www.youtube.com/thenbrhc
Alison Robinson, Director

***Sudbury:* Sudbury Mental Health and Addictions Centre**
Kirkwood Place
Affiliated with: Health Sciences North
680 Kirkwood Dr., Sudbury, ON P3E 1X3
Tel: 705-675-5900
www.hsnsudbury.ca
Note: Acute inpatient psychiatry services
Dr. Denis-Richard Roy, President & CEO, Health Sciences North
Dr. Chris Bourdon, Chief of Staff, Health Sciences North

***Thunder Bay:* Lakehead Psychiatric Hospital**
Affiliated with: St. Joseph's Care Group
580 Algoma St. North, Thunder Bay, ON P7B 5G4
Tel: 807-343-4300; *Fax:* 807-343-4387
Specialties: Mental Health
Tracey Buckler, President & CEO

***Toronto:* Bellwood Health Services**
Edgewood Health Network Inc.
Affiliated with: Toronto Central Local Health Integration Network
1020 McNicoll Ave., Toronto, ON M1W 2J6
Tel: 416-495-0926; *Fax:* 416-495-7943
Toll-Free: 800-387-6198
info@bellwood.ca
www.bellwood.ca
Social Media: www.facebook.com/bellwoodhealthservices; twitter.com/BellwoodHealth; www.youtube.com/user/BellwoodHealth
Note: Programs & services include: treatment & education for persons who struggle with addictions, such as alcohol & drugs, eating disorders, post traumatic stress disorder, problem gambling, & problematic sexual behaviour; assessment; withdrawal management services; residential treatment program for persons with alcohol addiction; 12-step education & support groups; life skills coaching; stress management; group therapy; & nutritional education & counselling.
M. Linda Bell, Co-Founder
Laura Bhoi, President
Janet Lansche, Vice-President, Finance & Administration
Susan McGrail, Director, Clinical Services
Dr. Mark Weiss, Medical Director
Grace Bautista, Manager, Nursing & Client Services
Michael Hartmann, Manager, PTSD & Trauma Services
Penny Lawson, Manager, Outpatient Services & Behavioural Addictions

***Toronto:* Community Outreach Services (COS)**
Affiliated with: Toronto East General Hospital
#203, 177 Danforth Ave., Toronto, ON M4K 1N2
Tel: 416-461-2000; *Fax:* 416-461-2222
ptrep@tegh.on.ca (Patients); community@tegh.on.ca (Community)
www.tegh.on.ca
Note: Specialties: Community based mental health services; Counselling to adults; Supported housing; Psychiatric treatment; Psycho-social rehabilitation; Family support program; Community & school outreach program

***Toronto:* Thistletown Regional Centre for Children & Adolescents**
51 Panorama Ct., Toronto, ON M9V 4L8
Tel: 416-326-0741; *Fax:* 416-326-9078
Note: Specialties: Counselling for children & youth up to 19 years of age; Family assessment & therapy; Treatment & education for youth with autism & developmental disorders; Sexual abuse treatment & family education; Home support; Outpatient services
Dr. Gail Gonda, Administrator

***Toronto:* Youthdale Treatment Centres**
227 Victoria St., Toronto, ON M5B 1T8
Tel: 416-368-4896; *Fax:* 406-368-5025
www.youthdale.ca
Year Founded: 1969
Note: Youthdale provides mental health services to approximately 5,000 children & their families each year. A crisis service line is available (416-363-9990). The non-profit, charitable community agency also offers clinical services that include psychiatric crisis response, residential treatment, & outpatient consultation.

***Whitby:* Ontario Shores Centre for Mental Health Sciences**
Former Name: Whitby Mental Health Centre
700 Gordon St., Whitby, ON L1N 5S9
Tel: 905-430-4055 *Toll-Free:* 800-341-6323
CentralizedReferralSystem@ontarioshores.ca
www.ontarioshores.ca
Year Founded: 1919
Number of Employees: 1200
Specialties: Mental Health
Note: Specialized, tertiary mental health care on an inpatien/outpatient basis. Residences in Stouffville, Oshawa; community service sites in Newmarket, Georgina, Maple, Uxbridge, Port Perry, Bowmanville, Lindsay & Whitby. Number of staff: 1,200
Karim Mamdani, President/CEO

Special Care Homes

***Aurora:* Kerry's Place Autism Services**
38B Berczy St., Aurora, ON L4G 1W9
Tel: 905-713-6808
tmansell@kerrysplace.org
www.kerrysplace.com
Info Line: 905-579-2720
Year Founded: 1974
Note: autistic adults home
Dr. Glenn Rampton, Executive Director
grampton@kerrysplace.org

***Belleville:* Cheshire Homes (Hastings - Prince Edward) Inc.**
41 Pinnacle St. South, Belleville, ON K8N 3A1
Tel: 613-966-2941; *Fax:* 613-966-2461
receptionist@cheshirehpe.ca
www.cheshirehpe.ca
Year Founded: 1973
Note: Cheshire Homes offers support housing & an outreach program to physically disabled adults.

***Brantford:* Participation House Brantford**
10 Bell Lane, Brantford, ON N3T 5W5
Tel: 519-756-1430
dhunt@participationhousebrantford.org
www.participationhousebrantford.org
Number of Beds: 30 beds
Note: Non-for-profit organization serving the needs of adults with physical disabilities
Steve Leighfield, Executive Director

***Cochrane:* Cochrane Community Living**
PO Box 2330, 18 2nd Ave., Cochrane, ON P0L 1C0
Tel: 705-272-2999
iccl@puc.net
www.communitylivingontario.ca
Number of Beds: 12 beds in 3 facilities
Mac Hiltz, Interim Executive Director

***Collingwood:* Canford House**
695 St. Marie St., Collingwood, ON L9Y 3L4
Tel: 705-445-5203; *Fax:* 705-445-7357
Number of Beds: 32 beds
Wayne Canning, Administrator

***Cornwall:* Open Hands Residential Services**
17383 South Branch Rd., Cornwall, ON K6K 1T3
Tel: 613-933-0012; *Fax:* 613-932-5134
www.ocapdd.on.ca
Note: The non-profit agency offers both residential & daytime community support services to persons with development disabilities. Open Hands is operated by the Ottawa Carleton Association for Persons with Developmental Disabilities (OCAPDD).
David A. Ferguson, Executive Director
dferguson@ocapdd.on.ca

***Dryden:* Patricia Gardens Care Home**
35 Van Horne Ave., Dryden, ON P8N 3B4
Tel: 807-223-5278; *Fax:* 807-223-5273
info@drydenseniorservices.ca
www.drydenseniorservices.ca
Penney Bradley, Program Coordinator
penney.bradley@drytel.net

***East Garafraxa:* Dufferin Association for Community Living**
065371 County Rd. 3, East Garafraxa, ON L9W 7J8
Tel: 519-941-8971; *Fax:* 519-941-9121
info@communitylivingdufferin.ca
www.communitylivingdufferin.ca
Social Media: www.facebook.com/communitylivingdufferin; twitter.com/cldufferin; www.youtube.com/user/CLDufferin/videos
Note: Dufferin Association for Community Living assists children & adults with developmental disabilities.
Residential services include supported independent living, the operation of group homes & a home for adults with Prader Willi Syndrome, a family home program, a transitional living co-operative, & respite care. The association's group homes provide accommodations for 56 adults with developmental disabilities.
Sheryl Chandler, Executive Director
sheryl@communitylivingdufferin.ca

Diane Slater, Director, Adult Services
diane@communitylivingdufferin.ca
Ann Somerville, Director, Business & Finance
ann@communitylivingdufferin.ca
Karen Bowen, Manager, Preschool Resource Program
karen@communitylivingdufferin.ca
Nadene Buck, Manager, Residential
nadene@communitylivingdufferin.ca
Joyce Cook, Manager, Options
joyce@communitylivingdufferin.ca
Teresa Donaldson, Manager, Systems
teresa@communitylivingdufferin.ca
Darlene Morrow, Manager, Residential
darlene@communitylivingdufferin.ca
Lindsay Pendleton, Manager, Residential
lindsay@communitylivingdufferin.ca
Catherine Ryan, Manager, Residential
cryan@communitylivingdufferin.ca
Denyse Small, Manager, Employment Services
denyse@communitylivingdufferin.ca

Gravenhurst: Doe Lake Residence
1750 Gravenhurst Pkwy., Gravenhurst, ON P1P 1R3
Tel: 705-687-6285; *Fax:* 705-687-0100
doelakeresidence@hotmail.com
Angie Joseph, Manager

Hamilton: Good Shepherd Centre
PO Box 1003, 10 Delaware Ave., Hamilton, ON L8N 3R1
Tel: 905-528-9109; *Fax:* 905-528-6967
info@goodshepherdcentres.ca
www.goodshepherdcentres.ca
Year Founded: 1961
Richard MacPhee, Executive Director

Hamilton: Lynwood Hall Child & Family Centre
526 Upper Paradise Rd., Hamilton, ON L9C 5E3
Tel: 905-389-1361
info@lynwoodhall.com
www.lynwoodhall.com
Note: Specialties: Mental health services, including day treatment, home-based services, & residential services
Alex Thomson, Executive Director

Hanmer: Kingsley Residential Home
PO Box 118, 36 Oscar St., Hanmer, ON P3P 1X6
Tel: 705-969-5538
Number of Beds: 6 beds
Jeannine Kingsley, Proprietor

Hanover: Community Living Hanover
521 - 11th Ave., Hanover, ON N4N 2J3
Tel: 519-364-6100; *Fax:* 519-364-7488
www.clhanover.com
Number of Beds: 15 beds
Charlie Caudle, Executive Director

Holland Landing: Cedar Lane Residential Home
19704 Holland Landing Rd., Holland Landing, ON L9N 1M8
Tel: 905-836-4272; *Fax:* 905-836-8277
Cathy Dowling, Contact

Holland Landing: Porter Place, Men's Shelter
18838 Hwy. 11, Holland Landing, ON L9N 0C5
Tel: 905-898-1015; *Fax:* 905-898-6414
Toll-Free: 888-554-5525
www.bluedoorshelters.ca
Number of Beds: 19 beds
Monica Auerbach, Executive Director

Keswick: Pipe & Slipper Home
2926 Old Homestead Rd., Keswick, ON L4P 3E9
Tel: 905-989-0907
Note: Residential care is provided for adults. Referral is necessary.

Kitchener: Sunbeam Lodge
389 Pinnacle Dr., Kitchener, ON N2G 3W5
Tel: 519-886-4222; *Fax:* 519-885-1580
teena@sunbeamlodge.com
www.sunbeamlodge.com
Info Line: 519-886-4700
Number of Beds: 22 beds
Note: Specialties: Lont-term residential care & treatment for children with special needs; Day program; Physiotherapy treatment; Kinesiology; Communications programs; Independent living skills program. Number of Employees: 9 Registered Nurses & Registered Practical Nurses + 2 Kinesiologists + 1 Program Coordinator + 21 Child Care Attendants + 1 Dietician + 2 Housekeepers + 1 Executive Secretary
John Vos, Administrator
Shabnam Vos, Administrator

Kitchener: Sunbeam Residential Development Centre
2749 Kingsway Dr., Kitchener, ON N2C 1A7
Tel: 519-893-6200; *Fax:* 519-893-9034
www.sunbeamcentre.com
Year Founded: 1956
Note: Specialties: Care for individuals with diverse & complex developmental challenges; Long-term & short-term support; Activation; Sensory stimulation
Dr. Shaune Lawton, Executive Director

Lucan: Crest Support Services
13570 Elginfield Rd., RR#1, Lucan, ON N0M 2J0
Tel: 519-227-6766; *Fax:* 519-227-6768
www.crestsupportservices.ca
Note: Specialties: Services for adults with mental health or developmental disabilities; Accommodation services; Operation of three small businesses to provide training & employment opportunities
David Ragobar, Executive Director
david@thecrestcentre.com

Markham: Kinark Child & Family Services
Corporate Office, #200, 500 Hood Rd., Markham, ON L3R 9Z3
Tel: 905-474-9595; *Fax:* 905-474-1448
Toll-Free: 800-230-8533
info@kinark.on.ca
www.kinark.on.ca
Social Media: www.facebook.com/kinark; twitter.com/mykinark; www.youtube.com/user/mykinark
Year Founded: 1916
Number of Employees: 800
Note: Services include crisis services, therapeutic family programs, child care, day treatment, residential treatment, adventure-based programming, autism services, & youth justice services.
Cathy Paul, President & CEO

Markham: Participation House
204 - 4261 Hwy. 7, Markham, ON L3R 9W6
Tel: 905-294-0944; *Fax:* 905-294-7834
postmaster@participationhouse.net
www.participationhouse.net
Number of Beds: 52 beds
Note: Provides services designed to enhance the qualify of life of people with disabilities
Sharon M. Lawlor, Executive Director

Nepean: Total Communication Environment (TCE)
#5, 203 Colonnade Rd. South, Nepean, ON K2E 7K3
Tel: 613-228-0999; *Fax:* 613-228-1402
TTY: 613-228-8669
tceadmin@tceottawa.org
www.tceottawa.org
Year Founded: 1979
Note: Specialties: Services for adults with multiple disabilities & special communication needs; Respite care; Day services; Outreach to long-term care homes
Karen Anderson, Executive Director

Newmarket: Brigitta's Residential Home Inc.
128 Arden Ave., Newmarket, ON L3Y 4H6
Tel: 905-895-5890
Number of Beds: 22 beds
Brigitta Miller, Administrator

Newmarket: Brown's Residential Home
399 Queen St., Newmarket, ON L3Y 2G9
Tel: 905-898-1955; *Fax:* 905-898-1955
Note: Supportive residential care is provided for adults.

Newmarket: Heritage Lodge
508 College St., Newmarket, ON L3Y 1C6
Tel: 905-853-1587; *Fax:* 905-853-1587
Note: Heritage Lodge is a home for special care to assist persons with a mental health disability.

North Bay: Community Living North Bay
161 Main St. East, North Bay, ON P1B 1A9
Tel: 705-476-3288; *Fax:* 705-476-4788
info@communitylivingnorthbay.org
www.communitylivingnorthbay.org
Year Founded: 1954
Jennifer Valenti, Executive Director

Ottawa: Roberts/Smart Centre
1199 Carling Ave., Ottawa, ON K1Z 8N8
Tel: 613-728-1946; *Fax:* 613-728-4986
Toll-Free: 800-279-9941
info@rsc-crs.com
www.robertssmartcentre.com
Number of Beds: 47 beds
Cameron Macleod, Executive Director

Owen Sound: Kent Residential Home
Former Name: Tucker's Residential Home
1065 - 9th Ave. West, Owen Sound, ON N4K 2G5
Tel: 519-371-5029; *Fax:* 519-371-3237
Number of Beds: 18 beds
Note: residential home for people with mental illness
Yvonne Kent

Oxford Mills: Old Mill Guest Home
12 Bridge St., Oxford Mills, ON K0G 1S0
Tel: 613-258-3366
Number of Beds: 22 beds
Note: Specialties: Residential services for post-psychiatric patients; Social programs

Peterborough: Community Living Peterborough
223 Aylmer St., Peterborough, ON K9J 3K3
Tel: 705-743-2411; *Fax:* 705-743-3722
www.communitylivingpeterborough.ca
Social Media: www.facebook.com/CommunityLivingPtbo; twitter.com/CLPeterborough; www.youtube.com/user/CommunityLivingPtbo
Year Founded: 1953
Note: The following services are provided: supported housing for adults over the age of 21; family support; community access; & employment options.
Jack Gillan, Chief Executive Officer
Barb Hiland, Director, Operations
Cindy Hobbins, Manager, Community Development, Communications, & Quality Enhancement
Pat McNamara, Manager
Edna O'Toole, General Manager, Supportive Housing

Petrolia: Lambton County Developmental Services
Former Name: Lambton County Association for Mentally Handicapped
PO Box 1210, 339 Centre St., Petrolia, ON N0N 1R0
Tel: 519-882-0933; *Fax:* 519-882-3386
administration@lcds.on.ca
www.lcds.on.ca
Number of Beds: 68 beds
Note: Provides services to persons with intellectual disabilities
Don Seymour, Executive Director

Powassan: Eide's Residential Home
532 Main St., Powassan, ON P0H 1Z0
Tel: 705-724-2748

Saint-Pascal-Baylon: St. Pascal Residential Home
2454 du Lac Rd., RR#1, Saint-Pascal-Baylon, ON K0A 3N0
Tel: 613-488-2626; *Fax:* 613-488-2626
admin@stpascalresidence.com
www.stpascalresidence.com

Severn Bridge: Trentview House
1647 Kilworthy Rd., RR#1, Severn Bridge, ON L0K 2B0
Tel: 705-689-5685
Year Founded: 1979
Number of Beds: 25 beds
Note: Specialties: Services for adults with mental health disabilities

St Thomas: Tara Hall Residential Care Home
38 Chester St., St Thomas, ON N5R 1V2
Tel: 519-631-4937; *Fax:* 519-631-1526
tarahall@rogers.com
Year Founded: 1988
Number of Beds: 36 beds
Note: Specialties: Assisted living for adults with an intellectual disability, brain injury, or mental illness
James Akey, Manager

St. Catharines: Montebello Place
Former Name: Horvath Residence
1 Montebello St., St. Catharines, ON L2R 6B5
Tel: 905-984-6506
caringplaces.ca/montebello-place.html
Year Founded: 1973
Number of Beds: 15 beds
Sharon Okum, Co-Owner
David Okum, Co-Owner

Thunder Bay: Marcinowsky Residential Home
601 Alice Ave., RR#14, Thunder Bay, ON P7G 1X1
Tel: 807-767-6199

***Toronto:* Community Head Injury Resource Services (CHIRS)**
Former Name: Ashby House
62 Finch Ave. West, Toronto, ON M2N 7G1
Tel: 416-240-8000; *Fax:* 416-240-1149
Chirs@chirs.com
www.chirs.com
Social Media: www.facebook.com/chirstoronto
Year Founded: 1974
Number of Employees: 160
Note: A range of residential services are offered for persons living with the effects of acquired brain injury. Community Head Injury Resource Services serves the Greater Toronto Area.
Hedy Chandler, Contact
hedyc@rogers.com

***Toronto:* Griffin Centre**
24 Silverview Dr., Toronto, ON M2M 2B3
Tel: 416-222-1153; *Fax:* 416-222-1321
contact@griffin-centre.org
www.griffin-centre.org
Number of Beds: 10 beds
Laurie Dart, Executive Director

***Toronto:* Hincks-Dellcrest Treatment Centre**
440 Jarvis St., Toronto, ON M4Y 2H4
Tel: 416-924-1164; *Fax:* 416-924-8208
info@hincksdellcrest.org
www.hincksdellcrest.org
Social Media: www.facebook.com/255128254500066; twitter.com/hincksdellcrest; www.youtube.com/thehincksdellcrest
Note: Children's mental health
John Spekkens, Executive Director

***Toronto:* Salvation Army Broadview Village**
1132 Broadview Ave., Toronto, ON M4K 2S5
Tel: 416-425-1052 *Toll-Free:* 888-333-1229
www.salvationarmy.ca
Number of Beds: 61 beds
Note: Facility for adults with developmental disabilities
Capt. Glenda Davis, Director

***Vars:* Pine Rest Residence**
PO Box 109, 5876 Bearbrook Rd., Vars, ON K0A 3H0
Tel: 613-835-2849; *Fax:* 613-835-9335
Number of Beds: 33 residential capacity
Note: Specialties: Residential care for persons with developmental disabilities, psychiatric disabilities, or those who suffer from alcoholism; Medication supervision; Respite care
Raymond Meloche, Administrator

***Vars:* Résidence Ste-Marie/Ste-Marie Residence**
5855, rue Buckland RR#2, Vars, ON K0H 3H0
Tel: 613-835-2525
Number of Beds: 40 lits
Note: Spécialisée à la prestation des soins aux personnes atteintes de maladie mentale grave; soins infirmiers, activités hebdomadaires
Gaétan Brisson, Propriétaire
Suzanne Brisson, Propriétaire

***Vineland:* Amber Lodge**
4024 Martin Rd., Vineland, ON L0R 2E0
Tel: 905-562-7272; *Fax:* 905-892-9700
William Ram, Administrator/Owner

***Vineland:* Bethesda Home for the Mentally Handicapped Inc.**
3950 Fly Rd., Vineland, ON L0R 2C0
Tel: 905-684-6918; *Fax:* 905-684-6918
info@bethesdaservices.com
www.bethesdaservices.com
Number of Beds: 42 beds
Donald Boese, Executive Director

***Waterloo:* Children's Mental Health Services Lutherwood**
285 Benjamin Rd., Waterloo, ON N2J 3Z4
Tel: 519-884-1470; *Fax:* 519-886-8479
www.lutherwood.ca
Number of Beds: 6 beds (Bridgelands program); 10 beds (Woodlands program)
Note: Specialties: Day treatment program; Residential treatment program; Group & individual skills training; Individual & family counselling; Home support; Community integration; Crisis support

***Waterloo:* Lutherwood**
285 Benjamin Rd., Waterloo, ON N2J 3Z4
Tel: 519-884-7755; *Fax:* 519-884-9071
www.lutherwood.ca
Social Media: www.facebook.com/lutherwoodjobs; twitter.com/lutherwood; www.youtube.com/user/LutherwoodCanada; www.linkedin.com/company/lutherwood
Year Founded: 1970
Number of Employees: 500
Note: Specialties: Mental health services for children & families, including assessment, a youth shelter, housing support services, residential treatment, family crisis & prevention counselling, a community services program, & school-based interventions; Senior services, including independent & supported living resources
John Colangeli, CEO

***Waterloo:* Underhill Residential Home**
127 Erb St. West, Waterloo, ON N2L 1T7
Tel: 519-884-7160; *Fax:* 519-884-5936
Note: Specialties: Residential & personal care services for seniors & persons with mental health concerns

Prince Edward Island

Government Departments in Charge

***Charlottetown:* Prince Edward Island Department of Health & Wellness**
PO Box 2000, 105 Rochford St., 4th Fl. North, Charlottetown, PE C1A 7N8
Tel: 902-368-6414; *Fax:* 902-368-4121
www.gov.pe.ca/health
Hon. Robert Henderson, Minister, Health & Wellness

Regional Health Authorities

***Charlottetown:* Health PEI**
PO Box 2000, 16 Garfield St., Charlottetown, PE C1A 7N8
Tel: 902-368-6130; *Fax:* 902-368-6136
healthinput@gov.pe.ca
www.healthpei.ca
Info Line: 811
Social Media: twitter.com/health_pei
Year Founded: 2010
Number of Beds: 575 long-term care beds
Population Served: 146105; *Number of Employees:* 3900
Note: Health PEI is responsible for the operation & delivery of publicly funded health services in Prince Edward Island.
Phyllis Horne, Board Chair
phorne@gov.pe.ca
Dr. Michael Mayne, Chief Executive Officer
Darlene Gillis, Senior Communications Officer
ddgillis@gov.pe.ca

Hospitals - General

***Alberton:* Western Hospital**
Affiliated with: Health PEI
PO Box 10, 148 Poplar St., Alberton, PE C0B 1B0
Tel: 902-853-8650; *Fax:* 902-853-8658
www.healthpei.ca/westernhospital
Number of Beds: 25 beds
Population Served: 8,000

***Charlottetown:* Queen Elizabeth Hospital Inc. (QEH)**
Affiliated with: Health PEI
PO Box 6600, 60 Riverside Dr., Charlottetown, PE C1A 8T5
Tel: 902-894-2111
TTY: 902-894-2204
www.healthpei.ca/qeh
Year Founded: 1982
Number of Beds: 243 beds
Note: Acute care hospital, with burn care services; coronary care; psychiatry; physiotherapy; occupational therapy; orthpedic & specialized gynecological surgery; eye surgery; plastic surgery; neonatal intensive care; cancer care; diagnostic imaging
Dr. Michael Mayne, Chief Executive Officer, Health PEI

***Montague:* King's County Memorial Hospital**
Affiliated with: Health PEI
PO Box 490, 409 McIntyre Ave., Montague, PE C0A 1R0
Tel: 902-838-0777; *Fax:* 902-838-0770
www.healthpei.ca/kcmh
Number of Beds: 30 beds

***O'Leary:* Community Hospital O'Leary**
Affiliated with: Health PEI
PO Box 160, 14 MacKinnon Dr., O'Leary, PE C0B 1V0
Tel: 902-859-8700; *Fax:* 902-859-8774
www.healthpei.ca/cho
Year Founded: 1957
Number of Beds: 13 extended care beds
Note: Specialties: Acute care; Immunization program; Lifeline emergency response system; Long-term care (Phone: 902-859-8750, Fax: 902-859-8756); Respite care

***Souris:* Souris Hospital**
Affiliated with: Health PEI
PO Box 640, 17 Knights Ave., Souris, PE C0A 2B0
Tel: 902-687-7150; *Fax:* 902-687-7175
www.healthpei.ca/sourishospital
Number of Beds: 17 beds
Population Served: 7,000
Note: Acute care rural facility. Services include acute and ambulatory care; x-ray; pyhsiotherapy; occupatioanl therapy; nutrition counseling; dialysis; diabetes programs; private dental clinic

***Summerside:* Prince County Hospital (PCH)**
Affiliated with: Health PEI
PO Box 3000, 65 Roy Boates Ave., Summerside, PE C1N 2A9
Tel: 902-432-2500; *Fax:* 902-438-4511
www.healthpei.ca/pch
Number of Beds: 110 beds
Note: Specialties: Emergency, surgery, internal medicine, obstetrics, pediatrics, psychiatry, radiology, rehabilitation, oncology
Arlene Gallant-Bernard, Chief Administrative Officer

***Tyne Valley:* Stewart Memorial Hospital**
Affiliated with: Health PEI
PO Box 10, 6926 RR#12, Tyne Valley, PE C0B 2C0
Tel: 902-831-7900; *Fax:* 902-831-7901
www.healthpei.ca/smh
Number of Beds: 23 beds
Note: Specialties: Acute care; Long-term care, Respite care; Palliative care

Community Health Care Centres

***Charlottetown:* Home Care Support - Hillsborough Hospital**
Affiliated with: Health PEI
Hillsborough Hospital Annex, 115 Deacon Grove Lane, Charlottetown, PE C1A 7N5
Tel: 902-368-4790

***Montague:* Home Care Support - Health PEI Montague**
Affiliated with: Health PEI
PO Box 490, 6 Harmony Lane, Montague, PE C0A 1R0
Tel: 902-838-0786

***O'Leary:* Home Care Support - Community Hospital**
Affiliated with: Health PEI
PO Box 160, 14 MacKinnon Dr., O'Leary, PE C0B 1V0
Tel: 902-859-8730

Special Treatment Centres

***Charlottetown:* Euston Street Group Home**
Affiliated with: Health PEI
190 Euston St., Charlottetown, PE C1A 1W8
Tel: 902-566-2964
Note: Respite care is available for adolescents who are in the care of the Director of Child Welfare.

***Charlottetown:* Provincial Addictions Treatment Facility**
PO Box 2000, 2814 Route 215, Mt. Herbert, Charlottetown, PE C1A 7N8
Tel: 902-368-4120; *Fax:* 902-368-6229
Toll-Free: 888-299-8399
www.healthpei.ca
Number of Beds: 24 withdrawal management beds, 16 rehab beds
Specialties: Medically supervised detoxification

***Tracadie Cross:* Provincial Adolescent Group Home**
171 Station Rd., Tracadie Cross, PE C1A 7N8
Tel: 902-676-3242; *Fax:* 902-676-3241
Number of Beds: 9 beds; 1 emergency 72-hour bed
Note: adolescent residential treatment
Scott Gregory, Contact

Long Term Care Facilities

***Alberton:* Partners in Action**
Affiliated with: Health PEI
120 Dufferin St., Alberton, PE C0B 1B0
Tel: 902-853-3109
Note: community care & beds

***Belfast:* Dr. John Gillis Memorial Lodge**
General Delivery, Belfast, PE C0A 1A0
Tel: 902-659-2337; *Fax:* 902-659-2865
www.gillislodge.com
Number of Beds: 62 beds
Douglas MacKenzie
douglas@gillislodge.com

***Charlottetown:* Andrews of Charlottetown**
Affiliated with: Health PEI
73 Malpeque Rd., Charlottetown, PE C1A 7J9
Tel: 902-368-2790; *Fax:* 902-894-3464
info@andrewsofpei.com
andrewsofpei.com/andrews-of-charlottetown.php
Number of Beds: 72 beds
Note: community care beds

***Charlottetown:* Champion Lodge**
Affiliated with: Health PEI
48 Green St., Charlottetown, PE C1A 2E8
Tel: 902-894-8968

***Charlottetown:* Charlotte Residence**
Affiliated with: Health PEI
39 All Souls Lane, Charlottetown, PE C1A 1P9
Tel: 902-894-8134

***Charlottetown:* Corrigan Lodge**
Affiliated with: Health PEI
8 Ellis Rd., Charlottetown, PE C1A 8N4
Tel: 902-894-7837
Note: community care beds
Noreen Corrigan, Contact

***Charlottetown:* Langille House**
Affiliated with: Health PEI
#212, 214 Kent St., Charlottetown, PE C1A 1P2
Tel: 902-628-8228
Note: community care beds

***Charlottetown:* McQuaid Lodge**
Affiliated with: Health PEI
36 Kent St., Charlottetown, PE C1A 1M8
Tel: 902-892-0791

***Charlottetown:* Old Rose Lodge**
Affiliated with: Health PEI
319 Queen St., Charlottetown, PE C1A 4C4
Tel: 902-368-8313; *Fax:* 902-368-8313

***Charlottetown:* Stamper Residence**
Affiliated with: Health PEI
29 Fitzroy St., Charlottetown, PE C1A 1R2
Tel: 902-894-3815
Joyce Pickles, Administrator

***Charlottetown:* Tenderwood Lodge Inc.**
Affiliated with: Health PEI
15 Hawthorne Ave., Charlottetown, PE C1A 5X8
Tel: 902-566-5174

***Crapaud:* South Shore Villa**
Affiliated with: Health PEI
PO Box 111, Sherwood Forest Dr., RR#2, Crapaud, PE C0A 1J0
Tel: 902-658-2228; *Fax:* 902-658-2576
info@southshorevilla.ca
www.southshorevilla.ca

***Georgetown:* Carroll's Lodge**
Affiliated with: Health PEI
PO Box 133, 110 Gordon St., Georgetown, PE C0A 1L0
Tel: 902-652-2369

***Hunter River:* Rosewood Residence**
Affiliated with: Health PEI
PO Box 97, 4260 Hopedale Rd., Route 13, Hunter River, PE C0A 1N0
Tel: 902-964-2436; *Fax:* 902-964-2436
www.rosewoodresidence.ca
Note: community care beds

***Kensington:* MacEwen Mews Seniors Residence**
Affiliated with: Health PEI
RR#6, Kensington, PE C0B 1M0
Tel: 902-836-4678

***Lower Montague:* French Creek Lodge**
Affiliated with: Health PEI
945 Rte. 17, Lower Montague, PE C0A 1R0
Tel: 902-838-4298; *Fax:* 902-838-2764
frenchcreeklodge@bellaliant.com
www.frenchcreeklodgepei.com
Social Media:
www.facebook.com/pages/French-Creek-Lodge/497232373712955
Number of Beds: 40 beds
Note: community care beds

***Miscouche:* Miscouche Community Care Villa**
Affiliated with: Health PEI
PO Box 40, 20 Lady Slipper Dr. North, Miscouche, PE C0B 1T0
Tel: 902-436-1946; *Fax:* 902-436-3215
Note: community care beds

***Montague:* MacKinnon Pines Lodge**
Affiliated with: Health PEI
PO Box 847, Montague, PE C0A 1R0
Tel: 902-838-2656; *Fax:* 902-838-3542

***O'Leary:* Lady Slipper Villa**
Affiliated with: Health PEI
490 Main St., O'Leary, PE C0B 1V0
Tel: 902-859-3544; *Fax:* 902-859-3255
ladyslippervilla@peiseniorshomes.com
ladyslippervilla.peiseniorshomes.com/ladyslippervilla
Note: community care beds
Karen Cook, Administrator

***Souris:* Bayview Lodge Community Care Facility**
Affiliated with: Health PEI
22 Washington St., Souris, PE C0A 2R0
Tel: 902-687-3122; *Fax:* 902-687-3512
Note: community care beds
Gerard Arsenault, Contact

***Summerside:* Andrews of Summerside**
Affiliated with: Health PEI
317 Pope Rd., Summerside, PE C1N 6G4
Tel: 902-436-0859; *Fax:* 902-436-1565
info@andrewsofpei.com
www.andrewsofpei.com/andrews-of-summerside.php
Note: community care facility

***Summerside:* MacDonald's Community Care Home Inc.**
Affiliated with: Health PEI
197 Cambridge St., Summerside, PE C1N 1N1
Tel: 902-436-7359; *Fax:* 902-436-7359
Gail MacDonald, Contact

***Tignish:* Tignish Seniors Home Care Cooperative Limited**
Affiliated with: Health PEI
116 MacLeod Lane, Tignish, PE C0B 2B0
Tel: 902-882-4663
Year Founded: 2002
Note: Specialty: Assisted living

Nursing Homes

***Alberton:* Maplewood Manor**
Affiliated with: Health PEI
PO Box 400, 405 Church St., Alberton, PE C0B 1B0
Tel: 902-853-8610; *Fax:* 902-853-8616
Number of Beds: 48 beds

***Charlottetown:* Beach Grove Home**
Affiliated with: Health PEI
200 Beach Grove Rd., Charlottetown, PE C1E 1L3
Tel: 902-368-6750; *Fax:* 902-368-6764
Number of Beds: 131 beds

***Charlottetown:* Garden Home**
Affiliated with: Health PEI
310 North River Rd., Charlottetown, PE C1A 3M4
Tel: 902-892-4131; *Fax:* 902-892-7326
office@peiseniorshomes.com
gardenhome.peiseniorshomes.com/gardenhome
Note: private
Phyllis Johnson, General Manager, Director of Care
generalmanager@peiseniorshomes.com

***Charlottetown:* Lennox Nursing Home**
140 Water St., Charlottetown, PE C1A 1A7
Tel: 902-894-4968; *Fax:* 902-368-2004
Note: private

***Charlottetown:* MacMillan Lodge Ltd.**
Affiliated with: Health PEI
215 Sydney St., Charlottetown, PE C1A 1J5
Tel: 902-894-7173; *Fax:* 902-894-3818
mlnursing@peiseniorshomes.com
Year Founded: 1999
Ann MacNeill, Director, Care

***Charlottetown:* Park West Lodge**
Affiliated with: Health PEI
22 Richmond St., Charlottetown, PE C1A 1H4
Tel: 902-566-2260; *Fax:* 902-894-7818
Gerry MacPhee, Contact

***Charlottetown:* PEI Atlantic Baptist Homes Inc.**
Affiliated with: Health PEI
16 Centennial Dr., Charlottetown, PE C1A 5C5
Tel: 902-566-5975
www.abschi.com
Note: Specialty: Long-term care by an interdisciplinary team

***Charlottetown:* The Prince Edward Home**
Affiliated with: Health PEI
75 Maypoint Rd., Charlottetown, PE C1E 3H1
Tel: 902-368-4607; *Fax:* 902-368-5646
www.healthpei.ca/pehome
Number of Beds: 120 beds
Note: Palliative care, convalescent, respite care; long-term care; day program for seniors; meals-on-wheels program

***Montague:* Riverview Manor**
Affiliated with: Health PEI
PO Box 820, 14 Rosedale Rd., Montague, PE C0A 1R0
Tel: 902-838-0772; *Fax:* 902-838-5294
www.healthpei.ca/riverviewmanor
Number of Beds: 49 beds
Note: Long-term & palliative care

***Souris:* Colville Manor**
Affiliated with: Health PEI
PO Box 640, 20 MacPhee Ave., Souris, PE C0A 2B0
Tel: 902-687-7090; *Fax:* 902-687-7103
www.healthpei.ca/colvillemanor
Number of Beds: 52 beds; 4 households, each with 13 residents in this facility

***Summerside:* Summerset Manor**
Affiliated with: Health PEI
15 Frank Mellish St., Summerside, PE C1N 0H3
Tel: 902-888-8310; *Fax:* 902-888-8338
Number of Beds: 82 beds
Note: Specialties: Long-term care; Operation of the Chapman Centre, a day program that provides therapeutic services to seniors who live in their own home; Physiotherapy; Occupational therapy; Foot care; Respite care

***Summerside:* Wedgewood Manor**
Affiliated with: Health PEI
310 Brophy St., Summerside, PE C1N 5N4
Tel: 902-888-8340; *Fax:* 902-888-8369
www.healthpei.ca/wedgewoodmanor
Number of Beds: 76 beds

Personal Care Homes

***Charlottetown:* Corrigan Lodge / Corrigan Home Inc.**
Affiliated with: Health PEI
8 Ellis Rd., Charlottetown, PE C1A 8N4
Tel: 902-894-7837
Note: The licensed community care facility is privately owned & operated.
Noreen Corrigan, Contact

***Charlottetown:* Elm Crest Lodge**
Affiliated with: Health PEI
267 Richmond St., Charlottetown, PE C1A 1J7
Tel: 902-566-5996
Note: Elm Crest Lodge is a privately owned community care facility, licensed in Prince Edward Island.

***Kensington:* Clinton View Lodge**
PO Box 8, Kensington, PE C0B 1M0
Tel: 902-866-2276; *Fax:* 902-886-2073
Note: The community care facility is privately owned. It is located at 30 Clinton View Court in Clinton.
Sherry Cole, Contact

***Wellington:* La Coopérative Le Chez-Nous Ltée**
Affiliated with: Health PEI
PO Box 40, 64 Sunset Dr., Wellington, PE C0B 2E0
Tel: 902-854-3426; *Fax:* 902-854-3055
cheznous@pei.aibn.com

Year Founded: 1993
Area Served: Évangéline region
Note: The community care facility is privately owned & operated. French is spoken at the housing complex.
Edgar Arsenault, Director

Mental Health Hospitals/Facilities

Charlottetown: **Hillsborough Hospital & Special Care Centre**
Affiliated with: Health PEI
PO Box 1929, 115 Murchison Lane, Charlottetown, PE C1A 7N5
Tel: 902-368-5400; *Fax:* 902-368-5467
Number of Beds: 75 beds
Note: Specialties: Psychiatry; Medical services for persons with acute or long-term mental illnesses or mental handicaps, & psychogeriatric patients; Day services for former patients; Assessment; Behavioural management

Charlottetown: **Sherwood Home**
Affiliated with: Health PEI
75 Murchison Lane, Charlottetown, PE C1N 7N5
Tel: 902-368-4141; *Fax:* 902-368-4931
Note: Sherwood Home is a provincial residential service for persons with physical and/or developmental disabilities. The home offers residential, respite and day program services.

Québec

Département gouvernemental responsable

Québec: **Ministère de la Santé et des services sociaux**
1075, ch Ste-Foy, Québec, QC G1S 2M1
Tél: 418-266-7171; *Téléc:* 418-266-7197
ministre@msss.gouv.qc.ca
www.msss.gouv.qc.ca
Hon. Gaétan Barrette, Ministre de la Santé et des Services sociaux
418-266-7171, ministre@msss.gouv.qc.ca

Agences de la santé et de services sociaux

Baie-Comeau: **Centre intégré de santé et de services sociaux de la Côte-Nord**
835, boul Jolliet, Baie-Comeau, QC G5C 1P5
Tél: 418-589-9845; *Téléc:* 418-589-8574
Ligne sans frais: 800-463-5142
www.cisss-cotenord.gouv.qc.ca
Info Line: 811
Média social: www.facebook.com/cisss.cotenord
Région desservi: Tadoussac à Blanc-Sablon, 1,300 km;
Population desservi: 94 752
Marc Fortin, Président-directeur général

Cap-aux-Meules: **Centre intégré de santé et de services sociaux des Iles**
430, ch Principal, Cap-aux-Meules, QC G4T 1R9
Tél: 418-986-2121
www.cisssdesiles.com
Info Line: 811
Média social: www.facebook.com/151244821567542
Population desservi: 80 353
Yvette Fortier, Présidente-directrice générale

Châteauguay: **Centre intégré de santé et de services sociaux de la Montérégie-Ouest**
200, boul Brisebois, Châteauguay, QC J6K 4W8
Tél: 450-699-2425
www.santemo.quebec
Info Line: 811
Population desservi: 430 000; *Personnel:* 8700
Yves Masse, Président-directeur général
Claude Jolin, Président, Conseil d'administration

Chibougamau: **Centre régional de santé et services sociaux de la Baie-James (CRSSSBJ)**
Également connu sous le nom de: CRSSS de la Baie-James
312, 3e rue, Chibougamau, QC G8P 1N5
Tél: 418-748-3575; *Téléc:* 418-748-6391
Ligne sans frais: 866-748-2676
info.crsssbj@ssss.gouv.qc.ca
www.crsssbaiejames.gouv.qc.ca
Média social: www.facebook.com/CRSSSBJ
Fondée en: 1996
Région desservi: Nord-du-Québec
Note: Centres de santé (CS): Centre de santé René-Ricard; Centre de santé de Chibougamau; Centre de santé Lebel; Centre de santé Isle-Dieu; Centre de santé de Radisson
Nathalie Boisvert, Présidente-directrice générale
Dr Éric Goyer, Directeur, Santé publique
Jean-Luc Imbeault, Directeur, ressources financières, techniques et informationnelles
Dr Jean Lemoyne, Directeur, services professionnels, et des services multidisciplinaires
Luc Néron, Directeur, soins infirmiers
Jean-Pierre Savary, Directeur, Ressources humaines

Chicoutimi: **Centre intégré universitaire de santé et de services sociaux du Saguenay-Lac-St-Jean**
Également connu sous le nom de: CIUSSS Saguenay-Lac-St-Jean
930, rue Jacques-Cartier est, Chicoutimi, QC G7H 7K9
Tél: 418-545-4980; *Téléc:* 418-545-0806
Ligne sans frais: 800-370-4980
info@santesaglac.gouv.qc.ca
santesaglac.com
Info Line: 811
Média social: www.facebook.com/SanteSagLac; twitter.com/CIUSSS_SLSJ
Population desservi: 278 560; *Personnel:* 8400
Martine Couture, Présidente-directrice générale
Gilles Gagnon, Président-directeur général adjoint
Julie Labbé, Directrice, Ressources humaines et communications
Michel Martel, Directeur, Ressources financières
Donald Aubin, Directeur, Santé publique
Marc Thibeault, Directeur général, adjoint aux programmes sociaux et de réadaptation

Chisasibi: **Conseil Cri de la santé et des services sociaux de la Baie James (CCSSSBJ)/Cree Board of Health & Social Services of James Bay**
PO Box 250, Chisasibi, QC J0M 1E0
Tél: 819-855-2744; *Fax:* 819-855-2098
ccsssbj-cbhssjb@ssss.gouv.qc.ca
www.creehealth.org
Social Media: www.facebook.com/creehealth; twitter.com/creehealth; youtube.com/creehealth
Year Founded: 1978
Area Served: Terres-Cries-de-la-Baie-James
Bella M. Petawabano, Président/représentant de l'Autorité regional des cris

Gaspé: **Centre intégré de santé et de services sociaux de la Gaspésie**
215, boul de York Ouest, Gaspé, QC G4X 2W2
Tél: 418-368-3301; *Téléc:* 418-368-6850
www.cisss-gaspesie.gouv.qc.ca
Info Line: 811
Fondée en: 2015
Population desservi: 80 353
Chantal Duguay, Présidente-directrice générale

Gatineau: **Centre intégré de santé et de services sociaux de l'Outaouais**
80, av Gatineau, Gatineau, QC J8T 4J3
Tél: 819-966-6000; *Téléc:* 819-966-6570
Ligne sans frais: 800-267-2325
relationaveclacommunauteagence07@ssss.gouv.qc.ca
santeoutaouais.qc.ca
Info Line: 811
Population desservi: 389 496
Note: Centres de santé et de services sociaux (CSSS): CSSS du Pontiac; CSSS de la Vallée-de-la-Gatineau; CSSS des Collines; CSSS de Gatineau; CSSS de Papineau
Jean Hébert, Président-directeur général

Greenfield Park: **Centre intégré de santé et de services sociaux de la Montérégie-Centre**
3120, boul Taschereau, Greenfield Park, QC J4V 2G9
Tél: 450-466-5000; *Téléc:* 450-466-8887
www.santemc.quebec
Info Line: 811
Population desservi: 383 000; *Personnel:* 8900
Richard Deschamps, Président-directeur général

Joliette: **Centre intégré de santé et de services sociaux de Lanaudière**
260, rue Lavaltrie Sud, Joliette, QC J6E 5X7
Tél: 450-759-1157; *Téléc:* 450-756-1157
Ligne sans frais: 800-668-9229
santelanaudiere@ssss.gouv.qc.ca
www.santelanaudiere.qc.ca
Info Line: 811
Population desservi: 502 846
Note: Centres de santé et de services sociaux (CSSS): CSSS du Sud de Lanaudière; CSSS du Nord de Lanaudière
Daniel Castonguay, Président-Directeur général
Jacques Perreault, Président, Conseil d'administration

Kuujjuaq: **Régie régionale de la santé et des services sociaux Nunavik (RRSSSN)/Nunavik Regional Board of Health & Social Services**
PO Box 900, Kuujjuaq, QC J0M 1C0
Tel: 819-964-2222; *Fax:* 819-964-2277
info@sante-services-sociaux.ca
www.sante-services-sociaux.ca
Social Media: www.facebook.com/perspectivenunavik; twitter.com/PNunavik; vimeo.com/user21609307; www.linkedin.com/company/3480026
Number of Beds: 50 lits; 12 lits (personnes en perte d'autonomie); 14 lits (direction régionale de la réadaptation)
Area Served: Nunavik; 14 communautés; sous-régions: Hudson et Ungava; *Number of Employees:* 65

Laval: **Centre intégré de santé et de services sociaux de Laval**
Également connu sous le nom de: CISSS de Laval
1755, boul René-Laennec, Laval, QC H7M 3L9
Tél: 450-688-1010
communications.cissslaval@ssss.gouv.qc.ca
www.lavalensante.com
Info Line: 811
Média social: www.facebook.com/cissslaval; twitter.com/cissslaval; www.youtube.com/csssdelaval
Fondée en: 2015
Population desservi: 429 430
Note: Centres de santé et de services sociaux (CSSS): CSSS de Laval
Caroline Barbir, Présidente-directrice générale
Yves Carignan, Président, Conseil d'administration

Montréal: **Centre intégré universitaire de santé et de services sociaux de l'Ouest-de-l'Ile-de-Montréal**
Institut universitaire en santé mentale Douglas, 6875, boul Lasalle, Pavillon Dobel, Montréal, QC H4H 1R3
Tél: 514-630-2123; *Téléc:* 514-888-4462
informations.comtl@ssss.gouv.qc.ca
www.ciusss-ouestmtl.gouv.qc.ca
Info Line: 811
Population desservi: 360 549
Benoît Morin, Président-directeur général

Montréal: **Centre intégré universitaire de santé et de services sociaux du Centre-Ouest-de-l'Ile-de-Montréal**
#119B, 3755, ch de la Côte Sainte-Cather, Montréal, QC H3T 1E2
Tél: 514-340-8222
www.ciusss-centreouestmtl.gouv.qc.ca
Info Line: 811
Population desservi: 368 740
Lawrence Rosenberg, Président-directeur général

Montréal: **Centre intégré universitaire de santé et de services sociaux du Centre-Sud-de-l'Ile-de-Montréal**
6161, rue Laurendeau, Montréal, QC H4E 3X6
Tél: 514-362-1000; *Téléc:* 514-732-5107
www.ciusss-centresudmtl.gouv.qc.ca
Média social: www.facebook.com/ciusss.csmtl; twitter.com/ciusss_csmtl; www.linkedin.com/company/ciusss-centre-sud-de-l'île-de-montréal
Population desservi: 299 555
Sonia Bélanger, Présidente-directrice générale

Montréal: **Centre intégré universitaire de santé et de services sociaux du Nord-de-l'Ile-de-Montréal**
555, boul Gouin ouest, Montréal, QC H3L 1K5
Tél: 514-336-6673
ciusss-nordmtl.gouv.qc.ca
Média social: fr-ca.facebook.com/CIUSSSnmtl
Population desservi: 436 177
Pierre Gfeller, Président-directeur général

Montréal: **Centre intégré universitaire de santé et de services sociaux de l'Est-de-l'Ile-de-Montréal**
5415, boul de l'Assomption, Montréal, QC H1T 2M4
Tél: 514-251-4000
www.ciusss-estmtl.gouv.qc.ca
Nombre de lits: 1279 lits de courte durée; 2502 lits d'hébergement de longue durée
Population desservi: 527 085
Yvan Gendron, Président-directeur général

Québec: Centre intégré universitaire de santé et de services sociaux de la Capitale-Nationale
Également connu sous le nom de: CIUSSS de la Capitale-Nationale
2915, av du Bourg-Royal, Québec, QC G1C 3S2
Tél: 418-266-1019; *Téléc:* 418-661-2845
www.ciusss-capitalenationale.gouv.qc.ca
Info Line: 811
Média social: www.facebook.com/538181276359816; twitter.com/CIUSSS_CN; www.youtube.com/channel/UCVtRERklhHKX0VTGRpL-mIA
Fondée en: 2015
Région desservi: Les territoires de Charlevoix et de Portneuf (69 municipalités); *Population desservi:* 736 787
Note: Le CIUSSS de la Capitale-Nationale est la fusion des Agence de la santé et des services sociaux de la Capitale-Nationale, Centre de réadaptation en déficience intellectuelle de Québec (CDRIQ), Centre de réadaptation en dépendance de Québec, CSSS de Charlevoix, CSSS de la Vieille-Capitale, CSSS de Portneuf, CSSS de Québec-Nord, Centre jeunesse de Québec-Institut universitaire, Institut de réadaptation en déficience physique de Québec (IRDPQ), Institut universitaire en santé mentale de Québec (IUSMQ) et Hôpital Jeffrey Hale-Saint Brigid's (établissement regroupé).
Michel Delamarre, Président-directeur général
Simon Lemay, Président, Conseil d'administration

Rimouski: Centre intégré de santé et de services sociaux du Bas-St-Laurent
Également connu sous le nom de: CISSS Bas-St-Laurent
355, boul Saint-Germain ouest, Rimouski, QC G5L 3N2
Tél: 418-724-3000
www.cisss-bsl.gouv.qc.ca
Info Line: 811
Nombre de lits: 476 lits de courte durée
Personnel: 8000
Isabelle Malo, Présidente-directrice générale
Hughes St-Pierre, Président, Conseil d'administration

Rouyn-Noranda: Centre intégré de santé et de services sociaux de l'Abitibi-Témiscamingue
1, 9e rue, Rouyn-Noranda, QC J9X 2A9
Tél: 819-764-3264; *Téléc:* 819-764-2948
info_sante-abitibi-temiscamingue@ssss.gouv.qc.ca
www.sante-abitibi-temiscamingue.gouv.qc.ca
Info Line: 811
Fondée en: 2015
Région desservi: La région de l'Abitibi-Témiscamingue (65 municipalités)
Note: Centres de santé et de services sociaux (CSSS): CSSS des Aurores-Boréales; CSSS les Eskers de l'Abitibi; CSSS de Rouyn-Noranda; CSSS de la Vallée-de-l'Or; CSSS du Témiscamingue
Jacques Boissonneault, Président-directeur général
Claude Morin, Président, Conseil d'administration

Saint-Hyacinthe: Centre intégré de santé et de services sociaux de la Montérégie-Est
2750, boul Laframboise, Saint-Hyacinthe, QC J2S 4Y8
Tél: 450-771-3333
santeme.quebec
Fondée en: 2015
Population desservi: 523 227; *Personnel:* 11800
Louise Potvin, Présidente-directrice générale

Saint-Jérôme: Centre intégré de santé et de services sociaux des Laurentides
290, rue Montigny, Saint-Jérôme, QC J7Z 5T3
Tél: 450-432-2777 *Ligne sans frais:* 866-963-2777
www.santelaurentides.qc.ca
Info Line: 811
Fondée en: 2015
Population desservi: 595 202; *Personnel:* 14000
Jean-François Foisy, Président-directeur général
André Poirier, Président, Conseil d'administration

Sainte-Marie: Centre intégré de santé et de services sociaux de Chaudière-Appalaches
363, rte Cameron, Sainte-Marie, QC G6E 3E2
Tél: 418-386-3363; *Téléc:* 418-386-3361
reception.cisss-ca@ssss.gouv.qc.ca
www.agencesss12.gouv.qc.ca
Info Line: 811
Population desservi: 423 065
Daniel Paré, Président-directeur général
Brigitte Busque, Présidente, Conseil d'administration

Sherbrooke: Centre intégré universitaire de santé et de services sociaux de l'Estrie
Également connu sous le nom de: CIUSSS de l'Estrie
375, rue Argyll, Sherbrooke, QC J1J 3H5
Tél: 819-780-2222
www.santeestrie.qc.ca
Info Line: 811
Média social: www.facebook.com/SanteEstrie; twitter.com/CIUSSSE_CHUS; www.youtube.com/channel/UCecOsAu7inOjWek_gpJDRtg; www.linkedin.com/company/2789705
Région desservi: Lac-Mégantic à Granby, environ 13,000 km2; *Population desservi:* 476 108; *Personnel:* 17000
Patricia Gauthier, Présidente-directrice générale

Trois-Rivières: Centre intégré universitaire de santé et de services sociaux de la Mauricie-et-du-Centre-du-Québec
858, terrasse Turcotte, Trois-Rivières, QC G9A 5C5
Tél: 819-375-3111
ciusssmcq.ca
Info Line: 811
Fondée en: 2015
Population desservi: 510 163
Note: Fournit des services dans les domaines suivants: Arthabask?a-et-de-l'Érable, Bécancour-Nicolet-Yamaska, Drummond, De l'Énergie (Shawinigan et les environs), Haut-Saint-Maurice, Maskinongé, Trois-Rivières et Vallée-de-la-Batiscan.
Martin Beaumont, Président-directeur général
Richard Desrochers, Président, Conseil d'administration

Centres de Santé et de Services Sociaux

Alma: CSSS de Lac-Saint-Jean-Est
Affiliée à: CIUSSS du Saguenay-Lac-Saint-Jean
CP 1300, 300, boul Champlain Sud, Alma, QC G8B 5W3
Tél: 418-669-2000; *Téléc:* 418-668-9695
www.santealma.qc.ca
Note: Les Installations (Services de CH, CHSLD, et CLSC): Hôpital d'Alma; CLSC Secteur-Centre (Alma); CLSC Secteur-Nord (L'Ascension-de-Notre-Seigneur); CLSC Secteur-Sud (Métabetchouan-Lac-à-la-Croix); Centre d'hébergement Isidore-Gauthier; Centre d'hébergement Métabetchouan-Lac-à-la-Croix; Centre d'hébergement Le normandie

Amos: CSSS Les Eskers de l'Abitibi (CSSSEA)
Affiliée à: CISSS de l'Abitibi-Témiscamingue
622, 4e rue ouest, Amos, QC J9T 2S2
Tél: 819-732-3341; *Téléc:* 819-732-7054
www.csssea.ca
Nombre de lits: 96 lits de courte durée; 103 lits d'hébergement; 24 lits en ressources intermédiaires
Région desservi: MRC d'Abitibi (19 municipalités); *Population desservi:* 25 000; *Personnel:* 900
Note: Les Installations (Services de CH, CHSLD, et CLSC): Hôpital Hôtel-Dieu d'Amos (819-732-3341); Centre d'hébergement Harricana (819-732-6521); CLSC Les Eskers (Amos, Barraute, Berry, Guyenne, La Corne, La Motte, Landrienne, Launay, Preissac, Rochebaucourt, Saint-Dominique-du-Rosaire, Saint-Félix-de-Dalquier, Saint-Marc-de-Figuery, Saint-Mathieu-d'Harricana, Sainte-Gertrude-Manneville, Trécesson - secteur La Ferme, Trécesson - secteur Villemontel).
Le Territoire desservi: 17 municipalités, deux territoires non organisés (TNO) et la communauté algonquine de Pikogan, MRC d'Abitibi

Amqui: CSSS de la Matapédia
135, av Gaétan-Archambeault, Amqui, QC G5J 2K5
Tél: 418-629-2211
www.csssmatapedia.qc.ca
Personnel: 502
Note: Services à la population: Services hospitaliers et urgence; Services diagnostiques; Services de réadaptation; Services ambulatoires; Services de pastorale; Services offerts en CLSC; Services de soutien à domicile; Services d'hébergement de longue durée; Services gériatriques

Chandler: CSSS du Rocher-Percé
Affiliée à: CISSS la Gaspésie
451, rue Monseigneur Ross est, Chandler, QC G0C 1K0
Tél: 418-689-2261; *Téléc:* 418-689-5551
www.csssrocherperce.com
Nombre de lits: 52 lits en soins de courte durée; 36 lits en soins de longue durée; 62 lits en hébergement de longue durée; 5 lits en psychiatrie
Région desservi: MRC du Rocher-Percé
Note: Les Installations (Services de CH, CHSLD, et CLSC): Hôpital de Chandler (418-689-2261); Centre d'hébergement Villa-Pabos (418-689-6621); CLSC Chandler (418-689-2572); CLSC Percé (418-782-2572); CLSC Gascons (418-396-2572)

Châteauguay: CSSS Jardins-Roussillon
Affiliée à: CISSS de la Montérégie-Ouest
200, boul Brisebois, Châteauguay, QC J6K 4W8
Tél: 450-699-2425
www.santemonteregie.qc.ca/jardins-roussillon
Population desservi: 189 000
Note: Les Installations (Services de CH, CHSLD, et CLSC): Hôpital Anna-Laberge (450-699-2425); Centre d'hébergement de Châteauguay (450-692-8231); Centre d'hébergement de La Prairie (450-659-9148); Centre d'hébergement de Saint-Rémi (450-454-4694); Centre de services Lauzon (450-699-7901); CLSC Châteauguay (450-699-3333); CLSC Jardin-du-Québec, Napierville (450-245-3336); CLSC Jardin-du-Québec, Saint-Rémi (450-454-4671); CLSC Kateri (450-659-7661); Centre d'hébergement Champlain Châteauguay (450-632-4451, poste 313); Centre d'hébergement Champlain Jean-Louis-Lapierre (450-632-4451, poste 313); Centre hospitalier Kateri Memorial (450-638-3930).
Le Territoire desservi: Candiac, Châteauguay, Delson, Hemmingford Canton et Village, La Prairie, Léry, Mercier, Napierville, Saint-Bernard-de-Lacolle, Saint-Constant, Saint-Cyprien de Napierville, Sainte-Catherine, Sainte-Clotilde, Saint-Édouard, Sainte-Martine, Saint-Isidore, Saint-Jacques-le-Mineur, Saint-Mathieu, Saint-Michel, Saint-Patrice-de-Sherrington, Saint-Philippe, Saint-Rémi, Saint-Urbain-Premier

Chicoutimi: CSSS de Chicoutimi
Affiliée à: CIUSSS du Saguenay-Lac-Saint-Jean
CP 5006, 305, rue Saint-Vallier, Chicoutimi, QC G7H 5H6
Tél: 418-541-1000; *Téléc:* 418-541-1144
www.csss-chicoutimi.qc.ca
Note: Les Installations (Services de CH, CHSLD, et CLSC): Hôpital de Chicoutimi (418-541-1000); Centre d'hébergement Beaumanoir (418-698-3900); Centre d'hébergement Mgr-Victor-Tremblay (418-698-3907); Centre d'hébergement de la Colline (418-549-5474); CLSC de Chicoutimi (418-543-2221); CLSC Maintien à domicile (418-693-3924). Médecins: 300

Coaticook: CSSS de la MRC de Coaticook
Affiliée à: CIUSSS de l'Estrie
163, rue Jeanne-Mance, Coaticook, QC J1A 1W3
Tél: 819-849-9102
info@csssscoaticook.ca
www.csssscoaticook.ca
Fondée en: 2005
Région desservi: MRC de Coaticook (12 municipalités);
Personnel: 300
Note: Les Installations (Services de CH, CHSLD, et CLSC): Centre hospitalier de Coaticook (819-849-9102); CLSC (1 point de service); 1 centre d'hébergement en soins de longue durée (92 lits); Clinique médicale GMF des Frontières (819-849-4808)

Cowansville: CSSS la Pommeraie
Affiliée à: CISSS de la Montérégie-Ouest
950, rue Principale, Cowansville, QC J2K 1K3
Tél: 450-266-4342; *Téléc:* 450-263-8669
www.santemonteregie.qc.ca/lapommeraie
Fondée en: 2004
Nombre de lits: 279 lits
Population desservi: 52 000; *Personnel:* 1 382
Note: Les Installations (Services de CH, CHSLD, et CLSC): Hôpital Brome-Missisquoi-Perkins (450-266-4342, option 5); Centre d'accueil de Cowansville (450-266-4342, option 3); CHSLD de Bedford (450-248-4304); Foyer Sutton (450-538-3332); Les Foyers Farnham (450-293-3167); CLSC de Bedford (450-248-4321 poste 0); CLSC de Cowansville (450-266-4342, option 4); CLSC de Farnham (450-293-3622); CLSC de Sutton (450-266-4342, option 4); CLSC de Vlle de Lac-Brome (450-242-2001); Service de soutien à domicile (450-266-4342, option 2).
Le Territoire desservi: La MRC de Brome-Missisquoi en plus des municipalités de Sainte-Brigide-d'Iberville et de l'Ange-Gardien

Dolbeau-Mistassini: CSSS Maria-Chapdelaine
Affiliée à: CIUSSS du Saguenay-Lac-Saint-Jean
L'Hôpital, 2000, boul Sacré-Coeur, Dolbeau-Mistassini, QC G8L 2R5
Tél: 418-276-1234; *Téléc:* 418-276-4355
www.csssmariachapdelaine.com
Nombre de lits: 292 lits
Population desservi: 28285; *Personnel:* 750
Note: Les Installations (Services de CH, CHSLD, et CLSC): L'Hôpital, Dolbeau-Mistassini; L'Oasis, Dolbeau-Mistassini; Les Jardins du Monastère, Dolbeau-Mistassini; Centre de Normandin, Normandin

***Donnacona:* CSSS de Portneuf**
Affiliée à: CIUSSS de la Capitale-Nationale
250, boul Gaudreau, Donnacona, QC G3M 1L7
Tél: 418-285-3025; *Téléc:* 418-285-3656
www.cssdeportneuf.qc.ca
Fondée en: 1999
Note: Les Installations (Services de CH, CHSLD, et CLSC): Hôpital régional de Portneuf (418-337-4611); Centre d'hébergement Donnacona (418-285-3025); Centre d'hébergement Pont-Rouge (418-873-4661); Centre d'hébergement Saint-Casimir (418-339-2861); Centre d'hébergement Saint-Marc-des-Carrières (418-268-3511); Centre d'hébergement Saint-Raymond (418-337-4661); CLSC Donnacona (418-285-2626); CLSC Pont-Rouge (418-873-6062); CLSC Rivière-à-Pierre (418-323-2253); CLSC Saint-Marc-des-Carrières (418-268-3571); CLSC Saint-Raymond (418-337-4611); CLSC Saint-Ubalde (418-277-2256). Médecins: 45

***Gaspé:* CSSS de La Côte-de-Gaspé**
Affiliée à: CISSS de la Gaspésie
215, boul de York Ouest, Gaspé, QC G4X 2W2
Tél: 418-368-3301 *Ligne sans frais:* 877-666-8766
www.cssscotedegaspe.ca
Note: Les Installations (Services de CH, CHSLD, et CLSC): Hôpital Hotel-Dieu de Gaspé (418-368-3301); Centre d'hébergement Mgr-Ross (418-368-3301); CLSC de Barachois (418-645-2572); CLSC de Gaspé (418-368-2572); CLSC de Grande-Vallée (418-393-2572); CLSC de Murdochville (418-784-2572); CLSC de Rivière-au-Renard (418-269-2572); Unité de médecine familiale (418-368-6663)

***Gatineau:* CSSS de Gatineau**
Affiliée à: CISSS de l'Outaouais
777, boul de la Gappe, Gatineau, QC J8T 8R2
Tél: 819-966-6550; *Téléc:* 819-966-6565
www.csssgatineau.qc.ca
Média social: twitter.com/csssgatineau
Fondée en: 2004
Population desservi: 230000; *Personnel:* 5500
Note: Les Installations (Services de CH, CHSLD, et CLSC): Hôpital de Gatineau (819-966-6100); Hôpital de Hull (819-966-6200); Hôpital de jour gériatrique (819-664-2060); Hôpital Pierre-Janet (819-771-7761); Centre d'hébergement - Foyer du Bonheur (819-966-6410); Centre d'hébergement - La Pietà (819-966-6420); Centre d'hébergement - Bon séjour (819-966-6450); Centre d'hébergement - Renaissance (819-966-6440); CLSC de Gatineau - boul de la Gappe (819-966-6550); CLSC de Gatineau - av Gatineau (819-966-6550); CLSC de Gatineau - rue Saint-Rédempteur (819-966-6510); CLSC de Gatineau - boul du Mont-Bleu (819-966-6530); CLSC de Gatineau - boul Saint-Raymond (819-966-6525); CLSC de Gatineau - rue LeGuerrier (819-966-6540); CLSC de Gatineau - Maison Bruyère (819-966-6540); CLSC de Gatineau - boul Alexandre-Taché (819-966-6580); Unité de médecine familiale (819-966-6380); Maison de naissance de l'Outaouais (819-966-6585); Pavillon Marcel D'amour (819-776-8093); Résidence de Hull (819-770-2992); Équipe de réadaptation (819-772-9777, poste 7221); Résidence Corbeil (819-777-2042); Résidence de Gatineau (819-568-3349)

***Gatineau:* CSSS de Papineau**
Affiliée à: CISSS de l'Outaouais
578, rue MacLaren Est, Gatineau, QC J8L 2W1
Tél: 819-986-3359
csss_papineau@ssss.gouv.qc.ca
www.csssppapineau.qc.ca
Note: Les Installations (Services de CH, CHSLD, et CLSC): Hôpital de Papineau (819-986-3341); Centre d'hébergement Vallée-de-la-Lièvre (819-986-4115); CLSC et Centre d'hébergement Petite-Nation (819-983-7341); CLSC Vallée-de-la-Lièvre (rue Maclaren est, Gatineau; av Buckingham, Gatineau; Val-des-Bois)

***Greenfield Park:* CSSS Champlain - Charles-Le Moyne (CSSSCCLM)**
Affiliée à: CISSS de la Montérégie-Centre
3120, boul Taschereau, Greenfield Park, QC J4V 2H1
Tél: 450-466-5000
www.santemonteregie.qc.ca/champlain
Nombre de lits: 473 lits d'hospitalisation et 195 en hébergement
Population desservi: 210 000; *Personnel:* 4 700
Note: Les Installations (Services de CH, CHSLD, et CLSC): Hôpital Charles-Le Moyne (450-466-5000); Centre d'hébergement Champlain (450-672-3320); Centre d'hébergement Henriette-Céré (450-672-3320); CLSC Saint-Hubert (450-443-7400); CLSC Samuel-de-Champlain (450-445-4452); Centre Saint-Lambert (450-672-3320); Centre de recherche appliquée (450-466-5433); Centre de recherche clinique (450-466-5024); Centre de prêt d'équipements Panama (450-462-5193); Centre externe de néphrologie Greenfield Park (450-466-5000, poste 3645); Centre externe de néphrologie Saint-Lambert (450-466-5000, poste 3646); Clinique externe de pédopsychiatrie (450-466-5000, poste 2414); Hôpital de jour pour adolescents (450-466-5000, poste 2008); Clinique externe de psychiatrie pour adultes (450-466-5620); Clinique externe de psychiatrie pour adultes (450-466-5453); Centre de jour, Clinique Labonté (450-466-5455); Maison Brodeur (450-448-4763); Suivi intensif dans la communauté (450-466-5605); Groupe de médecine familiale de l'Unité de médecine familiale Charles-Le Moyne (450-466-5630).
Le Territoire desservi: Arrondissements de Greenfield Park, du Vieux-Longueuil et de Saint-Hubert. Affilié à l'Université de Sherbrooke.

***Jonquière:* CSSS de Jonquière**
Affiliée à: CIUSSS du Saguenay-Lac-Saint-Jean
Centre administratif et hospitalier, CP 1200, 2230, rue de l'Hôpital, Jonquière, QC G7X 7X2
Tél: 418-695-7700
www.csssjonquiere.qc.ca
Nombre de lits: 294 lits d'hébergement; 5 lits d'hébergement temporaire; 70 lits d'hospitalisation; 15 lits en Unité de réadaptation fonctionnelle intensive
Personnel: 1500
Note: Les Installations (Services de CH, CHSLD, et CLSC): Centre administratif et hospitalier; CLSC Jonquière (St-Ambroise); Centre de réadaptation en déficience physique; Centre de réadaptation en dépendance; Centre d'hébergement Des Chênes; Centre d'hébergement Georges-Hébert; Centre d'hébergement Ste-Marie; Centre d'hébergement des Années d'Or

***La Baie:* CSSS Cléophas-Claveau**
Affiliée à: CIUSSS du Saguenay-Lac-Saint-Jean
Centre hospitalier, 1000, rue Docteur-Desgagné, La Baie, QC G7B 2Y6
Tél: 418-544-3381; *Téléc:* 418-544-0770
www.cssscleophasclaveau.qc.ca
Note: Les Installations (Services de CH, CHSLD, et CLSC): Centre hospitalier; Centre d'hébergement Bagotville; Centre d'hébergement St-Joseph; CLSC de La Baie; CLSC L'Anse-Saint-Jean

***La Sarre:* CSSS des Aurores-Boréales (CSSSAB)**
Affiliée à: CISSS de l'Abitibi-Témiscamingue
679, 2e rue Est, La Sarre, QC J9Z 2X7
Tél: 819-333-2311; *Téléc:* 819-333-4316
www.csssab.qc.ca
Population desservi: 21 308
Note: Les Installations (Services de CH, CHSLD, et CLSC): Centre de soins de courte durée (Centre hospitalier et siège social, 819-333-2311); Centre d'hébergement de soins de longue durée de Macamic (819-782-4661); Centre d'hébergement de soins de longue durée de La Sarre (819-333-5525); Centre d'hébergement de soins de longue durée de Palmarolle (819-787-2612); CLSC (Beaucanton, Duparquet, Dupuy, Gallichan, La Sarre, Macamic, Normétal, Palmarolle, Taschereau)
Paul Fortin, Directeur général

***La Tuque:* CSSS du Haut-Saint-Maurice (CSSSHSM)**
Affiliée à: CIUSSS de la Mauricie et du Centre-du-Québec
885, boul Ducharme, La Tuque, QC G9X 3C1
Tél: 819-523-4581
www.cssshsm.qc.ca
Note: Le Territoire desservi: Les régions du Centre-du-Québec, de Lanaudière, des Laurentides, de l'Abitibi-Témiscamingue, de la Baie-James, de Québec et du Saguenay-Lac Saint-Jean

***Lac-Mégantic:* CSSS du Granit**
Affiliée à: CIUSSS de l'Estrie
3569, rue Laval, Lac-Mégantic, QC G6B 1A5
Tél: 819-583-0330; *Téléc:* 819-583-5239
Ligne sans frais: 800-827-2572
info.granit@ssss.gouv.qc.ca
www.csssgranit.qc.ca
Note: Les Installations (Services de CH, CHSLD, et CLSC): CHSLD - Centre de jour (Point de service Lac-Mégantic); CLSC-CHSLD - Centre de jour (Point de service Lambton); CLSC (Point de chute Saint-Ludger); CLSC (Point de chute Notre-Dame des Bois)

***Lachine:* CSSS de Dorval-Lachine-LaSalle (CSSS DLL)**
Affiliée à: CIUSSS de l'Ouest-de-l'Île-de-Montréal
1900, rue Notre-Dame, Lachine, QC H8S 2G2
Tél: 514-639-0650
www.csssdll.qc.ca
Personnel: 2000
Note: Les Installations (Services de CH, CHSLD, et CLSC): Hôpital de LaSalle / Longue durée de l'hôpital de LaSalle (514-362-8000); CLSC de LaSalle (514-364-2572); CLSC de Dorval-Lachine (514-639-0650); Centre d'hébergement de Dorval (514-631-9094); Centre d'hébergement de Lachine (514-634-7161); Centre d'hébergement de LaSalle (514-364-6700); Centre d'hébergement Nazaire-Piché (514-637-2326).
Le Territoire desservi: Les arrondissements montréalais de LaSalle et Lachine; La municipalité de Dorval

***Laval:* CSSS de Laval**
Affiliée à: CISSS de Laval
1515, boul Chomedey, Laval, QC H7V 3Y7
Tél: 450-978-8300
www.cssslaval.qc.ca
Média social: www.facebook.com/cssslaval; twitter.com/cssslaval; www.youtube.com/csssdelaval
Fondée en: 2004
Nombre de lits: 751 lits d'hébergement longue durée; 512 lits d'hospitalisation courte durée; 489 lits au permis d'hospitalisation de courte durée
Note: Les Installations (Services de CH, CHSLD, et CLSC): Hôpital de la Cité-de-la-Santé, avec centre de prélèvements, UMF et CICL (450-668-1010); Centre ambulatoire (450-978-8300); Centre d'hébergement Fernand-Larocque (450-661-5440); Centre d'hébergement Idola-Saint-Jean (450-668-6750); Centre d'hébergement de La Pinière (450-661-3305); Centre d'hébergement Rose-de-Lima (450-622-6996); Centre d'hébergement de Sainte-Dorothée (450-689-0933); Centre intégré de services de première ligne de l'ouest de l'Ile (450-627-2530); CLSC du Marigot (450-668-1803); CLSC des Mille-Iles (450-661-2572, 450 972-6808); CLSC du Ruisseau-Papineau (450-687-5690); CLSC de Sainte-Rose (450-622-5110)

***Longueuil:* CSSS Pierre-Boucher**
Affiliée à: CISSS de la Montérégie-Est
1333, boul Jacques-Cartier Est, Longueuil, QC J4M 2A5
Tél: 450-468-8111
www.santemonteregie.qc.ca/cssspierreboucher
Fondée en: 2004
Population desservi: 250 000; *Personnel:* 4 400
Note: Les Installations (Services de CH, CHSLD, et CLSC): Hôpital Pierre-Boucher (450-468-8111); Centre d'hébergement de Contrecoeur (450-468-8410); Centre d'hébergement de Lajemmerais (450-463-2995); Centre d'hébergement de Mgr-Coderre (450-448-3111); Centre d'hébergement du Chevalier-De Lévis (450-670-5110); Centre d'hébergement du Manoir-Trinité (450-674-4948); Centre d'hébergement Jeanne-Crevier (450-641-0590); Centre d'hébergement René-Lévesque (450-651-2210); CLSC de Longueuil-Ouest (450-651-9830); CLSC des Seigneuries de Boucherville (450-655-3630); CLSC des Seigneuries de Contrecoeur (450-468-8413); CLSC des Seigneuries de Saint-Amable (450-468-5250); CLSC des Seigneuries de Sainte-Julie (450-468-3670); CLSC des Seigneuries de Varennes (450-677-2917); CLSC des Seigneuries de Verchères (450-448-3700); CLSC Simonne-Monet-Chartrand (450-463-2850); Centre d'accueil Saint-Laurent inc. (450-670-5480).
Le Territoire desservi: Arrondissement du Vieux-Longueuil, Boucherville, Calixa-Lavallée, Contrecoeur, Saint-Amable, Sainte-Julie, Varennes et Verchères

***Magog:* CSSS de Memphrémagog**
Affiliée à: CIUSSS de l'Estrie
50, rue Saint-Patrice Est, Magog, QC J1X 3X3
Tél: 819-843-2572 *Ligne sans frais:* 800-268-2572
www.csssm.santeestrie.qc.ca
Note: Les Installations (Services de CH, CHSLD, et CLSC): Hôpital de Memphrémagog; Point de service de Mansonville (450-292-3376); Point de service de Stanstead (819-876-7521)

***Maniwaki:* CSSS de la Vallée-de-la-Gatineau (CSSSVG)**
Affiliée à: CISSS de l'Outaouais
309, boul Desjardins, Maniwaki, QC J9E 2E7
Tél: 819-449-4690; *Téléc:* 819-449-7330
www.csssvg.qc.ca
Population desservi: 20 000
Note: Les Installations (Services de CH, CHSLD, et CLSC): L'hôpital de Maniwaki; Le Foyer Père Guinard de Maniwaki; Le Foyer d'accueil de Gracefield; Les CLSC de Low, Gracefield, et Maniwaki
Natalie Jobin, Direction santé physique
NathalieJobin@ssss.gouv.qc.ca

***Mansfield-et-Pontefract:* CSSS du Pontiac**
Affiliée à: CISSS de l'Outaouais
CP 430, 160, ch de la Chute, Mansfield-et-Pontefract, QC J0X 1V0
Tél: 819-683-3000; *Téléc:* 819-683-3682
Ligne sans frais: 800-567-9625
www.santepontiac.qc.ca
Média social: www.facebook.com/213024748134
Fondée en: 1996
Population desservi: 20000+
Note: Les Installations (Services de CH, CHSLD, et CLSC): Centre Hospitalier du Pontiac; Pavillon Centre d'accueil Pontiac; Pavillon Manoir Sacré Cour; CLSC Bryson; CLSC Chapeau; CLSC de Mansfield-et-Pontefract, Fort-Coulonge; CLSC Otter-Lake; CLSC Quyon; CLSC Rapides-des-Joachims
Jean-Guy Patenaude, Président, Conseil d'administration
Richard Grimard, Directeur général

***Maria:* CSSS de la Baie-des-Chaleurs (CSSSBC)**
Affiliée à: CISSS de la Gaspésie-Iles-de-la-Madeleine
Centre administratif, 419, boul Perron, Maria, QC G0C 1Y0
Tél: 418-759-3443; *Téléc:* 418-759-5063
csssbc@csssbc.qc.ca
www.csssbc.qc.ca
Média social: www.facebook.com/126574670696702
Fondée en: 2004
Nombre de lits: 77 lits
Région desservi: MRC d'Avignon; MRC de Bonaventure;
Population desservi: 32 591; *Personnel:* 1 100
Note: Les Installations (Services de CH, CHSLD, et CLSC): Hôpital de Maria (418-759-3443); Centre d'hébergement de Maria (418-759-3458); Centre d'hébergement de Matapédia (418-865-2221); Centre d'hébergement de New Carlisle (418-752-3386); CLSC Malauze de Matapédia (418-865-2221); CLSC de Pointe-à-la-Croix (418-788-5454); CLSC de Saint-Omer (418-364-7064); CLSC de Caplan (418-388-2572); CLSC de Paspébiac (418-752-2572); Unité de médecine familiale Baie-des-Chaleurs (418-759-1336, poste 2811).
Médecins: 67
Jean-Philippe Legault, Directeur général

***Matane:* CSSS de Matane**
Centre Administratif, Hôpital de Matane, 333, rue Thibault, Matane, QC G4W 2W5
Tél: 418-562-3135; *Téléc:* 418-562-9374
www.csssmatane.com
Population desservi: 22 057
Note: Les Installations (Services de CH, CHSLD, et CLSC): Hôpital de Matane (45 lits); Centre d'hébergement de Matane (106 lits); CLSC de Matane (Les Méchins, Baie-des-Sables)

***Montréal:* CSSS Cavendish**
Affiliée à: CIUSSS du Centre-Ouest-de-l'Ile-de-Montréal
Centre administratif, 5425, av Bessborough, Montréal, QC H4V 2S7
Tél: 514-484-7878; *Téléc:* 514-483-4596
www.csssscavendish.qc.ca
Fondée en: 2004
Population desservi: 121 900; *Personnel:* 1400
Note: Les Installations (Services de CH, CHSLD, et CLSC): Hôpital Richardson (514-484-7878); CLSC René-Cassin (514-484-7878); CLSC de Notre-Dame-de-Grâce - Montréal-Ouest (514-484-7878); Centre d'hébergement Henri-Bradet (514-484-7878); Centre d'hébergement St-Andrew (514-932-3630); Centre d'hébergement Father-Dowd (514-932-3630); Centre d'hébergement St-Margaret (514-932-3630)

***Montréal:* CSSS d'Ahuntsic et Montréal-Nord (CSSSAM-N)**
Affiliée à: CIUSSS du Nord-de-l'Ile-de-Montréal
1725, boul Gouin est, Montréal, QC H2C 3H6
Tél: 514-384-2000
www.csssamn.ca
Population desservi: 170 000
Note: Les Installations (Services de CH, CHSLD, et CLSC): Hôpital Fleury; Centre d'hébergement de Louvain; Centre d'hébergement Laurendeau; Centre d'hébergement Légaré; Centre d'hébergement Paul-Lizotte; CLSC d'Ahuntsic; CLSC de Montréal-Nord

***Montréal:* CSSS de l'Ouest-de-l'Ile/West Island Health & Social Services Centre**
Affiliée à: CIUSSS de l'Ouest-de-l'Ile-de-Montréal
160, av Stillview, Montréal, QC H9R 2Y2
Tél: 514-630-2225
www.csssouestdelile.qc.ca
Nombre de lits: 227 lits d'hospitalisation de courte durée; 155 lits d'hébergement de longue durée
Population desservi: 220000; *Personnel:* 2125
Note: Les Installations (Services de CH, CHSLD, et CLSC): Hôpital général du Lakeshore (514-630-2225); CLSC de Pierrefonds (514-626-2572); CLSC du Lac-Saint-Louis (514-697-4110); Centre d'hébergement Denis-Benjamin-Viger (514-620-6310).
Le Territoire desservi: Les arrondissments de de Pierrefonds-Roxboro et de L'Ile-Bizard-Sainte-Geneviève; Les villes de Baie d'Urfé, Beaconsfield, Dollard-des-Ormeaux, Kirkland, Pointe-Claire, Sainte-Anne-de-Bellevue, et Senneville

***Montréal:* CSSS de la Montagne**
Affiliée à: CIUSSS du Centre-Ouest-de-l'Ile-de-Montréal
1980, rue Sherbrooke Ouest, Montréal, QC H3H 1E8
Tél: 514-731-8531
www.csssdelamontagne.qc.ca
Média social: www.facebook.com/CSSSdelaMontagne
Note: Les Installations (Services de CH, CHSLD, et CLSC): CLSC de Côte-des-Neiges, Montréal (514-731-8531); CLSC de Côte-des-Neiges, Point de service Outremont; CLSC Métro (514-934-0354); CLSC de Parc-Extension (514-273-9591); Maison de naissance Côte-des-Neiges (514-736-2323); Programme régional d'accueil et d'intégration des demandeurs d'asile (PRAIDA).
Le Territoire desservi: Le quartier Côte-des-Neiges de l'arrondissement Côte-des-Neiges / Notre-Dame-de-Grâce; L'arrondissement Outremont; Le quartier Parc-Extension de l'arrondissement Villeray-Saint-Michel-Parc-Extension; Le district Peter-McGill de l'arrondissement Ville-Marie; Une partie de l'arrondissement Plateau Mont-Royal; Les villes de Mont-Royal et Westmount
Denis Sirois, Président, Conseil d'administration
Marc Sougavinski, Directeur général

***Montréal:* CSSS de la Pointe-de-l'Ile**
Affiliée à: CIUSSS de l'Est-de-l'Ile-de-Montréal
9503, rue Sherbrooke Est, Montréal, QC H1L 6P2
Tél: 514-356-2572
www.cssspointe.ca
Population desservi: 191 980
Note: Les Installations (Services de CH, CHSLD, et CLSC): Centre d'hébergement Biermans (514-351-9891); Centre d'hébergement François-Séguenot (514-642-4050); Centre d'hébergement Judith-Jasmin (514-354-5990); Centre d'hébergement Pierre-Joseph-Triest (514-353-1227); CLSC de Mercier-Est-Anjou (514-356-2572); CLSC de Pointe-aux-Trembles-Montréal-Est (514-642-4050); CLSC de Rivière-des-Prairies (514-494-4924); Manoir Claudette Barré (514-351-0200); Ressource intermédiaire Claudette Barré (514-351-0200); Ressource intermédiaire Limoges (514-852-3898)

***Nicolet:* CSSS de Bécancour-Nicolet-Yamaska (CSSSBNY)**
Affiliée à: CIUSSS de la Mauricie et du Centre-du-Québec
Centre administratif, Centre Christ-Roi, 675, rue St-Jean-Baptiste, Nicolet, QC J3T 1S4
Tél: 819-293-2071; *Téléc:* 819-293-6160
Ligne sans frais: 800-263-2572
www.csssbny.qc.ca
Info Line: 811
Population desservi: 44000; *Personnel:* 1000
Note: Les Installations (Services de CH, CHSLD, et CLSC): Centre Christ-Roi (819-293-2071); Centre Filles de la Sagesse (819-293-8337); Centre Fortierville (819-287-4442); Centre d'hébergement Deschaillons (819-292-2262); Centre d'hébergement Fortierville (819-287-4686); Centre d'hébergement Lucien-Shooner (450-568-2712); Centre d'hébergement Romain-Becquet (819-263-2245); Centre d'hébergement Saint-Célestin (819-229-3617); Point de service Gentilly (819-298-2144); Point de service Saint-Grégoire (819-233-2719); Point de service Saint-Léonard-d'Aston (819-399-3666)

***Notre-Dame-du-Lac:* CSSS de Témiscouata**
58, rue de l'Église, Notre-Dame-du-Lac, QC G0L 1X0
Tél: 418-899-6751
www.cssstemiscouata.com
Note: Les Installations (Services de CH, CHSLD, et CLSC): Hôpital de Notre-Dame-du-Lac; CLSC de Cabano; CLSC de Dégelis; CLSC de Lac-des-Aigles; CLSC de Pohénégamook; Clinique médicale de Squatec; Centre d'hébergement Squatec; Centre d'hébergement St-Louis; Centre d'hébergement Rivière-Bleue; La Maison du Lac; La Villa Saint-Louis; Résidence Dégelico; Les Habitations Jules Edouard; R.I. Véronique Lavoie; Le Manoir de l'Érable Argenté

***Ormstown:* CSSS du Haut-Saint-Laurent (CSSSHSL)**
Affiliée à: CISSS de la Montérégie-Ouest
28, rue Gale, Ormstown, QC J0S 1K0
Tél: 450-829-2321
www.santemonteregie.qc.ca/haut-saint-laurent
Nombre de lits: 125 lits (longue durée); 49 lits (courte durée); 9 lits (hébergement temporaire)
Note: Les Installations (Services de CH, CHSLD, et CLSC): Hôpital Barrie Memorial (450-829-2321); Centre d'hébergement d'Ormstown (450-829-2321); Centre d'hébergement du comté de Huntingdon (450-829-2321); CLSC Huntingdon (450-829-2321); Point de service du CLSC Huntingdon (450-829-2321).
Le Territoire desservi: La MRC du Haut Saint-Laurent (Dundee, Elgin, Franklin, Godmanchester, Havelock, Hinchinbrooke, Howick, Huntingdon, Ormstown, Saint-Anicet, Saint-Chrysostome, Sainte-Barbe, Très-Saint-Sacrement)

***Québec:* CSSS de la Vieille-Capitale**
Affiliée à: CIUSSS de la Capitale-Nationale
1, av du Sacré-Coeur, Québec, QC G1N 2W1
Tél: 418-529-4777
www.csssvc.qc.ca
Fondée en: 2004
Note: Les Installations (Services de CH, CHSLD, et CLSC): CLSC de Cap-Rouge-Saint-Augustin; CLSC de la Basse-Ville; CLSC de la Haute-Ville; CLSC de la Haute-Ville, édifice Courchesne; CLSC de Limoilou; CLSC de L'Ancienne-Lorette; CLSC de Sainte-Foy-Sillery; CLSC de Sainte-Foy-Sillery, Pavillon Marguerite-D'Youville; CLSC des Rivières; Centre d'hébergement Christ-Roi; Centre d'hébergement de Limoilou; Centre d'hébergement Hôpital général de Québec; Centre d'hébergement Le Faubourg; Centre d'hébergement Louis-Hébert; Centre d'hébergement Notre-Dame-de-Lourdes; Centre d'hébergement Sacré-Cour; Centre d'hébergement Saint-Antoine; Unité de médecine familiale de la Haute-Ville; Unité de médecine familiale Laurier; Unité de médecine familiale Laval; Unité de médecine familiale Saint-François d'Assise

***Québec:* CSSS Québec-Nord**
Affiliée à: CIUSSS de la Capitale-Nationale
Centre administratif, 2915, av du Bourg-Royal, 4e étage, Québec, QC G1C 3S2
Tél: 418-266-1019
www.csssqn.qc.ca
Fondée en: 2004
Nombre de lits: 900+ lits
Population desservi: 300 000; *Personnel:* 3,000
Note: Les Installations (Services de CH, CHSLD, et CLSC): Hôpital Ste-Anne-de-Beaupré; Hôpital Chauveau; Centre d'hébergement du Fargy; Centre d'hébergement Saint-Augustin; Centre d'hébergement Yvonne-Sylvain; Centre d'hébergement Roy-Rousseau; Centre d'hébergement Charlesbourg; Centre d'hébergement Alphonse-Bonenfant; Centre d'hébergement Loretteville; CLSC de la Jacques-Cartier (Loretteville, Sainte-Catherine-de-la-Jacques-Cartier); CLSC La Source Sud; CLSC La Source Nord; CLSC La Source La Maisonnée; CLSC Orléans (Beauport, Ile d'Orléans, Beaupré, Maizerets, Montmorency); Unité de médicine familiale

***Rivière-du-Loup:* CSSS de Rivière-du-Loup**
Le Centre hospitalier régional de Grand-Portage, 75, rue St-Henri, Rivière-du-Loup, QC G5R 2A4
Tél: 418-868-1010; *Téléc:* 418-868-1035
www.csssriviereduloup.qc.ca
Personnel: 1500
Note: Les Installations (Services de CH, CHSLD, et CLSC): Centre hospitalier régional de Grand-Portage ((CHRGP); Centre d'hébergement Saint-Joseph; Centre d'hébergement Saint-Antonin; Centre d'hébergement St-Cyprien; CLSC Rivière et Marées; L'Estran Centre de réadaptation en alcoolisme et toxicomanie du Bas-Saint-Laurent
Doris Laliberté-Kirouac, Présidente, Conseil d'administration
Daniel Lévesque, Directeur général et secrétaire

***Roberval:* CSSS Domaine-du-Roy**
Affiliée à: CIUSSS du Saguenay-Lac-Saint-Jean
Édifice Hôtel-Dieu de Roberval, 450, rue Brassard, Roberval, QC G8H 1B9
Tél: 418-275-0110; *Téléc:* 418-275-6202
www.csssdomaineduroy.com
Note: Les Installations (Services de CH, CHSLD, et CLSC): Hôtel-Dieu de Roberval; Centre d'hébergement Roberval; Centre d'hébergement Saint-Félicien; CLSC Saint-Félicien; CLSC Roberval; Mission de Centre de réadaptation en alcoolisme et autres toxicomanies (CRAT); Centre de réadaptation pour alcooliques et autres toxicomanes Saint-Antoine

***Rouyn-Noranda:* CSSS de Rouyn-Noranda (CSSSRN)**
Affiliée à: CIUSSS de l'Abitibi-Témiscamingue
4, 9e rue, Rouyn-Noranda, QC J9X 2B2
Tél: 819-764-5131
www.csssrn.qc.ca
Fondée en: 2004
Population desservi: 39 615; *Personnel:* 1 200
Note: Les Installations (Services de CH, CHSLD, et CLSC):

Hôpital, Rouyn-Noranda (819-764-5131); Centre d'hébergement, Rouyn-Noranda (819-762-0908); CLSC, Rouyn-Noranda (819-762-8144) (Beaudry-Cloutier, Cadillac, Cléricy-Mont-Brun, Montbeillard-Rollet, Destor)

Saint-Charles-Borromée: CSSS du Nord de Lanaudière
Affiliée à: CIUSSS de Lanaudière
1000, boul Sainte-Anne, Saint-Charles-Borromée, QC J6E 6J2
Tél: 450-759-8222
www.csssnl.qc.ca
Région desservi: MRC de D'Autray, de Joliette, de Matawinie, et de Montcalm; *Population desservi:* 200 000; *Personnel:* 4 700
Note: Les Installations (Services de CH, CHSLD, et CLSC): Centre hospitalier régional De Lanaudière; Centre d'hébergement Alphonse-Rondeau; Centre d'hébergement Desy; Centre d'hébergement Sainte-Élisabeth; Centre d'hébergement Parphilia-Ferland; Centre d'hébergement Saint-Eusèbe; Centre d'hébergement du Piedmont; Centre d'hébergement Saint-Donat; Centre d'hébergement Brassard; Centre d'hébergement Saint-Antoine de Padoue; Centre d'hébergement Saint-Jacques; Centre d'hébergement Saint-Liguori; CLSC de Berthier; CLSC de Lavaltrie; CLSC de Saint-Gabriel; CLSC de Joliette; CLSC de Chertsey; CLSC de Saint-Jean-de-Matha; CLSC de Saint-Donat; CLSC de Saint-Michel-des-Saints; CLSC de Saint-Esprit; Centre de réadaptation en dépendances Le Tremplin de Saint-Charles-Borromée; Centre de réadaptation en dépendances Le Tremplin de Repentigny; Centre de réadaptation en dépendances Le Tremplin de Terrebonne; Services externes psychiatriques intégrés pour adultes de Rawdon; Services psychiatriques pour enfants et adolescents; Unité de médecine familiale du Nord de Lanaudière.
Nombre de médecins, dentistes, et de pharmaciens: 350
Daniel Castonguay, Directeur général

Saint-Eustache: CSSS du Lac-des-Deux-Montagnes
Affiliée à: CISSS des Laurentides
Direction générale, 520, boul Arthur-Sauvé, Saint-Eustache, QC J7R 5B1
Tél: 450-473-6811; *Téléc:* 450-473-6966
Ligne sans frais: 888-234-3837
www.moncsss.com
Média social: www.facebook.com/Communications.CSSSLDDM; twitter.com/CSSS2Montagnes
Fondée en: 2004
Note: Les Installations (Services de CH, CHSLD, et CLSC): Hôpital de Saint-Eustache (450-473-6811); Centre d'hébergement de Saint-Eustache (450-472-0013); Centre d'hébergement de Saint-Benoît (450-258-2481); CLSC Jean-Olivier-Chénier (450-491-1233); CLSC Mirabel (450-475-7938); Clinique externe de psychiatrie (450-473-1533

Saint-Jean-sur-Richelieu: CSSS Haut-Richelieu - Rouville
Affiliée à: CISSS de la Montérégie-Centre
978, boul du Séminaire Nord, Saint-Jean-sur-Richelieu, QC J3A 1E5
Tél: 450-358-2572
www.santemonteregie.qc.ca/haut-richelieu-rouville
Fondée en: 2004
Population desservi: 182 000; *Personnel:* 4 000
Note: Les Installations (Services de CH, CHSLD, et CLSC): Hôpital du Haut-Richelieu, Saint-Jean-sur-Richelieu (450-359-5000); Centre d'hébergement Champagnat, Saint-Jean-sur-Richelieu (450-347-3769); Centre d'hébergement Georges-Phaneuf, Saint-Jean-sur-Richelieu (450-346-1133); Centre d'hébergement Gertrude-Lafrance, Saint-Jean-sur-Richelieu (450-359-5555); Centre d'hébergement Sainte-Croix, Marieville (450-460-4475); Centre d'hébergement Saint-Joseph, Chambly (450-658-6271); Centre d'hébergement Val-Joli, Saint-Césaire (450-469-3194); CLSC de Henryville (450-299-2828); CLSC de la Vallée-des-Forts, Saint-Jean-sur-Richelieu (450-358-2572); CLSC de Saint-Césaire (450-469-0269); CLSC du Richelieu (450-658-7561); Manoir Soleil, Chambly (450-658-4441); Clinique jeunesse 12-21 ans, Saint-Jean-sur-Richelieu (450-358-2572); Clinique jeunesse du Bassin de Chambly 12-24 ans, Chambly (450-658-2016); Point de chute de Lacolle (450-299-2828); Services de consultation externe - psychiatrie, réadaptation pédiatrique, clinique d'évaluation TED (450-346-2222).
Médecins: 300.
Le Territoire desservi: MRC de Rouville, MRC du Haut-Richelieu et MRC de la Vallée-du-Richelieu (21 municipalités)

Saint-Pascal: CSSS de Kamouraska
575, av Martin, Saint-Pascal, QC G0L 3Y0
Tél: 418-856-7000
www.cssskamouraska.ca
Note: Les Installations (Services de CH, CHSLD, et CLSC): Hôpital Notre-Dame-de-Fatima (49 lits); Centre d'hébergement D'Anjou, Saint-Pacôme (53 lits); Centre d'hébergement Thérèse-Martin, Rivière-Ouelle (46 lits); Centre d'hébergement Villa Maria, Saint-Alexandre (52 lits); CLSC, Saint-Pascal; CLSC, La Pocatière; CLSC, Saint-André

Sainte-Agathe-des-Monts: CSSS des Sommets
Affiliée à: CISSS des Laurentides
Pavillon administratif Jacques-Duquette, 234, rue Saint-Vincent, Sainte-Agathe-des-Monts, QC J8C 2B8
Tél: 819-324-4000 *Ligne sans frais:* 855-766-6387
www.csss-sommets.com
Nombre de lits: 217 lits de longue durée; 104 lits de courte durée
Région desservi: MRC des Laurentides et des environs;
Population desservi: 46 517; *Personnel:* 1 500
Note: Les Installations (Services de CH, CHSLD, et CLSC): Hôpital Laurentien (819-324-4000); Pavillon Philippe-Lapointe (819-324-4000); Centre d'hébergement de Mont-Tremblant (819-425-2793); Centre d'hébergement de Labelle (819-686-2372); CLSC de Sainte-Agathe-des-Monts (819-326-3111); CLSC de Mont-Tremblant (819-425-3771); CLSC de Labelle (819-686-2117)

Salaberry-de-Valleyfield: CSSS du Suroît
Affiliée à: CISSS de la Montérégie-Ouest
150, rue Saint-Thomas, Salaberry-de-Valleyfield, QC J6T 6C1
Tél: 450-371-9920 *Ligne sans frais:* 800-694-9920
www.santemonteregie.qc.ca/suroit/
Région desservi: Salaberry-de-Valleyfield; Beauharnois; Vaudreuil-Dorion
Note: Les Installations (Services de CH, CHSLD, et CLSC): Hôpital du Suroît (450-371-9920); Centre d'hébergement Cécile-Godin (450-429-6403); Centre d'hébergement Docteur-Aimé-Leduc (450-373-4818); CLSC de Beauharnois (450-429-6455); CLSC de Salaberry-de-Valleyfield (450-371-0143); Centre de jour pour adultes, Salaberry-de-Valleyfield (450-373-7321); Clinique externe pour adultes, Salaberry-de-Valleyfield (450-373-6252); Clinique externe pour jeunes, Salaberry-de-Valleyfield (450-373-5705); Clinique externe pour adultes, Vaudreuil-Dorion (450-455-7967); Clinique externe pour jeunes, Vaudreuil-Dorion (450-455-3356)

Shawinigan: CSSS de l'Énergie
Affiliée à: CIUSSS de la Mauricie et du Centre-du-Québec
Centre administratif, 243, 1e rue de la pointe, Shawinigan, QC G9N 1K2
Tél: 819-536-7500
info@cssse.qc.ca
www.etrehumain.ca
Note: Les Installations (Services de CH, CHSLD, et CLSC): Hôpital du Centre-de-la-Mauricie (819-536-7500); Centre d'hébergement Joseph-Garceau (819-537-5173); Centre d'hébergement Laflèche (819-533-2500); Centre d'hébergement Saint-Maurice (819-536-0071); CLSC du Centre-de-la-Mauricie (819-539-8371); CIC de Shawinigan (819-537-6647); Centre régional de santé mentale (819-536-7500)

Sherbrooke: CSSS Institut universitaire de gériatrie de Sherbrooke (CSSS IUG)
Affiliée à: CIUSSS de l'Estrie
375, rue Argyll, Sherbrooke, QC J1J 3H5
Tél: 819-780-2222
www.csss-iugs.ca
Média social: www.facebook.com/209159895905329; www.youtube.com/user/CSSSIUGS05
Fondée en: 2005
Nombre de lits: 750 lits
Note: Les Installations (Services de CH, CHSLD, et CLSC): CLSC Sherbrooke (5 points de service); Centre d'hébergement St-Vincent; Centre d'hébergement St-Joseph; Hôpital et centre d'hébergement Argyll; Hôpital et centre d'hébergement D'Youville; Centre de maternité de l'Estrie.
Médecins et médecins spécialistes: 100

Sorel-Tracy: CSSS Pierre-De Saurel
Affiliée à: CISSS de la Montérégie-Est
400, av Hôtel-Dieu, Sorel-Tracy, QC J3P 1N5
Tél: 450-746-6000
www.santemonteregie.qc.ca/sorel-tracy
Fondée en: 2004
Note: Les Installations (Services de CH, CHSLD, et CLSC): Hôtel-Dieu de Sorel (450-746-6000); Centre d'hébergement Élisabeth-Lafrance (450-746-5555); Centre d'hébergement de Tracy (450-743-4924); Centre d'hébergement J.-Arsène-Parenteau (450-742-5936); CLSC Gaston-Bélanger (450-746-4545); Résidence Sorel-Tracy inc. (450-742-9428); Centre de jour, Sorel-Tracy (450-743-5569); Hôpital de jour, Sorel-Tracy (450-743-5569).
Le Territoire desservi: Massueville; Saint-Gérard-de-Majella; Saint-Roch-de-Richelieu; Saint-Aimé; Saint-Joseph-de-Sorel; Sorel-Tracy; Saint-David; Sainte-Anne-de-Sorel; Saint-Ours; Yamaska; Sainte-Victoire-de-Sorel; Saint-Robert

St-Jérôme: CSSS de Saint-Jérôme
Affiliée à: CISSS des Laurentides
290, rue de Montigny, St-Jérôme, QC J7Z 5T3
Tél: 450-432-2777 *Ligne sans frais:* 866-963-2777
www.cdsj.org
Nombre de lits: 405 lits de courte durée dont 85 en psychiatrie; 305 lits répartis en trois centres d'hébergement
Note: Les Installations (Services de CH, CHSLD, et CLSC): Hôpital régional de Saint-Jérôme (450-432-2777); Centre d'hébergement Youville (450-432-2777, poste 26761); Centre d'hébergement L'Auberge (450-432-2777, poste 23621); Centre d'hébergement Lucien-G.-Rolland (450-432-2777, poste 23221); CLSC de Saint-Jérôme, famille, enfance, jeunesse, services à la collectivité (450-432-2777, poste 25000); CLSC de Saint-Jérôme, soutien à domicile (450-432-2777, poste 26221); CLSC de Saint-Jérôme, santé mentale et services psychosociaux (450-432-2777, poste 26500); Clinique de développement (450-432-2777, poste 23600); Maison de naissance du Boisé (450-432-2777, poste 23660); Centre de prélèvements (450-432-2777, poste 22197).
Médecins: 350

Terrebonne: CSSS du Sud de Lanaudière
Affiliée à: CISSS de Lanaudière
Centre administratif, 911, montée des Pionniers, Terrebonne, QC J6V 2H2
Tél: 450-654-7525 *Ligne sans frais:* 888-654-7525
www.csss.sudlanaudiere.ca
Note: Les Installations (Services de CH, CHSLD, et CLSC): Hôpital Pierre-Le Gardeur; CLSC Lamater; CLSC Meilleur; Centres d'hébergement; Centre de jour L'Escale; Hôpital de jour de psychiatrie de la MRC Les Moulins; Hôpital de jour de psychiatrie de la MRC de L'Assomption; Clinique externe de psychiatrie de Charlemagne; SIME (Suivi Intensif dans le Milieu en Équipe); Clinique externe de psychiatrie de L'Assomption

Trois-Pistoles: CSSS des Basques
550, rue Notre-Dame est, Trois-Pistoles, QC G0L 4K0
Tél: 418-851-1111
www.csssbasques.qc.ca
Personnel: 210

Trois-Rivières: CSSS de Trois-Rivières
Affiliée à: CIUSSS de la Mauricie et du Centre-du-Québec
731, rue Ste-Julie, Trois-Rivières, QC G9A 1Y1
Tél: 819-370-2100
www.cssstr.qc.ca
Média social: www.facebook.com/csss.trois.rivieres; www.youtube.com/cssstr
Note: Les Installations (Services de CH, CHSLD, et CLSC): Centre hospitalier affilié universitaire régional (819-697-3333); Centre Cloutier-du Rivage (819-370-2100); Centre St-Joseph (819-370-2100); Centre d'hébergement Cooke (819-370-2100); Centre d'hébergement Louis-Denoncourt (819-376-2566); Centre d'hébergement Roland-Leclerc (819-370-2100); Centre de services Les Forges (819-379-5650); Centre Ste-Geneviève (819-370-2200, poste 46101); Centre de l'Horloge (819-370-2100); Centre Arc-en-Ciel (pédopsychiatrie, 819-374-6291); Centre de prêt d'équipement (819-370-2100)

Val-d'Or: CSSS de la Vallée-de-l'Or (CSSSVO)
Affiliée à: CISSS de l'Abitibi-Témiscamingue
Pavillon Germain-Bigué, 725, 6e rue, Val-d'Or, QC J9P 3Y1
Tél: 819-825-5858; *Téléc:* 819-825-7873
www.csssvo.qc.ca
Média social: www.facebook.com/189290301107018
Fondée en: 2004
Nombre de lits: 88 lits (CH); 183 lits (CHSLD)
Population desservi: 43 000; *Personnel:* 1300
Note: Les Installations (Services de CH, CHSLD, et CLSC): Hôpital de Val-d'Or (819-825-5858); Hôpital psychiatrique de Malartic (819-825-5858); Centre d'hébergement de Val-d'Or (819-825-5858); Centre d'hébergement Saint-Martin de Malartic (819-825-5858); CLSC de Val-d'Or (819-825-5858); CLSC de Senneterre (819-825-5858); CLSC de Malartic (819-825-5858); Unité de médecine familiale de la Vallée-de-l'Or (819-825-5858, poste 3549); Clinique externe de psychiatrie (819-825-5858)

Victoriaville: CSSS d'Arthabaska-et-de-l'Érable
Affiliée à: CIUSSS de la Mauricie et du Centre-du-Québec
Centre administratif, 5, rue des Hospitalières, Victoriaville, QC G6P 6N2
Tél: 819-357-2030
www.csssae.qc.ca
Note: Les Installations (Services de CH, CHSLD, et CLSC): Hôtel-Dieu d'Arthabaska; CLSC Suzor-Coté; CLSC des Bois-Francs; CLSC de l'Érable; CLSC Saint-Louis; Centre

d'hébergement du Chêne; Centre d'hébergement du Roseau; Centre d'hébergement des Étoiles-d'Or; Centre d'hébergement du Sacré-Coeur; Centre d'hébergement des Quatre-Vents; Centre d'hébergement des Bois-Francs; Centre d'hébergement de Saint-Eusèbe; Centre d'hébergement du Tilleul

Ville-Marie: CSSS du Témiscamingue (CSSST)
Affiliée à: CISSS de l'Abitibi-Témiscamingue
Ancien nom: CSSS du Lac-Témiscamingue; CSSS de Témiscaming-et-de-Kipawa
Services administratifs, 22, rue Notre-Dame Nord, Ville-Marie, QC J9V 1W8
Tél: 819-629-2420; *Téléc:* 819-629-3257
www.cssst.ca
Fondée en: 2011
Population desservi: 17 000; *Personnel:* 600
Note: Les Installations (Services de CH, CHSLD, et CLSC): Pavillon Sainte-Famille (CH et CLSC); Pavillon Témiscaming-Kipawa (CH, CLSC, et CHSLD); Pavillon Duhamel (CHSLD). Points de services: Angliers; Laforce; Latulipe; Moffet; Nédélec; Notre-Dame-du-Nord; Rémigny

Wakefield: CSSS des Collines
Affiliée à: CISSS de l'Outaouais
101, ch Burnside, Wakefield, QC J0X 3G0
Tél: 819-459-1112; *Téléc:* 819-459-1894
www.santedescollines.qc.ca
Note: Les Installations (Services de CH, CHSLD, et CLSC): L'Hôpital Mémorial de Wakefield; Le Centre d'hébergement La Pêche; Le CLSC des Collines (Cantley, Chelsea, Masham, Val-des-Monts).
Les Municipalités: Cantley; Chelsea; La Pêche; Val-des-Monts (excluant le secteur Poltimore)
André Désilets, Directeur général

Weedon: CSSS du Haut-Saint-François
Affiliée à: CIUSSS de l'Estrie
460, 2e av, Weedon, QC J0B 3J0
Tél: 819-821-4000; *Téléc:* 819-877-3714
www.cssshsf.com
Région desservi: MRC du Haut-Saint-François (14 municipalités)
Note: Les Installations (Services de CH, CHSLD, et CLSC): Centre d'hébergement d'East Angus (819-832-2487); Centre d'hébergement de Weedon (819-877-2500); CLSC de Weedon (819-877-3434); CLSC de Cookshire (819-875-3373); CLSC de La Patrie (819-888-2811); CLSC d'East Angus (819-832-4961)

Windsor: CSSS du Val-Saint-François
Affiliée à: CIUSSS de l'Estrie
Centre administratif, 79, rue Allen, Windsor, QC J1S 2P8
Tél: 819-542-2777; *Téléc:* 819-845-5521
recrutement.vsf@ssss.gouv.qc.ca (services administratifs)
www.csssvsf.com
Média social: twitter.com/csssvsf; www.linkedin.com/company/1149395
Note: Les Installations (Services de CH, CHSLD, et CLSC): CLSC - Urgence mineure de Windsor; CLSC de Richmond; CLSC de Valcourt; Centre d'hébergement de Windsor; Centre d'hébergement de Richmond; Centre d'hébergement de Valcourt

Centres hospitaliers

Amos: Hôpital Hôtel-Dieu d'Amos
Affiliée à: CISSS de l'Abitibi-Témiscamingue
622, 4e rue Ouest, Amos, QC J9T 2S2
Tél: 819-732-3341
Note: Services diagnostiques; urgence et traumatologie; othopédie; rhumatologie; ophtalmologie; chirurgie plastique/reconstructive/maxillo-faciale; gynécologie; obstétrique; gériatrie; physiotherapie; réadaptation cardio-respiratoire.

Amqui: Le centre hospitalier d'Amqui
Affiliée à: CISSS du Bas-St-Laurent
135, av Gaétan-Archambault, Amqui, QC G5J 2K5
Tél: 418-629-2211; *Téléc:* 418-629-4498
www.chamqui.com
Population desservi: 21000
Alain Paquet, Directeur général

Baie-Comeau: Hôpital Le Royer
Affiliée à: CISSS de la Côte-Nord
635, boul Jolliet, Baie-Comeau, QC G5C 1P1
Tél: 418-589-3701; *Téléc:* 418-589-9654
Fondée en: 1951
Nombre de lits: 85 lits de santé physique; 21 lits de psychiatrie
Note: Pprogrammes et services comprennent: chirurgie; médecine nucléaire; pédopsychiatrie; radiologie; urologie

Baie-Saint-Paul: Hôpital de Baie-Saint-Paul
Affiliée à: CIUSSS de la Capitale-Nationale
74, rue Ambroise-Fafard, Baie-Saint-Paul, QC G3Z 2J6
Tél: 418-435-5150; *Téléc:* 418-435-3315
Nombre de lits: 40 lits hospitaliers; 56 lits de soins de longue durée
Note: Services: anesthésie, chirurgie, gériatrie, psychiatrie, radiologie, ophtalmologie, urologie; soins généraux et spécialisés; urgence.

Beaupré: Hôpital Sainte-Anne-de-Beaupré
Affiliée à: CIUSSS de la Capitale-Nationale
11000, rue des Montagnards, Beaupré, QC G0A 1E0
Tél: 418-827-3726; *Téléc:* 418-827-3563
Nombre de lits: 158 lits d'hébergement et de soins de longue durée; 9 lits UTRF; 3 lits de soins palliatifs; 2 lits de transition
Note: Services infirmiers, médicaux, et psychosociaux.
Lucie Lacroix, Directrice générale, CSSS de Québec-Nord

Cap-aux-Meules: Hôpital de l'Archipel
Affiliée à: CISSS des Iles
430, ch Principal, Cap-aux-Meules, QC G4T 1R9
Tél: 418-986-2121
Nombre de lits: 105 lits

Chandler: Hôpital de Chandler
Affiliée à: CISSS de la Gaspésie
451, rue Mgr Ross Est, Chandler, QC G0C 1K0
Tél: 418-689-2261; *Téléc:* 418-689-5551
Nombre de lits: 155 lits
Note: Soins hospitaliers; soins de longue durée; a fusionné avec le CLSC-CHSLD Pabok en 2004.

Châteauguay: Hôpital Anna-Laberge
Affiliée à: CISSS de la Montérégie-Ouest
200, boul Brisebois, Châteauguay, QC J6K 4W8
Tél: 450-699-2425
www.santemonteregie.qc.ca
Fondée en: 1988
Nombre de lits: 226 lits hospitaliers
Paul Moreau, Directeur général, CSSS Jardins-Roussillon

Chicoutimi: Hôpital de Chicoutimi
Affiliée à: CIUSSS du Saguenay-Lac-St-Jean
305, rue Saint-Vallier, Chicoutimi, QC G7H 5H6
Tél: 418-541-1000; *Téléc:* 418-541-1144
Ligne sans frais: 866-404-7468

Chisasibi: Hôpital de Chisasibi
Affiliée à: Conseil Cri de la santé et des services sociaux de la Baie James
21, rue Maamuu, Chisasibi, QC J0M 1E0
Tél: 819-855-2844; *Téléc:* 819-855-9060
www.creehealth.org/services/chisasibi-hospital
Nombre de lits: 17 servent aux soins actifs (5 en pédiatrie); 9 aux malades chroniques; 3 aux soins respiratoires; 9 hémodialyse
Personnel: 34

Coaticook: Centre hospitalier de Coaticook
Affiliée à: CIUSSS de l'Estrie
138, rue Jeanne-Mance, Coaticook, QC J1A 1W3
Tél: 819-849-9102
info@cssscoaticook.ca

Dolbeau-Mistassini: Hôpital de Dolbeau-Mistassini
Affiliée à: CIUSSS du Saguenay-Lac-Saint-Jean
2000, boul Sacré-Coeur, Dolbeau-Mistassini, QC G8L 2R5
Tél: 418-276-1234; *Téléc:* 418-276-4355

Donnacona: Centre hospitalier Portneuf
Affiliée à: CIUSSS de la Capitale-Nationale
250, boul Gaudreau, Donnacona, QC G3M 1L7
Tél: 418-285-3025; *Téléc:* 418-285-3508
csssdeportneuf.qc.ca
Nombre de lits: 369 lits
Lucie Gagnon, Directrice générale
Philippe Leboeuf, Président du conseil d'administration

Drummondville: Hôpital Sainte-Croix
Affiliée à: CIUSSS de la santé Mauricie-et-du-Centre-du-Québec
570, rue Heriot, Drummondville, QC J2B 1C1
Tél: 819-478-6464
www.csssdrummond.qc.ca
Note: Anatomopathologie, chirurgie générale, gynécologie-obstétrique, pédiatrie, médecine familiale/interne/nucléaire, ophtalmologie, orthopédie, psychiatrie, radiologie, urologie.

Gaspé: Hôpital Hôtel-Dieu de Gaspé
Affiliée à: CISSS de la Gaspésie
215, boul de York Ouest, Gaspé, QC G4X 2W2
Tél: 418-368-3301

Gatineau: Hôpital de Gatineau
Affiliée à: CISSS de l'Outaouais
909, boul de La Vérendrye, Gatineau, QC J8P 7H2
Tél: 819-966-6100 *Ligne sans frais:* 800-267-2325
www.csssgatineau.qc.ca
Info Line: 819-966-6333

Gatineau: Hôpital de Hull
Affiliée à: CISSS de l'Outaouais
116, boul Lionel-Émond, Gatineau, QC J8Y 1W7
Tél: 819-966-6200 *Ligne sans frais:* 866-595-2002
www.csssgatineau.qc.ca
Info Line: 819-966-6222

Gatineau: Hôpital de Papineau
Affiliée à: CISSS de l'Outaouais
155, rue Maclaren est, Gatineau, QC J8L 0C2
Tél: 819-986-3341
Nombre de lits: 63 lits hospitaliers; 55 lits soins longue durée

Greenfield Park: Hôpital Charles LeMoyne
Affiliée à: CISSS de la Montérégie-Centre
3120, boul Taschereau, Greenfield Park, QC J4V 2H1
Tél: 450-466-5000
Note: L'Hôpital est le centre hospitalier régional et universitaire de la Montéregie; affilié à l'Université de Sherbrooke; soins et services de court durée en santé physique, santé mentale, réadaptation; recherche; enseignement universitaire.

Jonquière: Hôpital de Jonquière
Affiliée à: CIUSSS du Saguenay-Lac-St-Jean
CP 1200, 2230, rue de l'Hôpital, Jonquière, QC G7X 7X2
Tél: 418-695-7700
csssjonquiere@ssss.gouv.qc.ca

La Baie: Hôpital de La Baie
Affiliée à: CIUSSS du Saguenay-Lac-St-Jean
CP 38, 1000, rue Docteur-Desgagné, La Baie, QC G7B 3P9
Tél: 418-544-3381; *Téléc:* 416-544-0770

La Malbaie: Hôpital de La Malbaie
Affiliée à: CIUSSS de la Capitale-Nationale
303, rue St-Étienne, La Malbaie, QC G5A 1T1
Tél: 418-665-1700; *Téléc:* 418-665-1732
Micheline Tremblay, Directrice générale, CSSS de Charlevoix
micheline.tremblay@ssss.gouv.qc.ca

La Pocatière: L'Hôpital Notre-Dame-de-Fatima
Affiliée à: CISSS du Bas-St-Laurent
1201, 6e Av Pilote, La Pocatière, QC G0R 1Z0
Tél: 418-856-7000; *Téléc:* 418-856-4737
Nombre de lits: 49 lits

La Sarre: Centre hospitalier de La Sarre
Affiliée à: CISSS de l'Abitibi-Témiscamingue
679, 2e rue Est, La Sarre, QC J9Z 2X7
Tél: 819-333-2311; *Téléc:* 819-333-4316

LaSalle: Hôpital de LaSalle
Affiliée à: CIUSSS de l'Ouest-de-l'Ile-de-Montréal
8585, Terrasse Champlain, LaSalle, QC H8P 1C1
Tél: 514-362-8000

Laval: Hôpital de la Cité-de-la-Santé
Affiliée à: CISSS de Laval
1755, boul René-Laennec, Laval, QC H7M 3L9
Tél: 450-668-1010

Laval: Jewish Rehabilitation Hospital (JRH)/Hôpital juif de réadaptation
Affiliée à: CISSS de Laval
3205, Place Alton-Goldbloom, Laval, QC H7V 1R2
Tél: 450-688-9550
www.hjr-jrh.qc.ca
Fondée en: 1962
Nombre de lits: 132
Personnel: 557
Gary Stoopler, Executive Director

Laval: Santé Courville inc.
5200, 80e rue, Laval, QC H7R 5T6
Tél: 450-627-7990; *Téléc:* 450-627-7993
santecourville.com
Fondée en: 1935
Nombre de lits: 120 lits
Christine Durocher, Directrice générale

Lévis: Hôtel-Dieu de Lévis
Affiliée à: CISSS de Chaudière-Appalache
143, rue Wolfe, Lévis, QC G6V 3Z1
Tél: 418-835-7121 *Ligne sans frais:* 888-835-7105
Note: Associé à l'Université Laval.
Hervé Moysan, Directeur général
Robert Amyot, Directeur, Services techniques

Diana Lancup, Responsable des services sanitaires et lingerie

Longueuil: Hôpital Pierre-Boucher
Affiliée à: CISSS de la Montérégie-Est
1333, boul Jacques-Cartier Est, Longueuil, QC J4M 2A5
Tél: 450-468-8111
Note: Services comprennent: urgence; soins intensifs; soins palliatifs; services médicaux; chirurgie; psychiatrie.

Maniwaki: Hôpital de Maniwaki
Affiliée à: CISSS de l'Outaouais
309, boul Desjardins, Maniwaki, QC J9E 2E7
Tél: 819-449-2300; *Téléc:* 819-449-6137
Fondée en: 1998
Nombre de lits: 36 lits de courte durée; 4 lits soins intermédiaires

Maria: Hôpital de Maria
Affiliée à: CISSS de la Gaspésie
419, boul Perron, Maria, QC G0C 1Y0
Tél: 418-759-3443; *Téléc:* 418-759-5063
csssbc.qc.ca
Nombre de lits: 77 lits
Note: Unité de médecine familiale Baie-des-Chaleurs: 418-759-1336, poste 2811.
Bernard Nadeau, Directeur général, CSSS de la Baie-des-Chaleurs

Matane: Hôpital de Matane
Affiliée à: CISSS du Bas-St-Laurent
333, rue Thibault, Matane, QC G4W 2W5
Tél: 418-562-3135; *Téléc:* 418-562-9374
Population desservi: 21000
Nicole Morin, Directrice générale

Mont-Laurier: Hôpital de Mont-Laurier
Affiliée à: CISSS des Laurentides
2561, ch de la Lièvre sud, Mont-Laurier, QC J9L 3G3
Tél: 819-623-1234; *Téléc:* 819-440-4299

Montmagny: Hôpital de Montmagny
Affiliée à: CISSS de Chaudière-Appalaches
350, boul Taché Ouest, Montmagny, QC G5V 3R8
Tél: 418-248-0630; *Téléc:* 418-248-6838
Spécialités: Oncologie; Radiologie; Psychiatrie; Physiothérapie; Ergothérapie; Inhalothérapie

Montréal: Centre hospitalier de l'Université de Montréal
Affiliée à: CIUSSS du Centre-Est-de-l'Ile-de-Montréal
3840, rue St-Urbain, Montréal, QC H2W 1T8
Tél: 514-890-8000
www.chumontreal.qc.ca
Média social: www.facebook.com/chum.montreal; twitter.com/chumontreal; www.youtube.com/user/chumontreal
Nombre de lits: 1217 lits hospitaliers, 170 lits longue durée
Fabrice Brunet, Président-Directeur général

Montréal: Centre hospitalier de St. Mary
Affiliée à: CIUSSS de l'Ouest-de-l'Ile-de-Montréal
3830, av Lacombe, Montréal, QC H3T 1M5
Tél: 514-345-3511
www.smhc.qc.ca
Nombre de lits: 271 lits hospitaliers
Ralph Dadoun, Directeur général

Montréal: Centre universitaire de santé McGill - Hôpital neurologique de Montréal/Montreal Neurological Institute & Hospital
Affiliée à: CIUSSS du Centre-Ouest-de-l'Ile-de-Montréal
3801, rue University, Montréal, QC H3A 2B4
Tél: 514-398-6644
www.mni.mcgill.ca
Nombre de lits: 65 lits de soins de courte durée; 14 lits de soins neurologiques intensifs
Guy Rouleau, Directeur général

Montréal: Hôpital Catherine Booth de l'Armée du Salut
Affiliée à: CIUSSS du Centre-Ouest-de-l'Ile-de-Montréal
4375, av Montclair, Montréal, QC H4B 2J5
Tél: 514-484-7878
Note: Réadaptation

Montréal: Hôpital de réadaptation Lindsay
6363, ch Hudson, Montréal, QC H3S 1M9
Tél: 514-737-3661
www.irglm.qc.ca
Fondée en: 1914
Note: Hôpital spécialisé de courte-durée

Montréal: Hôpital de Verdun
Affiliée à: CIUSSS du Centre-Est-de-l'Ile-de-Montréal
4000, boul LaSalle, Montréal, QC H4G 2A3
Tél: 514-362-1000
www.ciusss-centresudmtl.gouv.qc.ca

Montréal: Hôpital du Sacré-Coeur de Montréal
Affiliée à: CIUSSS du Nord-de-l'Ile-de-Montréal
5400, boul Gouin ouest, Montréal, QC H4J 1C5
Tél: 514-338-2222
www.hscm.ca
Nombre de lits: 554 lits hospitaliers
Note: outpatient services & trauma centre

Montréal: Hôpital Fleury
Affiliée à: CIUSSS du Nord-de-l'Ile-de-Montréal
2180, rue Fleury Est, Montréal, QC H2B 1K3
Tél: 514-384-2000
ciusss-nordmtl.gouv.qc.ca
Nombre de lits: 174 lits
Région desservi: Le territoire d'Ahuntsic et de Montréal-Nord, QC
Spécialités: Prélèvements; Urgence psychiatrique

Montréal: Hôpital général de Montréal/The Montreal General Hospital
1650, av Cedar, Montréal, QC H3G 1A4
Tél: 514-934-1934
www.muhc.ca
Fondée en: 1821
Nombre de lits: 533 beds
Normand Rinfret, Directeur général, MUHC

Montréal: Hôpital général juif Sir Mortimer B. Davis/Sir Mortimer B. Davis Jewish General Hospital
Affiliée à: CIUSSS du Centre-Ouest-de-l'Ile-de-Montréal
3755, ch Côte Ste-Catherine, Montréal, QC H3T 1E2
Tél: 514-340-8222; *Téléc:* 514-340-7510
jgh.ca
Nombre de lits: 637 lits hospitaliers
Personnel: 4869
Lawrence Rosenberg, Président-directeur général
Georges Bendavid, Directeur, Services techniques par intérim

Montréal: Hôpital Jean-Talon
Affiliée à: CIUSSS du Nord-de-l'Ile-de-Montréal
1385, rue Jean-Talon Est, Montréal, QC H2E 1S6
Tél: 514-495-6767
www.cssscoeurdelile.ca

Montréal: Hôpital Maisonneuve-Rosemont
Affiliée à: CIUSSS de l'Est-de-l'Ile-de-Montréal
5415, boul de l'Assomption, Montréal, QC H1T 2M4
Tél: 514-252-3400
www.maisonneuve-rosemont.org
Média social: www.facebook.com/351488907544; www.youtube.com/user/HMRmontreal

Montréal: Hôpital Mont-Sinai
Affiliée à: CIUSSS du Centre-Ouest-de-l'Ile-de-Montréal
5690, boul Cavendish, Montréal, QC H4W 1S7
Tél: 514-369-2222; *Téléc:* 514-369-2225
www.sinaimontreal.ca
Fondée en: 1909
Nombre de lits: 107 lits
Note: Services comprennent: soins respiratoires; soins palliatifs; soins long-terme; services de soutien. Affilié avec McGill University
Barbara Gold, Responable

Montréal: Hôpital Richardson
Affiliée à: CIUSSS du Centre-Ouest-de-l'Ile-de-Montréal
5425, rue Bessborough, Montréal, QC H4V 2S7
Tél: 514-484-7878; *Téléc:* 514-483-4596
www.cssscavendish.qc.ca
Anna Maria Malorni, Personne ressource
514-484-7878, annamaria.malorni.cvd@ssss.gouv.qc.c

Montréal: Hôpital Santa Cabrini
Affiliée à: CIUSSS de l'Est-de-l'Ile-de-Montréal
5655, rue St-Zotique est, Montréal, QC H1T 1P7
Tél: 514-252-6000
www.santacabrini.qc.ca
Nombre de lits: 472 lits hospitaliers
Jean-François Foisy, Directeur général

Montréal: Hôpital Shriners pour enfants (Quebec) inc.
1003, boul Decarie, Montréal, QC H4A 0A9
Tél: 514-842-4464; *Téléc:* 514-842-7553
Ligne sans frais: 800-361-7256
fr.shrinershospitalsforchildren.org/%C3%A9tablissements/lrf/canada
Céline Doray, Directrice générale

Montréal: Institut de cardiologie de Montréal
Affiliée à: CIUSSS de l'Est-de-l'Ile-de-Montréal
5000, rue Bélanger, Montréal, QC H1T 1C8
Tél: 514-376-3330 *Ligne sans frais:* 855-922-6387
www.icm-mhi.org
Média social: www.facebook.com/institutcardiologiemontreal; twitter.com/ICMtl; www.youtube.com/user/InstitutdeCardioMtl
Nombre de lits: 153 lits
Personnel: 1900
Dr. Denis Roy, Président-directeur général

Montréal: Institut Philippe Pinel de Montréal
10905, boul Henri-Bourassa est, Montréal, QC H1C 1H1
Tél: 514-648-8461
www.pinel.qc.ca
Fondée en: 1927
Nombre de lits: 292 lits
Personnel: 700
Dre Renée Fugère, Preésidente-Directrice générale
Anne Côté, Directrice, Services techniques

Montréal: Institut universitaire de gériatrie de Montréal (IUGM)
Affiliée à: CIUSSS du Centre-Est-de-l'Ile-de-Montréal
Pavillon Côte-des-Neiges, 4565, ch Queen-Mary, Montréal, QC H3W 1W5
Tél: 514-340-2800; *Téléc:* 514-340-2802
www.iugm.qc.ca
Nombre de lits: 446 lits
Note: Affilié à l'Université de Montréal.

Notre-Dame-du-Lac: Hôpital de Notre-Dame-du-Lac
Affiliée à: CISSS du Bas-St-Laurent
58, rue de l'Église, Notre-Dame-du-Lac, QC G0L 1X0
Tél: 418-899-6751; *Téléc:* 418-899-2809
Ligne sans frais: 855-899-2424
Nombre de lits: 35 lits
Marie-Claude Ouellet, Directrice générale par intérim

Ormstown: Hôpital Barrie Memorial
Affiliée à: CISSS de la Montérégie-Ouest
28, rue Gale, Ormstown, QC J0S 1K0
Tél: 450-829-2321; *Téléc:* 450-829-3582
www.santemonteregie.qc.ca/haut-saint-laurent
Fondée en: 2006
Note: Affilié à l'université McGill.

Pointe-Claire: Hôpital général du Lakeshore
Affiliée à: CIUSSS de l'Ouest-de-l'Ile-de-Montréal
160, av Stillview, Pointe-Claire, QC H9R 2Y2
Tél: 514-630-2225
www.csssouestdelile.qc.ca
Nombre de lits: 227 lits hospitaliers

Québec: Centre hospitalier de l'Université Laval (CHUL)
Centre hospitalier universitaire de Québec
Affiliée à: CIUSSS de la Capitale-Nationale
2705, boul Laurier, Québec, QC G1V 4G2
Tél: 418-525-4444; *Téléc:* 418-654-2762
www.chuq.qc.ca
Note: Affilié à l'Université Laval.
Gertrude Bourdon, Présidente-directrice générale

Québec: Centre hospitalier universitaire de Québec (CHUQ)
11, côte du Palais, Québec, QC G1R 2J6
Tél: 418-525-4444
www.chuq.qc.ca
Média social: www.facebook.com/chudequebec; twitter.com/chudequebec; www.youtube.com/user/chudequebec; linkedin.com/company/centre-hospitalier-universitaire-de-qu-bec
Personnel: 13500
Gertrude Bourdon, Présidente-Directrice générale

Québec: Hôpital Chauveau
Affiliée à: CIUSSS de la Capitale-Nationale
11999, rue de l'Hôpital, Québec, QC G2A 2T7
Tél: 418-842-3651; *Téléc:* 418-842-8660
www.csssqn.qc.ca
Note: Services: anesthésie, chirurgie, gériatrie, psychiatrie, radiologie, ophtalmologie, urologie; soins généraux et spécialisés; urgence.
Dr. Gilles Caron, Chef du service de l'urgence

***Québec:* Hôpital de l'Enfant-Jésus**
Affiliée à: CIUSSS de la Capitale-Nationale
1401, 18e rue, Québec, QC G1J 1Z4
Tél: 418-649-0252
www.cha.quebec.qc.ca
Note: Affilié à l'Université Laval et Université de Québec.
Marie Girard, Directrice générale

***Québec:* Hôpital du Saint-Sacrement**
Centre hospitalier affilié universitaire de Québec
Affiliée à: CIUSSS de la Capitale-Nationale
1050, ch Sainte-Foy, Québec, QC G1S 4L8
Tél: 418-682-7511
www.cha.quebec.qc.ca
Note: Affilié à l'Université Laval et Université de Québec.
Marie Girard, Directrice générale

***Québec:* Hôpital Jeffery Hale**
Affiliée à: CIUSSS de la Capitale-Nationale
1250, ch Ste-Foy, Québec, QC G1S 2M6
Tél: 418-684-5333 *Ligne sans frais:* 888-984-5333
www.jhsb.ca
Nombre de lits: 99 lits de soins de longue durée

***Québec:* Hôpital Saint-François d'Assise**
Centre hospitalier universitaire de Québec
Affiliée à: CIUSSS de la Capitale-Nationale
10, rue de l'Espinay, Québec, QC G1L 3L5
Tél: 418-525-4444; *Téléc:* 418-525-6338
www.chuq.qc.ca
Note: Affilié à l'Université Laval.

***Québec:* L'Hôtel-Dieu de Québec**
Centre hospitalier universitaire de Québec
Affiliée à: CIUSSS de la Capitale-Nationale
11, côte du Palais, Québec, QC G1R 2J6
Tél: 418-525-4444; *Téléc:* 418-691-5205
www.chuq.qc.ca
Note: Affilié à l'Université Laval.

***Québec:* Institut universitaire de cardiologie et de pneumologie de Québec (IUCPQ)**
Affiliée à: CIUSSS de la Capitale-Nationale
Ancien nom: Hôpital Laval
2725, ch Sainte-Foy, Québec, QC G1V 4G5
Tél: 418-656-8711; *Téléc:* 418-656-4829
iucpq.qc.ca
Média social: twitter.com/IUCPQ; www.youtube.com/IUCPQ; www.linkedin.com/company/iucpq
Fondée en: 1918
Personnel: 3000
Note: Spécialisé dans la santé des personnes souffrant de maladies cardio-pulmonaires et dans le traitement des troubles liés à l'obésité. Affilié à l'Université Laval.

***Rimouski:* Hôpital régional de Rimouski**
Affiliée à: CISSS du Bas-St-Laurent
150, av Rouleau, Rimouski, QC G5L 5T1
Tél: 418-724-3000; *Téléc:* 418-724-8632
Nombre de lits: 255 lits

***Rivière-Rouge:* Centre de services de Rivière-Rouge**
Affiliée à: CISSS des Laurentides
1525, rue L'Annonciation nord, Rivière-Rouge, QC J0T 1T0
Tél: 819-623-1234
mylene.perrier@ssss.gouv.qc.ca
www.csssal.org
Média social: fr.facebook.com/182385008476466
Jean-Pierre Urbain, Directeur général, CSSS d'Antoine-Labelle

***Rivière-du-Loup:* Le Centre hospitalier régional du Grand-Portage (CHRGP)**
Affiliée à: CISSS du Bas-St-Laurent
75, rue Saint-Henri, Rivière-du-Loup, QC G5R 2A4
Tél: 418-868-1000; *Téléc:* 418-868-1035
Nombre de lits: 145 lits
Daniel Lévesque, Directeur général

***Roberval:* Hôtel-Dieu de Roberval / Centre d'hébergement Roberval**
Affiliée à: CIUSSS du Saguenay-Lac-Saint-Jean
450, rue Brassard, Roberval, QC G8H 1B9
Tél: 418-275-0110; *Téléc:* 418-275-6202
Note: L'hôpital offre service d'urgence, médecine générale/interne/nucléaire, ophtalmologie, obstétrique, orthopédie, pédiatrie, chirurgie, psychiatrie, urologie, réadaptation physique.
Jacques Dubois, Directeur général, CSSS Domaine-du-Roy

***Rouyn-Noranda:* Hôpital de Rouyn-Noranda**
Affiliée à: CISSS de l'Abitibi-Témiscamingue
4, 9e rue, Rouyn-Noranda, QC J9X 2B2
Tél: 819-764-5131

***Saint-Charles-Borromée:* Centre hospitalier régional de Lanaudière (CHRDL)**
Affiliée à: CISSS de Lanaudière
1000, boul Sainte-Anne, Saint-Charles-Borromée, QC J6E 6J2
Tél: 450-759-8222

***Saint-Eustache:* Hôpital de Saint-Eustache**
Affiliée à: CISSS des Laurentides
520, boul Arthur-Sauvé, Saint-Eustache, QC J7R 5B1
Tél: 450-473-6811; *Téléc:* 450-473-6966
Ligne sans frais: 888-234-3837
Nombre de lits: 261 lits

***Saint-Georges:* Hôpital de Saint-Georges**
Affiliée à: CISSS de Chaudière-Appalaches
1515, 17e rue, Saint-Georges, QC G5Y 4T8
Tél: 418-228-2031; *Téléc:* 418-227-3825

***Saint-Hyacinthe:* Hôpital Honoré-Mercier**
Affiliée à: CISSS de la Montérégie-Est
2750, boul Laframboise, Saint-Hyacinthe, QC J2S 4Y8
Tél: 450-771-3333
Note: Services comprennent: centre mère-enfant-famille; Pédiatrie; Soins intensifs; Chirurgie.

***Saint-Jean-sur-Richelieu:* Hôpital du Haut-Richelieu**
Affiliée à: CISSS de la Montérégie-Centre
920, boul du Séminaire Nord, Saint-Jean-sur-Richelieu, QC J3A 1B7
Tél: 450-359-5000; *Téléc:* 450-359-5251
Ligne sans frais: 866-967-4825
Nombre de lits: 307 lits
Personnel: 1 500
Note: L'Hôpital, et le centre administratif du CSSS Haut-Richelieu-Rouville.

***Saint-Jérôme:* Hôpital régional de Saint-Jérôme**
Affiliée à: CISSS des Laurentides
290, rue de Montigny, Saint-Jérôme, QC J7Z 5T3
Tél: 450-432-2777 *Ligne sans frais:* 866-963-2777

***Saint-Raymond:* Hôpital régional de Portneuf**
Affiliée à: CIUSSS de la Capitale-Nationale
700, rue Saint-Cyrille, Saint-Raymond, QC G3L 1W1
Tél: 418-337-4611; *Téléc:* 418-337-8919

***Sainte-Agathe-des-Monts:* Hôpital Laurentien**
Affiliée à: CISSS des Laurentides
234, rue Saint-Vincent, Sainte-Agathe-des-Monts, QC J8C 2B8
Tél: 819-324-4000 *Ligne sans frais:* 855-766-6387

***Sainte-Anne-de-Bellevue:* Hôpital Sainte-Anne**
Le ministère des affaires des anciens combattants, 305, boul des Anciens-Combattants, Sainte-Anne-de-Bellevue, QC H9X 1Y9
Tél: 514-457-3440 *Ligne sans frais:* 800-361-9287
information@vac-acc.gc.ca
www.vac-acc.gc.ca
Nombre de lits: 590 lits
Rachel Corneille-Gravel, Directrice générale

***Salaberry-de-Valleyfield:* Hôpital du Suroît**
Affiliée à: CISSS de la Montérégie-Ouest
150, rue Saint-Thomas, Salaberry-de-Valleyfield, QC J6T 6C1
Tél: 450-371-9920

***Sept-Iles:* Hôpital de Sept-Iles**
Affiliée à: CISSS de la Côte-Nord
45, rue du Père-Divet, Sept-Iles, QC G4R 3N7
Tél: 418-962-9761; *Téléc:* 418-962-2701

***Shawinigan:* Hôpital du Centre-de-la-Mauricie**
Affiliée à: CIUSSS de la Mauricie-et-du-Centre-du-Québec
50, 119 rue, Shawinigan, QC G9P 5K1
Tél: 819-536-7500
www.etrehumain.ca

***Shawville:* Centre hospitalier du Pontiac**
Affiliée à: CISSS de l'Outaouais
200, rue Argue, Shawville, QC J0X 2Y0
Tél: 819-647-2211; *Téléc:* 819-647-2409

***Sherbrooke:* Centre hospitalier universitaire de Sherbrooke - Édifice Murray (CHUS)**
Affiliée à: CIUSSS de l'Estrie
500, rue Murray, Sherbrooke, QC J1G 2K6
Tél: 819-346-1110 *Ligne sans frais:* 866-638-2601
www.chus.qc.ca
Média social: www.facebook.com/CHUSherbrooke; twitter.com/CHUSherbrooke; www.youtube.com/user/CHUSherbrooke
Fondée en: 1995
Nombre de lits: 677 lits
Région desservi: Sherbrooke; Haut-St-François; Val-St-François; MRC de Coaticook; *Personnel:* 6202
Note: Programmes et services comprennent: chimiothérapie cérébrale; neurochirurgie par scalpel-gamma; neurochirurgie assistée par IRM 3D avancé; dépistage du cancer colorectal; production de radioisotopes par cyclotron (au Centre de recherche). Associé à l'Université de Sherbrooke.
Stéphane Tremblay, Directeur général
Patrice Laplante, Chef, Département de médecine générale par intérim
Céline E. Gervais, Directrice, Soins infirmiers

***Sherbrooke:* Centre hospitalier universitaire de Sherbrooke - Fleurimont (CHUS)**
Affiliée à: CIUSSS de l'Estrie
3001, 12e Av Nord, Sherbrooke, QC J1H 5N4
Tél: 819-346-1110 *Ligne sans frais:* 866-638-2601
www.chus.qc.ca
Média social: www.facebook.com/pages/Le-CHUS-Page-officielle/188395517869328; twitter.com/CHUSherbrooke; www.youtube.com/user/CHUSherbrooke
Fondée en: 1995
Nombre de lits: 677 lits
Région desservi: Sherbrooke; Haut-St-François; Val-St-François; MRC de Coaticook; *Personnel:* 6202
Note: Programmes et services comprennent: chimiothérapie cérébrale; neurochirurgie par scalpel-gamma; neurochirurgie assistée par IRM 3D avancé; dépistage du cancer colorectal; production de radioisotopes par cyclotron (au Centre de recherche). Associé à l'Université de Sherbrooke.

***Sherbrooke:* Centre hospitalier universitaire de Sherbrooke - Hôtel-Dieu (CHUS)**
Affiliée à: CIUSSS de l'Estrie
580, rue Bowen Sud, Sherbrooke, QC J1G 2E8
Tél: 819-346-1110 *Ligne sans frais:* 866-638-2601
www.chus.qc.ca
Média social: www.facebook.com/pages/Le-CHUS-Page-officielle/188395517869328; twitter.com/CHUSherbrooke; www.youtube.com/user/CHUSherbrooke
Fondée en: 1995
Nombre de lits: 677 lits
Région desservi: Sherbrooke; Haut-St-François; Val-St-François; MRC de Coaticook; *Personnel:* 6202
Note: Programmes et services comprennent: chimiothérapie cérébrale; neurochirurgie par scalpel-gamma; neurochirurgie assistée par IRM 3D avancé; dépistage du cancer colorectal; production de radioisotopes par cyclotron (au Centre de recherche). Associé à l'Université de Sherbrooke.

***Sherbrooke:* Hôpital et Centre d'hébergement Argyll**
Affiliée à: CIUSSS de L'Estrie
375, rue Argyll, Sherbrooke, QC J1J 3H5
Tél: 819-780-2222
Note: Programmes et services comprennent: centre d'hébergement; centre de prélèvements; cliniques ambulatoires gériatriques; unité de courte durée gériatrique.

***Sherbrooke:* Hôpital et centre d'hébergement D'Youville**
Affiliée à: CIUSSS de l'Estrie
1036, rue Belvédère Sud, Sherbrooke, QC J1H 4C4
Tél: 819-780-2222
Note: Programmes et services comprennent: centre d'hébergement; hôpital de jour; unité de réadaptation; centre de recherche sur le vieillissement.

***Sorel-Tracy:* Hôtel-Dieu de Sorel**
Affiliée à: CISSS de la Montérégie-Est
400, av de l'Hôtel-Dieu, Sorel-Tracy, QC J3P 1N3
Tél: 450-746-6000

***Terrebonne:* Hôpital Pierre-Le Gardeur**
Affiliée à: CISSS de Lanaudière
911, montée des Pionniers, Terrebonne, QC J6V 2H2
Tél: 450-654-7525 *Ligne sans frais:* 888-654-7525
Note: Programmes et services comprennent chirurgies, cliniques spécialisées, suppléance rénale, centre d'oncologie et soins en santé psychiatrique.

***Thetford Mines:* Hôpital de Thetford Mines**
Affiliée à: CISSS de Chaudière-Appalaches
1717, rue Notre-Dame Est, Thetford Mines, QC G6G 2V4
Tél: 418-338-7777
csssrt@ssss.gouv.qc.ca

***Trois-Pistoles:* Centre hospitalier Trois-Pistoles**
Affiliée à: CISSS du Bas-St-Laurent
550, rue Notre-Dame Est, Trois-Pistoles, QC G0L 4K0
Tél: 418-851-3700
Line Moisan, Directrice générale, CSSS des Basques

***Trois-Rivières:* Centre hospitalier affilié universitaire régional**
Affiliée à: CIUSSS de la Mauricie-et-du-Centre-du-Québec
1991, boul du Carmel, Trois-Rivières, QC G8Z 3R9
Tél: 819-697-3333
Note: Affilié à l'Université de Montréal en Mauricie.

***Trois-Rivières:* Centre St-Joseph**
Affiliée à: CIUSSS de la Mauricie-et-du-Centre-du-Québec
731, rue Sainte-Julie, Trois-Rivières, QC G9A 1Y1
Tél: 819-370-2100
www.cssstr.qc.ca
Média social: www.facebook.com/csss.trois.rivieres; www.youtube.com/cssstr
Nombre de lits: 198 lits hospitaliers; 100 lits de soins de longue durée
Note: Centre St-Joseph: services hospitaliers; Résidence La Providence: hébergement 819-370-2200, poste 43104.
Jacques Longval, Directeur général, CSSS de Trois-Rivières

***Val-d'Or:* Hôpital de Val-d'Or**
Affiliée à: CISSS de l'Abitibi-Témiscamingue
25, 6e rue, Val-d'Or, QC J9P 3Y1
Tél: 819-825-5858
Note: Programmes et services comprennent: audiologie; biochimie; chirurgie générale; gastro-entérologie; médecine nucléaire; néphrologie; pneumologie; féadaptation physique; santé mentale

***Verdun:* Centre d'hébergement du Manoir-de-Verdun**
Affiliée à: CIUSSS du Centre-Est-de-l'Île-de-Montréal
Ancien nom: CHSLD Champlain - Manoir de Verdun
5500, boul Lasalle, Verdun, QC H4H 1N9
Tél: 514-769-8801
www.sov.qc.ca
Nombre de lits: 220 lits

***Verdun:* Hôpital Douglas**
6875, boul Lasalle, Verdun, QC H4H 1R3
Tél: 514-761-6131
www.douglas.qc.ca
Média social: www.facebook.com/institutdouglas; twitter.com/institutdouglas; www.youtube.com/douglasinstitute
Nombre de lits: 210 lits hospitaliers, 192 lits longue durée
Note: mental hospital affiliated with McGill University; also community services, outpatient services, housing, social rehabilitation, specialized services (eating disorders, alcoholism & drug abuse, schizophrenia, aging, dementia & Alzheimer dementia)
Lynne McVey, Directrice générale

***Victoriaville:* Hôtel-Dieu d'Arthabaska**
Affiliée à: CIUSSS de la Mauricie-et-du-Centre-du-Québec
5, rue des Hospitalières, Victoriaville, QC G6P 6N2
Tél: 819-357-2030
www.csssae.qc.ca
Nombre de lits: 178 lits de santé physique; 21 lits de psychiatrie

***Ville-Marie:* Hôpital de CSSS du Témiscamingue**
Affiliée à: CISSS de l'Abitibi-Témiscamingue
22, rue Notre-Dame Nord, Ville-Marie, QC J9V 1W8
Tél: 819-629-2420; *Téléc:* 819-629-3257

***Wakefield:* Hôpital Mémorial de Wakefield**
Affiliée à: CISSS de l'Outaouais
101, ch Burnside, Wakefield, QC J0X 3G0
Tél: 819-459-1112; *Téléc:* 819-459-1894
Ligne sans frais: 877-459-1112
Nombre de lits: 16 lits

Hôpitaux privés

***Kahnawake:* Kateri Memorial Hospital Centre/Centre hospitalier Kateri Memorial**
Affiliated with: CISSS de la Montérégie-Ouest
Also Known As: Tehsakotitsén:tha
PO Box 10, Kahnawake, QC J0L 1B0
Tél: 450-638-3930; *Fax:* 450-638-4634
admin@kmhc.ca
www.kmhc.ca
Social Media: www.facebook.com/katerimemorialhospital.centre
Number of Beds: 43 beds/lits
Note: Family medicine, home care, community health, infection prevention and control, nutrition services, occupational therapy, physiotherapy, speech therapy, social services.
Susan Horne, Executive Director

***Montréal:* Brassard Plasticien**
Ancien nom: Centre métropolitain de Chirurgie Plastique Inc.
995, rue de Salaberry, Montréal, QC H3L 1L2
Tél: 514-288-2097; *Téléc:* 514-288-3547
information@drbrassard.com
www.drbrassard.com
Nombre de lits: 17 lits
Pierre Brassard, Directeur général

***Montréal:* Hôpital Marie-Clarac**
3530, boul Gouin est, Montréal, QC H1H 1B7
Tél: 514-321-8800; *Téléc:* 514-321-9626
ressourceshumaines.macl@ssss.gouv.qc.ca
www.hopitalmarie-clarac.qc.ca
Nombre de lits: 204 lits
Sr. Pierre-Anne Mandato, Directrice générale

***Montréal:* Hôpital Shriners pour enfants (Québec) inc./Shriners Hospital for Children**
1529, av Cedar, Montréal, QC H3G 1A6
Tél: 514-842-4464; *Téléc:* 514-842-7553
Nombre de lits: 40 lits
Maureen Brennan, Directrice générale
John Krisa, Superviseur, Installations matériels

***Sillery:* La Maison Michel Sarrazin**
Affiliée à: CIUSSS de la Capitale-Nationale
2101, ch St-Louis, Sillery, QC G1T 2P5
Tél: 418-688-0878; *Téléc:* 418-681-8636
info@michel-sarrazin.ca
www.michel-sarrazin.ca
Nombre de lits: 15 lits
Michel L'Heureux, Directeur général

Centres locaux des services communautaires (CLSC)

***Aupaluk:* Dispensaire d'Aupaluk**
Aupaluk, QC J0M 1X0
Tél: 819-491-9090; *Téléc:* 819-491-7020
clsc.aupaluk@ssss.gouv.qc.ca
Nombre de lits: 1 lit

***Barachois:* CLSC de Barachois**
Affiliée à: CISSS de la Gaspésie
1070, rte 132 Est, Barachois, QC G0C 1A0
Tél: 418-645-2572; *Téléc:* 418-645-2106
Note: CSSS Côte-de-Gaspé.

***Bassin:* CLSC de Bassin**
Affiliée à: CISSS des Iles
599, ch du Bassin, Bassin, QC G4T 0C8
Tél: 418-937-2572; *Téléc:* 418-937-5381

***Bedford:* CLSC de Bedford**
Affiliée à: CISSS de la Montérégie-Ouest
34, rue St-Joseph, Bedford, QC J0J 1A0
Tél: 450-248-4321; *Téléc:* 450-248-7435
www.santemonteregie.qc.ca/lapommeraie

***Beloeil:* CLSC des Patriotes**
Affiliée à: CISSS de la Montérégie-Est
300, rue Serge-Pepin, Beloeil, QC J3G 0B8
Tél: 450-536-2572; *Téléc:* 450-536-6367
www.santemonteregie.qc.ca/richelieu-yamaska
Fondée en: 1985
Région desservi: MRC de la Vallée-du-Richelieu
Spécialités: Cliniques de vaccination; Clinique du diabète; Programmes en périnatalité; Services à domicile aux personnes en perte d'autonomie

***Boucherville:* CLSC des Seigneuries de Boucherville**
Affiliée à: CISSS de la Montérégie-Est
160, boul De Montarville, Boucherville, QC J4B 6S2
Tél: 450-655-3630; *Téléc:* 450-655-8530
www.santemonteregie.qc.ca/cssspierreboucher

***Candiac:* CLSC Kateri**
Affiliée à: CISSS de la Montérégie-Ouest
90, boul Marie-Victorin, Candiac, QC J5R 1C1
Tél: 450-659-7661; *Téléc:* 450-444-6260
Nombre de lits: 340 lits

***Cantley:* CLSC Cantley**
Affiliated with: CISSS de l'Outaouais
850, Montée de la Source, Cantley, QC J8V 3H4
Tél: 819-459-1112; *Fax:* 819-827-5818
Toll-Free: 877-459-1112
www.santedescollines.qc.ca
Jean-Paul Racine, Président du conseil d'administration, CSSS des Collines

***Cap-Chat:* CLSC de Cap-Chat**
Affiliée à: CISSS de la Gaspésie
CP 415, 49, rue Notre-Dame, Cap-Chat, QC G0E 1E0
Tél: 418-786-5594; *Téléc:* 418-786-2638
www.cssshautegaspesie.qc.ca

***Cap-aux-Meules:* CLSC de Cap-aux-Meules**
Affiliée à: CISSS des Iles
420, ch Principal, Cap-aux-Meules, QC G4T 1S1
Tél: 418-986-2572; *Téléc:* 418-986-4911

***Caplan:* CLSC de Caplan**
Affiliée à: CISSS de la Gaspésie
96, rte 132, Caplan, QC G0C 1H0
Tél: 418-388-2572; *Téléc:* 418-388-5646

***Chandler:* CLSC de Chandler**
Affiliée à: CISSS de la Gaspésie
CP 1090, 633, av Daignault, Chandler, QC G0C 1K0
Tél: 418-689-2572; *Téléc:* 418-689-4707
csssrocherperce.org
Nombre de lits: 62 lits
Chantal Duguay, Directrice générale

***Châteauguay:* CLSC Châteauguay**
Affiliée à: CISSS de la Montérégie-Ouest
95, ave de la Verdure, Châteauguay, QC J6K 1C7
Tél: 450-699-3333; *Téléc:* 450-691-6202

***Chertsey:* CLSC de Chertsey**
Affiliée à: CISSS de Lanaudière
485, rue Dupuis, Chertsey, QC J0K 3K0
Tél: 450-882-2488

***Côte Saint-Luc:* CLSC René-Cassin**
Affiliée à: CIUSSS du Centre-Ouest-de-l'Île-de-Montréal
5800, boul Cavendish, Côte Saint-Luc, QC H4W 2T5
Tél: 514-484-7878; *Téléc:* 514-485-2978
www.cssscavendish.qc.ca
Spécialités: Services médicaux; Services psychosociaux; Centre d'éducation pour la santé; Clinique enfance - jeunesse; Services de nutrition; Vaccination

***Drummondville:* CLSC Drummond**
Affiliée à: CIUSSS de la Mauricie-et-du-Centre-du-Québec
350, rue Saint-Jean, Drummondville, QC J2B 5L4
Tél: 819-474-2572
csssdrummond@ssss.gouv.qc.ca
www.csssdrummond.qc.ca
Note: Santé au travail: 819-474-8428

***Forestville:* Pavillon Forestville**
Affiliée à: CISSS de la Côte-Nord
CP 790, 2, 7e rue, Forestville, QC G0T 1E0
Tél: 418-587-2212; *Téléc:* 418-587-2865
www.cssshcn.gouv.qc.ca
Nombre de lits: 20 lits
Daniel Côté, Directeur général

***Gascons:* CLSC Gascons**
Affiliée à: CISSS de la Gaspésie
CP 28, 63, rte 132, Gascons, QC G0C 1P0
Tél: 418-396-2572; *Téléc:* 418-396-2367
Note: CSSS du Rocher-Percé.

***Gaspé:* CLSC de Gaspé**
Affiliée à: CISSS de la Gaspésie
CP 6397, 205, boul de York ouest, 2e étage, Gaspé, QC G4X 2R8
Tél: 418-368-2572; *Téléc:* 418-368-1532

Note: CSSS Côte-de-Gaspé.

Gaspé: CLSC de Rivière-au-Renard
Affiliée à: CISSS de la Gaspésie
154, boul Renard Est, Gaspé, QC G4X 5R5
Tél: 418-269-2572; *Téléc:* 418-269-5294

Nombre de lits: 3 lits
Note: CSSS Côte-de-Gaspé.

Gatineau: CLSC de Gatineau - Point de service de la Gappe
Affiliée à: CISSS de l'Outaouais
777, boul de la Gappe, Gatineau, QC J8T 8R2
Tél: 819-966-6550; *Téléc:* 819-966-6552
www.csssgatineau.qc.ca
Note: Services généraux santé; soins infirmiers et ambulatoires; consulation médicale pour les clientèles vulnérables.

Gatineau: CLSC de Gatineau - Point de service Gatineau
Affiliée à: CISSS de l'Outaouais
80, av Gatineau, Gatineau, QC J8T 4J3
Tél: 819-966-6550; *Téléc:* 819-966-6572
www.csssgatineau.qc.ca
Note: Centre local de services communautaires.

Gatineau: CLSC de Gatineau - Point de service LeGuerrier
Affiliée à: CISSS de l'Outaouais
425, rue LeGuerrier, Gatineau, QC J9H 6N8
Tél: 819-966-6540; *Téléc:* 819-966-6541
www.csssdegatineau.qc.ca

Gatineau: CLSC Vallée-de-la-Lièvre
Affiliée à: CISSS de l'Outaouais
578, rue Maclaren est, Gatineau, QC J8L 2W1
Tél: 819-986-3359; *Téléc:* 819-986-5671
csss_papineau@ssss.gouv.qc.ca
www.cssspapineau.qc.ca

Grande-Vallée: CLSC de Grande-Vallée
Affiliée à: CISSS de la Gaspésie
71, rue St-François-Xavier est, Grande-Vallée, QC G0E 1K0
Tél: 418-393-2572; *Téléc:* 418-393-2952
Note: CSSS Côte-de-Gaspé.

Grosse-Ile: CLSC de l'Est
Affiliée à: CISSS des Iles
773, ch Principal, Grosse-Ile, QC G4T 6B5
Tél: 418-985-2572; *Téléc:* 418-985-2862

Huntingdon: CLSC Huntingdon
Affiliée à: CISSS de la Montérégie-Ouest
10, rue King, Huntingdon, QC J0S 1H0
Tél: 450-829-2321; *Téléc:* 450-264-6801
www.santemonteregie.qc.ca/haut-saint-laurent
Spécialités: Services médicaux; Santé mentale adulte et jeunesse; Santé publique; Clinique de vaccination; Soutien à domicile

Ile d'Entrée: CLSC de l'Ile d'Entrée
Affiliée à: CISSS des Iles
Ile d'Entrée, QC G4T 1Z1
Tél: 418-986-4299; *Téléc:* 418-986-4094

Joliette: CLSC de Joliette
Affiliée à: CISSS de Lanaudière
380, boul Base-de-Roc, Joliette, QC J6E 9J6
Tél: 450-755-2111
www.santelanaudiere.qc.ca
Spécialités: Clinique santé; Centre d'enseignement sur l'asthme; Clinique d'enseignement sur le diabète; Services de santé mentale; Cessation tabagique

Jonquière: CLSC de Jonquière
Affiliée à: CIUSSS du Saguenay-Lac-St-Jean
3667, boul Harvey, Jonquière, QC G7X 3A9
Tél: 418-695-2572

Kawawachikamach: CLSC Naskapi
Affiliée à: CISSS de la Côte-Nord
CP 5154, Kawawachikamach, QC G0G 2Z0
Tél: 418-585-2897; *Téléc:* 418-585-3126
Région desservi: La communauté autochtone de Kawawachikamach

Kipawa: Health Centre of Eagle Village
3 Omiga St., Kipawa, QC J0Z 2H0
Tél: 819-627-9060; *Téléc:* 819-627-1885
www.evfn.ca/HealthCentre.html

Kuujjuaq: Centre de santé Tulattavik de l'Ungava
Affiliée à: Régie régionale de la santé et des services sociaux Nunavik
CP 149, Kuujjuaq, QC J0M 1C0
Tél: 514-735-7645; *Téléc:* 514-735-7641
recrutement@ungava.info
www.ungava.info
Nombre de lits: 15 lits hospitaliers; 10 lits de soins de longue durée
Note: Urgence; soins médicaux; soins infirmiers; maternité; radiologie; pharmacie; électrocardiographie; laboratoire; physiothérapie.
Bruno Fréchette, Chef de programme, Point de service et santé communautaire

La Malbaie: CLSC de La Malbaie
Affiliée à: CIUSSS de la Capitale-Nationale
535, boul de Comporté, La Malbaie, QC G5A 1S8
Tél: 418-665-6413
www.cssscharlevoix.qc.ca
Micheline Tremblay, Directrice générale, CSSS de Charlevoix 418-435-5150, micheline.tremblay@ssss.gouv.qc.ca

LaSalle: CLSC de LaSalle
Affiliée à: CIUSSS de l'Ouest-de-l'Ile-de-Montréal
8550, boul Newman, LaSalle, QC H8N 1Y5
Tél: 514-364-2572; *Téléc:* 514-364-6365
www.santemontreal.qc.ca

Lachine: CLSC de Dorval-Lachine
Affiliée à: CIUSSS de l'Ouest-de-l'Ile-de-Montréal
1900, rue Notre-Dame, Lachine, QC H8S 2G2
Tél: 514-639-0650; *Téléc:* 514-639-0666
www.santemontreal.qc.ca
Note: Services de santé; services sociaux curatifs et préventifs.

Laval: CLSC des Mille-Iles
Affiliée à: CISSS de Laval
4731, boul Levesque Est, Laval, QC H7C 1M9
Tél: 450-661-2572; *Téléc:* 450-661-6177
Note: Les autres points de service CLSC: Marigot (2 sites), Mille-Iles (304, boul Cartier ouest), Ruisseau-Papineau (2 sites), et Sainte-Rose.

Longueuil: CLSC de Longueuil-Ouest
Affiliée à: CISSS de la Montérégie-Est
201, boul Curé-Poirier Ouest, Longueuil, QC J4J 2G4
Tél: 450-651-9830; *Téléc:* 450-651-4606
www.santemonteregie.qc.ca/cssspierreboucher

Longueuil: CLSC Simonne-Monet-Chartrand
Affiliée à: CISSS de la Montérégie-Est
1303, boul Jacques-Cartier est, Longueuil, QC J4M 2Y8
Tél: 450-463-2850; *Téléc:* 450-646-7552
www.santemonteregie.qc.ca/cssspierreboucher

Low: CLSC de Low
Affiliée à: CISSS de l'Outaouais
CP 130, 334, rte 105, Low, QC J0X 2C0
Tél: 819-422-3548; *Téléc:* 819-422-3568

Marsoui: CLSC de Marsoui
Affiliée à: CISSS de la Gaspésie
CP 415, 8, rte Principale Est, Marsoui, QC G0E 1S0
Tél: 418-288-5511; *Téléc:* 418-288-2572
www.cssshautegaspesie.qc.ca

Matapédia: CLSC Malauze de Matapédia
Affiliée à: CISSS de la Gaspésie
14, boul Perron Est, Matapédia, QC G0J 1V0
Tél: 418-865-2221; *Téléc:* 418-865-2317
Note: Services sociaux; programme petite enfance; clinique de vaccination et dépistage; programme de santé mentale; services aux personnes handicapées; soutien à domicile; service dentaire. Le centre d'hébergement est situé au deuxième étage du CLSC.

Métabetchouan-Lac-a-la-Cr: CLSC Secteur-Sud
Affiliée à: Centre de santé et de services sociaux de Lac-Saint-Jean-Est
1895, rte 169, Métabetchouan-Lac-a-la-Cr, QC G8G 1B4
Tél: 418-349-2861; *Téléc:* 418-349-8774
Nombre de lits: 168 lits

Mont-Louis: CLSC de Mont-Louis
Affiliée à: CISSS de la Gaspésie
CP 100, 19, 1e av Ouest, Mont-Louis, QC G0E 1T0
Tél: 418-797-2744; *Téléc:* 418-797-5173
www.cssshautegaspesie.qc.ca

Montréal: Clinique communautaire de Pointe St-Charles
500, av Ash, Montréal, QC H3K 2R4
Tél: 514-937-9251; *Téléc:* 514-937-3492
ccpsc.qc.ca
Marie-Claude Rose, Présidente
Luc Leblanc, Coordonnateur général de la Clinique

Montréal: CLSC d'Ahuntsic
Affiliée à: CIUSSS du Nord-de-l'Ile-de-Montréal
1165, boul Henri-Bourassa Est, Montréal, QC H2C 3K2
Tél: 514-384-2000
www.csssamn.ca
Spécialités: Prélèvements; Services sociaux courants; Réadaptation; Information sur les vaccins

Montréal: CLSC de Benny Farm
Affiliée à: CIUSSS du Centre-Ouest-de-l'Ile-de-Montréal
6484, av Monkland, Montréal, QC H4B 1H3
Tél: 514-484-7878; *Téléc:* 514-485-6406
www.cssscavendish.qc.ca
Note: Les Services: Centre de prélèvements; Clinique d'hypertension artérielle du CSSS Cavendish (514-484-7878, poste 3098); Maladie pulmonaire obstructive chronique (514-484-7878); Centre d'abandon du tabagisme (514 484-7878, poste 3068); Clinique de la santé des femmes (514-484-7878, poste 3067)

Montréal: CLSC de Bordeaux-Cartierville
Affiliée à: CIUSSS du Nord-de-l'Ile-de-Montréal
11822, av du Bois-de-Boulogne, Montréal, QC H3M 2X6
Tél: 514-331-2572; *Téléc:* 514-331-5827
info_bcstl@ssss.gouv.qc.ca
www.santemontreal.qc.ca

Montréal: CLSC de Côte-des-Neiges
Affiliée à: CIUSSS du Centre-Ouest-de-l'Ile-de-Montréal
5700, ch de la Côte-des-Neiges, Montréal, QC H3T 2A8
Tél: 514-731-8531; *Téléc:* 514-731-9600
www.santemontreal.qc.ca; www.clsccote-des-neiges.qc.ca

Montréal: CLSC de Hochelaga-Maisonneuve
Affiliée à: CIUSSS de l'Est-de-l'Ile-de-Montréal
4201, rue Ontario Est, Montréal, QC H1V 1K2
Tél: 514-253-2181
www.cssslucilleteasdale.qc.ca
Spécialités: Les services de santé; Les services sociaux

Montréal: CLSC de La Petite Patrie
Affiliée à: Centre de santé et de services sociaux du Coeur-de-l'Ile
6520, rue de Saint-Vallier, Montréal, QC H2S 2P7
Tél: 514-273-4508
www.cssscoeurdelile.ca
Spécialités: Service de santé; Services sociaux; Services de psychogériatrie; Services d'aide à domicile; Réadaptation; Services d'information

Montréal: CLSC de Mercier-Est — Anjou
Affiliée à: CIUSSS de l'Est-de-l'Ile-de-Montréal
9503, rue Sherbooke Est, Montréal, QC H1L 6P2
Tél: 514-356-2572
www.cssspointe.ca
Note: Les Services: Sevices de prélèvement; Services pour les futurs parents, nourrissons, enfant âgés de moins de 5 ans et leurs parents; Clinique des jeunes (jeunes âgés de 12 à 18 ans); Santé mentale; Radiologie

Montréal: CLSC de Montréal-Nord
Affiliée à: CIUSSS du Nord-de-l'Ile-de-Montréal
11441, boul Lacordaire, Montréal, QC H1G 4J9
Tél: 514-384-2000
www.csssamn.ca
Spécialités: Clinique des adultes; Clinique des jeunes; Informations et counselling; Clinique d'avortement; Pose de dispositifs intra-utérins (DIU)

Montréal: CLSC de Parc Extension
Affiliée à: CIUSSS du Centre-Ouest-de-l'Ile-de-Montréal
7085, rue Hutchison, Montréal, QC H3N 1Y9
Tél: 514-273-9591
www.csssdelamontagne.qc.ca
Spécialités: Soins infirmiers et médicaux; Services psychosociaux; Réadaptation; Aide domestique; Assistance personnelle

Montréal: CLSC de Rivière-des-Prairies
Affiliée à: CIUSSS de l'Est-de-l'Ile-de-Montréal
8655, boul Perras, Montréal, QC H1E 4M7
Tél: 514-494-4924

Spécialités: Les services de santé; Les services sociaux

Montréal: CLSC de Rosemont
Affiliée à: CIUSSS de l'Est-de-l'Ile-de-Montréal
Centre administratif, 2909, rue Rachel Est, Montréal, QC H1W 0A9
Tél: 514-524-3541
www.csssluciIleteasdale.qc.ca
Spécialités: Services de santé; Services psychosociaux; Services sociaux scolaires; Services de maintien à domicile; Service de santé dentaire

Montréal: CLSC de Saint-Henri
Affiliée à: CIUSSS du Centre-Est-de-l'Ile-de-Montréal
3833, rue Notre-Dame ouest, Montréal, QC H4C 1P8
Tél: 514-933-7541
www.sov.qc.ca

Montréal: CLSC de Saint-Michel
Affiliée à: CIUSSS de l'Est-de-l'Ile-de-Montréal
3355, rue Jarry est, Montréal, QC H1Z 2E5
Tél: 514-722-3000
www.csss-stleonardstmichel.qc.ca
Spécialités: Clinique médicale; Prélèvements; Vaccination (514-374-8223); Soutien à domicile

Montréal: CLSC de Villeray
Affiliée à: CIUSSS du Nord-de-l'Ile-de-Montréal
1425, rue Jarry est, Montréal, QC H2E 1A7
Tél: 514-376-4141
www.cssscoeurdelile.ca
Fondée en: 1985
Spécialités: Promotion de la santé; Intervention psychosociale; Services thérapeutiques; Vaccination des enfants; Support à l'allaitement; Soutien à domicile

Montréal: CLSC des Faubourgs - Visitation
Affiliée à: CIUSSS du Centre-Est-de-l'Ile-de-Montréal
1705, rue de la Visitation, Montréal, QC H2L 3C3
Tél: 514-527-2361; *Téléc:* 514-598-7754
www.csssjeannemance.ca

Montréal: CLSC du Plateau Mont-Royal
Affiliée à: CIUSSS du Centre-Est-de-l'Ile-de-Montréal
4625, av de Lorimier, Montréal, QC H2H 2B4
Tél: 514-521-7663
www.csssjeannemance.ca
Spécialités: Services psychosociaux; Services médicaux courants; Service en nutrition; Service d'échange de seringues pour personnes toxicomanes; Réadaptation

Montréal: CLSC Métro
Affiliée à: CIUSSS du Centre-Ouest-de-l'Ile-de-Montréal
1801, boul de Maisonneuve Ouest, Montréal, QC H3H 1J9
Tél: 514-934-0354
www.csssdelamontagne.qc.ca
Spécialités: Clinique médicale; Services sociaux; Programmes de santé pour les écoles et les garderies; Thérapie familiale et de couple

Montréal: CLSC Olivier-Guimond
Affiliée à: CIUSSS de l'Est-de-l'Ile-de-Montréal
5810, rue Sherbrooke Est, Montréal, QC H1N 1B2
Tél: 514-255-2365
www.csssluciIleteasdale.qc.ca
Spécialités: Maladies infectieuses; Santé mentale; Violence conjugale et familiale; Santé dentaire; Nutrition; Réadaptation

Montréal: CLSC Pointe-aux-Trembles - Montréal-Est
Affiliée à: CIUSSS de l'Est-de-l'Ile-de-Montréal
13926, rue Notre-Dame est, Montréal, QC H1A 1T5
Tél: 514-642-4050
www.cssspointe.ca
Spécialités: Services sociaux; Réadaptation; Aide domestique; Vaccination

Montréal: CLSC Saint-Louis-du-Parc
Affiliée à: CIUSSS du Centre-Est-de-l'Ile-de-Montréal
#100, 15, av du Mont-Royal Ouest, Montréal, QC H2T 2R9
Tél: 514-286-9657; *Téléc:* 514-286-9706
www.csssjeannemance.ca

Montréal: Santé au travail
#430, 75, rue de Port-Royal, Montréal, QC H3L 3T1
Tél: 514-858-2460; *Téléc:* 514-858-6568

Murdochville: CLSC de Murdochville
Affiliée à: CISSS de la Gaspésie
600, rue William-May, Murdochville, QC G0E 1W0
Tél: 418-784-2572; *Téléc:* 418-784-3629
Note: CSSS Côte-de-Gaspé.

Paspébiac: CLSC de Paspébiac
Affiliée à: CISSS de la Gaspésie
273, boul Gérard-D.-Lévesque ouest, Paspébiac, QC G0C 2K0
Tél: 418-752-2572; *Téléc:* 418-752-6734

Percé: CLSC de Percé
Affiliée à: CISSS de la Gaspésie
CP 269, 98, rte 132, Percé, QC G0C 2L0
Tél: 418-782-2727
Note: CSSS du Rocher-Percé.

Plessisville: CLSC-CHSLD de l'Érable
Affiliée à: CIUSSS de la Mauricie-et-du-Centre-du-Québec
1331, rue Saint-Calixte, Plessisville, QC G6L 1P4
Tél: 819-362-6301; *Téléc:* 819-362-6300
fondation_erable@ssss.gouv.qc.ca
www.csssae.qc.ca
Nombre de lits: 40 lits de soins de longue durée
Note: CLSC de l'Érable, et l'Unité de soins longue durée de l'Érable.
François Biron, Président

Pohénégamook: CLSC de Pohénégamook
Affiliée à: CISSS du Bas-St-Laurent
1922, rue St-Vallier, Pohénégamook, QC G0L 2T0
Tél: 418-859-2450; *Téléc:* 418-859-1285
www.cssstemiscouata.com

Pointe-Claire: CLSC du Lac-Saint-Louis
Affiliée à: CIUSSS de l'Ouest-de-l'Ile-de-Montréal
180, av Cartier, Pointe-Claire, QC H9S 4S1
Tél: 514-697-4110
www.csssouestdelile.qc.ca
Note: Les Services: Santé sexuelle (514-697-4110, poste 1313); Suivis post-natals (514-697-4110, poste 1346); Soutien à l'allaitement (514-697-4110, poste 1346); Suivi diététique (514-697-4110, poste 1346); Vaccination (514-697-4110); Suivis intensifs et continus pour la clientèle vulnérable (514-697-4110, poste 1346); Clinique des jeunes (514-697-4110, poste 1313); Services psychosociaux (514-697-4110, poste 1334); Santé dentaire (514-697-4110)

Pointe-à-la-Croix: CLSC de Pointe-à-la-Croix
Affiliée à: CISSS de la Gaspésie
48, boul Interprovincial, Pointe-à-la-Croix, QC G0C 1L0
Tél: 418-788-5454; *Téléc:* 418-788-2510

Puvirnituq: Centre de santé Inuulitsivik
Affiliated with: Régie régionale de la santé et des services sociaux Nunavik
ch Baie d'Hudson, Puvirnituq, QC J0M 1P0
Tél: 819-988-2957; *Fax:* 819-988-2796
recrutement.csi@ssss.gouv.qc.ca
www.inuulitsivik.ca
Number of Beds: 17 lits hospitaliers; 8 lits de soins de longue durée
Note: Soins médicaux, soins dentaires; sages-femmes; services en santé mentale; télémedicine; laboratoire; points de service: Akulivik, Inukjuak, Ivujivik, Kuujjuarapik, Puvirnituq, Salluit et Umiujuaq.
Jane Beaudoin, Directrice générale

Quaqtaq: Dispensaire de Quaqtaq
General Delivery, Quaqtaq, QC J0M 1J0
Tél: 819-492-9090
Région desservi: Nunavik (région sociosanitaire)
Spécialités: Services intégrés de dépistage et de prévention des infections transmissibles sexuellement et par le sang (SIDEP)

Québec: CLSC de la Basse-Ville
Affiliée à: CIUSSS de la Capitale-National
50, rue Saint-Joseph Est, Québec, QC G1K 3A5
Tél: 418-529-2572; *Téléc:* 418-521-5801

Québec: CLSC de la Haute-Ville
Affiliée à: CIUSSS de la Capitale-Nationale
55, ch Ste-Foy, Québec, QC G1R 1S9
Tél: 418-641-2572
www.csssvc.qc.ca
Note: Services: Consultations médicales (418-682-75940); Consultations psychosociales (418-641-2572); Clinique jeunesse (418-682-7594); Contraception orale d'urgence (418-682-7594); Cours prénataux (418-641-2572); Vaccination (418-682-7594); Soutien à domicile (418-651-3888)

Québec: CLSC de la Jacques-Cartier (Loretteville)
Affiliée à: CIUSSS de la Capitale-Nationale
11999A, rue de l'Hôpital, Québec, QC G2A 2T7
Tél: 418-843-2572; *Téléc:* 418-843-3880
www.csssqn.qc.ca

Spécialités: Clinique prénatale (418-661-7195); Soutien à domicile; Services infirmiers

Richelieu: CLSC du Richelieu
Affiliée à: CISSS de la Montérégie-Centre
300, ch de Marieville, Richelieu, QC J3L 3V8
Tél: 450-658-7561; *Téléc:* 450-658-4390
www.santemonteregie.qc.ca/haut-richelieu-rouville
Spécialités: Rencontres prénatales; Clinique de la petite enfance (450-658-7561, poste 4164)

Richmond: CLSC de Richmond
Affiliée à: CIUSSS de l'Estrie
110, rue Barlow, Richmond, QC J0B 2H0
Tél: 819-542-2777; *Téléc:* 819-826-3867
vsf.santeestrie.qc.ca

Rimouski: CLSC Rimouski
Affiliée à: CISSS du Bas-St-Laurent
165, rue des Gouverneurs, Rimouski, QC G5L 7R2
Tél: 418-724-7204; *Téléc:* 418-724-5494
courrierweb.crsssr@ssss.gouv.qc.ca
www.chrr.qc.ca
Personnel: 2200
Note: 3 autres points de service: Saint-Fabien, Saint-Marcellin, et Saint-Narcisse
Dre. Gabrielle Gagnon, Présidente

Rivière-du-Loup: CLSC de Rivière-du-Loup
22, rue Saint-Laurent, Rivière-du-Loup, QC G5R 4W5
Tél: 418-867-2642; *Téléc:* 418-867-4713
www.cssstiviereduloup.qc.ca

Rouyn-Noranda: CLSC de Rouyn-Noranda
Affiliée à: CISSS de l'Abitibi-Témiscamingue
1, 9e rue, Rouyn-Noranda, QC J9X 2A9
Tél: 819-762-8144; *Téléc:* 819-764-2948
www.sante-abitibi-temiscamingue.gouv.qc.ca; www.csssrn.qc.ca
Note: Point de service CLSC, et consultations externes CHSGS.
Huguette Lemay, Directrice générale, CSSS de Rouyn-Noranda

Saint-Félicien: CLSC Saint-Félicien - Édifice Bon-Conseil
Affiliée à: CIUSSS du Saguenay-Lac-St-Jean
CP 10, 1228, boul Sacré-Coeur, Saint-Félicien, QC G8K 2P8
Tél: 418-679-5270; *Téléc:* 418-679-1748

Saint-Félicien: CLSC Saint-Félicien - Édifice Hôtel de Ville
Affiliée à: CIUSSS du Saguenay-Lac-St-Jean
CP 10, 1209, boul Sacré-Coeur, Saint-Félicien, QC G8K 2P8
Tél: 418-679-5270; *Téléc:* 418-679-3510

Saint-Hubert: CLSC Saint-Hubert
Affiliée à: CISSS de la Montérégie-Centre
6800, boul Cousineau, Saint-Hubert, QC J3Y 8Z4
Tél: 450-443-7400
www.santemonteregie.qc.ca/champlain
Région desservi: L'arrondissement Saint-Hubert de la Ville de Longueuil
Spécialités: Rencontres prénatales (450-443-7400, option 6); Consultations psychosociales (450-443-7400, poste 7318)

Saint-Jean-sur-Richelieu: CLSC de la Vallée-des-Forts
Affiliée à: CISSS de la Montérégie-Centre
978, boul du Séminaire nord, Saint-Jean-sur-Richelieu, QC J3A 1E5
Tél: 450-358-2572; *Téléc:* 450-349-0724

Saint-Léonard: CLSC de Saint-Léonard
Affiliée à: CIUSSS de l'Est-de-l'Ile-de-Montréal
5540, rue Jarry Est, Saint-Léonard, QC H1P 1T9
Tél: 514-722-3000
csss-stleonardstmichel.qc.ca

Saint-Ludger: CLSC Saint-Ludger
Affiliée à: CIUSSS de l'Estrie
210-A, rue La Salle, Saint-Ludger, QC G0M 1W0
Tél: 819-548-5551; *Téléc:* 819-548-5553
www.csssgranit.qc.ca

Saint-Omer: CLSC de Saint-Omer
Affiliée à: CISSS de la Gaspésie
107, rte 132 Ouest, Saint-Omer, QC G0C 2Z0
Tél: 418-364-7064; *Téléc:* 418-364-7119

Saint-Paulin: CLSC de St-Paulin
Affiliée à: CIUSSS de la Mauricie-et-du-Centre-du-Québec
2841, rue Laflèche, Saint-Paulin, QC J0K 3G0
Tél: 819-268-2572
www.csssm.qc.ca
Spécialités: Services infirmiers courants; Vaccination

Saint-Rémi: **CLSC Jardin-du-Québec**
Affiliée à: CISSS de la Montérégie-Ouest
2, rue Sainte-Famille, Saint-Rémi, QC J0L 2L0
Tél: 450-454-4671; *Téléc:* 450-454-4538

Saint-Siméon: **CLSC-CHSLD de Saint-Siméon**
Affiliée à: CIUSSS de la Capitale-Nationale
CP 7, 371, rue Saint-Laurent, Saint-Siméon, QC G0T 1X0
Tél: 418-638-2414; *Téléc:* 418-638-2470
www.cssscharlevoix.qc.ca
Nombre de lits: 18 lits
Note: Centre local de services communautaires (418-638-2369); centre d'hébergement et centre de jour.
Micheline Tremblay, Directrice générale, CSSS de Charlevoix
micheline.tremblay@ssss.gouv.qc.ca

Sherbrooke: **CLSC de Sherbrooke - Point de service 50 rue Camirand**
Affiliée à: CIUSSS de l'Estrie
50, rue Camirand, Sherbrooke, QC J1H 4J5
Tél: 819-780-2222
www.csss-iugs.ca
Note: Autres points de service: 95, rue Camirand; 356, rue King ouest; 1200, rue King est; et 8, rue Speid.

Sorel-Tracy: **CLSC Gaston-Bélanger**
Affiliée à: CISSS de la Montérégie-Est
Également connu sous le nom de: CLSC du Havre
30, rue Ferland, Sorel-Tracy, QC J3P 3C7
Tél: 514-746-4545
Nombre de lits: 18 lits

Sorel-Tracy: **Hôpital Richelieu / CLSC du Havre**
30, rue Ferland, Sorel-Tracy, QC J3P 3C7
Tél: 450-743-5569; *Téléc:* 450-743-1803

Ste-Anne-des-Monts: **CLSC de Sainte-Anne-des-Monts**
Affiliée à: CISSS de la Gaspésie
50, rue Belvédère, Ste-Anne-des-Monts, QC G4V 1X4
Tél: 418-763-7771; *Téléc:* 418-763-7176
www.cssshautegaspesie.qc.ca

Ste-Catherine-de-la-J-Car: **CLSC de la Jacques-Cartier (Sainte-Catherine-de-la-Jacques-Cartier)**
Affiliée à: CIUSSS de la Capitale-Nationale
4570, rte de Fossambault, Ste-Catherine-de-la-J-Car, QC G3N 2T6
Tél: 418-843-2572; *Téléc:* 418-843-3880
www.csssqn.qc.ca
Spécialités: Soutien à domicile; Services infirmiers

Ste-Cécile-de-Masham: **CLSC des Collines**
Affiliée à: Centre de santé et de services sociaux des Collines
9, ch Passe-Partout, Ste-Cécile-de-Masham, QC J0X 2W0
Tél: 819-456-1112; *Téléc:* 819-456-4531
Ligne sans frais: 877-459-1112
www.santedescollines.qc.ca
Nombre de lits: Centre d'hébergement La Pêche: 32 lits.
Note: Y compris le Centre d'hébergement La Pêche et le CLSC Masham.

Terrebonne: **CLSC Lamater - boul des Seigneurs**
Affiliée à: CISSS de Lanaudière
2099, boul des Seigneurs, Terrebonne, QC J6X 4A7
Tél: 450-471-2881; *Téléc:* 450-471-8235
www.csss.sudlanaudiere.ca
Spécialités: Clinique médicale; Services sociaux scolaires; Service en santé mentale; Services dentaires préventifs; Clinique des jeunes; Vaccination

Trois-Rivières: **Centre de service Laviolette**
Affiliée à: CIUSSS de la Mauricie-et-du-Centre-du-Québec
1274, rue Laviolette, Trois-Rivières, QC G9A 1W4
Tél: 819-379-5650
www.cssstr.qc.ca
Spécialités: Soutien à domicile

Victoriaville: **CLSC Suzor-Côté**
Affiliée à: CIUSSS de la Mauricie-et-du-Centre-du-Québec
100, rue Ermitage, Victoriaville, QC G6P 9N2
Tél: 819-758-7281; *Téléc:* 819-758-5009
www.csssae.qc.ca
Fondée en: 1981

Centres de traitments spécialisés

Amos: **Centre Normand**
Affiliée à: CISSS de l'Abitibi-Témiscamingue
621, rue de l'Harricana, Amos, QC J9T 2P9
Tél: 819-732-8241; *Téléc:* 819-727-2210
www.centrenormand.org
Fondée en: 1981
Nombre de lits: 10 lits
Note: Offre des services de réadaptation aux personnes qui présentent une dépendance - à l'alcool, drogues illicites, médicaments, jeu; services de support psychosocial.
Pierre Michel Guay, Directeur général
pierremichel_guay@ssss.gouv.qc.ca

Amos: **CRDI Abitibi-Témiscamingue Clair-Foyer**
841, 3e rue Ouest, Amos, QC J9T 2T4
Tél: 819-732-6511; *Téléc:* 819-732-0922
www.sante-abitibi-temiscamingue.gouv.qc.ca
Nombre de lits: 31 lits
Note: Centre de réadaptation (déficience intellectuelle); services de support.
Sylvette Gilbert, Directrice générale
sylvette_gilbert@ssss.gouv.qc.ca

Baie-Comeau: **Centre de protection et de réadaptation de la Côte-Nord**
Affiliée à: CISSS de la Côte-Nord
835, boul Joliet, Baie-Comeau, QC G5C 1P5
Tél: 418-589-9927; *Téléc:* 418-589-4304
cprcn_dg@ssss.gouv.qc.ca
www.cprcn.qc.ca
Nombre de lits: 225 lits
Note: et centre jeunesse
Claude Montigny, Directeur général

Beauceville: **Centre de réadaptation en dépendance de Chaudière-Appalaches**
Affiliée à: CISSS de Chaudière-Appalaches
Ancien nom: Centre de réadaptation en alcoolisme et toxicomanie de Chaudière-Appalaches
253, rte 108, Beauceville, QC G5X 2Z3
Tél: 418-774-3329; *Téléc:* 418-774-4423
www.acrdq.qc.ca
Nombre de lits: 14 lits
Huguette Giroux, Directrice générale

Bonaventure: **Centre de réadaptation de la Gaspésie MRC de Bonaventure**
CP 667, 238, av Port-Royal, Bonaventure, QC G0C 1E0
Tél: 418-534-4243; *Téléc:* 418-534-2411
Note: Déficiences physiques et intellectuelles.

Bonaventure: **Centre jeunesse Gaspésie/Les Iles - Succursale Bonaventure-Avignon**
CP 308, 106, av Port-Royal, Bonaventure, QC G0C 1E0
Tél: 418-534-2272; *Téléc:* 418-534-4278

Bonaventure: **Centre jeunesse Gaspésie/Les Iles - Unité La Balise**
CP 308, 193, av Port Royal, Bonaventure, QC G0C 1E0
Tél: 418-534-3283; *Téléc:* 418-534-4024
www.cjgaspesielesiles.qc.ca
Nombre de lits: 12 lits
Note: Pour mésadaptées socio-affectifs.

Cap-aux-Meules: **Centre jeunesse Gaspésie/Les Iles - Succursale des Iles**
CP 268, 539-2, ch Principal, Cap-aux-Meules, QC G4T 1E7
Tél: 418-986-2230; *Téléc:* 418-986-5445

Carleton: **Centre de réadaptation de la Gaspésie MRC d'Avignon - Carleton**
CP 26, 314, boul Perron ouest, Carleton, QC G0C 1J0
Tél: 418-364-6037; *Téléc:* 418-364-7040
Note: Déficience intellectuelle.

Chandler: **Centre de réadaptation de la Gaspésie - MRC du Rocher-Percé**
CP 2168, 328, boul René-Lévesque ouest, Chandler, QC G0C 1K0
Tél: 418-689-4286; *Téléc:* 418-689-7155
Note: Déficiences physiques et intellectuelles.

Chandler: **Centre jeunesse Gaspésie/Les Iles - Succursale Rocher-Percé**
#102, 107, rue Commerciale Ouest, Chandler, QC G0C 1K0
Tél: 418-689-2286; *Téléc:* 418-689-4643

Charny: **Centre de réadaptation en déficience physique Chaudière-Appalaches**
Affiliée à: CISSS de Chaudière-Appalaches
9500, boul. du Centre-Hospitalier, Charny, QC G6X 0A1
Tél: 418-380-2064; *Téléc:* 418-380-2096
TTY: 418-360-2089
www.crdpca.qc.ca
Nombre de lits: 48 lits
Note: Programmes: Déficience auditive, Déficience du langage, Déficience motrice (enfant, adulte), Clinique de sclérose en plaques, Programme d'évaluation & de réadaptation en conduite automobile, Neurotraumatisme, Dépistage du traumatisme craniocérébral léger, Programme intensif de gestion autonome de la douleur, et Programme de suppléance à la communication. Points de service: Beauce-Etchemin (Beauceville), Montmagny-L'Islet (Montmagny), l'Amiante (Thetford Mines), et Littoral (Charny).

Chicoutimi: **Le Centre jeunesse du Saguenay — Lac-Saint-Jean**
Affiliée à: CIUSSS du Saguenay-Lac-Saint-Jean
1109, av Bégin, Chicoutimi, QC G7H 4P1
Tél: 418-549-4853; *Téléc:* 418 693-0765
www.cjsaglac.ca
Média social: www.facebook.com/cjsaglac
Laval Dionne, Président, Conseil d'administration
Marc Thibeault, Directeur général
Sylvie Mailhot, Commissaire aux plaintes et à la qualité des services
plaintes@cjsaglac.ca
Danielle Tremblay, Directrice de la protection de la jeunesse
Brigitte Savaria, Agente d'information

Dixville: **Centre d'accueil Dixville inc./Dixville Home CRDITED Estrie**
301, rue Saint-Alexandre, Dixville, QC J0B 1P0
Tél: 819-346-8471; *Téléc:* 819-849-6673
info.crditedestrie@ssss.gouv.qc.ca
www.crditedestrie.qc.ca
Fondée en: 1958
Note: Le centre de réadaptation en déficience intellectuelle et troubles envahissants du développement Estre (CRDITED Estrie) est composé de deux établissements du réseau de la santé et des services sociaux du Québec, soit le Centre d'accueil Dixville inc. et le Centre Notre-Dame de l'Enfant (Sherbrooke) inc.
Gaétan Duford, Président, Conseil d'administration
Danielle Lareau, Directrice générale, et secrétaire, conseil d'administration

Fatima: **Centre de réadaptation de la Gaspésie MRC des Iles-de-la-Madeleine**
CP 549, 695, ch des Caps, Fatima, QC G4T 2S9
Tél: 418-986-4870; *Téléc:* 418-986-2623
Note: Déficience physique.

Gaspé: **Centre de réadaptation de la Gaspésie - MRC de la Côte-de-Gaspé**
CP 6320, 150, rue Mgr Ross, aile 550, Gaspé, QC G4X 2R8
Tél: 418-368-2306; *Téléc:* 418-368-7761
Note: Déficiences physiques et intellectuelles.

Gaspé: **Centre jeunesse Gaspésie/Les Iles**
Affiliée à: CISSS de la Gaspésie
Pavillon Cantin, #100, 205, boul de York ouest, Gaspé, QC G4X 2V7
Tél: 418-368-1803; *Téléc:* 418-368-5478
Nombre de lits: 55 lits

Gaspé: **Centre jeunesse Gaspésie/Les Iles - Succursale Côte-de-Gaspé**
#100, 205, boul de York Ouest, Gaspé, QC G4X 2V7
Tél: 418-368-3381; *Téléc:* 418-368-5101

Gaspé: **Centre jeunesse Gaspésie/Les Iles - Unité La Rade**
#100, 205, boul de York Ouest, Gaspé, QC G4X 2V7
Tél: 418-368-1803; *Téléc:* 418-368-6303

Gaspé: **Centre jeunesse Gaspésie/Les Iles - Unité La Vigie**
205, boul York Ouest, bur. 100, Gaspé, QC G4X 2V7
Tél: 418-368-1803; *Téléc:* 418-368-8744
www.cjgaspesielesiles.qc.ca
Nombre de lits: 14 places
Note: Centre de réadaptation.

***Gatineau:* Centre Jellinek**
Ancien nom: Pavillon Jelinek
25, rue Saint-François, Gatineau, QC J9A 1B1
Tél: 819-776-5584; *Téléc:* 819-776-0255
Ligne sans frais: 866-776-5585
jellinek@jellinek.org
www.jellinek.org
Nombre de lits: 33 places
Note: centre de réadaptation des drogues, de l'alcool ou du jeu

***Gatineau:* Les Centres jeunesse de l'Outaouais**
Affiliée à: CISSS de l'Outaouais
105, boul Sacré-Coeur, Gatineau, QC J8X 1C5
Tél: 819-771-6631
cjoutaouais.qc.ca
Nombre de lits: 149 lits
Note: centre jeunesse, protection
Luc Cadieux, Directeur général
Luc.Cadieux@ssss.gouv.qc.ca

***Gatineau:* Pavillon du Parc inc.**
Affiliée à: CISSS de l'Outaouais
124, rue Lois, Gatineau, QC J8Y 3R7
Tél: 819-770-1022; *Téléc:* 819-770-1023
info@pavillonduparc.qc.ca
www.pavillonduparc.qc.ca
Nombre de lits: 92 lits
Note: centre de réadaptation
Jean Dansereau, Directeur général par intérim

***Joliette:* Centre de réadaptation La Myriade**
Affiliée à: CISSS de Lanaudière
339, boul Base-de-Roc, Joliette, QC J6E 5P3
Tél: 450-753-9600; *Téléc:* 450-753-1930
Ligne sans frais: 450-753-9622
www.crlamyriade.qc.ca
Nombre de lits: 38 lits
Robert Lasalle, Directeur général

***Joliette:* Les Centres jeunesse de Lanaudière (CJL)**
Affiliée à: CISSS de Lanaudière
260, rue Lavaltrie Sud, Joliette, QC J6E 5X7
Tél: 450-756-4555; *Téléc:* 450-756-0814
Ligne sans frais: 800-229-1152
www.centresjeunessedelanaudiere.qc.ca
Jacques Perreault, Président, Conseil d'administration
Richard Provost, Vice-président
Christian Gagné, Directeur général & Secrétaire

***Kuujjuaq:* Centre de santé Tulattavik de l'Ungava**
CP 149, Kuujjuaq, Kuujjuaq, QC J0M 1C0
Tél: 514-735-7645; *Téléc:* 514-735-7641
recrutement@ungava.info
www.ungava.info
Nombre de lits: 23 lits

***Lachine:* Centre de réadaptation de l'Ouest de Montréal (CROM/WMR)/West Montreal Readaptation Centre**
Affiliée à: CIUSSS de l'Ouest-de-l'Île-de-Montréal
8000, rue Notre-Dame, Lachine, QC H8R 1H2
Tél: 514-363-3025; *Téléc:* 514-364-0608
infocrom@ssss.gouv.qc.ca
www.crom-wmrc.ca
Média social: www.facebook.com/CROM.WMRC
Région desservi: CSSS de l'Ouest de l'Ile; CSSS Cavendish; CSSS de la Montagne
Spécialités: Services spécialisés pour des adultes et enfants présentant une déficience intellectuelle ou un trouble du spectre autistique
Dre. Katherine Moxness, Directrice générale

***Laval:* Centre Jeunesse de Laval**
Affiliée à: CISSS de Laval
308, boul Cartier Ouest, Laval, QC H7N 2J2
Tél: 450-975-4150
www.centrejeunessedelaval.ca
Guy Villeneuve, Président, Conseil d'administration
Jean-Guy Blanchet, Premier vice-président, Conseil d'administration
Danièle Dulude, Secrétaire, Conseil d'administration
Yvon Shedleur, Trésorier, Conseil d'administration
Mathieu Vachon, Responsable, services des communications

***Laval:* CRDI Normand-Laramée**
304, boul Cartier Ouest, Laval, QC H7N 2J2
Tél: 450-972-2099
crdinl@ssss.gouv.qc.ca
www.crdinl.qc.ca
Note: Le CRDI Normand-Laramée est membre actif du Consortium national de recherche sur l'intégration sociale.
Julie Vaillancourt, Directrice générale

Isabelle Portelance, Responsable, direction des services à la clientèle

***Lévis:* Centre de réadaptation en déficience intellectuelle de Chaudière-Appalaches**
Affiliée à: CISSS de Chaudière-Appalaches
55, rue du Mont-Marie, Lévis, QC G6V 0B8
Tél: 418-833-3218; *Téléc:* 418-833-9849
Ligne sans frais: 866-333-3218
crdi@chaudiere.appalaches@ssss.gouv.qc.ca
www.crditedca.com
Nombre de lits: 674 lits
Dominique Paquette, Directeur général

***Lévis:* Les Centres jeunesse Chaudière-Appalaches**
100, rue Mgr Ignace-Bourget, Lévis, QC G6V 2Y9
Tél: 418-837-9331; *Téléc:* 418-838-8860
Ligne sans frais: 800-461-9331
www.cj12.qc.ca
Nombre de lits: 146 lits
Note: Services de la protection de la jeunesse; service aux jeunes contrevenants; service d'adoption; services de réadaptation. Installations: Lévis, Saint-Romuald, Montmagny, Sainte-Marie, Saint-Joseph, Saint-Georges & Thetford Mines.
Patrick Simard, Directeur général

***Longueuil:* Centre de réadaptation en déficience intellectuelle Montérégie-est (CRDITED)**
1255, rue Beauregard, Longueuil, QC J4K 2M3
Tél: 450-679-6511; *Téléc:* 450-928-3315
16_crdime_information@ssss.gouv.qc.ca
www.crdime.qc.ca
Média social: www.facebook.com/CRDITEDME
Nombre de lits: 1157 lits
Johanne Gauthier, Directrice générale

***Longueuil:* Centre jeunesse de la Montérégie (CJM)**
Affiliée à: CISSS de la Montérégie-Est
575, rue Adoncour, Longueuil, QC J4G 2M6
Tél: 450-928-5125; *Téléc:* 450-679-3731
Ligne sans frais: 800-641-1315
www.centrejeunessemonteregie.qc.ca
Fondée en: 1992
Personnel: 1 906
Marc Rodier, Président
Catherine Lemay, Directrice générale & Secrétaire
Pierre Henrichon, Trésorier

***Montréal:* Atelier le Fil d'Ariane inc.**
#100, 4837, rue Boyer, Montréal, QC H2J 3E6
Tél: 514-842-5592; *Téléc:* 514-842-8343
atelier.bureau.ariane@ssss.gouv.qc.ca
www.atelierlefildariane.org
Nombre de lits: 20 places
Note: Un atelier de travail pour des adultes ayant des limitations fonctionnelles sur le plan intellectuel; l'atelier favorise l'intégration sociale & communautaire & l'autonomie personnelle & professionnelle des artisans.
Lisette Claveau, Directrice générale

***Montréal:* Centre d'accueil le programme de Portage inc.**
Également connu sous le nom de: Portage
885, square Richmond, Montréal, QC H3J 1V8
Tél: 514-939-0202
info@portage.ca
www.portage.ca
Média social: www.facebook.com/PortageCanada; twitter.com/PortageCanada
Fondée en: 1970
Note: Portage operates drug addiction treatment centres in the Québec cities of Montréal, Québec, Beaconsfield, Prévost, & Saint-Malachie. Centres in Atlantic Canada, Ontario, & British Columbia assist adolescents.

***Montréal:* Centre de réadaptation Constance-Lethbridge**
Affiliée à: CIUSSS du Centre-Ouest-de-l'Île-de-Montréal
7005, boul de Maisonneuve Ouest, Montréal, QC H4B 1T3
Tél: 514-487-1770 *Ligne sans frais:* 866-487-1891
www.constance-lethbridge.qc.ca
Média social: www.facebook.com/ConstanceLethbridge
Note: Déficience motrice

***Montréal:* Centre de réadaptation en déficience intellectuelle et en troubles envahissants du développement (CRDITED)**
#110, 75, rue de Port-Royal est, Montréal, QC H3L 3T1
Tél: 514-387-1234; *Téléc:* 514-387-8715
www.crditedmtl.ca
Fondée en: 2011
Joseph-Charles Giguère, Président, Conseil d'administration

Louis-Marie Marsan, Directeur général, et secrétaire, conseil d'administration

***Montréal:* Centre de réadaptation Mab-Mackay (CRMM)**
7000, rue Sherbrooke Ouest, Montréal, QC H4B 1R3
Tél: 514-488-5552; *Téléc:* 514-489-3477
info@mabmackay.ca
www.mabmackay.ca
Fondée en: 2006
Note: Fournit des services de réadaptation pour les personnes ayant une déficience visuelle et déficience auditive afin qu'ils puissent vivre de façon autonome. Le centre de réadaptation a été formé à la suite d'une fusion entre l'Association montréalaise pour les aveugles et le Centre de réadaptation Mackay.
Sara Saber-Freedman, Présidente
Christine Boyle, Directrice générale

***Montréal:* Centre Dollard-Cormier**
950, rue de Louvain est, Montréal, QC H2M 2E8
Tél: 514-385-3490; *Téléc:* 514-385-2462
cqdt.cdc@ssss.gouv.qc.ca
www.centredollardcormier.qc.ca
Nombre de lits: 55 lits
Madeleine Roy, Directrice générale

***Montréal:* Centre hospitalier universitaire Sainte-Justine**
Affiliée à: CIUSSS du Centre-Ouest-de-l'Île-de-Montréal
3175, ch de la Côte-Sainte-Catherine, Montréal, QC H3T 1C5
Tél: 514-345-4931; *Téléc:* 514-345-4808
www.chu-sainte-justine.org
Média social: www.facebook.com/ChuSteJustine; twitter.com/ChuSteJustine
Nombre de lits: 55 lits
Fabrice Brunet, Président-directeur général

***Montréal:* Centre jeunesse de Montréal - Institut universitaire**
Affiliée à: CIUSSS du Centre-Est-de-l'Île-de-Montréal
4675, rue Bélanger, Montréal, QC H1T 1C2
Tél: 514-593-3979
courrier@cjm-iu.qc.ca
www.centrejeunessedemontreal.qc.ca
Média social: www.facebook.com/cjmiu.fanpage; www.youtube.com/user/centrejeunessemtl
Nombre de lits: 826 admissions
Note: services psychosociaux et de réadaptation
Jean-Marc Potvin, Directeur général

***Montréal:* Centre Miriam/Miriam Home**
Affiliée à: CIUSSS du Centre-Ouest-de-l'Île-de-Montréal
8160, ch Royden, Montréal, QC H4P 2T2
Tél: 514-345-0210; *Téléc:* 514-345-8965
mircea.bruj.miriam@ssss.gouv.qc.ca
www.centremiriam.ca
Fondée en: 1960
Note: Soutient les personnes ayant une déficience intellectuelle.
Dr. Abraham Fuks, M.D., Président, Conseil d'administration
Daniel Amar, Directeur général

***Montréal:* La Corporation du centre de réadaptation Lucie-Bruneau**
Affiliée à: CIUSSS du Centre-Est-de-l'Île-de-Montréal
2275, av Laurier est, Montréal, QC H2H 2N8
Tél: 514-527-4527; *Téléc:* 514-527-0979
info@luciebruneau.qc.ca
www.luciebruneau.qc.ca
Nombre de lits: 50 lits
Note: centre de réadaptation (déficience motrice)
Pierre Paul Milette, Directeur général

***Montréal:* Hôpital de réadaptation Villa Medica**
225, rue Sherbrooke est, Montréal, QC H2X 1C9
Tél: 514-288-8201
rh@villamedica.ca
www.villamedica.ca
Nombre de lits: 150 lits
Note: centre hospitalier de réadaptation
Michel Duchesne, Directeur général

***Montréal:* Institut de réadaptation Gingras-Lindsay-de-Montréal**
Affiliée à: CIUSSS du Centre-Est-de-l'Île-de-Montréal
Ancien nom: Institut de réadaptation de Montréal
6300, av Darlington, Montréal, QC H3S 2J4
Tél: 514-340-2085; *Téléc:* 514-340-2091
www.irm.qc.ca
Média social: www.facebook.com/IRGLM; www.youtube.com/user/IRGLM

Fondée en: 1949
Nombre de lits: 200 lits
Note: centre de réadaptation
Michael Fortin, Directeur général
514-340-2135, michel.fortin.irglm@ssss.gouv.qc.ca

Montréal: Institut Raymond-Dewar
Affiliée à: CIUSSS du Centre-Est-de-l'Ile-de-Montréal
3600, rue Berri, Montréal, QC H2L 4G9
Tél: 514-284-2581; *Téléc:* 514-284-5086
ird@raymond-dewar.gouv.qc.ca
www.raymond-dewar.qc.ca
Note: centre de réadaptation (déficience auditive et de la parole et du language)

Montréal: Maison Elisabeth
2131, av de Marlowe, Montréal, QC H4A 3L4
Tél: 514-482-2488; *Téléc:* 514-482-9467
questions@maisonelizabethhouse.com
www.maisonelizabethhouse.com
Nombre de lits: 18 lits
Linda Schachtler, Directrice générale

Montréal: The Montréal Morgentaler Clinic/Clinique Morgentaler
#710, 30, boul St Joseph Est, Montréal, QC H2T 1G9
Tel: 514-844-4844; *Fax:* 514-844-7883
Toll-Free: 888-401-4844
mclinique@gmail.com
www.morgentalermontreal.ca
Year Founded: 1968
Note: Specialties: Pregnancy termination services; Post-abortion service

Puvirnituq: Centre de santé Inuulitsivik
ch Baie d'Hudson, Puvirnituq, QC J0M 1P0
Tél: 819-988-2957; *Téléc:* 819-988-2796
inuulitsivik@ssss.gouv.qc.ca
www.inuulitsivik.ca
Nombre de lits: 8

Québec: Centre de réadaptation en déficience intellectuelle de Québec (CRDIQ)
Affiliée à: CIUSSS de la Capitale-Nationale
7843, rue des Santolines, Québec, QC G1G 0G4
Tél: 418-683-2511; *Téléc:* 418-683-9735
infocrdiq@ssss.gouv.qc.ca
www.crdiq.qc.ca
Fondée en: 2001
Nombre de lits: 530 lits
Catherine Chagnon, Direction général

Québec: Centre de réadaptation Ubald-Villeneuve
2525, ch de la Canardière, Québec, QC G1J 2G3
Tél: 418-663-5008; *Téléc:* 418-663-6575
communication@cruv.qc.ca
www.cruv.qc.ca
Andrée Deschênes, Directrice générale

Québec: Institut de réadaptation en déficience physique de Québec
Affiliée à: CIUSSS de la Capitale-Nationale
525, boul Wilfrid Hamel, Québec, QC G1M 2S8
Tél: 418-529-9141; *Téléc:* 418-529-7318
TTY: 418-649-3733
communications@irdpq.qc.ca
www.irdpq.qc.ca
Média social: www.facebook.com/IRDPQ; www.youtube.com/user/VideosIRDPQ
Nombre de lits: 165 lits
Note: centre de réadaptation (déficience physique)
Louise Lavergne, Directrice générale

Restigouche: Centre jeunesse Gaspésie/Les Iles - Unité Gignu
CP 193, 4, Pacific Dr., Restigouche, QC G0C 2R0
Tél: 418-788-5605; *Téléc:* 418-788-2751

Rimouski: Centre de réadaptation en déficience intellectuelle du Bas St-Laurent (CRDIBSL)
Ancien nom: Centre de réadaptation intellectuelle du Bas St-Laurent
274, rue Potvin, Rimouski, QC G5L 7P5
Tél: 418-723-4425; *Téléc:* 418-722-6113
info.crditedbsl@sss.gouv.qc.ca
www.crdibsl.qc.ca
Nombre de lits: 348 lits
Guylaine Côté, Directrice générale

Rimouski: Centre jeunesse du Bas-St-Laurent
CP 3500, 287, rue Pierre-Saindon, 3e étage, Rimouski, QC G5L 8V5
Tél: 418-723-1255; *Téléc:* 418-722-0620
www.centrejeunessebsl.com
Nombre de lits: 73 lits

Roberval: Centre de réadaptation en déficience intellectuelle du Saguenay-Lac-Saint-Jean
Affiliée à: CIUSSS du Saguenay-Lac-Saint-Jean
835, rue Roland, Roberval, QC G8H 3J5
Tél: 418-275-1360; *Téléc:* 418-275-6595
www.crdited02.qc.ca
Média social: www.facebook.com/CRDITEDduSLSJ
Personnel: 600
Note: Centre de réadaptation pour personnes présentant une déficience intellectuelle
Johanne Houde, Directrice générale

Rouyn-Noranda: Centre de réadaptation La Maison
Affiliée à: CISSS de l'Abitibi-Témiscamingue
CP 1055, 100, ch Docteur-Lemay, Rouyn-Noranda, QC J9X 5C8
Tél: 819-762-6592; *Téléc:* 819-762-2049
info@crlm.qc.ca
www.crlm.qc.ca
Nombre de lits: 55 lits
Note: Centre de réadaptation (déficience physique, troubles envahissants du développement).
Line St-Amour, Directrice générale
Line_St-Amour@ssss.gouv.qc.ca

Saint-Jean-sur-Richelieu: Les services de réadaptation du Sud-Ouest et du Renfort
Affiliée à: CISSS de la Montérégie-Ouest
#105, 315, rue MacDonald, Saint-Jean-sur-Richelieu, QC J3B 8J3
Tél: 450-348-6121; *Téléc:* 450-348-8440
www.srsor.qc.ca
Nombre de lits: 581 lits
Gilles Bertrand, Directeur général

Saint-Jérôme: Centre du Florès
Affiliée à: CISSS de Laurentides
#252, 500, boul des Laurentides, Saint-Jérôme, QC J7Z 4M2
Tél: 450-569-2970; *Téléc:* 450-569-2961
Ligne sans frais: 877-569-2970
centreduflores@ssss.gouv.qc.ca
www.centreduflores.com
Fondée en: 1995
Note: centre de réadaptation
Lyse Beaudet, Direction générale

Saint-Jérôme: Centre jeunesse des Laurentides
Affiliée à: CISSS des Laurentides
#241, 500, boul des Laurentides, Saint-Jérôme, QC J7Z 4M2
Tél: 450-436-7607; *Téléc:* 450-436-4811
Ligne sans frais: 866-492-3263
www.cjlaurentides.qc.ca
Nombre de lits: 160 lits
France Trépanier, Direction général

Saint-Jérôme: Pavillon Ste-Marie inc.
45, rue Pavillon, Saint-Jérôme, QC J7Y 3R6
Tél: 450-438-3583; *Téléc:* 450-438-7481
Nombre de lits: 100 lits

Sept-Iles: Bande indienne des montagnes de Sept-Iles/Maliotenam
1089, rue Dequen, Sept-Iles, QC G4R 4L9
Tél: 418-962-0222; *Téléc:* 418-968-0935
Nombre de lits: 29 lits

Sherbrooke: Centre de réadaptation Estrie (CRE)
Affiliée à: CIUSSS de l'Estrie
#200, 300, rue King est, Sherbrooke, QC J1G 1B1
Tél: 819-346-8411; *Téléc:* 819-346-4580
Ligne sans frais: 800-361-1013
info.cre@ssss.gouv.qc.ca
www.centredereadaptationestrie.org
Média social: www.facebook.com/centredereadaptationestrie; www.youtube.com/user/readaptationestrie
Spécialités: Réadaptation fonctionnelle intensive; Ressources résidentielles et d'hébergement
Lucie Dumas, Directrice générale
nmarchand.cre@ssss.gouv.qc.ca

Sherbrooke: Centre Jean-Patrice Chiasson/Maison St-Georges
1930, rue King ouest, Sherbrooke, QC J1J 2E2
Tél: 819-821-2500
Nombre de lits: 40 places
Note: Centre de réadaptation des drogues
Murray McDonald, Directeur général

Sherbrooke: Centre jeunesse de l'Estrie (CJE)
Affiliée à: CIUSSS de l'Estrie
594, boul Queen Victoria, Sherbrooke, QC J1H 3R7
Tél: 819-564-7100; *Téléc:* 819-564-7109
Ligne sans frais: 800-567-3495
intranet.cje@ssss.gouv.qc.ca
www.cjestrie.ca
Média social: www.facebook.com/CJEstrie; twitter.com/CjEstrie
Personnel: 620
Marie Caron, Directrice générale

Sherbrooke: Centre Notre-Dame de l'Enfant (Sherbrooke) inc. (CNDE)
CRDITED Estrie
1621, rue Prospect, Sherbrooke, QC J1J 1K4
Tél: 819-346-8471; *Téléc:* 819-346-8473
info.crditedestrie@ssss.gouv.qc.ca
www.crditedestrie.qc.ca
Fondée en: 1965
Note: Le centre de réadaptation en déficience intellectuelle et troubles envahissants du développement Estre (CRDITED Estrie) est composé de deux établissements du réseau de la santé et des services sociaux du Québec, soit le Centre Notre-Dame de l'Enfant (Sherbrooke) inc. et le Centre d'accueil Dixville inc.
Danielle Lareau, Directrice générale

Sherbrooke: Villa Marie-Claire inc.
470, rue Victoria, Sherbrooke, QC J1H 3J2
Tél: 819-563-1622; *Téléc:* 819-563-6990

St-Philippe-de-Laprairie: Pavillon Foster
6 Foucreault St., St-Philippe-de-Laprairie, QC J0L 2K0
Tel: 450-659-8911; *Fax:* 450-659-7173
www.pavillonfoster.org
Year Founded: 1964
Number of Beds: 20 lits
Note: alcohol/drug rehabilitation
John Topp, Directeur général

Ste-Anne-des-Monts: Centre de réadaptation de la Gaspésie
Affiliée à: CISSS de la Gaspésie
CP 370, 230, rte du Parc, Ste-Anne-des-Monts, QC G4V 2C4
Tél: 418-763-3325; *Téléc:* 418-763-5631
Ligne sans frais: 855-763-3325
Nombre de lits: 131 lits
Jacques Tremblay, Directeur général

Ste-Anne-des-Monts: Centre de réadaptation de la Gaspésie - MRC de la Haute-Gaspésie
230, rte du Parc, Ste-Anne-des-Monts, QC G4V 2C4
Tél: 418-763-3325; *Téléc:* 418-763-5631
Note: Déficiences physiques et intellectuelles.

Ste-Anne-des-Monts: Centre de réadaptation L'Escale
Affiliée à: CISSS de la Gaspésie
52, rue Belvedere, Ste-Anne-des-Monts, QC G4V 1X4
Tél: 418-763-5000; *Téléc:* 418-763-9024
www.cssshautegaspesie.qc.ca
Note: Pour personnes toxicomanes. Le Centre relocalisera en 2010. Les nouvelles installations seront adjacentes à l'Hôpital des Monts.

Ste-Anne-des-Monts: Centre jeunesse Gaspésie/Les Iles - Succursale Haute-Gaspésie
#EB-132, 230, rte du Parc, Ste-Anne-des-Monts, QC G4V 2C4
Tél: 418-763-2251; *Téléc:* 418-763-2538

Trois-Rivières: Centre de réadaptation Interval
Affiliée à: CIUSSS de la Mauricie-et-du-Centre-du-Québec
1775, rue Nicolas-Perrot, Trois-Rivières, QC G9A 1C5
Tél: 819-378-4083; *Téléc:* 819-693-0237
www.centreinterval.qc.ca
Note: Centre de réadaptation (déficience motrice)
Bruno Landry, Directeur général

Trois-Rivières: Centre jeunesse de la Mauricie et Centre-du-Québec
Affiliée à: CIUSSS de la Mauricie-et-du-Centre-du-Québec
Centre administratif, 1455, boul du Carmel, Trois-Rivières, QC G8Z 3R7
Ligne sans frais: 855-378-5481
communications_cjmcq@ssss.gouv.qc.ca
www.cjmcq.qc.ca
Robert Nolin, Président, Conseil d'administration
Nathalie Garon, Directrice générale intérimaire

Gérald Milot, Vice-président, Conseil d'administration
Dorothée Leblanc, Secrétaire, Conseil d'administration

Trois-Rivières: CRDITED de la Mauricie et du Centre-du-Québec
3255, rue Foucher, Trois-Rivières, QC G8Z 1M6
Tél: 819-379-6868; *Téléc:* 819-379-5155
Ligne sans frais: 888-379-7732
www.crditedmcq.qc.ca
Média social: www.facebook.com/crditedmcq.iu; twitter.com/crditedmcqiu; www.youtube.com/channel/UCv3p3-3l6FoqZSX5sCDEGxQ
Région desservi: La région sociosanitaire de la Mauricie et du Centre-du-Québec
Note: Le Centre de réadaptation en déficience intellectuelle et en troubles envahissants du développement de la Mauricie et du Centre-du-Québec (CRDITED MCQ) est affilié à l'Université du Québec à Trois-Rivières (UQTR).
Sylvie Dupras, Directrice générale

Trois-Rivières: Domremy Mauricie-Centre-du-Québec
440, rue des Forges, Trois-Rivières, QC G9A 2H5
Tél: 819-374-4744
DomremyMCQ@ssss.gouv.qc.ca
www.domremymcq.qc.ca
Fondée en: 1958
Note: Centre de réadaptation des drogues
Nathalie Magnan, Directrice générale

Val-d'Or: Centre jeunesse de l'Abitibi-Témiscamingue
Affiliée à: CISSS de l'Abitibi-Témiscamingue
700, boul Forest, Val-d'Or, QC J9P 2L3
Tél: 819-825-0002; *Téléc:* 819-825-5132
www.cjat.qc.ca
Fondée en: 1996
Nombre de lits: 57 lits
Personnel: 450
Catherine Langlois, Direction générale
cathlang@ssss.gouv.qc.ca

Verdun: Teen Haven/Havre-jeunesse
4360, boul Lasalle, Verdun, QC H4G 2A8
Tel: 514-769-5050; *Fax:* 514-769-3510
teenhaven@b2b2c.ca
Number of Beds: 15 lits
Robert Johnson, Managing Director

Wemotaci: Conseil de la Nation Atikamekw
Wemotaci, QC G0X 3R0
Tél: 418-523-6153; *Téléc:* 418-676-8965
Nombre de lits: 9
Clément St-Cyr, Directeur général

Westmount: Les Centres de jeunesse Shawbridge
5, rue Weredale Park, Westmount, QC H3Z 1Y5
Tél: 514-989-1885
Nombre de lits: 138 lits
Note: centre de réadaptation (déficience motrice)

Westmount: Les centres de la jeunesse et de la famille Batshaw
Affiliée à: CIUSSS de l'Ouest-de-l'Ile-de-Montréal
Ancien nom: Les centres de la jeunesse et de la famille Saint-Georges
5, rue Weredale Park, Westmount, QC H3Z 1Y5
Tél: 514-989-1885
www.batshaw.qc.ca
Nombre de lits: 243 lits
Note: centre de réadaptation (déficience motrice) + déficience sensorielle
Margaret Douek, Directrice générale

Centres d'hébergement et des soins de longue durée (CHSLD)

Acton Vale: Centre d'hébergement de la MRC-d'Acton
Affiliée à: CISSS de la Montérégie-Est
1268, rue Ricard, Acton Vale, QC J0H 1A0
Tél: 450-546-3234; *Téléc:* 450-546-4811
communication.csssry16@ssss.gouv.qc.ca
www.santemonteregie.qc.ca/richelieu-yamaska
Nombre de lits: 81 lits

Akwesasne: Conseil Mohawk d'Akwesasne
CP 40, Akwesasne, QC H0M 1A0
Tél: 613-575-2507
Nombre de lits: 30 lits
Patti Jocko-Adia Conieti, Directrice générale

Amos: Centre d'hébergement Harricana
Affiliée à: CISSS de l'Abitibi-Témiscamingue
612, 5e av Ouest, Amos, QC J9T 4L3
Tél: 819-732-6521; *Téléc:* 819-732-7526
www.csssea.ca

Anjou: Centre Le Royer
7351, rue Jean-Desprez, Anjou, QC H1K 5A6
Tél: 514-493-9397; *Téléc:* 514-493-9103
Fondée en: 1989
Nombre de lits: 66 lits
Suzanne Larin
514-493-9397, suzanne.larin.groys@ssss.gouv.qc.ca

Baie-Saint-Paul: Centre d'hébergement Pierre-Dupré
Affiliée à: CIUSSS de la Capitale-Nationale
CP 1779, 10, rue Boivin, Baie-Saint-Paul, QC G3Z 1B0
Tél: 418-435-5562
Nombre de lits: 60 lits

Beaconsfield: Manoir Beaconsfield
34, av Woodland, Beaconsfield, QC H9W 4V9
Tél: 514-694-2000; *Téléc:* 514-694-5000
Nombre de lits: 23 lits

Beauharnois: Centre d'accueil le Vaisseau d'Or
55, rue Saint-André, Beauharnois, QC J6N 3G7
Tél: 450-429-6403; *Téléc:* 450-429-6602
Nombre de lits: 88 lits

Beauport: Centre d'hébergement du Fargy
Affiliée à: CIUSSS de la Capitale-Nationale
700, boul des Chutes, Beauport, QC G1E 2B7
Tél: 418-663-9934; *Téléc:* 418-663-1948
Nombre de lits: 60 lits, 4 lits d'hébergement temporaires

Beloeil: Centre d'hébergement Champlain-des-Pommetiers Groupe Champlain
Affiliée à: CIUSSS de la Mauricie-et-du-Centre-du-Québec
350, rue Serge Pepin, Beloeil, QC J3G 0C3
Tél: 450-464-7666; *Téléc:* 450-464-4144
www.groupechamplain.qc.ca
Nombre de lits: 132 lits

Beloeil: Centre d'hébergement Marguerite-Adam
Affiliée à: CISSS de la Montérégie-Est
425, rue Hubert, Beloeil, QC J3G 2T1
Tél: 450-467-1631; *Téléc:* 450-467-4210
communication.csssry16@ssss.gouv.qc.ca
www.santemonteregie.qc.ca/richelieu-yamaska
Nombre de lits: 70 lits

Berthierville: Centre d'hébergement Champlain Le Château
1231, rue Dr Olivier-M.-Gendron, Berthierville, QC J0K 1A0
Tél: 450-836-6241; *Téléc:* 450-836-4013
Nombre de lits: 64 lits
Marie-Claude Ouellet, Directeurice générale

Boucherville: Centre d'hébergement Jeanne-Crevier
Affiliée à: CISSS de la Montérégie-Est
151, rue De Muy, Boucherville, QC J4B 4W7
Tél: 450-641-0595; *Téléc:* 450-641-3082
www.santemonteregie.qc.ca/cssspierreboucher
Nombre de lits: 93 lits

Brossard: Centre d'accueil Marcelle Ferron inc.
8600, boul Marie Victorin, Brossard, QC J4X 1A1
Tél: 450-923-1430; *Téléc:* 450-923-1805
info@chsldmarcelleferron.com
www.chsldmarcelleferron.com
Nombre de lits: 175 lits

Brossard: CHSLD Vigi Brossard
Affiliée à: Vigi Santé Ltée
5955, boul Grande-Allée, Brossard, QC J4Z 3G4
Tél: 450-656-8500; *Téléc:* 450-656-8586
www.vigisante.com
Nombre de lits: 66 lits
Note: Agence/région administrative: Agence de la santé et des services sociaux de Montérégie.

Chambly: Manoir Soleil inc.
Affiliée à: CISSS de la Montérégie-Centre
125, rue Daigneault, Chambly, QC J3L 1G7
Tél: 450-658-4441; *Téléc:* 450-658-6521
Fondée en: 1983
Nombre de lits: 68 lits

Chandler: CHSLD Villa Pabos
Affiliée à: CISSS de la Gaspésie
CP 1088, 75, rue des Cèdres, Chandler, QC G0C 1K0
Tél: 418-689-6621; *Téléc:* 418-689-4860

Charlesbourg: Centre d'hébergement de Charlesbourg
Affiliée à: CIUSSS de la Capitale-Nationale
7150, boul Cloutier, Charlesbourg, QC G1H 5V5
Tél: 418-628-0456; *Téléc:* 418-622-8676
Nombre de lits: 64 lits
Note: Hébergement permanent, centre de jour

Châteauguay: Centre d'hébergement Champlain Châteauguay
Groupe Champlain Soins de Longue Durée
Affiliée à: CISSS de la Montérégie-Ouest
210, rue Salaberry sud, Châteauguay, QC J6K 3M9
Tél: 450-699-1694; *Téléc:* 450-699-1696
www.groupechamplain.qc.ca
Nombre de lits: 96 lits
Marie-Claude Ouellet, Directrice générale, Groupe Champlain Soins de Longue Durée

Chicoutimi: Centre d'hébergement Mgr-Victor-Tremblay
Affiliée à: CIUSSS du Saguenay-Lac-St-Jean
1236, rue D'Angoulême, Chicoutimi, QC G7H 6P9
Tél: 418-698-3907; *Téléc:* 418-549-5850
www.csss-chicoutimi.qc.ca
Nombre de lits: 50 lits

Chicoutimi: Centre d'hébergement Saint-François
Affiliée à: CIUSSS du Saguenay-Lac-Saint-Jean
912, rue Jacques-Cartier Est, Chicoutimi, QC G7H 2A9
Tél: 418-549-3727; *Téléc:* 418-543-2038
centrestfrancois.ca
Nombre de lits: 64 lits
Sonia Bergeron, Présidente et directrice générale

Chicoutimi: CHSLD de Chicoutimi
904, rue Jacques-Cartier Est, Chicoutimi, QC G7H 2A9
Tél: 418-698-3900; *Téléc:* 418-543-6285
Nombre de lits: 104 lits

Clermont: Centre d'hébergement de Clermont
Affiliée à: CIUSSS de la Capitale-Nationale
6, rue du Foyer, Clermont, QC G4A 1G8
Tél: 418-665-1712
Nombre de lits: 42 lits

Cleveland: Foyer Wales
506, rte 243, Cleveland, QC J0B 2H0
Tél: 819-826-3266; *Téléc:* 819-826-2549
info@waleshome.ca
waleshome.ca
Nombre de lits: 222 lits
Simms Stuart, Directeur général

Cleveland: Wales Home/Foyer Wales
506, rte 243 nord, Cleveland, QC J0B 2H0
Tél: 819-826-3266; *Téléc:* 819-826-3910
Ligne sans frais: 877-826-3266
info@waleshome.ca
www.waleshome.ca
Nombre de lits: 190 lits
Brendalee Piironen, Directrice générale
819-826-3266, bpiironen@waleshome.ca

Contrecoeur: CLSC des Seigneuries de Contrecoeur / Centre d'hébergement De Contrecoeur
Affiliée à: CISSS de la Montérégie-Est
4700, rte Marie-Victorin, Contrecoeur, QC J0L 1C0
Tél: 450-468-8413
Nombre de lits: 52 lits
Note: Centre d'hébergement, et le point de service CLSC des Seigneuries de Contrecoeur (450-652-2917).

Côte Saint-Luc: Centre d'hébergement Waldorf inc. Revera Living
7400, ch Côte Saint-Luc, Côte Saint-Luc, QC H4W 3J4
Tél: 514-369-1000; *Téléc:* 514-489-3968
lewaldorf@reveraliving.com
www.reveraliving.com
Nombre de lits: 20 lits
Jeffrey C. Lozon, President & CEO, Revera Living

Côte Saint-Luc: Les résidences montréalaises de l'église unie pour personnes agées
5790, av Parkhaven, Côte Saint-Luc, QC H4W 1Y1
Tél: 514-482-0590; *Téléc:* 514-482-2643
Nombre de lits: 216 beds

***Coteau-du-Lac:* Pavillon Laura Ferguson**
CP 909, 60, ch du Fleuve, Coteau-du-Lac, QC J0P 1B0
Tél: 514-267-3379

***Cowansville:* Résidence Manoir Beaumont (1988) Inc.**
430, rue Beaumont, Cowansville, QC J2K 1W1
Tél: 514-263-6235; *Téléc:* 514-263-8598
Nombre de lits: 36 lits
Note: Hébergement et soins de longue durée

***Deux-Montagnes:* CHSLD Vigi Deux-Montagnes inc.**
580, 20e av, Deux-Montagnes, QC J7R 7E9
Tél: 450-473-5111; *Téléc:* 450-491-4309
www.vigisante.com
Nombre de lits: 76 lits
Note: Agence/région administrative: Agence de la santé et des services sociaux des Laurentides.

***Disraéli:* Centre d'hébergement René-Lavoie**
Affiliée à: CISSS de Chaudière-Appalaches
CP 698, 260, av Champlain, Disraéli, QC G0N 1E0
Tél: 418-449-2020; *Téléc:* 418-449-4006
csssrt@ssss.gouv.qc.ca
www.centresantethetford.ca/sante-quebec/
Nombre de lits: 47 lits

***Dolbeau:* Maison du Bel Age**
2020, rue Provencher, Dolbeau, QC G8L 3E6
Tél: 418-276-1866; *Téléc:* 418-276-1866
Nombre de lits: 53 places
Note: Maison d'hébergement pour personnes agées autonomes

***Dollard-des-Ormeaux:* Vigi Santé Ltée**
197, rue Thornhill, Dollard-des-Ormeaux, QC H9B 3H8
Tél: 514-684-0930; *Téléc:* 514-684-0179
www.vigisante.com
Nombre de lits: 1,500 lits
Note: Propriétaire et administrateur de 15 centres d'hébergement, présente dans plusieurs régions du Québec. Le siège du CHSLD Vigi Dollard-des-Ormeaux, avec 160 lits.

***Dorval:* Chartwell Maison Herron**
Affiliée à: Chartwell Retirement Residence
2400, ch Herron, Dorval, QC H9S 5W3
Tél: 438-819-8468
chartwell.com

***Drummondville:* Centre d'hébergement Frederick-George-Heriot**
Affiliée à: CIUSSS de la Mauricie-et-du-Centre-du-Québec
75, rue Saint-Georges, Drummondville, QC J2C 4G6
Tél: 819-477-0544
csssdrummond@ssss.gouv.qc.ca
www.csssdrummond.qc.ca
Nombre de lits: 354 lits

***Farnham:* Les Foyers Farnham**
Affiliée à: CISSS de la Montérégie-Ouest
800, rue Saint-Paul, Farnham, QC J2N 2K6
Tél: 450-293-3167; *Téléc:* 450-293-7878
Nombre de lits: 61 lits

***Gaspé:* Centre d'hébergement Mgr-Ross**
Affiliée à: CISSS de la Gaspésie
150, rue Mgr Ross, Gaspé, QC G4X 2S7
Tél: 418-368-3301; *Téléc:* 418-368-6730
Nombre de lits: 129 lits
Note: CSSS Côte-de-Gaspé.

***Gatineau:* Centre d'hébergement - Bon Séjour**
Affiliée à: CISSS de l'Outaouais
134, rue Jean-René Monette, Gatineau, QC J8P 7C3
Tél: 819-966-6450; *Téléc:* 819-966-6453
www.csssgatineau.qc.ca
Nombre de lits: 100 lits

***Gatineau:* Centre d'hébergement - Foyer du Bonheur**
Affiliée à: CISSS de l'Outaouais
125, boul Lionel-Émond, Gatineau, QC J8Y 5S8
Tél: 819-966-6410; *Téléc:* 819-966-6414
www.csssgatineau.qc.ca
Nombre de lits: 263 lits

***Gatineau:* Centre d'hébergement - La Pietà**
Affiliée à: CISSS de l'Outaouais
273, rue Laurier, Gatineau, QC J8X 3W8
Tél: 819-966-6420; *Téléc:* 819-966-6427
www.csssgatineau.qc.ca
Nombre de lits: 158 lits
Denis Beaudoin, Directeur Général, CSSS Gatineau
819-966-6560

***Gatineau:* Centre d'hébergement Vallée-de-la-Lièvre**
Affiliée à: CISSS de l'Outaouais
111, rue Gérard-Gauthier, Gatineau, QC J8L 3C9
Tél: 819-986-4115
www.cssspapineau.qc.ca
Nombre de lits: 79 lits
Jacques Prud'Homme, Directeur général

***Gracefield:* Le Foyer d'accueil de Gracefield**
Affiliée à: CISSS de l'Outaouais
CP 317, 1, rue du Foyer, Gracefield, QC J0X 1W0
Tél: 819-463-2100; *Téléc:* 819-463-4721
Nombre de lits: 31 lits

***Granby:* Centre d'hébergement Villa Bonheur**
Affiliée à: CISSS de la Montérégie-Ouest
71, rue Court, Granby, QC J2G 4Y7
Tél: 450-776-5222; *Téléc:* 450-372-7617
Nombre de lits: 108 lits

***Grand-Mère:* Centre d'hébergement Laflèche**
Affiliée à: CIUSSS de la Mauricie-et-du-Centre-du-Québec
1650, 6e av, Grand-Mère, QC G9T 2K4
Tél: 819-533-2500
Nombre de lits: 319 places

***Huntingdon:* Centre d'hébergement du comté de Huntingdon**
Affiliée à: CISSS de la Montérégie-Ouest
198, rue Châteauguay, Huntingdon, QC J0S 1H0
Tél: 450-829-2321; *Téléc:* 450-264-4923
www.santemonteregie.qc.ca/haut-saint-laurent
Nombre de lits: 60 lits

***Ile-Bizard:* Centre d'hébergement Denis-Benjamin Viger**
Affiliée à: CIUSSS de l'Ouest-de-l'Ile-de-Montréal
3292, rue Cherrier, Ile-Bizard, QC H9C 1E4
Tél: 514-620-6310; *Téléc:* 514-620-6553
www.csssouestdelile.qc.ca
Nombre de lits: 125 lits

***Ile-Perrot:* Centre d'hébergement Laurent-Bergevin**
Affiliée à: CISSS de la Montérégie-Ouest
Également connu sous le nom de: Centre d'accueil Laurent-Bergevin
200, boul Perrot, Ile-Perrot, QC J7V 7M7
Tél: 514-453-5860; *Téléc:* 514-453-8939
Nombre de lits: 82 lits

***Joliette:* Centre d'hébergement de Saint-Eusèbe**
Affiliée à: CISSS de Lanaudière
585, boul Manseau, Joliette, QC J6E 3E5
Tél: 450-759-1662
www.csssnl.qc.ca
Nombre de lits: 159 lits

***Jonquière:* Centre d'hébergement Des Chênes**
Affiliée à: CIUSSS du Saguenay-Lac-St-Jean
CP 1200, 1841, rue Deschênes, Jonquière, QC G7S 4K6
Tél: 418-695-7727
www.csssjonquiere.qc.ca

***Jonquière:* Centre d'hébergement Georges-Hébert**
Affiliée à: CIUSSS du Saguenay-Lac-St-Jean
2841, rue Faraday, Jonquière, QC G7S 5C8
Tél: 418-695-7727; *Téléc:* 418-695-7737
www.csssjonquiere.qc.ca
Nombre de lits: 75 lits

***Jonquière:* Centre d'hébergement Sainte-Marie**
Affiliée à: CIUSSS du Saguenay-Lac-St-Jean
2184, rue Perrier, Jonquière, QC G7X 9C9
Tél: 418-695-7727
Nombre de lits: 66 lits
Note: Hébergement permanent et temporaire

***La Baie:* Centre d'hébergement Bagotville**
Affiliée à: CIUSSS Saguenay-Lac-St-Jean
562, rue Victoria, La Baie, QC G7B 3M6
Tél: 418-544-3381; *Téléc:* 418-544-6407

***La Baie:* Foyer St-Joseph de La Baie inc.**
Affiliée à: CIUSSS du Saguenay-Lac-St-Jean
1893, rue Alexis-Simard, La Baie, QC G7B 2K9
Tél: 418-544-2673; *Téléc:* 418-544-8936
Nombre de lits: 48 lits

***La Guadeloupe:* Centre d'hébergement de la Guadeloupe**
CP 490, 437, 15e rue ouest, La Guadeloupe, QC G0M 1G0
Tél: 418-459-3476; *Téléc:* 418-459-6428
Nombre de lits: 50 lits

***La Sarre:* CHSLD de La Sarre**
Affiliée à: CISSS de l'Abitibi-Témiscamingue
22, 1ère av Est, La Sarre, QC J9Z 1C4
Tél: 819-333-5525
www.cisssab.qc.ca
Nombre de lits: 25 chambres privées
Spécialités: Les services d'hébergement; Physiothéapie; Ergothérapie; Le service psychosocial

***LaSalle:* Centre d'hébergement de LaSalle**
Affiliée à: CIUSSS de l'Ouest-de-l'Ile-de-Montréal
8686, rue Centrale, LaSalle, QC H8P 3N4
Tél: 514-364-6700
www.csssdll.qc.ca
Nombre de lits: 202 lits
Isabelle Brault, Président

***Labelle:* Centre d'hébergement de Labelle**
Affiliée à: CISSS des Laurentides
CP 38, 50, rue de l'Église, Labelle, QC J0T 1H0
Tél: 819-686-2372; *Téléc:* 819-686-1950
www.csss-sommets.com
Nombre de lits: 46 lits
Jacques Morin, Président, Conseil d'administration, CSSS des Sommets

***Lac-Bouchette:* Centre d'hébergement de Lac-Bouchette**
Édifice Foyer de Lac-Bouchette, CP 39, 99, rte de l'Ermitage, Lac-Bouchette, QC G0W 1V0
Tél: 418-348-6313; *Téléc:* 418-348-6342
Nombre de lits: 14 lits

***Lac-Mégantic:* CHSLD / Centre de jour Lac-Mégantic**
Affiliée à: CIUSSS de l'Estrie
3675, rue du Foyer, Lac-Mégantic, QC G6B 2K2
Tél: 819-583-0330; *Téléc:* 819-583-0900
www.csssgranit.qc.ca
Nombre de lits: 46 lits
Pierre Latulippe, Directeur général, CSSS du Granit

***Lac-au-Saumon:* Centre d'hébergement Marie-Anne Ouellet**
Affiliée à: CISSS du Bas-St-Laurent
6, rue Turbide, Lac-au-Saumon, QC G0J 1M0
Tél: 418-778-5816; *Téléc:* 418-778-3391
www.csssmatapedia.qc.ca
Nombre de lits: 96 lits

***Lachine:* Centre d'hébergemen Nazaire-Piché**
Affiliée à: CIUSSS de l'Ouest-de-l'Ile-de-Montréal
150, 15e av, Lachine, QC H8S 3L9
Tél: 514-637-2326
www.csssdll.qc.ca
Nombre de lits: 100 lits
Personnel: 113

***Lachine:* Centre d'hébergement de Lachine**
Affiliée à: CIUSSS de l'Ouest-de-l'Ile-de-Montréal
650, place d'Accueil, Lachine, QC H8S 3Z5
Tél: 514-634-7161
www.csssdll.qc.ca
Nombre de lits: 187 lits
Personnel: 261

***Lambton:* CLSC / CHSLD de Lambton**
Affiliée à: CIUSSS de l'Estrie
310-A, rue Principale, Lambton, QC G0M 1H0
Tél: 418-486-7441; *Téléc:* 418-486-2172
www.csssgrant.qc.ca
Nombre de lits: 32 lits
Note: Le point de service Lambton regroupe un centre local de services communautaire (CLSC), un centre d'hébergement, et un centre de jour.
Pierre Latulippe, Directeur général, CSSS du Granit

***Lanoraie:* Centre d'hébergement Alphonse-Rondeau**
Affiliée à: CISSS de Lanaudière
419, rue Faust, Lanoraie, QC J0K 1E0
Tél: 450-887-2343
www.csssnl.qc.ca

***Laval:* Centre d'hébergement de la Rive Prodimax inc.**
4605, boul Sainte-Rose, Laval, QC H7R 5S9
Tél: 450-627-5599; *Téléc:* 450-627-5107
Nombre de lits: 79 lits
Note: Centre privé non-conventionné.

Laval: Centre d'hébergement de la Villa-des-Tilleuls inc.
5590, boul des Laurentides, Laval, QC H7K 2K2
Tél: 450-628-0322; *Téléc:* 450-622-3674
Nombre de lits: 68 lits
Note: Centre privé non-conventioné.

Laval: Centre d'hébergement de Sainte-Dorothée
Affiliée à: CISSS de Laval
350, boul Samson Ouest, Laval, QC H7X 1J4
Tél: 514-689-0933; *Téléc:* 514-689-3147
cucssslaval.ca
Nombre de lits: 277 lits
Note: Les autres centres d'hébergement: Fernand-Larocque, Idola-Saint-Jean, La Pinière, et Rose-de-Lima.

Laval: Centre d'hébergement l'Eden de Laval inc
8528, boul Lévesque Est, Laval, QC H7A 1W6
Tél: 450-665-6283; *Téléc:* 450-665-7127
Nombre de lits: 43 lits
Note: Centre privé non-conventioné.

Laval: Centre d'hébergement St-François inc.
Affiliée à: Groupe Champlain Soins de Longue Durée
4105, Montée Masson, Laval, QC H7B 1B6
Tél: 450-666-6541; *Téléc:* 450-666-1601
www.groupechamplain.qc.ca
Nombre de lits: 53 lits
Marie-Christine Moulin, Directrice générale, Groupe Champlain

Laval: CHSLD Saint-Jude inc.
Affiliée à: Siège social Age3
4410, boul St-Martin Ouest, Laval, QC H7T 1C3
Tél: 450-687-7714; *Téléc:* 450-682-0330
info@age-3.com
www.age-3.com
Fondée en: 1957
Nombre de lits: 204 lits
Daniel Leclair, Directeur général

Laval: Manoir St-Patrice inc.
3615, boul Perron, Laval, QC H7V 1P4
Tél: 450-681-1621; *Téléc:* 450-681-6120
www.chsldmanoirstpatrice.com
Nombre de lits: 132 lits

Laval: La Résidence du Bonheur
5855, rue Boulard, Laval, QC H7B 1A3
Tél: 450-666-1567; *Téléc:* 450-666-6387
info@residencedubonheur.com
www.residencedubonheur.com
Nombre de lits: 50 lits
Note: Centre privé non-conventionné.

Laval: Résidence Riviera inc.
2999, boul. Notre-Dame, Laval, QC H7V 4C4
Tél: 450-682-0111; *Téléc:* 450-682-0154
www.chsldresidenceriviera.com
Fondée en: 1959
Nombre de lits: 128 lits
Jean Nadon, Directeur général
450-682-0111, jnadon_riviera@ssss.gouv.qc.ca

Lévis: CLSC-CHSLD de la MRC Desjardins
15, rue de l'Arsenal, Lévis, QC G6V 4P6
Tél: 418-835-3400; *Téléc:* 418-835-1978
Nombre de lits: 95 lits
Renée Lachance-Auger, Directrice générale

Lévis: Pavillon Bellevue inc.
99, rue Monseigneur-Bourget, Lévis, QC G6V 9V2
Tél: 418-833-3490; *Téléc:* 418-833-6874
Nombre de lits: 50 lits

Lévis: Villa Mon Domaine inc.
109, rue du Mont-Marie, Lévis, QC G6V 8B4
Tél: 418-837-6408; *Téléc:* 418-837-2626
Nombre de lits: 57 lits

Longueuil: Centre d'accueil St-Laurent inc.
Affiliée à: CISSS de la Montérégie-Est
480, rue LeMoyne ouest, Longueuil, QC J4H 1X1
Tél: 450-670-5480; *Téléc:* 450-670-9874
Nombre de lits: 32 lits
Note: CHSLD privé non conventionné

Longueuil: Centre d'hébergement de Mgr-Coderre
Affiliée à: CISSS de la Montérégie-Est
2761, rue Beauvais, Longueuil, QC J4M 2A4
Tél: 450-448-3111; *Téléc:* 450-448-4322
www.santemonteregie.qc.ca/cssspierreboucher
Nombre de lits: 154 lits

Longueuil: Centre d'hébergement du Chevalier-De Lévis
Affiliée à: CISSS de la Montérégie-Est
40, rue Lévis, Longueuil, QC J4H 1S5
Tél: 450-670-5110; *Téléc:* 450-670-7292
www.santemonteregie.qc.ca/cssspierreboucher
Nombre de lits: 142 lits

Longueuil: Centre d'hébergement du Manoir-Trinité
Affiliée à: CISSS de la Montérégie-Est
1275, boul Jacques-Cartier Est, Longueuil, QC J4M 2Y8
Tél: 450-674-4948; *Téléc:* 450-674-8571
www.santemonteregie.qc.ca/cssspierreboucher
Spécialités: Un centre de jour offrant des services à des adultes en perte d'autonomie demeurant à domicile; Services de réadaptation

Longueuil: Centre d'hébergement René-Lévesque
Affiliée à: CISSS de la Montérégie-Est
1901, rue Claude, Longueuil, QC J4G 1Y5
Tél: 450-651-2210; *Téléc:* 450-670-7731
www.santemonteregie.qc.ca/cssspierreboucher
Nombre de lits: 224 lits

Loretteville: Centre d'hébergement Loretteville
Affiliée à: CIUSSS de la Capitale-Nationale
165, rue Lessard, Loretteville, QC G2B 2V9
Tél: 418-842-9191; *Téléc:* 418-842-4472
Nombre de lits: 74 lits

Lyster: Centre d'hébergement des Quatre-Vents
Affiliée à: CIUSSS de la Mauricie-et-du-Centre-du-Québec
Ancien nom: Le Foyer de Lyster
2180, rue Bécancour, Lyster, QC G0S 1V0
Tél: 819-389-5923; *Téléc:* 819-389-5969
www.csssae.qc.ca
Fondée en: 1969
Nombre de lits: 26 lits
Marcel Dubois, Président, Conseil d'administration, CSSS d'Arthabaska-et-de-l

Magog: Résidence Ste-Marguerite Marie
64, rue St-Pierre, Magog, QC J1X 3A2
Tél: 819-843-0202; *Téléc:* 819-843-9518
info@residencesmagog.ca
www.residencesmagog.ca

Malartic: Centre d'hébergement Saint-Martin de Malartic
Affiliée à: CISSS de l'Abitibi-Témiscamingue
CP 639, 701, rue de la Paix, Malartic, QC J0Y 1Z0
Tél: 819-825-5858; *Téléc:* 819-757-3309
www.csssvo.qc.ca
Nombre de lits: 57 lits
Note: Centre d'hébergement/centre de jour.
Marc Fillion, Président, CSSS de la Vallée-de-l'Or

Maria: Centre d'hébergement de Maria
Affiliée à: CISSS de la Gaspésie
491, boul Perron, Maria, QC G0C 1Y0
Tél: 418-759-3458; *Téléc:* 418-759-5103
www.csssbc.qc.ca
Nombre de lits: 91 lits

Marieville: Centre d'hébergement Sainte-Croix
Affiliée à: CISSS de la Montérégie-Centre
300, rue Docteur-Poulin, Marieville, QC J3M 1L7
Tél: 450-460-4475; *Téléc:* 450-460-4104
Nombre de lits: 128 lits

Matane: Centre d'hébergement de Matane
Affiliée à: CISSS du Bas-St-Laurent
150, av Saint-Jérôme, Matane, QC G4W 3A2
Tél: 418-562-4154; *Téléc:* 418-562-9281
www.agencesssbsl.gouv.qc.ca
Nombre de lits: 106 lits

Matapédia: Centre d'hébergement de Matapédia
Affiliée à: CISSS de la Gaspésie
14, boul Perron Est, Matapédia, QC G0J 1V0
Tél: 418-865-2221; *Téléc:* 418-865-2317
www.csssbc.qc.ca
Spécialités: Services d'hébergement; Réadaptation

Mont-Joli: CSSS de La Mitis
800, av du Sanatorium, Mont-Joli, QC G5H 3L6
Tél: 418-775-7261
info@csssmitis.ca
www.centremitissien.net
Média social: www.facebook.com/CSSSMitis; twitter.com/csssdelamitis
Nombre de lits: 136 lits

Manon Dufresne, Directrice générale

Mont-Laurier: Centre d'Hébergement Sainte-Anne
Affiliée à: CISSS de Laurentides
411, rue de la Madone, Mont-Laurier, QC J9L 1S1
Tél: 819-623-5940; *Téléc:* 819-623-7347
www.csssal.org
Nombre de lits: 128 lits

Mont-Royal: CHSLD Vigi Mont-Royal
Affiliée à: Vigi Santé Ltée
275, av Brittany, Mont-Royal, QC H3P 3C2
Tél: 514-739-5593; *Téléc:* 514-733-7973
www.vigisante.com
Nombre de lits: 273 lits
Note: Agence/région administrative: Agence de la santé et des services sociaux de Montréal.

Mont-Tremblant: Centre d'hébergement de Mont-Tremblant
Affiliée à: CISSS des Laurentides
925, rue de Saint-Jovite, Mont-Tremblant, QC J8E 3J8
Tél: 819-425-2793 *Ligne sans frais:* 855-766-6387

Montmagny: CLSC et Centre d'hébergement de Montmagny
Affiliée à: CISSS de Chaudière-Appalaches
168, rue Saint-Joseph, Montmagny, QC G5V 1H8
Tél: 418-248-1572; *Téléc:* 418-248-3374
www.csssml.qc.ca
Nombre de lits: 65 lits
Région desservi: Le territoire de Montmagny-L'Islet

Montréal: Les Cèdres - Le Centre d'accueil pour personnes âgées
#200, 1275, Côte-Vertu, Montréal, QC H4L 4V2
Tél: 514-389-1023; *Téléc:* 514-389-0581
info@centrelescedres.ca
www.centrelescedres.ca
Fondée en: 1960
Fadia El Khoury, Directrice générale

Montréal: Centre d'accueil Father Dowd/Father Dowd Home
6565, ch Hudson, Montréal, QC H3S 2T7
Tél: 514-341-1007; *Téléc:* 514-341-8988
www.chssn.org
Nombre de lits: 134 lits
Carole McDonough, Directrice générale

Montréal: Centre d'accueil Heritage Inc.
5716, ch de la Côte St-Antoine, Montréal, QC H4A 1R9
Tél: 514-484-2978; *Téléc:* 514-678-6928
info@centreheritage.com
www.centreheritage.com
Nombre de lits: 16 lits
William Sauvé, Président

Montréal: Centre d'hébergement Armand-Lavergne
Affiliée à: CIUSSS du Centre-Est-de-l'Ile-de-Montréal
3500, rue Chapleau, Montréal, QC H2K 4N3
Tél: 514-527-8921
www.csssjeannemance.ca
Nombre de lits: 182 lits
Note: Centre de jour; centre d'hébergement permanent.

Montréal: Centre d'hébergement Biermans
Affiliée à: CIUSSS du l'Est-de-l'Ile-de-Montréal
7905, rue Sherbrooke Est, Montréal, QC H1L 1A4
Tél: 514-351-9891
Fondée en: 1936

Montréal: Centre d'hébergement de Cartierville
Affiliée à: CIUSSS du Nord-de-l'Ile-de-Montréal
12235, rue Grenet, Montréal, QC H4J 2N9
Tél: 514-337-7300; *Téléc:* 514-337-4188
www.csssbcstl.qc.ca
Nombre de lits: 285 lits
Daniel Corbeil, Directeur général

Montréal: Centre D'Hébergement de la Maison-Saint-Joseph
5605, rue Beaubien est, Montréal, QC H1T 1X4
Tél: 514-254-4991; *Téléc:* 514-257-1742
www.ch-maison-saint-joseph.com
Nombre de lits: 80 lits

Montréal: Centre d'hébergement de Louvain
Affiliée à: CIUSSS du Nord-de-l'Ile-de-Montréal
9600, rue St-Denis, Montréal, QC H2M 1P2
Tél: 514-381-7256; *Téléc:* 514-381-6486
www.csssamn.ca
Nombre de lits: 155 lits

***Montréal:* Centre d'hébergement de Saint-Michel**
Affiliée à: CIUSSS de l'Est-de-l'Ile-de-Montréal
3130, rue Jarry Est, Montréal, QC H1Z 4N8
Tél: 514-722-3000; *Téléc:* 514-593-7400
dotation.slsm@ssss.gouv.qc.ca
csss-stleonardstmichel.qc.ca
Nombre de lits: 192 lits
Note: Centre administratif du CSSS, et centre d'hébergement.
Denis Blanchard, Directeur général, CSSS de Saint-Léonard et Saint-Michel

***Montréal:* Centre d'hébergement des Quatre-Temps**
Affiliée à: CIUSSS de l'Est-de-l'Ile-de-Montréal
7400, boul Saint-Michel, Montréal, QC H2A 2Z8
Tél: 514-722-3000
csss-stleonardstmichel.qc.ca
Nombre de lits: 192 lits

***Montréal:* Centre d'hébergement des Seigneurs**
Affiliée à: CIUSSS du Centre-Est-de-l'Ile-de-Montréal
1800, rue St-Jacques, Montréal, QC H3J 2R5
Tél: 514-935-4681; *Téléc:* 514-935-6189
www.sov.qc.ca

***Montréal:* Centre d'hébergement du Centre-Ville-de-Montréal**
Affiliée à: CIUSSS du Centre-Est-de-l'Ile-de-Montréal
66, boul René-Lévesque est, Montréal, QC H2X 1N3
Tél: 514-861-9331; *Téléc:* 514-861-8385
www.csssjeannemance.ca
Nombre de lits: 196 lits

***Montréal:* Centre d'hébergement du Manoir-de-l'Age-d'Or**
Affiliée à: CIUSSS du Centre-Est-de-l'Ile-de-Montréal
3430, rue Jeanne-Mance, Montréal, QC H2X 2J9
Tél: 514-842-1147; *Téléc:* 514-842-1146
www.csssjeannemance.ca
Nombre de lits: 189 lits

***Montréal:* Centre d'hébergement Émilie-Gamelin**
Affiliée à: CIUSSS du Centre-Est-de-l'Ile-de-Montréal
1440, rue Dufresne, Montréal, QC H2K 3J3
Tél: 514-527-8921; *Téléc:* 514-527-3587
www.csssjeannemance.ca
Nombre de lits: 184 lits

***Montréal:* Centre D'hebergement Jeanne-le Ber**
Ancien nom: gentre-hospitalier -Centre d'accueil Gouin-Rosemont; CHSLD Jeanne-Leber
7445, rue Hochelaga, Montréal, QC H1N 3V2
Tél: 514-251-6000
Nombre de lits: 351 lits

***Montréal:* Centre d'hébergement Jeanne-Le Ber**
Affiliée à: CIUSSS de l'Est-de-l'Ile-de-Montréal
7445, rue Hochelaga, Montréal, QC H1N 3V2
Tél: 514-251-6000
www.cssslucilleteasdale.qc.ca
Nombre de lits: 351 lits

***Montréal:* Centre d'hébergement Légaré**
Affiliée à: CIUSSS du Nord-de-l'Ile-de-Montréal
1615, av Émile-Journault, Montréal, QC H2M 2G3
Tél: 514-384-5490
www.csssamn.ca
Nombre de lits: 105 lits
Agnès Boussion, Directrice générale

***Montréal:* Centre d'hébergement Louis Riel**
Affiliée à: CIUSSS du Centre-Est-de-l'Ile-de-Montréal
2120, rue Augustin-Cantin, Montréal, QC H3K 3G3
Tél: 514-931-2263; *Téléc:* 514-931-2299
www.sov.qc.ca
Nombre de lits: 100 lits
Sonia Bélanger, Directrice générale

***Montréal:* Centre d'hebergement Marie-Rollet**
Affiliée à: CIUSSS de l'Est-de-l'Ile-de-Montréal
5003, rue Saint-Zotique est, Montréal, QC H1T 1N6
Tél: 514-729-5281; *Téléc:* 514-593-5568
www.cssslucilleteasdale.qc.ca
Nombre de lits: 110 lits
Note: Hébergement et soins de longue durée
Lise Tremblay, Présidente

***Montréal:* Centre d'hébergement Paul-Gouin**
Affiliée à: CIUSSS du Nord-de-l'Ile-de-Montréal
5900, rue de Saint-Vallier, Montréal, QC H2S 2P3
Tél: 514-273-3681; *Téléc:* 514-273-7645
Nombre de lits: 100 lits

***Montréal:* Centre d'hébergement Rousselot**
Affiliée à: CIUSSS de l'Est-de-l'Ile-de-Montréal
5655, rue Sherbrooke est, Montréal, QC H1N 1A4
Tél: 514-254-9421; *Téléc:* 514-254-3967
www.cssslucilleteasdale.qc.ca
Nombre de lits: 157 lits
Daniel Corbeil, Directeur général

***Montréal:* Centre d'hébergement St-Andrew**
Affiliée à: CIUSSS du Centre-Ouest-de-l'Ile-de-Montréal
3350, boul Cavendish, Montréal, QC H4B 2M7
Tél: 514-932-3630
www.cssscavendish.qc.ca
Nombre de lits: 300 lits

***Montréal:* Centre d'hébergement St-Margaret/St. Margaret Residence**
Affiliée à: CIUSSS du Centre-Ouest-de-l'Ile-de-Montréal
50, av Hillside, Montréal, QC H3Z 1V9
Tél: 514-932-3630

***Montréal:* Centre d'hébergement Yvon-Brunet**
Affiliée à: CIUSSS du Centre-Est-de-l'Ile-de-Montréal
6250, av Newman, Montréal, QC H4E 4K4
Tél: 514-765-8000; *Téléc:* 514-765-8064
www.sov.qc.ca
Fondée en: 1982
Nombre de lits: 185 lits

***Montréal:* Centre de soins prolongés Grace Dart**
Affiliée à: CIUSSS de l'Ouest-de-l'Ile-de-Montréal
5155, rue Ste-Catherine est, Montréal, QC H1V 2A5
Tél: 514-255-2833; *Téléc:* 514-255-0650
www.gracedart.ca
Nombre de lits: 381 lits
Marie-France Bodet, Directrice générale

***Montréal:* Centre Le Cardinal inc.**
12900, rue Notre-Dame est, Montréal, QC H1A 1R9
Tél: 514-645-2766; *Téléc:* 514-640-6267
Nombre de lits: 204 lits
Léonard Chevarie, Directeur général

***Montréal:* CHSLD Bourget inc.**
11570, rue Notre-Dame Est, Montréal, QC H1B 2X4
Tél: 514-645-1673; *Téléc:* 514-645-8451
Nombre de lits: 112 lits
Note: Un établissement privé.
Diane Girard, Directrice générale
diane_girard@ssss.gouv.qc.ca

***Montréal:* CHSLD Jean XXIII inc.**
6900, 15e av, Montréal, QC H1X 2V9
Tél: 514-725-2190; *Téléc:* 514-728-5901
www.chsldjean23.com
Nombre de lits: 24 lits

***Montréal:* CHSLD juif de Montréal**
Affiliée à: CIUSSS du Centre-Ouest-de-l'Ile-de-Montréal
5725, av Victoria, Montréal, QC H3W 3H6
Tél: 514-738-4500; *Téléc:* 514-738-2611
www.chsldjuif.ca
Nombre de lits: 160 beds
Barbara Gold, Dir. gén. (intérim)

***Montréal:* CHSLD Manoir Fleury inc.**
2145, rue Fleury est, Montréal, QC H2B 1J8
Tél: 514-388-1553; *Téléc:* 514-388-4161
Nombre de lits: 25 lits

***Montréal:* CHSLD Marie-Claret inc.**
Affiliée à: Vigi Santé Ltée
3345, boul Henri-Bourassa Est, Montréal, QC H1H 1H6
Tél: 514-322-4380; *Téléc:* 514-326-8811
www.vigisante.com
Nombre de lits: 78 lits
Note: Agence/région administrative: Agence de la santé et des services sociaux de Montréal.

***Montréal:* CHSLD Providence Notre-Dame-de-Lourdes**
1870, boul Pie-IX, Montréal, QC H1V 2C6
Tél: 514-527-4595; *Téléc:* 514-527-4475
communication.nddl@ssss.gouv.qc.ca
www.chsld-providence-notre-dame-lourdes.com
Fondée en: 1934
Nombre de lits: 162 lits

***Montréal:* Groupe Champlain Soins de Longue Durée**
Affiliée à: Groupe Santé Sedna inc.
7150, rue Marie-Victorin, Montréal, QC H1G 2J5
Tél: 514-324-2044; *Téléc:* 514-324-5900
www.groupechamplain.qc.ca
Fondée en: 1966
Nombre de lits: 1443 lits
Note: 15 établissements
Marie-Claude Ouellet, Présidente & Directrice Générale

***Montréal:* L'Hôpital Chinois de Montréal (1963)**
Affiliée à: CIUSSS du Centre-Est-de-l'Ile-de-Montréal
189, av Viger est, Montréal, QC H2X 3Y9
Tél: 514-871-0961; *Téléc:* 514-871-0966
montrealchinesehospital.ca
Nombre de lits: 128 lits
Anthony Shao, Directeur général

***Montréal:* Institut Canadien-Polonais du Bien-Etre inc.**
Affiliée à: CIUSSS de l'Est-de-l'Ile-de-Montréal
5655, rue Bélanger, Montréal, QC H1T 1G2
Tél: 514-259-2551; *Téléc:* 514-259-9948
instpol.com
Nombre de lits: 126 lits
M. Szpotowicz, Directrice générale

***Montréal:* Résidence Berthiaume-du Tremblay**
1635, boul Gouin est, Montréal, QC H2C 1C2
Tél: 514-381-1841; *Téléc:* 514-381-1090
www.residence-berthiaume-du-tremblay.com
Nombre de lits: 246 lits
Nicole Ouellet, Directrice générale
nicole_ouellet@sss.gouv.qc.ca

***Montréal:* La Résidence Fulford**
1221, rue Guy, Montréal, QC H3H 2K8
Tél: 514-933-7375; *Téléc:* 514-933-3773
fulford@fulfordresidence.com
www.fulfordresidence.com
Nombre de lits: 6 lits
Note: residence for women
Catherine Lackenbauer, First Directress

***Montréal:* Résidence Rive Soleil inc.**
15150, rue Notre-Dame Est, Montréal, QC H1A 1W6
Tél: 514-642-5509
Nombre de lits: 30 chambres

***Montréal:* Résidence Sainte-Claire inc.**
8950, rue Sainte-Claire est, Montréal, QC H1L 1Z1
Tél: 514-351-3877; *Téléc:* 514-352-5956
Nombre de lits: 38 lits

***Montréal:* Résidence St-Jacques**
8712, rue St-Hubert, Montréal, QC H2M 1Y5
Tél: 514-389-5880
Fondée en: 1989
Nombre de lits: 25 lits

***Montréal-Nord:* Centre d'hébergement Champlain Gouin**
Affiliée à: Groupe Champlain inc.
4445, boul Henri-Bourassa est, Montréal-Nord, QC H1H 5M4
Tél: 514-327-6209; *Téléc:* 514-327-9912
www.groupechamplain.qc.ca
Nombre de lits: 93 lits
Note: Agence/région administrative: Agence de la santé et des services sociaux de Montréal.

***Montréal-Nord:* CHSLD Villa Belle Rive**
5320, boul Gouin est, Montréal-Nord, QC H1G 1B4
Tél: 514-321-1367; *Téléc:* 514-322-4211
info@chsldvillabellerive.com
www.chsldvillabellerive.com
Nombre de lits: 27 lits

***Montréal-Nord:* Résidence Angelica inc.**
3435, boul Gouin est, Montréal-Nord, QC H1H 1B1
Tél: 514-324-6110; *Téléc:* 514-324-4005
www.angelica-residence.com
Nombre de lits: 400 lits

***New Carlisle:* Centre d'hébergement de New Carlisle**
Affiliée à: CISSS de la Gaspésie
108, rue Principale, New Carlisle, QC G0C 1Z0
Tél: 418-752-3386; *Téléc:* 418-752-6483
Nombre de lits: 75 lits

***Normandin:* Centre de Normandin**
Affiliée à: Centre de santé et de services sociaux Maria-Chapdelaine
1205, rue St-Cyrille, Normandin, QC G8M 4K1
Tél: 418-274-1234; *Téléc:* 418-274-6970
www.csssmariachapdelaine.com
Nombre de lits: 35 lits de soins de longue durée
Note: Centre d'hébergement; point de service CLSC; centre de jour.
Normand Brassard, Directeur général, CSSS Maria Chapdelaine

***North Hatley:* Connaught Home**
Affiliée à: Massawippi Christian Retirement Homes
77 Main St., North Hatley, QC J0B 2C0
Tél: 819-842-2164; *Téléc:* 819-842-2667
info@mcrh.ca
www.mcrh.ca
Nombre de lits: 41 lits

***Notre-Dame-du-Bon-Conseil:* Centre d'hébergement L'Accueil Bon-Conseil**
Affiliée à: CIUSSS de la Mauricie-et-du-Centre-du-Québec
91, rue Saint-Thomas, Notre-Dame-du-Bon-Conseil, QC J0C 1A0
Tél: 819-336-2122
csssdrummond@ssss.gouv.qc.ca
www.csssdrummond.qc.ca
Nombre de lits: 52 lits
Note: Centre d'hébergement; le point de service CLSC: 819-474-2572.
Yves Martin, Directeur général, CSSS Drummond
819-478-6401

***Notre-Dame-du-Nord:* CHSLD des premières nations du Timiskaming**
20, av Algonquin, Notre-Dame-du-Nord, QC J0Z 3B0
Tél: 819-723-2225; *Téléc:* 819-723-2112
wpp01.msss.gouv.qc.ca
Nombre de lits: 20 lits
Note: Établissement privé non conventionné

***Oka:* Manoir Oka inc.**
CP 567, 2083, ch Oka, Oka, QC J0N 1E0
Ligne sans frais: 800-251-9902
manoiroka@videotron.ca
manoiroka.com
Nombre de lits: 34 lits
Raynald Jean, Directeur général

***Ormstown:* Centre d'hébergement d'Ormstown**
Affiliée à: CISSS de la Montérégie-Ouest
65, rue Hector, Ormstown, QC J0S 1K0
Tél: 450-829-2321; *Téléc:* 450-829-3110
Fondée en: 1978
Nombre de lits: 74 lits

***Palmarolle:* CHSLD de Palmarolle**
Affiliée à: CISSS de l'Abitibi-Témiscamingue
136, rue Principale, Palmarolle, QC J0Z 3C0
Tél: 819-787-2612; *Téléc:* 819-787-3293
www.csssab.qc.ca
Nombre de lits: 22 chambres privées
Spécialités: Les services d'hébergement; Physiothérapie; Ergothéapie; Optométrie

***Pierrefonds:* Le Manoir Pierrefonds**
Affiliée à: Chartwell Résidences Pour Retraités
18465, boul Gouin Ouest, Pierrefonds, QC H9K 1A6
Tél: 514-626-6651; *Téléc:* 514-626-6415
www.chartwell.com
Nombre de lits: 183 unités

***Pierreville:* Centre d'hébergement Lucien Shooner**
Affiliée à: CIUSSS de la Mauricie-et-du-Centre-du-Québec
CP 220, 50, rue Lt-Gouv.-Paul-Comtois, Pierreville, QC J0G 1J0
Tél: 450-568-2712; *Téléc:* 450-568-3658
Www.csssbny.qc.ca
Nombre de lits: 38 lits
Danielle Gamelin, Directrice générale, CSSSBNY

***Plessisville:* Centre d'hébergement des Bois-Francs**
Affiliée à: CIUSSS de la Mauricie-et-du-Centre-du-Québec
1450, av Trudelle, Plessisville, QC G6L 3K4
Tél: 819-362-3558; *Téléc:* 819-362-9266
www.csssae.qc.ca
Nombre de lits: 40 lits
Claude Charland, Directeur général, CSSS d'Arthabaska-et-de-L'Érable

***Pointe-Claire:* CHSLD Bayview inc.**
Également connu sous le nom de: Centre Bayview
27, ch. du Bord-du-Lac, Pointe-Claire, QC H9S 4H1
Tél: 514-695-9384; *Téléc:* 514-695-5723
www.chsldbayview.com
Nombre de lits: 128 lits
Note: Un établissement privé de soins de longue durée.
George Guillon, Directeur général

***Princeville:* Centre d'hébergement de Saint-Eusèbe**
Affiliée à: CIUSSS de la Mauricie-et-du-Centre-du-Québec
Également connu sous le nom de: Foyer St-Eusèbe
CP 610, 435, rue Saint-Jacques, Princeville, QC G6L 5C5
Tél: 819-364-2355; *Téléc:* 819-364-7824
www.csssae.qc.ca
Nombre de lits: 26 lits
Marcel Dubois, Président, Conseil d'administration, CSSS d'Arthabaska-et-de-l

***Québec:* Centre d'accueil Nazareth inc.**
715, rue des Glacis, Québec, QC G1R 3P8
Tél: 418-694-0492; *Téléc:* 418-694-9452
Nombre de lits: 75 lits

***Quebec:* Centre d'hébergement Christ-Roi**
Affiliée à: CIUSSS de la Capitale-Nationale
900, boul Wilfrid-Hamel, Quebec, QC G1M 2R9
Tél: 418-682-1711; *Téléc:* 418-682-1770
Nombre de lits: 142 lits
Note: Hébergement permanent/soins de longue durée, hôpital de jour, hébergement temporaire, consultations externes

***Québec:* Centre d'hébergement Henri-Bradet**
Affiliée à: CIUSSS du Centre-Ouest-de-l'Ile-de-Montréal
6465, av Chester, Québec, QC H4V 2Z8
Tél: 514-484-7878; *Téléc:* 514-483-4596
www.cssscavendish.qc.ca

***Québec:* Centre d'hébergement Louis-Hebert**
Affiliée à: CIUSSS de la Capitale-Nationale
1550, rue de la Pointe-aux-Lièvres Nord, Québec, QC G1L 4M8
Tél: 418-529-5511; *Téléc:* 418-524-1143
Nombre de lits: 52 lits
M. Huges Mattes, Directeur général, CSSS de la Vieille-Capitale

***Québec:* Centre d'hébergement Saint-Antoine**
Affiliée à: CIUSSS de la Capitale-Nationale
1451, boul Père-Lelièvre, Québec, QC G1M 1N8
Tél: 418-683-2516; *Téléc:* 418-683-4031
www.csssvc.qc.ca
Nombre de lits: 284 lits
Note: Hébergement et soins de longue durée

***Québec:* Centre d'hébergement Saint-Augustin**
Affiliée à: CIUSSS de la Capitale-Nationale
2135, rue Terrasse-Cadieux, Québec, QC G1C 1Z2
Tél: 418-667-3910; *Téléc:* 418-667-3910
www.csssqn.qc.ca
Nombre de lits: 34 lits de gériatrie

***Québec:* Centre d'hébergement St-Jean-Eudes (CHSJE)**
Affiliée à: CIUSSS de la Capitale-Nationale
6000, 3e av Ouest, Québec, QC G1H 7J5
Tél: 418-627-1124; *Téléc:* 418-781-2604
www.chsje.qc.ca
Nombre de lits: 150 lits
Note: Le Centre d'hébergement St-Jean-Eudes est un établissement privé conventionné
Clémence Boucher, Directrice générale
clemence_boucher@ssss.gouv.qc.ca
Nicolas Labrèche, Directeur général-adjoint
nicolas.labreche@ssss.gouv.qc.ca
Louise Godin, Commissaire locale aux plaintes, et à la qualité des services
418-563-2917

***Québec:* Centre hospitalier Nôtre-Dame du Chemin inc.**
510, ch Ste-Foy, Québec, QC G1S 2J5
Tél: 418-681-7882; *Téléc:* 418-681-5387
Nombre de lits: 50 lits
Antoine Pichette, Directeur général

***Québec:* La Corporation Notre-Dame de Bon-Secours**
990, rue Gérard-Morisset, Québec, QC G1S 1X6
Tél: 418-681-4637
Nombre de lits: 20 lits
Michel Bilodrau, Directeur général

***Québec:* Foyer Ste-Marie-des-Anges Résidence**
2340, boul Masson, Québec, QC G1P 1J4
Tél: 418-871-5365; *Téléc:* 418-667-7537
www.cmafhaiti.org/foyer.htm
Nombre de lits: 14 chambres
Note: Pour personnes retraitées autonomes et en perte d'autonomie

***Québec:* Hôpital Ste-Monique inc.**
Affiliée à: CIUSSS de la Capitale-Nationale
4805, boul Wilfrid-Hamel, Québec, QC G1P 2J7
Tél: 418-871-8701; *Téléc:* 418-871-0105
www.chsld-ste-monique.com
Nombre de lits: 58 lits

***Rawdon:* CHSLD Bouleaux Argentés**
3567, rue Church, Rawdon, QC J0K 1S0
Tél: 450-834-2794; *Téléc:* 450-834-8286
Nombre de lits: 16 lits

***Rawdon:* Manoir Heather/Heather Lodge**
3462 - av. 3e, Rawdon, QC J0K 1S0
Tél: 450-834-2512; *Téléc:* 450-834-5805
www.manoirheather.com
Nombre de lits: 76 lits
Note: CHSLD Heather II: 3462, 3e av, Rawdon, QC J0K 1S0, 450-834-2512.
Paul Arbec, Directeur général
paul_arbec@ssss.gouv.qc.ca

***Richmond:* Centre d'hébergement de Richmond**
Affiliée à: CIUSSS de l'Estrie
110, rue Barlow, Richmond, QC J0B 2H0
Tél: 819-542-2777; *Téléc:* 819-826-3867
vsf.santeestrie.qc.ca
Nombre de lits: 54 lits
Pierre Lalande, Directeur général, CSSS du Val-Saint-François

***Rimouski:* Centre d'hébergement de Rimouski**
Affiliée à: CISSS du Bas-St-Laurent
645, boul Saint-Germain ouest, Rimouski, QC G5L 3S2
Tél: 418-724-4111; *Téléc:* 418-724-0604
courrierweb.crsssr@ssss.gouv.qc.ca
www.chrr.qc.ca
Nombre de lits: 246 lits
Michel Beaulieu, Directeur général, CSSS de Rimouski-Neigette

***Rimouski:* Foyer Ste-Bernadette inc.**
280, av Belzile, Rimouski, QC G5L 8K7
Tél: 418-723-0040; *Téléc:* 418-723-0615
Nombre de lits: 24 lits

***Rivière-Bleue:* Centre d'hébergement Rivière-Bleue**
Affiliée à: CISSS du Bas-St-Laurent
45, rue du Foyer, Rivière-Bleue, QC G0L 2B0
Tél: 418-893-5511; *Téléc:* 418-893-7151
www.ccsstemiscouata.com
Nombre de lits: 44 lits

***Rivière-Ouelle:* Centre d'hébergement Thérèse-Martin**
Affiliée à: CISSS du Bas-St-Laurent
100, ch. Petite-Anse, Rivière-Ouelle, QC G0L 2C0
Tél: 418-856-7000; *Téléc:* 418-856-4381
www.agencesssbsl.gouv.qc.ca

***Rivière-du-Loup:* Centre d'hébergement Saint-Joseph**
Affiliée à: CIUSSS du Bas-St-Laurent
28, rue Joly, Rivière-du-Loup, QC G5R 3H2
Tél: 418-862-6385; *Téléc:* 418-862-1986
www.cssrivieredulouop.qc.ca
Nombre de lits: 145 lits

***Rouyn-Noranda:* Centre d'hébergement de Rouyn-Noranda**
Affiliée à: CISSS de l'Abitibi-Témiscamingue
512, av Richard, Rouyn-Noranda, QC J9X 4M1
Tél: 819-762-0908; *Téléc:* 819-764-5036
www.csssrn.qc.ca
Nombre de lits: 157 lits
Note: Centre d'hébergement, centre de jour, hôpital de jour.
Jean-Pierre Lemire, Directrice générale, CSSS de Rouyn-Noranda
Annie Audet, Directrice, Programme des personnes en perte d'autonomie

***Saint-Alexandre:* Centre d'hébergement Villa Maria**
Affiliée à: CISSS du Bas-St-Laurent
404, av du Foyer, Saint-Alexandre, QC G0L 2G0
Tél: 418-856-7000; *Téléc:* 418-495-2829
www.cssskamouraska.ca

***Saint-André-Avellin:* CLSC et Centre d'hébergement Petite-Nation**
Affiliée à: CISSS de l'Outaouais
14, rue Saint-André, Saint-André-Avellin, QC J0V 1W0
Tél: 819-983-7341; *Téléc:* 819-983-7812
www.csssppapineau.qc.ca
Pierre Gagnon, Directeur général, CSSS de Papineau

***Saint-Antoine-sur-Richeli:* Accueil du Rivage inc.**
Affiliée à: CISSS de la Montérégie-Est
1008, ch du Rivage, Saint-Antoine-sur-Richeli, QC J0L 1R0
Tél: 450-787-3163; *Téléc:* 450-787-1156
www.accueildurivage.com
Nombre de lits: 36 lits
Jean Bergeron, Directeur général
jean.bergeron@rrsss16.gouv.qc.ca

***Saint-Antonin:* Centre d'hébergement de Saint-Antonin**
Affiliée à: CISSS du Bas-St-Laurent
CP 430, 286, rue Principale, Saint-Antonin, QC G0L 2J0
Tél: 418-862-7993; *Téléc:* 418-862-5278
www.csssrivierreduloup.qc.ca
Nombre de lits: 42 lits

***Saint-Augustin-de-Desmaur:* Jardins du Haut Saint-Laurent**
Affiliée à: CIUSSS de la Capitale-Nationale
4770, rue St-Felix, Saint-Augustin-de-Desmaur, QC G3A 1B1
Tél: 418-872-4936; *Téléc:* 418-872-4245
info@jardins-hsl.com
www.jardins-hsl.com
Nombre de lits: 140 lits

***Saint-Bernard-de-Lacolle:* Florence Groulx inc.**
7, rue Saint-Louis RR#2, Saint-Bernard-de-Lacolle, QC J0J 1V0
Tél: 450-246-3879; *Téléc:* 450-246-4111
Nombre de lits: 50 lits
Daniel Gaudette, Directeur général

***Saint-Bruno-de-Montarvill:* Centre d'hébergement de Montarville**
Affiliée à: CISSS de la Montérégie-Est
265, boul Seigneurial ouest, Saint-Bruno-de-Montarvill, QC J3V 2H4
Tél: 450-461-2650; *Téléc:* 450-461-2968
communication.csssry16@ssss.gouv.ac.ca
www.santemonteregie.qc.ca/richelieu-yamaska
Nombre de lits: 155 lits

***Saint-Casimir:* Centre d'hébergement Saint-Casimir**
Affiliée à: CIUSSS de la Capitale-Nationale
CP 10, 605, rue Fleury, Saint-Casimir, QC G0A 3L0
Tél: 418-339-2861; *Téléc:* 418-339-2875
www.csssdeportneuf.qc.ca
Nombre de lits: 64 lits

***Saint-Célestin:* Centre d'hébergement Saint-Célestin**
Affiliée à: CIUSSS de la Mauricie-et-du-Centre-du-Québec
CP 90, 475, rue Houde, Saint-Célestin, QC J0C 1G0
Tél: 819-229-3617; *Téléc:* 819-229-1165
www.csssbny.qc.ca
Nombre de lits: 52 lits
Danielle Gamelin, Directrice générale, CSSSBNY

***Saint-Constant:* Centre d'hébergement Champlain Jean-Louis Lapierre**
Groupe Champlain Soins de Longue Durée
Affiliée à: CISSS de la Montérégie-Ouest
199, rue St-Pierre, Saint-Constant, QC J5A 2N8
Tél: 450-632-4451; *Téléc:* 450-632-2004
www.santemonteregie.qc.ca/jardins-roussillon
Nombre de lits: 76 lits
Marie-Claude Ouellet, Directrice générale, Groupe Champlain Soins de Longue Durée

***Saint-Cyprien:* Centre d'hébergement de Saint-Cyprien**
Affiliée à: CIUSSS du Bas-St-Laurent
CP 325, 101-D, rue Collin, Saint-Cyprien, QC G0L 2P0
Tél: 418-963-7914; *Téléc:* 418-963-2274
www.csssrivierreduloup.qc.ca
Nombre de lits: 20 lits

***Saint-Eustache:* Centre d'hébergement de Saint-Eustache**
Affiliée à: CISSS des Laurentides
CP 850, 55, rue Chenier, Saint-Eustache, QC J7R 4Y8
Tél: 450-472-0013; *Téléc:* 450-472-3104
Nombre de lits: 194 lits

***Saint-Eustache:* Société en commandite centre d'accueil l'Ermitage**
112, 25e av, Saint-Eustache, QC J7P 2V2
Tél: 450-473-5961; *Téléc:* 450-491-1847

***Saint-Félicien:* Centre d'hébergement de Saint-Félicien**
Affiliée à: Centre de santé et de services sociaux Domaine-du-Roy
Édifice Foyer de la Paix, 1229, boul Sacré-Coeur, Saint-Félicien, QC G8K 1A5
Tél: 418-679-1585; *Téléc:* 418-679-2376
www.csssdomaineduroy.com
Nombre de lits: 46 lits
Note: Hébergement permanent et temporaire; centre de jour.
Jacques Dubois, Directeur général, CSSS Domaine-du-Roy

***Saint-Ferdinand:* Pavillon Morisset-Huppé Inc.**
Ancien nom: Ressource Intermédiare
CP 2060, 290, rte 165, Saint-Ferdinand, QC G0N 1N0
Tél: 418-428-3568
Fondée en: 1980
Note: Hébergement pour adultes en déficience intellectuels et handicapés physiques.

***Saint-Gabriel-de-Brandon:* Centre d'hébergement Desy**
Affiliée à: CISSS de Lanaudière
CP 840, 90, rue Maskinonge, Saint-Gabriel-de-Brandon, QC J0K 2N0
Tél: 450-835-4712; *Téléc:* 450-835-7606
www.csssnl.qc.ca
Nombre de lits: 54 lits
Martin Beaumont, Directeur Général

***Saint-Georges:* Centre hospitalier de l'Assomption**
16750, boul Lacroix, Saint-Georges, QC G5Y 2G4
Tél: 416-228-2041

***Saint-Georges-de-Beauce:* CHSLD L'Assomption**
Affiliée à: Groupe Champlain Soins de Longue Durée
16750, boul Lacroix, Saint-Georges-de-Beauce, QC G5Y 2G4
Tél: 418-228-2041; *Téléc:* 418-228-9366
www.groupechamplain.qc.ca
Nombre de lits: 96 lits
Note: Agence/région administrative: Agence de la santé et des services sociaux de Lanaudière.

***Saint-Hubert:* Centre d'hébergement Henriette Céré**
Affiliée à: CISSS de la Montérégie-Centre
6435, ch de Chambly, Saint-Hubert, QC J3Y 3R6
Tél: 450-672-3320

***Saint-Hubert:* Pavillon St-Hubert**
3823, rue Grand Boulevard, Saint-Hubert, QC J4T 2M3
Tél: 450-445-3598; *Téléc:* 450-462-3767

***Saint-Hyacinthe:* Centre d'hébergement Andrée-Perrault**
Affiliée à: CISSS de la Montérégie-Est
1955, av Pratte, Saint-Hyacinthe, QC J2S 7W5
Tél: 514-771-4536; *Téléc:* 450-771-5499
info@lesommetavotreportee.qc.ca
www.santemonteregie.qc.ca/richelieu-yamaska
Nombre de lits: 70 lits
Lise Pouliot, Directrice générale, CSSS Richelieu-Yamaska

***Saint-Hyacinthe:* CHSLD Résidence Bourg-Joli inc.**
2915, boul Laframboise, Saint-Hyacinthe, QC J2S 4Z3
Tél: 450-773-4197; *Téléc:* 450-773-6545
wpp01.msss.gouv.qc.ca
Nombre de lits: 24 lits

***Saint-Jean-sur-Richelieu:* Centre d'hébergement Georges-Phaneuf**
Affiliée à: CISSS de la Montérégie-Centre
230, rue Jacques-Cartier Nord, Saint-Jean-sur-Richelieu, QC J3B 6T4
Tél: 450-346-1133; *Téléc:* 450-346-2199
www.santemonteregie.qc.ca/haut-richelieu-rouville
Nombre de lits: 124 lits

***Saint-Jean-sur-Richelieu:* Centre d'hébergement Gertrude-Lafrance**
Affiliée à: CISSS de la Montérégie-Centre
150, boul. Saint-Luc, Saint-Jean-sur-Richelieu, QC J3A 1G2
Tél: 450-349-5555; *Téléc:* 450-348-7693
www.santemonteregie.qc.ca/haut-richelieu-rouville
Nombre de lits: 174 lits

***Saint-Jérome:* Centre d'hébergement L'Auberge**
Affiliée à: CISSS des Laurentides
66, rue Danis, Saint-Jérome, QC J7Y 2R3
Tél: 450-432-2777
Nombre de lits: 92 lits

***Saint-Jérome:* CHSLD de la Rivière du Nord**
531, rue Laviolette, Saint-Jérome, QC J7Y 2T8
Tél: 450-436-3061; *Téléc:* 450-436-8328
Nombre de lits: 305 lits
Note: Centres d'hébergement: Youville, l'Auberge, et Lucien G. Rolland.

***Saint-Lambert:* CHSLD de la MRC de Champlain**
831, av Notre-Dame, Saint-Lambert, QC J4R 1S1
Tél: 450-672-3320; *Téléc:* 450-672-3370
andree.ouellette@rrsss16.gouv.qc.ca
Nombre de lits: 313 lits
Gisèle Lacoste, Directrice générale
Real Guilbert, Directeur, Services techniques

***Saint-Laurent:* Les Cèdres - Centre d'accueil pour personnes âgées**
#200, 1275, boul de la C"te-Vertu, Saint-Laurent, QC H4L 4V2
Tél: 514-389-1023; *Téléc:* 514-389-0581
info@cedarshome.ca
www.centrelescedres.ca
Nombre de lits: 25 lits
Rose Khoury, Directrice générale

***Saint-Laurent:* Centre d'hébergement de Saint-Laurent**
Affiliée à: CIUSSS du Nord-de-l'Ile-de-Montréal
1055, av Ste-Croix, Saint-Laurent, QC H4L 3Z2
Tél: 514-744-4981; *Téléc:* 514-744-0895
Nombre de lits: 154 lits

***Saint-Liguori:* Centre d'hébergement Saint-Liguori**
Affiliée à: CISSS de Lanaudière
771, rue Principale, Saint-Liguori, QC J0K 2X0
Tél: 450-753-7062; *Téléc:* 450-753-3208
Nombre de lits: 48 lits
Paul-Yvon de Billy, Directeur général

***Saint-Louis-du-Ha!-Ha!:* Centre d'hébergement St-Louis**
Affiliée à: CISSS du Bas-St-Laurent
25, rue Saint-Philippe, Saint-Louis-du-Ha!-Ha!, QC G0L 3S0
Tél: 418-854-2631; *Téléc:* 418-854-0430
www.cssstemiscouata.com
Nombre de lits: 43 lits

***Saint-Michel-de-Bellechas:* CHSLD Vigi Notre-Dame de Lourdes**
CP 10, 80, rue Principale, Saint-Michel-de-Bellechas, QC G0R 3S0
Tél: 418-884-2811; *Téléc:* 418-884-3714
www.vigisante.com
Nombre de lits: 40 lits
Note: Agence/région administrative: Agence de la santé et des services sociaux de Chaudière-Appalaches.

***Saint-Michel-des-Saints:* Centre d'hébergement Brassard**
Affiliée à: CISSS de Lanaudière
CP 309, 390, rue Brassard, Saint-Michel-des-Saints, QC J0K 3B0
Tél: 514-833-6331; *Téléc:* 514-833-6093
Nombre de lits: 35 lits
Jean-Jacques Lamarche, Directeur général par intérim

***Saint-Michel-du-Squatec:* CHSLD de Squatec**
Affiliée à: CIUSSS du Bas-St-Laurent
Ancien nom: Domaine du Sommet
10, rue Saint-André, Saint-Michel-du-Squatec, QC G0L 4H0
Tél: 418-855-2442; *Téléc:* 418-855-2357
www.cssstemiscouata.com
Nombre de lits: 24 lits

***Saint-Pacôme:* Centre d'hébergement D'Anjou**
Affiliée à: CISSS du Bas-St-Laurent
127, rue Galarneau, Saint-Pacôme, QC G0L 3X0
Tél: 418-856-7000
www.agencesssbsl.gouv.qc.ca
Nombre de lits: 53 lits d'hébergement permanents
Mireille Drapeau, Coordonnatrice

***Saint-Pierre-les-Becquets:* Centre d'hébergement Romain-Becquet**
Affiliée à: CIUSSS de la Mauricie-et-du-Centre-du-Québec
255, rte Marie-Victorin, Saint-Pierre-les-Becquets, QC G0X 2Z0
Tél: 819-263-2245; *Téléc:* 819-263-2636
Nombre de lits: 35 lits
Note: Hébergement permanent et temporaire

***Saint-Raymond:* Centre hébergement Saint-Raymond**
Affiliée à: CISS de la Capitale-Nationale
324, rue Saint-Joseph, Saint-Raymond, QC G3L 1J7
Tél: 418-337-4611; *Téléc:* 418-337-4662
www.csssdeportneuf.qc.ca

***Saint-Rémi:* Centre d'hébergement de Saint-Rémi**
Affiliée à: CISSS de la Montérégie-Ouest
CP 820, 110, rue du Collège, Saint-Rémi, QC J0L 2L0
Tél: 450-454-4694; *Téléc:* 450-454-3614
Nombre de lits: 58 lits

***Saint-Romuald:* CHSLD Chanoine-Audet inc.**
Affiliée à: Groupe Champlain inc.
2155, ch du Sault, Saint-Romuald, QC G6W 2K7
Tél: 418-834-5322; *Téléc:* 418-834-5754
www.groupechamplain.qc.ca
Nombre de lits: 96 lits
Note: Agence/région administrative: Agence de la santé et des services sociaux de Chaudière-Appalaches.

***Saint-Timothée:* La Maison des Aîne(e)s**
1, rue des Aînes, Saint-Timothée, QC J6S 6M8
Tél: 450-377-3925; *Téléc:* 450-377-3490
Nombre de lits: 65 lits

***Saint-Tite:* Centre d'hébergement et CLSC Mgr Paquin**
Affiliée à: CIUSSS de la Mauricie-et-du-Centre-du-Québec
CP 400, 580, rue du Couvent, Saint-Tite, QC G0X 3H0
Tél: 418-365-5107; *Téléc:* 418-365-7914
www.csssvalleebatiscan.qc.ca
Nombre de lits: 55 lits

***Sainte-Adèle:* Centre d'hébergement des Hauteurs**
707, boul. Ste-Adèle, Sainte-Adèle, QC J8B 2N1
Tél: 450-229-6601
Nombre de lits: 112 lits

***Sainte-Anne-de-la-Pérade:* Centre multiservice Foyer de la Pérade**
CP 217, 60, rue de la Fabrique, Sainte-Anne-de-la-Pérade, QC G0X 2J0
Tél: 418-325-2313; *Téléc:* 418-325-3233
Nombre de lits: 42 lits

***Sainte-Cécile:* Pavillon Ste-Cécile**
4581, rue Principale, Sainte-Cécile, QC G0Y 1J0
Tél: 819-583-0400; *Téléc:* 819-583-0983
Nombre de lits: 15 lits

***Sainte-Foy:* Résidence Paul Triquet**
Affiliée à: CIUSSS de la Capitale-Nationale
Également connu sous le nom de: La Maison Paul-Triquet
789, rue de Belmont, Sainte-Foy, QC G1V 4V2
Tél: 418-657-6890; *Téléc:* 418-657-6894
maisonpaultriquet@mail.cuhq.qc.ca
www.chuq.qc.ca/maisonpaultriquet
Fondée en: 1987
Nombre de lits: 64 lits
Note: Centre d'hébergement de soins de longue durée pour anciens combattants

***Sainte-Sophie:* Villa du Nord**
2319, rang Sainte-Marie, Sainte-Sophie, QC J5J 1M8
Tél: 450-436-5627

***Sainte-Thérèse:* Centre d'hébergement Drapeau-Deschambault**
Affiliée à: CISSS des Laurentides
100, rue du Chanoine Lionel-Groulx, Sainte-Thérèse, QC J7E 5E1
Tél: 450-437-4267; *Téléc:* 450-437-0788
www.cssstheresedeblainville.qc.ca
Nombre de lits: 223 lits

***Sainte-Thérèse:* CHSLD Boise Ste-Thérèse Inc.**
179, Place Fabien-Drapeau, Sainte-Thérèse, QC J7E 5W6
Tél: 450-430-6767; *Téléc:* 450-430-6965
info@le-boise.com
www.le-boise.com
Nombre de lits: 41 CHSLD privé; 60 autonomes

***Saint-Éphrem-de-Beauce:* Résidence St-Éphrem inc.**
CP 310, 1, rue Plante, Saint-Éphrem-de-Beauce, QC G0M 1R0
Tél: 418-484-2121; *Téléc:* 418-484-2144
info@residencestephrem.com
www.residencestephrem.com
Nombre de lits: 40 lits
Lynda Roy, Directrice Générale

***Salaberry-de-Valleyfield:* Les Centres du Haut St-Laurent (CHSLD) Valleyfield**
80, rue de Marche, Salaberry-de-Valleyfield, QC J6T 1P5
Tél: 450-373-4818; *Téléc:* 450-373-0325
chsl@rocler.qc.ca
Nombre de lits: 177 lits
Claude Chayer, Directeur général

***Shawinigan:* CHSLD Vigi Les Chutes**
Affiliée à: Vigi Santé Ltée
5000, av Albert-Tessier, Shawinigan, QC G9N 8P9
Tél: 819-539-5408; *Téléc:* 819-539-5400
www.vigisante.com
Nombre de lits: 64 lits
Note: Agence/région administrative: Agence de la santé et des services sociaux de la Mauricie.

***Shawville:* Pavillon Centre d'accueil Pontiac**
Affiliée à: CISSS de l'Outaouais
CP 2001, 290, rue Marion, Shawville, QC J0X 2Y0
Tél: 819-647-5755; *Téléc:* 819-647-2453
Nombre de lits: 50 lits

***Sherbrooke:* Centre d'hébergement St-Joseph**
Affiliée à: CIUSSS de l'Estrie
611, boul Queen-Victoria, Sherbrooke, QC J1H 3R6
Tél: 819-780-2222
www.csss-iugs.ca
Nombre de lits: 144 lits
Carol Fillion, Directeur général, CSSS-Institut universitaire de gériatrie de Sherbro

***Sherbrooke:* CHSLD Vigi Shermont inc.**
Affiliée à: Vigi Santé Ltee
3220, 12e av Nord, Sherbrooke, QC J1H 5H3
Tél: 819-820-8900; *Téléc:* 819-820-8902
www.vigisante.com
Nombre de lits: 52 lits
Note: Agence/région administrative: Agence de la santé et des services sociaux de l'Estrie.

***Sherbrooke:* Les Dominicaines des saints anges gardiens**
Ancien nom: Mont St-Dominique
361, rue Moore, Sherbrooke, QC J1H 1C1
Tél: 819-346-5512

***Sillery:* Pavillon Saint-Dominique**
1045, boul René-Lévesque ouest, Sillery, QC G1S 1V3
Tél: 418-681-3561; *Téléc:* 418-687-9196
info@domaine-saint-dominique.com
www.domaine-saint-dominique.com
Nombre de lits: 152 lits

***Sillery:* Saint Brigid's Home Inc.**
Affiliée à: CIUSSS de la Capitale-Nationale
1645, ch Saint-Louis, Sillery, QC G1S 4M3
Tél: 418-681-4687; *Téléc:* 418-527-6862
www.jhsb.ca/fr/chsld-saint-brigids
Fondée en: 1856
Nombre de lits: 142 lits
Louis Hanrahan, Directeur général

***Sorel-Tracy:* Centre d'hébergement de Tracy**
Affiliée à: CISSS de la Montérégie-Est
4025, rue Frontenac, Sorel-Tracy, QC J3R 4G8
Tél: 450-742-9427; *Téléc:* 450-742-9668
Nombre de lits: 64 lits

***Sorel-Tracy:* Centre d'hébergement J.-Arsène-Parenteau**
Affiliée à: CISSS de la Montérégie-Est
Également connu sous le nom de: Foyer Richelieu
40, rue de Ramezay, Sorel-Tracy, QC J3P 3Y7
Tél: 514-742-5936; *Téléc:* 514-742-1613
Nombre de lits: 60 lits
Jacques Blais, Directeur général

***Sorel-Tracy:* CHSLD du Bas-Richelieu**
151, rue George, Sorel-Tracy, QC J3P 1C8
Tél: 450-746-5555; *Téléc:* 450-746-4897
www.soreltracyregion.net
Nombre de lits: 261 lits
René Legault, Directeur général (intérim)

***St-Charles-de-Bellechasse:* Résidence Charles Couillard Inc.**
20, av St-Georges, St-Charles-de-Bellechasse, QC G0R 2T0
Tél: 418-887-6455; *Téléc:* 418-887-1316
rcouillard1@hotmail.com
www.saint-charles.ca
Nombre de lits: 35 lits

***St-Pierre-de-l'Ile-d'Orlé:* Centre d'hébergement Alphonse-Bonenfant**
Affiliée à: CIUSSS de la Capitale-Nationale
1199, ch Royal, St-Pierre-de-l'Ile-d'Orlé, QC G0A 4E0
Tél: 418-828-1127
www.csssqn.qc.ca
Nombre de lits: 50 lits

***Sutton:* Foyer Sutton**
Affiliée à: CISSS de la Montérégie-Ouest
50, rue Western, Sutton, QC J0E 2K0
Tél: 514-538-3332; *Téléc:* 514-538-0514
Nombre de lits: 71 lits
Spécialités: Centre d'hébergement

***Terrebonne:* CHSLD de La Côte Boisée inc.**
4300, rue d'Angora, Terrebonne, QC J6X 4P1
Tél: 450-471-5877; *Téléc:* 450-471-7511
www.chslddelacoteboisee.org
Nombre de lits: 140 lits
Gerald Asselin, Directeur général

***Thetford Mines:* Résidence La Rosée d'Or**
736, boul Ouellet, Thetford Mines, QC G6G 4X5
Tél: 418-338-3774
Nombre de lits: 9 lits

***Trois-Rivières:* Centre d'hébergement Cooke**
Affiliée à: CIUSSS de la Mauricie-et-du-Centre-du-Québec
3450, rue Ste-Marguerite, Trois-Rivières, QC G8Z 1X3
Tél: 819-370-2100
www.cssstr.qc.ca
Nombre de lits: 190 lits

***Trois-Rivières:* Centre d'hébergement Louis-Denoncourt**
Affiliée à: CIUSSS de la Mauricie-et-du-Centre-du-Québec
435, rue Saint-Roch, Trois-Rivières, QC G9A 2L9
Tél: 819-376-2566; *Téléc:* 819-376-5620
www.cssstr.qc.ca
Nombre de lits: 75 lits
Note: Hébergement permanent
Lucie Letendre, Directrice générale, CSSS de Trois-Rivières

***Trois-Rivières:* Centre d'hébergement Roland-Leclerc**
Affiliée à: CIUSSS de la Mauricie-et-du-Centre-du-Québec
3500, rue Ste-Marguerite, Trois-Rivières, QC G8Z 1X3
Tél: 819-379-5650
www.cssstr.qc.ca
Note: Hébergement permanent et temporaire.
Lucie Letendre, Directrice générale, CSSS de Trois-Rivières

***Upton:* Domaine du Bel Age**
CP 89, 906, rue Lanoie, Upton, QC J0H 2E0
Tél: 514-549-4404
Nombre de lits: 9 lits
Jacqueline Gosslin, Directrice générale

***Varennes:* Centre d'hébergement de Lajemmerais**
Affiliée à: CISSS de la Montérégie-Est
60, rue D'Youville, Varennes, QC J3X 1R1
Tél: 450-463-2995; *Téléc:* 450-468-8329
www.santemonteregie.qc.ca/cssspierreboucher
Fondée en: 1971
Spécialités: Un centre de jour pour la clientèle en perte d'autonomie vivant à domicile; Une unité prothétique; éadaptation

***Vaudreuil-Dorion:* Le Manoir Harwood**
Affiliée à: CISSS de la Montérégie-Ouest
170, rue Boileau, Vaudreuil-Dorion, QC J7V 8A3
Tél: 450-424-6458; *Téléc:* 450-424-2074
manoir.harwood@rocler.com

Verdun: **Centre d'hébergement Réal Morel**
Affiliée à: CIUSSS du Centre-Est-de-l'Ile-de-Montréal
3500, rue Wellington, Verdun, QC H4G 1T3
Tél: 514-761-5874; *Téléc:* 514-761-7264
www.sov.qc.ca
Nombre de lits: 148 lits

Victoriaville: **Centre d'hébergement du Chêne**
Affiliée à: CIUSSS de la Mauricie-et-du-Centre-du-Québec
61, rue de l'Ermitage, Victoriaville, QC G6P 6X4
Tél: 819-758-7511; *Téléc:* 819-758-7967
www.csssae.qc.ca
Fondée en: 1971
Nombre de lits: 122 lits
Note: Les autres centres d'hébergement: Quatre-Vents, Saint-Eusèbe, Sacré-Coeur, Étoiles-d'Or, et Roseau.
Claude Charland, Directeur Général, CSSS d'Arthabaska-et-de-L'Érable

Victoriaville: **Centre d'hébergement du Roseau**
Affiliée à: CIUSSS de la Mauricie-et-du-Centre-du-Québec
Ancien nom: La Résidence le Roseau
45, rue de l'Ermitage, Victoriaville, QC G6P 6X4
Tél: 819-758-7511; *Téléc:* 819-758-7967
www.csssae.qc.ca
Fondée en: 1952
Nombre de lits: 88 lits d'hébergement permanent; 12 lits à l'URFI; 5 lits en soins posthospitaliers

Waterloo: **Santé Courville Waterloo**
CP 580, 5305, av Courville, Waterloo, QC J0E 2N0
Tél: 450-539-1821; *Téléc:* 450-539-1937
santecourville.com
Nombre de lits: 52 lits
Kenneth Courville, Président
kenneth.courville@santecourville.com
Christine Durocher, Directrice générale
christine.durocher@santecourville.co

Weedon: **Centre d'hébergement de Weedon**
Affiliée à: CIUSSS de l'Estrie
Également connu sous le nom de: CHSLD de Weedon
245, rue Saint-Janvier, Weedon, QC J0B 3J0
Tél: 819-877-2500; *Téléc:* 819-877-3089
www.cssshsf.com

Westmount: **Chateau Westmount inc.**
4860, boul de Maisonneuve ouest, Westmount, QC H3Z 3G2
Tél: 514-369-3000; *Téléc:* 514-369-0014
www.chateauwestmount.ca
Nombre de lits: 112 lits
Nancy Fournier, Contact, Ressources humaines
nancy.fournier@chateauwestmount.ca
Zara Pilian, Contact
zara.pilian@chateauwestmount.ca

Centres d'accueil et d'hébergement

Gatineau: **Manoir Ste-Marie**
156, boul Lorrain, Gatineau, QC J8P 2G2
Tél: 819-663-5736; *Téléc:* 819-643-1358
info@monoirstemaire.com
manoirstemarie.com
Nombre de lits: 23 lits

Grandes-Bergeronnes: **Pavillon Bergeronnes**
Affiliée à: CISSS de la Côte-Nord
CP 68, 450, rue de la Mer, Grandes-Bergeronnes, QC G0T 1G0
Tél: 418-232-6224; *Téléc:* 418-232-6771
www.cssshcn.gouv.qc.ca
Nombre de lits: 32 lits
Daniel Côté, Directeur général

Ham-Nord: **Foyer Saints-Anges de Ham-Nord inc.**
CP 269, 493, rue Principale, Ham-Nord, QC G0P 1A0
Tél: 819-344-2940; *Téléc:* 819-344-2584
chsldstsanges.ca
Nombre de lits: 38 lits
Alain Lavertu, Directeur général
alain_lavertu@ssss.gouv.qc.ca

La Doré: **Ressource intermédiaire de La Doré**
Également connu sous le nom de: Résidence La Doré
CP 190, 4921, rue des Peupliers, La Doré, QC G0W 2J0
Tél: 418-256-3851; *Téléc:* 418-256-3608
santesaglac.com
Nombre de lits: 21 lits

Montréal: **Centre d'hebergement Judith Jasmin**
Affiliée à: CIUSSS de l'Est-de-l'Ile-de-Montréal
8850, rue Bisaillon, Montréal, QC H1K 4N2
Tél: 514-354-5990; *Téléc:* 514-642-6381
www.cssspointe.ca
Nombre de lits: 75 lits

Montréal: **Centre hospitalier gériatrique Maimonides/Donald Berman Maimonides Geriatric Centre**
Affiliée à: CIUSSS du Centre-Ouest-de-l'Ile-de-Montréal
5795, av Caldwell, Montréal, QC H4W 1W3
Tél: 514-483-2121; *Téléc:* 514-483-1561
www.donaldbermanmaimonides.net
Média social: twitter.com/MaimonidesGC; www.youtube.com/user/MaimonidesGeriatric
Nombre de lits: 387 lits
Barbara Gold, Directrice générale
barbra.gold@ssss.gouv.qc.ca

Montréal: **Résidence Pie IX**
4090, rue Martial, Montréal, QC H1H 1X4
Tél: 514-327-2333; *Téléc:* 514-327-3276
Nombre de lits: 42 lits
Note: Centre de réadaptation

Montréal-Nord: **Château Beaurivage**
Affiliée à: Résidences Azur
6880, boul Gouin Est, Montréal-Nord, QC H1G 6L8
Tél: 514-323-7222; *Téléc:* 514-328-8987
chateaubeaurivage@residencesazur.com
www.residencesazur.com/39-residence-chateau-beaurivage.html
Média social: www.facebook.com/79262182077770
Julie Dagenais, Directrice générale

Pierrefonds: **CHSLD Manoir Ile de l'Ouest**
17725, boul Pierrefonds, Pierrefonds, QC H9J 3L1
Tél: 514-620-9850; *Téléc:* 514-620-3196
admin@westislandmanor.com
www.westislandmanor.com
Nombre de lits: 63 lits
Heather Karakas, Directrice générale

Roberval: **Résidence des Érables**
992, boul Saint-Joseph, Roberval, QC G8H 2L9
Tél: 418-275-4376
Nombre de lits: 23 lits
Note: déficience intellectuelle

Saint-Benoît-Labre: **Pavillon Baillargeon inc.**
#357, 271 Rte 1, Saint-Benoît-Labre, QC G0M 1P0
Tél: 418-228-9141; *Téléc:* 418-226-3772
Nombre de lits: 35 places

Saint-Eustache: **Domaine des Trois Pignons**
112, 25e av, Saint-Eustache, QC J7P 2V2
Tél: 450-473-5961

Saint-Fabien: **Foyer St-Fabien**
CP 520, 142, 1re rue, Saint-Fabien, QC G0L 2Z0
Tél: 418-869-2709

Saint-Zacharie: **Résidence l'Eden**
668, 12e av, Saint-Zacharie, QC G0M 2C0
Tél: 418-593-5200; *Téléc:* 418-593-5200
Fondée en: 1964
Nombre de lits: 30 lits

Sainte-Geneviève: **Château sur le Lac**
16289, boul Gouin ouest, Sainte-Geneviève, QC H9H 1E2
Tél: 514-620-9794; *Téléc:* 514-696-3196
info@chateausurlelac.com
chateausurlelac.com
Nombre de lits: 50 lits

Verdun: **Manoir des Floralies Verdun**
1050, av Gordon, Verdun, QC H4G 2S2
Tél: 514-766-2858; *Téléc:* 514-766-8701
www.floraliesverdun.com
Nombre de lits: 103 lits

Maisons de retraite

Baie-d'Urfé: **Maxwell Residence**
678, rue Surrey, Baie-d'Urfé, QC H9X 3S1
Tel: 514-457-3111; *Fax:* 514-457-7909
linda@maxwellresidence.com
www.maxwellresidence.com
Note: Specialties: Fitness center & health programs
R.W. Maxwell, Administrator

Laval: **Les Loggias et Villa Val des Arbres**
Chartwell Seniors Housing REIT
3241 - 3245 boul St. Martin est, Laval, QC H7E 4T6
Tel: 450-661-0911; *Fax:* 450-661-9820
www.chartwell.com
Number of Beds: 163
Note: Centre privé non-conventionné; 163 unités, 48 appartements, 115 chambres.
Denis Lagueux, Président, Chartwell-Québec

Rimouski: **Manoir Les Générations**
280, av Belzile, Rimouski, QC G5L 8K7
Tél: 418-723-0611; *Téléc:* 418-723-0615
www.manoirlesgenerations.com
Nombre de lits: 85 lits

Hôpitaux psychiatriques et assistance communautaire

Fatima: **Centre de réadaptation en DI-TED**
Affiliée à: CISSS des Iles
695, ch des Caps, Fatima, QC G4T 2S9
Tél: 418-986-3590; *Téléc:* 418-986-5778
www.cssdesiles.qc.ca

Gatineau: **Hôpital Pierre-Janet**
Affiliée à: CISSS de l'Outaouais
20, rue Pharand, Gatineau, QC J9A 1K7
Tél: 819-771-7761; *Téléc:* 819-771-2908
www.chpj.ca
Fondée en: 1965
Nombre de lits: 87 lits

Malartic: **Hôpital psychiatrique de Malartic**
Affiliée à: CISSS de l'Abitibi-Témiscamingue
1141, rue Royale, Malartic, QC J0Y 1Z0
Tél: 819-825-5858; *Téléc:* 819 825-7739
Nombre de lits: 34 lits
Note: Services de santé mentale et psychiatrie; soins aigus; soins de longue durée.

Montréal: **Hôpital Louis-H. Lafontaine**
7401, rue Hochelaga, Montréal, QC H1N 3M5
Tél: 514-251-4000
www.hlhl.qc.ca
Nombre de lits: 606 lits
Francine Décary, Présidente, Conseil d'administration
Pierre Miron, Vice-président, Conseil d'administration
Denise Fortin, Secrétaire générale, Conseil d'administration

Montréal: **Hôpital Rivière-des-Prairies**
Affiliée à: CIUSSS du Nord-de-l'Ile-de-Montréal
7070, boul Perras, Montréal, QC H1E 1A4
Tél: 514-323-7260; *Téléc:* 514-323-8622
www.hrdp.qc.ca
Média social: www.facebook.com/hrdp.qc; twitter.com/hopitalrdp
Nombre de lits: 125 lits

Québec: **Centre de réadaptation en santé mentale**
Également connu sous le nom de: La Maisonnée
855, boul Louis XIV, Québec, QC G1H 1A6
Tél: 418-628-2572; *Téléc:* 418-628-5440
www.csssqn.qc.ca
Région desservi: Région de la Capitale-Nationale

Quebec: **L'Institut universitaire en santé mentale de Québec/The Mental Health University Institute of Quebec**
Ancien nom: Centre hospitalier Robert Giffard
2601, ch. de la Canardière, Quebec, QC G1J 2G3
Tél: 418-663-5000; *Téléc:* 418-663-9774
www.institutsmq.qc.ca
Fondée en: 1976
Nombre de lits: 513 lits
Note: Affilié à l'Université Laval.
Dr. Simon Racine, Directeur général
Sylvie Laverdière, Directrice générale adjointe
Dr. Pierre Laliberté, Directeur des services professionnels et hospitaliers
Sylvain Pouliot, Directeur des Programmes-clientèles
Carl Parent, Directeur des ressources humaines
Dr. Philip Baruch, Directeur de l'enseignement
Dr. Evens Villeneuve, Chef du Département régional de psychiatrie
Dr. Yves de Koninck, Directeur de la recherche
Gilles Grondin, Directeur des ressources informationnelles

Rimouski: **L'hôpital de jour santé mentale et psychiatrie**
Affiliée à: CISSS du Bas-St-Laurent
95, rue de l'Évêché Ouest, Rimouski, QC G5L 4H4
Tél: 418-725-0544
Population desservi: 21000

Jocelyne Morissette, Responsable

Saskatchewan

Government Departments in Charge

Regina: Saskatchewan Health
T.C. Douglas Building, 3475 Albert St., Regina, SK S4S 6X6
Tel: 306-787-0146; *Fax:* 306-787-8310
Toll-Free: 800-667-7766
info@health.gov.sk.ca
www.saskatchewan.ca/health
Note: Establishes policy & standards, provides funding, supports regional health authorities, & ensures the provision of essential health services. Branches: acute & emergency services, communications, community care branch, Deputy Minister's Office, drug plan & extended benefits, financial services, Health Information Solutions Centre, health registration & vital statistics, human resources, medical services, policy & planning branch, population health, primary health services, regional accountability, regional policy, Saskatchewan Disease Control Laboratory, & workforce planning.
Hon. Dustin Duncan, Minister

Regional Health Authorities

Black Lake: Athabasca Health Authority (AHA)
PO Box 124, Black Lake, SK S0J 0H0
Tel: 306-439-2200; *Fax:* 306-439-2212
www.athabascahealth.ca
Info Line: 811
Population Served: 4500; *Number of Employees:* 82
Note: Provides health care services to the First Nations communities of Black Lake, Fond du Lac, Stony Rapids, Uranium City, Camsell Portage & Hatchet Lake.
Jennifer Conley, Chief Executive Officer

Buffalo Narrows: Keewatin Yatthé Regional Health Authority (KYRHA)
Metis Society Bldg., PO Box 40, Buffalo Narrows, SK S0M 0J0
Tel: 306-235-2220; *Fax:* 306-235-4604
Toll-Free: 866-274-8506
www.kyrha.ca
Info Line: 811
Area Served: Northwest Saskatchewan; 1/4 of the province;
Number of Employees: 350
Tina Rasmussen, Board Chair
Jean-Marc Desmeules, Chief Executive Officer
Edward Harding, Executive Director, Finance & Infrastructure
Rowena Materne, Executive Director, Corporate Services
Michael Quennell, Executive Director, Community Health Development

La Ronge: Mamawetan Churchill River Health Region
PO Box 6000, La Ronge, SK S0J 1L0
Tel: 306-425-2422; *Fax:* 306-425-5513
www.mcrrha.sk.ca
Info Line: 811
Social Media: www.facebook.com/MCRHealth; twitter.com/MCR_Health
Year Founded: 2002
Area Served: Northeastern Saskatchewan; 25% of the province;
Population Served: 24000; *Number of Employees:* 300
Note: Operates facilities in the following communities: Creighton, La Ronge, Pinehouse, Sandy Bay & Weyakwin
Ron Woytowich, Board Chair
Andrew McLetchie, Chief Executive Officer

Moose Jaw: Five Hills Health Region
55 Diefenbaker Dr., Moose Jaw, SK S6J 0C2
Tel: 306-694-0296; *Fax:* 306-694-0282
Toll-Free: 888-425-1111
inquiries@fhhr.ca
www.fhhr.ca
Info Line: 811
Area Served: South-central Saskatchewan; *Population Served:* 54000; *Number of Employees:* 1200
Note: Five Hills Health Region is home to 14 health facilities, including acute care, long term care & wellness centres.
Betty Collicott, Board Chair
Cheryl Craig, President & CEO
Dr. Fred Wigmore, Senior Medical Officer
Dr. Mark Vooght, Medical Health Officer
Georgia Hutchinson, Interim Vice-President, Continuing Care
Wayne Blazieko, Chief Financial Officer & Vice-President, Finance
Laurie Albinet, Vice-President, Clinical Services
Jim Allen, Vice-President, Environmental Services
Stuart Cunningham, Vice-President, Human Resources
Terry Hutchinson, Vice-President, Community Health Services
John Liguori, Vice-President, New Hospital Project
Kyle Matthies, Vice-President, Corporate Strategy & Communications

North Battleford: Prairie North Health Region (PNHR)
Battlefords Union Hospital, 1092 - 107 St., North Battleford, SK S9A 1Z1
Tel: 306-446-6606
www.pnrha.ca
Info Line: 811
Area Served: Northwest part of central Saskatchewan
Bonnie O'Grady, Chair
David Fan, Chief Executive Officer
Derek Miller, Vice-President, Finance & Operations
Irene Denis, Vice-President, People, Strategy & Performance
Gloria King, Vice-President, Integrated Health Services
Vikki Smart, Vice-President, Primary Health Services
Dr. Kevin Govender, Co-Senior Medical Officer
Dr. Wilhelm Retief, Co-Senior Medical Officer

Prince Albert: Prince Albert Parkland Health Region (PAPHR)
1521 - 6th Ave. West, Prince Albert, SK S6V 5K1
Tel: 306-765-6400; *Fax:* 306-763-6401
www.princealbertparklandhealth.com
Info Line: 811
Social Media: www.facebook.com/paphr
Area Served: North central Saskatchewan; *Population Served:* 80000
Brenda Abrametz, Board Chair
Cecile Hunt, President & CEO
Brett Enns, Vice-President, Primary Health Services
Don McKay, Vice-President, Human Resources
Cheryl Elliott, Vice-President, Finance & Corporate Support Services
Carol Gregoryk, Vice-President, Integrated Health Services
Pat Stuart, Vice-President, Clinical Support Services & Quality Performance
Dr. Brenda Hookenson, Co-Senior Medical Officer
Dr. Cecil Hammond, Co-Senior Medical Officer

Regina: Regina Qu'Appelle Health Region (RQHR)
2180 - 23 Ave., Regina, SK S4S 0A5
Tel: 306-766-5100; *Fax:* 306-766-5414
www.rqhealth.ca
Info Line: 811
Social Media: www.facebook.com/ReginaQuAppelleHealthRegion; twitter.com/rqhealth; www.youtube.com/user/rqhr; www.linkedin.com/company/regina-qu'appelle-health-region
Area Served: 26,663 sq km; *Population Served:* 260000;
Number of Employees: 9700
Dick Carter, Board Chair
Keith Dewar, President & CEO
keith.dewar@rqhealth.ca
Tania Diener, Medical Health Officer
tania.diener@rqhealth.ca

Rosetown: Heartland Regional Health Authority Also Known As: Heartland Health Region
PO Box 2110, 301 Centennial Dr., Rosetown, SK S0L 2V0
Tel: 306-882-4111; *Fax:* 306-882-1389
Toll-Free: 800-631-7686
heartland@hrha.sk.ca
www.hrha.sk.ca
Info Line: 811
Number of Beds: 481 long term care beds; 82 acute care; 58 program beds
Area Served: West-central Saskatchewan; 41,770 sq km;
Population Served: 44256
Note: Facilities in 16 communities, including a district hospital in Kindersley. Services include primary & acute health care, emergency services, telehealth, public health, dental health, counselling, addictions services, occupation therapy, speech & language therapy, nutrition.
Gregory Cummings, President & CEO
Stacey Bosch, Vice-President, Corporate Services
Jeannie Munro, Vice-President, Primary Health & Quality Services
Sheila Pajunen, Vice-President, Human Resources
Gayle Riendeau, Vice-President, Health Services
Dr. Lyle Williams, Senior Medical Officer
Wayne Pierrpont, Director, Environmental Services/Capital Projects

Saskatoon: Saskatoon Health Region (SRHA)
Saskatoon City Hospital, 701 Queen St., Level 1 Administration, Saskatoon, SK S7K 0M7
Tel: 306-655-7500
general.inquiries@saskatoonhealthregion.ca
www.saskatoonhealthregion.ca
Info Line: 811
Social Media: www.facebook.com/SaskatoonHealthRegion; twitter.com/SaskatoonHealth; www.youtube.com/user/SaskatoonHealthReg
Area Served: 34,120 sq km; *Population Served:* 342362
Note: The health region serves over 100 regional municipalities, cities, towns, villages, & First Nation communities in Saskatchewan. Facilities include hospitals, long term care facilities, primary health care sites, public health centres, mental health & addictions centres & community-based sites.
Mike Stensrud, Board Chair
Dan Florizone, President & CEO
Dr. Cory Neudorf, Chief Medical Health Officer
Jackie Mann, Vice-President, Integrated Health Services
Sandra Blevins, Vice-President
Diane Shendruk, Vice-President, Integrated Health Services
Petrina McGrath, Vice-President, People, Practice & Quality
Nilesh Kavia, Vice-President, Finance & Corporate Services
Dr. George Pylypchuk, Vice-President, Practitioner Staff Affairs

Swift Current: Cypress Regional Health Authority Also Known As: Cypress Health Region
429 - 4th Ave. NE, Swift Current, SK S9H 2J9
Tel: 306-778-5100; *Fax:* 306-773-9513
Toll-Free: 888-461-7443
info@cypressrha.ca
www.cypresshealth.ca
Info Line: 811
Social Media: www.facebook.com/cypresshealth; twitter.com/cypresshealth; www.youtube.com/user/cypresshealthsk
Year Founded: 2002
Area Served: Western Saskatchewan; 44,000 sq km; *Population Served:* 43000; *Number of Employees:* 1700
Lyle Quintin, Board Chair
Beth Vachon, Chief Executive Officer
Dr. Ivo Radevski, Senior Medical Officer
Beth Adashynski, Vice-President, Performance & Quality
Larry Allsen, CFO & Vice-President, Corporate Services
Bryce Martin, Vice-President, Primary Health Care
Brenda Schwan, Vice-President, Continuing Care
Kim Kruse, Director, Executive & Board Support

Tisdale: Kelsey Trail Regional Health Authority
PO Box 1780, Tisdale, SK S0E 1T0
Tel: 306-873-6600; *Fax:* 306-873-2372
TDemarsh@kthr.sk.ca
www.kelseytrailhealth.ca
Info Line: 811
Social Media: www.facebook.com/123342694465; twitter.com/kelseytrail; www.linkedin.com/company/kelsey-trail-health-region
Area Served: 44,369.62 sq km; *Population Served:* 42650;
Number of Employees: 1683
Rennie Harper, Board Chair
Shane Merriman, Chief Executive Officer

Weyburn: Sun Country Health Region (SCHR)
808 Souris Valley Rd., Weyburn, SK S4H 2Z9
Tel: 306-842-8339
info@schr.sk.ca
www.suncountry.sk.ca
Info Line: 811
Social Media: www.facebook.com/137459919728709
Year Founded: 2002
Area Served: Southeast portion of Saskatchewan; 33,239 sq km;
Population Served: 56529
Marilyn Charlton, Board Chair
Marga Cugnet, President & CEO
306-842-8718
Dean Biesenthal, Vice-President, Human Resources
306-842-8724
Janice Giroux, Vice-President, Community Health
306-842-8652
Murray Goeres, Interim Vice-President, Health Facilities
306-842-8706
John Knoch, Vice-President, Corporate & Finance
306-842-8714
Dr. Dimitri Louvish, Vice-President, Medical
306-842-8651

Yorkton: Sunrise Regional Health Authority
270 Bradbrooke Dr., Yorkton, SK S3N 2K6
Tel: 306-786-0100; *Fax:* 306-786-0122
Toll-Free: 800-505-9220
www.sunrisehealthregion.sk.ca
Info Line: 811
Social Media: twitter.com/SunriseRegion
Number of Employees: 2900
Note: Sunrise Health Region stretches from the Qu'Appelle Valley to the northern boreal forest, & from the parklands of the Manitoba border into the Saskatchewan prairie farmlands.
Don Rae, Interim Chair
Suann Laurent, President & CEO
Dr. Phillip Fourie, Senior Medical Officer & Vice-President, Medical Services
Christina Denysek, Vice-President, Strategy & Partnerships
Lorelei Stusek, Vice-President, Corporate Services
Sandy Tokaruk, Vice-President, Integrated Primary Health Services
Roberta Wiwcharuk, Vice-President, Integrated Health Services

Hospitals - General

Arcola: Arcola Health Centre
Affiliated with: Sun Country Health Region
PO Box 419, 607 Prairie Ave., Arcola, SK S0C 0G0
Tel: 306-455-2771
Note: Programs & services include: telehealth; palliative care; mental health services; acuate care services.
Marnelle Wyatt, Contact

Assiniboia: Assiniboia Union Hospital
Affiliated with: Five Hills Regional Health Authority
501 - 6 Ave., Assiniboia, SK S0H 0B0
Tel: 306-642-3351
Info Line: 306-642-9444
Number of Beds: 22 long term care; 12 acute care beds; 4 respite / palliative care beds
Note: Programs & services include: Emergency service; Acute care; Laboratory service; Respite care; Palliative care

Balcarres: Balcarres Integrated Care Centre
Affiliated with: Regina Qu'Appelle Health Region
PO Box 340, 100 South Elgin St., Balcarres, SK S0G 0C0
Tel: 306-334-6260; *Fax:* 306-334-2674
Year Founded: 1999
Number of Beds: 44 beds
Note: Programs & services include: emergency services; acute care; physiotherapy; diabetes education; mental health & drug & alcohol counselling; respite services; day care services; home care nursing; long term care

Big River: Big River Health Centre
Affiliated with: Prince Albert Parkland Regional Health Authority
PO Box 100, 220 - 1st Ave. North, Big River, SK S0J 0E0
Tel: 306-469-2220; *Fax:* 306-469-2193
Note: Programs & services include: emergency services; acute care; laboratory services; public health services; physiotherapy; occupational therapy; long term care; home care; respite care; palliative care

Biggar: Biggar Hospital
Affiliated with: Heartland Regional Health Authority
PO Box 130, 501 - 1 Ave. West, Biggar, SK S0K 0M0
Tel: 306-948-3323; *Fax:* 306-948-2011

Broadview: Broadview Hospital
Affiliated with: Regina Qu'Appelle Health Region
PO Box 100, 901 Nina St., Broadview, SK S0G 0K0
Tel: 306-696-2441; *Fax:* 306-696-2611
Note: Programs & services include: emergency services; diagnostic services; ambulatory care; native liaison work; respite care; palliative care

Canora: Canora Hospital
Affiliated with: Sunrise Regional Health Authority
PO Box 749, 1219 Main St., Canora, SK S0A 0L0
Tel: 306-563-5621; *Fax:* 306-563-5571
Year Founded: 1968
Number of Beds: 16 acute care beds
Note: Programs & services include: emergency services; laboratory services; radiology; acute care; occupational therapy; respite care; long term care

Central Butte: Central Butte Regency Hospital
Affiliated with: Five Hills Regional Health Authority
PO Box 40, Central Butte, SK S0H 0T0
Tel: 306-796-2190
Number of Beds: 7 respite/palliative/observation beds; 22 residents at special care home
Note: Programs & services include: Acute care; Special care home

Davidson: Davidson & District Health Centre
Affiliated with: Heartland Regional Health Authority
PO Box 758, 900 Government Rd., Davidson, SK S0G 1A0
Tel: 306-567-2801; *Fax:* 306-567-2073
Number of Employees: 70

Esterhazy: St. Anthony's Hospital
Affiliated with: Sunrise Regional Health Authority
PO Box 280, 216 Ancona St., Esterhazy, SK S0A 0X0
Tel: 306-745-3973; *Fax:* 306-745-3245
Year Founded: 1940
Number of Beds: 22 acute care beds
Note: Emergency & outpatient services; visiting primary care services & dietition; x-ray

Estevan: St. Joseph's Hospital
Affiliated with: Sun Country Health Region
PO Box 500, 1174 Nicholson Rd., Estevan, SK S4A 2V6
Tel: 306-637-2400
stjosephsestevan.ca
Note: Programs & services include: telehealth; spiritual care; child speech-language pathology; rehabilitation; parenting skills; palliative care; occupational therapy; dental education.
Greg Hoffort, Executive Director
Greg.Hoffort@schr.sk.ca

Fort Qu'Appelle: All Nations' Healing Hospital (ANHH)
Affiliated with: Regina Qu'Appelle Health Region
PO Box 300, 450 - 8th St., Fort Qu'Appelle, SK S0G 1S0
Tel: 306-332-5611; *Fax:* 306-332-5033
www.fortquappelle.com/anhh.html
Number of Beds: 14 acute care beds
Population Served: 2500
Note: Hospital Specialties: First Nations health services; acute care; emergency services; women's health; mental health; diabetes education; nutrition education.

Gravelbourg: St. Joseph's Hospital/Foyer d'Youville
Affiliated with: Five Hills Regional Health Authority
PO Box 810, 216 Bettez St., Gravelbourg, SK S0H 1X0
Tel: 306-648-3185
Number of Beds: 9 hospital beds, 49 long term care beds

Hafford: Hafford Special Care Centre
Affiliated with: Prince Albert Parkland Regional Health Authority
PO Box 130, 213 South Ave. East, Hafford, SK S0J 1A0
Tel: 306-549-2108; *Fax:* 306-549-2104
Doreen Madwid, Manager
dmadwid@paphr.sk.ca

Herbert: Herbert & District Integrated Health Facility
Affiliated with: Cypress Regional Health Authority
PO Box 520, 405 Herbert Ave., Herbert, SK S0H 2A0
Tel: 306-784-2466
Number of Beds: 40 long term care beds; 6 acute care beds; 1 respite care bed; 1 program bed
Note: Programs & services include: acute care; additions program; home care program; mental health services; palliative care; physiotherapy; respite care; speech language pathology.

Hudson Bay: Hudson Bay Health Care Facility
Affiliated with: Kelsey Trail Regional Health Authority
PO Box 940, 614 Prince St., Hudson Bay, SK S0E 0Y0
Tel: 306-865-5600; *Fax:* 306-865-2429
Number of Beds: 20 long term care; 2 Respite care
Note: Programs & services include: acute care; palliative care; radiology services; telehealth; day care services.

Humboldt: Humboldt District Health Complex (HDHC)
Affiliated with: Saskatoon Health Region
Former Name: St. Elizabeth's Hospital
PO Box 10, 515 - 14th. Ave., Humboldt, SK S0K 2A0
Tel: 306-682-2603
www.saskatoonhealthregion.ca
Year Founded: 2011
Note: Programs & services include: home care; mental health; addiction services

Ile-a-la-Crosse: St. Joseph's Hospital
Affiliated with: Keewatin Yatthé Regional Health Authority
PO Box 630, Ile-a-la-Crosse, SK S0M 1C0
Tel: 306-833-2016; *Fax:* 306-833-2556

Indian Head: Indian Head Union Hospital
Affiliated with: Regina Qu'Appelle Health Region
PO Box 340, 300 Hospital St., Indian Head, SK S0G 2K0
Tel: 306-695-4000; *Fax:* 306-695-4002

Kamsack: Kamsack Hospital/Kamsack Nursing Home
Affiliated with: Sunrise Regional Health Authority
PO Box 429, 341 Stewart St., Kamsack, SK S0A 1S0
Tel: 306-542-2635; *Fax:* 306-542-4360
Number of Beds: 20 acute care, 61 long-term care, 2 respite beds
Note: Services include: 24 emergency care; instensive care; laboratory services; cardiac services; outpatient services; physiotherapy; diagnostic imaging/x-ray
Chris Mayer, Hospital Administrator

Kelvington: Kelvington Hospital
Affiliated with: Kelsey Trail Regional Health Authority
PO Box 70, 512 - 1 Ave. South, Kelvington, SK S0A 1W0
Tel: 306-327-5500; *Fax:* 306-327-5115
www.kelseytrailhealth.ca
Note: Programs & services include: acute care; palliative care; radiology services; telehealth.
Denise Geck, Director, Health Services

Kindersley: Kindersley Integrated Health Care Facility
Affiliated with: Heartland Regional Health Authority
1003 - 1 St. West, Kindersley, SK S0L 1S2
Tel: 306-463-1000; *Fax:* 306-463-1117
Note: Long term care; acute care.

Kipling: Kipling Integrated Health Centre
Affiliated with: Sun Country Health Region
PO Box 420, 906 Industrial Dr., Kipling, SK S0G 2S0
Tel: 306-736-2552
Note: Programs & services include: respite care; rehabilitation services; palliative care.
Kelly Beattie, Contact

La Loche: La Loche Health Centre
Affiliated with: Keewatin Yatthé Regional Health Authority
Bag Service 1, La Loche, SK S0M 1G0
Tel: 306-822-3200; *Fax:* 306-822-2274
Toll-Free: 888-688-7087

Lanigan: Lanigan Hospital
Affiliated with: Saskatoon Health Region
PO Box 609, 36 Downing St. East, Lanigan, SK S0K 2M0
Tel: 306-365-1400; *Fax:* 306-365-3354
www.saskatoonhealthregion.ca
Year Founded: 1968
Number of Beds: 45 beds
Number of Employees: 88

Leader: Leader Hospital
Affiliated with: Cypress Regional Health Authority
PO Box 129, 423 Main St., Leader, SK S0N 1H0
Tel: 306-628-3845
Number of Beds: 10 acute

Lestock: St. Joseph's Integrated Care Centre
Affiliated with: Regina Qu'Appelle Health Region
PO Box 280, Lestock, SK S0A 2G0
Tel: 306-274-2215; *Fax:* 306-274-2045
Number of Beds: 10 beds

Lloydminster: Lloydminster Hospital
Affiliated with: Prairie North Health Region
3820 - 43 Ave., Lloydminster, SK S9V 1Y5
Tel: 306-820-6000; *Fax:* 306-825-6516
Note: Hospital Specialties: Cancer treatment & Care-Alberta Community Cancer Centres; Hemodialysis - Northern Alberta Renal Program; Surgical services & recovery; Obstetrics; Paediatrics; Special care unit.

Loon Lake: Loon Lake Hospital & Special Care Home
Affiliated with: Prairie North Health Region
PO Box 69, 510 - 2nd Ave., Loon Lake, SK S0M 1L0
Tel: 306-837-2114; *Fax:* 306-837-2268
Number of Beds: 12 long term; 4 short term; 1 respite; 1 palliative

Maidstone: Maidstone Health Complex
Affiliated with: Prairie North Health Region
PO Box 160, 214 - 5th Ave. East, Maidstone, SK S0M 1M0
Tel: 306-893-2622; *Fax:* 306-893-2922
Number of Beds: 11 acute beds; 24 long-term care beds; 2 respite beds
Note: Specialties: Community health services, including home care & counselling; Acute care; Long-term care wing; Respite care; Palliative care

Meadow Lake: **Meadow Lake Hospital**
Affiliated with: Prairie North Health Region
#2, 711 Centre St., Meadow Lake, SK S9X 1E6
Tel: 306-236-1500; *Fax:* 306-236-3244

Meadow Lake: **Northwest Health Facility**
Affiliated with: Prairie North Health Region
Also Known As: Meadow Lake Hospital
#2, 711 Centre St., Meadow Lake, SK S9X 1E6
Tel: 306-236-1500; *Fax:* 306-236-3244
Note: Specialty: Acute care; Diagnostic imaging

Melfort: **Melfort Hospital**
Affiliated with: Kelsey Trail Regional Health Authority
PO Box 1480, 510 Broadway Ave., Melfort, SK S0E 1A0
Tel: 306-752-8700; *Fax:* 306-752-8711
Note: Programs & services include: acute care; general surgery; radiology services; chemotherapy; mental health & addiction services; diabetes & heart health centre; palliative care
Judy Blair, Director, Health Services

Melville: **St. Peter's Hospital**
Affiliated with: Sunrise Regional Health Authority
PO Box 1810, 200 Heritage Dr., Melville, SK S0A 2P0
Tel: 306-728-5407; *Fax:* 306-728-4870
Year Founded: 1942
Number of Beds: 30 acute care beds
Note: Programs & services include: emergency services; outpatient services; physiotherapy; social work; Lifeline Response Centre; chemotherapy outreach program; pharmacy.

Moose Jaw: **Moose Jaw Union Hospital**
Affiliated with: Five Hills Regional Health Authority
455 Fairford St. East, Moose Jaw, SK S6H 1H3
Tel: 306-694-0200
www.fhhr.ca/MooseJawHospital.htm
Number of Beds: 31 medical unit; 20 surgery unit; 10 peadiatric; 12 mental health & addiction; 14 obstretrical; 5 intensive care

Moosomin: **Southeast Integrated Care Centre - Moosomin**
Affiliated with: Regina Qu'Appelle Health Region
Former Name: Moosomin Union Hospital
601 Wright Rd. East, Moosomin, SK S0G 3N0
Tel: 306-435-3303; *Fax:* 306-435-3211
Number of Beds: 27 in-patient; 58 long-term

Nipawin: **Nipawin Hospital**
Affiliated with: Kelsey Trail Regional Health Authority
PO Box 389, 800 - 6 St. East, Nipawin, SK S0E 1E0
Tel: 306-862-6100; *Fax:* 306-862-9310
www.kelseytrailhealth.ca
Note: Programs & services include: acute care; palliative care; radiology; chemotherapy; endoscopy; telehealth.

North Battleford: **Battlefords Union Hospital**
Affiliated with: Prairie North Health Region
1092 - 107 St., North Battleford, SK S9A 1Z1
Tel: 306-446-6600; *Fax:* 306-446-6561
Note: Hospital specialties: Emergency services; Acute care; Day patient clinic

Outlook: **Outlook & District Health Centre**
Affiliated with: Heartland Regional Health Authority
PO Box 369, 500 Semple St., Outlook, SK S0L 2N0
Tel: 306-867-8676; *Fax:* 306-867-9449
Year Founded: 2008
Note: Programs & services include: acute care; diagnostic services; therapies; community health; public health inspections; mental health services; home care; long-term care; respite care; adult day care; palliative care

Porcupine Plain: **Porcupine Carragana Hospital**
Affiliated with: Kelsey Trail Regional Health Authority
PO Box 70, Windsor Ave., Porcupine Plain, SK S0E 1H0
Tel: 306-278-6262; *Fax:* 306-278-3088
Number of Beds: 3 respite beds
Note: Programs & services include: acute care; palliative care; telehealth; radiology
Christine Pohl, Director, Health Services
Keith Butler, Supervisor, Physical Plant

Preeceville: **Preeceville & District Health Centre**
Affiliated with: Sunrise Regional Health Authority
Former Name: Preeceville Hospital; Preeceville & District Integrated Health Care Facility
PO Box 469, 712 - 7 St. NE, Preeceville, SK S0A 3B0
Tel: 306-547-2102; *Fax:* 306-547-2223
www.sunrisehealthregion.sk.ca
Number of Beds: 10 acute care, 38 long-term care beds, 2 respite beds
Note: Programs & services include: Doctors' medical clinic, acute & long-term care; consulting servicing; cardiac services; outpatient services; physiotherapy; diagnositic imaging/x-ray

Prince Albert: **Victoria Hospital**
Affiliated with: Prince Albert Parkland Regional Health Authority
1200 - 24 St. West, Prince Albert, SK S6V 5T4
Tel: 306-765-6000; *Fax:* 306-765-6401
Toll-Free: 800-922-1834
Note: Programs & services include: acute care; addiction services; dental services; diabetes education; early childhood program; long term care facility; mental health services; palliative care; telehealth.

Redvers: **Redvers Health Centre**
Affiliated with: Sun Country Health Region
PO Box 30, 18 Eichhorst St., Redvers, SK S0C 2H0
Tel: 306-452-3553
Note: Programs & services include: physical therapy; long-term care; dietitian services; child speech-language pathology.
Naomi Hjertaas, Contact

Regina: **Pasqua Hospital**
Affiliated with: Regina Qu'Appelle Health Region
4101 Dewdney Ave., Regina, SK S4T 1A5
Tel: 306-766-2222
www.rqhealth.ca/facilities/pasqua-hospital

Regina: **Regina General Hospital**
Affiliated with: Regina Qu'Appelle Health Region
Former Name: Victoria Hospital
1440 - 14 Ave., Regina, SK S4P 0W5
Tel: 306-766-4444
www.rqhealth.ca/facilities/regina-general-hospital
Year Founded: 1901
Note: Offers full-range acute care services; home to the Wasakaw Pisim Native Health Centre, Sleep Disorders Centre, and 50-bed mental health facility

Rosthern: **Rosthern Hospital**
Affiliated with: Saskatoon Health Region
2016 - 2 St., Rosthern, SK S0K 3R0
Tel: 306-232-4811
www.saskatoonhealthregion.ca
Year Founded: 1950
Number of Beds: 30 beds
Number of Employees: 60
Note: Acute care facility with six physicians on-staff.

Saskatoon: **Children's Hospital of Saskatchewan**
Affiliated with: Saskatoon Health Region
c/o Saskatoon Health Region - Royal Univ. Hospital, 103 Hospital Dr., 3rd Fl., Saskatoon, SK S7N 0W8
Tel: 306-655-2293
childrenshospitalsask@saskatoonhealthregion.ca
Social Media: www.facebook.com/childrenhospSK; twitter.com/childrenhospSK; www.pinterest.com/childrenshospsk
Note: Programs & services include: maternal services; children's sleep lab; children's Hemodialysis

Saskatoon: **Royal University Hospital**
Affiliated with: Saskatoon Health Region
103 Hospital Dr., Saskatoon, SK S7N 0W8
Tel: 306-655-1000
www.saskatoonhealthregion.ca
Year Founded: 1955
Note: Affiliated with the University of Saskatchewan.

Saskatoon: **St. Paul's Hospital**
Saskatchewan Catholic Health Corporation
Affiliated with: Saskatoon Health Region
1702 - 20 St., Saskatoon, SK S7M 0Z9
Tel: 306-655-5000; *Fax:* 306-655-5900
info@stpaulshospital.org
www.stpaulshospital.org
Jean Morrison, President & CEO

Saskatoon: **Saskatoon City Hospital**
Affiliated with: Saskatoon Health Region
701 Queen St., Saskatoon, SK S7K 0M7
Tel: 306-655-8000
www.saskatoonhealthregion.ca
Year Founded: 1909

Shaunavon: **Shaunavon Hospital & Care Centre**
Affiliated with: Cypress Regional Health Authority
PO Box 789, 660 - 4 St. East, Shaunavon, SK S0N 2M0
Tel: 306-297-2644; *Fax:* 306-297-1949
Number of Beds: 41 long term care beds; 10 acute/multidisciplinary beds; 1 respite beds; 2 program beds
Note: Programs & services include: acute care; addictions treatment; podiatry; long term care; mental health; physiotherapy; respite care; speech language pathology.

Shellbrook: **Shellbrook & District Hospital**
Affiliated with: Prince Albert Parkland Regional Health Authority
PO Box 70, 211 - 2nd Ave. West, Shellbrook, SK S0J 2E0
Tel: 306-747-2603; *Fax:* 306-747-3004

Spiritwood: **Spiritwood & District Health Complex**
Affiliated with: Prince Albert Parkland Regional Health Authority
PO Box 69, Spiritwood, SK S0J 2M0
Tel: 306-883-2133; *Fax:* 306-883-4440

Swift Current: **Cypress Regional Hospital**
Affiliated with: Cypress Regional Health Authority
Former Name: Swift Current Regional Hospital
2004 Saskatchewan Dr., Swift Current, SK S9H 5M8
Tel: 306-778-9400
www.cypressrha.ca
Year Founded: 1951
Note: Programs & services include: intensive care; long-term care; palliative care; inpatient and outpatient surgery; renal dialysis; pediatric care; CT scans; obstetrics/gynecology; midwifery and general medical care.

Tisdale: **Tisdale Hospital**
Affiliated with: Kelsey Trail Regional Health Authority
PO Box 1630, 2010 - 110th Ave. West, Tisdale, SK S0E 1T0
Tel: 306-873-2621; *Fax:* 306-873-5994
www.kelseytrailhealth.ca
Note: Specialties: Acute care; Diabetes & Heart Health Centre; Hemodialysis satellite unit; Mental health & addiction services; Home care; Palliative care
Anne Haley-Callaghan, Manager, Community Health

Tisdale: **Tisdale Hospital**
Affiliated with: Kelsey Trail Regional Health Authority
PO Box 1630, 2010 - 110th Ave. West, Tisdale, SK S0E 1T0
Tel: 306-873-6500; *Fax:* 306-873-5994
Note: Programs & services include: acute care; palliative care; radiology services; telehealth; sigmiodoscopy

Uranium City: **Uranium City Health Centre**
Affiliated with: Athabasca Health Authority
PO Box 360, Uranium City, SK S0J 2W0
Tel: 306-498-2412; *Fax:* 306-498-2577

Wadena: **Wadena Hospital**
Affiliated with: Saskatoon Health Region
PO Box 10, 533 - 5 St. NE, Wadena, SK S0A 4J0
Tel: 306-338-2515
www.saskatoonhealthregion.ca
Year Founded: 1967
Number of Beds: 52 beds
Population Served: 107
Note: Provides acute, respite, and long-term care

Wakaw: **Wakaw Health Centre**
Affiliated with: Saskatoon Regional Health Authority
Former Name: Wakaw Hospital
PO Box 309, 301 - 1 St. North, Wakaw, SK S0K 4P0
Tel: 306-233-4611
Year Founded: 1956
Note: Health centre; X-ray; Home care; Community services; Municipal medical clinic

Watrous: **Watrous Hospital**
Affiliated with: Saskatoon Health Region
PO Box 130, 702 - 4 St. East, Watrous, SK S0K 4T0
Tel: 306-946-1200
www.saskatoonhealthregion.ca

Wawota: **Wawota Memorial Health Centre**
Affiliated with: Sun Country Health Region
PO Box 60, 609 Choo Foo Cres., Wawota, SK S0G 5A0
Tel: 306-739-2306
Note: Programs & services include: diabetes program; mental health services; palliative care; telehealth
Holly Hodgson, Contact

Weyburn: **Weyburn General Hospital**
Affiliated with: Sun Country Health Region
201 - 1 Ave. NE, Weyburn, SK S4H 2Z9
Tel: 306-842-8400
Note: Programs & services include: acute care; addiction services; diabetes education program; mental health services; occupational therapy; palliative care; spiritual care.
Sylvia Danyluk, Contact

Wolseley: **Wolseley Memorial Hospital**
Affiliated with: Regina Qu'Appelle Health Region
PO Box 458, 801 Ouimet St., Wolseley, SK S0G 5H0
Tel: 306-698-4440; *Fax:* 306-698-4434

Wynyard: **Wynyard Integrated Facility**
Affiliated with: Saskatoon Health Region
PO Box 670, 300 - 10 St. East, Wynyard, SK S0A 4T0
Tel: 306-554-2586
www.saskatoonhealthregion.ca
Number of Beds: 58 beds

Yorkton: **Yorkton Regional Health Centre**
Affiliated with: Sunrise Regional Health Authority
270 Bradbrooke Dr., Yorkton, SK S3N 2K6
Tel: 306-782-2401; *Fax:* 306-786-6295
Number of Beds: 87 acute care beds

Federal Hospitals

Saskatoon: **Regional Psychiatric Centre (Prairies)**
PO Box 9243, 2520 Central Ave., Saskatoon, SK S7K 3X5
Tel: 306-975-5400; *Fax:* 306-975-6024
Year Founded: 1978
Number of Beds: 206 beds

Community Health Care Centres

Arborfield: **Arborfield & District Health Care Centre**
Affiliated with: Kelsey Trail Regional Health Authority
PO Box 160, 5 Ave., Arborfield, SK S0E 0A0
Tel: 306-769-4200; *Fax:* 306-769-8759
Number of Beds: 36 beds
Note: Programs & services include: clinic; laboratory; day care; health care.

Beauval: **Beauval Health Centre**
Affiliated with: Keewatin Yatthé Regional Health Authority
PO Box 68, Beauval, SK S0M 0G0
Tel: 306-288-4800; *Fax:* 306-288-2225
Toll-Free: 866-848-8022
Note: Addiction treatments; mental health; dentistry; ambulance.

Beechy: **Beechy Health Centre**
Affiliated with: Heartland Regional Health Authority
PO Box 68, 226 - 1st Ave. North, Beechy, SK S0L 0C0
Tel: 306-859-2118; *Fax:* 306-859-2206
Note: Programs & services include: primary health care; lab/radiology services; visiting community health services: public health, counselling, occupational health, nutrition.

Bengough: **Bengough Health Centre**
Affiliated with: Sun Country Health Region
PO Box 399, 400 - 2 St. West, Bengough, SK S0C 0K0
Tel: 306-268-2048
Note: Programs & services include: diabetes; home care; palliative care.

Biggar: **Biggar Home Care Office**
Affiliated with: Heartland Regional Health Authority
PO Box 130, Biggar, SK S0K 0M0
Tel: 306-948-3323; *Fax:* 306-948-2011

Biggar: **Eatonia Home Care Office**
Affiliated with: Heartland Regional Health Authority
PO Box 400, 205 - 2 Ave. West, Biggar, SK S0L 0Y0
Tel: 306-967-2985; *Fax:* 306-967-2373

Birch Hills: **Birch Hills Health Centre**
Affiliated with: Prince Albert Parkland Regional Health Authority
PO Box 578, 3 Wilson St., Birch Hills, SK S0J 0G0
Tel: 306-749-3331; *Fax:* 306-749-2440

Black Lake: **Athabasca Health Facility**
Affiliated with: Athabasca Health Authority
PO Box 124, 224 Chicken Indian Reserve, Black Lake, SK S0J 0H0
Tel: 306-439-2200; *Fax:* 306-439-2211
Year Founded: 2003
Note: Programs & services include: acute care, birthing services, long term care, emergency & ambulatory care, public health, mental health, addictions therapy, traditional healing, radiology & lab services.

Black Lake: **Black Lake Denesuline Health Centre/Nursing Station**
Affiliated with: Athabasca Health Authority
PO Box 135, Black Lake, SK S0J 0H0
Tel: 306-284-2020; *Fax:* 306-284-2090

Borden: **Borden Primary Health Centre**
Affiliated with: Saskatoon Health Region
Former Name: Borden Community Health Centre
PO Box 90, 308 Shepard St., Borden, SK S0K 0N0
Tel: 306-997-2110; *Fax:* 306-997-2114

Buffalo Narrows: **Buffalo Narrows Health Centre**
Affiliated with: Keewatin Yatthé Regional Health Authority
PO Box 40, Buffalo Narrows, SK S0M 0J0
Tel: 306-235-5800; *Fax:* 306-235-4500
Toll-Free: 866-848-8011
Note: Programs & services include: pharmacy; mental & public health; long term care; acute care; laboratory.

Cabri: **Prairie Health Care Centre**
Affiliated with: Cypress Regional Health Authority
PO Box 79, 517 - 1 St. North, Cabri, SK S0N 0J0
Tel: 306-587-2623
Number of Beds: 17 long term care beds; 3 multipurpose beds
Note: Programs & services include: outpatient procedures; lab/x-ray; physiotherapy; respite; speech language pathology

Canoe Narrows: **Canoe Narrows/Lake Health Centre & Nursing Station**
Affiliated with: Keewatin Yatthé Regional Health Authority
PO Box 229, Canoe Narrows, SK S0M 0K0
Tel: 306-829-2140; *Fax:* 306-829-4450

Carlyle: **Carlyle Community Health**
Affiliated with: Sun Country Health Region
PO Box 670, 206 Railway Ave. East, Carlyle, SK S0C 0R0
Tel: 306-453-6131; *Fax:* 306-453-6799

Carlyle: **Carlyle Medical Clinic**
Affiliated with: Sun Country Health Region
PO Box 1090, 214 Main St., Carlyle, SK S0C 0R0
Tel: 306-453-6795; *Fax:* 306-453-6796
Liette Hrabia, Contact

Carrot River: **Carrot River Health Centre**
Affiliated with: Kelsey Trail Regional Health Authority
PO Box 250, 4101 - 1 Ave. West, Carrot River, SK S0E 0L0
Tel: 306-768-3100; *Fax:* 306-768-3233
Number of Beds: 36 beds(35 long term care bed, 1 respite bed)
Bessie Lefebvre, Director, Health Services

Christopher Lake: **Little Red Health Centre**
Affiliated with: Prince Albert Parkland Health Region
PO Box 330, Christopher Lake, SK S0J 0N0
Tel: 306-982-4294; *Fax:* 306-982-3672

Clearwater River: **Clearwater River Dene First Nation Health Centre**
Affiliated with: Keewatin Yatthé Regional Health Authority
PO Box 5040, Clearwater River, SK S0M 3H0
Tel: 306-822-2378; *Fax:* 306-822-2297

Climax: **Border Health Centre**
Affiliated with: Cypress Regional Health Authority
PO Box 60, 301 - 1 St. West, Climax, SK S0N 0N0
Tel: 306-293-2222
Number of Beds: 4 beds

Coronach: **Coronach Health Centre**
Affiliated with: Sun Country Health Region
PO Box 150, 240 South Ave. East, Coronach, SK S0H 0Z0
Tel: 306-267-2022
Note: Programs & services include: diabetes program; dietitian services; home care; palliative care; rehabilitation services; respite care; telehealth; mental health services
Dawn Gold, Contact

Creighton: **Creighton Health Centre**
Affiliated with: Mamawetan Churchill River Health Region
PO Box 219, 298 - 1st St. East, Creighton, SK S0P 0A0
Tel: 306-688-8620; *Fax:* 306-688-8629

Cumberland House: **Cumberland House Health Centre**
Affiliated with: Kelsey Trail Regional Health Authority
PO Box 8, 2nd Ave., Cumberland House, SK S0E 0S0
Tel: 306-888-2244; *Fax:* 306-884-2269

Cupar: **Cupar Health Clinic**
Affiliated with: Regina Qu'Appelle Health Region
PO Box 100, 217 Stanley St., Cupar, SK S0G 0Y0
Tel: 306-723-4300; *Fax:* 306-723-4416

Note: Programs & services offered include: lab and x-ray services; system wide admission/discharge department (SWADD).

Cut Knife: **Cut Knife Health Complex**
Affiliated with: Prairie North Health Region
PO Box 220, 102 Dion Ave., Cut Knife, SK S0M 0N0
Tel: 306-398-4718; *Fax:* 306-398-2206
www.pnrha.ca
Number of Beds: 28 long-term care beds; 2 respite beds; 1 palliative care bed; 2 observation beds
Note: attached Special Care Home

Davidson: **Davidson Home Care Office**
Affiliated with: Heartland Regional Health Authority
PO Box 669, Davidson, SK S0G 1A0
Tel: 306-567-2302; *Fax:* 306-567-2073

Debden: **Big River First Nation Health Centre**
Affiliated with: Prince Albert Parkland Health Region
PO Box 160, Debden, SK S0J 0S0
Tel: 306-724-4664; *Fax:* 306-724-4555

Delisle: **Delisle Primary Health Centre**
Affiliated with: Saskatoon Health Region
PO Box 119, 305 - 1 St. West, Delisle, SK S0L 0P0
Tel: 306-493-2810; *Fax:* 306-493-2812

Dillon: **Buffalo River Health Centre**
Affiliated with: Keewatin Yatthé Regional Health Authority
PO Box 130, Dillon, SK S0M 0S0
Tel: 306-282-2132; *Fax:* 306-282-2117

Dinsmore: **Dinsmore Health Care Centre**
Affiliated with: Heartland Regional Health Authority
PO Box 219, 207 - 1st St. East, Dinsmore, SK S0L 0T0
Tel: 306-846-2222; *Fax:* 306-846-2225
Population Served: 375
Note: Programs & services include: long term care; visiting care services include physiotherapy, occupational therapy, mental health consultation, nutrition, child health.

Dodsland: **Dodsland Clinic**
Former Name: Dodsland Health Centre
4 Ave., Dodsland, SK S0L 0V0
Tel: 306-356-2104
Note: community-owned clinic

Eastend: **Eastend Wolf Willow Health Centre**
Affiliated with: Cypress Regional Health Authority
PO Box 490, 555 Redcoat Dr., Eastend, SK S0N 0T0
Tel: 306-295-3534
Number of Beds: 25 beds (23 long term care, 2 multipurpose)
Note: Programs & services include: lab/x-ray; mental health programs; physiotherapy; long term care; palliative beds; respite care.

Eatonia: **Eatonia Health Centre**
Affiliated with: Heartland Regional Health Authority
PO Box 400, 205 - 2nd Ave. West, Eatonia, SK S0L 0Y0
Tel: 306-967-2591; *Fax:* 306-967-2373
Note: Programs & services include: physician services; wellness program; lab/radiology; home care services; emergency services; occupational therapy; pharmacy deliveries.

Edam: **Lady Minto Health Care Centre**
Affiliated with: Prairie North Health Region
PO Box 330, Edam, SK S0M 0V0
Tel: 306-397-5560; *Fax:* 306-397-2225
Number of Beds: 14 long-term care beds; 3 respite beds; 2 convalescent beds; 1 palliative bed
Note: Programs & services include: laboratory/diagnostic imaging; home care; addictions; family counseling; occupational therapy.

Elrose: **Elrose Health Centre**
Affiliated with: Heartland Regional Health Authority
PO Box 100, 505 Main St., Elrose, SK S0L 0Z0
Tel: 306-378-2882; *Fax:* 306-378-2812
Note: Programs & services include: long term care; respite/palliative & convalescent.

Esterhazy: **Esterhazy Home Care Office**
Affiliated with: Sunrise Regional Health Authority
PO Box 1570, 216 Ancona St., Esterhazy, SK S0A 0X0
Tel: 306-745-6700; *Fax:* 306-745-3206

Esterhazy: **Esterhazy Public Health Office**
Affiliated with: Sunrise Regional Health Authority
PO Box 849, 216 Ancona St., Esterhazy, SK S0A 0X0
Tel: 306-745-3200; *Fax:* 306-745-3207

Eston: **Eston Health Centre**
Affiliated with: Heartland Regional Health Authority
PO Box 667, 800 Main St., Eston, SK S0L 1A0
Tel: 306-962-3667; *Fax:* 306-962-3900

Eston: **Eston Home Care Office**
Affiliated with: Heartland Regional Health Authority
PO Box 667, 822 Main St., Eston, SK S0L 1A0
Tel: 306-962-3215

Fillmore: **Fillmore Health Centre**
Affiliated with: Sun Country Health Region
PO Box 246, 100 Main St., Fillmore, SK S0G 1N0
Tel: 306-722-3315
Note: Programs & services include: ambulartory servicing; diabetes program; home care; palliative care; public health inspection
Linda Wilson, Contact

Foam Lake: **Foam Lake Health Centre**
Affiliated with: Sunrise Regional Health Authority
PO Box 190, 715 Saskatchewan Ave. East, Foam Lake, SK S0A 1A0
Tel: 306-272-3325; *Fax:* 306-272-4449

Fond du Lac: **Fond du Lac Denesuline Health Centre/Nursing Station**
Affiliated with: Athabasca Health Authority
PO Box 213, Fond du Lac, SK S0J 0W0
Tel: 306-686-2003; *Fax:* 306-686-2145

Fort Qu'Appelle: **Fort Qu'Appelle Community Health Services Centre**
Affiliated with: Regina Qu'Appelle Health Region
178 Boundary Ave. North, Fort Qu'Appelle, SK S0G 1S0
Tel: 306-332-3300

Gainsborough: **Gainsborough & Area Health Centre**
Affiliated with: Sun Country Health Region
PO Box 420, 312 Stephens St., Gainsborough, SK S0C 0Z0
Tel: 306-685-2277
Note: Programs & services include: telehealth; palliative care; respite care; long term care; home care; diabetes edcation program; convalescent care
Donna Davis, Contact

Goodsoil: **L. Gervais Memorial Health Centre**
Affiliated with: Prairie North Health Region
PO Box 100, Main St., Goodsoil, SK S0M 1A0
Tel: 306-238-2100; *Fax:* 306-238-4449
www.pnrha.ca
Number of Beds: 12 long-term care beds; 2 respite beds; 4 convalescent/palliative beds
Note: Health centre with a nursing home & attached special care home. Services include diagonistic imaging/laboratory; ambulatory services; home care; occupational therapy

Green Lake: **Green Lake Health Centre**
Affiliated with: Keewatin Yatthé Regional Health Authority
PO Box 29, Green Lake, SK S0M 1B0
Tel: 306-832-6257 *Toll-Free:* 877-800-0002

Grenfell: **Grenfell Health Centre**
Affiliated with: Regina Qu'Appelle Health Region
PO Box 243, 721 Stella St., Grenfell, SK S0G 2B0
Tel: 306-697-2853; *Fax:* 306-697-3459
Note: Programs & services include: laboratory and x-ray services; public and mental health programs; addiction; nutrition; community therapy

Gull Lake: **Gull Lake Special Care Centre**
Affiliated with: Cypress Regional Health Authority
PO Box 539, 751 Grey St., Gull Lake, SK S0N 1A0
Tel: 306-672-4700
Number of Beds: 36 beds
Note: Programs & services include lab/x-ray; child and youth counselling; dietitian; physiotherapy; day program; home care; palliative care; respite care.

Hodgeville: **Hodgeville Health Centre**
Affiliated with: Cypress Regional Health Authority
PO Box 232, 105 Main St., Hodgeville, SK S0H 2B0
Tel: 306-677-2292

Humboldt: **Humboldt Public Health Office**
Affiliated with: Saskatoon Health Region
PO Box 1930, 515 - 14th Ave., Humboldt, SK S0K 2A0
Tel: 306-682-2626 *Toll-Free:* 855-613-8205

Imperial: **Long Lake Valley Integrated Facility**
Affiliated with: Regina Qu'Appelle Health Region
PO Box 180, Imperial, SK S0G 2J0
Tel: 306-963-2210; *Fax:* 306-963-2518
Year Founded: 1992
Number of Beds: 15 long term care beds; 3 respite or palliative beds
Note: Programs & services include: short-term & long-term care; Respite & day care services; well baby clinics; foot care clinics; outreach programs; education programs

Invermay: **Invermay Health Centre**
Affiliated with: Sunrise Regional Health Authority
PO Box 160, 303 - 4 Ave. North, Invermay, SK S0A 1M0
Tel: 306-593-2133; *Fax:* 306-593-4566
www.sunrisehealthregion.sk.ca
Number of Beds: 26 beds (24 long term care beds, 2 respite beds)
Note: Programs & services include child and youth worker; drug and alcohol programs; visiting occupational therapy; behaviour management; public health office; adult day wellness program

Ituna: **Ituna Home Care Office**
Affiliated with: Sunrise Regional Health Authority
PO Box 130, 320 - 5 Ave. NE, Ituna, SK S0A 1N0
Tel: 306-795-2911; *Fax:* 306-795-3592

Ituna: **Ituna Pioneer Health Care Centre**
Affiliated with: Sunrise Regional Health Authority
PO Box 130, 320 - 5 Ave. East, Ituna, SK S0A 1N0
Tel: 306-795-2471; *Fax:* 306-795-3592
Number of Beds: 38 beds (35 long term care beds, 2 respite beds, 1 transition bed)
Note: Programs & services include adult day programs.

James Smith: **James Smith Health Centre**
Affiliated with: Prince Albert Parkland Health Region
PO Box 506, James Smith, SK S0J 1H0
Tel: 306-864-2454; *Fax:* 306-864-2536

Kamsack: **Kamsack Home Care Office**
Affiliated with: Sunrise Regional Health Authority
PO Box 1053, 341 Stewart St., Kamsack, SK S0A 1S0
Tel: 306-542-2212; *Fax:* 306-542-3902

Kamsack: **Kamsack Public Health Office**
Affiliated with: Sunrise Regional Health Authority
PO Box 218, 359 Queen Elizabeth Blvd., Kamsack, SK S0A 1S0
Tel: 306-542-4295; *Fax:* 306-542-2995

Kerrobert: **Kerrobert Health Centre**
Affiliated with: Heartland Regional Health Authority
PO Box 350, 365 Alberta Ave., Kerrobert, SK S0L 1R0
Tel: 306-834-2646; *Fax:* 306-834-1004
Year Founded: 1959
Number of Beds: 47 beds

Kerrobert: **Kerrobert Home Care Office**
Affiliated with: Heartland Regional Health Authority
PO Box 320, 365 Alberta Ave., Kerrobert, SK S0L 1R0
Tel: 306-834-2646; *Fax:* 306-834-1007

Kincaid: **Kincaid Wellness Centre**
Affiliated with: Five Hills Regional Health Authority
PO Box 179, Kincaid, SK S0H 2J0
Tel: 306-264-3233; *Fax:* 306-264-3878
www.fhhr.ca/Kincaid.htm

Kindersley: **Kindersley Home Care Office**
Affiliated with: Heartland Regional Health Authority
1003 - 1 St. West, Kindersley, SK S0L 1S2
Tel: 306-463-1000; *Fax:* 306-463-4550

Kinistino: **Kinistino Medical Clinic**
Affiliated with: Prince Albert Parkland Regional Health Authority
PO Box 100, 401 Meyers Ave., Kinistino, SK S0J 1H0
Tel: 306-864-2212; *Fax:* 306-864-3220

Kipling: **Kipling Community Health**
Affiliated with: Sun Country Health Region
PO Box 480, 602 Main St., Kipling, SK S0G 2S0
Tel: 306-736-2522; *Fax:* 306-736-2300

Kyle: **Kyle & District Health Centre**
Affiliated with: Heartland Regional Health Authority
PO Box 70, 208 - 3 Ave. East, Kyle, SK S0L 1T0
Tel: 306-375-2251; *Fax:* 306-375-2422

Kyle: **Kyle Home Care Office**
Affiliated with: Heartland Regional Health Authority
PO Box 68, Kyle, SK S0L 1T0
Tel: 306-375-2400; *Fax:* 306-375-2422

La Ronge: **La Ronge Health Centre**
Affiliated with: Mamawetan Churchill River Health Region
PO Box 6000, 227 Backlund St., La Ronge, SK S0J 1L0
Tel: 306-425-2422; *Fax:* 306-425-5513

Lafleche: **LaFleche & District Health Centre**
Affiliated with: Five Hills Regional Health Authority
PO Box 159, 315 Main St., Lafleche, SK S0H 2K0
Tel: 306-472-5230
www.fhhr.ca/Lafleche.htm
Number of Beds: 16 beds

Lampman: **Lampman Community Health Centre**
Affiliated with: Sun Country Health Region
PO Box 100, 309 - 2 Ave. East, Lampman, SK S0C 1N0
Tel: 306-487-2561
Note: Programs & services include: dietitian services; ambulartory services; home care; meergency medical services; palliative care; respite care
Cyndee Hoium, Contact

Langenburg: **Langenburg Health Care Complex**
Affiliated with: Sunrise Regional Health Authority
PO Box 370, 200 Heritage Dr., Langenburg, SK S0A 2A0
Tel: 306-743-2661; *Fax:* 306-743-5025

Langenburg: **Langenburg Home Care Office**
Affiliated with: Sunrise Regional Health Authority
PO Box 370, 200 Heritage Dr., Langenburg, SK S0A 2A0
Tel: 306-743-5005; *Fax:* 306-743-2844

Langenburg: **Langenburg Public Health Office**
Affiliated with: Sunrise Regional Health Authority
PO Box 160, 200 Heritage Dr., Langenburg, SK S0A 2A0
Tel: 306-743-2801; *Fax:* 306-743-2899

Leader: **Leader Primary Health Care Site**
Affiliated with: Cypress Regional Health Authority
PO Box 638, 519 Main St. East, Leader, SK S0N 1H0
Tel: 306-628-4584

Leask: **Mistawasis Health Centre**
Affiliated with: Prince Albert Parkland Health Region
PO Box 148, Leask, SK S0J 1M0
Tel: 306-466-4507; *Fax:* 306-466-2220

Leoville: **Evergreen Health Centre**
Affiliated with: Prince Albert Parkland Regional Health Authority
PO Box 160, Leoville, SK S0J 1N0
Tel: 306-984-2136; *Fax:* 306-984-2046

Leoville: **Pelican Lake (Chitek) Health Centre**
Affiliated with: Prince Albert Parkland Health Region
PO Box 361, Leoville, SK S0J 1N0
Tel: 306-984-4716; *Fax:* 306-984-4728

Leroy: **Leroy Community Health & Social Centre**
Affiliated with: Saskatoon Health Region
PO Box 7, 211 - 1 Ave. NE, Leroy, SK S0K 2P0
Tel: 306-286-3347; *Fax:* 306-286-3888
www.saskatoonhealthregion.ca

Lloydminster: **Lloydminster & Area Home Care Services**
Affiliated with: Prairie North Health Region
3830 - 43 Ave., Lloydminster, SK S9V 1Y3
Tel: 306-820-6200; *Fax:* 306-825-3666

Lloydminster: **Lloydminster & District Co-operative Health Services Ltd.**
PO Box 530, 4910 - 50 St., Lloydminster, SK S9V 0Y6
Tel: 306-825-4427

Lucky Lake: **Lucky Lake Health Centre**
Affiliated with: Heartland Regional Health Authority
PO Box 250, 1 Ave., Lucky Lake, SK S0L 1Z0
Tel: 306-858-2133; *Fax:* 306-858-2312

Macklin: **Macklin Home Care Office**
Affiliated with: Heartland Regional Health Authority
PO Box 190, Macklin, SK S0L 2C0
Tel: 306-753-3202; *Fax:* 306-753-2181

Macklin: **St. Joseph's Health Centre**
Affiliated with: Heartland Regional Health Authority
PO Box 190, Hwy. 31 North, Macklin, SK S0L 2C0
Tel: 306-753-2115; *Fax:* 306-753-2181

Marcelin: **Muskeg Lake Health Centre**
Affiliated with: Prince Albert Parkland Health Region
PO Box 224, Marcelin, SK S0J 1R0
Tel: 306-466-4914; *Fax:* 306-466-4919

Maryfield: **Maryfield Health Centre**
Affiliated with: Sun Country Health Region
PO Box 164, 233 Main St., Maryfield, SK S0G 3K0
Tel: 306-646-2133
Note: Programs & services include: diabetes program; mental health services; primary health care; palliative care.
Nikki Ford, Contact

Meadow Lake: **Meadow Lake Community Services**
Affiliated with: Prairie North Health Region
#9, 711 Centre St., Meadow Lake, SK S9X 1E6
Tel: 306-236-1570; *Fax:* 306-236-4974

Melfort: **Melfort Home Care Office**
Affiliated with: Kelsey Trail Regional Health Authority
PO Box 1480, 401 Burns Ave. East, Melfort, SK S0E 1A0
Tel: 306-752-1780; *Fax:* 306-752-1786

Melfort: **Melfort Public Health Office**
Affiliated with: Kelsey Trail Regional Health Authority
PO Box 6500, 107 Crawford Ave. East, Melfort, SK S0E 1A0
Tel: 306-752-6310; *Fax:* 306-752-6353

Melville: **Melville Public Health Office**
Affiliated with: Sunrise Regional Health Authority
PO Box 62, 200 Heritage Dr., Melville, SK S0A 2P0
Tel: 306-728-7310; *Fax:* 306-728-4925

Melville: **Melville/Ituna Home Care Office**
Affiliated with: Sunrise Regional Health Authority
PO Box 2348, 200 Heritage Dr., Melville, SK S0A 2P0
Tel: 306-728-7300; *Fax:* 306-728-4925

Midale: **Mainprize Manor & Health Centre**
Affiliated with: Sun Country Health Region
PO Box 239, 206 South St., Midale, SK S0C 1S0
Tel: 306-458-2300
Note: Programs & service offered: Doctor clinics; Outpatient service; Day respite care; Long-term care
Cyndee Hoium, Contact

Mont Nebo: **Ahtahkakoop Health Centre**
Affiliated with: Prince Albert Parkland Health Regionty
PO Box 64, Mont Nebo, SK S0J 1X0
Tel: 306-468-2747; *Fax:* 306-468-2967

Montmartre: **Montmartre Health Centre**
Affiliated with: Regina Qu'Appelle Health Region
PO Box 206, 237 - 2 Ave. East, Montmartre, SK S0G 3M0
Tel: 306-424-2222; *Fax:* 306-424-2227

Moose Jaw: **Crescent View Clinic**
Affiliated with: Five Hills Health Region
131A - 1st Ave. NE, Moose Jaw, SK S6H 0Y8
Tel: 306-691-2040

Mossbank: **Mossbank Health Centre**
Affiliated with: Five Hills Regional Health Authority
PO Box 322, Mossbank, SK S0H 3G0
Tel: 306-354-2300; *Fax:* 306-354-2819
www.fhhr.ca/Mossbank.htm

Muskoday: **Muskoday Health Centre**
Affiliated with: Prince Albert Parkland Health Region
PO Box 40, Muskoday, SK S0J 3H0
Tel: 306-764-6737; *Fax:* 306-764-4664

Naicam: **Naicam Home Care Office**
Affiliated with: Kelsey Trail Regional Health Authority
305 - 1 St. South, Naicam, SK S0K 2Z0
Tel: 306-874-2276

Neilburg: **Manitou Health Centre**
Affiliated with: Prairie North Health Region
PO Box 190, 105 - 2nd Ave. West, Neilburg, SK S0M 2C0
Tel: 306-823-4262; *Fax:* 306-823-4590
Note: Programs & services include: laboratory/diagnostic imaging; home care; public health; addictions

Neudorf: **Neudorf Health & Social Centre**
410 Main St., Neudorf, SK S0A 2T0
Tel: 306-748-2566; *Fax:* 306-748-2868
Note: Senior centre

Nipawin: **Nipawin Public Health Office**
Affiliated with: Kelsey Trail Regional Health Authority
PO Box 389, 210 - 2 St. West, Nipawin, SK S0E 1E0
Tel: 306-862-7230; *Fax:* 306-862-0763

Nokomis: **Nokomis Health Centre**
Affiliated with: Saskatoon Health Region
PO Box 98, 103 - 2 Ave. East, Nokomis, SK S0G 3R0
Tel: 306-528-2114; *Fax:* 306-528-4445
Number of Beds: 14 beds

Norquay: **Norquay Health Centre**
Affiliated with: Sunrise Regional Health Authority
PO Box 190, Norquay, SK S0A 2V0
Tel: 306-594-2133; *Fax:* 306-594-2488
Number of Beds: 30 long term care beds; 2 respite beds
Note: Programs & services include: laboratory/diagnostic imaging; home care; public health; addictions. Palliative care beds provided as needed.

Norquay: **Norquay Home Care Office**
Affiliated with: Sunrise Regional Health Authority
PO Box 535, 355 East Rd. Allowance South, Norquay, SK S0A 2V0
Tel: 306-594-2277; *Fax:* 306-594-2220

Outlook: **Outlook Home Care Office**
Affiliated with: Heartland Regional Health Authority
PO Box 1100, Outlook, SK S0L 2N0
Tel: 306-867-8676; *Fax:* 306-867-2069

Oxbow: **Galloway Health Centre**
Affiliated with: Sun Country Health Region
PO Box 268, 917 Tupper St., Oxbow, SK S0C 2B0
Tel: 306-483-2956
Note: Programs & services include: convalescent care; respite care; telehealth.
Caroline Hill, Contact

Pangman: **Pangman Health Centre**
Affiliated with: Sun Country Health Region
PO Box 90, 211 Keeler St., Pangman, SK S0C 2C0
Tel: 306-442-2044
Note: Programs & services include: rehabilitation services; public health inspection; mental health services; diabetes program; ambulance services; home care; palliative care

Paradise Hill: **Paradise Hill Health Centre**
Affiliated with: Prairie North Health Region
PO Box 179, Paradise Hill, SK S0M 2G0
Tel: 306-344-2255; *Fax:* 306-344-2277
Number of Beds: No patient/resident care beds
Note: Programs & services include: laboratory; clinic; dietician; addiction treatment.

Patuanak: **English River Health Services**
Affiliated with: Keewatin Yatthé Regional Health Authority
PO Box 60, Patuanak, SK S0M 2H0
Tel: 306-396-2072; *Fax:* 306-396-2177

Pinehouse: **Pinehouse Health Centre**
Affiliated with: Mamawetan Churchill River Health Region
PO Box 70, Pinehouse, SK S0J 2B0
Tel: 306-884-5670; *Fax:* 306-884-5699
Note: Programs & services include: public health; health education; primary care; addiction services; mental health services; home care services

Ponteix: **Ponteix Health Centre**
Affiliated with: Cypress Regional Health Authority
PO Box 600, 428 - 2 Ave., Ponteix, SK S0N 1Z0
Tel: 306-625-3382; *Fax:* 306-625-3764
Note: Programs & services include: Radiology, Laboratory Services, Home Care, Nutrition, Mental Health, Baby Clinic, Public Health, Foyer St. Joseph Nursing Home, Ambulance Service.

Preeceville: **Preeceville Home Care Office**
Affiliated with: Sunrise Regional Health Authority
PO Box 407, 712 - 7 Ave. NW, Preeceville, SK S0A 3B0
Tel: 306-547-4441; *Fax:* 306-547-5514

Preeceville: **Preeceville Public Health & Physiotherapy Office**
Affiliated with: Sunrise Regional Health Authority
PO Box 466, 239 Highway Ave. East, Preeceville, SK S0A 3B0
Tel: 306-547-2815; *Fax:* 306-547-2092

Prince Albert: **Associate Medical Clinic**
Affiliated with: Prince Albert Parkland Health Region
#400, 20 - 14 St. West, Prince Albert, SK S6V 3K8
Tel: 306-764-1513; *Fax:* 306-764-3091

Prince Albert: **Crescent Heights Family Medical Centre**
Affiliated with: Prince Albert Parkland Health Region
#114, 2805 - 6 Ave. East, Prince Albert, SK S6V 6Z6
Tel: 306-763-2681; *Fax:* 306-953-1024

Prince Albert: **First Nations & Inuit Health North Service Centre**
Affiliated with: Prince Albert Parkland Health Region
PO Box 5000, 3601 - 5 Ave. East, Prince Albert, SK S6V 7V6
Tel: 306-953-8600; *Fax:* 306-953-8566

Prince Albert: **Prince Albert Co-Operative Health Centre**
Affiliated with: Prince Albert Parkland Regional Health Authority
110 - 8th St. East, Prince Albert, SK S6V 0V7
Tel: 306-763-6464; *Fax:* 306-763-2101
www.coophealth.com
Year Founded: 1962
Frank Regel, Board Chair
Renee Danylczuk, Executive Director

Prince Albert: **Prince Albert Medical Clinic**
Affiliated with: Prince Albert Parkland Health Region
681 - 15th St. West, Prince Albert, SK S6V 7H9
Tel: 306-764-1505; *Fax:* 306-764-7751

Prince Albert: **South Hill Family Practice**
Affiliated with: Prince Albert Parkland Health Region
2685 - 2nd Ave. West, Prince Albert, SK S6V 5E3
Tel: 306-922-9570; *Fax:* 306-922-2464

Prince Albert: **West Hill Medical Clinic**
Affiliated with: Prince Albert Parkland Health Region
#1A, 2995 - 2nd Ave. West, Prince Albert, SK S6V 5V5
Tel: 306-765-8500; *Fax:* 306-765-8501

Quill Lake: **Quill Lake Community Health & Social Centre**
Affiliated with: Saskatoon Health Region
PO Box 126, Quill Lake, SK S0A 3E0
Tel: 306-383-2266

Radville: **Radville Marian Health Centre**
Affiliated with: Sun Country Health Region
PO Box 310, 840 Conrad Ave., Radville, SK S0C 0G0
Tel: 306-869-2224
Number of Beds: 25 beds
Note: Programs & services include: palliative care; home care; diabetes program; acute care services.

Radville: **Radville Public Health Office**
Affiliated with: Sun Country Health Region
PO Box 683, 840 Conrad Ave., Radville, SK S0C 2G0
Tel: 306-869-2555; *Fax:* 306-369-3118
Judy DeRoose, Contact

Raymore: **Raymore Community Health & Social Centre**
Affiliated with: Regina Qu'Appelle Health Region
PO Box 134, 806 - 2 Ave., Raymore, SK S0A 3J0
Tel: 306-746-2231; *Fax:* 306-746-4639
Year Founded: 1981

Regina: **Al Ritchie Health Action Centre**
Affiliated with: Regina Qu'Appelle Health Region
325 Victoria Ave., Regina, SK S4N 0P5
Tel: 306-766-7660
Note: Programs & services include: GED exam support services; skills registry; job search support; prenatal nutrition advice; community computer; Dad's Group; family crafts; quit smoking program; seniors' potluck lunch; community kitchen; foot care; primary care nurse (by appt); food bank referrals; video lending library.

Regina: **Four Directions Community Health Centre**
Affiliated with: Regina Qu'Appelle Health Region
3510 - 5 Ave., Regina, SK S4T 0M2
Tel: 306-766-7540

Regina: **Meadow Primary Health Care Centre**
Affiliated with: Regina Qu'Appelle Health Region
4006 Dewdney Ave., Regina, SK S4T 1A2
Tel: 306-766-6399 *Toll-Free:* 855-766-6399

Regina Beach: **Regina Beach Primary Health Care Centre**
Affiliated with: Regina Qu'Appelle Health Region
410 Centre St., Regina Beach, SK S0G 4C0
Tel: 306-729-3395; *Fax:* 306-729-3395
Toll-Free: 855-766-6399

Rockglen: **Grasslands Health Centre**
Affiliated with: Five Hills Regional Health Authority
PO Box 219, 1006 Hwy. 2, Rockglen, SK S0H 3R0
Tel: 306-476-2030
www.fhhr.ca
Number of Beds: 17 beds

Rose Valley: **Rose Valley Health Centre**
Affiliated with: Kelsey Trail Regional Health Authority
PO Box 310, 119 McCallum St., Rose Valley, SK S0E 1M0
Tel: 306-322-2115; *Fax:* 306-322-2037

Rosetown: **Rosetown & District Health Centre**
Affiliated with: Heartland Regional Health Authority
PO Box 850, Hwy. 4 North, Rosetown, SK S0L 2V0
Tel: 306-882-2672; *Fax:* 306-882-3335
Year Founded: 1964
Gail Adamowski, Facility Manager

Rosetown: **Rosetown Home Care Office**
Affiliated with: Heartland Regional Health Authority
PO Box 624, Rosetown, SK S0L 2V0
Tel: 306-882-4100; *Fax:* 306-882-4251

Rosthern: **Rosthern Public Health Office**
Affiliated with: Saskatoon Health Region
PO Box 216, 2014 - 6th St., Rosthern, SK S0K 3R0
Tel: 306-232-6001 *Toll-Free:* 888-301-4636

Sandy Bay: **Sandy Bay Health Centre**
Affiliated with: Mamawetan Churchill River Health Region
PO Box 210, Sandy Bay, SK S0P 0G0
Tel: 306-754-5400; *Fax:* 306-754-5429
Note: Programs & services include: primary care; public health; health education; telehealth; home care services

Saskatoon: **20th & Q Pediatric Specialists & Family Walk-In**
Affiliated with: Saskatoon Health Region
1631 - 20th St. West, Saskatoon, SK S7M 0Z9
Tel: 306-384-9888

Saskatoon: **Blairmore Medical Clinic**
Affiliated with: Saskatoon Health Region
225 Betts Ave., Saskatoon, SK S7M 1L2
Tel: 306-652-6400

Saskatoon: **Idylwyld Centre Public Health Office**
Affiliated with: Saskatoon Health Region
#101, 310 Idylwyld Dr. North, Saskatoon, SK S7L 0Z2
Tel: 306-655-4620

Saskatoon: **Lakeside Medical Clinic**
Affiliated with: Saskatoon Health Region
3919 - 8th St. East, Saskatoon, SK S7H 5M7
Tel: 306-374-6884; *Fax:* 306-374-2552
www.lakeside.ca
Social Media: twitter.com/LMCSaskatoon

Saskatoon: **Lenore Medical Clinic**
Affiliated with: Saskatoon Health Region
#4, 123 Lenore Dr., Saskatoon, SK S7K 7H9
Tel: 306-242-6700

Saskatoon: **MediClinic**
Affiliated with: Saskatoon Health Region
#101, 3333 - 8th St. East, Saskatoon, SK S7H 4K1
Tel: 306-955-1530
www.mediclinic-sk.com
Social Media: twitter.com/Mediclinicon8th
Year Founded: 1982

Saskatoon: **North East Public Health Office**
Affiliated with: Saskatoon Health Region
#108, 407 Ludlow St., Saskatoon, SK S7S 1P3
Tel: 306-655-4700

Saskatoon: **Our Neighbourhood Health Centre**
Affiliated with: Saskatoon Health Region
1120 - 20th St. West, Saskatoon, SK S7M 0Y8
Tel: 306-655-3250

Saskatoon: **Primary Health Centre South East - Scott-Forget Towers**
Affiliated with: Saskatoon Health Region
#100, 2501 Louise St., Saskatoon, SK S7J 3M1
Tel: 306-655-4550

Saskatoon: **Saskatoon Community Clinic**
Affiliated with: Saskatoon Health Region
455 - 2nd Ave. North, Saskatoon, SK S7K 2C2
Tel: 306-652-0300; *Fax:* 306-664-4120
member.relations@communityclinic.sk.ca
www.saskatooncommunityclinic.ca
Year Founded: 1962
Note: Health services are offered at the Downtown Clinic & the Westside Clinic.
Anne Doucette, President, Board of Directors

Saskatoon: **Saskatoon Minor Emergency Clinic**
Affiliated with: Saskatoon Health Region
3110 Laurier Dr., Saskatoon, SK S7L 5J7
Tel: 306-978-2200

Saskatoon: **South East Public Health Office**
Affiliated with: Saskatoon Health Region
3006 Taylor St. East, Saskatoon, SK S7H 4J2
Tel: 306-655-4730 *Toll-Free:* 855-613-8216

Shellbrook: **Shellbrook Doctors Office**
Affiliated with: Prince Albert Parkland Health Region
PO Box 1030, 206 - 2nd Ave. West, Shellbrook, SK S0J 2E0
Tel: 306-747-2552; *Fax:* 306-747-2141

Shellbrook: **Shellbrook Home Care**
Affiliated with: Prince Albert Parkland Health Region
PO Box 70, 211 - 2 Ave. West, Shellbrook, SK S0J 2E0
Tel: 306-747-4266; *Fax:* 306-747-3004

Shellbrook: **Shellbrook Medical Clinic**
Affiliated with: Prince Albert Parkland Health Region
PO Box 504, 208 - 2nd Ave. West, Shellbrook, SK S0J 2E0
Tel: 306-747-2171; *Fax:* 306-747-2173

Smeaton: **Smeaton Health Centre**
Affiliated with: Kelsey Trail Regional Health Authority
PO Box 158, 2nd Ave. West, Smeaton, SK S0J 2J0
Tel: 306-426-2051; *Fax:* 306-426-2299

Southey: **Southey Health Action Centre**
Affiliated with: Regina Qu'Appelle Health Region
PO Box 519, 280 Burns Ave., Southey, SK S0G 4P0
Tel: 306-726-2239; *Fax:* 306-726-4472
Year Founded: 1995

Spalding: **Spalding Community Health Centre**
Affiliated with: Saskatoon Health Region
PO Box 220, Spalding, SK S0K 4C0
Tel: 306-872-2011

Spiritwood: **Spiritwood Home Care**
Affiliated with: Prince Albert Parkland Health Region
PO Box 69, 400 - 1 St. East, Spiritwood, SK S0J 2M0
Tel: 306-883-4266; *Fax:* 306-883-4440

Spiritwood: **Spiritwood Indian Health Services**
Affiliated with: Prince Albert Parkland Health Region
PO Box 579, 100 Railroad Ave. West, Spiritwood, SK S0J 2M0
Tel: 306-883-2905; *Fax:* 306-883-2535

Spiritwood: **Spiritwood Medical Clinic**
Affiliated with: Prince Albert Parkland Health Region
PO Box 668, Spiritwood, SK S0J 2M0
Tel: 306-883-2140; *Fax:* 306-883-3211

Spiritwood: **Witchekan Lake Health Centre**
Affiliated with: Prince Albert Parkland Health Region
PO Box 359, Spiritwood, SK S0J 2M0
Tel: 306-883-2552; *Fax:* 306-883-2578

St Walburg: **St. Walburg Health Complex**
Affiliated with: Prairie North Health Region
PO Box 339, 410 - 3rd Ave. West, St Walburg, SK S0M 2T0
Tel: 306-248-6719; *Fax:* 306-248-3413
Number of Beds: 31 beds (28 long term care bed, 1 respite, 1 palliative, 1 convalescent)
Note: Attached special care home. Programs offered include diagnostic imaging; medical clinic services; dietitian; family counseling; mental health programs; physiotherapy; occupational therapy

Strasbourg: **Strasbourg & District Health Centre**
Affiliated with: Saskatoon Health Region
303 Edward St., Strasbourg, SK S0G 4V0
Tel: 306-725-3220
Year Founded: 1974
Note: Specialties: Physiotherapy; Counselling; Public health services

Sturgeon Lake: **Sturgeon Lake Health Centre**
Affiliated with: Prince Albert Parkland Health Region
Comp 5, Site 12, RR#1, Sturgeon Lake, SK S0J 2E0
Tel: 306-764-9352; *Fax:* 306-763-0767

Swift Current: **Cypress Health Region's Community Health Services**
Affiliated with: Cypress Regional Health Authority
350 Cheadle St. West, Swift Current, SK S9H 4G3
Tel: 306-778-5280

Theodore: **Theodore Public Health Office**
Affiliated with: Sunrise Regional Health Authority
PO Box 292, 615 Anderson Ave., Theodore, SK S0A 4C0
Tel: 306-647-2353; *Fax:* 306-647-2238

Tisdale: **Tisdale Public Health Office**
Affiliated with: Kelsey Trail Regional Health Authority
PO Box 1297, 800 - 1 St. East, Tisdale, SK S0E 1T0
Tel: 306-873-8282; *Fax:* 306-873-2168

Turtleford: **Riverside Health Complex**
Affiliated with: Prairie North Health Region
PO Box 10, Turtleford, SK S0M 2Y0
Tel: 306-845-2195; *Fax:* 306-845-2772
Number of Beds: 29 beds
Note: Attached special care home

Unity: **Unity & District Health Centre**
Affiliated with: Heartland Regional Health Authority
Former Name: Unity Hospital
PO Box 741, Airport Rd., Unity, SK S0K 4L0
Tel: 306-228-2666; *Fax:* 306-228-2292
Year Founded: 2001
Note: Programs & services include: acute care; diagnostic services; maternity services; community health services; public health nursing; mental health services; counselling; physiotherapy; occupational therapy; home care; long-term care; respite care; palliative care
Kim Halter, Facility Manager
Randy Scherr, Supervisor, Plant Maintenance

Unity: **Unity Home Care Office**
Affiliated with: Heartland Regional Health Authority
PO Box 1538, Unity, SK S0K 4L0
Tel: 306-228-2666; *Fax:* 306-228-2292

Vanguard: **Vanguard Health Centre**
Affiliated with: Cypress Regional Health Authority
PO Box 190, Division St., Vanguard, SK S0N 2V0
Tel: 306-582-2044

Wadena: **Wadena Primary Health Team**
Affiliated with: Saskatoon Health Region
533 - 5th St. NE, Wadena, SK S0A 4J0
Tel: 306-338-2597

Wadena: **Wadena Public Health Office**
Affiliated with: Saskatoon Health Region
PO Box 10, 533 - 5 St. NE, Wadena, SK S0A 4J0
Tel: 306-338-2538 *Toll-Free:* 855-338-9994

Wahpeton: **Wahpeton Health Centre**
Affiliated with: Prince Albert Parkland Health Region
PO Box 128, Wahpeton, SK S6V 5R4
Tel: 306-922-6772; *Fax:* 306-922-6774

Watrous: **Watrous Primary Health Centre**
Affiliated with: Saskatoon Health Region
403 Main St., Watrous, SK S0K 4T0
Tel: 306-946-2075

Watrous: **Watrous Public Health Office**
Affiliated with: Saskatoon Health Region
PO Box 130, 704 - 4th Ave., Watrous, SK S0K 4T0
Tel: 306-946-2102 *Toll-Free:* 877-817-9336

Watson: **Watson Community Health Centre**
Affiliated with: Saskatoon Health Region
PO Box 220, Watson, SK SOK 4VO
Tel: 306-287-3791

Weyakwin: **Weyakwin Health Centre**
Affiliated with: Mamawetan Churchill River Health Region
PO Box 8, Weyakwin, SK S0J 1W0
Tel: 306-663-6100; *Fax:* 306-663-6165

Weyburn: **Weyburn Community Health Services**
Affiliated with: Sun Country Health Region
PO Box 2003, 900 Saskatchewan Dr., Weyburn, SK S4H 2Z9
Tel: 306-842-8618; *Fax:* 306-842-8637

Note: Programs & services include: mental health services; telehealth.
Janice Giroux, Contact

Weyburn: Weyburn Primary Health Care Clinic
Affiliated with: Sun Country Health Region
#204, 117 - 3 St., Weyburn, SK S4H 0W3
Tel: 306-842-8790

Whitewood: Whitewood Community Health Centre
Affiliated with: Regina Qu'Appelle Health Region
PO Box 669, 921 Gambetta St., Whitewood, SK S0G 5C0
Tel: 306-735-2688; *Fax:* 306-735-2512
Specialties: Outpatient / ambulatory care services
Note: Programs & services: public health (306-435-6279); parenting plus (306-697-4048); mental health services for children (306-697-4021); mental health services for adults (306-697-4023); nutrition services (306-697-4037); home care services (306-696-2500).

Wilkie: Wilkie Health Centre
Affiliated with: Heartland Regional Health Authority
PO Box 459, 304 - 7 Ave. East, Wilkie, SK S0K 4W0
Tel: 306-843-2644; *Fax:* 306-843-3222

Wilkie: Wilkie Home Care Office
Affiliated with: Heartland Regional Health Authority
PO Box 459, 304 - 7 St. East, Wilkie, SK S0K 4W0
Tel: 306-843-2644; *Fax:* 306-843-3222

Willow Bunch: Willow Bunch Health Centre
Affiliated with: Five Hills Regional Health Authority
PO Box 6, Willow Bunch, SK S0H 4K0
Tel: 306-473-2310; *Fax:* 306-473-2677
www.fhhr.ca/WillowBunch.htm

Wynyard: Wynyard & District Community Health Centre
Affiliated with: Saskatoon Health Region
PO Box 1539, 210 Ave. B East, Wynyard, SK S0A 4T0
Tel: 306-554-3363

Yorkton: Sunrise Health & Wellness Centre
Affiliated with: Sunrise Regional Health Authority
#25, 259 Hamilton Rd., Yorkton, SK S3N 4C6
Tel: 306-786-6363; *Fax:* 306-786-6364

Yorkton: Yorkton Home Care Office
Affiliated with: Sunrise Regional Health Authority
PO Box 5016, 270 Bradbrooke Dr., Yorkton, SK S3N 3Z4
Tel: 306-786-0711; *Fax:* 306-786-0707

Yorkton: Yorkton Public Health Office
Affiliated with: Sunrise Regional Health Authority
150 Independent St., Yorkton, SK S3N 0S7
Tel: 306-786-0600; *Fax:* 306-786-0620

Nursing Stations

Stony Rapids: Black Lake Nursing Station
General Delivery, Stony Rapids, SK S0J 2R0
Tel: 306-439-2200

Special Treatment Centres

Melville: Saul Cohen Family Resource Centre
Affiliated with: Sunrise Regional Health Authority
PO Box 164, 200 Heritage Dr., Melville, SK S0A 2P0
Tel: 306-728-7320; *Fax:* 306-728-4925
Note: Outpatient counseling & support individuals & families affected by addictions
Sherry Shumay

North Battleford: Saskatchewan Hospital
Affiliated with: Prairie North Health Region
PO Box 39, North Battleford, SK S9A 2X8
Tel: 306-446-6800; *Fax:* 306-445-5392
Note: psychiatric rehabilitation hospital

Regina: Wascana Rehabilitation Centre
Affiliated with: Regina Qu'Appelle Health Region
2180 - 23 Ave., Regina, SK S4S 0A5
Tel: 306-766-5100
Year Founded: 1968
Number of Beds: 307 beds
Note: Programs & services include: rehabilitation centre; long term care centre.

Long Term Care Facilities

Big River: Big River Health Centre
PO Box 100, 220 - 1 Ave. North, Big River, SK S0J 0E0
Tel: 306-469-2333; *Fax:* 306-469-2193
Number of Beds: 29 beds

Cudworth: Cudworth Nursing Home/Health Centre
Affiliated with: Saskatoon Health Region
PO Box 190, Cudworth, SK S0K 1B0
Tel: 306-256-3423; *Fax:* 306-256-3343
Number of Beds: 32 beds

Cumberland House: Cumberland House Home Care
Affiliated with: Kelsey Trail Regional Health Authority
3 Cumberland St., Cumberland House, SK S0E 0S0
Tel: 306-888-2197; *Fax:* 306-888-2177

Hafford: Hafford Home Care
Affiliated with: Prince Albert Parkland Health Region
PO Box 130, 213 South Ave. East, Hafford, SK S0J 1A0
Tel: 306-549-4266; *Fax:* 306-549-2104

Lanigan: Central Parkland Lodge
Affiliated with: Saskatoon Health Region
PO Box 459, Lanigan, SK S0K 2M0
Tel: 306-365-1420; *Fax:* 306-365-3354
Number of Beds: 35 beds
Specialties: Long term health care for senior citizens

Lloydminster: Jubilee Home
Affiliated with: Prairie North Health Region
3902 - 45 Ave., Lloydminster, SK S9V 1Z2
Tel: 306-820-5950; *Fax:* 306-825-9869
Note: Respite care is available.

Middle Lake: Bethany Pioneer Village Inc.
Affiliated with: Saskatoon Health Region
PO Box 8, Middle Lake, SK S0K 2X0
Tel: 306-367-2033; *Fax:* 306-367-2155
bethanyvillage@sasktel.net
www.bethanypioneervillage.ca
Year Founded: 1956
Specialties: Care for seniors & others with similar needs
Note: Bethany Pioneer Village provides independent living suites, assisted living, & special care. The factility is recognized by Lutheran Church Canada as a service organization.
Sharon Carter, Chair
Sinikka Purmonen, Administrator

Prince Albert: Pine View Terrace Lodge
Affiliated with: Prince Albert Parkland Health Region
701 - 13 St. West, Prince Albert, SK S6V 3H2
Tel: 306-765-6570; *Fax:* 306-764-0212

St. Brieux: Chateau Providence
Affiliated with: Kelsey Trail Regional Health Authority
PO Box 340, 200 - 1 Ave. North, St. Brieux, SK S0K 3V0
Tel: 306-275-2400; *Fax:* 306-275-2027
Number of Beds: 29 Long Term Care beds; 1 respite bed

Wadena: Pleasant View Care Home
Affiliated with: Saskatoon Health Region
PO Box 10, 433 - 5 St. NE, Wadena, SK S0A 4J0
Tel: 306-338-2412; *Fax:* 306-338-2720
Year Founded: 1989
Number of Beds: 46 beds

Wakaw: Lakeview Pioneer Lodge
Affiliated with: Saskatoon Health Region
PO Box 189, Wakaw, SK S0K 4P0
Tel: 306-233-4621; *Fax:* 306-233-5225
Number of Beds: 46 beds

Nursing Homes

Assiniboia: Assiniboia Pioneer Lodge
Affiliated with: Five Hills Regional Health Authority
PO Box 1120, 800 - 1 St. West, Assiniboia, SK S0H 0B0
Tel: 306-642-3311; *Fax:* 306-642-3099
Number of Beds: 128 beds

Assiniboia: Ross Payant Centennial Home
Affiliated with: Five Hills Regional Health Authority
Former Name: Ross Payant Centennial Home
300 Jubilee Place, Assiniboia, SK S0H 0B0
Tel: 306-642-3330
Number of Beds: 38 beds

Biggar: Biggar Diamond Lodge
Affiliated with: Heartland Regional Health Authority
PO Box 340, 402 - 2nd Ave. West, Biggar, SK S0K 0M0
Tel: 306-948-3385; *Fax:* 306-948-5421

Birch Hills: Birchview Nursing Home
Affiliated with: Prince Albert Parkland Regional Health Authority
3 Wilson St., Birch Hills, SK S0J 0G0
Tel: 306-749-2288; *Fax:* 306-749-2406

Broadview: Broadview Centennial Lodge
Affiliated with: Regina Qu'Appelle Health Region
PO Box 670, 310 Calgary St., Broadview, SK S0G 0K0
Tel: 306-696-2458; *Fax:* 306-696-2577
Note: The facility offers an Adult Day Support Program.

Canwood: Whispering Pine Place Inc.
Affiliated with: Prince Albert Parkland Regional Health Authority
PO Box 418, 300 - 1st Ave., Canwood, SK S0J 0K0
Tel: 306-468-2900; *Fax:* 306-468-2199
Population Served: 1720

Carlyle: Moose Mountain Lodge
Affiliated with: Sun Country Health Region
PO Box 729, 801 Souris Ave., Carlyle, SK S0C 0R0
Tel: 306-453-2434
Trent Truscott, Contact

Carnduff: Sunset Haven
Affiliated with: Sun Country Health Region
PO Box 250, 415 Spencer St., Carnduff, SK S0C 0S0
Tel: 306-482-3424
Number of Beds: 40 beds
Note: Programs & services included: Long-term care; Home care; Palliative care
Cindy Simpson, Contact

Cupar: Cupar & District Nursing Home Inc.
Affiliated with: Regina Qu'Appelle Health Region
PO Box 310, 213 Mills St., Cupar, SK S0G 0Y0
Tel: 306-723-4666; *Fax:* 306-723-4248
Number of Beds: 48 beds

Duck Lake: Goodwill Manor
Affiliated with: Saskatoon Health Region
PO Box 370, Duck Lake, SK S0K 1J0
Tel: 306-467-4440; *Fax:* 306-467-2220
Number of Beds: 30 beds

Estevan: Estevan Regional Nursing Home
Affiliated with: Sun Country Health Region
1921 Wallock Rd., Estevan, SK S4A 2B5
Tel: 306-634-2689
Christine Stephany, Contact

Eston: Jubilee Lodge Inc.
Affiliated with: Heartland Regional Health Authority
PO Box 667, 800 Main St., Eston, SK S0L 1A0
Tel: 306-962-3667; *Fax:* 306-962-3900

Foam Lake: Foam Lake Jubilee Home
Affiliated with: Sunrise Regional Health Authority
PO Box 460, 421 Alberta Ave. East, Foam Lake, SK S0A 1A0
Tel: 306-272-4141; *Fax:* 306-272-4973
Number of Beds: 52 beds

Grenfell: Grenfell & District Pioneer Home
Affiliated with: Regina Qu'Appelle Health Region
PO Box 760, 710 Regina Ave., Grenfell, SK S0G 2B0
Tel: 306-697-2842; *Fax:* 306-697-2280

Indian Head: Golden Prairie Home
Affiliated with: Regina Qu'Appelle Health Region
PO Box 250, 916 Eden St., Indian Head, SK S0G 2K0
Tel: 306-695-3636; *Fax:* 306-695-2698
Number of Beds: 38 beds
Population Served: 1800

Kelvington: Kelvindell Lodge
Affiliated with: Kelsey Trail Regional Health Authority
PO Box 280, 701 - 6 Ave. West, Kelvington, SK S0A 1W0
Tel: 306-327-5505; *Fax:* 306-327-4504
Number of Beds: 46 beds

Kindersley: Heritage Manor
Affiliated with: Heartland Regional Health Authority
1003 - 1st St. West, Kindersley, SK S0L 1S2
Tel: 306-463-2611; *Fax:* 306-465-4550

Kinistino: Jubilee Lodge
Affiliated with: Prince Albert Parkland Regional Health Authority
PO Box 370, 410 Myers Ave., Kinistino, SK S0J 1H0
Tel: 306-864-2851; *Fax:* 306-864-3220
Number of Employees: 50

Kipling: Willowdale Lodge
Affiliated with: Sun Country Health Region
PO Box 537, 128 - 4 St. South, Kipling, SK S0G 2S0
Tel: 306-736-2218

Langham: Langham Senior Citizens Home
Affiliated with: Saskatoon Health Region
PO Box 287, 140 Main St. East, Langham, SK S0K 2L0
Tel: 306-283-4210; *Fax:* 306-283-4212
www.saskatoonhealthregion.ca
Year Founded: 1971
Number of Beds: 28 beds
Specialties: Restorative & supportive care

Leader: Western Senior Citizens Home
Affiliated with: Cypress Regional Health Authority
PO Box 69, 400 - 1 St. West, Leader, SK S0N 1H0
Tel: 306-628-3565
Number of Beds: 36 beds

Leask: Wheatland Lodge
Affiliated with: Prince Albert Parkland Health Region
PO Box 130, 971 - 2 St. North, Leask, SK S0J 1M0
Tel: 306-466-4949; *Fax:* 306-466-2209

Lumsden: Lumsden & District Heritage Home Inc.
Affiliated with: Regina Qu'Appelle Health Region
PO Box 479, Lumsden, SK S0G 3C0
Tel: 306-731-2247
Number of Beds: 30 long-term care beds
Note: Programs & services include: assisted living services for seniors; Adult day support program

Maple Creek: Cypress Lodge Nursing Home
Affiliated with: Cypress Regional Health Authority
PO Box 1330, 510 Hwy. 21 South, Maple Creek, SK S0N 1N0
Tel: 306-662-2671
Number of Beds: 48 beds
Specialties: Long term care services; Exercise maintenance programs

Melfort: Nirvana Pioneer Villa
300 Burns Ave. East, Melfort, SK S0E 1A0
Tel: 306-752-2116; *Fax:* 306-752-4099

Melfort: Parkland Place
Affiliated with: Kelsey Trail Regional Health Authority
Former Name: Parkland Care Centre
PO Box 2260, 402 Bemister Ave. East, Melfort, SK S0E 1A0
Tel: 306-752-1777; *Fax:* 306-752-3170
Number of Beds: 103 long-term care beds; 2 respite beds
Specialties: Acquired brain injury program

Melville: St. Paul Lutheran Home
Affiliated with: Sunrise Regional Health Authority
PO Box 1390, 100 Heritage Dr., Melville, SK S0A 2P0
Tel: 306-728-7340; *Fax:* 306-728-5471
Number of Beds: 128 long term care beds; 1 respite bed
Note: Long-term care facility affiliated with the Evangelical Lutheran Church in Canada

Moose Jaw: Extendicare - Moose Jaw
Extendicare Canada
1151 Coteau St. West, Moose Jaw, SK S6H 5G5
Tel: 306-693-5191; *Fax:* 306-692-1770
cnh_moosejaw@extendicare.com
www.extendicarecanada.com/moosejaw/index.aspx
Number of Beds: 127 beds
Specialties: Nursing & supportive care; Rehabilitation services; Therapeutic & social programs

Moose Jaw: Pioneer Housing Lodge & Village
Affiliated with: Five Hills Regional Health Authority
1000 Albert St., Moose Jaw, SK S6H 2Y2
Tel: 306-693-4616; *Fax:* 306-692-0771
Number of Beds: Long Term Care: 60; Convalescent, Palliate, Respite Care: 14; Seniors Housing Units: 24 Married, 37 Single

Moose Jaw: Providence Place
Affiliated with: Five Hills Regional Health Authority
100 - 2nd Ave. NE, Moose Jaw, SK S6H 1B8
Tel: 306-694-8081; *Fax:* 306-694-8804
www.provplace.ca
Number of Beds: 174 beds
Note: Geriatric long-term care, assessment & rehabilitation

Nipawin: Pineview Lodge
Affiliated with: Kelsey Trail Regional Health Authority
PO Box 2105, 400 - 6th Ave. East, Nipawin, SK S0E 1E0
Tel: 306-862-9828; *Fax:* 306-862-2400
Number of Beds: 95 long term care beds; 1 respite bed
Note: Program & services include: long-term care; dementia care unit; day care services; respite care

North Battleford: River Heights Lodge
Affiliated with: Prairie North Health Region
2001 - 99 St., North Battleford, SK S9A 0S3
Tel: 306-446-6950; *Fax:* 306-445-6032
Note: Special care home

Ponteix: Foyer St. Joseph Nursing Home
Affiliated with: Cypress Regional Health Authority
428 - 2 Ave., Ponteix, SK S0N 1Z0
Tel: 306-625-3366; *Fax:* 306-625-3764
Year Founded: 1958
Number of Beds: 32 beds
Number of Employees: 50

Porcupine Plain: Red Deer Nursing Home
Affiliated with: Kelsey Trail Regional Health Authority
PO Box 70, 330 Oak St., Porcupine Plain, SK S0E 1H0
Tel: 306-278-2469; *Fax:* 306-278-3088
Number of Beds: 38 long-term care beds

Preeceville: Preeceville & District Health Centre - Long Term Care Facility
Affiliated with: Sunrise Regional Health Authority
PO Box 348, 712 - 7 St. NE, Preeceville, SK S0A 3B0
Tel: 306-547-3112; *Fax:* 306-547-3215
Number of Beds: 38 long term care beds; 10 acute care beds; 2 respite beds

Redvers: Redvers Centennial Haven
Affiliated with: Sun Country Health Region
PO Box 30, 18 Eichhorst St., Redvers, SK S0C 2H0
Tel: 306-452-3553; *Fax:* 306-452-3556
Number of Beds: 24 beds

Regina: Extendicare - Elmview
Extendicare Canada
Affiliated with: Regina Qu'Appelle Health Region
4125 Rae St., Regina, SK S4S 3A5
Tel: 306-586-1787; *Fax:* 306-585-0255
www.extendicarecanada.com/reginaelmview
Number of Beds: 62 beds

Regina: Extendicare - Parkside
Extendicare Canada
Affiliated with: Regina Qu'Appelle Health Region
4540 Rae St., Regina, SK S4S 3B4
Tel: 306-586-0220; *Fax:* 306-585-0622
www.extendicarecanada.com/reginaparkside
Number of Beds: 228 beds

Regina: Extendicare - Sunset
Extendicare Canada
Affiliated with: Regina Qu'Appelle Health Region
260 Sunset Dr., Regina, SK S4S 2S3
Tel: 306-586-3355; *Fax:* 306-584-8082
www.extendicarecanada.com/reginasunset

Regina: Qu'Appelle House
Affiliated with: Regina Qu'Appelle Health Region
1425 College Ave., Regina, SK S4P 1B4
Tel: 306-522-0335; *Fax:* 306-522-4800

Regina: Regina Lutheran Home
Affiliated with: Eden Care Communities
1925 - 5 Ave. North, Regina, SK S4R 7W1
Tel: 306-543-4055; *Fax:* 306-543-4094
info@edencare.ca
www.myedencare.ca
Number of Beds: 91 beds
Note: Nursing home

Regina: Regina Pioneer Village Ltd.
Affiliated with: Regina Qu'Appelle Health Region
430 Pioneer Dr., Regina, SK S4T 6L8
Tel: 306-757-5646; *Fax:* 306-757-5001
Year Founded: 1955
Number of Beds: 390 beds

Regina: Santa Maria Senior Citizens Home
Affiliated with: Regina Qu'Appelle Health Region
4215 Regina Ave., Regina, SK S4S 0J5
Tel: 306-766-7100; *Fax:* 306-766-7115
SantaMariaGeneral@rqhealth.ca
santamariaregina.ca
Number of Beds: 147 beds
John Kelly, Executive Director

Rosetown: Wheatbelt Centennial Lodge
Affiliated with: Heartland Regional Health Authority
PO Box 250, Rosetown, SK S0L 2V0
Tel: 306-882-2672; *Fax:* 306-882-3335

Rosthern: Mennonite Nursing Home Inc.
Affiliated with: Saskatoon Health Region
PO Box 370, Hwy. 11 South, Rosthern, SK S0K 3R0
Tel: 306-232-4861; *Fax:* 306-232-5611
www.saskatoonhealthregion.ca
Year Founded: 1963
Number of Beds: 68
Note: Specialties: Long-term care; Adult Day Program
Joan Lemauviel, Administrator

Saltcoats: Lakeside Manor Care Home Inc.
Affiliated with: Sunrise Regional Health Authority
PO Box 340, 101 Crescent Lake Rd., Saltcoats, SK S0A 3R0
Tel: 306-744-2353; *Fax:* 306-744-2414
Number of Beds: 29 beds, 1 respite

Saskatoon: Central Haven Special Care Home
Affiliated with: Saskatoon Health Region
1020 Ave. I North, Saskatoon, SK S7L 2H7
Tel: 306-665-6180; *Fax:* 306-665-5540
www.sherbrookecommunitycentre.ca
Number of Beds: 60 beds

Saskatoon: Jubilee Residences
Affiliated with: Saskatoon Health Region
#25, 2602 Taylor St. East, Saskatoon, SK S7H 1X2
Tel: 306-955-0234; *Fax:* 306-373-8828
www.jubileeresidences.ca
Year Founded: 1955
Specialties: Nursing & personal care; Physical & occupational therapy
Note: Long term care is provided to 200 older adults at Stensrud & Porteous Lodges. Independent living suites are available for approximately 300 older adults at the Cosmopolitan, Eamer, & Mount Royal facilities.
Yvonne Morgan, CEO
Bob Cowan, Chair

Saskatoon: Oliver Lodge
Affiliated with: Saskatoon Health Region
1405 Faulkner Cres., Saskatoon, SK S7L 3R5
Tel: 306-986-5462; *Fax:* 306-382-9822
www.oliverlodge.ca
Year Founded: 1949
Number of Beds: 139 beds
Note: Specialties: Specialized services for persons with dementia; Day program for seniors; Respite care
Brandon Little, Executive Director
306-986-5462

Saskatoon: Parkridge Centre
Affiliated with: Saskatoon Health Region
110 Gropper Cres., Saskatoon, SK S7M 5N9
Tel: 306-655-3800; *Fax:* 306-655-3801
Number of Beds: 237 beds

Saskatoon: Porteous Lodge
Jubilee Residences
Affiliated with: Saskatoon Health Region
833 Ave. PN, Saskatoon, SK S7L 2W5
Tel: 306-382-2626; *Fax:* 306-382-2633
www.jubileeresidences.ca
Number of Beds: 95 beds

Saskatoon: St. Ann's Home
Affiliated with: Saskatoon Health Region
2910 Louise St., Saskatoon, SK S7J 3L8
Tel: 306-374-8900; *Fax:* 306-477-2623
catholichealth.ca
Year Founded: 1953
Number of Beds: 80 beds
Number of Employees: 135
Note: Affiliated with the Catholic Health Ministry of Saskatchewan
Rae Sveinbjornson, Executive Director
rae.sveinbjornson@saskatoonhealthreg

Saskatoon: St. Joseph's Home
Affiliated with: Saskatoon Health Region
33 Valens Dr., Saskatoon, SK S7L 3S2
Tel: 306-382-6306; *Fax:* 306-384-0140
Number of Beds: 85 beds

***Saskatoon:* Samaritan Place**
Affiliated with: Saskatoon Health Region
375 Cornish Rd., Saskatoon, SK S7T 0P3
Tel: 306-986-1460; *Fax:* 306-986-1464
reception@samaritanplace.ca
www.samaritanplace.ca
Social Media: www.facebook.com/pages/Samaritan-Place-Corp/181815878562092
Number of Beds: 100 beds
Lynne Kohle, Executive Director

***Saskatoon:* Saskatoon Convalescent Home**
Affiliated with: Saskatoon Health Region
101 - 31 St. West, Saskatoon, SK S7L 0P6
Tel: 306-244-7155; *Fax:* 306-244-2066
www.saskatoonconvalescenthome.com
Number of Beds: 60 beds
Gwen Peterson, Chief Executive Officer
gwen.peterson@saskatoonhealthregion.

***Saskatoon:* Sherbrooke Community Centre**
Affiliated with: Saskatoon Health Region
401 Acadia Dr., Saskatoon, SK S7H 2E7
Tel: 306-655-3600; *Fax:* 306-655-3727
www.sherbrookecommunitycentre.ca
Social Media: www.facebook.com/SherbrookeCommunityCentre; twitter.com/SherbrookeCC
Year Founded: 1966
Number of Beds: 263 beds
Number of Employees: 500
Note: Long-term care home. Also provides a Community Day Program for 100 local residents
Suellen Beatty, CEO

***Saskatoon:* Stensrud Lodge**
Jubilee Residences
Affiliated with: Saskatoon Health Region
2202 McEown Ave., Saskatoon, SK S7J 3L6
Tel: 306-373-5580; *Fax:* 306-477-0308
www.jubileeresidences.ca
Number of Beds: 100 beds

***Saskatoon:* Sunnyside Adventist Care Centre**
Affiliated with: Saskatoon Health Region
Former Name: Sunnyside Nursing Home
2200 St. Henry Ave., Saskatoon, SK S7M 0P5
Tel: 306-653-1267; *Fax:* 306-653-7223
www.sunnysidecare.ca
Year Founded: 1964
Note: Specialties: Nursing care; Physiotherapy; Activity program; Palliative care
Randy Kurtz, Adminstrator
Randy.Kurtz@saskatoonhealthregion.ca

***Spiritwood:* Idylwild Lodge**
PO Box 159, Spiritwood, SK S0J 2M0
Tel: 306-883-2267
Number of Beds: 35 beds
Carroll Joyes, Director, Care
Louis Willick, Director, Maintenance

***Stoughton:* New Hope Pioneer Lodge Inc.**
Affiliated with: Sun Country Health Region
PO Box 38, 123 Government Rd. North, Stoughton, SK S0G 4T0
Tel: 306-457-2552
Linda Wilson, Contact

***Swift Current:* Palliser Regional Care Centre**
Affiliated with: Cypress Regional Health Authority
440 Central Ave. South, Swift Current, SK S9H 3G6
Tel: 306-778-5160
Number of Beds: 94 beds

***Swift Current:* Prairie Pioneers Lodge**
Affiliated with: Cypress Regional Health Authority
302 Central Ave. South, Swift Current, SK S9H 3G3
Tel: 306-778-5192
Number of Beds: 41 beds

***Swift Current:* Swift Current Care Centre (SCCC)**
Affiliated with: Cypress Regional Health Authority
700 Aberdeen St. SE, Swift Current, SK S9H 3E3
Tel: 306-778-9371
Number of Beds: 63 beds
Note: Programs & services include: Nursing care from Registered Nurses, Registered Psychiatric Nurses, & Licensed Practical Nurses; Social work; Activity program; Respite care program

***Tisdale:* Newmarket Manor**
Affiliated with: Kelsey Trail Regional Health Authority
PO Box 2620, 2001 Newmarket Dr., Tisdale, SK S0E 1T0
Tel: 306-873-6550; *Fax:* 306-873-4822
Number of Beds: 40 beds

***Tisdale:* Sasko Park Lodge**
Affiliated with: Kelsey Trail Regional Health Authority
806 - 97 Ave., Tisdale, SK S0E 1T0
Tel: 306-873-4585; *Fax:* 306-873-2404
Number of Beds: 33 beds

***Waldheim:* Menno Homes of Saskatchewan Inc.**
PO Box 130, 4006 - 3 Ave. South, Waldheim, SK S0K 4R0
Tel: 306-945-2070; *Fax:* 306-945-4641
menno.homes@sasktel.net
mennohomes.ca
Year Founded: 1963
Number of Beds: 105 residential capacity
Note: Number of Employees: 105
Tanya Mitzel, Executive Director
306-945-2070, tmitzel@mennohomes.ca

***Watrous:* Manitou Lodge**
Affiliated with: Saskatoon Health Region
PO Box 130, Watrous, SK S0K 4T0
Tel: 306-946-1200; *Fax:* 306-946-2396
Number of Beds: 43 beds

***Wawota:* Deer View Lodge**
Affiliated with: Sun Country Health Region
PO Box 240, 201 Wilfred St., Wawota, SK S0G 5A0
Tel: 306-739-2400
Number of Beds: 30 beds
Note: Area Served: Regional Municipality of Walpole; Regional Municipality of Wawken; Regional Municipality of Maryfield; Wawota; Maryfield; Fairlight; half the villages of Kennedy & Kenosee, & half the Regional Municipality of Moose Mountain

***Wolseley:* Lakeside Home**
Affiliated with: Regina Qu'Appelle Health Region
PO Box 10, 710 Quimet St., Wolseley, SK S0G 5H0
Tel: 306-698-4400; *Fax:* 306-698-4401
Number of Beds: 80 beds
Area Served: Wolseley, SK
Specialties: Long term care
Note: Lakeside Home is linked to Wolseley Memorial Hospital.

***Wynyard:* Golden Acres**
Affiliated with: Saskatoon Health Region
300 - 10 St. East, Wynyard, SK S0A 4V0
Tel: 306-554-2586; *Fax:* 306-554-2247
Number of Beds: 59 beds
Population Served: 1800

***Yorkton:* Yorkton & District Nursing Home Corporation**
Affiliated with: Sunrise Regional Health Authority
200 Bradbrooke Dr., Yorkton, SK S3N 2K5
Tel: 306-786-0801; *Fax:* 306-786-0808
Number of Beds: 211 long term care beds; 5 respite beds; 5 program beds; 3 stroke beds; 4 transition beds

Personal Care Homes

***Avonlea:* Coteau Range Manor**
Affiliated with: Five Hills Regional Health Authority
PO Box 60, 210 New Warren Pl., Avonlea, SK S0H 0C0
Tel: 306-868-2033; *Fax:* 306-868-4790
Number of Beds: 30 beds
Note: Respite care is available at the personal care home.

***Bangor:* Morris Lodge Society Inc.**
PO Box 54, Lots 4-12, Block 6, Main St., Bangor, SK S0A 0E0
Tel: 306-728-5322; *Fax:* 306-728-2048
Number of Beds: 20 beds

***Beechy:* Beechy Community Care Home**
209 Railway Ave., Beechy, SK S0L 0C0
Tel: 306-859-4470; *Fax:* 306-859-4470
bcch@sasktel.net
www.beechysask.ca
Number of Beds: 10
Note: Personal care is provided to ten elderly residents.
Noel Taylor, Contact

***Codette:* Serenity Lane**
Affiliated with: Kelsey Trail Regional Health Authority
PO Box 152, Codette, SK S0E 0P0
Tel: 306-862-2579
Number of Beds: 10 beds
Debbie Karlee

***Eatonia:* Eatonia Oasis Living Inc.**
Former Name: Eatonia Personal Care Home
PO Box 217, 205, 2nd Ave. W, Eatonia, SK S0L 0Y0
Tel: 306-967-2447; *Fax:* 306-967-2373
eatoniaoasisliving.com
Number of Beds: 16 single rooms; 4 double rooms
Lorraine Bews, Chairperson

***Estevan:* Creighton Lodge**
1028 Hillcrest Dr., Estevan, SK S4A 1Y7
Tel: 306-634-4154; *Fax:* 306-634-2396
Number of Beds: 44 suites
Number of Employees: 11

***Herbert:* Herbert Heritage Manor**
Former Name: Herbert Senior Citizens Home
PO Box 10, Herbert, SK S0H 2A0
Tel: 306-784-3167; *Fax:* 306-784-3456
Year Founded: 1962
Note: Personal care home level 1 & 2

***Kamsack:* Eaglestone Lodge Personal Care Home Inc.**
PO Box 1330, 346 Miles St., Kamsack, SK S0A 1S0
Tel: 306-542-2620; *Fax:* 306-542-4342
eaglestone@sasktel.net
Number of Beds: 42 beds

***Moose Jaw:* Capilano Court**
Affiliated with: Five Hills Regional Health Authority
1236 - 3rd Ave. NW, Moose Jaw, SK S6H 3V3
Tel: 306-693-4518

***Moose Jaw:* Chez Nous Senior Citizens Home**
Affiliated with: Five Hills Regional Health Authority
1101 Grafton Ave., Moose Jaw, SK S6H 3S4
Tel: 306-693-4371
chez.nous@sasktel.net
www.cheznoushome.ca

***Moose Jaw:* Oxford Place Inc.**
1007 Main St. North, Moose Jaw, SK S6H 0X1
Tel: 306-692-2837

***Moose Jaw:* Valley View Centre**
PO Box 1300, 7th Ave., Moose Jaw, SK S6H 4R2
Tel: 306-694-3000; *Fax:* 306-694-3003
Number of Beds: 348 beds
Terry Hardy, Director

***Oxbow:* Bow Valley Villa Corp.**
319 Wylie Ave., Oxbow, SK S0C 2B0
Tel: 306-483-2744; *Fax:* 306-483-2915

***Pangman:* Deep South Personal Care Home**
PO Box 150, 211 Keeler St., Pangman, SK S0C 2C0
Tel: 306-442-2043; *Fax:* 306-442-4261
Number of Beds: 25 beds
Note: Deep South Care Home is a private personal care home for 25 residents.
Gail Santon, Administrator

***Ponteix:* Bridges Personal Care**
PO Box 148, 332 - 2 St. West, Ponteix, SK S0N 1Z0
Tel: 306-625-3511

***Prince Albert:* Nelson Care Home Ltd.**
Affiliated with: Prince Albert Parkland Regional Health Authority
1336 - 7th St. East, Prince Albert, SK S6V 0V1
Tel: 306-922-9506

***Rosthern:* Rosthern Mennonite Home for the Aged**
PO Box 370, Rosthern, SK S0K 3R0
Tel: 306-232-4861; *Fax:* 306-232-5611
joan.lemauviel@saskatoonhealthregion.ca
www.yfbc.ca
Number of Beds: 63 beds
Jacob Loewen, Chair

***Saskatoon:* Arbor Villa Care Home Inc.**
202 Lewis Cres., Saskatoon, SK S7L 7H5
Tel: 306-384-1419
yourcarehome@shaw.ca
www.arborvillacarehomeinc.ca
Note: The personal care home offers respite care.

Agnes Lopez, Operator

Saskatoon: Ashton Care Home Inc.
Affiliated with: Saskatoon Health Region
438 Ave. Y North, Saskatoon, SK S7L 3L2
Tel: 306-382-8975
Number of Beds: 7 single bedrooms; 2 double bedrooms
Note: Respite care is available.
Emyou Mekonnen, Contact

Saskatoon: Balicanta Personal Care Home
Affiliated with: Saskatoon Health Region
Also Known As: Balicanta Holdings Ltd.
510 Spencer Cres., Saskatoon, SK S7K 7T4
Tel: 306-934-5903; *Fax:* 306-934-5903
Number of Beds: 6 single bedrooms; 3 double bedrooms
Note: Personal care is provided for twelve residents. Respite care is available.
I. Balicanta, Contact

Saskatoon: Bergman's Private Home Care
Affiliated with: Saskatoon Health Region
333 LaRonge Rd., Saskatoon, SK S7K 4S1
Tel: 306-934-2031; *Fax:* 306-934-2031

Saskatoon: Betty Sandulak Personal Care Home
122 Adilman Dr., Saskatoon, SK S7K 7S5
Tel: 306-931-7859
Note: Respite care is available.

Saskatoon: Cabello Personal Care Home
518/520 Russell Rd., Saskatoon, SK S7K 6L6
Tel: 306-242-6501
Note: Specialties: Diabetic care; Respite care
Marionela Cabello, Contact

Saskatoon: Fairhaven Care Home Inc.
Affiliated with: Saskatoon Health Region
139 Olmstead Rd., Saskatoon, SK S7M 4L9
Tel: 306-974-1156
Number of Beds: 6 single rooms; 3 double rooms
Note: Respite care is available.

Saskatoon: Marg's Care Home Ltd.
Affiliated with: Saskatoon Health Region
310 Adilman Dr., Saskatoon, SK S7K 7K5
Tel: 306-222-2805
carolbrosnan7@hotmail.com
Info Line: 306-975-1189

Shellbrook: T.L.C. Personal Care Home
308 - 3rd Ave. East, Shellbrook, SK S0J 2E0
Tel: 306-747-3123
Year Founded: 1997

Speers: Oasis Personal Care Home
Affiliated with: Prince Albert Parkland Regional Health Authority
PO Box 26, Speers, SK S0M 2V0
Tel: 306-246-2067; *Fax:* 306-246-2028
info@oasiscarehome.ca
www.oasiscarehome.ca
Year Founded: 1993
Delbert Miller, Co-Owner; Operator
Sheila Miller, Co-Owner; Operator

St Louis: McDougall Wings Care Home
457 River Rd., St Louis, SK S0J 2C0
Tel: 306-422-8223
Lynn Regnier

Theodore: Theodore Health Centre
Affiliated with: Sunrise Regional Health Authority
PO Box 70, 615 Anderson Ave., Theodore, SK S0A 4C0
Tel: 306-647-2115; *Fax:* 306-647-2238
Number of Beds: 19 beds (18 long term care beds, 1 respite/palliative care bed)
Note: Specialties: Long-term care; Nursing services; Phlebotomy service; Respite care; Palliative care

Watson: Quill Plains Centennial Lodge
Affiliated with: Saskatoon Health Region
PO Box 459, Watson, SK S0K 4V0
Tel: 306-287-3791; *Fax:* 306-287-4444
Number of Beds: 53 beds

Weyburn: Crocus Plains Villa Ltd.
Affiliated with: Sun Country Health Region
1135 Park Ave., Weyburn, SK S4H 0K6
Tel: 306-842-0616; *Fax:* 306-842-2361
nickturanich@sasktel.net
www.crocusplainsvilla.com
Note: Care planning is provided by a multidisciplinary team. Crocus Plains Villa features a secured area for persons with a cognitive impairment. The personal care home also offers respite care.
Nick Turanich, President
nickturanich@sasktel.net

Weyburn: Parkway Lodge Personal Care Home
Affiliated with: Sun Country Health Region
420 - 8 Ave. SE, Weyburn, SK S4H 3N2
Tel: 306-842-7868; *Fax:* 306-842-6808
parkwaylodge@gmail.com
www.parkwaylodge.ca
Number of Beds: 23 suites

Weyburn: Tatagwa View
Affiliated with: Sun Country Health Region
Former Name: Souris Valley Extended Care Centre
PO Box 2003, 808 Souris Valley Rd., Weyburn, SK S4H 2Z9
Tel: 306-842-8398
Year Founded: 2005
Note: Programs & services include: long-term care; mental health services (10 beds); acquired brain injury services; diabetes program; rehabilitation services; day care centre; palliative care
Marnell Cornish, Administrator

Mental Health Hospitals/Facilities

Arcola: Arcola Mental Health Clinic
Affiliated with: Sun Country Health Region
PO Box 419, Arcola, SK S0C 0G0
Tel: 306-455-2159
Note: Programs & services include: children's mental health.

Cumberland House: Cumberland House Addiction Services
Affiliated with: Kelsey Trail Regional Health Authority
PO Box 218, Cumberland House, SK S0E 0S0
Tel: 306-888-2155; *Fax:* 306-888-4633

Estevan: Estevan Mental Health Clinic
Affiliated with: Sun Country Health Region
1174 Nicholson Rd., Estevan, SK S4A 2V3
Tel: 306-637-3610
Note: Programs & services include: children's mental health.

Kipling: Kipling Mental Health Clinic
Affiliated with: Sun Country Health Region
PO Box 420, Kipling, SK S0G 2S0
Tel: 306-736-2638
Note: Programs & services include: children's mental health.

Lloydminster: Lloydminster Mental Health & Addictions Services
Affiliated with: Prairie North Health Region
3830 - 43 Ave., Lloydminster, SK S9V 1Y3
Tel: 306-820-6250; *Fax:* 306-820-6256

Melfort: Sakwatamo Lodge
Affiliated with: Prince Albert Parkland Health Region
PO Box 3917, Melfort, SK S0E 1A0
Tel: 306-864-3631; *Fax:* 306-864-2204
Note: Programs & services include: addiction services; family support; suicide prevention.

Prince Albert: Addiction Services Prince Albert
Affiliated with: Prince Albert Parkland Health Region
101 - 15th St. East, Prince Albert, SK S6V 1G1
Tel: 306-765-6550; *Fax:* 306-765-6567

Prince Albert: White Buffalo Youth Inhalant Treatment Centre
Affiliated with: Prince Albert Parkland Health Region
PO Box 2350, Prince Albert, SK S6V 6Z1
Tel: 306-764-5250; *Fax:* 306-764-5255
Note: Programs & services include: family support; suicide prevention; addiction services.

Weyburn: Weyburn Mental Health Clinic
Affiliated with: Sun Country Health Region
PO Box 2003, Weyburn, SK S4H 2Z9
Tel: 306-842-8660
Note: Programs & services include: children's mental health.

Yorkton: Sunrise Regional Health Authority Mental Health & Addiction Services
Affiliated with: Sunrise Regional Health Authority
270 Bradbrooke Dr., Yorkton, SK S3N 2K6
Tel: 306-786-0558; *Fax:* 306-786-0556
Number of Beds: 18 inpatient and assessment beds
Note: Programs & services include: adult community services; rehabilitation services; child & youth services.

Special Care Homes

Arborfield: Arborfield Special Care Lodge
Affiliated with: Kelsey Trail Regional Health Authority
PO Box 160, 509 - 5th Ave., Arborfield, SK S0E 0A0
Tel: 306-769-8757; *Fax:* 306-769-8759
www.kelseytrailhealth.ca
Number of Beds: 36 beds
Sharon Frisky, Community Coordinator

Battleford: Battlefords District Care Centre
Affiliated with: Prairie North Health Region
PO Box 69, Battleford, SK S0M 0E0
Tel: 306-446-6900; *Fax:* 306-937-2258

Canora: Canora Gateway Lodge
Affiliated with: Sunrise Regional Health Authority
PO Box 1387, 212 Centre Ave. East, Canora, SK S0A 0L0
Tel: 306-563-5685; *Fax:* 306-563-5711
Number of Beds: 63 long-term beds; 1 respite

Carrot River: Pasquia Special Care Home
Affiliated with: Kelsey Trail Regional Health Authority
PO Box 250, 4101 - 1 Ave West, Carrot River, SK S0E 0L0
Tel: 306-768-2725; *Fax:* 306-768-3233
Number of Beds: 35 long-term care beds

Dalmeny: Spruce Manor Special Care Home
Affiliated with: Saskatoon Health Region
PO Box 190, 701 - 1st St., Dalmeny, SK S0K 1E0
Tel: 306-254-2101; *Fax:* 306-254-2178
sprucemanor.mennonite.net
Year Founded: 1950
Number of Beds: 36 beds

Esterhazy: Centennial Special Care Home
Affiliated with: Sunrise Regional Health Authority
PO Box 310, 300 James St., Esterhazy, SK S0A 0X0
Tel: 306-745-6444; *Fax:* 306-745-2741
Number of Beds: 52 long term care beds; 1 respite bed

Fort Qu'appelle: Echo Lodge Special Care Home
Affiliated with: Regina Qu'Appelle Health Region
PO Box 1790, 560 Broadway St. West, Fort Qu'appelle, SK S0G 1S0
Tel: 306-332-4300; *Fax:* 306-332-5708
Number of Beds: 50 beds
Note: Adult day care & respite care are available.

Herbert: Herbert Nursing Home Inc.
Affiliated with: Cypress Regional Health Authority
PO Box 520, 405 Herbert Ave., Herbert, SK S0H 2A0
Tel: 306-784-2466
Year Founded: 1951
Number of Beds: 48 beds

Humboldt: St. Mary's Villa
Affiliated with: Saskatoon Health Region
PO Box 1360, 1109 - 13 St. North, Humboldt, SK S0K 2A0
Tel: 306-682-2628; *Fax:* 306-682-3211
Number of Beds: 85 beds

Langenburg: Centennial Special Care Home
Affiliated with: Sunrise Regional Health Authority
PO Box 370, 407 - 2 St. South, Langenburg, SK S0A 2A0
Tel: 306-743-2232; *Fax:* 306-743-5025
Number of Beds: 44 long-term care beds; 2 respite beds; 1 palliative care bed

Mankota: Prairie View Health Centre
Affiliated with: Cypress Regional Health Authority
PO Box 390, 241 - 1 Ave., Mankota, SK S0H 2W0
Tel: 306-478-2200
Number of Beds: 20 beds

Meadow Lake: Northland Pioneers Lodge Inc.
Affiliated with: Prairie North Health Region
515 - 3 St. West, Meadow Lake, SK S9X 1L1
Tel: 306-236-5812

North Battleford: Villa Pascal
Affiliated with: Prairie North Health Region
Also Known As: Société Joseph Breton Inc.
1301 - 113 St., North Battleford, SK S9A 3K1
Tel: 306-445-8465; *Fax:* 306-445-5117

Prince Albert: Herb Bassett Home
Affiliated with: Prince Albert Parkland Regional Health Authority
PO Box 3000, 1220 - 25 St. West, Prince Albert, SK S6V 5T4
Tel: 306-765-6000; *Fax:* 306-765-6207

Note: Herb Basset Home hosts an adult day program.

Prince Albert: **Mont St. Joseph Home Inc.**
Affiliated with: Prince Albert Parkland Regional Health Authority
777 - 28 St. East, Prince Albert, SK S6V 8C2
Tel: 306-953-4500; *Fax:* 306-953-4550
montstjoseph.org
Social Media: www.facebook.com/pages/Mont-St-Joseph-Home/176717885855784
Year Founded: 1956
Number of Beds: 120 beds
Note: Special care home
Brian Martin, Executive Director

Raymore: **Silver Heights Special Care Home**
Affiliated with: Regina Qu'Appelle Health Region
PO Box 549, 402 McLean St., Raymore, SK S0A 3J0
Tel: 306-746-5744; *Fax:* 306-746-5747
Number of Beds: 29 beds
Population Served: 600

Regina: **Salvation Army William Booth Special Care Home**
Affiliated with: Regina Qu'Appelle Health Region
50 Angus Rd., Regina, SK S4R 8P6
Tel: 306-543-0655; *Fax:* 306-543-1292
www.williamboothregina.ca
Number of Beds: 53 beds
Ivy Scobie, Executive Director

Saskatoon: **Circle Drive Special Care Home Inc.**
Affiliated with: Saskatoon Health Region
3055 Preston Ave. South, Saskatoon, SK S7T 1C3
Tel: 306-955-4800; *Fax:* 306-955-2376
circlecare@saskatoonhealthregion.ca
circledrivespecialcarehome.ca
Number of Beds: 53 beds
Diane Martin, Director of Care
Clint Kinchen, Administrator
Brad Traill, Board Chair

Saskatoon: **Extendicare - Preston**
Extendicare Canada
Affiliated with: Saskatoon Health Region
2225 Preston Ave., Saskatoon, SK S7J 2E7
Tel: 306-374-2242; *Fax:* 306-373-2203
cnh_preston@extendicare.com
www.extendicarecanada.com/saskatoon/index.aspx
Number of Beds: 82 beds

Saskatoon: **Luther Seniors' Centre**
LutherCare Communities
1800 Alexandra Ave., Saskatoon, SK S7K 3C7
Tel: 306-664-0366; *Fax:* 306-664-0395
lsc@luthercare.com
www.luthercare.com
Year Founded: 1985
Note: Specialties: Day program for adults with irreversible dementia; Social services; Nursing; Personal care; Sensory stimulation

Saskatoon: **Luther Special Care Home**
LutherCare Communities
Affiliated with: Saskatoon Health Region
1212 Osler St., Saskatoon, SK S7N 0T9
Tel: 306-664-0300; *Fax:* 306-664-0311
www.luthercare.com
Year Founded: 1955
Number of Beds: 129 beds, including 49 special needs beds & 2 respite beds
Note: Specialties: Secure special needs unit for residents with cognitive impairment; Nursing care; Physio, occupational, & recreational therapy; Community day program for seniors at risk; Respite care

Saskatoon: **LutherCare Communities**
Affiliated with: Saskatoon Health Region
Former Name: Lutheran Sunset Home
Main Corporate Office, 1212 Osler St., Saskatoon, SK S7N 0T9
Tel: 306-664-0300; *Fax:* 306-664-0311
luthercare@shaw.ca
www.luthercare.com
Year Founded: 1955
Note: Specialties: Group living for young adults; Community day programs for adults; Home support; Intermediate care; Seniors' housing; Long-term nursing care

Strasbourg: **Last Mountain Pioneer Home**
Affiliated with: Saskatoon Health Region
PO Box 459, 700 Prospect Ave., Strasbourg, SK S0G 4V0
Tel: 306-725-3342; *Fax:* 306-725-3404
www.saskatoonhealthregion.ca
Number of Beds: 39 beds
Connie Fuessel, Manager

Tisdale: **Nipawin District Nursing Home**
Affiliated with: Kelsey Trail Regional Health Authority
PO Box 1780, Tisdale, SK S0E 1T0
Tel: 306-873-6600; *Fax:* 306-873-6605
tthompson@kthr.sk.ca
www.kelseytrailhealth.ca
Number of Beds: 96 beds

Warman: **Warman Mennonite Special Care Home**
Affiliated with: Saskatoon Health Region
PO Box 100, 201 Centennial Blvd., Warman, SK S0K 4S0
Tel: 306-933-2011; *Fax:* 306-933-2782
Number of Beds: 31 beds

Weyburn: **Weyburn Special Care Home**
Affiliated with: Sun Country Health Region
PO Box 2003, 704 - 5th St. NE, Weyburn, SK S4H 2Z9
Tel: 306-842-4455
Note: Programs & services include: dietician; home care; palliative care; respite care.
Debbie Obst, Contact

Yukon Territory

Government Departments in Charge

Whitehorse: **Yukon Health & Social Services**
PO Box 2703, Whitehorse, YT Y1A 2C6
Tel: 867-667-3673; *Fax:* 867-667-3096
Toll-Free: 800-661-0408
hss@gov.yk.ca
www.hss.gov.yk.ca
Social Media: www.facebook.com/yukonhss; twitter.com/HSSYukon; www.youtube.com/user/hssyukongovernment
Hon. Mike Nixon, Minister
Bruce McLennan, Deputy Minister

Hospitals - General

Dawson: **Dawson City Community Hospital**
Yukon Hospital Corporation
Former Name: Dawson City Health Centre
PO Box 870, 501 - 6th Ave., Dawson, YT Y0B 1G0
Tel: 867-993-4444; *Fax:* 867-993-4317
yukonhospitals.ca/dawson-city-hospital
Number of Beds: 6 beds
Number of Employees: 28
Note: Services offered by the Dawson Community Health Centre & Dawson Medical Clinic are now located within this facility. Programs & services include: ambulatory care; basic diagnostic & lab tests; communicable disease screening; diagnostic imaging; emergency; healthy lifestyle support; hearing services; house calls; immunizations; infant & preschool health exams; inpatient care; mental health services; palliative care; pharmacy; physiotherapy; pre & post-natal education; school health program; third party medical assessments; & travel health education & immunizations.
Jason Bilsky, Chief Executive Officer, Yukon Hospital Corporation

Watson Lake: **Watson Lake Hospital**
Yukon Hospital Corporation
817 Ravenhill Dr., Watson Lake, YT Y0A 1C0
Tel: 867-536-4444
yukonhospitals.ca/yukonhospitalsfacilities/watsonlake
Number of Beds: 6 beds
Number of Employees: 32
Note: Programs & services include: ambulatory care; convalescent care; diagnostic services (laboratory & medical imaging); emergency; First Nations health program; inpatient care; respite care; & stabilization, observation & monitoring.
Carol Chiasson, Facility Administrator
Jason Bilsky, Chief Executive Officer, Yukon Hospital Corporation

Whitehorse: **Whitehorse General Hospital (WGH)**
Yukon Hospital Corporation
5 Hospital Rd., Whitehorse, YT Y1A 3H7
Tel: 867-393-8700
www.whitehorsehospital.ca
Year Founded: 1902
Number of Beds: 55 beds
Number of Employees: 486
Specialties: Medical imaging services; Laboratory services; Diabetes Education Centre; Nutrition services; First Nations health programs; Therapy services
Note: Programs & services include: First Nations health programs; cancer care; cardiac stress testing; diabetes education; emergency; environmental; intensive care; laboratory; maternity; medical; medical imaging (CT scanning, digital mammography, MRI & ultrasound); nutrition; pediatrics; pharmacy; social work; specialists clinic; surgery; therapy; & pastoral care.
Dr. Sherillynne Himmelsbach, Medical Staff, Yukon Hospital Corporation

Community Health Care Centres

Beaver Creek: **Beaver Creek Health Centre**
General Delivery, Beaver Creek, YT Y0B 1A0
Tel: 867-862-4444; *Fax:* 867-862-7909

Carmacks: **Carmacks Health Centre**
PO Box 230, Carmacks, YT Y0B 1C0
Tel: 867-863-4444; *Fax:* 867-863-6612
carmacks.nic@gov.yk.ca
Number of Beds: 2 beds

Destruction Bay: **Destruction Bay Health Centre**
General Delivery, Destruction Bay, YT Y0B 1H0
Tel: 867-841-4444; *Fax:* 867-841-5274

Faro: **Faro Health Centre**
PO Box 99, Faro, YT Y0B 1K0
Tel: 867-994-4444; *Fax:* 867-994-3457

Haines Junction: **Haines Junction Health Centre**
PO Box 5334, Haines Junction, YT Y0B 1L0
Tel: 867-634-4444; *Fax:* 867-634-2733

Mayo: **Mayo Nursing Station**
PO Box 98, Mayo, YT Y0B 1M0
Tel: 867-996-4444; *Fax:* 867-996-2018
hc.mayo@gov.yk.ca
Note: Specialties: Public health services; Health promotion services; Home care services. Number of Employees: 1 doctor + 3 community nurse practitioners

Old Crow: **Old Crow Health Centre**
General Delivery, Old Crow, YT Y0B 1N0
Tel: 867-996-4444; *Fax:* 867-966-3614
www.oldcrow.ca/nursing
Year Founded: 1960
Note: Specialties: Nursing care; Health promotion; Home & community care

Pelly Crossing: **Pelly Crossing Health Centre**
General Delivery, Pelly Crossing, YT Y0B 1P0
Tel: 867-537-4444; *Fax:* 867-537-3611
hc.pelly-crossing@gov.yk.ca

Ross River: **Ross River Health Centre**
General Delivery, Ross River, YT Y0B 1S0
Tel: 867-969-4444; *Fax:* 867-969-2014

Teslin: **Teslin Health Centre**
General Delivery, Teslin, YT Y0A 1B0
Tel: 867-390-4444
Note: Specialties: Public health services; Health promotion; Clinical care by community nurses; Home care

Watson Lake: **Watson Lake Health Centre**
PO Box 500, Watson Lake, YT Y0A 1C0
Tel: 867-536-7483; *Fax:* 867-536-7011

Long Term Care Facilities

Dawson City: **Alexander McDonald Home for Seniors**
PO Box 310, 636 - 5th Ave., Dawson City, YT Y0B 1G0
Tel: 867-993-5345; *Fax:* 867-993-5849
Toll-Free: 800-661-0408
Number of Beds: 11 residential beds, including 2 respite beds
Note: Specialties: Residential care for seniors & physically challenged persons who require moderate assistance; Recreational & therapeutic activities; Respite care; Home support services; Palliative care

Whitehorse: **Copper Ridge Place**
60 Lazulite Dr., Whitehorse, YT Y1A 6S9
Tel: 867-393-7500; *Fax:* 867-393-7510
bev.oyler@gov.yk.ca
www.hss.gov.yk.ca/copperridgeplace.php
Number of Beds: 96 beds

***Whitehorse:* Norman D. Macaulay Lodge**
2 Klondike Rd., Whitehorse, YT Y1A 3L5
Tel: 867-667-5955; *Fax:* 867-393-6237
Number of Beds: 44 beds

Retirement Residences

***Whitehorse:* Front Street Senion's Residence**
1190 Front St., Whitehorse, YT Y1A 0P4
Year Founded: 2016
Number of Beds: 48 unites

SECTION 11
LAW FIRMS

Major Law Firms

Aird & Berlis LLP
Former Name: Aird, Zimmerman & Berlis
#1800, Brookfield Place, P.O. Box 754, 181 Bay St., Toronto, ON M5J 2T9
Tel: 416-863-1500; *Fax:* 416-863-1515
www.airdberlis.com
twitter.com/AirdBerlis,
www.linkedin.com/company/aird-&-berlis-llp
Profile: 1 Office, 137 Lawyers, Founded in: 1919
Legal services in the areas of Banking Law, Corporate & Commercial Law, Corporate Finance, Insolvency & Restructuring, Litigation, Real Estate Law, & Tax Law
Senior and Managing Partners:
Steven Zakem, Managing Partner
416-865-3440
szakem@airdberlis.com
Jack Bernstein, Senior Partner
416-865-7766
jbernstein@airdberlis.com
David Malach, Senior Partner
416-865-7702
dmalach@airdberlis.com
Leo F. Longo, Senior Partner
416-865-7778
llongo@airdberlis.com
Paul V. McCallen, Senior Partner
416-865-7723
pmccallen@airdberlis.com

BCF LLP - Montréal
Also Known As: Brouillette Charpentier Fortin
1100, boul René-Lévesque ouest, 25e étage, Montréal, QC H3B 5C9
Tél: 514-397-8500; *Téléc:* 514-397-8515
Ligne sans frais: 866-511-8501
info@bcf.ca
www.bcf.ca
twitter.com/bcf_avocats_law
Profile: 5 Offices, 91 Lawyers, Founded in: 1995
Expertise in both local & cross-border transactions by financial institutions & corporate borrowers.
Senior and Managing Partners:
P. Mario Charpentier, Managing Partner
514-397-6950
mario.charpentier@bcf.ca

BCF LLP - Québec
Complexe Jules-Dallaire, T1, 2828, boul Laurier, 12e étage, Québec, QC G1V 0B9
Tél: 418-266-4500; *Téléc:* 418-266-4515
Ligne sans frais: 866-925-4500
info@bcf.ca
www.bcf.ca
Profile: 23 Lawyers

BCF LLP - Sept-Iles
#202, 421, av Arnaud, Sept-Iles, QC G4R 3B3
Tél: 418-968-3073; *Téléc:* 418-961-1937
info@bcf.ca
www.bcf.ca

Bennett Jones LLP - Calgary
#4500, Bankers Hall East Tower, 855 - 2nd St. SW, Calgary, AB T2P 4K7
Tel: 403-298-3100; *Fax:* 403-265-7219
www.bennettjones.ca
twitter.com/BennettJonesLaw,
www.linkedin.com/company/bennett-jones-llp
Profile: 9 Offices, 362 Lawyers, Founded in: 1922
Senior and Managing Partners:
Blair C. Yorke-Slader, Q.C., Vice-Chair & Partner
403-298-3291
yorkesladerb@bennettjones.ca
Perry Spitznagel, Q.C., Vice-Chair & Managing Partner
403-298-3153
spitznagelp@bennettjones.com

Bennett Jones LLP - Edmonton
#3200, TELUS House, South Tower, 10020 - 100th St., Edmonton, AB T5J 0N3
Tel: 780-421-8133; *Fax:* 780-421-7951
www.bennettjones.ca
Profile: 36 Lawyers
Senior and Managing Partners:
Enzo J. Barichello, Q.C., Managing Partner
780-917-4269
barichelloe@bennettjones.com

Bennett Jones LLP - Ottawa
#1900, World Exchange Plaza, 45 O'Connor St., Ottawa, ON K1P 1A4
Tel: 613-683-2300; *Fax:* 613-683-2323
www.bennettjones.ca
Profile: 4 Lawyers
Senior and Managing Partners:
Edward S. Goldenberg, Managing Partner
613-683-2301
goldenberge@bennettjones.com

Bennett Jones LLP - Toronto
#3400, One First Canadian Place, P.O. Box 130, Toronto, ON M5X 1A4
Tel: 416-863-1200; *Fax:* 416-863-1716
www.bennettjones.ca
Profile: 136 Lawyers
Senior and Managing Partners:
Hugh L. MacKinnon, Chair/CEO
416-777-4810
mackinnonh@bennettjones.com
Stephen W. Bowman, Managing Partner
416-777-4624
bowmans@bennettjones.com

Bennett Jones LLP - Vancouver
#2200, 1055 West Hastings St., Vancouver, BC V6E 2E9
Tel: 604-891-7500; *Fax:* 604-891-5100
www.bennettjones.ca
Profile: 8 Lawyers

Blake, Cassels & Graydon LLP - Toronto
#4000, Commerce Court West, 199 Bay St., Toronto, ON M5L 1A9
Tel: 416-863-2400; *Fax:* 416-863-2653
toronto@blakes.com
www.blakes.com
www.facebook.com/Blakes, twitter.com/blakeslaw,
www.linkedin.com/company/13193
Profile: 12 Offices, 577 Lawyers, Founded in: 1856
The firm has experience successfully structuring, negotiating & documenting a wide variety of domestic & cross-border financing transactions. These include syndications, project finance, asset-based lending, trade finance, high-yield offerings, debt & debtor-in-possession financing, warehouse facilities credit arrangements, private placements, securitizations & structured financing, subordinated debt arrangements, as well as aircraft & other equipment finance & capital markets debt offerings.
Senior and Managing Partners:
Robert Granatstein, Firm Managing Partner
416-863-2748
robert.granatstein@blakes.com

Blake, Cassels & Graydon LLP - Calgary
#3500, Bankers Hall East Tower, 855 - 2nd St. SW, Calgary, AB T2P 4J8
Tel: 403-260-9600; *Fax:* 403-260-9700
calgary@blakes.com
www.blakes.com
Profile: 91 Lawyers
Senior and Managing Partners:
Ken Mills, Managing Partner
403-260-9648
ken.mills@blakes.com
Brock W. Gibson, Q.C., Firm Chair
403-260-9610
brock.gibson@blakes.com

Blake, Cassels & Graydon LLP - Montréal
#3000, 1 Place Ville Marie, Montréal, QC H3B 4N8
Tél: 514-982-4000; *Téléc:* 514-982-4099
montreal@blakes.com
www.blakes.com
Profile: 68 Lawyers
Senior and Managing Partners:
Robert Torralbo, ManagingPartner
514-982-4014
robert.torralbo@blakes.com

Blake, Cassels & Graydon LLP - Ottawa
#1750, Constitution Square, Tower 3, 340 Albert St., Ottawa, ON K1R 7Y6
Tel: 613-788-2200; *Fax:* 613-788-2247
ottawa@blakes.com
www.blakes.com
Profile: 13 Lawyers
Senior and Managing Partners:
Nancy Brooks, Managing Partner
613-788-2218
nancy.brooks@blakes.com

Blake, Cassels & Graydon LLP - Vancouver
#2600, Three Bentall Centre, P.O. Box 49314, 595 Burrard St., Vancouver, BC V7X 1L3
Tel: 604-631-3300; *Fax:* 604-631-3309
vancouver@blakes.com
www.blakes.com
Profile: 86 Lawyers
Senior and Managing Partners:
Bill S. Maclagan, Q.C., Managing Partner
604-631-3336
bill.maclagan@blakes.com

Blaney McMurtry LLP
#1500, 2 Queen St. East, Toronto, ON M5C 3G5
Tel: 416-593-1221; *Fax:* 416-593-5437
www.blaney.com
www.facebook.com/blaneymcmurtry,
twitter.com/blaneymcmurtry,
www.linkedin.com/company/blaney-mcmurtry-llp
Profile: 1 Office, 132 Lawyers, Founded in: 1954
Business Reorganization & Insolvency; Corporate & Commercial Law; Corporate Finance & Securities; Corporate Insurance; E-Commerce; Insurance Coverage Counsel; Insurance Litigation; International Trade and Business; Tax Law
Senior and Managing Partners:
Maria Scarfo, Managing Partner
416-593-3955
mscarfo@blaney.com

Borden Ladner Gervais LLP - Toronto
Also Known As: BLG
Bay Adelaide Centre, East Tower, 22 Adelaide St. West, Toronto, ON M5H 4E3
Tel: 416-367-6000; *Fax:* 416-367-6749
Toll-Free: 855-660-6003
info@blg.com
www.blg.com
www.facebook.com/BordenLadnerGervaisLLP,
twitter.com/blglaw, www.linkedin.com/company/blglaw
Profile: 6 Offices, 765 Lawyers, Founded in: 1936
The Financial Services Group, in conjunction with our other practice groups, provides comprehensive & specialized advice & legal services in all aspects of financial services law. The group is a large multidisciplinary team with expertise in all areas of financial services law, including banking, lending, structured finance, project finance, securitizations, regulatory matters, bankruptcy, insolvency, restructuring, & related disciplines. The multidisciplinary approach reflects the reality of financial services both domestically & internationally, where traditional financial sectors have become integrated & traditional activities require special expertise. The Financial Services Group provides a wide range of services to major Canadian & foreign banks, financial institutions, trust companies, credit unions, insurance companies & investment dealers. The Group represents numerous corporate borrowers & lessees in diverse sectors of the economy.
Senior and Managing Partners:
Sean Weir, National Managing Partner/CEO
416-367-6040
sweir@blg.com
William D.T. Carter, Senior Partner
416-367-6173
wcarter@blg.com
Barry H. Bresner, Senior Partner
416-367-6167
bbresner@blg.com
Christopher D. Bredt, Senior Partner
416-367-6165
cbredt@blg.com
Richard H. Shaban, Senior Partner
416-367-6262
rshaban@blg.com
Linda L. Bertoldi, Senior Partner
416-367-6647
lbertoldi@blg.com
J. Mark Rodger, Senior Partner
416-367-6190
mrodger@blg.com
Shane Freitag, Senior Partner
416-367-6137
sfreitag@blg.com
Murray B. Shopiro, Senior Partner
416-367-6264
mshopiro@blg.com
Stephen F. Waqué, Senior Partner
416-367-6275
swaque@blg.com

Borden Ladner Gervais LLP - Calgary
#1900, Centennial Place, East Tower, 520 - 3rd Ave. SW, Calgary, AB T2P 0R3
Tel: 403-232-9500; *Fax:* 403-266-1395
Toll-Free: 855-660-6003
info@blg.com
www.blg.com

Profile: 114 Lawyers
Senior and Managing Partners:
Alan Ross, Managing Partner
403-232-9656
aross@blg.com

Borden Ladner Gervais LLP - Montréal
#900, 1000, rue de la Gauchetière ouest, Montréal, QC H3B 5H4
Tel: 514-879-1212; *Fax:* 514-954-1905
Toll-Free: 855-660-6003
info@blg.com
www.blg.com

Profile: 123 Lawyers
Senior and Managing Partners:
John G. Murphy, Managing Partner
514-954-3155
jmurphy@blg.com

Borden Ladner Gervais LLP - Ottawa
#1300, World Exchange Plaza, 100 Queen St., Ottawa, ON K1P 1J9
Tel: 613-237-5160; *Fax:* 613-230-8842
Toll-Free: 855-660-6003
info@blg.com
www.blg.com

Profile: 91 Lawyers
Senior and Managing Partners:
Katherine Cooligan, Managing Partner
613-787-3565
kcooligan@blg.com

Borden Ladner Gervais LLP - Vancouver
#1200, Waterfront Centre, P.O. Box 48600, 200 Burrard St., Vancouver, BC V7X 1T2
Tel: 604-687-5744; *Fax:* 604-687-1415
Toll-Free: 855-660-6003
info@blg.com
www.blg.com

Profile: 136 Lawyers, Founded in: 1911
Senior and Managing Partners:
Graham Walker, Managing Partner
604-640-4045
gwalker@blg.com

Bull, Housser & Tupper LLP
#1800, 510 West Georgia St., Vancouver, BC V6B 0M3
Tel: 604-687-6575; *Fax:* 604-641-4949
www.bht.com
twitter.com/bullhousser,
www.linkedin.com/company/bull-housser-&-tupper
Profile: 1 Office, 89 Lawyers, Founded in: 1890
Industry groups include: Financial Services; Real Estate; & Wealth Preservation. Specialty groups include: Business Law; Corporate Finance & Securities; Insolvency & Restructuring; Insurance; Intellectual Property; Labour & Employment Law; Pension; & Tax.
Senior and Managing Partners:
Janet Grove, Managing Partner
604-641-4824
jpg@bht.com

Burnet, Duckworth & Palmer LLP
***Also Known As:* BD&P**
#2400, 525 - 8th Ave. SW, Calgary, AB T2P 1G1
Tel: 403-260-0100; *Fax:* 403-260-0332
www.bdplaw.com
Profile: 1 Office, 145 Lawyers, Founded in: 1905
Corporate; Commercial; Taxation; Real Estate; Securities
Senior and Managing Partners:
John A. Brussa, Partner; Vice-Chair
403-260-0131
jab@bdplaw.com
Grant A. Zawalsky, Managing Partner
403-260-0376
gaz@bdplaw.com
Harry S. Campbell, Q.C., Chair
403-260-0281
hsc@bdplaw.com

Cain Lamarre Casgrain Wells - Val-d'Or
#202, 855, 3e av, Val-d'Or, QC J9P 1T2
Tél: 819-825-4153; *Téléc:* 819-825-9769
info@clcw.ca
www.clcw.qc.ca
www.facebook.com/205419056171407,
twitter.com/Cain_Lamarre,
www.linkedin.com/company/cain-lamarre-casgrain-wells
Profile: 17 Offices, 158 Lawyers, Founded in: 1999
Senior and Managing Partners:
Pascal Porlier, Associé propriétaire
pascal.porlier@clcw.ca
Robert-André Adam, Associé propriétaire
robert.andre.adam@clcw.ca

Cain Lamarre Casgrain Wells - Alma
#03, Complexe Jacques-Gagnon, 100, rue St-Joseph Sud, Alma, QC G8B 7A6
Tél: 418-669-4580; *Téléc:* 418-669-0088
info@clcw.ca
www.clcw.qc.ca

Profile: 4 Lawyers
Senior and Managing Partners:
Christian Gendron, Associé propriétaire
christian.gendron@clcw.ca

Cain Lamarre Casgrain Wells - Amos
#201, 101, 1re av est, Amos, QC J9T 1H4
Tél: 819-727-4153; *Téléc:* 819-727-9769
info@clcw.ca
www.clcw.qc.ca

Profile: 2 Lawyers

Cain Lamarre Casgrain Wells - Amqui
20, rue Desbiens, Amqui, QC G5J 3P1
Tél: 418-629-3302; *Téléc:* 418-629-3333
info@clcw.ca
www.clcw.qc.ca
Profile: 1 Lawyer

Cain Lamarre Casgrain Wells - Drummondville
#201, 330, rue Cormier, Drummondville, QC J2C 8B3
Tél: 819-477-2544; *Téléc:* 819-477-4343
info@clcw.ca
www.clcw.qc.ca
Profile: 10 Lawyers
Senior and Managing Partners:
Jean Côté, Associé propriétaire
j.cote@clcw.ca
Jean-François Brouillard, Associé propriétaire
jean.francois.brouillard@clcw.ca

Cain Lamarre Casgrain Wells - Montréal
#2780, 630, boul René-Lévesque ouest, Montréal, QC H3B 1S6
Tél: 514-393-4580; *Téléc:* 514-393-9590
info@clcw.ca
www.clcw.qc.ca
Profile: 30 Lawyers
Senior and Managing Partners:
Denis Cloutier, Associé propriétaire
denis.cloutier@clcw.ca
Stéphane Gauthier, Associée propriétaire
stephane.gauthier@clcw.ca
Richard Gaudreault, Associé propriétaire
richard.gaudreault@clcw.ca
André Gauthier, Associé propriétaire
andre.gauthier@clcw.ca
Claude Mageau, Associé propriétaire
claude.mageau@clcw.ca
Stéphane Lamarre, Associé propriétaire
stephane.lamarre@clcw.ca
Alain Ménard, Associé propriétaire
alain.menard@clcw.ca
Marie-Josée Monfette, Associée propriétaire
mariejosee.monfette@clcw.ca

Cain Lamarre Casgrain Wells - Plessisville
2014, rue Saint-Calixte, Plessisville, QC G6L 1R9
Tél: 819-362-6699; *Téléc:* 819-362-2121
info@clcw.ca
www.clcw.qc.ca

Profile: 1 Lawyer
Senior and Managing Partners:
Frédéric Levasseur, Associé propriétaire
frederic.levasseur@clcw.ca

Cain Lamarre Casgrain Wells - Québec
#440, 580, Grande Allée est, Québec, QC G1R 2K2
Tél: 418-522-4580; *Téléc:* 418-529-9590
info@clcw.ca
www.clcw.qc.ca

Profile: 35 Lawyers
Senior and Managing Partners:
Sylvain Chabot, Associé propriétaire
sylvain.chabot@clcw.ca
Gaston Desrosiers, Associé propriétaire
gaston.desrosiers@clcw.ca
Jean Houle, Associé propriétaire
jean.houle@clcw.ca
Stéphane Martin, Associé propriétaire
stephane.martin@clcw.ca
Karl Jessop, Associé propriétaire
karl.jessop@clcw.ca
Normand Drolet, Associé propriétaire
normand.drolet@clcw.ca
Linda Lavoie, Associée propriétaire
linda.lavoie@clcw.ca
Frédéric Levasseur, Associé propriétaire
frederic.levasseur@clcw.ca

Cain Lamarre Casgrain Wells - Rimouski
#400, Edifice Trust General, CP 580, 2, boul St-Germain est, Rimouski, QC G5L 7C6
Tél: 418-723-3302; *Téléc:* 418-722-6939
info@clcw.ca
www.clcw.qc.ca

Profile: 9 Lawyers
Senior and Managing Partners:
Pierre Lévesque, Associé propriétaire
pierre.levesque@clcw.ca
Yvan Bujold, Associé propriétaire
yvan.bujold@clcw.ca
Eric Monfette, Associé propriétaire
eric.monfette@clcw.ca

Cain Lamarre Casgrain Wells - Rivière-du-Loup
#201, CP 1104, 299, rue Lafontaine, Rivière-du-Loup, QC G5R 4C3
Tél: 418-860-4580; *Téléc:* 418-860-4588
info@clcw.ca
www.clcw.qc.ca
Profile: 6 Lawyers
Senior and Managing Partners:
François Bérubé, Associé propriétaire
francois.berube@clcw.ca

Cain Lamarre Casgrain Wells - Roberval
814, boul St-Joseph, Roberval, QC G8H 2L5
Tél: 418-275-2472; *Téléc:* 418-275-6878
info@clcw.ca
www.clcw.qc.ca

Profile: 2 Lawyers
Senior and Managing Partners:
Benoît Amyot, Associé propriétaire
benoit.amyot@clcw.ca

Cain Lamarre Casgrain Wells - Rouyn-Noranda
#200, 33, av Horne, Rouyn-Noranda, QC J9X 4S1
Tél: 819-797-5222; *Téléc:* 819-762-6810
info@clcw.ca
www.clcw.qc.ca

Senior and Managing Partners:
Louis-Charles Bélanger, Associé propriétaire
louis.charles.belanger@clcw.ca

Cain Lamarre Casgrain Wells - Saguenay
#300, CP 0, 199, rue Racine est, Chicoutimi, QC G7H 1R9
Tél: 418-545-4580; *Téléc:* 418-549-9590
info@clcw.ca
www.clcw.qc.ca

Profile: 31 Lawyers
Senior and Managing Partners:
Richard Bergeron, Associé propriétaire
richard.bergeron@clcw.ca
Guy Wells, Associé propriétaire
guy.wells@clcw.ca
Jean Dauphinais, Associé propriétaire
jean.dauphinais@clcw.ca
Gina Doucet, Associée propriétaire
gina.doucet@clcw.ca
Chantal Lavallée, Associée propriétaire
chantal.lavallee@clcw.ca
Jean-Jacques Rancourt, Associé propriétaire
jean.jacques.rancourt@clcw.ca
François G. Tremblay, Associé propriétaire
francoisg.tremblay@clcw.ca
François Bouchard, Associé propriétaire
francois.bouchard@clcw.ca
Pierre Parent, Associé propriétaire
raphael.tremblay@clcw.ca

Cain Lamarre Casgrain Wells - Saint-Félicien
1067, boul du Sacré-Coeur, Saint-Félicien, QC G8K 1R3
Tél: 418-679-1331; *Téléc:* 418-679-9344
info@clcw.ca
www.clcw.qc.ca

Profile: 3 Lawyers

Cain Lamarre Casgrain Wells - Saint-Georges
#350, 11535, 1re av, Saint-Georges, QC G5Y 7H5
Tél: 418-228-2074; *Téléc:* 418-228-6016
info@clcw.ca
www.clcw.qc.ca
Profile: 3 Lawyers

Cain Lamarre Casgrain Wells - Sept-Iles
440, av Brochu, 2e étage, Sept-Iles, QC G4R 2W8
Tél: 418-962-6572; *Téléc:* 418-968-8576
info@clcw.ca
www.clcw.qc.ca
Profile: 6 Lawyers
Senior and Managing Partners:
Michel Claveau, Associé propriétaire
michel.claveau@clcw.ca

Cain Lamarre Casgrain Wells - Sherbrooke
#300, 455, rue King ouest, Sherbrooke, QC J1H 6E9
Tél: 819-780-1515; *Téléc:* 819-780-1341
info@clcw.ca
www.clcw.qc.ca
Profile: 6 Lawyers
Senior and Managing Partners:
Sophie Lapierre, Associée propriétaire
sophie.lapierre@clcw.ca

Cassels Brock & Blackwell LLP - Toronto
#2100, Scotia Plaza, 40 King St. West, Toronto, ON M5H 3C2
Tel: 416-869-5300; *Fax:* 416-360-8877
www.casselsbrock.com
twitter.com/casselsbrock,
www.linkedin.com/company/cassels-brock-&-blackwell-llp
Profile: 3 Offices, 209 Lawyers, Founded in: 1888
Full-service law firm, with an emphasis on tax & business law, both domestic & international
Senior and Managing Partners:
David R. Peterson, P.C., Q.C., Firm Chair
416-869-5451
dpeterson@casselsbrock.com
Cameron Mingay, Senior Partner
416-860-6615
cmingay@casselsbrock.com
Mark I. Young, Managing Partner
416-869-5380
myoung@casselsbrock.com
Wendy Berman, Senior Partner
416-860-2926
wberman@casselsbrock.com

Cassels Brock & Blackwell LLP - Calgary
#1250, Millenium Tower, 440 - 2nd Ave. SW, Calgary, AB T2P 5E9
Tel: 403-351-2920; *Fax:* 403-648-1151
www.casselsbrock.com
Profile: 5 Lawyers

Cassels Brock & Blackwell LLP - Vancouver
#2200, HSBC Building, 885 West Georgia St., Vancouver, BC V6C 3E8
Tel: 604-691-6100; *Fax:* 604-691-6120
www.casselsbrock.com
Profile: 16 Lawyers

Cox & Palmer - St. John's
#1100, Scotia Centre, 235 Water St., St. John's, NL A1C 1B6
Tel: 709-738-7800; *Fax:* 709-738-7999
stjohns@coxandpalmer.com
www.coxandpalmerlaw.com
twitter.com/CoxandPalmer
Profile: 10 Offices, 171 Lawyers
Senior and Managing Partners:
Alexander (Sandy) MacDonald, Q.C., Managing Partner
709-570-5512
amacdonald@coxandpalmer.com

Cox & Palmer - Alberton
P.O. Box 40, 347 Church St., Alberton, PE C0B 1B0
Tel: 902-853-3313; *Fax:* 902-853-3753
alberton@coxandpalmer.com
www.coxandpalmerlaw.com
Profile: 1 Lawyer
Senior and Managing Partners:
Mary Lynn Kane, Q.C., Managing Partner
902-629-3904
mkane@coxandpalmer.com

Cox & Palmer - Charlottetown
#600, 97 Queen St., Charlottetown, PE C1A 4A9
Tel: 902-628-1033; *Fax:* 902-566-2639
charlottetown@coxandpalmer.com
www.coxandpalmerlaw.com
Profile: 12 Lawyers
Senior and Managing Partners:
Mary Lynn Kane, Q.C., Managing Partner
902-629-3904
mkane@coxandpalmer.com

Cox & Palmer - Fredericton
#400, Phoenix Square, P.O. Box 310, Stn. A, 371 Queen St., Fredericton, NB E3B 4Y9
Tel: 506-453-7771; *Fax:* 506-453-9600
fredericton@coxandpalmer.com
www.coxandpalmerlaw.com
Profile: 25 Lawyers
Senior and Managing Partners:
Jamie C. Eddy, Managing Partner
506-462-4751
jeddy@coxandpalmer.com

Cox & Palmer - Halifax
#1100, Purdy's Wharf, Tower One, P.O. Box 2380, Stn. Central, 1959 Upper Water St., Halifax, NS B3J 3E5
Tel: 902-421-6262; *Fax:* 902-421-3130
halifax@coxandpalmer.com
www.coxandpalmerlaw.com
Profile: 56 Lawyers
Senior and Managing Partners:
Kevin Latimer, Q.C., Managing Partner
902-491-4212
klatimer@coxandpalmer.com

Cox & Palmer - Moncton
#500, Blue Cross Centre, 644 Main St., Moncton, NB E1C 1E2
Tel: 506-856-9800; *Fax:* 506-856-8150
moncton@coxandpalmer.com
www.coxandpalmerlaw.com
Profile: 17 Lawyers
Senior and Managing Partners:
George L. Cooper, Managing Partner
506-863-0793
gcooper@coxandpalmer.com

Cox & Palmer - Montague
P.O. Box 516, 4A Riverside Dr., Montague, PE C0A 1R0
Tel: 902-838-1033; *Fax:* 902-838-3440
montague@coxandpalmer.com
www.coxandpalmerlaw.com
Profile: 2 Lawyers
Senior and Managing Partners:
Mary Lynn Kane, Q.C., Managing Partner
902-629-3904
mkane@coxandpalmer.com

Cox & Palmer - Morell
29 Park St., Morell, PE C0A 1S0
Tel: 902-961-9300
www.coxandpalmerlaw.com
Senior and Managing Partners:
Mary Lynn Kane, Q.C., Managing Partner
902-629-3904
mkane@coxandpalmer.com

Cox & Palmer - Saint John
#1500, Brunswick Square, P.O. Box 1324, Stn. Main, 1 Germain St., Saint John, NB E2L 4H8
Tel: 506-632-8900; *Fax:* 506-632-8809
saintjohn@coxandpalmer.com
www.coxandpalmerlaw.com
Profile: 18 Lawyers
Senior and Managing Partners:
Joshua J.B. McElman, Managing Partner
506-633-2708
jmcelman@coxandpalmer.com

Cox & Palmer - Summerside
#401, Holman Centre, South Tower, 250 Water St., Summerside, PE C1N 1B6
Tel: 902-888-1033; *Fax:* 902-436-7131
summerside@coxandpalmer.com
www.coxandpalmerlaw.com
Profile: 3 Lawyers
Senior and Managing Partners:
Mary Lynn Kane, Q.C., Managing Partner
902-629-3904
mkane@coxandpalmer.com

Davies Ward Phillips & Vineberg LLP - Toronto
Former Name: Davies Ward & Beck
155 Wellington St. West, Toronto, ON M5V 3J7
Tel: 416-863-0900; *Fax:* 416-863-0871
www.dwpv.com
twitter.com/_Davies_,
ca.linkedin.com/company/davies-ward-phillips-&-vineberg-llp
Profile: 3 Offices, 246 Lawyers, Founded in: 1961
Business transactions & business operations including acquisitions, divestitures, financing, securities, real estate & land development. The firm also has an office in New York City.
Senior and Managing Partners:
William M. Ainley, Senior Partner
416-863-5509
wainley@dwpv.com
Gregory J. Howard, Senior Partner
416-863-5580
ghoward@dwpv.com
D. Shawn McReynolds, Managing Partner
416-863-5538
smcreynolds@dwpv.com
Patricia L. Olasker, SeniorPartner
416-863-5551
polasker@dwpv.com
Derek R.G. Vesey, CorporatePartner
416-367-6921
dvesey@dwpv.com
George N. Addy, Senior Partner
416-863-5588
gaddy@dwpv.com
Robert T. Bauer, Senior Partner
416-863-5552
rbauer@dwpv.com
Melanie Koszegi, Executive Director
416-863-5563
mkoszegi@dwpv.com

Davies Ward Phillips & Vineberg S.E.N.C.R.L., s.r.l. - Montréal
Former Name: Phillips & Vineberg
1501 McGill College Ave., 26th Fl., Montréal, QC H3A 3N9
Tel: 514-841-6400; *Fax:* 514-841-6499
www.dwpv.com
Profile: 85 Lawyers
The oldest office of Davies Ward Phillips & Vineberg, the Montreal location has a practice focus on Corporate Law, Tax Law, Securities Law, Real Estate Law, International Law, & Commercial Litigation
Senior and Managing Partners:
Pierre-André Themens, Managing Partner
514-841-6448
pathemens@dwpv.com
Richard Cherney, Senior Partner
514-841-6457
rcherney@dwpv.com
Elias Benhamou, Senior Partner
514-841-6427
ebenhamou@dwpv.com
Jacques P. Fournier, Executive Director
514-841-6435
jfournier@dwpv.com

Dentons Canada LLP - Toronto
Former Name: Fraser Milner Casgrain LLP
#400, 77 King St. West, Toronto, ON M5K 0A1
Tel: 416-863-4511; *Fax:* 416-863-4592
www.dentons.com
twitter.com/dentons, www.linkedin.com/company/dentons
Profile: 6 Offices, 400+ Lawyers
A large business & institutional client base, are active in the mid-market, & represent all facets of industry, including banking & financial services, public-private partnerships, renewable energy, retail, mining, consulting & professional firms, technology & real estate.
Senior and Managing Partners:
Michael N. (Mike) Kaplan, Managing Partner
416-863-4421
mike.kaplan@dentons.com

Dentons Canada LLP - Calgary
Bankers Court, 850 - 2nd St. SW, 15th Fl., Calgary, AB T2P 0R8
Tel: 403-268-7000; *Fax:* 403-268-3100
www.dentons.com
Profile: 100+ Lawyers
The firm offers legal services in the following areas: Financial Services; Project Finance; Mergers & Acquisitions; Restructuring & Insolvency; & Bankruptcy Matters
Senior and Managing Partners:
Donald R. Leitch, Managing Partner
403-268-3008
don.leitch@dentons.com

Dentons Canada LLP - Edmonton
#2900, Manulife Place, 10180 - 101 St., Edmonton, AB T5J 3V5
Tel: 780-423-7100; *Fax:* 780-423-7276
www.dentons.com
Profile: 100 Lawyers
The firm provides legal services to the financial services industry, & to the consumer products & services industry
Senior and Managing Partners:

Carman McNary, Q.C., Managing Partner
780-423-7236
carman.mcnary@dentons.com

Dentons Canada LLP - Montréal
1 Place Ville-Marie, 39th Fl., Montréal, QC H3B 4M7
Tel: 514-878-8800; *Fax:* 514-866-2241
www.dentons.com

Profile: 100+ Lawyers
The firm provides legal services in the areas of Real Estate, Competition & Antitrust Law, Litigation & Dispute Resolution, Employment & Labour Law; & Public-Private Partnerships
Senior and Managing Partners:
Claude Morency, Managing Partner
514-878-8870
claude.morency@dentons.com

Dentons Canada LLP - Ottawa
#1420, 99 Bank St., Ottawa, ON K1P 1H4
Tel: 613-783-9600; *Fax:* 613-783-9690
www.dentons.com

Profile: 34 Lawyers
The firm provides legal services in the areas of Competition & Antitrust Law, International Trade Law, Communications Law, Food & Drug Regulatory, Corporate & Commercial Law, Litigation & Dispute Resolution, Intellectual Property Law, Employment & Labour Law, Real Estate Law, Financial Services, Regulatory & Compliance, & Tax Law
Senior and Managing Partners:
DavidP. Little, Managing Partner
613-783-9639
david.little@dentons.com

Dentons Canada LLP - Vancouver
250 Howe St., 20th Fl., Vancouver, BC V6C 3R8
Tel: 604-687-4460; *Fax:* 604-683-5214
www.dentons.com

Profile: 60+ Lawyers, Founded in: 1980
The firm provides legal services in the areas of Business Law, Real Estate Law, Entertainment Law, Restructuring & Insolvency, & Public-Private Partnerships
Senior and Managing Partners:
Lori Anne Mathison, Managing Partner
604-443-7118
lori.mathison@dentons.com

DLA Piper (Canada) LLP - Vancouver
Former Name: Davis LLP; Davis & Company LLP
#2800, Park Place, 666 Burrard St., Vancouver, BC V6C 2Z7
Tel: 604-687-9444; *Fax:* 604-687-1612
www.dlapiper.com/en/canada
www.facebook.com/officialdlapiper,
twitter.com/DLA_PiperCanada,
www.linkedin.com/company/dla-piper

Profile: 6 Offices, 260 Lawyers, Founded in: 1892
DLA Piper (Canada) LLP was established in April 2015, with the merger of Davis LLP & DLA Piper LLP (US). Drawing on Davis LLP's resources & areas of specialty, the firm employs 260 Canadian lawyers working in more than 50 practice areas, with an emphasis on corporate & finance areas related to energy, natural resources, infrastructure, development, litigation & transportation. DLA Piper has over 4,000 lawyers worldwide.
Senior and Managing Partners:
Stuart B. Morrow, Senior Partner
604-643-2948
stuart.morrow@dlapiper.com
Catherine Gibson, Managing Partner
604-643-6468
c.gibson@dlapiper.com
David R. Reid, Senior Partner
604-643-6428
david.reid@dlapiper.com

DLA Piper (Canada) LLP - Calgary
Former Name: Davis LLP
#1000, Livingston Place West, 250 - 2nd St. SW, Calgary, AB T2P 0C1
Tel: 403-296-4470; *Fax:* 403-296-4474
www.dlapiper.com/en/canada

Profile: 60 Lawyers, Founded in: 2002
Practice areas emphasize corporate & finance areas related to energy, natural resources, infrastructure, development, litigation & transportation.
Senior and Managing Partners:
Heather Treacy, Q.C., Managing Partner
403-294-3589
heather.treacy@dlapiper.com
Laura M. Safran, Q.C., Senior Partner
403-698-8778
laura.safran@dlapiper.com
David J. Stratton, Q.C., Senior Partner
403-296-4470
david.stratton@dlapiper.com

DLA Piper (Canada) LLP - Edmonton
Former Name: Davis LLP
#1201, Scotia Tower 2, 10060 Jasper Ave., Edmonton, AB T5J 4E5
Tel: 780-426-5330; *Fax:* 780-428-1066
www.dlapiper.com/en/canada

Profile: 26 Lawyers, Founded in: 2002
Practice areas emphasize corporate & finance areas related to energy, natural resources, infrastructure, development, litigation & transportation.
Senior and Managing Partners:
Robert A. Seidel, Q.C., National ManagingPartner
780-429-6814
robert.seidel@dlapiper.com
Rachel J. Hamilton, Managing Partner
780-429-6633
r.hamilton@dlapiper.com

DLA Piper (Canada) S.E.N.C.R.L. - Montréal
Former Name: Davis LLP
#1400, 1501, av McGill College, Montréal, QC H3A 3M8
Tel: 514-392-1991; *Fax:* 514-392-1999
www.dlapiper.com/fr/canada

Profile: 17 Lawyers
Practice areas emphasize corporate & finance areas related to energy, natural resources, infrastructure, development, litigation & transportation.
Senior and Managing Partners:
Marc Philibert, Managing Partner
514-392-8442
marc.philibert@dlapiper.com

DLA Piper (Canada) LLP - Toronto
Former Name: Davis LLP
#6000, 1 First Canadian Place, P.O. Box 367, 100 King St. West, Toronto, ON M5X 1E2
Tel: 416-365-3500; *Fax:* 416-365-7886
www.dlapiper.com/en/canada

Profile: 65 Lawyers
Practice areas emphasize corporate & finance areas related to energy, natural resources, infrastructure, development, litigation & transportation.
Senior and Managing Partners:
Michael S. Richards, Managing Partner
416-941-5395
michael.richards@dlapiper.com
Dan MacDougall, Chief Operating Officer
604-643-2915
dan.macdougall@dlapiper.com

DLA Piper (Canada) LLP - Yellowknife
Former Name: Davis LLP
#802, Northwest Tower, 5201 - 50th Ave., Yellowknife, NT X1A 3S9
Tel: 867-669-8400; *Fax:* 867-669-8420
www.dlapiper.com/en/canada

Profile: 1 Lawyer
Practice areas emphasize corporate & finance areas related to energy, natural resources, infrastructure, development, litigation & transportation.

Fasken Martineau DuMoulin LLP - Toronto
Also Known As: Fasken Martineau
#2400, Bay Adelaide Centre, P.O. Box 20, 333 Bay St., Toronto, ON M5H 2T6
Tel: 416-366-8381; *Fax:* 416-364-7813
Toll-Free: 800-268-8424
toronto@fasken.com
www.fasken.com
www.facebook.com/154446131283771,
twitter.com/faskenmartineau,
www.linkedin.com/company/fasken-martineau-dumoulin

Profile: 9 Offices, 712 Lawyers, Founded in: 1863
Fasken Marineau provides legal services to the full array of participants in the financial services industry; our clients include leading Canadian & foreign banks, life & property & casualty insurance companies, loan & trust companies, cooperatives & credit unions, finance companies, insurance agents & brokers & other financial services providers; we pride ourselves on knowing each client's business & the current issues & trends affecting them; we work closely with our clients across the breadth of their transactional investment & other activities & in their relations with Canadian regulators; our group regularly provides advice regarding mergers & acquisitions, financings, restructurings, the establishment of financial services businesses, the development & distribution of financial services products & all manner of regulatory issues with both federal & provincial regulators
Senior and Managing Partners:
Martin K. Denyes, Managing Partner, Ontario
416-868-3489
mdenyes@fasken.com

Fasken Martineau DuMoulin LLP - Calgary
Also Known As: Fasken Martineau
#3400, First Canadian Centre, 350 - 7th Ave. SW, Calgary, AB T2P 3N9
Tel: 403-261-5350; *Fax:* 403-261-5351
Toll-Free: 877-336-5350
calgary@fasken.com
www.fasken.com/en/calgary

Profile: 28 Lawyers, Founded in: 2003
Senior and Managing Partners:
Peter Feldberg, Managing Partner, Firm
403-261-5364
pfeldberg@fasken.com
Robert D. Maxwell, Co-Managing Partner, Calgary
403-261-5503
rmaxwell@fasken.com
Clarke Barnes, Co-Managing Partner, Calgary
403-261-5374
clbarnes@fasken.com

Fasken Martineau DuMoulin LLP - Montréal
Also Known As: Fasken Martineau
#3700, Stock Exchange Tower, P.O. Box 242, 800 Victoria Sq., Montréal, QC H4Z 1E9
Tel: 514-397-7400; *Fax:* 514-397-7600
Toll-Free: 800-361-6266
montreal@fasken.com
www.fasken.com

Profile: 175 Lawyers, Founded in: 1907
Senior and Managing Partners:
Éric Bédard, Managing Partner, Québec
514-397-4314
ebedard@fasken.com

Fasken Martineau DuMoulin LLP - Ottawa
Also Known As: Fasken Martineau
Former Name: Johnston & Buchan LLP
#1300, 55 Metcalfe St., Ottawa, ON K1P 6L5
Tel: 613-236-3882; *Fax:* 613-230-6423
Toll-Free: 877-609-5685
ottawa@fasken.com
www.fasken.com

Profile: 28 Lawyers, Founded in: 2007
Senior and Managing Partners:
Stephen P. Whitehead, Managing Partner, Ottawa
613-969-6873
swhitehead@fasken.com

Fasken Martineau DuMoulin LLP - Québec
Also Known As: Fasken Martineau
#800, 140, Grande Allée est, Québec, QC G1R 5M8
Tel: 418-640-2000; *Fax:* 418-647-2455
Toll-Free: 800-463-2827
quebec@fasken.com
www.fasken.com

Profile: 41 Lawyers, Founded in: 1983
Senior and Managing Partners:
Guy C. Dion, Primary Contact
418-640-2016
gdion@fasken.com

Fasken Martineau DuMoulin LLP - Vancouver
Also Known As: Fasken Martineau
#2900, 550 Burrard St., Vancouver, BC V6C 0A3
Tel: 604-631-3131; *Fax:* 604-631-3232
Toll-Free: 866-635-3131
vancouver@fasken.com
www.fasken.com
www.linkedin.com/company/163768

Profile: 140 Lawyers, Founded in: 1889
Senior and Managing Partners:
William Westeringh, Q.C., Managing Partner, Vancouver
604-631-3155
wwesteringh@fasken.com

Field LLP - Edmonton
Also Known As: Field Law
#2000, 10235 - 101st St. NW, Edmonton, AB T5J 3G1
Tel: 780-423-3003; *Fax:* 780-428-9329
Toll-Free: 800-222-6479
info@fieldlaw.com
www.fieldlaw.com
www.facebook.com/fieldlaw, twitter.com/FieldLaw,
www.linkedin.com/companies/field-law

Profile: 3 Offices, 116 Lawyers, Founded in: 1915
Field Law offers the following financial services: negotiation; preparation & registration of security; foreclosures & collections; security realization; negotiation & finalization of loan agreements; regulatory compliance matters; financing agreements; security enforcement matters; loan restructuring; reorganizations & work-outs; bankruptcy; & insolvency & receivership.
Senior and Managing Partners:

Saunderson Doreen, Firm Managing Partner
dsaunderson@fieldlaw.com

Field LLP - Calgary
Also Known As: Field Law
#400, 604 - 1st St. SW, Calgary, AB T2P 1M7
Tel: 403-260-8500; *Fax:* 403-264-7084
Toll-Free: 877-260-6515
info@fieldlaw.com
www.fieldlaw.com
Profile: 49 Lawyers

Field LLP - Yellowknife
Also Known As: Field Law
#601, 4920 - 52 St., Yellowknife, NT X1A 3T1
Tel: 867-920-4542; *Fax:* 867-873-4790
Toll-Free: 800-753-1294
info@fieldlaw.com
www.fieldlaw.com
Profile: 4 Lawyers, Founded in: 2001

Fogler, Rubinoff LLP - Toronto
#3000, TD Centre, North Tower, P.O. Box 95, 77 King St. West, Toronto, ON M5K 1G8
Tel: 416-864-9700; *Fax:* 416-941-8852
Toll-Free: 866-861-9700
info@foglers.com
www.foglers.com
Profile: 2 Offices, 105 Lawyers, Founded in: 1982
Practice areas include: Banking & Financial; Capital Markets & Securities; Commercial Real Estate; Corporate Commercial; Employment & Labour; Insolvency & Restructuring; Intellectual Property; Tax; & Wills & Estates.
Senior and Managing Partners:
Michael S. Slan, Managing Partner
416-941-8857
mslan@foglers.com

Fogler, Rubinoff LLP - Ottawa
#701, 116 Albert St., Ottawa, ON K1P 5G3
Fax: 613-842-7445
Toll-Free: 866-363-8386
info@foglers.com
www.foglers.com
Profile: 3 Lawyers

Goodmans LLP
Former Name: Goodman Phillips & Vineberg
#3400, Bay Adelaide Centre, 333 Bay St., Toronto, ON M5H 2S7
Tel: 416-979-2211; *Fax:* 416-979-1234
info@goodmans.ca
www.goodmans.ca
twitter.com/GoodmansLLP
Profile: 1 Office, 211 Lawyers, Founded in: 1917
Goodmans is a leading Canadian law firm, well-recognized across Canada & internationally for its excellence & market leadership in large-scale corporate transactions. Goodmans is a full-service business law firm that offers clients a wide range of services & expertise in all of the major business law areas, including: Broadcasting, Telecommunications & New Media; Commercial Real Estate; Corporate & Commercial Law; Corporate Restructuring; Corporate Finance & Securities; Litigation; Mergers & Acquisitions; Municipal, Planning & Property Tax Law; Pensions; Trusts & Estates & Tax. With over 200 lawyers, Goodmans provides a complete spectrum of legal advice & representation to domestic & foreign business clients ranging from emerging technology companies to financial institutions & conglomerates
Senior and Managing Partners:
Dale Lastman, Chair
416-597-4129
dlastman@goodmans.ca
Byron Sonberg, Managing Director
416-597-4222
bsonberg@goodmans.ca

Gowling WLG (Canada) LLP - Toronto
Former Name: Gowling Lafleur Henderson LLP
#1600, 1 First Canadian Place, 100 King St. West, Toronto, ON M5X 1G5
Tel: 416-862-7525; *Fax:* 416-862-7661
www.gowlings.com
www.facebook.com/gowlinwlgcanada, twitter.com/GowlingWLG_CA, www.linkedin.com/company/gowlingwlg-canada
Profile: 7 Offices, Founded in: 2015
In 2015, Gowling Lafleur Henderson LLP merged with UK firm Wragge Lawrence Graham & Co to create the international firm Gowling WLG International Limited. With over 1400 professionals in offices across Canada, the UK, Europe, Asia & the Middle East, Gowling WLG offers comprehensive legal services & solutions in all areas of business & corporate law to key industries. In addition, the firm's practice groups are skilled & experienced in the areas of intellectual property law, advocacy, international trade law, technology law, administrative law, & government affairs. Both Gowling WLG (Canada) LLP & Gowling WLG (UK) LLP operate as independent & autonomous entities.
Senior and Managing Partners:
R. Scott Jolliffe, Head, Intl. Development
416-862-5400
scott.joliffe@gowlingwlg.com
Peter J. Lukasiewicz, Chief Executive Officer
416-862-4328
peter.lukasiewicz@gowlingwlg.com
Alan James, Co-Lead, Technology
416-369-6186
alan.james@gowlingwlg.com
Paul H. Harricks, Lead, Energy, Infr. & Mining
416-369-7296
paul.harricks@gowlingwlg.com
Michael Bussmann, Lead, Tax Group
416-369-4663
michael.bussmann@gowlings.com
Tina M. Woodside, Firm Managing Partner
416-369-4584
tina.woodside@gowlingwlg.com
Rob Landry, Chief Operating Officer
416-369-7389
rob.landry@gowlingwlg.com
Karyn Bradley, Managing Partner (Toronto)
416-862-5430
karyn.bradley@gowlinwlg.com
Shelagh Carnegie, Lead, Manuf. Sales & Dist.
416-862-4682
shelagh.carnegie@gowlingwlg.com

Gowling WLG (Canada) LLP - Calgary
Former Name: Code Hunter; Ballem MacInnes
#1600, 421 - 7 Ave. SW, Calgary, AB T2P 4K9
Tel: 403-298-1000; *Fax:* 403-263-9193
www.gowlings.com
Profile: 118 Lawyers
Financial services include: Business Law; Charities & Not-for-Profit Organizations; Commercial Insurance; Commercial Leasing; Competition Law/Antitrust; Construction Law; Corporate Finance & Mergers & Acquisition; Crisis Management; Employment & Labour Law; Entertainment Law; Executive Compensation; Financial Regulatory Law; Financial Services; Franchise & Distribution Law; Gaming Law; Global Business Integrity/Business Ethics; Insurance & Professional Liability; Product Liability; International Business (China, Russis/CIS, U.K., U.S.); International Trade; Private Equity & Venture Capital; Real Estate & Urban Development; Restructuring & Insolvency; Succession Planning & Estates; Tax; Intellectual Property; Securities Law; Litigation & Dispute Resolution
Senior and Managing Partners:
Regina M. Corrigan, Managing Partner
403-298-1964
regina.corrigan@gowlingwlg.com

Gowling WLG (Canada) LLP - Hamilton
One Main St. West, Hamilton, ON L8P 4Z5
Tel: 905-540-8208; *Fax:* 905-528-5833
www.gowlings.com
Profile: 32 Lawyers
Senior and Managing Partners:
Leigh Ann Sheather, Managing Partner
905-540-3269
leighann.sheather@gowlingwlg.com

Gowling WLG (Canada) LLP - Kitchener
#1020, P.O. Box 2248, 50 Queen St. North, Kitchener, ON N2H 6M2
Tel: 519-576-6910; *Fax:* 519-576-6030
www.gowlings.com
Profile: 38 Lawyers
Senior and Managing Partners:
Bryce Kraeker, Managing Partner
519-575-7545
bryce.kraeker@gowlingwlg.com

Gowling WLG (Canada) S.E.N.C.R.L./LLP
#3700, 1 Place Ville Marie, Montréal, QC H3B 3P4
Tel: 514-878-9641; *Fax:* 514-878-1450
www.gowlings.com
Profile: 88 Lawyers
Business Law; Banking Law; Financial Services; Securities; Corporate & Commercial Law; Corporate Finance; Mergers & Acquisitions; Corporate Reorganization; Insolvency & Restructuring; Corporate Governance; Intellectual Property Law
Senior and Managing Partners:
Joëlle Boisvert, Managing Partner
514-392-9580
joelle.boisvert@gowlingwlg.com

Gowling WLG (Canada) LLP - Ottawa
#2600, 160 Elgin St., Ottawa, ON K1P 1C3
Tel: 613-233-1781; *Fax:* 613-563-9869
www.gowlings.com
Profile: 182 Lawyers
Senior and Managing Partners:
Wayne B. Warren, Managing Partner
613-786-0191
wayne.warren@gowlingwlg.com

Gowling WLG (Canada) LLP - Vancouver
#2300, Bentall V, 550 Burrard St., Vancouver, BC V6C 2B5
Tel: 604-683-6498; *Fax:* 604-683-3558
www.gowlings.com
Profile: 66 Lawyers
Senior and Managing Partners:
Shayne P. Strukoff, Managing Partner
604-891-2280
shayne.strukoff@gowlingwlg.com

Hicks Morley Hamilton Stewart Storie LLP - Toronto
Also Known As: Hicks Morley
TD Centre, P.O. Box 371, 77 King St. West, 39th Fl., Toronto, ON M5K 1K8
Tel: 416-362-1011; *Fax:* 416-362-9680
www.hicksmorley.com
Profile: 5 Offices, 115 Lawyers
The firm is exclusively devoted to representing employers on human resources law & advocacy issues. Financial practice areas include pensions & benefits & workplace safety & insurance.
Senior and Managing Partners:
Stephen J. Shamie, Managing Partner
416-864-7304
stephen-shamie@hicksmorley.com

Hicks Morley Hamilton Stewart Storie LLP - Kingston
#310, 366 King St. East, Kingston, ON K7K 6Y3
Tel: 613-549-6353; *Fax:* 613-549-4068
www.hicksmorley.com
Profile: 4 Lawyers
Senior and Managing Partners:
Vince M. Panetta, Partner/Primary Contact
613-541-4003
vince-panetta@hicksmorley.com

Hicks Morley Hamilton Stewart Storie LLP - London
#1608, 148 Fullerton St., London, ON N6A 5P3
Tel: 519-433-7515; *Fax:* 519-433-8827
www.hicksmorley.com
Profile: 4 Lawyers
Senior and Managing Partners:
Robert J. Atkinson, Partner/Primary Contact
519-931-5601
atkinson@hicksmorley.com

Hicks Morley Hamilton Stewart Storie LLP - Ottawa
#2000, 150 Metcalfe St., Ottawa, ON K2P 1P1
Tel: 613-234-0386; *Fax:* 613-234-0418
www.hicksmorley.com
Profile: 8 Lawyers
Senior and Managing Partners:
Lisa J. Mills, Partner/Primary Contact
613-369-2112
lisa-mills@hicksmorley.com

Hicks Morley Hamilton Stewart Storie LLP - Waterloo
#200, Waterloo City Centre, 100 Regina St. South, Waterloo, ON N2J 4P9
Tel: 519-746-0411; *Fax:* 519-746-4037
www.hicksmorley.com
Profile: 9 Lawyers
Senior and Managing Partners:
D. Brent Labord, Partner/Primary Contact
519-883-3101
brent-labord@hicksmorley.com

Lavery, de Billy - Montréal
#4000, 1, Place Ville-Marie, Montréal, QC H3B 4M4
Tel: 514-871-1522; *Fax:* 514-871-8977
info@lavery.ca
www.lavery.ca
facebook.com/LaverydeBilly, twitter.com/LaverydeBilly, www.linkedin.com/company/797440
Profile: 4 Offices, 169 Lawyers, Founded in: 1913
Senior and Managing Partners:
Don McCarty, Firm Managing Partner
514-878-5555
dmccarty@lavery.ca

Lavery, de Billy - Ottawa
#1810, 360 Albert St., Ottawa, ON K1R 7X7
Tel: 613-594-4936; *Fax:* 613-594-8783
www.lavery.ca
Profile: 5 Lawyers, Founded in: 1913

Lavery, de Billy - Québec
#500, 925, Grande Allée ouest, Québec, QC G1S 1C1
Tel: 418-688-5000; *Fax:* 418-688-3458
www.lavery.ca
Profile: 22 Lawyers, Founded in: 1913

Lavery, de Billy - Trois-Rivières
#360, 1500, rue Royale, Trois-Rivières, QC G9A 6E6
Tel: 819-373-7000; *Fax:* 819-373-0943
www.lavery.ca
Profile: 10 Lawyers

Lawson Lundell LLP - Vancouver
Former Name: Lawson, Lundell, Lawson & McIntosh
#1600, Cathedral Place, 925 West Georgia St., Vancouver, BC V6C 3L2
Tel: 604-685-3456; *Fax:* 604-669-1620
www.lawsonlundell.com
twitter.com/LawsonLundell,
www.linkedin.com/companies/lawson-lundell-llp
Profile: 3 Offices, 119 Lawyers, Founded in: 1886
The firm's range of practice includes: corporate finance, mergers & acquisitions, general business & commercial matters, pensions, tax, labour & employment, real estate, Aboriginal issues, mining, energy, public utility, oil & gas, regulatory, & the resolution of disputes through negotiations, mediation arbitration or litigation.
Senior and Managing Partners:
Karen L. MacMillan, B.A., LL.B., Chief Inclusiveness Officer
604-631-9160
kmacmillan@lawsonlundell.com
Clifford G. Proudfoot, LL.B., LL.M., Managing Partner
604-631-9217
cproudfoot@lawsonlundell.com

Lawson Lundell LLP - Calgary
#3700, Bow Valley Square 2, 205 - 5th Ave. SW, Calgary, AB T2P 2V7
Tel: 403-269-6900; *Fax:* 403-269-9494
www.lawsonlundell.com
Profile: 18 Lawyers, Founded in: 1997

Lawson Lundell LLP - Yellowknife
Former Name: Gullberg, Weist, MacPherson & Kay
#200, P.O. Box 818, 4915 - 48 St., Yellowknife, NT X1A 2N6
Tel: 867-669-5500; *Fax:* 867-920-2206
Toll-Free: 888-465-7608
www.lawsonlundell.com
Profile: 4 Lawyers, Founded in: 2002

MacPherson Leslie & Tyerman LLP - Regina
Also Known As: MLT
#1500, Hill Centre I, 1874 Scarth St., Regina, SK S4P 4E9
Tel: 306-347-8000; *Fax:* 306-352-5250
www.mlt.com
twitter.com/MLT_Law,
www.linkedin.com/company/macpherson-leslie-&-tyerman-llp
Profile: 5 Offices, 121 Lawyers, Founded in: 1920
Client-centered & business-oriented law firm; experience extends from the more traditional practice areas of business law (such as corporate finance, mergers & acquisitions, tax, insolvency, commercial litigation) to other rapidly developing areas
Senior and Managing Partners:
Donald K. Wilson, Q.C., Firm Managing Partner
306-347-8437
dwilson@mlt.com

MacPherson Leslie & Tyerman LLP - Calgary
Also Known As: MLT
#1600, Centennial Place, 520 - 3rd Ave. SW, Calgary, AB T2P 0R3
Tel: 403-693-4300; *Fax:* 403-508-4349
www.mlt.com
Profile: 21 Lawyers, Founded in: 1920
The business law firm provides services in the areas of corporate/commercial law & insolvency law.

MacPherson Leslie & Tyerman LLP - Edmonton
Also Known As: MLT
#2200, Oxford Tower, 10235 - 101st St., Edmonton, AB T5J 3G1
Tel: 780-969-3500; *Fax:* 780-969-3549
www.mlt.com
Profile: 16 Lawyers

MacPherson Leslie & Tyerman LLP - Saskatoon
Also Known As: MLT
#1500, Saskatoon Square, 410 - 22nd St. East, Saskatoon, SK S7K 5T6
Tel: 306-975-7100; *Fax:* 306-975-7145
www.mlt.com
Profile: 37 Lawyers

MacPherson Leslie & Tyerman LLP - Vancouver
Also Known As: MLT
Former Name: Goodmans LLP - Vancouver
#1800, 355 Burrard St., Vancouver, BC V6C 2G8
Tel: 604-682-7737; *Fax:* 604-682-7131
www.mlt.com
Profile: 15 Lawyers, Founded in: 1996
Business law firm specializing in Corporate Finance, Mergers & Acquisitions, Securities, & Commercial Law

McCarthy Tétrault LLP - Toronto
#5300, TD Bank Tower, Box 48, 66 Wellington St. West, Toronto, ON M5K 1E6
Tel: 416-362-1812; *Fax:* 416-868-0673
Toll-Free: 877-244-7711
info@mccarthy.ca
www.mccarthy.ca
Profile: 6 Offices, 608 Lawyers, Founded in: 1855
One of their largest practice areas is in corporate finance, where they represent public issuers & underwriters in corporate finance matters involving the preparation of prospectuses & other offering documents for public & private offerings; they have extensive experience in dealing with mergers & acquisitions & corporate reorganizations; their practice has involved many significant takeovers, as well as the development & implementation of defensive strategies in hostile bid situations to improve shareholder value.
Senior and Managing Partners:
David E. Leonard, Partner & CEO
416-601-7694
dleonard@mccarthy.ca

McCarthy Tétrault LLP - Calgary
#4000, 421 - 7th Ave. SW, Calgary, AB T2P 4K9
Tel: 403-260-3500; *Fax:* 403-260-3501
Toll-Free: 877-244-7711
info@mccarthy.ca
www.mccarthy.ca
Profile: 7 Offices, 64 Lawyers
Senior and Managing Partners:
Sean S. Smyth, Managing Partner, Alberta
403-260-3698
ssmyth@mccarthy.ca

McCarthy Tétrault LLP - Montréal
#2500, 1000, rue de la Gauchetière ouest, Montréal, QC H3B 0A2
Tel: 514-397-4100; *Fax:* 514-875-6246
Toll-Free: 877-244-7711
info@mccarthy.ca
www.mccarthy.ca
Profile: 7 Offices, 150 Lawyers, Founded in: 1855
Provides advice to Canadian chartered banks & foreign banks, investment institutions, insurance companies & borrowers on matters concerning banking & financial services law, as well as regulation in Canada; practitioners advise on a broad range of issues, including financial institutions regulation, payments systems, personal property security, electronic securities, foreign exchange clearing & settlement systems, domestic & international capital funding programs, lending activities & major commercial projects & financings; assists in domestic & foreign banking groups & syndicates in significant Canadian project financings & auisitions, as well as corporate loan workouts
Senior and Managing Partners:
Kim Thomassin, Managing Partner, Québec
514-397-5685
kthomassin@mccarthy.ca

McCarthy Tétrault LLP - Québec
500, Grande Allée est, 9e étage, Québec, QC G1R 2J7
Tel: 418-521-3000; *Fax:* 418-521-3099
Toll-Free: 877-244-7711
info@mccarthy.ca
www.mccarthy.ca
Profile: 7 Offices, 25 Lawyers
Senior and Managing Partners:
Mathieu Laflamme, Lead Partner
418-521-3018
mlaflamme@mccarthy.ca
Kim Thomassin, Managing Partner, Québec
418-521-3010
kthomassin@mccarthy.ca

McCarthy Tétrault LLP - Vancouver
#2400, 745 Thurlow St., Vancouver, BC V6E 0C5
Tel: 604-643-7100; *Fax:* 604-643-7900
Toll-Free: 877-244-7711
info@mccarthy.ca
www.mccarthy.ca
Profile: 7 Offices, 100 Lawyers, Founded in: 1960
Senior and Managing Partners:
Sven Milelli, Managing Partner, BC
604-643-7125
smilelli@mccarthy.ca

McDougall Gauley - Regina
#1500, 1881 Scarth St., Regina, SK S4P 4K9
Tel: 306-757-1641; *Fax:* 306-359-0785
www.mcdougallgauley.com
Profile: 4 Offices, 75 Lawyers, Founded in: 1891

McDougall Gauley - Moose Jaw
330 Main St. North, Moose Jaw, SK S6H 3J9
Tel: 306-694-0052; *Fax:* 306-691-0445
moosejaw@mcdougallgauley.com
www.mcdougallgauley.com
Profile: 1 Lawyer

McDougall Gauley - Saskatoon
#500, 616 Main St., Saskatoon, SK S7H 0J6
Tel: 306-653-1212; *Fax:* 306-652-1323
www.mcdougallgauley.com
Profile: 37 Lawyers
Senior and Managing Partners:
Robert (Bob) G. Kennedy, Q.C., Senior Litigation Counsel
306-665-5441
rkennedy@mcdougallgauley.com

McInnes Cooper - Halifax
#1300, Purdy's Wharf Tower II, 1969 Upper Water St., Halifax, NS B3J 3R7
Tel: 902-425-6500; *Fax:* 902-425-6350
www.mcinnescooper.com
twitter.com/mcinnescooper
Profile: 7 Offices, 205 Lawyers, Founded in: 1859
Senior and Managing Partners:
Raymond G. Adlington, Managing Partner/CEO
902-444-8470
ray.adlington@mcinnescooper.com

McInnes Cooper - Charlottetown
#300, McInnes Cooper Bldg., 141 Kent St., Charlottetown, PE C1A 1N3
Tel: 902-368-8473; *Fax:* 902-368-8346
www.mcinnescooper.com
Profile: 13 Lawyers

McInnes Cooper - Fredericton
#600, Barker House, P.O. Box 610, Stn. A, 570 Queen St., Fredericton, NB E3B 5A6
Tel: 506-458-8572; *Fax:* 506-458-9903
www.mcinnescooper.com
Profile: 22 Lawyers

McInnes Cooper - Moncton
#400, Blue Cross Building, South Tower, P.O. Box 1368, 644 Main St., Moncton, NB E1C 8T6
Tel: 506-857-8970; *Fax:* 506-857-4095
www.mcinnescooper.com
Profile: 17 Lawyers

McInnes Cooper - Saint John
#1700, Brunswick Square, P.O. Box 6370, Stn. A, 1 Germain St., Saint John, NB E2L 4R8
Tel: 506-643-6500; *Fax:* 506-643-6505
www.mcinnescooper.com
Profile: 15 Lawyers

McInnes Cooper - St. John's
Baine Johnston Centre, P.O. Box 5939, 10 Fort William Place, 5th Fl., St. John's, NL A1C 5X4
Tel: 709-722-8735; *Fax:* 709-722-1763
www.mcinnescooper.com
Profile: 24 Lawyers, Founded in: 1859
Senior and Managing Partners:
Douglas B. Skinner, Deputy Managing Partner
709-724-8249
doug.skinner@mcinnescooper.com

McMillan LLP - Toronto
Former Name: McMillan Binch LLP/Mendelsohn GP; McMillan Binch Mendelsohn
#4400, Brookfield Place, 181 Bay St., Toronto, ON M5J 2T3
Tel: 416-865-7000; *Fax:* 416-865-7048
Toll-Free: 888-622-4624
info@mcmillan.ca
www.mcmillan.ca
Profile: 6 Offices, 376 Lawyers, Founded in: 1903
Senior and Managing Partners:
T.E. (Ted) Scott, Senior Partner
416-865-7183
ted.scott@mcmillan.ca
David Elenbaas, Chief Professional Partner
416-865-7232
david.elenbaas@mcmillan.ca
Teresa M. Dufort, Chief Executive Officer
416-865-7145
teresa.dufort@mcmillan.ca

Michael P. Whitcombe, Senior Partner
416-865-7126
michael.whitcombe@mcmillan.ca
Paul J. Avis, Senior Partner
416-865-7006
paul.avis@mcmillan.ca
Eric B. Friedman, Office Managing Partner
416-307-4030
eric.friedman@mcmillan.ca

McMillan LLP - Calgary
Former Name: Lang Michener LLP
#1700, TD Canada Trust Tower, 421 - 7 Avenue SW, Calgary, AB T2P 4K9
Tel: 403-531-4700; *Fax:* 403-531-4720
info@mcmillan.ca
www.mcmillan.ca

Profile: 16 Lawyers, Founded in: 1951
The Financial Services Law Group has considerable involvement in the structuring of loan transactions, drafting of loan & intercreditor agreements & the development of security documentation; it has expertise in factoring & asset-based lending
Senior and Managing Partners:
Michael A. Thackray, Q.C., Managing Partner
403-531-4710
michael.thackray@mcmillan.ca

McMillan S.E.N.C.R.L., s.r.l. - Montréal
Former Name: Lang Michener LLP
#2700, 1000 Sherbrooke St. West, Montréal, QC H3A 3G4
Tel: 514-987-5000; *Fax:* 514-987-1213
info@mcmillan.ca
www.mcmillan.ca

Profile: 36 Lawyers, Founded in: 1951
The Financial Services Law Group has considerable involvement in the structuring of loan transactions, drafting of loan & intercreditor agreements & the development of security documentation; it has expertise in factoring & asset-based lending
Senior and Managing Partners:
Charles Chevrette, Managing Partner
514-987-5003
charles.chevrette@mcmillan.ca

McMillan LLP - Ottawa
Former Name: Lang Michener LLP
#2000, World Exchange Plaza, 45 O'Connor St., Ottawa, ON K1P 1A4
Tel: 613-232-7171; *Fax:* 613-231-3191
info@mcmillan.ca
www.mcmillan.ca

Profile: 29 Lawyers, Founded in: 1984
McMillan's areas of practice related to financial services are as follows: tax law; securities law; real estate law; business law; franchising & distribution; mergers & acquisitions; business restructuring & insolvency; insurance law; & banking & project finance.
Senior and Managing Partners:
Ron Petersen, Senior Partner
613-691-6101
ron.petersen@mcmillan.ca

McMillan LLP - Vancouver
Former Name: Lang Michener LLP
#1500, Royal Centre, P.O. Box 11117, 1055 West Georgia St., Vancouver, BC V6E 4N7
Tel: 604-689-9111; *Fax:* 604-685-7084
info@mcmillan.ca
www.mcmillan.ca

Profile: 91 Lawyers, Founded in: 1926
Senior and Managing Partners:
Tom Theodorakis, Managing Partner
604-691-7492
tom.theodorakis@mcmillan.ca

Miller Thomson LLP - Toronto
#5800, Scotia Plaza, P.O. Box 1011, 40 King St. West, Toronto, ON M5H 3S1
Tel: 416-595-8500; *Fax:* 416-595-8695
Toll-Free: 888-762-5559
toronto@millerthomson.com
www.millerthomson.com
twitter.com/millerthomson,
www.linkedin.com/company/miller-thomson-llp

Profile: 11 Offices, 499 Lawyers, Founded in: 1957
Bankruptcy; Corporate Commercial; E-Commerce; Estates/Pensions; Financial Services; Franchising; Insolvency & Insurance; Mergers & Acquisitions; Securities; Tax Law
Senior and Managing Partners:
Barbara R.C. Doherty, Senior Partner
416-595-8621
bdoherty@millerthomson.com
E. Peter Auvinen, Managing Partner
416-595-8162
pauvinen@millerthomson.com

Miller Thomson LLP - Calgary
#3000, 700 - 9th Ave. SW, Calgary, AB T2P 3V4
Tel: 403-298-2400; *Fax:* 403-262-0007
Toll-Free: 888-298-2400
calgary@millerthomson.com
www.millerthomson.com

Profile: 46 Lawyers, Founded in: 1987
Miller Thompson's Financial Services Law Group consists of a multi-disciplinary team of lawyers with specific expertise in lending & real estate transactions, securities & insurance law, trusts, & taxation. The group has experience in the regulation of financial institutions. Clients include major Canadian & foreign banks, trust & insurance companies, pension funds, credit unions, finance companies, government loan agencies & governments, & numerous corporate borrowers from diverse sectors of the economy.
Senior and Managing Partners:
Shashi B. Malik, Managing Partner
403-298-2443
smalik@millerthomson.com

Miller Thomson LLP - Edmonton
#2700, Commerce Place, 10155 - 102nd St., Edmonton, AB T5J 4G8
Tel: 780-429-1751; *Fax:* 780-424-5866
Toll-Free: 800-215-1016
edmonton@millerthomson.com
www.millerthomson.com

Profile: 49 Lawyers, Founded in: 1953
Corporate/Commercial; Estate Planning; Financial Services; Insolvency & Restructuring; Insurance Litigation; Mergers & Acquisitions; Pension & Benefits; Securities & Corporate Finance; Securities Litigation & Enforcement; Taxation
Senior and Managing Partners:
Sandra L. Hawes, Managing Partner
780-429-9787
shawes@millerthomson.com
Kent H. Davidson, Q.C., Firm Chair & Partner
780-429-9790
kdavidson@millerthomson.com

Miller Thomson LLP - Guelph
#301, Ontario AGRICentre, 100 Stone Rd. West, Guelph, ON N1G 5L3
Tel: 519-822-4680; *Fax:* 519-822-1583
Toll-Free: 866-658-0092
guelph@millerthompson.com
www.millerthomson.com

Profile: 17 Lawyers, Founded in: 1906
The office offers advice and representation in labour and employment, family law, corporate and commercial, agri-business law, health professionals, estate planning, condominium law, as well as municipal and real estate development.
Senior and Managing Partners:
Thomas W.R. Manes, Managing Partner
519-780-4614
tmanes@millerthomson.com

Miller Thomson LLP - London
#2010, One London Place, 255 Queens Ave., London, ON N6A 5R8
Tel: 519-931-3500; *Fax:* 519-858-8511
Toll-Free: 877-319-3500
london@millerthomson.com
www.millerthomson.com

Profile: 15 Lawyers
Senior and Managing Partners:
John K. Downing, Managing Partner
519-931-3506
jdowning@millerthomson.com

Miller Thomson LLP - Markham
#600, 60 Columbia Way, Markham, ON L3R 0C9
Tel: 905-415-6700; *Fax:* 905-415-6777
Toll-Free: 866-348-2432
markham@millerthomson.com
www.millerthomson.com

Profile: 11 Lawyers, Founded in: 1957
Senior and Managing Partners:
E. Peter Auvinen, Managing Partner
416-595-8162
pauvinen@millerthomson.com
Andy Chan, Managing Partner
905-415-6751
achan@millerthomson.com

Miller Thomson LLP - Montréal
Also Known As: Miller Thomson Pouliot S.E.N.C.R.L.
#3700, 1000, rue de la Gauchetière ouest, Montréal, QC H3B 4W5
Tél: 514-875-5210; *Téléc:* 514-875-4308
Ligne sans frais: 888-875-5210
info@millerthomsonpouliot.com
www.millerthomson.com

Profile: 59 Lawyers, Founded in: 1952
Senior and Managing Partners:
Bernard Blouin, Associé directeur
514-871-5351
bblouin@millerthomson.com

Miller Thomson LLP - Regina
Former Name: Balfour Moss
#600, Bank of Montreal Building, 2103 - 11th Ave., Regina, SK S4P 3Z8
Tel: 306-347-8300; *Fax:* 306-347-8350
Toll-Free: 855-347-8300
regina@millerthomson.com
www.millerthomson.com

Profile: 21 Lawyers
Institutional lenders, local national and international businesses and is active in the real estate development sector, franchising, criminal law, mergers and acquisitions and environmental law and regulation.
Senior and Managing Partners:
Jeff N. Grubb, Q.C., Managing Partner
306-347-8393
jgrubb@millerthomson.com

Miller Thomson LLP - Saskatoon
Former Name: Balfour Moss
#300, 15 - 23rd St. East, Sasktoon, SK S7K 0H6
Tel: 306-665-7844; *Fax:* 306-652-1586
Toll-Free: 855-665-7844
saskatoon@millerthomson.com
www.millerthomson.com

Profile: 10 Lawyers, Founded in: 2010
A wide range of clients in joint ventures, financings, partnerships, shareholder agreements and other forms of commercial contracts.
Senior and Managing Partners:
Jeff N. Grubb, Q.C., Managing Partner
306-347-8393
jgrubb@millerthomson.com

Miller Thomson LLP - Vancouver
#1000, Robson Court, 840 Howe St., Vancouver, BC V6Z 2M1
Tel: 604-687-2242; *Fax:* 604-643-1200
Toll-Free: 800-794-6866
vancouver@millerthomson.com
www.millerthomson.com

Profile: 61 Lawyers, Founded in: 2000
Bankruptcy; Corporate; Real Estate; Securities; Taxation
Senior and Managing Partners:
Karen A.R. Dickson, Managing Partner
604-643-1210
kdickson@millerthomson.com

Miller Thomson LLP - Waterloo
#300, Accelerator Bldg., 295 Hagey Blvd., Waterloo, ON N2L 6R5
Tel: 519-579-3660; *Fax:* 519-743-2540
Toll-Free: 866-658-0091
waterloo@millerthomson.com
www.millerthomson.com

Profile: 41 Lawyers, Founded in: 1876
Advice and representation in commercial litigation, insurance defence, labour and employment law, patent and intellectual property law, and corporate law.
Senior and Managing Partners:
Patricia J. Forte, Managing Partner
519-593-3219
pforte@millerthomson.com

Norton Rose Fulbright Canada LLP - Montréal
Former Name: Ogilvy Renault LLP/S.E.N.C.R.L., s.r.l. - Montréal
#2500, 1, Place Ville Marie, Montréal, QC H3B 1R1
Tél: 514-847-4747; *Téléc:* 514-286-5474
www.nortonrosefulbright.com/ca
twitter.com/NLawGlobal,
www.linkedin.com/company/nortonrosefulbright

Profile: 6 Offices, 585 Lawyers, Founded in: 1879
Asset-based Lending; Banking & Financial Products; Corporate & Commercial Law; Insolvency & Restructuring; Mergers & Acquisitions; Projects & Project Finance; Securities; Tax
Senior and Managing Partners:
Jean R. Allard, Senior Partner
514-847-4400
jean.allard@nortonrosefulbright.com

R. Luc Beaulieu, Senior Partner
514-847-4428
luc.beaulieu@nortonrosefulbright.com
Jean G. Bertrand, Senior Partner
514-847-4401
jean.bertrand@nortonrosefulbright.com
Pierre Bienvenu, Senior Partner
514-847-4452
pierre.bienvenu@nortonrosefulbright.com
Robert G. Borduas, SeniorPartner
514-847-4524
robert.borduas@nortonrosefulbright.com
Danièle Boutet, Senior Partner
514-847-4527
daniele.boutet@nortonrosefulbright.com
Michel G. Carle, Senior Partner
514-847-4501
michel.carle@nortonrosefulbright.com
Mario M. Caron, Senior Partner
514-847-4525
mario.caron@nortonrosefulbright.com
Christine A. Carron, Senior Partner
514-847-4404
christine.carron@nortonrosefulbright.com
Jules Charette, Senior Partner
514-847-4450
jules.charette@nortonrosefulbright.com
John A. Coleman, Senior Partner
514-847-4503
john.coleman@nortonrosefulbright.com
Éric Dunberry, Senior Partner
514-847-4492
eric.dunberry@nortonrosefulbright.com
Marc Duquette, Senior Partner
514-847-4508
marc.duquette@nortonrosefulbright.com
François Fontaine, Senior Partner
514-847-4413
francois.fontaine@nortonrosefulbright.com
Pierre Hébert, Senior Partner
514-847-4474
pierre.hebert@nortonrosefulbright.com
William Hesler, Q.C., Senior Partner
514-847-4510
william.hesler@nortonrosefulbright.com
Olivier F. Kott, Senior Partner
514-847-4445
olivier.kott@nortonrosefulbright.com
Pierre Y. Lamarre, Senior Partner
514-847-4480
pierre.lamarre@nortonrosefulbright.com
Louise Laplante, Senior Partner
514-847-4433
louise.laplante@nortonrosefulbright.com
Hélène Lefebvre, Senior Partner
514-847-4457
helene.lefebvre@nortonrosefulbright.com
Bernard P. Quinn, Senior Partner
514-847-4518
bernard.quinn@nortonrosefulbright.com
Marianne Ignacz, Senior Partner
514-847-4511
marianne.ignacz@nortonrosefulbright.com
Michel G. Sylvestre, Senior Partner
514-847-4460
michel.sylvestre@nortonrosefulbright.com
Paul Raymond, Senior Partner
514-847-4479
paul.raymond@nortonrosefulbright.com
Martin Rochette, Senior Partner
514-847-4430
martin.rochette@nortonrosefulbright.com
Brian Mulroney, P.C., C.C., LL.D., Senior Partner
514-847-4779
brian.mulroney@nortonrosefulbright.com
Solomon Sananes, Managing Partner
514-847-4411
solomon.sananes@nortonrosefulbright.com
Claude Brunet, Senior Partner
514-847-4726
claude.brunet@nortonrosefulbright.com
Jean Piette, Senior Partner
514-847-4584
jean.piette@nortonrosefulbright.com
Jean-Pierre Colpron, Senior Partner
514-847-4880
jean-pierre.colpron@nortonrosefulbright.com
André Legrand, Senior Partner
514-847-4412
andre.legrand@nortonrosefulbright.com
François Côté, Senior Partner
514-847-4464
francois.cote@nortonrosefulbright.com
Wilfrid Lefebvre, Q.C., Senior Partner
514-847-4440
wilfrid.lefebvre@nortonrosefulbright.com

Norton Rose Fulbright Canada LLP - Calgary
Also Known As: Norton Rose
Former Name: Ogilvy Renault LLP; Macleod Dixon LLP
#3700, 400 - 3rd Ave. SW, Calgary, AB T2P 4H2
Tel: 403-267-8222; *Fax:* 403-264-5973
www.nortonrosefulbright.com/ca

Profile: 154 Lawyers
Asset-based Lending; Banking & Financial Products; Corporate & Commercial Law; Insolvency & Restructuring; Mergers & Acquisitions; Projects & Project Finance; Securities; Tax
Senior and Managing Partners:
Robert J. Engbloom, Deputy Chair; Senior Partner
403-267-9405
robert.engbloom@nortonrosefulbright.com
Daniel P. Hays, P.C., Senior Partner
403-267-8338
dan.hays@nortonrosefulbright.com
KevinE. Johnson, Q.C., Senior Partner
403-267-8250
kevin.johnson@nortonrosefulbright.com
Harry J. Ludwig, Senior Partner
403-267-8235
harry.ludwig@nortonrosefulbright.com
Jack MacGillivray, Senior Partner
403-267-9407
jack.macgillivray@nortonrosefulbright.com
Judson E. Virtue, Senior Partner
403-267-9541
jud.virtue@nortonrosefulbright.com
Everett L. Bunnell, Q.C., Senior Partner
403-267-9545
everett.bunnell@nortonrosefulbright.com
William Armstrong, Q.C., Senior Partner
403-267-8255
bill.armstrong@nortonrosefulbright.com
Richard P. Borden, Senior Partner
403-267-8362
rick.borden@nortonrosefulbright.com
John P. Carleton, Senior Partner
403-267-9406
john.carleton@nortonrosefulbright.com
James H. Coleman, Q.C., Senior Partner
403-267-8373
jim.coleman@nortonrosefulbright.com
Mary E. Comeau, Senior Partner
403-267-8156
mary.comeau@nortonrosefulbright.com
Don Davies, Q.C., Senior Partner
403-267-8183
don.davies@nortonrosefulbright.com
Samuel F. Durante, Senior Partner
403-267-8243
samuel.durante@nortonrosefulbright.com
Howard A. Gorman, Q.C., Senior Partner
403-267-8144
howard.gorman@nortonrosefulbright.com
Dave Guichon, Q.C., Senior Partner
403-267-9511
dave.guichon@nortonrosefulbright.com
Alan Harvie, Senior Partner
403-267-9411
alan.harvie@nortonrosefulbright.com
Terrance M. Hughes, Q.C., Senior Partner
403-267-8117
terry.hughes@nortonrosefulbright.com
Clarke Hunter, Q.C., Senior Partner
403-267-8292
clarke.hunter@nortonrosefulbright.com
Kerrie J. Logan, Senior Partner
403-267-8340
kerrie.logan@nortonrosefulbright.com
Howard E. MacKichan, Senior Partner
403-267-8388
howard.mackichan@nortonrosefulbright.com
Donald S. MacKimmie, Q.C., Senior Partner
403-267-9403
donald.mackimmie@nortonrosefulbright.com
Ian E. MacRae, Senior Partner
403-267-8153
ian.macrae@nortonrosefulbright.com
Stephen G. Raby, Q.C., Senior Partner
403-267-8226
steve.raby@nortonrosefulbright.com
Robert A. Rakochey, Senior Partner
403-267-8234
rob.rakochey@nortonrosefulbright.com
Alan Rudakoff, Senior Partner
403-267-8270
alan.rudakoff@nortonrosefulbright.com
Rick Skeith, Senior Partner
403-267-8165
rick.skeith@nortonrosefulbright.com
Thomas E. Valentine, Senior Partner
403-267-8154
tom.valentine@nortonrosefulbright.com

Norton Rose Fulbright Canada LLP - Ottawa
Also Known As: Norton Rose
Former Name: Ogilvy Renault LLP
#1500, 45 O'Connor St., Ottawa, ON K1P 1A4
Tel: 613-780-8661; *Fax:* 613-230-5459
www.nortonrosefulbright.com/ca

Profile: 35 Lawyers
Asset-based Lending; Banking & Financial Products; Corporate & Commercial Law; Insolvency & Restructuring; Mergers & Acquisitions; Projects & Project Finance; Securities; Tax
Senior and Managing Partners:
Norman B. Lieff, Senior Partner
613-780-8611
norman.lieff@nortonrosefulbright.com
Matthew J. Halpin, Senior Partner
613-780-8654
matthew.halpin@nortonrosefulbright.com
D. John Naccarato, Senior Partner
613-780-8608
john.naccarato@nortonrosefulbright.com
Richard A. Wagner, Senior Partner
613-780-8632
richard.wagner@nortonrosefulbright.com
Charles E. Hurdon, Managing Partner, Canada
613-780-8653
charles.hurdon@nortonrosefulbright.com
Andrew Pritchard, Senior Partner
613-780-8607
andrew.pritchard@nortonrosefulbright.com

Norton Rose Fulbright Canada LLP - Québec
Also Known As: Norton Rose
Former Name: Ogilvy Renault LLP
#1500, Complexe Jules-Dallaire/Tour Norton Rose Fulbright, 2828, boul Laurier, Québec, QC G1V 0B9
Tel: 418-640-5000; *Fax:* 418-640-1500
www.nortonrosefulbright.com/ca

Profile: 41 Lawyers
Asset-based Lending; Banking & Financial Products; Corporate & Commercial Law; Insolvency & Restructuring; Mergers & Acquisitions; Projects & Project Finance; Securities; Tax
Senior and Managing Partners:
Carl Tremblay, Managing Partner
418-640-5013
carl.tremblay@nortonrosefulbright.com

Norton Rose Fulbright Canada LLP - Toronto
Also Known As: Norton Rose
Former Name: Ogilvy Renault LLP
#3800, Royal Bank Plaza South Tower, P.O. Box 84, 200 Bay St., Toronto, ON M5J 2Z4
Tel: 416-216-4000; *Fax:* 416-216-3930
www.nortonrosefulbright.com/ca

Profile: 190 Lawyers
Asset-based Lending; Banking & Financial Products; Corporate & Commercial Law; Insolvency & Restructuring; Mergers & Acquisitions; Projects & Project Finance; Securities; Tax
Senior and Managing Partners:
Michael J. Lang, Senior Partner
416-216-3939
michael.lang@nortonrosefulbright.com
John B. West, Senior Partner
416-216-3976
john.west@nortonrosefulbright.com
Terence S. Dobbin, Senior Partner
416-216-3935
terence.dobbin@nortonrosefulbright.com
Richard J. Lachcik, Senior Partner
416-202-6711
richard.lachcik@nortonrosefulbright.com
Dawn P. Whittaker, Senior Partner
416-216-1895
dawn.whittaker@nortonrosefulbright.com
Janne Duncan, Senior Partner
416-202-6715
janne.duncan@nortonrosefulbright.com
Michael R. Moher, Senior Partner
416-202-6701
mike.moher@nortonrosefulbright.com

Peter S. Newell, Senior Partner
416-216-2963
peter.newell@nortonrosefulbright.com
David Knight, Senior Partner
416-203-4460
david.knight@nortonrosefulbright.com
Marvin Singer, Senior Partner
416-203-4426
marvin.singer@nortonrosefulbright.com
Robert A. Kozlov, Senior Partner
416-216-4810
robert.kozlov@nortonrosefulbright.com
Peter E. Lockie, Senior Partner
416-216-4813
peter.lockie@nortonrosefulbright.com
John Mastoras, Senior Partner
416-216-3905
john.mastoras@nortonrosefulbright.com
Mark A. Convery, Senior Partner
416-216-4803
mark.convery@nortonrosefulbright.com
Brian W. Gray, Senior Partner
416-216-1905
brian.gray@nortonrosefulbright.com
Rogers Watkiss, Senior Partner
416-202-6716
roger.watkiss@nortonrosefulbright.com
Ruth I. Wahl, Senior Partner
416-216-3910
ruth.wahl@nortonrosefulbright.com
James R. Cade, Senior Partner
416-216-4840
james.cade@nortonrosefulbright.com
Andrew Fleming, Managing Partner
416-216-4007
andrew.fleming@nortonrosefulbright.com
James A. Hodgson, Senior Partner
416-216-2989
jim.hodgson@nortonrosefulbright.com
Richard S. Sutin, Senior Partner
416-216-4821
richard.sutin@nortonrosefulbright.com
James H. Coleman, Q.C., Senior Partner
416-202-6748
jim.coleman@nortonrosefulbright.com
Patrick E. Kierans, Senior Partner
416-216-3904
patrick.kierans@nortonrosefulbright.com

Osler, Hoskin & Harcourt LLP - Toronto
Also Known As: Osler
#6200, One First Canadian Place, P.O. Box 50, 100 King St. West, Toronto, ON M5X 1B8
Tel: 416-362-2111; *Fax:* 416-862-6666
www.osler.com
twitter.com/osler_law,
www.linkedin.com/company/osler-hoskin-&-harcourt-llp
Profile: 6 Offices, 400 Lawyers
Advises many of Canada's corporate leaders as well as U.S. & international parties with extensive interests in Canada; has over 400 lawyers based in Toronto, Montréal, Ottawa, Calgary, Vancouver & New York; specializes in mergers & acquisitions, tax, competition & litigation, commercial property & infrastructure projects, IP & IT, & more
Senior and Managing Partners:
Dale R. Ponder, Managing Partner/CEO
416-862-6500
dponder@osler.com

Osler, Hoskin & Harcourt LLP - Calgary
#2500, TransCanada Tower, 450 - 1st St. SW, Calgary, AB T2P 5H1
Tel: 403-260-7000; *Fax:* 403-260-7024
www.osler.com
Profile: 52 Lawyers
Senior and Managing Partners:
Maureen Killoran, Managing Partner
403-260-7003
mkilloran@osler.com

Osler, Hoskin & Harcourt S.E.N.C.R.L./LLP
#2100, 1000, rue de la Gauchetière ouest, Montréal, QC H3B 4W5
Tel: 514-904-8100; *Fax:* 514-904-8101
www.osler.com
Profile: 66 Lawyers
Senior and Managing Partners:
Shahir Guindi, Managing Partner
514-904-8126
sguindi@osler.com

Osler, Hoskin & Harcourt LLP - Ottawa
#1900, 340 Albert St., Ottawa, ON K1R 7Y6
Tel: 613-235-7234; *Fax:* 613-235-2867
www.osler.com
Profile: 22 Lawyers
Senior and Managing Partners:
Donna White, Managing Partner
613-787-1061
dwhite@osler.com

Osler, Hoskin & Harcourt LLP - Vancouver
#1700, Guinness Tower, 1055 West Hastings St., Vancouver, BC V6E 2E9
Fax: 778-785-2745
Toll-Free: 888-675-3755
www.osler.com

Siskind LLP - London
Former Name: Siskind, Cromarty, Ivey & Dowler LLP
P.O. Box 2520, 680 Waterloo St., London, ON N6A 3V8
Tel: 519-672-2121; *Fax:* 519-672-6065
Toll-Free: 877-672-2121
hello@siskinds.com
www.siskinds.com
www.facebook.com/siskinds, twitter.com/SiskindsLLP
Profile: 4 Offices, 100 Lawyers, Founded in: 1933
Bankruptcy & Insolvency Law; Business Law; Commercial Litigation; Creditors Rights; Financial Institutions; Franchise Law; Insurance Law

Siskind LLP - Montreal
#501, 480, boul Saint-Laurent, Montréal, QC H2Y 3Y7
Tél: 514-849-1970; *Téléc:* 514-849-7934
www.siskinds.com

Siskind LLP - Québec
#320, 43, rue Buade, Québec, QC G1R 4A2
Tél: 418-694-2009; *Téléc:* 418-694-0281
www.siskinds.com

Siskind LLP - Toronto
#302, 100 Lombard St., Toronto, ON M5C 1M3
Tel: 416-362-8334; *Fax:* 416-362-2610
www.siskinds.com
Profile:
Insolvency, civil & commercial litigation; immigration litigation; defence litigation on behalf of financial institutions

Smart & Biggar/Fetherstonhaugh - Toronto
#1100, 150 York St., Toronto, ON M5H 3S5
Tel: 416-593-5514; *Fax:* 416-591-1690
toronto@smart-biggar.ca
www.smart-biggar.ca
Profile: 28 Lawyers
Senior and Managing Partners:
Mark Evans, Co-Managing Partner
416-593-5514
mkevans@smart-biggar.ca
Ronald Faggetter, Chair & Co-Managing Partner
416-593-5514
rdfaggetter@smart-biggar.ca

Smart & Biggar/Fetherstonhaugh - Calgary
#301, Burns Bldg., 237 - 8th Ave. SE, Calgary, AB T2G 5C3
Tel: 587-887-9997; *Fax:* 587-887-9998
calgary@smart-biggar.ca
www.smart-biggar.ca

Smart & Biggar/Fetherstonhaugh - Montréal
#3300, 1000, rue de la Gauchetière ouest, Montréal, QC H3B 4W5
Tél: 514-954-1500; *Téléc:* 514-954-1396
montreal@smart-biggar.ca
www.smart-biggar.ca
Profile: 15 Lawyers

Smart & Biggar/Fetherstonhaugh - Ottawa
#900, P.O. Box 2999, Stn. D, 55 Metcalfe St., Ottawa, ON K1P 5Y6
Tel: 613-232-2486; *Fax:* 613-232-8440
ottawa@smart-biggar.ca
www.smart-biggar.ca
twitter.com/smartbiggar,
www.linkedin.com/company/smart-&-biggar
Profile: 5 Offices, 111 Lawyers, Founded in: 1890
The firm specializes in intellectual property & technology law.

Smart & Biggar/Fetherstonhaugh - Vancouver
#2300, P.O. Box 11115, 1055 West Georgia St., Vancouver, BC V6E 3P3
Tel: 604-682-7780; *Fax:* 604-682-0274
vancouver@smart-biggar.ca
www.smart-biggar.ca
Profile: 17 Lawyers
Senior and Managing Partners:
John Knox, Managing Partner
jwknox@smart-biggar.ca

Stewart McKelvey - Halifax
Former Name: Stewart McKelvey Stirling Scales
#900, Purdy's Wharf Tower One, P.O. Box 997, 1959 Upper Water St., Halifax, NS B3J 2X2
Tel: 902-420-3200; *Fax:* 902-420-1417
halifax@stewartmckelvey.com
www.stewartmckelvey.com
twitter.com/SM_Law, www.linkedin.com/company/85897
Profile: 6 Offices, 221 Lawyers, Founded in: 1867
Tax Law; Insurance; Securities Law & Business Transactions; Bank and bankruptcy law; Insolvency and restructuring
Senior and Managing Partners:
Lydia S. Bugden, Managing Partner & CEO
902-420-3372
lbugden@stewartmckelvey.com

Stewart McKelvey - Charlottetown
P.O. Box 2140, 65 Grafton St., Charlottetown, PE C1A 8B9
Tel: 902-892-2485; *Fax:* 902-566-5283
charlottetown@stewartmckelvey.com
www.stewartmckelvey.com
Profile: 28 Lawyers
Senior and Managing Partners:
Spencer Campbell, Q.C., Managing Partner
902-629-4549
scampbell@stewartmckelvey.com

Stewart McKelvey - Fredericton
#600, Frederick Square, P.O. Box 730, 77 Westmorland St., Fredericton, NB E3B 5B4
Tel: 506-458-1970; *Fax:* 506-444-8974
fredericton@stewartmckelvey.com
www.stewartmckelvey.com
Profile: 13 Lawyers

Stewart McKelvey - Moncton
#601, Blue Cross Centre, P.O. Box 28051, 644 Main St., Moncton, NB E1C 9N4
Tel: 506-853-1970; *Fax:* 506-858-8454
moncton@stewartmckelvey.com
www.stewartmckelvey.com
Profile: 17 Lawyers

Stewart McKelvey - Saint John
#1000, Brunswick House, P.O. Box 7289, Stn. A, 44 Chipman Hill, Saint John, NB E2L 4S6
Tel: 506-632-1970; *Fax:* 506-652-1989
saint-john@stewartmckelvey.com
www.stewartmckelvey.com
Profile: 32 Lawyers
Senior and Managing Partners:
Catherine A. Lahey, Managing Partner
506-632-8307
clahey@stewartmckelvey.com

Stewart McKelvey - St. John's
#1100, Cabot Place, P.O. Box 5038, 100 New Gower St., St. John's, NL A1C 5V3
Tel: 709-722-4270; *Fax:* 709-722-4565
st-johns@stewartmckelvey.com
www.stewartmckelvey.com
Profile: 31 Lawyers
Senior and Managing Partners:
Neil L. Jacobs, Managing Partner
709-570-8888
njacobs@stewartmckelvey.com

Stikeman Elliott LLP - Montréal
1155, boul René-Lévesque ouest, 40th Fl., Montréal, QC H3B 3V2
Tel: 514-397-3000; *Fax:* 514-397-3222
www.stikeman.com
twitter.com/stikemanelliott,
www.linkedin.com/company/stikeman-elliott-llp
Profile: 8 Offices, 491 Lawyers, Founded in: 1952
Les spécialités du bureau de Montréal sont les fusions et les acquisitions, les restructurations financières transfrontalières, l'impartition, les valeurs mobilières, le droit bancaire, la fiscalité et les opérations sur les marchandises à l'échelle internationale, la technologie de l'information et le commerce électronique, le transport, le droit des assurances et le droit du travail. Le savoir-faire de Stikeman Elliott en droit civil et dans les opérations commerciales. La majorité du travail effectué par le bureau de Montréal porte principalement sur des activités internationales.
Senior and Managing Partners:
André J. Roy, Associé directeur
514-397-3119
aroy@stikeman.com

Stikeman Elliott LLP - Calgary
#4300, Bankers Hall West, 888 - 3rd St. SW, Calgary, AB T2P 5C5
Tel: 403-266-9000; *Fax:* 403-266-9034
www.stikeman.com

Profile: 50 Lawyers, Founded in: 1992
The office's practice is focused on M&A, securities, real estate, joint ventures, project financings, structured financings, tax, employment & banking. It also advises on foreign investment in the Canadian energy sector & cross-border trade in energy resources. It maintains a commercial litigation practice and has a reputation for its regulatory practice involving oil, gas & electricity.
Senior and Managing Partners:
Leland P. Corbett, Managing Partner
403-266-9046
lcorbett@stikeman.com

Stikeman Elliott LLP - Ottawa
#1600, 50 O'Connor St., Ottawa, ON K1P 6L2
Tel: 613-234-4555; *Fax:* 613-230-8877
Toll-Free: 877-776-2263
www.stikeman.com

Profile: 13 Lawyers, Founded in: 1981
Senior and Managing Partners:
Justine M. Whitehead, Managing Partner
613-566-0541
jwhitehead@stikeman.com

Stikeman Elliott LLP - Toronto
#5300, Commerce Court West, 199 Bay St., Toronto, ON M5L 1B9
Tel: 416-869-5500; *Fax:* 416-947-0866
Toll-Free: 877-973-5500
www.stikeman.com

Profile: 219 Lawyers
Senior and Managing Partners:
Jay Kellerman, Managing Partner
416-869-5201
jkellerman@stikeman.com
Kathleen G. Ward, Senior Partner
416-869-5617
kward@stikeman.com

Stikeman Elliott LLP - Vancouver
#1700, Park Place, 666 Burrard St., Vancouver, BC V6C 2X8
Tel: 604-631-1300; *Fax:* 604-681-1825
www.stikeman.com

Profile: 36 Lawyers, Founded in: 1988
Corporate Commercial Law; Corporate Finance; Mergers & Acquisitions; Commercial Litigation; Banking; Commercial Real Property
Senior and Managing Partners:
Ross A. MacDonald, Managing Partner
604-631-1367
rmacdonald@stikeman.com

Torys LLP - Toronto
Former Name: Tory Tory DesLauriers & Binnington
TD South Tower, P.O. Box 270, 79 Wellington St. West, 30th Fl., Toronto, ON M5K 1N2
Tel: 416-865-0040; *Fax:* 416-865-7380
www.torys.com
www.facebook.com/TorysLLP, twitter.com/torysllp,
www.linkedin.com/company/torys-llp

Profile: 5 Offices, 373 Lawyers, Founded in: 1941
Torys LLP is an international business law firm with offices in Toronto, New York & Calgary. Torys is known for its seamless cross-border services in a range of areas, including mergers & acquisitions; corporate & capital markets; litigation & dispute resolution; restructuring & insolvency; taxation; competition & antitrust; environmental, health & safety; debt finance & lending; project development & finance; managed assets; private equity & venture capital; financial institutions; pension & employment; intellectual property; technology, media & telecom; life sciences; real estate; infrastructure & energy; climate change & emissions trading; & personal client services.
Senior and Managing Partners:
Les M. Viner, Managing Partner
416-865-8107
lviner@torys.com

Torys LLP - Calgary
Eighth Avenue Place East, 525 - 8th Ave. SW, 46th Fl., Calgary, AB T2P 1G1
Tel: 403-776-3700; *Fax:* 403-776-3800
www.torys.com

Profile: 17 Lawyers, Founded in: 2011
Senior and Managing Partners:
Ron Deyholos, Partner; Head, Calgary
403-776-3718
rdeyholos@torys.com

Torys LLP - Halifax
Also Known As: Torys Legal Services Centre (LSC)
#200, 1871 Hollis St., Halifax, NS B3J 0C3
Tel: 902-720-3500
www.torys.com

Profile: 6 Lawyers, Founded in: 2014
The Legal Services Centre (LSC) supports Torys lawyers across all offices with the following services: drafting of documents; corporate reorganization implementation; due diligence; banking & security documentation; & more

Torys LLP - Montréal
#2880, 1 Place Ville Marie, Montréal, QC H3B 2C3
Tél: 514-868-5600; *Téléc:* 514-868-5700
www.torysmontreal.com

Profile: 7 Lawyers, Founded in: 2013
Senior and Managing Partners:
Sylvie Rodrigue, Partner
514-868-5601
srodrigue@torys.com
William McNamara, Partner
514-868-5622
wmcnamara@torys.com

Law Firms/By Province

Alberta

***Airdrie*: Warnock, Rathgeber & Company - *2**
Also Known As: Warnock Rathgeber & Company
Former Name: Warnock, Rathgeber & Hassett
225 First Ave. NW, Airdrie, AB T4B 2M8
Tel: 403-948-0009; *Fax:* 403-948-6740
office@wrlawyers.ca
www.wrlawyers.ca

***Banff*: Eric Harvie - *1**
#202, P.O. Box 3220, 216 Banff Ave., Banff, AB T1L 1C8
Tel: 403-762-3438; *Fax:* 403-762-8101
ericharvie@telus.net
www.ericharvielaw.ca

***Barrhead*: Driessen Law Office - *1**
P.O. Box 4220, Stn. Main, 5017 - 50 Ave., Barrhead, AB T7N 1A2
Tel: 780-674-2276; *Fax:* 780-674-4592
solutions@driessenlaw.ca

***Blairmore*: Valerie J. Danielson Law Office - *1**
P.O. Box 1620, 13143 - 20th Ave., Blairmore, AB T0K 0E0
Tel: 403-562-2132; *Fax:* 403-562-2700
valeriejdanielson@shaw.ca

***Bonnyville*: Allan Wayne Fraser, Professional Corporation - *1**
P.O. Box 6710, Stn. Main, 4816 - 50 Ave., Bonnyville, AB T9N 2H2
Tel: 780-826-3355; *Fax:* 780-826-6132
awfraser@telusplanet.net

***Bonnyville*: Wood & Wiebe - *2**
#101, P.O. Box 8060, Stn. Main, 4811 - 50 Ave., Bonnyville, AB T9N 2J3
Tel: 780-826-5767; *Fax:* 780-826-4654
woodwieb@telusplanet.net

***Brooks*: Douglas H. Bell Law Office - *1**
P.O. Box 670, Stn. Main, 103 - 2nd Ave. West, Brooks, AB T1R 1B6
Tel: 403-362-3447; *Fax:* 403-362-4379
dhb@telus.net

***Brooks*: Susan E. Robertson - *1**
411B Third Ave. West, Brooks, AB T1R 0B2
Tel: 403-362-4064; *Fax:* 403-362-4024
www.susanrobertsonlawoffice.ca

***Calgary*: Allen Hryniuk - *2**
Former Name: Laurie Allen & Associates
#403, 888 - 4 Ave. SW, Calgary, AB T2P 0V2
Tel: 403-266-5556; *Fax:* 403-266-5427
mail@allenhryniuk.com
allenhryniuk.com

***Calgary*: Robert J.E. Allen Law Office - *1**
1817 Crowchild Trail NW, Calgary, AB T3A 2L6
Tel: 403-216-5522; *Fax:* 403-216-5524
admin@calgarylawyer.net

***Calgary*: Anderson Law Firm - *1**
14 Strathridge Grove SW, Calgary, AB T3H 4M1
Tel: 403-253-4597; *Fax:* 403-253-4599
latitude@telus.net

***Calgary*: Linda A. Anderson - *1**
#16, 2439 - 54 Ave. SW, Calgary, AB T3E 1M4
Tel: 403-243-6400; *Fax:* 403-243-0126
linda@lindaandersonlaw.com

***Calgary*: Armstrong & Partners - *4**
#800, 736 - 6 Ave. SW, Calgary, AB T2P 3T7
Tel: 403-537-9950; *Fax:* 403-537-9951
lawyers@aplaw.com
www.aplaw.com

***Calgary*: Deborah L. Barron - *1**
Macleod Place II, 5940 Macleod Trail SW, 5th Fl., Calgary, AB T2H 2G4
Tel: 403-238-0000; *Fax:* 403-238-2255
dbarron@deborahbarronlaw.com
www.deborahbarronlaw.com

***Calgary*: Robert J. Batting - *1**
#2410, 645 - 7 Ave. SW, Calgary, AB T2P 4G8
Tel: 403-263-4949; *Fax:* 403-261-8977
rbatting@telus.net
www.rbattinglaw.com/en/

***Calgary*: Alan V.M. Beattie, Q.C. - *1**
3621 - 1A St. SW, Calgary, AB T2S 1R4
Tel: 403-245-5255; *Fax:* 403-228-0254
beattiea@shaw.ca

***Calgary*: Gary E. Bilyk Professional Corporation - *1**
#602, 706 - 7 Ave. SW, Calgary, AB T2P 0Z1
Tel: 403-266-2810; *Fax:* 403-264-1151
gebilyklawyer@shaw.ca

***Calgary*: Blake, Nichol Law Office - *1**
Former Name: Reich Nichol
#226, 4935 - 40 Ave. NW, Calgary, AB T3A 2N1
Tel: 403-288-6500; *Fax:* 403-288-6510
blake@blakenichol.ca
www.blakenichol.ca

***Calgary*: Blumell & Hartney - *2**
#203, 2411 - 4 St. NW, Calgary, AB T2M 2Z8
Tel: 403-282-4544; *Fax:* 403-284-4503

***Calgary*: Michael J. Bondar, Professional Corporation - *1**
#1840, 801 - 6 Ave. SW, Calgary, AB T2P 3W2
Tel: 403-266-5511; *Fax:* 403-237-6620
mjbondar@shaw.ca

***Calgary*: Burstall Winger LLP - *28**
#1600, Dome Tower, 333 - 7th Ave. SW, Calgary, AB T2P 2Z1
Tel: 403-264-1915; *Fax:* 403-266-6016
www.burstall.com
www.linkedin.com/company/burstall-winger-zammit-llp

***Calgary*: Richard Cairns, Q.C. - *1**
#1210, 630 - 6th Ave. SW, Calgary, AB T2P 0S8
Tel: 403-205-3155; *Fax:* 403-546-0034
counsel@echambers.ca
www.echambers.ca

***Calgary*: Calgary Legal Guidance**
#100, 840 - 7th Ave. SW, Calgary, AB T2P 3G2
Tel: 403-234-9266; *Fax:* 403-234-9299
clg@clg.ab.ca
www.clg.ab.ca

***Calgary*: Cameron Horne Law Office LLP - *2**
Former Name: A.B. Cameron
#820, 10201 Southport Rd. SW, Calgary, AB T2W 4X9
Tel: 403-531-2700; *Fax:* 403-531-2707
geoff@cameronhorne.ca
www.cameronhorne.ca

***Calgary*: Campbell O'Hara - *12**
Former Name: Campbell Taylor O'Hara
#1160, 1122 - 4th St. SW, Calgary, AB T2R 1M1
Tel: 403-294-0030; *Fax:* 403-229-2977
Assistant@CampbellOHara.com
www.campbellohara.com
www.facebook.com/pages/Campbell-OHara/150802634953217

***Calgary*: Caron & Partners LLP - *16**
#2100, Scotia Centre, 700 - 2 St. SW, 21st Fl., Calgary, AB T2P 2W1
Tel: 403-262-3000; *Fax:* 403-237-0111
legalservices@caronpartners.com
www.caronpartners.com

***Calgary*: Carscallen LLP**
#1500, 407 - 2 St. SW, Calgary, AB T2P 2Y3
Tel: 403-262-3775; *Fax:* 403-262-2952
www.carscallen.com

* *indicates number of lawyers*

Calgary: Castle & Associates - *5
#302, 221 - 10th Ave. SE, Calgary, AB T2G 0V9
Tel: 587-326-0128; Fax: 403-269-3217
Toll-Free: 800-653-6495
mailbox@castleandassociates.ca
www.castleandassociates.ca

Calgary: Chadi & Company - *1
1832 - 19th Ave. SW, Calgary, AB T2T 0J6
Tel: 403-777-1099; Fax: 403-777-1096
Toll-Free: 877-777-1099
info@chadilaw.ca
www.chadilaw.ca

Calgary: Clark & Associates - *2
Also Known As: Brian N. Clark Professional Corporation
#203, 136 - 17 Ave. NE, Calgary, AB T2E 1L6
Tel: 403-520-2011; Fax: 403-230-3509
bclark@clarkandassociates.ca
www.clarkandassociates.ca

Calgary: Clark Dymond McCaffery O'Brien-Kelly - *3
Former Name: Clark Dymond McCaffery
#300, 1122 - 4 St. SW, Calgary, AB T2R 1M1
Tel: 403-265-7070; Fax: 403-232-6750
lawcdmg@telusplanet.net

Calgary: Clayton Rice - *1
Former Name: Ouellette, Rice
#425, 630 - 6 Ave. SW, Calgary, AB T2P 0S8
Tel: 403-263-3855; Fax: 403-265-5855
claytonrice@claytonrice.com
www.claytonrice.com

Calgary: James K. Conley - *1
#210, The Burns Bldg., 237 - 8th Ave. SE, Calgary, AB T2G 5C3
Tel: 403-290-0994; Fax: 403-265-7680
jkconley@telus.net

Calgary: Timothy J. Corcoran - *1
#701, 4656 Westwinds Dr. NE, Calgary, AB T3J 3Z5
Tel: 403-263-6000; Fax: 403-280-7666
alberta@lawyer.com
albertalaw.wordpress.com

Calgary: Cornerstone Law Group LLP - *2
Former Name: Keeler Law Firm; Milne & Company
#225, 10655 Southport Rd. SW, Calgary, AB T2W 4Y1
Tel: 403-296-1700; Fax: 403-258-0020
jordan@cornerstonelaw.ca
www.cornerstonelaw.ca

Calgary: Craig Law LLP - *3
Former Name: Mullen Craig
3408 - 114 Ave. SE, Calgary, AB T2Z 3V6
Tel: 403-297-0130; Fax: 403-297-0133

Calgary: Cuming & Gillespie - *3
Former Name: McNally Cuming Raymaker; McNally Cuming
#210, 140-10th Ave. SE, Calgary, AB T2G 0R1
Tel: 403-571-0555; Fax: 403-232-8818
Toll-Free: 800-682-2480
james@cglaw.ca
www.cglaw.ca

Calgary: Damen Hoffman LLP - *2
Former Name: Arkell Damen Hoffman
109 - 14 Ave. SE, Calgary, AB T2G 1C6
Tel: 403-531-4151; Fax: 403-531-4153
info@damenhoffman.com

Calgary: Daniel J. Aberle Professional Corporation - *1
Former Name: Stirling, Aberle & Row
#305, 602 - 11 Ave. SW, Calgary, AB T2R 1J8
Tel: 403-229-1129; Fax: 403-245-9660
djalaw@aberle.ca
www.danieljaberle.com/en/

Calgary: Gary A. Daniels - *1
#200, 209 - 19 St. NW, Calgary, AB T2N 2H9
Tel: 403-297-0800; Fax: 403-283-7000
garyadaniels@shaw.ca

Calgary: Dartnell & Lutz - *2
Former Name: Dartnell, Wenngatz & Lutz
#840, 840 - 6 Ave. SW, Calgary, AB T2P 3E5
Tel: 403-264-8484; Fax: 403-263-9110
www.dartnellandlutz.com

Calgary: Daunais McKay Harms + Jones - *12
#2050, 645 - 7th Ave. SW, Calgary, AB T2P 4G8
Tel: 403-218-6275; Fax: 403-218-6299
contact@dmhjfamilylaw.com
www.dhjfamilylaw.com

Calgary: Dawe Law Office - *2
#200, 1409 Edmonton Trail NE, Calgary, AB T2E 3K8
Tel: 403-277-3100; Fax: 403-230-5855
terry@dawelawoffice.ca

Calgary: Demiantschuk Lequier Burke & Hoffinger LLP - *10
Also Known As: DLBH LLP
#1200, 1015 - 4th St. SW, Calgary, AB T2R 1J4
Tel: 403-252-9937; Fax: 403-263-8529
assistance@dlbhlaw.com
www.dlbhlaw.com
www.linkedin.com/company/dlbh-law

Calgary: Derburgis - *2
#2410, 645 - 7 Ave. SW, Calgary, AB T2P 4G8
Tel: 403-213-2999; Fax: 403-261-8977
lburgis@telus.net
www.derburgis.com

Calgary: Dixon Law Firm - *2
#501, 888 - 4 Ave. SW, Calgary, AB T2P 0V2
Tel: 403-297-9480; Fax: 403-266-1487

Calgary: Docken & Company - *2
#900, 800 - 6th Ave. SW, Calgary, AB T2P 3G3
Tel: 403-269-3612; Fax: 403-269-8246
info@docken.com
www.docken.com
www.facebook.com/pages/Docken-Company-Class-Action-Lawyers/250575991653402, twitter.com/dockenlaw

Calgary: Dunphy Best Blocksom LLP - *25
#800, 517 - 10 Ave. SW, Calgary, AB T2R 0A8
Tel: 403-265-7777; Fax: 403-269-8911
info@dbblaw.com
www.dbblaw.com
www.linkedin.com/company/dunphy-best-blocksom-llp

Calgary: Ellert Law - *2
#510, 706 - 7 Ave. SW, Calgary, AB T2P 0Z1
Tel: 403-269-3315; Fax: 403-269-3329
dale.ellert@ellertlaw.com

Calgary: P. Robert Enns - *1
#222, 1100 - 8 Ave. SW, Calgary, AB T2P 3T8
Tel: 403-262-6588; Fax: 403-262-6590
prenns@shaw.ca

Calgary: Patrick Fagan - *2
#304, 1117 - 1st St. SW, Calgary, AB T2R 0T9
Tel: 403-517-1777; Fax: 403-517-1776
www.patrickfagan.com

Calgary: Felesky Flynn LLP - Calgary - *22
#5000, Suncor Energy Centre, 150 - 6th Ave. SW, Calgary, AB T2P 3Y7
Tel: 403-260-3300; Fax: 403-263-9649
felesky@felesky.com
www.felesky.com

Calgary: Philip L. Fiess - *1
#312, 602 - 11 Ave. SW, Calgary, AB T2R 1J8
Tel: 403-266-0033; Fax: 403-261-4958
phillfeiss@hotmail.com

Calgary: Findlay Smith LLP - *8
Former Name: Millar Smith & Associates
#300, 1550 - 8th St. SW, Calgary, AB T2R 1K1
Tel: 403-283-1925; Fax: 403-270-8033
www.findlaysmith.com

Calgary: First West Law LLP - *6
Former Name: Butlin Oke Roberts Nobles Braun; Butlin Oke Roberts & Nobles; Butlin Oke & Roberts
#100, 1501 - 1 St. SW, Calgary, AB T2R 0W1
Tel: 403-543-7750; Fax: 403-543-7759
reception@firstwest.com
www.firstwest.com

Calgary: Foster Iovinelli Beyak - *6
#201, 224 - 11 Ave. SW, Calgary, AB T2R 0C3
Tel: 403-269-3655; Fax: 403-237-5109
Toll-Free: 800-884-4780
info@fiblaw.ca
www.fiblaw.ca

Calgary: Fric, Lowenstein & Co. LLP - *4
#420, 1925 - 18 Ave. NE, Calgary, AB T2E 7T8
Tel: 403-291-2594; Fax: 403-291-2668
friclow@telusplanet.net

Calgary: German Fong Albus, Barristers & Solicitors - *5
#418, Hewlett Packard Bldg., 715 - 5 Ave. SW, Calgary, AB T2P 2X6
Tel: 403-263-7880; Fax: 403-237-7075

Calgary: The Law Firm of W. Donald Goodfellow, Q.C. - *3
#715, 999 - 8th St. SW, Calgary, AB T2R 1J5
Tel: 403-228-7102; Fax: 403-228-7199
reception@goodfellowqc.com
www.goodfellowqc.com

Calgary: Sean W. Goodwin Prof Corporation
Former Name: Goodwin McKay
#222, 602 - 12th Ave. SW, Calgary, AB T2R 1J3
Tel: 403-203-0107; Fax: 403-203-0403
goodwinlaw.ca

Calgary: Gorman, Gorman, Burns & Watson - *2
#500, 1135 - 17 Ave. SW, Calgary, AB T2T 0B6
Tel: 403-244-5515; Fax: 403-244-5605

Calgary: Hadley & Davis - *2
#311, 1711 - 4 St. SW, Calgary, AB T2S 1V8
Tel: 403-264-1234; Fax: 403-264-0999
info@hadleydavis.com
www.hadleydavis.com

Calgary: Hansen & Company - *8
538 - 9 Ave. SE, Calgary, AB T2G 0S1
Tel: 403-261-6890; Fax: 403-263-1632
Toll-Free: 800-523-6162
info@hansen-company.com
www.hansen-company.com
www.facebook.com/profile.php?id=100000719988785, twitter.com/hansencompany, ca.linkedin.com/in/hansencompany

Calgary: Larry S. Heald - *1
#300, 840 - 6 Ave. SW, Calgary, AB T2P 3E5
Tel: 403-266-2131; Fax: 403-261-6862
heald@shaw.ca

Calgary: Stephen Graham Heinz - *1
#2900, 350 - 7 Ave. SW, Calgary, AB T2P 3N9
Tel: 403-262-4462; Fax: 403-265-4496
stephen.heinz@3web.net

Calgary: Alain Hepner - *4
Former Name: Ross, Hepner
921 - 18 Ave. SW, Calgary, AB T2T 0H2
Tel: 403-244-6800; Fax: 403-265-2455

Calgary: Clarence J. Hooksen
#218, Mayfair Place, 6707 Elbow Dr. SW, Calgary, AB T2V 0E4
Tel: 403-259-5041; Fax: 403-258-0719

Calgary: Horne Wytrychowski - *5
#14, 620 - 1st Ave. NW, Calgary, AB T4B 2R3
Tel: 403-912-3565
www.airdrielawyers.com

Calgary: Michael M. Jamison - *1
2503 - 22 St. SW, Calgary, AB T2T 5G3
Tel: 403-217-1250; Fax: 403-287-1968
mmjlaw2@shaw.ca

Calgary: Jensen Shawa Solomon Duguid Hawkes LLP - *24
Former Name: May Jensen Shawa Solomon LLP
#800, Lancaster Bldg., 304 - 8 Ave. SW, Calgary, AB T2P 1C2
Tel: 403-571-1520; Fax: 403-571-1528
inquiries@jssbarristers.ca
www.jssbarristers.ca

Calgary: Jivraj Knight & Pritchett, Barristers & Solicitors - *3
Also Known As: JKP Barristers & Solicitors
#1000, 444 - 5 Ave. SW, Calgary, AB T2P 2T8
Tel: 403-261-0017; Fax: 403-266-6030
mailbox@jkp-law.com

Calgary: Kelly & Kelly - *4
#220, 3505 - 32nd St. NE, Calgary, AB T1Y 5Y9
Tel: 403-266-6296; Fax: 403-264-2954
kellykp@telusplanet.net

* indicates number of lawyers

***Calgary*: Robert D. Kerr - *1**
#300, 840 - 6 Ave. SW, Calgary, AB T2P 3E5
Tel: 403-265-1331; *Fax:* 403-265-1332
bkerr@shaw.ca

***Calgary*: George R. Klatt - *1**
#400, Centre 70, 7015 Macleod Trail SW, Calgary, AB T2H 2K6
Tel: 403-255-3033; *Fax:* 403-255-0403

***Calgary*: John Kong - *2**
#330, 1324 - 17 Ave. SW, Calgary, AB T2T 5S8
Tel: 403-233-9432; *Fax:* 403-237-9614
leekong@canada.com

***Calgary*: Kre8tive Law - *1**
Former Name: Riccio Law
#800, 350 - 7th Ave. SW, Calgary, AB T2P 3S1
Tel: 403-289-3131; *Fax:* 403-289-2396
kre8tive@shaw.ca
www.kre8tivelaw.com

***Calgary*: Kubitz & Company - *2**
Former Name: Everard & Kubitz
1716-10th Ave. South West, Calgary, AB T3C 0J8
Tel: 403-250-7100; *Fax:* 403-291-5473
www.kubitzlaw.com

***Calgary*: Kuefler & Company - *3**
#12, 601 - 10th Ave. SW, Calgary, AB T2R 0B2
Tel: 403-237-0123; *Fax:* 403-237-0128
quinn.kuefler@kueflerlaw.com

***Calgary*: Catherine G. Langlois - *1**
4740 - 14th St. NE, Calgary, AB T2E 6L7
Tel: 403-531-9300; *Fax:* 403-261-8977
info@medicalmalpracticecalgary.com
www.medicalmalpracticecalgary.com

***Calgary*: Lauzon Law Office - *1**
#218, 5403 Crowchild Trail NW, Calgary, AB T3B 4Z1
Tel: 403-288-7601; *Fax:* 403-288-3689

***Calgary*: Laven & Company - *2**
#310, McFarlane Tower, 700 - 4th Ave. SW, Calgary, AB T2P 3J4
Tel: 403-263-2444; *Fax:* 403-263-3235
www.lavenco.com

***Calgary*: Corinna Lee - *1**
509 - 20th Ave. SW, Calgary, AB T2S 0E7
Tel: 403-228-2238; *Fax:* 403-228-5550

***Calgary*: Lenhardt Law Office - *1**
#301, 888 - 7 Ave. SW, Calgary, AB T2P 3J3
Tel: 403-237-6970; *Fax:* 403-237-6974

***Calgary*: Leon Bickman Brener - *8**
Former Name: Faber Gurevitch Bickman
#350, 603 - 7 Ave. SW, Calgary, AB T2P 2T5
Tel: 403-263-1540; *Fax:* 403-269-2653
www.fbllaw.ca
www.facebook.com/pages/Leon-Bickman-Brener/413706495344005?ref=hl, twitter.com/LBBLaw,
www.linkedin.com/company/leon-bickman-brener

***Calgary*: Lerner Sutherland - *1**
P.O. Box 32053, Stn. RPO Bankview, 2619 - 14 St. SW, Calgary, AB T2T 5X6
Tel: 403-282-1515; *Fax:* 403-220-1575

***Calgary*: Lord Russell - *6**
410 - 6th St. SW, Calgary, AB T2P 1X2
Tel: 403-262-7722
info@simonlord.ca
www.calgary-criminal-lawyer.ca

***Calgary*: Low, Glenn & Card - *6**
#120, 3636 - 23 St. NE, Calgary, AB T2E 8Z5
Tel: 403-291-2532; *Fax:* 403-291-2534
lawyer@lgc-law.com
www.lowglenncard.ca

***Calgary*: Birjinder P.S. Mangat**
#217, 3825 - 34 St. NE, Calgary, AB T1Y 6Z8
Tel: 403-735-6088; *Fax:* 403-735-6089
bmangat@cadvision.com

***Calgary*: Masuch Albert LLP - Calgary - *15**
Former Name: Masuch, Albert & Neale LLP
#209, 10836 - 24 St. SE, Calgary, AB T2Z 4C9
Tel: 403-543-1100; *Fax:* 403-543-1111
www.manlaw.com

***Calgary*: McCaffery Mudry Pritchard LLP**
#2200, 736 - 6 Ave. SW, Calgary, AB T2P 3T7
Tel: 403-260-1400; *Fax:* 403-260-1444
reception@mccafferylaw.ca
www.mccafferylaw.ca

***Calgary*: McConnell MacInnes - *7**
Former Name: McConnell, MacInnes, Graham
#4, 12110 - 40 St. SE, Calgary, AB T2Z 4K6
Tel: 403-278-7001; *Fax:* 403-271-2826
kfm@mcmaclaw.ca
mcmaclaw.com

***Calgary*: McGown Johnson - *5**
#120, 7260 - 12th St. SE, Calgary, AB T2H 2S5
Tel: 403-255-5114; *Fax:* 403-258-3840
www.mcgownjohnson.com

***Calgary*: McKenna Law Office - *1**
1505 - 5 St. SW, Calgary, AB T2R 1P2
Tel: 403-716-2092; *Fax:* 403-234-7911
paul@mckennalegal.com

***Calgary*: McKinnon Carstairs - *2**
#525, First Alberta Place, 777 - 8 Ave. SW, Calgary, AB T2P 3R5
Tel: 403-261-8822; *Fax:* 403-261-4892
rlmckinnon@mckinnoncarstairs.com

***Calgary*: McLeod & Company LLP - *46**
14505 Bannister Rd. SE, 3rd Fl., Calgary, AB T2X 3J3
Tel: 403-278-9411; *Fax:* 403-271-1769
www.mcleod-law.com
www.facebook.com/McLeodLawLLP,
www.linkedin.com/company/326750

***Calgary*: McManus & Hubler - *2**
63 Rockcliff Landing NW, Calgary, AB T3G 5Z5
Tel: 403-208-6099; *Fax:* 403-208-6018
Toll-Free: 877-423-6054
sean@mcmanus-hubler.ca
www.mcmanus-hubler.ca

***Calgary*: Anne E. McTavish - *1**
7410E - 5th St. SE, Calgary, AB T2H 2L9
Tel: 403-252-4965; *Fax:* 403-253-7743
anne.mctavish@telusplanet.net

***Calgary*: Miles, Davison LLP - *21**
Former Name: Miles, Davison, McCarthy; McNiven Kelly
#1600, Bow Valley Square II, 205 - 5th Ave. SW, Calgary, AB T2P 2V7
Tel: 403-298-0333; *Fax:* 403-263-6840
thefirm@milesdavison.com
www.milesdavison.com

***Calgary*: Milne, Davis & Young - *2**
#850, 933 - 17th Ave. SW, Calgary, AB T2T 5R6
Tel: 403-229-3000; *Fax:* 403-229-3282
milnedavisyoung@shaw.ca

***Calgary*: Moore Wittman Phillips - *6**
#850, 1015 - 4 St. SW, Calgary, AB T2R 1J4
Tel: 403-269-8500; *Fax:* 403-269-8515
mwp@nucleus.com

***Calgary*: Maureen Morgan - *1**
#206, P.O. Box 73001, Stn. RPO Woodbine, 2525 Woodview Dr. SW, Calgary, AB T2W 6E4
Tel: 403-233-2215; *Fax:* 403-264-1328
maureenmorgan96@hotmail.com

***Calgary*: Rick Muenz - *1**
#2410, 645 - 7 Ave. SW, Calgary, AB T2P 4G8
Tel: 403-543-6666; *Fax:* 403-261-8977
info@rickmuenz.ca
www.rickmuenz.ca

***Calgary*: Mullen & Company - *2**
Former Name: Peterson, Shields, Milne, Mullen & Galbraith
#120, 11012 Macleod Trail SE, Calgary, AB T2J 6A5
Tel: 587-331-8259; *Fax:* 403-271-3942
Toll-Free: 800-607-5676
www.mullenco.ca

***Calgary*: Munro & Wood - *2**
#500, 2424 - 4 St. SW, Calgary, AB T2S 2T4
Tel: 403-299-9285; *Fax:* 403-228-1389
katewood@telus.net
www.munrowood.ca

***Calgary*: Murray & Company - *1**
Also Known As: Murray & Company Law Office
#104, 2003 - 14 St. NW, Calgary, AB T2M 3N4
Tel: 403-297-9850; *Fax:* 403-297-9855
gmurray@murraylaw.ca
www.murraylaw.ca

***Calgary*: O'Brien, Devlin, Markey & Macleod - *3**
#1310, Watermark Tower, 530 - 8th Ave. SW, Calgary, AB T2P 3S8
Tel: 403-265-5616; *Fax:* 403-264-8146
nobrien@obriendevlin.com
www.obriendevlin.com

***Calgary*: Parlee McLaws LLP - *82**
#3400, Suncor Energy Centre, 150 - 6th Ave. SW, Calgary, AB T2P 3Y7
Tel: 403-294-7000; *Fax:* 403-265-8263
www.parlee.com

***Calgary*: Peacock Linder Halt & Mack LLP - *16**
Former Name: Mack Meagher LLP; Machida Mack Shewchuk Meagher LLP
#850, 400 - 3rd Ave. SW, Calgary, AB T2P 4H2
Tel: 403-296-2280; *Fax:* 403-296-2299
info@plhlaw.ca
www.plhlaw.ca

***Calgary*: Phipps Law Office - *1**
#303, 8180 MacLeod Trail SE, Calgary, AB T2H 2B8
Tel: 403-531-0182; *Fax:* 403-531-0180

***Calgary*: Pittman MacIsaac & Roy - *5**
#2600, West Tower, Sun Life Plaza, 144 - 4th Ave. SW, Calgary, AB T2P 3N4
Tel: 403-237-6566; *Fax:* 403-237-6594
gwp@pmrlaw.ca
www.pmrlaw.ca

***Calgary*: Pomerance & Company - *3**
#1430, 1122 - 4th St. SW, Calgary, AB T2R 1M1
Tel: 403-278-5840; *Fax:* 403-271-6929
Toll-Free: 866-278-5840
pomeranc@telus.net
www.pomerancelaw.ca

***Calgary*: Lawrence S. Portigal - *1**
6638 Bow Cres. NW, Calgary, AB T3B 2B9
Tel: 403-286-6380; *Fax:* 403-286-6821
lportig@yahoo.com

***Calgary*: ProVenture Law LLP - *5**
#700, 1300 - 8th St. SW, Calgary, AB T2R 1B2
Tel: 403-294-5710; *Fax:* 403-262-4860
www.proventurelaw.com

***Calgary*: Purdy & Purdy - *2**
#801, 1015 - 4th St. SW, Calgary, AB T2R 1J4
Tel: 403-777-4850; *Fax:* 403-777-4855

***Calgary*: Radke & Associates - *2**
#205, 5917 - 1A St. SW, Calgary, AB T2H 0G4
Tel: 403-252-4466; *Fax:* 403-258-0695
info@radkeandassociates.com
www.radkeandassociates.com

***Calgary*: Rae & Company - *4**
#2910, 715 - 5 Ave. SW, Calgary, AB T2P 2X6
Tel: 403-264-8389; *Fax:* 403-264-8399
reception@raeandcompany.com
www.raeandcompany.com

***Calgary*: Ridout Barron, Barristers & Solicitors - *4**
1827 - 14th St. SW, Calgary, AB T2T 3T1
Tel: 403-278-3730; *Fax:* 403-271-8016
info@ridoutbarron.com
www.ridoutbarron.com

***Calgary*: Rogers & Company, Barristers & Solicitors - *8**
#200, 815 - 10 Ave. SW, Calgary, AB T2R 0B4
Tel: 403-263-6805; *Fax:* 403-263-6800
reception@rogcolaw.com
rogcolaw.com

***Calgary*: A. Charles Ruff - *1**
#200, 683 - 10th St. SW, Calgary, AB T2P 5G3
Tel: 403-230-0999

***Calgary*: Salmon & Company - *1**
#577, 717 - 7 Ave. SW, Calgary, AB T2P 0Z3
Tel: 403-231-2705; *Fax:* 403-705-1214
david@salmonco.ca

** indicates number of lawyers*

Calgary: Sara Anand Law - *2
Former Name: Zinner & Sara
#145, 1935 - 32 Ave. NE, Calgary, AB T2E 7C8
Tel: 403-262-7363; *Fax:* 403-233-0392

Calgary: Schwartzberg Law Office - *1
#214, 222 - 16th Ave. NE, Calgary, AB T2E 1J8
Tel: 403-232-1302; *Fax:* 403-249-6655
schwartzberglaw@shaw.ca
www.sblawcalgary.com

Calgary: Scott Venturo LLP - *26
#203, Eau Claire Market, 200 Barclay Parade SW, Calgary, AB T2P 4R5
Tel: 403-261-9043; *Fax:* 403-265-4632
Toll-Free: 877-505-5651
www.scottventuro.com

Calgary: Sefcik & Company - *1
Former Name: Douglas M. Sefcik
#212, 20 Sunpark Plaza SE, Calgary, AB T2X 3T2
Tel: 403-258-1124; *Fax:* 403-640-1220

Calgary: William J. Shachnowich - *1
1700 Varsity Estates Dr. NW, Calgary, AB T3B 2W9
Tel: 403-269-1313; *Fax:* 403-210-0106
shachnow@telus.net

Calgary: Shea Nerland LLP - *16
Former Name: Shea Nerland Calnan LLP
#2800, 715 - 5th Ave. SW, Calgary, AB T2P 2X6
Tel: 403-299-9600; *Fax:* 403-299-9601
info@sheanerland.com
sheanerland.com

Calgary: Singh & Partner LLP - *7
#1101, 3961 - 52 Ave. NE, Calgary, AB T3J 0J7
Tel: 403-285-7070; *Fax:* 403-590-7800
splaw.ca

Calgary: Smith & Smith - *2
#503, 1300 - 8 St. SW, Calgary, AB T2R 1B2
Tel: 403-229-1727; *Fax:* 403-229-1730

Calgary: Smith Law Office - *2
348 - 14 St. NW, Calgary, AB T2N 1Z7
Tel: 403-283-8018; *Fax:* 403-270-3065
j.smith@smithlawoffice.ca
www.smithlawoffice.ca

Calgary: Smith Mack Lamarsh - *3
#450, United Place, 808 - 4 Ave. SW, Calgary, AB T2P 3E8
Tel: 403-234-7779; *Fax:* 403-263-7897
slamarsh@telusplanet.net

Calgary: W. Murray Smith - *1
348 - 14 St. NW, Calgary, AB T2N 1Z7
Tel: 403-283-8018; *Fax:* 403-270-3065

Calgary: Sparrow Law Office - *1
#10, 628 - 12 Ave. SW, Calgary, AB T2R 0H6
Tel: 403-234-9722; *Fax:* 403-237-8748
sparrow@nucleus.com

Calgary: Spier Harben - *9
#1400, Iveagh House, 707 - 7th St. SW, Calgary, AB T2P 3H6
Tel: 403-263-5130; *Fax:* 403-264-9600
asattin@spierharben.com
www.spierharben.com

Calgary: Stephens Holman Devraj - *2
Former Name: Stephens & Holman
412 - 16th Ave. NE, Calgary, AB T2E 1K2
Tel: 403-265-6400; *Fax:* 403-262-9294
rishmad@shdlawyers.ca
www.shdlawyers.ca
www.facebook.com/pages/Stephens-Holman-Devraj/126283444109348

Calgary: Stewart & McCullough - *4
#307, 1228 Kensington Rd. NW, Calgary, AB T2N 3P7
Tel: 403-270-2641; *Fax:* 403-670-7025
martin.meronek@shaw.ca

Calgary: Peter A. Stone - *1
Former Name: Paterson Foster
1923 - 5th St. SW, Calgary, AB T2S 2B2
Tel: 403-283-8460; *Fax:* 403-283-8461
peter@pastonelaw.com

Calgary: Stones Carbert Waite LLP - *18
Former Name: Stones Carbert Waite LLP
#2300, Encor Place, 645 - 7th Ave. SW, Calgary, AB T2P 4G8
Tel: 403-263-5656; *Fax:* 403-263-5553
info@scwlawyers.com
www.scwlawyers.com
www.linkedin.com/company/stones-carbert-waite-wells-llp

Calgary: Story Law Office - *1
#115, 1925 - 18th Ave. NE, Calgary, AB T2E 7T8
Tel: 403-250-1918; *Fax:* 403-250-3287
annestory@shaw.ca
www.storylawoffice.ca

Calgary: Sugimoto & Company - *5
#204, 2635 - 37 Ave. NE, Calgary, AB T1Y 5Z6
Tel: 403-291-4650; *Fax:* 403-291-4099
sugimoto@sugimotolaw.com
sugimotolaw.com

Calgary: Nancy A. Swanby - *1
#700, One Executive Place, 1816 Crowchild Trail NW, Calgary, AB T2M 3Y7
Tel: 403-520-5455; *Fax:* 403-220-1389
info@swanbylaw.com
www.swanbylaw.com

Calgary: Szabo & Company, Barristers & Solicitors
#200, 1115 - 11th Ave. SW, Calgary, AB T2R 0G5
Tel: 403-229-1111; *Fax:* 403-245-0569
info@szaboco.com
www.szaboco.com

Calgary: Michael J. Tadman - *1
#10, 628 - 12 Ave. SW, Calgary, AB T2R 0H6
Tel: 403-234-9722; *Fax:* 403-237-8748
tadman@nucleus.com

Calgary: Mark S. Takada - *1
#200, 604 - 1 St. SW, Calgary, AB T2P 1M7
Tel: 403-234-9477; *Fax:* 403-261-1839
www.albertacriminallawoffice.com

Calgary: Taylor Conway - *2
Former Name: Taylor, Zinkhofer & Conway
#440, 7220 Fisher St. SE, Calgary, AB T2H 2H8
Tel: 403-259-4028; *Fax:* 403-640-0103
www.taylorconway.ca
www.facebook.com/pages/Taylor-Conway-Barristers-Solicitors/289786387802529, www.twitter.com/taylorconwaybs/

Calgary: Thompson Laughlin - *2
Former Name: Thompson, Ball & Associates
#390, 11012 Macleod Trail SE, Calgary, AB T2J 6A5
Tel: 403-271-5050; *Fax:* 403-271-5298

Calgary: Thornborough, Smeltz - *8
Former Name: Thornborough, Smeltz, Gillis & Mebs
11650 Elbow Drive SW, Calgary, AB T2W 1S8
Tel: 403-271-3221; *Fax:* 403-271-6684
info@thornsmeltz.com
www.thornsmeltz.com

Calgary: TingleMerrett LLP - *12
#1250, Standard Life Bldg., 639 - 5th Ave. SW, Calgary, AB T2P 0M9
Tel: 403-571-8000; *Fax:* 403-571-8008
www.tinglemerrett.com

Calgary: Richard T. Tumanon - *1
#301, 5555 Falsbridge Dr. NE, Calgary, AB T3J 3E8
Tel: 403-262-3841; *Fax:* 403-269-7173

Calgary: Vickers Hendrix LLP - *4
#500, 707 - 7th Ave. SW, Calgary, AB T2P 3H6
Tel: 403-269-9400; *Fax:* 403-266-2447
office@vickershendrix.com
www.vickershendrix.com

Calgary: Vinci, Phillips - *2
1509 - 26 Ave. SW, Calgary, AB T2T 1C4
Tel: 403-265-4323; *Fax:* 403-262-8087

Calgary: Walsh LLP - *24
#2800, 801 - 6 Ave. SW, Calgary, AB T2P 4A3
Tel: 403-879-1502; *Fax:* 403-264-9400
Toll-Free: 800-682-4052
info@walshlaw.ca
walshlaw.ca

Calgary: Samuel D.C. Wan - *1
191 Edgepark Way NW, Calgary, AB T3A 4T2
Tel: 403-973-0678

Calgary: Peter M. Ward - *1
#300, 400 - 5th Ave. SW, Calgary, AB T2P 0L6
Tel: 403-263-1158; *Fax:* 403-264-9218

Calgary: Warren Tettensor Amantea LLP - *11
1413 - 2nd St. SW, Calgary, AB T2R 0W7
Tel: 403-228-7007; *Fax:* 403-244-1948
info@warren.ab.ca
www.warren.ab.ca

Calgary: Peggy A. Wedderburn - *1
#16, 2439 - 54th Ave. SW, Calgary, AB T3E 1M4
Tel: 403-242-8081; *Fax:* 403-246-2055
pwedderburn@shaw.ca

Calgary: Weeks Law - *1
#403, Willow Park Centre, 10325 Bonaventure Dr. SE, Calgary, AB T2J 7E4
Tel: 403-209-4988; *Fax:* 403-444-6827
info@weekslaw.com
www.weekslaw.com

Calgary: West End Legal Centre - *2
1705 - 10th Ave. SW, Calgary, AB T3C 0K1
Tel: 403-249-5297; *Fax:* 403-249-5001
info@westendlegalcentre.com
westendlegalcentre.com

Calgary: White & Company - *2
#204, 3716 - 61 Ave. SE, Calgary, AB T2C 1Z4
Tel: 403-236-2110; *Fax:* 403-279-4842

Calgary: Wilson Laycraft - *10
#1601, 333 - 11th Ave. SW, Calgary, AB T2R 1L9
Tel: 403-290-1601; *Fax:* 403-290-0828
www.wilcraft.com

Calgary: Dawn M. Wilson - *1
44 Bow Village Cres. NW, Calgary, AB T3B 4X2
Tel: 403-247-9090; *Fax:* 403-247-9090

Calgary: Wise Walden Barkauskas - *5
Former Name: Foster, Wise & Walden
#600, 700 - 4 Ave. SW, Calgary, AB T2P 3J4
Tel: 403-263-6601; *Fax:* 403-269-6785
law@divorceinc.com
www.wisedivorce.com

Calgary: Stephen R. Wojcik - *1
#200, The Lougheed Bldg., 604 - 1 St. SW, Calgary, AB T2P 1M7
Tel: 403-547-4415; *Fax:* 403-208-0717
wojicks@shaw.ca

Calgary: Wolch deWit Silverberg & Watts - *7
Former Name: Wolch, Ogle, Wilson, Hursh & deWit
#1500, 633 - 6 Ave. SW, Calgary, AB T2P 2Y5
Tel: 403-265-6500; *Fax:* 403-263-1111
msmale@calgarycriminaldefence.ca
calgarycriminaldefence.ca

Calgary: David I. Wolfman - *1
Former Name: Wolfman Ryder Barristers & Solicitors
328 Pumphill Gardens SW, Calgary, AB T2V 4M7
Tel: 403-266-4433; *Fax:* 403-266-4433
thewolfmans@telus.net

Calgary: Yanko & Popovic Law Firm - *6
Former Name: Yanko & Company
#302, 325 - 25 St. SE, Calgary, AB T2A 7H8
Tel: 403-262-0262; *Fax:* 403-204-0284
dgy@yplaw.ca
www.yankopopovic.com

Calgary: Your Lawyer Law Office - *6
Former Name: Lehan, Menzies, Walters & Abdi
9937 Fairmount Dr. SE, Calgary, AB T2J 0S2
Tel: 403-261-4010; *Fax:* 403-261-4040

Calgary: Youth Criminal Defence Office - Calgary - *9
#600, 444 - 5 Ave. SW, Calgary, AB T2P 2T8
Tel: 403-297-4400; *Fax:* 403-297-4201
sfellger@ycdo.ca
www.ycdo.ca

Camrose: Andreassen Borth, Barristers, Solicitors, Notaries, Mediators - *5
Former Name: Andreassen Olson Borth
#200, 4870 - 51 St., Camrose, AB T4V 1S1
Tel: 780-672-3181; *Fax:* 780-672-0682
aob@telusplanet.net
www.andreassenolsonborth.com

* indicates number of lawyers

***Camrose*: Farnham West Stolee LLP - *6**
Former Name: Farnham, Ziebart
5016 - 52 St., Camrose, AB T4V 1V7
Tel: 780-679-0444; *Fax:* 780-679-0958
camlaw@telusplanet.net
www.fwsllp.ca

***Camrose*: Fielding & Company LLP - *3**
#100, 4918 - 51 St., Camrose, AB T4V 1S3
Tel: 780-672-8851; *Fax:* 780-672-4707
lawyers@camroselaw.com
www.camroselaw.com

***Camrose*: Knaut Johnson - *2**
4925 - 51 St., Camrose, AB T4V 1S4
Tel: 780-672-5561; *Fax:* 780-672-5565
info@kjf-law.ca
www.kjf-law.ca/en/

***Canmore*: Canmore Legal Services - *1**
Also Known As: Schneider Law Office
909A Railway Ave., Canmore, AB T1W 1P3
Tel: 403-678-9818; *Fax:* 403-609-2333
johnschneider@shaw.ca

***Canmore*: Tannis J. Naylor - *1**
826B - 10th St., Canmore, AB T1W 2A7
Tel: 403-678-5777; *Fax:* 403-678-5679
t_naylor@telus.net

***Canmore*: Peter Perren - *1**
726 - 10 St., Canmore, AB T1W 2A6
Tel: 403-678-6988; *Fax:* 403-678-5952
pperren@telusplanet.net

***Carstairs*: Stiles Law Office - *1**
Former Name: Stiles & Naqi
P.O. Box 790, 209 - 10th Ave. South, Carstairs, AB T0M 0N0
Tel: 403-337-3357; *Fax:* 403-337-3359

***Coaldale*: Leonard D. Fast - *1**
P.O. Box 1360, Stn. Main, 1709 - 20 Ave., Coaldale, AB T1M 1N2
Tel: 403-345-4415; *Fax:* 403-345-2719
lfastlaw@telusplanet.net

***Coaldale*: Vincent A. Lammi - *1**
Also Known As: Lammi Law
P.O. Box 1329, Stn. Main, 1910 - 18 St., Coaldale, AB T1M 1N1
Tel: 403-345-3922; *Fax:* 403-345-2172
lammilaw@telusplanet.net

***Cochrane*: Fercho Law Offices - *1**
#14, 205 - 1 St. East, Cochrane, AB T4C 1X6
Tel: 403-932-4477; *Fax:* 403-932-4084
RFercho@FerchoLaw.com
www.ferncholaw.com

***Cochrane*: Mabbott & Company - *5**
#5, 201 Grand Blvd., Cochrane, AB T4C 2G4
Tel: 403-932-3066; *Fax:* 403-932-3076
reception@mabbott.ca
www.mabbott.ca

***Cochrane*: Rask Law Office - *1**
216 Sunterra Views, Cochrane, AB T4C 1W8
Tel: 403-981-7275; *Fax:* 403-981-7277
info@rasklaw.com
www.rasklaw.com

***Cold Lake*: Todd & Drake LLP - *6**
Former Name: Todd, Drake, Williams, Findlater LLP
P.O. Box 908, 4807 - 51 St., Cold Lake, AB T9M 1P2
Tel: 780-594-7151; *Fax:* 780-594-7155
Toll-Free: 877-594-7151
www.tdlaw.ca
www.facebook.com/pages/Todd-Drake-LLP/168339593224163,
www.twitter.com/toddrakellp

***Coronation*: E. Roger Spady - *1**
P.O. Box 328, 5015 Victoria Ave., Coronation, AB T0C 1C0
Tel: 403-578-3131; *Fax:* 403-578-2660

***Didsbury*: Brian M. Forestell - *1**
P.O. Box 625, 1701 - 20th Ave., Didsbury, AB T0M 0W0
Tel: 403-335-8491; *Fax:* 403-335-8589
briandid@telusplanet.net
brianforestelllaw.com

***Didsbury*: Roy D. Shellnutt - *1**
P.O. Box 898, 2021 - 19th Ave., Didsbury, AB T0M 0W0
Tel: 403-335-2145; *Fax:* 403-335-3185
shellnutlaw@hotmail.com

***Drumheller*: Herman, Kloot & Company - *5**
P.O. Box 970, 98 - 3 Ave. West, Drumheller, AB T0J 0Y0
Tel: 403-823-4000; *Fax:* 403-823-6407
reception@drumhellerlaw.com
www.drumhellerlaw.ca

***Drumheller*: Schumacher, Gough & Company - *2**
Former Name: Schumacher, Gough & Pedersen
P.O. Box 2800, 196 - 3rd Ave. West, Drumheller, AB T0J 0Y0
Tel: 403-823-2424; *Fax:* 403-823-6984
Toll-Free: 866-923-2424
enquiries@schumachergough.com
www.schumachergough.com

***Edmonton*: Abbey Hunter Davison - *4**
Former Name: Abbey Hunter Davison Spencer
9636 - 102A Ave., Edmonton, AB T5H 0G5
Tel: 587-400-5139; *Fax:* 780-425-0472
dhabbey@shaw.ca
www.abbeyhunterdavisonedmonton.ca

***Edmonton*: Abells Regan - *2**
Former Name: Elizabeth M. Regan
#2500, 10303 Jasper Ave. NW, Edmonton, AB T5J 3N6
Tel: 780-442-4420; *Fax:* 780-424-9370

***Edmonton*: Ackroyd LLP Barristers & Solicitors**
#1500, First Edmonton Place, 10665 Jasper Ave., Edmonton, AB T5J 3S9
Tel: 780-423-8905; *Fax:* 780-423-8946
info@ackroydlaw.com
www.ackroydlaw.com

***Edmonton*: Jack N. Agrios, Q.C., LL.B, O.C. - *1**
#1325, Manulife Place, 10180 - 101 St., Edmonton, AB T5J 3S4
Tel: 780-696-6915; *Fax:* 780-969-6901
jack@jackagrios.com

***Edmonton*: Anderson Haak & Engels - *2**
#102, 9811 - 34 Ave., Edmonton, AB T6E 5X9
Tel: 780-413-1763; *Fax:* 780-413-1734
info@ahelaw.com
www.albertarealestatelawyers.com

***Edmonton*: Andrew, March & Oake - *9**
#300, 10020 - 101A Ave. NW, Edmonton, AB T5J 3G2
Tel: 780-429-3391; *Fax:* 780-424-8483

***Edmonton*: Ares Law - *2**
LeMarchand Tower, 11507 - 100 Ave., Edmonton, AB T5K 2R2
Tel: 780-488-1951; *Fax:* 780-482-6048
reception@areslaw.com
www.areslaw.com

***Edmonton*: Attia, Reeves, Tensfeldt, Snow - *9**
Former Name: Attia, Reeves
#200, 10525 Jasper Ave. NW, Edmonton, AB T5J 1Z4
Tel: 780-424-3334; *Fax:* 780-424-4252
attia-reeves-tensfeldt-snow.alberta.canadab.com

***Edmonton*: Barr Picard - *12**
#1100, 10020 - 101A Ave. NW, Edmonton, AB T5J 3G2
Tel: 780-414-5400; *Fax:* 780-414-5509
info@barrpicard.com
www.barrpicard.com

***Edmonton*: Dennis E. Bayrak - *1**
#800, 10310 Jasper Ave. NW, Edmonton, AB T5J 2W4
Tel: 780-426-4884; *Fax:* 780-425-9358
bayrak@telus.net

***Edmonton*: Beresh Cunningham Aloneissi O'Neill Hurley - *10**
Former Name: Beresh DePoe Cunningham
#300, MacLean Block, Box 300, 10110 - 107 St., Edmonton, AB T5J 1J4
Tel: 780-421-4766; *Fax:* 780-429-0346
Toll-Free: 877-277-4766
info@libertylaw.ca
libertylaw.ca

***Edmonton*: Helmut Berndt - *1**
Former Name: Berndt & Associates
#1780, 10020 - 101A Ave. NW, Edmonton, AB T5J 3G2
Tel: 780-439-6643; *Fax:* 780-439-6696

***Edmonton*: Bhalla Law Offices - *1**
9360 - 34 Ave., Edmonton, AB T6E 5X8
Tel: 780-450-6155; *Fax:* 780-490-0116
bhallalawoffice@gmail.com
www.bhallalawoffice.com

***Edmonton*: Biamonte Cairo & Shortreed LLP - *13**
#1600, 10025 - 102A Ave., Edmonton, AB T5J 2Z2
Tel: 780-425-5800; *Fax:* 780-426-1600
Toll-Free: 888-425-2620
biamonte@biamonte.com
biamonte.com

***Edmonton*: Bishop & McKenzie LLP**
#2300, 10180 - 101 St. NW, Edmonton, AB T5J 1V3
Tel: 780-426-5550; *Fax:* 780-426-1305
bmllp.ca

***Edmonton*: Bitner & Associates Law Offices - *1**
6932 Roper Rd. NW, Edmonton, AB T6B 3H9
Tel: 780-461-6633; *Fax:* 780-461-9239
www.bitnerlaw.com

***Edmonton*: Kerry A. Bjarnason - *1**
#600, 9707 - 110 St., Edmonton, AB T5K 2L9
Tel: 780-433-4547; *Fax:* 780-482-6613
kbjarnason@telusplanet.net

***Edmonton*: Bosecke & Associates - *6**
Former Name: Bosecke Song LLP
#102, 9333 - 47 St. NW, Edmonton, AB T6B 2R7
Tel: 780-469-0494; *Fax:* 780-469-4181
www.edmontonlaw.ca
www.facebook.com/edmontonlaw

***Edmonton*: Braithwaite Boyle - *11**
11816 - 124 St. NW, Edmonton, AB T5L 0M3
Tel: 780-451-9191; *Fax:* 780-451-9198
Toll-Free: 800-661-4902
ken.braithwaite@accidentinjurylawyer.com
www.accidentinjurylawyer.com

***Edmonton*: Braul McEvoy & Gee - *3**
#2170, Sun Life Place, 10123 - 99 St., Edmonton, AB T5J 3H1
Tel: 780-423-2481; *Fax:* 780-423-2474
braulmcevoygee.yolasite.com

***Edmonton*: Brownlee LLP - Edmonton - *44**
#2200, Commerce Place, 10155 - 102 St., Edmonton, AB T5J 4G8
Tel: 780-497-4800; *Fax:* 780-424-3254
Toll-Free: 800-661-9069
contactus@brownleelaw.com
www.brownleelaw.com

***Edmonton*: Bryan & Company LLP - *48**
#2600, Manulife Place, Box 2600, 10180 - 101 St., Edmonton, AB T5J 3Y2
Tel: 780-423-5730; *Fax:* 780-428-6324
Toll-Free: 800-357-9265
info@bryanco.com
www.bryanco.com

***Edmonton*: Campbell & Van Doesburg - *2**
10938-124 St. NW, Edmonton, AB T5N 0H5
Tel: 780-451-2661; *Fax:* 780-452-1051

***Edmonton*: Adam F. Campbell - *1**
#2410, Oxford Tower, 10235 - 101 St. NW, Edmonton, AB T5J 3G1
Tel: 780-428-8882; *Fax:* 780-421-0818
pgl31416@telusplanet.net

***Edmonton*: J.K.J. Campbell - *1**
Also Known As: Whitemud Law
#208, Whitemud Business Park, 4245 - 97 St., Edmonton, AB T6E 5Y7
Tel: 780-434-8777; *Fax:* 780-436-6357
johncam@telusplanet.net
www.whitemudlaw.ca

***Edmonton*: Carr Law - *1**
Former Name: Carr & Company
#1296, First Edmonton Pl., 10665 Jasper Ave., Edmonton, AB T5J 3S9
Tel: 780-425-5959; *Fax:* 780-423-4728
www.carrlaw.com
www.linkedin.com/company/carr-&-company-lawyers

***Edmonton*: Chatwin Cox & Michalyshyn - *6**
#1000, Scotia Place Tower, 1, 10060 Jasper Ave. NW, Edmonton, AB T5J 3R8
Tel: 780-421-7667; *Fax:* 780-424-7231
lawyers@chatwin.ab.ca

***Edmonton*: Chomicki Baril Mah LLP - *20**
#1201, TD Tower, 10088 - 102 Ave., Edmonton, AB T5J 4K2
Tel: 780-423-3441; *Fax:* 780-420-1763
office_admin@cbmllp.com
www.cbmllp.com

** indicates number of lawyers*

***Edmonton*: Shirish P. Chotalia - *2**
Also Known As: Pundit & Chotalia
#1506, Edmonton City Centre, 10025 - 102A Ave., Edmonton, AB T5J 2Z2
Tel: 780-421-0861; *Fax:* 780-425-6048
info@shirishchotalia.com
www.shirishchotalia.com
ca.linkedin.com/pub/shirish-p-chotalia-queen-s-counsel/62/b4a/826

***Edmonton*: Michael H. Clancy - *1**
9844 - 106 St. NW, Edmonton, AB T5K 1B8
Tel: 780-424-9014; *Fax:* 780-424-9023
Toll-Free: 800-647-7723

***Edmonton*: Cochard Johnson - *3**
Former Name: Cochard Gordon
#607, Royal Bank Bldg., 10117 Jasper Ave., Edmonton, AB T5J 1W8
Tel: 780-429-9929; *Fax:* 780-429-9981

***Edmonton*: ColeColey Hennessy Cassis Ewasko - *4**
#212, 3132 Parsons Rd., Edmonton, AB T6N 1L6
Tel: 780-468-2551; *Fax:* 780-466-8006
Toll-Free: 877-460-2551
info@chclaw.ca
www.chclaw.ca

***Edmonton*: Combe & Kent - *2**
10614-124 St. NW, Edmonton, AB T5N 1S3
Tel: 780-425-4666; *Fax:* 780-425-9358

***Edmonton*: Coulter & Power - *2**
#2200, Metropolitan Pl., 10303 Jasper Ave., Edmonton, AB T5J 3N6
Tel: 780-413-2300; *Fax:* 780-420-0049

***Edmonton*: Charles D. Cousineau - *1**
#215, 11098 - 156 St. SW, Edmonton, AB T5P 4M8
Tel: 780-455-0485; *Fax:* 780-447-5853

***Edmonton*: Cox Trofimuk Campbell - Edmonton - South Side - *4**
#208, 4245 - 97 St., Edmonton, AB T6E 5Z9
Tel: 780-437-6600; *Fax:* 780-436-6357
Toll-Free: 866-282-4340
www.coxtrofimukcampbell.com

***Edmonton*: Ted R. Croll - *1**
#1300, 10665 Jasper Ave., Edmonton, AB T5J 3S9
Tel: 780-420-9903; *Fax:* 780-424-3631
croll_law@shaw.ca

***Edmonton*: Cummings Andrews Mackay LLP - *8**
#500, 10150 - 100 St. NW, Edmonton, AB T5J 0P6
Tel: 780-428-8222; *Fax:* 780-426-2670
Toll-Free: 800-565-5745
cam@cummings.ab.ca
www.cummings.ab.ca

***Edmonton*: Brock I. Dagenais - *1**
#1405, TD Tower, 10088 - 102 Ave., Edmonton, AB T5J 2Z1
Tel: 780-424-8519; *Fax:* 780-425-0931
brockd@bidlaw.ca

***Edmonton*: Davidson Gregory Danyliuk - *3**
10008 - 110 St., Edmonton, AB T5K 1J6
Tel: 780-993-6999 *Toll-Free:* 855-321-4111
rod.gregory@davidsongregory.com
www.thedefencelawyer.com

***Edmonton*: Dawson, Stevens, Duckett & Shaigec - *10**
Former Name: Anderson, Dawson, Knisely, Stevens & Shaigec
#300, Anderson Dawson Bldg., 9924 - 106 St., Edmonton, AB T5K 1C4
Tel: 780-424-9058; *Fax:* 780-425-0172
Toll-Free: 800-661-3176
www.dsscrimlaw.com

***Edmonton*: de Villars Jones - *5**
#300, Noble Bldg., 8540 - 109 St., Edmonton, AB T6G 1E6
Tel: 780-433-9000; *Fax:* 780-433-9780
www.devillarsjones.ca

***Edmonton*: Dean Duckett Carlson LLP - *10**
#700, Bell Tower, 10104 - 103 Ave. NW, Edmonton, AB T5J 0H8
Tel: 780-423-3366; *Fax:* 780-423-0505
office@deanduckett.com
www.deanduckett.com

***Edmonton*: Gary A. Dlin - *1**
7904 Gateway Blvd., Edmonton, AB T6E 6C3
Tel: 780-438-4972; *Fax:* 780-435-1037

***Edmonton*: Doherty Schuldhaus - *2**
#219, 6203 - 28 Ave., Edmonton, AB T6L 6K3
Tel: 780-450-1106; *Fax:* 780-461-8612

***Edmonton*: Duncan Craig LLP - Edmonton - *50**
Former Name: Duncan & Craig LLP, Lawyers & Mediators
#2800, 10060 Jasper Ave., Edmonton, AB T5J 3V9
Tel: 780-428-6036; *Fax:* 780-428-9683
Toll-Free: 800-782-9409
edmonton@dcllp.com
www.dcllp.com
ca.linkedin.com/company/duncan-&-craig-llp

***Edmonton*: Durocher Simpson Koehli & Erler - *6**
Former Name: Durocher Simpson
Old Strathcona Law Office, 7904 Gateway Blvd., Edmonton, AB T6E 6C3
Tel: 780-420-6850; *Fax:* 780-425-9185
mail@dursim.com
www.dursim.com

***Edmonton*: Edmonton Community Legal Centre**
#200, 10115 - 100A St., Edmonton, AB T5J 2W2
Tel: 780-702-1725; *Fax:* 780-702-1726
Intake@eclc.ca
www.eclc.ca

***Edmonton*: David C. Elliott - *1**
P.O. Box 1423, Stn. Main, Edmonton, AB T5J 2H5
Tel: 780-425-7337; *Fax:* 780-425-5710
words@davidelliott.ca
www.davidelliott.ca

***Edmonton*: Embury & McFayden - *1**
#602, Centre 104, 5241 Calgary Trail NW, Edmonton, AB T6H 5G8
Tel: 780-439-7302; *Fax:* 780-433-6510
emburymc@telus.net

***Edmonton*: Emery Jamieson LLP - *26**
#1700, 10235 - 101st St. NW, Edmonton, AB T5J 3G1
Tel: 780-426-5220; *Fax:* 780-420-6277
Toll-Free: 866-212-5220
general@emeryjamieson.com
www.emeryjamieson.com

***Edmonton*: Environmental Law Centre (ELC) - *4**
#410, 10115-100A St., Edmonton, AB T5J 2W2
Tel: 780-424-5099; *Fax:* 780-424-5133
Toll-Free: 800-661-4238
elc@elc.ab.ca
www.elc.ab.ca

***Edmonton*: Feehan Law Office - *2**
Former Name: Mark E. Feehan
10160 - 118 St., Edmonton, AB T5K 1Y4
Tel: 780-424-6425; *Fax:* 780-424-6477
markfeehan@shaw.ca
feehanlaw.ca

***Edmonton*: Fix & Smith - *2**
10277 - 97 St. NW, Edmonton, AB T5J 0L9
Tel: 780-424-2245; *Fax:* 780-423-0425
www.fixandsmith.com

***Edmonton*: Fleming & Gubbins - *2**
9636 - 102A Ave. NW, Edmonton, AB T5H 0G5
Tel: 780-424-9505; *Fax:* 780-425-0472

***Edmonton*: Galbraith Empson - *2**
#180, 10123 - 99 St., Edmonton, AB T5J 3H1
Tel: 780-424-9558; *Fax:* 780-424-5852
galson@shaw.ca

***Edmonton*: Galbraith Law - *2**
17318 - 106 Ave., Edmonton, AB T5S 1H9
Tel: 780-483-6111; *Fax:* 780-483-6411
Toll-Free: 866-483-6111
info@galbraith.ab.ca
www.galbraith.ab.ca

***Edmonton*: Richard Gariepy - *1**
Former Name: Gariepy & Lloyd
10039 - 117 St., Edmonton, AB T5K 1W7
Tel: 780-482-7370; *Fax:* 780-482-2553

***Edmonton*: Blair M. Geiger - *1**
7904 Gateway Blvd. NW, Edmonton, AB T6E 6C3
Tel: 780-438-4972; *Fax:* 780-436-7771
bgeiger@telusplanet.net

***Edmonton*: Dale Gibson Consulting Barrister - *1**
11018 - 125 St., Edmonton, AB T5M 0M1
Tel: 780-454-5081; *Fax:* 780-454-5081
giblaw@shaw.ca

***Edmonton*: Gledhill Larocque - *5**
#300, Wentworth Building, 10209 - 97 St., Edmonton, AB T5J 0L6
Tel: 780-425-3511; *Fax:* 780-426-5919
www.gledhill-larocque.com

***Edmonton*: Goldford Law Office - *2**
#200, 10735 - 107th St., Edmonton, AB T5H 0W6
Tel: 780-482-1000; *Fax:* 780-482-0963
Toll-Free: 877-438-2667
hgoldford@goldfordlaw.com

***Edmonton*: Gunn & Prithipaul - *5**
Also Known As: Gunn Law Group
Former Name: Gunn Prithipaul & Hatch
11210 - 142 St., Edmonton, AB T5M 1T9
Tel: 780-488-4460; *Fax:* 780-488-4783
www.gunnlawgroup.ca
twitter.com/GunnLawGroup

***Edmonton*: Hajduk Gibbs LLP - *6**
#202, Platinum Place Bldg., 10120 - 118 St. NW, 2nd Fl., Edmonton, AB T5K 1Y4
Tel: 780-428-4258; *Fax:* 780-425-9439
Toll-Free: 800-749-9989
info@hajdukandgibbs.com
www.hajdukandgibbs.com

***Edmonton*: Hall & Van Campenhout - *2**
12026 - 102 Ave. NW, Edmonton, AB T5K 0R9
Tel: 780-482-5732; *Fax:* 780-482-5736

***Edmonton*: Hansma Bristow Finlay LLP - *6**
13815 - 127 St. NW, 2nd Fl., Edmonton, AB T6V 1A8
Tel: 780-456-3661; *Fax:* 780-457-9381
www.hbf-law.ca

***Edmonton*: Hardman Law Office - *1**
18067 - 107 Ave., Edmonton, AB T5S 1K3
Tel: 780-484-2041; *Fax:* 780-484-8950
hardman@compusmart.ab.ca

***Edmonton*: R. Allan Harris Professional Corp. - *1**
#10109, 502 Energy Square, 106 St. NW, Edmonton, AB T5J 3L7
Tel: 780-421-1641; *Fax:* 780-421-1936

***Edmonton*: Haymour Kalil - *1**
#2031, 10060 Jasper Ave. NW, Edmonton, AB T5J 3R8
Tel: 780-429-4573

***Edmonton*: Christopher R. Head - *1**
#300, 10209 - 97 St. NW, Edmonton, AB T5J 0L6
Tel: 780-441-4758; *Fax:* 780-702-1552
chead@shawbiz.ca

***Edmonton*: Henning Byrne - *5**
Former Name: Henning Byrne Whitmore & McKall
#1450, Standard Life Centre, 10405 Jasper Ave. NW, Edmonton, AB T5J 3N4
Tel: 780-421-1707; *Fax:* 780-425-9438
Toll-Free: 888-702-1707
general@henningbyrne.com
www.henningbyrne.com

***Edmonton*: Heritage Law Offices - *3**
#108, 284 - 109 St., Edmonton, AB T6J 6B7
Tel: 780-436-0011; *Fax:* 780-436-7000
lawyers@heritagelaw.com
heritagelaw.com

***Edmonton*: Leroy N. Hiller - *1**
#1720, Sun Life Place, 10123 - 99th St., Edmonton, AB T5J 3H1
Tel: 780-424-6660; *Fax:* 780-426-2980
lhiller@leroyhiller.com
www.leroyhiller.com

***Edmonton*: John Hinton - *1**
5508 - 141 St. NW, Edmonton, AB T6H 4A2
Tel: 780-434-4710; *Fax:* 780-437-4281

***Edmonton*: Robert W. Hladun - *2**
#300, 10711 - 102 St., Edmonton, AB T5H 2T8
Tel: 780-423-1888; *Fax:* 780-424-0934

***Edmonton*: Terry E. Hofmann - *1**
P.O. Box 51070, Stn. Highlands, 6525 - 118 Ave., Edmonton, AB T5W 5G5
Tel: 780-448-3885; *Fax:* 780-448-5840

** indicates number of lawyers*

***Edmonton*: Holman & Tilleard - *2**
Former Name: Michael J. Tilleard
#720, 10150 - 100 St. NW, Edmonton, AB T5J 0P6
Tel: 780-429-3644; *Fax:* 780-429-3685

***Edmonton*: Douglas B. Holman - *1**
#720, 10150 - 100 St. NW, Edmonton, AB T5J 0P6
Tel: 780-429-3644; *Fax:* 780-429-3685

***Edmonton*: William K. Horwitz - *1**
#220, 8702 Meadowlarke Rd., Edmonton, AB T5R 5W5
Tel: 780-486-3100; *Fax:* 780-489-9671

***Edmonton*: Stanley V.T. Hum - *1**
#1003, 10010 - 106 St. SW, Edmonton, AB T5J 3L8
Tel: 780-453-8988; *Fax:* 780-424-7379
stan_hum@hotmail.com

***Edmonton*: Hustwick Payne - *3**
#600, Capital Pl., 9707 - 110 St. NW, Edmonton, AB T5K 2L9
Tel: 780-482-6555; *Fax:* 780-482-6613
reception@hhplegal.com
www.hplegal.ca

***Edmonton*: Jomha, Skrobot LLP**
10621 - 124 St. NW, Edmonton, AB T5N 1S5
Tel: 780-424-0688; *Fax:* 780-424-0695
www.jomhalaw.com

***Edmonton*: Kennedy Agrios LLP - *5**
#1325, 10180 - 101 St. NW, Edmonton, AB T5J 3S4
Tel: 780-969-6900; *Fax:* 780-969-6901
www.kennedyagrios.com

***Edmonton*: Kirwin LLP - *7**
Former Name: Kirwin & Kirwin
#200, 10339 - 124 St., Edmonton, AB T5N 3W1
Tel: 780-448-7401; *Fax:* 780-453-3281
www.kirwinllp.com

***Edmonton*: Robert A. Kiss - *1**
Former Name: Kiss & Davidson
17393 - 108 Ave, Edmonton, AB T5S 1G2
Tel: 780-447-7205; *Fax:* 780-481-6258

***Edmonton*: Kolthammer, Batchelor & Laidlaw LLP - *4**
#208, 11062 - 156 St. NW, Edmonton, AB T5P 4M8
Tel: 780-489-5003; *Fax:* 780-486-2107
www.kbllaw.com

***Edmonton*: K. June Koska Professional Corporation - *1**
#10209, 97 St. NW, Edmonton, AB T5J 0L6
Tel: 780-448-9137

***Edmonton*: I. Samuel Kravinchuk - *1**
#800, 10310 Jasper Ave. NW, Edmonton, AB T5J 2W4
Tel: 780-426-4884; *Fax:* 780-428-8259
isklaw@shaw.ca

***Edmonton*: Katherine A. Kubica Professional Corporation - *1**
10530 - 110 St., Edmonton, AB T5H 3C5
Tel: 780-425-8000; *Fax:* 780-425-8488

***Edmonton*: Kuckertz Law Office - *2**
#202, 8003 - 102 St., Edmonton, AB T6E 4A2
Tel: 780-432-9308; *Fax:* 780-439-9950
h.kuckertz@kuckertzlaw.com

***Edmonton*: Kulasa Campbell - *3**
#100, 10703 - 181 St. NW, Edmonton, AB T5S 1N3
Tel: 780-484-0665; *Fax:* 780-486-7282

***Edmonton*: Laurier Law Office - *3**
8623 - 149 St., Edmonton, AB T5R 1B3
Tel: 780-486-0207; *Fax:* 780-483-0848

***Edmonton*: Keith M. Leslie - *1**
1612 - 89 St. NW, Edmonton, AB T6K 2A9
Tel: 780-463-4019; *Fax:* 780-468-2976
kleslie@agt.net

***Edmonton*: Liddell Law Office - *2**
Former Name: Polack, Meindersma, Liddell
#320, Circle Square, 11808 St Albert Trail, Edmonton, AB T5L 4G4
Tel: 780-486-0926; *Fax:* 780-444-1393
www.liddelllaw.ca

***Edmonton*: Linton Law Office - *1**
Former Name: Kathleen S.V. Linton
#52, Commonwealth Bldg., 9912-106 St. NW, Edmonton, AB T5K 1C5
Tel: 780-415-5540; *Fax:* 780-415-5541
info@lintonlawoffice.com

***Edmonton*: Philip G. Lister Law Office - *1**
Former Name: Lister & Associate
#302, 10080 Jasper Ave. NW, Edmonton, AB T5J 1V9
Tel: 780-422-6114; *Fax:* 780-421-0818
phil@listerlaw.com

***Edmonton*: Julie C. Lloyd - *1**
#950, 10303 Jasper Ave. NW, Edmonton, AB T5J 3N6
Tel: 780-442-4417; *Fax:* 780-424-9370
jclloyd@telusplanet.net

***Edmonton*: Peter T.K. Loong - *1**
11440 Kingsway Ave. NW, Edmonton, AB T5G 0X4
Tel: 780-424-3200; *Fax:* 780-424-2369
peterloonglaw@telusplanet.net

***Edmonton*: Lyons Albert & Cook - *2**
#306, 10328 - 81 Ave. NW, Edmonton, AB T6E 1X2
Tel: 780-437-0743; *Fax:* 780-438-6695
www.lyonsalbertcook.com

***Edmonton*: Machida Mack Shewchuk Meagher LLP - *1**
#1300, 710-7 Ave. SW, Edmonton, AB T2P 3H6
Tel: 403-221-8322; *Fax:* 403-221-8339

***Edmonton*: Mah & Company - *2**
#1013, TD Tower, 10088 - 102 Ave., Edmonton, AB T5J 2Z1
Tel: 780-428-3888; *Fax:* 780-425-8383

***Edmonton*: Rajiv Malhotram - *1**
#315, 10909 Jasper Ave., Edmonton, AB T5J 3L9
Tel: 780-423-5792; *Fax:* 780-426-0081

***Edmonton*: James W. Mandick Professional Corporation - *1**
#1850, 10123 - 99 St. NW, Edmonton, AB T5J 3H1
Tel: 780-423-3311; *Fax:* 780-423-3321
jmandick@wmlaw.ca

***Edmonton*: Michael B. Marcovitch - *1**
#1300, 10665 Jasper Ave. NW, Edmonton, AB T5J 3S9
Tel: 780-453-4390; *Fax:* 780-424-3631

***Edmonton*: Matheson & Company LLP**
10410 - 81 Ave., Edmonton, AB T6E 1X5
Tel: 780-433-5881; *Fax:* 780-432-9453

***Edmonton*: McAllister LLP - *14**
Former Name: Cleall Barrsiters Solicitors; Cleall Pahl
#2500, Commerce Place, 10155 - 102nd St., Edmonton, AB T5J 4G8
Tel: 587-745-0195; *Fax:* 780-425-1222
mcallisterllp.com

***Edmonton*: McGee Richard - *3**
#1155, Weber Centre, 5555 Calgary Trail NW, Edmonton, AB T6H 5P9
Tel: 780-437-2240; *Fax:* 780-438-5788
www.mcgeerichard.com

***Edmonton*: McKay-Carey & Company - *1**
200-6928 Roper Rd., Edmonton, AB T6B 3H9
Tel: 780-424-0222; *Fax:* 780-421-0834

***Edmonton*: McKee & Company - *2**
#213, 14065 Victoria Trail, Edmonton, AB T5Y 2B6
Tel: 780-471-1100; *Fax:* 780-471-1150
terrymckee@mckeeandcompany.ca
www.mckeeandcompany.ca

***Edmonton*: Mckenzie House Law Group - *2**
Former Name: G.D. Honey
#8603, 104 St. NW, Edmonton, AB T6E 4G6
Tel: 780-428-4531

***Edmonton*: McLennan Ross LLP - Edmonton**
#600, West Chambers, 12220 Stony Plain Rd., Edmonton, AB T5N 3Y4
Tel: 780-482-9200; *Fax:* 780-482-9100
Toll-Free: 800-567-9200
info@mross.com
www.mross.com
www.twitter.com/mclennanrosslaw

***Edmonton*: Ingrid E. Meier - *1**
2406 Tegler Green NW, Edmonton, AB T6R 3K2
Tel: 780-436-5954; *Fax:* 780-401-3204
lawyer@meier.ca

***Edmonton*: Ron J. Meleshko - *1**
15412 - 55 St. NW, Edmonton, AB T5Y 2S4
Tel: 780-414-0298

***Edmonton*: Miller Boileau - *3**
11835 - 102nd Ave. NW, Edmonton, AB T5K 0R6
Tel: 780-482-2888; *Fax:* 780-482-4600
mail@millerboileau.com
www.millerboileau.com

***Edmonton*: Minsos Stewart Masson - *3**
#220, 8723 - 82 Ave., Edmonton, AB T6C 0Y9
Tel: 780-466-1175; *Fax:* 780-465-6717
www.realestatelawedmonton.com

***Edmonton*: Mintz Law - *6**
#400, 10357 - 109 St. NW, Edmonton, AB T5J 1N3
Tel: 780-425-2041; *Fax:* 780-425-2195
twitter.com/MintzLaw1

***Edmonton*: W. Robert Mitchell - *1**
#223, 6650 - 177th St., Edmonton, AB T5T 4J5
Tel: 780-486-8686; *Fax:* 780-486-0084

***Edmonton*: Moustarah & Company - *3**
#400, 10150 - 100 St., Edmonton, AB T5J 0P6
Tel: 780-428-6565; *Fax:* 780-428-6564
firm@moustarah.com
moustarah.com

***Edmonton*: Murray, Chilibeck & Horne - *3**
10605 - 172nd St. NW, Edmonton, AB T5S 1P1
Tel: 780-484-2323; *Fax:* 780-486-4289
lorne.mchlaw@telus.net
www.murraychilibeckandhorne.ca

***Edmonton*: Alann J. Nazarevich - *1**
#201, 9035 - 51 Ave., Edmonton, AB T6E 5X4
Tel: 780-430-0363; *Fax:* 780-435-9279

***Edmonton*: Neuman Thompson - *8**
#301, 550 - 91 St. SW, Edmonton, AB T6X 0V1
Tel: 780-482-7645; *Fax:* 780-488-0026
www.neumanthompson.com

***Edmonton*: Kenneth Ng - *1**
3234 Parsons Rd. NW, Edmonton, AB T6N 1M2
Tel: 780-988-9188; *Fax:* 780-496-9717

***Edmonton*: Nicholl & Akers - *7**
#200, 10187 - 104 St. NW, Edmonton, AB T5J 0Z9
Tel: 780-429-2771; *Fax:* 780-425-1665

***Edmonton*: Nickerson Roberts Holinski & Mercer - *13**
Former Name: Nickerson, Roberts
#100, 7712 - 104 St., Edmonton, AB T6E 4C5
Tel: 780-428-0041; *Fax:* 780-425-0272
reception@nrhmlaw.com
www.nrhmlaw.com

***Edmonton*: Gregory O'Laughlin - *1**
#300, 10209 - 97 St. NW, Edmonton, AB T5J 0L6
Tel: 780-424-9059; *Fax:* 780-429-2615

***Edmonton*: Ronald J. Obirek - *1**
#240, 6005 Gateway Blvd. NW, Edmonton, AB T6H 2H3
Tel: 780-496-9046; *Fax:* 780-436-9669
rjobirek@telusplanet.net

***Edmonton*: Ogilvie LLP - *31**
#1400, 10303 Jasper Ave., Edmonton, AB T5J 3N6
Tel: 780-421-1818; *Fax:* 780-429-4453
info@ogilvielaw.com
www.ogilvielaw.com

***Edmonton*: Kelly R. Palmer - *1**
#1800, 10250 - 101 St. NW, Edmonton, AB T5J 3P4
Tel: 780-448-9275; *Fax:* 780-423-0163

***Edmonton*: Phillip G. Parker - *1**
#12, 11440 Kingsway NW, Edmonton, AB T5G 0X4
Tel: 780-471-2244

***Edmonton*: Patrick & Patrick - *1**
#800, 10310 Jasper Ave. NW, Edmonton, AB T5J 2W4
Tel: 780-426-4884; *Fax:* 780-425-9358

** indicates number of lawyers*

Edmonton: Patrick Dolphin Professional Corporation - *1
Former Name: Edney, Hattersley & Dolphin
10621 - 124 St. NW, Edmonton, AB T5N 1S5
Tel: 780-423-4081; *Fax:* 780-425-5247

Edmonton: Penonzek Murray - *2
Former Name: Kenneth W. Penonzek Professional Corp
#147, 10403 - 122 St. NW, Edmonton, AB T5N 4C1
Tel: 780-482-1199; *Fax:* 780-482-1883
k.penonzek@shawbiz.ca

Edmonton: Patrick J. Phelan - *1
#1550, Sun Life Pl., 10123 - 99 St., Edmonton, AB T5J 3H1
Tel: 780-424-7730; *Fax:* 780-428-4484
patrick.phelan@telus.net

Edmonton: Roy A. Philion - *1
#880, 10020 - 101 Ave. NW, Edmonton, AB T5J 3G2
Tel: 780-423-2977; *Fax:* 780-424-8098

Edmonton: Ronald W. Poitras - *1
#300, 10209 - 97 St., Edmonton, AB T5J 0L6
Tel: 780-424-3270; *Fax:* 780-429-2615

Edmonton: Pringle Chivers Sparks - *5
Former Name: Pringle & Company
#300, Transalta Place, 10150 - 100 St. NW, Edmonton, AB T5J 0P6
Tel: 780-424-8866; *Fax:* 780-426-1470
Toll-Free: 877-424-8866
reception@pringlelaw.ca
www.pringlelaw.ca

Edmonton: Purdon Caskenette - *2
Former Name: Baker & Purdon
10263 - 178 St., Edmonton, AB T5S 1M3
Tel: 780-489-5566; *Fax:* 780-486-7735
www.purdonlaw.com

Edmonton: Rackel Belzil LLP - *4
#100, Westgrove Professional Building, 10230 - 142 St. NW, Edmonton, AB T5N 3Y6
Tel: 780-424-2929; *Fax:* 780-451-8460
rackelbelzil.ca

Edmonton: Rand Kiss Turner LLP - *3
Former Name: Frohlich Rand Kiss
#1600, 10316 - 124th St., Edmonton, AB T5J 3G2
Tel: 780-423-1984; *Fax:* 780-423-1969
randkissturner.com

Edmonton: M. Naeem Rauf
#300, 10209 - 97 St. NW, Edmonton, AB T5J 0L6
Tel: 780-453-4399; *Fax:* 780-429-2615

Edmonton: Peter E. Recto - *1
6423 - 154th Avenue, Edmonton, AB T5Y 2N7
Tel: 780-423-1283; *Fax:* 780-473-8324
recto2001@hotmail.com

Edmonton: James E. Redmond - *1
P.O. Box 67306, Edmonton, AB T6M 0J5
Tel: 780-444-3035; *Fax:* 780-481-9124
info@jimeredmond.com
www.jimeredmond.com

Edmonton: Hans Reich - *1
#207, 10110 - 124 St. NW, Edmonton, AB T5N 1P6
Tel: 780-424-7732; *Fax:* 780-428-4484
reichlaw@telus.net

Edmonton: Richard S. Rennick - *1
Former Name: Rennick & Di Pinto
2320 Sun Life Pl., Edmonton, AB T5J 3H1
Tel: 780-426-5510; *Fax:* 780-420-1645

Edmonton: Reynolds Mirth Richards & Farmer LLP
#3200, Manulife Pl., 10180 - 101 St., Edmonton, AB T5J 3W8
Tel: 780-425-9510; *Fax:* 780-429-3044
Toll-Free: 800-661-7673
www.rmrf.com

Edmonton: Richards Hunter Toogood - *4
Former Name: Worton Hunter & Callaghan, and Richard Wood Toogood
#1240, Weber Centre, 5555 Calgary Trail NW, Edmonton, AB T6H 5P9
Tel: 780-436-8554; *Fax:* 780-436-8566
www.rht-law.ca

Edmonton: Ritchie Mill Law Office - *4
Also Known As: RMLO
#101, 10301 - 109 St. NW, Edmonton, AB T5J 1N4
Tel: 780-431-1444; *Fax:* 780-431-1499
Toll-Free: 888-333-8818
office@rmlo.com
rmlo.com

Edmonton: James A. Robertson - *1
10735-42 Ave. NW, Edmonton, AB T6J 2P5
Tel: 780-423-1680; *Fax:* 780-421-7304
jamesrob@shaw.ca

Edmonton: Robinson LLP - *7
Former Name: Frieser Robinson MacKay
10410 - 81 Ave., Edmonton, AB T6E 1X5
Tel: 780-429-1717; *Fax:* 780-421-8335
Toll-Free: 877-302-1717
inquiries@robinsonllp.com
www.robinsonllp.com

Edmonton: Terry J. Romaniuk - *1
9743 - 89 Ave. NW, Edmonton, AB T6E 2S1
Tel: 780-433-8127

Edmonton: David W. Ross - *1
8623 - 149 St. NW, Edmonton, AB T5R 1B3
Tel: 780-425-1965; *Fax:* 780-483-0848
dwross@bigfoot.com

Edmonton: James D. Ross - *1
#1003, Highfield Place, 10010 - 106 St., Edmonton, AB T5J 3L8
Tel: 780-482-3144; *Fax:* 780-424-7379

Edmonton: Samy F. Salloum - *1
1341 Carter Crest Rd. NW, Edmonton, AB T6R 2L6
Tel: 780-426-7777; *Fax:* 780-426-7778

Edmonton: David L. Schwartz - *1
#324, 10909 Jasper Ave. NW, Edmonton, AB T5J 3L9
Tel: 780-424-0259; *Fax:* 780-424-0299
thebigkahuna@interbaun.com

Edmonton: Sharek Logan & van Leenen LLP - *7
Also Known As: Sharek&Co.
Former Name: Sharek Logan Collingwood van Leenen LLP
#701, Tower 2, Scotia Place, 10060 Jasper Ave. NW, Edmonton, AB T5J 3R8
Tel: 780-413-3100; *Fax:* 780-413-3152
www.yeglaw.ca

Edmonton: William Shim
#2000, 10123 - 99 St. NW, Edmonton, AB T5J 3H1
Tel: 780-423-8060; *Fax:* 780-425-4201

Edmonton: Shores Jardine LLP - *8
#2250, Bell Tower, 10104 - 103 Ave., Edmonton, AB T5J 0H8
Tel: 780-448-9275; *Fax:* 780-423-0163
info@shoresjardine.com
www.shoresjardine.com

Edmonton: Wialliam J. Shymko - *1
#200, 9602 - 111 Ave. NW, Edmonton, AB T5G 0A8
Tel: 780-425-6414; *Fax:* 780-425-6416

Edmonton: Simons & Stephens - *3
#750, First Edmonton Pl., 10665 Jasper Ave. NW, Edmonton, AB T5J 3S9
Tel: 780-482-1536; *Fax:* 780-488-1914
nsimons@lawsimons.com

Edmonton: Larry A. Sitko - *1
#201, 12907 - 97 St. NW, Edmonton, AB T5E 4C2
Tel: 780-476-7686; *Fax:* 780-476-7688

Edmonton: Snyder & Associates LLP - *16
#2500, Sun Life Pl., 10123 - 99 St., Edmonton, AB T5J 3H1
Tel: 780-426-4133; *Fax:* 780-424-1588
Toll-Free: 877-426-4148
inquiries@snyder.ca
www.snyder.ca

Edmonton: Stadnyk Law - Edmonton - 91 St. - *2
Former Name: Kobewka Stadnyk
#202, 1289 - 91 St. SW, Edmonton, AB T6X 1H1
Tel: 780-414-0222; *Fax:* 780-414-0002
Toll-Free: 877-414-0222
www.stadnyklaw.com

Edmonton: Stewart Law Offices - *2
11724 - 103 Ave. NW, Edmonton, AB T5K 0S7
Tel: 780-482-3800; *Fax:* 780-482-5600
stwlaw@telusplanet.net

Edmonton: Stillman LLP - *8
#300, 10335 - 172 St., Edmonton, AB T5S 1K9
Tel: 780-484-4445; *Fax:* 780-484-4184
Toll-Free: 888-258-2529
lawyers@stillmanllp.com
www.stillmanllp.com

Edmonton: André A. Szaszkiewicz - *1
#202, 1289 - 91 St., Edmonton, AB T6X 1H1
Tel: 780-452-2000; *Fax:* 780-455-7229
andresz@telusplanet.net

Edmonton: Tarrabain & Company - *9
Former Name: Tarrabain O'Byrne & Co
#2150, Tower One, Scotia Place, 10060 Jasper Ave., Edmonton, AB T5J 3R8
Tel: 780-429-1010; *Fax:* 780-429-0101
lawyers@tarrabain.com
www.tarrabain.com

Edmonton: Christopher G. Taskey - *1
16404-100 Ave, NW, Edmonton, AB T5P 4Y2
Tel: 780-424-3558; *Fax:* 780-423-5515

Edmonton: Taylor & Jewell - *2
#215, Tower One, Millbourne Market Mall, 38 Ave. NW, Edmonton, AB T6K 3L6
Tel: 780-450-5761; *Fax:* 780-468-4524

Edmonton: Sylvia O. Tensfeldt - *1
#200, 10525 Jasper Ave. NW, Edmonton, AB T5J 1Z4
Tel: 780-424-3334; *Fax:* 780-424-4252

Edmonton: Thom Law Office - *1
8506 - 104 St., Edmonton, AB T6E 4G4
Tel: 780-434-5870; *Fax:* 780-756-8008
len@thomlaw.com
www.thomlaw.com

Edmonton: Tkachuk & Patterson - *2
#590, 10621, 100 Ave. NW, Edmonton, AB T5J 0B3
Tel: 780-428-1593; *Fax:* 780-426-6679

Edmonton: Helen S. Tymoczko - *1
#106, 10108 - 125 St., Edmonton, AB T5N 4B6
Tel: 780-472-1758; *Fax:* 780-476-4085

Edmonton: Tyson Law - *1
#300, 10209 - 97th St. NW, Edmonton, AB T5J 0L6
Tel: 780-488-3333; *Fax:* 780-429-2615
brent@tysonlaw.ca
www.tysonlaw.ca

Edmonton: Venkatraman Purewal & Pillay - *4
Former Name: Venkatraman & Purewal
#303, 9811 - 34 Ave., Edmonton, AB T6E 5X9
Tel: 780-436-7060; *Fax:* 780-436-7064
lawyers@vplaw.ca

Edmonton: Wachowich & Company - *4
#555, 10310 Jasper Ave. NW, Edmonton, AB T5J 2W4
Tel: 780-429-0555; *Fax:* 780-425-4795
mail@wachowich.com
www.wachowich.com

Edmonton: Weir Bowen LLP - *14
#500, The Revillon Building, 10320 - 102 Ave. NW, Edmonton, AB T5J 4A1
Tel: 780-424-2030; *Fax:* 780-424-2323
weirbowen.com

Edmonton: Uwe Welz - *1
7904 - 103 St. NW, Edmonton, AB T6E 6C3
Tel: 780-432-7711; *Fax:* 780-439-1177
uwpc@telusplanet.net

Edmonton: Wheatley Sadownik - *3
#2000, 10123 - 99 St., Edmonton, AB T5J 3H1
Tel: 780-423-6671; *Fax:* 780-420-6327
mail@wheatleysadownik.com
www.wheatleysadownik.com

Edmonton: Willis Bokenfohr Thorsrud - *3
Former Name: Willis & Bokenfohr
#410, ATB Place, 9888 Jasper Ave., Edmonton, AB T5J 5C6
Tel: 780-452-2764; *Fax:* 780-452-3247

Edmonton: Witten LLP - *55
#2500, Canadian Western Bank Place, 10303 Jasper Ave., Edmonton, AB T5J 3N6
Tel: 780-428-0501; *Fax:* 780-429-2559
Toll-Free: 888-429-9900
lawyers@wittenlaw.com
www.wittenlaw.com

** indicates number of lawyers*

Edmonton: Collin Wong - *1
10704 - 108 St., Edmonton, AB T5H 3A3
Tel: 780-488-7003; Fax: 780-488-1593
cwongpf@compusmart.ab.ca

Edmonton: Peter S. Wong - *1
#204, Kingsdale Professional Centre, 9644 - 54 Ave. NW, Edmonton, AB T6E 5V1
Tel: 780-430-1070; Fax: 780-430-1773
pwong@sequiter.com

Edmonton: Wood Law Office - *2
#304, 10209 - 97 St. NW, Edmonton, AB T5J 0L6
Tel: 780-482-3291; Fax: 780-452-1821
www.wood-law.ca

Edmonton: Worobec Law Offices - *4
Heritage Crt., 268-150 Chippewa Rd., Edmonton, AB T8A 6A2
Tel: 780-467-6325; Fax: 780-467-6326

Edmonton: Hu Eliot Young Law Office - *1
#440, Hong Kong Bank, 10055-106 St. NW, Edmonton, AB T5J 2Y2
Tel: 780-425-8400; Fax: 780-424-3777
heyoung@telusplanet.net

Edmonton: Ronald J. Young - *1
#204, 10265 - 107 St., Edmonton, AB T5J 5G2
Tel: 780-424-3311; Fax: 780-425-9609

Edmonton: Zariwny Law Office - *1
9211-96 St. NW, Edmonton, AB T6C 3Y5
Tel: 780-433-5999; Fax: 780-439-6456
zlo@oanet.com

Edson: Robert W. Anderson - *1
P.O. Box 6748, 202B - 50 St., Edson, AB T7E 1V1
Tel: 780-723-3245; Fax: 780-723-5443
rwandlaw@telus.net

Edson: Dennis C. Calvert - *1
P.O. Box 6658, Stn. Main, 107 - 50 St., Edson, AB T7E 1V1
Tel: 780-723-6047; Fax: 780-723-3602

Fort McMurray: Campbell & Cooper - *6
Former Name: Campbell, Germain, Cooper & Jean
#212, 9714 Main St., Fort McMurray, AB T9H 1T6
Tel: 780-791-7787; Fax: 780-791-0750
lawyers@campbell-cooper-law.com
mcmurraylaw.com

Fort McMurray: Evelyn J Roblee - *1
#202A, Plaza Shopping Centre, 8706 Franklin Ave., Fort McMurray, AB T9H 2J6
Tel: 780-743-2860; Fax: 780-790-1618
frontdeskmiel@shaw.ca
www.evelynroblee.com

Fort McMurray: Wolff Taitinger - *2
10019R Franklin Ave., Fort McMurray, AB T9H 2K7
Tel: 780-790-9040; Fax: 780-743-1813
www.wolfftaitingerlawab.ca

Fort Saskatchewan: Fotty & Torok-Both - *4
10509 - 100 Ave., Fort Saskatchewan, AB T8L 1Z5
Tel: 780-998-4841; Fax: 780-998-4821

Fort Saskatchewan: Jenkins & Jenkins - *2
#200, 9906 - 102 St., Fort Saskatchewan, AB T8L 2C3
Tel: 780-998-4200; Fax: 780-998-4370

Grande Cache: Harry Arnesen - *1
P.O. Box 385, 2502 Pine Plaza, Grande Cache, AB T0E 0Y0
Tel: 780-827-2458; Fax: 780-827-3734

Grande Prairie: Dobko & Wheaton - *3
10022 - 102 Ave., Grande Prairie, AB T8V 0Z7
Tel: 780-539-6200; Fax: 780-532-9052
Toll-Free: 866-539-6200
receptionist@dwlaw.ca
www.dwlaw.ca

Grande Prairie: Gurevitch Burnham Law Office - *4
Former Name: Burgess & Gurevitch
9931 - 106 Ave., Grande Prairie, AB T8V 1J4
Tel: 780-539-3710; Fax: 780-532-2788
bplaw@telus.net
www.grandeprairielaw.ca

Grande Prairie: Howey Law Office - *1
#201, Professional Bldg., 9905 - 101 Ave., Grande Prairie, AB T8V 0X7
Tel: 780-539-0690; Fax: 780-539-3813

Grande Prairie: Kay McVey Smith & Carlstrom LLP - Grande Prairie - *12
#600, Windsor Court, 9835 - 101st Ave., Grande Prairie, AB T8V 5V4
Tel: 780-532-7771; Fax: 780-532-1158
Toll-Free: 888-531-7771
info@mylawteam.ca
www.mylawteam.ca

Grande Prairie: Lewis & Chrenek LLP - *5
#108, 9824 - 97 Ave., Grande Prairie, AB T8V 7K2
Tel: 780-539-6800; Fax: 780-539-7975
contact@lewischrenek.com
www.lewischrenek.com

Grande Prairie: Robert S. Pollick Professional Corporation - *1
#200, 10006 - 101 Ave., Grande Prairie, AB T8V 0Y1
Tel: 780-538-8290; Fax: 780-538-4515
enniski@telusplanet.net

Grande Prairie: Walisser Shavers LLP - *2
#202, Prairie Pl., 10027 - 101 Ave., Grande Prairie, AB T8V 0X9
Tel: 780-532-0315; Fax: 780-532-3369

Hanna: Ross, Todd & Company - *3
P.O. Box 1330, 124 - 2 Ave. West, Hanna, AB T0J 1P0
Tel: 403-854-4431; Fax: 403-854-2561
reception@drumhellerlaw.com

High Prairie: Harry J. Jong - *2
P.O. Box 1379, 5119 - 50 St., High Prairie, AB T0G 1E0
Tel: 780-523-4554; Fax: 780-523-5550
hjlaw@cablecomet.com

High River: A. George Dearing Professional Corp. - *1
#103, 14 - 2 Ave. SE, High River, AB T1V 2B8
Tel: 403-652-2771; Fax: 403-652-2699
info@ageorgedearing.ca
www.ageorgedearing.ca

Hinton: Johnson McClelland Murdoch - *4
213 Pembina Ave., Hinton, AB T7V 2B3
Tel: 780-865-2222; Fax: 780-865-8857
lawyer@jmmlaw.ca

Hinton: Woods & Robson - *2
110 Brewster Dr., Hinton, AB T7V 1B4
Tel: 780-865-3086; Fax: 780-865-7149
woodsrob@telusplanet.net

Innisfail: Tulloch Law Office - *1
P.O. Box 6099, Stn. Main, 5030 - 50 St., Innisfail, AB T4G 1S7
Tel: 403-227-5591; Fax: 403-227-1230
carolyntulloch@gmail.com

Lac La Biche: John W. Kozina - *1
Also Known As: Kozina Law Office
Former Name: Kozina & Gregory
P.O. Box 1439, 10130 Alberta Ave., Lac La Biche, AB T0A 2C0
Tel: 780-623-4818; Fax: 780-623-2933

Leduc: Arends Law Office - *1
4915-48 Ave., Leduc, AB T9E 7H9
Tel: 780-986-1443; Fax: 780-980-5385
arendslaw@shaw.ca

Leduc: Elgert & Company - *1
5206 - 50 St., Leduc, AB T9E 6Z6
Tel: 780-986-3487; Fax: 780-986-2040
herbelgert@shaw.ca

Leduc: Jackie, Handerek & Forester, Barristers & Solicitors - *8
4710 - 50th St., Leduc, AB T9E 6W2
Tel: 780-986-5081; Fax: 780-986-8807
www.leduclawyers.ab.ca

Leduc: Pahl Howard Rowland LLP - *4
#1, 5304 - 50 St., Leduc, AB T9E 6Z6
Tel: 780-986-8428; Fax: 780-986-2552

Lethbridge: Douglas N. Alger - *1
#230, 719 - 4 Ave. South, Lethbridge, AB T1J 0O1
Tel: 403-380-6005; Fax: 403-380-6088

Lethbridge: Connolly & Associates - *2
#203, P.O. Box 1207, Stn. Main, 506 - 7 St. South, Lethbridge, AB T1J 4A4
Tel: 403-329-8188; Fax: 403-328-7079

Lethbridge: Davidson & Williams LLP - *6
P.O. Box 518, 501 - 4 St. South, Lethbridge, AB T1J 4X2
Tel: 403-328-1766; Fax: 403-320-5434
lethbridge@davidsonandwilliams.com
www.davidsonandwilliams.com

Lethbridge: Frank de Walle - *1
323 - 7 St. South, Lethbridge, AB T1J 2G4
Tel: 403-328-8800; Fax: 403-328-8502
dewalle@telusplanet.net

Lethbridge: Dimnik & Company - *3
334 - 12 St. South, Lethbridge, AB T1J 2R1
Tel: 403-320-9800; Fax: 403-320-9124
info@lethbridgelawyers.com
www.lethbridgelawyers.com

Lethbridge: Huckvale Wilde Harvie MacLennan LLP - *8
410 - 6th St. South, Lethbridge, AB T1J 2C9
Tel: 403-328-8856; Fax: 403-380-4050
www.huckvalelaw.com

Lethbridge: MacLachlan McNab Hembroff LLP - *7
1003 - 4th Ave. South, Lethbridge, AB T1J 0P7
Tel: 403-381-4966; Fax: 403-329-9300
mmh@mmhlawyers.com
www.mmhlawyers.com

Lethbridge: Millar & Keith LLP - *2
Former Name: Millar, Thiessen & Keith
200 - 3rd St. South, Lethbridge, AB T1J 1Y7
Tel: 403-327-5716; Fax: 403-329-4063
mtklaw@telusplanet.net

Lethbridge: Milne Pritchard Law Office - *2
#807, 400 - 4 Ave. South, Lethbridge, AB T1J 4E1
Tel: 403-329-1133; Fax: 403-329-0395
bruce@milnepritchard.com
www.milnepritchard.com

Lethbridge: Harold N. Moodie Law Office - *1
#200, 424 - 7th St. South, Lethbridge, AB T1J 2G6
Tel: 403-328-0005; Fax: 403-329-0945
Toll-Free: 800-207-8482
hmoodie@moodielaw.com
www.moodielaw.com

Lethbridge: North & Company LLP - *19
#600, Chancery Court, 220 - 4th St., Lethbridge, AB T1J 4J7
Tel: 403-328-7781; Fax: 403-320-8958
Toll-Free: 800-552-8022
www.north-co.com

Lethbridge: Peterson & Purvis LLP - *6
P.O. Box 1165, 537 - 7th St. South, Lethbridge, AB T1J 4A4
Tel: 403-328-9667; Fax: 403-320-1393
p-plaw@telusplanet.net
www.petersonpurvislaw.ca

Lethbridge: Pollock & Company - *3
Former Name: Fletcher, Norton & Pollock
#200, P.O. Box 1386, 434 - 7th St. South, Lethbridge, AB T1J 4K1
Tel: 403-329-6900
dlplaw@lawpollock.com
www.lawpollock.com

Lethbridge: RMcD Law Offices - *1
243-12B St. N, Lethbridge, AB T1H 2K8
Tel: 403-328-9125; Fax: 403-328-9143
wfmlaw@telus.net

Lethbridge: Shapiro & Company - *1
#200, 427 - 5 St. South., Lethbridge, AB T1J 2B6
Tel: 403-328-9300; Fax: 403-328-9307
shapco@telusplanet.net

Lethbridge: Stringam LLP - *19
150 - 4 St. South, Lethbridge, AB T1J 5G4
Tel: 403-328-5577; Fax: 403-327-1141
info@stringam.ca
www.stringam.ca
www.facebook.com/stringamdenecky,
twitter.com/stringamdenecky,
www.linkedin.com/company/stringam-denecky-llp

Lethbridge: Thiessen Law Group - *3
1412 - 3rd Ave. South, Lethbridge, AB T1J 0K6
Tel: 403-381-7343; Fax: 403-381-7350
thiessenlaw@thiessenlaw.ca
www.thiessenlaw.ca
www.facebook.com/pages/Thiessen-Law_Group/171450492908177, twitter.com/ThiessenLaw

** indicates number of lawyers*

Lethbridge: Torry Lewis Abells LLP - *7
#110, Chancery Court, 220 - 4 St. South, Lethbridge, AB T1J 4J7
Tel: 403-327-4406; Fax: 403-328-4597
Toll-Free: 888-327-4406
ken.torry@tlalaw.com
www.tlalaw.com

Lloydminster: Clements & Smith - *3
#212, 5704 - 44 St., Lloydminster, AB T9V 2A1
Tel: 750-875-7999

Lloydminster: Kindrachuk Dobson - *2
Former Name: Kindrachuk Law Office
Stafford Building, 5014 - 48 St., 2nd fl., Lloydminster, AB T9V 0H8
Tel: 780-875-6600; Fax: 780-875-6601
info@kindrachukdobson.com
www.kindrachukdobson.com
www.linkedin.com/company/2269686

Lloydminster: Kirzinger, Wells Law Office - *2
#203, 5101 - 48 St., Lloydminster, AB T9V 0H9
Tel: 780-875-8400; Fax: 780-875-8499

Lloydminster: Knight Law Office - *1
P.O. Box 1500, Stn. Main, 4912 - 50th Ave., Lloydminster, AB S9V 1K5
Tel: 780-875-9555; Fax: 780-875-9557
bknight@silvercrest.ca

Lloydminster: Lonsdale Law Office - *1
P.O. Box 1248, 5117 - 48 St., Lloydminster, AB S9V 1G1
Tel: 780-875-5185; Fax: 780-875-6547
lonsdalelaw@lgl.cc
www.lgl.cc

Medicine Hat: Haynes, William L., Law Office - *1
#108, 1235 Southview Dr. SE, Medicine Hat, AB T1B 4K3
Tel: 403-528-8883; Fax: 403-526-7698
bill@hayneslaw.net

Medicine Hat: Hill & Hill - *2
#6, 3151 Dunmore Rd. SE, Medicine Hat, AB T1B 2H2
Tel: 403-527-1544; Fax: 403-526-2551

Medicine Hat: Leis, Wiese & Company - *3
#35, 7 St. SE, Medicine Hat, AB T1A 1J2
Tel: 403-527-7766; Fax: 403-527-7788

Medicine Hat: MacLean Wiedemann Lawyers LLP - *4
422 - 6th St. SE, Medicine Hat, AB T1A 1H5
Tel: 403-527-3343; Fax: 403-526-0473
www.mwllp.ca/mmllp

Medicine Hat: Niblock & Company LLP - *7
P.O. Box 609, Stn. Main, 420 Macleaod Trail SE, Medicine Hat, AB T1A 7G5
Tel: 403-526-2806; Fax: 403-526-2356
Toll-Free: 800-245-9411
reception@Niblock.ca
www.niblock.ca

Medicine Hat: Pritchard & Company LLP - *6
#204, P.O. Box 100, 430 - 6th Ave. SE, Medicine Hat, AB T1A 7E8
Tel: 403-527-4411; Fax: 403-527-9806
www.pritchardandcompany.ca
www.facebook.com/pages/Pritchard-and-Company-LLP/179232512100230, twitter.com/PCo_LLP

Medicine Hat: Schindel Law Office - *1
#1, 3295 Dunmore Rd. SE, Medicine Hat, AB T1B 3R2
Tel: 403-529-5548; Fax: 403-529-2694
ryan@schindellaw.com
schindellaw.com

Medicine Hat: Sihvon Carter Fisher & Berger LLP - *4
499 - 1st St. SE, Medicine Hat, AB T1A 0A7
Tel: 403-526-2600; Fax: 403-526-3217
info@scfb.ca
www.scfb.ca

Medicine Hat: Smith & Hersey Law Firm - Medicine Hat - *4
Former Name: Gordon, Smith & Company
#104, Westside Common, 2201 Box Springs Blvd. NW, Medicine Hat, AB T1C 0C8
Tel: 403-527-5506; Fax: 403-527-0577
Toll-Free: 800-598-7626
simon@smithhersey.com
smithhersey.com

Nanton: Laurie M. Gordon - *1
P.O. Box 586, 2213 - 20th St., Nanton, AB T0L 1R0
Tel: 403-646-6111; Fax: 403-646-6112
lmgordon@telusplanet.net

Nanton: Roddie Law Office - *1
P.O. Box 100, 2117 - 20 St., Nanton, AB T0L 1R0
Tel: 403-646-2211; Fax: 403-646-3159
rodmclaw@telusplanet.net

Okotoks: Brandi Aymount - *1
Also Known As: Okotoks Law
P.O. Box 669, 84 Elizabeth St., Okotoks, AB T1S 1A8
Tel: 403-938-2101; Fax: 403-938-6020
aymontb@okotokslaw.com
okotokslaw.com

Okotoks: Diane Luttmer Professional Corporation - *1
Former Name: Diane Dolsen
P.O. Box 267, Okotoks, AB T1S 1A5
Tel: 403-938-8296; Fax: 403-938-8286

Okotoks: Charles A. Dixon - *1
P.O. Box 1169, Stn. Main, 51 Riverside Gate, Okotoks, AB T1S 1B2
Tel: 403-938-8131; Fax: 403-938-6365

Olds: R. Brent Carlyle
P.O. Box 3755, Stn. Main, 4911 - 51 Ave., Olds, AB T4H 1P5
Tel: 866-279-2110; Fax: 866-619-2904
brentc@reveal.ca

Olds: Alvin F. Ganser - *1
P.O. Box 4040, Stn. Main, 4834 - 50 St., Olds, AB T4H 1P7
Tel: 403-556-8481; Fax: 403-556-3830
aganser@oldsnet.ca

Olds: Martinson & Harder - *3
#1, 5401 - 49 Ave., Olds, AB T4H 1G3
Tel: 403-556-8955; Fax: 403-556-8895
contact@martinsonharder.com
martinsonharder.com

Parksville: Evans & Company - *1
P.O. Box 40, 182 Memorial Ave., Parksville, AB V2P 2G3
Tel: 250-248-5748; Fax: 250-248-5758
evansandco@telus.net

Peace River: Mathieu Hryniuk LLP - Peace River - *6
P.O. Box 6210, 10012 - 101 St., Peace River, AB T8S 1S2
Tel: 780-624-2565; Fax: 780-624-5766
Toll-Free: 800-661-1962
mh@mhllp.ca
mhllp.ca

Ponoka: Noble & Kidd - *1
P.O. Box 4278, Stn. Main, Ponoka, AB T4J 1R7
Tel: 403-783-3325; Fax: 403-783-5080
noblekid@telus.net

Ponoka: Paterson & Company - *1
#4550, 5016 - 51 Ave., Ponoka, AB T4J 1S1
Tel: 403-783-5521; Fax: 403-783-2012
office@craigpatersonlaw.com
www.craigpatersonlaw.com

Priddis: Rath & Company - *3
P.O. Box 44, RR#1, Site 8, Priddis, AB T0L 1W0
Tel: 403-931-4047; Fax: 403-931-4048
rathco@rathandcompany.com
www.rathandcompany.com

Red Deer: Brian Adair - *1
#207, 4909 - 48 St., Red Deer, AB T4N 1S8
Tel: 403-342-1777; Fax: 403-341-4775
adair_law@hotmail.com
www.brianadair.ca

Red Deer: Susan K. Allison - *1
4919 - 48 St., 2nd Floor, Red Deer, AB T4N 1S8
Tel: 403-340-3136; Fax: 403-343-7016
sallison@reddeerlaw.com

Red Deer: Altalaw LLP - *12
Former Name: Duhamel Manning Feehan Warrender Glass LLP
5233 - 49 Ave., Red Deer, AB T4N 6G5
Tel: 403-343-0812; Fax: 403-340-3545
altalaw@altalaw.ca
www.altalaw.ca

Red Deer: Dunkle McBeath - *2
5004 - 48 Ave., Red Deer, AB T4N 3T6
Tel: 403-347-5522; Fax: 403-347-5632
dkm_law@telusplanet.net

Red Deer: C.E. Forgues - *1
#103, 4310-49 Ave., Red Deer, AB T4N 6M5
Tel: 403-342-7044; Fax: 403-342-7055

Red Deer: Gerig Hamilton Neeland LLP - *5
#501, 4901 - 48 St., Red Deer, AB T4N 6M4
Tel: 403-343-2444; Fax: 403-343-6522
info@ghnlawyers.ca
www.ghnlawyers.ca

Red Deer: Donald A. Gross - *1
#274, 4919 - 59 St., Red Deer, AB T4N 6C9
Tel: 403-343-3715; Fax: 403-343-7435

Red Deer: Johnston Ming Manning LLP - Red Deer - *13
Royal Bank Bldg., 4943 - 50th St., 3rd & 4th Fl., Red Deer, AB T4N 1Y1
Tel: 403-346-5591; Fax: 403-346-5599
info@jmmlawrd.ca
www.johnstonmingmanning.com

Red Deer: Gayle A. Langford - *1
#303, 5008 - 50th St., Red Deer, AB T4N 1Y3
Tel: 403-358-3559; Fax: 403-356-0397
gayle@galangford.ca
www.galangford.ca

Red Deer: Brian S. MacNairn - *1
#201, 5008 Ross St., Red Deer, AB T4N 1Y3
Tel: 403-347-2700; Fax: 403-346-5825
macnairn@telusplanet.net

Red Deer: P.E.B. MacSween - *1
4824 - 51 St., Red Deer, AB T4N 2A5
Tel: 403-342-5595; Fax: 403-342-7519

Red Deer: Peter C. McElhaney - *1
#5, 4801 - 51 Ave., Red Deer, AB T4N 4H2
Tel: 403-346-2026; Fax: 403-309-1969

Red Deer: Gerald W. Neufeld - *1
#504, 4909-49 St., Red Deer, AB T4N 1V1
Tel: 403-343-2202; Fax: 403-343-2203
gneufeld@telusplanet.net

Red Deer: Patrick A. Penny - *1
10 Reeves Cres., Red Deer, AB T4P 2Y4
Tel: 403-342-9595; Fax: 403-346-9778
pmanpenny@telus.net
red-deer-criminal-lawyer.ca

Red Deer: Schnell Hardy Jones LLP - Red Deer - *9
Former Name: Schnell, MacSween & Hardy
#504, 4909 - 49th St., Red Deer, AB T4N 1V1
Tel: 403-342-7400; Fax: 403-340-0520
Toll-Free: 800-342-7405
lawyers@schnell-law.com
www.schnell-law.com

Red Deer: Sully Chapman Beattie LLP - *3
Former Name: Flanagan, Sully, Surkan
#202, Park Place, 4825 - 47th St., Red Deer, AB T4N 1R3
Tel: 403-342-7715; Fax: 403-347-5955
info@scblaw.ca
www.scblaw.ca

Red Deer: Warren Sinclair LLP - *11
Former Name: Sisson Warren Sinclair
#600, First Red Deer Place, 4911 - 51 St., Red Deer, AB T4N 6V4
Tel: 403-343-3320; Fax: 403-343-6069
email@warrensinclair.com
www.warrensinclair.com

Red Deer: William D. Weiswasser - *1
#300, 4808-50 St., Red Deer, AB T4N 1X5
Tel: 403-343-0317; Fax: 403-343-0318
mediate@agt.net

Redwater: D. Lawrence McCallum - *1
4816-50 Ave., Redwater, AB T0A 2W0
Tel: 780-942-3040; Fax: 780-942-2003
Toll-Free: 800-390-2257

Rimbey: David R. Pfau - *1
P.O. Box 1009, 5001 - 50th Ave., Rimbey, AB T0C 2J0
Tel: 403-843-2296; Fax: 403-843-2344

** indicates number of lawyers*

Rocky Mountain House: Peter Crossley Law Office - *1
P.O. Box 1108, 4616 - 47 Ave., Rocky Mountain House, AB T4T 1A8
Tel: 403-845-2828; *Fax:* 403-845-4630
crossleylaw@shawbiz.ca

Rocky Mountain House: Dunsford & Scott - *2
5135 - 48 Ave., Rocky Mountain House, AB T4T 1A3
Tel: 403-845-7112; *Fax:* 403-845-4670
reception@dunsfordandscott.com
www.dunsfordandscott.com

Sherwood Park: Stanley H. King - *1
241 Kaska Rd., 2nd Fl., Sherwood Park, AB T8A 4E8
Tel: 780-449-1404; *Fax:* 780-449-1409
stan@westana.com

Sherwood Park: Wayne LeDrew - *1
#16, 140 Athabascan Ave., Sherwood Park, AB T8A 4E3
Tel: 780-467-3014; *Fax:* 780-464-8504
wledrew@telusplanet.net

Sherwood Park: Nigro & Company - *2
282 Kaska Rd., Sherwood Park, AB T8A 4G7
Tel: 780-467-9559; *Fax:* 780-467-0720
nigroco@shaw.ca

Sherwood Park: Thomas E. Spratlin - *1
Former Name: Spratlin Tonnellier
#120, 363 Sioux Rd., Sherwood Park, AB T8A 4W7
Tel: 780-464-5404; *Fax:* 780-417-1759
spratlinlaw.petrasite.com

Sherwood Park: Strathcona Law Group - *4
#132, Heritage Court, 150 Chippewa Rd., Sherwood Park, AB T8A 6A2
Tel: 780-417-9222; *Fax:* 780-449-1222
info@strathconalawgroup.com
www.strathconalawgroup.com

Slave Lake: Allan G. McMillan - *1
#107, P.O. Box 533, 201 - 2 St. NE, Slave Lake, AB T0G 2A0
Tel: 780-849-2227; *Fax:* 780-849-2143
mcmillan@telusplanet.net

Slave Lake: Twinn Barristers & Solicitors - *1
Former Name: Catherine M. Twinn
P.O. Box 1460, 810 Caribou Trail NE, Slave Lake, AB T0G 2A0
Tel: 780-849-4319; *Fax:* 780-805-3274
ctwinn@twinnlaw.com

Spruce Grove: Larry D. Ayers - *2
#210, P.O. Box 4372, Stn. Main, 215 McLeod Ave., Spruce Grove, AB T7X 3B5
Tel: 780-962-9500; *Fax:* 780-962-9535
ayers@ayerslawco.com
www.ayerslawco.com

Spruce Grove: Loretta (Lori) Edlund - *1
#35, 54023 SH 779, Spruce Grove, AB T7X 3V5
Tel: 780-968-1668; *Fax:* 780-968-1667
nlaedlund@gmail.com
sprucegrovelaywer.ca

Spruce Grove: Randall C. Heil - *1
#201, Cumbria Centre, 93 McLeod Ave., Spruce Grove, AB T7X 2Z9
Tel: 780-962-9700; *Fax:* 780-962-9329
rheil@telus.net
www.rcheillaw.ca/en/

Spruce Grove: Robert A. Joly - *1
#4, 20 McLeod Ave., Spruce Grove, AB T7X 3Y1
Tel: 780-962-4447; *Fax:* 780-962-3638
bbjoly@shaw.ca

Spruce Grove: Mainstreet Law Offices - *7
115 Main St., Spruce Grove, AB T7X 3A7
Tel: 780-960-8100
www.mainstreetlaw.ca

Spruce Grove: Robinson & Company - *2
P.O. Box 4113, 16 Westgrove Dr., Spruce Grove, AB T7X 3B3
Tel: 780-962-0660; *Fax:* 780-962-0622
office@sprucegrovelaw.com
www.sprucegrovelaw.com

St Albert: Cody Law Office - *1
#407, 22 Sir Winston Churchill Ave., St Albert, AB T8N 1B4
Tel: 780-470-0500; *Fax:* 780-670-0501
www.codylawoffice.com

St Albert: Oddleifson & Kaup - *2
#200, 39 St Thomas St., St Albert, AB T8N 6N8
Tel: 780-459-2220; *Fax:* 780-459-0621

St Albert: Quantz Law Group - *3
Former Name: Stonhouse & Downie
#220, 8 Perron St., St Albert, AB T8N 1E4
Tel: 780-458-7690; *Fax:* 780-458-5510
info@quantzlaw.com
www.quantzlaw.com

St Albert: Thomas A. Rowand Professional Corp. - *1
22 Perron St., St Albert, AB T8N 6B9
Tel: 780-458-9440; *Fax:* 780-458-9442
trowand@telusplanet.net

St Albert: Wallace Law Office - *1
#3, 30 Rayborn Cres., St Albert, AB T8N 5B7
Tel: 780-458-7717; *Fax:* 780-460-1818

St Albert: Weary & Company - *4
#400, 30 Green Grove Dr., St Albert, AB T8N 5H6
Tel: 780-459-5596; *Fax:* 780-459-6572
www.wearyandco.com

St Paul: Lamoureux Culham LLP - *3
Former Name: Lamoureux & Lawrence
4713 - 50th St., St Paul, AB T0A 3A4
Tel: 780-645-5202; *Fax:* 780-645-6507
www.stpaul-law.ca

Stony Plain: Birdsell Grant LLP
Former Name: Birdsell Grant Gardner Morck
#102, 5300 - 50 St., Stony Plain, AB T7Z 1T8
Tel: 780-963-8181; *Fax:* 780-963-9618
info@birdsell.ca
www.birdsell.ca

Stony Plain: Deborah A. Kay - *1
#104, 4310 - 33 St., Stony Plain, AB T7Z 0A8
Tel: 780-591-0225; *Fax:* 780-591-0223
info@kaylawandmediation.com
www.kaylawandmediation.com

Stony Plain: Glen G. McAllister - *1
#128, 5211 - 50 St., Stony Plain, AB T7Z 0C1
Tel: 780-968-2900; *Fax:* 780-968-2224
contact@mcallisterlawfirm.ca
www.mcallisterlawfirm.ca/en/

Strathmore: Getz & Associates - *2
P.O. Box 2370, Stn. Main, 225A Wheatland Trail, Strathmore, AB T1P 1K3
Tel: 403-934-2500; *Fax:* 403-934-2794
getzlaw@getzlaw.ca

Strathmore: Jarvis, Randal E.J. - *2
#110, 304 Third Ave., Strathmore, AB T1P 1Z1
Tel: 403-934-5000; *Fax:* 403-934-4853
rejarvis@shaw.ca

Sylvan Lake: Brian C. Flanagan - *1
#203, 5043 - 50A St., Sylvan Lake, AB T4S 1R1
Tel: 403-887-5441; *Fax:* 403-887-3010
burflan@telusplanet.net

Sylvan Lake: Vanden Brink Law Office - *1
Former Name: Vanden Brink & Madden
P.O. Box 9613, Stn. Main, Sylvan Lake, AB T4S 1S8
Tel: 403-885-2222; *Fax:* 403-885-2226
benbrink@hughes.net

Taber: Baldry Sugden LLP - *3
5401 - 50 Ave., Taber, AB T1G 1V2
Tel: 403-223-3585; *Fax:* 403-223-1732
balsug@telusplanet.net
baldrysugden.ca

Three Hills: Norman L. Tainsh Prof. Corp. - *7
P.O. Box 1234, 205 Main St., Three Hills, AB T0M 2A0
Tel: 403-443-2200; *Fax:* 403-443-2025
Toll-Free: 888-939-2200
ntainsh@tainsh.ca
www.tainsh.ca

Turner Valley: Beverly A.B. Broadhurst - *1
#2, P.O. Box 501, 101 Sunset Blvd. SW, Turner Valley, AB T0L 2A0
Tel: 403-933-3255; *Fax:* 403-933-4104

Vermilion: Reynolds & Flemke - *2
#11, Vermilion Prof. Bldg., 5125 - 50 Ave., Vermilion, AB T9X 1A8
Tel: 780-853-5339; *Fax:* 780-853-4200
rfverm@telusplanet.net

Vermilion: Wheat Law Office - *2
5042 - 49 Ave., Vermilion, AB T9X 1B7
Tel: 780-853-4707; *Fax:* 780-853-4499
wheatlaw@telusplanet.net

Wainwright: Peter Van Winssen - *1
1013 - 5 Ave., Wainwright, AB T9W 1L6
Tel: 780-842-5140; *Fax:* 780-842-3830

Westlock: ProperziTims - *5
#2, P.O. Box 490, 9831 - 107th St., Westlock, AB T7P 1R9
Tel: 780-349-5366; *Fax:* 780-349-6510
candice@properzitims.com
properzitims.com

Wetaskiwin: McDonald Street Law Office - *1
4408 - 51 St., Wetaskiwin, AB T9A 1K5
Tel: 780-352-0369; *Fax:* 780-352-0393

Wetaskiwin: SIRRS LLP - Wetaskiwin - *7
Former Name: Deckert Allen Cymbaluk Genest
5220 - 51st Ave., Wetaskiwin, AB T9A 2G3
Tel: 780-352-3301; *Fax:* 780-352-5976
wetaskiwin@sirrsllp.com
www.sirrsllp.com

Wetaskiwin: Sockett Law - *4
5118 - 50 Ave., Wetaskiwin, AB T9A 0S6
Tel: 780-352-6691; *Fax:* 780-352-0599
sockett@sockettlaw.com
www.facebook.com/pages/Sockett-Law/137438379708196,

Whitecourt: McConnell Law Office - *1
P.O. Box 1795, Stn. Main, 5115 Highway St., Whitecourt, AB T7S 1P5
Tel: 780-778-4945; *Fax:* 780-778-3851

British Columbia

100 Mile House: Centennial Law Corporation - *2
#1, P.O. Box 2169, 241 Birch Ave., 100 Mile House, BC V0K 2E0
Tel: 250-395-1080; *Fax:* 250-395-1088
centenniallaw@bcinternet.net
centenniallaw.com

100 Mile House: George J. Wool - *1
5741 Simon Lake Rd., One Hundred Mile House, BC V0K 2E1
Tel: 250-791-9295; *Fax:* 250-791-9228
gjwool@xplornet.ca

Abbotsford: Balakshin Hargrave Law Corporation - *2
#202, 2955 Gladwin Rd., Abbotsford, BC V2T 5T4
Tel: 604-859-1220
info@bhlawyers.ca
www.bhlawyers.ca
www.facebook.com/BalakshinHargraveLawCorporation

Abbotsford: Kenneth R. Beatch - *1
2459 Pauline St., Abbotsford, BC V2S 3S1
Tel: 604-853-9555; *Fax:* 604-859-3361
ken@drugdefence.com
www.drugdefence.com

Abbotsford: Conroy & Company - *3
2459 Pauline St., Abbotsford, BC V2S 3S1
Tel: 604-852-5110; *Fax:* 604-859-3361
Toll-Free: 877-852-5110
office@johnconroy.com
www.johnconroy.com

Abbotsford: Stanley T. Cope - *1
#205, 2692 Clearbrook Rd., Abbotsford, BC V2T 2Y8
Tel: 604-855-2089
stan@copeinjuryclaimlawyers.ca
www.copeinjuryclaimlawyers.ca/en/

Abbotsford: Dhami Narang & Company - *4
#301, 2975 Gladwin Rd., Abbotsford, BC V2T 5T4
Tel: 604-864-6131; *Fax:* 604-864-6116
Toll-Free: 877-864-6131
www.dnclaw.ca
www.facebook.com/dnclaw, www.twitter.com/injurylawyersbc

Abbotsford: Donald R. Gardner - *1
Abbotsford Registry & Judges' Chambers, 32203 South Fraset Way, Abbotsford, BC V2T 1W6
Tel: 604-855-3200; *Fax:* 604-855-3232

** indicates number of lawyers*

***Abbotsford*: Integra Law Group - *1**
#101, 2776 Bourquin Cres. West, Abbotsford, BC V2S 6A4
Tel: 604-859-7187; *Fax:* 604-859-7185
josh@integralaw.ca

***Abbotsford*: Just Law Corpoartion - *1**
#10, 2151 McCallum Rd., Abbotsford, BC V2S 3N8
Tel: 604-854-6689; *Fax:* 604-852-4789
mw.law@telus.net
www.justlawinc.com

***Abbotsford*: Kuhn LLP - *12**
#100, 2160 South Fraser Way, Abbotsford, BC V2T 1W5
Tel: 604-864-8877; *Fax:* 604-864-8867
Toll-Free: 888-704-8877
www.kuhnco.net

***Abbotsford*: Linley Welwood LLP - *7**
Former Name: Linley, Duignan & Company; Welwood Wiens Warkentin; Fast Welwood & Wiens; Linley Duignan
#305, 2692 Clearbrook Rd., Abbotsford, BC V2T 2Y8
Tel: 604-850-6640; *Fax:* 604-850-6616
info@linleywelwood.com
www.linleywelwood.com
www.facebook.com/LinleyWelwoodLLP

***Abbotsford*: MacAdams Law Firm - *3**
#205, Gladwin Centre, 2955 Gladwin Rd., Abbotsford, BC V2T 5T4
Fax: 604-850-1937
Toll-Free: 800-800-2967
www.macadamslaw.com
www.linkedin.com/company/macadams-law-firm

***Abbotsford*: Palmer Gillen - *2**
#1, 33775 Essendene Ave., Abbotsford, BC V2S 2H1
Tel: 604-859-3887; *Fax:* 604-859-3883
www.abbotsfordlawyers.com

***Abbotsford*: Robertson, Downe & Mullally**
Also Known As: RDM Lawyers
33695 South Fraser Way, Abbotsford, BC V2S 2C1
Tel: 604-853-0774; *Fax:* 604-852-3829
Toll-Free: 888-853-0774
info@rdmlawyers.com
www.rdmlawyers.com
www.facebook.com/RDMLawyers

***Abbotsford*: Rosborough & Company - *3**
#201, 33832 Fraser Way South, Abbotsford, BC V2S 2C5
Tel: 604-859-7171
MBurke@Rosborough.com
www.rosborough.com

***Abbotsford*: Valley Law Group - *4**
Former Name: Kuzminski & Haraldsen
#301, 2031 McCallum Rd., Abbotsford, BC V2S 3N5
Tel: 604-853-5401; *Fax:* 604-853-8358
inquiry@valleylawgroup.com
www.valleylawgroup.com

***Armstrong*: Blakely & Company Law Corporation - *1**
#201, P.O. Box 357, 2595 Pleasant Valley Blvd., Armstrong, BC V0E 1B0
Tel: 250-546-3188; *Fax:* 250-546-2677
Toll-Free: 888-838-9982
blakely@junction.net
www.blakelylaw.ca

***Armstrong*: Culos & Company - *1**
Former Name: Clarke & Company
#1, P.O. Box 70, 2516 Patterson Ave., Armstrong, BC V0E 1B0
Tel: 250-546-2448; *Fax:* 250-546-2621
robculos@telus.net

***Brentwood Bay*: Sandra E. Jenko - *1**
#112, P.O. Box 425, Stn. Main, 7088 West Saanich Rd., Brentwood Bay, BC V8M 1R3
Tel: 250-652-5151; *Fax:* 250-652-9687
jenkolaw@shaw.ca

***Burnaby*: Baily McLean, Barristers & Solicitors - *2**
Former Name: Greenbank Murdoch & Company; Baily, McLean, Greenbank & Murdoch
#900, Metrotower II, 4720 Kingsway, Burnaby, BC V5H 4M2
Tel: 604-437-6611; *Fax:* 604-437-3065
info@bmgm.com
www.bmgm.com

***Burnaby*: Cobbett & Cotton - *8**
#800, 410 Carleton Ave., Burnaby, BC V5C 6P6
Tel: 604-299-6251; *Fax:* 604-299-6627
mail@cobbett-cotton.com
cobbett-cotton.com

***Burnaby*: Eder Birgit - *2**
#216, 3989 Henning Dr., Burnaby, BC V5C 6P8
Tel: 604-687-0134; *Fax:* 604-687-5176
Toll-Free: 800-461-3455

***Burnaby*: Edwards & Co. - *2**
Former Name: Edwards, Edwards & Edwards
#510, 5021 Kingsway, Burnaby, BC V5H 4A5
Tel: 604-433-2445; *Fax:* 604-433-8209
eee@bcpersonalinjurylaw.com
www.bcpersonalinjurylaw.com

***Burnaby*: James K. Fitzsimmons - *1**
#200, 6960 Royal Oak Ave., Burnaby, BC V5J 4J2
Tel: 604-298-8939; *Fax:* 604-298-8956

***Burnaby*: James K. Fraser Law Corporation - *1**
#200, 4603 Kingsway, Burnaby, BC V5H 4M4
Tel: 604-433-0010; *Fax:* 604-435-0269
jkf@jkf.ca

***Burnaby*: Hawthorne, Piggott & Company - *7**
Also Known As: HP Law
#208, 1899 Willingdon Ave., Burnaby, BC V5C 5T1
Tel: 604-299-8371; *Fax:* 604-299-1523
info@hplaw.ca
www.hplaw.ca

***Burnaby*: O'Neill Rozenberg - *2**
#201, 4547 Hastings St., Burnaby, BC V5C 2K3
Tel: 604-294-8311
contact@oneillrozenberg.ca
www.oneillrozenberg.ca

***Burnaby*: Pihl & Company - *1**
#205, 5481 Kingsway, Burnaby, BC V5H 2G1
Tel: 604-437-8837; *Fax:* 604-437-3529

***Burnaby*: Sellens & Associates - *3**
#320, 9940 Lougheed Hwy., Burnaby, BC V3J 1N3
Tel: 604-421-0716; *Fax:* 604-421-7692

***Burnaby*: Maureen J. Wesley - *1**
4270 McGill St., Burnaby, BC V5C 1M9
Tel: 604-298-6555; *Fax:* 604-298-6540

***Burnaby*: Patricia Yaremovich - *1**
#105, 6540 East Hastings St., Burnaby, BC V5B 4Z5
Tel: 604-320-0688; *Fax:* 604-320-0007
pyaremovich@shaw.ca

***Burns Lake*: Warren Chapman - *1**
#17, P.O. Box 258, 343 16 Hwy. East, Burns Lake, BC V0J 1E0
Tel: 250-692-3339; *Fax:* 250-692-3342
chapmanlaw@telus.net
www.warrenchapmanlaw.com/en/

***Campbell River*: Frame & Co. Injury Law - *2**
#301, 1100 Island Hwy., Campbell River, BC V9W 8C6
Tel: 250-286-6691; *Fax:* 250-286-1191
Toll-Free: 800-661-0238
www.frameandcolaw.com

***Campbell River*: Claire I. Moglove - *1**
#201, 909 Island Hwy., Campbell River, BC V9W 2C2
Tel: 250-286-9946; *Fax:* 250-287-3592
cmoglove@shaw.ca

***Campbell River*: Shook, Wickham, Bishop & Field - *11**
Former Name: McVea, Shook, Wickham & Bishop
906 Island Hwy., Campbell River, BC V9W 2C3
Tel: 250-287-8355; *Fax:* 250-287-8112
info@crlawyers.ca
www.crlawyers.ca

***Campbell River*: Karen D. Stevan - *1**
748 Galerno Rd., Campbell River, BC V9W 5J3
Tel: 250-926-0120; *Fax:* 250-926-0121
kdstevan@yahoo.ca

***Campbell River*: Tees Kiddle Spencer - *6**
#200, 1260 Shoppers Row, Campbell River, BC V9W 2C8
Tel: 250-287-7755; *Fax:* 250-287-3999
Toll-Free: 800-224-7755
info@tkslaw.com
www.tkslaw.com

***Castlegar*: Polonicoff & Perehudoff - *2**
1115 - 3 St., Castlegar, BC V1N 2A1
Tel: 250-365-3343; *Fax:* 250-365-6307

***Chemainus*: Mary Lynn Bancroft - *1**
Box 168, 9834 Croft St., Chemainus, BC V0R 1K0
Tel: 250-246-4771; *Fax:* 250-246-2547
mbancroft@shaw.ca

***Chilliwack*: Baker Newby LLP - *23**
P.O. Box 390, 9259 Main St., Chilliwack, BC V2P 6K2
Tel: 604-792-1376; *Fax:* 604-792-8711
www.bakernewby.com

***Chilliwack*: Clearpath Law Group**
#101, 9123 Mary St., Chilliwack, BC V2P 4H7
Tel: 604-795-4522; *Fax:* 604-795-4522
info@clearpathlaw.com
clearpathlaw.com

***Chilliwack*: Fraser West Law Group LLP - *4**
Former Name: Kaye Thome Toews & Hansford
P.O. Box 372, 9202 Young Rd., Chilliwack, BC V2P 6J4
Tel: 604-792-1977 *Toll-Free:* 888-792-1977
www.fraserwestlaw.com

***Chilliwack*: Patten Thornton - *4**
P.O. Box 379, 9245 Main St., Chilliwack, BC V2P 6J4
Tel: 604-795-9188; *Fax:* 604-795-6340
Toll-Free: 877-529-9799
info@pattenthornton.com
www.pattenthornton.com

***Chilliwack*: Stander & Company - *1**
#108, 7491 Vedder Rd., Chilliwack, BC V2R 4E7
Tel: 604-847-9777; *Fax:* 604-847-9779
info@standerandcompany.ca
www.standerandcompany.com

***Clearwater*: John Kurta - *1**
P.O. Box 5171, 32 East Old North Thompson Hwy., Clearwater, BC V0E 1N0
Tel: 250-674-2126; *Fax:* 250-674-3493

***Comox*: Schaffrick & Sutton - *2**
1984 Comox Ave., Comox, BC V9M 3M7
Tel: 250-339-3363; *Fax:* 250-339-3315
Toll-Free: 877-778-8866

***Coquitlam*: David Boulding - *1**
2126 Elspeth, Coquitlam, BC V3C 1G3
Tel: 604-942-5301; *Fax:* 604-942-5302
dmboulding@shaw.ca
www.davidboulding.com

***Coquitlam*: Drysdale Bacon McStravick LLP - *10**
Former Name: Feller Bacon McStravick
#211, 1015 Austin Ave., Coquitlam, BC V3K 3N9
Tel: 604-939-8321; *Fax:* 604-939-7584
inquiries@dbmlaw.ca
www.dbmlaw.ca
www.facebook.com/DrysdaleBaconMcStravick,
www.linkedin.com/company/drysdale-bacon-mcstravick-llp

***Coquitlam*: The Spagnuolo Group of Real Estate Law Firms - *10**
#300, 906 Roderick Ave., Coquitlam, BC V3K 1R1
Tel: 604-527-4242; *Fax:* 604-527-8976
Toll-Free: 888-873-2829
info@bcrealestatelawyers.com
www.bcrealestatelawyers.com
www.facebook.com/pages/Spagnuolo-Company-Real-Estate-Lawyers/16830998985871, twitter.com/SpagnuoloLaw,
ca.linkedin.com/pub/tony-spagnuolo/27/745/961

***Coquitlam*: Spraggs & Company - *6**
#202, 1030 Westwood St., Coquitlam, BC V3C 4E4
Tel: 604-464-3333 *Toll-Free:* 866-939-3339
spraggslaw.ca
www.facebook.com/pages/Spraggs-Co/123830580985035,
twitter.com/spraggslaw,
www.linkedin.com/company/spraggs-&-co-

***Coquitlam*: Taylor Bardal - *3**
#220, 1024 Ridgeway Ave., Coquitlam, BC V3J 1S5
Tel: 604-931-3477; *Fax:* 604-931-1277

***Coquitlam*: Judy Wong - *1**
#205, 3030 Lincoln Ave., Coquitlam, BC V3B 6B4
Tel: 604-945-6982; *Fax:* 604-945-6819
www.judywonglawcorp.ca

** indicates number of lawyers*

***Courtenay*: Ansley & Company - *3**
#306, 576 England Ave., Courtenay, BC V9N 2N3
Tel: 250-338-0202; *Fax:* 250-338-0902
www.ansleyandcompany.com

***Courtenay*: Bush & Company - *5**
#101, 1350 England Ave., Courtenay, BC V9N 8X6
Tel: 250-338-6741; *Fax:* 250-338-6780
Toll-Free: 877-338-6741
info@bushandcompany.ca
bushandcompany.ca

***Courtenay*: Crispin Morris Law Corporation - *1**
Former Name: Morris, C.H.L.
5463 Headquarters Rd., Courtenay, BC V9J 1M3
Tel: 250-338-5311; *Fax:* 250-338-1818
crispinmorris@telus.net

***Courtenay*: James E. Dow - *1**
#7, 625 Cliffe Ave., Courtenay, BC V9N 2J6
Tel: 250-338-7701; *Fax:* 250-338-6641
jamesdow@shaw.ca

***Courtenay*: Ives Burger - *3**
Former Name: Gibson Kelly & Ives
505 - 5 St., Courtenay, BC V9N 1K2
Tel: 250-334-2416; *Fax:* 250-334-3198
info@ivesburgerlaw.com
www.ivesburgerlaw.com

***Courtenay*: Roy William Pouss - *1**
243 - 4th St., Courtenay, BC V9N 1G7
Tel: 250-334-3188; *Fax:* 250-334-3174

***Courtenay*: Swift Datoo Law Corporation - *11**
#201, 467 Cumberland Rd., Courtenay, BC V9N 2C5
Tel: 250-334-4461; *Fax:* 250-334-2335
Toll-Free: 877-334-4461
lawyers@swiftdatoo.com
www.swiftdatoo.com

***Cranbrook*: Patrick J. Dearden - *1**
#201, 129 - 10th Ave. South, Cranbrook, BC V1C 2N1
Tel: 250-426-7431; *Fax:* 250-426-3746

***Cranbrook*: Kelle M. Maag Law Corporation - *1**
1808-8th Ave. South, Cranbrook, BC V1C 7E7
Tel: 250-426-5508
kmaag@cyberlink.ca

***Cranbrook*: Murielle A. Matthews - *1**
801B Baker St., Cranbrook, BC V1C 1A3
Tel: 250-426-0601; *Fax:* 250-426-0642

***Cranbrook*: Miles, Daroux, Zimmer & Sheard - *4**
45 - 8th Ave. South, Cranbrook, BC V1C 2K4
Tel: 250-489-3350; *Fax:* 250-489-2235
mdza.ca

***Cranbrook*: Rella & Paolini - *2**
#6, 10 Ave. South, 2nd Fl., Cranbrook, BC V1C 2M8
Tel: 250-426-8981; *Fax:* 250-426-8987
Toll-Free: 866-426-8981

***Cranbrook*: Robertson & Co. - *1**
#200, 135 - 10 Ave. South, Cranbrook, BC V1C 2N1
Tel: 250-489-4346; *Fax:* 250-489-1899
robertson@cranbrooklaw.com
www.cranbrooklaw.com

***Cranbrook*: Darrel C. Symington - *1**
123 - 12th Ave. South, Cranbrook, BC V1C 2S2
Tel: 250-489-2800; *Fax:* 250-489-1173
dsymington@cyberllink.ca

***Dawson Creek*: Allen & Associates - *3**
#2, 933 - 103 Ave., Dawson Creek, BC V1G 2G4
Tel: 250-782-8155; *Fax:* 250-782-4525

***Dawson Creek*: Higson Apps - *3**
Former Name: Plenert Higson
#201, 1136 - 103 Ave., Dawson Creek, BC V1G 2G7
Tel: 250-782-9134; *Fax:* 250-782-9135
Toll-Free: 888-782-9134

***Delta*: James M. Antifay Law Corporation - *1**
#212, 7313 - 120 St., Delta, BC V4C 6P5
Tel: 604-572-8333; *Fax:* 604-572-6744
jantifay@dccnet.com

***Delta*: James Broad - *1**
9337 - Scott Rd., Delta, BC V4C 6R8
Tel: 604-585-3422; *Fax:* 604-585-3613

***Delta*: Delta Legal Office - *3**
4873 Delta St., Delta, BC V4C 6P5
Tel: 604-946-2199; *Fax:* 604-946-8818
Toll-Free: 877-203-1100
info@deltalawoffice.com
deltalawoffice.com

***Delta*: Lehal & Company - *1**
#200, 6905 - 120th St., Delta, BC V4E 2A8
Tel: 604-596-1321; *Fax:* 604-596-1320
info@lehallaw.ca
www.lehallaw.com

***Delta*: Millichamp & Company - *1**
#210, 1530 - 56 St., Delta, BC V4L 2A8
Tel: 604-943-7401; *Fax:* 604-943-7402
millichamplawco@gmail.com

***Delta*: Severide Law Group - *5**
#201, 5027 47A Ave., Delta, BC V4K 1T9
Tel: 604-940-8182; *Fax:* 604-940-9892
info@severide.com
www.severidelawgroup.com

***Duncan*: Donald S. Allan - *1**
1500 Kingsview Rd., Duncan, BC V9L 5P1
Tel: 250-748-2340; *Fax:* 250-748-2343
d.s.allan@shaw.ca

***Duncan*: Hugh J. Armstrong - *1**
157 Trunk Rd., Duncan, BC V9L 2P1
Tel: 250-746-4354; *Fax:* 250-746-8101
hugh@hugharmstronglaw.ca
www.hugharmstronglaw.ca

***Duncan*: Coleman Fraser Whittome Lehan - *4**
Former Name: Coleman Parceus Fraser Whittome
#202, 58 Station St., Duncan, BC V9L 1M4
Tel: 250-748-1013; *Fax:* 250-743-8318
Toll-Free: 888-748-1013
www.cowichanlaw.com

***Duncan*: Molnar Desjardins Arndt - *3**
Former Name: Molnar, Desjardins & Arndt
435 Trunk Rd., Duncan, BC V9L 2P5
Tel: 250-748-5253
arndtlaw.yolasite.com

***Duncan*: Robert W. Nelford - *1**
2340 Trillium Terrace, Duncan, BC V9L 3Z6
Tel: 250-478-5805; *Fax:* 250-748-1957
melford@shaw.ca

***Duncan*: Orchard & Company - *6**
321 St. Julian St., Duncan, BC V9L 3S5
Tel: 250-746-5899; *Fax:* 250-746-7182
admin@orchardandco.ca
www.orchardandco.ca

***Duncan*: Ridgway & Company - *5**
#200, 44 Queens Rd., Duncan, BC V9L 2W4
Tel: 250-746-7121; *Fax:* 250-746-4070
info@ridgco.com
www.ridgco.com

***Duncan*: Taylor Granitto Inc. - *3**
466 Trans Canada Hwy., Duncan, BC V9L 3R6
Tel: 250-748-4444; *Fax:* 250-748-5920
Toll-Free: 800-665-5414
dtaylor@taylor-co.com
www.taylor-co.com

***Fernie*: Ron W. Bentley - *1**
P.O. Box 2038, 642 - 2nd Ave., Fernie, BC V0B 1M0
Tel: 250-423-9241; *Fax:* 250-423-6440
bentleylaw@elkvalley.net

***Fernie*: Etheridge Law - *1**
P.O. Box 9, 401 - 2nd Ave., 2nd Fl., Fernie, BC V0B 1M0
Tel: 250-430-0007; *Fax:* 866-462-3992
angela@eastkootenaylaw.com
www.eastkootenaylaw.com

***Fernie*: Leffler Law Office - *2**
862 - 3rd Ave., Fernie, BC V0B 1M0
Tel: 250-423-3904; *Fax:* 250-423-7417
info@fernielaw.com
www.fernielaw.com

***Fernie*: Majic, Purdy Law Corpoartion - *3**
P.O. Box 369, 592 - 2nd Ave., Fernie, BC V0B 1M0
Tel: 250-423-4497; *Fax:* 250-423-6714
www.majicpurdy.com

***Fernie*: Rockies Law Corporation - Fernie - *7**
Former Name: Sliva & Summers
#202, P.O. Box 490, 502 - 3rd Ave., Fernie, BC V0B 1M0
Tel: 250-423-4446; *Fax:* 250-423-4065
Toll-Free: 866-427-0111
fernie@rockieslaw.com
rockieslaw.com

***Fort St John*: Rodney J. Strandberg Law Corp. - *1**
#320, 9900 - 100 Ave., Fort St John, BC V1J 5S7
Tel: 250-787-7760; *Fax:* 250-787-7752
strandberglaw@telus.net

***Fort St John*: Earmme & Associates - *3**
Former Name: Daley & Earmme
10740 - 101st Ave., Fort St John, BC V1J 2B4
Tel: 250-785-6961; *Fax:* 250-785-6967
info@delaw.ca
earmme.com

***Garibaldi Highlands*: Brian N. Hughes - *1**
#201, P.O. Box 557, 1364 Pemberton Ave., Garibaldi Highlands, BC V0N 1T0
Tel: 604-892-5114; *Fax:* 604-892-0114

***Gibsons*: Peter J. Holden - *1**
995 Grandview Rd., Gibsons, BC V0N 1V3
Tel: 604-630-3913
pholden@dccnet.com

***Gibsons*: J. Wayne Rowe - *2**
P.O. Box 1880, 758 School Rd., Gibsons, BC V0N 1V0
Tel: 604-886-2029; *Fax:* 604-886-9191

***Gibsons*: Leanne L. Turnbull - *1**
523 Central Ave., RR#1, Gibsons, BC V0N 1V1
Tel: 604-886-7666; *Fax:* 604-886-7636
leeturnbull@dccnet.com

***Golden*: William J. Alexander Law Corporation - *1**
#102, 509-9th Ave. North, Golden, BC V0A 1H0
Tel: 250-344-1472; *Fax:* 250-344-1543
alextax@shaw.ca

***Hope*: Kennedy, Jensen - *2**
#101, P.O. Box 1719, 400 Park St., Hope, BC V0X 1L0
Tel: 604-869-9981; *Fax:* 604-869-7640

***Hornby Island*: Sally Campbell - *1**
4505 Roburn Rd., Hornby Island, BC V0R 1Z0
Tel: 250-335-2272; *Fax:* 250-335-0895
scampbel@island.net
www.island.net/~scampbel/

***Hornby Island*: Sue M. Kelly - *1**
6165 Anderson Dr., Hornby Island, BC V0R 1Z0
Tel: 250-335-0735; *Fax:* 250-335-0732
smkelly@telus.net

***Invermere*: Kluge, Boyd - *2**
P.O. Box 2647, 906 - 8 Ave., Invermere, BC V0A 1K0
Tel: 250-342-4447; *Fax:* 250-342-3298
barnim@telus.net

***Invermere*: MacDonald Thomas Barristers & Solicitors - *2**
10188-7th Ave., Invermere, BC V0A 1K0
Tel: 250-342-6921; *Fax:* 250-342-3237
reception@macdonaldthomas.com
www.macdonaldthomas.com

***Kamloops*: Bilkey Law Corporation - *7**
Former Name: Bilkey Law LLP
#301, 186 Victoria St., Kamloops, BC V2C 5R3
Tel: 778-471-4350; *Fax:* 778-471-4351
admin@bilkeylaw.ca
www.bilkeylaw.ca

***Kamloops*: George Coutlee & Co. - *1**
1270 Salish Rd., Kamloops, BC V2H 1K1
Tel: 250-372-9922; *Fax:* 250-372-1114

***Kamloops*: Cundari & Company Law Corporation - *5**
#810, 175 - 2 Ave., Kamloops, BC V2C 5W1
Tel: 250-372-3368; *Fax:* 250-372-5554
cundari@cundarilaw.com
www.cundarilaw.com

* indicates number of lawyers

***Kamloops*: Epp Cates Oien - *9**
Former Name: Taylor Epp & Dolder; Cates Carroll Watt
#300, 125 - Fourth Ave., Kamloops, BC V2C 3N3
Tel: 250-372-8811; *Fax:* 250-828-6697
Toll-Free: 800-949-3362
info@eppcatesoien.com
www.eppcatesoien.com

***Kamloops*: Fulton & Company LLP, Lawyers & Trade-Mark Agents - *28**
#300, 350 Lansdowne St., Kamloops, BC V2C 1Y1
Tel: 250-372-5542; *Fax:* 250-851-2300
law@fultonco.com
www.fultonco.com

***Kamloops*: Gibraltar Law Group - *2**
#102, 418 St. Paul St., Kamloops, BC V2C 2J6
Tel: 250-374-3737; *Fax:* 250-374-0035
Toll-Free: 877-374-3737
mail@gibraltarlawgroup.com
www.gibraltarlawgroup.com

***Kamloops*: Gillespie & Company LLP - *4**
Former Name: Gillespie Renkema Barnett Broadway LLP
#200, 121 St. Paul St., Kamloops, BC V2C 3K8
Tel: 250-374-4463; *Fax:* 250-374-5250
Toll-Free: 855-374-4463
info@kamloopslawyers.com
www.kamloopslawyers.com

***Kamloops*: HMZ Law - *4**
Former Name: Horne Marr Zak
#600, 175 Second Ave., Kamloops, BC V2C 5W1
Tel: 250-372-1221; *Fax:* 250-372-8339
Toll-Free: 800-558-1933
hmz@hmzlaw.com
www.hmzlaw.com

***Kamloops*: Kahle & Co. Law Corporation - *1**
172 Battle St., Kamloops, BC V2C 2L2
Tel: 250-372-1234
kahleco@telus.net

***Kamloops*: Mary MacGregor - *1**
975 Victoria St., Kamloops, BC V2C 2C1
Tel: 250-828-0282; *Fax:* 250-828-0287
mary.macgregor@mmlc.ca
www.marymacgregor.ca

***Kamloops*: Mair Jensen Blair LLP - *14**
#700, 275 Lansdowne St., Kamloops, BC V2C 6H6
Tel: 250-374-3161; *Fax:* 250-374-6992
Toll-Free: 888-374-3161
info@mjblaw.com
www.mjblaw.com

***Kamloops*: David A. McMillan - *1**
#401, 286 St. Paul St., Kamloops, BC V2C 6G4
Tel: 250-828-0702; *Fax:* 250-828-0703
dmlawoff@telus.net

***Kamloops*: Morelli Chertkow LLP, Lawyers - Kamloops - *12**
#300, 180 Seymour St., Kamloops, BC V2C 2E3
Tel: 250-374-3344; *Fax:* 250-374-1144
info@morellichertkow.com
www.morellichertkow.com
www.facebook.com/MorelliChertkow, twitter.com/morellichertkow

***Kamloops*: Craig Nixon Law Corp. - *1**
#880, 175 Second Ave., Kamloops, BC V2C 5W1
Tel: 250-374-1555; *Fax:* 250-374-9992
onlc@direct.ca

***Kamloops*: Wozniak & Walker - *2**
533 Nicola St., Kamloops, BC V2C 2P9
Tel: 250-374-6226; *Fax:* 250-374-4485

***Kaslo*: T.R. Humphries - *1**
P.O. Box 636, Kaslo, BC V0G 1M0
Tel: 250-353-2292; *Fax:* 250-353-7430
trhlaw@telus.net

***Kelowna*: Bassett & Company - *5**
#221, 3011 Louie Dr., Kelowna, BC V4T 3E3
Tel: 250-768-0717; *Fax:* 250-768-5854
BobBassett@OkanaganLaw.com
www.okanaganlaw.com

***Kelowna*: Benson Law LLP - *7**
270 Hwy. 33 West, Kelowna, BC V1X 1X7
Tel: 250-491-0206; *Fax:* 250-491-0266
www.bensonlawllp.com

***Kelowna*: Burgess & Company - *2**
#202, 3528 Scott Rd., Kelowna, BC V1W 3H6
Tel: 250-861-5533; *Fax:* 250-861-4442
dblaw@live.ca
www.burgessandcompany.com/en/

***Kelowna*: Bev Churchill - *1**
Former Name: Tinker, Churchill, Wallis
#210, 347 Leon Ave., Kelowna, BC V1Y 8C7
Tel: 250-763-7333; *Fax:* 250-763-5507
Bev@BevChurchillFamilyLawyer.com
www.bevchurchillfamilylawyer.com

***Kelowna*: Doak Shirreff LLP - *13**
#200, Chancery Place, 537 Leon Ave., Kelowna, BC V1Y 2A9
Tel: 250-763-4323; *Fax:* 250-763-4780
Toll-Free: 800-661-4959
thefirm@doakshirreff.com
www.doakshirreff.com

***Kelowna*: FH&P Lawyers LLP - *14**
215 Lawrence Ave., 2nd Fl., Kelowna, BC V1Y 6L2
Tel: 250-762-4222; *Fax:* 250-762-8616
Toll-Free: 888-320-4488
info@fhplawyers.com
www.fhplawyers.com

***Kelowna*: Fischer & Company Law Corporation - *1**
#202, 1447 Ellis St., Kelowna, BC V1Y 2A3
Tel: 250-712-0066; *Fax:* 250-712-0061
matthew@fischerandcompany.ca
www.fischerandcompany.ca

***Kelowna*: Fraser Chris - *2**
#200, 1449 St Paul St., Kelowna, BC V1Y 7S5
Tel: 250-868-8306; *Fax:* 250-868-8301

***Kelowna*: Glazier Polley - *3**
Former Name: Wageman Glazier & Polley
1674 Bertram St., 2nd Fl., Kelowna, BC V1Y 9G4
Tel: 250-763-3343; *Fax:* 250-763-9524

***Kelowna*: Gordon & Company - *2**
#102, 1433 St. Paul St., Kelowna, BC V1Y 2E4
Tel: 250-860-9997; *Fax:* 250-860-9937
info@gordoncolaw.com
www.gordoncolaw.com/en/

***Kelowna*: Laura J. Gosset - *1**
#214, 440 Cascia Dr., Kelowna, BC V1W 4Y4
Tel: 250-717-1677; *Fax:* 250-862-5292
lauragosset@shaw.ca

***Kelowna*: Jenson & Co. - *1**
Also Known As: Wade D. Jenson
#200, 1460 Pandosy St., Kelowna, BC V1Y 1P3
Tel: 250-868-2239; *Fax:* 250-861-5079
www.jensonlaw.com
www.facebook.com/JensonandCo

***Kelowna*: Martin Johnson Law Corporation - *2**
Also Known As: The Heritage Law Group
830 Bernard Ave., Kelowna, BC V1Y 6P5
Tel: 250-868-2848; *Fax:* 250-868-3080
Toll-Free: 877-868-2848
office@heritagelawgroup.com
www.heritagelawgroup.com
www.facebook.com/pages/The-Heritage-Law-Group/165669196779086

***Kelowna*: Roberta L. Jordan - *1**
#16, 4524 Eldorado Ct., Kelowna, BC V1W 1G3
Tel: 250-764-0888; *Fax:* 250-764-0680

***Kelowna*: Kelly Christiansen & Company - *2**
Former Name: Christiansen, Newcombe
#208, 1470 St Paul St., Kelowna, BC V1Y 2E6
Tel: 250-862-2327

***Kelowna*: Kimmitt Wrzesniewski - *2**
#202, 1433 St. Paul St., Kelowna, BC V1Y 2E4
Tel: 250-763-6441; *Fax:* 250-763-1633
info@kimmitt.ca
www.kimmitt.ca

***Kelowna*: Robert O. Levin - *2**
#607, 1708 Dolphin Ave., Kelowna, BC V1Y 9S4
Tel: 250-868-2101; *Fax:* 250-868-2414
robert@rlevin.com
www.rlevin.com

***Kelowna*: M. Gail Miller - *1**
#904, 1708 Dolphin Ave., Kelowna, BC V1Y 9S4
Tel: 250-763-6767; *Fax:* 250-763-0980

***Kelowna*: Mission Law Group - *1**
#212, 2900 Pandosy St., Kelowna, BC V1Y 1V9
Tel: 250-868-8803; *Fax:* 250-868-8876
law@missionlawgroup.com
www.missionlawgroup.com

***Kelowna*: Oland & Company - *2**
803 Bernard Ave., Kelowna, BC V1Y 6P6
Tel: 250-762-8092; *Fax:* 250-762-2857
shiplaw@aboland.com
www.aboland.com

***Kelowna*: Pihl & Associates Law Corporation - *7**
#100, 1465 Ellis St., Kelowna, BC V1Y 2A3
Tel: 250-762-5434; *Fax:* 250-762-5450
lawyers@pihl.ca
www.pihl.ca

***Kelowna*: Porter Ramsay LLP - *9**
#200, 1465 Ellis St., Kelowna, BC V1Y 2A3
Tel: 250-763-7646; *Fax:* 250-762-9960
Toll-Free: 888-933-4411
lawyers@porterramsay.com
www.porterramsay.com

***Kelowna*: Pushor Mitchell LLP - *34**
#301, 1665 Ellis St., Kelowna, BC V1Y 2B3
Tel: 250-762-2108; *Fax:* 250-762-9115
Toll-Free: 800-558-1155
www.pushormitchell.com
www.twitter.com/pushormitchell,
www.linkedin.com/company/pushor-mitchell-llp

***Kelowna*: Rush Ihas Hardwick LLP - *5**
1368 St. Paul St., Kelowna, BC V1Y 2E1
Tel: 250-868-2313; *Fax:* 250-868-2659
info@rihlaw.com
www.rihlaw.com

***Kelowna*: Sabey Rule LLP - *4**
#201, 401 Glenmore Rd., Kelowna, BC V1V 1Z6
Tel: 250-762-6111; *Fax:* 250-762-6480
Toll-Free: 866-268-6383
lawyers@sabeyrule.ca
www.sabeyrule.ca

***Kelowna*: Smith Peacock - *2**
#201, 1180 Sunset Dr., Kelowna, BC V1Y 9W6
Tel: 250-860-7868; *Fax:* 250-860-7527
Toll-Free: 888-757-6484
www.smithpeacock.ca

***Kelowna*: Smithson Employment Law Corporation - *1**
#204, 1630 Pandosy St., Kelowna, BC V1Y 1P7
Tel: 778-478-0150; *Fax:* 778-478-0155
robert@smithsonlaw.ca
www.smithsonlaw.ca
www.facebook.com/146651752055816, twitter.com/youworkhere, ca.linkedin.com/pub/robert-smithson/28/443/3b1

***Kelowna*: Daniel E. Spelliscy - *1**
#1, 715 Sutherland Ave., Kelowna, BC V1Y 5X4
Tel: 250-862-9586; *Fax:* 250-862-2677
dspelliscy@yahoo.com

***Kelowna*: Tessmer Law Offices - *4**
272 Bernard Ave., Kelowna, BC V1Y 6N4
Tel: 250-762-6747; *Fax:* 250-762-3163
info@tessmerlaw.com
tessmerlaw.com
www.facebook.com/pages/Tessmer-Law-Office/121930751219109?sk=app_2257550907, twitter.com/TessmerLaw

***Kelowna*: Thomas Butler LLP - *2**
#700, 1708 Dolphin Ave., Kelowna, BC V1Y 9S4
Tel: 250-763-0200; *Fax:* 250-762-8848
Toll-Free: 800-483-0291
www.thomasbutlerllp.com

***Kelowna*: Touchstone Law Group LLP - *2**
#208, 1664 Richter St., Kelowna, BC V1Y 8N3
Tel: 250-448-2637; *Fax:* 250-484-7101
Toll-Free: 855-889-2637
info@touchstonelawgroup.com
touchstonelawgroup.com
www.facebook.com/TouchstoneLawGroupLlp, twitter.com/touchstonelaw

***Kelowna*: Douglas W. Welder - *1**
#200, 586 Leon Ave., Kelowna, BC V1Y 6J6
Tel: 250-868-8228; *Fax:* 250-868-8232
welder@okanagan.net

** indicates number of lawyers*

***Kelowna*: Marc R.B. Whittemore - *1**
830 Bernard Ave., Kelowna, BC V1V 6P5
Tel: 250-868-2202; *Fax:* 250-868-2270
marc@whittemorelawcorporation.com
whittemorelawcorporation.com

***Kimberley*: Robert E.C. Apps - *1**
230 Spokane St., Kimberley, BC V1A 2E4
Tel: 250-427-2235; *Fax:* 250-427-5168
bobapps@shaw.ca

***Kitimat*: Wozney & Company - *1**
46 Clifford St., Kitimat, BC V8C 1B4
Tel: 250-632-7151; *Fax:* 250-632-7100
rwozney@telus.net

***Ladysmith*: Robson, O'Connor - Ladysmith - *2**
P.O. Box 1890, 22 High St., Ladysmith, BC V9G 1B4
Tel: 250-245-7141; *Fax:* 250-245-2921
www.robsonoconnor.ca

***Langley*: Bryenton & Associates - *2**
#300, 20689 Fraser Hwy., Langley, BC V3A 4G4
Tel: 604-530-7135; *Fax:* 604-530-7118
lawyers@brylaw.net
www.brylaw.ca

***Langley*: Campbell, Burton & McMullan LLP - Langley - *15**
#200, 4769 - 222 St., Langley, BC V2Z 3C1
Tel: 604-533-3821; *Fax:* 604-533-5521
info@cbmlawyers.com
www.cbmlawyers.com

***Langley*: Darnell & Company Lawyers - *3**
#202, 6351 - 197 St., Langley, BC V2Y 1X8
Tel: 604-532-9119; *Fax:* 604-532-9127
www.langleylaw.ca

***Langley*: Fleming Olson Taneda & MacDougall - *3**
Former Name: Fleming, Olson & Taneda
4038 - 200B St., Langley, BC V3A 1N9
Tel: 604-533-3411; *Fax:* 604-533-8749
fotlawyers@aol.com

***Langley*: Carl D. Holm - *1**
#102, 20475 Douglas Cres., Langley, BC V3A 4B6
Tel: 604-533-4101; *Fax:* 604-533-2024

***Langley*: Bryce Jeffrey LLB - *1**
20450 Fraser Hwy., 2nd Fl., Langley, BC V3A 4G2
Tel: 604-530-3141; *Fax:* 604-530-9573
info@jefferymediation.com
www.jefferymediation.com

***Langley*: J. Michael Le Dressay & Associates - *13**
20689 - 56 Ave., Langley, BC V3A 7G9
Tel: 604-530-2191; *Fax:* 604-530-6282
michael@jmldlaw.com

***Langley*: Stephen G. Price Law Corp. - *1**
#300, 20644 Eastleigh Cres., Langley, BC V3A 4C4
Tel: 604-530-2191
info@stephengprice.com
stephengprice.com

***Langley*: Waterstone Law Group LLP**
#304, 20338 - 65th Ave., Langley, BC V2Y 2X3
Tel: 604-533-2300; *Fax:* 604-533-2387
Toll-Free: 800-880-1667
info@waterstonelaw.com
www.waterstonelaw.com

***Lantzville*: Kristin Rongve - *1**
Former Name: Loy & Rongve
7180 Lantzville Rd., Lantzville, BC V0R 2H0
Tel: 250-390-3157; *Fax:* 250-390-4857
info@kristinrongve.ca
www.kristinrongve.ca

***Lillooet*: R. Kendel Kaser - *1**
P.O. Box 1449, 416 Main St., Lillooet, BC V0K 1V0
Tel: 250-256-7519; *Fax:* 250-256-7554

***Madeira Park*: Michael C. Crowe - *1**
12874 Madeira Park Rd., Madeira Park, BC V0N 2H0
Tel: 604-883-9875; *Fax:* 604-883-9873
m_crowe@sunshine.net

***Maple Ridge*: Fowle & Company - *4**
#650, 22470 Dewdney Trunk Rd., Maple Ridge, BC V2X 5Z6
Tel: 604-476-2130; *Fax:* 604-476-2135
Toll-Free: 800-663-8996
randallfowle@fowleandcompany.com
www.fowleandcompany.com

***Maple Ridge*: Vernon & Thompson Law Group - *4**
22311 - 119 Ave., Maple Ridge, BC V2X 2Z2
Tel: 604-463-6281; *Fax:* 604-463-7497
vernon-thompson.com

***Mill Bay*: Hicks & Co. - *2**
#24, Mill Bay Shopping Centre, P.O. Box 83, 2720 Mill Bay Rd., Mill Bay, BC V0R 2P0
Tel: 250-743-3756; *Fax:* 250-743-3756

***Mission*: Jarrett & Company - *1**
9701 Dewdney Trunk Rd., Mission, BC V2V 7G5
Tel: 604-826-5582

***Mission*: Taylor, Tait, Ruley & Company - *6**
33066 First Ave., Mission, BC V2V 1G3
Tel: 604-826-1266; *Fax:* 604-826-4288
info@taylortait.com
www.taylortait.com

***Mission*: Taylor, Tait, Ruley & Company - *6**
33066 First Ave., Mission, BC V2V 1G3
Tel: 604-826-1266; *Fax:* 604-826-4288
info@taylortait.com
www.taylortait.com

***Nanaimo*: Carlson & Company - *3**
669 Terminal Ave. North, Nanaimo, BC V9S 4K1
Tel: 250-753-7582; *Fax:* 250-753-7583

***Nanaimo*: Fabris McIver Hornquist & Radcliffe - *4**
Former Name: Fabris McIver Hornquist
P.O. Box 778, 40 Cavan St., Nanaimo, BC V9R 5M2
Tel: 250-753-6661; *Fax:* 250-753-6648
Toll-Free: 800-811-3555
reception@fabris-law.com
www.fabris-law.com

***Nanaimo*: Geselbracht Brown - *2**
#3, 4488 Wellington Rd., Nanaimo, BC V9T 2H3
Tel: 250-758-2825; *Fax:* 250-758-7412
inquiry@gblaw.bc.ca
www.gblaw.bc.ca

***Nanaimo*: Heath Law LLP - *11**
#200, 1808 Bowen Rd., Nanaimo, BC V9S 5W4
Tel: 250-753-2202; *Fax:* 250-753-3949
Toll-Free: 866-753-2202
consult@nanaimolaw.com
www.nanaimolaw.com

***Nanaimo*: A. Peter Hertzberg - *1**
1687 Princess Royal Ave., Nanaimo, BC V9S 4A3
Tel: 250-753-1891

***Nanaimo*: Johnston Franklin - *7**
Former Name: Johnston, Lewis & Franklin
#210, 3260 Norwell Dr., Nanaimo, BC V9T 1X5
Tel: 250-756-3823; *Fax:* 250-756-6188
Toll-Free: 888-343-0782
lawyers@johnstonfranklin.ca
www.johnstonfranklin.ca
www.facebook.com/johnstonfranklin, twitter.com/jflaw_ca, www.linkedin.com/company/johnston-franklin

***Nanaimo*: Gary R. Korpan - *1**
3598 Hammond Bay Rd., Nanaimo, BC V9T 1E9
Tel: 250-758-9445; *Fax:* 250-754-8263
gkorpan@island.net

***Nanaimo*: Manning & Kirkhope - *2**
430 Wentworth St., Nanaimo, BC V9R 3E1
Tel: 250-753-6766; *Fax:* 250-753-0080
office@mannkirk.com
www.mannkirk.com

***Nanaimo*: Merrill, Long & Co. - *4**
201 Milton St., Nanaimo, BC V9R 2K5
Tel: 250-754-4441; *Fax:* 250-754-4286
ranlaw@telus.net
www.merrill-long.com
www.facebook.com/pages/Merrill-Long-and-Company/10150148290075641

***Nanaimo*: Mont & Walker Law Corporation - *4**
Former Name: Allin Anderson Mont & Walker Law Corp
201 Selby St., Nanaimo, BC V9R 2R2
Tel: 250-753-6435; *Fax:* 250-753-5285
mont@islandlaw.ca
www.islandlaw.ca

***Nanaimo*: Park Place Law - *3**
#100, 2124 Bowen Rd., Nanaimo, BC V9S 1H7
Tel: 250-758-7758; *Fax:* 250-758-7756
reception@parkplacelaw.ca
parkplacelaw.ca

***Nanaimo*: Petley-Jones & Co. Law Corp. - *1**
5732 Hammond Bay Rd., Nanaimo, BC V9T 5N2
Tel: 250-758-7370; *Fax:* 250-758-8703
info@petley-jones.net
www.petley-jones.net

***Nanaimo*: Ramsay Lampman Rhodes - *19**
Former Name: Ramsay Thompson Lampman
111 Wallace St., Nanaimo, BC V9R 5B2
Tel: 250-754-3321; *Fax:* 250-754-1148
Toll-Free: 800-263-3321
info@rlr-law.com
www.rlr-law.com

***Nanaimo*: Robert N. Stacey Law Corp. - *1**
Former Name: Old City Quarter Law Office
#10, 321 Wesley St., Nanaimo, BC V9R 2T5
Tel: 250-753-0844; *Fax:* 250-753-0877
rnstacey@telus.net
www.bcdivorceonline.com

***Nanaimo*: Strain & Company - *2**
#103, 360 Selby St., Nanaimo, BC V9R 2R5
Tel: 250-753-0860; *Fax:* 250-753-0861
reception@strain.ca
www.nanaimofamilylaw.com

***Nanaimo*: Victor Svacek - *1**
155 Commercial St., Nanaimo, BC V9R 5G5
Tel: 250-756-4765

***Nanaimo*: Vining, Senini**
P.O. Box 190, Stn. Main, 30 Front St., Nanaimo, BC V9R 5K9
Tel: 250-754-1234; *Fax:* 250-754-8080

***Nanaimo*: Eric L. Williams - *1**
#302, 240 Milton St., Nanaimo, BC V9R 2K6
Tel: 250-741-1100; *Fax:* 250-741-1094
Toll-Free: 888-959-1100
eric.williams@telus.net

***Nanaimo*: C.D. Wilson & Associates - *1**
630 Terminal Ave. North, Nanaimo, BC V9S 4K2
Tel: 250-741-1400; *Fax:* 250-741-1441
nanaimo@cdwilson.bc.ca
www.cdwilson.bc.ca

***Nelson*: Susan Kurtz - *1**
Sound Legal Solutions, 407 Nelson Ave., Nelson, BC V1L 2N1
Tel: 250-354-1881; *Fax:* 250-354-1808
Toll-Free: 866-926-1881
susan@resolutionplace.ca
www.resolutionplace.ca
www.facebook.com/207513745934475, ca.linkedin.com/pub/susan-kurtz/25/b64/560

***Nelson*: Nasmyth, Morrow & Bogusz - *2**
#105, 465 Ward St., Nelson, BC V1L 1S7
Tel: 250-352-3171; *Fax:* 250-352-1777
info@nbclegal.com

***Nelson*: Stacey, Trillo & Company - *2**
#1, 405 Baker St., Nelson, BC V1L 4H7
Tel: 250-352-3125; *Fax:* 250-352-3145
greg@stacey-trillo.com
www.stacey-trillo.com

***Nelson*: Terry Napora Law Offices - *1**
Former Name: Napora Underwood & Co.
608 Baker St., Nelson, BC V1L 4J4
Tel: 250-352-3321; *Fax:* 250-354-4547
Toll-Free: 800-579-5338
terry@naporalaw.ca
www.britishcolumbialaw.ca
www.facebook.com/group.php?gid=79045011682

***Nelson*: Susan E. Wallach - *1**
#4, 577 Baker St., Nelson, BC V1L 4J1
Tel: 250-352-6124; *Fax:* 250-352-3460

** indicates number of lawyers*

***New Westminster*: Amicus Lawyers - *4**
Former Name: Hwang, Pollock & Company
Westminster Building, 711 Columbia St., New Westminster, BC V3M 1B2
Tel: 604-889-7000; *Fax:* 604-526-7033
info@amicuslawyers.com
www.amicuslawyers.com
twitter.com/amicuslawyers,
www.linkedin.com/profile/view?id=17256273

***New Westminster*: Gordon J. Bondoreff - *1**
#202, 713 Columbia St., New Westminster, BC V3M 1B2
Tel: 604-526-4491; *Fax:* 604-526-5979
gbondoreff@telus.net

***New Westminster*: Browning Ray Soga Dunne & Mirsky - *5**
Former Name: Dickey, Browning, McShane, Dunne
#203, 668 Carnarvon St., New Westminster, BC V3M 5Y6
Tel: 604-526-4525; *Fax:* 604-526-8595
info@triallawyers.ca
www.triallawyers.ca

***New Westminster*: Raymond E. Drabik Law Corp. - *1**
#217, 713 Columbia St., New Westminster, BC V3M 1B2
Tel: 604-526-4875; *Fax:* 604-526-4879
red_law@telus.net

***New Westminster*: Goodwin & Mark - *5**
#217, 713 Columbia St., New Westminster, BC V3M 1B2
Tel: 778-727-0128; *Fax:* 604-526-8044
Toll-Free: 800-414-5097
www.goodmark.ca

***New Westminster*: Angela S. Kerslake - *1**
131 - 8th St., New Westminster, BC V3M 3P6
Tel: 604-520-6276; *Fax:* 604-520-5765
angela@angelakerslakelaw.com

***New Westminster*: Kinman Mulholland - *4**
Also Known As: KM Law
Former Name: Kinman Amlani Mulholland; Baumgartel Gould
#100, 624 Agnes St., New Westminster, BC V3M 1G8
Tel: 604-526-1805; *Fax:* 604-526-8056
info@kmlawoffice.com
www.kmlawoffice.com

***New Westminster*: Stan N. Lanyon - *1**
#217, 713 Columbia St., New Westminster, BC V3M 1B2
Tel: 604-522-5002; *Fax:* 604-522-5055
stan.lanyon@arboffices.com

***New Westminster*: Scarborough, Herman, Harvey & Bluekens - *4**
900 Quayside Dr., 10th Fl., New Westminster, BC V3M 6G1
Tel: 604-521-2223; *Fax:* 604-521-7772

***North Delta*: TNT Lawyers**
7929 - 120 St., North Delta, BC V4C 6P6
Tel: 604-502-5615; *Fax:* 604-591-8722
Toll-Free: 800-750-5122
info@icbcinjurylawyers.ca
www.icbcinjurylawyers.ca

***North Saanich*: Barbara J. Yates - *1**
430 Wain Rd., North Saanich, BC V8L 5P9
Tel: 250-656-5536; *Fax:* 250-656-4333

***North Vancouver*: Ardagh Hunter - *2**
#300, 1401 Lonsdale Ave., North Vancouver, BC V7M 2H9
Tel: 604-986-4366; *Fax:* 604-986-9286
account@ahtlaw.com

***North Vancouver*: Trevors R. Bjurman - *1**
#205, 1433 Lonsdale Ave., North Vancouver, BC V7M 2H9
Tel: 604-983-3728; *Fax:* 604-983-0148
bjurman@smartt.com

***North Vancouver*: Oren E. Breitman - *1**
1503 Dovercourt Rd., North Vancouver, BC V7K 1K6
Tel: 604-218-9480; *Fax:* 604-984-0502
orenb@shaw.ca

***North Vancouver*: Charlotte C. Gregory - *1**
205 St. Patrick's Ave., North Vancouver, BC V7L 3N3
Tel: 604-983-2886; *Fax:* 604-983-2886
cgregory@istar.ca

***North Vancouver*: Hollander Plazzer & Co. LLP - *3**
#300, 145 - 17th St. West, North Vancouver, BC V7M 3G4
Tel: 778-340-3353; *Fax:* 778-340-2848
reception@hollanderplazzer.ca
www.hollanderplazzer.ca

***North Vancouver*: Jabour, Sudeyko - *1**
#603, 145 East 13th St., North Vancouver, BC V7L 2L4
Tel: 604-986-8600; *Fax:* 604-986-4872
Toll-Free: 877-860-7575
dsudeyko@telus.net
www.jaboursudeyko.com
www.facebook.com/pages/Jabour-Sudeyko-Barristers-Solicitors/231071370335191, twitter.com/DanSudeyko

***North Vancouver*: Robert W. Johnson - *1**
#300, 1401 Lonsdale Ave., North Vancouver, BC V7M 2H9
Tel: 604-984-0305; *Fax:* 604-984-0304
robert.johnson@ahtlaw.com

***North Vancouver*: Lakes, Whyte LLP - *7**
#200, 879 Marine Dr., North Vancouver, BC V7P 1R7
Tel: 604-984-3646; *Fax:* 604-984-8573
Toll-Free: 800-488-7788
info@lakeswhyte.com
www.lakeswhyte.com

***North Vancouver*: Lee T. Lau Law Corp. - *1**
315 Mt. Hwy Ave., North Vancouver, BC V7J 2K7
Tel: 604-603-4907; *Fax:* 604-909-1699
www.leelau.net

***North Vancouver*: Judith C. Lee - *1**
#110, 223 Mountain Hwy., North Vancouver, BC V7J 3V5
Tel: 604-971-5107; *Fax:* 604-971-5109
www.judithleelaw.com

***North Vancouver*: Lynn Valley Law - *1**
#40, 1199 Lynn Valley Rd., North Vancouver, BC V7J 3H2
Tel: 604-985-8000; *Fax:* 604-985-5999
admin@lynnlaw.ca
www.lynnlaw.ca

***North Vancouver*: North Shore Law LLP - *15**
Former Name: Bradbrooke Crawford Green
171 West Esplanade, 6th Floor, North Vancouver, BC V7M 3J9
Tel: 604-980-8571; *Fax:* 604-980-4019
Toll-Free: 877-980-8571
inquiries@northshorelaw.com
www.northshorelaw.com
www.facebook.com/NorthShoreLaw, twitter.com/northshorelaw, ca.linkedin.com/company/north-shore-law-llp

***North Vancouver*: Ron Perrick Law Corp. - *2**
#913, 1641 Lonsdale Ave., North Vancouver, BC V7M 1V5
Tel: 604-984-9521; *Fax:* 604-984-9104

***North Vancouver*: Poyner & Company - *4**
Former Name: Poyner Baxter LLP
#101, 901 West 3rd St., North Vancouver, BC V7P 2P9
Tel: 604-988-6321; *Fax:* 604-988-0217
info@poynerlaw.ca
www.poynerlaw.ca

***North Vancouver*: Ratcliff & Company LLP - *30**
#500, 221 West Esplanade, North Vancouver, BC V7M 3J3
Tel: 604-988-5201; *Fax:* 604-988-1452
admin@ratcliff.com
www.ratcliff.com

***North Vancouver*: Robert C. Reid - *1**
#233, 1433 Lonsdale Ave., North Vancouver, BC V7M 2H9
Tel: 604-984-4357; *Fax:* 604-984-4326
robertcreid@hotmail.com

***North Vancouver*: D.A. Roper - *1**
334 West 15th St., North Vancouver, BC V7M 1S5
Tel: 604-986-0488; *Fax:* 604-984-3463
roperlaw@shawbiz.ca

***North Vancouver*: Thomas Immigration Law Group - *2**
Former Name: David L. Thomas Law Corporation
#8, 728 - 14th St. West, North Vancouver, BC V7M 0A8
Tel: 604-988-0795; *Fax:* 604-988-0718
info@executive-visa.com
www.executive-visa.com

***Okotoks*: James C. Lozinsky - *1**
#208, P.O. Box 509, 11 Elizabeth St., Okotoks, BC T1S 1A7
Tel: 403-995-7744; *Fax:* 403-995-7045
jclozinsky@jcl-law.ca
www.jcl-law.ca

***Oliver*: Alan P. Czepil - *1**
P.O. Box 1800, 6313 Main St., Oliver, BC V0H 1T0
Tel: 250-498-4901; *Fax:* 250-498-1400
aczepil@gordonandyoung.com

***Oliver*: Gordon & Young - *3**
P.O. Box 1800, 6313 Main St., Oliver, BC V0H 1T0
Tel: 250-498-4941; *Fax:* 250-498-4100
aczepil@gordonandyoung.com

***Parksville*: Davis & Avis - *2**
#201, P.O. Box 1600, 156 Morison Ave., Parksville, BC V9P 2H5
Tel: 250-248-5731; *Fax:* 250-248-5730
law@davis-avis.com
www.davis-avis.com

***Parksville*: John A. Hossack & Company - *1**
P.O. Box 1486, 311 McKinnon St., Parksville, BC V9P 2H4
Tel: 250-248-9241; *Fax:* 250-248-8375
john@hossack-law.com
www.hossack-law.com

***Peachland*: John E. Humphries Law Corporation - *1**
5848B Beach Ave., Peachland, BC V0H 1X7
Tel: 250-767-2221; *Fax:* 250-767-3477
johnehumphrieslaw@hotmail.com

***Penticton*: Boyle & Company - *8**
#201, 100 Front St., Penticton, BC V2A 1H1
Tel: 250-492-6100; *Fax:* 250-492-4877
Toll-Free: 800-665-8244
info@boyleco.bc.ca
www.boyleco.bc.ca

***Penticton*: Gilchrist & Company - *4**
#101, 123 Martin St., Penticton, BC V2A 7X6
Tel: 250-492-3033; *Fax:* 250-492-6162
info@gilchristlaw.com
www.gilchristlaw.com

***Penticton*: Kathryn J. Ginther - *1**
#301, 301 Main St., Penticton, BC V2A 5B7
Tel: 250-487-4355; *Fax:* 250-487-4356

***Penticton*: Halbauer & Company - *1**
Former Name: Halbauer & McAndrews
#104, 2504 Skana Lake Road, Penticton, BC V2A 6G1
Tel: 250-492-7225; *Fax:* 250-492-7395
larry@pentictonlawyers.com
www.pentictonlawyers.com

***Penticton*: Thomas A. Kampman - *1**
409 Ellis St., Penticton, BC V2A 4M1
Tel: 250-493-6786; *Fax:* 250-493-3964
tom@kokm.ca

***Penticton*: Zaseybida, Bonga - *2**
#101, 100 Nanaimo Ave. East, Penticton, BC V2A 1M4
Tel: 250-492-2244; *Fax:* 250-492-0090
zaseybida-bonga@telus.net

***Pitt Meadows*: Becker & Company Law Offices - *6**
#230, 19150 Lougheed Hwy., Pitt Meadows, BC V3Y 2H6
Tel: 604-465-9993; *Fax:* 604-465-0066
info@beckerlawyers.ca
www.beckerlawyers.ca

***Port Alberni*: Beckingham & Co. - *2**
5029 Argyle St., Port Alberni, BC V9Y 1V5
Tel: 250-724-0111; *Fax:* 250-724-4422
info@beckinghamandcompany.ca
www.beckinghamandcompany.ca

***Port Coquitlam*: John K. Bledsoe - *1**
2239B McAllister Ave., Port Coquitlam, BC V3C 2A9
Tel: 604-941-6162; *Fax:* 604-941-4369

***Port Coquitlam*: Darychuk Deane-Cloutier - *2**
Former Name: Macleod Thorson Darychuk
#310, 2755 Lougheed Hwy., Port Coquitlam, BC V3B 5Y9
Tel: 604-464-2644
www.pocolawyers.com

***Port Coquitlam*: David Greenbank - *1**
Former Name: Greenbank Murdoch & Company
#2300, 2850 Shaughnessy St., Port Coquitlam, BC V3C 6K5
Tel: 604-941-6215; *Fax:* 604-941-6207
dgreenbank@dgreenbank.com
dgreenbank.com

***Port Coquitlam*: Payne & Associates - *1**
#105, 1465 Salisbury Ave., Port Coquitlam, BC V3B 6J3
Tel: 604-944-4115; *Fax:* 604-944-4120

***Port Coquitlam*: Larry W. Pippard - *1**
#2, 3397 Hastings St., Port Coquitlam, BC V3B 4M8
Tel: 604-464-5615; *Fax:* 604-464-5615
larrywpippard@shaw.ca

** indicates number of lawyers*

***Port Coquitlam*: Smyth & Co. - *4**
#330, 2755 Lougheed Hwy., Port Coquitlam, BC V3B 5Y9
Tel: 604-942-6560; *Fax:* 604-942-1347
smythandcompany.ca

***Port Hardy*: Nowosad & Company - *1**
P.O. Box 1289, 8700 Market St., Port Hardy, BC V0N 2P0
Tel: 250-949-6031; *Fax:* 250-949-2633
nowosad1@telus.net
macisaacgroup.com/office/port-hardy/

***Port Moody*: Burke Tomchenko Morrison LLP - *5**
Also Known As: BTM Lawyers LLP
Former Name: Burke Tomchenko & Fraser
#530, 130 Brew St., Port Moody, BC V3H 0E3
Tel: 604-937-1166; *Fax:* 604-937-5577
firm@btmlawyers.com
www.btmlawyers.com

***Port Moody*: Judy S. Voss Law Corporation - *1**
2225 Clarke St., Port Moody, BC V3H 1Y6
Tel: 604-937-4757; *Fax:* 604-937-4714
Toll-Free: 866-944-8888
jsvoss@jsvlc.com

***Port Moody*: Maryn & Associates - *4**
2613 St. Johns St., Port Moody, BC V3H 2B5
Tel: 604-936-9600; *Fax:* 604-936-9800
info@marynlaw.com
www.marynlaw.com

***Powell River*: Garling Ostensen - *1**
4581 Marine Ave., Powell River, BC V8A 2K7
Tel: 604-485-2818; *Fax:* 604-485-7161
garost@powellriverlawyers.com

***Powell River*: James Garrett-Rempel - *1**
4766 Michigan Ave., Powell River, BC V8A 2S9
Tel: 604-485-9898; *Fax:* 604-485-9850
jgrlaw@shaw.ca
www.garrett-rempel.com

***Powell River*: F. Gregory Reif - *1**
#201, 4801 Joyce Ave., Powell River, BC V8A 3B7
Tel: 604-485-2056; *Fax:* 604-485-2196
gregreif@telus.net

***Powell River*: Villani & Company - *4**
Former Name: Whyard Villani
#103, 7020 Duncan St., Powell River, BC V8A 1V9
Tel: 604-485-6188; *Fax:* 604-485-6923
info@villaniandco.com
villaniandco.com

***Prince George*: G.R. Brown Law Corporation**
Former Name: Hope Heinrich, Barristers & Solicitors
#330, 500 Victoria St., Prince George, BC V2L 2J9
Tel: 250-563-0681; *Fax:* 250-562-3761
grb@grblaw.ca

***Prince George*: Dick Byl Law Corporation - *2**
#900, 550 Victoria St., Prince George, BC V2L 2K1
Tel: 250-564-3400; *Fax:* 250-564-7873
Toll-Free: 800-835-0088
dbyl@dbylaw.com
www.dbylaw.com

***Prince George*: Richard C. Gibbs - *1**
1134 - 3rd Ave., Prince George, BC V2L 3E5
Tel: 250-564-6460; *Fax:* 250-562-0671
rcgibbs@telus.net

***Prince George*: Heather Sadler Jenkins LLP - *18**
#700, Royal Bank Bldg., P.O. Box 4500, 550 Victoria St., Prince George, BC V2L 2K1
Tel: 250-565-8000; *Fax:* 250-565-8001
Toll-Free: 866-565-8777
hsj@hsjlawyers.com
www.hsjlawyers.com

***Prince George*: Andrew Kemp, Lawyer & Mediator - *1**
#204, 411 Quebec St., Prince George, BC V2L 1W5
Tel: 250-564-5544; *Fax:* 250-562-4104
Toll-Free: 877-964-5544
www.andrewkemp.ca

***Prince George*: Richard B. Krehbiel - *1**
1415 Douglas St., Prince George, BC V2M 2N1
Tel: 250-562-8935
rkrehbiel@shaw.ca

***Prince George*: Benjamin D. Levine - *2**
Former Name: Bill A. Coller.
1140 - 3rd Ave., Prince George, BC V2L 3E5
Tel: 250-960-2169; *Fax:* 250-960-2196
coller@collerlevine.ca
www.collerlevine.ca

***Prince George*: Ronald W. Madill - *1**
1033 - 3rd Ave., Prince George, BC V2L 3E3
Tel: 250-562-5000; *Fax:* 250-562-5105

***Prince George*: Marcotte Kerrigan - *2**
440 Brunswick St., Prince George, BC V2L 2B6
Tel: 250-564-0052; *Fax:* 250-564-0053
marcottekerrigan.ca

***Prince George*: Irene G. Peters Law Corp. - *2**
Former Name: Peters & O'Byrne
P.O. Box 23050, Stn. College Heights, 5240 Domano Blvd., Prince George, BC V2N 6Z2
Tel: 250-964-7844; *Fax:* 888-219-8502
Toll-Free: 877-365-4093
admin@igpeters.ca

***Prince George*: Traxler Haines - *6**
Former Name: Ramsay Nosè Traxler Haines
#614, 1488 - 4 Ave., Prince George, BC V2L 4Y2
Tel: 250-563-7741; *Fax:* 250-563-2953
info@traxlerhaines.com
www.traxlerhaines.com

***Prince George*: Tyo Law Corp. - *1**
P.O. Box 10130, Stn. Hart, Prince George, BC V2K 5Y1
Tel: 250-962-5755; *Fax:* 888-922-6010
tyolaw@shaw.ca

***Prince George*: Wilson King LLP - *9**
Former Name: Wilson, King & Company
#1000, HSBC Tower, 299 Victoria St., Prince George, BC V2L 5B8
Tel: 250-960-3200; *Fax:* 250-562-7777
Toll-Free: 800-365-4566
www.wilsonking.com

***Prince George*: Garth A. Wright Law Corporation - *1**
#204, 411 Quebec St., Prince George, BC V2L 1W5
Tel: 250-564-5544 *Toll-Free:* 877-964-5544
garthwright@shaw.ca
www.garthwrightlaw.ca

***Prince Rupert*: Johnston Law Office - *1**
Former Name: Punnett & Johnston
#7, 222 - 3rd Ave. West, Prince Rupert, BC V8J 1L1
Tel: 250-624-2106; *Fax:* 250-627-8805
gmjohnston@citytel.net

***Prince Rupert*: Marina C-K Kan - *1**
P.O. Box 722, Prince Rupert, BC V8J 3S1
Tel: 250-624-6060; *Fax:* 250-624-6451

***Prince Rupert*: Silversides, Merrick & McLean - *4**
Former Name: Silversides, Seidemann & Kucher
P.O. Box 188, Stn. Prince Rupert, 217 - 3rd Ave. West, Prince Rupert, BC V8J 3P7
Tel: 250-624-2116; *Fax:* 250-627-7786

***Qualicum Beach*: Marshall & Lamperson**
P.O. Box 879, 710 Memorial Ave., Qualicum Beach, BC V9K 1T2
Tel: 250-752-5615; *Fax:* 250-752-2055
doug@qualicumlaw.ca

***Qualicum Beach*: Rodway & Perry - *2**
#1, P.O. Box 138, 699 Beach Rd., Qualicum Beach, BC V9K 1S7
Tel: 250-752-9526; *Fax:* 250-752-9521
rodwayandperry@shaw.ca
macisaacgroup.com/office/qualicum-beach/

***Qualicum Beach*: Walker Hubbard - *4**
#2, 707 Primrose St., Qualicum Beach, BC V9K 2K1
Tel: 250-752-6951; *Fax:* 250-752-6022
kwalker@qblaw.ca
www.qblaw.ca

***Quesnel*: John B. Schmitz - *1**
633 Clark St., Quesnel, BC V2J 1L3
Tel: 250-992-6793; *Fax:* 250-992-6795

***Revelstoke*: Bernard C. Lavallée - *1**
Former Name: Lavallée, Rackel
109 Connaught Ave., Revelstoke, BC V0E 2S0
Tel: 250-837-5168; *Fax:* 250-837-5178
bcl59lawyer@rctvonline.net

***Revelstoke*: Robert A. Lundberg Law Corporation - *1**
P.O. Box 2490, 119 Campbell Ave., Revelstoke, BC V0E 2S0
Tel: 250-837-5196; *Fax:* 250-837-4746
robertlundberg@rctvonline.net

***Richmond*: Ash O'Donnell Hibbert Law Corporation**
#1, 11575 Bridgeport Rd., Richmond, BC V6X 1T5
Tel: 604-273-9111; *Fax:* 604-273-1117

***Richmond*: David G. Baker, Barrister - *1**
#210, 7340 Westminster Hwy., Richmond, BC V6X 1A1
Tel: 604-244-7587; *Fax:* 604-303-6922
davegbaker@yahoo.ca
www.davidgbaker.ca

***Richmond*: Berger & Company - *1**
#130, 8400 Granville Ave., Richmond, BC V6Y 1P6
Tel: 604-273-9959; *Fax:* 604-273-9910
eberger@telus.net
www.berger-and-company.com

***Richmond*: David W. Blinkhorn - *1**
#430, 5900 No. 3 Rd., Richmond, BC V6X 3P7
Tel: 604-244-7880; *Fax:* 604-244-9611

***Richmond*: Campbell Froh May & Rice LLP - *13**
#200, 5611 Cooney Rd., Richmond, BC V6X 3J6
Tel: 604-273-8481; *Fax:* 604-273-4729
Toll-Free: 800-883-8288
contact@cfmrlaw.com
richmondbclawyers.com

***Richmond*: V.N. Carvalho - *1**
13811 Gilbert Rd., Richmond, BC V7E 2H8
Tel: 604-274-5636; *Fax:* 604-275-5694
vncarvalho@shaw.ca

***Richmond*: Robert J. Charlton - *1**
Also Known As: Robert J. Charlton Personal Law Corporation
#816, 6081 No. 3 Rd., Richmond, BC V6Y 2B2
Tel: 604-214-7818; *Fax:* 604-214-7819
rjc@rjcharlton.com
www.rjcharlton.com

***Richmond*: Chouinard & Company - *2**
#816, 6081 No. 3 Rd., Richmond, BC V6Y 2B2
Tel: 604-284-5633; *Fax:* 604-284-5632
Toll-Free: 877-685-8999
ray@chouinardlaw.com
www.chouinardlaw.com

***Richmond*: Cohen, Buchan, Edwards LLP - *9**
#208, 4940 No. 3 Rd., Richmond, BC V6X 3A5
Tel: 604-273-6411; *Fax:* 604-273-4512
info@cbelaw.com
www.cbelaw.com

***Richmond*: John C. Fairburn**
#305, 5811 Cooney Rd., Richmond, BC V6X 3M1
Tel: 604-279-8283; *Fax:* 604-279-8243
fairburnlaw@execcentre.com

***Richmond*: Fast & Company, Barristers & Solicitors - *2**
#5080, 8171 Ackroyd Rd., Richmond, BC V6X 3K1
Tel: 604-273-6424; *Fax:* 604-273-2290
Toll-Free: 877-552-2323
mlfast@fastandco.ca
www.fastandco.ca

***Richmond*: Forbes & Boyle - *2**
#215, 8171 Cook Rd., Richmond, BC V6Y 3T8
Tel: 604-273-7575; *Fax:* 604-273-8475
info@forbesboyle.ca
www.forbesboyle.ca

***Richmond*: Douglas B. Graves - *1**
#218, 8055 Anderson Rd., Richmond, BC V6Y 1S2
Tel: 604-276-0069

***Richmond*: Guo Law Corporation - *1**
#120, 6068 - #3 Rd., Richmond, BC V6Y 4M7
Tel: 778-297-6560; *Fax:* 778-297-6561
office@guolaw.ca
www.guolaw.ca

***Richmond*: Henderson Law Group - *2**
Former Name: Henderson Livingston Stewart LLP
#280, Riverside Professional Centre, 11331 Coppersmith Way, Richmond, BC V7A 5J9
Tel: 604-639-5175; *Fax:* 604-639-5176
office@hlglaw.ca
hlglaw.ca

** indicates number of lawyers*

***Richmond*: Bernard Hoodekoff - *1**
#206, 5811 Cooney Rd., Richmond, BC V6X 3M1
Tel: 604-278-8451; *Fax:* 604-278-8453

***Richmond*: Humphry Paterson - *2**
#205, 8171 Park Rd., Richmond, BC V6Y 1S9
Tel: 604-278-3031; *Fax:* 604-278-3021

***Richmond*: INC Business Lawyers - *2**
Former Name: Moir & Moir
#1201, 11871 Horseshoe Way, Richmond, BC V7A 5H5
Tel: 604-272-6960; *Fax:* 604-272-6959
Toll-Free: 888-272-7771
info@incorporate.ca
www.incorporate.ca
twitter.com/INCLawyers

***Richmond*: Jang Cheung Lee Chu Law Corporation - *6**
Former Name: Jang, Cheung, Lee
#700, London Plaza, 5951 No. 3 Rd., Richmond, BC V6X 2E3
Tel: 604-276-8300; *Fax:* 604-276-8309
office@jclclawcorp.com
www.jclclawcorp.com

***Richmond*: Kahn Zack Ehrlich Lithwick LLP - *14**
#300, 10991 Shellbridge Way, Richmond, BC V6X 3C6
Tel: 604-270-9571; *Fax:* 604-270-8282
Toll-Free: 888-529-6368
general@kzellaw.com
www.kzellaw.com

***Richmond*: Nancy L. Kinsman - *1**
#315, 8171 Cook Rd., Richmond, BC V6Y 3T8
Tel: 604-273-4664; *Fax:* 604-273-7442
nkinsman@familylawbc.ca
www.familylawbc.ca

***Richmond*: Kenneth B. Krag - *1**
#228, 8055 Anderson Rd., Richmond, BC V6Y 1S2
Tel: 604-270-8702; *Fax:* 604-270-6708

***Richmond*: Susan Label - *1**
#250, 11590 Cambie Rd., Richmond, BC V6X 3Z5
Tel: 604-273-6448; *Fax:* 604-273-6998
www.susanlabel.com

***Richmond*: Levitt Law Office - *1**
Also Known As: Morley A. Levitt
#120, 11181 Voyageur Way, Richmond, BC V6X 3N9
Tel: 604-270-9611; *Fax:* 604-270-4588
morley@levittlaw.ca
www.protectmyestate.ca

***Richmond*: Lim & Company - *5**
#320, 7480 Westminster Hwy., Richmond, BC V6X 1A1
Tel: 604-303-0788; *Fax:* 604-303-0789
info@limcolawyers.com
www.limcolawyers.com

***Richmond*: V. Brent Louie, Personal Law Corporation - *1**
#203, 2680 Shell Rd., Richmond, BC V6X 4C9
Tel: 604-270-8708; *Fax:* 604-270-8735
vblouie@shaw.ca

***Richmond*: Peter Li & Company - *3**
Former Name: Peter S.K. Li
#110, 4400 Hazelbridge Way, Richmond, BC V6X 3R8
Tel: 604-273-6308; *Fax:* 604-273-6393
office@peterliandcompany.com
www.peterliandcompany.com

***Richmond*: Phillips Paul - *2**
#215, 4800 No. 3 Rd., Richmond, BC V6X 3A6
Tel: 604-273-5297; *Fax:* 604-273-1643
inquiries@phillipspaul.com
www.phillipspaul.com

***Richmond*: Susan L. Polsky Shamash - *1**
#150, 4600 Jacombs Rd., Richmond, BC V6V 3B1
Tel: 604-664-7800; *Fax:* 604-664-7898
Toll-Free: 800-663-2782

***Richmond*: Pryke Lambert Leathley Russell LLP - *19**
#500, North Tower, 5811 Cooney Rd., Richmond, BC V6X 3M1
Tel: 604-243-8912; *Fax:* 604-276-8045
Toll-Free: 800-733-8716
www.pllr.com

***Richmond*: Rees-Thomas & Company - *3**
#5080, 8171 Ackroyd Rd., Richmond, BC V6X 3K1
Tel: 604-279-9300; *Fax:* 604-273-2290
info@reesthomas.com
www.reesthomas.com

***Richmond*: Scardina & Co. - *1**
#215, 4800 No. 3 Rd., Richmond, BC V6X 3A6
Tel: 604-273-5558; *Fax:* 604-273-5550

***Richmond*: Spry Hawkins Micner - *6**
#440, VanCity Tower, 5900 No. 3 Rd., Richmond, BC V6X 3P7
Tel: 604-233-7001; *Fax:* 604-233-7017
www.willpowerlaw.com

***Richmond*: Bruce Allan Thompson Law Corporation - *1**
#215, Churchill Centre, 2nd Fl., 8171 Cook Rd., Richmond, BC V6Y 3T8
Tel: 604-270-7773; *Fax:* 604-273-8475

***Richmond*: Tsang & Company - *2**
Former Name: Wong & Tsang
#320, 8171 Cook Rd., Richmond, BC V6Y 3T8
Tel: 604-279-9023; *Fax:* 604-279-9025
www.TsangCo.com

***Richmond*: Webster & Associates - *4**
#550, 5900 No. 3 Rd., Richmond, BC V6X 3P7
Tel: 604-713-8030; *Fax:* 604-713-8038
info@braininjurylaw.ca
www.braininjurylaw.ca

***Richmond*: Mary E.B. Wood - *1**
#724, 6081 - No. 3 Rd., Richmond, BC V6Y 2B2
Tel: 604-273-5547; *Fax:* 604-273-3044
mebwood@telus.net
www.marywoodlawyer.com

***Roberts Creek*: Lynn Chapman - *1**
1947 Crystal Cr., Roberts Creek, BC V0N 2W1
Tel: 604-886-0382; *Fax:* 604-886-0366
lchapman@dccnet.com

***Saanichton*: Vahan A. Ishkanian - *1**
#6, 7855 East Saanich Rd., Saanichton, BC V8M 2B4
Tel: 778-426-4455; *Fax:* 250-508-6336
www.wcbbclawyer.com

***Saanichton*: C.J. Kip Wilson - *1**
#6, 7855 East Saanich Rd., Saanichton, BC V8M 2B4
Tel: 250-544-0727; *Fax:* 250-544-0728
Toll-Free: 800-785-3874
kipwilson@home.com
www.saanichtonlaw.com

***Salmon Arm*: Brooke, Jackson, Downs LLP - *4**
Centennial Building, P.O. Box 67, 51 - 3rd St. NE, Salmon Arm, BC V1E 4N2
Tel: 250-832-9311; *Fax:* 250-832-3801
bjdlaw@sunwave.net
www.bjdlaw.com

***Salmon Arm*: Derek McManus Law Corporation - *1**
P.O. Box 57, 450 Lakeshore Dr. NE, Salmon Arm, BC V1E 4N2
Tel: 250-833-4720; *Fax:* 250-832-4787
corp@salmonarmlaw.com
www.salmonarmlaw.com

***Salmon Arm*: Seale Law Corp. - *1**
#302, P.O. Box 3248, Stn. Main, 370 Kaleshore Dr. NE, Salmon Arm, BC V1E 4S1
Tel: 250-832-9301; *Fax:* 250-832-9300

***Salmon Arm*: Sivertz Kiehlbauch - *3**
Former Name: Sivertz, Kiehlbauch & Zachernuk
P.O. Box 190, Stn. Main, 351 Hudson Ave. NE, Salmon Arm, BC V1E 4N3
Tel: 250-832-8031; *Fax:* 250-832-6177

***Salmon Arm*: Verdurmen & Company - *1**
Former Name: Verdurmen & Lee
P.O. Box 826, 450 Lakeshore Dr. NE, Salmon Arm, BC V1E 4N9
Tel: 250-833-0914; *Fax:* 250-833-0924
Toll-Free: 855-833-0914
vlex@telus.net
www.verdurmenlaw.com

***Salt Spring Island*: Fisher, Murphy & Woodward - *1**
Also Known As: Orca Law Corp.
Former Name: Ian H. Clement Law Corporation
#1, 105 Rainbow Rd., Salt Spring Island, BC V8K 2V5
Tel: 250-537-5505; *Fax:* 250-537-5099
ianhclement@gmail.com
saltspringlawfirm.com
www.facebook.com/#!/pages/Fisher-Murphy-Woodward-Lawyers/253823191300084

***Salt Spring Island*: James Pasuta - *1**
P.O. Box 414, Stn. Ganges, 560 Fulford-Ganges Rd., Salt Spring Island, BC V8K 2W1
Tel: 250-537-9995; *Fax:* 250-537-9975

***Sechelt*: Narbonne Law Office - *1**
P.O. Box 762, Sechelt, BC V0N 3A0
Tel: 604-886-7972; *Fax:* 604-886-7147
www.narbonnelawoffice.com

***Sechelt*: William C. Prowse - *1**
6866 Island View Rd., Sechelt, BC V0N 3A8
Tel: 604-740-0303; *Fax:* 604-740-0306
transmed@telus.net

***Sechelt*: Robinson & Co. Law Office - *1**
P.O. Box 920, Sechelt, BC V0N 3A0
Tel: 604-885-7541; *Fax:* 604-885-7561
robco@telus.net

***Sidney*: Henley & Walden LLP - *5**
#201, 2377 Bevan Ave., Sidney, BC V8L 4M9
Tel: 250-656-7231; *Fax:* 250-656-0937
Toll-Free: 800-656-7231
inquiries@henleywalden.com
www.henleywalden.com

***Sidney*: McKimm & Lott - *9**
9830 - 4th St., Sidney, BC V8L 2Z3
Tel: 250-656-3961; *Fax:* 250-655-3329
reception@mclott.com
www.mclott.com

***Smithers*: Perry & Company - *6**
P.O. Box 790, 3875 Broadway Ave., Smithers, BC V0J 2N0
Tel: 250-847-4341; *Fax:* 250-847-5634
reception@perryco.ca
www.perryco.ca

***Smithers*: G. Ronald Toews, Q.C. - *1**
P.O. Box 970, 3835 - 10th Ave., Smithers, BC V0J 2N0
Tel: 250-847-2187; *Fax:* 250-847-2183
grt@buckley.net

***Sooke*: Hallgren & Faulkner - *2**
#104, 6739 West Coast Rd., Sooke, BC V9Z 1H9
Tel: 250-642-5271 *Toll-Free:* 877-358-5271
info@hallgrenfaulkner.ca
www.hallgrenfaulkner.ca

***Sorrento*: Begin & Company - *1**
P.O. Box 122, Sorrento, BC V0E 2W0
Tel: 250-835-4857; *Fax:* 250-835-2298
rb@zipitlaw.com

***Squamish*: Race & Company - *8**
#301, P.O. Box 1850, 37989 Cleveland Ave., Squamish, BC V8B 0B3
Tel: 604-892-5254; *Fax:* 604-892-5461
www.raceandcompany.com
www.facebook.com/RaceandCoLawyers

***Summerland*: Bell, Jacoe & Company - *3**
P.O. Box 520, 13211 Victoria Rd. North, Summerland, BC V0H 1Z0
Tel: 250-494-6621; *Fax:* 250-494-8055
Toll-Free: 800-663-0392
belljacoe@shaw.ca
www.bell-jacoe.com

***Surrey*: Alan J. Benson - *1**
#106, 15585 - 24 Ave., Surrey, BC V4A 2J4
Tel: 604-538-4911; *Fax:* 604-538-5754
info@alanbensonlaw.com
www.alanbensonlaw.com

***Surrey*: Roger S. Bhatti - *1**
#203, 8556 - 120th St., Surrey, BC V3W 3N5
Tel: 604-590-1177; *Fax:* 604-596-8800
rblaw@intergate.ca

***Surrey*: Spencer A. Bowers - *1**
8893 - 160 St., Surrey, BC V4N 2X8
Tel: 604-951-9224; *Fax:* 604-951-9224
sabowers@axionet.com

** indicates number of lawyers*

Surrey: Brawn, Karras & Sanderson - *4
#309, 1688 - 152nd St., Surrey, BC V4A 4N2
Tel: 604-259-1620; *Fax:* 604-542-5341
Toll-Free: 877-470-7535
www.bkslaw.com

Surrey: Buckley Hogan - *7
Former Name: Buckley & Buckley
#200, 8120 - 128th St., Surrey, BC V3W 1R1
Tel: 604-635-3000; *Fax:* 604-635-3311
lawyers@buckleyhogan.com
www.buckleyhogan.com

Surrey: Caissie & Company - *1
#205, 15127 - 100 Ave., Surrey, BC V3R 0N9
Tel: 604-586-7200; *Fax:* 604-583-5870
info@calaw.bc.ca
www.calaw.bc.ca

Surrey: James L. Davidson & Company - *2
#403, P.O. Box 271, 16033 - 108 Ave., Surrey, BC V4N 1P2
Tel: 604-951-2990; *Fax:* 604-951-2991
reception@jldlawyers.com
www.jldlawyers.com

Surrey: De Jager Volkenant & Company - *6
#5, 15243 - 91 Ave., Surrey, BC V3R 8P8
Tel: 604-953-1500; *Fax:* 604-953-1501
Toll-Free: 866-953-1500
dvc@dvclawyers.com
www.dvclawyers.com

Surrey: Paul E. Del Rossi - *1
#1012, 7445 - 132nd St., Surrey, BC V3W 1J8
Tel: 604-590-5600; *Fax:* 604-590-5626
pdelrossi@sternandalbert.com

Surrey: Fritz Shirreff & Vickers - *4
Former Name: Fritz Lail Shirreff & Vickers
#201, 15127 - 100th Ave., Surrey, BC V3R 0N9
Tel: 604-582-5157; *Fax:* 604-582-5167

Surrey: Gabbrel & Company - *1
#202, 15388 - 24 Ave., Surrey, BC V4A 2J2
Tel: 604-583-5776
gambrelandcompany.ca

Surrey: Hamilton Duncan Armstrong & Stewart Law Corporation - *20
#1450, Station Tower Gateway, 13401 - 108th Ave., Surrey, BC V3T 5T3
Tel: 604-581-4677; *Fax:* 604-581-5947
www.hdas.com
www.facebook.com/HamiltonDuncanLaw,
www.linkedin.com/company/812865

Surrey: Hittrich Family Law Group - *2
#300, 15230 - #10 Hwy., Surrey, BC V3S 5K7
Tel: 604-575-2274; *Fax:* 604-575-2357
info@hittrichlaw.com
www.hzfamilylaw.com

Surrey: Howard Smith & Company - *3
#111, 15272 Croydon Dr., Surrey, BC V3S 0Z5
Tel: 604-535-7688; *Fax:* 604-535-7699
info@howardsmithlawyers.com
www.howardsmithlawyers.com

Surrey: Sharen Janeson - *1
#456, 15355 - 24 Ave., Surrey, BC V4A 2H9
Tel: 604-536-6884; *Fax:* 604-618-9500
sjaneson@shaw.ca

Surrey: Kaminsky & Company - *6
#205, 15240 - 56 Ave., Surrey, BC V3S 5K7
Tel: 604-591-7877; *Fax:* 604-591-1978
inbox@kaminskyco.com
www.kaminskyco.com

Surrey: Kane, Shannon & Weiler - *21
#220, 7565 - 132nd St., Surrey, BC V3W 1K5
Tel: 604-591-7321; *Fax:* 604-591-7149
Toll-Free: 800-497-3069
www.ksw.bc.ca
www.facebook.com/kswlaw

Surrey: Kereluk & Company - *1
#125, 15225 - 104 Ave., Surrey, BC V3R 6Y8
Tel: 604-589-3278; *Fax:* 604-589-8473
mail@kereluklaw.com
www.kereluklaw.com

Surrey: James R. Kitsul - *1
19395 Langley Bypass, Surrey, BC V3S 6K1
Tel: 604-539-2610; *Fax:* 604-534-3811
kitsul@supersave.ca

Surrey: Leung, Arthur-Leung - *1
14340-57th Ave., Surrey, BC V3X 1B2
Tel: 604-572-2300

Surrey: MacMillan, Tucker & Mackay - *5
5690 - 176A St., Surrey, BC V3S 4H1
Tel: 604-574-7431; *Fax:* 604-574-3021
Toll-Free: 800-922-7431
mactuc@telus.net
www.mactuc.com

Surrey: Maier & Co. - *1
#310, 10524 King George Hwy., Surrey, BC V3S 2X2
Tel: 604-582-5951; *Fax:* 604-588-0779
maier@telus.net

Surrey: Malik Law Corporation - *2
Former Name: Unterman & Associates; South Fraser Law Group
#206, Khalsa Business Center, 8388 - 128th St., Surrey, BC V3W 4G2
Tel: 604-543-9111; *Fax:* 604-543-9112
info@maliklaw.ca
www.maliklaw.ca

Surrey: Manthorpe Law Offices - *3
#200, 10233 - 153 St., Surrey, BC V3R 0Z7
Tel: 604-582-7743; *Fax:* 604-582-7753
info@manthorpelaw.com
www.manthorpelaw.com

Surrey: Alistair L. McAndrew - *1
#240, 13711 - 72 Ave., Surrey, BC V3W 2P2
Tel: 604-591-2288; *Fax:* 604-591-7366

Surrey: Cameron C. McLeod - *1
#310, 10524 King George Hwy, Surrey, BC V3T 2X2
Tel: 604-583-6318; *Fax:* 604-588-0779
mcleodlaw@dccnet.com

Surrey: David C. McPhillips - *1
#199-800, 15355-24 Ave., Surrey, BC V4A 2H9
Tel: 604-535-7266; *Fax:* 604-535-6658
dmcphillips@shaw.ca

Surrey: McQuarrie Hunter LLP - *24
#1500, Central City Tower, 13450 - 102nd Ave., 15th Fl., Surrey, BC V3T 5X3
Tel: 604-581-7001; *Fax:* 604-581-7110
Toll-Free: 877-581-7001
www.mcquarrie.com
www.facebook.com/pages/McQuarrie-Hunter-LLP/180921071990015, twitter.com/McQuarrieHunter,
www.linkedin.com/company/2365673?trk=tyah

Surrey: Morrison & Co. - *1
#303, 15225 - 104th Ave., Surrey, BC V3R 6Y8
Tel: 604-930-9013; *Fax:* 604-930-9014
admin@morrocolaw.ca
morrocolaw.ca

Surrey: Murchison Thomson & Clarke LLP - *24
#101, Surrey Central Business Park, 7565 - 132 St., Surrey, BC V3W 1K5
Tel: 604-590-8855; *Fax:* 604-590-2000
info@mtclaw.ca
www.murchisonthomson.com

Surrey: Larry Nelson - *1
#309, 1656 Martin Dr., Surrey, BC V4A 6E7
Tel: 604-538-1511; *Fax:* 604-535-5344

Surrey: Nyack & Persad - *2
#201, 9380 - 120 St., Surrey, BC V3V 4B9
Tel: 604-588-9933; *Fax:* 604-588-2731

Surrey: Michael G. Parent, Law Corporation - *1
#203, 15225 - 104 Ave., Surrey, BC V3R 6Y8
Tel: 604-589-6437; *Fax:* 604-589-7238

Surrey: Peterson Stark Scott - *9
#300, 10355 - 136A St., Surrey, BC V3T 5R3
Tel: 604-588-9321; *Fax:* 604-589-5391
Toll-Free: 800-555-3288
sry@psslaw.ca
www.psslaw.ca

Surrey: Donald F. Porter - *1
#149, 6350 - 120 St., Surrey, BC V3X 3K1
Tel: 604-594-5155; *Fax:* 604-594-1304
dfporter@uniserve.com

Surrey: Richards & Richards - *3
10325 - 150 St., Surrey, BC V3R 4B1
Tel: 604-588-6844; *Fax:* 604-588-8800
Toll-Free: 877-588-1101
litigation@richardslaw.com
www.richardslaw.com

Surrey: Roxwal Lawyers LLP - *4
#212, 5455 - 152nd St., Surrey, BC V3S 5A5
Tel: 604-575-3718; *Fax:* 604-575-3719
info@roxwal.com
www.roxwal.com

Surrey: Sanghera Law Group - *3
#203, 7134 King George Blvd., Surrey, BC V3W 5A3
Tel: 604-543-8484; *Fax:* 604-543-8584
Toll-Free: 877-778-8484
info@slglawyers.com
www.slglawyers.com

Surrey: Sedai Law Office - *1
#110, 10768 Whalley Blvd., Surrey, BC V3T 0G1
Tel: 778-395-7810; *Fax:* 604-909-4859
msedai@immigrationcitizenshiplaw.com
www.immigrationcitizenshiplaw.com
www.facebook.com/immigrationcitizenshiplaw,
twitter.com/MarinaSedai, www.linkedin.com/in/marinasedai

Surrey: Shergill & Company, Trial Lawyers - *3
#286, Payal Business Center, 8128 - 128th St., Surrey, BC V3W 1R1
Tel: 604-597-8111; *Fax:* 604-597-8133
Toll-Free: 855-597-8111
main@shergilllaw.com
www.shergilllaw.com
www.facebook.com/pages/Shergill-Company-Trial-Lawyers/177500442309003, twitter.com/Shergill_law

Surrey: Sicotte & Henry Criminal Defence Lawyers - *3
#200, 10706 King George Blvd., Surrey, BC V3T 2X3
Tel: 604-585-8898; *Fax:* 604-585-8964
www.surreycriminallawyer.com/en/

Surrey: Siebenga & King Law Offices - *3
#288, 12899 - 76th Ave., Surrey, BC V3W 1E6
Tel: 604-592-3550; *Fax:* 604-592-3551
info@sklawoffices.com
www.sklawoffices.com

Surrey: South Coast Law Group - *3
#6, 15243 - 91st Ave., Surrey, BC V3R 8P8
Tel: 604-496-5096; *Fax:* 604-496-5196
info@southcoastlaw.ca
www.southcoastlaw.ca

Surrey: Starr & Company - *2
#203, 2383 King George Hwy., Surrey, BC V4A 5A4
Tel: 604-536-3393; *Fax:* 604-536-3115

Surrey: Swedahl & Company - *1
#11, 15243 - 91 Ave., Surrey, BC V3R 8P8
Tel: 604-581-3232; *Fax:* 604-589-3741

Surrey: Taylor, Bjorge & Company - *2
#205, 1676 Martin Dr., Surrey, BC V4A 6E7
Tel: 604-536-1117; *Fax:* 604-536-0445

Surrey: Trial Lawyers Advocacy Group - *3
Former Name: Guildford Law Group
#200, 8459 - 160 St., Surrey, BC V4N 0V6
Tel: 604-635-1330; *Fax:* 604-635-1340
sbobb@tlag.ca
www.tlag.ca

Surrey: Virk Law Group
#1005, 7495 - 132 St., Surrey, BC V3W 1J8
Tel: 604-596-4342; *Fax:* 604-596-4312
psv@virklawgroup.com
www.virklawgroup.com

Surrey: Gordon G. Walters - *1
12321 Beecher St., Surrey, BC V4A 3A7
Tel: 604-596-3300; *Fax:* 604-596-9111

** indicates number of lawyers*

***Surrey*: Wilson & Rasmussen LLP - *3**
Former Name: Greig, Wilson & Brajovic
#300, Guildford Landmark Bldg., 15127 - 100th Ave., Surrey, BC V3R 0N9
Tel: 604-583-7917; *Fax:* 604-583-7139
info@wilsonrasmussen.com
www.wilsonrasmussen.com
www.linkedin.com/company/wilson-rasmussen-llp

***Surrey*: Yearwood & Company - *2**
#2, 9613 - 192nd St., Surrey, BC V4N 4C7
Tel: 604-513-2333; *Fax:* 604-513-0211
pyearwood@bclaw.bc.ca
www.bclaw.bc.ca

***Terrace*: Crampton Personal Law Corporation - *2**
4623 Park Ave., Terrace, BC V8G 1V5
Tel: 250-635-6330; *Fax:* 250-635-4795
Toll-Free: 800-667-0080
bryan_crampton@telus.net

***Terrace*: Talstra Law Corporation - *6**
#101, 3219 Eby St., Terrace, BC V8G 4R3
Tel: 250-638-1137; *Fax:* 250-638-1306
Toll-Free: 877-998-4222
www.talstralaw.ca

***Terrace*: Warner Bandstra Brown - *5**
#200, 4630 Lazelle Ave., Terrace, BC V8G 1S6
Tel: 250-635-2622; *Fax:* 250-635-4998
Toll-Free: 800-665-5120
www.warnerbandstra.com

***Trail*: Ghilarducci & Cromarty - *2**
1309 Bay Ave., Trail, BC V1R 4A7
Tel: 250-368-6455; *Fax:* 250-368-6107

***Trail*: McEwan & Company - *7**
Also Known As: McEwan Law
Former Name: McEwan Harrison & Co.
1432 Bay Ave., Trail, BC V1R 4B1
Tel: 250-368-8211; *Fax:* 250-368-9401
Toll-Free: 888-354-4844
www.mcewanlawco.com

***Trail*: Thompson LeRose & Brown - *6 1**
1199 Cedar St., Trail, BC V1R 4B8
Tel: 250-368-3327; *Fax:* 250-368-4494

***Vancouver*: Aaron Gordon Daykin Nordlinger LLP - *11**
Former Name: Aaron, MacGregor, Gordon & Daykin
#1100, 777 Hornby St., Vancouver, BC V6Z 1S4
Tel: 604-689-7571; *Fax:* 604-685-8563
reception@agdnlaw.ca
www.agdnlaw.ca

***Vancouver*: Access Law Group - *6**
#1700, 1185 Georgia St. West, Vancouver, BC V6E 4E6
Tel: 604-689-8000; *Fax:* 604-689-8835
reception@accesslaw.ca
www.accesslaw.ca

***Vancouver*: Jack A. Adelaar - *1**
#1700, P.O. Box 12148, 808 Nelson St., Vancouver, BC V6Z 2H2
Tel: 604-687-8840; *Fax:* 604-687-8370
jadelaar@telus.net

***Vancouver*: Adrian & Company - *2**
5660 Yew St., Vancouver, BC V6M 3Y3
Tel: 604-266-7811; *Fax:* 604-266-5869

***Vancouver*: Alexander Holburn Beaudin & Lang, LLP - *72**
#2700, P.O. Box 10057, 700 West Georgia St., Vancouver, BC V7Y 1B8
Tel: 604-484-1700; *Fax:* 604-484-9700
Toll-Free: 877-688-1351
info@ahbl.ca
www.ahbl.ca
www.facebook.com/pages/Alexander-Holburn-Beaudin-Lang-LLP/310808898998791,
www.linkedin.com/company/alexander-holburn-beaudin-lang-llp

***Vancouver*: Allan & Lougheed - *2**
1622 - 7th Ave. W, 2nd Fl., Vancouver, BC V6J 1S5
Tel: 604-733-2411; *Fax:* 604-736-6225
aandllaw@telus.net

***Vancouver*: Alvin Hui Law Corp. - *1**
1606 Hornby St., Vancouver, BC V6Z 2T4
Tel: 604-732-3898; *Fax:* 604-739-2821

***Vancouver*: Andersen Paul - *2**
1662 - 8th Ave. West, Vancouver, BC V6J 4R8
Tel: 604-734-8411; *Fax:* 604-734-8511
info@AndersenPaulLaw.com
andersenpaullaw.com
twitter.com/andersenpaullaw

***Vancouver*: Brian W. Anderson Law Corporation - *1**
835 Granville St., 2nd Fl., Vancouver, BC V6Z 1K7
Tel: 604-684-5367

***Vancouver*: Jane Anderson - *1**
#1782, 808 Nelson St., Vancouver, BC V6Z 2H2
Tel: 604-488-1162; *Fax:* 604-488-0666
janeanderso@telus.net

***Vancouver*: Anfield Sujir Kennedy & Durno - *10**
Also Known As: ASKD Law
#1600, Pacific Centre, P.O. Box 10068, 609 Granville St., Vancouver, BC V7Y 1C3
Tel: 604-669-1322; *Fax:* 604-669-3877
www.askdlaw.com

***Vancouver*: Armstrong Simpson - *6**
Former Name: Armstrong & Company
#2080, 777 Hornby St., Vancouver, BC V6Z 1S4
Tel: 604-683-7361; *Fax:* 604-662-3231
www.armlaw.com

***Vancouver*: Aydin Bird - *6**
Former Name: Aydin & Co
#530, Oakridge Centre, North Office Tower, 650 - 41 Ave. West, Vancouver, BC V5Z 2M9
Tel: 604-266-5828; *Fax:* 604-266-3929
aydin@aydinco.com
www.aydinco.com

***Vancouver*: Baker & Baker - *2**
808 Nelson St., 17th Fl., Vancouver, BC V6Z 2H2
Tel: 604-642-0107; *Fax:* 604-681-3504
www.bakerbaker.ca

***Vancouver*: Barbeau, Evans & Goldstein, Barristers & Solicitors - *3**
#280, Park Place, 666 Burrard St., Vancouver, BC V6C 2X8
Tel: 604-688-4900; *Fax:* 604-688-0649
info@beg-law.com
www.beg-law.com

***Vancouver*: Gail Barnes - *1**
149 Main St., Vancouver, BC V6A 2S5
Tel: 604-684-1124; *Fax:* 604-684-1122
www.gailbarneslawyer.ca/en/

***Vancouver*: Beach Avenue Barristers, A Law Corporation - *3**
Former Name: Epstein Wood
#150, 1008 Beach Avenue, Vancouver, BC V6E 1T7
Tel: 604-629-0429; *Fax:* 604-689-4451
beachavenuebarristers.com

***Vancouver*: Beck, Robinson & Company - *5**
#700, 686 West Broadway, Vancouver, BC V5Z 1G1
Tel: 604-874-0204; *Fax:* 604-874-0820
rich@beckrobinson.com
www.beckrobinson.com

***Vancouver*: Patrick J. Beirne - *1**
157 Alexander St., 3rd Fl., Vancouver, BC V6A 1B8
Tel: 604-683-4311; *Fax:* 604-683-4317

***Vancouver*: David R. Bellamy - *1**
#101, 1012 Beach Ave., Vancouver, BC V6E 1T7
Tel: 604-800-5352; *Fax:* 604-662-8902
Toll-Free: 877-713-8239
www.bellamy.bc.ca

***Vancouver*: Benchmark Law Corpoartion - *1**
#600, 1285 Broadway West, Vancouver, BC V6H 3X8
Tel: 778-371-3446; *Fax:* 604-757-9904
info@benchmarklaw.ca
www.benchmarklaw.ca
www.facebook.com/benchmarklaw,
twitter.com/BenchmarkLawCo,
ca.linkedin.com/pub/dana-gordon/46/ab3/a55/

***Vancouver*: Bennett, Parkes - *2**
#460, 2609 Granville St., Vancouver, BC V6H 3H3
Tel: 604-734-6838; *Fax:* 604-738-6789
www.bennettparkes.com

***Vancouver*: Bernard LLP - *18**
#1500, 570 Granville St., Vancouver, BC V6C 3P1
Tel: 604-681-1700; *Fax:* 604-681-1788
info@bernardllp.ca
www.bernardllp.ca

***Vancouver*: Anthony Beruschi - *2**
#605, 889 West Pender St., Vancouver, BC V6C 3B2
Tel: 604-669-3116; *Fax:* 604-669-5886

***Vancouver*: Raymond J. Bianchin - *1**
#1410, 1130 Pender St. West, Vancouver, BC V6E 4A4
Tel: 604-683-8111; *Fax:* 604-685-0194
rjblawcorp@telus.net
www.icbcclaimslawyer.com

***Vancouver*: Birnie & Company**
#3334, Four Bentall Centre, P.O. Box 49116, Stn. Bentall, 1055 Dunsmuir St., Vancouver, BC V7X 1G4
Tel: 604-688-4511; *Fax:* 604-688-0511
www.linkedin.com/company/birnie-&-company

***Vancouver*: Pamela S. Boles - *1**
#210, 970 Burrard St., Vancouver, BC V6Z 2R4
Tel: 604-688-5001; *Fax:* 604-685-5006

***Vancouver*: Bolton Hatcher Dance Barristers and Solicitors - *3**
#360, 1122 Mainland St., Vancouver, BC V6B 5L1
Tel: 604-687-7078; *Fax:* 604-687-3022
info@bhd-law.com
www.bhd-law.com
ca.linkedin.com/pub/claire-hatcher/a/b78/b8a

***Vancouver*: Bond Ellen - *2**
#200, 157 Alexander St., Vancouver, BC V6A 1B8
Tel: 604-682-3621; *Fax:* 604-682-3919

***Vancouver*: Boughton Law Corporation - *54**
Also Known As: Boughton
Former Name: Boughton Peterson Yang Anderson
#700, P.O. Box 49290, 595 Burrard St., Vancouver, BC V7X 1S8
Tel: 604-687-6789; *Fax:* 604-683-5317
info@boughtonlaw.com
www.boughton.ca
www.facebook.com/boughtonlaw, twitter.com/boughtonlaw/,
www.linkedin.com/company/boughton-law-corporation

***Vancouver*: Joyce W. Bradley - *1**
P.O. Box 45565, Stn. Westside, Vancouver, BC V6S 2N5
Tel: 604-732-3886; *Fax:* 604-732-3781
jwbmediate@telus.net

***Vancouver*: W. Anita Braha - *1**
#300, Stn. F, 1275 West 6th Ave., Vancouver, BC V6H 1A6
Tel: 604-839-5594
wabraha@telus.net
www.wanitabraha.com

***Vancouver*: Bronson, Jones & Company - Vancouver - Broadway - *10**
Former Name: Bronson & Company
#720, 999 West Broadway, Vancouver, BC V5Z 1K3
Tel: 604-681-9666 *Toll-Free:* 855-852-5100
www.bronsonco.com

***Vancouver*: Brown Henry Keith - *3**
#1504, 100 West Pender St., 15th Fl., Vancouver, BC V6B 1R8
Tel: 604-684-1021; *Fax:* 604-688-6243
henrykbrownlawcorporation@telus.net

***Vancouver*: Peter W. Brown Law Corp. - *2**
#402, 1525 Robson St., Vancouver, BC V6G 1C3
Tel: 604-915-7075
peterwbrown@owblawcorp.com

***Vancouver*: John Buchanan - *1**
#788, 601 West Broadway, Vancouver, BC V5Z 4C2
Tel: 604-876-0343; *Fax:* 604-876-9035
johngbuchanan@telus.net
www.johnbuchananlaw.com
www.facebook.com/144703168966144,
twitter.com/CriminalLawVan

***Vancouver*: Susan P. Burak - *1**
1628 - 7th Ave West, 2nd Fl., Vancouver, BC V6J 1S5
Tel: 604-733-2411; *Fax:* 604-736-6225
ajzburak@shaw.ca

* indicates number of lawyers

***Vancouver*: Burke & Jones - *2**
687 - 20th Ave. East, Vancouver, BC V5V 1M9
Tel: 604-879-6365; *Fax:* 604-879-6367
acb@burkeandjones.com
www.burkeandjones.com

***Vancouver*: Burns Fitzpatrick LLP - *12**
Former Name: Burns, Fitzpatrick, Rogers, Schwartz & Turner LLP
#1400, 510 Burrard St., Vancouver, BC V6C 3A8
Tel: 604-602-5000; *Fax:* 604-685-2104
www.burnsfitz.com

***Vancouver*: Bradley M. Caldwell - *1**
#401, 815 Hornby St., Vancouver, BC V6Z 2E6
Tel: 604-689-8894; *Fax:* 604-689-5739
bcaldwell@admiraltylaw.com

***Vancouver*: Cawkell Brodie Glaister LLP - *4**
Former Name: Cawkell, Brodie
439 Helmcken St., Vancouver, BC V6B 2E6
Tel: 604-684-3323; *Fax:* 604-684-3350
www.cawkell.com

***Vancouver*: Chalke & Company - *1**
#708, 1155 Pender St. West, Vancouver, BC V6E 2P4
Tel: 604-980-4855; *Fax:* 604-980-6469
info@chalke.ca
www.chalke.ca

***Vancouver*: Chan Yue & Lee - *1**
#212, 475 Main St., Vancouver, BC V6A 2T7
Tel: 604-687-4576; *Fax:* 604-683-3258
chanyue@telus.net

***Vancouver*: Chen & Leung - *10**
#728, North Tower, Oakridge Centre, 650 - 41st Ave. West, Vancouver, BC V5Z 2M9
Tel: 604-264-8331; *Fax:* 604-264-8387
info@cllawyers.ca
www.cllawyers.ca

***Vancouver*: Chow & Company - *1**
378 Smithe St., Vancouver, BC V6B 1T7
Tel: 604-669-0268; *Fax:* 604-669-9863
n-chow@telus.net

***Vancouver*: Gregory T. Chu - *1**
#650, 1188 Georgia St. West, Vancouver, BC V6E 4A2
Tel: 604-628-5005; *Fax:* 604-987-9939
gtchu@telus.net

***Vancouver*: Clark Wilson LLP - *79**
#900, 885 Georgia St. West, Vancouver, BC V6C 3H1
Tel: 604-687-5700; *Fax:* 604-687-6314
www.cwilson.com
twitter.com/ClarkWilsonLLP

***Vancouver*: Cobb St. Pierre Lewis - *3**
#330, 233 West 1st St., Vancouver, BC V7M 1B3
Tel: 604-770-3311; *Fax:* 604-770-3389
info@acquit.ca
acquit.ca

***Vancouver*: Cochran Bradshaw - *3**
439 Helmcken St., Vancouver, BC V6B 2E6
Tel: 604-681-9200; *Fax:* 604-681-8339
cochranlaw@telus.net

***Vancouver*: Morley E. Cofman Law Corporation - *1**
#1500, 701 West Georgia St., Vancouver, BC V7Y 1C6
Tel: 604-696-6674; *Fax:* 604-801-5911
mcofman@shaw.ca

***Vancouver*: Leonard M. Cohen - *1**
#570, 999 West Broadway, Vancouver, BC V5Z 1K5
Tel: 604-731-8118; *Fax:* 604-731-5274
www.vancouvernotary.ca

***Vancouver*: Brian Coleman Q.C. - *1**
#320, 425 Carrall St., Vancouver, BC V6B 6E3
Tel: 604-683-5821; *Fax:* 604-683-9354
coleman@telus.net

***Vancouver*: Collette Parsons Harris - *8**
#1750, P.O. Box 10090, 700 Georgia St. West, Vancouver, BC V7Y 1B6
Tel: 604-662-7777; *Fax:* 604-669-4053
Toll-Free: 800-999-4991
info@colletteparsons.com
www.colletteparsons.com
www.facebook.com/pages/Vancouver-BC/Collette-Parsons/126892367346858, twitter.com/bcinjurylawyers

***Vancouver*: Collins & Cullen - *3**
#680, 999 West Broadway, Vancouver, BC V5Z 1K5
Tel: 604-259-2897; *Fax:* 604-730-2628
Toll-Free: 800-594-4252
www.collinscullen.com

***Vancouver*: Comparelli & Company - *2**
#704, 510 West Hastings St., Vancouver, BC V6B 1L8
Tel: 604-683-6888; *Fax:* 604-683-4497
james@comparelli.com
www.comparelli.com

***Vancouver*: Coric Adler Wener - *3**
Former Name: Simon Wener
#620, 1385 - 8 Ave. West, Vancouver, BC V6H 3V9
Tel: 604-736-5500
reception@cawlaw.ca
cawlaw.ca

***Vancouver*: Coristine Woodall - *2**
#540, 220 Cambie St., Vancouver, BC V6B 2M9
Tel: 604-689-3242; *Fax:* 604-689-3292

***Vancouver*: Carla Courtenay Law Office - *1**
#1160, 777 Hornby St., Vancouver, BC V6Z 1S4
Tel: 604-682-2200; *Fax:* 604-682-2246
lilias@cclaw.bc.ca
www.cclaw.bc.ca

***Vancouver*: Coutts Pulver LLP - *6**
Former Name: Schiller, Coutts, Weiler & Gibson
#1710, One Bentall Center, 505 Burrard St., Vancouver, BC V7X 1M6
Tel: 604-682-1866; *Fax:* 604-682-6947
reception@cplaw.ca
www.cplaw.ca

***Vancouver*: Raffaele Crescenzo - *1**
#206, 1651 Commercial Dr., Vancouver, BC V5L 3Y3
Tel: 604-255-9030; *Fax:* 604-255-9075

***Vancouver*: Flavio Crestani - *1**
5052 Victoria Dr., Vancouver, BC V5P 3T8
Tel: 604-251-1168; *Fax:* 604-253-7726

***Vancouver*: Kenneth Cristall - *1**
#610, P.O. Box 12110, 808 Nelson St., Vancouver, BC V6Z 2H2
Tel: 604-654-2250; *Fax:* 604-682-8879
cristall@shawcable.com
www.personalinjurybc.com/en/

***Vancouver*: Harry Crosby - *1**
5052 Victoria Dr., Vancouver, BC V5P 3T8
Tel: 604-321-6922; *Fax:* 604-323-0093

***Vancouver*: Cruickshank Huinink Zukerman - *3**
#250, 1122 Mainland St., Vancouver, BC V6B 5L1
Tel: 604-688-3933; *Fax:* 604-681-6677
Toll-Free: 888-553-2450
www.chzlaw.ca

***Vancouver*: Cummings Law Corporation - *1**
#320, North Tower, 650 West 41st Ave., Vancouver, BC V5Z 2M9
Tel: 604-264-7038; *Fax:* 604-264-7039
info@cummingslawcorp.com

***Vancouver*: Barbara J. Curran**
#407, 825 Granville St., Vancouver, BC V6Z 1K9
Tel: 604-689-4501; *Fax:* 604-689-5572
bjcurran@telus.net

***Vancouver*: Cuttler & Company - *1**
#1801, Nelson Sq., P.O. Box 12184, Stn. Nelson Square, 808 Nelson St., Vancouver, BC V6Z 2H2
Tel: 604-673-4225; *Fax:* 604-633-1838
info@cuttlerlegal.com
cuttlerlegal.com

***Vancouver*: Aspha J. Dada & Co. - *2**
2479 Kingsway, Vancouver, BC V5R 5G8
Tel: 604-433-3300; *Fax:* 604-436-3937
info-ajd@telus.net

***Vancouver*: Arthur DeMeulemeester - *1**
#411, 119 Pender St. West, Vancouver, BC V6B 1S5
Tel: 604-685-6610; *Fax:* 604-682-5687

***Vancouver*: Derpak White Spencer LLP - *2**
#901, 1788 Broadway West, Vancouver, BC V6J 1Y1
Tel: 604-736-9791; *Fax:* 604-736-7197
ls@dwslaw.ca
www.dwslaw.ca

***Vancouver*: David H. Doig & Associates - *2**
#1450, 1188 Georgia St. West, Vancouver, BC V6E 4A2
Tel: 604-687-8874; *Fax:* 604-687-8134
Toll-Free: 877-687-8844
www.daviddoig.com

***Vancouver*: Dolden Wallace Folick LLP - Vancouver - *34**
609 Granville St., 18th Fl., Vancouver, BC V7Y 1G5
Tel: 604-689-3222; *Fax:* 604-689-3777
reception@dolden.com
www.dolden.com
twitter.com/DWFinsurancelaw, www.linkedin.com/company/dolden-wallace-folick-llp

***Vancouver*: Donovan & Company - *10**
73 Water St., 6th Fl., Vancouver, BC V6B 1A1
Tel: 604-688-4272; *Fax:* 604-688-4282
www.aboriginal-law.com

***Vancouver*: Emil M. Doricic - *1**
195 Alexander St., 2nd Fl., Vancouver, BC V6A 1B8
Tel: 604-688-8338; *Fax:* 604-688-8356

***Vancouver*: Le Dressay & Company - *1**
#103, 1525 - 8th Ave. West, Vancouver, BC V6J 1T5
Tel: 604-739-0017; *Fax:* 604-739-0041
dan@ledressay.com
www.ledressay.com

***Vancouver*: DuMoulin Boskovich LLP - *15**
#1800, Manulife Place, P.O. Box 52, 1095 West Pender St., Vancouver, BC V6E 2M6
Tel: 604-669-5500; *Fax:* 604-688-8491
Toll-Free: 800-288-9893
info@dubo.com
www.dubo.com
www.linkedin.com/company/2293070

***Vancouver*: Dunnaway Marnie - *2**
Former Name: Dunnaway, Jackson & Hamilton
#1205, 808 Nelson St., Vancouver, BC V6Z 2H2
Tel: 604-682-0007; *Fax:* 604-682-8711

***Vancouver*: Edwards, Kenny & Bray LLP - *23**
#1900, 1040 West Georgia St., Vancouver, BC V6E 4H3
Tel: 604-689-1811; *Fax:* 604-689-5177
inquiry@ekb.com
www.ekb.com

***Vancouver*: Ellis Business Lawyers - *3**
#440, 319 West Pender St., Vancouver, BC V6B 1T3
Tel: 604-688-7374; *Fax:* 604-688-7385
info@ellislawyers.com
www.ellislawyers.com

***Vancouver*: Ellis, Nauss & Jones - *2**
#600, 1665 West Broadway, Vancouver, BC V6J 1X1
Tel: 604-731-9276; *Fax:* 604-734-0206

***Vancouver*: Ellis, Roadburg - *2**
#200, 853 Richards St., Vancouver, BC V6B 3B4
Tel: 604-669-7131; *Fax:* 604-669-7684

***Vancouver*: Embarkation Law Group - *5**
Also Known As: Larson Sohn
#600, Princess Building, P.O. Box 26, 609 West Hastings St., 6th Fl., Vancouver, BC V6B 4W4
Tel: 604-628-6375; *Fax:* 604-662-7466
Toll-Free: 877-804-3230
info@elgcanada.com
www.elgcanada.com
www.facebook.com/163198040402130

***Vancouver*: Dick W. Eng Law Corp. - *1**
#701, 601 Broadway West, Vancouver, BC V5Z 4C2
Tel: 604-877-2689; *Fax:* 604-877-0330
dick_eng@telus.net

***Vancouver*: Epstein Law - *2**
Former Name: Epstein Wood
#1900, 1177 West Hastings St., Vancouver, BC V6E 2K3
Tel: 604-283-1012 *Toll-Free:* 800-836-9323
www.epsteinlawcorp.com

***Vancouver*: Robert J. Falconer, Q.C. - *1**
#400, 409 Granville St., Vancouver, BC V6C 1T2
Tel: 604-683-5674; *Fax:* 604-682-8417
robert.falconer@axion.net

***Vancouver*: Fan & Company - *1**
#601, 609 Gore Ave., Vancouver, BC V6A 2Z8
Tel: 604-682-2123; *Fax:* 604-683-8748
info@harryfan.com
www.harr fan.com

** indicates number of lawyers*

***Vancouver*: Farris, Vaughan, Wills & Murphy LLP - *80**
Pacific Centre South, P.O. Box 10026, 700 West Georgia St., 25th Floor, Vancouver, BC V7Y 1B3
Tel: 604-684-9151; *Fax:* 604-661-9349
Toll-Free: 877-684-9151
info@farris.com
www.farris.com
www.linkedin.com/company/farris-vaughan-wills-&-murphy-llp

***Vancouver*: Fayers & Company - *2**
#380, 5740 Cambie St., Vancouver, BC V5Z 3A6
Tel: 604-325-1246; *Fax:* 604-325-1261

***Vancouver*: Robert S. Fleming - *1**
#915, 925 West Georgia, Vancouver, BC V6C 3L2
Tel: 604-682-1659; *Fax:* 604-568-8548
robbie@fleminglawyer.com
www.robertflemingIawyer.com

***Vancouver*: Constance C. Fogal - *1**
3570 Hull St., Vancouver, BC V5N 4R9
Tel: 604-872-2128

***Vancouver*: Forrester & Company - *3**
#600, Randall Building, 555 West Georgia St., Vancouver, BC V6B 1Z6
Tel: 604-682-1066; *Fax:* 604-682-8036
www.forresterbarristers.ca

***Vancouver*: Fowler & Smith - *3**
#502, 602 West Hastings St., Vancouver, BC V6B 1P2
Tel: 604-684-1311; *Fax:* 604-681-9797
rfowler@fowlersmithlaw.com
fowlersmithlaw.com

***Vancouver*: Fraser & Company**
#1200, 999 Hastings St. West, Vancouver, BC V6C 2W2
Tel: 604-669-5244; *Fax:* 604-669-5791

***Vancouver*: Gordon J. Fretwell Law Corp. - *1**
#1780, 400 Burrard St., Vancouver, BC V6C 3A6
Tel: 604-689-1280; *Fax:* 604-689-1288

***Vancouver*: Friesen & Epp, Barristers & Solicitors - *4**
5660 Yew St., Vancouver, BC V6M 3Y3
Tel: 604-264-8386; *Fax:* 604-264-8815
eepp@friesenandepp.com
www.friesenandepp.com

***Vancouver*: Gall Legge Grant & Munroe LLP - *16**
1199 West Hastings St., 10th Fl., Vancouver, BC V6E 3T5
Tel: 604-669-0011
info@glgmlaw.com
www.glgmlaw.com

***Vancouver*: Ganapathi & Company - *2**
#302, 1224 Hamilton St., Vancouver, BC V6B 2S8
Tel: 604-689-9222; *Fax:* 604-689-4888
Toll-Free: 866-689-9222
info@ganapathico.com
www.ganapathico.com

***Vancouver*: Alnoor R.S. Gangji - *1**
#788, 601 West Broadway, Vancouver, BC V5Z 4C2
Tel: 604-708-3783; *Fax:* 604-876-9035
aglawyer@smartt.com

***Vancouver*: Robert G. Gateman - *1**
#202, 1112 Brougton St., Vancouver, BC V6G 2A8
Tel: 604-687-4911
robert.gateman@ubc.ca

***Vancouver*: Te Hennepe Gerrit - *1**
#203, 4545 West 10th Ave., Vancouver, BC V6R 4N2
Tel: 604-228-1433; *Fax:* 604-228-9822
tehennepe@telus.net

***Vancouver*: Getz Prince Wells LLP - *5**
#530, 355 Burrard St., Vancouver, BC V6C 2G8
Tel: 604-685-6367; *Fax:* 604-685-9798
www.getzpw.com

***Vancouver*: Kenneth Glasner Q.C. Law Corp. - *1**
#318, 1275 West 6th Ave., Vancouver, BC V6H 1A6
Tel: 604-683-4181; *Fax:* 604-683-0226
glasnerqc@telus.net
glasnerqc.tripod.com

***Vancouver*: Goldman Zimmer Bray - *3**
Former Name: Goldman Lakhani Zimmer Bray
#950, 1111 Melville St., Vancouver, BC V6E 3V6
Tel: 604-682-6181; *Fax:* 604-683-5723
ezimmer@goldmath.com
www.goldmanzimmer.com

***Vancouver*: Paul D. Gornall - *1**
#1820, 355 Burrard St., Vancouver, BC V6C 2G8
Tel: 604-681-7932; *Fax:* 604-775-8555
pdg@telus.net

***Vancouver*: Granger & Co. - *2**
#1400, 777 Hornby St., Vancouver, BC V6Z 1S4
Tel: 604-685-1900; *Fax:* 604-685-2034

***Vancouver*: Granville Law Group - *2**
Former Name: Vertlieb Anderson
#200, 835 Granville St., Vancouver, BC V6Z 1K7
Tel: 604-669-6580; *Fax:* 604-688-7291

***Vancouver*: Grossman & Stanley - *3**
#800, Box 55, 1090 West Georgia St., Vancouver, BC V6E 3V7
Tel: 604-683-7454; *Fax:* 604-683-8602
info@grossmanstanley.com
www.grossmanstanley.com

***Vancouver*: Gudmundseth Mickelson LLP - *7**
#2525, 1075 West Georgia St., Vancouver, BC V6E 3C9
Tel: 604-685-6272; *Fax:* 604-685-8434
info@lawgm.com
www.lawgm.com

***Vancouver*: Wayne F. Guinn - *1**
671G Market Hill, Vancouver, BC V5Z 4B5
Tel: 604-872-6658; *Fax:* 604-876-3304

***Vancouver*: Guy & Company - *1**
#100, 190 Alexander St., Vancouver, BC V6A 1B5
Tel: 604-681-6164; *Fax:* 604-681-7420
guy_and_company@telus.net

***Vancouver*: Hammerberg Lawyers LLP - *17**
#1220, Airport Square, 1200 West 73rd Ave., Vancouver, BC V6P 6G5
Tel: 604-269-8500; *Fax:* 604-269-8511
Toll-Free: 888-529-5544
www.hammerco.net

***Vancouver*: Hara & Company - *2**
#301, 460 Nanaimo St., Vancouver, BC V5L 4W3
Tel: 604-255-4800; *Fax:* 604-255-8111
haraco@telus.net

***Vancouver*: Harper Grey LLP - *55**
Former Name: Harper Grey Easton
#3200, Vancouver Centre, 650 West Georgia St., Vancouver, BC V6B 4P7
Tel: 604-687-0411; *Fax:* 604-669-9385
info@harpergrey.com
www.harpergrey.com
twitter.com/harpergreyllp, www.linkedin.com/company/143149

***Vancouver*: Harris & Brun - *7**
#500, 555 West Georgia St., Vancouver, BC V6B 1Z5
Tel: 604-683-2466; *Fax:* 604-683-4541
www.harrisbrun.com

***Vancouver*: Harris & Company LLP - *38**
Bentall 5, 550 Burrard St., 14th Floor, Vancouver, BC V6C 2B5
Tel: 604-684-6633; *Fax:* 604-684-6632
info@harrisco.com
www.harrisco.com

***Vancouver*: John E. Helsing - *1**
#347, 1275 West 6th Ave., Vancouver, BC V6H 1A6
Tel: 604-739-7731; *Fax:* 604-738-7134

***Vancouver*: D. Brad Henry Law Corporation - *1**
Former Name: Epstein Wood
#1900, 1177 West Hastings St., Vancouver, BC V6E 2K3
Tel: 604-718-6891; *Fax:* 604-718-6873
bhenry@dbhlaw.ca

***Vancouver*: Hobbs Giroday - *4**
#908, 938 Howe St., Vancouver, BC V6Z 1N9
Tel: 604-669-6609; *Fax:* 604-669-6612
info@hobbsgiroday.com
www.hobbsgiroday.com
www.linkedin.com/company/2954352

***Vancouver*: Hogan & Company - *1**
#1730, 355 Burrard St., Vancouver, BC V6C 2G8
Tel: 604-687-8806; *Fax:* 604-687-7089

***Vancouver*: Holmes & Company - *2**
Former Name: Holmes & Greenslade
#1880, Oceanic Plaza, 1066 Hastings St. West, Vancouver, BC V6E 3X1
Tel: 604-688-7861; *Fax:* 604-688-0426
www.holmescompany.com
www.linkedin.com/company/holmes-and-company

***Vancouver*: Holmes & King - *4**
#1300, 1111 Georgia St. West, Vancouver, BC V6E 4M3
Tel: 604-681-1310; *Fax:* 604-681-1307
lawyers@mhklaw.com
www.holmesandking.com
www.facebook.com/pages/Holmes-and-King-Law/262297667115077, www.twitter.com/HolmesandKing, www.linkedin.com/pub/robert-holmes/22/4b1/68b

***Vancouver*: Hoogbruin & Company - *6**
#650, 1188 West Georgia St., Vancouver, BC V6E 4A2
Tel: 604-609-3783; *Fax:* 604-682-8348
www.hoogbruin.com

***Vancouver*: Hordo Bennett Mounteer LLP - *7**
Former Name: McAlpine & Hordo
#1400, Sun Tower Building, 128 West Pender St., Vancouver, BC V6B 1R8
Tel: 604-639-3680; *Fax:* 604-639-3681
info@complexlitigation.ca
www.complexlitigation.ca
twitter.com/HBMLaw

***Vancouver*: Wayne Hum & Co. - *1**
#1608, 1166 Alberni St., Vancouver, BC V6E 3Z3
Tel: 604-687-6806; *Fax:* 604-687-6809

***Vancouver*: Hunter Litigation Chambers - *22**
Former Name: Hunter Voith
#2100, 1040 West Georgia St., Vancouver, BC V6E 4H1
Tel: 604-891-2400; *Fax:* 604-647-4554
www.litigationchambers.com

***Vancouver*: Irwin, White & Jennings - *3**
Also Known As: Irwin, White & Jennings
Former Name: Alex Irwin Law Corp.
#2020, 1055 West Georgia St., Vancouver, BC V6E 3R5
Tel: 604-664-3723; *Fax:* 604-689-2806
www.iwjlaw.com

***Vancouver*: Law Offices of Jonathan J. Israels - *1**
#760, 475 West Georgia St., Vancouver, BC V6B 4M9
Tel: 604-488-1313
info@CriminalLawyerVancouver.ca
www.criminallawyervancouver.ca

***Vancouver*: Donald Jang - *1**
#701, 601 West Broadway, Vancouver, BC V5Z 4C2
Tel: 604-877-0880; *Fax:* 604-877-0330

***Vancouver*: Jarvis McGee Rice LLP - *7**
Former Name: Jarvis Burns McGee
#600, 1125 Howe St., Vancouver, BC V6Z 2K8
Tel: 604-682-3771; *Fax:* 604-682-0587
www.jarvismcgee.com
www.facebook.com/pages/Jarvis-McGee-Rice/200219480010862, twitter.com/icbccases, www.linkedin.com/company/jarvis-mcgee-rice

***Vancouver*: Jeffery & Calder - *5**
#601, 815 Hornby St., Vancouver, BC V6Z 2E6
Tel: 604-669-5534; *Fax:* 604-669-7563
contact@jefferycalder.com
www.jefferycalder.com

***Vancouver*: Jenkins Marzban Logan LLP - *19**
#900, 808 Nelson St., Vancouver, BC V6Z 2H2
Tel: 604-681-6564; *Fax:* 604-681-0766
info@jml.ca
www.jml.ca

***Vancouver*: J. Douglas Jevning - *1**
#420, The Standard Bldg., 625 Howe St., Vancouver, BC V6C 2T6
Tel: 604-688-7414; *Fax:* 604-688-6243
doug_jevning@telus.net

** indicates number of lawyers*

***Vancouver*: Josephson Litigation Counsel - *1**
Former Name: Josephson Associates Barristers; Josephson & Company
#906, Cathedral Pl., 925 West Georgia St., Vancouver, BC V6C 3L2
Tel: 604-684-9887; *Fax:* 604-684-3221
info@josephlitigation.ca
www.josephlitigation.ca
twitter.com/jabarristers,

***Vancouver*: Steven B. Jung - *1**
#701, 601 Broadway West, Vancouver, BC V5Z 4C2
Tel: 604-877-2684; *Fax:* 604-877-0330
stevenjung@telus.net

***Vancouver*: Ramzan N. Jussa - *1**
#204, 4676 Main St., Vancouver, BC V5V 3R7
Tel: 604-872-8191; *Fax:* 604-872-8217

***Vancouver*: Kaplan & Waddell - *3**
#102, 2590 Granville St., Vancouver, BC V6H 3H1
Tel: 604-736-8021; *Fax:* 604-736-3845
duffwaddell@kaplanwaddell.com
kaplanwaddell.com

***Vancouver*: David J. Karp Law Corporation - *1**
Former Name: Myers, Waddell, McMurdo & Karp
195 Alexander St., 5th Fl., Vancouver, BC V6A 1B8
Tel: 604-800-2686; *Fax:* 604-688-8350
Toll-Free: 877-421-4404
www.vancouverdefencelawyer.com

***Vancouver*: Katz & Company - *1**
#1018, Nelson Square, P.O. Box 12135, 808 Nelson St., Vancouver, BC V6Z 2H2
Tel: 604-669-6226; *Fax:* 604-669-6752

***Vancouver*: Peter M. Kendall - *1**
#850, 475 Georgia St. West, Vancouver, BC V6B 4M9
Tel: 604-685-3512; *Fax:* 604-681-9142

***Vancouver*: C. Robert Kennedy - *1**
#206, 190 Alexander St., Vancouver, BC V6A 1B5
Tel: 604-684-3927; *Fax:* 604-684-3228

***Vancouver*: Kerfoot Burroughs LLP - *7**
#300, 5687 Yew St., Vancouver, BC V6M 3Y2
Tel: 604-263-2565; *Fax:* 604-263-2737
www.kblawllp.com

***Vancouver*: Khanna & Co. - *3**
#1540, 1100 Melville St., Vancouver, BC V6E 4A6
Tel: 604-605-5500; *Fax:* 604-689-5596
khanna-law.com

***Vancouver*: Killam Cordell - *5**
#2000, 401 Georgia St. West, Vancouver, BC V6B 5A1
Tel: 604-622-5252; *Fax:* 604-622-5244

***Vancouver*: William N. King - *1**
5650 Kullahun Dr., Vancouver, BC V6N 2E5
Tel: 604-682-1245; *Fax:* 604-682-8417

***Vancouver*: Klein Lyons - *11**
#400, 1385 - 8th Ave. West, Vancouver, BC V6H 3V9
Tel: 604-874-7171; *Fax:* 604-874-7180
info@kleinlyons.com
www.kleinlyons.com
www.facebook.com/KleinLyons

***Vancouver*: Koffman Kalef LLP - *23**
885 West Georgia St., 19th Fl., Vancouver, BC V6C 3H4
Tel: 604-891-3688; *Fax:* 604-891-3788
info@kkbl.com
www.kkbl.com

***Vancouver*: Dimitri A. Kontou - *1**
#1550, 355 Burrard St., Vancouver, BC V6G 2C8
Tel: 604-662-7244; *Fax:* 604-687-3097
dkontou@telus.net
www.kontoulawcorporation.com
www.facebook.com/pages/Dimitri-Kontou-Law-Corporation/1481 98608576718, twitter.com/kontoulaw

***Vancouver*: Gordon Kopelow Law Offices - *2**
#208, 2475 Bayswater St., Vancouver, BC V6K 4N3
Tel: 604-684-0096; *Fax:* 604-734-0057
www.gordonjkopelow.com

***Vancouver*: Kornfeld & Company - *2**
#640, 943 West Broadway, Vancouver, BC V5Z 4E1
Tel: 604-689-3838; *Fax:* 604-689-0526

***Vancouver*: Kornfeld LLP - *15**
Former Name: Kornfeld Mackoff Silber LLP
#1100, Bentall Centre, P.O. Box 11, 505 Burrard St., Vancouver, BC V7X 1M5
Tel: 604-331-8300; *Fax:* 604-683-0570
info@kornfeldllp.com
www.kornfeldllp.com

***Vancouver*: Ron Y. Kornfeld - *1**
#630, Broadway Medical Bldg., 943 Broadway West, Vancouver, BC V5Z 4E1
Tel: 604-733-2448; *Fax:* 604-736-5131
rykornfeld@telus.net

***Vancouver*: Yoke Lam - *1**
#328, 88 East Pender St., Vancouver, BC V6A 1T1
Tel: 604-689-1123; *Fax:* 604-689-2003

***Vancouver*: Lando & Company LLP - *8**
#2010, Royal Centre, P.O. Box 11140, 1055 West Georgia St., Vancouver, BC V6E 3P3
Tel: 604-682-6821; *Fax:* 604-662-8293
www.lando.ca

***Vancouver*: Georgialee A. Lee & Associates - *4**
#1201, P.O. Box 12163, 808 Nelson St., Vancouver, BC V6Z 2H2
Tel: 604-669-2030; *Fax:* 604-669-2038
glang@georgialeelang.com

***Vancouver*: Laughton & Company - *2**
#1090, 1090 Georgia St. West, Vancouver, BC V6E 3V7
Tel: 604-683-6665; *Fax:* 604-683-6622

***Vancouver*: Laxton Gibbens & Company - *2**
Former Name: Laxton & Company
#1119, 808 Nelson St., Vancouver, BC V6Z 2H2
Tel: 604-682-3871; *Fax:* 604-682-3704
rgibbens@laxtonco.com
www.laxtongibbens.com

***Vancouver*: Valmon J. LeBlanc - *1**
#1400, 1125 Howe St., Vancouver, BC V6Z 2K8
Tel: 604-687-0909; *Fax:* 604-688-0933
vleblanc@domuslegis.com

***Vancouver*: Ledding Richard Law - *2**
#415, 1788 - 5th Ave. West, Vancouver, BC V6J 1P2
Tel: 604-731-1161; *Fax:* 604-731-6527

***Vancouver*: Lesperance Mendes - *7**
#410, 900 Howe St., Vancouver, BC V6Z 2M4
Tel: 604-685-3567; *Fax:* 604-685-7505
admin@lmlaw.ca
www.lmlaw.ca

***Vancouver*: Lew & Lee - *2**
#108, 329 Main St., Vancouver, BC V6A 2S9
Tel: 604-685-8331; *Fax:* 604-685-8334

***Vancouver*: Chuck Lew - *1**
#1010, 207 Hastings St. West, Vancouver, BC V6B 1H7
Tel: 604-688-3601; *Fax:* 604-688-7866
lewlaw@uniserve.com

***Vancouver*: Lex Pacifica Law Corporation - *3**
Former Name: John H. Shevchuk, Law Corporation
#1000, 543 Granville St., Vancouver, BC V6C 1X8
Tel: 604-689-1024; *Fax:* 604-689-1028
johnshevchuk@lexpacifica.com
www.lexpacifica.com

***Vancouver*: Carey Linde Personal Law Corporation - *2**
Also Known As: Divorce for Men
#605, 1080 Howe St., Vancouver, BC V6Z 2T1
Tel: 604-684-7794; *Fax:* 604-682-1243
lawyer@divorce-for-men.com
www.divorce-for-men.com
www.facebook.com/pages/Divorce-For-Men/201662089890907, twitter.com/Divorce_For_Men

***Vancouver*: Lindsay Kenney LLP - Vancouver - *35**
Also Known As: LK Law
#1800, 401 West Georgia St., Vancouver, BC V6B 5A1
Tel: 604-687-1323; *Fax:* 604-687-2347
Toll-Free: 866-687-1323
info@lklaw.ca
www.lklaw.ca

***Vancouver*: Lipetz & Company - *1**
#202, 2902 West Broadway, Vancouver, BC V6K 2G8
Tel: 604-733-5611; *Fax:* 604-738-5611

***Vancouver*: Keith A. Lo - *2**
#338, 237 Keefer St., Vancouver, BC V6A 1X6
Tel: 604-687-4315; *Fax:* 604-681-2289

***Vancouver*: Logan & Company**
#1119, 808 Nelson St., Vancouver, BC V6Z 2H2
Tel: 604-682-8521; *Fax:* 604-682-8753

***Vancouver*: Loh & Company - *4**
#802, 1788 West Broadway, Vancouver, BC V6J 1Y1
Tel: 604-261-1234; *Fax:* 604-261-1222
general@lohandco.com
lohandco.com

***Vancouver*: Ralph H. Long - *1**
865 - 46th Ave. West, Vancouver, BC V5Z 2R4
Tel: 604-876-0492; *Fax:* 604-876-3219
rhlong@shaw.ca

***Vancouver*: Lowe & Company - *5**
#900, 777 West Broadway, Vancouver, BC V5Z 4J7
Tel: 604-875-9338; *Fax:* 604-875-1325
info@canadavisalaw.com
www.canadavisalaw.com

***Vancouver*: Phillip R. Lundrie - *2**
#3, 2597 Hastings St. East, Vancouver, BC V5K 1Z2
Tel: 604-257-3588; *Fax:* 604-257-3511
www.lundrielaw.com

***Vancouver*: Lyons Hamilton - *4**
#404, 815 Hornby St., Vancouver, BC V6Z 2E6
Tel: 604-684-6718; *Fax:* 604-684-2501

***Vancouver*: Macaulay McColl LLP - *9**
#600, 840 Howe St., Vancouver, BC V6Z 2L2
Tel: 604-687-9811; *Fax:* 604-687-8716
Toll-Free: 800-233-4405

***Vancouver*: Macdonald Fahey - *2**
Former Name: Epstein Wood
#1900, 1177 West Hastings St., Vancouver, BC V6E 2K3
Tel: 604-718-6869; *Fax:* 604-629-2175
www.macdonaldfahey.com

***Vancouver*: MacKenzie Fujisawa LLP - *21**
#1600, 1095 West Pender St., Vancouver, BC V6E 2M6
Tel: 604-689-3281; *Fax:* 604-685-6494
lawyers@maclaw.bc.ca
www.mackenziefujisawa.com

***Vancouver*: MacKinlay Woodson Diebel - *2**
#1170, 1040 West Georgia St., Vancouver, BC V6E 4H1
Tel: 604-669-1511; *Fax:* 604-669-1566
corp@woodsonlaw.bc.ca

***Vancouver*: M. Diane MacKinnon - *1**
#2077, 37th Av.e. West, Vancouver, BC V6M 1N7
Tel: 604-263-7891; *Fax:* 604-263-5781
mdmac@telus.net

***Vancouver*: MacLean Family Law Group - *14**
Former Name: MacLean Nicol
#2010, 1075 West Georgia St., Vancouver, BC V6E 3C9
Tel: 604-602-9000; *Fax:* 604-682-0556
info@bcfamilylaw.ca
www.bcfamilylaw.ca

***Vancouver*: MacLeod & Company - *4**
#1900, 777 Hornby St., Vancouver, BC V6Z 1S4
Tel: 604-687-7287; *Fax:* 604-682-2534
Toll-Free: 866-997-7287
info@macleodlaw.com
www.macleodlaw.com

***Vancouver*: Morag M.J. MacLeod - *1**
#800, The Randall Building, 555 West Georgia St. West, Vancouver, BC V6B 1Z6
Tel: 604-430-8444; *Fax:* 604-430-1164
mmacleod@celtlaw.com

***Vancouver*: Martland & Saulnier Criminal Defence Counsel - *4**
Former Name: Smart & Williams
#506, 815 Hornby St., Vancouver, BC V6Z 2E6
Tel: 604-687-6278; *Fax:* 604-687-6298
vancrimlaw.com

***Vancouver*: Matthew Nathanson Law - *3**
#1000, Marine Building, 355 Burrard St., Vancouver, BC V6C 7G8
Tel: 604-608-6185; *Fax:* 604-677-5560
matthew@mnlaw.ca
www.mnlaw.ca

** indicates number of lawyers*

***Vancouver*: Maxwell Bulmer Hopman - *4**
#310, 1152 Mainland St., Vancouver, BC V6B 4X2
Tel: 604-669-1106

***Vancouver*: Joanne S. McClusky - *1**
#810, 675 Hastings St. West, Vancouver, BC V6B 1N2
Tel: 604-689-4010; *Fax:* 604-684-2349
jmcclusky@telus.net

***Vancouver*: McComb Witten - Vancouver - *8**
#210, 2730 Commercial Dr., Vancouver, BC V5N 5P4
Tel: 604-255-9018; *Fax:* 604-255-8588
info@mmw.bc.ca
www.mccombwitten.com
www.facebook.com/McCombWitten,
twitter.com/McComb_Witten

***Vancouver*: McCrea & Associates - *4**
#102, 1012 Beach Ave., Vancouver, BC V6E 1T7
Tel: 604-662-8200; *Fax:* 604-662-8225
lawyers@mccrealaw.ca
www.mccrealaw.ca

***Vancouver*: McCullough O'Connor Irwin LLP - *15**
Also Known As: MOI Solicitors
#2600, Oceanic Plaza, 1066 West Hastings St., Vancouver, BC V6E 3X1
Tel: 604-687-7077; *Fax:* 604-687-7099
moimail@moisolicitors.com
www.moisolicitors.com

***Vancouver*: Ruth E. McIntyre - *1**
#1520, 355 Burrard St., Vancouver, BC V6C 2G8
Tel: 604-688-5185; *Fax:* 604-688-5186
www.rmcintyre.com

***Vancouver*: McKenzie & Company - *2**
891 Helmcken St., Vancouver, BC V6Z 1B1
Tel: 604-687-7811; *Fax:* 604-685-4358
lawfirm@mckenzie-co.com

***Vancouver*: McLachlan Brown Anderson - *7**
938 Howe St., 10th Fl., Vancouver, BC V6Z 1N9
Tel: 604-331-6000; *Fax:* 604-331-6008
mbalawyers.ca

***Vancouver*: Bruce E. McLeod - *1**
#1120, 1040 Georgia St. West, Vancouver, BC V6E 4H1
Tel: 604-682-3133; *Fax:* 604-682-3161
bmcleod1@telus.net

***Vancouver*: McNeney & McNeney - *7**
#900, 1080 Howe St., Vancouver, BC V6Z 2T1
Tel: 604-867-1766; *Fax:* 604-687-0181
Toll-Free: 800-535-6565
info@McNeneyMcNeney.com
www.mcneneymcneney.com

***Vancouver*: Megan Ellis & Company - *2**
Former Name: Stowe Ellis
#700, 555 Georgia St. West, Vancouver, BC V6B 1Z6
Tel: 604-683-7144; *Fax:* 604-683-0207
info@ellisandcompany.ca
www.ellisandcompany.ca

***Vancouver*: MetroWest Law Corporation - *3**
#801, 938 Howe St., Vancouver, BC V6Z 1N9
Tel: 604-428-2211; *Fax:* 604-428-2212
www.vancouver-realestate-lawyer.com
www.facebook.com/metrowest.law, twitter.com/metrowestlaw,
ca.linkedin.com/in/metrowestlaw

***Vancouver*: Mickelson & Company Law Corporation - *2**
Sun Tower, 128 West Pender St., 10th Fl., Vancouver, BC V6B 1R8
Tel: 604-688-8588; *Fax:* 604-637-1617
Toll-Free: 866-688-8588
info@mwcrimlaw.com
www.criminallawyervancouver.com

***Vancouver*: John L. Mickelson - *7**
#300, 1120 Hamilton St., Vancouver, BC V6B 2S2
Tel: 604-684-0040; *Fax:* 604-684-0048
info@personalinjurylawbc.com
www.personalinjurylawbc.com

***Vancouver*: Miller Titerle LLP - *8**
#215, 209 Carrall St., Vancouver, BC V6B 2J2
Tel: 604-681-4112; *Fax:* 604-681-4113
info@millertiterle.com
www.millertiterle.com

***Vancouver*: Michael Mines - *2**
#1550, 355 Burrard St., Vancouver, BC V6C 2G8
Tel: 604-484-1940; *Fax:* 604-687-3097
Toll-Free: 877-467-1804
www.mineslaw.com

***Vancouver*: Morris & Co. - *2**
#460, 850 West Hastings St., Vancouver, BC V6C 1E1
Tel: 604-685-5175; *Fax:* 604-669-2744
info@vancouvermorrismen.org
www.vancouvermorrismen.org

***Vancouver*: Don Morrison - *1**
#1109, 207 West Hastings St., Vancouver, BC V6B 1H7
Tel: 604-685-7097; *Fax:* 604-662-7511
don.morrison@telus.net
www.donmorrisonlaw.com

***Vancouver*: Edward M. Mortimer, QC - *2**
#920, 777 Hornby St., Vancouver, BC V6Z 1S4
Tel: 604-669-0440; *Fax:* 604-669-0228

***Vancouver*: Murdy & McAllister - *7**
#1155, Two Bentall Centre, P.O. Box 49059, Stn. Bentall, 555 Burrard St., Vancouver, BC V7X 1C4
Tel: 604-689-5263; *Fax:* 604-689-9029
www.murdymcallister.com

***Vancouver*: Murphy Battista LLP - *12**
#2020, P.O. Box 11547, 650 West Georgia St., Vancouver, BC V6B 4N7
Tel: 604-683-9621; *Fax:* 604-683-5084
Toll-Free: 888-683-9621
www.murphybattista.com

***Vancouver*: Murray Jamieson Barristers & Solicitors - *4**
#200, 1152 Mainland St., Vancouver, BC V6B 4X2
Tel: 604-688-0777; *Fax:* 604-688-9700
www.murrayjamieson.com

***Vancouver*: James B. Myers Law Corporation - *1**
#619, 610 Granville St., Vancouver, BC V6C 3T3
Tel: 604-682-8670; *Fax:* 604-682-2348
myerslaw@telus.net

***Vancouver*: Nathanson, Schachter & Thompson LLP - *8**
#750, 900 Howe St., Vancouver, BC V6Z 2M4
Tel: 604-662-8840; *Fax:* 604-684-1598
info@nst.bc.ca
www.nst.bc.ca

***Vancouver*: Nexus Law Group LLP - *4**
777 Hornby St., Vancouver, BC V6Z 1S4
Tel: 604-689-1622; *Fax:* 604-689-8300
info@nexuslaw.ca
www.nexuslaw.ca

***Vancouver*: Ng Ariss Fong - *5**
Former Name: Ng & Ariss
#210, P.O. Box 160, 900 Howe St., Vancouver, BC V6Z 2M4
Tel: 604-331-1155; *Fax:* 604-677-5410
general@ngariss.com
www.ngariss.com

***Vancouver*: Kimball R. Nichols - *1**
1591 Bowser Ave., Vancouver, BC V7P 2Y4
Tel: 604-682-0541; *Fax:* 604-924-5541

***Vancouver*: Northwest Law Group**
Former Name: O'Neill & Company
#704, 595 Howe St., Vancouver, BC V6C 2T5
Tel: 604-687-5792; *Fax:* 604-687-6650

***Vancouver*: Norton Stewart Business Lawyers - *3**
#1850, Manulife Place, 1095 West Pender St., Vancouver, BC V6E 2M6
Tel: 604-687-0555; *Fax:* 604-689-1248
info@nortonstewart.com
www.nortonstewart.com

***Vancouver*: Glen Orris Q.C. Law Corporation - *1**
#500, 815 Hornby St., Vancouver, BC V6Z 2E6
Tel: 604-669-6711; *Fax:* 604-669-5180
glen@orrislawcorp.com
www.orrislawcorp.com

***Vancouver*: Osten & Osten**
#356, P.O. Box 11113, 5740 Cambie St., Vancouver, BC V6E 3A6
Tel: 604-683-9104; *Fax:* 604-688-0034

***Vancouver*: Owen Bird Law Corporation - *43**
#2900, Three Bentall Centre, P.O. Box 49130, 595 Burrard St., Vancouver, BC V7X 1J5
Tel: 604-688-0401; *Fax:* 604-688-2827
inquiries@owenbird.com
www.owenbird.com

***Vancouver*: Oyen Wiggs Green & Mutala LLP - *14**
#480, The Station, 601 West Cordova St., Vancouver, BC V6B 1G1
Tel: 604-669-3432; *Fax:* 604-681-4081
Toll-Free: 866-475-2922
mail@patentable.com
www.patentable.com

***Vancouver*: Paine Edmonds LLP - *14**
#1100, 510 Burrard St., Vancouver, BC V6C 3A8
Tel: 604-683-1211; *Fax:* 604-681-5084
Toll-Free: 800-669-8599
law@paine-edmonds.com
www.paine-edmonds.com

***Vancouver*: Pape Salter Teillet LLP - *7**
#460, 220 Cambie St., Vancouver, BC V6B 2M9
Tel: 604-681-3002; *Fax:* 604-681-3050
www.pstlaw.ca

***Vancouver*: Peck & Company - *9**
#610, 744 Hastings St. West, Vancouver, BC V6C 1A5
Tel: 604-669-0208; *Fax:* 604-669-0616
hmoore@peckandcompany.ca
www.peckandcompany.ca

***Vancouver*: Peter Altridge Mediation Services - *1**
Former Name: Altridge & Company
#741, 1489 Marine Dr., Vancouver, BC V7T 1B8
Tel: 604-688-3557; *Fax:* 604-688-0535
pga@altridge.com
www.altridge.com

***Vancouver*: Donald B. Phelps - *1**
#1200, 805 Broadway West, Vancouver, BC V5Z 1K1
Tel: 604-736-3722; *Fax:* 604-736-3725
www.donphelpsfamilylawvancouver.ca

***Vancouver*: Pierce Law Group - *2**
#850, 475 Georgia St. West, Vancouver, BC V6B 4M9
Tel: 604-681-4434; *Fax:* 604-681-9142
contact@bcdisabilitylaw.com
www.bcdisabilitylaw.com

***Vancouver*: Vincent E. Pigeon - *1**
#410, 688 Hastings St. West, Vancouver, BC V6B 1P1
Tel: 604-684-2889; *Fax:* 604-685-2900
vpigeon@telus.net
www.vincentpigeonlawyer.com

***Vancouver*: Sarah B. Pollard - *1**
#400, 1681 Chestnut St., Vancouver, BC V6J 4M6
Tel: 604-732-5667; *Fax:* 604-732-1262
lawoffice@sprint.ca

***Vancouver*: Lianne Potter Law Corporation - *1**
#218, 470 Granville St., Vancouver, BC V6C 1V5
Tel: 604-662-8373; *Fax:* 604-662-8321
lpotter@lwp-lawcorp.com

***Vancouver*: Poulsen & Co. - *3**
#1800, 999 West Hastings St., Vancouver, BC V6C 2W2
Tel: 604-681-0123; *Fax:* 604-683-1375
info@poulsenlaw.com
www.poulsenlaw.com

***Vancouver*: Quinlan Abrioux - *12**
Also Known As: QA Law
#1510, TD Tower, P.O. Box 10031, Stn. Pacific Centre, 700 West Georgia St., Vancouver, BC V7Y 1A1
Tel: 604-687-3711; *Fax:* 604-687-3741
Toll-Free: 877-545-9486
www.qalaw.com

***Vancouver*: Radelet & Company - *2**
#1625, 1075 Georgia St. West, Vancouver, BC V6E 3C9
Tel: 604-689-0878; *Fax:* 604-689-1386
james@radelet.com

***Vancouver*: Richard Raibmon - *1**
#560, 1125 Howe St., Vancouver, BC V6Z 2K8
Tel: 604-688-8551; *Fax:* 604-687-1799
rlrlaw@uniserve.com
richardraibmon.com

***Vancouver*: Rao McKercher & Co. - *2**
#908, 510 Burrard St., Vancouver, BC V6C 3A8
Tel: 604-664-7474; *Fax:* 604-664-7477

** indicates number of lawyers*

***Vancouver*: Raphanel & Courtenay - *2**
Former Name: Gayle M. Raphanel
#1160, 777 Hornby St., Vancouver, BC V6Z 1S4
Tel: 604-682-2200; *Fax:* 604-682-2246

***Vancouver*: Richards Buell Sutton LLP - *43**
#700, 401 West Georgia St., Vancouver, BC V6B 5A1
Tel: 604-682-3664; *Fax:* 604-688-3830
info@rbs.ca
www.rbs.ca

***Vancouver*: Ritchie Sandford - *2**
#502, 602 Hastings St. West, Vancouver, BC V6B 1P2
Tel: 604-684-0778; *Fax:* 604-684-0799

***Vancouver*: Roberts & Stahl - *4**
#500, 220 Cambie St., Vancouver, BC V6B 2M9
Tel: 604-684-6377; *Fax:* 604-684-6387
paulcoastmicro1.mydomain.com/robertsstahl/home.htm

***Vancouver*: Rogers, Bobert & Burton - *3**
#707, 1281 West Georgia St., Vancouver, BC V6E 3J7
Tel: 604-681-5600; *Fax:* 604-681-1475
info@rbblaw.ca
rbblaw.ca

***Vancouver*: Roper Greyell LLP, Employment & Labour Lawyers - *24**
Former Name: Greyell MacPhail
#800, Park Place, 666 Burrard St., Vancouver, BC V6C 3P3
Tel: 604-806-0922; *Fax:* 604-806-0933
info@ropergreyell.com
www.ropergreyell.com
twitter.com/RoperGreyell,
www.linkedin.com/company/roper-greyell-llp

***Vancouver*: Rosenberg & Rosenberg - *4**
671D Market Hill, Vancouver, BC V5Z 4B5
Tel: 604-879-4505; *Fax:* 604-879-4934
reception@rosenberglaw.ca
www.rosenberglaw.ca

***Vancouver*: J. Herbert Rosner - *1**
#770, 475 Georgia St. West, Vancouver, BC V6B 4M9
Tel: 604-687-6638; *Fax:* 604-682-2481
roslaw@telus.net

***Vancouver*: Robert D. Ross Q.C. - *1**
4741 West 2 Ave., Vancouver, BC V6T 1C1
Tel: 604-228-9701; *Fax:* 604-228-9055

***Vancouver*: Howard Rubin Law Corp. - *1**
405E - 4 St., Vancouver, BC V7L 1J4
Tel: 604-984-2030; *Fax:* 604-988-0068
howard@howard-rubin.com

***Vancouver*: RWE Law Corporation - *3**
Also Known As: Robert W. Evans Law Corpoartion
#1700, 808 Nelson St., Vancouver, BC V6Z 2H2
Tel: 778-899-7028; *Fax:* 604-608-5385
info@rwelaw.ca
www.rwelaw.ca

***Vancouver*: Morrie Sacks Law Corporation - *1**
#207, 1525 - 8th Ave. West, Vancouver, BC V6T 1T5
Tel: 604-685-7629; *Fax:* 604-685-7630

***Vancouver*: Salley Bowes Harwardt Law Corp. - *4**
#1750, 1185 Georgia St. West, Vancouver, BC V6E 4E6
Tel: 604-688-0788; *Fax:* 604-688-0778
www.sbh.bc.ca

***Vancouver*: Gary M. Salloum - *1**
286 - 21st Ave. West, Vancouver, BC V5Y 2E5

***Vancouver*: Gregory L. Samuels - *1**
#204, 1730 - 2nd Ave. West, Vancouver, BC V6J 1H6
Tel: 604-636-9157
gls@borderlaw.com

***Vancouver*: Charles A. Sandberg - *1**
#108, 2786 - 16 Ave. West, Vancouver, BC V6K 4M1
Tel: 604-734-7768; *Fax:* 604-733-1229

***Vancouver*: Michael D. Sanders - *1**
811 Drake St., Vancouver, BC V6Z 1C1
Tel: 604-669-5005; *Fax:* 604-669-1334
Toll-Free: 888-778-8803
www.sanderscriminallaw.com

***Vancouver*: Sangra Moller LLP - *12**
#1000, Cathedral Pl., 925 Georgia St. West, Vancouver, BC V6C 3L2
Tel: 604-662-8808; *Fax:* 604-669-8803
www.sangramoller.com

***Vancouver*: Scarlett Manson Angus - *4**
#1200, 777 Hornby St., Vancouver, BC V6Z 1S4
Tel: 604-684-4777; *Fax:* 604-684-7773
lawfirm@smalaw.com

***Vancouver*: Antya Schrack - *1**
#116, 970 Burrard St., Vancouver, BC V6Z 2R4
Tel: 604-682-2078; *Fax:* 604-682-6697
aschrack@immigrate-to-canada.ca
www.immigrate-to-canada.ca

***Vancouver*: Schuman Daltrop Basran & Robin - *8**
#1200, 777 Hornby St., Vancouver, BC V6Z 1S4
Tel: 604-669-4912; *Fax:* 604-669-4911
www.sdbrlaw.com

***Vancouver*: David A. Schwartz - *1**
#600, 890 West Pender St., Vancouver, BC V6C 1J9
Tel: 604-687-0811; *Fax:* 604-687-1327
Toll-Free: 855-687-0811
schwartzdav@gmail.com
www.davidschwartzsecuritieslaw.com

***Vancouver*: Anthony P. Serka, Q.C. - *1**
#788, Broadway Plaza, 601 West Broadway, Vancouver, BC V5Z 4C2
Tel: 604-876-8761; *Fax:* 604-876-9035
aserka@shaw.ca
www.serkaqc.com

***Vancouver*: Shandro Dixon Edgson**
#400, 999 Hastings St. West, Vancouver, BC V6C 2W2
Tel: 604-689-0400; *Fax:* 604-685-2009

***Vancouver*: Shapiro Hankinson & Knutson Law Corporation - *14**
#700, Two Bental Centre, 555 Burrard St., Vancouver, BC V7X 1M8
Tel: 604-684-0727; *Fax:* 604-684-7094
info@shk.ca
www.shk.ca
www.facebook.com/pages/Shapiro-Hankinson-Knutson-Law-Corporation/2546526545, twitter.com/SHKLaw

***Vancouver*: Murray H. Shapiro - *1**
694 West 19th Ave., Vancouver, BC V5Z 1X1
Tel: 604-879-6777; *Fax:* 604-879-6728

***Vancouver*: Shapray Cramer LLP - *5**
#670, World Trade Centre, 999 Canada Pl., Vancouver, BC V6C 3E1
Tel: 604-681-0900; *Fax:* 604-681-0920
enquiries@shapraycramer.com
shapraycramer.com

***Vancouver*: Sylvia S. Shelton - *1**
3469 Commercial St., Vancouver, BC V5N 4E8
Tel: 604-251-2144; *Fax:* 604-251-2781

***Vancouver*: George Shimizu - *1**
#718, P.O. Box 50959, 808 Nelson St., Vancouver, BC V6Z 2H2
Tel: 604-685-4467; *Fax:* 604-685-4408
geoshimizu@telus.net

***Vancouver*: Silbernagel & Company**
#700, 595 Howe St., Vancouver, BC V6C 2T5
Tel: 604-687-9621; *Fax:* 604-687-5960

***Vancouver*: Singleton Urquhart LLP - *43**
#1200, 925 West Georgia St., Vancouver, BC V6C 3L2
Tel: 604-682-7474; *Fax:* 604-682-1283
su@singleton.com
www.singleton.com

***Vancouver*: Skorah Doyle - *2**
#2100, 200 Granville St., Vancouver, BC V6C 1S4
Tel: 604-602-8502; *Fax:* 604-608-1660

***Vancouver*: Smith & Hughes - *2**
4472 James St., Vancouver, BC V5V 3J1
Tel: 604-683-4176; *Fax:* 604-683-2621
outlaw@smith-hughes.com
www.smith-hughes.com

***Vancouver*: Michael P.S. Spearing - *1**
#501, 1949 Beach Ave., Vancouver, BC V6G 1Z2
Tel: 604-681-0699
michaelspearing@telus.net

***Vancouver*: Specht & Pryer - *1**
#612, 475 Howe St., Vancouver, BC V6C 2B3
Tel: 604-681-2500; *Fax:* 604-736-0118
staff@spechtandpryer.com
www.spechtandpryer.com
www.facebook.com/bc.lawyer

***Vancouver*: Stephens & Holman - South Vancouver - *6**
#500, 1200 - 33 St. West, Vancouver, BC V6P 6Z6
Tel: 604-730-4100; *Fax:* 604-736-2867
Toll-Free: 866-394-7070
www.stephensandholman.com

***Vancouver*: John S. Stowe - *1**
#1109, 207 Hastings St. West, Vancouver, BC V6B 1H7
Tel: 604-684-1665; *Fax:* 604-687-3097
john_stowe@bc.sympatico.ca

***Vancouver*: Sugden, McFee & Roos LLP - *10**
#700, The Landing, 375 Water St., Vancouver, BC V6B 5N3
Tel: 604-687-7700; *Fax:* 604-687-5596
info@smrlaw.ca
www.smrlaw.ca

***Vancouver*: Sutherland & Company - *1**
Former Name: Sutherland Johnston
#1620, 401 Georgia St. West, Vancouver, BC V6B 5A1
Tel: 604-688-0047; *Fax:* 604-688-8880

***Vancouver*: Sutherland Jetté - *4**
#201, 128 West Pender St., Vancouver, BC V6B 1R8
Tel: 604-669-6699; *Fax:* 604-681-0652
info@sutherlandjette.com
www.sutherlandjette.com

***Vancouver*: David F. Sutherland & Associates - *1**
#1700, 1185 West Georgia St., Vancouver, BC V6E 4E6
Tel: 604-737-8711; *Fax:* 604-737-8655
www.djslaw.ca

***Vancouver*: Tao & Company**
#860, 999 West Broadway, Vancouver, BC V5Z 1K5
Tel: 604-730-8219; *Fax:* 604-730-2553

***Vancouver*: Taylor & Blair - Vancouver - *3**
#1607, 805 West Broadway, Vancouver, BC V5Z 1K1
Tel: 604-737-6900; *Fax:* 604-737-6901
graham@taylorandblair.com
taylorandblair.com

***Vancouver*: Taylor & Company - *2**
Former Name: Taylor Wray
#218, 470 Granville St., Vancouver, BC V6C 1V5
Tel: 604-662-8373; *Fax:* 604-662-8321
wtaylor@twlaw.ca

***Vancouver*: Taylor Jordan Chafetz - *8**
#1010, 777 Hornby St., Vancouver, BC V6Z 1S4
Tel: 604-683-2223; *Fax:* 604-683-2798
tsaumure@tjclaw.com
www.tjclaw.com

***Vancouver*: Colin Taylor Professional Corp.**
#203, 1275 - 6th Ave. West, Vancouver, BC V6H 1A6
Tel: 604-798-8775; *Fax:* 604-608-6117
colintaylor@telus.net
colintaylor.ca

***Vancouver*: Isaac Thau - *1**
#101, 1012 Beach Ave., Vancouver, BC V6E 1T7
Tel: 604-685-4220; *Fax:* 604-685-0400
ithau@orbitinc.net

***Vancouver*: Eric P. Thiessen - *1**
#702, 756 Great Northern Way, Vancouver, BC V5T 1E4
Tel: 604-876-6220; *Fax:* 604-876-6253

***Vancouver*: Thomas, Rondeau - *6**
#1780, 400 Burrard St., Vancouver, BC V6C 3A6
Tel: 604-688-6775; *Fax:* 604-688-6995
www.thomasrondeau.com

***Vancouver*: Tim Louis & Company - *1**
Also Known As: TL & Co.
#208, 175 East Broadway, Vancouver, BC V5T 1W2
Tel: 604-732-7678; *Fax:* 604-732-7579
timlouis@timlouislaw.com
www.timlouislaw.com

***Vancouver*: Timothy J. Vondette Law Corporation - *1**
#506, 1128 Hornby St., Vancouver, BC V6Z 2L4
Tel: 604-669-6990; *Fax:* 604-669-6944
tvondette@aol.com

** indicates number of lawyers*

***Vancouver*: Tobin & Associates - *1**
#816, 938 Howe St., Vancouver, BC V6Z 1N9
Tel: 604-331-1591; *Fax:* 604-688-8120
enquiries@endisputes.com
www.endisputes.com

***Vancouver*: Tupper, Jonsson & Yeadon - *6**
#1710, 1177 Hastings St. West, Vancouver, BC V6E 2L3
Tel: 604-683-9262; *Fax:* 604-681-0139
tupjon@globalserve.net

***Vancouver*: Winfred A. van der Sande - *1**
2774 Granville St., Vancouver, BC V6H 3J3
Tel: 604-739-7989; *Fax:* 604-909-4798

***Vancouver*: Varty & Company - *2**
#900, 555 Burrard St., Vancouver, BC V7X 1M8
Tel: 604-684-5356; *Fax:* 604-443-5001
dvarty@smartt.com
www.vartylaw.ca

***Vancouver*: Vector Corporate Finance Lawyers - *4**
Former Name: Scott, Bissett
#1040, 999 West Hastings St., Vancouver, BC V6C 2W2
Tel: 604-683-1102; *Fax:* 604-683-2643
www.vectorlaw.com

***Vancouver*: Vick, McPhee and Liu - *3**
#1025, 1185 West Georgia St., Vancouver, BC V6E 4E6
Tel: 604-682-0926; *Fax:* 604-688-8615
VML@pro.net
www.vickmcpheeandliu.com

***Vancouver*: Von Dehn & Company - *3**
#700, 595 Howe St., Vancouver, BC V6C 2T5
Tel: 604-688-4541; *Fax:* 604-687-5960
vondehnco@telus.net

***Vancouver*: T. Wing Wai - *1**
#205, 475 Main St., Vancouver, BC V6A 2T7
Tel: 604-688-2291; *Fax:* 604-688-8983

***Vancouver*: Walker & Company - *1**
#304, 1230 Haro St., Vancouver, BC V6E 4J9
Tel: 604-682-1147; *Fax:* 604-681-7705
agwalker@telus.net

***Vancouver*: Watson Goepel LLP - *33**
#1700, 1075 West Georgia St., Vancouver, BC V6E 3C9
Tel: 604-688-1301; *Fax:* 604-688-8193
info@watsongoepel.com
www.watsongoepel.com
www.facebook.com/WatsonGoepel, twitter.com/WatsonGoepel,
www.linkedin.com/company/200752

***Vancouver*: Elizabeth E. Watson - *1**
#4412, 349 Georgia St. West, Vancouver, BC V6B 3Z8
Tel: 604-877-1412; *Fax:* 604-877-0134
ewatson@telus.net

***Vancouver*: Webster Hudson & Coombe LLP - *14**
Former Name: Webster Hudson & Akerly LLP
#510, 1040 West Georgia St., Vancouver, BC V6E 4H1
Tel: 604-682-3488; *Fax:* 604-682-3438
www.wha.bc.ca

***Vancouver*: Westpoint Law Group - *1**
Former Name: Epstein Wood
#1900, 1177 West Hastings St., Vancouver, BC V6E 2K3
Tel: 604-718-6886; *Fax:* 604-629-1882
www.westpointlawgroup.com

***Vancouver*: Whitelaw Twining Law Corporation - *40**
#2400, 200 Granville St., Vancouver, BC V6C 1S4
Tel: 604-682-5466; *Fax:* 604-682-5217
Toll-Free: 866-982-9898
contact@wt.ca
www.whitelawtwining.com

***Vancouver*: Wilcox & Company Law Corporation - *3**
Former Name: Dale W. Wilcox Law Corporation
#1910, 777 Hornby St., Vancouver, BC V6Z 1S4
Tel: 604-687-1374; *Fax:* 604-687-2731
dwilcox@wilcoxlawcorp.com

***Vancouver*: Williamson Giesen Murray - *3**
Former Name: Williamson Giesen
#200, 1290 Homer St., Vancouver, BC V6B 2Y5
Tel: 604-681-1004; *Fax:* 604-684-1199
agiesen@wgmlaw.ca
www.laurieharrisdesign.com/wgm/

***Vancouver*: Wilson Butcher - *4**
#400, 744 West Hastings St., Vancouver, BC V6C 1A5
Tel: 604-684-4751; *Fax:* 604-684-8319
info@wbbslaw.com
wbbslaw.com

***Vancouver*: Andrew J. Winstanley - *1**
#410, 688 Hastings St. West, Vancouver, BC V6B 1P1
Tel: 604-682-2939; *Fax:* 604-682-2241
ajwinstanley@teleus.net

***Vancouver*: George Wong & Company - *1**
4423 Boundary Rd., Vancouver, BC V5R 2N3
Tel: 604-687-6166; *Fax:* 604-687-8002

***Vancouver*: Patrick L. Wong - *1**
#407, 1541 West Broadway, Vancouver, BC V6J 1W7
Tel: 604-731-5301; *Fax:* 604-731-1266

***Vancouver*: Robert Wood & Company - *2**
Former Name: Dawson, Wood & Company
#100, 2501 Spruce St., Vancouver, BC V6H 2P8
Tel: 604-731-1200; *Fax:* 604-266-0119
rwood@dawsonwood.com

***Vancouver*: Anthony K. Wooster - *1**
#570, 999 West Broadway, Vancouver, BC V5Z 1K5
Tel: 604-684-1204; *Fax:* 604-684-1206
akwoods@aol.com

***Vancouver*: Donlad W.H. Yerxa - *1**
#1200, 805 West Broadway, Vancouver, BC V5Z 1K1
Tel: 604-873-5225

***Vancouver*: Young & Noble - *1**
#1119, 808 Nelson St., Vancouver, BC V6Z 2H2
Tel: 604-669-9755; *Fax:* 604-921-4817
john.noble@youngnoble.com

***Vancouver*: Young Anderson Barristers & Solicitors - *21**
#1616, Nelson Square, P.O. Box 12147, 808 Nelson St., Vancouver, BC V6Z 2H2
Tel: 604-689-7400; *Fax:* 604-689-3444
Toll-Free: 800-665-3540
reception@younganderson.ca
www.younganderson.ca
www.facebook.com/YoungAndersonBC,
twitter.com/YoungAndersonBC

***Vancouver*: David L. Youngson - *1**
#10, 1656 - 11th Ave. West, Vancouver, BC V6J 2B9
Tel: 604-266-6588; *Fax:* 604-266-6393
saluspopuli@shaw.ca

***Vancouver*: Xiao Zheng - *1**
#248, 515 Pender St. West, Vancouver, BC V6B 6H5
Tel: 604-608-0387; *Fax:* 604-608-0385
zheng@axionet.com

***Vancouver*: Deborah Lynn Zutter - *1**
609 West Hastings, 6th Fl., Vancouver, BC V6B 4W4
Tel: 604-219-2259; *Fax:* 604-662-7466
deb@debzutter.com
www.debzutter.com

***Vanderhoof*: Steven F. Peleshok - *1**
P.O. Box 1128, 2608 Burrard Ave., Vanderhoof, BC V0J 3A0
Tel: 250-567-9277; *Fax:* 250-567-2657

***Vernon*: Allan Francis Pringle LLP - *6**
3009B - 28 St., Vernon, BC V1T 4Z7
Tel: 250-542-1177; *Fax:* 250-542-1105
info@afp-law.ca
www.afp-law.ca

***Vernon*: Crosby Lawyers**
3406 - 32nd Ave., Vernon, BC V1T 2N1
Tel: 250-558-5790; *Fax:* 250-558-3910
crosby@crosbylaw.ca

***Vernon*: Kenneth R. Fiddes - *1**
#2, 2908 - 31 Ave., Vernon, BC V1T 2G4
Tel: 250-542-5391; *Fax:* 250-542-4199
fiddes@shaw.ca

***Vernon*: Alan M. Gaudette - *1**
#9, 11341 Kidston Rd., Vernon, BC V1B 1Z4
Tel: 250-545-3132; *Fax:* 250-545-1617
amgaudette@shaw.ca
ca.linkedin.com/pub/alan-gaudette/44/3a8/375

***Vernon*: Jamie MacArthur Barrister & Solicitor - *1**
2608 - 48 Ave., Vernon, BC V1T 8K8
Tel: 250-549-6030
jamie@macarthurlaw.ca
www.jamiemacarthurlaw.ca

***Vernon*: Kern & Company Law Corp.**
#3, 2908 - 32 St., Vernon, BC V1T 5M1
Tel: 250-549-2184; *Fax:* 250-549-2207

***Vernon*: Kidston & Company LLP - Vernon - *6**
#200, 3005 - 30th St., Vernon, BC V1T 2M1
Fax: 250-545-4776
Toll-Free: 800-262-2678
info@kidston.ca
www.kidston.ca
www.facebook.com/KidstonandCo, twitter.com/kidstonandco,
www.linkedin.com/company/davidson-lawyers-llp

***Vernon*: John S. Maguire - *1**
Former Name: Sigalet, Maguire & Cole
3018 - 29 St., Vernon, BC V1T 5A7
Tel: 250-545-6054; *Fax:* 250-545-7227
jsmag@sigmag.com

***Vernon*: Nixon Wenger - *21**
#301, 2706 - 30th Ave., Vernon, BC V1T 2B6
Tel: 250-542-5353; *Fax:* 250-542-7273
Toll-Free: 800-243-5353
nw@nixonwenger.com
www.nixonwenger.com
twitter.com/NixonWengerLLP

***Vernon*: Robert Moffat Law Corp. - *1**
2912 - 29th St., Vernon, BC V1T 5A6
Tel: 250-542-1312; *Fax:* 250-542-2788
Toll-Free: 800-371-0181

***Vernon*: Steiner & Company - *1**
3107A - 31 Ave., Vernon, BC V1T 2G9
Tel: 250-545-1371; *Fax:* 250-542-5630
Toll-Free: 800-661-2600

***Victoria*: Acheson Whitley Sweeney Foley - *6**
Former Name: Acheson & Co
535 Yates St., 4th Fl., Victoria, BC V8W 2Z6
Tel: 250-384-6262; *Fax:* 250-384-5353
Toll-Free: 877-275-8766
info@awslaw.ca
www.achesonwhitley.com

***Victoria*: Robert D. Adair - *1**
#201, 4430 Chatterton Way, Victoria, BC V8X 5J2
Tel: 250-479-9367; *Fax:* 250-479-8316
adair@adairlaw.ca

***Victoria*: Anniko & Hunter - *2**
#201, 300 Gorge Rd. West, Victoria, BC V9A 1M8
Tel: 250-385-1233; *Fax:* 250-385-4078
ah@annikohunter-law.com
www.annikohunterlawyersnotaries.ca

***Victoria*: Jacqueline Beltgens - *1**
3929 Woodhaven Terrace, Victoria, BC V8N 1S7
Tel: 250-385-3909
jbeltgens@pinc.com

***Victoria*: Christopher Brennan - *1**
1027 Pandora Ave., Victoria, BC V8V 3P6
Tel: 250-388-9024; *Fax:* 250-388-9060
chrisbrennan@shaw.ca

***Victoria*: Browne & Associates - *1**
1633 Hillside Ave., Victoria, BC V8T 2C4
Tel: 250-598-1888; *Fax:* 250-598-9880
info@browneassociates.ca
www.browneassociates.ca

***Victoria*: Butterfield Law - *1**
#402, 2020 Richmond Rd., Victoria, BC V8R 6R5
Tel: 250-382-4529; *Fax:* 250-480-1896
reception@butterfieldlaw.ca
www.butterfieldlaw.ca

***Victoria*: Carfra & Lawton - *16**
395 Waterfront Cres., 6th Fl., Victoria, BC V8T 5K7
Tel: 250-381-7188; *Fax:* 250-381-7804
info@carlaw.ca
www.carlaw.ca
www.linkedin.com/company/carfra-&-lawton

** indicates number of lawyers*

***Victoria*: Carr Buchan & Co. - *7**
520 Comerford St., Victoria, BC V9A 6K8
Tel: 250-388-7571; *Fax:* 250-388-7327
Toll-Free: 888-313-7571
carrbuchan@esquimaltlaw.com
www.esquimaltlaw.com

***Victoria*: Clapp & Company - *1**
4599 Chatterton Way, Victoria, BC V8X 4Y7
Tel: 250-479-1422; *Fax:* 250-479-1667

***Victoria*: Clay & Company - *6**
837 Burdett Ave., Main Fl., Victoria, BC V8W 1B3
Tel: 250-386-2261; *Fax:* 250-389-1336
Toll-Free: 877-688-9634
lawyers@clay.bc.ca
www.clay.bc.ca

***Victoria*: Coad & Davidson - *2**
3200 Quadra St., Victoria, BC V8X 1G2
Tel: 250-388-9003; *Fax:* 250-388-3577
reception@coadlawcorp.com
www.coadlawcorp.com

***Victoria*: Donald R. Colborne - *1**
1125 Fort St., Victoria, BC V8V 3K9
Tel: 807-344-6628; *Fax:* 807-983-3079
drcolborne@shaw.ca

***Victoria*: Considine & Company, Barristers & Solicitors - *1**
30 Dallas Rd., Victoria, BC V8V 0A2
Tel: 250-381-7788; *Fax:* 250-381-1042
www.considinelaw.com

***Victoria*: Cook Roberts LLP - *14**
1175 Douglas St., 7th Fl., Victoria, BC V8W 2E1
Tel: 250-385-1411; *Fax:* 250-413-3300
www.cookroberts.bc.ca

***Victoria*: Cox Taylor - *10**
Burnes House, 26 Bastion Sq., 3rd Fl., Victoria, BC V8W 1H9
Tel: 250-388-4457; *Fax:* 250-382-4236
reception@coxtaylor.ca
www.coxtaylor.bc.ca
twitter.com/CoxTaylor_YYJ

***Victoria*: Crease Harman LLP - *13**
#800, 1070 Douglas St., Victoria, BC V8W 2S8
Tel: 250-388-5421; *Fax:* 250-388-4294
www.creaseharman.com

***Victoria*: Dinning Hunter Jackson Law - Victoria - Fort St. - *17**
Former Name: Dinning Hunter Lambert & Jackson; Dinning Crawford; Dinning Hunter
1202 Fort St., Victoria, BC V8V 3L2
Tel: 250-381-2151; *Fax:* 250-386-2123
info@dinninghunter.com
www.dinninghunter.com

***Victoria*: Jeremy S.G. Donaldson - *1**
2555 Sinclair Rd., Victoria, BC V8N 1B8
Tel: 250-721-5759; *Fax:* 250-721-5455

***Victoria*: Dwyer Tax Lawyers - *2**
#900, CIBC Tower, 1175 Douglas St., Victoria, BC V8W 2E1
Tel: 250-360-2110; *Fax:* 250-360-0440
inquiries@dwyertaxlaw.com
www.dwyertaxlaw.com

***Victoria*: Michael W. Egan - *1**
#101, 288 Eltham Rd., Victoria, BC V9B 1J9
Tel: 250-382-3426; *Fax:* 250-382-3427

***Victoria*: Frank A.V. Falzon Law Corporation - *1**
#200, 3561 Shelbourne St., Victoria, BC V8P 4G8
Tel: 250-384-3995; *Fax:* 250-384-4924
favf@islandnet.com

***Victoria*: Patrick S. Finnegan - *1**
#6, 1140 Fort St., Victoria, BC V8V 3K8
Tel: 250-384-4252; *Fax:* 250-384-4252
psfinnegan@shaw.ca

***Victoria*: Firestone & Tyhurst - *2**
#301, 919 Fort St., Victoria, BC V8V 3K3
Tel: 250-386-1112; *Fax:* 250-386-1124
firestone.tyhurst@shawbiz.ca

***Victoria*: Joseph Gereluk Law Office - *1**
#401, 1011 Fort St., Victoria, BC V8V 3K5
Tel: 250-380-1423; *Fax:* 250-380-0920

***Victoria*: Larry P. Gilbert - *1**
275 Pallisier Ave., Victoria, BC V9A 1C5
Tel: 250-478-8881; *Fax:* 250-478-8801

***Victoria*: Peter Golden - *1**
#218, 852 Fort St., Victoria, BC V8W 1H8
Tel: 250-361-3131
www.petergolden.ca

***Victoria*: Goult & Company - *1**
2185 Theatre Lane, Victoria, BC V8R 6T1
Tel: 250-595-1621; *Fax:* 250-595-5888
goultco@shaw.ca

***Victoria*: Green & Helme - *4**
Former Name: Green & Claus
1161 Fort St., Victoria, BC V8V 3K9
Tel: 250-361-9600; *Fax:* 250-361-9181
greenandhelme@greenclaus.com

***Victoria*: Lenore B. Harlton - *1**
215 Superior St., Victoria, BC V8V 2G7
Tel: 250-382-5161; *Fax:* 250-382-5160

***Victoria*: Hart Legal - *10**
Also Known As: Berge Hart Cassels LLP
Former Name: Berge, Hart & Cassels
#300, 1001 Wharf St., Victoria, BC V8W 1T6
Tel: 250-388-9477; *Fax:* 250-388-9470
hart-legal.com
www.facebook.com/HART.Legal, twitter.com/Hart_Legal, www.linkedin.com/company/2560603

***Victoria*: Hatter, Thompson, Shumka & McDonagh - *4**
#201, 919 Fort St., Victoria, BC V8V 3K3
Tel: 250-388-4931; *Fax:* 250-386-8088
Toll-Free: 800-667-0705

***Victoria*: James I. Heller - *1**
2090 Chauchher St., Victoria, BC V8R 1H7
Tel: 250-984-7037
www.jamesheller.ca

***Victoria*: Helm Legal - *1**
1027 Pandora Ave., Victoria, BC V8V 3P6
Tel: 250-588-4356; *Fax:* 250-483-1952
jordan@helmlegal.ca
helmlegal.ca

***Victoria*: Hemminger Schmid - *6**
#204, 388 Harbour Rd., Victoria, BC V9A 3S1
Tel: 250-220-8686; *Fax:* 250-385-8686
www.lawyersandmediators.ca
www.twitter.com/viclawyers

***Victoria*: Holmes & Isherwood - *1**
1190 Fort St., Victoria, BC V8V 3K8
Tel: 250-383-7157; *Fax:* 250-383-1535

***Victoria*: Horne Coupar - *12**
Royal Trust Building, 612 View St., 3rd Fl., Victoria, BC V8W 1J5
Tel: 250-388-6631; *Fax:* 250-388-5974
Toll-Free: 866-467-2490
www.hornecoupar.com
www.facebook.com/pages/Horne-Coupar/167656853298279, twitter.com/#HORNECOUPAR

***Victoria*: Raymond T. Horne - *1**
#46, 530 Marsett Pl., Victoria, BC V8Z 7J2
Tel: 250-658-8387

***Victoria*: Hutchison Oss-Cech Marlatt, Barristers & Solicitors - *5**
Former Name: The Seigel Law Group
#1, 505 Fisgard St., Victoria, BC V8W 1R3
Tel: 250-360-2500
info@hom-law.com
www.hom-law.com

***Victoria*: Jawl & Bundon - *8**
1007 Fort St., 4th Fl., Victoria, BC V8V 3K5
Tel: 250-385-5787; *Fax:* 250-385-4364
info@jawlbundon.com
www.jawlbundon.com

***Victoria*: Johns Southward Glazier Walton & Margetts - *9**
#204, 655 Tyee Rd., Victoria, BC V9A 6X5
Tel: 250-381-7321; *Fax:* 250-381-1181
Toll-Free: 888-442-4042
johnssouthward.com

***Victoria*: William S. Johnson Law Corp. - *1**
Former Name: W.S. Johnson
#309, 895 Fort St., Victoria, BC V8W 1H7
Tel: 250-382-2404; *Fax:* 250-382-2426

***Victoria*: Jones Emery Hargreaves Swan - *13**
#1212, 1175 Douglas St., Victoria, BC V8W 2E1
Tel: 250-382-7222; *Fax:* 250-382-5436
lawyers@jonesemery.com
www.jonesemery.com

***Victoria*: Kinar Curry Lawyers - *2**
#200, 852 Fort St., Victoria, BC V8W 1B9
Tel: 250-383-8685; *Fax:* 250-383-7973
gwk@kinarlaw.com
www.kinarlaw.com

***Victoria*: Lampion Pacific Law Corporation - *2**
Victoria, BC
Tel: 250-477-0129
cmorris@lampion.bc.ca
www.lampion.bc.ca

***Victoria*: Alice Shun Yee Lo - *1**
#401, 1011 Fort St., Victoria, BC V8V 3K5
Tel: 250-380-1423; *Fax:* 250-380-0920
alicelo@telus.net

***Victoria*: Susan J. Loney Law Office - *1**
1006 Russell St., Victoria, BC V9A 3X9
Tel: 250-384-1804; *Fax:* 250-384-1805
susan@vicwestlaw.ca

***Victoria*: Lovett Westmacott - *3**
Former Name: Lovett Westmacott & Clancy
#417, 645 Fort St., Victoria, BC V8W 1G2
Tel: 250-480-7481; *Fax:* 250-480-7455
www.lw-law.ca

***Victoria*: MacIsaac & Company - *11**
P.O. Box 933, 1117 Wharf St., 3rd Fl., Victoria, BC V8W 1T7
Tel: 250-381-5353; *Fax:* 250-380-7272
Toll-Free: 800-663-6299
victoria@macisaacandcompany.com
www.macisaacandcompany.com

***Victoria*: MacIsaac & MacIsaac - *4**
2227 Sooke Rd., Victoria, BC V9B 1W8
Tel: 250-478-1131; *Fax:* 250-478-3106
mac@macisaaclaw.ca
macisaaclaw.ca

***Victoria*: MacMinn & Company - *5**
846 Broughton St., Victoria, BC V8W 1E4
Tel: 250-381-6444; *Fax:* 250-381-7857
dtodd@macminnco.com
www.deborahtoddlaw.com

***Victoria*: Marshall Allen & Massey - *3**
Former Name: Brooks & Marshall
1519 Amelia St., Victoria, BC V8W 2K1
Tel: 250-920-0144; *Fax:* 250-920-0177
claudia@ameliastreetlawyers.com
www.ameliastreetlawyers.com

***Victoria*: McConnan, Bion, O'Connor & Peterson - *12**
#420, 880 Douglas St., Victoria, BC V8W 2B7
Tel: 250-385-1383; *Fax:* 250-385-2841
Toll-Free: 888-385-1383
info@mcbop.com
www.mcbop.com

***Victoria*: McCullough Blazina Dieno Gustafson & Watt - *10**
#200, 1011 Fort St., Victoria, BC V8V 3K5
Tel: 250-480-1529; *Fax:* 250-480-4910
Toll-Free: 800-360-6488
info@mbdglaw.com
www.mbdglaw.com

***Victoria*: McMicken & Bennett - *2**
303 - 1111 Blanshard St., Victoria, BC V8W 2H7
Tel: 250-385-9555; *Fax:* 250-385-9841
lawyer@mcmickenbennett.bc.ca

***Victoria*: Milton, Johnson - *2**
#204, 947 Fort St., Victoria, BC V8V 3K3
Tel: 250-385-5523; *Fax:* 250-385-7420
miltjohn@pacificcoast.net

***Victoria*: Robert Moore-Stewart - *1**
#616, 620 View St., Victoria, BC V8W 1J6
Tel: 250-380-1887; *Fax:* 250-380-9134
rmoorest@telus.net

** indicates number of lawyers*

***Victoria*: Jane B. Morley - *1**
Former Name: Morley & Ross
#7, 356 Simcoe St., Victoria, BC V8V 1L1
Tel: 250-480-7487; *Fax:* 250-480-7488
jbmorley@mrlaw.ca

***Victoria*: Mulroney & Company - *7**
#301, 852 Fort St., Victoria, BC V8W 1H8
Tel: 250-389-6022; *Fax:* 250-389-6033
reception@mulroneyco.com
www.mulroneyco.com

***Victoria*: John M. Orr Law Office - *1**
2368 The Esplanade, Victoria, BC V8R 2W2
Tel: 250-595-8675; *Fax:* 250-595-7421
orrlaw@shaw.ca
www.adrweb.ca/john-orr

***Victoria*: Pearlman Lindholm - *17**
#201, 19 Dallas Rd., Victoria, BC V8V 5A6
Tel: 250-388-4433; *Fax:* 250-388-5856
nphilpott@pearlmanlindholm.com
www.pearlmanlindholm.com

***Victoria*: Purves, Clark**
Former Name: Purves, Hickford, Horne & Curry
#203, 919 Fort St., Victoria, BC V8W 1H6
Tel: 250-388-7188

***Victoria*: Quadra Legal Centre - *6**
#101, 2750 Quadra St., Victoria, BC V8T 4E8
Tel: 250-380-1566; *Fax:* 250-380-3090
info@quadralegal.com
www.quadralegal.com

***Victoria*: Randall & Murrell LLP - *2**
Former Name: Randall & Company
#201, 1006 Fort St., Victoria, BC V8V 3K4
Tel: 250-382-9282; *Fax:* 250-382-0366
reception@viclawfirm.ca
www.viclawfirm.ca

***Victoria*: Reed Pope LLP - *6**
#202, 1007 Fort St., Victoria, BC V8V 3K5
Tel: 250-383-3838; *Fax:* 250-385-4324
rkreed@reedpope.ca
www.reedpope.ca

***Victoria*: Nichola Reid & Company - *2**
#214, 284 Helmcken Rd., Victoria, BC V9B 1T2
Tel: 250-744-1844; *Fax:* 250-744-1890

***Victoria*: Ross, Johnson & Associates - *2**
888 Fort St., 4th Fl., Victoria, BC V8W 1H8
Tel: 250-381-7677; *Fax:* 250-381-7657
kjohnson@rjalawyers.com
www.kimejohnson.com

***Victoria*: Marlene Russo - *1**
#110, 1175 Cook St., Victoria, BC V8V 4A1
Tel: 250-380-0076; *Fax:* 250-380-0092
marlenerusso@shaw.ca

***Victoria*: Salmond Ashurst - *4**
1620 Cedar Hill Cross Rd., Victoria, BC V8P 2P6
Tel: 250-477-4143; *Fax:* 250-477-4451
derek@salmondashurst.com
www.salmondashurst.ca

***Victoria*: Sihota & Starkey - *1**
1248 Esquimalt Rd., Victoria, BC V9A 3N8
Tel: 250-381-5111; *Fax:* 250-381-3947

***Victoria*: Smith Hutchison Law Corporation - *1**
#202, 1640 Oak Bay Ave., Victoria, BC V8W 1E5
Tel: 250-388-6666; *Fax:* 250-389-0400
mhutchqc@bclawfirm.com
www.bclawfirm.com

***Victoria*: Spier & Company Law - *1**
#208, 852 Fort St., Victoria, BC V8W 1H8
Tel: 250-590-1539; *Fax:* 250-590-2539
info@spierlaw.ca
www.spierlaw.ca
www.facebook.com/pages/Family-Law-BC-Spier-Company-Law/134424973247497, twitter.com/SpierLaw

***Victoria*: Stevenson, Doell Law Corporation - *5**
999 Fort St., Victoria, BC V8V 3K3
Tel: 250-388-7881; *Fax:* 250-388-7324
Toll-Free: 888-633-5567
stevensondoell@shawcable.com
www.stevensondoell.com

***Victoria*: Stevenson, Luchies & Legh - *15**
#300, 848 Courtney St., Victoria, BC V8W 1C4
Tel: 250-381-4040; *Fax:* 250-388-9406
Toll-Free: 888-381-8555
lawyers@sll.ca
www.sll.ca
www.facebook.com/VictoriaLawFirms, twitter.com/LawyersVictoria

***Victoria*: Stewart Johnston Law Corpoartion - *1**
1521 Amelia St., Victoria, BC V8W 2K1
Tel: 250-385-2975; *Fax:* 250-385-2977
goodadvice@sjlaw.ca
www.sjlaw.ca

***Victoria*: Christine A. Stretton - *1**
#202, 895 Fort St., Victoria, BC V8W 1H7
Tel: 250-388-5333; *Fax:* 250-382-8644
castretton@pacificcoast.net

***Victoria*: Thompson Cooper LLP - *2**
Also Known As: Barrigar Intellectual Property Law
#201, 1007 Fort St., Victoria, BC V8V 3KS
Tel: 250-389-0387; *Fax:* 250-389-2659
doug@bcpatents.ca
www.tcllp.ca
twitter.com/ThompsonCooper, www.linkedin.com/company/316566?trk=tyah

***Victoria*: Diane E. Tourell - *1**
#500, 645 Fort St., Victoria, BC V8W 1G2
Tel: 250-384-1443; *Fax:* 250-380-7299

***Victoria*: Dalmar F. Tracy - *1**
#206, 1005 Cook St., Victoria, BC V8V 3Z6
Tel: 250-384-5331; *Fax:* 250-384-5206
dalmartracy@shaw.ca
www.dalmartracy.com

***Victoria*: Jill K. Turner - *1**
#101, 4475 Viewmount Ave., Victoria, BC V8Z 6L8
Tel: 250-360-0983; *Fax:* 250-658-1949
jill@turnerlegal.com

***Victoria*: Turnham Woodland, Barristers & Solicitors - *4**
1002 Wharf St., Victoria, BC V8W 1T4
Tel: 250-385-1122; *Fax:* 250-385-6522
www.turnhamwoodland.ca

***Victoria*: Vangenne & Company**
Former Name: Skillings & Company
#B, 777 Blanshard St., Victoria, BC V8W 2G9
Tel: 250-388-5136; *Fax:* 250-388-5195
vangenne.com

***Victoria*: Velletta & Company - *7**
Former Name: Gordon & Velletta
#302, 852 Fort St., Victoria, BC V8W 1H8
Tel: 250-383-9104; *Fax:* 250-383-1922
Toll-Free: 866-383-9104
mail@victorialaw.ca
www.victorialaw.ca
www.facebook.com/pages/Velletta-Lawyers/176365079057666, twitter.com/VellettaLawyers

***Victoria*: Waddell Raponi LLP - *5**
Former Name: Waddell Raponi, Lawyers
1002 Wharf St., Victoria, BC V8W 1T4
Tel: 250-385-4311; *Fax:* 250-385-2012
www.waddellraponi.com

***Victoria*: Peter I. Waldmann - *1**
2582 Beach Dr., Victoria, BC V8R 6K4
Tel: 250-381-3113; *Fax:* 250-381-3122

***Victoria*: Wilson Marshall Law Corporation - *7**
#200, 911 Yates St., Victoria, BC V8V 4X3
Tel: 250-385-8741; *Fax:* 250-385-0433
Toll-Free: 877-385-8741
reception@wilsonmarshall.com
www.wilsonmarshall.com

***Victoria*: Wong & Doerksen - *2**
1618 Government St., Victoria, BC V8W 1Z3
Tel: 250-381-7799; *Fax:* 250-386-7799
info@wongdoerksen.com
www.wongdoerksen.com

***Victoria*: Woodward & Company - *18**
844 Courtney St., 2nd Fl., Victoria, BC V8W 1C4
Tel: 250-383-2356; *Fax:* 250-380-6560
reception@woodwardandcompany.com
www.woodwardandcompany.com

***Victoria*: Wendy K. Zimmerman - *1**
1006 Russell St., Victoria, BC V9A 3X9
Tel: 250-384-1804; *Fax:* 250-384-1805
Toll-Free: 800-313-9581
wendy@vicwestlaw.ca

***West Vancouver*: Christopher B. Chu - *1**
#200, 100 Park Royal South, West Vancouver, BC V7T 1A2
Tel: 604-925-5898; *Fax:* 604-648-8361
cbchu@mail.com

***West Vancouver*: David T. Forsyth - *1**
#1110, 100 Park Royal South, West Vancouver, BC V7T 1A2
Tel: 604-925-0045; *Fax:* 604-926-7782
dforsyth33@shaw.ca

***West Vancouver*: Goluboff & Mazzei, Barristers & Solicitors - *4**
#201, 585 - 16th St., West Vancouver, BC V7V 3R8
Tel: 604-229-4470; *Fax:* 604-926-7817
Toll-Free: 800-815-5894
info@goluboffmazzei.com
www.goluboffmazzei.com

***West Vancouver*: James C. Hutchinson - *1**
#200, 100 Park Royal South, West Vancouver, BC V7T 1A2
Tel: 604-926-2876; *Fax:* 604-926-2937
jch@jameschutchinson.com
www.jameschutchinson.ca

***West Vancouver*: Myrle L. Lawrence, Law Corporation - *1**
#203, 815 Main St., West Vancouver, BC V7T 2Z3
Tel: 604-925-9260; *Fax:* 604-925-9261
mlawrence@veritaslaw.ca

***West Vancouver*: McLean Armstrong LLP - *9**
#300, 1497 Marine Dr., West Vancouver, BC V7T 1B8
Tel: 604-925-0672; *Fax:* 604-925-8984
www.mcleanarmstrong.com

***West Vancouver*: David H. Stoller - *1**
#801, 100 Park Royal S., West Vancouver, BC V7T 1A2
Tel: 604-922-4702; *Fax:* 604-922-0374
stoller@stoller.ca
www.stoller.ca

***West Vancouver*: Ann Marie Sweeney - *1**
#201, 1590 Bellevue Ave., West Vancouver, BC V7V 1A7
Tel: 604-922-0131; *Fax:* 604-922-0171

***West Vancouver*: Yeager & Company Law Corporation - *2**
#202, 1555 Marine Dr., West Vancouver, BC V7V 1N9
Tel: 604-921-1295; *Fax:* 604-921-1297
Toll-Free: 855-921-1295
info@dismissal.ca
www.dismissal.ca

***Whistler*: Tom Docking - *1**
#338A, 4370 Lorimer Rd., Whistler, BC V0N 1B4
Tel: 604-905-5180; *Fax:* 866-974-7729
tom@whistlerlawyer.ca
whistlerrealestatelawyer.ca

***Whistler*: Mountain Law Corporation - *1**
Former Name: Shrimpton & Company
#200, 1410 Alpha Lake Rd., Whistler, BC V0N 1B1
Tel: 604-938-4947; *Fax:* 604-938-0471
shrimpco@direct.ca
www.mountainlaw.com

***Whistler*: Ian D. Reith - *1**
#14, 4227 Village Stroll, RR#4, Whistler, BC V0N 1B4
Tel: 604-932-6501; *Fax:* 604-932-5615

***Whistler*: Whistler Law Offices - *1**
Former Name: Davies & McLean
#201A, P.O. Box 449, 4230 Gateway Dr/, Whistler, BC V0N 1B0
Tel: 604-938-1763; *Fax:* 604-938-1764
Toll-Free: 877-938-1763
nick@whistlerlawoffices.com
www.whistlerlawoffices.com

***White Rock*: Cleveland Doan LLP - *3**
1321 Johnston Rd., White Rock, BC V4B 3Z3
Tel: 604-536-5002; *Fax:* 604-536-7002
lawyers@clevelanddoan.com
www.cleveland-doan.com

** indicates number of lawyers*

***White Rock*: Dawn Wattie Law Corporation - *1**
#2, 15621 Marine Dr., White Rock, BC V4B 1E1
Tel: 604-385-3952; *Fax:* 604-224-4068
info@dwlc.ca
www.dawnwattielawcorp.ca

***White Rock*: Medland & Company - *1**
14582 - 18th Ave., White Rock, BC V4A 5V5
Tel: 604-230-8476; *Fax:* 604-535-4145
medlandco@shaw.ca

***White Rock*: Joseph M. Prodor - *1**
15260 Thrift Ave., White Rock, BC V4B 2L2
Tel: 604-536-4676; *Fax:* 604-535-8981
Toll-Free: 877-577-6367
jprodor@axionet.com

***Williams Lake*: Vanderburgh & Company - *3**
#5, 123 Borland St., Williams Lake, BC V2G 1R1
Tel: 250-392-7161; *Fax:* 250-392-7060
aev@cariboolaw.com
www.cariboolaw.com

Manitoba

***Beausejour*: Middleton & Middleton - *1**
527 Park Ave., Beausejour, MB R0E 0C0
Tel: 204-268-4566; *Fax:* 204-268-4572
Toll-Free: 866-222-3259

***Brandon*: Terri E. Deller Law Office - *1**
801 Princess Ave., Brandon, MB R7A 0P5
Tel: 204-726-0128
questions@dellerlaw.com
www.dellerlaw.com

***Brandon*: Donald Legal Services - *3**
22 - Sixth St., Brandon, MB R7A 3N1
Tel: 204-729-4900; *Fax:* 204-728-4477
ld@donaldlegal.com
www.donaldlegal.com

***Brandon*: Meighen Haddad LLP - *17**
P.O. Box 22105, 110 - 11 St., Brandon, MB R7A 6Y9
Tel: 204-727-8461; *Fax:* 204-726-1948
mail@mhlaw.ca
www.mhlaw.ca

***Brandon*: Paterson Patterson Wyman & Abel**
#1, Carriage House, 1040 Princess Ave., Brandon, MB R7A 0P8
Tel: 204-727-2424; *Fax:* 204-728-4670
info@patersons.ca
www.patersons.ca

***Brandon*: James W. Potter - *1**
1202 Princess Ave., Brandon, MB R7A 0R3
Tel: 204-727-6431; *Fax:* 204-727-2818

***Brandon*: Roy, Johnston & Company - *8**
363 - 10 St., Brandon, MB R7A 4E9
Tel: 204-727-0761; *Fax:* 204-726-1339
www.royjohnston.ca

***Brandon*: Westman Community Law Centre**
236 - 11th St., Brandon, MB R7A 4J6
Tel: 204-729-3484; *Fax:* 204-726-1732
Toll-Free: 800-876-7326

***Carman*: Brown & Associates - *4**
P.O. Box 1240, 71 Main St. South, Carman, MB R0G 0J0
Tel: 204-745-2028; *Fax:* 204-745-3513
lawyers@brownlawoffice.org
www.brownlawoffice.org

***Carman*: Lee & Lee**
P.O. Box 656, 5 Centre Ave. West, Carman, MB R0G 0J0
Tel: 204-745-6751; *Fax:* 204-745-3481
bullsandbears@leeandlee.mb.ca

***Dauphin*: Amisk Community Law Centre**
202 Main St. South, Dauphin, MB R7N 1K6
Tel: 204-622-4660; *Fax:* 204-622-4679
Toll-Free: 877-622-4660

***Dauphin*: Dawson Law Office - *1**
34 - 1 Ave. NW, Dauphin, MB R7N 1G7
Tel: 204-638-4101; *Fax:* 204-638-8541

***Dauphin*: Hawkins & Sanderson - *1**
20 - 2nd Ave. NW, Dauphin, MB R7N 1H2
Tel: 204-638-4121

***Dauphin*: Irwin Law Office - *2**
122 Main St. North, Dauphin, MB R7N 1C2
Tel: 204-638-9249; *Fax:* 204-638-3647
irwinlaw@mymts.net

***Dauphin*: Johnston & Company - *5**
P.O. Box 551, 18 - 3 Ave. NW, Dauphin, MB R7N 2V4
Tel: 204-638-3211; *Fax:* 204-638-9646
www.johnstonlawoffice.ca

***Dauphin*: Johnston & Company - *5**
P.O. Box 551, 18 - 3rd Ave. NW, Dauphin, MB R7N 2V4
Tel: 204-638-3211; *Fax:* 204-638-9646
www.johnstonlawoffice.ca

***Dauphin*: Parklands Community Law Centre - *4**
31 - 3rd Ave. NE, Dauphin, MB R7N 0Y5
Tel: 204-622-7000; *Fax:* 204-622-7029
Toll-Free: 800-810-6977

***Deloraine*: Sheldon Lanchbery - *1**
P.O. Box 489, Deloraine, MB R0M 0M0
Tel: 204-747-2082; *Fax:* 204-747-2180
slanchbery@escape.ca

***Erickson*: Platt Law Office - *1**
Erickson Professional Centre, P.O. Box 70, 36 Main St., Erickson, MB R0J 1P0
Tel: 204-636-7838; *Fax:* 204-636-7861
ajp@plattlegal.ca
www.plattlegal.ca

***Flin Flon*: Ginnell, Bauman, Watt - *2**
47 Main St., Flin Flon, MB R8A 1N5
Tel: 204-687-3431

***Killarney*: Val Duke Law Office - *1**
514 Broadway Ave., Killarney, MB R0K 1G0
Tel: 204-523-4464; *Fax:* 204-523-5676

***Manitou*: Selby Law Office - *3**
P.O. Box 279, 351 Main St., Manitou, MB R0G 1G0
Tel: 204-242-2801; *Fax:* 204-242-2723
selbylaw@mts.net

***Minnedosa*: Sims & Company - *2**
P.O. Box 460, 76 Main St. South, Minnedosa, MB R0J 1E0
Tel: 204-867-2717; *Fax:* 204-867-2434
minnedosa@simsco.mb.ca
www.simsco.mb.ca

***Neepawa*: Taylor Law Office - *2**
P.O. Box 309, 269 Hamilton St, Neepawa, MB R0J 1H0
Tel: 204-476-2336; *Fax:* 204-476-5783
admin@taylorlawoffice.ca

***Portage la Prairie*: Miller Pressey Selinger - *1**
P.O. Box 368, 103 Saskatchewan Ave. East, Portage la Prairie, MB R1N 3B7
Tel: 204-857-3436; *Fax:* 204-857-9238
mpslaw@mts.net
millerpresseyselingerlawyer.com

***Roblin*: Marcel J.J.R. Gregoire - *1**
P.O. Box 1630, 158 Main St., Roblin, MB R0L 1P0
Tel: 204-937-2117; *Fax:* 204-937-4576
mgreg@mb.sympatico.ca

***Russell*: Mason D. Jardine - *1**
P.O. Box 1270, 346 Main St., Russell, MB R0J 1W0
Tel: 204-773-2165; *Fax:* 204-773-2920
mjardine@escape.ca

***Selkirk*: W. Douglas Kitchen - *1**
1202 River Rd., Selkirk, MB R1A 2E1
Tel: 204-482-8929

***Selkirk*: Kohaykewych & Associates - *1**
413 Main St., Selkirk, MB R1A 1V2
Tel: 204-482-7925; *Fax:* 204-482-7099
kohaykewych@mts.net

***Selkirk*: David L. Moore & Assoc. - *2**
407 Main St., Selkirk, MB R1A 1T9
Tel: 204-482-3921; *Fax:* 204-482-5564
Toll-Free: 877-482-3921
david@davidmoorelaw.ca

***Steinbach*: Loewen Henderson Banman Legault LLP - *4**
Former Name: Loewen Henderson Banman; Plett Goossen & Associates
#200, 250 Main St., Steinbach, MB R5G 1Y8
Tel: 204-326-6454; *Fax:* 204-326-6917

***Steinbach*: Smith Neufeld Jodoin LLP - *13**
P.O. Box 1267, 85 PTH 12 North, Steinbach, MB R5G 1M9
Tel: 204-326-3442; *Fax:* 204-326-2154
lawyers@snj.ca
www.snj.ca

***Stonewall*: Grantham Law Offices - *1**
#1, P.O. Box 1400, 333 Main St., Stonewall, MB R0C 2Z0
Tel: 204-467-5527; *Fax:* 204-467-5550

***Swan River*: Burnside & Ferriss - *2**
P.O. Box 340, 509 Main St. East, Swan River, MB R0L 1Z0
Tel: 204-734-3485; *Fax:* 204-734-2872
ggb@burnsideferris.com

***Swan River*: Palsson & Holmes Law Office - *2**
114 - 5th Ave. North, Swan River, MB R0L 1Z0
Tel: 204-734-4528; *Fax:* 204-734-5085

***Teulon*: Steven R. Shinnie - *1**
P.O. Box 149, 70 Main St., Teulon, MB R0C 3B0
Tel: 204-886-3959; *Fax:* 204-886-3962

***The Pas*: Bjornsson & Wight Law Office - *2**
#3, P.O. Box 1769, 314 Edwards Ave., The Pas, MB R9A 1L5
Tel: 204-627-1200; *Fax:* 204-627-1210

***The Pas*: Kelsey Community Law Centre**
P.O. Box 1770, 130 - 3rd St. West, The Pas, MB R9A 1L5
Tel: 204-627-4833; *Fax:* 204-627-4840
Toll-Free: 800-839-7946

***The Pas*: Northlands Community Law Centre**
P.O. Box 2429, 236 Edwards Ave., The Pas, MB R9A 1M2
Tel: 204-627-4820; *Fax:* 204-627-4838
Toll-Free: 800-268-9790

***Thompson*: Mayer, Dearman & Pellizzaro - *3**
7 Selkirk Ave., Thompson, MB R8N 0M4
Tel: 204-677-2393; *Fax:* 204-778-8125
www.mdplaw.ca

***Thompson*: McDonald, Huberdeau - *3**
Former Name: McDonald, Thompson, Huberdeau
Westwood Mall, 436 Thompson Dr. North, Thompson, MB R8N 0C6
Tel: 204-677-2366; *Fax:* 204-677-3249

***Thompson*: Ronald J. Nadeau Law Office - *1**
76 Severn Cres., Thompson, MB R8N 1M6
Tel: 204-774-8009; *Fax:* 204-778-6559
jrnadeau@mts.net

***Thompson*: Thompson Community Law Centre**
3 Station Rd., Thompson, MB R8N 0N3
Tel: 204-677-1211; *Fax:* 204-677-1220
Toll-Free: 800-665-0656

***Virden*: McNeill Harasymchuk McConnell - *3**
P.O. Box 520, Virden, MB R0M 2C0
Tel: 204-748-1220; *Fax:* 204-748-3007
ene@mhmlaw.ca

***Winnipeg*: Agrawal Law Office - *1**
Former Name: Ram Kishore Agrawal
#B, 83 Sherbrook St., Winnipeg, MB R3C 2B2
Tel: 204-779-7265; *Fax:* 204-779-6334

***Winnipeg*: Alexander Law Office - *1**
387 Broadway Ave., Winnipeg, MB R3C 0V5
Tel: 204-957-1717; *Fax:* 204-949-9232
dalaw_101@hotmail.com

***Winnipeg*: Antymniuk & Antymniuk**
Also Known As: Antymniuk van der Krabben
#200, 600 St. Anne's Rd., Winnipeg, MB R2M 2S2
Tel: 204-254-3511; *Fax:* 204-257-5139

***Winnipeg*: Scott Armstrong Law Office - *1**
64 Silver Springs Bay, Winnipeg, MB R2K 4L4
Tel: 204-667-3137; *Fax:* 204-667-1118
armstrong.scott@shaw.ca

***Winnipeg*: Assiniboia Law Office - *1**
Former Name: Barber Law Office
3651 Roblin Blvd., Winnipeg, MB R3R 0E2
Tel: 204-949-3240; *Fax:* 204-949-3249
algonline.ca

***Winnipeg*: Bernstein & Hirsch - *3**
883 Corydon Ave., Winnipeg, MB R3M 0W7
Tel: 204-942-0706; *Fax:* 204-957-1345

** indicates number of lawyers*

Winnipeg: Booth, Dennehy LLP - *15
387 Broadway Ave., Winnipeg, MB R3C 0V5
Tel: 204-957-1717; *Fax:* 204-943-6199
general@dek-law.com
www.boothdennehy.com

Winnipeg: Broadway Law Group - *5
#300, 326 Broadway Ave., Winnipeg, MB R3C 0S5
Tel: 204-984-9420; *Fax:* 204-947-2757

Winnipeg: Brodsky & Company - *5
#1212, 363 Broadway Ave., Winnipeg, MB R3C 3N9
Tel: 204-940-4433; *Fax:* 204-940-4435
www.gregbrodsky.ca

Winnipeg: Bradley J. Brooks - *1
P.O. Box 2461, Stn. Main, 360 Main St., Winnipeg, MB R6M 1C2
Tel: 204-992-4700; *Fax:* 866-744-2579
bbrooks@cite-on-site.ca

Winnipeg: Campbell, Marr LLP - *12
10 Donald St., Winnipeg, MB R3C 1L5
Tel: 204-942-3311; *Fax:* 204-943-7997
www.campbellmarr.com

Winnipeg: Michael Capozzi - *1
45 Wharton Blvd., Winnipeg, MB R2Y 0S9
Tel: 204-832-4807; *Fax:* 204-895-2336

Winnipeg: Cassidy Ramsay - *4
385 St. Mary Ave., 2nd Fl., Winnipeg, MB R3C 0N1
Tel: 204-943-7454; *Fax:* 204-943-9563
rcassidy@cassidyramsay.com
www.cassidyramsay.com

Winnipeg: Champagne Law Office - *1
390 Provencher Blvd., Unit F, Winnipeg, MB R2H 0H1
Tel: 204-956-1199; *Fax:* 204-956-5333

Winnipeg: Chapman Goddard Kagan - *8
1864 Portage Ave., Winnipeg, MB R3J 0H2
Tel: 204-888-7973; *Fax:* 204-832-3461
Toll-Free: 800-665-6119
info@cgklaw.ca
www.cgklaw.ca

Winnipeg: Jack M. Chapman & Associates - *1
#2250, 360 Main St., Winnipeg, MB R3C 3Z3
Tel: 204-942-9994; *Fax:* 204-885-7420

Winnipeg: Cherniack Smith - *7
#200, 100 Osborne St., Winnipeg, MB R3L 1Y5
Tel: 204-452-4000; *Fax:* 204-477-1856

Winnipeg: S. Cohan - *1
#607, 386 Broadway, Winnipeg, MB R3C 3R6
Tel: 204-944-1413; *Fax:* 204-943-5102

Winnipeg: Phillip F.B. Cramer Law Office - *1
390 York St., Winnipeg, MB R3C 0P3
Tel: 204-987-0070; *Fax:* 204-987-0076

Winnipeg: D'Arcy & Deacon LLP - Winnipeg - *46
Former Name: Swift, MacLeod, Deacon; D'Arcy, Irving, Haig & Smethurst
#2200, 1 Lombard Pl., Winnipeg, MB R3B 0X7
Tel: 204-942-2271; *Fax:* 204-943-4242
inquiries@darcydeacon.com
www.darcydeacon.com

Winnipeg: Deeley, Fabbri, Sellen - *15
#903, 386 Broadway, Winnipeg, MB R3C 3R6
Tel: 204-949-1710; *Fax:* 204-956-4457
info@dfslaw.ca
www.dfslaw.ca

Winnipeg: Dowhan & Dowhan - *2
#600, 63 Albert St., Winnipeg, MB R3B 1G4
Tel: 204-942-4235; *Fax:* 204-956-4560

Winnipeg: Duboff Edwards Haight & Schachter - *10
#1900, 155 Carlton St., Winnipeg, MB R3C 3H8
Tel: 204-942-3361; *Fax:* 204-942-3362
duboff@dehslaw.com

Winnipeg: Edmond & Associates - *4
#204, 1120 Grant Ave., Winnipeg, MB R3M 2A6
Tel: 204-452-5314; *Fax:* 204-452-5989
gedmond@edmond.ca

Winnipeg: Fillmore Riley LLP - *64
#1700, 360 Main St., Winnipeg, MB R3C 3Z3
Tel: 204-956-2970; *Fax:* 204-957-0516
frinfo@fillmoreriley.com
www.fillmoreriley.com
twitter.com/Fillmore_Riley, www.linkedin.com/company/142469

Winnipeg: Funk & Strell - *2
#1400, 1 Lombard Pl., Winnipeg, MB R3B 0X3
Tel: 204-957-5600; *Fax:* 204-949-1043
funk@mts.net

Winnipeg: George & Tweed Law Corporation - *3
Former Name: Abrams & Tweed
#4, 549 Regent Ave. West, Winnipeg, MB R2C 1R9
Tel: 204-949-3080; *Fax:* 204-949-3089
btweed@george-tweed.ca

Winnipeg: J. David George & Associates - *2
108 Regent Ave. East, Winnipeg, MB R2C 0C1
Tel: 204-982-7503; *Fax:* 204-222-4761
david-dg@shaw.ca

Winnipeg: Martin D. Glazer - *1
#1210, 363 Broadway, Winnipeg, MB R3C 3N9
Tel: 204-942-6560; *Fax:* 204-942-2696
mglazlaw@mymts.net
members.shaw.ca/Martinglazerlaw

Winnipeg: Martin R. Gutnik - *1
201 Portage Ave., 18th Fl., Winnipeg, MB R3B 3K6
Tel: 204-786-8924
martin@gutnik.com
www.gutnik.com

Winnipeg: Habing Laviolette - *3
2643 Portage Ave., Winnipeg, MB R3J 0P9
Tel: 204-832-8322; *Fax:* 204-832-3906
www.habinglaviolette.com

Winnipeg: Harrison Law Office - *6
#200, 99 Scurfield Blvd., Winnipeg, MB R3Y 1Y1
Tel: 204-989-8760; *Fax:* 204-989-8765
info@harrisonlaw.ca
www.harrisonlaw.ca

Winnipeg: Hill Sokalski Walsh Trippier LLP - *13
Former Name: Hill & Walsh
#2670, 360 Main St., Winnipeg, MB R3C 3Z3
Tel: 204-943-6740; *Fax:* 204-943-3934
lawyers@hillco.mb.ca
www.hillco.mb.ca

Winnipeg: Alain J. Hogue Law Office - *1
194 Provencher Blvd., Winnipeg, MB R2H 0G3
Tél: 204-237-9600; *Téléc:* 204-233-2689

Winnipeg: Hook & Smith - *4
#201, 3111 Portage Ave., Winnipeg, MB R3K 0W4
Tel: 204-885-4520; *Fax:* 204-837-9846
general@hookandsmith.com
hookandsmith.com

Winnipeg: D.R. Knight Law Office - *5
#202, 900 Harrow St. East, Winnipeg, MB R3M 3Y7
Tel: 204-948-0400; *Fax:* 204-948-0401
don.knight@knightlaw.ca
www.knightlawoffice.ca

Winnipeg: Krawchuk & Company - *2
#2250, 360 Main St., Winnipeg, MB R3C 3Z3
Tel: 204-943-4561; *Fax:* 204-947-5724
krawchukandco@mts.net

Winnipeg: Frank Lawrence - *1
#202, 1382 Henderson Hwy., Winnipeg, MB R2G 1M8
Tel: 204-338-9705

Winnipeg: Victoria E. Lehman Law Offices - *1
412 Wardlaw Ave., Winnipeg, MB R3L 0L7
Tel: 204-453-6416; *Fax:* 204-477-1379
www.vlehmanlawoffices.com

Winnipeg: Levene Tadman Golub Corporation - *17
#700, 330 St. Mary Ave., Winnipeg, MB R3C 3Z5
Tel: 204-957-0520; *Fax:* 204-957-1696
inquiries@ltglc.ca
www.ltgg.ca

Winnipeg: Liffman Soronow - *2
#210, 400 St. Mary Ave., Winnipeg, MB R3C 4K5
Tel: 204-925-6070; *Fax:* 204-944-0513
hal@escape.ca

Winnipeg: MacInnes, Burbidge - *1
Also Known As: Frank L. Cvitkovitch, Q.C.
#500, 177 Lombard Ave., Winnipeg, MB R3B 0W5
Tel: 204-942-5256; *Fax:* 204-942-5259
macinnesburbidge@gmail.com

Winnipeg: Hilary C. Maxim - *1
212B Regent Ave. West, Winnipeg, MB R2C 1R2
Tel: 204-224-2600; *Fax:* 204-222-2824

Winnipeg: McDonald Law Office - *1
258 Tache Ave., Winnipeg, MB R2H 1Z9
Tel: 204-927-3900; *Fax:* 204-927-3909
Toll-Free: 800-393-1110
info@mcdonaldlaw.ca
www.mcdonaldlaw.ca

Winnipeg: McJannet Rich - *6
#1308, Royal Bank Building, 220 Portage Ave., Winnipeg, MB R3C 0A5
Tel: 204-957-0951; *Fax:* 204-989-0688
www.mcjannetrich.com

Winnipeg: McRoberts Law Office LLP - *15
#200, Madison Square, 1630 Ness Ave., Winnipeg, MB R3J 3X1
Tel: 204-944-7907; *Fax:* 204-772-1684
consult@mcrobertslawoffice.com
www.mcrobertslawoffice.com

Winnipeg: Michaels & Stern - *2
#300, 326 Broadway Ave., Winnipeg, MB R3C 0S5
Tel: 204-989-5500; *Fax:* 204-989-5508
michaelsandstern@mts.net

Winnipeg: Mirwaldt & Gray - *2
#403, 171 Donald St., Winnipeg, MB R3C 1M4
Tel: 204-943-3040; *Fax:* 204-943-5135
Toll-Free: 866-630-4892
info@mirwaldtandgray.com
www.mirwaldtandgray.com

Winnipeg: Peter J. Moss - *5
1002 Pembina Hwy., Winnipeg, MB R3T 1Z5
Tel: 204-284-3221; *Fax:* 204-284-7960
mosslaw@shaw.ca

Winnipeg: Murray & Kovnats - *2
#100, 1600 Ness Ave., Winnipeg, MB R3J 3W7
Tel: 204-957-1700; *Fax:* 204-942-2325

Winnipeg: Myers Weinberg LLP - *29
#724, Cargill Bldg., 240 Graham Ave., Winnipeg, MB R3C 0J7
Tel: 204-942-0501; *Fax:* 204-956-0625
info@myersfirm.com
www.myersfirm.com

Winnipeg: Stanley S. Nozick - *1
Former Name: Nozick, Sinder & Associates
#1130, 386 Broadway, Winnipeg, MB R3C 3R6
Tel: 204-944-8227; *Fax:* 204-944-9246
snozick@escape.ca

Winnipeg: Orle, Bargen, Davidson LLP - *7
280 Stradbrook Ave., Winnipeg, MB R3L 0J6
Tel: 204-989-2760; *Fax:* 204-989-2774
reception@odgb.mb.ca
www.odgb.mb.ca

Winnipeg: Overall Grimes - *3
Former Name: Mutchmor, Violago, Overall, Grimes
390 York Ave., Winnipeg, MB R3C 0P3
Tel: 204-989-1300; *Fax:* 204-989-1301

Winnipeg: Murray S. Palay - *1
#703, 161 Portage Ave. East, Winnipeg, MB R3B 0Y4
Tel: 204-944-2491; *Fax:* 204-944-8046
mpalay@quadasset.com

Winnipeg: Parashin Law Office - *1
404 McGregor St., Winnipeg, MB R2W 4X5
Tel: 204-582-3558

Winnipeg: Phillips, Aiello - *14
668 Corydon Ave., Winnipeg, MB R3M 0X7
Tel: 204-949-7700; *Fax:* 204-452-0922
Toll-Free: 866-949-7701

** indicates number of lawyers*

***Winnipeg*: Pitblado LLP - *61**
#2500, Commodity Exchange Tower, 360 Main St., Winnipeg, MB R3C 4H6
Tel: 204-956-0560; *Fax:* 204-957-0227
firm@pitblado.com
www.pitblado.com
twitter.com/PitbladoLaw, www.linkedin.com/company/1049203

***Winnipeg*: Pollock & Company - *5**
#1120, 363 Broadway, Winnipeg, MB R3C 3N9
Tel: 204-956-0450; *Fax:* 204-947-0109
mail@pollockandcompany.com
www.pollockandcompany.com

***Winnipeg*: Prober Law Offices - *1**
#208, 387 Broadway Ave., Winnipeg, MB R3C 0V5
Tel: 204-957-1205; *Fax:* 204-943-6199

***Winnipeg*: Pullan Kammerloch Frohlinger - *10**
#300, 240 Kennedy St., Winnipeg, MB R3C 1T1
Tel: 204-956-0490; *Fax:* 204-947-3747
www.pkflawyers.com

***Winnipeg*: Radchuk & Company - *1**
10 Salvia Bay, Winnipeg, MB R2V 2L8
Tel: 204-338-8880; *Fax:* 204-334-5241

***Winnipeg*: Edward Rice - *1**
#301, 63 Albert St., Winnipeg, MB R3B 1G4
Tel: 204-944-1905; *Fax:* 204-947-5895
ricelaw@mts.net

***Winnipeg*: Russell Ridd - *1**
#6, 405 Broadway, Winnipeg, MB R3C 3L6
Tel: 204-945-2852; *Fax:* 204-945-1260
russ.ridd@gov.mb.ca

***Winnipeg*: Robertson Shypit Soble Wood - *7**
#202, 1555 St. Mary's Rd., Winnipeg, MB R2M 5L9
Tel: 204-257-6061; *Fax:* 204-254-7183
info@rsswlawyers.com
www.rsswlawyers.com

***Winnipeg*: James F.C. Rose - *1**
582 Bruce Ave., Winnipeg, MB R3J 0W5
Tel: 204-889-3885; *Fax:* 204-889-3885
Toll-Free: 800-414-8091
jamesrose@shaw.ca
www.members.shaw.ca/jamesrose/baddebt.htm

***Winnipeg*: Rosenbaum & Company - *1**
#201, 2211 McPhillips St., Winnipeg, MB R2V 3M5
Tel: 204-338-4663; *Fax:* 204-338-4667
racplan@mts.net
www.rosenbaumandco.ca

***Winnipeg*: Sheldon Rosenstock - *1**
848 Waterloo St., Winnipeg, MB R3N 0T6
Tel: 204-488-4121; *Fax:* 204-488-1869
sheldon@mymts.net

***Winnipeg*: St. Mary's Law LLP - *1**
Former Name: Inkster Christie Hughes LLP
619 St. Mary Rd., Winnipeg, MB R2M 3L8
Tel: 204-942-1799; *Fax:* 204-947-6800
pbruckshaw@stmaryslaw.com
www.divorcelawyerwinnipeg.com

***Winnipeg*: Mario J. Santos - *1**
#202, 1080 Wall Street, Winnipeg, MB R3E 2R9
Tel: 204-783-0554; *Fax:* 204-772-4231
mjsantos@mts.net
www.mariosantoslawoffice.com

***Winnipeg*: Shewchuk & Associates - *2**
2645 Portage Ave., Winnipeg, MB R3J 0P9
Tel: 204-889-4595

***Winnipeg*: Sinclair & Associates - *2**
#231, 1120 Grant Ave., Winnipeg, MB R3M 2A6
Tel: 204-474-2468; *Fax:* 204-474-2535

***Winnipeg*: Sidney Soronow - *1**
Former Name: Liffman Soronow
#210, 400 St. Mary Ave., Winnipeg, MB R3C 4K5
Tel: 204-925-6074; *Fax:* 204-944-0513

***Winnipeg*: J.S. Sukhan - *1**
1158 Clarence Ave., Winnipeg, MB R3T 1S9
Tel: 204-284-0728

***Winnipeg*: Tacium, Vincent, Orlikow - *1**
#200, 99A Scurfield Blvd., Winnipeg, MB R3Y 1G4
Tel: 204-989-4220; *Fax:* 204-254-7744
taciumvincentorlikow.com

***Winnipeg*: Tapper Cuddy LLP - *28**
Former Name: Scufield Tupper Cuddy
#1000, 330 St. Mary Ave., Winnipeg, MB R3C 3Z5
Tel: 204-944-8777; *Fax:* 204-947-2593
tc@tappercuddy.com
www.tappercuddy.com

***Winnipeg*: Taylor McCaffrey LLP - *62**
400 St. Mary Ave., 9th Fl., Winnipeg, MB R3C 4K5
Tel: 204-949-1312; *Fax:* 204-957-0945
www.tmlawyers.com

***Winnipeg*: Tepley Law Office - *1**
#401, 460 Main St., Winnipeg, MB R3B 1B6
Tel: 204-942-7218

***Winnipeg*: Teskey Legal & ADR Services - *1**
1905 One Evergreen Pl., Winnipeg, MB R3L 0E9
Tel: 204-943-8395; *Fax:* 204-943-1288
teskey@mb.sympatico.ca

***Winnipeg*: Thompson Dorfman Sweatman LLP - Winnipeg - *75**
Also Known As: TDS
#2200, 201 Portage Ave., Winnipeg, MB R3B 3L3
Tel: 204-957-1930; *Fax:* 204-934-0570
www.tdslaw.com
www.facebook.com/tdslaw, www.twitter.com/tdslaw,
www.linkedin.com/company/thompson-dorfman-sweatman-llp

***Winnipeg*: John F. Thullner - *1**
#102, 2200 McPhillips St., Winnipeg, MB R2V 3P4
Tel: 204-694-0161

***Winnipeg*: Tradition Law LLP - *4**
#200, 207 Donald St., Winnipeg, MB R3C 1M5
Tel: 204-947-6806; *Fax:* 204-947-3705
info@traditionlaw.ca
www.traditionlaw.ca

***Winnipeg*: Troniak Law - *2**
#1000, 444 St Mary Ave., Winnipeg, MB R3C 3T1
Tel: 204-947-1743; *Fax:* 204-947-0101
info@troniaklaw.com
www.troniaklaw.com

***Winnipeg*: Tupper & Adams - *3**
#201, 90 Garry St., Winnipeg, MB R3C 4H1
Tel: 204-942-0161; *Fax:* 204-943-2385
general@Tupper-Adams.mb.ca
www.tupper-adams.mb.ca

***Winnipeg*: W.R. Van Walleghem - *1**
#206, 1120 Grant Ave., Winnipeg, MB R3M 2A6
Tel: 204-477-0210; *Fax:* 204-452-9746

***Winnipeg*: Walsh & Company - *3**
426 Portage Ave., 2nd Fl., Winnipeg, MB R3C 0C9
Tel: 204-947-2282; *Fax:* 204-943-0211
paulwalsh@walshandco.com
www.walshandco.com

***Winnipeg*: Warkentin & Calver - *1**
3651 Roblin Blvd., Winnipeg, MB R3R 0E2
Tel: 204-949-3230; *Fax:* 204-949-3249

***Winnipeg*: Eugene Waskiw - *1**
441 Perth Ave., Winnipeg, MB R2V 0T9
Tel: 204-334-7372

***Winnipeg*: Arthur M. Werier - *1**
905 Corydon Ave., Winnipeg, MB R3M 0W8
Tel: 204-475-7923

***Winnipeg*: Wilder Wilder & Langtry - *6**
#1500, Richardson Bldg., 1 Lombard Pl., Winnipeg, MB R3B 0X3
Tel: 204-947-1456; *Fax:* 204-957-1368
www.wilderwilder.com

***Winnipeg*: Zaifman Associates - *4**
#500, 191 Lombard Ave., 5th Fl., Winnipeg, MB R3B 0X1
Tel: 204-944-8888; *Fax:* 204-956-2909
zaifman@zaifmanlaw.com
www.zaifmanlaw.com

***Winnipeg*: Saheel, Zaman Law Corporation - *4**
#1130, 363 Broadway, Winnipeg, MB R3C 3N9
Tel: 204-943-9922; *Fax:* 204-975-1802
szaman@szamanlaw.com

***Winnipeg*: Daria Zyla - *1**
1230 Hector Bay West, Winnipeg, MB R3M 3R9
Tel: 204-452-5626; *Fax:* 204-475-7979

New Brunswick

***Atholville*: Roger G. Gauvin - *1**
65 Fairview St., Atholville, NB E3N 4N3
Tel: 506-753-4545; *Fax:* 506-753-2006

***Bathurst*: Robert M. Boudreau - *1**
#100, 1154 St. Peter Ave., Bathurst, NB E2A 2Z9
Tél: 506-545-2099; *Téléc:* 506-546-4765
rboudro@nbnet.nb.ca

***Bathurst*: Chiasson & Roy - *4**
#203, Stn. Main, 216 Main St., Bathurst, NB E2A 3Z2
Tel: 506-548-3375; *Fax:* 506-548-4264
www.chiassonroy.ca

***Bathurst*: Riordon, Arseneault & Theriault - *5**
Former Name: Robichaud, Williamson, Theriault & Johnstone
#300, Keystone Place, P.O. Box 506, 270 Douglas Ave., Bathurst, NB E2A 3Z4
Tel: 506-548-8822; *Fax:* 506-548-5297

***Bouctouche*: Yvon J.G. LeBlanc - *2**
P.O. Box 310, 25, boul Irving, Bouctouche, NB E0A 1G0
Tel: 506-743-2427; *Fax:* 506-743-8314
lebbell@nbnet.nb.ca

***Bouctouche*: Mark Robere - *1**
#2, 6, rue Station, Bouctouche, NB E4S 3X1
Tel: 506-743-2262; *Fax:* 506-743-9014
roberem@nb.aibn.com

***Campbellton*: J.Yvon Arseneau C.P. Inc. - *3**
Former Name: Arseneau & Associés
114 Water St., Campbellton, NB E3N 1B3
Tel: 506-753-3000; *Fax:* 506-753-2393

***Campbellton*: Terrance H. Delaney, Q.C. - *2**
#206, P.O. Box 490, 123 Water St., Campbellton, NB E3N 3G9
Tel: 506-753-7618; *Fax:* 506-759-7315
terra1@nb.sympatico.ca

***Caraquet*: Alie A. LeBouthillier - *1**
CP 5661, 295, boul St-Pierre ouest, Caraquet, NB E1W 1B7
Tél: 506-727-3484; *Téléc:* 506-727-3484
alie@nb.aira.com

***Chipman*: Nicholas D. DiCarlo**
P.O. Box 489, Stn. Main, 131 Main St., Chipman, NB E4A 3N6
Tel: 506-339-6688; *Fax:* 506-339-5598
ndicarlo@nb.aibn.com

***Chipman*: Sharon R. Lockwood - *1**
28 Northrup Dr., Chipman, NB E4A 2P7
Tel: 506-339-6632; *Fax:* 506-339-5130
sharon.lockwood@nb.aibn.com

***Dieppe*: Martin J. Aubin - *1**
250 Acadie Ave., Dieppe, NB E1A 1G5
Tel: 506-856-6083; *Fax:* 506-853-0110

***Dieppe*: Jacques Gauthier - *1**
157 Lakeburn Ave., Dieppe, NB E1A 8N5
Tél: 506-383-4564
acadian22@hotmail.com

***Dieppe*: Thompson & Thompson - *2**
379 Champlain St., Dieppe, NB E1A 1P2
Tel: 506-859-7794; *Fax:* 506-859-1297
ttlaw@nbnet.nb.ca
www.thompsonandthompson.ca

***Edmundston*: Pilote Morin & Moreau - *3**
#304, 121, rue de l'Église, Edmundston, NB E3V 1J9
Tél: 506-739-7311
pmm@nb.aibn.com
www.pilotemorinmoreau.ca

***Fredericton*: Athey & Gregory - *2**
206 Rockwood Ave., Fredericton, NB E3B 2M2
Tel: 506-458-8060; *Fax:* 506-459-8288
gordon.gregory@nb.aibn.com
www.atyp.com/atheygregory/

***Fredericton*: Atkinson & Atkinson - *1**
108 Queen St., Fredericton, NB E3B 5B4
Tel: 506-451-7777; *Fax:* 506-451-1029

***Fredericton*: Barbara Hughes Campbell - *3**
186 Waterloo Row, Fredericton, NB E3B 4Y9
Tel: 506-458-8140; *Fax:* 506-450-6186
www.barbarahughescampbell.com

** indicates number of lawyers*

***Fredericton*: Carol H.Y. Boxill - *1**
57 Carleton St., Fredericton, NB E3B 6Y8
Tel: 506-454-5108; *Fax:* 506-450-3880

***Fredericton*: Le Cabinet Bertrand Law - *1**
Former Name: Bertrand & Bertrand
700 Mcleod Ave., Fredericton, NB E3B 1V5
Tel: 506-450-3325; *Fax:* 506-450-6333

***Fredericton*: Barbara Hughes Campbell - *1**
186 Waterloo Row, Fredericton, NB E3B 1Z2
Tel: 506-458-8140; *Fax:* 506-450-6186
www.barbarahughescampbell.com/en/

***Fredericton*: Collingwood Stephen Law Office - *1**
#5, Pepper Creek Plaza, 336, Rte. 10, Richibucto Rd., Fredericton, NB E3A 7E1
Tel: 506-458-1880; *Fax:* 506-458-9868
peppercreek@brunnet.net

***Fredericton*: Dean & McMath - *2**
406 Regent St., Fredericton, NB E3B 3X7
Tel: 506-458-8555; *Fax:* 506-444-0920
dwmcmath@deanmcmath.ca

***Fredericton*: Eddy & Downs**
#210, P.O. Box 1205, Stn. A, 65 Regent St., Fredericton, NB E3B 5C8
Tel: 506-443-9700; *Fax:* 506-443-9710

***Fredericton*: Elliott McCrea Hill - *8**
Former Name: Matthews McCrea Elliott; Matthews Teriault
197 Main St., Fredericton, NB E3A 1E1
Tel: 506-458-5959; *Fax:* 506-460-5934
office@emhlaw.com
emhlaw.com

***Fredericton*: Foster & Company - *9**
#200, 919 Prospect St., Fredericton, NB E3B 2T7
Tel: 506-462-4000; *Fax:* 506-462-4001
info@fandclaw.com
www.fandclaw.com

***Fredericton*: Glencross Ashford - *2**
288 Union St., Fredericton, NB E3A 1E5
Tel: 506-454-1256; *Fax:* 506-454-2365
www.glencrossashford.com

***Fredericton*: Daniel W. McCormack - *1**
P.O. Box 1356, Stn. A, 259 Brunswick St., Fredericton, NB E3B 5S3
Tel: 506-459-3331; *Fax:* 506-457-6332

***Fredericton*: McNally & Smart - *2**
P.O. Box 3152, Stn. LCD 1, 819 Union St., Fredericton, NB E3A 5G9
Tel: 506-472-4872; *Fax:* 506-472-9844

***Fredericton*: Donna E. Mitchell - *1**
#301, 358 Kng St., Fredericton, NB E3B 1E3
Tel: 506-451-1117; *Fax:* 506-459-2228
info@donnaemitchell.com
www.donnaemitchell.com

***Fredericton*: E.J. Mockler - *1**
495C Prospect St., Fredericton, NB E3B 9M4
Tel: 506-454-8200; *Fax:* 506-454-7300
pete@ejmockler.ca
www.ejmockler.com/en/

***Fredericton*: Murray Digdon Donovan - *3**
#102, 401 Biship Dr., Fredericton, NB E3C 2M6
Tel: 506-458-1108; *Fax:* 506-458-2645
amurray@mddlaw.ca
www.kennymurray.com

***Fredericton*: J. Shawn O'Toole - *1**
#201, 346 Queen St., Fredericton, NB E3B 1B2
Tel: 506-458-8833; *Fax:* 506-454-1999

***Fredericton*: Peters Rouse - *3**
Former Name: Mockler, Peters, Oley, Rouse & Williams
P.O. Box 547, Stn. A, 839 Aberdeen St., Fredericton, NB E3B 5A6
Tel: 506-444-6589; *Fax:* 506-444-6550
www.porlaw.com

***Fredericton*: Pink Larkin - *4**
Former Name: Pink Breen Larkin
#210, 1133 Regent St., Fredericton, NB E3B 3Z2
Tel: 506-458-1989; *Fax:* 506-458-1127
Toll-Free: 888-280-2777
jbartlett@pinklarkin.com
www.pinklarkin.com

***Fredericton*: Gerald R. Pugh - *1**
57 Carleton St., 4th Fl., Fredericton, NB E3B 3T2
Tel: 506-450-2666; *Fax:* 506-457-4295
info@easternlegal.ca
www.geraldpugh.com

***Fredericton*: Rowan McGrath Lawyers - *2**
#206, 403 Regent St., Fredericton, NB E3B 3X6
Tel: 506-451-0657; *Fax:* 506-451-8011
drowan@rowanmcgrath.ca
www.rowanmcgrath.ca

***Fredericton*: Michael J.F. Scully - *1**
9 Amanda St., Fredericton, NB E3G 0N5
Tel: 506-999-5035; *Fax:* 506-472-0240
scullylaw@gmail.com
scullylaw.ca

***Fredericton*: P. Lorrie Yerxa - *3**
Former Name: Yerxa, Stephenson
#102, Stn. A, 403 Regent St., Fredericton, NB E3B 4Y9
Tel: 506-459-1450; *Fax:* 506-459-2301

***Grand Falls*: Godbout, Ouellette - *2**
698 E.H. Daigle Blvd., Grand Falls, NB E3Z 2S1
Tel: 506-473-6272; *Fax:* 506-473-6065
godouel@nbnet.nb.ca

***Grand Falls*: Peter Seheult - *1**
275A Sheriff St., Grand Falls, NB E3Z 3A1
Tel: 506-473-2164; *Fax:* 506-473-5543
pdseheult@rogers.com

***Hampton*: Veniot Law Office - *1**
Former Name: Veniot Loughery Levine
71 Randall Dr., Hampton, NB E5N 6A4
Tel: 506-832-3418; *Fax:* 506-832-3755
vll@nb.aibn.com

***Lamèque*: Roger A. Noël - *2**
CP 2038, Stn. Main, 5120E, rte 113, Lamèque, NB E8T 3N4
Tél: 506-344-2217; *Téléc:* 506-344-5380
rogeranoel@nb.aibn.com
www.etudelegalenoel.com

***Minto*: Mario DiCarlo Law Office - *1**
255 Main St., Minto, NB E4B 3R8
Tel: 506-327-3777; *Fax:* 506-327-6080
mariodicarlo@bellaliant.net

***Minto*: Sheila R. Thorne - *1**
29 Queen St., Minto, NB E4B 3P2
Tel: 506-327-6120

***Miramichi*: Rosemary Losier - *1**
P.O. Box 112, Stn. Main, 173 Wellington St., Miramichi, NB E1N 3A5
Tel: 506-773-6817

***Miramichi*: Maynes Law - *4**
P.O. Box 518, 1723 Water St., Miramichi, NB E1N 3A8
Tel: 506-778-8336; *Fax:* 506-778-2103

***Moncton*: Michel C. Arsenault - *1**
1255 Main St., Moncton, NB E1C 1H9
Tel: 506-857-8008; *Fax:* 506-857-8885
mcalaw@nb.aibn.com

***Moncton*: Bingham Law - *16**
Former Name: Bingham Robinson McLennan Ehrhardt & Teed
#300, Heritage Court, 95 Foundry St., Moncton, NB E1C 5H7
Tel: 506-857-8856; *Fax:* 506-857-2017
info@bingham.ca
www.bingham.ca

***Moncton*: Robert N. Charman - *1**
170 Highfield St., Moncton, NB E1C 5P2
Tel: 506-854-8656; *Fax:* 506-854-8684
rcharman@nbnet.nb.ca
www.robertncharman.com

***Moncton*: Delehanty Rinzler Druckman - *2**
Former Name: Tedford Delehanty Rinzler
#101, P.O. Box 1083, 720 Main St., Moncton, NB E1C 8P6
Tel: 506-857-3030; *Fax:* 506-857-0085
mail@drdlaw.ca
www.drdlaw.ca

***Moncton*: Forbes Roth Basque - *5**
#300, P.O. Box 480, 814 Main St., Moncton, NB E1C 8L9
Tel: 506-857-4880; *Fax:* 506-857-0151
www.forbesrothbasque.nb.ca

***Moncton*: Fowler & Fowler - *2**
69 Waterloo St., Moncton, NB E1C 0E1
Tel: 506-857-8811; *Fax:* 506-857-9297
www.fowlerandfowler.ca

***Moncton*: groupe Murphy group - *4**
128 Highfield St., Moncton, NB E1C 5N7
Tel: 506-877-0077; *Fax:* 506-877-0079
info@murphygroup.ca
www.murphygroup.ca

***Moncton*: LeBlanc Boucher Rodger Bourque - *3**
740 Main St., Moncton, NB E1C 1E6
Tel: 506-858-0110; *Fax:* 506-858-9497

***Moncton*: LeBlanc Boudreau Maillet**
Former Name: LeBlanc Boudreau Desjardins Maillet
#200, 735 Main St., Moncton, NB E1C 1E5
Tel: 506-858-5666; *Fax:* 506-858-5570

***Moncton*: Susan D. LeBlanc - *1**
76 Albert St., Moncton, NB E1C 1B1
Tel: 506-859-4402; *Fax:* 506-859-9195

***Moncton*: Letcher & Murray - *3**
76 Albert St., Moncton, NB E1C 1B1
Tel: 506-857-2070; *Fax:* 506-859-9195

***Moncton*: Lise Lorrain - *1**
40 Edgett Ave., Moncton, NB E1C 7B2
Tel: 506-855-6084; *Fax:* 506-389-3867

***Moncton*: Kenneth Martin - *1**
51 Highfield St., Moncton, NB E1C 5N2
Tel: 506-867-2522
kennethmartinlaw.yolasite.com

***Moncton*: Mitchell Law Office - *1**
Former Name: MacPherson Mitchell
89 Church St., Moncton, NB E1C 4Z4
Tel: 506-853-1105; *Fax:* 506-857-9129

***Moncton*: Murphy Collette Murphy - *6**
250 Lutz St., Moncton, NB E1C 5G3
Tel: 506-856-8560; *Fax:* 506-856-8579
manager@murco.nb.ca
www.murco.nb.ca

***Moncton*: Murphy, Murphy & Mollins - *3**
89 Church St., Moncton, NB E1C 4Z4
Tel: 506-857-9120; *Fax:* 506-857-9129
mmmlaw@nb.aibn.com

***Moncton*: Alan D. Schelew - *1**
#100, P.O. Box 182, 803 Main St., Moncton, NB E1C 8K9
Tel: 506-857-2272; *Fax:* 506-857-2276
schelew@nb.aibn.com
www.monctonlawyer.com

***Moncton*: Sheehan Law - *1**
76 Albert St., Moncton, NB E1C 1B1
Tel: 506-387-7400; *Fax:* 506-859-9588

***Oromocto*: Blair W. McKay - *1**
#3, 291 Restigouche Rd., Oromocto, NB E2V 2H2
Tel: 506-446-3000; *Fax:* 506-446-9010

***Perth-Andover*: Mark C. Johnson - *1**
Former Name: Crocco, Hunter, Purvis, Johnson
P.O. Box 3066, 14A Beech Glen Rd., Perth-Andover, NB E7H 1J8
Tel: 506-273-6818; *Fax:* 506-273-6590
mjlaw@nb.aibn.com

***Riverview*: Grew MacDonald - *3**
Former Name: McAllister & Grew
704A Coverdale Rd., Riverview, NB E1B 3L1
Tel: 506-856-8870; *Fax:* 506-856-8879
hgrew@nbnet.nb.ca

***Riverview*: Wilbur Law Offices - *1**
Former Name: Wilbur & Wilbur
706B Coverdale Rd., Riverview, NB E1B 3L1
Tel: 506-387-7715; *Fax:* 506-387-5875
info@wilburlaw.ca
www.wilburlaw.ca

***Sackville*: Meldrum Law - *2**
7 Bridge St., Sackville, NB E4L 3N6
Tel: 506-536-3870; *Fax:* 506-536-2131
Toll-Free: 866-792-1416
meldrumk@nbnet.nb.ca

** indicates number of lawyers*

***Sackville*: Ove B. Samuelsen - *1**
1 Squire St., Sackville, NB E4L 4K8
Tel: 506-536-0511; *Fax:* 506-536-1169
www.ovesamuelsen.com

***Saint John*: Michael D. Bamford**
#420, 40 Charlotte St., Saint John, NB E2L 2H6
Tel: 506-634-8132; *Fax:* 506-633-0389

***Saint John*: Boyle, Dennis - *1**
345 Lancaster Ave. W, Saint John, NB E2M 2L3
Tel: 506-634-7575

***Saint John*: BretonKean Lawyers - *7**
Former Name: Barry Spalding
P.O. Box 6907, 75 Prince William St., 4th Fl., Saint John, NB E2L 4S3
Tel: 506-633-2556; *Fax:* 506-633-5902
info@brentonkean.com
www.brentonkean.com

***Saint John*: Carleton Law Group - *2**
Former Name: Sherwood & Flanagan
117 Carleton St., Saint John, NB E2L 2Z6
Tel: 506-634-0001; *Fax:* 506-634-0456
info@carletonlawgroup.com
www.carletonlawgroup.com

***Saint John*: Correia & Collins - *3**
Market Sq., 3rd Level Dockside, P.O. Box 6969, Stn. A, Saint John, NB E2L 4S4
Tel: 506-648-1700; *Fax:* 506-648-1701
chris.correia@correiaandcollins.com
www.correiaandcollins.com

***Saint John*: Allen G. Doyle Law Office - *1**
45 Canterbury St., Saint John, NB E2L 2C6
Tel: 506-633-4198; *Fax:* 506-633-1645

***Saint John*: Lynda D. Farrell - *4**
P.O. Box 1971, Stn. Main, 15 Market Sq., 8th Fl., Saint John, NB E2L 4L1
Tel: 506-658-2860; *Fax:* 506-649-7939

***Saint John*: Gilbert McGloan Gillis - *7**
Also Known As: GMC
P.O. Box 7174, 22 King St., 2nd Fl., Saint John, NB E2L 1G3
Tel: 506-634-3600; *Fax:* 506-634-3612
Toll-Free: 888-246-4529
www.gmglaw.com

***Saint John*: Gorman Nason Lawyers - *10**
P.O. Box 7286, Stn. A, 121 Germain St., Saint John, NB E2L 4S6
Tel: 506-634-8600; *Fax:* 506-634-8685
rec@gormannason.com
www.gormannason.com

***Saint John*: John M. Henderson - *1**
#410, 40 Charlotte St., Saint John, NB E2L 2H6
Tel: 506-652-5502; *Fax:* 506-634-1795
jmhlaw@nbnet.nb.ca

***Saint John*: Frank J. Hogan - *1**
491 Bay St. West, Saint John, NB E2M 7L3
Tel: 506-333-4646

***Saint John*: Mary Ann G. Holland - *1**
#2B, P.O. Box 7041, Stn. Brunswick Sq., 28 King St., Saint John, NB E2L 4S4
Tel: 506-652-3774; *Fax:* 506-633-0581
lawyer@nbnet.nb.ca

***Saint John*: Lisa A. Keenan - *1**
108 Prince William St., Saint John, NB E2L 2B3
Tel: 506-632-8999

***Saint John*: W. Rodney Macdonald - *1**
108 Prince William St., Saint John, NB E2L 3J5
Tel: 506-632-8999; *Fax:* 506-634-1532

***Saint John*: Elizabeth T. McLeod, QC - *1**
#5C, Brunswick Sq., P.O. Box 20045, 28 King St., Saint John, NB E2L 5B2
Tel: 506-632-4048; *Fax:* 506-652-6594

***Saint John*: Mosher Chedore - *9**
885 Danells Dr., Saint John, NB E2M 5A9
Tel: 506-634-1600; *Fax:* 506-634-0740
www.mosherchedore.ca

***Saint John*: Richard A. Northrup - *1**
#420, 40 Charlotte St., Saint John, NB E2L 2H6
Tel: 506-634-8134; *Fax:* 506-693-3473
nbrick@nb.aibn.com

***Saint John*: Riley, John G. - *1**
#410, 40 Charlotte St., Saint John, NB E2L 2H6
Tel: 506-634-1188; *Fax:* 506-634-1795

***Saint John*: Teed & Teed - *1**
P.O. Box 6639, Stn. A, 127 Prince William St., Saint John, NB E2L 4S1
Tel: 506-634-7320; *Fax:* 506-634-7423
info@teedandteed.com
www.teedandteed.com

***Saint John*: Whelly & Kelly - *4**
122 Carleton St., Saint John, NB E2L 2Z7
Tel: 506-634-1193; *Fax:* 506-693-9040

***Saint John*: Patrick R. Wilbur - *1**
15 Market Sq., 4th Fl., Saint John, NB E2L 1E8
Tel: 506-658-2580; *Fax:* 506-658-3061
patrick.wilbur@gnb.ca

***Saint John*: Theodore E. Wilson - *1**
#A-112, Prince Edward St., Saint John, NB E2L 4M5
Tel: 506-633-8788; *Fax:* 506-632-2023
theowil@nb.aibn.com

***Shediac*: Michel C. Leger - *2**
Also Known As: Hebert Leger
5, rue Mill, Shediac, NB E4P 2H8
Tél: 506-532-0100; *Téléc:* 506-532-6332
ca.linkedin.com/in/michelcleger

***Shippagan*: Godin, Lizotte, Robichaud, Guignard - *4**
239A J.D Gauthier Blvd., Shippagan, NB E8S 1N2
Tél: 506-336-0400; *Téléc:* 506-336-0409

***Shippagan*: Theriault, Larocque, Boudreau - *3**
Former Name: Theriault, Larocque & Associés
283 J.D. Gauthier Blvd., Shippagan, NB E8S 1N6
Tel: 506-336-4726; *Fax:* 506-336-1159
tla@nbnet.nb.ca

***St Andrews*: David A. Bartlett - *1**
Also Known As: Bartlett & Harrison
Former Name: Larsen & Bartlett
64 King St., St Andrews, NB E5B 1Y3
Tel: 506-529-9000; *Fax:* 506-529-9003
bartllaw@nb.aibn.com

***St George*: Peter A. Johnston Law Office - *2**
4 Main St., St George, NB E5C 3J1
Tel: 506-755-3376; *Fax:* 506-755-8044
larjon@nbnet.nb.ca

***Sussex*: Gary M. Fulton - *1**
30 Church Ave., Sussex, NB E4E 1Y7
Tel: 506-433-4215; *Fax:* 506-433-4216
lawyers@nbnet.nb.ca

***Sussex*: D. James Garrish - *1**
19 Maxwell Dr., Sussex, NB E4S 2S4
Tel: 506-433-8678; *Fax:* 506-433-6994
jgerrish1@rogers.com

***Sussex*: Palmer & Palmer - *2**
17 Queen St., Sussex, NB E4E 2A4
Tel: 506-433-2168; *Fax:* 506-433-4740
emily@palmerlaw.ca
www.palmerlaw.ca/en/

***Tracadie-Sheila*: Doiron, Lebouthillier, Boudreau, Allain - *4**
CP 3010, Stn. Bureau, 3674, rue Principale, Tracadie-Sheila, NB E1X 1G5
Tél: 506-395-0044; *Téléc:* 506-395-0050
dllb@nbnet.nb.ca

***Woodstock*: McCue Brewer Dickinson - *3**
179 Broadway St., Woodstock, NB E7M 1B7
Tel: 506-325-2835; *Fax:* 506-328-6248
mblaw@nbnet.nb.ca

***Woodstock*: Stephen L. Wilson - *1**
Former Name: Wilson & Kinney
#1, 733 Main St., Woodstock, NB E7M 2E6
Tel: 506-325-1100; *Fax:* 506-328-4873
stepwil@nbnet.nb.ca

Newfoundland & Labrador

***Bay Roberts*: Moores & Collins - *2**
Former Name: Moores, Andrews, Collins
P.O. Box 806, 268 Conception Bay Hwy., Bay Roberts, NL A0A 1G0
Fax: 709-786-6952
Toll-Free: 855-786-7114
mac@mac-law.ca
www.mac-law.ca

***Bay Roberts*: Morrow & Morrow - *2**
P.O. Box 870, 344 Conception Bay Hwy., Bay Roberts, NL A0A 1G0
Tel: 709-786-9207; *Fax:* 709-786-9507
Toll-Free: 888-786-9207
morrow@nf.aibn.com
www.morrow-law.ca

***Carbonear*: J. William Finn - *1**
66 Powell Dr., Carbonear, NL A1Y 1A5
Tel: 709-596-5143; *Fax:* 709-596-3208
www.legalservicescbn.com/en/

***Channel-Port-aux-Basques*: Marks & Parsons - *4**
174 Caribou Rd., Channel-Port-aux-Basques, NL A0M 1C0
Tel: 709-695-7341; *Fax:* 709-695-3944

***Clarenville*: Hughes & Brannan Law Offices - *2**
357 Memorial Dr., Clarenville, NL A5A 1R8
Tel: 709-466-3106; *Fax:* 709-466-3107
hughes.brannan@nfld.net

***Conception Bay South*: Robert R. Regular - *2**
P.O. Box 14002, Stn. Manuels, 131 Conception Bay Hwy., Conception Bay South, NL A1W 3J1
Tel: 709-834-2132; *Fax:* 709-834-3025
general@robertregularlaw.com
www.robertregularlaw.com

***Corner Brook*: Poole Althouse, Barristers & Solicitors - *10**
Former Name: Poole, Althouse, Thompson & Thomas
49 - 51 Park St., Corner Brook, NL A2H 2X1
Tel: 709-634-3136; *Fax:* 709-634-8247
Toll-Free: 877-634-3136
info@pa-law.ca
www.poolealthouse.ca

***Corner Brook*: Graham Watton - *1**
Noton Bldg., P.O. Box 188, 133 Riverside Dr., Corner Brook, NL A2H 6C7
Tel: 709-639-7490; *Fax:* 709-634-7229

***Gander*: Easton Hillier Lawrence Preston - *9**
Former Name: Easton Facey Hillier Lawrence
Polaris Bldg., 61 Elizabeth Dr., Gander, NL A1V 1G4
Tel: 709-256-4006; *Fax:* 709-651-2850
Toll-Free: 800-256-4006
info@ganderlawyers.com
www.ganderlawyers.com

***Labrador City*: Miller & Hearn - *2**
P.O. Box 129, Stn. Main, Labrador City, NL A2V 2K3
Tel: 709-944-3666; *Fax:* 709-944-5494
miller&hearn@crrstv.net

***Mount Pearl*: Budden, Morris - *4**
184 Park Ave., Mount Pearl, NL A1N 1K8
Tel: 709-747-0077; *Fax:* 709-747-0104
lawyers@buddenmorris.com
www.buddenmorris.com

***Paradise*: Aylward, Chislett & Whitten - *5**
#200, 1655 Topsail Road, Paradise, NL A1L 1V1
Tel: 709-722-6000; *Fax:* 709-726-1225
contact@acwlaw.ca
www.acwlaw.ca

***Paradise*: Susan L. Fisher - *1**
31 Deborah Lynn Hts., Paradise, NL A1L 3E6
Tel: 709-773-1806; *Fax:* 709-773-1807

***Springdale*: Shawn C.A. Colbourne Law Office - *1**
8 Juniper Rd., Springdale, NL A0J 1T0
Tel: 709-673-3693; *Fax:* 709-673-3991
colbourne.5@nf.sympatico.ca

** indicates number of lawyers*

***St. John's*: Benson Buffett - *14**
Former Name: Benson Myles
#900, Atlantic Place, P.O. Box 1538, 215 Water St., St. John's, NL A1C 5N8
Tel: 709-579-2081; *Fax:* 709-579-2647
Toll-Free: 888-325-3425
info@bensonbuffett.com
www.bensonbuffett.com

***St. John's*: Browne, Fitzgerald, Morgan & Avis - *4**
Terrace on the Square, Level II, P.O. Box 23135, RPO Churchill Sq., St. John's, NL A1B 4J9
Tel: 709-724-3800; *Fax:* 709-754-3800
info@bfma-law.com
www.bfma-law.com

***St. John's*: Ches Crosbie Barristers - *4**
169 Water St., St. John's, NL A1C 1B1
Tel: 709-579-4000; *Fax:* 709-579-9671
Toll-Free: 888-579-3262
www.chescrosbie.com

***St. John's*: Curtis Dawe Lawyers - *17**
Fortis Building, 139 Water St., 11th Fl., St. John's, NL A1C 5J9
Tel: 709-722-5181; *Fax:* 709-722-7521
curtisdawe@curtisdawe.com
www.curtisdawe.nf.ca

***St. John's*: Duffy & Associates**
640 Torbay Rd., St. John's, NL A1A 5G9
Tel: 709-726-5298; *Fax:* 709-726-8883
www.duffylawyers.com

***St. John's*: Fraize Law Offices - *2**
P.O. Box 5217, Stn. C, 268 Duckworth St., St. John's, NL A1C 5W1
Tel: 709-726-7978; *Fax:* 709-726-8201
tfraize@fraizelawoffices.nf.net

***St. John's*: French & Associates - *3**
Former Name: French, Noseworthy & Associates; French, Dunne & Associates
#122, Elizabeth Towers, 100 Elizabeth Ave., St. John's, NL A1B 1R8
Tel: 709-754-1800; *Fax:* 709-754-2701
info@french-associates.com
french-associates.com

***St. John's*: Lewis, Day - *2**
#A, 84 Airport Rd., 1st Fl., St. John's, NL A1A 4Y3
Tel: 709-753-2545; *Fax:* 709-753-2266
Toll-Free: 877-553-2545
admin@lewisday.ca
www.lewisday.ca

***St. John's*: Lewis, Sinnott, Shortall - *4**
#300, TD Place, P.O. Box 884, Stn. C, 140 Water St., St. John's, NL A1C 5L7
Tel: 709-753-7810; *Fax:* 709-738-2965
www.lssh.ca

***St. John's*: Martin Whalen Hennebury Stamp - *9**
P.O. Box 5910, 15 Church Hill, St. John's, NL A1C 5X4
Tel: 709-754-1400; *Fax:* 709-754-0915
info@mwhslaw.com
www.mwhslaw.com

***St. John's*: John W. Mcgrath - *2**
18 Argyle St., St. John's, NL A1A 1V3
Tel: 709-738-2190
jwmcgrath@nf.aibn.com

***St. John's*: Noonan Law - *2**
Former Name: Noonan, Oakley
P.O. Box 5303, 339 Duckworth St., St. John's, NL A1C 5W1
Tel: 709-726-9598; *Fax:* 709-726-9614
info@noonanlaw.ca
www.noonanlaw.ca

***St. John's*: O'Brien Anthony White - *3**
#300, 53 Bond St., St. John's, NL A1C 1S9
Tel: 709-722-0637; *Fax:* 709-722-6780
Toll-Free: 888-722-0638
info@obaw.ca
www.obaw.ca

***St. John's*: O'Dea Earle - *16**
P.O. Box 5955, 323 Duckworth St., St. John's, NL A1C 5X4
Tel: 709-726-3524; *Fax:* 709-726-9600
injury@odeaearle.ca
www.odeaearle.ca

***St. John's*: Ottenheimer Boone - *2**
8 Albany St., St. John's, NL A1E 3C5
Tel: 709-579-7180; *Fax:* 709-579-1647

***St. John's*: Roebothan, McKay & Marshall - *15**
Former Name: Williams, Roebothan, McKay & Marshall
Paramount Building, P.O. Box 5236, 34 Harvey Rd., 5th Fl., St. John's, NL A1C 5W1
Tel: 709-753-5805; *Fax:* 709-753-5221
Toll-Free: 800-563-5563
www.makethecall.ca

***St. John's*: Rogers Bussey - *7**
Stn. C, 102 Lemarchant Rd., St. John's, NL A1C 2H2
Tel: 709-738-8533; *Fax:* 709-738-8534
Toll-Free: 877-637-6837
info@rogersbussey.com
www.rogersbussey.com

***St. John's*: Wells & Company - *1**
10 Freshwater Rd., St. John's, NL A1E 0A5
Tel: 709-739-7768; *Fax:* 709-739-4434
www.wellsandcompanynl.com

***Stephenville*: Fred R. Stagg, Barrister & Solicitor - *1**
28 Main St., Stephenville, NL A2N 2Z4
Tel: 709-643-5651; *Fax:* 709-643-5369
fstagg@frs-law.com

Northwest Territories

***Hay River*: Stephen M. Shabala - *1**
Former Name: Stephen Simpson
#205, 31 Capital Dr., Hay River, NT X0E 1G2
Tel: 867-874-3365; *Fax:* 867-874-6955

***Yellowknife*: Denroche & Associates - *3**
P.O. Box 2910, Stn. Main, 5107 - 53rd. St., Yellowknife, NT X1A 2R2
Tel: 867-920-4151; *Fax:* 867-920-4252
reception@denrochelaw.ca
www.denrochelaw.ca

***Yellowknife*: Peter C. Fuglsang & Associates - *2**
P.O. Box 2459, Stn. Main, 4912 - 49 St., Yellowknife, NT X1A 2P8
Tel: 867-920-4344; *Fax:* 867-873-3386

***Yellowknife*: Keenan Bengts Law Office - *2**
P.O. Box 262, Stn. Main, 5018 - 47th St., Yellowknife, NT X1A 2N2
Tel: 867-873-8631; *Fax:* 867-920-2511
kbengtslaw@theedge.ca

***Yellowknife*: Marshall & Company - *1**
P.O. Box 1236, Stn. Main, 5125 - 48 St., Yellowknife, NT X1A 2N9
Tel: 867-873-4969; *Fax:* 867-873-6567
mmarshall@marshallyk.com
www.marshall.yk.com

***Yellowknife*: Phillips & Wright - *2**
#1008, 4920 - 52nd St., Yellowknife, NT X1A 3T1
Tel: 867-873-3335

***Yellowknife*: Wallbridge & Associates - *3**
P.O. Box 383, 5016 - 47th St., Yellowknife, NT X1A 2N3
Tel: 867-920-4000; *Fax:* 867-920-7389
garth@wallbridgelaw.net

Nova Scotia

***Amherst*: Beaton Blaikie - *3**
P.O. Box 295, 141 Victoria St. East, Amherst, NS B4H 3Z2
Tel: 902-667-0515; *Fax:* 902-667-6161
info@bbnflaw.com
www.bbnflaw.com

***Amherst*: Fairbanks Law Office - *1**
P.O. Box 103, 55 Church St., Amherst, NS B4H 3Y6
Tel: 902-667-7579; *Fax:* 902-667-0644
william.fairbanks@ns.aliantzinc.ca
www.fairbankslawoffice.com

***Amherst*: Hicks, LeMoine - *5**
P.O. Box 279, 15 Princess St., Amherst, NS B4H 3Z2
Tel: 902-667-7214; *Fax:* 902-667-5886
info@hickslemoine.ca
www.hickslemoine.ca

***Amherst*: Jerry Langille, Inc. - *1**
Also Known As: Cumberland Legal Services
P.O. Box 548, 55 Church St., Amherst, NS B4H 4A1
Tel: 902-667-3856; *Fax:* 902-667-0104
jerry@jlilaw.com

***Annapolis Royal*: Armstrong & Armstrong - *1**
P.O. Box 575, 240 St. George St., Annapolis Royal, NS B0S 1A0
Tel: 902-532-2155; *Fax:* 902-532-7211
armstrong@ns.aliantzinc.ca

***Annapolis Royal*: Patricia L. Reardon - *1**
P.O. Box 366, 234 St. George St., Annapolis Royal, NS B0S 1A0
Tel: 902-532-7904; *Fax:* 902-532-7775
preardon@ns.aliantzinc.ca

***Antigonish*: Daniel J. MacIsaac - *1**
P.O. Box 1478, Stn. Main, 30 Church St., Antigonish, NS B2G 2L7
Tel: 902-863-5398; *Fax:* 902-863-9440

***Antigonish*: MacPherson MacNeil Macdonald - *2**
188 Main St., Antigonish, NS B2G 2B9
Tel: 902-863-2925; *Fax:* 902-863-2925
mthree@eastlink.com

***Antigonish*: William F. Meehan, Q.C. - *1**
P.O. Box 1803, Stn. Main, 195 Main St., Antigonish, NS B2G 2M5
Tel: 902-863-3136; *Fax:* 902-863-6270
wmeehan@hotmail.com

***Arichat*: Ivo R. Winter - *1**
P.O. Box 180, 14 Bay St., Arichat, NS B0E 1A0
Tel: 902-226-3711; *Fax:* 902-226-1837
ivowinter@ns.sympatico.ca

***Baddeck*: Daniel T.L. Chiasson - *1**
P.O. Box 567, 137 Upper Twinning St., Baddeck, NS B0E 1B0
Tel: 902-295-1245; *Fax:* 902-295-2610
dan.baddeck@ns.aliantzinc.ca

***Barrington*: G. David Eldridge - *1**
P.O. Box 157, 2459 Hwy. 3, Barrington, NS B0W 1E0
Tel: 902-637-2878; *Fax:* 902-637-2025
eldridgeqc@eastlink.ca

***Bedford*: Atlantica Law Group - *22**
Also Known As: ALG Law Group
Atlantic Acres Industrial Park, 2 Bluewater Rd., Bedford, NS B4B 1G7
Tel: 902-835-6647; *Fax:* 902-835-3029
Toll-Free: 877-343-9894
halifax@algvip.com
www.algvip.com

***Bedford*: Bedford Law - *3**
#100, 1496 Bedford Hwy., Bedford, NS B4A 1E5
Tel: 902-832-2100; *Fax:* 902-832-2323
bedfordlawreception@gmail.com
www.bedfordlaw.com

***Bedford*: Cameron Rhindress - *1**
Former Name: Rusk & McCay
1394 Bedford Hwy., Bedford, NS B4A 1E2
Tel: 902-835-7444; *Fax:* 902-835-3819
crhindross@accesscable.net

***Bedford*: David G. Barrett Law Inc. - *1**
#404, Sun Tower, 1550 Bedford Hwy., Bedford, NS B4A 1E6
Tel: 902-835-6375; *Fax:* 902-835-4565
dgbarrett@eastlink.ca
www.barrett-law-inc.com

***Bedford*: Gillis & Associates - *2**
Former Name: Gillis & Walden
#310, Sun Tower, 1550 Bedford Hwy., Bedford, NS B4A 1E6
Tel: 902-835-6174; *Fax:* 902-835-1486
Toll-Free: 866-277-3863
admin@gillisassociates.ca
www.gillisassociates.ca

***Bedford*: Melnick, Doll, Condran - *3**
#302, 1160 Bedford Hwy., Bedford, NS B4A 1C1
Tel: 902-835-2300; *Fax:* 902-835-2303

***Bedford*: Pressé Mason, Barristers & Solicitors - *4**
1254 Bedford Hwy., Bedford, NS B4A 1C6
Tel: 902-832-1175; *Fax:* 902-832-1856
Toll-Free: 800-630-2254
lawyers@pressemason.ns.ca
www.pressemasonlaw.ca

* indicates number of lawyers

Bedford: Resolute Legal - *1
#204, Southgate Village Professional Centre, 540 Southgate Dr., Bedford, NS B4A 0C9
Fax: 888-694-7086
Toll-Free: 888-480-9050
resolutelegal.ca
facebook.com/ResoluteLegal, twitter.com/Resolute_Legal, www.linkedin.com/in/davidbrannen

Berwick: Stewart & Turner - *2
P.O. Box 208, 196 Cottage St., Berwick, NS B0P 1E0
Tel: 902-538-3123; *Fax:* 902-538-7933
stewart.turner@ns.sympatico.ca

Berwick: Waterbury Newton - *25
P.O. Box 475, 188 Commercial St., Berwick, NS B0P 1E0
Tel: 902-538-3168; *Fax:* 902-538-8680
Toll-Free: 877-559-8585
reception@wnns.ca
www.wnns.ca

Bridgewater: J. Patrick Morris - *1
344 King St., Bridgewater, NS B4V 1A9
Tel: 902-543-6661; *Fax:* 902-543-6639
morris@eastlink.ca

Bridgewater: Power, Dempsey, Power, Dempsey, Leefe & Reddy - *3
Former Name: Power, Dempsey, Cooper & Leefe
84 Dufferin St., Bridgewater, NS B4V 2G3
Tel: 902-543-7815; *Fax:* 902-543-3196
Reception@Lawpower.ca
lawpower.ca

Bridgewater: The Law Offices of Timothy A. Reid - *1
Also Known As: Reid Law Office
176 Aberdeen Rd., Bridgewater, NS B4V 2S9
Tel: 902-543-1303; *Fax:* 902-543-3243
tareid@ns.sympatico.ca

Bridgewater: Romneylaw Inc. - *2
Former Name: Romney & Romney
P.O. Box 368, Stn. Main, 136 Aberdeen Rd., Bridgewater, NS B4V 2W9
Tel: 902-543-4444; *Fax:* 902-543-0232
romneylaw1@eastlink.ca

Canning: Cornwallis Legal Services - *1
P.O. Box 69, 765 Canard St., Lower Canard, Canning, NS B0P 1H0
Tel: 902-582-3372; *Fax:* 902-582-3201

Cheticamp: Réjean Aucoin - *1
P.O. Box 328, 15957 Cabot Trail, Cheticamp, NS B0E 1H0
Tel: 902-224-1450; *Fax:* 902-224-2224
rejean.aucoin@ns.sympatico.ca

Cheticamp: Carmel A. Lavigne - *1
P.O. Box 579, 15595 Cabot Trail, Cheticamp, NS B0E 1H0
Tel: 902-224-2551; *Fax:* 902-224-2555
clavigne@ns.sympatico.ca

Dartmouth: Bailey & Associates - *3
#800, 46 Portland St., Dartmouth, NS B2Y 1H4
Tel: 902-465-4888; *Fax:* 902-465-4844
appointments@baileylawyers.com
www.baileylawyers.com

Dartmouth: Casey Rodgers Chisholm Penny Duggan - *10
Former Name: Casey Rodgers Chisholm Penny
#201, 219 Waverley Rd., Dartmouth, NS B2X 2C3
Tel: 902-434-6181; *Fax:* 902-434-7737
www.crcplawyers.com
www.facebook.com/caseyrodgerschisholmpennyduggan, twitter.com/crcplawyers

Dartmouth: David A. Grant - *1
63 Tacoma Dr., Dartmouth, NS B2W 3E7
Tel: 902-463-6300; *Fax:* 902-435-7910
davidgrant@ns.sympatico.ca

Dartmouth: Heritage House Law Office - *7
92 Ochterloney St., Dartmouth, NS B2Y 1C5
Tel: 902-465-6669; *Fax:* 902-466-4412
www.heritagelaw.ca

Dartmouth: Landry McGillivray - *10
#300, Quaker Landing, P.O. Box 1200, 33 Ochterloney St., Dartmouth, NS B2Y 4B8
Tel: 902-463-8800; *Fax:* 902-463-0590
slg@landrymcgillivray.ns.ca
www.landrymcgillivray.ca

Dartmouth: Langille & Associates - *1
#201, P.O. Box 767, Stn. Main, 56 Portland St., Dartmouth, NS B2Y 3Z3
Tel: 902-463-5200; *Fax:* 902-465-5200
ken.langille@ns.aliantzinc.ca

Dartmouth: Donald C. Murray - *1
#102, 277 Pleasant St., Dartmouth, NS B2Y 4B7
Tel: 902-466-7378; *Fax:* 902-466-7379
dcmurray@norestdefence.com
www.norestdefence.com

Dartmouth: Lester Pyne - *1
194 Caledonia Rd., Dartmouth, NS B2X 1L4
Tel: 902-434-6167; *Fax:* 902-434-5448

Dartmouth: Sealy Cornish Coulthard - *4
#200, 56 Portland St., Dartmouth, NS B2Y 1H2
Tel: 902-466-2500; *Fax:* 902-463-0500
info@scclaw.ca
scclaw.ca

Dartmouth: Serbu & Lumsden - *3
945 Cole Harbour Rd., Dartmouth, NS B2V 1E5
Tel: 902-434-7755; *Fax:* 902-434-7813
info@serbulumsden.com
www.serbulumsden.ca

Dartmouth: Smith Evans - *3
Former Name: Owen & Morrison
#604, Queen Sq., 45 Alderney Dr., Dartmouth, NS B2Y 2N6
Tel: 902-463-8100; *Fax:* 902-465-2581
info@smithevans.ns.ca
www.smithevans.ns.ca

Dartmouth: Weldon McInnis - *9
118 Ochterloney St., Dartmouth, NS B2Y 1C7
Tel: 902-469-2421; *Fax:* 902-463-4452
Toll-Free: 800-757-2421
office@weldonmcinnis.ca
www.weldonmcinnis.ca

Digby: Brian E. McConnell - *1
P.O. Box 1239, 3 Birch St., Digby, NS B0V 1A0
Tel: 902-245-5856; *Fax:* 902-245-6800
bmcconnell@ns.aliantzinc.ca

Digby: James L. Outhouse Q.C. - *1
P.O. Box 1567, 78 Water St., Digby, NS B0V 1A0
Tel: 902-245-2551; *Fax:* 902-245-6622
jamesouthouse@ns.aliantzinc.ca

Elmsdale: Quigley's Law Office - *1
P.O. Box 653, 214 Hwy. 214, Elmsdale, NS B2S 1J7
Tel: 902-883-2757; *Fax:* 902-883-4401
kquigleylaw@aol.com

Enfield: Blackburn English - *8
287 Hwy. 2, Enfield, NS B2T 1C9
Tel: 902-883-2264; *Fax:* 902-883-8744
enfield@blackburnenglish.com
www.blackburnenglish.com

Fall River: Fall River Law Office - *2
3161 Hwy. 2, Fall River, NS B2T 1K6
Tel: 902-886-0151; *Fax:* 902-860-1718
www.fallriverlawoffice.ca

Glace Bay: Crosby, Burke & Macrury
38 Union St., Glace Bay, NS B1A 2P5
Tel: 902-849-3971; *Fax:* 902-849-7009

Glace Bay: McIntyre, Gillis & O'Leary - *2
P.O. Box 187, Stn. Main, 65 Minto St., Glace Bay, NS B1A 5V2
Tel: 902-849-6507; *Fax:* 902-849-0555

Glace Bay: David H. Raniseth - *1
P.O. Box 249, 34 McKeen St., Glace Bay, NS B1A 5B9
Tel: 902-849-0960; *Fax:* 902-849-6512

Greenwood: Proudfoot Law Office Inc. - *1
Former Name: AndersonSinclair
P.O. Box 100, 811 Central Ave., Greenwood, NS B0P 1N0
Tel: 902-765-3301; *Fax:* 902-765-6493
amplaw2@ns.sympatico.ca
dap@davidproudfoot.com

Guysborough: Campbell & MacKeen - *2
P.O. Box 200, 146 Main St., Guysborough, NS B0H 1N0
Tel: 902-533-2644; *Fax:* 902-533-3526

Halifax: Frederick Angus - *1
#435, 5991 Spring Garden Rd., Halifax, NS B3H 1Y6
Tel: 902-420-9595; *Fax:* 902-423-8040

Halifax: Richard G. Arab - *1
Assessment Services, 5151 Terminal Rd., 4th Fl., Halifax, NS B3J 2L6
Tel: 902-424-6091; *Fax:* 902-424-0587
arabg@gov.ns.ca

Halifax: Auld Allen - *3
1452 Dresden Row, Halifax, NS B3J 3T5
Tel: 902-492-3633; *Fax:* 902-492-3655
info@auldallen.com
www.auldallen.com

Halifax: Barss, Hare & Turner - *1
#137, Roy Bldg., Stn. Central, 1657 Barrington St., Halifax, NS B3J 2A1
Tel: 902-423-1249

Halifax: Barteaux Durnford - *8
Former Name: Ritch Durnford, Lawyers
#L106, 1701 Hollis St., Halifax, NS B3J 3M8
Tel: 902-377-2233; *Fax:* 902-377-2234
www.barteauxdurnford.com

Halifax: Beveridge, MacPherson & Buckle - *4
Former Name: Beveridge, Lambert & Duncan
P.O. Box 547, Stn. Central, 1684 Barrington St., 4th Fl., Halifax, NS B3J 2R7
Tel: 902-423-9143; *Fax:* 902-422-7837
www.bmblaw.ca

Halifax: Blois, Nickerson & Bryson LLP - *14
#1100, P.O. Box 2147, 1645 Granville St., Halifax, NS B3J 3B7
Tel: 902-425-6000; *Fax:* 902-429-7347
www.bloisnickerson.com

Halifax: BOYNECLARKE LLP - *50
P.O. Box 876, Stn. Dartmouth Main, Halifax, NS B2Y 3Z5
Tel: 902-469-9500; *Fax:* 902-463-7500
Toll-Free: 866-339-3400
info@boyneclarke.ca
www.boyneclarke.ca
www.facebook.com/201499616532777, www.linkedin.com/company/boyneclarke-llp

Halifax: Burchells LLP - *23
#1800, 1801 Hollis St., Halifax, NS B3J 3N4
Tel: 902-423-6361; *Fax:* 902-420-9326
firm@burchells.ca
www.burchells.ca

Halifax: Burke Thompson - *5
#200, P.O. Box 307, 5162 Duke St., Halifax, NS B3J 2N7
Tel: 902-429-8590; *Fax:* 902-423-2968
www.bmtlaw.ns.ca

Halifax: Evangeline Cain-Grant - *1
6156 Quinpool Rd., Halifax, NS B3L 1A3
Tel: 902-422-3500; *Fax:* 902-422-9660

Halifax: Cantini Law Group
#1700, Purdy's Wharf Tower One, 1959 Upper Water St., Halifax, NS B3J 3N2
Tel: 902-420-9577; *Fax:* 902-482-5210
Toll-Free: 800-606-2529
contact@cantinilaw.com
www.atlanticcanadainjurylawyers.com

Halifax: Cassidy Nearing Berryman - *5
#401, 1741 Brunswick St., Halifax, NS B3J 3X8
Tel: 902-492-1770; *Fax:* 902-423-2485
Toll-Free: 800-792-1770
alexa@cnb.ca
cnb.ca

Halifax: Christie Cuffari Law Office - *1
Former Name: Clare Christie's Law Office
#310, 1657 Barrington St., Halifax, NS B3J 2A1
Tel: 902-422-2297; *Fax:* 902-422-2162

Halifax: Claman Legal Services Limited
#4004, 7071 Bayers Rd., Halifax, NS B3L 2C2
Tel: 902-492-4000; *Fax:* 902-492-4001

Halifax: Coady Filliter - *8
#208, 880 Spring Garden Rd., Halifax, NS B3H 1Y1
Tel: 902-429-6264; *Fax:* 902-423-3044
info@coadyfilliter.com
coadyfilliter.com

Halifax: Crowe Dillon Robinson - *9
#2000, 7075 Bayers Rd., Halifax, NS B3L 2C1
Tel: 902-453-1732; *Fax:* 902-454-9948
john.dillon@cdr.ns.ca
www.cdr.ns.ca

* *indicates number of lawyers*

Halifax: Gilles J. Deveau - *1
5336 Young St., Halifax, NS B3K 1Z4
Tel: 902-454-4551; *Fax:* 902-454-9154
gilles.deveau@ns.sympatico.ca

Halifax: Kevin P. Downie, Barrister & Solicitor - *1
#402, P.O. Box 580, Stn. Central, 5121 Sackville St., Halifax, NS B3J 2R7
Tel: 902-425-7233; *Fax:* 902-425-2252
kpdownie@accesswave.ca

Halifax: Elizabeth Wozniak Inc. - *2
P.O. Box 272, 1684 Barrington St., 5th Fl., Halifax, NS B3J 2N7
Tel: 902-446-4747; *Fax:* 902-446-4745
ewozniak@nsimmigration.ca
nsimmigration.ca
twitter.com/lizawoz

Halifax: Sally B. Faught - *1
#601, Duke Tower, 5251 Duke St., Halifax, NS B3J 1P3
Tel: 902-423-8200; *Fax:* 902-423-3100
s.faught@ns.sympatico.ca

Halifax: Michael F. Feindel - *1
Nolan Davis Bldg., P.O. Box 22162, Stn. Bayers, 7020 Mumford Rd., Halifax, NS B3L 4T7
Tel: 902-455-7730; *Fax:* 902-455-7739

Halifax: Garson Pink - *3
P.O. Box 1, 1741 Brunswick St., Halifax, NS B3J 3X8
Tel: 902-425-0222; *Fax:* 902-423-4690
info@garsonmacdonald.ca
www.garsonpink.ca

Halifax: Gavras & Associates - *2
Former Name: Pavey Gavras Associates
#201, The Maitland Terrace, 2085 Maitland St., Halifax, NS B3K 2Z8
Tel: 902-423-5711; *Fax:* 902-431-9444
jgavras@gavrasassociates.com
gavrasassociates.com

Halifax: Harvey Hebert & Manthorne - *5
Former Name: Harvey & Hebert Affiliated Law Practices
1492 Lower Water St., Halifax, NS B3J 1R9
Tel: 902-492-0614; *Fax:* 902-492-0634
Toll-Free: 877-492-0614
general@harveyhebert.com

Halifax: MacDonald Elliott Legal Services - *2
7071 Bayers Rd., Halifax, NS B3L 2C2
Tel: 902-454-9827; *Fax:* 902-454-7630
macdonaldlegal@hfx.eastlink.ca

Halifax: MacDonald Law Office, Paton & Paton - *1
12 Robert Allen Dr., Halifax, NS B3M 3G8
Tel: 902-457-5111; *Fax:* 902-457-5113
act1@eastlink.ca

Halifax: McGinty Doucet Walker - *4
Former Name: McGinty Law
#705, Park Lane, Box 227, 5657 Spring Garden Rd., Halifax, NS B3J 3R4
Tel: 902-422-5881; *Fax:* 902-422-5882
info@mdwlaw.ca
mdwlaw.ca

Halifax: McInnes Cooper Lawyers
#1300, 1969 Upper Water St., Halifax, NS B3J 2V1
Tel: 902-425-6500; *Fax:* 902-425-6350
www.mcinnescooper.com

Halifax: Medjuck & Medjuck - *2
#700, Summit Place, P.O. Box 1074, 1601 Lower Water St., Halifax, NS B3J 2X1
Tel: 902-429-4061; *Fax:* 902-422-7639
medjuck@ns.sympatico.ca

Halifax: Merrick Jamieson Sterns Washington & Mahody - *8
#503, 5475 Spring Garden Rd., Halifax, NS B3J 3T2
Tel: 902-429-3123; *Fax:* 902-429-3522
www.mjswm.com

Halifax: Metcalf & Company - *5
Benjamin Wier House, 1459 Hollis St., Halifax, NS B3J 1V1
Tel: 902-420-1990; *Fax:* 902-429-1171
frankmetcalf@metcalf.ns.ca
www.metcalf.ns.ca

Halifax: Morris Bureau - *3
#307, 6080 Young St., Halifax, NS B3K 5L2
Tel: 902-454-8070; *Fax:* 902-454-7070
www.morrisbureau.com

Halifax: John P. Nisbet - *1
142 Main Ave., Halifax, NS B3M 1B2
Tel: 902-445-3736

Halifax: Noseworthy, Di Costanzo, Diab - *3
Former Name: Thomson, Noseworthy, Di Costanzo
6470 Chebucto Rd., Halifax, NS B3L 1L4
Tel: 902-444-4747; *Fax:* 902-444-4301

Halifax: Patterson Law - *29
1718 Argyle St., 5th Fl., Halifax, NS B3J 3N6
Tel: 902-405-8000; *Fax:* 902-405-8001
Toll-Free: 888-897-2001
contactus@pattersonlaw.ca
www.pattersonlaw.ca

Halifax: Clyde A. Paul & Associates - *4
349 Herring Cove Rd., Halifax, NS B3R 1V9
Tel: 902-477-2518; *Fax:* 902-479-1482
info@clydepaul.ca
www.clydepaul.ca/en/

Halifax: Price Havlovic - *2
Former Name: Beatrice A. Havlovic
Halifax, NS
info@pricehavlovic.com
www.pricehavlovic.com

Halifax: Quackenbush, Thomson & Robbins - *5
2571 Windsor St., Halifax, NS B3K 5C4
Tel: 902-492-1655; *Fax:* 902-492-1697
qtrlawyershalifax.com

Halifax: Ritch Williams & Richards Insurance & Marine Law - *8
Former Name: Ritch Durnford, Lawyers; Huestis Ritch
#1200, CIBC Bldg., 1809 Barrington St., Halifax, NS B3J 3K8
Tel: 902-429-3400; *Fax:* 902-422-4713
Toll-Free: 877-896-0706
info@rwrlawyers.ca
www.rwrlawyers.ca

Halifax: Joseph S. Roza - *1
#210, 6021 Young St., Halifax, NS B3K 2A1
Tel: 902-425-5111; *Fax:* 902-425-5112
j.roza@ns.sympatico.ca
www.josephroza.com

Halifax: Scaravelli & Associates - *5
#2030, 1801 Hollis St., Halifax, NS B3J 3N4
Tel: 902-429-4104; *Fax:* 902-423-4009
lancescaravelli@eastlink.ca

Halifax: Singleton & Associates - *2
Former Name: Singleton Morrison
#204, 2000 Barrington St., Halifax, NS B3J 3K1
Tel: 902-492-7000; *Fax:* 902-492-4309
tsingleton@singleton.ns.ca
singleton.ns.ca

Halifax: Stockton, Maxwell & Elliott - *3
#402, 7020 Mumford Rd., Halifax, NS B3L 4S9
Tel: 902-422-6055; *Fax:* 902-429-7655
stockton@smelaw.ca
www.smelaw.ca

Halifax: Wagnes Law Firm - *6
#PH301, Pontac House, P.O. Box 756, Stn. RPO Central, 1869 Upper Water St., 3rd Fl., Halifax, NS B3J 1S9
Tel: 902-425-7330; *Fax:* 902-422-1233
Toll-Free: 800-465-8794
www.wagners.co

Halifax: Walker Dunlop - *6
1477 South Park St., Halifax, NS B3J 2L1
Tel: 902-423-8121; *Fax:* 902-429-0621
reception@walkerdunlop.ca
www.walkerdunlop.ca

Halifax: Walker Law Office Inc. - *1
Former Name: Walker & Associates
#200, 2742 Robie St., Halifax, NS B3K 4P2
Tel: 902-425-5297; *Fax:* 902-425-5095
reception@walkerlaw.ca
www.walkerlaw.ca

Halifax: Wickwire Holm
#2100, P.O. Box 1054, 1801 Hollis St., Halifax, NS B3J 2X6
Tel: 902-429-4111; *Fax:* 902-429-8215
Toll-Free: 866-429-4111
wh@wickwireholm.com
www.wickwireholm.com
www.facebook.com/pages/Wickwire-Holm/281421025262399,
twitter.com/WickwireHolm

Halifax: Wolfson, Schelew, Zatzman - *3
#500, Tacoma Tower, 73 Tacoma Dr., Halifax, NS B2W 3Y6
Tel: 902-435-7000; *Fax:* 902-435-4085

Halifax: Diane K. Zwicker - *1
1561 Vernon St., Halifax, NS B3H 3M8
Tel: 902-425-2193
dzwicker@sprint.ca

Kentville: Astek Legal Services - *1
P.O. Box 441, Stn. Main, Kentville, NS B4N 3X3
Tel: 902-679-0101; *Fax:* 902-679-0066

Kentville: Donald C. Fraser - *1
P.O. Box 668, Stn. Main, 35R Webster St., Kentville, NS B4N 3X9
Tel: 902-678-4006; *Fax:* 902-678-2999
fraser.law@ns.aliantzinc.ca

Kentville: Manning & Associates - *1
27 Cornwallis St., Kentville, NS B4N 2E2
Tel: 902-679-1600; *Fax:* 902-679-5122
chris.manning@manningassociates.ca

Kentville: Muttarts Law Firm - *6
Also Known As: Muttart Tufts Dewolfe & Coyle
P.O. Box 515, 20 Cornwallis St., Kentville, NS B4N 3X3
Tel: 902-678-2157; *Fax:* 902-678-9455
www.muttartslaw.ca

Kentville: Nathanson Seaman Watts - *8
Former Name: Forse, Nathanson
24 Webster Crt., Kentville, NS B4N 2E3
Tel: 902-678-1616; *Fax:* 902-678-1615
info@24webster.com
24webster.com

Kentville: Tayllor MacLellan Cochrane - *12
Also Known As: TMC Law
50 Cornwallis St., Kentville, NS B4N 2E4
Tel: 902-678-6156; *Fax:* 902-678-6010
Toll-Free: 888-486-2529
lawfirm@tmclaw.com
www.tmclaw.com

Liverpool: Fownes Law Offices Inc. - *1
#C, P.O. Box 1739, 190 Main St., Liverpool, NS B0T 1K0
Tel: 902-354-2744; *Fax:* 902-354-2746
acfownes@novascotialaw.com
www.novascotialaw.com

Lower Sackville: David F. Farwell - *1
Former Name: Farwell & Hines
#206, Vogue Optical Plaza, 405 Sackville Dr., Lower Sackville, NS B4C 2R9
Tel: 902-865-5537; *Fax:* 902-865-4354
davidfarwell@ns.sympatico.ca

Lower Sackville: Robert W. Newman & Associates - *1
85 Sackville Cross Rd., Lower Sackville, NS B4C 2M2
Tel: 902-864-2722; *Fax:* 902-864-3164
robert.newman@ns.sympatico.ca

Lower Sackville: Richardson's Law Office - *2
#100A, 800 Sackville Dr., Lower Sackville, NS B4E 1R8
Tel: 902-864-2300; *Fax:* 902-864-4410
Toll-Free: 877-304-2300
kim@novalawyer.com
www.novalawyer.com

Lunenburg: Burke, Macdonald & Luczak - *3
P.O. Box 549, 28 King St., Lunenburg, NS B0J 2C0
Tel: 902-634-8354; *Fax:* 902-634-4226
burkelaw@wolffhaus.com
wolffhaus.com

Middleton: Cole Sawler - *2
P.O. Box 400, 264 Main St., Middleton, NS B0S 1P0
Tel: 902-825-6288; *Fax:* 902-825-4340
officemanager@colesawlerlaw.ca
www.colesawlerlaw.ca

** indicates number of lawyers*

***Middleton*: Durland, Gillis & Schumacher, Associates - *2**
Also Known As: Durland, Gillis
Former Name: Durland Gillis Parker & Richter
P.O. Box 700, 74 Commercial St., Middleton, NS B0S 1P0
Tel: 902-825-3415; *Fax:* 902-825-2522

***Musquodoboit Harbour*: Eastern Shore Law Centre - *1**
1653 Ostrea Lake Rd., Musquodoboit Harbour, NS B0J 2L0
Tel: 902-889-2860
easternshorelaw@aol.com
easternshorelawcentre.ca

***New Glasgow*: R.A. Balmanoukian - *1**
137 McColl St., New Glasgow, NS B2H 4Z6
Tel: 902-755-3393; *Fax:* 902-755-6373
blackacre@north.nsis.com

***New Glasgow*: Goodman MacDonald Daley - *3**
P.O. Box 697, Stn. Main, 47 Riverside Dr., New Glasgow, NS B2H 5G2
Tel: 902-752-5090; *Fax:* 902-755-3545
Toll-Free: 888-253-5455
info@goodmanmacdonald.ca
www.gmpdlaw.ca

***New Glasgow*: MacIntosh, MacDonnell & MacDonald - *15**
#260, Aberdeen Business Centre, P.O. Box 368, Stn. Main, 610 East River Rd., 2nd Fl., New Glasgow, NS B2H 5E5
Tel: 902-752-8441; *Fax:* 902-752-7810
Toll-Free: 888-752-8441
office@macmacmac.ns.ca
macmacmac.ns.ca

***New Waterford*: M. Sweeney Hinchey - *1**
3383 Plummer Ave., New Waterford, NS B1H 1Z1
Tel: 902-862-2368; *Fax:* 902-862-9581
hinchems@yahoo.com

***North Sydney*: M. Mora B. Maclennan - *1**
33 Archibald Ave., North Sydney, NS B2A 2W6
Tel: 902-794-2060; *Fax:* 902-794-3558
moramaclennan@eastlink.ca

***North Sydney*: Michael A. Tobin - *1**
P.O. Box 1925, Stn. Main, 254 Commercial St., North Sydney, NS B2A 3S9
Tel: 902-794-8803; *Fax:* 902-794-9869
miketobinlaw@syd.eastlink.ca

***Pictou*: MacLean & MacDonald - *2**
P.O. Box 730, 90 Coleraine St., Pictou, NS B0K 1H0
Tel: 902-485-4347; *Fax:* 902-485-8887
law@macleanmacdonald.com

***Pictou*: Scanlan Graham Scanlan - *2**
P.O. Box 1720, 94 Water St., Pictou, NS B0K 1H0
Tel: 902-485-4313; *Fax:* 902-485-5083
sgslaw@ns.sympatico.ca

***Port Hawkesbury*: Pickup & MacDowell - *2**
302 Pitt St., Port Hawkesbury, NS B9A 2T8
Tel: 902-625-2500; *Fax:* 902-625-0500
pickupmacdowell@pkpmd.ca
www.pkpmd.ca

***Port Hawksberry*: Robin W. Archibald - *1**
202-15 Kennedy St., Port Hawksberry, NS B9A 2Y1
Tel: 902-625-2294; *Fax:* 902-625-3060
archibrw@gov.ns.ca

***Port Hood*: Francis X. Moloney - *1**
P.O. Box 122, 351 Main St., Port Hood, NS B0E 2W0
Tel: 902-787-3113; *Fax:* 902-787-3105

***Pubnico*: d'Entremont & Boudreau - *2**
P.O. Box 118, Pubnico, NS B0W 2W0
Tel: 902-762-3119; *Fax:* 902-762-3124

***Shelburne*: Celia J. Melanson, Barristor & Solicitor, Inc. - *1**
P.O. Box 562, 171 Water St., Shelburne, NS B0T 1W0
Tel: 902-875-4188; *Fax:* 902-875-1316
celia.melanson@ns.sympatico.ca
www.celiamelanson.com

***Shelburne*: Donald R. Miller - *1**
6767 Shore Rd. RR#3, Shelburne, NS B0T 1W0
Tel: 902-637-2527; *Fax:* 902-637-2165

***Shelburne*: Johanne L. Tournier - *1**
Shelburne Industrial Park, 9 Hero Rd., RR#2, Shelburne, NS B0T 1W0
Tel: 902-875-4365; *Fax:* 902-875-4365

***Shubenacadie*: Carruthers & MacDonell Law Office Inc. - *3**
#204, Chubenacadie Professional Centre, P.O. Box 280, 5 Mill Village Rd., Shubenacadie, NS B0N 2H0
Tel: 902-758-2591; *Fax:* 902-758-4022
office@carmaclaw.com
easthants.com/law/

***Stellarton*: Hector J. MacIsaac - *1**
P.O. Box 849, 195 Foord St., Stellarton, NS B0K 1S0
Tel: 902-752-5143; *Fax:* 902-928-1299

***Sydney*: The Breton Law Group - *8**
#300, 292 Charlotte St., Sydney, NS B1P 1C7
Tel: 902-563-1000; *Fax:* 902-563-1113
www.bretonlawgroup.com

***Sydney*: Cusack Law Office - *1**
174 Commercial St., Sydney, NS B2A 1B4
Tel: 902-544-0611

***Sydney*: Vincent A. Gillis - *1**
P.O. Box 847, Stn. A, 321 Townsend St., Sydney, NS B1P 6J1
Tel: 902-562-3222; *Fax:* 902-539-4199
vagillislaw@ns.sympatico.ca

***Sydney*: Khattar & Khattar - *4**
P.O. Box 387, 378 Charlotte St., Sydney, NS B1P 6H2
Tel: 902-539-9696; *Fax:* 902-562-7147
Toll-Free: 888-542-8827
law@khattar.ca
www.khattarandkhattarlaw.com

***Sydney*: John G. Khattar - *1**
463 Prince St., Sydney, NS B1P 5L6
Tel: 902-564-6611; *Fax:* 902-564-8805
jkhatter@syd.eastlink.ca

***Sydney*: LaFosse MacLeod - *5**
P.O. Box 297, 50 Dorchester St., Sydney, NS B1P 6H1
Tel: 902-563-0025; *Fax:* 902-563-0026
inquiries@lafossemacleod.ca
www.lafossemacleod.ca

***Sydney*: Lorway MacEachern - *3**
112 Charlotte St., Sydney, NS B1P 1B9
Tel: 902-539-4447; *Fax:* 902-564-9844
northlaw@syd.eastlink.ca
www.northlawcan.com

***Sydney*: MacDonald & MacLennan - *1**
P.O. Box 1148, Stn. A, 205 Charlotte St., 2nd Fl., Sydney, NS B1P 6J7
Tel: 902-564-4429; *Fax:* 902-539-2303

***Sydney*: H.F. MacIntyre & Associates - *2**
P.O. Box 788, Stn. A, 245 Charlotte St., Sydney, NS B1P 6J1
Tel: 902-562-4224; *Fax:* 902-562-0606
macintyre.assoc@ns.sympatico.ca

***Sydney*: Hugh R. McLeod - *1**
P.O. Box 306, 275 Charlotte St., Sydney, NS B1P 6H2
Tel: 902-539-2261; *Fax:* 902-539-3386
hugh.mcleod@ns.sympatico.ca

***Sydney*: John W. Morgan - *1**
#4, 29 Riverdale Dr., Sydney, NS B1R 1P2
Tel: 902-539-2800; *Fax:* 902-562-2554

***Sydney*: Ralph W. Ripley Barrister & Solicitor Inc. - *1**
#202, P.O. Box 7, Stn. A, 295 Charlotte St., Sydney, NS B1P 6G9
Tel: 902-564-4446; *Fax:* 902-539-7765
rripley@ns.aliantzinc.ca

***Sydney*: M. Joseph Rizzetto - *1**
#206, 275 Charlotte St., Sydney, NS B1P 1C6
Tel: 902-562-6262; *Fax:* 902-539-3567
info@rizzetto.ns.ca

***Sydney*: Sampson McDougall - *9**
#200, 66 Wentworth St., Sydney, NS B1P 6T4
Tel: 902-539-2425; *Fax:* 902-564-0954
mail@sampsonmcdougall.com
sampsonmcdougall.com

***Sydney*: Sheldon Nathanson Barristers & Solicitors - *5**
P.O. Box 79, Stn. Pier Post., 797 Victoria Rd., Sydney, NS B1N 3B1
Tel: 902-562-1929 *Toll-Free:* 800-868-1929
sheldonlaw@sheldonnathanson.ca
www.sheldonnathanson.com

***Tantallon*: Smith-Camp Law - *1**
104 Whynacht's Point Rd., Tantallon, NS B3Z 2K9
Tel: 902-826-2193; *Fax:* 902-826-1043
smithcamplaw@hotmail.com

***Truro*: Archibald Lederman Barristers - *2**
P.O. Box 1100, Stn. Main, 43 Walker St., Truro, NS B2N 5G9
Tel: 902-895-0524; *Fax:* 902-893-7608
plederman@archibaldlederman.ca
www.archibaldlederman.ca

***Truro*: Burchell MacDougall Lawyers - Truro - *27**
P.O. Box 1128, 710 Prince St., Truro, NS B2N 5H1
Tel: 902-895-1561; *Fax:* 902-895-7709
Toll-Free: 800-565-1200
truro@burchellmacdougall.com
www.burchellmacdougall.com
www.facebook.com/burmaclawyers, twitter.com/burmaclawyers, www.linkedin.com/company/burchell-macdougall-lawyers

***Truro*: David F. Curtis Q.C. - *1**
#202, 640 Prince St., Truro, NS B2N 1G4
Tel: 902-895-0528; *Fax:* 902-893-1158
dcurtislaw@ns.aliantzinc.ca

***Truro*: Melinda J. MacLean, Q.C. - *1**
779 Prince St., Truro, NS B2N 5B6
Tel: 902-895-2866; *Fax:* 902-897-9890

***Truro*: McLellan, Richards & Bégin - *3**
P.O. Box 1064, 779 Prince St., Truro, NS B2N 5G9
Tel: 902-895-4417; *Fax:* 902-897-9890
Toll-Free: 866-600-0011
www.truro-law.com

***Truro*: Gerard P. Scanlan - *1**
P.O. Box 1228, Stn. Main, 640 Prince St., Truro, NS B2N 5N2
Tel: 902-895-9249; *Fax:* 902-893-3078
scanpayn@eastlink.ca

***Truro*: Yuill Chisholm Killawee - *2**
541 Prince St., Truro, NS B2N 1E8
Tel: 902-893-0243; *Fax:* 902-897-0282

***Westville*: S. Charles Facey, Q.C. - *1**
P.O. Box 610, 1912 Drummond Rd., Westville, NS B0K 2A0
Tel: 902-396-4191; *Fax:* 902-396-3606
charles.facey@ns.sympatico.ca

***Windsor*: How Lawrence White Bowes - *3**
P.O. Box 3177, 98 Gerrish St., Windsor, NS B0N 2T0
Tel: 902-798-5997; *Fax:* 902-798-8925
jjwhite@scotialaw.com
www.scotialaw.com

***Windsor*: Nelson Law - *2**
Former Name: Nelson Gardiner
P.O. Box 2018, 258 King St., Windsor, NS B0N 2T0
Tel: 902-798-5797; *Fax:* 902-798-2332
office@nelson-law.ca

***Wolfville*: Kimball Law - Wolfville - *4**
Former Name: Kimball Brogan Law Office
121 Front St., Wolfville, NS B4P 1A6
Tel: 902-542-5757; *Fax:* 902-542-5759
Toll-Free: 800-294-7851
info@kimballlaw.ca
www.kimballlaw.ca

***Wolfville*: LJM Environmental Law & Consulting**
P.O. Box 2279, Wolfville, NS B4P 2N5
Tel: 902-670-1130; *Fax:* 902-542-7315
info@ljmenvironmental.ca
www.ljmenvironmental.ca

***Yarmouth*: R.K. Murray Judge - *1**
#201, 164 Main St., Yarmouth, NS B5A 1C2
Tel: 902-742-7827; *Fax:* 902-742-0676
murray.judge@nslegalaid.ca

Nunavut

***Iqaluit*: Michael Chandler - *1**
P.O. Box 2021, Iqaluit, NU X0A 0H0
Tel: 867-979-3505; *Fax:* 867-979-3506

** indicates number of lawyers*

***Iqaluit*: Crawford Law Office**
P.O. Box 747, Fred Coman Dr., Iqaluit, NU X0A 0H0
Tel: 867-979-0678; *Fax:* 867-979-0679
crawford@nunavutlegal.com
sites.google.com/a/nunavutlegal.com/www/

Ontario

***Ajax*: Ajax Law Chambers - *2**
#206, 158 Harwood Ave. South, Ajax, ON L1S 2H6
Tel: 905-683-1042; *Fax:* 905-683-7794
Toll-Free: 800-801-4602
johntlaw@rogers.com
alclaw.ca

***Ajax*: Daniel J. Balena - *1**
Hunt Street Professional Building, 110 Hunt St., Ajax, ON L1S 1P5
Tel: 905-897-4321; *Fax:* 905-683-4610
info@danielbalena.com
www.danielbalena.com

***Ajax*: Foden & Doucette - *2**
555 Kingston Rd. West, Ajax, ON L1S 6M1
Tel: 905-428-8200; *Fax:* 905-428-8666
wfoden@fodenanddoucette.com
www.fodenanddoucette.com

***Ajax*: Glover & Associates - Ajax - *3**
Former Name: Glover, Darryl T.G
562 Kingston Rd. West, Ajax, ON L1T 3A2
Tel: 905-619-3700; *Fax:* 905-619-0022
info@gloverlaw.ca
www.gloverlaw.ca

***Ajax*: Greening & Bucknam - *1**
#202, 50 Commercial Ave., Ajax, ON L1S 2H5
Tel: 905-683-7037; *Fax:* 905-683-7627
bucknam@rogers.com

***Ajax*: Jennifer Hirlehey & Associates - *1**
7 Mill St., Ajax, ON L1Z 6J8
Tel: 905-427-8082; *Fax:* 905-427-8084
info@hirleheylaw.ca
www.hirleheylaw.ca

***Ajax*: Reilly & Partners - *4**
Former Name: Reilly D'Heureux Lanzi LLP
555 Kingston Rd. West, 2nd Fl., Ajax, ON L1S 6M1
Tel: 905-427-4077; *Fax:* 905-427-4042
mreilly@reillyandpartners.com
www.reillyandpartners.com

***Ajax*: Juanita Wislesky - *1**
#202, 15 Harwood Rd. Ave. South, Ajax, ON L1S 2B9
Tel: 905-686-1686
juanita_wislesky@yahoo.ca

***Ajax*: George D. Wright - *1**
543 Kingston Rd. West, Ajax, ON L1S 6M1
Tel: 905-427-7200; *Fax:* 905-427-2999

***Alexandria*: Jean-Marc Lefebvre, Q.C. - *2**
32 Main St. North, Alexandria, ON K0C 1A0
Tel: 613-525-1358; *Fax:* 613-525-3411
lefebvre@bellnet.ca
www.lefebvrelaw.ca

***Allenford*: Richard R. Evans - *1**
P.O. Box 14, 7771 Hwy. 21, Allenford, ON N0H 1A0
Tel: 519-934-2875; *Fax:* 519-934-1460
rrevans@bmts.com

***Alliston*: John W. Clarke - *1**
#3, P.O. Box 408, Stn. Main, 103 Victoria St. West, Alliston, ON L9R 1V6
Tel: 705-435-4301; *Fax:* 705-435-3407

***Alliston*: Feehely, Gastaldi - *4**
P.O. Box 399, 2 Victoria St. East, Alliston, ON L9R 1V6
Tel: 705-435-4386; *Fax:* 705-435-9256
gastaldi@feehelygastaldi.com

***Alliston*: Mary L. Galbraith - *1**
Former Name: Darling, Smith, McLean
22 Church St. South, Alliston, ON L9R 1V9
Tel: 705-435-4324; *Fax:* 705-435-2628

***Alliston*: Gilmore & Gilmore - *2**
P.O. Box 250, 458 Victoria St. East, Alliston, ON L9R 1V5
Tel: 705-435-4339; *Fax:* 705-435-6520
Toll-Free: 877-855-3425
info@gilmoreandgilmore.com
www.gilmoreandgilmore.com
twitter.com/JamieMGilmore

***Alliston*: James W. Smith - *1**
P.O. Box 730, Stn. Main, 8 Victoria St. East, Alliston, ON L9R 1T4
Tel: 705-435-0160; *Fax:* 705-435-5049
jsmithl@bellnet.ca

***Almonte*: Canadian Hydro Components Ltd. - *1**
P.O. Box 640, 16 Main St., Almonte, ON K0A 1A0
Tel: 613-256-1983; *Fax:* 613-256-4235
plemay@canadianhydro.com

***Almonte*: Elizabeth A. Swarbrick - *4**
#107, P.O. Box 639, 83 Little Bridge St., Almonte, ON K0A 1A0
Tel: 613-256-9811; *Fax:* 613-256-9814
elizabeth@familyfocusedlaw.com
www.familyfocusedlaw.com

***Almonte*: Evelyn Wheeler - *1**
P.O. Box 1540, 38 Mill St., Almonte, ON K0A 1A0
Tel: 613-256-4148; *Fax:* 613-256-4708
www.evelynwheeler.com

***Amherstburg*: Baker Busch - *2**
41 Sandwich St. South, Amherstburg, ON N9V 1Z5
Tel: 519-736-2154; *Fax:* 519-736-2466
info@bakerbusch.ca
www.bakerbusch.com

***Amherstview*: William E.M. Vince - *1**
6 Speers Blvd., #G, Amherstview, ON K7N 1Z6
Tel: 613-389-6727; *Fax:* 613-389-6256
vincelaw@cogeco.net

***Ancaster*: G. Kevin Eggleton - *1**
#S110, 911 Golf Links Rd., Ancaster, ON L9K 1H9
Tel: 905-304-5297; *Fax:* 905-304-7711

***Ancaster*: Randy L. Levinson - *1**
58 Cumming Ct., Ancaster, ON L9G 1V3
Tel: 905-648-7239; *Fax:* 905-648-4437
randy@randylevinson.com
www.randylevinson.com

***Ancaster*: Wynne, Dingwall, Pringle & Kovacs - *4**
Former Name: Wynne, Dingwall & Pringle; Wynne & Dingwall
231 Wilson St. East, #B, Ancaster, ON L9G 2B8
Tel: 905-648-1851; *Fax:* 905-648-1715
www.anclaw.com

***Angus*: Gordon R. MacKenzie Professional Corporation - *1**
Former Name: MacKenzie, Greenfield
#A, P.O. Box 600, 189 Mill St., Angus, ON L0M 1B2
Tel: 705-424-1331; *Fax:* 705-424-6441
info@yourlocallawyer.com
www.yourlocallawyer.com

***Annan*: Alan E. Marsh - *1**
RR #2, Annan, ON N0H 1B0
Tel: 519-371-8373; *Fax:* 519-371-8971
alanmarsh@gbtel.ca

***Arnprior*: C.P. Merla - *1**
#4, 75 Elgin St. West, Arnprior, ON K7S 3T9
Tel: 613-623-6593; *Fax:* 613-623-8947

***Aurora*: Allan Law - *2**
15393 Yonge St., Aurora, ON L4G 1P1
Tel: 905-895-3425; *Fax:* 905-726-3098
www.allanlaw.ca

***Aurora*: Boland Howe Barristers LLP - *5**
130 Industrial Pkwy. North, Aurora, ON L4G 4C3
Tel: 905-841-5717; *Fax:* 905-841-7128
info@bolandhowe.com
www.bolandhowe.com

***Aurora*: Christie Saccucci Matthews - *1**
Former Name: Christie Lawyers; Christie, Saccucci, Matthews, Caskie & Chilco
74 Wellington St. East, Aurora, ON LFG 1H8
Tel: 416-367-0680; *Fax:* 905-780-8216
Toll-Free: 800-715-3516
www.ontarioconstructionlaw.ca

***Aurora*: Di Cecco Law - *2**
Former Name: Di Cecco, Jones
#205, 15171 Yonge St., Aurora, ON L4G 1M1
Tel: 905-751-1517; *Fax:* 905-751-1518
info@diceccolaw.com
www.diceccolaw.com

***Aurora*: Laurion Law Office - *1**
41 Wellington St. East, Aurora, ON L4G 1H6
Tel: 905-841-2222; *Fax:* 905-841-3388
jlaurion@laurionlaw.com

***Aurora*: McPherson & Lewis - *2**
Former Name: McPherson, Thomas & Associates
P.O. Box 338, 15220 Yonge St., Aurora, ON L4G 3H4
Tel: 905-727-3151; *Fax:* 905-841-2164

***Aurora*: Peddle & Pollard LLP - *2**
#102, 15449 Yonge St., Aurora, ON L4G 1P3
Tel: 905-727-1361; *Fax:* 905-727-9395
info@peddlepollard.ca
www.peddlepollard.ca

***Aurora*: Sorley & Still - *5**
15064 Yonge St., Aurora, ON L4G 1M2
Tel: 905-726-9956; *Fax:* 905-726-9957
www.sorleyandstill.com

***Aurora*: Barry W. Switzer - *1**
15187 Yonge St., Aurora, ON L4G 1L8
Tel: 905-727-9488; *Fax:* 905-841-8647
www.barrywswitzer.ca
www.facebook.com/Barry-W-Switzer-1500211470199211, twitter.com/barrywswitzer

***Aylmer*: Doyle & Prendergast - *2**
10 Sydenham St. East, Aylmer, ON N5H 1L2
Tel: 519-773-3105; *Fax:* 519-765-1728

***Aylmer*: Gloin, Hall & Shields - *5**
139 Talbot St. East, Aylmer, ON N5H 1H3
Tel: 519-773-9221; *Fax:* 519-765-1885
ghsaylaw@amtelecom.net

***Bancroft*: Lorne C. Plater - *1**
P.O. Box 1150, 129 Hastings St. North, Bancroft, ON K0L 1C0
Tel: 613-332-1605; *Fax:* 613-332-2619
lorne@bancroftlawyer.com
www.bancroftlawyer.ca

***Barrie*: Nancy Lee Allison - *1**
P.O. Box 163, Barrie, ON L0L 2X0
Tel: 705-353-0145
nancyallison79@yahoo.com

***Barrie*: John G. Alousis - *1**
76 Mulcaster St., Barrie, ON L4M 3M4
Tel: 705-735-0065; *Fax:* 705-735-0277
john@alousislaw.com
www.alousislaw.com

***Barrie*: Peter D. Archibald - *1**
P.O. Box 907, 59 Collier St., Barrie, ON L4M 4Y6
Tel: 705-726-4511; *Fax:* 705-726-0613
pda@bconnex.net

***Barrie*: Barriston Law - Barrie - Mulcaster St. - *28**
Former Name: Burgar Rowe Professional Corporation; Purser Dooley Cockburn Smith LLP
90 Mulcaster St., Barrie, ON L4M 4Y5
Tel: 705-792-9200; *Fax:* 705-721-4025
www.barristonlaw.com
www.facebook.com/pages/Barriston-LLP-Law-Firm/106985366002895, twitter.com/BarristonLLP, www.linkedin.com/company/barriston-llp

***Barrie*: Brian Bond**
25 Poyntz St., Barrie, ON L4M 3N8
Tel: 705-734-1550; *Fax:* 705-734-0306
bwb@bondlaw.ca
www.brianbondlaw.ca/en/

***Barrie*: Boswell Chapman - *2**
#301, 135 Bayfield St., Barrie, ON L4M 3B3
Tel: 705-719-2200; *Fax:* 705-719-2265
boswellchapman.com

***Barrie*: Thomas Bryson - *1**
11 Sophia St. West, Barrie, ON L4N 1H9
Tel: 705-728-2232; *Fax:* 705-728-7525
tbrysonlaw@bellnet.ca

* indicates number of lawyers

***Barrie*: Peter C. Card - *1**
#621, 80 Bradford St., Barrie, ON L4N 6S7
Tel: 705-737-9179; *Fax:* 705-737-1380

***Barrie*: Carroll Heyd Chown - *9**
P.O. Box 5481, 109 Ferris Lane, Barrie, ON L4M 4T7
Tel: 705-722-4400; *Fax:* 705-722-0704
admin@chcbarristers.com
www.chcbarristers.com
www.facebook.com/#!/pages/Carroll-Heyd-Chown-LLP/295907650441688?fref=ts, twitter.com/CHCBarristers

***Barrie*: Cowan & Carter - *1**
P.O. Box 722, 107 Collier St., Barrie, ON L4M 4Y5
Tel: 705-728-4521; *Fax:* 705-728-8744

***Barrie*: Cugelman & Eisen - *2**
#100, 89 Collier St., Barrie, ON L4M 1H2
Tel: 705-721-1888; *Fax:* 705-721-7755
help@cugelmaneisen.com
www.cugelmaneisen.com
www.facebook.com/pages/Cugelman-Eisen/190336767785823

***Barrie*: Alfred W.J. Dick - *1**
P.O. Box 758, 90 Mulcaster St., Barrie, ON L4M 4Y5
Tel: 705-725-4900; *Fax:* 705-721-4025
adick@barristonlaw.com

***Barrie*: Julianne Ecclestone - *1**
80 Worsley St., Barrie, ON L4M 1L8
Tel: 705-725-8050; *Fax:* 705-722-0189
sandra@jecclestone.ca

***Barrie*: Galbraith Family Law - *4**
Former Name: Brian G. Galbraith
124 Dunlop St. West, Barrie, ON L4N 1B1
Tel: 705-727-4242; *Fax:* 705-727-4240
Brian@GalbraithFamilyLaw.com
www.galbraithfamilylaw.com
www.facebook.com/GalbraithFamilyLaw?ref=ts, twitter.com/GalbraithFamLaw

***Barrie*: Jacoby & Jacoby - *2**
P.O. Box 350, 34 Clapperton St., Barrie, ON L4M 4T5
Tel: 705-726-0238; *Fax:* 705-726-9197
info@jacobylaw.ca

***Barrie*: Mark A. Kelly - *1**
43 Worsley St., Barrie, ON L4M 1L7
Tel: 705-739-6955; *Fax:* 705-739-6956
www.markkellylaw.ca

***Barrie*: Peter Lamprey - *1**
78 Worsley St., Barrie, ON L4M 1L8
Tel: 705-722-1114; *Fax:* 705-720-1155
peter@plamprey.com
www.plamprey.com

***Barrie*: Larry E. Lant - *1**
#5, 4 Simcoe St., Barrie, ON L4M 1A1
Tel: 705-726-1901

***Barrie*: R. John Mitchell - *1**
40 Clapperton St., Barrie, ON L4M 4S9
Tel: 705-726-8855; *Fax:* 705-721-0782
www.barrie.homemove.biz/r-john-mitchell

***Barrie*: Murray Ralston Lawyers - *3**
Also Known As: Murray Ralston Professional Corporation
576 Bryne Dr., #O, Barrie, ON L4N 9P6
Tel: 705-737-3229; *Fax:* 705-737-5380
admin@murrayralston.com
www.murrayralston.com
www.facebook.com/pages/Murray-Ralston-Lawyers/200839669967063, twitter.com/MurrayRalston

***Barrie*: Gerald E. Norman - *1**
P.O. Box 732, 99 Bayfield St., Barrie, ON L4M 4Y5
Tel: 705-726-2772; *Fax:* 705-734-1942
geraldnorman@normanlawoffice.ca
www.normanlawoffice.ca

***Barrie*: Owen, Harris-Lowe - *4**
Former Name: Owen, Dickey
P.O. Box 848, 26 Owen St., Barrie, ON L4M 4Y6
Tel: 705-726-1181; *Fax:* 705-726-1463
ohlaw@owenharrislowe.com
www.owenharrislowe.com

***Barrie*: Michael E. Reed - *1**
Also Known As: Michael Reed Law
105 Collier St., Barrie, ON L4M 1H2
Tel: 705-726-4300; *Fax:* 705-725-7910
michael@michaelreedlaw.com
www.michaelreedlaw.com

***Barrie*: Catherine A. Rogers - *1**
78 Mulcaster St., Barrie, ON L4M 3M4
Tel: 705-734-2800; *Fax:* 705-734-2807

***Barrie*: Charles F. Ruttan - *1**
23 Owen St., Barrie, ON L4M 3G8
Tel: 705-737-0688; *Fax:* 705-722-4749
chuckruttan@ruttanlaw.ca

***Barrie*: Mark Scharf - *1**
103 Collier St., Barrie, ON L4M 1H2
Tel: 705-728-0555; *Fax:* 705-722-3741
mscharf@bellnet.ca

***Barrie*: Eric C. Taves - *1**
P.O. Box 295, 86 Worsley St., Barrie, ON L4M 4T2
Tel: 705-728-4770; *Fax:* 705-728-7642
etaves@etaves-law.com

***Barrie*: Wall, Armstrong & Green - *3**
#B, 375 Yonge St., Barrie, ON L4N 4C9
Tel: 705-722-7272; *Fax:* 705-722-3568
info@wall-arm.ca
www.wall-arm.ca
www.facebook.com/wallarmstrongandgreen

***Beamsville*: Monty G. Vandeyar - *1**
#7, Lincoln Kingsway Plaza, P.O. Box 489, 5041 King St., Beamsville, ON L0R 1B0
Tel: 905-563-8818; *Fax:* 905-563-7750

***Beaverton*: Woodcock & Tomlinson - *1**
P.O. Box 512, 402 Simcoe St., Beaverton, ON L0K 1A0
Tel: 705-426-7317; *Fax:* 705-426-5740
stephenwoodcock@rogers.com
www.woodcockandtomlinson.ca/en/

***Belle River*: John L. Deziel - *1**
P.O. Box 909, 531 Notre Dame, Belle River, ON N0R 1A0
Tel: 519-728-2000; *Fax:* 519-728-4599
Toll-Free: 800-501-3494
jldeziel@cogeco.net

***Belleville*: Wendy J. Elliott - *1**
187B North Front St., Belleville, ON K8P 3C1
Tel: 613-966-0394; *Fax:* 613-966-1307
wjelliott@hotmail.com

***Belleville*: Hurley & Williams - *2**
112 Front St., Belleville, ON K8N 2Y7
Tel: 613-966-4614; *Fax:* 613-966-6182
www.hwlaw.ca

***Belleville*: Edward J. Kafka - *3**
P.O. Box 243, 309 Front St., Belleville, ON K8N 5A2
Tel: 613-968-3416; *Fax:* 613-968-3417

***Belleville*: Richard R. Ketcheson - *1**
#200, 199 Front St., Belleville, ON K8N 5H5
Tel: 613-966-1123; *Fax:* 613-966-0478

***Belleville*: O'Flynn Weese LLP - *10**
Former Name: O'Flynn, Weese & Tausendfreund LLP
65 Bridge St. East, Belleville, ON K8N 1L8
Tel: 613-966-5222; *Fax:* 613-966-7991
info@owtlaw.com
www.owtlaw.com

***Belleville*: Procter Professional Corporation - *4**
Former Name: Procter, Cameron
#204, P.O. Box 700, 365 Front St. North, Belleville, ON K8N 5B3
Tel: 613-962-2584; *Fax:* 613-962-0968
wprocter@procterlaw.ca

***Belleville*: Reynolds O'Brien LLP - *6**
P.O. Box 1327, 183 Front St., Belleville, ON K8N 5J1
Tel: 613-966-3031; *Fax:* 613-966-2390
info@reynoldsobrien.com
www.reynoldsobrien.com

***Belleville*: Peter A. Robertson - *1**
#101, 3 Applewood Dr., Belleville, ON K8P 4E3
Tel: 613-969-9611; *Fax:* 613-969-9775
Toll-Free: 800-561-6385
www.facebook.com/pages/Peter-A-Robertson-Professional-Corporation/113151782

***Belleville*: C. Roderick Rolston - *1**
#202, 175 Front St., Belleville, ON K8N 2Y9
Tel: 613-962-9154; *Fax:* 613-962-8109
Toll-Free: 800-361-4437
rrolston@reach.net

***Belleville*: Templeman Menninga LLP - Belleville - *24**
#200, P.O. Box 234, 205 Dundas St. East, Belleville, ON K8N 5A2
Tel: 613-966-2620; *Fax:* 613-966-2866
info@tmlegal.ca
www.tmlegal.ca

***Belleville*: Berend Van Huizen - *1**
210 Church St., Belleville, ON K8N 3C3
Tel: 613-962-8645; *Fax:* 613-962-7689
berend@berendvanhuizenlaw.com
www.berendvanhuizenlaw.com

***Blenheim*: Kerr & Wood - *1**
P.O. Box 1150, 15 George St., Blenheim, ON N0P 1A0
Tel: 519-676-5465; *Fax:* 519-676-3918
info@kwmlaw.ca

***Bobcaygeon*: Robert J. Walker - *1**
P.O. Box 243, 4 King St. West, Bobcaygeon, ON K0M 1A0
Tel: 705-738-3588; *Fax:* 705-738-4252
rjwalkerlaw@hotmail.com

***Bolton*: Jean P. Carberry - *1**
34 Queen St., Bolton, ON L4E 1B3
Tel: 905-857-2332; *Fax:* 905-857-2367
jpclaw@jpclaw.ca

***Bolton*: W. Ross Milliken - *1**
P.O. Box 225, 49 Queen St. North, Bolton, ON L7E 5T2
Tel: 905-857-2835; *Fax:* 905-857-0097
ross.milliken@boltonlaw.ca
www.rossmilliken.ca

***Bolton*: Neiman, Callegari - *3**
#H3, 18 King St. East, Bolton, ON L7E 1E8
Tel: 905-857-0095; *Fax:* 905-857-0488
neimancallegari@gmail.com
www.neimancallegari.ca

***Bolton*: Mark E. Penfold - *4**
49 Queen St. North, Bolton, ON L7E 5T2
Tel: 905-857-2835
mark.penfold@boltonlaw.ca
www.boltonlaw.ca

***Bowmanville*: William Brown - *1**
P.O. Box 1, 71 Mearns Court, Bowmanville, ON L1C 4N4
Tel: 905-623-3305; *Fax:* 905-623-3287

***Bowmanville*: Mervyn B. Kelly - *1**
42 Prince St., Bowmanville, ON L1C 1G6
Tel: 905-623-4444

***Bracebridge*: Ronald G. Burk - *1**
32 Wharf Rd., Bracebridge, ON P1L 2A7
Tel: 705-645-3007; *Fax:* 705-645-3998
rgburklaw@on.aibn.com

***Bracebridge*: Brian G. Jacques - *1**
P.O. Box 1227, 14 Ontario St., Bracebridge, ON P1L 1V4
Tel: 705-645-8743; *Fax:* 705-645-8895
brianjacqueslaw@bellnet.ca

***Bracebridge*: Lee, Roche & Kelly - *3**
P.O. Box 990, 6 Dominion St., Bracebridge, ON P1L 1V2
Tel: 705-645-2286; *Fax:* 705-645-5541
Toll-Free: 866-331-1100
nickroche@lrklaw.ca
www.lrklaw.ca

***Bracebridge*: Penelope A. Lithgow - *1**
58 Ontario St., Bracebridge, ON P1L 1S5
Tel: 705-645-8118

***Bracebridge*: Marshall MacLennan LLP - *2**
58 Ontario St., Bracebridge, ON P1L 2A6
Tel: 705-645-5251; *Fax:* 866-450-1819
www.marshallmaclennan.ca

***Bracebridge*: Brian E. Slocum - *1**
63 Quebec St., Bracebridge, ON P1L 2A4
Tel: 705-645-2900; *Fax:* 705-645-2549
slocum@slocumlaw.com

** indicates number of lawyers*

***Bracebridge*: Bruce McLeod Thompson - *1**
3 Dominion St., Bracebridge, ON P1L 1T5
Tel: 705-646-1000; *Fax:* 705-646-9510
Toll-Free: 800-661-8080

***Bracebridge*: Wyjad Fleming Associates - *2**
Former Name: Pinckard Wyjad Associates
P.O. Box 177, 39 Dominion St., Bracebridge, ON P1L 1T6
Tel: 705-645-8787; *Fax:* 705-645-3390
bracebridge@wylaw.ca
www.wylaw.ca

***Bradford*: Evans & Evans - *2**
P.O. Box 190, 21 Holland St. West, Bradford, ON L3Z 2A8
Tel: 905-775-3381; *Fax:* 905-775-8835
law@evansevans.ca

***Bradford*: Gaska & Ballantyne-Gaska - *2**
P.O. Box 1677, Stn. Main, 60 Barrie St., Bradford, ON L3Z 2B9
Tel: 905-775-0015; *Fax:* 905-775-7772
ballantyne.gaska@rogers.com

***Bradford*: E. Pauline Taylor - *1**
76 Holland St. West, Bradford, ON L3Z 2B6
Tel: 905-775-9606; *Fax:* 905-775-0692

***Brampton*: Linda B. Alexander - *1**
#201, 197 County Court Blvd., Brampton, ON L6W 4P6
Tel: 905-450-7757; *Fax:* 905-455-9190
lba@lindaalexander.com
lindaalexander.com

***Brampton*: Bowyer, Greenslade, Webster, Allison LLP, Barristers, Solicitors - *3**
#600, 24 Queen St. East, Brampton, ON L6V 1A3
Tel: 905-451-1300; *Fax:* 905-451-4451

***Brampton*: Edmond O. Brown - *1**
#100, 205 County Court Blvd., Brampton, ON L6W 4R6
Tel: 905-454-4141; *Fax:* 905-454-4463
edbrown@bellnet.ca
www.peelbarristers.com/edbrown

***Brampton*: Connon & Iacobelli - *2**
21 John St., Brampton, ON L6W 1Z1
Tel: 905-454-3070; *Fax:* 905-454-2964
connon-iacobelli@on.aibn.com
www.connoniacobelli.com/en/

***Brampton*: Crawford Chondon & Partners LLP - *11**
#500, 24 Queen St. East, Brampton, ON L6V 1A3
Tel: 905-874-9343; *Fax:* 905-874-1384
Toll-Free: 877-874-9343
info@ccpartners.ca
www.ccpartners.ca
twitter.com/CrawfordChondon,
www.linkedin.com/company/crawford-chondon-&-partners-llp

***Brampton*: Dale, Streiman & Kurz - *7**
480 Main St. North, Brampton, ON L6V 1P8
Tel: 905-455-7300; *Fax:* 905-455-5848
Toll-Free: 866-219-8109
reception@dsklaw.com
www.dsklaw.com

***Brampton*: Dalzell & Waite - *2**
Former Name: Dalzell, Inglis, Waite
#19, 1 Bartley Bull Pkwy., Brampton, ON L6W 3T7
Tel: 905-454-2288; *Fax:* 905-454-2297

***Brampton*: Davis Webb LLP - *8**
Former Name: Davis Webb Schulze & Moon LLP
#800, 24 Queen St. East, Brampton, ON L6V 1A3
Tel: 905-451-6714; *Fax:* 905-454-1876
info@daviswebb.ca
www.daviswebb.com

***Brampton*: Fader Furlan Moss LLP - *7**
#200, 134 Queen St. East, Brampton, ON L6V 1B2
Tel: 905-459-6160; *Fax:* 905-459-4606
Toll-Free: 877-468-8494
www.faderfurlanmoss.com

***Brampton*: Folkes Law Legal Professional Corporation - Brampton - *1**
Former Name: Folites Legal Professional Corporation; Ron E. Folkes
#900, 21 Queen St. East, Brampton, ON L6W 3P1
Tel: 905-457-2118; *Fax:* 905-457-3707
Toll-Free: 877-457-2118
ronefolkes@folkeslaw.ca
www.folkeslaw.ca
www.facebook.com/Folkes-Law-434236576667100,
twitter.com/FolkesLaw, www.linkedin.com/in/ronefolkes

***Brampton*: Pina Grella - *1**
#101, 8501 Mississauga Rd., Brampton, ON L6Y 5G8
Tel: 905-453-6000; *Fax:* 905-453-6016
pina@grellalaw.com

***Brampton*: Hillier & Hillier Personal Injury Lawyers - *4**
165 Main St. North, Brampton, ON L6X 1N1
Tel: 905-453-8636; *Fax:* 905-453-6267
www.avahillier.ca

***Brampton*: Stephen A. Holmes - *1**
180 Queen St. West, Brampton, ON L6X 1A8
Tel: 905-796-3030; *Fax:* 905-796-2157
sholmes@on.aibn.com
www.stephenholmeslawoffice.com

***Brampton*: Hope & Henderson Law Office - *2**
Former Name: Henderson Law Office
253 Main St. North, Brampton, ON L6X 1N3
Tel: 905-451-7700; *Fax:* 905-451-6620

***Brampton*: Vincent V. Houvardas - *1**
#1802, 83 Kennedy Rd. South, Brampton, ON L3W 3P3
Tel: 905-455-9970; *Fax:* 905-455-6148
vhlaw@rogers.com
www.vhlegal.ca

***Brampton*: Kania Lawyers - *7**
223 Main St. North, Brampton, ON L6X 1N2
Tel: 905-451-3222; *Fax:* 905-451-1267
Toll-Free: 877-485-2642
www.kanialawyers.com

***Brampton*: Lawrence, Lawrence, Stevenson LLP**
Also Known As: Lawrences Lawyers
43 Queen St. West, Brampton, ON L6Y 1L9
Tel: 905-451-3040; *Fax:* 905-451-5058
lls@lawrences.com
www.lawrences.com
www.linkedin.com/company/lawrence-lawrence-stevenson-llp

***Brampton*: Douglas R. Lent - *1**
38 Queen St. West, Brampton, ON L6X 1A1
Tel: 905-457-4215; *Fax:* 905-457-6454

***Brampton*: Ritchie J. Linton - *1**
182 Queen St. West, Brampton, ON L6X 1A8
Tel: 905-453-3145; *Fax:* 905-454-2270

***Brampton*: Mackay & Company - *1**
Former Name: Mackay, Alison R.
#202, 2 County Court Blvd., Brampton, ON L6W 3W8
Tel: 905-455-6000; *Fax:* 905-456-1209
mackaya@rogers.com
www.mississaugacriminallawyer.net/en/

***Brampton*: June A. Maresca - *1**
#100, Central West Region-Peel Regional Municipality, 7755 Hurontario St., Brampton, ON L6W 4T6
Tel: 905-456-4833; *Fax:* 905-456-4829

***Brampton*: McCabe, Filkin & Garvie - *5**
Former Name: James A. Garvie
#320, Plaza II, 350 Rutherford Rd. South, Brampton, ON L6W 4P7
Tel: 905-452-7400; *Fax:* 905-452-6444
mfa@mccabefilkin.com

***Brampton*: McClelland Law, A Professional Corporation, Lawyers - *2**
Former Name: McLelland & Novak
202 Main St. North, Brampton, ON L6V 1P1
Tel: 905-793-3026; *Fax:* 905-793-2446
info@mcclellandlaw.com
www.mcclellandlaw.com

***Brampton*: W. John McCulligh - *1**
#301, 197 County Court Blvd., Brampton, ON L6W 4P6
Tel: 905-459-1545; *Fax:* 905-459-2826
wjmcculligh@idirect.com
www.peelbarristers.com/mcculligh

***Brampton*: North Peel & Dufferin Community Legal Services - *4**
#601, 24 Queen St. East, Brampton, ON L6V 1A3
Tel: 905-455-0160; *Fax:* 905-455-0832
Toll-Free: 866-455-0160
www.legalclinicsinpeel.ca

***Brampton*: Laszlo Pandy - *1**
#6, 279 Queen St. East, Brampton, ON L6W 2C2
Tel: 905-457-0977; *Fax:* 905-457-8108

***Brampton*: Prouse, Dash & Crouch LLP - *12**
50 Queen St. West, Brampton, ON L6X 4H3
Tel: 905-451-6610; *Fax:* 905-451-1549
Toll-Free: 877-217-4732
pdc@pdclawyers.ca
www.prousedash.ca

***Brampton*: Richardson, Schnall & Sanderson - *1**
#402, 134 Queen St. East, Brampton, ON L6V 1B2
Tel: 905-451-1593; *Fax:* 905-451-3132
gschnall@bellnet.ca

***Brampton*: Simmons, Da Silva & Sinton - *11**
#200, 201 County Court Blvd., Brampton, ON L6W 4L2
Tel: 905-457-1660; *Fax:* 905-457-5641
www.sdslawfirm.com

***Brampton*: Mark E. Skursky - *1**
#101, 380 Bovaird Dr., Brampton, ON L6Z 2S8
Tel: 905-840-0001; *Fax:* 905-840-0002
skurskylawoffice@on.aibn.com

***Brampton*: George Paul Smith - *1**
280 Main St. North, Brampton, ON L6V 1P6
Tel: 905-457-9791; *Fax:* 905-457-9798
gpsmith@pathcom.com
www.peelbarristers.com/gpsmith/

***Brampton*: Victor E. Szumlanski - *1**
9610 McLaughlin Rd. North, Brampton, ON L6X 0B8
Tel: 905-456-1673; *Fax:* 905-456-1201
zoomer@on.aibn.com

***Brampton*: Alan Wainwright - *1**
#102, 197 County Court Blvd., Brampton, ON L6W 4P6
Tel: 905-453-9520; *Fax:* 905-450-7842
awainwright@bellnet.ca
www.peelbarristers.com/wainwright

***Brampton*: Cynthia K. Waite - *3**
Former Name: Waite and Associates
#102, 197 County Court Blvd., Brampton, ON L6W 4P6
Tel: 905-450-3800; *Fax:* 905-450-8376
cyndy@wjfamilylaw.com

***Brampton*: Michael J. Walsh - *1**
280 Main St. North, Brampton, ON L6V 1P6
Tel: 905-453-4105; *Fax:* 905-457-3075
walaw@on.aibn.com

***Brantford*: Douglas C. Ainsworth - *1**
Stn. Main, 120B Market St., Brantford, ON N3T 3A1
Tel: 519-756-4220; *Fax:* 519-756-3462

***Brantford*: Donald A. Archi - *1**
80 Brant Ave., Brantford, ON N3T 3G7
Tel: 519-751-3101; *Fax:* 519-751-0347
info@archilaw.ca
www.archilaw.ca

***Brantford*: Boddy Ryerson LLP - *5**
#101, P.O. Box 1265, 172 Dalhousie St., Brantford, ON N3T 5T3
Tel: 519-753-8417; *Fax:* 519-753-7421
trignani@boddy-ryerson.com
www.boddy-ryerson.com

***Brantford*: Donald C. Calder - *1**
40 Nelson St., Brantford, ON N3T 2M8
Tel: 519-759-1910; *Fax:* 519-759-2881
donald.calder@bellnet.ca

***Brantford*: DeLong Law - *2**
16 Darling St., Brantford, ON N3T 2K2
Tel: 519-720-6700; *Fax:* 519-720-6757
www.delonglaw.ca

***Brantford*: Stephen C, Frost - *1**
101 Wellington St., Brantford, ON N3T 2M1
Tel: 519-753-4113

** indicates number of lawyers*

***Brantford*: Gerry Smits Law Firm - *1**
#4, 45 Dalkeith Dr., Brantford, ON N3P 1M1
Tel: 519-720-6733; *Fax:* 519-720-0933
contact@smitslawfirm.com
www.smitslawfirm.com

***Brantford*: Sandra J. Harris - *1**
#102, 99 Chatham St., Brantford, ON N3T 2P3
Tel: 519-756-0350; *Fax:* 519-756-6611
sjharrison@on.aibn.com

***Brantford*: Hospodar, Davies & Goold - *3**
120 Market St., Brantford, ON N3T 3A1
Tel: 519-759-0082; *Fax:* 519-759-8490

***Brantford*: John Jakub - *1**
45 Peel St., Brantford, ON N3S 5L7
Tel: 519-754-0495; *Fax:* 519-754-1882
johnjakub@rogers.com

***Brantford*: Lefebvre & Lefebvre LLP - *9**
P.O. Box 488, 75 Chatham St., Brantford, ON N3T 5N9
Tel: 519-756-3350; *Fax:* 519-756-4727
info@lefebvrelawyers.ca
www.lefebvrelawyers.ca

***Brantford*: McIntosh & Pease - *2**
442 Grey St., #D, Brantford, ON N3S 7N3
Tel: 519-752-7733; *Fax:* 519-751-7526
Toll-Free: 800-601-6801
www.mcintosh-pease.com

***Brantford*: Melanie A. Peters - *1**
#109, Royal Victoria Place, 136 Dalhousie St., Brantford, ON N3T 2J3
Tel: 519-900-6055; *Fax:* 519-900-6058
mpeters@melaniepeterslaw.ca
www.melaniepeterslaw.ca

***Brantford*: Pipe Law Professional Corporation - *1**
387 Wellington St., Brantford, ON N3S 4A8
Tel: 226-400-0797; *Fax:* 815-572-0950
Brian@PipeLaw.Com
www.parisontariolawyer.com

***Brantford*: Staats Law - *2**
Former Name: Staats, Newton
P.O. Box 1417, 188 Mohawk St., Brantford, ON N3T 5T6
Tel: 519-756-5217; *Fax:* 519-756-4783

***Brantford*: Shelley M. Stanzlik - *1**
P.O. Box 691, 119 Brant Ave., Brantford, ON N3T 3H5
Tel: 519-756-7566; *Fax:* 519-756-7558
shelley.stanzlik@bellnet.ca

***Brantford*: Thomas H. Buck Law Office - *1**
Former Name: Reeves & Buck LLP
442 Grey St., #G, Brantford, ON N3S 7N3
Tel: 226-381-0900
info@thomasbuck.ca
www.thomasbuck.ca

***Brantford*: Trepanier Verity LLP - *6**
P.O. Box 144, Stn. Main, 63 Charlotte St., Brantford, ON N3T 2W6
Tel: 519-756-8700; *Fax:* 519-756-5454
info@trepanierverity.com
www.trepanierverity.com

***Brantford*: Underwood, Ion & Johnson LLP - *2**
Former Name: Underwood & Ion
P.O. Box 1536, 442 Grey St., Unit B, Brantford, ON N3T 5V6
Tel: 519-759-0920; *Fax:* 519-759-2122
dennis@uijlaw.com

***Brantford*: Paul Vandervet - *1**
P.O. Box 1495, 107 Wellington St., Brantford, ON N3T 5V6
Tel: 519-759-4240; *Fax:* 519-759-4863
vandervet@bellnet.ca

***Brantford*: Wayne P. Vipond - *1**
99 Chatham St., Brantford, ON N3T 2P3
Tel: 519-751-0240; *Fax:* 519-751-0251
wvipond@bellnet.ca

***Brantford*: Waterous, Holden, Amey, Hitchon LLP - *21**
P.O. Box 1510, 20 Wellington St., Brantford, ON N3T 5V6
Tel: 519-759-6220; *Fax:* 519-759-8360
law@waterousholden.com
www.waterousholden.com

***Brantford*: Michael R. White - *1**
#103, North Brantford Professional Centre, 525 Park Rd. North, Brantford, ON N3R 7K8
Tel: 519-752-9004; *Fax:* 519-752-0449
mrw@michaelrwhite.com

***Brantford*: Wyatt, Purcell, Stillman & Karkkainen - *3**
P.O. Box 1115, Stn. Main, 442 Grey St., Brantford, ON N3S 7N3
Tel: 519-756-5800; *Fax:* 519-756-3861
wyattpurcell@wyatturcell.com

***Brigden*: William E. Tennyson - *1**
P.O. Box 232, 3015 Brigden Rd., Brigden, ON N0N 1B0
Tel: 519-864-1189; *Fax:* 519-864-1966
tennysonlaw@bellnet.ca

***Brockville*: Barr & O'Brien - *2**
#206, 9 Broad St., Brockville, ON K6V 6Z4
Tel: 613-498-0800; *Fax:* 613-498-0001
Toll-Free: 800-673-3429
rabarr@barrobrien.com
www.barrobrien.com

***Brockville*: Michael P. Bird - *1**
#304, The Boardwalk, 9 Broad St., Brockville, ON K6V 6Z4
Tel: 613-342-1183; *Fax:* 613-342-0887
mpbird@ripnet.com

***Brockville*: Fitzpatrick & Culic - *1**
21 Pine St., Brockville, ON K6V 1E9
Tel: 613-342-6693; *Fax:* 613-342-8449
www.culiclaw.com

***Brockville*: Robert W. Flood - *1**
13 Hartley St., Brockville, ON K6V 3N2
Tel: 613-345-0087; *Fax:* 613-342-5294

***Brockville*: Fraser & Bickerton - *1**
#100, P.O. Box 692, 36 Broad St., Brockville, ON K6V 4V9
Tel: 613-345-3377; *Fax:* 613-345-3372

***Brockville*: David A. Hain - *1**
P.O. Box 757, 20 King St. West, Brockville, ON K6V 5W1
Tel: 613-342-5577; *Fax:* 613-342-1773
david@hainlaw.com
www.hainlaw.com

***Brockville*: Hammond Osborne - *3**
#207, 9 Broad St., Brockville, ON K6V 6Z4
Tel: 613-498-0944; *Fax:* 613-498-0946
Toll-Free: 877-498-0944
rob@hammondosborne.ca
www.hammondosborne.ca / www.hammondmediation.ca

***Brockville*: Henderson Johnston Fournier - *3**
Equity Bldg., 61 King St. East, Brockville, ON K6V 5V4
Tel: 613-345-5613; *Fax:* 613-345-6473
www.hendersonjohnstonfournier.com

***Brockville*: John M. Johnston - *1**
41 Court House Sq., Brockville, ON K6V 7N3
Tel: 613-341-2821; *Fax:* 613-341-2818
john.m.johnston@scj-csj.ca

***Brockville*: John H. Macintosh, Q.C. - *1**
2 Court House Ave., Brockville, ON K6V 4T1
Tel: 613-345-5653

***Brockville*: Michael J. O'Shaughnessy - *1**
P.O. Box 2121, Stn. Main, 21 Court House Ave., Brockville, ON K6V 6N5
Tel: 613-342-2010; *Fax:* 613-342-6405
mike@courthouse.ca
www.michaeloshaughnessy.ca

***Brockville*: Preston Lawyers - *2**
#201, P.O. Box 1814, Stn. Main, 68 King St. West, Brockville, ON K6V 3P9
Tel: 613-342-1866; *Fax:* 613-342-1634
preslaw@bellnet.ca

***Brockville*: Wilson Evely - *1**
P.O. Box 1, 3 Court Terrace, Brockville, ON K6V 4T4
Tel: 613-345-1907; *Fax:* 613-345-4604
wilson-evely@bellnet.ca

***Brooklin*: Mason Bennett Johncox - *5**
79 Baldwin St. North, Brooklin, ON L1M 1A4
Tel: 905-620-4499; *Fax:* 905-620-7738
www.whitbylawyers.com
twitter.com/whitbylawyers

***Bruce Mines*: Peterson & Peterson - *1**
2 Taylor St., Bruce Mines, ON P0R 1C0
Tel: 705-785-3491; *Fax:* 705-785-3768
larryd.peterson@sympatico.ca
www.petersonandpetersonlawfirm.com

***Burlington*: Christopher C. Breen - *1**
3400 Fairview St., Burlington, ON L7N 3G5
Tel: 905-634-1828; *Fax:* 905-634-9630
breenlaw@lawtel.ca
www.lawtel.ca

***Burlington*: Burgess Law Office - *1**
#27, 460 Brant St., Burlington, ON L7R 4B6
Tel: 905-632-9474; *Fax:* 905-632-3035
info@burgesslawoffice.com
burgesslawoffice.com

***Burlington*: Cleaver Crawford LLP - *3**
530 Brant St., Burlington, ON L7R 2G7
Tel: 905-634-5581; *Fax:* 905-634-1563
eldon.hunt@cleavercrawford.ca
www.cleavercrawford.ca

***Burlington*: Dunlop & Associates - *2**
Former Name: Daniel R. Pust Law Office
3556 Commerce Ct., Burlington, ON L7N 3L7
Tel: 905-681-3311; *Fax:* 905-681-3565
info@dunloplaw.com
www.dunloplaw.com

***Burlington*: Feltmate Delibato Heagle LLP - *15**
#200, 3600 Billings Ct., Burlington, ON L7N 3N6
Tel: 905-639-8881; *Fax:* 905-639-8017
Toll-Free: 800-636-6927
www.fdhlawyers.com

***Burlington*: Forbes Law Office - *1**
Former Name: Forbes, Conant, Barristers & Solicitors
#2, 3455 Harvester Rd., Burlington, ON L7N 3P2
Tel: 905-333-1622; *Fax:* 905-333-1624
robf@forbeslaw.ca

***Burlington*: Green Germann Sakran - *3**
P.O. Box 400, 411 Guelph Line, Burlington, ON L7R 3Y3
Tel: 905-639-1222; *Fax:* 905-632-6977
www.ggslaw.ca

***Burlington*: Gross, Shuman, Brizdle & Gilfillan, P.C. - *23**
#300, Hoover Business Park, 1100 Burloak Dr., Burlington, ON L7L 6B2
Tel: 416-221-5600
www.gross-shuman.com

***Burlington*: Haber & Associates - Burlington - *7**
3370 South Service Rd., 2nd Fl., Burlington, ON L7N 3M6
Tel: 905-639-8894; *Fax:* 905-639-0459
www.haber-lawyer.com
www.facebook.com/HaberAssociates, twitter.com/HaberLawyers

***Burlington*: Catherine A. Haber - *1**
3370 South Service Rd., 2nd Fl., Burlington, ON L7N 3M6
Tel: 905-333-4421; *Fax:* 905-333-0575
catherine@catherineahaber.com
www.catherineahaber.com

***Burlington*: Hastings, Charlebois - *2**
3513 Mainway Dr., Burlington, ON L7M 1A9
Tel: 905-332-1888; *Fax:* 905-332-0021
hjcharlebois@hclawyers.ca

***Burlington*: John Hicks Law Office - *1**
#7, 541 Brant St., Burlington, ON L7R 2G6
Tel: 905-681-3131; *Fax:* 905-333-6688
www.johnhickslaw.ca/en

***Burlington*: Hofbauer Professional Corporation - *1**
#3, 3350 Fairview St., Burlington, ON L7N 3L5
Tel: 905-634-0040; *Fax:* 905-349-0809
info@capatents.com
www.capatents.com

***Burlington*: Jaskot Family Law - *3**
#101, 4200 South Service Rd., Burlington, ON L7L 4X5
Toll-Free: 888-522-3517
info@jaskotfamilylaw.ca
www.jaskotfamilylaw.ca

***Burlington*: Richard R. Kosterski - *1**
394 Guelph Line, Burlington, ON L7R 3L4
Tel: 905-637-8249; *Fax:* 905-637-6015
richard@kosterskilaw.ca

** indicates number of lawyers*

***Burlington*: Martin & Hillyer Associates - *8**
Former Name: Lakeshore Law Chambers
2122 Old Lakeshore Rd., Burlington, ON L7R 1A3
Tel: 905-637-5641; *Fax:* 905-637-5404
info@mhalaw.ca
www.mhalaw.ca

***Burlington*: Gary Rich - *1**
#12, 460 Brant St., Burlington, ON L7R 4B6
Tel: 905-681-1521; *Fax:* 905-333-5075

***Burlington*: SimpsonWigle LAW LLP - *29**
Former Name: Simpson, Wigle LLP
#501, 390 Brant St., Burlington, ON L7R 4J4
Tel: 905-639-1052; *Fax:* 905-333-3960
Toll-Free: 800-434-4414
info@simpsonwigle.com
www.simpsonwigle.com

***Burlington*: Snelius, Redfearn LLP - *4**
Former Name: J. Douglas Redfearn
#105, 3410 South Service Rd., Burlington, ON L7N 3T2
Tel: 905-333-5322; *Fax:* 905-333-9835
info@familylawassociates.ca
www.familylawassociates.ca

***Burlington*: Thomas R. Sutherland Q.C. - *1**
3310 South Service Road, Burlington, ON L7N 3M6
Tel: 905-634-5521; *Fax:* 905-631-7914

***Burlington*: Harold Kim Taylor - *1**
3380 South Service Road, Burlington, ON L7N 3J5
Tel: 905-681-6400; *Fax:* 905-681-6510

***Burlington*: Thatcher & Wands - *2**
1457 Ontario St., Burlington, ON L7S 1G6
Tel: 905-681-0444; *Fax:* 905-681-2937
office@thatcherandwands.com
www.thatcherandwands.com

***Burlington*: Elizabeth A. Urban - *1**
3380 South Service Rd., Burlington, ON L7N 3J5
Tel: 905-333-6640; *Fax:* 905-681-6510
eaurban@urbanfamilylaw.ca
www.urbanfamilylaw.ca

***Caledon East*: George W. Jenney - *1**
P.O. Box 340, 15891 Airport Rd., Caledon East, ON L0N 1E0
Tel: 905-584-9300; *Fax:* 905-584-9233

***Caledon East*: Lockyer Law Professional Corporation - *1**
Former Name: Matheson, Holmes A.
#201, 15955 Airport Rd., Caledon East, ON L7C 1H9
Tel: 905-584-4545; *Fax:* 905-584-6565
info@lockyerlaw.ca
www.lockyerlaw.ca

***Caledonia*: Arrell Law LLP - *3**
Former Name: Arrell, Brown, Osier, Murray & Rosewell
2 Caithness St. West, Caledonia, ON N3W 2J2
Tel: 905-765-5414; *Fax:* 905-765-5144
paul.osier@arrelllaw.com
www.arrelllaw.com

***Caledonia*: Benedict & Ferguson - *2**
322 Argyle St. South, Caledonia, ON N3W 1K8
Tel: 905-765-4004; *Fax:* 905-765-3001

***Caledonia*: Larry S. Humenik - *1**
P.O. Box 2112, 19 Argyle St. North, Caledonia, ON N3W 1B6
Tel: 905-765-3162; *Fax:* 905-765-4313
www.humeniklaw.com

***Callander*: George D. Olah - *1**
492 Main St., Callander, ON P0H 1H0
Tel: 705-752-1323; *Fax:* 705-752-1283
georgeolah@bellnet.ca

***Cambridge*: Brownell & Reier - *2**
Former Name: Bond & Brownell
32 Grand Ave. South, Cambridge, ON N2S 2L6
Tel: 519-623-2311; *Fax:* 519-623-6957
info@brownellandreier.ca
www.brownellandreier.ca

***Cambridge*: Copp & Cosman - *2**
#409, Cambridge Place, P.O. Box 1729, Stn. Galt, 73 Water St. North, Cambridge, ON N1R 7G8
Tel: 519-623-4799; *Fax:* 519-623-7154
cosman@coppcosman.com

***Cambridge*: Teresa L. Fairborn - *1**
285 Fountain St. South, 2nd Fl., Cambridge, ON N3H 1J2
Tel: 519-653-1460; *Fax:* 519-653-4169

***Cambridge*: George R. Ingram - *1**
#206, P.O. Box 1447, Stn. Galt, 99 Main St., Cambridge, ON N1R 7G7
Tel: 519-621-9000; *Fax:* 519-621-9009
gringram@sentex.net

***Cambridge*: Rein Kao - *1**
#102, 24 Queens Square, Cambridge, ON N1S 1H6
Tel: 519-624-8722; *Fax:* 519-624-3589
r.kao@kaolawoffices.net

***Cambridge*: David A. Kinder - *1**
61 Cambridge St., Cambridge, ON N1R 3R8
Tel: 519-740-6676; *Fax:* 519-623-8545
Toll-Free: 888-779-9954
klo@Kinder.ca
www.kinder.ca

***Cambridge*: William Korz, Q.C. - *1**
Former Name: Korz & Associates
927 King St. East, Cambridge, ON N3H 3P4
Tel: 519-653-7174; *Fax:* 519-653-5222
wmkorz@execulink.com

***Cambridge*: George E. Loker - *1**
P.O. Box 1723, Stn. Galt, 108 Myers Rd., Cambridge, ON N1R 2Z8
Tel: 519-621-4300; *Fax:* 519-621-4300
eloker@golden.net

***Cambridge*: Paul M. Mann Professional Corp. - *1**
25 George St. South, Cambridge, ON N1S 2N3
Tel: 519-623-0700; *Fax:* 519-622-4091
info@paulmann.ca
www.paulmann.ca

***Cambridge*: McDonald Ross - *2**
9 Brant Rd. South, Cambridge, ON N1S 2W4
Tel: 519-622-0499; *Fax:* 519-740-6368
jwm@mcdonaldross.com

***Cambridge*: McSevney Law Offices - *2**
Former Name: Onorato Law Offices
708 Duke St., Cambridge, ON N3H 3T6
Tel: 519-653-3217; *Fax:* 519-653-3702
www.mcsevneylaw.com

***Cambridge*: Pavey, Law & Witteveen LLP - *7**
Also Known As: Pavey Law
Former Name: Pavey, Law & Wannop LLP
P.O. Box 1707, Stn. Galt, 19 Cambridge St., Cambridge, ON N1R 3R8
Tel: 519-621-7260; *Fax:* 519-621-1304
info@paveylaw.com
www.paveylaw.com

***Cambridge*: Pettitt Schwarz Hills - *3**
Also Known As: PSH Lawyers
#403, 73 Water St. North, Cambridge, ON N1R 7L6
Tel: 519-621-2450; *Fax:* 519-621-5750
www.pettittschwarz.com
www.facebook.com/pages/PSH-Lawyers/136696276391017

***Cambridge*: Henry R. Shields - *1**
2 Water St. North, Cambridge, ON N1R 3B1
Tel: 519-622-2150; *Fax:* 519-623-0997
henryshields@on.aibn.com

***Cambridge*: J. Craig Wilson - *1**
P.O. Box 1297, 2 Water St. North, Cambridge, ON N1R 3B1
Tel: 519-622-0192

***Cambridge*: William C. Wraight - *1**
P.O. Box 22103, Stn. RPO Water St., 15 Main St., Cambridge, ON N1R 8E3
Tel: 519-623-3330; *Fax:* 519-621-0136

***Campbellford*: Paul D.H. Burgess - *1**
P.O. Box 1540, 64 Front St. North, Campbellford, ON K0L 1L0
Tel: 705-653-5555; *Fax:* 705-653-5557
pdhburgess@xplornet.com

***Campbellville*: Robert B. Burgess - *1**
P.O. Box 86, 8220 MacArthur Dr., Campbellville, ON L0P 1B0
Tel: 905-854-2790; *Fax:* 905-854-1968
rbburgess@sympatico.ca

***Carleton Place*: Kenneth J. Bennett - *1**
32 Beckwith St., Carleton Place, ON K7C 2T2
Tel: 613-257-1655; *Fax:* 613-257-8837

***Carleton Place*: Paul D. Courtice - *1**
P.O. Box 29, 164 Bridge St., Carleton Place, ON K7C 2V7
Tel: 613-257-5001; *Fax:* 613-257-8797
pdclaw@on.aibn.com

***Carleton Place*: N. Alan Jones - *1**
92 Bridge St., Carleton Place, ON K7C 2V3
Tel: 613-257-3811; *Fax:* 613-253-0479
ajones@bellnet.ca

***Casselman*: Mireille C. LaViolette - *1**
CP 179, 719, rue Principale, Casselman, ON K0A 1M0
Tél: 613-764-3747; *Téléc:* 613-764-1000
info@mireillelaviolette.com
www.mireillelaviolette.com

***Chatham*: James E.S. Allin - *1**
128 Queen St., Chatham, ON N7M 2G6
Tel: 519-352-6540; *Fax:* 519-352-9097
www.allinlaw.ca

***Chatham*: Mark M. MacKew - *1**
Also Known As: The MacKew Law Firm
237 Wellington St. West, Chatham, ON N7M 1J9
Tel: 519-354-0407; *Fax:* 519-354-3250
mark@mackewlaw.com
www.mackewlaw.com

***Chatham*: Mayes Law Firm - *1**
Also Known As: Stanley G. Mayes
16 Victoria Ave., Chatham, ON N7L 2Z6
Tel: 519-436-1040; *Fax:* 519-436-2442
sgmayes@mayeslawfirm.ca
www.mayeslawfirm.ca

***Chatham*: Gudrun Mueller-Wilm - *1**
P.O. Box 554, Stn. C, 6 Harvey St., Chatham, ON N7M 1L6
Tel: 519-358-1822; *Fax:* 519-358-7406

***Chatham*: F. Vaughn Pugh - *1**
190 Wellington St. West, Chatham, ON N7M 1J6
Tel: 519-354-4360

***Chatham*: J. Quaglia Law Office - *1**
Former Name: Benoit, Van Raay, Spisani, Fuerth & Quaglia
P.O. Box 1087, 193 Queen St., Chatham, ON N7M 5L6
Tel: 519-352-8580; *Fax:* 519-352-4114
www.jquaglialaw.ca

***Chatham*: Jim Renick Law Office - *1**
Former Name: Walstedt Renick
78 Talbot St. North, Chatham, ON N8M 1A2
Tel: 519-776-9020; *Fax:* 519-776-9027
info@jamesrenick.com
www.jamesrenick.com

***Chatham*: John B. Trinca - *1**
P.O. Box 428, 75 Thames St., Chatham, ON N7L 1S4
Tel: 519-352-7750; *Fax:* 519-352-4159
jtrinca@mnsi.net

***Chatham*: Paul D. Watson - *1**
84 Dover St., Chatham, ON N7M 5K8
Tel: 519-351-7721; *Fax:* 519-351-7726
pwatson@cogeco.net

***Chelmsford*: Gerard E. Guimond**
3527 Errington Ave. North, Chelmsford, ON P0M 1L0
Tel: 705-855-4511; *Fax:* 705-855-5631
guimond12@bellnet.ca

***Chesley*: McClelland Law Office - *1**
159 - 1st Ave. South, Chesley, ON N0G 1L0
Tel: 519-363-3293; *Fax:* 519-363-2315

***Chesley*: McLean Lawyers - *2**
P.O. Box 118, 27 1st Ave. South, Chesley, ON N0G 1L0
Tel: 519-363-3190; *Fax:* 519-363-2213
r.mclean@mcleanlawyers.ca
www.mcleanlawyers.ca

***Clinton*: Philip B. Cornish - *1**
35 Ontario St., Clinton, ON N0M 1L0
Tel: 519-482-1434; *Fax:* 519-482-1481

***Clinton*: D. Gerald Hiltz - *1**
P.O. Box 1087, 52 Huron St., Clinton, ON N0M 1L0
Tel: 519-482-3414; *Fax:* 519-482-7525

***Coboconk*: Tyler P. Higgins**
P.O. Box 219, 6654 Hwy. 35, Coboconk, ON K0M 1K0
Tel: 705-454-2625

** indicates number of lawyers*

Cobourg: Rodger F. Cooper - *1
#102, 253 Division St., Cobourg, ON K9A 3P9
Tel: 905-372-8728; *Fax:* 905-372-0720

Cobourg: Ember Leigh Hamilton - *1
289 Lakeview Crt., Cobourg, ON K9A 5C3
Tel: 905-373-0589; *Fax:* 905-373-0928

Cobourg: Hustler & Kay - *2
301 Division St., Cobourg, ON K9A 3R2
Tel: 905-372-1991; *Fax:* 905-372-1995

Cobourg: Irvine & Irvine - *1
24 Covert St., Cobourg, ON K9A 2L6
Tel: 905-372-5449; *Fax:* 905-372-1707
rirvine@eagle.ca

Cobourg: SMM Law Professional Corp. - *5
Former Name: Stewart, Mitchell & Macklin.
#205, The Fleming Bldg., 1005 Elgin St., Cobourg, ON K9A 5J4
Tel: 905-372-3395; *Fax:* 905-372-1695
info@smmlaw.com
www.smmlaw.com

Cobourg: William J. Taggart - *1
#124, 148 Third St., Cobourg, ON K9A 5X2
Tel: 905-372-8700; *Fax:* 905-372-1943
info@taggartlaw.ca
www.taggartlaw.ca

Cochrane: Beaudoin Boucher
P.O. Box 1898, 174 - 4th Ave., Cochrane, ON P0L 1C0
Tel: 705-272-4346; *Fax:* 705-272-2991
bblaw@puc.net

Colborne: Carter Thompson Law Office - *1
Former Name: Carter, J.A.
P.O. Box 699, 26 King St. East, Colborne, ON K9A 1K7
Tel: 905-355-3322; *Fax:* 905-355-3104
carterthompson@bellnet.ca

Collingwood: Baulke Augaitis Stahr LLP - *4
Former Name: Baulke & Augaitis LLP
P.O. Box 100, 150 Hurontario St., Collingwood, ON L9Y 3Z4
Tel: 705-445-4930; *Fax:* 705-445-1871
Toll-Free: 866-230-9993
info@collingwoodlaw.com
www.collingwoodlaw.com

Collingwood: Besse, Merrifield & Cowan LLP - *3
47 Hurontario St., Collingwood, ON L9Y 2L7
Tel: 705-446-2000; *Fax:* 705-446-1044
Toll-Free: 888-879-3052
besse@blclawoffices.com
www.bmclawoffices.com

Collingwood: Christie/Cummings - *5
325 Hume St., Collingwood, ON L9Y 1W4
Tel: 705-444-3650; *Fax:* 705-444-0024
maccummings@christiecummings.com
www.christiecummings.com

Collingwood: Elstons - *2
#224, The Admiral Building, 1 First St., Collingwood, ON L9Y 1A1
Tel: 705-445-1200; *Fax:* 705-445-1209
Harold@Elstons.ca
elstons.ca

Collingwood: Brian Greasley - *1
P.O. Box 490, 33 Ste. Marie St., Collingwood, ON L9Y 4B2
Tel: 705-445-9300; *Fax:* 705-445-2269

Collingwood: Mumford Law Office - *1
Former Name: Neathery & Mumford
#202, 150 St. Paul St., Collingwood, ON L9Y 3P2
Tel: 705-444-6051; *Fax:* 705-444-0969
gailmumfordlaw@hotmail.com
www.mumfordlaw.ca

Concord: Bisceglia & Associates - *4
#200, 7941 Jane St., Concord, ON L4K 4L6
Tel: 905-695-5200; *Fax:* 905-695-5201
www.lawtoronto.com

Concord: Chehab & Khan
#206, 3100 Steeles Ave. West, Concord, ON L4K 3R1
Tel: 905-738-2463; *Fax:* 905-738-9638
info@cnklaw.ca
www.cnklaw.ca

Concord: John G. Chris - *1
8700 Dufferin St., Concord, ON L4K 4S6
Tel: 416-661-5989; *Fax:* 905-669-0444
www.jgc-law.com

Concord: D'Ambrosio Law Office - *1
#204, 3300 Steeles Ave. West, Concord, ON L4K 3R1
Tel: 905-761-7400; *Fax:* 905-738-4901
romeo36@cromeo@ontariowills.ca
ontariowills.ca

Concord: Gianfranco John De Matteis - *1
#204, 3300 Steeles Ave. West, Concord, ON L4K 2Y4
Tel: 905-738-4900; *Fax:* 905-738-4901
john@dematteis.ca

Concord: Di Monte & Di Monte LLP - *2
Former Name: Di Monte, Patrick
#211, 3100 Steeles Ave. West, Concord, ON L4K 3R1
Tel: 905-738-2101; *Fax:* 905-738-1168
patdimonte@on.aibn.com

Concord: Louis M. Fried - *1
#212, 2180 Steeles Ave. West, Concord, ON L4K 2Z5
Tel: 905-738-0180; *Fax:* 905-738-6203
Toll-Free: 866-306-3286
info@louismfried.com
louismfried.com

Concord: Okell & Weisman - *2
#218, 1600 Steeles Ave. West, Concord, ON L4K 4M2
Tel: 905-761-8711; *Fax:* 905-761-8633

Concord: Norman S. Panzica - *1
A, 9100 Jane St., 3rd Fl., Concord, ON L4K 4L8
Tel: 905-738-1078; *Fax:* 905-738-0528
npanzica@rogers.com
www.normanpanzica.com

Concord: Piersanti & Company - *2
#10, 445 Edgeley Blvd., Concord, ON L4K 4G1
Tel: 905-738-2176; *Fax:* 905-738-5182
piersanti@look.com
piersantico.com

Concord: Enzo Salvatori - *1
#4, 161 Pennsylvania Ave., Concord, ON L4K 1C3
Tel: 416-745-1777; *Fax:* 905-760-9503

Concord: Vito S. Scalisi - *1
#204, 3300 Steeles Ave. West, Concord, ON L4K 2Y4
Tel: 905-760-5588; *Fax:* 905-738-4901
vito@scalisilaw.ca
www.scalisilaw.ca

Cornwall: Bergeron Filion - *2
103 Sydney St., Cornwall, ON K6H 3H1
Tel: 613-932-2911; *Fax:* 613-932-2356
lfilion@cogeco.net
www.bergeronfilion.ca

Cornwall: Giovanniello, Bellefeuille - *2
340 - 2nd St. East, Cornwall, ON K6H 1Y9
Tel: 613-938-0294; *Fax:* 613-932-2374
law@gblawfirm.ca
www.gblawfirm.ca

Cornwall: Guindon, MacLean & Castle - *3
254 Pitts St., Cornwall, ON K6J 3P6
Tel: 613-933-3931; *Fax:* 613-933-6123
info@g-m-c.on.ca

Cornwall: Law Office of Diane M. Lahaie - *1
132 Second East, Cornwall, ON K6H 1Y4
Tel: 613-936-8833; *Fax:* 613-936-6717

Cornwall: Levesque, Grenkie - *2
233 Augustus St., Cornwall, ON K6J 3W2
Tel: 613-932-7654; *Fax:* 613-938-1692
info@levesquegrenkielaw.ca
www.levesquegrenkielaw.ca

Cornwall: Ian D. Paul - *1
5 Third St. East, Cornwall, ON K2H 2L6
Tel: 613-933-9455; *Fax:* 613-933-7566
ipaul@on.aibn.com
www.ianpaul.ca/lawyer
www.facebook.com/pages/Ian-Paul/353107988124632

Cornwall: D. Randolph Ross - *1
120 Sydney St., Cornwall, ON K6H 3H2
Tel: 613-932-2044; *Fax:* 613-937-0993
drandolphross@bellnet.ca

Cornwall: Donald J. White - *1
700 Montreal Rd., Cornwall, ON K6H 1C4
Tel: 613-933-6443; *Fax:* 613-933-6453
nwhite10@cogeco.ca

Cornwall: Wilson, Poirier, Byrne - *2
132 - 2nd St. West, Cornwall, ON K6J 1G5
Tel: 613-938-2224; *Fax:* 613-938-8005

Deep River: George W. LeConte - *1
P.O. Box 340, 8 Glendale Ave., Deep River, ON K0J 1P0
Tel: 613-584-3154; *Fax:* 613-584-4877
gleconte@bellnet.ca
www.georgewleconte.com

Deep River: Thomas E. Roche - *1
Former Name: Roche & Dakin
P.O. Box 1240, 27 Champlain St., Deep River, ON K0J 1P0
Tel: 613-584-3392; *Fax:* 613-584-4922
rochdaki@bellnet.ca

Delhi: John R. Hanselman - *1
138 Eagle St., Delhi, ON N4B 1S5
Tel: 519-582-0770; *Fax:* 519-582-1876

Dresden: Timothy D. Mathany - *1
P.O. Box 568, 423 St. George St. South, Dresden, ON N0P 1M0
Tel: 519-683-6219; *Fax:* 519-683-6548

Dryden: McAuley & Partners - *6
P.O. Box 159, 4 Whyte Ave., Dryden, ON P8N 2Y8
Tel: 807-223-2254; *Fax:* 807-223-3794
www.mcauleylaw.com

Dryden: Vermeer & Van Walleghem - *2
P.O. Box 938, Stn. Main, 65 King St., 2nd Fl., Dryden, ON P8N 2Z5
Tel: 807-223-3311; *Fax:* 807-223-4133
lawweb@vermeerlaw.com
www.vermeerlaw.com

Dundas: Lesperance & Associates - *1
Former Name: Lesperance, David S.
#202, 84 King St. West, Dundas, ON L9H 1T9
Tel: 905-627-3037; *Fax:* 905-627-9868
info@lesperanceassociates.com
lesperanceassociates.com

Dundas: William J. Wilkins - *2
63 King St. West, Dundas, ON L9H 1T5
Tel: 905-628-6321; *Fax:* 905-628-2767
Toll-Free: 888-556-3368
www.dundaslaw.ca

Dunrobin: Alan Pratt Law Firm - *2
Former Name: Pratt, Alan
P.O. Box 100, 3550 Torwood Dr., Dunrobin, ON K0A 1T0
Tel: 613-832-1261; *Fax:* 613-832-0856
Shirley@prattlaw.ca
www.prattlaw.ca

Dutton: Martin Joldersma - *1
P.O. Box 279, 159 Main St., Dutton, ON N0L 1J0
Tel: 519-762-2882; *Fax:* 519-762-2880
martinjoldersmalawoffice@yahoo.ca

Elliot Lake: Kearns Law Office - *1
13 Manitoba Rd., Elliot Lake, ON P5A 2A6
Tel: 705-848-3601; *Fax:* 705-848-8416
Toll-Free: 800-268-7733
kearn1@bellnet.ca

Elmira: Cynthia M. Rudavsky - *1
9 Church St. West, Elmira, ON N3B 1M2
Tel: 519-669-2200; *Fax:* 519-669-4349
rudavsky@sentex.net

Elmira: Woods, Clemens & Fletcher Professional Corporation - *4
Former Name: Woods & Clemens
P.O. Box 216, 9 Memorial Ave., Elmira, ON N3B 2R1
Tel: 519-669-5101; *Fax:* 519-669-5618
lawoffice@woodsclemens.ca

Elora: J.E. Morris - *2
149 Geddes St., Elora, ON N0B 1S0
Tel: 519-846-5366; *Fax:* 519-846-8170
john@johnmorrislaw.ca
johnmorrislaw.ca

Elora: Gregory A. Oakes - *1
155 Geddes St., Elora, ON N0B 1S0
Tel: 519-846-5555; *Fax:* 519-846-5554

** indicates number of lawyers*

Embrun: Campbell & Sabourin LLP/S.R.L. - *4
#1, 165 Bay St., Embrun, ON K0A 1W1
Tel: 613-443-5683; *Fax:* 613-443-3285
info@campbellaw.on.ca
www.campbellaw.on.ca

Embrun: Jean G. Martel - *1
800, rue Notre Dame, Embrun, ON K0A 1W1
Tel: 613-443-3267; *Fax:* 613-443-3857
jeanmartel@rogers.com

Essex: Hickey, Bryne - *2
14 Centre St., Essex, ON N8M 1N9
Tel: 519-776-7349; *Fax:* 519-776-8161

Exeter: Little, Masson & Reid - *3
71 Main St. North, Exeter, ON N0M 1S0
Tel: 519-235-0670; *Fax:* 519-235-1603
www.littlemassonreid.com

Exeter: Raymond & McLean - *1
P.O. Box 100, 387 Main St. South, Exeter, ON N0M 1S6
Tel: 519-235-2234; *Fax:* 519-235-2671
raymclea@quadro.net

Fenelon Falls: David J. Gowanlock - *1
P.O. Box 607, 16 May St., Fenelon Falls, ON K0M 1N0
Tel: 705-887-2582; *Fax:* 705-887-1871

Fenelon Falls: John D. Walden
57 Lindsay St., Fenelon Falls, ON K0M 1N0
Tel: 705-887-2941
walden-nagel@nexicom.net
johndwaldenlaw.ca

Fergus: Leigh G. Fishleigh - *1
169 St. Andrew St. West, Fergus, ON N1M 1N6
Tel: 519-843-7100; *Fax:* 519-843-3038
leigh.fishleigh@bellnet.ca
leighfishleighlaw.com

Fergus: Grant & Acheson LLP
265 Bridge St., Fergus, ON N1M 1T7
Tel: 519-843-1960; *Fax:* 519-843-6888
Toll-Free: 800-746-0685
fergusinfo@smithvaleriote.com
grant-acheson.com

Flesherton: John L. Ferris Law Offices - *2
P.O. Box 100, 15 Durham St., Flesherton, ON N0C 1E0
Tel: 519-923-2031; *Fax:* 519-924-3198
www.ferrislaw.ca

Fonthill: Jill Anthony - *1
P.O. Box 743, 10 Hwy. 20 East, Fonthill, ON L0S 1E0
Tel: 905-892-2621; *Fax:* 905-892-1022
janthony@jillanthony.com
www.jillanthony.com

Fort Erie: Hagan Law Firm - *1
Former Name: Hagan & McDowell
P.O. Box 68, 29 Jarvis St., Fort Erie, ON L2A 5M6
Tel: 905-871-4440; *Fax:* 905-871-9266

Fort Frances: Clare Allan Brunetta - *1
P.O. Box 656, 420 Victoria Ave., Fort Frances, ON P9A 3M9
Tel: 807-274-9809; *Fax:* 807-274-8760
cbrunetta@nwonet.net

Fort Frances: Lawrence A. Eustace - *1
510 Portage Ave., Fort Frances, ON P9A 2A3
Tel: 807-274-3247; *Fax:* 807-274-6447
www.eustace-law.com

Fort Frances: Lawrence G. Phillips - *1
406 Church St., Fort Frances, ON P9A 1E2
Tel: 807-274-8525; *Fax:* 807-274-5758
phillaw19@hotmail.com

Fort Frances: Donald A. Taylor - *1
504 Armit Ave., Fort Frances, ON P9A 2H7
Tel: 807-274-7811; *Fax:* 807-274-8485
dalaw@shaw.ca

Gananoque: Michael R. Eyolfson - *1
#5, 140 Garden St., Gananoque, ON K7G 1H9
Tel: 613-382-7772; *Fax:* 613-382-3030
eyolfso1@bellnet.ca

Gananoque: Steacy & Delaney - *1
Stn. Main, 110 Stone St., Gananoque, ON K7G 2A1
Tel: 613-382-2137; *Fax:* 613-382-7794
l.steacy@ganlaw.com
www.gananoque.com/steacyanddelaney

Georgetown: Banbury Law Office - *1
#2, 211 Guelph St., Georgetown, ON L7G 5B5
Tel: 905-877-5252; *Fax:* 905-877-4100
cbanbury@banburylaw.com

Georgetown: Jeffrey L. Eason - *1
P.O. Box 159, Stn. Main, 116 Guelph St., Georgetown, ON L7G 4T1
Tel: 905-846-1557; *Fax:* 905-877-9725
jeffreyleason@bellnet.ca
www.jeffreyleason.com

Georgetown: Helson Kogon Ashbee Schaljo & Associates LLP - *5
132 Mill St., Georgetown, ON L7G 2C6
Tel: 905-877-5200; *Fax:* 905-877-3948
info@helsons.ca
helsons.ca

Georgetown: W. Glen How & Associates - *3
P.O. Box 40, Stn. Main, Georgetown, ON L7G 4T1
Tel: 905-873-4545; *Fax:* 905-873-4522
wghow@wghow.ca

Georgetown: William H. Manderson - *1
#1004, 83 Mill St., Georgetown, ON L7G 5E9
Tel: 905-873-0121; *Fax:* 905-873-4114

Georgetown: R. Paul Millman - *1
116 Guelph St., Georgetown, ON L7G 4A3
Tel: 905-873-9481; *Fax:* 905-873-9483

Georgetown: Sopinka & Kort LLP - *2
145 Mill St., Georgetown, ON L7G 2C2
Tel: 905-877-0196; *Fax:* 905-877-0604
www.sopinka-kort.ca

Glencoe: Gary R. Merritt - *1
P.O. Box 309, 213 Main St., Glencoe, ON N0L 1M0
Tel: 519-287-3432; *Fax:* 519-287-2498
merritt@bellnet.ca

Gloucester: MacQuarrie Whyte Killoran - *4
#208, 1980 Ogilvie Rd., Gloucester, ON K1J 9L3
Tel: 613-748-1600; *Fax:* 613-748-0800
info@mwklaw.ca
www.ottawaorleanslawyers.com

Goderich: Mary E. Cull - *1
1 East St., Goderich, ON N7A 1N3
Tel: 519-524-1115
maryecull@hurontel.on.ca
marycull.com

Goderich: Donnelly & Murphy Lawyers - *8
18 The Square, Goderich, ON N7A 3Y7
Tel: 519-524-2154; *Fax:* 519-524-8550
Toll-Free: 800-332-7160
admin@dmlaw.on.ca
www.donnellymurphy.com

Goderich: Timothy G. Macdonald - *1
1 Nelson St. East, Goderich, ON N7A 1R7
Tel: 519-524-1120; *Fax:* 519-524-2576

Goderich: Norman B. Pickell - *1
58 South St., Goderich, ON N7A 3L5
Tel: 519-524-8335; *Fax:* 519-524-1530
pickell@normanpickell.com
www.normanpickell.com

Goderich: Troyan & Fincher - *2
44 North St., Goderich, ON N7A 2T4
Tel: 519-524-2115; *Fax:* 519-524-4481
enquiries@troyanfincher.on.ca

Gore Bay: Terence E. Land, Barrister & Solicitor - *1
Former Name: Armstrong & Land
P.O. Box 90, 4 Eleanor St., Gore Bay, ON P0P 1H0
Tel: 705-282-2710; *Fax:* 705-282-2205
landlaw@gorebaycable.com

Gore Bay: James E. Weppler - *1
P.O. Box 222, 65 Meredith St., Gore Bay, ON P0P 1H0
Tel: 705-282-3354; *Fax:* 705-282-3211
jamesweppler@bellnet.ca

Grand Bend: Forrester Law - *1
Former Name: Forrester, Michael G.
82 Ontario St. South, Grand Bend, ON N0M 1T0
Tel: 519-238-5297; *Fax:* 519-238-5234
www.forresterlaw.ca

Gravenhurst: Stuart & Cruickshank - *2
P.O. Box 1270, 195 Church St., Gravenhurst, ON P1P 1V4
Tel: 705-687-3441; *Fax:* 705-687-5405
info@stuartandcruickshank.com

Grimsby: George Krusell - *1
260 Main St. East, Grimsby, ON L3M 1P8
Tel: 905-945-2300; *Fax:* 905-945-8529

Grimsby: Donald C. Loney - *1
Former Name: Sinclair, Murakami, Loney & Van Velzen
55 Main St. East, Grimsby, ON L3M 1R3
Tel: 905-945-9271; *Fax:* 905-945-3066
Toll-Free: 800-363-5073

Guelph: Lynn Archbold - *1
27 Cork St. West, Guelph, ON N1H 2W9
Tel: 519-763-4748; *Fax:* 519-763-4207
info@archboldlaw.com
www.archboldlaw.com

Guelph: Andrea S. Clarke - *1
Stn. ain, 258 Woolwich St., Guelph, ON N1H 3W1
Tel: 519-763-3999; *Fax:* 519-763-5116
bgjorgieva@andreasclarke.com
andreasclarke.com

Guelph: Dason Law Office - *1
Former Name: Hugh Guthrie Q.C. Professional Corporation
367 Woolwich St., Guelph, ON N1H 3W4
Tel: 519-824-2020; *Fax:* 519-824-2023
www.dasonlaw.com

Guelph: David Doney Law Office - *1
20 Douglas St., Guelph, ON N1H 2S9
Tel: 519-837-3265; *Fax:* 519-837-1758
info@guelphcriminallawyer.com
guelphcriminallawyer.com

Guelph: Charles R. Davidson
172 Woolwich St., Guelph, ON N1H 3V5
Tel: 519-767-6637; *Fax:* 519-826-5212
charles@crdavidson.ca

Guelph: Guy D.E. Farb - *1
22 Paisley St., Guelph, ON N1H 2N6
Tel: 519-763-6644; *Fax:* 519-763-8091
lawguy@execulink.com
www.linkedin.com/pub/guy-farb/18/559/986

Guelph: Siobhan Ann Hanley - *1
98 Surrey St. East, Guelph, ON N1H 3P9
Tel: 519-824-2586; *Fax:* 519-827-1715
Toll-Free: 888-262-6333
shanley@bellnet.ca

Guelph: Jackman & Rowles - *2
P.O. Box 37, Stn. Main, 17 Cork St. West, Guelph, ON N1H 2W9
Tel: 519-824-4883; *Fax:* 519-821-2910
mmjr@on.aibn.com

Guelph: Maiocco & DiGravio - *2
230 Speedvale Ave. West, Guelph, ON N1H 1C4
Tel: 519-836-2710; *Fax:* 519-836-7312

Guelph: McElderry & Morris - *5
P.O. Box 875, 84 Woolwich St., Guelph, ON N1H 3T9
Tel: 519-822-8150; *Fax:* 519-822-1921
www.mcelderrymorris.com

Guelph: Bryna D. McLeod - *1
221 Woolwich St., Guelph, ON N1H 3V4
Tel: 519-767-2141; *Fax:* 519-763-2204
www.brynamcleod.com

Guelph: Peter A. McSherry - *1
343 Waterloo Ave., Guelph, ON N1H 3K1
Tel: 519-821-5465; *Fax:* 519-822-2867
www.petermcsherry.ca
www.facebook.com/profile.php?id=180598342086142, twitter.com/PeterMcSherry, www.linkedin.com/company/2853921

Guelph: Nelson, Watson LLP - *6
183 Norfolk St., Guelph, ON N1H 4K1
Tel: 519-821-9610; *Fax:* 519-821-8550
www.nelwat.com

Guelph: Kenneth H. Richardson - *1
#5, 340 Edinburgh Rd. North, Guelph, ON N1H 7Y4
Tel: 519-821-6036; *Fax:* 519-821-3317
richlaw@rogers.com
www.richlaw.ca

** indicates number of lawyers*

Guelph: Judith C. Sidlofsky Stoffman - *1
15 Wyndham St. South, Guelph, ON N1H 4C6
Tel: 519-824-1212; *Fax:* 519-822-0949
judith.stoffman@police.guelph.on.ca

Guelph: Smith Valeriote LLP - *23
#100, P.O. Box 1240, Stn. Main, 105 Silvercreek Pkwy. North, Guelph, ON N1H 6N6
Tel: 519-837-2100; *Fax:* 519-837-1617
Toll-Free: 800-746-0685
info@smithvaleriote.com
www.smithvaleriote.com

Guelph: Teresa Tummillo-Goy - *1
Also Known As: TTG Law
#3, 367 Woodlawn Rd. West, Guelph, ON N1H 7K9
Tel: 226-251-3008; *Fax:* 226-251-3009
teresa@ttglaw.ca
www.ttglaw.ca
www.facebook.com/pages/TTG-LAW-OFFICE/139477986107996, www.linkedin.com/pub/teresa-tummillo-goy/31/4a8/a63

Guelph: Vorvis, Anderson, Gray, Armstrong LLP - *4
353 Elizabeth St., Guelph, ON N1H 2X9
Tel: 519-824-7400; *Fax:* 519-824-7521
vaga@vaga.ca
www.vaga.ca

Hagersville: James R. Baxter - *1
19 King St. West, Hagersville, ON N0A 1H0
Tel: 905-768-3363; *Fax:* 905-768-1550
jrbaxter@mountaincable.net

Haileybury: Byck Law Office - Haileybury - *4
Former Name: Smith, Wowk
573 Lakeshore St., Haileybury, ON P0J 1K0
Tel: 705-647-8167; *Fax:* 705-647-8575
temlaw@nt.net
www.temlaw.com

Haliburton: Raymond G. Selbie - *1
P.O. Box 699, 34 Maple Ave., Haliburton, ON K0M 1S0
Tel: 705-457-2435; *Fax:* 705-457-3074
rselbie@on.aibn.com
www.selbielaw.com

Halton Hills: Steven C. Foster - *2
#201, 232A Guelph St., Halton Hills, ON L7G 4B1
Tel: 905-873-0204; *Fax:* 905-873-4962
sfoster@arnold-foster.com

Hamilton: John S. Abrams - *1
#300, 69 John St. South, Hamilton, ON L8N 2B9
Tel: 905-522-3600; *Fax:* 905-529-1570
jabrams@bellnet.ca
www.johnabrams.ca

Hamilton: Agro Zaffiro LLP - *26
1 James St. South, Hamilton, ON L8N 3G6
Tel: 905-527-6877; *Fax:* 905-527-6843
mail@agrozaffiro.com
www.agrozaffiro.com

Hamilton: Ballagh & Edward LLP - *2
#102, McMaster Innovation Park, 175 Longwood Rd. South, Hamilton, ON L8P 0A1
Tel: 905-572-9300; *Fax:* 905-572-9301
info@ballaghedward.ca
www.ballaghedward.ca

Hamilton: Deborah Lee Barfknecht - *1
#601, 25 Main St. West, Hamilton, ON L8P 1H1
Tel: 905-521-1898; *Fax:* 905-521-0486

Hamilton: R.B. Barrs - *1
#204, 640 Upper James St., Hamilton, ON L9C 2Z2
Tel: 905-387-9212; *Fax:* 905-387-6109

Hamilton: Bartolini, Berlingieri , Barrafato; Fortino LLP - *7
#101, 154 Main St. East, Hamilton, ON L8N 1G9
Tel: 905-577-6833; *Fax:* 905-577-6839
lawfirm@bbb-lawyers.on.ca
bbbflawyershamilton.ca

Hamilton: John A. Bland - *1
#801, Union Gas Bldg., 20 Hughson St. South, Hamilton, ON L8N 2A1
Tel: 905-524-3533; *Fax:* 905-524-5142

Hamilton: Peter Borkovich - *1
Former Name: Borkovich Ingrassia Macaluso
46 Jackson St. East, Hamilton, ON L8N 1L1
Tel: 905-527-0990; *Fax:* 905-521-1976

Hamilton: Brock Howard Bedford - *1
166 John St. South, Hamilton, ON L8N 2C4
Tel: 905-527-3867; *Fax:* 905-527-3860

Hamilton: Burns Associates - *2
Former Name: Burns, Vasan, Limberis, Vitulli LLP
#305, 21 King St. West, Hamilton, ON L8P 4W9
Tel: 905-522-1381; *Fax:* 905-522-0855
adouglasburns@balawllp.com

Hamilton: Camporese Sullivan Di Gregorio - *12
Former Name: Camporese & Associates
#1700, Commerce Place, 1 King St. West, Hamilton, ON L8P 1A4
Tel: 905-522-7068; *Fax:* 905-522-5734
contactus@csdlawyers.ca
www.csdlawyers.ca

Hamilton: Jerry J. Chaimovitz - *2
#250, 100 Main St. East, Hamilton, ON L8N 3W4
Tel: 905-526-7030; *Fax:* 905-526-0682
info@jjcfamilylaw.com
www.jjcfamilylaw.com

Hamilton: Michael P. Clarke - *1
#1221, 25 Main St. West, Hamilton, ON L8P 1H1
Tel: 905-527-4399; *Fax:* 905-521-0210
michaelpclarke@bellnet.ca

Hamilton: Clyde Halford - *1
336 Sanatorium Rd., Hamilton, ON L9C 2A4
Tel: 905-388-0973; *Fax:* 905-388-2797

Hamilton: Confente, Garcea - *2
#340, 69 John St. South, Hamilton, ON L8N 2B9
Tel: 905-529-9999; *Fax:* 905-529-1160
confentegarcea.com

Hamilton: Connor, Connor, Guyer & Araiche - *2
#210, 1104 Fennell Ave. East, Hamilton, ON L8T 1R9
Tel: 905-385-3229; *Fax:* 905-385-6182
ccga@araiche.ca

Hamilton: Rory J. Cornale - *1
#201, 4 Hughson St. South, Hamilton, ON L8N 3Z1
Tel: 905-521-9989; *Fax:* 905-525-7737
Rory.cornale@dcllaw.ca
www.rorycornalelaw.ca/en

Hamilton: Earl R. Cranfield Q.C. - *1
#608, 20 Hughson St. South, Hamilton, ON L8N 2A1
Tel: 905-528-0089; *Fax:* 905-528-7692
ecranfield@nas.net

Hamilton: Janis P. Criger - *1
#700, 25 Main St. West, Hamilton, ON L8P 1H1
Tel: 905-525-4639; *Fax:* 905-525-2103
jpcriger@crigerlaw.com
www.crigerlaw.ca

Hamilton: Stephen F. De Wetter - *1
#1215, 25 Main St. West, Hamilton, ON L8P 1H1
Tel: 905-521-8878; *Fax:* 905-577-0229
dewetterlaw@gmail.com

Hamilton: Dermody Law - *3
550 Concession St., Hamilton, ON L8V 1A9
Tel: 905-383-3331; *Fax:* 905-574-3299
info@dermody.ca
dermodylaw.com

Hamilton: DiCenzo & Associates - *2
#41, 1070 Stone Church Rd. East, Hamilton, ON L8W 3K8
Tel: 905-574-3300; *Fax:* 905-574-1766
adicenzo@dcalawyers.com
www.dcalawyers.com

Hamilton: Peter J. Dudzic - *2
#312, 883 Upper Wentworth St., Hamilton, ON L9A 4Y6
Tel: 905-318-4441; *Fax:* 905-318-7775
www.dudziclaw.ca

Hamilton: Duxbury Law Professional Corporation - *2
Former Name: Duxbury, Brian
#1500, 1 King St. West, Hamilton, ON L8P 1A4
Tel: 905-570-1242; *Fax:* 905-570-1955
brian@duxburylaw.ca

Hamilton: Paul H. Ennis, Q.C - *1
#203, P.O. Box 101, Stn. Main, 58 Jarvis St., Hamilton, ON L8N 1G6
Tel: 905-871-1888; *Fax:* 905-871-1881

Hamilton: Evans Philp LLP - *20
Commerce Place, P.O. Box 930, Stn. A, 1 King St. West, 16th Fl., Hamilton, ON L8N 3P9
Tel: 905-525-1200; *Fax:* 905-525-7897
www.evansphilp.com

Hamilton: Evans Sweeny Bordin LLP - *7
Former Name: Evans-Lawyers/Advocates
#1201, 1 King St. West, Hamilton, ON L8P 1A4
Tel: 905-523-5666; *Fax:* 905-523-8098
jfe@esblawyers.com
www.esblawyers.com

Hamilton: Foreman Rosenblatt & Lewis - *3
York Law Centre, 425 York Blvd., Hamilton, ON L8R 3M3
Tel: 905-525-3570; *Fax:* 905-523-0363
www.yorklawcentre.com

Hamilton: Frankel Law Offices - *1
#1001, 105 Main St. East, Hamilton, ON L8N 1G6
Tel: 905-522-3972; *Fax:* 905-528-2767
stephan@frankelaw.ca
www.frankelaw.ca

Hamilton: Fyshe McMahon LLP - *5
207 Locke St. South, Hamilton, ON L8P 2V3
Tel: 905-522-0600; *Fax:* 905-522-9101
info@lockelaw.net
www.lockelaw.net

Hamilton: Genesee & Clarke - *4
#2225, 25 Main St. West, Hamilton, ON L8P 1H1
Tel: 905-522-7066; *Fax:* 905-522-7085
www.geneseeclarke.com

Hamilton: Gerald A. Swaye & Associates Professional Corporation - *7
Also Known As: Swaye, Gerald A., Q.C., C.S.
#901, 105 Main St. East, Hamilton, ON L8N 1G6
Tel: 905-524-2861; *Fax:* 905-524-2313
contactus@swaye.ca
www.swaye.ca

Hamilton: Guyatt, Gaasenbeek & Millikin - *3
#250, 69 John St. South, Hamilton, ON L8N 2B9
Tel: 905-528-8369; *Fax:* 905-528-8066
keith@ggmlaw.ca

Hamilton: Harvey Katz Law Office - *4
14 Hess St. South, Hamilton, ON L8P 3M9
Tel: 905-523-1442; *Fax:* 905-525-3817
www.harveykatzlaw.ca

Hamilton: Michael E. Hinchey - *1
203 MacNab St. South, Hamilton, ON L8P 3C8
Tel: 905-525-1630; *Fax:* 905-527-3686

Hamilton: Inch Hammond Professional Corporation - *13
Former Name: Inch, Easterbrook & Shaker
#500, 1 King St. West, Hamilton, ON L8P 4X8
Tel: 905-525-4481; *Fax:* 905-525-0031
ies@inchlaw.com
www.inchlaw.com

Hamilton: Brian J. Inglis - *1
#803, 20 Hughson St. South, Hamilton, ON L8N 2A1
Tel: 905-527-6727; *Fax:* 905-527-6310
inglislaw@interlynx.net

Hamilton: Jaskula, Sherk - *2
#915, 25 Main St. West, Hamilton, ON L8P 1H1
Tel: 905-577-1040; *Fax:* 905-577-7775
csherk@jaskulasherk.com
jaskulasherk.com

Hamilton: George E. Johnson - *1
19 Augusta St., Hamilton, ON L8N 1P6
Tel: 905-523-7333; *Fax:* 905-523-1311

Hamilton: Kathryn A. Junger - *1
19 Augusta St., Hamilton, ON L8N 1P6
Tel: 905-523-7333; *Fax:* 905-523-1311

Hamilton: Michael W. Kelly - *1
#101, 154 Main St. East, Hamilton, ON L8N 1G9
Tel: 905-546-1920; *Fax:* 905-546-8471
mikelly@bellnet.ca

Hamilton: Mary Elizabeth Kneeland Barrister & Solicitor - *1
75 Young St., Hamilton, ON L8N 1V4
Tel: 905-572-7737; *Fax:* 905-529-8819
maryl@netscape.ca

** indicates number of lawyers*

Hamilton: John O. Krawchenko - *1
#111, 175 Hunter St. East, Hamilton, ON L8N 4E7
Tel: 905-546-0525; *Fax:* 905-546-0596
j.o.krawchenko@on.aibn.com

Hamilton: Landeg, Spitale - *2
#806, Union Gas Bldg., 20 Hughson St. South, Hamilton, ON L8N 2A1
Tel: 905-529-7462; *Fax:* 905-528-6787

Hamilton: Lees & Lees - *1
#2225, 25 Main St. West, Hamilton, ON L8P 1H1
Tel: 905-523-7830; *Fax:* 905-523-4677
leeslaw@leesandlees.ca

Hamilton: Mackesy Smye - *11
2 Haymarket St., Hamilton, ON L8N 1G7
Tel: 905-525-2341; *Fax:* 905-525-6300
maclaw@mackesysmye.com
www.mackesysmye.com

Hamilton: W.J.I. Malcolm - *1
#709, 20 Hughson St. South, Hamilton, ON L8N 2A1
Tel: 905-528-4291; *Fax:* 905-528-4292
wjimalcolm@bellnet.ca

Hamilton: Nicole Matthews - *1
#908, 20 Hughson St. South, Hamilton, ON L8N 2A1
Tel: 905-523-0017
nicoleblake@hotmail.com
www.nicolematthews.ca

Hamilton: McArthur, Vereschagin & Brown LLP - *4
195 James St. South, Hamilton, ON L8P 3A8
Tel: 905-527-6900; *Fax:* 905-527-5177
www.labourlaw.com

Hamilton: Anthony E. McCusker - *2
#1, 200 Aberdeen Avenue, Hamilton, ON L8P 2P9
Tel: 905-523-0593; *Fax:* 905-522-0988
amccusker@cogeco.ca

Hamilton: McLelland & Dean - *1
1 King St. West, 7th Fl., Hamilton, ON L8P 1A4
Tel: 905-546-0393; *Fax:* 905-527-6286

Hamilton: Millar, Alexander - *2
Plaza Level, 120 King St. West, Hamilton, ON L8P 4V2
Tel: 905-528-1186; *Fax:* 905-529-7073

Hamilton: Milligan Gresko Limberis LLP - *2
Former Name: Milligan Gresko Brown Vitulli Limberis LLP
#1060, Standard Life Building, 120 King St. West, Hamilton, ON L8P 4V2
Tel: 905-522-7700; *Fax:* 905-522-7794
contactus@mgllawyers.com
www.mgllawyers.com

Hamilton: Morris Law Group - *6
125 Main St. East, Hamilton, ON L8N 3Z3
Tel: 905-526-8080; *Fax:* 905-521-1927
Toll-Free: 877-464-4466
www.morrislawyers.com

Hamilton: Gordon F. Morton Q.C. - *1
#701, Commerce Place, 1 King St. West, Hamilton, ON L8P 1A4
Tel: 905-522-8147; *Fax:* 905-522-9548
info@gordmortonlaw.com
www.gordmortonlaw.com

Hamilton: Nolan Ciarlo LLP - *5
Former Name: Nolan Law Offices
#700, 1 King St. West, Hamilton, ON L8P 1A4
Tel: 905-522-9261; *Fax:* 905-525-5836
info@nolanlaw.ca
www.nolanlaw.ca

Hamilton: George J. Parker - *1
45 Main St. East, Hamilton, ON L8N 2B7
Tel: 905-645-5252; *Fax:* 905-522-9615

Hamilton: A. Pazaratz - *1
55 Main St. West, Hamilton, ON L8P 1H4
Tel: 905-645-6254; *Fax:* 905-645-6265

Hamilton: Pelech Otto & Powell Barristers & Solicitors - *3
#100, 12 Walnut St. South, Hamilton, ON L8N 2K7
Tel: 905-522-4696; *Fax:* 905-528-6608
dmorrison@poplaw.ca
www.poplaw.ca

Hamilton: Michael S. Puskas - *1
46 Jackson St. East, Hamilton, ON L8N 1L1
Tel: 905-527-4495; *Fax:* 905-527-4496
michael.puskas@bellnet.ca

Hamilton: Daniel P. Randazzo - *1
44 Hughson St. South, Hamilton, ON L8N 2A7
Tel: 905-777-1773; *Fax:* 905-777-1774
randazzo@liuna.ca

Hamilton: Geoffrey M. Read - *1
172 Main St. East, Hamilton, ON L8N 1G9
Tel: 905-529-2028; *Fax:* 905-522-6677

Hamilton: Robinson, McCallum, McKerracher, Graham - *1
#300, 69 John St. South, Hamilton, ON L8N 2B9
Tel: 905-528-1435; *Fax:* 905-529-1570
m.graham@on.aibn.com
www.malcolmgrahamlaw.ca

Hamilton: Ross & McBride - *40
Commerce Place, P.O. Box 907, 1 King St. West, 10th Fl., Hamilton, ON L8N 3P6
Tel: 905-526-9800; *Fax:* 905-526-0732
contact@rossmcbride.com
www.rossmcbride.com

Hamilton: Ross & McBride LLP - *37
Former Name: Martin, Martin, Evans, Husband
Commerce Place, P.O. Box 907, 1 King St. West, 10th Fl., Hamilton, ON L8N 3P6
Tel: 905-526-9800; *Fax:* 905-526-0732
contact@rossmcbride.com
www.rossmcbride.com

Hamilton: Michael N. Rubenstein - *1
#200, 242 James St. South, Hamilton, ON L8P 3B3
Tel: 905-525-9636; *Fax:* 905-521-0690
smerz@primus.ca

Hamilton: Linda Irvine Sapiano - *1
#601, 25 Main St. West, Hamilton, ON L8P 1H1
Tel: 905-522-2040; *Fax:* 905-528-8808
Toll-Free: 877-350-1109
linda@sapianolaw.com
sapianolaw.com

Hamilton: Scarfone Hawkins LLP - *18
P.O. Box 926, Stn. Depot 1, 1 James St. South, 14th Fl., Hamilton, ON L8N 3P9
Tel: 905-523-1333; *Fax:* 905-523-5878
info@shlaw.ca
www.scarfonehawkinsllp.com

Hamilton: Monica U.M. Scholz - *1
184 Jackson St. East, Hamilton, ON L8N 1L4
Tel: 905-577-6070; *Fax:* 905-577-6051
monica@scholzlaw.ca

Hamilton: Schreiber & Smurlick - *1
1219 Main St. East, Hamilton, ON L8K 1A5
Tel: 905-545-1107

Hamilton: Simpson & Watson - *3
950 King St. West, Hamilton, ON L8S 1K8
Tel: 905-527-1174; *Fax:* 905-577-0661
davidsimpson@simpsonwatson.com
www.simpsonwatson.com

Hamilton: Smith & Smith - *1
1416 King St. East, Hamilton, ON L8M 1H8
Tel: 905-544-6034

Hamilton: Frank P. Sondola - *1
#105, 124 James St. South, Hamilton, ON L8P 2Z4
Tel: 905-523-1970; *Fax:* 905-523-1971

Hamilton: Sullivan Festeryga LLP - *20
1 James St. South, 11th Fl., Hamilton, ON L8P 4R5
Tel: 905-528-7963; *Fax:* 905-577-0077
lawyers@sfllp.ca
www.sfllp.ca

Hamilton: Szpiech, Ellis, Skibinski, Shipton - *5
414 Main St. East, Hamilton, ON L8N 1J9
Tel: 905-524-2454; *Fax:* 905-523-1733
contact@sesslaw.ca
www.sesslaw.ca

Hamilton: Edward Tharen - *1
1243 Barton St. East, Hamilton, ON L8H 2V8
Tel: 905-547-1618; *Fax:* 905-549-5654

Hamilton: Stanley M. Tick & Associates - *3
108 John St. North, Hamilton, ON L8R 1H6
Tel: 905-523-6464; *Fax:* 905-523-8080
tickinfo@smtick.com
www.smtick.com

Hamilton: Donna Tiqui-Shebib - *1
#601, 20 Hughson St. South, Hamilton, ON L8N 2A1
Tel: 905-523-8049; *Fax:* 905-523-9368
Toll-Free: 888-523-8049
info@donnatiquishebiblaw.com
www.donnatiquishebiblaw.com
www.facebook.com/DonnaTiquiShebibLaw,
www.twitter.com/dtiquishebib,
www.linkedin.com/pub/donna-tiqui-shebib/29/890/6b7

Hamilton: Tkach & Tokiwa - *1
#126, Mountain Plaza Mall, 651 Upper James St., Hamilton, ON L9C 5R8
Tel: 905-383-3545; *Fax:* 905-574-3020
tkachlaw@shaw.ca

Hamilton: Turkstra Mazza Lawyers - *11
Former Name: Turkstra Mazza Shinehoft Mihailovich Associates
15 Bold St., Hamilton, ON L8P 1T3
Tel: 905-529-3476; *Fax:* 905-529-3663
reception@tmalaw.ca
www.tmalaw.ca

Hamilton: Jennifer M. Vandenberg - *1
172 Main St. East, Hamilton, ON L8N 1G9
Tel: 905-572-6611; *Fax:* 905-572-9440
jvandenberg@cogeco.ca

Hamilton: Wallace Law - *1
14 Mornington Dr., Hamilton, ON L9B 1Z3
Tel: 905-575-0732; *Fax:* 905-574-3406
info@wallacelaw.ca
www.wallacelaw.ca

Hamilton: Gary Leonard Waxman - *1
#234, 845 Upper James St., Hamilton, ON L9C 3A3
Tel: 905-388-0585; *Fax:* 905-575-1613
gary.waxman@shaw.ca
garywaxman.ca

Hamilton: Weisz, Rocchi & Scholes - *6
#200, 242 Main St. East, Hamilton, ON L8N 1H5
Tel: 905-523-1842; *Fax:* 905-523-4011

Hamilton: Wellenreiter & Wellenreiter - *3
Rastrick House, 46 Forest Ave., Hamilton, ON L8N 1X2
Tel: 905-525-4520; *Fax:* 905-525-7943
www.wellenreiter.ca

Hamilton: Nicholas R. White - *1
120 Jackson St. East, Hamilton, ON L8N 1L3
Tel: 905-521-8901; *Fax:* 905-521-9564
nwhite@netaccess.on.ca

Hamilton: Wissenz Law - *2
183 James St. South, Hamilton, ON L8P 3A8
Tel: 905-522-1102; *Fax:* 905-522-1122
reception@wissenzlaw.com
www.wissenzlaw.com

Hamilton: Yachetti, Lanza & Restivo - *5
#100, 154 Main St. East, Hamilton, ON L8N 1G9
Tel: 905-528-7534; *Fax:* 905-528-5275
info@ylrlawyers.com
www.ylrlawyers.com

Hanover: Kenneth P. Duffy - *1
414 - 10 St., Hanover, ON N4N 1P6
Tel: 519-364-1440; *Fax:* 519-364-6023

Hanover: Garcia & Donnelly Law Office - *2
325 - 10th St., Hanover, ON N4N 1P1
Tel: 519-364-3643; *Fax:* 519-364-6594

Hanover: Halpin & McMeeken - *1
Former Name: Kevin W. McMeeken Law Office
478 - 10 St., Hanover, ON N4N 1R1
Tel: 519-364-5505; *Fax:* 519-364-0165
www.hanoverlaw.ca

Harrow: Karl G. Melinz - *1
P.O. Box 880, 41A Centre St. West, Harrow, ON N0R 1G0
Tel: 519-738-2232; *Fax:* 519-738-9080
kgmelinz@mmsi.net

** indicates number of lawyers*

***Hawkesbury*: Lachapelle Professional Corporation - *1**
Former Name: Lachapelle Law Office
444 McGill St., Hawkesbury, ON K6A 1R2
Tel: 613-632-7032; *Fax:* 613-632-5472
lachapellelawoffice@bellnet.ca

***Hawkesbury*: Pilon Professional Corporation - *1**
Former Name: Smith Lacombe Marcotte
280 Main St. West, Hawkesbury, ON K6A 2H7
Tel: 613-632-0103; *Fax:* 613-632-2800
pilons@bellnet.ca

***Hawkesbury*: Woods Parisien - *1**
#200, 115 Main St. East, Hawkesbury, ON K6A 1A1
Tel: 613-632-8557; *Fax:* 613-632-8559
parisien@on.aibn.com

***Hillsburgh*: Robert P. Harper - *1**
P.O. Box 10, 115 Main St., Hillsburgh, ON N0B 1Z0
Tel: 519-855-4961; *Fax:* 519-855-4029
robertharper@bellnet.ca

***Huntsville*: James S. Anderson**
#5, 133 Hwy. 60, Huntsville, ON P1H 1C2
Tel: 705-789-8823; *Fax:* 705-789-1272
jamesanderson@sympatico.ca

***Huntsville*: Andrew B. Cochran - *1**
#5, 133 Hwy. 60, Huntsville, ON P1H 1C2
Tel: 705-789-5538; *Fax:* 705-789-1272
acochran@vianet.ca

***Huntsville*: Ryan and Lewis Professional Corporation - *2**
#301, 395 Centre St. North, Huntsville, ON P1H 2P5
Tel: 705-788-7077; *Fax:* 705-789-6309
david.ryan@ryanandlewis.com
www.ryanandlewis.com

***Huntsville*: G.A. Smith - *1**
Also Known As: Glen A. Smith
#1, 3 Fairy Ave., Huntsville, ON P1H 1G7
Tel: 705-789-8829; *Fax:* 705-789-2984
glensmith@bellnet.ca

***Huntsville*: Thoms & Currie - *7**
#1, 6 Main St. West, Huntsville, ON P1H 2E1
Tel: 705-789-8844; *Fax:* 705-789-6547
info@thomsandcurrie.com
thomsandcurrie.com

***Huntsville*: Peter N. Ward - *1**
46 West Rd., Huntsville, ON P1H 1L2
Tel: 705-788-0018; *Fax:* 705-788-2944

***Ingersoll*: Nesbitt Coulter LLP - *7**
183 Thames St. South, Ingersoll, ON N5C 2T6
Tel: 519-485-5651; *Fax:* 519-485-6582
mborndahl@nesbittlaw.com
www.nesbittlaw.com

***Innisfil*: Anderson Adams - *4**
Former Name: Gibson & Adams LLP
8000 Yonge St., Innisfil, ON L9S 1L5
Tel: 705-436-1701; *Fax:* 705-436-1710
info@andersonadams.ca
www.andersonadams.com

***Innisfil*: D. Anne Cheney - *1**
P.O. Box 7074, 1984 Wilkinson St., Innisfil, ON L9S 1A8
Tel: 705-734-9644; *Fax:* 705-734-0333

***Innisfil*: Duco & Duco LLP - *2**
2093 Lilac Dr., #B, Innisfil, ON L9S 1Z1
Tel: 705-436-1020; *Fax:* 705-436-1027
www.ducolaw.com

***Iroquois Falls*: J. Kenneth Alexander - *1**
P.O. Box 290, Stn. A, 283 Main St., Iroquois Falls, ON P0K 1G0
Tel: 705-232-4309; *Fax:* 705-232-5274

***Iroquois Falls*: Susan T. McGrath - *1**
97 Ambridge Dr., Iroquois Falls, ON P0K 1E0
Tel: 705-232-4055; *Fax:* 705-232-6301
mcgrath@nt.net

***Jarvis*: William E. Kelly - *1**
P.O. Box 430, 32 Main St. North, Jarvis, ON N0A 1J0
Tel: 519-587-4561; *Fax:* 519-587-5052

***Kapuskasing*: Bourgeault Brunelle Dumais Boucher - *5**
P.O. Box 446, 7 Cain Ave., Kapuskasing, ON P5N 1S8
Tel: 705-335-6121; *Fax:* 705-335-8127

***Kapuskasing*: J.M. Michel Majerovich - *1**
28 Kolb Ave., Kapuskasing, ON P5N 1G1
Tel: 705-335-5051; *Fax:* 705-337-5051

***Kapuskasing*: Perras Mongenais**
Former Name: Perras et Associés
10B Circle St., Kapuskasing, ON P5N 1T3
Tel: 705-335-3939; *Fax:* 705-335-3960

***Kapuskasing*: Guy A. Wainwright - *1**
19 Cain Ave., Kapuskasing, ON P5N 1T2
Tel: 705-335-8501; *Fax:* 705-337-1474
gwainrt@ntl.sympatico.ca

***Kenora*: Beamish & Associates - *1**
P.O. Box 1600, 50 Queen St., Kenora, ON P8T 1C3
Tel: 807-737-2809; *Fax:* 807-737-1211
cathyb@beamishlaw.ca

***Kenora*: Carten Law Office - *2**
#13, 208, 2nd St. South, Kenora, ON P9N 1G4
Tel: 807-468-3036; *Fax:* 807-468-7576

***Kenora*: David James Elliott - *1**
Stone House, 225 Main St. South, Kenora, ON P9N 1T3
Tel: 807-468-3355; *Fax:* 807-468-7858

***Kenora*: Gibson & Wexler - *2**
P.O. Box 2450, 111 Main St. South, Kenora, ON P9N 3X8
Tel: 807-468-3061; *Fax:* 807-468-7940

***Kenora*: Hook, Seller & Lundin, LLP - *7**
#204, Bannister Centre, 301 - 1 Ave. South, Kenora, ON P9N 1W2
Tel: 807-468-9831; *Fax:* 807-468-8384
www.hsllawyers.com

***Kenora*: Shewchuk, Ormiston, Richardt & Johnson LLP - *5**
Former Name: Shewchuk, MacDonell, Ormiston & Richardt LLP
214 Main St. South, Kenora, ON P9N 1T2
Tel: 807-468-5559; *Fax:* 807-468-5504
lawoffice@kmts.ca
www.kenoralaw.com
www.facebook.com/kenoralaw

***Keswick*: Altwerger Law - *2**
Former Name: Altwerger, Baker, Weinberg
187 Simcoe Ave., Keswick, ON L4P 2H6
Tel: 905-476-2555; *Fax:* 905-476-2560
stevea@lexpertor.com
www.altwergerlaw.com

***Keswick*: Donnell Law Group - *4**
183 Simcoe Ave., Keswick, ON L4P 2H6
Tel: 905-476-9100; *Fax:* 905-476-2027
Toll-Free: 888-307-9991
info@donnellgroup.ca
www.donnellandassociates.com

***Keswick*: Robert E. Pollock - *1**
#300, 449 The Queensway South, Keswick, ON L4P 2C9
Tel: 905-476-0021; *Fax:* 905-476-0134

***Kincardine*: Marshall & Mahood - *1**
Former Name: Mahood & Darcy
313 Lambton St., Kincardine, ON N2Z 2Y8
Tel: 519-396-8144; *Fax:* 519-396-9446
reception@marshallmahood.com
www.marshallmahood.com

***Kincardine*: William S. Mathers - *1**
226 Queen St., Kincardine, ON N2Z 2S5
Tel: 519-396-4147; *Fax:* 519-396-1872
wwmlawyer@bmts.com

***King City*: Margaret Black & Associates - *2**
2175 King Rd., King City, ON L7B 1G3
Tel: 905-833-9090; *Fax:* 905-833-9091
info@blackandassociates.ca
ww.blackandassociates.ca

***Kingston*: Bédard, Barrister & Solicitor Business Law - *1**
#2, P.O. Box 695, 159 Wellington St., Kingston, ON K7L 4X1
Tel: 613-542-3552; *Fax:* 613-542-1034
jb@bedardlegal.com
www.bedardlegal.com

***Kingston*: Bergeron Clifford LLP - *13**
1 Hyperion Crt., Kingston, ON K7K 7G3
Tel: 613-384-5886; *Fax:* 613-384-0501
Toll-Free: 877-485-3054
info@BergeronClifford.com
www.bergeronclifford.com
www.facebook.com/bergeron.clifford, www.twitter.com/bclawyers

***Kingston*: Caldwell & Moore - *1**
260 Barrie St., Kingston, ON K7L 3K7
Tel: 613-545-1860; *Fax:* 613-545-1862
caldwell-moore@cogeco.ca

***Kingston*: Jack W. Chong - *1**
Former Name: Chong & O'Neill
P.O. Box 1382, Stn. Main, 273 King St. East, Kingston, ON K7L 5C6
Tel: 613-549-1225; *Fax:* 613-549-3882
jackchong@chongoneill.ca

***Kingston*: Robert K. Cooper - *1**
11 Carruthers St., Kingston, ON K7L 1L9
Tel: 613-544-3634

***Kingston*: Cunningham, Swan, Carty, Little & Bonham LLP - *25**
#300, 27 Princess St., Kingston, ON K7L 1A3
Tel: 613-544-0211; *Fax:* 613-542-9814
info@cswan.com
www.cswan.com

***Kingston*: Ecclestone & Ecclestone LLP - *3**
Former Name: C.E. John Ecclestone
#100, 1480 Bath Rd., Kingston, ON K7M 4X6
Tel: 613-384-0735; *Fax:* 613-384-0731
email@ecclaw.net
www.ecclaw.net

***Kingston*: John R. Gale - *1**
2263 Princess St., Kingston, ON K7M 3G4
Tel: 613-546-4283; *Fax:* 613-546-9861
info@galeforlaw.ca
www.galeforlaw.ca

***Kingston*: Wayne C. Gay & Associate - *2**
P.O. Box 370, Stn. Main, 275 Ontario St., Kingston, ON K7L 4W2
Tel: 613-549-4300; *Fax:* 613-549-6948
waynegay@waynegay.com

***Kingston*: Good Elliott Hawkins LLP - *3**
Former Name: Good & Elliott
153 Brock St., Kingston, ON K7L 4Y8
Tel: 613-544-1330; *Fax:* 613-547-4538
www.geh.ca/mambo/

***Kingston*: Hickey & Hickey - *2**
P.O. Box 110, 93 Clarence St., Kingston, ON K7L 4V6
Tel: 613-548-3191; *Fax:* 613-548-8195
hickeym@on.aibn.com

***Kingston*: Mary Ann Higgs - *1**
#206, P.O. Box 700, 275 Ontario St., Kingston, ON K7L 4X1
Tel: 613-548-7399; *Fax:* 613-548-1862
maryannhiggs@on.aibn.com

***Kingston*: R. Wayne Keeler - *1**
23 Jane Ave., Kingston, ON K7M 3G6
Tel: 613-531-4600; *Fax:* 613-547-4577
keelerw@kos.net

***Kingston*: J. Bruce MacNaughton - *1**
P.O. Box 1621, 45 Johnson St., Kingston, ON K7L 5C8
Tel: 613-546-9990; *Fax:* 613-546-6176
bruce@macnaughtonlaw.com
www.macnaughtonlaw.com

***Kingston*: Douglas R. Macpherson, Q.C. - *1**
#102, Howard Maitland Building, 780 Midpark Dr., Kingston, ON K7M 7P6
Tel: 613-389-1999; *Fax:* 613-384-8777
macpherson@kingston-lawyers.ca
www.kingston-lawyers.ca

***Kingston*: Mary-Jo Maur - *1**
#3, 159 Wellington St., Kingston, ON K7L 3E1
Tel: 613-530-2665; *Fax:* 613-530-2241
mary-jo.maur@bellnet.ca

***Kingston*: M.A. McCue - *1**
#201A, 837 Princess St., Kingston, ON K7L 1G8
Tel: 613-542-3700; *Fax:* 613-542-5700
mamccue@kingston.net

** indicates number of lawyers*

Kingston: **Gordon Y. McDiarmid - *1**
P.O. Box 1010, Stn. Main, 3 Rideau St., Kingston, ON K7L 4X8
Tel: 613-546-3274; Fax: 613-546-1493
gmcdiarmid@on.aibn.com

Kingston: **Morley Law Office - *1**
211 Division St., Kingston, ON K7K 3Z2
Tel: 613-542-2192; Fax: 613-542-2393
Toll-Free: 800-743-7126
les@lesmorley.com
www.lesmorley.com
facebook.com/pages/Morley-Law-Office/303931516334604,
twitter.com/LesMorley, www.linkedin.com/in/lesmorley

Kingston: **Fergus J. (Chip) O'Connor - *1**
P.O. Box 1959, 104 Johnson St., Kingston, ON K7L 5J7
Tel: 613-546-5581; Fax: 613-546-5540
oconnor@kos.net

Kingston: **Elizabeth I. Ollson - *1**
1770 Bath Rd., Kingston, ON K7M 4Y2
Tel: 613-384-8122; Fax: 613-384-7056
eollson@kos.net

Kingston: **Philip M. Osanic - *1**
819 Blackburn Mews, Kingston, ON K7P 2N6
Tel: 613-634-4440; Fax: 613-634-4443

Kingston: **J. Yvonne Pelley - *1**
819 Blackburn Mews, Kingston, ON K7P 2N6
Tel: 613-634-4440; Fax: 613-634-4443
jypelley@on.aibn.com

Kingston: **RZCD Law Firm LLP - *22**
Also Known As: Racioppo Zuber Coetzee Dionne LLP
#210, 650 Dalton Ave., Kingston, ON K7M 8N7
Tel: 613-544-1482; Fax: 613-546-3633
info@rzcdlaw.com
www.rzcdlaw.com

Kingston: **Jennifer L. Sims - *1**
#207, 275 Ontario St., Kingston, ON K7K 2X5
Tel: 613-507-7467; Fax: 613-507-7468
jennifer@jennifersims.ca
www.jennifersims.ca

Kingston: **Douglas M. Slack - *1**
366 King East, Kingston, ON K7K 6Y3
Tel: 613-384-7260; Fax: 613-384-7262
dm.slack@utoronto.ca

Kingston: **Britton C. Smith - *1**
P.O. Box 1376, Stn. Main, 74 Johnson St., Kingston, ON K7L 5C6
Tel: 613-547-3798; Fax: 613-547-6814

Kingston: **Letitia M. Steele - *1**
P.O. Box 29013, Stn. Portsmouth, Kingston, ON K7M 8W6
Tel: 613-542-1795; Fax: 613-542-2471

Kingston: **Tepper Law Office - *1**
461 Princess St., Kingston, ON K7L 1C3
Tel: 613-546-1169; Fax: 613-546-6992
gtepper@kingston.net

Kingston: **Alan G. Thomson - *1**
232 Brock St., Kingston, ON K7L 1S4
Tel: 613-549-5111; Fax: 613-549-4074
thomson@kingston.net
www.thomsonlaw.ca

Kingston: **Thomas W. Troughton - *1**
#103, P.O. Box 668, Stn. Main, 780 Midpark Dr., Kingston, ON K7L 4X1
Tel: 613-634-0302; Fax: 613-384-8777
troughton@frontenaclaw.on.ca

Kingston: **Viner, Kennedy, Frederick, Allan & Tobias LLP - *8**
Also Known As: Viner Kennedy
#300, The Royal Block, 366 King St. East, Kingston, ON K7K 6Y3
Tel: 613-542-7867; Fax: 613-542-1279
www.vinerkennedy.com

Kingsville: **Dunnion, Dunmore & Schippel LLP - *1**
59 Main St. East, Kingsville, ON N9Y 1A1
Tel: 519-733-6573; Fax: 519-733-3172
pdunmore@cogeco.net

Kirkland Lake: **Gorman & Richard-Gorman - *2**
6 Government Rd. West, Kirkland Lake, ON P2N 2E1
Tel: 705-567-9500; Fax: 705-567-5014
reception@jrgormanlaw.ca
www.jrgormanlaw.ca

Kirkland Lake: **Gavin Shorrock - *1**
15 Gov't Rd. East, Kirkland Lake, ON P2N 2E6
Tel: 705-567-5213; Fax: 705-567-3987
shorlaw@ntl.sympatico.ca

Kitchener: **Derek K. Babcock - *1**
28 Weber St. West, Kitchener, ON N2H 3Z2
Tel: 519-742-3570; Fax: 519-576-7451
dbabcock@on.aibn.com

Kitchener: **Thomas L. Brock - *1**
17 Irvin St., Kitchener, ON N2H 1K6
Tel: 519-742-1270; Fax: 519-742-6973

Kitchener: **J. Mark Coffey - *1**
#705, 30 Duke St. West, Kitchener, ON N2H 3W5
Tel: 519-742-5100; Fax: 519-742-5229

Kitchener: **Harold J. Cox - *1**
#610, 50 Queen St. North, Kitchener, ON N2H 6M1
Tel: 519-744-6551; Fax: 519-744-9885
harold@hjcox.ca

Kitchener: **N.A. Crawford - *1**
1444 King St. East, Kitchener, ON N2G 2N7
Tel: 519-743-3615; Fax: 519-743-2212

Kitchener: **Dietrich Law Office - *2**
Former Name: G.B. Dietrich
141 Duke St. East, Kitchener, ON N2H 1A6
Tel: 519-749-0770; Fax: 519-749-0288
george.deitrich@sympatico.ca
www.dietrichlaw.ca

Kitchener: **Farhood Boehler Winny LLP - *2**
#510, Marsland Centre, 101 Frederick St., Kitchener, ON N2H 6R2
Tel: 519-744-9949; Fax: 519-744-7974
info@fblaw.ca
www.fblaw.ca

Kitchener: **Timothy C. Flannery - *1**
82 Weber St. East, Kitchener, ON N2P 1K3
Tel: 519-578-8017; Fax: 519-578-8327
flannery@flannerylaw.ca
www.flannerylaw.ca

Kitchener: **George C. Amos - *1**
276 Frederick St., Kitchener, ON N2H 2N4
Tel: 519-576-8480; Fax: 519-579-3042
george@amoslaw.ca

Kitchener: **Gerry V. Schaffer Law Office - *1**
Former Name: Roetsch & Schaffer
284 Frederick St., Kitchener, ON N2H 2N4
Tel: 519-576-5310; Fax: 519-576-2797

Kitchener: **Giesbrecht, Griffin, Funk and Irvine LLP - *7**
60 College St., Kitchener, ON N2H 5A1
Tel: 519-579-4300; Fax: 519-579-8745
ggfi@ggfilaw.com
www.ggfilaw.com

Kitchener: **Giffen LLP - *17**
Former Name: Giffen Lee LLP
#500, Commerce House, P.O. Box 2396, 50 Queen St. North, Kitchener, ON N2H 6M3
Tel: 519-578-4150; Fax: 519-578-8740
info@giffenlawyers.com
www.giffenlawyers.com

Kitchener: **R. Haalboom, Q.C. - *1**
#304, 7 Duke St. West, Kitchener, ON N2H 6N7
Tel: 519-579-2920; Fax: 519-576-0471
richard@haalboom.ca

Kitchener: **Robert J. Hare - *1**
741 King St. West, Kitchener, ON N2G 1E3
Tel: 519-576-6710; Fax: 519-576-0258
harelawoffice@on.aibn.com

Kitchener: **Richard H.F. Herold - *1**
53 Roy St., Kitchener, ON N2H 4B4
Tel: 519-749-0555; Fax: 519-741-9041
herold.legal@gmail.com

Kitchener: **Timothy Jansen - *1**
46 Brembel St., Kitchener, ON N2B 3T8
Tel: 519-741-1911; Fax: 519-741-5945
timjansen@bellnet.ca

Kitchener: **Jennifer Roggemann Law Office - *1**
1135 King St. East, Kitchener, ON N2G 2N3
Tel: 519-744-3570; Fax: 519-744-3571
www.jrlawoffice.com

Kitchener: **Kay Professional Corporation - *4**
Former Name: Kay, Bogdon
370 Frederick St., Kitchener, ON N2H 2P3
Tel: 519-579-1220; Fax: 519-743-8063
law@kaylaw.ca
www.kaylaw.ca

Kitchener: **Kelly & Co. - *3**
#903, 50 Queen St. North, Kitchener, ON N2H 6P4
Tel: 519-579-3360; Fax: 519-579-2556
www.kellylaw.com

Kitchener: **Kokila D. Khanna**
#101, 10 Duke St. West, Kitchener, ON N2H 3W4
Tel: 516-571-1542; Fax: 516-571-0945
kdkhanna@khannalaw.ca

Kitchener: **Sheldon Kosky - *1**
P.O. Box 2307, 71 Weber St. East, Kitchener, ON N2H 1C6
Tel: 519-578-1480; Fax: 519-579-2537
skosky@kosky.com

Kitchener: **Stephanie A. Krug - *1**
17 Irvin St., Kitchener, ON N2H 1K6
Tel: 519-743-1603; Fax: 519-742-6973
stephaniekrug@aol.com

Kitchener: **Madorin, Snyder LLP - *16**
P.O. Box 1234, 55 King St. West, 6th Fl., Kitchener, ON N2G 4G9
Tel: 519-744-4491; Fax: 519-741-8060
www.kw-law.com
twitter.com/MadorinSnyder,
www.linkedin.com/company/madorin-snyder-llp

Kitchener: **Richard V. Marchak - *1**
245 Frederick St., Kitchener, ON N2H 2M7
Tel: 519-570-3635; Fax: 519-570-4427
richardmarchak@hotmail.com

Kitchener: **McCarter Grespan - *12**
675 Riverbend Dr., Kitchener, ON N2K 3S3
Tel: 519-571-8800; Fax: 519-742-1841
jweir@mgbwlaw.com
www.mgbwlaw.com

Kitchener: **Jane A. McKenzie - *1**
55 King St. West, 7th Fl., Kitchener, ON N2G 4W1
Tel: 519-745-7614; Fax: 519-745-9778
jane.mckenzie@execulink.com
www.janemckenziefamilylawyer.com

Kitchener: **McLeod Green Dewar LLP & Associates - *4**
#605, 30 Duke St. West, Kitchener, ON N2H 3W6
Tel: 519-742-4297; Fax: 519-744-5526
reception@mgdlawyers.ca
www.mgdlawyers.ca
www.facebook.com/mgdlawyers,
ca.linkedin.com/pub/amy-a-green/16/a48/688

Kitchener: **Mollison, McCormick - *7**
P.O. Box 2307, Stn. C, 71 Weber St. East, Kitchener, ON N2H 6L2
Tel: 519-579-1040; Fax: 519-579-2537

Kitchener: **Morrison Reist - *3**
279 Queen St. South, Kitchener, ON N2G 1W4
Tel: 519-576-5351; Fax: 519-576-5411
Toll-Free: 800-354-5723
law@morrisonreist.com
www.morrisonreist.com

Kitchener: **Morscher & Morscher - *1**
85 Margaret Ave. N, Kitchener, ON N2J 3R2
Tel: 519-749-8100; Fax: 519-749-8141

Kitchener: **Jacqueline Mulvey - *1**
293 Frederick St., Kitchener, ON N2H 2N6
Tel: 519-744-3704; Fax: 519-744-3662
jmulvey@rogers.com

Kitchener: **Mark T. Nowak - *1**
370 Frederick St., Kitchener, ON N2H 2P3
Tel: 519-746-8340; Fax: 519-746-8144

** indicates number of lawyers*

Kitchener: John E. Opolko - *1
372 Queen St. South, Kitchener, ON N2G 1W7
Tel: 519-743-2670; Fax: 519-743-2670

Kitchener: Phillips Lytle LLP - *13
#152, The Tannery, 151 Charles St. West, Kitchener, ON N2G 1H6
Tel: 519-570-4800; Fax: 519-570-4858
www.phillipslytle.com

Kitchener: Bruce H. Ritter - *1
17 Irvin St., Kitchener, ON N2H 1K6
Tel: 519-744-1169; Fax: 519-742-6973
britter1@aol.com

Kitchener: Schmidt Law Office Professional Corporation
#1100, 305 King St. West, Kitchener, ON N2G 1B9
Tel: 519-578-1448; Fax: 519-578-1168
admin@schmidtlawoffices.net
www.schmidtlawoffices.net

Kitchener: John D. E. Shannon - *1
30 Spetz St., Kitchener, ON N2H 1K1
Tel: 519-743-3654; Fax: 519-578-9521
jdeslaw@bellnet.ca

Kitchener: Sloane & Pinchen - *2
#301, 824 King St. North, Kitchener, ON N2G 1G1
Tel: 519-578-3094; Fax: 519-578-3682
david@sloanepinchen.com

Kitchener: Smith, Hunt, Buck - *2
53 Roy St., Kitchener, ON N2H 4B4
Tel: 519-579-3400; Fax: 519-741-9041

Kitchener: Smyth, Hobson - *1
#206, 7 Duke St. West, Kitchener, ON N2H 6N7
Tel: 519-578-9400; Fax: 519-578-7482

Kitchener: Sorbara, Schumacher, McCann LLP - *29
Also Known As: Sorbara Law
300 Victoria St. North, Kitchener, ON N2H 6R9
Tel: 519-576-0460; Fax: 519-576-3234
info@sorbaralaw.com
www.sorbaralaw.com

Kitchener: Sutherland Mark Flemming Snyder-Penner Professional Corporation - *6
#100, 675 Queen St. South, Kitchener, ON N2M 1A1
Tel: 519-725-2500; Fax: 519-725-2525
info@sutherlandmark.com
www.sutherlandmark.com

Kitchener: Carolyn R. Thomas & Associate - *1
#900, 50 Queen St. North, Kitchener, ON N2H 6P4
Tel: 519-576-4459; Fax: 519-576-9349

Kitchener: Voll & Santos - *2
30 Spetz St., Kitchener, ON N2H 1K1
Tel: 519-578-3400; Fax: 519-578-9521

Kitchener: Colleen J. Winn - *1
604 Charles St. East, Kitchener, ON N2G 2R5
Tel: 519-743-3981; Fax: 519-743-3647

Kitchener: Stephen C. Woodworth - *1
#9, 300 Victoria St. North, Kitchener, ON N2H 6R9
Tel: 519-570-0033; Fax: 519-570-0104

Kitchener: Wilfrid R. Zalman - *1
#102, 684 Belmont Ave. West, Kitchener, ON N2M 1N6
Tel: 519-579-6170; Fax: 519-579-6171

L'Orignal: Tolhurst & Miller - *4
1030 King St., L'Orignal, ON K0B 1K0
Tel: 613-675-4512; Fax: 613-675-1103
Toll-Free: 866-752-8277

Lakefield: Baker & Cole - *2
Former Name: T.E. Cole
8 Bridge St., Lakefield, ON K0L 2H0
Tel: 705-652-8161; Fax: 705-652-7088
adam.baker@nexicom.net
www.bakerandcole.com

Lancaster: Paul D. Syrduk - *1
P.O. Box 9, 10 Oak St., Lancaster, ON K0C 1N0
Tel: 613-347-2423; Fax: 613-347-7118
syruduk@glen-net.ca

Leamington: Ricci, Enns & Rollier LLP - *5
Former Name: Reid, Reynolds, Collins, Ricci & Enns
60 Talbot St. West, Leamington, ON N8H 1M4
Tel: 519-326-3237; Fax: 519-326-8139
www.ricciennsrollier.ca

Lindsay: Brent Walmsley - *1
223 Kent St. West, Lindsay, ON K9V 2Z1
Tel: 705-878-8131; Fax: 705-878-4642

Lindsay: J.W. Evans - *1
P.O. Box 427, Stn. Main, 219 Kent St. West, Lindsay, ON K9V 4S5
Tel: 705-324-3207; Fax: 705-328-1128

Lindsay: Frost, Frost & Gorwill - *1
#217, 189 Kent St. West, Lindsay, ON K9V 5G6
Tel: 705-324-2193; Fax: 705-324-9879

Lindsay: Carol E. Jamieson - *1
18 Cambridge St. North, Lindsay, ON K9V 4C3
Tel: 705-878-8864; Fax: 705-878-1813
caroljamieson@cogeco.ca

Lindsay: Timothy W. Johnston - *2
#218, The Kent Place Mall, 189 Kent St. West, Lindsay, ON K9V 5G6
Tel: 705-328-2393; Fax: 705-328-2428
twj@nexicom.net

Lindsay: J. Scott McLeod - *1
16 Russell St. West, Lindsay, ON K9V 2W7
Tel: 705-324-6711; Fax: 705-324-5723

Lindsay: Leonard S. Siegel - *1
P.O. Box 997, 11 Adelaide St. North, Lindsay, ON K9V 5N4
Tel: 705-878-7990; Fax: 705-878-7992
lsiegel@kawarthalaw.ca

London: Ambrogio & Ambrogio - *2
200 Queens Ave., London, ON N6A 1J3
Tel: 519-438-7219; Fax: 519-438-5919

London: Anissimoff Mann Professional Corporation - *4
#101, Talbot Centre, 140 Fullarton St., London, ON N6A 5P2
Tel: 519-673-5591; Fax: 519-673-6784
info@anissimoff.on.ca
www.anissimoff.on.ca

London: Arvai Personal Injury Lawyers - *3
Former Name: Karl Arvai
#1508, 140 Fullarton St., London, ON N6A 5P2
Tel: 519-672-0911; Fax: 519-642-1272
info@arvailaw.ca
www.arvailaw.ca

London: Daniel S.J. Bangarth - *1
562 Waterloo St., London, ON N6B 2P9
Tel: 519-472-2340; Fax: 519-657-8173
darlene.howard@sympatico.ca

London: Bates Law Office - *1
Also Known As: Bates, Thomas A.
#1, 151 Pine Valley Blvd., London, ON N6K 3T6
Tel: 519-472-0330; Fax: 519-472-1814
tabates@rogers.com

London: Joanne G. Beasley & Associates - *2
Former Name: Joanne G. Beasley & Associates
525 South St., London, ON N6B 1C4
Tel: 519-642-1520; Fax: 519-673-3868
info@beasleylawoffice.com
www.beasleylawoffice.com

London: Behr Law Firm - *3
Former Name: Behr & Rady
#1105, 383 Richmond St., London, ON N6M 3C4
Tel: 519-438-4530; Fax: 519-679-6576
behrlawfirm@gmail.com
www.londoncriminallaw.com

London: Belanger, Cassino, Coulston & Gallagher - *4
#153, 759 Hyde Park Rd., London, ON N6H 3S2
Tel: 226-271-4372; Fax: 519-657-5189
m.bccglondon.ca

London: Belecky & Belecky - *3
95 Dufferin Ave., London, ON N6A 1K3
Tel: 519-673-5630; Fax: 519-667-4836
info@belecky.ca
www.belecky.ca

London: Brown, Beattie, O'Donovan LLP - *17
City Centre Tower, 380 Wellington St., 16th Fl., London, ON N6A 5B5
Tel: 519-679-0400; Fax: 519-679-6350
bboinfo@bbo.on.ca
www.bbo.on.ca

London: Mervin F. Burgard, Q.C. - *1
#203, 219 Oxford St. West, London, ON N6H 1S5
Tel: 519-679-9900; Fax: 519-679-8546

London: Carlyle Peterson Lawyers LLP - *4
#216, 700 Richmond St., London, ON N6A 5C7
Tel: 519-432-0632; Fax: 519-432-0634
Toll-Free: 800-610-9751
www.cplaw.com

London: Luigi E. Circelli - *1
557 Talbot St., London, ON N6A 2S9
Tel: 519-673-1850; Fax: 519-673-4966
lcircelli@bellnet.ca

London: Cohen Highley LLP - London - *25
One London Place, 255 Queens Ave., 11th Fl., London, ON N6A 5R8
Tel: 519-672-9330; Fax: 519-672-5960
www.cohenhighley.com

London: Cram & Associates - *5
#514, 200 Queens Ave., London, ON N6A 1J3
Tel: 519-673-1670; Fax: 519-439-5011
www.cramassociates.com
www.facebook.com/pages/Cram-Associates/219463871414493,
twitter.com/CramAssociates

London: William L. Dewar - *1
479 Talbot St., London, ON N6A 2S4
Tel: 519-672-1830; Fax: 519-661-0095
wildew@on.aibn.com

London: Kenneth Duggan - *1
#203, 111 Waterloo St., London, ON N6B 2M4
Tel: 519-672-5360; Fax: 519-433-6975
kvduggan@bellnet.ca

London: Family Law Group - *3
Also Known As: Brenda Barr, Barrister & Solicitor
Former Name: Barr Family Law
521 Colborne St., London, ON N6B 2T6
Tel: 519-672-5953; Fax: 519-672-8736
www.familylawgroup.ca
www.facebook.com/pages/Family-Law-Group/155767857939309

London: Foster, Townsend, Graham & Associates LLP - *22
#900, 150 Dufferin Ave., London, ON N6A 5N6
Tel: 519-672-5272; Fax: 519-672-9313
Toll-Free: 888-354-0448
www.ftgalaw.com

London: Frauts, Dobbie - *3
Former Name: Dobson & Dobbie
585 Talbot St., London, ON N6A 2T2
Tel: 519-679-4000; Fax: 519-679-7700
info@frautsdobbie.ca
www.frautsdobbie.ca

London: David G. Fysh - *1
520 Springbank Dr., London, ON N6J 1G8
Tel: 519-472-3974; Fax: 519-472-3756
david@davidfysh.com
www.davidfysh.com

London: Giffen & Partners - *4
465 Waterloo St., London, ON N6B 2P4
Tel: 519-679-4700; Fax: 519-432-8003

London: Gordon B. Good - *1
255 Queens Ave., London, ON N6A 5R8
Tel: 519-672-9330
gordongood@goodlawoffice.com

London: Gregory Willoughby Law - *1
Also Known As: Only Immigration
Former Name: Willoughby, MacLeod
100 Fullarton St., London, ON N6A 1K1
Tel: 519-645-1500; Fax: 519-645-1503
www.londonimmigrationlawyers.ca

* indicates number of lawyers

London: **Harrison Pensa LLP - *57**
P.O. Box 3237, 450 Talbot St., London, ON N6A 4K3
Tel: 519-679-9660; *Fax:* 519-667-3362
Toll-Free: 800-263-0489
reception@harrisonpensa.com
www.harrisonpensa.com
www.facebook.com/HarrisonPensa, twitter.com/harrisonpensa, http://ca.linkedin.com/company/harrison-pensa-llp

London: **Antin Jaremchuk - *1**
Also Known As: Jaremchuk Law Offices
100 Fullarton St., London, ON N6A 1K1
Tel: 519-432-2417; *Fax:* 519-663-1165
antin@jaremchuklaw.com
www.jaremchuklaw.com

London: **Michael J. Lamb - *1**
#102, 101 Cherryhill Blvd., London, ON N6H 4S4
Tel: 519-645-1104; *Fax:* 519-645-1107
lamblaw@on.aibn.com

London: **Therese D.P. Landry Law Office - *1**
#319, 148 York St., London, ON N6A 1A9
Tel: 519-438-4111; *Fax:* 519-438-4113

London: **The Lawhouse - Kirwin Fryday Medcalf Lawyers - *3**
Former Name: Fryday, Murphy, Brown
#104, 140 Fullarton St., London, ON N6A 5P2
Tel: 519-679-8800; *Fax:* 519-518-2362
Toll-Free: 877-633-6878
dkirwin@lawhouse.ca
www.lawhouse.ca

London: **Lerners LLP - London - *68**
P.O. Box 2335, 80 Dufferin Ave., London, ON N6A 4G4
Fax: 519-672-2044
Toll-Free: 800-263-5583
lerner.london@lerners.ca
www.lerners.ca
www.facebook.com/LernersLLP, twitter.com/LernersLLP, www.linkedin.com/company/lerners-llp

London: **Lexcor Business Lawyers LLP - *6**
629 Wellington St., London, ON N6A 3R8
Tel: 519-858-2222; *Fax:* 519-858-2323
Toll-Free: 877-772-2424
lexcor.ca
www.facebook.com/lexcor, www.linkedin.com/company/2455421

London: **V. Libis - *1**
93 Dufferin Ave., London, ON N6A 1K3
Tel: 519-434-6821
valdis.libis@odyssey.on.ca

London: **John R. Lisowski - *1**
607 Queens Ave., London, ON N6B 1Y9
Tel: 519-679-5000; *Fax:* 519-672-1717

London: **Little & Jarrett - *2**
#304, 200 Queens Ave., London, ON N6A 1J3
Tel: 519-672-8121; *Fax:* 519-432-0784
little@litjar.on.ca
www.litjar.on.ca

London: **Little, Inglis, Price & Ewer - *4**
Former Name: Little, Inglis & Price
148 Wortley Rd., London, ON N6C 3P5
Tel: 519-672-5415; *Fax:* 519-672-3906
admin@lip.on.ca
www.lipelaw.com

London: **Michael F. Loebach - *3**
#508, 171 Queens Ave., London, ON N6A 5J7
Tel: 519-439-3031; *Fax:* 519-439-3540
info@mloebachlaw.com

London: **MacKewn, Winder LLP - *2**
#300, P.O. Box 96, 376 Richmond St., London, ON N6A 3C7
Tel: 519-672-2040; *Fax:* 519-672-6583
mwk@mwk.on.ca
mwlaw.ca/partnerA.html

London: **Nancy Z. Magguilli - *1**
PO Box 29002, RPO Westmount Mall, London, ON N6K 4L9
Tel: 519-641-6255; *Fax:* 519-641-6255

London: **Edward J. Mann - *1**
#605, 137 Dundas St., London, ON N6A 1E9
Tel: 519-672-8707; *Fax:* 519-660-4678
ejmann@on.aibn.com

London: **McKenzie Lake Lawyers - *42**
#1800, 140 Fullarton St., London, ON N6A 5P2
Tel: 519-672-5666; *Fax:* 519-672-2674
www.mckenzielake.com

London: **McNamara, Pizzale - *3**
#220, 200 Queens Ave., London, ON N6A 1J3
Tel: 519-434-2174; *Fax:* 519-642-7654
mcpizz@execulink.com

London: **Menear Worrad & Associates - *4**
478 Waterloo St., London, ON N6B 2P6
Tel: 519-672-7370; *Fax:* 519-663-1165
info@menearlaw.com
www.menearlaw.com

London: **Armand Morrow - *1**
42 Hampton Cres., London, ON N6H 2N8
Tel: 519-471-7607; *Fax:* 519-471-9121

London: **Frederick A. Mueller - *1**
Former Name: Mueller & Reich
141 Wortley Rd., London, ON N6C 3P4
Tel: 519-673-1300; *Fax:* 519-673-1728
fred_mueller@rogers.com

London: **Barry F. Nelligan - *1**
#202, 145 Wharncliffe Rd. South, London, ON N6J 2K4
Tel: 519-438-1709; *Fax:* 519-438-1700
barry@barrynelliganlaw.com
www.barrynelliganlaw.com/en/

London: **Nicholson, Smith & Partners LLP - *6**
295 Central Ave., London, ON N6B 2C9
Tel: 519-679-3366; *Fax:* 519-679-0958
reception@nicholsonsmith.com
nicholsonsmith.com

London: **Suhas T. Nimkar - *1**
151 York St., London, ON N6A 1A8
Fax: 519-474-9578
Toll-Free: 866-551-5255
suhasnimkar@aol.com

London: **Michael R. Nyhof**
380 Queens Ave., London, ON N6B 1X6
Tel: 519-642-4015; *Fax:* 519-642-4034
michaelnyhof@on.aibn.com

London: **Patton Cormier & Associates - *4**
#1512, 140 Fullarton St., London, ON N6A 5P2
Tel: 519-432-8282; *Fax:* 519-432-7285
www.pattoncormier.ca

London: **Paul Lépine Law Office - *1**
570 Queens Ave., London, ON N6B 1Y8
Tel: 519-432-4155; *Fax:* 519-432-6861
wendy@paullepine.ca
www.paullepine.ca

London: **Judith M. Potter - *1**
54 Hunt Club Dr., London, ON N6H 3Y3
Tel: 519-432-8811; *Fax:* 519-663-1165
jpotter@start.ca

London: **Peter J. Quigley - *1**
924 Oxford East, London, ON N5Y 3J9
Tel: 519-453-3393
PeterQuigley@londonlawyer.ca
www.london-lawyer.ca

London: **Wayne G. Rabley - *1**
#Unit E., 80 Dundas St., 2nd Fl., London, ON N6A 6A5
Tel: 519-660-3014; *Fax:* 519-660-3024

London: **Michael Robertson - *1**
#105, 186 Albert St., London, ON N6A 1M1
Tel: 226-289-2119; *Fax:* 519-660-0840
Toll-Free: 800-813-9702
smrobertson.lawyer@bellnet.ca
www.londonlitigation.com

London: **Stambler & Mills - *1**
#111, 142 Fullarton St., London, ON N6A 0A4
Tel: 519-672-6240; *Fax:* 519-433-9593
rmills@bellnet.ca

London: **Szemenyei Kerwin MacKenzie LLP - *9**
Former Name: Bitz, Szemenyei, Ferguson & MacKenzie
376 Richmond St., London, ON N6A 3C7
Tel: 519-433-8155; *Fax:* 519-660-4857
www.smglaw.ca

London: **L. Kent Thomas - *1**
11 Stanley St., London, ON N6C 1A9
Tel: 519-438-4181; *Fax:* 519-433-5557

London: **Thomson Mahoney Dobson Delorey - *8**
Former Name: Thomson Mahoney Elliott Delorey
#200, 145 Wharncliffe Rd., London, ON N6J 2K4
Tel: 519-673-1151; *Fax:* 519-673-3632
tmd@londonlawyers.com
www.londonlawyers.com

London: **Underhill Joles - *1**
607 Princess Ave., London, ON N6B 2C1
Tel: 519-432-4644; *Fax:* 519-438-3936
cjoles@bellnet.ca

London: **Despina S. Valassis - *1**
579 Talbot St., London, ON N6A 2T2
Tel: 519-439-2768

London: **Watson Jacobs McCreary LLP - *8**
Former Name: Jesin, Watson & McCreary
507 Talbot St., London, ON N6A 2S5
Tel: 416-226-0055; *Fax:* 416-226-0910
www.wjm-law.ca

London: **Holly A. Watson - *1**
380 Queens Ave., London, ON N6B 1X6
Tel: 519-642-4015; *Fax:* 519-642-4034
hollywatson@on.aibn.com

London: **Kenneth J. Williams - *1**
902 Adelaide St. North, London, ON N6J 1H3
Tel: 519-641-2200; *Fax:* 519-641-7995
kwilliams@kenwlaw.ca

London: **David Winninger - *1**
557 Talbot St., London, ON N6A 2S9
Tel: 519-858-3152; *Fax:* 519-858-3182

Madoc: **Karen J. Yarrow - *1**
P.O. Box 340, 246 St. Lawrence St. East, Madoc, ON K0K 2K0
Tel: 613-473-2802; *Fax:* 613-473-4472
kyarrow@lks.net

Manotick: **Wilson Law Partners LLP - *3**
Also Known As: Wilson & Associates
P.O. Box 429, 5542 Main St., Manotick, ON K4M 1A4
Tel: 613-692-3547; *Fax:* 613-692-0826
andrew@wilsonlawpartners.com
www.wilsonlawpartners.com

Maple: **Judith Holzman Law Offices - *1**
2126 Major Mackenzie Dr., Maple, ON L6A 1P7
Tel: 905-303-1070; *Fax:* 905-303-4364
Toll-Free: 866-233-0945
judith@jhlawoffices.com
www.jhlawoffices.com

Maple: **M.D. Newman - *1**
62 Lancer Dr., Maple, ON L6A 1C9
Tel: 905-832-5602; *Fax:* 905-832-5446
mdnewman@rogers.com

Maple: **Walsh & Associates - *1**
Former Name: Walsh McLuskie Doyle
#215, 2535 Major Mackenzie Dr., Maple, ON L6A 1C6
Tel: 905-832-2611; *Fax:* 905-832-2611
www.wmdlawmaple.com

Markdale: **Johonson & Schnass P.C. - *3**
Former Name: Dunlop, Johnson & Pust
P.O. Box 433, 21 Main St. East, Markdale, ON N0C 1H0
Tel: 519-986-2100; *Fax:* 519-986-2904
johnslaw@on.aibn.com

Markdale: **McMeeken Law Office - *1**
Former Name: Harris, Willis
P.O. Box 466, 45 Main St. West, Markdale, ON N0C 1H0
Tel: 519-986-2740; *Fax:* 519-986-4205
kevin@mcmeeken-law.ca

Markdale: **Rodney T. O'Halloran - *1**
P.O. Box 522, RR#7, Markdale, ON N0C 1H0
Tel: 519-986-1428; *Fax:* 519-986-1471

Markham: **Akai Seto & Friend - *1**
Former Name: David G. Friend, Q.C.
#602, 7130 Warden Ave., Markham, ON L3R 1S2
Tel: 905-604-3015; *Fax:* 905-604-3095
akai_seto@lawyer.com

** indicates number of lawyers*

***Markham*: Susan M. Ambrose - *2**
#202, 5762 Hwy. 7, Markham, ON L3P 1A8
Tel: 905-477-0624; *Fax:* 905-477-5846
inquiries@lawgals.com
www.lawgals.com

***Markham*: Elliot Berlin - *1**
#101, 16 Esna Park Dr., Markham, ON L3R 5X1
Tel: 905-470-9444; *Fax:* 905-470-9449
eberlin@elliotberlin.com

***Markham*: Bigioni Barristers & Solicitors - *2**
#201, 6060 Hwy. 7 East, Markham, ON L3P 3A9
Tel: 905-294-5222; *Fax:* 905-294-1607

***Markham*: Marvin B. Bongard - *1**
Former Name: Bongard & Associate
P.O. Box 509, 10 Washington St., Markham, ON L3P 3R2
Tel: 905-294-7555; *Fax:* 905-294-8360
marvin@mbongard.com

***Markham*: Burstein & Greenglass LLP - *4**
#200, Royal Bank Bldg., 7481 Woodbine Ave., Markham, ON L3R 2W1
Tel: 905-475-1266; *Fax:* 905-475-7851
office@bglaw.ca
www.bglaw.ca

***Markham*: Cattanach Hindson Sutton VanVeldhuizen - *6**
52 Main St. North, Markham, ON L3P 1X5
Tel: 905-294-0666; *Fax:* 905-294-5688
Toll-Free: 888-258-9798
www.cattanach.ca

***Markham*: Annie A. Cheng - *1**
2919 Bur Oak Ave., Markham, ON L6B 1E6
Tel: 905-294-2289; *Fax:* 905-294-7836
aacheng@solutionsinlaw.ca

***Markham*: Anna Chung - *2**
#209, 80 Acadia Ave., Markham, ON L3R 9V1
Tel: 905-940-6802; *Fax:* 905-940-6804
Toll-Free: 877-213-2284

***Markham*: Marie Davison - *1**
182 Town Centre Blvd., Markham, ON L3R 5H9
Tel: 905-940-9701; *Fax:* 905-944-1397

***Markham*: Dotsikas Hawtin Professional Corporation - *2**
#1000, 5221 Highway #7 East, Markham, ON L3R 1N3
Toll-Free: 800-804-0441
www.dhlawyers.com

***Markham*: Sydney Gangbar, Q.C. - *1**
#303, 80 Tiverton Ct., Markham, ON L3R 0G4
Tel: 905-470-0272; *Fax:* 905-470-8365
sydneygangbar@rogers.com

***Markham*: E. Alan Garbe - *1**
7507 Kennedy Rd., Markham, ON L3R 0L8
Tel: 905-415-9100; *Fax:* 905-479-3625
eagarbe@garbe-law.com
www.garbe-law.com

***Markham*: Paul Gollom - *1**
7507 Kennedy Rd., Markham, ON L3R 0L8
Tel: 905-881-6200; *Fax:* 905-881-6200
pgollom@rogers.com

***Markham*: Jozefacki, Fielding - *2**
#200, 4961 Hwy. 7 East, Markham, ON L3R 1N1
Tel: 905-940-3141; *Fax:* 905-940-3139
realestate@jozefackifielding.ca
www.jozefackifielding.ca/en/

***Markham*: Barry M. Kaufman - *1**
#308, 3950 - 14th Ave., Markham, ON L3R 0A9
Tel: 905-477-8848; *Fax:* 905-477-8489
barrykaufman@rogers.com

***Markham*: Anthea Koon - *1**
#232, Commerce Gate, 505 Highway 7 East, Markham, ON L3T 7T1
Tel: 905-889-0698; *Fax:* 905-889-8390
antheakoon@rogers.com

***Markham*: Alan J. Luftspring - *1**
#236, 7181 Woodbine Ave., Markham, ON L3R 1A3
Tel: 905-479-1200; *Fax:* 905-479-9769

***Markham*: Irene L. Matthews - *1**
#104, 7225 Woodbine Ave., Markham, ON L3R 1A3
Tel: 905-475-9716; *Fax:* 905-475-9142

***Markham*: Mingay & Vereshchak - *3**
81 Main St. North, Markham, ON L3P 1X7
Tel: 905-294-0550; *Fax:* 905-294-9141
info@mvlaw.net
www.mvlaw.net

***Markham*: G. Arthur Moad - *1**
#206, 5762 Hwy. 7, Markham, ON L3P 1A8
Tel: 905-294-6446; *Fax:* 905-294-4436
gamoad@on.aibn.com

***Markham*: Paul Harte Professional Corporation - *1**
#404, 8920 Woodbine Ave., Markham, ON L3R 9W9
Tel: 905-754-3800; *Fax:* 905-754-3790
Toll-Free: 855-663-3800
pharte@hartelaw.com
www.hartelaw.com

***Markham*: Theodore B. Rotenberg Barrister - *1**
#303, 7461 Woodbine Ave., Markham, ON L3R 2W1
Tel: 905-475-1266
general@rogerlaw.com

***Markham*: Alan R. Smith - *1**
#207, 2800 - 14th Ave., Markham, ON L3R 0E4
Tel: 905-415-8858; *Fax:* 905-940-1285
alansmithlaw@on.aibn.com

***Markham*: Paul F. Smith - *1**
#202, 5762 Hwy. 7, Markham, ON L3P 1A8
Tel: 905-294-9955; *Fax:* 905-294-4004

***Markham*: A. Melvin Sokolsky - *1**
#3, 200 Riviera Dr., Markham, ON L3R 5M1
Tel: 905-944-9427; *Fax:* 905-479-7025
amelvinsokolsky@rogers.com

***Markham*: E. Bruce Solomon - *1**
7507 Kennedy Rd., Markham, ON L3R 0L8
Tel: 905-479-1900; *Fax:* 905-479-9793
ebs@markhamlaw.ca
www.markhamlaw.ca

***Markham*: Dennis M. Starzynski, Q.C. - *1**
20 Main St. North, Markham, ON L3P 1Y2
Tel: 905-294-3891; *Fax:* 905-471-2550
starzynski@sympatico.ca

***Markham*: Howard J. Stern - *1**
#308, 3621 Hwy. 7 East, Markham, ON L2R 0G6
Tel: 416-410-7880; *Fax:* 416-410-7880

***Markham*: Williams HR Law - *4**
#100, 11 Allstate Pkwy., Markham, ON L3R 9T8
Tel: 905-205-0496; *Fax:* 905-418-0147
info@williamshrlaw.com
www.williamshrlaw.com
www.facebook.com/pages/Williams-HR-Law/248693148539051, twitter.com/#!/williamshrlaw, www.linkedin.com/company/1661854?trk=tyah

***Markham*: Wilson Vukelich LLP - *18**
#710, Valleywood Corporate Centre, 60 Columbia Way, Markham, ON L3R 0C9
Tel: 905-940-8700; *Fax:* 905-940-8785
Toll-Free: 866-508-8700
information@wvllp.ca
www.wvllp.ca

***Markham*: Judith M. Wolf - *1**
#500, 7030 Woodbine Ave., Markham, ON L3R 6G2
Tel: 905-313-0568; *Fax:* 905-313-0569

***Markham*: Shirley Yee**
#200, 80 Acadia Ave., Markham, ON L3R 9V1
Tel: 905-940-6800; *Fax:* 905-305-7630
shirleyyeelaw@hotmail.com

***Markham*: Zwicker Dispute Resolution Inc. - *1**
#306, 7100 Woodbine Ave., Markham, ON L3R 5J2
Tel: 905-470-2544; *Fax:* 905-470-2571
jackzwicker@on.aibn.com
www.zwickerdisputeresolutions.com

***Matheson*: J.A. Barber - *1**
P.O. Box 189, 362 MacDougall St., Matheson, ON P0K 1N0
Tel: 705-273-2151; *Fax:* 705-273-2144

***Meaford*: Carol A. Allen - *1**
P.O. Box 3272, 54 Sykes St. South, Meaford, ON N4L 1A5
Tel: 519-538-9929; *Fax:* 519-538-9931
Toll-Free: 877-538-9929
contact@carolallen.ca
www.carolallen.ca/en/

***Meaford*: Kopperud Hamilton LLP - *2**
Former Name: Norman A. Kopperud Law Office
76 Sykes St. North, Meaford, ON N4L 1R2
Tel: 519-538-2044; *Fax:* 519-538-5323
Toll-Free: 877-593-1938
info@kohalaw.com
www.bluemountainlawyers.com

***Meaford*: Scheifele, Erskine & Renken - *4**
P.O. Box 3395, 39 Nelson St. West, Meaford, ON N4L 1A5
Tel: 519-538-2510; *Fax:* 519-538-1843
info@meafordlawyers.com
www.meafordlawyers.com

***Metcalfe*: Gary M. Chayko - *1**
P.O. Box 579, Metcalfe, ON K2P 1L5
Tel: 613-230-7260; *Fax:* 613-230-2163
gchayko@netscape.net

***Midland*: Chin & Orr Lawyers - *2**
#15, 9225 County Rd. #93, Midland, ON L4R 4K4
Tel: 705-526-5529; *Fax:* 705-526-3071
Toll-Free: 877-526-5529
sonyam@chinandorrlawyers.ca

***Midland*: Deacon Taws - *2**
476 Elizabeth St., Midland, ON L4R 1Z8
Tel: 705-526-3791; *Fax:* 705-526-2688
admin@deacontaws.com
www.deacontaws.com

***Midland*: Ferguson Barristers LLP - Midland - *5**
531 King St., Midland, ON L4R 3N6
Tel: 705-526-1471; *Fax:* 705-526-1067
Toll-Free: 800-563-6348
www.fergusonbarristers.ca
www.facebook.com/Ferguson-Barristers-LLP-143074919075604, www.twitter.com/fergusonlaw, www.linkedin.com/company/1712523

***Midland*: HGR Graham Partners LLP - Midland - *34**
Former Name: Hacker Gignac Rice LLP
518 Yonge St., Midland, ON L4R 2C5
Tel: 705-526-2231; *Fax:* 705-526-0313
info@hgrgp.ca
www.hgrgp.ca

***Midland*: Mark Kowalsky - *1**
P.O. Box 280, 8970 County Rd. #93, Midland, ON L4R 4K8
Tel: 705-526-1336; *Fax:* 705-526-8499

***Midland*: Prost Associates - *2**
P.O. Box 96, 323 Midland Ave., Midland, ON L4R 4K6
Tel: 705-526-9328; *Fax:* 705-526-1209
info@prostlaw.com
www.prostlaw.com

***Midland*: John F.L. Rose - *1**
476 Elizabeth St., Midland, ON L4R 1Z8
Tel: 705-527-1235; *Fax:* 705-527-0066
john@johnroselaw.com
www.johnroselaw.com

***Midland*: Wanda L. Warren - *2**
512 Dominion Ave., Midland, ON L4R 1P8
Tel: 705-538-2172; *Fax:* 705-526-3238
Toll-Free: 800-838-8706

***Milton*: Ingrid Hibbard - *1**
440 Harrop Dr., Milton, ON L9T 3H2
Tel: 905-875-3828; *Fax:* 905-875-3829
ihibbard@pelangio.com

***Milton*: Hutchinson, Thompson, Henderson & Mott - *3**
264 Main St. East, Milton, ON L9T 1P2
Tel: 905-878-2841; *Fax:* 905-878-3937
lawoffice@lawmilton.com
lawmilton.com

***Minden*: Donald J. Lange - *1**
Comp. 50, RR#2, Minden, ON K0M 2K0
Tel: 705-489-4974; *Fax:* 705-489-4975
donaldlange@donaldlange.com
www.donaldlange.com

***Mississauga*: Esther O. Abraham Law Office - *1**
#110A, 377 Burnhamthorpe Rd. East, Mississauga, ON L5A 3Y1
Tel: 905-270-3755; *Fax:* 905-270-3844
esther@dlaw.ca
www.dlaw.ca

** indicates number of lawyers*

Mississauga: David A. Aiken - *1
#200, 39 Lake Shore Rd. East, Mississauga, ON L5G 1C9
Tel: 905-602-5230; Fax: 905-871-8507
d.aiken.law@davidaaiken.com

Mississauga: J. Paul Bannon - *1
Former Name: Bannon & Falkeisen
#360, 33 City Centre Dr., Mississauga, ON L5B 2N5
Tel: 905-272-3412; Fax: 905-272-0142
paul@bannonlaw.ca

Mississauga: Richard S. Barrett - *1
1498 Lewisham Dr., Mississauga, ON L5J 3R4
Tel: 905-823-1487; Fax: 905-823-2529
lawyer@rogers.com
www.the-friendly-lawyer.com

Mississauga: N. Bartels - *1
#304, 470 Hensall Circle, Mississauga, ON L5A 1X7
Tel: 905-276-8286; Fax: 905-270-0130
nbartels@sympatico.ca
www.nbartels.com

Mississauga: Paula L. Bateman, Barrister & Solicitor - *2
#C, 6505 Mississauga Rd., Mississauga, ON L5N 1A6
Tel: 905-567-4440; Fax: 905-821-1572

Mississauga: Stephen I. Beck - *1
295 Matheson Blvd. E, Mississauga, ON L4Z 1X8
Tel: 905-568-8351
stephen@becklaw.ca
www.becklaw.ca

Mississauga: Richard T. Bennett - *2
82 Queen St. South., Mississauga, ON L5M 1K6
Tel: 905-826-1453; Fax: 905-826-7185
richard.rtb@sympatico.ca

Mississauga: Bhangal & Virk - *2
295 Derry Rd. West, Mississauga, ON L5W 1G3
Tel: 905-565-0655; Fax: 905-565-0649
asb@criminalcases.ca
www.criminalcases.ca

Mississauga: Eugene J. Bhattacharya - *1
295 Matheson Blvd. East, Mississauga, ON L4Z 1X8
Tel: 905-507-3796; Fax: 905-507-6011

Mississauga: Binsky Whittle - *4
Former Name: The Law Office of Howard Binsky
#200, 2345 Stanfield Rd., Mississauga, ON L4Y 3R3
Tel: 905-270-8811; Fax: 905-270-2977
rec@binskywhittle.com
www.binskywhittle.com

Mississauga: George F. Brant - *1
62 Queen St. S, Mississauga, ON L5M 1K4
Tel: 905-826-2511; Fax: 905-286-1335
gbrant@attglobal.net
www.georgebrant.com

Mississauga: Brian Chan Barrister, Solicitor & Notary Public - *1
#42, 145 Traders Blvd. East, Mississauga, ON L4Z 3L3
Tel: 905-712-2888; Fax: 905-712-3838

Mississauga: Burych Lawyers - *2
#204, 89 Queensway West, Mississauga, ON L5B 2V2
Tel: 905-896-8600; Fax: 905-896-9757
info@burychlawyers.com

Mississauga: Campbell Partners LLP - *6
2624 Dunwin Dr., Mississauga, ON L5L 3T5
Tel: 905-828-2247; Fax: 905-828-4311
info@campbelllawyers.net
www.campbelllawyers.net

Mississauga: Larry R. Plener - *2
Former Name: Larry R. Plener
#300, 2 Robert Speck Pkwy., Mississauga, ON L4Z 1S1
Tel: 905-897-8611; Fax: 905-897-8807
www.willsmart.ca

Mississauga: Carey McCallum & Nimjee - *1
1325 Burnhamthorpe Rd. East, Mississauga, ON L4Y 3V8
Tel: 905-624-1149

Mississauga: J.C. Chapman - *1
2572 Stanfield Rd., Mississauga, ON L4Y 1S2
Tel: 905-270-7034; Fax: 905-270-1001
jcchapman@on.aibn.com

Mississauga: Laurence R. Cutler - *1
Former Name: Cutler/Goldberg LLP
#1201, 90 Burnhamthorpe Rd. West, Mississauga, ON L5B 3C3
Tel: 905-275-6132; Fax: 905-276-2193

Mississauga: Wieslawa Dabrowska - *1
#405, 4310 Sherwoodtowne Blvd., Mississauga, ON L4Z 4C4
Tel: 905-281-0308; Fax: 905-281-3552
viesiad@istar.ca

Mississauga: Douglas M. Davidson - *1
#200, 1552 Dundas St. West, Mississauga, ON L5C 1E4
Tel: 905-279-3330; Fax: 905-279-2735

Mississauga: Day + Borg LLP - *6
Former Name: Day, Michael J.
93 Queen St. South, Mississauga, ON L5M 1K7
Tel: 905-826-5670; Fax: 905-826-5673
www.dayborg.com
www.facebook.com/i3dthemes/, www.twitter.com/i3dthemes/

Mississauga: DeRusha Law Firm - *5
#1, 1015 Matheson Blvd. East, Mississauga, ON L4W 3A4
Tel: 905-625-2874; Fax: 905-625-0614
contact@derushalawfirm.com
www.derushalawfirm.com

Mississauga: DH Professional Corporation, Barristers & Solicitors - *3
Also Known As: Daigle & Hancock
51 Village Centre Pl., Mississauga, ON L4Z 1V9
Tel: 905-273-3339; Fax: 905-273-5672
Toll-Free: 877-273-3339
lawyers@daiglehancock.com
www.mississaugalawyer.com

Mississauga: Eades Law Office - *1
7229 Pacific Circle, Mississauga, ON L5T 1S9
Tel: 905-795-4040; Fax: 905-564-2315

Mississauga: Richard Alan Fellman - *1
#100, 46 Village Centre Pl., Mississauga, ON L4Z 1V9
Tel: 905-275-2231; Fax: 905-275-8323
rfellman@on.aibn.com

Mississauga: Michael J. Fisher - *1
#4, 265 Queen St. South, Mississauga, ON L5M 1L9
Tel: 905-812-9700; Fax: 905-812-0770
mjfisher@globalserve.net

Mississauga: R. Brian Foster Q.C. - *1
92 Lakeshore Rd. East, Mississauga, ON L5G 4S2
Tel: 905-278-2900; Fax: 905-278-8677
info@brianfosterlaw.com
www.brianfosterlaw.com

Mississauga: David A. Fram - *1
810 Meadow Wood Road, Mississauga, ON L5J 2S6
Tel: 905-916-0130; Fax: 905-916-1600

Mississauga: Garvey & Garvey LLP - *3
972 Clarkson Rd. South, Mississauga, ON L5J 2V7
Tel: 905-823-4400; Fax: 905-823-5153

Mississauga: Jean Moenis P. Ghalioungui - *1
#11, 4040 Creditview Rd.., Mississauga, ON L5C 3Y8
Tel: 905-820-4442; Fax: 905-820-4442

Mississauga: Goodman & Griffin - *1
44 Village Centre Place, 3rd Fl., Mississauga, ON L4Z 1V9
Tel: 905-276-5050; Fax: 905-276-8917
Toll-Free: 888-333-3675
realestate@goodgriff.com
www.goodmangriffin.com
twitter.com/goodmangriffin

Mississauga: John L.Z. Gora - *1
893 Beechwood Ave., Mississauga, ON L5G 4E3
Tel: 905-278-7678; Fax: 905-271-5568

Mississauga: Harris & Harris LLP - *8
#300, 2355 Skymark Ave., Mississauga, ON L4W 4Y6
Tel: 905-629-7800; Fax: 905-629-4350
info@harrisandharris.com
www.harrisandharris.com

Mississauga: David L. Hynes - *1
#30, 1100 Central Pkwy. West, Mississauga, ON L5C 4E5
Tel: 905-361-2020; Fax: 905-361-2011
david@davidlhynes.com

Mississauga: William G., Jeffery Law Office - *1
#301, 8 Stavebank Rd. North, Mississauga, ON L5G 2T4
Tel: 905-278-7362; Fax: 905-278-7514

Mississauga: Kain & Ball - *7
#402, Erindale Corporate Centre, 1290 Central Pkwy. West, Mississauga, ON L5C 4R3
Tel: 905-855-4888; Fax: 905-855-3760
contact@kainfamilylaw.com
www.kainfamilylaw.com

Mississauga: John H. Kalina - *1
#210, 1325 Eglinton Ave. East, Mississauga, ON L4W 4L9
Tel: 416-900-6999; Fax: 416-410-5482
hjkalina@lawyer4u.ca
www.lawyer4u.ca

Mississauga: Julian B. Keller - *1
#301, 25 Watline Ave., Mississauga, ON L4Z 2Z1
Tel: 905-890-2211; Fax: 905-890-2246
juliankeller@rogers.com

Mississauga: Sami N. Kerba - *1
1093 Lakeshore Rd. East, Mississauga, ON L5E 1E8
Tel: 905-274-6073; Fax: 905-274-9876
samikerba@nskerba.com

Mississauga: Keyser Mason Ball LLP - *18
Also Known As: KMB Law
#1600, 4 Robert Speck Pkwy., Mississauga, ON L4Z 1S1
Tel: 905-276-9111; Fax: 905-276-2298
info@kmblaw.com
www.kmblaw.com
twitter.com/KeyserMasonBall,
www.linkedin.com/company/349986

Mississauga: Klein Law - *3
#38, 1100 Central Pkwy. West, Mississauga, ON L5C 4E5
Tel: 905-272-2540; Fax: 905-272-2100
contact@kleinlaw.ca
www.kleinlaw.ca

Mississauga: Kostyniuk & Bruggeman - *3
#213, 1515 Matheson Blvd. East, Mississauga, ON L4W 2P5
Tel: 905-602-5551; Fax: 905-602-9775
rkostyniuk@rogers.com

Mississauga: Kozlowski & Company - *1
5065 Foresthill Dr., Mississauga, ON L5M 5A7
Tel: 905-569-9400; Fax: 905-608-9400
Toll-Free: 877-569-9499
info@kozlowskiandcompany.com
www.kozlowskiandcompany.com

Mississauga: Barbara E. LaVieille - *1
#2A, 1325 Burnhamthorpe Rd. East, Mississauga, ON L4Y 2X3
Tel: 905-238-1411; Fax: 905-629-9277
www.lavieillelaw.com

Mississauga: Law Office of Janusz Puzniak - *1
295 Matheson Blvd. East, Mississauga, ON L4Z 1X8
Tel: 905-890-2112; Fax: 905-502-6982
janusz@polskiprawnik.com
www.polskiprawnik.com

Mississauga: Malicki & Malicki - *4
650 Lakeshore Rd. East, Mississauga, ON L5G 1J6
Tel: 905-274-1650; Fax: 905-274-1652
info@malicki-law.ca
www.malicki-law.ca
www.linkedin.com/company/malicki-&-malicki-law-firm

Mississauga: Marks & Ciraco - *2
#205, 120 Traders Blvd. East, Mississauga, ON L4Z 2H7
Tel: 905-712-8300; Fax: 905-712-8559
info@marksandciraco.com
www.marksandciraco.com

Mississauga: Martin C. Schulz - *1
Former Name: Schulz Pereira Fordjour
#500, 201 City Centre Dr., Mississauga, ON L5B 2T4
Tel: 905-897-2200; Fax: 905-897-1517
mschulz@bellnet.ca
www.schulzlaw.ca

Mississauga: Kevin McCallum - *1
1325 Burnhamthorpe Rd. East, Mississauga, ON L4Y 3V8
Tel: 905-624-1149; Fax: 905-624-0522

Mississauga: Cindy McGoldrick - *1
#103, 2691 Credit Valley Rd., Mississauga, ON L5M 7A1
Tel: 905-608-9967; Fax: 905-608-8206
cindy@cindymcgoldrick.com
www.cindymcgoldrick.com

Mississauga: Ronald F. Mossman - *1
#300, 34 Village Centre Pl., Mississauga, ON L4Z 1V9
Tel: 905-848-4020; Fax: 905-848-4026

* indicates number of lawyers

***Mississauga*: Kotak Nainesh - *1**
#120, 120 Traders Blvd. East, Mississauga, ON L4Z 2H7
Tel: 905-755-8900; *Fax:* 905-755-8901
Toll-Free: 877-945-6825
info@kotaklaw.com
www.mississaugapersonalinjurylawyers.ca

***Mississauga*: D.M. Nathwani - *1**
#129, 1250 Mississauga Valley Blvd., Mississauga, ON L5A 3R6
Tel: 905-273-7887

***Mississauga*: R. Geoffrey Newbury - *1**
#106, 150 Lakeshore Rd. West, Mississauga, ON L5H 3R2
Tel: 905-271-9600; *Fax:* 905-271-1638
newbury@mandamus.org

***Mississauga*: Niebler, Liebeck**
1462 Hurontario St., Mississauga, ON L5G 3H4
Tel: 905-271-3232; *Fax:* 905-271-3677
dniebler@nieblerlaw.com
www.nieblerlaw.com

***Mississauga*: O'Connor Zanardo - *2**
#300, 4230 Sherwoodtowne Blvd., Mississauga, ON L4Z 2G6
Tel: 905-896-4370; *Fax:* 905-896-4926
ozlaw.ca

***Mississauga*: O'Marra & Elliott - *2**
#203, 125 Lakeshore Rd. East, Mississauga, ON L5G 1E5
Tel: 905-278-7277; *Fax:* 905-278-5805
omarraelliott.com

***Mississauga*: Ovenden & Ovenden - *2**
#204, 130 Dundas St. East, Mississauga, ON L5A 3V8
Tel: 905-270-8544; *Fax:* 905-273-7386
www.ovendenandovenden.ca

***Mississauga*: Pallett Valo LLP - *29**
#300, West Tower, 77 City Centre Dr., Mississauga, ON L5B 1M5
Tel: 905-273-3300; *Fax:* 905-273-6920
Toll-Free: 800-323-3781
www.pallettvalo.com
www.linkedin.com/company/84491

***Mississauga*: Petrillo Law - *2**
#201, 2600 Skymark Ave., Unit 1, Mississauga, ON L4W 5B2
Tel: 905-949-9433; *Fax:* 905-949-1153
info@petrillolaw.com
www.petrillolaw.com
www.facebook.com/pages/Petrillo-Law/135489526520149, twitter.com/PetrilloLaw

***Mississauga*: Terry D. Richardson - *1**
18 Mississauga Rd. North, Mississauga, ON L5H 2H4
Tel: 905-891-0011; *Fax:* 905-891-1410

***Mississauga*: Ridout & Maybee LLP - *35**
#301, Plaza I, 2000 Argentia Rd., Mississauga, ON L5N 1P7
Tel: 905-363-3054; *Fax:* 905-363-0248
mail@ridoutmaybee.com
www.ridoutmaybee.com
twitter.com/RidoutMaybee, www.linkedin.com/company/45189

***Mississauga*: Roger Foisy Professional Corp. - *1**
#295, Meadowvale Corporate Centre, Plaza 4, 2000 Argentia Rd., Mississauga, ON L5N 1W1
Tel: 905-286-1110; *Fax:* 905-286-4381
Toll-Free: 877-286-0050
info@injurylawyercanada.com
www.injurylawyercanada.com
www.facebook.com/pages/Roger-R-Foisy/418618568158384, twitter.com/InjuryLawyerRRF, www.linkedin.com/company/2260920

***Mississauga*: Jerry Saltzman**
#15, 7205 Goreway Dr., Mississauga, ON L4T 2T9
Tel: 905-671-1178; *Fax:* 905-671-8030
jerry_westwood@hotmail.com

***Mississauga*: Edgar R. Schink - *1**
#405, 130 Dundas St. E, Mississauga, ON L5A 3V8
Tel: 905-270-8882; *Fax:* 905-270-7665
edgarrichards2002@yahoo.ca
www.edgarschink.yp.ca

***Mississauga*: Allan Shulman - *1**
#4, P.O. Box 204, 2225 Erin Mills Pkwy., Mississauga, ON L5K 1T9
Tel: 905-822-3563; *Fax:* 905-822-6342
ashulman@on.aibn.com

***Mississauga*: John F. Silvester - *1**
#544, 33 City Centre Dr., Mississauga, ON L5B 2N5
Tel: 905-275-2588; *Fax:* 905-275-0714
www.johnsilvesterlaw.ca

***Mississauga*: Speigel Nichols Fox LLP - *9**
#400, 30 Eglinton Ave. West, Mississauga, ON L5R 3E7
Tel: 905-366-9700; *Fax:* 905-366-9707
www.ontlaw.com
www.linkedin.com/company/speigel-nichols-fox-llp

***Mississauga*: Harvey A. Swartz - *1**
37 Wanita Rd., Mississauga, ON L5G 1B3
Tel: 416-665-0600; *Fax:* 416-665-2848
harvey@haslawfirm.com

***Mississauga*: Tannahill, Lockhart & Clark Law LLP - *3**
#10, 5805 Whittle Rd., Mississauga, ON L4Z 2J1
Tel: 905-502-5770; *Fax:* 905-502-5009
www.tlcl.ca

***Mississauga*: Thompson, MacColl & Stacy LLP - *8**
#5, 1020 Matheson Blvd. East, Mississauga, ON L4W 4J9
Tel: 905-625-5591; *Fax:* 905-238-3313
www.tmslaw.com

***Mississauga*: Brian M. Watson - *1**
#105, 3034 Palston Rd., Mississauga, ON L4Y 2Z6
Tel: 905-272-0942; *Fax:* 905-272-1682
watsonlaw@sympatico.ca

***Mississauga*: Annette Wilson - *1**
#203, 1325 Eglinton Ave. East, Mississauga, ON L4W 4L9
Tel: 905-602-1989; *Fax:* 905-602-8491

***Mississauga*: Michael Woods - *1**
#203, 120 Traders Blvd. E, Mississauga, ON L4Z 2H7
Tel: 905-568-3810; *Fax:* 905-568-1206
michaelwoods@on.aibn.com

***Mississauga*: Richard M. Woodside - *1**
2479 Burnford Trail, Mississauga, ON L5M 5E4
Tel: 905-567-4562; *Fax:* 905-564-5534
rwoodside@rogers.com

***Mississauga*: Janice E. Younker**
1370 Hurontario St., Mississauga, ON L5G 3H4
Tel: 905-271-2784; *Fax:* 905-271-5960
younkerlaw@rogers.com

***Monotick*: Alan C. Macleod - *1**
P.O. Box 1158, Stn. Main, 5576 Dickinson St., Monotick, ON K4M 1A9
Tel: 613-692-4180; *Fax:* 613-692-0073

***Moosonee*: Keewaytinok Native Legal Services - *2**
P.O. Box 218, 40 Revillon Rd. North, Moosonee, ON P0L 1Y0
Tel: 705-336-2981; *Fax:* 705-336-2577
www.facebook.com/193595124668

***Morrisburg*: Gorrell, Grenkie & Remillard - *2**
Former Name: Gorrell, Grenkie, Leroy & Rémillard
P.O. Box 820, Stn. Morrisburg, 67 Main St., Morrisburg, ON K0C 1X0
Tel: 613-543-2922; *Fax:* 613-543-4228
info@yourlawfirm.ca
www.yourlawfirm.ca

***Morrisburg*: Horner & Pietersma - *3**
Former Name: McInnis, MacEwen & Horner
P.O. Box 733, 777 Main St., Morrisburg, ON K0C 1X0
Tel: 613-543-2946; *Fax:* 613-543-3867

***Mount Albert*: Urquhart, Urquhart, Aiken & Medcof - *1**
P.O. Box 285, Mount Albert, ON L0G 1M0
Tel: 416-595-1111; *Fax:* 416-595-7312
tommax99@yahoo.com

***Mount Forest*: Fallis, Fallis & McMillan - *2**
150 Main St. South, Mount Forest, ON N0G 2L0
Tel: 519-323-2800; *Fax:* 519-323-4115
ffmlaw@wightman.ca
www.ffmlaw.ca

***Mount Forest*: Grant, Deverell & Lemaich LLP - *2**
Former Name: Grant Deverell Lemaich & Barclay
P.O. Box 460, Stn. Mount Forest, 166 Main St. South, Mount Forest, ON N0G 2L0
Tel: 519-323-1600; *Fax:* 519-323-3877
info@northwellington-law.ca
www.northwellington-law.ca

***Napanee*: Chris F. Doreleyers - *2**
P.O. Box 398, Stn. Main, 35 Dundas St. East, Napanee, ON K7R 3P5
Tel: 613-354-3375; *Fax:* 613-354-5641

***Nepean*: Michael G. Carey - *1**
84 Centrepointe Dr., Nepean, ON K2G 6B1
Tel: 613-723-4774; *Fax:* 613-723-2377
careylawoffice@bellnet.ca

***Nepean*: Chiarelli Cramer Witteveen - *4**
Centrepointe Chambers, 92 Centrepointe Dr., Nepean, ON K2G 6B1
Tel: 613-723-9100; *Fax:* 613-723-9105
www.centrepointelaw.com

***Nepean*: Clermont Clausi Gardiner & Associates - *4**
1447 Woodroffe Ave., Nepean, ON K2G 1W1
Tel: 613-225-0037; *Fax:* 613-225-0921
www.ccglawoffice.com

***Nepean*: E. Max Cohen, Q.C. - *1**
24 Kitimat Cres., Nepean, ON K2H 7G5
Tel: 613-828-5855; *Fax:* 613-237-0510

***Nepean*: Kathryn d'Artois - *1**
#100, 104 Centrepointe Dr., Nepean, ON K2G 1B6
Tel: 613-228-9292; *Fax:* 613-228-0005
dartois@dartoismediation.ca
www.dartoismediation.ca

***Nepean*: Pablo Fernandez-Davila - *1**
Also Known As: HC Law
Former Name: Raymond A. Baumgarten
#215, 35 Auriga Dr., Nepean, ON K2E 8B7
Tel: 613-565-8686; *Fax:* 613-565-8989
huntclublaw.com

***Nepean*: Rod A. Vanier - *1**
90 Centrepointe Dr., Nepean, ON K2G 6B1
Tel: 613-226-3336; *Fax:* 613-226-8767
vanier@vanierlaw.on.ca
www.vanierlaw.on.ca

***Nepean*: Stephen A. Ritchie - *1**
92 Centrepointe Dr., Nepean, ON K2G 6B1
Tel: 613-224-6674; *Fax:* 613-723-9105
stephen.ritchie@centrepointelaw.com

***Nepean*: Robin D. MacKay & Associates - *4**
Former Name: MacKay & Sanderson
#201, 1580 Merivale Rd., Nepean, ON K2G 4B5
Tel: 613-238-6180; *Fax:* 613-238-3288
www.robindmackay.com

***New Liskeard*: Ramsay Law Office - *2**
P.O. Box 160, 18 Armstrong St., New Liskeard, ON P0J 1P0
Tel: 705-647-4010; *Fax:* 705-647-4341
Toll-Free: 800-837-6648
ramsaypr@nt.net
www.nt.net/~ramsaypr

***Newcastle*: Michael F. Boland - *1**
P.O. Box 20051, 78 George St. West, Newcastle, ON L1B 1M3
Tel: 905-987-1288; *Fax:* 905-987-1416
mfboland@on.aibn.com

***Newcastle*: Richard J. Mazar Professional Corp. - *2**
115 King Ave. West, Newcastle, ON L1B 1L3
Tel: 905-987-1550; *Fax:* 905-987-1552
mazar@mazarlaw.com
www.mazarlaw.com

***Newcastle*: Valentine Lovekin - *1**
Former Name: Cureatz & Lovekin Law Office
35 King St. West, Newcastle, ON L1B 1H2
Tel: 905-987-3500; *Fax:* 905-987-3503
lovekin@lovekinlaw.com

***Newmarket*: Brown Law Firm - *3**
#21-22, 1228 Gorham St., Newmarket, ON L3Y 8Z1
Tel: 905-853-2529; *Fax:* 905-853-3539
cartwright@brownlawfirm.ca
brownlawfirm.ca

***Newmarket*: Paul H. Caroline - *1**
#300, 16775 Yonge St., Newmarket, ON L3Y 8J4
Tel: 905-836-4018; *Fax:* 905-836-4020

***Newmarket*: Criminal Law Associates - *4**
105 Eagle St., Newmarket, ON L3Y 1J2
Tel: 905-898-2686; *Fax:* 905-898-3957
general@criminallawassociates.ca
www.criminallawassociates.ca

** indicates number of lawyers*

Newmarket: **Epstein & Associates - *8**
71 Main St. South, Newmarket, ON L3Y 3Y5
Tel: 905-898-2266; *Fax:* 905-898-2216
www.epsteinlawyers.com

Newmarket: **GPS Law**
#217, 16775 Yonge St., Newmarket, ON L3Y 8J4
Tel: 905-952-0002; *Fax:* 905-952-0687
Toll-Free: 855-952-0002
admin@gpslaw.ca
www.gpslaw.ca
www.facebook.com/pages/GPS-Law/268397999865931, twitter.com/GPSLaw

Newmarket: **Hill Hunter Losell Law Firm LLP - *7**
#200, P.O. Box 324, Stn. Main, 17360 Yonge St., Newmarket, ON L3Y 4X7
Tel: 905-895-1007; *Fax:* 905-895-4064
www.hillhunterlosell.com

Newmarket: **Neal J. Kearney - *1**
#3, 320 Harry Walker Pkwy. North, Newmarket, ON L3Y 7B4
Tel: 905-898-3012; *Fax:* 905-853-9894
nkearney@kearneylaw.ca

Newmarket: **David Lakie - *1**
105 Eagle St., Newmarket, ON L3Y 1J2
Tel: 905-898-2686; *Fax:* 905-898-3957
davidlakie@rogers.com
www.davidlakie.com

Newmarket: **Debra L. McNairn - *1**
78 Main St. South, Newmarket, ON L3Y 3Y6
Tel: 905-836-1371; *Fax:* 905-898-2050
dmcnairn@mcnairnllb.ca

Newmarket: **Derrick McNamara - *1**
433 Eagle St. E, Newmarket, ON L3Y 1K5
Tel: 905-954-0593; *Fax:* 905-954-1827
dermcnamara@bellnet.ca

Newmarket: **Monteith Baker Johnston & Doodnauth - Professional Corporation - *5**
227 Eagle St. East, Newmarket, ON L3Y 4X1
Tel: 905-895-8600; *Fax:* 905-895-8269
info@monteithbaker.com
www.monteithbaker.com

Newmarket: **Paul E. Montgomery - *1**
#305, 16600 Bayview Ave., Newmarket, ON L3X 1Z9
Tel: 905-836-4018; *Fax:* 905-836-4020
paulmontgomery@rogers.com

Newmarket: **Murphy Law Chambers - *2**
#300, 390 Davis Dr., Newmarket, ON L3Y 7T8
Tel: 905-836-4750; *Fax:* 905-836-6691
info@murphylawchambers.ca
www.murphylawchambers.ca

Newmarket: **Alexander Schneider - *1**
291 Davis Dr., Newmarket, ON L3Y 2N6
Tel: 905-898-1342; *Fax:* 905-898-1344

Newmarket: **Steinberg, Bruce & Paterson - *3**
1091 Gorham St., Newmarket, ON L3Y 8X7
Tel: 905-830-9940; *Fax:* 905-830-9246

Newmarket: **Stiver Vale Barristers and Solicitor - *4**
195 Main St. South, Newmarket, ON L3Y 3Y9
Tel: 905-895-4571; *Fax:* 905-853-2958
www.stivervale.ca

Niagara Falls: **Calvin W. Beresh - *1**
4673 Ontario Ave., Niagara Falls, ON L2E 3R1
Tel: 905-357-5555
info@calvinberesh.com
www.calvinberesh.com

Niagara Falls: **Bev Hodgson Law - *1**
6057 Drummond Rd., Niagara Falls, ON L2G 4M1
Tel: 905-354-1600; *Fax:* 905-354-0171
bevh@bevhodgson.com

Niagara Falls: **Broderick & Partners - *9**
P.O. Box 897, 4625 Ontario Ave., Niagara Falls, ON L2E 6V6
Tel: 905-356-2621; *Fax:* 905-356-6904
www.broderickpartners.com

Niagara Falls: **David P. Czifra - *1**
P.O. Box 868, Stn. Main, 4786 Queen St., Niagara Falls, ON L2E 6V6
Tel: 905-357-6633; *Fax:* 905-357-0736
czifra@vaxxine.com

Niagara Falls: **Charles A. Galloway - *1**
5146 Victoria Ave., Niagara Falls, ON L2E 4E3
Tel: 905-356-2512; *Fax:* 905-356-2513

Niagara Falls: **Margaret A. Hoy - *1**
6617 Drummond Rd., Niagara Falls, ON L2G 4N4
Tel: 905-354-4414; *Fax:* 905-356-7772
hoy@bellnet.ca

Niagara Falls: **D. Ceri Hugill - *1**
6304 Stonefield Park, Niagara Falls, ON L2J 4K1
Tel: 905-353-1790; *Fax:* 905-353-1790
resolver@cogeco.ca

Niagara Falls: **Jaluvka & Sauer Lawyers - *2**
#101, 4701 St. Clair Ave., Niagara Falls, ON L2E 3S9
Tel: 905-356-6484; *Fax:* 905-356-3004
Toll-Free: 877-223-5071
www.jaluvka-sauer-niagara-lawyers.com

Niagara Falls: **Paul N. Krowchuk - *1**
3848 Main St., #A, Niagara Falls, ON L2G 6B2
Tel: 905-295-9995; *Fax:* 905-295-2037
pklaw@bellnet.ca
www.paulkrowchuk.com

Niagara Falls: **Patricia Lucas - *1**
4056 Dorchester Rd., Niagara Falls, ON L2E 6M9
Tel: 905-357-4510; *Fax:* 905-357-9757

Niagara Falls: **Martin Sheppard Fraser LLP - Niagara Falls - *12**
P.O. Box 900, 4701 St. Clair Ave., 2nd Fl., Niagara Falls, ON L2E 6V7
Tel: 289-271-0005; *Fax:* 905-354-5540
Toll-Free: 800-491-0147
www.msflawyers.com

Niagara Falls: **McBurney Durdan Henderson & Corbett - *4**
P.O. Box 177, 4759 Queen St., Niagara Falls, ON L2E 2M1
Tel: 905-356-4511
info@mdhclaw.com
www.mdhclaw.com/en/

Niagara Falls: **Daniel J. McDonald - *1**
Former Name: Knight, S. James, Q.C.
P.O. Box 726, 4683 Queen St., Niagara Falls, ON L2E 2L9
Tel: 905-356-1524; *Fax:* 905-357-9686

Niagara Falls: **Daniel J. McDonald - *1**
P.O. Box 726, Stn. Main, 4683 Queen St., Niagara Falls, ON L2E 6V5
Tel: 905-356-1524; *Fax:* 905-357-9686
danielmcdonald@bellnet.ca

Niagara Falls: **McKay & Heath - *2**
#102, 4701 St. Clair Ave., Niagara Falls, ON L2E 3S9
Tel: 905-357-0660; *Fax:* 905-357-5680
mckayandheathlaw.yolasite.com

Niagara Falls: **Gordon F. McNab, Q.C. - *1**
4056 Dorchester Rd., Niagara Falls, ON L2E 6M9
Tel: 905-357-4510; *Fax:* 905-357-9757
mcnablucas@on.aibn.com

Niagara Falls: **Sharpe, Beresh & Gnys - *4**
Elgin Block, 4673 Ontario Ave., 3rd Fl., Niagara Falls, ON L2E 3R1
Tel: 289-438-2127; *Fax:* 905-357-5760
sharpe@sharpelawyers.ca
www.sharplawyers.calls.net

Niagara Falls: **Brian N. Sinclair, Q.C. - *3**
6617 Drummond Rd., Niagara Falls, ON L2G 4N4
Tel: 905-356-7755
brian@briansinclair.com
www.briansinclair.com

Niagara Falls: **William Slovak, Q.C. - *1**
5627 Main St., Niagara Falls, ON L2G 5Z3
Tel: 905-374-6000; *Fax:* 905-374-9410
Toll-Free: 877-231-0011
mjs5627@hotmail.com

Niagara Falls: **Malcolm A.F. Stockton - *1**
P.O. Box 868, Stn. Main, 4786 Queen St., Niagara Falls, ON L2E 6V6
Tel: 905-357-3500; *Fax:* 905-356-3635
stockton@iaw.com

Niagara Falls: **Brian C. Wilcox - *1**
#118, 6150 Valley Way, Niagara Falls, ON L2E 1Y3
Tel: 905-358-0782; *Fax:* 905-356-7772
Toll-Free: 877-220-7211
office@bcwlawoffice.com
www.bcwlawoffice.com

Niagara South: **Wilson, Opatovsky - *2**
P.O. Box 99, Stn. Main, 190 Elm St., Niagara South, ON L3K 5V7
Tel: 905-835-1163; *Fax:* 905-835-2171
Toll-Free: 888-288-8338
cwilson@wilsonop.com

Niagara on the Lake: **Richard J.W. Andrews - *1**
#202, 111B Garrison Village Dr., Niagara on the Lake, ON L0S 1J0
Tel: 905-468-0081; *Fax:* 905-468-0087
rjwandrews@bellnet.ca
rjwandrews.ca

North Bay: **Bowness & Murray - *2**
P.O. Box 327, 348 Fraser St., North Bay, ON P1B 3W7
Tel: 705-474-9680; *Fax:* 705-474-4218
info@bownessandmurray.ca
bownessandmurray.ca

North Bay: **Clements Eggerts Professional Corporation - *1**
Former Name: Tafel, Trussler & Eggert
477 Sherbrooke St., North Bay, ON P1B 2C2
Tel: 705-472-4890; *Fax:* 705-472-9612
info@northbaylaw.com
www.northbaylaw.com

North Bay: **Colvin & Colvin Professional Corporation - *2**
P.O. Box 657, Stn. Main, 577 Main St. West, North Bay, ON P1B 8J5
Tel: 705-476-5161; *Fax:* 705-476-9902
Toll-Free: 877-268-8566
colvinlaw@cogeco.net

North Bay: **M. Lucie Laperriere - *1**
325 Ski Club Rd., North Bay, ON P1B 7R3
Tel: 705-495-8554; *Fax:* 705-495-6274
advice@northbaylawyer.ca

North Bay: **Larmer Stickland - *2**
Former Name: Larmer & Larmer Barristers
#401, 101 Worthington St. East, North Bay, ON P1B 1G5
Tel: 705-478-8200; *Fax:* 705-478-8100
Toll-Free: 888-947-2746
info@larmerstickland.com
www.larmerstickland.com

North Bay: **Lucenti, Orlando & Ellies Professional Corporation - *4**
#2nd Fl., 373 Main St. West, North Bay, ON P1B 2T9
Tel: 705-472-9500; *Fax:* 705-472-4814

North Bay: **James R. McIntosh - *1**
325 Main St. West, North Bay, ON P1B 2T9
Tel: 705-476-2500; *Fax:* 705-476-9347
maclaw@efni.com

North Bay: **McLachlan Froud & Rochon LLP - *3**
#202, 373 Main St. West, North Bay, ON P1B 2T9
Tel: 705-476-6333; *Fax:* 705-476-4397

North Bay: **Joe Sinicrope - *1**
495 Main St. West, North Bay, ON P1B 2V3
Tel: 705-495-1334; *Fax:* 705-495-7990
joesinicrope@neilnet.com

North Bay: **Wallace Klein Partners in Law LLP - *9**
P.O. Box 37, 225 McIntyre St. West, North Bay, ON P1B 8G8
Tel: 705-474-2920; *Fax:* 705-474-1758
info@partnersinlaw.net
www.partnersinlaw.net

Oakville: **John G. Cox - *1**
297 Church St., Oakville, ON L6J 1N9
Tel: 905-844-5600; *Fax:* 905-844-9100
www.jgcoxfamilylaw.com

Oakville: **Diane F. Daly - *1**
#301, 165 Cross Ave., Oakville, ON L6J 0A9
Tel: 905-844-5883; *Fax:* 905-844-9765
dianedaly@dalylaw.ca
www.oakvillelaw.ca

** indicates number of lawyers*

***Oakville*: Fabio Gazzola, Barrister, Solicitor & Notary - *1**
233 Robinson St., Oakville, ON L6J 1G5
Tel: 905-842-8600; *Fax:* 905-842-4774
gazzolaf@bellnet.ca
www.fabiogazzola.com

***Oakville*: Harrington LLP - *3**
#101, 2275 Upper Middle Rd. East, Oakville, ON L6H OC3
Fax: 888-829-5396
Toll-Free: 888-492-0336
help@harringtonllp.com
www.harringtonllp.com

***Oakville*: Stuart W. Henderson - *1**
228 Lakeshore Rd. East, Oakville, ON L6J 1H8
Tel: 905-844-3218; *Fax:* 905-844-3699
swhenderson@on.aibn.com

***Oakville*: Stuart W. Henderson - *1**
P.O. Box 249, 228 Lakeshore Rd. East, Oakville, ON L6J 5A2
Tel: 905-844-3218; *Fax:* 905-844-3699
jbg@quixnet.net

***Oakville*: Law Offices of Charles W. Pley - *1**
#102, 2660 Sherwood Heights Dr., Oakville, ON L6J 7Y8
Tel: 905-829-3888; *Fax:* 905-829-2100
info@pleylaw.com
www.pleylaw.com

***Oakville*: Lush, Bowker, Aird - *4**
P.O. Box 734, 261 Lakeshore Rd. East, Oakville, ON L6J 1H9
Tel: 905-844-0381; *Fax:* 905-849-4540
Toll-Free: 877-844-0381
info@scottaird.com
www.scottaird.com

***Oakville*: Thomas H. Marshall, Q.C., Barristers & Solicitors - *4**
#205, 1540 Cornwall Rd., Oakville, ON L6J 7W5
Tel: 905-844-0464; *Fax:* 905-844-3983
sanderson@oakvillefamilylawyer.ca
www.oakvillefamilylawyer.ca

***Oakville*: Terri L. McCarthy - *1**
#3A, 418 North Service Rd. East, Oakville, ON L6H 5R2
Tel: 905-842-4223; *Fax:* 905-842-7401
tlm.law@on.aibn.com

***Oakville*: David L. McKenzie - *1**
P.O. Box 906, Stn. Main, Oakville, ON L6J 5E8
Tel: 905-845-7591; *Fax:* 905-845-8876

***Oakville*: Keith D. Nelson - *1**
#205, North (Rear) Entrance, 243 North Service Rd. West, Oakville, ON L6M 3E5
Tel: 905-338-8481; *Fax:* 905-338-0748
kdnelson@nelsonlawyer.com
www.nelsonlawyer.com

***Oakville*: O'Connor MacLeod Hanna LLP - *17**
#300, 700 Kerr St., Oakville, ON L6K 3W5
Tel: 905-842-8030; *Fax:* 905-842-2460
info@omh.ca
www.omh.ca

***Oakville*: P. William Perras, Jr. - *2**
#210, 1540 Cornwall Rd., Oakville, ON L6J 7W5
Tel: 905-827-2700; *Fax:* 905-827-2766
billperras@on.aibn.com

***Oakville*: David J. Pilo - *1**
#301, 88 Dunn St., Oakville, ON L6J 3C7
Tel: 905-338-2002; *Fax:* 905-338-3810
dpilo@on.aibn.com

***Oakville*: Richard Day Law - *1**
164 Trafalgar Rd., Oakville, ON L6J 3G6
Tel: 905-844-8581; *Fax:* 905-842-6166
rick@daylaw.ca
www.daylaw.ca

***Oakville*: Martin A. Shanahan - *1**
#200, 2620 Bristol Circle, Oakville, ON L6H 6Z7
Tel: 905-829-2700

***Oakville*: Sweatman Law Firm - *3**
#11, 1400 Cornwall Rd., Oakville, ON L6J 7W5
Fax: 905-337-3309
Toll-Free: 888-389-2165
www.sweatmanlaw.com
www.facebook.com/profile.php?id=547341131973798,
www.linkedin.com/company/3192424

***Oakville*: Karen Thompson Law - *1**
#301, 165 Cross Ave., Oakville, ON L6J 0A9
Tel: 905-338-7941; *Fax:* 905-844-9765
karens@karenthompsonlaw.ca
www.karenthompsonlaw.ca

***Oakville*: Helen M. Thomson - *1**
#1160, 1011 Upper Middle Rd. East, Oakville, ON L6H 5Z9
Tel: 416-410-8895; *Fax:* 416-410-8895

***Oakville*: Townsend & Associates - *3**
Also Known As: Lynn Townend
Former Name: Townsend Renaud, Lynda J.
#10, 1525 Cornwall Rd., Oakville, ON L6J 0B2
Tel: 905-829-8600; *Fax:* 905-829-2035
lyn.townsend@ltownsend.ca

***Oakville*: William B. Kerr, Barrister & Solicitor - *1**
Former Name: Ryrie, Kerr, Davidson
233 Robinson St., Oakville, ON L6J 1G5
Tel: 905-842-8600; *Fax:* 905-842-4774

***Ohsweken*: Bucci Law Office - *2**
P.O. Box 819, 1721 Chiefswood Rd., Ohsweken, ON N0A 1M0
Tel: 519-751-0494; *Fax:* 519-751-1342
timbucci@buccilawoffice.net
www.buccilawoffice.net

***Orangeville*: Parkinson & Parkinson Associates - *1**
145 Broadway St., Orangeville, ON L9W 1K2
Toll-Free: 800-831-8106
parkinson@parkinsonparkinson.ca
www.parkinsonparkinson.ca

***Orangeville*: Patricia L. Sproule Ward Law Office - *1**
Former Name: Mullin, Thwaites, Ward LLP
P.O. Box 67, 30 Mill St., Orangeville, ON L9W 2M3
Tel: 519-941-4559; *Fax:* 519-941-4806
www.pswardlawoffice.ca

***Orangeville*: Anne Welwood - *1**
14 Zina St., Orangeville, ON L9W 1E1
Tel: 519-941-9710; *Fax:* 519-941-9244
Toll-Free: 800-919-4919
www.annewelwood.com

***Orangeville*: Stephen F. White, Barrister & Solicitor - *1**
30 Mill St., Orangeville, ON L9W 2M3
Tel: 519-941-9440; *Fax:* 519-941-3803
info@whitelaw.pro
www.whitelaw.pro

***Orillia*: Crawford McLean Anderson LLP - *2**
P.O. Box 520, 40 Coldwater St. East, Orillia, ON L3V 6K4
Tel: 705-325-2753; *Fax:* 705-325-4913
wmclean@mclaw.ca
www.mclaw.ca

***Orillia*: Brian D. Kinnear - *1**
#108, P.O. Box 656, 17 Colborne St. East, Orillia, ON L3V 6K7
Tel: 705-323-9386; *Fax:* 705-323-9388
bkinnearlaw@on.aibn.com
www.briankinnearlaw.ca

***Orillia*: Lisa Welch Madden Law Firm - *1**
Former Name: Bourne, Jenkins & Mulligan
#102, 32 Matchedash St. N, Orillia, ON L3V 4T5
Tel: 705-325-6439; *Fax:* 705-325-7058
madden@lwmlaw.com

***Orillia*: Allan C. Parslow - *1**
212 John St., Orillia, ON L3V 3H7
Tel: 705-329-2223; *Fax:* 705-329-0433

***Orillia*: Russell, Christie LLP - *7**
P.O. Box 158, 505 Memorial Ave., Orillia, ON L3V 6J3
Tel: 705-325-1326; *Fax:* 705-327-1811
rcmkw@russellchristie.com
www.russellchristie.com

***Orleans*: Galarneau & Associates Professional Corp. - *4**
2831 St. Joseph Blvd., Orleans, ON K1C 1G6
Tel: 613-830-7111; *Fax:* 613-830-7108
bjg@galarneauassoc.com
www.galarneauassoc.com

***Orleans*: Marc Nadon - *1**
#101, 3009 St. Joseph Blvd., Orleans, ON K1E 1E1
Tel: 613-837-4437; *Fax:* 613-837-4204
info@marcnadon.ca

***Orleans*: Sicotte Guilbault LLP - *12**
Former Name: Sicotte & Associates
4275 Innes Rd., 2nd Fl., Orleans, ON K1C 1T1
Tel: 613-837-7408; *Fax:* 613-837-8015
info@sicotte.ca
www.sicotte.ca

***Orléans*: Dust Evans Grandmaitre Professional Corporation - *5**
2589 St. Joseph Blvd., Orléans, ON K1C 1G4
Tel: 613-837-1010; *Fax:* 613-837-9670
Toll-Free: 800-379-6668
info@dustevans.com
www.dustevans.com
www.facebook.com/dustevansgrandmaitre

***Orléans*: Jacques Robert - *2**
2788, boul St-Joseph, Orléans, ON K1C 1G5
Tel: 613-837-7880; *Fax:* 613-837-7664
mail@jacquesrobert.com
www.jacquesrobert.com

***Orono*: W. Kay Lycett, Q.C. - *1**
P.O. Box 87, 5301 Main St., Orono, ON L0B 1M0
Tel: 905-983-5007; *Fax:* 905-983-9022
wklycett@look.ca

***Oshawa*: Aleksandr G. Bolotenko - *1**
P.O. Box 978, 225 King St. East, Oshawa, ON L1H 7H2
Tel: 905-433-1176; *Fax:* 905-433-0283
abolotenko@agblaw.com
www.agblaw.com

***Oshawa*: Boychyn & Boychyn - *1**
#1E, 57 Simcoe St. South, Oshawa, ON L1H 4G4
Tel: 905-576-2670; *Fax:* 905-576-0915

***Oshawa*: Julie Clark - *1**
P.O. Box 365, Stn. A, 32 Elgin St. East, Oshawa, ON L1H 7L5
Tel: 905-434-6411; *Fax:* 905-571-6114

***Oshawa*: Catherine Cornwall-Taylor - *1**
32 Elgin St. East, Oshawa, ON L1J 1T1
Tel: 905-434-6411; *Fax:* 905-571-6114

***Oshawa*: Creighton Victor Alexander Hayward Morison & Hall LLP - *5**
Also Known As: The Creighton Law Firm
Former Name: Hayward Morrison & Hall LLP
P.O. Box 26010, 235 King St. East, Oshawa, ON L1H 8R4
Tel: 905-723-3446; *Fax:* 905-432-2323
inquire@durhamlawyers.ca
www.durhamlawyers.ca

***Oshawa*: Diamond, Fischman & Pushman - *3**
P.O. Box 26008, Stn. 206, 179 King St. East, Oshawa, ON L1H 8R4
Tel: 905-723-5243; *Fax:* 905-436-6041
scott@dfplaw.com
www.dfplaw.com

***Oshawa*: Elliott & Hills - *2**
106 Stevenson Rd. South, Oshawa, ON L1J 5M1
Tel: 905-571-1774; *Fax:* 905-571-7706
Toll-Free: 877-272-5220
www.elliottandhills.com

***Oshawa*: Diane M. England - *1**
167 Simcoe St. North, Oshawa, ON L1G 4S8
Tel: 905-721-1277; *Fax:* 905-721-1217
mail@dianeengland.com
www.dianeengland.com

***Oshawa*: Farquharson, Adamson & Affleck LLP - *3**
201 Bond St. East, Oshawa, ON L1G 1B4
Tel: 905-404-1947; *Fax:* 905-404-9050
inquires@criminallawoshawa.com
www.criminallawoshawa.com

***Oshawa*: Shan K. Jain, Q.C. - *1**
#2, 215 Simcoe St. North, Oshawa, ON L1G 4T1
Tel: 905-432-7787; *Fax:* 905-432-2343
jainc@sprint.ca

***Oshawa*: Kelly Greenway Bruce - *8**
Former Name: Kelly, Greenway, Bruce, Korb
114 King St. East, Oshawa, ON L1H 7N1
Tel: 905-723-2278; *Fax:* 905-432-2663
mail@oshawalawyers.com
www.oshawalawyers.com

** indicates number of lawyers*

***Oshawa*: Kitchen Legal - *1**
P.O. Box 82, 95 Simcoe St. South, Oshawa, ON L1H 7K8
Tel: 905-436-8787; *Fax:* 905-721-0868
rkitchen@kitchenlegal.ca
www.kitchenlegal.ca

***Oshawa*: Kitchen Simeson Belliveau LLP - *3**
Former Name: Kitchen Simeson LLP
P.O. Box 428, 86 Simcoe St. South, Oshawa, ON L1H 7L5
Tel: 905-579-5302; *Fax:* 905-579-6073
Toll-Free: 888-669-6446
kslawfirm.ca
www.facebook.com/KitchenSimesonBelliveauLLP

***Oshawa*: Laskowsky & Laskowsky - *1**
73 Centre St. South, Oshawa, ON L1H 4A1
Tel: 905-579-0777; *Fax:* 905-576-9918

***Oshawa*: Mack Lawyers - *3**
Former Name: Mack, Kisbee & Greer
146 Simcoe St. North, Oshawa, ON L1G 4S7
Tel: 905-571-1405
www.macklawyers.ca

***Oshawa*: Elaine M. Forbes McCallum - *1**
174 Athol St. East, Oshawa, ON L1H 1K1
Tel: 905-579-8866; *Fax:* 905-579-8913
Toll-Free: 888-579-5252
elainemfmccallum@on.aibn.com

***Oshawa*: Sharon A. Moote - *1**
Former Name: Moote & Cocchetto
#210, 200 Bond St. West, Oshawa, ON L1J 2L7
Tel: 905-432-7880; *Fax:* 905-432-7674

***Oshawa*: Neal & Mara Barristers & Solicitors - *2**
142 Simcoe St. North, Oshawa, ON L1G 4S7
Tel: 905-436-9015; *Fax:* 905-436-6098

***Oshawa*: Josef Neubauer - *1**
106 Stevenson Rd. South, Oshawa, ON L1J 5M1
Tel: 905-433-1991; *Fax:* 905-433-7038
neubauer@bellnet.ca
www.josefneubauer.com

***Oshawa*: O'Brien, Balka & Elrick, Barristers & Solicitors - *6**
219 King St. East, Oshawa, ON L1H 1C5
Tel: 905-576-3402; *Fax:* 905-576-3915
Toll-Free: 866-245-5063
obe@oshawalaw.com
www.oshawalaw.com

***Oshawa*: Margot Poepjes - *1**
#217, 650 King St. East, Oshawa, ON L1H 1G5
Tel: 905-433-4020; *Fax:* 905-433-7028
mpoepjeslawoffice@rogers.com

***Oshawa*: Catherine L. Salmers - *1**
#101, McLaughlin Square, 55 William St. East, Oshawa, ON L1G 7C9
Tel: 905-723-1101; *Fax:* 905-723-1157
csalmers@ssf-oshawa.com
www.salmerslawoffices.com

***Oshawa*: Scott & Olver LLP - *3**
Former Name: Scott, Kimball, Olver
39 Bond St. East, Oshawa, ON L1G 1B2
Tel: 905-579-9400; *Fax:* 905-579-7400
scottolver@scottandolver.ca
scottandolver.ca

***Oshawa*: Sosna & Burch - *3**
#8, 500 King St. West, Oshawa, ON L1J 2K9
Tel: 905-668-6811; *Fax:* 905-668-6899
sosna-burch@sosnaburch.com

***Oshawa*: Frank H.M. Stolwyk - *1**
57 Simcoe St. South, Unit 1-F, Oshawa, ON L1H 4G4
Tel: 905-576-8100; *Fax:* 905-579-6762
franks4950@aol.com

***Oshawa*: Strike Furlong Ford - *6**
Former Name: Salmers, Strike & Furlong
P.O. Box 486, Stn. A, 282 King St. East, Oshawa, ON L1H 1C8
Tel: 905-448-4800; *Fax:* 905-448-4801
sff-law.ca

***Oshawa*: David B. Thomas - *1**
28B Albert St., Oshawa, ON L1H 8S5
Tel: 905-576-5666; *Fax:* 905-576-5289

***Oshawa*: The Law Office of Martin Tweyman - *3**
#101, 19 Celina St., Oshawa, ON L1H 4M9
Tel: 905-571-1500; *Fax:* 905-571-7528
www.tweymanlaw.com

***Oshawa*: Walters, Dizenbach, Ferguson - *3**
P.O. Box 2307, 218 Centre St. N, Oshawa, ON L1B 1H3
Tel: 905-579-1066

***Oshawa*: Ronald F. Worboy - *1**
153 Simcoe St. North, Oshawa, ON L1G 4S6
Tel: 905-723-2288; *Fax:* 905-576-1355

***Oshawa*: Yanch & Yanch - *1**
#1D, P.O. Box 154, 57 Simcoe St. South, Oshawa, ON L1H 7L1
Tel: 905-728-9495; *Fax:* 905-721-8044
yanchfirm@hotmail.com
yanchlawoffice.com

***Ottawa*: Douglas R. Adams - *1**
#1502, 222 Queen St., Ottawa, ON K1P 5V9
Tel: 613-238-8076; *Fax:* 613-238-5519

***Ottawa*: Addelman, Baum & Gilbert LLP - *4**
Former Name: Baum, Douglas M.
#800, 85 Albert St., Ottawa, ON K1P 6A4
Tel: 613-237-2673; *Fax:* 613-237-8146
Richard.Addelman@addelmanbaumgilbert.com
www.addelmanbaumgilbert.com

***Ottawa*: Ahmad-Yousuf & Assoc. - *3**
Former Name: Moore & Ahmad-Yousuf
#100, 180 Metcalfe St., Ottawa, ON K2P 1P5
Tel: 613-236-1111; *Fax:* 613-232-7763

***Ottawa*: Aitken Klee LLP - *15**
#300, 100 Queen St., Ottawa, ON K1P 1J9
Tel: 613-695-5858; *Fax:* 613-695-5854
info@aitkenklee.com
www.aitkenklee.com

***Ottawa*: Allan & Snelling LLP, Barristers & Solicitors - *7**
#104, Stealth Building, 303 Terry Fox Dr., Ottawa, ON K2K 3J1
Tel: 613-270-8600; *Fax:* 613-270-0900
info@compellingcounsel.com
www.compellingcounsel.com

***Ottawa*: Anders, Young, Strong & Jonah - *4**
Former Name: Anders, Young & Jonah
#401, 1580 Merivale Rd., Ottawa, ON K2G 4B5
Tel: 613-224-1621; *Fax:* 613-224-8827
info@aysj-law.com
www.aysj-law.com

***Ottawa*: Andrews Robichaud - *7**
#500, 1306 Wellington St., Ottawa, ON K1Y 3B2
Tel: 613-237-1512; *Fax:* 613-237-9580
info@andrewsrobichaud.com
www.andrewsrobichaud.com

***Ottawa*: Arbique & Ahde - *2**
Former Name: Fortey & Arbique
#210, 1335 Carling Ave., Ottawa, ON K1Z 8N8
Tel: 613-725-0303; *Fax:* 613-725-1292
info@forteyarbique.com
www.arbiqueahde.com
twitter.com/ArbiqueAhde,

***Ottawa*: Augustine Bater Binks LLP - *8**
#1100, 141 Laurier Ave. West, Ottawa, ON K1P 5J3
Tel: 613-569-9500; *Fax:* 613-569-9522
info@abblaw.ca
www.abblaw.ca
twitter.com/abblaw,
ca.linkedin.com/company/augustine-bater-binks-llp

***Ottawa*: Robert G. Bales - *1**
1041 Harkness Ave., Ottawa, ON K1V 6N9
Tel: 613-731-2129; *Fax:* 613-248-5151
rob.bales@adjudicate.ca

***Ottawa*: Barnes Barristers - *3**
#500, 200 Elgin St., Ottawa, ON K2P 1L5
Tel: 613-225-2529; *Fax:* 613-225-3930
barnesgary@rogers.com
www.barnesbarristers.com

***Ottawa*: Barnes, Sammon LLP - *15**
#400, 200 Elgin St., Ottawa, ON K2P 1L5
Tel: 613-594-8000; *Fax:* 613-235-7578
www.barnessammon.ca

***Ottawa*: Beament Green - *7**
979 Wellington St. West, Ottawa, ON K1Y 2X7
Tel: 613-241-3400; *Fax:* 613-241-8555
www.beament.com

***Ottawa*: Bell Baker LLP - *11**
#700, 116 Lisgar St., Ottawa, ON K2P 0C2
Tel: 613-237-3444; *Fax:* 613-237-1413
info@bellbaker.com
www.bellbaker.com

***Ottawa*: Bell, Unger, Riley, Morris - *4**
24 Bayswater Ave., Ottawa, ON K1Y 2E4
Tel: 613-235-1266; *Fax:* 613-230-2727

***Ottawa*: John E. Bogue - *1**
#802, 200 Elgin St., Ottawa, ON K2P 1L5
Tel: 613-234-4901; *Fax:* 613-236-8906

***Ottawa*: Bosada & Associates - *1**
#222, 280 Metcalfe St., Ottawa, ON K2P 1R7
Tel: 613-563-1001; *Fax:* 613-563-1031
richard@bosada.ca

***Ottawa*: Bradley, Hiscock, McCracken - *5**
Former Name: Bradley, Hiscock
1581 Greenbank Rd., Ottawa, ON K2J 4Y6
Tel: 613-825-4585; *Fax:* 613-825-5101
infow@bhlaw.ca
www.bhmlaw.ca

***Ottawa*: Alan Brass - *1**
#1002, 200 Elgin St., Ottawa, ON K2P 1L5
Tel: 613-238-5757; *Fax:* 613-688-1212
abrass@alanbrass.ca
www.alanbrass.ca

***Ottawa*: BrazeauSeller LLP - *18**
#750, 55 Metcalfe St., Ottawa, ON K1P 6L5
Tel: 613-237-4000; *Fax:* 613-237-4001
www.brazeauseller.com
www.facebook.com/BrazeauSeller, twitter.com/BrazeauSeller,
www.linkedin.com/company/brazeauseller.llp

***Ottawa*: C.P. Brett - *1**
70 Gloucester St., Ottawa, ON K2P 0A2
Tel: 613-230-2907; *Fax:* 613-235-4430
cpbrett@attglobal.net

***Ottawa*: Thomas W. Brooker - *1**
#208, 1400 Clyde Ave., Ottawa, ON K2G 3J2
Tel: 613-226-3265; *Fax:* 613-224-8943
tom@brookerlawoffice.ca
www.brookerlawoffice.ca

***Ottawa*: Bulger, Young - *3**
1493 Merivale Rd., Lower Level, Ottawa, ON K2E 5P3
Tel: 613-728-5881; *Fax:* 613-728-6158

***Ottawa*: Donald J. Byrne - *1**
#204, 1568 Carling Ave., Ottawa, ON K1Z 7M4
Tel: 613-722-5292; *Fax:* 613-729-6732
dbyrne@primus.ca

***Ottawa*: Callan Honeywell LLP - *2**
418 Preston St., Ottawa, ON K1S 4N2
Tel: 613-729-2460; *Fax:* 613-729-1710
www.callanhoneywell.ca
ca.linkedin.com/in/williamhoneywell

***Ottawa*: Campbell Clark Yemensky - *4**
Former Name: Mount Clark Yemensky
#208, 1400 Clyde Ave., Ottawa, ON K2G 3J2
Tel: 613-727-9698; *Fax:* 613-224-8943
gyemensky@familylaw-ottawa.ca
familylaw-ottawa.ca

***Ottawa*: Capelle Kane Professional Corporation - *3**
#300, 311 Richmond Rd., Ottawa, ON K1Z 6X3
Tel: 613-230-7070; *Fax:* 613-230-9444
contact@capellekane.com
www.capellekane.com

***Ottawa*: Diana Carr - *2**
#601, 225 Metcalfe St., Ottawa, ON K2P 1P9
Tel: 613-567-1431
info@dianacarrlawyer.com
www.parentcarrlawyers.com

***Ottawa*: Carroll & Wallace - *3**
#502, 66 Slater St., Ottawa, ON K1P 5H1
Tel: 613-236-5494; *Fax:* 613-232-7322

** indicates number of lawyers*

***Ottawa*: Edward Y.W. Cheung - *1**
#22, 5340 Canotek Rd., Ottawa, ON K1J 9C8
Tel: 613-748-9898; *Fax:* 613-748-1114
yw61@aol.com

***Ottawa*: Paul-Emile Chiasson - *1**
18 Nepean St., Ottawa, ON K2P 2L2
Tel: 613-230-8800; *Fax:* 613-236-3136
pechiasson@sympatico.ca

***Ottawa*: Conlin & Payette - *4**
Former Name: Conlin & McAlpin
#305, 1719 Bank St., Ottawa, ON K1V 7Z4
Tel: 613-737-4140; *Fax:* 613-737-7903
info@conlinpayette.com
www.conlinpayette.com/en/

***Ottawa*: Connolly Obagi LLP - *7**
Former Name: Cooligan/Ryan LLP
#1100, 200 Elgin St., Ottawa, ON K2P 1L5
Tel: 613-567-4412; *Fax:* 613-567-9751
Toll-Free: 855-683-2240
info@connollyobagi.com
www.connollyobagi.com

***Ottawa*: Law Office of Rosalind E. Conway - *2**
#320, 185 Somerset St. West, Ottawa, ON K2P 0J2
Tel: 613-594-0300; *Fax:* 613-594-8111
rosalind.conway@gmail.com
www.rosalindconway.com
www.facebook.com/pages/Law-Office-of-Rosalind-E-Conway

***Ottawa*: Delaney's Law Firm - *4**
352 Elgin St., 2nd Fl., Ottawa, ON K2P 1M8
Tel: 613-233-7000; *Fax:* 866-846-4191
info@delaneys.ca
www.delaneys.ca
www.facebook.com/pages/Delaneys-Law-Firm/120319207930?v=info

***Ottawa*: DioGuardi Tax Law - *3**
#600, 100 Gloucester St., Ottawa, ON K2P 0A4
Tel: 613-237-2222; *Fax:* 613-237-9463
Toll-Free: 877-829-7902
www.taxamnesty.ca
www.facebook.com/pages/DioGuardi-Tax/105831712772926, www.twitter.com/dioguarditax

***Ottawa*: Donald R. Good & Associates - *3**
#207, 43 Roydon Pl., Ottawa, ON K2E 1A3
Tel: 613-228-9676; *Fax:* 613-228-7404
farmlaw@on.aibn.com

***Ottawa*: Drache Aptowitzer LLP - *5**
226 Maclaren St., Ottawa, ON K2P 0L6
Tel: 613-237-3300; *Fax:* 613-237-2786
adamapt@drache.ca
www.drache.ca
twitter.com/charitytax

***Ottawa*: Dubuc-Osland - *4**
#204, Fitzsimmons Building, 265 Carling Ave., Ottawa, ON K1S 2E1
Tel: 613-236-3360; *Fax:* 613-236-3771
dubucosland.com

***Ottawa*: Daniel F. Dunlap - *1**
Stn. B, 111 Sherwood Dr,, Ottawa, ON K1Y 3V1
Tel: 613-722-7788; *Fax:* 613-722-8909
ddunlap@dunlaplaw.ca

***Ottawa*: Edelson Clifford D'Angelo Barristers LLP - *7**
#600, 200 Elgin St., Ottawa, ON K2P 1L5
Tel: 613-237-2290; *Fax:* 613-237-0071
mail@edelsonlaw.ca
www.edelsonlaw.ca

***Ottawa*: Emond Harnden SRL/LLP - *28**
707 Bank St., Ottawa, ON K1S 3V1
Tel: 613-563-7660; *Fax:* 613-563-8001
info@ehlaw.ca
www.ehlaw.ca

***Ottawa*: Engel & Associates - *2**
#210, 116 Lisgar St., Ottawa, ON K2P 0C2
Tel: 613-909-8152; *Fax:* 613-235-3159
www.bruceengel.com

***Ottawa*: Fanaian Law Office - *1**
30 Staten Way, Ottawa, ON K2C 4E5
Tel: 613-567-0833; *Fax:* 613-567-9549
fanaian@hotmail.com
fan.shojaei.us

***Ottawa*: Farber & Robillard - *3**
330 Churchill Ave. North, Ottawa, ON K1Z 5B9
Tel: 613-722-9418; *Fax:* 613-722-5981
www.frllplaw.com

***Ottawa*: Finlayson & Singlehurst - *6**
#700, 225 Metcalfe St., Ottawa, ON K2P 1P9
Tel: 613-232-0227; *Fax:* 613-232-0542
mail@FS.ca
www.fs.ca

***Ottawa*: Ann L. Flint - *1**
#203, 190 Somerset St. West, Ottawa, ON K2P 0J4
Tel: 613-594-5461; *Fax:* 613-594-5468

***Ottawa*: George Flumian - *1**
222 Argyle Ave., Ottawa, ON K2P 1B9
Tel: 613-236-8321; *Fax:* 613-230-6597

***Ottawa*: Steven A. Fried - *1**
303 Waverly St., Ottawa, ON K2P 0V9
Tel: 613-233-4420; *Fax:* 613-288-1554
sfried@stevenfried.com

***Ottawa*: Susan Gahrns Law Office - *1**
#401, 1580 Merivale Rd., Ottawa, ON K2G 4B5
Tel: 613-235-6299; *Fax:* 613-224-8827
susan@gahrns.com
www.gahrns.com

***Ottawa*: Goldberg Wiseman Stroud & Hollingsworth LLP - *4**
Former Name: Goldberg Stroud LLP; Goldberg, Kronick & Stroud LLP
176 Bronsons Ave., Ottawa, ON K1R 6K9
Tel: 613-237-4922; *Fax:* 613-237-2920
info@gwshlaw.com
www.gwshlaw.com

***Ottawa*: Donald J. Gormley - *1**
#204, 190 Somerset St. West, Ottawa, ON K2P 0J4
Tel: 613-237-7726; *Fax:* 613-237-1977
donald.gormley@sympatico.ca

***Ottawa*: Goss, McCorriston, Stel - *3**
#203, 2430 Bank St., Ottawa, ON K1V 0T7
Tel: 613-738-0023; *Fax:* 613-738-1294
www.gms-law.com

***Ottawa*: Grant & Dawn - *3**
226 MacLaren St., Ottawa, ON K2P 0L6
Tel: 613-235-2212; *Fax:* 613-235-5294
dawn@lexfix.ca

***Ottawa*: Greenspon, Brown & Associates - *4**
Former Name: Karam Greenspon
331 Somerset St. West, Ottawa, ON K2P 0J8
Tel: 613-288-2890; *Fax:* 613-288-2896
info@greensponbrown.ca
greensponbrown.ca

***Ottawa*: David R. Habib - *1**
18 Honeyood Ct., Ottawa, ON K1V 1Y4
Tel: 613-822-4100; *Fax:* 613-691-0656
david@habiblaw.ca
www.habiblaw.ca

***Ottawa*: Hale Criminal Law Office - *1**
#101, 116 Lisgar St., Ottawa, ON K2P 0C2
Tel: 613-230-4253; *Fax:* 613-230-6996
john.hclo@me.com
www.facebook.com/hclo.ca

***Ottawa*: Hewitt, Hewitt, Nesbitt, Reid LLP - *5**
#604, Fuller Bldg., 75 Albert St., Ottawa, ON K1P 5E7
Tel: 613-563-0202; *Fax:* 613-563-0445
info@hewitts-law.com
hewittslaw.com

***Ottawa*: Susan Hodgson - *1**
#307, 150 Isabella St., Ottawa, ON K1S 1V7
Tel: 613-237-0505; *Fax:* 613-567-3559
susan@hodgsonlaw.ca

***Ottawa*: Honey/MacMillan - *3**
146 Richmond Rd., Ottawa, ON K1Z 6W2
Tel: 613-722-2493; *Fax:* 613-722-2773
honeymac@rogers.com

***Ottawa*: Jay C. Humphrey Professional Corporation - *1**
2821 Riverside Dr., Ottawa, ON K1V 8N4
Tel: 613-733-3393; *Fax:* 613-733-3393
jay@humphreylaw.ca
humphreylaw.ca

***Ottawa*: Katsepontes Law - *2**
Former Name: Burton Katsepontes
#200, 283 Dalhousie St., Ottawa, ON K1N 7E5
Tel: 613-239-3064; *Fax:* 613-237-9181
nicholas@katsepontes law.com
www.katsepontes law.com

***Ottawa*: Kelly Santini LLP - Downtown Ottawa - *32**
#2401, 160 Elgin St., Ottawa, ON K2P 2P7
Tel: 613-238-6321; *Fax:* 613-233-4553
inquiries@kellysantini.com
www.kellysantini.com
www.facebook.com/pages/Kelly-Santini-LLP/131696316896954, www.twitter.com/KellySantiniLaw, www.linkedin.com/company/240452?trk=tyah

***Ottawa*: Kerr & Kerr - *1**
#607, 1755 Riverside Dr., Ottawa, ON K1G 3T6
Tel: 613-293-0852; *Fax:* 613-526-3511
akerr@kerr-kerr.com
www.kerr-kerr.com

***Ottawa*: LaBarge Weinstein LLP - Ottawa - *21**
#800, 515 Legget Dr., Ottawa, ON K2K 3G4
Tel: 613-599-9600; *Fax:* 613-599-0018
info@lwlaw.com
www.lwlaw.com
twitter.com/LWConnect, www.linkedin.com/company/labarge-weinstein

***Ottawa*: Lafleur & Associes/Associates - *1**
237 King Edward Ave., Ottawa, ON K1N 7L8
Tel: 613-241-7335; *Fax:* 613-241-5012
www.mjlafleurlaw.ca

***Ottawa*: Laird, Sheena - *1**
#110, 261 Cooper St., Ottawa, ON K2P 0G3
Tel: 613-232-3575; *Fax:* 613-232-6622
sheenalaird@asselmlaird.com
www.asselinlaird.com

***Ottawa*: Langevin Morris Smith LLP - Ottawa - *16**
Former Name: Lewis Langevin LLP
190 O'Connor St., 9th Fl., Ottawa, ON K2P 2R3
Tel: 613-230-5787; *Fax:* 613-230-8563
www.lmslawyers.com
www.facebook.com/langevinmorrissmith, twitter.com/310lawyer

***Ottawa*: Laveaux, Frank**
Also Known As: Cabinet Laveaux Law Office
#210, 1725 St-Laurent Blvd., Ottawa, ON K1G 3V4
Tel: 613-523-0307; *Fax:* 613-523-0377

***Ottawa*: Low Murchison Radnoff LLP - *77**
1565 Carling Ave., 4th Fl., Ottawa, ON K1Z 8R1
Tel: 613-236-9442; *Fax:* 613-236-7942
Toll-Free: 888-909-9442
lawyer@lmrlawyers.com
lmrlawyers.com

***Ottawa*: Macdonald, Affleck - *2**
#1100, 200 Elgin St., Ottawa, ON K2P 1L5
Tel: 613-236-8712; *Fax:* 613-236-5145

***Ottawa*: MacKinnon & Phillips - *7**
#802, 200 Elgin St., Ottawa, ON K2P 1L5
Tel: 613-236-0662; *Fax:* 613-236-8906
www.mackinnonphillips.com

***Ottawa*: Maclaren Corlett LLP - Ottawa - *5**
#1424, 50 O'Connor St., Ottawa, ON K1P 6L2
Tel: 613-233-1146; *Fax:* 613-233-7190
mail@macorlaw.com
www.macorlaw.com
www.facebook.com/MaclarenCorlett, twitter.com/maclarencorlett, www.linkedin.com/company/maclaren-corlett-llp

***Ottawa*: Mann Lawyers - Ottawa - Scott St. - *18**
Former Name: Mann & Partners LLP
#710, Tower B, 1600 Scott St., Ottawa, ON K1Y 4N7
Tel: 613-722-1500; *Fax:* 613-722-7677
Toll-Free: 800-420-0577
info@mannlawyers.com
www.mannlawyers.com
twitter.com/MannLawyers, www.linkedin.com/company/mann-&-partners-l-l-p-

***Ottawa*: Howard Mann - *1**
578 O'Connor St., Ottawa, ON K1S 3R3
Tél: 613-729-0621; *Téléc:* 613-729-0306
howard@howardmann.ca
www.howardmann.ca

** indicates number of lawyers*

***Ottawa*: Marks & Marks - *1**
#201, 190 Somerset St. West, Ottawa, ON K2P 0J4
Tel: 613-230-2123; *Fax:* 613-230-5707
bdm@marks-marks.com
www.marks-marks.com

***Ottawa*: Marks & Marks LLP - *2**
#201, 190 Somerset St. West, Ottawa, ON K2P 0J4
Tel: 613-230-2123; *Fax:* 613-230-5707
bdm@marks-marks.com
www.marks-marks.com

***Ottawa*: Leonard Max, Q.C.**
428 Kent St., Ottawa, ON K2P 2B3
Tel: 613-269-3872

***Ottawa*: May & Konyer - *5**
#305, 185 Somerset St. West, Ottawa, ON K2P 0J2
Tel: 613-230-6524; *Fax:* 613-230-2705
jmccausland@mayandkonyer.com
www.seanmaylaw.ca

***Ottawa*: Mazerolle & Lemay - *5**
#202, 1173 Cyrville Rd., Ottawa, ON K1J 7S6
Tel: 613-746-5700; *Fax:* 613-746-1783
www.mazerollelemay.com

***Ottawa*: MBM Intellectual Property Law LLP - *8**
Former Name: Marusyk Miller & Swain
270 Albert St., 14th Fl., Ottawa, ON K1P 5G8
Tel: 613-567-0762; *Fax:* 613-563-7671
MBMGeneral@mbm.com
www.mbm.com
www.facebook.com/mbmiplaw, www.twitter.com/mbmiplaw,
www.linkedin.com/company/mbm-intellectual-property-law-llp

***Ottawa*: McBride Bond Christian LLP - *11**
Former Name: *Doucet McBride LLP*
#500, 265 Caeling Ave., Ottawa, ON K1S 2E1
Tel: 613-233-4474; *Fax:* 613-233-8868
Toll-Free: 888-288-2033
reception@mbclaw.ca
mbclaw.ca

***Ottawa*: McCann & Lyttle - *2**
#800, 200 Elgin St., Ottawa, ON K2P 1L5
Tel: 613-236-1410; *Fax:* 613-563-1367
pmccann@mccannandlyttle.com
mccannandlyttle.com

***Ottawa*: McCloskey McCloskey - *2**
#202, 5307 Canotek Rd., Ottawa, ON K1J 9M2
Tel: 613-745-0395; *Fax:* 613-745-8007
ronald@mccloskey.ca
www.mccloskey.ca

***Ottawa*: McDonald & Quinn - *1**
#1, 1480 Woodward Ave., Ottawa, ON K1Z 7W6
Tel: 613-729-1005; *Fax:* 613-729-1176

***Ottawa*: McFadden, Fincham - *7**
#606, 225 Metcalfe St., Ottawa, ON K2P 1P9
Tel: 613-234-1907; *Fax:* 613-234-5233
mail@mcfaddenfincham.com
www.mcfaddenfincham.com

***Ottawa*: McGuinty Law Offices Professional Corporation - *3**
Former Name: McGuinty & McGuinty
1192 Rockingham Ave., Ottawa, ON K1H 8A7
Tel: 613-526-3858; *Fax:* 613-526-3187
mcguinty@mcguintylaw.ca
www.mcguintylaw.com

***Ottawa*: Robert F. Meagher - *1**
#502, 66 Slater St., Ottawa, ON K1P 5H1
Tel: 613-563-4278; *Fax:* 613-232-7322
rmeagher@bellnet.ca

***Ottawa*: Menzies Lawyers - *5**
Former Name: Menzies & Coulson
176 Gloucester St., 4th Fl., Ottawa, ON K2P 0A6
Tel: 613-722-1313; *Fax:* 613-722-4712
Toll-Free: 888-722-1313
info@menzieslawyers.com
www.menzieslawyers.com
www.facebook.com/home.php#!/pages/Menzies-Lawyers/26913
5529875143?fref=ts,
www.linkedin.com/company/2830426?trk=tyah

***Ottawa*: John E. Merner - *3**
Former Name: Merner Burton Massie
136 Lewis St., Ottawa, ON K2P 0S7
Tel: 613-567-6093; *Fax:* 613-567-7164

***Ottawa*: Merovitz Potechin LLP - *9**
#301, 200 Catherine St., Ottawa, ON K2P 2K9
Tel: 613-563-7544; *Fax:* 613-563-4577
mplaw@mpottawa.com
www.merovitzpotechin.com
www.facebook.com/#!/pages/Trial-page-Merovitz-Potechin-LLP/1
19359838144021,
www.linkedin.com/groups?gid=2888678&mostPopular=&trk=tya
h

***Ottawa*: Eric A. Milligan - *1**
#108, 55 Murray St., Ottawa, ON K1N 5M3
Tel: 613-562-4077; *Fax:* 613-562-4102
milligan@delsysresearch.com

***Ottawa*: Miltons IP Professional Corporation - *5**
Former Name: Milton, Geller LLP
#203, 2255 Carling Ave., Ottawa, ON K2B 7Z5
Tel: 613-567-7824; *Fax:* 613-567-4689
Toll-Free: 866-297-1179
info@miltonsip.com
www.miltonsip.com

***Ottawa*: Richard Minard - *1**
58 Clegg St., Ottawa, ON K1S 0H8
Tel: 613-237-6874; *Fax:* 613-234-1728
rminard@on.aibn.com

***Ottawa*: Moffat & Co., Macera & Jarzyna - *24**
Stn. D, 427 Laurier Ave. West, 12th Fl., Ottawa, ON K1R 7Y2
Tel: 613-238-8173; *Fax:* 613-235-2508
mail@macerajarzyna.com
www.macerajarzyna.com

***Ottawa*: Christopher A. Moore - *1**
63 Robert St., Ottawa, ON K2P 1G5
Tel: 613-230-9448; *Fax:* 613-230-3624
chalmo@istar.ca

***Ottawa*: More & McLeod - *1**
#212, 2249 Carling Ave., Ottawa, ON K2B 7E9
Tel: 613-820-7888; *Fax:* 613-820-3044
morelaw@bellnet.ca
moreandmcleod.ca

***Ottawa*: Kevin Murphy - *1**
112 Lisgar St., Ottawa, ON K2P 0C2
Tel: 613-238-1333

***Ottawa*: Robert Elmo Murray - *1**
#307, 150 Isabella St., Ottawa, ON K1S 1V7
Tel: 613-237-0505; *Fax:* 613-567-3559

***Ottawa*: Kenneth J. Naftel - *1**
#307, 150 Isabella St., Ottawa, ON K1S 1V7
Tel: 613-237-0505; *Fax:* 613-567-3559
ken@kennaftel.ca

***Ottawa*: Nelligan O'Brien Payne LLP - Ottawa - *46**
#1500, 50 O'Connor St., Ottawa, ON K1P 6L2
Tel: 613-238-8080; *Fax:* 613-238-2098
Toll-Free: 888-565-9912
info@nelligan.ca
www.nelligan.ca
www.facebook.com/nelliganobrienpayne,
twitter.com/NelliganLaw,
www.linkedin.com/company/nelligan-o%27brien-payne-llp_2

***Ottawa*: Nicol & Lazier - *3**
237 Somerset St. West, Ottawa, ON K2P 0J3
Tel: 613-232-4241; *Fax:* 613-236-9325

***Ottawa*: Paul Niebergall - *1**
34 Halldorson Cres., Ottawa, ON K2K 2C7
Tel: 613-232-8508; *Fax:* 613-232-9654
paulniebergall@rogers.com
www.paulniebergall.com

***Ottawa*: Wanda Noel Barrister & Solicitor - *1**
5496 Whitewood Ave., Ottawa, ON K4M 1C7
Tel: 613-794-1171; *Fax:* 613-692-1735
wanda.noel@bell.net

***Ottawa*: Michael B. Oliveira - *1**
#402, 280 Metcalfe St., Ottawa, ON K2P 1R7
Tel: 613-567-1016; *Fax:* 613-567-9126
moliveira@sprint.ca

***Ottawa*: Eugene L. Oscapella - *1**
70 MacDonald St., Ottawa, ON K2P 1H6
Tel: 613-238-5909; *Fax:* 613-238-2891
eugene@oscapella.ca

***Ottawa*: Overtveld & Associates - *1**
284 Wellington St., Ottawa, ON K1A 0H8
Tel: 613-941-6805; *Fax:* 613-957-4019
Overtveld@magma.ca
www.magma.ca/~overtvel/

***Ottawa*: Paradis, Jones, Horwitz, Bowles Associates - *4**
#900, 200 Elgin St., Ottawa, ON K2P 1L5
Tel: 613-238-5074; *Fax:* 613-230-3250

***Ottawa*: Lawrence S. Pascoe - *1**
Former Name: Mirsky, Pascoe
#300, 39 Robertson Rd., Ottawa, ON K2H 8R2
Tel: 613-828-2120; *Fax:* 613-596-0881
lspascoe@thepascoedifference.com
www.thepascoedifference.com

***Ottawa*: Francis K. Peddle - *1**
168 Henderson Ave., Ottawa, ON K1N 7P6
Tel: 613-232-1740; *Fax:* 613-232-0407
ftpeddle@bellnet.ca

***Ottawa*: Kimberley A. Pegg - *3**
#1, 200 Cooper St., Ottawa, ON K2P 0G1
Tel: 613-232-9331; *Fax:* 613-230-3551
kimberley.pegg@bellnet.ca
www.kimberleypeggbarristers.com

***Ottawa*: Pender & Leef - *2**
#1608, 130 Alber St., Ottawa, ON K1P 5G4
Tel: 613-569-0104; *Fax:* 613-569-6235
stephen@pender-leef.com

***Ottawa*: Perley-Robertson, Hill & McDougall LLP / s.r.l. - *51**
#1400, Constitution Square, 340 Albert St., Ottawa, ON K1R 0A5
Tel: 613-238-2022; *Fax:* 613-238-8775
Toll-Free: 800-268-8292
lawyers@perlaw.ca
www.perlaw.ca

***Ottawa*: Pfeiffer & Associates - *1**
157 McLeod St., Ottawa, ON K2P 0Z6
Tel: 613-238-4115; *Fax:* 613-563-8273
byron.pfeiffer@gmail.com

***Ottawa*: Piazza, Brooks - *2**
Former Name: Piazza, Brooks & Siddons
#202, 309 Cooper St., Ottawa, ON K2P 0G5
Tel: 613-238-2244; *Fax:* 613-238-3382
jpiazza@piazzalaw.com
www.piazzalaw.com

***Ottawa*: Plaskacz & Associates**
64 Glen Ave., Ottawa, ON K1S 2Z9
Tel: 613-299-0200
plaskacz@plaskacz.com
www.plaskacz.com

***Ottawa*: Prystupa Law Office - *2**
#400, 303 Moodie Dr., Ottawa, ON K2H 9R4
Tel: 613-729-4669; *Fax:* 613-729-4669
admin@prystupalaw.ca

***Ottawa*: Helene Bruce Puccini - *1**
247 Fourth Ave., Ottawa, ON K1S 2L9
Tel: 613-230-6295
helenebruce@gmail.com

***Ottawa*: Quinn Thiele Mineault Grodzki LLP - *15**
310 O'Connor St., Ottawa, ON K2P 1V8
Tel: 613-563-1131; *Fax:* 613-230-8297
reception@pqtlaw.com
www.ottawalawyers.com
www.facebook.com/QTMG.Lawyers,
twitter.com/QTMG_Lawyers

***Ottawa*: Ranger & Associés - *1**
#1000, 141 Laurier Ave. West, Ottawa, ON K1P 5J3
Tel: 613-234-2255; *Fax:* 613-234-2301

***Ottawa*: Rasmussen Starr Ruddy LLP - *12**
#660, 660 Carling Ave., Ottawa, ON K1Z 1G3
Tel: 613-232-1830; *Fax:* 613-232-2499
mail@rsrlaw.ca
www.rsrlaw.ca

** indicates number of lawyers*

Ottawa: **Raven, Cameron, Ballantyne, Yazbeck LLP - *12**
Former Name: Raven, Allen, Cameron & Ballantyne
#1600, 220 Laurier Ave. West, Ottawa, ON K1P 5Z9
Tel: 613-567-2901; *Fax:* 613-567-2921
info@ravenlaw.com
www.ravenlaw.com

Ottawa: **Karen Ann Reid - *1**
#202, 200 Elgin St., Ottawa, ON K2P 1L5
Tel: 613-238-8777; *Fax:* 613-238-4824
kareid@istop.com

Ottawa: **Frank I. Ritchie - *1**
2253 Alta Vista Dr., Ottawa, ON K1H 7L9
Tel: 613-731-8288

Ottawa: **Terrence M. Romanow - *1**
2038 Black Friars Rd., Ottawa, ON K2A 3K8
Tel: 613-722-8224; *Fax:* 613-722-0908
terryromanow@rogers.com

Ottawa: **Ross Talarico & Schwisberg Law Offices LLP - *4**
406 Queen St., Ottawa, ON K1R 5A7
Tel: 613-236-8000; *Fax:* 613-820-8818
info@talberglaw.com
www.talberglaw.com

Ottawa: **Glen F. Schruder - *1**
#505, 200 Elgin St., Ottawa, ON K2P 1L5
Tel: 613-235-9924; *Fax:* 613-235-1343
glenshruder@on.aibn.com

Ottawa: **Scott & Coulson - *1**
#420, 1335 Carling Ave., Ottawa, ON K1Z 8N8
Tel: 613-725-3723; *Fax:* 613-729-8613
rscott@scottcoulson.ca
www.lawottawa.com

Ottawa: **Sevigny Westdal - *4**
#300, 190 O'Connor St., Ottawa, ON K2P 2R3
Tel: 613-751-4459; *Fax:* 613-751-4471
info@sevignywestdal.com
www.sevignylaw.com

Ottawa: **Shapiro Cohen - *6**
#200, P.O. Box 13002, 411 Legget Dr., Ottawa, ON K2K 0E2
Tel: 613-232-5300; *Fax:* 613-563-9231
Toll-Free: 800-563-9390
info@shapirocohen.com
www.shapirocohen.com

Ottawa: **Sheppard & Claude - *2**
#200, 745A Montreal Rd., Ottawa, ON K1K 0T1
Tel: 613-748-3333; *Fax:* 613-748-1599
www.sheppardclaude.ca

Ottawa: **Shields & Hunt - *5**
68 Chamberlain Ave., Ottawa, ON K1S 1V9
Tel: 613-230-3232; *Fax:* 613-230-1664
jshields@shields-hunt.com
www.shields-hunt.com

Ottawa: **Paula M. Smith - *1**
450 Laurier Ave. East, Ottawa, ON K1N 6R3
Tel: 613-565-0490

Ottawa: **Soloway, Wright LLP - Ottawa - *32**
#900, 427 Laurier Ave. West, Ottawa, ON K1R 7Y2
Tel: 613-236-0111; *Fax:* 613-238-8507
Toll-Free: 800-207-5880
info@solowaywright.com
www.soloways.com
twitter.com/solowaywright,

Ottawa: **Stewart/Associates - *2**
#402, 200 Elgin St., Ottawa, ON K2P 1L5
Tel: 613-235-0453; *Fax:* 613-235-3304

Ottawa: **Jennifer A. Stiell - *1**
#307, 150 Isabella St., Ottawa, ON K1S 1V7
Tel: 613-237-0505; *Fax:* 613-567-3559
jstiell@cyberus.ca

Ottawa: **Sundin Law Office - *2**
276 Sunnyside Ave., Ottawa, ON K4R 1E2
Tel: 613-730-7476; *Fax:* 613-445-3424
annas@sundinlaw.com
www.sundinlaw.com

Ottawa: **Christopher C.C. Tan - *1**
70 Gloucester St., Ottawa, ON K2P 0A2
Tel: 613-235-2308; *Fax:* 613-235-6933

Ottawa: **Thompson Summers - *2**
Former Name: Steinberg Thompson d'Artois Rockman Summers
#730, 220 Laurier Ave. West, Ottawa, ON K1P 5Z9
Tel: 613-688-0433; *Fax:* 613-688-0437
www.thompsonsummers.com

Ottawa: **Tierney Stauffer LLP - *22**
#510, 1600 Carling Ave., Ottawa, ON K1Z 0A1
Tel: 613-728-8057; *Fax:* 613-728-9866
Toll-Free: 888-799-8057
info@tslawyers.ca
www.tierneystauffer.com
www.facebook.com/pages/Tierney-Stauffer-LLP/103214433106289, twitter.com/TSLawyers,
www.linkedin.com/company/tierney-stauffer

Ottawa: **Tom Curran Law - *2**
1704 Carling Ave., Ottawa, ON K2A 1C7
Tel: 613-596-2804; *Fax:* 613-596-2013
info@tomcurranlaw.com
www.tomcurranlaw.com
www.facebook.com/TomCurranLaw?bookmark_t=page

Ottawa: **Trudel Law Office - *1**
Also Known As: Roger P. Trudel
#103, 2828 St. Joseph Blvd., Ottawa, ON K1C 6E7
Tel: 613-837-2641; *Fax:* 613-830-5613
www.trudellawoffice.com

Ottawa: **Tunney, McMurray - *2**
#806, 200 Elgin St., Ottawa, ON K2P 1L5
Tel: 613-235-5660; *Fax:* 613-235-0805

Ottawa: **Gilad Vered - *1**
1801 Woodward Dr., Ottawa, ON K2C 0R3
Tel: 613-226-2000; *Fax:* 613-225-0391
gvered@arnon.ca

Ottawa: **Victor Ages Vallance LLP - *8**
Former Name: Kimmel, Victor & Ages
112 Lisgar St., Ottawa, ON K2P 0C2
Tel: 613-238-1333; *Fax:* 613-238-8949
www.vavlawyers.com

Ottawa: **Vincent Dagenais Gibson LLP/S.R.L. - *14**
#400, 260 Dalhousie St., Ottawa, ON K1N 7E4
Tel: 613-241-2701; *Fax:* 613-241-2599
info@vdg.ca
www.vdg.ca

Ottawa: **Ian H. Warren - *1**
#2000, 150 Metcalfe St., Ottawa, ON K2P 1P1
Tel: 613-565-3813; *Fax:* 613-234-0418
jacklaw@storm.ca

Ottawa: **Robert A. Whillans - *1**
540 Courtenay Ave., Ottawa, ON K2A 3B3
Tel: 613-238-1515; *Fax:* 613-238-1323

Ottawa: **Williams McEnery - *8**
Former Name: Williams, McEnery & Davis
169 Gilmour St., Ottawa, ON K2P 0N8
Tel: 613-237-0520; *Fax:* 613-237-3163
www.williamsmcenery.com

Ottawa: **David M. Wray - *1**
#310, P.O. Box 2760, Stn. D, 151 Slater St., Ottawa, ON K1P 5W8
Tel: 613-233-1322; *Fax:* 613-230-5168
dwray@wray-canada.com

Owen Sound: **Arnold & Arnold, LLP - *2**
Former Name: Arnold, Neil J.
935 - 2nd Ave. West, Owen Sound, ON N4K 4M8
Tel: 519-372-2218; *Fax:* 519-372-2599
arnoldlaw.os@gmail.com

Owen Sound: **Ian C. Boddy - *1**
195 - 9th St. West, Owen Sound, ON N4K 3N5
Tel: 519-372-9886; *Fax:* 519-372-1091
ianboddy@bellnet.ca

Owen Sound: **Herbert E. Boyce - *1**
#103, Dominion Place, P.O. Box 968, 887 Third Ave. East, Owen Sound, ON N4K 6H6
Tel: 519-371-4160; *Fax:* 519-371-1604

Owen Sound: **Chander G. Chaddah - *1**
P.O. Box 965, 712 - 2 Ave. East, Owen Sound, ON N4K 6H6
Tel: 519-376-4343; *Fax:* 519-376-2547

Owen Sound: **Andrew E. Drury - *1**
#5B, 945 - 3 Ave. East, Owen Sound, ON N4K 2K8
Tel: 519-372-1850; *Fax:* 519-372-1602

Owen Sound: **Douglas A. Grace - *1**
P.O. Box 952, Stn. Main, 949 - 2 Ave. West, Owen Sound, ON N4K 4M8
Tel: 519-371-9370; *Fax:* 519-371-5747
dougrace@bmts.com

Owen Sound: **Greenfield & Barrie - *2**
142 - 10 St. West, Owen Sound, ON N4K 3P9
Tel: 519-376-4930; *Fax:* 519-376-4010
gblaw@btms.com

Owen Sound: **Kirby Robinson Treslan Professional Corporation - *7**
Former Name: Kirby, Gordon & Robinson
P.O. Box 730, 930 - 1 Ave. West, Owen Sound, ON N4K 5W9
Tel: 519-376-7450; *Fax:* 519-376-8288
Toll-Free: 800-513-5559
info@owensoundlawyers.com
owensoundlawyers.com

Owen Sound: **Middlebro' & Stevens LLP - *5**
P.O. Box 100, 1030 - 2 Ave. East, Owen Sound, ON N4K 5P1
Tel: 519-376-8730; *Fax:* 519-376-7135
ms@mslaw.ca
www.mslaw.ca

Owen Sound: **Murray & Thomson - *4**
P.O. Box 1060, 912 - 2 Ave. West, Owen Sound, ON N4K 6K6
Tel: 519-376-6350; *Fax:* 519-376-0835
message@mtlaw.ca
www.mtlaw.ca

Owen Sound: **Scott C. Vining - *1**
1199 - 1st Ave. East, Owen Sound, ON N4K 2E2
Tel: 519-371-6210
office@vininglaw.ca
www.vininglaw.ca

Paris: **Tarrison & Hunter - *2**
19 William St., Paris, ON N3L 1K9
Tel: 519-442-2287
ghunter@tarrisonandhunter.com
www.tarrisonandhunter.ca/en/

Parry Sound: **Larry W. Douglas - *1**
22 Miller St., Parry Sound, ON P2A 1S8
Tel: 705-746-9471; *Fax:* 705-746-9606

Parry Sound: **David A. Holmes - *1**
2 William St., Parry Sound, ON P2A 1V1
Tel: 705-746-4223; *Fax:* 705-746-6368
daholmes@cogeco.ca

Parry Sound: **Oldham Law Firm - *3**
88 James St., Parry Sound, ON P2A 1T9
Tel: 705-746-8852; *Fax:* 705-746-6188
howard@oldhamlaw.ca
www.oldhamlaw.ca

Parry Sound: **Powell, Cunningham, Grandy - *1**
88 James St., Parry Sound, ON P2A 1T9
Tel: 705-746-4207; *Fax:* 705-746-2945
pcg@cogeco.net

Parry Sound: **D. Andrew Thomson - *1**
10 William St., Parry Sound, ON P2A 1V1
Tel: 705-746-5838; *Fax:* 705-746-4351
athomson@dathomsonbarrister.ca

Pembroke: **Blair Jones Professional Corporation - *1**
Former Name: Kelly Kelly & Jones
1064 Pembroke St. West, Pembroke, ON K8A 5R4
Tel: 613-735-8226; *Fax:* 613-735-8474
blair@jones-law.ca
www.jones-law.ca

Pembroke: **Adrian R. Cleaver - *1**
P.O. Box 1147, Stn. Main, 595 Pembroke St. East, Pembroke, ON K8A 6Y6
Tel: 613-732-1377; *Fax:* 613-732-3889
acleaver@nrtco.net

Pembroke: **Glen Price, Lawyers - *2**
Former Name: Garretto & Price
P.O. Box 697, Stn. Main, 141A Lake St., Pembroke, ON K8A 6X9
Tel: 613-732-2883; *Fax:* 613-732-3436
Toll-Free: 877-732-2884
glenpricelawyer.com

** indicates number of lawyers*

Pembroke: Huckabone, O'Brien, Instance, Bradley, Lyle - *5
Former Name: Huckabone, Shaw, O'Brien, Radley-Walters & Reimer
P.O. Box 487, 284 Pembroke St. East, Pembroke, ON K8A 6X7
Tel: 613-735-2341; Fax: 613-735-0920
admin@hsolawyers.com
www.hsolawyers.com

Pembroke: Johnson, Fraser & March - *3
P.O. Box 366, Stn. Main, 259 Pembroke St. East, Pembroke, ON K8A 6X6
Tel: 613-735-0624; Fax: 613-735-0625
jfmlawyers@nrtco.net
www.jfmlawyers.ca

Pembroke: Roy C. Reiche - *1
203 Nelson St., Pembroke, ON K8A 3N1
Tel: 613-735-2313; Fax: 613-735-2013

Perth: Anderson Foss - *2
10 Market Sq., Perth, ON K7H 1V7
Tel: 613-267-9898; Fax: 613-267-2741
www.andersonfoss.ca

Perth: Bond & Hughes Barristers & Solicitors - *2
Former Name: James M. Bond
10 Market Sq., Perth, ON K7H 1V7
Tel: 613-267-1212; Fax: 613-267-7059
www.bondhughes.ca

Perth: John J.S. Chalmers - *1
P.O. Box 2, Stn. Main, RR#3, Perth, ON K7H 3C5
Tel: 613-264-1505; Fax: 613-264-9259

Perth: Michael P. Reid - *1
#202, Code's Mill, 53 Herriott St., Perth, ON K7H 1T5
Tel: 613-267-7280; Fax: 613-267-7285
mike@reidlaw.ca
www.reidlaw.ca

Perth: Rubino & Chaplin - *1
P.O. Box 338, 10A Gore St. West, Perth, ON K7H 3E4
Tel: 613-267-5227; Fax: 613-267-3951
admin@rubinoandchaplin.ca

Perth: Woodwark Stevens Ireton - *3
Former Name: Woodwark & Stevens
8 Gore St. West, Perth, ON K7H 2L6
Tel: 613-264-8080; Fax: 613-264-8084
info@woodwarkstevens.com
www.woodwarkstevens.com

Peterborough: Gary E. Ainsworth - *1
#101, P.O. Box 1358, Stn. Main, 294 Rink St., Peterborough, ON K9J 7H6
Tel: 705-749-0628; Fax: 705-749-0633
gea@ainslaw.com
www.ainslaw.com

Peterborough: Aitken, Robertson Criminal Lawyers - *7
263 Charlotte St., Peterborough, ON K9J 7Y4
Tel: 705-742-0440 Toll-Free: 800-668-1657
freeconsult@callalawyer.ca
www.fightthecharges.com

Peterborough: Robert W. Beninger - *1
70 Simcoe St., Peterborough, ON K9H 7G9
Tel: 705-876-3834; Fax: 705-876-3847

Peterborough: W. Jelle Bosch - *1
#203, P.O. Box 2364, 130 Hunter St. West, Peterborough, ON K9J 7Y8
Tel: 705-741-3630; Fax: 705-741-6339
wj_bosch@on.aibn.com
ca.linkedin.com/pub/w-jelle-bosch/33/141/52b

Peterborough: John S. Crook - *1
Former Name: Crook & Collins
#5, P.O. Box 1539, Stn. Main, 261 George St. North, Peterborough, ON K9J 7H7
Tel: 705-742-5415; Fax: 705-742-1867

Peterborough: H. Girvin Devitt - *1
P.O. Box 1449, Stn. Main, 858 Chemong Rd., Peterborough, ON K9J 7H6
Tel: 705-742-5471
devitt@nexicom.net

Peterborough: Douglas F. Walker Professional Corporation - *2
243 Hunter St. West, Peterborough, ON K9H 2L4
Tel: 705-748-3012; Fax: 705-748-2746
dfwalker@lawyer.com
www.dfwalker.com

Peterborough: Dunn & Dunn - *1
469 Water St., Peterborough, ON K9H 3M2
Tel: 705-743-6460; Fax: 705-748-2675
info@dunnlaw.ca
www.dunnlaw.ca

Peterborough: Michael J. Dwyer - *1
P.O. Box 958, 359 Aylmer St. North, Peterborough, ON K9J 7A5
Tel: 705-743-4221; Fax: 705-743-2187
mdwyer@bellnet.ca

Peterborough: Farquharson Daly - *2
161 Hunter St. West, Peterborough, ON K9H 2L1
Tel: 705-742-9241; Fax: 705-741-1601

Peterborough: Gowland Boriss - *4
P.O. Box 1629, 371 Reid St., Peterborough, ON K9H 4G4
Tel: 705-743-7252; Fax: 705-743-1850
www.gowlandboriss.ca

Peterborough: Joan M. Guerin - *1
#4, P.O. Box 1420, Stn. Main, 193 Simcoe St., Peterborough, ON K9J 7H6
Tel: 705-743-9087; Fax: 705-743-8528

Peterborough: Harrison Law Office - *1
469 Water St., Peterborough, ON K9H 3M2
Tel: 705-741-5233; Fax: 705-741-2463

Peterborough: James S. Hauraney - *2
305 Reid St., Peterborough, ON K9J 3R2
Tel: 705-748-2333; Fax: 705-748-2618
jameshauraney.com

Peterborough: A. John Hodgins - *1
677 Brown Line, Peterborough, ON M8W 3V7
Tel: 416-251-9390; Fax: 416-251-0449
ajhodgins@hodginslaw.net

Peterborough: Rod E. Johnston - *1
P.O. Box 29, 521 George St. North, Peterborough, ON K9J 6Y5
Tel: 705-748-2244; Fax: 705-748-2540
info@rodjohnstonlaw.com

Peterborough: E.J. Jordan - *1
P.O. Box 958, 359 Aylmer St. North, Peterborough, ON K9J 7A5
Tel: 705-743-4221; Fax: 705-743-2187
jjordan@bellnet.ca

Peterborough: Lech, Lightbody & O'Brien - *2
116 Hunter St. West, Peterborough, ON K9H 2K6
Tel: 705-742-3844; Fax: 705-742-0121

Peterborough: Lillico Bazuk Kent Galloway - *4
P.O. Box 568, 163 Hunter St. West, Peterborough, ON K9J 6Z6
Tel: 705-743-3577; Fax: 705-743-0013
info@lbkglaw.com
www.lbkglaw.com

Peterborough: LLF Lawyers LLP - *12
P.O. Box 1146, 332 Aylmer St. North, Peterborough, ON K9J 7H4
Tel: 705-742-1674; Fax: 705-742-4677
info@llf.ca
www.llf.ca

Peterborough: J.M. Longworth - *1
P.O. Box 1747, Stn. Main, 310 Rubidge St., Peterborough, ON K9J 7X6
Tel: 705-749-0100; Fax: 705-742-8718

Peterborough: John E. McGarrity - *1
Stn. Main, 343 Stewart St., Peterborough, ON K9H 4A7
Tel: 705-743-1822; Fax: 705-743-4870
mcgarrity@trytel.net

Peterborough: McGillen Keay Cooper - *4
Former Name: McGillen Keay; McGillen, Ayotte, Dupuis
#202, P.O. Box 1718, 140 King St., Peterborough, ON K9J 7X6
Tel: 705-748-2241; Fax: 705-748-9125
www.mkclaw.ca

Peterborough: McMichael, Davidson - *1
223 Aylmer St. North, Peterborough, ON K9J 3K3
Tel: 705-745-0571; Fax: 705-745-0411
lawoffice@mcmichaeldavidson.com

Peterborough: Moldaver & McFadden - *3
Market Plaza, P.O. Box 1387, 121 George St. North, Peterborough, ON K9J 7H6
Tel: 705-743-1801
info@moldavermcfadden.ca
www.moldavermcfadden.ca

Peterborough: Christopher M. Spear - *1
430 Sheridan St., Peterborough, ON K9H 3J9
Tel: 705-741-2144; Fax: 705-741-2712

Peterborough: Richard J. Taylor - *1
P.O. Box 1963, Stn. Main, 193 Dalhousie St., Peterborough, ON K9J 7X7
Tel: 705-876-7791; Fax: 705-876-9280
richardtaylorlaw@cogeco.net

Peterborough: Gordon H. Usher - *1
P.O. Box 327, 359 Aylmer St. North, Peterborough, ON K9J 6Z3
Tel: 705-743-4221; Fax: 705-743-8692

Peterborough: J. Ross Whittington - *1
P.O. Box 327, Stn. Main, 359 Aylmer St. North, Peterborough, ON K9J 6Z3
Tel: 705-743-4221; Fax: 705-743-8692

Petrolia: Robert B. Gray - *1
#3, 4495 Petrolia Line, Petrolia, ON N0N 1R0
Tel: 519-882-0132; Fax: 519-336-3289

Petrolia: Wallace B. Lang - *1
Former Name: Kilby & Lang
4245 Petrolia Lane, Petrolia, ON N0N 1R0
Tel: 519-882-0770; Fax: 519-882-3144

Pickering: G.W. Edmiston - *1
1281 Commerce St., Pickering, ON L1W 1C7
Tel: 905-839-8270

Pickering: J Paul Fletcher Law - *2
3355 Brock Rd., R.R.#1, Pickering, ON L0H 1J0
Tel: 905-686-1329; Fax: 905-239-6204
info@jpaulfletcherlaw.com
www.jpaulfletcherlaw.com

Pickering: Brian R. Hawke - *1
1 Evelyn Ave., Pickering, ON L1V 1N3
Tel: 905-509-5267; Fax: 905-509-5270
bhawke@on.aibn.com
www.brianhawke.com

Pickering: John G. Howes - *1
#800, 1315 Pickering Pkwy., Pickering, ON L1V 7G5
Tel: 905-420-8628; Fax: 905-420-1073
john@howeslaw.com
howeslaw.com

Pickering: Murray Stroud Law Office - *2
356 Kingston Rd., Pickering, ON L1V 1A2
Tel: 905-509-1353; Fax: 905-509-2370
info@stroudlaw.ca
www.stroudlaw.ca

Pickering: Sherwood, Hunt - *2
364 Kingston Rd., Pickering, ON L1V 1A2
Tel: 905-509-5500; Fax: 905-509-0070

Pickering: Harvey Storm - *1
#11B, 1400 Bayly St., Pickering, ON L1W 3R2
Tel: 905-839-5121; Fax: 905-420-4062
Toll-Free: 888-876-5529
harvey@harveystorm.com
www.harveystorm.com

Pickering: Tim Vanular Lawyers Professional Corporation - *2
Former Name: Vanular, Timothy C.R.
#C10-C11, Brock North Plaza, 2200 Brock Rd. North, Pickering, ON L1X 2R2
Tel: 905-427-4886; Fax: 905-427-5542
Toll-Free: 800-243-4151
vanular@vanulaw.com
www.vanulaw.com
www.facebook.com/210973558915379, twitter.com/Vanulaw, ca.linkedin.com/pub/tim-vanular/33/546/a93

* indicates number of lawyers

***Pickering*: Walker, Head - *11**
#800, Corporate Centre, 1315 Pickering Pkwy., Pickering, ON L1V 7G5
Tel: 905-839-4484; *Fax:* 905-420-1073
Toll-Free: 877-839-4484
info@walkerhead.com
www.walkerhead.com

***Picton*: Bruce F. Campbell - *1**
194 Main St., Picton, ON K0K 2T0
Tel: 613-476-2366; *Fax:* 613-476-9821
bcampbl@kos.net

***Picton*: Mathers, Shelagh M. - *1**
#4, 6 Talbot St., Picton, ON K0K 2T0
Tel: 613-476-2733; *Fax:* 613-476-6064
matherslaw@kos.net
www.matherslaw.com

***Picton*: Donald T. Mowat - *1**
P.O. Box 2290, 165 Main St., Picton, ON K0K 2T0
Tel: 613-476-3261; *Fax:* 613-476-4417

***Point Edward*: Fleck Law - *5**
Former Name: *Fleck & Daigneault*
131 Kendall St., Point Edward, ON N7V 4G6
Tel: 519-337-5288; *Fax:* 519-337-5674
info@flecklaw.ca
flecklaw.ca
www.facebook.com/FleckDaigneault, twitter.com/flecklaw, ca.linkedin.com/pub/carl-e-fleck-q-c/2b/728/a2

***Point Edward*: C. Ed Gresham**
P.O. Box 84, 611 St. Clair St., Point Edward, ON N7V 1P2
Tel: 519-337-5007; *Fax:* 519-337-7440

***Point Edward*: Peter Westfall - *1**
#104, 805 Christina St. North, Point Edward, ON N7V 1X6
Tel: 519-344-1155; *Fax:* 519-344-1842
pwestfall@bellnet.ca

***Port Colborne*: Brian N. Lambie - *1**
151 Charlotte St., Port Colborne, ON L3K 4N6
Tel: 905-835-0404; *Fax:* 905-835-5966
blambie1@cogeco.ca

***Port Dover*: Lee Gaunt Law Office - *1**
Also Known As: Grant Law Office
Former Name: Driscoll & Gaunt
P.O. Box 580, Stn. Port Dover, Port Dover, ON N0A 1N0
Tel: 519-583-1411; *Fax:* 519-583-1110

***Port Elgin*: George D. Gruetzner - *1**
P.O. Box 10, 667 Goderich St., Port Elgin, ON N0H 2C0
Tel: 519-832-2482; *Fax:* 519-389-4617

***Port Hope*: Mann McCracken Bebee Ross & Schmidt - *6**
114 Walton St., Port Hope, ON L1A 1N5
Tel: 905-885-2451; *Fax:* 905-885-7474
Toll-Free: 866-964-4529
info@northumberlandlaw.com
northumberlandlaw.com

***Port Perry*: Michael L. Fowler - *2**
175 North St., Port Perry, ON L9L 1B7
Tel: 905-985-8411; *Fax:* 905-985-0029
www.fowlerlaw.ca

***Prescott*: Doris Law Office - Prescott - *2**
Also Known As: DLO Lawyers
P.O. Box 2019, 257 King St. West, Prescott, ON K0E 1T0
Tel: 613-925-9018; *Fax:* 613-925-1089
www.dorislaw.com

***Rama*: Nahwegahbow Corbiere - *5**
Former Name: Nahwegahbow, Nadjiwan, Corbiere
#109, 5884 Rama Rd., Rama, ON L3V 6H6
Tel: 705-325-0520; *Fax:* 705-325-7204
mail@nncfirm.ca
www.nncfirm.ca

***Renfrew*: Sharon L. Anderson-Olmstead - *1**
117 Raglan St. South, Renfrew, ON K7V 1P8
Tel: 613-432-5898; *Fax:* 613-432-5899
sharon_anderson@bellnet.ca

***Renfrew*: Chown & Smith - *2**
297 Raglan St. South, Renfrew, ON K7V 1R6
Tel: 613-432-3669; *Fax:* 613-432-2874
admin@chownandsmith.com
www.chownandsmith.com

***Renfrew*: Lawrence E. Gallagher - *1**
33 Renfrew Ave. East, Renfrew, ON K7V 2W6
Tel: 613-432-8537; *Fax:* 613-432-8538
legallagher@nrtco.net

***Renfrew*: Joseph D. Legris Professional Corp. - *1**
248 Argyle St. South, Renfrew, ON K7V 1T7
Tel: 613-432-3689; *Fax:* 613-432-3936
legris@legrislaw.com
www.legrislaw.com

***Renfrew*: McNab, Stewart & Prince - *2**
117 Raglan St. South, Renfrew, ON K7V 1P8
Tel: 613-432-5844; *Fax:* 613-432-7832
dstewart@mcnablaw.com
www.mcnablaw.com

***Richmond Hill*: Ronald A. Balinsky - *1**
96 Arnold Cres., Richmond Hill, ON L4C 3R8
Tel: 905-884-8161; *Fax:* 905-884-3155
info@balinskylawfirm.com
www.balinskylawfirm.com

***Richmond Hill*: Peter D. Bouroukis - *1**
#411, 15 Wertheim Ct., Richmond Hill, ON L4B 3H7
Tel: 905-771-7030; *Fax:* 905-771-7027
pbouroukis@rogers.com
www.bouroukis.com

***Richmond Hill*: Jay Chauhan - *1**
#309, 330 Hwy. 7 East, Richmond Hill, ON L4B 3P8
Tel: 905-771-1235; *Fax:* 905-771-1237
jayadvocate@yahoo.ca
www.jaychauhan.com

***Richmond Hill*: James H. Chow - *1**
#512, 330 Hwy. 7 East, Richmond Hill, ON L4B 3P8
Tel: 905-881-3363

***Richmond Hill*: Corinne M. Rivers - *1**
#104, 13311 Yonge St., Richmond Hill, ON L4E 3L6
Tel: 905-773-9911; *Fax:* 905-773-9927
corrine@cmrlaw.ca
cmrlaw.tel
www.linkedin.com/pub/corinne-rivers/4/b44/65

***Richmond Hill*: Perry H. Gruenberger - *1**
#7, 30 Wertheim Crt., Richmond Hill, ON L4B 1B9
Tel: 905-764-6411; *Fax:* 905-764-5616

***Richmond Hill*: Alla Koren - *1**
489 Worthington Ave., Richmond Hill, ON L4E 4R6
Tel: 905-780-1500; *Fax:* 905-773-7906
Toll-Free: 888-622-7673
alla@allakoren.com
www.allakoren.com

***Richmond Hill*: Shirley K.T. Lo - *1**
#PH 10, 330 Hwy. 7 East, Richmond Hill, ON L4B 3P8
Tel: 905-707-5707; *Fax:* 905-707-5752
kshirleylo@hotmail.com

***Richmond Hill*: Malach Fidler Sugar + Luxenberg LLP - *14**
#6, 30 Wertheim Ct., Richmond Hill, ON L4B 1B9
Tel: 905-889-1667; *Fax:* 905-889-1139
info@malach-fidler.com
www.malach-fidler.com

***Richmond Hill*: Parker Garber & Chesney LLP - *3**
#700, 1 West Pearce St., Richmond Hill, ON L4B 1L6
Tel: 905-764-0404; *Fax:* 905-764-0320
Toll-Free: 877-446-0404
info@pgcllp.com
www.pgcllp.com

***Richmond Hill*: Pazuki Wilkins LLP - *2**
#200, 10265 Yonge St., Richmond Hill, ON L4C 4Y7
Tel: 905-508-4878; *Fax:* 905-508-4879
info@pwlawyers.ca
pwlawyers.ca

***Richmond Hill*: Roselyn Pecus - *1**
2126 Major Mackenzie Dr., Richmond Hill, ON L6A 1P7
Tel: 905-303-1494; *Fax:* 905-303-1465
roselyn@pecus.ca

***Richmond Hill*: Rohmer & Fenn - *6**
#503, Park Place Corporate Centre, 15 Wertheim Ct., Richmond Hill, ON L4B 3H7
Tel: 905-763-6690; *Fax:* 905-763-6699
firm@rohmerfenn.com
www.rohmerfenn.com

***Richmond Hill*: Barry Seltzer - *1**
#204, 9140 Leslie St., Richmond Hill, ON L4B 0A9
Tel: 905-475-9001; *Fax:* 905-475-9004
barry@barryseltzer.com

***Richmond Hill*: Erwin S. Seltzer - *1**
#204, 9140 Leslie St., Richmond Hill, ON L4B 0A9
Tel: 905-474-4333; *Fax:* 905-474-4339
www.erwinseltzerdivorcefamilylaw.itgo.com

***Richmond Hill*: Virgilio Law - *1**
#500, 1 West Pearce St., Richmond Hill, ON L4B 3K3
Tel: 905-882-8666; *Fax:* 905-882-1082
jvirgilio@virgiliolaw.com
virgiliolaw.com

***Richmond Hill*: Gordon E. Watkin - *1**
#212A, 9350 Yonge St., Richmond Hill, ON L4C 5G2
Tel: 905-884-3778; *Fax:* 905-884-2655

***Ridgetown*: Edward T. Little - *1**
P.O. Box 700, 64 Main St. East, Ridgetown, ON N0P 2C0
Tel: 519-674-5436; *Fax:* 519-674-3352
etlittle@bellnet.ca

***Ridgetown*: Daniel B. Nicol - *1**
P.O. Box 700, 64 Main St. East, Ridgetown, ON N0P 2C0
Tel: 519-674-3372; *Fax:* 519-674-3352
dbnicol@bellnet.ca

***Ridgeway*: Community Legal Services of Niagara South - *1**
P.O. Box 430, 266 Ridge Rd. S, Ridgeway, ON L0S 1N0
Tel: 905-894-4775; *Fax:* 905-894-6101

***Rockland*: Charron Langlois LLP - Rockland - *10**
Former Name: Langlois/Gauthier
#1, P.O. Box 880, 2784 Laurier St., Rockland, ON K4K 1L5
Tel: 613-446-6411; *Fax:* 613-446-4513
clllp.ca
www.facebook.com/pages/Charron-Langlois-LLPsrl/3555401077 96575, www.linkedin.com/pub/stephane-langlois/52/707/619

***Rockwood*: Douglas S. Black - *1**
P.O. Box 95, 118 Main St. South, Rockwood, ON N0B 2K0
Tel: 519-856-4555; *Fax:* 519-856-4680
dblacklaw@cogeco.net

***Rockwood*: Judith P. Ryan - *1**
P.O. Box 550, Rockwood, ON N0B 2K0
Tel: 519-856-2223; *Fax:* 519-856-2047
jpmryan@aol.com

***Sarnia*: Paul R. Beaudet - *1**
251 Exmouth St., Sarnia, ON N7T 7M7
Tel: 519-337-1529; *Fax:* 519-336-2569
beaudet@ebtech.net

***Sarnia*: Terry L. Brandon - *1**
1069 London Rd., Sarnia, ON N7S 1P2
Tel: 519-337-4634; *Fax:* 519-337-5586
terrybrandon@sympatico.ca

***Sarnia*: Roderick Brown, Q.C. - *1**
555 Exmouth St., Sarnia, ON N7T 5P6
Tel: 519-336-7880; *Fax:* 519-336-6584
re_brown2927@hotmail.com

***Sarnia*: James J. Carpeneto - *1**
316 Christina St. North, Sarnia, ON N7T 5V5
Tel: 519-336-6955; *Fax:* 519-336-8401

***Sarnia*: Francis De Sena - *1**
422 East St. North, Sarnia, ON N7T 6Y4
Tel: 519-336-9999; *Fax:* 519-336-9131
francis@desenalaw.com
www.desenalaw.com

***Sarnia*: David A. Elliott - *2**
Former Name: Elliott, Porter, McFadyen & McFadyen
#101, St. Clair Corporate Centre, 265 Front St. North, Sarnia, ON N7T 7X1
Tel: 519-336-4600; *Fax:* 519-336-4640

***Sarnia*: George Murray Shipley Bell, LLP - *7**
P.O. Box 2196, 2 Ferry Dock Hill, Sarnia, ON N7T 7L8
Tel: 519-336-8770; *Fax:* 519-336-1811
www.sarnialaw.com

***Sarnia*: Gray, Bruce, Cimetta (Carlo Cimetta Professional Corporation) - *4**
P.O. Box 2259, 1166 London Rd., Sarnia, ON N7T 7L7
Tel: 519-336-9700; *Fax:* 519-336-3289

** indicates number of lawyers*

***Sarnia*: David G. Hockin - *1**
#101, 265 Front St. North, Sarnia, ON N7T 7X1
Tel: 519-336-4357; *Fax:* 519-336-4367
lawyer@ebtech.net

***Sarnia*: Pamela J. McLeod - *1**
1350 L'Heritage Dr., Sarnia, ON N7S 6H8
Tel: 519-542-7714; *Fax:* 519-542-5577
mcleodlaw@ebtech.net

***Sarnia*: Raymond A. Whitnall - *1**
#112, 560 Exmouth St., Sarnia, ON N7T 5P5
Tel: 519-336-9460; *Fax:* 519-336-8366

***Sarnia*: Wyrzykowski & Robb - *2**
P.O. Box 2200, Stn. Main, Sarnia, ON N7T 7L7
Tel: 519-336-6118; *Fax:* 519-336-9550
mars@ebtech.net

***Sault Ste Marie*: Aiello, Pawelek - *2**
#102, 123 March St., Sault Ste Marie, ON P6A 2Z5
Tel: 705-946-8590; *Fax:* 705-946-8589

***Sault Ste Marie*: Allemano & FitzGerald - *2**
#103, McCarda Bldg., P.O. Box 10, 139 Queen St. East, Sault Ste Marie, ON P6A 1Z4
Tel: 705-942-0142; *Fax:* 705-942-7188

***Sault Ste Marie*: Bisceglia Dumanski Romano & Johnson LLP - *4**
#202, 747 Queen St. East, Sault Ste Marie, ON P6A 2A8
Tel: 705-942-5856; *Fax:* 705-942-6493
info@ssmlawfirm.com
www.ssmlawfirm.com

***Sault Ste Marie*: Kenneth R. Davies**
#201, 111 Elgin St., Sault Ste Marie, ON P6A 6L6
Tel: 705-256-7839; *Fax:* 705-256-7837
kendavies@saultlawyer.com
www.saultlawyer.com

***Sault Ste Marie*: Laidlaw, Paciocco, Melville - *3**
Former Name: Kelleher, Laidlaw, Paciocco, Melville
#604, 421 Bay St., Sault Ste Marie, ON P6A 1X3
Tel: 705-949-7790; *Fax:* 705-949-5816

***Sault Ste Marie*: O. Kennedy Lawson - *1**
#104, 473 Queen St. East, Sault Ste Marie, ON P6A 1Z5
Tel: 705-759-5030; *Fax:* 705-942-5309
oklawson@bellnet.ca

***Sault Ste Marie*: Eric D. McCooeye - *1**
348 Albert St. East, Sault Ste Marie, ON P6A 2J6
Tel: 705-945-8868; *Fax:* 705-945-9051

***Sault Ste Marie*: O'Neill DeLorenzi & Mendes - *5**
116 Spring St., Sault Ste Marie, ON P6A 3A1
Tel: 705-949-6901; *Fax:* 705-949-0618
info@saultlawyers.com
www.saultlawyers.com

***Sault Ste Marie*: Orazietti, Kwolek, Walz - *4**
#200, 477 Queen St. East, Sault Ste Marie, ON P6A 1Z5
Tel: 705-256-5601; *Fax:* 705-945-9427

***Sault Ste Marie*: Rudolph C. Peres, Q.C. - *1**
#104, 212 Queen St. East, Sault Ste Marie, ON P6A 5X8
Tel: 705-949-9411; *Fax:* 705-949-3759

***Sault Ste Marie*: William R. Scott - *1**
#1, 224B Queen St. East, Sault Ste Marie, ON P6A 1Y7
Tel: 705-949-4333; *Fax:* 705-945-0958
wmrscottlaw@yahoo.com

***Sault Ste Marie*: Carol A. Shamess - *1**
#3, 553 Queen St. East, Sault Ste Marie, ON P6A 2A3
Tel: 705-942-2580; *Fax:* 705-942-5048
carola.shamess@shaw.ca

***Sault Ste Marie*: Jack Squire - *1**
191 Northern Ave. East, Sault Ste Marie, ON P6B 4H8
Tel: 705-949-0162; *Fax:* 705-541-9616

***Sault Ste Marie*: T. Frederick Baxter, Barrister & Solicitor - *1**
494 Albert St. East, Sault Ste Marie, ON P6A 2K2
Tel: 705-759-0948; *Fax:* 705-759-2042
kerriadmin@shaw.ca

***Sault Ste Marie*: Walker, Thompson - *1**
#506, 123 March St., Sault Ste Marie, ON P6A 2Z5
Tel: 705-949-7806; *Fax:* 705-759-0457
walkerlaw@shaw.ca

***Sault Ste Marie*: Willson, Carter - *3**
494 Albert St. East, Sault Ste Marie, ON P6A 2K2
Tel: 705-942-2000; *Fax:* 705-942-6511
willsoncarter.com

***Sault Ste Marie*: Wishart Law Firm LLP - *5**
#500, 390 Bay St., Sault Ste Marie, ON P6A 1X2
Tel: 705-949-6700; *Fax:* 705-949-2465
wishart@wishartlaw.com
www.wishartlaw.com

***Schomberg*: Clarke G. Smith - *1**
Brownsville Junction Plaza, P.O. Box 454, Schomberg, ON L0G 1T0
Tel: 905-939-2344; *Fax:* 905-727-7096
cgsmith@rogers.com

***Seaforth*: Devereaux Murray Professional Corporation - *2**
P.O. Box 220, 77 Main St. South, Seaforth, ON N0K 1W0
Tel: 519-527-0850; *Fax:* 519-527-2324
c4thlaw@devereauxmurray.ca
www.devereauxmurray.ca

***Seeleys Bay*: David J. Atkinson - *1**
RR#1, Seeleys Bay, ON K0H 2N0
Tel: 613-382-2692

***Shelburne*: Timmerman, Haskell & Mills LLP - *2**
P.O. Box 216, 305 Owen Sound St., Shelburne, ON L0N 1S0
Tel: 519-925-2608; *Fax:* 519-925-2268
lhaskell@shelburnelaw.ca
shelburnelaw.ca

***Simcoe*: Bachmann Personal Injury Law - *1**
P.O. Box 156, 39 Kent St. North, Simcoe, ON N3Y 4L1
Tel: 519-428-8090
www.bachmannlaw.ca
www.facebook.com/BachmannLaw

***Simcoe*: Brimage Law Group LLP - *9**
Former Name: Brimage, Tyrrell, Van Severen & Homeniuk
21 Norfolk St. North, Simcoe, ON N3Y 4L1
Tel: 519-426-5840; *Fax:* 519-426-7515
law@brimage.com
www.brimage.com
www.facebook.com/BrimageLawGroup, twitter.com/BrimageLawGroup, www.linkedin.com/company/2576968?trk=tyah

***Simcoe*: Cline Backus LLP - *8**
Former Name: Cline Backus Nightingale McArthur
P.O. Box 528, 39 Colborne St. North, Simcoe, ON N3Y 4N5
Tel: 519-426-6763; *Fax:* 519-426-2055
cbnmlaw@kwic.com
www.clinebackus.com

***Simcoe*: Cobb & Jones LLP - Simcoe - *8**
P.O. Box 548, 23 Argyle St., Simcoe, ON N3Y 4N5
Tel: 519-428-0170; *Fax:* 519-428-3105
cobblaw@cobbjones.ca
www.cobbjones.ca

***Simcoe*: Sheppard, MacIntosh, Lados & Nunn LLP - *4**
P.O. Box 677, 58 Peel St., Simcoe, ON N3Y 4T2
Tel: 519-426-1382; *Fax:* 519-426-1392
lawyers@sheppardmacintosh.com
www.sheppardmacintosh.com

***Simcoe*: Smelko Law Office - *1**
25 Norfolk St. North, Simcoe, ON N3Y 3N6
Tel: 519-426-1711; *Fax:* 519-426-7863
Toll-Free: 866-684-8527
smelkolaw@on.aibn.com

***Sioux Lookout*: Kevin W. Romyn - *1**
P.O. Box 99, 69 Queen St., Sioux Lookout, ON P8T 1A1
Tel: 807-737-2562; *Fax:* 807-737-2571
romynlaw@gosiouxlookout.com

***Smiths Falls*: G.W. Fournier - *1**
P.O. Box 752, 35 Daniel St., Smiths Falls, ON K7A 4W6
Tel: 613-283-8818; *Fax:* 613-283-8951
gwfournier@cogeco.ca

***Smiths Falls*: Howard Ryan Kelford Knott & Dixon - Smiths Falls - *5**
2 Main St. East, Smiths Falls, ON K7A 1A2
Tel: 613-283-6772; *Fax:* 613-283-8840
www.smithsfallslaw.ca

***Smiths Falls*: Kirkland & Murphy - *3**
Former Name: Kirkland, Murphy & Lee
P.O. Box 220, 15 Russell St. East, Smiths Falls, ON K7A 4T1
Tel: 613-283-0515; *Fax:* 613-283-8557
tblair@smithsfallslawyer.com
www.smithsfallslawyer.com

***Smiths Falls*: Ross Cliffen & Morrison - *3**
Former Name: Ross & Cliffen
P.O. Box 804, 30 Russell St. East, Smiths Falls, ON K7A 4W6
Tel: 613-283-7331; *Fax:* 613-283-6792
rosslaw@ripnet.com
www.rossandcliffen.com

***Southampton*: Robert E. Forsyth - *1**
P.O. Box 430, 243 High St., Southampton, ON N0H 2L0
Tel: 519-797-3223; *Fax:* 519-797-3192
forsyth3@bmts.com

***St Albert*: Ritzen Olivieri LLP - *3**
#302, 7 St Anne St., St Albert, ON T8N 2X4
Tel: 780-460-2900; *Fax:* 780-460-2466
dougr@rolaw.ca
www.rolaw.ca

***St Catharines*: Richard H. Barch - *1**
46 Ontario St., St Catharines, ON L2R 5J4
Tel: 905-641-1146; *Fax:* 905-641-1148

***St Catharines*: W.J. Garry Bracken - *1**
50 Dunvegan Rd., St Catharines, ON L2P 1H6
Tel: 905-988-9389
bracklaw@cogeco.ca
www.brackenlaw.ca

***St Catharines*: Jolanta B. Bula - *1**
#704, 1 St. Paul St., St Catharines, ON L2R 7L2
Tel: 905-938-5480; *Fax:* 905-938-5488
jbb@jolantabula.com
www.jolantabula.com

***St Catharines*: L. Jane Burbage - *1**
55 King Street, 4th Fl., St Catharines, ON L2R 3H5
Tel: 289-362-1322; *Fax:* 289-362-2487
ljb@burbagebarristers.com
www.burbagebarristers.com

***St Catharines*: Chown, Cairns LLP - *17**
#900, P.O. Box 760, 80 King St., St Catharines, ON L2R 6Y8
Tel: 905-346-0775; *Fax:* 905-688-0015
lawyers@chowlaw.com
www.chownlaw.com

***St Catharines*: Tracy J. Middleton Collini - *1**
123 Niagara St., St. Catharines, ON L2R 4L6
Tel: 905-937-9229; *Fax:* 905-937-9228
collinilaw@msn.com
collinilaw.vpweb.ca

***St Catharines*: Crossingham, Brady - *2**
P.O. Box 307, 63 Ontario St., St Catharines, ON L2R 6V2
Tel: 905-641-1621; *Fax:* 905-685-1461
cbo@crossinghambrady.com

***St Catharines*: Daniel & Partners LLP - *12**
P.O. Box 24022, 39 Queen St., St Catharines, ON L2R 7P7
Tel: 905-688-9411; *Fax:* 905-688-5747
Toll-Free: 800-263-3650
info@niagaralaw.ca
www.niagaralaw.ca
www.facebook.com/niagaralaw, twitter.com/niagaralaw

***St Catharines*: Mark F. Dedinsky - *1**
154 James St., St Catharines, ON L2R 5C5
Tel: 905-688-6275; *Fax:* 905-682-0264
mfd.lawoffice@gmail.com
www.mfdlawyer.com

***St Catharines*: Forster, Lewandowski & Cords - *2**
#2, 82 Lake St., St Catharines, ON L2R 7A7
Tel: 905-688-9110; *Fax:* 905-688-0901
Toll-Free: 866-715-9380
info@forsterlewandowskiandcords.ca
www.forsterlewandowskiandcords.ca/en/

***St Catharines*: Ralph H. Frayne - *1**
Former Name: Freeman, Frayne & Hummell
9 Raymond St., St Catharines, ON L2R 2S9
Tel: 905-684-1147; *Fax:* 905-684-7147

***St Catharines*: Graves Richard Harris LLP - *7**
#800, P.O. Box 1690, 55 King St., St Catharines, ON L2R 7K1
Tel: 289-438-2213; *Fax:* 905-641-0484
www.hurtline.ca

** indicates number of lawyers*

St Catharines: **Erik Grinbergs**
37 Church St., St Catharines, ON L2R 3B7
Tel: 905-688-9800; *Fax:* 905-684-0009
grinberg@vaxxine.com

St Catharines: **Hanna Injury Law - *2**
#300, P.O. Box 24044, 43 Church St., St Catharines, ON L2R 7P7
Tel: 905-687-9347; *Fax:* 905-687-3939
lawyers@hannainjurylaw.com
www.hannainjurylaw.com

St Catharines: **Heelis Little & Almas LLP, Barristers & Solicitors - *4**
Also Known As: HWL&A
Former Name: Heelis, Williams, Little & Almas LLP, Barristers & Solicitors
P.O. Box 1056, 14 Church St., St Catharines, ON L2R 7A3
Tel: 905-581-4242; *Fax:* 905-684-4844
www.14churchstlawoffice.com

St Catharines: **David R. House - *1**
31 Church St., St Catharines, ON L2R 3B7
Tel: 905-688-4650; *Fax:* 905-984-6314
dhouse@houselaw.ca
www.houselaw.ca
www.linkedin.com/pub/david-house/17/874/b13

St Catharines: **Lancaster, Brooks & Welch LLP - St Catharines - *19**
Former Name: Lancaster, Mix & Welch
#800, P.O. Box 790, 80 King St., St Catharines, ON L2R 6Z1
Tel: 905-641-1551; *Fax:* 905-641-1830
www.lbwlawyers.com
www.facebook.com/pages/Lancaster-Brooks-Welch-LLP/291713017639163,
www.linkedin.com/company/lancaster-brooks-&-welch-llp

St Catharines: **Leon & Fazari LLP - *1**
33 Maywood Ave., St Catharines, ON L2R 1C5
Tel: 905-658-0057
www.leonlaw.ca

St Catharines: **Frank M. Marotta - *1**
21 Duke St., St Catharines, ON L2R 5W1
Tel: 905-688-5401; *Fax:* 905-688-6204
fmarotta@vaxxine.com

St Catharines: **Martens, Lingard LLP - *7**
Former Name: Martens, Lingard, Maddalena, Robinson & Koke
#700, 43 Church St., St Catharines, ON L2R 7E1
Tel: 905-687-6551; *Fax:* 905-687-6553
reception@martenslingard.com
www.martenslingard.com/en/

St Catharines: **Joseph C. McCallum - *1**
#100, 205 King St., St Catharines, ON L2R 3J5
Tel: 289-362-5666; *Fax:* 289-434-0561
www.joemlaw.com

St Catharines: **Paula McPherson - *1**
51 Hillcrest Ave., St Catharines, ON L2R 4Y3
Tel: 905-641-3457
resolve@sympatico.ca

St Catharines: **Morgan, Dilts & Toppari Law - *2**
Box 216, 281 St Paul St., St Catharines, ON L2R 6S4
Tel: 905-685-7391; *Fax:* 905-685-9102
mdt@bellnet.ca
www.mdtlaw.ca

St Catharines: **O'Neill & Radford - *1**
154 James St., St Catharines, ON L2R 7A3
Tel: 905-641-2633; *Fax:* 905-682-0264
bmradford@bellnet.ca

St Catharines: **Ian G. Pearson - *1**
154 James St., 2nd Fl., St Catharines, ON L2R 5C5
Tel: 905-682-7882; *Fax:* 905-682-0264
ipearson@bellnet.ca

St Catharines: **Sullivan, Mahoney LLP - St Catharines - *31**
P.O. Box 1360, 40 Queen St., St Catharines, ON L2R 6Z2
Tel: 905-688-6655; *Fax:* 905-688-5814
www.sullivan-mahoney.com

St Catharines: **Wilson Spurr LLP - *3**
#168, 261 Martindale Rd., St Catharines, ON L2W 1A2
Tel: 905-682-2775; *Fax:* 905-682-2357
Toll-Free: 888-722-4193
contactus@wilsonspurrlaw.ca
www.wilsonspurrlaw.ca

St Catharines: **Virginia L. Workman - *1**
#1004, 1 St. Paul, St Catharines, ON L2R 7L2
Tel: 905-704-0804; *Fax:* 905-704-4464
lawoffice@virginiaworkman.ca
www.virginiaworkman.ca

St Marys: **William J. Galloway - *1**
P.O. Box 897, Stn. Main, 172 Queen St. East, St Marys, ON N4X 1B6
Tel: 519-284-2112; *Fax:* 519-284-3081

St Marys: **McCotter Law Office - St Marys - *6**
50 Water St. South, St Mary's, ON N4X 1C3
Tel: 519-284-2840
stmarys@lawtter.com
lawtter.com
twitter.com/MLOconnect,
www.linkedin.com/company/mccotter-law-office-p-c-

St Thomas: **Bowsher & Bowsher - *3**
112 Centre St., St Thomas, ON N5R 2Z9
Tel: 519-633-3301; *Fax:* 519-633-5995
sandyb@bowsherandbowsher.ca
www.bowsherandbowsher.com

St Thomas: **Jerome A. Collins - *1**
36 Hincks St., St Thomas, ON N5R 3N6
Tel: 519-633-3973; *Fax:* 519-633-7916

St Thomas: **Ferguson DiMeo Lawyers - *2**
#211, Canada Southern Railway Station, 750 Talbot St., St Thomas, ON N5P 1E2
Tel: 519-633-8838; *Fax:* 519-633-9361
www.fergusondimeolaw.com

St Thomas: **William Glover - *1**
P.O. Box 575, Stn. Main, 458 Talbot St., St Thomas, ON N5P 3V6
Tel: 519-633-2300; *Fax:* 519-633-0964
gloverlawyer@aol.com

St Thomas: **Gunn & Associates - *6**
108 Centre St., St Thomas, ON N5R 2Z7
Tel: 519-631-0700; *Fax:* 519-631-1468
lawyers@gunn.on.ca
www.gunn.on.ca

St Thomas: **Sanders, Cline - *3**
P.O. Box 70, 14 Southwick St., St Thomas, ON N5P 3T5
Tel: 519-633-0800; *Fax:* 519-633-9259
sanderscline@sandlawyers.ca
www.sandlawyers.ca

St Thomas: **Arnold B. Walker - *1**
P.O. Box 20022, Stn. Centre, 4 Elgin St., St Thomas, ON N5R 4H4
Tel: 519-633-3273; *Fax:* 519-633-8585

Stoney Creek: **Cicchi & Giangregorio - *2**
1-99 Hwy. 8, Stoney Creek, ON L8G 1C1
Tel: 905-664-6645; *Fax:* 905-664-6952

Stoney Creek: **Coombs & Lutz - *1**
6 Lake Ave. South, Stoney Creek, ON L8G 1P3
Tel: 905-664-6341; *Fax:* 905-664-8966
info@coombsandlutz.ca
www.coombsandlutz.ca/en/

Stoney Creek: **MacKinnon Law Associates - *2**
Former Name: MacKinnon, Mary J.
#10, 44 King St. East, Stoney Creek, ON L8G 1K1
Tel: 905-662-0046; *Fax:* 905-662-3339
info@mackinnonlaw.com
www.mackinnonlaw.com

Stoney Creek: **Murray Mazza - *1**
#1, 426 Hwy. 8, Stoney Creek, ON L8G 1G2
Tel: 289-273-0066
www.stoneycreekrealestatelaw.ca

Stoney Creek: **McHugh Mowat Whitmore Ionico MacPherson LLP - *9**
337 Queenston Rd., Stoney Creek, ON L8G 1B7
Tel: 905-662-6001; *Fax:* 905-662-6004
www.mmwimlawfirm.ca

Stoney Creek: **O'Brien & Skrtich - *1**
26 King St. East, Stoney Creek, ON L8G 1J8
Tel: 905-662-2855; *Fax:* 905-662-8881

Stoney Creek: **Mari-Anne Saunders - *1**
#303, 800 Queenston Rd., Stoney Creek, ON L8G 1A7
Tel: 905-664-6683; *Fax:* 905-664-4876

Stouffville: **Paul J. Crowe - *1**
#208, 86 Ringwood Dr., Stouffville, ON L4A 1C3
Tel: 905-640-8100; *Fax:* 905-640-6064
info@pauljcrowe.com
www.pauljcrowe.com

Stouffville: **Monica Farrell - *1**
P.O. Box 220, Stn. Main, 6361 Main St., Stouffville, ON L4A 7Z5
Tel: 905-640-3530
law@monicafarrell.com
www.monicafarrell.com

Stouffville: **Thomas & Pelman Professional Corporation - *1**
P.O. Box 940, 6131 Main St., Stouffville, ON L4A 3R6
Tel: 905-640-2211; *Fax:* 905-640-8161
thomasandpelman@thomasandpelman.com

Stratford: **Barenberg & Roth Professional Corporation - *3**
Former Name: Barenberg, McDonald
160 Erie St., Stratford, ON N5A 2M7
Tel: 519-271-6360; *Fax:* 519-271-3074
Toll-Free: 800-709-3849
info@barenbergandroth.com
www.barenbergandroth.com

Stratford: **John W. Buechler - *1**
488 Erie St., Stratford, ON N5A 2N6
Tel: 519-271-3520; *Fax:* 519-271-0097
wjblaw@wightman.ca

Stratford: **Michael F. Fair - *1**
10 Downie St., 2nd Fl., Stratford, ON N5A 7K4
Tel: 519-271-2912; *Fax:* 519-271-2732

Stratford: **W. Stirling Kenny Law Office - *1**
19 Ontario St., Stratford, ON N5A 3G7
Tel: 519-271-1005

Stratford: **Monteith Ritsma Phillips LLP - Stratford - *9**
P.O. Box 846, 56 Albert St., Stratford, ON N5A 6W3
Tel: 519-271-6770; *Fax:* 519-271-9261
www.stratfordlawyers.com

Stratford: **Skinner, Dunphy & Bantle LLP - *3**
Former Name: Skinner, Rogerson, Dunphy
P.O. Box 542, 1 Ontario St., Stratford, ON N5A 6T7
Tel: 519-271-7330; *Fax:* 519-271-1762
thefirm@stratfordlaw.com
www.stratfordlaw.com

Strathroy: **Robert J. Dack - *1**
16 Front St. East, Strathroy, ON N7G 1Y4
Tel: 519-245-0370; *Fax:* 519-245-0523
robertdack@bam.on.ca

Strathroy: **Jones, Gibbons & Reis - *2**
39 Front St. W, Strathroy, ON N7G 1X5
Tel: 519-245-0110

Strathroy: **Quinlan & Somerville - *2**
18 Front St. East, Strathroy, ON N7G 1Y4
Tel: 519-245-0342; *Fax:* 519-245-0108
cquinlan@quinlansomerville.com

Strathroy: **George E. Sinker - *2**
53 Front St. West, Strathroy, ON N7G 1X6
Tel: 519-245-1144; *Fax:* 519-245-6090
gsinker@bellnet.ca

Sudbury: **Michael G. Barnett - *1**
264 Elm St., Sudbury, ON P3C 1V4
Tel: 705-674-3210; *Fax:* 705-674-1265

Sudbury: **William G. Beach - *1**
224 Applegrove St., Sudbury, ON P3C 1N3
Tel: 705-675-5685; *Fax:* 705-675-6601

Sudbury: **D. Peter Best - *1**
125 Durham St., 2nd Fl., Sudbury, ON P3E 3M9
Tel: 705-674-9292; *Fax:* 705-674-8912
peterbest@peterbestlawoffices.com
www.peterbestlawoffices.com

Sudbury: **Gerald D. Brouillette - *1**
235 Elm St., Sudbury, ON P3C 1T8
Tel: 705-674-2822; *Fax:* 705-674-2975
gerry.brouillette@sympatico.ca

** indicates number of lawyers*

Sudbury: Conroy Trebb Scott Hurtubise LLP - *8
164 Elm St., Sudbury, ON P3C 1T7
Tel: 705-674-6441; Fax: 705-673-9567
Toll-Free: 800-627-1825
info@ctsh.ca
ctsh.ca

Sudbury: DeDiana, Eloranta & Longstreet - *1
219 Pine St., Sudbury, ON P3C 1X4
Tel: 705-674-4289; Fax: 705-671-1047

Sudbury: Desmarais, Keenan LLP - *11
#201, 62 Frood Rd., Sudbury, ON P3C 4Z3
Tel: 705-675-7521; Fax: 705-675-7390
Toll-Free: 800-290-5465
www.desmaraiskeenan.com

Sudbury: Hugh A. Doig, Q.C. - *1
296 Larc296 Regional Rd. 51, Sudbury, ON P3B 1M1
Tel: 705-674-4213; Fax: 705-671-1652
doig@on.aibn.com

Sudbury: Robbie D. Gordon - *1
Court House, 155 Elm St., Sudbury, ON P3C 1T9
Tel: 705-564-7799; Fax: 705-564-7252

Sudbury: Brian N. Howe - *1
235 Elm St. West, Sudbury, ON P3C 1T8
Tel: 705-674-8317; Fax: 705-674-2952

Sudbury: Elizabeth Kari - *1
293 Elm St., 2nd Fl., Sudbury, ON P3C 1V6
Tel: 705-670-2770; Fax: 705-670-9172
ekari@cyberbeach.net

Sudbury: Donald Kuyek - *1
229 Elm St. West, Sudbury, ON P3C 1T8
Tel: 705-675-1227; Fax: 705-675-5350
kuyek@vianet.ca

Sudbury: Lacroix Lawyers | Avocats - *2
#100, 161 Larch St., Sudbury, ON P3E 1C4
Tel: 705-674-1976; Fax: 705-674-6978
www.sudburylaw.com

Sudbury: Patricia L. Meehan - *1
293 Elm St. West, Sudbury, ON P3C 1V6
Tel: 705-674-2272; Fax: 705-674-5238
meehanlawoffice@bellnet.ca

Sudbury: Mensour & Mensour - *2
#101, 238 Elm St., Sudbury, ON P3C 1V3
Tel: 705-673-6787; Fax: 705-673-1418

Sudbury: Miller Maki LLP - *12
176 Elm St., Sudbury, ON P3C 1T7
Tel: 705-675-7503; Fax: 705-675-8669
email@millermaki.com
www.millermaki.com

Sudbury: Paquette-Renzini, Barristers, Solicitors & Notaries - *2
#202, 40 Larch St., Sudbury, ON P3E 5M7
Tel: 705-805-0403; Fax: 705-560-8072
mail@paquette-renzini.ca
www.paquette-renzini.ca

Sudbury: Parisé Law Office - *2
#200, 58 Lisgar St., 2nd Fl., Sudbury, ON P3E 3L7
Tel: 705-674-4042; Fax: 705-674-4242
pariselaw@unitz.ca

Sudbury: Stanley J. Thomas - *1
111 Durham St., Sudbury, ON P3E 3M9
Tel: 705-674-8306; Fax: 705-675-8466

Sudbury: Law Office of Serge F. Treherne - *1
P.O. Box 1269, 144 Elm St. West, Sudbury, ON P3C 1T7
Tel: 705-670-9689; Fax: 705-670-9141
Toll-Free: 877-550-5616

Sudbury: Violette Law Offices - *1
#1, 11 Elgin St., Sudbury, ON P3C 5B6
Tel: 705-674-1300; Fax: 705-671-1044
Toll-Free: 866-991-1300
office@violettelaw.com
violettelaw.com

Sudbury: Weaver - Simmons LLP - *34
#400, 233 Brady St., Sudbury, ON P3B 4H5
Tel: 705-674-6421; Fax: 705-674-9948
thefirm@weaversimmons.com
www.weaversimmons.com

Sutton: Fahey Crate Law Professional Corporation - *3
Former Name: Patrick J. Fahey Law Office
P.O. Box 487, 100 High St., Sutton, ON L0E 1R0
Tel: 905-722-3771; Fax: 905-722-9852
info@faheycratelaw.ca
www.faheycratelaw.ca

Thornhill: Arrigo Bros Ltd. - *1
Former Name: Augustine M. Arrigo, Q.C.
48 Guardsman Rd., Thornhill, ON L3T 6L4
Tel: 905-889-6131

Thornhill: Leslie (Masood) Brown - *1
#225B, Commerce Gate, 505 Hwy. 7 E, Thornhill, ON L3T 7T1
Tel: 905-731-5083; Fax: 905-731-4078
Toll-Free: 800-268-0314
info@torontolegalservices.ca
www.torontolegalservices.ca

Thornhill: Edward L. Burlew - *1
16 John St., Thornhill, ON L3T 1X8
Tel: 905-882-2422; Fax: 905-882-2431
Toll-Free: 888-486-5677

Thornhill: Crupi Law - *1
Former Name: D'Andrea, Crupi
#302, 305 Renfrew Dr., Thornhill, ON L3R 9S7
Tel: 905-415-8900; Fax: 905-415-8902
cacrupi@crupilaw.ca
www.crupilaw.ca

Thornhill: Iain Stewart Cunningham - *1
20 Cypress Point Ct., Thornhill, ON L3T 1V7
Tel: 905-764-7376; Fax: 905-707-5818

Thornhill: Stephen R. Dyment - *1
#216, 2900 Steeles Ave. E, Thornhill, ON L3T 4X1
Tel: 905-882-1277; Fax: 905-882-8536

Thornhill: Fish & Associates Professional Corporation - *2
7951 Yonge St., Thornhill, ON L3T 2C4
Tel: 905-881-1500 Toll-Free: 877-439-3999
www.familyfight.com

Thornhill: A.M. Flisfeder - *1
45 Janesville Rd., Thornhill, ON L4J 6Z9
Tel: 416-469-0375; Fax: 416-469-0375
sgt_lafourse@sympatico.ca

Thornhill: Gregory J. Gaglione - *1
#202, 7368 Yonge St., Thornhill, ON L4J 8H9
Tel: 905-882-0066; Fax: 905-882-2550

Thornhill: Elana P. Glass - *1
149 Langtry Pl., Thornhill, ON L4J 8L6
Tel: 416-587-5680

Thornhill: Seymour Iseman - *1
Former Name: Iseman & Associate
#216, 2900 Steeles Ave. East, Thornhill, ON L3T 4X1
Tel: 905-881-8800; Fax: 905-881-7391
siseman@allstream.net

Thornhill: Arthur Lundy - *1
#402, 300 John St., Thornhill, ON L3T 5W4
Tel: 905-886-3110; Fax: 905-886-0989

Thornhill: Carolyn L. MacDonald - *1
14 Morgan Ave., Thornhill, ON L3T 1R1
Tel: 905-707-7723; Fax: 905-707-5818

Thornhill: D. Todd Morganstein - *1
#110, 8111 Yonge St., Thornhill, ON L3T 4V9
Tel: 905-881-8289; Fax: 905-881-2696

Thornhill: Newton HR Law - *1
8 Waterloo Ct., Thornhill, ON L3T 6L9
Tel: 416-846-6855
www.newtonhrlaw.com
www.linkedin.com/profile/view?id=12179030

Thornhill: Tania Perlin - *1
P.O. Box 137, Stn. B10, 800 Steeles Ave. W, Thornhill, ON L4J 7L2
Tel: 416-225-5424; Fax: 416-225-3611
www.taniaperlin.com

Thornhill: Raphael Barristers - Thornhill - *5
#202, 1137 Centre St., Thornhill, ON L4J 3M6
Tel: 416-594-1812; Fax: 416-594-0868
Toll-Free: 877-217-1812
info@raphaelbarristers.com
www.raphaelbarristers.com

Thornhill: Thomas H. Riesz - *1
#218, 180 Steeles Ave. W, Thornhill, ON L4J 2L1
Tel: 905-881-5609; Fax: 905-881-9859

Thornhill: Alan G. Silverstein - *1
14 Windhaven Terrace, Thornhill, ON L4J 7N9
Tel: 905-886-0300; Fax: 647-795-9207
alan.silverstein@rogers.com
www.linkedin.com/in/alansilversteinlawyer

Thornhill: Stewart Floyd Sklar - *1
175 Newport Sq., Thornhill, ON L4J 7N6
Tel: 905-886-6802; Fax: 905-886-4482

Thornhill: Ben Weinstein - *1
#203, 1 Clark Ave. West, Thornhill, ON L4J 7Y6
Tel: 905-889-5364; Fax: 905-889-3231

Thornhill: Lawrence C. Wesson, Barrister & Solicitor - *1
300 John, Thornhill, ON L3T 5W4
Tel: 905-695-0290

Thornhill: Sheldon Wisener - *1
Former Name: Greenberg, Barry S.
7626A Yonge St., Thornhill, ON L4J 1V9
Tel: 905-886-9535; Fax: 905-886-9540
sheldon@wisenerlaw.com

Thorold: Jurmain Law Office
8A Clairmont St., Thorold, ON L2V 1R1
Tel: 905-227-2829; Fax: 905-227-9206
info@jurmainlaw.com
www.jurmainlaw.com

Thorold: John J. Simon - *1
P.O. Box 505, Stn. Thorold, 7 Front St. North, Thorold, ON L2V 4W1
Tel: 905-227-9191; Fax: 905-227-7234
john_smith@hotmail.com

Thorold: Young McNamara - *1
18 Albert St. East, Thorold, ON L2V 1P1
Tel: 905-227-3777; Fax: 905-227-5988
youngmcnamara@hotmail.com
www.youngmcnamara.com

Thunder Bay: Atwood Labine Arnone McCartney LLP - *8
501 Donald St. East, Thunder Bay, ON P7E 6N6
Tel: 807-623-4342; Fax: 807-623-2098
asl@asl-law.com
www.alamlaw.ca

Thunder Bay: David S. Bruzzese - *1
#320, Marina Park Centre, 180 Park Ave., Thunder Bay, ON P7B 6J4
Tel: 807-344-1020; Fax: 807-344-1433
dsb.law@shawlink.ca

Thunder Bay: Buset & Partners LLP - *14
1121 Barton St., Thunder Bay, ON P7B 5N3
Tel: 807-623-2500; Fax: 807-622-7808
Toll-Free: 866-532-8738
www.buset-partners.com

Thunder Bay: Carrel+Partners LLP - *6
1136 Alloy Dr., Thunder Bay, ON P7B 6M9
Tel: 807-346-3000; Fax: 807-346-3600
Toll-Free: 800-263-0578
www.carrel.com

Thunder Bay: Cheadles LLP - *5
Former Name: Cheadle Johnson Shanks MacIvor
#2000, P.O. Box 10429, 715 Hewitson St., Thunder Bay, ON P7B 6T8
Tel: 807-622-6821; Fax: 807-623-3892
info@cheadles.com
www.cheadles.com

Thunder Bay: Richard W. Courtis - *3
#300, 1119 Victoria Ave. East, Thunder Bay, ON P7C 3B7
Tel: 807-623-3000; Fax: 807-623-1251
Toll-Free: 877-266-6646
rcourtis@richardcourtis.com
www.richardcourtis.com

** indicates number of lawyers*

***Thunder Bay*: Cupello & Company - *4**
#104, 105 South May St., Thunder Bay, ON P7E 1B1
Tel: 807-622-8201; *Fax:* 807-622-3755
info.cupellolaw@shaw.ca

***Thunder Bay*: Erickson & Partners, Barristers, Solicitors, Notaries - *10**
Former Name: Erickson Larson
291 Court St. South, Thunder Bay, ON P7B 2Y1
Tel: 807-345-1213; *Fax:* 807-345-2526
Toll-Free: 800-465-3912
www.erickson-law.com

***Thunder Bay*: Filipovic, Conway & Associates - *4**
1020 East Victoria Ave., Thunder Bay, ON P7C 1B6
Tel: 807-343-9090; *Fax:* 807-345-1397
Toll-Free: 800-760-8694
www.filipovic.ca

***Thunder Bay*: Peter Heerema - *1**
44 Algoma St. South, Thunder Bay, ON P7B 3A9
Tel: 807-346-4053; *Fax:* 807-346-8714
peter.heerema@tbaytel.net

***Thunder Bay*: Illingworth & Illingworth - *2**
#201, 1151 Barton St., Thunder Bay, ON P7B 5N3
Tel: 807-623-7222; *Fax:* 807-622-5297
lawyers@tbaytel.net

***Thunder Bay*: Rick E. Lauder - *1**
217 Van Norman St., Thunder Bay, ON P7A 4B6
Tel: 807-683-4444; *Fax:* 807-345-0337

***Thunder Bay*: Martin Scrimshaw Scott LLP - *4**
Cumberland Park, 1 Cumberland St. South, Thunder Bay, ON P7B 2T1
Tel: 807-345-3600; *Fax:* 807-344-8152
msslaw@tbaytel.net

***Thunder Bay*: Thomas C. Mitton - *1**
123 Brodie St. South, Thunder Bay, ON P7E 1B8
Tel: 807-623-4320; *Fax:* 807-622-8038
tcmitton@tbaytel.net

***Thunder Bay*: Peter Mrowiec - *1**
#816, 34 Cumberland St. North, Thunder Bay, ON P7A 4L3
Tel: 807-344-0099 *Toll-Free:* 800-634-0660
www.pmlawoffice.ca

***Thunder Bay*: Robert D. Mullen - *1**
Former Name: Macgillivray-Poirier & Mullen In Association
395 Fort William Rd., Thunder Bay, ON P7B 2Z3
Tel: 807-344-5848; *Fax:* 807-344-5877
rmullen@shawbiz.ca

***Thunder Bay*: Seppo K. Paivalainen - *1**
275 Bay St., Thunder Bay, ON P7B 1R7
Tel: 807-343-9394; *Fax:* 807-344-1562

***Thunder Bay*: Petrone Hornak Garofalo Mauro - *7**
76 Algoma St. North, Thunder Bay, ON P7A 4Z4
Tel: 807-344-9191; *Fax:* 807-345-8391
Toll-Free: 800-465-3988
www.petronelaw.ca

***Thunder Bay*: Potestio Law - *1**
Former Name: Christie Potestio Freitag
#203, 920 Tungsten St., Thunder Bay, ON P7B 5Z6
Tel: 807-344-6651; *Fax:* 807-345-1105
tony@potestiolaw.com
www.potestiolaw.com
ca.linkedin.com/pub/tony-potestio/38/82/394

***Thunder Bay*: Kenneth A. Stewart - *1**
#112, 105 May St. North, Thunder Bay, ON P7C 3N9
Tel: 807-623-7852; *Fax:* 807-623-0014
astewart@807-city.on.ca

***Thunder Bay*: Thomas G. Watkinson - *1**
123 Brodie St. South, Thunder Bay, ON P7E 1B8
Tel: 807-624-5605; *Fax:* 807-623-6096

***Thunder Bay*: Weiler, Maloney, Nelson - *14**
#201, 1001 William St., Thunder Bay, ON P7B 6M1
Tel: 807-623-1111; *Fax:* 807-623-4947
Toll-Free: 866-934-5377
weilers@wmnlaw.com
www.weilers.ca

***Tilbury*: R.M. Jutras - *1**
P.O. Box 417, 50 Queen St. South, Tilbury, ON N0P 2L0
Tel: 519-682-3100 *Toll-Free:* 866-682-3100
www.progressivemediation.ca

***Tilbury*: Taylor & Delrue - *3**
P.O. Box 459, 40 Queen St. South, Tilbury, ON N0P 2L0
Tel: 519-682-0164; *Fax:* 519-682-2777
taydel@cogeco.net

***Tillsonburg*: James G. Battin - *1**
25 Bidwell St., Tillsonburg, ON N4G 3T4
Tel: 519-688-9033; *Fax:* 519-688-9036
jbattinlawoffice@gmail.com

***Tillsonburg*: Gibson Bennett Groom & Szorenyi - *2**
Former Name: Gibson, Linton, Toth, Campbell & Bennett
P.O. Box 5, Stn. Main, 36 Broadway, Tillsonburg, ON N4G 4H3
Tel: 519-842-3658; *Fax:* 519-842-5001
bbennett@gbgs.ca
tillsonburglawyers.com

***Tillsonburg*: Gibson Bennett Groom & Szorenyi - *2**
36 Broadway, Tillsonburg, ON N4G 4H3
Tel: 519-842-4205; *Fax:* 519-842-4261
tillsonburglawyers.com

***Tillsonburg*: Jenkins & Gilvesy - *3**
Former Name: Morris, Jenkins & Gilvesy
P.O. Box 280, Stn. Main, 107 Broadway St., Tillsonburg, ON N4G 4H5
Tel: 519-842-9017; *Fax:* 519-842-3394
info@jenkins-gilvesy.com
www.linkedin.com/pub/lisa-gilvesy/9/622/65a

***Tillsonburg*: Mandryk, Stewart & Morgan - *4**
65 Bidwell St., Tillsonburg, ON N4G 3T8
Tel: 519-842-4228; *Fax:* 519-842-7659
www.mandrykstewartandmorgan.com

***Timmins*: Barazzutti, Lisa F. - *2**
167 - 3rd Ave., Timmins, ON P4N IC7
Tel: 705-531-3200; *Fax:* 705-531-3202
lfbllblaw@eastlink.ca
www.barazzuttilaw.ca

***Timmins*: Sydney Brooks - *1**
Also Known As: Brooks & Associates
81 Balsam St. South, Timmins, ON P4N 2C9
Tel: 705-264-5341; *Fax:* 705-264-2550
sbrooks@ntl.sympatico.ca
www.sydbrookslaw.ca

***Timmins*: Suzanne Desrosiers Professional Corporation - *1**
92 Spruce St. North, Timmins, ON P4N 6M8
Tel: 705-268-6492; *Fax:* 705-264-1940
sd@suzannedesrosierslaw.com
suzannedesrosierslaw.com

***Timmins*: Evans, Bragagnolo & Sullivan LLP - Timmins - *9**
120 Pine St. South, Timmins, ON P4N 2K4
Tel: 705-264-1285; *Fax:* 705-264-7424
ebslawyers@ebslawyers.com
www.ebslawyers.com

***Timmins*: Maisonneuve Labelle LLP - *4**
Former Name: Racicot, Maisonneuve, Labelle, Cooper
15 Balsam St. South, Timmins, ON P4N 2C7
Tel: 705-264-2385; *Fax:* 705-268-3949
info@ml-law.ca
www.ml-law.ca

***Timmins*: Riopelle Group Professional Corporation - *9**
#202, 85 Pine St. South, Timmins, ON P4N 2K1
Tel: 705-264-9591; *Fax:* 705-264-1393
Toll-Free: 866-624-1614
www.rglaw.ca
www.facebook.com/RiopelleGriener

***Toronto*: Aaron & Aaron - *1**
#1400, 10 King St. East, Toronto, ON M5C 1C3
Tel: 416-364-9366; *Fax:* 416-364-3818
bob@aaron.ca
www.aaron.ca

***Toronto*: G.J. Abols - *1**
#2105, 700 Bay St., Toronto, ON M5G 1Z6
Tel: 416-598-8866; *Fax:* 416-971-7656
abolsgj@on.aibn.com

***Toronto*: Abrams & Krochak - Canadian Immigration Lawyers - *2**
#402, 250 Merton St., Toronto, ON M4S 1B1
Tel: 416-482-3387; *Fax:* 416-482-0647
www.abramsandkrochak.com

***Toronto*: Adair Morse LLP - *12**
#1800, 1 Queen St. East, Toronto, ON M5C 2W5
Tel: 416-863-1230; *Fax:* 416-863-1241
info@adairmorse.com
www.adairmorse.com

***Toronto*: Adams & Company - *2**
75 Mutual St., Toronto, ON M5B 2A9
Tel: 416-977-7373; *Fax:* 416-977-1722
reception@criminallawfirm.ca
www.criminallawfirm.ca
twitter.com/torontolawfirm

***Toronto*: G. Chalmers Adams - *1**
#245, 55 St. Clair Ave. West, Toronto, ON M4V 2Y7
Tel: 416-929-7232; *Fax:* 416-929-7225
info@gcadams.on.ca

***Toronto*: Adler Bytensky - *6**
#1708, 5000 Yonge St., Toronto, ON M2N 7E9
Tel: 416-365-3151; *Fax:* 416-365-0866
info@CrimLawCanada.com
www.crimlawcanada.com
www.facebook.com/CrimLawCanada, twitter.com/Prutschi, ca.linkedin.com/pub/edward-prutschi/4/289/a60

***Toronto*: Advocacy Centre for the Elderly - *5**
#701, 2 Carlton St., Toronto, ON M5B 1J3
Tel: 416-598-2656; *Fax:* 416-598-7924
www.advocacycentreelderly.org

***Toronto*: Affleck Greene McMurtry LLP - *13**
Former Name: Kelly Affleck Greene
#200, 365 Bay St., Toronto, ON M5H 2V1
Tel: 416-360-2800; *Fax:* 416-360-5960
info@agmlawyers.com
www.agmlawyers.com

***Toronto*: Claudio R. Aiello - *1**
#506, 330 University Ave., Toronto, ON M5G 1R7
Tel: 416-969-9900; *Fax:* 416-969-9060
claudio@aiellolaw.ca

***Toronto*: Irving J. Aiken - *1**
44 Charles St. West, Toronto, ON M4Y 1R7
Tel: 416-947-0199; *Fax:* 416-947-0379

***Toronto*: Alloway & Associates - *4**
64 Prince Andrew Place, Toronto, ON M3C 2H4
Tel: 416-971-9293; *Fax:* 416-971-9349
email@alloway.net
www.alloway.net

***Toronto*: Alpert Law Firm - *2**
#900, 1 St. Clair Ave. East, Toronto, ON M4T 2V7
Tel: 416-923-0809; *Fax:* 416-923-1549
halpert@alpertlawfirm.ca
www.alpertlawfirm.ca

***Toronto*: Harriet Altman - *1**
68 Garnier Court, Toronto, ON M2M 4C9
Tel: 416-224-5240; *Fax:* 416-224-0360
Toll-Free: 877-224-5229
haltman1@hotmail.com

***Toronto*: Altmid Roll & Associates - *3**
#600, 1120 Finch Ave. West, Toronto, ON M3J 3H7
Tel: 416-663-6888; *Fax:* 416-663-3442
www.altmidroll.com

***Toronto*: Jaikrishin R. Ambwani - *1**
#330, 100 Cowdray Ct., Toronto, ON M1S 5C8
Tel: 416-754-4404; *Fax:* 416-754-7746
jack@jackambwani.com
www.jackambwani.com

***Toronto*: Amnon Kestelman - *2**
245 Coxwell Ave., Toronto, ON M4L 3B4
Tel: 416-465-3561; *Fax:* 416-465-3563

***Toronto*: Julie Evelyn Amourgis - *1**
#2000, 393 University Ave., Toronto, ON M5G 1E6
Tel: 416-504-5844; *Fax:* 416-593-1352

***Toronto*: Anderson Bourdon Burgess**
#116, 295 The West Mall, Toronto, ON M9C 4Z4
Tel: 416-621-9644; *Fax:* 416-621-9668
PaulAnderson@andersonbb.com
www.andersonbb.com

** indicates number of lawyers*

***Toronto*: Dwight Anderson - *1**
1709 Bloor St. West, Toronto, ON M6P 4E5
Tel: 416-769-3522; *Fax:* 416-769-2302
dwightanderson@rogers.com

***Toronto*: Andriessen & Associates - *2**
#101, 703 Evans Ave., Toronto, ON M9C 5E9
Tel: 416-620-7020; *Fax:* 416-620-1398
info@andriessen.ca
www.andriessen.ca
twitter.com/andriessenlaw

***Toronto*: Philip Anisman Barrister & Solicitor - *1**
#1704, 80 Richmond St. West, Toronto, ON M5H 2A4
Tel: 416-363-4200; *Fax:* 416-363-6200

***Toronto*: Antflyck & Aulis LLP - *2**
***Former Name:* Antflyck & Mazin**
1501 Ellesmere Rd., Toronto, ON M1P 4T6
Tel: 647-693-6827
www.antflyckandaulislaw.com

***Toronto*: Dennis Apostolides - *1**
#201, 505 Danforth Ave., Toronto, ON M4K 1P5
Tel: 416-463-1147; *Fax:* 416-463-1762
apostolides@rogers.com

***Toronto*: Aronovitch Macaulay Rollo LLP - *20**
***Also Known As:* AMR LLP**
156 Front St. West, Toronto, ON M5J 2L6
Tel: 416-369-9393; *Fax:* 416-369-0665
info@amrlaw.ca
www.amrlaw.ca

***Toronto*: Harvey Ash - *1**
#900, 5799 Yonge St., Toronto, ON M2M 3V3
Tel: 416-250-0080; *Fax:* 416-225-1124
harveyash@yorklegal.ca

***Toronto*: William Ash - *1**
#801, 55 Eglinton Ave. East, Toronto, ON M4P 1G8
Tel: 416-486-8751; *Fax:* 416-486-8789
willash@bellnet.ca

***Toronto*: Ashbourne & Caskey - *1**
2077 Lawrence Ave. West, Toronto, ON M9N 1H7
Tel: 416-247-6677; *Fax:* 416-247-3519

***Toronto*: Atherton Barristers - *1**
#703, 357 Bay St., Toronto, ON M5H 2T7
Tel: 416-365-1030; *Fax:* 416-946-1619
Toll-Free: 866-237-1030
bcatherton@ablaw.com
www.athertonbarristers.com

***Toronto*: ATX Law - *1**
***Former Name:* Aprile Law**
#100, 174 Bedford Rd., Toronto, ON M5R 2K9
Tel: 416-218-5263
info@atxlaw.ca
atxlaw.ca
twitter.com/atxlaw,
www.linkedin.com/pub/peter-aprile/1b/678/a14

***Toronto*: S.J. AvRuskin - *1**
66 Charles St. East., Toronto, ON M4Y 2R3
Tel: 416-922-4147; *Fax:* 416-922-8022

***Toronto*: Azevedo & Nelson - *4**
892 College St., Toronto, ON M6H 1A4
Tel: 416-533-7133; *Fax:* 416-533-3114
aazevedo@azevedonelson.com
www.azevedonelson.com

***Toronto*: Babits, Wappel & Toome - *3**
#802, 480 University Ave., Toronto, ON M5G 1V2
Tel: 416-598-1333; *Fax:* 416-598-5024

***Toronto*: Denise Badley - *1**
#2, 2069 Danforth Ave., 2nd Fl., Toronto, ON M4C 1J8
Tel: 416-690-6195; *Fax:* 416-690-6271
dbadleylaw@rogers.com

***Toronto*: J. Waldo Baerg - *1**
#506, 372 Bay St., Toronto, ON M5H 2W9
Tel: 416-366-3705; *Fax:* 416-366-0157
waldobaerg@on.aibn.com

***Toronto*: Baker & Company - *6**
#3300, 130 Adelaide St. West, Toronto, ON M5H 3P5
Tel: 416-777-0100; *Fax:* 416-366-3992
info@bakerlawyers.com
www.bakerlawyers.com

***Toronto*: Baker & McKenzie LLP - *76**
#2100, Brookfield Place, P.O. Box 874, 181 Bay St., Toronto, ON M5J 2T3
Tel: 416-863-1221; *Fax:* 416-863-6275
www.bakermckenzie.com

***Toronto*: Gordon R. Baker, Q.C. - *1**
#200, 2 Lombard St., Toronto, ON M5C 1M1
Tel: 416-365-7203; *Fax:* 416-365-7204
gord@gordbaker.com
www.gordbaker.com

***Toronto*: Stanley Baker - *1**
#700, 55 Town Centre Ct., Toronto, ON M1P 4X4
Tel: 416-296-1794; *Fax:* 416-296-1259
stanleybaker@rogers.com

***Toronto*: Tony Baker - *1**
500 Danforth Ave., Toronto, ON M4K 1P6
Tel: 416-463-4411; *Fax:* 416-463-4562
tbaker1952@aol.com
www.tonybakerlaw.com

***Toronto*: Ahmad N. Baksh - *1**
#307, 1280 Finch Ave. West, Toronto, ON M3J 3K6
Tel: 416-667-1922; *Fax:* 416-667-0304
anbaksh@rogers.com

***Toronto*: Baldwin Sennecke Halman LLP - *7**
***Former Name:* Brans, Lehun, Baldwin**
#900, 25 Adelaide St. East, Toronto, ON M5C 3A1
Tel: 416-601-1040; *Fax:* 416-601-0655
info@bashllp.com
www.bashllp.com

***Toronto*: Banks & Starkman - *1**
#310, 200 Ronson Dr., Toronto, ON M9W 5Z9
Tel: 416-243-3394; *Fax:* 416-243-9692
lbanks@banksandstarkman.com
www.banksandstarkman.com

***Toronto*: Charles N. Barhydt - *1**
1199 The Queensway, Toronto, ON M8Z 1R7
Tel: 416-960-0049
info@barhydtcriminallaw.com
www.barhydtcriminallaw.com

***Toronto*: J.R. Barrs - *1**
23 Bedford Road, Toronto, ON M5R 2J9
Tel: 416-366-6466; *Fax:* 416-964-8067
randallbarrs.com

***Toronto*: Basman Smith LLP - *21**
#2400, P.O. Box 37, 1 Dundas St. West, Toronto, ON M5G 1Z3
Tel: 416-365-0300; *Fax:* 416-365-9276
Toll-Free: 855-815-0300
www.basmansmith.com

***Toronto*: Bastedo, Stewart, Smith - *8**
#1800, 180 Dundas St. West, Toronto, ON M5G 1Z8
Tel: 416-595-1916; *Fax:* 416-596-7538
www.bastedostewartsmith.com

***Toronto*: Batcher, Wasserman**
***Former Name:* Batcher, Wasserman & Associates**
#500, 718 Wilson Ave., Toronto, ON M3K 1E2
Tel: 416-635-6300; *Fax:* 416-635-6376
Toll-Free: 877-813-0820

***Toronto*: Batcher, Wasserman & Associates - *2**
***Former Name:* Robert G. Wasserman**
#500, 718 Wilson Ave., Toronto, ON M3K 1E2
Tel: 416-635-6300; *Fax:* 416-635-6376
tbatcher@rogers.com

***Toronto*: Bates Barristers - *1**
34 King St. East, 12th Fl., Toronto, ON M5C 2X8
Tel: 416-869-9898; *Fax:* 416-869-9405
info@batesbarristers.com
www.batesbarristers.com

***Toronto*: Jordan Battista LLP - *6**
#1000, 160 Bloor St. East, Toronto, ON M4W 1B9
Tel: 416-203-2899; *Fax:* 416-203-7949
info@jordanbattista.com
www.jordanbattista.com

***Toronto*: Beard Winter LLP - *64**
#701, 130 Adelaide St. West, Toronto, ON M5H 2K4
Tel: 416-593-5555; *Fax:* 416-593-7760
info@beardwinter.com
www.beardwinter.com

***Toronto*: Beber & Associates - *7**
#2900, 390 Bay St., Toronto, ON M5H 2Y2
Tel: 416-867-2280; *Fax:* 416-869-0321
www.beber.ca

***Toronto*: Sandra Bebris - *1**
#300, 1370 Don Mills Rd., Toronto, ON M3B 3N7
Tel: 416-510-1324
bebris@pathcom.com

***Toronto*: Steven Bellissimo - *1**
#802, 390 Bay St., Toronto, ON M5H 2Y2
Tel: 416-362-6437; *Fax:* 416-972-9940
steve@sblaw.ca

***Toronto*: Bellmore & Moore - *5**
#1600, 393 University Ave., Toronto, ON M5G 1E6
Tel: 416-581-1818; *Fax:* 416-581-1279
www.bellmoreandmoore.com

***Toronto*: Belmont, Fine & Associates - *2**
#601, 1120 Finch Ave. West, Toronto, ON M3J 3H7
Tel: 416-661-2066; *Fax:* 416-661-2116
www.belmontfine.com

***Toronto*: Belmore Neidrauer LLP - *10**
#2401, TD South Tower, 79 Wellington St. West, Toronto, ON M5K 1A1
Tel: 416-863-1771; *Fax:* 416-863-9171
info@belmorelaw.com
www.belmorelaw.com

***Toronto*: Bennett Bankruptcy Legal Counsel - *2**
***Former Name:* Bennett & Company**
#900, 25 Adelaide St. East, Toronto, ON M5C 3A1
Tel: 416-363-8688; *Fax:* 416-363-8083
bennett@ican.net
www.bennettonbankruptcy.ca

***Toronto*: Bennett Best Burn LLP - *12**
#1700, 150 York St., Toronto, ON M5H 3S5
Tel: 416-362-3400; *Fax:* 416-362-2211
info@bbburn.com
www.bbburn.com

***Toronto*: Benson Percival Brown LLP - *23**
#800, 250 Dundas St. West, Toronto, ON M5T 2Z6
Tel: 416-977-9777; *Fax:* 416-977-1241
www.bensonpercival.com

***Toronto*: Bereskin & Parr LLP - *60**
Scotia Plaza, 40 King St. West, 40th Fl., Toronto, ON M5H 3Y2
Tel: 416-364-7311; *Fax:* 416-361-1398
Toll-Free: 888-364-7311
info@bereskinparr.com
www.bereskinparr.com

***Toronto*: Bergel, Magence LLP - *4**
#501, 1018 Finch Ave. West, Toronto, ON M3J 3L5
Tel: 416-665-2000; *Fax:* 416-663-2348
Toll-Free: 866-492-3743
bergellaw.com

***Toronto*: Max Berger Professional Law Corporation - *2**
#207, 1033 Bay St., Toronto, ON M5S 3A5
Tel: 416-969-9263; *Fax:* 416-969-9098
max@maxberger.ca
www.maxberger.ca

***Toronto*: Berkow, Cohen LLP - *8**
#400, 141 Adelaide St. West, Toronto, ON M5H 3L5
Tel: 416-364-4900; *Fax:* 416-364-3865
reception@berkowcohen.com
www.berkowcohen.com

***Toronto*: Bradley F. Berns - *1**
554 Annette St., Toronto, ON M6S 2C6
Tel: 416-490-6456; *Fax:* 416-490-6439

***Toronto*: Bersenas Jacobsen Chouest Thomson Blackburn LLP - *11**
#201, 33 Yonge St., Toronto, ON M5E 1G4
Tel: 416-982-3800; *Fax:* 416-982-3801
info@lexcanada.com
www.lexcanada.com

***Toronto*: Myer Betel - *1**
7 Farrington Dr., Toronto, ON M2L 2B4
Tel: 416-447-4333; *Fax:* 416-447-3773
mbetel@rogers.com

* indicates number of lawyers

***Toronto*: Lynn Bevan Professional Corporation - *1**
1 Coulson Ave., Toronto, ON M4V 1Y3
Tel: 416-955-0400; *Fax:* 416-955-0410
lbevan@lynnbevan.com
www.lynnbevan.com

***Toronto*: Bhatia, Minipreet - *1**
#405, 3601 Victoria Park Ave., Toronto, ON M1W 3Y3
Tel: 416-493-1727; *Fax:* 416-756-3663

***Toronto*: Bigelow, Hendy - *4**
#200, 789 Don Mills Rd., Toronto, ON M3C 1T5
Tel: 416-429-3110; *Fax:* 416-429-3057
www.bigelowhendy.com

***Toronto*: Peter Bird - *1**
31 Prince Arthur Dr., Toronto, ON M5R 1B2
Tel: 416-929-9408; *Fax:* 416-960-5456
peterbird@on.aibn.com

***Toronto*: Birenbaum Gottlieb Professional Corporation - *2**
Also Known As: B&G Law
Former Name: Birenbaum & Bernstein
#21, 951 Wilson Ave., Toronto, ON M3K 2A7
Tel: 416-633-3720; *Fax:* 416-633-4546
info@bgtorontolaw.com
www.bgtorontolaw.com

***Toronto*: Birenbaum, Steinberg, Landau, Savin & Colraine LLP - *11**
#1000, 33 Bloor St. East, Toronto, ON M4W 3H1
Tel: 416-961-4100; *Fax:* 416-961-2531
info@bslsc.com
www.bslsc.com
twitter.com/bslsc/, ca.linkedin.com/pub/bslsc-llp/69/987/586/

***Toronto*: Birks, Langdon & Elliott - *2**
#329, 4195 Dundas St. West, Toronto, ON M8X 1Y4
Tel: 416-239-3431; *Fax:* 416-239-8259

***Toronto*: Donald H. Bitter, Q.C. - *1**
#607, 71 Charles St. East, Toronto, ON M4Y 2T3
Tel: 416-360-4357; *Fax:* 416-463-8259
notguilty@rogers.com

***Toronto*: Black, Sutherland LLP - *19**
Former Name: Black, Sutherland & Crabbe
#3425, P.O. Box 34, 130 Adelaide St. West, Toronto, ON M5H 3P5
Tel: 416-361-1500; *Fax:* 416-361-1674
Toll-Free: 866-902-7557
info@blacksutherland.com
www.blacksutherland.com

***Toronto*: Edith M. Blake - *1**
75 The Donway West, Toronto, ON M3C 2E9
Tel: 416-445-0310; *Fax:* 416-445-0316

***Toronto*: Jonathan A. Bliss - *1**
370 Bloor St. East, Toronto, ON M4W 3M6
Tel: 416-927-9000; *Fax:* 416-927-9069
jonbliss@sympatico.ca

***Toronto*: Bloom Lanys Professional Corporation - *2**
#200, 2171 Avenue Rd., Toronto, ON M5M 4B4
Tel: 416-486-9913; *Fax:* 416-485-6054
Toll-Free: 877-835-7658
barb@bloom-lanys.com; jessie@bloom-lanys.com

***Toronto*: Joseph L. Bloomenfeld - *1**
#2110, 120 Adelaide St. West, Toronto, ON M5H 1T1
Tel: 416-363-7315; *Fax:* 416-363-7697

***Toronto*: Blouin, Dunn LLP - *19**
#4805, P.O. Box 207, Stn. Commerce Court, 199 Bay St., Toronto, ON M5L 1E8
Tel: 416-365-7888; *Fax:* 416-365-7988
info@blouindunn.com
www.blouindunn.com

***Toronto*: Blumberg Segal LLP - *9**
#1202, 390 Bay St., Toronto, ON M5H 2Y2
Tel: 416-361-1982; *Fax:* 416-363-8451
Toll-Free: 866-961-1982
business@blumbergs.ca
www.blumbergs.ca
twitter.com/BlumbergSegal,
www.linkedin.com/company/blumberg-segal-llp

***Toronto*: Carla L. Bocci - *1**
#1917, 25 Adelaide St. East, Toronto, ON M5C 3A1
Tel: 416-365-2961; *Fax:* 416-365-1859

***Toronto*: Bodnaruk & Capone - *2**
53 Yonge St., 3rd Fl., Toronto, ON M5E 1J3
Tel: 416-593-7000; *Fax:* 416-593-5359

***Toronto*: Bogart Robertson & Chu - *5**
#303, 20 Adelaide St. East, Toronto, ON M5C 2T6
Tel: 416-601-1991; *Fax:* 416-601-0006
contact@brclaw.com
brclaw.com

***Toronto*: G.H. Bomza - *1**
#2303, 180 Dundas St. West, Toronto, ON M5G 1Z8
Tel: 416-598-2244; *Fax:* 416-598-3830
rosehallmgmt@bellnet.ca

***Toronto*: Sharon G.H. Bond - *1**
#1501, 5001 Yonge St., Toronto, ON M2N 6P6
Tel: 416-630-5600; *Fax:* 416-630-5906
sbond@rblawyers.ca

***Toronto*: Ira E. Book - *1**
#200, 85 Scarsdale Rd., Toronto, ON M3B 2R2
Tel: 416-447-2665; *Fax:* 416-447-0066
ira@irabook.com

***Toronto*: Norman H.R. Borski, Q.C. - *1**
34 Rivercres Rd., Toronto, ON M6S 4H3
Tel: 416-766-2441

***Toronto*: Y.R. Botiuk - *2**
#212, 2323 Bloor St. West, Toronto, ON M6S 4W1
Tel: 416-763-4333; *Fax:* 416-763-0613

***Toronto*: Bougadis, Chang LLP - *4**
#300, 555 Adelaide St. East, Toronto, ON M5C 1K6
Tel: 416-703-2402; *Fax:* 416-703-2406
office@bcbarristers.com
www.bcbarristers.com

***Toronto*: T. Sam Boutzouvis - *1**
#603, 1/2 Parliament St., Toronto, ON M4X 1P9
Tel: 416-591-0111; *Fax:* 416-591-0778
samboutzouvis@yahoo.ca

***Toronto*: Mary E.E. Boyce - *1**
69 Elm St., Toronto, ON M5G 1H2
Tel: 416-591-7588; *Fax:* 416-971-9092

***Toronto*: Boyle & Co. LLP - *2**
#1900, 25 Adelaide St. East, Toronto, ON M5C 3A1
Tel: 416-867-8800; *Fax:* 416-867-8833
www.boyleco.com

***Toronto*: Brannan Meiklejohn Barristers - *2**
#200, Rosedale Sq., 1055 Yonge St., Toronto, ON M4W 2L2
Tel: 416-926-3797; *Fax:* 416-926-3712

***Toronto*: Brauti Thorning Zibarras LLP - *17**
#1800, 151 Yonge St., Toronto, ON M5C 2W7
Tel: 416-362-4567; *Fax:* 416-362-8410
www.btlegal.ca

***Toronto*: Philip E. Brent - *1**
#210, 4800 Dundas St. West, Toronto, ON M9A 1B1
Tel: 416-203-1449; *Fax:* 416-203-1772
philip@brentayt.com

***Toronto*: Bresver Grossman Chapman & Habas LLP - *5**
Former Name: Bresver, Grossman, Scheininger & Chapman
#2900, 390 Bay St., Toronto, ON M5H 2Y2
Tel: 416-869-0366; *Fax:* 416-869-0321

***Toronto*: Daniel J. Brodsky - *1**
Barristers Chambers, 11 Prince Arthur Ave., Toronto, ON M5R 1B2
Tel: 416-964-2618; *Fax:* 416-964-8305
dbrodsky@daniel-brodsky.com

***Toronto*: Brown & Burnes - *6**
#1400, 390 Bay St., Toronto, ON M5H 2Y2
Tel: 416-366-7927; *Fax:* 416-363-9602
info@brownburnes.com
www.brownburnes.com

***Toronto*: Brown, Peck & Lubelsky - *4**
5287 Yonge St., Toronto, ON M2N 5R3
Tel: 416-223-8811; *Fax:* 416-223-8485

***Toronto*: Anthony G. Bryant - *2**
The Lumsden Bldg., 6 Adelaide St. East, 5th Fl., Toronto, ON M5C 1H6
Tel: 416-927-7441; *Fax:* 416-488-9802
info@bursteinbryant.com
www.bursteinbryant.com

***Toronto*: Buie Cohen LLP - *2**
Former Name: McPhail Buie & Cohen
#205, 250 Merton St., Toronto, ON M4S 1B1
Tel: 416-869-3400; *Fax:* 416-703-6522
cmbuie@buiecohen.com
www.buiecohen.com

***Toronto*: Harry R. Burkman - *1**
#5600, P.O. Box 129, 1 First Canadian Pl., Toronto, ON M5X 1A4
Tel: 416-364-3831; *Fax:* 416-364-3832
hburkman@burkman.com
www.burkman.com

***Toronto*: Burnett & Jacobson - *2**
44 St. Clair Ave. West, Toronto, ON M4V 3C9
Tel: 416-922-8710; *Fax:* 416-964-5840

***Toronto*: Burstein, Unger - *2**
Former Name: Paul Burstein & Associate
P.O. Box 180, 127 John St., Toronto, ON M5V 2E2
Tel: 416-204-1825; *Fax:* 416-204-1849
paul@127john.com

***Toronto*: Bernard Burton - *1**
#301, 120 Carlton St., Toronto, ON M5A 4K2
Tel: 416-922-1263; *Fax:* 416-922-1963
bburton@carltonlaw.ca

***Toronto*: Bussin & Bussin - *3**
#1410, 181 University Ave., Toronto, ON M5H 3M7
Tel: 416-364-4925; *Fax:* 416-868-1818
bruce@bussinlaw.com

***Toronto*: Paul Calarco - *1**
#405, P.O. Box 144, 700 Bay St., Toronto, ON M5G 1Z6
Tel: 416-598-1948; *Fax:* 416-596-7629
pcalarco@on.aibn.com
www.paulcalarco.com

***Toronto*: CaleyWray - *10**
#1600, 65 Queen St. West, Toronto, ON M5H 2M5
Tel: 416-366-3763; *Fax:* 416-366-3293
mail@caleywray.com
www.caleywray.com

***Toronto*: John Cannings, Barristers - *2**
#400, 425 University Ave., Toronto, ON M5G 1T6
Tel: 416-591-0703; *Fax:* 416-591-0710
info@jcannings.com
www.jcannings.com

***Toronto*: Ruth Canton - *1**
#302, 2489 Bloor St. West, Toronto, ON M6S 1R5
Tel: 416-769-5759; *Fax:* 416-769-3132

***Toronto*: Rochelle F. Cantor - *1**
180 Spadina Rd., Toronto, ON M5R 2T8
Tel: 416-861-1625; *Fax:* 416-861-1466
rochelle.cantor@bellnet.ca

***Toronto*: Capp, Shupak - *5**
#1703, 2 St. Clair Ave. West, Toronto, ON M4V 1L5
Tel: 416-944-2313; *Fax:* 416-323-0697
Toll-Free: 877-308-4878
mshupak@cappshupak.com
www.marilynshupak.com
ca.linkedin.com/pub/marilyn-shupak/34/74/470

***Toronto*: Cappell Parker LLP - *2**
#3000, 77 King St. West, Toronto, ON M5K 1K7
Tel: 416-367-0900
fecappell@cappell.com
www.cappell.com

***Toronto*: Cappellacci DaRoza LLP - *3**
#500, 462 Wellington St. West, Toronto, ON M5V 1E3
Tel: 416-955-9500; *Fax:* 416-955-9503
ecappellacci@capplaw.ca
www.capplaw.ca

***Toronto*: Caramanna, Friedberg LLP - *6**
#405, Lucliff Place, P.O. Box 144, 700 Bay St., Toronto, ON M5G 1Z6
Tel: 416-924-5969; *Fax:* 416-924-9973
info@cflaw.ca
www.cflaw.ca

** indicates number of lawyers*

***Toronto*: Michael W. Caroline - *1**
#505, 56 The Esplanade, Toronto, ON M5E 1A7
Tel: 416-203-2250; *Fax:* 416-203-2280
mwc@michaelcaroline.com
www.michaelcaroline.com

***Toronto*: John S.H. Carriere - *1**
#600, 330 Bay St., Toronto, ON M5H 2S8
Tel: 416-363-5594; *Fax:* 416-363-8492
johncarriere@bellnet.ca

***Toronto*: C. Anthony Carroll - *1**
#1807, 8 King St. East, Toronto, ON M5C 1B5
Tel: 416-361-0522; *Fax:* 416-361-0248
carrollt@istar.ca
tonycarroll-lawyer.com

***Toronto*: Gary M. Cass - *1**
Also Known As: Garry Cass
#302, 1200 Sheppard Ave. East, Toronto, ON M2K 2S5
Tel: 416-767-2277; *Fax:* 416-491-0273
www.garrycass.com

***Toronto*: Ceresney, Weisberg Associates - *2**
#202, 4651 Sheppard Ave. East, Toronto, ON M1S 3V4
Tel: 416-291-7701; *Fax:* 416-291-1766

***Toronto*: Chaitons LLP - *20**
Former Name: Chaiton & Chaiton
5000 Yonge St., 10th Fl., Toronto, ON M2N 7E9
Tel: 416-222-8888; *Fax:* 416-222-8402
info@chaitons.com
www.chaiton.com
ca.linkedin.com/company/chaitons-llp

***Toronto*: Evan Chang - *1**
#203, 1315 Lawrence Ave. East, Toronto, ON M3A 3R3
Tel: 416-449-1214
ww.evanchang.ca
www.evanchang.ca

***Toronto*: Peter P. Chang - *3**
#607, 220 Duncan Mill Rd., Toronto, ON M3B 3J5
Tel: 416-497-1575; *Fax:* 416-497-2261
peterchang@rogers.com

***Toronto*: Chapnick & Associates - *4**
228 Carlton St., Toronto, ON M5A 2L1
Tel: 416-968-2160; *Fax:* 416-975-9338
www.chapnick.ca

***Toronto*: Chappell Partners LLP - *10**
Former Name: Chappell, Bushell, Stewart LLP
#3310, 20 Queen St. West, Toronto, ON M5H 3R3
Tel: 416-351-0005; *Fax:* 416-351-0002
info@chappellpartners.ca
www.chappellpartners.ca
twitter.com/cp_llp

***Toronto*: Chiarotto Sultan LLP - *3**
#5700, First Canadian Place, 100 King St. West, Toronto, ON M5X 1C7
Tel: 416-214-1313; *Fax:* 416-214-0576
chiarottosultan.com

***Toronto*: Ronald W. Chisholm, Q.C. - *1**
85 Lonsdale Rd., Toronto, ON M4V 1W4
Tel: 416-586-0777; *Fax:* 416-586-0267

***Toronto*: Chitiz Pathak LLP - *14**
#1600, 320 Bay St. Ave., Toronto, ON M5H 4A6
Tel: 416-368-6200; *Fax:* 416-368-0300
info@chitizpathak.com
www.chitizpathak.com

***Toronto*: Christopher E. Chop - *1**
#2000, 1 Queen St. East, Toronto, ON M5C 2W5
Tel: 416-860-8015; *Fax:* 416-601-0206
choplaw@gmail.com

***Toronto*: Christie Law Office - *4**
750 Scarlett Rd., Toronto, ON M9P 2V1
Tel: 416-249-8300; *Fax:* 416-249-1480
rebecca@christielaw.ca
www.christielaw.ca

***Toronto*: Andrea E.K. Chun - *1**
#700, One Corporate Plaza, 2075 Kennedy Rd., Toronto, ON M1T 3V3
Tel: 416-754-3060; *Fax:* 416-754-3321
andreachun@bellnet.ca

***Toronto*: Cipollone & Cipollone Barristers - *1**
#2100, 130 Adelaide St. West, Toronto, ON M5H 3P5
Tel: 416-368-5366; *Fax:* 416-368-5361

***Toronto*: Dino J. Cirone - *1**
#2, 2084 Danforth Ave., Toronto, ON M4C 1J9
Tel: 416-423-8515; *Fax:* 416-423-4971

***Toronto*: S.G. Clapp - *1**
802 Eglington Ave. East, Toronto, ON M4G 2L1
Tel: 416-484-4840; *Fax:* 416-484-0821
stanleyclapp@on.aibn.com

***Toronto*: Clark Farb Fiksel LLP - *7**
188 Avenue Rd., Toronto, ON M5J 2J1
Tel: 416-599-7761; *Fax:* 416-324-4220
Toll-Free: 888-664-3779
www.cfflaw.com

***Toronto*: Deta J. Clark - *1**
#402, 5075 Yonge St., Toronto, ON M2N 6C6
Tel: 416-733-3135; *Fax:* 416-733-1081

***Toronto*: Clarke, Freeman, Miller & Ryan - *1**
1863 Danforth Ave., Toronto, ON M4C 1J3
Tel: 416-698-9323; *Fax:* 416-698-9110

***Toronto*: L. Peter Clyne - *1**
#207, Xerox Tower, 5650 Yonge St., Toronto, ON M2M 4G3
Tel: 416-922-0864; *Fax:* 416-922-6856
info@clynelawoffice.com
www.clynelawoffice.com

***Toronto*: Robert G. Coates - *1**
#307, 120 Carlton St., Toronto, ON M5A 4K2
Tel: 416-925-6490; *Fax:* 416-925-4492
robert@rgcoates.com
www.rgcoates.com

***Toronto*: Cognition LLP - *31**
#503, 263 Adelaide St. West, Toronto, ON M5H 1Y2
Tel: 416-348-0313; *Fax:* 416-479-0244
info@cognitionllp.com
www.cognitionllp.com
www.facebook.com/cognitionllp, twitter.com/cognitionllp,
www.linkedin.com/company/cognition-llp

***Toronto*: Cohen & Associate - *1**
#800, Yong-Norton Centre, 5255 Yonge St., Toronto, ON M2N 6P4
Tel: 416-323-0907; *Fax:* 416-324-8053
cohen@bellnet.ca

***Toronto*: Cohen, Sabsay LLP - *4**
#901, 350 Bay St., Toronto, ON M5H 2S6
Fax: 416-364-0083
Toll-Free: 888-626-1102
cohen@cohensabsay.com
www.cohensabsay.com

***Toronto*: David Cohn - *1**
#506, 330 University Ave., Toronto, ON M5G 1R7
Tel: 416-777-1100; *Fax:* 416-204-1849
david@davidcohn.ca
www.davidcohn.ca

***Toronto*: John Collins - *1**
#400, 357 Bay St., Toronto, ON M5H 2R7
Tel: 416-364-9006; *Fax:* 416-862-7911
john.collins@on.aibn.com

***Toronto*: Conway Davis Gryski - *6**
#601, 130 Adelaide St. West, Toronto, ON M5H 3P5
Tel: 416-214-4554; *Fax:* 416-214-9915
Toll-Free: 877-559-4554
contactus@cdglaw.net
www.conwaydavisgryski.com

***Toronto*: Conway Kleinman Kornhauser LLP - *3**
Former Name: Conway Kornhauser & Gotlieb
#1102, 390 Bay St., Toronto, ON M5H 2Y2
Tel: 416-368-5400; *Fax:* 416-368-5454

***Toronto*: Allen M. Cooper - *1**
#101, 15A Elm St., Toronto, ON M5G 1H1
Tel: 416-977-8070; *Fax:* 416-977-8151

***Toronto*: Kirk J. Cooper - *1**
207 Queen St. East, Toronto, ON M5A 1S2
Tel: 416-923-4277; *Fax:* 416-923-4144
kirkcooperlaw@rogers.com
www.kirkcooperlaw.com

***Toronto*: Cooper, Kleinman - *2**
3 Rowanwood Ave., Toronto, ON M4W 1Y5
Tel: 416-867-1400; *Fax:* 416-867-1873
gwcooper@cooperkleinman.ca

***Toronto*: Morris Cooper - *1**
99 Yorkville Ave., Toronto, ON M5R 3K5
Tel: 416-961-2626; *Fax:* 416-961-4000
cooper@cooperlaw.ca

***Toronto*: Robert A. Cooper - *1**
#208, 4211 Yonge St., Toronto, ON M2P 2A9
Tel: 416-222-8115; *Fax:* 416-222-8505

***Toronto*: Cooper, Sandler, Shime & Bergman LLP - *5**
#1900, 439 University Ave., Toronto, ON M5G 1Y8
Tel: 416-585-9191; *Fax:* 416-408-2372
www.criminal-lawyers.ca

***Toronto*: Copeland Duncan - *1**
31 Prince Arthur Ave., Toronto, ON M5R 1B2
Tel: 416-964-8126; *Fax:* 416-960-5456
paulcope9@yahoo.com

***Toronto*: Jack Copelovici - *1**
Former Name: Copelovici & Hanuk
#204, 1220 Sheppard Ave. East, Toronto, ON M2K 2S5
Tel: 416-494-0910; *Fax:* 416-494-5480
jack@copel-law.com

***Toronto*: Barry S. Corbin - *1**
#2000, 393 University Ave., Toronto, ON M5G 1E6
Tel: 416-593-4200; *Fax:* 416-593-1352
barry.corbin@corbinestateslaw.com
www.corbinestateslaw.com

***Toronto*: Cornerstone Group**
#1800, The Exchange Tower, P.O. Box 427, 130 King St. West, Toronto, ON M5X 1J8
Tel: 416-862-8000; *Fax:* 416-862-8001
Toll-Free: 888-268-6735
md@cornerstonegroup.com
www.cornerstonegroup.com

***Toronto*: Costa Law Firm - *4**
Former Name: David Costa & Associate
1015 Bloor St. West, Toronto, ON M6H 1M1
Tel: 416-535-6329; *Fax:* 416-535-4735
davidcosta@bell.blackberry.net
www.costalawfirm.ca
www.facebook.com/pages/Costa-Law-Firm/135772586482420,
twitter.com/costalawfirm

***Toronto*: Fernando D. Costa - *1**
#200, 1112 Dundas St. West, Toronto, ON M6J 1X2
Tel: 416-534-6357; *Fax:* 416-534-6219
fd.costa@bellnet.ca

***Toronto*: D.B. Cousins - *1**
#203, 425 University Ave., Toronto, ON M5G 1T6
Tel: 416-977-8871; *Fax:* 416-599-8075
david.b.cousins@bellnet.ca
www.davidbcousins.com

***Toronto*: Coutts Crane - *5**
#700, 480 University Ave., Toronto, ON M5G 1V2
Tel: 416-977-0956; *Fax:* 416-977-5331
info@couttscrane.com
www.couttscrane.com

***Toronto*: Ronald Cowitz - *1**
#308, 344 Bloor St. West, Toronto, ON M5S 3A7
Tel: 416-944-9594

***Toronto*: Christopher G. Cox - *1**
#209, 1711 McCowan Rd., Toronto, ON M1S 2Y3
Tel: 416-447-4274; *Fax:* 416-823-3215
cgcoxlaw@hotmail.com

***Toronto*: Cozen O'Connor - *8**
Former Name: Poss & Halfnight
#1920, 1 Queen St. East, Toronto, ON M5C 2W5
Tel: 416-361-3200; *Fax:* 416-361-1405
Toll-Free: 888-727-9948
www.cozen.com
www.facebook.com/CozenOConnor, twitter.com/cozen_oconnor,
www.linkedin.com/company/cozen-o%27connor

***Toronto*: Crane Davies Spina LLP - *4**
Former Name: Steven Allen Skurka
#205, 970 Lawrence Ave. West, Toronto, ON M6A 3B6
Tel: 416-787-6529; *Fax:* 416-787-7788
www.ssclawyers.com

***Toronto*: Crawley MacKewn Brush LLP - *10**
#800, 179 John St., Toronto, ON M5T 1X4
Tel: 416-217-0110; *Fax:* 416-217-0220
reception@cmblaw.ca
www.cmblaw.ca

** indicates number of lawyers*

***Toronto*: Cremer Barristers - *2**
Former Name: Cowan & Cremer
#216, 214 King St. West, Toronto, ON M5H 3S6
Tel: 416-322-3671; *Fax:* 416-971-5520
cremer@cremerbarristers.com
www.cremerbarristers.com

***Toronto*: F.H. Cremer - *1**
#201, 1593 Wilson Ave., Toronto, ON M3L 1A5
Tel: 416-244-5575; *Fax:* 416-247-3844

***Toronto*: Crewe & Marks - *2**
74 Riverdale Ave., Toronto, ON M4K 1C3
Tel: 416-967-9933; *Fax:* 416-967-9933
nsc@riv.com

***Toronto*: Frank D. Crewe - *2**
#500, 70 Bond St., Toronto, ON M5B 1X3
Tel: 416-362-2202; *Fax:* 416-363-9135
fcrewe@bondlaw.net

***Toronto*: Howard Crosner - *1**
190 Jarvis St., Toronto, ON M5B 2B7
Tel: 416-947-0455; *Fax:* 416-364-3818
crosner77@eol.ca
www.crosner.com

***Toronto*: Leroy A. Crosse - *1**
#203, 705 Lawrence Ave. West, Toronto, ON M6A 1B4
Tel: 416-785-8338; *Fax:* 416-785-9369

***Toronto*: Crum-Ewing & Poliacik - *3**
#412, 245 Fairview Mall Dr., Toronto, ON M2J 4T1
Tel: 416-733-9292; *Fax:* 416-733-9654
poliacik@ceplaw.ca

***Toronto*: Cummings Cooper Schusheim & Berliner LLP - *7**
#408, 4110 Yonge St., Toronto, ON M2P 2B5
Tel: 416-512-9500; *Fax:* 416-512-9501
info@ccsb-law.com
www.ccsb-law.com

***Toronto*: Gino A.J. Cundari - *1**
1179 St. Clair Ave. West, Toronto, ON M6E 1B5
Tel: 416-654-9000; *Fax:* 416-654-6688

***Toronto*: Peter Cusimano, Barrister & Solicitor - *1**
Former Name: Cusimano & Cusimano
#116, 185 Bridgeland Ave., Toronto, ON M6A 1Y7
Tel: 416-222-0588; *Fax:* 416-222-0239
peter@cusimano.com
www.cusimano.com/lawyer/
twitter.com/petercusimano

***Toronto*: J. Jerome Cusmariu - *1**
1310 Dundas St. West, Toronto, ON M6J 1Y1
Tel: 416-533-1173; *Fax:* 416-533-0761
jerry@cusmariulaw.com

***Toronto*: Andrew M. Czernik - *1**
#605, 920 Yonge St., Toronto, ON M4W 3C7
Tel: 416-920-4994; *Fax:* 416-920-5885
aczernik@on.aibn.com

***Toronto*: Czuma, Ritter - *2**
410 - 120 Carlton St., Toronto, ON M5A 4K2
Tel: 416-599-5799; *Fax:* 416-599-9981
czumamichael@gmail.com
www.michaelczuma.com

***Toronto*: Anthony D'Avella - *1**
#306, 4920 Dundas St. West, Toronto, ON M9A 1B7
Tel: 416-234-2198; *Fax:* 416-234-5142
anton.davella@on.aibn.com

***Toronto*: Dale & Lessmann LLP - *26**
#2100, 181 University Ave., Toronto, ON M5H 3M7
Tel: 416-863-1010; *Fax:* 416-863-1009
info@dalelessmann.com
www.dalelessmann.com

***Toronto*: Damien R. Frost & Associates - *2**
#103, 30 St. Clair Ave. West, Toronto, ON M4V 3A1
Tel: 647-800-6744; *Fax:* 866-235-6191
www.damienfrost.ca
www.linkedin.com/company/2633197?trk=tyah

***Toronto*: Danson Recht LLP - *5**
Former Name: Danson, Recht & Freedman
#2000, 700 Bay St., Toronto, ON M5G 1Z6
Tel: 416-929-2200; *Fax:* 416-929-2192
info@drlitigators.com
drlitigators.com

***Toronto*: Danson, Zucker & Connelly - *3**
#500, 70 Bond St., Toronto, ON M5B 1X3
Tel: 416-863-9955; *Fax:* 416-863-4896

***Toronto*: Daoust Vukovich LLP - *13**
#3000, 20 Queen St. West, Toronto, ON M5H 3R3
Tel: 416-597-6888; *Fax:* 416-597-8897
www.dv-law.com

***Toronto*: James Daris - *1**
#101, 8 Irwin Ave., Toronto, ON M4Y 1K9
Tel: 416-461-0395; *Fax:* 416-465-6042

***Toronto*: David Barristers Professional Corp. - *3**
Former Name: David Eklove Charles
#800, 1200 Bay St., Toronto, ON M5R 2A5
Tel: 416-923-7407; *Fax:* 416-923-6070
info@dcbfamilylaw.com
www.davidbarristers.com

***Toronto*: David Midanik & Associates - *1**
34 Shaftesbury Ave., Toronto, ON M4T 1A1
Tel: 416-967-1603; *Fax:* 416-967-1604
david@midaniklawoffice.com
www.midaniklawoffice.com

***Toronto*: Davies Howe Partners LLP - *18**
99 Spadina Ave., 5th Fl., Toronto, ON M5V 3P8
Tel: 416-977-7088; *Fax:* 416-977-8931
info@davieshowe.com
www.davieshowe.com

***Toronto*: Davies McLean Zweig Associates - *3**
1035 McNicoll Ave., Toronto, ON M1W 3W6
Tel: 416-756-7500; *Fax:* 416-512-1212

***Toronto*: Davis & Turk - *2**
#404, 3910 Bathurst St., Toronto, ON M3H 5Z3
Tel: 416-630-5541; *Fax:* 416-630-7724

***Toronto*: De Faria & De Faria - *2**
872 Dundas St. West, Toronto, ON M6J 1V7
Tel: 416-603-4440; *Fax:* 416-603-4441

***Toronto*: J.N. De Sommer - *1**
112 Adelaide St. East, Toronto, ON M5C 1K9
Tel: 416-341-7077; *Fax:* 416-368-2918
jndesommer@rbs.rogers.com

***Toronto*: Tilaka de Zoysa - *1**
#207, 2131 Lawrence Ave. East, Toronto, ON M1R 5G4
Tel: 416-752-2253; *Fax:* 416-752-6356

***Toronto*: DSFM - *8**
#2900, P.O. Box 2384, 2300 Yonge St., Toronto, ON M4P 1E4
Tel: 416-489-5677; *Fax:* 416-489-7794
info@condolaw.to
www.condolaw.to

***Toronto*: Deeth Williams Wall LLP - *21**
#400, 150 York St., Toronto, ON M5H 3S5
Tel: 416-941-9440; *Fax:* 416-941-9443
info@dww.com
www.dww.com
www.facebook.com/pages/DWW/170347319658865?v=info,
www.twitter.com/DWW_IPandITLaw,
www.linkedin.com/companies/deeth-williams-wall-llp

***Toronto*: DelZotto, Zorzi LLP - *11**
4810 Dufferin St., #D, Toronto, ON M3H 5S8
Tel: 416-665-5555; *Fax:* 416-665-9653
info@dzlaw.com
www.dzlaw.com

***Toronto*: Richard G.J. Desrocher - *1**
20 Leamington Ave., Toronto, ON M8Z 2W4
Tel: 416-236-5679; *Fax:* 416-236-7370

***Toronto*: Deverett Law Offices - *2**
163 Willowdale Ave., Toronto, ON M2N 4Y7
Tel: 416-222-6789; *Fax:* 416-222-7605
info@deverettlaw.com
www.deverettlaw.com

***Toronto*: Jane H. Devlin - *1**
#502, 121 Richmond St. West, Toronto, ON M5H 2K1
Tel: 416-366-3091; *Fax:* 416-366-0879
arbserv@istar.ca

***Toronto*: Devry Smith Frank LLP - Toronto - *51**
#100, 95 Barber Greene Rd., Toronto, ON M3C 3E9
Tel: 416-449-1400; *Fax:* 416-449-7071
Toll-Free: 866-474-1700
info@devrylaw.ca
www.devrylaw.ca
www.facebook.com/devrysmithfrank,
www.twitter.com/devrysmithfrank,
www.linkedin.com/companies/346809

***Toronto*: Diamond & Diamond - *8**
#701, 5075 Yonge St., Toronto, ON M2N 6C6
Tel: 416-850-7246; *Fax:* 416-256-0100
Toll-Free: 800-567-4878
jeremy@diamondlaw.ca
www.diamond-law.com
www.facebook.com/diamondanddiamondinjurylaw,
twitter.com/diamondlawtor

***Toronto*: Michael R. Diamond - *1**
#706, 55 Eglinton Ave. East, Toronto, ON M4P 1G8
Tel: 416-482-2666; *Fax:* 416-482-4165
syndicator@sympatico.ca

***Toronto*: Dickinson Wright (Canada) - Toronto - *33**
Former Name: Aylesworth LLP
#2200, Commerce Court West, 199 Bay St., Toronto, ON M5L 1G4
Tel: 416-777-0101; *Fax:* 416-865-1398
www.dickinson-wright.com
www.facebook.com/Dickinson-Wright-374489695906146,
twitter.com/dickinsonwright,
www.linkedin.com/company/dickinson-wright-pllc

***Toronto*: Dickson Appell LLP - *9**
Former Name: Dickson MacGregor Appell LLP; Dickson, MacGregor, Appell & Burton
#306, 10 Alcorn Ave., Toronto, ON M4V 3A9
Tel: 416-927-0891; *Fax:* 416-927-0385
www.dicksonlawyers.com

***Toronto*: Dimock Stratton LLP - *17**
P.O. Box 102, 20 Queen St. West, 32nd Fl., Toronto, ON M5H 3R3
Tel: 416-971-7202; *Fax:* 416-971-6638
firm@dimock.com
www.dimock.com

***Toronto*: Dion, Durrell & Associates - *2**
#2900, 250 Yonge St., Toronto, ON M5B 2L7
Tel: 416-408-2626; *Fax:* 416-408-3721
information@dion-durrell.com
www.dion-durrell.com

***Toronto*: Chris Dockrill - *1**
#2200, DBRS Tower, 181 University Ave., Toronto, ON M5H 3M7
Tel: 416-366-1881; *Fax:* 416-366-0608
chris@chris-dockrill.com
www.chris-dockrill.com

***Toronto*: Brian P. Donnelly - *1**
#2000, 393 University Ave., Toronto, ON M5G 1E6
Tel: 416-597-2191; *Fax:* 416-597-9808

***Toronto*: J. Brian Donnelly - *1**
#201, 1165A St. Clair Ave. West, Toronto, ON M6E 1B2
Tel: 416-653-0311; *Fax:* 416-653-6653
jbd@jbdonnelly.com

***Toronto*: Dorsey & Whitney LLP - *7**
#1600, TD Canada Trust Tower, 161 Bay St., Toronto, ON M5H 2Y4
Tel: 416-367-7370; *Fax:* 416-367-7371
toronto@dorsey.com
www.dorsey.com
www.facebook.com/DorseyWhitneyLLP,
twitter.com/DorseyWhitney,
www.linkedin.com/company/dorsey-&-whitney-llp

***Toronto*: Downtown Legal Services - *5**
Fasken Martineau Building, 655 Spadina Ave., Toronto, ON M5S 2H9
Tel: 416-934-4535; *Fax:* 416-934-4536
law.dls@utoronto.ca
dls.sa.utoronto.ca

***Toronto*: William C. Draimin - *1**
#101, 45 St. Clair Ave. West, Toronto, ON M4V 1K9
Tel: 416-920-4605; *Fax:* 416-960-0698
wdraimin@draiminlaw.com

** indicates number of lawyers*

Toronto: Dranoff & Huddart - *2
#314, 1033 Bay St., Toronto, ON M5S 3A5
Tel: 416-925-4500; *Fax:* 416-925-5197
info@dranoffhuddart.com
www.dranoffhuddart.com

Toronto: J. Blair Drummie - *1
326 Richmond St. West, Toronto, ON M5V 1X2
Tel: 416-921-0915; *Fax:* 416-925-6181
www.criminallawyer.to

Toronto: Du Markowitz LLP - *2
#2000, Madison Centre, 4950 Yonge St., Toronto, ON M2N 6K1
Tel: 416-590-1900; *Fax:* 416-590-1600
info@dumarkowitz.com
www.dumarkowitz.com

Toronto: Duncan-Morin LLP - *3
#701, The Fashion Bldg., 130 Spadina Ave., Toronto, ON M5V 2L4
Tel: 416-593-2513; *Fax:* 416-593-2514
info@duncanmorin.com
www.duncanmorin.com

Toronto: Thomas S. Dungey - *1
46 Fairview Blvd., Toronto, ON M4K 1L9
Tel: 416-469-3088; *Fax:* 416-469-6739
tsdungey@rogers.com

Toronto: Lloyd T. Duong - *1
2377 Dundas St. West, Toronto, ON M6P 1W7
Tel: 416-535-3463; *Fax:* 416-536-8279

Toronto: Norman L. Durbin - *1
Wycliffe-Jane Plaza, 2530 Jane St., Toronto, ON M3L 1S1
Tel: 416-743-2345; *Fax:* 416-743-0645

Toronto: Dutton Brock LLP - *41
Former Name: Dutton, Brock, MacIntyre & Collier
#1700, 438 University Ave., Toronto, ON M5G 2L9
Tel: 416-593-4411; *Fax:* 416-593-5922
info@duttonbrock.com
www.duttonbrock.com

Toronto: Diana C. Dzwiekowski - *1
260 Willard Ave., Toronto, ON M6S 3R2
Tel: 416-762-7251; *Fax:* 416-762-7252

Toronto: East Toronto Community Legal Services - *4
1320 Gerrard St. East, Toronto, ON M4L 3X1
Tel: 416-461-8102; *Fax:* 416-461-7497
www.etcls.ca

Toronto: Eccleston LLP - *4
#4020, Toronto-Dominion Centre, 66 Wellington St. West, Toronto, ON M5K 1J3
Tel: 416-504-2722; *Fax:* 416-504-2686
info@ecclestonllp.com
www.ecclestonllp.com

Toronto: Ecclestone, Hamer, Poisson & Neuwald & Freeman - *5
#900, The Sterling Tower, 372 Bay St., Toronto, ON M5C 1J3
Tel: 416-365-7135; *Fax:* 416-365-2189
www.ehpnf.com

Toronto: Ryan Edmonds Workplace Counsel - *1
#1600, 401 Bay St., Toronto, ON M5H 2Y4
Tel: 647-361-8228; *Fax:* 647-361-8229
ryan@torontoworkplacecounsel.com
torontoworkplacecounsel.com
twitter.com/ryanedmondslaw,
www.linkedin.com/in/ryanedmonds1

Toronto: Elliott Law Firm - *1
#1901, 5000 Yonge St., Toronto, ON M2N 7E9
Tel: 416-628-5598; *Fax:* 416-628-5597
elliottlawfirm@gmail.com
www.elliottlawfirm.ca

Toronto: Ellyn Law LLP - *5
#3000, 20 Queen St. West, Toronto, ON M5H 3R3
Tel: 416-365-3700; *Fax:* 416-368-2982
iellyn@ellynlaw.com
www.ellynlaw.com

Toronto: Mitch Engel - *1
#502, 1235 Bay St., Toronto, ON M5R 3K4
Tel: 416-944-8882; *Fax:* 416-925-4571
Toll-Free: 866-761-6904

Toronto: Epstein Cole LLP - *25
#2200, 393 University Ave., Toronto, ON M5G 1E6
Tel: 416-862-9888; *Fax:* 416-862-2142
www.epsteincole.com

Toronto: Norman Epstein - *1
#202, 745 Mount Pleasant Rd., Toronto, ON M4S 2N4
Tel: 416-225-5577; *Fax:* 416-483-5541

Toronto: Eric Lewis & Associates
164 Queen St. East, Toronto, ON M5A 1T9
Tel: 416-367-1918; *Fax:* 416-362-1918
lewis_smyth@hotmail.com

Toronto: EY Law LLP - *44
Former Name: Egan LLP; Couzin Taylor LLP; Donahue LLP
#2100, EY Tower, 222 Bay St., Toronto, ON M5K 1H6
Tel: 416-943-2400; *Fax:* 416-943-2735
www.eylaw.ca

Toronto: Charles A. Eyton-Jones - *3
1238 Kingston Rd., Toronto, ON M1N 1P3
Tel: 416-691-4529; *Fax:* 416-691-2563
info@eyton-jones.ca
www.eyton-jones.ca

Toronto: Fair & Siegel
#1002, 250 Heath St. West, Toronto, ON M5P 3L4
Tel: 416-948-1652; *Fax:* 416-483-9228
msiegel@rogers.com

Toronto: Falconer Charney - *7
8 Prince Arthur Ave., Toronto, ON M5R 1A9
Tel: 416-964-3408; *Fax:* 416-929-8179
falconercharney@fcbarristers.com
www.fcbarristers.com

Toronto: Ricardo G. Federico - *1
#506, 330 University Ave., Toronto, ON M5G 1R7
Tel: 416-928-1458; *Fax:* 416-322-3684
ricardo@federicolaw.ca
www.federicolaw.ca

Toronto: Frederick S. Fedorsen - *2
551 Gerrard St. East, Toronto, ON M4M 1X7
Tel: 416-463-6666; *Fax:* 416-463-8259
fred@fedorsennorth.com

Toronto: Jodi L. Feldman - *1
#205, 250 Merton St., Toronto, ON M4S 1B1
Tel: 416-922-3233
jfeldman@jfeldmanlaw.com

Toronto: Jane L. Ferguson - *1
41 Rosedale Rd., Toronto, ON M4W 2P5
Tel: 416-920-7533; *Fax:* 416-923-5576
jlferg@bellnet.ca

Toronto: Fernandes Hearn LLP - *9
Also Known As: Fernandes, Hearn, Theall
#700, 155 University Ave., Toronto, ON M5H 3B7
Tel: 416-203-9500; *Fax:* 416-203-9444
info@fernandeshearn.com
www.fernandeshearn.com
www.twitter.com/FernandesHearn,
www.linkedin.com/company/fernandes-hearn-llp?trk=fc_badge

Toronto: Filion Wakely Thorup Angeletti LLP - *37
#2601, P.O. Box 32, 150 King St. West, Toronto, ON M5H 4B6
Tel: 416-408-3221; *Fax:* 416-408-4814
toronto@filion.on.ca
www.filion.on.ca
www.linkedin.com/company/filion-wakely-thorup-angeletti-llp

Toronto: Filmlegals Entertainment Law Service - *1
7 Langley Ave., Toronto, ON M4K 1B4
Tel: 416-466-1487; *Fax:* 416-466-3094
mkrys@filmlegals.com
www.filmlegals.com

Toronto: Andrew Fine - *1
#306, 1000 Finch Ave. West, Toronto, ON M3J 2V5
Tel: 416-785-9499

Toronto: Fireman Steinmetz - *11
Former Name: Fireman Wolfe LLP
#415, P.O. Box 19, 55 St. Clair Ave. West, Toronto, ON M4V 2Y7
Tel: 416-967-9100; *Fax:* 416-967-1200
info@firemanlawyers.com
www.firemanlawyers.com

Toronto: Fisch & Antonette - *2
Former Name: S.J. Antonette
419 College St., 2nd Fl., Toronto, ON M5T 1T1
Tel: 416-920-6312; *Fax:* 416-920-1780
fa@torontorealestatelawyer.co
torontorealestatelawyer.co

Toronto: Steven M. Fishbayn - *1
#318, 100 Richmond St. West, Toronto, ON M5H 3K6
Tel: 416-361-9555; *Fax:* 416-862-7602
steven.fishbayn@sympatico.ca

Toronto: Barry B. Fisher - *1
#2000, Law Chambers, 393 University Ave., Toronto, ON M5G 1E6
Tel: 416-585-2330; *Fax:* 416-585-2105
barryfisher@rogers.com
barryfisher.ca

Toronto: Flancman & Frisch - *2
1286 Kennedy Rd., Toronto, ON M1P 2L5
Tel: 416-752-2221; *Fax:* 416-752-8434
Toll-Free: 877-468-1120
miskflan@hotmail.com & iifrisch@hotmail.com

Toronto: Fleischer & Kochberg - *1
#203, 77 Finch Ave. West, Toronto, ON M2N 2H5
Tel: 416-223-8102; *Fax:* 416-223-9502
www.fklawtorontolawyers.ca

Toronto: Fleming, Breen - *2
370 Bloor St. East, Toronto, ON M4W 3M6
Tel: 416-927-9000; *Fax:* 416-927-9069

Toronto: Fleming, White & Burgess - *2
#1002, 60 St. Clair Ave. East, Toronto, ON M4T 1N5
Tel: 416-961-2868; *Fax:* 416-961-2964
flemingwhite@bellnet.ca

Toronto: Fleury, Comery LLP - *4
#104, 215 Morrish Rd., Toronto, ON M1C 1E9
Tel: 416-282-5754; *Fax:* 416-282-9906
thefirm@fleurcom.on.ca
www.fleurcom.on.ca

Toronto: Ronald Flom - *2
#712, 2345 Yonge St., Toronto, ON M4P 2E5
Tel: 416-482-2777; *Fax:* 416-482-2599

Toronto: Forget Smith Morel - Toronto - *15
Former Name: Forget & Matthews LLP
#2802, P.O. Box 82, 401 Bay St., Toronto, ON M5H 2Y4
Tel: 416-368-4434; *Fax:* 416-368-7865
toronto@forgetsmith.com
www.forgetsmith.com

Toronto: Fournie Mickleborough LLP - *4
Former Name: Rogers, Campbell, Mickleborough
#701, 90 Adelaide St. West, Toronto, ON M5H 3V9
Tel: 416-366-3999; *Fax:* 416-366-2860
www.companylawyers.com

Toronto: Kevin Fox, Barrister & Solicitor - *1
Former Name: Fox Rovos
174 Davenport Rd., Toronto, ON M5R 1J2
Tel: 416-323-3252; *Fax:* 416-929-6885
kfox@davenportlaw.ca
www.kevinfoxlaw.ca
www.linkedin.com/pub/kevinfoxlaw

Toronto: Walter Fox - *3
#312, 100 Richmond St. West, Toronto, ON M5H 3K6
Tel: 416-363-9238; *Fax:* 416-363-9230
foxoffice@justlaw.ca

Toronto: Fraser Simms Reid & Spyrolpoulos LLP - *1
#4, 2011 Lawrence Ave. West, Toronto, ON M9N 3V3
Tel: 416-241-0111; *Fax:* 416-241-1911
vassili.fsrs@bellnet.ca
fsrslaw.ca

Toronto: Harvey Freedman - *3
#100, 79 Shuter St., Toronto, ON M5B 1B3
Tel: 416-363-1737; *Fax:* 416-861-9919
hfreedman@freedmans.ca

Toronto: Joel P. Freedman - *1
#200, 3200 Dufferin St., Toronto, ON M6A 2T3
Tel: 416-248-6231; *Fax:* 416-241-0080
www.freedmanlaw.ca

** indicates number of lawyers*

***Toronto*: Norman J. Freedman, Q.C.**
#2150, 121 King St. West, Toronto, ON M5H 3T9
Tel: 416-815-7767; *Fax:* 416-815-7722
elaine.freedman@sympatico.ca

***Toronto*: Randall R. Friedland - *1**
#1301, 2200 Yonge St., Toronto, ON M4S 2C6
Tel: 416-932-4969; *Fax:* 416-932-0541
friedland@jodlaw.com

***Toronto*: Fryer Levitt - *1**
#2, 421 Eglinton Ave. West, Toronto, ON M5N 1A4
Tel: 416-323-1377; *Fax:* 416-323-9355
jelevitt@fryerlevitt.com
www.fryerlevitt.com
www.facebook.com/fryerlevittlaw, twitter.com/jelevitt,
www.linkedin.com/pub/joel-levitt/1b/845/247

***Toronto*: Harry Frymer - *1**
#320, 100 Richmond St. West, Toronto, ON M5H 3K6
Tel: 416-869-1075; *Fax:* 416-869-1840

***Toronto*: Laurie A. Galway - *1**
712 Logan Ave., Toronto, ON M4K 3C6
Tel: 416-413-9466; *Fax:* 416-778-8364
laurie@lauriegalway.com

***Toronto*: Gardiner Miller Arnold LLP - *7**
#1202, 390 Bay St., Toronto, ON M5H 2Y2
Tel: 416-363-2614; *Fax:* 416-363-8451
gmainfo@gmalaw.ca
www.gmalaw.ca
www.facebook.com/pages/Toronto-ON/Gardiner-Miller-Arnold-LLP/11871502481799, twitter.com/gmalaw,
www.linkedin.com/companies/339366

***Toronto*: Gardiner Roberts LLP - *62**
#3600, Bay Adelaide Centre, East Tower, 22 Adelaide St. West, Toronto, ON M5H 4E3
Tel: 416-865-6600; *Fax:* 416-865-6636
contactGR@grllp.com
www.grllp.com

***Toronto*: Garfin Zeidenberg LLP - *13**
#800, Yonge Norton Centre, 5255 Yonge St., Toronto, ON M2N 6P4
Tel: 416-512-8000; *Fax:* 416-512-9992
Toll-Free: 877-529-9910
gzinfo@gzlegal.com
www.gzlegal.com

***Toronto*: Susan W. Garfin - *1**
#2000, 393 University Ave., Toronto, ON M5G 1E6
Tel: 416-599-9933; *Fax:* 416-599-5497
garfin@rogers.com

***Toronto*: Garfinkle, Biderman - *19**
#801, Dynamic Funds Tower, 1 Adelaide St. East, Toronto, ON M5C 2V9
Tel: 416-869-1234; *Fax:* 416-869-0547
www.garfinkle.com

***Toronto*: Gasee, Cohen & Youngman - *6**
#200, 65 Queen St. West, Toronto, ON M5H 2M5
Tel: 416-363-3351; *Fax:* 416-363-0252
www.gcylaw.com
www.facebook.com/GCYLaw

***Toronto*: Leon Gavendo - *1**
#2000, Law Chambers, University Centre, 393 University Ave., Toronto, ON M5G 1E6
Tel: 416-585-3109; *Fax:* 416-585-9668
lgavendo@on.aibn.com

***Toronto*: Gelfand & Co. - *2**
47 Harjolyn Dr., Toronto, ON M9B 3V3
Tel: 416-929-4949; *Fax:* 416-929-1996
Toll-Free: 877-286-4296

***Toronto*: Geller & Minster - *2**
2 Keewatin Ave., Toronto, ON M4P 1Z8
Tel: 416-480-2200; *Fax:* 416-480-2693
inquiry@gellerandminster.ca
gellerandminster.ca

***Toronto*: Genest Murray LLP - *9**
#1300, P.O. Box 45, 200 King St. West, Toronto, ON M5H 3T4
Tel: 416-368-8600; *Fax:* 416-360-2625
www.genestmurray.ca

***Toronto*: Basil L. Georgieff - *1**
3543A St. Clair Ave. East, Toronto, ON M1K 1L6
Tel: 416-464-6888; *Fax:* 416-267-1452
basgeo@msn.com

***Toronto*: Lorne Gershuny - *1**
1577 Bloor St. West, Toronto, ON M6P 1A6
Tel: 416-539-0989; *Fax:* 416-536-3618
lgershuny@hotmail.com

***Toronto*: Gertler & Associates - *2**
Also Known As: Robert Gertler LLB
#514, 1000 Finch St. West, Toronto, ON M3J 2V5
Tel: 416-410-8613; *Fax:* 416-231-9492
www.gertlerandassociates.com

***Toronto*: Ghose Law Office - *1**
Also Known As: Bassanio Ghose Professional Corporation
Former Name: Ghose & Malhotra
#308, 1620 Albion Rd., Toronto, ON M9V 4B4
Tel: 416-744-1480; *Fax:* 416-744-9855
gmreception@bellnet.ca
www.gmlawoffice.ca

***Toronto*: Gilbert & Yallen - *3**
Former Name: Howard Gilbert
204 St. George St., 3rd Fl., Toronto, ON M5R 2N5
Tel: 416-927-0001; *Fax:* 416-927-0930

***Toronto*: Gilbert's LLP - *13**
#2010, Toronto Dominion Centre, P.O. Box 301, 77 King st. West, Toronto, ON M5K 1K2
Tel: 647-560-2022; *Fax:* 416-703-7422
Toll-Free: 866-304-7054
www.gilbertslaw.ca
www.facebook.com/GilbertsLLP, twitter.com/GilbertsLLP

***Toronto*: Gilbert, Wright & Kirby LLP - *12**
#1920, 145 King St. West, Toronto, ON M5H 1J8
Tel: 416-363-3100; *Fax:* 416-363-1379
www.gkslawyers.com

***Toronto*: Gilbertson Davis Emerson LLP - *8**
#800, The Lumsden Bldg., 6 Adelaide St. East, Toronto, ON M5C 1H6
Tel: 416-979-2020; *Fax:* 416-979-1285
www.gilbertsondavis.com

***Toronto*: John D. Gilfillan, Q.C. - *1**
#1200, 20 Toronto St., Toronto, ON M5C 2B8
Tel: 416-861-1881; *Fax:* 416-861-1737
gilfillan@interware.net

***Toronto*: Leslie M. Giroday - *1**
190 Sixth St., Toronto, ON M8V 3A5
Tel: 416-255-1063; *Fax:* 416-251-8699
leslie.giroday@girodaylaw.ca

***Toronto*: Martin Gladstone LL.B. - *1**
#111, 579 Kingston Rd., Toronto, ON M4E 1R3
Tel: 416-693-9000; *Fax:* 416-693-9194
contact@gladstonelaw.ca
www.gladstonelaw.ca

***Toronto*: Glaholt LLP - *13**
#800, 141 Adelaide St. West, Toronto, ON M5H 3L5
Tel: 416-368-8280; *Fax:* 416-368-3467
Toll-Free: 866-452-4658
www.glaholt.com
twitter.com/GlaholtLLP

***Toronto*: Earl Glasner - *1**
#320, 100 Richmond St. West, Toronto, ON M5H 3K6
Tel: 416-869-1076; *Fax:* 416-869-1840
earlglasner@rogers.com

***Toronto*: Glass & Associates - *4**
50 Richmond St. East, 5th Fl., Toronto, ON M5C 1N7
Tel: 416-363-9295; *Fax:* 416-363-7659
lglass@glassassoc.com

***Toronto*: Alan A. Glass - *1**
#711, 505 Cummer Ave., Toronto, ON M2K 2L8
Tel: 416-222-0904; *Fax:* 416-222-0417
alanglass01@yahoo.ca

***Toronto*: Global Resolutions Inc. - *7**
45 St. Nicholas St., Toronto, ON M4Y 1W6
Tel: 416-964-7497; *Fax:* 416-925-8122
info@globalresolutions.com
globalresolutions.com

***Toronto*: Saul I. Glober - *3**
Former Name: Glober & Cohen, Associates
114 Scollard St., Toronto, ON M5R 1G2
Tel: 416-324-9994; *Fax:* 416-324-0966
www.sigestateplanning.com

***Toronto*: Gluckstein & Associates LLP - *7**
#301, P.O. Box 53, 595 Bay St., Toronto, ON M5G 2C2
Tel: 416-408-4252; *Fax:* 416-408-4235
Toll-Free: 866-308-7722
info@gluckstein.com
www.gluckstein.com
www.facebook.com/GlucksteinLLP, twitter.com/glucksteinlaw,

***Toronto*: Godfrey & Corcoran - *1**
#702, 55 Queen St. East, Toronto, ON M5C 1R6
Tel: 416-363-0484; *Fax:* 416-363-0485
ccorcoran@idirect.com

***Toronto*: Sydney L. Goldenberg - *1**
125 Highbourne Rd., Toronto, ON M5P 2J5
Tel: 416-482-3206; *Fax:* 416-482-8619
slgoldenberg@sympatico.ca

***Toronto*: Goldhar & Nemoy - *1**
#214, 120 Carlton St., Toronto, ON M5A 4K2
Tel: 416-928-1488; *Fax:* 416-924-7166

***Toronto*: Avra Goldhar - *1**
27 Abbeywood Trail, Toronto, ON M3B 3B4
Tel: 416-444-4378; *Fax:* 416-444-5721
agoldhar@rogers.com

***Toronto*: H.A. Goldkind - *1**
#320, 100 Richmond St. West, Toronto, ON M5H 3K6
Tel: 416-366-5280

***Toronto*: Goldman Sloan Nash & Haber LLP - *34**
#1600, 480 University Ave., Toronto, ON M5G 1V6
Tel: 416-597-9922; *Fax:* 416-597-3370
Toll-Free: 877-597-9922
urrego@gsnh.com
www.gsnh.com
twitter.com/GSNH_Law,
www.linkedin.com/company/143882?trk=tyah

***Toronto*: Goldman Sloan Nash & Haber LLP - Toronto - *5**
Former Name: Willson Lewis LLP
#1600, 480 University Ave., Toronto, ON M5G 1V2
Tel: 416-597-9922; *Fax:* 416-597-3370
Toll-Free: 877-597-9922
urrego@gsnh.com
www.gsnh.com
www.facebook.com/Goldman-Sloan-Nash-Haber-LLP-332939780108997, twitter.com/GSNH_Law,
www.linkedin.com/company/143882

***Toronto*: Jeffrey L. Goldman - *1**
#1600, 401 Bay St., Toronto, ON M5H 2Y4
Tel: 416-646-5164; *Fax:* 416-363-0406
jeffgoldmanlaw@gmail.com
jeffreygoldmanlaw.com

***Toronto*: Jeffrey W. Goldman - *1**
#400, 4580 Dufferin St., Toronto, ON M3K 5Y2
Tel: 416-787-1818; *Fax:* 416-661-4858
jeffreygoldmanlaw@gmail.com

***Toronto*: Goldman, Spring, Kichler & Sanders - *7**
#700, 40 Sheppard Ave. West, Toronto, ON M2N 6K9
Tel: 416-225-9400; *Fax:* 416-225-4805

***Toronto*: Goldstein & Grubner LLP - *2**
#212, 3459 Sheppard Ave. East, Toronto, ON M1T 3K5
Tel: 416-292-0414; *Fax:* 416-292-4508
info@gglawyers.ca
www.gglawyers.ca

***Toronto*: Goldstein, Rosen & Rassos LLP - *1**
#102, 1648 Victoria Park Ave., Toronto, ON M1R 1P7
Tel: 416-757-4156; *Fax:* 416-757-9318
trassos@grrlaw.ca
www.grrlaw.ca

***Toronto*: David Gomes - *1**
112 Adelaide St. East, Toronto, ON M5C 1K9
Tel: 416-361-0906; *Fax:* 416-368-2918
dgomes0604@rogers.com

***Toronto*: Goodman, Solomon & Gold - *2**
#1500, 439 University Ave., Toronto, ON M5G 1Y8
Tel: 416-595-5555; *Fax:* 416-595-7020

***Toronto*: Stanley Goodman, Q.C. - *1**
#1800, 4950 Yonge St., Toronto, ON M2N 6K1
Tel: 416-224-0224; *Fax:* 416-224-0758
stangoodman@torlaw.com

** indicates number of lawyers*

***Toronto*: Martin Z. Goose - *1**
#504, 555 Burnhamthorpe Rd., Toronto, ON M9C 2Y3
Tel: 416-239-4811; *Fax:* 416-239-1707
martingoose@bellnet.ca

***Toronto*: Nathan Gotlieb - *1**
#1800, Madison Centre, 4950 Yonge St., Toronto, ON M2N 6K1
Tel: 416-224-0200; *Fax:* 416-224-0758
ngotlieb@torlaw.com

***Toronto*: G.L. Gottlieb, Q.C. - *1**
#309, 600 Bay St., Toronto, ON M5G 1M6
Tel: 416-977-3835; *Fax:* 416-977-3807
glgqc@interlog.com
www.glgqc.com

***Toronto*: Max A. Gould - *1**
#1000, 30 St. Clair Ave. West, Toronto, ON M4V 3A1
Tel: 416-964-0290; *Fax:* 416-964-7102

***Toronto*: Deryk A. Gravesande - *1**
2 Carlton St., Toronto, ON M5B 1J3
Tel: 416-206-1110

***Toronto*: Green & Spiegel - *21**
#2800, 390 Bay St., Toronto, ON M5H 2Y2
Tel: 416-862-7880; *Fax:* 416-862-1698
www.gands.com

***Toronto*: David J. Green - *1**
#1, 399 Spadina Ave., Toronto, ON M5T 2G6
Tel: 416-979-2333; *Fax:* 416-597-8966

***Toronto*: Donald M. Greenbaum, Q.C. - *1**
#205, 265 Rimrock Rd., Toronto, ON M3J 3C6
Tel: 416-631-7504; *Fax:* 416-631-9895
baum@globility.com

***Toronto*: Greenberg & Levine - *2**
2223 Kennedy Rd., Toronto, ON M1T 3G5
Tel: 416-292-6500; *Fax:* 416-292-6559
reception@greenbergandlevine.com
www.greenbergandlevine.com

***Toronto*: Greenberg, Jack - *1**
#204, 181 Eglinton Ave. East, Toronto, ON M4P 1J4
Tel: 416-485-8833; *Fax:* 416-485-3246
jackgreenberg@greenberglawyers.ca

***Toronto*: Greenspan Partners LLP - *6**
Former Name: Greenspan, White
144 King St. East, Toronto, ON M5C 1G8
Tel: 416-366-3961; *Fax:* 416-366-7994
info@144king.com
www.greenspanpartners.com
twitter.com/GreenspanLLP

***Toronto*: Greenwood Lam LLP - *3**
Former Name: Greenwood Defense Law
#1240, 65 Queen St. West, Toronto, ON M5H 2M5
Tel: 416-686-4612; *Fax:* 416-362-3612
www.greenwooddefence.com

***Toronto*: E.J. Gresik - *1**
101 Scollard St., Toronto, ON M5R 1G4
Tel: 416-924-0781; *Fax:* 416-960-9650

***Toronto*: Jonathan G. Griffiths**
Also Known As: Griffiths Law
#710, 17 Wynford Dr., Toronto, ON M3C 1W1
Tel: 416-441-1253; *Fax:* 416-441-9757
Toll-Free: 866-412-2943
info@griffithslaw.com
griffithslaw.com

***Toronto*: Groia & Company Professional Corporation - *6**
#1100, 365 Bay St., Toronto, ON M5H 2V1
Tel: 416-203-2115; *Fax:* 416-203-9231
postmaster@groiaco.com
www.groiaco.com

***Toronto*: Bernard Gropper - *1**
#300, 261 Davenport Rd., Toronto, ON M5R 1K3
Tel: 416-962-3000; *Fax:* 416-487-3002

***Toronto*: Derek T. Ground - *1**
16 Oakview Avenue, Toronto, ON M6P 3J2
Tel: 416-604-3434; *Fax:* 416-604-3596
derek.ground@sympatico.ca

***Toronto*: Grundy, Cass & Campbell Professional Corporation - *3**
Former Name: Cass & Cass
#3150, Canadian Pacific Tower, P.O. Box 11, 100 Wellington St. West, Toronto, ON M5K 1A1
Tel: 416-849-8003; *Fax:* 416-849-8004
dgrundy@grundycass.com
www.grundycass.com

***Toronto*: Guberman Garson Immigration Lawyers - *5**
Former Name: Guberman Garson
#1920, 130 Adelaide St. West, Toronto, ON M5H 3P5
Tel: 416-363-1234; *Fax:* 416-363-8760
immlaw@ggilaw.com
www.ggilaw.com

***Toronto*: Lawrence Hadbavny - *1**
Law Society of Upper Canada, 130 Queen St. West, Toronto, ON M5H 2N6
Tel: 416-947-3394; *Fax:* 416-974-3924
Toll-Free: 800-668-7380
lhadbavn@lsuc.on.ca

***Toronto*: Michael P. Haddad - *1**
548 Parliament St., Toronto, ON M4X 1P6
Tel: 416-926-8151; *Fax:* 416-927-9005

***Toronto*: Hahn & Maian - *2**
664 Mount Pleasant Rd., Toronto, ON M4S 2N3
Tel: 416-486-9445; *Fax:* 416-486-1174
johnhahn@idirect.com

***Toronto*: Miles M. Halberstadt, Q.C. - *1**
120 Carlton St., Toronto, ON M5A 4K2
Tel: 416-944-0441; *Fax:* 416-944-8330
mileshalberstadt@hotmail.com

***Toronto*: Halfnight & McKinlay - *4**
#201, 65 Front St. East, Toronto, ON M5E 1B5
Tel: 416-361-3082; *Fax:* 416-361-0230
jhalfnight@halfnightlaw.com
www.halfnightlaw.com

***Toronto*: Hall Webber LLP - *3**
#400, 1200 Bay St., Toronto, ON M5R 2A5
Tel: 416-920-3849; *Fax:* 416-920-8373
info@hallwebber.com
www.ent-law.com

***Toronto*: David F. Halpenny - *1**
#403, 111 Peter St., Toronto, ON M5V 2H1
Tel: 416-867-9208; *Fax:* 416-867-9139
davetex@pathcom.com

***Toronto*: Allan S. Halpert - *1**
37 Maitland St., Toronto, ON M4Y 1C8
Tel: 416-968-7733; *Fax:* 416-968-7192
allan@halpertlaw.com

***Toronto*: Munyonzwe Hamalengwa**
#18A, 100 Westmore Dr., Toronto, ON M9V 5C3
Tel: 416-644-1106; *Fax:* 416-644-1126
munyonzweh@munyonzwehamalengwa.ca
www.munyonzwehamalengwa.ca

***Toronto*: Harvey L. Hamburg - *1**
#215, 120 Carlton St., Toronto, ON M5A 4K2
Tel: 416-968-9054; *Fax:* 416-968-9023
hhamburg@sympatico.ca

***Toronto*: Harasymowycz Law - *2**
#200, 2311 Bloor St. West, Toronto, ON M6S 1P1
Tel: 416-766-2472; *Fax:* 416-766-3297

***Toronto*: Murray P. Harrington - *1**
285 Pitfield Rd., Toronto, ON M1S 1Z2
Tel: 416-299-0477; *Fax:* 416-299-7570

***Toronto*: David E. Harris - *1**
#1900, 439 University Ave., Toronto, ON M5G 1Y8
Tel: 416-585-9329; *Fax:* 416-408-2372
delih@ca.inter.net

***Toronto*: Ricki D. Harris - *2**
#1800, 4950 Yonge St., Toronto, ON M2N 6K1
Tel: 416-224-0200; *Fax:* 416-224-0758
rdharris@torlaw.com

***Toronto*: Harris, Sheaffer LLP - *10**
#610, 4100 Yonge St., Toronto, ON M2P 2B5
Tel: 416-250-5800; *Fax:* 416-250-5300
www.harris-sheaffer.com

***Toronto*: Klaus Hartmann - *1**
391 Willowdale Ave., Toronto, ON M2N 5A8
Tel: 416-590-0311; *Fax:* 416-590-0312

***Toronto*: Peter L. Hatch - *1**
31 Prince Arthur Ave., Toronto, ON M5R 1B2
Tel: 416-972-6962; *Fax:* 416-960-5456

***Toronto*: Hazzard & Hore - *3**
#1220, 141 Adelaide St. West, Toronto, ON M5H 3L5
Tel: 416-868-0074; *Fax:* 416-868-1468
info@hazzardandhore.com
www.hazzardandhore.com

***Toronto*: Marian D. Hebb - *2**
6 Humewood Dr., Toronto, ON M6C 2W2
Tel: 416-971-6618; *Fax:* 866-513-5660
marian@hebbsheffer.ca

***Toronto*: Stephen H. Hebscher - *1**
#1800, 4950 Yonge St., Toronto, ON M2N 6K1
Tel: 416-224-0200; *Fax:* 416-224-0758
crimlaw@torlaw.com

***Toronto*: E.S. Heiber - *1**
#1, 197 Church St., Toronto, ON M5B 1Y7
Tel: 416-362-2768; *Fax:* 416-865-5328
esheiber@heiberlaw.com

***Toronto*: Heifetz, Crozier, Law Barristers and Solicitors - *3**
#600, 10 King St. East, Toronto, ON M5C 1C3
Tel: 416-863-1717; *Fax:* 416-368-3133
www.hclaw.com

***Toronto*: Julian Heller & Associates - *4**
#1905, 120 Adelaide St. West, Toronto, ON M5H 1T1
Tel: 416-364-2404; *Fax:* 416-364-0793

***Toronto*: Heller, Rubel - *8**
#1902, 120 Adelaide St. West, Toronto, ON M5H 1T1
Tel: 416-863-9311; *Fax:* 416-863-9465
bheller@hellerrubel.com
hellerrubel.com

***Toronto*: Heydary Law Firms - Toronto**
#4500, TD Bank Tower, P.O. Box 150, 66 Wellington St. West, Toronto, ON M5K 1H1
Tel: 416-972-9001; *Fax:* 416-972-9940
info@heydary.com
www.heydary.com

***Toronto*: John L. Hill - *1**
127 Bishop Ave., Toronto, ON M2M 1Z6
Tel: 416-226-3221; *Fax:* 416-226-3222
conlaw@pathcom.com

***Toronto*: Himelfarb Proszanski LLP - *16**
#1400, 480 University Ave., Toronto, ON M5G 1V2
Fax: 416-599-3131
Toll-Free: 877-820-1210
info@himprolaw.com
www.himprolaw.com

***Toronto*: Hinkson Sachak Mcleod**
Former Name: Steven M. Hinkson
#301, 366 Bay St., Toronto, ON M5H 4B2
Tel: 416-368-3476; *Fax:* 416-363-9917
shinkson@hinksonlaw.com

***Toronto*: Hodder Barristers - *3**
#2200, DBRS Tower, Adelaide Place, 181 University Ave., Toronto, ON M5H 3M7
Tel: 416-601-4818; *Fax:* 416-947-0909
www.torontolawyerlawfirm.com

***Toronto*: Hodgson Russ LLP - *3**
#2309, P.O. Box 30, 150 King St. West, Toronto, ON M5H 1J9
Tel: 416-595-5100; *Fax:* 416-595-5021
info@hodgsonruss.com
www.hodgsonruss.com
twitter.com/HodgsonRuss,
www.linkedin.com/company/hodgson-russ-llp

***Toronto*: Hoffer Adler LLP - *5**
#300, 425 University Ave., Toronto, ON M5G 1T6
Tel: 416-977-6666; *Fax:* 416-977-3332
www.hofferadler.com

***Toronto*: Hoffman, Sillery, Buckstein & Chuback - *3**
#200, 1810 Avenue Rd., Toronto, ON M5M 3Z2
Tel: 416-787-1161; *Fax:* 416-787-3894

** indicates number of lawyers*

Toronto: Gerri C. Holder - *1
#101, 703 Evans Ave., Toronto, ON M9C 5E9
Tel: 416-626-3069; Fax: 416-622-8952
gholder@rogers.com

Toronto: Christopher Holoboff - *1
#407, 1200 Sheppard Ave. East, Toronto, ON M2K 3C5
Tel: 416-868-0878; Fax: 416-868-0879
choloboff@aol.com

Toronto: Hooey Remus LLP - *4
#1410, 120 Adelaide St. West, 14th Fl., Toronto, ON M5H 1T1
Tel: 416-362-4000; Fax: 416-362-3646
asingh@hooeyremus.com
www.hooeyremus.com

Toronto: Houser Henry Syron LLP - *5
#2000, 145 King St. West, Toronto, ON M5H 2B6
Tel: 416-362-3411; Fax: 416-362-3757
inquiries@houserhenry.com
www.houserhenry.com
twitter.com/HouserHenry,
www.linkedin.com/company/houser-henry-&-syron-llp

Toronto: Howie, Sacks & Henry LLP - *14
#3500, 20 Queen St. West, Toronto, ON M5H 2R3
Tel: 416-361-5990; Fax: 416-361-0083
Toll-Free: 877-695-9440
www.hshlawyers.com

Toronto: John A. Howlett - *1
#850, 36 Toronto St., Toronto, ON M5C 2C5
Tel: 416-941-9444; Fax: 416-913-1444
jhowlett@bellnet.ca

Toronto: John P. Howorun - *1
1199 The Queensway, Toronto, ON M8Z 1R7
Tel: 416-363-9355; Fax: 416-363-6371

Toronto: Hrycyna Pothemont Hunter - *2
#200, 1081 Bloor St. West, Toronto, ON M6H 1M5
Tel: 416-532-8006; Fax: 416-532-2666
taras.hycyna@bellnet.ca

Toronto: Hughes, Amys LLP - Toronto - *45
#200, 48 Yonge St., Toronto, ON M5E 1G6
Tel: 416-367-1608; Fax: 416-367-8821
Toll-Free: 800-565-1713
www.hughesamys.com

Toronto: Edward F. Hung - *2
#319, 1033 Bay St., Toronto, ON M5S 3A5
Tel: 416-926-8777; Fax: 416-926-1799
info@torontolawteam.com
www.lawyersintoronto.com

Toronto: Peter D. Hutcheon - *1
#300, 55 Adelaide St. East, Toronto, ON M5C 1K6
Tel: 416-515-2049; Fax: 416-929-3204

Toronto: Nick Iannazzo - *1
Former Name: Iannazzo Onizuka Associates
#500, 425 University Ave., Toronto, ON M5G 1T6
Tel: 416-598-2002; Fax: 416-598-8183
niannazzo@on.aibn.com

Toronto: Iler Campbell LLP - *9
150 John St., 7th Fl., Toronto, ON M5V 3E3
Tel: 416-598-0103; Fax: 416-598-3484
www.ilercampbell.com

Toronto: Innovate LLP - *6
#120-E, MaRS Centre, 101 College St., Toronto, ON M5G 1L7
Toll-Free: 888-433-2030
info@innovatellp.com
www.innovatellp.com

Toronto: Joan M. Irwin - *1
#2200, P.O. Box 154, 4950 Yonge St., Toronto, ON M2N 6K1
Tel: 416-733-1990; Fax: 416-733-1992

Toronto: Isenberg & Shuman - *2
#804, 5075 Yonge St., Toronto, ON M2N 6C6
Tel: 416-225-5136; Fax: 416-225-6877
info@shumanlaw.ca
www.shumanlaw.ca
www.facebook.com/pages/Isenberg-Shuman/181620301889035

Toronto: Israel Foulon LLP - *6
#200, 65 St. Clair Ave. East, Toronto, ON M4T 2Y8
Tel: 416-640-1550; Fax: 416-640-1555
inquiries@israelfoulon.com
israelfoulon.com

Toronto: Cydney G. Israel - *1
61 Saint Nicholas St., Toronto, ON M4Y 1W6
Tel: 416-962-6188; Fax: 416-925-0162
cydisrael@rogers.com

Toronto: Carol E.F. Jackson - *1
#900, 60 Yonge St., Toronto, ON M5E 1H5
Tel: 416-363-3292; Fax: 416-868-6381

Toronto: Jacobson & Jacobson - *2
#222, 3089 Bathurst St., Toronto, ON M6A 2A4
Tel: 416-787-0611; Fax: 416-787-4873

Toronto: Jacqueline Bart & Associates - *3
Also Known As: Bart Law
#2200, Law Chambers, ING Tower, 181 University Ave., Toronto, ON M5H 3M7
Tel: 416-601-1346; Fax: 416-601-1357
info@bartlaw.ca
www.bartlaw.ca
twitter.com/Jbartlaw, ca.linkedin.com/in/jacquelinebart

Toronto: James, Siddall & Derzko - *4
#1305, 55 Queen St. East, Toronto, ON M5C 1R6
Tel: 416-860-0166; Fax: 416-860-0041

Toronto: Elham Jamshidi - *1
#920, 6 Adelaide St. East, Toronto, ON M5C 1H6
Tel: 416-363-7172; Fax: 416-363-9917
eej@criminallawlitigation.com
criminallawlitigation.com

Toronto: Jane Finch Community Legal Services - *3
#409, 1315 Finch Ave. West, Toronto, ON M3J 2G6
Tel: 416-398-0677; Fax: 416-398-7172
www.janefinchcommunitylegalservices.ca

Toronto: Janssen & Associates - *2
89 Scollard St., Toronto, ON M5R 1G4
Tel: 416-929-1103
enquiry@janssen-law.com
www.janssenlaw.ca

Toronto: Dale F. Jean-Pierre - *1
#700, 55 Town Centre Crt., Toronto, ON M1P 4X4
Tel: 416-290-0560; Fax: 416-290-1259

Toronto: Jellinek Law - *2
62A George St., Toronto, ON M5A 4K8
Tel: 416-955-4800; Fax: 416-972-1499
Info@JellinekLaw.com
www.jellineklaw.com

Toronto: Daphne Johnston - *1
#2000, 393 University Ave., Toronto, ON M5G 1E6
Tel: 416-599-9635; Fax: 416-599-6043
Toll-Free: 800-364-5793
daphnejohnston@rogers.com

Toronto: Joseph G. LoPresti, Barrister & Solicitor - *1
#1510, North York City Centre, 5140 Yonge St., Toronto, ON M2N 6L7
Tel: 416-218-5271; Fax: 416-250-7008
joseph@loprestilaw.ca
www.loprestilaw.ca

Toronto: Mary K.E. Joseph - *1
Hudson Bay Centre, 2 Bloor St. East, Toronto, ON M4W 1A8
Tel: 416-363-8048
mary@familylegalservices.ca
www.familylegalservices.ca

Toronto: Ron Jourard - *1
#504, 3200 Dufferin St., Toronto, ON M6A 3B2
Tel: 416-398-6685; Fax: 416-398-7396
Toll-Free: 888-257-0002
jourard@defencelaw.com
www.defencelaw.com

Toronto: Robert W. Judge - *1
44 Fairview Blvd., Toronto, ON M4K 1L9
Tel: 416-466-7007; Fax: 416-466-7050

Toronto: Steven W. Junger - *1
#14, 620 Supertest Rd., Toronto, ON M3J 2M8
Tel: 416-787-7247; Fax: 416-787-3021
s.junger@sympatico.ca

Toronto: Juriansz & Li - *1
#1709, North American Life Centre, 5650 Yonge St., Toronto, ON M2M 4G3
Tel: 416-226-2342; Fax: 416-222-6874
www.jurianszli.com

Toronto: Justice for Children & Youth - *6
#1203, 415 Yonge St., Toronto, ON M5S 2T9
Tel: 416-920-1633; Fax: 416-920-5855
Toll-Free: 866-999-5329
info@jfcy.org
www.jfcy.org

Toronto: JYJ Law - *1
Former Name: Swanick & Associates
#101, 225 Duncan Mill Rd., Toronto, ON M3B 3K9
Tel: 416-510-1888; Fax: 416-510-1945
info@jyjlaw.com
www.jyjlaw.com

Toronto: Kacaba & Associates - *2
#440, 100 Richmond St. West, Toronto, ON M5H 3K6
Tel: 416-361-1777; Fax: 416-361-1776

Toronto: Kagan Shastri LLP - *6
Former Name: Kagan, Zucker, Feldbloom, Shastri
188 Avenue Rd., Toronto, ON M5R 2J1
Tel: 416-368-2100; Fax: 416-368-8206
info@ksllp.ca
www.ksllp.ca

Toronto: The Kalen Group - *1
262 Avenue Rd., Toronto, ON M4V 2G7
Tel: 416-929-7781; Fax: 416-929-7784
kalen@mrgeenjeans.ca

Toronto: Speros Kanellos - *1
#202, 211 Consumers Rd., Toronto, ON M2J 4G8
Tel: 416-493-3100; Fax: 416-493-4377

Toronto: Chan Yeung Kang - *1
105 Sheppard Ave. East, Toronto, ON M2N 3A3
Tel: 416-221-1417; Fax: 416-221-1732
kang@cykanglaw.com

Toronto: William Kaplan - *1
#200, 70 Bond St., Toronto, ON M5B 1X3
Tel: 416-865-5341; Fax: 416-360-5746
william@williamkaplan.com
www.williamkaplan.com

Toronto: Kapoor Barristers - *4
#210, 20 Adelaide St. East, Toronto, ON M5C 2T6
Tel: 416-363-2700; Fax: 416-368-6811
info@kapoorbarristers.com
www.kapoorbarristers.com

Toronto: Joseph H. Kary - *1
90A Isabella St., Toronto, ON M4Y 1N4
Tel: 416-929-9656

Toronto: Sheldon L. Kasman & Associate - *2
#201, 1622 Eglinton Ave. West, Toronto, ON M6E 2G8
Tel: 416-789-1888; Fax: 416-789-5928
law@kasman.com
www.kasman.com

Toronto: Garen Kassabian - *1
#203, 8 Sampson Mews, Toronto, ON M3C 0H5
Tel: 416-443-9494; Fax: 416-443-0575
garen@bellnet.ca

Toronto: J.M. Kavanagh, Q.C. - *1
#340, 100 Cowdray Ct., Toronto, ON M1S 5C8
Tel: 416-265-3560; Fax: 416-265-1944

Toronto: Robert C. Kay - *1
#1108, 8 King St. East, Toronto, ON M5C 1B5
Tel: 416-362-9999

Toronto: Keel Cottrelle LLP - Toronto - *14
#920, 36 Toronto St., Toronto, ON M5C 2C5
Tel: 416-367-2900; Fax: 416-367-2791
www.keelcottrelle.com

Toronto: Kelly, Jennings & Lacy - *4
144 King St. East, 3rd Fl., Toronto, ON M5C 1G8
Tel: 416-366-1758; Fax: 416-366-1762
jennings@144king.com
www.144king.com/kjl/lawyers.htm

Toronto: Evan N. Kenley - *1
#301, 1352 Bathurst St., Toronto, ON M5K 3H7
Tel: 416-932-1148; Fax: 416-932-1108
evan@kenleylaw.com
www.kenleylaw.com

** indicates number of lawyers*

Toronto: Zachary Kerbel - *1
#501, 96 Spadina Ave., Toronto, ON M5V 2J6
Tel: 416-975-9660; Fax: 416-975-9868
zach@kerbel-law.com
www.kerbel-law.com

Toronto: Shayne G. Kert - *1
#1902, 120 Adelaide St. West, Toronto, ON M5H 1T1
Tel: 416-863-0141; Fax: 416-863-9465

Toronto: Kestenberg Siegal Lipkus LLP - *8
65 Granby St., Toronto, ON M5B 1H8
Tel: 416-597-0000; Fax: 416-597-6567
www.ksllaw.com

Toronto: El-Farouk A. Khaki - *1
315 Mutual St., Toronto, ON M4Y 1X6
Tel: 416-925-7227; Fax: 416-925-2450
elfin925@rogers.com

Toronto: King & King - *1
#2, 823 Millwood Rd., Toronto, ON M4G 1W3
Tel: 416-368-4678; Fax: 416-368-7234
aek@kingandking.net
www.kingandking.net

Toronto: Don P. Kirsh - *1
#207, 3500 Dufferin St., Toronto, ON M3K 1N2
Tel: 416-630-6136; Fax: 416-630-6135
dkirsh@bellnet.ca
www.donkirsh.ca

Toronto: Sheila Kirsh - *1
#3310, 20 Queen St. West, Toronto, ON M5H 3R3
Tel: 416-367-1765; Fax: 416-594-0868
sheila@kirsh-law.com
www.kirsh-law.com

Toronto: Howard Joshua Kirshenbaum - *1
#17, 1140 Sheppard Ave. West, Toronto, ON M3K 2A2
Tel: 416-865-5339; Fax: 416-777-9255
kirshenbaum@msn.com

Toronto: Klaiman, Edmonds - *3
#1000, 60 Yonge St., Toronto, ON M5E 1H5
Tel: 416-867-9600; Fax: 416-867-9783
www.klaimanedmonds.com
www.linkedin.com/company/klaiman-edmonds-llp

Toronto: Judi E. Klein - *1
#104, 2552 Finch Ave. West, Toronto, ON M9M 2G3
Tel: 416-749-7747; Fax: 416-749-9190
info@jkleinfamilylaw.com
www.judieklein.supersites.ca

Toronto: Paula Knopf Arbitrations Ltd. - *1
4 Biggar Ave., Toronto, ON M6H 2N4
Tel: 416-652-1516; Fax: 416-232-1175
paulaknopf@bellnet.ca
www.paulaknopf.ca

Toronto: Marc Koplowitz Associates - *2
#2900, 390 Bay St., Toronto, ON M5H 2Y2
Tel: 416-368-1100; Fax: 416-368-1998
marc@koplaw.com
www.koplaw.com

Toronto: Kopolovic, Strigberger - *1
#300, 69 Elm St., Toronto, ON M5G 1H2
Tel: 416-971-7272; Fax: 416-971-9092

Toronto: Korman & Company - *6
721 Queen St. East, Toronto, ON M4M 1H1
Tel: 416-465-4232; Fax: 416-465-6912
info@kormancompany.com
www.kormancompany.com

Toronto: Kornblum Law Professional Corporation - *1
#215, 3130 Bathurst St., Toronto, ON M6A 2A1
Tel: 647-496-2570
www.kornblumlawcorp.ca

Toronto: Koroloff & Huckins - *2
#304, 1110 Sheppard Ave. East, Toronto, ON M2K 2W2
Tel: 416-229-6226; Fax: 416-229-6517

Toronto: Koskie Minsky LLP - *48
#900, P.O. Box 52, 20 Queen St. West, Toronto, ON M5H 3R3
Tel: 416-977-8353; Fax: 416-977-3316
www.koskieminsky.com

Toronto: Kostyniuk & Greenside - *10
#300, 5468 Dundas St. West, Toronto, ON M9B 6E3
Tel: 416-762-8238; Fax: 416-762-5042
nkostyniuk@kglawyers.com
www.kostyniukandgreenside.com

Toronto: Kotler Law Firm - *1
#617, 1 Eglinton Ave. East, Toronto, ON M4P 3A1
Tel: 416-932-4949; Fax: 416-487-2992
hgk@koterlaw.ca

Toronto: S. Lenard Kotylo - *2
#300, 66 Gerrard St. East, Toronto, ON M5B 1G3
Tel: 416-585-9373; Fax: 416-585-9376

Toronto: Neil L. Kozloff - *1
#1900, 439 University Ave., Toronto, ON M5G 1Y8
Tel: 416-414-7031

Toronto: Alex Krakowitz - *1
#3101, P.O. Box 3, 250 Yonge St., Toronto, ON M5B 2L7
Tel: 416-596-4606; Fax: 416-599-8341
alex.krakowitz@lawpro.ca

Toronto: Kramer Simaan Dhillon LLP - *6
Former Name: Kramer Henderson Sidlofsky LLP
#2100, 120 Adelaide St. West, Toronto, ON M5H 1T1
Tel: 416-601-6820; Fax: 416-601-0712
info@kramersimaan.com
kramersimaan.com

Toronto: Krauss, Weinryb - *2
#502, 100 Shepard Ave. East, Toronto, ON M2N 6N5
Tel: 416-222-4446; Fax: 416-222-9788

Toronto: Gerald Kroll, Q.C. - *1
#1800, 4950 Yonge St., Toronto, ON M2N 6K1
Tel: 416-224-0200; Fax: 416-224-0758

Toronto: Kuretzky Vassos Henderson LLP - *10
#1404, 151 Yonge St., Toronto, ON M5C 2W7
Tel: 416-865-0504; Fax: 416-865-9567
info@kuretzkyvassos.com
www.kuretzkyvassos.com

Toronto: Grace F. Kwan - *1
90A Isabella St., 3rd Fl., Toronto, ON M4Y 1N4
Tel: 416-968-2014; Fax: 416-968-2054
gkwan@295.ca

Toronto: Stephen M. Labow - *1
#610, 480 University Ave., Toronto, ON M5G 1V2
Tel: 416-947-1172; Fax: 416-596-0808
stephen@labow.ca

Toronto: Lafontaine & Associates - *3
Former Name: Gregory L. Lafontaine
#506, 330 University Ave., Toronto, ON M5G 1R7
Tel: 416-204-1835; Fax: 416-204-1849
greg@127john.com

Toronto: Tikam K. Lalla - *1
1203 Bloor St. West, Toronto, ON M6H 1N4
Tel: 416-532-2801; Fax: 416-532-4942

Toronto: Mary L.F. Lam - *2
40 Binscarth Road, Toronto, ON M4W 1Y1
Tel: 416-383-0266; Fax: 416-383-0299
mary.lam@rogers.com

Toronto: Jack S. Lambert - *1
105 Sultana, Toronto, ON M6A 1T4
Tel: 416-226-6343; Fax: 416-226-6344
jacklamlaw@rogers.com

Toronto: Garry Lamourie - *1
#2000, 393 University Ave., Toronto, ON M5G 1E6
Tel: 416-597-9828; Fax: 416-597-9808
info@lamourie.ca
www.lamourie.ca/en/

Toronto: Landy Marr Kats LLP - *9
#900, 2 Sheppard Ave. East, Toronto, ON M2N 5Y7
Tel: 416-221-9343; Fax: 416-221-8928
lawyers@landymarr.com
www.thetorontolawyers.ca

Toronto: Wayne S. Laski - *1
197 Byng Ave., Toronto, ON M2N 4K8
Tel: 416-229-1166
wlaski@wlaski.com

Toronto: Law Office of Cynthia Mancia - *2
Former Name: Mancia & Mancia
#309, 14 Prince Arthur Ave., Toronto, ON M5R 1A9
Tel: 416-363-7422; Fax: 416-363-4975
cynthia@mancialaw.ca
www.mancialaw.ca

Toronto: Law Office of T. Edgar Reilly - *3
701 Coxwell Ave., Toronto, ON M4C 3C1
Tel: 416-461-7553; Fax: 416-461-2679
lawoffice@tedgarreilly.ca
www.reillylawofficeoftedgar.yp.ca

Toronto: John V. Lawer, Q.C. - *1
#306, 40 St. Clair Ave. East, Toronto, ON M4T 1M9
Tel: 416-922-0737; Fax: 416-922-1896
johnv@johnvlawer.on.ca

Toronto: L.B. Geffen - *1
#205, 2907 Kennedy Rd., Toronto, ON M1V 1S8
Tel: 416-292-6688; Fax: 416-292-6649
geffen02@bellnet.ca
lawrencebgeffen.com

Toronto: Lax O'Sullivan Lisus Gottlieb - *20
Former Name: Lax O'Sullivan Scott Lisus LLP
#2750, 145 King St. West, Toronto, ON M5H 1J8
Tel: 416-598-1744; Fax: 416-598-3730
info@counsel-toronto.com
www.counsel-toronto.com

Toronto: Laxton Glass LLP - *28
#200, 390 Bay St., Toronto, ON M5H 2Y2
Tel: 416-363-2353; Fax: 416-363-7112
info@laxtonglass.com
laxtonglass.com

Toronto: Sheldon S. Lazarovitz - *1
31 Westgate Blvd., Toronto, ON M3H 1N8
Tel: 416-638-6080; Fax: 416-638-6246
lazarovitz@rogers.com

Toronto: Timothy J. Leach - *1
#309, 658 Danforth Ave., Toronto, ON M4J 5B9
Tel: 416-868-0265; Fax: 416-868-0478

Toronto: Lee & Company - *4
#610, 255 Duncan Mill Rd., Toronto, ON M3B 3H9
Tel: 416-321-0100; Fax: 416-321-3528
info@leecompany.ca
www.leecompany.ca
www.facebook.com/leeandcompany,
twitter.com/leeandcompany, www.linkedin.com/company/447694

Toronto: John Y.C. Lee - *1
#418, 4002 Sheppard Ave. East, Toronto, ON M1S 1S6
Tel: 416-299-8900; Fax: 416-299-8232

Toronto: Paul Lee & Associates - *4
20 Maitland St., Toronto, ON M4Y 1C5
Tel: 416-961-2707; Fax: 416-961-5575
office@paullee.ca
paullee.ca

Toronto: Legal Aid Ontario
#200, Atrium on Bay, 40 Dundas St. West, Toronto, ON M5G 2H1
Tel: 416-979-1446; Fax: 416-979-8669
Toll-Free: 800-668-8258
info@lao.on.ca
www.legalaid.on.ca

Toronto: Legge & Legge - *5
#800, 65 St. Clair Ave. East, Toronto, ON M4T 2Y3
Tel: 416-923-1776; Fax: 416-925-5344
leggeandlegge.com

Toronto: Joseph C. Lemire - *1
#500, 70 Bond St., Toronto, ON M5B 1X3
Tel: 416-363-1097; Fax: 416-863-4896

Toronto: Lenczner Slaght LLP - *49
Former Name: Lenczner Slaght Royce Smith Griffin LLP
#2600, 130 Adelaide St., West, Toronto, ON M5H 3P5
Tel: 416-865-9500; Fax: 416-865-9010
Toll-Free: 877-805-7774
info@litigate.com
www.litigate.com

* indicates number of lawyers

Toronto: Frank Lento - *1
Former Name: Franco, Lento, D'Alimonte
#504, 3200 Dufferin St., Toronto, ON M3K 2A7
Tel: 416-398-4044; *Fax:* 416-398-7396
franklento@lentolaw.com
lentolaw.com

Toronto: George J. Leon - *1
29 Berwick Ave., Toronto, ON M5P 1G9
Tel: 416-487-1385; *Fax:* 647-348-1512
gleon@idirect.com

Toronto: Gérard Lévesque - *1
184 Lake Promenade, Toronto, ON M8W 1A8
Tel: 416-253-0129; *Fax:* 416-253-4737
levesque.gerard@sympatico.ca

Toronto: Levine Associates - *6
#1400, 10 King St. East, Toronto, ON M5C 1C3
Tel: 416-364-2345; *Fax:* 416-364-3818
www.levlaw.com
www.facebook.com/pages/Levine-Associates/114873891921144

Toronto: Lorne Levine - *1
401-55 Eglington Ave. E, Toronto, ON M4P 1G8
Tel: 416-483-1251; *Fax:* 416-483-1257
lornelevinelaw@bellnet.ca

Toronto: Levine, Sherkin, Boussidan - *4
#300, 23 Lesmill Rd., Toronto, ON M3B 3P6
Tel: 416-224-2400; *Fax:* 416-224-2408
larry@lsblaw.com
www.lsblaw.com

Toronto: Levinson & Associates - *1
#610, 480 University Ave., Toronto, ON M5G 1V2
Tel: 416-591-8484; *Fax:* 416-596-0808
levinson@levadvocate.net
www.levadvocate.net

Toronto: Levitan Lawyers - *1
22 Soho St., Toronto, ON M5T 1Z7
Tel: 416-368-4600; *Fax:* 416-368-1166
jerrylevitan@rogers.com

Toronto: Sherry Levitan - *1
#403, 1 Yorkdale Rd., Toronto, ON M6A 3A1
Tel: 416-784-1222
info@fertilitylaw.ca
www.fertilitylaw.ca
www.facebook.com/pages/Sherry-Levitan-Fertility-Law/1752172
52568557, twitter.com/sherrylevitan

Toronto: Levitt, Lightman, Dewar & Graham LLP - *4
#1, 16 Four Seasons Pl., Toronto, ON M9B 6E5
Tel: 416-620-0362; *Fax:* 416-620-5158
Toll-Free: 866-730-4919
www.lldg.ca
www.facebook.com/#!/pages/Levitt-Lightman-Dewar-Graham-LL
P/127863840638504, twitter.com/lldg_law,
www.linkedin.com/in/lldgrichard

Toronto: Alan D. Levy - *1
75 Robert St., Toronto, ON M5S 2K4
Tel: 416-929-8282; *Fax:* 416-929-9895

Toronto: Earl J. Levy, Q.C. - *1
#400, 100 Richmond St. West, Toronto, ON M5H 3K6
Tel: 416-364-7292; *Fax:* 416-364-7473

Toronto: Lewis & Associates - *5
41 Madison Ave., Toronto, ON M5R 2S2
Tel: 416-924-2227; *Fax:* 416-924-9993
lewisassociates@eol.ca

Toronto: Andrew C. Lewis - *1
#508, 1 Eglinton Ave. East, Toronto, ON M4P 3A1
Tel: 416-322-7010; *Fax:* 416-483-2737
andrew@andrewclewislaw.ca
www.andrewclewislaw.ca

Toronto: Joseph E. Lewis - *1
#202, 327 Eglinton Ave. E, Toronto, ON M4P 1L7
Tel: 416-486-0084; *Fax:* 416-486-7363

Toronto: Susan M.C. Libanio - *1
#617, 1 Summerhill Rd., Toronto, ON M8V 1R9
Tel: 416-533-6002; *Fax:* 416-533-6097
smel@rogers.com

Toronto: Yoel Lichtblau - *1
499 Wilson Heights Blvd., Toronto, ON M3H 2V7
Tel: 416-633-2465
yoel@yichtblaulaw.com
lichtblaulaw.com
ca.linkedin.com/pub/yoel-lichtblau/13/141/589

Toronto: Linden & Associates - *4
#2010, Royal Bank Plaza, North Tower, 200 Bay St., Toronto, ON M5J 2J1
Tel: 416-861-9338; *Fax:* 416-861-9973
www.lindenlex.com

Toronto: John Liss - *1
207 Brunswick Ave., Toronto, ON M5S 2M4
Tel: 416-968-2558; *Fax:* 416-961-7906

Toronto: John A.G. Lister - *1
167 Danforth Ave., Toronto, ON M4K 1N2
Tel: 416-461-0983; *Fax:* 416-462-3347
jaglister@on.aibn.com

Toronto: Nadia Liva - *1
Law Chambers, 15 Bedford Rd., Toronto, ON M5R 2J7
Tel: 416-598-0106; *Fax:* 416-868-0273
nadialiva@15bedford.com
www.nadialiva.com

Toronto: Locke & Associates - *3
#200, 37 Prince Arthur Ave., Toronto, ON M5R 1B2
Tel: 416-601-1525; *Fax:* 416-601-0392
david.locke@rogers.com
www.lockeandassociates.ca

Toronto: Lockyer Campbell Posner Barristers & Solicitors - *11
#103, 30 St. Clair Ave. West, Toronto, ON M4V 3A1
Tel: 416-847-2560; *Fax:* 416-847-2564
www.lcp-law.com

Toronto: Lofranco Corriero LLC - *10
Former Name: Rocco C. Lofranco, Barristers & Solicitors
#600, P.O. Box 174, 4950 Yonge St., Toronto, ON M2N 6K1
Tel: 416-223-8333; *Fax:* 416-223-3404
info@lofrancolawyers.com
www.lofrancolawyers.com

Toronto: Gerald P. Logan - *1
317 Grace St., Toronto, ON M6G 3A7
Tel: 416-535-8920; *Fax:* 416-537-6550

Toronto: Joachim M. Loh - *1
#10 b, 3880 Midland Ave., Toronto, ON M1V 5K4
Tel: 416-609-8289; *Fax:* 416-609-8857
jmloh@jmlohlaw.com

Toronto: Loopstra Nixon LLP Barristers & Solicitors - *23
#600, Woodbine Place, 135 Queen's Plate Dr., Toronto, ON M9W 6V7
Tel: 416-746-4710; *Fax:* 416-746-8319
www.loopstranixon.com

Toronto: Lorne Waldman & Associates - *6
281 Eglinton Ave. East, Toronto, ON M4P 1L3
Tel: 416-482-6501; *Fax:* 416-489-9618
lorne@lornewaldman.ca
www.lornewaldman.ca

Toronto: Francisco B. Luna - *1
1919 Lawrence Ave. East, Toronto, ON M1R 2Y6
Tel: 416-977-3249

Toronto: Karen D. Lundy - *1
#2400, P.O. Box 22, 1 Dundas St. West, Toronto, ON M5G 1Z3
Tel: 416-866-8858; *Fax:* 416-364-3866
karenlundy@waldin.ca

Toronto: Lawrence M. Lychowyd - *1
236A Bain Ave., Toronto, ON M4K 1G3
Tel: 416-466-8063; *Fax:* 416-694-3367
www.larrythelawyer.ca

Toronto: Bryan A. MacBride - *1
#612, 55 Lombard St., Toronto, ON M5C 2R7
Tel: 416-601-9222; *Fax:* 416-601-9223
bamc@rogers.com

Toronto: MacDonald & Partners LLP - *14
#1700, 155 University Ave., Toronto, ON M5H 3B7
Tel: 416-971-4802; *Fax:* 416-971-9584
famlaw@mpllp.com
www.macdonaldpartners.com

Toronto: MacDonald Geraldine - *1
80 Richmond St. West, Toronto, ON M5H 2A4
Tel: 416-366-7985; *Fax:* 416-366-4670

Toronto: Macdonald Sager Manis LLP - *22
#800, 150 York St., Toronto, ON M5H 3S5
Tel: 416-364-1553; *Fax:* 416-364-1453
www.msmlaw.ca
twitter.com/MSM_law,
www.linkedin.com/company/macdonald-sager-manis-llp

Toronto: Mary-Douglass MacDonald - *1
122 Prince George Dr., Toronto, ON M9B 2Y2
Tel: 416-231-4899; *Fax:* 647-438-4494
mdmacdonald@rogers.com

Toronto: Carolyn A. MacLean - *1
#102, 40 Isabella St., Toronto, ON M4Y 1N1
Tel: 416-925-4008; *Fax:* 416-920-0367
camaclean@hotmail.com

Toronto: Theresa M. MacLean - *1
#202, 40 Isabella St., Toronto, ON M4Y 1N1
Tel: 416-964-9224; *Fax:* 416-920-0367
theresa.m.maclean@gmail.com

Toronto: Thmoas J. MacLennan - *1
#201, 27 Yorkville Ave., Toronto, ON M4W 1L1
Tel: 416-591-1354; *Fax:* 416-925-3514
www.maclennanlaw.com

Toronto: MacLeod Law Firm
#1700, 22 St Clair Ave. East, Toronto, ON M4T 2S3
Tel: 416-977-9894; *Fax:* 416-977-7337
inquiry@macleodlawfirm.ca
www.macleodlawfirm.ca
www.facebook.com/dougmacleodCAN,
www.twitter.com/dougmacleodCAN,
ca.linkedin.com/in/dougmacleodcan

Toronto: Paul A. MacLeod - *1
32 Elm St., Toronto, ON L3M 1H3
Tel: 905-945-9659; *Fax:* 905-945-0838
office@macleod-barr.com

Toronto: S.G.R. MacMillan
#2110, 120 Adelaide St. West, Toronto, ON M5H 1T1
Tel: 416-363-0100

Toronto: Dan Malamet - *1
10 Audubon Ct., Toronto, ON M2N 1T9
Tel: 416-865-6952; *Fax:* 416-863-6275
dan.malamet@bakernet.com

Toronto: Malo Pilley Lehman - *2
1067 Bloor St. West, Toronto, ON M6H 1M5
Tel: 416-534-3555; *Fax:* 416-534-7625
Toll-Free: 855-534-3555
info@mpllaw.ca
www.mpllaw.ca

Toronto: Harvey Mandel - *1
#203, 55 Queen St. East, Toronto, ON M5C 1R6
Tel: 416-364-7717; *Fax:* 416-364-4813
harvey-mandel.com

Toronto: Mantas Bouwer & Rosen
10 King St. East, Toronto, ON M5C 1C3
Tel: 416-777-1400

Toronto: Pierre F. Marchildon - *1
#308, Dundas-Lambton Centre, 4195 Dundas St. West, Toronto, ON M8X 1Y4
Tel: 416-236-0686; *Fax:* 416-236-0650
Toll-Free: 866-236-0686
pfmlaw@on.aibn.com

Toronto: Marcos Associates - *2
1718 Dundas St. West, Toronto, ON M6K 1V5
Tel: 416-537-3151; *Fax:* 416-537-3153
eamarcos.office@gmail.com

Toronto: Marin, Evans & Bell - *2
#500, 200 Adelaide St. West, Toronto, ON M5H 1W7
Tel: 416-408-2177; *Fax:* 416-408-1718

Toronto: Charles C. Mark, Q.C. - *1
#2010, 401 Bay St., Toronto, ON M5H 2Y4
Tel: 416-869-0929; *Fax:* 416-869-9118
ccmark@on.aibn.com

** indicates number of lawyers*

***Toronto*: Markes Lawyers - *3**
Former Name: Beach, Hepburn
#506, 1090 Don Mills Rd., Toronto, ON M3C 3R6
Tel: 416-350-3500; *Fax:* 416-350-3510
www.markeslawyers.com

***Toronto*: Markle Reid Munoz LLP - *3**
Former Name: Markle, May, Phibbs
#300, 500 Sheppard Ave. East, Toronto, ON M2N 6H7
Tel: 416-593-4385; *Fax:* 416-593-4478
Toll-Free: 800-332-4033
www.marklelawyers.com
twitter.com/MarkleReidMunoz

***Toronto*: H. David Marks, Q.C. - *1**
#1600, 480 University Ave., Toronto, ON M5G 1V2
Tel: 416-863-1550; *Fax:* 416-863-9670
marks@gsnh.com

***Toronto*: Larry M. Marshall - *1**
#1017, 250 Consumers Rd., Toronto, ON M2J 4V6
Tel: 416-497-2526; *Fax:* 416-497-3143
lmarshal@idirect.com

***Toronto*: Malcolm M. Martin - *1**
#209, 29 Gervaid Dr., Toronto, ON M3C 1Z1
Tel: 416-449-4111; *Fax:* 416-449-7879
mmartin@malcolmmartin.com

***Toronto*: Martinello & Associates - *3**
#208, United Centre, 255 Duncan Mill Rd., Toronto, ON M3B 3H9
Tel: 416-800-1377
www.martinelloandassociates.ca

***Toronto*: Ville K. Masalin - *1**
#309, 191 Eglinton Ave. East, Toronto, ON M4P 1K1
Tel: 416-484-9347; *Fax:* 416-484-9027

***Toronto*: Masters & Masters - *2**
#440, 65 Queen St. West, Toronto, ON M5H 2M5
Tel: 416-361-1399; *Fax:* 416-361-6181
masterslaw@sympatico.ca
www.masterslaw.com

***Toronto*: Mathews, Dinsdale & Clark LLP - Toronto - *40**
#3600, RBC Centre, 155 Wellington St. West, Toronto, ON M5V 3H1
Tel: 416-862-8280; *Fax:* 416-862-8247
Toll-Free: 800-411-2900
www.mathewsdinsdale.com
www.facebook.com/mathewsdinsdale, twitter.com/mdclaw, www.linkedin.com/company/mathews-dinsdale-&-clark-llp

***Toronto*: Gaetano P. Matteazzi - *1**
#400, 340 College St., Toronto, ON M5T 3A9
Tel: 416-534-8881; *Fax:* 416-972-1885

***Toronto*: Matthew Wilton & Associates - *3**
#1503, 65 Queen St. West, Toronto, ON M5H 2M5
Tel: 416-860-9889; *Fax:* 416-860-1034
reception@wiltonlaw.com
wiltonlaw.com

***Toronto*: McBride Wallace Laurent & Cord LLP - *10**
#200, 5464 Dundas St. West, Toronto, ON M9B 1B4
Tel: 416-231-6555; *Fax:* 416-231-6630

***Toronto*: McCague Borlack LLP - Toronto - *74**
#2700, The Exchange Tower, P.O. Box 136, Stn. 1st, 130 King St. West, Toronto, ON M5X 1C7
Tel: 416-860-0001; *Fax:* 416-860-0003
Toll-Free: 888-960-0010
mccagueborlack.com

***Toronto*: Robert L. McClelland - *1**
#313, 2498 Yonge St., Toronto, ON M4P 2H8
Tel: 416-481-7360
robmcc@ca.inter.net

***Toronto*: John D. McCrie - *1**
#9, 15 Belfield Rd., Toronto, ON M9W 1E8
Tel: 416-243-9501; *Fax:* 416-243-2990
johndmccrie@rogers.com

***Toronto*: David J. McGhee - *1**
390 Bay St., 30th Fl., Toronto, ON M5H 2Y2
Tel: 416-362-9736; *Fax:* 416-362-9435
djmcghee@on.aibn.com

***Toronto*: McGregor & Martin Associates - *1**
Former Name: McGregor, David R.
#316, 18 Wynford Dr., Toronto, ON M3C 3S2
Tel: 416-485-1123; *Fax:* 416-485-8742

***Toronto*: McInnis, Nicoll - *2**
#507, 330 Bay St., Toronto, ON M5H 2S8
Tel: 416-362-1354; *Fax:* 416-362-1465

***Toronto*: McIver & McIver - *2**
#700, 1 Richmond St. West, Toronto, ON M5H 3W4
Tel: 416-864-9000; *Fax:* 416-864-9190

***Toronto*: Michael A. McKee - *1**
53 Widdicombe Hill Blvd., Toronto, ON M9R 1Y3
Tel: 416-928-6619; *Fax:* 416-928-9515
mckeelawoffice@yahoo.ca
www.torontooncriminallawyer.ca

***Toronto*: Michael G. McLachlan - *1**
Former Name: McLachlan Winter Freeman
#103, 30 St. Clair Ave. West, Toronto, ON M4V 3A1
Tel: 416-596-7077; *Fax:* 416-596-7629
info@mgmlaw.ca
www.mgmlaw.ca

***Toronto*: McLean & Kerr LLP - *26**
#2800, 130 Adelaide St. West, Toronto, ON M5H 3P5
Tel: 416-364-5371; *Fax:* 416-366-8571
mail@mcleankerr.com
www.mcleankerr.com

***Toronto*: McMaster, McIntyre & Smyth, LLP - *6**
2777 Dundas St. West, Toronto, ON M6P 1Y4
Tel: 647-547-9865; *Fax:* 416-769-4147
Toll-Free: 800-530-7597
www.mmslawyers.com

***Toronto*: McPhadden Samac Tuovi LLP - *4**
Former Name: McPhadden, Samac, Merner, Darling
#300, 8 King St. East, Toronto, ON M5C 1B5
Tel: 416-363-5195; *Fax:* 416-363-7485
www.mcst.ca

***Toronto*: Deborah L. Meldazy - *1**
426 Davenport Rd., Toronto, ON M4V 1B5
Tel: 416-929-8524; *Fax:* 416-929-4042
dmeldazy@sympatico.ca

***Toronto*: Menzies, von Bogen - *1**
Former Name: J. Alexander Menzies, Q.C.
1071B Bloor St. West, Toronto, ON M6H 1M5
Tel: 416-532-2833; *Fax:* 416-532-6553
Toll-Free: 877-218-0084
vonbogen@bellnet.ca

***Toronto*: Paul Mergler - *1**
1199 The Queensway, Toronto, ON M8Z 1R7
Tel: 416-232-9589; *Fax:* 416-232-9522
pabkon@interlog.com

***Toronto*: Clarke A. Merritt - *2**
#3300, Box 33, 20 Queen St. West, Toronto, ON M5H 3R3
Tel: 416-971-3306; *Fax:* 416-971-4849
cmerrittl@aol.com
twitter.com/clarkemerritt

***Toronto*: Jack A. Mikolajko - *1**
#506, P.O. Box 31, 2333 Dundas St. West, Toronto, ON M9R 3A6
Tel: 416-538-8493; *Fax:* 416-538-2274
jmikolajko@bellnet.ca

***Toronto*: Millar Kreklewetz LLP - *2**
Former Name: Millar Wyslobicky Kreklewetz LLP
24 Duncan St., 3rd Fl., Toronto, ON M5V 2B8
Tel: 416-864-6200; *Fax:* 416-864-6201
www.taxandtradelaw.com

***Toronto*: Miller & Miller - *2**
1577 Bloor St. West, Toronto, ON M6P 1A6
Tel: 416-536-1159; *Fax:* 416-536-3618
info@millerandmiller.ca
www.millerandmiller.ca

***Toronto*: Glen M.A. Miller - *1**
#211, 3850 Finch Ave. East, Toronto, ON M1T 3T6
Tel: 416-299-6785
info@glenmillerlaw.ca
www.glenmillerlaw.ca

***Toronto*: Mills & Mills LLP - *27**
#700, 2 St. Clair Ave. West, Toronto, ON M4V 1L5
Tel: 416-863-0125; *Fax:* 416-863-3997
mills@millsandmills.ca
www.millsandmills.ca

***Toronto*: Douglas J. Millstone - *1**
#309, 2100 Ellesmere Rd., Toronto, ON M1H 3B7
Tel: 416-289-7996; *Fax:* 416-289-7998
Toll-Free: 888-437-7996
dmilldtone@bellnet.ca
www.dmillstonelaw.com

***Toronto*: Minden Gross LLP - *53**
Also Known As: Minden Gross Grafstein & Greenstein LLP
#2200, 145 King St. West, Toronto, ON M5H 4G2
Tel: 416-362-3711; *Fax:* 416-864-9223
info@mindengross.com
www.mindengross.com
twitter.com/mindengross, www.linkedin.com/company/minden-gross-llp

***Toronto*: Iqbal I. Dewji - *1**
#201, 161 Frederick St., Toronto, ON M5A 4P3
Tel: 416-848-0704
dewlaw@gmail.com

***Toronto*: Paul Minz - *1**
#1, 3520 Pharmacy Ave., Toronto, ON M1W 2T8
Tel: 416-499-9350; *Fax:* 416-499-1463

***Toronto*: Mircheff & Mircheff - *1**
#2B, 3030 Midland Ave., Toronto, ON M1S 5C9
Tel: 416-321-2885; *Fax:* 416-321-3345
nick@mircheff-law.com
mircheff-law.com

***Toronto*: Misir & Company - *6**
880 St. Clair Ave. West, Toronto, ON M6C 1C5
Tel: 416-653-8600; *Fax:* 416-653-9639
www.misirandcompany.com

***Toronto*: Mitchell, Bardyn & Zalucky LLP - *14**
Also Known As: MBZ Law
#200, 3029 Bloor St. West, Toronto, ON M8X 1C5
Tel: 416-234-9111; *Fax:* 416-234-9114
info@mbzlaw.com
www.mbzlaw.com

***Toronto*: Heather Mitchell - *1**
#300, 165 Avenue Rd., Toronto, ON M5R 3S4
Tel: 416-927-6565; *Fax:* 416-975-3999
hhmitchell@heathermitchelllaw.com

***Toronto*: Said Mohammedally - *1**
#2, 45 Overlea Blvd., Toronto, ON M4H 1C3
Tel: 416-425-7695; *Fax:* 416-425-7596
saidmoha@bellnet.ca

***Toronto*: Bernard J. Monaghan - *1**
#4084, 3080 Yonge St., Toronto, ON M4N 3N1
Tel: 416-486-9919; *Fax:* 416-486-1885

***Toronto*: Barbara Morgan - *1**
#216, 4195 Dundas St. West, Toronto, ON M8X 1Y4
Tel: 416-234-8248; *Fax:* 416-234-8252
barbara.morgan@sympatico.ca
www.barbaramorganlaw.ca

***Toronto*: Morris & Morris LLP - *3**
#920, 390 Bay St., Toronto, ON M5H 2Y2
Tel: 416-366-2277; *Fax:* 416-366-5988
bmorris@mmlaw.ca
www.mmlaw.ca

***Toronto*: Dennis S. Morris - *1**
129 John St., Toronto, ON M5V 2E2
Tel: 416-977-4799; *Fax:* 416-977-4472

***Toronto*: Leslie J. Morris - *1**
101 Scollard St., Toronto, ON M5R 1G4
Tel: 416-924-0711; *Fax:* 416-960-9650

***Toronto*: Morrison Brown Sosnovitch - *11**
#910, P.O. Box 28, 1 Toronto St., Toronto, ON M5C 2V6
Tel: 416-368-0600; *Fax:* 416-368-6068
bizlaw@businesslawyers.com
www.businesslawyers.com

***Toronto*: Sam Moskowitz - *1**
60 Bloor West, Toronto, ON M5S 1X1
Tel: 416-961-8864; *Fax:* 416-961-7654

***Toronto*: Mostyn & Mostyn - *2**
845 St. Clair Ave. West, 4th Fl., Toronto, ON M6C 1C3
Tel: 416-653-3819; *Fax:* 416-653-3891
info@mostyn.ca
www.mostyn.ca

** indicates number of lawyers*

***Toronto*: Anthony Moustacalis - *1**
#1000, 121 Richmond St. West, Toronto, ON M5H 2K1
Tel: 416-363-2656; *Fax:* 416-363-4920

***Toronto*: Moyal & Moyal - *2**
North American Centre, 8 Finch Ave. West, Toronto, ON M2N 6L1
Tel: 416-733-3193; *Fax:* 416-250-1818
Toll-Free: 888-847-2078
canada@moyal.com
www.moyal.com

***Toronto*: Matthew Moyal - *1**
Also Known As: Moyal & Moyal
8 Finch Ave. West, Toronto, ON M2N 6L1
Tel: 416-733-0330; *Fax:* 416-250-1818
matthew@moyalandassociates.com

***Toronto*: J. Naumovich**
#101, 813 Broadview Ave., Toronto, ON M4K 2P8
Tel: 416-466-2119; *Fax:* 416-466-2581

***Toronto*: William E. Naylor - *1**
#203, 637 College St., Toronto, ON M6G 1B5
Tel: 416-532-9940; *Fax:* 416-532-9983
naylor-william@on.aibn.com

***Toronto*: Neal and Smith - *2**
#300, 3443 Finch Ave. East, Toronto, ON M1W 2S1
Tel: 416-494-4545; *Fax:* 416-494-4660
nealsmith@bellnet.ca
www.nealandsmith.com

***Toronto*: Neinstein & Associates LLP - *13**
#700, 1200 Bay St., Toronto, ON M5R 2A5
Tel: 416-920-4242; *Fax:* 416-923-8358
Toll-Free: 866-920-4242
info@neinstein.com
www.neinstein.com
www.facebook.com/pages/Toronto-ON/Personal-Injury-Lawyers-Toronto-Ontario-N, www.twitter.com/neinsteinlaw, www.linkedin.com/companies/449070/Neinstein%20&%20Associates

***Toronto*: C. Ann Nelson - *1**
#400, 2490 Bloor St. West, Toronto, ON M6S 1R4
Tel: 416-760-7076; *Fax:* 416-760-7338

***Toronto*: Theodore Nemetz - *1**
#801, 1 St. Clair Ave. E, Toronto, ON M4T 2V7
Tel: 416-961-6560; *Fax:* 416-964-2494
nemetz@bellnet.ca

***Toronto*: Newman Weinstock - *1**
#201, 3625 Dufferin St., Toronto, ON M3K 1Z2
Tel: 416-630-3220; *Fax:* 416-630-7632
rawein@on.aibn.com

***Toronto*: Alexandra Ngan - *1**
#306, 1033 Bay St., Toronto, ON M5S 3A5
Tel: 416-925-3333; *Fax:* 416-925-3339

***Toronto*: Metz L. Ngan - *1**
#209, 155 Gordon Baker Rd., Toronto, ON M2H 3N7
Tel: 416-502-9232; *Fax:* 416-502-3061
metznga@ipoline.com

***Toronto*: Peter J. Ngan - *1**
#207, 738 Sheppard Ave. East, Toronto, ON M2K 1C4
Tel: 416-298-1828; *Fax:* 416-298-2186
Toll-Free: 855-575-5557
pjngan@yahoo.ca
www.peterngan.com

***Toronto*: Trang T. Nguyen - *1**
#12, 3585 Keele St., Toronto, ON M3J 3H5
Tel: 416-638-9422; *Fax:* 416-398-8358

***Toronto*: Cynthia A. Nicholas - *1**
17 Annis Rd., Toronto, ON M1M 2Y8
Tel: 416-264-2875; *Fax:* 416-264-2330

***Toronto*: Nigel P. Watson Law Firm - *2**
#1812, 2 Carlton St., Toronto, ON M5B 1J3
Tel: 416-977-7700; *Fax:* 416-977-8570
nwatson@sympatico.ca
www.nigelpwatson.com

***Toronto*: Howard Nightingale - *1**
#302, 4580 Dufferin St., Toronto, ON M3H 5Y2
Tel: 416-663-4423; *Fax:* 416-663-4424
Toll-Free: 877-224-8225
info@howardnightingale.com
www.howardnightingale.com
www.facebook.com/pages/Howard-Nightingale-Professional-Corporation/25235607, twitter.com/HNPCLawyerBlog, ca.linkedin.com/pub/howard-nightingale/3/882/87b

***Toronto*: Niman Zemans Gelgoot Barristers LLP - *16**
#300, 10 Price St., Toronto, ON M4W 1Z4
Tel: 416-921-1700; *Fax:* 416-921-8936
niman@nzgfamlaw.com
www.nzgfamlaw.com

***Toronto*: Noik & Associates - *4**
#400, 3410 Sheppard Ave. E, Toronto, ON M1T 3K4
Tel: 416-754-1020; *Fax:* 416-754-1784

***Toronto*: O'Neill, Browning, Pineau - *2**
#302, 372 Bay St., Toronto, ON M5H 2W9
Tel: 416-868-0544; *Fax:* 416-868-0724
browninglaw@rigers

***Toronto*: O'Sullivan Estate Lawyers Professional Corporation - *3**
Also Known As: O'Sullivan Estate Lawyers
#1410, P.O. Box 68, 222 Bay St., Toronto, ON M5K 1E7
Tel: 416-363-3336; *Fax:* 416-363-9570
Toll-Free: 888-365-6235
www.osullivanlaw.com

***Toronto*: Oatley, Vigmond, Personal Injury Lawyers LLP - Downtown Toronto - *13**
#1052, 66 Wellington St. West, Toronto, ON M5K 1P2
Tel: 416-651-2421; *Fax:* 416-225-8935
Toll-Free: 888-662-2481
info@oatleyvigmond.com
www.oatleyvigmond.com
www.facebook.com/pages/Oatley-Vigmond-LLP/204132516298097, twitter.com/OatleyVigmond, www.linkedin.com/company/oatley-vigmond-personal-injury-lawyers

***Toronto*: Office of the Children's Lawyer - *23**
c/o MGS Mail Delivery Services, 2B-88 Macdonald Block, 77 Wellesley St. West, Toronto, ON M7A 1N3
Tel: 416-314-8000; *Fax:* 416-314-8050
www.attorneygeneral.jus.gov.on.ca/english/family/ocl/

***Toronto*: Oiye, Henderson - *2**
#1805 & 1812, 2 Carlton St., Toronto, ON M5B 1J3
Tel: 416-977-7700; *Fax:* 416-977-8570

***Toronto*: Olch, Torgov, Cohen LLP - *2**
#901, 111 Richmond St. West, Toronto, ON M5H 2G4
Tel: 416-363-8366; *Fax:* 416-363-0783
otc@otclaw.ca

***Toronto*: Olthuis Kleer Townshend LLP - *1**
Former Name: Olthuis Kleer Townshend
229 College St., 3rd Fl., Toronto, ON M5T 1R4
Tel: 416-981-9330; *Fax:* 416-981-9350
www.oktlaw.com

***Toronto*: Orbach, Katzman & Herschorn - *2**
#1001, 317 Adelaide St. West, Toronto, ON M5V 1P9
Tel: 416-967-6777; *Fax:* 416-967-1506
sender@okhlaw.ca

***Toronto*: Mark M. Orkin, Q.C. - *1**
1 Dundas St. West, Toronto, ON M5G 1Z3
Tel: 416-363-4108; *Fax:* 416-365-9276
mmorkin@look.ca

***Toronto*: Ormston, Bellissimo, Younan - *3**
#900, 1000 Finch Ave. West, Toronto, ON M3J 2V5
Tel: 416-787-6505; *Fax:* 416-787-0455

***Toronto*: Samuel Osak - *1**
6 Bitteroot Rd., Toronto, ON M3H 4J4
Tel: 416-630-1041; *Fax:* 416-630-1043
sosak@sympatico.ca

***Toronto*: Oster Wolfman LLP - *4**
Former Name: Kerr, Oster & Wolfman
#200, 133 Berkeley St., Toronto, ON M5A 2X1
Tel: 416-365-7163; *Fax:* 416-365-1270
kow@kow.on.ca

***Toronto*: Otis & Korman - *4**
41 Madison Ave., Toronto, ON M5R 2S2
Tel: 416-979-0670; *Fax:* 416-979-3778
info@otisandkorman.com
www.liveincanada.com
www.twitter.com/OtisandKorman

***Toronto*: Samy Ouanounou - *1**
#352, 1111 Finch Ave. West, Toronto, ON M3J 2E5
Tel: 416-222-3434; *Fax:* 416-222-3629
solaw@on.aibn.com

***Toronto*: Owens, Wright LLP - *17**
#300, 20 Holly St., Toronto, ON M4S 3B1
Tel: 416-486-9800; *Fax:* 416-486-3309
owenswright@owenswright.com
www.owenswright.com

***Toronto*: Pace Law Firm - *17**
295 The West Mall, 6th Fl., Toronto, ON M9C 4Z4
Tel: 416-236-3060; *Fax:* 416-236-1809
Toll-Free: 877-236-3060
lawyers@pacelawfirm.com
www.pacelawfirm.com
www.facebook.com/pages/Canada-Immigration/72362699107?ref=ts, twitter.com/paceimmigration

***Toronto*: Demetrius Pantazis - *1**
#204, 1315 Lawrence Ave. East, Toronto, ON M3A 3R3
Tel: 416-469-5355; *Fax:* 416-469-8136
dpantazis@on.aibn.com

***Toronto*: Pape Barristers Professional Corporation - *7**
#1910, P.O. Box 69, 1 Queen St. East, Toronto, ON M5C 2W5
Tel: 416-364-8765; *Fax:* 416-364-8855
info@papebarristers.com
www.papebarristers.com

***Toronto*: Allan Papernick, Q.C. - *1**
#203, 1200 Eglinton Ave. East, Toronto, ON M3C 1H9
Tel: 416-445-1273; *Fax:* 416-445-1678
allan@allanpapernick.com
www.allanpapernick.com

***Toronto*: Ado Park Q.C. - *1**
#604, 357 Bay St., Toronto, ON M5H 2T7
Tel: 416-363-4451; *Fax:* 416-363-9256

***Toronto*: Parkdale Community Legal Services - *6**
1266 Queen St. West, Toronto, ON M6K 1L3
Tel: 416-531-2411; *Fax:* 416-531-0885
www.parkdalelegal.org
www.facebook.com/pages/Parkdale-Community-Legal-Services/185810351443057, twitter.com/parkdalelegal

***Toronto*: Mary Lou Parker - *1**
#800, 2 St. Clair Ave. East, Toronto, ON M4T 2T5
Tel: 416-920-4708; *Fax:* 416-920-3819
mlparker@marylouparker.ca
www.marylouparker.ca/en/

***Toronto*: Paterson, MacDougall LLP - *9**
#900, P.O. Box 100, 1 Queen St. East, Toronto, ON M5C 2W5
Tel: 416-366-9607; *Fax:* 416-366-3743
info@pmlaw.com
www.pmlaw.com
twitter.com/pmlawcanada

***Toronto*: Philip Patterson - *1**
#305, 1033 Bay St., Toronto, ON M5S 3A5
Tel: 416-968-9188; *Fax:* 416-925-2860
ppaterson@on.aibn.com

***Toronto*: Paul & Paul - *2**
Former Name: Paul & Kanellos
39 Hayden St., Toronto, ON M4Y 2P2
Tel: 416-968-1777; *Fax:* 416-968-1211
npaul@bellnet.ca

***Toronto*: Murray E. Payne - *1**
3329 Bloor St. West, Toronto, ON M8X 1E7
Tel: 416-232-1242; *Fax:* 416-231-1280

***Toronto*: Peace, Burns, Halkiw & Manning LLP - *2**
#100, 25 Morrow Ave., Toronto, ON M6R 2H9
Tel: 416-533-1025; *Fax:* 416-516-5305

***Toronto*: Peirce, McNeely Associates - *3**
25 Lesmill Rd., Toronto, ON M3B 2T3
Tel: 416-449-2060; *Fax:* 416-449-2068

***Toronto*: Michael Pelensky - *1**
#300, 2 Toronto St., Toronto, ON M5C 2B6
Tel: 416-863-1300; *Fax:* 416-863-4942

** indicates number of lawyers*

***Toronto*: Penman Vona Professional Corporation, Barristers & Solicitors - *2**
Former Name: Penmam & Penman
#307A, 4195 Dundas St. West, Toronto, ON M8X 1Y4
Tel: 416-231-5696; *Fax:* 416-231-5697
gvona@penman-vona.ca
www.penman-vona.ca/en/
www.facebook.com/people/George-Vona/547477354,
www.linkedin.com/pub/george-vona/5/243/7b4

***Toronto*: Glenn B. Peppiatt - *1**
939 Mt. Pleasant Rd., Toronto, ON M4P 2L7
Tel: 416-323-3232; *Fax:* 416-323-9350
glenn@glennbpeppiattlaw.com
www.glennbpeppiattlaw.com

***Toronto*: Peterson Law - *5**
#806, 390 Bay St., Toronto, ON M5H 2Y2
Tel: 647-259-1790; *Fax:* 647-259-1785
dhp@petelaw.com
petelaw.com

***Toronto*: Petropoulos & Rapos - *1**
#305, 1920 Ellesmere Rd., Toronto, ON M1H 2V6
Tel: 416-431-5870; *Fax:* 416-289-4144

***Toronto*: V. Walter Petryshyn - *1**
1247 Dundas St. West, Toronto, ON M6J 1X6
Tel: 416-534-8431; *Fax:* 416-531-2455

***Toronto*: Philip Horgan Law Office - *3**
#301, 120 Carlton St., Toronto, ON M5A 4K2
Tel: 416-777-9994; *Fax:* 416-777-9921

***Toronto*: Phillips Gill LLP - *7**
Former Name: Doane Phillips Yonge LLP
#200, 33 Jarvis St., Toronto, ON M5E 1N3
Tel: 416-703-1900; *Fax:* 416-703-1955
www.phillipsgill.com

***Toronto*: Douglas N. Phillips - *1**
13 Reno Dr., Toronto, ON M1K 2V5
Tel: 416-757-3445; *Fax:* 416-759-8036
dnplaw@rogers.com

***Toronto*: Piasetzki Nenniger Kvas LLP - *9**
#2308, 120 Adelaide St. West, Toronto, ON M5H 1T1
Tel: 416-955-0050; *Fax:* 416-955-0053
office@pnklaw.ca
www.pnklaw.ca

***Toronto*: Picov & Kleinberg Barristers & Solicitors - *2**
#100, 110 Eglinton Ave. West, Toronto, ON M4R 1A3
Tel: 416-488-2100; *Fax:* 416-488-2794
kpicov@picovkleinberg.com
www.picovkleinberg.net

***Toronto*: Piller & Ross - *2**
#2200, 181 University Ave., Toronto, ON M5H 3M7
Tel: 416-601-1622; *Fax:* 416-363-7239

***Toronto*: Pinto Wray James LLP - *6**
#2000, 393 University Ave., Toronto, ON M5G 1E6
Tel: 416-703-2067; *Fax:* 416-593-4923
info@pintowrayjames.com
www.pintowrayjames.com

***Toronto*: Jillian M. Pivnick - *1**
#410, 350 Lonsdale Rd., Toronto, ON M5P 1R6
Tel: 416-484-6306

***Toronto*: D.V. Pledge, Barrister & Solicitor - *1**
#203, 1013 Wilson Ave., Toronto, ON M3K 1G1
Tel: 416-630-8702; *Fax:* 416-630-8714
donnav.pledge@bellnet.ca
www.dvpledge.ca

***Toronto*: Harry Poch - *1**
20 Beaverhall Dr., Toronto, ON M2L 2C7
Tel: 416-444-7971; *Fax:* 416-444-8971
harrypoch@rogers.com

***Toronto*: Podrebarac Barristers Professional Corporation - *3**
#701, 151 Bloor St. West, Toronto, ON M5S 1S4
Tel: 416-348-7500; *Fax:* 416-348-7505
podrebaracbarristers.com

***Toronto*: Stephen P. Ponesse - *1**
#3000, 390 Bay St., Toronto, ON M5H 2Y2
Tel: 416-361-3582; *Fax:* 416-368-7217
stephenponesse@on.aibn.com

***Toronto*: Porjes Employment Law - *2**
Former Name: M. Dawn McConnell; Porjes Walsh
#200, 30A Hazelton Ave., Toronto, ON M5R 2E2
Tel: 416-601-0500
mary@porjeslaw.com
www.porjeslaw.com

***Toronto*: Don Poscente - *1**
683 Mt. Pleasant Rd., Toronto, ON M4S 2N2
Tel: 416-410-3333; *Fax:* 416-410-3333

***Toronto*: Gary M. Posesorski - *1**
5 Wembley Rd., Toronto, ON M6C 2E8
Tel: 416-780-9655; *Fax:* 416-783-4574

***Toronto*: Wietse G. Posthumus - *1**
#2700, West Tower, 55 Avenue Rd., Toronto, ON M5R 3L2
Tel: 416-929-3030; *Fax:* 416-961-9898

***Toronto*: Potts, Weisberg & Musil - *3**
#206, 90 Eglinton Ave. East, Toronto, ON M4P 2Y3
Tel: 416-485-7366; *Fax:* 416-485-7368
pwmlaw@interlog.com

***Toronto*: Powell Weir, Barristers & Solicitors - *2**
#506, 50 Gervais Dr., Toronto, ON M3C 1Z3
Tel: 416-441-6840; *Fax:* 416-441-0330
mike@powellweir.com
www.powellweir.com

***Toronto*: Harry Preisman - *2**
#307, 885 Progress Ave., Toronto, ON M1H 3G3
Tel: 416-439-9559; *Fax:* 416-439-9553
pklaw@on.aibn.com
henrypreisman.synthasite.com

***Toronto*: Preobrazenski & Associates - *2**
#414, Sherman Centre, 100 Richmond St. West, Toronto, ON M5H 3K6
Tel: 416-964-1717; *Fax:* 416-964-0823
marie@interware.com

***Toronto*: Price Altman Barristers - *3**
Former Name: Sheldon Altman
#1708, 5000 Yonge St., Toronto, ON M2N 7E9
Tel: 416-365-0766; *Fax:* 416-365-0866
contact@over80law.com
over80law.com

***Toronto*: Stephen Price & Associates - *3**
Former Name: Price, Stephen & Associates
#1708, 5000 Yonge St., Toronto, ON M2N 7E9
Tel: 416-365-0766; *Fax:* 416-365-0866
contact@over80law.com
over80law.com

***Toronto*: David R. Proctor, Q.C. - *1**
#8A, 1921 Eglinton Ave. East, Toronto, ON M1L 2L6
Tel: 416-751-3958; *Fax:* 416-751-3770

***Toronto*: Richard G. Pyne - *1**
3329 Bloor St. West, Toronto, ON M8X 1E7
Tel: 416-231-3339; *Fax:* 416-231-1280

***Toronto*: Quirk, McGillicuddy & Sutton - *1**
1604 Dufferin St., Toronto, ON M6H 3L7
Tel: 416-652-3543; *Fax:* 416-652-2730
fran@qmsutton.ca

***Toronto*: R.L. & J.H. Webster - *2**
2600 Danforth Ave., Toronto, ON M4C 1L3
Tel: 416-699-9644; *Fax:* 416-699-8905
admin@websterlaw.ca
www1.websterlaw.ca/en/

***Toronto*: Rachlin & Wolfson LLP - *11**
#1500, 390 Bay St., Toronto, ON M5H 2Y2
Tel: 416-367-0202; *Fax:* 416-367-1820
enquiry@rachlinlaw.com
www.rachlinlaw.com

***Toronto*: Danuta H. Radomski - *1**
351 Castlefield Ave., Toronto, ON M5N 1L4
Tel: 416-322-6134; *Fax:* 416-489-1462
dradomski@on.aibn.com

***Toronto*: R. Sam Ramlall - *1**
#700, 5799 Yonge St., Toronto, ON M2M 3V3
Tel: 416-512-6465; *Fax:* 416-512-6042
rsamramlall@bellnet.ca

***Toronto*: Rawana & Rawana Barristers & Solicitors - *2**
11721 Sheppard Ave. East, 2nd Fl., Toronto, ON M1B 1G3
Tel: 416-281-8505; *Fax:* 416-286-4353

***Toronto*: Rayson & Associates - *4**
#302, 3845 Bathurst St., Toronto, ON M3H 3N2
Tel: 416-630-5600; *Fax:* 416-630-5906

***Toronto*: John L. Razulis - *1**
362 Glengarry Ave., Toronto, ON M5M 1E6
Tel: 416-787-1918; *Fax:* 416-787-7161
counsel@lawfulwork.ca
www.lawfulwork.ca

***Toronto*: Refugee Law Office - *4**
#202, 20 Dundas St. West, Toronto, ON M5G 2H1
Tel: 416-977-8111; *Fax:* 416-977-5567
rlo@lao.on.ca
www.legalaid.on.ca

***Toronto*: Regan Desjardins LLP - *11**
Former Name: Regan Kram Desjardins LLP
#1502, P.O. Box 2069, 20 Eglinton Ave. West, Toronto, ON M4R 1K8
Tel: 416-601-1000; *Fax:* 416-601-9255
reception@rkdlaw.com
www.regandesjardins.com

***Toronto*: Terrence S. Reiber - *1**
#211, 1110 Sheppard Ave. East, Toronto, ON M2K 2W2
Tel: 416-927-9841; *Fax:* 416-975-1531
terry@reiber.ca
www.reiber.ca

***Toronto*: Reingold & Reingold - *1**
#3028, P.O. Box 17, 3080 Yonge St., Toronto, ON M4N 3N1
Tel: 416-483-3364; *Fax:* 416-440-1942
jrqc58@bellnet.ca

***Toronto*: Arn C.J. Reisler - *1**
161 Bridgeland Ave., Toronto, ON M6A 1Z1
Tel: 416-781-4002; *Fax:* 416-781-7797
areisler@wastecogroup.com

***Toronto*: Stanley Reisman - *1**
#308, 360 Bloor St. West, Toronto, ON M5S 1X1
Tel: 416-961-8864; *Fax:* 416-961-7654

***Toronto*: Reiter-Nemetz - *2**
#100, 298 Sheppard Ave. West, Toronto, ON M2N 1N5
Tel: 416-665-1458; *Fax:* 416-665-0895
www.reiternemetz.com

***Toronto*: Rekai LLP - *5**
Former Name: Rekai Somerleigh Berezowski
#1605, 33 Bloor St. East, 16th Fl., Toronto, ON M4W 3H1
Tel: 416-960-8876; *Fax:* 416-924-2371
eleanor@mobilitylaw.com
www.mobilitylaw.com

***Toronto*: David J.M. Rendeiro - *2**
#200, 1201 Dundas St. West, Toronto, ON M6J 1X3
Tel: 416-588-8000; *Fax:* 416-588-8002

***Toronto*: Reznick, Parsons - *2**
#1917, 25 Adelaide St. E, Toronto, ON M5C 3A1
Tel: 416-863-6026; *Fax:* 416-863-9334

***Toronto*: Richman & Richman - *1**
#404, 255 Duncan Mill Rd., Toronto, ON M3B 3H9
Tel: 416-510-8866

***Toronto*: Nina S. Richmond - *1**
148 Brookdale Ave., Toronto, ON M5M 1P5
Tel: 416-489-4191; *Fax:* 416-489-5822
nina.richmond@rogers.com

***Toronto*: Ricketts, Harris LLP - *20**
#800, DBRS Tower, 181 University Ave., Toronto, ON M5H 2X7
Tel: 416-364-6211; *Fax:* 416-364-1697
www.rickettsharris.com

***Toronto*: Gerald Rifkin - *1**
#500, 1000 Finch Ave. West, Toronto, ON M3J 2V5
Tel: 416-667-9796; *Fax:* 416-667-8048

***Toronto*: Riley Aikins - *3**
#1509, 180 Dundas St. West, Toronto, ON M5G 1Z8
Tel: 416-364-7611; *Fax:* 416-596-7562
ariley@rileyaikins.ca
www.rileyaikins.ca

***Toronto*: Riverdale Law Group - *3**
167 Danforth Ave., Toronto, ON M4K 1N2
Tel: 416-466-6264; *Fax:* 416-466-8465

** indicates number of lawyers*

***Toronto*: Riverdale Mediation - *3**
#2000, 393 University Ave., Toronto, ON M5G 1E6
Tel: 416-593-0210; *Fax:* 416-593-1352
hello@riverdalemediation.com
www.riverdalemediation.com
www.facebook.com/RiverdaleMediation?sk=wall,
www.twitter.com/riverdaleADR,
www.linkedin.com/company/875109

***Toronto*: William H. Roberts - *1**
#201, 34 Southport St., Toronto, ON M6S 3N3
Tel: 416-769-3162; *Fax:* 416-762-8972

***Toronto*: Robertson & Keith - *1**
2481 Kingston Rd., Toronto, ON M1N 1V4
Tel: 416-261-1220; *Fax:* 416-261-1716

***Toronto*: Robins, Appleby & Taub LLP - *23**
#2600, 120 Adelaide St. West, Toronto, ON M5H 1T1
Tel: 416-868-1080; *Fax:* 416-868-0306
info@robapp.com
www.robinsapplebyandtaub.com
twitter.com/RobAppTaubLLP

***Toronto*: Rogers & Rowland - *1**
#400, 1235 Bay St., Toronto, ON M5R 3K4
Tel: 416-364-2333; *Fax:* 416-864-0271
mail@rogersrowland.com

***Toronto*: Rogers Law Office - *1**
Also Known As: RLO
#3B, 4 Deer Park Cres., Toronto, ON M4V 2C3
Tel: 416-363-6626; *Fax:* 416-363-6628
file@rlo.ca
www.rlo.ca

***Toronto*: Rogers Partners LLP - *23**
#1900, P.O. Box 255, 100 Wellington St. West, Toronto, ON M5K 1J5
Tel: 416-594-4500; *Fax:* 416-594-9100
info@rogerspartners.com
www.rogersmoore.com

***Toronto*: Nelson Roland - *1**
333 Adelaide St. West, 3rd Fl., Toronto, ON M5V 1R5
Tel: 416-351-1591; *Fax:* 416-340-9250
nroland@allstream.net

***Toronto*: Norman W. Ronka - *1**
946 College St., Toronto, ON M6H 1A5
Tel: 416-969-0917; *Fax:* 416-905-8221

***Toronto*: Law Office of Christopher J. Roper - *1**
#3300, The Cadillac Fairview Tower, 20 Queen St. W, Toronto, ON M5H 3R3
Tel: 416-368-6788; *Fax:* 416-368-5705
cjroper@interhop.net
www.cjroperlaw.com

***Toronto*: Rose, Persiko, Rakowsky, Melvin LLP - *2**
#600, 390 Bay St., Toronto, ON M5H 2Y2
Tel: 416-868-1900; *Fax:* 416-868-1708

***Toronto*: Rosen Nastor LLP - *3**
Former Name: Rosen & Company
#504, 330 University Ave., Toronto, ON M5G 1R7
Tel: 416-205-9700; *Fax:* 416-205-9970
reception@rosenlaw.ca
www.rosennaster.com

***Toronto*: Allan C. Rosen - *1**
#904, 27 Queen St. East, Toronto, ON M5C 2M6
Tel: 416-363-1601; *Fax:* 416-363-5620

***Toronto*: Elliot F. Rosenberg - *1**
#201, 4949 Bathurst St., Toronto, ON M2R 2T4
Tel: 416-512-7373; *Fax:* 416-512-7374
tlpress@patncom.com

***Toronto*: Irving Rosenberg - *1**
#507, 1000 Finch Ave. West, Toronto, ON M3J 2V5
Tel: 416-398-0102; *Fax:* 416-398-0103
irose@on.aibn.com

***Toronto*: Rosenblatt Immigration Law - *2**
#201, 645 King St. West, Toronto, ON M5V 1M5
Tel: 416-644-4000; *Fax:* 416-861-1215
contact@immigrate.net
www.immigrate.net

***Toronto*: Stanley Rosenfarb - *1**
#800, 2001 Sheppard Ave. East, Toronto, ON M2J 4Z8
Tel: 416-494-4899; *Fax:* 416-494-3024
stan@srlaw.com

***Toronto*: Ross & Bank - *2**
#300, 123 John St., Toronto, ON M5V 2E2
Tel: 416-572-4910; *Fax:* 416-551-8808
info@rossandbank.com
www.rossandbank.com

***Toronto*: Larry H. Ross - *1**
#200, 609 Bloor St. West, Toronto, ON M6G 1K5
Tel: 416-535-6211; *Fax:* 416-535-7698

***Toronto*: Aubrey M. Rossman - *1**
124 Laird Dr. East, Toronto, ON M4G 3V3
Tel: 416-444-2201; *Fax:* 416-444-0571

***Toronto*: Cecil L. Rotenberg - *3**
#308, 245 Fairveiw Dr., Toronto, ON M2J 4T1
Tel: 416-449-8866; *Fax:* 416-510-9090
cclrqc@yahoo.com
www.cecilrotenberg.org

***Toronto*: Rotenberg Shidlowski Jesin - *1**
144 King St. East, 3rd Fl., Toronto, ON M5C 1G8
Tel: 416-591-9100; *Fax:* 416-591-9008
robert@rsjlaw.ca
www.robertrotenberg.com
twitter.com/RobertRotenberg

***Toronto*: Frank L. Roth - *1**
#500, 70 Bond St., Toronto, ON M5B 1X3
Tel: 416-963-8776; *Fax:* 416-863-4896
flr@bondlaw.net

***Toronto*: Neal H. Roth - *1**
#401, 60 St. Clair Ave. East, Toronto, ON M4T 1N5
Tel: 416-351-7706; *Fax:* 416-351-7684
www.nealhroth.com

***Toronto*: Rothman & Rothman - *1**
#638, 121 Richmond St. W, Toronto, ON M5H 2K1
Tel: 416-367-9901; *Fax:* 416-367-9979
rothman@sympatico.ca

***Toronto*: Nancy-Gay Rotstein - *1**
#202, 40 Holly St., Toronto, ON M4S 3C3
Tel: 416-488-0800; *Fax:* 416-488-8350
nrotstein@municipal.ca

***Toronto*: Roy O'Connor LLP - *7**
#2300, 200 Front St. West, Toronto, ON M5V 3K2
Tel: 416-362-1989; *Fax:* 416-362-6204
info@royoconnor.ca
royoconnor.ca

***Toronto*: Rubenstein, Siegel - *2**
#402, 1200 Sheppard Ave. E, Toronto, ON M2K 2S5
Tel: 416-499-5252; *Fax:* 416-499-2290

***Toronto*: Rubin Thomlinson LLP - *7**
#1104, 20 Adelaide St. East, Toronto, ON M5C 2T6
Tel: 416-847-1814; *Fax:* 416-847-1815
info@rubinthomlinson.com
www.rubinthomlinson.com
twitter.com/RubinThomlinson

***Toronto*: Barry Rubinoff - *1**
488 Huron St., Toronto, ON M5R 2R3
Tel: 416-966-4884; *Fax:* 416-966-6768

***Toronto*: Ruby Shiller Chan Hasan Barristers - *5**
Former Name: Ruby & Edwardh
11 Prince Arthur Ave., Toronto, ON M5R 1B2
Tel: 416-964-9664; *Fax:* 416-964-8305
www.rubyshiller.com

***Toronto*: Ruderman Shaw - *2**
#1820, P.O. Box 2037, 20 Eglinton Ave. West, Toronto, ON M4R 1K8
Tel: 416-484-8558; *Fax:* 416-484-6918
info@rudermanshaw.com

***Toronto*: Victor E. Rudinskas - *1**
27 John St., 2nd Fl., Toronto, ON M9N 1J4
Tel: 416-240-0594; *Fax:* 416-248-5922
Toll-Free: 877-888-8390
vrudinskas@trebnet.com

***Toronto*: George A. Rudnik - *1**
#1901, 260 Queens Quay West, Toronto, ON M5J 2N3
Tel: 416-927-7788; *Fax:* 416-925-9963

***Toronto*: Rueter Scargall Bennett LLP - *16**
Also Known As: RSB
#2200, P.O. Box 4, 250 Yonge St., Toronto, ON M5B 2L7
Tel: 416-869-9090; *Fax:* 416-869-3411
rslawyers.com

***Toronto*: Martin K.I. Rumack - *1**
#202, 2 St. Clair Ave. East, Toronto, ON M4T 2T5
Tel: 416-961-3441; *Fax:* 416-961-1045
martin@martinrumack.com
www.martinrumack.com
twitter.com/MKIRumack, www.linkedin.com/company/3548583

***Toronto*: Brian A. Rumanek - *1**
#201, 200 Evans Ave., Toronto, ON M8Z 1J7
Tel: 416-252-9115; *Fax:* 416-253-0494
thelawman@rogers.com

***Toronto*: Richard E. Rusek - *1**
1623 Bloor St. West, Toronto, ON M6P 1A6
Tel: 416-533-8563

***Toronto*: Rusonik, O'Connor, Robbins, Ross, Gorham & Angelini, LLP - *28**
#100, 36 Lombard St., Toronto, ON M5C 2X3
Tel: 416-598-1811; *Fax:* 416-598-3384
www.criminaltriallawyers.ca

***Toronto*: Rebecca J. Rutherford - *1**
Ontario Court of Justice, 444 Yonge St., 2nd Fl., Toronto, ON M5B 2H4
Tel: 416-325-8972; *Fax:* 416-325-8944

***Toronto*: Ryder Wright Blair and Holmes LLP - *10**
333 Adelaide St. West, 3rd Fl., Toronto, ON M5V 1R5
Tel: 416-340-9070; *Fax:* 416-340-9250
www.rwbh.ca

***Toronto*: Lawrence D. Ryder - *1**
#502, 1235 Bay St., Toronto, ON MR5 3K4
Tel: 416-862-5557; *Fax:* 416-862-5551
www.ryderlitigationlawyer.com

***Toronto*: Rye & Partners - *3**
#1200, 65 Queen St. West, Toronto, ON M5H 2M5
Tel: 416-362-4901; *Fax:* 416-362-8291
partners@ryeandpartners.com
www.ryeandpartners.com

***Toronto*: Nadir Sachak - *1**
#920, 6 Adelaide St. East, Toronto, ON M5C 1H6
Tel: 416-363-7172; *Fax:* 416-363-9917
Toll-Free: 877-878-7206
baylawoffice@gmail.com

***Toronto*: Sack Goldblatt Mitchell LLP - *47**
Former Name: Engelmann Gottheil
#1100, 20 Dundas St. West, Toronto, ON M5G 2G8
Tel: 416-977-6070; *Fax:* 416-591-7333
Toll-Free: 800-387-5422
mailbox@eglaw.com
www.sgmlaw.com

***Toronto*: Howard Saginur - *1**
#1300, 5255 Yonge St., Toronto, ON M2N 6P4
Tel: 416-512-1912; *Fax:* 416-512-1989
howard@saginur.com
www.saginur.com

***Toronto*: Firoz G. Salehmohamed - *1**
#202, 747 Don Mills Rd., Toronto, ON M3C 1T2
Tel: 416-421-7000; *Fax:* 416-421-5388

***Toronto*: Maureen K. Saltman Arbitrations Ltd. - *1**
#502, 121 Richmond St. West, Toronto, ON M5H 2K1
Tel: 416-366-3091; *Fax:* 416-366-0879
mksaltman@bellnet.ca

***Toronto*: Samis & Company - *15**
#1600, 400 University Ave., Toronto, ON M5G 1S5
Tel: 416-365-0000; *Fax:* 416-365-9993
info@samislaw.com
www.samislaw.com

***Toronto*: Sanderson Entertainment Law - *4**
#303, 577 Kingston Rd., Toronto, ON M4E 1R3
Tel: 416-971-6616; *Fax:* 416-971-4144
info@sandersonlaw.ca
www.sandersonlaw.ca

***Toronto*: Sandler, Gordon - *2**
#260, 1027 Yonge St., Toronto, ON M4W 2K9
Tel: 416-971-5102; *Fax:* 416-971-5305
mzarnett@sandlergordon.com
www.sandlergordon.com

***Toronto*: Shil K. Sanwalka, Q.C. - *1**
#602, 18 Wynford Dr., Toronto, ON M3C 3S2
Tel: 416-449-7755; *Fax:* 416-449-6969
skslaw@sanwalka.org

** indicates number of lawyers*

Toronto: Umberto Sapone - *2
#201, 3200 Dufferin St., Toronto, ON M6A 2T3
Tel: 416-789-2689; Fax: 416-789-0454
www.saponeandcautillo.com

Toronto: Dianne Saxe, Ph.D. - *3
Also Known As: Saxe Law Office
720 Bathurst St., Toronto, ON M5S 2R4
Tel: 416-962-5009; Fax: 416-962-8817
admin@envirolaw.com
envirolaw.com
twitter.com/envirolaw1, www.linkedin.com/in/envirolaw

Toronto: Peter M. Scandiffio, Q.C. - *1
#308, 344 Bloor St. West, Toronto, ON M5S 3A7
Tel: 416-515-1660; Fax: 416-515-1526

Toronto: Scher Law Professional Corporation - Toronto - *2
175 Bloor St. East, Toronto, ON M4W 3R8
Tel: 416-515-9686 Toll-Free: 855-246-0243
info@lostjobs.ca
www.lostjobs.ca

Toronto: Schneider Ruggiero LLP - *8
#1000, 120 Adelaide St. West, Toronto, ON M5H 3V1
Tel: 416-363-2211; Fax: 416-363-0645
Toll-Free: 800-268-2111
info@srlawpractice.com
srlawpractice.com

Toronto: Schnurr Kirsh Schnurr Oelbaum Tator LLP - *7
Former Name: Schnurr Kirsh Stephens
#1700, Thomson Building, 65 Queen St., Toronto, ON M5H 2M5
Tel: 416-860-1057; Fax: 416-367-2502
www.estatelitigation.net

Toronto: Cecil Schwartz - *1
#2108, Madison Centre, 4950 Yonge St., Toronto, ON M2N 6K1
Tel: 416-250-0083; Fax: 416-512-8275
cecil@cecilschwartz.com

Toronto: Scott & Oleskiw - *2
Former Name: Diane Oleskiw
#235, 215 Spadina Ave., Toronto, ON M5T 2C7
Tel: 416-591-1261
admin@scottoleskiw.com

Toronto: Peter B. Scully - *1
56 Tranby St., Toronto, ON M5R 1N5
Tel: 416-929-2909; Fax: 416-929-2909
scullylaw@sympatico.ca

Toronto: Alexander Sennecke - *1
#900, Victoria Tower, 25 Adelaide St. East, Toronto, ON M5C 3A1
Tel: 416-410-2113; Fax: 416-410-9423
asennecke@sennecke.com
www.sennecke.com

Toronto: Seon Gutstadt Lash LLP - *6
#1800, 4950 Yonge St., Toronto, ON M2N 6K1
Tel: 416-224-0224; Fax: 416-224-0758
www.torlaw.com/sgl

Toronto: Sera Associates - *2
Former Name: Sera, Harrison Associates
#1800, 4950 Yonge St., Toronto, ON M2N 6K1
Tel: 416-224-0200; Fax: 416-224-0758

Toronto: Frederick J. Shanahan - *1
#414, 100 Richmond St. West, Toronto, ON M5H 3K6
Tel: 416-972-6449; Fax: 416-964-0823
f_shanny@hotmail.com

Toronto: Share Lawyers - *9
Former Name: David Share Associates
3442 Yonge St., Toronto, ON M4N 2M9
Tel: 416-488-9000; Fax: 416-488-9004
Toll-Free: 877-777-1109
www.sharelawyers.com
www.facebook.com/pages/Share-Lawyers/281913208534425, twitter.com/sharelaw, www.linkedin.com/company/share-lawyers

Toronto: Chet Sharma - *1
#7, 1658 Victoria Park Ave., Toronto, ON M1R 1P7
Tel: 416-285-1550; Fax: 416-285-1698
chetsharma@aol.com

Toronto: Roop N. Sharma - *2
942 Gerrard St. East, Toronto, ON M4M 1Z2
Tel: 416-461-0467; Fax: 416-461-5817

Toronto: Shearman & Sterling LLP - *8
#4405, Commerce Court West, P.O. Box 247, 199 Bay St., Toronto, ON M5L 1E8
Tel: 416-360-8484
www.shearman.com
www.facebook.com/shearmanandsterlingllp, twitter.com/ShearmanLaw, www.linkedin.com/company/shearman-&-sterling-llp

Toronto: Shekter, Dychtenberg LLP - *4
#2900, 390 Bay St., Toronto, ON M5H 2Y2
Tel: 416-941-9995; Fax: 416-869-0321
Toll-Free: 855-347-8177
richard@shekter.com
www.shekter.com

Toronto: Shell Lawyers - *2
Former Name: Shell Jacobs Lawyers
#401, 672 Dupont St., Toronto, ON M6G 1Z6
Tel: 416-539-0226; Fax: 416-539-0565
inquiry@shelllawyers.ca
www.shelllawyers.ca

Toronto: Shelton Associates - *2
#810, 439 University Ave., Toronto, ON M5G 1Y8
Tel: 416-977-8888; Fax: 416-977-1964

Toronto: Sheppard Shalinksy Brown - *3
488 Huron St., Toronto, ON M5R 2R3
Tel: 416-966-6885; Fax: 416-966-6837
Ysheppard@sfmlaw.com

Toronto: Sheridan, Ippolito & Associates - *2
#506, 2 Jane St., Toronto, ON M6S 4W3
Tel: 416-763-3399; Fax: 416-763-3443
info@sheridanippolito.com
www.sheridanippolito.com

Toronto: Sherman, Brown, Dryer, Karol, Gold, Lebow - *9
Also Known As: Sherman Brown Barristers & Solicitors
#900, 5075 Yonge St., Toronto, ON M2N 6C6
Tel: 416-224-9800; Fax: 416-222-3091
www.shermanbrown.com

Toronto: Sheldon L. Sherman - *1
2645 Eglinton Ave. East, Toronto, ON M1K 2S2
Tel: 416-261-7161; Fax: 416-261-7163

Toronto: Sherrard Kuzz LLP, Employment & Labour Lawyers - *24
#3300, 250 Yonge St., Toronto, ON M5B 2L7
Tel: 416-603-0700; Fax: 416-603-6035
info@sherrardkuzz.com
www.sherrardkuzz.com
twitter.com/sherrardkuzz

Toronto: Shibley Righton LLP - *37
#700, 250 University Ave., Toronto, ON M5H 3E5
Tel: 416-214-5200; Fax: 416-214-5400
Toll-Free: 877-214-5200
admin@shibleyrighton.com
www.shibleyrighton.com

Toronto: Shields O'Donnell MacKillop LLP - *9
Also Known As: Shields O'Donnell MacKillop LLP
Former Name: Hodgson Shields DesBrisay O'Donnell MacKillop Squire LLP
#1800, 65 Queen St. West, Toronto, ON M5H 2M5
Tel: 416-304-6400; Fax: 416-304-6406
info@somlaw.ca
www.somlaw.ca
twitter.com/Som_Law_, www.linkedin.com/company/1175232

Toronto: Bernard S. Shier - *1
219 Carlton St., Toronto, ON M5A 2L2
Tel: 416-923-8997; Fax: 416-923-8380

Toronto: Stanley I. Shier, Q.C. - *1
65 Queen St. West, 17th Fl., Toronto, ON M5H 2M5
Tel: 416-366-9591; Fax: 416-366-2107
stanleyshier@shierlaw.com

Toronto: Shoihet Earle Israel - *1
100 Adelaide St. West, Toronto, ON M5H 1S3
Tel: 416-863-9594

Toronto: Geary B. Shorser Law - *1
#2000, 393 University Ave., Toronto, ON M5G 1E6
Tel: 416-977-7749; Fax: 416-593-1352
shorserlaw.petrasite.com

Toronto: Ian C. Shoub - *1
1000 Finch Ave. West, 4th Fl., Toronto, ON M3J 2V5
Tel: 416-661-0990; Fax: 416-663-3236
ishoub@on.aibn.com

Toronto: Robert Shour - *1
#2000, 393 University Ave., Toronto, ON M5G 1E6
Tel: 416-977-4492; Fax: 416-977-4971
ralshour@on.aibn.com

Toronto: Louis D. Silver, Q.C. - *1
15 Silvergrove Rd., Toronto, ON M2L 2N5
Tel: 416-445-2795; Fax: 416-445-7243
louisdsilverqc@rogers.com

Toronto: Sheldon N. Silverman - *1
#638, 121 Richmond St. West, Toronto, ON M5H 2K1
Tel: 416-363-6295; Fax: 416-363-3047
ssilverman@sympatico.ca
www.sheldonsilverman.com

Toronto: Sim & McBurney - *17
330 University Ave., 6th Fl., Toronto, ON M5G 1R7
Tel: 416-595-1155; Fax: 416-595-1163
simip.com

Toronto: Sim, Lowman, Ashton & McKay LLP - *17
330 University Ave., 6th Fl., Toronto, ON M5G 1R7
Tel: 416-595-1155; Fax: 416-595-1163
simip.com

Toronto: Michael S. Simrod - *1
#500, 1000 Finch Ave. West, Toronto, ON M3J 2V5
Tel: 416-667-0980; Fax: 416-487-1091
fireblade4.8.11@gmail.com

Toronto: Isaac Singer - *1
2424 Bloor St. West, Toronto, ON M6S 1P9
Tel: 416-766-1135; Fax: 416-769-5365
isinger@bellnet.ca

Toronto: Singer, Keyfetz, Crackower & Saltzman - *2
532 Eglinton Ave. East, Toronto, ON M4P 1N6
Tel: 416-488-6900; Fax: 416-488-7530

Toronto: Singer, Kwinter LLP - *6
#214, 1033 Bay St., Toronto, ON M5S 3A5
Tel: 416-961-2882; Fax: 416-961-6760
Toll-Free: 866-285-6927
info@singerkwinter.com
www.singerkwinter.com
www.facebook.com/Singer-Kwinter-Personal-Injury-Lawyers-342779048517, twitter.com/Singer_Kwinter, www.linkedin.com/groups/2526865/profile

Toronto: Yaso Sinnadurai - *1
#202, 2100 Ellesmere Rd., Toronto, ON M1H 3B7
Tel: 416-265-3456; Fax: 416-265-2770

Toronto: Regina Sinukoff - *1
#507, 1000 Finch Ave. West, Toronto, ON M3J 2V5
Tel: 416-739-7272; Fax: 416-739-7770
rsinukoff@on.aibn.com

Toronto: Steven H. Sinukoff - *1
127 Orchard View Blvd., Toronto, ON M4R 1C1
Tel: 416-489-7997; Fax: 416-256-9244
stevensinukoff@bellnet.ca

Toronto: Skadden, Arps, Slate, Meagher & Flom LLP - Toronto - *11
Also Known As: Skadden
#1750, P.O. Box 258, 222 Bay St., Toronto, ON M5K 1J5
Tel: 416-777-4700; Fax: 416-777-4747
www.skadden.com
www.facebook.com/skadden, twitter.com/SkaddenArps, www.linkedin.com/company/4862

Toronto: Skapinker & Shapiro LLP - *2
#904, 180 Bloor St. West, Toronto, ON M5S 2V6
Tel: 416-214-1500; Fax: 416-214-0658
divorcelawyer@bellnet.ca
www.ontariofamilylaw.com

Toronto: Steven H. Skolnik - *1
#318, 4002 Sheppard Ave. East, Toronto, ON M1S 4R5
Tel: 416-297-7300; Fax: 416-298-7142

** indicates number of lawyers*

Toronto: Slater & Wells - *2
Sherway Executive Centre, 300 North Queen St., Toronto, ON M9C 5K4
Tel: 416-259-4293; *Fax:* 416-259-1286

Toronto: Andrea M. Smart - *1
8 Rolston Ave., Toronto, ON M5A 3Z2
Tel: 416-961-8829; *Fax:* 416-961-8829

Toronto: Cindy L. Smith
P.O. Box 43514, Stn. Leaside, 1531 Bayview Ave., Toronto, ON M4G 4G8
Tel: 416-408-0008

Toronto: Kenneth D. Smith - *1
#500, 70 Bond St., Toronto, ON M5B 1X3
Tel: 416-361-0232; *Fax:* 416-863-4896

Toronto: Raymond I. Smith - *1
#1507, 8 King St. East., Toronto, ON M5C 1B5
Tel: 416-861-8695; *Fax:* 416-861-9074
raylaw@on.aibn.com

Toronto: Smitiuch Injury Law - *3
#600, 21 Four Seasons Place, Toronto, ON M9B 6J8
Tel: 647-799-2735; *Fax:* 416-621-1558
Toll-Free: 800-528-6489
www.smitiuchinjurylaw.com
www.facebook.com/pages/Personal-Injury-Lawyers-Toronto-Ontario-Smitiuch-Inj, twitter.com/SmitiuchLaw, www.linkedin.com/company/smitiuch-injury-law

Toronto: Snider & Digregorio - *2
Former Name: Snider, D.B.
978 Kingston Rd., Toronto, ON M4E 1S9
Tel: 416-699-0424; *Fax:* 416-699-0285
info@sdlegal.ca
www.sdlegal.ca

Toronto: Kenneth E. Snider - *1
#309, 2100 Ellesmere Rd., Toronto, ON M1H 3B7
Tel: 416-438-4515
www.kennethsnider.ca

Toronto: Irving Snitman - *1
554 Annette St., Toronto, ON M6S 2C2
Tel: 416-767-0805; *Fax:* 416-767-4619
irv@irvingsnitman.com
www.irvingsnitman.com

Toronto: Solnik & Solnik Professional Corp. - *2
2991 Dundas St. West, Toronto, ON M6P 1Z4
Tel: 416-767-7506; *Fax:* 416-767-4738
info@solnikandsolnik.com
www.solnikandsolnik.com

Toronto: Solomon, Grosberg LLP - *2
#410, 20 Toronto St., Toronto, ON M5C 2B8
Tel: 416-366-7828; *Fax:* 416-366-3513
lawyers@solgro.com
www.solgro.com

Toronto: Somjen & Peterson - *1
#810, 1240 Bay St., Toronto, ON M5R 2A7
Tel: 416-922-8083; *Fax:* 416-922-4234
info@somjen.com
www.somjen.com

Toronto: Sommers & Roth - *4
268 Avenue Rd., Toronto, ON M4V 2G7
Tel: 416-961-1212; *Fax:* 416-961-2827
Toll-Free: 866-802-3789
www.sommersandroth.com

Toronto: Larry S. Sonenberg - *1
1123 Albion Rd., Toronto, ON M9V 1A9
Tel: 416-749-6000; *Fax:* 416-749-6004
Toll-Free: 877-388-5962
info@sonenberglaw.ca
www.sonenberglaw.ca/en/

Toronto: Sosa & Associates - *1
#600, 161 Eglinton Ave. East, Toronto, ON M4P 1J5
Tel: 416-480-2324; *Fax:* 416-480-2923

Toronto: Sotos LLP - *16
#1200, 180 Dundas St. West, Toronto, ON M5G 1Z8
Tel: 416-977-0007; *Fax:* 416-977-0717
Toll-Free: 888-977-9806
info@sotosllp.com
www.sotosllp.com
www.facebook.com/sotosllp, www.twitter.com/sotosllp, www.linkedin.com/company/sotos-llp

Toronto: Spencer Law Firm - *1
Former Name: Spencer Romberg Associates
#300, 162 Cumberland St., Toronto, ON M5R 3N5
Tel: 416-967-1571; *Fax:* 416-966-1161

Toronto: Spiegel Rosenthal - *1
#2410, P.O. Box 24, 401 Bay St., Toronto, ON M5H 2Y4
Tel: 416-865-9677; *Fax:* 416-363-7781
david@drlaw.ca
www.drlaw.ca

Toronto: Belva Spiel - *1
#12, 245 Eglington Ave., Toronto, ON M4P 3B7
Tel: 416-486-1688; *Fax:* 416-486-2274
spiel@on.aibn.com

Toronto: Michael Spiro - *1
#207, 3625 Dufferin St., Toronto, ON M3K 1Z2
Tel: 416-630-1370; *Fax:* 416-633-2229

Toronto: Sprigings Intellectual Property Law - *6
Former Name: Hitchman & Sprigings
#715, Sun Life Financial Centre, East Tower, 3250 Bloor St. West, Toronto, ON M8X 2X9
Tel: 416-777-0888; *Fax:* 416-777-0881
info@sprigings.com
www.sprigings.com

Toronto: Harvey Spring - *1
#488, 22 College St., Toronto, ON M5G 1K2
Tel: 416-967-0800; *Fax:* 416-967-2783
harveyspring@bellnet.ca

Toronto: Jerome Stanleigh - *1
#100, 20 York Mills Rd., Toronto, ON M2P 2C2
Tel: 416-924-0151; *Fax:* 416-924-2887
jerome@stanleigh.com / jhstanleigh@gmail.com
www.stanleigh.com

Toronto: James Stefoff - *1
#1505, 80 Richmond St. W, Toronto, ON M5H 2A4
Tel: 416-366-7984

Toronto: Maxwell Steidman, Q.C. - *1
#201, 1013 Wilson Ave., Toronto, ON M3K 1G1
Tel: 416-366-7661; *Fax:* 416-360-6868

Toronto: Larry C. Stein - *1
#625, 4211 Yonge St., Toronto, ON M2P 2A9
Tel: 416-636-8100; *Fax:* 416-636-6545

Toronto: Lorisa Stein - *1
#800, 150 York St., Toronto, ON M5H 3S5
Tel: 416-596-8081
lorisa@idirect.com
www.lorisastein.com

Toronto: Steinberg Morton Hope & Israel LLP - *13
#1100, 5255 Yonge St., Toronto, ON M2N 6P4
Tel: 416-225-2777; *Fax:* 416-225-7112
www.smhilaw.com

Toronto: Steinecke Maciura LeBlanc, Barristers & Solicitors - *9
#2308, P.O. Box 23, 401 Bay St., Toronto, ON M5H 2Y4
Tel: 416-599-2200; *Fax:* 416-593-7867
Toll-Free: 877-498-1630
rsteinecke@sml-law.com
www.sml-law.com

Toronto: Stern Landesman Clark LLP - *3
#1724, 390 Bay St., Toronto, ON M5H 2Y2
Tel: 416-869-3422; *Fax:* 416-869-3449
Toll-Free: 800-882-9635
jclark@sternlaw.ca
www.sternlaw.ca

Toronto: Gary A. Stern - *1
1938 Avenue Rd., Toronto, ON M5M 4A2
Tel: 416-780-0199; *Fax:* 416-780-0155
Toll-Free: 800-678-6705
gastern@torlaw.com

Toronto: Stevenson Whelton MacDonald & Swan LLP - *8
Former Name: Stevensons LLP
#202, 15 Toronto St., Toronto, ON M5C 2E3
Tel: 416-599-7900; *Fax:* 416-599-7910
www.stevensonlaw.net

Toronto: Deborah L. Stewart - *1
106 Glencairn Ave., Toronto, ON M4R 1M9
Tel: 416-226-9340; *Fax:* 416-226-5341

Toronto: Stikeman Keeley Spiegel Pasternack LLP - *6
#2300, 200 Front St. West, Toronto, ON M5V 3K2
Tel: 416-367-1930; *Fax:* 416-365-1813
www.stikeman.to

Toronto: Stockwoods LLP - *17
#4130, TD North Tower, P.O. Box 140, 77 King St. West, Toronto, ON M5K 1H1
Tel: 416-593-7200; *Fax:* 416-593-9345
reception@stockwoods.ca
www.stockwoods.ca
twitter.com/stockwoodsllp, www.linkedin.com/company/stockwoods-llp

Toronto: Stone & Osborne - *2
#201, 100 Sheppard Ave. West, Toronto, ON M2N 1M6
Tel: 416-225-1145; *Fax:* 416-225-0832

Toronto: Stone & Wenus - *2
330 Broadview Ave., Toronto, ON M4M 2G9
Tel: 416-469-4125; *Fax:* 416-469-2877
www.stoneandwenus.com

Toronto: David S. Strashin - *1
#702, 55 Eglinton Ave. East, Toronto, ON M4P 1G8
Tel: 416-482-8171; *Fax:* 416-485-4174

Toronto: Michael Strathman - *1
219 Carlton St., Toronto, ON M5A 2L2
Tel: 416-922-2424; *Fax:* 416-923-8380
michael@strathmanlaw.ca
www.strathmanlaw.ca

Toronto: Stringer LLP - *7
#800, 390 Bay St., Toronto, ON M5H 2Y2
Tel: 416-862-1616; *Fax:* 416-363-7358
Toll-Free: 866-821-7306
info@stringerllp.com
www.stringerllp.com
twitter.com/stringerLLP

Toronto: John F. Stroz, Q.C. - *1
2275 Dundas St. West, Toronto, ON M6R 1X6
Tel: 416-536-2131; *Fax:* 416-536-5451

Toronto: Robert P. Sullivan - *1
#1807, 8 King St. East, Toronto, ON M5C 1B5
Tel: 416-361-0390; *Fax:* 416-361-0248
rpsullivan@on.aibn.com

Toronto: Suter Law
102 Annette St., Toronto, ON M6P 1N6
Tel: 416-760-0529; *Fax:* 416-760-9967

Toronto: Ian Sutherland Barrister & Solicitor - *1
554 Annette St., Toronto, ON M6S 2C2
Tel: 416-763-0787; *Fax:* 416-763-0563
ian@sutherland.com
www.iansutherland.com

Toronto: Swadron Associates - *8
115 Berkeley St., Toronto, ON M5A 2W8
Tel: 416-362-1234; *Fax:* 416-362-1232
www.swadron.com

Toronto: Kenneth P. Swan - *1
P.O. Box 1284, Stn. K, 2384 Yonge St., Toronto, ON M4P 3E5
Tel: 416-368-5279; *Fax:* 888-547-0595
kpswan@bondlaw.net

Toronto: Eric J. Swetsky - *1
25 Sylvan Valley Way, Toronto, ON M5M 4M4
Tel: 416-787-4376; *Fax:* 416-787-3538
www.advertisinglawyer.ca

Toronto: Mimi Tang - *1
#202, 1210 Sheppard Ave. East, Toronto, ON M2K 1E3
Tel: 416-491-2929; *Fax:* 416-491-0990

Toronto: Tatham, Pearson & Malcolm LLP - *3
5524 Lawrence Ave. East, Toronto, ON M1C 3B2
Tel: 416-284-4749; *Fax:* 416-284-3086
Toll-Free: 800-970-5670
info@tathampearson.com
www.tathampearson.com

Toronto: Stanley Taube - *1
#503, 33 Jackes Ave., Toronto, ON M4T 1E2
Tel: 416-513-1233

Toronto: Taveroff & Associates - *2
#900, 2 Sheppard Ave. E, Toronto, ON M2N 5Y7
Tel: 416-221-9343; *Fax:* 416-221-8928

** indicates number of lawyers*

Toronto: Fred Tayar & Associates, Professional Corporation
#1200, 65 Queen St. West, Toronto, ON M5H 2M5
Tel: 416-363-1800; Fax: 416-363-3356
fred@fredtayar.com

Toronto: Ted Yoannou & Associates - *2
#600, 1000 Finch Ave. West, Toronto, ON M3J 2V5
Tel: 416-650-1011; Fax: 416-650-1980
info@tyalaw.ca
www.torontocriminallawyers.com

Toronto: Stephen Thom - *1
#300, 19 Yorkville Ave., Toronto, ON M4W 1L1
Tel: 416-364-3371; Fax: 416-863-4896

Toronto: Thomson, Rogers - *35
#3100, 390 Bay St., Toronto, ON M5H 1W2
Tel: 416-868-3100; Fax: 416-868-3134
Toll-Free: 888-223-0448
info@thomsonrogers.com
www.thomsonrogers.com
www.facebook.com/pages/Thomson-Rogers-Lawyers/406181779461781, twitter.com/thomsonrogers, www.linkedin.com/companies/1121502

Toronto: Ian Thornhill - *1
#406, 255 Duncan Mill Rd., Toronto, ON M3B 3H9
Tel: 416-224-2004; Fax: 416-224-2101
ithornhilllaw@rogers.com

Toronto: Thornton Grout Finnigan LLP - *18
#3200, Toronto-Dominion Centre, P.O. Box 329, 100 Wellington St. West, Toronto, ON M5K 1K7
Tel: 416-304-1616; Fax: 416-304-1313
info@tgf.ca
www.tgf.ca

Toronto: Thorsteinssons LLP - Toronto - *46
Brookfield Place, P.O. Box 786, 181 Bay St., 33rd Fl., Toronto, ON M5J 2T3
Tel: 416-864-0829; Fax: 416-864-1106
www.thor.ca

Toronto: Lorne B. Tick - *1
54 Misty Cres., Toronto, ON M3B 1T2
Tel: 416-444-9146; Fax: 416-444-9146
ltick@rogers.com

Toronto: Philip Tinianov - *1
#1800, 4950 Yonge St., Toronto, ON M2N 6K1
Tel: 416-363-0866; Fax: 416-224-0758
ptinianov@torlaw.com

Toronto: Michael K. Titherington - *1
#635, 60 Heintzman St., Toronto, ON M6P 5A1
Tel: 416-656-6465; Fax: 416-551-0488

Toronto: Tkatch & Associates - *2
#200, 464 Yonge St., Toronto, ON M4Y 1W9
Tel: 416-968-0333; Fax: 416-968-0232
mtkatch@tkatchlaw.ca
www.tkatchlaw.ca

Toronto: Norman W. Tomas - *1
954A Royal York Rd., Toronto, ON M8X 2E5
Tel: 416-233-5567; Fax: 416-233-9779
ntomas@bellnet.ca

Toronto: James Tomlinson - *1
#234A, 85 Ellesmere Rd., Toronto, ON M1R 4B9
Tel: 416-447-0476; Fax: 416-447-8611
tomlin09@bellnet.ca
www.jtomlinsonlaw.com

Toronto: Toomath & Associates - *1
Also Known As: Toomath, E.H.
100 Richmond St. West, Toronto, ON M5H 3K6
Tel: 416-869-0900; Fax: 416-366-4711

Toronto: Torkin Manes LLP - *77
#1500, 151 Yonge St., Toronto, ON M5C 2W7
Tel: 416-863-1188; Fax: 416-863-0305
Toll-Free: 800-665-1555
info@torkinmanes.com
www.torkinmanes.com
twitter.com/TorkinManesLLP, www.linkedin.com/company/torkin-manes

Toronto: Traub Moldaver
#1801, 4 King St. West, Toronto, ON M5H 1B6
Tel: 416-214-6500; Fax: 416-214-7275
Toll-Free: 877-727-6500

Toronto: Philip J. Traversy - *1
20 Flaming Roseway, Toronto, ON M2N 5W8
Tel: 647-271-4741
p.traversy@rogers.com

Toronto: Quoc Toan Trinh - *1
1577 Bloor St. W, Toronto, ON M6P 1A6
Tel: 416-533-8987; Fax: 416-536-3618

Toronto: William M. Trudell - *2
#100, 116 Simcoe St., Toronto, ON M5H 4E2
Tel: 416-598-2019; Fax: 416-596-2599
wtrudell@simcoechambers.com

Toronto: Constantine Tsantis - *1
69 Elm St., Toronto, ON M5G 1H2
Tel: 416-599-6689; Fax: 416-971-9092

Toronto: Maureen L. Tucker - *1
43 Madawaska Ave., Toronto, ON M2M 2R1
Tel: 416-221-5122; Fax: 416-226-9737
Toll-Free: 877-580-2049
maureen@mltuckerlaw.com
www.mltuckerlaw.com/en/

Toronto: Howard Ungerman - *1
37 Maitland St., Toronto, ON M4Y 1C8
Tel: 416-924-4111; Fax: 416-924-4112

Toronto: Ursel Phillips Fellows Hopkinson LLP - *17
Former Name: Green & Chercover
#1200, 555 Richmond St. West, Toronto, ON M5V 3B1
Tel: 416-968-3333; Fax: 416-968-0325
www.upfhlaw.ca

Toronto: S. Van Duffelen - *1
188 Coxwell Ave., Toronto, ON M4L 3B2
Tel: 416-598-5667; Fax: 416-971-7721
vanduffelenlaw@on.aibn.com

Toronto: Michael B. Vaughan Q.C.
#3100, 130 Adelaide St. West, Toronto, ON M5H 3P5
Tel: 416-363-9611; Fax: 416-363-9672
michaelbvaughan@yahoo.ca

Toronto: David R. Vine, QC - *1
#1604, 80 Richmond St. West, Toronto, ON M5H 2A4
Tel: 416-863-9341; Fax: 416-863-9342

Toronto: Mark H. Viner - *1
70 Bowring Walk, Toronto, ON M3H 5Z6
Tel: 416-785-7469; Fax: 416-785-1581
vinerlaw@gmail.com

Toronto: Julia M. Viva - *1
58 Plymbridge Rd., Toronto, ON M2P 1A3
Tel: 416-488-7222; Fax: 416-489-6258

Toronto: James D. Vlasis - *1
Crown Attorney's Office, 1911 Eglington Ave. E, Toronto, ON M1L 4P4
Tel: 416-325-0342; Fax: 416-325-0353

Toronto: Wagman, Sherkin - *2
#200, 756A Queen St. East, Toronto, ON M4M 1H4
Tel: 416-465-1102; Fax: 416-465-3941
charles_wagman@wagmansherkin.ca

Toronto: Waldin, de Kenedy - *3
1 Dundas St. West, Toronto, ON M5G 1Z3
Tel: 416-364-6761; Fax: 416-364-3866
waldin@waldin.ca

Toronto: Walker & Wood - *1
#1800, 181 University Ave., Toronto, ON M5H 3M7
Tel: 416-591-6832; Fax: 416-591-7513

Toronto: Walker Poole Nixon LLP - *7
#515, North York City Centre, 5160 Yonge St., Toronto, ON M2N 6L9
Tel: 416-225-5160; Fax: 416-225-0072
propertytax@wpnlaw.com
www.wpnlaw.com
www.facebook.com/pages/Walker-Poole-Nixon-LLP/190023941008835?sk=wall, www.twitter.com/@assessmentlaw, www.linkedin.com/company/2490703?trk=tyah

Toronto: Walker, Ellis - *2
390 Bay St., 30th Fl., Toronto, ON M5H 1W2
Tel: 416-363-2144; Fax: 416-363-1541

Toronto: James H.G. Wallace - *1
551 Gerrard St. East, Toronto, ON M4M 1X7
Tel: 416-463-6666; Fax: 416-463-8259

Toronto: The Rose & Thistle Group Ltd. - *5
30 Hazelton Ave., Toronto, ON M5R 2E2
Tel: 416-489-9790; Fax: 416-489-9973
info@roseandthistle.ca
www.roseandthistlegroup.com

Toronto: Walton, Brigham & Kelly - *2
301 Donlands Ave., Toronto, ON M4J 3R8
Tel: 416-425-4300; Fax: 416-425-4310
tkelly@bellnet.ca

Toronto: Warren Bergman Associates - *2
Former Name: Farb, Warren LLP
2925 Bathurst St., Toronto, ON M6S 3B1
Tel: 416-763-4183; Fax: 416-763-1310
dwarren@warrenbergman.com

Toronto: Warren Mediation Group - *1
#802, 2 Sheppard Ave. East, Toronto, ON M2N 5Y7
Tel: 647-890-3384; Fax: 416-598-4316
howard@warrenmediationgroup.com
www.warrenmediationgroup.com

Toronto: Robert D. Warren
15 Bedford Rd., Toronto, ON M5R 2J7
Tel: 416-368-5393; Fax: 416-905-7736

Toronto: Weatherhead, Weatherhead - *2
#500, 27 Queen St. East, Toronto, ON M5C 2M6
Tel: 416-362-1369; Fax: 416-362-5013
weatherhead@bellnet.ca

Toronto: John Weingust, Q.C. - *1
Penthouse, 481 University Ave., 10th Fl., Toronto, ON M5G 2E9
Tel: 416-977-7786; Fax: 416-340-0064

Toronto: F. Sheldon Weinles - *1
104 Caribou Rd., Toronto, ON M5N 2A9
Tel: 416-780-1330; Fax: 416-780-1331
sheldonweinles@rogers.com

Toronto: Joyce R. Weinman - *1
51 Cardiff Rd., Toronto, ON M4P 2P1
Tel: 416-848-1019; Fax: 416-486-3309
joyce@jwdental.com
www.jwdental.com

Toronto: Gilbert Weinstock - *1
#401, 1850 Victoria Park Ave., Toronto, ON M1R 1T1
Tel: 416-759-1354; Fax: 416-759-3256
gilbertweinstock@gmail.com

Toronto: WeirFoulds LLP - *78
#4100, Toronto-Dominion Centre, P.O. Box 35, 66 Wellington St. West, Toronto, ON M5K 1B7
Tel: 416-365-1110; Fax: 416-365-1876
firm@weirfoulds.com
www.weirfoulds.com
twitter.com/WeirFoulds, www.linkedin.com/company/weirfoulds-llp

Toronto: Weisdorf McCallum & Tatsiou: Associates - *2
#1000, 121 Richmond St. West, Toronto, ON M5H 2K1
Tel: 416-861-1000; Fax: 416-861-8166

Toronto: Wells Criminal Law - *2
#202, 559 College St. 2nd Fl., Toronto, ON M6G 1A9
Tel: 416-944-1485
www.torontocriminallawyer.ca

Toronto: Stephen Werbowyj Professional Corporation - *1
1199 The Queensway, Toronto, ON M8Z 1R2
Tel: 416-233-9461; Fax: 416-233-1524
werbowyj@bellnet.ca
www.werbowyj.com

Toronto: Ian D. Werker - *1
#2000, 393 University Ave., Toronto, ON M5G 1E6
Tel: 416-593-7552; Fax: 416-593-0668
ian@werkerlaw.com
www.werkerlaw.com

Toronto: West Scarborough Community Legal Services - *4
#201, 2425 Eglinton Ave. E., Toronto, ON M1K 5G8
Tel: 416-285-4460; Fax: 416-285-1070

Toronto: Lionel B. White, Q.C. - *1
65 Duggan Ave., Toronto, ON M4V 1Y1
Tel: 416-364-1127; Fax: 416-364-6903
lex.white@rogers.com

** indicates number of lawyers*

***Toronto*: Robin J. Wigdor - *1**
#901, 159 Frederick St., Toronto, ON M5A 4P1
Tel: 416-504-7237; *Fax:* 647-723-0197
robin@wigdor.com
www.wigdor.com/robin/

***Toronto*: Wildeboer Dellelce LLP - *37**
Former Name: Wildeboer Rand Thomson Apps & Dellelce LLP
#800, Wildeboer Dellelce Place, 365 Bay St., Toronto, ON M5H 2V1
Tel: 416-361-3121; *Fax:* 416-361-1790
Toll-Free: 866-945-3529
www.wildlaw.ca
twitter.com/wildlaw,
www.linkedin.com/company/wildeboer-dellelce-llp

***Toronto*: Will Davidson LLP - Toronto - *19**
Former Name: MacMillan Rooke Boeckle
#1400, 401 Bay St., Toronto, ON M5H 2Y4
Tel: 416-360-1194; *Fax:* 416-360-8469
Toll-Free: 800-661-7606
www.willdavidson.ca

***Toronto*: Willard & Devitt - *1**
155 Roncesvalles Ave., Toronto, ON M6R 2L3
Tel: 416-531-1136; *Fax:* 416-531-4096
robert@robertbeaumont.ca

***Toronto*: W.M. Sharpe - *3**
#307, 40 Wynford Dr., Toronto, ON M3C 1J5
Tel: 416-482-5321; *Fax:* 416-322-2083
info@shippinglaw.ca
www.shipping-law.ca

***Toronto*: Paul T. Willis - *1**
#308, 120 Carlton St., Toronto, ON M5A 4K2
Tel: 416-926-9806; *Fax:* 416-926-9737
paul.t.willis@on.aibn.com
www.paulwillis-law.com

***Toronto*: Willms & Shier Environmental Lawyers LLP - *13**
#900, 4 King St. West, Toronto, ON M5H 1B6
Tel: 416-863-0711; *Fax:* 416-863-1938
info@willmsshier.com
www.willmsshier.com
www.linkedin.com/company/willms-&-shier-environmental-lawyers-llp

***Toronto*: Willowdale Community Legal Services - *2**
#106, 245 Fairview Mall Dr., Toronto, ON M2J 4T1
Tel: 416-492-2437; *Fax:* 416-492-6281
willowdalelegal.com

***Toronto*: Norman H. Winter - *1**
#801, 1 St. Clair Ave. East, Toronto, ON M4T 2V7
Tel: 416-964-0325; *Fax:* 416-964-2494
nw@nwinlaw.com

***Toronto*: Wise & Associates Professional Corporation - *3**
Former Name: Wise, Roy
#602, 80 Bloor St. West, Toronto, ON M5S 2V1
Tel: 416-866-4144; *Fax:* 416-866-7946
roy.wise@wiseandassociates.com

***Toronto*: Gerald R. Wise - *1**
3329 Bloor St. West, Toronto, ON M8X 1E7
Tel: 416-231-7399; *Fax:* 416-231-1280

***Toronto*: Gary L. Wiseman - *1**
#1800, Madison Centre, 4950 Yonge St., Toronto, ON M2N 6K1
Tel: 416-224-0200; *Fax:* 416-224-0758
gwiseman@idirect.com

***Toronto*: Newton Wong & Associates - *2**
#307, 1033 Bay St., Toronto, ON M5S 3A5
Tel: 416-971-9118; *Fax:* 416-971-7210

***Toronto*: Wing H. Wong - *1**
#202, 4433 Sheppard Ave. East, Toronto, ON M1S 1V3
Tel: 416-298-6767; *Fax:* 416-298-3844

***Toronto*: Cynthia J. Woods - *1**
#8, 1 Chestnut Hills Cres., Toronto, ON M9A 2W3
Tel: 416-763-3065; *Fax:* 866-607-2510
info@woodslaw.ca
www.woodslaw.ca

***Toronto*: Woolgar VanWiechen Ketcheson Ducoffe LLP - *12**
Former Name: Ducoffe, Stuart M.
#401, 70 The Esplanade, Toronto, ON M5E 1R2
Tel: 416-867-1666; *Fax:* 416-867-1434
info@woolvan.com
www.woolvan.com

***Toronto*: George A. Wootten, Q.C. - *1**
1199 The Queensway, Toronto, ON M8Z 1R7
Tel: 416-621-7470; *Fax:* 416-621-6838
queenswaylaw@yahoo.ca

***Toronto*: Keith E. Wright - *1**
370 Bloor St. East, Toronto, ON M4W 3M6
Tel: 416-364-1157; *Fax:* 416-363-4978
keith.wright@rogers.com

***Toronto*: Peter J. Wuebbolt - *1**
1554A Bloor St. West, Toronto, ON M6P 1A4
Tel: 416-516-4621; *Fax:* 416-516-1679

***Toronto*: Sara Wunch - *1**
#1102, 1166 Bay St., Toronto, ON M5S 2X8
Tel: 416-595-7001; *Fax:* 416-595-5663

***Toronto*: Nicholas A. Xynnis - *1**
#318, 100 Richmond St. West, Toronto, ON M5H 3K6
Tel: 416-862-1010; *Fax:* 416-862-7602
naxynnis@istar.ca

***Toronto*: Arthur Yallen - *1**
204 St. George St., Toronto, ON M5R 2N5
Tel: 416-927-0001; *Fax:* 416-927-0930

***Toronto*: Gerald B. Yasskin - *1**
#402, 1183 Finch Ave. West, Toronto, ON M3J 2G2
Tel: 416-667-0982; *Fax:* 416-665-4291

***Toronto*: Yee & Lee - *2**
#109, 40 Wynford Dr., Toronto, ON M3C 1J5
Tel: 416-977-0091; *Fax:* 416-977-6335

***Toronto*: David P. Yerzy - *1**
#108, 14 Prince Arthur Ave., Toronto, ON M5R 1A9
Tel: 416-972-6957; *Fax:* 416-972-6427
werzy@planeteer.com

***Toronto*: Yeti Law Professional Corporation - *4**
Former Name: Agnew, Gladstone LLP
215 Carlton St., Toronto, ON M5A 2K9
Tel: 416-964-0021; *Fax:* 416-964-0744
info@yetilaw.com
www.yetilaw.com

***Toronto*: Hyun Soo Yi - *1**
#204, 640 Bloor St. West, Toronto, ON M6G 1K9
Tel: 416-534-7711; *Fax:* 416-534-7714

***Toronto*: Joseph R. Young - *1**
#200, 20 Cumberland St., Toronto, ON M4W 1J5
Tel: 416-969-8887; *Fax:* 416-969-8866
jryoung@globalmigration.com
www.globalmigration.com

***Toronto*: D.R. Zadorozny - *1**
#216, 4195 Dundas St. West, Toronto, ON M8X 1Y4
Tel: 416-239-2333; *Fax:* 416-239-1752
Toll-Free: 866-396-7251
drz@drzlaw.com

***Toronto*: Silvie Zakuta - *1**
#850, 36 Toronto St., Toronto, ON M5C 2C5
Tel: 416-923-1656; *Fax:* 416-368-2918
szakuta@aol.com

***Toronto*: Zaldin & Fine LLP - *3**
#900, 60 Yonge St., Toronto, ON M5E 1H5
Tel: 416-868-1431; *Fax:* 416-868-6381
sueking@zaldinandfine.ca

***Toronto*: Zammit Semple LLP - *2**
#200, 129 Yorkville Ave., Toronto, ON M5R 1C4
Tel: 416-923-2601
info@zds.on.ca
www.zds.on.ca

***Toronto*: Zarek Taylor Grossman Hanrahan LLP - *45**
#1301, 20 Adelaide St. East, Toronto, ON M5C 2T6
Tel: 416-777-2811; *Fax:* 416-777-2050
reception@ztgh.com
www.ztgh.com

***Toronto*: M. David Zbarsky - *1**
#1001, 85 Thorncliffe Park Dr., Toronto, ON M4H 1L6
Tel: 416-421-6252; *Fax:* 416-467-6780

***Toronto*: Zeldin, Collin - *1**
23 Bedford Rd., Toronto, ON M5R 2J9
Tel: 416-964-7914; *Fax:* 416-964-8067
collin@zecol.com

***Toronto*: David L. Zifkin - *1**
90A Isabella St., 1st Fl., Toronto, ON M4Y 1N4
Tel: 416-927-7720; *Fax:* 416-964-9348
dzifkin@zifkin.com
www.zifkin.com

***Trenton*: Bonn Law Office - *4**
Former Name: G.W. Bonn
80 Division St., Trenton, ON K8V 5S5
Tel: 613-392-9207; *Fax:* 613-392-6367
Toll-Free: 888-266-6529
www.bonnlaw.ca
www.facebook.com/pages/Bonn-Law/201504043200778,
www.linkedin.com/company/2387251

***Trenton*: Fleming Garrett Sioui - *3**
P.O. Box 397, Stn. Main, 21 Quinte St., Trenton, ON K8V 5R6
Tel: 613-965-6430; *Fax:* 613-965-6400
Toll-Free: 800-616-1294
www.fgslaw.net

***Tweed*: Bart F. Lackie - *1**
2718 Mallbank Rd., RR#4, Tweed, ON K0K 3J0
Tel: 613-478-9940; *Fax:* 613-478-6061
bart@linesat.com

***Unionville*: Janet L. Gillespie - *1**
178 Main St., Unionville, ON L3R 2G9
Tel: 905-479-6352; *Fax:* 905-479-1991
jlgillespie@rogers.com

***Unionville*: Minken Employment Lawyers - *4**
Former Name: Minken & Associates Professional Corporation
#200, 190 Main St., Unionville, ON L3R 2G9
Tel: 905-477-7011; *Fax:* 905-477-7010
Toll-Free: 866-477-7011
contact@minken.com
www.minkenemploymentlawyers.com
www.facebook.com/pages/Minken-Employment-Lawyers/206524622691440, twitter.com/MinkenLaw,
www.linkedin.com/company/684523?trk=tyah

***Uxbridge*: Bailey & Sedore - *2**
11 Brock St. East, Uxbridge, ON L9P 1M4
Tel: 905-852-3363; *Fax:* 905-852-3480
rwsedore@bellnet.ca
www.baileyandsedore.ca

***Uxbridge*: Paul D. Fox - *1**
6749 Concession 6, RR#1, Uxbridge, ON L9P 1R1
Tel: 905-852-4560; *Fax:* 905-852-4435
paulfox@bellnet.ca

***Uxbridge*: Randall B. Hoban - *3**
20 Bascom St., Uxbridge, ON L9P 1J3
Tel: 905-852-3900; *Fax:* 905-852-3666
www.stadamdesign.com

***Uxbridge*: P. Douglas Turner, Q.C. - *1**
P.O. Box 760, 63 Albert St., Uxbridge, ON L9P 1E5
Tel: 905-852-6196; *Fax:* 905-852-6197
doug@pdturner.com

***Uxbridge*: Wilson Associates - *2**
22 Brock St. East, Uxbridge, ON L9P 1P1
Tel: 905-852-3353; *Fax:* 905-852-5120
dwilson@uxbridgelaw.com
www.uxbridgelaw.com

***Vaughan*: Bianchi Presta LLP - *9**
Bldg. A, 9100 Jane St., 3rd Fl., Vaughan, ON L4K 0A4
Tel: 905-738-1078; *Fax:* 905-738-0528
contact@bianchipresta.com
www.bianchipresta.com

***Vaughan*: Bortolussi Family Law - *6**
#210, 3300 Hwy. 7 West, Vaughan, ON L4K 4M3
Tel: 416-987-3300; *Fax:* 905-907-0707
www.bortolussifamilylaw.com

** indicates number of lawyers*

***Vaughan*: Bratty & Partners, LLP Barristers & Solicitors - *15**
#200, 7501 Keele St., Vaughan, ON L4K 1Y2
Tel: 905-760-2600; *Fax:* 905-760-2900
info@bratty.com
www.bratty.com

***Vaughan*: Corsianos Lee - *3**
#203W, 3800 Steeles Ave. West, Vaughan, ON L4L 4G9
Tel: 905-370-1091; *Fax:* 905-370-1095
gcorsianos@cl-law.ca
www.cl-law.ca

***Vaughan*: Drudi, Alexiou, Kuchar LLP - *8**
#307, 7050 Weston Rd., Vaughan, ON L4L 8G7
Tel: 905-850-6116; *Fax:* 905-850-9146
www.dakllp.com

***Vaughan*: Fine & Deo - *12**
#300, 3100 Steeles Ave. West, Vaughan, ON L4K 3R1
Tel: 905-760-1800; *Fax:* 905-760-0050
Toll-Free: 888-346-3336
info@finedeo.com
finedeo.com

***Vaughan*: RDQ Law - *10**
Also Known As: Rotundo Dilorio Quaglietta LLP
Former Name: Gambin RDQ LLP
#400, 3901 Hwy. 7, Vaughan, ON L4L 8L5
Tel: 905-264-7800; *Fax:* 905-264-7808
info@rdqlaw.com
www.rdqlaw.com
www.facebook.com/RdqLaw, twitter.com/RDQLaw,
www.linkedin.com/company/669514?trk=tyah

***Vaughan*: P.M. Valenti - *1**
#300, West Bldg., 3800 Steeles Ave., Vaughan, ON L4L 4G9
Tel: 905-850-8550; *Fax:* 905-850-9998

***Vermilion Bay*: Shirley D. Gauthier - *1**
P.O. Box 490, Stn. Main, Vermilion Bay, ON P0V 2V0
Tel: 807-227-2445; *Fax:* 807-227-2902
sdg@mail.drytel.net

***Walkerton*: Van De Vyvere & Grove-McClement LLP**
Former Name: Magwood, Van De Vyvere, Thompson, & Grove-McClement LLP
P.O. Box 880, 215 Durham St. East, Walkerton, ON N0G 2V0
Tel: 519-881-3230; *Fax:* 519-881-3595

***Wallaceburg*: Carscallen, Reinhart, Mathany, Maslak - *3**
P.O. Box 409, Stn. Main, 619 James St., Wallaceburg, ON N8A 4X1
Tel: 519-627-2261; *Fax:* 519-627-1030

***Wallaceburg*: Hyde, Hyde & McGregor - *2**
233 Creek St., Wallaceburg, ON N8A 4C3
Tel: 519-627-2081; *Fax:* 519-627-1615
hhmlaw.ca

***Wasaga Beach*: Maurice Loton - *1**
P.O. Box 500, 802 Mosley St., Wasaga Beach, ON L9Z 2H4
Tel: 705-429-4332; *Fax:* 705-429-4683

***Waterdown*: Jansen Personal Injury Law - *1**
#3, P.O. Box 1436, 20 Main St. North, Waterdown, ON L0R 2H0
Tel: 905-690-2929; *Fax:* 905-690-2920
info@jansenlaw.ca
jansenlaw.ca

***Waterford*: Birnie & Gaunt - *2**
P.O. Box 429, 70 Alice St., Waterford, ON N0E 1Y0
Tel: 519-443-8676; *Fax:* 519-443-5596

***Waterford*: Cornelius A. Brennan - *1**
P.O. Box 1229, 19 Main St. South, Waterford, ON N0E 1Y0
Tel: 905-443-8643; *Fax:* 905-443-4489
neilbrennan@bellnet.ca

***Waterloo*: Amy, Appleby & Brennan - *3**
Former Name: William R. Appleby, Amy Appleby Brennan
372 Erb St. West, Waterloo, ON N2L 1W6
Tel: 519-884-7330; *Fax:* 519-884-7390
www.aab-lawoffice.com

***Waterloo*: Biggs & Gadbois - *2**
Former Name: Biggs, Richard C.
500 Dutton Dr., Waterloo, ON N2L 4C6
Tel: 519-886-1678; *Fax:* 519-886-1791
biggslaw@bellnet.ca

***Waterloo*: Blair L. Botsford - *1**
92 Erb St. East, Waterloo, ON N2J 1L9
Tel: 519-594-0936; *Fax:* 519-594-0937
blair@botsfordlaw.ca
botsfordlaw.webs.com

***Waterloo*: Chris & Volpini - *2**
375 University Ave. East, Waterloo, ON N2K 3M7
Tel: 519-888-0999; *Fax:* 519-888-0995
cvlaw@chrisvolpinilawyers.com

***Waterloo*: Dueck, Sauer, Jutzi & Noll LLP - *8**
Former Name: Dueck, Sauer, Jutzi & Noll
403 Albert St., Waterloo, ON N2L 3V2
Tel: 519-884-2620; *Fax:* 519-884-0254
info@dsjnlaw.com
www.dsjnlaw.com

***Waterloo*: W. Marlene Fitzpatrick - *1**
420 Weber St. North, Waterloo, ON N2L 4E7
Tel: 519-725-9500; *Fax:* 519-725-2379
marlenefitzpatrick@on.aibn.com

***Waterloo*: Haney, Haney & Kendall - *3**
P.O. Box 185, 41 Erb St. East, Waterloo, ON N2J 3Z9
Tel: 519-747-1010
reception@haneylaw.com
www.haneylaw.com

***Waterloo*: Fred J. Heimbecker - *1**
295 Weber St. North, Waterloo, ON N2J 3H8
Tel: 519-886-1750; *Fax:* 519-886-0503
heim@bellnet.ca

***Waterloo*: William C. Hoskinson - *1**
234 Westcourt Place, Waterloo, ON N2L 2R7
Tel: 519-571-1022; *Fax:* 519-743-0490
whoskinson@rogers.com

***Waterloo*: John E. Lang - *1**
21 Post Horn Place, Waterloo, ON N2L 5E8
Tel: 519-578-3330; *Fax:* 519-578-3337
johnelang@rogers.com

***Waterloo*: Kominek, Gladstone - *1**
28 Weber St. West, Waterloo, ON N2H 3Z2
Tel: 519-886-1050; *Fax:* 519-747-9565
glynne.gladstone2@sympatico.ca

***Waterloo*: Eric M. Kraushaar - *1**
#5, 620 Davenport Rd., Waterloo, ON N2V 2C2
Tel: 519-886-0088; *Fax:* 519-746-1122
eric@churchill-homes.com

***Waterloo*: Levesque & Deane - *2**
#5B, 490 Dutton Dr., Waterloo, ON N2L 6H7
Tel: 519-725-2929; *Fax:* 519-725-2920

***Waterloo*: Lowes, Salmon & Gadbois - *3**
500 Dutton Dr., Waterloo, ON N2L 4C6
Tel: 519-884-0800; *Fax:* 519-884-1026
Toll-Free: 877-258-2575
tlowes@watlaw.ca
www.watlaw.ca

***Waterloo*: Joe Mattes - *1**
#200, 24 Dupont St. East, Waterloo, ON N2J 2G9
Tel: 519-884-5600; *Fax:* 519-884-9963
joe@matteslaw.com
www.mattesevans.com

***Waterloo*: Peter M. Miller - *1**
15 Westmount Rd. South, Waterloo, ON N2L 2K2
Tel: 519-884-1332; *Fax:* 519-884-1161
pmiller@rogers.com
www.petermillerlaw.ca

***Waterloo*: Oldfield, Greaves, D'Agostino, Billo & Nowak - *6**
P.O. Box 16580, 172 King St. South, Waterloo, ON N2J 4X8
Tel: 519-576-7200; *Fax:* 519-576-0131
watlaw@watlaw.com
www.watlaw.com

***Waterloo*: Paquette Travers & Deutschmann - *5**
295 Weber St. North, Waterloo, ON N2J 3H8
Tel: 519-744-2281; *Fax:* 519-744-8008
Toll-Free: 877-744-2281
info@paquettetravers.com
www.paquettetravers.com

***Waterloo*: Petker & Associates - *3**
295 Weber St. North, Waterloo, ON N2J 3H8
Tel: 226-240-7736; *Fax:* 519-886-5674
Toll-Free: 800-617-5864
www.petkerlaw.com

***Waterloo*: James E. Pitcher - *1**
420 Weber St. N, Waterloo, ON N2J 4E7
Tel: 519-725-9444; *Fax:* 519-725-2379

***Waterloo*: Richard B. Strype - *2**
P.O. Box 547, 92 Erb St. East, Waterloo, ON N2J 4B8
Tel: 519-886-1590; *Fax:* 519-886-8545
rstrype@strypelaw.com

***Waterloo*: Verbanac Law Firm - *2**
#205B, 470 Weber St. North, Waterloo, ON N2L 6J2
Tel: 519-744-5588; *Fax:* 519-744-5533
info@vlawfirm.ca
www.vlawfirm.ca

***Waterloo*: White, Duncan & Linton LLP - *8**
P.O. Box 457, 45 Erb St. East, Waterloo, ON N2J 4B5
Tel: 519-886-3340; *Fax:* 519-886-8651
www.kwlaw.net

***Watford*: Wallace B. Lang - *1**
5290 Nauvoo Rd., Watford, ON N0M 2S0
Tel: 519-876-2742; *Fax:* 519-876-2073
info@wallacelang.ca
www.wallacelang.ca/en/

***Welland*: Vince Bellantino - *1**
8 East Main St., Welland, ON L3B 3W3
Tel: 905-788-3881; *Fax:* 905-788-3885
vincebel@iaw.on.ca

***Welland*: Beresh & Associates - *1**
P.O. Box 127, Stn. Main, 191 Division St., Welland, ON L3B 5P2
Tel: 905-735-1770; *Fax:* 905-735-7031

***Welland*: Blackadder Marion Wood LLP - *2**
P.O. Box 580, 136 East Main St., Welland, ON L3B 5R3
Tel: 905-735-3620; *Fax:* 905-735-1577
www.sterlingwood.ca

***Welland*: Flett Beccario - *8**
P.O. Box 340, Stn. Main, 190 Division St., Welland, ON L3B 5P9
Tel: 905-732-4481; *Fax:* 905-732-2020
Toll-Free: 866-473-5388
flett@flettbeccario.com
www.flettbeccario.com

***Welland*: William V. Frith - *1**
#301, 76 Division St., Welland, ON L3B 3Z7
Tel: 905-735-7582; *Fax:* 905-735-0093
w_firth@iaw.com

***Welland*: Houghton, Sloniowski & Stengel**
170 Division St., Welland, ON L3B 4A2
Tel: 905-734-4577; *Fax:* 905-732-3765
Toll-Free: 888-483-9770

***Welland*: Rodney J. Kajan - *1**
60 King St., Welland, ON L3B 5P2
Tel: 905-732-1352; *Fax:* 905-732-0531

***Welland*: Kormos & Evans Law Office - *1**
14 Niagara St., Welland, ON L3C 1H9
Tel: 905-732-4424; *Fax:* 905-732-7574
markevans@on.aibn.com
www.markevanslaw.com

***Welland*: Pylypuk & Associates - *2**
Former Name: Pylypuk, Anthony W.
P.O. Box 605, 80 King St., Welland, ON L3B 5R4
Tel: 905-735-2300; *Fax:* 905-735-9230
www.pylypuk.com

***Welland*: Talmage & DiFiore**
P.O. Box 97, 221 Division St., Welland, ON L3B 5P2
Tel: 905-732-4477; *Fax:* 905-732-4718
talstradi@iaw.on.ca

***Welland*: Douglas R. Thomas - *1**
9 East Main St., Welland, ON L3B 5R3
Tel: 905-732-5529; *Fax:* 905-732-2211
thomform@iaw.com

** indicates number of lawyers*

***Westport*: Barker Willson Professional Corporation - *1**
P.O. Box 309, 30 Main St., Westport, ON K0G 1X0
Tel: 613-273-3166; *Fax:* 613-273-3676
bwoffice@barkerwillson.com
www.barkerwillson.com

***Wheatley*: Joyce H. Eaton - *1**
26 Erie St. South, Wheatley, ON N0P 2P0
Tel: 519-825-7032; *Fax:* 519-825-9570
joyce.eaton@3web.net

***Whitby*: David J. Gillespie - *1**
P.O. Box 208, Stn. Main, 214 Dundas St. East, 2nd Fl., Whitby, ON L1N 5S1
Tel: 905-666-2221; *Fax:* 905-666-2344
Toll-Free: 888-880-6786
info@davidgillespie.ca
www.davidgillespie.ca/en/

***Whitby*: Howard Schneider - *1**
107 Kent St., Whitby, ON L1N 4Y1
Tel: 905-668-1677; *Fax:* 905-668-2023

***Whitby*: Stacy Howell**
916 Brock St. South, Whitby, ON L1N 8R1
Tel: 905-668-7747; *Fax:* 905-668-7787
showell@bellnet.ca

***Whitby*: Jenkins & Newman - *3**
106 Colborne St. East, Whitby, ON L1N 1V8
Tel: 905-666-8588; *Fax:* 905-666-4873
info@jenkinsandnewman.com
www.jenkinsandnewman.com

***Whitby*: Johnston Montgomery - Whitby - *3**
201 Byron St. South, Whitby, ON L1N 4P7
Tel: 905-666-2252; *Fax:* 905-430-0878
www.lawhitby.com

***Whitby*: Michaels & Michaels - *1**
#201, 1450 Hopkins St., Whitby, ON L1N 2C3
Tel: 905-665-7711; *Fax:* 905-430-9100
info@michaelslaw.ca

***Whitby*: Rosenberg, Pringle - *2**
#214, 185 Brock St. North, Whitby, ON L1N 4H3
Tel: 905-665-9594; *Fax:* 905-665-7124

***Whitby*: Edward P. Schein - *1**
107 Kent St., Whitby, ON L1N 4Y1
Tel: 905-666-1266; *Fax:* 905-668-2023

***Whitby*: Siksay & Fraser - *2**
618 Athol St., Whitby, ON L1N 3Z8
Tel: 905-666-4772; *Fax:* 905-666-3233
siksayd@rogers.com
www.siksayandfraser.com

***Whitby*: Sims Thomson & Babbs - *3**
P.O. Box 358, Stn. Main, 117 King St., Whitby, ON L1N 5S4
Tel: 905-668-7704; *Fax:* 905-668-1268

***Whitby*: B.P. Stelmach - *1**
#201, 1614 Dundas St. East, Whitby, ON L1N 8Y8
Tel: 905-430-6611; *Fax:* 905-430-6828
stelmach@bellnet.ca

***Whitby*: Debra J. Sweetman - *1**
340 Byron St. South, Whitby, ON L1N 4P8
Tel: 905-666-8166; *Fax:* 905-666-8163
debrajsweetman@aol.com
www.debrajsweetman.ca

***Wiarton*: Peter Pegg - *1**
P.O. Box 569, 647 Berford St., Wiarton, ON N0H 2T0
Tel: 519-534-2011; *Fax:* 519-534-4494
pegg@bmts.com

***Winchester*: David J. Barnhart - *1**
P.O. Box 730, 489 Main St., Winchester, ON K0C 2K0
Tel: 613-774-2808; *Fax:* 613-774-5731

***Windsor*: Ballance & Melville - *2**
#100, 251 Goyeau St., Windsor, ON N9A 6V2
Tel: 519-255-1414; *Fax:* 519-255-7404

***Windsor*: Barat, Farlam, Millson - *5**
#510, Westcourt Place, 251 Goyeau St., Windsor, ON N9A 6V2
Tel: 519-258-2424; *Fax:* 519-258-2451
reception@bfmlaw.ca
www.windsorlawyer.com

***Windsor*: Bartlet & Richardes LLP - *17**
#1000, Canada Bldg., 374 Ouellette Ave., Windsor, ON N9A 1A9
Tel: 519-253-7461; *Fax:* 519-253-2321
mail@bartlet.com
www.bartlet.com

***Windsor*: Belowus Easton English - *3**
100 Ouellette Ave., 7th Fl., Windsor, ON N9A 6T3
Tel: 519-973-1900; *Fax:* 519-973-0225

***Windsor*: Bondy, Riley, Koski LLP**
#310, 176 University Ave. West, Windsor, ON N9A 5P1
Tel: 519-258-1641; *Fax:* 519-258-1725

***Windsor*: A.J. Bradie - *2**
691 Ouellette Ave., Windsor, ON N9A 4J4
Tel: 519-255-1542; *Fax:* 519-255-9888
abradie@mnsi.net

***Windsor*: Mario Carnevale Law Office - *2**
2488 McDougall Ave., Windsor, ON N8X 3N7
Tel: 519-969-8855; *Fax:* 519-969-0085
carnevalelaw@cogeco.net
www.clolawoffice.com

***Windsor*: Maria Carroccia - *1**
#602, Canada Bldg., 374 Ouellette Ave., Windsor, ON N9A 1A8
Tel: 519-258-0905; *Fax:* 519-258-8755
Toll-Free: 888-959-9917

***Windsor*: F. Michael Cervi - *1**
#400, 1500 Ouellette Ave., Windsor, ON N8X 1K7
Tel: 519-258-9494; *Fax:* 519-258-9985
michaelcervi@on.aibn.com

***Windsor*: Chodola Reynolds Binder - *6**
720 Walker Rd., Windsor, ON N8Y 2N3
Tel: 519-254-6433; *Fax:* 519-254-7990
www.crblaw.ca
www.facebook.com/pages/Windsor-Lawyers/130689596945631,
www.linkedin.com/company/chodola-reynolds-binder

***Windsor*: Clarks LLP - *7**
Former Name: Clarks, Barristers & Solicitors
#1200, Canada Bldg., 374 Ouellette Ave., Windsor, ON N9A 1A8
Tel: 519-254-4990; *Fax:* 519-254-2294
www.clarkslaw.com

***Windsor*: Robert J. Comartin - *1**
350 Devonshire Rd., Windsor, ON N8Y 2L4
Tel: 519-253-7050; *Fax:* 519-253-7049

***Windsor*: Crown Attorney's Office - *1**
200 Chatham St. E, 5th Fl., Windsor, ON N9A 2W3
Tel: 519-253-1104; *Fax:* 519-253-1813
russ.cornett@ontario.ca

***Windsor*: John Paul Corrent - *5**
Former Name: Corrent & Macri
#201, 2485 Ouellette Ave., Windsor, ON N8X 1L5
Tel: 519-255-7332; *Fax:* 519-255-9123
jcorrent@correntmacri.com
www.jpcorrent.com
www.facebook.com/pages/John-Paul-Corrent-BA-LLB-Barrister/244754925562764,
ca.linkedin.com/pub/john-paul-corrent/3b/469/b8a

***Windsor*: Culmone Law - *1**
410 Giles Blvd. East, Windsor, ON N9A 4C6
Tel: 519-258-3632; *Fax:* 519-977-1199
floro@culmonelaw.com
www.culmonelaw.com

***Windsor*: D'hondt & Connor - *3**
#260, 2109 Ottawa St., Windsor, ON N8Y 1R8
Tel: 519-258-8220; *Fax:* 519-258-7788

***Windsor*: David Deluzio Law Firm - *1**
#200, 52 Chatham St. West, Windsor, ON N9A 5M6
Tel: 519-256-1994; *Fax:* 519-256-7233

***Windsor*: Robert M. DiPietro - *1**
#302, 380 Ouellette Ave., Windsor, ON N9A 6X5
Tel: 519-258-8248; *Fax:* 519-255-7685
robertdipietro@bellnet.ca

***Windsor*: Jon Dobrowolski - *1**
#309, Westcourt Place, 251 Goyeau St., Windsor, ON N9A 6V2
Tel: 519-258-0034; *Fax:* 519-258-9133

***Windsor*: Donaldson, Donaldson, Greenaway - *5**
547 Devonshire Rd., Windsor, ON N8Y 2L6
Tel: 519-255-7333; *Fax:* 519-255-7173
ddglaw@on.aibn.com

***Windsor*: Ducharme Fox LLP - *4**
800 University Ave. West, Windsor, ON N9A 5R9
Tel: 519-259-1800; *Fax:* 519-259-1830
info@ducharmefox.com
www.ducharmefox.com

***Windsor*: Fazio Giorgi LLP - *3**
333 Wyandotte St. East, Windsor, ON N9A 3H7
Tel: 519-258-5030; *Fax:* 519-971-9051
accounting@faziogiorgi.com
www.faziogiorgi.com

***Windsor*: Julie Fodor - *1**
3085 Longfellow Ave., Windsor, ON N9E 2L4
Tel: 519-256-8238; *Fax:* 519-258-5780
jfoder.law@bellnet.ca

***Windsor*: Gatti Law Professional Corporation - *2**
Also Known As: Lisa Carnelos
#400, 267 Pelissier St., Windsor, ON N9A 4K4
Tel: 519-258-1010; *Fax:* 519-258-0163
arg@argatti.com

***Windsor*: Goldstein DeBiase Manzocco, The Personal Injury Law Firm - *5**
#900, 176 University Ave. West, Windsor, ON N9A 5P1
Tel: 519-253-5242; *Fax:* 519-253-0218
gdm@thepersonalinjurylawfirm.net
www.thepersonalinjurylawfirm.net

***Windsor*: Goulin & Patrick - *1**
500 Windsor Ave., Windsor, ON N9A 6Y5
Tel: 519-258-8073; *Fax:* 519-977-0694
www.goulinpatricklawyer.com

***Windsor*: Greg Monforton and Partners - *8**
Former Name: Monforton, Robitaille, & Skipper
#801, 1 Riverside Dr. West, Windsor, ON N9A 5K3
Tel: 519-258-6490; *Fax:* 519-258-4104
Toll-Free: 800-663-1145
www.gregmonforton.com
www.facebook.com/GregMonfortonPartners?ref=hl,
twitter.com/GregMonforton,
www.linkedin.com/pub/greg-monforton/6b/954/b73

***Windsor*: Jason P. Howie - *1**
350 Devonshire Rd., Windsor, ON N8Y 2L4
Tel: 519-800-1039; *Fax:* 519-973-9905
Toll-Free: 800-335-7511
www.jasonpaulhowie.com
www.facebook.com/profile.php?id=390984134328940,
www.linkedin.com/company/1605795

***Windsor*: Hulka Porter LLP - *3**
#200, 110 Tecumseh Rd. East, Windsor, ON N8X 2P8
Tel: 519-254-5952; *Fax:* 519-254-3957
Toll-Free: 800-263-8723
enquire@hulkaporter.com
www.hulkaporter.com

***Windsor*: Kamin, Fisher, Burnett, Ziriada & Robertson - *5**
#200, 176 University Ave. West, Windsor, ON N9A 5P1
Tel: 519-252-1123; *Fax:* 519-977-6503
info@kaminlaw.ca

***Windsor*: Katzman, Wylupek LLP - *5**
1427 Ouellette Ave., Windsor, ON N8X 1K1
Tel: 519-254-4878; *Fax:* 519-254-6774
www.katzman-wylupek.com

***Windsor*: Kirwin Partners LLP - *10**
423 Pelissier St., Windsor, ON N9A 4L2
Tel: 519-255-9840; *Fax:* 519-255-1413
www.kirwinpartners.com

***Windsor*: Kyrtsakas Law Office - *1**
5655 Tecumseh Rd. East, Windsor, ON N8T 1C8
Tel: 519-974-6303; *Fax:* 519-974-8644
www.kyrtsakaslaw.com

***Windsor*: Lisa S. Labute - *1**
#444, 251 Goyeau St., Windsor, ON N9A 6V2
Tel: 519-252-6822; *Fax:* 519-252-2638
lslabute@mnsi.net

** indicates number of lawyers*

***Windsor*: Legal Assistance of Windsor - *3**
Former Name: Brian Rodenhurst
85 Pitt St. East, Windsor, ON N9A 2V3
Tel: 519-256-7831; *Fax:* 519-256-1387
www.uwindsor.ca/legalassistanceofwindsor

***Windsor*: Anthony R. Mariotti - *1**
#202, 176 University Ave. West, Windsor, ON N9A 5P1
Tel: 519-258-1931; *Fax:* 519-973-7575
arm.law@sympatico.ca

***Windsor*: Brenda A. McGinty - *1**
518 Victoria Ave., Windsor, ON N9A 4M8
Tel: 519-255-1535; *Fax:* 519-255-1719

***Windsor*: McTague Law Firm LLP - *31**
455 Pelissier St., Windsor, ON N9A 6Z9
Tel: 519-255-4300; *Fax:* 519-255-4360
info@mctaguelaw.com
www.mctaguelaw.com

***Windsor*: Melanie J. McWilliams - *1**
#710, 100 Ouellette Ave., Windsor, ON N9A 6T3
Tel: 519-258-1100; *Fax:* 519-258-7384
mjmcwilliams@winlaw.ca

***Windsor*: Tullio Meconi - *1**
349 Wyandotte St. East, Windsor, ON N9A 3H7
Tel: 519-252-7274

***Windsor*: Donald D. Merritt - *1**
#103, 525 Windsor Ave., Windsor, ON N9A 1J4
Tel: 519-258-8060; *Fax:* 519-258-9877
merritt2@mnsi.net

***Windsor*: Miller Canfield LLP (Ontario) - *21**
Former Name: Miller Canfield Paddock & Stone LLP; Miller Canfield Paddock & Stone - Wilson Walker
#1300, 100 Ouellette Ave., Windsor, ON N9A 6T3
Tel: 519-946-2123; *Fax:* 519-946-2133
www.millercanfield.com
www.facebook.com/MillerCanfield, twitter.com/millercanfield, www.linkedin.com/company/miller-canfield

***Windsor*: S. Frank Miller - *1**
560 Chatham St. West, Windsor, ON N9A 5N2
Tel: 519-258-3044; *Fax:* 519-258-2350
frankmilleratlaw@earthlink.net

***Windsor*: Joana G. Miskinis - *1**
518 Victoria Ave., Windsor, ON N9A 4M8
Tel: 519-254-3757; *Fax:* 519-255-1719
joanamiskinis@hotmail.com

***Windsor*: Mousseau DeLuca McPherson Prince LLP - *11**
#500, Westcourt Place, 251 Goyeau, Windsor, ON N9A 6V2
Tel: 519-258-0615; *Fax:* 519-258-6833
lawyers@mousseaulaw.com
www.mousseaulaw.com

***Windsor*: Michael P. O'Hearn - *1**
#A-1, P.O. Box 1212, Stn. A, 75 Riverside Dr. East, Windsor, ON N9A 6P8
Tel: 519-255-1250; *Fax:* 519-971-9607
mike.ohearn@sympatico.ca

***Windsor*: John G. Ohler - *2**
101 Tecumseh Rd. West, Windsor, ON N8X 1E8
Tel: 519-256-5496; *Fax:* 519-256-1492
ohlerlawfirm@bellnet.ca

***Windsor*: James W. Oxley**
1854 Kildare Rd., Windsor, ON N8W 2W7
Tel: 519-258-7211

***Windsor*: Paroian Skipper Lawyers - *3**
2510 Ouellette Ave., Windsor, ON N8X 1L4
Tel: 519-250-0894; *Fax:* 519-966-1869
skipper@therightcall.ca
therightcall.ca

***Windsor*: Peter Hrastovec Professional Corporation - *1**
2510 Ouellette Ave., Windsor, ON N8X 1L4
Tel: 519-966-1300; *Fax:* 519-966-1079
www.peterlaw.ca

***Windsor*: Derek R. Revait - *1**
#209, Royal Windsor Terrace, 380 Pelissier, Windsor, ON N9A 6W8
Tel: 519-258-7030; *Fax:* 519-258-2629
derek.revait@bellnet.ca

***Windsor*: Salem, McCullough & Gibson Professional Corp. - *2**
2828 Howard Ave., Windsor, ON N8X 3Y3
Tel: 519-966-3633; *Fax:* 519-972-7788
info@salemmcculloughgibson.com
www.salemmcculloughgibson.com

***Windsor*: Daniel W. Scott - *1**
#302, 380 Ouellette Ave., Windsor, ON N9A 6X5
Tel: 519-258-8248; *Fax:* 519-255-7685
donscott@bellnet.ca

***Windsor*: Stephen L. Shanfield - *1**
#333, 880 Ouellette Ave., Windsor, ON N9A 1C7
Tel: 519-258-3338; *Fax:* 519-258-3335

***Windsor*: Brian Sherwell - *1**
827 Pillette Rd., Windsor, ON N8Y 3B4
Tel: 519-945-1109; *Fax:* 519-948-0003

***Windsor*: Sorensen Baker Professional Corporation - *2**
1600 Wyandotte St. East, Windsor, ON N8Y 1C7
Tel: 519-256-3111; *Fax:* 519-256-5468
baker@cogeco.net
www.facebook.com/Sorensen.Baker

***Windsor*: R. Craig Stevenson - *1**
#18A, 25 Amy Croft Dr.., Windsor, ON N9K 1C7
Tel: 519-735-0777; *Fax:* 519-735-2999
rcslaw@mnsi.net
www.rcraigstevensonlawoffice.com

***Windsor*: Stipic, Arpino, Weisman LLP - *14**
1574 Ouellette Ave., Windsor, ON N8X 1K7
Tel: 519-258-3201; *Fax:* 519-258-2665
sawlawyers.com

***Windsor*: Tamara Stomp & Associate - *2**
721 Walker Rd., Windsor, ON N8Y 2N2
Tel: 519-948-9778; *Fax:* 519-948-9773
stomp@mnsi.net

***Windsor*: Sutts, Strosberg LLP - *17**
#600, 251 Goyeau St., Windsor, ON N9A 6V4
Tel: 519-258-9333; *Fax:* 519-258-9527
Toll-Free: 866-316-5311
www.strosbergco.com

***Windsor*: Gary V. Wortley - *1**
2490 Talbot Rd., Windsor, ON N9H 1A6
Tel: 519-967-9410; *Fax:* 519-967-9431
wortley@jet2.net

***Windsor*: Martin Wunder, Q.C. - *1**
#908, 100 Ouellette Ave., Windsor, ON N9A 6T3
Tel: 519-252-1121

***Woodbridge*: Gary A. Beaulne - *2**
#401, 3700 Steeles Ave. West, Woodbridge, ON L4L 8K8
Tel: 905-850-5060; *Fax:* 905-850-5066
Toll-Free: 866-850-5006
gary@garyabeaulne.com
www.garyabeaulne.com

***Woodbridge*: Frank Borgatti - *1**
7135 Islington Ave., 2nd Fl., Woodbridge, ON L4L 1V9
Tel: 905-851-2883; *Fax:* 905-851-2887

***Woodbridge*: Roger Bourque - *1**
#300, 3800 Steeles Ave. West, Woodbridge, ON L4L 4G9
Tel: 905-856-7101; *Fax:* 905-856-1524
rogerbourque@bellnet.ca

***Woodbridge*: Capo Sgro LLP - *13**
#400, 7050 Weston Rd., Woodbridge, ON L4L 8G7
Tel: 905-850-7000; *Fax:* 905-850-7050
www.csllp.ca

***Woodbridge*: Ralph Ciccia - *1**
#400, 7050 Weston Rd., Woodbridge, ON L4L 8G7
Tel: 905-850-6408; *Fax:* 905-850-7050
rciccia@ciccia.ca

***Woodbridge*: Cosman & Associates - *2**
Former Name: Cosman, Gray LLP
#37, 111 Zenway, Woodbridge, ON L4H 3H9
Tel: 905-850-3110; *Fax:* 905-850-3123
cosmanlaw.com
www.facebook.com/CosmanAssociates, twitter.com/infocosman

***Woodbridge*: D'Alimonte Law - *1**
#27, 4300 Steeles Ave. W, Woodbridge, ON L4L 4C2
Tel: 905-264-1553; *Fax:* 905-264-5450
jdalimonte@bellnet.ca

***Woodbridge*: M. DiPaolo - *1**
#400, 7050 Weston Rd., Woodbridge, ON L4L 8G7
Tel: 905-850-7575; *Fax:* 905-850-7050
mdipaolo@di-paolo.ca

***Woodbridge*: Michael A. Handler - *1**
#101, 10 Director Crt., Woodbridge, ON L4L 7E8
Tel: 905-265-2252; *Fax:* 905-265-2235
mhandler@mhandlerlaw.com

***Woodbridge*: Hans Law Firm - *1**
#305, 216 Chrislea Rd., Woodbridge, ON L4L 8S5
Tel: 905-790-0092; *Fax:* 905-605-1079
hanslaw.com

***Woodbridge*: Thomas F. Kowal - *1**
#906, 3700 Steeles Ave. West, Woodbridge, ON L4L 8K8
Tel: 905-856-5855

***Woodbridge*: Mancini Associates LLP - *3**
#505, 7050 Weston Rd., Woodbridge, ON L4L 8G7
Tel: 905-851-7717; *Fax:* 905-851-7718

***Woodbridge*: Massimo Panicali - *1**
#4, 253 Jevlan Dr., Woodbridge, ON L4L 7Z6
Tel: 905-850-2642; *Fax:* 905-850-8544
mass.pan-demonium@on.aibn.com

***Woodbridge*: Paradiso & Associates - *1**
#504, 216 Chrislea Rd., Woodbridge, ON L4L 8S5
Tel: 905-850-6006; *Fax:* 905-850-5616
Toll-Free: 800-429-735
mail@paradisolaw.com
www.paradisolaw.com

***Woodbridge*: Piccin Bottos - *6**
#201, 4370 Steeles Ave. West, Woodbridge, ON L4L 4Y4
Tel: 905-850-0155; *Fax:* 905-850-0498
pb@piccinbottos.com
www.piccinbottos.com

***Woodbridge*: Felix Rocca - *1**
#302, 7050 Weston Rd., Woodbridge, ON L4L 8G7
Tel: 905-851-7747; *Fax:* 905-851-7834
felixrocca@rogers.com

***Woodbridge*: Rovazzi, Pallotta - *3**
#901, 3700 Steeles Ave. West, Woodbridge, ON L4L 8K8
Tel: 905-850-2468; *Fax:* 905-850-4066

***Woodbridge*: Devi D. Sharma - *1**
#625, 7050 Weston Rd., Woodbridge, ON L4L 8G7
Tel: 905-856-6404; *Fax:* 905-856-6264

***Woodbridge*: Stabile Professional Corporation - *2**
Former Name: Stabile Partners
#905, 3700 Steeles Ave. West, Woodbridge, ON L4L 8K8
Tel: 905-851-6711; *Fax:* 905-851-5773
vista@stablaw.com

***Woodbridge*: Tanzola & Sorbara - *3**
#101, 10 Director Ct., Woodbridge, ON L4L 7E8
Tel: 905-265-2252; *Fax:* 905-265-0667
www.tanzola-sorbara.net

***Woodbridge*: Turner, Brooks - *1**
Former Name: Turner, Brooks Associates
#15, 4220 Steeles Ave. West, Woodbridge, ON L4L 3S8
Tel: 416-213-0524
sturner.barrister@bellnet.ca

***Woodbridge*: Weston Law Chambers - *9**
Also Known As: Weston Law
#600, 3700 Steeles Ave. West, Woodbridge, ON L4L 8K8
Tel: 905-856-3700; *Fax:* 905-856-1213
info@westonlaw.ca
www.westonlaw.ca

***Woodstock*: George H. Bishop - *1**
557 Adelaide St., Woodstock, ON N4S 4B7
Tel: 519-539-8559; *Fax:* 519-539-2401
angie-bishoplaw@rogers.com

***Woodstock*: Gregory W. Boddy - *1**
Former Name: Beatty Stock & Lemon
P.O. Box 336, 487 Princess St., Woodstock, ON N4S 7X6
Tel: 519-537-6629; *Fax:* 519-539-2459

***Woodstock*: Debra A. Brown - *1**
94 Graham St., Woodstock, ON N4S 6J7
Tel: 519-539-9870; *Fax:* 519-539-9248
debra@dabrownlaw.com

** indicates number of lawyers*

***Woodstock*: Peter H. Kratzmann - *1**
372 Hunter St., Woodstock, ON N4S 6E2
Tel: 519-537-2221; *Fax:* 519-537-5150
phklaw@primus.ca

***Woodstock*: Gordon Lemon - *1**
530 Adelaide St., Woodstock, ON N4S 8X8
Tel: 519-537-5555; *Fax:* 519-537-8609
glemon@beattylaw.on.ca

***Woodstock*: Gary D. McQuaid - *1**
380 Hunter St., Woodstock, ON N4S 4G2
Tel: 519-539-1310

***Woodstock*: White Coad LLP - *3**
P.O. Box 1059, 5 Wellington St. North, Woodstock, ON N4S 6P1
Tel: 519-421-1500; *Fax:* 519-539-6926
main@whitecoad.com
www.whitecoad.com

***Woodstock*: R.B. Wolyniuk - *3**
19 Riddell St., Woodstock, ON N4S 6L9
Tel: 519-539-7431; *Fax:* 519-539-4975

Prince Edward Island

***Charlottetown*: Campbell Lea Barristers & Solicitors - *9**
#400, P.O. Box 429, 15 Queen St., Charlottetown, PE C1A 7K7
Tel: 902-566-3400; *Fax:* 902-367-3713
www.campbelllea.com

***Charlottetown*: Carr, Stevenson & MacKay - *9**
Peake House, P.O. Box 522, 50 Water St., Charlottetown, PE C1A 7L1
Tel: 902-892-4156; *Fax:* 902-566-1377
csm@csmlaw.com
www.csmlaw.com

***Charlottetown*: Kenneth A. Clark Law Office - *1**
P.O. Box 2831, Stn. Central, 155 Queen St., 2nd Fl., Charlottetown, PE C1A 4B4
Tel: 902-566-9996; *Fax:* 902-566-9997

***Charlottetown*: Peter C. Ghiz - *1**
240 Pownal St., Charlottetown, PE C1A 3X1
Tel: 902-628-6300; *Fax:* 902-628-6399
Toll-Free: 800-399-3221
peterghiz@peterghizlawyer.com
www.petercghizlawcorporation.com

***Charlottetown*: Macnutt & Dumont - *3**
P.O. Box 965, 57 Water St., Charlottetown, PE C1A 7M4
Tel: 902-894-5003; *Fax:* 902-368-3782
www.macnuttdumont.ca

***Charlottetown*: Matheson & Murray - *9**
#202, P.O. Box 875, 119 Queen St., Charlottetown, PE C1A 7I9
Tel: 902-894-7051; *Fax:* 902-368-3762
charlottetown@keymurraylaw.com
www.mathesonandmurray.com

***Charlottetown*: Philip Mullally Q.C. - *1**
P.O. Box 2560, Stn. Central, 51 University Ave., Charlottetown, PE C1A 8C2
Tel: 902-892-5452; *Fax:* 902-892-7013
mullallyphiliplawoffice-charlottetown.onlinepei.com

***Charlottetown*: Paul J.D. Mullin Q.C. - *1**
P.O. Box 604, Stn. Central, 14 Great George St., Charlottetown, PE C1A 7L3
Tel: 902-368-3221; *Fax:* 902-894-7491
mullinlaw@pei.aibn.com

***Charlottetown*: Brenda J. Picard - *1**
P.O. Box 2000, Stn. Central, 40 Great George St., Charlottetown, PE C1A 7N8
Tel: 902-368-6043; *Fax:* 902-368-6122
bjpicard@gov.pe.ca

***Charlottetown*: Elizabeth S. Reagh Q.C. - *1**
17 West St., Charlottetown, PE C1A 3S3
Tel: 902-892-7667; *Fax:* 902-368-8629
reagh@isn.net

***Mount Stewart*: Marlene R. Clarke Q.C. - *1**
P.O. Box 63, Mount Stewart, PE C0A 1T0
Tel: 902-676-2954

***Summerside*: Kathleen Loo Craig - *1**
P.O. Box 11, Stn. Main, Summerside, PE C1N 4P6
Tel: 902-887-2900; *Fax:* 902-887-2100

***Summerside*: Lyle & McCabe - *2**
P.O. Box 300, 193 Arnett Ave., Summerside, PE C1N 4Y8
Tel: 902-436-4296; *Fax:* 902-436-4072
www.lylemccabelawoffice.com

***Summerside*: Robert McNeill - *1**
251 Water St., Summerside, PE C1N 1B5
Tel: 902-436-4847; *Fax:* 902-436-8183

Québec

***Alma*: Sandra Bouchard, Avocate - *1**
Palais de Justice, 725 Harvey ouest, Alma, QC G8B 1P5
Tél: 418-668-3334; *Téléc:* 418-662-3697

***Alma*: Larouche Lalancette Pilote, Avocats s.e.n.r.c.l. - *7**
Former Name: Larouche, Lalancette, Pilote & Bouchard
660, boul de Quen nord, Alma, QC G8B 6H5
Tél: 418-662-6475; *Téléc:* 418-662-9239
www.llpavocats.com

***Amos*: Bigué avocats - *6**
Former Name: Bigué & Bigué
91, 1re av ouest, Amos, QC J9T 1T7
Tél: 819-732-8911; *Téléc:* 819-732-1470
www.bigueavocats.com

***Amos*: McGuire Dussault et Associés - *2**
39A, av 1re ouest, Amos, QC J9T 1T7
Tél: 819-732-5258; *Téléc:* 819-732-0394

***Asbestos*: Denis Beaubien Avocat - *1**
601, boul Simoneau, Asbestos, QC J1T 4G7
Tél: 819-879-7177; *Téléc:* 819-879-2962
beaubienavocat@cgicavke.ca

***Beauport*: Blouin & Associés - *3**
1217, av Royal, Beauport, QC G1E 2B2
Tél: 418-663-2931; *Téléc:* 418-663-3792

***Beloeil*: Bastien, Morand & Associés - *7**
201, boul Laurier, Beloeil, QC J3G 4G8
Tél: 450-467-5849; *Téléc:* 450-467-3152
Ligne sans frais: 877-467-5849
info@bastienmorand.com
www.bastienmorand.com/en/

***Beloeil*: Doré, Tourigny, Mallette & Associés - *5**
#201, 347 rue Duvernay, Beloeil, QC J3G 5S8
Tél: 450-446-8474; *Téléc:* 450-467-7134

***Berthierville*: André Sylvestre**
1300, rue Notre Dame, Berthierville, QC J0K 1A0
Tél: 450-836-6213; *Téléc:* 450-836-7712
andre_sylvestre@bellnet.ca

***Boucherville*: Lecompte Deguire Avocats - *2**
1019, rue de la Ventrouze, Boucherville, QC J4B 5V3
Tél: 450-641-0065; *Téléc:* 450-641-3721
lecomptedeguire@videotron.ca

***Brossard*: Lord & Associes - *6**
#204, 5855 boul Taschereau, Brossard, QC J4Z 1A5
Tél: 514-990-2803; *Téléc:* 450-672-5320

***Chicoutimi*: Allard Gaston - *3**
Former Name: Girard Allard Guimond Avocats
#202, 200, rue Racine est, Chicoutimi, QC G7H 1S1
Tél: 418-543-0725; *Téléc:* 418-543-1765

***Châteauguay*: Marie-Andrée Mallette - *1**
272, boul St-Jean-Baptiste, Châteauguay, QC J6K 3C2
Tél: 450-699-9499; *Téléc:* 450-699-9710
marieandreemallette@videotron.ca

***Cowansville*: Claude Boulet - *1**
#330, 104, rue du Sud, Cowansville, QC J2K 2X2
Tél: 450-263-0061; *Téléc:* 450-263-9468
c.boulet@endirect.qc.ca

***Dolbeau-Mistassini*: Bouchard Voyer Boily - *3**
Former Name: Bouchard & Voyer
1273, boul Wallberg, Dolbeau-Mistassini, QC G8L 1H3
Tél: 418-276-2234; *Téléc:* 418-276-3582
bvb@bellnet.ca

***Dolbeau-Mistassini*: Simard Boivin Lemieux Avocats - *5**
Former Name: Boivin, Lussier, Hébert
112, av de l'Église, Dolbeau-Mistassini, QC G8L 4W4
Tél: 418-276-2570; *Téléc:* 418-276-8797
Ligne sans frais: 877-276-2570
dolmis@sblavocats.com
www.sblavocats.com

***Donnacona*: Bernatchez Associés - Avocats - *1**
Former Name: Yves Bernatchez
#120, 100, rte 138, Donnacona, QC G3M 1B5
Tél: 418-462-1010; *Téléc:* 418-462-1011
avocats@avoc.ca
www.avoc.ca
www.facebook.com/BernatchezAssociesAvocats,
www.twitter.com/BernatchezAvoc,
www.linkedin.com/company/2655304

***Donnacona*: Claude Dussault - *1**
220, av Ste-Marie, Donnacona, QC G3M 2M2
Tél: 418-284-4841

***Dorval*: Amaron, Viberg & Pecho - *1**
#200, 280, av Dorval, Dorval, QC H9S 3H4
Tél: 514-636-4992; *Téléc:* 514-636-8122

***Drummondville*: Paul Biron, Avocat - *1**
Former Name: Biron, Nilsson
#202, 150, rue Marchand, Drummondville, QC J2C 4N1
Tél: 819-477-8741; *Téléc:* 819-477-7166

***Drummondville*: Boudreau, Méthot, Tourigny - *2**
Former Name: Boudreau, Méthot
83, rue St-Damase, Drummondville, QC J2B 6E5
Tél: 819-477-3517; *Téléc:* 819-477-0700

***Drummondville*: Hinse Tousignant et Associés - *3**
360, rue Marchand, Drummondville, QC J2C 4N9
Tél: 819-477-3424; *Téléc:* 819-477-7728
Ligne sans frais: 888-488-3424
hinsetousignant@bellnet.ca
www.hinsetousignantavocats.com

***Drummondville*: Jutras et Associés - *4**
449, rue Hériot, Drummondville, QC J2B 1B4
Tél: 819-477-6321; *Téléc:* 819-474-5691
info@jutras.ca
www.jutras.ca

***Gatineau*: Jean-Paul Aubry - *1**
175, rue Champlain, Gatineau, QC J8X 3R3
Tél: 819-771-8645; *Téléc:* 819-771-9338

***Gatineau*: Christine M. Auger - *1**
#200, 525 boul Maloney est, Gatineau, QC J8P 1E8
Tél: 819-770-4022; *Téléc:* 819-669-9627

***Gatineau*: Beaudry, Bertrand, s.e.n.c.r.l.**
#107, 160, boul de l'Hôpital, Gatineau, QC J8T 8J1
Tel: 819-770-4880; *Fax:* 819-595-4979
www.beaudry-bertrand.com

***Gatineau*: Robert Bélanger, Avocat - *1**
307, boul Saint-Joseph, Gatineau, QC J8Y 3Y6
Tél: 819-771-6679; *Téléc:* 819-771-9675
robert.belanger.avocat@sympatico.ca

***Gatineau*: Pierre Fontaine - *1**
25, rue Bernier, Gatineau, QC J8Z 1E7
Tél: 819-771-6578
pierre14f@yahoo.ca

***Gatineau*: Gaudreau - *2**
167, rue Notre-Dame-de-l'Ile, Gatineau, QC J8X 3T3
Tél: 819-770-7928; *Téléc:* 819-770-1424
bergeron.gaudreau@qc.aira.com

***Gatineau*: André Gingras - *1**
30, rue Maricourt, Gatineau, QC J29 1R9
Tél: 819-595-4748; *Téléc:* 819-772-4193
mariannamerica@videotron.ca

***Gatineau*: Leduc, Bouthillette - *9**
#301, 200, rue Montcalm, Gatineau, QC J8Y 3B5
Tél: 819-778-1870; *Téléc:* 819-778-8860
LB@auocats.ca

***Gatineau*: Letellier - Gosselin - *8**
#127, 139, boul de l'Hôpital, Gatineau, QC J8T 8A3
Tél: 819-243-1336; *Téléc:* 819-243-9425
mgosselin@letellier.com
www.letellier.com

** indicates number of lawyers*

***Gatineau*: Lora, Houle, Jacques - *3**
Former Name: Lora, E. Wayne
175, rue Champlain, Gatineau, QC J8X 3R3
Tél: 819-778-6511; *Téléc:* 819-770-5703
wlora@mac.com

***Gatineau*: Pharand Joyal - *5**
166, rue Wellington, Gatineau, QC J8X 2J4
Tél: 819-771-7781; *Téléc:* 819-771-0608
pharand.joyal@qc.aira.com

***Gatineau*: Ste-Marie & Lacombe - *2**
175, rue Champlain, Gatineau, QC J8X 3R3
Tél: 819-770-7800; *Téléc:* 819-770-5703

***Gatineau*: Sarrazin & Charlebois - *2**
162, rue Wellington, Gatineau, QC J8X 2J4
Tél: 819-770-4888; *Téléc:* 819-770-0712
sarrazin-charlebois@videotron.ca

***Gracefield*: Louise Major - *1**
40, rue Principale, Gracefield, QC J0X 1W0
Tél: 819-463-3477; *Téléc:* 819-463-4603
lmajor@notarius.net

***Granby*: Gaudet Galipeau Parcel - Avocats - *5**
Former Name: Gaudet & Associés
18, rue Court, Granby, QC J2G 4Y5
Tél: 450-777-1070; *Téléc:* 450-777-5960
www.gaudetavocats.com

***Granby*: Daniel Laflamme - *1**
#200, 328, rue Principale, Granby, QC J2G 2W4
Tél: 450-372-3545

***Granby*: Gilles Viens - *1**
#204, 160 rue Principale, Granby, QC J2G 2V6
Tél: 450-770-2121; *Téléc:* 450-770-0088
gilles@fournierleclerc.ca

***Hampstead*: Judith Lifshitz - *1**
30, ch Belsize, Hampstead, QC H3X 3J8
Tél: 514-488-8561; *Téléc:* 514-488-0121

***Joliette*: Asselin, Asselin & Germain - *4**
569, rue Archambault, Joliette, QC J6E 2W7
Tél: 450-755-5050; *Téléc:* 450-755-5111
info@asgavocats.ca
www.asgavocats.ca

***Joliette*: Boulard & Richer - Avocates - *2**
198, rue St-Joseph, Joliette, QC J6E 5C6
Tél: 450-753-8360; *Téléc:* 450-753-8359
boulard_richer_sb@videotron.ca
www.boulardetricheravocates.com

***Joliette*: Claudette Vincelette - *1**
Former Name: Vincelette, Marois
125, rue Beaudry nord, Joliette, QC J6E 6A4
Tél: 450-759-3958; *Téléc:* 450-756-2933

***Kahnawake*: Mohawk Council of Kahnawake Legal Services - *4**
CP 720, Kahnawake, QC J0L 1B0
Tél: 450-632-7500; *Téléc:* 450-638-3663
communications@mck.ca
www.kahnawake.com
www.facebook.com/profile.php?id=100001092086286,
www.twitter.com/mckahnawake

***L'Île-Perrot*: Aumais Chartrand - Avocats - *6**
#12, 100, boul Don Quichotte, L'Île-Perrot, QC J7V 6L7
Tél: 514-425-2233; *Téléc:* 514-453-0977

***La Malbaie*: Marie-Claude Dallaire - *1**
#220, CP 237, 251, rue John-Nairne, La Malbaie, QC G5A 1M4
Tél: 418-665-6417; *Téléc:* 418-665-6174
marieclaude.dallaire@ccjg.qc.ca

***Lac-Beauport*: Alain Baccigalupo - *1**
27, ch le Tour du Lac, Lac-Beauport, QC G0A 2C0
Tél: 418-849-0396; *Téléc:* 418-656-7861

***Lac-Mégantic*: Daniel Drouin - *1**
4927, rue Laval, Lac-Mégantic, QC G6B 1E2
Tél: 819-583-0787; *Téléc:* 819-583-4631
ddrouin@notarius.net

***Lac-Simon*: Sylvie Savoie - *1**
1428, ch Du Tour-Du-Lac, Lac-Simon, QC J5A 2G9
Tél: 819-428-9366

***Lachine*: Louise Saint-Amour - *1**
#3, 1375, rue Notre-Dame, Lachine, QC H8S 2C9
Tél: 514-634-8243; *Téléc:* 514-634-3044
saintamourlouise@yahoo.ca

***Lachute*: William M.C. Steeves - *1**
18, boul de la Providence, Lachute, QC J8H 3K9
Tél: 450-562-2465; *Téléc:* 450-562-2467

***Laval*: Alepin Gauthier Avocats Inc - *20**
#601, 3080, boul Le Carrefour, Laval, QC H7T 2R5
Tél: 450-681-3080; *Téléc:* 450-681-1476
info@alepin.com
www.alepin.com
www.facebook.com/pages/Montreal-QC/Alepin-Gauthier-Avocats/142951296656, twitter.com/AlepinGauthier

***Laval*: Bélanger, Garceau - *2**
#309, 400, boul St-Martin ouest, Laval, QC H7M 3Y8
Tél: 450-669-1313; *Téléc:* 450-669-1122
belangergarceau@videotron.ca

***Laval*: François Bordeleau - *1**
60, rue Alexandre, Laval, QC H7G 3K9
Ligne sans frais: 877-975-2060

***Laval*: Cholette Côté & associés Avocats - *6**
#650, 1, Place Laval, Laval, QC H7N 1A1
Tél: 450-668-0888; *Téléc:* 450-668-0048
info@cholettecote.com
www.cholettecote.com

***Laval*: France Cormier - *1**
3682, rue Isabelle, Laval, QC H7P 4Z6
Tél: 450-622-7616; *Téléc:* 450-622-5254
francecormier@videotron.ca

***Laval*: Dagenais, Poupart - *3**
#650, 2550, boul Daniel-Johnson, Laval, QC H7T 2L1
Tél: 450-978-2442; *Téléc:* 450-973-4010

***Laval*: Fournier, Diamond - *2**
#1102, 2500, boul Daniel-Johnson, Laval, QC H7T 2P6
Tél: 450-682-7011; *Téléc:* 450-686-8566

***Laval*: Michel B. Fournier - *1**
#204, 4150, boul St-Martin ouest, Laval, QC H7T 1C1
Tél: 450-686-2600; *Téléc:* 450-681-8642
mb.fournier@sympatico.ca

***Laval*: Massicott & Guérard - *3**
134, boul. des Laurentides, Laval, QC H7G 2T3
Tél: 450-663-0851

***Laval*: Jean Mignault - *1**
#2020, 400 boul. Armand Frappier, Laval, QC H7V 4B4
Tél: 514-332-4110; *Téléc:* 514-334-6043
jean.mignault@2020.net

***Laval*: Pierre Lamarche - *1**
237A, boul des Prairies, Laval, QC H7N 2T8
Tél: 450-667-9802; *Téléc:* 450-667-5740
plamarche@g1bonavocat.com
www.g1bonavocat.com

***Laval*: Turcotte, Nolet - *5**
#470, 500, boul St. Martin ouest, Laval, QC H7M 3Y2
Tél: 450-901-0151; *Téléc:* 450-901-0152
turcotte.nolet@qc.aira.com

***Longueuil*: Bernard & Brassard LLP - *17**
#400, 555, boul Roland-Therrien, Longueuil, QC J4H 4E7
Tél: 450-670-7900; *Téléc:* 450-670-0673
Ligne sans frais: 888-670-7900
info@bernard-brassard.com
www.bernard-brassard.com
www.linkedin.com/company/2067921

***Longueuil*: Jacques Boissonnault - *1**
630, ch de Chambly, Longueuil, QC J4H 3L8
Tél: 514-831-3052; *Téléc:* 866-462-3192
avocat.jb@videotron.ca

***Longueuil*: Dubois et Associés - *3**
#97, 45, Place Charles-Lemoyne, Longueuil, QC J4K 5G5
Tél: 450-646-2613; *Téléc:* 450-646-4225

***Longueuil*: Monique Fortier - *2**
#95, 45, Place Charles Lemoyne, Longueuil, QC J4K 5G5
Tél: 450-651-4418; *Téléc:* 450-442-1125
me.mfortier@bellnet.ca

***Lorraine*: André J. Courtemanche - *1**
107, boul Val D'Ajol, Lorraine, QC J6Z 4G4
Tél: 514-758-6884; *Téléc:* 450-965-6958
andre.courtemanche@videotron.ca

***Lévis*: Gosselin, Lagueux, Roy, notaires s.e.n.c.r.l. - *9**
CP 1247, Stn. Lévis, 67, Côte-du-Passage, Lévis, QC G6V 6R8
Tél: 418-833-0311; *Téléc:* 418-833-1749
info@glrnotaires.com
www.glrnotaires.com

***Lévis*: Pelletier D'Amours - *8**
Former Name: Pelletier, Kronstro@#m, Giguère
CP 3500, 6300, boul de la Rive sud, Lévis, QC G6V 6P9
Tél: 418-835-4944; *Téléc:* 418-835-8847
Ligne sans frais: 800-314-4944

***Matane*: Deschenes & Doiron, Avocats, s.e.n.c. - *2**
352, av St-Jérôme, Matane, QC G4W 3B1
Tél: 418-562-2097; *Téléc:* 418-562-2926
desdoiron@cgocable.ca

***Mont-Laurier*: Maitre Marc-André Simard - *4**
Former Name: Simard, Deschênes et Barrette
445, rue du Pont, Mont-Laurier, QC J9L 2R8
Tél: 819-623-1715

***Mont-Laurier*: Roger Rancourt, Avocat - *1**
673, Carré Laurier, Mont-Laurier, QC J9L 2W4
Tél: 819-623-4485

***Montmagny*: Robert Daveluy, Q.C. - *1**
#22, 46, rue St-Jean-Baptiste est, Montmagny, QC G5V 1J8
Tél: 418-248-1072

***Montmagny*: Marcel Guimont - *2**
134, rue St-Jean Baptiste est, Montmagny, QC G5V 1K6
Tél: 418-248-1530; *Téléc:* 418-248-4157

***Montréal*: Adessky Lesage - *2**
#525, 4150, rue Ste-Catherine ouest, Montréal, QC H3Z 2Y5
Tél: 514-288-8070; *Téléc:* 514-288-8655
general@adesskylesage.com

***Montréal*: L'Agence Goodwin - *3**
#2, 839, rue Sherbrooke est, Montréal, QC H2L 1K6
Tél: 514-598-5252; *Téléc:* 514-598-1878
artistes@goodwin.agent.ca
www.agencegoodwin.com

***Montréal*: Joseph W. Allen - *1**
#203, 6855, av de l'Epée, Montréal, QC H3N 2C7
Tél: 514-274-9393; *Téléc:* 514-274-5614
jwallenimmlaw@bellnet.ca

***Montréal*: Amar & Associés - *3**
625, boul René Lévesque ouest, Montréal, QC H3B 1R2
Tél: 514-878-1532; *Téléc:* 514-878-4761
michael@amar.ca

***Montréal*: Arsenault, Lemieux - *2**
2328, rue Ontario est, Montréal, QC H2K 1W1
Tél: 514-527-8903; *Téléc:* 514-527-1410
arsenault.lemieux@qc.aira.com

***Montréal*: Aster & Aster - *2**
5274, av Ponsard, Montréal, QC H3W 2A8
Tél: 514-483-2445; *Téléc:* 514-483-0009
asterma@asterlaw.com
www.asterlaw.com

***Montréal*: Baron Abrams - *9**
#200, 4141, rue Sherbrooke ouest, Montréal, QC H3Z 1B8
Tél: 514-935-7783; *Téléc:* 514-989-1811

***Montréal*: Barsalou Lawson - *13**
#1500, 2000, av McGill College, Montréal, QC H3A 3H3
Tel: 514-982-3355; *Fax:* 514-982-2550
www.barsalou.ca

***Montréal*: Howard A. Barza - *2**
#450, 2015, rue Peel, Montréal, QC H3A 1T8
Tél: 514-288-9322; *Téléc:* 514-288-2562

***Montréal*: Bastien & Champagne - *2**
#100, 6621, rue Sherbrooke est, Montréal, QC H1N 1C7
Tél: 514-253-0876; *Téléc:* 514-253-2578

***Montréal*: Jacques Bazinet - *1**
4276, rue Fabre, Montréal, QC H2J 3T6
Tél: 514-527-1702; *Téléc:* 514-597-1352

***Montréal*: Beaudry Dessurealt - *3**
#304, 480, boul St-Laurent, Montreal, QC H2Y 3Y7
Tél: 514-282-0727; *Téléc:* 514-282-9363

***Montréal*: Belanger, Fiore - *2**
#300, 685, boul Décarie, Saint-Laurent, QC H4L 5G4
Tél: 514-744-0825; *Téléc:* 514-744-9861

** indicates number of lawyers*

***Montréal*: Bélanger Sauvé - *46**
#900, 5, Place Ville Marie, Montréal, QC H3B 2G2
Tél: 514-878-3081; *Fax:* 514-878-3053
info@belangersauve.com
www.belangersauve.com

***Montréal*: Peter J. Bellan - *1**
#1A, 5130, rue Charleroi, Montréal, QC H1G 2Z8
Tél: 514-955-0691; *Téléc:* 514-955-6921

***Montréal*: Nicole Benchimol - *1**
#1200, 2015, rue Peel, Montréal, QC H3A 1T8
Tél: 514-844-1515; *Téléc:* 514-845-4472

***Montréal*: Bérard Avocats - *2**
417, rue des Seigneurs, 2e étage, Montréal, QC H3J 1X7
Tél: 514-934-1760; *Téléc:* 514-934-1212

***Montréal*: Berger & Winston - *2**
#1150, 615, boul René-Lévesque ouest, Montréal, QC H3B 1P5
Tél: 514-288-4177; *Téléc:* 514-876-1090

***Montréal*: Jean Bernier - *1**
425, rue Saint-Sulpice, Montréal, QC H2Y 2V7
Tél: 514-395-2290

***Montréal*: Elaine Bissonnette - *1**
3892, rue Monselet, Montréal, QC H1H 2C1
Tél: 514-323-8770; *Téléc:* 514-323-8700
ebissonnette@sympatico.ca
www.avocatebissonnette.com

***Montréal*: Marc Bissonnette - *1**
4, rue Notre-Dame est, Montréal, QC H2Y 1B8
Tél: 514-871-8250
marc.bissonnette@sympatico.ca
www.marcbissonnette.com

***Montréal*: Harry Blank, Q.C. - *1**
#1416, 1255, rue University, Montréal, QC H3B 3X1
Tél: 514-866-1125; *Téléc:* 514-866-6898
hablank@videotron.ca

***Montréal*: Blitt Héroux - *2**
4770, av de Kent, Montréal, QC H3W 1H2
Tél: 514-483-2444; *Téléc:* 514-483-2477

***Montréal*: Harry J.F. Bloomfield - *1**
#1310, 1155, rue University, Montréal, QC H3B 3A7
Tél: 514-871-9571; *Téléc:* 514-397-0816
hbloomfield@fieldbloom.com
www.bloomfieldandassociates.ca

***Montréal*: Sonia, Bogdaniec - *1**
#400, 460, rue St-Gabriel, Montréal, QC H2Y 2Z9
Tél: 514-393-3326; *Téléc:* 514-392-7766

***Montréal*: Rika Bohbot - *1**
555, rue Chabanel ouest, Montréal, QC H2N 2L1
Tél: 514-385-3000; *Téléc:* 514-385-6625

***Montréal*: Gaston E. Bouchard - *1**
1015, rue Champigny, Saint-Laurent, QC H4L 4P3
Tél: 514-744-0918; *Téléc:* 514-345-4718

***Montréal*: Boucher Harper - *6**
#610, 630, rue Sherbrooke ouest, Montréal, QC H3A 1E4
Tél: 514-878-1900; *Téléc:* 514-878-3679

***Montréal*: Pierre-Paul Boucher - *1**
7568, rue St-Denis, Montréal, QC H2R 2E6
Tél: 514-495-8900; *Téléc:* 514-495-8367

***Montréal*: François Bourdon - *1**
2308, rue Sherbrooke est, Montréal, QC H2K 1E5
Tél: 514-526-0821; *Téléc:* 514-521-5397

***Montréal*: Jacques Bourgault - *1**
7575, rue des Ecores, Montréal, QC H2E 2W5
Tél: 438-490-3903
jacques.bourgault@videotron.ca
www.jacquesbourgaultavocatlawyer.com

***Montréal*: Boyer Gariépy - *4**
#200, 417, rue St-Nicolas, Montréal, QC H2Y 2P4
Tél: 514-287-9585; *Téléc:* 514-844-5243
boga@bellnet.ca

***Montréal*: Diane Brais - *1**
Former Name: Brais, Shindler
282 rue Notre-Dame ouest, Montréal, QC H2Y 1T7
Tél: 514-985-5454; *Téléc:* 514-985-5433
info@braislaw.ca
www.braislaw.ca

***Montréal*: Sarto Brisebois - *2**
#301, 60, rue St-Jacques, Montréal, QC H2Y 1L5
Tél: 514-849-9444; *Téléc:* 514-849-0119

***Montréal*: Brisset Bishop - *5**
#2020, 2020, rue University, Montréal, QC H3A 2A5
Tél: 514-393-3700; *Fax:* 514-393-1211
general@brissetbishop.com
www.brissetbishop.com

***Montréal*: Jacques Brunet - *1**
#103, 3714, rue Ontario est, Montréal, QC H1W 1R9
Tél: 514-524-6638

***Montréal*: Rebecca Butovsky - *1**
3562, av de Vendome, Montréal, QC H4A 3M7
Tél: 514-484-2942

***Montréal*: Diane G. Cameron - *1**
#206, 4700, av Bonavista, Montréal, QC H3W 2C5
Tél: 514-483-2619; *Téléc:* 514-483-3616

***Montréal*: Campbell Cohen Law Firm Inc. - *4**
#800, 1980, rue Sherbrooke ouest, Montréal, QC H3H 1E8
Tél: 514-937-9445; *Téléc:* 514-937-2618

***Montréal*: Andre Carbonneau - *1**
2567, rue Ontario est, Montréal, QC H2K 1W6
Tél: 514-528-2600

***Montréal*: Pauline Cazelais, Q.C. - *1**
2339, Terrasse Guindon, Montréal, QC H1H 1L7
Tél: 514-522-5427

***Montréal*: Cerundolo & Maiorino - *3**
1807, rue Jean-Talon est, Montréal, QC H1E 1T4
Tél: 514-376-0335; *Téléc:* 514-376-6334
gm.cema@bellnet.ca
avocatscema.com

***Montréal*: Chalifoux Montpetit Vaillancourt Paradis & Ass SENCRL - *12**
Former Name: Chalifoux, Carette & Montpetit
#200, 28, rue Notre-Dame est, Montréal, QC H2Y 1B9
Tél: 514-842-1006; *Téléc:* 514-842-1811

***Montréal*: Chapados Avocats - *1**
#2350, 1010, rue Sherbrooke ouest, Montréal, QC H3A 2R7
Tél: 514-849-2350; *Téléc:* 514-549-3589

***Montréal*: Charbonneau SA Adovats - *2**
#345, 32, rue Saint-Charles ouest, Montréal, QC J4H 1C6
Tél: 514-527-4561
nathalie@charbonneau-sa.com
www.charbonneau-sa.com
www.facebook.com/charbonneau.sa

***Montréal*: Charness, Charness & Charness - *9**
#500, 614 St-Jacques, Montréal, QC H3C 1E2
Tél: 514-878-1808; *Téléc:* 514-871-1149
info@charnesslaw.com
charnesslaw.com
www.facebook.com/jordancharness
www.twitter.com/jordancharness

***Montréal*: Maurice Chevalier - *1**
#1407, 3555, rue Berri, Montréal, QC H2L 4G4
Tél: 514-845-5551

***Montréal*: Choquette Beaupré Rheaume - *3**
#200, 5316, av du Parc, Montréal, QC H2V 4G7
Tél: 514-270-3192; *Téléc:* 514-270-8876

***Montréal*: Clyde & Cie Canada, S.E.N.C.R.L / LLP - *47**
#1700, 630, boul Rene-Levesque ouest, Montréal, QC H3B 1S6
Tél: 514-843-3777; *Téléc:* 514-843-6110
info@clydeco.ca
www.clydeco.ca

***Montréal*: Colby, Monet, Demers, Delage & Crevier - *16**
#2900, Tour McGill College, 1501, av McGill College, Montréal, QC H3A 3M8
Tél: 514-284-3663; *Fax:* 514-284-1961
cmddc@colby-monet.com
www.colby-monet.com

***Montréal*: Commission des services juridiques**
CP 123, Stn. Desjardins, Montréal, QC H5B 1B3
Tél: 514-873-3562
info@csj.qc.ca
www.csj.qc.ca

***Montréal*: Lulu Cornellier - *1**
#2821, 1, Place Ville Marie, Montréal, QC H3B 4R4
Tél: 514-842-1822; *Téléc:* 514-842-0052
lulucor@videotron.ca

***Montréal*: Côté Benoit - *1**
1252, rue Beaubien est, Montréal, QC H2S 1T9
Tél: 514-272-5755
benoit.cote@bellnet.ca

***Montréal*: Daigneault, avocats inc. - *4**
Also Known As: Daigneault, Lawyers Inc.
Former Name: Robert Daigneault, Cabinet D'Avocats
#400, Place D'Youville, 353, rue Saint-Nicolas, Montréal, QC H2Y 2P1
Tél: 514-985-2929; *Téléc:* 514-985-0595
Ligne sans frais: 888-228-5834
enviro@daigneaultinc.com
www.daigneaultinc.com

***Montréal*: Jean-Louis Daunais - *1**
#100, 10550, rue Iberville, Montréal, QC H2B 2V1
Tél: 514-385-1601

***Montréal*: David & Touchette - *2**
#1500, 1255 University St., Montréal, QC H3B 3X2
Tél: 514-871-8174; *Téléc:* 514-871-8052
mdavid@davidtouchette.com
www.davidtouchette.com

***Montréal*: De Grandpré Chait SENCRL-LLP - *68**
Former Name: De Grandpré Godin
#2900, 1000, rue de la Gauchetière ouest, Montréal, QC H3B 4W5
Tel: 514-878-4311; *Fax:* 514-878-4333
info@degrandpre.com
www.degrandpre.com

***Montréal*: Claude de la Madeleine - *1**
3600, boul Henri-Bourassa est, Montréal, QC H1H 1J4
Tél: 514-323-2112

***Montréal*: Charles Derome - *1**
5064, av du Parc, Montréal, QC H2V 4G1
Tél: 514-271-4700; *Téléc:* 514-271-4708
charles.derome@videotron.ca
www.facebook.com/pages/Charles-Derome-avocat/2526012181 77492?sk=info

***Montréal*: Claude Des Marais - *1**
1206, boul St. Joseph est, Montréal, QC H2J 1L6
Tél: 514-521-0047; *Téléc:* 514-521-0047

***Montréal*: Desjardins, Lapointe, Mousseau, Bélanger - *6**
#2185, 600, rue de la Gauchetière ouest, Montréal, QC H3B 4L8
Tél: 514-875-5404; *Téléc:* 514-875-5647

***Montréal*: Desrosiers, Joncas, Massicotte, Avocats - *6**
Former Name: Desrosiers, Turcotte, Marachand, Massicotte
#503, 480, boul St. Laurent, Montréal, QC H2Y 3Y7
Tél: 514-387-9284; *Téléc:* 514-397-9922

***Montréal*: Donato Di Tullio - *1**
7647, boul Gouin est, Montréal, QC H1E 1A7
Tél: 514-648-1048; *Téléc:* 514-648-1048
donatoditullio@gmail.com

***Montréal*: M. Diamond & Associates Inc. - *3**
#140, 8250 Decarie Blvd., Montréal, QC H4P 2P5
Tél: 514-483-2303
mdiamond.ca

***Montréal*: Doyon Izzi Nivoix - *5**
#501, 6455, rue Jean-Talon est, Montréal, QC H1S 3E8
Tél: 514-253-3338; *Téléc:* 514-251-0560
info@dinlex.com
www.dinlex.com

***Montréal*: Druker, Narvey, Green, Schwartz - *1**
#605, 1255, carré Phillips, Montréal, QC H3B 3G5
Tél: 514-871-1300; *Téléc:* 514-871-1304
inarvey@dngslaw.com
irvingnarvey.com
www.facebook.com/IrvingNarveylaw

***Montréal*: Mario Du Mesnil - *1**
1595, rue St-Hubert, 4e étage, Montréal, QC H2L 3Z2
Tél: 514-526-6625; *Téléc:* 514-524-4341

** indicates number of lawyers*

***Montréal*: Duceppe, Théoret & Associés - *3**
1595, rue St-Hubert, 4e étage, Montréal, QC H2L 3Z2
Tél: 514-526-6621; *Téléc:* 514-524-4341

***Montréal*: Dupuis Brodeur S.E.N.C. - *2**
315 Du Saint-Sacrement, 3è étage, Montréal, QC H2Y 1Y1
Tél: 514-849-5140; *Téléc:* 514-849-3633
dubro@depuisbrodeur.com
www.renaudbrodeur.com

***Montréal*: Emile J. Fattal - *1**
#705, 1134, rue Ste-Catherine ouest, Montréal, QC H3B 1H4
Tél: 514-861-4545; *Téléc:* 514-874-1639
occidental@europe.com

***Montréal*: Jon M. Feldman - *1**
#1500, 1 Westmount Sq., Montréal, QC H3Z 2P9
Tél: 514-935-6222; *Téléc:* 514-935-2314
jfeldman@jlaw.ca

***Montréal*: Ferland Marois Lanctot Avocats - *18**
#1610, 1080, Côte du Beaver Hall, Montréal, QC H2Z 1S8
Tél: 514-861-1110; *Téléc:* 514-861-1310
info@fml.ca
www.fml.ca

***Montréal*: Filteau & Belleau - *2**
Former Name: Filteau, Belleau, Normandeau & Daudelin
#301, 28, rue Notre-Dame est, Montréal, QC H2Y 1B9
Tél: 514-843-7877; *Téléc:* 514-499-1889

***Montréal*: Finkelberg, Light - *2**
#1200, 1, Westmount Sq., Montréal, QC H3Z 2P9
Tél: 514-932-7392; *Téléc:* 514-932-0990
plight@sympatico.ca

***Montréal*: Fishman Flanz Meland Paquin LLP - *14**
Former Name: Goldstein, Flanz & Fishman SENCRL/LLP
#4100, 1250, boul René-Lévesque ouest, Montréal, QC H3B 4W8
Tél: 514-932-4100; *Fax:* 514-932-4170
info@ffmp.ca
www.ffmp.ca

***Montréal*: Frankel & Spina - *2**
#401, 60, rue St-Jacques, Montréal, QC H2Y 1L5
Tél: 514-849-3544; *Téléc:* 514-849-4457
plvspina@frankelspina.ca

***Montréal*: Franklin & Franklin - *9**
#545, 4141, rue Sherbrooke ouest, Montréal, QC H3Z 1B8
Tél: 514-935-3576; *Téléc:* 514-935-6862
Ligne sans frais: 800-935-3576
info@franklinlegal.com
franklinlegal.com

***Montréal*: Frumkin, Feldman & Glazman - *3**
#2270, Place du Canada, 1010, rue de la Gauchetière ouest, Montréal, QC H3Z 1T3
Tél: 514-861-2812; *Téléc:* 514-861-6062
ffg@bellnet.ca

***Montréal*: Gasco Goodhue St-Germain - *19**
Former Name: Gasco Goodhue Provost
#800, 1000, rue Sherbrooke ouest, Montréal, QC H3A 3G4
Tél: 514-397-0066; *Téléc:* 514-397-0393
info@gasco.qc.ca
www.gasco.qc.ca

***Montréal*: Ulrich Gautier - *1**
#2350, 500, place D'Armes, Montréal, QC H2Y 2W2
Tél: 514-288-3344; *Téléc:* 514-288-7772
ugautier@videotron.ca

***Montréal*: Gendron, Carpentier, S.E.N.C - *2**
#300, 615, boul René-Lévesque ouest, Montréal, QC H3B 1P5
Tél: 514-395-4527; *Téléc:* 514-395-6031
cargen@bellnet.ca

***Montréal*: Gervais & Gervais - *1**
#2100, 500, place d'Armes, Montréal, QC H2Y 2W2
Tél: 514-288-4241; *Téléc:* 514-849-9984

***Montréal*: Gingras Ouellet - *2**
4141, av Pierre-de-Coubertin, Montréal, QC H1V 3N7
Tél: 514-252-4638; *Téléc:* 514-252-6906

***Montréal*: Goldwater, Dubé - *12**
#2310, 3500, de Maisonneuve ouest, Montréal, QC H3Z 3C1
Tél: 514-861-4367; *Téléc:* 514-861-7601
inquiries@goldwaterdube.com
www.goldwaterdube.com

***Montréal*: Gottlieb & Assciés - *4**
#1920, 2020, rue University, Montréal, QC H3A 2A5
Tél: 514-288-1744; *Téléc:* 514-288-6629
gottliebtradeandcustoms.com

***Montréal*: Gouveia, Gouveia - *3**
#1704, 507, Place d'Armes, Montréal, QC H2Y 2W8
Tél: 514-844-0116; *Téléc:* 514-844-9053

***Montréal*: Elizabeth Greene - *1**
#650, 4141, rue Sherbrooke ouest, Montréal, QC H3Z 1B8
Tél: 514-934-4852; *Téléc:* 514-935-3559

***Montréal*: Grenier, Gagnon - *3**
#1410, 625 boul René-Lévesque Ouest, Montréal, QC H3B 1R2
Tél: 514-875-4949; *Téléc:* 514-875-0313
info@greniergagnon.com
www.greniergagnon.com

***Montréal*: Gurman, Crevier Inc. - *2**
#200, 5000 Jean-Talon St. ouest, Montréal, QC H4P 1W9
Tél: 514-858-1118; *Téléc:* 514-858-1121
agurman@gurman-crevier.com

***Montréal*: Hadjis & Hadjis - *2**
#707, 1117, rue Ste-Catherine ouest, Montréal, QC H3B 1H9
Tél: 514-849-3526; *Téléc:* 514-849-1595
www.hadjislaw.ca

***Montréal*: Martine Hamel - *1**
#300, 13301, rue Sherbrooke est, Montréal, QC H1A 1C2
Tél: 514-642-4473; *Téléc:* 514-642-1663
martinehamel@vocate.com

***Montréal*: Hamilton, Cooper, Ashkenazy - *3**
#401, 4226, boul St-Jean, Montréal, QC H9G 1X5
Tél: 514-626-0266; *Téléc:* 514-626-0011
info@hcalaw.ca

***Montréal*: Handelman, Handelman & Schiller - *2**
#630, 5160, boul Decarie, Montréal, QC H3X 2H9
Tél: 514-866-5071; *Téléc:* 514-866-4210
ih@hhslaw.ca
www.hhslaw.ca

***Montréal*: Hanna Glasz & Sher - *5**
#2260, 1010, rue de la Gauchetière ouest, Montréal, QC H3B 2N2
Tél: 514-284-9551; *Téléc:* 514-284-3419

***Montréal*: Linda Hoddes - *3**
1070, rue Mathieu, Montréal, QC H3H 2S8
Tél: 514-842-1714; *Téléc:* 514-842-1718

***Montréal*: Hutchins Caron & Associates, Barristers & Solicitors - *16**
Also Known As: Hutchins Caron & Associates, Barristers & Solicitors
Former Name: Hutchins Grant & Associates; Hutchins, Soroka & Grant
#300, 204, rue du Saint-Sacrement, Montréal, QC H2Y 1W8
Tél: 514-849-2403; *Téléc:* 514-849-4907
admin@hutchinslegal.ca
www.hutchinslegal.ca
twitter.com/hutchinslegal

***Montréal*: Michel A. Iacono - *1**
#2001, 1 place Ville Marie, Montréal, QC H3B 2C4
Tél: 514-288-1414; *Téléc:* 514-288-0328
mmc.iacono@sympatico.ca

***Montréal*: Irving Mitchell Kalichman, SENCRL/LLP - *19**
#1400, Place Alexis Nihon, Tower 2, 3500, boul de Maisonneuve ouest, Montréal, QC H3Z 3C1
Tél: 514-935-4460; *Téléc:* 514-935-2999
info@imk.ca
www.imk.ca

***Montréal*: Jeansonne Avocats inc. - *7**
1401, av McGill College, Montréal, QC H3A 1Z4
Tél: 514-907-6175; *Téléc:* 514-840-9040
www.jeansonnelaw.ca

***Montréal*: Kierans & Guay - *2**
#440, 606, rue Cathcart, Montréal, QC H3B 1K9
Tél: 514-866-3394; *Téléc:* 514-866-3398

***Montréal*: Leonard Kliger - *3**
#808, 1255, carré Phillips, Montréal, QC H3B 3G1
Tél: 514-281-1720; *Téléc:* 514-281-0678
info@leonardkliger.com
leonardkliger.com

***Montréal*: Kounadis Perreault - *6**
#2000, 300, av Leo-Pariseau, Montréal, QC H2X 4B3
Tél: 514-844-8631; *Téléc:* 514-844-6691
info@kpa-law.com
www.kounadisperreault.com

***Montréal*: Kravitz & Kravitz - *2**
#350, 750, boul Marcel-Laurin, Saint-Laurent, QC H4M 2M4
Tél: 514-748-2889; *Téléc:* 514-748-5191
kravitz@centra.ca

***Montréal*: Kugler Kandestin - *14**
#1170, 1, Place Ville-Marie, Montréal, QC H3B 2A7
Tél: 514-878-2861; *Téléc:* 514-875-8424
info@kklex.com
kklex.com

***Montréal*: Lucien Lachapelle - *1**
5971, rue St-Hubert, Montréal, QC H2S 2L8
Tél: 514-277-2164; *Téléc:* 514-227-1120

***Montréal*: Gaetan Lagarde - *2**
#201, 1554, boul Mont-Royal est, Montréal, QC H2J 1Z2
Tél: 514-521-2442; *Téléc:* 514-525-5561
gaela@videotron.ca

***Montréal*: Lamarre Perron Lambert Vincent - *6**
Also Known As: LPLV
#200, 480, boul St-Laurent, Montréal, QC H2Y 3Y7
Tél: 514-798-1515; *Téléc:* 514-798-5599
info@lplv.com
www.lplv.com

***Montréal*: Raymond Landry - *1**
#404, 505 boul René-Lévesque ouest, Montréal, QC H2Z 1Y7
Tél: 514-908-2171; *Fax:* 514-940-7044
info@raymondlandry-avocat.com
www.raymondlandry-avocat.com

***Montréal*: Lapointe Rosenstein Marchand Melançon - *70**
Former Name: Lapointe Rosenstein; Marchand Melançon Forget
#1400, 1250, boul René-Lévesque ouest, Montréal, QC H3B 5E9
Tel: 514-925-6300; *Fax:* 514-925-9001
Toll-Free: 800-728-6228
www.lrmm.com

***Montréal*: LaSalle Sokol - *2**
Former Name: Moisan Lasalle Perreault
#280, 450, rue Sherbrooke est, Montréal, QC H2L 1J8
Tél: 514-844-3077; *Téléc:* 514-844-1018
lasallesokol.com

***Montréal*: LaTraverse Avocats - *4**
#1510, 1010, rue Sherbrooke ouest, Montréal, QC H3A 2R7
Tél: 514-938-1313; *Téléc:* 514-938-3691
latraverse@latraverse.ca
www.latraverse.ca

***Montréal*: Laurier, Cêré & Couturier - *3**
356, 90e av, LaSalle, QC H8R 2Z7
Tél: 514-363-0220; *Téléc:* 514-363-9495

***Montréal*: Lauzon Bélanger Lespérance inc. - *4**
#100, 286, Saint-Paul ouestWest, Montréal, QC H2Y 2A3
Tél: 514-844-4646; *Fax:* 514-844-7009
info@lblavocats.ca
lblavocats.ca

***Montréal*: Lazare & Altschuler - *2**
#2210, 1010, rue Sherbrooke ouest, Montréal, QC H3A 2R7
Tél: 514-878-3341; *Téléc:* 514-878-3314
lazare@lazalt.com

***Montréal*: John E. Lechter - *1**
2015, rue Drummond, Montréal, QC H3G 1W7
Tél: 514-845-4287; *Téléc:* 514-845-1803

***Montréal*: Legros, St-Gelais, Charbonneau, avocats - *7**
Former Name: Dugas & Legros
CP 1000, Stn. M, 4545, av Pierre-de-Coubertin, Montréal, QC H1V 3R2
Tél: 514-252-3000; *Téléc:* 514-252-0242
juridique@loisirquebec.qc.ca

* *indicates number of lawyers*

***Montréal*: Lepage Carette - *5**
Former Name: Hébert, Downs, Lepage, Soulière & Carette
#2830, 500, place d'Armes, Montréal, QC H2Y 2W2
Tél: 514-284-2351; *Téléc:* 514-284-2354
mlepage@lepagecarette.com
www.lepagecarette.com

***Montréal*: Liebman Légal Inc. - *1**
#1500, 1, carré Westmount, Montréal, QC H3Z 2P9
Tél: 514-846-0666; *Téléc:* 514-935-2314
info@liebmanlegal.com
www.liebmanlegal.com

***Montréal*: Robert Loulou - *1**
#1, 7924, rue St-Denis, Montréal, QC H2R 2G1
Tél: 514-388-3511; *Téléc:* 514-388-3211

***Montréal*: Lozeau Gonthier Masse Richard - *9**
#1900, 1010, rue de la Gauchetière ouest, Montréal, QC H3B 2N2
Tél: 514-981-5600; *Téléc:* 514-981-5601

***Montréal*: Mannella & Associés - *3**
3055, boul de l'Assomption, Montréal, QC H1N 2H1
Tél: 514-899-5375; *Téléc:* 514-899-0476
mannella@qc.aira.com

***Montréal*: Marchi Bellemare - *2**
#200, 400, av McGill, Montréal, QC H2Y 2G1
Tél: 514-288-5753; *Téléc:* 514-284-6606
www.marchibellemare.com

***Montréal*: Martin Camirand Pelletier Lawyers - *7**
#600, 460, rue St-Gabriel, Montréal, QC H2Y 2Z9
Tél: 514-847-8989; *Téléc:* 514-847-8990
mcp@mcp-avocats.com
www.mcp-avocats.com

***Montréal*: Melançon, Marceau, Grenier & Sciortino - *20**
#300, 1717, boul René-Lévesque est, Montréal, QC H2L 4T3
Tél: 514-525-3414; *Téléc:* 514-525-2803
www.mmgs.qc.ca

***Montréal*: Jean Mercier - *1**
#202, 4059, rue Hochelaga, Montréal, QC H1W 1K4
Tél: 514-252-0888; *Téléc:* 514-252-5010

***Montréal*: Miller & Khazzam - *2**
#525, 4150, Ste-Catherine ouest, Montréal, QC H3Z 2Y5
Tél: 514-875-8040; *Téléc:* 514-875-8044

***Montréal*: Monette Barakett, Avocats S.E.N.C. - *24**
Former Name: Monette, Barakett, Lévesque, Bourque, Pedneault
#2100, 1010, rue de la Gauchetière ouest, Montréal, QC H3B 2R8
Tél: 514-878-9381; *Téléc:* 514-878-3957
info@monette-barakett.com
www.monette-barakett.com

***Montréal*: Myszka & Tepner - *2**
#204, 4781, av Van Horne, Montréal, QC H3W 1J1
Tél: 514-737-4069

***Montréal*: Nudleman Lamontagne - *2**
Former Name: Nudleman, Lamontagne & Grenier
#716, 1010, Sherbrooke ouest, Montréal, QC H3A 2R7
Tél: 514-866-6674; *Téléc:* 514-866-9822
info@nlglegal.ca
www.nlglegal.ca

***Montréal*: O'Reilly & Associés - *4**
#1007, 1155, rue University, Montréal, QC H3B 3A7
Tél: 514-871-8117; *Téléc:* 514-871-9177

***Montréal*: Pasquin Viens - *15**
204, Place d'Youville, Montréal, QC H2Y 2B4
Tél: 514-845-5171; *Téléc:* 514-845-5578
info@pasquinviens.com
www.pasquinviens.com

***Montréal*: Pateras & Iezzoni - *5**
#2314, B.C. nord Bldg., 500, place d'Armes, Montréal, QC H2Y 2W2
Tél: 514-284-0860; *Téléc:* 514-843-7990

***Montréal*: Yvan Pelletier - *1**
#600, CP 1390, Stn. Succ., 1801, ave. McGill Collège, Montréal, QC H3B 3L2
Tél: 514-879-2901; *Téléc:* 514-879-1923

***Montréal*: John J. Pepper, Q.C & Associates - *1**
CP 2500, 1155, boul René-Lévesque ouest, Montréal, QC H3B 2K4
Tél: 514-875-5454; *Téléc:* 514-282-0053

***Montréal*: Gregoire Perron & Associes - *4**
Former Name: Perron & Associés
#1538, 507, Place d'Armes, Montréal, QC H2Y 2W8
Tél: 514-285-6441; *Fax:* 514-285-8589
Toll-Free: 888-285-6441
info@gregoireperron.com
www.gregoireperron.com

***Montréal*: Phillips, Friedman, Kotler - *16**
#900, Place du Canada, 1010, rue de la Gauchetière ouest, Montréal, QC H3B 2P8
Tél: 514-878-3371; *Téléc:* 514-878-4676
info@pfklaw.com
www.pfklaw.com

***Montréal*: Marcel Plante - *1**
6915, rue Saint-Denis, Montréal, QC H2S 2S3
Tél: 514-272-8217

***Montréal*: Polisuk, Lord - *2**
#2650, 1155, boul René-Lévesque ouest, Montréal, QC H3B 4S5
Tél: 514-861-8546; *Téléc:* 514-861-1298
info@polisuklord.com
www.polisuklord.com

***Montréal*: Jacques Ranger - *1**
5694, av Laurendeau, Montréal, QC H4E 3W4
Tél: 514-766-0756

***Montréal*: Robic LLP - *40**
Centre CDP Capital, Bloc E, 8e étage, 1001, Square-Victoria, Montréal, QC H2Z 2B7
Tél: 514-987-6242; *Téléc:* 514-845-7874
info@robic.com
www.robic.ca
fr-fr.facebook.com/pages/ROBIC-SENCRL-LLP/129420547115946?sk=info, twitter.com/robiccanada, www.linkedin.com/company/robic

***Montréal*: Robinson Sheppard Shapiro LLP - *71**
#4600, 800, du Square Victoria, Montréal, QC H4Z 1H6
Tél: 514-878-2631; *Fax:* 514-878-1865
info@rsslex.com
www.rsslex.com

***Montréal*: Rougeau Lambert Leborgne Avocats - *6**
#200, 402, rue Notre-Dame est, Montréal, QC H2Y 1C8
Tél: 514-840-9119; *Téléc:* 514-840-0177

***Montréal*: Johanne St. Pierre - *1**
#101, 1395, rue Fleury est, Montréal, QC H2C 1R7
Tél: 514-388-8922; *Téléc:* 514-388-3672
johannestpierre47@gmail.com

***Montréal*: Jean Saulnier - *1**
7190, rue St-Denis, Montréal, QC H2R 2E2
Tél: 514-273-1525; *Téléc:* 514-273-1673

***Montréal*: Seal Seidman G.P. - *3**
#1050, 2015, rue Drummond, Montréal, QC H3G 1W7
Tél: 514-842-8861; *Téléc:* 514-288-1708
info@sealseidman.com
www.sealseidman.com

***Montréal*: Ian M. Solloway - *1**
#1700, 700, rue Sherbrooke ouest, Montréal, QC H3A 1G1
Tél: 514-906-1701; *Téléc:* 514-844-7290
info@sollaw.ca
www.sollaw.ca
twitter.com/sollowaylaw

***Montréal*: Spiegel Sohmer - *49**
#1000, 1255, rue Peel, Montréal, QC H3B 2T9
Tél: 514-875-2100; *Téléc:* 514-875-8237
www.spiegelsohmer.com
www.facebook.com/Spiegel-Sohmer-Inc-128016573934088/, twitter.com/SpiegelSohmerl, www.linkedin.com/company/108294

***Montréal*: Stern & Blumer - *2**
#1825, 300, av Leo-Pariseau, Montréal, QC H3L 1R9
Tél: 514-842-1133; *Téléc:* 514-842-3105

***Montréal*: Sternthal Katznelson Montigny - *13**
#1020, Place du Canada, 1010, rue de la Gauchetière ouest, Montréal, QC H3B 2N2
Tél: 514-878-1011; *Téléc:* 514-878-9195
info@skm.ca
www.skm.ca

***Montréal*: Mark Sumbulian - *1**
Former Name: Sumbulian & Sumbulian; Sumbulian, Hayk
#1610, 1350, rue Sherbrooke ouest, Montréal, QC H3G 1J1
Tél: 514-281-1955; *Téléc:* 514-281-1956

***Montréal*: Tassé & Vescio - *2**
Former Name: Tassé & Themens
2421, rue Allard, Montréal, QC H4E 2L3
Tél: 514-769-9654; *Téléc:* 514-769-7363

***Montréal*: Tiger Goldman - *7**
#716, 1010, rue Sherbrooke ouest, Montréal, QC H3A 2R7
Tél: 514-284-8401; *Téléc:* 514-284-8408
info#tigergoldman.com
www.tigergoldman.com

***Montréal*: Harvey Toulch - *1**
Former Name: Toulch & Associates
#406, 1117, rue Ste-Catherine ouest, Montréal, QC H3B 1H9
Tél: 514-849-1289; *Téléc:* 514-849-3101
harvey.toulch@videotron.ca

***Montréal*: Trudel Nadeau Avocats S.E.N.C.R.L. - *26**
#2500, Place du Parc, 300, av Léo-Pariseau, Montréal, QC H2X 4B7
Tél: 514-849-5754; *Téléc:* 514-499-0312
info@trudelnadeau.com
www.trudelnadeau.com

***Montréal*: Tucci & Associés - *3**
Former Name: Sergio Tucci & Associates
201, rue St-Zotique est, Montréal, QC H2S 1L2
Tél: 514-271-0650; *Téléc:* 514-270-2164
tucci@tucci.ca
www.tucci.ca

***Montréal*: Peter H. Turner - *1**
256, rue Devon, Montréal, QC H3R 1B9
Tél: 514-731-3544; *Téléc:* 514-737-3770

***Montréal*: Unterberg, Carisse, Labelle, Dessureault, Lebeau & Petit**
Former Name: Unterberg, Labelle, Lebeau
#700, 1980, rue Sherbrooke ouest, Montréal, QC H3H 1E8
Tél: 514-934-0841; *Téléc:* 514-937-6547

***Montréal*: Woods LLP - *24**
#1700, 2000, av McGill College, Montréal, QC H3A 3H3
Tél: 514-982-4545; *Téléc:* 514-284-2046
general@woods.qc.ca
www.litigationboutique.com

***Paspébiac*: Gilles Moulin - *1**
CP 880, Paspébiac, QC G0C 2K0
Tél: 418-752-2244

***Pointe-Claire*: Stanley Gelfand - *1**
#306, 189, boul Hymus, Pointe-Claire, QC H9R 1E9
Tél: 514-695-4542; *Téléc:* 514-695-7975

***Québec*: Beauvais Truchon - *31**
#200, CP 1000, 79, boul René-Lévesque est, Québec, QC G1R 4T4
Tél: 418-692-4180; *Téléc:* 418-692-5321
www.beauvaistruchon.com
www.linkedin.com/company/beauvais-truchon-s-e-n-c-r-l-

***Québec*: Herman Bedard - *2**
#206, 51, rue des Jardins, Québec, QC G1R 4L6
Tél: 418-692-2425; *Téléc:* 418-692-2528
hermanbedard@qc.aira.com
www.hermanbedard.com

***Québec*: Claude Berlinguette - *1**
1429, rue du Nordet, Sainte-Foy, QC G2G 2C2
Tél: 418-871-1478

***Québec*: André Bernatchez - *1**
#220, 157, rue des Chênes ouest, Québec, QC G1L 1K6
Tél: 418-628-4575

***Québec*: Maurice Bernatchez - *1**
#2, 1460, av de la Verendrye, Québec, QC G1J 4V8
Tél: 418-667-7830

***Québec*: Yvan Bilodeau - *1**
#180, 801, ch St-Louis, Québec, QC G1S 1C1
Tél: 418-686-4875; *Téléc:* 418-686-6160

** indicates number of lawyers*

***Québec*: Bouchard Pagé Tremblay, S.E.N.C. - Avocats - *10**
#510, 825, boul Lebourgneuf, Québec, QC G2J 0B9
Tél: 418-622-6699; *Téléc:* 418-628-1912
bouchardpagetremblay@bptavocats.com
www.bouchardpagetremblay.com
www.facebook.com/pages/Bouchard-Page-Tremblay-avocats/195809217098870

***Québec*: J. Michel Bouchard - *1**
1753 ave. Industrielle, Québec, QC G3K 1L8
Tél: 418-842-0996

***Québec*: Roland Cote - *1**
1445, rue Maine, Québec, QC G1G 2J6
Tél: 418-628-2321

***Québec*: Norman Dumais - *1**
#7, CP 18500, Stn. Terminus, 400 boul Jean-Lesage, Québec, QC G1K 7Z5
Tél: 418-643-4933; *Téléc:* 418-646-3678
norman.dumais@cnt.gouv.qc.ca

***Québec*: Dussault Gervais Thivierge - *13**
Former Name: Brochet Dussault Lemieux Larochelle
#450, 2795, boul Laurier, Québec, QC G1V 4M7
Tél: 418-657-2424; *Téléc:* 418-657-1793
avocats@dlgt.ca
www.lesavocats.ca

***Québec*: Gagné Letarte S.E.N.C.R.L. - Québec - *8**
#400, 79, boul René-Lévesque est, Québec, QC G1R 5N5
Tél: 418-522-7900; *Téléc:* 418-523-7900
www.gagneletarte.qc.ca

***Québec*: Gagnon Girard Julien & Matte Avocats Avocates - *7**
#301, 1535, ch Ste-Foy, Québec, QC G1S 2P1
Tél: 418-681-0037; *Téléc:* 418-681-0539
www.ggjmavocats.ca

***Québec*: La Société d'Avocats Garneau, Verdon, Michaud, Samson - *10**
67, rue Ste-Ursule, Québec, QC G1R 4E7
Tél: 418-692-3010; *Téléc:* 418-692-1742
gvm@qc.aira.com

***Québec*: Giasson et Associés - *24**
#551, 2, rue des Jardins, Québec, QC G1R 4S9
Tél: 418-641-6156; *Téléc:* 418-641-6353

***Québec*: Gosselin, Bussières, Bedard, Ouellet - *4**
#315, 400, boul Jean-Lesage, Québec, QC G1K 8W1
Tél: 418-529-9968; *Téléc:* 418-524-5243

***Québec*: Hickson, Martin, Blanchard - *6**
Former Name: Hickson Noonan
1170 Grande Allée ouest, Québec, QC G1S 1E5
Tél: 418-681-9671; *Téléc:* 418-527-6938
wnoonan@oricom.ca
hickson-noonan.com

***Québec*: Joli-Coeur Lacasse Avocats - Québec - *59**
#600, 1134, Grande-Allée ouest, Québec, QC G1S 1E5
Tél: 418-681-7007; *Téléc:* 418-681-7100
infos@jolicoeurlacasse.com
www.jolicoeurlacasse.com
www.facebook.com/jolicoeurlacasse,
www.linkedin.com/company/joli-coeur-lacasse-avocats

***Québec*: Langlois Kronström Desjardins - *81**
Complexe Jules-Dallaire, T3, 2820, boul. Laurier, 13e étage, Québec, QC G1V 0C1
Tel: 418-650-7000; *Fax:* 418-650-7075
Toll-Free: 888-650-7001
info@lkd.ca
www.langloiskronstromdesjardins.com

***Québec*: Micheline Anne Montreuil - *1**
1050, rue François-Blondeau, Québec, QC G1H 2H2
Tél: 418-621-5032; *Téléc:* 418-621-5092
micheline@maitremontreuil.ca
www.maitremontreuil.ca

***Québec*: Morency Société d'Avocats - Québec - *58**
Former Name: Pothier Delisle Societé D'Avocats
#400, 3075, ch des Quatre-Bourgeois, Québec, QC G1W 4X5
Tél: 418-651-9900; *Téléc:* 418-651-5184
avocats@morencyavocats.com
www.morencyavocats.com
www.facebook.com/218984404818137,
twitter.com/morencyavocats,
ca.linkedin.com/pub/avocats-morency/3a/2b7/300

***Québec*: O'Brien avocats, S.E.N.C.R.L. - *11**
#600, 140, Grande Allée est, Québec, QC G1R 5M8
Tél: 418-648-1511; *Téléc:* 418-648-9335
dobrien@obrienavocats.qc.ca
obrienavocats.qc.ca

***Québec*: Poudrier Bradet - Québec - *25**
#100, 70, rue Dalhousie, Québec, QC G1K 4B2
Tél: 418-780-3333; *Téléc:* 418-780-3334
www.poudrierbradet.com

***Québec*: Provencal Breton Murray - *5**
#204, 2500, rue Jean-Pérrin, Québec, QC G2C 1X1
Tél: 418-871-2955; *Téléc:* 418-871-7352

***Québec*: Tremblay Bois Mignault Lemay S.E.N.C.R.L. - *31**
#200, Iberville Un, 1195, av Lavigerie, Québec, QC G1V 4N3
Tél: 418-658-9966; *Téléc:* 418-658-6100
avocats@tremblaybois.qc.ca
www.tremblaybois.qc.ca

***Repentigny*: Robert Toupin - *1**
#307, 579A, rue Notre-Dame, Repentigny, QC J6A 7L4
Tél: 450-654-9661; *Téléc:* 450-654-9657

***Rimouski*: Jean Blouin - *1**
216, av de la Cathedrale, Rimouski, QC G5L 5J2
Tél: 418-724-2031; *Téléc:* 418-723-4621

***Rivière-du-Loup*: Belzile & Associés - *3**
110, rue Lafontaine, Rivière-du-Loup, QC G5R 3A1
Tél: 418-862-9460; *Téléc:* 418-862-9939

***Rivière-du-Loup*: Moreau Avocats inc. - *6**
CP 487, 12, rue de la Cour, Rivière-du-Loup, QC G5R 3Z1
Tél: 418-862-3565; *Téléc:* 418-862-4408
www.moreauavocats.com

***Rouyn-Noranda*: Daoust, Boulianne, Parayre avocats - Rouyn-Noranda - *4**
Former Name: Martineau, Daoust, Boulianne, Pelletier, Geoffroy, Matte, Kélada
201, av Murdoch, Rouyn-Noranda, QC J9X 1E5
Tél: 819-762-8294; *Téléc:* 819-762-8296
info@mdbpavocats.com
mdbpavocats.com

***Saint-Hyacinthe*: Claude L. Bédard Avocat - *1**
1782, rue Girouard ouest, Saint-Hyacinthe, QC J2S 3A1
Tél: 450-774-2749; *Téléc:* 450-774-9533
claudebedardavocat@cgocable.ca

***Saint-Hyacinthe*: Sylvestre & Associés Avocats S.E.N.C. - Saint-Hyacinthe - *16**
#236, 1600, rue Girouard ouest, Saint-Hyacinthe, QC J2S 2Z8
Tél: 450-773-8445; *Téléc:* 450-773-2112
etude@jurisylvestre.ca
www.jurisylvestre.ca

***Saint-Jean-Port-Joli*: Les Avocats Blanchet Gaudreault - *2**
512, route de l'Eglise, Saint-Jean-Port-Joli, QC G0R 3G0
Tél: 418-598-7004; *Téléc:* 418-598-7390
blanchet.gaudreault@globetrotter.net

***Saint-Jean-sur-Richelieu*: Paul Claude Bérubé**
#225, 145, boul St-Joseph, Saint-Jean-sur-Richelieu, QC J3B 1W5
Tél: 450-359-7171; *Téléc:* 450-359-9957

***Saint-Jean-sur-Richelieu*: Lachance & Morin - *2**
108, rue St-Charles, Saint-Jean-sur-Richelieu, QC J3B 2C1
Tél: 450-346-4464; *Téléc:* 450-346-5824

***Saint-Jean-sur-Richelieu*: Claude Lauzon - *1**
160, rue Longueuil, Saint-Jean-sur-Richelieu, QC J3B 6P1
Tél: 450-347-2344; *Téléc:* 450-347-4132

***Saint-Joseph-de-Beauce*: Bureau d' Aide juridique - Saint-Joseph-de-Beauce - *3**
#100, 700, av Robert-Cliche, Saint-Joseph-de-Beauce, QC G0S 2V0
Tél: 418-397-7288; *Téléc:* 418-397-7283
bajstjoseph@ccjq.qc.ca

***Saint-Joseph-de-Beauce*: Cliche, Laflamme & Loubier - *8**
CP 160, 109, rue Verreault, Saint-Joseph-de-Beauce, QC G0S 2V0
Tél: 418-397-5264; *Téléc:* 418-397-5269
info@clichelaflamme.com
clichelaflamme.com

***Saint-Jérôme*: Lalonde Geraghty Riendeau Avocats - *8**
Former Name: Lalonde Geraghty Riendeau Lapierre Avocats
44, rue de Martigny ouest, Saint-Jérôme, QC J7Z 2E9
Tél: 450-436-8022; *Téléc:* 450-436-5185
info@lgra.ca
www.lgra.ca

***Saint-Jérôme*: Prévost Fortin D'Aoust - *41**
Former Name: Prévost Auclair Fortin D'Aoust
#400, 55, rue Castonguay, Saint-Jérôme, QC J7Y 2H9
Tél: 450-436-8244; *Fax:* 450-436-9735
info@pfdlex.com
www.pfdlex.com

***Saint-Lambert*: André Demers - *1**
439, av Notre-Dame, Saint-Lambert, QC J4P 2K5
Tél: 514-875-2007; *Téléc:* 450-466-7315

***Saint-Lambert*: Paul Joffe - *1**
360, av Putney, Saint-Lambert, QC J4P 3B6
Tél: 450-465-3654; *Téléc:* 450-465-5730
pjoffe@joffelaw.ca

***Sainte-Julie*: Roland Boyer - *1**
69, av Mont Bruno, RR#3, Sainte-Julie, QC J3E 3A1
Tél: 450-649-3772; *Téléc:* 450-649-0101
rolandboyer@yahoo.com

***Sainte-Marie*: Sylvain Parent Gobeil Simard S.E.N.C.R.L.**
225, av du College, Sainte-Marie, QC G6E 3X9
Tél: 418-387-2727; *Téléc:* 418-387-7070
spgs@globetrotter.net
www.spgs.ca

***Salaberry-de-Valleyfield*: Rancourt Legault Joncas - *6**
Former Name: Les Avocats Rancourt, Legault & St-Onge; Rancourt, Legault, Boucher & St-Onge
303, rue Victoria, Salaberry-de-Valleyfield, QC J6T 1B2
Tél: 450-371-2221; *Téléc:* 450-371-2094
info@rancourtlegault.com
www.rancourtlegault.com

***Salaberry-de-Valleyfield*: Vachon, Martin & Besner Avocats - *4**
57, rue St-Jean-Baptiste, Salaberry-de-Valleyfield, QC J6T 1Z6
Tél: 514-371-7771; *Téléc:* 514-371-2438
info@vmbavocats.com
www.vmbavocats.com

***Sept-Îles*: Besnier, Dion, Rondeau - *5**
865, boul Laure, Sept-Îles, QC G4R 1Y6
Tél: 418-962-9775; *Téléc:* 418-968-6806

***Sept-Îles*: Desrosiers & Associés - *3**
#201, 440, av Brochu, Sept-Îles, QC G4R 2W8
Tél: 418-962-7392; *Téléc:* 418-962-6100
desricar@globetrotter.qc.ca

***Sherbrooke*: Claude R. Beauchamp - *1**
#101, 380, rue King ouest, Sherbrooke, QC J1H 1R4
Tél: 819-563-7733; *Téléc:* 819-563-7734

***Sherbrooke*: Pierre Belhumeur - *1**
53 rue Peel, Sherbrooke, QC J1H 4J9
Tél: 819-566-1676; *Téléc:* 819-575-0610
pbelhumeuravocat@videotron.ca

***Sherbrooke*: Gerard G. Boudreau - *1**
2571, boul Portland, Sherbrooke, QC J1J 1V6
Tél: 819-562-0848; *Téléc:* 819-569-3580

***Sherbrooke*: Delorme, LeBel, Bureau, Savoie - *11**
#100, 2355, rue King ouest, Sherbrooke, QC J1J 2G6
Tél: 819-566-6222; *Téléc:* 819-566-4221
dlb@dlbavocats.com
www.dlbavocats.com

***Sherbrooke*: Fontaine, Panneton & Associes - *8**
#220, 2050, rue King ouest, Sherbrooke, QC J1J 2E8
Tél: 819-564-1222; *Téléc:* 819-822-2180

***Sherbrooke*: Gallant Morin Avocats**
731, rue Galt ouest, Sherbrooke, QC J1H 1Z1
Tél: 819-565-1808; *Téléc:* 819-565-2729
gcgm@globetrotter.net

***Sherbrooke*: Gérin Custeau Francoeur - *3**
100, rue Richmond, Sherbrooke, QC J1H 6E1
Tél: 819-348-0274

** indicates number of lawyers*

***Sherbrooke*: Hackett, Campbell & Bouchard - *5**
80, rue Peel, Sherbrooke, QC J1H 4K1
Tél: 819-565-7885; *Téléc:* 819-566-0888
info@hcblegal.com

***Sherbrooke*: Frédéric-Antoine Lemieux - *2**
18, rue Wellington nord, Sherbrooke, QC J1H 5B7
Tél: 819-566-3939
m.mefrederic-antoinelemieux.ca

***Sherbrooke*: Linda Boulanger - *1**
#3, 30, rue Vaudry, Sherbrooke, QC J1M 1B2
Tél: 819-820-2661; *Téléc:* 819-820-8330
lindaboulangeravocate@yahoo.ca

***Sherbrooke*: Monty Coulombe s.e.n.c. - Sherbrooke - *20**
#200, 234, rue Dufferin, Sherbrooke, QC J1H 4M2
Tél: 819-566-4466; *Téléc:* 819-565-2891
legal@montycoulombe.com
www.montycoulombe.com

***Sorel-Tracy*: Carole Lepage - *1**
96, rue George, Sorel-Tracy, QC J3P 1C3
Tél: 450-742-3766; *Téléc:* 450-742-1133

***St-Georges-de-Beauce*: Jérôme Poirier - *1**
Former Name: Lebel, Poirier
11720, 1re av, St-Georges-de-Beauce, QC G5Y 2C8
Tél: 418-228-3123; *Téléc:* 418-228-0494
jerome.poirier@globetrotter.net

***St-Léonard*: DiPace, Mercadente - *6**
#202, 5450, rue Jarry est, St-Léonard, QC H1P 1T9
Tél: 514-326-3300; *Téléc:* 514-326-4706

***St-Léondard*: Carmelo Morabito - *1**
#3001, 5095, rue Jean-Talon est, St-Léondard, QC H1S 3G4
Tél: 514-727-0332; *Téléc:* 514-727-9315
carmorab@total.net

***St-Romuald-d'Etchemin*: Huguette Gagnon - *1**
CP 2096, St-Romuald-d'Etchemin, QC G6W 5M3
Tél: 418-839-2045; *Téléc:* 418-839-2061
gagnonh@videotron.ca

***Terrebonne*: Talbot Kingsbury Avocats - *2**
#101, 227 boul Braves, Terrebonne, QC J6W 3H6
Tél: 450-964-0414; *Téléc:* 450-964-5739
tude@tkavocats.com
www.tkavocats.com

***Trois-Rivières*: Biron Spain - *3**
Former Name: Biron, Spain & Associés
CP 444, 154, rue Radisson, Trois-Rivières, QC G9A 5G4
Tél: 819-375-4187; *Téléc:* 819-375-7395
www.bironspainavocats.com

***Trois-Rivières*: Braun & Bélisle - *2**
#4, 1185, rue Hart, Trois-Rivières, QC G9A 4S4
Tél: 819-691-1390; *Téléc:* 819-378-7344

***Trois-Rivières*: Godin, Brunet - *2**
190, rue Bonaventure, Trois-Rivières, QC G9A 2B1
Tél: 819-379-5225; *Téléc:* 819-379-4545
dgodin@godinbrunet.comm

***Trois-Rivières*: Louis Hénaire - *1**
Also Known As: Hénaire, Avocats
983, rue Hart, Trois-Rivières, QC G9A 4S3
Tél: 819-379-3355; *Téléc:* 819-379-1227

***Val-d'Or*: Cliche Lortie Ladouceur inc. - *11**
1121, 6e rue, Val-d'Or, QC J9P 3W8
Tél: 819-825-3010; *Téléc:* 819-825-7375
Ligne sans frais: 800-692-3010
info@cll-avocats.ca
www.clicheavocats.com

***Val-d'Or*: Cossette, Claude - *1**
795, 3e av, Val-d'Or, QC J9P 1S8
Tél: 819-825-2787; *Téléc:* 819-874-4160

***Verdun*: Robert Beaudet - *2**
5331, rue Bannantyne, Verdun, QC H4H 1E8
Tél: 514-769-8527; *Téléc:* 514-769-7466

***Westmount*: Robert Berger - *1**
#220, 4823 rue Sherbrooke ouest, Westmount, QC H3Z 1G7
Tél: 514-931-5660; *Téléc:* 514-932-6570
rberger@segberg.com

***Westmount*: Luisa Biasutti - *1**
#410, 4115, rue Sherbrooke ouest, Westmount, QC H3Z 1K9
Tél: 514-933-3838; *Téléc:* 514-933-2668
biasutti@groupeteq.com

***Westmount*: Morris Chaikelson - *1**
#400, 4120, rue Sainte-Catherine ouest, Westmount, QC H3Z 1P4
Tél: 514-288-3838; *Téléc:* 415-288-3433
chaimor@videotron.ca

***Westmount*: Paul B. Cohen - *1**
#809, 4000, boul de Maisonneuve ouest, Westmount, QC H3Z 1J9
Tél: 514-931-3691; *Téléc:* 514-931-3637
paulcohen@bellnet.ca

***Westmount*: A. Barry Coleman - *1**
#660, 4141, rue Sherbrooke ouest, Westmount, QC H3Z 1B8
Tél: 514-620-6002; *Téléc:* 514-935-3559

***Westmount*: André R. Dorais Avocats - *3**
#2000, 1, carré Westmount, Westmount, QC H3Z 2P9
Tél: 514-938-0808; *Téléc:* 514-938-8888
adorais@ardavocats.com

***Westmount*: Linda Hammerschmid - *4**
#1290, 1 Westmount Sq., Westmount, QC H3Z 2P9
Tél: 514-846-1013; *Téléc:* 514-846-1803

***Westmount*: Orna & Hilberger - *2**
#939, 1, Carré Westmount, Westmount, QC H3Z 2P9
Tél: 514-932-7392; *Téléc:* 514-932-0990
info@montrealdivorcelaw.ca
www.montrealdivorcelaw.ca

***Westmount*: Stein & Stein Inc. - *3**
4101, rue Sherbrooke ouest, Westmount, QC H3Z 1A7
Tél: 514-866-9806; *Téléc:* 514-875-8218
www.steinandstein.com

***Westmount*: Rosalie Szewczuk - *1**
4420, rue Ste-Catherine ouest, Westmount, QC H3Z 1R2
Tél: 514-933-4453; *Téléc:* 514-934-3134
rosiesz@videotron.ca

Saskatchewan

***Assiniboia*: Lewans & Ford - *2**
P.O. Box 759, 228 Centre St., Assiniboia, SK S0H 0B0
Tel: 306-642-3543; *Fax:* 306-642-5777

***Assiniboia*: Marlin Law Office - *1**
P.O. Box 1088, 200 Centre St., Assiniboia, SK S0H 0B0
Tel: 306-642-3933; *Fax:* 306-642-5399

***Assiniboia*: Mountain & Mountain - *2**
P.O. Box 459, 101 - 4 Ave. West, Assiniboia, SK S0H 0B0
Tel: 306-642-3866; *Fax:* 306-642-5848
lee.mountain@sasktel.net

***Biggar*: Busse Law Professional Corporation - *2**
Former Name: bmwlaw.sasktelwebsite.net
Credit Union Bldg., P.O. Box 669, 302 Main St., Biggar, SK S0K 0M0
Tel: 306-948-3346; *Fax:* 306-948-3366
busselaw.ofc@sasktel.net
busselaw.net

***Broadview*: Gary G. Moore - *1**
P.O. Box 610, 616 Main St., Broadview, SK S0G 0K0
Tel: 306-696-2454; *Fax:* 306-696-3105

***Davidson*: Dellene S. Church - *1**
P.O. Box 724, 200 Garfield St., Davidson, SK S0G 1A0
Tel: 306-567-5554; *Fax:* 306-567-2831
dsc-law@sasktel.net

***Estevan*: Kohaly, Elash & Ludwig Law Firm LLP - *2**
P.O. Box 580, 1312 - 4th St., Estevan, SK S4A 0X2
Tel: 306-634-3631; *Fax:* 306-634-6901
www.kohalyelash.com

***Estevan*: Orlowski Law Office - *2**
1215 - 5th St., Estevan, SK S4A 0Z5
Tel: 306-634-3353; *Fax:* 306-634-7714
orlowski.law@sasktel.net

***Eston*: Hughes Law Office - *1**
P.O. Box 729, 305 Main St. South, Eston, SK S0L 1A0
Tel: 306-962-4111; *Fax:* 306-962-3302
hugheseston@hotmail.com
www.hughesagencies.saskbrokers.com

***Fort Qu'appelle*: Halford Law Office - *1**
P.O. Box 617, Fort Qu'appelle, SK S0G 1S0
Tel: 306-332-5661; *Fax:* 306-332-4293

***Humboldt*: Behiel, Will & Biemans - *4**
Former Name: Behiel, Munkler & Will
P.O. Box 878, 602 - 9 St., Humboldt, SK S0K 2A0
Tel: 306-682-2642; *Fax:* 306-682-5165
office_bmwlaw@sasktel.net
www.behielwill.com

***Kamsack*: Rosowsky, Campbell & Seidle - *3**
P.O. Box 399, 445 2nd St., Kamsack, SK S0A 1S0
Tel: 306-542-2646; *Fax:* 306-542-2510

***Kindersley*: Ard Law Office - *1**
P.O. Box 1898, Kindersley, SK S0L 1S0
Tel: 306-463-2626; *Fax:* 306-463-4917
ard.law@sasktel.net

***Kindersley*: Sheppard & Millar - *2**
P.O. Box 1510, 113 - 1 Ave. East., Kindersley, SK S0L 1S0
Tel: 306-463-4647; *Fax:* 306-463-6133
kindersley.law@sasktel.net

***La Ronge*: Buckle Law Office - *1**
P.O. Box 960, La Ronge, SK S0J 1L0
Tel: 306-425-5959; *Fax:* 306-425-2840

***Langenburg*: Layh & Associates - *3**
Former Name: Layh Law Office
Welke House, P.O. Box 250, 216 Road Ave. East, Langenburg, SK S0A 2A0
Tel: 306-743-5520; *Fax:* 306-743-5589
info@layhlaw.com
www.layhlaw.com

***Lloydminster*: Fox Wakefield - *2**
Former Name: Bennett Fox Wakefield
P.O. Box 500, Stn. Main, 5105 - 49 St., Lloydminster, SK S9V 0Y6
Tel: 780-875-9105; *Fax:* 780-875-6748

***Meadow Lake*: Francis & Company - *2**
Former Name: Francis
P.O. Box 310, Stn. Main, 822 - 9th Ave. West, Meadow Lake, SK S9X 1Y3
Tel: 306-236-5540; *Fax:* 306-236-5571
info@franciscolaw.ca

***Meadow Lake*: Gerald R. Perkins - *1**
#2, 132 Centre St., Meadow Lake, SK S9X 1Z7
Tel: 306-236-4040; *Fax:* 306-236-4878
perkinslawoffice@sasktel.net

***Melfort*: Annand Law Office - *4**
P.O. Box 69, 208 Main St., Melfort, SK S0E 1A0
Tel: 306-752-2707; *Fax:* 306-752-4484
info@annandlawoffice.com
www.annandlawoffice.com

***Melfort*: Carson Law Office - *1**
803 Main St., Melfort, SK S0E 1A0
Tel: 306-752-5781

***Melfort*: Kapoor Selnes Klimm - *4**
Former Name: Kapoor Selnes Klimm
417 Main St., Melfort, SK S0E 1A0
Tel: 306-752-5777; *Fax:* 306-752-2712

***Melfort*: Ronald Price-Jones - *1**
P.O. Box 129, #3 Hwy. East, Melfort, SK S0E 1A0
Tel: 306-752-5701; *Fax:* 306-752-2444
ronp-j@sasktel.net

***Melville*: Bell, Kreklewich & Company - *3**
P.O. Box 2000, 147 - 3 Ave. East, Melville, SK S0A 2P0
Tel: 306-728-5468; *Fax:* 306-728-4444
bell.kreklewich_bkc@sasktel.net
bkc-law.ca

***Melville*: Schmidt Law Office - *1**
P.O. Box 160, 101c 3rd Ave. West, Melville, SK S0A 2P0
Tel: 306-728-5481; *Fax:* 306-728-4201
solaw@sasktel.net
schmidtlaw.ca

***Moose Jaw*: Curran & Fielding - *2**
#108, 54 Ominica St. West, Moose Jaw, SK S6H 1W9
Tel: 306-693-7181; *Fax:* 306-691-0187

** indicates number of lawyers*

***Moose Jaw*: Grayson & Company - *7**
Former Name: Grayson, Rushford, Cooper, Arendt, Cornea & Patterson
350 Langdon Cres., Moose Jaw, SK S6H 0X4
Tel: 306-693-6176; *Fax:* 306-693-1515
admin@graysonandcompany.com
www.graysonandcompany.com

***Moose Jaw*: Terrance Ocrane Law Office - *1**
#414, 310 Main St. North, Moose Jaw, SK S6H 3K1
Tel: 306-694-4922; *Fax:* 306-692-6386
ocranelawoffice@sasktel.net

***Moose Jaw*: Walper-Bossence Law Office Prof. Corp. - *1**
84 Athabasca St. West, Moose Jaw, SK S6H 2B5
Tel: 306-693-7288; *Fax:* 306-692-6760
brenda@walperlaw.ca
www.walperlaw.ca

***Moose Jaw*: Wheatley Law Firm - *1**
P.O. Box 1648, Stn. Main, Moose Jaw, SK S6H 7K7
Tel: 306-692-0113; *Fax:* 306-692-0113

***Moose Jaw*: Whittaker, Craik, MacLowich & Hughes - *3**
P.O. Box 1178, 109 Ominica St. West, Moose Jaw, SK S6H 4P9
Tel: 306-694-4677; *Fax:* 306-694-5747

***Moosomin*: Osman & Co.**
Former Name: Osman, Gordon & Co.
1103 Broadway Ave., Moosomin, SK S0G 3N0
Tel: 306-435-3851; *Fax:* 306-435-3962

***Nipawin*: Eremko & Eremko - *1**
P.O. Box 250, Nipawin, SK S0E 1E0
Tel: 306-862-4422; *Fax:* 306-862-4477

***North Battleford*: Cawood Demmans Baldwin Friedman - *5**
#201, P.O. Box 905, 1291 - 102 St., North Battleford, SK S9A 2Z3
Tel: 306-445-6177; *Fax:* 306-445-7076
cawood.et.al@sasktel.net
cdbf.ca

***North Battleford*: Holm Meiklejohn Law Office - *1**
Former Name: Jones & Hudec
#103, 1501 - 100th St., North Battleford, SK S9A 0W3
Tel: 306-445-7300; *Fax:* 306-445-7302
holmlaw@sasktel.net
www.holmlaw.ca

***North Battleford*: Hudec Law Office - *2**
#10211, 12th Ave., 2nd Fl., North Battleford, SK S9A 3X5
Tel: 306-446-2555; *Fax:* 306-446-2556
hudeclaw@sasktel.net

***North Battleford*: Lindgren, Blais, Frank & Illingworth**
P.O. Box 940, 1301 - 101 St., North Battleford, SK S9A 2Z3
Tel: 306-445-2421; *Fax:* 306-445-2313

***North Battleford*: Migneault Greenwood - *3**
1391 - 101st St., North Battleford, SK S9A 2Y8
Tel: 306-445-4436; *Fax:* 306-445-6444
info@mglawoffice.com
www.migneaultgreenwood.com

***Preeceville*: Peet Law Firm - *1**
P.O. Box 1210, 17 First Ave. NW, Preeceville, SK S0A 3B0
Tel: 306-547-3322

***Prince Albert*: Abrametz & Eggum - *2**
#101, 88 - 13th St. East, Prince Albert, SK S6V 1C6
Tel: 306-763-7441; *Fax:* 306-764-2882
www.abrametzandeggum.com

***Prince Albert*: Balon Krishan - *2**
1335B - 2nd Ave. West, Prince Albert, SK S6V 5B2
Tel: 306-922-5151; *Fax:* 306-763-1755

***Prince Albert*: Cherkewich, Ronald, Legal Services - *1**
#202, 1000 - 1st Ave. East, Prince Albert, SK S6V 2A7
Tel: 306-764-1537; *Fax:* 306-763-0505

***Prince Albert*: Novus Law Group - Central Ave. - *14**
Also Known As: Wilcox Holash Chovin McCullagh
Former Name: Holash Logue McCullagh Law Office; Wilcox & Chovin Law Office; Harradence Logue Holash; Holash Logue
1200 Central Ave., Prince Albert, SK S6V 4V8
Tel: 306-922-4700
princealbert@novuslaw.ca
www.novuslaw.ca

***Prince Albert*: Sanderson Balicki Parchomchuk - *8**
110 - 11 St. East, Prince Albert, SK S6V 1A1
Tel: 306-764-2222; *Fax:* 306-764-2221
sbp.sbp@sasktel.net
www.sbplaw.ca

***Prince Albert*: Stephens Law Office - *1**
Former Name: Stephens Arnot Heffernan
#3, 27 - 11th St. West, Prince Albert, SK S6V 3A8
Tel: 306-764-3456; *Fax:* 306-922-3772

***Prince Albert*: West, Siwak - *2**
1109 Central Ave., Prince Albert, SK S6V 4V7
Tel: 306-763-7467; *Fax:* 306-763-7469

***Prince Albert*: Zatlyn Law Office - *4**
#231, 1061 Central Ave., Prince Albert, SK S6V 4V4
Tel: 306-922-1444; *Fax:* 306-922-5848
zatlyn@sasktel.net

***Regina*: Beke Law Firm - *1**
#700, 2103 - 11th Ave., Regina, SK S4P 4G1
Tel: 306-347-8325
bekelaw@sasktel.net

***Regina*: Dahlem Findlay - *1**
2100 Smith St., Regina, SK S4P 2P2
Tel: 306-522-3631; *Fax:* 306-565-2616
don.findlay@sasktel.net
www.donfindlay.ca

***Regina*: Duchin, Bayda & Kroczynski - *4**
Also Known As: DBK Law
2515 Victoria Ave., Regina, SK S4P 0T2
Tel: 306-359-3131; *Fax:* 306-359-3372
www.dbklaw.com

***Regina*: Duncan Bonneau Law - *2**
#1580, 2002 Victoria Ave., Regina, SK S4P 0R7
Tel: 306-525-8500; *Fax:* 306-525-8585
www.duncanbonneaulaw.com

***Regina*: Duncan Reimber Canham - *3**
116 Albert St., Regina, SK S4R 2N2
Tel: 306-791-2503; *Fax:* 306-543-9655

***Regina*: Gates & Company - *4**
Avonhurst Plaza, 3132 Avonhurst Dr., Regina, SK S4R 3J7
Tel: 306-949-5544; *Fax:* 306-775-2995
office@gateslaw.ca

***Regina*: Gerrand Rath Johnson LLP - *17**
Former Name: Gerrand Mulatz
#700, Toronto Dominion Bank Bldg., 1914 Hamilton St., Regina, SK S4P 3N6
Tel: 306-522-3030; *Fax:* 306-522-3555
grj@grj.ca
www.grj.ca

***Regina*: Griffin Toews Maddigan Brabant - *6**
Former Name: Griffin Toews Maddigan
1530 Angus St., Regina, SK S4T 1Z1
Tel: 306-525-6125; *Fax:* 306-525-5226
griffin.toews@sasktel.net

***Regina*: Cindy M. Haynes Law Office - *1**
320 Gardiner Park Crt., Regina, SK S4V 1R9
Tel: 306-789-2242; *Fax:* 306-789-4950
cindym.haynes@sasktel.net

***Regina*: Jaques Law Office - *2**
2912 Rae St., Regina, SK S4S 1R5
Tel: 306-359-3041; *Fax:* 306-525-4173
jaques@hierlaw.com
www.hierlaw.com

***Regina*: Kanuka Thuringer LLP, Barristers & Solicitors - *25**
#1400, 2500 Victoria Ave., Regina, SK S4P 3X2
Tel: 306-525-7200; *Fax:* 306-359-0590
firm@ktllp.ca
www.kanukathuringer.com

***Regina*: kmpLaw - Regina - *8**
2600 Victoria Ave., Regina, SK S4T 1K2
Tel: 306-761-6200; *Fax:* 306-761-6222
kmplaw.com

***Regina*: Kowalishen Law Firm**
1954 Angus St., Regina, SK S4T 1Z6
Tel: 306-525-2385; *Fax:* 306-525-2386

***Regina*: MacKay & McLean Barristers & Solicitors - *3**
2042 Cornwall St., Regina, SK S4P 2K5
Tel: 306-569-1301; *Fax:* 306-569-8560
dgmackay@sasktel.net
www.mackaymclean.com

***Regina*: MacLean Keith - *4**
Nicol Ct., 2398 Scarth St., Regina, SK S4P 2J7
Tel: 306-757-1611; *Fax:* 306-757-0712
pnm@macleankeith.com
www.macleankeith.com

***Regina*: Mellor Law Firm - *1**
The Anson House, 1547 Anson Rd., Regina, SK S4P 0E1
Tel: 306-569-5299; *Fax:* 306-546-4411
k.mellor@mellorlaw.net
mellorlaw.net

***Regina*: Merchant Law Group LLP - Regina - *35**
#100, Saskatchewan Drive Plaza, 2401 Saskatchewan Dr., Regina, SK S4P 4H8
Tel: 306-359-7777; *Fax:* 306-522-3299
Toll-Free: 888-567-7777
info@merchantlaw.com
www.merchantlaw.com

***Regina*: Mercier Law Office - *1**
#1, 2080 Rae St., Regina, SK S4T 2E5
Tel: 306-551-8001; *Fax:* 877-408-9431
louis@mercierlaw.ca
www.mercierlaw.ca

***Regina*: Donald R. Morgan - *1**
#361, Legislative Bldg., Minister's Office, 2405 Legislative Dr., Regina, SK S4S 0B3
Tel: 306-787-0613; *Fax:* 306-787-6946
minister.ae@gov.sk.ca

***Regina*: Morgan, Khaladkar & Skinner - *2**
2510 - 13 Ave., Regina, SK S4P 0W2
Tel: 306-525-9191; *Fax:* 306-525-0006

***Regina*: Noble, Johnston & Associates - *5**
1143 Lakewood Ct. North, Regina, SK S4X 3S3
Tel: 306-949-5616; *Fax:* 306-775-2234
info@noblejohnston.com
www.noblejohnston.com

***Regina*: Olive, Waller, Zinkhan & Waller LLP - *17**
#1000, 2002 Victoria Ave., Regina, SK S4P 0R7
Tel: 306-359-1888; *Fax:* 306-352-0771
owzw@owzw.com
www.owzw.com

***Regina*: Phillips & Co. - *2**
Haldane House, 2100 Scarth St., Regina, SK S4P 2H6
Tel: 306-569-0811; *Fax:* 306-565-3434
phillipsco@phillipsco.ca

***Regina*: Ann Phillips - *1**
#205, 2022 Cornwall St., Regina, SK S4P 2K5
Tel: 306-791-2626; *Fax:* 306-352-2020
annphillips@attglobal.net

***Regina*: Richmond Nychuk - *8**
#100, 2255 Albert St., Regina, SK S4P 2V5
Tel: 306-359-0202; *Fax:* 306-359-0330
lawoffice@richmondnychuk.com
www.richmondnychuk.com

***Regina*: Sheppard, Braun, Muma - *2**
#204, 3988 Albert St., Regina, SK S4S 3R1
Tel: 306-586-6020; *Fax:* 306-586-8525
sbmlaw@sasktel.net

***Regina*: Silversides & Cox - *2**
Former Name: Woloshyn & Company
#280, Saskatchewan Pl., 1870 Albert St., Regina, SK S4P 4B7
Tel: 306-337-4560; *Fax:* 306-337-4568

** indicates number of lawyers*

***Regina*: Tulloch, Tulloch & Horvath Law Firm - *4**
Also Known As: TTH Law
Former Name: Willows Tulloch & Howe
2012 McIntyre St., Regina, SK S4P 2R6
Tel: 306-924-8600; *Fax:* 306-924-8601
info@tthlaw.ca
tthlaw.ca

***Regina*: Walker, Singer & McCannell - *3**
1872 Angus St., Regina, SK S4T 1Z4
Tel: 306-352-8109; *Fax:* 306-352-7339

***Regina*: Willows Wellsch Orr & Brundige LLP - *14**
Former Name: Rendek McCrank; Stewart Johnson Brundige
#401, 1916 Dewdney Ave., Regina, SK S4R 1G9
Tel: 306-525-2191; *Fax:* 306-757-8138
www.willowswellsch.com

***Rosetown*: Skelton Turner Mescall - *2**
P.O. Box 1120, 314 Main St., Rosetown, SK S0L 2V0
Tel: 306-882-4244; *Fax:* 306-882-3969

***Saskatoon*: A.S.K. Law - *2**
#210, 75 - 24th St. East, Saskatoon, SK S7K 0K3
Tel: 306-933-3933; *Fax:* 306-933-9505
www.asklaw.ca

***Saskatoon*: Murray D. Acton - *1**
Also Known As: Acton Law Office
520 Spadina Cres. East, Saskatoon, SK S7K 3G7
Tel: 306-933-5155; *Fax:* 306-933-5725

***Saskatoon*: Agnew & Company**
279 - 3rd Avenue North, Saskatoon, SK S7K 2H7
Tel: 306-244-7966

***Saskatoon*: Bodnar & Campbell - *2**
Former Name: Bodnar, Wanhella & Cutforth
#400, 245 - 3 Ave. South, Saskatoon, SK S7K 1M4
Tel: 306-664-3314; *Fax:* 306-664-3354
mbodnarlaw@sasktel.net

***Saskatoon*: Bodnar & Campbell - *1**
#400, 235 - 3 Ave. South, Saskatoon, SK S7K 1M4
Tel: 306-664-3314; *Fax:* 306-664-3354
wjcampbell@sasktel.net

***Saskatoon*: Brayford Shapiro - *2**
311 - 21 St. East., Saskatoon, SK S7K 0C1
Tel: 306-244-5656; *Fax:* 306-244-5644
www.brayfordshapiro.ca

***Saskatoon*: Burlingham Cuelenaere Legal Prof. Corp. - *3**
1043 - 8 St. East, Saskatoon, SK S7H 0S2
Tel: 306-343-9581; *Fax:* 306-343-1947
burlinghamcuelenaere@sasktel.net

***Saskatoon*: Cuelenaere, Kendall, Katzman & Watson - *24**
#500, Standard Life Bldg., 128 - 4th Ave. South, Saskatoon, SK S7K 1M8
Tel: 306-653-5000; *Fax:* 306-652-4171
www.cuelenaere.com

***Saskatoon*: Halyk Kennedy Knox - *3**
321 - 6 Ave. North, Saskatoon, SK S7K 2S3
Tel: 306-665-3434; *Fax:* 306-652-1915
halyk@sasktel.net

***Saskatoon*: Hnatyshyn Gough - *8**
#601, 402 - 21st St. East, Saskatoon, SK S7K 0C3
Tel: 306-653-5150; *Fax:* 306-652-5859
hglaw@hglaw.ca
www.hglaw.ca
www.facebook.com/272144306219714

***Saskatoon*: Kloppenburg & Kloppenburg - *2**
#2, 527 Main St., Saskatoon, SK S7N 0C2
Tel: 306-665-7600; *Fax:* 306-665-7800
juristen@kloppenburg.ca
www.kloppenburg.ca

***Saskatoon*: Knott den Hollander - *3**
215 Wall St., Saskatoon, SK S7K 1N5
Tel: 306-664-6900; *Fax:* 306-653-4599
kddlaw@sasktel.net
www.kdqsaskatoonlaw.com

***Saskatoon*: Koskie Helms - *2**
Former Name: Koskie & Company
#3, 501 Gray Ave., Saskatoon, SK S7N 2H8
Tel: 306-242-8478; *Fax:* 306-653-2120
firm@koskie.com
www.koskie.com

***Saskatoon*: Leland Kimpinski LLP - *8**
#800, 230 - 22nd St. East, Saskatoon, SK S7K 0E9
Tel: 306-244-6686; *Fax:* 306-653-7008
info@lelandlaw.ca
www.lelandlaw.ca

***Saskatoon*: MacDermid Lamarsh - *6**
301 - 3rd Ave. South, Saskatoon, SK S7K 1M6
Tel: 306-652-9422; *Fax:* 306-242-1554
macmarsh@macmarsh.com
www.macdermidlamarsh.com

***Saskatoon*: Martel Law Office - *1**
811 Bayview Cres., Saskatoon, SK S7V 1B7
Tel: 306-652-6830; *Fax:* 306-652-6836
martellawoffice@sasktel.net
www.martellawoffice.ca

***Saskatoon*: Mathiason, Valkenburg & Polishchuk - *1**
Former Name: Mathiason, Valkenburg & McLeod
#705, 230 - 22nd St. East, Saskatoon, SK S7K 0E9
Tel: 306-242-1202; *Fax:* 306-244-4423
mvplaw@sasktel.net

***Saskatoon*: McKercher LLP - Saskatoon - *59**
374 Third Ave. South, Saskatoon, SK S7K 1M5
Tel: 306-653-2000; *Fax:* 306-653-2669
info@mckercher.ca
www.mckercher.ca
www.linkedin.com/company/mckercher-llp

***Saskatoon*: Nussbaum & Company - *2**
#204, 2102 - 8 St. East, Saskatoon, SK S7H 0V1
Tel: 306-955-8890; *Fax:* 306-955-1293
nussbaum@sasktel.net

***Saskatoon*: Piche & Company - *1**
#204, 611 University Dr., Saskatoon, SK S7N 3Z1
Tel: 306-955-7667; *Fax:* 306-955-7727
Toll-Free: 866-234-3444
pichelaw@sasktel.net

***Saskatoon*: Plaxton & Company Lawyers - *2**
Former Name: Walker, Plaxton & Co
#500, 402 - 21 St. East, Saskatoon, SK S7K 0C3
Tel: 306-653-1500; *Fax:* 306-664-6659
contactus@plaxtonlaw.com
www.plaxtonlaw.com

***Saskatoon*: Quon Ferguson - *2**
Former Name: Quon Ferguson Owens
#704, 224 - 4th Ave. South, Saskatoon, SK S7K 5M5
Tel: 306-665-8828; *Fax:* 306-665-8835

***Saskatoon*: Robertson Stromberg LLP - *27**
#600, Canada Building, 105 - 21st St. East, Saskatoon, SK S7K 0B3
Tel: 306-652-7575; *Fax:* 306-652-2445
Toll-Free: 800-667-0070
www.rslaw.com
www.facebook.com/Robertsonstromberg, twitter.com/RSLLP, www.linkedin.com/company/robertson-stromberg-llp

***Saskatoon*: Roe & Company - *3**
Former Name: Roe & Olson
#400, 245 Third Ave. South, Saskatoon, SK S7K 1M4
Tel: 306-244-9865; *Fax:* 306-934-6827
nfarenick@hotmail.com
www.roeandcompany.ca

***Saskatoon*: Rozdilsky, Baniak - *2**
#301, 220 - 3rd Ave. South, Saskatoon, SK S7K 1M1
Tel: 306-664-9900

***Saskatoon*: Scharfstein Gibbings Walen & Fisher LLP - *17**
#500, Scotiabank Bldg., 111 - 2 Ave. South, Saskatoon, SK S7K 1K6
Tel: 306-653-2838; *Fax:* 306-652-4747
lawyers@scharfsteinlaw.com
www.scharfsteinlaw.com

***Saskatoon*: Scott & Beaven Law Office - *3**
Former Name: Scott, Ludlow, Fehr
211A - 33 St. West, Saskatoon, SK S7L 0V2
Tel: 306-955-6822; *Fax:* 306-955-6823
www.sblo.ca

***Saskatoon*: Scott Phelps & Mason Barristers & Solicitors - *6**
306 Ontario Ave., Main Fl., Saskatoon, SK S7K 2H5
Tel: 306-244-2201; *Fax:* 306-244-2420
barristers@spmlaw.ca
www.spmlaw.ca

***Saskatoon*: Sonnenschein Law Office - *1**
Lincoln's Inn, 313 - 20th St. East, Saskatoon, SK S7K 0A9
Tel: 306-652-4730; *Fax:* 306-653-5760
sonnenschein@sasktel.net

***Saskatoon*: Stevenson Hood Thornton Beaubier LLP - *17**
#500, 123 - 2nd Ave. South, Saskatoon, SK S7K 7E6
Tel: 306-244-0132; *Fax:* 306-653-1118
info@shtb-law.com
www.shtb-law.com

***Saskatoon*: Stooshinoff Law Office - *2**
#300, 416 - 21st St. East, Saskatoon, SK S7K 0C2
Tel: 306-653-9000; *Fax:* 306-653-5284

***Saskatoon*: The W Law Group - *15**
Former Name: Woloshyn & Company
#300, 110 - 21st St. East, Saskatoon, SK S7K 0B6
Tel: 306-244-2242; *Fax:* 306-652-0332
Toll-Free: 888-244-2242
info@wlawgroup.com
wlawgroup.com

***Saskatoon*: Wallace Meschishnick Clackson Zawada - *19**
#410, 475 - 2nd Ave. South, Saskatoon, SK S7K 1P4
Tel: 306-933-0004; *Fax:* 306-933-2006
info@wmcz.com
www.wmcz.com
twitter.com/wmcz, www.linkedin.com/company/1772083

***Saskatoon*: Steven J. Wilson - *1**
2120 York Ave., Saskatoon, SK S7J 1H8
Tel: 306-956-3345; *Fax:* 306-955-1699

***Shaunavon*: Coralie O. Geving - *1**
Also Known As: Geving Law Office
23 - 3 Ave. East, Shaunavon, SK S0N 2M0
Tel: 306-297-2205; *Fax:* 306-297-2411

***Swift Current*: Anderson & Company - *8**
51 - 1st Ave. NW, Swift Current, SK S9H 0M5
Tel: 306-773-2891; *Fax:* 306-778-3364
anderson.company@sasktel.net
www.andersonandcompany.ca

***Swift Current*: Holland Law Office - *1**
#15, 600 Chaplin St. East, Swift Current, SK S9H 1J3
Tel: 306-773-0661; *Fax:* 306-773-9630

***Swift Current*: MacBean Tessem - Swift Current - *4**
P.O. Box 550, 151 First Ave. NE, Swift Current, SK S9H 2B1
Tel: 306-773-9343; *Fax:* 306-778-3828
macbeantessem@macbeantessem.com
www.macbeantessem.com

***Unity*: Neil Law Office - *1**
Former Name: Hepting Neil & Jeanson
P.O. Box 600, 206 - 2nd Ave. West, Unity, SK S0K 4L0
Tel: 306-228-2631; *Fax:* 306-228-4449
neillawoffice@saktel.net

***Weyburn*: Nimegeers Schuck Wormsbecker Bobbitt - *3**
Also Known As: NSWB Law Firm
Former Name: Nimegeers & Schuck; Nimegeers & Grant
P.O. Box 8, 319 Souris Ave., Weyburn, SK S4H 2J8
Tel: 306-842-4654; *Fax:* 306-842-0522
law@nswb.com
www.nswb.com
www.facebook.com/pages/NSWB-Law-Firm/195047653897186

***Wynyard*: Klebeck Law Office - *1**
P.O. Box 1120, 115 Ave. B East, Wynyard, SK S0A 4T0
Tel: 306-554-2523; *Fax:* 306-554-2099
klebeck.law.office@sasktel.net

** indicates number of lawyers*

***Wynyard*: Paulson & Ferraton - *1**
P.O. Box 460, 106 Main St., Wynyard, SK S0A 4T0
Tel: 306-554-2134; *Fax:* 306-554-2342
paulson.ferraton@sasktel.net

***Yorkton*: Leland Campbell LLP - *8**
P.O. Box 188, 36 - 4 Ave. North, Yorkton, SK S3N 2V7
Tel: 306-783-8541; *Fax:* 306-786-7484
reception@lelandcampbell.com
www.lelandcampbell.com

***Yorkton*: Tourney, Dellow - *2**
#2, 16 - 3rd Ave. North, Yorkton, SK S3N 0A1
Tel: 306-782-2211; *Fax:* 306-782-2213
tourneydellow@sasktel.net

Yukon Territory

***Whitehorse*: Austring, Fendrick & Fairman - *7**
3081 - 3 Ave., Whitehorse, YT Y1A 4Z7
Tel: 867-668-4405; *Fax:* 867-668-3710
info@lawyukon.com
www.lawyukon.com

***Whitehorse*: Cabott & Cabott - *5**
#101, 2131 - 2nd Ave., Whitehorse, YT Y1A 1C3
Tel: 867-456-3100; *Fax:* 867-456-7093
Toll-Free: 877-456-3105
tina.escareal@northwestel.net
www.cabottandcabott.com

***Whitehorse*: Lackowicz & Hoffman**
Former Name: Preston Lackowicz & Shier
#300, 204 Black St., Whitehorse, YT Y1A 2M9
Tel: 867-668-5252; *Fax:* 867-668-5251

***Whitehorse*: Lamarche Pearson**
505 Lambert St., Whitehorse, YT Y1A 1Z8
Tel: 867-456-3300
slamarche@lamarchepearson.com

***Whitehorse*: Macdonald & Company**
#200, 204 Lambert St., Whitehorse, YT Y1A 3T2
Tel: 867-667-7885; *Fax:* 867-667-7600

***Whitehorse*: Roothman & Company - *2**
#203, 4133 - 4th Ave, Whitehorse, YT Y1A 1H8
Tel: 867-667-4664
info@roothmanlaw.ca
www.roothmanlaw.ca/en/

***Whitehorse*: Tucker & Company - *5**
#102, 205 Hawkins St., Whitehorse, YT Y1A 1X3
Tel: 867-667-2099; *Fax:* 867-667-2109
info@tuckerandcompany.ca
tuckerandcompany.ca
www.facebook.com/tuckerandcompany,
www.linkedin.com/company/tucker-&-company

***Whitehorse*: Whittle & Company**
#203, 107 Main St., Whitehorse, YT Y1A 2A7
Tel: 867-633-4199

** indicates number of lawyers*

SECTION 12
LIBRARIES

Library & Archives Canada: 1735

Government Departments in Charge of Libraries: 1735

Library listings are arranged by province. Each province includes the following categories

Regional Systems

Public Libraries

Archives

Library & Archives Canada / Bibliothèque et Archives Canada
395 Wellington St., Ottawa ON K1A 0N4
613-996-5115; Fax: 613-995-6274
Toll-Free 866-578-7777; TTY 613-992-6969
www.bac-lac.gc.ca
Librarian & Archivist of Canada, Guy Berthiaume
Social Media: www.facebook.com/LibraryArchives; twitter.com/@LibraryArchives; www.youtube.com/user/LibraryArchiveCanada

AMICUS Services: 819-934-5851; Fax: 819-934-4388; bureauservicegiti-imitservicedesk@bac-lac.gc.ca; union.catalogue@bac-lac.gc.ca; reference@bac-lac.gc.ca; amicus.collectionscanada.gc.ca/aaweb/aalogine.htm; Symbol: OONL

Canadian Cataloguing in Publications Program (CIP): 819-994-6881; Fax: 819-997-7517; cip@bac-lac.gc.ca; www.bac-lac.gc.ca/eng/services/cip; Symbol: OONL

Canadian Subject Headings (CSH): 819-953-6810; Fax: 819-953-0291; standards@bac-lac.gc.ca; www.bac-lac.gc.ca/eng/services/canadiansubject-headings; Symbol: OONL

Canadiana: The National Bibliography of Canada: 819-994-6913; Fax: 819-953-0291; standards@bac-lac.gc.ca; www.bac-lac.gc.ca/eng/services/canadiana; Symbol: OONL; Acting Director, Published Canadiana, Susan Haigh, susan.haigh@canada.ca

Cataloguing & Metadata: 819-994-6900; Fax: 819-934-4388; standards@bac-lac.gc.ca; BAC.Normesdecatalogage-Cataloguingstandards.LAC@canada.ca; www.bac-lac.gc.ca/eng/services/cataloguing-metadata; Symbol: OONL

Electronic Collection: A Virtual Collection of Monographs & Periodicals: 819-997-9565; Fax: 819-953-8508; epe@bac-lac.gc.ca; Symbol: OONL; Information & Legal Deposit Technician, Rachel Trepanier, rachel.trepanier@canada.ca

Gifts: 819-934-5793; Fax: 819-997-2395; gifts@bac-lac.gc.ca; www.bac-lac.gc.ca/eng/about-us/about-collection/Pages/gifts-archives-published-materials.aspx; Symbol:OONL

Government Records Appraisal & Disposition Program: 819-934-7519; Fax: 819-934-7534; centre.liaison.centre@bac-lac.gc.ca; Symbol: OONL

Information Management: 819-934-7519; Fax: 819-934-7534; centre.liaison.centre@bac-lac.gc.ca; Symbol: OONL

Interlibrary Loan (ILL): 613-996-7527; Fax: 613-996-4424; illservicespeb@bac-lac.gc.ca; www.bac-lac.gc.ca/eng/services/loans-other-institutions/Pages/loans-other-institutions.aspx; Symbol: OONL; Manager, Interlibrary Loan Services, Elizabeth Onyszko, elizabeth.onyszko@lac-bac.gc.ca

International Standard Book Number (ISBN): 819-994-6872; Fax: 819-997-7517; BAC.ISBN.LAC@canada.ca; www.bac-lac.gc.ca/eng/services/isbn-canada; Symbol: OONL; ISBN Technician, Heidi Poapst, heidi.poapst@canada.ca

International Standard Music Number (ISMN): 819-994-6872; Fax: 819-997-7517; BAC.ISBN.LAC@canada.ca; www.bac-lac.gc.ca/eng/services/isbn-canada; Symbol: OONL; Supervisor, Serials & Music, Ivan Baser, ivan.basar@canada.ca

International Standard Serial Number (ISSN): 819-994-6895; Fax: 819-997-6209; BAC.ISSN.LAC@canada.ca; www.bac-lac.gc.ca/eng/services/issn-canada; Symbol: OONL; Supervisor, Serials & Music, Ivan Baser, ivan.basar@canada.ca

Jacob M. Lowy Collection: 613-995-7960; Fax: 613-943-1112; lowy@lac-bac.gc.ca; www.bac-lac.gc.ca/eng/lowy-collection; Symbol: OONL; Librarian, English Monographs, Leah Cohen, leah.cohen@canada.ca

Legal Deposit: 819-997-9565; Fax: 819-997-7019; BAC.Depotlegal-LegalDeposit.LAC@canada.ca; www.bac-lac.gc.ca/eng/services/legal-deposit; Symbol: OONL

Literary Archives: 819-934-8331; Fax: 819-934-8333; reference@bac-lac.gc.ca; www.bac-lac.gc.ca/eng/discover/archives-literary; Symbol: OONL

MARC Records Distribution Service (MRDS): 819-994-6913; Fax: 819-934-6777; BAC.SDNM-MRDS.LAC@canada.ca; Symbol: OONL

MARC 21 Standards: 819-994-6936; Fax: 819-934-4388; marc@bac-lac.gc.ca; www.marc21.ca/index-e.html; Symbol: OONL

The Rare Book Collection: 819-934-8334; Fax: 819-995-6274; rare.books@bac-lac.gc.ca; www.bac-lac.gc.ca/eng/discover/rare-book; Symbol: OONL

Recordkeeping: 819-934-7519; Fax: 819-934-7534; centre.liaison.centre@bac-lac.gc.ca; Symbol: OONL

Reference Services: 613-996-5115; Fax: 613-995-6274; reference@lac-bac.gc.ca; www.bac-lac.gc.ca/eng/services-public; Symbol: OONL; Reference Librarian, Megan Butcher, megan.butcher@canada.ca

Services to Federal Institutions: 819-934-7519; Fax: 819-934-7534; centre.liaison.centre@bac-lac.gc.ca; Symbol: OONL

Theses Canada: 819-994-6882; Fax: 819-997-2395; BAC.ThesesCanada-ThesesCanada.LAC@canada.ca; www.bac-lac.gc.ca/eng/services/theses; Symbol: OONL

Union Catalogue: 819-934-5851; Fax: 819-934-4388; union.catalogue@bac-lac.gc.ca; www.collectionscanada.gc.ca/union-catalogue/index-e.html; Symbol: OONL; Librarian, Myriam Beauchemin, myriam.beauchemin@canada.ca

Government Departments in Charge of Libraries

ALBERTA: Alberta Public Library Services, #803, Standard Life Centre, 10405 Jasper Ave., Edmonton, AB T5J 4R7, 780-427-4871; Fax: 780-415-8594, libraries@gov.ab.ca, www.municipalaffairs.alberta.ca/alberta_libraries

BRITISH COLUMBIA: Ministry of Education, Libraries Branch, PO Box 9831, Stn. Provincial Government, Victoria, BC V8W 9T1, 250-356-1791; Fax: 250-953-4985; Toll Free: 800-663-7051, llb@gov.bc.ca, www.bced.gov.bc.ca/pls; twitter.com/MyBCLibrary; Director, Library Services, Mari Martin

MANITOBA: Manitoba Public Library Services, #300, 1011 Rosser Ave., Brandon, MB R7A 0L5, 204-726-6590, Fax: 204-726-6868, pls@gov.mb.ca, www.gov.mb.ca/chc/pls/index; Director, Trevor Surgenor

NEW BRUNSWICK: New Brunswick Public Library Service, Provincial Office, #2, 570 Two Nations Crossing, Fredericton, NB E3A 0X9, 506-453-2354, Fax: 506-444-4064, sbpnb-nbpls@gnb.ca, www.gnb.ca/publiclibraries; Executive Director, Sylvie Nadeau, sylvie.nadeau@gnb.ca

NEWFOUNDLAND & LABRADOR: Newfoundland & Labrador Public Libraries, 48 St. George's Ave., Stephenville NL A2N 1K9, 709-643-0900, Fax: 709-643-0925, URL: www.nlpl.ca; Executive Director, Andrew Hunt, ahunt@nlpl.ca

NORTHWEST TERRITORIES: Northwest Territories Public Library Services, 75 Woodland Dr., Hay River NT X0E 1G1, 867-874-6531, Fax: 867-874-3321, Toll Free: 866-297-0232, www.nwtpls.gov.nt.ca; Territorial Librarian, Brian Dawson, Brian_Dawson@gov.nt.ca

NOVA SCOTIA: Nova Scotia Provincial Library, 1741 Brunswick St., 2nd Fl., Halifax NS B3J 2R5, 902-424-2457, Fax: 902-424-0633, Email: nspl@novascotia.ca, URL: library.novascotia.ca; Director, Jennifer Evans, evansjl@gov.ns.ca

NUNAVUT: Nunavut Public Library Services, PO Box 270, Baker Lake NU X0C 0A0, 867-793-3353, Fax: 867-793-3360, www.publiclibraries.nu.ca; Manager, Library Services, Ron Knowling, rknowling@gov.nu.ca

ONTARIO: Ontario Public Libraries, #1700, 401 Bay St., Toronto, ON M7A 0A7, 416-314-7620, Fax: 416-212-1802, www.mtc.gov.on.ca/en/libraries/libraries.shtml; Library Services Advisor, Rod Sawyer, rod.sawyer@ontario.ca

PRINCE EDWARD ISLAND: Provincial Library Service, PO Box 7500, Morell PE C0A 1S0, 902-961-7320, Fax: 902-961-7322, plshq@gov.pe.ca, www.library.pe.ca; twitter.com/PEILibrary; www.facebook.com/PEILibrary; Director, Libraries & Archives, Kathleen Eaton, keeaton@gov.pe.ca

QUÉBEC: Ministère de la culture et communications, Bibliothèque ministérielle, Direction de la coordination et du soutien à la gestion des programmes, Édifice Guy-Frégault, 225, Grande Allée est, Bloc C, RC, Québec QC G1R 5G5, 418-380-2325, Téle: 418-380-2326, biblio@mcc.gouv.qc.ca; www.mcc.gouv.qc.ca; Responsable, Jonathan Gailloux

SASKATCHEWAN: Provincial Library, 409A Park St., Regina, SK S4N 5B2, 306-787-2976, www.education.gov.sk.ca/Provincial-Library; Provincial Librarian & Executive Director, Alison Hopkins, alison.hopkins@gov.sk.ca

YUKON: Yukon Public Libraries, PO Box 2703, Whitehorse YT Y1A 2C6, 867-667-5239, Fax: 867-393-6333, Toll Free (in Yukon): 800-661-0408, whitehorse.library@gov.yk.ca, www.ypl.gov.yk.ca; Director, Public Libraries, Aimee Ellis, aimee.ellis@gov.yk.ca

Alberta

Regional Systems

***Elk Point:* Northern Lights Library System**
5615 - 48 St., Elk Point, AB T0A 1A0
Tel: 780-724-2596; *Fax:* 780-724-2597
Toll-Free: 800-561-0387
www.nlls.ab.ca
Social Media: www.facebook.com/220912134588039
Julie Walker, Interim Executive Director
780-724-2596 ext. 247
Wei Xuan, Library Consultant, Information Technology
780-724-2596 ext. 239

***Grande Prairie:* Peace Library System**
8301 - 110 St., Grande Prairie, AB T8W 6T2
Tel: 780-538-4656; *Fax:* 780-539-5285
Toll-Free: 800-422-6875
peacelib@peacelibrarysystem.ab.ca
www.peacelibrarysystem.ab.ca
Social Media: pinterest.com/peacelibrarysys; twitter.com/PeaceLibrarySys; www.facebook.com/peacelibrarysystem
Linda Duplessis, Director
lduples@peacelibrarysystem.ab.ca
Carol Downing, Assistant Director, Tech Services & School Library Consultant
cdowning@peacelibrarysystem.ab.ca

***Lacombe:* Parkland Regional Library**
5404 - 56 Ave., Lacombe, AB T4L 1G1
Tel: 403-782-3850; *Toll-Free:* 800-567-9024
www.prl.ab.ca
Social Media: www.youtube.com/user/PRLLibrary; twitter.com/PrlLibrary; www.facebook.com/prl.library
Ronald Sheppard, Director
rsheppard@prl.ab.ca

***Lethbridge:* Chinook Arch Regional Library System**
2902 - 7th Ave. North, Lethbridge, AB T1H 5C6
Tel: 403-380-1500; *Fax:* 403-380-3550
Toll-Free: 888-458-1500
Other Numbers: ILL Desk: 403-942-8027; Toll-Free: 1-866-941-9262
arch@chinookarch.ab.ca
www.chinookarch.ab.ca
Social Media: twitter.com/chinooklibs; www.facebook.com/149361021750600
Maggie Macdonald, CEO
mmacdonald@chinookarch.ca
403-380-1505
Robin Thiessen Hepher, Associate Director
rhepher@chinookarch.ca
403-380-1507
Lauren Jessop, Senior Manager, Public Services
ljessop@chinookarch.ca
403-380-1506
Trevor Haugen, IT Team Leader
thaugen@chinookarch.ca
403-380-1522

***Medicine Hat:* Shortgrass Library System**
2375 - 10th Ave. SW, Medicine Hat, AB T1A 8G2
Tel: 403-529-0550; *Fax:* 403-528-2473
Toll-Free: 866-529-0550
www.shortgrass.ca
Social Media: www.youtube.com/user/ShortgrassLibrary; twitter.com/shortgrassnews; www.facebook.com/shortgrasslibsystem
Petra Mauerhoff, CEO & Director
petra@shortgrass.ca
Chris Field, Manager, Technical Services
chris@shortgrass.ca
Peggy Curthoys, Acquisitions Officer
peggy@shortgrass.ca

***Spruce Grove:* Yellowhead Regional Library**
433 King St., Spruce Grove, AB T7X 2Y1
Tel: 780-962-2003; *Fax:* 780-962-2770
Toll-Free: 877-962-2003
www.yrl.ab.ca
Social Media: twitter.com/YRLnow

Kevin Dodds, Director
kdodds@yrl.ab.ca
780-982-2003 ext. 226
Wendy Sears Ilnicki, Assistant Director
wsears@yrl.ab.ca
780-962-2003 ext. 225

Strathmore: Marigold Library System
710 - 2nd St., Strathmore, AB T1P 1K4
Tel: 403-934-5334; _Toll-Free:_ 855-934-5334
admin@marigold.ab.ca
www.marigold.ab.ca
Social Media: twitter.com/MarigoldLibSys; www.facebook.com/pages/Marigold-Library-System/143659609025785
Michelle Toombs, CEO
michelle@marigold.ab.ca
403-934-5334 ext. 224
Lynne Thorimbert, Manager, Service Delivery
lynne@marigold.ab.ca
403-934-5334 ext. 248
Richard Kenig, Manager, Information Technology
richard@marigold.ab.ca
403-934-5334 ext. 240
Carlee Pilikowski, Communications & Marketing Specialist
carlee@marigold.ab.ca
403-934-5334 ext. 237

Public Libraries

Acadia Valley: Acadia Municipal Library
Warren Peers School, 103 - 1st Ave. North, Acadia Valley, AB T0J 0A0
Tel: 403-972-3744
aavalibrary@marigold.ab.ca
www.acadialibrary.ca

Acme: Acme Municipal Library
610 Walsh Ave., Acme, AB T0M 0A0
Tel: 403-546-3879
aamlibrary@marigold.ab.ca
www.acmelibrary.ca
Social Media: www.facebook.com/pages/Acme-Municipal-Library/377216215627149

Airdrie: Airdrie Public Library
#111, 304 Main St. SE, Airdrie, AB T4B 3C3
Tel: 403-948-0600; _Fax:_ 403-912-4002
info@airdriepubliclibrary.ca
www.airdriepubliclibrary.ca
Social Media: youtube.com/user/aplvids; twitter.com/AirdrieLibrary; www.facebook.com/AirdriePublicLibrary
Janine Jevne, Director
janine.jevne@airdriepubliclibrary.ca

Alberta Beach: Alberta Beach Public Library
4815 - 50th Ave., Alberta Beach, AB T0E 0A0
Tel: 780-924-3491
ablibrary@yrl.ab.ca
www.albertabeachlibrary.ca
Sylvia McGinley, Chair

Alder Flats: Alder Flats Public Library
Hwy. 13, Alder Flats, AB T0C 0A0
Tel: 780-388-3881; _Fax:_ 780-388-3887
alderflatslibrary@yrl.ab.ca
www.alderflatslibrary.ab.ca
Social Media: www.facebook.com/alderflatslibrary
Linda Volk, Library Director

Alix: Alix Public Library
4928 - 50th St., Alix, AB T0C 0B0
Tel: 403-747-3233
alixpublic@libs.prl.ab.ca
alixpublic.prl.ab.ca
Social Media: www.facebook.com/alixlibrary
Terry Holdstock, Library Manager

Alliance: Alliance Community Library
101 - 1st Ave. East, Alliance, AB T0B 0A0
Tel: 780-879-3733
alliance.prl.ab.ca
Tracy Rombough, Library Manager

Amisk: Amisk Municipal Library
5005 - 50 St., Amisk, AB T0B 0B0
Tel: 780-628-5457
amisklibrary.prl.ab.ca
Carmen Toma, Library Manager

Andrew: Andrew Municipal Public Library
5021 - 50 St., Andrew, AB T0B 0C0
Tel: 780-365-3501; _Fax:_ 780-365-3734
public@mcsnet.ca
www.andrewschool.ca

Arrowwood: Arrowwood Municipal Library
PO Box 88, Arrowwood, AB T0L 0B0
Tel: 403-534-3932; _Fax:_ 403-534-3932
help@arrowwoodlibrary.ca
www.arrowwoodlibrary.ca
Dawn Holoboff, Library Manager

Ashmont: Ashmont Community Library
Ashmont School, Main St., Ashmont, AB T0A 0C0
Tel: 780-726-3877; _Fax:_ 780-726-3777
www.ashmontlibrary.ab.ca
Tonya Hlushko, Contact

Athabasca: Alice B. Donahue Library & Archives
4716 - 48th St., Athabasca, AB T9S 2B6
Tel: 780-675-2735; _Fax:_ 780-675-2735
www.athabascalibrary.ab.ca
Social Media: www.facebook.com/AliceB.DonahueLibrary

Banff: Banff Public Library
101 Bear St., Banff, AB T1L 1H3
Tel: 403-762-2661; _Fax:_ 403-762-3805
info@banfflibrary.ab.ca
www.banfflibrary.ab.ca
Social Media: www.facebook.com/banfflibrary

Barnwell: Barnwell Municipal Library
500 - 2nd St. West, Barnwell, AB T0K 0B0
Tel: 403-223-3626
help@barnwelllibrary.ca
www.barnwelllibrary.ca
Social Media: twitter.com/Chinooklibs; www.facebook.com/pages/Barnwell-Public-Library/149942341759892
Maggie Macdonald, CEO
mmacdonald@chinookarch.ca
403-380-1505

Barrhead: Barrhead Public Library
5103 - 53 Ave., Barrhead, AB T7N 1N9
Tel: 780-674-8519; _Fax:_ 780-674-8520
library@barrheadpubliclibrary.ca
www.barrheadpubliclibrary.ca
Social Media: www.pinterest.com/barrheadl; www.facebook.com/BarrheadPublicLibrary
Elaine Dickie, Library Director

Bashaw: Bashaw Municipal Library
5020 - 52nd St., Bashaw, AB T0B 0H0
Tel: 780-372-4055
bashawlibrary@libs.prl.ab.ca
bashawlibrary.prl.ab.ca

Bassano: Bassano Memorial Library
522 - 2nd Ave., Bassano, AB T0J 0B0
Tel: 403-641-4065
bassano.shortgrass.ca
Social Media: www.facebook.com/BassanoMemorialLibrary

Bawlf: David Knipe Memorial Library
203 Hanson St., Bawlf, AB T0B 0J0
Tel: 780-373-3882
bawlflibrary.prl.ab.ca
Social Media: twitter.com/BawlfLibrary
Fern Reinke, Library Manager

Bear Canyon: Bear Point Community Library
PO Box 43, Bear Canyon, AB T0H 0B0
Tel: 780-595-3771
librarian@bearpointlibrary.ab.ca
www.bearpointlibrary.ab.ca

Beaumont: Bibliothèque de Beaumont Library
5700 - 49th St., Beaumont, AB T4X 1S7
Tel: 780-929-2665; _Fax:_ 780-929-1291
library@beaumontlibrary.com
www.beaumontlibrary.com
Social Media: www.facebook.com/BeaumontLibrary
Martin Walters, Library Director
martin@beaumontlibrary.com
Andrea Ciochetti, Program Coordinator
andrea@beaumontlibrary.com

Beaverlodge: Beaverlodge Public Library
406 - 10th St., Beaverlodge, AB T0H 0C0
Tel: 780-354-2569; _Fax:_ 780-354-3078
librarian@beaverlodgelibrary.ab.ca
www.beaverlodgelibrary.ab.ca
Social Media: www.facebook.com/BeaverlodgeLibrary

Beiseker: Beiseker Municipal Library
401 - 5th St., Beiseker, AB T0M 0G0
Tel: 403-947-3230
abemlibrary@marigold.ab.ca
www.beisekerlibrary.ca

Bentley: Bentley Municipal Library
5014 - 49 Ave., Bentley, AB T0C 0J0
Tel: 403-748-4626
bentleylibrary.prl.ab.ca
Social Media: www.facebook.com/582865878467285
Suzanne Moore, Library Manager

Berwyn: Berwyn W.I. Municipal Library
PO Box 89, Berwyn, AB T0H 0E0
Tel: 780-338-3616; _Fax:_ 780-338-3616
librarian@berwynlibrary.ab.ca
www.berwynlibrary.ab.ca
Kim Byard, Library Manager

Big Valley: Big Valley Municipal Library
29 - 1st Ave. South, Big Valley, AB T0J 0G0
Tel: 403-876-2642
bvlibrary.prl.ab.ca
Linda Stillinger, Library Manager

Blackfalds: Blackfalds Public Library
5018 Waghorn St., Blackfalds, AB T0M 0J0
Tel: 403-885-2343; _Fax:_ 403-885-4353
Other Numbers: 403-885-6251 program room
www.blackfaldslibrary.com
Social Media: twitter.com/blkfaldslibrary
Carley Binder, Librarian

Blairmore: Crowsnest Pass Municipal Library - Blairmore
2114 - 127 St., Blairmore, AB T0K 0E0
Tel: 403-562-8393; _Fax:_ 403-562-8397
help@crowsnestpasslibrary.ca
www.crowsnestpasslibrary.ca
Social Media: twitter.com/Chinooklibs; www.facebook.com/164362500321554
Maggie Macdonald, CEO

Blue Ridge: Blue Ridge Community Library
24A Main St., Blue Ridge, AB T0E 0B0
Tel: 780-648-7323
blueridgelibrary@yrl.ab.ca
www.blueridgelibrary.ab.ca

Bodo: Bodo Public Library
PO Box 93, Bodo, AB T0B 0M0
Tel: 780-753-6079
bodolibrary.prl.ab.ca
Roxanna Wotschell, Library Manager

Bon Accord: Bon Accord Public Library
PO Box 749, Bon Accord, AB T0A 0K0
Tel: 780-921-2540; _Fax:_ 780-921-2580
www.bonaccordlibrary.ab.ca
Brenda Gosbjorn, Chair
Peggy Teneycke, Library Manager

Bonanza: Bonanza Municipal Library
PO Box 53, Bonanza, AB T0H 0K0
Tel: 780-353-3067
librarian@bonanzalibrary.ca
www.bonanzalibrary.ca

Bonnyville: Bonnyville Municipal Library
4804 - 49th Ave., Bonnyville, AB T9N 2J3
Tel: 780-826-3071; _Fax:_ 780-826-2058
www.bonnyvillelibrary.ab.ca
Ina Smith, Library Director
Linda Smiley, Assistant Library Manager
Kim Dechaine, Programmer
Brigitte Stewart, Contact, Public Services & Interlibrary Loan

Bow Island: Bow Island Municipal Library
510 Centre St., Bow Island, AB T0K 0G0
Tel: 403-545-2828; _Fax:_ 403-545-6642
bowisland.shortgrass.ca
Social Media: www.facebook.com/BowIslandLibrary
Susan Andersen, Library Manager

***Bowden:* Bowden Public Library**
PO Box 218, Bowden, AB T0M 0K0
Tel: 403-224-3688
bowdenlibrary.prl.ab.ca
Social Media: www.facebook.com/123488397714713
Linda Toews, President

***Boyle:* Boyle Public Library**
5002 - 3 St., Boyle, AB T0A 0M0
Tel: 780-689-4161; *Fax:* 780-689-5660
librarian@boylepublib.ab.ca
www.boylepublib.ab.ca

***Breton:* Breton Public Library**
4916 - 50th Ave., Breton, AB T0C 0P0
Tel: 780-696-3740; *Fax:* 780-696-3590
bretonlibrary@yrl.ab.ca
www.bretonlibrary.ab.ca
Social Media:
www.facebook.com/pages/Breton-Municipal-Library/7783359088
61665
Diane Shave, Library Director
Alice Fenton, Contact
Cheryl Buck-Joudrey, Contact

***Brooks:* Berry Creek Community School Library**
Berry Creek Community School, RR#2, Brooks, AB T1R 1E2
Tel: 403-566-3743
www.berrycreeklibrary.ca
Social Media: www.facebook.com/berrycreekcommunitylibrary

***Brooks:* Brooks Public Library**
420 - 1st Ave. West, Brooks, AB T1R 1B9
Tel: 403-362-2947; *Fax:* 403-362-8111
brooks.shortgrass.ca
Social Media: www.youtube.com/user/BrooksPublicLibrary;
twitter.com/brookslibrary;
www.facebook.com/BrooksPublicLibrary
George Hawtin, Head Librarian

***Brownfield:* Brownfield Community Library**
PO Box 63, Brownfield, AB T0C 0R0
Tel: 403-578-2247
brownfieldlibrary.prl.ab.ca
Darvy Gilbertson, Librarian

***Brownvale:* Brownvale Community Library**
PO Box 407, Brownvale, AB T0H 1W0
Tel: 780-597-2250
brownvalelibrary@wispernet.ca

***Bruderheim:* Metro Kalyn Community Library**
5017 - 49th St., Bruderheim, AB T0B 0S0
Tel: 780-796-3032; *Fax:* 780-796-3032
librarian@bruderheimpl.ab.ca
www.bruderheimpl.ab.ca

***Cadogan:* Cadogan Public Library**
PO Box 10, Cadogan, AB T0B 0T0
Tel: 780-753-6933
cadoganlibrary.prl.ab.ca

***Calgary:* Calgary Public Library**
616 MacLeod Trail SE, 6th Fl., Calgary, AB T2G 2M2
Tel: 403-260-2600
calgarylibrary.ca
Social Media: youtube.com/user/CPLibrary;
twitter.com/calgarylibrary;
www.facebook.com/calgarypubliclibrary
Bill Ptacek, CEO
Cathy Freer-Leszczynski, Director, Partnership Development
Paul Lane, Director, Corporate Services
Scott Stanley, Senior Manager, Information Technology
Patrick Ulrich, Senior Manager, Facilities Planning & Operations
Ellen Humphrey, Deputy CEO
Elrose Klause, Controller
Heather Robertson, Director, Service Design
Mark Asberg, Director, Service Delivery
Paul McIntyre Royston, Director, External Relations

***Calling Lake:* Calling Lake Public Library**
PO Box 129, Calling Lake, AB T0G 0H0
Tel: 780-331-3027; *Fax:* 780-331-3029
librarian@callinglakelibrary.ab.ca
www.callinglakelibrary.ab.ca

***Calmar:* Calmar Public Library**
4705 - 50th Ave., Calmar, AB T0C 0V0
Tel: 780-985-3472; *Fax:* 780-985-2859
calmarlibrary@yrl.ab.ca
www.calmarpubliclibrary.ca

***Camrose:* Camrose Public Library**
4710 - 50th Ave., Camrose, AB T4V 0R8
Tel: 780-672-4214; *Fax:* 780-672-9165
cpl@libs.prl.ab.ca
cpl.prl.ab.ca
Social Media: twitter.com/CamroseLibrary1;
www.facebook.com/CamroseLibrary
Elizabeth Luck, Chair
Deb Cryderman, Library Manager
deb@prl.ab.ca

***Canmore:* Canmore Public Library**
#101, 700 Railway Ave., Canmore, AB T1W 1P4
Tel: 403-678-2468
staff@canmorelibrary.ab.ca
www.canmorelibrary.ab.ca
Social Media: www.pinterest.com/canmorelibrary;
twitter.com/CanmoreLibrary; www.facebook.com/canmorelibrary
Susan Beckett, Chair

***Carbon:* Carbon Municipal Library**
Community Centre, PO Box 70, Carbon, AB T0M 0L0
Tel: 403-572-3440
acarmlibrary@marigold.ab.ca
www.carbonlibrary.ca
Social Media: www.facebook.com/carbonmunicipallibrary
Holly Laffin, Chair
Jay-Lynn Boutin, Library Manager

***Cardston:* Jim & Mary Kearl Library of Cardston**
25 - 3rd Ave. West, Cardston, AB T0K 0K0
Tel: 403-653-4775; *Fax:* 403-653-4716
help@cardstonlibrary.ca
www.cardstonlibrary.ca
Social Media: twitter.com/Chinooklibs;
www.facebook.com/pages/Jim-and-Mary-Kearl-Library/2574449
74415851
Donna Beazer, Manager
403-653-4775
Michele Snyder, Children's Programming Specialist

***Carmangay:* Carmangay & District Municipal Library**
414 Grand Ave., Carmangay, AB T0L 0N0
Tel: 403-643-3777; *Fax:* 403-643-3777
help@carmangaylibrary.ca
www.carmangaylibrary.ca
Marian Schibbelhute, Library Manager

***Caroline:* Caroline Municipal Library**
5023 - 50 Ave., Caroline, AB T0M 0M0
Tel: 403-722-4060
carolinelibrary@prl.ab.ca
carolinelibrary.prl.ab.ca
Social Media: www.facebook.com/443310695699998
Sheryl Holmstrom, Chair

***Carseland:* Carseland Community Library**
Carseland Community Hall, 330 Railway Ave. West, Carseland, AB T0J 0M0
Tel: 403-934-6007; *Fax:* 403-934-9230
carselandlibrary@abnet.ca
www.carselandlibrary.ca

***Carstairs:* Carstairs Public Library**
1402 Scarlett Ranch Rd., Carstairs, AB T0M 0N0
Tel: 403-337-3943
www.carstairspublic.prl.ab.ca
Social Media: pinterest.com/carstairslibrar;
twitter.com/CarstairsL; www.facebook.com/222408391104566
Joanne Merrick, Library Manager

***Castor:* Castor Public Library**
5103 - 51 St., Castor, AB T0C 0X0
Tel: 403-882-3999
castorlibrary.prl.ab.ca
Wendy Bozek, Library Manager

***Cereal:* Cereal & District Municipal Library**
415 Main St., Cereal, AB T0J 0N0
Tel: 403-326-3883
acermlibrary@marigold.ab.ca
www.cereallibrary.ca
Social Media: www.facebook.com/318045288265934

***Champion:* Champion Municipal Library**
132A - 2 St. South, Champion, AB T0L 0R0
Tel: 403-897-3099; *Fax:* 403-897-3099
help@championlibrary.ca
www.championlibrary.ca
Patty Abel, Librarian

***Chauvin:* Chauvin Municipal Library**
Dr. Folkins Community School, 5200 - 4th Ave. North, Chauvin, AB T0B 0V0
Tel: 780-858-3746; *Fax:* 780-858-2392
www.chauvinmunicipallibrary.ab.ca
Jennifer Waters, Library Manager

***Chestermere:* Chestermere Public Library**
105B Marina Rd., Chestermere, AB T1X 1V7
Tel: 403-272-9025
acheslibrary@marigold.ab.ca
www.chestermerepubliclibrary.com
Social Media: www.pinterest.com/marigoldlibsys;
twitter.com/ChestermereLib;
www.facebook.com/ChestermerePublicLibrary
Marilyn King, Contact
marilyn@littleacorns.ca

***Claresholm:* Claresholm Municipal Library**
211 - 49 Ave. West, Claresholm, AB T0L 0T0
Tel: 403-625-4168; *Fax:* 403-625-2939
help@claresholmlibrary.ca
www.claresholmlibrary.ca
Social Media: www.facebook.com/clarlibrary
Kathy Davies, Library Manager
Shelley Ford, Library Clerk & Program Coordinator
Jay Sawatzky, Library Clerk
Brenda Fogarty, Library Clerk
Charley Waters, Library Clerk

***Cleardale:* Menno-Simons Public Library**
PO Bag 100, Cleardale, AB T0H 3Y0
Tel: 780-685-2340; *Fax:* 780-685-3665
Sylvia Gula, Librarian

***Clive:* Clive Public Library**
Clive Village Office, 5115 - 50 St., Clive, AB T0C 0Y0
Tel: 403-784-3131
www.clivepublib.prl.ab.ca
Wanda Wagner, President
Sandra Ward, Librarian

***Coaldale:* Coaldale Public Library**
2014 - 18 St., Coaldale, AB T1M 1E9
Tel: 403-345-1340; *Fax:* 403-345-1342
help@coaldalelibrary.ca
www.coaldalelibrary.ca
Social Media: twitter.com/CoaldaleLibrary;
www.facebook.com/pages/Coaldale-Public-Library/17726194232
9108
Heather Nicholson, Head Librarian
hnicholson@coaldalelibrary.ca
403-345-1341

***Cochrane:* Cochrane Nan Boothby Memorial Library**
405 Railway St. West, Cochrane, AB T4C 2E2
Tel: 403-932-4353
www.cochranepubliclibrary.ca
Social Media: www.pinterest.com/nanboothby;
twitter.com/Nanboothbee;
www.facebook.com/202620799775893
Marcia Johnston, Executive Director
marcia.johnston@cochranepubliclibrary.ca

***Cold Lake:* Cold Lake Public Library**
5513B - 48 Ave., Cold Lake, AB T9M 1X9
Tel: 780-594-5101; *Fax:* 780-594-7787
www.library.coldlake.ab.ca
Social Media: twitter.com/CLPublicLibrary
Mary Anne Penner, Library Director
director@library.coldlake.ab.ca

***Consort:* Consort Municipal Library**
Consort School, 5215 - 50th St., Consort, AB T0C 1B0
Tel: 403-577-2501
aconmlibrary@marigold.ab.ca
www.consortlibrary.ca

***Coronation:* Coronation Memorial Library**
5001 Royal St., Coronation, AB T0C 1C0
Tel: 403-578-3445
coronationlib.prl.ab.ca
Social Media: www.facebook.com/CoronationLibrary
Marilyn Polege, Chair
Lauren Reid, Manager

***Coutts:* Coutts Municipal Library**
218 - 1st Ave. South, Coutts, AB T0K 0N0
Tel: 403-344-3804; *Fax:* 403-344-3815
help@couttslibrary.ca
www.couttslibrary.ca
Sharon Wollersheim, Librarian

Cremona: **Cremona Municipal Library**
Village of Cremona Municipal Bldg., 205 - 1 St. East, Cremona, AB T0M 0R0
Tel: 403-637-3100
cremonalibrary@prl.ab.ca
cremonalibrary.prl.ab.ca
Sandra Herbert, Library Manager

Crossfield: **Crossfield Municipal Library**
1026 Chisholm Ave., Crossfield, AB T0M 0S0
Tel: 403-946-4232; *Fax:* 403-946-4212
admin@crossfieldlibrary.ca
www.crossfieldlibrary.ca
Social Media: twitter.com/CrossfieldLib; www.facebook.com/156681641025114

Czar: **Czar Municipal Library**
PO Box 127, Czar, AB T0B 0Z0
Tel: 780-857-3740
czarlibrary.prl.ab.ca
Jackie Almberg, Library Manager

Darwell: **Darwell Public Library**
Darwell Community Hall, #54, 225B Hwy. 765, Darwell, AB T0E 0L0
Tel: 780-892-3746; *Fax:* 780-892-3743
adarlibrary@yrl.ab.ca
www.darwellpubliclibrary.ab.ca
Social Media: www.facebook.com/DarwellPublicLibrary
Sandra Stepaniuk, Library Manager

Daysland: **Daysland Public Library**
5130 - 50th St., Daysland, AB T0B 1A0
Tel: 780-781-0005
dayslandlibrary.prl.ab.ca
Pat Malone, Library Manager

Debolt: **DeBolt Public Library**
PO Box 480, Debolt, AB T0H 1B0
Tel: 780-957-3770; *Fax:* 780-957-3770
librarian@deboltlibrary.ab.ca
www.deboltlibrary.ab.ca

Delburne: **Delburne Municipal Library**
2210 Main St., Delburne, AB T0M 0V0
Tel: 403-749-3848
delburnelibrary@prl.ab.ca
delburnelibrary.prl.ab.ca
Judy Nicklom, Library Manager

Delia: **Delia Municipal Library**
Delia School, 205 - 3 Ave. North, Delia, AB T0J 0W0
Tel: 403-364-3777
adm.library@plrd.ab.ca
www.delialibrary.ca
Social Media: www.pinterest.com/delialibrary; twitter.com/DeliaLibrary; www.facebook.com/admlibrary
Bob Marshall, Chair
Leah Hunter, Library Manager

Devon: **Devon Public Library**
Devon Shopping Center, #101, 17 Athabasca Ave., Devon, AB T9G 1G5
Tel: 780-987-3720
devon@devonpubliclibrary.ca
www.devonpubliclibrary.ca
Social Media: www.facebook.com/110715152303134
Joy Monsma, Chair
Audrey Benjamin, Library Director
audrey@devonpubliclibrary.ca
Linda Garez, Library Assistant
Holly Gilmour, Early Childhood/Seniors Program Co-ordinator

Didsbury: **Didsbury Municipal Library**
2033 - 19 Ave., Didsbury, AB T0M 0W0
Tel: 403-335-3142
didsburylibrary@prl.ab.ca
dml.prl.ab.ca
Social Media: pinterest.com/didsburylibrary; twitter.com/DidsburyLibrary; www.facebook.com/210993855623
Inez Kosinski, Librarian

Dixonville: **Dixonville Community Library**
PO Box 206, Dixonville, AB T0H 1E0
Tel: 780-971-2593; *Fax:* 780-971-2048
librarian@dixonvillelibrary.ab.ca
www.dixonvillelibrary.ab.ca
Cayley Cartwright, Library Manager

Donalda: **Donalda Municipal Library**
5001 Main St., Donalda, AB T0B 1H0
Tel: 403-883-2345; *Fax:* 403-883-2022
donaldalibrary.prl.ab.ca
Social Media: www.pinterest.com/dmunicipal; twitter.com/DonaldaLibrary; www.facebook.com/221607057874579
Shaleah Fox, Library Manager

Drayton Valley: **Drayton Valley Municipal Library**
5120 - 50 St., Drayton Valley, AB T7A 1R7
Tel: 780-514-2228
www.draytonvalleylibrary.ca
Social Media: twitter.com/dvlibrary; www.facebook.com/dvlibrary
Sandy Faunt, Librarian
sfaunt@draytonvalley.ca

Drumheller: **Drumheller Public Library**
80 Veterans Way, Drumheller, AB T0J 0Y2
Tel: 403-823-1371; *Fax:* 403-823-1374
www.drumhellerlibrary.ca
Social Media: www.pinterest.com/drumpublibrary; twitter.com/DrumPubLibrary; www.facebook.com/110077339080350

Duchess: **Duchess & District Public Library**
256a Louise Ave., Duchess, AB T0J 0Z0
Tel: 403-378-4369
duchess.shortgrass.ca
Social Media: www.facebook.com/www.shortgrass.ca
Shannon Vanderloh, Library Manager
Sandra Peers, Chair

Duffield: **Duffield Community Library**
1 Main St., Duffield, AB T0E 0N0
Tel: 780-892-2644
duffieldlibrary@yrl.ab.ca
www.pcmlibraries.ab.ca
Social Media: www.facebook.com/pcmlibraries
Kathy Gardiner, Library Manager
kgardiner@yrl.ab.ca

Duffield: **Keephills Community Library**
#15, 51515 RR#32A, Duffield, AB T0E 0N0
Tel: 780-731-0000
keephillslibrary@yrl.ab.ca
www.pcmlibraries.ab.ca
Social Media: www.facebook.com/pcmlibraries

Eaglesham: **Eaglesham Public Library**
PO Box 206, Eaglesham, AB T0H 1H0
Tel: 780-359-3792; *Fax:* 780-359-3745
librarian@eagleshamlibrary.ab.ca
www.eagleshamlibrary.ab.ca

Eckville: **Eckville Public Library**
4855 - 51 Ave., Eckville, AB T0M 0X0
Tel: 403-746-3240
eckvillelibrary.prl.ab.ca
Social Media: www.facebook.com/eckvilledistrictpubliclibrary
Carol Griner, Library Manager

Edberg: **Edberg Public Library**
48 - 1st Ave. West, Edberg, AB T0B 1J0
Tel: 780-678-5606
www.edberglibrary.prl.ab.ca
Pam Fankhanel, Library Manager

Edgerton: **Edgerton Public Library**
5037 - 50 Ave., Box 180, Edgerton, AB T0B 1K0
Tel: 780-755-2666; *Fax:* 780-755-2667
www.edgertonlibrary.ab.ca

Edmonton: **Alberta Public Library Services**
Standard Life Centre, #803, 10405 Jasper Ave., Edmonton, AB T5J 4R7
Tel: 780-427-4871; *Fax:* 780-415-8594
Toll-Free: -310-0000
libraries@gov.ab.ca
www.municipalaffairs.alberta.ca/alberta_libraries
Social Media: twitter.com/AB_Libraries
Diana Davidson, Director
diana.davidson@gov.ab.ca
Grant Tolley, Manager, Strategic Library Planning & Policy
grant.tolley@gov.ab.ca

Edmonton: **Edmonton Public Library**
7 Sir Winston Churchill Sq., Edmonton, AB T5J 2V4
Tel: 780-496-7000; *Fax:* 780-496-1885
TTY: 780-496-183
www.epl.ca
Social Media: www.youtube.com/user/edmontonpl; twitter.com/EPLdotCA; www.facebook.com/EPLdotCA
Pilar Martinez, Chief Executive Officer
780-496-7050
Gastone Monai, Chief Financial Officer
780-496-1840
Linda Garvin, Executive Director, Customer Experience
780-442-6851
Tina Thomas, Executive Director, Strategy & Innovation
780-496-7046
Mike Lewis, Director, Human Resource Services
780-496-7066
Johnny Nielsen, Director, Facilities & Operations
780-496-1848
Louise Reimer, Director, Library Services
780-442-6850

Edson: **Edson & District Public Library**
4726 - 8th Ave., Edson, AB T7E 1S8
Tel: 780-723-6691; *Fax:* 780-723-9728
www.edsonlibrary.ca
Social Media: twitter.com/edsonlibrary; www.facebook.com/pages/Edson-Public-Library/202333883135366
Helen Prosser, Library Manager
Debra Halterman, Chair

Elk Point: **Elk Point Public Library**
5123 - 50 Ave., Elk Point, AB T0A 1A0
Tel: 780-724-3737; *Fax:* 780-724-3739
www.elkpointlibrary.ab.ca

Elmworth: **Elmworth Community Library**
PO Box 23, Elmworth, AB T0H 1J0
Tel: 780-354-2930; *Fax:* 780-354-3639
librarian@elmworthlibrary.ab.ca
www.elmworthlibrary.ab.ca

Elnora: **Elnora Public Library**
210 Main St., Elnora, AB T0M 0Y0
Tel: 403-773-3966
elnoralibrary@prl.ab.ca
elnoralibrary.prl.ab.ca
Wanda Strandquist, Library Manager

Empress: **Empress Municipal Library**
PO Box 188, Empress, AB T0J 1E0
Tel: 403-565-3936
aemlibrary@marigold.ab.ca
www.empresslibrary.ca

Enchant: **Enchant Community Library**
PO Box 3000, Enchant, AB T0K 0V0
Tel: 403-739-3835; *Fax:* 403-739-2585
help@enchantlibrary.ca
www.enchantlibrary.ca
Sharon Hagen, Librarian

Entwistle: **Entwistle Municipal Library**
5232 - 50th St., Entwistle, AB T0E 0S0
Tel: 780-727-3811
entwistlelibrary@yrl.ab.ca
www.pcmlibraries.ab.ca

Evansburg: **Evansburg & District Municipal Library**
4707 - 46th Ave., Evansburg, AB T0E 0T0
Tel: 780-727-2030; *Fax:* 780-727-2060
www.evansburglibrary.ab.ca
Melissa Ronayne, Library Manager
melirona@gypsd.ca

Exshaw: **Bighorn Library**
2 Heart Mountain Dr., Exshaw, AB T0L 2C0
Tel: 403-673-3571; *Fax:* 403-673-3571
aexclibrary@marigold.ab.ca
www.bighornlibrary.ca
Social Media: twitter.com/bighornlibrary
Michelle Eve, Chair

Fairview: **Fairview Public Library**
10209 - 109 St., Fairview, AB T0H 1L0
Tel: 780-835-2613; *Fax:* 780-835-2613
librarian@fairviewlibrary.ab.ca
www.fairviewlibrary.ab.ca

Falher: **Bibliothèque Dentinger/Falher Library/ Dentinger Library**
CP 60, Falher, AB T0H 1M0
Tél: 780-837-2776; *Téléc:* 780-837-8755
librarian@falherlibrary.ab.ca
www.falherlibrary.ab.ca
Jocelyne Gervais, Gestionnaire

Flatbush: **Flatbush Community Library**
General Delivery, Flatbush, AB T0G 0Z0
Tel: 780-681-3756; *Fax:* 780-681-3756
librarian@flatbushlibrary.ab.ca
www.flatbushlibrary.ab.ca

Foremost: **Foremost Municipal Library**
103 - 1st Ave., Foremost, AB T0K 0X0
Tel: 403-867-3855
foremost.shortgrass.ca
Social Media: www.facebook.com/115060978577693

Forestburg: **Forestburg Municipal Library**
Farvolden Centre, 4901 - 50th St., Forestburg, AB T0B 1N0
Tel: 780-582-4110
forestburglibrary.prl.ab.ca
Social Media: www.facebook.com/230711340306287
Cathy Kells, Librarian

Fort Assiniboine: **Fort Assiniboine Public Library**
Fort Assiniboine School, 35 State Ave., Fort Assiniboine, AB T0G 1A0
Tel: 780-584-2227; *Fax:* 780-674-8575
www.fortassiniboinelibrary.ab.ca
Louise Davison, Library Manager

Fort MacLeod: **Fort MacLeod Municipal Library**
264 - 24 St., Fort MacLeod, AB T0L 0Z0
Tel: 403-553-3880; *Fax:* 403-553-2643
help@fortmacleodlibrary.ca
www.fortmacleodlibrary.ca
Darlene Hofer, Librarian
Laurie Huestis, Librarian

Fort McMurray: **Wood Buffalo Regional Library**
1 C.A. Knight Way, Fort McMurray, AB T9H 5C5
Tel: 780-743-7800
wbrl.ca
Social Media: instagram.com/wbrl_ab; twitter.com/wbrl_ab; www.facebook.com/wbrlab

Fort Saskatchewan: **Fort Saskatchewan Public Library**
10011 - 102 St., Fort Saskatchewan, AB T8L 2C5
Tel: 780-998-4275; *Fax:* 780-992-3255
fsasklib@fspl.ca
www.fspl.ca
Social Media: twitter.com/FSaskLib; www.facebook.com/117991368229430
Stacey Wenger, Public Services Librarian
swenger@fspl.ca
David Larsen, Director
dlarsen@fspl.ca
Susan Schulz, Operations Manager
sschulz@fspl.ca

Fort Vermilion: **Fort Vermilion Community Library**
5103 River Rd., Fort Vermilion, AB T0H 1N0
Tel: 780-927-4279; *Fax:* 780-927-4746
afvclibrary@incentre.net
www.fvclibrary.com
Debbie Bucckert, Library Manager

Fox Creek: **Fox Creek Municipal - School Library**
501 - 8 St., Fox Creek, AB T0H 1P0
Tel: 780-622-2343; *Fax:* 780-622-4160
foxcreeklibrary@yahoo.com
www.foxcreeklibrary.ca
Social Media: www.youtube.com/channel/UCsbGz9q-0q0i-WI5EMj_DCQ; www.facebook.com/383125811771324
Leslie Ann Sharkey, Head Librarian

Galahad: **Galahad Municipal Library**
PO Box 58, Galahad, AB T0B 1R0
Tel: 780-583-3917
galahadpublic.prl.ab.ca
Jocelynne Loeppky, Library Manager

Gem: **Gem Jubilee Library**
PO Box 6, Gem, AB T0J 1M0
Tel: 403-641-3245

Gibbons: **Gibbons Municipal Library**
5111 - 50 Ave., Gibbons, AB T0A 1N0
Tel: 780-923-2004; *Fax:* 780-923-2015
www.gibbonslibrary.ab.ca
Grail Rubin, Library Manager

Gleichen: **Gleichen & District Library Society**
404 Main St., Gleichen, AB T0J 1N0
Tel: 403-734-2390
agmlibrary@marigold.ab.ca
www.gleichenlibrary.ca
Social Media: www.facebook.com/pages/Gleichen-District-Library/111462155589014

Glenwood: **Glenwood Municipal Library**
59 Main Ave., Glenwood, AB T0K 2R0
Tel: 403-393-7260
help@glenwoodlibrary.ca
www.glenwoodlibrary.ca
Melissa Lybbert, Library Manager

Grande Cache: **Grande Cache Municipal Library**
10601 Shand Ave., Grande Cache, AB T0E 0Y0
Tel: 780-827-2081; *Fax:* 780-827-3112
www.grandecachelibrary.ab.ca
Laurel A. Kelsch, Library Director

Grande Prairie: **Grande Prairie Public Library**
#101, 9839 - 103 Ave., Grande Prairie, AB T8V 6M7
Tel: 780-532-3580; *Fax:* 780-538-4983
gplib@gppl.ab.ca
www.gppl.ab.ca
Social Media: twitter.com/GPPublicLibrary; www.facebook.com/16350654747
Maureen Curry, Library Director
mcurry@gppl.ab.ca
780-357-7463
Jacob Fehr, Head, Children's & Teen Services
jfehr@gppl.ab.ca
780-357-7477
Kelly Dickinson, Head, Adult Services
kdickinson@gppl.ab.ca
780-357-7474
Belinda Blackbourn, Technical Services Manager
bblackbourn@gppl.ab.ca
780-357-7460
Heather Willner, Customer Services Manager
780-357-7462

Granum: **Granum Public Library**
310 Railway Ave., Granum, AB T0L 1A0
Tel: 403-687-3912; *Fax:* 403-687-3914
help@granumpubliclibrary.ca
www.granumpubliclibrary.ca

Grassland: **Grassland Public Library**
Hwy. 63, Grassland, AB T0A 1V0
Tel: 780-525-3733; *Fax:* 780-525-3750
www.grasslandlibrary.ab.ca

Grassy Lake: **Grassy Lake Public Library**
PO Box 790, Grassy Lake, AB T0K 0Z0
Tel: 403-655-2232; *Fax:* 403-655-2259
help@grassylakelibrary.ca
www.grassylakelibrary.ca

Grimshaw: **Grimshaw Municipal Library**
5007 - 47 Ave., Grimshaw, AB T0H 1W0
Tel: 780-332-4553
read@grimshawlibrary.ab.ca
www.grimshawlibrary.ab.ca

Gunn: **Rich Valley Public Library**
Rich Valley Community Hall, RR#1, Gunn, AB T0E 1A0
Tel: 780-967-3525
rvpublib@yrl.ab.ca
www.richvalleylibrary.ab.ca
Social Media: www.facebook.com/pages/Rich-Valley-Public-Library/380070102110426
Betti-Ann Laporte, Librarian

Hanna: **Hanna Municipal Library**
202 - 1st Ave. West, Hanna, AB T0J 1P0
Tel: 403-854-3865
library@hanna.ca
www.hannalibrary.ca
Social Media: www.facebook.com/pages/Hanna-Municipal-Library/126902540827761

Hardisty: **Hardisty & District Public Library**
5027 - 50 St., Hardisty, AB T0B 1V0
Tel: 780-888-3947
hardistylib.prl.ab.ca
Billi-Jo Wildeboer, Library Manager

Hay Lakes: **Hay Lakes Municipal Library**
106 Main St., Hay Lakes, AB T0B 1W0
Tel: 780-878-2665
haylakeslibrary.prl.ab.ca
Amanda Barth, Library Manager
Sharmarann Myers, Chair

Hays: **Hays Public Library**
PO Box 36, Hays, AB T0K 1B0
Tel: 403-725-3744; *Fax:* 403-725-3744
help@hayslibrary.ca
www.hayslibrary.ca

Heinsburg: **Heinsburg Community Library**
General Delivery, Heinsburg, AB T0A 1X0
Tel: 780-943-3913; *Fax:* 780-943-3773
hcs@sperd.ca
www.heinsburgcapsite.8k.com
Rayma Isaac, Library Clerk

Heisler: **Heisler Municipal Library**
100 Haultain Ave., Heisler, AB T0B 2A0
Tel: 780-889-3925
heislerlibrary.prl.ab.ca
Marvis Zimmer, Library Manager

High Level: **High Level Municipal Library**
10601 - 103 St., High Level, AB T0H 1Z0
Tel: 780-926-2097; *Fax:* 780-926-4268
librarian@highlevellibrary.ab.ca
www.highlevellibrary.ab.ca
Social Media: twitter.com/HL_LibraryAB; www.facebook.com/373315752685440
Amanda Ebert, Library Director

High Prairie: **High Prairie Municipal Library**
4723 - 53 Ave., High Prairie, AB T0G 1E0
Tel: 780-523-3838; *Fax:* 780-523-2537
librarian@highprairielibrary.ab.ca
www.highprairielibrary.ab.ca
Social Media: www.facebook.com/194353513915591
Tracy Roberts, Library Manager
Karen Harris, Assistant Librarian (Interlibrary Loans)
Kayla Killoran, Assistant Librarian (Programming)

High River: **High River Library**
909 - 1st St. SW, High River, AB T1V 1A5
Tel: 403-652-2917
director@highriverlibrary.ca
www.highriverlibrary.ca
Social Media: twitter.com/hrclibrary; www.facebook.com/pages/High-River/29442446989
Deb Gardiner, Director

Hines Creek: **Hines Creek Municipal Library**
PO Box 750, Hines Creek, AB T0H 2A0
Tel: 780-494-3879; *Fax:* 780-494-3605
librarian@hinescreeklibrary.ab.ca
hinescreeklibrary.ab.ca

Hinton: **Hinton Municipal Library**
803 Switzer Dr., Hinton, AB T7V 1V1
Tel: 780-865-2363; *Fax:* 780-865-4292
www.hintonlibrary.org
Social Media: www.facebook.com/pages/Hinton-Municipal-Library/117588374933796
Tara Million, Manager
taramill@hintonlibrary.org
780-865-6051

Holden: **Holden Municipal Library**
4912 - 50 St., Holden, AB T0B 2C0
Tel: 780-688-3838; *Fax:* 780-688-3838
www.holdenlibrary.ab.ca

Hughenden: **Hughenden Public Library**
7 Mackenzie Ave., Hughenden, AB T0B 2E0
Tel: 780-856-2435
hughendenlibrary.prl.ab.ca
Karen Carson, Chair
Patricia Mackie, Library Manager

Hussar: **Hussar Municipal Library**
102 - 2 St. NW, Hussar, AB T0J 1S0
Tel: 403-787-3781; *Fax:* 403-787-3922
ahumlibrary@marigold.ab.ca
www.hussarlibrary.ca

Hythe: **Hythe Public Library**
10013 - 100 St., Hythe, AB T0H 2C0
Tel: 780-356-3014; *Fax:* 780-356-3014
manager@hythelibrary.ab.ca
www.hythelibrary.ab.ca

Innisfail: **Innisfail Public Library**
5300A - 55 St. Close, Innisfail, AB T4G 1A5
Tel: 403-227-4407
ipl.prl.ab.ca
Social Media:
www.youtube.com/channel/UC53tKtXsPKjWAQIG8KVfBzg;
twitter.com/Innisfail_Lib;
www.facebook.com/pages/Innisfail-Public-Library/206107056099442

Innisfree: **Innisfree Public Library**
Box 121, Innisfree, AB T0B 2G0
Tel: 780-853-7250
librarian@innisfreelibrary.ca
www.innisfreelibrary.ca
Social Media: twitter.com/innisfreelibrar
Marilyn Newton, Library Manager

Irma: **Irma Municipal Library**
PO Box 340, Irma, AB T0B 2H0
Tel: 780-754-3746; *Fax:* 780-754-3802
www.irmalibrary.ca

Irricana: **Irricana Municipal Library**
Curling Rink, 302 - 2 St., Irricana, AB T0M 1B0
Tel: 403-935-4818; *Fax:* 403-935-4818
ailibrary@marigold.ab.ca
www.irricanalibrary.ca
Social Media: www.pinterest.com/IrricanaLibrary;
twitter.com/IrricanaLibrary; www.facebook.com/irricanalibrary
Elysse Reicheneder, Library Manager

Jasper: **Jasper Municipal Library**
303 Bonhomme St., Jasper, AB T0E 1E0
Tel: 780-852-3652; *Fax:* 780-852-5841
www.jasperlibrary.ab.ca
Social Media: www.flickr.com/photos/18294679@N00;
twitter.com/jasperlib; www.facebook.com/jaspermunicipallibrary
Angie Thom, Library Director

Keg River: **Keg River Community Library**
PO Box 68, Keg River, AB T0H 2G0
Tel: 780-841-8841
Betty Hasenack, Library Manager

Killam: **Killam Community Library**
5017 - 49th Ave., Killam, AB T0B 2L0
Tel: 780-385-3032
www.killamlibrary.prl.ab.ca
Barb Cox, Library Manager

Kinuso: **Kinuso Municipal Library**
PO Box 60, Kinuso, AB T0G 1K0
Tel: 780-775-3694; *Fax:* 780-775-3650
librarian@kinusolibrary.ab.ca
kinusolibrary.ab.ca

Kitscoty: **Kitscoty Public Library**
4910 - 51 St., Kitscoty, AB T0B 2P0
Tel: 780-846-2822; *Fax:* 780-846-2215
librarian@kitscotypubliclibrary.ab.ca
www.kitscotypubliclibrary.ab.ca

La Crete: **La Crete Community Library**
10001 - 99 Ave., La Crete, AB T0H 2H0
Tel: 780-928-3166; *Fax:* 780-928-3166
www.lacretelibrary.com

La Glace: **La Glace Community Library**
9924 - 97 Ave., La Glace, AB T0H 2J0
Tel: 780-568-4696; *Fax:* 780-568-4707
librarian@laglacelibrary.ab.ca
www.laglacelibrary.ab.ca
Social Media: www.facebook.com/LaGlaceCommunityLibrary

Lac La Biche: **Stuart MacPherson Library**
Bold Center, 8702 - 91 St., Lac La Biche, AB T0A 2C0
Tel: 780-623-7467; *Fax:* 780-623-7497
www.stuartmacphersonlibrary.ca
Maureen Penn, Librarian

Lacombe: **Mary C. Moore Public Library**
#101, 5214 - 50 Ave., Lacombe, AB T4L 0B6
Tel: 403-782-3433; *Fax:* 403-782-3329
mcmpl@libs.prl.ab.ca
www.lacombelibrary.org
Social Media: twitter.com/MCM_PubLibrary;
www.facebook.com/MCMPL

Lamont: **Lamont Municipal Library**
PO Box 180, Lamont, AB T0B 2R0
Tel: 780-895-2299; *Fax:* 780-895-2600
www.lamontpubliclibrary.ca

Lancaster Park: **Edmonton Garrison Community Library**
#32, Bldg. 161, Lancaster Park, AB T0A 2H0
Tel: 780-973-4011; *Fax:* 780-973-1598
librarian@garrisonlibrary.ab.ca
www.garrisonlibrary.ab.ca
Shawna Murphy, Supervisor

Leduc: **Leduc Public Library**
2 Alexandra Park, Leduc, AB T9E 4C4
Tel: 780-986-2637; *Fax:* 780-986-3462
www.leduclibrary.ca
Social Media: pinterest.com/leduclibrary;
twitter.com/LeducLibrary;
www.facebook.com/pages/Leduc-Public-Library/303841479652730
Carla Frybort, Head Librarian
cfrybort@leduclibrary.ca
Sharon McAmmond, Public Services Coordinator
smcammond@leduclibrary.ca

Lethbridge: **Lethbridge Public Library**
810 - 5th Ave. South, Lethbridge, AB T1J 4C4
Tel: 403-380-7310; *Fax:* 403-329-1478
questions@lethlib.ca
www.lethlib.ca
Social Media: pinterest.com/lethlib; twitter.com/lethlib;
www.facebook.com/lethlib
Vic Mensch, Board Chair
Tony Vanden Heuvel, Chief Executive Officer

Lethbridge: **Médiathèque Françophone Emma Morrier**
2104, 6e av sud, Lethbridge, AB T1J 1C3
Tél: 403-388-2921
mediatheque@scfl.ca
www.mfem.ca
Sophie Morley, Bibliothécaire
Sophie Morley

Linden: **Linden Municipal Library**
c/o Dr. Elliot School, 215 - 1 St. SE, Linden, AB T0M 1J0
Tel: 403-546-3757; *Fax:* 403-546-4220
almlibrary@marigold.ab.ca
www.lindenlibrary.ca

Lomond: **Lomond Community Library**
2 Railway Ave. North, Lomond, AB T0L 1G0
Tel: 403-792-3934; *Fax:* 403-792-3934
help@lomondlibrary.ca
www.lomondlibrary.ca

Longview: **Longview Municipal Library**
128 Morrison Place, Longview, AB T0L 1H0
Tel: 403-558-3927; *Fax:* 403-558-3927
alomlibrary@marigold.ab.ca
www.longviewlibrary.ca
Social Media: www.facebook.com/LongviewLibrary

Lougheed: **Lougheed Public Library**
5004 - 50 St., Lougheed, AB T0B 2V0
Tel: 780-386-2498
www.lougheed.prl.ab.ca
Barb McConnell, Library Manager

Ma-Me-O Beach: **Pigeon Lake Public Library**
603 - 2 Ave., Ma-Me-O Beach, AB T0C 1X0
Tel: 780-586-3778; *Fax:* 780-586-3558
pigeonlakelibrary@yrl.ab.ca
www.pigeonlakepubliclibrary.ab.ca
Opal Taylor, Library Manager

Magrath: **Magrath Public Library**
6N - 1 St. W., Magrath, AB T0K 1J0
Tel: 403-758-6498; *Fax:* 403-758-6442
help@magrathlibrary.ca
www.magrathlibrary.ca

Mallaig: **Mallaig Public Library**
1st St. East, Mallaig, AB T0A 2K0
Tel: 780-635-3858; *Fax:* 780-635-3938
www.mallaiglibrary.ab.ca

Manning: **Manning Municipal Library**
PO Box 810, Manning, AB T0H 2M0
Tel: 780-836-3054; *Fax:* 780-836-0071
librarian@manninglibrary.ab.ca
www.manninglibrary.ab.ca

Mannville: **Mannville Municipal Library**
5029 - 50 St., Mannville, AB T0B 2W0
Tel: 230-663-3611; *Fax:* 306-663-3688
librarian@mannvillelibrary.ab.ca
www.mannvillelibrary.ab.ca

Marwayne: **Marwayne Public Library**
105 - 2nd St. South, Marwayne, AB T0B 2X0
Tel: 780-847-3930; *Fax:* 780-847-3796
www.marwaynelibrary.ab.ca
Carmen Smart, Library Manager

Mayerthorpe: **Mayerthorpe Public Library**
4911 - 52nd St., Mayerthorpe, AB T0E 1N0
Tel: 780-786-2404
www.mayerthorpelibrary.ab.ca
Social Media: www.facebook.com/Mayerthorpe.Public.Library

McLennan: **McLennan Municipal Library**
19 - 1st Ave. NW, McLennan, AB T0H 2L0
Tel: 780-324-3767; *Fax:* 780-324-2288
librarian@mclennanlibrary.ab.ca
www.mclennanlibrary.ab.ca

Medicine Hat: **Medicine Hat Public Library**
414 - 1st St. SE, Medicine Hat, AB T1A 0A8
Tel: 403-502-8525
www.mhpl.info
Social Media: www.youtube.com/user/MHPublicLibrary;
twitter.com/mhpubliclibrary; www.facebook.com/MHPublicLibrary
Shelley Ross, Chief Librarian
403-502-8528
Sheila Drummond, Head, Fiction Services
403-502-8533
Carol Ann Cross-Roen, Head, Youth Services
403-502-8532
Annette Ziegler, Manager, Circulation Services
403-502-8539

Milk River: **Milk River Municipal Library**
321 - 3rd Ave. NE, Milk River, AB T0K 1M0
Tel: 403-647-3793
help@milkriverlibrary.ca
www.milkriverlibrary.ca

Millarville: **Millarville Community Library**
Box 59, Millarville, AB T0L 1K0
Tel: 403-931-3919
amclibrary@marigold.ab.ca
www.millarvillelibrary.ca

Millet: **Millet Public Library**
5031 - 49th Ave., Millet, AB T0C 1Z0
Tel: 780-387-5222; *Fax:* 780-387-5224
millet@yrl.ab.ca
www.milletlibrary.ca
Margaret Blackstock, Library Manager

Milo: **Milo Municipal Library**
116 Centre St., Milo, AB T0L 1L0
Tel: 403-599-3850; *Fax:* 403-599-3924
help@milolibrary.ca
www.milolibrary.ca

Mirror: **Mirror Public Library**
5202 - 50 Ave., Mirror, AB T0B 3C0
Tel: 403-788-3044

Morinville: **Morinville Public Library**
10119 - 100 Ave., Morinville, AB T8R 1P8
Tel: 780-939-3292; *Fax:* 780-939-2757
www.morinvillelibrary.ca
Social Media: twitter.com/MoriLibrary;
www.facebook.com/pages/Morinville-Public-Library/124554254228030
Keith Norris, Chair
Isabelle Cramp, Library Manager

Morrin: **Morrin Municipal Library**
113 Main St., Morrin, AB T0J 2B0
Tel: 403-772-3922
amomlibrary@marigold.ab.ca
www.morrinlibrary.ca
Social Media: www.pinterest.com/amomlibrary;
www.facebook.com/pages/Village-of-Morrin-Library/152196974828164

Mundare: **Mundare Municipal Public Library**
5128 - 50 St., Mundare, AB T0B 3H0
Tel: 780-764-3929; *Fax:* 780-764-2003
www.mundarelibrary.ab.ca

Myrnam: **Myrnam Community Library**
New Myrnam School, 5105 - 50 St., Myrnam, AB T0B 3K0
Tel: 780-366-3801; *Fax:* 780-366-2332
www.myrnamlibrary.ab.ca

***Nampa:* Nampa Municipal Library**
10203 - 99 Ave., Nampa, AB T0H 2R0
Tel: 780-322-3805; *Fax:* 780-322-3955
librarian@nampalibrary.ab.ca
www.nampalibrary.ab.ca
Social Media: www.facebook.com/NampaMunicipalLibrary

***Nanton:* Nanton Municipal Library / Thelma Fanning Memorial Library**
1907 - 21 Ave., Nanton, AB T0L 1R0
Tel: 403-646-5535; *Fax:* 403-646-2653
help@nantonlibrary.ca
www.nantonlibrary.ca
Social Media: www.flickr.com/photos/nanton_library; www.facebook.com/pages/Nanton-Library/242719735785773

***Neerlandia:* Neerlandia Public Library**
PO Box 10, Neerlandia, AB T0G 1R0
Tel: 780-674-5384; *Fax:* 780-674-2927
www.neerlandialibrary.ab.ca
Brenda Gelderman, Library Assistant
Dagmar Visser, Library Assistant

***New Sarepta:* New Sarepta Community Library**
c/o New Sarepta Community High School, 5150 Center St., New Sarepta, AB T0B 3M0
Tel: 780-975-7513; *Fax:* 780-941-2224
www.newsareptalibrary.ca
Social Media: www.facebook.com/pages/New-Sarepta-Public-Library/315981572
Willow Schnell, Library Director

***Newbrook:* Newbrook Public Library**
Box 208, Newbrook, AB T0A 2P0
Tel: 780-576-3772; *Fax:* 780-576-2115
www.newbrooklibrary.ab.ca

***Niton Junction:* Green Grove Public Library**
53521A Range Rd. 130, Niton Junction, AB T0E 1S0
Tel: 780-795-2474; *Fax:* 780-795-3933
www.greengrovelibrary.ab.ca
Toni Smigelski, Library Manager

***Nordegg:* Nordegg Public Library**
General Delivery, Nordegg, AB T0M 2H0
Tel: 403-800-3667
nordegglibrary@libs.prl.ab.ca
nordegglibrary.prl.ab.ca
Heather Clement, Librarian

***Okotoks:* Okotoks Public Library**
7 Riverside Dr. West, Okotoks, AB T1S 1A6
Tel: 403-938-2220; *Fax:* 403-938-4317
www.okotokslibrary.ca
Social Media: www.pinterest.com/okotokslibrary; twitter.com/OkotoksLibrary; www.facebook.com/OkotoksPublicLibrary
Tessa Nettleton, Director
Lara Grunow, Acting Assistant Librarian

***Olds:* Olds & District Municipal Library**
5217 - 52 St., Olds, AB T4H 1H7
Tel: 403-556-6460
oml@prl.ab.ca
oml.prl.ab.ca
Social Media: www.pinterest.com/oldslibrary; twitter.com/oldslibrary; www.facebook.com/oldslibrary
Lesley Winfield, Head Librarian
lwinfield@prl.ab.ca
403-438-0454

***Onoway:* Onoway Public Library**
4708 Lac Ste., Anne Trail North, Onoway, AB T0E 1V0
Tel: 780-967-2445; *Fax:* 888-467-1389
onowaylibrary@yrl.ab.ca
www.onowaylibrary.ab.ca
Social Media: www.facebook.com/pages/Onoway-Public-Library/403901992978065
Kelly Huxley, Librarian
Lorrie Hafermehl, Chair

***Oyen:* Oyen Municipal Library**
105 - 3rd Ave. West, Oyen, AB T0J 2J0
Tel: 403-664-3580
aoymlibrary@marigold.ab.ca
www.oyenlibrary.ca

***Paddle Praire:* Paddle Praire Public Library**
PO Box 58, Paddle Praire, AB T0H 2W0
Tel: 780-981-3100; *Fax:* 780-981-3737
librarian@paddleprairielibrary.ab.ca
www.paddleprairielibrary.ab.ca

***Paradise Valley:* Three Cities Public Library**
PO Box 89, Paradise Valley, AB T0B 3R0
Tel: 780-745-2277; *Fax:* 780-745-2641
librarian@paradisevalleylibrary.ab.ca
www.paradisevalleylibrary.ab.ca
Social Media: www.facebook.com/281191885224423

***Peace River:* Peace River Municipal Library**
9807 - 97 Ave., Peace River, AB T8S 1H6
Tel: 780-624-4076; *Fax:* 780-624-4086
communications@prmlibrary.ab.ca
www.prmlibrary.ab.ca
Social Media: twitter.com/PRiverLibrary; www.facebook.com/137649962923374
Leslie Ayre-Jaschke, Chair

***Penhold:* Penhold & District Public Library**
1 Waskasoo Ave., Penhold, AB T0M 1R0
Tel: 403-886-2636; *Fax:* 403-886-2638
penholdlibrary@libs.prl.ab.ca
penholdlibrary.prl.ab.ca
Myra Binnendyk, Head of Library

***Picture Butte:* Picture Butte Municipal Library**
120 - 4th St. South, Picture Butte, AB T0K 1V0
Tel: 403-732-4141
help@picturebuttelibrary.ca
www.picturebuttelibrary.ca

***Pincher Creek:* Pincher Creek Municipal Library**
899 Main St., Pincher Creek, AB T0K 1W0
Tel: 403-627-3813; *Fax:* 403-627-2847
help@pinchercreeklibrary.ca
www.pinchercreeklibrary.ca
Social Media: twitter.com/pincherlibrary; www.facebook.com/42049238516

***Plamondon:* Plamondon Municipal Library**
9814 - 100th St., Plamondon, AB T0A 2T0
Tel: 780-798-3852
www.plamondonlibrary.ab.ca
Maureen Penn, Director, Library Services

***Ponoka:* Ponoka Jubilee Library**
5110 - 48 Ave., Ponoka, AB T4J 1R6
Tel: 403-783-3843
ponokalibrary.prl.ab.ca
Social Media: twitter.com/PonokaJubilee; www.facebook.com/pages/Ponoka-Jubilee-Library/305525409564207
Jaclyn Berry, Library Manager
jberry@prl.ab.ca

***Provost:* Provost Municipal Library**
5035 - 51 Ave., Provost, AB T0B 3S0
Tel: 780-753-2801
provostlibrary.prl.ab.ca
Donna Engel, Library Manager

***Radway:* Radway Public Library**
4915 - 50th St., Radway, AB T0A 2V0
Tel: 780-736-3548; *Fax:* 780-736-3858
www.radwaylibrary.ab.ca

***Rainbow Lake:* Rainbow Lake Municipal Library**
1 Atco Rd., Rainbow Lake, AB T0H 2Y0
Tel: 780-956-3656; *Fax:* 780-956-3858
librarian@rainbowlakelibrary.ab.ca
www.rainbowlakelibrary.ab.ca

***Rainier:* Alcoma Community Library**
c/o Alcoma School, Box 120, Rainier, AB T0J 2M0
Tel: 403-362-3741
alcoma.shortgrass.ca
Connie Waddle, Library Manager

***Ralston:* Graham Community Library**
Community Centre, R35 Dugway Dr., Ralston, AB T0J 2N0
Tel: 403-544-3670
graham.shortgrass.ca
Social Media: www.facebook.com/pages/Graham-Community-Library/105715752884381

***Raymond:* Raymond Public Library**
15 Broadway South, Raymond, AB T0K 2S0
Tel: 403-752-4785; *Fax:* 403-752-4710
rlibrary@chinookarch.ab.ca
www.raymondlibrary.ca

***Red Deer:* Red Deer Public Library**
4818 - 49th St., Red Deer, AB T4N 1T9
Tel: 403-346-4576; *Fax:* 403-341-3110
Other Numbers: 403-346-4688 (Children's department)
www.rdpl.org
Social Media: plus.google.com/102986604597427599978; twitter.com/rdpl; www.facebook.com/reddeerpubliclibrary

***Red Earth Creek:* Red Earth Public Library**
PO Box 390, Red Earth Creek, AB T0G 1X0
Tel: 780-694-3898
librarian@redearthlibrary.ab.ca
www.redearthlibrary.ab.ca
Social Media: www.facebook.com/redearthlibrary

***Redcliff:* Redcliff Public Library**
131 Main St. South, Redcliff, AB T0J 2P0
Tel: 403-548-3335
redcliff.shortgrass.ca
Social Media: www.facebook.com/pages/Redcliff-Public-Library/136650276405594

***Redwater:* Redwater Public Library**
4915 - 48th St., Redwater, AB T0A 2W0
Tel: 780-942-3464; *Fax:* 780-942-2013
director@redwaterlibrary.ab.ca
www.redwaterlibrary.ab.ca
Social Media: www.pinterest.com/redwaterpublicl; twitter.com/redwaterlibrary; www.facebook.com/RedwaterLibrary
Gayle Boyd, Director, Library Services
director@redwaterlibrary.ab.ca

***Rimbey:* Rimbey Municipal Library**
4938 - 50 Ave., Rimbey, AB T0C 2J0
Tel: 403-843-2841
rimbeylibrary.prl.ab.ca
Social Media: pinterest.com/RimbeyLibrary; twitter.com/RimbeyLibrary; www.facebook.com/pages/Rimbey-Municipal-Library/344392373862
Jean Keetch, Librarian

***Rochester:* Rochester Community Library**
Rochester School, Hwy. 661, Rochester, AB T0G 1Z0
Tel: 780-698-3970; *Fax:* 780-698-2290
librarian@rochesterlibrary.ab.ca
www.rochesterlibrary.ab.ca
Tammy Morey, Librarian

***Rocky Mountain House:* Rocky Mountain House Public Library**
4922 - 52nd St., Rocky Mountain House, AB T4T 1B1
Tel: 403-845-2042
rmhlibrary.prl.ab.ca
Social Media: www.pinterest.com/rmhlibrary; twitter.com/RockyLibrary; www.facebook.com/pages/Rocky-Public-Library/132801823443316
Cathie MacDonald, Library Manager

***Rockyford:* Rockyford Municipal & District Library**
Community Centre, 412 Serviceberry Trail, Rockyford, AB T0J 2R0
Tel: 403-533-3964
armlibrary@marigold.ab.ca
www.rockyfordlibrary.ca
Social Media: www.pinterest.com/rockyfordlib; twitter.com/Rockyford_AB

***Rolling Hills:* Rolling Hills Public Library**
302 - 4th St., Rolling Hills, AB T0J 2S0
Tel: 403-964-2186
rollinghills.shortgrass.ca
Johnene Amulung, Library Manager

***Rosemary:* Rosemary Community Library**
Rosemary Academic School, Block 6, Dahlia St., Rosemary, AB T0J 2W0
Tel: 403-378-4493
rosemary.shortgrass.ca
Social Media: www.facebook.com/214733181922638

***Rumsey:* Rumsey Community Library**
Main St., Rumsey, AB T0J 2Y0
Tel: 403-368-3939
arumlibrary@marigold.ab.ca
www.rumseylibrary.ca
Social Media: www.facebook.com/pages/Rumsey-Community-Library/113046358725666

Rycroft: **Rycroft Municipal Library**
PO Box 248, Rycroft, AB T0H 3A0
Tel: 780-765-3973; *Fax:* 780-765-2500
librarian@rycroftlibrary.ab.ca
www.rycroftlibrary.ab.ca

Ryley: **McPherson Public Library**
5113 - 50 St., Ryley, AB T0B 4A0
Tel: 780-663-3999; *Fax:* 780-663-3909
www.mcphersonlibrary.ab.ca
Laura Hill, Contact

Sangudo: **Sangudo Public Library**
5131 - 53rd Ave., Sangudo, AB T0E 2A0
Tel: 780-785-3431; *Fax:* 780-785-3179
sangudolibrary@yrl.ab.ca
www.sangudolibrary.ca
Social Media: www.facebook.com/pages/Sangudo-Public-Library/217520651640964
Marica Wierda, Library Manager

Seba Beach: **Seba Beach Public Library**
140 - 3rd St., Seba Beach, AB T0E 2B0
Tel: 780-797-3940; *Fax:* 780-797-3800
www.sebabeachlibrary.ab.ca
Social Media: www.facebook.com/pages/Seba-Beach-Public-Library/162751823790796
Judy Watts-Mott, Library Manager

Sedgewick: **Sedgewick Municipal Library**
5011 - 51 Ave., Sedgewick, AB T0B 4C0
Tel: 780-384-3003
sedgpublib.prl.ab.ca
Barb McConnell, Library Manager

Sexsmith: **Shannon Municipal Library**
Sexsmith Civic Centre, 9917 - 99th Ave., Sexsmith, AB T0H 3C0
Tel: 780-568-4333; *Fax:* 780-568-7249
librarian@shannonlibrary.ab.ca
www.shannonlibrary.ab.ca
Sheryl Pelletier, Library Manager

Sherwood Park: **Strathcona County Library (SCL)**
Community Centre, 401 Festival Lane, Sherwood Park, AB T8A 5P7
Tel: 780-410-8600; *Fax:* 780-467-6861
info@sclibrary.ab.ca
www.sclibrary.ab.ca
Social Media: www.flickr.com/photos/strathcona-county-library; twitter.com/sc_library; www.facebook.com/StrathconaCountyLibrary
Anna Pandos, Chair

Silver Valley: **Savanna Municipal Library**
PO Box 49, Silver Valley, AB T0H 3E0
Tel: 780-351-3771; *Fax:* 780-864-1623
librarian@savannalibrary.ca
www.savannalibrary.ca

Slave Lake: **Rotary Club of Slave Lake Public Library**
101 Main St. East, 1st Fl, Slave Lake, AB T0G 2A0
Tel: 780-849-5250; *Fax:* 780-849-3275
librarian@slavelakelibrary.ab.ca
www.slavelakelibrary.ab.ca
Shane Parmar, Library Manager

Smith: **Smith Community Library**
PO Box 134, Smith, AB T0G 2B0
Tel: 780-829-2389; *Fax:* 780-829-2389
librarian@smithlibrary.ab.ca
www.smithlibrary.ab.ca

Smoky Lake: **Smoky Lake Municipal Public Library**
5010 - 50th St., Smoky Lake, AB T0A 3C0
Tel: 780-656-4212; *Fax:* 780-656-4212
www.smokylakelibrary.ab.ca
Melody Kaban, Library Manager

Spirit River: **Spirit River Municipal Library**
4816 - 44 Ave., Spirit River, AB T0H 3G0
Tel: 780-864-4038
librarian@spiritriverlibrary.ab.ca
www.spiritriverlibrary.ab.ca

Spruce Grove: **Spruce Grove Public Library**
Melcor Cultural Centre, 35 - 5th Ave., Spruce Grove, AB T7X 2C5
Tel: 780-962-4423; *Fax:* 780-962-4826
library@sgpl.ca
www.sgpl.ca
Social Media: www.youtube.com/user/SpruceGroveLibrary61; twitter.com/SG_Library; www.facebook.com/pages/Spruce-Grove-Public-Library/100622914545
Tammy Svenningsen, Library Director

Spruce View: **Spruce View Community Library**
Hwy. 54, Spruce View, AB T0M 1V0
Tel: 403-728-0012
svlibrary.prl.ab.ca
Paddy Birkeland, Library Manager

St Albert: **St Albert Public Library**
5 St Anne St., St Albert, AB T8N 3Z9
Tel: 780-459-1530; *Fax:* 780-458-5772
sapl@sapl.ca
www.sapl.ca
Social Media: twitter.com/stalbertlibrary; www.facebook.com/stalbertpubliclibrary
Peter Bailey, Director
pbailey@sapl.ca
780-459-1681
Heather Dolman, Manager, Public Services
hdolman@sapl.ca
780-459-1686
Marlice Schmidt-Want, Manager, Collections & Technology
mswant@sapl.ca
780-459-1684
Barbara Moreau, Children's Department Coordinator
bmoreau@sapl.ca
780-459-1536

St Isidore: **St Isidore Community Library/ Bibliothèque de St Isidore**
PO Box 1168, St Isidore, AB T0H 3B0
Tel: 780-624-8182; *Fax:* 780-624-8192
www.bibliothequestisidore.ab.ca

St Paul: **St Paul Municipal Library**
PO Box 1328, St Paul, AB T0A 3A0
Tel: 780-645-4904; *Fax:* 780-645-5198
librarian@stpaullibrary.ab.ca
www.stpaullibrary.ab.ca

Standard: **Standard Municipal Library**
822 The Broadway, Standard, AB T0J 3G0
Tel: 403-644-3995
astmlibrary@marigold.ab.ca
www.standardlibrary.ca
Social Media: www.pinterest.com/lilmissbookworm; www.facebook.com/pages/Standard-Library/101036936653357
Adreena Harder, Librarian

Standoff: **Kainai Public Library**
PO Box 788, Standoff, AB T0L 1Y0
Tel: 403-737-8350
help@kainailibrary.ca
www.kainailibrary.ca

Stavely: **Stavely Municipal Library**
4823 - 49th St., Stavely, AB T0L 1Z0
Tel: 403-549-2190; *Fax:* 403-549-2190
help@stavelylibrary.ca
www.stavelylibrary.ca

Stettler: **Stettler Public Library**
6202 - 44th Ave., Stettler, AB T0C 2L1
Tel: 403-742-2292
spl@prl.ab.ca
spl.prl.ab.ca
Social Media: pinterest.com/stettlerlibrary; www.facebook.com/StettlerPublicLibrary

Stirling: **Stirling Theodore Brandley Municipal Library**
229 - 4th Ave., Stirling, AB T0K 2E0
Tel: 403-756-3665; *Fax:* 403-756-3665
help@stirlinglibrary.ca
www.stirlinglibrary.ca

Stony Plain: **Stony Plain Public Library**
#112, 4613 - 52nd Ave., Stony Plain, AB T7Z 1E7
Tel: 780-963-5440; *Fax:* 780-963-1746
info@stonyplainlibrary.org
www.stonyplainlibrary.org
Social Media: twitter.com/stonyplainlib; www.facebook.com/pages/Stony-Plain-Public-Library/137277601910

Shauna Johnstone, Chair

Strathmore: **Strathmore Municipal Library**
85 Lakeside Blvd., Strathmore, AB T1P 1A1
Tel: 403-934-5440; *Fax:* 403-934-1908
asmlibrary@marigold.ab.ca
www.strathmorelibrary.ca
Social Media: www.pinterest.com/strathmorelib; twitter.com/StrathmoreLib; www.facebook.com/strathmorelibrary
Rachel Dick Hughes, Director, Library Services

Sundre: **Sundre Municipal Library**
#2, 96 - 2nd Ave. NW, Sundre, AB T0M 1X0
Tel: 403-638-4000; *Fax:* 403-638-5755
sundrelibrary@prl.ab.ca
www.sundre.prl.ab.ca
Social Media: twitter.com/SundreLibrary; www.facebook.com/pages/Sundre-Municipal-Library/101147606607098
Jamie Syer, Library Manager

Swan Hills: **Swan Hills Public Library**
5536 Main St., Swan Hills, AB T0G 2C0
Tel: 780-333-4505; *Fax:* 780-333-4551
www.swanhillslibrary.ab.ca
Nancy Keough, Head Librarian
nkeough@yrl.ab.ca

Sylvan Lake: **Sylvan Lake Public Library**
4715 - 50 Ave., Sylvan Lake, AB T4S 1C5
Tel: 403-887-2130; *Fax:* 403-887-0537
sylvan.library@prl.ab.ca
www.sylvanlibrary.prl.ab.ca
Social Media: www.youtube.com/user/SylvanLibrary; twitter.com/SylvanLib; www.facebook.com/group.php?gid=109719189059777
Caroline Vandriel, Director

Taber: **Taber Public Library**
5415 - 50 Ave., Taber, AB T1G 1V2
Tel: 403-223-4343; *Fax:* 403-223-4314
libtab@taberlibrary.ca
www.taberlibrary.ca
Social Media: twitter.com/TaberLibrary; www.facebook.com/pages/Taber-Public-Library/21094305918
Diane Zelenka, Library Manager
manager@taberlibrary.ca
Dawn Kondas, Program Coordinator
dkondas@taberlibrary.ca

Tangent: **Tangent Community Library**
PO Box 63, Tangent, AB T0H 3J0
Tel: 780-359-2666
librarian@tangentlibrary.ab.ca
www.tangentlibrary.ab.ca

Thorhild: **Thorhild & District Municipal Library**
PO Box 658, Thorhild, AB T0A 3J0
Tel: 780-398-3502; *Fax:* 780-398-3504
www.thorhildlibrary.ab.ca

Thorsby: **Thorsby Municipal Library**
4901 - 48 Ave., Thorsby, AB T0C 2P0
Tel: 780-789-3808
thorsbypublib@yrl.ab.ca
www.thorsbymunicipallibrary.ab.ca

Three Hills: **Three Hills Municipal Library**
122 - 3rd Ave. South, Three Hills, AB T0M 2A0
Tel: 403-443-2360
athmlibrary@marigold.ab.ca
www.3hillslibrary.com
Social Media: www.pinterest.com/3HillsLibrary; www.facebook.com/ThreeHillsLibrary
Karen Nickel, Library Manager

Tilley: **Tilley Public Library**
1st Ave. East, Tilley, AB T0J 3K0
Tel: 403-377-2233
tilley.shortgrass.ca

Tofield: **Tofield Municipal Library**
5407 - 50 St., Tofield, AB T0B 4J0
Tel: 780-662-3838; *Fax:* 780-662-3929
www.tofieldlibrary.ca
Connie Forst, Library Manager

Tomahawk: **Tomahawk Public Library**
Tomahawk School, 6119 Township Rd. 512, Tomahawk, AB T0E 2H0
Tel: 780-339-3935
tomahawklibrary@yrl.ab.ca
www.pcmlibraries.ab.ca
Kathy Gardiner, Library Manager

Lisa Smith, Chair, Parkland County Library Board

Trochu: **Trochu Municipal Library**
317 Main St., Trochu, AB T0M 2C0
Tel: 403-442-2458
atrmlibrary@marigold.ab.ca
www.trochulibrary.ca

Turner Valley: **Sheep River Community Library**
129 Main St. NE, Turner Valley, AB T0L 2A0
Tel: 403-933-3278; *Fax:* 403-933-3298
www.sheepriverlibrary.ca
Social Media: twitter.com/SheepRvrLibrary; www.facebook.com/SheepRiverLibrary
Jan Burney, Librarian

Two Hills: **Alice Melnyk Public Library**
5009 Diefenbaker (50th) Ave., Two Hills, AB T0B 4K0
Tel: 780-657-3553; *Fax:* 780-657-3553
www.twohillslibrary.ab.ca
Cheryl Paulichuk, Library Manager

Valhalla Centre: **Valhalla Community Library**
PO Box 68, Valhalla Centre, AB T0H 3M0
Tel: 780-356-3834; *Fax:* 780-356-3834
librarian@valhallalibrary.ab.ca
www.valhallalibrary.ab.ca

Valleyview: **Valleyview Municipal Library**
4804 - 50 Ave., Valleyview, AB T0H 3N0
Tel: 780-524-3033; *Fax:* 780-524-4563
librarian@valleyviewlibrary.ab.ca
www.valleyviewlibrary.ab.ca
Social Media: www.facebook.com/ValleyviewMunicipalLibrary

Vauxhall: **Vauxhall Public Library**
314 - 2nd Ave. North, Vauxhall, AB T0K 2K0
Tel: 403-654-2370; *Fax:* 403-654-2370
help@vauxhalllibrary.ca
www.vauxhalllibrary.ca
Social Media: twitter.com/Chinooklibs

Vegreville: **Vegreville Centennial Library**
4709 - 50 St., Vegreville, AB T9C 1R1
Tel: 780-632-3491; *Fax:* 780-603-2338
www.vegrevillelibrary.ab.ca
Social Media: twitter.com/VegLibrary; www.facebook.com/Veglibrary
Natalia Toroshenko, Chair

Vermilion: **Vermilion Public Library**
5001 - 49th Ave., Vermilion, AB T9X 1B8
Tel: 780-853-4288; *Fax:* 780-853-1783
info@vplibrary.ca
www.vermilionpubliclibrary.ca
Social Media: www.facebook.com/vermilionpl
Stuart Paul, Library Manager

Veteran: **Veteran Municipal Library**
205 Luckow St., Veteran, AB T0C 2S0
Tel: 403-575-3915

Viking: **Viking Municipal Library**
Viking Carena Complex, 5120 - 45 St., Viking, AB T0B 4N0
Tel: 780-336-4992; *Fax:* 780-336-4992
www.vikinglibrary.ab.ca
Social Media: www.facebook.com/pages/Viking-Municipal-Library/180715135371094
Barb Chrystian, Library Manager
Betty Lou Weder, Assistant Library Manager

Vilna: **Vilna Municipal Library**
Cultural Center, 5431 - 50th St., Vilna, AB T0A 3L0
Tel: 780-636-2077; *Fax:* 780-636-2077
www.vilnapubliclibrary.ab.ca
Roxanne Loberg, Library Manager

Vulcan: **Vulcan Municipal Library**
303 Centre St., Vulcan, AB T0L 2B0
Tel: 403-485-2571; *Fax:* 403-485-5013
help@vulcanlibrary.ca
www.vulcanlibrary.ca
Social Media: www.facebook.com/621307437895021
Kim Armstrong, Library Manager
Dorothy Way, Assistant Librarian

Wabamun: **Wabamun Public Library**
Jubilee Hall, 5132 - 53 Ave., Wabamun, AB T0E 2K0
Tel: 780-892-2713; *Fax:* 780-892-7294
www.wabamunlibrary.ca
Social Media: www.facebook.com/187395764655501
Betty Lalonde, Library Manager

Wabasca: **Wabasca Public Library**
PO Box 638, Wabasca, AB T0G 2K0
Tel: 780-891-2203; *Fax:* 780-891-2402
librarian@wabascalibrary.ab.ca
www.wabascalibrary.ab.ca

Wainwright: **Wainwright Public Library**
921 - 3rd Ave., Wainwright, AB T9W 1C5
Tel: 780-842-2673; *Fax:* 780-842-2340
librarian@wainwrightlibrary.ab.ca
www.wainwrightlibrary.ab.ca
Social Media: www.facebook.com/WainwrightPublicLibrary
Jodi Dahlgren, Library Manager

Wandering River: **Wandering River Women's Institute Community Library**
Wandering River School, Wandering River, AB T0A 3M0
Tel: 780-771-3939; *Fax:* 780-771-2117
librarian@wanderingriverlibrary.ab.ca
www.wanderingriverlibrary.ab.ca
Jennifer Batiuk, Library Manager
780-623-0409

Warburg: **Warburg Public Library**
5212 - 50th Ave., Warburg, AB T0C 2T0
Tel: 780-848-2391; *Fax:* 780-848-2296
warburglibrary@yrl.ab.ca
www.warburglibrary.ab.ca
Gail O'Neil, Library Manager

Warner: **Warner Memorial Municipal Library**
206 - 3rd Ave., Warner, AB T0K 2L0
Tel: 403-642-3988
help@warnerlibrary.ca
www.warnerlibrary.ca

Waskatenau: **Anne Chorney Public Library**
PO Box 130, Waskatenau, AB T0A 3P0
Tel: 780-358-2777; *Fax:* 780-358-2777
www.waskatenaulibrary.ab.ca
Julia Krahulec, Library Manager

Water Valley: **Water Valley Public Library**
PO Box 250, Water Valley, AB T0M 2E0
Tel: 403-637-3899
watervalleylibrary.prl.ab.ca
Katherina Herman, Librarian

Wembley: **Wembley Public Library**
PO Box 926, Wembley, AB T0H 3S0
Tel: 780-766-3553; *Fax:* 780-776-3543
librarian@wembleypubliclibrary.ab.ca
www.wembleypubliclibrary.ab.ca

Westlock: **Westlock Libraries**
#1, 10007 - 100 Ave., Westlock, AB T7P 2H5
Tel: 780-349-3060; *Fax:* 780-349-5291
www.westlocklibrary.ca
Social Media: pinterest.com/westlocklibrary; twitter.com/westlocklibrary; www.facebook.com/westlocklibraries
Doug Whistance-Smith, Director
dwhistance@westlocklibrary.ca
Wendy Hodgson-Sadgrove, Assistant Director
hodgsonw@westlocklibrary.ca
Carey Whistance-Smith, Cataloging Clerk
cwhistance@westlocklibrary.ca

Wetaskiwin: **Wetaskiwin Public Library**
5002 - 51st Ave., Wetaskiwin, AB T9A 0V1
Tel: 780-361-4446; *Fax:* 780-352-3266
library@wetaskiwin.ca
www.wetaskiwinpubliclibrary.ab.ca
Rachelle Kuzyk, Manager, Library Services
780-361-4458
Svea Benson, Coordinator, Information Services

Whitecourt: **Whitecourt & District Public Library**
5201 - 49th St., Whitecourt, AB T7S 1N3
Tel: 780-778-2900
www.whitecourtlibrary.ab.ca
Social Media: www.pinterest.com/whitecourtlib; twitter.com/WhitecourtLib; www.facebook.com/642227655796206
Richard Bangma, Library Director

Wildwood: **Wildwood Public Library**
5112 - 50th St., Wildwood, AB T0E 2M0
Tel: 780-325-3882; *Fax:* 780-325-3880
wildwoodlibrary@yrl.ab.ca
www.wildwoodlibrary.ab.ca
Terrie Stone, Library Manager

Winfield: **Winfield Community Library**
PO Box 390, Winfield, AB T0C 2X0
Tel: 780-682-2498
winfieldlibrary@yrl.ab.ca
www.winfieldlibrary.ab.ca
Joyce Brown, Library Manager
Heidi Untinen, Library Assistant

Woking: **Woking Municipal Library**
PO Box 27, Woking, AB T0H 3V0
Tel: 780-774-3932
librarian@wokinglibrary.ca
www.wokinglibrary.ca

Worsley: **Worsley & District Library**
216 Alberta Ave., Worsley, AB T0H 3W0
Tel: 780-685-3842; *Fax:* 780-685-3766
awdlib@hotmail.com
www.worsleylibrary.ab.ca
Social Media: www.facebook.com/WorsleyLibrary

Wrentham: **Wrentham Library**
PO Box 111, Wrentham, AB T0K 2P0
Tel: 403-222-2485; *Fax:* 403-222-2101
help@wrenthamlibrary.ca
www.wrenthamlibrary.ca

Youngstown: **Youngstown Municipal Library**
218 Main St., Youngstown, AB T0J 3R0
Tel: 403-779-3864
aymlibrary@marigold.ab.ca
www.youngstownlibrary.ca

Zama City: **Zama Community Library**
1025 Aspen Dr., Zama City, AB T0H 4E0
Tel: 780-683-2888

Archives

Banff: **The Banff Centre (Paul D. Fleck Library & Archives)**
107 Tunnel Mountain Dr., Banff, AB T1L 1H5
Tel: 403-762-6265; *Fax:* 403-762-6266
library@banffcentre.ca
www.banffcentre.ca/library

Banff: **Whyte Museum of the Canadian Rockies**
111 Bear St., Banff, AB T1L 1A3
Tel: 403-762-2291; *Fax:* 403-762-2339
archives@whyte.org
www.whyte.org/archives
Social Media: www.youtube.com/user/WhyteMuseum; www.twitter.com/whytemuseum; www.facebook.com/WhyteMuseum
Jennifer Rutkair, Head Archivist
jrutkair@whyte.org

Brooks: **Eastern Irrigation District**
550 Industrial Rd. West, Brooks, AB T1R 1B2
Tel: 403-362-1400
www.eid.ca

Calgary: **Calgary Highlanders Regimental Museum & Archives**
4520 Crowchild Trail SW, Calgary, AB T3E 1T8
Tel: 403-410-2340
museum@calgaryhighlanders.com
www.calgaryhighlanders.com/organizations/museum/museum.htm
Mike Henry, Archivist

Calgary: **The City of Calgary**
Admin Bldg., 313 - 7th Ave. SE, Main Fl., Calgary, AB T2G 0J1
Tel: 403-268-8180; *Fax:* 403-268-6731
archives@calgary.ca
www.calgary.ca

Calgary: **Glenbow Museum**
130 - 9th Ave. SE, Calgary, AB T2G 0P3
Tel: 403-268-4204; *Fax:* 403-232-6569
glenbow@glenbow.org
www.glenbow.org/collections/archives
Lindsay Moir, Senior Librarian
Susan Kooyman, Archivist
Lynette Walton, Imperial Oil Archivist
lwalton@glenbow.org
403-268-4232

***Calgary:* Heritage Park Society**
1900 Heritage Dr. SW, Calgary, AB T2V 2X3
Tel: 403-268-8500; *Fax:* 403-268-8501
info@heritagepark.ab.ca
www.heritagepark.ca
Social Media: twitter.com/HeritageParkYYC;
www.facebook.com/pages/Heritage-Park/177397676028

***Calgary:* Legal Archives Society of Alberta**
#400, 1015 - 4th St. SW, Calgary, AB T2R 1J4
Tel: 403-244-5510; *Fax:* 403-454-4419
lasa@legalarchives.ca
www.legalarchives.ca
Everett L. Bunnell, President
Stacy F. Kaufeld, Executive Director
Brenda McCafferty, Archivist

***Calgary:* Lord Strathcona's Horse Regimental Museum**
4520 Crowchild Trail SW, Calgary, AB T2T 5J4
Tel: 403-410-2340; *Fax:* 403-410-2359
museum@strathconas.ca
www.strathconas.ca/archives
Social Media: twitter.com/LdSHRC

***Calgary:* The Military Museums**
4520 Crowchild Trail SW, Calgary, AB T2T 5J4
Tel: 403-410-2340
www.themilitarymuseums.ca/gallery-uofc
Jerremie Clyde, Head Librarian/Senior Archivist
jvclyde@ucalgary.ca

***Calgary:* Naval Museum of Alberta**
4520 Crowchild Trail SW, Calgary, AB T2T 5J4
Tel: 403-410-2340
www.themilitarymuseums.ca/gallery-uofc
Jerremie Clyde, Head Librarian/Senior Archivist

***Calgary:* Sisters Faithful Companions of Jesus**
219 - 19th Ave. SW, Calgary, AB T2S 0C8
Tel: 403-228-3623; *Fax:* 403-541-9297
www.fcjsisters.org
Social Media: twitter.com/fcjsisters;
www.facebook.com/57766155162

***Calgary:* YouthLink Calgary**
5151 - 47 St. NE, Calgary, AB T3J 3R2
Tel: 403-428-4566; *Fax:* 403-974-0508
info@youthlinkcalgary.com
www.youthlinkcalgary.com
Social Media: instagram.com/YouthLinkYYC;
twitter.com/YouthLinkCGY; www.facebook.com/YouthLinkCGY
Tara Robinson, Executive Director
trobinson@calgarypolice.ca
Noreen Barros, Museum Director
nbarros@calgarypolice.ca

***Edmonton:* Canadian Moravian Archives**
2304 - 38 St., Edmonton, AB T6L 4K9
Tel: 780-440-3050; *Fax:* 780-463-2143

***Edmonton:* City of Edmonton Archives**
10440 - 108 Ave., Edmonton, AB T5H 3Z9
Tel: 780-496-8711
cms.archives@edmonton.ca
www.edmonton.ca/archives
Kim Christie-Milley, Archivist
780-496-8716

***Edmonton:* Edmonton Public Schools**
McKay Avenue School, 10425 - 99 Ave. NW, Edmonton, AB T5K 0E5
Tel: 780-422-1970; *Fax:* 780-426-0192
archivesmuseum@epsb.ca
archivesmuseum.epsb.ca
Social Media: twitter.com/EPSB_McKay
Cindy Davis, Manager

***Edmonton:* The Edmonton Sun**
10006 - 101 St., Edmonton, AB T5J 0S1
Tel: 780-468-0100; *Toll-Free:* 877-624-1463
licensing@Postmedia.com
www.edmontonsun.com
Social Media: twitter.com/Edmontonsun;
www.facebook.com/edmontonsun

***Edmonton:* Provincial Archives of Alberta**
8555 Roper Rd., Edmonton, AB T6E 5W1
Tel: 780-427-1750
paa@gov.ab.ca
www.culture.alberta.ca/paa
Social Media:
www.facebook.com/www.provincialarchivesofalberta

Leslie Latta, Executive Director
leslie.latta@gov.ab.ca
Susan Stanton, Director, Access & Preservation Services
susan.stanton@gov.ab.ca
Wayne Murdoch, Director, Collections Management
wayne.murdoch@gov.ab.ca

***Edmonton:* Ukrainian Canadian Archives & Museum of Alberta**
9543 - 110th Ave. NW, Edmonton, AB T5H 1H3
Tel: 780-424-7580; *Fax:* 780-420-5062
ucama@shaw.ca
www.ucama.com
Paul Teterenko, President

***Jasper:* Jasper-Yellowhead Museum & Archives**
400 Bonhomme St., Jasper, AB T0E 1E0
Tel: 780-852-3013
archives@jaspermuseum.org
www.jaspermuseum.org
Social Media:
www.facebook.com/pages/Jasper-Museum/123561747657136

***Lethbridge:* Sir Alexander Galt Museum & Archives**
502 - 1st St. South, Lethbridge, AB T1J 1Y4
Tel: 403-329-7302; *Fax:* 403-329-4958
Toll-Free: 866-320-3898
archives@galtmuseum.com
www.galtmuseum.com/archives
Social Media: www.flickr.com/photos/galtmuseum;
twitter.com/GaltMuseum; www.facebook.com/GaltMuseum
Andrew Chernevych, Archivist

***Medicine Hat:* Esplanade Arts & Heritage Centre**
401 - 1st St. SE, Medicine Hat, AB T1A 8W2
Tel: 403-502-8582; *Fax:* 403-502-8589
archives@medicinehat.ca
www.esplanade.ca/archives
Social Media: twitter.com/MedHatEsplanade;
www.facebook.com/MedHatEsplanade

***Millet:* Millet & District Museum & Archives**
5120 - 50 St., Millet, AB T0C 1Z0
Tel: 780-387-5558; *Fax:* 780-387-5548
info@milletmuseum.ca
www.milletmuseum.ca
Social Media: twitter.com/milletmuseum;
www.facebook.com/221092931274232

***Olds:* Mountain View Museum & Archives**
5038 - 50th St., Olds, AB T4H 1P6
Tel: 403-556-8464
archives@oldsmuseum.ca
www.oldsmuseum.ca
Social Media: twitter.com/mvmuseum_olds;
www.facebook.com/646167382075285
Chantal Marchildon, Program Director
mountainviewmuseum@gmail.com
Jeffery Kearney, Archivist
archivist@oldsmuseum.ca

***Red Deer:* Red Deer & District Archives**
4525 - 47A Ave., Red Deer, AB T4N 6Z6
Tel: 403-309-8403; *Fax:* 403-340-8728
archives@reddeer.ca
www.reddeer.ca

***St Albert:* Musée Héritage Museum**
5 St Anne St., St Albert, AB T8N 3Z9
Tel: 780-459-1528; *Fax:* 780-459-1232
archives@artsandheritage.ca
museeheritage.ca
Social Media: twitter.com/artsandheritage;
www.facebook.com/ArtsAndHeritageStAlbert
Vinothaan Vipulanantharajah, Archivist
vinov@artsandheritage.ca
Shari Strachan, Director
sharis@artsandheritage.ca

***Stony Plain:* The Multicultural Heritage Centre**
5411 - 51st St., Stony Plain, AB T7Z 1X7
Tel: 780-963-2777; *Fax:* 780-963-0233
info@multicentre.org
www.multicentre.org
Social Media: twitter.com/MultiCentre;
www.facebook.com/MultiCentre1974
Rebecca Still, Museum Manager
rebecca@multicentre.org

***Taber:* Taber & District Museum Society**
4702 - 50th St., Taber, AB T1G 2B6
Tel: 403-223-5708; *Fax:* 403-223-0529
tiimchin@telusplanet.net
Social Media: www.facebook.com/569300306428531

***Wetaskiwin:* City of Wetaskiwin**
4904 - 51 St., Wetaskiwin, AB T9A 1L2
Tel: 780-361-4423
archives@wetaskiwin.ca
www.wetaskiwin.ca/Index.aspx?NID=107

British Columbia

Regional Systems

***Abbotsford:* Fraser Valley Regional Library**
34589 DeLair Rd., Abbotsford, BC V2S 5Y1
Tel: 604-859-7141; *Fax:* 604-852-5701
Toll-Free: 888-668-4141
www.fvrl.bc.ca
Social Media: www.youtube.com/user/FraserValleyLibrary;
twitter.com/readlearnplay;
www.facebook.com/FraserValleyLibrary
Scott Hargrove, CEO
scott.hargrove@fvrl.bc.ca
Heather Scoular, Director, Customer Experience
heather.scoular@fvrl.bc.ca
Devan Mitchell, Deputy Manager, Information Technology & Finance
devan.mitchell@fvrl.bc.ca
Jeff Narver, Director, Infrastructure & Resources
jeff.narver@fvrl.bc.ca
Cathy Wurtz, Director, Organizational Development
cathy.wurtz@fvrl.bc.ca
Mary Kierans, Manager, Support Services
mary.kierans@fvrl.bc.ca

***Burnaby:* Public Library InterLINK**
#158, 5489 Byrne Rd., Burnaby, BC V5J 3J1
Tel: 604-437-8441; *Fax:* 604-437-8410
info@interlinklibraries.ca
www.interlinklibraries.ca
Michael Burns, Executive Director
michael.burris@interlinklibraries.ca
Rita Avigdor, Manager of Operations
rita.avigdor@interlinklibraries.ca
Colleen Smith, Office Assistant

***Castlegear:* Kootenay Library Federation (KLF)**
PO Box 3125, Castlegar, BC V1N 3H4
Fax: 250-304-1832
Toll-Free: 888-664-4553
KLF-ofc@telus.net
klf.bc.libraries.coop
Joanne Richards, Director

***Kamloops:* Thompson-Nicola Regional District Library System**
#100, 465 Victoria St., Kamloops, BC V2C 2A9
Tel: 250-372-5145; *Toll-Free:* 877-377-8673
www.tnrdlib.ca
Social Media: twitter.com/TNRD;
www.facebook.com/TNRDLibrarySystem

***Kelowna:* Okanagan Regional Library**
1430 KLO Rd., Kelowna, BC V1W 3P6
Tel: 250-860-4033; *Fax:* 250-861-8696
Other Numbers: 250-860-4652 (Telecirc for account access)
www.orl.bc.ca
Social Media: www.youtube.com/OKRegLibrary;
twitter.com/OKRegLib; www.facebook.com/OKRegLib
Stephanie Hall, Executive Director
shall@orl.bc.ca
250-860-4033 ext. 2491

***Nanaimo:* Vancouver Island Regional Library**
6250 Hammond Bay Rd., Nanaimo, BC V9T 6M9
Tel: 250-758-4697; *Fax:* 250-758-2482
Toll-Free: 877-415-8475
Other Numbers: 250-753-1154 (Books By Mail)
info@virl.bc.ca
www.virl.bc.ca
Social Media: twitter.com/VI_Library;
www.facebook.com/MyVIRL
Rosemary Bonanno, Executive Director
rbonanno@virl.bc.ca
250-729-2313
Jamie Anderson, Director, Library Services & Planning
janderson@virl.bc.ca
250-729-2304
Joel Adams, Director of Finance
jadams@virl.bc.ca
250-729-2312
Harold Kamikawaji, Director of Human Resources
hkamikawaji@virl.bc.ca
250-729-2306

***New Westminster:* Northwest Library Federation**
432 Third St., New Westminster, BC V3L 2S2
Tel: 604-802-7996; *Toll-Free:* 800-276-1804
director@nclf.ca
nwlf.ca
Lauren Wolf, Manager

***Pender Island:* IslandLink Library Federation**
4446 Hooson Rd., Pender Island, BC V0N 2M1
Tel: 250-629-6015; *Fax:* 855-361-7297
Toll-Free: 855-927-2005
islandlink.bclibrary.ca

***Pender Island:* Southern Gulf Islands Community Libraries**
4407 Bedwell Harbour Rd., Pender Island, BC V0N 2M1
Tel: 250-629-3722
penderislandlibrary@crd.bc.ca
sgicl.bc.libraries.coop
Carmen Oleskevich, Library Manager

***Victoria:* North East Library Federation**
PO Box 44113, RPO Gorge, Victoria, BC V9A 7K1
Tel: 250-383-9409; *Fax:* 866-901-8509
nelf.bclibrary.ca

***Williams Lake:* Cariboo Regional District Library**
180 - 3rd Ave. North, #A, Williams Lake, BC V2G 2A4
Tel: 250-392-3630; *Toll-Free:* 800-665-1636
www.cln.bc.ca
Wanda Davis, Manager, Library Services
wdavis@cariboord.bc.ca
Katherine Anderson, Manager
kanderson@nelf.bclibrary.ca

Public Libraries

***Alert Bay:* Alert Bay Public Library & Museum**
118 Fir St., Alert Bay, BC V0N 1A0
Tel: 250-974-5721; *Fax:* 250-974-5026
abplb@island.net
alertbay.bc.libraries.coop
Joyce Wilby, Head Librarian/ Archivist
Steven Wong, Community Librarian

***Atlin:* Atlin Library**
Courthouse Bldg., 2nd St., Atlin, BC V0W 1A0
Linda Brown, Contact

***Bowen Island:* Bowen Island Public Library**
430 Bowen Trunk Rd., Bowen Island, BC V0N 1G0
Tel: 604-947-9788
info@bowenlibrary.ca
www.bowenlibrary.ca
Tina Nielsen, Chief Librarian

***Burnaby:* Burnaby Public Library**
6100 Willingdon Ave., Burnaby, BC V5H 4N5
Tel: 604-436-5427; *Fax:* 604-436-2961
Other Numbers: 604-293-0034 Telecirc
bpl@bpl.bc.ca
www.bpl.bc.ca
Social Media: twitter.com/burnabypl;
www.facebook.com/burnabypubliclibrary
Edel Toner-Rogala, Chief Librarian
edel.toner-rogala@bpl.bc.ca
604-436-5431
Deb Thomas, Deputy Chief Librarian
deb.thomas@bpl.bc.ca
604-436-5432

***Burns Lake:* Burns Lake Public Library**
585 Government St., Burns Lake, BC V0J 1E0
Tel: 250-692-3192; *Fax:* 250-692-7488
libraryn@burnslakelibrary.com
burnslake.bclibrary.ca
Social Media:
www.facebook.com/pages/Burns-Lake-Public-Library/57217083503
Elaine Wiebe, Library Director
Tenille Woskett, Assistant Director

***Castlegar:* Castlegar & District Public Library**
1005 - 3rd St., Castlegar, BC V1N 2A2
Tel: 250-365-6611; *Fax:* 250-365-7765
info@castlegarlibrary.com
www.castlegarlibrary.com
Social Media: www.facebook.com/castlegarlibrary
Heather Maisel, Library Director
director@castlegarlibrary.com
250-365-7751
Julie Kalesnikoff, Librarian
Vera Terpin, Office Manager

***Chetwynd:* Chetwynd Public Library**
5012 - 46th St., Chetwynd, BC V0C 1J0
Tel: 250-788-2559; *Fax:* 250-788-2186
cpl@chetwynd.bclibrary.ca
chetwynd.bclibrary.ca
Social Media: www.pinterest.com/chetwyndp;
twitter.com/ChetwyndLibrary;
www.facebook.com/pages/chetwynd-public-library/4619008040
Fay Asleson, Librarian
Margaret Movold, Chair

***Coquitlam:* Coquitlam Public Library**
575 Poirier St., Coquitlam, BC V3J 6A9
Tel: 604-937-4130; *Fax:* 604-931-6739
askalibrarian@coqlibrary.ca
www.coqlibrary.ca
Social Media:
www.pinterest.com/CoqLibrary/what-are-we-reading;
twitter.com/CoqLibrary; www.facebook.com/175241429202024
Todd Gnissios, Director
tgnissios@coqlibrary.ca
604-937-4132
Silvana Harwood, Deputy Director
sharwood@library.coquitlam.bc.ca
604-937-4131

***Cranbrook:* Cranbrook Public Library**
1212 - 2nd St. North, Cranbrook, BC V1C 4T6
Tel: 250-426-4063
staff@cranbrookpubliclibrary.ca
cranbrook.bibliocommons.com
Social Media: www.facebook.com/CranbrookPublicLibrary

***Crawford Bay:* Eastshore Community Library (Reading Centre)**
16234 King St., Crawford Bay, BC V0B 1E0
Tel: 250-227-9457
escomlib@theeastshore.net
Cathy Poch, Director

***Creston:* Creston & District Public Library**
531 - 16th Ave. South, Creston, BC V0B 1G5
Tel: 250-428-4141; *Fax:* 250-428-4703
info@crestonlibrary.com
www.crestonlibrary.com
Social Media: twitter.com/crestonlibrary;
www.facebook.com/pages/Creston-Public-Library/118409721541035
Cherine Klassen, Chair
Aaron Francis, Chief Librarian

***Dawson Creek:* Dawson Creek Municipal Public Library**
1001 McKellar Ave., Dawson Creek, BC V1G 4W7
Tel: 250-782-4661; *Fax:* 250-782-4667
dclib@pris.ca
dawsoncreek.bclibrary.ca
Social Media: www.facebook.com/183700895048680
Jenny Snyder, Head Librarian
Pamela Morris, Assistant Librarian/Children's Librarian/Acquisitions

***Edgewood:* Inonoaklin Valley Reading Centre**
409 Monashee Ave., Edgewood, BC V0G 1J0
Tel: 250-269-7212; *Fax:* 250-269-7633
Susan Bampton, Librarian
sbampton@hotmail.com
Kathy Watson, Chair

***Elkford:* Elkford Public Library**
816 Michel Rd., Elkford, BC V0B 1H0
Tel: 250-865-2912; *Fax:* 250-865-2460
library@elkfordlibrary.org
www.elkfordlibrary.org
Diane Andrews, Director
Rosalie Atherton, Assistant Librarian

***Fernie:* Fernie Heritage Library**
492 - 3rd Ave., Fernie, BC V0B 1M0
Tel: 250-423-4458; *Fax:* 250-423-7906
information@ferniheritagelibrary.com
www.fernieheritagelibrary.com
Social Media: twitter.com/FernieLibrary;
www.facebook.com/pages/Fernie-Heritage-Library/238888446209918
Emma Dressler, Librarian

***Fort Nelson:* Fort Nelson Public Library**
Town Square, 5315 - 50th Ave. South, Fort Nelson, BC V0C 1R0
Tel: 250-774-6777; *Fax:* 250-774-6777
fnpl@fortnelson.bclibrary.ca
fortnelson.bclibrary.ca
Social Media: twitter.com/FNLibrary;
www.facebook.com/123316444364744
Flora Clark, Chair
Joan Davidson, Managing Librarian
Sylvia Bramhill, Assistant Librarian, Interlibrary Loans
Linda Novotny, Assistant Librarian, Technical Support
lnovotny@fortnelson.bclibrary.ca

***Fort St James:* Fort St James Public Library**
425 Manson St., Fort St James, BC V0J 1P0
Tel: 250-996-7431; *Fax:* 250-996-7484
fortlib@fsjames.com
fortstjames.bclibrary.ca
Social Media: twitter.com/FtStJamesLibr;
www.facebook.com/pages/Fort-St-James-Public-Library/106264649600
Wayne Briscoe, Head Librarian
Flora Arias Molina, Assistant Librarian

***Fort St John:* Fort St John Public Library**
10015 - 100th Ave., Fort St John, BC V1J 1Y7
Tel: 250-785-3731; *Fax:* 250-785-7982
fortstjohn.bclibrary.ca
Social Media: instagram.com/fsjpl; twitter.com/fsjlibrary;
www.facebook.com/fsjlibrary
Kerry France, Director

***Fraser Lake:* Fraser Lake Public Library**
228 Endako Ave., Fraser Lake, BC V0J 1S0
Tel: 250-699-8888; *Fax:* 250-699-8899
flibrarian@bcgroup.net
fraserlake.bclibrary.ca
Audrey Fennema, Chief Librarian
Wendy Bailey, Library Assistant
Hazel Thomas, Library Assistant

***Fruitvale:* Beaver Valley Public Library**
1847 - 1st St., Fruitvale, BC V0G 1L0
Tel: 250-367-7114; *Fax:* 250-367-7130
bvpublic@telus.net
beavervalley.bclibrary.ca
Social Media: www.facebook.com/527274463973725
Marie Onyett, Head Librarian

***Galiano Island:* Galiano Island Community Library**
#2, 1290 Sturdies Bay Rd., Galiano Island, BC V0N 1P0
Tel: 250-539-2141
galianolibrary@shaw.ca
Social Media: www.facebook.com/galianolibrary

***Gibsons:* Gibsons & District Public Library**
470 South Fletcher Rd., Gibsons, BC V0N 1V0
Tel: 604-886-2130; *Fax:* 604-886-2689
gdplinfo@gibsons.bclibrary.ca
www.gibsons.bclibrary.ca
Social Media: twitter.com/LibraryGibsons;
www.facebook.com/116298521716163
Tracey Therrien, Chief Librarian
Heather Evans-Cullen, Outreach Coordinator

***Grand Forks:* Grand Forks & District Public Library**
7342 - 5th St., Grand Forks, BC V0H 1H0
Tel: 250-442-3944
library@gfpl.ca
grandforks.bclibrary.ca
Social Media: www.facebook.com/237995746243162
Avi Silberstein, Library Director

***Granisle:* Granisle Public Library**
#2 Village Sq., McDonald Ave., Granisle, BC V0J 1W0
Tel: 250-697-2713
library@granisle.net
granisle.bclibrary.ca
Sherry Smith, Chief Librarian

***Grasmere:* Grasmere Reading Centre**
PO Box 75, Grasmere, BC V0B 1R0
Tel: 250-887-3412; *Fax:* 250-887-3274
Bonnie Crosson, Head of Library

***Greenwood:* Greenwood Public Library**
346 South Copper Ave., Greenwood, BC V0H 1J0
Tel: 250-445-6111; *Fax:* 250-445-6111
greenlib@shaw.ca
greenwood.bclibrary.ca
Judy Foucher, Library Director
Clare Folvik, Assistant Librarian

Hazelton: Hazelton & District Public Library
4255 Government St., Hazelton, BC V0J 1Y0
Tel: 250-842-5961; *Fax:* 250-842-2176
hazlib@bulkley.net
hazelton.bclibrary.ca
Social Media: www.facebook.com/hazeltonpubliclibrary
Ruth Cooper, Acting Head Librarian

Houston: Houston Public Library
3150 - 14th St., Houston, BC V0J 1Z0
Tel: 250-845-2256; *Fax:* 250-845-2088
houston.bc.libraries.coop
Social Media: www.facebook.com/Gr8reads
Toni McKilligan, Library Director
Sara Lewis, Library Assistant

Hudson's Hope: Hudson's Hope Public Library
9905 Dudley Dr., Hudson's Hope, BC V0C 1V0
Tel: 250-783-9414; *Fax:* 250-783-5272
director.hhpl@pris.ca
hudsonshope.bc.libraries.coop

Invermere: Invermere Public Library
201 - 7th Ave., Invermere, BC V0A 1K0
Tel: 250-342-6416; *Fax:* 250-342-6416
publiclibrary@invermere.net
invermere.bclibrary.ca
Social Media: www.pinterest.com/InvLibrary;
twitter.com/invermerelib; www.facebook.com/invermerelibrary
Nicole Pawlak, Library Director

Kaslo: Kaslo & District Public Library
Kaslo Village Hall, Ground Fl., 413 - 4th St., Kaslo, BC V0G 1M0
Tel: 250-353-2942; *Fax:* 250-252-2943
info@kaslo.bclibrary.ca
www.kaslo.bclibrary.ca
Eva Kelemen, Library Director
Annie Reynolds, Coordinator, Library Services

Kimberley: Kimberley Public Library
115 Spokane St., Kimberley, BC V1A 2E5
Tel: 250-427-3112; *Fax:* 250-427-7157
staff@kimberleylibrary.net
kimberley.bc.libraries.coop
Social Media: twitter.com/Library_KPL
Karin von Wittgenstein, Director
Director@kimberleylibrary.net
Sharon Seward, Cataloguer Library Assistant
sharon.seward@kimberleylibrary.net
Traci Illes, Interlibrary Loans Library Assistant
traci.illes@kimberleylibrary.net

Kitimat: Kitimat Public Library
940 Wakashan Ave., Kitimat, BC V8C 2G3
Tel: 250-632-8985; *Fax:* 250-632-2630
ask@kitimatpubliclibrary.org
www.kitimatpubliclibrary.org
Virginia Charron, Chief Librarian

Kitwanga: Gitanyow Independent School Reading Centre
PO Box 369, Kitwanga, BC V0J 2A0
Tel: 250-849-5528; *Fax:* 250-849-5870
Other Numbers: 250-849-5384 administration
Bernadette McLean, Chair

Lillooet: Lillooet & Area Public Library Association
930 Main St., Lillooet, BC V0K 1V0
Tel: 250-256-7944; *Fax:* 866-704-3340
lala@lillooet.bclibrary.ca
lillooet.bclibrary.ca
Social Media: www.facebook.com/LillooetPublicLibrary
Betty Weaver, Chief Librarian
Toby Mueller, Children's Outreach Librarian
Sherry Rhodenizer, Community Adult Literacy Coordinator

Lions Bay: Lions Bay Library (Reading Centre)
400 Centre Rd., Lions Bay, BC V0N 2E0
Tel: 604-921-6944
www.lionsbay.ca/Library.html

Mackenzie: MacKenzie Public Library
Recreation Centre, 400 Skeena Dr., Mackenzie, BC V0J 2C0
Tel: 250-997-6343; *Fax:* 250-997-5792
mackenziepubliclibrary@gmail.com
www.mackenzie.bclibrary.ca
Wanda Davis, Head Librarian

Madeira Park: Pender Harbour Reading Centre
12952 Madeira Park Rd., Madeira Park, BC V0N 2H0
Tel: 604-883-2983
phrclibrary@gmail.com
penderharbourlibrary.ca

Lori Rhymes, Chair

Mayne Island: Mayne Island Public Library
411 Naylor Rd., Mayne Island, BC V0N 2J0
Tel: 250-539-2597
MIPL@shaw.ca

McBride: McBride & District Public Library
241 Dominion St., McBride, BC V0J 2E0
Tel: 250-569-2411
library@mcbridebc.org
www.mcbride.bclibrary.ca
Naomi Balla-Boudreau, Library Director
Doreen Beck, Library Assistant
Dawn Phillips, Library Assistant
Martina Wall, Library Assistant

Midway: Midway Public Library
612 - 6th Ave., Midway, BC V0H 1M0
Tel: 250-449-2620; *Fax:* 250-449-2389
midwaypubliclibrary@gmail.com
midway.bc.libraries.coop
Nicole Ferrier, Librarian

Nakusp: Nakusp Public Library
92 - 6th Ave. NW, Nakusp, BC V0G 1R0
Tel: 250-265-3363
nakusplibrary@netidea.com
nakusp.bclibrary.ca
Social Media: www.facebook.com/NakuspPublicLibrary
Susan Rogers, Librarian
250-265-3363

Nelson: Nelson Municipal Library
602 Stanley St., Nelson, BC V1L 1N4
Tel: 250-352-6333; *Fax:* 250-354-1799
library@nelson.ca
nelson.bclibrary.ca
Social Media: twitter.com/NelsonPLibrary;
wwww.facebook.com/186684484714424
June Stockdale, Chief Librarian
Nancy Radonich, Children's Services
Joanne Harris, Lieracy Coordinator

New Denver: New Denver Reading Centre
521 - 6 Ave., New Denver, BC V0G 1R0
Tel: 250-358-2221

New Westminster: New Westminster Public Library
716 - 6th Ave., New Westminster, BC V3M 2B3
Tel: 604-527-4660
reference@nwpl.ca
www.nwpl.ca
Social Media: twitter.com/nwplibrary;
www.facebook.com/newwestminsterpubliclibrary
Julie Spurrell, Chief Librarian
jspurrell@nwpl.ca
604-527-4675
Susan Buss, Deputy Chief Librarian
sbuss@nwpl.ca
604-527-4669
Faith Jones, Manager, Public Services
fjones@nwpl.ca
604-527-4661
Erin Watkins, Manager, Programs & Community Development
ewatkins@nwpl.ca
604-527-4678

North Vancouver: North Vancouver City Library
120 West 14th St., North Vancouver, BC V7M 1N9
Tel: 604-998-3450; *Fax:* 604-983-3624
Other Numbers: Renewals: 604-982-3917
nvcl@cnv.org
www.cnv.org/nvcl
Social Media: pinterest.com/nvcitylibrary/;
twitter.com/NorthVanCityLib;
www.facebook.com/NorthVanCityLibrary?sk=wall
Jane Watkins, Chief Librarian
jwatkins@cnb.org
604-990-4226
Wai-Lin Chee, Deputy Chief Librarian
wchee@cnv.org
604-990-4222

North Vancouver: North Vancouver District Public Library
1277 Lynn Valley Rd., North Vancouver, BC V7J 2A1
Tel: 604-990-5800; *Fax:* 604-984-7600
Other Numbers: 604-984-0286 ext. 8140 (Circulation)
www.nvdpl.ca
Social Media: twitter.com/nvdpl; www.facebook.com/nvdpl
Jacqueline van Dyk, Director, Library Services
jvandyk@nvdpl.ca
604-990-3740
Alison Campbell, Manager, Community Connections
alicam@nvdpl.ca
604-990-5800 ext. 88118

Pemberton: Pemberton & District Public Library
7390A Cottonwood St., Pemberton, BC V0N 2L0
Tel: 604-894-6916
library@pemberton.bclibrary.ca
pemberton.bc.libraries.coop
Social Media: instagram.com/pembylibrary;
twitter.com/pembylibrary; www.facebook.com/75469770237
Emma Gillis, Library Director
egillis@pemberton.bclibrary.ca
Marilyn Marinus, Senior Library Assistant
mmarinus@pemberton.bclibrary.ca
Niocole MacPhee, Library/Children's Programming Assistant
nmacphee@pemberton.bclibrary.ca
Valerie Fowler, Library Assistant
vfowler@pemberton.bclibrary.ca

Pender Island: Pender Island Public Library Association
4407 Bedwell Harbour Rd., Pender Island, BC V0N 2M1
Tel: 250-629-3722
penderislandlibrary@crd.bc.ca
pender.bclibrary.ca
Carmen Oleskevich, Library Manager

Penticton: Penticton Public Library
785 Main St, Penticton, BC V2A 5E3
Tel: 250-770-7781
Other Numbers: InfoDesk: 250-770-7782; Kids' Library: 250-770-7783
library@summer.com
www.library.penticton.bc.ca
Larry R. Little, Chief Librarian
Karen Kellerman, Public Services Librarian
Shelley Murphy, Systems Librarian
Julia Cox, Youth Services Librarian

Port Moody: Port Moody Public Library
100 Newport Dr., Port Moody, BC V3H 5C3
Tel: 604-469-4686; *Fax:* 604-469-4576
askthelibrary@portmoody.ca
library.portmoody.ca
Social Media: twitter.com/PoMoLibrary
Lynne Russell, Library Director
lrussell@portmoody.ca
604-469-4580

Pouce Coupe: Pouce Coupe Public Library
5010 - 52nd Ave., Pouce Coupe, BC V0C 2C0
Tel: 250-786-5765; *Fax:* 250-786-5761
bpoc.ill@pris.bc.ca
poucecoupe.bclibrary.ca
Social Media: www.facebook.com/PouceCoupePublicLibrary
Courtenay Johnston, Community Librarian

Powell River: Powell River Public Library
4411 Michigan Ave., Powell River, BC V8A 2S3
Tel: 604-485-4796; *Fax:* 604-485-5320
powellriverlibrary@shaw.ca
www.powellriverlibrary.ca
Social Media: twitter.com/PRPublicLibrary/;
facebook.com/170400112972465
Stephanie Hall, Head Librarian

Prince George: Prince George Public Library
888 Canada Games Way, Prince George, BC V2L 5T6
Tel: 250-563-9251
www.lib.pg.bc.ca
Social Media: www.youtube.com/pglibrary;
twitter.com/pg_library; www.facebook.com/pglibrary
Janet Marren, Chief Librarian
Shane Parmar, Manager, Public Services
Paul Burry, Manager, Support & Circulation Services

Prince Rupert: Prince Rupert Public Library
101 - 6th Ave. West, Prince Rupert, BC V8J 1Y9
Tel: 250-627-1345; *Fax:* 250-627-7851
info@princerupertlibrary.ca
www.princerupertlibrary.ca
Social Media: pinterest.com/princerupertlib;
twitter.com/princerupertlib;
www.facebook.com/pages/Prince-Rupert-Library/151774774872173
Joe Zelwietro, Chief Librarian

Radium Hot Springs: Radium Public Library
#2, 7585 Main St. West, Radium Hot Springs, BC V0A 1M0
Tel: 250-347-2434
radiumpubliclibrary@hotmail.com
radium.bclibrary.ca
Social Media: www.facebook.com/RadiumPublicLibrary

Jane Jones, Head Librarian

Richmond: Richmond Public Library
#100, 7700 Minoru Gate, Richmond, BC V6Y 1R8
Tel: 604-231-6422
Other Numbers: Adult Ask Me Desk: 604-231-6413
www.yourlibrary.ca
Social Media: www.youtube.com/user/YourLibraryRichmond; twitter.com/RPL_YourLibrary; www.facebook.com/yourlibraryRichmond
Greg Buss, Chief Librarian & Secretary to the Board
Susan Walters, Deputy Chief Librarian
Mark Ellis, Manager, Information Technology
Wendy Jang, Coordinator, Chinese Community Services
Melanie Au, Coordinator, Children & Family Services
Shaneena Rahman, Coordinator, Circulation & Merchandising

Riondel: Riondel Community Library
PO Box 29, Riondel, BC V0B 2B0
Tel: 250-225-3242
library55@riondel.ca
www.riondel.ca/library

Roberts Creek: Roberts Creek Community Library
1044 Roberts Creek Rd., Roberts Creek, BC V0N 2W0
Tel: 604-885-9401

Rossland: Rossland Public Library
2180 Columbia Ave., Rossland, BC V0G 1Y0
Tel: 250-362-7611
info@rossland.bclibrary.ca
rosslib.kics.bc.ca
Social Media: pinterest.com/rosslandlibrary; twitter.com/RosslandLibrary; www.facebook.com/RosslandPublicLibrary
Beverley Rintoul, Library Director
Lynn Amann, Children's Librarian & Assistant Librarian

Salmo: Salmo Public Library
106 - 4th St., Salmo, BC V0G 1Z0
Tel: 250-357-2312; Fax: 250-357-2312
salmopubliclibrary@telus.net
salmo.bclibrary.ca
Social Media: www.facebook.com/pages/Salmo-Public-Library/364282173581985
Taylor Caron, Library Director

Salt Spring Island: Salt Spring Island Public Library
129 McPhillips Ave., Salt Spring Island, BC V8K 2T6
Tel: 250-537-4666; Fax: 250-537-4666
info@saltspringlibrary.com
saltspring.bclibrary.ca
Social Media: pinterest.com/ssilibrary/; twitter.com/ssilibrary; facebook.com/104520346249533
Karen Hudson, Chief Librarian
khudson@saltspringlibrary.com
Nicole McCarville, Librarian
nmccarville@saltspringlibrary.com

Saturna Island: Saturna Island Library (Eddie Reid Memorial)
140 East Point Rd., Saturna Island, BC V0N 2Y0
Tel: 250-539-5312
saturnaislandlibrary@gmail.com

Sechelt: Sechelt Public Library
5797 Cowrie St., Sechelt, BC V0N 3A0
Tel: 604-885-3260; Fax: 604-885-5183
info@sechelt.bclibrary.ca
sechelt.bc.libraries.coop
Social Media: www.pinterest.com/bclibrary2; twitter.com/SecheltLibrary; www.facebook.com/pages/Sechelt-Public-Library/240370396078882
Margaret Hodgins, Chief Librarian

Sidney: Piers Island Library
PO Box 2223, Sidney, BC V8L 3S8
Tel: 250-656-3694
Other Numbers: 250-655-4812
piersislandreads@gmail.com

Smithers: Smithers Public Library
3817 Alfred Ave., Smithers, BC V0J 2N0
Tel: 250-847-3043; Fax: 250-847-1533
contact@smitherslibrary.ca
smithers.bclibrary.ca
Social Media: pinterest.com/smitherslibrary; twitter.com/smitherslibrary; www.facebook.com/107866782746?ref=ts
Wendy Wright, Library Director
director@smitherslibrary.ca

Sparwood: Sparwood Public Library
110 Pine Ave., Sparwood, BC V0B 2G0
Tel: 250-425-2299; Fax: 250-425-0229
sparwood.bclibrary.ca
James Bertoia, Head Librarian
jb@sparwoodlibrary.ca

Squamish: Squamish Public Library Association
37907 - 2nd Ave., Squamish, BC V8B 0A7
Tel: 604-892-3110; Fax: 604-892-9376
www.squamish.bclibrary.ca
Social Media: www.pinterest.com/squamishlibrary; twitter.com/squamishlibrary; www.facebook.com/pages/Squamish-Public-Library/98609473295
Hilary Bloom, Director, Library Services

Stewart: Stewart Public Library
824A Main St., Stewart, BC V0T 1W0
Tel: 250-636-2380; Fax: 250-636-2380
stewartpubliclibrary@gmail.com
stewart.bclibrary.ca
Social Media: www.facebook.com/stewart.spl
Galina Dyrant, Librarian
Billie Belcher, Chair

Surrey: Surrey Public Library
City Centre Library, 10350 University Dr., 3rd Fl., Surrey, BC V3T 4B8
Tel: 604-598-7300; Fax: 604-598-7310
www.surreylibraries.ca
Social Media: www.youtube.com/user/surreylibrary; twitter.com/surreylibrary; www.facebook.com/surreylibraries
Melanie Houlden, Chief Librarian

Taylor: Taylor Public Library
10008 - 104 Ave., Taylor, BC V0C 2K0
Tel: 250-789-9878
library@districtoftaylor.com
taylor.bc.libraries.coop
Social Media: twitter.com/TaylorBCLibrary; www.facebook.com/pages/Taylor-Public-Library/325257110840343
Sherry Murphy, Librarian

Terrace: Terrace Public Library Association
4610 Park Ave., Terrace, BC V8G 1V6
Tel: 250-638-8177; Fax: 250-635-6207
library@terracelibrary.ca
www.terracelibrary.ca
Social Media: www.facebook.com/pages/Terrace-Public-Library/121600227855422
David Try, Chair
Margo Schiller, Chief Librarian

Trail: Trail & District Public Library
Trail Memorial Centre, 1051 Victoria St., Trail, BC V1R 3T3
Tel: 250-364-1731; Fax: 250-364-2176
director@traillibrary.com
www.traillibrary.com
Social Media: www.facebook.com/TrailLibrary

Tumbler Ridge: Tumbler Ridge Public Library
340 Front St., Tumbler Ridge, BC V0C 2W0
Tel: 250-242-4778; Fax: 250-242-4707
tumblerridge.bclibrary.ca
Social Media: www.facebook.com/153075328086545
Paula Coutts, Head Librarian
Sharon Bray, Children's Librarian
Tim Stewart, Technical Services

Valemount: Valemount Public Library
1090A Main St., Valemount, BC V0E 2Z0
Tel: 250-566-4367; Fax: 250-566-4278
library@valemount.ca
valemount.bclibrary.ca
Social Media: www.facebook.com/pages/Valemount-Public-Library/218260084896402
Wendy Cinnamon, Chief Librarian
Elli Haag, Assistant Librarian/Interlibrary Loan Librarian
Hollie Blanchette, Technology
Giovanna Gislimberti, Clerk

Vancouver: Isaac Waldman Jewish Public Library
Jewish Community Centre of Greater Vancouver, 950 West 41st Ave., 2nd Fl., Vancouver, BC V5Z 2N7
Tel: 604-257-5111
library@jccgv.bc.ca
www.jcclibrary.ca
Social Media: www.facebook.com/IWJPL
Helen Pinsky, Librarian
Erica Pezim, Library Technician

Vancouver: Vancouver Public Library
350 West Georgia St., Vancouver, BC V6B 6B1
Tel: 604-331-3603
info@vpl.ca
www.vpl.ca
Social Media: flickr.com/photos/vancouverpubliclibrary; twitter.com/VPL; www.facebook.com/vancouverpubliclibrary
Sandra Singh, Chief Librarian
sandra.singh@vpl.ca
604-331-4003
Sandra Singh, Chief Librarian
Sandra.Singh@vpl.ca
604-331-4003
Diana Guinn, Director, Community Engagement & Partnerships
diana.guinn@vpl.ca
604-331-4005
Eric Smith, Director, Finance & Facilities Development
eric.smith@vpl.ca
604-331-4018
Ingrid Van Kemenade, Director, Human Resource Development
ingrid.vankemenade@vpl.ca
604-331-4052
Amanda Pitre-Hayes, Director, Planning & Projects
amanda.pitre-hayes@vpl.ca
604-331-4006
Stephen Barrington, Manager, Marketing & Communications
Stephen.Barrington@vpl.ca
604-331-3895

Vanderhoof: Vanderhoof Public Library
2300 Stewart St. East, Vanderhoof, BC V0J 3A0
Tel: 250-567-4060
vhpl@telus.net
vanderhoof.bclibrary.ca
Social Media: twitter.com/vhoofpublib; facebook.com/109105738170
Jane Gray, Librarian

Victoria: British Columbia Ministry of Education Libraries & Literacy
PO Box 9831, Stn. Provincial Government, Victoria, BC V8W 9T1
Tel: 250-356-1791; Fax: 250-953-4985
Toll-Free: 800-663-2165
llb@gov.bc.ca
www.bced.gov.bc.ca/pls
Social Media: twitter.com/MyBCLibrary
Mari Martin, Director
Mari.Martin@gov.bc.ca

Victoria: Greater Victoria Public Library
735 Broughton St., Victoria, BC V8W 3H2
Tel: 250-940-4875
www.gvpl.ca
Social Media: twitter.com/gvpl
Maureen Sawa, CEO
msawa@gvpl.ca
250-413-0353
Lynne Jordan, Deputy CEO/Director of Strategic Development
ljordon@gvpl.ca
250-413-0354
Daniel Phillips, Manager, IT Solutions
dphillips@gvpl.ca
250-413-0357
Terri Chyzowski, Manager, Human Resources
tchyzowski@gvpl.ca
250-413-0359
Jennifer Windecker, Manager, Public Services
jwindecker@gvpl.ca
250-413-0382

Victoria: View Royal Reading Centre
#103B, 1497 Admirals Rd., Victoria, BC V9A 2P8
Tel: 250-479-2723; Fax: 250-479-2723
vivr.ill@shaw.ca
viewroyal.bclibrary.ca
Doreen Jackman, Library Manager

West Vancouver: West Vancouver Memorial Library
1950 Marine Dr., West Vancouver, BC V7V 1J8
Tel: 604-925-7400; Fax: 604-925-5933
info@westvanlibrary.ca
www.westvanlibrary.ca
Social Media: twitter.com/westvanlibrary; www.facebook.com/WestVancouverMemorialLibrary
Jenny Benedict, Director, Library Services
jbenedict@westvanlibrary.ca
604-925-7424
Deb Hutchison Koep, Deputy Director & Head, Technology & Technical Services
dkoep@westvanlibrary.ca
604-925-7443

Pat Cumming, Head, Information Services
pcumming@westvanlibrary.ca
604-925-7439
Lesley Child, Acting Head, Circulation
lchild@westvanlibrary.ca
604-925-7430
Lauren Henderson, Manager, Operations
lhenderson@westvanlibrary.ca
604-925-7431

Whistler: Whistler Public Library
4329 Main St., Whistler, BC V0N 1B4
Tel: 604-935-8433; *Fax:* 604-935-8434
Other Numbers: 604-935-8436 (Youth Services)
www.whistlerlibrary.ca
Social Media: twitter.com/WhistlerPL;
www.facebook.com/whistlerpubliclibrary
Lindsay Debou, Library Director
604-935-8438
Suzanne Thomas, Coordinator, Technical Services
604-935-8433 ext. 8722
Nadine White, Librarian, Public Services
604-935-8433 ext. 8725
Libby McKeever, Youth Services Librarian
604-935-8433 ext. 8726
Julie Burrows, Supervisor, Materials Management
604-935-8433 ext. 8729

Archives

Abbotsford: Matsqui-Sumas-Abbotsford Museum Archives
2313 Ware St., Abbotsford, BC V2S 3C6
Tel: 604-853-0313; *Fax:* 866-373-2771
www.msamuseum.ca
Social Media: twitter.com/MSAMuseum;
www.facebook.com/people/Trethewey-House/100001845282384
Dorothy Van der Ree, Executive Director
Christina Reid, Collections Manager

Alert Bay: U'mista Cultural Centre
1 Front St., Alert Bay, BC V0N 1A0
Tel: 250-974-5403; *Fax:* 250-974-5499
Toll-Free: 800-690-8222
info@umista.ca
www.umista.ca
Social Media: www.facebook.com/Umista.Cultural.Society

Ashcroft: Ashcroft Museum
402 Brink St., Ashcroft, BC V0K 1A0
Tel: 250-453-9232; *Fax:* 250-453-9664
www.ashcroftbc.ca
Kathie Paulos, Curator

Barkerville: Barkerville Historic Town
14301 Hwy 26 East, Barkerville, BC V0K 1B0
Tel: 604-994-3332; *Fax:* 250-994-3435
Toll-Free: 888-994-3332
barkerville@barkerville.ca
www.barkerville.ca
Social Media: twitter.com/BarkervilleBC
Mandy Kilsby, Curator
mandy.kilsby@barkerville.ca

Bella Bella: Heiltsuk Cultural Education Centre
PO Box 880, Bella Bella, BC V0T 1Z0
Tel: 250-957-2626; *Fax:* 250-957-2780
www.hcec.ca
Jennifer Carpenter, Director
jgcarp@hcec.ca
Terri Reid, Resource Centre Assistant
treid@hcec.ca

Burnaby: Nikkei National Museum & Cultural Centre
6688 Southoaks Cres., Burnaby, BC V5E 4M7
Tel: 604-777-7000; *Fax:* 604-777-7001
info@nikkeiplace.org
centre.nikkeiplace.org
Social Media: www.youtube.com/user/nikkeimuse;
twitter.com/nikkeimuse; www.facebook.com/NNMCC
Roger Lemire, Executive Director
rlemire@nikkeiplace.org
604-777-7000 ext. 105
Sherri Kajiwara, Director-Curator
skajiwara@nikkeiplace.org
604-777-7000 ext. 112

Campbell River: Museum at Campbell River
470 Island Hwy., Campbell River, BC V9W 2B7
Tel: 250-287-3103; *Fax:* 250-286-0109
general.inquiries@crmuseum.ca
www.crmuseum.ca/archives-research-library
Social Media: www.instagram.com/museumatcampbellriver;
twitter.com/crmuseum1;
www.facebook.com/Campbell-River-Museum-100483307218
Megan Purcell, Collections Manager
megan.purcell@crmuseum.ca
Beth Boyce, Curator & Education Manager
beth.boyce@crmuseum.ca

Chilliwack: Chilliwack Archives
Evergreen Hall, 9291 Corbould St., Chilliwack, BC V2P 4A6
Tel: 604-795-9255; *Fax:* 604-795-5291
www.chilliwackmuseum.ca
Social Media: twitter.com/Chwkmuseandarch
Shannon Bettles, Archivist
shannon@chilliwackmuseum.ca
604-795-9255

Cranbrook: Canadian Museum of Rail Travel
57 Van Horne St. South, Cranbrook, BC V1C 4H9
Tel: 604-489-3918; *Fax:* 250-486-5744
archives@trainsdeluxe.com
www.trainsdeluxe.com/archives.html
Garry Anderson, Executive Director
mail@trainsdeluxe.com
Michelle Barocca, Archives Consultant

Cumberland: Cumberland Museum & Archives
2680 Dunsmuir Ave., Cumberland, BC V0R 1S0
Tel: 250-336-2445
info@cumberlandmuseum.ca
www.cumberlandmuseum.ca

Delta: Delta Museum & Archives Society
4450 Clarence Taylor Cres., Delta, BC V4K 3W3
Tel: 604-940-3832; *Fax:* 604-946-5791
info@deltamuseum.ca
www.deltamuseum.ca
Social Media:
www.facebook.com/DeltaMuseumAndArchivesSociety
Robert McLelland, Archivist

Duncan: Cowichan Valley Museum & Archives
Duncan City Hall, 3rd Fl., Duncan, BC V9L 3Y2
Tel: 250-746-6612; *Fax:* 250-746-6612
www.cowichanvalleymuseum.bc.ca

Esquimalt: Township of Esquimalt
1149A Esquimalt Rd., Esquimalt, BC V9A 3N6
Tel: 250-412-8540; *Fax:* 250-414-7111
www.esquimalt.ca/cultureHeritage/archives
Gregory Evans, Municipal Archivist

Fort Langley: Langley Centennial Museum & National Exhibition Centre
9135 King St., Fort Langley, BC V1M 2S2
Tel: 604-532-3536
museum@tol.ca
museum.tol.ca

Fort St John: Fort St John - North Peace Museum
9323 - 100th St., Fort St John, BC V1J 4N4
Tel: 250-787-0430
fsjnpmuseum@fsjmail.com
www.fsjmuseum.com
Social Media: www.facebook.com/102713059806910
Heather Sjoblom, Manager/Curator

Fort Steele: Fort Steele Heritage Town
9851 Hwy. 93/95, Fort Steele, BC V0B 1N0
Tel: 250-417-6000; *Fax:* 250-489-2624
fortsteele.ca
Social Media: www.facebook.com/fortsteeleheritagetown
Kathy Allison, Administration Manager
Kathy.Allison@FortSteele.bc.ca

Harrison Mills: Kilby Store & Farm Museum
215 Kilby Rd., Harrison Mills, BC V0M 1L0
Tel: 604-796-9576; *Fax:* 604-796-9592
info@kilby.ca
www.kilby.ca
Jo-Anne Leon, Sales & Marketing Manager
info@kilby.ca

Hazelton: 'Ksan Historical Village & Museum
PO Box 440, Hazelton, BC V0J 1Y0
Tel: 250-842-5544; *Fax:* 250-842-6533
Toll-Free: 877-842-5518
ksan@gitanmaax.com
www.ksan.org

Kamloops: Kamloops Museum & Archives
207 Seymour St., Kamloops, BC V2C 2E7
Tel: 250-828-3576; *Fax:* 250-828-3760
museum@kamloops.ca
www.kamloops.ca/museum
Social Media: twitter.com/kamloopsmuseum;
facebook.com/kamloopsmuseum
Scott Owens, Archivist

Kamloops: Secwepemc Cultural Education Society
#311, 355 Yellowhead Hwy., Kamloops, BC V2H 1H1
Tel: 250-828-9749; *Fax:* 250-372-8833
www.secwepemc.org/museum/archives
Daniel Saul, Museum Manager
dsaul@kib.ca

Kaslo: Kootenay Lake Archives
312 - 4th St., Kaslo, BC V0G 1M0
Tel: 250-353-3204
archives@klhs.bc.ca
klhs.bc.ca/archives
Elizabeth Scarlett, Archivist

Kelowna: Kelowna Public Archives
470 Queensway Ave., Kelowna, BC V1Y 6S7
Tel: 250-763-2417
info@kelownamuseums.ca
www.kelownamuseums.ca/archives/kelowna-public-archives-2
Social Media: twitter.com/kelownamuseums
Tara Hurley, Community Archivist
thurley@kelownamuseums.ca
250-763-2417 ext. 25

Kelowna: Roman Catholic Diocese of Nelson
3665 Benvoulin Rd., Kelowna, BC V1L 4M7
Tel: 250-448-2725
www.nelsondiocese.org
Phyllis Giroux, Archivist
phyllis.giroux@nelsondiocese.org
250-448-2725 ext. 140

Kitimat: Kitimat Centennial Museum & Archives
293 City Centre, Kitimat, BC V8C 1T6
Tel: 250-632-8950; *Fax:* 250-632-7429
info@kitimatmuseum.ca
www.kitimatmuseum.ca
Social Media:
www.facebook.com/pages/Kitimat-Museum-Archives/161440070544293
Louise Avery, Curator
lavery@kitimatmuseum.ca
Angela Eastman, Assistant Curator
aeastman@kitimatmuseum.ca

Lake Cowichan: Kaatza Historical Society
125 South Shore Rd., Lake Cowichan, BC V0R 2G0
Tel: 250-749-6142
kaatzamuseum@shaw.ca
www.kaatzastationmuseum.ca
Barbara Simkins, Curator/Manager

Maple Ridge: Maple Ridge Museum & Community Archives
22520 - 116th Ave., Maple Ridge, BC V2X 0S4
Tel: 604-463-5311
www.mapleridgemuseum.org
Social Media:
www.flickr.com/photos/mrcommunityarchives/5902226789;
www.facebook.com/106860626035721
Allison White, Curator

Merritt: Nicola Tribal Association
#202, 2090 Coutlee Ave., Merritt, BC V1K 1B8
Tel: 250-378-4235; *Fax:* 250-378-9119
www.nicolatribal.com
Arlene Johnston, Executive Director
250-378-4235
Sharon Joe, Manager, Research
250-378-4235 ext. 104

Merritt: Nicola Valley Museum & Archives
1672 Tutill Ct., Merritt, BC V1K 1B8
Tel: 250-378-4145; *Fax:* 250-378-4145
www.nicolavalleymuseum.org
Social Media: www.facebook.com/123292923631
Barb Watson, Office Administrator
Jo Atkinson, Assistant Administrator

Mission: Mission Community Archives
33215 - 2nd Ave., Mission, BC V2V 4L1
Tel: 604-820-2621
mca@missionarchives.com
www.missionarchives.com

Nakusp: Arrow Lakes Historical Society
92 - 6 Ave. NW, Nakusp, BC V0G 1R0
Tel: 250-265-0110; *Fax:* 250-265-0110
Other Numbers: Off-Hours Phone: 250-265-3323
alhs1234@telus.net
www.alhs-archives.com

Nelson: Touchstones Nelson Museum of Art & History
502 Vernon St., Nelson, BC V1L 4E7
Tel: 250-352-9813
collections@touchstonesnelson.ca
www.touchstonesnelson.ca/archives
Social Media: www.flickr.com/photos/touchstonesnelson; www.facebook.com/group.php?gid=62908084663
Laura Fortier, Archivist & Collections Manager

New Westminster: New Westminster Museum & Archives
777 Columbia St., New Westminster, BC V3M 1B6
Tel: 604-527-4640
museum@newwestcity.ca
newwestpcr.ca/culture/museums/new-westminster-museum
Social Media: www.facebook.com/NWMuseumandArchives
Barry Dykes, Assistant Archivist
bdykes@newwestcity.ca
604-527-4642

North Vancouver: North Vancouver Museum & Archives
Community History Centre, 3203 Institute Rd., North Vancouver, BC V7K 3E5
Tel: 604-990-3700
www.northvanmuseum.ca/collections3.htm
Social Media: twitter.com/NorthVanMuseum; www.facebook.com/NorthVancouverMuseumArchives
Janet Turner, Archivist
turnerj@dnv.org
Daien Ide, Reference Historian
ided@dnv.org

Penticton: Penticton Museum & Archives
785 Main St., Penticton, BC V2A 5E3
Tel: 250-490-2451; *Fax:* 250-490-2442
museum@city.penticton.bc.ca
www.pentictonmuseum.com
Social Media: www.facebook.com/Penticton-Museum-and-Archives-108559494129
Dennis Oomen, Museum Manager/Curator
Manda Maggs, Museum Assistant

Port Alberni: Alberni District Historical Society
4255 Wallace St., Port Alberni, BC V9Y 3Y6
Tel: 250-723-2181
aadhs1@gmail.com
www.alberniheritage.com/alberni-valley-museum/archives

Port Clements: Port Clements Historical Society
45 Bayview Dr., Port Clements, BC V0T 1R0
Tel: 250-557-4576
www.portclementsmuseum.ca
Social Media: www.facebook.com/pages/The-Port-/175359227203

Powell River: Powell River Historical Museum & Archives
4798 Marine Ave., Powell River, BC V8A 4Z5
Tel: 604-485-2222; *Fax:* 604-485-2327
info@powellrivermuseum.ca
www.powellrivermuseum.ca
Teedie Kagume, Collections Manager
604-485-2222

Prince George: Exploration Place
333 Becott Pl., Prince George, BC V2L 4V7
Tel: 250-562-1612; *Fax:* 250-562-6395
Toll-Free: 866-562-1612
info@theexplorationplace.com
www.theexplorationplace.com
Social Media: instagram.com/theexplorationplace; twitter.com/ExplorationPG; www.facebook.com/TheExplorationPlace
Alyssa Tobin, Curator
alyssa.tobin@theexplorationplace.com
250-562-1612 ext. 230
Alisha Rubadeau, Assistant Curator
Chad Hellenius, Assistant Archivist
archive@theexplorationplace.com

Prince Rupert: Prince Rupert City & Regional Archives
424 - 3rd Ave. West, Prince Rupert, BC V8J 1L7
Tel: 250-624-3326; *Fax:* 250-624-3706
info@princerupertarchives.ca
www.princerupertarchives.ca

Quesnel: Quesnel & District Museum & Archives
705 Carson Ave., Quesnel, BC V2J 2B6
Tel: 250-992-9580
www.quesnelmuseum.ca
Social Media: www.facebook.com/350659608390264
Elizabeth Hunter, Museum & Heritage Manager
ehunter@quesnel.ca
250-992-9580
Brandee Shutz, Museum Assistant
bshutz@quesnel.ca
250-992-9580

Revelstoke: Revelstoke Museum & Archives
315 - 1st St. West, Revelstoke, BC V0E 2S0
Tel: 250-837-3067; *Fax:* 250-837-3094
info@revelstokemuseum.ca
www.revelstokemuseum.ca
Social Media: twitter.com/revmuseum; www.facebook.com/144528853796

Richmond: City of Richmond Archives
7700 Minoru Gate, Richmond, BC V6Y 1R9
Tel: 604-247-8305; *Fax:* 604-231-6464
archives@richmond.ca
www.richmond.ca/cityhall/archives/about/about.htm
Social Media: www.youtube.com/user/richmondarchives; www.facebook.com/FriendsofTheRichmondArchives

Sooke: Sooke Region Museum & Visitor Centre
2070 Phillips Rd., Sooke, BC V9Z 0Y3
Tel: 250-642-6351; *Fax:* 250-642-7089
Toll-Free: 866-888-4748
info@sookeregionmuseum.com
www.sookeregionmuseum.com/archives.htm
Social Media: www.facebook.com/group.php?gid=118482471530145

Summerland: Summerland Museum & Heritage Society
9521 Wharton St., Summerland, BC V0H 1Z0
Tel: 250-494-9395; *Fax:* 250-494-9326
info@summerlandmuseum.org
www.summerlandmuseum.org
Amy McCroy, Curator/Administrator
info@summerlandmuseum.org

Surrey: City of Surrey Archives
17671 - 56 Ave., Surrey, BC V3S 1C9
Tel: 604-502-6459
archives@surrey.ca
www.surrey.ca/culture-recreation/2394.aspx
Social Media: youtube.com/surreyarchives; twitter.com/SurreyArchives

Trail: Trail Historical Society
Trail City Hall, 1394 Pine Ave., 2nd Fl., Trail, BC V1R 4E6
Tel: 250-364-0829; *Fax:* 250-364-0830
history@trail.ca
www.trailhistory.com/archives.html

Vancouver: British Columbia Sports Hall of Fame & Museum
777 Pacific Blvd. South, Vancouver, BC V6B 4Y8
Tel: 604-687-5520; *Fax:* 604-687-5510
sportsinfo@bcsportshalloffame.com
www.bcsportshalloffame.com
Social Media: twitter.com/BCSportsHall; www.facebook.com/bcsportshall
Jason Beck, Curator
jason.beck@bcsportshalloffame.com

Vancouver: City of Vancouver Archives
1150 Chestnut St., Vancouver, BC V6J 3J9
Tel: 604-736-8561
archives@vancouver.ca
www.vancouver.ca/archives
Social Media: www.youtube.com/user/VancouverArchives; twitter.com/VanArchives; www.facebook.com/pages/City-of-Vancouver-Archives/222020581254652
Heather Gordon, City Archivist

Vancouver: Institute of Indigenous Government / Union of BC Indian Chiefs
#500, 342 Water St., Vancouver, BC V6B 1B6
Tel: 604-684-0231; *Fax:* 604-684-5726
library@ubcic.bc.ca
www.ubcic.bc.ca/library
Social Media: twitter.com/UBCIC; www.facebook.com/UBCIC

Vancouver: Jewish Historical Society of BC
6184 Ash St., Vancouver, BC V5Z 3G9
Tel: 604-257-5199
info@jewishmuseum.ca
www.jewishmuseum.ca
Social Media: instagram.com/jewishmuseumbc; twitter.com/JMA_BC; www.facebook.com/JewishBC
Alysa Routtenberg, Archivist

Vancouver: Roman Catholic Archdiocese of Vancouver
4885 Saint John Paul II Way, Vancouver, BC V5Z 0G3
Tel: 604-683-0281; *Fax:* 604-683-4288
www.rcav.org/archives

Vancouver: Satellite Video Exchange Society
2625 Kaslo St., Vancouver, BC V5M 3G9
Tel: 604-872-8337; *Fax:* 604-876-1185
library@vivomediaarts.com
www.vivomediaarts.com
Emma Hendrix, General Manager
admin@vivomediaarts.com

Vancouver: Vancouver Ballet Society
677 Davie St., 6th Fl., Vancouver, BC V6B 2G6
Tel: 604-681-1525; *Fax:* 604-681-7732
vbs@telus.net
vancouverballetsociety.com/about/library-archives
Social Media: www.facebook.com/vancouverballetsocietyvbs

Vernon: Greater Vernon Museum & Archives
3009 - 32nd Ave., Vernon, BC V1T 2L8
Tel: 250-542-3142
mail@vernonmuseum.ca
www.vernonmuseum.ca
Social Media: www.facebook.com/vernonmuseum
Barbara Bell, Archivist
barbara.bell@vernonmuseum.ca
Liz Ellison, Database Manager & Assistant Archivist
liz.ellison@vernonmuseum.ca

Victoria: City of Victoria Archives
8 Centenial Sq., Victoria, BC V8W 1P6
Tel: 250-361-0375; *Fax:* 250-361-0394
archives@victoria.ca
victoria.ca/EN/main/departments/legislative-services/archives.html

Victoria: Roman Catholic Diocese of Victoria
#1, 4044 Nelthorpe St., Victoria, BC V8X 2A1
Tel: 250-479-1331; *Fax:* 250-479-5423
www.rcdvictoria.org
Social Media: twitter.com/RCDVictoria
Cynthia Bouchard-Williams, Chancellor, Archives
250-479-1331 ext. 225

Victoria: Saanich Municipal Archives
3100 Tillicum Rd., Victoria, BC V9A 6T2
Tel: 250-475-1775; *Fax:* 250-388-7819
archives@saanich.ca
www.saanicharchives.ca
Social Media: www.facebook.com/137902079636927
Caroline Duncan, Archivist
250-475-1775 ext. 3478
Sonia Nicholson, Archives Specialist
250-475-1775 ext. 3479
Evelyn Wolfe, Archives Specialist
250-475-1775 ext. 3477

Victoria: Sisters of St Ann
675 Belleville St., Victoria, BC V8R 9W2
Tel: 250-592-0685
archives@ssabc.ca
royalbcmuseum.bc.ca/bcarchives/sisters-of-st-ann
Social Media: www.facebook.com/SSAArchives1858
Carey Pallister, Archivist

West Vancouver: West Vancouver Archives
680 - 17th St., West Vancouver, BC V7V 3T2
Tel: 604-925-7298
archives@westvancouver.ca
westvancouver.ca/archives

White Rock: **White Rock Museum & Archives Society**
14970 Marine Dr., White Rock, BC V4B 1C4
Tel: 604-541-2221; *Fax:* 604-541-2223
archives@whiterockmuseum.ca
www.whiterockmuseum.ca
Hugh Ellenwood, Archives Manager
archives@whiterockmuseum.ca
604-541-2225
Kate Petrusa, Curator
curator@whiterockmuseum.ca
604-541-2230

Manitoba

Regional Systems

Brandon: **Western Manitoba Regional Library**
#1, 710 Rosser Ave., Brandon, MB R7A 0K9
Tel: 204-727-6648; *Fax:* 204-727-4447
brandon@wmrl.ca
www.wmrl.ca
Social Media: twitter.com/wmrlibrary
Shelley Mortensen, Chief Librarian

Dauphin: **Parkland Regional Library**
504 Main St. North, Dauphin, MB R7N 1C9
Tel: 204-638-6410; *Fax:* 204-638-9483
prlhq@parklandlib.mb.ca
www.parklandlib.mb.ca
Jean-Louis Guillas, Director
jguillas@parklandlib.mb.ca

Gimli: **Evergreen Regional Library**
65 - First Ave., Gimli, MB R0C 1B0
Tel: 204-642-7912; *Fax:* 204-642-8319
gimli.library@mts.net
www.erlibrary.ca
Valerie Eyolfson, Head Librarian
Sandy Reykdal, Assistant Librarian

Killarney: **Lakeland Regional Library**
318 Williams Ave., Killarney, MB R0K 1G0
Tel: 204-523-4949; *Fax:* 204-523-7460
lrl@mts.net
www.lakelandregionallibrary.ca
Gloria Kinsley, Librarian

Lac du Bonnet: **Lac du Bonnet Regional Library**
84 - 3rd St., Lac du Bonnet, MB R0E 1A0
Tel: 204-345-2653; *Fax:* 204-345-6827
mldb@mts.net
www.lacdubonnetlibrary.ca
Vickie Short, Head Librarian
Janice Hoffman, Assistant Librarian
Joanna Sokal, Assistant Librarian
Michelle Grimmelt, Library Clerk

Melita: **Southwestern Manitoba Regional Library**
149 Main St., Melita, MB R0M 1L0
Tel: 204-522-3923; *Fax:* 284-522-3923
Swmblib@mts.net
www.swmblib.wix.com/library-page

Virden: **Border Regional Library**
312 - 7th Ave., Virden, MB R0M 2C0
Tel: 204-748-3862; *Fax:* 204-748-3862
brlcoord@rfnow.com
www.borderregionallibrary.ca
Social Media:
www.facebook.com/pages/Border-Regional-Library/558622490862434

Winkler: **South Central Regional Library**
160 Main St., Winkler, MB R6W 4B4
Tel: 204-325-7174; *Fax:* 204-331-1847
winklerlib@gmail.com
scrl.mb.libraries.coop
Social Media: twitter.com/SCRL_Library;
www.facebook.com/scrllibrary
Mikaela MacDonald, Branch Librarian

Public Libraries

Baldur: **Regional Municipality of Argyle Public Library**
627 Elizabeth St. East, Baldur, MB R0K 0B0
Tel: 204-535-2314; *Fax:* 204-535-2242
rmargyle@gmail.com
rmargyle.wix.com/rmargyle
Social Media: twitter.com/RMArgyleLibrary
Cheri McLaren, Librarian

Beausejour: **Brokenhead River Regional Library**
427 Park Ave., Beausejour, MB R0E 0C0
Tel: 204-268-7570
brokenheadriverregionallibrary.ca
Debbie Winnicki, Head Librarian
Debbiewinnickibrrl@mts.net

Boissevain: **Boissevain & Morton Regional Library**
409 South Railway St., Boissevain, MB R0K 0E0
Tel: 204-534-6478; *Fax:* 204-534-3710
mail@bmlibrary.ca
bmlibrary.ca

Brandon: **Manitoba Public Library Services**
#300, 1011 Rosser Ave., Brandon, MB R7A 0L5
Tel: 204-726-6590; *Fax:* 204-726-6868
Toll-Free: 800-252-9998
pls@gov.mb.ca
www.gov.mb.ca/chc/pls/index

Carman: **Boyne Regional Library**
15 - 1st Ave. SW, Carman, MB R0G 0J0
Tel: 204-745-3504
boynereg@mymts.net
www.boyneregionallibrary.com
Sandra Yeo, Head Librarian
Diane Cohoe, Assistant Librarian

Cartwright: **Cartwright Branch Library**
483 Veteran Dr., Cartwright, MB R0K 0L0
Tel: 204-529-2261
cartlib@mymts.net
www.lakelandregionallibrary.ca
Andrea Trembath, Branch Librarian

Churchill: **Churchill Public Library**
59 Husdon Square, Churchill, MB R0B 0E0
Tel: 204-675-2731

Deloraine: **Bren Del Win Centennial Library**
PO Box 584, Deloraine, MB R0M 0M0
Tel: 204-747-2415; *Fax:* 204-747-3446
bdwlib@gmail.com
www.delorainelibrary.com
Lorraine Stovin, Librarian

Easterville: **Chemawawin Public Library**
1A Cree Cres., Easterville, MB R0C 0V0
Tel: 204-329-2115
soar.ucn.ca/ICS/Library/Chemawawin__(Easterville)/CH_Home.jnz
Anthony Zong, Librarian

Eriksdale: **Eriksdale Public Library**
9 Main St., Eriksdale, MB R0C 0W0
Tel: 204-739-2668
epl1@mymts.net
www.eriksdalepl.org

Flin Flon: **Flin Flon Public Library**
58 Main St., Flin Flon, MB R8A 1J8
Tel: 204-687-3397; *Fax:* 204-687-4233
ffpl@mts.net
www.flinflonpubliclibrary.ca
Social Media: www.facebook.com/FlinFlonPublicLibrary
Cindy McLean, Library Administrator
Buz Trevor, Library Board Chair

Gillam: **Bette Winner Public Library**
Gillam Recreation Centre, Gillam, MB R0B 0L0
Tel: 204-652-2617; *Fax:* 204-652-2617
library@townofgillam.com
Social Media: www.facebook.com/160167924017586
Ricci Bangle, Head Librarian
Dawna Gray McDonald, Assistant Librarian

Headingley: **Headingley Public Library**
49 Alboro St., Headingley, MB R4J 1A3
Tel: 204-888-5410
hml@mymts.net
www.headingleylibrary.ca

Holland: **Victoria Municipal Library**
102 Stewart Ave., Holland, MB R0G 0X0
Tel: 204-526-2011
victorialibrary@rmofvictoria.com

Ile-des-Chênes: **Bibliothèque Ritchot Library**
École Gabrielle-Roy, 310, ch Lamoureux, Ile-des-Chênes, MB R0A 0T0
Tél: 204-878-2147
ritchotlib@hotmail.com
brl.fbmb.ca

La Broquerie: **Bibliothèque Saint-Joachim Library**
29, baie Normandeau, La Broquerie, MB R0A 0W0
Tel: 204-424-9533; *Fax:* 204-424-5610
bsjl@bsjl.ca
www.bsjl.ca
Yolande Tétrault, Présidente, Conseil d'administration

Lorette: **Bibliothèque Taché Library**
1082, ch Dawson, Lorette, MB R0A 0Y0
Tel: 204-878-9488
btl@srsd.ca
www.bibliotachelibrary.ca
Susan Berry, Chair/Archivist

Lundar: **The Pauline Johnson Public Library**
23 Main St., Lundar, MB R0C 1Y0
Tel: 204-762-5367; *Fax:* 204-762-5367
mlpj@mts.net
mlpj.mb.ca

Lynn Lake: **Lynn Lake Centennial Library**
503 Sherritt Ave., Lynn Lake, MB R0B 0W0
Tel: 204-356-8222
lynnlakelibrarian@yahoo.ca
David Campbell, Contact

MacGregor: **North Norfolk MacGregor Regional Library**
35 Hampton St. East, MacGregor, MB R0H 0R0
Tel: 204-685-2796; *Fax:* 204-685-2478
maclib@mts.net
nnmrl.net
Social Media: twitter.com/nn_mac;
www.facebook.com/258806540802238

Manitou: **Manitou Regional Library**
418 Main St., Manitou, MB R0G 1G0
Tel: 204-242-3134; *Fax:* 204-242-3184
manitoulibrary@mymts.net

Minnedosa: **Minnedosa Regional Library**
45 - 1st Ave. SE, Minnedosa, MB R0J 1E0
Tel: 204-867-2585; *Fax:* 204-867-6140
mmr@mts.net
www.discoverminnedosa.ca
Social Media: www.facebook.com/103641533063836
Linda Cook, Head Librarian

Morris: **Valley Regional Library**
141 Main St. South, Morris, MB R0G 1K0
Tel: 204-746-2136
valleylib@mts.net
Diane Ali, Librarian

Norway House: **Ayamiscikawikamik Public Library/ Norway House Public Library**
University College of the North (UCN), Norway House, MB R0B 1B0
Tel: 204-359-6296; *Fax:* 204-359-6262
sduncan@ucn.ca
manitoba.cioc.ca/record/VMB4500
Violet Ouellette, Librarian

Notre-Dame-de-Lourdes: **Bibliothèque Père Champagne/ Père Champagne Library**
44, rue Rodgers, Notre-Dame-de-Lourdes, MB R0G 1M0
Tel: 204-248-2386
bpcndlib@gmail.com
bpcl.fbmb.ca

Pilot Mound: **Pilot Mound Library**
219 Broadway Ave. West, Pilot Mound, MB R0G 1P0
Tel: 204-825-2035
pmlibrary@mymts.net
www.pilotmoundlibrary.ca
Allison MacAulay, Librarian

Pinawa: **Pinawa Public Library**
Community Centre, Vanier Ave., Pinawa, MB R0E 1L0
Tel: 204-753-2496
email@pinawapubliclibrary.com
www.pinawapubliclibrary.com
Social Media:
www.facebook.com/pages/Pinawa-Public-Library/166929396717731

Portage la Prairie: **Portage la Prairie Regional Library**
40B Royal Rd. North, Portage la Prairie, MB R1N 1V1
Tel: 204-857-4271; *Fax:* 204-239-4387
portlib@portagelibrary.com
www.portagelibrary.com

Rapid City: **Rapid City Regional Library**
125 - 3rd Ave., Rapid City, MB R0K 1W0
Tel: 204-826-2732
rcreglib@mts.net
www.rclibrary.ca
Shirley Martin, Head Librarian

Reston: **Reston District Library**
220 - 4th St., Reston, MB R0M 1X0
Tel: 204-877-3673
restonlib@yahoo.ca
www.restonlibrary.ca

Rivers: **Prairie Crocus Regional Library**
137 Main St., Rivers, MB R0K 1X0
Tel: 204-328-7613
pcrl@mts.net
www.prairiecrocuslibrary.ca
Dora M. Irvine, Librarian

Rossburn: **Rossburn Regional Library**
53 Main St. North, Rossburn, MB R0J 1V0
Tel: 204-859-2687
rrl@mts.net
www.rossburnregionallibrary.ca
Stephanie Parkinson, Librarian/Book-Keeper
rrl@mts.net
Ivy Phelps, Library Assistant
rrl@mts.net

Saint Jean Baptiste: **Bibliothèque Montcalm Library**
113, 2e av, Saint Jean Baptiste, MB R0G 2B0
Tél: 204-758-3137; *Téléc:* 204-758-3574
bibliomontcalm@hotmail.ca
bml.fbmb.ca

Saint-Claude: **Bibliothèque Saint-Claude/ St. Claude Library**
50 - 1st St., Saint-Claude, MB R0G 1Z0
Tel: 204-379-2524
stclib@mts.net
www.stclaude.ca
Lynn Gobin, Librarian

Selkirk: **Gaynor Family Regional Library**
806 Manitoba Ave., Selkirk, MB R1A 2H4
Tel: 204-482-3522; *Fax:* 204-482-6166
library@gfrl.org
www.gfrl.org
Social Media: www.facebook.com/123919044304982
Ken Kuryliw, Director, Library Services
Darlene Phillips, Technical Services Coordinator
Katherine Anderson, Public Services & Information Technology Coordinator

Shilo: **Shilo Community Library**
Community Centre Bldg., 114 Notre Dame Ave., #T, Shilo, MB R0K 2A0
Tel: 204-765-3000
shilocommunitylibrary@yahoo.ca

Snow Lake: **Snow Lake Community Library**
Joseph H. Kerr School, 201 Cherry Ave., Snow Lake, MB R0B 1M0
Tel: 204-358-2322; *Fax:* 204-358-2116
dslibrary@hotmail.com
Social Media: www.facebook.com/SnowLakeCommunityLibrary

Somerset: **Somerset Library/ Bibliothèque Somerset**
289 Carlton Ave., Somerset, MB R0G 2L0
Tel: 204-744-2170

Souris: **Glenwood & Souris Regional Library**
#18, 114 - 2nd St. South, Souris, MB R0K 2C0
Tel: 204-483-2757
frontdesk@sourislibrary.mb.ca
sourislibrary.mb.ca
Gayle O'Greysik, Chair
Connie Bradshaw, Librarian
Lynda Luptak, Assistant Librarian

St Pierre Jolys: **Jolys Regional Library/ Bibliothèque régionale Jolys**
505 Hébert Ave., St Pierre Jolys, MB R0A 1V0
Tel: 204-433-7729; *Fax:* 204-433-7412
stplibrary@jrlibrary.mb.ca
www.jrlibrary.mb.ca

St. Georges: **Bibliothèque Allard Regional Library**
104086 PTH 11, St. Georges, MB R0E 1V0
Tel: 204-367-8443; *Fax:* 204-367-1780
info@allardlibrary.com
www.allardlibrary.com
Bruce Morrison, Chairperson

Ste Rose du Lac: **Ste Rose Regional Library**
580 Central Ave., Ste Rose du Lac, MB R0L 1S0
Tel: 204-447-2527
sroselib@mts.net
www.steroseregionallibrary.info
Social Media: pinterest.com/steroselibrary; twitter.com/steroselibrary; www.facebook.com/steroseregionallibrary

Ste-Anne-des-Chênes: **Bibliothèque Ste-Anne Library**
16, rue de l'Eglise, Ste-Anne-des-Chênes, MB R5H 1H8
Tél: 204-422-9958
steannelib@steannemb.ca
www.bibliothequesteannelibrary.ca
Mona Gauthier, Bibliothécaire

Steinbach: **Jake Epp Library**
255 Elmdale St., Steinbach, MB R5G 0C9
Tel: 204-326-6841; *Fax:* 204-326-6859
jakeepplibrary@yahoo.com
www.jakeepplibrary.com
Carolyn Graham, Head Librarian

Stonewall: **South Interlake Regional Library**
419 Main St., Stonewall, MB R0C 2Z0
Tel: 204-467-8415; *Fax:* 204-467-9809
sirl@mts.net
www.sirlibrary.com
Darlene Dallman, Head Librarian

Swan River: **North-West Regional Library**
610 - 1st St. North, Swan River, MB R0L 1Z0
Tel: 204-734-3880; *Fax:* 204-734-3880
email@swanriverlibrary.ca
www.swanriverlibrary.ca
Social Media: www.facebook.com/184968444852313
Kathy Sterma, Head Librarian

The Pas: **The Pas Regional Library**
53 Edwards Ave., The Pas, MB R9A 1R2
Tel: 204-623-2023; *Fax:* 204-623-4594
library@mts.net
www.thepasregionallibrary.com
Lauren Wadelius, Library Administrator
Keith Paquette, Head Librarian
Kristin Nolan, Library Assistant

Thompson: **Thompson Public Library**
81 Thompson Dr. North, Thompson, MB R8N 0C3
Tel: 204-677-3717
info@thompsonlibrary.com
www.thompsonlibrary.com
Social Media: facebook.com/Library.Thompson
Cheryl Davies, Administrator
admin@thompsonlibrary.com

Winnipeg: **Winnipeg Public Library**
251 Donald St., Winnipeg, MB R3C 3P5
Tel: 204-986-6462; *Fax:* 204-942-5671
wpl.winnipeg.ca/library
Social Media: www.youtube.com/user/winnipegpublibrary; twitter.com/wpglibrary; www.facebook.com/winnipegpubliclibrary
Rick Walker, Manager of Library Services
Gail Doherty, Central Services Coordinator
Betty Parry, Coordinator of Public Services & Collection Development
Kathleen Williams, Coordinator of Community Outreach & Marketing

Archives

Boissevain: **Boissevain Community Archives**
409 South Railway St., Boissevain, MB R0K 0E0
Tel: 204-534-6478; *Fax:* 204-534-3710
mail@bmlibrary.ca
bmlibrary.ca/resources/community-archives
Social Media: www.facebook.com/bmlibrary

Brandon: **Brandon General Museum & Archives Inc.**
#101, 19 - 9th St., Brandon, MB R7A 4A3
Tel: 204-717-1514
bgmainfo@wcgwave.ca
Social Media: twitter.com/TheBGMA; www.facebook.com/541456719235325

Brandon: **Magnacca Research Centre**
122 - 18th St., Brandon, MB R7A 5A4
Tel: 204-727-1722; *Fax:* 204-727-1722
dalymuseum@wcgwave.ca
www.dalyhousemuseum.ca/archives.htm
Social Media: twitter.com/DalyHouseMuseum; www.facebook.com/dalyhouse

Brandon: **X11 Manitoba Dragoons & 26 Field Regiment Museum**
Brandon Armoury, 1116 Victoria Ave., 1st Fl., Brandon, MB R7A 1B2
Tel: 204-717-4579; *Fax:* 204-725-1766
26fdlibrary@wcgwave.ca
www.12mbdragoons.com
Ed McArthur, Curator
26fdregCurator@wcgwave.ca
204-717-4579
Gord Sim, Researcher
26fdregmuseum@wcgwave.ca
204-727-7691

Carberry: **Carberry Plains Archives**
115 Main St., Carberry, MB R0K 0H0
Tel: 204-834-6614; *Fax:* 204-834-6604
cparchives@mts.net
www.mts.net/~archives/

Churchill: **Diocese of Churchill - Hudson Bay**
Eskimo Museum, 242 La Verendrye Ave., Churchill, MB R0B 0E0
Tel: 204-675-2252
Social Media: www.facebook.com/519341644800065

Killarney: **J.A.V. David Museum**
414 William St., Killarney, MB R0K 1G0
Tel: 204-523-7325
Social Media: www.facebook.com/JAV-David-Museum-721336597902552

Leaf Rapids: **Leaf Rapids Community Archives**
PO Box 190, Leaf Rapids, MB R0B 1W0
Tel: 204-473-2742; *Fax:* 204-473-2566
lrlib@mts.net
leafrapidslibrary.tripod.com

Selkirk: **Selkirk Mental Health Centre Archives Collection Inc.**
825 Manitoba Ave., Selkirk, MB R1A 2B5
Tel: 204-482-3810
smhc-archives.com
Brian Kaltenberger, Archival Request Contact

Shilo: **Royal Canadian Artillery Museum/ Le Musée de l'artillerie du Canada**
Building N, Canadian Forces Base Shilo, 118 Patricia Rd., Shilo, MB R0K 2A0
Tel: 204-765-3000
RCAMuseum@intern.mil.ca
www.rcamuseum.com

Steinbach: **Mennonite Heritage Village**
231 PTH 12 North, Steinbach, MB R5G 1T8
Tel: 204-326-9661; *Fax:* 204-326-5046
Toll-Free: 866-280-8741
info@mhv.ca
www.mennoniteheritagevillage.com
Social Media: twitter.com/MHVSteinbach; www.facebook.com/pages/Mennonite-Heritage-Village/107997272562045
Andrea Dyck, Curator
andread@mhv.ca
204-326-9661 ext. 226

Thompson: **Heritage North Museum**
162 Princeton Dr., Thompson, MB R8N 2A4
Tel: 204-677-2216
hnmuseum@mts.net
www.heritagenorthmuseum.ca
Tanna Teneycke, Executive Director

Winnipeg: **Archevêché de St-Boniface**
622, av Taché, Winnipeg, MB R2H 0B4
Tél: 204-237-9851; *Téléc:* 204-237-9942
secretariat@archsaintboniface.ca
Agata Johns, Secrétaire de la chancelerie
secretariat@archsaintboniface.ca

Winnipeg: **Archives of Manitoba/ Archives du Manitoba**
#130, 200 Vaughan St., Winnipeg, MB R3C 1T5
Tel: 204-945-3971; *Fax:* 204-948-2672
Toll-Free: 800-617-3588
archives@gov.mb.ca
www.gov.mb.ca/chc/archives
Social Media: twitter.com/MBGovArchives

***Winnipeg:* Centre for Mennonite Brethren Studies**
1310 Taylor Ave., Winnipeg, MB R3M 3Z6
Tel: 204-669-6575; *Fax:* 204-654-1865
Toll-Free: 888-669-6575
cmbs@mbchurches.ca
www.mennonitebrethren.ca/ministry/cmbs
Jon Isaak, Director
jon.isaak@mbchurches.ca
888-669-6575 ext. 695
Conrad Stoesz, Archivist
conrad.stoesz@mbchurches.ca
888-669-6575 ext. 769

***Winnipeg:* City of Winnipeg**
50 Myrtle St., Winnipeg, MB R3E 2R2
Tel: 204-986-5325; *Fax:* 204-986-7133
www.winnipeg.ca/clerks/toc/archives.stm

***Winnipeg:* Costume Museum of Canada**
#301, 250 McDermot Ave., Winnipeg, MB R3B 0S5
Tel: 204-989-0072
costumemuseumcanada@gmail.com
www.costumemuseumcanada.com
Social Media: costumemuseum.tumblr.com; twitter.com/costumemuseumca; www.facebook.com/pages/Costume-Museum-of-Canada/94897456640
Maralyn MacKay Hussain, President

***Winnipeg:* Fire Fighters Historical Society of Winnipeg**
56 Maple St., Winnipeg, MB R3B 0Y8
Tel: 204-942-4817; *Fax:* 204-885-1306
firemuseum@gatewest.net
www.winnipegfiremuseum.ca

***Winnipeg:* Fort Garry Horse Museum & Archives**
551 Machray Ave., Winnipeg, MB R2W 1A8
Tel: 204-586-6298
www.fortgarryhorse.ca
Gordon Crossley, Museum Director

***Winnipeg:* Grand Lodge of Manitoba**
420 Corydon Ave., Winnipeg, MB R3L 0N8
Tel: 204-832-6062; *Fax:* 204-284-3527
rkiv@mts.net
www.glmb.ca/archives.html
Allan G. Brock, Grand Archivist
rkiv@mts.net

***Winnipeg:* Jewish Heritage Centre of Western Canada**
#C140, 123 Doncaster St., Winnipeg, MB R3N 2B2
Tel: 204-477-7460; *Fax:* 204-477-7465
jewishheritage@jhcwc.org
www.jhcwc.org/archives
Ilana Abrams, General Manager

***Winnipeg:* Manitoba Museum**
190 Rupert Ave., Winnipeg, MB R3B 0N2
Tel: 204-988-0692; *Fax:* 204-942-3679
info@manitobamuseum.ca
www.manitobamuseum.ca
Cindi Steffan, Manager, Information Services
csteffan@manitobamuseum.ca

***Winnipeg:* Mennonite Heritage Centre**
600 Shaftesbury Blvd., Winnipeg, MB R3P 0M4
Tel: 204-888-6781; *Fax:* 204-831-5675
Toll-Free: 866-888-6785
archives.mennonitechurch.ca
Korey Dyck, Director
kdyck@mennonitechurch.ca
Connie Wiebe, Archives Secretary
cwiebe@mennonitechurch.ca
Conrad Stoesz, Archivist
cstoesz@mennonitechurch.ca

***Winnipeg:* Rainbow Resource Centre**
170 Scott St., Winnipeg, MB R3L 0L3
Tel: 204-474-0212; *Fax:* 204-478-1160
Toll-Free: 855-437-8523
info@rainbowresourcecentre.org
www.rainbowresourcecentre.org/library
Social Media: instagram.com/rainbowresourcecentre; twitter.com/RainbowResCtr; www.facebook.com/rrclibrary
Mike Tutthill, Executive Director
executivedirector@rainbowresourcecentre.org
204-474-0212 ext. 208
Craig Gibb, Coordinator, Information & Intake Assessment
204-474-0212 ext. 201

***Winnipeg:* Royal Aviation Museum of Western Canada**
Hangar T-2, 958 Ferry Rd., Winnipeg, MB R3H 0Y8
Tel: 204-786-5503; *Fax:* 204-775-4761
Info@RoyalAviationMuseum.com
www.royalaviationmuseum.com
Shirley Render, Executive Director
Shirley.Render@RoyalAviationMuseum.com
204-786-0733

***Winnipeg:* Sisters of Our Lady of the Missions/ Religieuses de Notre Dame des Missions**
310 Provencher Blvd., Winnipeg, MB R2H 0G7
Tel: 204-786-6054; *Fax:* 204-775-3224
canrndm@mts.net
www.rndmcanada.org

***Winnipeg:* Soeurs Missionnaires Oblates du Sacré-Coeur et de Marie Immaculée/ Missionary Oblate Sisters of the Sacred Heart & of Mary Immaculate**
Missionary Oblate Sisters of Saint Boniface, #111, 420, rue DesMeurons, Winnipeg, MB R2H 2N9
Tél: 204-233-7287; *Téléc:* 204-235-7418
generaladministration@missionaryoblatesisters.ca
www.missionaryoblatesisters.ca

***Winnipeg:* Transcona Historical Museum**
141 Regent Ave. West, Winnipeg, MB R2C 1R1
Tel: 204-222-0423; *Fax:* 204-222-0208
info@transconamuseum.mb.ca
www.transconamuseum.mb.ca/archives.htm
Social Media: www.youtube.com/user/TransconaMuseum; www.facebook.com/transconamuseum
Alanna Horejda, Curator

***Winnipeg:* Ukrainian Catholic Church Archeparchy of Winnipeg**
233 Scotia St., Winnipeg, MB R2V 1V7
Tel: 204-338-7801; *Fax:* 204-339-4006
chancery@archeparchy.ca
www.archeparchy.ca
Gloria Romaniuk, Archivist
Natalia Radawetz, Museum Curator

***Winnipeg:* Ukrainian Cultural & Educational Centre**
184 Alexander Ave. East, Winnipeg, MB R3B 0L6
Tel: 204-942-0218
ucec@mymts.net
www.ukrainianwinnipeg.ca/oseredok

New Brunswick

Regional Systems

***Campbellton:* Chaleur Library Regional Office/ Région de bibliothèques Chaleur**
113A Roseberry St., Campbellton, NB E3N 2G6
Tel: 506-789-6599; *Fax:* 506-789-7318
www.gnb.ca
Sylvie Nadeau, Acting Regional Director
Georgette Laval, Assistant Director
Anouck Vigneau, Public Services Librarian
Francis Hébert, Collections Management Librarian
Chantal Levesque, Regional Office Secretary

***Edmundston:* Haut-Saint-Jean Library Regional Office/ Région de bibliothèques Haut-Saint-Jean**
#102, 15 de l'Église St., Edmundston, NB E3V 1J3
Tel: 506-735-2074; *Fax:* 506-735-2193
www.gnb.ca/publiclibraries
Patrick Provencher, Regional Director
Marc Cool, Acting Assistant Regional Director
Edith Routhier, Public Services Librarian
Amy Sutherland, Acting Collections Management Librarian

***Fredericton:* York Library Regional Office/ Région de bibliothèques York**
#1, 570 Two Nations Crossing, Fredericton, NB E3A 0X9
Tel: 506-453-5380; *Fax:* 506-457-4878
www.gnb.ca
Sarah Kilfoil, Regional Director
Tyler Griffin, Acting Assistant Regional Director
Mark McCumber, Acting Public Services Librarian
Alexandra Ferguson, Collections Management Librarian
Jenna Knoetze, Coordinator, Interlibrary Loan

***Moncton:* Albert-Westmorland-Kent Library Regional Office/ Région de bibliothèques AWK**
#101, 644 Main St., Moncton, NB E1C 1E2
Tel: 506-869-6032; *Fax:* 506-869-6022
www.gnb.ca/publiclibraries
Tina Bourgeois, Regional Director
Nadine Goguen, Assistant Regional Director
Mathieu Lanteigne, Acting Public Services Librarian
Sophie Doiron, Collections Management Librarian

***Saint John:* Fundy Library Regional Office/ Région de bibliothèques de Fundy**
1 Market Sq., Saint John, NB E2L 4Z6
Tel: 506-643-7222; *Fax:* 506-643-7225
www.gnb.ca
Brian Steeves, Regional Director
Alexandra Brooks Robinson, Assistant Regional Director
Nora Kennedy, Public Services Librarian
Daniel Teed, Collections Management Librarian
Josée Thibault, Regional Office Secretary
Lucy Harrigan, Administrative Assistant

Public Libraries

***Atholville:* Bibliothèque publique de Raymond Lagacé/ Raymond Lagacé Public Library**
275, rue Notre-Dame, Atholville, NB E3N 4T1
Tél: 506-789-2914; *Téléc:* 506-789-2056
biblioda@gnb.ca
Média social: twitter.com/Athol_Library; www.facebook.com/251895744940066
Kevin Soussana, Directeur par intérim

***Bas-Caraquet:* Bibliothèque publique Claude-LeBouthillier/ Claude LeBouthillier Public Library**
#8185, 2, rue St-Paul, Bas-Caraquet, NB E1W 6C4
Tél: 506-726-2775; *Téléc:* 506-726-2770
bibliobc@gnb.ca
Mylène May Gionet, Directrice

***Bathurst:* Bibliothèque publique de Bathurst/ Bathurst Public Library**
#1, 150, rue St. George, Bathurst, NB E2A 1B5
Tél: 506-548-0706; *Téléc:* 506-548-0708
bibliocn@gnb.ca
Média social: twitter.com/librarybathurst; www.facebook.com/BiblioBathurst
Judith Lagacé, Directrice

***Beresford:* Bibliothèque publique Mgr-Robichaud/ Mgr. Robichaud Public Library**
#3, 855, rue Principale, Beresford, NB E8K 1T3
Tél: 506-542-2704; *Téléc:* 506-542-2714
bibliomr@gnb.ca
Marie-Claude Gagnon, Directrice par interim

***Bouctouche:* Bibliothèque publique Gérald-Leblanc/ Gérald Leblanc Public Library**
#100, 84, boul Irving, Bouctouche, NB E4S 3L4
Tél: 506-743-7263; *Téléc:* 506-743-7263
bibliopb@gnb.ca
Média social: www.facebook.com/184329614941091
Sylvie LeBlanc, Responsable

***Campbellton:* Campbellton Centennial Library/ Bibliothèque du Centenaire de Campbellton**
#100, 19 Aberdeen St., Campbellton, NB E3N 2J6
Tel: 506-753-5253; *Fax:* 506-753-3803
bibliocc@gnb.ca
Social Media: www.facebook.com/bibliocampbellton
Jocelyn Paquette, Manager
Caroline Jolicoeur, Acting Head, Young Adult & Adult Services
Otilia Cojocariu, Head, Children's Services
Eva Fischer, Head, Reference Services

***Campobello:* Campobello Public Library**
3 Welshpool St., Campobello, NB E5E 1G3
Tel: 506-752-7082; *Fax:* 506-752-7083
CampboPL@gnb.ca
www.campobello.com/library/library.html
Social Media: www.facebook.com/CampobelloLibrary
Stephanie Milbury, Manager

***Cap-Pelé:* Cap-Pelé Public Library**
2638 Acadie Rd., Cap-Pelé, NB E4N 1E3
Tel: 506-577-2090; *Fax:* 506-577-2094
bibliothequepublique.cap-pele@gnb.ca
Social Media: www.facebook.com/cappelepubliclibrary
Michele-Ann Goguen, Library Manager

***Caraquet:* Bibliothèque publique Mgr-Paquet/ Mgr. Paquet Public Library**
10A, du rue Colisée, Caraquet, NB E1W 1A5
Tél: 506-726-2681; *Téléc:* 506-726-2685
bibliock@gnb.ca
Irène Guraliuc, Directrice par interim

***Chipman:* Chipman Public Library**
8 King St., Chipman, NB E4A 2H3
Tel: 506-339-5852; *Fax:* 506-339-9804
chipman.publiclibrary@gnb.ca
Social Media:
www.facebook.com/pages/Chipman-Public-Library/3363931731 48889
Krista Blyth, Manager

***Dalhousie:* Bibliothèque du centenaire de Dalhousie/ Dalhousie Centennial Library**
403, rue Adelaide, Dalhousie, NB E8C 1B6
Tél: 506-684-7370; *Téléc:* 506-684-7374
bibliocd@gnb.ca
Média social: www.facebook.com/bibliodalhousie
Sandra B. Carter, Directrice

***Dieppe:* Bibliothèque publique de Dieppe/ Dieppe Public Library**
333, av Acadie, Dieppe, NB E1A 1G9
Tél: 506-877-7945; *Téléc:* 506-877-7897
bibliopd@gnb.ca
Média social: www.facebook.com/dieppepubliclibrary
Nathalie Brun, Directrice

***Doaktown:* Doaktown Community - School Library**
Doaktown Consolidated High School, 430 Main St., Doaktown, NB E9C 1E8
Tel: 506-365-2018; *Fax:* 506-365-2054
dtcslib@gnb.ca
Social Media:
www.facebook.com/DoaktownCommunitySchoolLibrary
Belva Brown, Library Manager
belva.brown@gnb.ca

***Dorchester:* Dorchester Public Library**
3516 Cape Rd., Dorchester, NB E4K 2X5
Tel: 506-379-3032; *Fax:* 506-379-3033
dorchPL@gnb.ca
Krista Johansen, Manager

***Edmundston:* Mgr. W.J. Conway Public Library/ Bibliothèque publique Mgr-W.-J. Conway**
33 Irène St., Edmundston, NB E3V 1B7
Tel: 506-735-4713; *Fax:* 506-737-6848
biblioed@gnb.ca
www.bibliotheque-edmundston.ca
Social Media: www.facebook.com/243972915711048
Stéphane Dupuy, Library Director
Tanya Eindiguer, Head, Young Adult & Adult Services
Jewel McLatchy, Head, Children's Services
Sarah Dereumetz, Head, Reference Services
Louis Roy, Supervisor, Circulation

***Florenceville:* Andrew & Laura McCain Public Library/ Bibliothèque publique Andrew-et-Laura-McCain**
8 McCain St., Florenceville, NB E7L 3H6
Tel: 506-392-5294; *Fax:* 506-392-8108
florenpl@gnb.ca
Social Media: www.facebook.com/47844016961
Julie Craig, Manager

***Fredericton:* Dre Marguerite Michaud Library/ Bibliothèque Dr Marguerite Michaud**
Centre communautaire Sainte-Anne, 715 Priestman St., Fredericton, NB E3B 5W7
Tél: 506-453-7100; *Téléc:* 506-453-3958
BiblioDMM@gnb.ca
www.franco-fredericton.com/bibliomm
Média social: twitter.com/BiblioMichaud
Françoise Caron, Manager

***Fredericton:* Fredericton Public Library**
12 Carleton St., Fredericton, NB E3B 5P4
Tel: 506-460-2800; *Fax:* 506-460-2801
FtonPub@gnb.ca
Social Media: twitter.com/FredLibrary;
www.facebook.com/FredLibrary
Julia Stewart, Library Director
Stephanie Furrow, Head, Reference Services
Jessica Larocque, Acting Head, Young Adult & Adult Services
Sheila Grondin-Lyons, Supervisor, Circulation

***Fredericton:* Fredericton Public Library - Nashwaaksis**
324 Fulton Ave., Fredericton, NB E3A 5J4
Tel: 506-453-3241; *Fax:* 506-444-4129
nashwaaksis.library@gnb.ca
Social Media: twitter.com/NasisLibrary;
www.facebook.com/NasisLibrary
Candace Hare, Manager

***Fredericton:* New Brunswick Public Library Service (NBPLS)/ Service des bibliothèques publiques du Nouveau-Brunswick**
Provincial Office, #2, 570 Two Nations Crossing, Fredericton, NB E3A 0X9
Tel: 506-453-2354; *Fax:* 506-444-4064
NBPLS-SBPNB@gnb.ca
www.gnb.ca/publiclibraries
Sylvie Nadeau, Executive Director

***Grand Falls:* Grand Falls Public Library/ Bibliothèque publique de Grand-Sault**
Town Hall, #201, 131 Pleasant St., Grand Falls, NB E3Z 1G6
Tel: 506-475-7781; *Fax:* 506-475-7783
gfplib@gnb.ca
Social Media: www.facebook.com/bibliograndsault.grandfallslib
Edith Routhier, Manager

***Grand Manan:* Grand Manan Library**
1144 Rte. 776, Grand Manan, NB E5G 4E8
Tel: 506-662-7099; *Fax:* 506-662-7094
GrandMananLibrary@gnb.ca
Kendra Neves, Manager

***Hartland:* Dr. Walter Chestnut Public Library/ Bibliothèque publique Dr-Walter-Chestnut**
#1, 395 Main St., Hartland, NB E7P 2N3
Tel: 506-375-4876; *Fax:* 506-375-6816
hartlandl@gnb.ca
Social Media: www.facebook.com/165459630180967
Jean Haywood, Manager

***Harvey:* Harvey Community Library**
Harvey High School, 2055 Rte. 3, Harvey, NB E6K 1L1
Tel: 506-366-2206; *Fax:* 506-366-2210
harvey.library@gnb.ca
Social Media:
www.facebook.com/pages/Harvey-Community-Library/43328841 6758301
Julian Christie, Acting Manager

***Hillsborough:* Hillsborough Public Library**
#2, 2849 Main St., Hillsborough, NB E4H 2X7
Tel: 506-734-3722; *Fax:* 506-734-3711
Hillsborough.publiclibrary@gnb.ca
Social Media: www.facebook.com/hillsboroughpubliclibrary
Barbara Alcorn, Manager

***Kedgwick:* Kedgwick Public Library/ Bibliothèque publique de Kedgwick**
116 Notre-Dame St., #P, Kedgwick, NB E8B 1H8
Tel: 506-284-2757; *Fax:* 506-284-4557
bibliopk@gnb.ca
Diane Thompson, Manager

***Lamèque:* Bibliothèque publique de Lamèque/ Lamèque Public Library**
46, rue du Pêcheur nord, Lamèque, NB E8T 1J3
Tél: 506-344-3262; *Téléc:* 506-344-3263
bibliopl@gnb.ca
Lison Gaudet, Directrice

***McAdam:* McAdam Public Library**
Municipal Bldg., 146 Saunders Rd., McAdam, NB E6J 1L2
Tel: 506-784-1403; *Fax:* 506-784-1402
mcadam.library@gnb.ca
Social Media: www.facebook.com/McAdamPublicLibrary
Amy Heans, Manager

***Memramcook:* Memramcook Public Library/ Bibliothèque publique de Memramcook**
#1, 540, rue Centrale, Memramcook, NB E4K 3S6
Tel: 506-758-4029; *Fax:* 506-758-4030
bibliopm@gnb.ca
Social Media:
www.facebook.com/pages/Memramcook-Public-Library/2331999 96690537
Jocelyne LeBlanc, Directrice

***Minto:* Minto Public Library**
Municipal Bldg., #2, 420 Pleasant Dr., Minto, NB E4B 2T3
Tel: 506-327-3220; *Fax:* 506-327-3041
minto.publiclibrary@gnb.ca
Social Media: www.facebook.com/MintoPublicLibrary
Mary Lambropoulos, Manager

***Miramichi:* Chatham Public Library**
24 King St., Miramichi, NB E1N 2N1
Tel: 506-773-6274; *Fax:* 506-773-6963
chathmpl@gnb.ca
Social Media: www.facebook.com/chathampubliclibrary
Jennifer Wilcox, Manager

***Miramichi:* Médiathèque Père-Louis-Lamontagne**
Centre communautaire Carrefour Beausoleil, 300 Beaverbrook Rd., Miramichi, NB E1V 1A1
Tel: 506-627-4084; *Fax:* 506-627-4592
mediathequeP@gnb.ca
www.mpll.nb.ca
Geneviève Thériault-McGraw, Manager

***Miramichi:* Newcastle Public Library**
100 Fountain Head Lane, Miramichi, NB E1V 4A1
Tel: 506-623-2450; *Fax:* 506-623-2335
Npublib@gnb.ca
Social Media: www.facebook.com/NewcastlePublicLibrary
Catherine Reid, Manager

***Moncton:* Moncton Public Library/ Bibliothèque publique de Moncton**
#101, 644 Main St., Moncton, NB E1C 1E2
Tel: 506-869-6000; *Fax:* 506-869-6040
mplib@gnb.ca
www.monctonpubliclibrary.ca
Social Media: twitter.com/MonctonLibrary;
www.facebook.com/monctonpubliclibrary
Chantale Bellemare, Manager
David Collette, Circulation Supervisor
Beatrice Houston, Head, Young Adult & Adult Services
Laura Mason, Head, Reference Services

***Nackawic:* Nackawic Public - School Library/ Bibliothèque publique-scolaire de Nackawic**
30 Landegger Dr., Nackawic, NB E6G 1E9
Tel: 506-572-2136; *Fax:* 506-575-2336
nackawic.library@gnb.ca
Social Media: www.facebook.com/173718052683180
Paulette Tonner, Manager

***New Bandon, Northumberland:* Upper Miramichi Community Library**
#1, 7263 Rte. 8, New Bandon, Northumberland, NB E9C 2A7
Tel: 506-365-2096; *Fax:* 506-365-2052
uppermiramichi.communitylibrary@gnb.ca
Social Media:
www.facebook.com/UpperMiramichiCommunityLibrary
Gail Ross, Manager

***Oromocto:* Oromocto Public Library**
54 Miramichi Rd., Oromocto, NB E2V 1S2
Tel: 506-357-3329; *Fax:* 506-357-5161
oromocto.publiclibrary@gnb.ca
Social Media:
www.facebook.com/OromoctoPublicLibraryBibliotequePubliqueO romocto
Christin Sheridan, Acting Library Manager

***Perth-Andover:* Perth-Andover Public Library/ Bibliothèque publique de Perth-Andover**
642 East Riverside Dr., Perth-Andover, NB E7H 1Z6
Tel: 506-273-2843; *Fax:* 506-273-1913
paplib@gnb.ca
Social Media: www.facebook.com/173921195993003
Tammie Wright, Manager

***Petit-Rocher:* Bibliothèque publique de Petit-Rocher/ Petit-Rocher Public Library**
#110, 702, rue Principale, Petit-Rocher, NB E8J 1V1
Tél: 506-542-2744; *Téléc:* 506-542-2745
bibliopr@gnb.ca
Sonia Godin, Directrice

***Petitcodiac:* Petitcodiac Public Library**
#101, 6 Kay St., Petitcodiac, NB E4Z 4K6
Tel: 506-756-3144; *Fax:* 506-756-3142
petitcodiac.publiclibrary@gnb.ca
Social Media: twitter.com/PetitcodiacLib;
www.facebook.com/PetitcodiacPublicLibrary
Danny Jacobs, Manager

***Plaster Rock:* Plaster Rock Public - School Library/ Bibliothèque publique-scolaire de Plaster Rock**
290A Main St., Plaster Rock, NB E7G 2C6
Tel: 506-356-6018; *Fax:* 506-356-6019
prplib@gnb.ca
Social Media: www.facebook.com/221659757862270
Patricia Corey, Manager

***Port Elgin:* Port Elgin Public Library**
1 Station St., Port Elgin, NB E4M 1C6
Tel: 506-538-2118; *Fax:* 506-538-2126
PortEPL@gnb.ca
Social Media: www.facebook.com/141475192561048
Kathleen Grigg, Manager

Quispamsis: **Kennebecasis Public Library**
1 Landing Ct., Quispamsis, NB E2E 4R2
Tel: 506-849-5314; *Fax:* 506-849-5318
kennebpl@gnb.ca
Social Media: twitter.com/kvlibrary; www.facebook.com/kennebpl
Tiffany Bartlett, Director

Richibucto: **Bibliothèque publique de Richibucto/ Richibucto Public Library**
9376, rue Main, Richibucto, NB E4W 4C9
Tél: 506-523-7851; *Téléc:* 506-523-2019
bibliori@gnb.ca
Média social: www.facebook.com/richibuctopubliclibrary
Sylvie Bourque, Directrice de bibliothèque par intérim

Riverview: **Riverview Public Library**
34 Honour House Ct., Riverview, NB E1B 3Y9
Tel: 506-387-2108; *Fax:* 506-387-7120
rplib@gnb.ca
Social Media: www.facebook.com/riverviewpubliclibrary
Lynn Cormier, Manager

Rogersville: **Rogersville Public Library**
#1, 65 École St., Rogersville, NB E4Y 1V4
Tel: 506-775-2102; *Fax:* 506-775-2087
bibliotheque.publiquedeRogersville@gnb.ca
Annick Goguen, Manager

Sackville: **Sackville Public Library**
66 Main St., Sackville, NB E4L 4A7
Tel: 506-364-4915; *Fax:* 506-364-4915
spublib@gnb.ca
Social Media: www.facebook.com/sackvillepubliclibrary
Allan J. Alward, Manager

Saint John: **Le Cormoran Library**
67 Ragged Point Rd., Saint John, NB E2K 5C3
Tel: 506-658-4610; *Fax:* 506-658-3984
BiblioLC@gnb.ca
Mireille Mercure, Manager

Saint John: **Saint John Free Public Library**
1 Market Sq., Saint John, NB E2L 4Z6
Tel: 506-643-7236; *Fax:* 506-643-7225
sjfpl@gnb.ca
saintjohnlibrary.com
Social Media: twitter.com/saintjohnfpl; www.facebook.com/345086335525976
Joann Hamilton-Barry, Library Director
Keith MacKinnon, Head, Reference Services
Carole MacFarquhar, Head, Young Adult & Adult Services
Heather McKend, Head, Children's Services
Mark Goodfellow, Supervisor, Circulation

Saint John: **Saint John Free Public Library, East Branch**
55 McDonald St., Saint John, NB E2J 0C7
Tel: 506-643-7250; *Fax:* 506-643-7225
EastBranch.PublicLibrary@gnb.ca
saintjohnlibrary.com
Social Media: twitter.com/EastSJLibrary; www.facebook.com/290748454326495
Emily King, Manager

Saint John: **Saint John Free Public Library, West Branch**
Lancaster Mall, 621 Fairville Blvd., Saint John, NB E2M 4X5
Tel: 506-643-7260; *Fax:* 506-643-7225
westbranch.publiclibrary@gnb.ca
saintjohnlibrary.com
Social Media: twitter.com/LibraryWest; www.facebook.com/410284008999650
Robin Sexton-Mayes, Manager

Saint-Antoine: **Bibliothèque publique de Omer-Léger/ Omer-Léger Public Library**
#100, 4556, rue Principale, Saint-Antoine, NB E4V 1R3
Tél: 506-525-4028; *Téléc:* 506-525-4199
bibliosa@gnb.ca
Média social: www.facebook.com/SALibrary
Paulette Léger, Directrice

Saint-François-de-Madawaska: **Mgr. Plourde Public Library/ Bibliothèque publique Mgr-Plourde**
15 Bellevue St., Saint-François-de-Madawaska, NB E7A 1A4
Tel: 506-992-6052; *Fax:* 506-992-6047
stfplib@gnb.ca
Tania St-Onge, Manager

Saint-Léonard: **Dr. Lorne J. Violette Public Library/ Bibliothèque publique Dr.-Lorne-J.-Violette**
180 St-Jean St., Saint-Léonard, NB E7E 2B9
Tel: 506-423-3025; *Fax:* 506-423-3026
stlplib@gnb.ca

Sophie-Michele Cyr, Manager

Saint-Quentin: **La Moisson Public Library/ Bibliothèque publique La Moisson de Saint-Quentin**
Municipal Bldg., 206 Canada St., Saint-Quentin, NB E8A 1H1
Tel: 506-235-1955; *Fax:* 506-235-1957
biblioIm@gnb.ca
Hélène DuRepos Thériault, Manager

Salisbury: **Salisbury Public Library**
3215 Main St., Salisbury, NB E4J 2K7
Tel: 506-372-3240; *Fax:* 506-372-3261
salisbury.publiclibrary@gnb.ca
Social Media: www.facebook.com/SalisburyPublicLibrary
Cathy MacDonald, Manager

Shediac: **Shediac Public Library/ Bibliothèque publique de Shediac**
#100, 290 Main St., Shediac, NB E4P 2E3
Tel: 506-532-7014; *Fax:* 506-532-8400
Other Numbers: Alternate Phone: 506-532-7000
bibliosh@gnb.ca
biblioshediaclibrary.ca
Social Media: www.facebook.com/pages/241960232493805
Gabrielle LeBlanc, Directrice

Shippagan: **Bibliothèque publique Laval Goupil/ Laval Goupil Public Library**
128, rue Mgr-Chiasson, Shippagan, NB E8S 1X7
Tél: 506-336-3920; *Téléc:* 506-336-3921
bibliops@gnb.ca
Pauline Godin, Directrice

St Andrews: **Ross Memorial Library**
110 King St., St Andrews, NB E5B 1Y6
Tel: 506-529-5125; *Fax:* 506-529-5129
standrpl@gnb.ca
www.rossmemlibrary.org
Social Media: www.facebook.com/pages/Ross-Memorial-Library/308783412497146
Lesley Wells, Manager

St Stephen: **St Croix Public Library**
11 King St., St Stephen, NB E3L 2C1
Tel: 506-466-7529; *Fax:* 506-466-7574
ststeppl@gnb.ca
Social Media: www.facebook.com/pages/St-Croix-Public-Library/337115176428142
Elva Hatt, Library Manager

Stanley: **Stanley Community Library**
#2, 28 Bridge St., Stanley, NB E6B 1B2
Tel: 506-367-2492; *Fax:* 506-367-2764
stanley.library@gnb.ca
Social Media: www.facebook.com/StanleyCommunityLibrary
Tim Sarty, Acting Manager

Sussex: **Sussex Regional Library**
46 Magnolia Ave., Sussex, NB E4E 2H2
Tel: 506-432-4585; *Fax:* 506-432-4583
sussexpl@gnb.ca
Social Media: twitter.com/Sussex_Library; www.facebook.com/pages/Sussex-Regional-Library/130299950376215
Vanessa Black, Manager

Tracadie-Sheila: **Bibliothèque publique de Tracadie/ Tracadie Public Library**
3620, rue Principale, Tracadie-Sheila, NB E1X 1G5
Tél: 506-394-4005; *Téléc:* 506-394-4009
bibliots@gnb.ca
Amel Boudina, Directrice par interim

Woodstock: **L.P. Fisher Public Library/ Bibliothèque publique L.-P.-Fisher**
679 Main St., Woodstock, NB E7M 2E1
Tel: 506-325-4777; *Fax:* 506-325-4811
lpfisher.library@gnb.ca
Social Media: www.facebook.com/222019507823690
Jennifer Carson, Manager

Archives

Bathurst: **Herman J. Good, VC, Royal Canadian Legion**
575 St Peters Ave., Bathurst, NB E2A 2Y5
Tel: 506-546-3135; *Fax:* 506-546-1011
hermanjgoodvc.tripod.com/museum.html

Bouctouche: **Musée de Kent**
150, ch du Couvent, Bouctouche, NB E4S 3C1
Tél: 506-743-5005
admin@museedekent.ca
www.museedekent.ca

Dalhousie: **Restigouche Regional Museum**
115 George St., Dalhousie, NB E8C 1R6
Tel: 506-684-7490; *Fax:* 506-684-7490
gurrm@nbnet.nb.ca
Social Media: www.facebook.com/restigoucheregionalmuseum

Edmundston: **Centre de documentation et d'études Madawaskayennes**
165, boul Hébert, Edmundston, NB E3V 2S8
Tél: 506-737-5058; *Téléc:* 506-737-5373
www.umce.ca/biblio/cdem/
Pierrette Fortin, Responsable
Claire Charest, Assistance aux chercheures
claire.d.charest@umoncton.ca

Fredericton: **Provincial Archives of New Brunswick/ Archives provinciales du Nouveau-Brunswick**
University of New Brunswick, Bonar Law-Bennett Bldg., 23 Dineen Dr., Fredericton, NB E3B 5H1
Tel: 506-453-2122; *Fax:* 506-457-4992
provincial.archives@gnb.ca
www.gnb.ca/Archives
Tom McCaffrey, Supervisor
Tom.mccaffrey@gnb.ca
506-453-2122
Roger Drummond, Archivist
roger.drummond@gnb.ca
506-453-2122
Lynn Hale Sears, Archivist
lynn.halesears@gnb.ca
506-453-7476
William Vinh-Doyle, Archivist
william.vinh-doyle@gnb.ca
506-453-2122

Grand Falls: **Grand Falls Museum/ Musée de Grand-Sault**
68 Madawaska Rd., Grand Falls, NB E3Y 1C6
Tel: 506-473-5265

Grand Manan: **Grand Manan Museum**
1141 Rte. 776, Grand Manan, NB E5G 4E9
Tel: 506-662-3424; *Fax:* 506-662-3009
gmadmin@grandmananmuseum.ca
www.grandmananmuseum.ca
Social Media: twitter.com/GMMuseum; www.facebook.com/GrandMananMuseum
M.J. Edwards, Director/Curator
mjedwards454@gmail.com
Ava Sturgeon, Archivist

Miramichi: **St Michael's Museum & Genealogical Centre**
10 Howard St., Miramichi, NB E1N 3A7
Tel: 506-778-5152; *Fax:* 506-778-5156
mmuseum@nbnet.nb.ca
www.saintmichaelsmuseum.com

Saint John: **New Brunswick Museum**
277 Douglas Ave., Saint John, NB E2K 1E5
Tel: 506-643-2322; *Fax:* 506-643-2360
Toll-Free: 888-268-9595
archives@nbm-mnb.ca
www.nbm-mnb.ca
Social Media: twitter.com/nbmmnb; www.facebook.com/nbmmnb
Felicity Osepchook, Head
506-643-2324
Christine Little, Archives & Research Library
506-643-2397

Saint John: **Roman Catholic Diocese of Saint John**
1 Bayard Dr., Saint John, NB E2L 3L5
Tel: 506-653-6807; *Fax:* 506-653-6812
archives@dioceseofsaintjohn.org
www.dioceseofsaintjohn.org
Mary McDevitt, Archivist

Saint John: **Saint John Jewish Historical Museum**
91 Leinster St., Saint John, NB E2L 1J2
Tel: 506-633-1833; *Fax:* 506-642-9926
sjjhm@nbnet.nb.ca
jewishmuseumsj.com

Shippagan: **Société historique Nicolas-Denys**
Université de Moncton, Campus de Shippagan, #PIL061, 218, boul J.-D.-Gauthier, Shippagan, NB E8S 1P6
Tél: 506-336-3461; *Téléc:* 506-336-3603
shnd@umoncton.ca
www.umoncton.ca/umcs-bibliotheque/node/6
Philippe Basque, Président
Nathalie Lanteigne, Responsable
Odette Haché, Vice-présidente
Lison Gaudet, Secrétaire

St Andrews: **Charlotte County Historical Society, Inc.**
123 Frederick St., St Andrews, NB E5B 1Z1
Tel: 506-529-4248
contact@ccarchives.ca
www.ccarchives.ca
Social Media: www.twitter.com/ccarchives1; www.facebook.com/pages/Charlotte-/494468727279390

Woodstock: **Carleton County Historical Society**
128 Connell St., Woodstock, NB E7M 1L5
Tel: 506-328-9706; *Fax:* 506-328-2942
cchs@nb.aibn.com
www.cchs-nb.ca

Newfoundland & Labrador

Regional Systems

Corner Brook: **Newfoundland & Labrador Public Libraries - West Newfoundland-Labrador Division**
4 West St., Corner Brook, NL A2H OC1
Tel: 709-634-7333; *Fax:* 709-634-7313
www.nlpl.ca
Sandy Chilcote, Manager
schilcote@nlpl.ca

Gander: **Newfoundland & Labrador Public Libraries - Central Division**
6 Bell Pl., Gander, NL A1V 1X2
Tel: 709-651-5351; *Fax:* 709-256-2194
Tina Murphy, Central Division Manager
tmurphy@nlpl.ca
709-651-5351

St. John's: **Provincial Information & Library Resources Board - Eastern Division**
Arts & Culture Centre, St. John's, NL A1B 3A3
Tel: 709-737-3508; *Fax:* 709-737-3571
www.nlpl.ca
John White, Division Manager
johnwhite@nlpl.ca
709-737-3508

Public Libraries

Arnold's Cove: **Arnold's Cove Public Library**
5 Highliner Dr., Arnold's Cove, NL A0B 1A0
Tel: 709-463-8707
www.nlpl.ca
Social Media: www.facebook.com/202329123122799
Beverly Best, Librarian

Baie Verte: **Baie Verte Public Library**
Hwy. 410, Baie Verte, NL A0K 1B0
Tel: 709-532-8361
www.nlpl.ca
Eileen Cooper, Librarian

Bay Roberts: **Bay Roberts Public Library**
76 Cross Rd., Bay Roberts, NL A0A 1G0
Tel: 709-786-9629
www.nlpl.ca
Social Media: www.facebook.com/bayrobertspubliclibrary
Marilyn Clarke, Librarian

Bay St George: **Bay St George South Public Library**
PO Box 70, Bay St George, NL A0N 1Y0
Tel: 709-645-2186
www.nlpl.ca
Leanda Shears, Librarian

Bell Island: **Bell Island Public Library**
Provincial Government Bldg., 20 Bennett St., Bell Island, NL A0A 4H0
Tel: 709-488-2413
www.nlpl.ca
Lois Clarke, Librarian

Bishop's Falls: **Bishop's Falls Public Library**
445 Main St., Bishop's Falls, NL A0H 1C0
Tel: 709-258-6244
www.nlpl.ca
Elizabeth John, Librarian

Bonavista: **Bonavista Memorial Public Library**
PO Box 400, Bonavista, NL A0C 1B0
Tel: 709-468-2185
www.nlpl.ca
Brenda Wilton, Librarian

Botwood: **Botwood Kinsmen Public Library**
240 Water St., Botwood, NL A0H 1E0
Tel: 709-257-2091
www.nlpl.ca
Social Media: www.facebook.com/277034772326408
Phyllis Coates, Librarian

Brigus: **Brigus Public Library**
South St., Brigus, NL A0A 1K0
Tel: 709-528-3156
www.nlpl.ca
Social Media: www.facebook.com/BrigusCAP
Raelene Wall, Librarian

Buchans: **Buchans Public Library**
Lakeside Academy, Buchans Hwy., PO Box 99, Buchans, NL A0H 1G0
Tel: 709-672-3859
www.nlpl.ca
Dawn Pennell, Librarian

Burgeo: **Burgeo Public Library**
1 School Rd., Burgeo, NL A0M 2H0
Tel: 709-886-2730
www.nlpl.ca
Social Media: www.facebook.com/pages/Burgeo-Public-Library/126797334057661
Freda MacDonald, Librarian

Burin: **Burin Public Library**
Pearce Junior High School, 48 Main Rd., Burin, NL A0E 1G0
Tel: 709-891-1924
www.nlpl.ca
Social Media: www.facebook.com/164399110273548
Patricia Peddle, Librarian

Cape St George: **Cape St George Public Library**
879 Oceanview Dr., Cape St George, NL A0N 1T1
Tel: 709-644-2852
www.nlpl.ca
Elizabeth Cornect, Librarian

Carbonear: **Carbonear Public Library**
256 Water St., Carbonear, NL A1Y 1C4
Tel: 709-596-3382
www.nlpl.ca
Social Media: www.facebook.com/pages/Carbonear-Public-Library/180339618708886
Tracey Vaughan-Evans, Librarian

Carmanville: **Carmanville Public Library**
Phoenix Academy, 95-97 Main St., Carmanville, NL A0G 1N0
Tel: 709-534-2370
www.nlpl.ca
Daphne Brown, Librarian

Cartwright: **Cartwright Public Library**
Henry Gordon Academy, Cartwright, NL A0K 1V0
Tel: 709-938-7219
www.nlpl.ca
Hazel Dyson, Librarian

Catalina: **Trinity Bay North Public Library**
PO Box 69, Catalina, NL A0C 1J0
Tel: 709-469-3045
www.nlpl.ca
Kimberley Johnson, Librarian

Centreville: **Centreville Public Library**
c/o Centreville Academy, 2 Memory Lane, PO Box 100, Centreville, NL A0G 4P0
Tel: 709-678-2700
www.nlpl.ca
Veronica Rogers, Librarian

Change Islands: **Change Islands Public Library**
c/o A.R. Scammell Academy, Main St. North, Main St. North, Change Islands, NL A0G 1R0
Tel: 709-621-5566
www.nlpl.ca
Wendy LeDrew, Librarian

Churchill Falls: **Churchill Falls Public Library**
E. Donald Gordon Town Centre, Ressigieu Dr., Churchill Falls, NL A0R 1A0
Tel: 709-925-3281
www.nlpl.ca
Social Media: www.facebook.com/169595486419342
Christine Young, Librarian

Clarenville: **Clarenville Public Library**
98 Manitoba Dr., Clarenville, NL A5A 1K7
Tel: 709-466-7634
www.nlpl.ca
Social Media: www.facebook.com/ClarenvillePublicLibrary
Tanya Cull, Librarian

Conception Bay South: **Conception Bay South Public Library**
110 Conception Bay Hwy., Conception Bay South, NL A1W 3A5
Tel: 709-834-4241
www.nlpl.ca
Social Media: www.facebook.com/CBSPublicLibrary
Rebecca Stone, Librarian

Cormack: **Cormack Public Library**
280A Veterans Dr., Cormack, NL A8A 2R4
Tel: 709-635-7022
www.nlpl.ca
Social Media: www.facebook.com/205158306213208
Chantille Coles, Librarian

Corner Brook: **Corner Brook Public Library**
4 West St., Corner Brook, NL A2H 0C1
Tel: 709-634-0013
www.cornerbrooklibrary.org
Social Media: www.facebook.com/CornerBrookPublicLibrary
Trivina Saunders, Librarian

Cow Head: **Cow Head Public Library**
119 Main St., Cow Head, NL A0K 2A0
Tel: 709-243-2467
www.nlpl.ca
Nora Shears, Librarian

Daniels Harbour: **Daniels Harbour Public Library**
15 Church Lane, Daniels Harbour, NL A0K 2C0
Tel: 709-898-2283
www.nlpl.ca
Social Media: www.facebook.com/110178682390214
Sharon Humber, Librarian

Deer Lake: **Deer Lake Public Library**
4 Poplar Rd., Deer Lake, NL A8A 1Z4
Tel: 709-635-3671
www.nlpl.ca
Social Media: www.facebook.com/130449280349655
Worneta Cramm, Librarian

Doyles: **Codroy Valley Public Library**
Belanger Memorial School, Doyles, NL A0N 1J0
Tel: 709-955-3158
www.nlpl.ca
Deanna Martin, Librarian

Fogo: **Fogo Island Public Library**
Fogo Island Central Academy, Main St., Fogo, NL A0G 2B0
Tel: 709-266-2210
www.nlpl.ca
Sarah Engram, Librarian

Fortune: **Fortune Public Library**
Municipal Centre, Temple St., PO Box 400, Fortune, NL A0E 1P0
Tel: 709-832-0232
www.nlpl.ca
Fay Herridge, Librarian

Fox Harbour: **Fox Harbour Public Library**
PO Box 139, Fox Harbour, NL A0B 1V0
Tel: 709-227-2135
www.nlpl.ca
Catherine Murray, Librarian

Gambo: **Gambo Public Library**
6 Centennial Rd., Gambo, NL A0G 1T0
Tel: 709-674-5052
www.nlpl.ca
Sarah Holloway, Librarian

Gander: **Gander Public Library**
6 Bell Pl., Gander, NL A1V 1X2
Tel: 709-651-5354
www.nlpl.ca
Social Media: www.facebook.com/pages/Gander-Public-Library/169210156452499
Michelle Stuckless, Librarian

Garnish: **Garnish (Greta Hollett) Memorial Library**
PO Box 40, Garnish, NL A0E 1T0
Tel: 709-826-2371
www.nlpl.ca
Linda Nolan, Librarian

Gaultois: **Gaultois Public Library**
Gaultlois Town Council Bldg., Valley Rd., Gaultois, NL A0H 1N0
Tel: 709-841-3311
www.nlpl.ca

Glenwood: **Glenwood Public Library**
26 Main St., Glenwood, NL A0G 2K0
Tel: 709-679-5700
www.nlpl.ca
Kelly Gillingham, Librarian

Glovertown: **Glovertown Public Library**
Glovertown Academy, Penney's Brook Rd., Glovertown, NL A0G 2L0
Tel: 709-533-6688
www.nlpl.ca
Rose Sweetapple, Librarian

Grand Bank: **Grand Bank Public Library**
PO Box 1000, Grand Bank, NL A0E 1W0
Tel: 709-832-0310
www.nlpl.ca
Jane Matthews, Librarian

Grand Falls-Windsor: **Grand Falls-Windsor Public Library**
Gordon Pinsent Centre for the Arts, 1 Cromer Ave., Grand Falls-Windsor, NL A2A 1W9
Tel: 709-489-2303
www.nlpl.ca
Madonna Crant, Librarian

Greenspond: **Greenspond Memorial Library**
Main St., Greenspond, NL A0G 2N0
Tel: 709-269-3434
www.nlpl.ca
Roxanne Hounsell, Librarian

Happy Valley-Goose Bay: **Happy Valley-Goose Bay Public Library**
Elizabeth Goudie Bldg., 141 Hamilton River Rd., Happy Valley-Goose Bay, NL A0P 1E0
Tel: 709-896-8045
www.nlpl.ca
Hyra Skoglund, Librarian

Harbour Breton: **Harbour Breton Public Library**
King Academy High School, 2nd Fl., Harbour Breton, NL A0H 1P0
Tel: 709-885-2165
www.nlpl.ca
Kerri Hunt, Librarian

Harbour Grace: **Harbour Grace Public Library**
Harvey St., Harbour Grace, NL A0A 2M0
Tel: 709-596-3894
www.nlpl.ca
Doreen Quinn, Librarian

Hare Bay: **Hare Bay Public Library**
Jane Collins Academy, 22 Anstey's Rd., Hare Bay, NL A0G 2P0
Tel: 709-537-2391
www.nlpl.ca
Jane Rogers-Willis, Librarian

Harry's Harbour: **Harry's Harbour Public Library**
Main Rd., Harry's Harbour, NL A0J 1E0
Tel: 709-624-5464
www.nlpl.ca
Beverly Batstone, Librarian

Hermitage: **Hermitage Public Library**
John Watkins Academy, PO Box 159, Hermitage, NL A0H 1S0
Tel: 709-883-2421
www.nlpl.ca
Bernice Willmott, Librarian

Holyrood: **Holyrood Public Library**
PO Box 263, Holyrood, NL A0A 2R0
Tel: 709-229-7852
www.nlpl.ca
Social Media: www.facebook.com/HolyroodPublicLibrary
Marianne King, Librarian

Kings Point: **King's Point Public Library**
PO Box 100, Kings Point, NL A0J 1J0
Tel: 709-268-2282
www.nlpl.ca
Patsy Bowers, Librarian

L'Anse au Loup: **L'Anse Au Loop Public Library**
Lawrence D. O'Brien Town Center, 11 Branch Rd., L'Anse au Loup, NL A0K 3L0
Tel: 709-927-5542
www.nlpl.ca
Pauline O'Dell, Librarian

La Scie: **La Scie Public Library**
Town Hall, Church Rd., La Scie, NL A0K 3M0
Tel: 709-675-2004
www.nlpl.ca
Karen Drover, Librarian

Labrador City: **Labrador City Public Library**
306 Hudson Dr., Labrador City, NL A2V 1L5
Tel: 709-944-2190
www.nlpl.ca
Trudy Andrews, Librarian

Lark Harbour: **Lark Harbour Public Library**
St. James All Grade School, Main St., Lark Harbour, NL A0L 1H0
Tel: 709-681-2147
www.nlpl.ca
Lesley Sheppard, Librarian

Lewisporte: **Lewisporte Public Library**
Town Hall, 152 Main St., Lewisporte, NL A0G 3A0
Tel: 709-535-2519
www.nlpl.ca
Bobbi Benson, Librarian

Lourdes: **Lourdes Public Library**
Lourdes Elementary School, 82 Main St., Lourdes, NL A0N 1R0
Tel: 709-642-5388
www.nlpl.ca
Alicia Drake, Librarian

Lumsden: **Lumsden Public Library**
Lumsden School Complex, PO Box 119, Lumsden, NL A0G 3E0
Tel: 709-530-2617
www.nlpl.ca
Kay Stagg, Librarian

Marystown: **Marystown Public Library**
Sacred Heart Elementary School, Marystown, NL A0E 2M0
Tel: 709-279-1507
www.nlpl.ca
Patricia Mayo, Librarian

Mount Pearl: **Mount Pearl (Ross King) Memorial Public Library**
65 Olympic Dr., Mount Pearl, NL A1N 5H6
Tel: 709-368-3603
www.nlpl.ca
Yvonne Gillard, Librarian

Musgrave Harbour: **John B. Wheeler Public Library**
PO Box 130, Musgrave Harbour, NL A0G 3J0
Tel: 709-655-2730
www.nlpl.ca
Eunice Abbott, Librarian

Norris Arm: **Norris Arm Public Library**
65 Norris Ave., PO Box 100, Norris Arm, NL A0G 3M0
Tel: 709-653-2531
www.nlpl.ca
Leona Rowsell, Librarian

Norris Point: **Norris Point Public Library**
Julia Ann Walsh Centre, Lower Level, #2, 6 Hospital Rd., Norris Point, NL A0K 3V0
Tel: 709-458-3368
www.nlpl.ca
Judy Samms, Librarian

North West River: **North West River Library & CAP Site**
PO Box 410, North West River, NL A0P 1M0
Tel: 709-497-8705; *Fax:* 709-497-8705
nwrvollibrary@hotmail.com
northwestriverlibrary.weebly.com
Wendy Mitchell, Librarian

Old Perlican: **Old Perlican Public Library**
PO Box 265, Old Perlican, NL A0A 3G0
Tel: 709-587-2028
www.nlpl.ca
Social Media: www.facebook.com/148308438552459
Cathy Hatch, Librarian

Pasadena: **Pasadena Public Library**
Town Council Building, 16 - 10th Ave., Pasadena, NL A0L 1K0
Tel: 709-686-2792
www.nlpl.ca
Social Media: www.facebook.com/pages/Pasadena-Public-Library/150799238311310
Angela Menchion, Librarian

Placentia: **Placentia Public Library**
14 Atlantic Ave., Placentia, NL A0B 2Y0
Tel: 709-227-3621
www.nlpl.ca
Melinda Bowering, Librarian

Point Leamington: **Point Leamington Public Library**
Point Leamington Academy, Point Leamington, NL A0H 1Z0
Tel: 709-484-3541
www.nlpl.ca
Beverley Warford, Librarian

Port au Port: **Port au Port Public Library**
St. Thomas Aquinas School, Main St., Port au Port, NL A0N 1T0
Tel: 709-648-2472
www.nlpl.ca
Janice Clarke, Librarian

Port Saunders: **Port Saunders (Ingornachoix) Public Library**
Main St., Port Saunders, NL A0K 4H0
Tel: 709-861-3690
www.nlpl.ca
Evelyn Biggin, Librarian

Port-aux-Basques: **Port aux Basques Public Library**
8 Grand Bay Rd., Port-aux-Basques, NL A0M 1C0
Tel: 709-695-3471
www.nlpl.ca
Tammy Musseau, Librarian

Pouch Cove: **Pouch Cove Public Library**
PO Box 40, Pouch Cove, NL A0A 3L0
Tel: 709-335-2652
www.nlpl.ca
Social Media: www.facebook.com/pages/Pouch-Cove-Public-Library/125102087554464
Laura Bragg, Librarian

Ramea: **Ramea Public Library**
c/o St. Boniface All Grade School, 10 School Rd., Ramea, NL A0N 2J0
Tel: 709-625-2344
www.nlpl.ca
Frances Lushman, Librarian

Robert's Arm: **Robert's Arm Public Library**
Town Hall, PO Box 119, Robert's Arm, NL A0J 1R0
Tel: 709-652-3100
Helen Suley, Librarian

Rocky Harbour: **Rocky Harbour Public Library**
Gros Morne Academy, 5 Parson's Lane, Rocky Harbour, NL A0K 4N0
Tel: 709-458-2900
www.nlpl.ca
Judy Samms, Librarian

Seal Cove: **Seal Cove Public Library**
Seal Cove Town Council, Council Rd., Seal Cove, NL A0K 5E0
Tel: 709-531-2505
www.nlpl.ca
Karen Pinksen, Librarian

***Sop's Arm:* Sop's Arm Public Library**
Main River Academy, Main St., Sop's Arm, NL A0K 5K0
Tel: 709-482-2225
www.nlpl.ca
Diane White, Librarian

***Southern Harbour:* Southern Harbour Public Library**
Community Centre, Municipal Dr., 1 Municipal Dr., Southern Harbour, NL A0B 3H0
Tel: 709-463-8814
www.nlpl.ca
Social Media: www.facebook.com/187626111269277
Bride Whiffen, Librarian

***Springdale:* Springdale Public Library**
Indian River High School, PO Box 1714, Springdale, NL A0J 1T0
Tel: 709-673-4169
www.nlpl.ca
Judy Hamilton, Librarian

***St Alban's:* St Alban's Public Library**
Town Hall Building, 14 Church Rd., St Alban's, NL A0H 2E0
Tel: 709-538-3034
www.nlpl.ca
Kerri-Ann King, Librarian

***St Anthony:* St Anthony Public Library**
St Anthony Town Council Bldg., West St., St Anthony, NL A0K 4S0
Tel: 709-454-3025
www.nlpl.ca
Jocelyn Elliott, Librarian

***St Bride's:* St Brides Public Library**
Council Bldg. Main Rd, St Bride's, NL A0B 2Z0
Tel: 709-337-2360
www.nlpl.ca
Jacqueline Nash, Librarian

***St George's:* St George's Public Library**
Town Office, 93 Main St., St George's, NL A0N 1Z0
Tel: 709-647-3808
www.nlpl.ca
Heather Parsons, Librarian

***St Lawrence:* St Lawrence Public Library**
St. Lawrence Academy, PO Box 366, St Lawrence, NL A0E 2V0
Tel: 709-873-2650
www.nlpl.ca
Social Media: facebook.com/pages/St-Lawrence-Public-Library/149095271806633
Vicki Lockyer, Librarian

***St Lunaire-Griquet:* St Lunaire-Griquet Public Library**
48 St. George Ave., St Lunaire-Griquet, NL A2N 1K9
Tel: 709-643-0900
www.nlpl.ca

***St. John's:* St John's Public Libraries**
Arts & Culture Centre, 125 Allendale Rd., St. John's, NL A1B 3A3
Tel: 709-737-2133; *Fax:* 709-737-2660
reference@nlpl.ca
www.nlpl.ca
Social Media: www.facebook.com/ACHunterPublicLibrary
Vicki Murphy, Manager, Provincial Resource Division
vmurphy@nlpl.ca
709-737-3418

***Stephenville:* Newfoundland & Labrador Public Libraries**
48 St Georges Ave., Stephenville, NL A2N 1K9
Tel: 709-643-0900; *Fax:* 709-643-0925
www.nlpl.ca
Andrew Hunt, Executive Director
ahunt@nlpl.ca
Lynn Cuff, Director, Regional Services
lcuff@nlpl.ca
Newman George, Director, Information Management
ngeorge@nlpl.ca

***Stephenville:* Stephenville Public Library**
45 Carolina Ave., Stephenville, NL A2N 3P8
Tel: 709-643-4262
www.nlpl.ca
Monica White, Librarian

***Stephenville Crossing:* Stephenville Crossing Public Library**
Town Council Office, 73 West St., Stephenville Crossing, NL A0N 2C0
Tel: 709-646-2173
www.nlpl.ca
Wanda Downey, Librarian

***Summerford:* Summerford Public Library**
Summerford Community Bldg., Main St., Summerford, NL A0G 4E0
Tel: 709-629-3244
www.nlpl.ca
Mavis Boyd, Librarian

***Torbay:* Torbay Public Library**
1339C Torbay Rd., Torbay, NL A1K 1B2
Tel: 709-437-6571
www.nlpl.ca
Marcia Deibel, Librarian

***Trepassey:* Trepassey Public Library**
PO Box 183, Trepassey, NL A0A 4B0
Tel: 709-438-2224
www.nlpl.ca
Patricia McCormack, Librarian

***Twillingate:* Twillingate Public Library**
J.M. Olds Collegiate, 97 Main St., Twillingate, NL A0G 4M0
Tel: 709-884-2353
www.nlpl.ca
Barbara Hamlyn, Librarian

***Victoria:* Victoria Public Library**
PO Box 190, Victoria, NL A0A 4G0
Tel: 709-596-3682
www.nlpl.ca
Shona Colbourne, Librarian

***Wabush:* Wabush Public Library**
Wabush Town Hall, Wabush, NL A0R 1B0
Tel: 709-282-3479
www.nlpl.ca
Kelly Roberts, Librarian

***Wesleyville:* New-Wes-Valley Public Library**
Lester Pearson High, Main St., Wesleyville, NL A0G 4R0
Tel: 709-536-5777
www.nlpl.ca
Beverley Hounsell, Librarian

***Whitbourne:* Whitbourne Public Library**
PO Box 400, Whitbourne, NL A0B 3K0
Tel: 709-759-2461
www.nlpl.ca
Social Media: www.facebook.com/pages/Whitbourne-Public-Library/144844512243474
Gloria Somerton, Librarian

***Winterton:* Winterton Public Library**
PO Box 119, Winterton, NL A0B 3M0
Tel: 709-583-2119
www.nlpl.ca
Glennys Coates, Librarian

***Woody Point:* Woody Point Public Library (E.L. Roberts Memorial Library)**
Water St., Woody Point, NL A0K 1P0
Tel: 709-453-2556
www.nlpl.ca
Michelle Harris, Librarian

Archives

***Bonavista:* Bonavista Historical Society**
PO Box 2957, Bonavista, NL A0C 1B0
Tel: 709-468-7747; *Fax:* 709-468-2495
bonavistaarchives@nf.aibn.com
www.townofbonavista.com

***Botwood:* Botwood Heritage Society Archive**
12 Airbase Place, Botwood, NL A0H 1E0
Tel: 709-257-4612
botwoodheritage@hotmail.com
Social Media: www.facebook.com/pages/Botwood-Heritage-Society/21744933206

***Happy Valley-Goose Bay:* Them Days Incorporated**
3 Courte Manche St., Happy Valley-Goose Bay, NL A0P 1E0
Tel: 709-896-8531; *Fax:* 709-896-4970
www.themdays.com
Shirley Mullins, Adminisrator
Aimee Chaulk, Editor & Archival Contact
editor@themdays.com

***Harbour Grace:* Conception Bay Museum**
PO Box 298, Harbour Grace, NL A0A 2M0
Tel: 709-596-5465; *Fax:* 709-596-5465
Other Numbers: Off season: 709-595-2261
cbm1870@gmail.com
Social Media: www.facebook.com/187284814810868

***Musgrave Harbour:* Fisherman's Museum**
4 Marine Dr., Musgrave Harbour, NL A0G 3J0
Tel: 709-655-2589; *Fax:* 709-655-2064
bantinghti@nf.aibn.com
www.musgraveharbour.com/museum.html
Mitzi Abbott, Town Clerk

***St. John's:* City of St John's Archives**
495 Water St., 3rd Fl., St. John's, NL A1C 5M2
Tel: 709-576-8167; *Fax:* 709-576-8254
archives@stjohns.ca
ngb.chebucto.org/Research/city.shtml
Social Media: twitter.com/CityofStJohns; www.facebook.com/cityofstjohns
Helen Miller, Archivist

***St. John's:* Congregation of Sisters of Mercy of Newfoundland**
Littledale Complex, Waterford Bridge Rd., St. John's, NL A1C 5P5
Tel: 709-726-7320; *Fax:* 709-726-4414
mercygeneralate@sistersofmercynf.org
www.sistersofmercynf.org
Elizabeth Davis, Congregational Leader

***St. John's:* Newfoundland Historical Society**
Churchill Square, St. John's, NL A1B 4J9
Tel: 709-722-3191; *Fax:* 709-722-9035
nhs@nf.aibn.com
www.nlhistory.ca
Social Media: www.twitter.com/nfhistsoc; www.facebook.com/nfhistsoc
Alan Byrne, President
Larry Dohey, Vice-President
Uli Brown, Office Manager

***St. John's:* Presentation Congregation Archives**
Cathedral Sq., Presentation Convent, St. John's, NL A1C 5L4
Tel: 709-753-7291; *Fax:* 709-753-1578
ngb.chebucto.org/Research/cong.shtml
Mary Perpetua Kennedy, Archivist

***St. John's:* Provincial Archives of Newfoundland & Labrador**
9 Bonaventure Ave., PO Box 1800, Stn. C, St. John's, NL A1C 5P9
Tel: 709-757-8030; *Fax:* 709-757-8031
archives@therooms.ca
www.therooms.ca/archives
Greg Walsh, Director/Provincial Archivist

***St. John's:* Queen's College**
Archives & Special Collections, Queen Elizabeth II Library, Memorial University of Newfoundland, St. John's, NL A1B 3Y1
Tel: 709-864-4349; *Fax:* 709-864-2153
Toll-Free: 877-753-0116
archives@mun.ca
queenscollegenl.ca
Colleen Quigley, Acting Head, Archives & Special Collections
csquigley@mun.ca
709-864-3238

***St. John's:* Roman Catholic Archdiocese of St John's**
200 Military Rd., St. John's, NL A1C 5N5
Tel: 709-726-3660; *Fax:* 709-729-8021
rcsj.org/archives-research
Rene Estrada, Archivist
restrada@rcsj.org
709-726-3660 ext. 223

***St. John's:* Sport Archives of Newfoundland & Labrador**
The Rooms Provincial Archives Division, 9 Bonaventure Ave., PO Box 1800, Stn. C, St. John's, NL A1C 5P9
Tel: 709-757-8088; *Fax:* 709-757-8031
archives@therooms.ca
www.therooms.ca/collections-research/our-collections

***Trinity TB:* Trinity Historical Society Archives**
Lester-Garland House, 3rd Fl., Trinity TB, NL A0C 2S0
Tel: 709-464-3599; *Fax:* 709-464-3599
info@trinityhistoricalsociety.com
www.trinityhistoricalsociety.com

***Wesleyville:* Bonavista North Regional Museum & Gallery**
12 Memorial Dr., Wesleyville, NL A0G 4R0
Tel: 709-536-2110; *Fax:* 709-536-3039
museum@nf.aibn.com
bonavistanorth.blogspot.ca
Social Media: twitter.com/BonavistaNorth

Northwest Territories

Regional Systems

***Hay River:* NWT Public Library Services**
75 Woodland Dr., Hay River, NT X0E 1G1
Tel: 867-874-6531; *Fax:* 867-874-3321
Toll-Free: 866-297-0232
www.nwtpls.gov.nt.ca

Brian Dawson, Territorial Librarian
brian_dawson@gov.nt.ca
Anne Walsh, Head, Technical Services
anne_walsh@gov.nt.ca
Janine Hoff, Acquisitions Clerk
janine_hoff@gov.nt.ca

Public Libraries

***Aklavik:* Aklavik Community Library**
Moose Kerr School, Aklavik, NT X0E 0A0
Tel: 867-978-2536; *Fax:* 867-978-2829

***Behchoko:* Behchoko Community Library**
c/o Chief Jimmy Bruneau School, Behchoko, NT X0E 0Y0
Tel: 867-371-4511

***Deline:* Deline Community Library**
Ehtseo Ayha School, Deline, NT X0E 0G0
Tel: 867-589-3391; *Fax:* 867-589-4020

***Fort Good Hope:* Fort Good Hope Community Library**
Chief T'Selehye School, Fort Good Hope, NT X0E 0H0
Tel: 867-598-2288

***Fort Liard:* Fort Liard Community Library**
c/o Hamlet Office, Fort Liard, NT X0G 0A0
Tel: 867-770-4004

***Fort McPherson:* Fort McPherson Community Library**
c/o Chief Julius School, Fort McPherson, NT X0E 0J0
Tel: 867-952-2131; *Fax:* 867-952-2847

***Fort Providence:* Zhahti Koe Community Library**
Deh Gáh Elementary & Secondary School, Fort Providence, NT X0E 0L0
Tel: 867-699-3131; *Fax:* 867-699-3525

***Fort Resolution:* Fort Resolution Community Library**
c/o Deninu School, Fort Resolution, NT X0E 0M0
Tel: 867-394-4501; *Fax:* 867-394-3201

***Fort Simpson:* John Tsetso Memorial Library**
PO Box 443, Fort Simpson, NT X0E 0N0
Tel: 867-695-3276; *Fax:* 867-695-3276
FortSimpson_Library@gov.nt.ca

Diane McIntosh, Librarian

***Fort Smith:* Mary Kaeser Library**
170 McDougal Rd., Fort Smith, NT X0E 0P0
Tel: 867-872-2296; *Fax:* 867-872-5303
www.fortsmith.ca/municipal/library
Social Media: www.facebook.com/MKLibrary

Chris Bird, Director, Community Services
cbird@fortsmith.ca

***Gameti:* Gameti Community Library**
c/o Jean Wetrade Gameti School, Gameti, NT X0E 1R0
Tel: 867-997-3600

***Hay River:* Hay River Centennial Library**
75 Woodland Dr., Hay River, NT X0E 1G1
Tel: 867-874-6486
hrlibrar@hotmail.com
Social Media:
www.facebook.com/pages/Hay-River-Public-Library/117573528267995

***Hay River:* Hay River Dene Reserve Community Library**
Chief Sunrise Education Centre, Hay River, NT X0E 1G4
Tel: 867-874-3678
Other Numbers: 867-874-6444

***Inuvik:* Inuvik Centennial Library**
100 MacKenzie Rd., Inuvik, NT X0E 0T0
Tel: 867-777-8620; *Fax:* 867-777-8621
IK_Library@gov.nt.ca
inuvik.ca/town-hall/library-services

Beverly Garven, Head Librarian

***Norman Wells:* Norman Wells Community Library**
Mackenzie Mountain School, Norman Wells, NT X0E 0V0
Tel: 867-587-3714; *Fax:* 867-587-2193

***Tuktoyaktuk:* Tuktoyaktuk Community Library**
c/o Mangilaluk School, Tuktoyaktuk, NT X0E 1C0
Tel: 867-977-2255
Social Media:
www.facebook.com/TuktoyaktukCommunityLibrary

***Tulita:* Tulita Community Library**
Chief Albert Wright School, Tulita, NT X0E 0K0
Tel: 867-588-4361

***Ulukhaktok:* Ulukhaktok Community Library**
Helen Kalvak Elihakvik School, Ulukhaktok, NT X0E 0S0
Tel: 867-396-3804

***Wha Ti:* Wha Ti Community Library**
c/o Mezi Community School, Wha Ti, NT X0E 1P0
Tel: 867-573-3131

***Yellowknife:* Yellowknife Public Library**
Centre Square Mall, 5022 - 49th St., 2nd Fl., Yellowknife, NT X1A 3R8
Tel: 867-920-5642
www.yellowknife.ca
Social Media: www.facebook.com/187241917965175

Deborah Bruser, Library Manager
dbruser@yellowknife.ca
867-669-3401
Kris Solowy, Library Technician
867-669-3402

Archives

***Fort Smith:* Northern Life Museum & Cultural Centre**
110 King St., Fort Smith, NT X0E 0P0
Tel: 867-872-2859
info@nlmcc.ca
nlmcc.ca
Social Media: www.twitter.com/NorthernLifeMus; www.facebook.com/NLMCC

Diane Seals, Manager

***Yellowknife:* Prince of Wales Northern Heritage Centre**
4750 - 48th St., Yellowknife, NT X1A 2L9
Tel: 867-767-9347; *Fax:* 867-873-0660
nwtarchives@gov.nt.ca
www.nwtarchives.ca

Ian Moir, Territorial Archivist
ian_moir@gov.nt.ca
867-767-9347 ext. 71210
Kate Guay, Senior Archivist
kate_guay@gov.nt.ca
867-767-9347 ext. 71212

Nova Scotia

Regional Systems

***Amherst:* Cumberland Regional Library**
21 Acadia St., 2nd Fl., Amherst, NS B4H 4W3
Tel: 902-667-2135; *Fax:* 902-667-1360
information@cumberlandpubliclibraries.ca
www.crl.library.ns.ca
Social Media: twitter.com/CumberlandPL; www.facebook.com/195505467145534

Frank Balcom, Chair
Denise Corey, Chief Librarian & Board Secretary
Chantelle Taylor, Deputy Chief Librarian
Jennifer Calder, Youth Services Librarian

***Bridgetown:* Annapolis Valley Regional Library**
26 Bay Rd., Bridgetown, NS B0S 1C0
Tel: 902-665-2995; *Fax:* 902-665-4899
Toll-Free: 866-922-0229
administration@valleylibrary.ca
www.valleylibrary.ca
Social Media: pinterest.com/valleylibrary; twitter.com/valleylibs; www.facebook.com/AVRLibrary

Lorraine McQueen, Interim CEO
lmcqueen@valleylibrary.ca
Charlotte Janes, Head, Systems & Administration
cjanes@valleylibrary.ca
Patricia Milner, Head, Reference Services
reference@valleylibrary.ca

***Bridgewater:* South Shore Regional Library**
135 North Park St., Bridgewater, NS B4V 9B3
Tel: 902-543-2548; *Toll-Free:* 877-455-2548
info@southshorepubliclibraries.ca
www.southshorepubliclibraries.ca
Social Media: twitter.com/ssplibraries; www.facebook.com/southshorepubliclibraries

Troy Myers, Chief Executive Officer & Chief Librarian

***Dartmouth:* Halifax Public Libraries**
60 Alderney Dr., Dartmouth, NS B2Y 4P8
Tel: 902-490-5744
Other Numbers: 902-490-5753 (Accounts); 903-490-5710 (Research)
www.halifaxpubliclibraries.ca
Social Media: twitter.com/hfxpublib; www.facebook.com/hfxpublib

Paul W. Bennett, Chair
Asa Kachan, Chief Librarian & CEO
Duncan Macpherson, Director, Information Technology & Collection Management
Kathleen Peverill, Director, Community Branch Services
Bruce Gorman, Director, Central Library & Regional Services
Margaret Barry, Director, Finance & Facilities
Cathy Maddigan, Director, Human Resources
Paula Saulnier, Director, Corporate Services
Darlene Beck, Manager, Adult Services
Karen Dahl, Manager, Youth Services
Heather MacKenzie, Manager, Diversity and Accessibility
Sara Gillis, Manager, Community Engagement
Kevin Crick, Manager, Information Technology
Denis Cunningham, Manager, Communications & Marketing
Debbie LeBel, Manager, Collection Development & Access

***Halifax:* Nova Scotia Provincial Library**
1741 Brunswick St., 2nd Fl., Halifax, NS B3J 2R5
Tel: 902-424-2457; *Fax:* 902-424-0633
nspl@novascotia.ca
library.novascotia.ca

***Mulgrave:* Eastern Counties Regional Library**
390 Murray St., Mulgrave, NS B0E 2G0
Tel: 902-747-2597; *Toll-Free:* 855-787-7323
www.ecrl.library.ns.ca
Social Media: www.facebook.com/153045861388306

***New Glasgow:* Pictou-Antigonish Regional Library**
182 Dalhousie St., PO Box 276, New Glasgow, NS B2H 5E3
Tel: 902-755-6031; *Fax:* 902-755-6775
Toll-Free: 866-779-7761
info@parl.ns.ca
www.parl.ns.ca
Social Media: twitter.com/parlevents; www.facebook.com/Pictou-Antigonish-Regional-Library-16057718490

Eric Stackhouse, Chief Librarian, Systems Librarian, & Board Secretary
Kristel Fleuren-Hunter, Children's Services Librarian
Trecia Schell, Community Services Librarian
Fern MacDonald, Manager, Web Services
Melanie Pauls, Coordinator, Community Access to Technology

***Sydney:* Cape Breton Regional Library**
50 Falmouth St., Sydney, NS B1P 6X9
Tel: 902-562-3279; *Fax:* 902-564-0765
Other Numbers: 902-562-3279 (Bookmobile services)
inssc@nssc.library.ns.ca
www.cbrl.ca
Social Media: www.pinterest.com/cbrlpinterest; twitter.com/CBRLibrary; www.facebook.com/cbrlibrary

Michael Milburn, Chair
Faye MacDougall, Regional Librarian
fmacdoug@nssc.library.ns.ca
Ian R. MacIntosh, Deputy Regional Librarian & Collections Librarian
imacinto@nssc.library.ns.ca
Theresa MacDonald, Librarian, Technical Services
tmacdona@nssc.library.ns.ca

Clare MacKillop, Supervisor, Cape Breton County Branch Libraries
cmackill@nssc.library.ns.ca
Erin Phillips, Supervisor, Victoria County Library Services
ephillip@nssc.library.ns.ca
Rosalie Gillis, Coordinator, Community Support
rgillis@nssc.library.ns.ca
Tara MacNeil, Coordinator, Programs
tmacneil@nssc.library.ns.ca

***Truro:* Colchester-East Hants Public Library**
754 Prince St., Truro, NS B2N 1G9
Tel: 902-895-0235; *Fax:* 902-895-7149
Toll-Free: 888-632-9088
anstc@cehpubliclibrary.ca
lovemylibrary.ca
Social Media: www.youtube.com/CEHPL; twitter.com/cehpl; www.facebook.com/161034847272531
Janet Pelley, Library Director
Lesley Brann, Administrator, Adult & Outreach Services
Lynda Marsh, Administrator, Youth Services
Bill Morgan, Administrator, Automated & Technical Services
Norma Johnson-MacGregor, Librarian, Electronic Services

***Yarmouth:* Western Counties Regional Library**
405 Main St., Yarmouth, NS B5A 1G3
Tel: 902-742-2486; *Fax:* 902-742-6920
ansy@nsy.library.ns.ca
www.westerncounties.ca
Social Media: www.youtube.com/irwhite62; twitter.com/wcrlibrary; www.facebook.com/62520112493
Erin Comeau, Regional Library Director
ecomeau@nsy.library.ns.ca
Joanne Head, Deputy Director
jhead@nsy.library.ns.ca
Deborah Duke, Coordinator, Library Services
dduke@nsy.library.ns.ca
Yvonne LeBlanc, Manager, Office
ansy@nsy.library.ns.ca
Ian White, Manager, Public Relations
iwhite@nsy.library.ns.ca
Carol Surette, Bookkeeper
csurette@nsy.library.ns.ca

Archives

***Amherst:* Cumberland County Museum & Archives**
150 Church St., Amherst, NS B4H 3C4
Tel: 902-667-2561
www.cumberlandcountymuseum.com
Social Media: www.facebook.com/148688355199338
Natasha Richard, Manager/Curator

***Annapolis Royal:* Historic Restoration Society of Annapolis County**
O'Dell House Museum, 136 St. George St., Annapolis Royal, NS B0S 1A0
Tel: 902-532-7754; *Fax:* 902-532-0700
annapolisheritage@gmail.com
www.annapolisheritagesociety.com

***Antigonish:* Antigonish Heritage Museum**
20 East Main St., Antigonish, NS B2G 2E9
Tel: 902-863-6160
antheritage@parl.ns.ca
www.heritageantigonish.ca
Social Media: www.youtube.com/user/AntigonishHeriMuseum; twitter.com/antheritage; www.facebook.com/AntigonishHeritageMuseum
Jocelyn Gillis, Manager

***Baddeck:* Alexander Graham Bell National Historic Site/ Lieu Historique National Alexander Graham Bell**
559 Chebucto St., Baddeck, NS B0E 1B0
Tel: 902-295-2069; *Fax:* 902-295-3496
information@pc.gc.ca
www.pc.gc.ca/eng/lhn-nhs/ns/grahambell
Social Media: www.facebook.com/AGBNHS

***Barrington:* Cape Sable Historical Society Centre**
2402 Hwy. 3, Barrington, NS B0W 1E0
Tel: 902-637-2185
barmuseumcomplex@eastlink.ca
www.capesablehistoricalsociety.com

***Bridgetown:* Bridgetown & Area Historical Society**
12 Queen St., Bridgetown, NS B0S 1C0
Tel: 902-665-4530
www.jameshousemuseum.com
Social Media: www.facebook.com/jameshousemuseum1835

***Bridgewater:* DesBrisay Museum**
130 Jubilee Rd., Bridgewater, NS B4V 2A7
Tel: 902-543-4033; *Fax:* 902-543-4713
museum@bridgewater.ca
www.desbrisaymuseum.ca
Social Media: www.youtube.com/desbrisaybridgewater; www.facebook.com/pages/DesBrisay-Museum/190907454254694
Linda Bedford, Curator
lbedford@bridgewater.ca

***Canso:* Canso Historical Society**
90 Union St., Canso, NS B0H 1H0
Tel: 902-366-2170

***Centreville:* Archelaus Smith Museum**
915 Hwy. 330, Centreville, NS B0W 1P0
Tel: 902-745-3361
archelaussmithmuseum@hotmail.ca
Social Media: www.facebook.com/ArchelausSmithMuseum

***Cherry Brook:* Black Cultural Centre for Nova Scotia**
10 Cherry Brook Rd., Cherry Brook, NS B2Z 1A8
Tel: 902-434-6223; *Fax:* 902-434-2306
Toll-Free: 800-465-0767
contact@bccns.com
www.bccns.com
Social Media: www.youtube.com/bccnsvideo; twitter.com/BCC_NS; facebook.com/pages/Black-Cultural-/188265867860941
Russell Grosse, Executive Director

***Church Point:* St Mary's Museum/ Le Musée Sainte Marie**
1713 Hwy 1, Church Point, NS B0W 1M0
Tel: 902-769-2378; *Fax:* 902-769-0048
www.museeeglisesaintemariemuseum.ca

***Dartmouth:* Cole Harbour Rural Heritage Society**
471 Poplar Dr., Dartmouth, NS B2W 4L2
Tel: 905-434-0222
coleharbourfarmmuseum.ca
Social Media: twitter.com/coleharbourfarm; www.facebook.com/ColeHarbourHeritageFarmMuseum

***Dartmouth:* Dartmouth Heritage Museum**
26 Newcastle St., Dartmouth, NS B2Y 3M5
Tel: 902-464-2300; *Fax:* 902-464-8210
www.dartmouthheritagemuseum.ns.ca
Social Media: www.facebook.com/pages/Dartmouth-Heritage-Museum/205574426126756
Bonnie Elliott, Executive Director
elliottb@bellaliant.com
902-464-2916

***Dartmouth:* Genealogical Association of Nova Scotia**
#100, Ochterloney St., Dartmouth, NS B2Y 4P5
Tel: 902-454-0322
info@novascotiaancestors.ca
www.novascotiaancestors.ca/libraryRecords.php
Pamela Wile, President

***Halifax:* Canadian Museum of Immigration at Pier 21**
1055 Marginal Rd., Halifax, NS B3H 4P7
Tel: 902-425-7770; *Fax:* 902-423-4045
Toll-Free: 855-526-4721
info@pier21.ca
www.pier21.ca
Cara MacDonald, Manager, Reference Services
caramacdonald@pier21.ca
902-425-7770 ext. 224
Steve Schwinghamer, Historian
sschwinghamer@pier21.ca
902-425-7770 ext. 250
Emily Burton, Oral Historian
eburton@pier21.ca
902-425-7770 ext. 241

***Halifax:* Halifax Regional Municipality**
Burnside Industrial Park, #11, 81 Isley Ave., Halifax, NS B3B 1L5
Tel: 902-490-4643; *Fax:* 902-490-6299
archives@halifax.ca
www.halifax.ca/archives
Susan McClure, Municipal Archivist

***Halifax:* Nova Scotia Archives & Records Management**
6016 University Ave., Halifax, NS B3H 1W4
Tel: 902-424-6060; *Fax:* 902-424-0628
archives@novascotia.ca
archives.novascotia.ca
Social Media: www.youtube.com/NSArchives; twitter.com/NS_Archives; www.facebook.com/novascotiaarchives

***Halifax:* Nova Scotia Sport Hall of Fame**
#446, 1800 Argyle St., Halifax, NS B3J 3N8
Tel: 902-421-1266; *Fax:* 902-425-1148
sporthalloffame@eastlink.ca
www.novascotiasporthalloffame.com
Social Media: twitter.com/NSSHF; www.facebook.com/116064731766960; linkedin.com/company/nova-scotia-sport-hall-of-fame
Bill Robinson, CEO
bill@nsshf.com
Shane Mailman, Programs & Facility Manager
shane@nsshf.com
Katie Wooler, Museum & Communications Coordinator
katie@nsshf.com

***Halifax:* Shambhala Archives**
1084 Tower Rd., Halifax, NS B3H 2Y5
Tel: 902-420-1118
archives@shambhala.org
fundshambhalaarchives.org
Social Media: www.facebook.com/ShambhalaArchives

***Halifax:* Sisters of Charity of St. Vincent de Paul - Halifax**
Sisters of Charity Centre, 215 Seton Rd., Halifax, NS B3M 0C9
Tel: 902-406-8077
communications@schalifax.ca
www.schalifax.ca
Social Media: instagram.com/schalifax; www.facebook.com/schalifax

***Kentville:* King's County Historical Society**
c/o The Genealogy & Family History Committee, The Kings County Museum, 37 Cornwallis St., Kentville, NS B4N 2E2
Tel: 902-678-6237; *Fax:* 902-678-2764
info@kingscountymuseum.ca
kingscountymuseum.ca
Social Media: twitter.com/Kings_Co_Museum; www.facebook.com/kingscountymuseum

***Liverpool:* Thomas H. Raddall Research Centre**
109 Main St., Liverpool, NS B0T 1K0
Tel: 902-354-4058; *Fax:* 902-354-2050
www.raddallresearchcentre.com
Social Media: www.facebook.com/223194214399105
Linda Rafuse, Director
rafusela@gov.ns.ca
902-354-4058
Kathy Stitt, Administrative Assistant
stittkim@gov.ns.ca

***Maplewood:* Parkdale-Maplewood Community Museum**
3005 Barss Corner Rd., RR#1, Maplewood, NS B0R 1A0
Tel: 902-644-2893; *Fax:* 902-644-3422
Other Numbers: Off-season: 902-644-3421
p-mcm@hotmail.com
parkdale.ednet.ns.ca
Social Media: www.facebook.com/94020106181
Donna Arenburg, Curator
Suzanne Isaacs, Museum Assistant

***Middleton:* Macdonald Museum**
21 School St., Middleton, NS B0S 1P0
Tel: 902-825-6116; *Fax:* 902-825-0531
macdonald.museum@ns.sympatico.ca
www.macdonaldmuseum.ca
Social Media: www.facebook.com/1438057503100139

***Parrsboro:* Parrsborough Shore Historical Society**
1155 Whitehall Rd., Parrsboro, NS B0M 1S0
Tel: 902-254-2376
ottawa.house@ns.sympatico.ca
www.parrsboroughshorehistoricalsociety.ca
Harriet McCready, President

Pictou: **McCulloch Heritage Centre**
86 Haliburton Rd., Pictou, NS B0K 1H0
Tel: 902-485-4563
pcghs@novascotia.ca
www.mccullochcentre.ca
Social Media: twitter.com/McCullochCentre;
www.facebook.com/mccullochcentre
Michelle Davey, Curator
Michelle.Davey@novascotia.ca

Port Hastings: **Port Hastings Historical Museum & Archives**
24 Rte. 19, Port Hastings, NS B9A 1M1
Tel: 902-625-1295
porthastingsmuseum@gmail.com
Social Media: www.facebook.com/PortHastingsMuseum

Shearwater: **Shearwater Aviation Museum**
34 Bonaventure St., Shearwater, NS B0J 3A0
Tel: 902-720-2165; *Fax:* 902-720-2037
library@shearwateraviationmuseum.ns.ca
www.shearwateraviationmuseum.ns.ca
Social Media: twitter.com/YAWmuseum;
www.facebook.com/shearwateraviationmuseum

Shelburne: **Shelburne County Museum**
20 Dock St., Shelburne, NS B0T 1W0
Tel: 902-875-3219; *Fax:* 902-875-4141
shelburne.museum@ns.sympatico.ca
www.historicshelburne.com
Social Media: www.facebook.com/364893103570881

Truro: **Colchester Historical Society Museum & Archives**
29 Young St., Truro, NS B2N 3W3
Tel: 902-895-6284; *Fax:* 902-895-9530
colchesterhistoreum.ca
Social Media: twitter.com/Col_Historeum
Nan D. Harvey, Archivist
902-895-9530

Tusket: **Argyle Township Court House Archives**
8162 Hwy. 3, Tusket, NS B0W 3M0
Tel: 902-648-2493
www.argylecourthouse.com
Social Media: www.facebook.com/Argylecourthouse
Peter Crowell, Municipal Historian & Archivist
pcrowell@argylecourthouse.com

Windsor: **West Hants Historical Society**
281 King St., Windsor, NS B0N 2T0
Tel: 902-798-4706
whhs@ns.aliantzinc.ca
www.westhantshistoricalsociety.ca
Social Media: www.youtube.com/user/westhantshistorical;
www.twitter.com/whhswindsor;
www.facebook.com/westhantshistoricalsociety;
ca.linkedin.com/in/west-hants-historical-society-2a693449

Yarmouth: **Yarmouth County Museum & Archives**
22 Collins St., Yarmouth, NS B5A 3C8
Tel: 902-742-5539; *Fax:* 902-749-1120
ycarchives@eastlink.ca
yarmouthcountymuseum.ca
Social Media: www.facebook.com/92402018979
Nadine Gates, Director & Curator
ycmuseum@eastlink.ca
Lisette Gaudet, Archivist
ycarchives@eastlink.ca
Gary Gaudet, Assistant Director
ycm.asst.dir@eastlink.ca

Ontario

Regional Systems

Sudbury: **Ontario Library Service North/ Service des bibliothèques de l'Ontario nord**
334 Regent St., Sudbury, ON P3C 4E2
Tel: 705-675-6467; *Fax:* 705-675-2285
Toll-Free: 800-461-6348
Other Numbers: Fax Toll-Free: 800-398-8890
www.olsn.ca
Social Media: www.facebook.com/olsnorth
Leanne Clendening, Chief Executive Offcier
lclendening@olsn.ca

Southern Ontario Library Service (SOLS)
#1504, 1 Yonge St., Tornoto, ON M5E 1E5
Tel: 416-961-1669; *Fax:* 416-961-5122
Toll-Free: 800-387-5765
helpdesk@sols.org
www.sols.org
Social Media: twitter.com/solslib
Barbara Franchetto, CEO
bfranchetto@sols.org
Karen Reid, Director, Operations
kreid@sols.org

Public Libraries

Ajax: **Ajax Public Library**
55 Harwood Ave. South, Ajax, ON L1S 2H8
Tel: 905-683-4000; *Fax:* 905-683-6944
TTY: 866-460-448
www.ajaxlibrary.ca
Social Media: youtube.com/user/ajaxlibrary;
twitter.com/ajax_library
Phill White, Chair
Donna Bright, Chief Librarian/CEO
905-683-4000 ext. 8825
Dan Gioiosa, Access Services Manager
905-683-4000 ext. 8824
Cindy Poon, Public Service Manager
cindy.poon@ajax.ca
905-683-4000 ext. 8801
Susan Burrill, Manager of Corporate Services
905-683-4000 ext. 8822

Alban: **French River Public Library/ Bibliothèque publique de la Rivière-des-français**
796 Hwy. 64, #A, Alban, ON P0M 1A0
Tel: 705-857-1771; *Fax:* 705-857-1771
www.olsn.ca/frenchriverpl
Linda Keenan, CEO

Alfred: **Bibliothèque publique du Canton d'Alfred et Plantagenet/ Alfred & Plantagenet Public Library**
330, rue St-Phillipe, Alfred, ON K0B 1A0
Tél: 613-679-2663
peladeaug@yahoo.ca
www.alfred-platagenet.com
Catherine Bélisle, Directrice
Anne St-Pierre, Aide

Alliston: **New Tecumseth Public Library**
17 Victoria St. East, Alliston, ON L9R 1V6
Tel: 705-435-0250; *Fax:* 705-435-0750
www.ntpl.ca
Social Media: www.youtube.com/user/NewTecumsethLibrary;
twitter.com/NewTecumsethPL;
www.facebook.com/139887459474221
Mark Gagnon, Chief Executive Officer
mgagnon@ntpl.ca
705-435-0250

Almonte: **Mississippi Mills Public Library**
155 High St., Almonte, ON K0A 1A0
Tel: 613-256-1037
missmillslibrary.com
Social Media: www.facebook.com/mississippimillspubliclibrary
Pam Harris, CEO/Chief Librarian
pharris@mississippimills.ca
Monica Blackburn, Branch Services Supervisor
mblackburn@mississippimills.ca

Angus: **Essa Public Library**
#1, 8505 County Road 10, Angus, ON L0M 1B1
Tel: 705-424-6531; *Fax:* 705-424-5512
essalib@essa.library.on.ca
www.essa.library.on.ca
Social Media: twitter.com/essalibrary;
www.facebook.com/essapubliclibrary
Laura Wark, CEO
Mark Stewart, Manager, Public Service
Angie Wishart, Coordinator of Support Services

Apsley: **North Kawartha Public Library**
175 Burleigh St., Apsley, ON K0L 1A0
Tel: 705-656-4333; *Fax:* 705-656-2538
www.northkawarthalibrary.com
Social Media: twitter.com/NorthKawartha;
www.facebook.com/NorthKawartha
Carolyn Amyotte, Chair
Shannon Hunter, Chief Executive Officer
Debbie Hall, Librarian, Apsley & Woodview Branches
Susan Suhr, Coordinator, Technical Services, Apsley & Woodview Branches

Arnprior: **Arnprior Public Library**
21 Madawaska St., Arnprior, ON K7S 1R6
Tel: 613-623-2279; *Fax:* 613-623-0281
library@arncap.com
www.arnprior.library.on.ca
Social Media: twitter.com/arnpriorlibrary;
www.facebook.com/197513506955476

Astorville: **East Ferris Public Library/ Bibliothèque publique d'East Ferris**
1257 Village Rd., PO Box 160, Astorville, ON P0H 1B0
Tel: 705-752-2042; *Fax:* 705-752-0365
efpl@ontera.net
www.efpl.ca
Social Media: pinterest.com/efpl; twitter.com/EF_pub_library;
www.facebook.com/EastFerrisPublicLibrary
Jennifer Laporte, CEO

Athens: **Township of Athens Public Library**
5 Central St., Athens, ON K0E 1B0
Tel: 613-924-2048
athenspl@bellnet.ca
www.athenslibrary.ca
Julianna McAleese, Chair
Freda Schaafsma, CEO / Head Librarian
Diane Benschop, Children's Librarian

Atherley: **Ramara Township Public Library**
5482 Hwy. 12 South, Atherley, ON L3V 6H7
Tel: 705-325-5776; *Fax:* 705-325-8176
info@ramarapubliclibrary.org
www.ramarapubliclibrary.org
Social Media: www.twitter.com/RamaraPL;
www.facebook.com/ramarapl
Jane Banfield, CEO
banfieldj@ramarapubliclibrary.org

Atikokan: **Atikokan Public Library**
Civic Centre, Atikokan, ON P0T 1C0
Tel: 807-597-4406; *Fax:* 807-597-1514
www.aplibrary.org
Social Media: www.facebook.com/139703726078003
Jonathan Lewis, CEO/Librarian
Tracey Sinclair, Head of Children's Services

Aurora: **Aurora Public Library**
15145 Yonge St., Aurora, ON L4G 1M1
Tel: 905-727-9494
Other Numbers: Telecirc 905-727-0314
www.library.aurora.on.ca
Social Media: www.youtube.com/AuroraPubLib;
twitter.com/APLtweets; www.facebook.com/aurorapubliclibrary
Jill Foster, CEO
jfoster@library.aurora.on.ca

Baden: **Region of Waterloo Library**
2017 Nafziger Rd., RR#2, Baden, ON N3A 3H4
Tel: 519-575-4590; *Fax:* 519-634-5371
libhq@regionofwaterloo.ca
www.rwlibrary.ca
Social Media: twitter.com/rwlibrary;
www.facebook.com/RegionofWaterlooLibrary
Kelly Bernstein, Manager, Library Services
kbernstein@regionofwaterloo.ca

Bala: **Wahta Mohawks Public Library**
2664 Muskoka Rd. 38, Bala, ON P0C 1A0
Tel: 705-756-2354; *Fax:* 705-756-2376
Carol Holmes, Education Coordinator

Bancroft: **Bancroft Public Library**
14 Flint St., Bancroft, ON K0L 1C0
Tel: 613-332-3380; *Fax:* 613-332-5473
info@bancroftpubliclibrary.ca
www.bancroftpubliclibrary.ca
Noreen Tinney, Chair
Vanessa Holm, CEO/Library Manager
Beverly Creighton, Librarian/InterLibrary Loan Officer
Shirley McRandall, Library Collection Maintenance Officer
Sheri Plumbe, Library Events Officer

Barrie: **Barrie Public Library**
60 Worsley St., Barrie, ON L4M 1L6
Tel: 705-728-1010; *Fax:* 705-728-4322
barlib@barrie.ca
library.barrie.ca
Social Media: twitter.com/BPL_inthecity;
www.facebook.com/pages/Barrie-Public-Library/4560242280
Al Davis, Director of Library Services
adavis@barrie.ca
705-728-1010 ext. 7500
Jaime Griffis, Manager, Branch & Public Services
Jaime.Griffis@barrie.ca
705-728-1010 ext. 7805

Jane Salmon, Acting Director, Service Delivery
Jane.Salmon@barrie.ca
705-728-1010 ext. 7017
Karen Barratt, Manager, Collections & Technology
Karen.Barratt@barrie.ca
705-728-1010 ext. 7010
Chris Vanderkruys, Director, Business & Development
Christopher.Vanderkruys@barrie.ca
705-728-1010 ext. 7137

***Barry's Bay:* Barry's Bay & Area Public Library**
19474 Opeongo Line, Barry's Bay, ON K0J 1B0
Tel: 613-756-2000; *Fax:* 613-756-2000
admin@madawaskavalleylibrary.ca
library.barrys-bay.ca
Karen Filipkowski, CEO/Head Librarian

***Baysville:* Lake of Bays Public Library**
Community Centre, 10 University Ave., Baysville, ON P0B 1A0
Tel: 705-767-2361; *Fax:* 705-767-2361
www.lakeofbayslibrary.ca
Social Media: www.facebook.com/BaysvillePublicLibrary
Linda Lacroix, CEO
linla@vianet.on.ca

***Beachburg:* Township of Whitewater Region Public Libraries**
20 Cameron St., Beachburg, ON K0J 1C0
Tel: 613-582-7090
libraries.whitewaterregion.ca
Marilyn Labow, CEO/Chief Librarian
mlabow@nrtco.net

***Beamsville:* Lincoln Public Library**
4996 Beam St., Beamsville, ON L0R 1B0
Tel: 905-563-7014; *Fax:* 905-563-1810
info@lincoln.library.on.ca
www.lincoln.library.on.ca
Social Media: www.facebook.com/115678635175024
John Kralt, Chair
Jill Nicholson, CEO
Janice Coles, Deputy CEO
Elisabeth Peters, Children's Services Coordinator

***Bear Island:* Temagami First Nation Public Library/ Bibliothèque publique de Tribu Temagami**
General Delivery, Bear Island, ON P0H 1C0
Tel: 705-237-8005; *Fax:* 705-237-8959
tfnpl@onlink.net
www.temagamifirstnation.ca
Virginia Mackenzie, CEO

***Bearskin Lake:* Bearskin Lake Public Library/ Bibliotheque Publique de Bearskin**
General Delivery, Bearskin Lake, ON P0V 1E0
Tel: 807-363-2518; *Fax:* 807-363-1066
Other Numbers: Alternate Phone: 807-363-2598
Rodney McKay, Chief

***Beaverton:* Brock Township Public Libraries**
401 Simcoe St., Beaverton, ON L0K 1A0
Tel: 705-426-9283; *Fax:* 705-426-9353
info@brocklibraries.ca
www.brocklibraries.ca
Social Media: twitter.com/brocklibrary;
www.facebook.com/201313729933754
Joe Allin, Chair
Susan Dalton, CEO
susandalton@brocklibraries.ca
705-426-9283

***Belleville:* Belleville Public Library (BPL)**
254 Pinnacle St., Belleville, ON K8N 3B1
Tel: 613-968-6731; *Fax:* 613-968-6841
Toll-Free: 866-979-5877
infoserv@bellevillelibrary.com
www.bellevillelibrary.com
Social Media: twitter.com/BellevillePL;
www.facebook.com/219197338115817
Trevor Pross, CEO
tpross@bellevillelibrary.com
613-968-6731 ext. 2222
Holly Dewar, Manager, Public Services
hdewar@bellevillelibrary.com
613-968-6731 ext. 2241
Fanny Tom, Head of Circulation
ftom@bellevillelibrary.com
613-968-6731 ext. 2243
Suzanne Humphreys, Coordinator, Children's, Youth & Readers' Services
shumphreys@bellevillelibrary.ca
613-968-6731 ext. 2246
Susan Holland, John M. Parrot Art Gallery Curator
gallery@bellevillelibrary.com
613-986-6731 ext. 2239

***Birch Island:* Whitefish River First Nation Public Library**
46 Bay of Islands Rd., Birch Island, ON P0P 1A0
Tel: 705-285-1888; *Fax:* 705-285-4532
whitefishriverfirstnationlibrary@hotmail.com
Social Media: www.facebook.com/WrfnLibrarian

***Blind River:* Blind River Public Library/ Bibliothèque de Blind River**
8 Woodward Ave., Blind River, ON P0R 1B0
Tel: 705-356-7616
www.olsn.ca/blindriverlibrary

***Blind River:* Mississauga First Nation Public Library**
148 Village Rd., Blind River, ON P0R 1B0
Tel: 705-356-3590; *Fax:* 705-356-1867
www.mississaugi.com
Social Media: www.facebook.com/MississaugaFirstNationLibrary

***Bolton:* Caledon Public Library**
150 Queen St. South, Bolton, ON L7E 1E3
Tel: 905-587-1400
bolton@caledon.library.on.ca
www.caledon.library.on.ca
Social Media: www.youtube.com/user/caledonpubliclibrary;
twitter.com/caledonlibrary; www.facebook.com/304312508343
Colleen Lipp, CEO/Chief Librarian
clipp@caledon.library.on.ca
519-927-5662
Gillian Booth-Moyle, Contact, Technical Services
gboothmoyle@caledon.library.on.ca
905-584-1456 ext. 224
Mary Maw, Contact, Communications & Community Development
mmaw@caledon.library.on.ca
905-857-1400 ext. 228
Kelley Potter, Contact, Juvenile & Young Adult Services
kpotter@caledon.library.on.ca
905-857-1400 ext. 238
Mojgan Schmalenberg, Contact, Technology Services
mschmale@caledon.library.on.ca
905-857-1400 ext. 237

***Bonfield:* Bonfield Public Library**
365 Hwy. 531, Bonfield, ON P0H 1E0
Tel: 705-776-2396; *Fax:* 705-776-1154
bpl@ontera.net
www.ontera.net/~bpl
Greg Boxwell, Chair

***Borden:* Borden Public & Military Library/ Bibliothèque publique et militaire de Borden**
Bldg. E-102, 41 Kapyong Rd., Borden, ON L0M 1C0
Tel: 705-424-1200
Donald Allen, Chief Librarian

***Bowmanville:* Clarington Public Library**
163 Church St., Bowmanville, ON L1C 1T7
Tel: 905-623-7322
Other Numbers: 905-623-7322, ext. 731 (Interlibrary loans)
info@clarington-library.on.ca
www.clarington-library.on.ca
Social Media: www.youtube.com/ClaringtonPL;
twitter.com/ClaringtonLib;
www.facebook.com/ClaringtonPublicLibrary
Linda Kent, Library Director
lkent@clarington-library.on.ca
905-623-7322 ext. 2702
Melissa Scott, Manager, Public Service
mscott@clarington-library.on.ca
905-623-7322 ext. 2714

***Bracebridge:* Bracebridge Public Library**
94 Manitoba St., Bracebridge, ON P1L 2B5
Tel: 705-645-4171; *Fax:* 705-645-6551
info@bracebridgelibrary.ca
bracebridgelibrary.ca
Social Media: twitter.com/bracebridgepl;
www.facebook.com/BracebridgePublicLibrary
Arlie Freer, Chair
Cathryn Rodney, CEO/Chief Librarian
Carolyn Dawkins, Library Assistant/Office Manager
Nancy Beasley, Interlibrary Loan Coordinator
Caroline Goulding, Children's & Youth Services Librarian

***Bradford:* Bradford-West Gwillimbury Public Library**
425 Holland St. West, Bradford, ON L3Z 0J2
Tel: 905-775-3328
www.bradford.library.on.ca
Social Media: www.youtube.com/user/BWGLibrary;
twitter.com/BWGLibrary; www.facebook.com/203251287495
Milt Calder, Chair
Terri Watman, CEO

***Brampton:* Brampton Library**
65 Queen St. East, Brampton, ON L6W 3L6
Tel: 905-793-4636
TTY: 866-959-999
www.bramlib.on.ca
Social Media: twitter.com/BramptonLibrary;
www.facebook.com/bramptonlibrary
Rebecca Raven, CEO
chieflib@bramlib.on.ca
905-793-4636 ext. 4311

***Brantford:* Brantford Public Library**
173 Colborne St., Brantford, ON N3T 2G8
Tel: 519-756-2220; *Fax:* 519-756-4979
info@brantford.library.on.ca
brantford.library.on.ca
Social Media: www.youtube.com/user/BrantfordLibrary;
twitter.com/BtfdLibrary; www.facebook.com/112507975464133
Craig Mann, Chair
Kathryn Goodhue, Chief Executive Officer
kgoodhue@brantford.library.on.ca
519-756-2220 ext. 319
Kathryn Drury, Manager, Community Focus
kdrury@brantford.library.on.ca
519-756-2220 ext. 309
Mike Olejnik, Manager, Technologies & Collections
molejnik@brantford.library.on.ca
519-756-2220 ext. 307

***Bridgenorth:* Selwyn Public Library**
836 Charles St., Bridgenorth, ON K0L 1H0
Tel: 705-292-5065; *Fax:* 705-292-6695
www.mypubliclibrary.ca
Social Media: pinterest.com/mypubliclibrary;
www.facebook.com/21180475746
Joan MacDonald, Librarian
jmacdonald@mypubliclibrary.ca

***Brighton:* Brighton Public Library**
35 Alice St., Brighton, ON K0K 1H0
Tel: 613-475-2511
brightonpl@gmail.com
www.brighton.library.on.ca
Robert Burke, Chair
bpburke@cogeco.ca
Mellissa D'Onofrio-Jones, CEO
Sharon Bugg, Assistant Librarian
Jeni Dyment, Contact, Children's Library

***Britt:* Britt Public Library**
841 Riverside Dr., Britt, ON P0G 1A0
Tel: 705-383-2292; *Fax:* 705-383-0077
www.olsn.ca/BrittPL
Terrilynn Gibson, Librarian

***Brockville:* Augusta Township Public Library**
4500 County Rd. 15, RR#2, Brockville, ON K6V 5T2
Tel: 613-926-2449; *Fax:* 613-702-0441
augusta@augustalibrary.com
www.augustalibrary.com

***Brockville:* Brockville Public Library**
23 Buell St., Brockville, ON K6V 5T7
Tel: 613-342-3936; *Fax:* 613-342-9598
info@brockvillelibrary.ca
www.brockvillelibrary.ca
Social Media: plus.google.com/114357656967318658573;
twitter.com/BrockvillePL;
www.facebook.com/BrockvillePublicLibrary
Nancy Bowman, Chair
Linda Chadwick, CEO
613-342-3936 ext. 27
Margie Bentley, Contact, Homebound Service & Local History Files
margie@brockvillelibrary.ca
613-342-3936 ext. 21
Lisa Cirka, Contact, Children's & Young Adult Services
lisa@brockvillelibrary.ca
613-342-3936 ext. 21
Laura Julien, Contact, Interlibrary Loan & Book Club Service
interlibrary@brockvillelibrary.ca
613-342-3936 ext. 21
Amanda Robinson, Manager, Access Services/IT Department/Webmaster/Donations

amanda@brockvillelibrary.ca
613-342-3936 ext. 24

Brockville: **Elizabethtown-Kitley Township Public Library**
4103 Country Rd. 29, Brockville, ON K6V 5T4
Tel: 613-498-3338; *Fax:* 613-345-7235
elizndub@elizabethtown-kitley.on.ca
www.elizabethtown-kitley.on.ca/content/public-library
C. Hoy, Chair

Bruce Mines: **Bruce Mines & Plummer Additional Union Public Library**
33 Desbarats St., Bruce Mines, ON P0R 1C0
Tel: 705-785-3370; *Fax:* 705-785-3370
bmpaupl@gmail.com
www.bruceminesandplummerlibrary.ca
Crystal Burch, CEO
Jackie Bloye, Clerk

Buckhorn: **Trent Lakes Public Libraries**
5 George St., Buckhorn, ON K0L 1J0
Tel: 705-657-3695; *Fax:* 705-657-3695
trentlakeslibrary.ca/
Social Media:
www.facebook.com/group.php?gid=374519655929786
Maria Bradburn, Chief Executive Officer
mbradburn@nexicom.net

Burks Falls: **Burks Falls, Armour & Ryerson Union Public Library**
39 Copeland St., Burks Falls, ON P0A 1C0
Tel: 705-382-3327
burksfallslibrary@gmail.com
www.burksfallslibrary.com
Social Media: twitter.com/BurksFallsLibra;
www.facebook.com/151818654228
Nieves Guijarro, CEO

Burlington: **Burlington Public Library**
2331 New St., Burlington, ON L7R 1J4
Tel: 905-639-3611; *Fax:* 905-681-7277
www.bpl.on.ca
Social Media: www.youtube.com/user/BPLStaffer;
twitter.com/BurlingtonPL;
www.facebook.com/pages/Burlington-Public-Library/245349649340
Nancy Douglas, Chair
board@bpl.on.ca
905-639-3611 ext. 1103
Maureen Barry, CEO
barrym@bpl.on.ca
905-639-3611 ext. 1100
Amanda Freeman, Manager, Central Branch
freemana@bpl.on.ca
905-639-3611 ext. 1211

Calabogie: **Greater Madawaska Public Library**
4984 Calabogie Rd., Calabogie, ON K0J 1H0
Tel: 613-752-2317; *Fax:* 613-752-1720
gmpl@bellnet.ca
Social Media:
www.facebook.com/GreaterMadawaskaPublicLibrary
Sharon Shalla, CEO/Librarian

Callander: **Callander Public Library**
30 Catherine St. West, Callander, ON P0H 1H0
Tel: 705-752-2544; *Fax:* 705-752-2819
cplstaff@ontera.net
www.mycallander.ca/library/home
Social Media: twitter.com/ourcplibrary;
www.facebook.com/callanderpubliclibrary
Helen McDonnell, CEO/Librarian
hemcdonnell@ontera.net

Cambridge: **Idea Exchange**
1 North Sq., Cambridge, ON N1S 2K6
Tel: 519-621-0460; *Fax:* 519-621-2080
askalibrarian@ideaexchange.org
www.cambridgelibraries.ca
Social Media: twitter.com/IdeaXchng;
www.facebook.com/161803547206997
Gary Price, Chair
board@ideaexchange.org
Helen Kelly, CEO
hkelly@ideaexchange.org
Aidan Ware, Gallery Director
aware@ideaexchange.org
Cathy Kiedrowski, Director, Branch Services
ckiedrowski@ideaexchange.org
Betty Wilson, Director, Digital Services
bwilson@ideaexchange.org
Jaime Griffis, Director, Programming & Promotion
jgriffis@ideaexchange.org

Campbellford: **Trent Hills Public Library**
98 Bridge St. East, Campbellford, ON K0L 1L0
Tel: 705-653-3611; *Fax:* 705-653-4611
campbellford@trenthillslibrary.ca
www.trenthillslibrary.ca
Donna Wilson, CEO

Carleton Place: **Carleton Place Public Library**
101 Beckwith St., Carleton Place, ON K7C 2T3
Tel: 613-257-2702
carletonplace.ca/library-c234.php
Social Media: twitter.com/CPLibrary101;
www.facebook.com/CarletonPlacePublicLibrary

Casselman: **Bibliothèque publique de Casselman/ Casselman Public Library**
764, rue Brébeuf, Casselman, ON K0A 1M0
Tél: 613-764-5505; *Téléc:* 613-764-5507
www.bibliocasselman.ca
Rachel Boucher, Directrice
rboucher@casselman.ca

Castleton: **Cramahe Township Public Library**
Castleton Town Hall, 1780 Percy St., Castleton, ON K0K 1M0
Tel: 905-344-7320
castleton@cramahelibrary.ca
www.cramahelibrary.ca
Social Media: www.facebook.com/476983602328692

Chapleau: **Chapleau Public Library**
20 Pine St. East, Chapleau, ON P0M 1K0
Tel: 705-864-0852; *Fax:* 705-864-0295
plchapleau@hotmail.com
www.olsn.ca/chapleau
Social Media:
www.facebook.com/pages/Chapleau-Public-Library/138198009599471
Maureen Travis, Chief Librarian
Gisele Robitaille, Assistant Librarian
Julie Hayes-Ruffo, Assistant Librarian

Chatham: **Chatham-Kent Public Library**
120 Queen St., Chatham, ON N7M 2G6
Tel: 519-354-2940; *Fax:* 519-354-2602
cklibrary@chatham-kent.ca
www.chatham-kent.ca/PublicLibraries
Social Media: www.youtube.com/user/CKPublicLibrary;
twitter.com/cklibrary; www.facebook.com/ChatKentPubLib
Chandra K. Clarke, Chair
Tania Sharpe, CEO/Chief Librarian
tanias@chatham-kent.ca
519-354-2940 ext. 241
Cassey Beauvais, Manager, Public Services
casseyb@chatham-kent.ca
519-354-2940 ext. 236
Sarah Hart, Maanger, Marketing, Outreach & Programs
sarah.hart@chatham-kent.ca
519-354-2940 ext. 242
Heidi Wyma, Coordinator, Support Services
heidiw@chatham-kent.ca
519-354-2940 ext. 257

Christian Island: **Beausoleil First Nation Library**
150 Mkade Kegwin Miikaan, Christian Island, ON L9M 0A9
Tel: 705-247-2255; *Fax:* 705-247-2772
www.olsn.ca/bfnlibrary
Kathy Monague, Contact

Clinton: **Huron County Library**
77722B London Rd., Hwy. 4 South, RR#5, Clinton, ON N0M 1L0
Tel: 519-482-5457; *Fax:* 519-482-7820
libraryadmin@huroncounty.ca
www.huroncounty.ca/library
Dorothy Kelly, Chair
Beth Ross, County Librarian
Meighan Wark, Branch Services Librarian
mwark@huroncounty.ca

Cobalt: **Cobalt Public Library/ Bibliothèque publique du Cobalt**
30 Lang St., Cobalt, ON P0J 1C0
Tel: 705-679-8120; *Fax:* 705-679-8119
cobaltlibrary@ntl.sympatico.ca
cobaltlibrary.com
Margaret Leaper, Chief Executive Officer
Ian Borean, Assistant Librarian

Cobourg: **Cobourg Public Library**
200 Ontario St., Cobourg, ON K9A 5P4
Tel: 905-372-9271; *Fax:* 905-372-4538
info@cobourg.library.on.ca
www.cobourg.library.on.ca
Social Media: www.flickr.com/photos/cobourgpubliclibrary;
twitter.com/cobourgPL; www.facebook.com/CobourgPublicLibrary
Tammy Robinson, Chief Executive Officer
kdavis@cobourg.library.on.ca
905-372-9271 ext. 6200
Rhonda Perry, Coordinator, Youth Services
rperry@cobourg.library.on.ca
Heather Viscount, Manager, Access Services

Cochrane: **Cochrane Public Library/ Bibliothèque publique de Cochrane**
178 - 4th Ave., Cochrane, ON P0L 1C0
Tel: 705-272-4178; *Fax:* 705-272-4165
library@cochraneontario.com
www.olsn.ca/cochrane
Social Media: www.facebook.com/CochraneLibrary
Christina Blazecka, Chief Executive Officer
christina.blazecka@cochraneontario.com

Coe Hill: **Wollaston & Limerick Public Library**
2149 Hwy. 620, Coe Hill, ON K0L 1P0
Tel: 613-337-5183; *Fax:* 613-337-5183
info@wollaston-limericklibrary.ca
www.wollaston-limericklibrary.ca
Bonnie Purdy, CEO/Librarian
Bonnie Weise, Library Assistant

Coldwater: **Coldwater Memorial Public Library**
31 Coldwater Rd., Coldwater, ON L0K 1E0
Tel: 705-686-3601; *Fax:* 705-686-3741
library@coldwater.library.on.ca
www.coldwater.library.on.ca
Social Media: www.pinterest.com/coldwaterlib;
twitter.com/ColdwaterLib;
www.facebook.com/ColdwaterMemorialPublicLibrary

Collingwood: **Collingwood Public Library**
55 Ste. Marie St., Collingwood, ON L9Y 0W6
Tel: 705-445-1571; *Fax:* 705-445-3704
www.collingwoodpubliclibrary.ca
Social Media: twitter.com/collingwoodpl;
www.facebook.com/collingwoodpubliclibrary
Chris Cable, Chair
Ken Haigh, CEO
khaigh@collingwood.ca
Lynda Reid, Manager, Collection & Facility Services
lreid@collingwood.ca
705-445-1571 ext. 6223

Constance Lake: **Constance Lake First Nation Public Library**
2 Musko St., Constance Lake, ON P0L 1B0
Tel: 705-463-1199; *Fax:* 705-463-2077
Lizzie Sutherland, CEO
lizzie.sutherland@clfn.on.ca

Cornwall: **Cornwall Public Library (Ontario)/ Bibliothèque publique de Cornwall**
45 - 2nd St. East, Cornwall, ON K6H 5V1
Tel: 613-932-4796; *Fax:* 613-932-2715
generalmail@library.cornwall.on.ca
www.library.cornwall.on.ca
Social Media: twitter.com/CornwallPubLibr
James G. Sallie, Chair

Cornwall: **Stormont, Dundas & Glengarry County Library/ Bibliothèque des comtés unis Stormont, Dundas et Glengarry**
#106, 26 Pitt St., Cornwall, ON K6J 3P2
Tel: 613-936-8777; *Fax:* 613-936-2532
generalinfo@sdglibrary.ca
www.sdglibrary.ca
Social Media: www.youtube.com/user/sdgcountylibrary;
twitter.com/sdglibrary;
www.facebook.com/pages/SDG-County-Library/250998401616550
Bill McGimpsey, Chair
mcgimpsey@ontarioeast.net
Karen Franklin, Manager, Library Services
kfranklin@sdglibrary.ca
613-936-8777 ext. 211
Susan Wallwork, Communications & Marketing Librarian
swallwork@sdglibrary.ca
613-936-8777 ext. 226

Curve Lake: **Curve Lake First Nation Public Library**
22 Winookeedaa St., Curve Lake, ON K0L 1R0
Tel: 705-657-3217; *Fax:* 705-657-8708
clfnlibrary@gmail.com
www.clfnpubliclibrary.webs.com

Cutler: **Serpent River First Nation Public Library**
49 Village Rd., Cutler, ON P0P 1B0
Tel: 705-844-2009; *Fax:* 705-844-2736
www.olsn.ca/proofs/serpent_river

Deep River: **Deep River Public Library**
55 Ridge Rd., Deep River, ON K0J 1P0
Tel: 613-584-4244
www.deepriverlibrary.ca

Deep River: **Laurentian Hills Public Library**
34465 Hwy. 17, RR#1, Deep River, ON K0J 1P0
Tel: 613-584-2714; *Fax:* 613-584-9145
library@laurentianhills.ca
library.laurentianhills.ca
Maureen L. Bakewell, CEO

Deseronto: **Deseronto Public Library**
358 Main St., Deseronto, ON K0K 1X0
Tel: 613-396-2744
info@deserontopubliclibrary.ca
www.deserontopubliclibrary.ca
Social Media: www.facebook.com/deseronto.dpl
Jean Rixen, Chair
Frances Smith, CEO & Librarian
Amy McDonald, Librarian Assistant

Devlin: **Naicatchewenin First Nations Library**
Rainy Lake Indian Reserve, RR#1, Devlin, ON P0W 1C0
Tel: 807-486-3407; *Fax:* 807-486-3704
naicatchewenin firstnation.ca
Darlene Smith, Director of Administration
darlene.smith@bellnet.ca

Dobie: **Dobie Public Library**
92 McPherson St., Dobie, ON P0K 1B0
Tel: 705-568-8951; *Fax:* 705-568-8951
Dianne Quinn, CEO

Dokis: **Dokis First Nation Public Library**
930 Main St., Dokis, ON P0M 2N1
Tel: 705-763-2511
dokislibrary@hotmail.com
www.dokisfirstnation.com
Social Media: www.facebook.com/dokislib
Jason Restoule, Librarian

Dorion: **Dorion Public Library**
170 Dorion Loop Rd., Dorion, ON P0T 1K0
Tel: 807-857-2289; *Fax:* 807-857-2203
dorlib@tbaytel.net
Betty Chambers, Head Librarian

Douglas: **Admaston-Bromley Public Library**
Hwy. 60, Douglas, ON K0J 1S0
Tel: 613-649-2576; *Fax:* 613-649-2676
info@admastonbromleylibrary.com
www.admastonbromleylibrary.com
Social Media: www.facebook.com/120297281409518

Douro: **Douro-Dummer Public Library**
435 Fourth Line, Douro, ON K0L 1S0
Tel: 705-652-8599
library@dourodummer.on.ca
www.dourodummer.on.ca/library
Social Media: www.youtube.com/DouroDummerLibrary;
twitter.com/DDPLibrarian
Edna Latone, Librarian

Dryden: **Dryden Public Library**
36 Van Horne Ave., Dryden, ON P8N 2A7
Tel: 807-223-1475; *Fax:* 807-223-4312
library@dryden.ca
www.dryden.ca/city_services/library
Social Media: twitter.com/DrydenLibrary;
www.facebook.com/322522094446779
Dayna DeBenedet, CEO

Dubreuilville: **Bibliothèque publique de Dubreuilville/ Dubreuilville Public Library**
120, rue Magpie, Dubreuilville, ON P0S 1B0
Tél: 705-884-1435; *Téléc:* 705-884-1437
Ligne sans frais: 877-637-8010
dpl@dubreuilville.ca

Dunchurch: **Whitestone Hagerman Memorial Public Library**
2206 Hwy. 124, Dunchurch, ON P0A 1G0
Tel: 705-389-3311; *Fax:* 705-389-3311
whitestonelibrary@vianet.ca
www.olsn.ca/whitestonelibrary
Social Media: twitter.com/whitestonelib;
www.facebook.com/whitestonelib
Lori Guillemette, Library Administrator

Dundalk: **Southgate Public Library**
80 Proton St. North, Dundalk, ON N0C 1B0
Tel: 519-923-3248
library@southgate.ca
southgate-library.com
Social Media: www.pinterest.com/southgatepl;
twitter.com/southgatepl; www.facebook.com/113603805368473
Jenna Helder, CEO

Dunnville: **Haldimand County Public Library**
111 Broad St. East, Dunnville, ON N1A 1E8
Tel: 905-774-7595; *Fax:* 905-774-4294
library@haldimandcounty.on.ca
www.haldimandcounty.on.ca
Linda Van Ede, Chair
Debra Jackson, CEO
Paul Diette, Deputy CEO

Durham: **West Grey Library System**
240 Garafraxa St. North, Durham, ON N0G 1R0
Tel: 519-369-2107; *Fax:* 519-369-9966
info@westgreylibrary.com
www.westgreylibrary.com
Social Media: www.facebook.com/west.greylibrary
Kim Priestman, CEO/Chief Librarian
kim@westgreylibrary.com

Eabamet Lake: **Fort Hope First Nation Public Library**
John C. Yesno Education Centre, PO Box 297, Eabamet Lake, ON P0T 1L0
Tel: 807-242-8421; *Fax:* 807-242-1592
Social Media: www.facebook.com/jcyschool

Ear Falls: **Ear Falls Public Library**
2 Willow Cres., Ear Falls, ON P0V 1T0
Tel: 807-222-3209; *Fax:* 807-222-3432
efpl@hotmail.ca
www.olsn.ca/earfallspl

Earlton: **Township of Armstrong Public Library/ Bibliothèque publique d'Armstrong**
35 - 10th St., Earlton, ON P0J 1E0
Tel: 705-563-2717
earltonlibrary@ntl.sympatico.ca
www.olsn.ca/armstrong
Ginette Hack, Head Librarian
Bernice Lockhart, Assistant Librarian

Eganville: **Bonnechere Union Public Library**
74A Maple St., Eganville, ON K0J 1T0
Tel: 613-628-2400; *Fax:* 613-628-5377
info@bonnechereupl.com
www.bonnechereupl.com
Social Media: www.facebook.com/BonnechereUPL
Jennifer Coleman-Davidson, CEO/CFO
ceo@bonnechereupl.com

Elgin: **Rideau Lakes Public Library**
26 Halladay St., Elgin, ON K0G 1E0
Tel: 613-359-5315
elgin@rideaulakeslibrary.ca
www.rideaulakeslibrary.ca
Social Media: twitter.com/rideaulibrary1;
www.facebook.com/rideaulakespubliclibrary
Sue Warrne, Library CEO
swarren@ripnet.com
Doug Franks, Library Chair
djfranks@uottawa.ca

Elk Lake: **Elk Lake Public Library**
First St., Elk Lake, ON P0J 1G0
Tel: 705-678-2340; *Fax:* 705-678-2340
elklake@ontera.net
www.olsn.ca/elklake
Cyndi Stockman, Librarian/CEO

Elliot Lake: **Elliot Lake Public Library**
White Mountain Academy, 99 Spine Rd., Elliot Lake, ON P5A 3S9
Tel: 705-461-7204; *Fax:* 705-848-2120
www.elliotlakelibrary.com
Pat McGurk, Chief Librarian

Emo: **Emo Public Library**
PO Box 490, Emo, ON P0W 1E0
Tel: 807-482-2575; *Fax:* 807-482-2575
emolib@bellnet.ca
www.twspemo.on.ca/library

Emo: **Emo Toy Library/Resource Centre**
36 Front St., Emo, ON P0W 1E0
Tel: 807-482-2946
emotoylibrary@bellnet.ca

Emsdale: **Perry Township (Emsdale) Public Library**
25 Joseph St., Emsdale, ON P0A 1J0
Tel: 705-636-5454; *Fax:* 705-636-5454
perrylib@ontera.net
www.olsn.ca/perrylibrary
Social Media: www.facebook.com/191662771194
Patricia Aitchison, CEO
Annette Gilpin, Assistant

Englehart: **Englehart Public Library/ Bibliothèque publique d'Englehart**
71 - 4th Ave., Englehart, ON P0J 1H0
Tel: 705-544-2100; *Fax:* 705-544-2238
www.englehartpubliclibrary.ca
Sharon Williams, Librarian/CEO
Liz Robitaille, Clerk
Karen Watchorn, Clerk

Espanola: **Espanola Public Library**
245 Avery Dr., Espanola, ON P5E 1S4
Tel: 705-869-2940; *Fax:* 705-869-6463
library@espanola.ca
www.espanola.library.on.ca
Charles Grayson, Chief Executive Officer

Essex: **Essex County Library**
#101, 360 Fairview Ave. West, Essex, ON N8M 1Y3
Tel: 519-776-5241; *Fax:* 519-776-6851
www.essexcountylibrary.ca
Social Media: twitter.com/EssexCountyLib;
www.facebook.com/pages/Essex-County-Library/109132675785815
Robin Greenall, Chief Librarian, CEO
Jennifer Franklin-McInnis, Deputy Chief Librarian/Manager of Branches
jfranklin@essexcountylibrary.ca

Fauquier: **Bibliothèque publique de Fauquier-Strickland/ Fauquier-Strickland Public Library**
25, rue Grzela, Fauquier, ON P0L 1G0
Tél: 705-339-2521; *Téléc:* 705-339-2421
fauquierbibliotheque@gmail.com
bibliofauquier.weebly.com
Claudie Tremblay-Blais, Directrice générale
Jocelyne Ratté, Aide-bibliothécaire

Fergus: **Wellington County Library**
190 St. Andrews St. West, Fergus, ON N1M 1N5
Tel: 519-846-0918; *Fax:* 519-846-2066
www.wellington.ca/en/discover/aboutus_library.asp
Murray McCabe, Chief Librarian
519-787-7805 ext. 6224
Janice Ellison, Library Technician
519-787-7805 ext. 6227

Flesherton: **Grey Highlands Public Library**
101 Highland Dr., Flesherton, ON N0C 1E0
Tel: 519-924-2241; *Fax:* 519-924-2562
fleshertonlibrary@greyhighlands.ca
www.greyhighlandspubliclibrary.com
Social Media: twitter.com/ghplconnect;
www.facebook.com/120056264709502
Jim Harrold, Chair
Wilda Allen, CEO/Chief Librarian

Flinton: **Addington Highlands Public Library**
3641 Flinton Rd., Flinton, ON K0H 1P0
Tel: 613-333-1091
flintonl@hotmail.com
www.addingtonhighlandspubliclibrary.ca
Social Media: www.facebook.com/445455308804599
Carol Lessard, Chair
June Phillips, CEO & Head Librarian

Foleyet: **Foleyet Public Library**
145 Sherry St., Foleyet, ON P0M 1T0
Tel: 705-899-2280

Fonthill: Pelham Public Library
43 Pelham Town Sq., Fonthill, ON L0S 1E0
Tel: 905-892-6443; *Fax:* 905-892-3392
admin@pelhamlibrary.on.ca
www.pelhamlibrary.on.ca
Social Media: www.facebook.com/pelham.ibrary
Kirk Weaver, CEO
kweaver@pelhamlibrary.on.ca
Jennifer Bennett, Children & Youth Services Coordinator
jbennett@pelhamlibrary.on.ca
Melanie Taylor-Ridgway, Development & Volunteer Coordinator
mtaylorridgway@pelhamlibrary.on.ca

Forest: Chippewas of Kettle & Stony Point Library
RR#2, 6218 Indian Lane, Forest, ON N0N 1J0
Tel: 519-786-2955; *Fax:* 519-786-6904

Fort Erie: Fort Erie Public Library
136 Gilmore Rd., Fort Erie, ON L2A 2M1
Tel: 905-871-2546; *Fax:* 905-871-2191
www.fepl.ca
Social Media: twitter.com/fepl;
www.facebook.com/135750286529152
Craig Shufelt, Chief Executive Officer
905-871-2546 ext. 303
Maria Brigantino, Business Administrator
905-871-2546 ext. 307
Michael Schell, Systems Administrator
905-871-2546 ext. 301
Joel Nash, Coordinator, Public Services
905-871-2546 ext. 310
Amy Roebuck, Coordinator, Community Services
905-871-2546 ext. 309

Fort Frances: Fort Frances Library Technology Centre
601 Red Ave., Fort Frances, ON P9A 0A2
Tel: 807-274-9879; *Fax:* 807-274-4496
ffpltc@gmail.com
library.fort-frances.com
Social Media: twitter.com/ffpltc; www.facebook.com/ffpltc
Andy Hallikas, Library Chair

Gananoque: Gananoque Public Library
100 Park St., Gananoque, ON K7G 2Y5
Tel: 613-382-2436
gplp@bellnet.ca
gplibrary.wordpress.com
Social Media: twitter.com/townofgananoque;
www.facebook.com/TownOfGananoque
John Love, Librarian

Garden River: Garden River First Nation Public Library
48 Syrette Lake Rd., Garden River, ON P6A 7A1
Tel: 705-946-3933; *Fax:* 705-946-0413
Toll-Free: 866-518-7806
Irene Gray, Resource Centre Coordinator

Garden Village: Nipissing First Nation Public Library
36 Semo Rd., Garden Village, ON P2B 3K2
Tel: 705-753-2050; *Fax:* 705-753-0571
www.kendaaswin.ca
Glenna Beaucage, Culture & Heritage Manager
glennab@nfn.ca
Christina Beaucage, Library Supervisor
christinab@nfn.ca

Georgetown: Halton Hills Public Library
9 Church St., Georgetown, ON L7G 2A3
Tel: 905-873-2681; *Fax:* 905-873-6118
www.hhpl.on.ca
Social Media: www.youtube.com/user/haltonhillspubliclib;
twitter.com/HaltonHillsPL; www.facebook.com/12169735434
Geoff Cannon, Director, Library Services
geoff.cannon@haltonhills.ca
905-873-2681 ext. 2513
Jane Diamanti, Commissioner, Community Services
jane.diamanti@haltonhills.ca
905-873-2681 ext. 2501

Georgina Island: Chippewas of Georgina Island First Nation Public Library
830 Joseph Snake Rd., Georgina Island, ON L0E 1L0
Tel: 705-437-4327
Karen Foster, Librarian
705-437-4327
Lynn Mooney, Literacy Coordinator
705-437-4327

Geraldton: Greenstone Public Library
405 - 2nd St. West, Geraldton, ON P0T 1M0
Tel: 807-854-2421; *Fax:* 807-854-2421
greenstonepl@hotmail.com
www.olsn.ca/greenstone
Mari Mannisto, CEO
greenstonepl@hotmail.com

Gilmour: Tudor & Cashel Baverstock Memorial Public Library
371 Weslemkoon Lake Rd., Gilmour, ON K0L 1W0
Tel: 613-474-1096; *Fax:* 613-474-0664
tudorandcashellibrary@yahoo.ca
www.tudorandcashel.com
Mary Hawkins, CEO, Secretary-Treasurer, & Librarian
Barb Sanderson, Assistant Librarian

Gogama: Gogama Public Library/ Bibliothèque publique de Gogama
15 Low Ave., Gogama, ON P0M 1W0
Tel: 705-894-2448; *Fax:* 705-894-2448
Sue Primeau, Volunteer Head Librarian

Gore Bay: Gore Bay Union Public Library
15 Water St., Gore Bay, ON P0P 1H0
Tel: 705-282-2221; *Fax:* 705-282-2221
gorebaylibrary@gorebaycable.com
www.olsn.ca/gorebay
Margaret Lane, Chair
Johanna Allison, CEO

Grafton: Alnwick-Haldimand Public Libraries
10836 County Rd. #2, Grafton, ON K0K 2G0
Tel: 905-349-2822; *Fax:* 905-349-3259
www.alnwickhaldimand.ca
Social Media: www.facebook.com/190046424350622
Carol Dempsey, Chief Executive Officer

Grand Valley: Grand Valley Public Library
4 Amaranth St. East, Grand Valley, ON L9W 5L2
Tel: 519-928-5622; *Fax:* 519-928-2586
info@grandvalley.org
www.grandvalley.org
Social Media:
www.facebook.com/pages/Grand-Valley-Public-Library/1289384 1499
Shann Leighton, CEO
sleighton@grandvalley.org

Gravenhurst: Gravenhurst Public Library
180 Sharpe St. West, Gravenhurst, ON P1P 1J1
Tel: 705-687-3382; *Fax:* 705-687-7016
library@gravenhurst.ca
www.gravenhurst.ca/library
Social Media: twitter.com/gravenhurstlib;
www.facebook.com/242143099195701
Marg Nicholson, Chair
Rita Orr, CEO/Chief Librarian

Grimsby: Grimsby Public Library
18 Carnegie Lane, Grimsby, ON L3M 1Y1
Tel: 905-945-5142
gen-library@town.grimsby.on.ca
www.town.grimsby.on.ca/Library
Social Media: twitter.com/GrimsbyLibrary;
www.facebook.com/236752953060009
Linda Henry, Board Chair
Lita Barrie, CEO/Chief Librarian & Secretary-Treasurer

Guelph: Guelph Public Library
100 Norfolk St., Guelph, ON N1H 4J6
Tel: 519-824-6220
askus@library.guelph.on.ca
www.guelphpl.ca
Social Media: www.youtube.com/user/GuelphPublicLibrary;
twitter.com/GuelphLibrary;
www.facebook.com/155431451134898
Anne MacKay, Chair
Steven Kraft, CEO
skraft@guelphpl.ca
Philip Kirby, Contact, Interlibrary Loans
pkirby@guelphpl.ca
Andrea Curtis, Contact, Children & Youth Services
acurtis@guelphpl.ca
Karen Cafarella, Contact, Extension Services
kcafarella@guelphpl.ca
Meg Forestell-Page, eLibrarian
mforestell@guelphpl.ca
Darcy Hiltz, Archivist
dhiltz@guelphpl.ca

Hagersville: Mississaugas of the New Credit First Nation Public Library
2789 Missisauga Rd., RR#6, Hagersville, ON N0A 1H0
Tel: 905-768-5686; *Fax:* 905-768-4592
www.newcreditfirstnation.com
Cynthia Jamieson, Executive Director
cjamieson@newcreditfirstnation.com

Haileybury: Temiskaming Shores Public Library
545 Lakeshore Rd., Haileybury, ON P0J 1K0
Tel: 705-672-3707; *Fax:* 705-672-5966
Haileybury@temisklibrary.com
www.temisklibrary.com
Social Media: www.facebook.com/TemiskamingShoresLibrary
Donald Bisson, Chair
Rebecca Hunt, Library CEO & Haileybury Branch Librarian

Haliburton: Haliburton County Public Library
78 Maple Ave., Haliburton, ON K0M 1S0
Tel: 705-457-2241; *Fax:* 705-457-9586
info@haliburtonlibrary.ca
www.haliburtonlibrary.ca
Social Media: haliburtonlibrary.wordpress.com;
twitter.com/HaliburtonCPL;
www.facebook.com/216747128340069
Nancy McLuskey, Chair
Bessie Sullivan, CEO/County Librarian
Susan Robinson, Supervisor, Community Partnerships & Administration
Sherrill Sherwood, Supervisor, Collections Development & Promotions
Catherine Coles, Branch Services Librarian

Hamilton: Hamilton Public Library
55 York Blvd., Hamilton, ON L8N 4E4
Tel: 905-546-3200; *Fax:* 905-546-3202
TTY: 905-546-347
askhpl@hpl.ca
www.hpl.ca
Social Media: pinterest.com/hamiltonlibrary;
twitter.com/HamiltonLibrary;
www.facebook.com/hamiltonpubliclibrary
Paul Takala, Chief Librarian & CEO
ptakala@hpl.ca
905-546-3200 ext. 3215
Tony Del Monaco, Director, Finance & Facilities
tdelmona@hpl.ca
905-546-3200 ext. 3226
Lisa DuPelle, Director, Human Resources
ldupelle@hpl.ca
905-546-3200 ext. 3290
Karen Anderson, Director, Public Service
kjanders@hpl.ca
905-546-3200 ext. 3285
Susan Kun, Interim Director, Collections
skun@hpl.ca
905-546-3200 ext. 3213
Melanie Southern, Director, Public Service, Partnerships & Communications
Lita Barrie, Director, Digital Technology

Hanover: Hanover Public Library
Civic Centre, 451 - 10th Ave., Hanover, ON N4N 2P1
Tel: 519-364-1420; *Fax:* 519-364-1747
hanpub@hanover.ca
hanoverlibrary.ca
Social Media: twitter.com/hanoverlibrary;
www.facebook.com/216793488339895
Agnes Rivers-Moore, Chief Librarian
arm@hanover.ca

Havelock: Havelock-Belmont-Methuen Township Public Library
13 Quebec St., Havelock, ON K0L 1Z0
Tel: 705-778-2621; *Fax:* 705-778-2621
habellib@nexicom.net
www.hbmlibrary.on.ca
Sandra Harris, CEO/Chief Librarian

Hawkesbury: Bibliothèque publique de Hawkesbury/ Hawkesbury Public Library
550 Higginson St., Hawkesbury, ON K6A 1H1
Tél: 613-632-0106
Other Numbers: 613-632-0106 x 2264 (Reference)
info@bibliotheque.hawkesbury.on.ca
www.bibliotheque.hawkesbury.on.ca
Yvon Leonard, Président
Lynn Belle-Isle, Directrice générale
Nathalie St-Jacques, Bibliotechnicienne
Jennifer Beaulieu, Bibliotechnicienne
Michel Bruneau, Commis à la référence

Hearst: Bibliothèque publique de Hearst/ Hearst Public Library
801 George St., Hearst, ON P0L 1N0
Tel: 705-372-2843; Fax: 705-372-2833
hearstpl@ontera.net
www.bibliohearst.on.ca
Francine D'aigle, Director, Library Services
Julie Portelance, Library Services Technician

Hermon: Carlow-Mayo Public Library
124 Fort Stewart Rd., Hermon, ON K0L 1C0
Tel: 613-332-2544
library@carlowmayo.ca

Heron Bay: Ojibways of the Pic River First Nation Public Library
Pic River Elementary School, 21 Rabbit Dr., Heron Bay, ON P0T 1R0
Tel: 807-229-0630; Fax: 807-229-1944
Glenda Michano-Nabigon, Chief Executive Officer

Hilton Beach: Hilton Union Public Library
3085 Marks St., Hilton Beach, ON P0R 1G0
Tel: 705-255-3520
hiltonlibrary@hotmail.ca
hiltonunion.library.on.ca
Melanie Dorscht, CEO/Librarian/Treasurer

Holland Landing: East Gwillimbury Public Library
19513 Yonge St., Holland Landing, ON L9N 1P2
Tel: 905-836-6492; Fax: 905-836-6499
info@egpl.ca
www.egpl.ca
Social Media: www.pinterest.com/egpubliclibrary; twitter.com/EGPublicLibrary; www.facebook.com/24029821550
Loretta Whiteman, Chair
Michelle Alleyne, CEO

Hornepayne: Hornepayne Township Public Library
68 Front St., Hornepayne, ON P0M 1Z0
Tel: 807-868-2332; Fax: 807-868-3111
hpl1@ontera.net
www.olsn.ca/hornepayne
Cheryl Fort, Chair
Darnelle Hill, CEO
Lily Jones, Circulation Clerk
Margarita LeFort, Circulation Clerk

Huntsville: Huntsville Public Library
7 Minerva St. East, Huntsville, ON P1H 1W4
Tel: 705-789-5232
Other Numbers: 705-789-5232 x 3402 (Information Desk)
www.huntsvillelibrary.net
Social Media: www.youtube.com/user/HuntsvillePL; twitter.com/HuntsvillePL; www.facebook.com/huntsvillelibrary
Barb Stephen, Chair
Deborah Duce, Chief Executive Officer & Chief Librarian
705-789-5232 ext. 3407
Roberta Green, Contact, Interlibrary Loan & Technical Services
705-789-5232 ext. 3405
Julie Manczak, Contact, Adult & Senior Services
705-789-5232 ext. 3410
Amber McNair, Contact, Youth Services - Children & Teens
705-789-5232 ext. 3406

Ignace: Ignace Public Library
36 Main St., Ignace, ON P0T 1T0
Tel: 807-934-2280; Fax: 807-934-6452
ceoignacelibrary@gmail.com
www.olsn.ca/ignace
Herman Dost, CEO
Tracey Stanley, Chair

Ilderton: Middlesex County Libraries
10227 Ilderton Rd., Ilderton, ON N0M 2A0
Tel: 519-666-1201
coldstream_circ@middlesex.ca
library.middlesex.ca
Social Media: www.facebook.com/MiddlesexCountyLibrary
Lindsay Brock, CEO/Chief Librarian
519-245-8237 ext. 4022

Innisfil: Innisfil ideaLAB & Library
967 Innisfil Beach Rd., Innisfil, ON L9S 1Y8
Tel: 705-431-7410; Fax: 705-431-4898
lakeshore@innisfil.library.on.ca
www.innisfil.library.on.ca
Social Media: www.youtube.com/user/InnsfilLibrary; twitter.com/InnisfilPL; www.facebook.com/InnisfilPublicLibrary
Susan Downs, Chief Librarian & CEO
sdowns@innisfil.library.on.ca
Jayne Asselstine, Deputy Chief Librarian & Recording Secretary
Kathy Hammer, Children's Services Librarian
khammer@innisfil.library.on.ca
Debra Mann, Reference Librarian
dmann@innisfil.library.on.ca

Iron Bridge: Huron Shores Public Library
10 Main St., Iron Bridge, ON P0R 1H0
Tel: 705-843-2192
hslibrary@hotmail.ca
www.olsn.ca/huronshores
Terri Beharriell, CEO/Librarian
Pat Walker, CAP Chair

Iroquois Falls: Bibliothèque publique d'Iroquois Falls Public Library
725 Synagogue Ave., Iroquois Falls, ON P0K 1G0
Tel: 705-232-5722
ifplibrary@hotmail.com
www.olsn.ca/iroquoisfallsp
Social Media: www.facebook.com/760929243946992
Lina Joseph, CEO
Diane Gagnon, Assistant Librarian
Elaine Lutz, Clerk

Kagawong: Billings Township Public Library
18 Upper St., Kagawong, ON P0P 1J0
Tel: 705-282-2944
billingslibrary@vianet.ca
www.olsn.ca/billingslibrary

Kakabeka Falls: Conmee Public Library
Conmee Community Centre, 19 Holland Rd. West, RR#1, Kakabeka Falls, ON P0T 1W0
Tel: 807-475-5229
info@conmee.com
www.conmee.com
Social Media: www.facebook.com/conmeelibrary

Kapuskasing: Kapuskasing Public Library/ Bibliothèque publique de Kapuskasing
24 Mundy Ave., Kapuskasing, ON P5N 1P9
Tel: 705-335-3363; Fax: 705-335-2464
ibrary@kapuskasing.ca
www.kapuskasinglibrary.ca
Social Media: www.facebook.com/pages/Kapuskasing-Public-Library/123240394393542
Nicole Audet, CEO/Secretary-Treasurer
Johane Fullum-Kosowan, Manager, Library Services

Kearney: Kearney & Area Public Library
Kearney Community Centre, 8 Main St., Kearney, ON P0A 1M0
Tel: 705-636-5849; Fax: 705-636-7060
kearneylibrary@hotmail.ca
www.olsn.ca/kearney
Brandi Nolan, CEO/Librarian

Keene: Otonabee-South Monaghan Public Library
3252 County Rd. 2, Keene, ON K0L 2G0
Tel: 705-295-6814
keene_library@nexicom.net
www.otosoumon.library.on.ca
Social Media: twitter.com/LibraryOtonSMon; www.facebook.com/OSMLIBRARY
Michael Gillespie, Chair
705-295-6156
Carolanne Nadeau, Chief Executive Officer

Kemptville: North Grenville Public Library
1 Water St., Kemptville, ON K0G 1J0
Tel: 613-258-4711; Fax: 613-258-4134
info@ngpl.ca
www.ngpl.ca
Social Media: twitter.com/NGPLStaff; www.facebook.com/NorthGrenvillePL
Joan Simpson, Chair
JSimpson@ripnet.com
Susan Higgins, CEO
shiggins@ngpl.ca
Patricia Evans, Manager, Information Services
pevans@ngpl.ca
Sierra Jones, Manager, Service Delivery
sjones@ngpl.ca

Kenora: City of Kenora Public Library
24 Main St. South, Kenora, ON P9N 1S7
Tel: 807-467-2081; Fax: 807-467-2085
www.kenorapubliclibrary.org
Social Media: pinterest.com/kenoralibrary; twitter.com/KenoraLibraries; www.facebook.com/175478409525
Cathy Peacock, CEO/Librarian
cpeacock@kenora.ca
Lori Jackson, Head of Reference
ljackson@kenora.ca
Crystal Alcock, Childrens Services
cralcock@kenora.ca

Keswick: Georgina Public Libraries
90 Wexford Dr., Keswick, ON L4P 3P7
Tel: 905-476-5762; Fax: 905-476-8724
www.georginalibrary.ca
Social Media: www.flickr.com/photos/44103929@N07; twitter.com/georginalibrary; www.facebook.com/GeorginaPL
Mary Baxter, CEO/Director, Library Services & eBranch Head
905-476-7233 ext. 4522

Killaloe: Killaloe & District Public Library
1 John St., Killaloe, ON K0J 2A0
Tel: 613-757-2211
info@killaloelibrary.ca
www.killaloelibrary.ca
Social Media: twitter.com/KillaloeLibrary; www.facebook.com/166579606709402
Megan Hazelton, Chair
Nicole Zummach, Librarian/CEO
Holly Snook, Assistant Librarian

King City: King Township Public Library
1970 King Rd., King City, ON L7B 1A6
Tel: 905-833-5101
www.king-library.on.ca
Social Media: twitter.com/KingLibraries; www.facebook.com/KTPLibrary
Rona O'Banion, CEO
r.obanion@kinglibrary.ca

Kingston: Kingston Frontenac Public Library
130 Johnson St., Kingston, ON K7L 1X8
Tel: 613-549-8888
publiclibrary@kfpl.ca
www.kfpl.ca
Social Media: www.youtube.com/user/kfplweb; twitter.com/KFPL; www.facebook.com/KingstonFrontenacPL
Patricia Enright, CEO/Chief Librarian
Doug Brown, Director, Facilities & Projects
Laura Carter, Manager, Branch Operations
Shelagh Quigley, Director, Human Resources
Lester Webb, Director, Outreach & Technology

Kirkland Lake: Teck Centennial Library
10 Kirkland St. East, Kirkland Lake, ON P2N 1P1
Tel: 705-567-7966
library@tkl.ca
www.olsn.ca/kirklandlakepl
Social Media: www.facebook.com/TeckCentennialLibrary
Cheryl Lafreniere, Head Librarian

Kirkland Lake: Teck Centennial Library (Kirkland Lake)
10 Kirkland St. East, Kirkland Lake, ON P2N 1P1
Tel: 705-567-7966
library@tkl.ca
www.olsn.ca/kirklandlakepl
Social Media: www.facebook.com/TeckCentennialLibrary
Cheryl Lafreniere, CEO

Kitchener: Kitchener Public Library
85 Queen St. North, Kitchener, ON N2H 2H1
Tel: 519-743-0271; Fax: 519-743-1261
TTY: 877-614-483
Other Numbers: InfoLink: 519-743-7502
askus@kpl.org
www.kpl.org
Social Media: www.youtube.com/user/kitchenerlibrary; twitter.com/KitchLibrary; www.facebook.com/kitchenerlibrary
Mary Chevreau, CEO
mary.chevreau@kpl.org
Penny-Lynn Fielding, Director, Customer & Community Engagement
penny-lynn.fielding@kpl.org
Lesa Balch, Director, Technologies & Content
lesa.balch@kpl.org

Lanark Village: Lanark Highlands Public Library
75 George St., 2nd Fl., Lanark Village, ON K0G 1K0
Tel: 613-259-3068
lanarklibrary@gmail.com
www.lanarklibrary.ca
Ken Sinclair, Chair
Wanda Proulx, CEO
Romalda Park, Assistant Librarian

Lansdowne: Leeds & the Thousand Islands Public Library
1B Jessie St., Lansdowne, ON K0E 1L0
Tel: 613-659-3885; Fax: 613-659-4192
leeds.admin@ltipl.net
www.ltipl.net
Social Media: twitter.com/ltipl; www.facebook.com/leeds1000islandspubliclibrary
Pat Stephenson, Chair
Tara Mendez, CEO
Lisa Marston, Contact
lisa@ltipl.net

Larder Lake: Larder Lake Public Library
Larder Lake Municipal Complex, 69 Fourth Ave., Larder Lake, ON P0K 1L0
Tel: 705-643-2222; Fax: 705-643-2222
www.larderlakepubliclibrary.ca
Social Media: www.facebook.com/pages/Larder-Lake-Public-Library/196291357068815
Tracey Reid, Board Chair
Patricia Bodick, Librarian

Latchford: Latchford Public Library
66 Main St., Latchford, ON P0J 1N0
Tel: 705-676-2030
lpl@ontera.net

Leamington: Caldwell First Nation Library
14 Orange St., Leamington, ON N8H 1P5
Tel: 519-322-1766; Fax: 519-322-1533
Donna Dodge, Library Coordinator

Lindsay: City of Kawartha Lakes Public Library
190 Kent St. West, Lindsay, ON K9V 2Y6
Tel: 705-324-9411; Fax: 705-878-1859
Toll-Free: 888-822-2225
libraryadministration@city.kawarthalakes.on.ca
www.city.kawarthalakes.on.ca/residents/library-services
Social Media: facebook.com/CKLPublicLibrary
Jamie Morris, Chair
David Harvie, CEO & Chief Librarian
dharvie@city.kawarthalakes.on.ca
705-324-9411 ext. 1260

Listowel: North Perth Public Library
260 Main St. West, Listowel, ON N4W 1A1
Tel: 519-291-4621; Fax: 519-291-2235
npl@northperth.library.on.ca
www.northperth.library.on.ca
Social Media: www.facebook.com/NorthPerthPublicLibrary
Rebecca Dechert Sage, Chief Executive Officer

Little Current: Aundeck Omni Kaning First Nation Library
RR#1, Comp 21, Little Current, ON P0P 1K0
Tel: 705-368-2228; Toll-Free: 705-368-3563

Little Current: Northeastern Manitoulin & the Islands Public Library
50 Meredith St. West, Little Current, ON P0P 1K0
Tel: 705-368-2444; Fax: 705-368-0708
nemilib@vianet.on.ca
www.olsn.ca/nemi
Social Media: www.facebook.com/NEMILibrary
Judith Kift, Librarian & CEO

London: London Public Library
251 Dundas St., London, ON N6A 6H9
Tel: 519-661-4600; Fax: 519-663-5396
ceo@lpl.ca
www.londonpubliclibrary.ca
Social Media: www.youtube.com/user/LondonPublicLibrary; twitter.com/londonlibrary; www.facebook.com/londonlibrary
Gloria Leckie, Chair
gloria.leckie@lpl.london.on.ca
Susanna Hubbard Krimmer, CEO & Chief Librarian
ceo@lpl.ca
519-661-4600
Barbara Jessop, Director, Financial Services
barbara.jessop@lpl.london.on.ca
519-661-4600 ext. 5144
Anne Baker, Director, Planning & Research
anne.baker@lpl.london.on.ca
519-661-5114
Tom Travers, Director, Information Technology Services
tom.travers@lpl.london.on.ca
519-661-5100 ext. 6475
Margaret Wilkinson, Director, Customer Services & Branch Operations
margaret.wilkinson@lpl.london.on.ca
519-661-5100 ext. 5135
Ellen Hobin, Manager, Communications
ellen.hobin@lpl.london.on.ca
519-661-6403
Julie Gonyou, Senior Director, Administration & Special Projects

M'Chigeeng: M'Chigeeng First Nation Public Library
18 Lakeview Dr., M'Chigeeng, ON P0P 1G0
Tel: 705-377-5540; Fax: 705-377-5080
mchigeeng.ca
Linda Debassige, CEO

MacTier: Township of Georgian Bay Public Library
12 Muskoka Rd., MacTier, ON P0C 1H0
Tel: 705-375-5430
info@gbpl.ca
www.gbpl.ca
Social Media: twitter.com/gbpl; www.facebook.com/200394210063297
Barbara Swyers, Chief Executive Officer
705-756-8851

Madoc: Madoc Public Library
20 Davidson St., Madoc, ON K0K 2K0
Tel: 613-473-4456
www.madocpubliclibrary.com
Gayle Ketcheson, Chair
Susan Smith, Librarian
Terry Pritchard, Assistant Librarian

Magnetawan: Magnetawan Public Library
Municipal Building, 4304 North Sparks St., Magnetawan, ON P0A 1P0
Tel: 705-387-4411; Fax: 705-387-0636
magcap@ontera.net
www.magnetawanlibrary.ca
Social Media: twitter.com/MagnetawanPL; www.facebook.com/41591429313
Shirley Dorig, Board Chair
Bonnie Davidson, CEO & Head Librarian
Lorinda Makoviczki, Library Assistant

Mallorytown: Front of Yonge Public Library
76 County Rd. 5 South, Mallorytown, ON K0E 1R0
Tel: 613-923-1790; Fax: 613-923-2691
foylibrary@ripnet.com
www.library.frontofyonge.com
Donna Hunt, Chief Executive Officer

Manitouwadge: Manitouwadge Public Library
Community Centre, 2 Manitou Road, Manitouwadge, ON P0T 2C0
Tel: 807-826-3913; Fax: 807-826-4640
Janis Lamothe, Librarian/CEO

Manitowaning: Assiginack Public Library
25 Spragge St., Manitowaning, ON P0P 1N0
Tel: 705-859-2110
aplgoodtomes@email.com
assiginacklibrary.wordpress.com
Debbie Robinson, CEO/Librarian

Marathon: Marathon Public Library
22 Peninsula Rd., Marathon, ON P0T 2E0
Tel: 807-229-0740; Fax: 807-229-3336
tneedham@tbaytel.net
www.marathon.ca/article/public-library-178.asp
Tamara Needham, Head Librarian

Markham: Markham Public Library
6031 Hwy. 7, Markham, ON L3P 3A7
Tel: 905-513-7977
comments@markham.library.on.ca
www.markhampubliclibrary.ca
Social Media: twitter.com/markhamlibrary; www.facebook.com/markhamlibrary
Catherine Biss, Chief Executive Officer
cbiss@markham.library.on.ca
905-513-7977 ext. 5999
Deborah Walker, Director, Library Strategy
dwalker@markham.library.on.ca
905-513-7977 ext. 4414
Larry Pogue, Director, Administration
lpogue@markham.library.on.ca
905-513-7977 ext. 5986
Andrea Cecchetto, Manager, Learning & Growth
acecch@markham.library.on.ca
905-513-7977 ext. 4997

Markstay: Markstay Public Library
7 Pioneer St. East, Markstay, ON P0M 2W0
Tel: 705-599-3009
library@markstay-warren.ca
www.olsn.ca/markstay-warrenpl
Social Media: www.facebook.com/MarkstayWarrenLibrary

Marmora: Marmora & Lake Public Library
37 Forsyth St., Marmora, ON K0K 2M0
Tel: 613-472-3122
info@marmoralibrary.ca
www.marmoralibrary.ca
Social Media: www.facebook.com/marmoralibrary
Joan Kennedy, Chair
Sheryl Price, Chief Executive Officer
Tammie Adams, Assistant Librarian

Massey: Massey & Township Public Library
185 Grove St., Massey, ON P0P 1P0
Tel: 705-865-2641; Fax: 705-865-2641
infomasseylibrary@gmail.com
www.masseylibrary.com
Social Media: www.facebook.com/masseyandtownshippubliclibrary
Elizabeth Gamble, CEO
Ruth DeClerck, Assistant Librarian

Massey: Sagamok Anishnawbek First Nation Public Library
4007 Espaniel Rd., Massey, ON P0P 1P0
Tel: 705-865-2034; Fax: 705-865-3307
Colleen Eshkakogan, CEO
eshkakogan_colleen@sagamok.ca

Matheson: Black River-Matheson Public Library
352 Second St., Matheson, ON P0K 1N0
Tel: 705-273-2760
brmlibrary@hotmail.com
www.olsn.ca/blackriver-matheson/
Karen Ukrainetz, CEO/Librarian

Mattagami: Mattagami First Nation Public Library
1 White Pine St., Mattagami, ON P0M 1W0
Tel: 705-894-2003; Fax: 705-894-2386
reception@mattagami.com
Patsy Mckay, Librarian

Mattawa: Mattawa Public Library
370 Pine St., Mattawa, ON P0H 1V0
Tel: 705-744-5550; Fax: 705-744-1714
mplibrary@efni.com
www.olsn.ca/mattawa
Social Media: www.facebook.com/JohnDixonPublicLibrary
Lise Moore Asselin, CEO

Mattice: Mattice - Val Côté Public Library/ Bibliothèque publique de Mattice - Val Côté
500 Hwy. 11, Mattice, ON P0L 1T0
Tel: 705-364-5301; Fax: 705-364-6431
biblimat@ntl.sympatico.ca
www.olsn.ca/mattice-valcote
Michelle Salonen, Librarian
Nancy Boucher, Library Assistant

Maynooth: Hastings Highlands Public Library
33011 Hwy. 62 North, Maynooth, ON K0L 2S0
Tel: 613-338-2262; Fax: 613-338-3292
hastingshighlandslibrary@gmail.com
www.hastingshighlandslibrary.ca
Social Media: www.facebook.com/HastingsHighlandsPublicLibrary
Kathy Irwin, Chair
Kimberly McMunn, CEO/Librarian
Kristin Seaborn, Assistant Librarian

McKellar: McKellar Township Public Library
701 Hwy. 124, McKellar, ON P0G 1C0
Tel: 705-389-2611; Fax: 705-389-2611
mckellarlib@vianet.ca
www.mckellarpubliclibrary.ca
Joan Ward, Librarian
Terri Short, Assistant Librarian

Meaford: Meaford Public Library
15 Trowbridge St. West, Meaford, ON N4L 1V4
Tel: 519-538-1060; Fax: 519-538-1808
info@meafordlibrary.on.ca
www.meafordlibrary.on.ca
Social Media: www.pinterest.com/meafordlibrary/; www.facebook.com/meafordpubliclibrary
Cathie Lee, Acting CEO
Michael Crowley, Children's Coordinator
Lynne Fascinato, Contact, Interlibrary Loan
David Port, Chair

Merrickville: Merrickville Public Library
446 Main St. West, Merrickville, ON K0G 1N0
Tel: 613-269-3326; Fax: 613-269-3326
merrickville_library@bellnet.ca
www.village.merrickville-wolford.on.ca/mpl/index.html
Mary Kate Laphen, Librarian

Midhurst: Springwater Township Public Library
12 Finlay Mill Rd., Midhurst, ON L0L 1X0
Tel: 705-737-5650; *Fax:* 705-737-3594
midhurst.library@springwater.ca
springwater.library.on.ca
Social Media: pinterest.com/springwaterpl; twitter.com/SpringwaterLib; www.facebook.com/82039213514
Lynn Patkau, Chief Librarian

Midland: Midland Public Library
320 King St., Midland, ON L4R 3M6
Tel: 705-526-4216; *Fax:* 705-526-1474
www.midlandlibrary.com
Social Media: twitter.com/midland_library; www.facebook.com/midlandlibrary
John E. Swick, Chair
Bill Molesworth, Chief Executive Officer
bmolesworth@town.midland.on.ca
Betty Fullerton, Head, Technical Services
Gail Griffith, Head, Adult & Information Services
Bonnie Reynolds, Head, Juvenile Services

Millbrook: Cavan Monaghan Libraries
Old Millbrook School, 1 Dufferin St., Millbrook, ON L0A 1G0
Tel: 705-932-2919
www.cavanmonaghanlibraries.ca
Social Media: twitter.com/CMLibraries; www.facebook.com/CavanMonaghanLibraries

Milton: Milton Public Library
1010 Main St. East, Milton, ON L9T 6H7
Tel: 905-875-2665; *Fax:* 905-875-4324
TTY: 905-875-155
information@mpl.on.ca
www.mpl.on.ca
Social Media: twitter.com/Milton_Library
Ken Jacobsen, Chair
h_kjaco@cogeco.ca
Leslie Fitch, Chief Executive Officer
leslie.fitch@mpl.on.ca
905-875-2665 ext. 3252

Milverton: Perth East Public Library
19 Mill St. East, Milverton, ON N0K 1M0
Tel: 519-595-8395; *Fax:* 519-595-2943
pel@pcin.on.ca
www.pertheast.library.on.ca
Social Media: facebook.com/PerthEastPublicLibrary
Cindy Dunbar, CEO

Mindemoya: Central Manitoulin Public Libraries
6020 Hwy. 542, Mindemoya, ON P0P 1S0
Tel: 705-377-5334
bookworm@amtelecom.net
www.centralmanitoulin.ca/central-manitoulin/library
Penny George, Chair
Claire Cline, CEO/Chief Librarian
Mel Delange, Assistant Librarian
Geraldine Carlisle, Library Assistant

Mine Centre: Seine River First Nation Public Library
c/o Public Library, Mine Centre, ON P0W 1H0
Tel: 807-599-2870; *Fax:* 807-599-2871
srlibrary@bellnet.ca
www.seineriverfirstnation.ca
Glenda Potson, Librarian
Susan Johnson, Librarian

Mississauga: Mississauga Library System
301 Burnhamthorpe Rd. West, Mississauga, ON L5B 3Y3
Tel: 905-615-3500; *Fax:* 905-615-3625
info.library@mississauga.ca
www.mississauga.ca/portal/residents/library
Social Media: twitter.com/mississaugalib; www.facebook.com/mississaugalibrary
Rose Vespa, Director, Library Services
rose.vespa@mississauga.ca
905-615-3200 ext. 3601

Mitchell: West Perth Public Library
105 St. Andrew St., Mitchell, ON N0K 1N0
Tel: 519-348-9234; *Fax:* 519-348-4540
wpl@pcin.on.ca
www.westperth.library.on.ca
Social Media: www.facebook.com/310691049146
Charles Fitzsimmons, Chair
Caroline Shewburg, Chief Librarian

Mobert: Pic Mobert First Nation Public Library
PO Box 634, Mobert, ON P0M 2J0
Tel: 807-822-1594; *Fax:* 807-822-1578
principal@picmobert.ca

Moonbeam: Bibliothèque publique de Moonbeam/ Moonbeam Public Library
53, av St-Aubin, Moonbeam, ON P0L 1V0
Tel: 705-367-2462; *Fax:* 705-367-2120
biblio@moonbeam.ca
biblio.moonbeam.ca
Gisèle Belisle, Directrice-Responsable
Angèle Albert, Directrice adjointe

Morson: Big Grassy First Nation Public Library
Pegamigaabo School, 513 Beach Rd., Morson, ON P0W 1J0
Tel: 807-488-5916; *Fax:* 807-488-5345
Toll-Free: 800-265-3379
library@biggrassy.ca
biggrassy.ca/library
Amanda Morrison, CEO

Muncey: Chippewas of the Thames
RR#1, 328 Chippewa Rd., Muncey, ON N0L 1Y0
Tel: 519-289-0008
cottfn.com/library
Kodi Chrisjohn, Librarian

Murillo: Oliver Paipoonge Public Library
1 Baxendale Rd., Murillo, ON P0T 2G0
Tel: 807-935-2729; *Fax:* 807-935-2161
oplibrary@tbaytel.net
www.olsn.ca/OliverPaipoonge
Social Media: www.facebook.com/317003395098369
Maxine McCulloch, CEO/Librarian

Napanee: Lennox & Addington County Library
97 Thomas St. East, Napanee, ON K7R 4B9
Tel: 613-354-4883; *Fax:* 613-354-3112
www.countylibrary.ca
Social Media: instagram.com/countylibraries; twitter.com/LAPubLib; www.facebook.com/LandALibrary
Catherine Coles, Manager of Library Services
ccoles@lennox-addington.on.ca
Julie Wendland, Readers' Services Coordinator
jwendland@lennox-addington.on.ca
613-354-4883 ext. 3371
Patricia Richard, Programming & Outreach Coordinator
Prichard@lennox-addington.on.ca
613-354-4883 ext. 3510
Coleen McFarlane, Technical Assistant
cmcfarlane@lennox-addington.on.ca
613-354-4883 ext. 3232

Naughton: Atikameksheng Anishnawbek First Nation Public Library
212 Maani St., RR#1, Naughton, ON P0M 2M0
Tel: 705-692-9901; *Fax:* 705-692-5010
library@wlfn.com
www.wlfn.com
Mary Fraser, Librarian

Nestor Falls: Ojibways of Onigaming First Nation Public Library
Mikinaak Onigaming School, 212 Mikinaak Rd., Nestor Falls, ON P0X 1K0
Tel: 807-484-2612; *Fax:* 807-484-2737
onigaming@hotmail.com
Geraldine Kelly, Librarian

Newmarket: Newmarket Public Library
438 Park Ave., Newmarket, ON L3Y 1W1
Tel: 905-953-5110; *Fax:* 905-953-5104
npl@newmarketpl.ca
www.newmarketpl.ca
Social Media: www.youtube.com/user/NewmarketLibrary; twitter.com/newmarktlibrary; www.facebook.com/pages/Newmarket-Public-Library/247080242075
Todd Kyle, CEO
Todd Kyle, Chief Executive Officer
Linda Peppiatt, Deputy Chief Executive Officer
Simon Chong, Contact, Systems
Heather Halliday, Contact, Adult Services
Susan Hoffman, Contact, Children's Services
Jennifer Leveridge, Contact, Community Services
Michael Russell, Contact, Digital Services

Neyaashiinigmiing: Ninda Kikaendjigae Wigammik Library
25 Maadookii Subdivision, RR#5, Neyaashiinigmiing, ON N0H 2T0
Tel: 519-534-1508; *Fax:* 519-534-2130
www.nawash.ca/index.cfm?page=library
Daphne Johnston, Supervisor
daphnejohnston@nawashfn.ca

Niagara Falls: Niagara Falls Public Library
4848 Victoria Ave., Niagara Falls, ON L2E 4C5
Tel: 905-356-8080; *Fax:* 905-356-7004
Other Numbers: Children's Department, Phone: 905-356-4053
nfpl@nflibrary.ca
www.nflibrary.ca
Social Media: facebook.com/8352228860
Monika Seymour, Chief Librarian
Susan DiBattista, Manager, Public Services
Janet Martin, Manager, Audiovisual & Technical Services
Keith Muma, Manager, Buildings & Property
Andrew Porteus, Manager, Reference & Information Services
Inge Saczkowski, Manager, Children's Services

Niagara on the Lake: Niagara on the Lake Public Library
10 Anderson Lane, Niagara on the Lake, ON L0S 1J0
Tel: 905-468-2023; *Fax:* 905-468-3334
www.notlpubliclibrary.org
Social Media: pinterest.com/notlpl; twitter.com/notl_library; www.facebook.com/210765253379
Cathy Simpson, Chief Librarian
csimpson@notl.org
905-468-2023 ext. 203
Laura Tait, Library Manager
ltait@notl.org
905-468-2023 ext. 206

Nipigon: Nipigon Public Library
52 Front St., Nipigon, ON P0T 2J0
Tel: 807-887-3142
nipigonpl@gmail.com
www.nipigon.net/residents/nipigon-public-library
Sumiye Sugawara, CEO/Librarian

Nobel: Shawanaga First Nation Public Library
2 Church St., Nobel, ON P0G 1G0
Tel: 705-366-2029; *Fax:* 705-366-2013
Chelsie Sousa, CEO
csousa_20@hotmail.com

North Bay: North Bay Public Library
271 Worthington St. East, North Bay, ON P1B 1H1
Tel: 705-474-4830; *Fax:* 705-495-4010
library@cityofnorthbay.ca
www.cityofnorthbay.ca/library
Social Media: twitter.com/North_BayPL; www.facebook.com/NorthBayPublicLibrary
Ravil Veli, CEO
ravil.veli@cityofnorthbay.ca
Rebecca Larocque, Head, Information Services
Judith Bouman, Head, Adult Services
Nora Elliott-Coutts, Head, Children's Services

Norwood: Asphodel-Norwood Public Library
2363 County Rd. #45, Norwood, ON K0L 2V0
Tel: 705-639-2228
norwood@anpl.org
www.anpl.org
Social Media: www.facebook.com/175172212505525
Krisandra Van Luven, CEO/ Head Librarian

Oakville: Oakville Public Library
120 Navy St., Oakville, ON L6J 2Z4
Tel: 905-815-2042; *Fax:* 905-815-2024
Other Numbers: Renewals & Holds, Phone: 905-815-2044
oplreference@oakville.ca
www.opl.on.ca
Social Media: twitter.com/OakvilleLibrary; www.facebook.com/184886721537133
Charlotte Meissner, Chief Executive Officer
charlotte.meissner@oakville.ca
905-815-2031
Janice Kullas, Director, Branch Services & Deputy CEO
janice.kullas@oakville.ca
905-815-2035
Tara Wong, Director, Collections & Technologies
tara.wong@oakville.ca
905-815-2027
Melanie Burgess, Director, Community Engagement
melanie.burgess@oakville.ca
905-815-2014
Susan Kun, Manager, Branch Support
susan.kun@oakville.ca
905-815-2042 ext. 5141
Nancy LeGrow, Supervisor, Cataloguing & Acquisitions
nancy.legrow@oakville.ca
905-815-2042 ext. 5049
Leslie Sutherland, Manager, Collections
leslie.sutherland@oakville.ca
905-815-2042 ext. 2029

Florence De Dominicis, Manager, Programs & Outreach
florence.dedominicis@oakville.ca
905-815-2042 ext. 5189

Ohsweken: **Six Nations Public Library**
1679 Chiefswood Rd., Ohsweken, ON N0A 1M0
Tel: 519-445-2954; *Fax:* 800-788-5289
info@snpl.ca
www.snpl.ca
Social Media: twitter.com/@6NationsLibrary;
www.facebook.com/pages/Six-Nations-Public-Library/30295313882
Sabrina Redwing Saunders, CEO
saunders@snpl.ca

Opasatika: **La Bibliothèque d'Opasatika/ Opasatika Public Library**
6, rue St-Antione, Opasatika, ON P0L 1Z0
Tél: 705-369-3421; *Téléc:* 705-369-3098
opasatikabiblio@hotmail.ca
opasatika.net
Joanne Lallier, Bibliothécaire

Orangeville: **Orangeville Public Library**
1 Mill St., Orangeville, ON L9W 2M2
Tel: 519-941-0610; *Fax:* 519-941-4698
TTY: 519-942-051
infolibrary@orangeville.ca
www.orangeville.library.on.ca
Social Media: twitter.com/orangevilleont;
www.facebook.com/pages/Orangeville-Ontario/359934204153
Darla Fraser, Chief Librarian
dfraser@orangeville.ca
Kathryn Creelman, Coordinator, Public Services
kcreelman@orangeville.ca
519-941-0610 ext. 5232

Orillia: **Orillia Public Library**
36 Mississaga St. West, Orillia, ON L3V 3A6
Tel: 705-325-2338; *Fax:* 705-327-1744
Other Numbers: Circulation: 705-325-2552; Child Svs.: 705-325-2559
info@orilliapubliclibrary.ca
www.orilliapubliclibrary.ca
Social Media: twitter.com/orillialibrary;
www.facebook.com/OrilliaPublicLibrary
Suzanne Campbell, CEO
Suzanne Campbell, Chief Executive Officer
Kelli Absalom, Contact, Adult Services
Joyce Dempsey, Contact, Circulation Services
David Rowe, Contact, Technical Services & Systems
Amanda Sist, Contact, Children's Services
Jayne Turvey, Contact, Community Services

Oshawa: **Oshawa Public Library**
65 Bagot St., Oshawa, ON L1H 1N2
Tel: 905-579-6111; *Fax:* 905-433-8107
admin@oshawalibrary.on.ca
www.oshawalibrary.on.ca
Social Media: twitter.com/OshawaLibraries;
www.facebook.com/oshawapubliclibrary
Frances Newman, CEO
Margaret Wallace, Director, Collection Management
Marc Bower, Manager, Information Technology

Ottawa: **Ottawa Public Library/ Bibliothèque publique d'Ottawa**
120 Metcalfe St., Ottawa, ON K1P 5M2
Tel: 613-580-2940
InfoService@BiblioOttawaLibrary.ca
www.biblioottawalibrary.ca
Social Media: www.pinterest.com/oplbpo; twitter.com/opl_bpo;
www.facebook.com/BiblioOttawaLibrary
Danielle McDonald, Chief Executive Officer
Danielle.McDonald@biblioottawalibrary.ca
Elaine Condos, Division Manager, Central Library Project
Elaine.Condos@biblioottawalibrary.ca
Vacant , Division Manager, Corporate Services
Catherine Seaman, Division Manager, Branch Operations
catherine.seaman@BiblioOttawaLibrary.ca
Monique Brûlé, Acting Division Manager, Content & Technology
monique.brule@biblioottawalibrary.ca
Anna Basile, Manager, Planning & Board Support
anna.basile@BiblioOttawaLibrary.ca
Ann Archer, Acting Manager, Content Services
ann.archer@biblioottawalibrary.ca
Craig Ginther, Manager, Technology Services
Craig.Ginther@biblioottawalibrary.ca
Otto Dos Santos, ActingManager, Materials Handling
Micheline McTiernan, Manager, Organizational Development
Matthew Pritz, Manager, Finance and Business Services
Matthew.Pritz@ottawa.ca
Richard Stark, Manager, Facilities Development
Richard.Stark@biblioottawalibrary.ca
Elizabeth Thornley, Manager, Program Development
elizabeth.thornley@BiblioOttawaLibrary.ca
Alexandra Yarrow, Manager, Alternative Services
alexandra.yarrow@BiblioOttawaLibrary.ca

Owen Sound: **Owen Sound & North Grey Union Public Library**
824 - 1st Ave. West, Owen Sound, ON N4K 4K4
Tel: 519-376-6623; *Fax:* 519-376-7170
info@owensound.library.on.ca
www.owensound.library.on.ca
Social Media: www.facebook.com/OSNGUPL
Tim Nicholls, Chief Librarian/CEO

Paris: **County of Brant Public Library**
12 William St., Paris, ON N3L 1K7
Tel: 519-442-2433; *Fax:* 519-442-7582
www.brant.library.on.ca
Gay Kozak Selby, CEO
Larry Stewart, Chair, Library Board
Christine Scrivener, Branch Coordinator

Parry Sound: **Parry Sound Public Library**
29 Mary St., Parry Sound, ON P2A 1E3
Tel: 705-746-9601
pspl@vianet.ca
www.parrysoundlibrary.ca
Social Media:
www.facebook.com/pages/Parry-Sound-Public-Library/346576685525
Andrea Gasper, CEO

Parry Sound: **Seguin Township Public Library**
15 Humphrey Dr., Parry Sound, ON P2A 2W8
Tel: 705-732-4526
humphreylibrary@gmail.com
www.seguinpubliclibraries.ca
Social Media: twitter.com/SeguinPL;
www.facebook.com/SeguinPublicLibraries
Rosemary Rae, Chief Executive Officer
ceoseguinlibrary@gmail.com

Parry Sound: **Wasauksing First Nation Public Library**
1126 Geewadin Rd, Lane G, Parry Sound, ON P2A 2X1
Tel: 705-746-1052; *Fax:* 705-746-2933
librarian@wasauksing.ca
firstnation.ca/wasauksing/wasauksing-public-library
Fran King, CEO
Tina Tabobandung, Education Director
705-726-2531

Pawitik: **Naotkamegwanning Public Library**
1004 Baibombeh Rd., Pawitik, ON P0X 1L0
Tel: 807-226-5710; *Fax:* 807-226-1066
nfnpl2014@live.ca
Natalie Durette, Librarian
807-226-5710

Pembroke: **Pembroke Public Library**
237 Victoria St., Pembroke, ON K8A 4K5
Tel: 613-732-8844; *Fax:* 613-732-1116
fineprint@pembrokelibrary.ca
www.pembroke.library.on.ca
Social Media: www.facebook.com/30360225984
Margaret Mau, CEO/Secretary-Treasurer
mmau@pembrokelibrary.ca

Penetanguishene: **Penetanguishene Public Library**
24 Simcoe St., Penetanguishene, ON L9M 1R6
Tel: 705-549-7164; *Fax:* 705-549-3932
www.penetanguishene.library.on.ca
Cynthia Coté, CEO
ccote@penetanguishene.library.on.ca
Jenet Ryan, Head, Public & Technical Services

Perth: **Perth & District Union Public Library**
30 Herriott St., Perth, ON K7H 1T2
Tel: 613-267-1224; *Fax:* 613-267-7899
info@perthunionlibrary.ca
www.perthunionlibrary.ca
Elizabeth Goldman, CEO/Head Librarian
egoldman@perthunionlibrary.ca

Petawawa: **Petawawa Public Library**
16 Civic Centre Rd., Petawawa, ON K8H 3H5
Tel: 613-687-2227; *Fax:* 613-687-2527
info@petawawapubliclibrary.ca
www.petawawapubliclibrary.ca
Social Media: www.facebook.com/102474823136454
C.M. Goldsmith, Librarian

Peterborough: **Peterborough Public Library**
345 Aylmer St. North, Peterborough, ON K9H 3V7
Tel: 705-745-5382; *Fax:* 705-745-8958
comments@city.peterborough.on.ca
www.peterborough.library.on.ca
Social Media: www.facebook.com/PeterboroughLibrary
Jennifer Jones, Head Librarian
jjones@city.peterborough.on.ca
705-745-5382 ext. 2382
Becky Waldman, Marketing & Communications Coordinator
bwaldman@city.peterborough.on.ca
705-745-5382 ext. 2324

Pickerel: **Henvey Inlet First Nation Public Library**
354B Pickerel River Rd., Pickerel, ON P0G 1J0
Tel: 705-857-2222; *Fax:* 705-857-3021
Debbie Fox, Librarian
maheengun12@hotmail.com
705-857-2331 ext. 225

Pickering: **Pickering Public Library**
1 The Esplanade, Pickering, ON L1V 6K7
Tel: 905-831-6265; *Fax:* 905-831-6927
Toll-Free: 888-831-6266
TTY: 905-831-278
Other Numbers: Renewals: 905-831-8209
help@picnet.org
www.picnet.org
Social Media: www.youtube.com/user/PickeringLibrary;
twitter.com/pickeringpublib; www.facebook.com/PPLibrary
Cathy Grant, CEO
cathyg@picnet.org
905-831-6265 ext. 6236
Elaine Bird, Director of Support Services
elaineb@picnet.org
905-831-6265 ext. 6231
Kathy Williams, Director of Public Services
kathyw@picnet.org
905-831-6265 ext. 6251

Picton: **County of Prince Edward Public Library**
208 Main St., Picton, ON K0K 2T0
Tel: 613-476-5962; *Fax:* 613-476-3325
crenaud@peclibrary.org
www.peclibrary.org
Barbara Sweet, CEO
Dianne Cranshaw, Assistant CEO & Contact, Interlibrary Loan
613-399-2023
Krista Richardson, Manager, Archives
613-399-2023
Kate Konkin, Coordinator, Seniors Programs
613-476-5962
Eric Pierce, Coordinator, Information Technology & Computer Training
613-476-5962
Liz Zylstra, Coordinator, Youth Programs
613-476-5962
Christine Renaud, Branch Manager
crenaud@peclibrary.org
613-476-5962

Pikwàkanagàn: **Algonquins of Pikwakanagan Library**
c/o 1657A Mishomis Inamo, Pikwàkanagàn, ON K0J 1X0
Tel: 613-625-2402; *Fax:* 613-625-2332
library@pikwakanagan.ca
algonquinsofpikwakanagan.com/library.php
Estelle Amikons, Librarian

Port Carling: **Township of Muskoka Lakes Libraries**
69 Joseph St., Port Carling, ON P0B 1J0
Tel: 705-765-5650; *Fax:* 705-765-0422
MuskokaLakes@pclib.ca
users.muskoka.com/library
Social Media: twitter.com/MuskokaLakesPL;
www.facebook.com/155634271143907
Linda McAuley, Chair
Sheila Durand, Chief Executive Officer & Chief Librarian
Nancy Doran, Library Assistant
Cathy Duck, Library Assistant
Lorna MacFarlane, Library Assistant
Barb Neibert, Library Assistant

Port Colborne: **Port Colborne Public Library**
310 King St., Port Colborne, ON L3K 4H1
Tel: 905-834-6512; *Fax:* 905-835-5775
library@portcolborne.ca
www.portcolbornelibrary.org
Social Media: www.facebook.com/340178134131
Jennifer R. Parry, Director of Library Services
Derek Miller, Chair
Robert Heil, Chief Administrative Office
CAO@portcolborne.ca

Port Elgin: Bruce County Public Library
1243 MacKenzie Rd., Port Elgin, ON N0H 2C6
Tel: 519-832-6935; *Fax:* 519-832-9000
libraryinfo@brucecounty.on.ca
library.brucecounty.on.ca
Social Media: instagram.com/brucecountypubliclibrary; twitter.com/BruceCountyLib; www.facebook.com/138293532885246
Melissa Legacy, Director
mlegacy@brucecounty.on.ca
Nicole Charles, Assistant Director, Branch Services
ncharles@brucecounty.on.ca
519-832-6935
Dan Blacklock, Collection Development Coordinator
dblacklock@brucecounty.on.ca
Donna Morey, Interlibrary Loan Coordinator
dmorey@brucecounty.on.ca
Christine Wood, Technical Services Coordinator
cwood@brucecounty.on.ca
Lorrainee Noseworthy, Administrative Assistant
lnoseworthy@brucecounty.on.ca

Port Hope: Port Hope Public Library
31 Queen St., Port Hope, ON L1A 2Y8
Tel: 905-885-4712; *Fax:* 905-885-4181
library@porthope.ca
www.phpl.ca
Social Media: www.facebook.com/pages/Port-Hope-Public-Library/301945576498428
Margaret Scott, CEO/Chief Librarian
mscott@porthope.ca
Alison M.B. Houston, Deputy Chief Librarian
ahouston@porthope.ca

Port Loring: Port Loring & District (Argyle) Public Library
11767 Hwy. 522, Port Loring, ON P0H 1Y0
Tel: 705-472-8170
ArgyleCommunityLibrary@hotmail.com
www.olsn.ca/argylecommunitylibrary
Social Media: www.facebook.com/pages/Argyle-Community-Library/139348189451348
Jennifer Fry, Library Services Contact

Port McNicoll: Tay Township Public Libraries
715 - 4th Ave., Port McNicoll, ON L0K 1R0
Tel: 705-534-3511; *Fax:* 705-534-3511
library@tay.ca
www.tay.library.on.ca
Heather Delong, Head Librarian

Port Perry: Mississaugas of Scugog Island First Nation Library
Health & Resource Centre, 22600 Island Rd., Port Perry, ON L9L 1B6
Tel: 905-985-1826; *Fax:* 905-985-7958
Toll-Free: 877-688-0988
library@scugogfirstnation.com
M. McLean, Library Contact
mmclean@scugogfirstnation.com
905-985-1826 ext. 221

Port Perry: Scugog Memorial Public Library
231 Water St., Port Perry, ON L9L 1A8
Tel: 905-985-7686
info@scugoglibrary.ca
www.scugoglibrary.ca
Social Media: youtube.com/watch?v=jmDAerNnNOw; twitter.com/ScugogLibrary; www.facebook.com/scugoglibrary
Betty Somerville, Chair
Amy Caughlin, Chief Librarian
acaughlin@scugoglibrary.ca

Powassan: Powassan & District Union Public Library
324 Clark St., Powassan, ON P0H 1Z0
Tel: 705-724-3618; *Fax:* 705-724-5525
mrosset@ontera.net
powlib.www2.onlink.net
Social Media: twitter.com/powassanlibrary; www.facebook.com/powassanlibrary
Marie Rosset, CEO

Prescott: Prescott Public Library
360 Dibble St. West, Prescott, ON K0E 1T0
Tel: 613-925-4340; *Fax:* 613-925-0100
library@prescott.ca
www.prescott.ca/residential/library
Jane McGuire, Chief Librarian/CEO
Susen Kaylo Raas, Assistant Librarian
Linda Doris, Library Assistant
Roxanne Brown, Library Assistant

Rainy River: Rainy River Public Library
334 - 4th St., Rainy River, ON P0W 1L0
Tel: 807-852-3375; *Fax:* 807-852-3375
libraryrr@gmail.com
www.rainyriverlibrary.com
Social Media: facebook.com/164559081453
Michael Dawber, Librarian/CEO

Rama: Chippewas of Rama First Nation Public Library
6147 Rama Rd., Rama, ON L3V 6H6
Tel: 705-325-3611; *Fax:* 705-325-2801
Sherry Lawson, Administrator of Heritage Services
sherryl@ramafirstnation.ca
705-325-3611 ext. 1437

Red Lake: Red Lake Public Library
117 Howey St., Red Lake, ON P0V 2M0
Tel: 807-727-2230; *Fax:* 807-727-2230
redlakepubliclibraries@hotmail.com
www.olsn.ca/redlake

Red Rock: Red Rock Public Library
42 Salls St., Red Rock, ON P0T 2P0
Tel: 807-886-2558
rrocklib@gmail.com
www.olsn.ca/redrock/
Social Media: www.pinterest.com/redrocklib; twitter.com/RedRockLibrary; www.facebook.com/pages/Red-Rock-Public-Library/142529769158602
Nancy Carrier, Chief Librarian

Redbridge: Phelps Public Library
9311 Hwy. 63, Redbridge, ON P0H 2A0
Tel: 705-663-2220
phelpspubliclibrary@intera.net
phelpstownship.com/Library/Phelps_Library.htm
Beverly Reynolds, Librarian

Renfrew: Renfrew Public Library
13 Railway Ave. East, Renfrew, ON K7V 3A9
Tel: 613-432-8151; *Fax:* 613-432-7680
renlib@renfrew.library.on.ca
www.town.renfrew.on.ca/library/
Social Media: twitter.com/renfrewreads; www.facebook.com/291766994831
Bettijane O'Neill, Chief Librarian
Susan Klinck, Head, Children Services

Richard's Landing: St Joseph Township Public Library
1240 Richard St., Richard's Landing, ON P0R 1J0
Tel: 705-246-2353
sjtlibrary@gmail.com
www.olsn.ca/stjoseph
Kristina Leith, Librarian/Treasurer/CEO

Richmond Hill: Richmond Hill Public Library
1 Atkinson St., Richmond Hill, ON L4C 0H5
Tel: 905-884-9288; *Fax:* 905-884-6544
Other Numbers: Administrative: 905-770-0310
www.rhpl.richmondhill.on.ca
Social Media: twitter.com/rhpltweets; www.facebook.com/rhpl.news
Louise Procter Maio, CEO
Catherine Charles, Corporate Relations Officer
ccharles@rhpl.ca
905-770-0310 ext. 300

Rockland: Clarence-Rockland Public Library/ Bibliothèque publique de Clarence-Rockland
#2, 1525 du Parc Ave., Rockland, ON K4K 1C3
Tel: 613-446-5680
biblioinfo@biblibclarence-rockland.ca.
www.clarence-rockland.com
Nancie Bolduc, President, Library Board
Daniel Noel, Chief Executive Officer
Danielle Denis, Libary Technician

Roseneath: Alderville Learning Centre & Library
11696 - 2nd Line Rd., Roseneath, ON K0K 2X0
Tel: 905-352-2488; *Fax:* 905-352-1080
Other Numbers: Learning Centre, Phone: 905-352-2793
aldervillelearningcentre@eagle.ca
www.aldervillelearningcentre.com
Shannon Catherwood, Librarian
Keri Gray, Learning Centre Coordinator

Russell: Bibliothèque publique du Canton de Russell/ Russell Township Public Library
1053 Concession St., Russell, ON K4R 1E1
Tel: 613-445-5331; *Fax:* 613-445-8014
mylibrary@russellbiblio.com
www.russellbiblio.com
Social Media: www.flickr.com/photos/russellbiblio; twitter.com/russellbiblio; www.facebook.com/159607974060274
Claire Dionne, CEO
claire.dionne@russellbiblio.com
613-445-5331
Hélène Quesnel, Branch Head, Russell
helene.quesnel@russellbiblio.com
613-445-5331

Sachigo Lake: Sachigo Lake First Nation Public Library
c/o Martin McKay Memorial School, Sachigo Lake, ON P0V 2P0
Tel: 807-595-2526; *Fax:* 807-595-1305
olsn.ent.sirsidynix.net/client/en_US/sachigo
Annie Tait, Librarian
taitannie@gmail.com

Saint-Isidore: Bibliothèque publique de la municipalité de La Nation/ Nation Municipality Public Library
25, rue de l'Aréna, Saint-Isidore, ON K0C 2B0
Tel: 613-524-2252; *Fax:* 613-524-2545
biblioinfo@nationmun.ca
www.nationmunbiblio.ca
Social Media: www.flickr.com/photos/librarybooks; twitter.com/BiblioLaNation; www.facebook.com/109251539103571
France Lamoureux, Chair
Jeanne Leroux, Directrice général
jeanneleroux@nationmun.ca
613-254-2252
Monique Thèorêt Quesnel, Bibliotechnienne, Services techniques
mtheoret@nationmun.ca
Lyne Paquette, Assistante de bibliothèque
lpaquette@nationmun.ca

Saugeen: Saugeen First Nation Library
812 French Bay Rd., Saugeen, ON N0H 2L0
Tel: 519-797-5986; *Fax:* 519-797-5987
www.saugeenfirstnation.ca
Theresa Gill, CEO

Sault Ste Marie: Batchewana First Nation
236 Frontenac St., Sault Ste Marie, ON P6A 5K9
Tel: 705-759-0914; *Fax:* 705-759-9171
Toll-Free: 877-236-2632
www.batchewana.ca

Sault Ste Marie: Prince Township Library/ Bibliothèque publique du Canton Prince
3042 - 2nd Line West, RR#6, Sault Ste Marie, ON P6A 6K4
Tel: 705-779-3653; *Fax:* 705-779-2725
ptpl@twp.prince.on.ca
www.olsn.ca/ptpl
Social Media: www.facebook.com/107899082570057
Rita Wagner, Chief Executive Officer

Sault Ste Marie: Sault Ste Marie Public Library
50 East St., Sault Ste Marie, ON P6A 3C3
Tel: 705-759-5230; *Fax:* 705-759-8752
admin.library@cityssm.on.ca
www.ssmpl.ca
Social Media: www.facebook.com/SSMPL
Christopher Rous, Chair
Roxanne Toth-Rissanen, Director, Public Libraries
r.rissanen@cityssm.on.ca
Mark Jones, Deputy Director
m.jones@cityssm.on.ca
Chris Rumas, Manager, Digital Literacy
c.rumas@cityssm.on.ca
Matthew MacDonald, Manager, Public Service
m.macdonald@cityssm.on.ca

Savant Lake: Savant Lake Community Library
General Delivery, Savant Lake, ON P0V 2S0
Tel: 807-584-2242

Schreiber: Schreiber Public Library
314 Scotia St., Schreiber, ON P0T 2S0
Tel: 807-824-2477; *Fax:* 807-824-2996
libinfo@schreiber.ca
www.schreiberlibrary.ca
Social Media: www.youtube.com/user/schreiberlibrary; www.facebook.com/160900397294463
Rona Godin, Chair

Donna Mikeluk, Head Librarian/CEO
Linda Williamson, Assistant Librarian

***Shannonville:* Tyendinaga Township Public Library**
852 Melrose Rd., RR#1, Shannonville, ON K0K 3A0
Tel: 613-967-0606; *Fax:* 613-967-0606
tyendinagatwplibrary@xplornet.ca
www.ttpl.ca
Tanya Stapley-Wilson, Librarian/CEO

***Shelburne:* Shelburne Public Library**
201 Owen Sound St., Shelburne, ON L9V 3L2
Tel: 519-925-2168; *Fax:* 519-925-6555
info@shelburnelibrary.ca
www.shelburnelibrary.ca
Social Media: www.facebook.com/195224210500255
Rose Dotten, CEO/Head Librarian
rdotten@shelburnelibrary.ca

***Sheshegwaning:* Sheshegwaning Public Library**
PO Box 1, Sheshegwaning, ON P0P 1X0
Tel: 705-283-3014; *Fax:* 705-283-4038
www.olsn.ca/sheshegwaning
Debra Cada, Librarian

***Shoal Lake:* Iskutewisakaggun #39 First Nation Community Public Library**
Kejick Post Office, Shoal Lake, ON P0X 1E0
Tel: 807-733-3621; *Fax:* 807-733-3635
i_ross38@hotmail.com
Irene Ross, CEO
i_ross38@hotmail.com

***Simcoe:* Norfolk County Public Library**
46 Colborne St. South, Simcoe, ON N3Y 4H3
Tel: 519-426-3506; *Fax:* 519-426-8918
norfolk.library@norfolkcounty.ca
www.ncpl.ca
Social Media: twitter.com/norfolklibrary;
www.facebook.com/NorfolkLibrary
Heather King, Chief Executive Officer
heather.king@norfolkcounty.ca
519-426-3506 ext. 1253
Heidi Goodale, Manager, Collection Development & Technology
heidi.goodale@norfolkcounty.ca
519-426-3506 ext. 1250
Beverley Slater, Manager, Programming & Communications
beverley.slater@norfolkcounty.ca
519-426-3506 ext. 1252
Janet Cowan, Manager, Facilities & Operations
janet.cowan@norfolkcounty.ca
519-426-3506 ext. 1251
Kasey Whitwell, Coordinator, Administration
kasey.whitwell@norfolkcounty.ca
519-426-3506 ext. 1258

***Sioux Lookout:* Sioux Lookout Public Library**
21 - 5th Ave., Sioux Lookout, ON P8T 1B3
Tel: 807-737-3660; *Fax:* 807-737-4046
publiclibrary@siouxlookout.ca
www.slpl.on.ca
Social Media: twitter.com/SLPublicLibrary;
www.facebook.com/SiouxLookoutPublicLibrary
Wendy MacDonald, Chief Executive Officer & Chief Librarian

***Sioux Narrows:* Sioux Narrows Public Library**
Sioux Narrows Public School, Hwy 71, Sioux Narrows, ON P0X 1N0
Tel: 807-226-5204; *Fax:* 807-226-5712
library@kmts.ca
Alice Motlong, Head Librarian
807-226-5204

***Smiths Falls:* Smiths Falls Public Library**
81 Beckwith St. North, Smiths Falls, ON K7A 2B9
Tel: 613-283-2911; *Fax:* 613-283-9834
smithsfallslibrary@vianet.ca
www.smithsfallslibrary.ca
Social Media: www.facebook.com/SmithsFallsLibrary
William Widenmaier, Chair
Karen Schecter, Chief Librarian

***Smithville:* West Lincoln Public Library**
Town Hall Complex, 318 Canboro St., Smithville, ON L0R 2A0
Tel: 905-957-3756
westlincolnlibrary@yahoo.ca
www.westlincolnlibrary.ca
Social Media: twitter.com/WLPLibrary;
www.facebook.com/pages/West-Lincoln-Library/119491941625

***Smooth Rock Falls:* Smooth Rock Falls Public Library/ Bibliothèque publique de Smooth Rock Falls**
120 Ross Rd., Smooth Rock Falls, ON P0L 2B0
Tel: 705-338-2318; *Fax:* 705-338-2330
smooth@ntl.sympatico.ca
www.townofsmoothrockfalls.ca
Lise Gagnon, CEO
Lynne Pelletier, Contact, ILL & Children's Services

***South River:* South River-Machar Union Public Library**
63 Marie St., South River, ON P0A 1X0
Tel: 705-386-0222; *Fax:* 705-386-0222
osrmlibrary@hotmail.com
www.olsn.ca/srmupl
Social Media: www.facebook.com/288691530122
Jan Heinonen, Chief Executive Officer

***Southwold:* Oneida Community Library**
2315 Keystone Pl., Southwold, ON N0L 2G0
Tel: 519-652-3977
www.oneida.on.ca

***Spanish:* Spanish Public Library/ Bibliothèque publique du Spanish**
8 Trunk Rd., Spanish, ON P0P 2A0
Tel: 705-844-2555; *Fax:* 705-844-2555
library@town.spanish.on.ca
www.olsn.ca/spanish
Social Media: www.facebook.com/613288855385408
Hanne Sauvé, CEO

***Spencerville:* Edwardsburgh/Cardinal Public Library**
5 Henderson St., Spencerville, ON K0E 1X0
Tel: 613-658-5575
library@spencerville.ca
www.spencervillelibrary.ca
Kathy Colwell, Head Librarian

***St Catharines:* St Catharines Public Library**
54 Church St., St Catharines, ON L2R 7K2
Tel: 905-688-6103; *Fax:* 905-688-6292
admin@stcatharines.library.on.ca
www.stcatharines.library.on.ca
Social Media: www.pinterest.com/stcathlibrary;
twitter.com/stcathlibrary; www.facebook.com/298407173635
A. Carruthers, Chair

***St Charles:* St. Charles Public Library**
22 Ste. Anne St., St Charles, ON P0M 2W0
Tel: 705-867-5332; *Fax:* 705-867-2511
stcharles_library@yahoo.ca
www.olsn.ca/stcharles
Nicole Lafontaine, Chief Librarian
Carmen Ethier, Assistant Librarian

***St Marys:* St Marys Public Library**
15 Church St. North, St Marys, ON N4X 1B4
Tel: 519-284-3346; *Fax:* 519-284-2630
libraryinfo@stmaryspubliclibrary.ca
www.townofstmarys.com/public-library
Social Media: twitter.com/stmaryspl;
www.facebook.com/group.php?gid=33345900699
Shannan Sword, Chief Executive Officer
Rebecca Webb, Coordinator, Library Services

***St Thomas:* St Thomas Public Library**
153 Curtis St., St Thomas, ON N5P 3Z7
Tel: 519-631-6050; *Fax:* 519-631-1987
rdenham@st-thomas.library.on.ca
www.st-thomas.library.on.ca
Social Media: www.facebook.com/302831323082900
Rudi Denham, CEO / Head Librarian
rdenham@st-thomas.library.on.ca
Paul Blower, Head, Reference/Adult Services
pblower@st-thomas.library.on.ca
Heather Robinson, Head, Children & Teens Services
hrobinson@st-thomas.library.on.ca
Terri Scott, Acting Head of Circulation
tscott@st-thomas.library.on.ca

***St. Thomas:* Elgin County Library**
450 Sunset Dr., St. Thomas, ON N5R 5V1
Tel: 519-631-1460
www.library.elgin-county.on.ca
Social Media: www.youtube.com/user/ElginLibrary;
twitter.com/LibrElginCounty;
www.facebook.com/ElginCountyLibrary
Laura Molnar, Library Coordinator
lmolnar@elgin.ca
Brian Masschaele, Director, Community & Cultural Events
bmasschaele@elgin-county.on.ca

***Stayner:* Clearview Public Library**
201 Huron St., Stayner, ON L0M 1S0
Tel: 705-428-3595
interlibraryloans@clearview.ca
www.clearview.library.on.ca
Social Media:
www.facebook.com/pages/Clearview-Public-Library/285803031750
Robert Charlton, Chair
705-428-6943

***Stirling:* Stirling-Rawdon Public Library**
43 West Front St., Stirling, ON K0K 3E0
Tel: 613-395-2837
www.stirlinglibrary.com
Social Media: www.facebook.com/172294119529138
Sue Winfield, CEO/Head Librarian
sue@stirlinglibrary.com
Theresa Brennan, Assistant Librarian
Jaye Bannon, Children's Librarian

***Stonecliffe:* Head, Clara & Maria Public Library**
15 Township Hall Rd., Stonecliffe, ON K0J 2K0
Tel: 613-586-2526; *Fax:* 613-586-2596
hcmlibra@xplornet.com
www.hcmpubliclibrary.ca
Gayle Watters, CEO/Librarian

***Stouffville:* Whitchurch-Stouffville Public Library**
2 Park Dr., Stouffville, ON L4A 4K1
Tel: 905-642-7323; *Fax:* 905-640-1384
Toll-Free: 888-603-4292
www.wsplibrary.ca
Social Media: twitter.com/WhitStoufLibrar;
www.facebook.com/WSPLibrary
Lloyd Pinnock, Chair
Carolyn Nordheimer James, Chief Executive Officer

***Stratford:* Stratford Public Library**
19 St Andrew St., Stratford, ON N5A 1A2
Tel: 519-271-0220; *Fax:* 519-271-3843
askspl@pcin.on.ca
www.stratford.library.on.ca
Social Media: pinterest.com/splibrary; twitter.com/SPLibrary;
www.facebook.com/stratfordpubliclibrary;
www.linkedin.com/company/stratford-public-library
Jeff Orr, Chair
Julia Merritt, Library Director & CEO
jmerritt@stratfordcanada.ca
519-271-0220 ext. 110
Wendy Hicks, Director, Public Service
whicks@stratfordcanada.ca
519-271-0220 ext. 111
Krista Robinson, Systems Librarian
krobinson@stratfordcanada.ca
519-271-0220 ext. 112

***Stratton:* Stratton Community Library**
11331 Hwy. 11, Stratton, ON P0W 1N0
Tel: 807-483-5455
Anna H.M. Boily, Clerk-Treasurer

***Sturgeon Falls:* West Nipissing Public Library/ Bibliothèque publique de Nipissing Ouest**
#107, 225 Holditch St., Sturgeon Falls, ON P2B 1T1
Tel: 705-753-2620; *Fax:* 705-753-2131
mail@wnpl.ca
www.wnpl.ca
Social Media: twitter.com/wnpubliclibrary;
www.facebook.com/205021066285255
Carole Marion, Chief Executive Officer
cmarion@wnpl.ca
Frances Cockburn, Head, Archives

***Sudbury:* Greater Sudbury Public Library/ Bibliothèque publique du grand Sudbury**
74 Mackenzie St., Sudbury, ON P3C 4X8
Tel: 705-673-1155; *Fax:* 705-673-0554
www.sudbury.library.on.ca
Social Media: www.youtube.com/gsplibrary;
twitter.com/GSPLibrary; www.facebook.com/GSPLibrary
Brian Harding, Manager, Libraries & Heritage Museums
705-673-1155 ext. 4756
Ron Henderson, Director, Citizen Services
705-673-1155 ext. 4759

***Sundridge:* Sundridge-Strong Union Public Library**
110 Main St., Sundridge, ON P0A 1Z0
Tel: 705-384-7311; *Fax:* 705-384-7311
sundridgelibrary@gmail.com
www.olsn.ca/sundridgestronglibrary
Social Media: www.facebook.com/332738433516395
Denise Rogers, Librarian

Tehkummah: **Tehkummah Township Public Library**
Municipal Offices Bldg., RR#1, Tehkummah, ON P0P 2C0
Tel: 705-859-3301; *Fax:* 705-859-2605
tehklib@yahoo.ca
Judy McDermid, CEO

Temagami: **Temagami Public Library**
Welcome Centre, 7 Lakeshore Dr., Temagami, ON P0H 2H0
Tel: 705-569-2945
library@temagami.ca
www.temagami.library.on.ca
Shelley Rowland, Chief Executive Officer & Librarian

Terrace Bay: **Terrace Bay Public Library**
13 Selkirk Ave., Terrace Bay, ON P0T 2W0
Tel: 807-825-3315; *Fax:* 807-825-1249
terracebay.library.on.ca
Social Media: www.facebook.com/TerraceBayPL
Mary Deschatelets, CEO
807-825-3315 ext. 234
Justina Pelto, Assistant Librarian

Thamesville: **Delaware Nation Public Library**
RR#3, Thamesville, ON N0P 2K0
Tel: 519-692-3411; *Fax:* 519-692-5522
delawarenationlibrary@hotmail.com
Darryl Stonefish, CEO

Thessalon: **Thessalon First Nation Public Library**
35 Sugarbush Rd., Thessalon, ON P0R 1L0
Tel: 705-842-1258; *Fax:* 705-842-2332
thessalonfirstnationlibrary@hotmail.com
www.olsn.ca/thessalonfirstnationpl
Julie Bisaillon, Chief Executive Officer

Thessalon: **Thessalon Public Library**
187 Main St., Thessalon, ON P0R 1L0
Tel: 705-842-2306; *Fax:* 705-842-5690
library@thesslibcap.com
www.thesslibcap.com
Social Media: twitter.com/ThessalonPublic;
www.facebook.com/104998919541074
Sandra McKee, CEO/Librarian
Sharon Couvillon, Contact, Technical Services

Thornbury: **The Blue Mountains Public Library**
173 Bruce St. South, Thornbury, ON N0H 2P0
Tel: 519-599-3681; *Fax:* 519-599-7951
libraryinfo@thebluemountains.ca
www.thebluemountainslibrary.ca
Social Media: twitter.com/le_shore;
facebook.com/thebluemountainslibrary
Cathy Innes, Chair
Carol Cooley, CEO
Elisa Chandler, Coordinator, Technical Services
Jennifer Perks, Coordinator, Children & Youth Services
Donna St. Jacques, Coordinator, Desk Services
Emma Barker, Library Assistant, Administrative Services

Thorold: **Thorold Public Library**
14 Ormond St. North, Thorold, ON L2V 1Y8
Tel: 905-227-2581; *Fax:* 905-227-2311
thoroldpubliclibrary@cogeco.net
www.thoroldpubliclibrary.ca
Social Media:
www.facebook.com/pages/Thorold-Public-Library/156082714436307
Patti Bronson, Chief Librarian
pbronson@cogeco.net
905-227-2581
Tony Vandermaas, Chair
Cheryl Bowman, Contact, Information Desk

Thunder Bay: **Thunder Bay Public Library**
285 Red River Rd., Thunder Bay, ON P7B 1A9
Tel: 807-345-8275
www.tbpl.ca
Social Media: www.facebook.com/TBayPL
John Pateman, CEO/Chief Librarian
jpateman@tbpl.ca
807-684-6803
Tina Tucker, Director, Communities
ttucker@tbpl.ca
807-684-6813
Cherri Braye, Acting Director, People
cbraye@tbpl.ca
807-684-6804
Joanna Aegard, Head, Virtual Library Services
jaegard@tbpl.ca
807-684-6819
Stephen Hurrell, Head, Automated Support Systems
shurrell@tbpl.ca
807-684-6807
Angela Meady, Head, Children's & Youth Services
ameady@tbpl.ca
807-684-6810
Barb Philp, Head, Adult Services
bphilp@tbpl.ca
807-684-6811
Sylvia Renaud, Head, Technical Services
srenaud@tbpl.ca
807-684-6808
Jesse Roberts, Head, Reference Services
jroberts@tbpl.ca
807-624-4203

Timmins: **Timmins Public Library/ Bibliothèque municipale de Timmins**
320 - 2nd Ave., Timmins, ON P4N 8A4
Tel: 705-360-2623; *Fax:* 705-360-2688
library@timmins.ca
tpl.timmins.ca
Carole-Ann Churcher, CEO
caroleann.churcher@timmins.ca
Chantal Benson, Head, Technical Support & Services
chantal.benson@timmins.ca

Toronto: **Holocaust Eduation Centre**
Sarah & Chaim Neuberger Holocaust Education Centre, UJA Federation, 4600 Bathurst St., 4th Fl., Toronto, ON M2R 3V3
Tel: 416-635-2996; *Fax:* 416-633-7535
www.holocaustcentre.com/AnitaEkstein
Anna Skorupsky, Librarian
askorupsky@ujafed.org

Toronto: **Ontario Public Libraries**
Hearst Block, 9th Fl., 900 Bay St., Toronto, ON M7A 2E1
Tel: 416-326-9326; *Fax:* 416-326-9338
Toll-Free: 800-668-2746
TTY: 800-700-004
www.mtc.gov.on.ca/en/libraries/libraries.shtml
Rod Sawyer, Advisor, Library Services
rod.sawyer@ontario.ca
416-314-7627 ext. 41621

Toronto: **Toronto Public Library/ Bibliothèque publique de Toronto**
789 Yonge St., Toronto, ON M4W 2G8
Tel: 416-393-7131; *Fax:* 416-393-7083
TTY: 416-393-703
www.torontopubliclibrary.ca
Social Media: www.youtube.com/torontopubliclibrary;
twitter.com/torontolibrary;
www.facebook.com/torontopubliclibrary;
www.linkedin.com/company/422295
Vickery Bowles, City Librarian
citylibrarian@torontopubliclibrary.ca
416-393-7032
Fernando Lopez, Director, Research & Reference Libraries
flopez@torontopubliclibrary.ca
416-393-7207
Joe Colangelo, Senior Manager, Information Technology
jcolangelo@torontopubliclibrary.ca
416-393-0775
Elizabeth Glass, Director, Planning, Policy & Performance Management
eglass@torontopubliclibrary.ca
416-395-5602
Linda Hazzan, Director, Communications, Programming & Engagement
lhazzan@torontopubliclibrary.ca
416-393-7214
Moe Hosseini-Ara, Director, Branch Operations & Customer Experience
mhoss@torontopubliclibrary.ca
416-397-5944
Michele Melady, Manager, Collections
mmelady@torontopubliclibrary.ca
416-395-5503
Dan Keon, Director, Human Resources
dkeon@torontopubliclibrary.ca
416-395-5850
Heather Rumball, President/Director of Development, Toronto Public Library Foundation
416-393-7134

Trenton: **Quinte West Public Library**
7 Creswell Dr., Trenton, ON K8V 6X5
Tel: 613-394-3381; *Fax:* 613-394-2079
www.library.quintewest.ca
Social Media: www.facebook.com/QuinteWestPublicLibrary
Bob Wannamaker, Chair
Rita Turtle, Chief Exectuive Officer
rturtle.qwpl@city.quintewest.on.ca
613-394-3381 ext. 3315
Robert Amesse, Coordinator, Adult Information & Reference
ramesse.qwpl@city.quintewest.on.ca
613-394-3381 ext. 3325
Rosemary Kirby, Contact, Children's Information & Reference
rkirby.qwpl@city.quintewest.on.ca
613-394-3381 ext. 3311
Linda Lafond, Contact, Interlibrary Loan Information
illo.qwpl@city.quintewest.on.ca
613-394-3381 ext. 3316
Kim Vivian, Contact, Homeward Bound
kvivian.qwpl@city.quintewest.on.ca
613-394-3381 ext. 3325

Tweed: **Municipality of Tweed Public Library**
230 Metcalf St., Tweed, ON K0K 3J0
Tel: 613-478-1066; *Fax:* 613-478-6457
tweedlibrary@vianet.ca
tweedlibrary.ca
Social Media: twitter.com/Tweed_Library;
www.facebook.com/110745655657043
Catherine Anderson, CEO

Tyendinaga: **Kanhiote / Tyendinaga Territory Public Library**
1658 York Rd., RR#1, Tyendinaga, ON K0K 1X0
Tel: 613-967-6264; *Fax:* 613-396-3627
kanhiote@gmail.com
www.kanhiote.ca
Karen Lewis, CEO

Uxbridge: **Uxbridge Township Public Library**
9 Toronto St. South, Uxbridge, ON L9P 1P7
Tel: 905-852-9747
uxlib@powergate.ca
www.uxlib.com
Social Media: www.flickr.com/photos/uxbridgepubliclibrary;
twitter.com/uxbridgelibrary;
www.facebook.com/pages/Uxbridge-Public-Library/181717581870540
Alexandra Hartmann, CEO / Chief Librarian
ahartmann@uxlib.com
905-852-9747 ext. 26
Pamela Noble, Outreach/Program Coordinator
pnoble@uxlib.com
905-852-9747 ext. 24
Leslie Nagle, Contact, Interlibrary Loans
leslie.nagle@uxlib.com
905-852-9747 ext. 27

Val Rita: **Val Rita-Harty Public Library/ Bibliothèque municipale de Val Rita-Harty**
106, ch Gouvernement, Val Rita, ON P0L 2G0
Tel: 705-335-8700; *Fax:* 705-335-8700
bibliovalrita@ntl.sympatico.ca
www.olsn.ca/valrita
Cecile Lamontagne, Directrice

Vankleek Hill: **Champlain Township Public Library/ Bibliothèque Champlain**
94 Main St. East, Vankleek Hill, ON K0B 1R0
Tel: 613-678-2216; *Fax:* 613-678-2216
library@champlaintwplibrary.ca
www.champlaintwplibrary.ca
Lise Béliveau, Chair
Lynda Poyser, CEO & Head Librarian
lpoyser@champlaintwplibrary.ca
Diane Bourgault, Circulation Clerk & Library Assistant
dianeb@champlaintwplibrary.ca
Margaret MacMillan, Circulation Clerk & Library Assistant
marg@champlaintwplibrary.ca
Cynthia Martin, Circulation Clerk & Library Assistant
cynthia@champlaintwplibrary.ca

Vaughan: **Vaughan Public Libraries**
900 Clark Ave. West, Vaughan, ON L4J 8C1
Tel: 905-653-7323; *Fax:* 905-709-1530
www.vaughanpl.info
Social Media: www.youtube.com/user/VaughanPL;
twitter.com/vaughanpl; www.facebook.com/133050006764886
Margie Singleton, Chief Executive Officer
margie.singleton@vaughan.ca
905-653-7323 ext. 4601
Aleksandra Dowiat Vine, Director, Growth & Communications
aleksandra.dowiat-vine@vaughan.ca
905-653-7323 ext. 4620
Marilyn Guy, Director, Innovative Technologies & Collections
marilyn.guy@vaughan.ca
905-653-7323 ext. 4114

***Virginiatown:* McGarry Township Public Library/ Bibliothèque publique de McGarry**
1 - 27 St. East, Virginiatown, ON P0K 1X0
Tel: 705-634-2312
mcgarry@onlink.net
www.mcgarrypubliclibrary.8m.com
Anne-Marie Boucher, CEO/Librarian

***Wainfleet:* Wainfleet Township Public Library**
31909 Park St., Wainfleet, ON L0S 1V0
Tel: 905-899-1277; *Fax:* 905-899-2495
www.wainfleetlibrary.ca
Lorrie Atkinson, CEO/Chief Librarian
latkinson@wainfleetlibrary.ca
905-899-1277 ext. 280
Carrie Mayr, Library Programmer
cmayr@wainfleetlibrary.ca
905-899-1277 ext. 281
Cheryl Davis-Catchpaw, Secretary/Library Clerk
cdavis-catchpaw@wainfleetlibrary.ca
905-899-1277 ext. 282
Dariusz Zelichowski, IT/Systems Specialist
darius@wainfleet.ca
905-899-1277 ext. 220

***Walker's Point:* Walker's Point Volunteer Community Book Exchange**
Walker's Point Community Centre, 1074 Walker's Point Rd., Walker's Point, ON P0C 1M0
Tel: 705-687-9965

***Wallaceburg:* Bkejwanong First Nation Public Library**
Walpole Island First Nation, 136 Tecumseh Road, RR #3, Wallaceburg, ON N8A 4K9
Tel: 519-627-7034; *Fax:* 519-627-7035
library@wifn.org
www.bkejwanonglibrary.ca
Social Media: www.facebook.com/bkejwanong.fnpl

***Wasaga Beach:* Wasaga Beach Public Library**
120 Glenwood Dr., Wasaga Beach, ON L9Z 2K5
Tel: 705-429-5481; *Fax:* 705-429-5481
wblibrary@georgian.net
www.wasagabeach.library.on.ca
Social Media:
youtube.com/channel/UCkRdBrQIDgDRnDxWt8zm9xA;
twitter.com/BeyondBooksWBPL;
facebook.com/400499330043065
Jackie Beaudin, CEO
705-429-5481 ext. 2404

***Waterloo:* Waterloo Public Library**
35 Albert St., Waterloo, ON N2L 5E2
Tel: 519-886-1310; *Fax:* 519-886-7936
TTY: 866-786-394
Other Numbers: TeleRenew: 519-886-5480
www.wpl.ca
Social Media: www.youtube.com/user/WaterlooLibrary;
twitter.com/waterloolibrary;
www.facebook.com/124917584192823
Laurie Clarke, CEO
lclarke@wpl.ca
519-886-1310 ext. 123
Gloria Van Eek-Meijers, Deputy CEO
gvaneek@wpl.ca
519-886-1310 ext. 125
Alannah d'Ailly, Manager, Library Collections
adailly@wpl.ca
519-886-1310 ext. 127
Sue Klopchic, Human Resources
jobs@wpl.ca
519-889-1310 ext. 164

***Wawa:* Michipicoten First Nation Public Library**
107 Hiawatha Dr., RR#1, Wawa, ON P0S 1K0
Tel: 705-856-1993; *Fax:* 705-856-1642
library@michipicoten.com
www.michipicoten.com
Lee-Ann Andre-Swanson, Librarian
landreswanson@michipicoten.com
705-856-1993 ext. 219

***Wawa:* Wawa Public Library**
40 Broadway Ave., Wawa, ON P0S 1K0
Tel: 705-856-2244; *Fax:* 705-856-1488
Other Numbers: Circulation Desk, ext. 290
mtpl@wawa.cc
www.mtpl.on.ca
Jayne Griffith, Head Librarian
jgriffith@wawa.cc
705-856-2062 ext. 291
Chantal Magi, Assistant Librarian
Jude Charbonneau, Circulation Technician
Joanne DeVries, Circulation Technician

***Weagamow Lake:* North Caribou First Nation Public Library**
PO Box 158, Weagamow Lake, ON P0V 2Y0
Tel: 807-469-1288; *Fax:* 807-469-1315
northcariboulakefirstnation@knet.ca
Beatrice Kanate, Librarian

***Welland:* Welland Public Library**
50 The Boardwalk, Welland, ON L3B 6J1
Tel: 905-734-6210; *Fax:* 905-734-8955
info@welland.library.on.ca
www.welland.library.on.ca
Social Media: twitter.com/wellandlib;
www.facebook.com/wellandpubliclibrary
Qingyi (Ken) Su, CEO & Secretary-Treasurer
qksu@wellandlibrary.ca
905-734-6210 ext. 2500
Julianne Brunet, Manager, Public Services
jbrunet@wellandlibrary.ca
905-734-6210 ext. 2502

***Westport:* Westport Public Library**
3 Spring St., Westport, ON K0G 1X0
Tel: 613-273-3223; *Fax:* 613-273-3223
library@rideau.net
village.westport.on.ca/about-westport/westport-public-library
Social Media: www.facebook.com/155845464448129
Pamela Stuffles, CEO

***Whitby:* Whitby Public Library**
405 Dundas St. West, Whitby, ON L1N 6A1
Tel: 905-668-6531; *Fax:* 905-668-7445
Other Numbers: Holds & Renewals, Phone: 905-430-7913
admin@whitbylibrary.on.ca
www.whitbylibrary.on.ca
Social Media: www.youtube.com/whitbypubliclibrary;
twitter.com/whitbylibrary; www.facebook.com/whitbylibrary
Eva Reti, Chair
Ian Ross, CEO/Chief Librarian
Rhonda Jessup, Public Services Manager
Elaine Yatulis Dobbin, Manager, Technical Services & Systems Support
Michelle Frenette, Manager, Support Services

***White River:* White River Public Library**
123 Superior St., White River, ON P0M 3G0
Tel: 807-822-1113; *Fax:* 807-822-1113
whiteriverlibrary@bellnet.ca
www.whiteriverlibrary.com
Jan Ramage, CEO

***Whitedog:* Wabaseemoong First Nation Public Library**
General Delivery, Whitedog, ON P0X 1P0
Tel: 807-927-2000; *Fax:* 807-927-2176

***Whitney:* South Algonquin Public Library**
33 Medical Centre Rd., Whitney, ON K0J 2M0
Tel: 613-637-5471; *Fax:* 613-637-5471
whitneylibrary@gmail.com
www.olsn.ca/southalgonquin
Charlene Alexander, CEO

***Wikwemikong:* Wikwemikong First Nation Public Library**
34A Henry St., Wikwemikong, ON P0P 2J0
Tel: 705-859-2692; *Fax:* 705-859-3851
wikylibrary@hotmail.com
www.olsn.ca/wpl

***Windsor:* Windsor Public Library**
850 Ouellette Ave., Windsor, ON N9A 4M9
Tel: 519-255-6770; *Fax:* 519-255-7207
TTY: 866-488-931
feedback@windsorpubliclibrary.com
www.windsorpubliclibrary.com
Social Media: www.youtube.com/wplwindsor;
twitter.com/windsorpublib; www.facebook.com/windsorpl
Kathleen Pope, Chief Executive Officer

***Woodstock:* Oxford County Library**
Oxford County Administration Bldg., 21 Reeve St., Woodstock, ON N4S 3G1
Tel: 519-539-9800; *Fax:* 519-421-4712
www.ocl.net
Social Media: twitter.com/_OCL;
www.facebook.com/OxfordCountyLibrary
Margaret Lupton, Chair
mlupton@zorra.on.ca
519-475-4443
Lisa Miettinen, Chief Executive Officer & Chief Librarian
lmiettinen@ocl.net
519-539-9800 ext. 4712

***Woodstock:* Woodstock Public Library**
445 Hunter St., Woodstock, ON N4S 4G7
Tel: 519-539-4801; *Fax:* 519-539-5246
gbaumbach@woodstock.library.on.ca
www.woodstock.library.on.ca
Social Media: pinterest.com/mywpl/; twitter.com/WoodstockLib;
www.facebook.com/myWPL
Brian Crockett, Chair
Gary Baumbach, CEO/Chief Librarian
gbaumbach@woodstock.library.on.ca
Susan Start, Head, Information & Adult Services
sstart@woodstock.library.on.ca
Darlene Pretty, Head, Children's & Youth Services
dpretty@woodstock.library.on.ca
Carolyn Veenstra, Head, Circulation Services
cmveenstra@woodstock.library.on.ca
Karen Scott, eBranch Manager
kscott@woodstock.library.on.ca
Judi Meadows, Administration & Room Bookings
jmeadows@woodstock.library.on.ca

***Wyoming:* Lambton County Library Headquarters**
787 Broadway St., Wyoming, ON N0N 1T0
Tel: 519-845-3324; *Fax:* 519-845-0700
Toll-Free: 866-324-6912
Other Numbers: Overdues, Phone: 519-845-3324, ext. 5229
library.contact@county-lambton.on.ca
www.lclibrary.ca
Social Media: www.youtube.com/user/lambtonlibrary;
twitter.com/LamLib; www.facebook.com/271179146270568
Robert Tremain, General Manager
robert.tremain@county-lambton.on.ca
519-845-0801 ext. 5236

Archives

***Toronto:* St James' Cathedral Archives**
65 Church St., Toronto, ON M5C 2E9
Tel: 416-364-7865; *Fax:* 416-364-0295
archives@stjamescathedral.on.ca
www.stjamescathedral.on.ca
Nancy Mallett, Archivist & Museum Curator

***Alexandria:* Glengarry Historical Society**
212 Main St. North, Alexandria, ON K0C 1A0
Tel: 613-525-1336
archives@glengarryhistory.ca
www.glengarryhistory.ca
Allan MacDonald, Contact
613-525-1336

***Ameliasburgh:* Quinte Educational Museum & Archives**
13 Coleman St. Group Box 14, Ameliasburgh, ON K0K 1A0
Tel: 613-966-5501
info@qema1978.com
www.qema1978.com
Lynda Sommer, President

***Amherstburg:* Marsh Collection Society**
235A Dalhousie St., Amherstburg, ON N9V 1W4
Tel: 519-736-9191
research@marshcollection.org
www.marshcollection.org
Social Media:
www.facebook.com/Marsh-Historical-Collection-968976766461303

***Amherstburg:* North American Black Historical Museum**
277 King St., Amherstburg, ON N9V 2C7
Tel: 519-736-5433
blackhistoricalmuseum.ca
Terran Fader, Curator
Terran.Fader@amherstburgfreedom.org
Mary-Katherine Whelan, Assistant Curator

***Aylmer:* Aylmer & District Museum Association**
14 East St., Aylmer, ON N5H 1W2
Tel: 519-773-9723
aylmermuseum@amtelecom.net
www.amtelecom.net/~aylmermuseum
Social Media: twitter.com/AylmerMuseum;
facebook.com/AylmerMalahideMuseumArchives
Amanda Vandenwyngaert, Curator

***Bayfield:* Bayfield Archives Room**
20 Main St. North, Bayfield, ON N0M 1G0
Tel: 519-441-3224
bayarchives@tcc.on.ca
www.bayfieldhistorical.ca
Ralph Laviolette, Archivist

***Bowmanville:* Clarington Museums & Archives**
Sarah Jane Williams Heritage Centre, 62 Temperance St., Bowmanville, ON L1C 3A8
Tel: 905-623-2734; *Fax:* 905-623-5684
info@claringtonmuseums.com
www.claringtonmuseums.com
Michael Adams, Executive Director
madams@claringtonmuseums.com
Heather Ridge, Curator
hridge@claringtonmuseums.com

***Brampton:* Region of Peel Art Gallery, Museum, & Archives**
The Peel Heritage Complex, 9 Wellington St. East, Brampton, ON L6W 1Y1
Tel: 905-791-4055; *Fax:* 905-451-4931
pama.peelregion.ca
Social Media: www.flickr.com/photos/peelheritage;
www.facebook.com/visitPAMA
Kyle Neill, Senior Achivist
905-791-4055 ext. 4677
Marty Brent, Manager
905-791-4055 ext. 4676

***Brantford:* Brant Historical Society**
57 Charlotte St., Brantford, ON N3T 2W6
Tel: 519-752-2483
information@brantmuseum.ca
www.brantmuseum.ca
Social Media: www.youtube.com/user/branthistorical;
twitter.com/branthistorical;
www.facebook.com/BrantHistoricalSociety
Nathan Etherington, Administrator
nathan.etherington@brantmuseums.ca
Sarah Thomas, Education Officer
sarah.thomas@brantmusems.ca

***Bridgenorth:* Smith Ennismore Historical Society**
826 Ward St., Bridgenorth, ON K0L 1H0
Tel: 705-292-9430
feedback@sehs.on.ca
sehs.on.ca/hlc.htm

***Brockville:* Brockville Museum**
5 Henry St., Brockville, ON K6V 6M4
Tel: 613-342-4397
Other Numbers: Leeds/Grenville Genealogical Society: 613-342-7773
museum@brockville.com
www.brockvillemuseum.com
Amy Mackie, Museum Educator
awhitehorne@brockville.com
Margaret Mulkins, Librarian, Leeds & Grenville Genealogical Society
cmulkins@bell.net

***Burlington:* Joseph Brant Museum**
1240 North Shore Blvd. East, Burlington, ON L7S 1C5
Tel: 905-634-3556; *Fax:* 905-634-4498
Toll-Free: 888-748-5386
www.museumsofburlington.com
Social Media: twitter.com/BurlingtonMuse;
facebook.com/BurlingtonMuseums
Barbara E. Teatero, Director
barbara.teatero@burlington.ca
Kimberly Watson, Community Curator
Kimberly.Watson@burlington.ca
Alicia Pettey, Assistant Curator
Alicia.Pettey@burlington.ca

***Cambridge:* Cambridge Archives**
46 Dickson St., 2nd Fl., Cambridge, ON N1R 1T7
Tel: 519-740-4680
archives@cambridge.ca
www.cambridge.ca

***Cannington:* Cannington & Area Historical Society**
21 Laidlaw St. South, Cannington, ON L0E 1E0
Tel: 705-432-3136
canningtonhistoricalsociety@hotmail.com
www.canningtonhistoricalsociety.ca

***Chatham:* Chatham-Kent Museum**
75 William St. North, Chatham, ON N7M 4L4
Tel: 519-360-1998; *Fax:* 519-354-4170
Toll-Free: 800-714-7497
ckcccmuseum@chatham-kent.ca
www.chatham-kent.ca/Chatham-KentMuseum
Social Media: www.twitter.com/culturalcentre1;
www.facebook.com/pages/The-Cultural-Centre/2315010202339
0

***Combermere:* Madonna House**
2888 Dafoe Rd. RR#2, Combermere, ON K0J 1L0
Tel: 613-756-3713; *Fax:* 613-756-0211
www.madonnahouse.org
Social Media: www.youtube.com/MadonnaHouseCanada;
twitter.com/madonnahouse; www.facebook.com/MadonnaHouse

***Delhi:* Delhi Tobacco Museum & Heritage Centre**
200 Talbot Rd., Delhi, ON N4B 2A2
Tel: 519-582-0278; *Fax:* 519-582-0122
delhi.museum@norfolkcounty.ca
www.delhimuseum.ca

***Fergus:* Wellington County Museum & Archives**
0536 County Rd. 18, RR#1, Fergus, ON N1M 2W3
Tel: 519-846-0916; *Fax:* 519-846-9630
Toll-Free: 800-663-0750
wellington.ca/en/museum.asp
Karen Wagner, Archivist

***Fort Frances:* Fort Frances Museum & Cultural Centre**
259 Scott St., Fort Frances, ON P9A 1G8
Tel: 807-274-7891
ffmuseum@fort-frances.com
museum.fort-frances.com
Sherry George, Curator

***Gatineau:* Canadian Museum of Nature/ Musée canadien de la nature**
1740, rue Pink, Gatineau, ON J9J 3N7
Tel: 613-364-4042; *Fax:* 613-364-4026
cmnlib@mus-nature.ca
nature.ca/en/research-collections/library-archives
Shannon Asencio, Head, Collections Services & Information Management
sasencio@mus-nature.ca
613-566-4255

***Georgetown:* Esquesing Historical Society**
9 Church St., Georgetown, ON L7G 2A3
Tel: 905-877-9510
www.esquesinghistoricalsociety.ca/archives.html
Stephen Blake, President, Esquesing Historical Society
905-877-8251
J. Mark Rowe, Archivist
mrowe6@sympatico.ca

***Goderich:* Huron County Museum Archives**
110 North St., Goderich, ON N7A 2T8
Tel: 519-524-2686; *Fax:* 519-524-1922
www.huroncounty.ca/museum
Social Media: instagram.com/huroncountymuseum;
twitter.com/hcmuseum;
www.facebook.com/huroncountymuseum

***Gravenhurst:* Gravenhurst Archives**
Gravenhurst Public Library, 180 Sharpe St. West, Gravenhurst, ON P1P 1J1
Tel: 705-687-6289
gravenhurstarchives@vianet.ca
www.gravenhurst.ca/en/library/library.asp
Julia Reinhart, Chief Executive Officer & Chief Librarian
705-687-3382

***Guelph:* Guelph Civic Museum**
52 Norfolk St., Guelph, ON N1H 4H8
Tel: 519-836-1221; *Fax:* 519-836-5280
museum@guelph.ca
www.guelph.ca/museum
Social Media: twitter.com/guelphmuseums;
www.facebook.com/guelphmuseums
Bev Dietrich, Curator
bev.dietrich@guelph.ca
519-836-1221 ext. 2774
Kathleen Wall, Curatorial Coordinator
kathleen.wall@guelph.ca
519-836-1221 ext. 2776

***Haliburton:* Haliburton Highlands Museum**
66 Museum Rd., Haliburton, ON K0M 1S0
Tel: 705-457-2760
info@haliburtonhighlandsmuseum.com
www.haliburtonhighlandsmuseum.com
Social Media: twitter.com/HH_Museum;
www.facebook.com/498191436905810
Kate Butler, Director
Stephen Hill, Curator

***Hamilton:* Canadian Baptist Archives/ Archives baptistes canadiennes**
c/o McMaster Divinity College, 1280 Main St. West, Hamilton, ON L8S 4K1
Tel: 905-525-9140
cbarch@mcmaster.ca
www.mcmasterdivinity.ca/welcome/canadian-baptist-archives
Gordon Heath, Director
Adam McCulloch, Archivist
amccull@mcmaster.ca
905-525-9140 ext. 23511

***Kenora:* Lake of the Woods Museum**
300 Main St. South, Kenora, ON P9N 3X5
Tel: 807-467-2105; *Fax:* 807-467-2109
museum@kmts.ca
www.lakeofthewoodsmuseum.ca
Social Media: www.facebook.com/LakeOfTheWoodsMuseum
Lori Nelson, Director
Lynn Halley, Museum Community Coordinator
Braden Murray, Museum Educator

***Kingston:* Marine Museum of the Great Lakes at Kingston**
55 Ontario St., Kingston, ON K7L 2Y2
Tel: 613-542-2261; *Fax:* 613-542-0043
marmus@marmuseum.ca
www.marmuseum.ca/index.php/research/research-facilities
Sandrena Raymond, Curator
curator@marmuseum.ca

***Kingston:* The Original Hockey Hall of Fame & Museum**
1350 Gardiners Rd., 2nd Fl., Kingston, ON K7P 0E5
Tel: 613-507-1943
info@originalhockeyhalloffame.com
www.originalhockeyhalloffame.com
Social Media: twitter.com/ihhof43;
www.facebook.com/207141552735961
Mark Potter, President
mpotter1@cogeco.ca

***Kingston:* Sisters of Providence of St. Vincent de Paul**
1200 Princess St., Kingston, ON K7L 4W4
Tel: 613-544-4525; *Fax:* 613-531-9805
archives@providence.ca
www.providence.ca
Social Media: www.youtube.com/srsofprovidence;
twitter.com/srsofprovidence;
www.facebook.com/Providence.Kingston

***Kitchener:* Waterloo Region Museum**
10 Huron Rd., Kitchener, ON N2P 2R7
Tel: 519-748-1914; *Fax:* 519-748-0009
TTY: 519-575-460
waterlooregionmuseum@regionofwaterloo.ca
waterlooregionmuseum.com/doon-heritage-village.aspx
Social Media: youtube.com/user/WaterlooRegionMuseum;
twitter.com/WRegionMuseum;
facebook.com/WaterlooRegionMuseum
Tom Reitz, Manager/Curator
treitz@regionofwaterloo.ca
519-748-1914 ext. 3270
Stacy McLennan, Registrar/Researcher
smclennan@regionofwaterloo.ca
519-748-1914 ext. 3268
James Jensen, Supervisor of Collections & Exhibits
jjensen@regionofwaterloo.ca
519-748-1914 ext. 3685
Richard Fuller, Conservator
rfuller@regionofwaterloo.ca
519-748-1914 ext. 3267

***Kleinburg:* McMichael Canadian Art Collection/ Collection McMichael d'Art Canadien**
10365 Islington Ave., Kleinburg, ON L0J 1C0
Tel: 905-893-1121; *Fax:* 905-893-0692
Other Numbers: www.youtube.com/mcmichaelgallery
library@mcmichael.com
www.mcmichael.com
Social Media: www.twitter.com/mcacgallery;
www.facebook.com/mcacgallery

Sarah Stanners, Director, Curatorial & Collections

London: Museum London
421 Ridout St. North, London, ON N6A 5H4
Tel: 519-661-0333
www.museumlondon.ca
Social Media: plus.google.com/+MuseumlondonCa; twitter.com/MuseumLondon; www.facebook.com/MuseumLondon
Janette Cousins Ewan, Art Registrar

London: The Royal Canadian Regiment Museum
Wolseley Hall, Wolseley Barracks, 701 Oxford St. East, London, ON N5Y 4T7
Tel: 519-660-5275; *Fax:* 519-660-5344
info@thercrmuseum.ca
www.thercrmuseum.ca
Georgiana Stanciu, Director & Curator
director@thercrmuseum.ca
519-660-5275 ext. 5015

Midland: Huronia Museum
549 Little Lake Park, Midland, ON L4R 4P4
Tel: 705-526-2844; *Fax:* 705-527-6622
info@huroniamuseum.com
www.huroniamuseum.com
Social Media: www.flickr.com/photos/huroniamuseum; twitter.com/HuroniaMuseum; www.facebook.com/huroniamuseum

Milton: Halton Region Heritage Services
5181 Kelso Rd., RR#3, Milton, ON L9T 2X7
Tel: 905-825-6000; *Toll-Free:* 866-442-5866
museum@halton.ca
www.halton.ca/discovering_halton/heritage_services
John Summers, Manager/Curator
john.summers@halton.ca
Claire Bennett, Assistant Curator/Collections Coordinator
claire.bennett@halton.ca

Milton: Ontario Electric Railway Historical Association
13629 Guelph Line, Milton, ON L9T 5A2
Tel: 519-856-9802; *Fax:* 519-856-1399
archives@hcry.org
www.hcry.org/archives.html

Minesing: County of Simcoe
1149 Hwy. 26, RR#2, Minesing, ON L0L 1Y2
Tel: 705-726-9331; *Fax:* 705-725-5341
Toll-Free: 866-893-9300
archives@simcoe.ca
www.simcoe.ca/dpt/arc
Ellen Millar, Assistant Archivist
ellen.millar@simcoe.ca

Mississauga: Pentecostal Assemblies of Canada
2450 Milltower Ct., Mississauga, ON L5N 5Z6
Tel: 905-542-7400; *Fax:* 905-542-7313
archives@paoc.org
www.paoc.org/about/archives
James Craig, Archivist

Napanee: Lennox & Addington County Museum & Archives
97 Thomas St. East, Napanee, ON K7R 4B9
Tel: 613-354-3027; *Fax:* 613-354-3112
archives@lennox-addington.on.ca
www.lennox-addington.on.ca/must-see/l-a-museum-archives.html
Social Media: www.facebook.com/158030467740667
Jane Foster, Manager
jfoster@lennox-addington.on.ca
613-354-3027 ext. 23
JoAnne Himmelman, Curatorial Assistant
jhimmelman@lennox-addington.on.ca
613-354-3027
Kim Kerr, Archivist
kkerr@lennox-addington.on.ca

Niagara on the Lake: Shaw Festival Theatre Foundation Library
PO Box 774, 10 Queen's Parade, Niagara on the Lake, ON L0S 1J0
Tel: 905-468-2153; *Fax:* 905-468-5438
Toll-Free: 800-657-1106
www.shawfest.com
Nancy Butler, Head Librarian

North Bay: Discovery North Bay Museum
100 Ferguson St., North Bay, ON P1B 1W8
Tel: 705-476-2323
www.discoverynorthbay.com
Social Media: twitter.com/discoverynbay; www.facebook.com/discovery.n.bay
Naomi Rupke, Director/Curator
naomi.rupke@heritagenorthbay.com

Norwich: Norwich & District Historical Society
91 Stover St. North, RR#3, Norwich, ON N0J 1P0
Tel: 519-863-3638; *Fax:* 519-863-2343
archives@norwichdhs.ca
www.norwichdhs.ca
Social Media: twitter.com/norwichdhs; www.facebook.com/418827451485779
Janet Hilliker, Archivist

Oil Springs: Oil Museum of Canada
2324 Kelly Rd., Oil Springs, ON N0N 1P0
Tel: 519-834-2840; *Fax:* 519-834-2840
www.lambtonmuseums.ca/oil

Orillia: Mariposa Folk Foundation
10 Peter St. South, Orillia, ON L3V 5A9
Tel: 705-326-3655; *Fax:* 705-326-5963
www.mariposafolk.com
Social Media: twitter.com/mariposafolk; www.facebook.com/MariposaFolkFestivalOfficial
Pam Carter, President

Orillia: Stephen Leacock Museum
50 Museum Dr., Orillia, ON L3V 7T9
Tel: 705-329-1908; *Toll-Free:* 705-326-5578
admin@leacockmuseum.com
www.leacockmuseum.com
Social Media: facebook.com/pages/Stephen-Leacock/104044192964809
Jenny Martynyshyn, Administrative Contact
admin@leacockmuseum.com

Oshawa: Oshawa Community Museum & Archives
1450 Simcoe St. South, Lakeview Park, Oshawa, ON L1H 8S8
Tel: 905-436-7624; *Fax:* 905-436-7625
info@oshawamuseum.org
www.oshawamuseum.org
Social Media: twitter.com/oshawamuseum; www.facebook.com/21181410334

Oshawa: Robert McLaughlin Gallery
Civic Centre, 72 Queen St., Oshawa, ON L1H 3Z3
Tel: 905-576-3000; *Fax:* 905-576-9774
communications@rmg.on.ca
www.rmg.on.ca
Social Media: www.youtube.com/RMGOshawa; twitter.com/theRMG; www.facebook.com/TheRMG
Linda Jansma, Senior Curator
ljansma@rmg.on.ca
905-576-3000 ext. 111
Alessandra Cirelli, Assistant Curator
acirelli@rmg.on.ca
905-576-3000 ext. 110
Jason Dankel, Preparator
jdankel@rmg.on.ca
905-576-3000 ext. 112

Ottawa: Archives Deschâtelets
175, rue Main, Ottawa, ON K1S 1C3
Tel: 613-237-0580
archives@ustpaul.ca

Ottawa: Bytown Railway Society
PO Box 47076, Ottawa, ON K1B 5P9
Tel: 613-745-1201; *Fax:* 613-745-1201
www.bytownrailwaysociety.ca
Social Media: youtube.com/user/bytownrailwaysociety; twitter.com/BytownRSociety; facebook.com/bytownrailwaysociety

Ottawa: C. Robert Craig Memorial Library
Ottawa City Archives, 100 Tallwood Dr., Ottawa, ON K2G 4R7
knowlesdc@bell.net
www.ovar.ca/CraigLibrary/craiglib.htm
Dennis Peters, President

Ottawa: Canadian Institute of Geomatics/ Association canadienne des sciences géomatiques
#100D, 900 Dynes Rd., Ottawa, ON K2C 3L6
Tel: 613-224-9851; *Fax:* 613-224-9577
www.cig-acsg.ca
Laura Duke, Manager, Production & Advertising for Geomatica
editgeo@magma.ca

Ottawa: Canadian Intergovernmental Conference Secretariat/ Secrétariat des conférences intergouvernementales Canadiennes
222 Queen St., 10th Fl., Ottawa, ON K1P 5V9
Tel: 613-995-2341; *Fax:* 613-996-6091
info@scics.gc.ca
www.scics.gc.ca

Ottawa: Canadian Women's Movement Archives/ Archives canadiennes du mouvement des femmes
Archives Special Collections, Morisset Hall, University of Ottawa, #039, 65 University Pvt, Ottawa, ON K1N 6N5
Tel: 613-562-5910
arcs@uottawa.ca
www.biblio.uottawa.ca
Michael Prévost, Chief Archivist
michel.prevost@uOttawa.ca
613-562-5825
Lucie Desjardins, Assistant to the Chief Archivist
lucie.desjardins@uottawa.ca
613-562-5800 ext. 6465

Ottawa: Chaise de recherche en histoire religieuse du Canada/ Research Chair in Religious History of Canada
Université St-Paul, 223, rue Main, Ottawa, ON K1S 1C4
Tél: 613-236-1393; *Téléc:* 613-782-3005
Ligne sans frais: 800-637-6859
crh-rc-rhc@ustpaul.ca
www.ustpaul.ca
Pierre Hurtubise, Titulaire
Denis Castonguay, Secrétaire

Ottawa: City of Ottawa Archives/ Archives municipales d'Ottawa
100 Tallwood Dr., Ottawa, ON K2G 4R7
Tel: 613-580-2857; *Fax:* 613-580-2614
archives@ottawa.ca
ottawa.ca/archives
Social Media: www.facebook.com/OttawaArchives
Paul Henry, City Archivist
paul.henry@ottawa.ca
613-580-2424 ext. 13181

Ottawa: National Archival Appraisal Board/ Conseil national d'évaluation des archives
c/o CCA, #1201, 130 Albert St., Ottawa, ON K1P 5G4
Tel: 613-565-1222; *Fax:* 613-565-5445
Toll-Free: 866-254-1403
naab@archivescanada.ca
www.naab.ca

Ottawa: Ottawa Jewish Archives
21 Nadolny Sachs Private, Ottawa, ON K2A 1R9
Tel: 613-798-4696; *Fax:* 613-798-4695
archives@jewishottawa.com
jewishottawa.com/ottawa-jewish-archives
Social Media: www.facebook.com/ottawajewisharchives
Saara Mortensen, Archivist
smortensen@jewishottawa.com
613-798-4696 ext. 260

Ottawa: Parent Finders of Canada & Parent Finders of Ottawa
PO Box 21025, Ottawa South Postal Outlet, Ottawa, ON K1S 5N1
Tel: 613-730-8305; *Fax:* 613-730-0345
pfncr@yahoo.com
www.parentfindersottawa.ca
Social Media: twitter.com/ParentFinders; facebook.com/120530528033309
Patricia McCarron, President

Ottawa: Roman Catholic Archdiocese of Ottawa/ Corporation Episcopale Catholique Romaine d'Ottawa
1247 Kilborn Pl., Ottawa, ON K1H 6K9
Tel: 613-738-5025; *Fax:* 613-738-0130
reception@archottawa.ca
archottawa.ca

Ottawa: The Royal College of Physicians & Surgeons of Canada
774 Echo Dr., Ottawa, ON K1S 5N8
Tel: 613-730-8177; *Fax:* 613-730-8830
Toll-Free: 800-668-3740
www.royalcollege.ca

Ottawa: Scouts Canada
1345 Baseline Rd., Ottawa, ON K2C 0A7
Tel: 613-224-5134
www.scouts.ca

Owen Sound: Grey Roots Museum & Archives
102599 Grey Rd. 18, RR#4, Owen Sound, ON N4K 5N6
Tel: 519-376-3690; Fax: 519-376-4654
Toll-Free: 877-473-9766
info@greyroots.com
www.greyroots.com
Karin Noble, Archivist
karin.noble@greyroots.com
519-376-3690 ext. 6113
Kate Jackson, Assistant Archivist
kate.jackson@greyroots.com
519-376-3690 ext. 6111

Pembroke: Grey Sisters of the Immaculate Conception
Marguerite Centre, 700 MacKay St., Pembroke, ON K8A 1G6
Tel: 613-735-4111; Fax: 613-735-3163
www.margueritecentre.com

Perth: The Perth Museum & Archives
11 Gore St. East, Perth, ON K7H 1H4
Tel: 613-267-1947
www.perth.ca/content/perth-museummatheson-house

Peterborough: Peterborough Museum & Archives
Ashburnham Memorial Park, 300 Hunter Hunter St. East, Peterborough, ON K9H 6Y5
Tel: 705-743-5180; Fax: 705-743-2614
Toll-Free: 855-738-3755
www.peterboroughmuseumandarchives.ca
Social Media:
www.facebook.com/pages/Peterborough-Museum-Archives/112608310308

Prescott: Grenville County Historical Society
500 Railway Ave., Prescott, ON K0E 1T0
Tel: 613-925-0489
gchs@ripnet.com
www.grenvillecountyarchives.ca
Bonnie Gaylord, Research Chair

Sault Ste Marie: Sault Ste Marie & 49th Field Regiment R.C.A. Historical Society, Sault Ste Marie Museum
690 Queen St. East, Sault Ste Marie, ON P6A 2A4
Tel: 705-759-7278; Fax: 705-759-3058
saultmuseum@gmail.com
www.saultmuseum.com
Social Media: www.youtube.com/user/saultmuseum;
twitter.com/SaultMuseum;
www.facebook.com/pages/Sault-Ste-Marie-Museum/143320129039949

Simcoe: Norfolk Historical Society
109 Norfolk St. South, Simcoe, ON N3Y 2W3
Tel: 519-426-1583
office@norfolklore.com
www.norfolklore.com
Social Media: www.twitter.com/museumnorfolk;
www.facebook.com/evabrookdonly
Helen Bartens, Curator
curator@norfolklore.com

Southampton: Bruce County Museum & Cultural Centre
33 Victoria St. North, Southampton, ON N0H 2L0
Tel: 519-797-2080; Fax: 519-797-2191
Toll-Free: 866-318-8889
museum@brucecounty.on.ca
www.brucemuseum.ca
Social Media: twitter.com/brucemuseum;
www.facebook.com/BruceCountyMuseum
Ann-Marie Collins, Archivist
acollins@brucecounty.on.ca
Susan Schlorff, Archival Assistant
sschlorff@brucecounty.on.ca
Deb Sturdevant, Archival Assistant
dsturdevant@brucecounty.on.ca

St Catharines: St Catharines Museum at Lock 3
1932 Welland Canals Pkwy., St Catharines, ON L2R 7K6
Tel: 905-984-8880; Fax: 905-984-6910
Toll-Free: 800-305-5134
TTY: 905-688-488
museum@stcatharines.ca
www.stcatharines.ca
Social Media: twitter.com/stcmuseum;
www.facebook.com/stcatharinesmuseum
Kathleen Powell, Supervisor & Curator
kpowell@stcatharines.ca
905-688-5601 ext. 5250

Stratford: Stratford Shakespeare Festival
350 Douro St., Stratford, ON N5A 3ST
Tel: 519-271-4040
www.stratfordfestival.ca
Social Media: www.flickr.com/photos/48668126@N07/;
twitter.com/stratfest; www.facebook.com/StratfordFestival
Liza Giffen, Archives Director
lgiffen@stratfordfestival.ca
Christine Schindler, Archives Coordinator
cschindler@stratfordfestival.ca
Nora Polley, Archives Assistant
npolley@stratfordfestival.ca

Stratford: Stratford-Perth Archives
4273 Line 34, RR#5, Stratford, ON N5A 6S6
Tel: 519-271-0531; Fax: 519-273-5746
archives@perthcounty.ca
www.stratfordpertharchives.on.ca

Teeterville: Teeterville Pioneer Museum
194 Teeter St., Teeterville, ON N0E 1S0
Tel: 519-426-5870; Fax: 519-428-3069
Other Numbers: Summer Hours, Phone: 519-443-4400
teeterville.museum@norfolkcounty.ca
www.teetervillemuseum.ca
Social Media: www.facebook.com/teetervillemuseum

Thunder Bay: City of Thunder Bay
235 Vickers St. North, Thunder Bay, ON P7C 6A3
Tel: 807-625-2270; Fax: 807-622-4212
archives@thunderbay.ca
www.thunderbay.ca/City_Government/City_Records_and_Archives.htm
Social Media: www.flickr.com/photos/thunderbayarchives
Matt Szybalski, Manager, Corporate Records & City Archivist
807-625-3390

Thunder Bay: Northwestern Ontario Sports Hall of Fame
219 May St. South, Thunder Bay, ON P7E 1B5
Tel: 807-622-2852; Fax: 807-622-2736
nwosport@tbaytel.net
www.nwosportshalloffame.com
Social Media: www.youtube.com/user/nwosport;
twitter.com/nwosports; www.facebook.com/259816551287
Diane Imrie, Executive Director
Kathryn Dwyer, Curator

Thunder Bay: Thunder Bay Historical Museum
425 Donald St. East, Thunder Bay, ON P7E 5V1
Tel: 807-623-0801; Fax: 807-622-6880
info@thunderbaymuseum.com
www.thunderbaymuseum.com
Social Media: instagram.com/thunderbaymuseum;
twitter.com/TBayMuseum;
www.facebook.com/pages/Thunder-Bay-Museum/40813019102
Thorold Tronrud, Curator

Toronto: Anglican General Synod Archives
80 Hayden St., Toronto, ON M4Y 3G2
Tel: 416-924-9199; Fax: 416-968-7983
archives@national.anglican.ca
www.anglican.ca/resources/gsarchives
Nancy Hurn, Librarian

Toronto: Archives of Ontario
134 Ian Macdonald Blvd., Toronto, ON M7A 2C5
Tel: 416-327-1600; Fax: 416-327-1999
Toll-Free: 800-668-9933
reference@ontario.ca
www.archives.gov.on.ca
Social Media: www.youtube.com/ArchivesOfOntario;
twitter.com/ArchivesOntario
Janice Orlando-Sottile, Acting Director
Janice.Orlando-Sottile@ontario.ca
416-327-1577

Toronto: Art Gallery of Ontario/ Musée des beaux-arts de l'Ontario
317 Dundas St. West, Toronto, ON M5T 1G4
Tel: 416-979-6642; Fax: 416-979-6602
library_archives@ago.net
www.ago.net
Social Media: twitter.com/agotoronto;
www.facebook.com/AGOToronto

Toronto: Arts & Letters Club
14 Elm St., Toronto, ON M5G 1G7
Tel: 416-597-0223; Fax: 416-597-9544
info@artsandlettersclub.ca
www.artsandlettersclub.ca
Scott James, Archivist

Toronto: Burgee Data Archives
117 Airdrie Rd., Toronto, ON M4G 1M6
Tel: 416-423-9979; Fax: 416-423-9979
Peter B. Edwards, Director

Toronto: Calgary Sun
333 King St. East, Toronto, ON M5A 3X5
Tel: 416-947-2258; Fax: 416-947-2043
Toll-Free: 877-624-1463
licensing@Postmedia.com
www.calgarysun.ca

Toronto: Canadian Children's Book Centre
#217, 40 Orchard View Blvd., Toronto, ON M4R 1B9
Tel: 416-975-0010; Fax: 416-975-8970
info@bookcentre.ca
www.bookcentre.ca/library
Charlotte Teeple, Executive Director
charlotte@bookcentre.ca
Meghan Howe, Library Coordinator
meghan@bookcentre.ca

Toronto: Canadian Lesbian & Gay Archives
34 Isabella St., Toronto, ON M4Y 1N1
Tel: 416-777-2755
queeries@clga.ca
www.clga.ca
Social Media: canadianlesbianandgayarchives.tumblr.com;
twitter.com/clgarchives; www.facebook.com/CLGArchives
Dennis Findlay, President
Glen Brown, Interim Executive Director
executivedirector@clga.ca

Toronto: Canadian Opera Company/ La compagnie d'opéra canadienne
227 Front St. East, Toronto, ON M5A 1E8
Tel: 416-363-6671; Fax: 416-363-5584
www.coc.ca
Social Media: twitter.com/canadianopera;
www.facebook.com/canadianoperacompany
Birthe Joergensen, Archivist
birthej@coc.ca

Toronto: Canadian Royal Heritage Trust
2708 Yonge St., Toronto, ON M4P 3J4
Tel: 716-482-4157
info@crht.ca
www.crht.ca/Resources

Toronto: City of Toronto Archives
255 Spadina Rd., Toronto, ON M5R 2V3
Tel: 416-397-0778; Fax: 416-392-9685
archives@toronto.ca
www.toronto.ca/archives
Social Media: flickr.com/photos/torontohistory;
twitter.com/TorontoArchives

Toronto: College of Physicians & Surgeons of Ontario
80 College St., Toronto, ON M5G 2E2
Tel: 416-967-2600; Fax: 416-961-3330
Toll-Free: 800-268-7096
www.cpso.on.ca

Toronto: Etobicoke Historical Society
c/o Montgomery's Inn, 4709 Dundas St. West, Toronto, ON M9A 1A8
www.etobicokehistorical.com
Social Media: twitter.com/EtobHistory;
facebook.com/pages/Etobicoke-/427420737349716
James Geneau, President
Denise Harris, Chief Historian

Toronto: Exhibition Place
#1, 100 Princes' Blvd., Toronto, ON M6K 3C3
Tel: 416-263-3658
www.explace.on.ca/about_us/archives/index.php
Social Media: twitter.com/explaceTO;
www.facebook.com/pages/Exhibition-Place/159377337482707
Linda Cobon, Manager, Records & Archives
lcobon@explace.on.ca

Toronto: The Film Reference Library
TIFF Bell Lightbox, 350 King St. West, Toronto, ON M5V 3X5
Tel: 416-599-8433; Fax: 416-967-0628
libraryservices@tiff.net
www.tiff.net/education/filmreferencelibrary
Sylvia Frank, Director

Toronto: General Archives of the Basilian Fathers
95 St Joseph St., Toronto, ON M5S 3C2
Tel: 416-925-4368
www.basilian.org

***Toronto:* Hockey Hall of Fame**
400 Kipling Ave., Toronto, ON M8V 3L1
Tel: 416-360-7735; *Fax:* 416-251-5770
acquisitions@hhof.com
www.hhof.com/htmlrescentre/rc00.shtml
Miragh Bitove, Archivist & Collections Registrar
mbitove@hhof.com
Craig Campbell, Manager, Resource Centre & Archives
campbellc@hhof.com
Steve Poirier, Coordinator, HHOF Images & Archival Services
Spoirier@hhof.com
Izak Westgate, Manager, Outreach Exhibits & Assistant Curator
Iwestgate@hhof.com

***Toronto:* Holy Blossom Temple**
1950 Bathurst St., Toronto, ON M5P 3K9
Tel: 416-789-3291
templemail@holyblossom.org
www.holyblossom.org
Social Media: youtube.com/user/holyblossomtemple; twitter.com/holyblossom; facebook.com/pages/Holy-Blossom-Temple/98017462501; linkedin.com/groups?gid=4507427
Russ Joseph, Executive Director
rjoseph@holyblossom.org
416-789-3291 ext. 226
Sara Novak, Education Department Administrator
snovak@holyblossom.org
416-789-3291 ext. 237

***Toronto:* Institute of the Blessed Virgin Mary in North America (Loretto Sisters)**
101 Mason Blvd., Toronto, ON M5M 3E2
Tel: 416-483-2238; *Fax:* 416-485-9884
ibvmadm@rogers.com
www.ibvm.ca

***Toronto:* Montgomery's Inn Museum**
4709 Dundas St. West, Toronto, ON M9A 1A8
Tel: 416-394-8113; *Fax:* 416-394-6027
montinn@toronto.ca
montgomerysinn.com
Social Media: twitter.com/MontINNTO; facebook.com/montgomerysinn

***Toronto:* Multicultural History Society of Ontario**
#307, 901 Lawrence Ave. West, Toronto, ON M6A 1C3
Tel: 416-979-2973; *Fax:* 416-979-7947
info@mhso.ca
www.mhso.ca

***Toronto:* National Ballet of Canada/ Ballet national du Canada**
470 Queens Quay West, Toronto, ON M5V 3K4
Tel: 416-345-9686; *Fax:* 416-345-8323
archives@national.ballet.ca
national.ballet.ca/Archives
Caitlin Dyer, Archives Manager

***Toronto:* Ontario Genealogical Society**
Humanities and Social Sciences Dept., Toronto Reference Library, 789 Yonge St., Toronto, ON M4W 2G8
Tel: 416-393-7175
trlhss@torontopubliclibrary.ca
www.ogs.on.ca

***Toronto:* Ontario Jewish Archives**
Sherman Campus, UJA Federation of Greater Toronto, 4600 Bathurst St., Toronto, ON M2R 3V2
Tel: 416-635-5391; *Fax:* 416-849-1006
www.ontariojewisharchives.org
Social Media: twitter.com/oja_toronto; www.facebook.com/OntarioJewishArchives
Dora Solomon, Director
Melissa Caza, Archivist
Donna Bernardo-Ceriz, Archivist
Elizabeth Banks, Assistant Archivist

***Toronto:* The Presbyterian Church in Canada**
50 Wynford Dr., Toronto, ON M3C 1J7
Tel: 416-441-1111; *Toll-Free:* 800-619-7301
www.presbyterianarchives.ca
Kim Arnold, Archivist & Records Administrator
karnold@presbyterian.ca
416-441-1111 ext. 310
Bob Anger, Assistant Archivist
banger@presbyterian.ca
416-441-1111 ext. 266

***Toronto:* Queen's Own Rifles of Canada Regimental Museum**
1 Austin Terrace, Toronto, ON M5R 1X8
museum@qormuseum.org
qormuseum.org
Social Media: www.flickr.com/photos/qormuseum; twitter.com/qormuseum; www.facebook.com/qormuseum
John Stephens, Curator

***Toronto:* Queen's York Rangers (1st American Regiment) Museum**
CFA Fort York, 660 Fleet St. West, Toronto, ON M5V 1A9
Tel: 416-203-4622
QYRangCENTRALREGISTRY@intern.mil.ca
www.qyrang.ca
Diane Kruger, Curator

***Toronto:* Roman Catholic Archdiocese of Toronto**
Catholic Pastoral Centre, #505, 1155 Yonge St., Toronto, ON M4T 1W2
Tel: 416-934-3400; *Fax:* 416-934-3434
archives@archtoronto.org
www.archtoronto.org/archives
Marc Lerman, Director
416-934-3400 ext. 505

***Toronto:* The Royal Canadian Yacht Club**
141 St George St., Toronto, ON M5R 2L8
Tel: 416-967-7245; *Fax:* 416-967-5710
heritage@rcyc.ca
www.rcyc.ca
Beverley Darville, Archivist
Beverley.Darville@rcyc.ca

***Toronto:* Royal Ontario Museum/ Musée royal de l'Ontario**
100 Queen's Park Cres., Toronto, ON M5S 2C6
Tel: 416-586-5595; *Fax:* 416-586-5519
info@rom.on.ca
www.rom.on.ca/en/collections-research/library-archives
Social Media: twitter.com/ROMLibrary; www.facebook.com/ROMLibrary
Arthur Smith, Head, Librarian
416-586-5740

***Toronto:* St John's Rehabilitation Hospital**
#S-325, 285 Cummer Ave., 3rd Fl, Toronto, ON M2M 2G1
Tel: 416-226-6780; *Fax:* 416-226-6265
www.stjohnsrehab.com

***Toronto:* The Salvation Army**
26 Howden Rd., Toronto, ON M1R 3E4
Tel: 416-285-4344
heritage_centre@can.salvationarmy.org
www.salvationist.ca/about-us/history/museum-archives
Social Media: twitter.com/salvationist

***Toronto:* Scarboro Mission Society**
2685 Kingston Rd., Toronto, ON M1M 1M4
Tel: 416-261-7135; *Fax:* 416-261-0820
Toll-Free: 800-260-4815
info@scarboromissions.ca
www.scarboromissions.ca
John Carten, Councillor
jcarten@scarboromissions.ca

***Toronto:* Scarborough Historical Society**
6282 Kingston Rd., Toronto, ON M1C 1K9
Tel: 416-995-6930
info@scarboroughhistorical.ca
scarboroughhistorical.ca/?page_id=55

***Toronto:* Sculptors Society of Canada/ La Société des sculpteurs du Canada**
500 Church St., Toronto, ON M4Y 2C8
Tel: 647-435-5858
gallery@cansculpt.org
www.cansculpt.org

***Toronto:* The Sisterhood of St. John the Divine Convent**
233 Cummer Ave., Toronto, ON M2M 2E8
Tel: 416-226-2201; *Fax:* 416-226-2131
convent@ssjd.ca
www.ssjd.ca/libraries.html

***Toronto:* Sisters of St. Joseph of Toronto**
101 Thorncliffe Park Dr., Toronto, ON M4H 1M2
Tel: 416-467-2643; *Fax:* 416-429-7921
info@csj-to.ca
www.csj-to.ca
Social Media: www.youtube.com/user/CSJTO; twitter.com/csjto; www.facebook.com/csjto
Linda Wicks, Archivist
lwicks@csj-to.ca

***Toronto:* Sisters Servants of Mary Immaculate**
5 Austin Terrace, Toronto, ON M5R 1Y1
Tel: 416-924-7422; *Fax:* 416-928-9261
ssmi.org@rogers.com
www.ssmi.org

***Toronto:* Tartu Institute**
310 Bloor St. West, Toronto, ON M5S 1W4
Tel: 416-925-9405; *Fax:* 416-925-2295
vemu@tartucollege.ca
www.tartuinstitute.ca
Piret Noorhani, Head Archivist
piret@tartucollege.ca
Roland Weiler, Archivist
rweiler7@cogeco.ca
905-627-3856

***Toronto:* Todmorden Mills Heritage Museum & Art Centre**
67 Pottery Rd., Toronto, ON M4K 2B9
Tel: 416-396-2819
todmorden@toronto.ca

***Toronto:* Toronto Port Authority**
60 Harbour St., Toronto, ON M5J 1B7
Tel: 416-863-2011; *Fax:* 416-863-0391
www.torontoport.com

***Toronto:* The Toronto Sun**
365 Bloor St. East, 3rd Fl., Toronto, ON M4W 3L4
Tel: 416-947-2258
licensing@Postmedia.com
www.torontosun.com

***Toronto:* Toronto Symphony Orchestra**
212 King St. West, 6th Fl., Toronto, ON M5H 1K5
Tel: 416-593-7769; *Fax:* 416-977-2912
www.tso.ca
Social Media: twitter.com/TorontoSymphony; www.facebook.com/pages/Toronto-Symphony-Orchestra/52219459772
John Dunn, Volunteer Archivist

***Toronto:* United Church of Canada Archives**
40 Oak St., Toronto, ON M5A 2C6
Tel: 416-644-3140; *Fax:* 416-321-3103
archives@united-church.ca
www.united-church.ca/local/archives/on
Social Media: www.facebook.com/UnitedChurchCda

***Toronto:* Upper Canada College Archives**
200 Lonsdale Rd., Toronto, ON M4V 1W6
Tel: 416-488-1125
www.ucc.on.ca
Jill Spellman, Archivist
jspellman@ucc.on.ca

***Toronto:* Weston Historical Society**
1901 Weston Rd., Toronto, ON M9N 3P1
Tel: 416-249-6663
info@heritageweston.com
heritageweston.com
Cherri Hurst, President

***Toronto:* York Pioneer & Historical Society**
2482 Yonge St., Toronto, ON M4P 3E3
Tel: 416-656-2954
yorkpioneers@gmail.com
www.yorkpioneers.org

***Tweed:* Tweed & Area Heritage Centre**
40 Victoria St. North, Tweed, ON K0K 3J0
Tel: 613-478-3989
tweedheritageinfo@on.aibn.com

***Uxbridge:* Uxbridge Historical Centre**
7239 Concession 6, Uxbridge, ON L9P 1N5
Tel: 905-852-5854
museum@town.uxbridge.on.ca
uxbridgehistoricalcentre.com
Social Media: twitter.com/UxbridgeMuseum; www.facebook.com/uxbridgehistoricalcentre

***Vaughan:* City of Vaughan Archives**
City Hall, Level 000, 2141 Major Mackenzie Dr., Vaughan, ON L6A 1T1
Tel: 905-832-2281
archives@vaughan.ca
www.vaughan.ca/services/vaughan_archives

***Vernon:* Osgoode Township Historical Society & Museum**
7814 Lawrence St., Vernon, ON K0A 3J0
Tel: 613-821-4062; *Fax:* 613-821-3140
osgoodemuseum.ca
Social Media: twitter.com/osgoodemuseum; www.facebook.com/125725207465630
Robin Cushnie, Museum Manager
manager@osgoodemuseum.ca
Ann Robinson, Administrator
administration@osgoodemuseum.ca

***Waterford:* Waterford Heritage & Agricultural Museum**
159 Nichol St., Waterford, ON N0E 1Y0
Tel: 519-443-4211
waterford.museum@norfolkcounty.ca
waterfordmuseum.ca

***Waterloo:* Evangelical Lutheran Church in Canada**
Wilfred Laurier University, 75 University Ave. West, Waterloo, ON N2L 3C5
Tel: 519-884-0710
www.easternsynod.org
Julia Hendry, Head, Archives & Special Collections
jhendry@wlu.ca
519-884-0710 ext. 3825
Cindy Preece, Archives Administrator
cpreece@wlu.ca
519-884-0710 ext. 3906

***Waterloo:* Mennonite Archives of Ontario**
Conrad Grebel University College, 140 Westmount Rd. North, Waterloo, ON N2L 3G6
Tel: 519-885-0220
marchive@uwaterloo.ca
uwaterloo.ca/mennonite-archives-ontario
Laureen Harder-Gissing, Librarian & Archivist

***Wellington:* Prince Edward County Archives**
261 Main St., Wellington, ON K0K 3L0
Tel: 613-399-2023
pecarchives.org
Krista Richardson, Archives Manager, County of Prince Edward Archives
krichardson@peclibrary.org

***Whitby:* Town of Whitby Archives**
Whitby Public Library, 405 Dundas St., Whitby, ON L1N 6A1
Tel: 905-668-6531; *Fax:* 905-668-7445
archives@whitbylibrary.on.ca
www.whitbylibrary.on.ca
Social Media: www.flickr.com/people/whitbyarchives
Sarah Ferencz, Archivist

***Windsor:* Assumption University Archives**
400 Huron Church Rd., Windsor, ON N9C 2J9
Tel: 519-973-7033; *Fax:* 519-973-7089
info@assumptionu.ca
www.assumptionu.ca
Cécile Bertrand, Executive Administrative Assistant/Archivist
cbertrand@assumptionu.ca

***Windsor:* Serbian Heritage Museum**
6770 Tecumseh Rd. East, Windsor, ON N8T 1E6
Tel: 519-944-4884; *Fax:* 519-974-3963
info@serbianheritagemuseum.com
www.serbianheritagemuseum.com
Social Media: youtube.com/user/shmuseum; facebook.com/shmuseum

***Windsor:* Windsor's Community Museum/ Le Musée communautaire de Windsor**
François Baby House, 254 Pitt St. West, Windsor, ON N9A 5L5
Tel: 519-253-1812
wmuseum@city.windsor.on.ca
www.citywindsor.ca
Madelyn Della Valle, Museum Curator
mdellavalle@citywindsor.ca

***Woodstock:* County of Oxford**
82 Light St., Woodstock, ON N4S 6H1
Tel: 519-539-9800
archives@oxfordcounty.ca
www.oxfordcounty.ca
Marion Baker, Archives Clerk
Liz Mayville, Assistant Archivist

Prince Edward Island

Regional Systems

***Morell:* Prince Edward Island Public Library Service**
89 Red Head Rd., Morell, PE C0A 1S0
Tel: 902-961-7320; *Fax:* 902-961-7322
plshq@gov.pe.ca
www.library.pe.ca
Social Media: pinterest.com/peilibrary; twitter.com/PEILibrary; www.facebook.com/PEILibrary

Public Libraries

***Alberton:* Alberton Public Library**
11 Railway St., Alberton, PE C0B 1B0
Tel: 902-231-2090
alberton@gov.pe.ca
www.library.pe.ca/index.php3?number=1031782&lang=E
Social Media: www.facebook.com/albertonpubliclibrary

***Borden:* Borden-Carleton Public Library**
244 Borden Ave., Borden, PE C0B 1X0
Tel: 902-437-6492
borden-carleton@gov.pe.ca

***Breadalbane:* Breadalbane Public Library**
4023 Dixon Rd., Breadalbane, PE C0A 1E0
Tel: 902-964-2520
breadalbane@gov.pe.ca

***Charlottetown:* Bibliothèque publique Dr. J. Edmond Arsenault**
5 Acadian Dr., Charlottetown, PE C1C 1M2
Tél: 902-368-6092
carrefour@gov.pe.ca

***Charlottetown:* Confederation Centre Public Library**
145A Richmond St., Charlottetown, PE C1A 8G8
Tel: 902-368-4642; *Fax:* 902-368-4652
ccpl@gov.pe.ca

***Cornwall:* Cornwall Public Library (PEI)**
39 Lowther Dr., Cornwall, PE C0A 1H0
Tel: 902-629-8415
cornwall@gov.pe.ca

***Crapaud:* Crapaud Public Library**
20424 Trans Canada Hwy., Crapaud, PE C0A 1J0
Tel: 902-658-2297
crapaud@gov.pe.ca

***Georgetown:* Georgetown Genevieve Soloman Memorial Library**
36 Kent St., Georgetown, PE C0A 1L0
Tel: 902-652-2832
georgetown@gov.pe.ca

***Hunter River:* Hunter River Public Library**
19816 Rte. 2, Hunter River, PE C0A 1N0
Tel: 902-964-2800
hunter_river@gov.pe.ca

***Kensington:* Kensington Public Library**
6 Commercial St., Kensington, PE C0B 1M0
Tel: 902-836-3721
kensington@gov.pe.ca

***Kinkora:* Kinkora Public Library**
45 Anderson Rd., Kinkora, PE C0B 1N0
Tel: 902-887-2172
kinkora@gov.pe.ca

***Montague:* Montague Rotary Library**
53 Wood Islands Rd., Montague, PE C0A 1R0
Tel: 902-838-2928
montague@gov.pe.ca

***Morell:* Morell Public Library**
89 Red Head Rd., Morell, PE C0A 1S0
Tel: 902-961-3389
morell@gov.pe.ca

***Mount Stewart:* Mount Stewart Public Library**
104 Main St., Mount Stewart, PE C0A 1T0
Tel: 902-676-2050
mtstewart@gov.pe.ca

***Murray Harbour:* Murray Harbour Public Library**
27 Park St., Murray Harbour, PE C0A 1V0
Tel: 902-962-3875
murray_harbour@gov.pe.ca

***Murray River:* Murray River Leona Giddings Memorial Library**
1066 McInnis Rd., Murray River, PE C0A 1V0
Tel: 902-962-2667
murray_river@gov.pe.ca

***O'Leary:* O'Leary Public Library**
18 Community St., O'Leary, PE C0B 1V0
Tel: 902-859-8788
o'leary@gov.pe.ca

***Souris:* Souris Public Library**
75 Main St., Souris, PE C0A 2B0
Tel: 902-687-2157
souris@gov.pe.ca

***St. Peters:* St. Peters Public Library**
1968 Cardigan Rd., St. Peters, PE C0A 2A0
Tel: 902-961-3415
st_peter's@gov.pe.ca

***Stratford:* Stratford Public Library (PEI)**
25 Hopeton Rd., Stratford, PE C1B 1T6
Tel: 902-569-7441
stratford@gov.pe.ca

***Summerside:* Bibliothèque J.-Henri-Blanchard**
5, av Maris Stella, Summerside, PE C1N 3Y5
Tél: 902-432-2748
blanchard@gov.pe.ca

***Summerside:* Summerside Rotary Library**
192 Water St., Summerside, PE C1N 1B1
Tel: 902-436-7323
summerside@gov.pe.ca

***Tignish:* Tignish Public Library**
103 School St., Tignish, PE C0B 2B0
Tel: 902-882-7363
tignish@gov.pe.ca

***Tyne Valley:* Tyne Valley Public Library**
19 Allen Rd., Tyne Valley, PE C0B 2C0
Tel: 902-831-3338
tyne_valley@gov.pe.ca

***Wellington:* Bibliothèque publique d'Abram-Village**
a/s École Évangéline, 1596 Rte. 124, Wellington, PE C0B 2E0
Tél: 902-854-2491; *Téléc:* 902-854-2981
abram@gov.pe.ca

Archives

***Charlottetown:* Prince Edward Island Public Archives & Records Office**
Hon. George Coles Building, 4th Fl., 175 Richmond St., Charlottetown, PE C1A 7M4
Tel: 902-368-4290
archives@gov.pe.ca
www.gov.pe.ca/archives
Jill MacMicken Wilson, Provincial Archivist
jswilson@gov.pe.ca
902-368-4351
Ann-Marie McIsaac, Provincial Records Manager
902-368-6093

Québec

Regional Systems

***Alma:* Réseau BIBLIO du Saguenay-Lac-Saint-Jean**
100, rue Price ouest, Alma, QC G8B 4S1
Tél: 418-662-6425; *Téléc:* 418-662-7593
Ligne sans frais: 800-563-6425
info@reseaubiblioslsj.qc.ca
www.reseaubiblioslsj.qc.ca
Média social: twitter.com/reseaubiblio; www.facebook.com/reseaubiblioSLSJ
Sophie Bolduc, Directrice générale
sbolduc@reseaubiblioslsj.qc.ca
Keven Rousseau, Conseiller aux bibliothèques - Informatique
krousseau@reseaubiblioslsj.qc.ca
Julie Dubé, Responsable services aux bibliothèques
jdube@reseaubiblioslsj.qc.ca

***Cap-Chat:* Réseau BIBLIO de la Gaspésie-Iles-de-la-Madeleine**
31, rue des Écoliers, Cap-Chat, QC G0J 1E0
Tél: 418-786-5597; *Téléc:* 418-786-2024
Ligne sans frais: 855-737-3281
info@reseaubibliogim.qc.ca
Média social: www.facebook.com/ReseauBIBLIOGIM

Julie Blais, Directrice générale
julie.blais@reseaubibliogim.qc.ca
Monique Demers, Responsable, soutien aux bibliothèques affiliées
monique.demers@reseaubibliogim.qc.ca
Carole Bernatchez, Responsable, service de prêt entre bibliothèques
carole.bernatchez@reseaubibliogim.qc.ca

***Charny:* Réseau BIBLIO de la Capitale-Nationale et de la Chaudière-Appalaches**
3189, rue Albert-Demers, Charny, QC G6X 3A1
Tél: 418-832-6166; *Téléc:* 418-832-6168
Ligne sans frais: 866-446-6166
info@reseaubibliocnca.qc.ca
www.reseaubiblioduquebec.qc.ca
Isabelle Poirier, Directrice générale
ipoirier@reseaubibliocnca.qc.ca
Marc Hébert, Agent culturel et de développement
mhebert@reseaubibliocnca.qc.ca

***Gatineau:* Réseau BIBLIO de l'Outaouais**
2295, rue Saint-Louis, Gatineau, QC J8T 5L8
Tél: 819-561-6008; *Téléc:* 819-561-6767
biblio@crsbpo.qc.ca
www.reseaubibliooutaouais.qc.ca
Sylvie Thibault, Directrice générale
sylvie.thibault@crsbpo.qc.ca
Claudette Deschênes, Agente de bureau
claudette.deschenes@crsbpo.qc.ca
Jonathan Careau, Responsable des services au réseau s
jonathan.careau@crsbpo.qc.ca

***La Prairie:* Réseau BIBLIO de la Montérégie**
275, rue Conrad-Pelletier, La Prairie, QC J5R 4V1
Tél: 450-444-5433; *Téléc:* 450-659-3364
crsaide@reseaubibliomonteregie.qc.ca
www.reseaubibliomonteregie.qc.ca
Média social: www.youtube.com/user/RBMonteregie; twitter.com/RBMonteregie; www.facebook.com/ReseauBiblioMonteregie; www.linkedin.com/company/réseau-biblio-de-la-montérégie
Jacqueline Labelle, Directrice générale
Josée Audet, Directrice, Services techniques

***Rivière-du-Loup:* Réseau BIBLIO du Bas-Saint-Laurent**
465, rue St-Pierre, Rivière-du-Loup, QC G5R 4T6
Tél: 418-867-1682; *Téléc:* 418-867-3434
crsbp@crsbp.net
www.reseaubibliobsl.qc.ca
Jacques Côté, Directeur général
jacques.cote@crsbp.net

***Rouyn-Noranda:* Réseau BIBLIO de l'Abitibi-Témiscamingue-Nord-du-Québec**
20, av Québec, Rouyn-Noranda, QC J9X 2E6
Tél: 819-762-4305; *Téléc:* 819-762-5309
info@reseaubiblioatnq.qc.ca
mabiblio.quebec
Louis Dallaire, Directeur général
louis.dallaire@reseaubiblioatnq.qc.ca

***Sainte-Agathe-des-Monts:* Ma BIBLIO à moi**
29, rue Brissette, Sainte-Agathe-des-Monts, QC J8C 3L1
Tél: 819-326-6440; *Téléc:* 819-326-0885
info@crsbpl.qc.ca
www.mabibliotheque.ca
JoAnne Turnbull, Directrice générale
jturnbull@crsbpl.qc.ca
Julie Filion, Directrice, Soutien aux bibliothèques
jfilion@crsbpl.qc.ca
Norbert Morveau, Directeur, Soutien informatique
nmorneau@crsbpl.qc.ca

***Sept-Îles:* Réseau BIBLIO de la Côte-Nord**
59, rue Napoléon, Sept-Îles, QC G4R 5C5
Tél: 418-962-1020; *Téléc:* 418-962-5124
www.reseaubiblioduquebec.qc.ca
Jean-Roch Gagnon, Directeur général
jrgagnon@reseaubibliocn.qc.ca
Chantal Hould, Responsable, Services techniques
chantalh@reseaubibliocn.qc.ca

***Sherbrooke:* Réseau BIBLIO de l'Estrie**
4155, rue Brodeur, Sherbrooke, QC J1L 1K4
Tél: 819-565-9744; *Téléc:* 819-565-9157
crsbpe@reseaubiblioestrie.qc.ca
www.reseaubiblioestrie.qc.ca
Joelle Thivierge, Directrice générale
jthivierge@reseaubiblioestrie.qc.ca
819-565-9744 ext. 102
France Lachance, Service à la clientele
flachance@reseaubiblioestrie.qc.ca
819-565-9744 ext. 103

***Trois-Rivières:* Réseau BIBLIO du Centre-du-Québec, de Lanaudière et de la Mauricie**
3125, rue Girard, Trois-Rivières, QC G8Z 2M4
Tél: 819-375-9623; *Téléc:* 819-375-0132
Ligne sans frais: 877-324-2546
crsbp@reseaubibliocqlm.qc.ca
www.mabibliotheque.ca
Média social: www.flickr.com/photos/reseaubibliocqlm; www.facebook.com/184614871577283
Hélène Arseneau, Directrice générale
helene.arseneau@reseaubibliocqlm.qc.ca
Chantal Bourgoing, Chef d'équipe, Services gestion et diffusion des collections
Chantal.bourgoing@reseaubibliocqlm.qc.ca
Valérie Simard, Directrice, technologies de l'information
valerie.simard@reseaubibliocqlm.qc.ca
Lauren Duchemin, Directrice, Services administratifs
lauren.duchemin@reseaubibliocqlm.qc.ca
Francine Allen, Directrice, Services techniques coopératifs
francine.allen@reseaubibliocqlm.qc.ca

Public Libraries

***Montréal:* Bibliothèque de Baie-D'Urfé**
20551, boul Lakeshore, Montréal, QC H9X 1R3
Tél: 514-457-3274
biblio@baie-durfe.qc.ca
www.bibliobaiedurfe.com

***Montréal-Est:* Bibliothèque Micheline-Gagnon**
11370, rue Notre-Dame Est, Montréal-Est, QC H1B 2W6
Tél: 514-905-2145

***Dégelis:* Bibliothèque municipale de Dégelis**
384, av Principale, Dégelis, QC G5T 1L3
Tél: 418-853-2332
biblio.degelis@crsbp.net
ville.degelis.qc.ca/bibliotheque-municipale
Média social: www.facebook.com/biblio.degelis
Gertrude Leclerc, Responsable

***Acton Vale:* Bibliothèque Acton Vale**
1093A, rue Saint-André, Acton Vale, QC J0H 1A0
Tél: 450-546-2703; *Téléc:* 450-642-1165
acton.vale@reseaubibliomonteregie.qc.ca
Média social: www.pinterest.com/BiblioActonVale; www.facebook.com/biblioActonVale

***Aguanish:* Bibliothèque d'Aguanish**
106, rue Jacques-Cartier, Aguanish, QC G0G 1A0
Tél: 418-533-2323; *Téléc:* 418-533-2012
Johanne Cormier, Responsable

***Albanel:* Bibliothèque publique d'Albanel**
153A, rue Principale, Albanel, QC G8M 3J3
Tél: 613-279-5250
albanel@reseaubiblioslsj.qc.ca
Hélène Théberge, Responsable
418-279-3355

***Albertville:* Bibliothèque d'Albertville**
1058, rue Principale, Albertville, QC G0J 1A0
Tél: 418-756-6015
biblio.albert@crsbp.net
www.reseaubiblioduquebec.qc.ca
Sabrina Raymond, Responsable

***Alma:* Bibliothèque municipale d'Alma**
500, rue Collard Ouest, Alma, QC G8B 1N2
Tél: 418-669-5140
www.ville.alma.qc.ca/biblio
Média social: www.facebook.com/biblio.alma
Emilie Guertin, Coordonnatrice des bibliothèques
emilie.guertin@ville.alma.qc.ca

***Alma:* Bibliothèque publique de Delisle**
221, rue des Bruyères, Alma, QC G8E 1J9
Tél: 418-668-2697
delisle@reseaubiblioslsj.qc.ca

***Alma:* Bibliothèque publique de Saint-Coeur-de-Marie**
#105, 5791, av du Pont nord, Alma, QC G8E 1X1
Tél: 418-347-3729
stcoeur@reseaubiblioslsj.qc.ca
www.reseaubiblioduquebec.qc.ca/portail/index.aspx?page=3&BID=558

***Amherst:* Bibliothèque de Saint-Rémi**
124, rue St-Louis, Amherst, QC J0T 2L0
Tél: 819-687-3372; *Téléc:* 819-687-8430
bibliostremi@municipalite.amherst.qc.ca

***Amqui:* Bibliothèque Madeleine-Gagnon**
24, promenade de l'Hôtel de Ville, Amqui, QC G5J 3E1
Tél: 418-629-4242
bibliotheque@ville.amqui.qc.ca
www.ville.amqui.qc.ca

***Angliers:* Bibliothèque d'Angliers**
14, rue Baie Miller, Angliers, QC J0Y 1A0
Tél: 819-949-4351; *Téléc:* 819-949-4321
angliers@reseaubiblioatnq.qc.ca
Isabelle Galant, Responsable

***Armagh:* Bibliothèque municipale d'Armagh**
9, rue de la Salle, Armagh, QC G0R 1A0
Tél: 418-466-3004; *Téléc:* 418-466-2409
www.mabibliotheque.ca/armagh
Lyse Roy, Responsable

***Arundel:* Bibliothèque d'Arundel/ Arundel Library**
2, rue du Village, Arundel, QC J0T 1A0
Tél: 819-687-8246; *Téléc:* 819-687-8760
biblio@municipalite.arundel.qc.ca
www.reseaubiblioduquebec.qc.ca

***Asbestos:* Bibliothèque municipale d'Asbestos**
351, boul Saint-Luc, Asbestos, QC J1T 2W4
Tél: 819-879-7171; *Téléc:* 819-879-2343
bibliotheque@ville.asbestos.qc.ca
ville.asbestos.qc.ca/bibliotheque-municipale
Julie Fontaine, Responsable

***Aston-Jonction:* Bibliothèque d'Aston-Jonction**
210, rue Lemire, Aston-Jonction, QC G0Z 1A0
Téléc: 819-226-3459
biblio070@reseaubibliocqlm.qc.ca
www.reseaubiblioduquebec.qc.ca
Léa Houle, Responsable

***Auclair:* Bibliothèque Auclair**
777, rue du Clocher, Auclair, QC G0L 1A0
Tél: 418-899-0847
biblio.auclair@crsbp.net
Gilles Lagrois, Responsable

***Aumond:* Bibliothèque de Aumond**
664, rue Principale, Aumond, QC J0W 1W0
Tél: 819-441-2300; *Téléc:* 819-449-7448
admaumond@crsbpo.qc.ca
Linda Lemieux, Responsable

***Baie-Comeau:* Bibliothèque municipale Alice-Lane**
6, av Radisson, Baie-Comeau, QC G4Z 1W4
Tél: 418-296-8304
biblio@ville.baie-comeau.qc.ca
www.ville.baie-comeau.qc.ca
Marie Amiot, Superviseur responsable
mamiot@ville.baie-comeau.qc.ca
418-396-8361

***Baie-des-Sables:* Bibliothèque de Baie-des-Sables**
20, rue de Couvent, Baie-des-Sables, QC G0J 1C0
Tél: 418-772-6218
biblio.sables@crsbp.net
www.reseaubiblioduquebec.qc.ca
Liliane Ferland, Responsable

***Baie-du-Febvre:* Bibliothèque de Baie-du-Febvre**
23, rue de l'Église, Baie-du-Febvre, QC J0G 1A0
Tél: 450-783-6484
Carole Fortin, Responsable

***Baie-Johan-Beetz:* Bibliothèque Baie-Johan-Beetz**
18, rue Tanguay, Baie-Johan-Beetz, QC G0G 1B0
Tél: 418-539-0125; *Téléc:* 418-539-0205
munbjb@globetrotter.net
Sylvain Roy, Responsable

***Baie-Saint-Paul:* Bibliothèque René-Richard**
9, rue Forget, Baie-Saint-Paul, QC G3Z 1T4
Tél: 418-435-5858; *Téléc:* 418-435-0010
Denise Ouellet, Responsable
deniseouellet@baiesaintpaul.com

***Baie-Sainte-Catherine:* Bibliothèque Ali-Baba**
308, rue Leclerc, Baie-Sainte-Catherine, QC G0T 1A0
Tél: 418-237-4241; *Téléc:* 418-237-4223
www.reseaubiblioduquebec.qc.ca/baie-sainte-catherine

***Baie-Trinité:* Bibliothèque de Baie-Trinité**
28, route des Baleines, Baie-Trinité, QC G0H 1A0
Tél: 418-939-2231; *Téléc:* 418-939-2616
Pierrette Bureau, Responsable

***Barraute:* Bibliothèque Barraute**
600, 1re rue Ouest, Barraute, QC J0Y 1A0
Tél: 819-734-6762; *Téléc:* 819-734-6762
barraute@reseaubiblioatnq.qc.ca
Claire Voyer, Responsable

***Bassin:* Bibliothèque de L'Ile-du-Havre-Aubert**
#104, 280, ch de Bassin, Bassin, QC G4T 0B5
Tél: 418-937-2279; *Téléc:* 418-937-5558
bibliohavre@muniles.ca
Christiane Turbide, Responsable

***Beaconsfield:* Bibliothèque de Beaconsfield**
303, boul Beaconsfield, Beaconsfield, QC H9W 4A7
Tél: 514-428-4460; *Téléc:* 514-428-4477
bibliotheque@beaconsfield.ca
www.beaconsfield.ca/fr/services-de-la-bibliotheque
Michèle Janis, Chef de division
michele.janis@beaconsfield.ca
514-482-4400 ext. 4482
Beverley Gilbertson, Chef bibliothécaire
beverley.gilbertson@beaconsfield.ca
514-428-4400 ext. 4466
Anne Bourel, Responsable, service du prêt
anne.bourel@beaconsfield.ca
514-428-4400 ext. 4472
Beverley Price, Responsable, services techniques
beverley.price@beaconsfield.ca
514-428-4400 ext. 4474

***Beaucanton:* Bibliothèque Beaucanton**
2709, boul McDuff, #C, Beaucanton, QC J0Z 1H0
Tél: 819-941-2101
Annie Lavoie, Responsable

***Beauceville:* Bibliothèque Madeleine-Doyon**
100, Place de l'Église, Beauceville, QC G5X 1X3
Tél: 418-774-2466; *Téléc:* 418-774-2499
biblio@ville.beauceville.qc.ca
www.reseaubiblioduquebec.qc.ca/beauceville

***Beauharnois:* Bibliothèque Dominique-Julien**
#100, 600, rue Ellice, Beauharnois, QC J6N 3P7
Tél: 450-429-3546
ville.beauharnois.qc.ca
Caroline Ménard, Bibliotechnicienne
caroline.menard@ville.beauharnois.qc.ca

***Beaumont:* Bibliothèque Luc-Lacourcière**
64, ch du Domaine, Beaumont, QC G0R 1C0
Tél: 418-837-2658; *Téléc:* 418-837-4666
bibl.l.lacourciere@videotron.ca

***Beaupré:* Bibliothèque La Plume d'Oie (Bibliothèque de Beaupré et Saint-Joachim)**
11298, rue de La Salle, Beaupré, QC G0A 1E0
Tél: 418-827-8483; *Téléc:* 418-827-3818
bibliotheque@ville.beaupre.qc.ca
www.reseaubiblioduquebec.qc.ca/beaupre/

***Bedford:* Bibliothèque Léon-Maurice-Côté**
52, rue Du Pont, Bedford, QC J0J 1A0
Tél: 450-248-4625
bedford@reseaubibliomonteregie.qc.ca

***Belcourt:* Bibliothèque de Belcourt**
219A, rue Communautaire, Belcourt, QC J0Y 2M0
Tél: 819-737-8894; *Téléc:* 819-737-4084
belcourt@reseaubiblioatnq.qc.ca
www.reseaubiblioduquebec.qc.ca/belcourt
Guylaine Labbée, Responsable

***Belleterre:* Bibliothèque de Belleterre**
265, 1e av, Belleterre, QC J0Z 1L0
Tél: 819-722-2052; *Téléc:* 819-722-2527
belleterre@reseaubiblioatnq.qc.ca
www.reseaubiblioduquebec.qc.ca/belleterre
Claudette Rioux Gauthier, Responsable

***Beloeil:* Bibliothèque municipale de Beloeil**
620, rue Richelieu, Beloeil, QC J3G 5E8
Tél: 450-467-7872
bibliothèque.ville.beloeil.qc.ca

***Berthier-sur-Mer:* Bibliothèque Camille-Roy**
5, rue du Couvent, Berthier-sur-Mer, QC G0R 1E0
Tél: 418-259-2353; *Téléc:* 418-259-2038

***Biencourt:* Bibliothèque de Biencourt**
#1, 2, rue Saint-Marc, Biencourt, QC G0K 1T0
Tél: 418-499-1041
biblio.biencourt@crsbp.net
www.reseaubiblioduquebec.qc.ca

***Blainville:* Bibliothèque municipale de Blainville**
1000, ch du Plan-Bouchard, Blainville, QC J7C 3S9
Tél: 450-434-5275; *Téléc:* 450-434-5378
bibliotheque@ville.blainville.qc.ca
biblio.ville.blainville.qc.ca

***Blue Sea:* Bibliothèque Blue Sea**
2, ch Blue Sea Nord, Blue Sea, QC J0X 1C0
Tél: 819-463-3919; *Téléc:* 819-463-4345
admbluesea@crsbpo.qc.ca
Vicky Martin, Responsable

***Bois-Franc:* Bibliothèque de Bois-Franc**
466, rte 105, Bois-Franc, QC J9E 3A9
Tél: 819-441-0645; *Téléc:* 819-449-4407
admboisfranc@crsbpo.qc.ca
www.reseaubiblioduquebec.qc.ca/BoisFranc
Francine Marenger, Bibliothécaire

***Boisbriand:* Bibliothèque municipale de Boisbriand**
901, boul. de la Grande-Allée, Boisbriand, QC J7G 1W6
Tél: 450-435-7466; *Téléc:* 450-435-0627
www.ville.boisbriand.qc.ca

***Bonaventure:* Bibliothèque Françoise-Bujold**
95A, av Port-Royal, Bonaventure, QC G0C 1E0
Tél: 418-534-4238; *Téléc:* 418-534-4336
bonapret@globetrotter.net
www.villebonaventure.ca/bibliotheque-bona.html
Média social: www.facebook.com/121517131205916

***Boucherville:* Bibliothèque Montarville-Boucher-De la Bruère**
501, ch du Lac, Boucherville, QC J4B 6V6
Tél: 450-449-8650; *Téléc:* 450-449-6865
bibliothèque@boucherville.ca
www.boucherville.ca
Média social: twitter.com/boucherville_;
www.facebook.com/pages/Ville-de-Boucherville/47679369584

***Bouchette:* Bibliothèque de Bouchette**
36, rue Principale, Bouchette, QC J0X 1E0
Tél: 819-465-5782; *Téléc:* 819-465-2318
admbouchette@crsbpo.qc.ca
www.reseaubiblioduquebec.qc.ca/Bouchette
Janick Patry, Responsable

***Boulanger:* Bibliothèque publique de Sainte-Jeanne-d'Arc**
#13, 400, rue Verreault, Boulanger, QC G0W 1E0
Tél: 418-276-3166
jeanne@reseaubiblioslsj.qc.ca
www.reseaubiblioduquebec.qc.ca

***Brigham:* Bibliothèque municipale de Brigham**
118, av des Cèdres, Brigham, QC J2K 4K4
Tél: 450-538-5843
brigham@reseaubibliomonteregie.qc.ca

***Bristol:* Bibliothèque de Bristol/ Bristol Library**
32, ch Aylmer, Bristol, QC J0X 1G0
Tél: 819-647-5555; *Téléc:* 819-647-2424
admbristol@crsbpo.qc.ca
www.reseaubiblioduquebec.qc.ca/Bristol
Kelly Dowe, Responsable

***Brossard:* Bibliothèque de Brossard (Georgette-Lepage)**
7855, av San-Francisco, Brossard, QC J4X 2A4
Tél: 450-923-6350; *Téléc:* 450-923-7042
bibliotheque@brossard.ca
www.ville.brossard.qc.ca/biblio
Média social: www.youtube.com/user/bibliobrossard;
twitter.com/Bibliobrossard; www.facebook.com/bibliobrossard
Suzanne Payette, Directrice
suzanne.payette@brossard.ca

***Brownsburg-Chatham:* Bibliothèque de Brownsburg-Chatham**
200, rue MacVicar, Brownsburg-Chatham, QC J8G 2Z6
Tél: 450-533-5355
biblio@brownsburgchatham.ca
www.reseaubiblioduquebec.qc.ca
Média social: www.facebook.com/BiblioBrownsburgChatham

***Bryson:* Bibliothèque de Bryson**
833, rue Principale, Bryson, QC J0X 1H0
Tél: 819-648-2543; *Téléc:* 819-648-5297
admbryson@crsbpo.qc.ca
www.commercepontiac.ca/services/libraries.html

***Brébeuf:* Bibliothèque M.-A. Grégoire-Coupal**
217, rte 323, Brébeuf, QC J0T 1B0
Tél: 819-425-9833; *Téléc:* 819-425-6611
biblio@brebeuf.ca
www.brebeuf.ca/loisirs-et-culture/bibliotheque
Ginette Bernard, Responsable

***Buckland:* Bibliothèque Biblio Buck**
4340, rue Principale, Buckland, QC G0R 1G0
Tél: 418-789-3119
www.buckland.qc.ca
Diane Laflamme, Préposée

***Béarn:* Bibliothèque de Béarn**
38, rue Principale nord, Béarn, QC J0Z 1G0
Tél: 819-726-2251; *Téléc:* 819-726-2121
bearn@reseaubiblioatnq.qc.ca
www.reseaubiblioduquebec.qc.ca/bearn
Annie Drolet, Responsable

***Bécancour:* Bibliothèque publique de Bécancour**
1295, av Nicolas-Perrot, Bécancour, QC G9H 1A1
Tél: 819-294-4455
www.becancour.net/fr/activites_et_loisirs/reseau_des_bibliotheques

***Bégin:* Bibliothèque publique de Bégin**
120B, rue Tremblay, Bégin, QC G0V 1B0
Tél: 418-672-4503
begin@reseaubiblioslsj.qc.ca

***Calixa-Lavallée:* Bibliothèque municipale de Calixa-Lavallée**
771, rang Beauce, Calixa-Lavallée, QC J0L 1A0
Tél: 450-583-6470
calixa.lavallee@reseaubibliomonteregie.qc.ca

***Campbell's Bay:* Bibliothèque de Campbell's Bay/Litchfield**
4, rue Patterson, CP 444, Campbell's Bay, QC J0X 1K0
Tél: 819-648-5676; *Téléc:* 819-648-2045
biblio-cb@mrcpontiac.qc.ca
www.reseaubiblioduquebec.qc.ca/CampbellsBay
Média social: www.facebook.com/172200822806575
Jean-Pierre Landry, Directeur général

***Candiac:* Bibliothèque municipale de Candiac**
Centre Claude-Hébert, 59, ch Haendel, Candiac, QC J5R 1R7
Tél: 450-635-6032; *Téléc:* 450-635-0900
biblio@ville.candiac.qc.ca
www.ville.candiac.qc.ca
Patricia Lemieux, Directrice

***Cantley:* Bibliothèque municipale de Cantley**
8, ch River, Cantley, QC J8V 2Z9
Tél: 819-827-3434; *Téléc:* 819-827-4328
www.cantley.ca/fr/bibliotheque
Christian Lesieur, Responsable
Mélanie Vigneault, Adjointe

***Cap-aux-Meules:* Bibliothèque de Cap-aux-Meules**
#3, 315, ch Principal, Cap-aux-Meules, QC G4T 1E2
Tél: 418-986-6821; *Téléc:* 418-986-6231
biblio.cam@muniles.ca
Suzanne Chevrier, Responsable

***Cap-Chat:* Bibliothèque La ruche littéraire**
27, rue des Écoliers, Cap-Chat, QC G0J 1E0
Tél: 418-786-2068

***Cap-d'Espoir:* Bibliothèque de Cap-d'Espoir**
52, rue du Curé-Poirier, Cap-d'Espoir, QC G0C 1G0
Tél: 581-353-2019
bbocesp@ville.perce.qc.ca
Média social: www.facebook.com/bibliotheque.capdespoir

***Cap-Saint-Ignace:* Bibliothèque Léo-Pol-Morin**
100, Place de l'Église, Cap-Saint-Ignace, QC G0R 1H0
Tél: 418-246-3037; *Téléc:* 418-246-5663
biblicap@globetrotter.qc.ca
www.reseaubiblioduquebec.qc.ca/cap-saint-ignace

***Cap-Santé:* Bibliothèque municipale de Cap-Santé**
15, rue Marie-Fitzbach, Cap-Santé, QC G0A 1L0
Tél: 418-285-6891; *Téléc:* 418-285-0009
bibliocapsante@hotmail.com
www.reseaubiblioduquebec.qc.ca/cap-sante

Caplan: **Bibliothèque Jeanne-Ferlatte**
17, boul Perron Est, Caplan, QC G0C 1H0
Tél: 418-388-2545; *Téléc:* 418-388-2429
bibliocaplan@hotmail.com

Capucins: **Bibliothèque de Capucins**
294, rte du Village, Capucins, QC G0J 1H0
Tél: 418-786-2013; *Téléc:* 418-786-2013
bbocapu@globetrotter.net

Carleton-sur-Mer: **Bibliothèque Gabrielle-Bernard-Dubé**
774, boul Perron, Carleton-sur-Mer, QC G0C 1J0
Tél: 418-364-7103; *Téléc:* 418-364-7103
livre1@globetrotter.net
Média social: www.facebook.com/283352675052837

Causapscal: **Bibliothèque de Causapscal**
3, Place de la Fabrique, Causapscal, QC G0J 1J0
Tél: 418-756-3522
biblio.causap@crsbp.net
www.reseaubiblioduquebec.qc.ca
Thérèse Audit, Responsable

Chambly: **Bibliothèque municipale de Chambly**
1691, av Bourgogne, Chambly, QC J3L 1Y8
Tél: 450-658-2711; *Téléc:* 450-447-4525
biblio@ville.chambly.qc.ca
www.ville.chambly.qc.ca/index.php/bibliotheque
Carole Mainville-Bériault, Directrice

Chambord: **Bibliothèque publique de Chambord**
#72, 1, boul de la Montagne, Chambord, QC G0W 1G0
Tél: 418-342-6274
chambord@reseaubiblioslsj.qc.ca
Média social: fr-ca.facebook.com/bibliothequepublique.dechambord

Champlain: **Bibliothèque de Champlain**
963, rue Notre-Dame, Champlain, QC G0X 1C0
Tél: 819-840-0407; *Téléc:* 819-295-3032
biblio005@reseaubibliocqlm.qc.ca
Isabelle Vézina, Coordonnatrice

Chandler: **Bibliothèque municipale-scolaire de Chandler**
183, rue Commerciale ouest, Chandler, QC G0C 1K0
Tél: 418-689-3808; *Téléc:* 418-689-3639
chandbbo@globetrotter.net
www.reseaubiblioduquebec.qc.ca
Gisele Cyr, Directeur

Chapais: **Bibliothèque publique de Chapais**
45, 5e av, Chapais, QC G0W 1H0
Tél: 418-745-3244
chapais@reseaubiblioslsj.qc.ca
www.reseaubiblioduquebec.qc.ca
Line Lambert, Responsable

Charette: **Bibliothèque de Charette (Armance-Samson)**
390, rue Saint-Édouard, Charette, QC G0X 1E0
Tél: 819-221-2095
biblio023@reseaubibliocqlm.qc.ca
Marie Fitzgerald, Coordonnatrice

Charlemagne: **Bibliothèque Camille-Laurin de Charlemagne**
84, rue du Sacré-Coeur, Charlemagne, QC J5Z 1W8
Tél: 450-581-7243; *Téléc:* 450-581-0597
biblio@ville.charlemagne.qc.ca
www.ville.charlemagne.qc.ca/biblio.htm

Chelsea: **Bibliothèque de Chelsea/ Chelsea Library**
100, ch Old Chelsea Road, Chelsea, QC J9B 1C1
Tél: 819-827-4019
bibliotheque@chelsea.ca
www.chelsea.ca
Média social: www.facebook.com/pages/Chelsea-Library/117427068307837
Béatrice O'Byrne, Bibliothécaire

Chertsey: **Bibliothèque de Chertsey**
333, av de l'Amitié, Chertsey, QC J0K 3K0
Tél: 450-882-4738
mpicard@municipalite.chertsey.qc.ca
www.reseaubiblioduquebec.qc.ca

Chesterville: **Bibliothèque de Chesterville**
474, rue de l'Accueil, Chesterville, QC G0P 1J0
Tél: 819-382-2997
biblio146@reseaubibliocqlm.qc.ca
www.reseaubiblioduquebec.qc.ca
Louise Lefebvre, Responsable

Chevery: **Bibliothèque de Chevery**
CP 92, Chevery, QC G0G 1G0
Tél: 418-787-2244; *Téléc:* 418-787-2241
Ana Osborne, Responsable

Chibougamau: **Bibliothèque municipale de Chibougamau**
601, 3e rue, Chibougamau, QC G8P 0A8
Tél: 418-748-2688
bibliotheque@ville.chibougamau.qc.ca
www.ville.chibougamau.qc.ca

Chicoutimi: **Bibliothèques de Saguenay**
155, rue Racine est, Chicoutimi, QC G7H 1R5
Tél: 418-698-5350; *Téléc:* 418-698-5359
webbiblio@ville.saguenay.qc.ca
www.ville.saguenay.qc.ca/biblio
Luc-Michel Belley, Chef de division, Arts, culture, communautaire et bibliothèques

Chute-aux-Outardes: **Bibliothèque de Chute-aux-Outardes**
4, rue de l'École, Chute-aux-Outardes, QC G0H 1C0
Tél: 418-567-2144; *Téléc:* 418-567-4478
Manon Finn, Responsable

Chute-Saint-Philippe: **Bibliothèque de Chute-Saint-Philippe**
592, ch du Progrès, Chute-Saint-Philippe, QC J0W 1A0
Tél: 819-585-3397; *Téléc:* 819-585-2209
bibliotheque@chute-saint-philippe.ca
www.reseaubiblioduquebec.qc.ca/chute-saint-philippe

Chénéville: **Bibliothèque Albert-Ferland**
77, rue Hôtel-de-Ville, Chénéville, QC J0V 1E0
Tél: 819-428-3583; *Téléc:* 819-428-4838
biblio.cheneville@mrcpapineau.com
Madeleine Tremblay, Responsable

Châteauguay: **Bibliothèque municipale de Châteauguay/ Châteauguay Municipal Library**
25, boul Maple, Châteauguay, QC J6J 3P7
Tél: 450-698-3080
www.ville.chateauguay.qc.ca

Clarenceville: **Bibliothèque municipale de Saint-Georges-de-Clarenceville**
1340, ch Middle, Clarenceville, QC J0J 1B0
Tél: 450-294-3200
clarenceville@reseaubibliomonteregie.qc.ca
Nicole Prud'homme, Responsable

Clermont: **Bibliothèque municipale de Clermont**
11, rue Jean Talon, Clermont, QC G4A 1A4
Tél: 418-439-2903
lachutedemots63@hotmail.com
www.reseaubiblioduquebec.qc.ca/clermont

Clerval: **Bibliothèque de Clerval**
579, rang 2-3, Clerval, QC J0Z 1R0
Tél: 819-783-2069; *Téléc:* 819-783-2640
clerval@reseaubiblioatnq.qc.ca
www.reseaubiblioduquebec.qc.ca/clerval
Germaine Thibault, Responsable

Cloridorme: **Bibliothèque de Cloridorme**
472, rte 132, Cloridorme, QC G0E 1G0
Tél: 418-395-2609; *Téléc:* 418-395-2228
munclori@globetrotter.net
www.mabibliotheque.ca/cloridorme

Cléricy: **Bibliothèque de Cléricy**
8002A, rue du Souvenir, Cléricy, QC J0Z 1P0
Tél: 819-797-7110; *Téléc:* 819-637-2133
clericy@reseaubiblioatnq.qc.ca
www.reseaubiblioduquebec.qc.ca/cléricy
Lise Robin Boucher, Responsable

Coaticook: **Bibliothèque Françoise-Maurice de Coaticook**
34, rue Main est, Coaticook, QC J1A 1N2
Tél: 819-849-4013; *Téléc:* 819-849-0479
biblcoat@bibliotheque.coaticook.qc.ca
bibliotheque.coaticook.qc.ca
Patrick Falardeau, Directeur

Colombier: **Bibliothèque de Colombier**
568, rue Principale, Colombier, QC G0H 1P0
Tél: 418-565-3013; *Téléc:* 418-565-3289
Isabelle Maltais, Responsable

Coteau-du-Lac: **Bibliothèque Jules-Fournier**
3, rue du Parc, Coteau-du-Lac, QC J0P 1B0
Tél: 450-763-2763; *Téléc:* 450-763-2495
bibliotheque@coteau-du-lac.com
www.coteau-du-lac.com/services-et-citoyens/bibliotheque
Christine Gauthier, Responsable
Sylvie Cloutier, Préposée au prêt

Cowansville: **Bibliothèque Gabrielle-Giroux-Bertrand**
608, rue du Sud, Cowansville, QC J2K 2X9
Tél: 450-263-4071; *Téléc:* 450-263-7477
cultureetpatrimoine@ville.cowansville.qc.ca
www.ville.cowansville.qc.ca

Crabtree: **Bibliothèque de Crabtree**
59, 16e rue, Crabtree, QC J0K 1B0
Tél: 450-754-4332
biblio114@reseaubibliocqlm.qc.ca
www.reseaubiblioduquebec.qc.ca
Média social: www.facebook.com/186371856677
Marjolaine Bertrand, Responsable
450-754-4332

Côte-Saint-Luc: **Bibliothèque publique Eleanor London Côte-Saint-Luc**
5851, boul Cavendish, Côte-Saint-Luc, QC H4W 2X8
Tél: 514-485-6900; *Téléc:* 514-485-6966
reference@cotesaintluc.org
www.elcslpl.org
Média social: www.facebook.com/group.php?gid=123100031035453
Janine West, Directrice de la bibliothèque
jwest @ cotesaintluc.org
514-485-6900 ext. 4202

Danford Lake: **Bibliothèque de l'Alleyn-et-Cawood**
10, ch Jondee, Danford Lake, QC J0X 1P0
Tél: 819-467-2941; *Téléc:* 819-467-3133
www.reseaubiblioduquebec.qc.ca/Alleyn-et-Cawood

Danville: **Bibliothèque municipale de Danville**
42, rue Daniel Johnson, Danville, QC J0A 1A0
Tél: 819-839-3236; *Téléc:* 819-839-2918
biblio053@reseaubiblioestrie.qc.ca
danville.ca/bottin/services/bibliotheque
Média social: www.facebook.com/168555559872384

Daveluyville: **Bibliothèque de Daveluyville**
111, 7e av, Daveluyville, QC G0Z 1C0
Tél: 819-367-3645; *Téléc:* 819-367-3550
biblio057@reseaubibliocqlm.qc.ca

Delson: **Bibliothèque municipale de Delson**
1, 1re av, Delson, QC J5B 1M9
Tél: 450-632-1050
biblio@ville.delson.qc.ca

Desbiens: **Bibliothèque publique de Desbiens**
1058, rue Marcellin, Desbiens, QC G0W 1N0
Tél: 418-346-5739
desbiens@reseaubiblioslsj.qc.ca

Deschaillons: **Bibliothèque de Deschaillons-sur-Saint-Laurent**
1042A, rue Marie-Victorin, CP 234, Deschaillons, QC G0S 1G0
Tél: 819-292-2483; *Téléc:* 819-292-3194
biblio101@reseaubibliocqlm.qc.ca
www.reseaubiblioduquebec.qc.ca
Odette Gilbert, Responsable

Deschambault-Grondines: **Bibliothèque Du Bord de l'Eau**
#1, 115, rue de l'Église, Deschambault-Grondines, QC G0A 1S0
Tél: 418-286-6938; *Téléc:* 418-286-6511
bibdesch@globetrotter.qc.ca
Jacqueline Gignac, Responsable

Deux-Montagnes: **Bibliothèque de Deux-Montagnes/ Deux-Montagnes Library**
200, rue Henri-Dunant, Deux-Montagnes, QC J7R 4W6
Tél: 450-473-2702; *Téléc:* 450-473-2816
biblio@ville.deux-montagnes.qc.ca
bibliotheque.ville.deux-montagnes.qc.ca
Pascale Dupuis, Directrice, culture et bibliothèque
pdupuis@ville.deux-montagnes.qc.ca
Guylaine Lemire, Technicienne en documentation
glemire@ville.deux-montagnes.qc.ca
Louise St-Laurent, Technicienne en documentation
lsaint-laurent@ville.deux-montagnes.qc.ca

***Dolbeau-Mistassini:* Bibliothèque de Dolbeau-Mistassini**
175, 4e av, Dolbeau-Mistassini, QC G8L 2W6
Tél: 418-276-1317; *Téléc:* 418-276-8265
www.dolbeau.biblio.qc.ca
Pauline Lapointe, Responsable
plapointe@ville.dolbeau-mistassini.qc.ca
418-276-1317
Liette Caron, Technicienne en documentation
lcaron@ville.dolbeau-mistassini.qc.ca
Annie Lamontagne, Technicienne en documentation
alamontagne@ville.dolbeau-mistassini.qc.ca

***Dollard-des-Ormeaux:* Bibliothèque publique de Dollard-des-Ormeaux**
12001, boul De Salaberry, Dollard-des-Ormeaux, QC H9B 2A7
Tél: 514-684-1496; *Téléc:* 514-684-9569
bibliotheque@ddo.qc.ca
www.ville.ddo.qc.ca
Média social: www.facebook.com/biblioddo

***Dorval:* Bibliothèque de Dorval**
1401, ch du Bord-du-Lac, Dorval, QC H9S 2E5
Tél: 514-633-4170; *Téléc:* 514-633-4177
biblio@ville.dorval.qc.ca
www.ville.dorval.qc.ca

***Dosquet:* Bibliothèque La Bouquinerie/Dosquet**
1, rue Viger, Dosquet, QC G0S 1H0
Tél: 418-728-3994; *Téléc:* 418-728-3338
bibliothequedosquet@videotron.ca
Média social: www.facebook.com/labouquineriededosquet

***Drummondville:* Bibliothèque municipale Côme-Saint-Germain**
545, rue des Écoles, Drummondville, QC J2B 1J6
Tél: 819-478-6573; *Téléc:* 819-478-0399
biblio@ville.drummondville.qc.ca
www.ville.drummondville.qc.ca
Martin Dubé, Chef de division
819-478-6588

***Drummondville:* Centre de lecture Réal-Rochefort**
Pavillon Jean Coutu, 565, rue Victorin, Drummondville, QC J2C 6G8
Tél: 819-477-2326
Guylaine Dion-Daneault, Responsable

***Duhamel:* Bibliothèque Duhamel**
1899, rue Principale, Duhamel, QC J0V 1G0
Tél: 819-428-7100; *Téléc:* 819-428-1941
admduhamel@crsbpo.qc.ca
Roselyne Bernard, Responsable

***Dunham:* Bibliothèque municipale de Dunham/ Dunham Municipal Library**
3638, rue Principale, Dunham, QC J0E 1M0
Tél: 450-295-2621
dunham@reseaubibliomonteregie.qc.ca

***Duparquet:* Bibliothèque Duparquet**
54, rue Principale, Duparquet, QC J0Z 1W0
Tél: 819-948-2266; *Téléc:* 819-948-2266
duparquet@reseaubiblioatnq.qc.ca
Carmen Lacroix, Responsable

***Dupuy:* Bibliothèque de Dupuy**
63, rue Principale, Dupuy, QC J0Z 1X0
Tél: 819-783-2147; *Téléc:* 819-783-2147
dupuy@reseaubiblioatnq.qc.ca
www.reseaubiblioduquebec.qc.ca/dupuy
Huguette Huot, Responsable

***Durham-Sud:* Bibliothèque de Durham-Sud**
77, rue de l'Église, Durham-Sud, QC J0H 2C0
Tél: 819-858-1156; *Téléc:* 819-858-2044
biblio153@reseaubibliocqlm.qc.ca

***Dégelis:* Bibliothèque Élisabeth-Turgeon**
663, 6e rue ouest, Dégelis, QC G5T 1Y3
Tél: 418-853-2332
biblio.degelis@crsbp.net
www.reseaubiblioduquebec.qc.ca
Gertrude Leclerc, Responsable

***East Broughton:* Bibliothèque La Bouquinerie/East Broughton/Sacré-Coeur-de-Jésus**
372A, av du Collège, East Broughton, QC G0N 1G0
Tél: 418-427-4900; *Téléc:* 418-427-3514
bouquinerieeb@hotmail.com

***Entrelacs:* Bibliothèque d'Entrelacs**
2351, ch Entrelacs, Entrelacs, QC J0T 2E0
Tél: 450-228-2529; *Téléc:* 450-228-4866
biblient@entrelacs.com
www.reseaubiblioduquebec.qc.ca

***Esprit-Saint:* Bibliothèque d'Esprit-Saint**
1, rue des Érables, Esprit-Saint, QC G0K 1A0
Tél: 418-779-2016
biblio.esprit@crsbp.net
www.reseaubiblioduquebec.qc.ca
Sylvie Boucher, Responsable

***Fabre:* Bibliothèque Le Coquelicot de Fabre**
620, av de l'Église, Fabre, QC J0Z 1Z0
Tél: 819-634-2745; *Téléc:* 819-634-2646
fabre@reseaubiblioatnq.qc.ca
www.reseaubiblioduquebec.qc.ca/fabre
Jacinthe Breton Desrochers, Responsable

***Farnham:* Bibliothèque de Farnham inc.**
479, rue de l'Hôtel de Ville, Farnham, QC J2N 2H3
Tél: 450-293-3178; *Téléc:* 450-293-2989
bibliotheque@ville.farnham.qc.ca
www.bibliofarnham.com

***Fassett:* Bibliothèque Fassett/Notre-Dame-de-Bonsecours**
19, rue Gendron, Fassett, QC J0V 1H0
Tél: 819-423-6943; *Téléc:* 819-423-5388
biblio.fassett@mrcpapineau.com
Mireille Dupuis, Responsable

***Fatima:* Bibliothèque de Fatima**
#2, 730, ch des Caps, Fatima, QC G4T 2T3
Tél: 418-986-4736
biblio.fatima@hotmail.com
Thérèse Harvie, Responsable

***Ferme-Neuve:* Bibliothèque de Ferme-Neuve**
144, 12e rue, Ferme-Neuve, QC J0W 1C0
Tél: 819-587-3102
bibliotheque@municipalite.ferme-neuve.qc.ca
www.reseaubiblioduquebec.qc.ca

***Fermont:* Bibliothèque publique de Fermont**
100, place Daviault, Fermont, QC G0G 1J0
Tél: 418-287-3227; *Téléc:* 418-287-3274
biblio@villedefermont.qc.ca
Aline Martel, Responsable

***Forestville:* Bibliothèque Camille-Bouchard**
10, 10e rue, Forestville, QC G0T 1E0
Tél: 418-587-4482
bibliotheque@forestville.ca
Sophie Gagnon, Coordonnatrice

***Fort-Coulonge:* Bibliothèque de Fort-Coulonge**
134, rue Principale, Fort-Coulonge, QC J0X 1V0
Tél: 819-683-3421; *Téléc:* 819-683-3627
biblio.fc@fortcoulonge.qc.ca
www.fortcoulonge.qc.ca
Sandra Gendron, Responsable

***Fortierville:* Bibliothèque de Fortierville**
198A, rue de la Fabrique, Fortierville, QC G0S 1J0
Tél: 819-287-4309; *Téléc:* 819-287-5922
biblio015@reseaubibliocqlm.qc.ca
Denise Lemay, Responsable

***Fossambault-sur-le-Lac:* Bibliothèque municipale de Fossambault-sur-le-Lac ("La Source")**
145, rue Gingras, Fossambault-sur-le-Lac, QC G3N 0K2
Tél: 418-875-3133
www.fossambault-sur-le-lac.com
Monique Blouin, Responsable

***Franquelin:* Bibliothèque municipale de Franquelin**
27, rue des Érables, Franquelin, QC G0H 1E0
Tél: 418-294-6170

***Fugèreville:* Bibliothèque de Fugèreville**
33A, rue Principale, Fugèreville, QC J0Z 2A0
Tél: 819-748-2276; *Téléc:* 819-748-2422
fugereville@reseaubiblioatnq.qc.ca
www.reseaubiblioduquebec.qc.ca/fugereville
Gaétane Cloutier, Responsable

***Gallix:* Bibliothèque municipale de Gallix**
524, av Lapierre, Gallix, QC G0G 1L0
Tél: 418-766-6152; *Téléc:* 418-766-3264
Lyne Porlier, Responsable

***Gaspé:* Bibliothèque Alma-Bourget-Costisella**
10, Côte Cater, Gaspé, QC G4X 1V2
Tél: 418-368-2104; *Téléc:* 418-368-8532
biblio.gaspe@globetrotter.net
Adrienne Bisson, Responsable

***Gaspé:* Bibliothèque de Cap-aux-Os**
1826, boul Forillon, Gaspé, QC G4X 6L4
Tél: 418-368-2104
biblio.cao@globetrotter.net

***Gaspé:* Bibliothèque de L'Anse-au-Griffon**
465, boul du Griffon, Gaspé, QC G4X 6A3
Tél: 418-368-2104; *Téléc:* 418-368-6962
bboaag@globetrotter.qc.ca

***Gaspé:* Bibliothèque de L'Anse-à-Valleau**
6, rue Mathurin, Gaspé, QC G4X 4A8
Tél: 418-368-2104
Priscillia Poirier, Responsable
priscillia.poirier@globetrotter.net

***Gaspé:* Bibliothèque de Petit-Cap**
439, boul Petit-Cap, Gaspé, QC G4X 4L1
Tél: 418-368-2104
bibliopetitcap@globetrotter.net

***Gaspé:* Bibliothèque de Saint-Majorique**
3-1, montée de Corte-Réal, Gaspé, QC G4X 6R7
Tél: 418-368-2104
biblio.stmajorique@globetrotter.net
www.reseaubiblioduquebec.qc.ca
Gracia Cabot, Responsable

***Gatineau:* Bibliothèque municipale de Gatineau**
25, rue Laurier, Gatineau, QC J8X 4C8
Tél: 819-595-7460
bibliotheque.gatineau.ca
Média social: twitter.com/ville_gatineau; www.facebook.com/villegatineau

***Girardville:* Bibliothèque publique de Girardville**
180, rue Principale, Girardville, QC G0W 1R0
Tél: 418-258-3222
girardv@reseaubiblioslsj.qc.ca

***Godbout:* Bibliothèque municipale de Godbout**
101, rue Levack, Godbout, QC G0H 1G0
Tél: 418-568-7670
biblio.godbout@hotmail.com
Claudia Michaud-Tremblay, Responsable

***Gracefield:* Bibliothèque de Gracefield**
3, rue de la Polyvalente, CP 312, Gracefield, QC J0X 1W0
Tél: 819-463-1180; *Téléc:* 819-463-4236
admgracefield@crsbpo.qc.ca
www.reseaubiblioduquebec.qc.ca/Gracefield
Denise Pelletier Rochon, Responsable

***Granby:* Bibliothèque Paul-O.-Trépanier**
11, rue Dufferin, Granby, QC J2G 2T8
Tél: 450-776-8320; *Téléc:* 450-776-8313
Other Numbers: Horaire (btc vocale): (450) 776-8310
bibliotheque@ville.granby.qc.ca
www.biblio.ville.granby.qc.ca

***Grand-Remous:* Bibliothèque de Grand-Remous**
1508, rte Transcanadienne, Grand-Remous, QC J0W 1E0
Tél: 819-438-2168; *Téléc:* 418-438-2364
admgrandremous@crsbpo.qc.ca
www.reseaubiblioduquebec.qc.ca/Grand-Remous
Christiane Gagnon, Responsable

***Grande-Entrée:* Bibliothèque de Grande-Entrée**
214, route 199, Grande-Entrée, QC G4T 7A4
Tél: 418-985-2277; *Téléc:* 418-985-2149
biblioge@muniles.ca
www.reseaubiblioduquebec.qc.ca
Raoul Cyr, Responsable

***Grande-Rivière:* Bibliothèque La Détente/Grande-Rivière**
210, rue du Carrefour, Grande-Rivière, QC G0C 1V0
Tél: 418-385-3833; *Téléc:* 418-385-2290
Marie-Paule Berger, Responsable

***Grande-Vallée:* Bibliothèque de Grande-Vallée**
18A, rue St-François-Xavier Est, Grande-Vallée, QC G0E 1K0
Tél: 418-393-2811; *Téléc:* 418-393-2274
bbogrval@globetrotter.net

Grandes-Piles: **Bibliothèque de Grandes-Piles**
650, 4e av, Grandes-Piles, QC G0X 1H0
Tél: 819-533-3697; *Téléc:* 819-538-6947
biblio030@reseaubibliocqlm.qc.ca
www.reseaubiblioduquebec.qc.ca
Line Blanchard, Responsable

Grenville: **Bibliothèque de Grenville**
18, rue Tri-Jean, Grenville, QC J0V 1J0
Tél: 819-242-2146; *Téléc:* 819-242-5891
biblio@grenville.ca

Grenville-sur-la-Rouge: **Bibliothèque de Calumet**
435, rue Principale, Grenville-sur-la-Rouge, QC J0V 1B0
Tél: 819-242-8088; *Téléc:* 819-242-1232
biblio5@crsbpl.qc.ca
www.reseaubiblioduquebec.qc.ca

Grenville-sur-la-Rouge: **Bibliothèque de Pointe-au-Chêne**
2714, rte 148, Grenville-sur-la-Rouge, QC J0V 1B0
Tél: 819-242-3232
bibliopac@xplornet.ca
www.reseaubiblioduquebec.qc.ca

Grondines: **Bibliothèque L'Ardoise**
490, chemin du Roy, Grondines, QC G0A 1W0
Tél: 418-268-4375
Michelle Trottier, Responsable

Gros-Morne: **Bibliothèque de Gros-Morne**
1, rue de l'Église Ouest, Gros-Morne, QC G0E 1L0
Tél: 418-797-2610
www.reseaubiblioduquebec.qc.ca

Grosse-Ile: **Bibliothèque de Grosse-Ile**
448, ch Principal, Grosse-Ile, QC G4T 6A8
Tél: 418-986-2885; *Téléc:* 418-985-2955
Holly Burke, Secrétaire
gis.admin@essb.qc.ca

Guyenne: **Bibliothèque de Guyenne**
1255-F, rang 5, Guyenne, QC J0Y 1L0
Tél: 819-732-9128; *Téléc:* 819-732-0904
guyenne@reseaubiblioatnq.qc.ca
www.reseaubiblioduquebec.qc.ca/guyenne
Francine Simard, Responsable

Ham-Nord: **Bibliothèque de Ham-Nord**
474, rue Principale, CP 1271, Ham-Nord, QC G0P 1A0
Tél: 819-344-2805; *Téléc:* 819-344-2806
biblio150@reseaubibliocqlm.qc.ca
www.reseaubiblioduquebec.qc.ca

Harrington Harbour: **Bibliothèque de Harrington Harbour**
CP 7, Harrington Harbour, QC G0G 1N0
Tél: 418-787-2244; *Téléc:* 418-787-2241
Judi Ransom, Responsable

Havre-aux-Maisons: **Bibliothèque de Havre-aux-Maisons**
37, ch Central, Havre-aux-Maisons, QC G4T 5H1
Tél: 418-969-2100
biblioham@muniles.ca
Marcel Thériault, Responsable

Havre-Saint-Pierre: **Bibliothèque municipale de Havre-St-Pierre**
1045, rue Dulcinée, Havre-Saint-Pierre, QC G0G 1P0
Tél: 418-538-3301; *Téléc:* 418-538-3439
biblio.havrest-pierre@globetrotter.net
Liliane Drolet, Responsable

Hemmingford: **Bibliothèque municipale d'Hemmingford/ Hemmingford Community Library**
552, av Goyette, Hemmingford, QC J0L 1H0
Tél: 450-247-0010
hemmingford@reseaubibliomonteregie.qc.ca

Henryville: **Bibliothèque municipale d'Henryville**
#104, 854, rue St-Jean-Baptiste, Henryville, QC J0J 1E0
Tél: 450-346-4116

Honfleur: **Bibliothèque La Livrothèque**
320, rue Saint-Jean, Honfleur, QC G0R 1N0
Tél: 418-885-8212; *Téléc:* 418-885-9195
livro@globetrotter.qc.ca

Huberdeau: **Bibliothèque d'Huberdeau**
101, rue Du Pont, Huberdeau, QC J0T 1G0
Tél: 819-687-1164; *Téléc:* 819-687-8808
biblio@municipalite.huberdeau.qc.ca
www.reseaubiblioduquebec.qc.ca

Huntingdon: **Little Green Library/ La Petite Bibliothèque Verte**
#103, 4, rue Lorne, Huntingdon, QC J0S 1H0
Tel: 450-264-4872
pbv.lgl@gmail.com
www.pbv-lgl.org
Social Media:
www.facebook.com/PetiteBibliothequeVerteLittleGreenLibrary
Louise Charlebois, President

Hérouxville: **Bibliothèque de Hérouxville**
1060, rue Saint-Pierre, Hérouxville, QC G0X 1J0
Tél: 418-365-7337; *Téléc:* 418-365-7041
biblio090@reseaubibliocqlm.qc.ca
www.reseaubiblioduquebec.qc.ca
Julie L'Heureux, Responsable

Ile d' Anticosti: **Bibliothèque municipale de l'Ile d'Anticosti**
4B, Rue Savoy, Ile d' Anticosti, QC G0G 2Y0
Tél: 418-535-0381
biblioanticosti@xplornet.com
Wendy Tremblay, Responsable
418-535-0048

Ile-du-Grand-Calumet: **Bibliothèque Ile-du-Grand-Calumet**
2, rue Brizard, Ile-du-Grand-Calumet, QC J0X 1J0
Tél: 819-648-5966; *Téléc:* 819-648-2659
admcalumet@crsbpo.qc.ca
Chantal Corriveau, Responable

Inverness: **Bibliothèque de Inverness (L'Inverthèque)**
1801, rue Dublin, Inverness, QC G0S 1K0
Tél: 418-453-2867; *Téléc:* 418-453-2554
biblio145@reseaubibliocqlm.qc.ca
www.reseaubiblioduquebec.qc.ca

Issoudun: **Bibliothèque La Rêverie/Notre-Dame-de-Sacré-Coeur-d'Issoudun**
268, rue Principale, Issoudun, QC G0S 1L0
Tél: 418-728-9061; *Téléc:* 418-728-2303
Mèdia social:
www.facebook.com/Bibliotheque.la.reverie.issoudun
Nicole Deschênes, Responsable

Kiamika: **Bibliothèque de Kiamika**
3, ch Valiquette, Kiamika, QC J0W 1G0
Tél: 819-585-3225; *Téléc:* 819-585-3992
biblio@kiamika.ca
www.mabibliotheque.ca/kiamika
Mèdia social: www.facebook.com/bibliotheque.dekiamika

Kingsey Falls: **Bibliothèque de Kingsey Falls**
13, rue Caron, Kingsey Falls, QC J0A 1B0
Tél: 819-363-3818
biblio040@reseaubibliocqlm.qc.ca

Kinnear's Mills: **Bibliothèque La Boukinnerie**
120, rue des Églises, Kinnear's Mills, QC G0N 1K0
Tél: 418-424-0082; *Téléc:* 418-424-3015
biblio@kinnearsmills.com
www.mabibliotheque.ca/kinnears

Kirkland: **Bibliothèque de Kirkland**
17100, boul Hymus, Kirkland, QC H9J 2W2
Tél: 514-630-2726; *Téléc:* 514-630-2716
www.ville.kirkland.qc.ca
Sonia Djevalikian, Chef de division
SDjevalikian@ville.kirkland.qc.ca
514-694-4100 ext. 3200

L'Anse-Saint-Jean: **Bibliothèque publique de L'Anse-St-Jean**
3, rue du Couvent, L'Anse-Saint-Jean, QC G0V 1J0
Tél: 418-272-2633
anse@reseaubiblioslsj.qc.ca
www.reseaubiblioduquebec.qc.ca
Germaine Boudreault, Responsable
Marie Thibeault, Adjointe

L'Ascension: **Bibliothèque de l'Ascension**
58, rue de l'hôtel-de-ville, L'Ascension, QC J0T 1W0
Tél: 819-275-3027; *Téléc:* 819-275-3489
bibliotheque@municipalite-lascension.qc.ca
Lyne Beaulieu, Responsable

L'Ascension: **Bibliothèque publique de L'Ascension**
900, 4e av Est, L'Ascension, QC G0W 1Y0
Tél: 418-347-3482; *Téléc:* 418-347-4253
ascens@reseaubiblioslsj.qc.ca
Lyne Beaulieu, Coordonnatrice

L'Assomption: **Bibliothèque Christian-Roy**
375, rue St-Pierre, L'Assomption, QC J5W 2B6
Tél: 450-589-5671; *Téléc:* 450-589-6882
bibliotheque@ville.lassomption.qc.ca
bibliotheque.ville.lassomption.qc.ca

L'Isle-aux-Coudres: **Bibliothèque 'Pour la suite du monde'**
1026, ch des Coudriers, L'Isle-aux-Coudres, QC G0A 3J0
Tél: 418-438-2602; *Téléc:* 418-438-2750
www.reseaubiblioduquebec.qc.ca/coudres

L'Isle-aux-Grues: **Bibliothèque La Rose des Vents/L'Isle-aux-Grues**
107, ch de la Volière, L'Isle-aux-Grues, QC G0R 1P0
Tél: 418-248-4680

L'Islet: **Bibliothèque Jean-Paul-Bourque/L'Islet-sur-Mer**
16, rte des Pionniers Est, L'Islet, QC G0R 2B0
Tél: 418-247-7576; *Téléc:* 418-247-5009
Jacqueline C. Kirouac, Responsable

L'Islet: **Bibliothèque Léon-Laberge**
284, boul Nilus-Leclerc, L'Islet, QC G0R 2C0
Tél: 418-247-5345; *Téléc:* 418-247-5085
bleonl@globetrotter.qc.ca

L'Épiphanie: **Bibliothèque de L'Épiphanie**
83, rue Amireault, L'Épiphanie, QC J5X 1A1
Tél: 450-588-4470
biblio061@reseaubibliocqlm.qc.ca

L'Étang-du-Nord: **Bibliothèque de l'Étang-du-Nord**
1589, ch Étang-du-Nord, L'Étang-du-Nord, QC G4T 3C1
Tél: 418-986-3321; *Téléc:* 418-986-6231
biblio.edn@muniles.ca
Georgette Chevarie, Responsable

La Conception: **Bibliothèque de La Conception**
1373, boul du Centenaire, La Conception, QC J0T 1M0
Tél: 819-686-3016; *Téléc:* 819-686-5808
biblio@municipalite.laconception.qc.ca
www.reseaubiblioduquebec.qc.ca

La Doré: **Bibliothèque publique de la Doré**
4450, rue des Peupliers, La Doré, QC G8J 1E5
Tél: 418-256-3545; *Téléc:* 418-307-8003
ladore@reseaubiblioslsj.qc.ca

La Macaza: **Bibliothèque de La Macaza**
53, rue des Pionniers, La Macaza, QC J0T 1R0
Tél: 819-275-2077; *Téléc:* 819-275-3429
biblio@munilamacaza.ca
Mèdia social: www.facebook.com/545160822205187

La Malbaie: **Bibliothèque Laure-Conan**
395, rue St-Etienne, La Malbaie, QC G5A 1S8
Tél: 418-665-3747; *Téléc:* 418-665-6481
respo.biblio@ville.lamalbaie.qc.ca
ville.lamalbaie.qc.ca/fr/bibliotheques/
Mèdia social: www.facebook.com/BibliothequeLaMalbaie

La Minerve: **Bibliothèque de La Minerve**
100, ch des fondateurs, La Minerve, QC J0T 1S0
Tél: 819-274-2313; *Téléc:* 819-274-2031
biblio@municipalite.laminerve.qc.ca
www.municipalite.laminerve.qc.ca
Mèdia social:
www.facebook.com/pages/Bibliothèque-La-Minerve/1423606051235164

La Motte: **Bibliothèque de La Motte**
349, ch St-Luc, La Motte, QC J0Y 1T0
Tél: 819-732-0505; *Téléc:* 819-727-4248
lamotte@reseaubiblioatnq.qc.ca
www.reseaubiblioduquebec.qc.ca/la motte
Nicole Richard, Responsable

La Pocatière: **Bibliothèque municipale de La Pocatière**
#4, 900, 6e av, La Pocatière, QC G0R 1Z0
Tél: 418-856-3459
biblio@lapocatiere.ca
www.reseaubiblioduquebec.qc.ca
Julie Garon, Responsable

La Prairie: **Bibliothèque Léo-Lecavalier**
Complexe Saint-Laurent, 500, rue Saint-Laurent, La Prairie, QC J5R 5X2
Tél: 450-444-6710; *Téléc:* 450-444-6708
biblio@ville.laprairie.qc.ca
www.ville.laprairie.qc.ca/bibliotheque
Brigitte Tremblay, Responsable

***La Reine:* Bibliothèque La Reine**
1, 3e av Ouest, La Reine, QC J0Z 2L0
Tél: 819-947-5271; *Téléc:* 819-947-5271
lareine@reseaubiblioatnq.qc.ca
Angèle Thouin, Responsable

***La Romaine:* Bibliothèque de La Romaine**
École Marie-Sarah, Poste Restante, La Romaine, QC G0G 1M0
Tél: 418-787-2241

***La Sarre:* Bibliothèque municipale Richelieu de La Sarre**
195, rue Principale, La Sarre, QC J9Z 1Y3
Tél: 819-333-2294; *Téléc:* 819-333-2296
www.ville.lasarre.qc.ca/culture/fr/lecture/details.cfm?ID=7
Média social: www.facebook.com/333704643348589
Noëlline Marcoux, Responsable
nmarcoux@ville.lasarre.qc.ca
819-333-2294 ext. 288
Johanne Audet, Adjointe à la technique
jaudet@ville.lasarre.qc.ca
819-333-2294 ext. 293

***La Trinité-des-Monts:* Bibliothèque de La Trinité-des-Monts**
12, rue Principale ouest, La Trinité-des-Monts, QC G0K 1B0
Tél: 418-779-2426
biblio.trinite@crsbp.net
www.reseaubiblioduquebec.qc.ca

***La Tuque:* Bibliothèque municipale, Ville de La Tuque**
575, rue St-Eugène, La Tuque, QC G9X 2T5
Tél: 819-523-3100; *Téléc:* 819-523-4487
bibliotheque@ville.latuque.qc.ca
www.ville.latuque.qc.ca
Média social: www.facebook.com/bibliotheque.latuque

***Labelle:* Bibliothèque de Labelle**
7393, boul du Curé-Labelle, Labelle, QC J0T 1H0
Tél: 819-681-3371; *Téléc:* 819-686-3820
biblio@municipalite.labelle.qc.ca
www.mabibliotheque.ca/labelle
Nathalie Robson, Directrice

***Labrecque:* Bibliothèque publique de Labrecque**
3425, rue Ambroise, Labrecque, QC G0W 2S0
Tél: 418-481-1618
labrecque@reseaubiblioslsj.qc.ca

***Lac-a-la-Croix:* Bibliothèque publique de Lac-a-la-Croix**
#002, 335, rue de Rouillac, Lac-a-la-Croix, QC G8G 2B5
Tél: 418-349-8495
lac.croix@reseaubiblioslsj.qc.ca
www.reseaubiblioduquebec.qc.ca

***Lac-au-Saumon:* Bibliothèque Bertrand-Leblanc**
20, Place de la Municipalité, Lac-au-Saumon, QC G0J 1M0
Tél: 418-778-3008
biblio.saumon@crsbp.net
www.reseaubiblioduquebec.qc.ca

***Lac-aux-Sables:* Bibliothèque de Lac-aux-Sables**
820, rue Saint-Alphonse, Lac-aux-Sables, QC G0X 1M0
Tél: 418-336-3299; *Téléc:* 418-336-2500
biblio045@reseaubibliocqlm.qc.ca
www.reseaubiblioduquebec.qc.ca
Louise Veillette, Responsable

***Lac-Beauport:* Bibliothèque L'Écrin**
50, ch du Village, Lac-Beauport, QC G0A 2C0
Tél: 418-849-7141; *Téléc:* 418-849-0361
bibliothequeecrin@lacbeauport.net

***Lac-Bouchette:* Bibliothèque publique de Lac-Bouchette**
#110, 258, rue Principale, Lac-Bouchette, QC G0W 1V0
Tél: 418-348-6306
lac.bouchett@reseaubiblioslsj.qc.ca
Lucie Tremblay, Responsable

***Lac-Brome:* Bibliothèque Commémorative Pettes/ Pettes Memorial Library**
276, ch Knowlton, Lac-Brome, QC J0E 1V0
Tél: 450-243-6128
pettes.ca
Média social: www.facebook.com/petteslibrary
Jana Valasek, Directrice générale
jana@pettes.ca

***Lac-Cayamant:* Bibliothèque municipale de Cayamant**
6, ch Lachapelle, Lac-Cayamant, QC J0X 1Y0
Tél: 819-463-4171; *Téléc:* 819-463-4020
info@cayamant.ca

***Lac-des-Aigles:* Bibliothèque Lac-des-Aigles**
75A, rue Principale, Lac-des-Aigles, QC G0K 1V0
Tél: 418-779-2300
biblio.aigles@crsbp.net
Lise Leblanc, Responsable

***Lac-des-Loups:* Bibliothèque Lac-des-Loups (La Pêche)**
275, rue Pontbriand, Lac-des-Loups, QC J0X 3K0
Tél: 819-456-3222; *Téléc:* 819-456-4534
admlac-des-loups@crsbpo.qc.ca
Michelle Archambault, Responsable

***Lac-des-Plages:* Bibliothèque Lac-des-Plages**
2053, ch Tour-du-Lac, Lac-des-Plages, QC J0T 1K0
Tél: 819-426-2391; *Téléc:* 819-426-2085
admdesplages@crsbpo.qc.ca
Micheline Tessier, Responsable

***Lac-des-Seize-Iles:* Bibliothèque de Lac-des-Seize-Iles**
47, rue de l'Église, Lac-des-Seize-Iles, QC J0T 2M0
Tél: 450-630-3044
bibliotheque@lac-des-seize-iles.com

***Lac-des-Écorces:* Bibliothèque de Lac-des-Écorces**
570, boul St-François, Lac-des-Écorces, QC J0W 1H0
Tél: 819-585-2555
bibliolde@lacdesecorces.ca
www.reseaubiblioduquebec.qc.ca

***Lac-des-Écorces:* Bibliothèque de Val-Barrette**
135, rue St-Joseph, Lac-des-Écorces, QC J0W 1H0
Tél: 819-585-3131
bibliovb@lacdesecorces.ca
Média social: www.facebook.com/biblio.valbarrette

***Lac-du-Cerf:* Bibliothèque de Lac-du-Cerf**
15, rue Émard, Lac-du-Cerf, QC J0W 1S0
Tél: 819-597-4163; *Téléc:* 819-597-4163
biblio@lac-du-cerf.ca
www.reseaubiblioduquebec.qc.ca
Francine Boismenu-St-Louis, Responsable

***Lac-Etchemin:* Bibliothèque L'Élan**
208A, 2e av, Lac-Etchemin, QC G0R 1S0
Tél: 418-625-5325; *Téléc:* 418-625-3175
biblio@sogetel.net

***Lac-Mégantic:* Médiathèque municipale Nelly-Arcan**
3700, rue Lemieux, Lac-Mégantic, QC G6B 1S7
Tél: 819-583-0876; *Téléc:* 819-583-0878
mediathequenellyarcan.ca
Daniel Lavoie, Directeur/Bibliothécaire
daniel.lavoie@mediathequenellyarcan.ca
Frédéric Lafrenière, Technicienne en documentation
frederic.lafreniere@mediathequenellyarcan.ca
Mike Roy, Technicienne en documentation
mike.roy@mediathequenellyarcan.ca
Michèle Guérard, Préposé à l'entretien

***Lac-Saguay:* Bibliothèque de Lac-Saguay**
257A, rte 117, Lac-Saguay, QC J0W 1L0
Tél: 819-278-3972; *Téléc:* 819-278-0260
biblio@lacsaguay.qc.ca
www.reseaubiblioduquebec.qc.ca
Micheline Bouliane, Responsable

***Lac-Saint-Paul:* Bibliothèque de Lac-Saint-Paul**
384A, rue Principale, Lac-Saint-Paul, QC J0W 1K0
Tél: 819-587-4283; *Téléc:* 819-587-4892
biblio@lac-saint-paul.ca
Solange Quévillon, Responsable

***Lac-Sainte-Marie:* Bibliothèque municipale de Lac-Sainte-Marie**
121, ch Lac-Sainte-Marie, Lac-Sainte-Marie, QC J0X 1Z0
Tél: 819-467-5437
admstemarie@crsbpo.qc.ca

***Lac-Supérieur:* Bibliothèque de Lac-Supérieur**
1277, ch du Lac-Supérieur, Lac-Supérieur, QC J0T 1J0
Tél: 819-681-3370; *Téléc:* 819-688-3010
biblio@muni.lacsuperieur.qc.ca
Thérèse Gaucher, Responsable

***Lac-à-la-Tortue:* Bibliothèque de Lac-à-la-Tortue**
1082, 37e av, Lac-à-la-Tortue, QC G0X 1L0
Tél: 819-538-5882
www.shawinigan.ca
Charlotte Lecours, Responsable des bibliothèques

***Lac-Édouard:* Bibliothèque de Lac-Édouard**
195, rue Principale, Lac-Édouard, QC G0X 3N0
Tél: 819-653-2238; *Téléc:* 819-653-2238
biblio024@reseaubibliocqlm.qc.ca

***Lachute:* Bibliothèque Jean-Marc-Belzile**
378, rue Principale, Lachute, QC J8H 1Y2
Tél: 450-562-4578; *Téléc:* 450-562-1431
biblio@ville.lachute.qc.ca
www.ville.lachute.qc.ca/bibliotheque
Média social: twitter.com/BiblioLachute; facebook.com/BiblioLachute
Claudia Tremblay, Chef de service de la bibliothèque et des activités culturelles
450-562-3781 ext. 255
Chantal Bélisle, Technicienne en documentation
cbelisle@ville.lachute.qc.ca
450-562-3781 ext. 214

***Lacolle:* Bibliothèque municipale de Lacolle**
3, rue de Collège, Lacolle, QC J0J 1J0
Tél: 450-515-8050
www.lacolle.com/citoyens/services-municipaux

***Laforce:* Bibliothèque Laforce**
703, rue Principale, Laforce, QC J0Z 2J0
Tél: 819-722-2461; *Téléc:* 819-722-2462
laforce@reseaubiblioatnq.qc.ca
Lise Bray, Responsable

***Lamarche:* Bibliothèque publique de Lamarche**
102, rue Principale, Lamarche, QC G0W 1X0
Tél: 418-481-2861
lamarche@reseaubiblioslsj.qc.ca
www.reseaubiblioduquebec.qc.ca

***Landrienne:* Bibliothèque Landrienne**
158, rue Principale Est, Landrienne, QC J0Y 1V0
Tél: 819-732-4357; *Téléc:* 819-732-3866
landrienne@reseaubiblioatnq.qc.ca
www.reseaubiblioduquebec.qc.ca/landrienne
Linda Perron, Responsable

***Lanoraie:* Bibliothèque de Lanoraie (Ginette-Rivard-Tremblay)**
#100, 12, rue Louis-Joseph-Doucet, Lanoraie, QC J0K 1E0
Tél: 450-887-1100; *Téléc:* 450-836-5229
biblio@lanoraie.ca
www.lanoraie.ca/index.jsp?p=67
C. Beland, Coordonnatrice
cbeland@lanoraie.ca

***Larouche:* Bibliothèque publique de Larouche**
#214, 610, rue Lévesque, Larouche, QC G0W 1Z0
Tél: 418-695-2201
larouche@reseaubiblioslsj.qc.ca
Média social: www.facebook.com/547293838619940

***Latulipe:* Bibliothèque Latulipe-et-Gaboury**
#5, rue du Carrefour Nord, Latulipe, QC J0Z 2N0
Tél: 819-747-4521
latulipe@reseaubiblioatnq.qc.ca
www.reseaubiblioduquebec.qc.ca/latulipe

***Laurier-Station:* Bibliothèque Wilfrid Laurier**
147, rue Saint-Denis, Laurier-Station, QC G0S 1N0
Tél: 418-728-5939; *Téléc:* 418-728-4801
bwlaurier@globetrotter.net
www.reseaubiblioduquebec.qc.ca/bay-station
Média social: www.facebook.com/bibliothequelaurier

***Laurierville:* Bibliothèque de Laurierville**
148A, rue Grenier, Laurierville, QC G0S 1P0
Tél: 819-365-4646; *Téléc:* 819-365-4936
biblio122@reseaubibliocqlm.qc.ca
Média social: www.facebook.com/246000148875253

***Laval:* Bibliothèques Ville de Laval**
1535, boul Chomedey, 1e étage, Laval, QC H7V 3Z4
Tél: 450-978-6888; *Téléc:* 450-978-5835
www.biblio.ville.laval.qc.ca
Média social: twitter.com/Laval331; www.facebook.com/bibliothequeslaval

***Lavaltrie:* Bibliothèque de Lavaltrie**
241, rue Saint-Antoine-Nord, Lavaltrie, QC J5T 2G7
Tél: 450-586-2921; *Téléc:* 450-586-0124
bibliotheque@ville.lavaltrie.qc.ca

Rachel-Kim Lebeau, Responsable

***Laverlochère:* Bibliothèque de Laverlochère**
3, rue Principale sud, Laverlochère, QC J0Z 2P0
Tél: 819-765-2549; *Téléc:* 819-765-2089
laverlochere@reseaubiblioatnq.qc.ca
www.reseaubiblioduquebec.qc.ca/laverlochere
Lauriane Rivest, Responsable

***Lebel-sur-Quévillon:* Bibliothèque Lebel-sur-Quévillon**
500, Place Quévillon, Lebel-sur-Quévillon, QC J0Y 1X0
Tél: 819-755-4826; *Téléc:* 819-755-8124
lebel@reseaubiblioatnq.qc.ca
Ghislaine Blouin, Responsable

***Lefebvre:* Bibliothèque de Lefebvre**
193, 10e rang, Lefebvre, QC J0H 2C0
Tél: 819-394-3354; *Téléc:* 819-394-2782
biblio081@reseaubibliocqlm.qc.ca
www.reseaubiblioduquebec.qc.ca

***Lejeune:* Bibliothèque de Lejeune**
69, rue de la Grande-Coulée, Lejeune, QC G0L 1S0
Tél: 418-855-2428
biblio.lejeune@crsbp.net
www.reseaubiblioduquebec.qc.ca

***Lemieux:* Bibliothèque de Lemieux**
526, rue de l'Eglise, CP 530, Lemieux, QC G0X 1S0
Tél: 819-283-2506
biblio138@reseaubibliocqlm.qc.ca
www.reseaubiblioduquebec.qc.ca
Lucie Blanchette, Responsable

***Les Bergeronnes:* Bibliothèque Les Bergeronnes**
514, rue du Boisé, Les Bergeronnes, QC G0T 1G0
Tél: 418-232-1134
Valérie Hovington, Responsable

***Les Coteaux:* Bibliothèque municipale Des Coteaux**
65, rte 338, Les Coteaux, QC J7X 1A2
Tél: 450-267-1414; *Téléc:* 450-267-3532
coteaux@reseaubibliomonteregie.qc.ca

***Les Cèdres:* Bibliothèque des Cèdres (Bibliothèque Gaby-Farmer-Denis)**
141, rue Valade, Les Cèdres, QC J7T 1A1
Tél: 450-452-4250
cedres@reseaubibliomonteregie.qc.ca
Média social: www.facebook.com/220101384695188

***Les Escoumins:* Bibliothèque municipale des Escoumins**
2, de la Rivère, Les Escoumins, QC G0T 1K0
Tél: 581-322-1080; *Téléc:* 418-233-3273
biblioescoumins@bellnet.ca
Odile Boisvert, Responsable

***Les Méchins:* Bibliothèque municipale de Les Méchins**
162, rue Principale, Les Méchins, QC G0J 1T0
Tél: 418-729-1346
biblio.lesmechins@mrcdematane.qc.ca
Louise Farand, Responsable

***Les Éboulements:* Bibliothèque Félix-Antoine-Savard**
#210, 2335, route du Fleuve, Les Éboulements, QC G0A 2M0
Tél: 418-489-2990; *Téléc:* 418-489-2989
bibliotheque@leseboulements.com

***Longue-Pointe-de-Mingan:* Bibliothèque de Longue-Pointe-de-Mingan**
878, ch du Roi, Longue-Pointe-de-Mingan, QC G0G 1V0
Tél: 418-949-2437; *Téléc:* 418-949-2166
Andrée Legault, Responsable

***Longueuil:* Bibliothèques publiques de Longueuil**
1100, rue Beauregard, Longueuil, QC J4K 2L1
Tél: 450-463-7180
www.longueuil.ca/bibliotheques/
Média social: www.facebook.com/BibliothequesLongueuil
Martin Dubois, Chef du Service des bibliothèques

***Lorraine:* Bibliothèque municipale de Lorraine**
31, boul de Gaulle, Lorraine, QC J6Z 3W9
Tél: 450-621-1071; *Téléc:* 450-621-6585
bibliotheque@ville.lorraine.qc.ca
www.ville.lorraine.qc.ca
Josianne Messier, Chef de service par intérim

***Lorrainville:* Bibliothèque Lorrainville**
8, rue de l'Église Sud, Lorrainville, QC J0Z 2R0
Tél: 819-625-2401; *Téléc:* 819-625-2380
lorrainville@reseaubiblioatnq.qc.ca
Alain Guimond, Responsable

***Lotbinière:* Bibliothèque 'Au fil des pages'**
#100, 30, rue Joly, Lotbinière, QC G0S 1S0
Tél: 418-796-2912; *Téléc:* 418-796-2198
Lucille Beaudet, Responsable

***Lourdes-de-Blanc-Sablon:* Bibliothèque de Blanc-Sablon**
20, rue Mgr Scheffer, Lourdes-de-Blanc-Sablon, QC G0G 1W0
Tél: 418-461-2030; *Téléc:* 418-461-2529
Vincent Joncas, Responsable

***Low:* Bibliothèque municipale de Low**
4A, ch D'Amour, Low, QC J0X 2C0
Tél: 819-422-3218; *Téléc:* 819-422-3796
admlow@crsbpo.qc.ca
Lise Legros, Responsable

***Lyster:* Bibliothèque de Lyster (Graziella-Ouellet)**
2375, rue Bécancour, Lyster, QC G0S 1V0
Tél: 819-389-5787; *Téléc:* 819-389-5981
biblio144@reseaubibliocqlm.qc.ca
Pierrette Fradette, Coordonnatrice

***Lévis:* Bibliothèques Lévis**
7, rue Monseigneur-Gosselin, Lévis, QC G6V 5J9
Tél: 418-835-8570
bibliolevis@ville.levis.qc.ca
bibliotheques.ville.levis.qc.ca
Suzanne Rochefort, Chef du service des bibliothèques

***Macamic:* Bibliothèque de Colombourg**
705, Rang 2-3 ouest, Macamic, QC J0Z 2S0
Tél: 819-333-5783; *Téléc:* 819-333-1075
colombourg@reseaubiblioatnq.qc.ca
www.reseaubiblioduquebec.qc.ca/colombourg
Noëlla Royer, Responsable

***Macamic:* Bibliothèque de Macamic**
34A, 6e av ouest, Macamic, QC J0Z 2S0
Tél: 819-782-4604; *Téléc:* 819-782-4464
macamic@reseaubiblioatnq.qc.ca
www.reseaubiblioduquebec.qc.ca/macamic
Ginette Labbé, Responsable

***Madeleine-Centre:* Bibliothèque Jacques-Ferron**
104, rue Principale, Madeleine-Centre, QC G0E 1P0
Tél: 418-393-3269; *Téléc:* 418-393-2869
bbostema@globetrotter.qc.ca

***Magog:* Bibliothèque municipale Memphrémagog**
90, rue Saint-David, Magog, QC J1X 0H9
Tél: 819-843-1330; *Téléc:* 819-843-1594
biblio@ville.magog.qc.ca
www.ville.magog.qc.ca
Média social: www.facebook.com/pages/Bibliothèque-Memphrémagog/189961484388618

***Malartic:* Bibliothèque Malartic**
640, De la Paix, Malartic, QC J0Y 1Z0
Tél: 819-757-3611; *Téléc:* 819-757-3084
malartic@reseaubiblioatnq.qc.ca
Maurice Bélanger, Responsable

***Manawan:* Bibliothèque de Manawan**
470, rue Otapi, Manawan, QC J0K 1M0
Tél: 819-971-1379; *Téléc:* 819-971-1266
Janette Ottawa, Responsable

***Mandeville:* Bibliothèque municipale de Mandeville**
162A, rue Desjardins, Mandeville, QC J0K 1L0
Tél: 514-835-2055
bibliomandeville@intermonde.net
www.mandeville.qc.ca/bibliotheque
Monique Bessette, Coordonnatrice

***Maniwaki:* Bibliothèque de Maniwaki/Déléage/Egan-Sud**
14, rue Comeau, Maniwaki, QC J9E 2R8
Tél: 819-449-2738; *Téléc:* 819-449-7626
admmaniwaki@crsbpo.qc.ca
Colette Archambault, Coordinatrice

***Manseau:* Bibliothèque de Manseau**
200A, rue Roux, CP 260, Manseau, QC G0X 1V0
Tél: 819-356-2450; *Téléc:* 819-356-2721
biblio084@reseaubibliocqlm.qc.ca
www.reseaubiblioduquebec.qc.ca

Denise Bernier, Responsable

***Mansfield:* Bibliothèque Mansfield-et-Pontefract**
314, rue Principale, Mansfield, QC J0X 1R0
Tél: 819-683-3491; *Téléc:* 819-683-3590
admmansfield@crsbpo.qc.ca
www.reseaubiblioduquebec.qc.ca/Mansfield
Martine Laroche, Responsable

***Maria:* Bibliothèque Noël-Audet**
#475, 1, rue des Chardonnerets, Maria, QC G0C 1Y0
Tél: 418-759-3832; *Téléc:* 418-759-5035
bbomaria@globetrotter.qc.ca

***Marieville:* Bibliothèque Commémorative Desautels**
603, rue Claude-De Ramezay, Marieville, QC J3M 1J7
Tél: 450-460-4444; *Téléc:* 450-460-3526
www.ville.marieville.qc.ca/bibliotheque
Daniel Lalonde, Directeur

***Marsoui:* Bibliothèque de Marsoui**
2, rue des Écoliers, Marsoui, QC G0E 1S0
Tél: 418-288-5508

***Mascouche:* Bibliothèque municipale de Mascouche**
3015, ave des Ancêtres, Mascouche, QC J7K 1X6
Tél: 450-474-4133
biblio@ville.mascouche.qc.ca
www.ville.mascouche.qc.ca

***Mashteuiatsh:* Bibliothèque publique de Mashteuiatsh**
507, rue Uapileu, Mashteuiatsh, QC G0W 2H0
Tél: 418-275-5386; *Téléc:* 418-275-0097
masht@reseaubiblioslsj.qc.ca
Johane Langlais, Responsable

***Maskinongé:* Bibliothèque de Maskinongé**
11, rue Marcel, Maskinongé, QC J0K 1N0
Tél: 819-227-4656
biblio059@reseaubibliocqlm.qc.ca
www.reseaubiblioduquebec.qc.ca
Andrée Livernoche, Responsable

***Massueville:* Bibliothèque municipale de Massueville/St-Aimé**
846A, rue de l'Église, Massueville, QC J0G 1K0
Tél: 450-788-3120
aime@reseaubibliomonteregie.qc.ca

***Matane:* Bibliothèque municipale de Matane (Fonds de Solidarité FTQ)**
Complexe culturel Joseph-Rouleau, 520, av Saint-Jérôme, Matane, QC G4W 3B5
Tél: 418-562-9233; *Téléc:* 418-566-2064
www.ville.matane.qc.ca
Christiane Melançon, Responsable
c.melancon@ville.matane.qc.ca

***Matapédia:* Bibliothèque de Matapédia**
5, rue Hôtel-de-Ville, Matapédia, QC G0J 1V0
Tél: 418-865-2717; *Téléc:* 418-865-2828
bbomatap@globetrotter.net

***Mercier:* Bibliothèque municipale de Mercier**
16, rue du Parc, Mercier, QC J6R 1E5
Tél: 450-691-6090
bibliotheque@ville.mercier.qc.ca
www.ville.mercier.qc.ca

***Messines:* Bibliothèque de Messines**
3, ch de la Ferme, Messines, QC J0X 2J0
Tél: 819-465-2637; *Téléc:* 819-465-2943
admmessines@crsbpo.qc.ca
www.reseaubiblioduquebec.qc.ca/Messines
Claire Lacroix, Responsable

***Mirabel:* Bibliothèque municipale de Mirabel**
17710, rue du Val-d'Espoir, Mirabel, QC J7J 1V7
Tél: 450-475-2011
biblio@ville.mirabel.qc.ca
www.ville.mirabel.qc.ca
Média social: www.facebook.com/152931024748094
Sarah Germain, Directrice
s.germain@ville.mirabel.qc.ca
450-475-2082
Carole Gaudet, Technicienne en documentation
c.gaudet@ville.mirabel.qc.ca
Diane Girouard, Bibliothécaire adjointe par intérim et technicienne en documentation
d.girouard@ville.mirabel.qc.ca
Fanny Laberge, Technicienne en documentation
f.laberge@ville.mirabel.qc.ca

Sylvie Labelle, Secrétaire
s.labelle@ville.mirabel.qc.ca

Moisie: **Bibliothèque de Moisie**
250, ch des Forges, Moisie, QC G0G 2B0
Tél: 418-927-2279

Mont-Brun: **Bibliothèque Mont-Brun**
9985, rang du Berger, Mont-Brun, QC J0Z 2Y0
Tél: 819-637-7101
montbrun@reseaubiblioatnq.qc.ca
Noëlla Thibault, Responsable

Mont-Carmel: **Bibliothèque Odile-Boucher**
22, rue de la Fabrique, Mont-Carmel, QC G0L 1W0
Tél: 418-498-2050
Média social: www.facebook.com/293122370741022
Huguette Massé, Responsable

Mont-Joli: **Bibliothèque Jean-Louis-Desrosiers de Mont-Joli**
1477, boul Jacques-Cartier, Mont-Joli, QC G5H 3L3
Tél: 418-775-4106; *Téléc:* 418-775-4037
bibliotheque@ville.mont-joli.qc.ca
ville.mont-joli.qc.ca
Julie Bélanger, Responsable
julie.belanger@ville.mont-joli.qc.ca

Mont-Laurier: **Bibliothèque de Des Ruisseaux**
1269, boul Des Ruisseaux, Mont-Laurier, QC J9L 0H6
Tél: 819-623-6748
biblio.villemontlaurier.qc.ca
Sophie Monette, Bibliothécaire

Mont-Laurier: **Bibliothèque de Mont-Laurier**
385, rue Du Pont, Mont-Laurier, QC J9L 2R5
Tél: 819-623-1833
biblio.villemontlaurier.qc.ca

Mont-Laurier: **Bibliothèque de Val-Limoges**
3620, ch Val-Limoges, Mont-Laurier, QC J9L 3G6
Tél: 819-623-9124
biblio.villemontlaurier.qc.ca
Sophie Monette, Bibliothécaire

Mont-Louis: **La Bibliothèque Liratou de Mont-Louis**
1A, 1re av Ouest, Mont-Louis, QC G0E 1T0
Tél: 418-797-2310; *Téléc:* 418-797-2928

Mont-Saint-Hilaire: **Bibliothèque Armand-Cardinal**
150, rue du Centre Civique, Mont-Saint-Hilaire, QC J3H 3M8
Tél: 450-467-2854
bibliotheque@villemsh.ca
www.ville.mont-saint-hilaire.qc.ca

Mont-Saint-Michel: **Bibliothèque de Mont-Saint-Michel**
73, rue Principale, Mont-Saint-Michel, QC J0W 1P0
Tél: 819-587-3093; *Téléc:* 819-587-3781
biblio55@lino.com
www.reseaubiblioduquebec.qc.ca
Média social: www.facebook.com/pages/Biblio-Mont-St-Michel/144550454903 1298
Marlène Paquin, Responsable

Mont-Saint-Pierre: **Bibliothèque Kevin Pouliot-Bernatchez**
102, rue Cloutier, Mont-Saint-Pierre, QC G0E 1V0
Tél: 418-797-2898; *Téléc:* 418-797-2307
bbomtsp@globetrotter.qc.ca

Mont-Tremblant: **Bibliothèque Samuel-Ouimet**
1147, rue de St-Jovite, Mont-Tremblant, QC J8E 1V1
Tél: 819-425-8614; *Téléc:* 819-425-1391
biblio.samuel-o@villedemont-tremblant.qc.ca
www.villedemont-tremblant.qc.ca

Montcalm: **Bibliothèque de Montcalm**
30, rte du Lac-Rond nord, Montcalm, QC J0T 2V0
Tél: 819-681-3383; *Téléc:* 819-687-2374
biblio@municipalite.montcalm.qc.ca

Montcerf-Lytton: **Bibliothèque Montcerf-Lytton**
16, rue Principale nord, 2e étage, Montcerf-Lytton, QC J0W 1N0
Tél: 819-449-2065; *Téléc:* 819-449-7310
admmontcerf@crsbpo.qc.ca
Angèle Lacaille, Responsable

Montebello: **Bibliothèque de Montebello**
516, rue Notre-Dame, Montebello, QC J0V 1L0
Tél: 819-423-6213; *Téléc:* 819-423-5703
biblio.montebello@videotron.ca
Diane Thivierge, Responsable

Montpellier: **Bibliothèque de Montpellier**
4B, rue du Bosquet, Montpellier, QC J0V 1M0
Tél: 819-428-3663; *Téléc:* 819-428-1221
admmontpellier@crsbpo.qc.ca
Nicole Touchette, Responsable

Montréal: **Atwater Library & Computer Centre/ Bibliothèque et centre d'informatique Atwater**
1200, av Atwater, Montréal, QC H3Z 1X4
Tél: 514-935-7344; *Fax:* 514-935-1960
info@atwaterlibrary.ca
www.atwaterlibrary.ca
Social Media: www.facebook.com/Atwaterlibraryandcomputercentre
Lynn Verge, Executive Director
Aude McDermott, Library Manager
Tanya Mayhew, Administration and Development Manager

Montréal: **Bibliothèque et Archives nationales du Québec**
2275, rue Holt, Montréal, QC H2G 3H1
Tél: 514-873-1100; *Téléc:* 514-873-9312
Ligne sans frais: 800-363-9028
collectionspeciale@banq.qc.ca
www.banq.qc.ca
Média social: www.youtube.com/user/BAnQweb20; twitter.com/_BAnQ; www.facebook.com/banqweb20
Christiane Barbe, Présidente-directrice générale

Montréal: **Bibliothèque Reginald J.P. Dawson**
1967, boul Graham, Montréal, QC H3R 1G9
Tél: 514-734-2967; *Téléc:* 514-734-3089
bibliotheque@ville.mont-royal.qc.ca
www.ville.mont-royal.qc.ca/index.php?id=112
Denis Chouinard, Chef de division
denis.chouinard@ville.mont-royal.qc.ca
514-734-2966

Montréal: **The Fraser-Hickson Institute/ Institut Fraser-Hickson**
2165 Madison Ave., 2nd Floor, Montréal, QC H4B 2T2
Tél: 514-489-5301
info@fraserhickson.ca
www.fraserhickson.qc.ca
Frances W. Ackerman, Library Director & Secretary to the Board

Montréal: **Jewish Public Library (Montréal)/ La Bibliothèque publique juive (Montréal)**
5151, Côte Ste-Catherine Rd., Montréal, QC H3W 1M6
Tél: 514-345-2627
www.jewishpubliclibrary.org
Social Media: twitter.com/jpl_montreal; www.facebook.com/jpl.montreal
Michael Crelinsten, Executive Director

Montréal: **Réseau des bibliothèques publiques de Montréal/ Montreal Public Libraries Network**
Pavillon Prince, 801, rue Brennan, 5e étage, Montréal, QC H3C 0G4
Tél: 514-872-0311
public_biblio@ville.montreal.qc.ca
bibliomontreal.com
Média social: www.youtube.com/user/BiblioMontreal; twitter.com/bibliomontreal; www.facebook.com/bibliomontreal
Louise Guillemette-Labory, Directrice-associée
lglabory@ville.montreal.qc.ca

Morin-Heights: **Bibliothèque de Morin-Heights**
823, ch du Village, Morin-Heights, QC J0R 1H0
Tél: 450-226-3232; *Téléc:* 450-226-8786
bibliomh@cgocable.ca
www.morinheights.com
Lois Russell, Coordonnatrice

Murdochville: **Bibliothèque de Murdochville**
635, 5e rue, Murdochville, QC G0E 1W0
Tél: 418-784-2866; *Téléc:* 418-784-2607
bbomurd@globetrotter.net

Métabetchouan-Lac-à-la-Croi: **Bibliothèque publique de Métabetchouan**
87, rue Saint-André, Métabetchouan-Lac-à-la-Croi, QC G8G 1Z2
Tél: 418-349-8495
metabet@reseaubiblioslsj.qc.ca
www.reseaubiblioduquebec.qc.ca

Métis-sur-Mer: **Bibliothèque Métis-sur-Mer**
130, rue Principale, Métis-sur-Mer, QC G0J 1S0
Tél: 418-936-3231
biblio.metis@crsbp.net
www.reseaubiblioduquebec.qc.ca/metis-sur-mer
Ginette Laflamme, Responsable

Namur: **Bibliothèque Namur/ Namur Library**
331, rue Hôtel-de-Ville, Namur, QC J0V 1N0
Tél: 819-426-2996; *Téléc:* 819-426-3074
namur03@mrcpapineau.com
Tammie Leggett, Responsable

Napierville: **Bibliothèque municipale de Napierville**
290, rue St-Alexandre, Napierville, QC J0J 1L0
Tél: 450-245-0030; *Téléc:* 450-245-3777
napierville@reseaubibliomonteregie.qc.ca
Média social: www.facebook.com/biblionapierville

Natashquan: **Bibliothèque de Natashquan**
29, ch d'en Haut, Natashquan, QC G0G 2E0
Tél: 418-726-3362; *Téléc:* 418-726-3698
Guillaume Hubermont, Responsable

Neuville: **Bibliothèque Félicité-Angers**
716, rue des Érables, Neuville, QC G0A 2R0
Tél: 418-876-4636
www.reseaubiblioduquebec.qc.ca/neuville
Suzanne Lemieux, Responsable

New Richmond: **Bibliothèque du Vieux-Couvent**
99, Place Suzanne-Guité, New Richmond, QC G0C 2B0
Tél: 418-392-7070; *Téléc:* 418-392-5331
biblio@villenewrichmond.com
www.reseaubiblioduquebec.qc.ca/portail/index.aspx?page=3&BID=726
Média social: www.facebook.com/185950867540

Newport: **Bibliothèque de Newport**
208, rte 132, Newport, QC G0C 2A0
Tél: 418-777-2523; *Téléc:* 418-689-3639
bbonewpt@globetrotter.qc.ca

Nicolet: **Bibliothèque de Nicolet**
116, rue Evariste-Lecomte, Nicolet, QC J3T 1G8
Tél: 819-293-6007; *Téléc:* 819-293-6767
biblio072@reseaubibliocqlm.qc.ca
www.reseaubiblioduquebec.qc.ca
Serge Rousseau, Responsable

Nicolet: **Bibliothèque Solidarité rurale**
204, 85, rue Notre-Dame, Nicolet, QC J3T 1V8
Tél: 819-293-6825; *Téléc:* 819-293-4181
www.reseaubiblioduquebec.qc.ca/solidarite-rurale

Nominingue: **Bibliothèque de Nominingue**
2112, ch du Tour du Lac, Nominingue, QC J0W 1R0
Tél: 819-278-3384; *Téléc:* 819-278-4967
biblio51@crsbpl.qc.ca
Sylvie Gendron, Responsable

Normandin: **Bibliothèque municipale de Normandin**
1156, rue Valois, Normandin, QC G8M 3Z8
Tél: 418-274-2004
bibliotheque@ville.normandin.qc.ca
Média social: www.facebook.com/460082477400331
Gilles Ouellet, Président
Éric Bhérer, Directeur des loisirs et de la culture

Normétal: **Bibliothèque Normétal**
36A, rue Principale, Normétal, QC J0Z 3A0
Tél: 819-788-2505; *Téléc:* 819-788-2730
normetal@reseaubiblioatnq.qc.ca
Louise Nolet, Responsable

North Hatley: **Bibliothèque de North Hatley/ North Hatley Library**
165, rue Main, North Hatley, QC J0B 2C0
Tél: 819-842-2110
biblio@nhlibrary.qc.ca
www.nhlibrary.qc.ca

Notre-Dame-de-Ham: **Bibliothèque de Notre-Dame-de-Ham**
25, rue de l'Église, Notre-Dame-de-Ham, QC G0P 1C0
Tél: 819-344-5010
biblio149@reseaubibliocqlm.qc.ca

Notre-Dame-de-la-Merci: **Bibliothèque de Notre-Dame-de-la-Merci**
1900, Montée de la Réserve, Notre-Dame-de-la-Merci, QC J0T 2A0
Tél: 819-424-2113; *Téléc:* 819-424-7347
biblio42@crsbpl.qc.ca
www.reseaubiblioduquebec.qc.ca

Notre-Dame-de-la-Paix: **Bibliothèque Notre-Dame-de-la-Paix**
10, rue Saint-Jean-Baptiste, Notre-Dame-de-la-Paix, QC J0V 1P0
Tél: 819-522-6610; *Téléc:* 819-522-6710
admpaix@crsbpo.qc.ca
Suzon Côté, Responsable

Notre-Dame-de-la-Salette: **Bibliothèque de Notre-Dame-de-la-Salette**
68, rue des Saules, Notre-Dame-de-la-Salette, QC J0X 2L0
Tél: 819-766-2872; *Téléc:* 819-766-2983
admsalette@crsbpo.qc.ca
www.reseaubiblioduquebec.qc.ca/Notre-Dame-de-la-Salette
Julie Bégin, Responsable

Notre-Dame-de-Lorette: **Bibliothèque publique de Notre-Dame-de-Lorette**
Couvent Maria-Goretti, 22, rue Principale, Notre-Dame-de-Lorette, QC G0W 1B0
Tél: 418-276-1934
ndlorette@reseaubiblioslsj.qc.ca

Notre-Dame-de-Lourdes: **Bibliothèque Notre-Dame-de-Lourdes**
3971, rue Principale, Notre-Dame-de-Lourdes, QC J0K 1K0
Tél: 450-759-7864
www.notredamedelourdes.ca/services-biblio.asp
Média social:
www.facebook.com/pages/Bibliothèque-NDL/622069297872428
Johanne Vincent, Responsable

Notre-Dame-de-Montauban: **Bibliothèque de Notre-Dame-de-Montauban**
545A, rue des Loisirs, Notre-Dame-de-Montauban, QC G0X 1W0
Tél: 418-336-1211; *Téléc:* 418-336-2353
biblio058@reseaubiblioqlm.qc.ca
www.reseaubiblioduquebec.qc.ca
Denise Villemure, Responsable

Notre-Dame-de-Pontmain: **Bibliothèque de Notre-Dame-de-Pontmain**
1027, rue Principale, Notre-Dame-de-Pontmain, QC J0W 1S0
Tél: 819-597-2382; *Téléc:* 819-597-2144
bibliotheque@munpontmain.qc.ca

Notre-Dame-de-Portneuf: **Bibliothèque La Découverte/Notre-Dame-de-Portneuf**
500A, rue Notre-Dame, Notre-Dame-de-Portneuf, QC G0A 2Z0
Tél: 418-286-4452
bibliodecouv@globetrotter.net
www.reseaubiblioduquebec.qc.ca/portneuf

Notre-Dame-des-Monts: **Bibliothèque La Girouette**
87, rue Notre-Dame, Notre-Dame-des-Monts, QC G0T 1L0
Tél: 418-489-2011; *Téléc:* 418-439-0883

Notre-Dame-des-Pins: **Bibliothèque Le Signet/Notre-Dame-des-Pins**
2755, 1e av, Notre-Dame-des-Pins, QC G0M 1K0
Tél: 418-774-9454
biblnddp@sogetel.net

Notre-Dame-du-Bon-Conseil: **Bibliothèque de Notre-Dame-du-Bon-Conseil**
541, rue Notre-Dame, Notre-Dame-du-Bon-Conseil, QC J0C 1A0
Tél: 819-336-2967
biblio096@reseaubiblioqlm.qc.ca
www.reseaubiblioduquebec.qc.ca
Véronique Montesinos, Responsable

Notre-Dame-du-Laus: **Bibliothèque de Notre-Dame-du-Laus**
4, rue de l'Église, Notre-Dame-du-Laus, QC J0X 2M0
Tél: 819-767-2772
biblio057@crsbpl.qc.ca
www.reseaubiblioduquebec.qc.ca
France Drouin, Responsable

Notre-Dame-du-Nord: **Bibliothèque Notre-Dame-du-Nord**
15A, rue Desjardins, Notre-Dame-du-Nord, QC J0Z 3B0
Tél: 819-723-2695; *Téléc:* 819-723-2483
nord@reseaubiblioatnq.qc.ca
Carmen Laliberté, Responsable

Notre-Dame-du-Portage: **Bibliothèque de Notre-Dame-du-Portage**
539, rte du Fleuve, Notre-Dame-du-Portage, QC G0L 1Y0
Tél: 418-862-9163
biblio.portage@crsbp.net
www.reseaubiblioduquebec.qc.ca

Nouvelle: **Bibliothèque de Nouvelle**
14, rue de l'Église, B.P. 6, Nouvelle, QC G0C 2E0
Tél: 418-794-2244; *Téléc:* 418-794-2254
bbonouv@globetrotter.net

Noyan: **Bibliothèque municipale de Noyan/ Noyan Public Library**
1312, ch de la Petite-France, Noyan, QC J0J 1B0
Tél: 450-291-4504; *Téléc:* 450-291-4505
noyan@reseaubibliomonteregie.qc.ca
Média social: www.facebook.com/128784550520545

Nédélec: **Bibliothèque de Nédélec**
68, rue Principale, Nédélec, QC J0Z 2Z0
Tél: 819-784-3351; *Téléc:* 819-784-2126
nedelec@reseaubiblioatnq.qc.ca
www.reseaubiblioduquebec.qc.ca/nedelec
Jacqueline Aylwin, Responsable

Obedjiwan: **Bibliothèque d'Obedjiwan**
22, rue Tcikatnaw, Obedjiwan, QC G0W 3B0
Tél: 819-974-1221; *Téléc:* 819-974-1224
biblio065@reseaubiblioqlm.qc.ca
www.reseaubiblioduquebec.qc.ca
Rachelle Chachai, Responsable

Odanak: **Bibliothèque de Odanak**
58, rue Waban-Aki, Odanak, QC J0G 1H0
Tél: 450-568-0107; *Téléc:* 450-568-0107
biblio139@reseaubiblioqlm.qc.ca
Média social:
www.facebook.com/pages/Bibliothèque-dOdanak/119556601459
Marcelle O'Bomsawin, Responsable

Old Fort: **Bibliothèque de Old Fort**
Livraison Generale, Old Fort, QC G0G 2G0
Tél: 418-379-2911; *Téléc:* 418-379-2959
René Fequet, Responsable

Ormstown: **Bibliothèque municipale d'Ormstown**
85, rue Roy, Ormstown, QC J0S 1K0
Tél: 450-829-3249
ormstown@reseaubibliomonteregie.qc.ca
Média social: www.facebook.com/1448920602061184

Otter Lake: **Bibliothèque Otter Lake**
340, av Martineau, Otter Lake, QC J0X 2P0
Tél: 819-453-7344; *Téléc:* 819-453-7311
admotterlake@crsbpo.qc.ca
www.reseaubiblioduquebec.qc.ca/OtterLake
Esther Dubeau, Responsable

Packington: **Bibliothèque Packington**
115, rue Soucy, Packington, QC G0L 1Z0
Tél: 418-853-5362
biblio.packing@crsbp.net
Denis Moreau, Responsable

Padoue: **Bibliothèque de Padoue**
215, rue Beaulieu, Padoue, QC G0J 1X0
Tél: 418-775-8188
Line Fillion, Responsable

Palmarolle: **Bibliothèque Palmarolle**
115, rue Principale, Palmarolle, QC J0Z 3C0
Tél: 819-787-3459; *Téléc:* 819-787-2412
palmarolle@reseaubiblioatnq.qc.ca
Ghislaine Bégin, Responsable

Papineauville: **Bibliothèque de Papineauville**
294, rue Papineau, Papineauville, QC J0V 1R0
Tél: 819-427-5511; *Téléc:* 819-427-8318
biblio.papineauville@mrcpapineau.com
Média social: www.facebook.com/284798808312015
Francine Denis, Responsable

Parisville: **Bibliothèque de Parisville**
1260, rue St-Jacques, Parisville, QC G0S 1X0
Tél: 819-292-2644; *Téléc:* 819-292-2214
biblio103@reseaubiblioqlm.qc.ca
Colette Ouellet, Responsable

Paspébiac: **Bibliothèque de Paspébiac**
95, boul Gérard-D.-Levesque ouest, Paspébiac, QC G0C 2K0
Tél: 418-752-3014; *Téléc:* 418-752-6747
pretpas@globetrotter.qc.ca
villepaspebiac.ca/bibliotheque

Percé: **Bibliothèque de Percé**
137, rte 132 Ouest, Percé, QC G0C 2L0
Tél: 418-782-2922; *Téléc:* 418-782-5347
bboperce@ville.perce.qc.ca
www.reseaubiblioduquebec.qc.ca
Média social: www.facebook.com/1401154396824528

Petit-Saguenay: **Bibliothèque publique de Petit-Saguenay**
50, rue Tremblay, Petit-Saguenay, QC G0V 1N0
Tél: 418-272-3083
petitsag@reseaubiblioslsj.qc.ca

Petite-Rivière-St-François: **Bibliothèque Gabrielle-Roy/Petite-Rivière-Saint-François**
1069, rue Principale, Petite-Rivière-St-François, QC G0A 2L0
Tél: 418-760-1050; *Téléc:* 418-760-1051
biblioprsf@hotmail.com
Suzanne Lapointe, Responsable
Viviane Guay, Adjointe
Martine Lavoie, Responsable, Animation

Petite-Vallée: **Bibliothèque de Petite-Vallée**
45, rue Principale, Petite-Vallée, QC G0E 1Y0
Tél: 418-393-2949; *Téléc:* 418-393-2949
bibliopv@globetrotter.net

Pierreville: **Bibliothèque de Pierreville (Jean-Luc-Précourt)**
26, rue Ally, Pierreville, QC J0G 1J0
Tél: 450-568-3500; *Téléc:* 450-568-0689
biblio051@reseaubiblioqlm.qc.ca
www.reseaubiblioduquebec.qc.ca
Chantale Bellamy, Responsable

Pincourt: **Bibliothèque de Pincourt/ Pincourt Library**
École secondaire du Chêne-Bleu, 225, boul Pincourt, Pincourt, QC J7V 9T2
Tél: 514-425-1104; *Téléc:* 514-425-6668
bibliotheque@villepincourt.qc.ca
www.villepincourt.qc.ca
Média social: www.facebook.com/villedepincourt
Sylvie de Repentigny, Régisseure
514-425-1104 ext. 6242
Mireille Péladeau, Technicienne en documentation

Plaisance: **Bibliothèque de Plaisance**
281, rue Desjardins, Plaisance, QC J0V 1S0
Tél: 819-427-5363; *Téléc:* 819-427-5015
admplaisance@crsbpo.qc.ca
www.reseaubiblioduquebec.qc.ca/Plaisance
Martine Prud'homme, Responsable

Plessisville: **Bibliothèque municipale de la Ville de Plessisville**
1800, rue Saint-Calixte, Plessisville, QC G6L 1R6
Tél: 819-362-6628; *Téléc:* 819-362-6421
bibliotheque@ville.plessisville.qc.ca
www.ville.plessisville.qc.ca
Suzanne Bédard, Coordonnatrice culturelle
sbedard@ville.plessisville.qc.ca

Pointe-aux-Outardes: **Bibliothèque de Pointe-aux-Outardes**
481, ch Principale, Pointe-aux-Outardes, QC G0H 1H0
Tél: 418-567-9529; *Téléc:* 418-567-4409
www.pointe-aux-outardes.ca
Guylaine Chouinard, Responsable

Pointe-Calumet: **Bibliothèque La Sablière**
190, 41e av, Pointe-Calumet, QC J0N 1G2
Tél: 450-473-5918; *Téléc:* 450-473-6571
bibliotheque@municipalite.pointe-calumet.qc.ca
www.reseaubiblioduquebec.qc.ca
Brigitte Lessard, Directrice

Pointe-Claire: **Bibliothèque publique de Pointe-Claire**
100, av Douglas-Shand, Pointe-Claire, QC H9R 4V1
Tél: 514-630-1218; *Téléc:* 514-630-1261
bibliotheque@ville.pointe-claire.qc.ca
www.ville.pointe-claire.qc.ca/fr_1046_index
Céline Laperrière, Chef de division, Bibliothèque
laperrierec@ville.pointe-claire.qc.ca
514-630-1218 ext. 1217

Pointe-des-Cascades: **Bibliothèque Adrienne Demontigny-Clément**
52, ch du Fleuve, Pointe-des-Cascades, QC J0P 1M0
Tél: 450-455-5310
pointe.cascades@reseaubibliomonteregie.qc.ca

Pointe-Lebel: **Bibliothèque de Pointe-Lebel**
380, rue Granier, Pointe-Lebel, QC G0H 1N0
Tél: 418-589-2325
bpleb@hotmail.ca
Lise Therrien, Responsable

Pointe-à-la-Croix: **Bibliothèque de La Petite-Rochelle**
44A, rue Lasalle, Pointe-à-la-Croix, QC G0C 1L0
Tél: 418-788-2931; *Téléc:* 418-788-1305
biblio.41@hotmail.com

Pont-Rouge: **Bibliothèque Auguste-Honoré-Gosselin**
41, rue du Collège, Pont-Rouge, QC G3H 3A4
Tél: 418-873-4067; *Téléc:* 418-873-4141
Other Numbers: Bureau: 418-873-4052
bibliotheque@ville.pontrouge.qc.ca
www.ville.pontrouge.qc.ca
Denyse Simard, Responsable
Gilberte Gallant, Responsable, activités

Pontiac: **Bibliothèque de Luskville**
2024, rte 148, Pontiac, QC J0X 2G0
Tél: 819-455-2370; *Téléc:* 819-455-9756
admluskville@crsbpo.qc.ca
www.reseaubiblioduquebec.qc.ca/Luskville
Louise Ramsay, Responsable

Pontiac: **Bibliothèque municipale de Quyon**
12, rue Saint-John, Pontiac, QC J0X 2V0
Tél: 819-458-1227; *Téléc:* 819-458-9756
admquyon@pioneerwireless.ca
Bernadette Milks, Coordonnateur

Port-Cartier: **Bibliothèque municipale de Port-Cartier (Le Manuscrit)**
21, rue des Cèdres, Port-Cartier, QC G5B 2W5
Tél: 418-766-3366
www.villeport-cartier.com

Portneuf-sur-Mer: **Bibliothèque de Portneuf-sur-Mer**
170, rue Principale, Portneuf-sur-Mer, QC G0T 1P0
Tél: 418-238-2642
Christine Olivier, Responsable

Poularies: **Bibliothèque Poularies**
990, rue Principale, Poularies, QC J0Z 3E0
Tél: 819-782-5159; *Téléc:* 819-782-5063
poularies@reseaubiblioatnq.qc.ca
Sophie Dallaire, Responsable

Price: **Bibliothèque de Price**
1, rue du Centre, Price, QC G0J 1Z0
Tél: 418-775-5596
biblio.price@crsbp.net
www.reseaubiblioduquebec.qc.ca

Princeville: **Bibliothèque de Princeville (Madeleine-Bélanger)**
140, rue Saint-Jean-Baptiste Sud, Princeville, QC G6L 5A5
Tél: 819-364-3333
biblio079@reseaubibliocqlm.qc.ca
Madeleine Beaudoin, Directrice

Préissac Nord: **Bibliothèque de Préissac-des-Rapides**
6, rue Des Rapides, Préissac Nord, QC J0Y 2E0
Tél: 819-732-4938; *Téléc:* 819-732-4909
preissacn@reseaubiblioatnq.qc.ca
www.reseaubiblioduquebec.qc.ca/preissac-des-rapides
Huguette Béland, Responsable

Préissac Sud: **Bibliothèque de Preissac Sud**
186, av du Lac, Préissac Sud, QC J0Y 2E0
Tél: 819-759-4138; *Téléc:* 819-759-4138
preissacs@reseaubiblioatnq.qc.ca
www.reseaubiblioduquebec.qc.ca/preissac sud
Yolande P. Gagné, Responsable

Prévost: **Bibliothèque Jean-Charles-Des Roches**
2945, boul du Curé-Labelle, Prévost, QC J0R 1T0
Tél: 450-224-8888; *Téléc:* 450-224-3024
www.ville.prevost.qc.ca

Péribonka: **Bibliothèque publique de Péribonka**
296A, Édouard-Niquet, Péribonka, QC G0W 2G0
Tél: 418-374-2967
peribonk@reseaubiblioslsj.qc.ca
Média social: www.facebook.com/BiblioPeribonka

Québec: **Réseau des bibliothèques de la Ville de Québec**
350, rue Saint-Joseph est, Québec, QC G1K 3B2
Tél: 418-641-6789
courrier@institutcanadien.qc.ca
www.bibliothequesdequebec.qc.ca
Rémy Vézina, Directeur général

Ragueneau: **Bibliothèque municipale Amaury-Tremblay**
13, rue des Loisirs, Ragueneau, QC G0H 1S0
Tél: 418-567-2291
biblio@municipalite.ragueneau.qc.ca
Média social: www.facebook.com/biblioragueneau

Ragueneau: **Bibliothèque Ragueneau**
13, rue des Loisirs, Ragueneau, QC G0H 1S0
Tél: 418-567-2291; *Téléc:* 418-567-2344
biblio@municipalite.ragueneau.qc.ca
www.reseaubiblioduquebec.qc.ca/rageneau
Média social: www.facebook.com/bibliorageneau
Édith Martel, Responsable

Ravignan: **Bibliothèque Liratu**
108A, rue de l'Église, Ravignan, QC G0R 2L0
Tél: 418-267-5931; *Téléc:* 418-267-5930

Rawdon: **Bibliothèque de Rawdon (Alice-Quintal)**
3643, rue Queen, Rawdon, QC J0X 1S0
Tél: 450-834-2596
Chantal Émard, Directrice

Repentigny: **Bibliothèque municipale de Repentigny**
1, Place d'Evry, Repentigny, QC J6A 8H7
Tél: 450-470-3420
bibliotheque@ville.repentigny.qc.ca
www.ville.repentigny.qc.ca/bibliotheque

Richelieu: **Bibliothèque municipale Simonne-Monet-Chartrand**
200, boul Richelieu, Richelieu, QC J3L 3R4
Tél: 450-658-1157
richelieu@reseaubibliomonteregie.qc.ca

Richmond: **Bibliothèque municipale de Richmond-Cleveland**
820, rue Gouin, Richmond, QC J0B 2H0
Tél: 819-826-5814
bibliormc@ville.richmond.qc.ca
www.ville.richmond.qc.ca/fr/bibliotheque

Rigaud: **Bibliothèque municipale de Rigaud**
102, rue Saint-Pierre, Rigaud, QC J0P 1P0
Tél: 450-451-0869
biblio@ville.rigaud.qc.ca
www.ville.rigaud.qc.ca
Média social: www.facebook.com/BiblioRigaud

Rimouski: **Bibliothèque de Le Bic**
149, rue Sainte-Cécile, Rimouski, QC G0L 1B0
Tél: 418-736-5325
biblio.lebic@crsbp.net
www.reseaubiblioduquebec.qc.ca
Martine Fournier, Bibliothécaire

Rimouski: **Bibliothèque de Sainte-Blandine**
22, rue Lévesque, Rimouski, QC G5N 5S6
Tél: 418-735-5055
biblio.blandine@crsbp.net
www.reseaubiblioduquebec.qc.ca

Rimouski: **Bibliothèque Lisette-Morin**
110, rue de l'Évêché E, Rimouski, QC G5L 7C7
Tél: 418-724-3164; *Téléc:* 418-724-3139
bibliotheque.lisette-morin@ville.rimouski.qc.ca
ville.rimouski.qc.ca/fr/citoyens/bibliotheques/lisettemorin.html
Nicole Gagnon, Responsable

Rimouski: **Bibliothèque Pointe-au-Père**
315, av Thomas-Dionne, Rimouski, QC G5M 1M7
Tél: 418-722-4748
biblio.pere@crsbp.net
Isabelle Boisvert, Responsable

Ripon: **Bibliothèque de Ripon**
31, rue Coursol, Ripon, QC J0V 1V0
Tél: 819-983-2000; *Téléc:* 819-983-1327
admripon@crsbpo.qc.ca
www.reseaubiblioduquebec.qc.ca/Ripon
Céline Derouin, Responsable

Rivière-au-Tonnerre: **Bibliothèque de Rivière-au-Tonnerre**
473, rue Jacques-Cartier, Rivière-au-Tonnerre, QC G0G 2L0
Tél: 418-465-2255; *Téléc:* 418-465-2956
Marie-Josée Lapierre, Responsable

Rivière-du-Loup: **Bibliothèque municipale Françoise-Bédard**
67, rue du Rocher, Rivière-du-Loup, QC G5R 1J8
Tél: 418-862-4252
bibliotheque@ville.riviere-du-loup.qc.ca
www.ville.riviere-du-loup.qc.ca/biblio
Média social: www.facebook.com/bibliothequefrancoisebedard
Sylvie Michaud, Bibliothécaire responsable
sylvie.michaud@ville.riviere-du-loup.qc.ca
418-867-6669
Marie-France April, Technicienne en documentation
418-867-6670
Annie Rodrigue, Technicienne en documentation (aide à la recherche)
annie.rodrigue@ville.riviere-du-loup.qc.ca
418-862-6529
Isabelle Moffet, Coordonnatrice à l'animation
isabelle.moffet@ville.riviere-du-loup.qc.ca
418-867-6668

Rivière-Héva: **Bibliothèque Rivière-Héva**
15A, rue du Parc, Rivière-Héva, QC J0Y 2H0
Tél: 819-735-2306; *Téléc:* 819-735-4251
heva@reseaubiblioatnq.qc.ca
Nicole Turcotte, Responsable

Rivière-Pentecôte: **Bibliothèque de Rivière-Pentecôte**
4344, rue Jacques-Cartier, Rivière-Pentecôte, QC G0H 1R0
Tél: 418-799-2262; *Téléc:* 418-799-2263
Hélène Jean, Responsable

Rivière-Rouge: **Bibliothèque de Sainte-Véronique**
2167, boul Fernand-Lafontaine, Rivière-Rouge, QC J0T 1T0
Tél: 819-275-3759; *Téléc:* 819-275-3759
bibliolannon@riviere-rouge.ca
www.reseaubiblioduquebec.qc.ca
Média social: www.facebook.com/bibliotheque.marchand
Ginette Terreault, Responsable

Rivière-St-Paul: **Bibliothèque Rivière-St-Paul**
Livraison Generale, Rivière-St-Paul, QC G0G 2G0
Tél: 418-379-2911; *Téléc:* 418-379-2959
Amanda Griffin, Responsable

Rivière-à-Claude: **Bibliothèque de Rivière-à-Claude**
520, rue Principale Est, Rivière-à-Claude, QC G0E 1Z0
Tél: 418-797-2455
Marie-Claude Rioux, Responsable
mcrioux@globetrotter.net

Rivière-Éternite: **Bibliothèque publique de Rivière Eternité**
404, rue Principale, Rivière-Éternite, QC G0V 1P0
Tél: 418-272-1052
eternite@reseaubiblioslsj.qc.ca
www.reseaubiblioduquebec.qc.ca

Roberval: **Bibliothèque Georges-Henri-Lévesque**
829, boul St-Joseph, Roberval, QC G8H 2L6
Tél: 418-275-0202; *Téléc:* 418-275-7045
www.roberval.biblio.qc.ca
Tania Loisirs, Directrice
tdesbiens@ville.roberval.qc.ca
Lise Morin, Technicienne
lmorin@ville.roberval.qc.ca

Rock Forest: **Bibliothèque du secteur de Rock Forest**
968, rue du Haut-Bois sud, Rock Forest, QC J1N 2C8
Tél: 819-823-8676; *Téléc:* 819-823-8345
Bibliotheque.rockforest@ville.sherbrooke.qc.ca
www.bibliotheque.ville.sherbrooke.qc.ca

Rosemère: **Bibliothèque municipale H J Hemens de Rosemère**
339, ch de la Grande-Côte, Rosemère, QC J7A 1K2
Tél: 450-621-3500
ville.rosemere.qc.ca
Marc Bineault, Bibliothécaire - Chef de service
mbineault@ville.rosemere.qc.ca

Rougemont: **Bibliothèque municipale de Rougemont**
839, rue Principale, Rougemont, QC J0L 1M0
Tél: 450-469-3213
rougemont@reseaubibliomonteregie.qc.ca

Rouyn-Noranda: **Biblio Rollet**
12570, boul Rideau, Rouyn-Noranda, QC J0Z 3J0
Tél: 819-797-7110; *Téléc:* 819-493-1210
rollet@reseaubiblioatnq.qc.ca
www.crsbpat.qc.ca/rollet/
Liliane Monderie, Responsable

Rouyn-Noranda: **Bibliothèque Cadillac**
2, rue Dumont Est, Rouyn-Noranda, QC J0Y 1C0
Tél: 819-797-7110; *Téléc:* 819-759-3607
cadillac@reseaubiblioatnq.qc.ca
Kim Flageole, Responsable

Rouyn-Noranda: **Bibliothèque de Arntfield**
15, rue Fugère, Rouyn-Noranda, QC J0Z 1B0
Tél: 819-797-7110; *Téléc:* 819-279-2481
arntfield@reseaubiblioatnq.qc.ca
Jeannine Drouin, Responsable

Rouyn-Noranda: **Bibliothèque de Beaudry**
6884, boul Témiscamingue, Rouyn-Noranda, QC J9Y 1N1
Tél: 819-797-2543; *Téléc:* 819-797-2108
beaudry@reseaubiblioatnq.qc.ca
Marguerite Petit, Responsable

Rouyn-Noranda: **Bibliothèque de Bellecombe**
2471, rte des Pionniers, Rouyn-Noranda, QC J0Z 1K0
Tél: 819-797-7110; *Téléc:* 819-797-6585
bellecombe@reseaubiblioatnq.qc.ca
mabiblio.quebec/bellecombe
Marie Aubin, Responsable

Rouyn-Noranda: **Bibliothèque de Cloutier**
10232, boul Témiscamingue, Rouyn-Noranda, QC J0Z 1S0
Tél: 819-797-8613; *Téléc:* 819-797-1299
cloutier@reseaubiblioatnq.qc.ca
Josée Falardeau, Responsable

Rouyn-Noranda: **Bibliothèque Destor**
7292, rang du parc, Rouyn-Noranda, QC J9Y 0C8
Tél: 819-637-2279; *Téléc:* 819-637-5512
destor@reseaubiblioatnq.qc.ca
www.reseaubiblioduquebec.qc.ca/destor
Rita Tremblay, Responsable
Guylaine Pelletier, Adjointe

Rouyn-Noranda: **Bibliothèque Montbeillard**
9632C, boul Rideau, Rouyn-Noranda, QC J0Z 2X0
Tél: 819-797-7110; *Téléc:* 819-797-2390
montbeillard@reseaubiblioatnq.qc.ca
Diane St-Onge, Responsable

Rouyn-Noranda: **Bibliothèque municipale de Rouyn-Noranda**
201, av Dallaire, Rouyn-Noranda, QC J9X 4T5
Tél: 819-762-0944; *Téléc:* 819-797-7564
info@biblrn.qc.ca
www.biblrn.qc.ca
Média social: www.facebook.com/BibliRN
Esther Labrie, Directrice générale
esther.labrie@biblrn.qc.ca
Ginette Montigny, Responsable, Services techniques
ginette.montigny@biblrn.qc.ca
Diane Brazeau, Secrétaire de direction
diane.brazeau@biblrn.qc.ca

Roxton Pond: **Bibliothèque municipale de Roxton Pond**
905, rue Saint-Jean, Roxton Pond, QC J0E 1Z0
Tél: 450-372-6875
www.roxtonpond.ca/bibliotheque
Média social: www.facebook.com/biblioroxtonpond
Julie Labbé, Responsable

Rémigny: **Bibliothèque de Rémigny**
1304, ch de l'Église, Rémigny, QC J0Z 3H0
Tél: 819-761-2331; *Téléc:* 819-761-2421
remigny@reseaubiblioatnq.qc.ca
www.reseaubiblioduquebec.qc.ca/rémigny
Jocelyne Savignac, Responsable

Sabrevois: **Bibliothèque municipale de Sainte-Anne-de-Sabrevois**
1218, rte 133, Sabrevois, QC J0J 2G0
Tél: 450-346-0899
sabrevois@reseaubibliomonteregie.qc.ca
www.reseaubiblioduquebec.qc.ca
Guylaine Marchand, Responsable

Sacré-Coeur-Saguenay: **Bibliothèque de Sacré-Coeur**
89-A, Principale nord, Sacré-Coeur-Saguenay, QC G0T 1Y0
Tél: 418-236-4460; *Téléc:* 418-236-9144
Vanessa Deschênes, Responsable

Saint-Adelphe: **Bibliothèque de Saint-Adelphe (Roger-Fontaine)**
150, rue Baillargeon, Saint-Adelphe, QC G0X 2G0
Tél: 418-322-6634; *Téléc:* 418-322-5434
biblio004@reseaubibliocqlm.qc.ca
www.reseaubiblioduquebec.qc.ca
Lyne Deshaies, Responsable

Saint-Adolphe-d'Howard: **Bibliothèque de Saint-Adolphe-d'Howard**
1881, ch du Village, Saint-Adolphe-d'Howard, QC J0T 2B0
Tél: 819-327-2117; *Téléc:* 819-327-2282
biblio24@crsbpl.qc.ca
www.reseaubiblioduquebec.qc.ca

Saint-Aimé-des-Lacs: **Bibliothèque La Plume d'Or**
123B, rue Principale, Saint-Aimé-des-Lacs, QC G0T 1S0
Tél: 418-439-2006; *Téléc:* 418-439-1475

Saint-Alban: **Bibliothèque Biblio-Chut!/Saint-Alban**
179, rue Principale, Saint-Alban, QC G0A 3B0
Tél: 418-268-3557; *Téléc:* 418-268-5073
Francine Lanouette, Responsable
Louise Lauzière, Responsable des expositions, décoration, fabrication de signets
Monette Perreault, Responsable rotation et prêt

Saint-Alexis-de-Matapédia: **Bibliothèque de Saint-Alexis-de-Matapédia**
190, rue Principale, Saint-Alexis-de-Matapédia, QC G0J 2E0
Tél: 418-299-2520; *Téléc:* 418-299-3011
plateau1@globetrotter.net
www.reseaubiblioduquebec.qc.ca
Rachel Lebrun, Responsable

Saint-Alexis-de-Montcalm: **Bibliothèque de Saint-Alexis**
232, rue Principale, Saint-Alexis-de-Montcalm, QC J0K 1T0
Tél: 450-839-7277; *Téléc:* 450-831-2108
biblio110@reseaubibliocqlm.qc.ca

Saint-Alexis-des-Monts: **Bibliothèque de Saint-Alexis-des-Monts (Léopold-Bellemare)**
105, rue Hôtel-de-Ville, Saint-Alexis-des-Monts, QC J0K 1V0
Tél: 819-265-2046
biblio028@reseaubibliocqlm.qc.ca
Média social: www.facebook.com/bibliotheque.stalexisdesmonts
Audrey Vallières, Responsable

Saint-Alphonse-de-Caplan: **Bibliothèque de ABC du savoir**
134A, rue Principale Ouest, Saint-Alphonse-de-Caplan, QC G0C 2V0
Tél: 418-388-5577; *Téléc:* 418-388-2435
bbostal@globetrotter.net
Média social: www.facebook.com/204499129733271

Saint-Alphonse-de-Granby: **Bibliothèque municipale de Saint-Alphonse-de-Granby**
360, rue Principale, Saint-Alphonse-de-Granby, QC J0E 2A0
Tél: 450-375-7229; *Téléc:* 450-375-4570
alphonse@reseaubibliomonteregie.qc.ca
Nancy Bouvier, Responsable

Saint-Alphonse-Rodriguez: **Bibliothèque de Saint-Alphonse-Rodriguez (Docteur-Jacques-Olivier)**
99, rue de la Plage, Saint-Alphonse-Rodriguez, QC J0K 1W0
Tél: 450-883-2264; *Téléc:* 450-883-3959
biblio062@reseaubibliocqlm.qc.ca
Hélène Bombardier, Responsable

Saint-Amable: **Maison de la culture Jacqueline Gemme**
575, rue Principale, Saint-Amable, QC J0L 1N0
Tél: 450-649-3555; *Téléc:* 450-649-0203
amable@reseaubibliomonteregie.qc.ca
www.reseaubiblioduquebec.qc.ca
France Therrien, Responsable

Saint-Ambroise: **Bibliothèque publique de Saint-Ambroise**
156, rue Gaudreault, Saint-Ambroise, QC G7P 2J9
Tél: 418-672-2253
stambr@reseaubiblioslsj.qc.ca
www.reseaubiblioduquebec.qc.ca
Carole Gagné, Responsable

Saint-André: **Bibliothèque publique de Saint-André**
74, rue Pricipale, Saint-André, QC G0W 2K0
Tél: 418-349-1196
standre@reseaubiblioslsj.qc.ca
www.reseaubiblioduquebec.qc.ca

Saint-André-Avellin: **Bibliothèque de Saint-André-Avellin**
532, rue Charles-Auguste Montreuil, Saint-André-Avellin, QC J0V 1W0
Tél: 819-983-2840; *Téléc:* 819-983-2344
admavellin@crsbpo.qc.ca
www.reseaubiblioduquebec.qc.ca/St-Andre-Avellin
Adéodat Bernard, Responsable

Saint-André-de-Restigouche: **Bibliothèque de Saint-André-de-Restigouche**
163, rue Principale, Saint-André-de-Restigouche, QC G0J 1G0
Tél: 418-865-2234; *Téléc:* 418-865-1393
m.st.and.restigouche@globetrotter.net

Saint-Anicet: **Bibliothèque municipale de Saint-Anicet**
1547, rte 132, Saint-Anicet, QC J0S 1M0
Tél: 450-264-9431; *Téléc:* 450-264-3544
anicet@reseaubibliomonteregie.qc.ca
Média social: www.facebook.com/547785058683707

Saint-Antoine-de-Tilly: **Bibliothèque La Corne de brume**
943, rue de l'Église, Saint-Antoine-de-Tilly, QC G0S 2C0
Tél: 819-799-2365; *Téléc:* 819-799-3571
lacorne@reseaubiblioatnq.qc.ca
Chantal Lessard, Responsable

Saint-Antoine-sur-Richelieu: **Bibliothèque Hélène-Dupuis-Marion**
#2, 1060, rue du Moulin Payet, Saint-Antoine-sur-Richelieu, QC J0L 1R0
Tél: 450-787-3140; *Téléc:* 450-787-2852
antoine@reseaubibliomonteregie.qc.ca

Saint-Antonin: **Bibliothèque Saint-Antonin**
261, rue Principale, Saint-Antonin, QC G0L 2J0
Tél: 418-862-1056
biblio.antonin@crsbp.net
Sylvie Ratté, Responsable

Saint-Apollinaire: **Bibliothèque Au Jardin des livres/Saint-Apollinaire**
#102, 94, rue Principale, Saint-Apollinaire, QC G0S 2E0
Tél: 418-881-2447
bibliotheque@st-apollinaire.com
www.mabibliotheque.ca/saint-apollinaire
Kim Picard, Responsable

Saint-Arsène: **Bibliothèque Saint-Arsène**
#104, 49, rue de l'Église, Saint-Arsène, QC G0L 2K0
Tél: 418-867-2205
biblio.arsene@crsbp.net
Marie-Jeanne Gagnon, Responsable

Saint-Athanase: **Bibliothèque Saint-Athanase**
6081, ch de l'Église, Saint-Athanase, QC G0L 2L0
Tél: 418-859-2575
biblio.athanase@crsbp.net
Diane Dumont, Responsable

Saint-Aubert: **Bibliothèque Charles-E.-Harpe**
14, rue des Loisirs, Saint-Aubert, QC G0R 2R0
Tél: 418-598-3623; *Téléc:* 418-598-3369

Saint-Augustin: **Bibliothèque publique de St-Augustin**
710, rue Principale, Saint-Augustin, QC G0W 1K0
Tél: 418-374-2147
augustin@reseaubiblioslsj.qc.ca
www.reseaubiblioduquebec.qc.ca

Saint-Augustin-Saguenay: **Bibliothèque de Saint-Augustin**
École de Saint-Augustin, 710, rue Principale, Saint-Augustin-Saguenay, QC G0W 1K0
Tél: 418-374-2147
augustin@reseaubiblioslsj.qc.ca

Saint-Barthélemy: **Bibliothèque de Saint-Barthélemy**
601 rue Dusablé, Saint-Barthélemy, QC J0K 1X0
Tél: 450-885-3232; *Téléc:* 450-885-2165
www.saint-barthelemy.ca
Média social: www.facebook.com/104244999653520
Louise Belhumeur, Responsable

Saint-Basile: **Bibliothèque Au fil des mots**
41, rue Caron, Saint-Basile, QC G0A 3G0
Tél: 418-329-2858; *Téléc:* 418-329-3743
www.reseaubiblioduquebec.qc.ca

Saint-Basile: **Bibliothèque Au fil des mots/Saint-Basile**
41, rue Caron, Saint-Basile, QC G0A 3G0
Tél: 418-329-2858; *Téléc:* 418-329-3743
biblio@saintbasile.qc.ca
Lise Bélanger, Responsable

Saint-Basile-le-Grand: **Bibliothèque Roland Leblanc**
40, rue Savaria, Saint-Basile-le-Grand, QC J3N 1L8
Tél: 450-461-8000
bibliotheque@villesblg.qc.ca
www.ville.saint-basile-le-grand.qc.ca

Saint-Benjamin: **Bibliothèque La Détente/Saint-Benjamin**
440B, rue du Collège, Saint-Benjamin, QC G0M 1N0
Tél: 418-594-6068; *Téléc:* 418-594-6068
Maryse Trépanier, Responsable

Saint-Benoît-Labre: **Bibliothèque L'Envolume**
216, rte 271, Saint-Benoît-Labre, QC G0M 1P0
Tél: 418-228-9250; *Téléc:* 418-228-0518
biblstbe@globetrotter.qc.ca
Nadia Lebel, Responsable
Suzanne Legroulx, Responsable, Échanges/Animation
Carmen Talbot, Responsable, PEB

Saint-Bernard: **Bibliothèque Liratout/Saint-Bernard**
540, rue Vaillancourt, Saint-Bernard, QC G0S 2G0
Tél: 418-475-4669; *Téléc:* 418-475-5136
bibliost-bernard@nouvellebeauce.com
Carolle Larochelle, Responsable

Saint-Bernard-de-Michaudvil: **Bibliothèque municipale de Saint-Bernard-de-Michaudville**
390, rue Principale, Saint-Bernard-de-Michaudvil, QC J0H 1C0
Tél: 450-792-3190; *Téléc:* 450-792-3591
bernard.sud@reseaubibliomonteregie.qc.ca
saintbernarddemichaudville.qc.ca/pages/o_bibliotheque.htm
Marie-Sylvie Lavallée, Responsable

Saint-Blaise-sur-Richelieu: **Bibliothèque municipale de Saint-Blaise-sur-Richelieu**
#6, 795, rue des Loisirs, Saint-Blaise-sur-Richelieu, QC J0J 1W0
Tél: 450-291-5944; *Téléc:* 450-291-5095
blaise@reseaubibliomonteregie.qc.ca
Laure Desrochers, Responsable
l.desrochers82@hotmail.com

Saint-Bonaventure: **Bibliothèque de Saint-Bonaventure**
110, rue Cyr, Saint-Bonaventure, QC J0C 1C0
Tél: 819-396-1676; *Téléc:* 819-396-2335
biblio120@reseaubibliocqlm.qc.ca
www.reseaubiblioduquebec.qc.ca
Gisèle Corbin, Responsable

Saint-Boniface: **Bibliothèque de Saint-Boniface**
155, rue Langevin, Saint-Boniface, QC G0X 2L0
Tél: 819-535-3330; *Téléc:* 819-535-1242
biblio021@reseaubibliocqlm.qc.ca
www.reseaubiblioduquebec.qc.ca
Chantal Gélinas, Responsable

Saint-Bruno: **Bibliothèque publique de Saint-Bruno**
550, rue des 4H, Saint-Bruno, QC G0W 2L0
Tél: 418-212-8007
stbruno@reseaubibliosIsj.qc.ca

Saint-Bruno-de-Guigues: **Bibliothèque de Saint-Bruno-de-Guigues**
23B, rue Principale nord, Saint-Bruno-de-Guigues, QC J0Z 2G0
Tél: 819-728-2910; *Téléc:* 819-728-2404
guigues@reseaubiblioatnq.qc.ca
www.reseaubiblioduquebec.qc.ca/s
Louise Gagnon, Responsable

Saint-Bruno-de-Kamouraska: **Bibliothèque des Brûlots**
6, rue Du Couvent, Saint-Bruno-de-Kamouraska, QC G0L 2M0
Tél: 418-856-7053
biblio.bruno@crsbp.net
www.reseaubiblioduquebec.qc.ca

Saint-Bruno-de-Montarville: **Bibliothèque municipale de Saint-Bruno-de-Montarville**
82, boul Seigneurial ouest, Saint-Bruno-de-Montarville, QC J3V 5N7
Tél: 450-645-2950; *Téléc:* 450-441-8485
bibliotheque@stbruno.ca
www.ville.stbruno.qc.ca

Saint-Calixte: **Bibliothèque de Saint-Calixte**
6250, rue Hôtel-de-Ville, Saint-Calixte, QC J0K 1Z0
Tél: 450-222-2782; *Téléc:* 450-222-2789
biblio@mscalixte.qc.ca
Céline Boucher, Responsable

Saint-Casimir: **Bibliothèque Jean-Charles-Magnan**
510, boul de la Montagne, Saint-Casimir, QC G0A 3L0
Tél: 418-339-2909; *Téléc:* 418-339-3105
jcmagnan@csportneuf.qc.ca
Ange-Aimée Asselin, Responsable
Nicole Tessier, Responsable, PEB

Saint-Charles-de Bourget: **Bibliothèque publique de Saint-Charles-de-Bourget**
357, rang 2, Saint-Charles-de Bourget, QC G0V 1G0
Tél: 418-672-2624
stcharle@reseaubibliosIsj.qc.ca
Claire Chayer, Responsable

Saint-Charles-Garnier: **Bibliothèque de Saint-Charles-Garnier**
38, de Saint-Charles-Garnier, Saint-Charles-Garnier, QC G0K 1K0
Tél: 418-798-4820
biblio.garnier@crsbp.net
www.reseaubiblioduquebec.qc.ca

Saint-Clet: **Bibliothèque municipale de Saint-Clet**
25, rue Piché, Saint-Clet, QC J0P 1S0
Tél: 450-465-3175
clet@reseaubibliomonteregie.qc.ca
Anne Renaut, Responsable

Saint-Clément: **Bibliothèque de Saint-Clément**
25A, rue Saint-Pierre, Saint-Clément, QC G0L 2N0
Tél: 418-963-2258
biblio.clement@crsbp.net
bww.reseaubiblioduquebec.qc.ca
Thérèse St-Pierre, Responsable

Saint-Cléophas-de-Brandon: **Bibliothèque de Saint-Cléophas-de-Brandon**
750, rue Principale, Saint-Cléophas-de-Brandon, QC J0K 2A0
Tél: 450-889-5683; *Téléc:* 450-889-8007
biblio107@reseaubibliocqlm.qc.ca
www.reseaubiblioduquebec.qc.ca
Marie-Line Gingras, Responsable

Saint-Cléophas-de-Brandon: **Bibliothèque de Saint-Cléophas-de-Brandon**
750, rue Principale, Saint-Cléophas-de-Brandon, QC J0k 2A0
Tél: 418-889-5683
biblio.cleophas@crsbp.net
www.reseaubiblioduquebec.qc.ca
Hélène Dumont, Responsable
Linda Hudon, Bénévole

Saint-Colomban: **Bibliothèque de Saint-Colomban**
347, montée de l'Église, Saint-Colomban, QC J5K 1B1
Tél: 450-436-1453; *Téléc:* 450-432-1863
biblio@st-colomban.qc.ca
www.st-colomban.qc.ca
Lucie Jubinville, Directrice

Saint-Constant: **Bibliothèque municipale de Saint-Constant**
#200, 121, rue Saint-Pierre, Saint-Constant, QC J5A 2G9
Tél: 450-638-2010
bibliotheque@ville.saint-constant.qc.ca

Saint-Cuthbert: **Bibliothèque de Saint-Cuthbert**
1891, rue Principale, Saint-Cuthbert, QC J0K 2C0
Tél: 450-836-4852; *Téléc:* 450-836-4833
biblio126@reseaubibliocqlm.qc.ca
Céline Denis, Responsable

Saint-Cyprien: **Bibliothèque de Saint-Cyprien (Alphonse-Desjardins)**
187, rue Principale, Saint-Cyprien, QC G0L 2P0
Tél: 418-963-2730
biblio.cyprien@crsbp.net
www.reseaubiblioduquebec.qc.ca
Ginette Gagné, Responsable

Saint-Cyprien-des-Etchemins: **Bibliothèque municipale de Saint-Cyprien**
187, rue Principale, Saint-Cyprien-des-Etchemins, QC G0L 2P0
Tél: 418-963-2226
biblio.cyprien@crsbp.net
Ginette Gagné, Responsable

Saint-Célestin: **Bibliothèque de Saint-Célestin (Claude-Bouchard)**
450B, rue Marquis, Saint-Célestin, QC J0C 1G0
Tél: 819-229-3403
biblio130@reseaubibliocqlm.qc.ca
Média social: www.facebook.com/928764117191372
Nicole Cameron, Responsable

Saint-Côme: **Bibliothèque de Saint-Côme**
1677, 55e rue, Saint-Côme, QC J0K 2B0
Tél: 450-883-2726; *Téléc:* 450-883-6431
biblio054@reseaubibliocqlm.qc.ca
www.reseaubiblioduquebec.qc.ca
Josée Blanchard, Responsable

Saint-Côme-Linière: **Bibliothèque municipale de Saint-Côme-Linière**
1375, 18e rue, Saint-Côme-Linière, QC G0M 1J0
Tél: 418-685-3825; *Téléc:* 418-685-2566
bibliostcome@hotmail.com

Saint-Damase: **Bibliothèque municipale de Saint-Damase**
113, rue St-Étienne, Saint-Damase, QC J0H 1J0
Tél: 418-797-3341; *Téléc:* 450-797-3543
damase@reseaubibliomonteregie.qc.ca
Média social:
fr-ca.facebook.com/people/Bibliothèque-St-Damase/100003966751596
Élyse Dolbec, Responsable

Saint-Damase-de-Matapédia: **Bibliothèque de Saint-Damase-de-Matapédia**
377, rue de l'Église, Saint-Damase-de-Matapédia, QC G0J 2J0
Tél: 418-776-2103
biblio.damase@crsbp.net

Saint-Damien: **Bibliothèque de Saint-Damien**
2045, rue Taschereau, Saint-Damien, QC J0K 2E0
Tél: 450-835-7519; *Téléc:* 450-835-5538
biblio041@reseaubibliocqlm.qc.ca
www.reseaubiblioduquebec.qc.ca
Josée St-Martin, Responsable

Saint-Damien-de-Buckland: **Bibliothèque Le Bouquin d'Or/Saint-Damien-de-Buckland**
75, rue Saint-Gérard, Saint-Damien-de-Buckland, QC G0R 2Y0
Tél: 418-789-2127; *Téléc:* 418-789-2125
biblio@saint-damien.com
Marie-Hélène Labbé, Responsable

Saint-Denis: **Bibliothèque de Saint-Denis**
5, rue 287, Saint-Denis, QC G0L 2R0
Tél: 418-498-2968
biblio.denis@crsbp.net
www.reseaubiblioduquebec.qc.ca
Doris Rivard, Responsable

Saint-Didace: **Bibliothèque de Saint-Didace**
530A, rue Principale, Saint-Didace, QC J0K 2G0
Tél: 450-835-3933; *Téléc:* 450-835-0602
biblio@saint-didace.com
www.saint-didace.com
Monique Guay, Coordonnatrice
450-835-4184 ext. 8205

Saint-Dominique: **Bibliothèque municipale de Saint-Dominique**
488, Saint-Dominique, Saint-Dominique, QC J0H 1L0
Tél: 450-771-0256
dominique@reseaubibliomonteregie.qc.ca

Saint-Donat: **Bibliothèque de Saint-Donat**
510, rue Desrochers, Saint-Donat, QC J0T 2C0
Tél: 819-424-3044; *Téléc:* 819-424-5020
biblio@saint-donat.ca

Saint-Donat: **Bibliothèque de Saint-Donat**
510, Desrochers, Saint-Donat, QC J0T 2C0
Tél: 418-424-5020
biblio@saint-donat.ca
www.reseaubiblioduquebec.qc.ca

Saint-Edmond-les-Plaines: **Bibliothèque publique de Saint-Edmond**
561, rue Principale, Saint-Edmond-les-Plaines, QC G0W 2M0
Tél: 418-274-3069
stedmond@reseaubiblioslsj.qc.ca
Josée Lavoie, Responsable

Saint-Edouard-de-Lotbinière: **Bibliothèque municipale de Saint-Édouard-de-Lotbinière**
105, rue de L'École, Saint-Edouard-de-Lotbinière, QC G0S 1Y0
Tél: 418-796-2433; *Téléc:* 418-796-2228
biblioalachance@hotmail.com
www.mabibliotheque.ca/saint-edouard

Saint-Elzéar: **Bibliothèque de Saint-Elzéar**
144B, ch Principal, Saint-Elzéar, QC G0C 2W0
Tél: 418-534-2637
biblio.stelzear@hotmail.com

Saint-Elzéar: **Bibliothèque de Saint-Elzéar (Saint-Elzéar-de-Témiscouata)**
144B, ch Principale, Saint-Elzéar, QC G0L 2W0
Tél: 418-534-2637
biblio.stelzear@hotmail.com
www.reseaubiblioduquebec.qc.ca

Saint-Esprit: **Bibliothèque de Saint-Esprit (Alice-Parizeau)**
45, rue des Écoles, Saint-Esprit, QC J0K 2L0
Tél: 450-831-2274; *Téléc:* 450-839-6070
biblio125@reseaubibliocqlm.qc.ca
Média social: www.facebook.com/343413225730969

Saint-Eugène: **Bibliothèque publique de Saint-Eugène**
469, du Pont, Saint-Eugène, QC G0W 1B0
Tél: 418-276-7790
steugene@reseaubiblioslsj.qc.ca
www.reseaubiblioduquebec.qc.ca

Saint-Eugène-de-Guigues: **Bibliothèque de Saint-Eugène-de-Guigues**
4, 1ère av ouest, Saint-Eugène-de-Guigues, QC J0Z 3L0
Tél: 819-785-4441; *Téléc:* 819-785-2301
eugene@reseaubiblioatnq.qc.ca
www.reseaubiblioduquebec.qc.ca/St-Eugene
Lorraine Falardeau, Responsable

Saint-Eustache: **Bibliothèque municipale Guy-Bélisle**
12, ch de la Grande-Côte, Saint-Eustache, QC J7P 1A2
Tél: 450-974-5035
biblio.ville.saint-eustache.qc.ca
Média social: fr-ca.facebook.com/AZ.SaintEustache

Saint-Eusèbe: **Bibliothèque de Saint-Eusèbe**
222B, rue Principale, Saint-Eusèbe, QC G0L 2Y0
Tél: 418-899-0194
biblio.eusebe@crsbp.net
www.reseaubiblioduquebec.qc.ca
Gisèle Lebrun Bolduc, Responsable

Saint-Fabien: **Bibliothèque de Saint-Fabien**
30, 7e av, Saint-Fabien, QC G0L 2Z0
Tél: 418-869-2602
biblio.fabien@crsbp.net
www.reseaubiblioduquebec.qc.ca
Média social: www.facebook.com/1408791249432954
Raynald Beaulieu, Responsable

Saint-Fabien-de-Panet: **Bibliothèque Fabiothèque/Saint-Fabien-de-Panet**
199, rue Bilodeau, Saint-Fabien-de-Panet, QC G0R 2J0
Tél: 418-249-4417; *Téléc:* 418-249-2507
www.reseaubiblioduquebec.qc.ca/saint-fabien-de-panet

Saint-Faustin-Lac-Carré: **Bibliothèque du Lac**
64, rue de la Culture, Saint-Faustin-Lac-Carré, QC J0T 1J1
Tél: 819-688-5434; *Téléc:* 819-688-5644
bibliodulac@municipalite.stfaustin.qc.ca
www.reseaubiblioduquebec.qc.ca

Saint-Ferdinand: **Bibliothèque de Saint-Ferdinand (Onil-Garneau)**
621, rue Notre-Dame, Saint-Ferdinand, QC G0N 1N0
Tél: 418-428-9607
biblio@minfo.net
Martine St-Pierre, Responsable

Saint-Ferréol-les-Neiges: **Bibliothèque Aux Sources/Saint-Ferréol-les-Neiges**
33, rue de l'Église, Saint-Ferréol-les-Neiges, QC G0A 3R0
Tél: 418-826-3540; *Téléc:* 418-826-0489
biblio@saintferreollesneiges.qc.ca
Danielle Houde, Responsable

Saint-Flavien: **Bibliothèque La Flaviethèque/Saint-Flavien**
12A, rue Roberge, Saint-Flavien, QC G0S 2M0
Tél: 418-728-3697; *Téléc:* 418-728-4190
flavietheque@gmail.com
Média social: www.facebook.com/flavietheque
Marie Pradet, Responsable

Saint-Fortunat: **Bibliothèque municipale de Saint-Fortunat**
173, rue Principale, Saint-Fortunat, QC G0P 1G0
Tél: 819-344-5399; *Téléc:* 819-344-5399
Huguette Garneau, Responsable

Saint-François-d'Assise: **Bibliothèque de Saint-François-d'Assise**
399, ch Central, Saint-François-d'Assise, QC G0J 2N0
Tél: 418-299-2099; *Téléc:* 418-299-3037
munstfrs@globetrotter.net

Saint-François-de-Sales: **Bibliothèque publique de Saint-François-de-Sales**
255, rue de l'Église, Saint-François-de-Sales, QC G0W 1M0
Tél: 418-348-6736
franco@reseaubiblioslsj.qc.ca
Myriam Simard, Responsable
418-348-6736 ext. 5210

Saint-François-du-Lac: **Bibliothèque de Saint-François-du-Lac**
480, rue Notre-Dame, Saint-François-du-Lac, QC J0G 1M0
Tél: 450-568-1130
bibliotheque@saint-francois-du-lac.ca
www.saint-francois-du-lac.ca/bibliotheque_saint-francois.php
Ghislaine Lachapelle, Responsable

Saint-Fulgence: **Bibliothèque publique de Saint-Fulgence**
12, rue Saint-Basile, Saint-Fulgence, QC G0V 1S0
Tél: 418-615-0059
stfulgence@reseaubiblioslsj.qc.ca
Lise Gauthier, Responsable

Saint-Félicien: **Bibliothèque municipale de Saint-Félicien**
#200, 1209, boul Sacré Coeur, Saint-Félicien, QC G8K 2R5
Tél: 418-679-2100; *Téléc:* 418-679-1449
www.stfelicien.biblio.qc.ca
Johanne Laprise, Responsable
Francine Ménard, Technicienne en documentation

Saint-Félicien: **Bibliothèque publique de Saint-Méthode**
3159, rue Saint-Méthode, Saint-Félicien, QC G8K 3C2
Tél: 418-679-0757
stmethode@reseaubiblioslsj.qc.ca

Saint-Félix-d'Otis: **Bibliothèque publique de Saint-Félix-d'Otis**
455, rue Principale, Saint-Félix-d'Otis, QC G0V 1M0
Tél: 418-544-5543
stfelix@reseaubiblioslsj.qc.ca
Nathalie Simard, Responsable

Saint-Félix-de-Kingsey: **Bibliothèque de Saint-Félix-de-Kingsey**
6115B, rue Principale, Saint-Félix-de-Kingsey, QC J0B 2T0
Tél: 819-848-1400
biblio152@reseaubibliocqlm.qc.ca
www.reseaubiblioduquebec.qc.ca
Pauline Roy, Responsable

Saint-Félix-de-Valois: **Bibliothèque de Saint-Félix-de-Valois**
4863, rue Principale, Saint-Félix-de-Valois, QC J0K 2M0
Tél: 450-889-5589; *Téléc:* 450-889-7911
biblio010@reseaubibliocqlm.qc.ca

Saint-Gabriel-de-Brandon: **Bibliothèque de Saint-Gabriel (Au fil des pages)**
53, rue Beausoleil, Saint-Gabriel-de-Brandon, QC J0K 2N0
Tél: 450-835-2212; *Téléc:* 450-835-1493
biblio013@reseaubibliocqlm.qc.ca
Noëlla Ganley, Coordonnatrice

Saint-Gabriel-de-Rimouski: **Bibliothèque Le Bouquinier**
103, rue Leblanc, Saint-Gabriel-de-Rimouski, QC G0K 1M0
Tél: 418-798-8310; *Téléc:* 418-798-4108
biblio.gabriel@crsbp.net
www.reseaubiblioduquebec.qc.ca
Nicole Leblanc, Responsable
Julie Lepage, Bénévole
Olivette Parent, Bénévole

Saint-Geneviève-de-Batiscan: **Bibliothèque municipale de Batiscan**
91, rue de l'Église, Saint-Geneviève-de-Batiscan, QC G0X 2R0
Tél: 418-362-2078; *Téléc:* 418-362-2111
biblio036@reseaubibliocqlm.qc.ca
www.reseaubiblioduquebec.qc.ca

Saint-Germain: **Bibliothèque de Saint-Germain**
506, rue de la Fabrique, Saint-Germain, QC G0L 3G0
Tél: 418-492-5767
biblio.germain@crsbp.net
www.reseaubiblioduquebec.qc.ca
Simone Lévesque, Responsable

Saint-Germain-de-Grantham: **Bibliothèque de Saint-Germain-de-Grantham (Le Signet)**
299, rue Notre-Dame, Saint-Germain-de-Grantham, QC J0C 1K0
Tél: 819-395-2644
biblio100@reseaubibliocqlm.qc.ca
www.reseaubiblioduquebec.qc.ca
Louise Gaillard-Simoneau, Responsable

Saint-Gervais: **Bibliothèque Faubourg de la Cadie**
36A, rue de la Fabrique Est, Saint-Gervais, QC G0R 3C0
Tél: 418-887-3628; *Téléc:* 418-887-3628
bibliger@globetrotter.qc.ca
Média social: www.facebook.com/faubourgdelacadie

Saint-Gilles: **Bibliothèque Le Signet**
1540, rue du Couvent, Saint-Gilles, QC G0S 2P0
Tél: 418-888-5178; *Téléc:* 418-888-5486
Pascale Bélanger, Responsable
Nicole Aubert, Adjointe

Saint-Guillaume: **Bibliothèque de Saint-Guillaume**
106, rue Saint-Jean-Baptiste, Saint-Guillaume, QC J0C 1L0
Tél: 819-396-3754; *Téléc:* 819-396-0184
biblio087@reseaubibliocqlm.qc.ca
www.reseaubiblioduquebec.qc.ca
Jocelyne Taillon, Responsable

Saint-Guy: **Bibliothèque de Saint-Guy**
54, ch Principal, Saint-Guy, QC G0K 1W0
Tél: 418-963-1490
biblio.guy@crsbp.net
Normande Rioux, Responsable

Saint-Gédéon: **Bibliothèque publique de Saint-Gédéon**
208, rue De Quen, Saint-Gédéon, QC G0W 2P0
Tél: 418-345-8001
stgedeon@reseaubiblioslsj.qc.ca
www.reseaubiblioduquebec.qc.ca

Saint-Henri: **Bibliothèque La Reliure/Saint-Henri**
217, rue Commerciale, Saint-Henri, QC G0R 3E0
Tél: 418-882-0694; *Téléc:* 418-882-0302
bibhenri@globetrotter.qc.ca
Média social: www.facebook.com/129584063807782

Saint-Henri-de-Taillon: **Bibliothèque publique de Saint-Henri-de-Taillon**
401, rue Hôtel-de-Ville, Saint-Henri-de-Taillon, QC G0W 2X0
Tél: 418-669-6001; *Téléc:* 418-347-1138
sthenri@reseaubiblioslsj.qc.ca
www.reseaubiblioduquebec.qc.ca

Saint-Hilarion: **Bibliothèque aux Quatre Vents de Saint-Hilarion**
#1, 247, ch Principal, Saint-Hilarion, QC G0A 3V0
Tél: 418-489-2999
biblioquatrevents@gmail.com
www.reseaubiblioduquebec.qc.ca/saint-hilarion

Saint-Hippolyte: **Bibliothèque de Saint-Hippolyte**
2258, ch des Hauteurs, Saint-Hippolyte, QC J8A 3P4
Tél: 450-224-4137; *Téléc:* 450-563-1085
biblio@saint-hippolyte.ca

Saint-Honoré-de-Chicoutimi: **Bibliothèque publique de Saint-Honoré**
100, rue Paul-Aimé Hudon, Saint-Honoré-de-Chicoutimi, QC G0V 1L0
Tél: 418-673-3790; *Téléc:* 418-673-3871
bibliothequesthonore@hotmail.com

Saint-Honoré-de-Témiscouata: **Bibliothèque Les Moussaillons**
6, rue de l'Église, Saint-Honoré-de-Témiscouata, QC G0L 3K0
Tél: 418-854-8450
biblio.honore@crsbp.net
www.reseaubiblioduquebec.qc.ca
Hélène Paradis, Responsable

Saint-Hugues: **Bibliothèque municipale de Saint-Hugues**
207, rue Saint-Germain, Saint-Hugues, QC J0H 1N0
Tél: 450-794-2630; *Téléc:* 450-794-2630
hugues@reseaubibliomonteregie.qc.ca
Marie Bernier Lavigne, Responsable

Saint-Hyacinthe: **Médiathèque maskoutaine**
2720, rue Dessaulles, Saint-Hyacinthe, QC J2S 2V7
Tél: 450-773-1830; *Téléc:* 450-773-3398
info@mediatheque.qc.ca
www.mediatheque.qc.ca
Média social: www.facebook.com/mediathequemaskoutaine
Yves Tanguay, Directeur général
tanguayy@mediatheque.qc.ca
450-773-1830 ext. 23
Nathalie Lespérance, Responsable, Services publics Bibliothèque T.-A.-St-Germain
lesperancen@mediatheque.qc.ca
450-773-1830 ext. 25
Marie-France Pineault, Secrétaire administrative
pineaultmf@mediatheque.qc.ca
450-773-1830 ext. 21

Saint-Ignace-de-Loyola: **Bibliothèque de Saint-Ignace-de-Loyola**
621, rue de l'Église, Saint-Ignace-de-Loyola, QC J0K 2P0
Tél: 450-836-3376; *Téléc:* 450-836-1400
biblio156@reseaubibliocqlm.qc.ca
www.reseaubiblioduquebec.qc.ca
Andrée Bergeron, Responsable

Saint-Irénée: **Bibliothèque Adolphe-Basile-Routhier**
400, rue Principale, Saint-Irénée, QC G0T 1V0
Tél: 418-620-5015; *Téléc:* 418-452-8221

Saint-Isidore: **Bibliothèque Laurette-Nadeau-Parent**
101, rue des Aigles, Saint-Isidore, QC G0S 2S0
Tél: 418-882-6470
www.reseaubiblioduquebec.qc.ca/saint-isidore
Média social: www.facebook.com/521370084539684

Saint-Isidore: **Bibliothèque municipale de Saint-Isidore**
693, rang St-Régis, Saint-Isidore, QC J0L 2A0
Tél: 450-992-1323
isidore@reseaubibliomonteregie.qc.ca

Saint-Jacques: **Bibliothèque municipale Marcel-Dugas**
16, rue Maréchal, Saint-Jacques, QC J0K 2R0
Tél: 450-839-2296; *Téléc:* 450-839-2387
biblio@st-jacques.org
www.st-jacques.org

Saint-Jacques-de-Leeds: **Bibliothèque La Ressource**
425, rue Principale, Saint-Jacques-de-Leeds, QC G0N 1J0
Tél: 418-424-3181; *Téléc:* 418-424-0126
Pierrette Routhier, Responsable

Saint-Jacques-le-Mineur: **Bibliothèque municipale de Saint-Jacques-le-Mineur**
89, rue Principale, Saint-Jacques-le-Mineur, QC J0J 1Z0
Tél: 450-347-5446; *Téléc:* 450-347-5754
jacques@reseaubibliomonteregie.qc.ca
Média social: www.facebook.com/bibliosjlm

Saint-Janvier-de-Joly: **Bibliothèque Adrien-Lambert/Saint-Janvier-de-Joly**
729, rue des Loisirs, Saint-Janvier-de-Joly, QC G0S 1M0
Tél: 418-728-2984; *Téléc:* 418-728-2984
adrienlambert1936@hotmail.com
Média social: www.facebook.com/bibliothequeadrienlambert

Saint-Jean-Baptiste: **Bibliothèque municipale de Saint-Jean-Baptiste**
3090, rue Principale, Saint-Jean-Baptiste, QC J0L 2B0
Tél: 450-467-1786
jean.baptiste@reseaubibliomonteregie.qc.ca
Média social: www.facebook.com/521970421194985
Sylvie Sweeney, Responsable

Saint-Jean-de-Brébeuf: **Bibliothèque Saint-Jean-de-Brébeuf(Bibliothèque Bibliomagie)**
844, rue de l'Église, Saint-Jean-de-Brébeuf, QC G6G 0A1
Tél: 418-453-2571; *Téléc:* 418-453-2339
www.reseaubiblioduquebec.qc.ca/saint-jean-de-brebeuf

Saint-Jean-de-Dieu: **Bibliothèque de Saint-Jean-de-Dieu**
75, rue Principale Nord, Saint-Jean-de-Dieu, QC G0L 3M0
Tél: 418-963-3529
biblio.jeandieu@crsbp.net
www.reseaubiblioduquebec.qc.ca
Francine Rioux, Responsable

Saint-Jean-de-Matha: **Bibliothèque de Saint-Jean-de-Matha**
81, rue Sainte-Louise, Saint-Jean-de-Matha, QC J0K 2S0
Tél: 450-886-5855
biblio047@reseaubibliocqlm.qc.ca
www.reseaubiblioduquebec.qc.ca
Nicole Léonard, Responsable

Saint-Jean-Port-Joli: **Bibliothèque Marie-Bonenfant/Saint-Jean-Port-Joli**
7B, place de l'Église, Saint-Jean-Port-Joli, QC G0R 3G0
Tél: 418-598-3187; *Téléc:* 418-598-3085
biblio.stjean@globetrotter.net

Saint-Jean-sur-Richelieu: **Bibliothèques municipales de Saint-Jean-sur-Richelieu**
180, rue Laurier, Saint-Jean-sur-Richelieu, QC J3B 7B2
Tél: 450-357-2111
biblio@ville.saint-jean-sur-richelieu.qc.ca
www.ville.saint-jean-sur-richelieu.qc.ca
Johanne Jacob, Chef, Division bibliothèques
j.jacob@ville.saint-jean-sur-richelieu.qc.ca

Saint-Joseph-de-Beauce: **Bibliothèque de Saint-Joseph-de-Beauce**
139, rue Sainte-Christine, Saint-Joseph-de-Beauce, QC G0S 2V0
Tél: 418-397-6160; *Téléc:* 418-397-5715
biblio@vsjb.ca

Saint-Joseph-de-Kamouraska: **Bibliothèque de Saint-Joseph-de-Kamouraska**
298A, rue Principale Est, Saint-Joseph-de-Kamouraska, QC G0L 3P0
Tél: 418-493-2214
biblio.joseph@crsbp.net
www.reseaubiblioduquebec.qc.ca
Élise Garneau-Roussel, Responsable

Saint-Joseph-de-Lepage: **Bibliothèque de Saint-Joseph-de-Lepage**
70, rue de la Rivière, Saint-Joseph-de-Lepage, QC G5H 3N8
Tél: 418-775-4607
biblio.lepage@crsbp.net
www.reseaubiblioduquebec.qc.ca
Noëlla Dupont, Responsable

Saint-Joseph-du-Lac: **Bibliothèque de Saint-Joseph-du-Lac**
70, Montée du Village, Saint-Joseph-du-Lac, QC J0N 1M0
Tél: 450-623-7833; *Téléc:* 450-623-2889
biblio@sjdl.qc.ca
www.reseaubiblioduquebec.qc.ca
Katerine Douville, Technicienne en documentation

Saint-Jude: **Bibliothèque St-Jude**
940, rue de Centre, Saint-Jude, QC J0H 1P0
Tél: 450-792-3855
www.saint-jude.ca/pages/s_bibliotheque.html
Élise Courville, Responsable

Saint-Julien: **Bibliothèque municipale de Saint-Julien**
794, ch Saint-Julien, Saint-Julien, QC G0N 1B0
Tél: 418-423-7474; *Téléc:* 418-423-3410
bibliotheque@st-julien.ca
Michel Tremblay, Responsable

Saint-Juste-du-Lac: **Bibliothèque de Saint-Juste-du-Lac**
37, ch Principal, Saint-Juste-du-Lac, QC G0L 3R0
Tél: 418-899-0374
biblio.juste@crsbp.net
Jeanne Benoist, Responsable

Saint-Juste-du-Lac: **Bibliothèque Lots-Renversés**
Route 295, Saint-Juste-du-Lac, QC G0L 1V0
Tél: 418-899-2356
biblio.lotsren@crsbp.net
Laurel Shiells, Responsable

Saint-Justin: **Bibliothèque de Saint-Justin**
590, rue Lafrenière, Saint-Justin, QC J0K 2V0
Tél: 819-227-2775
biblio056@reseaubibliocqlm.qc.ca

Saint-Jérôme: **Bibliothèque Marie-Antoinette-Foucher**
101, place du Curé-Labelle, Saint-Jérôme, QC J7Z 1X6
Tél: 450-432-0569; *Téléc:* 450-436-1211
www.vsj.ca/fr/bibliotheques.aspx

Saint-Lambert: **Bibliothèque de St-Lambert**
490, avenue Mercille, Saint-Lambert, QC J4P 2L5
Tél: 450-466-3910; *Téléc:* 819-788-2491
bibliotheque@saintlambert.ca
www.reseaubiblioduquebec.qc.ca/st-lambert
Jeanne D'Arc Fluet, Responsable

Saint-Lambert: **Bibliothèque municipale de Saint-Lambert**
490, av Mercille, Saint-Lambert, QC J4P 2L5
Tél: 450-466-3910
bibliotheque@saint-lambert.ca
www.ville.saint-lambert.qc.ca
Guylaine Pellerin, Directrice

Saint-Lazare: **Bibliothèque Biblio-Culture**
116B, rue de la Fabrique, Saint-Lazare, QC G0R 3J0
Tél: 418-883-2551; *Téléc:* 418-883-2551
biblio-st-lazare@globetrotter.net

Saint-Liboire: **Bibliothèque municipale de Saint-Liboire**
21, Place Mauriac, Saint-Liboire, QC J0H 1R0
Tél: 450-793-4751
liboire@reseaubibliomonteregie.qc.ca

Saint-Liguori: **Bibliothèque de Saint-Liguori**
741, rue Principale, Saint-Liguori, QC J0K 2X0
Tél: 450-753-4446; *Téléc:* 450-753-4638
biblio006@reseaubibliocqlm.qc.ca
www.reseaubiblioduquebec.qc.ca
Jeanne Gagné-Richard, Responsable

Saint-Lin-Laurentides: **Bibliothèque de Saint-Lin-Laurentides**
920, 12e av, Saint-Lin-Laurentides, QC J5M 2W2
Tél: 450-439-2486; *Téléc:* 450-439-1525
biblio@saint-lin-laurentides.com

Saint-Louis-de-Blandford: **Bibliothèque de Saint-Louis-de-Blandford**
80, rue Principale, Saint-Louis-de-Blandford, QC G0Z 1B0
Tél: 819-364-7007; *Téléc:* 819-364-2781
biblio116@reseaubibliocqlm.qc.ca
Françoise Lafond, Responsable

Saint-Louis-de-Gonzague: **Bibliothèque municipale de Saint-Louis-de-Gonzague**
140, rue Principale, Saint-Louis-de-Gonzague, QC J0S 1T0
Tél: 450-371-0523; *Téléc:* 450-371-6229
louis.gonzague@reseaubibliomonteregie.qc.ca
Marc-André Dumouchel, Responsable

Saint-Louis-du-Ha!Ha!: **Bibliothèque de Saint-Louis-du-Ha!Ha!**
234, rue Commerciale, Saint-Louis-du-Ha!Ha!, QC G0L 3S0
Tél: 418-854-4031
Laurette Lavoie, Responsable

Saint-Luc-de-Bellechasse: **Bibliothèque L'Éveil/Saint-Luc-de-Bellechasse**
115, rue de la Fabrique, Saint-Luc-de-Bellechasse, QC G0R 1L0
Tél: 418-636-2776; *Téléc:* 418-636-2776
bibliotheque@sogetel.net
Lisette Bilodeau, Responsable

Saint-Luc-de-Vincennes: **Bibliothèque de Saint-Luc-de-Vincennes**
660, rue Principale, Saint-Luc-de-Vincennes, QC G0X 3K0
Tél: 819-295-3608; *Téléc:* 819-295-3608
biblio097@reseaubibliocqlm.qc.ca
Média social: www.facebook.com/1415295512024049
Louise Lemire, Coordonnatrice

Saint-Ludger-de-Milot: **Bibliothèque publique de Saint-Ludger-de-Milot**
739, rue Gaudreault, Saint-Ludger-de-Milot, QC G0W 2B0
Tél: 418-373-2266; *Téléc:* 418-373-2554
stludger@reseaubibliosIsj.qc.ca
Média social: www.facebook.com/301721619937159
Karine Boutot, Responsable

Saint-Léon-le-Grand: **Bibliothèque de Saint-Léon-le-Grand (Bas-Saint-Laurent)**
241, rue Gendron, Saint-Léon-le-Grand, QC G0J 2W0
Tél: 418-743-2914
biblio.granleon@crsbp.net
Lise Fournier, Responsable

Saint-Léon-le-Grand: **Bibliothèque de Saint-Léon-le-Grand (Mauricie)**
44, rue de la Fabrique, Saint-Léon-le-Grand, QC J0K 2W0
Tél: 819-228-3236; *Téléc:* 819-228-8088
biblio029@reseaubibliocqlm.qc.ca

Saint-Léonard-d'Aston: **Bibliothèque de Saint-Léonard-d'Aston (Lucille-M.-Desmarais)**
440, rue de l'Exposition, Saint-Léonard-d'Aston, QC J0C 1M0
Tél: 819-399-3368
biblio089@reseaubibliocqlm.qc.ca
Média social: fr-fr.facebook.com/564046327004218

Saint-Léonard-de-Portneuf: **Bibliothèque Biblio 'Fleur de lin'**
260, rue Pettigrew, Saint-Léonard-de-Portneuf, QC G0A 4A0
Tél: 418-337-3961; *Téléc:* 418-337-6742
bibliofleurdelin@hotmail.com
Martine Girard, Responsable

Saint-Malachie: **Bibliothèque J.-A.-Kirouac**
1184, rue Principale, Saint-Malachie, QC G0R 3N0
Tél: 418-642-5127; *Téléc:* 418-642-2231
jakir@globetrotter.qc.ca
Louise Guénette, Responsable
Francine Moore, Responsable, PIB
Lise Gagnon, Responsable, Animation

Saint-Marc-du-Lac-Long: **Bibliothèque Saint-Marc-du-Lac-Long**
14A, rue de l'Église, Saint-Marc-du-Lac-Long, QC G0L 1T0
Tél: 418-893-1075; *Téléc:* 418-893-1339
biblio.laclong@crsbp.net
Jeanne-D'Arc Poliquin, Responsable

Saint-Marc-sur-Richelieu: **Bibliothèque municipale Archambault-Trépanier/Saint-Marc-sur-Richelieu**
102, rue de la Fabrique, Saint-Marc-sur-Richelieu, QC J0L 2E0
Tél: 450-584-2258
marc@reseaubibliomonteregie.qc.ca

Saint-Marcel: **Bibliothèque municipale de Saint-Marcel**
48, ch Taché Est, Saint-Marcel, QC G0R 3R0
Tél: 418-356-2635
www.saintmarcel.qc.ca
Solange Pelletier, Responsable
Laurence Bélanger, Responsable
418-356-5554

Saint-Marcel-de-Richelieu: **Bibliothèque Saint-Marcel-de-Richelieu**
117, rue St-Louis, Saint-Marcel-de-Richelieu, QC J0H 1T0
Tél: 450-794-2832; *Téléc:* 450-794-1140
munst-marcel@mrcmaskoutains.qc.ca
Nicole Beauchamp, Responsable
450-794-2706

Saint-Marcellin: **Fautoulire**
336, rte 234, Saint-Marcellin, QC G0K 1R0
Tél: 418-798-8164
biblio.marcellin@crsbp.net
www.reseaubiblioduquebec.qc.ca
Nathalie Chouinard, Responsable

Saint-Mathias-sur-Richelieu: **Bibliothèque municipale de Saint-Mathias-sur-Richelieu**
50, rue Lussier, Saint-Mathias-sur-Richelieu, QC J3L 6A4
Tél: 450-658-2841
mathias@reseaubibliomonteregie.qc.ca

Saint-Mathieu: **Bibliothèque municipale de Saint-Mathieu**
299, ch Saint-Édouard, Saint-Mathieu, QC J0L 2H0
Tél: 450-659-9528
biblio70@reseaubibliomonteregie.qc.ca
municipalite.saint-mathieu.qc.ca/bibliotheque
Média social: www.facebook.com/970409509643579

Saint-Mathieu-de-Beloeil: **Bibliothèque municipale Ryane-Provost**
5000, rue des Loisirs, Saint-Mathieu-de-Beloeil, QC J3G 2C9
Tél: 450-467-7490
mathieu.beloeil@reseaubibliomonteregie.qc.ca

Saint-Mathieu-de-Rioux: **Bibliothèque de Saint-Mathieu-de-Rioux**
41, rue de l'Église, Saint-Mathieu-de-Rioux, QC G0L 3T0
Tél: 418-738-3057
biblio.mathieu@crsbp.net
www.reseaubiblioduquebec.qc.ca
Michelyne Caron, Responsable

Saint-Mathieu-du-Parc: **Bibliothèque de Saint-Mathieu-du-Parc (Micheline H.- Gélinas)**
600, ch Saint-Marc, Saint-Mathieu-du-Parc, QC G0X 1N0
Tél: 819-299-3830
biblio093@reseaubibliocqlm.qc.ca
www.reseaubiblioduquebec.qc.ca

Saint-Maurice: **Bibliothèque de Saint-Maurice**
1544, rue Notre-Dame, Saint-Maurice, QC G0X 2X0
Tél: 819-378-7315
biblio026@reseaubibliocqlm.qc.ca

Saint-Michel: **Bibliothèque municipale Claire-Lazure**
440, place Saint-Michel, Saint-Michel, QC J0L 2J0
Tél: 450-454-7995
michel@reseaubibliomonteregie.qc.ca

Saint-Michel-de-Bellechasse: **Bibliothèque Benoît-Lacroix**
8, av Saint-Charles, Saint-Michel-de-Bellechasse, QC G0R 3S0
Tél: 418-884-2766; *Téléc:* 418-884-2866
biblistmic@globetrotter.net

Saint-Michel-des-Saints: **Bibliothèque de Saint-Michel-des-Saints (Antonio-Saint-Georges)**
390B, rue Matawin, Saint-Michel-des-Saints, QC J0K 3B0
Tél: 450-833-5471
biblio044@reseaubibliocqlm.qc.ca
Média social: www.facebook.com/327213797353672
Julie Picard, Responsable

Saint-Michel-du-Squatec: **Bibliothèque Alma-Durand**
149C, rue St-Joseph, Saint-Michel-du-Squatec, QC G0L 4H0
Tél: 418-855-5228; *Téléc:* 418-855-5228
biblio.squatec@crsbp.net
Céline Morin, Responsable

Saint-Modeste: **Bibliothèque municipale de Saint-Modeste**
312, rue Principale, Saint-Modeste, QC G0L 3W0
Tél: 418-867-2352
biblio.modeste@crsbp.net
www.reseaubiblioduquebec.qc.ca
Solange Chouinard, Responsable

Saint-Médard: **Bibliothèque de Saint-Médard**
1, rue Principale est, Saint-Médard, QC G0L 3V0
Tél: 418-963-1588
biblio.medard@crsbp.net
www.reseaubiblioduquebec.qc.ca
Kathy Bélisle, Responsable

Saint-Narcisse: **Bibliothèque de Saint-Narcisse (Gérard-Desrosiers)**
509, rue Massicotte, Saint-Narcisse, QC G0X 2Y0
Tél: 418-328-4430; *Téléc:* 418-328-4348
biblio001@reseaubibliocqlm.qc.ca

Saint-Narcisse-de-Beaurivag: **Bibliothèque municipale de Saint-Narcisse-de-Beaurivage**
510, rue de l'École, Saint-Narcisse-de-Beaurivag, QC G0S 1W0
Tél: 418-475-6464; *Téléc:* 418-475-6880
biblio.st-narcisse@globetrotter.net
Média social: www.facebook.com/bibliosn
Rachel Bêty, Responsable
418-475-6750

Saint-Nazaire: **Bibliothèque publique de St-Nazaire**
220, rue Principale, Saint-Nazaire, QC G0W 2V0
Tél: 418-662-1422; *Téléc:* 418-662-5467
nazaire@reseaubibliosIsj.qc.ca

Saint-Nazaire-d'Acton: **Bibliothèque municipale de Saint-Nazaire-d'Acton**
715, rue des Loisirs, Saint-Nazaire-d'Acton, QC J0H 1V0
Tél: 819-392-2090
nazaire@reseaubibliomonteregie.qc.ca
Média social: www.facebook.com/saintnazairedacton

Saint-Noël: **Bibliothèque de Saint-Noël**
25, rue de l'Église, Saint-Noël, QC G0J 3A0
Tél: 418-776-2549
biblio.noel@crsbp.net

Saint-Nérée: **Bibliothèque Biblio Du Centenaire**
2139, route Principale, Saint-Nérée, QC G0R 3V0
Tél: 418-243-3649; *Téléc:* 418-243-2136
Louis-Philippe Pelletier, Responsable
Julie Drapeau, Adjointe

Saint-Odilon: **Bibliothèque L'Intello/Saint-Odilon-de-Cranbourne**
111, rue de l'Hôtel-de-Ville, Saint-Odilon, QC G0S 3A0
Tél: 418-464-4803; *Téléc:* 418-464-4800
Mariette Vachon, Responsable
418-464-2463

Saint-Omer: **Bibliothèque de Saint-Omer**
106B, rte 132 Est, Saint-Omer, QC G0C 2Z0
Tél: 418-364-6485
bibliostomer@globetrotter.net

Saint-Ours: **Bibliothèque municipale de Saint-Ours**
2636, rue de l'Immaculée-Conception, Saint-Ours, QC J0G 1P0
Tél: 450-785-2779
ours@reseaubibliomonteregie.qc.ca

Saint-Pacôme: **Bibliothèque de Saint-Pacôme**
201, boul Bégin, Saint-Pacôme, QC G0L 3X0
Tél: 418-852-2356
biblio.pacome@crsbp.net
www.reseaubiblioduquebec.qc.ca
Yvonne Tremblay, Responsable

Saint-Pamphile: **Bibliothèque Marie-Louise-Gagnon/Saint-Pamphile**
3, rte Elgin sud, Saint-Pamphile, QC G0R 3X0
Tél: 418-356-5403
Micheline Leclerc, Responsable

Saint-Pascal: **Bibliothèque de Saint-Pascal**
470, rue Notre-Dame, Saint-Pascal, QC G0L 3Y0
Tél: 418-492-2312
biblio.pascal@crsbp.net
www.reseaubiblioduquebec.qc.ca
Cécile Joseph, Responsable

Saint-Patrice-de-Beaurivage: **Bibliothèque Florence-Guay/Saint-Patrice-de-Beaurivage**
470, du Manoir, Saint-Patrice-de-Beaurivage, QC G0S 1B0
Tél: 418-596-2439; *Téléc:* 418-596-2430
borivage@globetrotter.qc.ca

Saint-Paul: **Bibliothèque de Saint-Paul**
18, boul Brassard, Saint-Paul, QC J0K 3E0
Tél: 450-759-3333; *Téléc:* 450-759-6396
biblio071@reseaubibliocqlm.qc.ca

Saint-Paul de l'île-aux-Noi: **Bibliothèque municipale Lucile-Langlois-Éthier**
959C, rue Principale, Saint-Paul de l'ile-aux-Noi, QC J0J 1G0
Tél: 450-291-5585
paul.ile.noix@reseaubibliomonteregie.qc.ca

Saint-Paul-de-la-Croix: **Bibliothèque de Saint-Paul-de-la-Croix**
1B, rue du Parc, Saint-Paul-de-la-Croix, QC G0L 3Z0
Tél: 418-898-3095
biblio.croix@crsbp.net
www.reseaubiblioduquebec.qc.ca
Johanne Lagacé, Responsable

Saint-Paulin: **Bibliothèque de Saint-Paulin (Jeannine-Julien)**
3051, rue Bergeron, Saint-Paulin, QC J0K 3G0
Tél: 819-268-2425; *Téléc:* 819-268-2890
biblio118@reseaubibliocqlm.qc.ca
Louise Boucher, Responsable

Saint-Philippe: **Bibliothèque Saint-Philippe/Le Vaisseau d'Or**
2223, rte Édouard VII, Saint-Philippe, QC J0L 2K0
Tél: 450-659-7701; *Téléc:* 450-659-5354
commis@municipalite.saint-philippe.qc.ca
Josée Beaudet, Responsable

Saint-Philippe-de-Néri: **Bibliothèque Claude-Béchard**
11, Côte de l'Église, Saint-Philippe-de-Néri, QC G0L 4A0
Tél: 418-551-0314
biblio.philip@crsbp.net
www.reseaubiblioduquebec.qc.ca
Mariette Dumais, Responsable

Saint-Philippe-de-Néri: **Bibliothèque Claude-Béchard**
11 de la Côte, Saint-Philippe-de-Néri, QC G0L 4A0
Tél: 418-551-0314
biblio.philip@crsbp.net
www.reseaubiblioduquebec.qc.ca/claude-bechard
Mariette Dumais, Responsable

Saint-Philémon: **Bibliothèque des Sous-Bois**
1460, rue St-Louis, Saint-Philémon, QC G0R 4A0
Tél: 418-469-2443

Saint-Pie: **Bibliothèque municipale de Saint-Pie**
309, rue Notre-Dame, Saint-Pie, QC J0H 1W0
Tél: 450-772-2332; *Téléc:* 450-772-2332
biblio@villest-pie.ca
Martine Garon, Responsable

Saint-Pie-de-Guire: **Bibliothèque de Saint-Pie-de-Guire**
445C, rue Principal, Saint-Pie-de-Guire, QC J0G 1R0
Tél: 450-784-0232
biblio132@reseaubibliocqlm.qc.ca
Sylvie Courchesne, Responsable

Saint-Pierre-de-Broughton: **Bibliothèque Maurice-Couture/Saint-Pierre-de-Broughton**
6, du Couvent, Saint-Pierre-de-Broughton, QC G0N 1T0
Tél: 418-424-3450; *Téléc:* 418-424-0389
biblio.m.couture@cgocable.ca
Mèdia social: www.facebook.com/BibliothequeMauriceCoutureStPierreDeBroughton

Saint-Pierre-de-l'Île-d'Orl: **Bibliothèque Oscar-Ferland**
515, rte des Prêtres, Saint-Pierre-de-l'Île-d'Orl, QC G0A 4E0
Tél: 418-828-2962; *Téléc:* 418-828-0724

Saint-Pierre-les-Becquets: **Bibliothèque de Saint-Pierre-les-Becquets**
108, rue des Loisirs, Saint-Pierre-les-Becquets, QC G0X 2Z0
Tél: 819-263-0797; *Téléc:* 819-263-0798
biblio086@reseaubibliocqlm.qc.ca
Mèdia social: www.facebook.com/biblioslesbecquets
Francine Bergeron, Responsable

Saint-Placide: **Bibliothèque de Saint-Placide**
73, rue de l'Église, Saint-Placide, QC J0V 2B0
Tél: 450-258-1780; *Téléc:* 450-258-0364
biblio@municipalite.saint-placide.qc.ca
www.reseaubiblioduquebec.qc.ca

Saint-Polycarpe: **Bibliothèque municipale de Saint-Polycarpe**
7, rue Ste-Catherine, Saint-Polycarpe, QC J0P 1X0
Tél: 450-265-3444; *Téléc:* 450-265-3010
polycarpe@reseaubibliomonteregie.qc.ca

Saint-Prime: **Bibliothèque publique de Saint-Prime**
616, rue Principale, Saint-Prime, QC G8J 1T4
Tél: 418-251-2116
stprime@reseaubiblioslsj.qc.ca

Saint-Prosper: **Bibliothèque de Saint-Prosper (Livresque)**
2885, 25e av, Saint-Prosper, QC G0M 1Y0
Tél: 418-594-5197; *Téléc:* 418-594-8865
bibliostpros@globetrotter.net

Saint-Raphaël: **Bibliothèque Jeannine-Marquis-Garant**
88, rue du Foyer, Saint-Raphaël, QC G0R 4C0
Tél: 418-243-3437; *Téléc:* 418-243-2605
www.reseaubiblioduquebec.qc.ca/saint-raphael/

Saint-René-de-Matane: **Bibliothèque de Saint-René-de-Matane**
178, av Saint-René, Saint-René-de-Matane, QC G0J 3E0
Tél: 418-224-1339
www.saintrene.ca

Saint-Robert: **Bibliothèque municipale de Saint-Robert**
1, rue Aggée-Pelletier, Saint-Robert, QC J0G 1S0
Tél: 450-782-2562
strobert@pierredesaurel.com
Nathalie Cheney, Responsable

Saint-Roch-de-l'Achigan: **Bibliothèque de Saint-Roch-de-l'Achigan**
31, rue Gariepy, Saint-Roch-de-l'Achigan, QC J0K 3H0
Tél: 450-588-5838; *Téléc:* 450-588-4478
biblio109@reseaubibliocqlm.qc.ca
Jocelyne Allard, Responsable

Saint-Roch-de-Mékinac: **Bibliothèque de Saint-Roch-de-Mékinac**
1216, rue Principale, Saint-Roch-de-Mékinac, QC G0X 2E0
Tél: 819-507-9868; *Téléc:* 819-646-5635
biblio033@reseaubibliocqlm.qc.ca
Lise Bérubé, Responsable

Saint-Roch-de-Richelieu: **Bibliothèque municipale de Saint-Roch-de-Richelieu**
1111, rue du Parc, Saint-Roch-de-Richelieu, QC J0L 2M0
Tél: 450-785-2755
roch@reseaubibliomonteregie.qc.ca
Média social: www.facebook.com/bibliostrochderichelieu

Saint-Roch-des-Aulnaies: **Bibliothèque Bibli-Aulnaies/Saint-Roch-des-Aulnaies**
1028, rte de la Seigneurie, Saint-Roch-des-Aulnaies, QC G0R 4E0
Tél: 418-856-7045; *Téléc:* 418-354-2059
stroch@globetrotter.qc.ca

Saint-Rosaire: **Bibliothèque de Saint-Rosaire**
205, rang 6, Saint-Rosaire, QC G0Z 1K0
Tél: 819-795-4861; *Téléc:* 819-795-4861
biblio088@reseaubibliocqlm.qc.ca

Saint-Rémi: **Bibliothèque municipale de Saint-Rémi**
25, rue Saint-Sauveur, Saint-Rémi, QC J0L 2L0
Tél: 450-454-3993; *Téléc:* 450-454-4083
bibliotheque@ville.saint-remi.qc.ca
www.ville.saint-remi.qc.ca/05bibliotheque
Monique Black, Technicienne en documentation

Saint-Samuel: **Bibliothèque de Saint-Samuel**
141, rue de l'Église, Saint-Samuel, QC G0Z 1G0
Tél: 819-353-2642; *Téléc:* 819-353-1499
biblio137@reseaubibliocqlm.qc.ca
Érick Bergeron, Responsable
ebergeron@telwarwick.net

Saint-Sauveur: **Bibliothèque de Saint-Sauveur**
33, av de l'Église, Saint-Sauveur, QC J0R 1R0
Tél: 450-227-2669; *Téléc:* 450-227-3362
bibliotheque@ville.saint-sauveur.qc.ca
www.reseaubiblioduquebec.qc.ca

Saint-Simon: **Bibliothèque de Saint-Simon**
39, rue de l'Église, Saint-Simon, QC G0L 4C0
Tél: 418-738-2249
biblio.simon@crsbp.net
www.reseaubiblioduquebec.qc.ca
France Beauchesne, Responsable

Saint-Simon: **Bibliothèque municipale Lise-Bourque-St-Pierre**
46, rue des Loisirs, Saint-Simon, QC J0H 1Y0
Tél: 450-798-2276
simon@reseaubibliomonteregie.qc.ca

Saint-Siméon: **Bibliothèque Henri-Brassard**
505A, rue Saint-Laurent, Saint-Siméon, QC G0T 1X0
Tél: 418-471-0550

Saint-Siméon-de-Bonaventure: **Bibliothèque de Saint-Siméon**
116, rue Bélanger, Saint-Siméon-de-Bonaventure, QC G0C 3A0
Tél: 418-534-2606; *Téléc:* 418-534-3830
bbostsim@globetrotter.net
www.stsimeon.ca/bibliotheque

Saint-Stanislas: **Bibliothèque publique de Saint-Stanislas**
953, rue Principale, Saint-Stanislas, QC G8L 7B4
Tél: 418-276-4476; *Téléc:* 418-276-4476
stanisla@reseaubiblioslsj.qc.ca

Saint-Stanislas-de-Kostka: **Bibliothèque municipale Maxime-Raymond**
115, rue Centrale, Saint-Stanislas-de-Kostka, QC J0S 1W0
Tél: 450-370-4650
www.st-stanislas-de-kostka.ca/fr/bibliotheque

Saint-Sulpice: **Bibliothèque de Saint-Sulpice**
215, rue des Loisirs, Saint-Sulpice, QC J5W 6C9
Tél: 450-589-7816
biblio133@reseaubibliocqlm.qc.ca

Saint-Sylvestre: **Bibliothèque municipale de Saint-Sylvestre**
824, rue Principale, Saint-Sylvestre, QC G0S 3C0
Tél: 418-596-2427
larencontre@axion.ca

Saint-Sylvère: **Bibliothèque de Saint-Sylvère**
260, rte de l'École, Saint-Sylvère, QC G0Z 1H0
Tél: 819-285-2699; *Téléc:* 819-285-2040
biblio037@reseaubibliocqlm.qc.ca
www.reseaubiblioduquebec.qc.ca
Linda Searles, Responsable

Saint-Sébastien: **Bibliothèque municipale de Saint-Sébastien**
595, rue de La Fabrique, Saint-Sébastien, QC G0Y 1M0
biblio092@reseaubiblioestrie.qc.ca

Saint-Séverin: **Bibliothèque de Saint-Séverin**
1986, place du Centre, Saint-Séverin, QC G0X 2B0
Tél: 418-365-5844; *Téléc:* 418-365-7544
biblio008@reseaubibliocqlm.qc.ca

Saint-Séverin-de-Beauce: **La Voluthèque**
900, rue des Lacs, Saint-Séverin-de-Beauce, QC G0N 1V0
Tél: 418-426-2423; *Téléc:* 418-426-1274
biblioseverin@novicomfusion.com
www.mabibliotheque.ca/st-severin

Saint-Sévère: **Bibliothèque de Saint-Sévère (Denise L. Noël)**
47, rue Principale, Saint-Sévère, QC G0X 3B0
Tél: 819-264-5656; *Téléc:* 819-264-6013
biblio119@reseaubibliocqlm.qc.ca
www.reseaubiblioduquebec.qc.ca
Jocelyne Lavigne, Responsable

Saint-Tharcisius: **Bibliothèque de Saint-Tharcisius**
55, rue Principale, Saint-Tharcisius, QC G0J 3G0
Tél: 418-629-4727
biblio.tharci@crsbp.net
www.reseaubiblioduquebec.qc.ca
Maryse Rioux, Responsable

Saint-Thomas-de-Joliette: **Bibliothèque de Saint-Thomas (Jacqueline-Plante)**
#941, 10, rue Principale, Saint-Thomas-de-Joliette, QC J0K 3L0
Tél: 450-759-8173
biblio117@reseaubibliocqlm.qc.ca
Média social: www.facebook.com/263931613689729
Gisèle Bonin, Responsable

Saint-Thomas-Didyme: **Bibliothèque publique de Saint-Thomas-de-Didyme**
#31, 1, av du Moulin, Saint-Thomas-Didyme, QC G0W 1P0
Tél: 418-274-3638
thomas@reseaubiblioslsj.qc.ca
Denise Bergeron, Responsable

Saint-Théodore-d-Acton: **Bibliothèque autonome de Saint-Théodore-d'Acton**
1803, rue Principale, Saint-Théodore-d-Acton, QC J0H 1Z0
Tél: 450-546-5643
biblio.st-theodore@mrcacton.qc.ca
www.st-theodore.com

Saint-Tite: **Bibliothèque de Saint-Tite (Marielle-Brouillette)**
330, rue du Moulin, Saint-Tite, QC G0X 3H0
Tél: 418-365-6203
biblio017@reseaubibliocqlm.qc.ca
Denise Groleau, Responsable

Saint-Ubalde: **Bibliothèque Guy-Laviolette**
425, rue St-Paul, Saint-Ubalde, QC G0A 4L0
Tél: 418-277-2124; *Téléc:* 418-277-2055

Pauline Tessier, Responsable

Saint-Valentin: **Bibliothèque municipale de Saint-Valentin**
790, 4e Ligne, Saint-Valentin, QC J0J 2E0
Tél: 450-291-3948
valentin@reseaubibliomonteregie.qc.ca
Réjane Hébert Olivier, Responsable

Saint-Vallier: **Bibliothèque Marie-Josephte-Corrivaux**
365, av de l'Église, Saint-Vallier, QC G0R 4J0
Tél: 418-884-3190; *Téléc:* 418-884-2454
biblstva@globetrotter.qc.ca
Monique Rochefort, Responsable
Suzanne Alain, Adjointe

Saint-Valérien: **Bibliothèque de Saint-Valérien**
159, rue Principale, Saint-Valérien, QC G0L 4E0
Tél: 418-736-8170
biblio.valerien@crsbp.net
www.reseaubiblioduquebec.qc.ca
Chantal Paquet, Responsable

Saint-Valère: **Bibliothèque de Saint-Valère**
2A, rue du Parc, Saint-Valère, QC G0P 1M0
Tél: 819-353-3464; *Téléc:* 819-353-3465
biblio127@reseaubibliocqlm.qc.ca
www.msvalere.qc.ca/bibliotheque-horaire.php

Saint-Vianney: **Bibliothèque de Saint-Vianney**
170-B, av Centrale, Saint-Vianney, QC G0J 3J0
Tél: 418-629-4082
biblio.vianney@crsbp.net
Estelle Allaire, Responsable

Saint-Victor: **Bibliothèque Biblio Luc-Lacourcière**
287, rue Marchand, Saint-Victor, QC G0M 2B0
Tél: 418-588-6689; *Téléc:* 418-588-6855
saint-vic@telvic.net

Saint-Wenceslas: **Bibliothèque de Saint-Wenceslas**
1035, rue Hébert, Saint-Wenceslas, QC G0Z 1J0
Tél: 819-224-4169
biblio073@reseaubibliocqlm.qc.ca
Marise Ouellet, Coordonnatrice

Saint-Zotique: **Bibliothèque municipale de Saint-Zotique**
30, av des Maîtres, Saint-Zotique, QC J0P 1Z0
Tél: 450-267-9335
biblio@st-zotique.com
www.st-zotique.com/bibliotheque
Lyne Cadieux, Responsable

Saint-Zénon: **Bibliothèque de Saint-Zénon (Danièle-Bruneau)**
6191, rue Principale, Saint-Zénon, QC J0K 3N0
Tél: 450-884-0328; *Téléc:* 450-884-5285
biblio048@reseaubibliocqlm.qc.ca

Saint-Zéphirin-de-Courval: **Bibliothèque de Saint-Zéphirin-de-Courval**
950B, rue des Loisirs, Saint-Zéphirin-de-Courval, QC J0G 1V0
Tél: 450-564-2401; *Téléc:* 450-564-2339
biblio092@reseaubibliocqlm.qc.ca
www.saint-zephirin.ca/bibliotheque.asp
Angèle Lefebvre, Responsable

Saint-Édouard: **Bibliothèque municipale de Saint-Édouard**
405B, Montée Lussier, Saint-Édouard, QC J0L 1Y0
Tél: 450-454-2056
edouard@reseaubibliomonteregie.qc.ca
www.reseaubiblioduquebec.qc.ca
Fleurette Michaud, Responsable

Saint-Édouard-de-Maskinongé: **Bibliothèque de Saint-Édouard-de-Maskinongé**
3851, rue Notre-Dame, Saint-Édouard-de-Maskinongé, QC J0K 2H0
Tél: 819-268-2883
biblio123@reseaubibliocqlm.qc.ca
www.reseaubiblioduquebec.qc.ca
Hélène Robert, Responsable

Saint-Élie-de-Caxton: **Bibliothèque de Saint-Élie-de-Caxton**
50, ch des Loisirs, Saint-Élie-de-Caxton, QC G0X 2N0
Tél: 819-221-2839
biblio115@reseaubibliocqlm.qc.ca
www.reseaubiblioduquebec.qc.ca
Charline Plante, Responsable

Saint-Éloi: **Bibliothèque de Saint-Éloi**
456, rue Principale, Saint-Éloi, QC G0L 2V0
Tél: 418-898-2734
biblio.eloi@crsbp.net
www.reseaubiblioduquebec.qc.ca
Rachel Tardif, Responsable

Saint-Émile-de-Suffolk: **Bibliothèque de Saint-Émile-de-Suffolk**
299, route des Cantons, Saint-Émile-de-Suffolk, QC J0V 1Y0
Tél: 819-426-2987; *Téléc:* 819-426-3447
biblio.stemile@mrcpapineau.com
Georgette Haineault, Responsable

Saint-Éphrem-de-Beauce: **Bibliothèque La Voûte de l'Imaginaire**
#14, 34, rte 271 Sud, Saint-Éphrem-de-Beauce, QC G0M 1R0
Tél: 418-484-5716
www.reseaubiblioduquebec.qc.ca/saint-ephrem

Saint-Épiphane: **Bibliothèque de Saint-Épiphane**
216, rue du Couvent, Saint-Épiphane, QC G0L 2X0
Tél: 418-862-0052
biblio.epiphane@crsbp.net
www.reseaubiblioduquebec.qc.ca
Jacqueline Jalbert, Responsable

Saint-Étienne-de-Beauharnoi: **Bibliothèque municipale de Saint-Étienne-de-Beauharnois**
430, rue de l'Église, Saint-Étienne-de-Beauharnoi, QC J0S 1S0
Tél: 450-429-6384; *Téléc:* 450-429-6384
etienne@reseaubibliomonteregie.qc.ca
www.reseaubiblioduquebec.qc.ca
Carole Lalande, Responsable
Francine Boyer, Gestion du PIB et Administration des systèmes informatiques

Saint-Étienne-des-Grès: **Bibliothèque de Saint-Étienne-des-Grès**
#300, 190, rue Saint-Honoré, Saint-Étienne-des-Grès, QC G0X 2P0
Tél: 819-299-3854
biblio019@reseaubibliocqlm.qc.ca
Denis Boisvert, Responsable

Saint-Étienne-des-Grès: **Bibliothèque de Saint-Thomas-de-Caxton**
338, av Saint-Thomas-de-Caxton, Saint-Étienne-des-Grès, QC G0X 2P0
Tél: 819-296-3004; *Téléc:* 819-535-1246
biblio105@reseaubibliocqlm.qc.ca
France Bournival, Responsable

Sainte-Adèle: **Bibliothèque Claude-Henri-Grignon**
#118, 555 boul de Sainte-Adèle, Sainte-Adèle, QC J8B 1A7
Tél: 450-229-2921
ville.sainte-adele.qc.ca/bibliotheque.php
Mijanou Dubuc, Responsable
mdubuc@ville.sainte-adele.qc.ca

Sainte-Adèle: **Bibliothèque Jean-Baptiste-Rolland**
1200, rue Claude Grégoire, Sainte-Adèle, QC J8B 1E9
Tél: 450-229-2921; *Téléc:* 450-229-2283
mjfortier@ville.sainte-adele.qc.ca

Sainte-Agathe-de-Lotbinière: **Bibliothèque municipale Rayons d'Art**
402A, rue Gosford ouest, Sainte-Agathe-de-Lotbinière, QC G0S 2A0
Tél: 418-599-2830; *Téléc:* 418-599-2905
rayons@coopsteagathe.com
www.mabibliotheque.ca/sainte-agathe
Denise Allard-Martineau, Responsable

Sainte-Agathe-des-Monts: **Bibliothèque municipale de Sainte-Agathe-des-Monts**
10, rue St-Donat, Sainte-Agathe-des-Monts, QC J8C 1P5
Tél: 819-326-4595
culture@ville.sainte-agathe-des-monts.qc.ca
ville.sainte-agathe-des-monts.qc.ca/fr/services-bibliotheque.php

Sainte-Angèle-de-Monnoir: **Bibliothèque Sainte-Angèle-de-Monnoir**
7, ch du Vide, Sainte-Angèle-de-Monnoir, QC J0L 1P0
Tél: 450-460-3644; *Téléc:* 450-460-3853
biblio@sainte-angele-de-monnoir.ca
François Lachance, Responsable

Sainte-Angèle-de-Prémont: **Bibliothèque de Sainte-Angèle-de-Prémont**
2451, rue Camirand, Sainte-Angèle-de-Prémont, QC J0K 1R0
Tél: 819-268-5526; *Téléc:* 819-268-5536
biblio124@reseaubibliocqlm.qc.ca
Média social: www.facebook.com/192313390956865
Diane Lessard, Responsable

Sainte-Anne-de-Bellevue: **Bibliothèque de Sainte-Anne-de-Bellevue**
40, rue Saint-Pierre, Sainte-Anne-de-Bellevue, QC H9X 1Y6
Tél: 514-457-1940; *Téléc:* 514-457-7146
anne.bellevue@reseaubibliomonteregie.qc.ca

Sainte-Anne-de-la-Pérade: **Bibliothèque de Sainte-Anne-de-la-Pérade (Armand-Goulet)**
100, rue de la Fabrique, Sainte-Anne-de-la-Pérade, QC G0X 2J0
Tél: 418-325-2216; *Téléc:* 418-325-3070
biblio014@reseaubibliocqlm.qc.ca
www.sainteannedelaperade.net/culture/bibliotheque

Sainte-Anne-des-Lacs: **Bibliothèque de Sainte-Anne-des-Lacs**
723, ch Ste-Anne-des-Lacs, Sainte-Anne-des-Lacs, QC J0R 1B0
Tél: 450-224-2675; *Téléc:* 450-224-8672
www.reseaubiblioduquebec.qc.ca
Hélène Limoges, Responsable

Sainte-Anne-des-Monts: **Bibliothèque municipale Blanche-Lamontagne**
120, 7e rue ouest, Sainte-Anne-des-Monts, QC G4V 2L2
Tél: 418-763-3810; *Téléc:* 418-763-3811
maisondelaculture@globetrotter.net
www.maisondelaculture.net/bibliothèque-blanche-lamontagne

Sainte-Anne-des-Plaines: **Bibliothèque publique de Sainte-Anne-des-Plaines**
155, rue des Cèdres, Sainte-Anne-des-Plaines, QC J0N 1H0
Tél: 450-478-4337; *Téléc:* 450-478-6733
bibliotheque@villesadp.ca
www.villesadp.ca/biblio
Média social: twitter.com/BiblioSADP
Chantal Bélisle, Responsable

Sainte-Anne-du-Lac: **Bibliothèque de Sainte-Anne-du-Lac**
1B, rue St-François-Xavier, Sainte-Anne-du-Lac, QC J0W 1V0
Tél: 819-586-2051; *Téléc:* 819-586-2203
biblio@steannedulac.ca
www.reseaubiblioduquebec.qc.ca
Sylvie Giard, Responsable

Sainte-Aurélie: **Bibliothèque Le Maillon**
151B, ch des Bois-Francs, Sainte-Aurélie, QC G0M 1M0
Tél: 418-593-3021; *Téléc:* 418-593-3961
maillon@sogetel.net
JoAnne Leclerc, Responsable
Pierrette Morin, Adjointe

Sainte-Barbe: **Bibliothèque municipale Lucie Benoît**
468, ch de l'Église, Sainte-Barbe, QC J0S 1P0
Tél: 450-371-2324
barbe@reseaubibliomonteregie.qc.ca
Lucie Benoît, Responsable

Sainte-Brigide-d'Iberville: **Bibliothèque de Sainte-Brigide-d'Iberville**
Centre municipal, 510, 9e rang, Sainte-Brigide-d'Iberville, QC J0J 1X0
Tél: 450-293-4604; *Téléc:* 450-293-1243
administration@sainte-brigide.qc.ca
www.sainte-brigide.qc.ca
Francine Belzile, Responsable

Sainte-Brigitte-de-Laval: **Bibliothèque Le Trivent**
3, rue du Couvent, Sainte-Brigitte-de-Laval, QC G0A 3K0
Tél: 418-666-4666; *Téléc:* 418-825-3114
trivent.bibli@csdps.qc.ca

Sainte-Brigitte-des-Saults: **Bibliothèque de Sainte-Brigitte-des-Saults (Michel-David)**
400, rue Principale, Sainte-Brigitte-des-Saults, QC J0C 1E0
Tél: 819-336-7145; *Téléc:* 819-336-4410
biblio043@reseaubibliocqlm.qc.ca
Média social: www.facebook.com/466708776680988
Jocelyne Guilbault, Responsable

***Sainte-Béatrix:* Bibliothèque de Sainte-Béatrix**
861, rue de l'Église, Sainte-Béatrix, QC J0K 1Y0
Tél: 450-883-2245; *Téléc:* 450-883-1772
biblio069@reseaubibliocqlm.qc.ca
www.sainte-beatrix.com
Carole Lasalle, Responsable

***Sainte-Catherine:* Bibliothèque publique de Sainte-Catherine**
5365, boul St-Laurent, Sainte-Catherine, QC J5C 1A6
Tél: 450-632-0590; *Téléc:* 450-632-9908
bibliotheque@ville.sainte-catherine.qc.ca
www.ville.sainte-catherine.qc.ca/francais/biblio_accueil.html
Lise Forcier, Directrice
lise.forcier@ville.sainte-catherine.qc.ca

***Sainte-Christine:* Bibliothèque municipale de Sainte-Christine**
629, rue des Loisirs, Sainte-Christine, QC J0H 1H0
Tél: 819-858-2828
christine@reseaubibliomonteregie.qc.ca
www.reseaubiblioduquebec.qc.ca
Rosalie Proulx, Responsable

***Sainte-Claire:* Bibliothèque municipale de Sainte-Claire**
55, rue de la Fabrique, Sainte-Claire, QC G0R 2V0
Tél: 418-883-2275; *Téléc:* 418-883-3845
www.municipalite.sainte-claire.qc.ca
Josée Morin, Responsable
josee.m@globetrotter.net

***Sainte-Clotilde-de-Beauce:* Bibliothèque Jeanne-Édith-Audet**
307C, rue du Couvent, Sainte-Clotilde-de-Beauce, QC G0N 1C0
Tél: 418-427-2181; *Téléc:* 418-427-2495
pp307@hotmail.com
www.reseaubiblioduquebec.qc.ca/sainte-clotilde

***Sainte-Cécile-de-Lévrard:* Bibliothèque de Sainte-Cécile-de-Lévrard**
234, rue Principale, Sainte-Cécile-de-Lévrard, QC G0X 2M0
Tél: 819-263-0368; *Téléc:* 819-263-1023
biblio113@reseaubibliocqlm.qc.ca
Média social: www.facebook.com/SteCecileDeLevrard

***Sainte-Cécile-de-Masham:* Bibliothèque de Sainte-Cécile-de-Masham (La Pêche)**
5, rue Principale ouest, Sainte-Cécile-de-Masham, QC J0X 2W0
Tél: 819-456-2627; *Téléc:* 819-456-4228
admmasham@crsbpo.qc.ca
www.reseaubiblioduquebec.qc.ca/Masham
Gisèle Duguay, Responsable

***Sainte-Elisabeth-de-Proulx:* Bibliothèque publique de Sainte-Elisabeth-de-Proulx**
1254, rue Principale, Sainte-Elisabeth-de-Proulx, QC G8M 4V2
Tél: 418-276-9494
elisabeth@reseaubibliosIsj.qc.ca

***Sainte-Elizabeth:* Bibliothèque de Sainte-Elisabeth (Françoise-Allard-Bérard)**
2270, rue Principale, Sainte-Elizabeth, QC J0K 2J0
Tél: 450-759-2875
biblio068@reseaubibliocqlm.qc.ca

***Sainte-Eulalie:* Bibliothèque de Sainte-Eulalie**
757A, rue des Bouleaux, Sainte-Eulalie, QC G0Z 1E0
Tél: 819-225-8069; *Téléc:* 819-225-4078
biblio074@reseaubibliocqlm.qc.ca

***Sainte-Famille:* Bibliothèque municipale de Sainte-Famille/Saint-François-de-l'île-d"Orléans**
#3912, 1, ch Royal, Sainte-Famille, QC G0A 3P0
Tél: 418-666-4666; *Téléc:* 418-829-2513
www.mabibliotheque.ca/sainte-famille

***Sainte-Flavie:* Bibliothèque Olivar-Asselin**
505, rte de la Mer, Sainte-Flavie, QC G0J 2L0
Tél: 418-775-7050; *Téléc:* 418-775-5672
biblio.flavie@crsbp.net
Liz Fortin, Responsable

***Sainte-Florence:* Bibliothèque de Sainte-Florence**
29, rue des Loisirs, Sainte-Florence, QC G0J 2M0
Tél: 418-756-5079
biblio.florence@crsbp.net
www.reseaubiblioduquebec.qc.ca
Gaétane Morin, Responsable

***Sainte-Françoise:* Bibliothèque de Sainte-Françoise (Bas-Saint-Laurent)**
31, rue Principale, Sainte-Françoise, QC G0L 3B0
Tél: 418-851-3878
biblio.francoise@crsbp.net
Johanne Morin, Responsable

***Sainte-Françoise:* Bibliothèque de Sainte-Françoise (Centre-du-Québec)**
563, rue Principale, Sainte-Françoise, QC G0S 2N0
Tél: 819-287-0126; *Téléc:* 819-287-5838
biblio104@reseaubibliocqlm.qc.ca

***Sainte-Germaine-Boulé:* Bibliothèque de Sainte-Germaine-Boulé**
240, rue Roy, Sainte-Germaine-Boulé, QC J0Z 1M0
Tél: 819-787-6477; *Téléc:* 819-787-6477
boule@reseaubiblioatnq.qc.ca
www.reseaubiblioduquebec.qc.ca/ste-germaine-boule
Odette Rancourt Audet, Responsable

***Sainte-Hedwidge:* Bibliothèque publique de Sainte-Hedwidge**
1090, rue Principale, Sainte-Hedwidge, QC G0W 2R0
Tél: 418-275-3020
hedwidge@reseaubibliosIsj.qc.ca

***Sainte-Hélène:* Bibliothèque de Sainte-Hélène**
707, rue du Couvent, Sainte-Hélène, QC G0L 3J0
Tél: 418-856-7057
biblio.helene@crsbp.net
www.reseaubiblioduquebec.qc.ca
Lucie Bérubé, Responsable

***Sainte-Hélène-de-Bagot:* Bibliothèque municipale de Sainte-Hélène-de-Bagot**
384, 6e av, Sainte-Hélène-de-Bagot, QC J0H 1M0
Tél: 450-791-2618
helene@reseaubibliomonteregie.qc.ca
www.reseaubiblioduquebec.qc.ca
France Vachon, Responsable

***Sainte-Hénédine:* Bibliothèque La Détente/Sainte-Hénédine**
111D, rue Principale, Sainte-Hénédine, QC G0S 2R0
Tél: 418-935-3993; *Téléc:* 418-935-3113
bibliohenedine@hotmail.com
Doris Drouin-Dubreuil, Responsable

***Sainte-Irène:* Bibliothèque de Sainte-Irène**
362, rue de la Fabrique, Sainte-Irène, QC G0J 1P0
Tél: 418-629-5705

***Sainte-Julie:* Bibliothèque municipale de Sainte-Julie**
1600, ch du Fer-à-Cheval, Sainte-Julie, QC J3E 2M1
Tél: 450-922-7070; *Téléc:* 450-922-7077
biblio@ville.sainte-julie.qc.ca
www.ville.sainte-julie.qc.ca
Média social: www.facebook.com/bibliosaintejulie
Marie-Hélène Parent, Bibliothécaire en chef

***Sainte-Julienne:* Bibliothèque Gisèle-Paré**
2550, rue Eugène-Marsan, Sainte-Julienne, QC J0K 2T0
Tél: 450-831-3811; *Téléc:* 450-831-4433
biblio43@crsbpl.qc.ca
Francine Huard, Responsable

***Sainte-Justine:* Bibliothèque Roch-Carrier**
250, rue Principale, Sainte-Justine, QC G0R 1Y0
Tél: 418-383-5399
bibliorochcarrier@sogetel.net
ww.mabibliotheque.ca/roch-carrier

***Sainte-Louise:* Bibliothèque Idée-Lire**
506, rue Principale, Sainte-Louise, QC G0R 3K0
Tél: 418-354-7730
www.reseaubiblioduquebec.qc.ca/sainte-louise

***Sainte-Luce:* Bibliothèque de Luceville**
67, rue Saint-Pierre est, Sainte-Luce, QC G0K 1P0
Tél: 418-739-3534
biblio.luceville@crsbp.net
www.reseaubiblioduquebec.qc.ca

***Sainte-Luce:* Bibliothèque de Sainte-Luce**
#200, 1 rue Langlois, Sainte-Luce, QC G0K 1P0
Tél: 418-739-4420
biblio.luce@crsbp.net
www.reseaubiblioduquebec.qc.ca
Luc Bourassa, Responsable

***Sainte-Lucie-de-Beauregard:* Bibliothèque A la Bouquinerie**
21, rte des Chutes, Sainte-Lucie-de-Beauregard, QC G0R 3L0
Tél: 418-223-3125; *Téléc:* 418-223-3121
alabouquinerie@hotmail.com
Huguette Rouillard, Responsable
418-223-3613

***Sainte-Madeleine:* Bibliothèque municipale de Sainte-Madeleine**
1040A, rue Saint-Simon, Sainte-Madeleine, QC J0H 1S0
Tél: 450-795-3959; *Téléc:* 450-795-3736
madeleine@reseaubibliomonteregie.qc.ca

***Sainte-Marguerite:* Biblio La Bouquine**
235, rue Saint-Jacques, Sainte-Marguerite, QC G0S 2X0
Tél: 418-935-7089; *Téléc:* 418-935-3709
Adrienne Gagné, Responsable

***Sainte-Marguerite:* Bibliothèque de Sainte-Marguerite**
15, rue de la Vérendrye, Sainte-Marguerite, QC G0J 2Y0
Tél: 418-756-3364
biblio.margot@crsbp.net
Colette Marquis, Responsable

***Sainte-Marie:* Bibliothèque Honorius-Provost**
80, rue St-Antoine, Sainte-Marie, QC G6E 4B8
Tél: 418-387-2240
info-biblio@sante-marie.ca
sainte-marie.ca/bibliotheque-honorius-provost
Johanne Labbé, Responsable de la bibliothèque

***Sainte-Marie-de-Blandford:* Bibliothèque de Sainte-Marie-de-Blandford**
492, rue des Bosquets, Sainte-Marie-de-Blandford, QC G0X 2W0
Tél: 819-283-2127; *Téléc:* 819-283-2169
biblio108@reseaubibliocqlm.qc.ca
Josée Fortier, Responsable

***Sainte-Marie-Salomé:* Bibliothèque de Sainte-Marie-Salomé**
650, ch Saint-Jean, Sainte-Marie-Salomé, QC J0K 2Z0
Tél: 450-839-6212; *Téléc:* 450-753-5236
biblio050@reseaubibliocqlm.qc.ca
Média social: fr-fr.facebook.com/BibliothequeSTE.MARIE.SALOME
Diane Éthier, Responsable

***Sainte-Marthe-sur-le-Lac:* Bibliothèque municipale de Sainte-Marthe-sur-le-Lac**
#103, 3003, ch d'Oka, Sainte-Marthe-sur-le-Lac, QC J0N 1P0
Tél: 450-974-7111
bibliotheque@ville.sainte-marthe-sur-le-lac.qc.ca
www.ville.sainte-marthe-sur-le-lac.qc.ca/bibliotheque

***Sainte-Monique:* Bibliothèque de Sainte-Monique**
247, rue Principale, Sainte-Monique, QC J0G 1N0
Tél: 819-289-2051; *Téléc:* 819-289-2344
biblio052@reseaubibliocqlm.qc.ca

***Sainte-Monique-Lac-St-Jean:* Bibliothèque publique de Sainte-Monique**
138, rue Honfleur, Sainte-Monique-Lac-St-Jean, QC G0W 2T0
Tél: 418-347-4391
monique@reseaubibliosIsj.qc.ca

***Sainte-Mélanie:* Bibliothèque de Sainte-Mélanie (Louise-Amélie-Panet)**
940, rue Principale, Sainte-Mélanie, QC J0K 3A0
Tél: 450-889-5871
biblio111@reseaubibliocqlm.qc.ca
Martin Alarie, Responsable

***Sainte-Paule:* Bibliothèque de Sainte-Paule**
102, rue Banville, Sainte-Paule, QC G0J 3C0
Tél: 418-737-1378
biblio.paule@crsbp.net
www.reseaubiblioduquebec.qc.ca
Carmen Côté-D'Amour, Responsable

***Sainte-Perpétue:* Bibliothèque de Sainte-Perpétue**
2504, rang St-Joseph, Sainte-Perpétue, QC J0C 1R0
Tél: 819-336-6275
www.sainte-perpetue.com
Louiselle Robichaud, Responsable

Sainte-Pétronille: **Bibliothèque municipale de Sainte-Pétronille**
3, ch de l'Église, Sainte-Pétronille, QC G0A 4C0
Tél: 418-828-8888; *Téléc:* 418-828-1364
bibliospetro@qc.aira.com
Lise Paquet, Responsable

Sainte-Rita: **Bibliothèque Sainte-Rita**
5, rue de L'Église Ouest, Sainte-Rita, QC G0L 4G0
Tél: 418-963-2967
biblio.rita@crsbp.net
Lucille Turcotte, Responsable

Sainte-Rose-de-Watford: **Bibliothèque municipale de Sainte-Rose-de-Watford**
693, rue Carrier, Sainte-Rose-de-Watford, QC G0R 4G0
Tél: 418-267-5264; *Téléc:* 418-267-5812
biblioste-rose@sogetel.net
www.mabibliotheque.ca/sainte-rose

Sainte-Rose-du-Nord: **Bibliothèque publique de Ste-Rose-du-Nord**
126, rue Descente-des-Femmes, Sainte-Rose-du-Nord, QC G0V 1T0
Tél: 418-675-2250
ste-rose@reseaubibliosIsj.qc.ca
Rachelle Simard, Responsable

Sainte-Sabine: **Bibliothèque Sabithèque**
#203, 4, rue St-Charles, Sainte-Sabine, QC G0R 4H0
Tél: 418-383-5788; *Téléc:* 418-383-5488
sabitheque@hotmail.com

Sainte-Sophie-de-Lévrard: **Bibliothèque de Sainte-Sophie-de-Lévrard**
184A, rue St-Antoine, Sainte-Sophie-de-Lévrard, QC G0X 3C0
Tél: 819-288-0334; *Téléc:* 819-288-5804
biblio102@reseaubibliocqlm.qc.ca
Daniel Désilets, Responsable

Sainte-Thérèse: **Bibliothèque municipale de Sainte-Thérèse**
150, boul du Séminaire, Sainte-Thérèse, QC J7E 1Z2
Tél: 450-434-1440; *Téléc:* 450-434-6070
biblio@sainte-therese.ca
www.ville.sainte-therese.qc.ca/biblio
Lise Thériault, Directrice
l.theriault@sainte-therese.ca

Sainte-Thècle: **Bibliothèque de Sainte-Thècle**
301, rue St-Jacques, Sainte-Thècle, QC G0X 3G0
Tél: 418-289-3717; *Téléc:* 418-289-3014
biblio016@reseaubibliocqlm.qc.ca
Diane Proulx, Responsable

Sainte-Ursule: **Bibliothèque de Sainte-Ursule (C.-J. Magnan)**
215, rue Lessard, Sainte-Ursule, QC J0K 3M0
Tél: 819-228-4345; *Téléc:* 819-228-8326
biblio031@reseaubibliocqlm.qc.ca
Suzanne Pilon, Responsable

Sainte-Victoire-de-Sorel: **Bibliothèque municipale de Sainte-Victoire-de-Sorel**
519, ch Ste-Victoire, Sainte-Victoire-de-Sorel, QC J0G 1T0
Tél: 450-782-3111
victoire@reseaubibliomonteregie.qc.ca
www.reseaubiblioduquebec.qc.ca
Micheline Lamoureux, Responsable
Josée Paquette, Responsable, Échanges
Lucille Ayotte, Responsable, Collection locale

Sainte-Élizabeth-de-Warwick: **Bibliothèque de Sainte-Élizabeth-de-Warwick**
228, rue Principale, Sainte-Élizabeth-de-Warwick, QC J0A 1M0
Tél: 819-358-2429; *Téléc:* 819-358-9192
biblio141@reseaubibliocqlm.qc.ca

Sainte-Émélie-de-l'Énergie: **Bibliothèque de Sainte-Émélie-de-l'Énergie**
241, rue Coutu, Sainte-Émélie-de-l'Énergie, QC J0K 2K0
Tél: 450-886-3823; *Téléc:* 450-886-9175
biblio053@reseaubibliocqlm.qc.ca
Diane Durand, Responsable

Saints-Martyrs-Canadiens: **Bibliothèque de Saints-Martyrs-Canadiens**
13, ch du Village, Saints-Martyrs-Canadiens, QC G0P 1A1
Tél: 819-344-5171
biblio157@reseaubibliocqlm.qc.ca

Sayabec: **Bibliothèque Quilit**
8B, rue Keable, Sayabec, QC G0J 3K0
Tél: 418-536-5431
biblio.sayabec@crsbp.net
www.reseaubiblioduquebec.qc.ca
Charline Metcalfe, Responsable

Scott: **Bibliothèque municipale de Scott**
1, 8e rue, Scott, QC G0S 3G0
Tél: 418-386-2736; *Téléc:* 418-387-1837
www.reseaubiblioduquebec.qc.ca/scott

Senneterre: **Bibliothèque de Senneterre**
121, 1e rue est, Senneterre, QC J0Y 2M0
Tél: 819-737-8829; *Téléc:* 819-737-4215
senneterre@reseaubiblioatnq.qc.ca
www.reseaubiblioduquebec.qc.ca/senneterre
Denise Dufour, Responsable

Sept-Doleurs: **Bibliothèque de Notre-Dame-des-Sept-Douleurs**
6201, chemin de L'Ile, Sept-Doleurs, QC G0L 1K0
Tél: 418-898-3451
biblio.douleurs@crsbp.net
www.reseaubiblioduquebec.qc.ca

Sept-Îles: **Bibliothèque Louis-Ange-Santerre**
500, av Jolliet, Sept-Îles, QC G4R 2B4
Tél: 418-964-3355; *Téléc:* 418-964-3353
bibliotheque@ville.sept-iles.qc.ca
www.ville.sept-iles.qc.ca
Média social: www.facebook.com/bibliothequelouisangesanterre
Isabelle Bond, Superviseur
isabelle.bond@ville.sept-iles.qc.ca

Shannon: **Bibliothèque municipale de Shannon**
40, rue St-Patrick, Shannon, QC G0A 4N0
Tél: 418-844-1622; *Téléc:* 418-844-2111
bibliotheque@shannon.ca
www.reseaubiblioduquebec.qc.ca

Shawinigan: **Bibliothèque Fabian-LaRochelle**
550, av de l'Hôtel-de-Ville, Shawinigan, QC G9N 6V3
Tél: 819-536-7218
shawinigan.ca/Citoyens/bibliotheques_29.html

Shawinigan: **Bibliothèque Fabien-LaRochelle**
550, av de l'Hôtel-de-Ville, Shawinigan, QC G9N 6V3
Tél: 819-536-7218
www.shawinigan.ca
Charlotte Lecours, Responsable des bibliothèques

Shawville: **Bibliothèque Shawville/Clarendon/Thorne/ Shawville/Clarendon/Thorne Library**
356, rue Main, Shawville, QC J0X 2Y0
Tél: 819-647-3732
admshawville@crsbpo.qc.ca
Média social: www.facebook.com/sclibrary
Jennifer Davies, Responsable

Sherbrooke: **Bibliothèque de Lennoxville/ Lennoxville Library**
101, rue Queen, Sherbrooke, QC J1M 1J7
Tél: 819-562-4949
www.bibliolennoxvillelibrary.ca
Média social: www.facebook.com/BibliothequeLennoxvilleLibrary

Sherbrooke: **Bibliothèque du Gisèle-Bergeron**
#1, 81, rue du Curé-LaRocque, Sherbrooke, QC J1C 0T2
Tél: 819-846-6645; *Téléc:* 819-846-2299
biblio028@reseaubiblioestrie.qc.ca
www.ville.sherbrooke.qc.ca

Sherbrooke: **Bibliothèque du secteur de Sainte-Élie**
4505, ch Saint-Roch Nord, Sherbrooke, QC J1H 5H9
Tél: 819-566-8312
www.ville.sherbrooke.qc.ca

Sherbrooke: **Bibliothèque municipale Éva-Senécal**
450, rue Marquette, Sherbrooke, QC J1H 1M4
Tél: 819-821-5861; *Téléc:* 819-822-6110
bibliotheque@ville.sherbrooke.qc.ca
qww.bibliotheque.ville.sherbrooke.qc.ca/es

Sorel-Tracy: **Bibliothèque municipale de Sorel-Tracy**
145, rue George, Sorel-Tracy, QC J3P 1C7
Tél: 450-780-5600
bibliotheque@ville.sorel-tracy.qc.ca
www.ville.sorel-tracy.qc.ca
Andrée Martin, Responsable
andree.martin@ville.sorel-tracy.qc.ca

St-Aimé-du-Lac-des-Iles: **Bibliothèque de Saint-Aimé-du-Lac-des-Iles**
871, ch Diotte, St-Aimé-du-Lac-des-Iles, QC J0W 1J0
Tél: 819-597-4174; *Téléc:* 819-597-2554
biblio59@crsbpl.qc.ca
www.reseaubiblioduquebec.qc.ca
Johanne Coté, Responsable

St-Alexandre-de-Kamouraska: **Bibliothèque Saint-Alexandre**
480, av de l'École, St-Alexandre-de-Kamouraska, QC G0L 2G0
Tél: 418-495-3123
biblio.alexi@crsbp.net
Hélène Therrien, Responsable

St-Barnabé-Nord: **Bibliothèque de Saint-Barnabé**
70, rue Duguay, St-Barnabé-Nord, QC G0X 2K0
Tél: 819-264-2085; *Téléc:* 819-264-2079
biblio027@reseaubibliocqlm.qc.ca
www.reseaubiblioduquebec.qc.ca
Luc Gélinas, Responsable

St-Charles-de-Bellechasse: **Bibliothèque Jacques-Labrie/Saint-Charles-de-Bellechasse**
2829A, av Royale, St-Charles-de-Bellechasse, QC G0R 2T0
Tél: 418-887-6561; *Téléc:* 418-887-6779
biblstch@globetrotter.qc.ca

St-David-de-Falardeau: **Bibliothèque publique Saint-David-de-Falardeau**
124, boul St-David, St-David-de-Falardeau, QC G0V 1C0
Tél: 418-673-6395
stdavid@reseaubibliosIsj.qc.ca
www.reseaubiblioduquebec.qc.ca
Francine Allard, Responsable

St-Dominique-du-Rosaire: **Bibliothèque de St-Dominique-du-Rosaire**
235, rue Principale, St-Dominique-du-Rosaire, QC J0Y 2K0
Tél: 819-727-4144; *Téléc:* 819-727-4344
dominique@reseaubiblioatnq.qc.ca
www.reseaubiblioduquebec.qc.ca/st-dominique
Marcelle Gravelle, Responsable
Lucie Mercier, Adjointe
Isabelle Payette, Adjointe

St-François-Xavier-de-Viger: **Bibliothèque de Saint-François-Xavier-de-Viger**
125A, rue Principale, St-François-Xavier-de-Viger, QC G0L 3C0
Tél: 418-868-6855
biblio.xavier@crsbp.net
www.reseaubiblioduquebec.qc.ca
Suzie Lemelin, Responsable

St-Jean-de-l'Ile-d'Orléans: **Bibliothèque Vents et Marées**
10, ch des Côtes, St-Jean-de-l'Ile-d'Orléans, QC G0A 3W0
Tél: 418-829-3336
info.ventsetmarees@gmail.com
Patrick Plante, Responsable

St-Laurent-de-l'Ile-d'Orléa: **Bibliothèque David-Gosselin/Saint-Laurent-de-l'Ile-d'Orléans**
#1, 1330, ch Royal, St-Laurent-de-l'Ile-d'Orléa, QC G0A 3Z0
Tél: 418-828-2529; *Téléc:* 418-828-2170
biblio@saintlaurentio.com
Guy Delisle, Responsable

St-Nazaire-d'Acton: **Bibliothèque municipale de St-Nazaire-d'Acton**
715, rue des Loisirs, St-Nazaire-d'Acton, QC G0R 3T0
Tél: 418-392-2090
nazaire@reseaubibliomonteregie.qc.ca
www.reseaubiblioduquebec.qc.ca
Média social: www.facebook.com/saintnazairedacton

St-Pierre-de-la-Riv.-du-Sud: **La Volumineuse**
620, rue Principale, St-Pierre-de-la-Riv.-du-Sud, QC G0R 4B0
Tél: 418-241-5396; *Téléc:* 418-241-1477
lavolumineuse@stpierrerivieresud.ca
www.reseaubiblioduquebec.qc.ca/saint-pierre-r-s

St-Stanislas: **Bibliothèque Saint-Stanislas (Émile-Bordeleau)**
33A, rue du Pont, St-Stanislas, QC G0X 3E0
Tél: 819-840-0703; *Téléc:* 418-328-4121
biblio002@reseaubibliocqlm.qc.ca
www.reseaubiblioduquebec.qc.ca

Stanbridge East: **Bibliothèque Denise-Larocque-Duhamel/ Denise Larocque Duhamel Library**
12A, rue Maple, Stanbridge East, QC J0J 2H0
Tél: 450-248-4662
stanbridge@reseaubibliomonteregie.qc.ca

Standon: **Bibliothèque l'Étincelle**
514B, rue Principale, Standon, QC G0R 4L0
Tél: 418-642-2708; *Téléc:* 418-642-2570
etincel@globetrotter.qc.ca
www.reseaubiblioduquebec.qc.ca/saint-leon

Stanstead: **Haskell Free Library Inc./ Bibliotheque Haskell**
1 Church St., Stanstead, QC J0B 3E2
Tel: 819-876-2471
Other Numbers: Derby Line Phone: 802-873-3022
haskellopera.com/library
Social Media: www.youtube.com/user/Haskell1901; www,facebook.com/218080494874390
Nancy Rumery, Director of Library, Head Librarian

Ste-Catherine-de-la-J-Carti: **Bibliothèque Anne-Hébert**
22, rue Louis-Jolliet, Ste-Catherine-de-la-J-Carti, QC G3N 2V3
Tél: 418-875-2758; *Téléc:* 418-875-2699
bibliotheque@villescjc.com
Média social: fr-ca.facebook.com/157324597630077

Ste-Geneviève-de-Batiscan: **Bibliothèque de Sainte-Geneviève-de-Batiscan (Clément-Marchand)**
91, rue de l'Église, Ste-Geneviève-de-Batiscan, QC G0X 2R0
Tél: 418-363-2078; *Téléc:* 418-362-2111
biblio036@reseaubibliocqlm.qc.ca

Ste-Geneviève-de-Berthier: **Bibliothèque de Sainte-Geneviève-de-Berthier (Léo-Paul-Desrosiers)**
391, rang de la Rivière-Bayonne sud, Ste-Geneviève-de-Berthier, QC J0K 1A0
Tél: 450-836-4333; *Téléc:* 450-836-7260
biblio066@reseaubibliocqlm.qc.ca
Mèdia social: www.facebook.com/biblioleopauldesrosiers
Jeannette Plourde, Responsable

Ste-Gertrude-Mannville: **Bibliothèque de Sainte-Gertrude**
391, rte 395, Ste-Gertrude-Mannville, QC J0Y 2L0
Tél: 819-727-2248; *Téléc:* 819-727-2244
gertrude@reseaubiblioatnq.qc.ca
Geneviève Michaud, Responsable

Ste-Hélène-de-Mancebourg: **Bibliothèque de Sainte-Hélène-de-Mancebourg**
459, ch des Rangs 2 et 3, Ste-Hélène-de-Mancebourg, QC J0Z 2T0
Tél: 819-333-4609; *Téléc:* 819-333-9591
mancebourg@reseaubiblioatnq.qc.ca
www.reseaubiblioduquebec.qc.ca
Ginette Fortin, Responsable

Ste-Jeanne-d'Arc: **Bibliothèque de Sainte-Jeanne-d'Arc**
207, rue Principale, Ste-Jeanne-d'Arc, QC G0J 2T0
Tél: 418-776-5814
biblio.jeanne@crsbp.net
www.reseaubiblioduquebec.qc.ca
Raymonde Lévesque, Responsable

Ste-Lucie-des-Laurentides: **Bibliothèque de Sainte-Lucie-des-Laurentides**
2057, ch des Hauteurs, Ste-Lucie-des-Laurentides, QC J0T 2J0
Tél: 819-326-3228; *Téléc:* 819-326-0592
biblio@municipalite.sainte-lucie-des-laurentides.qc.ca
www.municipalite.sainte-lucie-des-laurentides.qc.ca
Lorraine Beauchamp, Responsable

Ste-Marcelline-de-Kildare: **Bibliothèque de Sainte-Marcelline-de-Kildare (Bibliothèque Gisèle Labine)**
435, 1èr av Pied-de-la-Montagne, Ste-Marcelline-de-Kildare, QC J0K 2Y0
Tél: 450-883-0247; *Téléc:* 450-883-2242
biblio135@reseaubibliocqlm.qc.ca
Vanessa Arbour, Responsable

Ste-Marguerite-du-Lac-Masso: **Bibliothèque de Sainte-Marguerite-Estérel**
4, rue des Lilas, Ste-Marguerite-du-Lac-Masso, QC J0T 1L0
Tél: 450-228-4442; *Téléc:* 450-228-4442
biblio031@crsbpl.qc.ca

Joane Grandmaison, Responsable

Ste-Séraphine: **Bibliothèque de Sainte-Séraphine**
2660, rue Centre communautaire, Ste-Séraphine, QC J0A 1E0
Tél: 819-336-3222; *Téléc:* 819-336-3800
biblio085@reseaubibliocqlm.qc.ca

Ste-Thérèse-de-la-Gatineau: **Bibliothèque municipale de Sainte-Thérèse-de-la-Gatineau**
29, rue Principale, Ste-Thérèse-de-la-Gatineau, QC J0X 2X0
Tél: 819-449-7964
Julie Richard, Bibliothécaire

Stoneham: **Bibliothèque Jean-Luc-Grondin**
325, ch du Hibou, Stoneham, QC G0A 4P0
Tél: 418-848-2381; *Téléc:* 418-848-1748
mairie@villestoneham.com
Mèdia social: www.facebook.com/pages/Ville-de-Stoneham/107069949315255
Éliane Ouellet, Coordonnatrice
eouellet@villestoneham.com

Sutton: **Bibliothèque municipale de Sutton**
19, rue Highland, Sutton, QC J0E 2K0
Tél: 450-538-5843; *Téléc:* 450-538-4286
sutton@reseaubibliomonteregie.qc.ca
www.reseaubiblioduquebec.qc.ca
Lisa Charbonneau, Responsable

Tadoussac: **Bibliothèque municipale de Tadoussac**
162, des Jésuites, Tadoussac, QC G0T 2A0
Tél: 418-235-4446
www.tadoussac.com/fr/loisirs/bibliotheque-municipale-de-tadoussac
Johanne Hovington, Responsable

Taschereau: **Bibliothèque de Taschereau**
50B, rue Morin, Taschereau, QC J0Z 3N0
Tél: 819-796-2219; *Téléc:* 819-796-3226
taschereau@reseaubiblioatnq.qc.ca
www.reseaubiblioduquebec.qc.ca/taschereau
Francine Laplante, Responsable

Terrasse-Vaudreuil: **Bibliothèque Terrasse-Vaudreuil**
74, 7e av, Terrasse-Vaudreuil, QC J7V 3M9
Tél: 514-425-0430
Média social: www.facebook.com/bibliotv

Terrebonne: **Bibliothèque publique de Terrebonne**
3425, place Camus, Terrebonne, QC J6Y 1L2
Tél: 450-961-2001
www.ville.terrebonne.qc.ca/loisirs_bibliotheques-publiques.php
Céline Paquette, Coordonnatrice aux bibliothèques

Thetford Mines: **Bibliothèque de Black Lake**
499, rue St-Désiré, Thetford Mines, QC G6H 1L7
Tél: 418-423-4291

Thetford Mines: **Bibliothèque de l'Amitié**
#3, 5785, boul Frontenac est, Thetford Mines, QC G6H 4H8
Tél: 418-332-4548
biblioamitie@ville.thetfordmines.qc.ca
www.ville.thetfordmines.qc.ca

Thetford Mines: **Bibliothèque L'HIBOUCOU**
5, rue de la Fabrique, Thetford Mines, QC G6G 2N4
Tél: 418-335-6111
bibliolhiboucou@ville.thetfordmines.qc.ca
www.ville.thetfordmines.qc.ca

Thurso: **Bibliothèque de Thurso/Lochaber-Partie-Ouest/Lochaber**
341A, rue Victoria, Thurso, QC J0X 3B0
Tél: 819-985-2200; *Téléc:* 819-386-0134
biblio.thurso@mrcpapineau.com
Lysette Boyer, Responsable

Tingwick: **Bibliothèque de Tingwick**
1266, rue St-Joseph, Tingwick, QC J0A 1L0
Tél: 819-359-3225; *Téléc:* 819-359-2233
biblio083@reseaubibliocqlm.qc.ca
Maureen Martineau, Responsable

Tring-Jonction: **Bibliothèque Livre-en-train**
208, rue Principale, Tring-Jonction, QC G0N 1X0
Tél: 418-426-1500
www.reseaubiblioduquebec.qc.ca/tring-jonction
Média social: www.facebook.com/BibliothequeLivresentrain

Trois-Pistoles: **Bibliothèque Anne-Marie-D'Amours**
145, rue de l'Aréna, Trois-Pistoles, QC G0L 4K0
Tél: 418-851-2374; *Téléc:* 418-851-3567
www.ville-trois-pistoles.ca
Karen Dionne, Responsable
k.dionne@ville-trois-pistoles.ca
418-851-2374

Trois-Rives: **Bibliothèque de Saint-Joseph-de-Mékinac**
258, rue St-Joseph, Trois-Rives, QC G0X 2C0
Tél: 819-646-5686; *Téléc:* 819-646-5686
biblio034@reseaubibliocqlm.qc.ca
www.reseaubiblioduquebec.qc.ca
Georgette Doucet, Responsable

Trois-Rivières: **Bibliothèques de Trois-Rivières**
1425, place de l'Hôtel-de-Ville, Trois-Rivières, QC G9A 5L9
Tél: 819-372-4615
bglreference@v3r.net
www.biblio.v3r.net
Mèdia social: www.facebook.com/bibliothequesdetroisrivieres
Julie Moreau, Chef d'équipe
jmoreau@v3r.net
Odette Pelletier, Coordination, Services techniques
opelletier@v3r.net
819-372-4641 ext. 4251

Très-Saint-Rédempteur: **Bibliothèque municipale de Très-Saint-Rédempteur**
769, rte Principale, Très-Saint-Rédempteur, QC J0P 1P1
Tél: 450-451-5203
redempteur@reseaubibliomonteregie.qc.ca
www.reseaubiblioduquebec.qc.ca
Carolle Lalonde, Responsable

Témiscaming: **Bibliothèque de Témiscaming**
40, rue Boucher, Témiscaming, QC J0Z 3R0
Tél: 819-627-3273; *Téléc:* 819-627-3019
biblioTEM@hotmail.com
www.temiscaming.net/bibliotheque
Suzelle Plante, Responsable
Claudie Gaudet, Responsable écolière

Témiscouata-sur-le-Lac: **Bibliothèque Cabano**
34A, rue Vieux Chemin, Témiscouata-sur-le-Lac, QC G0L 1E0
Tél: 418-854-5568
biblio.cabano@crsbp.net
Huguette Nadeau, Responsable

Témiscouata-sur-le-Lac: **Bibliothèque Notre-Dame-du-Lac**
2448, rue Commerciale Sud, Témiscouata-sur-le-Lac, QC G0L 1X0
Tél: 418-899-6004
biblio.ndlac@crsbp.net
Suzanne Morin, Responsable

Tête-à-la-Baleine: **Bibliothèque municipale de Tête-à-la-Baleine**
Centre Communautaire, Tête-à-la-Baleine, QC G0G 2W0
Tél: 418-787-2244; *Téléc:* 418-787-2241
Olive Marcoux, Responsable

Upton: **Bibliothèque municipale d'Upton**
784, rue Saint-Éphrem, Upton, QC J0H 2E0
Tél: 450-549-4537
Francine Savoie, Responsable

Val-Alain: **Bibliothèque L'Hiboucou**
1298, rue de l'Église, Val-Alain, QC G0S 3H0
Tél: 418-744-3313; *Téléc:* 418-744-1330
hiboucou@globetrotter.qc.ca
val-alain.com/loisirs-et-culture/bibliotheque

Val-Brillant: **Bibliothèque Val-Brillant**
2, rue Champagnat, Val-Brillant, QC G0J 3L0
Tél: 418-742-3279
biblio.brillant@crsbp.net
Josée Lauzier, Responsable

Val-d'Espoir: **Bibliothèque de Val-d'Espoir**
1240, ch de Val d'Espoir, Val-d'Espoir, QC G0C 3G0
Tél: 418-782-2005

Val-d'Or: **Bibliothèque municipale de Val-d'Or**
600, 7e rue, Val-d'Or, QC J9P 3P3
Tél: 819-824-2666
www.ville.valdor.qc.ca
Brigitte Richard, Responsable
Élaine Gauthier, Bibliotechnicienne
819-824-2666 ext. 4226

Diane Naud, Bibliotechnicienne
819-824-2666 ext. 4221

Val-David: **Bibliothèque de Val-David**
1355, rue de l'Académie, Val-David, QC J0T 2N0
Tél: 819-324-5680; *Téléc:* 819-322-6327
bibliotheque@valdavid.com
www.valdavid.com/citoyens-loisirs-biblio.php

Val-des-Bois: **Bibliothèque de Val-des-Bois/Bowman**
593, rte 309, Val-des-Bois, QC J0X 3C0
Tél: 819-454-2280; *Téléc:* 819-454-2211
biblio.valdesbois@mrcpapineau.com
www.reseaubiblioduquebec.qc.ca/Val-des-Bois
Shirley Raymond, Responsable

Val-des-Lacs: **Bibliothèque Val-des-Lacs**
349, ch Val-des-Lacs, Val-des-Lacs, QC J0T 2P0
Tél: 819-326-5624; *Téléc:* 819-326-7065
bibliotheque@municipalite.val-des-lacs.qc.ca

Val-des-Monts: **Bibliothèque de Perkins (Val-des-Monts)**
17, ch du Manoir, Val-des-Monts, QC J8N 7E8
Tél: 819-671-1476; *Téléc:* 819-457-4141
admperkins@crsbpo.qc.ca
www.reseaubiblioduquebec.qc.ca/Perkins
Denise Cécyre, Responsable

Val-des-Monts: **Bibliothèque de Poltimore/Denholm (Val-des-Monts)**
2720, rte Principale, Val-des-Monts, QC J8N 3B6
Tél: 819-457-4467; *Téléc:* 819-457-4141
bibliopoltimore@crsbpo.qc.ca
www.reseaubiblioduquebec.qc.ca/Poltimore
France Landry, Responsable

Val-des-Monts: **Bibliothèque de Saint-Pierre-de-Wakefield (Val-des-Monts)**
24, ch du Parc, Val-des-Monts, QC J8N 4H8
Tél: 819-457-1911; *Téléc:* 819-457-9113
admstpierre@crsbpo.qc.ca
www.reseaubiblioduquebec.qc.ca/St-Pierre-de-Wakefield
Colette Prud'Homme, Responsable

Val-Morin: **Bibliothèque Francine Paquette**
6160, rue Morin, Val-Morin, QC J0T 2R0
Tél: 819-324-5672
biblio@val-morin.ca
www.reseaubiblioduquebec.qc.ca

Val-Saint-Gilles: **Bibliothèque de Val-Saint-Gilles**
801, rue Principale, Val-Saint-Gilles, QC J0Z 3T0
Tél: 819-333-5676; *Téléc:* 819-333-3116
gilles@reseaubiblioatnq.qc.ca
www.reseaubiblioduquebec.qc.ca
Média social: www.youtube.com/user/reseaubiblioatnq; www.facebook.com/335729189842131
Nicole Richer, Responsable

Valcourt: **Bibliothèque publique Yvonne L. Bombardier**
1002, av J.A. Bombardier, Valcourt, QC J0E 2L0
Tél: 450-532-2250
bylb@fjab.qc.ca
www.centreculturelbombardier.com/bibliotheque.htm
Média social: www.facebook.com/CentreCulturelBombardier
Karine Corbeil, Directrice

Varennes: **Bibliothèque Jacques-Lemoyne-de-Sainte-Marie**
2221, boul René-Gaultier, Varennes, QC J3X 1E3
Tél: 450-652-3949
biblio@ville.varennes.qc.ca
ville.varennes.qc.ca/activites-bibliotheque/bibliotheque
Michèle Lamoureux, Bibliothécaire

Vaudreuil-Dorion: **Bibliothèque municipale de Vaudreuil-Dorion**
51, rue Jeannotte, Vaudreuil-Dorion, QC J7V 6E6
Tél: 450-455-3371; *Téléc:* 450-455-5653
biblio@ville.vaudreuil-dorion.qc.ca
www.ville.vaudreuil-dorion.qc.ca
Média social: www.youtube.com/user/vaudreuildorioninfos; twitter.com/ville_vd; www.facebook.com/villevaudreuildorion
Michel Vallée, Directeur, Arts et Culture

Vendée: **Bibliothèque de Vendée**
1816, ch du Village, Vendée, QC J0T 2T0
Tél: 819-681-3372
bibliovendee@municipalite.amherst.qc.ca
www.reseaubiblioduquebec.qc.ca

Verchères: **Bibliothèque municipale-scolaire Dansereau-Larose**
36, rue Dalpé, Verchères, QC J0L 2R0
Tél: 450-583-3309; *Téléc:* 450-583-3637
biblio@ville.vercheres.qc.ca
www.reseaubiblioduquebec.qc.ca/vercheres

Victoriaville: **Bibliothèque publique de Victoriaville**
2, rue de l'Ermitage, Victoriaville, QC G6P 6T2
Tél: 819-758-8441; *Téléc:* 819-758-9432
bibliotheque@victoriaville.ca
www.ville.victoriaville.qc.ca/bibliotheque
Média social: www.facebook.com/175715469175682

Ville-Marie: **Bibliothèque Ville-Marie 'La Bouquine'**
50, rue Notre-Dame de Lourdes, Ville-Marie, QC J9V 1X9
Tél: 819-629-2881
villemarie@reseaubiblioatnq.qc.ca
Cécile Boily, Responsable

Villebois: **Bibliothèque de Villebois**
3889, rue de l'Église, Villebois, QC J0Z 3V0
Tél: 819-941-2040; *Téléc:* 819-941-2685
villebois@reseaubiblioatnq.qc.ca
www.reseaubiblioduquebec.qc.ca/villebois
Marie-Pierre Desbiens, Responsable
Nathalie Simard, Adjointe

Wakefield: **Wakefield Library/ Bibliothèque de Wakefield (La Pêche)**
38 Valley Dr., Wakefield, QC J0X 3G0
Tél: 819-459-3266; *Fax:* 819-459-8832
contact@wakefieldlibrary.ca
bibliowakefieldlibrary.ca

Warwick: **Bibliothèque de Warwick (P.-Rodolphe-Baril)**
181, rue St-Louis, Warwick, QC J0A 1M0
Tél: 819-358-4325; *Téléc:* 819-358-4326
bibliotheque@ville.warwick.qc.ca
www.ville.warwick.qc.ca/content/s2_bibliotheque.aspx
France Gendron, Responsable
Diane Provencher, Animatrice et commis

Waterloo: **Bibliothèque publique de Waterloo**
650, rue de la Cour, Waterloo, QC J0E 2N0
Tél: 450-539-2268
biblio@cacwaterloo.qc.ca

Weedon: **Bibliothèque Saint-Gérard**
#249A, rue Principale, Weedon, QC J0B 3J0
Tél: 819-877-5704
biblio024@reseaubiblioestrie.qc.ca

Wemotaci: **Bibliothèque de Wemotaci**
CP 222, Wemotaci, QC G0X 3R0
Tél: 819-666-2232; *Téléc:* 819-666-2233
biblio064@reseaubibliocqlm.qc.ca

Wentworth-Nord: **Bibliothèque de Wentworth-Nord**
3470, rte Principale, Wentworth-Nord, QC J0T 1Y0
Tél: 450-226-2416

Westmount: **Bibliothèque publique de Westmount**
4574, rue Sherbrooke ouest, Westmount, QC H3Z 1G1
Tél: 514-989-5299
Other Numbers: 514-989-5368 (Audiovisuel)
refdesk@westmount.org
www.westlib.org/library
Média social: www.facebook.com/bibliowestmount
Julie-Anne Cardella, Directrice
jacardella@westmount.org
514-989-5429
Wendy Wayling, Bibliothécaire des enfants
wwayling@westmount.org
514-989-5357
Benoît Morin, Bibliothécaire de référence
bmorin@westmount.org
514-989-5517

Wickham: **Bibliothèque de Wickham**
893, rue Moreau, Wickham, QC J0C 1S0
Tél: 819-741-0202
biblio154@reseaubibliocqlm.qc.ca
Pierrette Courchesne, Responsable

Windsor: **Bibliothèque municipale Patrick-Dignan de Windsor**
52, rue St-Georges, Windsor, QC J1S 1J5
Tél: 819-845-7888; *Téléc:* 819-845-5516
bibliwin@abacom.com
www.bibliotheque.windsor.qc.ca
Jacynthe Dubois, Technicienne en documentation
duboisj2@abacom.com

Wotton: **Bibliothèque Wotton**
#398 Mgr. l'Heureaux, Wotton, QC J0A 1N0
Tél: 819-828-0693; *Téléc:* 819-828-3594
biblio055@reseaubiblioestrie.qc.ca

Yamachiche: **Bibliothèque de Yamachiche (J.-Alide-Pellerin)**
440, rue Sainte-Anne, Yamachiche, QC G0X 3L0
Tél: 819-296-3580; *Téléc:* 819-296-3542
biblio020@reseaubibliocqlm.qc.ca
Média social: www.facebook.com/117341625021483

Archives

Alma: **Société d'histoire du Lac-Saint-Jean**
1671, av du Pont nord, Alma, QC G8B 5G2
Tél: 418-668-2606; *Téléc:* 418-668-5851
Ligne sans frais: 866-668-2606
info@shlsj.org
www.shlsj.org
Média social: www.facebook.com/OdysseeDesBatisseurs
Allyson D'Amours, Archiviste et directrice
adamours@shlsj.org
418-668-2606 ext. 231

Amos: **Société d'histoire d'Amos**
Édifice de la Maison de la culture, 222, 1re av est, Amos, QC J9T 1H3
Tél: 819-732-6070
societe.histoire@cableamos.com
www.societehistoireamos.com
Média social: www.youtube.com/c/societehistoireamos1980; twitter.com/SHistoireAmos; www.facebook.com/societehistoireamos
Guillaume Trottier, Archiviste responsable

Baie-Comeau: **Société historique de la Côte-Nord**
2, place La Salle, Baie-Comeau, QC G4Z 1K3
Tél: 418-296-8228; *Téléc:* 418-294-4187
shcn@globetrotter.net
www.shcote-nord.org
Média social: www.facebook.com/215657145115493
Raphaël Hovington, Président
raphael.hovington@cgocable.ca
Marc Champagne, Vice-Président
marcus_spartacus@hotmail.com
Hélène Grenier, Secrétaire
gre-co@globetrotter.net
Catherine Pellerin, Archiviste
catherine.pellerin@shcote-nord.org

Baie-Comeau: **Ville de Baie-Comeau**
2, place La Salle, Baie-Comeau, QC G4Z 1K3
Tél: 418-296-8298; *Téléc:* 418-296-8120
Annick Tremblay, Greffière
antremblay@ville.baie-comeau.qc.ca

Chambly: **Société d'histoire de la Seigneurie de Chambly**
2445, rue Bourgogne, Chambly, QC J3L 2A5
Tél: 450-658-2666
shsc@societehistoirechambly.org
www.societehistoirechambly.org
Paul-Henri Hudon, Président

Chicoutimi: **Evêché de Chicoutimi**
602, rue Racine Est, Chicoutimi, QC G7H 1V1
Tél: 418-543-0783; *Téléc:* 418-543-2141
diocese.chicoutimi@evechedechicoutimi.qc.ca
www.evechedechicoutimi.qc.ca

Chicoutimi: **Séminaire de Chicoutimi**
679, rue Chabanel, Chicoutimi, QC G7H 1Z7
Tél: 418-549-0190; *Téléc:* 418-549-1524
www.sdec.qc.ca

Chicoutimi: **Société historique du Saguenay**
930, rue Jacques Cartier est, Chicoutimi, QC G7H 7K9
Tél: 418-549-2805; *Téléc:* 418-698-3758
shs@shistoriquesaguenay.com
www.shistoriquesaguenay.com
Laurent Thibeault, Directeur général
Myriam Gilbert, Archiviste

Gaspé: **Centre d'archives du Musée de la Gaspésie**
80, boul de Gaspé, Gaspé, QC G4X 1A9
Tel: 418-368-1534; *Fax:* 418-368-1535
www.museedelagaspesie.ca/fr
Social Media: www.youtube.com/user/musee1534; twitter.com/MG1534; facebook.com/pages/Musée-de-la-Gaspésie/110724575624365s

***Gatineau:* Archives municipales de la Ville de Gatineau**
855, boul de la Gappe, Gatineau, QC J8T 8H9
Tél: 819-243-2329
www.ville.gatineau.qc.ca/archives/

***Gatineau:* Western Québec School Board**
15, rue Katimavik, Gatineau, QC J9J 0E9
Tel: 819-864-2336; *Fax:* 819-684-1328
Toll-Free: 800-363-9111
wqsb@wqsb.qc.ca
cswq.wqsb.qc.ca

***Granby:* Société d'histoire de la Haute-Yamaska**
135, rue Principale, Granby, QC J2G 2V1
Tél: 450-372-4500
info@shhy.org
www.shhy.info/fonds-et-collections-d-archives
Johanne Rochon, Directrice générale
johanne.rochon@shhy.info
Mario Gendron, Historien
mario.gendron@shhy.info

***Jonquière:* La Commission scolaire de la Jonquière**
1955, rue Bourassa, Jonquière, QC G7X 4E1
Tél: 418-695-1801; *Téléc:* 418-695-2549
gdocuments@csjonquiere.qc.ca
www.csjonquiere.qc.ca
Christian St-Gelais, Directeur

***Knowlton:* Brome County Historical Society**
130, ch Lakeside, Knowlton, QC J0E 1V0
Tel: 450-243-6782
www.bromemuseum.com
Arlene Royea, Managing Director

***La Pocatière:* Evêché de Sainte-Anne-de-la-Pocatière**
#1200, 4, av Painchaud, La Pocatière, QC G0R 1Z0
Tél: 418-856-1811; *Téléc:* 418-856-5863
www.diocese-ste-anne.net

***La Pocatière:* Société historique de la Côte-du-Sud**
100, 4e av Painchaud, La Pocatière, QC G0R 1Z0
Tél: 418-856-2104; *Téléc:* 418-856-2104
archsud@bellnet.ca
www.shcds.org
Mèdia social: www.facebook.com/shcds
François Taillon, Directeur, Centre des archives

***La Prairie:* Archives des Frères de l'Instruction chrétienne**
870, ch de Saint-Jean, La Prairie, QC J5R 2L5
Tél: 450-659-1922
www.provincejdlm.com/Archives.htm
François Boutin, Archiviste
boutinf@jdlm.qc.ca

***La Prairie:* Société d'histoire de La Prairie de la Magdeleine**
249, rue Sainte-Marie, La Prairie, QC J5R 1G1
Tél: 450-659-1393
info@shlm.info
www.shlm.info
Johanne Doyle, Coordonnatrice

***Lachine:* Musée de Lachine**
1, ch du Musée, Lachine, QC H8S 4L9
Tél: 514-634-3478; *Téléc:* 514-637-6784
museedelachine@ville.montreal.qc.ca
lachine.ville.montreal.qc.ca/musee
Média social: www.flickr.com/photos/132134993@N02;
www.facebook.com/museedelachine

***Laval:* Société d'histoire et de généalogie de l'Ile Jésus**
4300, boul Samson, Laval, QC H7W 2G9
Tél: 450-681-9096; *Téléc:* 450-686-8270
info-cal@shgij.org
www.shgij.org
Dominique Bodeven, Directrice générale
Catherine Dugas, Archiviste

***Lennoxville:* Lennoxville-Ascot Historical & Museum Society**
9 Speid St., Lennoxville, QC J1M 1Z3
Tel: 819-564-0409; *Fax:* 819-564-8951
info@uplands.ca
www.uplands.ca/centre/?q=en/historyoflahms
Nancy Robert, Director

***Longueuil:* Soeurs des Saints Noms de Jésus et de Marie, Longueuil**
80, rue Saint-Charles est, Longueuil, QC J4H 1A9
Tél: 450-651-8104
centremarie-rose@yahoo.ca
www.snjm.qc.ca

***Magog:* Société d'histoire du Lac Memphrémagog/ Historic Society of Lake Memphremagog**
#002, 95, rue Merry nord, Magog, QC J1X 2E7
Tél: 819-868-6779
info@histoiremagog.com
www.histoiremagog.com
Média social: facebook.com/SocieteDhistoireDeMagog
Christine Marchand, Archiviste

***Montréal:* The Archive of the Jesuits in Canada/ Archives des jésuites au Canada**
25, rue Jarry ouest, Montréal, QC H2P 1S6
Tel: 514-387-2541; *Fax:* 514-387-5637
archives@jesuites.org
www.jesuites.org/archives
Theresa Rowat, Director
Sylvain Bouchard, Librarian
sbouchard@jesuites.org
Jacques Monet, Historian
Jasmin Miville Allard, Contact, Art Collection

***Montréal:* Archives de Montréal**
#108R, 275 rue Notre-Dame est, Montréal, QC H2Y 1C6
Tél: 514-872-2615; *Téléc:* 514-872-3475
consultation_archives@ville.montreal.qc.ca
www.archivesdemontreal.com
Mèdia social: www.youtube.com/user/ArchivesMtl;
twitter.com/Archives_Mtl; www.facebook.com/ArchivesMontreal
Suzanne Galaise, Directrice générale

***Montréal:* Les archives gais du Québec/ The Quebec Gay Archives**
#103, 1000 rue Amherst, Montréal, QC H2L 3K4
Tél: 514-287-9987
www.agq.qc.ca
Mèdia social: www.facebook.com/189505941096316

***Montréal:* Bank of Montreal**
129, rue Saint-Jacques, étage D, Montréal, QC H2Y 1L6
Tel: 514-877-6810; *Fax:* 514-877-7341

***Montréal:* Bell Canada/ Le Service de la documentation historique**
6055 Monkland Ave., 2nd Fl., Montréal, QC H4A 1H3
Tel: 514-870-5214; *Fax:* 514-484-4429
Lise Noël, Manager, Historical Records & Artifacts
lise.noel@bell.ca

***Montréal:* Canadian Jewish Congress, Charities Committee/ Congrès juif canadien, Comité des charités**
1590, av Docteur Penfield, Montréal, QC H3G 1C5
Tel: 514-931-7531
archives@cjarchives.ca
www.cjccc.ca
Norma Joseph, Chair, CJCCC National Archives
Janice Rosen, Director, CJCCC National Archives

***Montréal:* La Compagnie de Jésus Province du Canada français**
25, rue Jarry Ouest, Montréal, QC H2P 1S6
Tél: 514-387-2541; *Téléc:* 450-387-5637
www.jesuites.org

***Montréal:* Concordia University Archives**
Hall Bldg., #H1015, 1455, boul de Maisonneuve ouest, Montréal, QC H3G 1M8
Tel: 514-848-2424; *Fax:* 514-848-2857
archives@concordia.ca
www.concordia.ca/offices/archives.html
Marie-Pierre Aubé, Director, Records Management & Archives
Marie-Pierre.Aube@concordia.ca
514-848-2424 ext. 7776
Nathalie Hodgson, Lead, Historical Archives
Nathalie.Hodgson@concordia.ca
514-848-2424 ext. 5851
Rachel Marion, Archivist/Records Officer, Records Management
Rachel.Marion@concordia.ca
514-848-2424 ext. 3487

***Montréal:* Congrégation de Notre-Dame de Montréal**
2330, rue Sherbrooke ouest, Montréal, QC H3H 1G8
Tél: 514-931-5891; *Téléc:* 514-931-2915
archivesvirtuelles@cnd-m.org
Marie-Josée Morin, Coordinnatrice du service des archives
mjmorin@cnd-m.org

***Montréal:* Congrégation de Ste-Croix, Montréal**
4994, ch Côte-des-Neiges, Montréal, QC H3V 1A4
Tél: 514-735-1526; *Téléc:* 514-735-7813
archivescsc@religieuxcsc.qc.ca
www.ste-croix.qc.ca/index.php
Marie-Josée Vadnais, Archiviste
514-735-1526 ext. 420

***Montréal:* Frères de St Gabriel, Province de Montréal**
1601, boul Gouin est, Montréal, QC H2C 1C2
Tél: 514-387-7337; *Téléc:* 514-387-0735
www.saintgabriel.ca

***Montréal:* The Montréal Gazette**
#200, 1010, rue Ste-Catherine ouest, Montréal, QC H3B 5L1
Tel: 514-987-2583; *Fax:* 514-987-2399
library@thegazette.canwest.com
www.montrealgazette.com/index.html
Social Media: twitter.com/mtlgazette;
www.facebook.com/montrealgazette

***Montréal:* Montréal Holocaust Memorial Centre/ Centre commémoratif de l'holocauste à Montréal**
Cummings House, 5151, ch de la Côte-Sainte-Catherine, Montréal, QC H3W 1M6
Tel: 514-345-2605; *Fax:* 514-344-2651
info@mhmc.ca
www.mhmc.ca
Social Media: www.facebook.com/78382729139
Alice Herscovitch, Executive Director

***Montréal:* Musée du Château Ramezay Museum**
280, rue Notre-Dame est, Montréal, QC H2Y 1C5
Tél: 514-861-3708; *Téléc:* 514-861-8317
info@chateauramezay.qc.ca
www.chateauramezay.qc.ca
André Delisle, Directeur général et conservateur

***Montréal:* Musée McCord/ McCord Museum**
690, rue Sherbrooke ouest, Montréal, QC H3A 1E9
Tel: 514-398-7100; *Fax:* 514-398-5045
reference.mccord@mccord-stewart.ca
www.musee-mccord.qc.ca
Christian Vachon, Chef, Gestion des collections
Cynthia Cooper, Chef, Collections et recherche et Conservatrice
Céline Widmer, Conservatrice, Histoire et archives
Hélène Samson, Conservatrice, Archives photographiques Notman

***Montréal:* Oratoire Saint-Joseph**
3800, ch Queen Mary, Montréal, QC H3V 1H6
Tél: 514-733-8211
archives@osj.qc.ca
www.saint-joseph.org/fr/services-complementaires/archives

***Montréal:* Pères Dominicains, Montréal**
2715, ch. de la Côte-Sainte-Catherine, Montréal, QC H3T 1B6
Tél: 514-341-2244; *Téléc:* 514-341-3233
www.dominicains.ca

***Montréal:* Port de Montréal/ Port of Montreal**
Édifice du port de Montréal, 2100, av Pierre-Dupuy, aile 1, Montréal, QC H3C 3R5
Tél: 514-283-7011; *Téléc:* 514-283-0829
info@port-montreal.com
www.port-montreal.com

***Montréal:* Religious Hospitallers of St. Joseph, St Joseph Province**
245, av des Pins ouest, Montréal, QC H2W 1R5
Tel: 514-735-6585
contact@rhsj.org
www.rhsj.org

***Montréal:* Séminaire de Saint-Sulpice de Montréal**
116, rue Notre-Dame ouest, Montréal, QC H2Y 1T2
Tél: 514-849-6561; *Téléc:* 514-286-9021
ucss.archives@sulpc.org
www.sulpc.org/sulpc_univers_culturel_archives_en.php
Marc Lacasse, Archiviste, Coordinateur du service

***Montréal:* Soeurs Grises de Montréal**
138, rue Saint-Pierre, Montréal, QC H2Y 2L7
Tél: 514-842-9411; *Téléc:* 514-842-0142
asscong@sgm.ca
www.sgm.qc.ca

***Montréal:* Vidéographe inc**
4550, rue Garnier, Montréal, QC H2J 3S7
Tél: 514-521-2116; *Téléc:* 514-521-1676
info@videographe.qc.ca
www.videographe.qc.ca
Média social: twitter.com/Videographe;
www.facebook.com/pages/Vidéographe/124501969721

Julie Tremble, Directrice générale
direction@videographe.org
Karine Boulanger, Conservatrice
collection@videographe.org
Denis Vaillancourt, Coordonnateur de la distribution
distribution@videographe.org

Nicolet: Séminaire de Nicolet
645, boul Louis-Fréchette, Nicolet, QC J3T 1L6
Tél: 819-293-4838; *Téléc:* 819-293-4543
seminairedenicolet@sogetel.net
archivesseminairenicolet.wordpress.com

Nicolet: Les Soeurs de l'Assomption de la Sainte-Vierge
160, rue du carmel, Nicolet, QC J3T 1Z8
Tél: 819-293-2011
archives.sasv@sogetel.net
sasv.ca

Isabelle Périgny, Archiviste

Oka: Société d'histoire d'Oka
2017, ch d'Oka, Oka, QC J0N 1E0
Tél: 450-479-8556
www.histoiredoka.ca

Oka: Tsi Ronterihwanonhnha ne Kanienkeha/ Kanehsatake Resource Centre
14A, rue Joseph Swan, RR#1, Oka, QC J0N 1E0
Tél: 450-479-1651

Outremont: Fondation Lionel-Groulx
261, av Bloomfield, Outremont, QC H2V 3R6
Tél: 514-271-4759; *Téléc:* 514-271-6369
www.fondationlionelgroulx.org
Média social: www.youtube.com/user/fondlionelgroulx; twitter.com/fondlgroulx; www.facebook.com/fondationlionelgroulx
Pierre Graveline, Directeur général

Pierrefonds: Montréal Arrondissement Pierrefonds/Roxboro
13665, boul Pierrefonds, Pierrefonds, QC H9A 2Z4
Tél: 514-624-1011; *Fax:* 514-624-1300

Pointe-Claire: Canadian Ski Hall of Fame & Museum
317, ch du Bord-du-Lac, Pointe-Claire, QC H9S 4L6
Tel: 514-429-8444
info@skimuseum.ca
www.skimuseum.ca
Social Media: facebook.com/pages/Canadian-Ski-Museum/59397511258; www.linkedin.com/groups/Canadian-Ski-Hall-Fame-Museum-4174287

Stephen Finestone, Chair

Québec: Les Archives de la Ville de Québec
350, rue St-Joseph est, 4e étage, Québec, QC G1K 3B2
Tél: 418-641-6214
archives@ville.quebec.qc.ca
www.ville.quebec.qc.ca/culture_patrimoine/archives

Québec: Archives des Augustines du Monastère de l'Hôpital Général de Québec
260, boul Langelier, Québec, QC G1K 5N1
Tél: 418-529-0931
www.augustines.ca

Juliette Cloutier, Archiviste
418-529-0931 ext. 217

Québec: Centrale des syndicats du Québec
#100, 320, rue St-Joseph est, Québec, QC G1K 9E7
Tél: 418-649-8888; *Téléc:* 418-649-8800
Ligne sans frais: 877-850-0897
www.csq.qc.net

François Gagnon, Conseiller
gagnon.francois@lacsq.org
418-649-8888 ext. 3146

Québec: Église catholique de Québec
3, rue de la Vieille-Université, Québec, QC G1R 5K1
Tél: 418-688-1211
archives@ecdq.org
archivesacrq.org

Pierre Lafontaine, Archiviste diocésain
pierre.lafontaine@ecdq.org

Québec: Monastère des Augustines de l'Hôtel-Dieu de Québec
75, rue des Remparts, Québec, QC G1R 3R9
Tél: 418-780-4800; *Téléc:* 418-692-2668
Ligne sans frais: 855-780-4800
info@augustines.ca
www.augustines.ca

Québec: Musée de la Civilisation
85, rue Dalhousie, Québec, QC G1K 8R2
Tél: 418-643-2158; *Ligne sans frais:* 866-710-8031
renseignements@mcq.org
www.mcq.org
Média social: www.facebook.com/museedelacivilisation

Québec: Musée du Royal 22e Régiment/ Museum of the Royal 22e Régiment
La Citadelle, 1, Côte de la Citadelle, Québec, QC G1R 4V7
Tel: 418-694-2815; *Fax:* 418-694-2853
information@lacitadelle.qc.ca
www.lacitadelle.qc.ca
Social Media: www.youtube.com/user/museeroyal; www.facebook.com/193043460745807

Marie-Hélène St-Cyr Prémont, Archiviste
archives@lacitadelle.qc.ca
418-694-2800 ext. 2885
Miriam Schurman, Archiviste des collections
collections@lacitadelle.qc.ca
418-694-2800 ext. 2744

Québec: Pères Eudistes
6125, 1re av, Québec, QC G1H 2V9
Tél: 418-626-6494
archives.eudistes@eudistes.org
www.eudistes.org/French/archives_eudistes.html
André Samson, Coordonnateur du service

Québec: Religieux de St-Vincent-de-Paul (Canada)
2555, ch Ste-Foy, Québec, QC G1V 1T8
Tél: 418-650-3441
info@r-s-v.org
relsv.qc.ca

Québec: Société d'histoire de Sainte-Foy
Centre communautaire Claude-Allard, #107-1, 3200, av D'Amours, Québec, QC G1X 1L9
Tél: 418-641-6301
histoiresaintefoy@gmail.com
www.societeshistoirequebec.qc.ca

Alain Côté, Président
418-641-6301 ext. 4082

Québec: Soeurs de Saint-Joseph-de-Saint-Vallier, Québec
560, ch Sainte-Foy, Québec, QC G1S 2J6
Tél: 418-681-7361
info@patrimoine-religieux.com

Québec: Soeurs Servantes du Saint-Coeur-de-Marie, Québec
30, av des Cascades, Québec, QC G1E 2J8
Tél: 418-663-6280
archivesscm@qc.aira.com
www.soeurs-sscm.org

Québec: Soeurs Ursulines de Québec
1358, rue Barrin, Québec, QC G1S 2G8
Tél: 418-692-2523
archives@vmuq.com
www.ursulines-uc.com

Repentigny: Commission scolaire des Affluents, Affaires corporatives et gestion de l'information
80, rue Jean-Baptiste-Meilleur, Repentigny, QC J6A 6C5
Tél: 450-492-9400; *Téléc:* 450-492-3720
www.csaffluents.qc.ca

Marie-Josée Lorion, Secrétaire général et directeur des communications
marie-josee.lorion@csda.ca
450-492-9400 ext. 1310

Richelieu: Oblats de Marie Immaculée
#600, 460, 1re rue, Richelieu, QC J3L 4B5
Tél: 450-658-8761
info@archivesdndc.com
www.omi-qc-on.com
Elaine Sirois, Archiviste et directrice

Rimouski: Archevêché de Rimouski
34, rue de l'Évêché ouest, Rimouski, QC G5L 4H5
Tél: 418-723-3320; *Téléc:* 418-722-8978
www.dioceserimouski.com/ch/diocese.html

Sylvain Gosselin, Archiviste
diocriki@globetrotter.net

Rivière-du-Loup: Commission scolaire de Kamouraska - Rivière du Loup
464, rue Lafontaine, Rivière-du-Loup, QC G5R 3Z5
Tél: 418-862-8201; *Téléc:* 418-862-0964
www.cskamloup.qc.ca
Média social: twitter.com/cskamloup; www.facebook.com/cskamloup.qc.ca

Saint-Hyacinthe: Centre d'histoire de Saint-Hyacinthe
650, rue Girouard est, Saint-Hyacinthe, QC J2S 2W2
Tél: 450-774-0203; *Téléc:* 450-250-8127
infos@chsth.com
www.chsth.com
Média social: twitter.com/histoiredemaska; facebook.com/histoiremaskoutaine

Luc Cordeau, Archiviste
Luc Cordeau, Archiviste

Saint-Jean-sur-Richelieu: Société d'histoire du Haut-Richelieu
203, rue Jacques Cartier nord, Saint-Jean-sur-Richelieu, QC J3B 6Z4
Tél: 450-358-5220
shhr@qc.aira.com
www.genealogie.org/club/shhr
Nicole Poulin, Présidente

Saint-Joseph-de-Beauce: Société du patrimoine des Beaucerons/ Beauce Historical Society
#400, 139, rue Sainte-Christine, Saint-Joseph-de-Beauce, QC G0S 2V0
Tel: 418-397-6379; *Fax:* 418-397-6379
spb@axion.ca
www.spbbeauce.ca

Saint-Jérome: Commission scolaire de la Rivière-du-Nord
795, rue Melançon, Saint-Jérome, QC J7Z 4L1
Tél: 450-438-3131
archives@csrdn.qc.ca
www.csrdn.qc.ca

Saint-Laurent: Arrondissement de Saint-Laurent
777, boul Marcel-Laurin, Saint-Laurent, QC H4M 2M7
Tel: 514-855-6000; *Fax:* 514-855-5939

Saint-Laurent: Soeurs de Sainte-Croix, Saint-Laurent
900, boul de la cote-Vertu, Saint-Laurent, QC H4L 1Y4
Tél: 514-747-0100

Sainte-Agathe-des-Monts: Commission scolaire des Laurentides
13, rue Sainte-Antoine, Sainte-Agathe-des-Monts, QC J8C 2C3
Tél: 819-326-0333; *Téléc:* 819-326-2121
info@cslaurentides.qc.ca
www.cslaurentides.qc.ca

Sainte-Anne-de-Beaupré: Pères rédemptoristes, Sainte-Anne-de Beaupré
10018, av Royale, Sainte-Anne-de-Beaupré, QC G0A 3C0
Tél: 418-827-4629
info@redemptoristes.ca
www.redemptoristes.ca

Shawinigan: Commission scolaire de l'Énergie
2072, rue Gignac, Shawinigan, QC G9N 6V7
Tél: 819-539-6971; *Téléc:* 819-539-7797
Ligne sans frais: 888-711-0013
cse@csenergie.qc.ca
www.csenergie.qc.ca

Sherbrooke: Archevêché de Sherbrooke
130, rue de la Cathédrale, Sherbrooke, QC J1H 4M1
Tél: 819-563-9934; *Téléc:* 819-562-0125
www.diosher.org

Sherbrooke: Commission scolaire de la Région-de-Sherbrooke
2955, boul de l'Université, Sherbrooke, QC J1K 2Y3
Tél: 819-822-5540; *Téléc:* 819-822-5530
www.csrs.qc.ca
Média social: twitter.com/cssherbrooke; facebook.com/CSsherbrooke

Sherbrooke: Société d'histoire de Sherbrooke
275, rue Dufferin, Sherbrooke, QC J1H 4M5
Tél: 819-821-5406; *Téléc:* 819-821-5417
info@histoiresherbrooke.com
www.histoiresherbrooke.com

Karine Savary, Archiviste
karine.savary@histoiresherbrooke.org

Sorel-Tracy: Société historique Pierre-de-Saurel inc
6A, rue Saint-Pierre, Sorel-Tracy, QC J3P 3S2
Tél: 450-780-5739; *Téléc:* 450-780-5743
histoire.archives@shps.qc.ca
www.shps.qc.ca
Média social: www.facebook.com/shpierre.de.saurel
Luc Poirier, Président du Conseil d'Administration

Stanbridge East: **Missisquoi Historical Society**
Cornell Bldg., Missisquoi Museum, 2, rue River, Stanbridge East, QC J0J 2H0
Tel: 450-248-3153
info@missisquoimuseum.ca
www.museemissisquoi.ca
Rolande Laduke, Archivist
rladuke@missisquoimuseum.ca
450-248-3153
Heather Darch, Curator
hdarch@museemissisquoi.ca
450-248-3153

Stanstead: **Stanstead Historical Society/ Société historique de Stanstead**
535 Dufferin St., Stanstead, QC J0B 3E0
Tel: 819-876-7322; *Fax:* 819-876-7936
info@colbycurtis.ca
colbycurtis.ca/shs/archives.php
Chloe Southam, Director/Curator
chloe@colbycurtis.ca

Thetford Mines: **Société des archives historiques de la région de l'Amiante**
671, boul Frontenac ouest, Thetford Mines, QC G6G 1N1
Tél: 418-338-8591; *Téléc:* 418-338-3498
archives@cegepth.qc.ca
www.sahra.qc.ca
Mèdia social: www.facebook.com/100320283355855
Stéphane Hamann, Directeur - Archiviste
Patrick Houde, Archiviste-Historien

Trois-Rivières: **Evêché de Trois-Rivières**
362, rue Bonaventure, Trois-Rivières, QC G9A 5J9
Tél: 819-374-1432; *Téléc:* 819-375-6382
archives@evechetr.org
diocese-trois-rivieres.org
Denise Maltais, Archiviste
819-379-1432 ext. 2308

Trois-Rivières: **Sanctuaire Notre-Dame du Cap**
626, rue Notre-Dame est, Trois-Rivières, QC G8T 4G9
Tél: 819-374-2441
sanctuaire-ndc.ca
Mèdia social: www.facebook.com/193784683998487

Trois-Rivières: **Soeurs Ursulines, Trois-Rivières**
784, rue des Ursulines, Trois-Rivières, QC G9A 5B5
Tel: 819-375-7922; *Fax:* 819-375-0238
info@musee-ursulines.qc.ca
www.ursulines-uc.com/le-musee-des-ursulines-de-trois-rivieres

Trois-Rivières: **Ville de Trois-Rivières**
1325 place de l'Hôtel-de-Ville, Trois-Rivières, QC G9A 5H3
Tél: 819-372-4647; *Téléc:* 819-372-4648
archives@v3r.net
www.laville.v3r.net

Val-d'Or: **Société d'histoire et de généalogie de Val-d'Or**
600, 7e rue, Val-d'Or, QC J9P 3P3
Tél: 819-825-6352; *Téléc:* 819-825-3062
shvd@ville.valdor.qc.ca
www.telebecinternet.com/histoirevd/

Victoriaville: **Commission scolaire des Bois-Francs**
40, boul Bois-Francs, Victoriaville, QC G6P 6S5
Tél: 819-758-6453; *Téléc:* 819-758-2613
bulletin@csbf.qc.ca
www.csbf.qc.ca
Michael Provencher, Secrétariat général

Westmount: **Avataq Cultural Institute**
#360, 4150, rue Ste-Catherine ouest, Westmount, QC H3Z 2Y5
Tel: 514-989-9031; *Fax:* 514-989-8789
Toll-Free: 800-361-5029
avataq@avataq.qc.ca
www.avataq.qc.ca

Saskatchewan

Regional Systems

Moose Jaw: **Palliser Regional Library**
366 Coteau St. West, Moose Jaw, SK S6H 5C9
Tel: 306-693-3669; *Fax:* 306-692-5657
palliser@palliserlibrary.ca
www.palliserlibrary.ca
Social Media: twitter.com/PalliserLibrary
Jan Smith, Director & Systems Librarian
Arwen Rudolph, Rural Branch Supervisor
Wanda Burton, Office Manager
Melissa Silzer-Frank, Contact, Technical Support
Jackie Bochek, Contact, Interlibrary Loan

North Battleford: **Lakeland Library Region**
1302 - 100th St., North Battleford, SK S9A 0V8
Tel: 306-445-6108; *Fax:* 306-445-5717
info@lakeland.lib.sk.ca
www.lakeland.lib.sk.ca
Social Media: twitter.com/LakelandLR;
www.facebook.com/lakelandlibraryregion
Eleanor Crumblehulme, Director
ecrumblehulme@lakeland.lib.sk.ca
306-445-6108 ext. 222
Lane Jackson, Rural Branch Supervisor
ljackson@lakeland.lib.sk.ca
306-445-6108 ext. 230
Jacky Bauer, Business/HR Manager
jbauer@lakeland.lib.sk.ca
306-445-6108 ext. 228

Prince Albert: **Wapiti Regional Library**
145 - 12th St. East, Prince Albert, SK S6V 1B7
Tel: 306-764-0712; *Fax:* 306-922-1516
wapiti@wapitilibrary.ca
www.wapitilibrary.ca
Social Media: pinterest.com/wapitiregion;
twitter.com/WapitiLibrary; www.facebook.com/wapitilibrary
Tony Murphy, Regional Director/CEO
director@wapitilibrary.ca

La Ronge: **Pahkisimon Nuyeáh Library System**
118 Avro Pl., La Ronge, SK S0J 1L0
Tel: 306-425-4525; *Fax:* 306-425-4572
Toll-Free: 866-396-8818
pnlsoffice@pnls.lib.sk.ca
www.pnls.lib.sk.ca
Social Media: www.facebook.com/pahkisimon
Audrey Mark, Director
ae.mark@pnls.lib.sk.ca
Graham Guest, Archival Historian
archives@pnls.lib.sk.ca
Harriet Roy, Assistant Director
hroy@pnls.lib.sk.ca
Allan Johnson, CEO & Library Director
ajohnson@southeastlibrary.ca

Saskatoon: **Wheatland Regional Library**
806 Duchess St., Saskatoon, SK S7K 0R3
Tel: 306-652-5077; *Fax:* 306-931-7611
Toll-Free: 866-652-5077
branchmanager@wheatland.sk.ca
www.wheatland.sk.ca
Social Media: twitter.com/WheatlandRL;
www.facebook.com/WheatlandRegionalLibrary
Gayle Brown, Chair

Swift Current: **Chinook Regional Library**
1240 Chaplin St. West, Swift Current, SK S9H 0G8
Tel: 306-773-3186; *Fax:* 306-773-0434
chinook@chinook.lib.sk.ca
www.chinooklibrary.ca
Heather Walker, Director

Weyburn: **Southeast Regional Library**
49 Bison Ave., Weyburn, SK S4H 0H9
Tel: 306-848-3100; *Fax:* 306-842-2665
library.srl@southeastlibrary.ca
www.southeastlibrary.ca
Social Media:
www.youtube.com/channel/UC-I7YqMlgrmvrdWXzYPONXg;
twitter.com/srlhq; www.facebook.com/229926867063700

Yorkton: **Parkland Regional Library**
PO Box 5049, Yorkton, SK S3N 3Z4
Tel: 706-783-7022; *Fax:* 306-782-2844
parklandlibrary.ca

Public Libraries

Air Ronge: **Senator Myles Venne School / Public Library**
Box 268, Air Ronge, SK S0J 3G0
Tel: 306-425-2478; *Fax:* 306-425-2815
smvs10@sasktel.net
www.llribschools.ca/smvs.html
Edna Mirasty, Librarian
306-425-2478
Betsy Dorion, Library Assistant

Alameda: **Alameda Branch Library**
200 - 5th St., Alameda, SK S0C 0A0
Tel: 306-489-2066
alameda@southeast.lib.sk.ca
www.southeast.lib.sk.ca
Dee Anne Schiestel, Chair
Diane Miller, Librarian

Arcola: **Arcola Branch Library**
127 Main St., Arcola, SK S0C 0G0
Tel: 306-455-2321
arcola@southeast.lib.sk.ca
www.southeast.lib.sk.ca
Tanya Pongracz, Librarian

Assiniboia: **Assiniboia & District Public Library**
201 - 3rd Ave. West, Assiniboia, SK S0H 0B0
Tel: 306-642-3631
assiniboia@palliserlibrary.ca
www.palliserlibrary.ca
Nancy Young, Branch Librarian

Avonlea: **Avonlea Branch Library**
201 Main St. West, Avonlea, SK S0H 0C0
Tel: 306-868-2076; *Fax:* 306-868-2075
avonlea@palliserlibrary.ca
www.palliserlibrary.ca
Randi Edmonds, Librarian

Balgonie: **Balgonie Branch Library**
129 Railway St., Balgonie, SK S0G 0E0
Tel: 306-771-2332; *Fax:* 306-771-2332
balgonie@southeast.lib.sk.ca
www.southeast.lib.sk.ca
Diana Pflueger, Librarian

Beauval: **Beauval Public Library**
PO Bag 9000, Beauval, SK S0M 0G0
Tel: 306-288-2022; *Fax:* 306-288-2202
sb@pnls.lib.sk.ca
Carol Edguist, Librarian

Bengough: **Bengough Branch Library**
301 Main St., Bengough, SK S0C 0K0
Tel: 306-268-2022; *Fax:* 306-268-2022
bengough@southeast.lib.sk.ca
www.southeast.lib.sk.ca
Fay Adam, Librarian

Bethune: **Bethune Branch Library**
Community Hall, 524 East St., Bethune, SK S0G 0H0
Tel: 306-638-3046
bethune@palliserlibrary.ca
www.palliserlibrary.ca
Robbie Curtis, Librarian

Bienfait: **Bienfait Branch Library**
414 Main St., Bienfait, SK S0C 0M0
Tel: 306-388-2995; *Fax:* 306-388-2995
bienfait@southeast.lib.sk.ca
www.southeast.lib.sk.ca
Sheila Farstad, Librarian

Briercrest: **Briercrest Branch Library**
Community Center, Main St., Briercrest, SK S0H 0K0
Tel: 306-799-2137
briercrest@palliser.lib.sk.ca
www.palliserlibrary.ca
Julie Cockburn, Chair
Krista Nash, Branch Librarian

Broadview: **Broadview Branch Library**
515 Main St., Broadview, SK S0G 0K0
Tel: 306-696-2414; *Fax:* 306-696-2414
broadview@southeast.lib.sk.ca
www.southeast.lib.sk.ca
Pat Gerke, Chair
Christine Judy, Librarian

Broadview: **Kahkewistahaw First Nation**
PO Box 609, Broadview, SK S0G 0K0
Tel: 306-696-3291; *Toll-Free:* 888-691-0188
education@kahkewistahaw.com
www.kahkewistahaw.com
Iris Taypotat, Resource Coordinator

Buffalo Narrows: **Wisewood Public Library**
PO Box 309, Buffalo Narrows, SK S0M 0J0
Tel: 306-235-4240; *Fax:* 306-235-4511
sbn@pnls.lib.sk.ca
Darlene Petit, School Librarian
Marci Desjarlaos, Public Librarian
sbn@pnls.lib.sk.ca

***Carlyle:* Carlyle Branch Library**
119 Souris Ave. West, Carlyle, SK S0C 0R0
Tel: 306-453-6120; *Fax:* 306-453-6120
carlyle@southeast.lib.sk.ca
www.southeast.lib.sk.ca
Lauren Hume, Chair
306-453-2824
Jonathan Nicoll, Librarian

***Carnduff:* Carnduff Branch Library**
Carnduff Education Complex, PO Box 6, Carnduff, SK S0C 0S0
Tel: 306-482-3255; *Fax:* 306-482-3255
carnduff@southeast.lib.sk.ca
www.southeast.lib.sk.ca
Elizabeth Henger, Chair
306-482-3270
Linda Kimball, Librarian

***Coronach:* Coronach Branch Library**
111A Center St., Coronach, SK S0H 0Z0
Tel: 306-267-3260
coronach@palliser.lib.sk.ca
www.palliserlibrary.ca
Social Media: www.facebook.com/50610228952
Marlene McBurney, Branch Librarian
Giselle Wilson, Assistant Librarian

***Craik:* Craik Branch Library**
611 - 1st Ave., PO Box 339, Craik, SK S0G 0V0
Tel: 306-734-2388
craik@palliser.lib.sk.ca
www.palliserlibrary.ca
Jody Kearns, Chair
Jo McAlpine, Branch Librarian

***Davidson:* Davidson Branch Library**
314 Washington Ave., PO Box 754, Davidson, SK S0G 1A0
Tel: 306-567-2022; *Fax:* 306-567-2081
davidson@palliser.lib.sk.ca
www.palliserlibrary.ca
Audrey Hamm, Co-Chair
September Brooke, Librarian
Debbie Shearwood, Assistant

***Elbow:* Elbow Branch Library**
402 Minto St., Elbow, SK S0H 1J0
Tel: 306-854-2220; *Fax:* 306-854-2230
elbow@palliser.ca
www.palliserlibrary.ca
Leeanne Hurlburt, Branch Librarian

***Estevan:* Estevan Public Library**
701 Souris Ave. North, Estevan, SK S4A 2T1
Tel: 306-636-1620; *Fax:* 306-634-5830
estevan@southeast.lib.sk.ca
estevanlibrary.weebly.com
Social Media: twitter.com/estevanlibrary; www.facebook.com/EstevanPublicLibraryBranch

***Fillmore:* Fillmore Branch Library**
51 Main St., Fillmore, SK S0G 1N0
Tel: 306-722-3369; *Fax:* 306-722-3369
fillmore@southeast.lib.sk.ca
www.southeast.lib.sk.ca
Tracey Jones, Librarian

***Fort Qu'appelle:* Fort Qu'Appelle Branch Library**
140 Company Ave. South, Fort Qu'appelle, SK S0G 1S0
Tel: 306-332-6411; *Fax:* 306-332-6411
fort.quappelle@southeast.lib.sk.ca
www.fortquappelle.com/library
Social Media: twitter.com/FtQuAppelleLib; www.facebook.com/235064119879968
Crystal Clarke, Librarian

***Fort Qu'appelle:* Standing Buffalo Library**
Standing Buffalo Reserve School, Fort Qu'appelle, SK S0G 1S0
Tel: 306-332-4414
Eleice Bear, Librarian

***Gainsborough:* Gainsborough Branch Library**
401 Railway Ave., Gainsborough, SK S0C 0Z0
Tel: 306-685-2229; *Fax:* 306-685-2229
gainsborough@southeast.lib.sk.ca
www.southeast.lib.sk.ca
Leah Bishop, Librarian

***Glenavon:* Glenavon Branch Library**
311 Railway Ave., Glenavon, SK S0G 1Y0
Tel: 306-429-2180; *Fax:* 306-429-2180
glenavon@southeast.lib.sk.ca
www.southeast.lib.sk.ca
Angela Englot, Librarian

***Grenfell:* Grenfell Branch Library**
710 Desmond Ave., Grenfell, SK S0G 2B0
Tel: 306-697-2455; *Fax:* 306-697-2455
grenfell@southeast.lib.sk.ca
www.southeast.lib.sk.ca
Anne Neuls, Librarian

***Holdfast:* Holdfast Branch Library**
125 Roberts St., Holdfast, SK S0G 2H0
Tel: 306-488-2101
holdfast@palliserlibrary.ca
www.palliserlibrary.ca
Katherine Middleton, Librarian

***Ile-a-la-Crosse:* Ile-a-la-Crosse Public Library**
PO Box 540, Ile-a-la-Crosse, SK S0M 1C0
Tel: 306-833-3027; *Fax:* 306-833-2189
216.174.135.221/library.html
Linda Ryckman, Public Library Administrator
lpryckman@hotmail.com

***Imperial:* Imperial Branch Library**
Town Office, Main St., 310 Royal St., Imperial, SK S0G 2J0
Tel: 306-963-2272; *Fax:* 306-963-2445
imperial@palliserlibrary.ca
www.palliserlibrary.ca
Leanne Antufeaff, Branch Librarian

***Indian Head:* Indian Head Branch Library**
421 Grand Ave., Indian Head, SK S0G 2K0
Tel: 306-695-3922; *Fax:* 306-695-3922
indianhead@southeast.lib.sk.ca
www.southeast.lib.sk.ca
Colleen Reynard, Librarian

***Island Lake:* Island Lake Library**
Island Lake First Nations School, Island Lake, SK S0M 3G0
Tel: 306-837-4868; *Fax:* 306-837-4558

***Kennedy:* Kennedy Branch Library**
235 Scott St., Kennedy, SK S0G 2R0
Tel: 306-538-2020; *Fax:* 306-538-2020
kennedy@southeast.lib.sk.ca
www.southeast.lib.sk.ca
Carolyn McMillan, Librarian

***Kipling:* Kipling Branch Library**
207 - 6th Ave., Kipling, SK S0G 2S0
Tel: 306-736-2911; *Fax:* 306-736-2911
kipling@southeast.lib.sk.ca
www.southeast.lib.sk.ca
Traci Trail, Board Chair
Dawn Manns, Librarian

***La Loche:* Dave O'Hara Community Library**
Bag Service #4, La Loche, SK S0M 1G0
Tel: 306-822-2151; *Fax:* 306-822-2151
sll@pnls.lib.sk.ca
Priscilla Wolverine, Librarian

***La Ronge:* La Ronge Public Library**
1212 Hildebrand Dr., La Ronge, SK S0J 1L0
Tel: 306-425-2160; *Fax:* 306-425-3883
sla@pnls.lib.sk.ca
www.pnls.lib.sk.ca
Jocelyn Provost, Library Administrator
libadmin.nlr@pnls.lib.sk.ca

***Lake Alma:* Lake Alma Branch Library**
Hwy. 18, Lake Alma, SK S0C 1M0
Tel: 306-447-2061; *Fax:* 306-447-2061
lake.alma@southeast.lib.sk.ca
www.southeast.lib.sk.ca
Bernice Bloor, Librarian

***Lampman:* Lampman Branch Library**
302 Main St., Lampman, SK S0C 1N0
Tel: 306-487-2202; *Fax:* 306-487-2202
lampman@southeast.lib.sk.ca
www.southeast.lib.sk.ca
Krista Mack, Librarian

***Loreburn:* Loreburn Branch Library**
528 Main St., Loreburn, SK S0H 2S0
Tel: 306-644-2026
loreburn@palliserlibrary.ca
www.palliserlibrary.ca
Sue Ann Abbott, Branch Librarian

***Lumsden:* Lumsden Branch Library**
20 - 3rd Ave., Lumsden, SK S0G 3C0
Tel: 306-731-1431; *Fax:* 306-731-1431
lumsden@southeast.lib.sk.ca
www.lumsden.ca
Carol Fisher, Librarian

***Manor:* Manor Library**
23 Main St., Manor, SK S0C 1R0
Tel: 306-448-2266; *Fax:* 306-448-2266
manor@southeast.lib.sk.ca
www.southeast.lib.sk.ca
Tracy Brimmer, Board Chair
Pari Mahangoo, Librarian

***Maryfield:* Maryfield Branch Library**
21 Barrows St., Maryfield, SK S0G 3K0
Tel: 306-646-2148; *Fax:* 306-646-2148
maryfield@southeast.lib.sk.ca
www.southeast.lib.sk.ca
Jan Percy, Librarian

***Midale:* Midale Branch Library**
Civic Centre, 128 Haslem St., Midale, SK S0C 1S0
Tel: 306-458-2263; *Fax:* 306-458-2263
midale@southeast.lib.sk.ca
www.southeast.lib.sk.ca
Vanessa Lund, Librarian

***Milestone:* Milestone Library**
112 Main St., Milestone, SK S0G 3L0
Tel: 306-436-2112; *Fax:* 306-436-2112
milestone@southeast.lib.sk.ca
www.southeast.lib.sk.ca
Shelley Sentes, Librarian

***Montmartre:* Montmartre Regional Library**
136 Central St., Montmartre, SK S0G 3M0
Tel: 306-424-2029; *Fax:* 306-424-2029
montmartre@southeast.lib.sk.ca
www.southeast.lib.sk.ca
Lillian Ripplinger, Librarian

***Montreal Lake:* Montreal Lake Community Library**
PO Box 150, Montreal Lake, SK S0J 1Y0
Tel: 306-663-5602; *Fax:* 306-663-5652
sml@pnls.lib.sk.ca
Social Media: www.facebook.com/490295864364911
Blanche Bird, Librarian

***Moose Jaw:* Moose Jaw Public Library**
Crescent Park, 461 Langdon Cres., Moose Jaw, SK S6H 0X6
Tel: 306-692-2787; *Fax:* 306-692-3368
reference.smj@sasktel.net
www.moosejawlibrary.ca
Social Media: www.facebook.com/pages/Moose-Jaw-Public-Library/233647406694668
Karon Selzer, Head Librarian
Gwen Fisher, Asst. Head Librarian
Cristina Dolcetti, Children's Librarian
childrens.smj@sasktel.net

***Moosomin:* Moosomin Branch Library**
701 Main St., Moosomin, SK S0G 3N0
Tel: 306-435-2107; *Fax:* 306-435-2107
moosomin@southeast.lib.sk.ca
www.southeast.lib.sk.ca
Maegan Nielsen, Librarian

***Mortlach:* Mortlach Branch Library**
118 Rose St., Mortlach, SK S0H 3E0
Tel: 306-355-2202
mortlach@palliser.lib.sk.ca
www.palliserlibrary.ca
Joanne Williams, Branch Librarian

***Mossbank:* Mossbank Branch Library**
310 Main St., Mossbank, SK S0H 3G0
Tel: 306-354-2474
mossbank@palliser.lib.sk.ca
www.palliserlibrary.ca
Kimberly Miller, Branch Librarian

***Ogema:* Ogema Branch Library**
117 Main St., Ogema, SK S0C 1Y0
Tel: 306-459-2985; *Fax:* 306-459-2985
ogema@southeast.lib.sk.ca
www.southeast.lib.sk.ca
Sherri Jackson Mead, Librarian

***Oungre:* Oungre Branch Library**
Lyndale School, Oungre, SK S0C 1Z0
Tel: 306-456-2662; *Fax:* 306-456-2662
oungre@southeast.lib.sk.ca
www.southeast.lib.sk.ca
Allison Newton, Librarian

***Oxbow:* Oxbow Branch Library/Ada Staples Library**
516 Prospect Ave., Oxbow, SK S0C 2B0
Tel: 306-483-5175; *Fax:* 306-483-5175
oxbow@southeast.lib.sk.ca
www.oxbow.ca
Social Media: www.facebook.com/305162472833058
Janell Rempel, Librarian

***Pangman:* Pangman Library**
120 Mergens St., Pangman, SK S0C 2C0
Tel: 306-442-2119; *Fax:* 306-442-2119
pangman@southeast.lib.sk.ca
www.southeast.lib.sk.ca
Carolyn Colbow, Librarian

***Pelican Narrows:* Tawowikamik Public Library**
PO Box 100, Pelican Narrows, SK S0P 0E0
Tel: 306-632-2022; *Fax:* 306-632-2161
spn@pnls.lib.sk.ca
Merle Bighetty-Michel, School Library Clerk
Margaret Brass, Library Administrator

***Pilot Butte:* Pilot Butte Branch Library**
Rec. Complex, 3rd St. & 2nd Ave., Pilot Butte, SK S0G 3Z0
Tel: 306-781-3403; *Fax:* 306-781-3403
pilot.butte@southeast.lib.sk.ca
www.southeast.lib.sk.ca
Connie LaRonge-Mohr, Librarian

***Pinehouse Lake:* Peayamechikee Public Library**
PO Box 299, Pinehouse Lake, SK S0J 2B0
Tel: 306-884-4888; *Fax:* 306-884-2164
splm@pnls.lib.sk.ca
Sophie McCallum, Public Library Support

***Qu'Appelle:* Qu'Appelle Branch Library**
Town Hall, 25 - 9th Ave., Qu'Appelle, SK S0G 4A0
Tel: 306-699-2902
quappelle@southeast.lib.sk.ca
www.southeast.lib.sk.ca
Social Media: www.facebook.com/180194542061737
Elizabeth Fries, Librarian

***Radville:* Radville Branch Library**
420 Floren St., Radville, SK S0C 2G0
Tel: 306-869-2742; *Fax:* 306-869-2742
radville@southeast.lib.sk.ca
www.southeast.lib.sk.ca
Janine Mazenc, Librarian

***Redvers:* Redvers Library**
53B Railway Ave., Redvers, SK S0C 2H0
Tel: 306-452-3255; *Fax:* 306-452-3255
redvers@southeast.lib.sk.ca
www.southeast.lib.sk.ca
Windell Seargeant, Librarian

***Regina:* Regina Public Library**
2311 - 12th Ave., Regina, SK S4P 0N3
Tel: 306-777-6000; *Fax:* 306-949-7260
Other Numbers: 306-777-6120 (Info Svs); 306-777-6024 (ILL)
www.reginalibrary.ca
Social Media: www.flickr.com/photos/reginapubliclibrary; twitter.com/OfficialRPL; www.facebook.com/ReginaPublicLibrary
Jeff Barber, CEO & Library Director
jbarber@reginalibrary.ca
306-777-6099
Julie McKenna, Deputy Library Director
jmckenna@reginalibrary.ca
306-777-6074
Kevin Saunderson, Senior Manager, Corporate Services
ksaunderson@reginalibrary.ca
306-777-6222
Robert Borges, Manager, Information Technology
rborges@reginalibrary.ca
306-777-6056
Nancy MacKenzie, Manager, Community Engagement & Programming
nmackenzie@reginalibrary.ca
306-777-6071

***Regina:* Saskatchewan Provincial Library & Literacy Office**
409A Park St., Regina, SK S4N 5B2
Tel: 306-787-2976; *Fax:* 306-787-2029
www.education.gov.sk.ca/Provincial-Library
Alison Hopkins, Provincial Librarian
alison.hopkins@gov.sk.ca
Barbara Bulat, Director, Library Accountability & Administration
barbara.bulat@gov.sk.ca
306-787-6032
Julie Arie, Director, Public Library Planning
julie.arie@gov.sk.ca
306-787-3005
Maureen Johns, Director, Literacy Office
Maureen.Johns@gov.sk.ca
306-787-8020
Jack Ma, Coordinator, Multitype Library Development
Jack.Ma@gov.sk.ca
306-787-1306
Debbie Kraus, Executive Coordinator
Debbie.Kraus@gov.sk.ca
306-787-2514
Catherine Howett, Coordinator, Literacy & Learning Partnerships
catherine.howett@gov.sk.ca
306-787-9144
Jian Wang, Coordinator, Multilingual Library Services
Jian.Wang@gov.sk.ca
306-787-0984
Calvin Sadowski, Manager, Library Network Development
csadowski@library.gov.sk.ca
306-787-6299

***Regina Beach:* Regina Beach Branch Library**
133 Donovel Cres., Regina Beach, SK S0G 4C0
Tel: 306-729-2062; *Fax:* 306-729-2062
regina.beach@southeast.lib.sk.ca
www.southeast.lib.sk.ca
Krista Hannan, Librarian

***Riverhurst:* Riverhurst Branch Library**
The Village Square, 324 Teck St., Riverhurst, SK S0H 3P0
Tel: 306-353-2130
riverhurst@palliserlibrary.ca
www.palliserlibrary.ca
Winnie Hockman, Board Chair
Donna Miner, Librarian

***Rocanville:* Rocanville Branch Library**
218 Ellice St., Rocanville, SK S0A 3L0
Tel: 306-645-2088; *Fax:* 306-645-2088
rocanville@southeast.lib.sk.ca
www.southeast.lib.sk.ca
Kim Gulka, Board Chair
Carol Greening, Librarian

***Rockglen:* Rockglen Branch Library**
1018 Centre St., Rockglen, SK S0H 3R0
Tel: 306-476-2350
rockglen@palliserlibrary.ca
www.palliserlibrary.ca
Kendra Loucks, Board Chair
Angela Stewart, Branch Librarian

***Rouleau:* Rouleau Branch Library**
204 Main St., Rouleau, SK S0G 4H0
Tel: 306-776-2322; *Fax:* 306-776-0003
rouleau@palliserlibrary.ca
www.palliserlibrary.ca
Dee Colibaba, Branch Librarian

***Sandy Bay:* Ayamicikiwikamik Public Library**
PO Box 240, Sandy Bay, SK S0P 0G0
Tel: 306-754-2139; *Fax:* 306-754-2130
ssbpP@pnls.lib.sk.ca
Gwen Bear, Librarian

***Saskatoon:* Saskatoon Public Library**
311 - 23rd St. East, Saskatoon, SK S7K 0J6
Tel: 306-975-7558; *Fax:* 306-975-7542
askus@saskatoonlibrary.ca
www.saskatoonlibrary.ca
Social Media: www.flickr.com/photos/spl-photo; twitter.com/stoonlibrary; www.facebook.com/saskatoonpubliclibrary
Zenon Zuzak, Director of Libraries

***Sedley:* Sedley Branch Library**
224 Broadway, Sedley, SK S0G 4K0
Tel: 306-885-4505; *Fax:* 306-885-4506
sedley@southeast.lib.sk.ca
www.southeast.lib.sk.ca
Marnie Pope, Librarian
Shauna Forbes, Chair

***Spruce Home:* Spruce Home Branch Library**
Spruce Home School Library, Spruce Home, SK S0J 2N0
Tel: 306-764-8377

***Stanley Mission:* Keethanow Public Library**
PO Box 70, Stanley Mission, SK S0J 2P0
Tel: 306-635-2104; *Fax:* 306-635-2050
ssk@pnls.lib.sk.ca
Lucy Ratt, Branch Librarian

***Stoughton:* Stoughton Branch Library**
232 Main St., Stoughton, SK S0G 4T0
Tel: 306-457-2484
stoughton@southeast.lib.sk.ca
www.southeast.lib.sk.ca
Social Media: www.facebook.com/292105920817879?
Laura Sabados, Librarian

***Tugaske:* Tugaske Branch Library**
106 Ogema St., Tugaske, SK S0H 4B0
Tel: 306-759-2215
tugaske@palliserlibrary.ca
www.palliserlibrary.ca
Morgan Freeman, Branch Librarian

***Turtleford:* Thunderchild Branch Library**
PO Box 600, Turtleford, SK S0M 2Y0
Tel: 306-845-4325
www.lakeland.lib.sk.ca
Susan Wapass, Librarian

***Vibank:* Vibank Branch Library**
101 - 2nd Ave., Vibank, SK S0G 4Y0
Tel: 306-762-2270; *Fax:* 306-762-2270
vibank@southeast.lib.sk.ca
www.southeast.lib.sk.ca
Betty Kuntz, Librarian

***Wapella:* Wapella Branch Library**
519 Railway St. South, Wapella, SK S0G 4Z0
Tel: 306-532-4419; *Fax:* 306-532-4419
wapella@southeast.lib.sk.ca
www.southeast.lib.sk.ca
Sharon Matheson, Librarian

***Waskesiu Lake:* Waskesiu Lake Library**
1225 Montreal, Waskesiu Lake, SK S0J 2Y0
Tel: 306-663-5999

***Wawota:* Wawota Branch Library**
308 Railway Ave., Wawota, SK S0G 5A0
Tel: 306-739-2375; *Fax:* 306-739-2375
wawota@southeast.lib.sk.ca
www.southeast.lib.sk.ca
Social Media: www.facebook.com/286787141339067
Sylvia Jewkes, Librarian

***Weyburn:* Weyburn Public Library**
45 Bison Ave., Weyburn, SK S4H 0H9
Tel: 306-842-4352; *Fax:* 306-842-1255
weyburn@southeast.lib.sk.ca
weyburnpubliclibrary.weebly.com
Social Media: twitter.com/WeyburnPublic; www.facebook.com/189593097722161
Kam Teo, Librarian

***White City:* White City Branch Library**
White City Community Centre, 12 Ramm Ave., White City, SK S0G 5B0
Tel: 306-781-2118; *Fax:* 306-781-2118
white.city@southeast.lib.sk.ca
www.southeast.lib.sk.ca
Lori Lee Harris, Branch Librarian

***Whitewood:* Whitewood Library**
731 Lalonde St., Whitewood, SK S0G 5C0
Tel: 306-735-4233; *Fax:* 306-735-4233
whitewood@southeast.lib.sk.ca
www.southeast.lib.sk.ca
Krista Williams, Librarian

***Willow Bunch:* Willow Bunch Branch Library**
2 Ave. F South, Willow Bunch, SK S0H 4K0
Tel: 306-473-2393
willowbunch@palliserlibrary.ca
www.palliserlibrary.ca
Social Media: www.facebook.com/223931024328192
Jeanette Mondor, Chair
Barb Gibbons, Branch Librarian

***Windthorst:* Windthorst Branch Library**
202 Angus St., Windthorst, SK S0G 5G0
Tel: 306-224-2159; *Fax:* 306-224-2159
windthorst@southeast.lib.sk.ca
www.southeast.lib.sk.ca
Jill Taylor, Librarian

Wolseley: **Wolseley Branch Library**
500 Front St., Wolseley, SK S0G 5H0
Tel: 306-698-2221; *Fax:* 306-698-2221
wolseley@southeast.lib.sk.ca
www.southeast.lib.sk.ca

Sharon Jeeves, Librarian

Wood Mountain: **Wood Mountain Branch Library**
2 - 2nd Ave., Wood Mountain, SK S0H 4L0
Tel: 306-266-2110
woodmountain@palliser.lib.sk.ca
www.palliserlibrary.ca

Gus Gere, Branch Librarian

Yellow Grass: **Yellow Grass Branch Library**
213 Souris St., Yellow Grass, SK S0G 5J0
Tel: 306-465-2574; *Fax:* 306-465-2574
yellow.grass@southeast.lib.sk.ca
www.southeast.lib.sk.ca

Betty Guest, Librarian

Archives

Duck Lake: **Duck Lake Historical Museum**
PO Box 328, Duck Lake, SK S0K 1J0
Tel: 306-467-2057; *Toll-Free:* 866-467-2057
duckmuf@sasktel.net
www.dlric.org/museum.html

Prince Albert: **Prince Albert Historical Society**
10 River St. East, Prince Albert, SK S6V 8A9
Tel: 306-764-2992
historypa@citypa.com
www.historypa.com
Social Media: twitter.com/historypa;
www.facebook.com/PrinceAlbertHistoricalSociety

Regina: **RCMP Heritage Centre/ Centre du Patrimoine de la GRC**
5907 Dewdney Ave., Regina, SK S4T 0P4
Tel: 306-522-7333; *Fax:* 306-522-7340
Toll-Free: 866-567-7267
info@rcmphc.com
www.rcmpheritagecentre.com

Regina: **Regina Firefighters' Museum**
1205 Ross Ave., Regina, SK S4P 3C8
Tel: 306-777-7837

Regina: **Saskatchewan Archives Board**
3303 Hillsdale St., Regina, SK S4P 4B7
Tel: 306-787-4068; *Fax:* 306-787-1197
Other Numbers: Information Management Inquiry Line: 306-787-0734
www.saskarchives.com

Mark Docherty, Minister-in-Charge
minister.pcs@gov.sk.ca
Linda McIntyre, Provincial Archivist
lMcIntyre@archives.gov.sk.ca
Lenora Toth, Executive Director, Archival Programs & Information Management
ltoth@archives.gov.sk.ca

Regina: **Saskatchewan Genealogical Society**
#110, 1514 - 11th Ave., Regina, SK S4P 0H2
Tel: 306-780-9207; *Fax:* 306-780-3615
sgslibrary@sasktel.net
www.saskgenealogy.com
Social Media: www.facebook.com/216892188363312

Deanne Cairns, Executive Director
ed.sgs@sasktel.net

Saskatoon: **City of Saskatoon Archives**
224 Cardinal Cr., Saskatoon, SK S7L 6H8
Tel: 306-975-7811; *Fax:* 306-975-2612
city.archives@saskatoon.ca
www.saskatoon.ca
Social Media: www.youtube.com/saskatooncitynews;
twitter.com/cityofsaskatoon;
www.facebook.com/saskatooncitynews

Saskatoon: **Diefenbaker Canada Centre**
University of Saskatchewan, 101 Diefenbaker Pl., Saskatoon, SK S7N 5B8
Tel: 306-966-8384; *Fax:* 306-966-1967
dief.centre@usask.ca
www.usask.ca/diefenbaker
Social Media: twitter.com/DiefCentre;
www.facebook.com/diefenbakercentre

Saskatoon: **Mohyla Institute**
1240 Temperance St., Saskatoon, SK S7N 0P1
Tel: 306-653-1944; *Fax:* 306-653-1902
admin@mohyla.ca
www.mohyla.ca
Social Media: www.facebook.com/StPetroMohylaInstitute

Verigin: **National Doukhobour Heritage Village Inc.**
PO Box 99, Verigin, SK S0A 4H0
Tel: 306-542-4441
ndhv@yourlink.ca
www.ndhv.ca

Weyburn: **Soo Line Historical & Technical Society**
411 Industrial Lane, Weyburn, SK S4H 2L2
Tel: 306-842-2922
slhm@sasktel.net
Social Media:
www.facebook.com/pages/Soo-Line-Historical-Museum/118758801502753

Yukon Territory

Public Libraries

Whitehorse: **Yukon Public Libraries**
1171 Front St., Whitehorse, YT Y1A 2C6
Tel: 867-667-5239; *Fax:* 867-393-6333
Toll-Free: 800-661-0408
Other Numbers: 867-667-3668 (Reference); 867-667-5228 (Programs)
whitehorse.library@gov.yk.ca
www.ypl.gov.yk.ca/wpl.html
Social Media: yukonpubliclibraries.tumblr.com;
twitter.com/YukonLibraries;
www.facebook.com/yukonpubliclibraries

Archives

Dawson: **Dawson City Museum**
595 - 5th Ave., 2nd Fl., Dawson, YT Y0B 1G0
Tel: 867-993-5291; *Fax:* 867-993-5839
info@dawsonmuseum.ca
www.dawsonmuseum.ca
Social Media: twitter.com/dcmuseum;
www.facebook.com/pages/Dawson-City-Museum/118073228250444

Alex Somerville, Executive Director
asomerville@dawsonmuseum.ca
867-993-5291 ext. 21
Benjamin Peddle, Archivist
bpeddle@dawsonmuseum.ca
867-993-5291 ext. 24

Whitehorse: **Yukon Tourism & Culture**
400 College Dr., Whitehorse, YT Y1A 3K5
Tel: 867-667-5321; *Fax:* 867-393-6253
Toll-Free: 800-661-0408
yukon.archives@gov.yk.ca
www.yukonarchives.ca

Ian Burnett, Territorial Archivist
867-667-5321
Donna Darbyshire, Archives Reference Assistant
donna.darbyshire@gov.yk.ca
867-667-8064
Peggy D'Orsay, Archives Librarian
867-667-5625
Wendy Sokolon, Government Records Archivist
wendy.sokolon@gov.yk.ca
867-667-5926
Jennifer Roberts, Private Records Archivist
867-667-5625

SECTION 13
PUBLISHING

Publishers

Book Publishers

Aaspirations Publishing Inc.
6424 Longspur Rd, Mississauga, ON L5N 6E3
Fax: 416-850-5221
Toll-Free: 888-850-6277
www.aaspirationspublishing.com

AB collector publishing
5835 Grant St., Halifax, NS B3H 1C9
Tel: 902-429-5768; *Fax:* 506-385-1981
Toll-Free: 888-748-5514
darklady@nbnet.nb.ca
www.abcollectorpublishing.ca
Publisher of poetry, short stories, biography, drama, works relating to photography, ceramics, art & history, in English, French, German
Astrid Brunner, Publisher

ABC Publishing (Anglican Book Centre)
Owned By: Augsburg Fortress Canada
80 Hayden St., Toronto, ON M4Y 3G2
Tel: 416-924-9199; *Fax:* 416-968-7983
www.abcpublishing.com
ISBNs: 0-919030, 0-919891, 0-921846
ABC Publishing (Anglican Book Centre) produces liturgical resources (prayer books, hymn books, lectionary aids), institutional materials, and parish leadership resources (congregational development, biblical reflection, church school materials).

Able Sense Publishing
2585 Connaught Ave., Halifax, NS B3L 2Z5
Tel: 902-442-9356
info@ablesensepublishing.com
ablesensepublishing.com
Social Media: www.linkedin.com/company/able-sense-publishing
twitter.com/AbleSensePub
www.facebook.com/ablesensepublishing

Acadiensis Press
Campus House, University of New Brunswick, PO Box 4400, Fredericton, NB E3B 5A3
Tel: 506-453-4978
acadnsis@unb.ca
www.lib.unb.ca/Texts/Acadiensis
ISSN: 0044-5871
Publisher of ACADIENSIS: The Journal of the History of the Atlantic Region, & books on the culture & history of Atlantic Canada
Stephen Dutcher, Managing Editor

Acorn Press
PO Box 22024, Charlottetown, PE C1A 9J2
Tel: 902-221-1061
info@acornpresscanada.com
www.acornpresscanada.com
Social Media:
twitter.com/AcornPress
www.facebook.com/pages/The-Acorn-Press/146624385354176?re
ISBNs: 1-894838014-9; 1-894838-16-5-64
Publishing books about Prince Edward Island, with emphasis on Prince Edward Island authors, Acorn Press lists works of fiction, poetry, folklore, history & literature for children
Laurie Brinklow, Publisher

Alexander Press
2875, av Douglas, Montréal, QC H3R 2C7
Tel: 514-738-5517; *Fax:* 514-738-4718
Toll-Free: 866-303-5517
alexanderpress@gmail.com
www.alexanderpress.com
Other information: Alternate Telephone: 514-738-4018
ISBNs: 1-896800
Publishes Christian Orthodox books & media in Greek, English & French

Alpine Book Peddlers
#140, 105 Bow Meadows Cres., Canmore, AB T1W 2W8
Tel: 403-678-2280; *Fax:* 403-678-2840
Toll-Free: 866-478-2280
alpinebk@aeontech.ca
alpinebookpeddlers.ca
Other information: Toll Free Fax: 866-978-2840
ISBNs: 0-9699368, 0-9692631, 0-919934, 0-9692457; SAN: 1187546
Distributors of books, journals, maps, posters & cards

The Alternate Press
Owned By: Life Media
#52, B2-125 The Queensway, Toronto, ON M8Y 1H6
altpress@lifemedia.ca
www.lifemedia.ca/altpress
ISBNs: 0-920118-04-6; 978-0-920118-15-3;0-920118-00-3
An imprint of Life Media, The Alternate Press publishes materials promoting home schooling & natural learning, natural parenting, natural business (home-based & green), & poetry
Wendy Priesnitz, Publisher
Ron Priesnitz, Publisher

The Althouse Press
Faculty of Education, University of Western Ontario, 1137 Western Rd., London, ON N6G 1G7
Tel: 519-661-2096; *Fax:* 519-661-3714
press@uwo.ca
www.edu.uwo.ca/althousepress
ISBNs: 0-920354; SAN: 115-1142
Dr. Greg Dickinson, Director
K. Butson, Contact, kbutson@uwo.ca

Ampersand Inc.
Previous Name: Kate Walker & Company
2440 Viking Way, Richmond, BC V6V 1N2
Tel: 604-448-7111; *Fax:* 604-448-7118
Toll-Free: 800-561-8583
ampersandinc.ca
Other information: Toll Free Fax: 888-323-7118
Social Media: www.linkedin.com/company/ampersand-inc-
twitter.com/ampersandinc
www.f acebook.com/AmpersandCanada
ISBNs: 0-919591, 1-896095
Cheryl Fraser, Vice President & National Sales Manager, Sales, 604-448-7111 x403, cherylf@ampersandinc.ca

Annick Press Ltd.
15 Patricia Ave., Toronto, ON M2M 1H9
Tel: 416-221-4802; *Fax:* 416-221-8400
annickpress@annickpress.com
www.annickpress.com
Social Media: www.youtube.com/AnnickPress
twitter.com/AnnickPress
www.facebook.co m/AnnickPress
ISBNs: 0-920236, 920303, 1-55037; SAN: 115-0065
Publishers of fiction and nonfiction for children and young adults. Editorial offices in Toronto and Vancouver.

Anvil Press
278 East First Ave., Vancouver, BC V5T 1A6
Tel: 604-876-8710; *Fax:* 604-879-2667
info@anvilpress.com
www.anvilpress.com
Social Media:
twitter.com/AnvilPress
www.facebook.com/AnvilPress
ISBNs: 1-895636
Brian Kaufman, Publisher

Apple Press Publishing
810 Landresse Ct., Newmarket, ON L3X 1M6
Tel: 905-853-7979; *Fax:* 905-853-1175
Toll-Free: 866-222-8883
ISBNs: 0-919972
George Quinn, President, 905-853-7979

Aquila Communications Ltd.
2642, rue Diab, Montréal, QC H4S 1E8
Tel: 514-338-1065; *Fax:* 514-338-1948
Toll-Free: 800-667-7071
www.aquilacommunications.com
ISBNs: 0-88510, 2-89054; SAN: 115-2483, 115-8295
Publishes French as a Second Language reading materials from grades 4 through college
Mike Kelada, Vice-President & General Manager, mike@aquilacommunications.com
Sami Kelada, President/CEO

Arbeiter Ring Publishing
#201E, 121 Osborne St., Winnipeg, MB R3L 1Y4
Tel: 204-942-7058; *Fax:* 204-944-9198
info@arpbooks.org
arpbooks.org
Social Media: www.youtube.com/ArbeiterRing
twitter.com/arpbooks
www.facebook.com/arp books
ISBNs: 1-894037
Publishers of books on contemporary politics, culture, and social issues.

Arsenal Pulp Press Ltd.
#101, 211 East Georgia St., Vancouver, BC V6A 1Z6
Tel: 604-687-4233; *Fax:* 604-687-4283
info@arsenalpulp.com
www.arsenalpulp.com
Social Media:
twitter.com/arsenalpulp
www.facebook.com/arsenalpulp
ISBNs: 0-88978, 1-55152; SAN: 115-0847
Publisher with over 200 titles in print, including literary fiction & non-fiction; cultural & gender studies; gay, lesbian & multicultural literature; cookbooks & guidebooks.
Brian Lam, Publisher
Robert Ballantyne, Associate Publisher
Cynara Geisser, Marketing Director

Art Global
#960, 507 Place d'Arms, Montréal, QC H2Y 2W8
Tél: 514-272-6111; *Téléc:* 514-272-6111
artglobal@videotron.ca
www.artglobal.ca
Médias sociaux:
www.facebook.com/137924119586653
ISBNs: 2-920718
Art Global se consacre d'abord à la publication de livres d'artistes à tirage limité, tels Kamouraska, d'Anne Hébert ou Prochain Épisode d'Hubert Aquin. Plusieurs de ces ouvrages se retrouvent aujourd'hui dans les collections de livres rares de plusieurs universités et musées québécois.
Mireille Kermoyan, Administratrice & Éditrice
Robery Côté, Président
Christine Rebours, Coordonnatrice à L'édition

Art Metropole
1490 Dundas St. W, Toronto, ON M6K 1T5
Tel: 416-703-4400; *Fax:* 416-703-4404
info@artmetropole.com
www.artmetropole.com
Publishers of art books & publications
Corinn Gerbern, Director, Editor, corinn@artmetropole.com

Artel Educational Resources Ltd.
5528 Kingsway, Burnaby, BC V5H 2G2
Tel: 604-435-4949; *Fax:* 604-435-1955
Toll-Free: 800-665-9255
www.arteleducational.ca
Publishes educational resources for schools, institutions, home schoolers & the general public; Includes material for all levels of education, ESL & Special Education

Artexte / Centre d'information Artexte
#301, 2 Sainte-Catherine est, Montréal, QC H2X 1K4
Tél: 514-874-0049
info@artexte.ca
www.artexte.ca
Médias sociaux: www.artactuelcentreville.com
twitter.com/artexte
www.facebook.com/page s/ARTEXTE/260885753456
Artexte est attachée à la compréhension et à la promotion des arts visuels grâce à des sources d'information fiables.
Sarah Watson, Director, swatson@artexte.ca

Artistic Warrior
#207, 2475 Dobbin Rd., #22, West Kelowna, BC V4T 2E9
publisher@artisticwarrior.com
www.artisticwarrior.com
Publisher of new & emerging Canadian authors with a focus on BC authors.
Darcy Nybo, Publisher

Asteroid Publishing Inc.
PO Box 3, Richmond Hill, ON L4C 4X9
Tel: 416-352-1561
info@asteroidpublishing.ca
asteroidpublishing.ca
Social Media:
www.twitter.com/asteroidpublish
Publisher of literary fiction & non-fiction books.

Athabasca University Press
Edmonton Learning Centre, Peace Hills Trust Tower, #1200, 10011 - 109 St., Edmonton, AB T5J 3S8
Tel: 780-497-3412; *Fax:* 780-421-3298
aupress@athabascau.ca
www.aupress.ca
Social Media: www.youtube.com/user/aupresst
twitter.com/au_press
www.facebook.com/pa ges/AU-Press/189461926898
ISBNs: 0-919737
Kathy Killoh, Acting Director, director.aupress@athabascau.ca

Augsburg Fortress Publishers Canadian Office
500 Trillium Dr., Kitchener, ON N2G 4Y4
Tel: 519-748-2200; *Fax:* 519-748-9835
Toll-Free: 800-265-6397
info@afcanada.com
www.afcanada.com
Other information: kitchenerstore@augsburgfortress.org
Social Media: www.youtube.com/user/AugsburgFortress
www.twitter.com/augsburgfortres
www.facebook.com/augsburgfortress
The publishing wing of the Evangelical Lutheran Church in America, Augsburg Fortress also services the Evangelical Lutheran Church in Canada & publishes Bibles, Bible study resources, multicultural materials, music, & seasonal & special occasion books.
Larry N. Willard, Canadian Operations Director

Augustine Hand Press
62 Walter Copp Cres., Winnipeg, MB R2K 4H6
ISBNs: 0973151900, 0973151919

Aviation Publishers Co. Ltd.
PO Box 1361 B, Ottawa, ON K1P 5R4
www.aviationpublishers.com
ISBNs: 0-9690054
Publishers of the ground school flight training manual "From the Ground Up" as well as other books on flight training & aeronautical theory.
William N. Peppler, Publisher & Chief Editor

Backroad Mapbooks
Owned By: Mussio Ventures Ltd.
#106, 1500 Hartley Ave., Coquitlam, BC V3K 7A1
Tel: 604-521-6277; *Fax:* 604-521-6260
Toll-Free: 877-520-5670
info@backroadmapbooks.com
www.backroadmapbooks.com
Social Media:
twitter.com/backroadmapbook
www.facebook.com/backroadmapbooks
Backroad Mapbooks produces up-to-date outdoor recreation Canadian maps & guidebooks.
Russell Mussio, President, 250-766-9354, rmussio@backroadmapbooks.com
Chris Taylor, National Sales Manager, National Sales, 604-521-6277 ext. 205, ctaylor@backroadmapbooks.com

Bacon & Hughes Limited
#30, 81 Auriga Dr., Ottawa, ON K2E 7Y5
Tel: 613-226-8136; *Fax:* 613-226-8121
Toll-Free: 800-563-2468
sales@baconandhughes.ca
www.baconandhughes.ca
Bacon & Hughes Limited provides learning resources from early childhood to the secondary level. Teacher resources & French literature are also available.

Bahá'í Distribution Service
Previous Name: Unity Arts Inc.
#9, 945 Middlefield Rd., Toronto, ON M1V 5E1
Tel: 416-609-9900; *Fax:* 416-609-9600
Toll-Free: 800-465-3287
orders@bahaibooksonline.com
www.bds-canada.com
Publishes books about the Bahái faith

Banff Centre Press
The Banff Centre, PO Box 1020 21, 107 Tunnel Mountain Dr., Banff, AB T1L 1H5
Tel: 403-762-6408; *Fax:* 403-762-6334
Toll-Free: 800-565-9989
press@banffcentre.ca
www.banffcentre.ca/press
Social Media:
twitter.com/BanffCentreLit
www.facebook.com/TheBanffCentre
The Banff Centre Press publishes books of contemporary art, culture, & literature.
Jeff Melanson, President
Leanne Johnson, Managing Editor, leanne_johnson@banffcentre.ca
Devyani Saltzman, Director, Literary Arts, devyani_saltzman@banffcentre.ca

The Battered Silicon Dispatch Box
PO Box 50, R,R, #4, Euginia, ON N0C 1E0
Tel: 519-925-3027; *Fax:* 519-925-3482
gav@cablerocket.com
www.batteredbox.com
ISBNs: 1-55246
Publishers of Sherlock Holmes and other out-of-print works by Canadian & international authors
George A. Vanderhurgh, Publisher, gav@cablerocket.com

Bayeux Arts Inc.
119 Stratton Cres. SW, Calgary, AB T3H 1T7
mail@bayeux.com
bayeux.com
Ashis Gupta, Publisher, agupta@bayeux.com

Be That Books Publishing
#91033, 125 - 8888 Country Hills Blvd. NW, Calgary, AB T3G 5T0
Tel: 403-699-8845
admin@bethatbooks.com
bethatbooks.com
Social Media: www.pinterest.com/bethatbooks
twitter.com/BeThatBooks
www.facebook. com/BeThatBooks
Tina O'Connor, President & CEO

Béliveau Éditeur
Anciennement: Éditions Sciences et Culture inc.; Iris Diffusion
920, rue Jean-Neveu, Longueuil, QC J4G 2M1
Tél: 450-679-1933; *Téléc:* 450-679-6648
admin@beliveauediteur.com
www.beliveauediteur.com
ISBNs: 2-89092
Spécialités: Affaires, finances, biographies, psychologie et sciences humaines, religion, mathématiques, physique, chimie
Mathieu Béliveau, Président-directeur général, 450-679-1933, admin@beliveauediteur.com

Bendall Books Educational Publishers
PO Box 115, Mill Bay, BC V0R 2P0
Tel: 250-743-2946; *Fax:* 250-743-2910
admin@bendallbooks.com
www.bendallbooks.com
Bendall Books is a publisher & distributor of educational materials college & university students
Mary Moore, Publisher

The Best of Bridge Publishing Ltd.
Owned By: Robert Rose Inc.
#800, 120 Eglington Ave. E, Toronto, ON M4P 1E2
Tel: 416-322-6552; *Fax:* 416-322-6936
www.bestofbridge.com
Social Media: pinterest.com/robertrosebooks
twitter.com/thebestofbridge
www.facebook .com/102901496565355
ISBNs: 0-9690425
Publishers of cookbooks

Between the Lines (BTL)
#277, 401 Richmond St. West, Toronto, ON M5V 3A8
Tel: 416-535-9914; *Fax:* 416-535-1484
Toll-Free: 800-718-7201
info@btlbooks.com
www.btlbooks.com
Social Media: www.youtube.com/BTLbooks
twitter.com/readBTLbooks
facebook.com/BTLbooks
Between the Lines provides books with critical perspectives on culture, economics, & society.
Amanda Crocker, Managing Editor, editor@btlbooks.com
Paula Brill, Accounts Manager
Renée Knapp, Marketing & Sales Manager
Jennifer Tiberio, Art Director & Production Manager

Biblioasis
1520 Wyandotte St. East, Windsor, ON N9A 3L2
Tel: 519-968-2206; *Fax:* 519-250-5713
info@biblioasis.com
www.biblioasis.com
Social Media:
twitter.com/biblioasis
www.facebook.com/groups/2409174840
Publisher of poetry, fiction & non-fiction.
Daniel Wells, Publisher/Editor, dwells@biblioasis.com

Bibliothèque nationale du Québec
2275, rue Holt, Montréal, QC H2G 3H1
Tel: 514-873-1100; *Fax:* 514-873-9312
Toll-Free: 800-363-9028
www.bnquebec.ca
Social Media: www.youtube.com/user/BAnQweb20
twitter.com/_BAnQ
www.facebook.com/2391 06374115
ISBNs: 2-550, 2-551
Guy Berthiaume, Président-directeur général

Black Moss Press
2450 Byng Rd., Windsor, ON N8W 3E8
Tel: 519-252-2551
blackmosspress.com
Social Media: www.youtube.com/blackmosswindsor
twitter.com/READBLACKMOSS
www.face book.com/group.php?gid=118907923236
The literary press publishes Canadian literature, including poetry & short story anthologies.
Marty Gervais, Publisher

Black Rose Books
PO Box 35788 Leo Pariseau, Montréal, QC H2X 0A4
www.blackrosebooks.net
Social Media:
twitter.com/blackrosebooks
www.facebook.com/169914786530
Black Rose Books publishes critical writing on topics such as philosophy, politics, history, sociology, & the environment.
Robert Dollins, Editorial Administrator

Blue Heron Press
160 Greenlees Dr., Kingston, ON K7K 6P4
Tel: 613-549-4334
lorne.blueheron@gmail.com
www.blueheronpress.ca
The literary press specializes in Canadian literature.

Bodhi Publishing
PO Box 144, Kinmount, ON K0M 2A0
kcw@bodhipublishing.org
www.bodhipublishing.org
The charitable organization publishes books by Venerable Namgyal Rinpoche.

BookLand Press
#600, 15 Allstate Pkwy., Markham, ON L3R 5B4
Tel: 905-943-0950; *Fax:* 905-248-1215
Toll-Free: 800-535-1774
books@booklandpress.com
www.booklandpress.com
Social Media:
www.twitter.com/booklandpress

Boomerang Éditeur Jeunesse inc.
2, place de Domèvre, Lorraine, QC J6Z 4K6
Tél: 450-640-1234; *Ligne sans frais:* 800-771-3022
info@boomerangjeunesse.com
www.boomerangjeunesse.com
Publie des livres pour la jeunesse
Marion Bergeron, Édition & Production, mbergeron@boomerangjeunesse.com
Danielle Lalande, Gestion & Administration, dlalande@boomerangjeunesse.com
Caroline Lafrance, Promotion & Marketing, clafrance@boomerangjeunesse.com

Borealis Book Publishers
8 Mohawk Cres., Nepean, ON K2H 7G6
Tel: 613-829-0150; *Fax:* 613-829-7783
Toll-Free: 877-696-2585
drt@borealispress.com
www.borealispress.com
Borealis Book Publishers consists of Borealis Books, Tecumseh Books, Publishing Advisors Inc., Journal of Canadian Poetry, Canadian Critical Editions, & the Parliamentary Handbook / Répertoire Parlementaire Canadien.

Boston Mills Press
ON L4B 1H1
Tel: 416-499-8412; *Fax:* 416-499-8313
Toll-Free: 800-387-6192
service@fireflybooks.com
www.fireflybooks.com/BostonMi lls
ISBNs: 0-919783; 0-919822
Boston Mills Press publishes nonfiction books for adults, including nature, history, travel, & transportation titles. It is a client publisher of Firefly Books.

Boulder Publications Ltd.
198 Neary's Pond Rd., Portugal Cove-St. Philip's, NL A1M 2Y5
Tel: 709-895-6483; *Fax:* 709-895-8047
info@boulderpublications.ca
boulderpublications.ca
Social Media:
twitter.com/boulderpub
www.facebook.com/pages/Boulder-Publications/1771773556680

Breakwater Books Ltd.
Previous Name: Summerhill Books
PO Box 2188, 1 Stamp's Lane, St. John's, NL A1C 6E6
Tel: 709-722-6680; *Fax:* 709-753-0708
Toll-Free: 800-563-3333
info@breakwaterbooks.com
www.breakwaterbooks.com
Social Media:
twitter.com/BreakwaterBooks
www.facebook.com/pages/Breakwater-Books-Ltd/29596022506
ISBNs: 0-919519, 0-920911, 1-55081; SAN 115-0154
Newfoundland's first publishing house; specializing in educational & curriculum materials, and resources with an emphasis on the history & unique culture of Newfoundland & Labrador
Rebecca Rose, President

Brendan Kelly Publishing Inc.
2122 Highview Dr., Burlington, ON L7R 3X4
Tel: 905-335-3359; *Fax:* 905-335-5104
mail@brendankellypublishing.com
www.brendankellypublishing.com
ISBNs: 1-895997, 0-9695244
Specialists in the subject areas of mathematics, business, sports & psychology
Brendan Kelly, President Ph.D.; Ed.D.

Brick Books
PO Box 20081, 431 Boler Rd., London, ON N6K 4G6
Tel: 519-657-8579
brick.books@sympatico.ca
www.brickbooks.ca
Social Media: www.youtube.com/brickbooks
twitter.com/brickbooks
www.facebook.com/brickbooks
ISBNs: 0-919626, 1-894078; SAN: 115-0162
Small literary press devoted to the work of Canadian poets
Kitty Lewis, General Manager

Brighter Books Publishing House
4825 Fairbrook Cres., Nanaimo, BC V9T 6M6
Tel: 250-585-7372
info@brighterbooks.com
www.brighterbooks.com
Social Media:
twitter.com/BrighterBooks
www.facebook.com/pages/Brighter-Books/11734289 8278140
Angela Jurgensen, Chief Editor, Angela@brighterbooks.com

Brindle & Glass Publishing Ltd.
#103, 1075 Pendergast St., Victoria, BC V8V 0A1
Tel: 250-360-0829; *Fax:* 250-386-0829
info@brindleandglass.com
www.brindleandglass.com
Social Media:
twitter.com/BrindleAndGlass
www.facebook.com/BrindleandGlass
Publish a set of books: regional and national titles; new editions of books that should still be available; books for adults and for young readers; fiction, drama and poetry.
Ruth Linka, Publisher

Broadview Press
PO Box 1243, #5, 280 Perry St., Peterborough, ON K9J 7H5
Tel: 705-743-8990; *Fax:* 705-743-8353
customerservice@broadviewpress.com
www.broadviewpress.com
Social Media:
twitter.com/broadviewpress
www.facebook.com/pages/Broadview-Press/316561361724692
ISBNs: 0-921149, 1-55111; SAN: 115-6772
With additional offices in Guelph, Nanaimo, Wolfville & Calgary; specializing in English Studies & Philosophy
Don LePan, President

Broken Jaw Press Inc. (BJP)
Previous Name: Maritimes Arts Projects Productions
PO Box 596 A, Fredericton, NB E3B 5A6
Tel: 506-454-5127; *Fax:* 506-454-5134
editors@brokenjaw.com
www.brokenjaw.com
Social Media: brokenjawpress.blogspot.ca
www.facebook.com/190837609905
ISBNs: 0-921411, 1-896647, 1-55391; SAN: 117-1437
Joe Blades, Publisher

Broquet inc. / Broquet Publishing Company Inc.
97-B, Montee des Bouleaux, Saint-Constant, QC J5A 1A9
Tél: 450-638-3338; *Téléc:* 450-638-4338
Ligne sans frais: 800-363-2864
info@broquet.qc.ca
www.broquet.qc.ca
ISBNs: 2-89000
Ouvrages qui traitent des sciences de la nature, d'horticulture, d'hornithologie, de cuisine, de santé, de bricolage, de sport, de techniques artistiques, de livres jeunesse et de tout autres sujets pratiques.
Antoine Broquet, Propriétaire

The Brucedale Press
Owned By: Broad Horizons Books
PO Box 2259, Port Elgin, ON N0H 2C0
Tel: 519-832-6025; *Toll-Free:* 866-832-6025
info@brucedalepress.ca
www.brucedalepress.ca
ISBNs: 0-9698716, 1-896922
Specializing in Bruce Peninsula & Queen's Bush writers, artists & photographers

Brush Education
Previous Name: Detselig Enterprises Ltd.
#6531, 111th St. NW, Edmonton, AB T6H 3R5
Tel: 780-989-0910; *Fax:* 855-283-6947
Toll-Free: 855-283-0900
contact@brusheducation.ca
www.brusheducation.ca
ISBNs: 0-920490, 1-55059; SAN: 115-0324
Specializing in general trade & academic books written by authors from Canada, the U.S., Austria and The Netherlands
Glenn Rollans, Partner
Lauri Seidlitz, Managing Editor

Bungalo Books
#337, 829 Norwest Rd., Kingston, ON K7P 2N3
Tel: 613-374-1243
publisher@bungalobooks.com
www.bungalobooks.com
Social Media:
twitter.com/FrankBEdwards
www.facebook.com/BungaloBooks
ISBNs: 0-921285
Books for children
Frank Edwards, Publisher

Bunker to Bunker Books
PO Box 914 T, Calgary, AB T2H 2H4
Tel: 403-475-3882
bunkertobunkerbooks@yahoo.com
www.bunkertobunkerbooks.com
ISBNs: 0-9699039
Military firearms books, British & Canadian military collectible books, WW II history

BuschekBooks
PO Box 74053, 5 Beechwood Ave., Ottawa, ON K1M 2H9
Tel: 613-744-2589; *Fax:* 613-744-2967
contact@buschekbooks.com
www.buschekbooks.com
ISBNs: 0-9699904, 1-894543
Publishers of poetry, fiction & translations by first time authors & translators.

Caitlin Press Inc.
8100 Alderwood Rd., Halfmoon Bay, BC V0N 1Y1
Tel: 604-885-9194; *Toll-Free:* 877-964-4953
admin@caitlin-press.com
www.caitlin-press.com
Social Media:
twitter.com/caitlinpress
www.facebook.com/caitlinbooks
ISBNs: 1-894759, 0-920576; SAN: 115-2793
Specializing in BC authors, poetry, stories of the Central Interior and in works by and about BC women.
Vici Johnstone, Publisher, vici@caitlin-press.com
Rebecca Hendry, Publicist, admin@caitlin-press.com

Callawind Publications Inc. / Publications Callawind inc.
#179, 3551, boul St. Charles, Kirkland, QC H9H 3C4
Tel: 514-685-9109; *Fax:* 514-685-7952
info@callawind.com
www.callawind.com
ISBNs: 1-896511
Specializing in cookbooks & children's books; also available in the U.S. from #200, 4501 Forbes Blvd., Lanham, MD, 20706, Tel: 800-462-6420, www.bibliodistribution.com.

Canada Law Book
Owned By: Thomson Reuters
Toronto, ON
Tel: 416-609-3800; *Toll-Free:* 800-387-5164
carswell.customerrelations@thomsonreuters.com
www.canadalawbook.ca
ISBNs: 0-88804
Specializing in legal resources (print & online), & current awareness services

Canadian Bible Society (CBS)
10 Carnforth Rd., Toronto, ON M4A 2S4
Tel: 416-757-4171; *Toll-Free:* 800-465-2425
info@biblesociety.ca
www.biblesociety.ca
Social Media:
www.facebook.com/CanadianBibleSociety
ISBNs: 0-88834; SAN: 112-5559
The Society translates, publishes & distributes the Bible throughout Canada
Rev. Ted Seres, National Director, tseres@biblesociety.ca
Dennis Hillis, Director, Operations, dhillis@biblesociety.ca

Canadian Government Publishing
350 Albert St., 4th Fl., Ottawa, ON K1A 0S5
Tel: 613-941-5995; *Fax:* 613-998-1450
Toll-Free: 800-635-7943
publications@pwgsc.gc.ca
publications.gc.ca
ISBNs: 0-660, 0-662; SAN: 115-2882
The official publisher for the Government of Canada. As of March 7, 2014, Publishing and Depository Services is no longer selling or distributing Government of Canada publications in tangible formats.

The Canadian Institute for Law, Theology & Public Policy
89 Douglasview Rise SE, Calgary, AB T2Z 2P5
Tel: 403-720-8714; *Fax:* 403-720-8746
ciltpp@cs.com
www.ciltpp.com
ISBNs: 1-896363
Publishes books and taps which seek to integrate in depth the Christian faith with public policy issues

Canadian Institute of Strategic Studies
#064S, 1 Devonshire Pl., Toronto, ON M5S 3K7
Tel: 416-946-7209
info@opencanada.org
www.onlinecic.org
Social Media: opencanada.tumblr.com
twitter.com/TheCIC
www.facebook.com/CanadianInternationalCouncil
ISBNs: 1-894736, 0-919769; SAN: 115-2912
The Institute publishes books, papers & journals devoted to the research & analysis of Canadian Military Affairs, security affairs & international relations in general.
Jennifer Jeffs, President, 416-946-7209
Taylor Owen, Editor-in-Chief, towen@opencanada.org

Canadian Institute of Ukrainian Studies Press (CIUS Press)
University of Toronto, #308, 256 McCaul St., Toronto, ON M5T 1W5
Tel: 780-492-2973
cius@ualberta.ca
www.ciuspress.com
ISBNs: 0-920862, 1-895571, 1-894301, 1-894865; SAN: 115-2920
The Institute is the publishing arm of the Canadian Institute of Ukranian Studies. It focuses on original research in English on Ukrainian history, language, literature, contemporary Ukraine, and Ukrainians in Canada. It also publishes English translations of Ukrainian monographs and memoirs.

Canadian Scholars' Press Inc. (CSPI)
#200, 425 Adelaide St. West, Toronto, ON M5V 3C1
Tel: 416-929-2774; *Fax:* 416-929-1926
info@cspi.org
www.cspi.org
Social Media: www.linkedin.com/company/701428
twitter.com/CanadianScholar
www.facebook.com/120771713511
ISBNs: 1-55130, 0-921627, 1-894184
CSPI is an independent publisher of texts, scholarly works, and titles that present themes and issues of interest to the general Canadian market. It also imprints Women's Press and Sumach Press, both with a focus on feminist work which contributes to the social identity of Canada, and also Kellom Books which carries poetry, fiction and non-fiction by men.
Andrew Wayne, President, awayne@cspi.org
Lily Bergh, Publishing Director, lily.bergh@cspi.org

Canadian University Press
376 Bathurst St., Toronto, ON M5S 2M8
Tel: 416-962-2287; *Fax:* 416-966-3699
Toll-Free: 866-250-5595
president@cup.ca
www.cup.ca
Social Media: www.youtube.com/user/CUPonline
twitter.com/canunipress
www.facebook.com/canadianuniversitypress
Canadian University Press is a national, non-profit co-operative, owned & operated by more than 80 student newspapers from coast to coast.
Jane Lytvynenko, National Executive, executive@cup.ca

Canadian Urban Institute / Institut urbain du Canada
PO Box 612, #402, 555 Richmond St. W, Toronto, ON M5V 3B1
Tel: 416-365-0816; *Fax:* 416-365-0650
www.canurb.com
Social Media:
www.youtube.com/user/canurborg?feature=results_main
twitter.com/canurb
www.facebook.com/265253496954
ISBNs: 1-895446
Non-profit organization with annual publications to improve urban regions
John Farrow, Chairman of the Board
Caryl Arundel, Vice-Chair

CANAV Books (CANAV)
51 Balsam Ave., Toronto, ON M4E 3B6
Tel: 416-698-7559
www.canavbooks.com
ISBNs: 0-9690703, 0-91022; SAN: 115-3021
Publishers of books on aviation history
Larry Milberry, Publisher, larry@canavbooks.com

Cape Breton Catalogue
Previous Name: Breton Books & Music
Wreck Cove, NS B0C 1H0
Tel: 902-539-5140; *Fax:* 902-539-9117
Toll-Free: 800-565-5140
bretonbooks@ns.sympatico.ca
www.capebretonbooks.ca
ISBNs: 1-895415
Showcasing Cape Breton authors
Ronald Caplan, President

Cape Breton University Press (CBU)
Previous Name: University College of Cape Breton Press
PO Box 5300, 1250 Grand Lake Rd., Sydney, NS B1P 6L2
Tel: 902-563-1955; *Fax:* 902-563-1177
cbu_press@cbu.ca
cbup.ca
Social Media:
twitter.com/cbupress
www.facebook.com/CapeBretonUniversityPress
ISBNs: 0-920336; 1-897009; 1-927492
Publishing arm of Cape Breton University.
Mike R. Hunter, Editor-in-Chief, 902-563-1955, mike_hunter@cbu.ca

Captus Press
 # 14-15, 1600 Steeles Ave. W, Concord, ON L4K 4M2
Tel: 416-736-5537; *Fax:* 416-736-5793
info@captus.com
www.captus.com
ISBNs: 0-921801, 1-895712, 1-896691, 1-55322
Captus is a publisher of textbooks which provide a Canadian context for university and college courses in the subjects of business, law, disability studies, and Aboriginal economic development.

CBC Learning
Previous Name: CBC Non-Broadcast Sales
PO Box 500 A, Toronto, ON M5W 1E6
Fax: 416-205-2376
Toll-Free: 866-999-3072
www.cbceds.ca
Social Media: www.youtube.com/watchcbclearning
twitter.com/CBCLearning
www.facebook.com/102839444139?ref=ts
ISBNs: 0-660; SAN: 115-2777
Publishes resources related to CBC programs & programming

CCH Canadian Limited
Owned By: Wolters Kluwer
#300, 90 Sheppard Ave. E, Toronto, ON M2N 6X1
Tel: 416-224-2248; *Fax:* 416-224-2243
Toll-Free: 800-268-4522
cservice@cch.ca
www.cch.ca
Other information: Toll Free Fax: 800-461-4131
ISBNs: 1-55367, 1-55141, 0-88796, 1-55496; SAN: 115-2785
Publishers of professional information products involving tax, accounting, law, financial planning & human resources

CCSP Press
Simon Fraser University at Harbour Centre, 515 West Hastings Street, Vancouver, BC V6B 5K3
Tel: 778-782-5242; *Fax:* 778-782-5239
publishing.sfu.ca/read/ccsp-press/
CCSP Press publishes works that examine publishing (excluding newspapers), report the results of research into publishing, and inform students of the practicalities of publishing.

Cedar Cave Books
Newmarket, ON
info@cedarcave.com
www.cedarcave.com
Cedar Cave Books are publishers of Canadian writers & titles, with a self & e-publishing department

Centax Books & Distribution
Owned By: Printwest
1111 - 8th Ave., Regina, SK S4R 1E1
Fax: 800-853-6829
Toll-Free: 800-667-5595
centax@printwest.com
www.centaxbooks.com
ISBNs: 0-919845, 1-895292, 1-894022, 1-897010
Produces and markets cookbooks, RCMP history books, business and family management books, family lifestyle, gardening, self-help and sports books.
Jill Jensen, Office Manager, 800-664-6695

Centre for Addiction & Mental Health (CAMH)
Previous Name: Addiction Research Foundation
33 Russell St., Toronto, ON M5S 2S1
Tel: 416-595-6059; *Toll-Free:* 800-661-1111
info@camh.net.
www.camh.net
Other information: 1-800-463-627
Social Media: www.linkedin.com/company/camh
twitter.com/CAMHnews
www.facebook.com/CentreforAddictionandMentalHealth
ISBNs: 978-1-77052-003-5
CAMH publishes resources for therapists, doctors, nurses, front-line workers, and other professionals in the fields of addictions & mental health. Materials include research papers, pamphlets, newsletters and journals.
Dr. Catherine Zahb, President, CEO

Centre for Continuing & Distance Education (CCDE)
#237 Williams Bldg., University of Saskatchewan, 221 Cumberland Ave. N, Saskatoon, SK S7N 1M3
Tel: 306-966-5539; *Fax:* 306-966-5590
Toll-Free: 866-966-5563
ccde.reg@usask.ca
www.ccde.usask.ca
Social Media:
twitter.com/usask
www.facebook.com/CCDEUniversityofSaskatchewan
Bob Cram, Executive Director, 306-966-5536, Fax: 306-966-5590, bob.cram@usask.ca
Jim Greuel, Finance & IT Officer, Finance & IT, 306-966-5538, jim.greuel@usask.ca

Centre for Reformation & Renaissance Studies (CRRS)
Previous Name: Dovehouse Editions Inc.
17 Queen's Park Cres. E, Toronto, ON M5S 1K7
Tel: 416-585-4465; *Fax:* 416-585-4430
crrs.info@vicu.utoronto.ca
www.crrs.ca
Social Media:
twitter.com/CRRS_Toronto
www.facebook.com/pages109176085775329
ISBNs: 0-919473, 1-895537
Researches, teaches, & publishes series about time period between 1350-1700
Lynne Magnusson, Director, 416-585-4461

Centre FORA
#0103, 450, av Notre-Dame, Sudbury, ON P3C 5K8
Tél: 705-524-3672; *Téléc:* 705-524-8535
Ligne sans frais: 888-814-4422
info@centrefora.on.ca
www.centrefora.on.ca
ISBNs: 2-921706
Centre francophone d'édition en éducation de base des adultes, et de diffusion de matériel éducatif pour tout âge. Service d'édition: coordination de projects, production, impression, rédaction, etc. Service de diffusion. Bureaux: Sudbury, North Bay.
Liane Romain, Directrice générale, lianer@centrefora.on.ca

Centre franco-ontarien de ressources pédagogiques
435, rue Donald, Ottawa, ON K1K 4X5
Tél: 613-747-8000; *Téléc:* 613-747-2808
Ligne sans frais: 877-742-3677
cforp@cforp.ca
www.cforp.on.ca
Médias sociaux:
twitter.com/CFORP
Centre multiservices en éducation; développement, édition; production multimedia; programmation; formation professionnelle; imprimerie
Gilles Leroux, Directeur général, 613-747-8000 x253, gilles.leroux@cforp.ca

CGS Communications, Inc.
Previous Name: Canadian Guidance Services
2521 Nicklaus Ct., Burlington, ON L7M 4V1
Tel: 905-332-0083; *Fax:* 905-319-1641
info@cgscommunications.com
www.cgscommunications.com
ISBNs: 0-929079
Publishes materials include books on career/educational planning and scholarship informaton.
Brian Harris, Editor, 905-332-0083, brian@cgscommunications.com

CHA Press
#100, 17 York St., Ottawa, ON K1N 9J6
Tel: 613-241-8005; *Fax:* 613-241-5055
Toll-Free: 855-236-0213
info@cha.ca
www.cha.ca/publications
Social Media:
twitter.com/CHA_ACS
www.facebook.com/CanadianHealthcareAssociation
ISBNs: 0-919100, 1-896151
Publishes research about health system improvement

The Charlton Press
PO Box 69509, 5845 Younge St., Toronto, ON M2M 4K3
Tel: 416-488-1418; *Fax:* 416-488-4656
Toll-Free: 800-442-6042
chpress@charltonpress.com
www.charltonpress.com
Publishers of catalogues on 20th century collectables including coins, bank notes & others
Jean Dale, Publisher

Chenelière Éducation
Anciennement: Éditions de la Chenelière inc.
#900, 5800 rue Saint-Denis, Montréal, QC H2S 3L5
Tél: 514-273-1066; *Téléc:* 514-276-0324
Ligne sans frais: 800-565-5531
info@cheneliere.ca
www.cheneliere.ca
Autre information: Toll Free Fax: 800-814-0324
Médias sociaux: www.linkedin.com/company/cheneli-re-ducation
twitter.com/cheneliere
www.facebook.com/143896708843
ISBNs: 2-89310, 2-89461
Y compris Groupe Beauchemin, Gaëtan Morin Éditeur, et les Publications Graficor
Jacques Rochefort, Président-directeur général, jrochefort@cheneliere.ca
Michel Carl Perron, Vice-président, Production, mcperron@cheneliere.ca

Chestnut Publishing Group Inc.
#610, 4005 Bayview Ave, Toronto, ON M2M 3Z9
Tel: 416-224-5824; *Fax:* 416-224-0595
sharkstark@sympatico.ca
www.chestnutpublishing.com
ISBNs: 1-894601, 0-9731237, 0-9689552, 0-9688946
CPG publishes educational material for both adult & children, ESL materials, as well as novels & teacher's guides targeted at reluctant readers. It has 4 imprints: Chestnut Publishing, High Interest Publishing (HIP), Lynx Publishing and Patnor Books with its New Start Suspense Series.

Stanley Starkman, President & CEO, 416-224-5824, sharkstark@sympatico.ca

ChiZine Publications (CZP)
67 Alameda Ave., Toronto, ON M6C 3W4
Tel: 416-652-3482
www.chizinepub.com
CZP publishes weird, subtle, surreal, disturbing dark fiction and fantasy.

Claudiere Books
2423 Alta Vista Dr., Ottawa, ON K1H 7M9
info@chaudierebooks.com
www.chaudierebooks.com
Social Media: www.myspace.com/chaudierebooks
twitter.com/ChaudiereBooks
Christine McNair, Publisher/Production Manager, christine@chaudierebooks.com
Robert McLennan, Publisher/Senior Editor, rob@chaudierebooks.com

Clifford Ford Publications
#2004, 530 Laurier Ave. W, Ottawa, ON K1R 7T1
Tel: 613-699-7694
crford@cliffordfordpublications.ca
www.cliffordfordpublications.ca
ISBNs: 0-919883
This is a publisher of a wide range of sheet music, including Canadian historical anthologies, choral collections and pedagogical music, as well as those works composed by Clifford Ford.
Clifford Ford, Publisher

CMP Publications
PO Box 34097, Halifax, NS B3J 3S1
Tel: 902-425-1320; *Fax:* 902-425-1325
cmp@cmppublications.com
www.cmppublications.com
ISBNs: 0-9693595, 0-9739494
The company is dedicated to researching, publishing and / or distributing information and books related to the natural and social sciences. Titles include themes on fisheries, agriculture, construction, environment, recycling and more.

Coach House Books
80 bpNichol Lane, Toronto, ON M5S 3J4
Tel: 416-979-2217; *Fax:* 416-977-1158
Toll-Free: 800-367-6360
mail@chbooks.com
www.chbooks.com
Social Media:
www.goodreads.com/2578586-coach-house-books
twitter.com/coachhousebooks
www.facebook.com/groups/2260058751
ISBNs: 1-55245, 1-897439, 1-77056
Coach House Books publishes Canadian content across a variety of fields: fiction, poetry, art & architecture, drama & performing arts, children's, social science & travel, including a series of books about Toronto. It has been nominated for a slew of literary awards, such as Griffin Poetry Prizes, Governor General's Awards, Trillium Book Awards, and the Ontario Premier's Award for Excellence in the Arts.
Stan Bevington, Publisher, stan@chbooks.com
Alana Wilcox, Editorial Director, alana@chbooks.com

Colombo & Company
42 Dell Park Ave., Toronto, ON M6B 2T6
Tel: 416-782-6853; *Fax:* 416-782-0285
jrc@colombo.ca
www.colombo.ca
ISBNs: 1-894540, 0-9695092, 1-896308
This is the publishing imprint for books by John Robert Colombo & colleagues, including poetry & poetry anthologies, Canadiana, reference works & quotation collections, mysteries, humour & translations.
John Robert Colombo, Publisher

Commodore Books
6079 Academic Quadrangle, English Dept., Simon Fraser University, 8888 University Dr., Burnaby, BC V5A 1S6
Tel: 778-782-4988; *Fax:* 604-291-5737
info@commodorebooks.com
www.commodorebooks.com
The first and only black literary press in western Canada.

Commoners' Publishing Society Inc.
631 Tubman Cres., Ottawa, ON K1V 8L5
Tel: 613-523-2444; *Fax:* 888-613-0329
sales@commonerspublishing.com
www.commonerspublishing.com
ISBNs: 0-88970; SAN: 115-0243
Although by no means limited to men's issues, Commoners' publishes books on parenting, marriage and divorce policy from a male perspecitive.

Company's Coming Publishing Limited
#5, 2910 Commercial Dr., Vancouver, BC V5N 4C9
Tel: 780-450-6223; *Fax:* 780-450-1857
info@companyscoming.com
www.companyscoming.com
Social Media:
www.facebook.com/pages/Companys-Coming/59216157574
ISBNs: 1-896891, 1-897069, 1-895455, 0-9690695, 0-9693322, 1-897477
Publishes an extensive array of cookbooks, including a selection of series, with Kids Cooking, Pint Size, & Focus as examples. In addition, Company's Coming publishes a series of craft books.

Conundrum Press
10224 Highway #1, Wolfville, NS B4P 2R2
Toll-Free: 800-591-6250
conpress@ns.sympatico.ca
www.conundrumpress.com
Social Media:
twitter.com/ConundrumCanada
www.facebook.com/ConundrumPressCanada

Copp Clark Professional
Owned By: Pearson Plc
#1, 1675 Sismet Rd., Mississauga, ON L4W 4K8
Tel: 905-889-8458
www.coppclark.com
ISBNs: 0-7730, 0-273
The oldest, continuously active publisher in Canada, Copp Clark publishes resources for the financial trading community, authoritative reference data on holiday observances.
Ronald S. Marr, President & Publisher
Grace D'Alfonso, Editorial Director

Cormorant Books Inc.
#615, 10 St. Mary St., Toronto, ON M4Y 1P9
Tel: 416-925-8887
www.cormorantbooks.com
Social Media: www.youtube.com/user/cormorantbooks
www.twitter.com/cormorantbooks
www.facebook.com/pages/Cormorant-Books/27 6145292065
ISBNs: 0-920953, 1-896951, 1-897151; SAN: 115-4176
Cormorant Books specializes in fiction emerging Canadian writers, reissues of Canadian literary classics, and English translations of works by Quebec writers. There is a selection of gay & lesbian literature, as well as non-fiction titles, including historical biographies and memoirs.
Marc Coté, President & Publisher

Coteau Books
Owned By: Thunder Creek Publishing Cooperative
2517 Victoria Ave., Regina, SK S4P 0T2
Tel: 306-777-0170; *Fax:* 306-522-5152
Toll-Free: 800-440-4471
coteau@coteaubooks.com
www.coteaubooks.com
Other information: www.goodreads.com/profile/Coteau_Books
Social Media: pinterest.com/coteaubooks
twitter.com/CoteauBooks
www.facebook.com/pages/Coteau-Books/21207050660
ISBNs: 0-919926, 1-55050
Coteau Books is a not-for-profit, cooperatively run press specializing in fiction, poetry, drama & fiction for young readers, with some emphasis on Saskatchewan writers.
Nik L. Burton, Managing Editor
Amber Goldie, Marketing Manager, marketing@coteaubooks.com

Crabtree Publishing
616 Welland Ave., St. Catharines, ON L2M 5V6
Tel: 905-682-5221; *Fax:* 800-355-7166
Toll-Free: 800-387-7650
custserv@crabtreebooks.com
www.crabtreebooks.com
ISBNs: 0-7787, 0-86505, 1-4271; SAN: 115-1436
With offices in the U.S., Canada, the U.K. and Australia, Crabtreespecializes in children's non-fiction work & educational products on many curriculum subjects. Material is published in an audio format and in several languages, including Spanish and French. Imprints include: A Bobbie Kalman Book; Leaps and Bounds Books; and Look, Listen, & Learn.

Cranberry Tree Press
#173, 5060 Tecumseh Rd. E, Windsor, ON N8T 1C1
Fax: 519-945-6207
mail@cranberrytreepress.com
www.cranberrytreepress.com
ISBNs: 0-9681325, 0-9684218, 1-894668
Cranberry Tree Press is a contract, co-operative publishing service with editors & designers on staff.
Lenore Langs, Publisher & Editor
Laurie Smith, Publisher & Editor

Creative Book Publishing Ltd.
PO Box 8660 A, St. John's, NL A1B 3T7
Tel: 709-748-0813; *Fax:* 709-579-6511
nl.books@transcontinental.ca
www.creativebookpublishing.ca
ISBNs: 0-920021, 1-895387, 1-894294, 1-897174, 0-920884
Creative Book Publishing specializes in works by Newfoundland & Labrador authors, promoting them to national & international markets. Genres include fiction, poetry, memoirs, history, women's studies and more. Books are published under 3 imprints: Creative Publishers, Killick Press, & Tuckamore Books.
Russell Wangersky, General Manager, rwanger@thetelegram.com
Donna Francis, Editor & Marketing Manager, donna.francis@transcontinental.ca

Crisp Learning Canada
Previous Name: Reid Publishing Ltd.
Owned By: Course Technology, a Thomson company
60 Briarwood Ave., Mississauga, ON L5G 3N6
Tel: 905-274-5678; *Fax:* 905-278-2801
Toll-Free: 800-446-4797
info@crisplearning.ca
www.crisplearning.ca
Other information: Toll Free Fax: 866-722-1822
ISBNs: 0-921601; SAN: 116-0478
Crisp Learning publishes a library of books & training manuals specializing in: communication, conflict resolution, presentation skills, telephone skills, sales & marketing, customer service, managing, organizational development, and personal improvement.

Crown Publications Inc.
563 Superior St., Victoria, BC V8W 1T7
Tel: 250-387-6409; *Fax:* 250-387-1120
Toll-Free: 800-663-6105
crownpub@gov.bc.ca
www.crownpub.bc.ca
ISBNs: 0-9696417
Crown Publications is the authorized distributor of British Columbia acts, regulations & related legislative publications, and an authorized agent for Canadian Federal Government publications.

Culture Concepts Books
69 Ashmount Cres., Toronto, ON M9R 1C9
Tel: 416-245-8119
cultureconcepts@rogers.com
www.cultureconceptsbooks.ca
ISBNs: 0-921472
Culture Concepts Books publishes academic titles in adult education, food, nutrition and culture. Also offered are professional editing services & manuscript evaluation, selected literary agency & book production.
Thelma Barer-Stein, President Ph.D.

Cyclops Press
PO Box 206 Cordyon, Winnipeg, MB R3M 3S7
Tel: 204-779-7803; *Fax:* 204-779-6970
Toll-Free: 800-591-6250
mail@cyclopspress.com
www.cyclopspress.com
ISBNs: 1-894177
An independent, artist-run, multimedia, literary micro- publisher specializing in poetry, novels, feature films & videos, CDs, interdisciplinary art projects. Material is distributed through Signature Editions, www.signature-editions.com.

Dance Collection Danse Publishing
#301, 149 Church St., Toronto, ON M5B 1Y4
Tel: 416-365-3233; *Toll-Free:* 800-665-5320
talk@dcd.ca
www.dcd.ca
Social Media:
www.twitter.com/DanceCollection
www.facebook.com/pages/Dance-Collection-Danse/14927618346
ISBNs: 0-929003
Publisher of "Dance Collection Danse Magazine," & books on dance.
Francisco Alvarez, Chair

Database Directories
588 Dufferin St., London, ON N6B 2A4
Tel: 519-433-1666; *Fax:* 519-430-1131
mail@databasedirectory.com
www.databasedirectory.com
ISBNs: 1-896537
Publisher of current contact information on Canadian schools, libraries, book retailers & municipalities
Lesley Classic, CEO
Robert Kasher, President

Davus Publishing
150 Norfolk St. South, Simcoe, ON N3Y 2W2
Tel: 519-426-2077; *Fax:* 519-426-0105
davuspub@sympatico.ca
www.davuspublishing.com
ISBNs: 0-915317
Featuring the works of David Beasley, and Major John Richardson, Canada's first novelist.
David R. Beasley, President & Publisher,
davuspub@sympatico.ca

DC Books
PO Box 666 St. Laurent, 950, rue Décarie, Montréal, QC H4L 4V9
Tel: 514-939-3990; *Fax:* 514-939-0569
Toll-Free: 800-591-6250
dcbooks@videotron.ca
www.dcbooks.ca
ISBNs: 0-919688, 1-897190; SAN: 115-8988
DC Books publishes poetry & prose with innovative Canadian emphasis, histories, memoirs, & drama. Also offered are Railfare DC Books about railways & Moosehead Anthology. The house is a Member of the Association of English Editors of Quebec, & the Literary Press Group.
Keith Henderson, Managing Editor

Decker Publishing Inc.
#310, 69 John St. S, Hamilton, ON L8N 2B9
Tel: 905-522-8526; *Fax:* 905-522-9273
Toll-Free: 800-647-6511
customerccustomercare@deckerip.com
www.deckerpublishing.com
Publishes the ACP Medicine & ACS Surgery book products in both print & digital editions, as well as ten specialty medical journals, to serve the informational needs of health care professionals & students.

Demeter Press
PO Box 13022, 140 Holland St. West, Bradford, ON L3Z 2Y5
Tel: 905-775-9089
info@demeterpress.org
www.demeterpress.org
Social Media:
www.twitter.com/DemeterPress
www.facebook.com/PressDemeter
Demeter Press is an independent feminist press focused specifically on the topic of mothering/ motherhood.

Deux Voiliers Publishing (DVP)
Gatineau, QC
Tel: 819-684-7688
deuxvoiliers@gmail.com
www.deuxvoilierspublishing.com
Social Media: www.linkedin.com/pub/deux-voiliers/41/76b/134
www.facebook.com/DeuxVoili ersPublishing?ref=hl
A small print press specializing in first-time Canadian novelists.
Ian Thomas Shaw, Owner

Diffusion Dimedia inc.
539, boul Lebeau, Saint-Laurent, QC H4N 1S2
Tel: 514-336-3941; *Fax:* 514-331-3916
general@dimedia.qc.ca
www.dimedia.qc.ca
Diffuse & distribue des livres de langue française au Canada
Johanne Paquette, Contact

Diffusion du Livre Mirabel
Détenteur: Éditions du Renouveau Pédagogique Inc.
5757, rue Cypihot, Saint-Laurent, QC H4S 1R3
Tél: 514-334-2690; *Téléc:* 514-334-4720
Ligne sans frais: 800-263-3678
editorial@pearsonelt.ca
www.erpi.com
ISBNs: 0-88527
Division d'Éditions du Renouveau Pédagogique Inc.; livres jeunesse & imagerie, informatique, littérature, livres de cuisine, bandes dessinées
Normand Cleroux, Président

Diffusion Inter-Livres
1701, rue Belleville, Lemoyne, QC J4P 3M2
Tél: 450-465-0037; *Téléc:* 450-923-8966
Ligne sans frais: 866-465-5579
interlivres@llbquebec.ca
www.inter-livres.ca
Ministère de la Ligue pour la lecture de la Bible et du Canada français dans le but principal d'aider les librairies chrétiennes qui étaient de fournir des livres en langue française directement à partir de l'Europe.
Joël Coppieter

Doubleday Canada Ltd.
c/o Random House of Canada Limited, #300, One Toronto St., Toronto, ON M5C 2V6
Tel: 416-364-4449; *Fax:* 416-364-6863
www.randomhouse.ca
Social Media: www.youtube.com/user/BookLounge
twitter.com/RandomHouseCA
www.facebook .com/RandomHouseOfCanada
Publishes Canadian literary & commercial fiction from new & established writers, memoirs, history, business, & social & political journalism
John Neale, President
Evaughn Moffat, Vice-President, Sales & Marketing

Douglas & McIntyre (2013) Ltd.
PO Box 219, 4437 Rondeview Rd., Madeira Park, BC V0N 2H0
Toll-Free: 800-667-2988
info@douglas-mcintyre.com
www.douglas-mcintyre.com
Social Media:
twitter.com/DMPublishers
www.facebook.com/DMPublishers
ISBNs: 0-88894, 1-55054, 1-55365; SAN: 115-1886, 115-026X
Specializing in Canadian fiction & non-fiction. Harbour Publishing acquired Douglas & McIntyre in 2013 from D&M Publishers Inc.
Howard White, Publisher

Dragon Hill Publishing Ltd.
5474 Thibault Wynd NW, Edmonton, AB T6R 3P9
Tel: 780-239-4996
info@dragonhillpublishing.com
www.dragonhillpublishing.com
ISBNs: 1-896124
Publishing for the popular adult and youth markets, in the subject areas of self-help, biography, success guides, and traditional cultures
Gary Whyte, Publisher

Drawn & Quarterly
PO Box 48056, #800, 400, av Atlantic, Montréal, QC H2V 4S8
Tel: 514-279-2221
info@drawnandquarterly.com
www.drawnandquarterly.com
ISBNs: 1-896597
Publisher of comic books & graphic novels.
Chris Oliveros, Publisher, chris@drawnandquarterly.com

Dundurn Group
#500, 3 Church St., Toronto, ON M5E 1M2
Tel: 416-214-5544; *Fax:* 416-214-5556
info@dundurn.com
www.dundurn.com
Social Media:
twitter.com/dundurnpress
www.facebook.com/dundurnpress
Kirk Howard, President & Publisher
C. Dick Yu, Director of Finance
Margaret Bryant, Director of Sales & Marketing

eastendbooks
45 Fernwood Park Ave., Toronto, ON M4E 3E9
info@eastendbooks.com
www.eastendbooks.com
ISBNs: 1-896973
A small-press with an Ontario focus, publishing material in a range of subjects, including fiction, travel, current events, modern jazz
Jeanne MacDonald, Managing Partner,
macdonald@eastendbooks.com

Écrits des Forges
992-A, rue Royale, Trois-Rivières, QC G9A 4H9
Tél: 819-840-8492
ecritsdesforges.com
Médias sociaux:
facebook.com/editions.ecritsdesforges
ISBNs: 2-89046
Poésie, et essais en poésie

ECW Press (ECW)
#200, 2120 Queen St. East, Toronto, ON M4E 1E2
Tel: 416-694-3348; *Fax:* 416-698-9906
info@ecwpress.com
www.ecwpress.com
Social Media:
www.facebook.com/ecwpress
Jack David, Co-Publisher, Business, Sports, Mysteries,
jack@ecwpress.com
Michael Holmes, Sr. Editor, Literary fiction, poetry, wrestling,
michael@ecwpress.com
Crissy Calhoun, Managing Editor, crissy@ecwpress.com

Édifice Steel
#3000, 4080 rue Wellington, Montréal, QC H4G 1V4
Tél: 514-284-2622; *Téléc:* 514-284-2625
www.actualisation.com
Médias sociaux: www.linkedin.com/company/actualisation-idh
twitter.com/ActualisationRH
Matériel pour animer des formations, destiné aux formateurs, éducateurs et conseillers en ressources humaines: guides, manuels, questionnaires.

Éditions Anne Sigier inc.
Détenteur: Éditions Médiaspaul
a/s Éditions Médiaspaul, 3965, boul Henri-Bourassa est, Montréal, QC H1H 1L1
Tél: 514-322-7341; *Téléc:* 514-322-4281
mediaspaul@mediaspaul.qc.ca
www.annesigier.qc.ca
ISBNs: 2-89129
Bibles, livres de spiritualité chrétienne, beaux-livres
Anne Sigier

Les Éditions Ariane / Ariane Editions Inc.
#101, 1217 ave Bernard ouest, Outremont, QC H2V 1V7
Tél: 514-276-2949; *Téléc:* 514-279-4121
www.ariane.qc.ca
ISBNs: 2-920987
Offre une variété de cours liés à la spiritualité, le développement personnel, la santé mondiale et l'émergence d'un nouveau monde et un monde plus juste, durable et société plus verte
Marc Vallée, Éditeur

Les Éditions Brault & Bouthillier / Brault & Bouthillier Publishing
#275, 4823, rue Sherbrooke ouest, Montréal, QC H3Z 1G7
Tel: 514-932-9466; *Fax:* 514-932-5929
Toll-Free: 866-750-9466
editions@ebbp.ca
www.ebbp.ca
Other information: Toll Free Fax: 866-988-5929
Social Media:
www.facebook.com/218526381540151
ISBNs: 0-88537, 2-7615
Manuels scolaires, ouvrages pédagogiques/parascolaires; français et anglais
Christiane Beullac, Québec Contact, 866-750-9466

Les Éditions Cap-aux-Diamants Inc.
CP 26 Haute-Ville, #212, 3, rue de la Vieille-Université, Québec, QC G1R 5K1
Tél: 418-656-5040; *Téléc:* 418-656-7282
revue.cap-aux-diamants@hst.ulaval.ca
www.capauxdiamants.org
ISBNs: 2-920069
Yves Beauregard, revue.cap-aux-diamants@hst.ulaval.ca

Les Éditions CEC inc.
Une compagnie de Quebecor Media
Owned By: Quebecor Media
9001, boul Louis-H.-La Fontaine, Anjou, QC H1J 2C5
Tel: 514-351-6010; *Fax:* 514-351-3534
Toll-Free: 800-363-0494
infoped@ceceditions.com
www.editionscec.com
Other information: Toll Free Fax: 877-913-5920
ISBNs: 0-7751, 2-7617
Ouvrages pour tous les ordres d'enseignement - manuels scolaires, ouvrages de référence, grammaires, anthologies littéraires

Éditions CERES
CP 1089 B, Montréal, QC H5B 3K9
Téléc: 514-937-9875
editionsceres@gmail.com
www.editionsceres.ca
ISBNs: 0-919089
Les éditions CERES publient exclusivement des livres érudits

Les Éditions Chouette
#B-238, 1001, rue Lenoir, Montréal, QC H4C 2Z6
Tel: 514-925-3325; *Fax:* 514-925-3323
info@editions-chouette.com
www.chouettepublishing.com
Livres Caillou
Christine L'Heureux, Présidente-fondatrice

Les Éditions Cornac
Anciennement: Les Éditions du Loup de Gouttière
5, rue Sainte-Ursule, Québec, QC G1R 4C7
Tél: 418-692-0377; *Téléc:* 418-692-0605
editionscornac.com
Médias sociaux:
www.facebook.com/529976497028348

ISBNs: 2-921310, 2-89529
Livres jeunesse; poésie; essais; albums illustrés; a pour mission d'encourager l'expression des Premières Nations
Michel Brûlé, Éditeur, michel@editionscornac.com
Anne Peyrouse, Directrice de collection, poésie, poesie@editionscornac.com

Les Éditions de l'Hexagone
Une compagnie de Quebecor Media
Détenteur: Quebecor Media/Groupe VML
1010, rue de la Gauchetière est, Montréal, QC H2L 2N5
Tél: 514-523-7993; *Téléc:* 514-282-7530
adpcommandes@messageries-adp.com
www.edhexagone.com
Médias sociaux:
www.facebook.com/vlbediteur
ISBNs: 2-89006, 2-89295
Littérature québécoise
Martin Balthazar, Vice-président, Édition

Les Éditions de l'Homme
Une compagnie de Quebecor Media
Détenteur: Quebecor Media
955, rue Amherst, Montréal, QC H2L 3K4
Tél: 514-523-1182; *Téléc:* 514-597-0370
adpcommandes@messagies-adp.com
www.editions-homme.com
ISBNs: 2-7619, 2-89005, 2-89006
Livres de sciences humaines

Éditions de L'instant même
865, av Moncton, Québec, QC G1S 2Y4
Tél: 418-527-8690; *Téléc:* 418-681-6780
info@instantmeme.com
www.instantmeme.com
ISBNs: 2-921197, 2-9800635, 2-89502
Romans, essais, nouvelles

Les Éditions de la courte échelle
#404, 160 rue Saint-Viateur Est, Montréal, QC H2T 1A8
Tél: 514-274-2004; *Téléc:* 514-270-4160
info@courteechelle.com
www.courteechelle.com
Médias sociaux:
twitter.com/Courte_echelle
www.facebook.com/courteechelle
ISBNs: 2-89021; SAN: 116-0249
Un leader de la littérature jeunesse francophone - livres pour les trois à six ans; collection adulte
Hélène Derome, Présidente

Éditions de la Paix
412, rue Maupassant, Chicoutimi, QC G7J 4P6
Tél: 418-690-2335
info@editpaix.qc.ca
www.editpaix.qc.ca
Jeunesse, patrimoine, romans, poésie, spiritualité
Janine Perron, Éditrice
Pierre Tuinstra, Éditeur

Les Éditions de la Pleine Lune
223, 34e av, Lachine, QC H8T 1Z4
Tél: 514-637-6366
editpllune@videotron.ca
www.pleinelune.qc.ca
ISBNs: 978-2-89024
Ouvrages québécois et canadiens
Marie-Madeleine Raoult, Directrice

Éditions de Mortagne
CP 116, Boucherville, QC J4B 5E6
Tél: 450-641-2387; *Téléc:* 450-655-6092
www.editionsdemortagne.com
ISBNs: 2-89074
Biographies, romans, collection 'Lime et citron', guides pratiques, santé, psychologie, astrologie, motivation
Max Permingeat, Président

Les Éditions des Plaines
CP 123, Saint-Boniface, MB R2H 3B4
Tél: 204-235-0078; *Téléc:* 204-233-7741
admin@plaines.mb.ca
www.plaines.ca
Médias sociaux:
www.facebook.com/editionsdesplaines
ISBNs: 0-920944, 2-921353, 2-89611
La maison s'applique à donner la parole aux écrivains de l'Ouest canadien
Joanne Therrien, Éditrice, direction@plaines.mb.ca

Les Éditions du Blé
Détenteur: A Vos Livres
340, boule Provencher, Saint-Boniface, MB R2H 0G7
Tél: 204-237-8200
direction@editionsduble.ca
www.ble.avoslivres.ca
Médias sociaux:
www.facebook.com/EditionsduBle
ISBNs: 0-920640, 2-921347
La première maison d'édition francophone de l'Ouest canadien; ouvrages des auteurs de la région - poésie, romans, essais, théâtre, livres pour enfants & adolescents

Éditions du Bois-de-Coulonge
1140, av De Montigny, Sillery, QC G1S 3T7
Tél: 418-683-6332; *Téléc:* 418-683-6332
www.ebc.qc.ca
ISBNs: 2-9801397
Services aux collectivités & vente directe au grand public
Richard Leclerc, Président Ph.D., rleclerc@ebc.qc.ca

Éditions du Boréal
4447, rue Saint-Denis, Montréal, QC H2J 2L2
Tél: 514-287-7401; *Téléc:* 514-287-7664
boreal@editionsboreal.qc.ca
www.editionsboreal.qc.ca
Médias sociaux: www.youtube.com/user/EditionsduBoreal
twitter.com/editionsBoreal
www.facebook.com/126468671573?ref=ts
ISBNs: 2-89052, 0-7646
Fiction, poésie, essais, histoire, biographies, livres pratiques, collections jeunesse

Les Éditions du Noroît
#202, 4609, rue d'Iberville, Montréal, QC H2H 2L9
Tél: 514-727-0005; *Téléc:* 514-723-6660
lenoroit@lenoroit.com
www.lenoroit.com
ISBNs: 2-89018
Livres de poésie et essais littéraires
Paul Bélanger, Directeur

Les Éditions du Remue-Ménage inc.
La Maison Parent-Roback, #501, 110, rue Ste-Thérèse, Montréal, QC H2Y 1E6
Tél: 514-876-0097; *Téléc:* 514-876-7951
info@editions-remuemenage.qc.ca
www.editions-remuemenage.qc.ca
Médias sociaux:
twitter.com/remue_menage
www.facebook.com/editionsrm
ISBNs: 2-89091
Livres sur les femmes: biographie, culture, développement international, éducation, études féministes, poésie, politique, santé

Éditions du Renouveau Pédagogique inc.
Anciennement: Editions Pierre Tisseyre
5757, rue Cypihot, Saint-Laurent, QC H4S 1R3
Tél: 514-334-2690; *Téléc:* 514-334-4720
Ligne sans frais: 800-263-3678
info@erpi.com
www.erpi.com
Autre information: Télécopieur: 800-643-4720
ISBNs: 2-7613
Maison d'édition scolaire; matériel didactique pour tous les niveaux d'enseignement

Les Éditions du Septentrion
1300, av Maguire, Québec, QC G1T 1Z3
Tél: 418-688-3556; *Téléc:* 418-527-4978
sept@septentrion.qc.ca
www.septentrion.qc.ca
Spécialisée en histoire, archéologie, science politique, ethnographie, et aux sciences humaines
Denis Vaugeois, Président

Les Éditions du Trécarré
Une compagnie de Quebecor Media
Détenteur: Quebecor Media
La Tourelle, #800, 1055, boul René-Lévesque est, Montréal, QC H2L 4S5
Tél: 514-849-5259; *Téléc:* 514-849-1388
adpcommandes@messageries-adp.com
www.edtrecarre.com
ISBNs: 2-89249, 2-89568
Livres pratiques (cuisine, santé); cahiers d'exercices; littérature jeunesse

Éditions du Vermillon
305, rue Saint-Patrick, Ottawa, ON K1N 5K4
Tél: 613-241-4032
leseditionsduvermillon@rogers.com
www.leseditionsduvermillion.ca
ISBNs: 0-919925, 1-895873, 1-894547, 1-897058
Romans, poésie, bandes dessinées, guides pédagogiques, essais

Éditions Fides
#100, 7333 place des Roseraies, Anjou, QC H1M 2X6
Tél: 514-745-4290; *Téléc:* 514-745-4299
editions@groupefides.com
www.editionsfides.com
Médias sociaux:
twitter.com/editionsFides
www.facebook.com/344202282311782
ISBNs: 2-7621
Littérature (collection de poche 'Bibliothèque québécoise'), essais, livres religieux, ouvrages de référence, beaux livres; collection Éditions Bellarmin
Stéphane Lavoie, Directeur général

Les Éditions Flammarion Ltée
375, av Laurier ouest, Montréal, QC H2V 2K3
Tél: 514-277-8807; *Téléc:* 514-278-2085
info@flammarion.qc.ca
www.flammarion.qc.ca
Médias sociaux: www.youtube.com/user/Flammarionbref
www.facebook.com/288439417866015
ISBNs: 2-89077
Une maison d'édition généraliste
Louise Louiselle, Éditrice

Éditions Ganesha
CP 484 Youville, Montréal, QC H2P 2W1
Tél: 450-621-8167
courriel@editions-ganesha.qc.ca
www.editions-ganesha.qc.ca
Ouvrages diverses: philosophie, religion/cultes, psychologie

Les Éditions Héritage
1101, av Victoria, Saint-Lambert, QC J4R 1P8
Tél: 514-875-0327
dominiqueetcie@editionsheritage.com
dominiqueetcompagnie.com
Jacques Payette, Président

Éditions Hurtubise inc
1815, av De Lorimier, Montréal, QC H2K 3W6
Tél: 514-523-1523; *Téléc:* 514-523-9969
Ligne sans frais: 800-361-1664
www.editionshurtubise.com
Médias sociaux:
www.youtube.com/profile?user=livreshmh#grid/uploads
twitter.com/_Hurtubise
www.facebook.com/EditionsHurtubise
ISBNs: 2-89045, 2-89428
Littérature, beaux livres, jeunesse, éducation
Hervé Foulon, Président-directeur général
Amaud Foulon, Vice-président Éditions et Opérations, Éditions et Opérations, arnaud.foulon@editionshurtubise.com

Les Éditions JCL inc. / JCL Publishing
930, rue Jacques-Cartier est, Chicoutimi, QC G7H 7K9
Tél: 418-696-0536; *Téléc:* 418-696-3132
jcl@jcl.qc.ca
www.jcl.qc.ca
Médias sociaux:
www.facebook.com/pages/Les-%C3%A9ditions-JCL/119470338132
ISBNs: 2-89431, 2-920176
Éditeur généraliste: romans, histoire, culture, jeunesse
Jean-Claude Larouche, Président, jclarouche@jcl.qc.ca

Les Éditions JML inc.
1150, chemin des Patriotes nord, Mont-St-Hilaire, QC J3G 4S6
Tél: 450-536-1565; *Téléc:* 450-536-2565
infos@editionsjml.com
www.editionsjml.com
ISBNs: 2-89234
Cahiers de préparation de cours, cahiers de titularisat, relevés de notes, relevés d'absences

Éditions l'Artichaut inc.
355, rue Dubé, Rimouski, QC G5L 4W6
Tél: 418-723-1554; *Téléc:* 418-725-4828
artichaut@editionslartichaut.com
www.editionslartichaut.com
ISBNs: 2-921288; 2-922998
Matériel didactique axé sur le développement des compétences en langue française (niveaux primaire, secondaire)

Les Éditions La Pensée Inc.
4370, rue de l'Hôtel de Ville, Montréal, QC H2W 2H5
Tél: 514-848-9042; *Téléc:* 514-848-9836
Ligne sans frais: 800-667-5442
information@editions-lapensee.qc.ca
www.editions-lapensee.qc.ca

ISBNs: 978-2-89458; 978-2-91287
Les distributeurs de livres éducatifs pour les élèves du primaire et du secondaire
Claude Legault, Directeur Administratif, 514-848-9042, Fax: 514-848-9836, information@éditions-legensee.qc.ca

Éditions Les 400 Coups
#300, 4609 rue d'Iberville, Montréal, QC H2H 2L9
Tél: 514-381-1422; *Téléc:* 514-487-8811
info@editions400coups.com
www.editions400coups.ca
Médias sociaux:
twitter.com/Les400coups
www.facebook.com/editionsles400coups

ISBNs: 2-920993, 2-89540
Albums jeunesse, livres d'art, bandes dessinées. Publient également sous les noms de Mille-Iles, de Zone convective, et de Mécanique générale

Éditions Liber
2318, rue Bélanger, Montréal, QC H2G 1C8
Tél: 514-522-3227; *Téléc:* 514-522-2007
info@editionsliber.org
www.editionsliber.org
Médias sociaux:
twitter.com/EditionsLiber
www.facebook.com/EditionsLiber

ISBNs: 2-921569, 2-89578
Études & essais en philosophie, sciences humaines, littérature

Éditions Libre Expression
Détenteur: Quebecor Media
#800, 1055, boul. René-Lévesque E, Montréal, QC H2L 4S5
Tél: 514-849-5259; *Téléc:* 514-849-1388
www.edlibreexpression.com

ISBNs: 2-89111, 2-7648
Fiction, biographie, essais, histoire, culture, guides, beaux livres, livres de poche
Carole Boutin, Directrice des contrats et des droits dérivés, 514-373-2743, carole.boutin@groupelibrex.com

Les Éditions Logiques
Une compagnie de Quebecor Media
Anciennement: Logidisque inc.
Détenteur: Quebecor Media
La Tourelle, #800, 1055, boul René-Lévesque est, Montréal, QC H2L 4S5
Tél: 514-849-5259; *Téléc:* 514-849-1388
adpcommandes@messageries-adp.com
www.edlogiques.com

ISBNs: 2-89381
Gestion des affaires, économie, pédagogie, psychologie populaire, philosophie, sociologie

Éditions Marie-France
9900, av des Laurentides, Montréal, QC H1H 4V1
Tél: 514-329-3700; *Téléc:* 514-329-0630
Ligne sans frais: 800-563-6644
editions@marie-france.qc.ca
www.marie-france.qc.ca
Médias sociaux: www.linkedin.com/company/1234624
twitter.com/EdMarieFrance
www.faceboo k.com/editions.marie.france

ISBNs: 2-89168
Informatique, littérature, mathématique, français, français immersion
Jean H. Lachapelle, Président

Les Éditions Michel Quintin
CP 340, 4770, rue Foster, Waterloo, QC J0E 2N0
Tél: 450-539-3774; *Téléc:* 450-539-4905
info@editionsmichelquintin.ca
editionsmichelquintin.ca
Médias sociaux:
twitter.com/EditionsQuintin
www.facebook.com/#!/EditionsQuintin

ISBNs: 2-920438, 2-89435; SAN: 116-5356
Michel Quintin, Président-directeur général
Johanne Ménard, Édition scientifique, jmenard@editionsmichelquintin.ca
Colette Dufresne, Vice-présidente / Éditrice

Éditions MultiMondes
1815, av De Lorimier, Montréal, QC H2K 3W6
Tél: 514-523-1523; *Ligne sans frais:* 800-361-1664
www.multim.com

ISBNs: 2-921146, 2-89544
Environnement, santé, jeunesse, muséologie, pédagogie, science et technologie
Jean-Marc Gagnon, Président, jmgagnon@multim.com
Lise Morin, Vice-présidente, lmorin@multim.com

Éditions Paulines
5610, rue Beaubien est, Montréal, QC H1T 1X5
Tél: 514-253-5610
fsp-paulines@videotron.ca
www.paulines.qc.ca

ISBNs: 0-920912
Ouvrages de spiritualité

Les Éditions Perce-Neige ltée
#22, 140 Botsford St., Moncton, NB E1C 4X4
Tél: 506-383-4446
perceneige@nb.aibn.com
editionsperceneige.ca
Médias sociaux:
www.facebook.com/EditionsPerceNeige

ISBNs: 2-920221
Essaies historiques, études littéraires, contes traditionnels et récits, poésie, romans

Éditions Phidal inc./Phidal Publishing Inc.
5740, rue Ferrier, Montréal, QC H4P 1M7
Tel: 514-738-0202; *Fax:* 514-738-5102
Toll-Free: 800-738-7349
info@phidal.com
www.phidal.com

ISBNs: 2-89393, 2-7643
Ouvrages pour enfants

Les Éditions Prosveta / Prosveta Inc.
3950, Albert Mines, Canton-de-Hatley, QC J0B 2C0
Tel: 819-564-8212; *Fax:* 819-564-1823
Toll-Free: 800-854-8212
prosveta@prosveta-canada.com
www.prosveta-canada.com
Social Media:
www.facebook.com/461625167227233

ISBNs: 1-895978
Huguette Paquin, Vice-Presidente

Les Éditions Québec Amérique
329, rue de la Commune ouest, 3e étage, Montréal, QC H2Y 2E1
Tél: 514-499-3000; *Téléc:* 514-499-3010
courrier@quebec-amerique.com
www.quebec-amerique.com
Médias sociaux:
twitter.com/QuebecAmerique

ISBNs: 0-88552, 2-89037, 2-7644
Ouvrages de référence, littérature, jeunesse

Les Éditions Québec-Livres
Détenteur: Quebecor Media
#1100, 1001 boul de Maisonneuve est, Montréal, QC H2L 4P9
Tél: 514-270-1746; *Téléc:* 514-270-5313
www.quebecoreditions.com

ISBNs: 0-88617, 2-89089, 2-9801107
Affaires, alimentation, astrologie, biographie, guides pratiques, littérature, santé, sports, nouvel âge
Jacques Simard, Éditeur

Les Éditions Reynald Goulet inc.
40, rue Mireault, Repentigny, QC J6A 1M1
Tél: 450-654-2626; *Téléc:* 450-654-5433
Ligne sans frais: 800-663-3021
info@goulet.ca
www.goulet.ca

ISBNs: 2-89377
Ouvrages de bureautique, d'informatique, de dessin assisté par ordinateur, et l'autoformation au niveau post-secondaire
Reynald Goulet, Président & Directeur Général, reynald@goulet.ca
Alain Goulet, Commercialisation, alain@goulet.ca
Isabelle Goulet, Édition, isabelle@goulet.ca

Les Éditions Stanké
Une compagnie de Quebecor Media
Détenteur: Quebecor Media
La Tourelle, #800, 1055, boul René-Lévesque Est, Montréal, QC H2L 4S5
Tél: 514-849-5259; *Téléc:* 514-849-1388
info@groupelibrex.com
www.edstanke.com

ISBNs: 2-7604, 0-88566
Ouvrages grand public: romans, essais, récits
Alain Stanké, Président & Dir.-gén.
Patrick Leimgruber, Directeur commercial

Les Éditions Thémis
Faculté de droit, Université de Montréal, CP 6128 Centre-Ville, Montréal, QC H3C 3J7
Tél: 514-343-6627; *Téléc:* 514-343-6779
info@editionsthemis.com
www.themis.umontreal.ca

ISBNs: 978-2-89400
Livres juridiques; Revue juridique Thémis
Stéphane Rousseau, Président, CEO, stephane.rousseau@umontreal.ca

Les Éditions Un Monde différent ltée
#101, 3905, rue Isabelle, Brossard, QC J4Y 2R2
Tél: 450-656-2660; *Téléc:* 450-659-9328
Ligne sans frais: 800-443-2582
info@umd.ca
www.umd.ca

ISBNs: 2-89225, 2-92000
Traductions et adaptations de best-sellers américains, ouvrages d'auteurs canadiens et internationaux
Michel Ferron, Éditeur, info@umd.ca

Les Éditions Vents d'Ouest
#202, 109 Wright St., Gatineau, QC J8X 2G7
Tél: 819-770-6377; *Téléc:* 819-770-0559
info@ventsdouest.ca
www.ventsdouest.ca
Ado, histoire, romans, essais, nouvelles
Benoît Cazabon, Président

Les Éditions XYZ inc. / XYZ Publishing
1815, av De Lorimier, Montréal, QC H2K 3W6
Tél: 514-525-2170; *Téléc:* 514-525-7537
info@editionsxyz.com
www.editionsxyz.com
Médias sociaux:
www.youtube.com/profile?user=livreshmh#grid/upload/
twitter.com/editions xyz
www.facebook.com/EditionsXYZ

ISBNs: 2-89261 French; 0-9683601 Eng.
Pascal Genêt, Directeur général et éditeur, 514-525-2170 x260, pascal.genet@editionsxyz.com
Marie-Pierre Barathon, Éditrice, 514-525-2170 x270, marie-pierre.barathon@editionsxyz.com

Éditions Yvon Blais
Détenteur: Thomson Reuters
CP 180, Cowansville, QC J2K 3H6
Téléc: 450-263-9256
Ligne sans frais: 800-363-3047
www.editionsyvonblais.com

ISBNs: 2-89451
Éditeur juridique; textes des conférences des formations continues du Barreau du Québec; fiscalité; ressources humaines

EDU Reference Publishers Direct Inc.
Previous Name: EDU Reference Distribution; C. Kirkness Press
#3, 109 Woodbine Downs Blvd., Toronto, ON M9W 1Y6
Tel: 416-674-8622; *Fax:* 416-674-6215
Toll-Free: 877-647-8622
eduref@edureference.com
www.edureference.com

ISBNs: 0-86596, 0-04150
A distributor - bringing publishers & buyers in the Canadian education community together
Orland Kirkness, President, 416-647-8622 ext. 222

8th House Publishing
Montréal, QC
Tel: 438-338-8657
info@8thHousePublishing.com
www.8thHousePublishing.com
Social Media: www.youtube.com/user/8thHouseBooks
twitter.com/8thhouse
www.facebook.c om/pages/8th-House-Publishing/72137082479
Publisher of fiction.

Ekstasis Editions
PO Box 8474 Main, Victoria, BC V8W 3S1
Tel: 250-361-9941; *Fax:* 250-385-3378
Toll-Free: 866-361-9951
ekstasis@islandnet.com
www.ekstasiseditions.com
Ekstasis Editions is a literary publisher of fiction, poetry, criticism, & nonfiction books about spirituality. Children's books are published under the Cherubim Books imprint. Over 200 titles have been published.

Elsevier Inc.
905 King St. West, 4th Fl., Toronto, ON M6K 3G9
Tel: 416-253-3640; *Fax:* 866-290-5590
Toll-Free: 866-896-3331
salescdn.inquiry@elsevier.com
www.elsevier.ca; www.lb.ca
ISBNs: 0-3230, 0-3974, 0-3998, 0-4430, 0-4160, 1-5566, 1-5605,
Providing educational print reference information for the medical sector in pring & online formats
Ron Mobed, Chief Executive Officer

emc notes, inc.
PO Box 61507, 1119 Fennell St. E., Hamilton, ON L8T 5A1
Tel: 905-575-4449; *Fax:* 866-551-5382
Toll-Free: 877-246-1763
sales@emcnotes.com
www.emcnotes.com
Publishers of music curriculum products.

Emond Montgomery Publications Limited (EMP)
60 Shaftesbury Ave., Toronto, ON M4T 1A3
Tel: 416-975-3925; *Fax:* 416-975-3924
Toll-Free: 888-837-0815
info@emp.ca; orders@emp.ca
www.emp.ca
ISBNs: 978-1-55239
Specialists in legal publishing & textbooks
Paul Edmond, President, 416-975-3925 ext. 233, pemond@emp.ca

Engage Books
1666 - 160th St., Surrey, BC V4A 4X2
Tel: 604-901-8194
www.engagebooks.ca

Ergo Books
PO Box 1439 B, London, ON N6A 5M2
Tel: 519-432-4357
ergopro@ergobooks.com
www.ergobooks.com
ISBNs: 0-920516; SAN: 115-3374
Specializing in fiction, poetry, humour, local history & memoirs by Southwestern Ontario writers

Essence Publishing
20 Hanna Ct., Belleville, ON K8P 5J2
Tel: 613-962-2360; *Toll-Free:* 800-238-6376
info@essence-publishing.com
www.essence-publishing.com
ISBNs: 1-896400, 1-894169, 1-55306
Specializing in short-run publishing, with emphasis on Christian themes & perspectives

Everyday Publications Inc. (EPI)
310 Killaly St. W, Port Colborne, ON L3K 6A6
Tel: 905-834-5552; *Fax:* 905-834-8045
books@everydaypubications.org
www.everydaypublications.org
ISBNs: 978-0-88873
Specializing in books about the Bible, in English, French, Spanish, Portuguese, Swahili & Chinese
Gertrud Harlow, Publisher

Exile Editions Ltd.
144483 Southgate Rd. 14-GD, Holstein, ON N0G 2A0
Tel: 519-334-3634; *Toll-Free:* 800-888-4741
the.exile.writers@gmail.com
www.theexilewriters.com
Specializing in fiction, poetry, drama, non-fiction & translations, from established and new writers
Michael Callaghan, Publisher

Exportlivre
#223, 505 rue Bélanger, Montréal, QC H2S 1G5
Tel: 450-671-3888; *Fax:* 450-671-2121
order@exportlivre.com
www.exportlivre.com
Exportlivre est une agence d'exportation qui peut fournir, partout dans le monde, tous les livres québécois et canadiens disponibles, qu'il s'agisse de titres publiés en français ou en anglais
René Bonenfant, Direction, 450-671-3888 ext. 112

Fernwood Publishing Company Limited
Previous Name: Roseway Publishing Co. Ltd.
32 Oceanvista Lane, Site 2A, Box 5, Black Point, NS B0T 1B0
Tel: 902-857-1388; *Fax:* 902-857-1328
info@fernpub.ca
www.fernwoodpublishing.ca
Social Media:
twitter.com/fernpub
www.facebook.com/fernwood.publishing?ref=sgm
ISBNs: 0-9694180, 1-896496
Small publishing house; Publishes plays & fiction & non-fiction books of local interest
Beverly Rach, Publisher; Managing Editor & Acquisitions, 902-857-1388, Fax: 902-857-1328, roseway@fernpub.ca
Candida Hadley, Managing Editor, 902-857-1388, Fax: 902-857-1382, candida@fernpub.ca

Fierce Ink Press Co-op Ltd.
Halifax, NS
submissions@fierceinkpress.com
fierceinkpress.com
Social Media: www.flickr.com/photos/79201546@N03/
twitter.com/fierceinkpress
face book.com/FierceInkPress
Publisher and author collective of young adult books of fiction and short non-fiction.
Allister Thompson, Editorial Director, Allister@fierceinkpress.com

Fifth House Publishers
Owned By: Fitzhenry & Whiteside Limited
195 Allstate Pkwy., Markham, ON L3R 4T8
Fax: 800-260-9777
Toll-Free: 800-387-9776
bookinfo@fitzhenry.ca
www.fifthhousepublishers.ca
Social Media:
twitter.com/FifthHouseBooks
www.facebook.com/home.php?#/group.php?gid=167708953994&re
ISBNs: 0-920079, 1-894004, 1-894856, 1-895618; SAN: 115-1134
Specializing in non-fiction with a Western Canadian emphasis
Stephanie Stewart, Publisher, stewart@fifthhousepublishers.ca

Firefly Books Ltd.
#1, 50 Staples Ave., Richmond Hill, ON L4B 0A7
Tel: 416-499-8412; *Fax:* 416-499-8313
Toll-Free: 800-387-6192
service@fireflybooks.com
www.fireflybooks.com
ISBNs: 0-920668 ; 1-895565 ; 1-55209 ; 1-55297; 1-55407
Firefly Books publishes non-fiction books & distributes non-fiction & children's books.

Fitzhenry & Whiteside Limited
195 Allstate Pkwy., Markham, ON L3R 4T8
Tel: 905-477-9700; *Fax:* 800-260-9777
Toll-Free: 800-387-9776
godwit@fitzhenry.ca
www.fitzhenry.ca
Social Media:
twitter.com/FitzWhits
www.facebook.com/FitzWhits
ISBNs: 0-55041, 0-88902, 1-55005, 1-894004, 1-895618, 0-7737, 0
Specializing in history, biography, poety, sports, photography, reference resources, and children's and young adult material. Owner of Red Deer Press Inc., and Fifth House Publishers
Sharon Fitzhenry, CEO, sfitz@fitzhenry.ca

Fitzhenry & Whiteside Limited, Publishers
Previous Name: Trifolium Books Inc.
195 Allstate Pkwy., Markham, ON L3R 4T8
Tel: 905-477-9700; *Fax:* 800-260-9777
Toll-Free: 800-387-9776
bookinfo@fitzhenry.ca
www.fitzhenrty.ca
Social Media:
twitter.com/FitzWhits
www.facebook.com/FitzWhits
ISBNs: 1-895579, 1-55244
Publishes practical resources in science, technology, information technology, mathematics, careers, general business and life skills, for schools (elementary and secondary), trade professional and reference and library markets.
Sharon Fitzhenry, President, sfitz@fitzhenry.ca

Flanker Press Ltd.
PO Box 2522 C, #A, 1243 Kenmount Rd., St. John's, NL A1C 6K1
Tel: 709-739-4477; *Fax:* 709-739-4420
Toll-Free: 866-739-4420
info@flankerpress.com
www.flankerpress.com
Social Media: www.flickr.com/photos/111805560@N03/sets/
twitter.com/FlankerPress
www.facebook.com/pages/Flanker-Press-Ltd/430191 950460
ISBNs: 0-9698767, 1-894463
Specializing in regional Newfoundland & Labrador historical fiction & non-fiction titles; imprints include Pennywell Books, & Brazen Books
Garry Cranford, President, 709-739-4477 x23

Fleurbec
QC G0R 3E0
Tél: 418-882-0843; *Téléc:* 418-882-6133
melilot@videotron.ca
www.fleurbec.com
ISBNs: 2-920174
Guides d'identification, ouvrages scientifiques, guide culinaire - plantes sauvages, flore
Gisèle Lamoureux, Dirigeante, melilot@videotron.ca

Folklore Publishing
9731 - 42 Ave. NW, Edmonton, AB T6E 5P8
Tel: 780-435-2376; *Fax:* 780-435-0674
fboer@folklorepublishing.com
www.folklorepublishing.com
History
Faye Boer, Publisher

Formac Publishing Company Limited
5502 Atlantic St., Halifax, NS B3H 1G4
Tel: 902-421-7022; *Fax:* 902-425-0166
Toll-Free: 800-565-1975
orderdesk@formac.ca
www.formac.ca
ISBNs: 0-8878, 0-921921; SAN: 115-1371
Publishers & distributors of cooking, travel, regional interest, biographical, fiction, historical, nature, Maritime politics, natural history, children, & teen books
James Lorimer, Publisher, 902-421-7022 ext. 29, jlorimer@formac.ca

The Fraser Institute
1770 Burrard St., 4th Fl., Vancouver, BC V6J 3G7
Tel: 604-688-0221; *Fax:* 604-688-8539
Toll-Free: 800-665-3558
info@fraserinstitute.ca
www.fraserinstitute.org
ISBNs: 0-88975; SAN: 115-3498
Offices in Vancouver, Calgary, Toronto, Montreal; engaged in research & publication with emphasis on economics, public policy and other issues that affect Canadians
Niels Veldhuis, President, niels.veldhuis@fraserinstitute.org

The Frederick Harris Mucic Co. Limited
273 Bloor St. W, Toronto, ON M5S 1W2
Tel: 416-673-1426; *Fax:* 416-408-1542
Toll-Free: 800-387-4013
fhmc@frederickharris.com
www.frederickharris.com
Catalogues of music repertoire for ear training, sight reading, technique, theory, harmony, & music history
Ellen Reeves, Account Executive, 416-673-1426 ext. 235, ereeves@frederickharrismusic.com

Free World Publishing Inc.
#1304, 250 Lett St., Ottawa, ON K1R 0A8
Tel: 613-909-1694
fwp@freeworldpublishing.com
www.freeworldpublishing.com
Free World Publishing's is a Canadian publishing house with Academic and Fiction divisions.

Freehand Books
#515, 815 1st St. SW, Calgary, AB T2P 1N3
Tel: 403-452-5662
customerservice@broadviewpress.com
www.freehand-books.com
Social Media:
twitter.com/fhbooks
www.facebook.com/freehandbooks
Kelsey Attard, Managing Editor, kattard@broadviewpress.com

Frontenac House
1138 Frontenac Ave. SW, Calgary, AB T2T 1B6
Tel: 403-245-8588
connect@frontenachouse.com
frontenachouse.com
Rose Scollard, Owner
David Scollard, Owner

Full Blast Productions
70 Allan Dr., St. Catherines, ON L2N 1E9
Tel: 905-397-5479
fbp@cogeco.ca
fullblastproductions.highwire.com
ISBNs: 1-895451
Publisher of English & Spanish language teaching resources

The Fundy Guild Inc.
#2, 8642, RR#114, Fundy National Park, NB E4H 4V2
Tel: 506-887-6094; *Fax:* 506-887-6008
info@fundyguild.ca
www.fundyguild.ca
ISBNs: 0-920383
Publishes books related to the bay of Fundy & Fundy National Park

Gaspereau Press Ltd.
47 Church Ave., Kentville, NS B4N 2M7
Tel: 902-678-6002; *Fax:* 902-678-7845
Toll-Free: 877-230-8232
info@gaspereau.com
www.gaspereau.com
Social Media:
www.facebook.com/gaspereaupress
ISBNs: 1-894031
Specializing in contemporary literature by emerging & established Canadian authors, with publishing & printing under one roof
Gary Dunfield, Co-publisher
Andrew Steeves, Co-publisher

General Store Publishing House (GSPH)
PO Box 415, 499 O'Brien Rd., Renfrew, ON K7A 4A6
Tel: 613-432-7697; *Fax:* 613-432-7184
Toll-Free: 800-465-6072
submissions@gsph.com
www.gsph.com
Social Media:
twitter.com/GeneralStorePH
www.facebook.com/GeneralStorePH
ISBNs: 0-919431, 1-896182, 1-894263, 1-897113 SAN: 115-6853
Tim Gordon, President

Georgetown Publications Inc.
34 Armstrong Ave., Georgetown, ON L7G 4R9
Tel: 905-873-8498; *Fax:* 888-595-3009
Toll-Free: 888-595-3008
info@georgetownpublications.com
www.georgetownpublications.com
Social Media:
twitter.com/georgetownpubl
www.facebook.com/pages/Georgetown-Publications/2020572398
ISBNs: 0-9731994, 0-9733149
Distributor for Allison & Busby, American Girl Pubishing, Hampton Roads Publishing, & Large Print Press, among others

Gilpin Publishing
PO Box 597, Alliston, ON L9R 1V7
Tel: 705-424-6507; *Fax:* 705-424-6507
Toll-Free: 800-867-3281
mail@gilpin.ca
www.gilpin.ca
Music publishing - MP3s, CDs, piano methods, instrumental & choral arrangements, sheet music

The Ginger Press
848 - 2 Ave. East, Owen Sound, ON N4K 2H3
Tel: 519-376-4233; *Fax:* 519-376-9871
Toll-Free: 800-463-9937
www.gingerpress.com
ISBNs: 0-921773
A bookshop, café, & publishing house, specializing in Owen Sound & area writers & subjects
Maryann Thomas, Publisher, maryann@gingerpress.com

Godwin Books
PO Box 50021, #15, 1594 Fairfield Mall, Victoria, BC V8S 5L8
Tel: 250-370-7753
rthomson@islandnet.com
www.godwinbooks.com
ISBNs: 0-9696774
Featuring books by Robert Thomson & George Godwin
Robert Stuart Thomson, Editor Ph.D., 250-370-7753, rthomson@islandnet.com

The Good Medine Cultural Foundation
PO Box 844, Skookumchuck, BC V0B 2E0
canadiancaboose@yahoo.com
goodmedicinefoundation.com
ISBNs: 0-920698
Good Medicine Cutural Foundation publishes a collection of material on a theme of trains, as well documentation & accounts on First Nations People, in particular, the Pikunni.
Adolf Hungry Wolf, Publisher

Goose Lane Editions
Previous Name: Fiddlehead Poetry Books
#330, 500 Beaverbrook Ct., Fredericton, NB E3B 5X4
Tel: 506-450-4251; *Fax:* 506-459-4991
Toll-Free: 888-926-8377
info@gooselane.com
www.gooselane.com
Social Media:
twitter.com/goose_lane
ISBNs: 0-919197, 0-86492, 0-920110; SAN: 115-3420
Small independent publisher of high-quality, award-winning books.
Susanne Alexander, Publisher, s.alexander@gooselane.com

Gordon Soules Book Publishers Ltd.
1359 Ambleside Lane, West Vancouver, BC V7T 2Y9
Tel: 604-922-6588; *Fax:* 604-922-6574
books@gordonsoules.com
www.gordonsoules.com
Publisher of self-help, fitness & natural medicine books; cookbooks; tarot decks & tarot books; travel books & maps

Granville Island Publishing
#212, 1656 Duranleau St., Vancouver, BC V6H 3S4
Tel: 604-688-0320; *Fax:* 604-668-0132
Toll-Free: 877-688-0320
info@granvilleislandpublishing.com
www.granvilleislandpublishing.com
Social Media:
twitter.com/GIPLbooks
Granville Island Publishing manages book projects for clients such as individuals, corporations, & other orgnaizations.
Jo Blackmore, Publisher

Grass Roots Press
Owned By: Literacy Services of Canada Ltd.
6520 - 82 Ave., Main Fl., Edmonton, AB T6B 0E7
Tel: 780-413-6491; *Fax:* 780-413-6582
Toll-Free: 888-303-3213
info@grassrootsbooks.net
www.grassrootsbooks.net
Social Media:
www.facebook.com/pages/Grass-Roots-Press/187241824635013
Specializing in adult literacy & ESL resources
Dr Pat Campbell, President, 780-413-7323, Fax: 780-413-6512, pat@grassrootsbooks.net
Lisa Zohar, Manager, 780-413-6491, Fax: 780-413-6582, lisa@grassrootsbooks.net
Linda Kita-Bradley, linda@grassrootsbooks.net

Great Plains Publications Ltd.
233 Garfield St. South, Winnipeg, MB R3G 2M1
Tel: 204-475-6799
info@greatplains.mb.ca
www.greatplains.mb.ca
Social Media:
twitter.com/GreatPlainsPub
www.facebook.com/GreatPlainsPublications
ISBNs: 0-9697804, 1-894283
Specializing in the best books from the Prairies & authors from across Canada
Gregg Shilliday, Publisher

Green Dragon Press
#1009, 2267 Lakeshore Blvd. W, Toronto, ON M8V 3X2
Tel: 416-251-6366; *Fax:* 416-251-6365
greendragonpress.com
ISBNs: 1-896781
Publishes books & materials on women's equity

Grey House Publishing Canada
PO Box 1207, #512, 555 Richmond St. West, Toronto, ON M5V 3B1
Tel: 416-644-6479; *Fax:* 416-644-1904
Toll-Free: 866-433-4739
info@greyhouse.ca
www.greyhouse.ca
Other information: circ.greyhouse.ca
Social Media:
www.linkedin.com/company/grey-house-publishing-canada
twitter.com/greyhousecanada
www.facebook.com/GreyHouseCanada
ISBNs: 978-1-61925
Publisher of a number of comprehensive Canadian directories including the Canadian Almanac & Directory, Canadian Who's Who, Associations Canada, Libraries Canada & the Canadian Parliamentary Guide.
Bryon Moore, General Manager
Stuart Paterson, Managing Editor

Greystone Books Ltd.
#201, 343 Railway St., Vancouver, BC V6A 1A4
Tel: 604-875-1550; *Fax:* 604-254-9099
Toll-Free: 800-667-6902
info@greystonebooks.com
www.greystonebooks.com
Social Media:
twitter.com/greystonebooks
www.facebook.com/GreystoneBooks
Books about nature, the environment, travel, sports, popular culture & current issues. Greystone Books was acquired by Heritage House Publishing in 2013.
Rob Sanders, Publisher

Groupe Éducalivres inc.
Anciennement: Éditions Agence d'Arc
955, rue Bergar, Laval, QC H7L 4Z6
Tél: 514-334-8466; *Téléc:* 514-334-8387
Ligne sans frais: 800-567-3671
infoservice@grandduc.com
www.educalivres.com
ISBNs: 2-7607, 0-88586, 0-289022, 0-03-92
Conçoivent, publient et distribuent du matériel pédagogique destiné aux élèves du primaire, du secondaire et de l'éducation aux adultes.

Groupe Fides Inc.
#100, 7333, place des Roseraies, Anjou, QC H1M 2X6
Tél: 514-745-4290; *Téléc:* 514-745-4299
editions@groupefides.com
www.groupefides.com
Médias sociaux:
twitter.com/editionsFides
www.facebook.com/pages/%C3%89ditions-Fides/344202282311178
ISBNs: 2-89137, 2-89035, 2-7621, 2-923694, 2-923989
Maison d'édition dont les spécialités sont : ouvrages de fiction, de référence, de spiritualité, essais, beaux livres, manuels d'enseignment collégial et universitaire.
Claude Rhéaume, Directeur général
Guylaine Girard, Directrice de l'édition, Éditions Fides, guylaine.girard@groupefides.com
Marie-Andrée Lamontagne, Éditrice littéraire

Groupe Modulo Inc.
Previous Name: Modulo Publisher
Owned By: Nelson Education
#900, 5800 rue St-Denis, Montréal, QC H2S 3L5
Tel: 514-738-9818; *Fax:* 514-738-5838
Toll-Free: 888-738-9818
www.moduloediteur.com
Other information: Toll Free Fax: 800-273-5247
Social Media: pinterest.com/groupemodulo
www.facebook.com/508846245806167
ISBNs: 2-89113, 2-920210, 2-920922, 2-89443, 2-920190, 2-921363
Éditeur au préscolaire et au primaire

Groupe Modus
Previous Name: Les Éditions Modus Vivendi inc
55 rue Jean-Talon Ouest, Montréal, QC H2R 2W8
Tel: 514-272-0433; *Fax:* 514-272-7234
info@groupemodus.com
www.modusaventure.com
Social Media:
twitter.com/groupemodus
www.facebook.com/GroupeModus
ISBNs: 2-921556, 2-92155, 2-89523, 2-922148 (Presses Aventure)
Publishers of books covering topics such as arts & crafts, cooking, food & wine, diet & health, games & activities, home renovations and others.
Marc Alain, Chief Executive Officer

GTK Press
#109, 18 Wynford Dr., Toronto, ON M3C 3S2
Tel: 416-385-1313; *Fax:* 416-385-1319
Toll-Free: 866-485-7737
info@gtkpress.com
www.gtkpress.com
ISBNs: 1-894318, 1-55137
Publisher of curriculum resources, notably science, technology, mathematics
K.L. Kwong, President

Guérin éditeur ltée
4501, rue Drolet, Montréal, QC H2T 2G2
Tél: 514-842-3481; *Téléc:* 514-842-4923
Ligne sans frais: 800-398-8337
france.larochelle@guerin-editeur.qc.ca
www.guerin-editeur.qc.ca

ISBNs: 2-7601
L'éditeur des écoles. Groupe Guérin: Guérin, éditeur limitée, Les Éditions La Pensée Inc., et LIDEC Inc.
Marc-Aimé Guérin, President

Guernica Editions Inc.
489 Strathmore Blvd., Toronto, ON M4C 1N8
Tel: 416-658-9888; *Fax:* 416-657-8885
Toll-Free: 800-565-9523
www.guernicaeditions.com
Social Media: www.youtube.com/user/guernicaed
twitter.com/guernica_ed
www.facebook.c om/guernicaed
ISBNs: 0-919349, 2-89135, 0-920717, 1-55071; SAN: 115-0421
Michael Mirolla, Editor-in-Chief/Publisher, michaelmirolla@guernicaeditions.com
Connie McParland, Publisher & Chief Administrative Officer, conniemcparland@guernicaeditions.com

Guy Saint-Jean Éditeur
3440, boul Industriel, Laval, QC H7L 4R9
Tél: 450-663-1777; *Téléc:* 450-663-6666
info@saint-jeanediteur.com
www.saint-jeanediteur.com
ISBNs: 2-920340, 2-89455
Guides pratiques sur la santé, la psychologie populaire, le sport, le jardinage; beaux-livres; littérature; Green Frog Publishing (www.greenfrogpublishing.com) et MarieGray (www.mariegray.com)
Nicole Saint-Jean, Présidente, nicole@saint-jeanediteur.com

GWEV Publishing Inc.
PO Box 565, Stittsville, ON K2S 1A6
Tel: 613-831-9154; *Fax:* 613-831-4291
Toll-Free: 866-747-3797
Sylvia@gwevpublishing.com
www.gwevpublishing.com
Social Media: www.facebook.com/49467845278
ISBNs: 0-9681414, 0-9731300
Publisher of children's books
Sylvia Vincent, Publisher, sylvia@gwevpublishing.com

H.B. Fenn & Company Ltd.
34 Nixon Rd., Bolton, ON L7E 1W2
Tel: 905-951-6600; *Fax:* 905-951-6601
Toll-Free: 800-267-3366
administrator@hbfenn.com
www.hbfenn.com
ISBNs: 0-919768, 1-55168; SAN: 115-1746
Book distributor
Harold B. Fenn, President

Hades Publications, Inc.
PO Box 1414 M, Calgary, AB T2P 2L6
Tel: 403-254-0160; *Fax:* 403-254-0456
admin@hadespublications.com
www.trickster.com
ISBNs: 0-919230, 0-921298
Publishes books and other materials on Magic, Illusion, Conjuring & Variety Arts
Brian Hades, Publisher, admin@hadespublications.com

Hagios Press
PO Box 33024, Regina, SK S4T 7X2
Tel: 306-522-5055
hagiospress@myaccess.ca
www.hagiospress.com
Social Media: twitter.com/hagiospress
www.facebook.com/pages/Hagios-Press/260545 433980082
Publisher of poetry, art books, short-fiction, and literary non-fiction, with a particular focus on books that advance a spiritual connection with the world.
Eric Greenway, Co-Publisher
Donald Ward, Co-Publisher/Co-Founder
Paul Wilson, Co-Publisher

Hancock House Publishers Ltd.
19313 Zero Ave., Surrey, BC V3S 9R9
Tel: 604-538-1114; *Fax:* 604-538-2262
Toll-Free: 800-938-1114
sales@hancockhouse.com
www.hancockhouse.com
Publishers of nonfiction regional titles, focussing on western and northern hisory, biography, wildlife & nature
David Hancock, President

Hans Schafler & Co. Ltd.
#2, 1184 Speers Rd., Oakville, ON L6L 2X4
Tel: 905-827-2949; *Fax:* 905-827-2524
Toll-Free: 877-646-9323
info@schafler.com
www.schafler.com
Publishes curriculum books for schools
Lisbeth Schafler, Owner

Happy Landings
851 Heritage Dr., RR#4, Merrickville, ON K0G 1N0
Tel: 613-269-2552
books@happylandings.com
www.happylandings.com
ISBNs: 0-9697322
Publisher of aviation books by Garth Wallace
Liz Wallace, Publisher

Harbour Publishing Co. Ltd.
PO Box 219, Madeira Park, BC V0N 2H0
Tel: 604-883-2730; *Fax:* 604-883-9451
Toll-Free: 800-667-2988
info@harbourpublishing.com
www.harbourpublishing.com
Social Media: twitter.com/Harbour_Publish
www.facebook.com/group.php?gid=2284749935
ISBNs: 0-920080, 1-55017
Specializing in BC authors & books of the Pacific Northwest
Howard White, President

Harlequin Enterprises Limited
Owned By: Torstar
225 Duncan Mill Rd., Toronto, ON M3B 3K9
Tel: 416-445-5860; *Toll-Free:* 800-432-4879
CustomerService@Harlequin.com
www.harlequin.com
Social Media: www.linkedin.com/company/harlequin
twitter.com/harlequinbooks
www.f acebook.com/HarlequinBooks
ISBNs: 978-0-778
Specializing in series romance & fiction for women, in 31 languages, and 111 international markets.
Donna Hayes, Publisher, Chief Executive Officer

HarperCollins Publishers Ltd.
1995 Markham Rd., Toronto, ON M1B 5M8
Tel: 416-321-2241; *Fax:* 416-321-3033
Toll-Free: 800-387-0117
hcorder@harpercollins.com
www.harpercollins.ca
Other information: 416-975-9334
Social Media: www.youtube.com/harpercollinscanada
twitter.com/harpercollinsca
www.fa cebook.com/HarperCollinsCanada
ISBNs: 978-1-44341; 1-44341
Canadian imprints include Avon, Greenwillow Books, HarperAudio, HarperBusiness, HarperLargePrint, William Morrow, among many others; specializing in Canadian fiction & non-fiction, for adults & children

Hartley & Marks Group
#400, 948 Homer St., Vancouver, BC V6B 2W7
Fax: 800-707-5887
Toll-Free: 800-277-5887
pbdesk@hartleyandmarks.com
www.hartleyandmarksgroup.com
Book publishing & notebooks

Hedgerow Press
PO Box 2471, Sidney, BC V8L 3Y3
Tel: 250-656-9320
hedgep@telus.net
www.hedgerowpress.com
Joan Coldwell, Publsiher

Herald Press
Owned By: MennMedia
#C8, 490 Dutton Dr., Waterloo, ON N2L 6H7
Tel: 519-747-5722; *Fax:* 519-747-5721
Toll-Free: 800-631-6535
info@MennoMedia.org
www.mpn.net
Social Media: www.youtube.com/user/mennomedia
twitter.com/MennoMedia
www.facebook.com/MennoMedia
ISBNs: 978-8-08361
Specializing in resources with emphasis on the Anabaptist perspective, biblical studies, mission, family & church life
Amy Gingerich, Editorial Director, AmyG@MennoMedia.org

Heritage House Publishing Co. Ltd.
#103, 1075 Pendergast St., Victoria, BC V8V 0A1
Tel: 250-360-0829; *Fax:* 250-386-0829
Toll-Free: 800-665-3302
heritage@heritagehouse.ca
www.heritagehouse.ca
Social Media: www.facebook.com/pages/Heritage-House-Publishing/15190894
ISBNs: 0-919214, 1-895811, 1-894384; SAN: 115-8287
Specializing in Western Canadian non-fiction subjects & authors
Rodger Touchie, President/Publisher

HikingCamping.com
PO Box 8563, Canmore, AB T1W 2V3
Fax: 866-431-3894
nomads@hikingcamping.com
www.hikingcamping.com
Social Media: twitter.com/nomadhikers
Specializing in guidebooks for hikers & campers, works of inspiration, insight & philosophy, & photography

Historical Trails West/Historical Research Centre
1115 - 8th Ave. S, Lethbridge, AB T1J 1P7
Tel: 403-328-3824
hrc@ourheritage.net
www.ourheritage.net
Specializing in books & resources of Western Canadian interest
Bruce A. Haig, Director

Hogrefe Publishing
Previous Name: Hogrefe & Huber Publishers
#119-514, 660 Eglington Ave. E, Toronto, ON M4G 2K2
hhpub@hogrefe.com
www.hogrefe.com
Publishes books and journals on psychology, mental health, & tests
Dr. G.Jürgen Hogrefe, Publisher & CEO, juergen.hogrefe@hogrefe.com

Home Builder Magazine
4819 St. Charles Blvd, Pierrefonds, QC H9H 3C7
Tel: 514-620-2200; *Fax:* 514-620-6300
homebuilder@work4.ca
www.homebuildercanada.com
Magazine for Canadian residential construction industry

House of Anansi Press & Groundwood Books
Owned By: Stoddart Publishing
Lower Level, 128 Sterling Rd., Toronto, ON M5V 2K4
Tel: 416-363-4343; *Fax:* 416-363-1017
Toll-Free: 800-663-5714
customerservice@houseofanansi.com
www.houseofanansi.com
Social Media: youtube.com/HouseOfAnansi
twitter.com/houseofanansi
www.facebook.com/houseofanansi?ref=ts
ISBNs: 0-88784; SAN: 115-0391
Specializing in new & established Canadian writers of fiction, non-fiction & poetry, & French-Canadian works in translation
Sarah MacLachlan, President & Publisher

House of Parlance
5230 Marguerite St., Vancouver, BC V6M 3K2
www.houseofparlance.com
Cathy Barrett, Co-founder/Publisher

Human Kinetics Canada
#100, 475 Devonshire Rd., Windsor, ON N8Y 2L5
Tel: 519-971-9500; *Fax:* 519-971-9797
Toll-Free: 800-465-7301
info@khcanada.com
www.humankinetics.com
Publishes information about psychology & phisiology of physical activity

Hungry I Books
#215, 1590 Dr. Penfield Ave., Montréal, QC H3G 1C5
Tel: 514-848-2424
hungryibooks@hotmail.com
cjs.concordia.ca/publications/hungry-i-books
Hungry I Books is a publishing arm of the Institute for Canadian Jewish Studies.

Iguana Books
CSI Annex, 720 Bathurst St., 3rd Fl., Toronto, ON M5S 2R4
Tel: 416-214-0760
info@iguanabooks.com
iguanabooks.com
Social Media: plus.google.com/105947237335899768242?prsrc=3
twitter.com/#!/Iguana_Book s
www.facebook.com/pages/Iguana-Books/146245292128679
Greg Ioannou, President
Meghan Behse, Publisher

Inanna Publications
210 Founders College, York University, 4700 Keele Street, Toronto, ON M3J 1P3
Tel: 416-736-5356; *Fax:* 416-736-5765
inanna.publications@inanna.ca
www.inanna.ca
Social Media: pinterest.com/readinannabooks/
twitter.com/InannaPub
www.facebook.com/ pages/Inanna-Publications/9971851861
Independent feminist press.
Luciana Ricciutelli, Editor-in-Chief, luciana@inanna.ca

Inclusion Press International
47 Indian Trail, Toronto, ON M6R 1Z8
Tel: 416-658-5363; *Fax:* 416-658-5067
inclusionpress@inclusion.com
www.inclusion.com
ISBNs: 1-895418; *ISSN:* 978-1-927771
Resource materials with emphasis on diversity, inclusion & community, for educational institutions, government agencies, human service agencies, First Nations organizations
Jack Pearpoint, Co-publisher, jack@inclusion.com
Lynda Kahn, Director of Marketing, Marketing, lynda@inclusion.com
Cathy Hollands, Managing Director, cathy@inclusion.com

Inhabit Media
PO Box 11125, Iqaluit, NU X0A 1H0
Tel: 647-344-3540
info@inhabitmedia.com
inhabitmedia.com
Social Media:
twitter.com/Inhabit_Media
www.facebook.com/inhabitmedia
An Inuit-owned publishing company whose aim is to preserve and promote the stories, knowledge and talent of Inuit and northern Canada.

Inner City Books
PO Box 1271 Q, Toronto, ON M4T 2P4
Tel: 416-927-0355; *Fax:* 416-924-1814
info@innercitybooks.net
www.innercitybooks.net
ISBNs: 0-919123, 1-894574; SAN: 115-3870
Publishers of studies in Jungian Psychology by Jungian Analysts.
Daryl Sharp, President

Insomniac Press
520 Princess Ave., London, ON N6B 2B8
www.insomniacpress.com
ISBNs: 1-895837, 1-894663
Independent press that publishes non-fiction, poetry & fiction
Mike O'Connor, Publisher, mike@insomniacpress.com
Dan Varrette, Managing Editor, dan@insomniacpress.com

Institut de recherches psychologiques, inc. / Institute of Psychological Research Inc.
1304 Fleury est, Montréal, QC H2C 1R3
Tel: 514-382-3000; *Toll-Free:* 800-363-7800
info@irpcanada.com
www.irpcanada.com
ISBNs: 0-88509, 2-89109
Un institut de recherche axée sur le développement d'outils d'évaluation psychométrique
Patricia Bergeron, Partner
Paul-Julien Groleau, Partner

The Institute for Research on Public Policy / L'Institut de recherche en politiques publiques
#200, 1470, rue Peel, Montréal, QC H3A 1T1
Tel: 514-985-2461
irpp@irpp.org
www.irpp.org
Social Media:
twitter.com/irpp
www.facebook.com/IRPP.org
ISBNs: 0-920380, 0-88645; SAN: 115-3889, 115-0537
Specializing in research & publication with emphasis on Canadian public policy, Canadian federalism, economic policy, international relations; publisher of Policy Options journal
Graham Fox, President & CEO, 514-787-0741, gfox@irpp.org
Suzanne Ostiguy-McIntyre, Vice President, Operations, 514-787-0740, smcintyre@irpp.org

Institute for Risk Research
University of Waterloo, 200 University Ave. West, Waterloo, ON N2L 3G1
Tel: 519-888-4567; *Fax:* 519-725-4834
irr-neram@uwaterloo.ca
www.irr-neram.ca
ISBNs: 0-88898, 0-9696747, 0-9684982
Along with The Network for Environmental Risk Assessment and Management (NERAM), the Institute for Risk Research specializes in research & publications in the areas of risk, risk management for the environment, human health, industrial safety & transportation
Dr. Paul Guild, Vice President-Research, Research

International Development Research Centre (IDRC) / Le Centre de recherches pour le développement international
150 Kent St., Ottawa, ON K1P 0B2
Tel: 613-236-6163; *Fax:* 613-238-7230
info@idrc.ca
www.idrc.ca
Social Media: www.youtube.com/user/IDRCCRDI
twitter.com/idrc_crdi
www.facebook.com/I DRC.CRDI
ISBNs: 0-88936, 1-55250
Publishers of IDRC Bulletin, & resources with emphasis on international development, sustainable development, food, health, social issues
Jean Lebeln, President, Ottawa

Invisible Publishing
2578 Maynard St., Halifax, NS B3K 3V5
info@invisiblepublishing.com
invisiblepublishing.com
Social Media:
twitter.com/invisibooks
www.facebook.com/invisibooks?ref=ts&fref=ts

Irwin Law Inc.
#206, 14 Duncan St., Toronto, ON M5H 3G8
Tel: 416-862-7690; *Fax:* 416-862-9236
Toll-Free: 888-314-9014
www.irwinlaw.com
Social Media:
twitter.com/irwinlaw
www.facebook.com/144205078960918
ISBNs: 1-55221
Publishes books on law for students & legal practitioners
Jeffrey Miller, Publisher

Is Five Communications
Owned By: Is Five Foundation
#302, 161 Eglinton Ave. E, Toronto, ON M4P 1J5
Tel: 416-480-2408; *Fax:* 416-480-2546
tom@isfive.com
www.isfive.com
ISBNs: 0-920934; SAN: 115-3943
Writes, designs, & produces funcraising, educational materials, brochures, annual reports, posters, & other material needed for businesses
Tom Scanlan, Director, 416-278-2408, tom@isfive.com
Laura Scanlan, Project Coordinator, laura.isfive@gmail.com
Monica Scanlan, Office Manager, monica@isfive.com

ISER Books
Memorial University
Arts Publications, 297 Mount Scio Rd., St. John's, NL A1C 5S7
Tel: 709-864-3453; *Fax:* 709-864-4342
iser-books@mun.ca
www.mun.ca/iser
ISBNs: 1-894725, 0-919666; SAN: 115-3897
Research social economic questions regarding historic, geographic & economic circumstances in Newfoundland and Labrador

Island Studies Press (ISP)
University of Prince Edward Island, 550 University Ave., Charlottetown, PE C1A 4P3
Tel: 902-566-0386; *Fax:* 902-566-0756
ispstaff@upei.ca
www.islandstudies.com
ISBNs: 0-919013
Publisher of books on the history, literature, culture and environment of Prince Edward Island
Joan Sinclair, Publishing Coordinator, 902-566-0356, Fax: 902-566-0756, ispstaff@upei.ca

ITMB Publishing Ltd.
12300 Bridgeport Rd., Richmond, BC V6V 1J5
Tel: 604-273-1400; *Fax:* 604-273-1488
itmb@itmb.com
www.itmb.ca
Social Media: www.linkedin.com/company/itmb-canada
twitter.com/ITMBCanada
www.facebook.com/pages/ITMB-Publishing-Ltd/1897699310444 6
ISBNs: 978-1-55341
Publisher of travel maps
Jack Joyce, President

J. Gordon Shillingford Publishing Inc.
Previous Name: The Muses' Company
Box 86, RPO Corydon Avenue, Winnipeg, MB R3M 3S3
Tel: 204-779-6967
jgshill2@mymts.net
jgshillingford.com
ISBNs: 1-896239, 0-919754, 0-969761, 0-920486, 0-968942
Primarily a literary publisher; publishes on average 14 titles/year.
J. Gordon Shillingford, President
Karen Green, Marketing Director
Glenda MacFarlane, Drama Editor
Catherine Hunter, Poetry Editor

Jack The Bookman Ltd.
C/O Jack the Bookman Route E, #4, 1150 Kerrisdale Blvd., Newmarket, ON L3Y 8Z9
Tel: 905-836-5999; *Fax:* 905-836-1152
Toll-Free: 800-563-5168
info@jackthebookman.com
www.jackthebookman.com
Library wholesalers
Markt Davey, President, markd@jackthebookman.com
Scott Davey, Vice President, scottd@jackthebookman.com

James Lorimer & Co. Ltd., Publishers
#1002, 317 Adelaide St. W, Toronto, ON M5V 1P9
Tel: 416-362-4762; *Fax:* 416-362-3939
Toll-Free: 800-565-1975
info@lorimer.ca
www.lorimer.ca
Social Media:
www.facebook.com/LorimerBooks
ISBNs: 0-88862, 1-55028; SAN: 115-1134
Literature for children and adults.
Lynn Schellenberg, Acquisitions Editor, acquisitions@lorimer.ca
Faye Smailes, Children's Book Editor, childrenseditor@lorimer.ca
James Lorimer, Publisher, jlorimer@lorimer.ca
Allison McDonald, Editorial & Marketing Coordinator, promotion@lorimer.ca

John Wiley & Sons Inc.
6045 Freemont Blvd., Mississauga, ON L5R 4J3
Tel: 416-236-4433; *Fax:* 416-236-8743
Toll-Free: 800-567-4797
canada@wiley.com
www.wiley.com
Other information: Toll Free Fax: 800-565-6802
ISBNs: 0-471; SAN: 115-1185
Scientific, mechanical, technical & scholarly content in articles, journals, books & databases
Stephen M. Smith, President & CEO
Ellis E. Cousens, Executive Vice President & CFOO, Finance & Operations
William J. Arlington, Senior Vice President, Human Resources

Kegedonce Press
Neyaashiinigmiing, Chippewas of Nawash First Nation, 11 Park Rd/, Neyaashiinigmiing, ON N0H 2T0
info@kegedonce.com
www.kegedonce.com
Social Media:
twitter.com/KegedoncePress
www.facebook.com/Kegedonce
Publishes the work of Indigenous writers nationally and internationally.
Kateri Akiwenzie-Damm, Owner/Managing Editor

Ken Haycock & Associates Inc
Previous Name: Rockland Press
4839 Vaulfeild Crt., Vancouver, BC V7W 3B3
Tel: 778-689-5938
www.kenhaycock.com
ISBNs: 0-920175
Ken Haycock, President & Publisher, 778-689-5938, ken@kenhaycock.com
Shelley Jackson, Director, Client Services, shelley@kenhaycock.com

Keng Seng Enterprises Inc.
#103, 4000, rue St-Ambroise, Montréal, QC H4C 2C7
Tel: 514-939-3971; *Fax:* 514-989-1922
canada@kengseng.com
www.kengseng.com
ISBNs: 1-895494

Kerrwil Publications Ltd.
538 Elizabeth St., Midland, ON L4R 2A3
Toll-Free: 877-620-9373
www.kerrwil.com
Market resource publishers of Canadian Yachting; Trailer Boating Canada; Boating Industy Canada; Sail-World Cruising; Powerboat-World Canada & Marine Business World

John W. Kerr, Chief Executive Officer, 705-527-7677, johnkerr@kerrwil.com
Elizabeth A. Kerr, President, 416-258-9948, eakerr@kerrwil.com
Greg Nicoll, Vice President, 416-620-9373, gnicoll@kerrwil.com

The Key Publishing House Inc. (KPH)
#A102/230, 1075 Bay St., Toronto, ON M5S 2B2
Tel: 416-935-1790; *Fax:* 416-935-1790
info@thekeypublish.com
www.thekeypublish.com
The Key publishes a wide variety of academic, non-fiction, literary fiction and young adults and children books.

Kids Can Press Ltd.
Owned By: Corus Entertainment Inc.
25 Dockside Dr., Toronto, ON M5A 0B5
Tel: 416-479-7000; *Fax:* 416-960-5437
customerservice@kidscan.com
www.kidscanpress.com
Social Media: www.youtube.com/KidsCanPressMovies
twitter.com/KidsCanPress
www.fac ebook.com/KidsCanBooks
ISBNs: 0-919964, 0-55337, 1-55074; SAN: 115-4001
Specializes in children's literature & children's books

Kindred Productions
1310 Taylor Ave., Winnipeg, MB R3M 3Z6
Tel: 204-669-6575; *Fax:* 204-654-1865
Toll-Free: 800-545-7322
www.kindredproductions.com
ISBNs: 0-919797, 0-921788, 1-894791
Publishing & distribution arm of the Mennonite Bretheren Churches in North America.

Kirkton Press Ltd.
396 Grills Rd., RR#2, Baltimore, ON K0K 1C0
Tel: 905-349-3443; *Fax:* 905-349-3420
kirkton@eagle.ca
www.breakingtheviciouscycle.info
ISBNs: 0-9692768
Publishers of "The Vicious Cycle" series of diet/health books.
Elaine Gottschall, Author

Lancaster House
#200, 17 Dundonald St., Toronto, ON M4Y 1K3
Tel: 416-977-6618; *Fax:* 416-977-5873
Toll-Free: 888-298-8841
customerservice@lancasterhouse.com
www.lancasterhouse.com
Social Media: www.linkedin.com/company/1332214?trk=tyah
twitter.com/LancasterCanada
ISBNs: 0-920450
Publishes information & hosts conferences in the areas of labour & employment law.
Kristina Mark, General Manager
Paula Chapman, Senior Editor
Vanessa Scotts, Editorial Administrator

LandOwner Resource Centre
PO Box 599, 3889 Rideau Vally Dr., Manotick, ON K4M 1A5
Tel: 613-692-3571; *Fax:* 613-692-0831
Toll-Free: 800-267-3504
info@lrconline.com
www.lrconline.com
ISBNs: 0-9680992
Publishes information on forestry, agriculture, wildlife, water, soil and other land management issues.

Lazara Press
PO Box 2269 VMPO, Vancouver, BC V6B 3W2
Tel: 604-872-1134
www.lazarapress.ca
ISBNs: 0-920999
Small, progressive publishing house located in Vancouver. Publishers of poetry, literature, broadsides & chapbooks. Committed to publishing & distributing works that might not otherwise be available.
Penny Goldsmith, Owner

Leaf Press
PO Box 416, Lantzville, BC V0R 2H0
poems@leafpress.ca
www.leafpress.ca
Social Media:
www.facebook.com/Leaf.Press
Poetry chapbook publisher.
Ursula Vaira, Founder/Publisher

Left Field Press
3105 Cowie Rd., Hornby Island, BC V0R 1Z0
Tel: 250-335-0005
info@leftfieldpress.com
www.leftfieldpress.com
Dan Bruiger, Editor

Legacy Project
The Legacy Centre, 9 Lobraico Lane, Whitchurch-Stouffville, ON L4A 7X5
Tel: 905-640-8914; *Fax:* 905-640-2922
Toll-Free: 800-772-7765
admin@legacyproject.org
www.legacyproject.org
Social Media: www.linkedin.com/groups/LegacyCubed-4321233
twitter.com/legacycubed
www.facebook.com/legacycubed
ISBNs: 1-896232
A research & education group, with an independent press, dedicated to quality books for children & adults in the areas of literacy, science education, life course, & intergenerational relationships
Susan V. Bosak, Legacy Project Chair

Leméac Éditeur
4609, rue d'Iberville, 1er étage, Montréal, QC H2H 2L9
Tél: 514-524-5558; *Téléc:* 514-524-3145
lemeac@lemeac.com
www.lemeac.com
ISBNs: 2-7609, 0-7761
Notre politique éditoriale essentiellement à caractère littéraire s'inscrit surtout dans les domaines du roman, du théâtre contemporain, de l'essai, de la biographie de personalités ayant marqué le secteur culturel.
Lise P. Bergevin, Directrice générale

LexisNexis Canada Inc.
Previous Name: Lexis Nexis Butterworths; Butterworths Canada Ltd
#700, 123 Commerce Valley Dr. E, Markham, ON L3T 7W8
Tel: 905-479-2665; *Toll-Free:* 800-668-6481
info@lexisnexis.ca
www.lexisnexis.ca
Social Media: www.linkedin.com/company/lexisnexis-canada-inc.
twitter.com/lexisnexisca n
www.facebook.com/lexisnexiscanada
Provider of invormation & services to law professionals, corporations, government & academic institutions through online products.
Mark Kelsey, Chief Executive Officer, Risk Solutions
Mike Walsh, Chief Executive Officer, Legal & Professional

Libra Information Services Co-op Inc.
PO Box 353 A, Toronto, ON M5W 1C2
Tel: 416-707-3509; *Fax:* 416-861-0520
libra@web.ca
2ww.web.ca/~libra
Publishers of material on Innovative Health Care methods, and for Social Investors & Conscious Consumers

Librairie Gallimard de Montréal
3700, boul Saint-Laurent, Montréal, QC H2X 2V4
Tél: 514-499-2012; *Téléc:* 514-499-1535
librairie@gallimardmontreal.com
www.gallimardmontreal.com
Médias sociaux:
www.facebook.com/LibrairieGallimardMontreal
La librairie Gallimard de Montréal est un lieu pour poésie, théâtre, philosophie, histoire, littérature, sciences humaines sont de véritables niches qui révèlent un fonds accumulé par une longue expérience

Librairie Wilson & Lafleur Ltée
40, rue Notre-Dame est, Montréal, QC H2Y 1B9
Tél: 514-875-6326; *Téléc:* 514-875-8356
Ligne sans frais: 800-363-2327
libraire@wilsonlafleur.com
www.wilsonlafleur.com
ISBNs: 2-89127
Éditeur en droit et législation

Library Bound
#2, 100 Bathurst Dr., Waterloo, ON N2V 1V6
Tel: 519-885-3233; *Fax:* 519-885-2662
www.librarybound.com
ISBNs: SAN: 116-9203
Also provide services for shelf-ready materials
Heather Bindseil, President, 5198853233 ext. 28, heatherb@librarybound.com
Lisa Bendig, Accounting Department, 5198853233 ext. 36, lisab@librarybound.com
Ron Stadnik, Print Collections Development, 5198853233 ext. 26, ron@librarybound.com

Lidec Inc.
4350, av de l'Hôtel-de-Ville, Montréal, QC H2W 2H5
Tél: 514-843-5991; *Téléc:* 514-843-5252
Ligne sans frais: 800-350-5991
lidec@lidec.qc.ca
www.lidec.qc.ca
ISBNs: 2-7608, 0-7762
Éditeurs des manuels de base et du matériel complémentaire adaptés aux différents programmes du ministère de l'Éducation, du Loisir et du Sport du Québec et des autres provinces canadiennes.
Claude Legault, Directeur Général, 514-843-5991, Fax: 514-843-5252, claude.legault@lidec.qc.ca

Life Cycle Books Ltd.
#20, 1085 Bellamy Rd. N, Toronto, ON M1H 3C7
Tel: 416-690-5860; *Fax:* 866-260-8172
Toll-Free: 866-880-5860
support@lifecyclebooks.ca
www.lifecyclebooks.ca
ISBNs: 0-919225; SAN: 115-8417
Publisher of pro-life & abstinence books and other educational materials.

Linda Leith Publishing (LLP)
PO Box 322 Victoria, Westmount, QC H3Z 2V8
linda@lindaleith.com
www.lindaleith.com
LLP is a trade publisher specializing in literary fiction, non-fiction, our innovative short Singles essays and occasionally cartoons.
Linda Leith, Publisher/Owner

Lingo Media Corporation
#703, 151 Bloor St. W, Toronto, ON M5S 1S4
Tel: 416-927-7000; *Fax:* 416-927-1222
Toll-Free: 866-927-7011
info@lingomedia.com
www.lingomedia.com
Other information: Toll Free Fax: 866-927-1222
Social Media:
www.linkedin.com/company/lingo-media-corporation
twitter.com/LingoMediaC orp
www.facebook.com/LingoMedia
Develops and publishes English Language Learning materials for use in China.
Michael Kraft, President & Chief Executive Officer
Khurram Qureshi, Chief Financial Officer

Linguatech éditeur inc.
CP 26026 Salaberry, Montréal, QC H3M 1L0
Tél: 514-336-5207; *Téléc:* 514-336-4736
information@linguatechediteur.com
www.linguatechediteur.com
ISBNs: 2-920342
Publications: dictionnaires et vocabulaires; Actes de congrès; Ouvrages didactiques; Langues de spécialité
Line Mailhot, CEO, 514-336-5207, Fax: 514-336-4936, editeur@linguatechediteur.com
Lucie Dubuc, Éditrice, information@linguatechediteur.com

Little Brick Schoolhouse Inc.
PO Box 84001, 1235 Trafalgar Rd., Oakville, ON L6H 3J0
Tel: 905-690-3400; *Fax:* 905-690-3400
schoolhouse@littlebrick.com
www.littlebrick.com
ISBNs: 0-919788
Publisher of Educational entertainment products dealing with Canadian & American History.

Lone Pine Publishing
23115 - 96 St., Edmonton, AB T6N 1G3
Tel: 780-450-6223; *Fax:* 780-450-1857
Toll-Free: 800-875-7108
info@lonepinepublishing.com
www.lonepinepublishing.com
ISBNs: 0-919433, 1-55105; SAN: 115-4125
Focus as a regional publisher in the Rocky Mountains, West Coast & Great Lakes. Focus on nature, outdoor recreation & popular history.

Loon Books Publishing
722 Lipton St., Winnipeg, MB R3E 2L3
Tel: 204-772-2527; *Fax:* 204-783-6944
loonbooksltd@yahoo.ca
loonbooks.ca

Louise Courteau, éditrice inc.
481, Lac St-Louis est, Saint-Zénon, QC J0K 3N0
Tél: 450-884-5958; *Téléc:* 450-884-5913
editions@louisecourteau.com
www.louisecourteau.com
Publie dans les domaines du développement personnel, de la psychologie, de la santé "autrement", des aliénigènes (extraterrestres), de l'au-delà, des sociétés secrètes, et plus encore.
Louise Courteau, Éditrice, editions@louisecourteau.com

Lynx Images Inc.
PO Box 2463 C, St. John's, NL A1C 6E8
Tel: 709-579-3366; *Fax:* 709-576-3367
website@lynximages.com
www.lynximages.com

ISBNs: 0-9698427, 1-894073
Documentary Film production company & publisher. Publishes books dealing with Canadian History & companion books to documentaries.
Russell Floren, President
Barbara Chisolm, Producer, Director, Writer
Andrea Gutsche, Director, Writer, Graphics

Maa Press
1-4925 Marello Rd., Nelson, BC V1L 6X4
info@maapress.ca
www.maapress.ca

K. Linda Kivi

MacIntyre Purcell Publishing Inc.
194 Hospital Rd., Lunenburg, NS B0J 2C0
Tel: 902-640-3350; *Fax:* 902-640-3075
info@macintyrepurcell.com
www.macintyrepurcell.com
Social Media: www.youtube.com/macintyrepurcell
twitter.com/mpp_inc
www.facebook.com/macintyrepurcell

Madison Press Books
TTC Distributing Inc., 45 Tyler St., Aurora, ON L4G 3L5
Tel: 905-841-9300; *Fax:* 905-841-3026
info@madisonpressbooks.com
www.madisonpressbooks.com
Other information: Toronto Phone Number: 416-923-5027
Independent publishers of illustrated non-fiction titles; Catalog includes a number of international best-sellers including Robert D. Ballard's 'Discovery of the Titanic'; Also publish children's books & custom publishing programs for corporate clients
Oliver Salzmann, Publisher, ext. 223, osalzmann@madisonpressbooks.com

Madonna House Publications
Madonna House, 2888 Dafoe Rd., Combermere, ON K0J 1L0
Tel: 613-756-3728; *Fax:* 613-756-0103
Toll-Free: 888-703-7110
publications@madonnahouse.org
www.madonnahouse.org/publications

ISBNs: 0-921440
Non-profic Catholic Christian publisher of religious books, audiobooks, videos, music & cards.
Linda Lambeth

Malcolm Lester & Associates
#605, 50 Prince Arthur Ave., Toronto, ON M5R 1B5
Tel: 416-921-6637
malcolm@malcolmlester.com
www.malcolmlester.com

ISBNs: 1-9659415
Publisher & publishing consultant; Develop books for other publishers; Develops custom books for corporate clients, individuals & organizations.
Malcolm Lester, malcolm@malcolmlester.com

Mansfield Press
25 Mansfield Ave., Toronto, ON M6J 2A9
Tel: 416-532-2086
info@mansfieldpress.net
www.mansfieldpress.net
Social Media:
twitter.com/MansfieldPress
www.facebook.com/group.php?gid=5479869165
Denis De Klerck, Publisher, denis@mansfieldpress.net

MapArt Publishing Corporation
70 Bloor St. E, Oshawa, ON L1H 3M2
Tel: 905-436-2525; *Toll-Free:* 877-231-6277
www.mapartmaps.com
Social Media:
twitter.com/mapartmaps
Leading publishers of Maps, Atlases, Wall Maps & Street Guides.

Master Point Press (MPP)
331 Douglas Ave., Toronto, ON M5M 1H2
Tel: 416-781-0351; *Fax:* 416-781-1831
info@masterpointpress.com
www.masterpointpress.com

ISBNs: 0-9698461, 1-894154, 1-897106
Publisher of a variety of books on the topic of the card game Bridge; also publishes books on other games, as well as software
Ray Lee, Co-Owner
Linda Lee, Co-Owner

MBooks of BC
Richmond Gardens, #307, Birchwood Ct., 6311 Gilbert Rd., Richmond, BC V7C 3V7
Tel: 778-822-3864
www.mbooksofbc.com

ISBNs: 0-9694933
MBooks of BC has published books by Joe Ruggier (Publisher / Author) as well as titles by many other authors (mostly poets) using print-on-demand technology.
Joe M. Ruggier, Managing Editor, Publisher, Author, jrmbooks@hotmail.com

McClelland & Stewart Ltd. (M&S)
Owned By: Penguin Random House Canada
1 Toronto St., Toronto, ON M5C 2V6
Tel: 416-364-4449; *Fax:* 416-957-1587
editorial@mcclelland.com
www.mcclelland.com

ISBNs: 0-7710; SAN: 115-4192
Publisher of over 100 titles annually, both fiction & non-fiction. Publishers of authors such as Margaret Atwood, Alistair MacLeod, Rohinton Mistry & Jane Urquhart. Publishers of political memoirs, including Pierre Elliott Trudeau's.
Jared Bland, Pubisher

McGill-Queen's University Press
Previous Name: Carleton University Press Inc
#1720, 1010, rue Sherbrooke ouest, Montréal, QC H3A 2R7
Tel: 514-398-3750; *Fax:* 514-398-4333
Toll-Free: 877-864-8477
mqup@mcgill.ca
www.mqup.mcgill.ca
Social Media: www.youtube.com/user/McGillQueens
twitter.com/scholarmqup
www.facebook .com/McGillQueens
ISBNs: 0-88629, 0-7735, 0-88911, 1-55339; SAN: 106-4206
Publisher of non-fiction books, with over 1800 books in print and numerous awards & bestsellers.
Jonathan Crago, Editor-in-Chief, 514-398-7480, jonathan.crago@mcgill.ca
Philip Cercone, Executive Director, 514-398-2910, philip.cercone@mcgill.ca
Ryan van Huijstee, Managing Editor, 514-398-3922, ryan.vanhuijstee@mcgill.ca
Natalie Blachere, Rights & Special Projects Manager, 514-398-2121, natalie.blachere@mcgill.ca

McGill-Queen's University Press
Douglas Library, 93 University Ave., Kingston, ON K7L 5C4
Tel: 613-533-2155; *Fax:* 613-533-6822
mqup@post.queensu.ca
www.mqup.mcgill.ca
Social Media: www.youtube.com/user/McGillQueens
twitter.com/scholarmqup
www.facebook .com/McGillQueens

ISBNs: 0-7735
Scholarly publisher with aims to advance scholarship, promote public debate, and contribute to culture

McGraw-Hill Ryerson Limited
300 Water St., Whitby, ON L1N 9B6
Tel: 800-245-2914; *Fax:* 800-463-5885
Toll-Free: 800-565-5758
cs_queries@mcgrawhill.ca
www.mcgrawhill.ca

ISBNs: 0-07; SAN: 115-060X
Publishers of a large quantity of education materials, including textbooks

McKellar & Martin Publishing Group
5256 Prince Edward St., Vancouver, BC V5W 2X5
Tel: 778-833-1499
www.mckellarmartin.com

Meghan Spong, Publisher / CEO, meghan@mckellarmartin.com
Tonya Martin, Publisher /Editor-In-Chief, tonya@mckellarmartin.com

MDAG Publishing
Tel: 604-502-0796
contact@mdag.com
www.mdag.com

ISBNs: 0-9682039
Released tools & publications produced by the Minesite Drainage Assessment Group
Kevin A. Morin, President Ph.D.,P.Geo.

Mediacorp Canada Inc.
21 New St., Toronto, ON M5R 1P7
Tel: 416-964-6069; *Fax:* 416-964-3202
www.mediacorp.ca
Social Media:
twitter.com/top_employers

ISBNs: 0-9681447, 1-894450
Publishers of data & publications regarding employment, employers & labour

Messageries ADP inc.
Une compagnie de Quebecor Media
Détenteur: Quebecor Media
2315, rue de la Province, Longueuil, QC J4G 1G4
Tél: 450-640-1234; *Téléc:* 450-640-1251
Ligne sans frais: 800-771-3022
www.messageries-adp.com
Autre information: Télécopieur sans frais: 800-603-0433
Diffuseur et distributeur de livres francophones au Canada; partenaire de 139 maisons d'édition québécoises, françaises, belges et suisses

Mile Oak Publishing Inc.
#81, 20 Mineola Rd. East, Mississauga, ON L5G 4N9
Tel: 905-274-4356; *Fax:* 905-274-8656
mile_oak@compuserve.com
www.i75online.com

ISBNs: 1-896819
Publishers of the "Along Interstate-75" travel guide.
Dave Hunter, Publisher
Kathy Hunter, Editor & Researcher

Mini Mocho Press
PO Box 57424 Jackson, Hamilton, ON L8P 4X2
Tel: 905-523-1518
jamesstrecker@sympatico.ca
www.jamesstrecker.com

ISBNs: 0-921980
Publishes a catalog of 26 titles featuring primarily authors from Southern Ontario
James Strecker, Co-Publisher

Misthorn Press
2069 Galleon Way, Comox, BC V9M 3Z2
Tel: 250-339-5202
www.lindsayelms.ca

ISBNs: 0-9680159
Lindsay Elms, Owner

MOD Publishing
4 Fairview Blvd., Toronto, ON M4K 1L9
Tel: 416-466-9275
jean.weihs@rogers.com
www.modpublishing.com
ISBNs: 0-9684559, 0-9683974, 1-894461
Publishes supplemental educational aids that covers material not covered within current circiculum
Shirley Lewis, Founder & Publisher, shirleylewis6@yahoo.com

Monarch Books of Canada
5000 Dufferin St., Toronto, ON M3H 5T5
Tel: 416-663-8231; *Fax:* 416-736-1702
customer_service@monarchbooks.ca
www.monarchbooks.ca
Social Media: monarchbooks.tumblr.com
twitter.com/monarch_books
www.facebook.com/340625476012713
Specializes in distributing Children's books, Teacher Resources, Special Needs, Sports, Reference, Cookbooks & audiobooks

Moose Hide Books
684 Walls Side Rd., Sault Ste Marie, ON P6A 5K6
Tel: 705-779-3331; *Fax:* 705-779-3331
mooseenterprises@on.aibn.com
www.moosehidebooks.com

ISBNs: 0-9698319, 0-9681852, 0-9684909, 0-9686086, 1-894650
To assist and nurture new and up and coming authors and present works by new and established authors.
Richard Mousseau, Owner; Publisher; Editor, 705-779-3331, rmousseau@moosehidebooks.com
Edmond Alcid, Editor, 705-779-3331, ealcid@moosehidebooks.com

Mosaic Press
#1 & 2, 1252 Speers Rd., Oakville, ON L6L 5M1
Tel: 905-825-2130; *Fax:* 905-825-2130
info@mosaic-press.com
www.mosaic-press.com

ISBNs: 0-88962; SAN: 115-4362, 115-4370
Publishes over 20 original titles each year, with a back catalog of over 500 books covering all genres. Literature; The Arts; Social Studies & International Studies
Michael Walsh, Founder

Mother Tongue Publishing Ltd.
290 Fulford-Ganges Rd., Salt Spring Island, BC V8K 2K6
Tel: 250-537-4155; *Fax:* 250-537-4725
info@mothertonguepress.com
www.mothertonguepublishing.com
Social Media:
www.facebook.com/153416691391280
ISBNs: 1-896949, 0-9698904
Publishers of local authors as well as books on British Columbia art history, art & literature.

Multicultural History Society of Ontario
#307, 901 Lawrence Ave. W, Toronto, ON M6A 1C3
Tel: 416-979-2973; *Fax:* 416-979-7947
info@mhso.ca
www.mhso.ca
ISBNs: 0-919045
Publishers of a number of journals and non-fiction books dealing with Multicultural History in Ontario
Cathy Leekam, Program Manager, cathy.leekam@mhso.ca

Native Law Centre of Canada
University of Saskatchewan, 15 Campus Dr., Saskatoon, SK S7N 5A6
Tel: 306-966-6189; *Fax:* 306-966-6207
native.law@usask.ca
www.usask.ca/nativelaw
ISBNs: 0-88880; SAN: 115-4540
Publishers of materials relating to First Nations & Aboriginal Law in Canada.
James (Sákéj) Youngblood Henderson, Research Director, Research, 306-966-6191, Sakej.Henderson@usask.ca

Nelson Education Ltd.
1120 Birchmount Rd., Toronto, ON M1K 5G4
Tel: 416-752-9100; *Fax:* 416-752-8101
Toll-Free: 800-668-0671
www.nelson.com
Other information: Toll Free Fax: 800-430-4445
Social Media:
www.linkedin.com/company/nelson-education?trk=fc_badge
www.facebook.com/ nelsoneducation
ISBNs: 0-176; SAN: 115-0669
Canada's leading Educational Publisher. Publishes K-12 textbooks and educational products, as well as higher education, professional learning & business education publications
Greg Nordal, President & Chief Executive Officer
Michael Andrews, Senior Vice-President, Finance & Chief Financial Offic
Jonathan Abrams, Senior Vice-President & Managing Director, Higher Educa
Susan Cline, Senior Vice-President, Media & Production Services
Jessica Phinn, Vice-President, People & Engagement

New Society Publishers
PO Box 189, Gabriola Island, BC V0R 1X0
Tel: 250-247-9737; *Fax:* 250-247-7471
Toll-Free: 800-567-6772
info@newsociety.com
www.newsociety.com
Social Media:
twitter.com/NewSocietyPub
www.facebook.com/NewSocietyPublishers
ISBNs: 1-55092, 0-86571
Progressive publishing company that specializes in books about activism & ecological sustainability
Judith Plant, Acting Publisher

New Star Books Ltd.
#107, 3477 Commercial St., Vancouver, BC V5N 4E8
Tel: 604-738-9429; *Fax:* 604-738-9332
info@newstarbooks.com
www.newstarbooks.com
ISBNs: 0-919573, 0-921586, 1-55420; SAN: 115-1908
Publishes 6-10 titles annually covering politically- and socially-based non-fiction as well as fiction, poetry and books on local history & culture.
Rolf Maurer, President/Publisher

New World Publishing
PO Box 36075, Halifax, NS B3J 3S9
Tel: 902-576-2055; *Fax:* 902-576-2095
Toll-Free: 877-211-3334
www.newworldpublishing.com
ISBNs: 1-895814
Francis Mitchell, Managing Editor

NeWest Publishers Ltd.
#201, 8540 - 109 St., Edmonton, AB T6G 1E6
Tel: 780-432-9427; *Fax:* 780-433-3179
Toll-Free: 866-796-5473
info@newestpress.com
www.newestpress.com
Social Media:
twitter.com/newestpress
www.facebook.com/group.php?gid=5242749678
ISBNs: 0-920316, 0-920897, 1-896300
Western regional press publishing 10-12 books annually
Paul Matwychuk, General Manager
Matt Bowes, Marketing & Production Coordinator

Newport Bay Publishing Limited
356 Cyril Owen Pl., Victoria, BC V9E 2B6
Tel: 250-479-4616; *Fax:* 250-479-3836
info@newportbay.ca
www.newportbay.ca/publishing
ISBNs: 0-921513
Publishers of a small number of books covering the following subjects: biography, world governance, alternative economics, alternative health and world medicine, home and garden, media/journalism, Native peoples, nature/environment, philosophy, social sciences, and women/feminism.

Nightwood Editions
PO Box 1779, Gibsons, BC V0N 1V0
Toll-Free: 800-667-2988
info@nightwoodeditions.com
www.nightwoodeditions.com
Social Media:
twitter.com/nightwooded
www.facebook.com/pages/Nightwood-Editions/250167 265022217
ISBNs: 0-88971; SAN: 115-2661
Publishers of new poetry & fiction by Canadian writers; Also publishes non-fiction works

Nimbus Publishing Ltd.
Previous Name: Petheric Press Ltd.
PO Box 9166, 3731 MacKintosh St., Halifax, NS B3K 5M8
Tel: 902-455-4286; *Fax:* 902-455-5440
Toll-Free: 800-646-2879
info@nimbus.ns.ca
www.nimbus.ns.ca
Social Media: www.youtube.com/user/NimbusPublishing
www.twitter.com/NimbusPub
www.fa cebook.com/nimbuspub
ISBNs: 0-920852, 0-921054, 1-55109; SAN: 115-0685
Nimbus produces more than thirty new titles a year relevant to the Atlantic Provinces. Vagrant Press is Nimbus Publishing's fiction imprint.
John S. Marshall, President
Terrilee Bulger, Sales & Marketing Manager, tbulger@nimbus.ns.ca

North Shore Publishing Inc.
2351 Sinclair Circle, Burlington, ON L7P 3C1
Tel: 905-336-2364; *Fax:* 905-336-5110
info@canadianheritagebooks.com
www.canadianheritagebooks.com
Social Media: pinterest.com/canadianbooks
twitter.com/Canadian_Books
www.facebook.com/345338745530110
ISBNs: 1-896899
Publishers of local heritage books in Southern Ontario

Northern Canada Mission Distributors
PO Box 3030, Prince Albert, SK
Tel: 306-764-4490; *Fax:* 306-764-3390
missiondist@ncem.ca
www.ncem.ca
Social Media:
www.facebook.com/129747593747605
ISBNs: 0-920731, 1-896968
Art Wanuch, Governing Board

The North-South Institute / L'Institut Nord-Sud
#500, 55 Murray St., Ottawa, ON K1N 5M3
Tel: 613-241-3535; *Fax:* 613-241-7435
nsi@nsi-ins.ca
www.nsi-ins.ca
Social Media:
twitter.com/nsi_ins
www.facebook.com/NSIINS
ISBNs: 1-896770; SAN: 115-4605
Publishers of findings made by the North-South Institute
Roy Culpepper, President, rculpepper@nsi-ins.ca
Ann Weston, Vice-President & Coordinator of Research, aweston@nsi-ins.ca

Novalis Publishing
#400, 10 Lower Spadina Ave., Toronto, ON M5V 2Z2
Tel: 416-363-3303; *Fax:* 416-363-9409
Toll-Free: 877-702-7773
books@novalis.ca
www.novalis.ca
Social Media: www.youtube.com/user/novalisbooks
twitter.com/bayardcanada
www.face book.com/pages/Novalis-Books/122209491151036
ISBNs: 2-89088, 2-89507; SAN: 115-4621
Religious publishing house in the Catholic Tradition; Publishes in the areas of liturgy, prayer, spirituality, sacramental practice, catechetics, religious education and personal growth.
Joesph Sinasac, Publishing Director, joseph.sinasac@novalis.ca
Anne Louise Mahoney, Managing Editor, anne-louise.mahoney@novalis.ca

Now Or Never Publishing
#313, 1255 Seymour St., Vancouver, BC V6B 0H1
Tel: 604-992-9960
www.nonpublishing.com
Social Media:
www.facebook.com/noworneverpublishing
Chris Needham, Publisher, chris@nonpublishing.com
Sidney Shapiro, Editor, editor@nonpublishing.com

Oberon Press
#205, 145 Spruce St., Ottawa, ON K1R 6P1
Tel: 613-238-3275; *Fax:* 613-238-3275
oberon@sympatico.ca
www.oberonpress.ca
ISBNs: 0-88750, 0-7780; SAN: 115-0723
Publishers of fiction by Canadian Authors. Publishes 10 new titles annually, and has 650 titles in print.
Nicholas Macklem, President

OCAPT Business Books
539 Turner Dr., Burlington, ON L7L 2W8
Tel: 905-632-9374; *Fax:* 905-639-4099
Toll-Free: 888-579-3013
www.ocapt.com
ISBNs: 0-915299, 1-56327, 0-527, 0-9667843
Publishes books & visual learning products for the manufacturing & service industries

Ontario Nature (FON)
#612, 214 King St. W, Toronto, ON M5H 3S6
Tel: 416-444-8419; *Fax:* 416-444-9866
Toll-Free: 800-440-2366
info@ontarionature.org
www.ontarionature.org
Social Media: www.youtube.com/user/ONNature
twitter.com/ontarionature
www.facebook.com/OntarioNature?ref=ts
Publisher of ON Nature; other resources available through the online Shop
Angela Martin, President

Oolichan Books
PO Box 2278, Fernie, BC V0B 1M0
Tel: 250-423-6113
info@oolichan.com
www.oolichan.com
Social Media:
twitter.com/OolichanBooks
www.facebook.com/pages/Oolichan-Books/18 1252759556
ISBNs: 0-88982; SAN: 115-4680
Publishes poetry, fiction & non-fiction titles including literary criticism, memoirs & books on regional history
Randal Macnair, Publisher
Ron Smith, Managing Editor
Pat Smith, Consulting Editor

Orca Book Publishers Canada
PO Box 5626 B, Victoria, BC V8R 6S4
Fax: 877-408-1551
Toll-Free: 800-210-5277
orca@orcabook.com
www.orcabook.com
Social Media:
twitter.com/orcabook
www.facebook.com/OrcaBook
ISBNs: 0-920501, 1-55143; SAN: 115-7485
Publishers of children's books; with ovr 350 titles in print & 60 new titles per year. Picturebooks, Early chapter books, teen novels
Bob Tyrrell, President
Andrew Wooldridge, Publisher

Organisation for Economic Cooperation & Development (OECD)
#650, 2001 L St. NW, Washington, DC
Tel: 202-785-6323; *Fax:* 202-785-0350
Toll-Free: 800-456-6323
washington.contact@oecd.org
www.oecdwash.org
ISBNs: 92-64
Publisher of books in the fields of economics & public affairs; also publishes statistical tables & databases
Gabriela Ramos, Chief of Staff

Owlkids Books
Previous Name: Maple Tree Press Inc.
#400, 10 Lower Spadina Ave., Toronto, ON M5V 2Z2
Tel: 416-340-2700; *Fax:* 416-340-9769
owlkids@owlkids.com
owlkidsbooks.com
Social Media:
twitter.com/owlkids
www.facebook.com/owlkids
ISBNs: 0-919872, 0-920775, 1-895688, 1-897066, 1-894379; SAN: 1
Publishers of non-fiction books for children covering a wide variety of topics including Sports, Humor, Science, Crafts, Canada, History & Culture.
Jennifer Canham, Group Publisher, Owlkids
Karen Boersma, Publisher, Owlkids Books

Oxford University Press - Canada
#204, 8 Sampson Mews, Toronto, ON M3C 0H5
Tel: 416-441-2941; *Fax:* 416-444-0427
Toll-Free: 800-387-8020
customer.service@oup.com
www.oupcanada.com
ISBNs: 0-19; SAN: 115-731
One of the oldest publishing companies in the world; Publishers of non-fiction & educational material
Geoff Forguson, General Manager
Sophia Fortier, VP/Director, Higher Education Division
Julie Wade, Associate Director, ESL Department

P.D. Meany Publishers
Owned By: Joseph Norman Editions
145 Westminster Ave., Toronto, ON M6R 1N8
Tel: 416-516-2903; *Fax:* 416-516-7632
info@pdmeany.com
www.pdmeany.com
ISBNs: 0-88835; SAN: 115-4273
Publishers of a variety of fiction, non-fiction & scholarly titles

Pacific Edge Publishing Ltd.
1773 El Verano Dr., Gabriola, BC V0R 1X6
Tel: 250-247-9093
www.pacificedgepublishing.com
ISBNs: 1-895110
Publisher & distributor of educational resources for K-12 teachers

Pacific Educational Press
University of British Columbia, Faculty of Education, 411-2389 Health Sciences Mall, Vancouver, BC V6T 1Z3
Tel: 604-822-5385; *Fax:* 604-822-6603
pep.admin@ubc.ca
pacificedpress.ca
Social Media:
twitter.com/PacificEdPress
ISBNs: 0-88865, 1-895766; SAN: 115-1266
Publishing house of the Faculty of Education at the University of British Columbia; Publishes educational resources
Catherine Edwards, Director

Pajama Press
#207, 181 Carlaw Ave., Toronto, ON M4M 2S1
Tel: 647-221-7120
info@pajamapress.ca
pajamapress.ca
Social Media: www.youtube.com/user/PajamaPress
twitter.com/PajamaPress1
www.faceb ook.com/PajamaPress
Publisher of all formats of children's books including the following genres: picture books, board books, middle grade novels, young adult novels, non-fiction for all juvenile categories.
Gail Winskill, Publisher, gailwinskill@pajamapress.ca
Richard Jones, President

Pandora Press
47 Water St. North, Kitchener, ON N2H 5A6
Tel: 519-745-1560; *Fax:* 519-578-1826
Toll-Free: 866-696-1678
christian@pandorapress.com
www.pandorapress.com
ISBNs: 0-9698762, 0-9685543, 1-894710
Angie Hostetler, Manager, angie@pandorapress.com

Paperplates Books
Toronto, ON
info@paperplates.org
www.paperplates.org
Small Publishing House; Publishes short fiction & personal essays

Parkland Publishing
501 Mount Allison Pl., Saskatoon, SK S7H 4A9
Tel: 306-242-7731
info@parklandpublishing.com
www.parklandpublishing.com
Social Media:
www.facebook.com/pages/Parkland-Publishing/1612394872512 7
Publishes non-fiction books about Saskatchewan, hiking in Saskatchewan & trivia about Saskatchewan
Robin Kaplan, Co-founder
Arlene Kaplan, Co-founder

Pearson Canada Inc.
Previous Name: Prentice-Hall Canada; Addison-Wesley Publishers
Owned By: Pearson Canada
26 Prince Andrew Pl., Don Mills, ON M3C 2T8
Tel: 416-447-5101; *Fax:* 416-443-0948
Toll-Free: 800-263-9965
www.pearsoncanada.ca
ISBNs: 9780131113497; 9780131228436; 9780131280397
A Pearson Canada imprint, Pearson Education Canada Inc. is the largest publisher of print & electronic curriculum materials in Canada
Dan Lee, President & CEO, Pearson Canada

Pearson Education Canada
Owned By: Pearson Canada
26 Prince Andrew Pl., Toronto, ON M3C 2T8
Tel: 416-447-5101; *Fax:* 416-443-0948
Toll-Free: 800-263-9965
www.pearsoncanada.ca
Social Media:
twitter.com/pearsonplc
www.facebook.com/pearsonplc
Pearson is a publisher of technical resources of particular interest to computer programmers, engineers & system administrators. Academic titles include astronomy, mathematics & statistics, economics & finance
Allan T. Reynolds, President & CEO

Pedlar Press
113 Bond St., St. John's, NL A1C 1T6
feralgrl@interlog.com
www.pedlarpress.com
ISBNs: 0-9681884, 0-9686522, 0-9732140
Publishes contemporary Canadian fiction & poetry

Pembroke Publishers Limited
538 Hood Rd., Markham, ON L3R 3K9
Tel: 905-477-0650; *Fax:* 905-477-3691
Toll-Free: 800-997-9807
mary@pembrokepublishers.com
www.pembrokepublishers.com
Social Media:
www.twitter.com/PembrokePublish
www.facebook.com/PembrokePublishers
ISBNs: 0-921217, 1-55138
Publisher of educational resources for parents & teachers covering: Reading & Writing; Grammar & Speaking; Thinking & drama; Classroom management & major issues in education
Claudia Connolly, General Manager
Mary Macchiusi, President

Pemmican Publications Inc.
150 Henry Ave., Winnipeg, MB R3B 0J7
Tel: 204-589-6346; *Fax:* 204-589-2063
pemmican@pemmican.mb.ca
www.pemmicanpublications.ca
ISBNs: 0-91943, 0-921827; SAN: 115-1657
Published more than 150 titles, including history, biography, Canadian cultural and linguistic studies, adult fiction, poetry and illustrated stories for young and early readers. Pemmican is the only dedicated Metis publishing house in Canada.
Randal McIlroy, Managing Editor, 204-944-9620

Penguin Random House
Previous Name: Random House Canada Ltd. & Penguin Canada
Owned By: Bertelsmann & Pearson PLC
Penguin Random House Canada, #1400, 320 Front St. W, Toronto, ON M5V 3B6
Tel: 416-364-4449; *Fax:* 416-364-6863
penguinrandomhouse@penguinrandomhouse.com
www.penguinrandomhouse.com
Social Media:
twitter.com/PenguinRH_News
ISBNs: 0-394, 0-679; SAN: 115-088X
After merging with Penguin in July 2013, Random House has become Penguin Random House & still publishes numerous titles each month

Penumbra Press
PO Box 20011, Newcastle, ON L1B 1M3
Tel: 613-692-5590
john@penumbrapress.ca
www.penumbrapress.com
Social Media:
plus.google.com/117234084307813147497?prsrc=3
twitter.com/Penumbra_Press
ISBNs: 0-921254, 0-929806, 1-894131; SAN: 115-0774
Small fine-art & literary publishing house; Publishes Northern and Native literatures; children's literature; poetry; translations of Scandinavian literature; history; mythology; art books
John Flood, President, john@penumbrapress.ca

Pippin Publishing Corp.
5201 Dufferin St., Toronto, ON M3H 5T8
Tel: 416-667-7791; *Fax:* 416-667-7832
Toll-Free: 800-565-9523
utpbooks@utpress.utoronto.ca
www.pippinpub.com
Other information: Toll Free Fax: 800-221-9985
ISBNs: 0-88751; SAN: 115-3293
Toronto-based publisher of books for students, teachers & parents

Playfort Publishing
PO Box 576, Salmon Arm, BC V1E 4N7
Tel: 250-833-5554; *Fax:* 250-833-4915
louise@playfortpublishing.ca
playfortpublishing.ca
Social Media: pinterest.com/playfort/
twitter.com/#!/FriendlyFiction
www.facebook.com/pages/Playfort-Publishing/31847411151314
Children's publisher.
Louise Wallace-Richmond, Publisher

Playwrights Canada Press
Previous Name: Playwrights Union of Canada
#202, 269 Richmond St. West, Toronto, ON M5V 1X1
Tel: 416-703-0013; *Fax:* 416-408-3402
info@playwrightscanada.com
www.playwrightscanada.com
Social Media:
twitter.com/PlayCanPress
www.facebook.com/PLCNP
ISBNs: 0-88754, 0-919834
Publishes roughly 32 books of plays, theatre history & criticism annually
Annie Gibson, Publisher, annie@playwrightscanada.com
Blake Sproule, Managing Editor, blake@playwrightscanada.com

Pokeweed Press
Owned By: Bungalo Books
#337, 829 Norwest Rd., Kingston, ON K7P 2N3
Tel: 613-374-2494
publisher@pokeweed.com
www.pokeweed.com
ISBNs: 1-894323
Publishers of picture books
Frank B. Edwards, Publisher, 613-374-1243, fedwards@pokeweed.com
John Bianchi, Illustrator, 520-977-0645, ArtDrew@gmail.com

Polar Bear Press
35 Price Andrew Pl., Toronto, ON M3C 2H2
Tel: 416-449-4000; *Fax:* 416-449-9924
Toll-Free: 800-490-4049
north49@idirect.com
www.polarbearpress.com
ISBNs: 1-896757
Publishers of children's, business & sign writing books

Pontifical Institute of Mediaeval Studies, Dept. of Publications
59 Queen's Park Cres. E, Toronto, ON M5S 2C4
Tel: 416-926-7142
www.pims.ca

ISBNs: 0-88844; SAN: 115-0804
Small University Press publishing the results of research carried out by all medievalists
Richard M.H. Alway, President

Porcupine's Quill Inc.
PO Box 160, 68 Main St., Erin, ON N0B 1T0
Tel: 519-833-9158; *Fax:* 519-833-9845
pql@sentex.net
porcupinesquill.ca
Social Media: pinterest.com/porcupinesquill
twitter.com/porcupinesquill
www.facebook .com/theporcupinesquill
ISBNs: 0-88984; SAN: 115-0820
Small publishing house; Publishers of Canadian poetry & literature
Tim Inkster, Publisher
Elke Inkster, Publisher

Portage & Main Press
Previous Name: Peguis Publishers Limited
#100, 318 McDermot Ave., Winnipeg, MB R3A 0A2
Tel: 204-987-3500; *Fax:* 866-734-8477
Toll-Free: 800-667-9673
books@pandmpress.com
www.portageandmainpress.com
ISBNs: 0-919566, 1-89110, 1-895411, 1-55379
Publishers of educational books & resources for teachers

Potlatch Publications Limited
30 Berryhill Ave., Waterdown, ON L0R 2H4
Tel: 905-689-2104; *Fax:* 905-689-1632
www.potlatchpublications.wordpress.com
ISBNs: 0-919676; SAN: 115-1355
Robert Nielsen, President & Editor In Chief
Mary Trach-Holadyk, Art Director & Illustrator

Pottersfield Press
83 Leslie Rd., East Lawrencetown, NS B2Z 1P8
Tel: 902-827-4517; *Fax:* 902-455-3652
Toll-Free: 800-646-2879
www.pottersfieldpress.com
Social Media:
twitter.com/PottersPress
ISBNs: 0-919001, 1-895900; SAN: 115-0790
Publishers of a number of non-fiction books, including local history & geography; memoirs; & biographies
Lesley Choyce

Power Engineering Books Ltd.
7 Perron St., St Albert, AB T8N 1E3
Tel: 780-458-3155; *Fax:* 780-460-2530
Toll-Free: 800-667-3155
www.powerengbooks.com
Other information: Phone Number: 780-459-2525
ISBNs: SAN: 115-4850
Publshers of technical books & suppliers of codes & standards to private, trade, and public businesses across Canada

Prentice-Hall Canada Inc.
Previous Name: Ginn Publishing Canada Inc.
Owned By: Pearson Canada
26 Prince Andrew Place, Don Mills, ON M3C 2T8
Tel: 416-447-5101; *Fax:* 416-443-0948
Toll-Free: 800-263-9965
www.pearsoncanada.ca
ISBNs: 9780137149445; 9780205608171
A Pearson Canada (Pearson Education) imprint.

The Press of the Nova Scotia College of Art & Design (NSCAD)
5163 Duke St., Halifax, NS B3J 3J6
Tel: 902-494-8221; *Fax:* 902-425-4021
thepress@nscad.ca
www.nscad.ca
ISBNs: 0-919616
Publishers of scholarly works in the fields of contemporary art, craft & design

Les Presses de l'Université de Montréal
306, rue Saint-Zotique est, Montréal, QC H2S 1L6
Tél: 514-343-6933; *Téléc:* 514-343-2232
pum@umontreal.ca
www.pum.umontreal.ca
Médias sociaux:
twitter.com/umontreal_news
ISBNs: 2-7606
A pour mandat le diffusion des résultats de la recherche universitaire (livres, revues, édition électronique); la transférence des connaissances scientifiques à un large public; participation à la vie de la Cité; et contribution au rayonnement national et international de l'Université de Montréal

Presses de l'Université du Montréal
#6010, 3744, rue Jean-Brillant, Montréal, QC H3T 1P1
Tél: 514-343-6933; *Téléc:* 514-343-2232
Ligne sans frais: 800-859-7474
pum@umontreal.ca
www.pum.umontreal.ca
Médias sociaux:
twitter.com/PressesUdeM
www.facebook.com/1485468251667307?ref=hl
ISBNs: 0-7770, 2-7605, 2-920073
Antoine Del Busso, Directeur générale, adb@editionspum.ca

Les Presses de l'Université Laval
Pavillon de l'Est, 2180, chemin Sainte-Foy, 1é, Québec, QC G1V 0A6
Tél: 418-656-2803; *Téléc:* 418-656-3305
presses@pul.ulaval.ca
www.pulaval.com
Médias sociaux: www.youtube.com/user/PressesUL
www.facebook.com/pulaval
ISBNs: 2-7637, 2-89224
Ouvrages didactiques, manuels, travaux savants; diffuseur et distributeur
Denis Dion, Directeur général, denis.dion@pul.ulaval.ca
Émilie Pineau, Secrétaire, emilie.pineau@pul.ulaval.ca

Presses de l'Université Laval de l'Est
1er étage, 2180, chemin Saint-Foy, Québec, QC G1V 0A6
Tél: 418-656-2803; *Téléc:* 418-656-3305
presses@pul.ulaval.ca
www.pulaval.com
Médias sociaux: www.youtube.com/user/PressesUL
www.facebook.com/pulaval
ISBNs: 2-89224
Américana, bioéthique critique, cinéma et société, culture québécoise, éducation, géographie, histoire sociale, lectures, politique
Denis Dion, Directeur général, denis.dion@pul.ulaval.ca
André Baril, Édution Générale, andr.baril@sympatico.ca

Prise de Parole
#205, 109, rue Elm, Sudbury, ON P3C 1T4
Tél: 705-675-6491; *Téléc:* 705-673-1817
info@prisedeparole.ca
www.prisedeparole.ca
Médias sociaux:
twitter.com/prisedeparole
www.facebook.com/editionsPrisedeparole
ISBNs: 0-920814, 0-921573, 2-89423
Bandes dessinées, beaux livres, contes traditionnels, enfants, ados, études littéraires, poésie, revues, romans
Denise Truax, Directrice générale, dtruax@prisedeparole.ca
Sylvie Lessard, Agente de commercialisation, slessard@prisedeparole.ca
Alain Mayotte, Directeur administratif, amayotte@prisedeparole.ca

Probe International
225 Brunswick Ave., Toronto, ON M5S 2M6
www.probeinternational.org
Social Media:
twitter.com/ProbeIntl
www.facebook.com/ProbeInternational
ISBNs: 0-919849, 1-85383, 0-7656
Promotes social, economi & environmental well=being in Canada
Gail Regan, Chair

Productive Publications
PO Box 7200 A, Toronto, ON M5W 1X8
Tel: 416-483-0634; *Fax:* 416-322-7434
productivepublications@rogers.com
www.productivepublications.ca
ISBNs: 0-920847, 1-896210, 1-55270; SAN: 117-1712
Iain Williamson, Owner

Ptarmigan Press
1372 - 16th Ave., Campbell River, BC V9W 2E1
Tel: 250-286-0878; *Fax:* 250-286-9749
info@kaskgraphics.com
www.kaskgraphics.com/ptarmigan
ISBNs: 0-919537; SAN: 116-0281
Small publishing house; Publisher of non-fiction covering Fishing; Hiking; Local history; Autobiography; Cooking; How To; Health; Sexual Abuse

Public Works & Government Services Canada - Depository Services Program / Travaux public et services gouvernement aux Canada
Anciennement: Canada Communications Group Publishing
Public Works & Government Services Canada, Ottawa, ON K1A 0S5
Tél: 613-941-5995; *Téléc:* 613-954-5779
Ligne sans frais: 800-635-7943
publications@tpsgc-pwgsc.gc.ca
dsp-psd.pwgsc.gc.ca
Publishes federal government publications and distribute them to oublic & academic libraries.
Christine Leduc, Director, Publishing & Depository Services, 613-996-5959, Fax: 613-947-6949, Christine.Leduc@pwgsc.gc.ca

Publishers Group Canada
Previous Name: Publishers Group West
#300, 76 Stratford St., Toronto, ON M6J 2S1
Tel: 416-934-9900; *Fax:* 416-934-1410
Toll-Free: 800-747-8147
info@pgcbooks.ca
www.pgcbooks.ca
Social Media:
twitter.com/pgcanada
www.facebook.com/pages/Publishers-Group-Canada/16271343
24
ISBNs: SAN: 117-0171
Distributors of a large number of non-fiction, fiction & children's books for a large number of publishers.
Graham Fidler, Exec. Vice-President, ext. 203, graham@pgcbooks.ca
Suzanne Wice, Director, Sales & Marketing, ext. 207, suzanne@pgcbooks.ca

Purich Publishing Ltd.
PO Box 23032 Market Mall, Saskatoon, SK S7J 5H3
Tel: 306-373-5311; *Fax:* 306-373-5315
purich@sasktel.net
www.purichpublishing.com
Social Media:
www.facebook.com/Purich.Publishing
ISBNs: 1-895830
Publishers of books dealing with Aboriginal & Social Justice Issues; Law & Western Canadian History; Focus on the university, college & reference market
K. Bolstad
D. Purich

Qualitas Publishing
195 Cardiff Dr. NW, Calgary, AB T2K 1S1
Tel: 403-618-3830
info@qualitaspublishing.com
www.qualitaspublishing.com

Quarry Press
20 Hatter St., Kingston, ON K7M 2L5
Tel: 613-548-8429; *Fax:* 613-548-1556
Social Media:
www.facebook.com/QuarryPress
ISBNs: 0-919627, 1-55082; SAN: 115-4958
Bob Hilderley, Publisher

Quattro Books
Centre for Social Innovation, 720 Bathurst St., 2nd Fl., Toronto, ON M5S 2R4
Tel: 647-748-7484
info@quattrobooks.ca
www.quattrobooks.ca
Social Media: www.youtube.com/quattrobooks
twitter.com/quattrobooks
www.facebook. com/group.php?gid=132166700599&ref=ts
Allan Briesmaster, Vice-Presidnet/Publisher, allan@quattrobooks.ca

Québec dans le Monde
CP 8503 Sainte-Foy, #404, 1001, route de l'Eglise, Québec, QC G1V 4N5
Tél: 418-659-5540; *Téléc:* 418-659-4143
info@quebecmonde.com
www.quebecmonde.com
Médias sociaux:
twitter.com/Quebec_Monde
www.facebook.com/282129985132094
ISBNs: 2-921309, 2-89525, 2-9801130; SAN: 116-8657
Une organisation à but non lucratif livres de l'édition de référence sur le Québec, la promotion des entreprises locales du Québec et a récemment ouvert une école internationale d'immersion en français à Québec
M. Alain Prujiner, Président
Mme. Juliette Champagne, Vice-Présidente

Québec Science
1251 rue Rachel E, Montréal, QC H2L 2J9
Tél: 514-521-5356; *Ligne sans frais:* 800-567-5356
courrier@quebecscience.qc.ca
www.quebecscience.qc.ca/a -propos
Médias sociaux:
twitter.com/quebecscience
www.facebook.com/280257226593

ISBNs: 2-920073
Québec Science aborde toutes les questions liées à la science et à la technologie et est un regard scientifique sur les grandes questions
Pierre Sormany, Éduteur, jypoirier@velo.qc.ca
Raymond Lemieux, Rédacteur en chef

Rattling Books
Owned By: Alca Productions Inc.
Tors Cove, NL A0A 4A0
Tel: 709-334-3911
www.rattlingbooks.com
Social Media: myspace.com/rattlingbooks
www.facebook.com/groups/2427995853

Audio Book publisher.

Reach for Unbleached
PO Box 1270, Commox, BC V9M 7Z8
reach@rfu.org
www.rfu.org

ISBNs: 0-9680431
Publishers of environmental education material about paper & pulp mill monitoring

Red Deer Press
195 Allstate Pkwy., Markham, ON L3R 4T8
Toll-Free: 800-387-9776
bookinfo@fitzhenry.ca
www.reddeerpress.com

ISBNs: 0-88995; SAN: 115-0871
Publishes picture books, junior, juvenile, Young Adult fiction and non-fiction and adult non-fiction titles. Was purchased by Fitzhenry & Whiteside in 2005.
Richard Dionne, Publisher, dionne@reddeerpress.com
Peter Carver, Children's Editor

Reference Press
PO Box 70, Teeswater, ON N0G 2S0
Tel: 519-392-6634
www.libris.ca/refpress

ISBNs: 0-919981; SAN: 115-687X
Publisher of Canadian reference materials & software for use in school & public libraries
Gordon Ripley, Contact, 519-392-6634

Renouf Publishing Co. Ltd. / Éditions Renouf limitées
#22, 1010 Polytek St., Ottawa, ON K1J 9J3
Tel: 613-745-2665; *Fax:* 613-745-7660
Toll-Free: 866-767-6766
orders@renoufbooks.com
www.renoufbooks.com
Other information: Alternate E-mails:
accounting@renoufbooks.com; serials@renoufbooks.com
Social Media:
twitter.com/renoufbooks

ISBNs: 0-88852; SAN: 170-8066
Publishers of over 35 international organizations' publiations & documents
Gordon Grahame, President

The Resource Centre
PO Box 190, Waterloo, ON N2J 3Z9
Tel: 519-885-0826; *Fax:* 519-747-5629
Toll-Free: 800-923-0330
sales@theresourcecentre.com
www.theresourcecentre.com

ISBNs: 0-920701; SAN: 115-5032
Publishers of educational resources, including books on ESL, Language & Writing among other subjects

Retromedia Inc.
PO Box 471, Charlottetown, PE C1A 7L1
Tel: 902-394-3855
www.retromediastore.ca

Larry Resnitzky, Owner, larry@retromedia.ca

Riverwood Publishers Ltd.
471 Eagle St., Newmarket, ON L3Y 1K7
Tel: 905-853-8887; *Fax:* 905-853-3330
info@riverwoodpub.com
www.riverwoodpub.com

ISBNs: 1-895121; SAN: 116-1288
Publishers of children's books & Canadian distributors of Usborne Books, a respected children's book publisher.

Ron Charlesworth, President

RK Publishing Inc.
#308, 3089 Bathurst St., Toronto, ON M6A 2A4
Tel: 416-785-0312; *Fax:* 416-785-0317
Toll-Free: 866-696-9549
frenchtextbooks@rkpublishing.com
www.rkpublishing.com
Social Media:
twitter.com/#!/RKPublishing
www.facebook.com/pages/RK-Publishing-Inc/196868130385973
Publishing company that specializes in developing Grades 1 to 12 teaching and learning resources for French as a Second Language.
Greg Pilon, Director of Sales, 905-665-3210, greg.pilon8@sympatico.ca

Robert Rose, Inc.
#800, 120 Eglinton Ave. East, Toronto, ON M4P 1E2
Tel: 416-322-6552; *Fax:* 416-322-6936
www.robertrose.ca

Publisher of cookbooks and health books.

Robin Brass Studio Inc.
PO Box 335 du Parc, Montréal, QC H2S 3M0
Tel: 514-272-7463
rbrass@sympatico.ca
www.rbstudiobooks.com

ISBNs: 1-896941; SAN: 115-5040
Small publishing house producing primarily non-fiction, especially within the area of military history & other Canadian history; Also designs and produces books under contract for other publishers & organizations

Rocky Mountain Books
#103, 1075 Pendergast St., Victoria, BC V8V 0A1
Tel: 250-360-0829; *Fax:* 250-386-0829
Toll-Free: 800-665-3302
distribution@heritagehouse.ca
www.rmbooks.com
Social Media: www.youtube.com/rmbooks1
twitter.com/rmbooks
www.facebook.com/rmboo ks

ISBNs: 0-921102; SAN: 115-5040
Publisher of outdoor activity guidebooks, historical accounts of Canadian mountaineering and other adventures, biographies & related non-fiction
Don Gorman, Publisher, don@rmbooks.com

Ronsdale Press
Previous Name: Cacanadadada Press
3350 West 21st Ave., Vancouver, BC V6S 1G7
Tel: 604-738-4688; *Fax:* 604-731-4548
ronsdale@shaw.ca
www.ronsdalepress.com
Social Media:
twitter.com/ronsdalepress
www.facebook.com/ronsdalepress

ISBNs: 0-921870, 1-55380; SAN: 116-2454
Publishers of fiction, poetry, regional history, biography & autobiography, books of ideas about Canada, as well as children's books.
Ronald B. Hatch, Director

Roseway Publishing
Fernwood Publishing
32 Oceanvista Lane, Black Point, NS B0J 1B0
Tel: 902-857-1388; *Fax:* 902-857-1328
roseway@fernpub.ca
www.fernwoodpublishing.ca/roseway
Social Media:
twitter.com/fernpub
www.facebook.com/fernwood.publishing?ref=sgm
ISBNs: 1-895686, 1-55266
Errol Sharpe, Publisher/Editor, errol@fernpub.ca
Nancy Malek, Promotions, promotions@fernpub.ca

The Royal Astronomical Society of Canada (RASC)
#203, 4920 Dundas St. W, Toronto, ON M9A 1B7
Tel: 416-924-7973; *Fax:* 416-924-2911
Toll-Free: 888-924-7272
www.rasc.ca

Publishes journals and guides to astronomy
Colin Haig, Chair, Committee

Rubicon Publishing Inc.
PO Box 69596, 281 Wyecroft Rd., Oakville, ON L6J 7R4
Tel: 905-849-8777; *Fax:* 905-849-7579
contact@rubiconpublishing.com
www.rubiconpublishing.com

ISBNs: 0-921156; SAN: 115-432X
Publisher of educational resources for students and educators for grades K-12.

Sandhill Book Marketing Ltd.
#4, 3308 Appaloosa Rd., Kelowna, BC V1V 2G9
Tel: 250-491-1446; *Fax:* 250-491-4066
Toll-Free: 800-667-3848
info@sandhillbooks.com
www.sandhillbooks.com

ISBNs: 0-920923; SAN: 115-2181
Distributor for Small Press & Independent Publishers

Sara Jordan Publishing
Owned By: Jordan Music Productions Inc.
PO Box 28105, RPO Lakeport, 600 Ontario St., St Catharines, ON L2N 7P8
Tel: 905-938-9555; *Fax:* 905-938-9970
Toll-Free: 800-567-7733
sjordan@sara-jordan.com
www.SongsThatTeach.com
Social Media: www.myspace.com/funtoteach
twitter.com/SongsThatTeach
www.facebook.com/406506519407554
ISBNs: 1-895523, 1-894262, 1-533860; SAN: 118-959X
Publisher & producer of educational songs & music

Saunders Book Company
PO Box 308, Collingwood, ON L9Y 3Z7
Tel: 705-445-4777; *Fax:* 705-445-9569
Toll-Free: 800-461-9120
info@saundersbook.ca
www.librarybooks.com
Social Media:
www.facebook.com/190537359741

ISBNs: SAN: 169-9768
Publishers of books for educational books & fiction for K-12 schools & libraries
James Saunders, Sales, james.saunders@saundersbook.ca

Scholar's Choice
2323 Trafalgar St., London, ON N5Y 5S7
Tel: 519-453-7470; *Fax:* 800-363-3398
Toll-Free: 800-265-1095
web@scholarschoice.ca
www.scholarschoice.ca
Social Media: pinterest.com/scholarschoice
twitter.com/scholarschoice
www.facebook.com/scholarschoice.ca
ISBNs: 0-88809; SAN: 170-0014
Publisher & retailer of educational materials
Scott Webster, President
Cindy Webster, Executive Vice-President

Scholastic Canada Ltd. / Éditions Scholastic
175 Hillmount Rd., Markham, ON L6C 1Z7
Tel: 905-887-7323; *Fax:* 800-387-4944
Toll-Free: 800-268-3660
custserve@scholastic.ca
www.scholastic.ca
Social Media:
twitter.com/scholasticcda
www.facebook.com/ScholasticCanada
ISBNs: 0-590; SAN: 115-5164
Leading publishers & distributors of children's books & educational materials in French & English
Richard Robinson, Chairman of the Board, President, & CEO
Maureen O'Connell, Executive Vice President, CAO, & CFO

Scrivener Press
465 Loach's Rd., Sudbury, ON P3E 2R2?
Tel: 705-522-5126
www.scrivenerpress.com

Second Story Press
#401, 20 Maud St., Toronto, ON M5S 2R4
Tel: 416-537-7850; *Fax:* 416-537-0588
info@secondstorypress.ca
secondstorypress.ca
Social Media:
twitter.com/_secondstory
www.facebook.com/pages/Second-Story-Press /10623359005
ISBNs: 0-929005, 1-896764; SAN: 115-1134
Publishers of roughly 8 titles per season, spanning adult fiction & non-fiction; children's fiction, non-fiction & picture books; Young Adult fiction & non-fiction. Special interest areas include Judaica, Ability Issues, Coping with Cancer & Queer rights

The Secret Mountain
3816 Royal Ave., Montréal, QC H4A 2M2?
Tel: 514-483-9281
info@thesecretmountain.com
www.thesecretmountain.com
The Secret Mountain publishes children's books, videos and audio recordings.

Self-Counsel Press Ltd.
1481 Charlotte Rd., North Vancouver, BC V7J 1H1
Tel: 604-986-3366; *Fax:* 604-986-3947
Toll-Free: 800-663-3007
orders@self-counsel.com
www.self-counsel.com
Social Media: www.linkedin.com/company/self-counsel-press
twitter.com/SelfCounsel
www.facebook.com/selfcounselpress
ISBNs: 0-88908, 1-55180; SAN: 115-0545
Publisher of self-help law books & books for small business
Diana R. Douglas, President

September Dreams Publishing
viktor@septemberdreams.com
www.septemberdreams.com
ISBNs: 0-9695763
Publishers of four books covering business, computer, humour & lifestyle
Viktor E. Oey

Septembre éditeur inc.
#101, 2200 rue Cyrille-Duquet, Québec, QC G1N 2G3
Tél: 418-658-7272; *Téléc:* 418-652-0986
Ligne sans frais: 800-361-7755
www.septembre.com
Médias sociaux:
twitter.com/Septembre_
www.facebook.com/septembre.editeur
ISBNs: 2-930433, 2-89471
Matériel didactique; éducation; emplois; formation; littérature jeunesse; management; ressources humaines; métiers; orientation; outils pédagogiques

Seraphim Editions
54 Bay St., Woodstock, ON N4S 3K9
Tel: 519-290-5509; *Fax:* 519-290-5509
info@seraphimeditions.com
www.seraphimeditions.com
Maureen Whyte, Publisher

ServiceOntario Publications
50 Grosvenor St., Toronto, ON M7A 1N8
Tel: 416-326-5300; *Toll-Free:* 800-668-9938
webpubont@ontario.ca
www.publications.serviceontario.ca
ISBNs: 0-7743, 0-7729, 0-7778
Publishers of government publications, including driver's handbook, fire codes, building codes, agricultural publications, employment standards & occupational health & safety

Services documentaires multimedia inc. (SDM)
#620, 5650, rue d'Iberville, Montréal, QC H2G 2B3
Tel: 514-382-0895; *Fax:* 514-384-9139
informations@sdm.qc.ca
www.sdm.qc.ca
ISBNs: 2-89059, 0-88523
SDM a des bases de données et d'autres produits de pointe pour aider à gérer les documents publiés dans le monde de langue française
Philippe Sauvageau, Chef de Direction, philippe.sauvageau@sdm.qc.ca
Diane Dallaire-Talbot, Directrice, L'exploitation, diane.dallaire-talbot@sdm.qc.ca

Shoreline Press
23, rue Sainte-Anne, Sainte-Anne-de-Bellevue, QC H9X 1L1
Tel: 514-457-5733
info@shorelinepress.ca
www.shorelinepress.ca
Social Media:
www.facebook.com/200539666667166
ISBNs: 0-9695180, 0-9698752, 1-896754; SAN 116-9564
Independent press publishing specializing in memoirs & titles of local interest
Judith Isherwood, Owner & Senior Editor

Signature Editions
Previous Name: Nuage Éditions
PO Box 206, RPO Corydon, Winnipeg, MB R3M 3S7
Tel: 204-779-7803; *Fax:* 204-779-6970
signature@allstream.net
www.signature-editions.com
Social Media:
twitter.com/SigEditions
www.facebook.com/pages/Signature-Editions/154009474633646
ISBNs: 0-921833, 1-897109; SAN: 115-0723
Signature Editions is a literary press with an eclectic list of fiction, non-fiction, poetry and drama.
Karen Haughian, Publisher

Simon & Schuster Canada
Owned By: Simon & Schuster
#300, 166 King St. E, Toronto, ON M5A 1J3
Tel: 647-427-8882; *Fax:* 641-430-9446
Toll-Free: 800-387-0446
info@simonandschuster.ca
www.simonandschuster.ca
Social Media:
twitter.com/SimonSchusterCA
www.facebook.com/simonandschustercanada
Publishers of a large catalog of books covering all aspects of fiction & non-fiction; while the company was originally restricted to distributing foreign titles, they can now publish Canadian content domestically as of May 2013.
Carolyn Reidy, President, Chief Executive Officer
Jon Anderson, Executive Vice President & Publisher, Children's Publishing

Simply Read Books
#501, 5525 West Blvd., Vancouver, BC V6M 3W6
go@simplyreadbooks.com
www.simplyreadbooks.com
Publishers of fiction for children

Socadis Inc.
420, rue Stinson, Ville Saint-Laurent, QC H4N 3L7
Tel: 514-331-3300; *Fax:* 514-745-3282
Toll-Free: 800-361-2847
socinfo@socadis.com
www.socadis.com
Other information: Toll Free Fax: 866-803-5422
Publishes & distributes French books to Canadian retailers

Sono Nis Press
PO Box 160, Winlaw, BC V0G 2J0
Tel: 250-226-0077; *Fax:* 250-226-0074
Toll-Free: 800-370-5228
books@sononis.com
www.sononis.com
A literary house specializing in poetry, fiction & regional non-fiction.
Diane Morriss, Publisher

Spotted Cow Press
4216 - 121 St., Edmonton, AB T6J 1Y8
Tel: 780-434-3858
www.spottedcowpress.ca
Jerome Martin, Publisher, jmartin@spottedcowpress.ca

Stanton Atkins & Dosil Publishers (SA&D)
2632 Bronte Dr., North Vancouver, BC V7H 1M4
Tel: 604-881-7067; *Fax:* 604-881-7068
Toll-Free: 800-665-3302
info@s-a-d-publishers.ca
www.s-a-d-publishers.ca

Statistics Canada
150 Tunney's Pasture Driveway, Ottawa, ON K1A 0T6
Tel: 800-263-1136; *Fax:* 877-287-4369
Toll-Free: 800-363-7329
infostats@statcan.gc.ca
www.statcan.ca
ISBNs: 0-660, 0-662
Publishes research and information conducted by Statistics Canada

Sumach Press
Owned By: Three O'Clock Press
#20, 425 Adelaide St. West, Toronto, ON M5V 3C1
Tel: 416-929-2964; *Fax:* 416-929-1926
info@sumachpress.com
www.threeoclockpress.com/tags/sumach-press
Social Media:
twitter.com/3oclockpress
www.facebook.com/pages/Three-OClock-Press/139452176099151
ISBNs: 1-894549, 1-896764, 0-929005; SAN: 115-1134
Publishers of feminist writing

Summerthought Publishing
PO Box 2309, Banff, AB T1L 1C1
Tel: 403-762-0535; *Fax:* 403-762-3095
info@summerthought.com
www.summerthought.com
Social Media:
www.facebook.com/TheCanadianRockies
ISBNs: 0-919934; SAN: 115-2149
Specializing in the publication of Canadian Rockies non fiction books.
Andrew Hempstead, Publisher

Summit Educational Services
PO Box 149, Richmond Hill, ON L4C 4X9
Tel: 905-883-9427; *Fax:* 905-770-8576
Toll-Free: 800-741-5956
admin@summit-ed.com
www.summit-ed.com
ISBNs: 1-895187
Arlene Marks, President

Sybertooth Inc.
59 Salem St., Sackville, NB E4L 4J6
sybertooth.ca
A publisher of fiction, non-fiction, poetry, and plays.

Talon Books Ltd.
PO Box 2076, 278 East 1st Ave., Vancouver, BC V6B 3S3
Tel: 604-444-4889; *Fax:* 604-444-4119
Toll-Free: 888-445-4176
info@talonbooks.com
www.talonbooks.com
Social Media:
twitter.com/Talonbooks
www.facebook.com/pages/Talonbooks/139312703339
ISBNs: 0-88922; SAN: 115-5334; Telebook: S1150391
Publishers specializing in poetry, drama & literary criticism. Also publishes fiction & non-fiction
Kevin Williams, President/Publisher, kevin@talonbooks.com
Greg Gibson, Managing Editor, production@talonbooks.com

TechnoKids Inc.
2097 Bates Common, Burlington, ON L7R 0A5
Fax: 905-631-9113
Toll-Free: 800-221-7921
information@technokids.com
www.technokids.com
Social Media: www.technokids.com/blog
twitter.com/technokidsinc
www.facebook.com/ technokidscomputercurriculum
ISBNs: 1-894995
Publisher of technology cirriculum for schools. Publish K-12 Microsoft Office technology projects. Over 60 titles available.

Ten Speed Press
Random House Inc.
1745 Broadway, New York, NY 10019
Tel: 212-782-9000
tenspeed.com
Social Media:
twitter.com/TenSpeedPress
ISBNs: 0-89815, 1-58008, 0-89087, 1-883672, 1-58246, 1-58761
Division of Random House & part of The Crown Publishing Group, Ten Speed Press publishes cookbooks

Theytus Books
Green Mountain Rd., Lot 45, RR#2, Comp. 8, Site 50, Penticton, BC V2A 6J7
Tel: 250-493-7181; *Fax:* 250-493-5302
info@theytus.com
www.theytus.com
Social Media:
twitter.com/theytusbooks
www.facebook.com/245963905424764
ISBNs: 0-919441, 1-894778; SAN: 115-1517
Aboriginal-owned & operated publishing house; Focus is on publishing books of Aboriginal literature, children's books, history, culture, politics & educational materials
Sarah Dickie, Operations Manager, operations@theytus.com

Third Sector Publishing
14 Matchedash St. North, Orillia, ON L3V 4T5
Tel: 705-325-5552; *Fax:* 705-325-5596
info@thirdsectorpublishing.ca
www.thirdsectorpublishing.ca
Social Media: www.linkedin.com/company/third-sector-publishing
twitter.com/thirdsector_
www.facebook.com/thirdsectorpublishing
Publisher of information regarding Canada's registered charities and those who donate to them.
Anderson Charters, Owner / Publisher

Thistledown Press Ltd.
410 - 2nd Ave., Saskatoon, SK S7K 2C3
Tel: 306-244-1722; *Fax:* 306-244-1762
tdpress@thistledownpress.com
www.thistledownpress.com
Social Media:
twitter.com/ReadThistledown
www.facebook.com/pages/Thistledown-Press/115752538043
ISBNs: 0-920066, 1-894345, 0-920633, 1-895449
Publishes poetry & fiction for adults & young adults by Canadian writers; Also publishes resources for teachers
Allan Forrie, Publisher, editorial@thistledownpress.com
Jackie Forrie, Publishing & Production Manager

Thomas Allen & Son Ltd.
390 Steelcase Rd. E, Markham, ON L3R 1G2
Tel: 905-475-9126; *Toll-Free:* 800-387-4333
info@t-allen.com
www.thomasallen.ca
ISBNs: 0-919028, 088762; SAN: 115-1762
Publishers of award-winning bestsellers; Publish a small, highly-focused list of no more than 10-12 books a year, both fiction & non-fiction
Darryl Scott, National Sales Manager, 905-475-9126 ext. 327, Fax: 905-475-4255, darryl.scott@t-allen.com

Thompson Educational Publishing, Inc.
20 Ripley Ave., Toronto, ON M6S 3N9
Tel: 416-766-2763; *Fax:* 416-766-0398
Toll-Free: 877-366-2763
info@thompsonbooks.com
thompsonbooks.com
ISBNs: 1-55077; SAN: 115-0391
Publishes educational texts in the social sciences & humanities
Keith Thompson, President
Faye Thompson, Vice-President, faye@thompsonbooks.com

Three O'Clock Press
#200, 425 Adelaide St. West, Toronto, ON M5V 3C1
Tel: 416-929-2964; *Fax:* 416-929-1926
info@threeoclockpress.com
threeoclockpress.com
Social Media:
twitter.com/3oclockpress
www.facebook.com/pages/Three-OClock-Press/139452176099151
Feminist writing.

Tikka Books
3866 Claude, Verdun, QC H4G 1H1
Tel: 450-658-6205
leila@tikkabooks.com
www.tikkabooks.com
ISBNs: 1-896106; 0-921993
Independent publishing house specializing in how-to books for crafts, sewing, cooking, & Halloween
Leila Pelposaari, Publisher, leila@tikkabooks.com

Timeless Books
PO Box 9, Walker's Landing Rd., Kootenay, BC V0B 1X0
Tel: 250-227-9224; *Fax:* 250-227-9224
Toll-Free: 800-661-8711
contact@timeless.org
www.timeless.org
ISBNs: 0-931454, 2-9044616
Publishers of teachings on yoga, including poetry & spiritual biography; Also publishes classic books & audio

TouchWood Editions Ltd.
Previous Name: Horsdal & Schubart Publishers Ltd.
#103, 1075 Pendergast St., Victoria, BC V8V 0A1
Tel: 250-360-0829; *Fax:* 250-386-0829
info@touchwoodeditions.com
www.touchwoodeditions.com
Social Media:
twitter.com/TouchWoodEd
www.facebook.com/TouchWoodEditions
ISBNs: 0-920663, 1-894898
Publishes books with a focus on history, historical fiction, biography, food, nautical subjects, mysteries & art/architecture
Pat Touchie, Publisher

Tradewind Books
#202, 1807 Maritime Mews, Vancouver, BC V6H 3W7
Tel: 604-662-4405; *Fax:* 604-730-0454
tradewindbooks@eudoramail.com
www.tradewindbooks.com
Social Media:
twitter.com/tradewindbooks
www.facebook.com/pages/Tradewind-Books/164946283181
ISBNs: 1-896580
Publishers of children's literature recognized internationally
R. David Stephens, Sr. Editor

Tralco Educational Services Inc.
#101, 1030 Upper James St., Hamilton, ON L9C 6X6
Tel: 905-575-5717; *Fax:* 905-575-1783
Toll-Free: 888-487-2526
sales@tralco.com
www.tralco.com
ISBNs: 0-921376, 1-894738, 1-55409
Publishes supplementary materials for second-language education; Publishes in French, German, Spanish, ESL & Italian. Also produces activity books, videos, audio cassettes, games & software
Karen Traynor, President

Tree House Press Inc.
#2, 110 Lansing Dr., Hamilton, ON L8W 3A1
Tel: 905-574-3399; *Fax:* 905-574-0228
Toll-Free: 800-776-8733
contact@treehousepress.com
www.treehousepress.com
Social Media: www.youtube.com/mytreehousepress
twitter.com/treehousepress
www.fac ebook.com/treehousepress
ISBNs: 1-895165
Publishes educational resources specifically made for each province's educational standards
Patrick Lashmar, President & Chief Executive Officer
David Lashmar, Vice President

Trillistar Books
PO Box 50002 South Slope, Burnaby, BC V5J 5G3
Tel: 778-433-5340
editor@trillistar.com
trillistar.com
Books to alter the cultural landscape through evolving ideas, both educational and aesthetic.

TSAR Publications
PO Box 6996 A, Toronto, ON M5W 1X7
Tel: 416-483-7191; *Fax:* 416-486-0706
inquiries@tsarbooks.com
www.tsarbooks.com
Social Media:
twitter.com/TSARbooks
www.facebook.com/pages/TSAR-Publications/211176882248465
ISBNs: 0-929661, 1-894770
Publishes 6-8 titles of fiction, poetry & non-fictoin (literary criticism, history) annually.

Tundra Books
Owned By: McClelland & Stewart Ltd.
#300, 1 Toronto St., Toronto, ON M5C 2V6
Tel: 416-364-4449; *Toll-Free:* 800-788-1074
tundra@mcclelland.com
www.tundrabooks.com
Imprint of McClelland & Stewart.
Kathryn Cole, Editorial Director
Alison Morgan, Managing Director

Tuns Press
Faculty of Architecture & Planning, Dalhousie University, PO Box 15000, Halifax, NS B3J 2X4
Tel: 902-494-3925; *Fax:* 902-423-6672
tuns.press@dal.ca
tunspress.dal.ca
ISBNs: 0-929112
Publishing arm of the Faculty of Architecture & Planning at Dalhousie University
Essy Beniassad, Editorial
Sarah Bonnemaison, Editorial

Turnstone Press
#018, 100 Arthur St., Winnipeg, MB R3B 1H3
Tel: 204-947-1555; *Fax:* 204-942-1555
editor@turnstonepress.com
www.turnstonepress.com
Social Media: www.pinterest.com/turnstonepress/
twitter.com/turnstonepress
www.fa cebook.com/TurnstonePress
ISBNs: 0-88801; SAN: 115-1096
Publishers of fiction, literary criticism, poetry & non-fiction; Imprints include Turnstone Press which publishes mysteries, thrillers & noir fiction
Manuela David, Managing Editor
Patrick Gunter, Marketing Director

Ulverscroft Large Print Books Ltd. Canada
PO Box 1230, West Seneca, NY
Tel: 905-637-8734; *Fax:* 905-333-6788
Toll-Free: 888-860-3365
sales@ulverscroftcanada.com
www.ulverscroft.com
ISBNs: 0-7089
Publishers of large print books, producing 84 large print books monthly.

Ulysses Travel Guides Inc. / Éditions Ulysse
4176, rue Saint-Denis, Montréal, QC H2W 2M5
Tel: 514-843-9447; *Fax:* 514-843-9448
info@ulysses.ca
www.ulyssesguides.com
ISBNs: 2-921444, 2-89464; SAN: 115-7167
Publishers of Canadian travel guides covering all areas of the country with a focus on Québec

United Church Publishing House
#300, 3250 Bloor St. West, Toronto, ON M8X 2Y4
Tel: 416-231-5931; *Fax:* 416-231-3103
Toll-Free: 800-288-7365
bookpub@united-church.ca
www.united-church.ca/ucph
Other information: Toll Free Fax: 888-858-8358
Social Media: www.youtube.com/unitedchurchofcanada
twitter.com/UnitedChurchCda
www.facebook.com/UnitedChurchCda
ISBNs: 0-919000, 1-55134; SAN: 111-6002
Rebekah Chevalier, Director, Publishing
416-231-7680 ext 4034, rchevali@united-church.ca

University of Alberta Press
Ring House 2, University of Alberta, Edmonton, AB T6G 2E1
Tel: 780-492-3662; *Fax:* 780-492-0719
www.uap.ualberta.ca
ISBNs: 0-88864; SAN: 118-9794
Publishes culturally significant works of high quality & creative excellence. Also using new technologies & methods to offer digital titles
Linda D. Cameron, Director, 780-492-0717, linda.cameron@ualberta.ca
Peter Midgley, Senior Editor, Acquisitions, 780-492-7714, pmidgley@ualberta.ca

University of British Columbia Press
2029 West Mall, Vancouver, BC V6T 1Z2
Tel: 604-822-5959; *Fax:* 604-822-6083
Toll-Free: 877-377-9378
frontdesk@ubcpress.ca
www.ubcpress.ca
Other information: Toll Free Fax: 800-668-0821
ISBNs: 0-7748; SAN: 115-1118
Publishing branch of the University of British Columbia; Largest scholarly press in Western Canada; Publishes 50-60 books annually with over 800 published since establishment; Specialties include political science, native studies, forestry, Asian studies, Canadian history, environmental studies, planning & urban studies.
Melissa Pitts, Director, 604-822-6376, pitts@ubcpress.ca
Peter Milroy, Director, Emeritus, 604-822-3807, milroy@ubcpress.ca

University of Calgary Press
2500 University Dr. NW, Calgary, AB T2N 1N4
Fax: 403-282-0085
ucpbooks@ucalgary.ca
www.uofcpress.com
Publishing arm of the University of Calgary
John King, Senior Editor, 403-220-4208, jking@ucalgary.ca
Karen Buttner, Editorial Secretary, 403-220-3979, kbuttner@ucalgary.ca

University of Manitoba Press
301 St. John's College, University of Manitoba, Winnipeg, MB R3T 2M5
Tel: 204-474-6465; *Fax:* 204-474-7566
uofmpress@umanitoba.ca
www.umanitoba.ca/publications/uofmpress
ISBNs: 0-88755; SAN: 115-5474
Publishing arm of the University of Manitoba; Publishes 6-8 scholarly works annually; Best known for Native History, Canadian History, Native Studies & Canadian literary studies.
David Carr, Director, 204-474-9242, carr@cc.umanitoba.ca
Jean Wilson, Senior Acquisitions Editor, jeanl.wilson@shaw.ca
Glenn Bergen, Managing Editor, 204-474-7338, bergeng@cc.umanitoba.ca

University of Ottawa Press (UOP/PUO) / Presses de l'Université d'Ottawa
542 King Edward Ave., Ottawa, ON K1N 6N5
Tel: 613-562-5246; *Fax:* 613-562-5247
Toll-Free: 800-565-9523
puo-uop@uottawa.ca
www.press.uottawa.ca
Social Media:
twitter.com/uOttawaPress
www.facebook.com/uOttawaPress
ISBNs: 0-7766, 2-7603
Canada's oldest French Language university press & the only Bilingual University press in North America.
Lara Mainville, Director, 613-562-5663, lara.mainville@uottawa.ca

University of Regina Press (CPRCP Press)
Previous Name: Canadian Plains Research Center Press
University of Regina, 3737 Wascana Pkwy., Regina, SK S4S 0A2
Tel: 306-585-4758; *Fax:* 306-585-4699
Toll-Free: 866-874-2257
canadian.plains@uregina.ca
www.uofrpress.ca
ISBNs: 0-88977; SAN: 115-0278
The University of Regina Press is the publishing arm of the University of Regina. It publishes scholarly manuscripts on aspects of life in the Prairie region, as well as non-fiction trade titles concerning the Prairies.
Bruce Walsh, Executive Director, bruce.walsh@uregina.ca
Donna Grant, Senior Editor, 306-585-4787, donna.grant@uregina.ca

University of Toronto Press (UTP)
#700, 10 St. Mary St., Toronto, ON M4Y 2W8
Tel: 416-978-2239; *Fax:* 416-978-4738
info@utpress.utoronto.ca
www.utpress.utoronto.ca
Social Media:
twitter.com/utpress
www.facebook.com/utpress
ISBNs: ISBN: 0-8020; SAN: 115-1134, 115-3234
UTP publishes scholarly, reference and general interest books in Canadian history and literature, medieval studies, social sciences, etc., as well as scholarly journals.
John Yates, President; Publisher & Chief Executive Officer, 416-978-2239 ext. 222, jyates@utpress.utoronto.ca
Katheryn Bennett, Senior Vice President, HR & Administration, 416-978-2239 ext. 224, kbennett@utpress.utoronto.ca

Véhicule Press
CP 42094 Roy, Montréal, QC H2W 2T3
Tél: 514-844-6073; *Téléc:* 514-844-7543
admin@vehiculepress.com
www.vehiculepress.com
Médias sociaux:
www.twitter.com/VehiculePress
www.facebook.com/VehiculePress?ref=h l
ISBNs: 0-919890, 1-55065; SAN: 115-1150
Simon Dardick, Co-Publisher
Nancy Marrelli, Co-Publisher

VLB Éditeur
Une compagnie de Quebecor Media
Anciennement: Editions Quinze
Détenteur: Quebecor Media
1010, rue de la Gauchetière est, Montréal, QC H2L 2N5
Tél: 514-523-7993; *Téléc:* 514-282-7530
adpcommandes@messageries-adp.com
www.edvlb.com
Médias sociaux:
www.facebook.com/vlbediteur
ISBNs: 2-89005
Publie des romans, des essais et des nouvelles.
Martin Balthazar, Éditeur

Voyageur Publishing
C/O Paula Marquis, 1474 Clayton Rd., RR1, Almonte, ON K0A 1A0
Tel: 613-256-8166
www.voyageurpublishing.weebly.com
ISBNs: 0-921842
Publishers of Canadian History books with a Christian Perspective
Paula Marquis, President, paulemarquis@gmail.com

Wall & Emerson, Inc.
#533, 21 Dale Ave., Toronto, ON M4W 1K3
Fax: 416-352-5368
wall@wallbooks.com
www.wallbooks.com
ISBNs: 1-895131, 0-921332; SAN: 116-0486
Client publisher of the University of Toronto Press; Publishes textbooks for universities & colleges, primarily in adult education, science, history of science, mathematics, English as a second language, and industrial engineering
Byron E. Wall, President
Martha Wall, Vice President

Whitecap Books Ltd.
Owned By: Fitzhenry & Whiteside Ltd.
#210, 314 West Cordova St., Vancouver, BC V6B 1E8
Tel: 604-681-6181
whitecap@whitecap.ca
www.whitecap.ca
ISBNs: 1-895099, 1-55110, 1-55285; SAN: 115-1290
Currently publishes more than 300 Canadian & foreign titles; Primary emphasis is in the areas of food & wine, but also publish children's fiction & non-fiction; travel sports & transportation.
Nick Rundall, Publisher, nickr@whitecap.ca
Jordie Yow, Editor

Whitlands Publishing Ltd.
4444 Tremblay Dr., Victoria, BC V8N 4W5
Tel: 250-477-0192
info@whitlands.com
www.whitlands.com
Social Media:
www.linkedin.com/pub/joyce-sandilands/33/a73/129
twitter.com/twoauthors
www.facebook.com/JRobertWhittleAuthor?ref=hl
ISBNs: 0-9685061, 0-9734383
Publishers of novels by J. Robert Whittle & Joyce Sandilands-Whittle
Joyce Sandilands-Whittle, Publisher
Robert Whittle, Publisher

Wilfrid Laurier University Press
75 University Ave. W, Waterloo, ON N2L 3C5
Tel: 519-884-0710; *Fax:* 519-725-1399
press@wlu.ca
www.wlupress.wlu.ca
Social Media:
twitter.com/wlupress
www.facebook.com/wlupress
ISBNs: 0-88920; SAN: 115-1525
Publishing arm of Wilfrid Laurier University; Publishes 28-30 titles annually in the fields of history, literature, sociology, social work, life writing, film and media studies, aboriginal studies, women's studies, philosophy, & religious studies
Lisa Quinn, Director, Rights & Permissions, lquinn@wlu.ca
Rob Kohlmeier, Managing Editor, rkohlmeier@wlu.ca

Wilson et Lafleur
40, rue Notre-Dame, Montréal, QC H2Y 1B9
Tél: 514-875-6326; *Téléc:* 514-875-8356
librarie@wilsonlafleur.com
www.wilsonlafleur.com
ISBNs: 2-89127
Distribue la majorité des ouvrages de droit publiés au Québec et de nombreux autres titres canadiens et étrangers.
Claude Wilson, Directeur

Winding Trail Press
1304 St-Jacques Rd., Toronto, ON K0A 1W0
Tel: 416-443-4484; *Fax:* 800-221-9985
Toll-Free: 800-565-9523
contact@windingtrailpress.com
windingtrailpress.geliefan.net
Publishes Canadian literature and non-fiction.
Ruth Bradley-St. Cyr, Publisher

Wolsak & Wynn Publishers Ltd.
280 James St. North, Hamilton, ON L8R 2L3
Tel: 905-972-9885; *Fax:* 905-972-8589
info@wolsakandwynn.ca
www.wolsakandwynn.ca
Social Media: www.flickr.com/photos/95805497@N04/
twitter.com/wolsakandwynn
www.face book.com/groups/24466746964/
ISBNs: 0-919897
Publishers mostly poetry and non-fiction.
Noelle Allen, Publisher

Women's Press
Owned By: Canadian Scholars' Press
#200, 245 Adelaide St. West, Toronto, ON M5V 3C1
Tel: 416-929-2774; *Fax:* 416-929-1926
info@cspi.org
cspi.org/womens_press
Social Media: www.linkedin.com/company/701428
twitter.com/WomensPressCA
www.facebook .com/WomensPress
ISBNs: 0-88961, 0-921881, 0-7737, 0-921556; SAN: 115-5628
Publishes high-quality feminist writing

Wood Lake Publishing Inc.
485 Beaver Lake Rd., Kelowna, BC V4V 1S5
Tel: 250-766-2778; *Fax:* 250-766-2736
Toll-Free: 800-299-2926
info@woodlake.com
www.woodlakebooks.com
Social Media: www.youtube.com/woodlakepublishing
twitter.com/woodlakebooks
www.faceb ook.com/WoodLakePublishingInc
ISBNs: 1-55145, 1-896836; SAN: 117-7436
Publishers of religious books and religious education tools. Imprints: WoodLake | Northstone | CopperHouse | Seasons of the Spirit | The Best of Whole People of God Online.
Bonnie Schlosser, Publisher
Lois Huey Heck, Marketing Manager

Wordwrights Canada
Tel: 416-752-0689; *Fax:* 416-752-0689
wordwrights@sympatico.ca
www.wordwrights.ca
ISBNs: 0-920835
Wordwrights Canada provides resources for writers, including the online course Lessons in Writing the Poem, and publishes books and eBooks.
Susan Ioannou, Director, 416-752-0689, Fax: 416-752-0689, wordwrights@sympatico.ca

YYZ Books
#140, 401 Richmond St. W, Toronto, ON M5V 3A8
Tel: 416-598-4546; *Fax:* 416-598-2282
publish@yyzartistsoutlet.org
www.yyzbooks.com
Social Media:
twitter.com/YYZ_YYZBOOKS
www.facebook.com/yyzartistsoutlet
ISBNs: 0-920397
Publishes a variety of current writing focusing on art & culture
Ana Barajas, Director, abarajas@yyzartistsoutlet.org

Zygote Publishing
PO Box 4049, Edmonton, AB T6E 4S8
Tel: 780-439-7580; *Fax:* 780-439-7529
publish@zygotepublishing.com
www.zygotepublishing.com

e-Reading Service Providers

Munsey Music
PO Box 511, Richmond Hill, ON L4C 4Y8
web@MunseyMusic.com
www.pathcom.com/~munsey/MunseyMusic
ISBNs: 0-9697066, 0-9685152; SAN: 116-967X
Electronic copies of Mystery, Fantasy & Self-Help books

Star Dispatches
Owned By: Toronto Star
1 Yonge St., Toronto, ON M5E 1E6
Tel: 416-945-8725; *Toll-Free:* 855-945-8725
customersupport@stardispatches.com
www.stardispatches.com
A cross between a newspaper & a book, Star Dispatches offers weekly stories, written by the same journalists that published them in the newspaper, but that go more in-depth.

Magazine & Newspaper Publishers

Aberdeen Publishing Inc.
2562C Main St., West Kelowna, BC V4T 2N5
Tel: 778-754-5722; *Fax:* 778-754-5721
webads@aberdeenpublishing.com
www.aberdeenpublishing.com
Social Media:
twitter.com/aberdeenpublish
www.facebook.com/1414195442182278
Robert W. Doull, President, rdoull@aberdeenpublishing.com

Acadie Média
860 Main St., Moncton, NB E1C 1G2
Tél: 506-383-1955; *Téléc:* 506-383-7440
Francis Sonier, Publisher & CEO

Advocate Printing & Publishing Co.
PO Box 1000, 181 Brown's Point Rd., Pictou, NS B0K 1H0
Tel: 902-485-1990; *Fax:* 902-485-6353
Toll-Free: 800-236-9526
advocateprinting.com
Social Media:
twitter.com/Advocate1891
www.facebook.com/groups/advocatefamily
Divisions include Advocate Media Inc. & Metro Guide Publishing.
Sean Murray, President & CEO, seanmurray@advocateprinting.com

AgMedia Inc.
Previous Name: AgMedia Co-operative Inc.
58 Teal Dr., Guelph, ON N1C 1G4
Tel: 519-763-4044; *Fax:* 519-763-4482
www.betterfarming.com
Focus on the Ontario agricultural community, with industry magazines, trade show guides, custom publishing and database services.

Alta Newspaper Group LP
Owned By: Glacier Media Inc.
#920, 1200 - 73rd Ave. West, Vancouver, BC V6P 6G5
Tel: 604-732-4443

Andrew John Publishing Inc.
#220, 115 King St. West, Dundas, ON L9H 1V1
Tel: 905-628-4309; *Fax:* 866-849-1266
Toll-Free: 877-245-4080
info@andrewjohnpublishing.com
www.andrewjohnpublishing.com
Andrew John Publishing Inc. is a trade oriented publishing house with a focus on health sciences and specializing in association and society publishing. They publish, for example, "Wavelength", "Caslpo", "Canadian Hearing Report", "College Contact" and "Listen Ecoute".
John D. Birkby, Publisher, 905-628-4309, jbirkby@andrewjohnpublishing.com
Brenda Robinson, Sales & Circulation Coordinator, Sales & Circulation, 905-628-4309, brobinson@andrewjohnpublishing.com

Annex Media & Printing Inc.
Previous Name: AIS Communications Ltd.
Owned By: Annex Business Media
PO Box 530, 105 Donly Dr. South, Simcoe, ON N3Y 4N5
Tel: 519-429-3966; *Fax:* 519-429-3094
Toll-Free: 800-265-2827
salesprint@annexweb.com
www.annexweb.com
Michael Fredericks, President & CEO, mfredericks@annexweb.com
Diane Kleer, VP Production/Group Publisher, dkleer@annexweb.com

Annex-Newcom
Previous Name: Southam Business Communications Inc.
80 Valleybrook Dr., Toronto, ON M3B 2S9
Tel: 416-442-5600; *Fax:* 416-442-2191
Toll-Free: 800-668-2374
www.businessinformationgroup.ca
ISBNs: 1-55257, 0-919217, 0-919378, 0-9693221, 0-911448
Specializes in business magazines, directories and databases.
Mike Fredericks, CEO

Armadale Publications Inc.
#203, 10544 - 106SE, Edmonton, AB T5H 2X6
Tel: 780-429-1073
armadale@global-serve.net
www.albertaoilandgas.com
Publishers of the Alberta Oil & Gas Directory

Bale Communications Inc.
#1463, 1011 Upper Middle Rd. East, Oakville, ON L6H 5Z9
info@adnews.com
www.adnews.com
Bale Communications publishes Adnews, a Canadian publication that offers daily advertising & marketing news.
Robert Bale, Publisher
Derek Winkler, Editor

Baum Publications Ltd.
124-2323 Boundary, Vancouver, BC V5M 4V8
Tel: 604-291-9900; *Fax:* 604-291-1906
circulation@baumpub.com
www.baumpub.com
Baum Publications Ltd. publishes specialty trade publications, such as Contractors Magazine, Heavy Equipment Guide, Oil & Gas Product News, & Recycling Product News.
Engelbert J. Baum, President, ebaum@baumpub.com
Ken Singer, Publisher & Vice-President, ksinger@baumpub.com
Melvin Date Chong, Controller & Vice-President, mdatechong@baumpub.com
Tina Anderson, Manager, Production, tanderson@baumpub.com

Baxter Publications Inc.
310 Dupont St., Toronto, ON M5R 1V9
Tel: 416-968-7252; *Fax:* 416-968-2377
info@baxter.net
www.baxter.net
Social Media: www.linkedin.com/company/baxter-travel-media
twitter.com/CdnTravelPress
Baxter Publications is the publisher of education products & travel industry products. Services include web design & development, web hosting, & digital publishing.

Bayard Presse Canada Inc.
4475, rue Frontenac, Montréal, QC H2H 2S2
Tel: 514-522-3936; *Fax:* 514-522-1761
www.bayardcanada.ca

Becker Associates
Previous Name: Publishing & Printing Services
#202, 10 Morrow Ave., Toronto, ON M6R 2J1
Tel: 416-538-1650; *Fax:* 416-489-1713
info@beckerassociates.ca
www.beckerassociates.ca
Other information: Montréal Phone: 514-274-0742
Social Media: www.linkedin.com/company/becker-associates
twitter.com/BeckerAssoc
facebook.com/pages/Becker-Associates/123404977701883
Becker Associates offers services such as editorial management, production management, & web-based publishing for publications & scholarly journals.
Adam Becker, President, Publications & Web, abecker@beckerassociates.ca

Black Press
#309, 5460 - 152nd St., Surrey, BC V3S 5J9
Tel: 604-575-2744
www.blackpress.ca
Publishes over 100 newspapers throughout British Columbia
David H. Black, Chairman
Rick O'Connor, President & CEO

Breton Communications Inc.
#202, 495 boul. St-Martin ouest, Laval, QC H7M 1Y9
Tel: 450-629-6005; *Fax:* 450-629-6044
Toll-Free: 888-462-2112
info@bretoncom.com
www.bretoncom.com
Social Media: www.linkedin.com/in/4748794
twitter.com/BretonCom
www.facebook.com/BretonCom
Publishers specialising in optometry
Martine Breton, President & Publisher, 450-629-6005, martine@bretoncom.com
Nicky Fambois, Assistant Publisher, nicky@bretoncom.com

Brunico Communications Ltd.
#100, 366 Adelaide St. W, Toronto, ON M5V 1R9
Tel: 416-408-2300; *Fax:* 416-408-0870
www.brunico.com
Through print, electronic publications and industry events, Brunico connects indiciduals and organizations, building communities specializing in the entertainment and marketing sectors. Brunico Marketing Inc., the California subsidiary of Brunico Communications Ltd., produces Brunico's entertainment and marketing conferences in New York, Washington, Los Angeles and other U.S. cities.
Russell Goldstein, President & Chief Executive Officer, rgoldstein@brunico.com
Omri Tintpulber, Vice President & Chief Investments Officer, otintpulver@brunico.com
Linda Lovegrove, Vice President Finance & Administration, llovegrove@brunico.com

Brunswick News Inc.
PO Box 1001, 939 Main St., Moncton, NB E1C 8P3
Tel: 506-859-4900; *Fax:* 506-859-4899
Toll-Free: 888-923-4900
Jamie Irving, Vice-President

Business Link Media Group
#200, 36 Hiscott St., St Catharines, ON L2R 1C8
Tel: 905-646-9366; *Fax:* 905-646-5486
info@businesslinkmedia.com
www.businesslinkmedia.com
Social Media:
twitter.com/TheBusinessLink
www.facebook.com/BusinessLinkMedia
Publishes the following: "Business Link Niagara", "Business Link Hamilton", "Health, Wellness & Safety Magazine", "All in the Family", "Profiles in Business", & "The Golden Highway".

Byrne Publishing Group Inc.
814 Lawrence Ave., Kelowna, BC V1Y 6L9
Tel: 250-861-5399; *Fax:* 250-868-3040
info@okanaganlife.com
www.okanaganlife.com
Publishes Okanagan Life magazine
Paul Byrne, Publisher & Editor, paul@okanaganlife.com
Laurie Carter, Senior Editor, laurie@okanaganlife.com

Canada Wide Media Limited
Previous Name: Canada Wide Magazines & Communications Ltd.
4180 Lougheed Hwy., 4th Fl., Burnaby, BC V5C 6A7
Tel: 604-299-7311; *Fax:* 604-299-9188
cwm@canadawide.com
www.canadawide.com
Canada Wide Media provides a range of media services and products, in printed publications and digital media.
Peter Legge, President & Publisher LL.D, plegge@canadawide.com
Heather Parker, Senior Vice-President CGA, hparker@canadawide.com
Samantha Legge, Vice-President, Marketing, slegge@canadawide.com
Corinne Smith, Vice-President, Production, csmith@canadawide.com

Canadian Circumpolar Institute
CCI Press
1 - 42 Pembina Hall, University of Alberta, Edmonton, AB T6G 2H8
Tel: 780-492-4512; *Fax:* 780-492-1153
ccinst@gpu.srv.ualberta.ca
www.cci.ualberta.ca/en/CCIPress
ISBNs: 1-896445, 0-919058
Academic publishing house with a focus on peer-reviewed publishing
Elaine Maloney, Managing Editor, elaine.maloney@ualberta.ca
Cindy S. Mason, Business Manager, 780-492-4512, cindy.mason@ualberta.ca

Canadian Committee on Labour History
Peace Hills Trust Tower, Athabasca University, 1200, 10011 - 109 St., Edmonton, AB T5J 3S8
cclh@athabascau.ca
www.cclh.ca
ISBNs: 0-9692060, 0-9695835, 1-894000; SAN: 115-4168
Publisher of Labour/Le Travail: Journal of Canadian Labour Studies, as well as books & bulletins around the subject of labour history.
Janis Thiessen, President, ja.thiessen@uwinnipeg.ca
Gregory S. Kealey, Treasurer, gkealey@unb.ca

Canadian Controlled Media Communications
#101, 5397 Eglinton Ave. W, Toronto, ON M9C 5K6
Tel: 416-928-2909; *Fax:* 416-966-1181
Toll-Free: 800-320-6420
www.ccmc.ca
CCMC is a sports and entertainment marketing company with ventures in publishing, radio and television, internet, event production and media creation. Published products include SCOREGolf and CFL Illustrated.
Kim Locke, President, SCOREGolf, 416-928-2909 ext. 229, Fax: 416-966-1181, kiml@ccmc.ca
Ryan Hudecki, Director Corporate Parternships, Corporate Parternships, 416-928-2909 ext. 242, Fax: 416-966-1181, ryan@ccmc.ca

Canadian Energy Research Institute (CERI)
#150, 3512 - 33rd St. NW, Calgary, AB T2L 2A6
Tel: 403-282-1231; *Fax:* 403-284-4181
info@ceri.ca
www.ceri.ca
Social Media:
twitter.com/ceri_canada
ISBNs: 0-920522, 1-896091; SAN: 115-2866
CERI is an independent, not-for-profit research establishment created through a partnership of industry, academia, and government. It aims to provide relevant, objective economic research in energy and related environmental issues. CERI's publications are categorized into Studies and Periodicals. Studies are reports published by the Institute on completion of study projects.
Peter Howard, President & CEO, 403-220-2379, phoward@ceri.ca
Megan Murphy, Executive Assistant, mmurphy@ceri.ca

Canadian House & Home
#120, 511 King St. W, Toronto, ON M5V 2Z4
Tel: 416-593-0204; *Fax:* 416-591-1630
Toll-Free: 800-559-8868
advertising@hhmedia.com
www.houseandhome.com
Social Media:
twitter.com/HouseandHome
www.facebook.com/houseandhomemagazine
Publishes interiors of beautiful & unique homes across Canada
Lynn Reeves, President & Publisher
Kirby Miller, VP & General Manager

Canadian Institute of Mining, Metallurgy & Petroleum (CIM) / Institut canadien des mines, de la métallurgie et du pétrol
#1250, 3500 boul de Maisonneuve ouest, Westmount, QC H3Z 3C1
Tel: 514-939-2710; *Fax:* 514-939-2714
cim@cim.org
www.cim.org
ISBNs: 1-894475, 0-919086, 1-926872
Publishes magazines, journals & books about Canada's mining industry

Angela Hamlyn, Editor-in-Chief & Communications Director, 514-939-2710, ahamlyn@cim.org
Ryan Bergen, Editor-in-Chief, rbergen@cim.org

Canadian Institute of Resources Law
#3353 MFH, University of Calgary, 2500 University Dr. NW, Calgary, AB T2N 1N4
Tel: 403-220-3200; *Fax:* 403-282-6182
cirl@ucalgary.ca
www.cirl.ca
ISBNs: 0-919269; SAN: 115-2904
The Institute publishes the results of its research & proceedings of conferences that it sponsors, on the topic of Natural Resources Law. Titles include, "Canada Energy Law Service."
Dr. Ian Halloway, Chairman
Nigel Bankes, Vice Chairman

Canadian Science Publishing
#203, 65 Auriga Dr., Ottawa, ON K2E 7W6
Tel: 613-656-9846; *Fax:* 613-656-9838
pubs@nrcresearchpress.com
www.nrcresearchpress.com
Social Media:
www.linkedin.com/company/canadian-science-publishing
twitter.com/cdnsciencepub
www.facebook.com/NRCResearchPress
Publisher of scholarly journals since 1929. They are part of the Canada Institute for Scientific and Technical Information and publish 16 journals, monographs, conference proceedings, and allied publications.
Bruce P. Dancik, Editor-in-Chief, pubs@nrc-cnrc.gc.ca

Canstar Community News Ltd.
Owned By: FP Canadian Newspapers
1355 Mountain Ave., Winnipeg, MB R2X 3B6
Tel: 204-697-7000; *Fax:* 204-953-4300
www.winnipegfreepress.com
Published titles include such community newspapers as The Herald, The Lance, The Metro and The Times.

Capemara Communications Inc.
4623 William Head Rd., Victoria, BC V9C 3Y7
Tel: 250-474-3935; *Fax:* 250-478-3979
Toll-Free: 800-661-0368
info@capamara.com
capamara.com
This publisher offers specialty magazines and trade newspapers for various industries in Canada and around the world. Titles include: Aquaculture, Hatchery International, Small Farm Canada, Crane & Hoist Canada.

Carswell
Owned By: Thomson Reuters
One Corporate Plaza, 2075 Kennedy Rd., Toronto, ON M1T 3V4
Tel: 416-609-3800; *Fax:* 416-298-5082
Toll-Free: 800-387-5164
carswell.customerrelations@thomson.com
www.carswell.com
Other information: Toll Free Fax: 877-750-9041
ISBNs: 0-459, 0-7798, 0-88820
Carswell publishes information and electronic research solutions to the legal, tax, finance, accounting and human resources markets. Its material is integrated information available in a range of formats, including books, looseleaf services, journals, newsletters, CD-ROMS and online.

Chronicle Companies
#306, 555 Burnhamthorpe Rd., Toronto, ON M9C 2Y3
Tel: 416-916-2476; *Fax:* 416-352-6199
Toll-Free: 866-632-4766
health@chronicle.org
chronicle.ca
ISBNs: 0-9685848
A privately-held independent producer of periodicals, newsletters, websites and information for medical practitioners, and for the pharmaceutical and biotech industries. Publications include, "The Chronicle of Cancer Therapy," "The Chronicle Neurology Network," and "The Skin Book."
R.Allan Ryan, Editorial Director, allan.ryan@chronicle.ca

CNIB
1929 Bayview Ave., Toronto, ON M4G 3E8
Tel: 416-486-2500; *Fax:* 416-480-7700
Toll-Free: 800-563-2642
www.cnib.ca
Social Media: www.youtube.com/cnibnatcomm
twitter.com/CNIB
www.facebook.com/myCNIB
ISBNs: 0-616, 0-921122
CNIB reproduces materials in alternative formats, including DAISY audio, Braille

Continental Newspapers
Previous Name: Continental Newspapers Canada Ltd.
550 Doyle Ave., Kelowna, BC V1Y 7V1

Cottage Life Media
Owned By: Blue Ant Media
54 St. Patrick St., Toronto, ON M5T 1V1
Tel: 416-599-2000; *Toll-Free:* 800-465-6183
cottagelife@cdsglobal.ca
www.cottagelife.com
Social Media: pinterest.com/cottagelife
twitter.com/cottagelife
www.facebook.com/cot tagelife
ISBNs: 0-9696922
In addition to keeping a website with a plethora of information about cottage lifestyle, the company publishes Cottage Life magazine and distributes a small selection of cottage-related books and television shows.
Al Zikovitz, President & Chief Executive Officer

Craig Kelman & Associates
2020 Portage Ave., Winnipeg, MB R3J 0K4
Tel: 866-985-9780; *Fax:* 866-985-9799
info@kelman.ca
www.kelman.ca
Social Media: www.linkedin.com/company/1058679
www.facebook.com/Kelman.Publishing
Craig Kelman & Associates is a contract publisher of magazines, directories, & newsletters.
Chris Kelman, Contact, 866-985-9781, chris@kelman.ca

CTC Communications Corporation
#200, 2110 Matheson Blvd. E, Mississauga, ON L4W 5E1
Tel: 905-712-3636; *Fax:* 905-712-1679
info@ctccomm.com
www.ctccomm.com
Medical communications company with a focus on branding through education

DBC Communications Inc.
655, av Sainte-Anne, Saint-Hyacinthe, QC J2S 5G4

Department of National Defence
National Defence Headquarters, 101 Colonel By Dr., Ottawa, ON K1A 0K2
www.forces.gc.ca

E.J. Lewchuck & Associates Ltd.
45 South Ave., Bay C, Spruce Grove, AB T7X 3A8
Tel: 780-962-9228

Les Éditions Apex inc. / Apex Publications Inc.
185, rue Saint-Paul, Québec, QC G1K 3W2
Fax: 800-664-2739
Toll-Free: 800-905-7468
info@photolife.com
www.photolife.com
Éditeur de périodiques: "Photo Life", et "Photo Solution"
Guy J. Poirier, Publisher, 800-905-9468 ext. 101, gpoirier@photolife.com
Valérie Racine, Rédactrice en chef, editor@photolife.com

Les Editions du Journal de l'Assurance
#100, 321, rue de la Commune ouest, Montréal, QC H2Y 2E1
Tél: 514-289-9595; *Téléc:* 514-289-9527
reception@journal-assurance.ca
www.journal-assurance.ca
Publications: "FlashFinance.ca", "Le Journal de l'assurance", "Répertoire des services en assurance des dommages" & "The Insurance & Investment Journal". Conventions: "Le Congrès de l'assurance et de l'investissement", "Canada Sales Conference" et "Journée de l'assurance de dommages".
Serge Therrien, Président et éditeur, serge.therrien@journal-assurance.ca

Les Éditions forestières
#203, 1175, rue Lavigerie, Québec, QC G1V 4P1
Tél: 418-877-4583; *Téléc:* 418-877-6449
www.lemondeforestier.ca
Médias sociaux:
twitter.com/MondeForestier
www.facebook.com/LeMondeForestier
Le Monde Forestier est le journal mensuel québécois dédié à la foresterie
Guy Lavoie, Directeur Général, direction@lemondeforestier.ca
Roger Robitaille, Directeur des Ventes, roger@lemondeforestier.ca

Les Éditions Rogers Limitée
Anciennement: Maclean Hunter Publishing
Détenteur: Rogers Media inc.
1200, av McGill College, 8e étage, Montréal, QC H3B 4G7
Tél: 514-845-5141
www.leseditionsrogers.ca

Ken Whyte, Président/Chef de la direction

EGS Press
#118, 283 Danforth Ave., Toronto, ON M4K 1N2
Tel: 416-829-8014
info@egspress.com
www.egspress.com
ISBNs: 0-9685330
Publisher of research material in the fields of media, the arts & therapy from the European Graduate School, Switzerland, & the annual journal "Poiesis: A Journal of the Arts & Communication."
Steve Levine, Editor-in-Chief, editor@egspress.com
Shara Claire, Assistant Poetry Editor, Poetry, shara@egspress.com
Kristin Briggs, Art Submissions Co-ordinator, Art, egspress.design@yahoo.com.

Family Communications Inc. / Communications Famille inc.
65 The East Mall, Toronto, ON M8Z 5W3
Tel: 416-537-2604; *Fax:* 416-538-1794
Social Media:
www.linkedin.com/company/family-communications-inc-
Family Communications is Canada's largest privately-held, independent publisher of women's magazines, holding a leading position in Canada's bridal, new parent and home buying markets through its flagship titles: Today's Bride, Best Wishes, Mon Bébé, Expecting, C'est Pour Quand?, The Baby & Child Care Encyclopedia, Parents Canada and Canadian Home Planning.
Donald G. Swinburne, President

Farm Business Communications
Owned By: Glacier Media Group
PO Box 9800, 1666 Dublin Ave., Winnipeg, MB R3H 0H1
Tel: 204-954-1400; *Fax:* 204-945-4142
Bob Willcox, Publisher, 204-944-5751, bob.willcox@fbcpublishing.com
John Morriss, Associate Publisher / Editorial director, 204-944-5754, john.morriss@fbcpublishing.com

FP Newspapers Inc.
PO Box 11583, #2900, 650 West Georgia St., Vancouver, BC V6B 4N8
www.fpnewspapers.com
Daniel Koshowski, CFO

Friday Circle
Dept. of English, University of Ottawa, Ottawa, ON K1N 6N5
www.fridaycircle.uottawa.ca
ISBNs: 1-896362, 1-9697391
Publishing works by faculty, students & alumni of the Creative Writing Program, University of Ottawa

Fulcrum Media Inc.
Previous Name: Fulcrum Publishing Inc.
#201, 508 Lawrence Ave. West, Toronto, ON M6A 1A1
Tel: 416-504-0504; *Fax:* 416-256-3002
Toll-Free: 866-688-0504
info@fulcrum.ca
fulcrum.ca
Other information: Vancouver E-mail: info@eat-vancouver.com
New media company targeting the food & beverage industries, with print & digital publications, social media & live events.
Alan Fogel, Group Publisher, afogel@fulcrum.ca
Russell Hoffman, Genreal Manager, rhoffman@fulcrum.ca

Glacier Media Inc.
2188 Yukon St., Vancouver, BC V5Y 3P1
www.glaciermedia.ca
Jonathon Kennedy, President & CEO

The Globe and Mail Inc.
Owned By: The Woodbridge Company Limited
444 Front St. West, Toronto, ON M5V 2S9

Great West Newspapers LP
Owned By: Glacier Media Inc. / Jamison Newspapers Inc.
340 Carleton Dr., St. Albert, AB T8N 7L3
Tel: 780-460-5500; *Fax:* 780-460-8220
www.greatwest.ca
Social Media:
twitter.com/StAlbertGazette
www.facebook.com/stalbertgazettenews
Great West Newspapers Limited Partnership is a Canadian community newspaper publishing company.
Duff Jamison, President & CEO, 780-460-5519, djamison@greatwest.ca

Groupe Bomart
#204, 905 Michèle-Bohec, Blainville, QC J7C 5J6
Tél: 450-435-3131; *Téléc:* 450-435-3884
www.bomartgroup.com
Spécialisée dans l'édition de magazines dans le domaine du camionnage, de transport, de la logistique et des affaires

Groupe Capitales Médias Inc.
CP 1547, Succ. Terminus, 410, boul Charest est, Québec, QC G1K 7J6
Tél: 418-686-3233
www.gcmedias.com

Groupe Constructo
Détenteur: TC Transcontinental
#200, 1500, boul Jules-Poitras, Saint-Laurent, QC H4N 1X7
Tél: 514-745-5720; *Téléc:* 514-339-2267
Ligne sans frais: 800-363-0910
www.constructo.ca
Manon Bouchard, Marketing contact, 514-856-6609, manon.bouchard@tc.tc

Halifax Herald Ltd.
2717 Joseph Howe St., Halifax, NS B3J 2T2
Tel: 902-426-2811

HOMES Publishing Group (HPG)
178 Main St., Unionville, ON L3R 2G9
Tel: 905-479-4663; *Toll-Free:* 800-363-4663
info@homesmag.com
www.homespublishinggroup.com
Social Media:
twitter.com/HOMESPublishing
www.facebook.com/pages/HOMES-Publishing-Group/11773177455
Homes Publishing Group publishes titles such as "Homes Magazines", "Active Adult Magazine", "Condo Life Magazine", and "Moving To Magazines".
Michael Rosset, President & Publisher, cleo@homesmag.com

Horse Publications Group
Previous Name: Corinthian Publishing Co. Ltd.
PO Box 670, Aurora, ON L4G 4J9
Tel: 905-727-0107; *Fax:* 905-841-1530
Toll-Free: 800-505-7428
info@horse-canada.com
www.horse-canada.com
Publications includes Horse Sport, Horse-Canada & Canadian Thoroughbred, and Horsepower.
Jennifer Anstey, Publisher, janstey@horse-canada.com
Susan Strafford, Managing Editor, editor@horse-canada.com

IG Publications (Banff) Ltd.
100 Owl St., Banff, AB T1L 1C7
Tel: 403-760-3484
www.visitors-info.com
Publishes travel information for B.C.

Infopresse
4310, boul St-Laurent, Montréal, QC H2W 1Z3
Tél: 514-842-5873; *Téléc:* 514-842-2422
redaction@infopresse.com
www.infopresse.com
Le mensuell du marketing, de la publicité et des communications
Bruno Gautier, Président et éditeur
Clodine Chartrand, Directrice générale, clodine.chartrand@infopresse.com

Institute of Intergovernmental Relations
Room 301, School of Policy Studies, 138 Union St., Kingston, ON K7L 3N6
Tel: 613-533-2080; *Fax:* 613-533-6868
iigr@queensu.ca
www.iigr.ca
ISBNs: 0-88911, 1-55339
Specializing in research & publication, with emphasis on Canadian federalism, intergovernmental relations, constitutional reform & social union
André Juneau, Director, 613-533-6000, john.allan@queensu.ca

Insurancewest Media Ltd.
PO Box 3311 Terminal, 661 Market Hill, Vancouver, BC V6B 3Y3
Tel: 604-874-1001; *Fax:* 604-874-3922
Toll-Free: 800-888-8811
manager@insurancewest.ca
www.insurancewest.ca
Publishes a variety of publications such as "The BC Broker", "Insurance People", "Prairies Insurance Directory", & "British Columbia Insurance Directory".
Bill Earle, Publisher, 604-875-7766

Investment Executive
100 - 25 Sheppard Ave. West, Toronto, ON M2N 6S7
Tel: 416-733-7600; *Fax:* 416-218-3624
sales@investmentexecutive.com
www.investmentexecutive.com

Ishcom Publications Ltd.
#201, 2065 Dundas St. East, Mississauga, ON L4X 2W1
Tel: 905-206-0150; *Fax:* 905-206-9972
Toll-Free: 800-201-8596
canadianrestaurantnews.com/canada
Social Media: www.linkedin.com/company/ishcom-publications
Steven Isherwood, Publisher, 905-206-0150 x236, sisherwood@canadianrestaurantnews.com

Issues Ink
#403, 313 Pacific Ave., Winnipeg, MB R3A 0M2
Tel: 204-453-1965; *Fax:* 204-475-5247
Toll-Free: 877-710-3222
issues@issuesink.com
www.issuesink.com
Social Media:
www.facebook.com/IssuesInk
Issues Ink is a Winnipeg-based publishing and consulting company with extensive experience in the agricultural sector.
Shawn Brook, President, sbrook@issuesink.com

Jamison Newspapers Inc.
#10, 25 Chisholm Ave., St. Albert, AB T8M 5A5
Tel: 780-460-5500
Duff Jamison, President

Journal la Nouvelle Édition
Anciennement: L'Edition Commerciale
#400, 11905 rue Notre-Dame E, Montréal, QC H1V 2Y4
Tél: 514-257-1000; *Téléc:* 514-257-7505
www.journaledition.com
"Journal des gens d'affaires de Montréal"; actualités économiques
Alain Dulong, Président/Éditeur, a.dulong@journaledition.com

JuneWarren-Nickle's Energy Group
Previous Name: JuneWarren Publishing Ltd.
Owned By: Glacier Media Inc.
816 - 55 Ave. NE, 2nd Fl., Calgary, AB T2E 6Y4
Tel: 403-209-3500; *Fax:* 403-245-8666
Toll-Free: 800-387-2446
www.nickles.com
Social Media:
www.facebook.com/92980312678
Bill Whitelaw, Publisher

Kenilworth Media Inc.
#710, 15 Wertheim Ct., Richmond Hill, ON L4B 3H7
Tel: 905-771-7333; *Fax:* 905-771-7336
Toll-Free: 800-409-8688
www.kenilworth.com
Ellen Kral, Group Publisher & CEO

Kenilworth Publishing Inc.
#710, 15 Wertheim Ct., Richmond Hill, ON L4B 3H7
Tel: 905-771-7333; *Fax:* 905-771-7336
Toll-Free: 800-409-8688
www.kenilworthpublishing.com
Magazines include "Sign Media" & "Construction Canada".
Ellen Kral, Group Publisher & CEO

Kerrwil Publications Ltd.
538 Elizabeth St., Midland, ON L4R 2A3
www.kerrwil.com
John W. Kerr, Presidentor, 705-527-7677, johnkerr@kerrwil.com
Andy Adams, Managing Editor, 416-574-7313, aadams@kerrwil.com

Key Media Inc. (KMI)
#800, 312 Adelaide St. West, Toronto, ON M5V 1R2
Tel: 416-644-8740; *Fax:* 416-203-9083
www.kmipublishing.com
Specializes in business-to-business and consumer publications.

Kingston Publications
Owned By: Sun Media Corporation
18 St. Remy Pl., Kingston, ON K7K 6C4
Tel: 613-389-7400; *Fax:* 613-389-7507
www.kingstonpublications.com
Liza Nelson, Publisher, 613-549-8442 ext 135, liza.nelson@sunmedia.ca
Jane Deacon, Editor, 613-549-8442 ext 108

Koocanusa Publications Inc.
#100, 100 - 7th Ave. South, Cranbrook, BC V1C 2J4
Tel: 250-426-7253; *Fax:* 250-426-4125
Toll-Free: 800-663-8555
info@kpimedia.com
www.koocanusapublications.com
Magazine and directory publishing.
Keith Powell, Publisher, keith@kpimedia.com
Kerry Shellborn, Editorial Coordinator, kerry@kpimedia.com

Kostuch Media Ltd. (KML)
Previous Name: Kostuch Publications Ltd.
101-23 Lesmill Rd., Toronto, ON M3B 3P6
Tel: 416-447-0888; *Fax:* 416-447-5333
web@kostuchmedia.com
www.kostuchmedia.com
Publisher serving the foodservice and hospitality markets in Canada such as "Foodservice and Hospitality" and "Hotelier".
Rosanna Caira, Editor and Publisher, rcaira@foodservice.ca

Kylix Media Inc
5165, rue Sherbrooke Ouest, Montréal, QC H4A 1T6
Tél: 514-481-5892; *Téléc:* 514-481-9699
Aldo Parise, Editorial Director

LexisNexis Canada Ltd.
#900, 111 Gordon Baker Rd., Toronto, ON M2H 3R1
Tel: 905-479-2665; *Toll-Free:* 800-668-6481
www.lexisnexis.ca
Social Media: www.linkedin.com/company/lexisnexis-canada-inc-
twitter.com/lexisnexisca n
www.facebook.com/lexisnexiscanada
Loik Amis, Chief Executive Officer

Lighthouse Publishing Limited
353 York St., Bridgewater, NS B4V 3K2
Tel: 902-543-2457; *Fax:* 902-543-2228
hello@lighthousenow.ca
Social Media:
twitter.com/lhnownews
www.facebook.com/731074106985943
Lynn Hennigar, General Manager

Lloydmedia, Inc.
137 Main St. North, 3rd Fl., Markham, ON L3P 1Y2
Tel: 905-201-6600; *Fax:* 905-201-6601
Toll-Free: 800-668-1838
Media company with an audience of more than 100,000 readers; publishes four magazines & three industry directories.
Steve Lloyd, President, 905-201-6600 ext. 225, steve@paymentsbusiness.ca

Mackenzie Report Inc.
10006 - 97th St., High Level, AB T0H 1Z0
Tel: 780-926-2000; *Fax:* 780-926-2001
echo@mrnews.ca
www.mrnews.ca

Martin Charlton Communications
Previous Name: Charlton Communications
#300, 1914 Hamilton St., Regina, SK S4N 3N6
Tel: 306-584-1000; *Fax:* 306-352-4110
www.martincharlton.ca
This is a public relations consultant with services including writing, graphic design, media training, communications planning, among others.
Marylynn Charlton, marylynn@martincharlton.ca

MediaEdge Inc.
c/o MediaEdge Inc., 5255 Yonge St., Toronto, ON M2N 6P4
Tel: 416-512-8186; *Fax:* 416-512-8344
www.mediaedge.ca
Publications including Building Strategies, Canadian Apartment Magazine, CondoBusiness, Construction Business, & Design Quarterly.
Kevin Brown, President, kevinb@mediaedge.ca

Mediconcept Inc.
#300, 3333, boul Cote-Vertu, Saint-Laurent, QC H4R 2N1
Tél: 514-331-4561; *Fax:* 514-336-1129
www.mediconcept.ca

Mercury Publications Ltd.
1740 Wellington Ave., Winnipeg, MB R3H 0E8
Tel: 204-954-2085; *Fax:* 204-954-2057
Toll-Free: 800-337-6372
mp@mercury.mb.ca
www.mercury.mb.ca
Specializes in business-to-business communications.
Frank Yeo, President & CEO, fyeo@mercury.mb.ca

Metro Guide Publishing
Owned By: Advocate Printing & Publishing Co.
162 Trider Cres., Dartmouth, NS B3B 1R6
Tel: 902-420-9943; *Fax:* 902-429-9058
publishers@metroguide.ca
www.metroguide.ca
Patty Baxter, Publisher, 902-420-9943 x1810, pbaxter@metroguide.ca

Metroland Media Group Ltd.
Owned By: Torstar Corp.
#6, 3715 Laird Rd., Mississauga, ON L5L 0A3
Tel: 905-281-5656; *Fax:* 905-281-5630
www.metroland.com
Ian Oliver, President

Moorshead Magazines Ltd.
#500, 505 Consumers Rd., Toronto, ON M2J 4V8
Toll-Free: 888-326-2476
www.moorshead.com
Publications include Family Chronicle; Internet-genealogy; History Magazine.

Moving to Magazines Ltd.
Previous Name: Moving Publications Ltd.
Owned By: Homes Publishing Group
178 Main St., Unionville, ON L3R 2G9
Tel: 905-479-4663; *Toll-Free:* 800-363-4663
info@movingto.com
www.movingto.com
ISBNs: 1-895020
Publishers of the "Moving to" series of publications geared towards people moving to new cities in Canada.
Anita Wood, President/Publisher

Multimedia Nova Corporation
101 Wingold Ave., North York, ON M6B 1P8
Tel: 416-785-4300; *Fax:* 416-785-7350
Lori Abittan, President & CEO

Naylor (Canada) Inc.
Previous Name: Naylor Communications Ltd.
Owned By: Naylor, LLC
#300, 1630 Ness Ave., Winnipeg, MB R3J 3X1
Fax: 204-947-2047
Toll-Free: 800-665-2456
www.naylor.com
Social Media: www.linkedin.com/company/naylor-publications
twitter.com/naylorllc
www .facebook.com/naylorllc
Provides customized association marketing communications, including magazines, member directories, online buyers' guides, e-newsletters, digital magazines, show guides, & event marketing & promotion materials. Publications includes "Icon," "The Clarifier," "Who's Who," "Connections," "Pace," & "Association Leadership."
Robert Thompson, Publisher

The Neepawa Press
Previous Name: Sundance Publications Ltd.
PO Box 939, 423 Mountain Ave., Neepawa, MB ROJ 1HO
Tel: 204-476-2309; *Fax:* 204-476-5802
office@neepawapress.com
www.neepawapress.com
Publications such as the Neepawa Press.
Brent Fitzpatrick, Regional Publisher, pub@sasktel.net
Darren Graham, General Manager, advertising@neepawapress.com

Néomédia
9085, boul Lacroix, Saint-Georges, QC G5Y 2B4
Ligne sans frais: 866-327-0660
Médias sociaux:
www.facebook.com/neomedia.ca?fref=ts
Néomédia publishes 17 100% Web-based daily newspapers in Québec.

Nesbitt Publishing Ltd.
PO Box 160, Shoal Lake, MB R0J 1Z0
Tel: 204-759-2644; *Fax:* 204-759-2521
www.crossroadsthisweek.com
Greg Nesbitt, Manager, gnesbitt@mb.sympatico.ca

News Canada Inc.
Head Office
#509, 920 Yonge St., Toronto, ON M4W 3C7
Tel: 416-599-9900; *Fax:* 416-599-9700
Toll-Free: 888-855-6397
www.newscanada.com
Provides print editors with feature news stories of interest to their readers, as well as video & radio segments for broadcasters.
Ruth Douglas, President/Publisher

Norris-Whitney Communications Inc.
#202, 4056 Dorchester Rd., Niagara Falls, ON L2E 6M9
Tel: 905-374-8878; *Fax:* 888-665-1307
info@nor.com
www.nor.com
Norris-Whitney Communications publishes Canadian Musician, Professional Sound, Professional Lighting & Production and Canadian Music Trade magazines and Music Directory Canada.
Jim Norris, President, 905-374-9012, jnorris@nor.com

North Huron Publishing Inc.
PO Box 429, 404 Queen St., Blyth, ON N0M 1H0
Tel: 519-523-4792
info@northhuron.on.ca
www.northhuron.on.ca
Publications include; The Citizen, The Rural Voice, and Stops Along the Way.

North Island Publishing Ltd.
Previous Name: North Island Sound Ltd.
#8, 1606 Sedlescomb Dr., Mississauga, ON L4X 1M6
Tel: 905-625-7070; *Fax:* 905-625-4856
Toll-Free: 800-331-7408
www.northisland.ca
Sandy Donald, Publisher
Doug Bennet, Editor

North Superior Publishing Inc.
1402- 590 Beverly St., Thunder Bay, ON P7B 5N3
Tel: 807-623-2348; *Fax:* 807-623-7515
nspinc@tbaytel.net
www.northsuperiorpublishing.com
Publishes "Golfing News", "Business", and "Snowmobile News".
Scott A. Sumner, Publisher & Editor

Northern Star Communications Ltd.
900 - 6 Ave. SW, 5th Fl., Calgary, AB T2P 3K2
Tel: 403-263-6881; *Fax:* 403-263-6886
Toll-Free: 800-052-6417
editor@northernstar.ab.ca
www.northernstar.ab.ca
Four oilpatch magazines- "The Roughneck", "Energy Processing Canada", "Propane Canada" and "The Roughneck Buy and Sell", as well as the annual "Alberta Gas Plant Directory" and volume one of the "Roughneck Joke Book".
Scott Jeffrey, Publisher & Owner, scott@northernstar.ab.ca

The Ontario Historical Society
34 Parkview Ave., Toronto, ON M2N 3Y2
Tel: 416-226-9011; *Fax:* 416-226-2740
ohs@historicalsociety.ca
www.ontariohistoricalsociety.ca
Social Media:
twitter.com/OntarioHistory
www.facebook.com/pages/The-Ontario-Historical-Society/146

OP Media Group Ltd.
#802, 1166 Alberni St., Vancouver, BC V6E 3Z3
Tel: 604-998-3316; *Fax:* 604-998-3326
Toll-Free: 800-816-0747
info@oppublishing.com
www.oppublishing.com
Publishes magazines such as "Fishing", "Cottage", "Pacific Yachting", "Western Sportsman", "Outdoor Edge", "Canadian Aviator", "BC Marine Parks Guide", and "BC Fishing".
Mark Yelic, Publisher

OT Communications
1025-101 Sixth Ave. SW, Calgary, AB T2P 3P4
Tel: 403-264-3270; *Fax:* 403-264-3276
Toll-Free: 800-465-0322
info@otcommunications.com
www.otcommunications.com

Our Kids Publications Ltd.
4242 Rockwood Rd., Mississauga, ON L4W 1L8
Toll-Free: 877-272-1845
info@ourkids.net
www.ourkids.net
Other information: communications@ourkids.net
Social Media: www.youtube.com/ourkidsnet
www.twitter.com/ourkidsnet
www.facebook.com /ourkidsnet
Magazine "Our Kids Go to Camp" is devoted to helping parents find the right camp for their children and "Our Kids Go To School" is devoted to helping parents find the "best education for their kids".
Agatha Stawicki, Publisher, 905-272-1843 x24.

Parents Canada Group
Owned By: Family Communications Inc.
65 The East Mall, Toronto, ON M8Z 5W3
Tel: 416-537-2604; *Fax:* 416-538-1794
www.parentscanada.com
Social Media:
twitter.com/#%21/ParentsCanada
www.facebook.com/ParentsCanada
Publishes 9 parenting magazines.
Donald G. Swinburne, President
Amy Bielby, Contact, 416-537-2604 x238, amyb@parentscanada.com

Parkhurst Publishing
Previous Name: C.M.E. Publishing
400 McGill St., 3rd Fl., Montréal, QC H2Y 2G1
Tel: 514-397-8833; *Fax:* 514-397-0228
www.parkpub.com
ISBNs: 0-9688648, 0-9698972, 0-9732870
Parkhurst is a medical publishing house providing a wide range of medical media journals and educational communications to physicians and patients
Dr. Steven Blitzer, Medical Editor-in-Chief

Paton Publishing
Owned By: Metroland Media Group Ltd.
3145 Wolfedale Rd., Mississauga, ON L5C 1A9
Tel: 905-273-8145; *Fax:* 905-273-4991
info@patonpublishing.com
www.patonpublishing.com
Publisher of children's magazines, including What's UP, POP!, and Whoa!.
Erin Ruddy, Editor-in-Chief

Pink Triangle Press
#1600, 2 Carlton St., Toronto, ON M5B 1J3
Tel: 416-925-5221; *Fax:* 416-925-4817
pinktrianglepress@dailyxtra.com
pinktrianglepress.com

Playhouse Publications
Owned By: Suggitt Group Ltd.
10177 - 105 St. NW, Edmonton, AB T5J 1E2
Tel: 780-423-5834; *Fax:* 780-413-6185
info@playhousepublications.ca
www.playhousepublications.ca
Specializes in playbills for theatre & opera companies.

Post City Magazines Inc.
30 Lesmill Rd., Toronto, ON M3B 2T6
Tel: 416-250-7979; *Fax:* 416-250-1737
editorial@postcity.com
www.postcity.com
Social Media:
twitter.com/PostCity
Lorne London, Publisher, lornelondon@postcity.com

Postmedia Network Canada Corp.
365 Bloor St. East, Toronto, ON M4W 3L4
Tel: 416-383-2300
www.postmedia.com
Social Media:
www.linkedin.com/company/postmedia-network-inc.
twitter.com/postmedianet
www.facebook.com/Postmedia

Postmedia Network Inc.
Owned By: Postmedia Network Canada Corp.
365 Bloor St. East, Toronto, ON M4W 3L4
Tel: 416-383-2300
www.postmedia.com
Social Media:
www.linkedin.com/company/postmedia-network-inc.
twitter.com/postmedianet
www.facebook.com/Postmedia
Postmedia Network Inc. is a wholly owned subsidiary of Postmedia Network Canada Corporation and is the largest publisher, by circulation, of English-language daily newspapers in Canada.
Paul Godfrey, President & CEO

Power Corporation of Canada
161 Bay St., Toronto, ON M5J 2S1
www.powercorporation.com/en
Paul Desmarais Jr., Chairman & Co-CEO

Powershift Communications Inc.
245 Fairview Mall Dr., 5th Fl., Toronto, ON M2J 4T1
Tel: 416-494-1066; *Fax:* 416-494-2536
dbmckerchar@sympatico.ca
www.powershift.ca
A business-to-business publishing corporation.

Premier Publications and Shows
Owned By: Metroland Media Group Ltd.
#4, 447 Speers Rd., Oakville, ON L6K 3S7
Tel: 905-842-6591; *Toll-Free:* 800-693-7986
premierconsumershows.com
Vicki Dillane, General Manager, vdillane@metroland.com

Pulsus Group Inc.
2902 South Sheridan Way, Oakville, ON L6J 7L6
Tel: 905-829-4770; *Fax:* 905-829-4799
pulsus@pulsus.com
www.pulsus.com
Privately owned Canadian company which publishes "The Canadian Journal of Cardiology", "The Canadian Journal of Gastroenterology", "The Canadian Journal of Infectious Diseases & Medical Microbiology", "The Canadian Journal of Plastic Surgery", "Canadian Respiratory Journal", "Pain Research & Management", "Paediatrics & Child Health", and "Experimental & Clinical Cardiology".
LeBlanc Ann, Vice-President, 905-829-4770 ext 124
Lisa Robb, Director of Advertising Sales, 905-829-4770 ext 143

Québecor Media Inc.
612, rue Saint-Jacques, Montréal, QC H3C 4M8
Tel: 514-380-1999
www.quebecor.com/en
Social Media: twitter.com/Quebecor
Pierre Dion, President & CEO

Rogers Media Inc.
One Mount Pleasant Rd., Toronto, ON M4Y 2Y5
Tel: 416-764-2000
www.rogersmedia.com
Publications include "Canadian Business", "Chatelaine", "Flare", "Todays' Parents", "Macleans", "Money Sense", "Profit", "Marketing", "Lou Lou" and "Ontario Out of Doors" as well as Quebec magazines "L'actualité", "Le Bulletin", "Châtelaine", et "Lou Lou".
Ken Whyte, President
Garth S. Thomas, Senior Executive Publisher
Amanda Hudswell, Director, Human Resources

Salon Communications Inc.
#1902, 365 Bloor St. East, Toronto, ON M4W 3L4
Tel: 416-869-3131; *Fax:* 416-869-3008
info@salonmagazine.ca
www.saloncommunications.com
Salon Communications Inc. publishes Salon Magazine (English and French Editions), salonmagazine.ca, beautynet.com, Elevate Magazine, and elevatemagazine.com.
Laura Dunphy, President, 416-869-3131 x110, laura@salonmagazine.ca

Shoetrades Publications
Montréal, QC
Tel: 514-457-8787; *Fax:* 514-457-5832
books@shoetrades.com
www.shoetrades.com
Lumina Fillion, Editor & Art Director

Sing Tao Newspapers Ltd.
417 Dundas St. West, Toronto, ON M5T 1G6
Tel: 416-596-8140
news.singtao.ca/toronto

snapd Inc.
505 Queen St., Newmarket, ON L3Y 2H3
Tel: 905-953-7977; *Toll-Free:* 866-953-8509
info@snapnewspapers.com
snapnewspapers.com
Social Media: twitter.com/getsnapd
www.facebook.com/getsnapd

Solstice Publishing Inc.
47 Soho Sq., Toronto, ON M5T 2Z2
Toll-Free: 800-263-5295
ISSN: 0702-701X
Publisher of Ski Canada Magazine.
Paul Green, President

STA Communications Inc.
#310, 6500 Trans-Canada Hwy., Pointe-Claire, QC H9R 0A5
Tel: 514-695-7623; *Fax:* 514-695-8554
www.stacommunications.com
Journals include "Diagnosis", "CME", "Clinicien", Cardiology", and"Pharmaceutical".
Paul Brand, Contact (Montreal office), 541-695-8393 ext. 220, paulb@sta.ca

Stagnito Business Information & Edgell Communications
#1510, 2300 Yonge St., Toronto, ON M4P 1E4
Tel: 416-256-9908; *Fax:* 888-889-9522
Toll-Free: 877-687-7321
stagnito-edgell.com
Social Media: www.linkedin.com/company/stagnito-media
Provides business resources for retailers, retail suppliers, & technology vendors, including a variety of trade publications.
Kollin Stagnito, Chief Executive Officer, KollinStagnito@stagnitomail.com
Korry Stagnito, Chief Brand Officer, korrystagnito@stagnitomail.com

Suggitt Publishing Ltd.
10177 105 St. NW, Edmonton, AB T5J 1E2
Tel: 780-413-6163; *Fax:* 780-413-6185
Toll-Free: 877-784-4488
reception@suggitt.com
www.suggitt.com
Other information: Alternate Fax: 780-428-6100
Consumer magazines.
Tom Suggitt, President & CEO, tom@suggitt.com
Rob Suggitt, President & CFO, rob@suggitt.com

Sun Media Corporation
Previous Name: Bowes Publishing Ltd.
Owned By: Québecor Media Inc.
333 King St. East, Toronto, ON M5A 3X5
Tel: 416-947-2222
Forty-three dailies and more than 250 community weekly newspapers make Sun Media Corporation the largest press group in Canada.
Julie Tremblay, President & CEO
Eric Morrison, Vice-President, Editorial

Sunrise Publishing
Previous Name: Saskatchewan Business Magazine
2213B Hanselman Ct., Saskatoon, SK S7L 6A8
Tel: 306-244-5668; *Fax:* 306-244-5679
Toll-Free: 800-247-5743
sunrisepublish.com
Publishing information on Saskatchewan's businesses
Twila Reddekopp, Publisher
Matt Josdal, Account Executive, Accounts

Swan-Erickson Publishing Inc.
#355, 4261 - A14 Highway #7 East, Markham, ON L3R 9W6
Tel: 905-649-8966
Michael Swan, President

Taylor Publishing Group (TPG)
#2, 1121 Invicta Dr., Oakville, ON L6H 2R2
Tel: 905-844-8218
www.taylorpublishinggroup.com
William Taylor, Owner & Publisher

TC Transcontinental
Previous Name: Transcontinental Inc.
#3315, 1 Place Ville Marie, Montreal, QC H3B 3N2
Tel: 514-954-4000; *Fax:* 514-954-4016
communications@tc.tc
tctranscontinental.com

Torstar Corporation
One Yonge St., Toronto, ON M5E 1E6
www.torstar.com/index.cfm
Lorenzo DeMarchi, Executive Vice-President & CFO

Town Media Inc.
Previous Name: Town Publishing Inc.
Owned By: Sun Media
1074 Cooke Blvd., Burlington, ON L7T 4A8
Tel: 905-634-8003; *Fax:* 905-634-7661
TM.info@sunmedia.ca
www.townmedia.ca

Trajan Publishing Corp.
PO Box 28103 Lakeport, #10, 600 Ontario St., St Catharines, ON L2N 7P8
Tel: 905-646-7744; *Fax:* 905-646-0995
Toll-Free: 800-408-0352
office@tranjan.ca
www.trajan.com
Produces "Antique & Collectibles Showcase" and "Canadian Coin News& Canadian Stamp News".
Bret Evans, Managing Editor, bret@trajan.ca

Tribute Publishing Inc.
71 Barber Greene Rd., Toronto, ON M3C 2A2
Tel: 416-445-0544; *Fax:* 416-445-2894
info@tribute.ca
www.tribute.ca

Entertainment magazine

TVA Publications inc.
Anciennement: Trustar Ltd
Détenteur: Québecor Média
1010, rue de Sérigny, Longueuil, QC J4K 5G7
Tél: 514-848-7000; *Téléc:* 514-848-9854
Ligne sans frais: 888-535-8634
www.tvapublications.com
Julie Tremblay, Présidente et chef de la direction, Groupe TVA Inc.
Lucie Dumas, Éditrice en chef, Groupe Magazines

University of Calgary Press
2500 University Dr. NW, Calgary, AB T2N 1N4
Tel: 403-220-7578; *Fax:* 403-282-0085
ucpmail@ucalgary.ca
www.uofcpress.com
Michelle Lipp, Operations Manager, mlipp@ucalgary.ca

University of Toronto Centre of Criminology
14 Queen's Park Cres. W, Toronto, ON M5S 3K9
Tel: 416-978-7068
criminology.library@utoronto.ca
www.criminology.utoronto.ca
ISBNs: 0-919584
In-house publishing facility to showcase research of Centre faculty & graduate students

Up Here Publishing Ltd.
Previous Name: Outcrop, The Northern Publishers
PO Box 1350, Yellowknife, NT X1A 2N9
Tel: 867-766-6710; *Fax:* 867-873-9876
Toll-Free: 866-572-1757
www.uphere.ca
Social Media: instagram.com/upheremag
twitter.com/upheremag
www.facebook.com/uphere
Matthew Mallon, Editor-in-Chief, matthew@uphere.ca

Velo Québec Éditions
Maison des Cyclistes, 1251, rue Rachel est, Montréal, QC H2J 2J9
Tél: 514-521-8356; *Téléc:* 514-521-5711
www.velo.qc.ca/fr/publication.php
Médias sociaux: twitter.com/VeloQuebec
www.facebook.com/VeloQuebec

York Region Media Group
Owned By: Metroland Media Group Ltd.
580B Steven Crt., Newmarket, ON L3Y 4X1
Tel: 905-773-7627
www.yorkregion.com
Social Media: twitter.com/yorkregion
www.facebook.com/pages/YRMG-On-The-Town/165976160160967
Ian Proudfoot, Group Publisher, iproudfoot@yrmg.com
Robert Lazurkot, Business Director

Youth Culture Inc.
#100, 163 Queen St. East, Toronto, ON M5A 1S1
Tel: 416-363-1411; *Fax:* 416-595-1312
info@youthculture.com
www.youthculture.com
Social Media: twitter.com/vervegirlmag
www.facebook.com/vervegirlcanada
Magazines are directed and marketed towards teens and "tweens".
Kaaren Whitney-Vernon, President, CEO, and Group Publisher, kaaren@youthculture.com
Joanna Whitney, Editor, joanna@youthculture.com

Newspapers

Alberta

Daily Newspapers in Alberta

***Calgary:* Calgary Herald**
Owned By: Postmedia Network Inc.
PO Box 2400 M, Calgary, AB T2P 0W8
Tel: 403-235-7100; *Fax:* 403-235-7379
Toll-Free: 800-372-9219
submit@calgaryherald.com
www.calgaryherald.com
Social Media: www.linkedin.com/company/calgary-herald
twitter.com/calgaryherald
www.facebook.com/yycherald
Circulation: 680,009 total; *Frequency:* Monday-Saturday

Lorne Motley, Editor
403-235-7546
lmotley@calgaryherald.com
Monica Zurowski, Executive Producer
403-235-7291
mzurowski@calgaryherald.com

***Calgary:* Calgary Sun**
Owned By: Postmedia Network Inc.
2615 - 12 St. NE, Calgary, AB T2E 7W9
Tel: 403-410-1010; *Fax:* 403-250-4176
www.calgarysun.com
Other information: Classified, E-mail: calgarysun.classifieds@sunmedia.ca
Social Media: twitter.com/calgarysun
www.facebook.com/thecalgarysun
Circulation: 319,838 total; *Frequency:* Daily
Calgary's daily newspaper
Jose Rodriguez, Editor-in-chief
jose.rodriguez@sunmedia.ca
Martin Hudson, Managing Editor
martin.hudson@sunmedia.ca
Ty Pilson, Assistant Managing Editor
ty.pilson@sunmedia.ca
Tony Seskus, City Editor
dave.naylor@sunmedia.ca
Craig Ellingson, Sports Editor
todd.saelhof@sunmedia.ca

***Calgary:* Daily Oil Bulletin**
Owned By: Glacier Media Group
816 - 55 Ave. NE, 2nd Fl., Calgary, AB T2E 6Y4
Tel: 403-209-3500; *Fax:* 403-245-8666
editor@dailyoilbulletin.com
www.dailyoilbulletin.com
Circulation: 12,000; *Frequency:* Monday-Friday
Stephen Marsters, Publisher/Editor

***Calgary:* Metro Calgary**
Owned By: Torstar Corp.
#120, 3030 - 3 Ave. NE, Calgary, AB T2A 6T7
Tel: 403-444-0136
calgaryletters@metronews.ca
metronews.ca/news/calgary
Circulation: 315,284 total; *Frequency:* Monday-Friday

***Edmonton:* The Edmonton Journal**
Owned By: Postmedia Network Inc.
The Edmonton Journal's Downtown Building, PO Box 2421, 10006 - 101 St., Edmonton, AB T5J 0S1
Tel: 780-429-5100
City Desk Tip Line: 780-429-5330
www.edmontonjournal.com
Other information: Customer Service: 780-498-5500; Classified Advertising: 800-232-9486
Social Media: twitter.com/EJ_Life; twitter.com/EJ_Arts
www.facebook.com/edmontonjournal
Circulation: 597,789; *Frequency:* Monday-Saturday
A print edition & a digital edition are available.
Margo Goodhand, Editor-in-Chief
780-429-5452
mgoodhand@edmontonjournal.com
Stephanie Coombs, Managing Editor
scoombs@edmontonjournal.com

***Edmonton:* Edmonton Sun**
Owned By: Postmedia Network Inc.
#350, 4990 - 92 Ave., Edmonton, AB T6B 3A1
Tel: 780-468-0100
www.edmontonsun.com
Other information: News tips, E-mail: edm.citydesk@sunmedia.ca
Social Media: twitter.com/edmontonsun
www.facebook.com/edmontonsun
Circulation: 286,693 total; *Frequency:* Daily
Edmonton's daily newspaper
Dave Breakenridge, Editor in chief
dave.breakenridge@sunmedia.ca
Donna Harker, Managing Editor
donna.harker@sunmedia.ca
Nicole Bergot, City Editor
nicole.bergot@sunmedia.ca
Tom Braid, Photo Editor
tom.braid@sunmedia.ca

***Edmonton:* Metro Edmonton**
Owned By: Torstar Corp.
#2070, 10123 - 99 St. NW, Edmonton, AB T5J 3H1
Tel: 780-702-0592
edmontonletters@metronews.ca
metronews.ca/news/edmonton
Circulation: 307,172 total; *Frequency:* Monday-Friday

***Fort McMurray:* Fort McMurray Today**
Owned By: Postmedia Network Inc.
8223 Manning Ave., Fort McMurray, AB T9H 1V8
Tel: 780-743-8186; *Fax:* 780-715-3820
www.fortmcmurraytoday.com
Social Media: twitter.com/Fortmactoday
www.facebook.com/FortMacToday
Circulation: 9,508 total; *Frequency:* Monday-Friday
Erika Beauchesne, Managing Editor
erika.beauchesne@sunmedia.ca

***Grande Prairie:* Grande Prairie Daily Herald-Tribune**
Owned By: Postmedia Network Inc.
PO Box 3000, 10604 - 100 St., Grande Prairie, AB T8V 6V4
Tel: 780-532-1110; *Fax:* 780-532-2120
www.dailyheraldtribune.com
Social Media: twitter.com/GPHeraldTribune
www.facebook.com/DailyHeraldTribune
Circulation: 18,640 total; *Frequency:* Monday-Friday
Peter Meyerhoffer, Publisher
peter.meyerhoffer@sunmedia.ca
Fred Rinne, Editor-in-Chief
fred.rinne@sunmedia.ca

***Lethbridge:* Lethbridge Herald**
Owned By: Alta Newspaper Group LP
PO Box 670, 504 - 7th St. South, Lethbridge, AB T1J 2H1
Tel: 403-328-4411; *Fax:* 403-328-4536
www.lethbridgeherald.com
Social Media: www.youtube.com/user/lethbridgeherald
twitter.com/Leth_Herald
www.face book.com/LethbridgeHerald
Circulation: 115,942 total; *Frequency:* Daily
Garrett Simmons, Assistant Managing Editor
gsimmons@lethbridgeherald.com

***Medicine Hat:* The Medicine Hat News**
Owned By: Continental Newspapers Canada Ltd. / Glacier Media Inc.
3257 Dunmore Rd. SE, Medicine Hat, AB T1B 3R2
Tel: 403-527-1101; *Fax:* 403-528-5696
www.medicinehatnews.com
Social Media: www.youtube.com/user/MedicineHatNews
twitter.com/medicinehatnews
www.f acebook.com/MedicineHatNews
Circulation: 73,938 total; *Frequency:* Monday-Saturday

***Red Deer:* Red Deer Advocate**
Owned By: Black Press
2950 Bremner Ave., Red Deer, AB T4R 1M9
Tel: 403-343-2400
editorial@reddeeradvocate.com
www.reddeeradvocate.com
Social Media: twitter.com/RedDeerAdvocate
www.facebook.com/RDAdvocate
Circulation: 66,214 total; *Frequency:* Monday-Saturday
Central Alberta's news
Mary Kemmis, Publisher
403-314-4311
mary.kemmis@blackpress.ca
John Stewart, Editor
403-314-4328
jstewart@reddeeradvocate.com

Other Newspapers in Alberta

***Airdrie:* Airdrie City View**
Owned By: Great West Newspapers LP
#403, 2903 Kingview Blvd., Airdrie, AB T4A 0C4
Tel: 403-948-1885; *Fax:* 403-948-2554
sales@airdrie.greatwest.ca
www.airdriecityview.com
Social Media: facebook.com/airdriecityviewnewspaper
Circulation: 17,000; *Frequency:* Thurs.
Cameron Christianson, Publisher
cchristianson@airdrie.greatwest.ca
Stacie Snow, Editor
ssnow@airdrie.greatwest.ca

***Airdrie:* Airdrie Echo**
Owned By: Sun Media Corporation
112 - 1st Ave. NE, Airdrie, AB T4B 0R6
Tel: 403-948-7280; *Fax:* 403-912-2341
www.airdrieecho.com
Social Media: twitter.com/Airdrie_Echo
www.facebook.com/AirdrieEcho
Circulation: 17,035; *Frequency:* Wednesday
Airdrie's weekly newspaper
Ed Huculak, Publisher
403-250-4240
ed.huculak@sunmedia.ca

***Airdrie:* Rocky View Weekly**
Owned By: Great West Newspapers LP
#403, 2903 Kingsview Blvd., Airdrie, AB T4A 0C4
Tel: 403-948-1885; *Fax:* 403-948-2554
www.rockyviewweekly.com
Social Media: twitter.com/RV_Publishing
www.facebook.com/rockyviewweekly
Circulation: 18,079; *Frequency:* Weekly; Tuesday
Shows local news around Airdrie & Rocky View, AB.

***Athabasca:* Athabasca Advocate**
Owned By: Great West Newspapers LP
4917B - 49th St., Athabasca, AB T9S 1C5
Tel: 780-675-9222; *Fax:* 780-675-3143
advocate@athabasca.greatwest.ca
www.athabascaadvocate.com
Other information: Subscriptions & Classified Ads: reception@athabasca.greatwest.ca
Social Media: twitter.com/athaadvocate
www.facebook.com/pages/The-Athabasca-Advocate/1 2260854447
Circulation: 2,800; *Frequency:* Tues.
The newspaper serves the Alberta communities of Athabasca & Boyle, & the surrounding area.
Ross Hunter, Publisher
rhunter@athabasca.greatwest.ca
Meghan McIvor, Manager, Production
production@athabasca.greatwest.ca

***Barrhead:* The Barrhead Leader**
Previous Name: Barrhead News
Owned By: Great West Newspapers LP
PO Box 4520, 5015 - 51 St., Barrhead, AB T7N 1A4
Tel: 780-674-3823; *Fax:* 780-674-6337
www.barrheadleader.com
Social Media: www.youtube.com/barrheadleader
twitter.com/barrheadleader
www.facebook.com/BarrheadLeader
Circulation: 3,737; *Frequency:* Weekly
Barrhead's weekly newspaper
Carol Farnalls, Publisher
farnalls@barrhead.greatwest.ca
Marcus Day, Editor
mday@barrhead.greatwest.ca
Amy Newton, Manager, Sales
sales@barrhead.greatwest.ca

***Beaumont:* La Nouvelle Beaumont News**
Owned By: Sun Media Corporation
4908 - 50th Ave., Beaumont, AB T4X 1J9
Tel: 780-929-6632; *Fax:* 780-929-6634
www.thebeaumontnews.ca
Social Media: twitter.com/BeaumontNews
www.facebook.com/LaNouvelleBeaumontNews
Circulation: 6,305; *Frequency:* Friday
Beaumont's weekly news
Bobby Roy, Regional Managing Editor
leducrep.editor@sunmedia.ca

***Blairmore:* Crowsnest Pass Herald**
Owned By: The Pass Herald Ltd.
PO Box 960, 12925 - 20th Ave., Blairmore, AB T0K 0E0
Tel: 403-562-2248; *Fax:* 403-562-8379
news@passherald.ca
www.passherald.ca
Social Media: www.facebook.com/398857086794980
Circulation: 1,966; *Frequency:* Tuesday
Blairmore's weekly newspaper
Lisa Sygutek, Publisher
Trevor Slapak, Editor

***Bonnyville:* Bonnyville Nouvelle**
Owned By: Great West Newspapers LP
5304 - 50 Ave., Bonnyville, AB T9N 1Y4
Tel: 780-826-3876; *Fax:* 780-826-7062
nouvelle@bonnyville.greatwest.ca
www.bonnyvillenouvelle.ca
Other information: Advertising, E-mail: advertising@bonnyville.greatwest.ca
Social Media:
twitter.com/BvilleNouvelle
www.facebook.com/pages/Bonnyville-Nouvelle/29 4955134326
Circulation: 2,808; *Frequency:* Tuesday
The Bonnyville Nouvelle serves communities in northeastern Alberta, including Bonnyville, Cold Lake, Ardmore, La Corey, Fort Kent, Glendon, & Iron River.
Clare Gauvreau, Publisher
Melissa Barr, Editor & Reporter
Nora Chachula, Manager, Production
Brandon MacLeod, Sports Reporter
Amber Cook, Sales Associate
Breanna Ernst, Sales Associate

***Bow Island:* The 40-Mile County Commentator**
Previous Name: County Commentator & Cypress Courier
Owned By: Alta Newspaper Group
PO Box 580, 147 - 5th Ave., Bow Island, AB T0K 0G0
Tel: 403-545-2258; *Fax:* 403-545-6886
www.bowislandcommentator.com
Circulation: 5,700; *Frequency:* Tues.
Coleen Campbell, Publisher
403-545-2258
ccampbell@tabertimes.com
Jamie Rieger, Editor
editor@bowislandcommentator.com

***Brooks:* Brooks & County Chronicle**
PO Box 1568 Main, 619 - 1st St. West, Brooks, AB T1R 1C4
Tel: 403-793-2252; *Fax:* 403-793-2288
thechronicle@telusplanet.net
www.brooksinthenews.com
Social Media:
www.facebook.com/group.php?gid=179545068732938
Circulation: 11,300; *Frequency:* Sun.
The newspaper serves Brooks, Alberta & the surrounding communities.
M. Joan Brees, Publisher & Editor

***Brooks:* The Brooks Bulletin**
Owned By: Nesbitt Publishing Ltd.
PO Box 1450, Brooks, AB T1R 1C3
Tel: 403-362-5571; *Fax:* 403-362-5080
editor@brooksbulletin.com
www.brooksbulletin.com
Frequency: Weekly
Part of the Alberta Weekly Newspaper's Association

***Camrose:* The Camrose Booster**
4925 - 48 St., Camrose, AB T4V 1L7
Tel: 780-672-3142; *Fax:* 780-672-2518
ads@camrosebooster.com
www.camrosebooster.com
Circulation: 12,729; *Frequency:* Weekly; Tuesday
Daily newspaper in Camrose, Alberta
Blain Fowler, Publisher
Ron Pilger, Sales Manager

***Camrose:* The Camrose Canadian**
Owned By: Sun Media Corporation
4610 - 49 Ave., Camrose, AB T4V 0M6
Tel: 780-672-4421; *Fax:* 780-672-5323
editor@camrosecanadian.com
www.camrosecanadian.com
Social Media:
twitter.com/CamroseCanadian
www.facebook.com/CamroseCanadian
Circulation: 14,776; *Frequency:* Weekly; Thursday
The Camrose Canadian is a member of Canoe Sun Media Community Newspapers.
Mark Crown, Editor
mark.crown@sunmedia.ca

***Canmore:* Rocky Mountain Outlook**
Owned By: Great West Newspapers LP
PO Box 8610, #201, 1001 - 6th Ave., Canmore, AB T1W 2V3
Tel: 403-609-0220
www.rmoutlook.com
Social Media:
twitter.com/rmoutlook
Circulation: 9,400; *Frequency:* Thurs.
The newspaper serves the communities of Banff, Lake Louise, Canmore, & Kananaskis.
Jason Lyon, Publisher
jlyon@outlook.greatwest.ca
Dave Whitfield, Editor
dwhitfield@outlook.greatwest.ca
Craig Douce, Photojournalist
cdouce@outlook.greatwest.ca
Erin Buehler, Contact, Sales
swhite@outlook.greatwest.ca

***Cardston:* Temple City Star**
PO Box 2060, 311 Main St., Cardston, AB T0K 0K0
Tel: 403-653-4664; *Fax:* 403-653-3162
info@templecitystar.net
www.templecitystar.net
Circulation: 803; *Frequency:* Weekly; Thursday
Cardston & Area newspaper
Robert T. Smith, Owner & Publisher

***Carstairs:* Carstairs Courier**
Owned By: Great West Newspapers LP
PO Box 114, 320 - 10th St. South, Carstairs, AB T0M 0N0
Tel: 403-337-2806; *Fax:* 403-337-3160
www.carstairscourier.ca
Circulation: 3,257; *Frequency:* Weekly; Tuesday

***Claresholm:* Claresholm Local Press**
PO Box 520, Claresholm, AB T0L 0T0
Tel: 403-625-4474; *Fax:* 403-625-2828
info@claresholmlocalpress.ca
www.claresholmlocalpress.ca
Social Media:
www.facebook.com/ClaresholmLocalPress
Circulation: 1,610; *Frequency:* Weekly; Wednesday
The newspaper serves the Alberta communities of Claresholm, Stavely, & Granum.
Roxanne Thompson, Owner & Publisher

***Coaldale:* Sunny South News**
Owned By: Alta Newspaper Group LP
1802 - 20th Ave., Coaldale, AB T1M 1M2
Tel: 403-732-4045
office@sunnysouthnews.com
www.sunnysouthnews.com
Social Media:
twitter.com/SunnySouthNews
Circulation: 3,713; *Frequency:* Weekly; Tuesday
Serves the towns of Coaldale and Picture Butte as well as the villages and hamlets within the County of Lethbridge.
Coleen Campbell, Publisher
403-223-9659
ccampbell@abnewsgroup.com

***Cochrane:* Cochrane Eagle**
Owned By: Great West Newspapers LP
126A River Ave., Cochrane, AB T4C 2C2
Tel: 403-932-6588; *Fax:* 403-851-6520
letters@cochrane.greatwest.ca
www.cochraneeagle.com
Other information: Advertising, E-mail: advertising@cochrane.greatwest.ca
Social Media:
twitter.com/CochraneEagle
facebook.com/pages/Cochrane-Eagle/175941871603
Circulation: 10,600; *Frequency:* Thurs.
Brenda Tennant, Publisher
btennant@cochrane.greatwest.ca
Derek Clouthier, Editor
dclouthier@cochrane.greatwest.ca
Lindsay Seewalt, Reporter
lseewalt@cochrane.greatwest.ca
Brendan Nagle, Reporter, Sports
sports@cochrane.greatwest.ca
Carrie Anderson, Contact, Administration & Circulation
classifieds@cochrane.greatwest.ca
Jodi Collins, Contact, Accounting
accounting@cochrane.greatwest.ca

***Cochrane:* The Cochrane Times**
Bay 8, 206 - 5th Ave. West, Cochrane, AB T4C 1X3
Tel: 403-932-3500; *Fax:* 403-932-3935
www.cochranetimes.com
Social Media:
www.twitter.com/CochraneTimes
Frequency: Wednesday
The Cochrane Times is a member of Canoe Sun Media Community Newspapers.
Shawn Cornell, Publisher
403-932-3500 ext. 245
shawn.cornell@sunmedia.ca
Noel Edey, City Editor
403-932-3500 ext. 227
noel.edey@sunmedia.ca

***Cold Lake:* Cold Lake Sun**
Owned By: Sun Media Corporation
PO Box 268, Cold Lake, AB T9M 1P1
Tel: 780-594-5881; *Fax:* 780-594-2120
www.coldlakesun.com
Social Media:
twitter.com/ColdLakeSun
www.facebook.com/ColdLakeSun
Circulation: 6,458; *Frequency:* Weekly; Tuesday
The Cold Lake Sun is a member of Canoe Sun Media Community Newspapers. A PDF version of the newspaper is produced each week.
Peter Lozinski, Editor
peter.lozinski@sunmedia.ca

***Cold Lake:* The Courier**
Owned By: Department of National Defence
Centennial Bldg. #67, PO Box 6190 Forces, Cold Lake, AB T9M 2C5
Tel: 780-594-5206; *Fax:* 780-594-2139
thecourier@telus.net
www.thecouriernewspaper.ca
Circulation: 2,126; *Frequency:* Weekly; Tuesday
The Courier serves the military community of Cold Lake, Alberta.
Connie Lavigne, Manager
780-840-8000; Fax: 780-594-2139
Connie.Lavigne@forces.gc.ca
Jeff Gaye, Editor & Reporter
780-594-5206; Fax: 780-594-2139
thecourier@telus.net

***Consort:* Consort Enterprise**
PO Box 129, Consort, AB T0C 1B0
Tel: 403-577-3337; *Fax:* 403-577-3611
www.consortenterprise.com
Circulation: 1,080; *Frequency:* Weekly; Wednesday
The Consort Enterprise serves the Alberta communities of Consort, Monitor, Altario, Veteran, Kirriemuir, & Compeer.
Carol Bruha, Co-publisher
Dave Bruha, Co-publisher

***Coronation:* East Central Alberta Review**
Owned By: Coronation Review Limited
PO Box 70, 4923 Victoria Ave., Coronation, AB T0C 1C0
Tel: 403-578-4111; *Fax:* 403-578-2088
www.ecareview.com
Social Media:
twitter.com/ECA_review
www.facebook.com/EcaReview
Circulation: 26,826; *Frequency:* Weekly; Thursday
ECA Review provides a source of for news and entertainment in Central Alberta.
Joyce Webster, Publisher & Editor
publisher@ecareview.com

***Didsbury:* Didsbury Review**
Owned By: Great West Newspapers LP
PO Box 760, 2017 - 19th Ave., Didsbury, AB T0M 0W0
Tel: 403-335-3301; *Fax:* 403-335-8143
www.didsburyreview.ca
Social Media:
twitter.com/didsburyreview
Circulation: 3,101; *Frequency:* Weekly; Tuesday
Part of Mountain View Publishing Inc.

***Drayton Valley:* Drayton Valley Western Review**
Owned By: Sun Media Corporation
PO Box 6960, 4905 - 52nd Ave., Drayton Valley, AB T7A 1S3
Tel: 780-542-5380; *Fax:* 780-542-9200
www.draytonvalleywesternreview.com
Social Media:
twitter.com/Western_Review
www.facebook.com/group.php?gid=269245220567
The Drayton Valley Western Review is a member of Canoe Sun Media Community Newspapers. A digital edition of the newspaper is also produced each week.
Courtney Whalen, City Editor
courtney.whalen@sunmedia.ca

***Drumheller:* Drumheller Mail**
Previous Name: The Munson Mail
PO Box 1629, 515 Hwy. 10 East, Drumheller, AB T0J 0Y0
Tel: 403-823-2580; *Fax:* 403-823-3864
www.drumhellermail.com
Social Media:
twitter.com/DrumhellerMail
www.facebook.com/drumhellermail
Circulation: 4,104; *Frequency:* Weekly; Wednesday
Online & print editions of weekly news in Drumheller
Ossie Sheddy, Publisher
Bob Sheddy, Managing Editor

Edmonton: The Edmonton Examiner
Previous Name: West Edmonton Examiner
Owned By: Sun Media Corporation
#350, 4990 - 92nd Ave., Edmonton, AB T6B 3A1
Tel: 780-468-0100; *Fax:* 780-451-4574
www.edmontonexaminer.com
Social Media:
twitter.com/edm_examiner
www.facebook.com/edmontonexaminer
Circulation: 125,824; *Frequency:* Weekly; Wednesday
The Edmonton Examiner is a member of Canoe Sun Media Community Newspapers. Each week, seven versions of the newspaper are published for seven city zones. The newspaper employs over 90 people.
Dave Breakenridge, Editor-in-Chief
dave.breakenridge@sunmedia.ca

Edmonton: Le Franco
#312, 8627 - rue 91, Edmonton, AB T6C 3N1
Tél: 780-465-6581; *Téléc:* 780-469-1129
journal@lefranco.ab.ca
www.lefranco.ab.ca
Autre information: Autre Site Web: journaux.apf.ca/lefranco
Médias sociaux:
twitter.com/#!/JournalLeFranco
www.facebook.com/pages/Le-Franco-journal/ 225495297491230
Tirage: 3 508; *Fréquence:* Weekly; Thursday
Le Franco est un journal indépendant sur les plans administratif et rédactionnel.
Étienne Alary, Director
direction@lefranco.ab.ca
Lysane Sénécal Mastropaolo, Journaliste
redaction@lefranco.ab.ca

Edson: The Edson Leader
Owned By: Sun Media Corporation
4820 - 3rd Ave., Edson, AB T7E 1T8
Tel: 780-723-3301; *Fax:* 780-723-5171
leadernews@telusplanet.net
www.edsonleader.com
Social Media:
twitter.com/Edson_Leader
www.facebook.com/edsonleader
Circulation: 5,831; *Frequency:* Weekly; Monday
The Edson Leader is a member of Canoe Sun Media Community Newspapers. A PDF version of the newspaper is produced each week.
Ian Mcinnes, Editor
ian.mcinnes@sunmedia.ca

Edson: The Weekly Anchor
PO Box 6870, 5040 - 3rd Ave., Edson, AB T7E 1V2
Tel: 780-723-5787; *Fax:* 780-723-5725
anchorwk@telusplanet.net
www.weeklyanchor.com
Social Media:
www.facebook.com/weeklyanchor
Circulation: 5,796; *Frequency:* Weekly; Monday
The independent newspaper serves the Alberta communities of Edson, Robb, Evansburg, Marlboro, Entwistle, Nojack, Wildwood, Carrot Creek, Peers, & Niton Junction.

Fairview: Fairview Post
Owned By: Sun Media Corporation
PO Box 1900, 10915 - 102 Ave., Fairview, AB T0H 1L0
Tel: 780-835-4925; *Fax:* 780-835-4227
www.fairviewpost.com
Social Media:
twitter.com/fairviewpost
www.facebook.com/fairviewpost
Circulation: 1,672; *Frequency:* Weekly; Wednesday
The Fairview Post is a member of Canoe Sun Media Community Newspapers. A digital edition of the newspaper is available each week.
Chris Eakin, Editor
chris.eakin@sunmedia.ca

Falher: Smoky River Express
Owned By: South Peace News Ltd.
PO Box 644, Falher, AB T0H 1M0
Tel: 780-837-2585; *Fax:* 780-837-2102
www.smokyriverexpress.com
Social Media:
www.facebook.com/SmokyRiverExpress
Circulation: 2,063; *Frequency:* Weekly; Wednesday
The newspaper serves the Municipal District of Smoky River.
Mary Burgar, Publisher
spn@cablecomet.com

Fort Macleod: The Macleod Gazette
PO Box 720, 310 Col. Macleod Blvd., Fort Macleod, AB T0L 0Z0
Tel: 403-553-3391; *Fax:* 403-553-2961
ftmgazet@telusplanet.net
www.fortmacleodgazette.com
Circulation: 1,192; *Frequency:* Weekly; Wednesday
Independent newspaper published weekly
Frank McTighe, Publisher & Editor
Emily McTighe, Manager

Fort Saskatchewan: Fort Saskatchewan Record
Owned By: Sun Media Corporation
#168A, 10404 - 99 Ave., Fort Saskatchewan, AB T8L 3W2
Tel: 780-998-7070; *Fax:* 780-998-5515
www.fortsaskatchewanrecord.com
Social Media:
www.twitter.com/Fort_Record
www.facebook.com/FortSaskatchewanRecord?ref= hl
Circulation: 8,750; *Frequency:* Weekly; Thursday
Fort Saskatchewan's weekly newspaper
Ben Proulx, Editor
ben.proulx@sunmedia.ca

Grande Prairie: Peace Country Sun
Owned By: Sun Media Corporation
PO Box 3000, 10604 - 100th St., Grande Prairie, AB T8V 6V4
Tel: 780-532-1110; *Fax:* 780-532-2120
www.peacecountrysun.com
Social Media:
twitter.com/peacecountrysun
www.facebook.com/PeaceCountrySun
Circulation: 18,668; *Frequency:* Weekly; Friday
The Peace Country Sun is a member of Canoe Sun Media Community Newspapers.
Fred Rinne, Regional Managing Editor
fred.rinne@sunmedia.ca

Grimshaw: The Mile Zero News
Owned By: Mackenzie Report Inc.
4921 - 54th Ave., Grimshaw, AB T0H 1W0
Tel: 780-332-2215
www.mrnews.ca/mile-zero-news
Circulation: 1,672; *Frequency:* Weekly; Wednesday
Tom Mihaly, Publisher

Hanna: Hanna Herald
Owned By: Sun Media Corporation
PO Box 790, 113 - 1st Ave., Hanna, AB T0J 1P0
Tel: 403-854-3366; *Fax:* 403-854-3256
www.hannaherald.com
Social Media:
twitter.com/HannaHerald
www.facebook.com/pages/Hanna-Herald/134487 243289016
Circulation: 900; *Frequency:* Weekly; Wednesday
The Hanna Herald is a member of Canoe Sun Media Community Newspapers. A PDF version of the newspaper is produced each week.

High Level: The Echo-Pioneer
Owned By: Mackenzie Report Inc.
10006 - 97th St., High Level, AB T0H 1Z0
Tel: 780-926-2000
www.mrnews.ca/the-echo-mrnews-pioneer
Circulation: 2,000; *Frequency:* Weekly; Wednesday

High Prairie: South Peace News
Owned By: South Peace News Ltd.
PO Box 1000, High Prairie, AB T0G 1E0
Tel: 780-523-4484; *Fax:* 780-523-3039
www.southpeacenews.com
Social Media:
twitter.com/SouthPeaceNews
Circulation: 1,358; *Frequency:* Weekly; Wednesday
Mary Burgar, Publisher
spn@cablecomet.com

High River: High River Times
Owned By: Sun Media Corporation
618 Centre St. South, High River, AB T1V 1E9
Tel: 403-652-2034; *Fax:* 403-652-3962
www.highrivertimes.com
Social Media:
twitter.com/HighRiverTimes
www.facebook.com/HighRiverTimes
Circulation: 13,231; *Frequency:* Tuesday, Friday
The High River Times is a member of Canoe Sun Media Community Newspapers. The newspaper serves the Alberta communities of High River, Cayley, Blackie, & Longview.
Kevin Rushworth, Editor
kevin.rushworth@sunmedia.ca

Hinton: The Hinton Parklander
Owned By: Sun Media Corporation
387 Drinnan Way, Hinton, AB T7V 2A3
Tel: 780-865-3115; *Fax:* 780-865-1252
news@hintonparklander.com
www.hintonparklander.com
Social Media:
twitter.com/H_Parklander
www.facebook.com/group.php?gid=113936721972274
Circulation: 4,078; *Frequency:* Weekly; Monday
The Hinton Parklander is a member of Canoe Sun Media Community Newspapers. The newspaper serves the town of Hinton in Alberta & its surrounding area.
Gord Fortin, Editor
780-723-3301
gord.fortin@sunmedia.ca

Innisfail: Innisfail Province
Owned By: Great West Newspapers LP
5036 - 48th St., Innisfail, AB T4G 1M8
Tel: 403-227-3477; *Fax:* 403-227-3330
www.innisfailprovince.ca
Social Media:
twitter.com/innisfailprovin
www.facebook.com/pages/Innisfail-Province/62 1035251342433
Circulation: 8,306; *Frequency:* Tuesday
Ray Brinson, Publisher
Lea Smaldon, Managing Editor
Johnnie Bachusky, Editor

La Crete: The Northern Pioneer
Owned By: Mackenzie Report Inc.
PO Box 571, 10303 - 100 St., La Crete, AB T0H 2H0
Tel: 780-928-4000; *Fax:* 780-928-4001
pioneer@mackreport.ab.ca
mrnews.ca/the-northern-pioneer-mrnews
Circulation: 900; *Frequency:* Wed.
The Northern Pioneer serves the Alberta communities of La Crete & Fort Vermilion.
Tom Mihaly, Publisher & Editor
publisher@mrnews.ca
Lisa Neufeld, Contact, Office, Advertising
northernpioneer@mrnews.ca

Lac La Biche: The Lac La Biche Post
Owned By: Great West Newspapers LP
PO Box 508, 10211 - 101st St., Lac La Biche, AB T0A 2C0
Tel: 780-623-4221; *Fax:* 780-623-4230
production@llb.greatwest.ca
www.laclabichepost.com
Social Media: www.youtube.com/user/LLBPostNews
twitter.com/LLBPOSTnews
www.facebook.com/group.php?gid=157459007605036
Circulation: 2,218; *Frequency:* Weekly; Tuesday
Covering events & businesses in Lac La Biche, Plamondon, Owl River, Wandering River, Kikino, Beaver Lake, Buffalo Lake, Hylo, Casian, Atmore, Rich Lake & Heart Lake
Rob McKinley, Publisher

Lacombe: Lacombe Globe
Owned By: Sun Media Corp.
5019 - 50th St., Lacombe, AB T4L 1W9
Tel: 403-782-3498; *Fax:* 403-782-5850
www.lacombeglobe.com
Social Media:
twitter.com/LacombeGlobe
facebook.com/lacombe.globe
Circulation: 7,100; *Frequency:* Thurs.
Nick Goetz, Publisher
nick.goetz@sunmedia.ca
Vince Burke, Editor
vince.burke@sunmedia.ca

Lamont: Lamont Farm 'n' Friends
Owned By: W & E Cowley Publishing Ltd.
PO Box 800, Lamont, AB T0B 2R0
Tel: 780-943-2032; *Fax:* 780-942-2515
redwater@shaw.ca
www.cowleynewspapers.com/farm-n-friends
Circulation: 19,200; *Frequency:* Fri.
Serves the counties of Sturgeon, Thorhild, Smoky Lake, Lamont & Beaver.
Ed Cowley, Publisher & Editor

Leduc: **The Leduc Rep**
Previous Name: Leduc Representative
Owned By: Sun Media Corporation
4504 - 61st Ave., Leduc, AB T9E 3Z1
Tel: 780-986-2271; *Fax:* 780-986-6397
www.leducrep.com
Social Media:
www.twitter.com/LeducRep
www.facebook.com/LeducRep
Circulation: 16,795; *Frequency:* Weekly; Friday
The Leduc Representative is a member of Canoe Sun Media Community Newspapers. The newspaper serves Leduc & Leduc County in Alberta.
Bobby Roy, Editor
leducrep.editor@sunmedia.ca

Lethbridge: **The Lethbridge Shopper**
234A - 12B St. North, Lethbridge, AB T1H 2K7
Tel: 403-329-8225; *Fax:* 403-329-8211
www.shoppergroup.com
Frequency: Weekly
The Lethbridge Shopper publishes classifieds for Lethbridge and surrounding area

Lloydminster: **Lloydminster Meridian Booster**
Owned By: Sun Media Corp.
5714 - 44th St., Lloydminster, AB T9V 0B6
Tel: 780-875-3362; *Fax:* 780-875-3423
www.meridianbooster.com
Social Media:
twitter.com/meridianbooster
facebook.com/pages/Lloydminster-Meridian-Boo ster/17048705
Circulation: 39,800; *Frequency:* Mon., Wed., Fri.
Mary-Ann Kostiuk, Publisher
mary-ann.kostiuk@sunmedia.ca
Dana Smith, Managing Editor
dana.smith@sunmedia.ca

Manning: **The Banner Post**
Owned By: Mackenzie Report Inc.
413 Main St., Manning, AB T0H 2M0
Tel: 780-836-3588
www.mrnews.ca/the-banner-post
Circulation: 1,125; *Frequency:* Weekly; Wednesday

Medicine Hat: **Holmes Publishing Co. Ltd.**
1577 Dunmore Rd. SE, Medicine Hat, AB T1A 1Z8
Tel: 403-526-5937

Medicine Hat: **Medicine Hat Shopper**
922 Allowance Ave. SE, Medicine Hat, AB T1A 3G7
Tel: 403-527-5777; *Fax:* 403-526-7352
www.shoppergroup.com
Frequency: Weekly
Classified advertisements also appear on the web site.

Morinville: **The Free Press Newspaper**
Owned By: W & E Cowley Publishing Ltd.
PO Box 3005, 10126 - 100th Ave., Morinville, AB T8R 1R9
Tel: 780-939-3309; *Fax:* 780-939-3093
morinville@shaw.ca
www.cowleynewspapers.com
Circulation: 11,987; *Frequency:* Weekly; Tuesday
The newspaper serves residents of Alberta's Sturgeon County.

Morinville: **The Morinville News**
PO Box 3135, Morinville, AB T8R 1S1
Tel: 780-800-3619
editor@morinvillenews.com
morinvillenews.com
Social Media: youtube.com/user/MorinvilleNews
twitter.com/MorinvilleNews
www.faceboo
k.com/pages/MorinvilleNewscom/116150388429696
Stephen A. Dafoe, Owner & Publisher

Nanton: **Nanton News**
Owned By: Sun Media Corporation
1902 - 21st Ave., Nanton, AB T0L 1R0
Tel: 403-646-2023; *Fax:* 403-646-2848
www.nantonnews.com
Social Media:
twitter.com/NantonNews
www.facebook.com/224526534248789
Circulation: 560; *Frequency:* Weekly; Wednesday
Nanton community news
Sheena Read, City Editor
sheena.read@sunmedia.ca

Okotoks: **Okotoks Western Wheel**
Owned By: Great West Newspapers LP
PO Box 150, Okotoks, AB T1S 2A2
Tel: 403-938-6397; *Fax:* 403-938-2518
www.westernwheel.com
Circulation: 16,284; *Frequency:* Weekly; Wednesday
Okotoks' weekly newspaper
Matt Rockley, Publisher
mrockley@okotoks.greatwest.ca

Olds: **Mountain View Gazette**
Owned By: Great West Newspapers LP
5013 - 51st St., Olds, AB T4H 1P6
Tel: 403-556-7510; *Fax:* 403-556-7515
www.mountainviewgazette.ca
Social Media:
twitter.com/mtnviewgazette
Circulation: 23,000; *Frequency:* Weekly; Tuesday
Alberta's Mountain View & Red Deer Counties are served by the Mountain View Gazette.
Dan Singleton, Editor
dsingleton@olds.greatwest.ca

Olds: **Olds Albertan**
Owned By: Great West Newspapers LP
5013 - 51st St., Olds, AB T4H 1P6
Tel: 403-556-7510; *Fax:* 403-556-7515
www.oldsalbertan.ca
Social Media:
twitter.com/oldsalbertan
www.facebook.com/OldsAlbertan
Circulation: 6,611; *Frequency:* Weekly; Tuesday
The free newspaper serves the Alberta communities of Olds, Wimborne, Torrington, & Bowden & the surrounding region.
Doug Collie, Editor
dcollie@olds.greatwest.ca

Oyen: **Oyen Echo**
Owned By: Holmes Publishing Co. Ltd.
PO Box 420, Oyen, AB T0J 2J0
Tel: 403-664-3622
oyenecho@telusplanet.net
www.oyenecho.ca
Circulation: 1,306; *Frequency:* Weekly; Tuesday
Oyen Echo's classifieds

Peace River: **Peace River Record-Gazette**
Owned By: Sun Media Corp.
PO Box 6870, 10002 - 100 St., Peace River, AB T8S 1S6
Tel: 780-624-2591; *Fax:* 780-624-8600
www.prrecordgazette.com
Social Media:
twitter.com/PRRecordGazette
facebook.com/peaceriverrecordgazette
Circulation: 1,500; *Frequency:* Wed.
Peter Meyerhoffer, Publisher
peter.meyerhoffer@sunmedia.ca
Fred Rinne, Editor, City
fred.rinne@sunmedia.ca

Pincher Creek: **Pincher Creek Echo**
Owned By: Sun Media Corporation
PO Box 1000, Pincher Creek, AB T0K 1W0
Tel: 403-627-3252; *Fax:* 403-627-3949
www.pinchercreekecho.com
Social Media:
twitter.com/PCEcho
www.facebook.com/pinchercreekecho1
Circulation: 1,091; *Frequency:* Weekly; Friday
Pincher Creek's weekly newspaper
Greg Cowan, Managing Editor
greg.cowan@sunmedia.ca

Ponoka: **Ponoka News**
Owned By: Black Press
PO Box 4217, Ponoka, AB T4J 1R6
Tel: 403-783-3311; *Fax:* 403-783-6300
www.ponokanews.com
Social Media:
twitter.com/PonokaNews
www.facebook.com/476641985724647
Circulation: 5,885; *Frequency:* Weekly; Wednesday
Free weekly publication
Mustafa Eric, Editor
403-783-3311
editorial@ponokanews.com

Provost: **The Provost News**
Owned By: Holmes Publishing Co. Ltd.
PO Box 180, 5111 - 50th St., Provost, AB T0B 3S0
Tel: 780-753-2564; *Fax:* 780-753-6117
advertising@provostnews.ca; news@provostnews.ca
www.provostnews.ca

Circulation: 1,746; *Frequency:* Weekly; Wednesday
Richard Holmes, Managing Editor
rcholmes@agt.net

Red Deer: **Red Deer Express**
Owned By: Black Press Group Ltd.
#121, 5301 - 43 St., Red Deer, AB T4N 1C8
Tel: 403-346-3356
advertising@reddeerexpress.com
www.reddeerexpress.com
Social Media:
twitter.com/reddeerexpress
www.facebook.com/pages/The-Red-Deer-Express-N ews-Wire/121
Circulation: 25,000; *Frequency:* Wednesday
The Red Deer Express is a community newspaper & online news source that serves Red Deer & central Alberta.
Tracy Scheveers, Publisher
tscheveers@reddeerexpress.com
Erin Fawcett, Co-Editor
1-403-309-5457
efawcett@reddeerexpress.com
Mark Weber, Co-Editor
1-403-309-5455
editor@reddeerexpress.com

Red Deer: **Red Deer Life**
2950 Bremner Ave., Red Deer, AB T4R 1M9
Tel: 403-343-2400
editorial@reddeeradvocate.com
www.reddeeradvocate.com
Social Media:
twitter.com/RedDeerAdvocate
facebook.com/RDAdvocate
Circulation: 26,000+; *Frequency:* Sun.
The community newspaper is delivered to homes in Red Deer & rural regions.
Fred Gorman, Publisher
fgorman@reddeeradvocate.com
John Stewart, Managing Editor
jstewart@reddeeradvocate.com

Redwater: **The Review**
Owned By: W & E Cowley Publishing Ltd.
PO Box 850, 4720 - 50th Ave., Redwater, AB T0A 2W0
Tel: 780-942-2023; *Fax:* 780-942-2515
redwater@shaw.ca
www.cowleynewspapers.com
Circulation: 4,437; *Frequency:* Weekly; Tuesday
Redwater's The Review serves residents in the Counties of Smoky Lake & Thorhild.

Rimbey: **Rimbey Review**
Owned By: Black Press Group Ltd.
PO Box 244, 5001 - 50 Ave., Rimbey, AB T0C 2J0
Tel: 403-843-4909
www.rimbeyreview.com
Social Media:
twitter.com/RedDeerAdvocate
facebook.com/pages/Rimbey-Review/397611640365446
Circulation: 5,500; *Frequency:* Tues.
The free community newspaper provides news & information to readers in Rimbey & west central Alberta.
Michele Rosenthal, Publisher
publisher@sylvanlakenews.com
Treena Mielke, Editor
reporter@rimbeyreview.com
Treena Mielke, Reporter
reporter@rimbeyreview.com
Susan Whitecotton, Contact, Classifieds
sales@rimbeyreview.com

Rocky Mountain House: **The Mountaineer**
Owned By: The Mountaineer Publishing Company
4814 - 49th St., Rocky Mountain House, AB T4T 1S8
Tel: 403-845-3334; *Fax:* 403-845-5570
advertising@mountaineer.bz
www.rock-e.ca
Social Media:
twitter.com/RMH_Mountaineer
www.facebook.com/RMHMountaineer
Circulation: 3,353; *Frequency:* Weekly; Tuesday
The newspapers covers news from Clearwater County, the Town of Rocky Mountain House, & the Village of Caroline.
Glen Mazza, Publisher
publish@mountaineer.bz

Rycroft: **The Central Peace Signal**
PO Box 250, Rycroft, AB T0H 3A0
Tel: 780-765-3604
signalnews@abnorth.com
Circulation: 2,650; *Frequency:* Tues.
Danny Zahara, Publisher

***Sedgewick:* The Community Press**
Previous Name: The Sedgewick Sentinel
Owned By: Caribou Publishing
PO Box 99, Sedgewick, AB T0B 4C0
Tel: 780-385-6693; *Fax:* 780-385-3107
news@thecommunitypress.com
www.thecommunitypress.com
Other information: Phone: 780-384-3641; Fax: 780-384-2244
Social Media:
twitter.com/CPresstweet
www.facebook.com/TheCommPress?ref=s
Circulation: 2,468; *Frequency:* Weekly; Tuesday
The newspaper serves Alberta's Flagstaff County & the surrounding region. The Community Press is part of a multi-newspaper collective known as Caribou Publishing.
Eric Anderson, Publisher
Leslie Cholowsky, Editor

***Sherwood Park:* The Sherwood Park/Strathcona County News**
Owned By: Sun Media Corporation
168 Kaska Rd., Sherwood Park, AB T8A 4G7
Tel: 780-464-0033; *Fax:* 780-464-8512
www.sherwoodparknews.com
Social Media:
twitter.com/SHPk_News
www.facebook.com/SherwoodParkNews
Circulation: Tues. 25,869; Fri. 27,981; *Frequency:* Tuesday, Friday
The two newspapers, Sherwood Park News & Strathcona County This Week, merged in 2007 to become Sherwood Park - Strathcona County News. The newspaper is a member of Canoe Sun Media Community Newspapers.
Michael Di Massa, Regional Managing Editor
michael.dimassa@sunmedia.ca

***Slave Lake:* Lakeside Leader**
Owned By: South Peace News Ltd.
PO Box 849, 103 - 3rd St. NE, Slave Lake, AB T0G 2A0
Tel: 780-849-4380; *Fax:* 780-849-3903
lsleader@telusplanet.net
www.lakesideleader.com
Circulation: 2,775; *Frequency:* Weekly; Wednesday
Slave Lake's weekly newspaper
Mary Burgar, Publisher
spn@cablecomet.com

***Smoky Lake:* Smoky Lake Signal**
PO Box 328, Smoky Lake, AB T0A 3C0
Tel: 780-656-4114; *Fax:* 780-656-4361
signal@mcsnet.ca
www.smokylake.com
Circulation: 1,347; *Frequency:* Weekly; Wednesday
Smoky Lake's local news
Lorne Taylor, Publisher

***Spruce Grove:* Calmar Community Voice**
Owned By: E.J. Lewchuck & Associates Ltd.
c/o E.J. Lewchuck & Associates Ltd., PO Box 3595, 45 South Ave., Bay C, Spruce Grove, AB T7X 3A3
Tel: 780-962-9228; *Fax:* 780-962-1021
news@com-voice.com
www.com-voice.com
Other information: Classifieds Phone: 780-962-9229
Circulation: 4,000; *Frequency:* Biweekly
Bi-weekly newspaper

***Spruce Grove:* Onoway Community Voice**
Owned By: E.J. Lewchuck & Associates Ltd.
c/o E.J. Lewchuck & Associates Ltd., PO Box 3595, 45 South Ave., Bay C, Spruce Grove, AB T7X 3A3
Tel: 780-962-9228; *Fax:* 780-962-1021
news@com-voice.com
www.com-voice.com
Other information: Classifieds Phone: 780-962-9229
Circulation: 6,000; *Frequency:* Biweekly
Bi-weekly newspaper

***Spruce Grove:* The Spruce Grove Examiner**
Owned By: Sun Media Corporation
PO Box 4206, #1, 420 King St., Spruce Grove, AB T7X 3B4
Tel: 780-962-4257; *Fax:* 780-962-0658
www.sprucegroveexaminer.com
Social Media:
twitter.com/RepEx1
www.facebook.com/153508004671004
Circulation: 10,970; *Frequency:* Weekly; Friday
The Grove Examiner is Spruce Grove's weekly newspaper
Thomas Miller, Publisher
thomas.miller@sunmedia.ca

***Spruce Grove:* The Stony Plain Reporter**
Owned By: Sun Media Corporation
PO Box 4206, #1, 420 King St., Spruce Grove, AB T7X 3B4
Tel: 780-962-4257; *Fax:* 780-962-0658
www.stonyplainreporter.com
Social Media:
twitter.com/StonyPlain
www.facebook.com/153508004671004
Circulation: 10,195; *Frequency:* Weekly; Friday
Spruce Grove's weekly newspaper
Thomas Miller, Publisher
thomas.miller@sunmedia.ca

***Spruce Grove:* Wabamun Community Voice**
Owned By: E.J. Lewchuck & Associates Ltd.
c/o E.J. Lewchuck & Associates Ltd., PO Box 3595, 45 South Ave., Bay C, Spruce Grove, AB T7X 3A3
Tel: 780-962-9228; *Fax:* 780-962-1021
news@com-voice.com
www.com-voice.com
Other information: Classifieds Phone: 780-962-9229
Circulation: 6,000; *Frequency:* Biweekly
Bi-weekly newspaper

***St. Albert:* St. Albert Gazette**
Owned By: Great West Newspapers LP
340 Carleton Dr., St. Albert, AB T8N 7L3
Tel: 780-460-5500; *Fax:* 780-460-8220
www.stalbertgazette.com
Social Media:
twitter.com/StAlbertGazette
www.facebook.com/stalbertgazettenews
Circulation: 28,314; *Frequency:* Weekly; Wednesday
St. Albert's weekly newspaper
Brian Bachynski, Publisher
bbachynski@greatwest.ca

***St. Paul:* St. Paul Journal**
Owned By: Great West Newspapers LP
PO Box 159, 4813 - 50th Ave., St. Paul, AB T0A 3A0
Tel: 780-645-3342; *Fax:* 780-645-2346
www.spjournal.com
Social Media:
twitter.com/StPaulJournal
www.facebook.com/pages/St-Paul-Journal/3 12421611441?ref=t
Circulation: 3,599; *Frequency:* Weekly; Tuesday
The community newspaper provides news & information about the County & Town of St. Paul.
Janani Whitfield, Publisher
jwhitfield@stpaul.greatwest.ca

***Stettler:* Stettler Independent**
Owned By: Black Press
PO Box 310, 4810 - 50th St., Stettler, AB T0C 2L0
Tel: 403-742-2395
editorial@reddeeradvocate.com
www.stettlerindependent.com
Social Media:
twitter.com/RedDeerAdvocate
www.facebook.com/RDAdvocate
Circulation: 2,163; *Frequency:* Weekly; Wednesday
Settler's weekly newspaper
Randy Holt, Publisher
Mustafa Eric, Editor

***Strathmore:* Strathmore Standard**
Owned By: Sun Media Corporation
#A, 510 Hwy. 1, Strathmore, AB T1P 1M6
Tel: 403-934-3021; *Fax:* 403-934-5011
www.strathmorestandard.com
Social Media:
twitter.com/S_Standard
www.facebook.com/209809935701875
Circulation: 11,264; *Frequency:* Weekly; Thursday
The Strathmore Standard is Strathmore's weekly newspaper
Josh Chalmers, Regional Managing Editor
josh.chalmers@sunmedia.ca

***Sundre:* Sundre Round Up**
Owned By: Great West Newspapers LP
PO Box 599, 103 - 2nd St. NW, Sundre, AB T0M 1X0
Tel: 403-638-3577; *Fax:* 403-638-3077
www.sundreroundup.ca
Social Media:
twitter.com/sundreroundup
www.facebook.com/1469549416644673
Circulation: 1,487; *Frequency:* Weekly; Tuesday
Sundre Round Up is one of six newspapers published by Mountain View Publishing, which is a subsidiary of Great West Newspapers LP. The newspaper features information from the town of Sundre & the surrounding region in west central Alberta.
Simon Ducatel, Editor
sducatel@sundre.greatwest.ca

***Swan Hills:* Swan Hills Grizzly Gazette**
Owned By: Grizzly Gazette (1990) Inc.
PO Box 1000, 5435 Plaza Ave., Swan Hills, AB T0G 2C0
Tel: 780-333-2100; *Fax:* 780-333-2111
sgazette@telusplanet.net
Circulation: 526; *Frequency:* Weekly; Tuesday
Carol Webster, Publisher

***Sylvan Lake:* Eckville Echo**
Owned By: Sylvan Lake News Ltd.
#103, 5020 - 50A St., Sylvan Lake, AB T4S 1R2
Tel: 403-887-2331; *Fax:* 403-887-2081
Toll-Free: 888-882-2331
Other information: Toll-Free Fax: 1-888-999-2081
Circulation: 2,500; *Frequency:* Thurs.
Sylvan Lake News Ltd. publishes the Eckville Echo.
Michele Rosenthal, Publisher
publisher@sylvanlakenews.com

***Sylvan Lake:* Sylvan Lake News**
Owned By: Black Press
#103, 5020 - 50A St., Sylvan Lake, AB T4S 1R2
Tel: 403-887-2331
www.sylvanlakenews.com
Social Media:
twitter.com/RedDeerAdvocate
www.facebook.com/SylvanLakeNews
Circulation: 7,778; *Frequency:* Weekly; Friday
News is presented from the town of Sylvan Lake & the surrounding region, from Red Deer to Benalto.
Randy Holt, Publisher
Stuart Fullarton, Editor

***Taber:* The Taber Times**
Owned By: Alta Newspaper Group LP
4822 - 53rd St., Taber, AB T1G 1W4
Tel: 403-223-2266; *Fax:* 403-223-1408
www.tabertimes.com
Other information: Alternate Phone: 403-223-9659
Social Media: www.youtube.com/user/TheTaberTimes
twitter.com/tabertimes
www.faceb ook.com/TheTaberTimes
Circulation: 2,104; *Frequency:* Weekly; Wednesday
Coleen Campbell, Publisher
ccampbell@abnewsgroup.com
Greg Price, Editor
gprice@tabertimes.com

***Three Hills:* The Capital**
Owned By: Capital Printers Ltd.
411 Main St., Three Hills, AB T0M 2A0
Tel: 403-443-5133; *Fax:* 403-443-7331
info@threehillscapital.com
www.threehillscapital.com
Circulation: 3,744; *Frequency:* Weekly; Wednesday
The Capital is also available through electronic subscription.
Timothy J. Shearlaw, Publisher & Editor

***Tofield:* The Tofield Mercury**
Owned By: Caribou Publishing
PO Box 150, 5312 - 50th St., Tofield, AB T0B 4J0
Tel: 780-662-4046; *Fax:* 780-662-3735
adsmercury@gmail.com
www.tofieldmerc.com
Social Media:
twitter.com/tofieldmercury
www.facebook.com/TofieldMercury
Circulation: 1,106; *Frequency:* Weekly; Tuesday
The newspaper is part of Caribou Publishing. It serves the Alberta communities of Tofield, Ryley, & Holden & the surrounding region.
Kerry Anderson, Publisher
Patricia Harcourt, Editor

***Two Hills:* Two Hills & County Chronicle**
PO Box 668, 4708 - 50 St., Two Hills, AB T0B 4K0
Tel: 780-657-2524; *Fax:* 780-657-2534
Circulation: 1,300; *Frequency:* Tuesday
Ruven Rajoo, Publisher
Sonny Rajoo, Editor

***Vauxhall:* The Vauxhall Advance**
Owned By: Alta Newspaper Group LP
516 - 2nd Ave. North, Vauxhall, AB T0K 2K0
Tel: 403-654-2122
office@vauxhalladvance.com
www.vauxhalladvance.com
Circulation: 496; *Frequency:* Weekly; Thursday
Weekly paper published by the Alta Newspaper Group Ltd. Partnership
Coleen Campbell, Publisher
ccampbell@abnewsgroup.com

Greg Price, Editor
gprice@tabertimes.com

Vegreville: Vegreville News Advertiser Ltd.
PO Box 810, 5110 - 50th St., Vegreville, AB T9C 1R9
Tel: 780-632-2861; *Fax:* 780-632-7981
Toll-Free: 800-522-4127
editor@newsadvertiser.com
www.newsadvertiser.com
Other information: Alternative E-mail:
news@newsadvertiser.com
Circulation: 7,433; *Frequency:* Weekly; Wednesday
Weekly newspaper for Vegreville
Dan Beaudette, Publisher & Editor
dan@newsadvertiser.com
Michael Simpson, Editorial Manager
michael@newsadvertiser.com

Vermilion: Vermilion Standard
Owned By: Sun Media Corporation
4917 - 50th Ave., Vermilion, AB T9X 1A6
Tel: 780-853-5344; *Fax:* 780-853-5203
www.vermilionstandard.com
Social Media:
twitter.com/Vermstand
www.facebook.com/VermilionStandard
Circulation: 4,098; *Frequency:* Weekly; Tuesday
Vermillion weekly newspaper
Chris Roberts, Regional Managing Editor
chris.roberts@sunmedia.ca

Veteran: The Veteran Eagle
PO Box 322, Veteran, AB T0C 2S0
Tel: 403-575-5632
veteraneagle@gmail.com
Social Media:
www.facebook.com/theveteraneagle
Circulation: 525; *Frequency:* Weekly; Thursday
Veteran weekly newspaper

Viking: The Weekly Review
Owned By: Caribou Publishing
PO Box 240, 5311 - 50th St., Viking, AB T0B 4N0
Tel: 780-336-3422; *Fax:* 780-336-3223
vikingreview@gmail.com
www.weeklyreview.ca
Social Media:
twitter.com/vikingweekly
www.facebook.com/VikingWeeklyReview
Circulation: 1,097; *Frequency:* Weekly; Tuesday
The newspaper reports on the Alberta communities of Viking, Ryley, Kinsella, Irma, Holden, & Bruce. Both regular & online subscriptions are available. The Weekly Review is part of Caribou Publishing.
Kerry Anderson, Owner & Publisher
Lorraine Poulsen, Managing Editor

Vulcan: Vulcan Advocate
Owned By: Sun Media Corporation
112 - 3rd Ave. North, Vulcan, AB T0L 2B0
Tel: 403-485-2036; *Fax:* 403-485-6938
www.vulcanadvocate.com
Social Media:
twitter.com/Vulcanadvocate
www.facebook.com/177296522292461
Circulation: 1,043; *Frequency:* Weekly; Wednesday
Vulcan Alberta's daily newspaper for citizens and Star Trek fans alike
Josh Chalmers, Assistant Manager
josh.chalmers@sunmedia.ca

Wainwright: Star News Inc.
1027 - 3rd Ave., Wainwright, AB T9W 1T6
Tel: 780-842-4465; *Fax:* 780-842-2760
info@starnews.ca
www.starnews.ca
Rogers Holmes, Publisher
roger@starpress.ca
Kelly Clemmer, Editor-in-Chief
kelly@starnews.ca

Wainwright: Wainwright StarEDGE
Owned By: Star News Inc.
1027 - 3rd Ave., Wainwright, AB T9W 1T6
Tel: 780-842-4465; *Fax:* 780-842-2760
classifieds@starnews.ca
www.starnews.ca
Social Media:
facebook.com/WainwrightStarNews
Circulation: 6,650; *Frequency:* Fri.
Roger Holmes, Publisher
roger@starpress.ca

Patrick Moroz, Associate Publisher & Manager, Sales
patrick@starnews.ca
Kelly Clemmer, Editor-in-Chief
kelly@starnews.ca
Terry Hunka, Manager, Composition
terry@starnews.ca
Sandy Olejnik, Manager, Finance
sandy@starnews.ca
Carrie Baumgartner, Graphic Designer
carrie@starnews.ca
Sherry Schatz, Contact, Sales & Promotions
sherry@starnews.ca

Westlock: The Westlock News
Owned By: Great West Newspapers LP
9871 - 107th St., Westlock, AB T7P 1R9
Tel: 780-349-3033; *Fax:* 780-349-3677
www.westlocknews.com
Social Media: www.youtube.com/user/WestlockNews
twitter.com/westlocknews
www.faceboo k.com/130628693670762
Circulation: 3,085; *Frequency:* Weekly; Tuesday
The town & county of Westlock & the village of Clyde are served by the newspaper.
George Blais, Publisher
gblais@westlock.greatwest.ca
Doug Neuman, Editor
dneuman@westlock.greatwest.ca

Wetaskiwin: Wetaskiwin Times
Owned By: Sun Media Corporation
5013 - 51st St., Wetaskiwin, AB T9A 1L4
Tel: 780-352-2231; *Fax:* 780-352-4333
www.wetaskiwintimes.com
Social Media:
twitter.com/WetaskiwinTimes
Circulation: 10,689; *Frequency:* Weekly; Wednesday
Wetaskiwin's weekly newspaper
Jerold Leblanc, City Editor
wtimes.editor@sunmedia.ca

Whitecourt: Mayerthorpe Freelancer
Owned By: Sun Media Corporation
PO Box 630, 4732 - 50th Ave., Whitecourt, AB T7S 1N7
Tel: 780-778-3977; *Fax:* 780-778-6459
www.mayerthorpefreelancer.com
Social Media:
twitter.com/M_Freelancer
www.facebook.com/145871818816228
Circulation: 671; *Frequency:* Weekly; Wednesday
Mayerthore's weekly newspaper
Ann Harvey, Editor
ann.harvey@sunmedia.ca

Whitecourt: The Whitecourt Star
Owned By: Sun Media Corporation
PO Box 630, 4732 - 50th Ave., Whitecourt, AB T7S 1N7
Tel: 780-778-3977; *Fax:* 780-778-6459
www.whitecourtstar.com
Social Media:
twitter.com/Whitecourtstar
www.facebook.com/244728762259644
Circulation: 1,643; *Frequency:* Weekly; Wednesday
Weekly newspaper for Whitecourt
Pam Allain, Regional Director of Advertising
pamela.allain@sunmedia.ca
Christopher King, Editor
christopher.king@sunmedia.ca

British Columbia

Daily Newspapers in British Columbia

Fort St. John: Alaska Highway News
Previous Name: Dawson Creek Daily News; Peace River Block News
Owned By: Glacier Media Inc.
9916 - 98th St., Fort St. John, BC V1J 3T8
Tel: 250-782-5631; *Fax:* 250-782-3522
www.alaskahighwaynews.ca
Social Media:
twitter.com/AHNnewspaper
www.facebook.com/AlaskaHighwayNews
Circulation: 10,715 total; *Frequency:* Monday-Friday
Serving Dawson Creek, Fort St. John and surrounding communities
William Julian, Regional Manager
wj@ahnfsj.ca
Nicole Palfy, Associate Publisher
250-782-4888 ext 101
npalfy@dcdn.ca

Matt Lamers, Managing Editor
250-785-5631
editor@ahnfsj.ca

Kelowna: The Daily Courier
Owned By: Continental Newspapers Canada Ltd.
550 Doyle Ave., Kelowna, BC V1Y 7V1
Tel: 250-762-4445; *Fax:* 250-762-3866
csr@ok.bc.ca
www.kelownadailycourier.ca
Other information: Classifieds, Phone: 250-763-3228; Circulation: 250-763-4000
Social Media:
twitter.com/KelownaCourier
www.facebook.com/KelownaDailyCourier
Circulation: 73,399 total; *Frequency:* Daily
The Daily Courier is distributed Monday to Friday, & the Okanagan Saturday & the Okanagan Sunday are distributed on weekends.
Terry Armstrong, Publisher & Vice-President
250-470-0721
terry.armstrong@ok.bc.ca
Dave Trifunov, Managing Editor
250-470-0741
dave.trifunov@ok.bc.ca

Kimberley: The Bulletin
Owned By: Black Press
335 Spokane St., Kimberley, BC V1A 1Y9
Tel: 250-427-5333; *Fax:* 250-427-5336
bulletin@cyberlink.bc.ca
www.dailybulletin.ca
Social Media:
twitter.com/@kbulletin
www.facebook.com/TownsmanBulletin
Circulation: 15,215 total; *Frequency:* Monday-Friday
Karen Johnston, Publisher
250-426-5201
kjohnston@dailytownsman.com
Carolyn Grant, Editor
250-427-5333
editor@dailybulletin.ca

Nanaimo: Nanaimo Daily News
Owned By: Black Press
2575 McCullough Rd., Nanaimo, BC V9S 5W5
Tel: 250-729-4200
circulation@nanaimodailynews.com
www.nanaimodailynews.com
Other information: Subscription & delivery enquiries, Phone: 250-729-4266
Social Media:
twitter.com/NanaimoDaily
www.facebook.com/pages/Nanaimo-Daily-News/150301821648264
Circulation: 57,421 total; *Frequency:* Monday-Saturday
The Nanaimo Daily News serves central Vancouver Island.
Philip Wolf, Managing Editor
pwolf@nanaimodailynews.com

Penticton: Penticton Herald
Previous Name: Penticton Press
Owned By: Continental Newspapers Canada Ltd.
#101, 186 Nanaimo Ave. West, Penticton, BC V2A 1N4
Tel: 250-492-4002; *Fax:* 250-492-2403
csr@ok.bc.ca
www.pentictonherald.ca
Other information: Classified, Phone: 250-493-4332; Circulation: 250-493-6737
Social Media: linkedin.com/company/penticton-herald
twitter.com/pentictonherald
www.facebook.com/pentictonherald
Circulation: 38,884 total; *Frequency:* Daily
The Herald is delivered Monday to Friday. The Okanagan, which is published jointly with The Daily Courier of Kelowna, is delivered on Saturday & Sunday.
Ed Kennedy, General Manager & Publisher
ed.kennedy@ok.bc.ca
James Miller, Managing Editor
editor@pentictonherald.ca

Port Alberni: Alberni Valley Times
Previous Name: West Coast Advocate, Twin Cities Times
Owned By: Black Press
4918 Napier St., Port Alberni, BC V9Y 3H5
Tel: 250-723-8171; *Fax:* 250-723-0586
news@avtimes.net
www.avtimes.net
Social Media:
twitter.com/albernitimes
www.facebook.com/AVTimes?sk=wall

Circulation: 23,965 total; *Frequency:* Monday-Friday
The newspaper reaches communities in the Alberni Valley on Vancouver Island Monday to Friday.
Keith Currie, Publisher
keith.currie@avtimes.net

***Prince George:* The Prince George Citizen**
Owned By: Glacier Media Inc.
150 Brunswick St., Prince George, BC V2L 2B3
Tel: 250-562-2441; *Fax:* 250-562-7453
info@pgcitizen.ca
www.princegeorgecitizen.com
Social Media:
twitter.com/pgcitizen
www.facebook.com/pgcitizen
Circulation: 68,502 total; *Frequency:* Monday-Saturday
Colleen Sparrow, Publisher
csparrow@pgcitizen.ca

***Trail:* Trail Daily Times**
Owned By: Black Press
1163 Cedar Ave., Trail, BC V1R 4B8
Tel: 250-368-8551
www.traildailytimes.ca
Social Media:
twitter.com/traildailytimes
www.facebook.com/trailtimes
Circulation: 10,924 total; *Frequency:* Tuesday-Friday
The British Columbia communities of Trail, Rossland, Montrose, Warfiels, & Fruitvale are served by the newspaper.
Barb Blatchford, Publisher
publisher@trailtimes.ca
Guy Bertrand, Editor
editor@trailtimes.ca
Michelle Bedford, Circulation Manager, Circulation
circulation@trailtimes.ca

***Vancouver:* Metro Vancouver**
Owned By: Torstar Corp.
#405, 375 Water St., Vancouver, BC V6B 5C6
Tel: 604-602-1002; *Fax:* 866-254-6504
vancouver@metronews.ca
metronews.ca/news/vancouver
Social Media:
twitter.com/metrovancouver
facebook.com/metrovancouver
Circulation: 578,419 total; *Frequency:* Monday-Friday
Mary Kemmis, Publisher/Managing Director

***Vancouver:* The Province**
Owned By: Postmedia Network Inc.
#1, 200 Granville St., Vancouver, BC V6C 3N3
Tel: 604-605-2000; *Fax:* 604-605-2308
Toll-Free: 800-663-2662
info@png.canwest.com
www.theprovince.com
Other information: Letters to the Editor, E-mail: provletters@theprovince.com
Social Media: www.youtube.com/user/TheProvinceOnline
twitter.com/theprovince
www.fac ebook.com/TheProvince
Circulation: 760,874 total; *Frequency:* Monday-Friday, Sunday
The Province is a tabloid that publishes daily, except for Saturdays & holidays.
Wayne Moriarty, Editor-in-Chief
wmoriarty@theprovince.com

***Vancouver:* Sing Tao Daily**
Owned By: Sing Tao Newspapers / Torstar Corp.
1296 Kingsway, Vancouver, BC V5V 3E1
Tel: 604-321-1111; *Fax:* 604-321-1178
vanadmin@singtao.ca
news.singtao.ca/vancouver
Other information: Editorial email: editorial@singtao.ca
Frequency: Daily
News is presented in Cantonese for Chinese Canadians.
Amy Mui, Contact, Advertising
amui@singtao.ca

***Vancouver:* The Vancouver Sun**
Owned By: Postmedia Network Inc.
#1, 200 Granville St., Vancouver, BC V6C 3N3
Tel: 604-605-2000; *Fax:* 604-605-2308
www.vancouversun.com
Other information: Letters to the editor: sunletters@vancouversun.com
Social Media: pinterest.com/vancouversun
twitter.com/VanSunReporters/vancouver-sun-mas ter-list
www.facebook.com/VancouverSun
Circulation: 869,571 total; *Frequency:* Monday-Saturday
Gordon Fisher, President
604-605-2480; Fax: 604-605-2633
gfisher@postmedia.com
Harold Munro, Editor-in-Chief
604-605-2185; Fax: 604-605-2323
hmunro@vancouversun.com

***Victoria:* Times Colonist**
Previous Name: Victoria Daily Times, British Colonist
Owned By: Glacier Media Inc.
2621 Douglas St., Victoria, BC V8T 4M2
Tel: 250-380-5211 *Toll-Free:* 800-663-6384
customerservice@timescolonist.com
www.timescolonist.com
Other information: Classified Inquiries, E-mail: classified@timescolonist.com
Social Media:
twitter.com/timescolonist
www.facebook.com/timescolonist
Circulation: 330,301 total; *Frequency:* Tuesday-Sunday
The oldest daily newspaper in Western Canada.
Dave Obee, Editor-in-Chief
dobee@timescolonist.com

Other Newspapers in British Columbia

***100 Mile House:* 100 Mile House Free Press**
Owned By: Black Press Group Ltd.
PO Box 459, 100 Mile House, BC V0K 2E3
Tel: 250-395-2219; *Fax:* 250-395-3939
circulation@100milefreepress.net
www.100milefreepress.net
Social Media:
twitter.com/100mile
www.facebook.com/pages/100-Mile-Free-Press/1172529983540
4
Frequency: Wednesday
The 100 Mile House Free Press covers the South Cariboo region, from Lac la Hache to Clinton.
Chris Nickless, Publisher & Manager, Sales
publisher@100milefreepress.net
Ken Alexander, Editor
newsroom@100milefreepress.net
Heather Nelson, Contact, Advertising Sales
heather@100milefreepress.net

***Abbotsford:* Abbotsford News**
Owned By: Black Press
34375 Gladys Ave., Abbotsford, BC V2S 2H5
Tel: 604-853-1144
www.abbynews.com
Social Media:
twitter.com/abbynews
www.facebook.com/myabbynews
Circulation: Wed. 44,800; Fri. 46,000; *Frequency:* Biweekly
Full printed editions of the newspaper are also available online.
Andrew Franklin, Publisher
publisher@abbynews.com
Andrew Holota, Editor
604-851-4522
newsroom@abbynews.com

***Agassiz:* The Agassiz-Harrison Observer**
Owned By: Black Press
PO Box 129, 7167 Pioneer Ave., Agassiz, BC V0M 1A0
Tel: 604-796-4300
www.agassizharrisonobserver.com
Social Media:
twitter.com/agassizobserver
www.facebook.com/AgassizHarrisonObserver
Circulation: 2,884; *Frequency:* Thursday
Community news from Agassiz, Harrison Hot Springs, & Hope, is featured in the newspaper.
Carly Ferguson, Publisher
604-702-5560
publisher@theprogress.com
Lorene Keitch, Editor
604-796-4302
news@ahobserver.com

***Aldergrove:* Aldergrove Star**
Previous Name: Aldergrove Echo
Owned By: Black Press
27118 Fraser Hwy., Aldergrove, BC V4W 3P6
Tel: 604-856-8303
www.aldergrovestar.com
Social Media:
twitter.com/aldergrovestar
www.facebook.com/186177368124190
Circulation: 8,970; *Frequency:* Weekly; Thursday
Aldergrove's weekly newspaper
Dwayne Weidendorf, Publisher
publisher@aldergrovestar.com
Kurt Langmann, Editor
604-856-8303
newsroom@aldergrovestar.com

***Armstrong:* Okanagan Advertiser**
PO Box 610, 3400 Okanagan St., Armstrong, BC V0E 1B0
Tel: 250-546-3121
www.okanaganadvertiser.com
Other information: Enderby Office, Phone: 250-838-6017
Circulation: 1,974; *Frequency:* Weekly; Wednesday
The Okanagan Advertiser serves the British Columbia communities of Armstrong, Enderby, & the Spallumcheen Valley.

***Ashcroft:* Ashcroft-Cache Creek Journal**
Previous Name: The Ashcroft Journal; British Columbia Mining Journal
Owned By: Black Press
PO Box 190, 130 - 4th St., Ashcroft, BC V0K 1A0
Tel: 250-453-2261
www.ash-cache-journal.com
Social Media:
twitter.com/ashcroftnews
www.facebook.com/272576022776823
Circulation: 965; *Frequency:* Weekly; Thursday
Subscriptions are available for print & the online edition.
Terry Daniels, Publisher & Sales, Sales
250-453-2261
sales@accjournal.ca
Wendy Coomber, Editor
250-453-2261
editorial@accjournal.ca

***Barriere:* Barriere Star Journal**
Previous Name: Barriere Bulletin
Owned By: Black Press
PO Box 1020, Barriere, BC V0E 1E0
Tel: 250-672-5611
news@starjournal.net
www.starjournal.net
Social Media:
twitter.com/barrierenews
www.facebook.com/233231670068900
Circulation: 649; *Frequency:* Weekly; Thursday
Barrier's first weekly newspaper
Al Kirkwood, Publisher
al@starjournal.net
Jill Hayward, Editor
news@starjournal.net

***Bella Coola:* Coast Mountain News (CMN)**
Owned By: Black Press
442 Mackenzie St., Bella Coola, BC V0T 1C0
Tel: 250-799-5699
cmnews@cariboadvisor.com
www.coastmountainnews.com
Social Media:
twitter.com/CoastMtNews
www.facebook.com/CoastMountainNews
Circulation: 366; *Frequency:* Bi-monthly
Bi-monthly publication for Bella Coola Valley
Lorie Williston, Publisher
250-392-2331
Caitlin Thompson, Editor
250-982-2696
cmnews@cariboadvisor.com

***Bowen Island:* Undercurrent**
Owned By: Glacier Media Inc.
PO Box 130, Bowen Island, BC V0N 1G0
Tel: 604-947-2442
Ads: ads@bowenislandundercurrent.com
www.bowenislandundercurrent.com
Social Media:
twitter.com/BIUndercurrent
www.facebook.com/292053204139974
Circulation: 850; *Frequency:* Fri.
A print edition & and e-edition of the newspaper are available.
Doug Foot, Publisher
604-998-3550
dfoot@nsnews.com
Meribeth Deen, Editor
editor@bowenislandundercurrent.com

***Burnaby:* Burnaby NewsLeader**
Owned By: Glacier Media Inc.
7438 Fraser Park Dr., Burnaby, BC V5J 5B9
Tel: 604-438-6397
newsroom@burnabynewsleader.com
www.burnabynewsleader.com
Social Media:
twitter.com/burnabynews
www.facebook.com/burnabynews
Circulation: 45,211; *Frequency:* Weekly; Thursday
The newspaper publishes a print & online edition.
Nigel Lark, Publisher
publisher@tricitynews.com

Ian Jacques, Editor
editor@burnabynewsleader.com

Burnaby: Burnaby Now
Previous Name: The Columbian
Owned By: Glacier Media Inc.
#201A, 3430 Brighton Ave., Burnaby, BC V5A 3H4
Tel: 604-444-3451
editorial@burnabynow.com
www.burnabynow.com
Social Media:
twitter.com/BurnabyNOW_News
www.facebook.com/BurnabyNOW
Circulation: Wed. 47,779; Fri. 47,715; *Frequency:* Wednesday, Friday
Burnaby's biweekly newspaper
Alvin Brouwer, Publisher
abrouwer@glaciermedia.ca
Pat Tracy, Editor
editor@burnabynow.com

Burnaby: New Westminster Record
Previous Name: Royal City Record
Owned By: Glacier Media Inc.
#201A, 3430 Brighton Ave., Burnaby, BC V5A 3H4
Tel: 604-444-3451
editorial@royalcityrecord.com
www.royalcityrecord.com
Circulation: 16,641; *Frequency:* Biweekly; Wednesday, Friday
Shows local news around New Westminster, BC.
Alvin Brouwer, Publisher
abrouwer@glaciermedia.ca

Burnaby: The Record
Owned By: Glacier Media Inc.
#201A, 3430 Brighton Ave., Burnaby, BC V5A 3H4
Tel: 604-444-3451; *Fax:* 604-444-3460
production@royalcityrecord.com
www.royalcityrecord.com
Other information: Classified, Phone: 604-444-3000; Circulation: 604-942-3081
Social Media:
twitter.com/TheRecord
www.facebook.com/RoyalCityRecord
Circulation: 16,000+; *Frequency:* Wednesday, Friday
The community newspaper focuses upon New Westminster, British Columbia.
Brad Alden, Publisher
604-444-3010
balden@van.net
Pat Tracy, Editor
604-444-3007
editorial@royalcityrecord.com
Lara Graham, Director, Sales & Marketing
604-444-3030
lgraham@royalcityrecord.com

Burns Lake: Burns Lake District News
Owned By: Black Press
PO Box 309, Burns Lake, BC V0J 1E0
Tel: 250-692-7526
newsroom@ldnews.net
www.ldnews.net
Social Media:
twitter.com/burnslakenews
www.facebook.com/150524125018658
Circulation: 1,323; *Frequency:* Weekly; Wednesday
Weekly newspaper in Burns Lake
Laura Blackwell, Publisher
laura@ldnews.net
Flavio Nienow, Editor
newsroom@ldnews.net

Campbell River: Campbell River Mirror
Owned By: Black Press
#104, 250 Dogwood St., Campbell River, BC V9W 5Z5
Tel: 250-287-9227
www.campbellrivermirror.com
Social Media:
twitter.com/crmirror
www.facebook.com/251551478191572
Circulation: Wed. 15,746; Fri. 15,435; *Frequency:* Biweekly
News is presented from Campbell River & the central region of Vancouver Island. The newspaper is available in print & as an e-edition.
David Hamilton, Publisher
publisher@campbellrivermirror.com
Alistair Taylor, Managing Editor
editor@campbellrivermirror.com

Castlegar: Castlegar News
Owned By: Black Press Group Ltd.
#2, 1810 - 8th Ave., Castlegar, BC V1N 2Y4
Tel: 250-365-6397
www.castlegarnews.com
Social Media:
twitter.com/castlegarnews
www.facebook.com/castlegarnews
Circulation: 6,600; *Frequency:* Thurs.
A print edition & an e-edition are available. The free newspaper is distributed from Genelle to Playmor Junction, British Columbia.
Chris Hopkyns, Publisher
publisher@castlegarnews.com
Jim Sinclair, Editor
newsroom@castlegarnews.com
Cindy Amaral, Manager, Production
creative@castlegarnews.com
Theresa Hodge, Manager, Office
circulation@castlegarnews.com
Craig Lindsay, Reporter
reporter@castlegarnews.com

Chetwynd: Chetwynd Echo
Owned By: Draper, Dobie & Company Inc.
5016 - 50th Ave., Chetwynd, BC V0C 1J0
Tel: 250-788-2246
editor@chetwyndecho.net
www.chetwyndecho.net
Social Media:
twitter.com/ChetwyndEcho
www.facebook.com/161898250528779
Circulation: 1,300; *Frequency:* Weekly; Friday
The newspaper is available in print & online.
Naomi Larsen, Editor
editor@chetwyndecho.net

Chilliwack: Chilliwack Progress
Owned By: Black Press
45860 Spadina Ave., Chilliwack, BC V2P 6H9
Tel: 604-702-5550
www.theprogress.com
Social Media:
twitter.com/theprogress
www.facebook.com/chilliwackprogress
Circulation: 27,466; *Frequency:* Weekly; Thursday
Daily newspaper for Chilliwack
Carly Ferguson, Publisher
604-702-5560
publisher@theprogress.com
Gregg Knill, Editor
editor@theprogress.com

Chilliwack: Chilliwack Times
Owned By: Black Press
45951 Trethewey Ave., Chilliwack, BC V2P 1K4
Tel: 604-792-9117; *Fax:* 604-792-9300
editorial@chilliwacktimes.com
www.chilliwacktimes.com
Other information: Alternate Phone: 604-795-4417
Social Media:
twitter.com/chilliwacktimes
www.facebook.com/ChilliwackTimes
Circulation: 27,466; *Frequency:* Weekly; Thursday
Biweekly news in Chilliwack, BC
Nick Bastaja, Publisher
604-854-5244
nbastaja@chilliwacktimes.com

Clearwater: Clearwater Times
Owned By: Black Press
Brookfield Mall, #14, 74 Young Rd., Clearwater, BC V0E 1N1
Tel: 250-674-3343
newsroom@clearwatertimes.com
www.clearwatertimes.com
Social Media:
twitter.com/clearwaternews
www.facebook.com/302066023142345
Circulation: 1,250; *Frequency:* Weekly; Thursday
The weekly community newspaper covers events in Clearwater, Upper Clearwater, Wells Gray Park, Blue River, Roundtop, Avola, East Blackpool, Vavenby, & Birch Island, British Columbia.
Al Kirkwood, Publisher
classifieds@clearwatertimes.com
Keith McNeill, Editor
newsroom@clearwatertimes.com

Courtenay: Comox Valley Echo
Owned By: Glacier Media Inc.
407 - 5th St., Courtenay, BC V9N 1J7
Tel: 250-334-4722; *Fax:* 250-334-3172
echo@comoxvalleyecho.com
www.comoxvalleyecho.com
Social Media:
twitter.com/comoxvalleyecho
www.facebook.com/ComoxValleyEcho?v=wal l
Circulation: Tues. 22,141; Fri. 22,143; *Frequency:* Tuesday, Friday
The newspaper covers the Vancouver Island communities of Courtenay, Cumberland, Comox, Black Creek, Denman, Merville, Fanny Bay, Royston, & the Hornby Islands.
Keith Currie, Publisher
keith.currie@comoxvalleyecho.com
Debra Martin, Editor
debra.martin@comoxvalleyecho.com

Courtenay: Comox Valley Record
Owned By: Black Press
765 McPhee Ave., Courtenay, BC V9N 2Z7
Tel: 250-338-5811
www.comoxvalleyrecord.com
Social Media:
twitter.com/cvrecord
www.facebook.com/173357482636
Circulation: Tues. 21,417; Thurs. 21,168; *Frequency:* Tuesday, Thursday
The newspaper is available in print & online.
Chrissie Bowker, Publisher
publisher@comoxvalleyrecord.com
Terry Farrell, Editor
editor@comoxvalleyrecord.com

Cranbrook: Cranbrook Daily Townsman
Previous Name: Cranbrook Courier
Owned By: Black Press
822 Cranbrook St. North, Cranbrook, BC V1C 3R9
Tel: 250-426-5201
www.dailytownsman.com
Social Media:
twitter.com/@crantownsman
www.facebook.com/TownsmanBulletin
Frequency: Monday - Friday
The daily newspaper is distributed to communities throughout British Columbia's Columbia Valley.
Karen Johnston, Publisher
kjohnston@dailytownsman.com
Barry Coulter, Editor
barry@dailytownsman.com

Cranbrook: Kootenay News Advertiser
Owned By: Black Press
1510 - 2nd St. North, Cranbrook, BC V1C 3L2
Tel: 250-489-3455; *Fax:* 250-984-7744
Toll-Free: 800-665-2382
editor@kootenayadvertiser.com
www.kootenayadvertiser.com
Social Media:
twitter.com/cranbrooknews
www.facebook.com/110173431596
Circulation: Mon. 14,942; Fri. 21,505; *Frequency:* Monday, Friday
Cranbrook's weekly newspaper
Zena Williams, Publisher
publisher@kootenayadvertiser.com

Creston: Creston Valley Advance
Owned By: Black Press Group Ltd.
PO Box 1279, 1018 Canyon St., Creston, BC V0B 1G0
Tel: 250-428-2266; *Fax:* 250-428-3320
editor@crestonvalleyadvance.ca
www.crestonvalleyadvance.ca
Social Media:
twitter.com/crestonadvance
www.facebook.com/cvadvance?v=wall
Circulation: 3,500; *Frequency:* Weekly
Serving the communities of Creston, Erickson, Lister, Canyon, Yahk, West Creston and Wynndel, as well as the East Shore of Kootenay Lake.
Brian Lawrence, Editor
editor@crestonvalleyadvance.ca
Lorne Eckersley, Publisher
250-428-2266
publisher@crestonvalleyadvance.ca

Delta: South Delta Leader
Owned By: Black Press Group Ltd.
#207, 4840 Delta St., Delta, BC V4K 2T6
Tel: 604-948-3640
editor@southdeltaleader.com
www.southdeltaleader.com
Social Media:
twitter.com/sdleader
www.facebook.com/sdleader
Circulation: 16,600; Frequency: Fri.
The community newspaper is available in print & online. The print edition is delivered to homes & businesses in Tsawwassen, Ladner, & Tilbury, British Columbia.
Alvin Brouwer, Publisher
abrouwer@glaciermedia.ca
Ted Murphy, Editor
tmurphy@delta-optimist.com
Dave Hamilton, General Manager
dhamilton@delta-optimist.com

Duncan: Cowichan News Leader Pictorial
Owned By: Black Press Group Ltd.
#2, 5380 Trans Canada Hwy., Duncan, BC V9L 6W4
Tel: 250-746-4471; Fax: 250-746-8529
editor@cowichannewsleader.com
www.cowichannewsleader.com
Social Media:
twitter.com/duncannews
www.facebook.com/group.php?gid=196266000414293
Circulation: 23,400; Frequency: Wed., Fri.
The newspaper covers Vancouver Island's Cowichan Valley.
Simon Lindley, Publisher
250-856-0051
publisher@cowichannewsleader.com
John McKinley, Managing Editor
Lara Stuart, Manager, Circulation
circulation@cowichannewsleader.com
Kim Sayer, Supervisor, Office
office@cowichannewsleader.com

Duncan: Cowichan Valley Citizen
Owned By: Black Press
251 Jubilee St., Duncan, BC V9L 1W8
Tel: 250-748-2666
classifieds@van.net
www.cowichanvalleycitizen.com
Social Media: pinterest.com/cowichancitizen
twitter.com/CowichanCitizen
www.facebook .com/CowichanValleyCitizen
News & information is provided about British Columbia's Cowichan Valley.
Shirley Skolos, Publisher
sskolos@cowichanvalleycitizen.com

Fernie: Fernie Free Press
Owned By: Black Press Group Ltd.
PO Box 2350, Fernie, BC V0B 1M0
Tel: 250-423-4666; Fax: 250-423-3110
Toll-Free: 866-337-6437
freepress@shawcable.com
www.thefreepress.ca
Social Media:
twitter.com/FernieFreePress
www.facebook.com/freepressbc
Circulation: 1,851; Frequency: Weekly; Thursday
Serves Elkford, Fernie, Sparwood and the South Country.
Andrea Horton, Publisher
250-430-2168
publisher@thefreepress.ca
Nicole Obre, Editor
250-423-4666
editor@thefreepress.ca

Fort Nelson: Fort Nelson News
Owned By: Fort Nelson News Ltd.
PO Box 600, #3, 4448 - 50th Ave. North, Fort Nelson, BC V0C 1R0
Tel: 250-774-2357; Fax: 250-774-3612
www.fnnews.ca
Social Media:
twitter.com/fortnelsonnews
www.facebook.com/fortnelsonnews
Circulation: 1,961; Frequency: Weekly; Wednesday
Judith Kenyon, Editor
editorial@fnnews.ca

Fort Nelson: Fort Nelson News Ltd.
PO Box 600, Fort Nelson, BC V0C 1R0
Tel: 250-774-2357
www.fnnews.ca

Fort St James: Caledonia Courier
Owned By: Black Press Group Ltd.
PO Box 1298, Fort St James, BC V0J 1P0
Tel: 250-996-8482
newsroom@caledoniacourier.com
www.caledoniacourier.com
Social Media:
twitter.com/fortstjamesnews
www.facebook.com/207583255934276
Circulation: 575; Frequency: Wednesday
Pam Berger, Publisher & Manager, Sales
250-567-9258
advertising@ominecaexpress.com
Ruth Lloyd, Editor
250-996-8482
newsroom@caledoniacourier.com
Anne Stevens, Manager, Classified, Circulation, & Front Office
250-567-9258
office@ominecaexpress.com
Wendy Haslam, Contact, Production Department

Fort St John: The Northerner
Owned By: Glacier Media Inc.
9916 - 98A Ave., Fort St John, BC V1J 3T8
Tel: 250-785-5631
www.thenortherner.ca
Circulation: 8657; Frequency: Friday
William Julian, Publisher
Alison McMeans, Editor

Fort St. John: North Peace Express
9916 - 98th St., Fort St. John, BC V1J 3T8
Tel: 250-785-5631; Fax: 250-785-3522
ahnews@awink.com
Circulation: 10,400; Frequency: Weekly
William Julian, Publisher

Gabriola: Gabriola Sounder
Owned By: Gabriola Sounder Media Inc.
PO Box 62, #1, 510 North Rd., Gabriola, BC V0R 1X0
Tel: 250-247-9337; Fax: 250-247-8147
derek@soundernews.com
www.soundernews.com
Social Media:
twitter.com/News4Gabriola
Circulation: 3,227; Frequency: Monday
Derek Kilbourn, Editor
derek@soundernews.com
Sarah Holmes, Publisher
sarah@soundernews.com

Gold River: The Record
PO Box 279, Gold River, BC V0P 1G0
Tel: 250-283-2324
record@island.net
www.island.net/~record
Social Media:
www.facebook.com/pages/The-Record/131808520232076?sk=wall
Circulation: 700; Frequency: Bi-weekly; Wednesday
The Record is an independent newspaper that serves the Nootka Sound communities of British Columbia. Both print & web editions are available.
Jerry West, Editor
Suzanne Trevis, Contact
strevis@cablerocket.com

Grand Forks: Boundary Weekender
7255 Riverside Dr., Grand Forks, BC V0H 1H5
Tel: 250-442-2191

Grand Forks: Grand Forks Gazette
Owned By: Black Press Group Ltd.
PO Box 700, Grand Forks, BC V0H 1H0
Tel: 250-442-2191; Fax: 250-442-3336
editor@grandforksgazette.ca
www.grandforksgazette.ca
Social Media:
twitter.com/grandforksgaz
www.facebook.com/pages/Grand-Forks-Gazette/17401365933631
Circulation: 2,218; Frequency: Weekly; Wednesday
Chuck Bennett, Publisher
2504422191
chuckbennett@blackpress.ca
Karl Yu, Editor
Della Mallette, Manager, Production
production@grandforksgazette.ca

Greenwood: Boundary Creek Times Mountaineer
Previous Name: Boundary Creek Times
Owned By: Black Press Ltd.
PO Box 99, Greenwood, BC V0H 1J0
Tel: 250-445-2233; Fax: 250-445-2243
bctimes@direct.ca
Circulation: 501; Frequency: Thursday, Weekly
Chuck Bennett, Publisher
Karen Bennett, Editor

Hope: Hope Standard
Owned By: Black Press Group Ltd.
PO Box 1090, 540 Wallace St., Hope, BC V0X 1L0
Tel: 604-869-2421
www.hopestandard.com
Social Media:
twitter.com/hopestandard
www.facebook.com/HopeStandard
Circulation: 1381; Frequency: Thursday, Weekly
Carly Ferguson, Publisher
604-869-2421
publisher@hopestandard.com
Kerrie-Ann Schoenit, Editor
604-869-4992
news@hopestandard.com
Pattie Desjardins, Contact, Advertising Sales
604-869-4990
sales@hopestandard.com
Janice McDonald, Contact, Classified Advertising
604-869-2421
classifieds@hopestandard.com

Houston: Houston Today Newspaper
Owned By: Black Press Group Ltd.
PO Box 899, 3232 Hwy. 16, Houston, BC V0J 1Z1
Tel: 250-845-2890
newsroom@houston-today.com
www.houston-today.com
Social Media:
twitter.com/houstonnews1
www.facebook.com/pages/Houston-Today/2302454737 00891
Circulation: 1020; Frequency: Wednesday, Weekly
Andrew Hudson, Reporter

Invermere: The Valley Echo
Owned By: Black Press Group Ltd.
PO Box 70, #8, 1008- 8th Ave., Invermere, BC V0A 1K0
Tel: 250-341-6299
nicole@invermerevalleyecho.com
www.invermerevalleyecho.com
Social Media:
twitter.com/TheValleyEcho
www.facebook.com/InvermereValleyEcho
Circulation: 1397; Frequency: Wednesday, Weekly
The Valley Echo serves the British Columbia communities of Invermere, Fairmont Hot Springs, Windermere, Radium Hot Springs, & Wilmer.
Rose-Marie Regitnig, Publisher
publisher@invermerevalleyecho.com
Nicole Trigg, Editor
nicole@invermerevalleyecho.com

Kamloops: Kamloops This Week
Owned By: Aberdeen Publishing Inc.
1365B Dalhousie Dr., Kamloops, BC V2C 5P6
Tel: 250-374-7467
www.kamloopsthisweek.com
Social Media: youtube.com/user/KamloopsThisWeek
twitter.com/kamthisweek
www.faceb ook.com/kamloopsthisweek
Circulation: 58,650; Frequency: Biweekly
Kelly Hall, Publisher
publisher@kamloopsthisweek.com
Christopher Foulds, Editor
editor@kamloopsthisweek.com

Kelowna: Capital News
Owned By: Black Press Group Ltd.
2495 Enterprise Way, Kelowna, BC V1X 7K2
Tel: 250-763-3212
nlark@kelownacapnews.com
www.kelownacapnews.com
Social Media:
twitter.com/kelownacapnews
www.facebook.com/newskelowna
Circulation: 144,660; Frequency: Tuesday, Thursday, & Friday
Kelowna & its surrounding communities of Peachland, the Westside, & Lake Country are served by the newspaper.
Karen Hill, Publisher
2507633212
khill@kelownacapnews.com

Barry Gerding, Managing Editor & Columnist
2057633212
bgerding@kelownacapnews.com
Alistair Waters, Assistant Editor
awaters@kelownacapnews.com
Glenn Beaudry, Manager, Circulation
2507633212
gbeaudry@kelownacapnews.com
Sean Connor, Photographer
photodesk@kelownacapnews.com

Kelowna: Lake Country Calendar
Owned By: Black Press Group Ltd.
2495 Enterprise Way, Kelowna, BC V1X 7K2
Tel: 250-766-4688; *Fax:* 250-766-4645
production@lakecountrynews.net
www.lakecountrycalendar.com
Other information: Classifieds & Community Events, E-mail: classified@lakecountrynews.net
Social Media:
twitter.com/winfieldnews
www.facebook.com/pages/Lake-Country-Calendar/30 1407309875
Circulation: 3,600; *Frequency:* Wednesday
The area covered by the Lake Country Calendar includes the communities of Winfield, Oyama, Okanagan Centre, & Carr's Landing.
Barry Gerding, Editor
2509797302
newsroom@lakecountrynews.net

Kelowna: Westside Weekly
Owned By: Continental Newspapers Canada Inc.
550 Doyle Ave., Kelowna, BC V1Y 7V1
Tel: 250-762-4445; *Fax:* 250-762-3866
westside@ok.bc.ca
www.kelownadailycourier.ca
Social Media:
twitter.com/Westside_Weekly
www.facebook.com/westsideweekly
Circulation: 13,600; *Frequency:* Thurs., Sun.
The Westside Weekly serves West Kelowna, Peachland, & the Westbank First Nation.
Terry Armstrong, Group Publisher
terry.armstrong@ok.bc.ca
Dave Trifunov, Editor

Keremeos: The Review
Owned By: Black Press Group Ltd.
PO Box 130, 605 - 7th Ave., Keremeos, BC V0X 1N0
Tel: 250-499-2653; *Fax:* 250-499-2645
www.keremeosreview.com
Social Media:
twitter.com/keremeosnews
www.facebook.com/pages/Keremeos-Review/14483434 8947774
Circulation: 850; *Frequency:* Thurs.
Don Kendall, Publisher
1-250-492-0444
dkendall@blackpress.ca
Tammy Sparkes, Associate Publisher
publisher@keremeosreview.com
Steve Arstad, Editor
news@keremeosreview.com
Tammy Hartfield, Manager, Composing
ads@keremeosreview.com
Sandi Nolen, Representative, Advertising Sales
sales@keremeosreview.com

Kitimat: Northern Sentinel
Owned By: Black Press Group Ltd.
626 Enterprise Ave., Kitimat, BC V8C 2E4
Tel: 250-632-6144
newsroom@northernsentinel.com
www.northernsentinel.com
Social Media:
twitter.com/kitimatnews
www.facebook.com/pages/Kitimat-Northern-Sentinel /20302058
Circulation: 805; *Frequency:* Wednesday
Louisa Genzale, Publisher & Contact, Ad Management
2506326144
publisher@northernsentinel.com
Cameron Orr, Editor
2506326144
newsroom@northernsentinel.com

Ladner: The Delta Optimist
Owned By: Glacier Media Inc.
5008 - 47A Ave., Ladner, BC V4K 1T8
Tel: 604-946-4451; *Fax:* 604-946-5680
production@delta-optimist.com
www.delta-optimist.com
Other information: Classifieds, Phone: 604-630-3300; Distribution: 604-249-3332
Social Media:
twitter.com/DeltaOptimist
www.facebook.com/128177527229189
Circulation: Wed. 17,140; Fri. 17,050; *Frequency:* Wednesday, Friday
The newspaper covers community news & events in Ladner & Tsawwassen.
Alvin Brouwer, Publisher
abrouwer@delta-optimist.com
Ted Murphy, Editor
tmurphy@delta-optimist.com

Ladysmith: Ladysmith-Chemainus Chronicle
Owned By: Black Press Group Ltd.
PO Box 400, 940 Oyster Bay Dr., Ladysmith, BC V9G 1A3
Tel: 250-245-2277
www.ladysmithchronicle.com
Social Media:
twitter.com/LC_Chronicle
www.facebook.com/group.php?gid=173359166022754
Circulation: 1431; *Frequency:* Tuesday, Weekly
A print edition & an e-edition of the newspaper are available.
Teresa McKinley, Publisher
2502452277
publisher@ladysmithchronicle.com
Lindsay Chung, Editor
2502452277
editor@ladysmithchronicle.com
Doug Kent, Manager, Production
2502452277
Colleen Wheeler, Manager, Circulation & Office
2502452277
circulation@ladysmithchronicle.com
Niomi Pearson, Reporter
news@ladysmithchronicle.com

Lake Cowichan: Lake Cowichan Gazette
Owned By: Black Press Group Ltd.
PO Box 10, 170 Cowichan Lake Rd., Lake Cowichan, BC V0R 2G0
Tel: 250-749-4383
office@lakecowichangazette.com
www.lakecowichangazette.com
Social Media:
twitter.com/lakecowichannew
www.facebook.com/pages/Lake-Cowichan-Gazette /117628711667
Circulation: 730; *Frequency:* Wed.
Local news is provided for the British Columbia communities of Lake Cowichan, Honeymoon Bay, Caycuse, Skutz Falls, Youbou, & Mesachie Lake. A print edition & an e-dition of the newspaper are available.
Dennis Skalicky, Publisher & Editor
publisher@lakecowichangazette.com
Karen Brouwer, Office Manager

Langley: Langley Advance
Owned By: Glacier Media Inc.
#112, 6375 - 202nd St., Langley, BC V2Y 1N1
Tel: 604-534-8641; *Fax:* 604-534-0824
editorial@langleyadvance.com
www.langleyadvance.com
Social Media:
twitter.com/LangleyAdvance
facebook.com/LangleyAdvance
Circulation: 80125; *Frequency:* Tuesday, Thursday
The City of Langley, Langley Township, & Cloverdale are served by the newspaper.
Ryan McAdams, General Manager
rmcadams@langleyadvance.com
Bob Groeneveld, Editor
6049941050
editorial@langleyadvance.com
Jackie McKinley, Contact, Delivery
6049941045
jmckinley@langleyadvance.com

Langley: Langley Times
Owned By: Black Press Group Ltd.
PO Box 3097, 20258 Fraser Hwy., Langley, BC V3A 4E6
Tel: 604-533-4157
newsroom@langleytimes.com
www.langleytimes.com
Social Media:
twitter.com/langleytimes
www.facebook.com/pages/Langley-Times/1204 74554691065
Circulation: 35,823; *Frequency:* Tuesday, Thursday
Dwane Weidendorf, Publisher
6045146750
publisher@langleytimes.com
Frank Bucholtz, Editor
6045146751
newsroom@langleytimes.com

Lantzville: The Lantzville Log
PO Box 214, Lantzville, BC V0R 2H0
Tel: 250-390-5336; *Fax:* 250-390-2847
editor@thelog.ca
www.thelog.ca
Social Media:
facebook.com/LantzvilleLoggers
Circulation: 2,000; *Frequency:* 11 times a year
Julie Winkel, Owner & Publisher

Lazo: Totem Times
Owned By: Department of National Defence
PO Box 1000 Main, 19 Wing Comox, Lazo, BC V0R 2K0
Tel: 250-339-2541
totemtimes@gmail.com
www.cg.cfpsa.ca
Circulation: 1,800; *Frequency:* Semimonthly; Tuesday
The newspaper is distributed at 19 Wing in the Comox Valley, Canadian Forces bases throughout Canada, & Canadian Forces deployments around the world.
Camille Douglas, Managing Editor
camille.douglas@forces.gc.ca

Lillooet: Bridge River-Lillooet News
Owned By: Glacier Newspaper Group
PO Box 709, 979 Main St., Lillooet, BC V0K 1V0
Tel: 250-256-4219; *Fax:* 250-256-4210
Toll-Free: 877-300-8569
lillooetnews@cablelan.net
www.lillooetnews.net
Social Media:
twitter.com/lillooetnews
www.facebook.com/BridgeRiverLillooetNews
Circulation: 1,058; *Frequency:* Wednesday
Bruce MacLennan, Publisher
pub@lillooetnews.net
Wendy Fraser, Editor
editor@lillooetnews.net

Lumby: Lumby Valley Times
PO Box 408, 2062 Park Ave., Lumby, BC V0E 2G0
Tel: 250-307-0163
lvt@telus.net
www.lumbyvalleytimes.ca
Circulation: 2,700; *Frequency:* Fri.
Rod Neufeld, Publisher

Mackenzie: Mackenzie Times
PO Box 609, #125, 403 Mackenzie Blvd., Mackenzie, BC V0J 2C0
Tel: 250-997-6675; *Fax:* 250-997-4747
ads@mackenzietimes.com; news@mackenzietimes.com
Circulation: 1,000; *Frequency:* Wednesday
Jackie Benton, Editor
Kathy Dugan, Contact, Advertising

Maple Ridge: Maple Ridge - Pitt Meadows Times
Owned By: Glacier Media Inc.
#2, 22345 North Ave., Maple Ridge, BC V2X 8T2
Tel: 604-463-2281; *Fax:* 604-463-9943
www.mrtimes.com
Other information: Classified Advertising, Phone: 604-998-0218
Social Media:
twitter.com/mapleridgetimes
www.facebook.com/group.php?gid=153740064640252
Circulation: 30,089; *Frequency:* Tuesday, Thursday
The newspaper is a division of Postmedia Nework Inc.
Shannon Balla, Publisher
sballa@mrtimes.com
Bob Groeneveld, Editor
bgroeneveld@mrtimes.com
Roxanne Hooper, Assistant Editor
rhooper@mrtimes.com
Ralph DeAdder, Advertising Representative
rdeadder@mrtimes.com

Wendy Bradley, Contact, Delivery
wbradley@van.net

***Maple Ridge:* The News**
Owned By: Black Press Group Ltd.
22611, Dewdney Trunk Rd., Maple Ridge, BC V2X 3K1
Tel: 604-467-1122
newsroom@mapleridgenews.com
www.mapleridgenews.com
Social Media:
www.twitter.com/mapleridgenews
www.facebook.com/MapleRidgeNews
Circulation: 30,500; *Frequency:* Wed., Fri.
The News is distributed in the communities of Maple Ridge & Pitt Meadows, British Columbia. An e-edition is also available.
Jim Coulter, Publisher
1-604-476-2720
publisher@mapleridgenews.com
Michael Hall, Editor
1-604-476-2733
editor@mapleridgenews.com
Lisa Prophet, Manager, Advertising & Creative Services
admanager@mapleridgenews.com
Brian Yip, Manager, Circulation
circulation@mapleridgenews.com

***Merritt:* Merritt Herald**
Owned By: Black Press Group Ltd.
PO Box 9, 2090 Granite Ave., Merritt, BC V1K 1B8
Tel: 250-378-4241; *Fax:* 250-378-6818
www.merrittherald.com
Social Media:
twitter.com/merrittherald
www.facebook.com/pages/Merritt-Herald/30030671 6649720
Circulation: 6054; *Frequency:* Thursday, Weekly
News, community events, & sports are presented from Merritt & the Nicola Valley.
Theresa Arnold, Publisher
publisher@merrittherald.com
Emily Wessel, Editor
newsroom@merrittherald.com
Carol Soames, Manager, Office & Classifieds
classifieds@merrittherald.com

***Mission:* Mission City Record**
Owned By: Black Press Group Ltd.
33047 First Ave., Mission, BC V2V 1G2
Tel: 604-826-6221
Front Office: adcontrol@missioncityrecord.com
www.missioncityrecord.com
Social Media:
twitter.com/missionrecord
www.facebook.com/pages/Mission-Record/123079451105629
Circulation: 10,000+; *Frequency:* Thursday
A print edition & an e-edition are available.
Andrew Franklin, Publisher
1-604-851-4538
publisher@missioncityrecord.com
Andrew Holota, Editor
editor@abbynews.com
Carol Aun, Editor, Arts
arts@missioncityrecord.com
Crystal Orchison, Contact, Advertising
crystal@missioncityrecord.com

***Nakusp:* Arrow Lakes News**
Owned By: Black Press Group Ltd.
PO Box 189, 203 Broadway, Nakusp, BC V0G 1R0
Tel: 250-265-3823
www.arrowlakesnews.com
Social Media:
twitter.com/nakuspnews
www.facebook.com/pages/Arrow-Lakes-News/11825902487615 8
Circulation: 605; *Frequency:* Wednesday, Weekly
The British Columbia communities of Naskusp, New Denver, Trout Lake, Silverton, Burton, Fauquier, Arrow Park, & Edgewood are served by the newspaper.
Mavis Cann, Publisher & Manager, Ads
publisher@arrowlakesnews.com
Aaron Orlando, Editor
newsroom@arrowlakesnews.com

***Nanaimo:* Harbour City Star**
Owned By: Glacier Newspaper Group
c/o Nanaimo Daily News, 2575 McCullough Rd., #B1, Nanaimo, BC V9S 5W5
Tel: 250-729-4200; *Fax:* 250-729-4256
www.nanaimodailynews.com
Other information: Classifieds, Phone: 250-729-4222; Circulation: 250-729-4266
Social Media:
twitter.com/NanaimoDaily
facebook.com/pages/Nanaimo-Daily-News/150301821 648264
Circulation: 27,800; *Frequency:* Fri.
Hugh Nicholson, Publisher
250-729-4257
hnicholson@glaciermedia.ca
Mark MacDonald, Managing Editor
mamacdonald@nanaimodailynews.com
Wendy King, Manager, Production
wking@nanaimodailynews.com
Rachel Mason, Manager, Business
rmason@nanaimodailynews.com
Andrea Rosato-Taylor, Manager, Advertising
arosato-taylor@nanaimodailynews.com

***Nanaimo:* Nanaimo News Bulletin**
Owned By: Black Press Group Ltd.
777 Poplar St., Nanaimo, BC V9S 2H7
Tel: 250-753-3707
editor@nanaimobulletin.com
www.nanaimobulletin.com
Social Media:
twitter.com/nanaimobulletin
www.facebook.com/nanaimobulletin
Circulation: 30,000; *Frequency:* Tuesday, Thursday, Saturday
The Nanaimo New Bulletin is available in print & online.
Maurice Donn, Publisher
2507344600
publisher@nanaimobulletin.com
Melissa Fryer, Editor
2507344621
editor@nanaimobulletin.com
Michael Kelly, Manager, Circulation
2507344605
circulation@nanaimobulletin.com
Sean McCue, Manager, Sales
salesmgr@nanaimobulletin.com
Chris Bush, Photographer
2507344625
photos@nanaimobulletin.com

***Nelson:* Express**
554 Ward St., Nelson, BC V1L 1S9
Tel: 250-354-3910; *Fax:* 250-352-5075
Toll-Free: 800-665-3288
express@expressnews.bc.ca
www.expressnews.ca
Other information: Editorial, Phone: 250-354-1118
Social Media: www.youtube.com/user/expressnewsupdate
www.facebook.com/group.php?gid=28 1836361276
Frequency: Weekly
Nelson Becker, Publisher

***Nelson:* Nelson Star**
Owned By: Black Press
514 Hall St., Nelson, BC V1L 1Z2
Tel: 250-352-1890
www.nelsonstar.com
Social Media:
twitter.com/nelsonstarnews
www.facebook.com/nelsonstarnews
Circulation: 9,000; *Frequency:* Wednesday, Friday
Twice weekly newspaper for Nelson, BC
Karen Bennett, Publisher
250-352-1890
advertising@nelsonstar.com
Greg Nesteroff, Editor
250-551-4137
editor@nelsonstar.com

***North Vancouver:* North Shore News**
Owned By: Glacier Newspaper Group
#100, 126 East 15th St., North Vancouver, BC V7L 2P9
Tel: 604-985-2131; *Fax:* 604-985-3227
distribution@nsnews.com
www.nsnews.com
Other information: Classified, Phone: 604-630-3300; Real Estates Ads: 604-985-6982
Social Media:
twitter.com/NorthShoreNews
www.facebook.com/northshorenews
Circulation: 62,725; *Frequency:* Wednesday, Friday, Sunday
Doug Foot, Publisher
604-998-3550
dfoot@nsnews.com
Terry Peters, Managing Editor
604-998-3530
tpeters@nsnews.com
Vicki Magnison, Director, Sales & Marketing
604-998-3520
vmagnison@nsnews.com
Rick Anderson, Manager, Real Estate
604-998-3580
randerson@nsnews.com

***Oliver:* Oliver Chronicle**
Owned By: Tydeman Publishing Ltd.
PO Box 880, 6379 Main St., Oliver, BC V0H 1T0
Tel: 250-498-3711; *Fax:* 250-498-3966
www.oliverchronicle.com
Social Media:
twitter.com/OliverChronicle
facebook.com/OliverChronicle
Circulation: 1722; *Frequency:* Wednesday
Both paper & online editions are available.
Steve Ceron, Publisher
publisher@oliverchronicle.com
Lyonel Doherty, Editor
editor@oliverchronicle.com
Derrick Robson, Contact, Production
production@oliverchronicle.com
Marilyn Swartz, Contact, Sales
sales@oliverchronicle.com

***Osoyoos:* Osoyoos Times**
Owned By: Aberdeen Publishing Group
PO Box 359, 8712 Main St., Osoyoos, BC V0H 1V0
Tel: 250-495-7225; *Fax:* 250-495-6616
ads@osoyoostimes.com
www.osoyoostimes.com
Circulation: 1911; *Frequency:* Wednesday
Steve Ceron, Publisher
sceron@osoyoostimes.com
Keith Lacey, Editor
news@osoyoostimes.com
Richard McGuire, Reporter & Photographer
reporter@osoyoostimes.com
Jocelyn Merit, Office Administrator
admin@osoyoostimes.com
Sherry Anderson, Contact, Newspaper Circulation & Delivery
Ken Baker, Contact, Advertising Sales & Layout
sales@osoyoostimes.com

***Parksville:* The Parksville Qualicum Beach News**
Previous Name: Oceanside Star
Owned By: Black Press
PO Box 1180, #4, 154 Middleton, Parksville, BC V9P 2H2
Tel: 250-248-4341
www.pqbnews.com
Circulation: 16,243; *Frequency:* Weekly; Thursday
Peter McCully, Publisher
250-905-0018
publisher@pqbnews.com
John Harding, Editor
editor@pqbnews.com

***Parksville:* Parksville Qualicum News**
Owned By: Black Press Group Ltd.
PO Box 1180, #4, 154 Middleton Ave., Parksville, BC V9P 2H2
Tel: 250-248-4341
www.pqbnews.com
Social Media:
twitter.com/parksvillenews
www.facebook.com/PQBNews
Circulation: 15800+; *Frequency:* Tuesday, Friday, Thursday
The Parksville Qualicum News is available inprint & online. The newspaper serves the City of Parksville, the Town of Qualicum Beach, & the Vancouver Island communities of Deep Bay, Qualicum Bay, Errington, Hilliers, Coombs, & Whiskey Creek.
Peter McCully, Publisher
250-905-0018
publisher@pqbnews.com
John Harding, Editor
250-905-0019
editor@pqbnews.com
Lissa Alexander, Reporter
250-905-0028
reporter@pqbnews.com
Auren Ruvinsky, Reporter
250-905-0026
writer@pqbnews.com

Peggy Sidbeck, Manager, Production
250-905-0016
production@pqbnews.com
Grant DeGagne, Representative, Advertising
250-905-0015
gdegagne@pqbnews.com

***Peachland:* The Peachland Signal**
PO Box 800, #3, 4478 Third St., Peachland, BC V0H 1X0
Tel: 250-767-2004; *Fax:* 250-767-3306
signal@cablelan.net

Circulation: 1,308; *Frequency:* Weekly
Darren Bayrack, Publisher

***Peachland:* Peachland View**
***Owned By:* Aberdeen Publishing Group**
PO Box 1150, 4437 - 3rd St., Peachland, BC V0H 1X7
Tel: 250-767-7771
publisher.peachlandview@shaw.ca
www.peachlandview.com
Social Media:
twitter.com/peachlandview
facebook.com/ThePeachlandView

Circulation: 3,100; *Frequency:* Fri.
The independently owned, free community newspaper is distributed to Peachland's residences & businesses, as well as businesses in Westbank.
Steve Ceron, Group Publisher
sceron@aberdeenpublishing.com
Erin Christie, Editor
editor@peachlandview.ca
Joanne Layh, Manager, Sales
sales@peachlandview.ca

***Pender Island:* Island Tides**
PO Box 55, Pender Island, BC V0N 2M1
Tel: 250-216-2267; *Fax:* 250-629-3838
islandtides@islandtides.com; news@islandtides.com
www.islandtides.com

Circulation: 14,600; *Frequency:* Thurs., bi-weekly
Island Tides presents news & views from British Columbia's west coast. The newspaper is available around the Strait of Georgia.
Christa Grace-Warrick, Publisher

***Penticton:* Penticton Western News**
***Owned By:* Black Press Group Ltd.**
2250 Camrose St., Penticton, BC V2A 8R1
Tel: 250-492-3636
region@pentictonwesternnews.com
www.pentictonwesternnews.com
Other information: Classified Department, E-mail: classifieds@pentictonwesternnews.com
Social Media:
twitter.com/pentictonnews
www.facebook.com/pentictonnews
Circulation: 20,000+; *Frequency:* Wednesday, Friday
News, sports, & entertainment in Penticton & the South Okanagan are covered by the newspaper.
Don Kendall, Publisher
2504920444
dkendall@blackpress.ca
Percy Hébert, Editor & Columnist
editor@pentictonwesternnews.com
Emanuel Sequeira, Sports Editor & Columnist
2504923636
sports@pentictonwesternnews.com
Larry Mercier, Manager, Sales
2504920444
larry@pentictonwesternnews.com
Kirk Myltoft, Composing Manager, Creative Services
kirk@pentictonwesternnews.com
Sue Kovacs, Manager, Circulation
circulation@pentictonwesternnews.com
Mark Brett, Photographer
photos@pentictonwesternnews.com

***Port Coquitlam:* The Tri-City News**
***Owned By:* Glacier Media Inc.**
#115, 1525 Broadway St., Port Coquitlam, BC V3C 6L6
Tel: 604-525-6397
www.tricitynews.com
Social Media:
twitter.com/tricitynews
www.facebook.com/73945744787
Circulation: Wed. 52,310; Fri. 52,297; *Frequency:* Wednesday, Friday
The newpaper covers happenings in the British Columbia communities of Port Coquitlam, Coquitlam, Anmore, Port Moody, & Belcarra.
Nigel Lark, Publisher
publisher@tricitynews.com
Richard Dal Monte, Editor
newsroom@tricitynews.com

***Port Hardy:* North Island Gazette**
***Owned By:* Black Press Group Ltd.**
PO Box 458, 7305 Market St., Port Hardy, BC V0N 2P0
Tel: 250-949-6225
viads@bcclassified.com (classified advertising)
www.northislandgazette.com
Social Media:
twitter.com/nigazette
www.facebook.com/pages/North-Island-Gazette/188989 2344453
Circulation: 1,500; *Frequency:* Thursday
The newspaper serves the northern part of Vancouver Island, including the communities of Port McNeill, Port Hardy, Port Alice, Sointula, & Alert Bay.
Sandy Grenier, Publisher
publisher@northislandgazette.com
J.R. Rardon, Editor
editor@northislandgazette.com
Annae Marchand, Manager, Production
production@northislandgazette.com
Aidan O'Toole, Reporter
reporter@northislandgazette.com
Lisa Harrison, Representative, Sales
sales@northislandgazette.com

***Port Moody:* The Tri-Cities Now**
***Owned By:* Glacier Media Inc.**
#216, 3190 St. Johns St., Port Moody, BC V3H 2C7
Tel: 604-492-4492
www.thenownews.com
Other information: Classified Advertising, E-mail: classified@van.net
Social Media:
twitter.com/TheTriCitiesNow
www.facebook.com/TheTriCitiesNOW
Circulation: 54,989; *Frequency:* Wednesday, Friday
News is provided for the British Columbia communities of Coquitlam, Port Moody & Port Coquitlam.
Shannon Balla, Publisher
604-492-4229
publisher@thenownews.com
Leneen Robb, Editor
604-492-4967
editorial@thenownews.com

***Powell River:* Powell River Peak**
***Owned By:* Glacier Media Inc.**
4400 Marine Ave., Powell River, BC V8A 2K1
Tel: 604-485-5313; *Fax:* 604-485-5007
Editor: editor@prpeak.com
www.prpeak.com
Other information: Administration email: admin@prpeak.com
Social Media:
twitter.com/Peak_Aboo
www.facebook.com/pages/Peak-Publishing/16876744017 3
Circulation: 2,850; *Frequency:* Wed.
Joyce Carlson, Publisher

***Prince George:* Pipeline News North**
***Owned By:* Glacier Media Inc.**
PO Box 5700, Prince George, BC V2L 5K9
Tel: 250-785-5631
editor@pipelinenewsnorth.ca
www.pipelinenewsnorth.ca
Social Media:
twitter.com/PipelineNN
www.facebook.com/PipelineNewsNorth
Circulation: 14,000; *Frequency:* Monthly
Discusses petroleum news in northern British Columbia & Alberta.
Matt Prepost, Managing Editor
editor@ahnfsj.ca

***Prince George:* Prince George Free Press**
***Owned By:* Black Press Group Ltd.**
1773 South Lyon St., Prince George, BC V2N 1T3
Tel: 250-564-0005; *Fax:* 250-562-0025
editor@pgfreepress.com
pgfreepress.com
Social Media:
twitter.com/pgfreepress
www.facebook.com/pages/Prince-George-Free-Press/ 140123662
Circulation: 56,000; *Frequency:* Wed., Fri.
Ron Drillen, General Manager
publisher@pgfreepress.com
Bill Phillips, Editor

***Princeton:* Similkameen News Leader**
***Owned By:* Black Press Ltd.**
PO Box 956, 226A Bridge St., Princeton, BC V0X 1W0
Tel: 250-295-4149; *Fax:* 250-295-4103
Toll-Free: 888-350-9969
editor@thenewsleader.ca
www.thenewsleader.ca
Other information: Advertising Department, E-mail: ads@thenewsleader.ca
Social Media:
twitter.com/PrincetonBCNews
facebook.com/thenewsleader1

Circulation: 1,000; *Frequency:* Wed.
The tabloid newspaper is distributed in the Similkameen Valley, including Princeton, Cawston, Coalmont, Keremeos, Hedley, & Tulameen.
W. George Elliott, Publisher
george@thenewsleader.ca
Brenda Engel, Office Administrator
brenda@thenewsleader.ca

***Princeton:* Similkameen Spotlight**
***Owned By:* Black Press Group Ltd.**
PO Box 340, 282 Bridge St., Princeton, BC V0X 1W0
Tel: 250-295-3535
classifieds@similkameenspotlight.com
www.similkameenspotlight.com
Social Media:
twitter.com/similkameennews
www.facebook.com/pages/Similkameen-Spotlight/12566867052 9

Circulation: 1000+; *Frequency:* Wednesday, Weekly
The Similkameen Spotlight serves the Similkameen Valley, including Coalmont, Princeton, Tulameen, Keremeos, & Hedley.
Lisa Carleton, Editor & Associate Publisher
lisa@similkameenspotlight.com
Sandi Nolan, Consultant, Advertising
advertising@similkameenspotlight.com

***Queen Charlotte:* Haida Gwaii Observer**
***Owned By:* Observer Publishing Co. Ltd.**
PO Box 205, 623 - 7th St., Queen Charlotte, BC V0T 1S0
Tel: 250-559-4680; *Fax:* 250-559-8433
Toll-Free: 888-529-4747
observer@haidagwaii.ca
www.qciobserver.com
Social Media:
facebook.com/haidagwaiiobserver
Circulation: 900; *Frequency:* Thursday, Weekly
Formerly the Queen Charlotte Islands Observer
Jeff King, Manager, Publishing

***Quesnel:* Cariboo Observer**
***Owned By:* Black Press Group Ltd.**
188 Carson Ave., Quesnel, BC V2J 2A8
Tel: 250-992-2121
editor@quesnelobserver.com
www.quesnelobserver.com
Social Media:
twitter.com/quesnelnews
www.facebook.com/pages/Quesnel-Cariboo-Observer/ 258929627
Circulation: 9000+; *Frequency:* Wednesday, Friday
News is provided about Quesnel & area, British Columbia.
Tracey Roberts, Publisher & Manager, Sales
publisher@quesnelobserver.com
Autumn MacDonald, Editor
editor@quesnelobserver.com
Whitney Griffiths, Reporter, Sports
sports@quesnelobserver.com

***Revelstoke:* Revelstoke Times Review**
***Owned By:* Black Press Group Ltd.**
PO Box 20, 518 - 2nd St. West, Revelstoke, BC V0E 2S0
Tel: 250-837-4667
www.revelstoketimesreview.com
Social Media:
twitter.com/revelstoketimes
www.facebook.com/RevelstokeTimesReview
Circulation: 1,200+; *Frequency:* Wednesday
The Revelstoke Review, which was founded in 1914, merged with the Revelstoke Times in 2003 to create the Revelstoke Times Review.
Mavis Cann, Publisher
mavis@revelstoketimesreview.com
Alex Cooper, Editor
editor@revelstoketimesreview.com
Fran Carlson, Manager, Office
circulation@revelstoketimesreview.com
Rob Stokes, Contact, Production
production@revelstoketimesreview.com

***Richmond:* Richmond News**
Owned By: Glacier Media Inc.
5731, No. 3 Road, Richmond, BC V6X 2C9
Tel: 604-270-8031; *Fax:* 604-270-2248
editor@richmond-news.com
www.richmond-news.com
Frequency: Biweekly; Wednesday, Friday
Discusses local news in & around Richmond.
Pierre Pelletier, Publisher
604-249-3336
ppelletier@richmond-news.com

***Richmond:* Richmond Review**
Owned By: Black Press Group Ltd.
#1, 3671 Viking Way, Richmond, BC V6V 2J5
Tel: 604-247-3700
news@richmondreview.com
www.richmondreview.com
Other information: Newsroom, Phone: 604-247-3730; Classified Advertising: 604-575-5555
Social Media:
twitter.com/richmondreview
www.facebook.com/richmondreview
Circulation: 93,500; *Frequency:* Wed., Fri.
Mary Kemmis, Publisher
publisher@richmondreview.com
Bhreandain Clugston, Editor
Jaana Bjork, Manager, Creative Services
jaana@richmondreview.com
Kristene Murray, Manager, Circulation
circulation@richmondreview.com
Elana Gold, Assistant Manager, Advertising
admanager@richmondreview.com

***Salmon Arm:* Salmon Arm Observer**
Owned By: Black Press Group Ltd.
PO Box 550, 171 Shuswap St., Salmon Arm, BC V1E 4H7
Tel: 250-832-2131
circulation@saobserver.net
www.saobserver.net
Social Media:
twitter.com/salmonarm
www.facebook.com/pages/Salmon-Arm-Observer/126369231201
Circulation: 2400+; *Frequency:* Wednesday
Tracy Hughes, Editor & Columnist
newsroom@saobserver.net
Penny Brown, Contact, Advertising Sales
pennyjb@saobserver.net

***Salmon Arm:* The Shuswap Market News**
Owned By: Black Press Group Ltd.
171 Shuswap St., Salmon Arm, BC V1E 4H7
Tel: 250-832-2131
www.saobserver.net
Circulation: 14,000; *Frequency:* Friday
The Shuswap Market News is a free paper.
Tracy Hughes, Editor & Columnist
newsroom@saobserver.net
Sherry Kaufmam, Contact, Advertising Sales
sherry@saobserver.net

***Salt Spring Island:* Gulf Islands Driftwood**
Owned By: Black Press Group Ltd.
328 Lower Ganges Rd., Salt Spring Island, BC V8K 2V3
Tel: 250-537-9933
info@driftwoodgimedia.com
www.gulfislandsdriftwood.com
Social Media:
twitter.com/gidriftwood
www.facebook.com/gulfislandsdriftwood
Circulation: 2996; *Frequency:* Wednesday
The community newspaper is available in print & online. The Gulf Island Driftwood serves the British Columbia islands of Mayne, Salt Spring, Pender, Saturna, & Galiano.
Amber Ogilvie, Publisher
aogilvie@gulfislandsdriftwood.com
Gail Sjuberg, Managing Editor
gsjuberg@gulfislands.net
Lorraine Sullivan, Manager, Production
production@gulfislands.net

***Sechelt:* Coast Reporter**
Previous Name: Coast Independent
Owned By: Glacier Media Inc.
PO Box 1388, 5485 Wharf Rd., Sechelt, BC V0N 3A0
Tel: 604-885-4811; *Fax:* 604-885-4818
www.coastreporter.net
Social Media:
twitter.com/coast_reporter
www.facebook.com/coastreporter
Circulation: 11,900; *Frequency:* Fri.
Peter Kvarnstrom, Publisher
pkvarnstrom@coastreporter.net
Ian Jacques, Editor
editor@coastreporter.net

***Sicamous:* Eagle Valley News**
Owned By: Black Press Group Ltd.
PO Box 113, 1133 Parksville St., Sicamous, BC V0E 2V0
Tel: 250-836-2570; *Fax:* 250-836-2661
classifieds@eaglevalleynews.com
www.eaglevalleynews.com
Circulation: 500; *Frequency:* Wednesday
Lavigne Laura, Contact, Sales
laura@saobserver.net
Lachlan Labere, Reporter
circulation@saobserver.net

***Sidney:* Peninsula News Review**
Previous Name: Sidney Review
Owned By: Black Press Group Ltd.
#6, 9843 Second St., Sidney, BC V8L 3C7
Tel: 250-656-1151
victorianews.com
Social Media:
twitter.com/peninsulanews
www.facebook.com/PeninsulaNewsReview
The newspaper serves the British Columbia communities of Sidney, North Saanich, & Central Saanich.
Jim Parker, Publisher
publisher@peninsulanewsreview.com
Steven Heywood, Editor
editor@peninsulanewsreview.com
Arlene Smith, Manager, Circulation
circulation@peninsulanewsreview.com
Devon MacKenzie, Reporter
reporter@peninsulanewsreview.com

***Smithers:* Interior News**
Owned By: Black Press Group Ltd.
PO Box 2560, 3764 Broadway, Smithers, BC V0J 2N0
Tel: 250-847-3266; *Fax:* 250-847-2995
advertising@interior-news.com
www.interior-news.com
Social Media:
twitter.com/smithersnews
www.facebook.com/pages/Smithers-Interior-News/22646570738
Circulation: 2,700; *Frequency:* Wednesday
Grant Harris, Publisher
publisher@interior-news.com
Ryan Jensen, Editor
editor@interior-news.com

***Sooke:* Sooke News Mirror**
Owned By: Black Press Group Ltd.
#4, 6631 Sooke Rd., Sooke, BC V9Z 0A3
Tel: 250-642-5752; *Fax:* 250-642-4767
www.sookenewsmirror.com
Social Media:
twitter.com/sookenews
www.facebook.com/SookeNewsMirror
Circulation: 5700+; *Frequency:* Wednesday
The Sooke News Mirror serves the District of Sooke & its surrounding area.
Rod Sluggett, Publisher
publisher@sookenewsmirror.com
Pirjo Raits, Editor
editor@sookenewsmirror.com
Britt Santowski, Reporter
news@sookenewsmirror.com
Harla Eve, Contact, Office Administration
office@sookenewsmirror.com
Joan Gamache, Advertising Representative & Contact, Circulation
sales@sookenewsmirror.comm

***Squamish:* Squamish Chief**
Owned By: Glacier Newspapers Group
PO Box 3500, 38117 - 2nd Ave., Squamish, BC V8B 0B9
Tel: 604-892-9161; *Fax:* 604-892-8483
lpasko@squamishchief.com
www.squamishchief.com
Social Media:
youtube.com/channel/UCPhqqWAiRSno3glg7vSqpAA
twitter.com/squamishchie f
facebook.com/squamishchief
Circulation: 2,846; *Frequency:* Friday
Darren Roberts, Publisher
publisher@squamishchief.com
David Burke, Editor
dburke@squamishchief.com

***Summerland:* Summerland Review**
Owned By: Black Press Group Ltd.
PO Box 309, Summerland, BC V0H 1Z0
Tel: 250-494-5406
www.summerlandreview.com
Social Media:
twitter.com/summerlandnews
www.facebook.com/pages/Summerland-Review/149061881826182
Circulation: 1,700; *Frequency:* Thursday
A print edition & an e-edition are available.
Don Kendall, Publisher
dkendall1@hotmail.com
John Arendt, Editor
news@summerlandreview.com
Nan Cogbill, Manager, Circulation & Classified
class@summerlandreview.com
Jo Freed, Manager, Sales
ads@summerlandreview.com

***Surrey:* Cloverdale Reporter**
Owned By: Black Press Group Ltd.
17586 - 56A Ave., Surrey, BC V3S 1G3
Tel: 604-575-2405
editor@cloverdalereporter.com
www.cloverdalereporter.com
Social Media:
twitter.com/cloverdalenews
www.facebook.com/CloverdaleReporter
Circulation: 20,000; *Frequency:* Thurs.
News is reported from the Cloverdale area of Surrey, British Columbia in both print & e-editions.
Jennifer Lang, Editor
editor@cloverdalereporter.com
Ursula Maxwell-Lewis, Founding Editor
604-575-2405
Lyliane Ward, Consultant, Advertising
604-575-2423
sales@cloverdalereporter.com

***Surrey:* The Indo-Canadian Voice**
#102-9360 - 120 St., Surrey, BC V3V 4B9
Tel: 604-502-6100; *Fax:* 604-501-6111
editor@voiceonline.com
www.voiceonline.com
Social Media:
twitter.com/indocanvoice
facebook.com/indocanadianvoice
Circulation: 18,500; *Frequency:* Weekly
The VOICE caters to the South Asian population of Vancouver and British Columbia
Rattan Mall, Editor
newsdesk@voiceonline.com
Vinnie Combow, General Manager
rcombow@gmail.com

***Surrey:* The Leader**
Owned By: Black Press Group Ltd.
#200, 5450 - 152nd St., Surrey, BC V3S 5J9
Tel: 604-575-2744
newsroom@surreyleader.com
www.surreyleader.com
Social Media:
twitter.com/surreyleader
www.facebook.com/surreyleader
Circulation: 80,000+; *Frequency:* Tuesday, Thursday
The Leader covers news for Surrey & North Delta, British Columbia. Editions are available in print & online.
Jim Mihaly, Publisher
publisher@surreyleader.com
Paula Carlson, Editor
6045755337
pcarlson@surreyleader.com
Sheila Reynolds, Assistant Editor
6045755332
sreynolds@surreyleader.com
Jeff Nagel, Regional Reporter
6045755334
jnagel@surreyleader.com
Boaz Joseph, Multimedia Journalist
6045755340
bjoseph@surreyleader.com

***Surrey:* The Link**
#203, 12725 - 80th Ave., Surrey, BC V3W 3A6
Tel: 604-591-5160; *Fax:* 604-591-2113
ads@thelinkpaper.ca
www.thelinkpaper.ca
Focus on both British Columbia & international South Asian news & issues
Paul R. Dhillon, Editor-in-chief
editor@thelinkpaper.ca

***Surrey:* The Now**
Owned By: Glacier Newspapers Group
#201, 7889 - 132nd St., Surrey, BC V3W 4N2
Tel: 604-572-0064
delivery@thenownewspaper.com
www.thenownewspaper.com
Other information: Distribution, Phone: 604-534-6493; Classifieds: 604-444-3000
Social Media:
twitter.com/TheNowNewspaper
www.facebook.com/thesurreynow
Circulation: 116,000+; *Frequency:* Tuesday, Friday
The area covered by the newspaper includes Surrey, Whiterock, & Noth Delta, British Columbia.
Gary Hollick, Publisher
ghollick@thenownewspaper.com
Beau Simpson, Editor
bsimpson@thenownewspaper.com

***Surrey:* The Peace Arch News**
Owned By: Black Press Group Ltd.
#200, 2411 - 160 St., Surrey, BC V3S 0C8
Tel: 604-531-1711
www.peacearchnews.com
Social Media:
twitter.com/whiterocknews
www.facebook.com/pages/Peace-Arch-News/135146319865795
Circulation: 37,000+; *Frequency:* Tuesday, Thursday
The Peace Arch News serves communities on the Semiahmoo Peninsula, including South Surrey & White Rock.
Rita Walters, Publisher
publisher@peacearchnews.com
Lance Peverley, Editor & Columnist
604-542-7402
lpeverley@peacearchnews.com
Jim Chmelyk, Manager, Creative Services
604-542-7420
jim@peacearchnews.com
Marilou Pasion, Manager, Circulation
604-542-7430
marilou@peacearchnews.com

***Terrace:* Terrace Standard**
Owned By: Black Press Group Ltd.
3210 Clinton Ave., Terrace, BC V8G 5R2
Tel: 250-638-7283; *Fax:* 250-638-8432
www.terracestandard.com
Social Media:
twitter.com/terracestandard
www.facebook.com/pages/Terrace-Standard/1715 47382936857
Circulation: 8,000; *Frequency:* Wednesday
The newspaper employs fifteen staff members in its Terrace office.
Rod Link, Publisher & Editor
rodlink@terracestandard.com
Brian Lindenbach, Manager, Sales
brianl@terracestandard.com
Margaret Speirs, Community Reporter
newsroom@terracestandard.com

***Tumbler Ridge:* Tumbler Ridge News**
#120, 230 Main St., Tumbler Ridge, BC V0C 2W0
Tel: 250-242-5343; *Fax:* 250-242-5340
mail@tumblerridgenews.com
www.tumblerridgenews.com
Social Media:
www.facebook.com/TumblerRidgeNews
Circulation: 1,500; *Frequency:* Wednesday
Loraine Funk, Publisher
Trent Ernst, Editor
2502425597
editor@tumblerridgenews.com
Colette Ernst, Manager
2502425300
sales@tumblerridgenews.com
Roxanne Braam, Contact, Classifieds
2502425343
frontdesk@tumblerridgenews.com

***Ucluelet:* Tofino-Ucluelet Westerly News**
Owned By: Glacier Newspapers Group
PO Box 317, #1, 1920 Lyche Rd., Ucluelet, BC V0R 3A0
Tel: 250-726-7029; *Fax:* 250-726-4282
office@westerlynews.ca; reporter@westerlynews.ca
www.westerlynews.ca
Other information: Classified Advertising, E-mail: classifieds@van.net
Social Media:
twitter.com/WesterlyNews
www.facebook.com/group.php?gid=1980561569 72097
Circulation: 987; *Frequency:* Thursday

Hugh Nicholson, Publisher
2507294257
hnicholson@glaciermedia.ca
Jacqueline Carmichael, Editor

***Valemount:* The Valley Sentinel**
Owned By: Aberdeen Publishig Group
PO Box 688, 1012 Commercial Dr., Valemount, BC V0E 2Z0
Tel: 250-566-4425; *Fax:* 250-566-4528
Toll-Free: 800-226-2129
ads@thevalleysentinel.com
www.thevalleysentinel.com
Social Media: www.linkedin.com/company/the-valley-sentinel
twitter.com/@ValleySentinel
facebook.com/valleysentinelnewspaper
Circulation: 690; *Frequency:* Wednesday
The Valley Sentinel Robson Valley communities, including Valemount & McBride.
Kelly Hall, Publisher
publisher@thevalleysentinel.com
Daniel Betts, Editor
editor@thevalleysentinel.com

***Vancouver:* Apna Roots**
PO Box 2296, Vancouver, BC V6B 3W5
Tel: 604-599-5408; *Fax:* 604-599-5415
indo@telus.net
www.apnaroots.com
Circulation: 15,000; *Frequency:* Fri., bi-weekly
Published for an Indo-Canadian/South Asian audience; covers developments in Science & Technology, Education & Careers, Health & Fitness, Parenting, & Beauty & Lifestyle. Also features editorials that discuss serious issues confronting ethnic communities, e.g. terrorism, the role of women, gangs, drug problems, etc.
Rue Hayer Bains, Publisher

***Vancouver:* Country Life in BC**
1120 East 13th Ave., Vancouver, BC V5T 2M1
Tel: 250-871-0001; *Fax:* 250-871-0003
countrylifeinbc@shaw.ca
www.countrylifeinbc.com
Frequency: Monthly
Country Life in BC provides agricultural news for farmers in British Columbia.
Peter Wilding, Publisher & Editor
604-871-0001; Fax: 604-871-0003
David Schmidt, Associate Editor
604-793-9193
davidschmidt@shaw.ca
Cathy Glover, Contact
604-328-3814; Fax: 604-946-5919
cathyglover@telus.net

***Vancouver:* L'Express du Pacifique**
#227A, 1555, 7e av ouest, Vancouver, BC V6J 1S1
Tél: 604-736-3734; *Téléc:* 604-736-3740
administration@lexpress.org
www.lexpress.org
Tirage: 1 800; *Fréquence:* Lundi; aux deux semaines
Stéphanie Descôteaux
Raphael Perdrau, directeur de la publication
Cécil Lepage, journaliste

***Vancouver:* Indo-Canadian Times**
PO Box 2296, Vancouver, BC V6B 3W5
Tel: 604-599-5408; *Fax:* 604-599-5415
indo@telus.net
blogs.vancouversun.com/tag/indo-canadian-times
Circulation: 32,000; *Frequency:* Wed.
Oldest and largest circulating Punjabi newspaper in Canada
Rupinder Hayer, Publisher

***Vancouver:* Jewish Independent**
Previous Name: Jewish Western Bulletin
#99, 291 East 2nd Ave., Vancouver, BC V5T 1B8
Tel: 604-689-1520
editor@jewishindependent.ca
jewishindependent.ca
Social Media:
twitter.com/jiviews
www.facebook.com/pages/Jewish-Independent/1835431450065 90
Circulation: 5,000; *Frequency:* Weekly
Cynthia Ramsay, Publisher
cramsay@jewishindependent.ca
Basya Laye, Editor
editor@jewishindependent.ca
Leanne Jacobsen, Contact, Advertising
sales@jewishindependent.ca
Steve Freedman, Contact, Classified Advertising
sfreedman@jewishindependent.ca

***Vancouver:* The Vancouver Courier**
Owned By: Glacier Newspapers Group
1574 - West 6th Ave., Vancouver, BC V6J 1R2
Tel: 604-738-1411
delivery@vancourier.com; releases@vancourier.com
www.vancourier.com
Other information: Community Events: events@vancourier.com
Social Media:
twitter.com/VanCourierNews
www.facebook.com/TheVancouverCourierNewspaper
Circulation: 123,092; *Frequency:* Wednesday, Friday
Dee Dhaliwal, Publisher
604-630-3521
ddhaliwal@vancourier.com
Barry Link, Editor
blink@vancourier.com
Tara Lalanne, Director
tlalanne@vancourier.com

***Vancouver:* WestEnder**
Owned By: Black Press Group Ltd.
#205, 1525 8th Ave. West, Vancouver, BC V6J 1T5
Tel: 604-606-8686
www.westender.com
Social Media:
twitter.com/wevancouver
www.facebook.com/WEVancouver
Circulation: 53,000+; *Frequency:* Thursday
Dee Dhaliwal, Publisher
604-630-3521
ddhaliwal@vancourier.com
Robert Mangelsdorf, Editor
604-742-8695
editor@wevancouver.com
Kelsey Klassen, Reporter
604-742-8699
kelsey@wevancouver.com
Miguel Black, Manager, Circulation
604-742-8676
circulation@wevancouver.com
Gail Nugent, Director, Management
604 742-8678
gnugent@wevancouver.com

***Vancouver:* Westside Revue**
1736A East 33rd Ave., Vancouver, BC V5N 3E2
Tel: 604-327-1665
Circulation: 7,600; *Frequency:* Bi-weekly
Rod Raglin, Publisher & Editor

***Vanderhoof:* Omineca Express**
Owned By: Black Press Group Ltd.
PO Box 1007, 150 Columbia St. West, Vanderhoof, BC V0J 3A0
Tel: 250-567-9258; *Fax:* 250-567-2070
newsroom@ominecaexpress.com
www.ominecaexpress.com
Social Media:
twitter.com/vanderhoofnews
www.facebook.com/pages/Vanderhoof-Omineca-Express/11349 81
Circulation: 890; *Frequency:* Wednesday
The newspaper serves the British Columbia communities of Vanderhoof, Fraser Lake, & Fort Fraser.
Pam Berger, Publisher & Manager, Sales
publisher@ominecaexpress.com
Sam Redding, Editor
newsroom@ominecaexpress.com
Wendy Haslam, Contact, Production Department
wendy@ominecaexpress.com
Anne Stevens, Contact, Front Office, Circulation Sales & Classified Sales
office@ominecaexpress.com

***Vernon:* The Morning Star**
Owned By: Black Press Group Ltd.
4407 - 25th Ave., Vernon, BC V1T 1P5
Tel: 250-545-3322
newsroom@vernonmorningstar.com
www.vernonmorningstar.com
Social Media:
twitter.com/vernonnews
www.facebook.com/pages/Vernon-Morning-Star/192507 09412252
Circulation: 30,000+; *Frequency:* Sunday, Wednesday, Friday
News is covered in the North Okanagan communities of Vernon, Oyama, Cherryville, Lavington, Coldstream, Silver Star, Armstrong, Falkland Lumby, Enderby, North Westside, Grindrod, Kingfisher, Ashton Creek, Mabel Lake, the Okanagan Indian Band, Spallumcheen, & the Splatsin First Nation.

Ian Jensen, Publisher
250-550-7906
publisher@vernonmorningstar.com
Glenn Mitchell, Managing Editor & Columnist
250-550-7920
glenn@vernonmorningstar.com
Kristin Froneman, Entertainment Editor & Columnist
250-550-7923
entertainment@vernonmorningstar.com
Roger Knox, Web Editor & Columnist
250-550-7922
roger@vernonmorningstar.com
Kevin Mitchell, Sports Editor
250-550-7902
sports@vernonmorningstar.com
Tammy Stelmachowich, Circulation Manager
250-550-7901
circulation@vernonmorningstar.com
Carol Williment, Classified Manager
250-550-7900
classifieds@vernonmorningstar.com
Lisa VanderVelde, Reporter & Photographer
250-550-7909
lisa@vernonmorningstar.comtar.com

Victoria: Lookout
c/o CFB Esquimalt, PO Box 17000 Forces, 1522 Esquimalt Rd., Victoria, BC V9A 7N2
Tel: 250-363-3127; *Fax:* 250-363-3015
frontoffice@lookoutnewspaper.com
www.lookoutnewspaper.com
Social Media:
twitter.com/Lookout_news
www.facebook.com/lookout.newspaper
Frequency: Monday
The newspaper contains news & information about the Canadian Navy.
Melissa Atkinson, Publisher
melissa.atkinson@forces.gc.ca
Shawn O'Hara, Writer
250-363-3672
shawn.ohara3@forces.gc.ca
Raquel Tirado, Supervisor, Office Accounts
raquel.tirado@forces.gc.ca
Ivan Groth, Sales Representative
sales@lookoutnewspaper.com

Victoria: Oak Bay News
Previous Name: Oak Bay Star
Owned By: Black Press Group Ltd.
818 Broughton St., Victoria, BC V8W 1E4
Tel: 250-381-3484
viads@bcclassified.com (classified advertising)
www.oakbaynews.com
Social Media:
twitter.com/oakbaynews
www.facebook.com/OakBayNews
Circulation: 6304; *Frequency:* Wednesday, Friday
Laura Lavin, Editor
editor@oakbaynews.com

Victoria: Saanich News
Owned By: Black Press News Group Ltd.
818 Broughton St., Victoria, BC V8W 1E4
Tel: 250-381-3484
www.vicnews.com
Social Media:
twitter.com/saanichnews
facebook.com/saanichnews
Circulation: 30,000+; *Frequency:* Wednesday & Friday, Weekly
News is featured from the Vancouver Island municipality of Saanich. A print & an e-edition are available. Formerly Saanich News.
Penny Sakamoto, Publisher
2504803204
publisher@saanichnews.com
Edward Hill, Editor
2504803238
editor@saanichnews.com
Oliver Sommer, Contact, Advertising
2504803274
osommer@saanichnews.com

Victoria: Victoria News
Owned By: Black Press Group Ltd.
818 Broughton St., Victoria, BC V8W 1E4
Tel: 250-386-3484
editor@vicnews.com
www.vicnews.com
Social Media:
twitter.com/victorianews
www.facebook.com/victorianews
News is provided about Victoria & Equimalt, British Columbia. An e-edition is available.
Penny Sakamoto, Publisher
psakamoto@blackpress.ca
Don Descoteau, Editor
editor@vicnews.com
Bruce Hogarth, Director, Circulation
distribution@vicnews.com
Oliver Sommer, Director, Sales
osommer@blackpress.ca

Whistler: The Whistler Question
Owned By: Glacier Newspapers Group
#103, 1390 Alpha Lake Rd., Whistler, BC V0N 1B1
Tel: 604-932-5131; *Fax:* 604-932-2862
Toll-Free: 877-419-8866
www.whistlerquestion.com
Social Media:
twitter.com/whistlernews
www.facebook.com/whistlerquestion
Circulation: 6,900; *Frequency:* Tuesday
Serves the communities of Whistler, Pemberton, and Mt. Currie with select distribution in Greater Vancouver.
Stephanie Matches, Publisher
smatches@whistlerquestion.com
Alyssa Noel, Editor
editor@whistlerquestion.com

Williams Lake: The Cariboo Advisor
Owned By: Black Press Group Ltd.
68 North Broadway Ave., Williams Lake, BC V2G 1C1
Tel: 250-398-5516
wltribune.com
Social Media:
www.facebook.com/pages/The-Cariboo-Advisor/2841481549468 7
Circulation: 10,200; *Frequency:* Fri.
Amalgamated with the Williams Lake Tribune (Wed., weekly) in 2013
Kathy McLean, Publisher
Rob DeMone, Editor

Williams Lake: Williams Lake Tribune
Owned By: Black Press Group Ltd.
188 North First Ave., Williams Lake, BC V2G 1Y8
Tel: 250-392-2331
editor@wltribune.com
www.wltribune.com
Social Media:
twitter.com/williamslnews
www.facebook.com/pages/Williams-Lake-Tribune/232460703435
Circulation: 7,200; *Frequency:* Wednesday
The Williams Lake Tribune employs 45 full & part-time people.
Lisa Bowering, Publisher & Manager, Advertising
publisher@wltribune.com
Angie Mindus, Acting Editor
editor@wltribune.com
Gaeil Farrar, Community Editor
community@wltribune.com
Lynn Bolt, Contact, Classifieds
classifieds@wltribune.com

Manitoba

Daily Newspapers in Manitoba

Brandon: Brandon Sun
Owned By: FP Newspapers Inc.
501 Rosser Ave., Brandon, MB R7A 0K4
Tel: 204-727-2451
circ@brandonsun.com; opinion@brandonsun.com
www.brandonsun.com
Other information: Classified Advertising, Phone: 204-571-7400; Newsroom: 204-571-7430
Social Media:
twitter.com/thebrandonsun
www.facebook.com/thebrandonsun
Circulation: 68,410 total; *Frequency:* Daily
The Brandon Sun publishes seven day a week & serves Brandon & southwestern Manitoba.
Eric Lawson, Publisher
204-571-7401

Flin Flon: The Reminder
Owned By: Glacier Media Inc.
14 North Ave., Flin Flon, MB R8A 0T2
Tel: 204-687-3454
ads@thereminder.ca
www.thereminder.ca
Social Media:
www.facebook.com/FlinFlonReminder
Circulation: 1300 M; 1300 W; 1600 F; 4200 total; *Frequency:* Monday, Wednesday, Friday
Communities served by The Reminder include Flin Flon, Denare Beach, Snow Lake, Creighton, & Cranberry Portage, Manitoba.
Valerie Durnin, Publisher
publisher@thereminder.ca
Jonathon Naylor, Editor
news@thereminder.ca
John Bettger, Production Manager, Production
production@thereminder.com

Portage la Prairie: Portage Daily Graphic
Owned By: Postmedia Network Inc.
1941 Saskatchewan Ave. West, Portage la Prairie, MB R1N 0R7
Tel: 204-857-3427; *Fax:* 204-239-1270
www.portagedailygraphic.com
Social Media:
twitter.com/TheDailyGraphic
www.facebook.com/pages/Portage-Daily-Graphic/217303238304
Frequency: Weekly, Tuesday
Johnna Ruocco, Editor
cphl.editor@sunmedia.ca
Daria Zmiyiwsky, Director of Advertising
daria.zmiyiwsky@sunmedia.ca

Winnipeg: Winnipeg Free Press
Owned By: FP Newspapers Inc.
1355 Mountain Ave., Winnipeg, MB R2X 3B6
Tel: 204-697-7000; *Fax:* 204-697-7412
letters@freepress.mb.ca (letters to the editor)
www.winnipegfreepress.com
Other information: News Tips: city.desk@freepress.mb.ca
Social Media: www.youtube.com/user/WinnipegFreePress
twitter.com/WinnipegNews
www.fa cebook.com/winnipegfreepress
Circulation: 663,431 total; *Frequency:* Monday-Saturday
Bob Cox, Publisher
204-697-7547
bob.cox@freepress.mb.ca
Paul Samyn, Editor
204-697-7295
paul.samyn@freepress.mb.ca

Winnipeg: The Winnipeg Sun
Owned By: Postmedia Network Inc.
1700 Church Ave., Winnipeg, MB R2X 3A2
Tel: 204-632-2780
wpgsun.citydesk@sunmedia.ca
www.winnipegsun.com
Social Media:
twitter.com/WinnipegSun
www.facebook.com/wpgsun
Circulation: 375,876 total; *Frequency:* Daily
Mark Hamm, Editor
mark.hamm@sunmedia.ca
Daria Zmiyiwsky, Director of Advertising
daria.zmiyiwsky@sunmedia.ca

Other Newspapers in Manitoba

Altona: The Red River Valley Echo
Owned By: Sun Media Corp.
PO Box 700, Altona, MB R0G 0B0
Tel: 204-324-5001; *Fax:* 204-324-1402
www.altonaecho.com
Social Media:
twitter.com/AltonaEcho
facebook.com/RedRiverValleyEcho
Circulation: 4,500; *Frequency:* Thursday
Darcie Morris, Publisher
darcie.morris@sunmedia.ca
Don Radford, Regional Managing Editor
winkler.news@sunmedia.ca
Greg Vandermeulen, City Editor
altona.news@sunmedia.ca

Baldur: Baldur-Glenboro Gazette
Previous Name: Baldur Gazette; Baldur Gazette News
PO Box 280, 223 Elizabeth Ave., Baldur, MB R0K 0B0
Tel: 204-535-2127; *Fax:* 204-535-2350
gazette@mts.net
www.baldur-glenborogazette.ca
Other information: Glenboro Office, Phone: 204-827-2343, E-mail: gazette2@mts.net
Circulation: 1,500; *Frequency:* Tuesday
The Baldur Gazette News amalgamated with the Glenboro Gazette in 2003 to create the Baldur-Glenboro Gazette. The newspaper serves the southwestern Manitoba communities of Baldur, Glenboro, Belmont, Glenora, Cypress River, Stockton, Ninette, Wawanesa, & Treesbank.
Mike Johnson, Co-Publisher & Editor

Travis Johnson, Co-Publisher & Assistant Editor

Beausejour: **The Clipper Weekly**
Owned By: Clipper Publishing Corp.
PO Box 2033, 27A - 3rd St. South, Beausejour, MB R0E 0C0
Tel: 204-268-4700; *Fax:* 204-268-3858
mail@clipper.mb.ca
www.clipper.mb.ca
Social Media:
www.facebook.com/group.php?gid=227001374012429
Circulation: 12,000+; *Frequency:* Thurs.
Community news is provided to the North Eastman Region of Manitoba, including the communities of Beausejour, Dugald, Tyndall, Whitemouth, Oakbank, Anola, Garson, & Lac du Bonnet. Readership stands at 83%.
Kim MacAulay, Publisher
macaulay@clipper.mb.ca
Mark T. Buss, Editor
news@clipper.mb.ca
Jennifer Kuhn, Manager, Office
Traci Klimchuk, Contact, Display Advertising
traci@clipper.mb.ca

Boissevain: **Boissevain Recorder**
Boissevain Recorder Inc., PO Box 220, 425 South Railway St., Boissevain, MB R0K 0E0
Tel: 204-534-6479; *Fax:* 204-534-2977
news@therecorder.ca; subscribe@therecorder.ca
www.therecorder.ca
Other information: Classified Advertising: classifieds@therecorder.ca
Circulation: 1,200; *Frequency:* Friday
Lorraine Houston, Editor
editor@therecorder.ca
Paul Rayner, Reporter
prayner@therecorder.ca
Julie Watt, Contact, Circulation & Accounts
mail@therecorder.ca
Christie Paskewitz-Smith, Contact, Advertising & Printing
ads@therecorder.ca

Brandon: **Westman Journal**
Previous Name: Wheat City Journal
Owned By: Glacier Newspapers Group
315 College Ave., Unit D, Brandon, MB R7A 1E7
Tel: 204-725-0209; *Fax:* 204-725-3021
info@wheatcityjournal.ca
www.westmanjournal.com
Social Media:
twitter.com/ChrisTataryn
www.facebook.com/pages/Westman-Journal/22 2064044474022
Circulation: 15,000; *Frequency:* Wed.
Todd Hamilton, Editor
newsroom@wheatcityjournal.ca
Lorraine Dillabough, Manager, Production
ldillabough@wheatcityjournal.ca

Carberry: **The Carberry News-Express**
Owned By: FP Newspapers Inc.
Carberry News-Express Ltd., 34 Main St., Carberry, MB R0K 0H0
Tel: 204-834-2153; *Fax:* 204-834-2714
info@carberrynews.ca
www.carberrynews.ca
Circulation: 930; *Frequency:* Weekly; Monday
Kathy Carr, General Manager
kathy@carberrynews.ca

Carman: **The Valley Leader**
Owned By: Sun Media Corp.
70 Main St., Carman, MB R0G 0J0
Tel: 204-745-2051; *Fax:* 204-745-3976
www.carmanvalleyleader.com
Circulation: 5,852; *Frequency:* Friday
Darcie Morris, Publisher
darcie.morris@suntimes.ca
Don Radford, Regional Managing Editor
winkler.news@suntimes.ca
Gene Still, City Editor
carmanvl.news@suntimes.ca

Cartwright: **Southern Manitoba Review**
PO Box 249, Cartwright, MB R0K 0L0
Tel: 204-529-2342; *Fax:* 204-529-2029
cartnews@mts.net
www.southernmanitobareview.com
Circulation: 785; *Frequency:* Thursday
Vicky M. Wallace, Publisher

Darlingford: **The Southern Shopper & Review**
RR#2, Darlingford, MB R0G 0L0
Tel: 204-362-2666; *Fax:* 204-246-2018
southernshopper@mts.net
www.southernshopperonline.ca
Frequency: Bi-weekly
The Southern Shopper & Review serves communities in southern Manitoba.

Dauphin: **The Dauphin Herald**
Previous Name: The Weekly News; The Spectator; Dauphin Herald & Press
Owned By: Gilroy Publishing
PO Box 548, 120 - 1st Ave. NE, Dauphin, MB R7N 1A5
Tel: 204-638-4420; *Fax:* 204-638-8760
dherald@mts.net
www.dauphinherald.com
Circulation: 4,143; *Frequency:* Tuesday
Shawn Bailey, Editor
shawn@dauphinherald.com
Mandy Carberry, Manager, Circulation & Distribution
circ@dauphinherald.com
Bob Gilroy, Manager, Print Shop
bob@dauphinherald.com
Brent Wright, Manager, Advertising
displayads@dauphinherald.com
Samantha Gallaway-Boulbria, Contact, Classified Advertising
classifieds@dauphinherald.com

Deloraine: **Deloraine Times & Star**
Owned By: Glacier Newspaper Group
PO Box 407, 122 Broadway St. North, Deloraine, MB R0M 0M0
Tel: 204-747-2249; *Fax:* 204-747-3999
Circulation: 746; *Frequency:* Friday
Judy Wells, Publisher
cpocket@mts.net
Marlene Tilbury, Contact, Sales
204-522-3491
ads.cpocket@mts.net

Emerson: **The Southeast Journal**
PO Box 68, 104 1/2 Dominion St., Emerson, MB R0A 0L0
Tel: 204-373-2493; *Fax:* 204-373-2084
sej@mts.net
www.southeastjournal.ca
Circulation: 3,390; *Frequency:* Sat.
News is covered in the Manitoba communities of Emerson, Morris, Dominion City, Tolstoi, Woodmore, Riverside/Rosenort, & Ridgeville.
Brenda Piett, Co-Publisher & Contact, Sales & Circulation
Don Piett, Co-Publisher & Editor

Grandview: **Grandview Exponent**
Owned By: Chaloner Publishers
PO Box 39, Grandview, MB R0L 0Y0
Tel: 204-546-2555; *Fax:* 204-546-3081
expos@mts.net
www.grandviewexponent.com
Circulation: 1,000; *Frequency:* Tuesday
Clayton Chaloner, Publisher & Editor

Killarney: **The Guide**
Struth Publishing Ltd., PO Box 670, 336 Park St. East, Killarney, MB R0K 1G0
Tel: 204-523-4611; *Fax:* 204-523-4445
info@killarneyguide.ca
www.killarneyguide.ca
Circulation: 1,655; *Frequency:* Friday
The newspaper is available in print & online.
Jay Struth, Editor
news@killarneyguide.ca
Curt Struth, Manager, Printing & Advertising
printing@killarneyguide.ca

Manitou: **Manitou Western Canadian**
Owned By: BKS Publishing Ltd.
PO Box 190, 424 Ellis Ave. East, Manitou, MB R0G 1G0
Tel: 204-242-2555; *Fax:* 204-242-3137
westerncanadian@goinet.ca
Circulation: 1,245; *Frequency:* Tuesday
Grant Howatt, Publisher

Melita: **Corner Pocket**
Owned By: Glacier Media Inc.
PO Box 820, 128 Main St., Melita, MB R0M 1L0
Tel: 204-522-3491; *Fax:* 204-522-3648
cpocket@mts.net
www.glaciermedia.ca/advertisers/local-newspapers/corner-pocket
Circulation: 20,000; *Frequency:* Monthly
Sent to households in Southwestern Manitoba & Southeastern Saskatchewan.

Melita: **Melita New Era**
Owned By: Glacier Newspaper Group
PO Box 820, 128 Main St. South, Melita, MB R0M 1L0
Tel: 204-522-3491; *Fax:* 204-522-3648
Circulation: 1,104; *Frequency:* Friday
The newspaper serves southwestern Manitoba & southeastern Saskatchewan.
G. Longmuir, Manager
cpocket@mts.net
Marlene Tilbury, Contact, Sales
ads.cpocket@mts.net

Minnedosa: **Minnedosa Tribune**
PO Box 930, 14 - 3rd Ave. SW, Minnedosa, MB R0J 1E0
Tel: 204-867-3816; *Fax:* 204-867-5171
www.minnedosatribune.com
Circulation: 2,480; *Frequency:* Friday
Darryl Holyk, Publisher & Editor
editor@minnedosatribune.com
Gloria Kerluke, Office Manager & Contact, Classifieds
class@minnedosatribune.com
Jennifer Page, Reporter & Photographer
reporter@minnedosatribune.com
Nathalie Loughlin, Contact, Graphic Design & Ad Sales
adsales@minnedosatribune.com

Morden: **The Morden Times**
Owned By: Sun Media Corp.
104 - 8th St., Morden, MB R6M 1Y7
Tel: 204-822-4421; *Fax:* 204-822-4079
www.mordentimes.com
Social Media:
twitter.com/MordenTimes
facebook.com/mordentimes
Circulation: 5,600; *Frequency:* Thursday
Jack Neufeld, Publisher & Advertising Director
jack.neufeld@sunmedia.ca
Lorne Stelmach, City Editor
mordentimes.new@sunmedia.ca

Neepawa: **Neepawa Banner**
Owned By: 3259545 (Manitoba) Ltd.
PO Box 699, 243 Hamilton St., Neepawa, MB R0J 1H0
Tel: 204-476-3401; *Fax:* 204-476-5073
Toll-Free: 888-436-4242
www.neepawabanner.com
Social Media: www.youtube.com/TheNeepawaBanner
twitter.com/NeepawaBanner
www.faceboo k.com/neepawabanner
Circulation: 8,228; *Frequency:* Friday
Ken Waddell, Owner, Publisher, & Contact, Sales
kwaddell@neepawabanner.com
Kate Jackman-Atkinson, Reporter & Photographer
news@neepawabanner.com
Kay De'Ath, Contact, Accounts & Circulation
accounts@neepawabanner.com
Lanny Stewart, Contact, Sports
sports@neepawabanner.com
Sandra Unger, Contact, Front Desk
print@neepawabanner.com

Neepawa: **Neepawa Press**
Owned By: Glacier Newspaper Group
PO Box 939, 423 Mountain Ave., Neepawa, MB R0J 1H0
Tel: 204-476-2309; *Fax:* 204-476-5802
office@neepawapress.com
www.neepawapress.com
Other information: Classified Advertising, E-mail: classified@neepawapress.com
Circulation: 7,200; *Frequency:* Wednesday
Brent Fitzpatrick, Regional Publisher
pub@sasktel.net
Darren Graham, General Manager
advertising@neepawapress.com
Jean Seaborn, Manager, Office
office@neepawapress.com

Pilot Mound: **The Sentinel Courier**
PO Box 179, 13 Railway St. South, Pilot Mound, MB R0G 1P0
Tel: 204-825-2772; *Fax:* 204-825-2439
sentinel@sentinelcourier.com
www.sentinelcourier.com
Circulation: 1,100; *Frequency:* Tuesday
The Sentinel Courier serves the Manitoba communities of Pilot Mound, Clearwater, Mariapolis, La Riviere, & Crystal City.
Susan Peterson, Publisher

***Portage la Prairie:* Central Manitoba Shopper & News**
1943 Saskatchewan Ave. West, Portage la Prairie, MB R1N 0R7
Tel: 204-857-7582; *Fax:* 204-239-5437
cmshopper@shawcable.com
Frequency: Weekly

***Reston:* Reston Recorder**
Owned By: Glacier Newspaper Group
PO Box 10, 330 - 4th St., Reston, MB R0M 1X0
Tel: 204-877-3321; *Fax:* 204-522-3648
Circulation: 570; *Frequency:* Friday
Dolores Caldwell, Manager
cpocket@mts.net
Donna Anderson, Contact, Sales
ads.cpocket@mts.net

***Rivers:* Gilroy Publishing**
526 - 2nd Ave., Rivers, MB R0K 1X0
Tel: 204-328-7494

***Rivers:* Rivers Banner**
Owned By: 3259545 (Manitoba) Ltd.
PO Box 70, Rivers, MB R0K 1X0
Tel: 204-328-7494; *Fax:* 204-328-5212
info@riversbanner.com
www.riversbanner.com
Social Media: www.youtube.com/TheNeepawaBanner
Circulation: 1,683; *Frequency:* Weekly; Friday
Ken Waddell, Owner & Publisher

***Rivers:* 3259545 (Manitoba) Ltd.**
526 - 2nd Ave., Rivers, MB R0K 1X0
Tel: 204-328-7494

***Roblin:* The Roblin Review**
Owned By: Gilroy Publishing
PO Box 938, 119 - 1st Ave., Roblin, MB R0L 1P0
Tel: 204-937-8377; *Fax:* 204-937-8212
rreview@mts.net; reviewads@mts.net
www.theroblinreview.com
Circulation: 1,635; *Frequency:* Tuesday
Robert Gilroy, Publisher
Brent Wright, General Manager
Ed Doering, Editor

***Russell:* Russell Banner**
Owned By: Gilroy Publishing
PO Box 100, 455 Main St. North, Russell, MB R0J 1W0
Tel: 204-773-2069; *Fax:* 204-773-2645
www.russellbanner.com
Circulation: 1,411; *Frequency:* Tuesday
Terrie Welwood, Editor & Reporter
rbeditor@mts.net
Jessica Shaw, Contact, Advertising
rbanner@mts.net
Jenna Simard, Contact, Subscriptions & Accounts
russellbanner@mts.net

***Selkirk:* The Selkirk Journal**
Owned By: Sun Media Corp.
PO Box 352, 510 Greenwood Ave., Selkirk, MB R1A 2B3
Tel: 204-467-2421; *Fax:* 204-482-3336
www.selkirkjournal.com
Social Media:
twitter.com/SelkirkJournal
facebook.com/pages/Selkirk-/373966049285954
Circulation: 15,700; *Frequency:* Thursday
Jenifer Bilsky, Publisher
jenifer.bilsky@sunmedia.ca
Glen Hallick, Group Editor
glen.hallick@sunmedia.ca
Amanda Lefley, City Editor
amanda.lefley@sunmedia.ca

***Shilo:* Shilo Stag**
PO Box 5000 Main, CFB Shilo, Shilo, MB R0K 2A0
Tel: 204-765-3000; *Fax:* 204-765-3814
stag@mymts.net
www.cfcommunitygeteway.ca
Other information: Phone ext. 3093
Social Media:
www.facebook.com/ShiloSTAG
Circulation: 3,000; *Frequency:* Bi-weekly; Thursday
The Canadian Forces newspaper serves the military & civilian communities of CFB Shilo, Wawanesa, Sprucewoods, Cottonwoods, & Douglas.
Jules Xavier, Managing Editor
204-765-3000; Fax: 204-765-3814
jules.xavier@forces.gc.ca
Jillian Driessen, Reporter & Photographer, Editorial
204-365-3000; Fax: 204-765-3814
jillian.driessen@forces.gc.ca

***Shoal Lake:* Crossroads This Week**
Previous Name: Birtle Eye-Witness
Owned By: Nesbitt Publishing Ltd.
PO Box 160, 353 Station Rd., Shoal Lake, MB R0J 1Z0
Tel: 204-759-2644; *Fax:* 204-759-2521
ctwnews@mts.net
www.crossroadsthisweek.com
Circulation: 2,525; *Frequency:* Weekly; Friday
Greg Nesbitt, Publisher
ctwnews@mts.net

***Souris:* Souris Plaindealer**
Owned By: Glacier Media Inc.
PO Box 488, 35 Crescent Ave. West, Souris, MB R0K 2C0
Tel: 204-483-2070; *Fax:* 204-483-3866
Circulation: 789; *Frequency:* Friday
Darci Semeschuk, Manager
204-483-2070
cpocket@mts.net
Marlene Tilbury, Contact, Sales
204-522-3491
ads.cpocket@mts.net

***St-Boniface:* La Liberté**
Owned By: Presse Ouest Ltée.
PO Box 190, #105, 420 rue des Meurons, St-Boniface, MB R2H 3B4
Tel: 204-237-4823; *Fax:* 204-231-1998
Toll-Free: 800-523-3355
la-liberte@la-liberte.mb.ca
www.la-liberte.mb.ca/le-journal
Social Media:
www.youtube.com/user/LaLiberteMB?feature=mhum
twitter.com/LaLiberteMB
www.facebook.com/LaLiberteManitoba
Circulation: 5000; *Frequency:* Weekly
La Liberté is a French language newspaper.
Sophie Gaulin, Editor
la-liberte@la-liberte.mb.ca
Lysiane Romain, Assistant Editor & Coordinator, Special Projects
promotions@la-liberte.mb.ca
Véronique Togneri, Production Manager & Graphics Specialist

***Steinbach:* The Carillon**
377 Main St., Steinbach, MB R5G 1A5
Tel: 204-326-3421; *Fax:* 204-326-4860
info@thecarillon.com
www.thecarillon.com
Other information: Advertising, E-mail: ads@thecarillon.com
Social Media:
facebook.com/thecarillon
Circulation: 6,000; *Frequency:* Thursday
The Carillon serves Steinbach southeastern Manitoba. Derksen Printers & Publishers publishes the newspaper.
Glenn Buffie, Publisher & General Manager
gbuffie@thecarillon.com
Grant Burr, Editor
gburr@thecarillon.com
Terry Frey, Editor, Sports
tfrey@thecarillon.com
Carol Martens, Editor, Community News
cmartens@thecarillon.com
Kelsey Wynn, Manager, Circulation
kwynn@thecarillon.com

***Stonewall:* The Interlake Spectator**
Owned By: Sun Media Corp.
PO Box 190, #3, 411 - 3rd Ave., Stonewall, MB R0C 2Z0
Tel: 204-642-2421
www.interlakespectator.com
Circulation: 14,341; *Frequency:* Friday
Jenifer Bilsky, Publisher
jenifer.bilsky@sunmedia.ca
Glen Hallick, Group Editor
glen.halick@sunmedia.ca

***Stonewall:* The Stonewall Argus & Teulon Times**
Owned By: Sun Media Corp.
PO Box 190, #3, 411 - 3rd Ave. South, Stonewall, MB R0C 2Z0
Tel: 204-467-2421; *Fax:* 204-467-5967
stonewallargusteulontimes.com
Social Media:
twitter.com/Stonewall_argus
facebook.com/pages/Stonewall-/36283422706123 2
Circulation: 6,700; *Frequency:* Thursday
Jenifer Bilsky, Publisher
jenifer.bilsky@sunmedia.ca
Glen Halick, Group Editor
glen.halick@sunmedia.ca
Brook Jones, City Editor
brook.jones@sunmedia.ca

***Swan River:* The Swan Valley Star & Times**
Owned By: Gilroy Publishing
PO Box 670, 704 Main St., Swan River, MB R0L 1Z0
Tel: 204-734-3858; *Fax:* 204-734-4935
info@starandtimes.ca; office@starandtimes.ca
www.starandtimes.ca
Circulation: 2,985; *Frequency:* Tuesday
Brian Gilroy, Publisher & General Manager
brian@starandtimes.ca
Danielle Gordon-Broome, Editor
editor@starandtimes.ca
Tara Grey, Reporter & Photographer
reporter@starandtimes.ca
Kelley Hagglund, Contact, Classified Advertising
classifieds@starandtimes.ca

***The Pas:* Opasquia Times**
Owned By: Gilroy Publishing
PO Box 750, 148 Fischer Ave., The Pas, MB R9A 1K8
Tel: 204-623-3435; *Fax:* 204-623-5601
opads@mts.net (advertising)
www.opasquiatimes.com
Other information: Classified Advertising, E-mail: opclass@mts.net
Circulation: 2,609; *Frequency:* Biweekly; Wednesday, Friday
Opasquia Times presents news & information from the Opaskwayak Cree Nation, The Pas, the Rural Municipality of Kelsey, & the surrounding region.
Jennifer Cook, General Manager
optimes@mts.net
Trent Allen, Editor
opeditor@mts.net

***Thompson:* Nickel Belt News**
Owned By: Glacier Media Inc.
PO Box 887, 141 Commercial Pl., Thompson, MB R8N 1N8
Tel: 204-677-4534
Circulation: 7,000; *Frequency:* Friday
The Nickel Belt News is a free publication that circulates in Thompson & throughout northern Manitoba.
Brent Fitzpatrick, Publisher
Lynn Taylor, General Manager
generalmanager@thompsoncitizen.net
John Barker, Editor
editor@thompsoncitizen.net

***Thompson:* Thompson Citizen**
Owned By: Glacier Media Inc.
PO Box 887, 141 Commercial Pl., Thompson, MB R8N 1N8
Tel: 204-677-4534; *Fax:* 204-677-3681
ads@thompsoncitizen.net
www.thompsoncitizen.net
Social Media:
twitter.com/ThompsonCitizen
Circulation: 4,500; *Frequency:* Wednesday
Brent Fitzpatrick, Regional Publisher
pub@sasktel.net
Lynn Taylor, General Manager
generalmanager@thompsoncitizen.net
John Barker, Editor
editor@thompsoncitizen.net
Ryan Lynds, Manager, Production
production@thompsoncitizen.net
Ian Graham, Contact, Sports
sports@thompsoncitizen.net
Ashley Rust-McIvor, Contact, Classified Advertising
classified@thompsoncitizen.net

***Treherne:* The Times**
PO Box 50, 194 Broadway St., Treherne, MB R0G 2V0
Tel: 204-723-2542; *Fax:* 204-723-2754
trehernetimes@mts.net
www.trehernetimes.ca
Circulation: 2500; *Frequency:* Monday
The Times circulates in the Manitoba rural municipalities of South Norfolk, Victoria, Lorne, & Grey. The newspaper is available in print & online.
Daxley Lodwick, Editor

***Virden:* Virden Empire-Advance**
Owned By: Glacier Media Inc.
PO Box 250, #4, 585 Seventh Ave. South, Virden, MB R0M 2C0
Tel: 204-748-3931; *Fax:* 204-748-1816
www.empireadvance.ca

Circulation: 2,158; *Frequency:* Weekly; Friday
The newspaper serves the southwestern Manitoba communities of Virden, Elkhorn, Oak Lake, Reston, Pipestone, Miniota, Kenton, & Lenore.
Cheryl Rushing, General Manager
manager@empireadvance.ca

***Winkler:* The Winkler Times**
Owned By: Sun Media Corporation
PO Box 1356, Winkler, MB R6W 4B3
Tel: 204-325-4771; *Fax:* 204-325-5059
www.winklertimes.com
Social Media:
facebook.com/pages/Winkler-/223143737748598
Circulation: 7430; *Frequency:* Thursday
Darcie Morris, Publisher
darcie.morris@sunmedia.ca
Don Radford, Publisher
winkler.news@sunmedia.ca

***Winnipeg:* Headingley Headliner**
1355 Mountain Ave., Winnipeg, MB R2X 3B6
Tel: 204-697-7009; *Fax:* 204-953-4300
www.winnipegfreepress.com/our-communities/headliner
Circulation: 5,500; *Frequency:* Friday
Michelle Pereira, Publisher
John Kendle, Editor

***Winnipeg:* The Herald**
Owned By: FP Newspapers Inc.
1355 Mountain Ave., Winnipeg, MB R2X 3B6
Tel: 204-697-7009; *Fax:* 204-953-4300
classifieds@canstarnews.com
www.winnipegfreepress.com/our-communities/he rald
Social Media:
twitter.com/HeraldWPG
facebook.com/TheHeraldWpg
Circulation: 44,300; *Frequency:* Wednesday
Laurie Finley, Vice President, Sales, Marketing
204-697-7044
John Kendle, Managing Editor
204-697-7093

***Winnipeg:* The Jewish Post & News**
#11, 395 Berry St., Winnipeg, MB R3J 1N6
Tel: 204-694-3332; *Fax:* 204-694-3916
jewishp@mymts.net
www.jewishpostandnews.ca
Social Media: youtube.com/user/JewishPostWpg
twitter.com/JewishPostWpg
facebook.com/ TheJewishPost
Circulation: 2,779; *Frequency:* Weekly
The newspaper features local news & news from Israel, as well as features & opinions of interest to the Jewish community.
Bernie Bellan, Publisher
Matt Bellan, Publisher & Editor

***Winnipeg:* The Lance**
Owned By: FP Newspapers Inc.
1355 Mountain Ave., Winnipeg, MB R2X 3B6
Tel: 204-697-7009; *Fax:* 204-953-4300
www.winnipegfreepress.com/our-communities/lance
Social Media:
twitter.com/lanceWPG
facebook.com/TheLanceWpg
Circulation: 38,000; *Frequency:* Wed.
Laura Finley, Vice President, Sales & Marketing
laurie.finley@winnipegfreepress.com
John Kendle, Editor
john.kendle@canstarnews.com

***Winnipeg:* The Metro**
Owned By: FP Newspapers Inc.
1355 Mountain Ave., Winnipeg, MB R2X 3B6
Tel: 204-697-7009; *Fax:* 204-953-4300
www.winnipegfreepress.com/our-communities/metro
Social Media:
twitter.com/metroWPG
facebook.com/TheMetroWPG
Circulation: 35,500; *Frequency:* Wed.
Laurie Finley, Vice President, Sales & Marketing
laurie.finley@winnipegfreepress.com
John Kendle, Managing Editor
204-697-7093
john.kendle@canstarnews.com

***Winnipeg:* The Times**
Owned By: FP Newspapers Inc.
1355 Mountain Ave., Winnipeg, MB R2X 3B6
Tel: 204-697-7009; *Fax:* 204-953-4300
www.winnipegfreepress.com/our-communities/times
Social Media:
twitter.com/timesWPG
facebook.com/TheTimesWpg
Circulation: 37,400; *Frequency:* Wednesday
Laurie Finley, Vice President, Sales & Marketing
204-697-7164
laurie.finley@winnipegfreepress.com
John Kendle, Managing Editor
204-697-7093
john.kendle@canstarnews.com

***Winnipeg:* The Voxair**
PO Box 17000 Forces, #105, Bldg. 63, 17 Wing Winnipeg, Winnipeg, MB R3J 3Y5
Tel: 204-833-2500; *Fax:* 204-833-2809
voxair@mymts.net
www.thevoxair.ca
Other information: Accounting: accountsvoxair@gmail.com
Social Media:
www.facebook.com/thevoxair
Frequency: Bi-weekly; Wednesday
The Voxair is a community newspaper for Royal Canadian Air Force personnel at 17 Wing Winnipeg.
Michael Sherby, Voxair Manager
Michael.Sherby@forces.gc.ca

New Brunswick

Daily Newspapers in New Brunswick

***Caraquet:* L'Acadie Nouvelle**
Détenteur: Acadie Média
CP 5536, 476, boul Saint-Pierre ouest, Caraquet, NB E1W 1A3
Tél: 506-727-4444; *Téléc:* 506-727-7620
Ligne sans frais: 800-561-2255
info@acadiemedia.com
www.acadienouvelle.com
Autre information: Bureau du Sud-Est, Téléphone: 800-561-2255, Télécopieur: 506-383-7440
Médias sociaux:
twitter.com/acadienouvelle
www.facebook.com/acadienouvelle
Tirage: 108 612 total; *Fréquence:* lundi-samedi
Le journal L'Acadie Nouvelle est le seul quotidien francophone du Nouveau-Brunswick.
Francis Sonier, Éditeur-directeur général
francis.sonier@acadiemedia.com
Gaétan Chiasson, Directeur de la salle des nouvelles
gaetan.chiasson@acadienouvelle.com

***Fredericton:* The Daily Gleaner**
Owned By: Brunswick News Inc.
PO Box 3370, 984 Prospect St. West, Fredericton, NB E3B 2T8
Tel: 506-452-6671; *Fax:* 506-452-7405
Toll-Free: 800-565-9399
news@dailygleaner.com
www.telegraphjournal.com/daily-g leaner
Social Media:
twitter.com/dailygleaner
www.facebook.com/DailyGleaner
Circulation: 96,612 total; *Frequency:* Monday-Saturday
The Daily Gleaner serves Fredericton & the surrounding region with local & international news.
Nancy Cook, Publisher
Catherine Metcalfe, Managing Editor

***Moncton:* Times & Transcript**
Previous Name: Moncton Weekly Times; Moncton Daily Transcript
Owned By: Brunswick News Inc.
PO Box 1001, 939 Main St., Moncton, NB E1C 8P3
Tel: 506-859-4905 *Toll-Free:* 800-322-3329
news@timestranscript.com
www.telegraphjournal.com/times-transcript
Circulation: 173,328 total; *Frequency:* Monday-Saturday
Southeastern New Brunswick
Jessie Robichaud, Legislative Reporter
506-450-4132

***Saint John:* The Telegraph-Journal**
Owned By: Brunswick News Inc.
PO Box 2350, 210 Crown St., Saint John, NB E2L 2X7
Tel: 506-632-8888; *Fax:* 506-633-5741
Toll-Free: 877-389-6397
newsroom@telegraphjournal.com
www.telegraphjournal.com
Circulation: 161,742 total; *Frequency:* Monday-Saturday
New Brunswick's provincial newspaper
David Stonehouse, Senior Editor
506-645-3226

Other Newspapers in New Brunswick

***Bathurst:* The Northern Light**
Owned By: Brunswick News Inc.
355 King Ave., Bathurst, NB E2A 1P4
Tel: 506-546-4491; *Fax:* 506-546-1491
www.telegraphjournal.com
Circulation: 3,358; *Frequency:* Tuesday
Maurice Aube, Publisher
Greg Mulock, Editor

***Campbellton:* The Tribune**
Owned By: Brunswick News Inc.
PO Box 486, 6 Shannon St., Campbellton, NB E3N 2G6
Tel: 506-753-4413; *Fax:* 506-759-9595
www.telegraphjournal.com
Circulation: 2,700; *Frequency:* Friday
Subscriptions are available for both the print & online edition,
Peter MacIntosh, Publisher
Tim Jaques, Editor

***Edmundston:* Le Journal Madawaska**
Détenteur: Brunswick News Inc.
20, rue St. François, Edmundston, NB E3V 1E3
Tél: 506-735-5575; *Téléc:* 506-735-8086
www.telegraphjournal.com
Tirage: 2700; *Fréquence:* Mercredi
Hermel Volpé, Publisher
Christine Theriault, Editor

***Grand Falls:* The Victoria Star**
Owned By: Brunswick News Inc.
PO Box 7363, 229 Broadway Blvd., Grand Falls, NB E3Z 2K1
Tel: 506-473-3083
www.telegraphjournal.com
Circulation: 2,270; *Frequency:* Wednesday
The Victoria Star provides community news & information to the northwestern New Brunswick town of Grand Falls & Victoria County.
Matt Hemphill, Publisher
Mark Rickard, Editor

***Grand Sault:* La Cataracte**
Détenteur: Brunswick News Inc.
CP 7363, 229, boul Broadway, Grand Sault, NB E3Z 2K1
Tél: 506-473-3083
Tirage: 6 300; *Fréquence:* Thursday
Jamie Irving, Publisher
Madeleine Leclerc, Editor

***Hampton:* Ossekeag Publishing Co. Ltd.**
242 Main St., Hampton, NB E5N 6B8
Tel: 506-832-5613; *Fax:* 506-832-3353
info@ossekeag.ca
www.ossekeag.ca
The newspaper is distributed in the Town of Hampton & the neighbouring communities of Hatfield Point, Titusville, Belleisle, Smithtown, Bloomfield, Norton, Nauwigewauk, & Bloomfield.
Debbie Hickey, President
506-832-5613
debbie@ossekeag.ca
Mike Hickey, Vice-president
506-832-5613
mike@ossekeag.ca

***Hampton:* The Sussex Herald**
242 Main St., Hampton, NB E5N 6B8
Tel: 506-832-5613; *Fax:* 506-832-3353
Toll-Free: 888-289-2555
info@ossekeag.ca
www.ossekeag.ca
Social Media:
facebook.com/Ossekeag
Circulation: 10,794; *Frequency:* Bi-weekly
The Sussex Herald serves Sussex, New Brunswick & the neighbouring communities of Petitcodiac, Havelock, Cambridge-Narrows, Apohaqui, & Salisbury.
Debbie Hickey, Co-Owner & Operator, Ossekeag Publishing
debbie@ossekeag.ca
Mike Hickey, Co-Owner & Operator, Ossekeag Publishing
mike@ossekeag.ca

***Miramichi:* Miramichi Leader**
Owned By: Brunswick News Inc.
2428 King George Hwy., Miramichi, NB E1V 6V9
Tel: 506-622-2600 *Toll-Free:* 888-295-8665
www.telegraphjournal.com
Circulation: 3900; *Frequency:* Monday, Wednesday; Friday (Miramichi Weekend)
The Miramichi Leader & the Miramichi Weekend provide news for residents of New Brunswick's Miramichi Valley.
Bill MacIntosh, Publisher
Gail Savoy, Editor

***Oromocto:* The Post-Gazette**
Owned By: Brunswick News Inc.
281 Restigouche Rd., Oromocto, NB E2V 2H5
Tel: 506-357-9813
Circulation: 12,844; *Frequency:* Thursday
The greater Fredericton area of New Brunswick is served by Oromocto's community newspaper.
Shelley Wood, Publisher
Heather Gratton, Editor

***Richibucto:* L'Étoile de Kent**
#2, 9406, rue Principale, Richibucto, NB E4W 4E1
Tél: 506-523-6231; *Téléc:* 506-523-6520
redaction@journaletoile.com
Tirage: 100 000+; *Fréquence:* Weekly, Thursday
Mario Tardiff

***Sackville:* Sackville Tribune Post**
Owned By: TC Transcontinental
80 Main St., Sackville, NB E4L 4A7
Tel: 506-536-2500; *Fax:* 506-536-4024
www.sackvilletribunepost.com
Social Media:
www.facebook.com/pages/Sackville-Tribune-Post/14581003216
Circulation: 2,250; *Frequency:* Wednesday
Richard Russell, Publisher
Scott Doherty, Editor
sdoherty@sackvilletribunepost.com

***Shediac:* Le Moniteur Acadien**
Détenteur: Les Editions de Moniteur Acadien Inc.
CP 5191, 817 Boudreau Oest, Rt. 133, Shediac, NB E4P 8T9
Tél: 506-532-6680; *Téléc:* 506-532-6681
moniteur@rogers.com
www.moniteuracadien.com
Tirage: 5000; *Fréquence:* Mercredi
Gilles Hache, Éditeur

***St Stephen:* International Money Saver**
57 King St., St Stephen, NB E3L 2L4
Tel: 506-466-5072; *Fax:* 506-466-9950
moneysav@nbnet.nb.ca
Circulation: 15,000; *Frequency:* Saturday

***St Stephen:* St. Croix Courier**
PO Box 250, Milltown Blvd., St Stephen, NB E3L 2X2
Tel: 506-466-3220; *Fax:* 506-466-9950
www.stcroixcourier.com
Social Media:
facebook.com/pages/The-Saint-Croix-/113338125360812
Circulation: 3,324 Tu; 2,193 F; *Frequency:* Tuesday; Friday (Courier Weekend)
Vern Faulkner, Editor
506-467-5203
editor@stcroixcourier.ca
Heather Cunningham, Director, Advertising
heather@stcroixcourier.ca
Shelley McKeeman, Director, Business Operations
shelley@stcroixcourier.ca

***Sussex:* Kings County Record**
Owned By: Brunswick News Inc.
593 Main St., Sussex, NB E4E 7H5
Tel: 506-433-1070; *Fax:* 506-432-3532
www.telegraphjournal.com
Frequency: Tuesday; Friday (Kings County Record Weekender)
David Kelly, Editor
Bill Ballard, Manager, Sales
ballard.william@brunswicknews.com

***Woodstock:* Bugle-Observer**
Previous Name: The Bugle; The Observer
Owned By: Brunswick News Inc.
110 Carleton St., Woodstock, NB E7M 1E4
Tel: 506-328-8863
www.telegraphjournal.com
Social Media:
twitter.com/BugleObserver1
Circulation: 2,700; *Frequency:* Tuesday; Friday (Bugle-Observer Weekend)
The Bugle-Observer provides news to New Brunswick's Carleton County.
Peter Macintosh, Publisher
Jim Dumville, Editor

Newfoundland & Labrador

Daily Newspapers in Newfoundland & Labrador

***Corner Brook:* The Western Star**
Owned By: TC Media
106 West St., Corner Brook, NL A2H 2Z3
Tel: 709-634-4348; *Fax:* 709-634-9824
newsroom@thewesternstar.com
www.thewesternstar.com
Other information: Advertising, Fax: 709-637-4675
Social Media: www.youtube.com/thewesternstardotcom
twitter.com/western_star
www.face book.com/thewesternstar
Circulation: 32,863 total; *Frequency:* Monday-Saturday
The Western Star provides news & information for Corner Brook & western Newfoundland.
Trina Burden, Publisher & General Manager
tburden@thewesternstar.com

***St. John's:* The Telegram**
Owned By: TC Media
PO Box 8660 A, 36 Austin St., St. John's, NL A1B 3T7
Tel: 709-364-6300; *Fax:* 709-364-3939
telegram@thetelegram.com; circ@thetelegram.com
www.thetelegram.com
Other information: Advertising, Phone: 709-748-0829; News Tips: 709-364-2323
Social Media:
twitter.com/StJohnsTelegram
www.facebook.com/StJohnsTelegram
Circulation: 198,815 total; *Frequency:* Monday-Saturday
Gordon Brewerton, Publisher
gordon.brewerton@tc.tc
Steve Bartlett, Managing Editor
sbartlett@thetelegram.com

Other Newspapers in Newfoundland & Labrador

***Carbonear:* The Compass**
Owned By: TC Transcontinental
PO Box 760, 176 Water St., Carbonear, NL A1Y 1C3
Tel: 709-596-6458; *Fax:* 709-596-1700
www.cbncompass.ca
Social Media:
twitter.com/cbncompass
Circulation: 3,200; *Frequency:* Tuesday
Kevin Hiscock, General Manager, NL Weeklies
khiscock@cbncompass.ca
Terry Roberts, Senior Editor
editor@cbncompass.ca
Bill Bowman, Editor
editor@cbncompass.ca
Nicholas Mercer, Reporter
nmercer@cbncompass.ca
Amanda Pike, Coordinator, Sales & Circulation
apike@cbncompass.ca
Shelleen Emberley, Representative, Customer Service & Circulation
semberley@cbncompass.ca
Daphne Hearn, Representative, Advertising Sales
dhearn@cbncompass.ca

***Channel-Port-aux-Basques:* The Gulf News**
Owned By: TC Transcontinental
PO Box 1090, 17 Grand Bay Rd., Channel-Port-aux-Basques, NL A0M 1C0
Tel: 709-695-3671; *Fax:* 709-695-7901
editor@gulfnews.ca
www.gulfnews.ca
Social Media:
twitter.com/thegulfnews
Circulation: 2,300; *Frequency:* Monday
The Gulf News provides news & information to Channel-Port-aux-Basques & communities in southwestern Newfoundland & Labrador.
Brodie Thomas, Editor
Chantelle MacIsaac, Reporter
reporter@gulfnews.ca
Charlene Blackmore, Manager, Circulation
circulation@gulfnews.ca

***Clarenville:* The Packet**
Owned By: TC Transcontinental
8B Thompson St., Clarenville, NL A5A 1Y9
Tel: 709-466-2243; *Fax:* 709-466-2717
editor@thepacket.ca
www.thepacket.ca
Social Media:
twitter.com/nlpacket
facebook.com/packet.newspapers
Circulation: 3,500; *Frequency:* Thursday
Newfoundland & Labrador communities on Trinity Bay, Bonavista Bay, & Placentia Bay are served by The Packet.
Barbara Dean-Simmons, Editor
bsimmons@thepacket.ca
Bonnie Goodyear, Manager, Business
bgoodyear@thepacket.ca
Shalyn Penney, Circulation Representative
shalyn.penney@tc.tc

***Gander:* The Beacon**
Owned By: TC Transcontinental
PO Box 420, 61 Elizabeth Dr., Gander, NL A1V 1W8
Tel: 709-256-4371; *Fax:* 709-256-3826
info@ganderbeacon.ca
www.ganderbeacon.ca
Social Media:
www.facebook.com/pages/The-Beacon/111859792188557
Circulation: 2,800; *Frequency:* Thursday
The newspaper serves the town of Gander & communities in the Terra Nova & Bonavista North regions of Newfoundland & Labrador.
Kevin Higgins, Editor
khiggins@ganderbeacon.ca
Matt Molloy, Editor, Sports
mmolloy@ganderbeacon.ca
Lori Anstey, Representative, Circulation
circulation@ganderbeacon.ca
Paula Clark, Senior Account Executive
pclark@ganderbeacon.ca

***Grand Falls-Windsor:* Advertiser**
Owned By: TC Transcontinental
PO Box 129, 6 Hardy Ave., Grand Falls-Windsor, NL A2A 2P9
Tel: 709-489-2162; *Fax:* 709-489-4817
editor@advertisernl.ca
www.gfwadvertiser.ca
Social Media:
twitter.com/gfwadvertiser
Circulation: 1,800; *Frequency:* Monday, Thursday
Renell LeGrow, Editor
editor@advertisernl.ca
Krysta Carroll, Associate Editor
kcarroll@gfwadvertiser.ca
Andrea Gunn, Reporter & Photographer
agunn@advertisernl.ca
Kitty Dean, Office Manager
kitty.dean@transcontinental.ca
Karla King, Sales Executive
kingk@gfwadvertiser.ca

***Happy Valley-Goose Bay:* The Labradorian**
Owned By: TC Transcontinental
PO Box 39 B, 2 Hillcrest Rd., Happy Valley-Goose Bay, NL A0P 1E0
Tel: 709-896-3341; *Fax:* 709-896-8781
www.thelabradorian.ca
Social Media:
twitter.com/labradoriannl
Circulation: 1,500; *Frequency:* Monday
The newspaper serves coastal & central Labrador.
Jamie Lewis, Editor
editor@thelabradorian.ca
Derek Montague, Reporter
reporter@thelabradorian.ca
Sharon Gallant, Business Manager, Sales
sgallant@thelabradorian.ca
Melissa Rumbolt, Contact, Circulation
mrumbolt@thelabradorian.ca

***Labrador City:* The Aurora**
Owned By: TC Transcontinental
PO Box 423, Labrador City, NL A2V 2K7
Tel: 709-944-2957; *Fax:* 709-944-2958
www.theaurora.ca
Social Media:
twitter.com/auroranl
Circulation: 1,200; *Frequency:* Monday
The Aurora serves residents of western Labrador.
Michelle Stewart, Editor
editor@theaurora.ca
Paula Hillier, Office Manager
phillier@theaurora.ca

Cheryl Little, Representative, Advertising & Sales
ads@theaurora.ca

***Lewisporte:* The Pilot**
Owned By: TC Transcontinental
PO Box 1210, 151 Main St., Lewisporte, NL A0G 3A0
Tel: 709-535-6910; *Fax:* 709-535-8640
editor@pilotnl.ca
www.lportepilot.ca
Social Media:
twitter.com/lportepilot
facebook.com/pages/The-Lewisporte-Pilot/11010554 2347855
Circulation: 2,500; *Frequency:* Wednesday
The Pilot serves the Lewisporte - Twillingate area of Newfoundland & Labrador.
Karen Wells, Editor
Pam Snow, Reporter & Photographer
psnow@pilotnl.ca
Joanne Chaffey, Office Manager & Contact, Sales
jchaffey@pilotnl.ca

***Marystown:* The Southern Gazette**
Owned By: TC Transcontinental
PO Box 1116, Ville Marie Dr., Marystown, NL A0E 2M0
Tel: 709-279-3188; *Fax:* 709-279-2628
www.southerngazette.ca
Social Media:
twitter.com/southerngazette
Circulation: 2,800; *Frequency:* Tues.
George MacVicar, Manager & Editor
editor@southerngazette.ca
Paul Herridge, Reporter & Photographer
pherridge@southerngazette.ca
Maxine Drake, Consultant, Sales
mdrake@southerngazette.ca

***Paradise:* The Shoreline News**
PO Box 3065, Paradise, NL A1L 3W2
Tel: 709-834-2169
tsnews@nf.aibn.com
www.theshorelinenews.com
Circulation: 16,000; *Frequency:* Saturday
The Shoreline News serves the residents of Paradise, Conception Bay South, Conception Bay Centre, & St. Mary's Bay. Subscriptions are available for both the print & online editions of the newspaper.
Frank Petten, Publisher

***Placentia:* The Charter**
Owned By: TC Transcontinental
PO Box 450, Placentia, NL A0B 2Y0
Tel: 709-227-5240; *Fax:* 709-227-3892
adsales@thecharter.ca
www.thecharter.ca
Circulation: 4,636; *Frequency:* Thursday
Elizabeth MacDonald, Editor

***Springdale:* The Nor'Wester**
Owned By: TC Transcontinental
PO Box 28, 4 Juniper Lane, Springdale, NL A0J 1T0
Tel: 709-673-3721; *Fax:* 709-673-4171
info@thenorwester.ca; adsales@thenorwester.ca
www.thenorwester.ca
Social Media:
twitter.com/thenorwester
facebook.com/thenorwester
Circulation: 1,900; *Frequency:* Thursday
Rudy Norman, Editor
709-252-2954
editor@thenorwester.ca
Christine Saunders, Manager, Office & Circulation
709-673-3721

***St. Anthony:* The Northern Pen**
Owned By: TC Transcontinental
PO Box 520, 10-12 North St., St. Anthony, NL A0K 4S0
Tel: 709-454-2191; *Fax:* 709-454-3718
info@northernpen.ca
www.northernpen.ca
Social Media:
twitter.com/northernpen
facebook.com/pages/Northern-Pen/206446989387790
Circulation: 4,144; *Frequency:* Monday
Newfoundland & Labrador's northern peninsula & southern Labrador are served by The Northern Pen newspaper.
Kevin Hiscock, General Manager, NL Weeklies
khiscock@cbncompass.ca
Kathy Parsons, Manager, Advertising
kparsons@northernpen.ca
Frances Reardon, Manager, Office & Circulation
freardon@northernpen.ca
Wavey Pilgrim, Account Executive
wpilgrim@northernpen.ca

***St-Jean:* Le Gaboteur**
Détenteur: Le Gaboteur Inc.
#254, 65 chemin Ridge, St-Jean, NL A1B 4P5
Tél: 709-753-9585; *Téléc:* 709-753-9586
gaboteur@nf.sympatico.ca
www.gaboteur.ca
Médias sociaux: www.youtube.com/Legaboteur
www.facebook.com/gaboteur
Tirage: 731; *Fréquence:* Lundi, bi-mensuel
Jacinthe Tremblay, Codirectrice (rédaction)
jacinthe@gaboteur.ca
Steven Watt, Corecteur (administration)
steven@gaboteur.ca
Jordan Elliott, Adjoint administratif
jordan@gaboteur.ca

Northwest Territories

***Fort Smith:* Northern Journal**
Owned By: Cascade Publishing Limited
PO Box 990, 207 McDougall Rd., Fort Smith, NT X0E 0P0
Tel: 867-872-2784
news@norj.ca
www.srji.com
Social Media:
twitter.com/NorthernJournal
facebook.com/NorthernJournal
Circulation: 4,346; *Frequency:* Tuesday
Formerly the Slave River Journal
Don Jaque, Publisher
don@norj.ca
Meagan Wohlberg, Managing Editor
news@norj.ca

***Hay River:* The Hub**
Owned By: Northern News Services Ltd.
PO Box 2820, 8-4 Courtoreille St., Hay River, NT X0E 1G2
Tel: 867-874-6577; *Fax:* 867-874-2679
advertise@hayriverhub.com
www.hayriverhub.com
Other information: Classified Advertising, E-mail: classifieds@hayriverhub.com
Social Media:
twitter.com/hayriverhub
www.facebook.com/hayriverhub
Circulation: 1,800; *Frequency:* Wednesday
J.W. Sigvaldason, Publisher
Mike Bryant, Editor

***Yellowknife:* L'Aquilon**
CP 456, Yellowknife, NT X1A 2N4
Tél: 867-873-6603; *Téléc:* 867-873-6663
ykjournaliste@northwestel.net
www.aquilon.nt.ca
Tirage: 1 000; *Fréquence:* Vendredi
Alain Bessette, Publisher
Denis Lord, Reporter
ykjournaliste@northwestel.net
Alain Bessette, Officer, Administration
direction_aquilon@northwestel.net

***Yellowknife:* Deh Cho Drum**
Owned By: Northern News Services Ltd.
PO Box 2820, Yellowknife, NT X1A 2R1
Tel: 867-695-3786; *Fax:* 867-695-3766
dehchodrum@nnsl.com
www.nnsl.com/dehcho/dehcho.html
Social Media:
twitter.com/nnslonline
www.facebook.com/NnslOnline
Circulation: 1,150; *Frequency:* Thurs.
Jack Sigvaldason, Publisher
Petra Ehrke, Manager, National/Territorial Advertising

***Yellowknife:* Den Cho Drum**
Owned By: Northern News Services Ltd.
PO Box 2820, Yellowknife, NT X1A 2R1
Tel: 867-873-4031; *Fax:* 867-873-8507
nnsl@nnsl.com; circulation@nnsl.com
www.nnsl.com/dehcho
Other information: Advertising: advertising@nnsl.com; Editorial: editorial@nnsl.com
Social Media:
twitter.com/nnslonline
www.facebook.com/NnslOnline
Circulation: 1,160; *Frequency:* Thursday
J.W. Sigvaldson, Publisher
Michael Scott, General Manager
Bruce Valpy, Managing Editor
Petra Ehrke, Manager, Advertising

***Yellowknife:* Nunavut News North**
Owned By: Northern News Services Ltd.
PO Box 2820, 5108 - 50th St., Yellowknife, NT X1A 2R1
Tel: 867-873-4031; *Fax:* 867-873-8507
nnsl@nnsl.com
www.nnsl.com/publish/nunavutpromo.html
Circulation: 5,300; *Frequency:* Mon.
Special issues include Year in Review (January), Iqaluit Visitors' Guide (February), Degrees of Success (a special report on post-secondary occupations) (March), Construction (May), Nunavut/NWT Graduation (June), Opportunities North (a comprehensive all-industry report covering Nunavut and Northwest Territories on an industry-by-industry basis) (June), Nunavut/NWT Mining, Nunavut Mining Symposium, Nunavut Holiday Songbook (a translated version of the most popular holiday sing-along songs and activities) (November), Addictions (a special, sobering report on the effects of addictions in the North) (November), Holiday Gift Guide (November/December), Don't Drink and Drive (December).
Jack Sigvaldason, Publisher

***Yellowknife:* NWT News North**
Owned By: Northern News Services Ltd.
PO Box 2820, 5108 - 50th St., Yellowknife, NT X1A 2R1
Tel: 867-873-4031; *Fax:* 867-873-8507
nnsl@nnsl.com
www.nnsl.com/nwtnewsnorth/nwt.html
Other information: Advertising: advertising@nnsl.com; Circulation: circulation@nnsl.com
Social Media:
twitter.com/nnslonline
www.facebook.com/NnslOnline
Circulation: 5,800; *Frequency:* Monday
Jack (Sig) Sigvaldason, Publisher
Bruce Valpy, Managing Editor
editorial@nnsl.com

***Yellowknife:* Yellowknifer**
Owned By: Northern News Services Ltd.
PO Box 2820, 5108 - 50th St., Yellowknife, NT X1A 2R1
Tel: 867-873-4031; *Fax:* 867-873-8507
editorial@nnsl.com
www.nnsl.com/publish/yellowkniferpromo.html
Circulation: 7,900; *Frequency:* Bi-weekly: Wednesday, Friday
J.W. Sigvaldason, Publisher
Bruce Valpy, Editor

Nova Scotia

Daily Newspapers in Nova Scotia

***Amherst:* Amherst News**
Owned By: TC Media
147 South Albion St., Amherst, NS B4H 2X2
Tel: 902-667-5102; *Fax:* 902-667-0419
darrell.cole@tc.tc
cumberlandnewsnow.com
Other information: Advertising, Phone: 902-661-5427, Fax: 902-667-0419
Social Media:
twitter.com/amherstdaily
www.facebook.com/pages/Amherst-Daily-News/131375826905362
Richard Russell, Group Publisher
rrussell@ngnews.ca
Darrell Cole, Managing Editor
darrell.cole@tc.tc

***Halifax:* The Chronicle Herald**
Owned By: Halifax Herald Ltd.
PO Box 610, 2717 Joseph Howe Dr., Halifax, NS B3J 2T2
Tel: 902-426-2811; *Fax:* 902-426-1164
reception@herald.ca
thechronicleherald.ca
Other information: Classifieds: classified@herald.ca
Social Media:
twitter.com/chronicleherald
www.facebook.com/thechronicleherald
Circulation: 548,938; *Frequency:* Monday-Saturday
Atlantic Canada
Fred Buckland, General Manager
902-426-2811
fbuckland@herald.ns.ca

***Halifax:* Metro Halifax**
Owned By: Torstar Corp.
#102, 3260 Barrington St., Halifax, NS B3K 0B5
Tel: 902-444-4444
halifaxletters@metronews.ca
metronews.ca/news/halifax
Circulation: 219,638 total; *Frequency:* Monday-Friday

***Kentville:* The Kings County Advertiser**
Owned By: TC Transcontinental
#6, 28 Aberdeen St., Kentville, NS B4N 2N1
Tel: 902-681-2121; *Fax:* 902-681-0830
events@kentvilleadvertiser.ca
www.kingscountynews.ca
Social Media:
twitter.com/KingsNSnews
facebook.com/KingsCountyNews
Circulation: 3,400; *Frequency:* Tuesday
Don Brander, Publisher
Jason Malloy, Editor

***Kentville:* Kings County Register**
Owned By: TC Transcontinental
#6, 28 Aberdeen St., Kentville, NS B4N 2N1
Tel: 902-681-2121; *Fax:* 902-681-0830
events@kentvilleadvertiser.ca
www.kingscountynews.ca
Social Media:
twitter.com/KingsNSnews
facebook.com/KingsCountyNews
Circulation: 3,600; *Frequency:* Thurs.
Jennifer Little, Editor
jlittle@kingscountynews.ca
Jennifer Hoegg, Associate Editor
jhoegg@kingscountynews.ca

***New Glasgow:* The News**
Previous Name: The Evening News
Owned By: TC Media
PO Box 159, 352 East River Rd., New Glasgow, NS B2H 5E2
Tel: 902-752-3000
news@ngnews.ca; classified@ngnews.ca
www.ngnews.ca
Other information: Newsroom, Phone: 902-928-3514;
Classifieds: 902-928-3515
Social Media:
twitter.com/ngnews
www.facebook.com/pages/The-News/137537789618902
Circulation: 31,920 total; *Frequency:* Monday-Saturday
Nova Scotia's Pictou County is served by the daily newspaper.
Richard Russell, Group Publisher
rrussell@ngnews.ca

***Sydney:* Cape Breton Post**
Owned By: TC Media
PO Box 1500, 255 George St., Sydney, NS B1P 6K6
Tel: 902-564-5451; *Fax:* 902-562-7077
news@cbpost.com; edit@cbpost.com
www.capebretonpost.com
Other information: Advertising, Phone: 902-563-3873, Fax:
902-564-6280
Social Media:
twitter.com/capebretonpost; twitter.com/cbpost_sports
www.facebook.com/thecapebretonpost
Circulation: 109,927 total; *Frequency:* Monday-Saturday
The Cape Breton Post is Cape Breton Island's only local daily newspaper. Offers broad coverage of Cape Breton county with growing coverage in the remaining counties of the island.
Anita DeLazzer, Publisher & General Manager
adelazzer@cbpost.com
Helen MacCoy, Director, Reader Sales & Distribution
hmaccoy@cbpost.com
Scott MacQuarrie, Manager, Sales & Marketing
smacquarrie@cbpost.com
Shaun Robinson, Manager, Business & Operation
srobinson@cbpost.com

***Truro:* Truro Daily News**
Owned By: TC Media
PO Box 220, 6 Louise St., Truro, NS B2N 5C3
Tel: 902-893-9405; *Fax:* 902-895-6104
Toll-Free: 800-939-4992
news@trurodaily.com
www.trurodaily.com
Other information: Newsroom, Phone: 902-896-7527; Classified
Advertising: 902-896-7529
Social Media:
twitter.com/trurodaily
www.facebook.com/pages/Truro-Daily-News/108 404435879900
Circulation: 29,274 total; *Frequency:* Monday-Saturday
The newspaper covers Truro, Tatamagouche, & Colchester County.
Richard Russell, Group Publisher
rrussell@ngnews.ca
Sherry Martell, Managing Editor
smartell@trurodaily.com

Other Newspapers in Nova Scotia

***Amherst:* The Citizen-Record**
Owned By: TC Transcontinental
147 South Albion St., Amherst, NS B4H 2X2
Tel: 902-667-5102; *Fax:* 902-667-0419
darrell.cole@tc.tc
www.cumberlandnewsnow.com
Other information: Advertising, Phone: 902-661-5439
Social Media:
twitter.com/ADNandrew
facebook.com/pages/Amherst-131375826905362
Frequency: Thursday
In 2011, The Citizen & The Record community newspapers merged to create The Citizen-Record. The newspaper covers Nova Scotia's Cumberland County. The Citizen-Record is available in print & online.
Richard Russell, Group Publisher, Transcontinental Nova Scotia Media Group Inc.
902-896-7526
rrussell@ngnews.ca
Christopher Gooding, Co-Editor
902-597-3731
Andrew Wagstaff, Co-Editor
902-661-5440
Gladys Coish, Regional Manager, Sales
gcoish@amherstdaily.com

***Antigonish:* The Casket**
Owned By: Halifax Herald Ltd.
88 College St., Antigonish, NS B2G 2L7
Tel: 902-863-4370; *Fax:* 902-863-1943
www.thecasket.ca
Social Media:
twitter.com/casketeditor
www.facebook.com/99987897299
Circulation: 3,427; *Frequency:* Weekly; Wednesday
The Casket serves the town & county of Antigonish in Nova Scotia.
Brian Lazzuri, General Manager & Managing Editor
editor@thecasket.ca

***Bass River:* The Shoreline Journal**
Previous Name: West Colchester Free Press
PO Box 41, RR#1, Bass River, NS B0M 1B0
Tel: 902-647-2968
www.theshorelinejournal.com
Social Media:
twitter.com/mauricerees
www.facebook.com/theshorelinejournal
Circulation: 1,363; *Frequency:* Monthly
The community newspaper serves Nova Scotia's Fundy Shore, including the communities of Bass River, Truro, Parrsboro, Belmont, Masstown, Debert, & Onslow.
Dorothy Rees, Co-Manager
Maurice Rees, Co-Manager
maurice@theshorelinejournal.com

***Bridgetown:* Monitor-Examiner**
Previous Name: Bridgetown Monitor
PO Box 250, 29 Queen St., Bridgetown, NS B0S 1C0
Tel: 902-665-4441; *Fax:* 902-665-4014
Frequency: Weekly
Susanne Wagner, Publisher

***Bridgewater:* Lunenburg County Progress Bulletin**
Previous Name: Bridgewater Bulletin, Lunenburg Progress Enterprise
Owned By: Lighthouse Publishing Limited
353 York St., Bridgewater, NS B4V 3K2
Tel: 902-543-2457; *Fax:* 902-634-3572
mail@southshorenow.ca
www.southshorenow.ca
Social Media: www.youtube.com/user/southshorenowca/featured
twitter.com/southshorenow
www.facebook.com/171604385422
Circulation: 7,959; *Frequency:* Weekly; Wednesday

***Digby:* The Digby County Courier**
Owned By: TC Transcontinental
PO Box 430, 124 Water St., Digby, NS B0V 1A0
Tel: 902-245-4715; *Fax:* 902-245-6136
info@digbycourier.ca
www.digbycourier.ca
Social Media:
twitter.com/DigbyNews
Circulation: 1,280; *Frequency:* Thursday
John DeMings, Editor
editor@digbycourier.ca
Leanne Delong, Reporter
ldelong@digbycourier.ca
Chris Frost, Representative, Sales
cfrost@digbycourier.ca

***Enfield:* The Laker**
Owned By: Advocate Media Inc.
287 Hwy. 2, Enfield, NS B2T 1C9
Tel: 902-883-3181; *Fax:* 902-883-3180
advertising@enfieldweeklypress.com
www.thelaker.ca
Social Media:
twitter.com/TheLakerNews
Circulation: 7,600; *Frequency:* Monthly, first Thursday
The community newspaper serves Nova Scotia's Lakes area, including Waverley, Windsor Junction, Beaver Bank, Fall River, & Wellington. The Laker is published the first week of each month.
Leith Orr, Publisher
leith@advocatemediainc.com
Abby Cameron, Editor
editor@enfieldweeklypress.com
Scott MacKinnon, Manager, Advertising
scott@advocatemediainc.com om
Angela Isenor, Contact, Design & Production
design@enfieldweeklypress.com
Danielle Shreenan, Contact, Classified & Circulation
admin@enfieldweeklypress.com

***Enfield:* The Weekly Press**
Owned By: Advocate Printing & Publishing Co.
287 Hwy. 2, Enfield, NS B2T 1C9
Tel: 902-883-3181; *Fax:* 902-883-3180
editor@enfieldweeklypress.com
www.enfieldweeklypress.com
Circulation: 1,458; *Frequency:* Weekly; Wednesday
Fred Fiander, Publisher
fredfiander@advocatemediainc.com
Abby Cameron, Editor
editor@enfieldweeklypress.com

***Greenwood:* The Aurora**
Owned By: Department of National Defence
PO Box 99, 14 Wing, Greenwood, NS B0P 1N0
Tel: 902-765-1494; *Fax:* 902-765-1717
www.auroranewspaper.com
Circulation: 5,900; *Frequency:* Monday
The Aurora is a free newspaper that serves the personnel of 14 Wing Greenwood, Nova Scotia.
Sara Keddy, Managing Editor
auroraeditor@ns.aliantzinc.ca
LT. Sylvain Rousseau, Editorial Advisor
9027651494
Brian Graves, Coordinator, Production
auroraproduction@ns.aliantzinc.ca
Anne Kempton, Contact, Business & Advertising
auroramarketing@ns.aliantzinc.ca
Candance May Timmins, Administrative Clerk
auroranews@ns.aliantzinc.ca

***Guysborough:* Guysborough Journal**
Owned By: Addington Publications
PO Box 210, 48 Main St., Guysborough, NS B0H 1N0
Tel: 902-533-2851; *Fax:* 902-533-2750
news@guysboroughjournal.ca
www.guysboroughjournal.com
Other information: Subscriptions, E-mail:
subscribe@guysboroughjournal.ca
Social Media:
twitter.com/GysboroJournal
Circulation: 970; *Frequency:* Wed.
The community newspaper covers Nova Scotia's Guysborough County. Print & digital editions are available.
Helen Murphy, Publisher, Manager, & Editor
Sharon Heighton, Manager, Office & Circulation
Dorothy Ostewig, Coordinator, Production
Navneet Kaur, Contact, Advertising
advertising@guysboroughjournal.ca

***Halifax:* The Coast**
5567 Cunard St., Halifax, NS B3K 1C5
Tel: 902-422-6278; *Fax:* 902-425-0013
frontdesk@thecoast.ca; coast@thecoast.ca
www.thecoast.ca
Social Media:
twitter.com/TwitCoast
www.facebook.com/TheCoastHalifax
Circulation: 22,000; *Frequency:* Thursday
The Coast is an independent, locally owned paper that features news, reports on the arts, & movie, theatre, music, gallery, & museum listings for Halifax, Nova Scotia. The free newspaper is distributed each week at over 650 locations. The Coast is a member of the international Association of Alternative Newsweeklies.

Catherine Salisbury, President
cathsalis@thecoast.ca
Christine Oreskovich, Publisher
christineo@thecoast.ca
Kyle Shaw, Editor
editor@thecoast.ca
Stephanie Johns, Editor, Arts
arts@thecoast.ca
Lindsay Raining Bird, Editor, Listings
listings@thecoast.ca
Jessica Tasker, Manager, Distribution
distribution@thecoast.ca
Bethany Stout, Director, Advertising
bethanys@thecoast.ca

***Inverness:* The Inverness Oran**
Owned By: Inverness Communications Ltd.
PO Box 100, 15767 Central Ave., Inverness, NS B0E 1N0
Tel: 902-258-2253; *Fax:* 902-258-2632
oran@ns.aliantzinc.ca
www.oran.ca
Other information: Advertising e-mail: oran-advertising@ns.aliantzinc.ca
Social Media:
facebook.com/invernessoran
Circulation: 3,500; *Frequency:* Wednesday
Rankin MacDonald, President & Editor
editor@oran.ca
Eleanor MacDonald, Publisher & Secretary
Bill Dunphy, Editor, Sports
oran-sports@ns.aliantzinc.ca
Ann Morrison, Accountant
ann@oran.ca
Kelly MacGillivray, Contact, Advertising & Circulation
Diane Mouland, Contact, Production

***Liverpool:* The Queens County Advance**
Owned By: TC Transcontinental
271 Main St., Liverpool, NS B0T 1K0
Tel: 902-354-3441; *Fax:* 902-354-2455
info@theadvance.ca
www.theadvance.ca
Social Media:
www.linkedin.com/company/the-queens-county-advance
facebook.com/QueensCo untyAdvance
Circulation: 1,560; *Frequency:* Tuesday
Mark Roberts, Editor

***Meteghan River:* Le Courrier de la Nouvelle-Écosse**
9250, rte 1, Meteghan River, NS B0W 2L0
Tél: 902-769-3078; *Téléc:* 902-769-3869
adminstration@lecourrier.com
www.lecourrier.com
Médias sociaux:
twitter.com/CourrierNE1937
facebook.com/lecourrier
Tirage: 1 325; *Fréquence:* vendredi
Denise Comeau-Desautels, Directrice générale; Rédactrice en chef; Directrice, des ventes

***Middleton:* The Annapolis County Spectator**
Owned By: TC Transcontinental
PO Box 880, 87 Commercial St., Middleton, NS B0S 1P0
Tel: 902-825-3457; *Fax:* 902-825-6707
info@annapolisspectator.ca
www.annapoliscountyspectator.ca
Social Media:
twitter.com/SpectatorNS
facebook.com/AnnapolisCountySpectator
Circulation: 1,800; *Frequency:* Thursday
Larry Powell, Editor
editor@annapolisspectator.ca
Heather Killen, Reporter
hkillen@annapolisspectator.ca
Al Simpson, Representative, Sales
hkillen@annapolisspectator.ca

***Oxford:* The Oxford Journal**
Owned By: Oxford Journal Ltd.
PO Box 10, 111 Rideau St., Oxford, NS B0M 1P0
Tel: 902-447-2051; *Fax:* 902-447-2055
www.oxfordjournal.ca
Circulation: 1,750; *Frequency:* Wednesday
The Oxford Journal serves central & eastern Cumberland County in Nova Scotia.
Paul Marchant, Publisher
Charles Weeks, Editor

***Pictou:* The Advocate**
Owned By: Advocate Media Inc.
PO Box 1000, 21 George St., Pictou, NS B0K 1H0
Tel: 902-485-8014; *Fax:* 902-752-4816
www.pictouadvocate.com
Other information: Advertising: mark@pictouadvocate.com, doug@pictouadvocate.com
Social Media:
twitter.com/pictouadvocate
www.facebook.com/pages/The-Pictou-Advocate/11500838191033
Circulation: 2,624; *Frequency:* Wednesday
Leith Orr, Publisher
leith@advocatemediainc.com
Jackie Jardine, Editor
editor@pictouadvocate.com
Lorraine Van Veen, Manager, Circulation
circul@pictouadvocate.com

***Pictou:* The Light**
Owned By: Advocate Media Inc.
PO Box 1000, 21 George St., Pictou, NS B0K 1H0
Tel: 902-956-8099; *Fax:* 902-257-2832
circul@advocateprinting.ns.ca (circulation)
www.tatamagouchelight.com
Other information: Subscriptions, Phone: 902-485-8014; Advertising: 902-657-2593
Social Media:
twitter.com/TheLightNews
Circulation: 4,412; *Frequency:* Monthly, first Wednesday
The Light is a free newspaper that provides news & information to the Nova Scotia communities of Tatamagouche, Pugwash, Malagash, Earltown, River John, Wentworth, & Wallace.
Leith Orr, Publisher
leith@advocatemediainc.com
Scott MacKinnon, Manager, Advertising
scott@advocatemediainc.com

***Port Hawkesbury:* The Reporter**
Owned By: Reporter Publishing Ltd.
2 MacLean Ct., Port Hawkesbury, NS B9A 3K2
Tel: 902-625-3300; *Fax:* 902-625-1701
www.porthawkesburyreporter.com
Social Media:
twitter.com/thereporternews
Circulation: 2,100; *Frequency:* Wednesday
Rick Cluett, Publisher
rickc@porthawkesburyreporter.com
Jake Boudrot, Editor
jake@porthawkesburyreporter.com
Anne Cluett, Manager, Advertising
annec@porthawkesburyreporter.com

***Shelburne:* The Shelburne County Coast Guard**
Owned By: TC Transcontinental
164 Water St., Shelburne, NS B0T 1W0
Tel: 902-875-3244; *Fax:* 902-875-3454
info@thecoastguard.ca
www.thecoastguard.ca
Social Media:
twitter.com/ShelburneCoastG
facebook.com/pages/The-Shelburne-/2377 96249638696
Circulation: 2,500; *Frequency:* Tuesday
Greg Bennett, Editor
editor@thecoastguard.ca
Fred Fiander, General Manager

***Windsor:* The Hants Journal**
Owned By: TC Transcontinental
PO Box 550, 86 Gerrish St., Windsor, NS B0N 2T0
Tel: 902-798-8371; *Fax:* 902-798-5451
info@hantsjournal.ca
www.hantsjournal.ca
Social Media:
twitter.com/HantsJournal
www.facebook.com/pages/The-Hants-Journal/132834683453645
Circulation: 2,251; *Frequency:* Thursday
The Hants Journal covers Windsor, Hantsport, & Hants County in Nova Scotia.
Carole Morris-Underhill, Editor
editor@hantsjournal.ca
Ashley Thompson, Reporter
athompson@hantsjournal.ca
Michele White, Representative, Sales
mwhite@hantsjournal.ca

***Yarmouth:* The Yarmouth County Vanguard**
Owned By: TC Transcontinental
2 Second St., Yarmouth, NS B5A 4B1
Tel: 902-742-7111; *Fax:* 902-742-2311
info@thevanguard.ca
www.thevanguard.ca
Other information: Advertising, Fax: 902-742-6527
Social Media:
twitter.com/YarVanguardnews
facebook.com/pages/Yarmouth-Vanguard/1658156 26810474
Circulation: 3,800; *Frequency:* Tuesday
Don Brander, Publisher
Fred A. Hatfield, Managing Editor
editor@thevanguard.ca

Nunavut

***Iqaluit:* Nunatsiaq News**
Owned By: Nortext Publishing Corporation
PO Box 8, Iqaluit, NU X0A 0H0
Tel: 867-979-5357; *Fax:* 867-979-4763
editor@nunatsiaqonline.ca; ads@nunatsiaqonline.ca
www.nunatsiaqonline.ca
Other information: Advertising, Toll-Free: 1-800-263-1452, ext. 131, Fax: 1-800-417-2474
Social Media:
twitter.com/nunatsiaqnews
www.facebook.com/pages/Nunatsiaq-News/100174284441
Circulation: 6,228; *Frequency:* Friday
The newspaper of the eastern Arctic is published weekly in English & Inuktitut. Stories are published online each day, and a virtual paper delivered by email is also available weekly.
Steven Roberts, Publisher
Jim Bell, Editor

***Yellowknife:* Kivalliq News**
Owned By: Northern News Services Ltd.
PO Box 2820, Yellowknife, NU X1A 2R1
Tel: 867-645-3223; *Fax:* 867-645-3225
kivalliqnews@nnsl.com
www.nnsl.com/publish/kivpromo.html
Circulation: 1,400; *Frequency:* Wed.
Bilingual Inuktitut & English newspaper serving communities in the Kivalliq region (Central Arctic).
J.W. Sigvaldason, Publisher
Petra Ehrke, Advertising Manager

Ontario

Daily Newspapers in Ontario

***Belleville:* The Belleville Intelligencer**
Owned By: Postmedia Network Inc.
#535, 199 Front St., Belleville, ON K8N 5H5
Tel: 613-962-9171; *Fax:* 613-962-9652
newsroom@intelligencer.ca
www.intelligencer.ca
Social Media:
twitter.com/theintell
www.facebook.com/TheBellevilleIntelligencer
Circulation: 43,399 total; *Frequency:* Monday-Saturday
Brice McVicar, Managing Editor
brice.mcvicar@sunmedia.ca

***Brantford:* Brantford Expositor**
Owned By: Postmedia Network Inc.
#1, 195 Henry St., Building 4, Brantford, ON N3S 5C9
Tel: 519-756-2020; *Fax:* 519-756-3285
www.brantfordexpositor.ca
Social Media:
twitter.com/theexpositor
www.facebook.com/BrantfordExpositor
Circulation: 108,676 total; *Frequency:* Monday-Saturday
Jeff Dertinger, Managing Editor
jeff.dertinger@sunmedia.ca

***Brockville:* The Recorder & Times**
Owned By: Postmedia Network Inc.
2479A Parkedale Ave., Brockville, ON K6V 3H2
Tel: 613-342-4441; *Fax:* 613-342-4456
Toll-Free: 800-267-4434
www.recorder.ca
Social Media:
twitter.com/recordertimes
www.facebook.com/recorder.newsroom
Circulation: 53,979 total; *Frequency:* Tuesday-Saturday
Bob Doornenbal, Publisher
Liza Nelson, Publisher
Bob Pearce, Publisher
bobpearce@recorder.ca

***Chatham:* Chatham Daily News**
Owned By: Postmedia Network Inc.
138 King St. West, Chatham, ON N7M 1E3
Tel: 519-354-2000; *Fax:* 519-354-3448
www.chathamdailynews.ca
Social Media:
twitter.com/ChathamNews
www.facebook.com/ChathamDailyNews
Circulation: 32,372 total; *Frequency:* Monday-Saturday
Rod Hilts, Managing Editor
rod.hilts@sunmedia.ca

***Cobourg:* Northumberland Today**
Owned By: Postmedia Network Inc.
PO Box 400, 99 King St. West, Cobourg, ON K9A 4L1
Tel: 905-372-0131; *Fax:* 905-372-4966
www.northumberlandtoday.com
Social Media:
twitter.com/northumbtoday
www.facebook.com/NorthumberlandToday
Circulation: 34,290 total; *Frequency:* Monday-Friday
Northumberland Today combines the Cobourg Daily Star, the Port Hope Evening Guide, & the Colborne Chronicle into one paper for the Northumberland County area.
Darren Murphy, Regional Publisher
darren.murphy@sunmedia.ca

***Cornwa ll:* Standard-Freeholder**
Owned By: Postmedia Network Inc.
1150 Montreal Rd., Cornwall, ON K6H 1E2
Tel: 613-933-3160; *Fax:* 613-933-7521
www.standard-freeholder.com
Social Media:
twitter.com/northumbtoday
www.facebook.com/standardfreeholder
Circulation: 45,067 total; *Frequency:* Monday-Saturday
Hugo Rodrigues, Managing Editor
hugo.rodrigues@sunmedia.ca

***Fort Frances:* Fort Frances Times**
Owned By: Independent
PO Box 339, 116 First St. East, Fort Frances, ON P9A 1K2
Tel: 807-274-5373; *Fax:* 807-274-7286
Toll-Free: 800-465-8508
news@fortfrances.com
www.fftimes.com
Social Media:
twitter.com/fftimes
www.facebook.com/fortfrancestimes
Circulation: 3,559; *Frequency:* Weekly, Wednesday
News from Fort Frances & the Rainy River District
James R. Cumming, Publisher
jcumming@fortfrances.com
Mike Behan, Editor
mbehan@fortfrances.com

***Guelph:* Guelph Mercury**
Owned By: Torstar Corp.
#8, 14 Macdonell St., Guelph, ON N1H 6P7
Tel: 519-823-6066 *Toll-Free:* 866-871-9868
editor@guelphmercury.com
www.guelphmercury.com
Social Media:
twitter.com/guelphmercury
www.facebook.com/guelphmercury
Circulation: 68,014 total; *Frequency:* Monday-Saturday
Dave Kruse, General Manager
dkruse@guelphmercury.com

***Hamilton:* The Hamilton Spectator**
Owned By: Torstar Corp.
44 Frid St., Hamilton, ON L8N 3G3
Tel: 905-526-3333
www.thespec.com
Social Media:
twitter.com/TheSpec
facebook.com/hamiltonspectator
Circulation: 686,450 total; *Frequency:* Monday-Saturday
Neil Oliver, Publisher
noliver@metroland.com
Paul Berton, Editor-in-Chief
pberton@metroland.com

***Kenora:* Daily Miner & News**
Owned By: Postmedia Network Inc.
PO Box 1620, 33 Main St. South, Kenora, ON P9N 3X7
Tel: 807-468-5555; *Fax:* 807-468-4318
www.kenoradailyminerandnews.com
Social Media:
twitter.com/Kenora_Daily
www.facebook.com/KenoraDailyMiner
Circulation: 8,308 total; *Frequency:* Monday, Wednesday, Friday
Lloyd Mack, Regional Managing Editor
lloyd.mack@sunmedia.ca

***Kingston:* The Kingston Whig-Standard**
Owned By: Postmedia Network Inc.
6 Cataraqui St., Kingston, ON K7L 4Z7
Tel: 613-544-5000; *Fax:* 613-530-4122
whig.local@sunmedia.ca
www.thewhig.com
Social Media:
twitter.com/whigstandard
www.facebook.com/KingstonWhigStandard
Circulation: 104,053 total; *Frequency:* Monday-Saturday
Steve Serviss, Managing Editor
steve.serviss@sunmedia.ca

***Kirkland Lake:* Northern News**
Owned By: Postmedia Network Inc.
8 Duncan Ave., Kirkland Lake, ON P2N 3L4
Tel: 705-567-5321; *Fax:* 705-567-6162
news@northernnews.ca
www.northernnews.ca
Social Media:
www.twitter.com/NorthernTimes
www.facebook.com/klnorthernnews
Joe O'Grady, Managing Editor
joe.ogrady@sunmedia.ca

***Kitchener:* The Record**
Previous Name: Kitchener Daily Record
Owned By: Torstar Corp.
160 King St. East, Kitchener, ON N2G 4E5
Tel: 519-894-2250 *Toll-Free:* 800-265-8261
www.therecord.com
Social Media:
twitter.com/WR_Record
facebook.com/waterlooregionrecord
Circulation: 338,441 total; *Frequency:* Monday-Saturday
Donna Luelo, Publisher
dluelo@therecord.com
Lynn Haddrall, Editor-in-Chief
lhaddrall@therecord.com

***London:* The London Free Press**
Owned By: Postmedia Network Inc.
369 York St., London, ON N6A 4G1
Tel: 519-679-1111; *Fax:* 519-667-4523
www.lfpress.com
Social Media:
twitter.com/lfpress
www.facebook.com/lfpress
Circulation: 417,901 total; *Frequency:* Monday-Saturday
Joe Ruscitti, Editor-in-chief
joe.ruscitti@sunmedia.ca

***Niagara Falls:* Niagara Falls Review**
Owned By: Postmedia Network Inc.
4424 Queen St., Niagara Falls, ON L2R 2L3
Tel: 905-358-5711; *Fax:* 905-356-0785
www.niagarafallsreview.ca
Social Media:
twitter.com/niafallsreview
www.facebook.com/niagarafallsreview
Circulation: 78,890 total; *Frequency:* Monday-Saturday
Peter Conradi, Editor-in-Chief
peter.conradi@sunmedia.ca

***North Bay:* The North Bay Nugget**
Owned By: Postmedia Network Inc.
259 Worthington St. West, North Bay, ON P1B 3B5
Tel: 705-472-3200; *Fax:* 705-472-1438
nbay.news@sunmedia.ca
www.nugget.ca
Social Media:
twitter.com/northbaynugget
www.facebook.com/NBNugget
Circulation: 51,055 total; *Frequency:* Monday-Saturday
Steve Page, Advertising Director
steve.page@sunmedia.ca

***Orillia:* The Packet & Times**
Owned By: Postmedia Network Inc.
#15, 425 West St. North, Orillia, ON L3V 7R2
Tel: 705-325-1355; *Fax:* 705-325-4033
www.orilliapacket.com
Social Media:
twitter.com/OrilliaPacket
www.facebook.com/OrilliaPacketTimes
Circulation: 51,924 total; *Frequency:* Monday-Saturday
Brian Rodnick, Editor
brian.rodnick@sunmedia.ca
Nathan Taylor, City Editor
nathan.taylor@sunmedia.ca

***Ottawa:* Le Droit**
Détenteur: Groupe Capitales Médias Inc.
CP 8860 T, #222, 47 Clarence St., Ottawa, ON K1N 3J9
Tél: 613-562-0111; *Téléc:* 613-562-7572
nouvelles@ledroit.com
www.lapresse.ca/le-droit/
Médias sociaux:
twitter.com/LeDroitca
Tirage: 205 136 total; *Fréquence:* lundi-samedi
Jacques Pronovost, Président et éditeur
Jean Gagnon, Rédacteur

***Ottawa:* Metro Ottawa**
Owned By: Torstar Corp.
#100, 130 Slater St., Ottawa, ON K1P 6E2
Tel: 613-236-5058; *Fax:* 866-253-2024
ottawaletters@metronews.ca
metronews.ca/news/ottawa
Other information: Toll Free Fax: 1-866-253-2024
Circulation: 238,651 total; *Frequency:* Monday-Friday
Dara Mottahed, Publisher

***Ottawa:* Ottawa Citizen**
Owned By: Postmedia Network Inc.
PO Box 5020, 1101 Baxter Rd., Ottawa, ON K2C 3M4
Tel: 613-829-9100; *Fax:* 613-726-1198
Toll-Free: 800-267-6100
letters@ottawacitizen.com
www.ottawacitizen.com
Circulation: 626,272 total; *Frequency:* Monday-Saturday
Andrew Potter, Editor
apotter@ottawacitizen.com

***Ottawa:* The Ottawa Sun**
Previous Name: Ottawa Sun and Sunday Sun
Owned By: Postmedia Network Inc.
PO Box 9729 T, 18A Antares Dr., Ottawa, ON K2E 1A9
Tel: 613-739-7000; *Fax:* 613-739-8041
ottsun.city@sunmedia.ca
www.ottawasun.com
Social Media:
twitter.com/ottawasuncom
www.facebook.com/OttawaSun
Circulation: 266,777; *Frequency:* Daily
Michelle Walters, Managing Editor
michelle.walters@sunmedia.ca

***Owen Sound:* The Sun Times**
Owned By: Postmedia Network Inc.
290 - 9th St. East, Owen Sound, ON N4K 5P2
Tel: 519-376-2250; *Fax:* 519-376-7190
osst.news@sunmedia.ca
www.owensoundsuntimes.com
Social Media:
twitter.com/OwenSoundST
www.facebook.com/pages/Owen-Sound-Sun-Time s/1058115027839
Circulation: 84,457 total; *Frequency:* Monday-Saturday
Doug Edgar, Managing Editor
doug.edgar@sunmedia.ca

***Pembroke:* The Daily Observer**
Previous Name: Pembroke Observer
Owned By: Postmedia Network Inc.
100 Crandall St., Pembroke, ON K8A 0B1
Tel: 613-732-3691; *Fax:* 613-732-2226
pem.editorial@sunmedia.ca
www.thedailyobserver.ca
Social Media:
twitter.com/Pemobserver
www.facebook.com/TheDailyObserver
Circulation: 16,655 total; *Frequency:* Tuesday-Saturday
Anthony Dixon, Managing Editor
anthony.dixon@sunmedia.ca

***Peterborough:* The Peterborough Examiner**
Owned By: Postmedia Network Inc.
PO Box 3890, 60 Hunter St. East, Peterborough, ON K9J 3L4
Tel: 705-745-4641; *Fax:* 705-745-3361
exam.newsroom@sunmedia.ca
www.thepeterboroughexaminer.com
Circulation: 92,301 total; *Frequency:* Monday-Saturday
Kennedy Gordon, Managing Editor
kennedy.gordon@sunmedia.ca

***Sarnia:* The Sarnia Observer**
Owned By: Postmedia Network Inc.
140 South Front St., Sarnia, ON N7T 7M8
Tel: 519-344-3641; *Fax:* 519-332-2951
editorial@theobserver.ca
www.theobserver.ca
Social Media:
twitter.com/sarniaObserver
www.facebook.com/sarniaobserver
Circulation: 55,904 total; *Frequency:* Monday-Saturday
Peter Epp, Managing Editor
peter.epp@sunmedia.ca

***Sault Ste. Marie:* The Sault Star**
Owned By: Postmedia Network Inc.
145 Old Garden River Rd., Sault Ste. Marie, ON P6A 5M5
Tel: 705-759-3030; *Fax:* 705-759-5947
ssmstar@saultstar.com
www.saultstar.com
Social Media:
twitter.com/SaultStar
www.facebook.com/SaultStar
Circulation: 59,680 total; *Frequency:* Monday-Saturday
Frank Rupnik, Regional Managing Editor
frank.rupnik@sunmedia.ca

***Simcoe:* Simcoe Reformer**
Owned By: Postmedia Network Inc.
50 Gilberston Dr., Simcoe, ON N3Y 4L2
Tel: 519-426-5710
www.simcoereformer.ca
Social Media:
twitter.com/simcoe_reformer
www.facebook.com/simcoereformer
Circulation: 47,341 total; *Frequency:* Tuesday-Saturday
Kim Novak, Regional Managing Editor
kim.novak@sunmedia.ca

***St Catharines:* The St. Catharines Standard**
Owned By: Postmedia Network Inc.
#10, 1 St. Paul St., St. Catharines, ON L2R 7L4
Tel: 905-684-7251; *Fax:* 905-684-6032
standard@stcatharinesstandard.ca
www.stcatharinesstandard.ca
Social Media:
twitter.com/stcatstandard
www.facebook.com/stcatharinesstandard
Circulation: 138,961 total; *Frequency:* Monday-Saturday
Peter Conradi, Editor-in-Chief
peter.conradi@sunmedia.ca
Erica Bajer, Managing Editor
erica.bajer@sunmedia.ca

***St Thomas:* The St. Thomas Times-Journal**
Owned By: Postmedia Network Inc.
16 Hincks St., St. Thomas, ON N5R 5Z2
Tel: 519-631-2790
www.stthomastimesjournal.com
Social Media:
twitter.com/Timesjournal
www.facebook.com/stthomastimesjournal
Circulation: 16,465 total; *Frequency:* Tuesday-Saturday
Ian McCallum, Page Editor
ian.mccallum@sunmedia.ca

***Stratford:* Stratford Beacon Herald**
Owned By: Postmedia Network Inc.
789 Erie St., Stratford, ON N4Z 1A1
Tel: 519-271-2222
www.stratfordbeaconherald.com
Social Media:
twitter.com/ThebeaconHerald
www.facebook.com/stratfordbeaconherald
Circulation: 40,080 total; *Frequency:* Monday-Saturday
Dave Carter, Group Advertising Director
dave.carter@sunmedia.ca

***Sudbury:* The Sudbury Star**
Owned By: Postmedia Network Inc.
#201, 128 Pine St., Sudbury, ON P3C 1X3
Tel: 705-674-5271; *Fax:* 705-674-0624
editorial@thesudburystar.com
www.thesudburystar.com
Social Media:
www.twitter.com/sudburystar
www.facebook.com/thesudburystar
Circulation: 57,435 total; *Frequency:* Monday-Saturday
Don MacDonald, Managing Editor
don.macdonald@sunmedia.ca

***Thunder Bay:* The Chronicle-Journal**
Previous Name: Times-News
Owned By: Continental Newspapers Canada Ltd.
75 South Cumberland St., Thunder Bay, ON P7B 1A3
Tel: 807-343-6200
www.chroniclejournal.com
Social Media:
twitter.com/cj_thunderbay
www.facebook.com/chroniclejournal
Circulation: 143,679 total; *Frequency:* Daily
Clint Harris, Publisher & General Manager
Greg Giddens, Managing Editor
ggiddens@chroniclejournal.com

***Timmins:* Timmins Daily Press**
Owned By: Postmedia Network Inc.
187 Cedar St. South, Timmins, ON P4N 7G1
Tel: 705-268-5050; *Fax:* 705-268-7373
news@thedailypress.ca
www.timminspress.com
Social Media:
twitter.com/TimminsPress
www.facebook.com/TimminsDailyPress
Circulation: 42,726 total; *Frequency:* Monday-Saturday
Thomas Perry, Managing Editor
thomas.perry@sunmedia.ca

***Toronto:* The Globe and Mail**
Owned By: The Globe and Mail Inc.
444 Front St. West, Toronto, ON M5V 2S9
Tel: 416-585-5000; *Fax:* 416-585-5102
Newsroom@globeandmail.com
www.theglobeandmail.com
Circulation: 2,149,124 total; *Frequency:* Monday-Saturday
Phillip Crawley, Publisher
David Walmsley, Editor-in-Chief
dwalmsley@globeandmail.com

***Toronto:* Metro Toronto**
Previous Name: Metro Today
Owned By: Torstar Corp.
1 Yonge St., 2nd Fl., Toronto, ON M5E 1E6
Tel: 416-486-4900; *Fax:* 416-482-8097
Toll-Free: 888-916-3876
torontoletters@metronews.ca
metronews.ca/news/toronto
Other information: News tips: toronto@metronews.ca; Ads: adinfotoronto@metronews.ca
Social Media:
twitter.com/metrotoronto
facebook.com/metrotoronto
Circulation: 1,103,886 total; *Frequency:* Monday-Friday

***Toronto:* National Post**
Owned By: Postmedia Network Inc.
365 Bloor St. East, 3rd Fl., Toronto, ON M4W 3L4
Tel: 416-383-2300; *Fax:* 416-383-2305
Toll-Free: 800-267-6568
www.nationalpost.com
Social Media: pinterest.com/nationalpost
twitter.com/nationalpost
www.facebook.com/N ationalPost
Circulation: 1,097,080 total; *Frequency:* Monday-Saturday
Toronto's daily news
Anne Marie Owens, Editor-in-Chief

***Toronto:* The Toronto Star**
Owned By: Torstar Corp.
1 Yonge St., Toronto, ON M5E 1E6
Tel: 416-367-2000; *Fax:* 416-869-4328
Toll-Free: 800-268-9213
city@thestar.ca
www.thestar.com
Social Media:
twitter.com/TorontoStar
www.facebook.com/torontostar
Circulation: 2,397,691 total; *Frequency:* Daily
Canada's largest daily newspaper
David Holland, Acting Publisher
Michael Cooke, Editor

***Toronto:* The Toronto Sun**
Owned By: Postmedia Network Inc.
333 King St. East, Toronto, ON M5A 3X5
Tel: 416-947-2222; *Fax:* 416-368-0374
torsun.citydesk@sunmedia.ca
www.torontosun.com
Other information: Circulation: webservices@sunmedia.ca. Ads: torsun.retail@sunmedia.ca
Social Media:
twitter.com/TheTorontoSun
www.facebook.com/torontosun
Circulation: 171,639 Sunday, 967,574 total; *Frequency:* Daily
Mike Power, Publisher

***Toronto:* 24 Hours Toronto**
Owned By: Postmedia Network Inc.
333 King St. East, Toronto, ON M5A 3X5
Tel: 416-350-6400; *Fax:* 416-350-6523
eedition.toronto.24hrs.ca
Circulation: 1,095,994 total; *Frequency:* Monday-Friday

***Welland:* Welland Tribune**
Previous Name: Welland-Port Colborne Tribune
Owned By: Postmedia Network Inc.
228 East Main St., Welland, ON L3B 5P5
Tel: 905-732-2411
welland.tribune@sunmedia.ca
www.wellandtribune.ca
Social Media:
twitter.com/wellandtribune
www.facebook.com/wellandtribune
Circulation: 62,762 total; *Frequency:* Monday-Saturday
Peter Conradi, Managing Editor
peter.conradi@sunmedia.ca

***Windsor:* The Windsor Star**
Owned By: Postmedia Network Inc.
300 Ouellette Ave., Windsor, ON N9A 7B4
Tel: 519-255-5711; *Fax:* 519-255-5515
Toll-Free: 800-265-5647
letters@windsorstar.com; news@windsorstar.com
www.windsorstar.com
Social Media:
twitter.com/TheWindsorStar
facebook.com/windsorstar
Circulation: 325,360 total; *Frequency:* Monday-Saturday
Marty Beneteau, Editor-in-Chief
519-255-5714
mbeneteau@windsorstar.com

***Woodstock:* The Woodstock Sentinel Review**
Previous Name: Woodstock-Ingersoll Daily Sentinel Review
Owned By: Postmedia Network Inc.
16 Brock St., Woodstock, ON N4S 3B4
Tel: 519-537-2341
www.woodstocksentinelreview.com
Social Media:
twitter.com/woodstocksr
www.facebook.com/sentinelreview
Circulation: 22,278 total; *Frequency:* Monday-Saturday
Bruce Urquhart, Managing Editor
bruce.urquhart@sunmedia.ca

Other Newspapers in Ontario

***Ailsa Craig:* Middlesex Banner**
Owned By: Banner Publications
PO Box 433, 175 Main St., Ailsa Craig, ON N0M 1A0
Tel: 519-293-1095; *Fax:* 519-293-1095
editor@banner.on.ca
www.banner.on.ca
Circulation: 1,170; *Frequency:* Wed.
Brad Harness, Publisher & Editor

***Alexandria:* Glengarry News**
Owned By: Glengarry News Ltd.
PO Box 10, 3 Main St., Alexandria, ON K0C 1A0
Tel: 613-525-2020; *Fax:* 613-525-3824
gnews@glengarrynews.ca
www.glengarrynews.ca
Social Media:
www.facebook.com/pages/The-Glengarry-News/128432023877168
Circulation: 4,700; *Frequency:* Wednesday
Kevin Macdonald, President
J.T. Grossmith, Publisher
Steven Warburton, Managing Editor

***Alliston:* Alliston Herald**
Owned By: Metroland Media Group Ltd.
PO Box 280, #22, 169 Dufferin St. South, Alliston, ON L9R 1E6
Tel: 705-435-6228; *Fax:* 705-435-3342
www.simcoe.com/community/alliston
Social Media:
twitter.com/allistonherald
facebook.com/AllistonHerald
Circulation: 22,000; *Frequency:* Tuesday, Thursday
Ian Proudfoot, Publisher
Elise Allain, General Manager
eallain@simcoe.com
Amanda Smug, Manager, Sales
asmug@simcoe.com

Maija Hoggett, Editor
mhoggett@simcoe.com
Heather Harris, Manager, Distribution
hharris@simcoe.com

Arnprior: Arnprior Chronicle-Guide
Owned By: Metroland Media Group Ltd.
8 McGonigal St. West, Arnprior, ON K7S 1L8
Tel: 613-623-6571
issuu.com/arnpriorchronicleguide
Circulation: 7,941; *Frequency:* Thursday
Cindy Manor, General Manager
cmanor@metroland.com
Ryland Coyne, Editor-in-Chief
rcoyne@metroland.com

Arnprior: West Carleton Review
Previous Name: West Carleton Review, West Carleton
8 McGonigal St., Arnprior, ON K7S 1L8
Tel: 613-623-6571
issuu.com/westcarletonreview
Social Media:
twitter.com/emcnews
www.facebook.com/emcnewspaper
Frequency: Weekly
Mike Tracy, General Manager
mike.tracy@metroland.com
Ryland Coyne, Editor-in-Chief
rcoyne@metroland.com

Atikokan: Atikokan Progress
Owned By: Atikokan Printing (1994) Ltd.
PO Box 220, 109 Main St. East, Atikokan, ON P0T 1C0
Tel: 807-597-2731; *Fax:* 807-597-6103
info@atikokanprogress.ca
www.atikokanprogress.ca
Social Media:
www.facebook.com/pages/Atikokan-Progress/101501558551702
4
Circulation: 1,260; *Frequency:* Monday
Eve Shine, Publisher
Michael P. McKinnon, Editor

Aurora: Aurora Banner
Owned By: York Region Media Group
250 Industrial Pkwy. North, Aurora, ON L4G 4C3
Tel: 905-727-0819; *Fax:* 905-727-2909
yrcustomerservice@yrmg.com
www.yorkregion.com
Frequency: Twice a week, Thursday and Sunday
Tracy Kibble, Managing Editor

Aurora: The Auroran
#8, 15213 Yonge St., Aurora, ON L4G 1L8
Tel: 905-727-3300
support@theauroran.com (technical department)
www.auroran.com
Circulation: 19,160; *Frequency:* Wed.
The Auroran is an independent community newspaper.
Bob Ince, General Manager & Contact, Advertising
bob@auroran.com
Cynthia Proctor, Manager, Production
cynthia@auroran.com
Zach Shoub, Manager, Operations
zach@auroran.com
Brock Weir, Editor
brock@auroran.com

Aylmer: Aylmer Express
Owned By: Aylmer Express
PO Box 160, 390 Talbot St. East, Aylmer, ON N5H 2R9
Tel: 519-773-3126; *Fax:* 519-773-3147
Toll-Free: 800-465-9433
www.aylmerexpress.com
Circulation: 3,400; *Frequency:* Wednesday
John Hueston, Publisher & Editor

Ayr: The Ayr News
Owned By: Ayr News Ltd.
PO Box 1173, 40 Piper St., Ayr, ON N0B 1E0
Tel: 519-632-7432; *Fax:* 519-632-7743
ayrnews@golden.net
www.ayrnews.ca
Circulation: 3,100; *Frequency:* Wednesday
Heidi Schmidt, President & Editor
James W. Schmidt, Publisher
jw.schmidt@ayrnews.ca

Bancroft: Bancroft This Week
Previous Name: Bancroft Times
PO Box 1254, 254 Hastings St., Bancroft, ON K0L 1C0
Tel: 613-332-2002; *Fax:* 613-332-1710
bancroft-times@sympatico.ca
www.bancroftthisweek.com
Other information: Letters to editor: nate@haliburtonpress.com
Social Media:
twitter.com/BancroftTWeek
facebook.com/bancroftthisweek
Circulation: 7,870; *Frequency:* Friday
David Zilstra, Publisher
david.zilstra@gmail.com
Jenn Watt, Managing Editor
jenn@haliburtonpress.com

Barrie: Barrie Advance
Owned By: Metroland Media Group Ltd.
21 Patterson Rd., Barrie, ON L4N 7W6
Tel: 705-726-0573; *Fax:* 705-726-9350
www.simcoe.com
Social Media:
twitter.com/barrieadvance
facebook.com/newsbarrieadvance
Circulation: 104,800; *Frequency:* Tuesday, Thursday
Ian Proudfoot, Publisher
iproudfoot@metroland.com
Elise Allain, General Manager
eallain@simcoe.com
Lori Martin, Editor-in-Chief
lmartin@simcoe.com

Barrie: Barrie Examiner
Owned By: Sun Media Corp.
571 Bayfield St., Barrie, ON L4M 4Z9
Tel: 705-726-6537; *Fax:* 705-726-5148
www.thebarrieexaminer.com
Social Media:
twitter.com/BarrieExaminer
www.facebook.com/pages/Barrie-Examiner/335403 395723
Circulation: Tu, W, F, Sa 6000; Th 44,000; *Frequency:* Tues.-Sat.
Sandy Davies, Publisher
sandy.davies@sunmedia.ca
Brian Rodnick, Editor
brian.rodnick@sunmedia.ca

Barrie: Innisfil Examiner
Owned By: Simcoe-York Printing & Publishing Ltd.
571 Bayfield St., Barrie, ON L4M 4Z9
Tel: 705-726-6537; *Fax:* 705-726-5148
www.innisfilexaminer.ca
Social Media:
twitter.com/Innisfilexamin1
facebook.com/pages/Innisfil-Examiner/1928014 37495824
Circulation: 11,000; *Frequency:* Friday
Sandy Davies, Publisher
sandy.davies@sunmedia.ca
Brian Rodnick, Editor
brian.rodnick@sunmedia.ca

Barry's Bay: The Valley Gazette
PO Box 375, 19574 Opeongo Line, Barry's Bay, ON K0J 1B0
Tel: 613-756-0256
www.thevalleygazette.ca
Social Media: youtube.com/user/ValleyGazette
twitter.com/valleygazette1
facebook. com/pages/The-Valley-/128742167181043
Circulation: 1,400; *Frequency:* Wednesday
Michel Lavigne, Publisher & Editor
michel@thevalleygazette.ca

Beamsville: Lincoln Post Express
PO Box 400, 4309 Central Ave., Beamsville, ON L0R 1B0
Tel: 905-563-5393; *Fax:* 905-563-7977
Circulation: 16,000; *Frequency:* Weekly
Tim Dundas, Publisher
Tom Wilkinson, Editor

Beeton: Beeton/New Tecumseth Times
Previous Name: Tottenham Times, New Tecumseth Times
Owned By: Simcoe-York Printing and Publishing Ltd.
34 Main St. West, Beeton, ON L0G 1A0
Tel: 905-729-2287; *Fax:* 905-729-2541
editor.syp@rogers.com
newspapers-online.com/tecumseth
Other information: Front office email: sylvia@simcoeyorkprinting.com
Social Media:
twitter.com/NewTecTimes
facebook.com/newtectimes
Circulation: 1,400; *Frequency:* Thurs.
John Miles, General Manager
Wendy Soloduik, News Editor
wendy@simcoeyorkprinting.com
Annette Derraugh, Contact, Advertising
annette@simcoeyorkprinting.com

Beeton: Woodbridge Advertiser
PO Box 379, 2 Main St. West, Beeton, ON L0G 1A0
Tel: 905-729-4501 *Toll-Free:* 888-285-4501
wa@csolve.net
auctionsontario.ca
Social Media:
twitter.com/OntarioAuctions
facebook.com/WoodbridgeAdvertiser
Circulation: 5,500; *Frequency:* Thu.
Karl Mallette, Publisher
info@ontariosauctionpaper.com
Tina Dedels, Editor

Belle River: Lakeshore News
Previous Name: North Essex News
Owned By: Postmedia Network Inc.
473 Notre Dame, Belle River, ON N0R 1A0
Tel: 519-728-1082; *Fax:* 519-728-4551
lakeshore@windsoressexnews.com
lakeshore-news-belle-river.windsordirect. info
Circulation: 9,300; *Frequency:* Thursday
Bob Thwaites, Publisher
William Harris, Editor
Wendie Conliffe, Contact

Belleville: Belleville News
Owned By: Metroland Media Group Ltd.
PO Box 25009, 250 Sidney St., Belleville, ON K8P 5E0
Tel: 613-966-2034; *Fax:* 613-966-8747
www.emcbelleville.com
Social Media:
twitter.com/emcnews
www.facebook.com/emcnewspaper
Circulation: 24,100; *Frequency:* Thurs.
Mike Mount, Vice-President & Regional Publisher
John Kearns, Publisher
jkearns@theemc.ca
Terry Bush, Regional Managing Editor
tbush@theemc.ca

Belleville: Belleville Shopper's Market
PO Box 446, 365 North Front St., Belleville, ON K8N 5A5
Tel: 866-541-6757; *Fax:* 866-757-0227
www.shoppersmarket.on.ca
Circulation: 42,800; *Frequency:* Saturday
Charles Parker, General Manager

Belleville: The Community Press
Owned By: Sun Media Corp.
#33, 199 Front St., Belleville, ON K8N 5H5
Tel: 613-962-9171; *Fax:* 613-962-9652
www.communitypress.ca
Social Media:
twitter.com/community_press
www.facebook.com/TheCommunityPress
Circulation: 45,400; *Frequency:* Thurs.
THe Community Press is a member of Canoe Sun Media Community Newspapers.
Darren Murphy, Publisher
Bill Glisky, Regional Managing Editor
bill.glisky@sunmedia.ca
Janet Richards, City Editor
janet.richards@sunmedia.ca

Belleville: Trentonian
Owned By: Sun Media Corp.
#535, 199 Front St., Belleville, ON K8V 5H5
Tel: 613-392-6501; *Fax:* 613-392-0505
tren.newsroom@sunmedia.ca
www.trentonian.ca
Social Media:
twitter.com/TheTrentonian
www.facebook.com/pages/The-Trentonian/16 4324826919177
Circulation: 14,000; *Frequency:* Thurs.
Bill Glisky, Regional Managing Editor
bill.glisky@sunmedia.ca
Tim Meeks, City Editor
tim.meeks@sunmedia.ca

Blenheim: Blenheim News-Tribune
Owned By: Blenheim Publishers
PO Box 160, 62 Talbot St. West, Blenheim, ON N0P 1A0
Tel: 519-676-3321; *Fax:* 519-676-3454
tribune@southkent.net
Circulation: 2,270; *Frequency:* Wednesday
Peter Laurie, Editor

Blyth: The Citizen
Owned By: North Huron Publishing Inc.
PO Box 429, Blyth, ON N0M 1H0
Tel: 519-523-4792; *Fax:* 519-523-9140
info@northhuron.on.ca
www.northhuron.on.ca

Circulation: 1,800; *Frequency:* Thursday
Keith Roulston, Publisher
Shawn Loughlin, Editor

Bolton: Caledon Citizen
Owned By: Caledon Publishing Ltd.
25 Queen St., Bolton, ON L7E 1C1
Tel: 905-857-6626; *Fax:* 905-857-6363
admin@caledoncitizen.com
www.caledoncitizen.com

Circulation: 17,000; *Frequency:* Thursday
Alan Claridge, Publisher
publisher@citizen.on.ca
Bill Rea, Editor
4164583944
editor@caledoncitizen.com

Bolton: Caledon Enterprise
Previous Name: Bolton Entrprise
Owned By: Metroland Media Group Ltd.
PO Box 99, #4A, 12612 Hwy. 50, Bolton, ON L7E 5T1
Tel: 905-454-4344
Ads: advertising@caledonenterprise.com
caledonenterprise.com
Other information: Classifieds email:
classified@caledonenterprise.com
Social Media:
twitter.com/CaledonNews
facebook.com/pages/Caledon-/197774103574450
Circulation: 30,000; *Frequency:* Tuesday, Thursday
Steve Foreman, General Manager
Chris Vernon, Regional Managing Editor
editorial@caledonenterprise.com

Bolton: King Weekly Sentinel
Previous Name: King Township Sentinel
Owned By: Simcoe-York Printing & Publishing Ltd.
25 Queen St. North, Bolton, ON L7E 1C1
Tel: 905-857-6626; *Fax:* 905-729-2541
www.kingsentinel.com
Social Media:
facebook.com/thekingsentinel
Circulation: 7,800; *Frequency:* Wed.
Mark Pavilons, Editor
editor@kingsentinel.com

Bracebridge: Bracebridge Examiner
Owned By: Metroland Media Group Ltd.
PO Box 1049, 34 E.P. Lee Dr., Bracebridge, ON P1L 1V2
Tel: 705-645-8771; *Fax:* 705-645-1718
examnews@muskoka.com
www.muskokaregion.com/bracebridge-on
Social Media:
twitter.com/BracebridgeExam
www.facebook.com/examinerbannernews
Circulation: 9,400; *Frequency:* Wednesday
Maureen Christie, Publisher
mchristie@metroland.com
Jack Tynan, Editor-in-Chief
jtynan@metrolandnorthmedia.com
Kim Good, Sub-editor
kgood@metrolandmedia.com

Bracebridge: Muskoka Sun
Previous Name: Muskoka Sun
Owned By: Metroland Media
34 E.P. Lee Dr., Bracebridge, ON P1L 1V2
Tel: 705-645-4463; *Fax:* 705-645-1718
sun@muskoka.com
www.cottagecountrynow.ca/topic/MuskokaSun
Social Media:
twitter.com/TheMuskokaSun
Circulation: 11,000; *Frequency:* Weekly
Shaun Sauve, Regional General Manager
ssauve@metroland.com
Kim Good, Sub-editor
kgood@metrolandmedia.com

Bracebridge: The Muskokan
Owned By: Metroland Media
PO Box 1049, 34 E.P. Lee Dr., Bracebridge, ON P1L 1V2
Tel: 705-645-8771; *Fax:* 705-645-1718
www.muskokaregion.com/muskokaregion
Circulation: 25,000; *Frequency:* Weekly; Thursday
Maureen Christie, General Manager
mchristie@metroland.com
Jack Tynan, Editor-in-Chief
jtynan@metrolandnorthmedia.com
Kim Good, Sub-editor
kgood@metrolandnorthmedia.com

Bradford: Bradford West Gwillimbury Times
PO Box 1570, 74 John St. West, Bradford, ON L3Z 2B8
Tel: 905-775-4471; *Fax:* 905-775-4489
www.bradfordtimes.ca

Circulation: 11,000; *Frequency:* Saturday
Miriam King, Editor
905-775-4471 ext 223
David Zilstra, Publisher
905-775-4471 ext 263

Brantford: The Paris Star
Owned By: Sun Media Corp.
#1, 195 Henry St., Brantford, ON N3S 5C9
Tel: 519-442-7866; *Fax:* 519-442-3100
www.parisstaronline.com
Social Media:
twitter.com/ParisStar
www.facebook.com/pages/The-Paris-Star/114234 248620217
Circulation: 775; *Frequency:* Wednesday
Ken Koyama, Publisher
ken.koyama@sunmedia.ca
Michael Peeling, Editor
michael.peeling@sunmedia.ca

Bridgebridge: Gravenhurst Banner
Owned By: Metroland Media Group Ltd.
34 E.P. Lee Dr., Bridgebridge, ON P1L 1V2
Tel: 705-687-6674
www.cottagecountrynow.ca/community/southmuskoka
Social Media:
www.facebook.com/examinerbannernews/examinerbannernews
Circulation: 3,043; *Frequency:* Wednesday
Joe Anderson, Publisher

Brighton: The Independent
Owned By: Metroland Media Group Ltd.
PO Box 1030, 1 Young St., Brighton, ON K0K 1H0
Tel: 613-475-0255; *Fax:* 613-475-4546
www.northumberlandnews.com

Circulation: 17,000; *Frequency:* Thursday
Tim Whittaker, Publisher
Crystal Crimi, Editor

Brockville: St. Lawrence News
Owned By: Metroland Media
7712 Kent Blvd., Brockville, ON K6V 7H6
Tel: 613-342-0305; *Fax:* 613-498-0307
Toll-Free: 866-242-0262
www.emcstlawrence.ca
Social Media:
twitter.com/emcnews
www.facebook.com/emcnewspaper
Circulation: 29,500; *Frequency:* Thurs.
Richard Squires, Supervisor, Distribution
richard.rquires@metroland.com
Marla Dowdall, News Editor
mdowdall@perfprint.ca

Burks Falls: Almaguin News
Previous Name: Burks Falls-Powasson Almaguin News
Owned By: Metroland Media Group Ltd.
59 Ontario St., Burks Falls, ON P0A 1C0
Tel: 705-382-9996; *Fax:* 705-382-9997
Toll-Free: 800-731-6397
www.almaguinnews.com

Circulation: 2,500; *Frequency:* Thursday
Scott Sauve, Regional General Manager
ssauve@metrolandmedia.com
Jack Tynan, Editor-in-Chief
jtynan@metrolandmedia.com

Burlington: Burlington Post
Owned By: Metroland Media Group Ltd.
#1, 5040 Mainway, Burlington, ON L7L 7G5
Tel: 905-632-4444; *Fax:* 905-632-9162
Letters to editor: letters@burlingtonpost.com
insidehalton.com/burlington-on
Other information: Classifieds: classified@haltonsearch.com
Social Media:
twitter.com/InsideHalton
facebook.com/HaltonPhotog
Circulation: 60,000; *Frequency:* Wednesday, Thursday, Friday
Neil Oliver, Publisher
Jill Davis, Editor-in-Chief
jdavis@burlingtonpost.com
Debbi Koppejan, Director, Advertising
dkoppejan@metroland.com

Burlington: The Oakville Beaver
Owned By: Metroland Media Group Ltd.
#2, 5046 Mainway, Burlington, ON L7L 7G5
Tel: 905-845-3824
www.insidehalton.com
Social Media:
twitter.com/oakvillebeaver
www.facebook.com/OakvilleBeav
Circulation: 147,652; *Frequency:* Wednesday - Friday
Oakville's community newspaper; print and online editions
Angela Blackburn, Contact

Caledonia: The Sachem
Owned By: Metroland Media Group Ltd.
3 Sutherland St. West, Caledonia, ON N3W 1C1
Tel: 905-765-4441; *Fax:* 905-765-3651
news@sachem.ca; advertising@sachem.ca
www.sachem.ca
Social Media:
twitter.com/sachemnews
facebook.com/thesachem
Circulation: 21,200; *Frequency:* Thursday
Neil Dring, Associate Publisher
ndring@sachem.ca
Katie Dawson, Editor

Cambridge: Cambridge Times
Owned By: Metroland Media Group Ltd.
#1-4, 475 Thompson Dr., Cambridge, ON N1T 2K7
Tel: 519-623-7395; *Fax:* 519-623-9155
www.cambridgetimes.ca
Social Media:
twitter.com/cambridgetimes
facebook.com/pages/Cambridge-/267977793339111
Circulation: 48,000; *Frequency:* Tuesday, Thursday, Friday
Peter Winkler, Publisher
pwinkler@cambridgetimes.ca
Richard Vivian, Editor
rvivian@cambridgetimes.ca

Cannington: Brock Citizen
Owned By: Metroland Media Group Ltd.
2D Cameron St. East, Cannington, ON L0E 1E0
Tel: 705-432-8842; *Fax:* 705-432-2942
www.mykawartha.com
Social Media:
twitter.com/BrockCitizen
Circulation: 5,400; *Frequency:* Thursday
Mike Mount, Publisher
mike.mount@mykawartha.com
Scott Howard, Editor
showard@mykawartha.com

Chatham: Chatham Smart Shopper
Owned By: Sun Media Corp.
138 King St. West, 2nd Fl., Chatham, ON N7M 1E3
Tel: 519-351-4362; *Fax:* 519-351-7774
Toll-Free: 877-351-7331
classifieds.chathamsmartshopper.com
Dean Muharrem, Manager, Advertising
dean.muharrem@sunmedia.ca

Chatham: Chatham This Week
Owned By: Sun Media Corp.
138 King St. West, Chatham, ON N7M 1E3
Tel: 519-351-7331; *Fax:* 519-351-7774
www.chathamthisweek.com
Social Media:
twitter.com/ctw_news
www.facebook.com/pages/Chatham-This-Week/1119 10658860951
Circulation: 19,600; *Frequency:* Wednesday
Dean Muharrem, Publisher
519-598-4700
dead.muharrem@sunmedia.ca
Peter Epp, Editor
519-598-4727
peter.epp@sunmedia.ca

Chatham: Wallaceburg Courier Press
Owned By: Sun Media Corp.
138 King St. West, Chatham, ON N7M 1E3
Tel: 519-351-7331; *Fax:* 519-351-7334
www.wallaceburgcourierpress.com
Social Media:
twitter.com/w_courierpress
www.facebook.com/pages/Wallaceburg-Courier-Press/15259469

Circulation: 8,900; *Frequency:* Thurs.
Dean Muharrem, Publisher
dean.muharrem@sunmedia.ca
Peter Epp, Editor
peter.epp@sunmedia.ca

***Chesterville:* Chesterville Record**
Owned By: Etcetera Publications
PO Box 368, 7 King St., Chesterville, ON K0C 1H0
Tel: 613-448-2322 *Toll-Free:* 866-307-3541
chestervillerecord.com
Circulation: 1,900; *Frequency:* Wednesday
Robin Morris, Publisher
record@storm.ca
Nelson Zandbergen, Editor

***Chesterville:* The Villager**
Previous Name: Russell Villager
Owned By: County Media
PO Box 368, 7 King St. St., Chesterville, ON K0C 2K0
Tel: 613-445-3804
adsrussellvillager@gmail.com
russellvillager.com
Social Media:
www.facebook.com/TheRussellVillager
Circulation: 800; *Frequency:* Wed.
Serving Russell Village and Township and surrounding areas.
Robin Morris, Managing Publisher
record@storm.ca
Nelson Zandbergen, Editor
thevillager.editor@gmail.com

***Clinton:* Clinton News-Record**
Owned By: Sun Media Corp.
53 Albert St., Clinton, ON N0M 1L0
Tel: 519-482-3443
www.clintonnewsrecord.com
Social Media:
twitter.com/clintonnewsreco
www.facebook.com/ClintonNewsRecord
Circulation: 1,400; *Frequency:* Wednesday
Neil H. Clifford, Publisher
neil.clifford@sunmedia.ca
Cheryl Heath, Editor
clinton.news@sunmedia.ca

***Cobden:* The Pulse**
Owned By: The Cobden Sun Ltd.
PO Box 100, Crawford St., Cobden, ON K0J 1K0
Tel: 613-646-2380; *Fax:* 613-628-3291
Circulation: 1,374; *Frequency:* Wednesday
Formerly the Cobden Sun
Ron Tracey, Publisher

***Cobourg:* The Northumberland News**
Owned By: Metroland Media Group Ltd.
#212, 884 Division St., Cobourg, ON K9A 5V6
Tel: 905-373-7355; *Fax:* 905-373-4719
northnews@northumberlandnews.com
www.northumberlandnews.com
Social Media:
twitter.com/north_news
www.facebook.com/Northnews
Circulation: 22,800; *Frequency:* Thurs., Fri.
The Ontario communities of Cobourg & Port Hope, & the Townships of Cramahe, Hamilton, & Alnwick/Haldimand are served by The Northumberland News.
Tim Whittaker, Publisher
Joanne Burghardt, Editor in Chief
Fred Eismont, Director, Advertising
Abe Fakhourie, Manager, Distribution
Lillian Hook, Manager, Office
Peter Dounoukos, Senior Sales Representative
pdounoukos@northumberlandnews.com
Carol Chapple, Contact, Classifieds
cchapple@northumberlandnews.com
Layla Dounoukos, Contact, Distribution
ldounoukos@northumberlandnews.com

***Cochrane:* Cochrane Times-Post**
Previous Name: Cochrane Times
Owned By: Sun Media Corp.
143 - 6th Ave., Cochrane, ON P0L 1C0
Tel: 705-272-3344; *Fax:* 705-272-3434
www.cochranetimespost.com
Social Media:
twitter.com/CTimesPost
Circulation: 11,300; *Frequency:* Wed.
Wayne Major, Publisher
wayne.major@sunmedia.ca
Kevin Anderson, Regional Managing Editor
kevin.anderson@sunmedia.ca

***Collingwood:* Collingwood Connection**
Previous Name: Collingwood Connection
Owned By: Metroland Media Group Ltd.
#B, 11 Ronell Cres., Collingwood, ON L9Y 4J6
Tel: 705-444-1875; *Fax:* 705-444-1876
www.simcoe.com
Circulation: 11,000; *Frequency:* Thursday
Carol Lamb, Regional General Manager
clamb@simcoe.com
Erika Engel, Editor
eengel@simcoe.com

***Collingwood:* The Enterprise-Bulletin**
Owned By: Sun Media Corp.
PO Box 98, 77 Simcoe St., Collingwood, ON L9Y 3J9
Tel: 705-445-4611; *Fax:* 705-444-6477
www.theenterprisebulletin.com
Social Media:
twitter.com/EnterpriseBulle
www.facebook.com/theenterprisebulletin
Circulation: 18,800; *Frequency:* Tuesday, Friday
Sandy Davies, Publisher
Ian Adams, Managing Editor
ian.adams@sunmedia.ca

***Cornwall:* Le Journal de Cornwall**
Détenteur: Campagnie d'Edition André Paquette
113 rue de Montréal, Cornwall, ON K6H 1B2
Tél: 613-938-1433; *Téléc:* 613-938-2798
jcornwall@eap.on.ca
editionap.ca/en/newspaper/35
Tirage: 23 000; *Fréquence:* Jeudi
Roger Duplantie, President
roger.duplantie@eap.on.ca

***Cornwall:* Seaway News**
Owned By: J.G.F. Holdings Inc.
29 - 2nd St. East, Cornwall, ON K6H 1Y2
Tel: 613-933-0014; *Fax:* 613-933-0024
diane@cornwallseawaynews.com
www.cornwallseawaynews.com
Social Media:
twitter.com/SeawayNews
facebook.com/cornwallseawaynews
Circulation: 36,500; *Frequency:* Thursday
Rick Shaver, Editor & General Manager
rshaver@conwallseawaynews.com
Joel Herrington, Editor

***Deep River:* North Renfrew Times**
Owned By: Deep River Community Assn. Inc.
PO Box 310, 21 Champlain St., Deep River, ON K0J 1P0
Tel: 613-584-4161; *Fax:* 613-584-1062
nrt@magma.ca
www.northrenfrewtimes.com
Circulation: 1,845; *Frequency:* Wednesday
Terry Myers, Editor-in-Chief
Kelly Lapping, General Manager

***Delhi:* Delhi News-Record**
Owned By: Sun Media Corp.
237 Main St., Delhi, ON N4B 2M4
Tel: 519-582-2510
www.delhinewsrecord.com
Social Media:
twitter.com/DelhiNewsRecord
www.facebook.com/DelhiNewsRecord
Circulation: 503; *Frequency:* Wednesday
Ken Koyama, Publisher
ken.koyama@sunmedia.ca
Kim Novak, Managing Editor
kim.novak@sunmedia.ca

***Dorchester:* Dorchester Signpost**
Owned By: Dorchester Signpost
15 Bridge St., Dorchester, ON N0L 1G2
Tel: 519-268-7337; *Fax:* 519-268-3260
info@dorchestersignpost.com; signpost@rogers.com
www.dorchestersignpost.com
Circulation: 1,670; *Frequency:* Wednesday
Fred Huxley, Publisher
Wendy Spence, Editor
news@dorchestersignpost.com

***Drayton:* The Community News**
Owned By: W.H.A. Publications Ltd.
PO Box 169, 41 Wellington St. North, Drayton, ON N0G 1P0
Tel: 519-638-3066; *Fax:* 519-638-3066
Toll-Free: 800-708-9555
news@wellingtonadvertiser.com
www.wellingtonadvertiser.com
Other information: Ads: advertising@wellingtonadvertiser.com
Circulation: 5,400; *Frequency:* Friday
William H. Adsett, Publisher
David L. Adsett, Editor & General Manager
editor@wellingtonadvertiser.com

***Dryden:* Dryden Observer**
Owned By: Alex Wilson Coldstream Ltd.
PO Box 3009, #1, 32 Colonization Ave, Dryden, ON P8N 2Y9
Tel: 807-223-2381; *Fax:* 807-223-2907
Toll-Free: 800-465-7230
www.drydenobserver.ca
Social Media:
twitter.com/DrydenObserver
facebook.com/pages/Dryden-/169413476422982
Circulation: 2,460; *Frequency:* Wednesday
Chris Marchand, Editor
807-221-7334
chrism@drydenobserver.ca
Graham Mackenzie, General Manager

***Dundalk:* Dundalk Herald**
Owned By: Dundalk Herald Publishing
PO Box 280, 260 Main St. East, Dundalk, ON N0C 1B0
Tel: 519-923-2203; *Fax:* 519-923-2747
dundalk.heraldnews@gmail.com
dundalkherald.ca
Other information: Ads: dundaldkherald@gmail.com
Circulation: 1,700; *Frequency:* Wednesday
Matthew Walls, Publisher
Mary Fowler, Editor

***Dundalk:* The Flesherton Advance**
PO Box 280, 260 Main St. East, Dundalk, ON N0C 1B0
Tel: 519-923-2203; *Fax:* 519-923-2747
dundalk.heraldnews@gmail.com
www.dundalkherald.ca
Other information: Ads: dundalk.herald@gmail.com
Circulation: 1,700; *Frequency:* Wednesday
Matt Walls, Publisher
Cathy Walls, General Manager

***Eganville:* Eganville Leader**
Owned By: The Eganville Leader Publishing Ltd.
PO Box 310, 150 John St., Eganville, ON K0J 1T0
Tel: 613-628-2332; *Fax:* 613-628-3291
leader@nrtco.net
www.eganvilleleader.com
Circulation: 5,800; *Frequency:* Wednesday
Gerald Tracey, Editor & Co-Publisher

***Elliot Lake:* Elliot Lake Standard**
Owned By: Sun Media Corp.
14 Hillside Dr. South, Elliot Lake, ON P5A 1M6
Tel: 705-848-7195; *Fax:* 705-848-0249
news@elliotlakestandard.ca
www.elliotlakestandard.ca
Social Media:
twitter.com/ELStandard
www.facebook.com/pages/Elliot-Lake-Standard/1186295215427
Circulation: 3,400; *Frequency:* Wednesday
Karsten Johansen, Publisher
karsten.johansen@sunmedia.ca
Kevin McSheffrey, Editor
kevin.mcsheffrey@sunmedia.ca

***Elmira:* Elmira Independent**
Owned By: Metroland Media Group Ltd.
PO Box 128, 13A Industrial Dr., Elmira, ON N3B 2Z5
Tel: 519-669-5155; *Fax:* 519-669-5928
editor@elmiraindependent.com
www.elmiraindependent.com
Social Media:
twitter.com/Indyupdates
facebook.com/ElmiraIndependent
Circulation: 1,970; *Frequency:* Thursday
Doug Rowe, General Manager
519-291-1660 ext 116
drowe@southwesternontario.ca
Gail Martin, Editor
519-669-5155 ext 206
gmartin@elmiraindependent.com

***Elmira:* Observer**
20B Arthur St. North, Elmira, ON N3B 1Z9
Tel: 519-669-5790; *Fax:* 519-669-5753
Toll-Free: 888-966-5942
info@woolwichobserver.com
www.observerxtra.com
Other information: Advertising, E-mail: sales@woolwichobserver.com
Social Media: www.flickr.com/photos/observerxtra
twitter.com/woolwichnews
www.facebook.com/pages/The-Woolwich-Observer/4358114228
5

Circulation: 15,200; *Frequency:* Sat.
The community newspaper serves Woolwich & Wellesley Townships in Ontario.
Joe Merlihan, Publisher
jmerlihan@woolwichobserver.com
Steve Kannon, Editor
skannon@woolwichobserver.com

Erin: Erin Advocate
Owned By: Metroland Media Group Ltd.
PO Box 578, #1A, Spring St., Erin, ON N0B 1T0
Tel: 519-833-9603; *Fax:* 519-833-9605
www.metroland.com
Circulation: 1,900; *Frequency:* Thursday
Dana Robbins, Vice President & Regional Publisher
Joan Murray, Managing Editor

Espanola: Mid-North Monitor
Owned By: Sun Media Corp.
#1, 46 Mead Blvd., Espanola, ON P5E 1E8
Tel: 705-869-0588; *Fax:* 705-869-0587
www.midnorthmonitor.com
Social Media:
twitter.com/MidNorthMonitor
facebook.com/MidNorthMonitor
Circulation: 1,000; *Frequency:* Thursday
Karsten Johansen, Publisher
karsten.johansen@sunmedia.ca
Kevin McSheffery, Editor
mnm.editor@sunmedia.ca

Essex: Essex Free Press
Owned By: The Essex Free Press Limited
PO Box 115, 16 Centre St., Essex, ON N8M 2Y1
Tel: 519-776-4268; *Fax:* 519-776-4014
essexfreepress@on.aibn.com
sxfreepress.com; essexfreepress.blogspot.ca
Social Media: youtube.com/user/essexfreepress
twitter.com/essexfreepress
facebook.co m/theessexfreepress
Circulation: 9,950; *Frequency:* Thursday
Richard Parkinson, Editor & Co-Publisher

Exeter: Exeter Times-Advocate
Owned By: Metroland Media Group Ltd.
PO Box 850, 365 Main St., Exeter, ON N0M 1S0
Tel: 519-235-1331; *Fax:* 519-235-0766
www.southwesternontario.ca
Circulation: 2,650; *Frequency:* Wednesday
Deb Lord, Manager
dlord@southhuron.com
Scott Nixon, Editor
snixon@southhuron.com

Fergus: The Wellington Advertiser
Owned By: W.H.A. Publications Ltd.
PO Box 252, 905 Gartshore St., Fergus, ON N1M 2W8
Tel: 519-843-5410; *Fax:* 519-843-7607
News: news@wellingtonadvertiser.com
www.wellingtonadvertiser.com
Other information: Ads: advertising@wellingtonadvertiser.com
Social Media:
twitter.com/WellyAdvertiser
Circulation: 40,470; *Frequency:* Friday
David L. Adsett, Publisher
Chris Daponte, Editor
editor@wellingtonadvertiser.com

Fonthill: The Voice
#8, 209 Hwy. 20 East, Fonthill, ON L0S 1E6
Tel: 905-892-8690; *Fax:* 905-892-0823
classified@thevoiceofpelham.ca
www.thevoiceofpelham.ca
Social Media:
facebook.com/voiceofpelham
Circulation: 5,500; *Frequency:* Wed.
Sarah Murrell, Publisher & Editor
Stephen Dyell, Reporter
editor@thevoiceofpelham.ca
Leslie Chiappetta, Manager, Office
office@thevoiceofpelham.ca
Warren Mason, Contact, Advertising Sales
advertising@thevoiceofpelham.ca

Forest: Forest Standard
Owned By: Hayter-Walden Publications Inc.
1 King St. West, Forest, ON N0N 1J0
Tel: 519-786-5242; *Fax:* 519-786-4884
standard@execulink.com
hayterwalden.com
Circulation: 1,900; *Frequency:* Thursday
Dale Hayter, Publisher
Kimberly Powell, Editor

Fort Erie: Fort Erie Times
Previous Name: Fort Erie Times Review
Owned By: Sun Media Corp.
PO Box 1219, #1, 450 Garrison Rd., Fort Erie, ON L2A 1N2
Tel: 905-871-3100; *Fax:* 905-871-5243
www.forterietimes.com
Social Media:
twitter.com/FortErieTimes
facebook.com/pages/Fort-Erie-Times/10878509916 0935
Circulation: 12,349; *Frequency:* Thursday
Tim Dundas, Publisher
tim.dundas@sunmedia.ca
Kris Dube, Editor
kris.dube@sunmedia.ca

Fort Frances: Fort Frances Times
Owned By: Fort Frances Times Ltd.
116 - 1st St. East, Fort Frances, ON P9A 3M7
Tel: 807-274-5373; *Fax:* 807-274-7286
Toll-Free: 800-465-8508
fftimes.com
Social Media:
twitter.com/hashtag/fortfrances
facebook.com/fortfrancestimes
Circulation: 3,990; *Frequency:* Wednesday
Jim Cumming, Publisher
jcumming@fortfrances.com
Mike Behan, Editor
mbehan@fortfrances.com

Gananoque: Gananoque Reporter
Owned By: Sun Media Corp.
79 King St. East, Gananoque, ON K7G 1E8
Tel: 613-389-7400; *Fax:* 613-382-3010
editor@gananoquereporter.com
www.gananoquereporter.com
Social Media:
twitter.com/GanReporter
www.facebook.com/pages/Gananoque-Reporter/197634110311148
Circulation: 7,500; *Frequency:* Wednesday
Liza Nelson, Publisher
liza.nelson@sunmedi.ca
Mike Beaudin, Managing Editor
mike.beaudin@sunmedi.ca

Georgetown: Georgetown Independent/Acton Free Press
Owned By: Metroland Media Group Ltd.
#77, 280 Guelph St., Georgetown, ON L7G 4B1
Tel: 905-873-0301; *Fax:* 905-873-0398
www.independentfreepress.com
Social Media:
twitter.com/IFP_11
facebook.com/pages/The-Independent-/226903397341755
Circulation: 22,000; *Frequency:* Tuesday, Thursday
Chris Vernon, Managing Editor
cvernon@metroland.com
Steve Foreman, General Manager
sforeman@theifp.ca

Geraldton: Times Star
Owned By: Time Star Publishing
PO Box 340, 401 Main St., Geraldton, ON P0T 1M0
Tel: 807-854-1919; *Fax:* 807-854-1682
web@thetimestar.ca
thetimesstar.ca
Circulation: 938; *Frequency:* Wednesday
Eric Pietsch, Publisher & Editor
editor@thetimestar.ca

Glencoe: Transcript & Free Press
Owned By: Hayter-Walden Publications Inc.
PO Box 400, 243 Main St., Glencoe, ON N0L 1M0
Tel: 519-287-2615; *Fax:* 519-287-2408
tfp@execulink.com
hayterwalden.com
Circulation: 1,100; *Frequency:* Thursday
Dale Hayter, Publisher
Marie Williams-Gagnon, Editor

Gloucester: Orléans Star / Orleans Express
CP 46009, #30, 5300 Canotek Rd., Gloucester, ON K1J 8R7
Tél: 613-323-2801; *Téléc:* 613-744-8232
orleansstar@transcontinental.ca
www.orleansstar.ca
Médias sociaux:
twitter.com/orleansstar
Tirage: 40 000; *Fréquence:* Jeudi
Madeleine Joanisse, Éditeur
Anne Moralejo, Éditeur

Goderich: The Goderich Signal-Star
Owned By: Sun Media Corp.
120 Huckins St., Goderich, ON N7A 3X8
Tel: 519-524-2614; *Fax:* 519-524-9175
www.goderichsignalstar.com
Social Media:
twitter.com/goderichsignals
www.facebook.com/pages/Goderich-Signal-Star/ 284282905213
Circulation: 4000; *Frequency:* Wed; also Focus (every other Fri.)
John Bauman, Publisher
john.bauman@sunmedia.ca
Paul Cluff, Editor

Grand Bend: The Lakeshore Advance
Owned By: Sun Media Corp.
PO Box 1195, 58 Ontario St. North, Grand Bend, ON N0M 1T0
Tel: 519-238-5383; *Fax:* 519-238-5131
lakeshore.advance@sunmedia.ca
www.lakeshoreadvance.com
Social Media:
twitter.com/lakeshoreadvanc
www.facebook.com/pages/Lakeshore-Advance/180897961958469
Circulation: 1,000; *Frequency:* Wednesday
Neil H. Clifford, Publisher
neil.clifford@sunmedia.ca
Lynda Hillman-Rapley, Editor
lakeshore.advance@sunmedia.ca

Gravenhurst: Muskoka Today
PO Box 34, Gravenhurst, ON P1P 1H5
Tel: 705-687-5777 *Toll-Free:* 800-240-2329
news@muskokatoday.com
www.muskokatoday.com
Other information: Advertising email: ads@muskokatoday.com
Circulation: 10,000
Mark Clairmont, Publisher

Grimsby: Grimsby Lincoln News
Owned By: Metroland Media Group Ltd.
32 Main St. West, Grimsby, ON L3M 1R4
Tel: 905-945-8392; *Fax:* 905-945-3916
www.niagarathisweek.com/community/grimsby
Social Media:
facebook.com/GrimsbyLincolnNews
Circulation: 161,000; *Frequency:* Wed., Fri.
The Grimsby Lincoln News is a free tabloid newspaper delivered to every home in the region.
Neil Oliver, Publisher
David Bos, General Manager
Joel Billinghurst, Manager, Production
Melissa Duemo, Manager, Business
Tracy Travis-Scott, Manager, Circulation
Dave Hawkins, Director, Advertising

Grimsby: newsnow
Owned By: 16002207 Ontario Ltd.
49 Main St. West, Grimsby, ON L3M 1R3
Tel: 289-235-9500
wn3.ca
Social Media:
twitter.com/MikesNiagara
Circulation: 25,733; *Frequency:* Thursday
100% Niagara owned, operated & printed
Mike Williscraft, Publisher
289-442-4244

Guelph: The Guelph Tribune
Owned By: Metroland Media Group Ltd.
#7, 367 Woodlawn Rd. West, Guelph, ON N1H 7K9
Tel: 519-763-3333; *Fax:* 519-763-4814
www.guelphtribune.ca
Social Media:
twitter.com/guelphtribune
facebook.com/pages/Guelph-Tribune/106266629404 548
Circulation: 44,700; *Frequency:* Tuesday, Thursday
Chris Clark, Editor
519-763-3333 ext 230
cclark@guelphtribune.ca
Peter Winkler, Publisher

Haliburton: Haliburton Echo
Previous Name: Haliburton County Echo
Owned By: Sun Media Corp.
PO Box 136, 146 Highland St., Haliburton, ON K0M 1S0
Tel: 705-457-1037; *Fax:* 705-457-3275
info@haliburtonecho.on.ca
www.haliburtonecho.ca
Social Media:
twitter.com/haliburtonecho
www.facebook.com/HaliburtonEcho
Circulation: 2,100; *Frequency:* Tuesday

David Zilstra, Publisher
david.zilstra@gmail.com
Jenn Watt, Editor
jenn@haliburtonpress.com

Hamilton: Le Régional Hamilton Branch
970 rue King Est, Hamilton, ON L8M 1C4
Tél: 905-549-7002; *Téléc:* 905-790-9127
info@leregional.com
www.leregional.com
Médias sociaux:
facebook.com/leregionalontario
Tirage: 10 000; *Fréquence:* Mercredi
Christiane Beaupré, Rédactrice en chef

Hanover: The Post (Hanover)
Owned By: Sun Media Corp.
413 - 18th Ave., Hanover, ON N4N 3S5
Tel: 519-364-2001; *Fax:* 519-364-6950
postedit@thepost.on.ca
www.thepost.on.ca
Social Media:
twitter.com/hanoverthepost
www.facebook.com/pages/The-Post-Hanover/28286 2818943
Circulation: 15,500; *Frequency:* Thursday
Patrick Bales, Managing Editor
patrick.bales@sunmedia.ca
Marie David, Publisher
marie.david@sunmedia.ca

Harrow: Harrow News
Owned By: Harrownews Publishing Co. Inc.
PO Box 310, 563 Queen St., Harrow, ON N0R 1G0
Tel: 519-738-2542; *Fax:* 519-738-3874
harnews@mnsi.net
Circulation: 1,300; *Frequency:* Tuesday
Cecil MacKenzie, Publisher & Co-Editor

Hawkesbury: Le Carillon
Détenteur: La Comp. D'Edition Andre Paquette Inc.
CP 1000, 1100 Aberdeen, Hawkesbury, ON K6H 3H1
Tél: 613-632-4155; *Téléc:* 613-632-6122
nouvelles@eap.on.ca
www.lecarillon.ca
Médias sociaux:
facebook.com/LeCarillonTribuneExpress
Tirage: 19 500; *Fréquence:* Mercredi
Yvan Joly, Directeur
yvan.joly@eap.on.ca

Hawkesbury: Le/The Regional
124, rue Principale est, Hawkesbury, ON K6A 1A3
Tel: 613-632-0112; *Fax:* 613-632-0277
Toll-Free: 888-477-3566
pub@le-regional.ca; news@le-regional.ca
www.le-regional.ca
Social Media:
facebook.com/pages/Journal-Le-Régional/266630786710813
Circulation: 27,000; *Frequency:* Fri.
André Cayer
Sylvain Roy

Hawkesbury: Tribune-Express édition Ontario
Previous Name: Hawkesbury Tribune/Express
PO Box 1000, 1100 Aberdeen, Hawkesbury, ON K6H 3H1
Tel: 613-632-4155; *Fax:* 613-632-8601
nouvelles@eap.on.ca
editionap.ca/fr/newspaper/32
Social Media:
facebook.com/LeCarillonTribuneExpress
Circulation: 24,100; *Frequency:* Friday
Yvan Joly, Directeur
yvan.joly@eap.on.ca

Hearst: Le Nord
Détenteur: Le Nord Inc.
CP 2320, 813, rue Georges, Hearst, ON P0L 1N0
Tél: 705-372-1233; *Téléc:* 705-362-5954
lenord@lenord.on.ca
www.lenord.on.ca
Médias sociaux:
www.facebook.com/pages/Journal-Le-Nord-de-Hearst/14860381
Tirage: 1 480; *Fréquence:* Mercredi
Omer Cantin, Éditeur
705-372-1234 ext 222
ocantin@lenord.on.ca
Marlène Bélanger, Gérante
705-372-1237 ext 229
mbelanger@lenord.on.ca

Huntsville: Huntsville Forester
Owned By: Metroland Media Group Ltd.
11 Main St. West, Huntsville, ON P1H 2C5
Tel: 705-789-5541; *Fax:* 705-789-9381
www.muskokaregion.com
Circulation: 10,300; *Frequency:* Wednesday
Shaun Sauve, Regional General Manager
705-645-8771 ext 227
ssauve@metroland.com
Jack Tynan, Editor-in-Chief
705-645-8771 ext 247
jtynan@metrolandnorthmedia.com

Ingersoll: Ingersoll Times
Owned By: Sun Media Corp.
16 Brock St., Ingersoll, ON N4S 3B4
Tel: 519-537-2341; *Fax:* 519-537-3049
www.ingersolltimes.com
Social Media:
twitter.com/IngersollTimes
www.facebook.com/IngersollTimes
Circulation: 728; *Frequency:* Wednesday
Andrea DeMeer, Publisher
ademeer@bowesnet.com
Jennifer Vandermeer, Editor
jennifer.vandermeer@sunmedia.ca

Iroquois Falls: The Enterprise
Owned By: William C. Cavell Enterprises Ltd.
PO Box 834, 727 Synagogue St., Iroquois Falls, ON P0K 1G0
Tel: 705-232-4081
Circulation: 2,130; *Frequency:* Thursday
William C. Cavell, Publisher
Tony Delaurier, General Manager

Johnstown: Barrhaven Independent
Owned By: The Morris Group
3201 County Rd. 2, Johnstown, ON K0E 1T0
Tel: 613-692-6000
advert@bellnet.ca; newsfile@bellnet.ca
www.barrhavenindependent.on.ca
Social Media:
www.facebook.com/142393275816516
Circulation: 17,138; *Frequency:* Semimonthly
Now available only online.
Jeffrey Morris, Publisher & Editor

Johnstown: Prescott Journal
Owned By: St. Lawrence Printing Co. Ltd.
PO Box 549, 3201 - 2 County Rd., Johnstown, ON K0E 1T0
Tel: 613-925-4265; *Fax:* 613-925-2837
editor@prescottjournal.com
www.prescottjournal.com
Other information: Ads: jnurse@slpprint.ca; Classifieds: classifieds@prescottjournal.com
Social Media:
facebook.com/pages/The-Prescott-Journal/108117515962137
Circulation: 1,400; *Frequency:* Wed.
Lisa D. Taylor, Publisher
Jeff Morris, Editor
newsfile@bellnet.ca

Kapuskasing: Kapuskasing Times
Owned By: Sun Media Corp.
51 Riverside Dr., Kapuskasing, ON P5N 1A7
Tel: 705-335-2283; *Fax:* 705-337-1222
kaptimes.news@sunmedia.ca
www.kapuskasingtimes.com
Social Media:
twitter.com/northerntimes
www.facebook.com/pages/The-Northern-Times/1365879097003 33
Circulation: 1,700; *Frequency:* Vendredi; aussi Le/The Weekender (Vendredi)
Wayne Major, Publisher
wayne.major@sunmedia.ca
Kevin Anderson, Regional Managing Editor
kevin.anderson@sunmedia.ca

Kenora: Lake of the Woods Enterprise
Owned By: Sun Media Corp.
33 Main St., Kenora, ON P9N 3X7
Tel: 807-468-5555; *Fax:* 807-468-4318
info@kenoraenterprise.com
www.kenoradailyminerandnews.com
Circulation: 8,700; *Frequency:* Thurs.
Daria Zmiyiwsky, Publisher
daria.zmiyiwsky@sunmedia.ca
Lloyd Mack, Regional Managing Editor
lloyd.mack@sunmedia.ca

Keswick: Georgina Advocate
Owned By: York Region Media Group
184 Simcoe Ave., Keswick, ON L4P 2H7
Tel: 905-476-7753; *Fax:* 905-476-5785
www.yorkregion.com
Circulation: 28,500; *Frequency:* Thursday, Sunday
Ian Proudfoot, Publisher
Tracy Kibble, Editor
tkibble@yrmg.com
Tanya Pacheco, Director, Circulation
tpacheco@yrmg.com

Kincardine: The Kincardine Independent
Owned By: Kincardine Publishing Company Ltd.
PO Box 1240, 840 Queen St., Kincardine, ON N2Z 2Z4
Tel: 519-396-3111; *Fax:* 519-396-3899
indepen@bmts.com
www.independent.on.ca
Circulation: 2,368; *Frequency:* Wednesday
Eric Howald, Publisher
John Miles, Regional Manager

Kincardine: Kincardine News
Owned By: Sun Media Corp.
719 Queen St., Kincardine, ON N2Z 1Z9
Tel: 519-396-2963; *Fax:* 519-396-6865
kincardine.news@sunmedia.ca
www.kincardinenews.com
Social Media:
twitter.com/Kincardinenews
www.facebook.com/pages/Kincardine-News/120117654724117
Circulation: 5,676; *Frequency:* Thursday
Marie David, Publisher
marie.david@sunmedia.ca
Troy Patterson, Editor
kincardine.news@sunmedia.ca

Kingston: Kingston This Week
Owned By: Sun Media Corp.
18 St Remy Place, Kingston, ON K7K 6C4
Tel: 613-389-7400; *Fax:* 613-389-7507
news@kingstonthisweek.com
www.kingstonthisweek.com
Social Media:
twitter.com/ktwchat
www.facebook.com/pages/Kingston-This-Week/92511562310
Circulation: 50,200; *Frequency:* Thursday
Liza Nelson, Publisher
liza.nelson@sunmedia.ca
Mike Beaudin, Managing Editor
mike.beaudin@sunmedia.ca

Kingsville: Kingsville Reporter
Owned By: Postmedia Community Publishing
17 Chestnut St., Kingsville, ON N9Y 1J9
Tel: 519-733-2211; *Fax:* 519-733-6464
kingsvillereporter@kingsvillereporter.com
kingsvillereporter.com
Other information: Ads: rsims@kingsvillereporter.com
Circulation: 1,420; *Frequency:* Tuesday
Nelson Santos, Editor
519-733-2211 ext 24
nsantos@kingsvillereporter.com

Lakefield: Lakefield Herald
Previous Name: Katchewanooka Herald
Owned By: Lakefield Herald Ltd.
PO Box 1000, 74 Bridge St., Lakefield, ON K0L 2H0
Tel: 705-652-6594; *Fax:* 705-652-6912
Toll-Free: 877-652-5114
info@lakefieldherald.com
www.lakefieldherald.com
Social Media:
twitter.com/LakefieldHerald
facebook.com/pages/Lakefield-Herald/225838317450949
Circulation: 940; *Frequency:* Friday
Simon Conolly, Publisher
sconolly@lakefieldherald.com

Listowel: Listowel Banner & Independent Plus
Owned By: Metroland Media Group Ltd.
PO Box 97, 185 Wallace Ave. North, Listowel, ON N4W 1K8
Tel: 519-291-1660; *Fax:* 519-291-3771
www.southwesternontario.ca
Circulation: 2,500; *Frequency:* Wednesday
Bill Huether, General Manager
bhuether@northperth.com
Shannon Burrows, Editor
sburrows@metroland.com

***Little Current:* The Manitoulin Expositor**
Previous Name: The Manitoulin West Recorder
Owned By: Manitoulin Publishing Co. Ltd.
PO Box 369, 1 Manitowaning Rd., Little Current, ON P0P 1K0
Tel: 705-368-2744; *Fax:* 705-368-3822
expositor@manitoulin.ca
www.manitoulin.ca
Social Media:
twitter.com/man_expositor
facebook.com/ManitoulinExpositor

Circulation: 5,480; *Frequency:* Wednesday
Rick McCutcheon, Publisher
Alicia McCutcheon, Editor
editor@manitoulin.ca

***London:* London Pennysaver**
PO Box 2280, 369 York St., London, ON N6A 4G1
Tel: 519-685-2020; *Fax:* 519-667-4573
pennyreaderads@londonpennysaver.com
www.londonpennysaver.com

Frequency: Friday
Cathy Forster, Manager, Sales
cforster@lfpress.com

***London:* The Londoner**
Owned By: Sun Media Corp.
1147 Gainsborough Rd., London, ON N6H 5L5
Tel: 519-673-5005; *Fax:* 519-673-4624
www.thelondoner.ca
Social Media:
twitter.com/londoneronline
www.facebook.com/LondonerOnline

Circulation: 140,000; *Frequency:* Thurs.
Linda LeBlanc, Publisher
linda.leblanc@sunmedia.ca
Don Biggs, Editor
don.biggs@sunmedia.ca

***Lucknow:* Lucknow Sentinel**
Owned By: Sun Media Corp.
619 Campbell St., Lucknow, ON N0G 2H0
Tel: 519-528-2822; *Fax:* 519-528-3529
lucknow.editorial@sunmedia.ca
www.lucknowsentinel.com
Social Media:
twitter.com/LucknowSentine1
www.facebook.com/LucknowSentinel

Circulation: 1,160; *Frequency:* Wednesday
Marie David, Publisher
519-364-2001 ext 24
marie.david@sunmedia.ca

***Manotick:* Manotick Messenger**
Owned By: The Morris Group
PO Box 567, 1165 Beaverwood Rd., Manotick, ON K4M 1A5
Tel: 613-692-6000; *Fax:* 613-692-3758
publish@bellnet.ca; newsfile@bellnet.ca
www.manotickmessenger.on.ca
Other information: Classified Advertising, Phone: 613-925-4265
Social Media:
twitter.com/ManotickMessngr
facebook.com/pages/Manotick-Messenger/267448403344583
Circulation: 8,000; *Frequency:* Thurs.
Beth Morris, Owner
Jeff Morris, Publisher
Bev McRae, Journalist & Photographer
Gary Coulombe, Representative, Advertising
advert@bellnet.ca

***Markham:* Markham Economist & Sun**
Owned By: York Region Media Group
#115, 50 McIntosh Dr., Markham, ON L3R 9T3
Tel: 905-294-2200; *Fax:* 905-294-1538
www.yorkregion.com
Circulation: 135,000; *Frequency:* Thursday, Saturday
Ian Proudfoot, Publisher
Bernie O'Neill, Editor
boneill@yrmg.com

***Markham:* Richmond Hill/Thornhill Liberal**
Owned By: York Region Media Group
115, 50 McIntosh Dr., Markham, ON L3R 9T3
Tel: 905-881-3373; *Fax:* 905-881-9924
ycustomerservice@yrmg.com
www.yorkregion.com
Social Media:
facebook.com/pages/Richmond-Hill-Liberal/656576374383875
Circulation: 131,000; *Frequency:* Thurs., Sat.
Marney Beck, Managing Editor
mbeck@urmg.com
Anne Beswick, Manager, Advertising
abeswick@yrmg.com

***Mattawa:* Mattawa Recorder**
PO Box 64, 341 McConnell St., Mattawa, ON P0H 1V0
Tel: 705-744-5361; *Fax:* 705-744-5361
recorder@bellnet.ca
mattawa.ca
Social Media:
facebook.com/mattawa.recorder

Circulation: 1,050; *Frequency:* Sunday
Heather Edwards, Publisher
Tom Edwards, Publisher

***Meaford:* Blue Mountains Courier-Herald**
Previous Name: The Courier Herald
Owned By: Metroland Media
#6, 24 Trowbridge St., Meaford, ON N4L 1Y1
Tel: 519-599-3760; *Fax:* 519-538-5028
courierherald@simcoe.com
simcoe.com/bluemountains-on
Circulation: 480; *Frequency:* Wed.; also Meaford Express (Wed., circ. 2,521)
Carol Lamb, General Manager
clamb@simcoe.com
Scott Woodhouse, Editor
swoodhouse@simcoe.com

***Meaford:* Meaford Express**
Owned By: Metroland Media Group Ltd.
#6, 24 Trowbridge St. West, Meaford, ON N4L 1Y1
Tel: 519-538-1421; *Fax:* 519-538-5028
www.simcoe.com/community/meaford
Social Media:
twitter.com/meafordexpress
www.facebook.com/TheMeafordExpress

Circulation: 1,200; *Frequency:* Wed.
Ian Proudfoot, Publisher
iproudfoot@metroland.com
Chris Fell, Editor
cfell@simcoe.com
Carol Lamb, General Manager
clamb@simcoe.com
Cheryl McMenemy, Manager, Sales
cmcmenemy@simcoe.com

***Midland:* Midland & Penetanguishene Mirror**
Previous Name: Penetanguishene Mirror
Owned By: Metroland Media Group Ltd.
PO Box 391, 174 Pillsbury Dr., Midland, ON L4R 4L1
Tel: 705-527-5500; *Fax:* 705-527-5467
simcoe.com

Circulation: 31,500; *Frequency:* Thursday, Tuesday
Travis Mealing, Editor
tmealing@simcoe.com
Maureen Christie, General Manager
mchristie@simcoe.com

***Mildmay:* Mildmay Town & Country Crier**
Owned By: Mildmay Town and Country Crier
PO Box 190, 100 Elora St., Mildmay, ON N0G 2J0
Tel: 519-367-2681; *Fax:* 519-367-5417
thecrier@wightman.ca

Circulation: 1,350; *Frequency:* Wednesday
Susan Bross, Publisher

***Millbrook:* Millbrook Times**
Owned By: Millbrook Times
PO Box 285, 1 King St. West, Millbrook, ON L0A 1G0
Tel: 705-932-3001; *Fax:* 705-932-8816
thetimes@nexicom.net
themillbrooktimes.ca
Social Media:
facebook.com/themillbrooktimes

Circulation: 1,816; *Frequency:* Thu.
Karen Graham, Publisher
Celia Hunter, Editor

***Milton:* Milton Canadian Champion**
Owned By: Metroland Media Group Ltd.
555 Industrial Dr., Milton, ON L9T 5E1
Tel: 905-878-2341
www.insidehalton.com
Circulation: 28,600; *Frequency:* Tuesday, Thursday
Jill Davis, Editor-in-Chief
jdavis@metroland.com
David Harvey, Regional Group Manager
dharvey@metroland.com
Karen Miceli, Editor
kmiceli@metroland.com

***Minden:* Minden Times**
Owned By: Sun Media Corp.
PO Box 97, 2 IGA Rd., Minden, ON K0M 2K0
Tel: 705-286-1288; *Fax:* 705-286-4768
www.mindentimes.ca
Social Media:
twitter.com/mindentimes
www.facebook.com/MindenTimes

Circulation: 1,500; *Frequency:* Wednesday
Jenn Watt, Editor
jenn.watt@sunmedia.ca
David Zilstra, Publisher
david.zilstra@gmail.com
Don Smith, Publisher

***Mississauga:* The Mississauga News**
Owned By: Metroland Media Group Ltd.
3145 Wolfedale Rd., Mississauga, ON L5C 3A9
Tel: 905-273-8111; *Fax:* 905-277-0146
www.mississauga.com
Social Media:
twitter.com/MissiNewsRoom
www.facebook.com/MissiNewsRoom
Circulation: 124,000; *Frequency:* Wed., Fri.
The News is a perennial newspaper award winner, including best newspaper in Ontario & Canada, on several occasions. The Mississauga News is delivered three times a week to houses. A separate edition called The Mississauga News This Week is delivered Thursdays to apartments.
Dana Robbins, Publisher
dana.robbins@metroland.com
Bill Anderson, General Manager
banderson@metroland.com

***Mississauga:* The Weekly Voice**
#16, 7015 Tranmere Dr., Mississauga, ON L5S 1T7
Tel: 905-795-8282; *Fax:* 905-795-9801
info@weeklyvoice.com
www.weeklyvoice.com
Circulation: 10,100 W; 29,900 Sa; 40,000 total; *Frequency:* Wed., Sat.
The free newspaper presents information & views of interest to the South Asian community of the Greater Toronto Area. The Weekly Voice is distributed at major South Asian grocery stores, transit stations, libraries, & community centres.
Sudhir Anand, Publisher
sudhir@weeklyvoice.com
Binoy Thomas, Editor in Chief
Dhruv Ghosh, General Manager
dhruv@weeklyvoice.com
Harsimrat Panfer, Contact, Classifieds
admin@weeklyvoice.com
Asha Singhh, Contact, Accounts
accounts@weeklyvoice.com

***Mitchell:* Mitchell Advocate**
Owned By: Sun Media Corp.
PO Box 669, 42 Montreal St., Mitchell, ON N0K 1N0
Tel: 519-348-8431; *Fax:* 519-348-8836
www.mitchelladvocate.com
Social Media:
twitter.com/mitchellpaper
www.facebook.com/pages/The-Mitchell-Advocate/274629353636

Circulation: 2,050; *Frequency:* Wednesday
Andy Bader, Publisher/Editor
andy.bader@sunmedia.ca

***Morrisburg:* Morrisburg Leader**
Owned By: The Morrisburg Leader Ltd.
PO Box 891, 41 Main St., Morrisburg, ON K0C 1X0
Tel: 613-543-2987
info@morrisburgleader.ca
www.morrisburgleader.ca
Social Media:
twitter.com/theleader_ca
facebook.com/morrisburgleader

Circulation: 1,900; *Frequency:* Wednesday
Sam Laurin, Publisher & Editor
Bonnie McNairn, Managing Editor

***Mount Forest:* Arthur Enterprise-News**
Owned By: Metroland Media Group Ltd.
PO Box 130, 277 Main St. South, Mount Forest, ON N0G 2L0
Tel: 519-323-1550; *Fax:* 519-323-4548
www.southwesternontario.ca

Circulation: 420; *Frequency:* Wednesday
Bill Huether, General Manager
bhuether@mountforest.com
Dianne Hatch, Manager, Classifieds, Circulation
dhatch@mountforest.com

Mount Forest: Fergus-Elora News Express
Previous Name: Ferguse-Elora News Express
Owned By: Metroland Media Group Ltd.
PO Box 130, Mount Forest, ON N0G 2L0
Tel: 519-843-1550; *Fax:* 519-323-4548
www.southwesternontario.ca
Social Media:
facebook.com/pages/Fergus-Elora-/561584510603572
Circulation: 8,071; *Frequency:* Wednesday
Lynne Turner, Publisher
Chris Holden, Editor
Ann Hepburn, Representative, Advertising
ahepburn@wellingtonnorth.com

Mount Forest: Mount Forest Confederate
Owned By: Metroland Media Group Ltd.
PO Box 130, 277 Main St. South, Mount Forest, ON N0G 2L0
Tel: 519-323-1550; *Fax:* 519-323-4548
dhatch@wellingtonnorth.com
www.mountforest.com
Circulation: 1,900; *Frequency:* Wednesday
Bill Huether, General Manager
bhuether@northperth.com
Shannon Burrows, Editor
sburrows@metroland.com

Napanee: Napanee Beaver
Owned By: 543570 Ont. Inc.
72 Dundas St. East, Napanee, ON K7R 1H9
Tel: 613-354-6641; *Fax:* 613-354-2622
www.napaneebeaver.com
Circulation: 15,700; *Frequency:* Thursday
Jean Morrison, Publisher
Seth Duchene, Editor

Napanee: The Napanee Guide
Owned By: Sun Media Corp.
#11, 2 Dairy Ave., Napanee, ON K7R 3T1
Tel: 613-354-6648; *Fax:* 613-354-6708
www.napaneeguide.com
Social Media:
twitter.com/napaneeguide
www.facebook.com/groups/208529789177838
Circulation: 14,900; *Frequency:* Thursday
Liza Nelson, Publisher
liza.nelson@sunmedia.ca

Nepean: Alta Vista Canterbury News
Previous Name: Alta Vista News
Owned By: Ottawa News Publishing
#3B, 15 Antares Dr., Nepean, ON K2E 7Y9
Tel: 613-723-5970; *Fax:* 613-723-1862
Circulation: 36,000; *Frequency:* Every other Thu.; also Britannia/Lincoln Heights News, Carlingwood/Baseline News, Glebe & Ottawa South News, Westboro/Hampton Park News
Michael Wollock, Publisher
Tom Collins, Editor

Nepean: Nepean/Barrhaven News
Owned By: Metroland Media Group Ltd.
#4, 80 Colonnade Rd. North, Nepean, ON K2E 7L2
Tel: 613-224-3330; *Fax:* 613-224-2265
www.yourottawaregion.com; www.emcbarrhaven.ca
Social Media:
twitter.com/emcnews
www.facebook.com/emcnewspaper
Circulation: 50,000; *Frequency:* Thurs.
In 2011, the Nepean / Barrhaven EMC merged with the Nepean & Barrhaven editions of Ottawa This Week.
Mike Mount, Vice-President & Regional Publisher
Theresa Fritz, Managing Editor
theresa.fritz@metroland.com
Mike Tracy, General Manager
mtracy@perfprint.ca

Nepean: Ottawa South News
Owned By: Metroland Media Group Ltd.
#4, 80 Colonnade Rd., Nepean, ON K2E 7L2
Tel: 613-224-3330; *Fax:* 613-723-1862
www.emcottawasouth.ca/news
Social Media:
twitter.com/emcnews
www.facebook.com/emcnewspaper
Circulation: 41,500; *Frequency:* Thurs.
Mike Tracy, Publisher & General Manager
613-283-3182 x164
dweir@perfprint.ca
Theresa Fritz, Managing Editor
theresa.fritz@metroland.com

Nepean: Stittsville News
Previous Name: Stittsville EMC
Owned By: Metroland Media Group Ltd.
#4, 80 Colonnade Rd., Nepean, ON K2E 7L2
Tel: 613-224-3330; *Fax:* 613-224-2265
metroland.com/Communities/100094/Stittsville_News_EMC
Circulation: 13,446; *Frequency:* Weekly; Thursday
Mike Tracy, General Manager
mike.tracy@metroland.com
Ryland Coyne, Editor-in-Chief
rcoyne@metroland.com

New Hamburg: New Hamburg Independent
Owned By: Metroland Media Group Ltd.
77 Peel St., New Hamburg, ON N3A 1B7
Tel: 519-662-1240; *Fax:* 519-662-3521
Toll-Free: 800-563-3578
editor@newhamburgindependent.ca
www.newhamburgindependent.ca
Social Media:
twitter.com/newhamburgindy
facebook.com/NewHamburgIndependent
Circulation: 2,250; *Frequency:* Wednesday
Peter Winkler, Publisher
Doug Coxson, Managing Editor
dcoxson@newhamburgindependent.ca

New Liskeard: The Temiskaming Speaker
Owned By: Temiskaming Printing Co.
PO Box 580, 18 Wellington St. South, New Liskeard, ON P0J 1P0
Tel: 705-647-6791; *Fax:* 705-647-9669
www.northernontario.ca
Social Media:
facebook.com/pages/Temiskaming-Speaker/113689282130374
Circulation: 3,150; *Frequency:* Wednesday
Dave Armstrong, Publisher
Gordon Black, Editor
Lois Perry, General Manager

Newmarket: King Connection
Owned By: York Region Media Group
580B Steven Ct., Newmarket, ON L3Y 4X1
Tel: 905-853-8888; *Fax:* 905-853-4626
yrcustomerservice@yrmg.com .
www.yorkregion.com
Kim Champion, Editor

Newmarket: Newmarket Era Banner
Previous Name: Era Banner
Owned By: York Region Media Group
580B Steven Ct., Newmarket, ON L3Y 4X1
Tel: 416-798-7284; *Fax:* 905-853-5379
www.yorkregion.com
Circulation: 174,637; *Frequency:* Twice a week, Thursday and Sunday
Debora Kelly, Editor-in-Chief
Ian Proudfoot, Regional General Manager
iproudfoot@yrmg.com

Niagara Falls: Niagara Falls Review
Previous Name: Niagara Falls News
Owned By: Sun Media Corp.
4801 Valley Way, Niagara Falls, ON L2E 1W4
Tel: 905-358-5711
www.niagarafallsreview.ca
Social Media:
twitter.com/niafallsreview
www.facebook.com/niagarafallsreview
Michael Cressman, Publisher
905-358-5711 x1111
michael.cressman@sunmedia.ca
Peter Conradi, Editor-in-Chief
peter.conradi@sunmedia.ca

Niagara Falls: Niagara Shopping News
Owned By: Sun Media
4949 Victoria Ave., Niagara Falls, ON L2E 4C7
Tel: 905-357-2440; *Fax:* 905-357-1620
placeit@classifiedextra.ca
niagarashoppingnews.classifiedextra.ca
Circulation: 28,000; *Frequency:* Friday
Mark Munson

Nipigon: Nipigon-Red Rock Gazette
Owned By: Lakeshore Community Publishing Ltd.
PO Box 1057, 20 Riverview St., Nipigon, ON P0T 2J0
Tel: 807-887-3583; *Fax:* 807-887-3720
nipigongazette@shaw.ca
Circulation: 810; *Frequency:* Tuesday
Linda Harbison, Publisher
Paulette Forsythe, Editor

Oakville: Milton Shopping News
c/o The Shopping News, 467 Speers Rd., 2nd Fl., Oakville, ON L6K 3S4
Tel: 905-878-8855; *Fax:* 905-878-6727
smillen@haltonsearch.com
miltonshoppingnews.com
Circulation: 16,500; *Frequency:* Thursday
Lars Melander, General Manager
905-337-5555

Oakville: Oakville Beaver
Owned By: Metroland Media Group Ltd.
467 Speers Rd., 2nd Fl., Oakville, ON L6K 3S4
Tel: 905-825-2229; *Fax:* 905-825-8315
www.insidehalton.com/community/oakvilletoday
Social Media:
twitter.com/OakvilleBeaver
facebook.com/OakvilleBeav
Circulation: 50,000; *Frequency:* Wed., Thurs., Fri.
The newspaper is delivered to residences in northern Oakville.
Neil Oliver, Publisher
noliver@metroland.com
David Harvey, Regional Group Manager
dharvey@metroland.com
Jill Davis, Editor-in-Chief
jdavis@metroland.com
Charlene Hall, Manager, Distribution
charlenehall@metroland.com
Sandy Pare, Manager, Business
spare@metrolandwest.com
Manuel Garcia, Manager, Production
mgarcia@metroland.com

Oakville: Oakville Shopping News
2526 Speers Rd., Oakville, ON L6L 5M2
Tel: 905-827-6090; *Fax:* 905-827-7318
Bill Whitaker Sr.

Orangeville: Orangeville Banner
Owned By: Metroland Media Group Ltd.
37 Mill St., Orangeville, ON L9W 2M4
Tel: 519-941-1350; *Fax:* 519-941-9600
banner@orangevillebanner.com
www.orangeville.com
Circulation: 42,000; *Frequency:* Tuesday, Thursday
Steve Foreman, General Manager
sforeman@metroland.com
Chris Vernon, Managing Editor
cvernon@metroland.com

Orangeville: Orangeville Citizen
Owned By: Claridge Community Newspaper Ltd.
10 - 1st St., Orangeville, ON L9W 2C4
Tel: 519-941-2230; *Fax:* 519-941-9361
www.citizen.on.ca
Social Media:
twitter.com/OvilleCitizen
facebook.com/Citizen.on.ca
Circulation: 17,300; *Frequency:* Thursday
Tom Claridge, Editor
editor@citizen.on.ca
Alan Claridge, Publisher
publisher@citizen.on.ca

Orillia: Orillia Today
Owned By: Metroland Media Group Ltd.
25 Ontario St., Orillia, ON L3V 6H2
Tel: 705-329-2058; *Fax:* 705-329-2059
www.simcoe.com
Social Media:
twitter.com/orilliatoday
facebook.com/orilliatodaynews
Circulation: 24,100; *Frequency:* Thursday
Maureen Christie, Regional General Manager
mchristie@simcoe.com
Martin Melbourne, Editor
mmelbourne@simcoe.com

Orono: Orono Weekly Times
Owned By: Orono Weekly Times
PO Box 209, 5310 Main St., Orono, ON L0B 1M0
Tel: 905-983-5301; *Fax:* 905-983-5301
oronotimes@rogers.com
www.oronoweeklytimes.com
Social Media:
twitter.com/oronotimes
www.facebook.com/oronotimes
Circulation: 930; *Frequency:* Wednesday
Margaret Zwart, Publisher

***Oshawa:* Ajax/Pickering News Advertiser**
Owned By: Metroland Media Group Ltd.
865 Farewell Ave., Oshawa, ON L1H 7L5
Tel: 905-579-4400; *Fax:* 905-579-2238
www.durhamregion.com/community/ajax
Social Media:
twitter.com/newsdurham
www.facebook.com/newsdurham
Circulation: 54,400; *Frequency:* Wednesday, Thursday
Tim Whittaker, Publisher
Joanne Burghardt, Editor-in-Chief

***Oshawa:* Clarington This Week**
Owned By: Metroland Media Group Ltd.
PO Box 481, 865 Farewell Ave., Oshawa, ON L1H 7L5
Tel: 905-579-4400; *Fax:* 905-579-2238
www.durhamregion.com
Circulation: 24,550; *Frequency:* Thursday, Wednesday

***Oshawa:* Oshawa Express**
Owned By: Dowellman Publishing Corp.
774 Simcoe St. South, Oshawa, ON L1H 4K6
Tel: 905-571-7334; *Fax:* 905-571-0255
editor@oshawaexpress.ca
www.oshawaexpress.ca
Social Media:
www.facebook.com/pages/The-Oshawa-Express/218913348146 817
Circulation: 35,000; *Frequency:* Wed.
Greg McDowell, Publisher
Lindsey Cole, Editor

***Oshawa:* Oshawa This Week**
Owned By: Metroland Media Group Ltd.
PO Box 481, 865 Farewell Ave., Oshawa, ON L1H 7L5
Tel: 905-579-4400; *Fax:* 905-579-2238
www.durhamregion.com
Circulation: 121,000; *Frequency:* Wednesday, Thursday, Friday
Tim Whittaker, Publisher
Joanne Burghardt, Editor-in-chief

***Oshawa:* Whitby This Week**
Owned By: Metroland Media Group Ltd.
865 Farewell Ave., Oshawa, ON L1H 7L5
Tel: 905-579-4400; *Fax:* 905-579-2238
www.durhamregion.com
Circulation: 121,000; *Frequency:* Wednesday, Thursday, Friday

***Ottawa:* Centretown News**
St. Patrick's Building, #303, 1125 Colonel By Dr., Ottawa, ON K1S 5B6
Tel: 613-520-7410; *Fax:* 613-520-4068
ctown@carleton.ca
www.centretownnews.ca
Other information: Advertising, E-mail: ctownads@carleton.ca
Social Media:
twitter.com/CentretownNews
facebook.com/CentretownNews
Circulation: 17,000; *Frequency:* Fri., bi-weekly from Sept.-April
The content of Centretown News is produced by third & fourth year students from Carleton University's School of Journalism & Communication. The community newspaper is deliverd to homes & businesses in the Ottawa-Carleton region between September & April.
Klaus Pohle, Publisher
Brian Platt, Editor
Hanna Lange-Chenier, Editor, Photos
Meagan Curran, Editor, Insight
Francesa Weigensberg, Editor, Sports
Sara Louden, Editor, Online
Mireille Sylvester, Editor, News
Julia Green, Editor, Business
Kelly Fleck, Editor, Arts
Sara Louden, Manager, Advertising

***Ottawa:* The Hill Times**
Owned By: The Hill Times Publishing Inc.
69 Sparks St., Ottawa, ON K1P 5A5
Tel: 613-232-5952; *Fax:* 613-232-9055
news@hilltimes.com
www.thehilltimes.ca
Social Media:
twitter.com/thehilltimes
www.facebook.com/thehilltimes
Circulation: 8,370; *Frequency:* Monday
Independently-owned political & government newspaper.
Andrew Morrow, General Manager
613-688-8844
amorrow@hilltimes.com
Kate Malloy, Editor
613-688-8838
kmalloy@hilltimes.com

***Ottawa:* The Star**
Owned By: TC Transcontinental
#400, 303 Moodie Dr., Ottawa, ON K2J 9R4
Tel: 613-744-4800; *Fax:* 613-744-1976
editor@ottawastar.com
ottawastar.com
Circulation: 35,000; *Frequency:* Tues.
A newspaper for Ottawa's new & ethnic Canadians, concentrating on international news
Chandrakanth Arya, Publisher
Sangeetha Arya, Editor-in-Chief
Ellen O'Connor, Editor

***Palmerston:* Minto Express**
Previous Name: Harriston Review
Owned By: Metroland Media Group Ltd.
PO Box 757, 171 William St., Palmerston, ON N0G 2P0
Tel: 519-343-2440; *Fax:* 519-343-2267
www.southwesternontario.ca
Social Media:
twitter.com/TheMintoExpress
facebook.com/pages/The-Minto-Express/1968442 63730454
Circulation: 737; *Frequency:* Wednesday
Bill Huether, General Manager
519-291-1660 ext 103
bhuether@metroland.com
Shannon Burrows, Editor
519-343-2440
editor@mintoexpress.com

***Parkhill:* Parkhill Gazette**
Owned By: Hayter-Walden Publications Inc.
PO Box 400, 165 Parkhill King St., Parkhill, ON N0M 2K0
Tel: 519-294-6264; *Fax:* 519-294-6391
gazette@execulink.com
hayterwalden.com
Circulation: 890; *Frequency:* Thurs.
Dale Hayter, Publisher
Terry Heffernan, Editor

***Parry Sound:* Parry Sound Beacon Star**
Owned By: Metroland Media Group Ltd.
PO Box 370, 66A Bowes St., Parry Sound, ON P2A 2L3
Tel: 705-746-2104; *Fax:* 705-746-8369
parrysound.com
Circulation: 7,700; *Frequency:* Friday
Shaun Sauve, Regional General Manager
705-645-8771 ext 227
ssauve@metroland.com
Janice Heidman, General Manager
jheidman@metroland.com
Jack Tynan, Editor-in-Chief
jtynan@metroland.com

***Parry Sound:* Parry Sound North Star**
Owned By: Metroland Media Group Ltd.
PO Box 370, 66A Bowes St., Parry Sound, ON P2A 2L3
Tel: 705-746-2104; *Fax:* 705-746-8369
parrysound.com
Social Media:
www.facebook.com/PSNorthStar
Circulation: 2,600; *Frequency:* Wednesday
Shaun Sauve, Regional General Manager
ssauve@metroland.com
Janice Heidman, General Manager
jheidman@metroland.com
Jack Tynan, Editorin-Chief
jtynan@metroland.com

***Perth:* Perth Courier**
Owned By: Metroland Media Group Ltd.
PO Box 158, 65 Lorne St., Perth, ON K7A 4T1
Tel: 613-283-3182; *Fax:* 613-267-3986
insideottawavalley.com/perth-on
Circulation: 12,800; *Frequency:* Thursday
Duncan Weir, Group Publisher
Cindy Manor, General Manager
cmanor@metroland.com
Marla Dowdall, Managing Editor
mdowdall@perfprint.ca

***Petawawa:* Petawawa Post**
Bldg. P-106, CFB Petawawa, Petawawa, ON K8H 2X3
Tel: 613-687-5511; *Fax:* 613-588-6966
petawawapost@bellnet.ca
cg.cfpsa.ca
Circulation: 7,700; *Frequency:* Tuesday
Bruce Peever, Manager
bruce.peever@forces.gc.ca
Lisa Brazeau, Assistant Editor

***Peterborough:* Kawartha Lakes This Week**
Owned By: Metroland Media Group Ltd.
884 Ford St., Peterborough, ON K9V 5V3
Tel: 705-749-3383; *Fax:* 705-749-0074
www.mykawartha.com
Circulation: 29,400; *Frequency:* Tues., Thurs.
Mike Mount, Publisher
mike.mount@metroland.com
Mary Babcock, Regional General Manager
mbabcock@mykawartha.com

***Peterborough:* Peterborough This Week**
Owned By: Metroland Media Group Ltd.
884 Ford St., Peterborough, ON K9J 5V3
Tel: 705-749-3383; *Fax:* 705-749-0074
www.mykawartha.com
Social Media: pinterest.com/rellman
twitter.com/kawarthanews
www.facebook.com/mykawartha.peterboroughnews
Circulation: 91,100; *Frequency:* Wed., Fri.
Mike Mount, Publisher
mike.mount@metroland.com
Mary Babcock, Regional General Manager
mbabcock@mykawartha.com
Lois Tuffin, Editor-in-Chief
ltuffin@mykawartha.com

***Picton:* Picton Gazette**
Owned By: Picton Gazette
267 Main St., Picton, ON K0K 2T0
Tel: 613-476-3201; *Fax:* 613-476-3464
gazette@connect.reach.net
www.pictongazette.com
Social Media:
twitter.com/Gazettenews
facebook.com/PictonGazette
Circulation: 12,000; *Frequency:* Thursday; The Picton Gazette Regional (Sat., circ. 10,602)
Jean Morrison, Publisher
dmccann1@bellnet.ca
Adam Bramburger, Editor

***Port Dover:* Port Dover Maple Leaf**
Owned By: Port Dover Maple Leaf Limited
PO Box 70, 351 Main St., Port Dover, ON N0A 1N0
Tel: 519-583-0112; *Fax:* 519-583-3200
news@portdovermapleleaf.com
www.portdovermapleleaf.com
Social Media:
twitter.com/PDMapleLeaf
facebook.com/PortDoverMapleLeaf
Circulation: 3,163; *Frequency:* Wed.
Stan Morris, Publisher

***Port Elgin:* Shoreline Beacon**
Previous Name: Shoreline News
Owned By: Sun Media Corp.
694 Goderich St., Port Elgin, ON N0H 2C0
Tel: 519-832-9001; *Fax:* 519-389-4793
shorelinebeacon.news@sunmedia.ca
www.shorelinebeacon.com
Social Media:
twitter.com/shorelinebeacon
www.facebook.com/shorelinebeacon?sk=wall
Circulation: 3,250; *Frequency:* Tuesday
Kiera Merriam, Publisher
kiera.merriam@sunmedia.ca
Patrick Bales, Editor
patrick.bales@sunmedia.ca

***Port Perry:* Port Perry Star**
Owned By: Metroland Media Group Ltd.
#11, 180 Mary St., Port Perry, ON L9L 1C4
Tel: 905-985-7383; *Fax:* 905-985-3708
www.metroland.com/Communities/100390/Port_Perry_Star
Circulation: 12,000; *Frequency:* Thursday
Tim Whittaker, Publisher
Joanne Burghardt, Editor

***Rainy River:* Rainy River Record**
Owned By: Fort Frances Times Ltd.
PO Box 280, 312 - 3rd St., Rainy River, ON P0W 1L0
Tel: 807-852-3366; *Fax:* 807-852-4434
info@rainyriverrecord.com
www.rainyriverrecord.com
Other information: Ads: advertising@rainyriverrecord.com
Social Media:
facebook.com/rainyriverrecord
Circulation: 600; *Frequency:* Tuesday
J.R. Cumming, Publisher
Ken Johnston, Editor

Rainy River: The Westend Weekly
PO Box 66, Rainy River, ON P0W 1L0
Tel: 807-852-3815; *Fax:* 807-852-1863
westendweekly@tbaytel.net
www.westendweekly.ca
Circulation: 8,600; *Frequency:* Wed.
Jacquie Dufresne, Editor-in-chief

Renfrew: Renfrew Mercury
Previous Name: Renfrew Mercury/Mercury Weekender
Owned By: Metroland Media Group Ltd.
35 Opeongo Rd., Renfrew, ON K7V 2T2
Tel: 613-432-3655; *Fax:* 613-432-6689
www.metroland.com/communities/100092/renfrew_mercury
Social Media:
facebook.com/pages/The-Renfrew-Mercury/191489104221461
Circulation: 15,300; *Frequency:* Tuesday
Mike Tracy, Publisher
Tom O'Malley, Regional Manager

Ridgetown: The Ridgetown Independent News
PO Box 609, 1 Main St. West, Ridgetown, ON N0P 2C0
Tel: 519-674-5205; *Fax:* 519-674-2573
Circulation: 1,850; *Frequency:* Wed.
Jim Brown, Owner & Publisher
Gord Brown, General Manager
Barb Brown, Editor

Rockland: Le Journal Vision
PO Box 897, 1315 rue Laurier, Rockland, ON K4K 1L5
Tel: 613-446-6456; *Fax:* 613-446-1381
Toll-Free: 800-365-9970
vision@eap.on.ca
editionap.ca
Social Media:
www.facebook.com/group.php?gid=199878750108078
Circulation: 28,100; *Frequency:* Weekly
The newspaper is bilingual.
Paulo Casimiro, Director & Editor
paulo.casimiro@eap.on.ca

Sarnia: The Petrolia Topic
Owned By: Sun Media Corp.
140 Front St. South, Sarnia, ON N7T 7M8
Tel: 519-336-1100; *Fax:* 519-336-1833
www.petroliatopic.com
Social Media:
twitter.com/petroliatopic
www.facebook.com/pages/Petrolia-Topic/15152106 1568151
Circulation: 1,300; *Frequency:* Wednesday
Linda Leblanc, Publisher
linda.leblanc@sunmedia.ca

Sarnia: The Sarnia & Lambton County This Week
Previous Name: Sarnia This Week
Owned By: Sun Media Corp.
140 Front St. South, Sarnia, ON N7T 7M8
Tel: 519-336-1100; *Fax:* 519-336-1833
www.sarniathisweek.com
Social Media:
twitter.com/STW_Heather
www.facebook.com/185718368129719
Circulation: 40,240; *Frequency:* Wed.
Linda Leblanc, Publisher
linda.leblanc@sunmedia.ca
Peter Epp, Editor

Sault Ste Marie: Sault Ste Marie This Week
Owned By: Sun Media Corp.
145 Old Garden River Rd., Sault Ste Marie, ON P6A 5M5
Tel: 705-759-3030; *Fax:* 705-942-8596
www.saultthisweek.com
Circulation: 30,800; *Frequency:* Wed.
Mike Kennedy, Publisher
mike.kennedy@sunmedia.ca
Frank Rupnik, Regional Managing Editor
frank.rupnik@sunmedia.ca

Schreiber: Terrace Bay Schreiber News
Owned By: Lakeshore Community Publishing Ltd.
PO Box 930, 303 Scotia St., Schreiber, ON P0T 2S0
Tel: 807-824-2021; *Fax:* 807-824-2162
Circulation: 328; *Frequency:* Tues.
The Ontario community newspaper publishes local stories of interest to readers in Terrace Bay, Schreiber, Rossport, & the surrounding area.
Linda Harbinson, Publisher
Paulette Forsythe, Editor

Seaforth: The Huron Expositor
Owned By: Sun Media Corp.
8 Main St., Seaforth, ON N0K 1W0
Tel: 519-527-0240; *Fax:* 519-527-2858
www.seaforthhuronexpositor.com
Social Media:
twitter.com/C4thExp
www.facebook.com/TheHuronExpositor
Circulation: 1,400; *Frequency:* Wed.
Neil H. Clifford, Publisher
neil.clifford@sunmedia.ca
Susan Hundertmark, Editor
seaforth.news@sunmedia.ca

Shelburne: Shelburne Free Press & Economist
Owned By: Claridge Community Newspapers Ltd.
PO Box 100, #1, 143 Main St. West, Shelburne, ON L9V 3K3
Tel: 519-925-2832; *Fax:* 519-925-5500
email@shelburnefreepress.ca
shelburnefreepress.ca
Social Media:
facebook.com/ShelburneFreePress
Circulation: 3,400; *Frequency:* Thurs.
Karin Rossi, Publisher
Wendy Gabrek, Editor
wendy@simcoeworkprinting.com

Sioux Lookout: Sioux Lookout Bulletin
Owned By: 948892 Ontario Inc.
PO Box 1389, 40 Front St., Sioux Lookout, ON P8T 1B9
Tel: 807-737-3209; *Fax:* 807-737-3084
bulletin@siouxbulletin.com
www.siouxbulletin.com
Other information: Accounts: office@siouxbulletin.com; Ads: advertising@siouxbulletin.com
Circulation: 4,460; *Frequency:* Wed.
Dick MacKenzie, Editor
dick@siouxbulletin.com

Sioux Lookout: Wawatay News
Owned By: Wataway Native Communications Society
Wawatay Native Communications Society, PO Box 1180, 16 - 5th Ave., Sioux Lookout, ON P8T 1B7
Tel: 807-737-2951; *Fax:* 807-737-3224
editor@wawatay.on.ca
www.wawatay.on.ca
Social Media:
twitter.com/wawataynews
Circulation: 6,500; *Frequency:* Every other Thu.; English, Ojibwe & Cree
Distributed by the Sioux Lookout
Lenny Carpenter, Publisher/Editor
lennyc@wataway.on.ca

Smiths Falls: Carleton Place-Almonte Canadian Gazette
Owned By: Metroland Media Group Ltd.
PO Box 158, 65 Lorne St., Smiths Falls, ON K7A 4T1
Tel: 613-283-3182
ottawacommunitynews.com/ottawaregion
Social Media:
twitter.com/cdngazette
facebook.com/canadiangazette
Circulation: 12,800; *Frequency:* Thurs.
In 2011, The Carleton Place EMC & The Canadian merged to create the Carleton Place EMC & Canadian-Gazette newspaper.
Mike Mount, Publisher
Marla Dowdall, Managing Editor
mdowdall@perfprint.ca
Cindy Manor, General Manager
cmanor@metroland.com

Smiths Falls: Smiths Falls Record News
Owned By: Performance Printing Ltd.
PO Box 158, 65 Lorne St., Smiths Falls, ON K7A 4T1
Tel: 613-283-6222; *Fax:* 613-267-3986
insideottawavalley.com
Social Media:
twitter.com/ljweir
facebook.com/pages/Smiths-Falls-Record-News/535833289857 0
Circulation: 12,600; *Frequency:* Tuesday
Duncan Weir, Publisher
Ryland Coyne, Regional Editor
Marla Dowdall, Managing Editor
mdowdall@perfprint.ca

St Catharines: Thorold Niagara News
Owned By: Sun Media Corp.
#10, 1 St Paul St., St Catharines, ON L2R 7L4
Tel: 905-688-4332; *Fax:* 905-688-6313
stcatharinesnews@bellnet.ca
www.thoroldedition.ca
Social Media:
twitter.com/ThoroldNews
www.facebook.com/pages/Thorold-Niagara-New s/1003918167460
Circulation: 7,300; *Frequency:* Thurs.
Mark Cressman, Publisher
Tom Wilkinson, Editor

St Marys: St Marys Journal-Argus
Owned By: Metroland Media Group Ltd.
PO Box 103, 11 Wellington St. North, St Marys, ON N4X 1B7
Tel: 519-284-2440; *Fax:* 519-284-3650
www.stmarys.com
Social Media:
facebook.com/pages/The-St-Marys-Journal-Argus/33634736639
Circulation: 1,800; *Frequency:* Wed.
Doug Rowe, Regional Group Manager
drowe@southwesternontario.ca
Stew Slater, News Editor
sslater@stmarys.com

St Thomas: Elgin County Market
Owned By: Sun Media Corp.
16 Hincks St., St Thomas, ON N5R 5Z2
Tel: 519-631-3782; *Fax:* 519-631-3759
www.elgincountymarket.com
Circulation: 30,600
Linda Axelson, Publisher

Stoney Creek: Ancaster News
Owned By: Metroland Media Group Ltd.
333 Arvin Ave., Stoney Creek, ON L8E 2M6
Tel: 905-664-8800; *Fax:* 905-523-4014
www.hamiltonnews.com/community/ancaster
Circulation: 12,900; *Frequency:* Thursday
Debra Downey, Editor
ddowney@hamiltonnews.com

Stoney Creek: Dundas Star News
Owned By: Metroland Media Group Ltd.
333 Arvin Ave., Stoney Creek, ON L8E 2M6
Tel: 905-523-4014
hamiltonnews.com/community/dundas
Circulation: 15,700; *Frequency:* Thursday
Neil Oliver, Publisher
Debra Downey, Editor
ddowney@hamiltonnews.com

Stoney Creek: Hamilton Mountain News
Owned By: Metroland Media Group Ltd.
333 Arvin Ave., Stoney Creek, ON L8E 2M6
Tel: 905-523-5800; *Fax:* 905-523-4014
www.hamiltonmountainnews.com
Circulation: 50,500; *Frequency:* Thursday
Gord Bowes, Senior Editor
editor@hamiltonmountainnews.com
Neil Oliver, Publisher

Stoney Creek: Stoney Creek News
Owned By: Metroland Media Group Ltd.
333 Arvin Ave., Stoney Creek, ON L6E 2M6
Fax: 905-523-4014
www.hamiltonnews.com
Social Media:
twitter.com/StoneyCreekNews
facebook.com/StoneyCreekNews
Circulation: 30,500; *Frequency:* Thurs.
Neil Oliver, Publisher
Mike Pearson, News Editor
mpearson@hamiltonnews.com

Stouffville: Stouffville Sun-Tribune
Previous Name: Stouffville Tribune
Owned By: York Region Media Group
6290 Main St., Stouffville, ON L4A 1H2
Tel: 905-640-2612; *Fax:* 905-640-8778
www.yorkregion.com
Social Media:
twitter.com/stouffeditor
facebook.com/stouffvillesuntribune
Circulation: 38,300; *Frequency:* Thu., Sat.
Ian Proudfoot, Publisher
Jim Mason, Managing Editor
jmason@yrmg.com

***Stratford:* Inside Stratford / Perth**
PO Box 23016, 285 Lorne Ave. East, Stratford, ON N5A 7V8
Tel: 519-272-0051; *Fax:* 519-272-0067

Circulation: 24,000+; *Frequency:* Weekly
The community newspaper serves Stratford & Perth County.
Richard Johnson, Publisher & Editor

***Stratford:* Stratford Gazette**
Owned By: Metroland Media Group Ltd.
#106, 10 Downie St., Stratford, ON N5A 7K4
Tel: 519-271-8002; *Fax:* 519-271-5636
www.southwesternontario.ca/community/stratford-gazette
Social Media:
twitter.com/StratGazette
facebook.com/pages/Stratford-Gazette/188314707972056
Circulation: 19,500; *Frequency:* Fri.
Doug Rowe, Regional Managing Editor
drowe@southwesternontario.ca
Laura Carter, Manager, Distribution

***Strathroy:* Strathroy Age Dispatch**
Owned By: Sun Media Corp.
73 Front St. West, Strathroy, ON N7G 1X6
Tel: 519-245-2370; *Fax:* 519-245-1647
www.strathroyagedispatch.com
Social Media:
twitter.com/AgeDispatch
www.facebook.com/pages/Strathroy-Age-Dispatch/12098118126

Circulation: 1,800; *Frequency:* Thurs.
Linda LeBlanc, Publisher
linda.leblanc@sunmedia.ca
Don Biggs, Editor
don.biggs@sunmedia.ca

***Sturgeon Falls:* West Nipissing Tribune**
Previous Name: Sturgeon Falls Tribune
Owned By: 1102282 Ontario Inc.
206 King St., Sturgeon Falls, ON P2B 1R7
Tel: 705-753-2930; *Fax:* 705-753-5231
tribune@westnipissing.com
westnipissing.com
Social Media:
facebook.com/pages/Tribune-West-/282577981766818
Circulation: 1,800; *Frequency:* Wednesday
Suzanne Gammon, Publisher & Editor

***Sudbury:* Journal Le Voyageur**
Détenteur: Publications Voyageur Inc.
302-336, rue Pine, Sudbury, ON P3C 5L1
Tél: 705-673-3377; *Téléc:* 705-673-5854
Ligne sans frais: 866-688-7027
levoyageur@levoyageur.ca
www.levoyageur.ca
Médias sociaux:
twitter.com/voyageursudbury
facebook.com/pages/Journal-Le-Voyageur/130564328071
Tirage: 8 400; *Fréquence:* Mercredi
Paul Lefebvre, Editor

***Sudbury:* Northern Life**
Owned By: Laurentian Media Group
158 Elgin St., Sudbury, ON P3E 3N5
Tel: 705-673-5667; *Fax:* 705-673-4652
www.northernlife.ca
Social Media:
twitter.com/northern_life
facebook.com/northernlife.ca
Circulation: 85,900; *Frequency:* Tue., Thu.
Abbas Homayed, Publisher
Mark Gentili, Managing Editor

***Tavistock:* Tavistock Gazette**
Owned By: Tavistock Gazette Ltd.
PO Box 70, 119 Woodstock South, Tavistock, ON N0B 2R0
Tel: 519-655-2341; *Fax:* 519-655-3070
gazette@tavistock.on.ca
www.tavistock.on.ca

Circulation: 1,250; *Frequency:* Wed.
William Gladding, Publisher

***Tecumseh:* LaSalle Post**
Owned By: Postmedia Network Inc.
1116 Lesperance Rd., Tecumseh, ON N8N 1X2
Tel: 519-735-2080; *Fax:* 519-735-2082
lasallepost@postmedia.com
www.windsoressexnews.com/LasallePost.aspx
Social Media:
twitter.com/TheLaSallePost
facebook.com/LaSallePost

Circulation: 11,100; *Frequency:* Fri.
Bob Thwaites, Publisher
Kari Bowden, Editor

***Tecumseh:* Shoreline Week**
Owned By: Postmedia Community Publishing
1116 Lesperance Rd., Tecumseh, ON N8N 1X2
Tel: 519-735-2080; *Fax:* 519-735-2082
mamcleod@postmedia.com
www.windsoressexnews.com

Circulation: 15,024; *Frequency:* Fri.
David Calibaba, Publisher
Bill England, Editor

***Tecumseh:* Tilbury Times**
Owned By: Postmedia Community Publishing
1116 Lesperance Rd., Tecumseh, ON N8N 1X2
Tel: 519-753-2080; *Fax:* 519-682-3633
tilburytimes@postmedia.com
Social Media:
facebook.com/TilburyTimes

Circulation: 1,170; *Frequency:* Tue.
Garry Baxter, General Manager
Gerry Harvieux, Editor

***Thamesville:* Thamesville Herald**
PO Box 580, 105 Elizabeth St., Thamesville, ON N0P 2K0
Tel: 519-692-3825; *Fax:* 519-692-9515
thamesvilleherald@sympatico.ca

Circulation: 670; *Frequency:* Wed.
Allison Humphrey, Publisher

***Thessalon:* The North Shore Sentinel**
Owned By: Rankin Publications
359 River Rd. North, Thessalon, ON P0R 1L0
Tel: 705-842-2504; *Fax:* 705-842-2679
ns-sentinel@bellnet.ca

Circulation: 1,950; *Frequency:* Wed.
Randy Rankin, Publisher

***Thorold:* Fort Erie Post**
Owned By: Metroland Media Group Ltd.
#1B, 3300 Merrittville Hwy., Thorold, ON L2V 4Y6
Tel: 905-688-2444
www.niagarathisweek.com/forterie-on/
Circulation: 161,000; *Frequency:* Weekly, Thurs.
David Bos, General Manager

***Thorold:* Niagara This Week**
Owned By: Metroland Media Group Ltd.
#1B, 3300 Merrittville Hwy., Thorold, ON L2V 4Y6
Tel: 905-688-2444
www.niagarathisweek.com
Social Media:
twitter.com/NiagarathisWeek
facebook.com/pages/Niagara-this-Week/163184140529
Circulation: 180,000; *Frequency:* Wed., Thurs.
David Bos, General Manager
dbos@niagarathisweek.com
Melissa Duemo, Manager, Office
mduemo@niagarathisweek.com
Neil Oliver, Publisher
noliver@metroland.com

***Thunder Bay:* Thunder Bay Source**
Owned By: Dougall Media
87 North Hill St., Thunder Bay, ON P7A 5V6
Tel: 807-346-2600; *Fax:* 807-345-9923
www.tbnewswatch.com
Social Media:
twitter.com/tbnewswatch
facebook.com/tbnewswatch
Circulation: 43,700; *Frequency:* Thurs.
Free weekly
Leith Dunick, Publisher
ldunick@dougallmedia.com

***Tillsonburg:* Tillsonburg News**
Owned By: Sun Media Corp.
25 Townline Rd., Tillsonburg, ON N4G 4H6
Tel: 519-688-6397
www.tillsonburgnews.com
Social Media:
twitter.com/TillsonburgNews
www.facebook.com/TillsonburgNews

Circulation: 4,150; *Frequency:* Mon., Fri.
Ken Koyama, Publisher
ken.koyama@sunmedia.ca
Kim Novak, Editor
kim.novak@sunmedia.ca

***Timmins:* Les Nouvelles**
187, rue Cedar, Timmins, ON P4N 7G1
Tél: 705-268-2955; *Téléc:* 705-268-3614
lesnouv@vianet.ca
journaux.apf.ca/lesnouvelles
Fréquence: Mercredi
Doris Bouchard, Rédactrice en chef
Bruce Cowan, Publisher

***Timmins:* Timmins Times**
Owned By: Sun Media Corp.
187 Cedar St. South, Timmins, ON P4N 7G1
Tel: 705-268-6252; *Fax:* 705-268-2255
www.timminstimes.com
Social Media:
twitter.com/timminspress
facebook.com/pages/The-Timmins-/213004885 393148
Circulation: 16,300; *Frequency:* Thurs.
Lisa Wilson, Publisher
lisa.wilson@sunmedia.ca
Thomas Perry, Regional Managing Editor
thomas.perry@sunmedia.ca

***Tiny:* Le Goût de Vivre**
Détenteur: Comité d'action Place Lafontaine
343 rue Lafontaine ouest, Tiny, ON L9M 0H1
Tél: 705-533-3349; *Téléc:* 705-533-3422
legoutdevivre@bellnet.ca
legoutdevivre.com

Tirage: 912; *Fréquence:* 1er et 3e jeudi du mois

***Tobermory:* The Bruce Peninsula Press**
PO Box 89, 39 Legion St., Tobermory, ON N0H 2R0
Tel: 519-596-2658; *Fax:* 519-596-8030
Toll-Free: 800-794-4480
info@tobermorypress.com
brucepeninsulapress.com
Circulation: 3,000; *Frequency:* Tuesday (bi-monthly)
The community newspaper serves the northern Bruce Peninsula.
John Francis, Publisher & Editor
Trudy Watson, Contact, Advertising & Sales

***Toronto:* Annex Gleaner**
581 Bloor St. West, Toronto, ON M6G 1K3
Tel: 416-504-6987; *Fax:* 416-504-8792
gleanereditor@gmail.com
www.gleanernews.ca
Other information: Display & Classified Advertising, E-mail: gleanerpub@gmail.com
Social Media:
twitter.com/gleanernews

Circulation: 33,500; *Frequency:* Monthly
Community news is provided to Toronto western downtown neighbourhood. The Annex Gleaner is a free publication that is delivered to residents & businesses.
Rebecca Payne, Editor-in-Chief
Justin Crann, Contributing Editor
justin.gleaner@gmail.com
Monika Warzecha, Online Editor
monika.gleaner@gmail.com

***Toronto:* The Bay Street Times**
#514, 5334 Yonge St., Toronto, ON M2N 6V1
Tel: 416-949-6332; *Fax:* 416-997-6697
editor@baystreetimes.com
www.baystreetimes.com

Frequency: Monthly

***Toronto:* Beach Metro Community News**
2196 Gerrard St. East, Toronto, ON M4E 2C7
Tel: 416-698-1164; *Fax:* 416-698-1253
admin@beachmetro.com
www.beachmetro.com
Social Media: www.youtube.com/BeachMetroNews
twitter.com/BeachMetroNews
www.facebook .com/BeachMetroNews?v=wall
Circulation: 30,000; *Frequency:* 23 per year
Phil Lameira, General Manager
phil@beachmetro.com
Jon Muldoon, Editor
jon@beachmetro.com

***Toronto:* Bloor West Villager**
Owned By: Metroland Media Group Ltd.
175 Gordon Baker Rd., Toronto, ON M2H 0A2
Tel: 416-675-4390; *Fax:* 416-675-9262
www.insidetoronto.com
Social Media:
twitter.com/BWVillager
facebook.com/BloorWestVillager

Circulation: 33,100; *Frequency:* Thurs.
The Toronto neighbourhoods of Bloor West, Roncesvalles, & The Juncion are served by the newspaper.
Ian Proudfoot, Publisher
Grace Peacock, Managing Editor
gpeacock@insidetoronto.com

Toronto: Downtown Bulletin
Previous Name: Toronto St. Lawrence & Downtown Community Bulletin
Owned By: Community Bulletin Newspaper Group Inc.
#121, 260 Adelaide St. East, Toronto, ON M5A 1N1
Tel: 416-929-0011
info@communitybulletin.ca
www.thebulletin.ca
Social Media:
twitter.com/TheBulletinca
facebook.com/pages/TheBulletinca/3628780 1341
Circulation: 51,300; *Frequency:* Monthly, Mon.
Frank Touby, Editor
Paulette Touby, Publisher

Toronto: East York Mirror
Owned By: Metroland Media Group Ltd.
175 Gordon Baker Rd., Toronto, ON M2H 0A2
Tel: 416-493-4400; *Fax:* 416-493-6190
wwww.insidetoronto.com
Social Media:
twitter.com/EastYorkMirror
facebook.com/EastYorkMirror
Circulation: 34,820; *Frequency:* Thurs.
The newspaper covers the Toronto neighbourhoods of East York, Riverdale, & Leaside.
Ian Proudfoot, Publisher
Alan Shackleton, Managing Editor
asackleton@insidetoronto.com

Toronto: Etobicoke Guardian
Previous Name: Etobicoke Advertiser-Guardian
Owned By: Metroland Media Group Ltd.
175 Gordon Baker Rd., Toronto, ON M2H 0A2
Tel: 416-493-4400; *Fax:* 416-675-9262
etg@insidetoronto.com
insidetoronto.com/etobicoke-toronto-on
Social Media:
twitter.com/ETGuardian
facebook.com/EtobicokeGuardian
Circulation: 71,000; *Frequency:* Thurs.
Grace Peacock, Managing Editor
gpeacock@insidetoronto.com
Ian Proudfoot, Publisher
iproudfoot@yrmg.com
Marg Middleton, General Manager

Toronto: L'Express
888 ave. Eastern, Toronto, ON M4L 1A3
Tél: 416-465-2107; *Téléc:* 416-465-3778
info@lexpress.to
www.lexpress.to
Médias sociaux:
twitter.com/LExpressToronto
facebook.com/LExpressDeToronto
Tirage: 22 000; *Fréquence:* Mardi
Jean-Pierre Mazare, Publisher
Francois Bergeron, Editor

Toronto: Hi-Rise
Owned By: Val Publications Ltd.
#121, 95 Leeward Glenway, Toronto, ON M3C 2Z6
Tel: 416-424-1393; *Fax:* 416-467-8262
sec.valdunn@vif.com
www.hi-risenews.com
Circulation: 50,000+; *Frequency:* Monthly
Distributed free of charge to the apartment/townhouse community of the GTA
Valerie Dunn

Toronto: The Korea Times Daily
287 Bridgeland Ave., Toronto, ON M6A 1Z6
Tel: 416-787-1111; *Fax:* 416-781-8434
www.koreatimes.net
Social Media:
twitter.com/ktimesca
www.facebook.com/ktimesca

Toronto: North York Mirror
Owned By: Metroland Media Group Ltd.
175 Gordon Baker Rd., Toronto, ON M2H 0A2
Tel: 416-495-6526; *Fax:* 416-493-6190
www.insidetoronto.com/community/northyork
Social Media:
twitter.com/NorthYorkMirror
facebook.com/northyorkmirror
Circulation: 94,700; *Frequency:* Thurs., Fri.
The community newspaper is deistributed to homes in the former city of North York, Ontario.
Ian Proudfoot, Publisher
Paul Futhey, Managing Editor
pfuthey@insidetoronto.com

Toronto: Our Toronto Free Press
#202, 49 Elm St., Toronto, ON M5G 1H1
Tel: 416-977-0183
letters@torontofreepress.com
www.torontofreepress.com
Frequency: Tues.
Judi McLeod, Editor & Owner
tfp@torontofreepress.com

Toronto: Scarborough Mirror
Owned By: Metroland Media Group Ltd.
175 Gordon Baker Rd., Toronto, ON M2H 0A2
Tel: 416-493-4400; *Fax:* 416-493-6190
insidetoronto.com/scarborough-toronto-on
Social Media:
twitter.com/SCMirror
facebook.com/ScarboroughMirror
Circulation: 234,000; *Frequency:* Thurs., Fri.
Alan Shackleton, Managing Editor
ashackleton@insidetoronto.com
Ian Proudfoot, Publisher
iproudfoot@yrmg.com
Marg Middleton, General Manager

Toronto: Share
658 Vaughan Rd., Toronto, ON M6E 2Y5
Tel: 416-656-3400; *Fax:* 416-656-3711
share@interlog.com
www.sharenews.com
Social Media:
twitter.com/sharenews
www.facebook.com/pages/Share-Newspaper/35798374757 7821
Circulation: 50,000; *Frequency:* Weekly
Serves the Black and Caribbean community in the GTA.
Arnold A. Auguste, Publisher

Toronto: Toronto Street News
c/o LoveCry, 1024 Queen St. East, Toronto, ON M4M 1K4
Tel: 416-406-0099
info@torontostreetnews.net
www.torontostreetnews.net
Circulation: 3,000; *Frequency:* Weekly
Available free to homeless, handicapped, underemployed and dying so that they can sell for income.
Victor Fletcher, Publisher

Toronto: Town Crier
Owned By: Streeter Publications
c/o Streeter Publications, #204, 46 St. Clair Ave. East, Toronto, ON M4T 1M9
Tel: 416-901-8182
news@MyTownCrier.ca
www.mytowncrier.ca
Social Media:
twitter.com/mytowncrier
www.facebook.com/TownCriersTownSports
Circulation: 60,000; *Frequency:* Bimonthly
Serving the neighbourhoods of Leaside-Rosedale, North Toronto and Forest Hill.
Lori Abittan, President & Publisher
Eric McMillan, Managing Editor

Toronto: Village Living Magazines
Toronto, ON
Toll-Free: 866-933-1652
villagelivingmagazine.ca
Social Media: pinterest.com/villagelivinmag
twitter.com/villagelivinmag
www.facebook .com/VillageLivingMagazines
Frequency: Bi-Monthly
Free community newspaper serving the areas of Forest Hill, Hillcrest Village, Wychwood Heights, Regal Heights, and Upper Village.
Andrew Fishman, Publisher
1-866-933-1652 ext 2
Iris Zimmer-Fishman, Associate Publisher
1-866-933-1652 ext 3

Toronto: The Women's Post
#214, 501 Yonge St., Toronto, ON M4Y 1Y4
Tel: 416-900-1088; *Fax:* 416-645-7046
www.womenspost.ca
Social Media:
youtube.com/channel/UCNHnMz-3IISR7JzVYwcmzjg
twitter.com/womenspost
fa cebook.com/womenspost
Circulation: 71,818; *Frequency:* Bi-monthly
Sarah Whatmough-Thomson, Editor
editor@womenspost.ca
Greg Thomson, Chief Financial Officer
gthomson@womenspost.ca

Toronto: York Guardian
Owned By: Metroland Media Group Ltd.
175 Gordon Baker Rd., Toronto, ON M2H 0A2
Tel: 416-493-4400
wwww.insidetoronto.com
Social Media:
twitter.com/YorkGuardian
facebook.com/yorkguardian
Circulation: 28,550; *Frequency:* Thurs.
The newspaper is delivered to homes in Toronto.
Ian Proudfoot, Publisher
Paul Futhey, Managing Editor
pfuthey@insidetoronto.com

Tweed: Tweed News
Owned By: Tweed News Publishing Co. Ltd.
PO Box 550, 242 Victoria St. North, Tweed, ON K0K 3J0
Tel: 613-478-2017; *Fax:* 613-478-2749
info@thetweednews.ca
www.thetweednews.ca
Social Media:
twitter.com/TheTweedNews
facebook.com/pages/The-Tweed-News/5451096655873 54
Circulation: 900; *Frequency:* Wed.
Rodger Hanna, Publisher & Editor

Uxbridge: Uxbridge Times-Journal
Previous Name: Uxbridge Times-Journal
Owned By: Metroland Media Group Ltd.
PO Box 459, 16 Bascom St., Uxbridge, ON L9P 1M9
Tel: 905-852-9141; *Fax:* 905-852-9341
www.durhamregion.com
Circulation: 9,000; *Frequency:* Thurs.
Tim Whittaker, Publisher
twhittaker@durhamregion.com
Joanne Burghardt, Editor-in-Chief
jburghardt@durhamregion.com

Vankleek Hill: The Review
Previous Name: Vankleek Hill Review
Owned By: The Review (996963 Ontario Inc.)
PO Box 160, 76 Main St. East, Vankleek Hill, ON K0B 1R0
Tel: 613-678-3327; *Fax:* 613-937-2591
Toll-Free: 877-678-3327
review@thereview.ca
www.thereview.on.ca
Social Media: youtube.com/user/VKHReview
twitter.com/vkhreview
facebook.com/vkhre view
Circulation: 3,200; *Frequency:* Wed.
Louise Sproule, Publisher
lsproule@thereview.ca
Richard Mahoney, Editor
editor@thereview.ca

Vaughan: Vaughan Citizen
Owned By: York Region Media Group
#29, 8611 Weston Rd., Vaughan, ON L4L 9P1
Tel: 905-264-8703; *Fax:* 905-264-9453
www.yorkregion.com
Social Media:
twitter.com/VaughanEditor
facebook.com/TheVaughanCitizen
Circulation: 51,000; *Frequency:* Wed., Thurs.
Kim Champion, Editor
kchampion@yrmg.com
John Willems, Regional General Manager
john.willems@metroland.com
Robert Lazurko, Manager, Business

Virgil: Niagara Advance
Owned By: Sun Media Corp.
PO Box 430, 1501 Niagara Stone Rd., Virgil, ON L0S 1T0
Tel: 905-468-3283; *Fax:* 905-468-3137
www.niagaraadvance.ca
Social Media:
twitter.com/NiagaraAdvance
www.facebook.com/pages/Niagara-Advance/121004 834576571

Circulation: 7,600; Frequency: Thursday
Michael Cressman, Publisher
Penny Coles, Editor
Tim Dundas, General Manager

Walkerton: Walkerton Herald-Times
Owned By: Metroland Media Group Ltd.
PO Box 190, 10 Victoria St., Walkerton, ON N0G 2V0
Tel: 519-881-1600; Fax: 519-881-0276
southwesternontario.ca/community/walkerton-herald-times
Social Media:
facebook.com/WHTnews

Circulation: 1,600; Frequency: Wed.
John McPhee, General Manager
editor@walkerton.com
Doug Rowe, General Manager, Southwestern Division
drowe@southwesternontario.ca
Cathy Spitzig, Contact, Circulation
classifieds@walkerton.com

Wallaceburg: Wallaceburg News
538 James St., Wallaceburg, ON N8A 2N9
Tel: 519-627-2557; Fax: 519-627-1261
www.thewallaceburgnews.ca

Frequency: Wed.
Wayne Snider, Managing Editor
Daryl Smith, Publisher

Wasaga Beach: Stayner Sun
Previous Name: Angus-Borden Sun
Owned By: Metroland Media
#10, 1 Market Lane, Wasaga Beach, ON L9Z 0B6
Tel: 705-428-2638; Fax: 705-422-2446
www.simcoe.com/community/stayner
Social Media:
twitter.com/staynersun
facebook.com/pages/Stayner-Sun/145839558780312
Circulation: 4000; Frequency: Thurs.
Carol Lamb, General Manager
clamb@simcoe.com
Mike Gennings, Editor
mgennings@simcoe.com

Wasaga Beach: The Wasaga Sun
Owned By: Metroland Media Group Ltd.
#10, 1 Market Lane, Wasaga Beach, ON L9Z 2B9
Tel: 705-429-1688; Fax: 705-422-2446
www.simcoe.com/community/wasagabeach
Social Media:
twitter.com/WasagaSun
facebook.com/WasagaSunnews

Circulation: 8,200; Frequency: Thurs.
Carol Lamb, General Manager
clamb@simcoe.com
Mike Gennings, Editor
mgennings@simcoe.com

Waterdown: Flamborough Review
Owned By: Metroland Media Group Ltd.
PO Box 20, 30 Main St. North, Waterdown, ON L0R 2H0
Tel: 905-689-4841; Fax: 905-689-3110
www.flamboroughreview.com
Social Media:
twitter.com/FlamReview
facebook.com/FlamboroughReview

Circulation: 13,700; Frequency: Thurs.
Neil Oliver, Publisher
noliver@metroland.com
Brenda Jeffries, Editor
editor@flamboroughreview.com

Waterloo: Waterloo Chronicle
Owned By: Metroland Media Group Ltd.
#20, 279 Weber St. North, Waterloo, ON N2J 3H8
Tel: 519-886-2830; Fax: 519-886-9383
www.waterloochronicle.ca
Social Media:
twitter.com/wlchronicle
facebook.com/pages/Waterloo-Chronicle/1999810433 71187
Circulation: 30,500; Frequency: Wed.
Peter Winkler, Publisher
Bob Vrbanac, Editor
bvrbanac@waterloochronicle.ca

Watford: Watford Guide-Advocate
Owned By: Hayter-Walden Publications Inc.
PO Box 99, 5292 Nauvoo Rd., Watford, ON N0M 2S0
Tel: 519-876-2809; Fax: 519-876-2322
guideadvocate@execulink.com
hayterwalden.com

Circulation: 920; Frequency: Thurs.
Dale Hayter, Publisher
Stephanie Cattrysee, Editor

West Lorne: The West Elgin Chronicle
Owned By: Sun Media Corp.
168 Main St., West Lorne, ON N0L 2P0
Tel: 519-768-2220; Fax: 519-768-2221
www.thechronicle-online.com
Social Media:
twitter.com/WE_TheChronicle
www.facebook.com/TheWestElginChronicle

Circulation: 5,500; Frequency: Thu.
Linda Leblanc, Publisher
519-474-5371 x242
linda.leblanc@sunmedia.ca
Ian McCallum, Editor
519-631-2790 x248
ian.mccallum@sunmedia.ca

Westport: The Review-Mirror
Owned By: The Mirror Group
PO Box 130, 43 Bedford St., Westport, ON K0G 1X0
Tel: 613-273-8000; Fax: 613-273-8001
Toll-Free: 800-387-0796
info@review-mirror.com; editor@review-mirror.com
www.review-mirror.com
Other information: News Tips: newsroom@review-mirror.com
Circulation: 1,550; Frequency: Thursday
The Review Mirror serves Westport, the Rideau Valley, & the Rideau Lakes in Ontario. Print & electronic subscriptions are available.
Howard Crichton, Publisher & Managing Editor
Margaret Brand, Reporter & Photographer
mbrand@review-mirror.com
Marco Smits, Reporter & Photographer
msmits@review-mirror.com
Louise Haughton, Contact, Office
lhaughton@review-mirror.com
Bill Ritchie, Contact, Advertising Sales
advertising@review-mirror.com

Wheatley: Wheatley Journal
Owned By: Wheatley Journal
PO Box 10, 14 Talbot West, Wheatley, ON N0P 2P0
Tel: 519-825-4541; Fax: 519-825-4546
journal@mnsi.net
Social Media:
facebook.com/wheatleyjournal
Circulation: 700; Frequency: Wed.
Jim Heynes, Publisher
jim@southpoint.ca
Sheila McBrayne, Editor
sheila@southpointsun.ca

Wiarton: Wiarton Echo
Owned By: Sun Media Corp.
PO Box 220, 573 Berford St., Wiarton, ON N0H 2T0
Tel: 519-534-1560; Fax: 519-534-4616
www.wiartonecho.com
Social Media:
twitter.com/wiartonecho
www.facebook.com/pages/Wiarton-Echo/334537 066702
Circulation: 1,700; Frequency: Tues.
Nelson Phillips, Publisher
nelson.phillips@sunmedia.ca
Keith Gilbert, Managing Editor
keith.gilbert@sunmedia.ca

Winchester: Winchester Press
Owned By: Manotick Messenger Inc.
PO Box 399, 545 Lawrence St., Winchester, ON K0C 2K0
Tel: 613-774-2524; Fax: 613-774-3967
Ads: advert@winchesterpress.on.ca
www.winchesterpress.on.ca
Other information: Front office email: accounts@winchesterpress.on.ca
Social Media:
facebook.com/WinchesterPress
Circulation: 3,200; Frequency: Wed.
Beth Morris, Owner & President
Matthew Uhrig, Editor
news@winchesterpress.on.co

Windsor: Journal Le Rempart
Anciennement: Le Rempart
7515, ch. Forest Glade, Windsor, ON N8T 3P5
Tél: 519-948-4139; Téléc: 519-948-0628
info@lerempart.ca
www.lerempart.ca
Médias sociaux:
facebook.com/pages/Le-Rempart/184833808388836
Tirage: 6 500; Fréquence: Mercredi
Denis Poirier, Publisher

Windsor: Windsor Pennysaver
4525 Rhodes Dr., Windsor, ON N8W 5R8
Tel: 519-966-4500; Fax: 519-966-3660
classified@windsorpennysaver.com
shopinwindsor.com/Windsor-Essex-County-Pennysaver/344420.htm

Circulation: 119,000; Frequency: Fri.
Shannon Ricker, Publisher
Rod Hilts, Regional Managing Editor

Wingham: Wingham Advance-Times
Owned By: Metroland Media Group Ltd.
PO Box 390, 11 Veterans Rd., Wingham, ON N0G 2W0
Tel: 519-357-2320; Fax: 519-357-2900
www.southwesternontario.ca
Social Media:
facebook.com/WinghamAdvanceTimes
Circulation: 1,200; Frequency: Wed.
Pauline Kerr, Editor
pkerr@wingham.com
Bill Huether, General Manager
bhuether@northperth.com

Woodstock: Norwich Gazette
Owned By: Sun Media Corp.
16 Brock St., Woodstock, ON N4S 3B4
Tel: 519-537-2341
norwich.gazette@sunmedia.ca
www.norwichgazette.ca
Social Media:
twitter.com/NorwichGazette
www.facebook.com/NorwichGazette
Circulation: 800; Frequency: Wednesday
Andrea DeMeer, Publisher
ademeer@bowesnet.com
Jennifer Vandermeer, Editor
jennifer.vandermeer@sunmedia.ca

Woodstock: Oxford Shopping News
Owned By: Sun Media Group
16 Brock St., Woodstock, ON N4S 3B4
Tel: 519-537-6657; Fax: 519-537-8542
www.oxfordshoppingnews.com
Circulation: 26,800; Frequency: Tues.
Distributed by the Woodstock Sentinel Review
Ken Koyama, Publisher
ken.koyama@sunmedia.ca
Gord McCreary, Director, Advertising
gord.mccreary@sunmedia.ca

Multicultural Newspapers in Ontario

Brampton: Gujarat Express
Corporate Office, 20 Eldwood Pl., Brampton, ON L6V 3N3
Tel: 905-457-7096; Fax: 905-457-7096
abgujaratexpress@yahoo.ca

Frequency: Weekly
Gujarat Express serves new immigrants to Canada & the South Asian community.
Amit Bhatt, Publisher & Editor
Haresh Kumar, Sub Editor
Chinmay Dave, Contact, Sales & Marketing

Toronto: Sing Tao Daily
Owned By: Sing Tao Newspapers / Torstar Corp.
417 Dundas St. West, Toronto, ON M5T 1G6
Tel: 416-596-8140; Fax: 416-599-6688
singtaoadmin@singtao.ca
news.singtao.ca/toronto

Frequency: Daily; Chinese
Chinese daily newspaper.
Robert Lang, Chief Editor

University & College Newspapers in Ontario

Belleville: QNet News
Owned By: Loyalist College
PO Box 4200, Belleville, ON K8N 5B9
Tel: 613-969-1913; Fax: 613-962-1376
Toll-Free: 888-569-2547
qnetnewsdesk@gmail.com
www.qnetnews.ca
Social Media:
twitter.com/QNetNews
www.facebook.com/qnetnews

Frequency: Weekly
News and information site for the journalism program of Loyalist College.

Hamilton: Ignite
Owned By: Mohawk College
#F172H, 135 Fennell Ave. West, G108K, Hamilton, ON L8N 3T2
Tel: 905-575-1212; Fax: 905-575-2385
ignitenewsca@gmail.com
www.satelliteonline.ca
Social Media: youtube.com/user/IgniteNewsCanada
twitter.com/IgniteOnline
facebook .com/IgniteNews
Mohawk College newspaper.

Kingston: The Navigator
Owned By: St. Lawrence College
King & Portsmouth, 100 Portsmouth Ave., Kingston, ON K7L 5A6
Tel: 613-544-5400; Fax: 613-545-3923
www.stlawrencecollege.ca
St. Lawrence College newspaper.

Kitchener: Spoke
Owned By: Conestoga College
299 Doon Valley Dr., Kitchener, ON N2G 4M4
Tel: 519-748-5220; Fax: 519-748-3505
spoke@conestogac.on.ca
spokeonline.com
Social Media:
twitter.com/SpokeOnline
facebook.com/spokeonline
Frequency: Weekly
The newspaper of Conestoga College's journalism program produced by second-year print journalism students
Christina Jones, Faculty Adviser
Chris Martin, New Media Technologist

London: The Interrobang
Owned By: Fanshawe College
PO Box 7005, 1001 Fanshawe College Blvd., London, ON N5Y 5R6
Tel: 519-452-4430; Fax: 519-452-4420
fsu.ca/interrobang_main.php
Social Media:
twitter.com/interrobang_fsu
facebook.com/fsuinterrobang
Frequency: Weekly
Fanshawe College newspaper.
Stephanie Lai, Editor
s_lai6@fanshawac.ca
John Said, Manager, Publications & Communications
jsaid@fanshawec.ca

Oakville: The Sheridan Sun
Owned By: Sheridan College Institute of Technology & Advanced Learning
Trafalgar Road Campus, PO Box 2500 Main, 9430 Trafalgar Rd., Oakville, ON L6H 2L1
Tel: 905-845-9430; Fax: 905-815-4148
sheridan.sun@sheridanc.on.ca
thesheridansun.ca
Social Media:
twitter.com/thesheridansun
facebook.com/thesheridansun
Sheridan College Institute of Technology & Advanced Learning newspaper, maintained by the students in the Journalism-Print program.

Oshawa: The Chronicle
Owned By: Durham College
PO Box 385, 2000 Simcoe St. North, Oshawa, ON L1H 7K4
Tel: 905-721-3068; Fax: 905-721-3113
chronicle.news@dc.uoit.ca
chronicle.durhamcollege.ca
Social Media:
twitter.com/DCUOITChronicle
Durham College newspaper.
Gerald Rose, Editor-in-Chief
gerald.rose@durhamcollege.ca
Dawn Salter, Manager, Advertising
dawn.salter@durhamcollege.ca

Ottawa: The Charlatan
Owned By: Carleton University
Unicentre Building, Rm. 531, 1125 Colonel By Dr., Ottawa, ON K1S 5B6
Tel: 613-520-6680
editor@charlatan.ca
www.charlatan.ca
Social Media:
twitter.com/CharlatanLive
www.facebook.com/CharlatanLive
Carleton University newspaper.

Peterborough: The Three Penny Beaver
Owned By: Sir Sandford Fleming College
Sutherland Campus, 599 Brealey Dr., Peterborough, ON K9J 7B1
Tel: 705-749-5530; Fax: 705-749-5507
Toll-Free: 866-353-6464
info@flemingc.on.ca
flemingcollege.ca
Sir Sandford Fleming College newspaper.

Sarnia: Lion's Tale
Owned By: Lambton College
1457 London Rd., Sarnia, ON N7S 6K4
Tel: 519-542-7751
info@lambton.on.ca
www.lambton.on.ca
Social Media:
twitter.com/LionsTale
www.facebook.com/LambtonCollegeSAC
Lambton College newspaper.

Scarborough: The Underground
Owned By: University of Toronto at Scarborough
#SL-243, 1265 Military Trail, Scarborough, ON M1C 1A4
Tel: 416-287-7054
info@the-underground.ca
www.the-underground.ca
Other information: Editor: editor@the-underground.ca
Social Media:
twitter.com/utscUNDERGROUND
facebook.com/utscUNDERGROUND
Frequency: Bi-weekly
University of Toronto at Scarborough newspaper.
Ranziba Nehrin, Editor-in-Chief
editor@the-underground.ca

St Catharines: Brock Press
Owned By: Brock University
Alumni Student's Centre, Rm. 204a, 500 Glenridge Ave., St Catharines, ON L2S 3A1
Tel: 905-688-5550; Fax: 905-984-4853
editor@brockpress.com
www.brockpress.com
Social Media:
twitter.com/TheBrockPress
facebook.com/BrockPress
Brock University newspaper.
Gaylynn Janzen, Manager
manager@brockpress.com

Sudbury: The Shield
Owned By: Cambrian College of Applied Arts & Technology
1400 Barrydowne Rd., Sudbury, ON P3A 3V8
Tel: 705-566-8101 Toll-Free: 800-461-7145
Cambrian College of Applied Arts & Technology newspaper.

Thunder Bay: The Argus
Owned By: Lakehead University
#UC-2014B, 955 Oliver Rd., Thunder Bay, ON P7B 5E1
Tel: 807-766-7251; Fax: 807-343-8803
editor@theargus.ca
www.theargus.ca
Social Media:
twitter.com/TheArgusNews
facebook.com/theargus
Circulation: 3000+
Lakehead University newspaper.

Thunder Bay: Opus
Owned By: Confederation College
PO Box 398, 1450 Nakina Dr., Thunder Bay, ON P7C 4W1
Tel: 807-475-6110; Fax: 807-623-4512
Toll-Free: 800-465-5493
www.confederationc.on.ca
Confederation College student newspaper

Toronto: The Buzz
Owned By: Seneca College of Applied Arts & Technology
c/o Newnham Campus, 1750 Finch Ave. East, Toronto, ON M2J 2X5
Tel: 416-491-5050
buzzinfo@senecac.on.ca
www.senecacollege.ca
Seneca College of Applied Arts & Technology newspaper.

Toronto: Dialog Newspaper
Owned By: George Brown College
PO Box 1015 B, #E122, 142 Kendal Ave., Toronto, ON M5R 1M3
Tel: 416-415-5000 Toll-Free: 800-265-2002
dialog@georgebrown.ca
dialog.studentassociation.ca
Social Media:
twitter.com/dialoggbc
facebook.com/thedialogonline
Frequency: Monthly, from Aug.-April
George Brown College student newspaper.
Mick Sweetman, Managing Editor

Toronto: EtCetera
Owned By: Humber Institute of Technology and Advanced Learning
North Campus, 205 Humber College Blvd., Toronto, ON M9W 5L7
Tel: 416-675-6622; Fax: 416-675-2427
etc.humber@gmail.com
www.humber.ca
Social Media:
twitter.com/humberetc
facebook.com/pages/Humber-Et-Cetera/14701161869319 8
Humber Institute of Technology and Advanced Learning newspaer.
Victoria Quiroz, Editor-in-Chief

Welland: Niagara News
Owned By: Niagara College
Welland Campus, 300 Woodlawn Rd., Welland, ON L3C 7L3
Tel: 905-735-2211; Fax: 905-736-6000
news@niagaracollege.ca
www.niagaracollege.ca/newspaper
Niagara College newspaper.

Windsor: The Converged Citizen
Owned By: St. Clair College
South Campus, 2000 Talbot Rd. West, Windsor, ON N9A 6S4
Tel: 519-972-2727; Fax: 519-972-3811
media.converged@gmail.com
themediaplex.com/convergedcitizen
Social Media:
facebook.com/pages/Converged-Citizen/257301984308571
St. Clair College newspaper.
Jason Viau, Staff Member

Prince Edward Island

Daily Newspapers in Prince Edward Island

Charlottetown: The Guardian
Previous Name: The Evening Patriot
Owned By: TC Media
165 Prince St., Charlottetown, PE C1A 4R7
Tel: 902-629-6000; Fax: 902-566-3808
Toll-Free: 800-267-6397
newsroom@theguardian.pe.ca
www.theguardian.pe.ca
Social Media:
twitter.com/peiguardian
www.facebook.com/PEI.Guardian
Circulation: 89,958 total; Frequency: Monday-Saturday
Don Brander, Publisher
d.brander@theguardian.pe.ca
Gary MacDougall, Managing Editor

Summerside: The Journal Pioneer
Owned By: TC Media
PO Box 2480, 316 Water St., Summerside, PE C1N 4K5
Tel: 902-436-2121 Toll-Free: 800-841-2527
newsroom@journalpioneer.com
www.journalpioneer.com
Social Media:
twitter.com/journalpioneer
www.facebook.com/journalpioneer
Circulation: 36,169 total; Frequency: Monday-Saturday
Brad Works, Managing Editor
902-432-8212
bworks@journalpioneer.com
Sandy Rundle, Publisher
902-432-8203; Fax: 902-436-3736

Other Newspapers in Prince Edward Island

***Montague:* The Eastern Graphic**
Owned By: Island Press Ltd.
PO Box 790, 567 Main St. South, Montague, PE C0A 1R0
Tel: 902-838-2515; *Fax:* 902-838-4392
subscribe@peicanada.com; accounts@peicanada.com
peicanada.com/content/eastern_graphic
Social Media:
twitter.com/graphicnews
www.facebook.com/peicanada
Circulation: 5,100; *Frequency:* Wed.
The publication covers news for eastern Prince Edward Island.
Paul MacNeill, Publisher
paul@peicanada.com
Heather Moore, Editor
editor@peicanada.com
Jan MacNeill, Manager, Advertising
jan@peicanada.com
Aura Lee Shepard, Coordinator, Production
auralee@peicanada.com
Sharon Riley, Account Executive
sharon@peicanada.com

***Montague:* West Prince Graphic**
Owned By: Island Press Ltd.
PO Box 790, 4 Railway St., Montague, PE C0B 1B0
Tel: 902-838-2515; *Fax:* 902-838-4392
Toll-Free: 800-806-5443
accounts@peicanada.com
www.peicanada.com
Social Media:
twitter.com/graphicnews
facebook.com/peicanada
Circulation: 5,800; *Frequency:* Weds.
Paul MacNeill, Publisher
902-838-2515 x 201
paul@peicanada.com
Cindy Chant, Editor

***Summerside:* La Voix Acadienne**
Détenteur: La Voix Acadienne
5, av Maris Stella, Summerside, PE C1N 6M9
Tél: 902-436-6005; *Téléc:* 902-888-3976
pub@lavoixacadienne.com
www.lavoixacadienne.com
Médias sociaux:
twitter.com/lavoixacadienne
www.facebook.com/pages/La-Voix-Acadienne/246332682050424
Tirage: 2 200; *Fréquence:* Mercredi
Marcia Enman, Directrice général
marcia.enman@lavoixacadienne.com

Québec

Daily Newspapers in Québec

***Granby:* La Voix de L'Est**
Détenteur: Groupe Capitales Médias Inc.
76, rue Dufferin, Granby, QC J2G 9L4
Tél: 450-375-4555; *Téléc:* 450-777-7221
redaction@lavoixdelest.ca
www.lavoixdelest.ca
Médias sociaux:
twitter.com/lavoixdelest
www.facebook.com/lavoixdelest
Tirage: 94 765 total; *Fréquence:* lundi-samedi
Louise Boisvert, Présidente et éditrice
François Beaudoin, Rédacteur en chef

***Montréal:* Le Devoir**
Détenteur: Independent
2050, de Bleury, 9e étage, Montréal, QC H3A 3M9
Tél: 514-985-3333 *Ligne sans frais:* 800-463-7559
redaction@ledevoir.com
www.ledevoir.com
Médias sociaux:
twitter.com/LeDevoir
www.facebook.com/ledevoir
Tirage: 214 263 total; *Fréquence:* lundi-samedi
Le Devoir est une référence en matière d'information.
Jean Lamarre, Président

***Montréal:* Le Journal de Montréal**
Détenteur: Québecor Media Inc. / Sun Media Corporation
4545, rue Frontenac, Montréal, QC H2H 2R7
Tél: 514-521-4545
www.journaldemontreal.com
Médias sociaux:
twitter.com/JdeMontreal
www.facebook.com/jdemontreal
Tirage: 1 633 726 total; *Fréquence:* quotidien
Lyne Robitaille, Présidente et éditrice

***Montréal:* Journal Métro de Montréal**
Détenteur: TC Media
1100 boul. René-Lévesque ouest, 24e étage, Montréal, QC H3B 4X9
Tél: 514-286-1066; *Téléc:* 514-286-9310
info@journalmetro.com
journalmetro.com
Médias sociaux: foursquare.com/journalmetro
twitter.com/metromontreal
www.facebook.com /journalmetro
Tirage: 1,633,726 total; *Fréquence:* quotidien
Nicolas Faucher, Éditeur
Yves Bédard, Éditeur adjoint

***Montréal:* Montreal 24 heures**
Détenteur: Québecor Media Inc. / Sun Media Corporation
4545, rue Frontenac, Montréal, QC H2H 2R7
Tél: 514-521-4545
www.journaldemontreal.com/24heures
Tirage: 751,193 total; *Fréquence:* lundi-vendredi

***Montreal:* Montreal Gazette**
Previous Name: The Gazette
Owned By: Postmedia Network Inc.
#200, 1010 Ste-Catherine St. W, Montreal, QC H3B 5L1
Tel: 514-987-2222; *Fax:* 514-987-2640
Toll-Free: 800-361-8478
www.montrealgazette.com
Social Media:
twitter.com/mtlgazette
www.facebook.com/montrealgazette
Circulation: 547,445 total; *Frequency:* Monday-Saturday
Michelle Richardson, Managing Editor
514-987-2598
mrichardson@montrealgazette.com

***Québec:* Le Journal de Québec**
Détenteur: Québecor Media Inc. / Sun Media Corporation
450, rue Béchard, Québec, QC G1M 2E9
Tél: 418-683-1573
commentaires@journaldequebec.com
www.journaldequebec.com
Médias sociaux:
twitter.com/JdeQuebec
www.facebook.com/JdeQuebec
Tirage: 1 055 490 total; *Fréquence:* quotidien
Louise Cordeau, Éditrice
louise.cordeau@journaldequebec.com

***Québec:* Le Soleil**
Détenteur: Groupe Capitales Médias Inc.
CP 1547 Terminus, 410, boul Charest est, Québec, QC G1K 7J6
Tél: 418-686-3394; *Téléc:* 418-686-3374
Ligne sans frais: 866-686-3344
nouvelles@lesoleil.com
www.lapresse.ca/le-soleil
Tirage: 553 309 total; *Fréquence:* quotidien
Journal hebdomadaire du Québec
Claude Gagnon, Président & éditeur
Pierre-Paul Norreau, Éditeur adjoint

***Saguenay:* Le Quotidien**
Détenteur: Groupe Capitales Médias Inc.
1051, boul Talbot, Saguenay, QC G7H 5C1
Tél: 418-545-4474; *Téléc:* 418-690-8824
redaction@lequotidien.com
www.lapresse.ca/le-quotidien
Médias sociaux:
twitter.com/LeQuotidien_Cyb
facebook.com/LeQuotidienProgresDimanche
Tirage: 189 527 total; *Fréquence:* quotidien
Michel Simard, Président et éditeur

***Sainte-Marie-de-Beauce:* Beauce Média**
Anciennement: Journal de Beauce-Nord
Détenteur: TC Media
1147, boul Vachon Nord, Sainte-Marie-de-Beauce, QC G6E 1M8
Tél: 418-387-8000; *Téléc:* 418-387-4495
redaction.beauce@tc.tc
www.editionbeauce.com
Médias sociaux:
twitter.com/editionbeauce
Tirage: 24 000; *Fréquence:* mercredi

***Sherbrooke:* The Record**
Owned By: Glacier Media Inc.
1195 rue Galt Est, Sherbrooke, QC J1G 1Y7
Tel: 819-569-9525; *Fax:* 819-821-3179
www.sherbrookerecord.com
Social Media:
twitter.com/recordnewspaper
www.facebook.com/sherbrookerecord
Circulation: 21,715 total; *Frequency:* Monday-Friday
Sharon McCully, Publisher
outletjournal@sympatico.ca
John Edwards, Editor
newsroom@sherbrookerecord.com

***Sherbrooke:* La Tribune**
Détenteur: Groupe Capitales Médias Inc.
1950, rue Roy, Sherbrooke, QC J1K 2X8
Tél: 819-564-5450 *Ligne sans frais:* 800-567-6955
redaction@latribune.qc.ca
www.lapresse.ca/la-tribune
Médias sociaux:
www.facebook.com/quotidienlatribune
Tirage: 181 785 total; *Fréquence:* lundi-samedi
Louise Boisvert, Présidente et éditrice

***Trois-Rivières:* Le Nouvelliste**
Détenteur: Groupe Capitales Médias Inc.
CP 668, 1920, rue Bellefeuille, Trois-Rivières, QC G9A 3Y2
Tél: 819-376-2501
information@lenouvelliste.qc.ca
www.lapresse.ca/le-nouvelliste
Médias sociaux:
twitter.com/le_nouvelliste
www.facebook.com/lenouvelliste
Tirage: 256 565 total; *Fréquence:* lundi-samedi
Alain Turcotte, Président et éditeur
Stéphan Frappier, Rédacteur en chef

Other Newspapers in Québec

***Acton Vale:* La Pensée de Bagot**
Détenteur: DBC Communications Inc.
800, rue de Roxton, Acton Vale, QC J0H 1A0
Tél: 450-546-3271; *Téléc:* 450-546-3491
publicite@lapensee.qc.ca
www.lapensee.qc.ca
Tirage: 14 797; *Fréquence:* mercredi
Benoit Chartier, Éditeur
Michel Dorais, Directeur
mdorais@lapensee.qc.ca

***Alma:* Le Lac Saint-Jean**
#01, 100, rue St-Joseph sud, Alma, QC G8B 7A6
Tél: 418-668-4545; *Téléc:* 418-668-8522
redaction_alma@tc.tc
www.lelacstjean.com
Médias sociaux:
twitter.com/lelacstjean
facebook.com/lelacstjean
Fréquence: Samedi

***Amos:* Le Citoyen de L'Harricana**
Détenteur: TC Transcontinental
92, rue Principale Sud, Amos, QC J9T 2J6
Tél: 819-732-6531; *Téléc:* 819-732-3764
lecitoyendelharricana.ca
Médias sociaux:
twitter.com/LechoAbitibien
facebook.com/lechoabitibien
Tirage: 11 400; *Fréquence:* Mercredi
Caroline Couture, Éditrice
caroline.couture@tc.tc

***Asbestos:* Les Actualités**
Détenteur: Les Hebdos Régionaux Québecor Média
572, 1è ave, Asbestos, QC J1T 4R4
Tél: 819-879-6681; *Téléc:* 819-879-7235
nathalie.hurdle@quebecormedia.com
journallesactualites.ca
Médias sociaux:
twitter.com/LesActualites
www.facebook.com/actuasbestos

Tirage: 14 800; *Fréquence:* Samedi
Carole Pellerin, Éditrice
carole.pellerin@quebecormedia.com
Jean-Marc Bourque, Directeur régional, Québec-Est
jean-marc.bourque@tc.tc

***Baie-Comeau:* Plein Jour de Baie-Comeau**
Anciennement: Plein-Jour Charlevoix, Le Plein-Jour en Haute Côte-Nord
Détenteur: Les Hebdos Régionaux Québecor Média
#309, 625, boul Laflèche, Baie-Comeau, QC G5C 1C5
Tél: 418-589-5900; *Téléc:* 418-589-8216
bco.redaction@tc.tc
pleinjourdebaiecomeau.ca
Médias sociaux:
twitter.com/PJbaiecomeau
www.facebook.com/pleinjourbaiecomeau

Tirage: 16 366; *Fréquence:* Vendredi; aussi Plein jour sur la Manicouagan (mercredi, tirage 15 866)
Sebastien Rouillard, Éditeur
sebastien.rouillard@tc.tc
Alain Saint-Amand, Directeur général régional, Québec-Est
alain.saint-amand@tc.tc

***Baie-Saint-Paul:* L'Hebdo Charlevoisien**
Détenteur: Néomedia
45, boul Raymond Mailloux, Baie-Saint-Paul, QC G3Z 1W2
Tél: 418-435-0220; *Téléc:* 418-435-3349
hebdo@charlevoix.net
www.charlevoixendirect.com

Tirage: 13 033; *Fréquence:* Saturday
Charles Warren, Directeur
418-665-1299
charles@hebdocharlevoisien.ca
Guy Charlebois, Directeur de production

***Beaulac-Garthby:* Journal Le Contact**
9, rue de la Chapelle, Beaulac-Garthby, QC G0Y 1BO
Tél: 418-458-2737; *Téléc:* 418-458-1142
contactbg2002@yahoo.ca
www.beaulac-garthby.com

Tirage: 475; *Fréquence:* vendredi
Guy St-Onge, Rédacteur

***Beaupré:* Journal L'Autre Voix**
Détenteur: TC Media
#101, 10 989, boul Sainte-Anne, Beaupré, QC G0A 1E0
Tél: 418-827-1511; *Téléc:* 418-827-1513
redaction.lautrevoix@tc.tc
www.lautrevoix.com

Tirage: 14 390; *Fréquence:* mercredi
Michel Chalifour, Directeur général régional

***Beloeil:* L'Oeil Régional**
Détenteur: Les Hebdos Régionaux Québecor Média
393, boul Sir-Wilfrid-Laurier, Beloeil, QC J3G 4H6
Tél: 450-467-1821; *Téléc:* 450-467-3087
bel.redaction@tc.tc
www.oeilregional.com
Autre information: Publicité: genevieve.robert@tc.tc
Médias sociaux:
twitter.com/oeilregional
www.facebook.com/oeilregional

Tirage: 35 000+; *Fréquence:* Samedi
Serge Landry, Éditeur; Directeur général régional, Montérégie-Est
serge.landry@tc.tc
Gilbert Desrosiers, Directeur des projets spéciaux
gilbert.desrosiers@quebecormedia.com

***Blainville:* Journal Le Courrier**
Anciennement: Courrier Le Courrier
Détenteur: TC Transcontinental
#103, 31, boul de la Seigneurie est, Blainville, QC J7C 4G6
Tél: 450-434-4144; *Téléc:* 450-434-3142
louis.sauvageau@transcontinental.ca
www.journallecourrier.com
Médias sociaux:
twitter.com/journalcourrier
www.facebook.com/JournalCourrier

Tirage: 55 014; *Fréquence:* Mercredi
Claudine Mainville, Rédactrice en chef
André Juteau, Directeur général régional

***Boucherville:* Journal La Relève Inc.**
Détenteur: TC Transcontinental
528, rue St-Charles, Boucherville, QC J4B 3M5
Tél: 450-641-4844; *Téléc:* 450-641-4849
lareleve@lareleve.qc.ca
www.lareleve.qc.ca

Tirage: 54 650; *Fréquence:* Jeudi et Vendredi
Bernard Desmarteau, Représentant
Michel Desmarteau, Représentant

***Boucherville:* La Seigneurie**
Détenteur: Les Hebdos Régionaux Québecor Média
391, boul de Montagne, Boucherville, QC J4B 1B7
Tél: 450-641-3360; *Téléc:* 450-655-9752
bou.redaction@tc.tc
www.la-seigneurie.qc.ca
Médias sociaux:
twitter.com/LSeigneurie
www.facebook.com/laseigneurie

Tirage: 29 421; *Fréquence:* Samedi
Sylvain Bouchard, Éditeur
450-641-3360
sylvain.bouchard.a@tc.tc
Serge Landry, Directeur général régional, Montérégie-Est
serge.landry@tc.tc

***Cantley:* L'Écho de Cantley / The Echo of Cantley**
188, montée de la Source, Boîte 1, Comp. 9, Cantley, QC J8V 3J2
Tel: 819-827-2828
info@echocantley.ca
www.echocantley.ca

Circulation: 2 400
Joël Deschênes, Rédacteur en chef
editor@echocantley.ca

***Cap-aux-Meules:* Le Radar**
CP 8183, 110, ch Gros-Cap, Cap-aux-Meules, QC G4T 1R3
Tél: 418-986-2345; *Téléc:* 418-986-6358
Ligne sans frais: 866-986-2345
secretaire@leradar.qc.ca
www.leradar.qc.ca
Médias sociaux:
www.facebook.com/radar.hebdomadaire

Tirage: 2 136; *Fréquence:* mardi
Adèle Arseneau, Rédactrice en chef
redacteur@leradar.qc.ca

***Chambly:* Le Journal de Chambly**
Détenteur: Les Hebdos Régionaux Québecor Média
CP 175, 1685, rue Bourgogne, Chambly, QC J3L 1Y8
Tél: 450-658-6516; *Téléc:* 450-658-3785
cly.redaction@tc.tc
journaldechambly.com
Médias sociaux:
twitter.com/JournalChambly
www.facebook.com/journaldechambly

Tirage: 21 237; *Fréquence:* Mardi
Daniel Noiseux, Éditeur
daniel.noiseux@tc.tc
Serge Landry, Directeur général régional, Montérégie-Est
serge.landry@tc.tc

***Châteauguay:* Le Soleil de Châteauguay**
Anciennement: Le Soleil du Samedi
Détenteur: Les Hebdos Régionaux Québecor Média
82, boul Salaberry sud, Châteauguay, QC J6J 4J6
Tél: 450-692-8552; *Téléc:* 450-692-3460
ctg.redaction@tc.tc
cybersoleil.com
Médias sociaux:
twitter.com/cybersoleil
www.facebook.com/cybersoleil

Tirage: 36 350; *Fréquence:* Mercredi
Robert Fichaud, Éditeur
robert.fichaud@tc.tc
Michel Thibault, Directeur de l'information
michel.thibault@tc.tc

***Chibougamau:* La Sentinelle et le Jamésien**
Détenteur: TC Media
317, 3e rue, Chibougamau, QC G8P 1N4
Tél: 418-748-6406; *Téléc:* 418-748-2421
www.lasentinelle.ca

Tirage: 1 968; *Fréquence:* mercredi
Ralph Pilote, Directeur général Québecor Média Saguenay-Lac-Saint-Jea
ralph.pilote@quebecormedia.ca

***Chibougamau:* La Sentinelle et le Jamésien**
Détenteur: TC Media
317, rue 3e, Chibougamau, QC G8P 1N3
Tél: 418-748-6406; *Téléc:* 418-748-2421
www.lasentinelle.ca

Tirage: 1 772; *Fréquence:* mercredi

***Coaticook:* Le Progrès de Coaticook**
Détenteur: TC Transcontinental
20, rue de Manège, Coaticook, QC J1A 3B3
Tél: 819-849-9846; *Téléc:* 819-849-1041
dany.jacques@tc.tc
www.leprogres.net
Médias sociaux:
twitter.com/HebdoCoaticook
facebook.com/LeProgresDeCoaticook

Tirage: 8 600; *Fréquence:* Samedi
Monique Côté, Éditrice
monique.cote@tc.tc
Dany Jacques, Chef de pupitre
dany.jacques@transcontinental.ca

***Cookshire-Eaton:* Journal Le Haut-Saint-François**
#101, 57, rue Craig nord, Cookshire-Eaton, QC J0B 1M0
Tél: 819-875-5501
info@journalhsf.com
www.estrieplus.com/section-0404040431353537-la_une__accueil.html
Médias sociaux:
www.facebook.com/JournalHSF?ref=hl

Tirage: 11 200; *Fréquence:* mercredi
Pierre Hébert, Directeur général

***Courcelette:* Adsum**
CP 1000 Forces, #516, Garnison Valcartier, Courcelette, QC G0A 4Z0
Tél: 418-844-6934; *Téléc:* 418-844-6934
adsum@forces.gc.ca
www.journaladsum.com
Médias sociaux:
www.journaladsum.com/contact.php#

Tirage: 4 200; *Fréquence:* semi-mensuelle, mercredi
Caroline Charest, Editor
caroline.charest@forces.gc.ca

***Daveluyville:* Le Causeur**
337, rue Principale, Daveluyville, QC G0Z 1C0
Tél: 819-367-3395; *Téléc:* 819-367-3550
info@ville.daveluyville.qc.ca
www.ville.daveluyville.qc.ca/causeur_journ al_municipal.php
Médias sociaux:
www.facebook.com/pages/Le-Causeur/351233864932287

Tirage: 1 100; *Fréquence:* mensuel
Pauline Vrain, Directrice générale
dg@ville.daveluyville.qc.ca

***Delson:* Le Reflet**
Détenteur: Les Hebdos Régionaux Québecor Média
11, rte 132, Delson, QC J5B 1G9
Tél: 450-635-9146; *Téléc:* 450-635-4619
info@lereflet.qc.ca
lereflet.qc.ca
Médias sociaux:
twitter.com/lereflet
www.facebook.com/journallereflet

Tirage: 40 000+; *Fréquence:* Samedi
Robert Fichaud, Éditeur
robert.fichaud@quebecormedia.com
Hélène Gingras, Directrice de l'information
helene.gingras@quebecormedia.com

***Disraéli:* Le Cantonnier**
888, rue St-Antoine, Disraéli, QC G0N 1E0
Tél: 418-449-1888; *Téléc:* 418-449-1889
lecantonnier@lino.com
www.lecantonnier.com

Jean-Denis Grimard, Rédacteur

***Dolbeau-Mistassini:* Journal Nouvelles Hebdo**
Détenteur: TC Media
1741, rue des Pins, Dolbeau-Mistassini, QC G8L 1J7
Tél: 418-276-6211; *Téléc:* 418-276-6166
redaction.dolbeau@tc.tc
www.nouvelleshebdo.com
Médias sociaux:
twitter.com/NouvellesHebdo
www.facebook.com/Nouvelleshebdo?ref=ts& sk=wall

Tirage: 12 596; *Fréquence:* mercredi
Claudia Turcotte, Directrice générale
claudia.turcotte@tc.tc

Donnacona: Le Courrier de Portneuf
CP 1030, 276, rue Notre-Dame, Donnacona, QC G3M 1G7
Tél: 418-285-0211 *Ligne sans frais:* 866-577-0211
www.courrierdeportneuf.com
Médias sociaux:
twitter.com/CourrierdePnf

Tirage: 27 700; *Fréquence:* Samedi
Josee-Anne Fiset, Directrice general
josee-anne.fiset@courrierdeportneuf.com

Dorval: The Chronicle
Détenteur: TC Transcontinental
#303, 455, boul Fénelon, Dorval, QC H9S 5T8
Tél: 514-636-7314; *Téléc:* 514-636-7317
info.chronicle@transcontinental.ca
www.westislandchronicle.com
Médias sociaux:
twitter.com/WestIslandChron
www.facebook.com/wichronicle

Tirage: 43 400; *Fréquence:* Wednesday
Denis Therrien, Publisher
denis.therrien@tc.tc
Marc Lalonde, Editor-in-chief
marc.lalonde@tc.tc

Dorval: Cités Nouvelles / City News
Owned By: TC Transcontinental
#303, 455, boul Fenelon, Dorval, QC H9S 5T8
Tel: 514-636-7314; *Fax:* 514-636-7317
cites.nouvelles@tc.tc
www.citesnouvelles.com
Social Media:
twitter.com/CitesNouvelles
www.facebook.com/CitesNouvelles

Circulation: 44 400; *Frequency:* Dimanche
Sylviane Lussier, Directrice régionale
Denis Therrien, Directeur général

Dorval: Magazine Ile des Soeurs / Nuns Island Magazine
Détenteur: TC Transcontinental
#303, 455, boul Fénelon, Dorval, QC H9S 5T8
Tél: 514-636-7314; *Téléc:* 514-636-7315
redaction_lemagazineids@tc.tc
www.lemagazineiledessoeurs.com
Médias sociaux:
twitter.com/LeMagazineIDS
www.facebook.com/278830125519919

Tirage: 8 148; *Fréquence:* Mercredi
Patricia-Ann Beaulieu, Éditrice
patriciaann.beaulieu@tc.tc
Normand Sauvé, Chef de pupitre
normand.sauve@tc.tc

Dorval: Le Messager de LaSalle
Détenteur: TC Transcontinental
#303, 455, boul Fénelon, Dorval, QC H9S 5T8
Tél: 514-636-7314; *Téléc:* 514-636-7315
redaction_lasalle@tc.tc
www.messagerlasalle.com
Médias sociaux:
twitter.com/MessagerLaSalle
www.facebook.com/166724190111906

Tirage: 32 200; *Fréquence:* Sunday
Patricia-Ann Beaulieu, Éditrice
patriciaann.beaulieu@tc.tc
Normand Sauvé, Chef de pupitre
normand.sauve@tc.tc

Dorval: Le Messager Lachine Dorval
Détenteur: TC Transcontinental
#303, 455, boul Fénelon, Dorval, QC H9S 5T8
Tél: 514-636-7314; *Téléc:* 514-636-7315
redaction_lachine-dorval@transcontinental.ca
www.messagerlachine.com
Médias sociaux:
twitter.com/MessagerLachine
www.facebook.com/166241803496061

Tirage: 23 100; *Fréquence:* Sunday
Robert Leduc, Rédacteur en chef
robert.leduc@tc.tc
Dennis Therrien, Directeur général. ouest de Montréal
denis.therrien@tc.tc

Dorval: Le Messager Verdun
Détenteur: TC Transcontinental
#303, 455, boul Fénelon, Dorval, QC H9S 5T8
Tél: 514-636-7314; *Téléc:* 514-636-7315
redaction_verdun@tc.tc
www.messagerverdun.com
Médias sociaux:
twitter.com/MessagerVerdun
www.facebook.com/379058848771978

Tirage: 24 443; *Fréquence:* Jeudi
Stéphane Desjardins, Directeur général
stephane.desjardins@tc.tc
Daniel Beaudin, Conseiller en solutions médias
daniel.beaudin@tc.tc

Dorval: La Voix Pop
Anciennement: La Voix Populaire
Détenteur: TC Transcontinental
#303, 455, boul Fénelon, Dorval, QC H9S 5T8
Tél: 514-636-7314; *Téléc:* 514-636-7315
redaction_lavoixpop@tc.tc
www.lavoixpopulaire.com
Médias sociaux:
twitter.com/VoixPop
www.facebook.com/lavoixpop

Tirage: 29 170; *Fréquence:* Dimanche
Stéphane Desjardins, Directeur général - Sud ouest de Montréal
stephane.desjardins@tc.tc
Olivier Laniel, Directeur du contenu et des relations avec la communaut
olivier.laniel@tc.tc

Drummondville: L'Express
Détenteur: TC Transcontinental
1050, rue Cormier, Drummondville, QC J2C 2N6
Tél: 819-478-8171; *Téléc:* 819-478-4306
redaction_dr@tc.tc
www.journalexpress.ca
Médias sociaux:
twitter.com/JournalExpress
facebook.com/JournalExpressDrummond

Tirage: 48 000+; *Fréquence:* Dimanche
Jean Morisette, Directeur général
jean.morissette@tc.tc
Lise Tremblay, Chef de pupitre
lise.tremblay@tc.tc

Drummondville: L'Impact de Drummondville
Détenteur: TC Transcontinental
2345, rue St-Pierre, Drummondville, QC J2C 5A7
Tél: 819-445-7000; *Téléc:* 819-445-7001
dmv.redaction@tc.tc
limpact.ca
Médias sociaux:
twitter.com/impactdrummond

Tirage: 46 300; *Fréquence:* Mercredi
Jean Crépeau, Éditeur
jean.crepeau@tc.tc
Jocelyn Ouellet, Chef de nouvelles
jocelyn.ouellet@tc.tc

Egan-Sud: La Gatineau
Détenteur: Les Éditions La Gatineau Ltée
135-B, route 105, Egan-Sud, QC J9E 3A9
Tél: 819-449-1725; *Téléc:* 819-449-5108
reception@lagatineau.com
www.lagatineau.com
Médias sociaux:
facebook.com/lagatineau

Tirage: 11 100; *Fréquence:* Vendredi
Philippe Patry, Directeur général
ppatry@lagatineau.com
Sylvie Dejouy, Rédaction
ppatry@lagatineau.com

Fermont: Journal Le Trait D'union du Nord
Détenteur: Le Trait d'union
850 Place Daviault, local 159, Fermont, QC G0G 1J0
Tél: 418-287-3655; *Téléc:* 418-287-3874
info.journaltdn@gmail.com
www.journaltdn.ca

Tirage: 1 800; *Fréquence:* mercredi
Le journal des villes nordiques
Sandra Carter, Directrice générale
Véronique Dumais, Rédactrice en chef et journaliste

Forestville: Journal Haute Côte-Nord Ouest
Détenteur: Journal Haute Côte-Nord Inc.
31, rte 138, Forestville, QC G0T 1E0
Tél: 418-587-2090; *Téléc:* 418-587-6407
pub@journalhcn.com
www.journalhcnouest.com

Tirage: 5 604; *Fréquence:* mercredi
Luc Brisson, Éditeur
luc.brisson@journalhcn.com

Fort-Coulonge: Pontiac Journal du Pontiac / Le Journal de Pontiac
289, Manoir Mansfield, #RR 148, Fort-Coulonge, QC J0X 1V0
Tél: 819-683-3582; *Téléc:* 819-683-2977
editor@journalpontiac.com
journalpontiac.com

Tirage: 9 319; *Fréquence:* Bi-weekly
Journal is the only local newspaper that has both French & English editors. / C'est le seul journal local qui a des rédacteurs francophone et anglophone
Lynne Lavery, Directrice générale
info@journalpontiac.com
Fred Ryan, Éditeur
Nancy Hunt, Editor / rédactrice (English/anglais)
editor@journalpontiac.com
Andre Macron, Editor / rédacteur (French/français)
editor@journalpontiac.com

Gaspé: L'Aviron
Détenteur: TC Transcontinental
144, rue Jacques Cartier, Gaspé, QC G4X 1M9
Tél: 506-753-7637
www.hebdosregionaux.ca/est-du-quebec/lecho-de-la-baie-et-laviron
Médias sociaux:
twitter.com/LEchoDeLaBaie
facebook.com/echobaie

Tirage: 6 100; *Fréquence:* Vendredi
Bernard Johnson, Éditeur
bernard.johnson@hebdosquebecor.com

Gaspé: L'Écho de la Baie
Détenteur: TC Transcontinental
144, rue Jacques Cartier, Gaspé, QC G4X 1M9
Tél: 418-392-5083; *Téléc:* 418-392-6605
nrm.redaction@tc.tc
lechodelabaie.ca
Médias sociaux:
twitter.com/LEchoDeLaBaie
www.facebook.com/echobaie

Tirage: 18 390; *Fréquence:* Mercredi
Bernard Johnson, Éditeur
bernard.johnson@tc.tc
Frédéric Durand, Directeur de l'information

Gaspé: Le Havre
Détenteur: TC Transcontinental
144, rue Jacques Cartier, Gaspé, QC G4X 1M9
Tél: 418-689-6686
can.redaction@tc.tc
journallehavre.ca
Médias sociaux:
twitter.com/LeHavre
www.facebook.com/lehavre

Tirage: 8 230; *Fréquence:* Mercredi
Bernard Johnson, Éditeur
bernard.johnson@tc.tc
Alain Lavoie, Chef de nouvelles
alain.lavoie@tc.tc

Gaspé: Le Pharillon
Détenteur: Les Hebdos Régionaux Québecor Média
144, rue Jacques-Cartier, Gaspé, QC G4X 1M9
Tél: 418-368-3242
gas.redaction@tc.tc
lepharillon.ca
Médias sociaux:
twitter.com/LePharillon
www.facebook.com/pharillon

Tirage: 8 466; *Fréquence:* Dimanche
Alain Saint-Amand, Directeur général régional, Est du Québec
alain.saint-amand@quebecormedia.com
Bernard Johnson, Éditeur
bernard.johnson@hebdosquebecor.com

Gatineau: Bulletin d'Aylmer
#C-10, 181, rue Principale, Gatineau, QC J9H 6A6
Tel: 819-684-4755; *Fax:* 819-684-6428
Toll-Free: 800-486-7678
www.bulletinaylmer.com

Circulation: 24,700; *Frequency:* Wed.
Lynne Lavery, Office Manager
l.lavery@bulletinaylmer.com
Fred Ryan, Editor
abawqp@videotron.ca

Gatineau: Bulletin d'Aylmer
Previous Name: The West Québec Post
#C-10, 181, rue Principale, Gatineau, QC J9H 6A6
Tel: 819-684-4755; *Fax:* 819-684-6428
Toll-Free: 800-486-7678
info@bulletinaylmer.com
www.bulletinaylmer.com

Circulation: 24 543; *Frequency:* mercredi
Lily Ryan, Éditrice
info@bulletinaylmer.com

***Gatineau:* L'Etoile de l'Outaouais**
Détenteur: TC Transcontinental
160, boul de l'Hôpital, Gatineau, QC J8T 8J1
Tél: 819-568-7544; *Téléc:* 819-568-7038
redaction.outaouais@transcontinental.ca
www.letudiantoutaouais.ca
Tirage: 34 324; *Fréquence:* Mercredi

***Gatineau:* La Revue**
Anciennement: La Revue de Gatineau
Détenteur: TC Transcontinental
1885, rue St-Louis, Gatineau, QC J8T 6G4
Tél: 819-568-7544; *Téléc:* 819-568-7038
pascal.laplante@tc.tc
www.journallarevue.com
Médias sociaux:
twitter.com/LaRevue1
facebook.com/LaRevueGatineau
Tirage: 41 174; *Fréquence:* Mercredi
Yves Blondin, Éditeur

***Granby:* L'Avenir et des Rivières**
Détenteur: TC Media
#127, 100, rue Robinson sud, Granby, QC J2G 7L4
Ligne sans frais: 800-363-4542
jacqueline.noiseux@tc.tc
www.laveniretdesrivieres.com
Médias sociaux:
twitter.com/HebdoFarnham
www.facebook.com/lAveniretDesRivieres
Tirage: 10 885; *Fréquence:* mercredi

***Granby:* Granby Express**
Anciennement: Samedi Express
Détenteur: TC Media
#127, 100, rue Robinson Sud, Granby, QC J2G 7L4
Tél: 450-777-4515
jacqueline.noiseux@tc.tc
www.granbyexpress.com
Médias sociaux:
www.facebook.com/GranbyExpress
Tirage: 43 245; *Fréquence:* mercredi
Cathy Bernard, Éditrice
cathy.bernard@tc.tc

***Grande-Vallée:* Journal le Phare**
Anciennement: Le Phare, l'autre vision
1A, rue du Vieux Pont est, Grande-Vallée, QC G0E 1K0
Tél: 418-393-2205
redaction@journallephare.org
journallephare.org
Médias sociaux:
twitter.com/journallephare
www.facebook.com/pages/Journal-le-Phare/22590 5758286
Tirage: 1 300

***Hudson:* Gazette Vaudreuil-Soulanges**
Previous Name: Lake of Two Mountains Gazette
Owned By: Lake of Two Mountains Gazette Ltd.
PO Box 70, 397 Main Rd., Hudson, QC J0P 1H0
Tél: 450-458-5482; *Fax:* 450-458-3337
hudsongazette@videotron.ca
gazettevaudreuilsoulanges.com
Social Media:
www.facebook.com/437408105332
Circulation: 16,000; *Frequency:* Wed.
First English Quebec weekly on the web.

***Huntingdon:* The Gleaner/La Source**
Détenteur: TC Transcontinental
66, rue Châteauguay, Huntingdon, QC J0S 1H0
Tél: 450-264-5364; *Téléc:* 450-264-9521
hun.redaction@tc.tc
gleaner-source.com
Médias sociaux:
facebook.com/gleaner.source
Tirage: 4 000; *Fréquence:* Lundi
Sheri Graham, Éditrice
sheri.sheri.graham@tc.tc

***Joliette:* L'Action**
Détenteur: TC Transcontinental
342, Beaudry nord, Joliette, QC J6E 6A6
Tél: 450-759-3664; *Téléc:* 450-759-3190
infolanaudierre@tc.tc
www.laction.com
Médias sociaux:
twitter.com/journalaction
facebook.com/journallaction
Tirage: 46 700; *Fréquence:* Dimanche

***Knowlton:* Brome County News**
Owned By: Sherbrooke Record
5 Victoria, Knowlton, QC J0E 1V0
Tel: 450-242-1188; *Fax:* 450-243-5155
Toll-Free: 800-463-9525
Editorial: newsroom@sherbrookerecord.com
www.sherbrookerecord.com/brome
Other information: Ads: classad@sherbrookerecord.com
Social Media:
www.facebook.com/sherbrookerecord
Circulation: 12,297; *Frequency:* Tuesday
Daniel Coulombe, Editor
dcoulombe@sherbrookerecord.com
Sharon McCully, Publisher
outletjournal@sympatico.ca

***L'Islet:* Journal le Hublot**
Détenteur: Les Éditions des Trois Clochers
#202, 16, ch des Pionniers est, L'Islet, QC G0R 2B0
Tél: 418-247-3333; *Téléc:* 418-247-3336
clochers@globetrotter.net
www.lehublot.ca
Tirage: 1 900; *Fréquence:* mensuel
Guylaine Hudon, Directrice Générale

***La Sarre:* Le Citoyen Abitibi-Ouest**
Détenteur: TC Transcontinental
29, avenue 8e est, La Sarre, QC J9Z 1N5
Tél: 819-333-5507; *Téléc:* 819-333-4537
www.hebdosregionaux.ca/abitibi-temiscamingue
Médias sociaux:
twitter.com/LaFrontiere
facebook.com/lafrontiere
Tirage: 10 480; *Fréquence:* Mercredi
Joël Caya, Éditeur
joel.caya@tc.tc

***La Tuque:* L'Écho de La Tuque**
Détenteur: TC Transcontinental
324, rue St-Joseph, La Tuque, QC G9X 1L2
Tél: 819-523-6141; *Téléc:* 819-523-6143
redaction_latuque@tc.tc
www.lechodelatuque.com
Médias sociaux:
twitter.com/lechodelatuque
facebook.com/pages/Écho-de-La-Tuque/246 902629754
Tirage: 6 802
Michel Scarpino, Directeur du journal

***Lac-Etchemin:* La Voix du Sud**
1516A, rte 277, Lac-Etchemin, QC G0R 1S0
Tél: 418-625-7471; *Téléc:* 418-625-5200
Ligne sans frais: 866-325-8649
redaction_lacetchemin@tc.tc
www.lavoixdusud.com
Médias sociaux:
twitter.com/voixdusud
facebook.com/lavoixdusud
Tirage: 30 000+; *Fréquence:* Samedi
Caroline Gilbert, Éditeur
caroline.gilbert@tc.tc

***Lac-Mégantic:* L'Écho de Frontenac**
5040, boul des Vétérans, Lac-Mégantic, QC G6B 2G5
Tél: 819-583-1630; *Téléc:* 819-583-1124
www.echodefrontenac.com
Médias sociaux:
twitter.com/echodefrontenac
www.facebook.com/308170576707
Tirage: 9 134; *Fréquence:* Dimanche
Gaétan Poulin, Éditeur
Rémi Tremblay, Rédacteur-en-chef

***Lachute:* L'Argenteuil**
Détenteur: La Compagnie d'édition André Paquette inc
52, rue Principale, Lachute, QC J8H 3A8
Tél: 450-562-2494; *Téléc:* 450-562-1434
argenteuil@eap.on.ca
editionap.ca
Tirage: 16 500; *Fréquence:* Mercredi
François Leblanc, Directeur
francois.leblanc@eap.on

***Lachute:* Tribune Express Progrès Watchman**
Anciennement: The Watchman
52, rue Principale, Lachute, QC J8H 3A8
Tél: 450-562-8593; *Téléc:* 450-562-1434
Ligne sans frais: 800-561-5738
Tirage: 13 000; *Fréquence:* Samedi
Evelyne Bergeron, Editor

***Laval:* Courrier Laval**
Détenteur: TC Media
#200, 2700, av Francis-Hughes, Laval, QC H7S 2B9
Tél: 450-667-4360; *Téléc:* 450-667-0845
redactionlaval@tc.tc
www.courrierlaval.com
Médias sociaux:
twitter.com/#!/LeCourrierLaval
www.facebook.com/courrierlaval
Tirage: 132 838; *Fréquence:* mercredi
Benoit Caron, Directeur général régional

***Laval:* L'Écho de Laval**
Détenteur: TC Transcontinental
#200, 2700, ave Francis-Hughes, Laval, QC H7S 2B9
Tél: 450-667-4360; *Téléc:* 450-667-6193
lav.redaction@tc.tc
lechodelaval.ca
Médias sociaux:
twitter.com/LEchodeLaval
www.facebook.com/echolaval
Tirage: 142 135; *Fréquence:* Mercredi
Eric Mercier, Éditeur
eric.mercier@tc.tc
Marie-Eve Courchesne, Chef des nouvelles
marie-eve.courchesne@tc.tc

***Laval:* The Laval News**
Previous Name: The Chomedey News
Owned By: Newsfirst Multimedia
3860, boul Notre-Dame, Laval, QC H7V 1S1
Tel: 450-978-9999; *Fax:* 450-687-6330
lavalnews.ca
Circulation: 33 164; *Frequency:* samedi
Laval's English newspaper since 1993
George Bakoyannis, Co-publisher
George Guzmas, Co-publisher

***Laval:* Nouvelles Parc-Extension News**
#304, 3860, boul Notre-Dame, Laval, QC H7V 1S1
Tel: 450-978-9999; *Fax:* 450-687-6330
editor@the-news.ca
www.px-news.com
Frequency: Saturday, bi-weekly
George Bakoyannis, Co-Publisher, General Director
georgeb@the-news.ca
George S. Guzmas, Co-Publisher, Advertising Director
georgeg@the-news.ca

***Laval:* Vivre**
828, av 79, Laval, QC H7V 3J1
Tél: 450-973-8787; *Téléc:* 450-973-8414
poste@ccvm.org
www.ccvm.org/journal-vivre
Médias sociaux:
www.facebook.com/ccvm.org
Tirage: 1 000; *Fréquence:* deux fois par an
Manon Rousseau, Directrice générale

***Lennoxville:* The Townships Sun**
PO Box 28, Lennoxville, QC J1M 1Z3
Tel: 819-566-7424
townsun@netrevolution.com
Social Media:
twitter.com/TownshipsSun
facebook.com/TheTownshipsSun
Circulation: 570; *Frequency:* Monthly
Gordon Lambie, Editor

***Lévis:* Le Peuple Lévis**
Anciennement: Le Peuple-Tribune
Détenteur: Les Hebdos Régionaux Québecor Média
#103B, 5790, boul Étienne-Dallaire, Lévis, QC G6V 8V6
Tél: 418-833-9398; *Téléc:* 418-833-8177
redaction.levis@hebdosquebecor.com
lepeuplelevis.ca
Médias sociaux:
twitter.com/LePeupleLevis
www.facebook.com/peuplelevis
Tirage: 57 087; *Fréquence:* Samedi
Paul Lessard, Éditeur
paul.lessard@quebecormedia.com
Mathieu Galarneau, Directeur de l'information
mathieu.galarneau@tc.tc

***Lévis:* Le Peuple Lotbinière**
#103B, 5790, boul Étienne-Dallaire, Lévis, QC G6V 8V6
Tél: 418-728-2131; *Téléc:* 418-728-4819
ltd.redaction@tc.tc
www.peuplelotbiniere.com
Médias sociaux:
twitter.com/Plotbiniere
www.facebook.com/plotbiniere

Tirage: 15 000; *Fréquence:* Dimanche
Paul Lessard, Éditeur
paul.lessard@tc.tc
Mathieu Galarneau, Directeur de l'information
mathieu.galarneau@tc.tc

Lingwick: Le Reflet du canton de Lingwick
72, rte 108, Lingwick, QC J0B 2Z0
Tél: 819-877-3560
info@lereflet.org
lereflet.org

Tirage: 275; *Fréquence:* neuf fois par an
Chantal Lapointe, Présidente

Longueuil: Brossard-Eclair
Détenteur: Les Hebdos Régionaux Québecor Média
267, rue Saint-Charles ouest, Longueuil, QC J4H 1E3
Tél: 450-646-3333; *Téléc:* 450-674-0205
cds.redaction@tc.tc
www.lecourrierdusud.ca

Tirage: 148 500; *Fréquence:* Mardi
Lucie Masse, Rédacteur-en-chef
450-616-8080
lucie.masse@tc.tc

Longueuil: Le Courrier du Sud
Détenteur: Les Hebdos Régionaux Québecor Média
267, rue Saint-Charles ouest, Longueuil, QC J4H 1E3
Tél: 450-646-3333; *Téléc:* 450-674-0205
publicite@courrierdusud.com
lecourrierdusud.ca
Médias sociaux:
twitter.com/LeCourrierDuSud
www.facebook.com/lecourrierdusud

Tirage: 145 815; *Fréquence:* Mercredi
Lucie Masse, Éditrice
lucie.masse@tc.tc
Geneviève Michaud, Directrice de l'information

Longueuil: Le Journal de Saint-Hubert
Détenteur: TC Transcontinental
267, rue Saint-Charles ouest, Longueuil, QC J4H 1E3
Tél: 450-646-3333; *Téléc:* 450-674-0205
cds.redaction@tc.tc
www.lejournaldesainthubert.ca

Lucie Masse, Éditrice
lucie.masse@tc.tc

Longueuil: Point Sud
#1, 674 rue Saint-Jean, Longueuil, QC J4H 2Y4
Tél: 450-677-2626; *Téléc:* 450-442-2663
info@pointsud.ca
www.pointsud.ca
Médias sociaux:
twitter.com/Point_Sud
www.facebook.com/pointsud

Louiseville: L'Écho de Maskinongé
Anciennement: L'Écho D'Autray et de Maskinongé
43, St-Louis, Louiseville, QC J5V 2C7
Tél: 819-228-5532; *Téléc:* 819-228-9379
redaction_em@transcontinental.ca
www.lechodemaskinonge.com
Médias sociaux:
twitter.com/EchoMaski
facebook.com/echomaskinonge

Tirage: 13 652; *Fréquence:* Dimanche
André Juteau, Directeur général régional
Pierre Bergeron, Directeur régional
André Juteau, Directeur général régional
Marie-Ève Veillette, Chef de nouvelles

Magog: Le Reflet du Lac
Détenteur: TC Transcontinental
#104, 101, rue Du Moulin, Magog, QC J1X 4A1
Tél: 819-843-3500; *Téléc:* 819-843-3085
Ligne sans frais: 866-637-5236
www.lerefletdulac.com
Médias sociaux:
twitter.com/refletdulac
www.facebook.com/LeRefletduLac

Tirage: 26 639; *Fréquence:* Samedi
Monique Côté, Éditrice
monique.cote@tc.tc
Dany Jacques, Chef de pupitre
dany.jacques@tc.tc

Malartic: Le Courrier de Malartic
CP 4020, Malartic, QC J0Y 1Z0
Tél: 819-757-4712; *Téléc:* 819-757-4712

Tirage: 1 200; *Fréquence:* Mardi
Denyse Roberge, Éditrice

Maniwaki: Le Choix
Détenteur: Les Hebdos Régionaux Québecor Média
139, rue Principale sud, Maniwaki, QC J9E 1Z8
Tél: 819-441-2225; *Téléc:* 819-623-7148
journallechoix.ca
Médias sociaux:
facebook.com/JournalLeChoix

Tirage: 12 600; *Fréquence:* Mercredi
Laure Voilquin, Éditrice
laure.voilquin@journallechoix.ca
Steve Ross, Directeur de l'information
steve.ross@journallechoix.ca

Matane: L'Avant-Poste
Détenteur: TC Media
305, rue de la Gare, Matane, QC G4W 3J2
Tél: 418-629-3443; *Téléc:* 418-562-4607
www.lavantposte.ca
Médias sociaux:
twitter.com/LAvantPoste
www.facebook.com/lavantposte

Tirage: 8 241; *Fréquence:* mercredi

Matane: La Voix Gaspesienne
Détenteur: Les Hebdos Régionaux Québecor Média
#107, 305, rue de la Gare, Matane, QC G4W 3J2
Tél: 418-562-4040; *Téléc:* 418-562-4607
voixgaspesienne@hebdosquebecor.com
www.hebdosregionaux.ca/est-du-quebec/la-voix-gaspesienne-et-la-voix-de-la-m
Médias sociaux:
twitter.com/VoixGaspeMatane
www.facebook.com/voixgaspematane

Tirage: 5 013; *Fréquence:* Mercredi; aussi La Voix du dimanche
Alain Saint-Amand, Directeur régional Bas Saint-Laurent / Gaspésie
alain.saint-amand@quebecormedia.com
Jean Gagnon, Éditeur
jean.gagnon@hebdosquebecor.com

Mont-Laurier: L'Écho de la Lievre
Détenteur: Les Hebdos Régionaux Québecor Média
369, boul Albiny-Paquette, Mont-Laurier, QC J9L 1K5
Tél: 819-623-5250; *Téléc:* 819-623-7148
mla.redaction@tc.tc
lechodelalievre.ca
Médias sociaux:
twitter.com/LEchoDeLaLievre
www.facebook.com/lecholievre

Tirage: 20 633; *Fréquence:* Samedi
André Guillemette, Directeur général régional Laurentides
andre.guillemette@tc.tc
Carole Simard, Éditrice
richard.charbonneau@tc.tci

Mont-Royal: Le Journal de Mont-Royal
Détenteur: Proxima Publications Inc.
#206, 8180, Devonshire, Mont-Royal, QC H4P 2K3
Tél: 514-736-1133; *Téléc:* 514-736-7855
redaction@proxima-p.qc.ca
www.proxima-p.qc.ca
Médias sociaux:
www.facebook.com/pages/Proxima-Publications/1134087120217
Tristan Roy, Éditeur

Mont-Tremblant: L'Information du Nord Mont-Tremblant
Détenteur: Les Hebdos Régionaux Québecor Média
1107, rue de Saint-Jovite, Mont-Tremblant, QC J8E 3J9
Tél: 819-425-8658; *Téléc:* 819-425-7713
infonord.journal@tc.tc
linformationdunordmonttremblant.ca
Médias sociaux:
twitter.com/linfodunordmt
www.facebook.com/linfodunordmt

Tirage: 14 300; *Fréquence:* Vendredi
Johanne Régimbald, Éditrice
johanne.regimbald@tc.tc
André Guillemette, Directeur général régional, Laurentides
andre.guillemette@tc.tc

Mont-Tremblant: L'Information du Nord Sainte-Agathe
Détenteur: TC Transcontinental
1107, rue de Saint-Jovite, Mont-Tremblant, QC J8E 3J9
Tél: 819-425-8658; *Téléc:* 819-425-7713
infonnord.journal@tc.tc; infonord.redaction@tc.tc
linformationdunordsainteagathe.ca
Médias sociaux:
twitter.com/linfodunordsa
www.facebook.com/linfodunordsa

Tirage: 15 430; *Fréquence:* Mercredi

Johanne Régimbald, Éditrice
johanne.regimbald@tc.tc
Éric Busque, Chef des nouvelles
eric.busque.a@tc.tc

Mont-Tremblant: L'Information du Nord Valée de la Rouge
Détenteur: TC Transcontinental
1107, rue de Saint-Jovite, Mont-Tremblant, QC J8E 3J9
Tél: 819-425-8658; *Téléc:* 819-425-7713
infonord.journal@tc.tc; infonord.redaction@tc.tc
linformationdunordvalleedelarouge.ca

Tirage: 8 055; *Fréquence:* Mercredi
Johanna Régimbald, Éditrice
johanne.regimbald@tc.tc
Éric Busque, Chef des nouvelles
eric.busque.a@tc.tc

Montmagny: L'Oie Blanche
70, rue de l'Anse, Montmagny, QC G5V 3S7
Tél: 418-248-8820; *Téléc:* 418-248-4033
oieblanc.sec@globetrotter.net
www.oieblanc.com
Médias sociaux:
twitter.com/oieblanc
www.facebook.com/166453626708427

Tirage: 19 672; *Fréquence:* Samedi
Michel Montminy, Directeur général
mmontminy@groupermmedias.com
José Soucy, Journaliste
nouvelles@cmatv.ca

Montmagny: Le Peuple Côte-du-Sud
Détenteur: Les Hebdos Régionaux Québecor Média
#200, 80, boul Taché est, Montmagny, QC G5V 3S7
Tél: 418-248-0415; *Téléc:* 418-248-2377
www.hebdosregionaux.ca/chaudiere-appalaches/le-peuple-cote-sud

Tirage: 21 073; *Fréquence:* Samedi
Claudette Tardif, Éditrice
claudette.tardif@quebecormedia.com

Montréal: L'Avenir de l'Est
#210, 8770 boul Langelier, Montréal, QC H1P 3C6
Tél: 514-899-5888; *Téléc:* 514-899-5001
redaction_est@tc.tc
www.avenirdelest.com
Médias sociaux:
twitter.com/avenirdelest
www.facebook.com/avenirdelest

Tirage: 28 090; *Fréquence:* Mardi
Véronique Gauthier, Éditrice

Montréal: Le Couac
6940, rue Jogues, Montréal, QC H4E 2W8
Tél: 514-596-1017
info@lecouac.org
www.lecouac.org

Montréal: Courrier Ahuntsic
Détenteur: TC Media
8000, Blaise Pascal, Montréal, QC H1E 2S7
Tél: 514-643-0013; *Téléc:* 514-899-5001
courrierahuntsic@tc.tc
www.courrierahuntsic.com
Médias sociaux:
twitter.com/InfoAhuntsicBC
www.facebook.com/courrierahuntsicbc

Tirage: 33 552; *Fréquence:* vendredi
Denis Filion, Directeur général

Montréal: Échos Montréal
387, rue Saint-Paul ouest, Montréal, QC H2Y 2A7
Tél: 514-844-2133; *Téléc:* 514-844-5858
info@echosmontreal.com
Médias sociaux:
www.youtube.com/watch?v=77tQjl7SJjk&feature=youtu.be
www.facebook.com/pages/Échos-Montréal/365501026942053?fre

Denise Di Candido, Chief Editor
Vincent Di Candido, Président

Montréal: Le Flambeau Mercier-Anjou
Détenteur: TC Media
8000, Blaise Pascal, Montréal, QC H1E 2S7
Tél: 514-643-0013; *Téléc:* 514-899-5001
redaction_est@tc.tc
www.flambeaudelest.com
Médias sociaux:
twitter.com/Flambeaudelest
www.facebook.com/leflambeaudelest

Tirage: 56 718; *Fréquence:* mardi
Véronique Gauthier, Directrice générale

***Montréal:* Greek Canadian Reportage**
8060, rue Birnam, Montréal, QC H3N 2T7
Tel: 514-279-7772
pages.globetrotter.net/gcradb
Circulation: 15,000; *Frequency:* Weekly
Anthony Bartzakos, Publisher & Editor

***Montréal:* Guide de Montréal-Nord**
Détenteur: TC Media
8000, Blaise Pascal, Montréal, QC H1E 2S7
Tél: 514-643-0013; *Téléc:* 514-899-5001
redaction_est@tc.tc
www.guidemtlnord.com
Médias sociaux:
twitter.com/Guidemtlnord
www.facebook.com/guidemtlnord
Tirage: 34 730; *Fréquence:* mardi
Véronique Gauthier, Directrice générale

***Montréal:* L'Informateur de Rivières-des-Prairies**
Détenteur: TC Media
8000, Blaise Pascal, Montréal, QC H1E 2S7
Tél: 514-643-0013; *Téléc:* 514-899-5001
redaction_est@tc.tc
www.linformateurrdp.com
Médias sociaux:
twitter.com/LinformateurRDP
www.facebook.com/linformateurrdp
Tirage: 21 276; *Fréquence:* mardi
Véronique Gauthier, Directrice générale
Marie-Josée Chouinard, Directrice de l'information

***Montréal:* L'Itinéraire**
2103, rue Ste-Catherine est, 3e étage, Montréal, QC H2K 2H9
Tél: 514-597-0238; *Téléc:* 514-597-1544
itineraire@itineraire.ca
itineraire.ca
Médias sociaux: www.youtube.com/user/itineraire1
twitter.com/LItineraire
www.facebook. com/pages/Itinéraire/115888658426315
Tirage: 13 000; *Fréquence:* bimensuel
Serge Lareault, Éditeur

***Montréal:* Journal de Rosemont - La Petite-Patrie**
Détenteur: TC Media
1100, boul René-Lévesque ouest, 24e étage, Montréal, QC H3B 4X9
Tél: 514-643-2300
info@journalmetro.com
journalmetro.com/local/rosemont-la-petite-patrie
Médias sociaux:
twitter.com/JournalRosemont
www.facebook.com/JournaldeRosemont
Tirage: 60 041; *Fréquence:* mardi
Nicolas Faucher, Éditeur

***Montréal:* Montréal Express**
Anciennement: Nouvelles de l'Est
Détenteur: TC Transcontinental
#210, 8770 boul Langelier, Montréal, QC H1P 3C6
Tél: 514-899-5885
redaction_est@tc.tc
www.montrealexpress.ca
Tirage: 24 629

***Montréal:* Les Nouvelles Saint-Laurent / Saint-Laurent News**
Détenteur: TC Transcontinental
#210, 8770, boul Langelier, Montréal, QC H1P 3C6
Tél: 514-855-1292; *Téléc:* 514-855-1855
nouvellessaint-laurent@tc.tc
www.nouvellessaint-laurent.com
Médias sociaux:
twitter.com/InfoStLaurent
www.facebook.com/NouvellesSaintLaurent
Tirage: 31 660; *Fréquence:* Jeudi
Denis Therrien, Directeur général
Serge Labrosse, Directeur de l'information

***Montréal:* Le Plateau Mont-Royal**
Détenteur: TC Media
1100, boul René-Lévesque ouest, 24e étage, Montréal, QC H3B 4X9
Tél: 514-643-2300
info@journalmetro.com
journalmetro.com/local/le-plateau-mont-royal
Médias sociaux:
twitter.com/Journalplateau
www.facebook.com/journalduplateau
Tirage: 36 268; *Fréquence:* jeudi
Nicolas Faucher, Éditeur

***Montréal:* La Presse**
Détenteur: Power Corp. of Canada
7, rue Saint-Jacques, Montréal, QC H2X 1K9
Tél: 514-285-7000 *Ligne sans frais:* 800-361-5013
nouvelles@lapresse.ca
www.lapresse.ca
Médias sociaux: plus.google.com/110605183489279609207
twitter.com/LP_LaPresse
www.face book.com/LaPresseFB
Tirage: 1 734 445 total; *Fréquence:* samedi
Guy Crevier, Président et éditeur
Éric Trottier, Vice-président et éditeur adjoint

***Montréal:* Reflet de Société**
Anciennement: Journal de la Rue
4233, rue Ste-Catherine est, Montréal, QC H1V 1X4
Tél: 514-256-9000; *Téléc:* 514-256-9444
journal@journaldelarue.ca
www.journaldelarue.com
Raymond Viger, Éditeur et rédacteur en chef

***Montréal:* The Suburban**
Owned By: Michael Publishing Co. Inc.
#105, 7575 Trans-Canada Hwy., Montréal, QC H4T 1V6
Tel: 514-484-1107; *Fax:* 514-484-9616
www.thesuburban.com
Circulation: East End: 26,746; West Island: 40,239; City Edition: 63,319; *Frequency:* East End: Thursday; West Island: Wednesday; City Edition: Wednesday
The largest English-language weekly in Quebec.
Sari Medicoff, Associate Publisher
sari@thesuburban.com
Beryl Wajsman, Editor-in-Chief
editor@thesuburban.com

***Montréal:* Westmount Examiner**
Owned By: TC Transcontinental
#210, 245, av Victoria, Montréal, QC H3Z 2M6
Tel: 514-484-5610; *Fax:* 514-484-6028
Toll-Free: 866-637-5236
examiner@tc.tc
www.westmountexaminer.com
Social Media:
twitter.com/WestmountExam
facebook.com/westmountexaminer
Circulation: 9,530; *Frequency:* Thursday
Sylviane Lussier, General Manager
sylviane.lussier@tc.tc
Mark Lalonde, Contact, Editorial
marc.lalonde@tc.tc

***Natashquan:* Le Portageur**
50, ch d'en Haut, Natashquan, QC G0G 2E0
Tél: 418-726-3736; *Téléc:* 418-726-3714
secom@globetrotter.net
leportageur.jimdo.com
Tirage: 551; *Fréquence:* mercredi

***New Carlisle:* The Gaspé Spec**
Détenteur: Sea-Coast Publications Inc.
CP 99, 128, boul Gerard D. Levesque, New Carlisle, QC G0C 1Z0
Tél: 418-752-5400; *Téléc:* 418-752-6932
specs@globetrotter.net
www.gaspespec.com
Autre information: Alternate Phone: 418-752-5070
Tirage: 2 580; *Fréquence:* Wednesday
Sharon Renouf-Farrell, Publisher
Gilles Gagné, News Editor

***Nicolet:* Le Courrier-Sud**
Anciennement: Nicolet Courrier-Sud
Détenteur: TC Transcontinental
Medias Trancontinental, 3255, boul Louis-Fréchette, Nicolet, QC J3T 1X5
Tél: 819-293-4551
redaction_cs@tc.tc
www.lecourriersud.com
Médias sociaux:
twitter.com/journalcs
facebook.com/LeCourrierSud
Tirage: 20 850; *Fréquence:* Mercredi
Patrick Dumais, Directeur de journal
patrick.dumas@tc.tc
Marie-Eve Veillette, Chef de nouvelles

***Outremont:* L'Express d'Outremont & Mont-Royal**
Anciennement: L'Express d'Outremont/de Mont-Royal
Détenteur: TC Transcontinental
#203, 1500, boul Jules-Poitras, Outremont, QC H4N 1X7
Tél: 514-855-1292; *Téléc:* 514-855-1855
redactionexpress@transcontinental.ca
www.expressoutremont.com
Médias sociaux:
twitter.com/InfoOutremontMR
www.facebook.com/372191966155544
Tirage: 11 560; *Fréquence:* Jeudi, hebdo
Stéphane Desjardins, Directeur général - Sud-ouest de Montréal
stephane.desjardins@tc.tc
Marilaine Bolduc-Jacob, Rédactrice en chef
Michel-Joanny Furtin, Rédacteur-en-chef
michel.joanny-furtin@tc.tc

***Preissac:* Journal L'Alliance de Preissac**
180, av du Lac, Preissac, QC J0Y 2E0
Tél: 819-759-4141
www.preissac.com
Médias sociaux:
www.facebook.com/preissac
Fréquence: mensuel
Estelle Gelot, Président

***Québec:* L'Actuel**
Détenteur: TC Media
#107, 710, Bouvier, Québec, QC G2J 1C2
Tél: 418-628-7460
redaction_quebec@tc.tc
www.lactuel.com
Médias sociaux:
twitter.com/l_actuel
www.facebook.com/lactuel
Tirage: 57 669; *Fréquence:* vendredi
Michel Chalifour, Directeur général régional

***Québec:* L'Appel**
#107, 710 boul Bouvier, Québec, QC G2J 1C2
Tél: 418-686-6400; *Téléc:* 418-686-1086
redaction_quebec@tc.tc
www.lappel.com
Médias sociaux:
twitter.com/quebechebdo
facebook.com/journallappel
Tirage: 44 360; *Fréquence:* Mercredi
Lilianne Laprise, Éditrice
Michel Chalifour, Directeur général régional

***Québec:* Beauport Express**
Détenteur: TC Transcontinental
Hebdos Transcontinental à Québec, #107, 710 Bouvier, Québec, QC G2J 1C2
Tél: 418-686-6400; *Téléc:* 418-686-1086
redaction_quebec@tc.tc
www.beauportexpress.com
Médias sociaux:
twitter.com/quebechebdo
www.facebook.com/quebechebdo
Tirage: 38 700; *Fréquence:* Hebdomadaire
Lilianne Laprise, Directrice des ventes
Michel Chalifour, Directeur général régional
Lynda Drouin, Directrice administrative

***Québec:* Le Carrefour de Québec**
Détenteur: Journal Le Carrefour de Québec
799, rue 5e, Québec, QC G1J 2S9
Tél: 418-649-0775; *Téléc:* 418-649-7531
www.carrefourdequebec.com
Médias sociaux:
twitter.com/LeCarrefourQc
www.facebook.com/LeCarrefourQc
Tirage: 70 000; *Fréquence:* mercredi

***Québec:* Charlesbourg Express**
Détenteur: TC Transcontinental
Médias-Transcontinental, #107, 710 boul Bouvier, Québec, QC G2J 1C2
Tél: 418-686-6400; *Téléc:* 418-686-4841
redaction_quebec@tc.tc
www.charlesbourgexpress.com
Médias sociaux:
twitter.com/quebechebdo
facebook.com/pages/Charlesbourg-Express/295346853862208
Tirage: 27 095; *Fréquence:* Mercredi
Lilianne Laprise, Éditrice

***Québec:* Droit de Parole**
Détenteur: Communications Basse-ville
266, Saint-Vallier Ouest, Québec, QC G1K 1K2
Tél: 418-648-8043
droitdeparole.org

Tirage: 16 000; *Fréquence:* mensuel

***Québec:* Journal le Jacques-Cartier**
Détenteur: TC Media
#107, 710, rue Bouvier, Québec, QC G2J 1C2
Tél: 418-628-7460; *Téléc:* 418-622-1511
redaction_quebec@transcontinental.ca
www.lejacquescartier.com
Médias sociaux:
twitter.com/#!/quebechebdo
www.facebook.com/LeJacquesCartier

Tirage: 9 500
Michel Chalifour, Directeur général régional

***Québec:* Journal Le Québec Express**
Détenteur: TC Media
#107, 710, rue Bouvier, Québec, QC G2J 1C2
Tél: 418-628-7460; *Téléc:* 418-622-1511
redaction_quebec@tc.tc
www.lequebecexpress.com
Médias sociaux:
twitter.com/quebechebdo
www.facebook.com/lequebecexpress?fref=ts

Tirage: 30 259; *Fréquence:* vendredi
Michel Chalifour, Directeur général régional

***Québec:* Quebec Chronicle-Telegraph**
Owned By: 1764 Publications Inc.
#218, 1040 av Belvédère, Québec, QC G1S 3G3
Tél: 418-650-1764; *Fax:* 418-650-5172
info@qctonline.com
www.qctonline.com
Social Media:
twitter.com/QCTonline
www.facebook.com/64677421759

Circulation: 1,300; *Frequency:* Wednesday
Stacie Stanton, Editor/Publisher
editor@qctonline.com

***Québec:* La Quête**
Détenteur: L'Archipel d'Entraide (The Archipelago of Assistance)
190, rue Saint-Joseph est, Québec, QC G1K 3A7
Tél: 418-649-9145; *Téléc:* 418-649-7770
laquetejournal@yahoo.ca

Tirage: 2 500; *Fréquence:* mensuel
Francine Chatigny, Contact

***Repentigny:* Hebdo Rive Nord**
Anciennement: L'Artisan
Détenteur: TC Transcontinental
1004, rue Notre-Dame, Repentigny, QC J5Y 1S9
Tél: 450-581-5120; *Téléc:* 450-581-4515
equiperedaction@transcontinental.ca
www.hebdorivenord.com
Médias sociaux:
twitter.com/hebdorivenord
facebook.com/hebdorn

Tirage: 56 780; *Fréquence:* Mardi
Louise Bourget, Chef de nouvelles
Olivia Nguonly, Rédactrice en chef

***Richelain:* Journal Servir**
Détenteur: Department of National Defence
Garnison Saint-Jean, CP 100 Bureau-Chef, Richelain, QC J0J 1R0
Tél: 450-358-7099; *Téléc:* 450-358-7423
servir@forces.gc.ca
www.journalservir.com

Tirage: 3 500; *Fréquence:* mercredi
Gaëtane Dion, Rédactrice-en-chef

***Rimouski:* L'Avantage votre journal**
Détenteur: TC Media
#6-D, 217, av Léonidas sud, Rimouski, QC G5L 2T5
Ligne sans frais: 877-722-0205
redaction_rimouski@tc.tc
www.lavantage.qc.ca
Médias sociaux: www.youtube.com/user/journallavantage
twitter.com/lavantageqcca
www.facebook.com/lavantageqcca

Tirage: 42 803; *Fréquence:* mercredi
Mélina de Champlain, Directrice générale
melina.dechamplain@tc.tc

***Rimouski:* Le Rimouskois**
Détenteur: TC Transcontinental
CP 3217, 271, av Leónidas, Rimouski, QC G5L 9G6
Tél: 418-721-1212; *Téléc:* 418-723-1855
rim.redaction.tc.tc
rimouskois.ca
Médias sociaux:
twitter.com/RimouskoisPecho
facebook.com/progresecho

Tirage: 29 130; *Fréquence:* Mercredi
Marc Pitre, Rédacteur-en-chef
marc.pitre@tc.tc
Ernie Wells, Directeur de l'information

***Rivière-du-Loup:* Info Dimanche**
72, rue Fraser, Rivière-du-Loup, QC G5R 1C6
Tél: 418-862-1911; *Téléc:* 418-862-6165
journal@infodimanche.com
www.infodimanche.com
Médias sociaux: www.youtube.com/infodimanche
twitter.com/infodimanche
www.facebook. com/infodimanche

Tirage: 31 420; *Fréquence:* Mercredi
Hugo Levasseur, Éditeur
Mario Pelletier, Rédacteur-en-chef
mario@infodimanche.com

***Rivière-du-Loup:* Info Dimanche**
Détenteur: Néomédia
72, rue Fraser, Rivière-du-Loup, QC G5R 1C6
Tél: 418-862-1911; *Téléc:* 418-862-6165
journal@infodimanche.com
www.infodimanche.com
Médias sociaux:
twitter.com/infodimanche
www.facebook.com/infodimanche

Tirage: 31 860; *Fréquence:* dimanche
Hugo Levasseur, Éditeur
418-862-1911

***Rivière-du-Loup:* L'Information**
Détenteur: Les Hebdos Régionaux Québecor Média
55-A, rue de l Hôtel-de-ville, Rivière-du-Loup, QC G5R 1L4
Tél: 418-775-4381; *Téléc:* 418-775-7768
info.montjoli@hebdosquebecor.com
linformation.ca
Médias sociaux:
twitter.com/Linformation
www.facebook.com/infomontjoli

Tirage: 9 901; *Fréquence:* Dimanche
Francis Desrosiers, Éditeur
francis.desrosiers@tc.tc

***Rivière-du-Loup:* Saint-Laurent Portage**
Anciennement: Le Portage
Détenteur: TC Transcontinental
55-A, rue de l Hôtel-de-ville, Rivière-du-Loup, QC G5R 1L4
Tél: 418-862-1774; *Téléc:* 418-862-4387
rdl.redaction@tc.tc
lesaintlaurentportage.ca
Médias sociaux:
twitter.com/SLPortage
www.facebook.com/slportage

Tirage: 35 670; *Fréquence:* Mercredi
Francis Desrosiers, Éditeur
francis.desrosiers@tc.tc
Alain Saint-Amand, Directeur général régional, Est du Quebec
alain.saint-amand@tc.tc

***Roberval:* L'Étoile du Lac**
Détenteur: TC Media
#101, 797 boul Saint-Joseph, Roberval, QC G8H 2L4
Tél: 418-275-2911; *Téléc:* 418-275-2834
redaction_roberval@tc.tc
www.letoiledulac.com
Médias sociaux:
www.twitter.com/letoiledulac
www.facebook.com/letoiledulac

Tirage: 14 636; *Fréquence:* mercredi
Claudia Turcotte, Directrice générale
claudia.turcotte@tc.tc

***Rouyn-Noranda:* Le Citoyen Rouyn-Noranda**
Anciennement: Le Citoyen
Détenteur: TC Transcontinental
1, rue du Terminus est, Rouyn-Noranda, QC J9X 3B5
Tél: 819-762-4361; *Téléc:* 819-797-2450
rou.redaction@tc.tc
lafrontiere.ca
Médias sociaux:
twitter.com/LaFrontiere
facebook.com/lafrontiere

Tirage: 19 620; *Fréquence:* Mercredi; supplement, Journal du Nord-Ouest
Joël Caya, Éditeur
joel.caya@tc.tccormedia.com

***Rouyn-Noranda:* La Frontière**
Détenteur: TC Transcontinental
1, rue du Terminus est, Rouyn-Noranda, QC J9X 3B5
Tél: 819-762-4361; *Téléc:* 819-797-2450
rou.redaction@tc.tc
lafrontiere.ca
Médias sociaux:
twitter.com/lafrontiere
www.facebook.com/lafrontiere

Tirage: 5 000; *Fréquence:* Vendredi
Joël Caya, Éditeur
joel.caya@tc.tc
David Prince, Chef des nouvelles, Abitibi
david.prince@tc.tc

***Rouyn-Noranda:* Journal Ensemble pour bâtir**
CP 424, 200, rue Leblanc, Rouyn-Noranda, QC J0Z 1Y0
Tél: 819-797-7110
ensemblepb1@tlb.sympatico.ca
www.journal-ensemble.org

Tirage: 1 400
Diane Gaudet-Bergeron, Présidente

***Saguenay:* Le Progrès Dimanche**
1051, boul Talbot, Saguenay, QC G7H 5C1
Tél: 418-545-4474
redaction@lequotidien.com
www.lapresse.ca/le-quotidien/progres-dimanche

Tirage: 44 500; *Fréquence:* Dimanche
Michel Sinard, Président et éditeur
Denis Bouchard, Rédacteur en chef

***Saint-André-Avellin:* La Petite-Nation**
Détenteur: TC Transcontinental
3A, rue Principale, Saint-André-Avellin, QC J0V 1W0
Tél: 819-983-2725; *Téléc:* 819-983-6844
pascal.laplante@tc.tc
www.lapetitenation.com
Médias sociaux:
twitter.com/LaPetiteNation1
facebook.com/pages/La-Petite-Nation/11 6015295181711

Tirage: 10 010; *Fréquence:* Mercredi
Eric Lacfleur, Directeur général
eric.lafleur@tc.tc
Sylvain Dupras, Directeur régional de l'information, région Ouest TC Me
sylvain.dupras@tc.tc

***Saint-Basile-le-Grand:* L'Action Régionale**
Détenteur: TC Transcontinental
#101, 155, boul Sir-Wilfrid-Laurier, Saint-Basile-le-Grand, QC J3N 1A9
Tél: 450-441-7252; *Téléc:* 450-441-4497
direction@journalactionregionale.com
journalactionregionale.com
Médias sociaux:
www.facebook.com/journalactionregionale

Tirage: 50 640; *Fréquence:* Mercredi
Isabelle Bergeron, Éditrice
direction@journalactionregionale.com
Vincent Guilbault, Directeur de l'information

***Saint-Bruno:* Journal les Versants**
Détenteur: TC Media
1488, rue Montarville, Saint-Bruno, QC J3V 3T5
Tél: 450-441-5300
info@versants.com
www.versants.com
Médias sociaux:
twitter.com/JournalVersants
www.facebook.com/VersantsMontBruno

Tirage: 18 000
Philippe Clair, Éditeur
pclair@versants.com

***Saint-Bruno-de-Kamouraska:* Le Trait d'Union**
Détenteur: Le Trait d'Union de Saint-Bruno inc.
CP 3, 4, rue du Couvent, Saint-Bruno-de-Kamouraska, QC G0L 2M0
Tél: 418-492-9432; *Téléc:* 418-492-9076
trdunion@globetrotter.net
www.stbrunokam.qc.ca

Diane Bossé, Présidente

Saint-Bruno-de-Montarville: Le Journal de Saint-Bruno/Saint-Basile
Détenteur: Les Hebdos Régionaux Québecor Média
1507, rue Roberval, Saint-Bruno-de-Montarville, QC J3V 3P8
Tél: 450-653-3685; Téléc: 450-653-6967
bru@redaction@tc.tc
journaldest-bruno.qc.ca
Médias sociaux:
twitter.com/JournalStBruno
www.facebook.com/journaldestbruno
Tirage: 19 010; Fréquence: Mercredi
Sylvain Bouchard, Éditeur
sylvain.bouchard@tc.tc
Serge Landry, Directeur général régional, Montérégie-Est
serge.landry@tc.tc

Saint-Charles-de-Bellechasse: Au fil de La Boyer
8B ave Commerciale, Saint-Charles-de-Bellechasse, QC G0R 2T0
Tél: 418-948-0741
laboyer@laboyer.com
www.laboyer.com
Médias sociaux:
www.facebook.com/journal.la.boyer
Tirage: 1 200; Fréquence: mensuel
Jean-Pierre Lamonde, Président

Saint-Denis-de-Brompton: Le Saint-Denisien
CP 244, Saint-Denis-de-Brompton, QC J0B 2P0
www.lesaintdenisien.ca
Tirage: 1 175
René Coupal, Président
819-846-3267

Saint-Donat: Journal Altitude
365, rue Principale, Saint-Donat, QC J0T 2C0
Tél: 819-424-2610; Téléc: 819-424-3615
journalaltitude@cgocable.ca
www.st-donat.com/journal.html
Tirage: 3 700; Fréquence: Vendredi
Martin Lafortune, Éditeur et chef
Nathalie Bouisson, Éditeur et chef

Saint-Eustache: La Concorde
Détenteur: Les Éditions Blainville-Deux-Montagnes Inc.
53, rue Saint-Eustache, Saint-Eustache, QC J7R 2L2
Tél: 450-472-3440; Téléc: 450-472-1638
infojournaux@groupejcl.com
www.leveil.com
Médias sociaux:
www.facebook.com/JOURNAL.LEVEIL
Tirage: 52 470; Fréquence: Mercredi; aussi L'Eveil (dimanche; tirage 37 400)
Jean-Claude Langlois, Président-Éditeur
Benoît Bilodeau, Rédacteur en chef

Saint-Eustache: L'Éveil
Détenteur: TC Media
53, rue St-Eustache, Saint-Eustache, QC J7R 2L2
Tél: 450-472-3440; Téléc: 450-472-1638
infojournaux@groupejcl.com
www.leveil.com
Médias sociaux:
twitter.com/#!/LeveilConcorde
www.facebook.com/JOURNAL.LEVEIL
Tirage: 56 735; Fréquence: samedi
Jean-Claude Langlois, Éditeur

Saint-Fabien-de-Panet: Journal Le Réveil
195, rue Bilodeau, Saint-Fabien-de-Panet, QC G0R 2J0
Tél: 418-249-4471; Téléc: 418-249-4470
saintfabiendepanet.com
Tirage: 515; Fréquence: mensuel

Saint-François-de-la-Rivière du Sud: L'Écho de St-François
534, ch St-François ouest, Saint-François-de-la-Rivière du Sud, QC G0R 3A0
Tél: 418-717-2659; Téléc: 418-259-2177
echosf@videotron.ca
Tirage: 725; Fréquence: mensuel
Raynald Laflamme, Directeur

Saint-Georges: L'Écho de la Rive-Nord
Détenteur: Néomédia
9085, boul Lacroix, Saint-Georges, QC G5Y 2B4
Tél: 450-818-7575; Téléc: 418-222-5699
Médias sociaux:
twitter.com/LEchoRiveNord
www.facebook.com/lechorivenord

Saint-Georges: Le Journal de Joliette
Détenteur: Néomédia
9085, boul Lacroix, Saint-Georges, QC G5Y 2B4
Téléc: 418-222-5699
Ligne sans frais: 866-327-0660
www.lejournaldejoliette.ca
Médias sociaux:
twitter.com/JdeJoliette
www.facebook.com/jdejoliette
Claude Poulin, Président et directeur général
cpoulin@neomedia.com

Saint-Georges: Le Point du Lac Saint-Jean
Détenteur: Néomédia
9085, boul Lacroix, Saint-Georges, QC G5Y 2B4
Tél: 418-695-2601; Téléc: 418-222-5699
www.lepoint.ca
Médias sociaux:
twitter.com/PointLacStJean
www.facebook.com/pointlacstjean
Guy Dallaire, Directeur des ventes
guy.dallaire@lepoint.ca

Saint-Georges: Le Réveil du Saguenay
Détenteur: Néomédia
9085, boul Lacroix, Saint-Georges, QC G5Y 2B4
Tél: 418-695-2601; Téléc: 418-222-5699
www.lereveil.ca
Médias sociaux:
twitter.com/LeReveil
www.facebook.com/lereveil
Guy Dallaire, Directeur des ventes
guy.dallaire@lepoint.ca

Saint-Georges-de-Beauce: L'Éclaireur Progrès
Détenteur: Les Hebdos Régionaux Québecor Média
710, 98e rue, Saint-Georges-de-Beauce, QC G5Y 8G1
Tél: 418-228-8858; Téléc: 418-227-0268
sgb.redaction@tc.tc
leclaireurprogres.ca
Médias sociaux:
twitter.com/EclairProgres
www.facebook.com/leclaireurprogres
Tirage: 38 147; Fréquence: Mercredi, Vendredi
Gilbert Bernier, Éditeur
gilbert.bernier@tc.tc
Simon Busque, Chef des nouvelles, Chaudière-Appalaches
simon.bisque@tc.tc

Saint-Hippolyte: Le Sentier
2264, ch des Hauteurs, Saint-Hippolyte, QC J8A 3C5
Tél: 450-563-5151; Téléc: 450-563-1059
redaction@journal-le-sentier.ca
www.journal-le-sentier.ca
Tirage: 4 000; Fréquence: mensuel
Michel Bois, Président
michel.bois@journal-le-sentier.ca

Saint-Hyacinthe: Le Clairon Regional de St-Hyacinthe
Détenteur: DBC Communications inc.
655, av Ste-Anne, Saint-Hyacinthe, QC J2S 5G4
Tél: 450-773-6028; Téléc: 450-773-3115
redaction@leclairon.qc.ca
www.leclairon.qc.ca
Tirage: 39 730; Fréquence: Mardi
Benoit Chartier, Éditeur
Guillaume Bédard, Directeur, Ventes

Saint-Hyacinthe: Le Courrier de Saint-Hyacinthe
Détenteur: DBC Communications inc.
655, rue Ste-Anne, Saint-Hyacinthe, QC J2S 5G4
Tél: 450-773-6028; Téléc: 450-773-3115
redaction@lecourrier.qc.ca
www.lecourrier.qc.ca
Médias sociaux:
twitter.com/LeCourrier1853
Tirage: 13 605; Fréquence: Quotidien
Benoit Chartier, Éditeur
Martin Bourassa, Rédacteur en chef et éditorialiste
mbourassa@lecourrier.qc.ca

Saint-Jean-Port-Joli: L'Attisée
Maison Communautaire Joly, CP 954, 318, rue Verreault, Saint-Jean-Port-Joli, QC G0R 3G0
Tél: 418-598-9590; Téléc: 418-598-7588
journal.attisee@videotron.ca
www.lattisee.com
Tirage: 2 750; Fréquence: mensuel
Benedict Levesques, Président

Saint-Jean-sur-Richelieu: Le Canada Français
84, rue Richelieu, Saint-Jean-sur-Richelieu, QC J3B 6X3
Tél: 450-347-0323; Téléc: 450-347-4539
canadaf@canadafrancais.com
www.canadafrancais.com
Médias sociaux:
twitter.com/Canada_Francais
www.facebook.com/lecanadafrancais
Tirage: 18 955; Fréquence: Mercredi; aussi Le Richelieu Dimanche (dimanche)
Gilles Lévesque, Rédacteur en chef
Charles Couture, Directeur général régional

Saint-Jérome: Journal Le Nord
Anciennement: L'Annonceur
Détenteur: TC Media
393, des Laurentides, Saint-Jérome, QC J7Z 4L9
Tél: 450-438-8383; Téléc: 450-438-4174
mychel.lapointe@transcontinental.ca
www.journallenord.com
Médias sociaux:
twitter.com/#!/journallenord
www.facebook.com/Journallenord
Tirage: 55 388; Fréquence: mercredi

Saint-Jérome: Le Mirabel
Détenteur: TC Transcontinental
179, rue St-Georges, Saint-Jérome, QC J7Z 4Z8
Tél: 450-436-8200; Téléc: 450-436-5904
jer.redaction.tc.tc
lechodunord.ca
Médias sociaux:
twitter.com/EchoNordMirabel
www.facebook.com/echonordmirabel
Tirage: 52 220; Fréquence: Vendredi
André Guillemette, Éditeur / Directeur général régional des Laurentides
andre.guillemette@quebecormedia.com
Marc Fradellin, Directeur de l'information
marc.fradellin@tc.tc

Saint-Laurent: Progrés Villeray
Détenteur: TC Transcontinental
#203, 1500, boul Jules-Poitras, Saint-Laurent, QC H4N 1X7
Tél: 514-855-1292; Téléc: 514-855-1855
redactionprogres@transcontinental.ca
www.leprogresvilleray.com
Médias sociaux:
twitter.com/InfoVillerayPE
www.facebook.com/ProgresVillerayParcExtension
Tirage: 21 630; Fréquence: Mardi
Séverine Galus, Directrice du contenu et des relations avec la communau

Saint-Pamphile: L'Écho d'en Haut
Détenteur: Journal l'Écho d'en Haut Inc.
#209, 35, rue Principale, Saint-Pamphile, QC G0R 3X0
Tél: 418-356-5491; Téléc: 418-356-5491
echo.den.haut@globetrotter.net
www.echodenhaut.org
Tirage: 3 100; Fréquence: mensuel
Diane Bérubé, Directrice Générale

Saint-Pascal: Le Placoteux
Détenteur: Néomédia
491, av d'Anjou, Saint-Pascal, QC G0L 3Y0
Tél: 418-492-2706; Téléc: 418-492-9706
association@leplacoteux.qc.ca
www.leplacoteux.com
Médias sociaux:
twitter.com/LPlacoteux
www.facebook.com/LePlacoteux
Tirage: 18 530; Fréquence: mercredi
Maurice Gagnon, Rédacteur en chef
journaliste@leplacoteux.com

Saint-Pierre-de-l'île-d'Orléans: Autour de l'île
115, 517 rte des Prêtres, Saint-Pierre-de-l'île-d'Orléans, QC G0A 4E0
Tél: 418-828-0330; Téléc: 418-828-0741
info@autourdelile.com
www.autourdelile.com
Médias sociaux:
www.facebook.com/autourdelile
Tirage: 4 500; Fréquence: mensuel
Sylvain Delisle, Rédacteur en chef

Saint-Sauveur: **Le Journal des Pays D'en Haut La Vallée**
Détenteur: TC Transcontinental
#104, 94, de la Gare, Saint-Sauveur, QC J0R 1R6
Tél: 450-227-4646; *Téléc:* 450-227-8144
ssm.redaction@tc.tc
lejournaldespaysdenhautlavallee.ca
Médias sociaux:
twitter.com/JdesPaysdEnHaut
www.facebook.com/journalpdh
Tirage: 30 230; *Fréquence:* Mercredi
André Guillemette, Éditeur / Directeur général régional des Laurentides
andre.guillemette@tc.tc
Josée Girard, Éditrice / Directrice régional des ventes
josee.girard@tc.tc

Saint-Siméon: **Le Goéland**
CP 250, 127-C, boul Perron ouest, Saint-Siméon, QC G0C 3A0
Tél: 418-534-2123; *Téléc:* 418-534-4353
journalgoeland@globetrotter.net
www.stsimeon.ca/journal-communautaire
Tirage: 650
Journal communautaire de Saint-Siméon
Antoinette Lepage, Présidente

Saint-Tite: **L'Hebdo Mekinac-des Chenaux**
CP 4057, Saint-Tite, QC G0X 3H0
Tél: 819-537-5111; *Téléc:* 819-537-5471
Ligne sans frais: 866-637-5236
redaction.hmc@transcontinental.ca
www.lhebdomekinacdeschenaux.com
Médias sociaux:
www.facebook.com/hebdomekinacdeschenaux
Tirage: 13 081; *Fréquence:* Samedi
Nancy Allaire, Éditeur

Sainte-Anne-des-Plaines: **Journal Le Point d'Impact**
194B, boul Sainte-Anne, Sainte-Anne-des-Plaines, QC J0N 1H0
Tél: 450-478-3538
journallepoint@qc.aira.com
www.journallepoint.com
Tirage: 6 000; *Fréquence:* samedi
Serge Blondin, Éditeur

Sainte-Brigitte-de-Laval: **Le Lavalois**
CP 1020, Sainte-Brigitte-de-Laval, QC G0A 3K0
Tél: 418-907-7172
lelavalois@ccapcable.com
www.lelavalois.com
Tirage: 1 300; *Fréquence:* dix fois par an
Lucille Thomassin, Présidente
lucille@ccapcable.com

Sainte-Geneviève-de-Batiscan: **Le Bulletin des Chenaux**
44, chemin Rivière-à-Veillet, Sainte-Geneviève-de-Batiscan, QC G0X 2R0
Tél: 819-840-3091; *Téléc:* 418-362-2861
info@lebulletindeschenaux.com
www.lebulletindeschenaux.com
Médias sociaux:
twitter.com/BullDesChenaux
www.facebook.com/pages/Bulletin-des-Chenaux/213099518727 2
Tirage: 9 000
Lucien Gélinas, Directeur général

Sainte-Julie: **L'Information Sainte-Julie**
Détenteur: TC Transcontinental
566, rue Jules-Choquet, Sainte-Julie, QC J3E 1W6
Tél: 450-649-0719; *Téléc:* 450-649-7748
jul.redaction@tc.tc
infodeste-julie.qc.ca
Médias sociaux:
twitter.com/InfoSteJulie
www.facebook.com/infodestejulie
Tirage: 20 545; *Fréquence:* Mercredi
Sylvain Bouchard, Éditeur
sylvain.bouchard@tc.tc
Nathalie Gilbert, Directrice de l'information
nathalie.gilbert@tc.tc

Sainte-Marie-de-Beauce: **Beauce Média**
Détenteur: TC Transcontinental
1147, boul Vachon nord, Sainte-Marie-de-Beauce, QC G6E 3B6
Tél: 418-387-8000; *Téléc:* 418-387-4495
smb.redaction@tc.tc
www.hebdosregionaux.ca/chaudiere-appalaches/beauce-m edia
Médias sociaux:
twitter.com/BeauceMedia
www.facebook.com/beaucemedia
Tirage: 25 120; *Fréquence:* Mercredi
Gilbert Bernier, Éditrice
gilbert.berner@tc.tc
André Boutin, Directeur de l'information
andre.boutin@tc.tc

Sainte-Thérèse: **L'Écho de la Rive-Nord**
Détenteur: TC Transcontinental
#208, 204, boul Labelle, Sainte-Thérèse, QC J7E 2X7
Tél: 450-818-7575; *Téléc:* 450-818-7582
sat.redaction@tc.tc
lechodelarivenord.ca
Médias sociaux:
twitter.com/LEchoRiveNord
www.facebook.com/lechorivenord
Tirage: 64 580; *Fréquence:* Mercredi
Serge Cameron, Éditeur
serge.cameron@tc.tc

Sainte-Thérèse: **L'Écho de Saint-Eustache**
Détenteur: TC Transcontinental
#208, 204, boul Labelle, Sainte-Thérèse, QC J7E 2X7
Tél: 450-818-7575; *Téléc:* 450-818-7582
redaction.saint-eustache@hebdosquebecor.com
Médias sociaux:
twitter.com/LEchoStEustache
www.facebook.com/lechosteustache
Serge Cameron, Éditeur
serge.cameron@quebecormedia.com

Sainte-Thérèse: **Le Nord Info**
Détenteur: Les Éditions Blainville-Deux-Montagnes Inc.
50B, rue Turgeon, Sainte-Thérèse, QC J7E 3H4
Tél: 450-435-6537; *Téléc:* 450-435-0588
infojournaux@groupejcl.com
www.nordinfo.com
Médias sociaux:
twitter.com/NordInfoVoix
www.facebook.com/NordInfoCom
Tirage: 60 033; *Fréquence:* Samedi
Jean-Claude Langlois, Président-Éditeur
Claude Desjardins, Rédacteur en chef

Sainte-Thérèse: **Nord Info et Voix des Mille-Iles**
Détenteur: TC Media
50B, rue Turgeon, Sainte-Thérèse, QC J7E 3H4
Tél: 450-435-6537; *Téléc:* 450-435-0588
infojournaux@groupejcl.com
www.nordinfo.com
Médias sociaux:
twitter.com/NordInfoVoix
www.facebook.com/NordInfoCom
Tirage: 65 536; *Fréquence:* mercredi
Jean-Claude Langlois, Éditeur

Salaberry-de-Valleyfield: **Journal le Suroît**
Détenteur: Les Publications du Sud-Ouest
52, rue Nicholson, Salaberry-de-Valleyfield, QC J6T 4M8
Tél: 450-371-8051; *Téléc:* 450-371-4237
Ligne sans frais: 877-371-8051
journal@media-sudouest.com
www.publications-sudouest.com

Salaberry-de-Valleyfield: **Le Journal Saint-François**
Détenteur: TC Media
55, rue Jacques-Cartier, Salaberry-de-Valleyfield, QC J6T 4R4
Tél: 450-371-6222; *Téléc:* 450-371-7254
www.journalsaint-francois.ca
Médias sociaux:
www.facebook.com/journalsaintfrancois
Tirage: 34 722; *Fréquence:* mercredi

Salaberry-de-Valleyfield: **Le Journal Saint-François**
Anciennement: Le Soleil de Salaberry-de-Valleyfield
Détenteur: TC Media
55, rue Jacques-Cartier, Salaberry-de-Valleyfield, QC J6T 4R4
Tél: 450-371-6222; *Téléc:* 450-371-7254
www.journalsaint-francois.ca
Tirage: 36 326; *Fréquence:* samedi

Sept-Îles: **Le Nord-Est**
Détenteur: TC Transcontinental
365, boul Laure, Sept-Iles, QC G4R 1Y2
Tél: 418-962-9441
sis.redaction@tc.tc
lenordest.ca
Médias sociaux:
twitter.com/JournalNordEst
www.facebook.com/lenordest
Tirage: 19 090; *Fréquence:* Mercredi; aussi Le Nord-Est Plus (mercredi)
Catherine Martin, Éditrice
catherine.martin@tc.tc
Jean Saint-Pierre, Directeur de l'information
jean.st-pierre@tc.tc

Sept-Îles: **Le Port-Cartois**
Détenteur: TC Transcontinental
781, boul Laure, Sept-Iles, QC G4R 1Y2
Tél: 418-766-5321; *Téléc:* 418-766-5329
sis.redaction@tc.tc
leportcartois.ca
Tirage: 19 090; *Fréquence:* Mercredi
Catherine Martin, Éditrice
catherine.martin@tc.tc
Jean Saint-Pierre, Directeur de l'information
jean.st-pierre@tc.tc

Shawinigan: **L'Hebdo du St-Maurice**
CP 10, 2102, av Champlain, Shawinigan, QC G9N 6T8
Tél: 819-537-5111; *Téléc:* 819-537-5471
redaction_shawinigan@transcontinental.ca
www.lhebdodustmaurice.com
Médias sociaux:
twitter.com/HebdoStMaurice
facebook.com/lhebdodustmaurice
Tirage: 30 511; *Fréquence:* Samedi
Bernard Lepage, Éditeur
bernard-lepage@tc.tc
André Juteau, Directeur général régional
andre.juteau@tc.tc

Shawville: **The Equity**
Owned By: Pontiac Printshop Ltd.
133 Centre St., Shawville, QC J0X 2Y0
Tel: 819-647-2204; *Fax:* 819-647-2206
news@theequity.ca
www.theequity.ca
Social Media: www.youtube.com/equitynewspaper
twitter.com/equitynewspaper
www.facebook.com/EquityNewspaper
Circulation: 3,362
Heather Dickson, Publisher
Charles Dickson, Publisher & Editor
charles.dickson@theequity.ca

Sherbrooke: **Entrée Libre**
#317, 187, rue Laurier, Sherbrooke, QC J1H 4Z4
Tél: 819-821-2270; *Téléc:* 819-566-2664
journal@entreelibre.info
www.entreelibre.info
Médias sociaux:
www.facebook.com/journalentreelibre
Tirage: 9 500; *Fréquence:* jeudi
Produit par le collectif du même nom selon une démarche d'éducation populaire autonome, est accessible aux gens du quartier centre-sud-ouest de Sherbrooke.
Claude Dostie, Rédacteur en chef

Sherbrooke: **L'Info**
CP 157, Succ. Saint-Élie d'Orford, Sherbrooke, QC J1R 1A1
Tél: 819-820-9663
journalinfo@cooptel.qc.ca
linfodesaintelie.org/Site_Journal_Linfo/Bienvenue.html
Tirage: 3 966; *Fréquence:* mensuel
Josée Dostie, Directrice générale

Sherbrooke: **Le Journal de Magog**
Détenteur: TC Transcontinental
270, rue Principale Est, Sherbrooke, QC J1X 4X5
Tél: 819-573-2322; *Téléc:* 819-573-0643
mag.redaction@tc.tc
lejournaldemagog.ca
Autre information: 819-575-7575
Médias sociaux:
twitter.com/JdeMagog
www.facebook.com/jdemagog
Tirage: 28 000; *Fréquence:* Mercredi
Ghislain Allard, Directeur de l'information
ghislain.allard@tc.tc

Sherbrooke: **Le Journal de Sherbrooke**
Détenteur: TC Transcontinental
3330 boul Industriel, Sherbrooke, QC J1L 2S7
Tél: 819-566-8585; *Téléc:* 819-566-8442
she.redaction@tc.tc
lejournaldesherbrooke.ca
Autre information: 819-575-7575
Médias sociaux:
twitter.com/jdesherbrooke
www.facebook.com/journaldesherbrooke
Tirage: 63 500; *Fréquence:* Mercredi
Ghislain Allard, Chef des nouvelles
ghislain.allard@tc.tc

Sherbrooke: **La Nouvelle de Sherbrooke**
1950, rue Roy, Sherbrooke, QC J1K 2X8
Tél: 819-564-5450
redaction@lanouvelle.ca
www.lapresse.ca/la-tribune/la-nouvelle
Médias sociaux:
twitter.com/HebdoLaNouvelle
facebook.com/LaPresseFB
Tirage: 52 000; *Fréquence:* Mercredi
Louise Boisvert, Présidente-éditrice
Maurice Cloutier, Rédacteur-en-chef

Shipshaw: **Journal La Vie d'Ici**
4681, rue Saint-Léonard, Shipshaw, QC G7P 1J4
Téléc: 418-213-0701
informations@laviedici.com
www.laviedici.com
Fréquence: mensuel
Claire Duchesne, Présidente

Sorel-Tracy: **Les 2 Rives et La Voix**
Détenteur: Les Hebdos Régionaux Québecor Média
58, rue Charlotte, Sorel-Tracy, QC J3P 1G3
Tél: 450-742-9408; *Téléc:* 450-742-2493
str.redaction@tc.tc
les2riveslavoix.ca
Médias sociaux:
twitter.com/Voix2RivesSorel
www.facebook.com/les2rives
Tirage: 30 950; *Fréquence:* Mardi
Jean Curadeau, Éditeur
jean.curadeau@tc.tc
Jean-Philippe Morin, Directeur de l'information
jean-philippe.morin@tc.tc

St-André-Avellin: **Le Bulletin**
Détenteur: TC Transcontinental
3A, rue Principale, St-André-Avellin, QC J0V 1W0
Tél: 819-986-5089; *Téléc:* 819-986-2073
pascal.laplante@tc.tc
www.lebulletin.net
Médias sociaux:
twitter.com/LeBulletin1
facebook.com/pages/Le-Bulletin/20679933940 2133
Tirage: 11 351; *Fréquence:* Dimanche
Michel Blais, Éditeur
Eric Lafleur, Contact, Ventes
eric.lafleur@tc.tc

St-Laurent: **Courrier Bordeaux-Cartierville**
Détenteur: TC Transcontinental
#203, 1500, boul Jules-Poitras, St-Laurent, QC H4N 1X7
Tél: 514-855-1292; *Téléc:* 514-855-1855
courrierahuntsic@tc.tc
www.courrierahuntsic.com
Médias sociaux:
twitter.com/InfoAhuntsicBC
www.facebook.com/courrierahuntsicbc
Tirage: 18 100; *Fréquence:* Jeudi

St-Léonard: **Guide de Montréal-Nord**
Détenteur: TC Transcontinental
#210, 8770, boul Lanaelier, St-Léonard, QC H1P 3C6
Tél: 514-899-5888; *Téléc:* 514-899-5001
redaction_est@tc.tc
www.guidemtlnord.com
Médias sociaux:
twitter.com/Guidemtlnord
www.facebook.com/guidemtlnord
Tirage: 34 680; *Fréquence:* Mardi
Véronique Gauthier, Éditrice
Marie-Joseé Chouinard, Directrice du content et des relations avec la communau

St-Léonard: **Progrès Saint-Léonard**
Détenteur: TC Transcontinental
#212, 8770, boul Langelier, St-Léonard, QC H1P 3C6
Tél: 514-899-5888; *Téléc:* 514-899-5984
redaction_est@tc.tc
www.progresstleonard.com
Médias sociaux:
twitter.com/progresstleo
www.facebook.com/progresstleonard
Tirage: 32 220; *Fréquence:* Mardi
Véronique Gauthier, Directrice générale
Sylviane Lussier, Directrice générale régionale pour l'île de Montréal

St-Pierre-de-la-Rivière-du-Sud: **Journal Le Pierr'Eau**
645, 2e av, St-Pierre-de-la-Rivière-du-Sud, QC G0R 4B0
Tél: 418-248-8277; *Téléc:* 418-248-7068
journal@stpierrerivieresud.ca
www.pierreau.ca
Médias sociaux:
www.facebook.com/groups/stpierrerivieredusud
Christian Collin, Président

Stanstead: **Stanstead Journal**
269 Dufferin St., Stanstead, QC J0B 3E2
Tél: 819-876-7514 *Ligne sans frais:* 800-567-1259
reception@stanstead-journal.com
www.stanstead-journal.com
Tirage: 2,700; *Fréquence:* Wednesday
Jean-Yves Durocher, President & Publisher
jy.durocher@stanstead-journal.com

St-Étienne-des-Grès: **Le Stéphanois**
CP 282, St-Étienne-des-Grès, QC G0X 2P0
Tél: 819-299-3858
lestephanois@cgocable.ca
www.lestephanois.ca
Tirage: 2 000
Gérard Levesque, Président

Témiscaming: **Le Contact**
PO Box 566, 32, rue Simon, Témiscaming, QC J0Z 3R0
Tel: 819-627-9050; *Fax:* 819-627-1794
contact@cablevision.qc.ca
temiscamingcontact.org
Circulation: 1 000; *Frequency:* mercredi
Élaine Ouellet, Éditrice

Terrebonne: **La Revue de Terrebonne**
231, rue Ste-Marie, Terrebonne, QC J6W 3E4
Tél: 450-964-4444; *Téléc:* 450-471-1023
larevue@larevue.qc.ca; ventes@larevue.qc.ca
www.larevue.qc.ca
Autre information: Montréal: 514-990-7314
Médias sociaux:
www.linkedin.com/pub/gilles-bordonado/12/a66/556
twitter.com/revueterreb onne
www.facebook.com/revueterrebonne
Tirage: 60 000; *Fréquence:* Mercredi
Gilles Bordonado, Président-Directeur général
gbordonado@larevue.qc.ca
Daniel Soucy, Directeur développement et marketing
dsoucy@larevue.qc.ca

Terrebonne: **Le Trait d'Union**
Détenteur: TC Media
#210, 1300, Grande Allée, Terrebonne, QC J6W 4M4
Tél: 450-964-4400; *Téléc:* 450-964-4403
letraitdunion@transcontinental.ca
www.letraitdunion.com

Thetford Mines: **Le Courrier Frontenac**
CP 789, 541, boul Frontenac est, Thetford Mines, QC G6G 5V3
Tél: 418-338-5181; *Téléc:* 418-338-5482
courrier.frontenac@tc.tc
www.courrierfrontenac.qc.ca
Médias sociaux:
twitter.com/CourFrontenac
facebook.com/CourrierFrontenac
Tirage: 22 950; *Fréquence:* Mercredi
Pascal Gourdeau, Rédacteur-en-chef
pascal.gourdeau@tc.tc
Laurent Raby, Directeur général
laurent.raby@tc.tc

Trois-Rivières: **Le Bulletin**
Détenteur: Le Tour d'y Voir
991, rue Champflour, Trois-Rivières, QC G9A 1Z8
Tél: 819-375-0484
www.tourdyvoir.ca
Tirage: 1 000

Trois-Rivières: **L'Écho de Trois-Rivières**
Détenteur: TC Transcontinental
3406, boul Gene H Kruger, Trois-Rivières, QC G9A 4M3
Tél: 819-379-1490; *Téléc:* 819-379-0705
trr.redaction@tc.tc
lechodetroisrivieres.ca
Médias sociaux:
twitter.com/lecho3rivieres
www.facebook.com/lecho3rivieres
Tirage: 68 580; *Fréquence:* Mercredi
Jocelyn Ouellet, Directeur de l'information
jocelyn.ouellet@tc.tc

Trois-Rivières: **L'Hebdo-Journal**
Détenteur: TC Transcontinental
635, rue du Père-Daniel, Trois-Rivières, QC G9A 5Z7
Tél: 819-379-1490; *Téléc:* 819-379-0705
reception.hj@tc.tc
www.lhebdojournal.com
Médias sociaux:
twitter.com/hebdojournal
facebook.com/hebdojournal
Tirage: 44 870; *Fréquence:* Samedi
Marie-Eve Veillette, Éditrice
819-379-1492 ext 242
marie-eve.veillette@tc.tc
Éric Maltais, Directeur général régional
eric.maltais@tc.tc
Carole Béliveau, Secrétaire de direction
carole.beliveau@tc.tc

Val-David: **Le Journal Ski-se-Dit**
#200, 2496, rue de l'Église, Val-David, QC J0R 2N0
Tél: 819-322-7969; *Téléc:* 819-322-7904
ski-se-dit@cgocable.ca
www.ski-se-dit.info
Médias sociaux:
www.facebook.com/skisedit
Tirage: 3 000; *Fréquence:* mensuel

Val-d'Or: **Le Citoyen**
Détenteur: TC Media
1462, rue de la Québécoise, Val-d'Or, QC J9P 5H4
Tél: 819-825-3755
www.lechoabitibien.ca
Médias sociaux:
twitter.com/LechoAbitibien
www.facebook.com/lechoabitibien
Tirage: 19 979; *Fréquence:* mercredi
Louis Lavoie, Directeur général
louis.lavoie@tc.tc

Val-d'Or: **L'Écho Abitibien**
Détenteur: TC Media
1462, rue de la Québécoise, 2e étage, Val-d'Or, QC J9P 5H4
Tél: 819-825-3755; *Téléc:* 819-825-0361
vld.redaction@tc.tc
lechoabitibien.ca
Médias sociaux:
twitter.com/LechoAbitibien
www.facebook.com/lechoabitibien
Tirage: 4 102; *Fréquence:* mercredi
Louis Lavoie, Directeur général
louis.lavoie@tc.tc
David Prince, Chef des nouvelles
david.prince@tc.tc

Val-des-Monts: **Journal l'Envol**
Previous Name: L'Envol des Monts
12, Potvin, Val-des-Monts, QC J8N 7B2
Tel: 819-671-1502; *Fax:* 819-671-7463
envol.desmonts@sympatico.ca
Circulation: 11 500; *Frequency:* bimensuelle
Nicole A. Thibodeau, Éditrice

Vaudreuil-Dorion: **L'Étoile**
Anciennement: 1ère Edition du Sud-Ouest
Détenteur: TC Transcontinental
469, av St-Charles, Vaudreuil-Dorion, QC J7V 2N4
Tél: 450-455-6111; *Téléc:* 450-455-3028
webmestre@hebdosdusuroit.com
www.journalletoile.com
Médias sociaux:
twitter.com/journalletoile
www.facebook.com/journalletoile
Tirage: 61 750; *Fréquence:* Mercredi
Marie-Andrée Prévost, Directrice générale
maprevost@hebdosdusuroit.com

Vaudreuil-Dorion: **Journal Première Édition**
Détenteur: VIVA ID
469, av St-Charles, Vaudreuil-Dorion, QC J7V 2N4
Tél: 450-455-7955; *Téléc:* 450-455-3028
id.viva-media.ca/fr/medias/publications/journal-premiere-edition
Médias sociaux:
twitter.com/journal1edition
www.facebook.com/journalpremiereedition
Tirage: 61 000; *Fréquence:* samedi
Yanick Michaud, Directeur de l'information

Victoriaville: **La Nouvelle Union**
Anciennement: L'Union
Détenteur: TC Media
43, rue Notre-Dame est, 2e étage, Victoriaville, QC G6P 3Z4
Tél: 819-758-6211; *Téléc:* 819-758-2759
redaction_victo@tc.tc
www.lanouvelle.net
Tirage: 35 999; *Fréquence:* mercredi

Victoriaville: **La Nouvelle Union**
Détenteur: TC Media
43, rue Notre-Dame est, 2e étage, Victoriaville, QC G6P 3Z4
Tél: 819-758-6211; *Téléc:* 819-758-0417
redaction_victo@tc.tc
www.lanouvelle.net
Médias sociaux:
twitter.com/LaNouvelleNet
www.facebook.com/lanouvellenet
Tirage: me. 37 349; vend. 42 104; *Fréquence:* mercredi, vendredi
Sylvie Côté, Éditrice
Manon Samson, Rédactrice-en-chef

Ville-Marie: **Journal Le Reflet**
Anciennement: Le Témiscamien
22, rue Sainte-Anne, Ville-Marie, QC J9V 2B7
Tél: 819-622-1313; *Téléc:* 819-622-1333
information@journallereflet.com
www.journallereflet.com
Tirage: 8 500; *Fréquence:* Mercredi
Karen Lachapelle, Directrice générale
dg@journallereflet.com

Wakefield: **The Low Down to Hull & Back News**
Owned By: Performance Printing Ltd.
PO Box 99, 815 Riverside Dr., Wakefield, QC J0X 3G0
Tel: 819-459-2222; *Fax:* 819-459-3831
general@lowdownonline.com
www.lowdownonline.com
Social Media:
twitter.com/TrevorGreenway; twitter.com/lucyannescholey
www.facebook.com/152335818154890
Circulation: 2,990; *Frequency:* Wednesday
Nikki Mantell, Publisher
nmantell@lowdownonline.com
Liette Robert, General Manager

Windsor: **L'Etincelle**
193, rue St-Georges, Windsor, QC J1S 1J7
Tél: 819-845-2705; *Téléc:* 819-845-5520
journal@letincelle.qc.ca
www.letincelle.qc.ca
Tirage: 10 500; *Fréquence:* Mercredi
Claude Frenette, Éditeur
cfrenette@letincelle.qc.ca
Chantal Darveau, Directrice
cdarveau@letincelle.qc.ca

Saskatchewan

Daily Newspapers in Saskatchewan

Moose Jaw: **The Moose Jaw Times Herald**
Owned By: TC Media
44 Fairford St. West, Moose Jaw, SK S6H 1V1
Tel: 306-692-6441
editorial@mjtimes.sk.ca
www.mjtimes.sk.ca
Social Media:
twitter.com/MJTimesHerald
facebook.com/MJTHerald
Circulation: 88,950 total; *Frequency:* Monday-Saturday
On Wednesdays, publishes with the TMC supplement FYI (circ. 24,000). The newspaper provides local content & subscribes to the Saskatchewan News Network & the Canadian Press.
Nancy Johnson, Publisher
306-691-1254; Fax: 306-692-2101
nancy.johnson@tc.tc
Lyndsay McCready, Managing Editor
306-691-1262; Fax: 306-692-2101
editorial@mjtimes.sk.ca

Prince Albert: **The Prince Albert Daily Herald**
Owned By: TC Media
30 - 10th St. East, Prince Albert, SK S6V 0Y5
Tel: 306-764-4276; *Fax:* 306-763-3331
editorial@paherald.sk.ca
www.paherald.sk.ca
Other information: Advertising, Phone: 306-764-4276, ext. 238, Fax: 306-763-6747
Social Media:
twitter.com/padailyherald
www.facebook.com/pages/Prince-Albert-Daily-Herald/1405868
Circulation: 31,425 total; *Frequency:* Monday-Saturday
Darryl Mills, Managing Editor
darryl.mills@paherald.sk.ca

Regina: **The Leader-Post**
Owned By: Postmedia Network Inc.
PO Box 2020, Regina, SK S4P 3G4
Tel: 306-781-5211; *Fax:* 306-565-2588
citydesk@leaderpost.com
www.leaderpost.com
Social Media:
twitter.com/leaderpost
www.facebook.com/reginaleaderpost
Circulation: 220,031 total; *Frequency:* Monday-Saturday
Tim Switzer, City Coordinator
citydesk@leaderpost.com
Cindy Zawislak, Manager
czawislak@postmedia.com

Saskatoon: **The StarPhoenix**
Previous Name: The Saskatoon Phoenix; Saskatoon Capital; Daily Star; Daily Phoenix
Owned By: Postmedia Network Inc.
204 - 5th Ave. North, Saskatoon, SK S7K 2P1
Tel: 306-657-6231; *Fax:* 306-657-6437
Toll-Free: 800-667-2002
citydesk@thestarphoenix.com
www.thestarphoenix.com
Other information: Advertising, Phone: 306-657-6340, Fax: 306-657-6208
Social Media:
twitter.com/thestarphoenix
www.facebook.com/thestarphoenix
Circulation: 261,691 total; *Frequency:* Monday-Saturday
Six editions of the newspapers are published each week. TheStarPhoenix.com offers news each day.
Heather Persson, Editor
306-657-6315
hpersson@thestarphoenix.com

Other Newspapers in Saskatchewan

Assiniboia: **Assiniboia Times**
Owned By: Glacier Media Group Ltd.
PO Box 910, 410 - 1st Ave. East, Assiniboia, SK S0H 0B0
Tel: 306-642-5901; *Fax:* 306-642-4519
Circulation: 3,400; *Frequency:* Fri.
Joyce Simard, Editor
joyce@assiniboiatimes.ca
Kevin Rasmussen, General Manager
kevin@assiniboiatimes.ca

Biggar: **The Biggar Independent**
Owned By: Independent Printers Ltd.
PO Box 40, 102 - 3rd Ave. West, Biggar, SK S0K 0M0
Tel: 306-948-3344; *Fax:* 306-948-2133
info@biggarindependent.ca
www.biggarindependent.ca
Circulation: 1,600; *Frequency:* Thurs.
Daryl Hasein, Co-Publisher
Margaret Hasein, Co-Publisher
Kevin Brautigam, Editor
Urla Tyler, Consultant, Advertising
tip@sasktel.net
Delta Fay Cruickshank, Contact, Production

Canora: **The Canora Courier**
Owned By: Glacier Media Inc.
123 First Ave. East, Canora, SK S0A 0L0
Tel: 306-563-5131; *Fax:* 306-563-5131
canoracourier@sasktel.net
Circulation: 1,200; *Frequency:* Wed.
The Saskatchewan town of Canora & the villages in its municipal district are served by the weekly newspaper.
Ken Lewchuk, General Manager
k.lewchuk@sasktel.net
Gary Lewchuk, Editor
kamsacktimes@sasktel.net
Dan Daoust, Contact, Sales
sales.canoracourier@sasktel.net
Sonia Lewchuk, Contact, Administration
office.canoracourier@sasktel.net

Canora: **Kamsack Times**
Owned By: Glacier Newspaper Group
PO Box 746, 123 First Ave. East, Canora, SK S0A 0L0
Tel: 306-563-5131; *Fax:* 306-563-6144
office.canoracourier@sasktel.net
Circulation: 1,400; *Frequency:* Wed.
The Times presents community affairs for the towns of Norquay & Kamsack, as well as nearby villages & hamlets.
Ken Lewchuk, General Manager
k.lewchuk@sasktel.net
William Koreluik, Editor
kamsacktimes@sasktel.net
Dan Daoust, Contact, Sales
sales.canoracourier@sasktel.net

Canora: **Norquay North Star**
PO Box 746, 18 - 1st Ave. South East, Canora, SK S0A 0L0
Tel: 306-563-5131; *Fax:* 306-563-6144
Circulation: 762; *Frequency:* Weekly
Ken Sopkow, Publisher & Editor

Canora: **The Preeceville Progress**
Owned By: Glacier Newspaper Group
PO Box 746, 123 First Ave. East, Canora, SK S0A 0L0
Tel: 306-563-5131; *Fax:* 306-563-5131
Circulation: 1,000; *Frequency:* Thurs.
The towns of Preeceville & Sturgis, plus nearby villages & hamlets, are served by The Preeceville Progress.
Ken Lewchuk, General Manager
k.lewchuk@sasktel.net
Gary Lewchuk, Editor
canoracourier@sasktel.net
Dan Daoust, Contact, Sales
sales@canoracourier@sasktel.net

Carlyle: **Carlyle Observer**
Owned By: Glacier Newspaper Group
PO Box 160, 132 Main St., Carlyle, SK S0C 0R0
Tel: 306-453-2525; *Fax:* 306-453-2938
observer@saskte.net
www.carlyleobserver.com
Social Media:
facebook.com/CarlyleObserver
Circulation: 3,200; *Frequency:* Fri.
Cindy Moffatt, Publisher
sasknew3@yahoo.com

Carnduff: **Gazette Post-News**
PO Box 220, 106 Broadway St., Carnduff, SK S0C 0S0
Tel: 306-482-3252; *Fax:* 306-482-3373
gazettepost.news@sasktel.net
Circulation: 1,000; *Frequency:* Fri.
Bruce Schwanke, Publisher
Bill Grass, Editor

Coronach: **Triangle News**
Owned By: TC Transcontinental
PO Box 689, Coronach, SK S0H 0Z0
Tel: 306-267-3381
trianglenews@sasktel.net
www.trianglenews.sk.ca
Circulation: 920; *Frequency:* Mon.
The Triangle News serves the community of Coronach with a weekly newspaper & a daily web site.
Rob Clark, Group Publisher
rob.clark@mjtimes.sk.ca
Kelly Elder, Editor
Denise Skinner, Contact, Office & Sales

Craik: **Craik Weekly News**
PO Box 360, 221 - 3rd St., Craik, SK S0G 0V0
Tel: 306-734-2313; *Fax:* 306-734-2789
craiknews@sasktel.net
Circulation: 880; *Frequency:* Monday
Harve Freidel, Publisher & Editor

Cut Knife: **Highway 40 Courier**
PO Box 639, 200 Steele St., Cut Knife, SK S0M 0N0
Tel: 306-398-4901; *Fax:* 306-398-4909
ckcouriernews@sasktel.net
Circulation: 490; *Frequency:* Wed.
Lorie Gibson, Publisher & Editor

***Davidson:* The Davidson Leader**
Owned By: Davidson Publishing Ltd.
PO Box 786, 205 Washington Ave., Davidson, SK S0G 1A0
Tel: 306-567-2047; *Fax:* 306-567-2900
theleaderonline@gmail.com
www.leaderonline.ca
Social Media:
twitter.com/davidsonleader
www.facebook.com/DavidsonLeader
Circulation: 1,200; *Frequency:* Mon.
The Davidson Leader covers the Saskatchewan communities of Davidson, Kenaston, Elbow, Imperial, Bladworth, Dundurn, Craik, & Loreburn. The newspaper is available in print & as as e-paper.
Tara de Ryk, Publisher & Editor

***Emerald Park:* The Star**
Owned By: Star News Inc.
8 Percival Dr., Emerald Park, SK S4L 1B7
Tel: 306-352-3393
www.TheStarNewspaper.ca
Social Media:
twitter.com/StarNewspaperSK
www.facebook.com/StarNewspaperSaskatchewan
Frequency: Weekly
Michelle Nicholson, Managing Editor
michelle@starnews.ca

***Esterhazy:* The Miner-Journal**
Owned By: Koskie Publications Ltd.
PO Box 1000, 606 Veterans Ave., Esterhazy, SK S0A 0X0
Tel: 306-745-6669; *Fax:* 306-745-2699
miner.journal@sasktel.net
www.minerjournal.com
Social Media:
facebook.com/pages/The-Miner-Journal/122690607744257
Circulation: 1,530; *Frequency:* Mon.
The Miner-Journal covers news for the Saskatchewan communities of Esterhazy, Bredenbury, Stockholm, Langenburg, Dubuc, Churchbridge, Atwater, Rocanville, Bangor, Gerald, Spy Hill, Yarbo, & Tantallon.
Brenda Matchett, Publisher
Christina Holmberg, General Manager
Helen Solmes, Editor

***Estevan:* Estevan Lifestyles**
Owned By: Glacier Interactive Media
PO Box 816, 300 Kensington Ave., Estevan, SK S4A 2A7
Tel: 306-634-5112; *Fax:* 306-634-2588
lifestyles@sasktel.net
www.sasklifestyles.com
Social Media:
www.facebook.com/lifestyles.estevan
Circulation: 7,500; *Frequency:* Fri.
Teresa Howie, Publisher
David Willberg, Editor

***Estevan:* Estevan Mercury**
Owned By: Glacier Interactive Media
PO Box 730, 68 Souris Ave. North, Estevan, SK S4A 2A6
Tel: 306-634-2654; *Fax:* 306-634-3934
classifieds@estevanmercury.ca
www.estevanmercury.ca
Social Media:
twitter.com/estevan_mercury
www.facebook.com/EstevanMercury
Circulation: 3,100; *Frequency:* Wed.
Peter Ng, Publisher
Brant Kersey, General Manager
bkersey@estevanmercury.ca
Jordan Baker, Editor
editor@estevanmercury.ca
Norm Park, Co-Editor
normpark@estevanmercury.ca

***Estevan:* Pipeline News**
Owned By: Glacier Media Inc.
68 Souris Ave., Estevan, SK S4A 2M3
Tel: 306-634-2654; *Fax:* 306-634-3934
www.pipelinenews.ca
Social Media:
twitter.com/PipelineNewsSK
www.facebook.com/pipelinenews
Circulation: 28,600; *Frequency:* Monthly
Discusses petroleum news in Saskatchewan.
Brant Kersey, Publisher
bkersey@estevanmercury.ca

***Estevan:* The Southeast Trader Express**
Owned By: Glacier Newspapers Group
PO Box 730, 68 Souris Ave. North, Estevan, SK S4A 2A6
Tel: 306-634-2654; *Fax:* 306-634-3934
mercury_merc1@sasktel.net
www.estevanmercury.ca
Circulation: 6,700; *Frequency:* Friday
Free weekly publication put out by the Estevan Mercury office. Serves the region of Southwest Saskatchewan
Peter Ng, Publisher
Brant Kersey, General Manager
bkersey@estevanmercury.ca
Jordan Baker, Editor
editor@estevanmercury.ca

***Eston:* The Press Review**
Owned By: Jamac Publishing Ltd.
PO Box 787, 112 Main St. West, Eston, SK S0L 1A0
Tel: 306-962-3221; *Fax:* 306-962-4445
estonpress@sasktel.net
Circulation: 840; *Frequency:* Tuesday
Stewart Crump, Publisher & General Manager
Kevin McBain, Editor

***Foam Lake:* Foam Lake Review**
Owned By: Foam Lake Review Ltd.
PO Box 550, 325 Main St., Foam Lake, SK S0A 1A0
Tel: 306-272-3262; *Fax:* 306-272-4521
review.foamlake@sasktel.net
foamlakereview.com
Circulation: 1,370; *Frequency:* Mon.
Bob Johnson, Publisher & Editor

***Fort Qu'Appelle:* Fort Qu'Appelle Times**
PO Box 940, 141 Broadway St. West, Fort Qu'Appelle, SK S0G 1S0
Tel: 306-332-5526; *Fax:* 306-332-5414
forttimes@sasktel.net
bit.ly/185lou0
Circulation: 1,100; *Frequency:* Tues.
Chris Ashfield, Publisher
George Brown, Editor

***Gravelbourg:* Gravelbourg Tribune**
PO Box 1017, 611 Main St., Gravelbourg, SK S0H 1X0
Tel: 306-648-3479; *Fax:* 306-648-2520
gravelbourgtribune@sasktel.net
Circulation: 1,000; *Frequency:* Mon.
Paul Boisvert, Publisher & Editor
trib.editorial@sasktel.net

***Grenfell:* The Broadview Express**
Owned By: TC Transcontinental
PO Box 189, Grenfell, SK S0G 2B0
Tel: 306-697-2722
sunnews@sasktel.net
www.grenfellsun.sk.ca
Social Media:
facebook.com/GrenfellSun
Circulation: 340; *Frequency:* Tues.
Rob Clark, Group Publisher
rob.clark@mjtimes.sk.ca
Dwayne Stone, Publisher
sunnews@sasktel.net

***Grenfell:* Grenfell Sun**
Owned By: TC Transcontinental
PO Box 189, Grenfell, SK S0G 2B0
Tel: 306-697-2722
sunnews@sasktel.net
www.grenfellsun.sk.ca
Social Media:
facebook.com/GrenfellSun
The newspaper covers happenings in Grenfell & the surrrounding area.
Rob Clark, Group Publisher
rob.clark@mjtimes.sk.ca
Dwayne Stone, Publisher
Annie Savage, Reporter

***Gull Lake:* The Gull Lake Advance**
Owned By: Winquist Ventures Ltd.
PO Box 628, 1462 Conrad Ave., Gull Lake, SK S0N 1A0
Tel: 306-672-3373; *Fax:* 306-672-3573
glad12@sasktel.net
gulllakeadvance.com
Social Media:
twitter.com/GullLakeAdvance
www.facebook.com/pages/Gull-Lake-Advance/126675707344759
Circulation: 1,200; *Frequency:* Tuesday
The weekly newspaper provides news & information for Gull Lake & southwestern Saskatchewan.
Kate Winquist, Publisher
kate.winquistventures@sasktel.net
Devin Beck, Contact, Sales & Marketing
sales.winquistventures@sasktel.net

***Herbert:* Herbert Herald**
PO Box 399, 716 Herbert Ave., Herbert, SK S0H 2A0
Tel: 306-784-2422; *Fax:* 306-784-3246
herbertherald@sasktel.net
Circulation: 1,500; *Frequency:* Tuesday
Rhonda Ens, Owner

***Hudson Bay:* Hudson Bay Post Review**
Owned By: Glacier Newspaper Group
20 Railway Ave., Hudson Bay, SK S0E 0Y0
Tel: 306-865-2771; *Fax:* 306-865-2340
Circulation: 987; *Frequency:* Thursday
Sherry Pilon, General Manager
postreview2@sasktel.net
Brent Fitzpatrick, Publisher
pub@sasktel.net

***Humboldt:* Humboldt Journal**
Owned By: Glacier Newspaper Group
PO Box 970, 535 Main St., Humboldt, SK S0K 2A0
Tel: 306-682-2561; *Fax:* 306-682-3322
humboldt.journal@sasktel.net
www.humboldtjournal.ca
Social Media:
facebook.com/pages/Humboldt-Journal-/122759507869764
Circulation: 3,000; *Frequency:* Friday
Al Guthro, Publisher
aguthro@humboldtjournal.ca
Kelly Friesen, Editor
kfriesen@humboldtjournal.ca

***Indian Head:* Indian Head - Wolseley News**
PO Box 70, 508 Grand Ave., Indian Head, SK S0G 2K0
Tel: 306-695-3565; *Fax:* 306-695-3448
ihwnews@sasktel.net
Circulation: 1,190; *Frequency:* Mon.
Jodi Gendron, Publisher & Editor

***Ituna:* The Ituna News**
Owned By: Foam Lake Review Ltd.
PO Box 413, 303 Main St. North, Ituna, SK S0A 1N0
Tel: 306-795-2412; *Fax:* 306-795-3621
news.ituna@sasktel.net
Circulation: 770; *Frequency:* Mon.
Bob Johnson, Publisher
Heidi Spilchuk, Editor

***Kindersley:* The Clarion**
PO Box 1150, 919 Main St., Kindersley, SK S0L 1S0
Tel: 306-463-4611; *Fax:* 306-463-6505
ads.jamac@gmail.com
Circulation: 1,500; *Frequency:* Wed.
Stewart Crump, Publisher
Kevin McBain, Editor

***Kindersley:* Kerrobert Citizen**
Owned By: Jamac Publishing
PO Box 1150, 919 Main St., Kindersley, SK S0L 1S0
Tel: 306-463-4611; *Fax:* 306-463-6505
ads.jamac@gmail.com
Circulation: 430; *Frequency:* Wed.
Stewart Crump, Publisher
Kevin McBain, Editor
publishing_jamac@sasktel.net

***Kindersley:* West Central Crossroads**
Owned By: Jamac Publishing
PO Box 1150, 919 Main St., Kindersley, SK S0L 1S0
Tel: 306-463-4611; *Fax:* 306-463-6505
ads.jamac@gmail.com
Circulation: 15,300; *Frequency:* Fri.
Stewart Crump, Publisher
Kevin McBain, Editor
publishing_jamac@sasktel.net

***Kipling:* Kipling Citizen**
Owned By: Glacier Newspapers Group
PO Box 329, 521 Main St., Kipling, SK S0J 2S0
Tel: 306-736-2535; *Fax:* 306-736-8445
thecitizen@sasktel.net
Circulation: 930; *Frequency:* Fri.
News & advertising from the Saskatchewan communities of Kipling, Corning, Peebles, Kennedy, Wawota, Windthorst, Glenavon, & Langbank are featured in the Kipling Citizen.
Laura Kish, General Manager
Terry Curzon, Representative, Advertising Sales

La Ronge: La Ronge Northerner
Owned By: Glacier Newspapers Group
PO Box 1350, 715 La Ronge Ave., La Ronge, SK S0J 1L0
Tel: 306-425-3344; *Fax:* 306-425-2827
northerner@sasktel.net
Other information: Sales: kdfith@sasktel.net
Circulation: 950; *Frequency:* Thurs.
Covers a geography of 30 communities in the northern area of Saskatchewan
Brenda Fitch, Publisher
Debbie Parkinson, Manager, Office, Circulation
ads.northerner@sasktel.net

Langenburg: The Four-Town Journal
PO Box 68, 102 Carl Ave. West, Langenburg, SK S0A 2A0
Tel: 306-743-2617; *Fax:* 306-743-2299
fourtown@sasktel.net
Circulation: 1,300; *Frequency:* Wed.
Langenburg, Saltcoats, Bredenbury, & Churchbridge are the communities served by The Four-Town Journal.
Bill Johnston, Publisher & Editor
Lynda Johnston, Contact, Office

Lanigan: Lanigan Advisor
PO Box 1029, 42 Main St., Lanigan, SK S0K 2M0
Tel: 306-365-2010; *Fax:* 306-365-3388
laniganadvisor@sasktel.net
Circulation: 880; *Frequency:* Mon.
Linda Mallett, Publisher & Editor

Lumsden: Lumsden Waterfront Press Regional Newspaper
PO Box 507, 635 James St. North, Lumsden, SK S0G 3C0
Tel: 306-731-3143; *Fax:* 306-731-2277
watpress@sasktel.net
www.waterfrontpress.com
Circulation: 4,160; *Frequency:* Thurs.
Lucien Chouinard, Co-Publisher & Editor
Jacqueline Chouinard, Co-Publisher & Editor

Macklin: Macklin Mirror
Owned By: Holmes Publishing
PO Box 100, 4701 Herald St., Macklin, SK S0L 2C0
Tel: 306-753-2424; *Fax:* 306-753-2424
macklinmirror@sasktel.net
Circulation: 875; *Frequency:* Wed.
Stewart Crump, Publisher

Maple Creek: Maple Creek News
Owned By: Alta Newspaper Group Limited Partnership
PO Box 1328, 116 Harder St., Maple Creek, SK S0N 1N0
Tel: 306-662-2133; *Fax:* 306-662-3092
editorial@maplecreeknews.com
www.maplecreeknews.com
Other information: Ads: ads@maplecreeknews.com
Social Media:
twitter.com/maplecreeknews
www.facebook.com/pages/Maple-Creek-News/150542211683094
Circulation: 1,700; *Frequency:* Thurs.
Angela Litke, Manager
Della Fournier, Contact, Advertising, Sales
dfournier@maplecreeknews.com

Meadow Lake: Northern Pride
219 Centre St., Meadow Lake, SK S9X 1Z4
Tel: 306-236-5353; *Fax:* 306-236-5962
northern.pride@sasktel.net
www.northernprideml.com
Social Media:
twitter.com/NorthernPrideML
facebook.com/northern.pride.5?sk=wall
Circulation: 4,800; *Frequency:* Tues.
The newspaper serves Meadow Lake & northwestern Saskatchewan.
Terry Villeneuve, Publisher
Phil Ambroziak, Editor

Melfort: The Melfort Journal
Owned By: Sun Media Corp.
PO Box 1300, 901 Main St., Melfort, SK S0E 1A0
Tel: 306-752-5737; *Fax:* 306-752-5358
www.melfortjournal.com
Social Media:
twitter.com/MelfortJournal
facebook.com/pages/Melfort-Journal/330748053648867
Circulation: 1,500; *Frequency:* Tues.
Ken Sorenson, Publisher, Advertising
ken.sorensen@sunmedia.ca
Greg Wiseman, Regional Managing Editor
greg.wiseman@sunmedia.ca
Greg Wiseman, Editor

Melville: Melville Advance
PO Box 1420, 218 - 3rd Ave. West, Melville, SK S0A 2P0
Tel: 306-728-5448; *Fax:* 306-728-4004
melvilleadvance@sasktel.net
www.melvilleadvance.com
Social Media:
twitter.com/MelvilleAdvance
facebook.com/TheMelvilleAdvance
Circulation: 2,400; *Frequency:* Wed.
Print & online subscriptions are available.
Chris Ashfield, Publisher & Contact, Advertising
George Brown, Managing Editor
editor.melvilleadvance@sasktel.net
Darcy Gross, Sports Reporter
sports.melvilleadvance@sasktel.net
Lloyd Schmidt, Computer Graphic Artist

Moose Jaw: The Moose Jaw Times Herald
Previous Name: Moose Jaw This Week
Owned By: Star News Publishing Inc.
44 Fairford St. West, Moose Jaw, SK S6H 1V1
Tel: 306-692-6441; *Fax:* 306-692-2101
www.mjtimes.sk.ca
Social Media:
twitter.com/MJTimesHerald
facebook.com/MJTHerald?fref=ts
Circulation: 24,000; *Frequency:* Wed.
Nancy Johnson, Publisher
306-691-1254; Fax: 3066922101
nancy.johnson@tc.tc
Lyndsay McCready, Managing Editor
editorial@mjtimes.sk.ca

Moosomin: The World-Spectator
Owned By: McKay Publications Ltd.
PO Box 250, 624 Main St., Moosomin, SK S0G 3N0
Tel: 306-435-2445; *Fax:* 306-435-3969
world_spectator@sasktel.net
www.world-spectator.com
Other information: Advertising, E-mail: ads@world-spectator.com
Social Media:
www.facebook.com/worldspectator
Circulation: 3,400; *Frequency:* Mon.
The following Saskatchewan communities are served by The World-Spectator: Moosomin, Wawota, Maryfield, Tantallon, St. Lazare, Elkhorn, Fleming, Manson, Kennedy, Rocanville, Wapella, Spy Hill, Welwyn, McAuley, Kola, Kelso, Fairlight, & Langbank.
Kevin Weedmark, Publisher & Editor
kevin@world-spectator.com

Muenster: Prairie Messenger
PO Box 190, 100 College Dr., Muenster, SK S0K 2Y0
Tel: 306-682-1772; *Fax:* 306-682-5285
pm@stpeterspress.ca
www.prairiemessenger.ca
Circulation: 4,800; *Frequency:* Wed.
Maureen Weber, Editor
pm.canadian@stpeterspress.ca
Donald Ward, Local News Editor
pm.local@stpeterspress.ca
Gail Kleefeld, Contact, Circulation
pm.circulation@stpeterspress.ca

Nipawin: The Nipawin Journal
Previous Name: Nipawin N.E. Region Community Booster.
Owned By: Sun Media Corp.
117 - 1st St. West, Nipawin, SK S0E 1E0
Tel: 306-862-4618; *Fax:* 306-862-4566
www.nipawinjournal.com
Social Media:
twitter.com/NipawinJournal
facebook.com/nipawin.journal
Circulation: 1,100; *Frequency:* Wed.
Ken Sorensen, Publisher
ken.sorensen@sunmedia.ca
Greg Wiseman, Regional Managing Editor
greg.wiseman@sunmedia.ca

Nokomis: Last Mountain Times
Owned By: Last Mountain Times Ltd.
PO Box 340, 103 - 1st Ave. West, Nokomis, SK S0G 3R0
Tel: 306-528-2020; *Fax:* 306-528-2090
Classifieds: inbox@lastmountaintimes.ca
lastmountaintimes.ca
Social Media:
facebook.com/lastmountaintimes
Circulation: 1,100; *Frequency:* Tues.
David Degenstien, Owner/Editor/Publisher
editor@lastmountaintimes.ca
Lynn Sonmor, Contact, Advertising
sales@lastmountaintimes.ca

Nokomis: The Market Connection
PO Box 340, Nokomis, SK S0G 3R0
Tel: 306-528-2020; *Fax:* 306-528-2090
editor@lastmountaintimes.ca
lastmountaintimes.ca
Other information: Classifieds email: inbox@lastmountaintimes.ca
Circulation: 10,600; *Frequency:* 4 times a year
The Market Connection is published concurrently with an issue of Last Mountain Times.
Dave Degenstien, Publisher/Editor/Owner

North Battleford: The Battlefords News-Optimist
Owned By: Glacier Newspapers Group
PO Box 1029, 892 - 104 St., North Battleford, SK S9A 3E6
Tel: 306-445-7261; *Fax:* 306-445-3223
Toll-Free: 866-549-9979
battlefords.publishing@sasktel.net
www.newsoptimist.ca
Other information: Sales, Fax: 306-445-1977; Composition, Fax: 306-445-7281
Social Media:
twitter.com/BfordsNewsOpt
Circulation: 2,350; *Frequency:* Tues.
Alana Schweitzer, Publisher
newsoptimist.alana@sasktel.net
Becky Doig, Editor
newsoptimist.editor@sasktel.net
John Cairns, Staff Reporter
newsoptimist.john@sasktel.netet

North Battleford: Maidstone Mirror
Owned By: Battlefords Publishing Ltd.
PO Box 1029, 892 - 104th St., North Battleford, SK S9A 3E6
Tel: 306-445-7261; *Fax:* 306-445-3223
Toll-Free: 866-549-9979
battlefords.publishing@sasktel.net
Circulation: 777; *Frequency:* Weekly
John Webster, Publisher
Becky Doig, Editor

Outlook: The Outlook
Owned By: Glacier Media Inc.
PO Box 1717, Outlook, SK S0L 2N0
Tel: 306-867-8262; *Fax:* 306-867-9556
theoutlook@sasktel.net
Circulation: 1,437; *Frequency:* Thursdays
The Outlook offers news & information to west central Saskatchewan.
Delwyn Luedtke, Publisher

Oxbow: The Oxbow Herald
Owned By: TC Transcontinental
219 Main St., Oxbow, SK S0C 2B0
Tel: 306-483-2323
oxbow.herald@sasktel.net
www.oxbowherald.sk.ca
Social Media:
facebook.com/pages/The-Oxbow-Herald/167990390043290
Circulation: 970; *Frequency:* Mon.
The Oxbow Herald reports the happenings of Oxbow, Saskatchewan & the surrounding area through a weekly newspaper & a daily web site.
Nancy Johnson, Group Publisher
nancy.johnson@tc.tc
Lizz Bottrell, Contact, Editorial
lizz@oxbowherald.sk.ca
Lorena Wolensky, Contact, Advertising
lorena@oxbowherald.sk.ca

Pierceland: The Beaver River Banner
PO Box 700, 171 - 2nd St. West, Pierceland, SK S0M 2K0
Tel: 306-839-4496; *Fax:* 306-839-2306
br.banner@outlook.com
www.beaverriverbanner.com
Circulation: 2,600; *Frequency:* Tues.
Dan Birsebois, Publisher/Editor

Radville: Radville & Deep South Star
Owned By: TC Transcontinental
PO Box 370, Radville, SK S0C 2G0
Tel: 306-869-2202; *Fax:* 306-869-2533
editorial@rdstar.sk.ca
www.rdstar.sk.ca
Social Media:
facebook.com/pages/The-Radville-Star/111164815576277
Circulation: 615; *Frequency:* Thurs.
Nancy Johnson, Group Publisher
nancy.johnson@tc.tc

Melissa Aspen, Contact, Advertising
circulation@rdstar.sk.ca
Ernie Wilson, Manager, Regional Sales
wilsone@transcontinental.ca

Redvers: Redvers Optimist
Owned By: Glacier Newspaper Group
PO Box 490, 10 Broadway St., Redvers, SK S0C 2H0
Tel: 306-452-3363; *Fax:* 306-452-6408
the.optimist@sasktel.net
Social Media:
www.facebook.com/RedversOptimist
Circulation: 932; *Frequency:* Saturday
Evelyn Smith, Office Manager
Ellen Skulmoski, Contact, Sales

Regina: Journal L'eau vive
Détenteur: La Coopérative de publ. fransaskoises
#210, 1440 9e Avenue Nord, Regina, SK S4R 8B1
Tél: 306-347-0481; *Téléc:* 306-565-3450
Ligne sans frais: 888-644-3236
www.leau-vive.ca
Médias sociaux:
twitter.com/leauvive
facebook.com/leauvive.CPF
Tirage: 1 400; *Fréquence:* Thurs.
Jean-Pierre Picard, Directeur/Rédacteur
direction@leau-vive.ca

Regina: Sunday Post
Previous Name: Regina Sun
Owned By: The Leader-Post
PO Box 2020, 1964 Park St., Regina, SK S4P 3G4
Tel: 306-565-8250; *Fax:* 306-565-8350
Social Media:
facebook.com/reginaleaderpost
Circulation: 78,350; *Frequency:* Sun.
A free weekly newspaper focusing on features, analysis and lengthier, weekend-style reads.
Marty Klyne, Publisher

Rosetown: Rosetown Eagle
Owned By: Rosetown Publishing Co. Ltd.
PO Box 130, Rosetown, SK S0L 2V0
Tel: 306-882-4202; *Fax:* 306-882-4204
editor.eagle@gmail.com
Circulation: 1,790; *Frequency:* Mon.
Stewart Crump, Publisher
Ian McKay, Editor

Rosthern: Saskatchewan Valley News
Previous Name: The Enterprise
PO Box 10, Rosthern, SK S0K 3R0
Tel: 306-232-4865; *Fax:* 306-232-4694
Toll-Free: 800-601-7858
info@saskvalleynews.com
www.saskvalleynews.com
Circulation: 1,750; *Frequency:* Thurs.
The Saskatchewan Valley News covers Rosthern & rural communities in the surrounding area.
Renay Kowalczyk, General Manager & Editor

Saskatoon: The Saskatoon Express
Previous Name: Saskatoon Neighbourhood Express
#15, 2220 Northridge Dr., Saskatoon, SK S7L 6X8
Tel: 306-244-5050; *Fax:* 306-244-5053
general@saskatoonexpress.com
www.saskatoonexpress.com
Social Media:
twitter.com/Sask_Express
www.facebook.com/165460726849382
Circulation: 55,000; *Frequency:* Weekly
Ryan McAdams, Publisher
Cam Hutchinson, Editor
chutchinson@saskatoonexpress.com

Shaunavon: The Shaunavon Standard
Owned By: Alta Newspaper Group Limited Partnership
PO Box 729, Shaunavon, SK S0N 2M0
Tel: 306-297-4144; *Fax:* 306-297-3357
www.theshaunavonstandard.com
Social Media:
twitter.com/The_SStandard
facebook.com/pages/The-Shaunavon-Standard/118598378227507
Circulation: 1,150; *Frequency:* Tues.
Paul MacNeil, Editor
standard@sasktel.net
Joanne Gregoire, Contact, Advertising & Sales
jgregoire@theshaunavonstandard.com

Shellbrook: Shellbrook Chronicle
Owned By: Pepperfram Limited Publications
PO Box 10, Shellbrook, SK S0J 2E0
Tel: 306-747-2442; *Fax:* 306-747-3000
chads@shellbrookchronicle.com (advertising)
www.shellbrookchronicle.com
Social Media:
twitter.com/ShellbrookChron
facebook.com/SBChronicle
Circulation: 3,950; *Frequency:* Fri.
The following Saskatchewan communities are covered by the Shellbrook Chronicle: Shellbrook, Debden, Parkside, Marcelin, Holbein, Mayview, Mont Nebo, Canwook, Big River, Leask, & Blaine Lake.
C.J. Pepper, Publisher
Flavio Nienow, Editor
chnews@shellbrookchronicle.com
Madeleine Wrigley, Contact, Advertising Sales
chroniclesales@sasktel.net
Cheryl Mason, Contact, Reception & Bookkeeping

Shellbrook: Spiritwood Herald
Owned By: Pepperfram Limited Publications
PO Box 10, 44 Main St., Shellbrook, SK S0J 2E0
Tel: 306-747-2442; *Fax:* 306-747-3000
Advertising: chads@sbchron.com
spiritwoodherald.com
Social Media:
www.facebook.com/pages/Spiritwood-Herald/253716234680672
Circulation: 2,570; *Frequency:* Fri.
Clark Pepper, Publisher
Tom Pierson, Editor
chnews@sbchron.com

Swift Current: The Southwest Booster
Owned By: TC Transcontinental
30 - 4th Ave. NW, Swift Current, SK S9H 3X4
Tel: 306-773-9321; *Fax:* 306-773-9136
www.swbooster.com
Social Media:
twitter.com/swbooster
www.facebook.com/pages/The-Southwest-Booster/163689647007
Circulation: 18,400; *Frequency:* Thurs.
Nancy Johnson, Publisher
nancy.johnson@tc.tc
Scott Anderson, Managing Editor
sanderson@swbooster.com
Bridget Denys, Manager, Business
bdenys@swbooster.com
Mark Soper, Manager, Sales
msoper@swbooster.com
Morgan Reil, Supervisor, Commercial Print
mreil@swbooster.com
Steven Mah, Sports Reporter
smah@swbooster.com
Valerie McLearn, Coordinator, Ads
vmclearn@swbooster.com

Tisdale: Tisdale Recorder & Parkland Review
Owned By: Glacier Newspaper Group
PO Box 1660, 1004 - 102nd Ave., Tisdale, SK S0E 1T0
Tel: 306-873-4515; *Fax:* 306-873-4712
Social Media:
www.facebook.com/199458986756467
Circulation: 13,288; *Frequency:* Wed.
Brent Fitzpatrick, Publisher
pub@sasktel.net
James Tarrant, Editor
newsrecorder@sasktel.net

Unity: The Unity-Wilkie Press Herald
Owned By: Glacier Media Inc.
PO Box 309, 310 Main St., Unity, SK S0K 4L0
Tel: 306-228-2267; *Fax:* 306-228-2767
northwest.herald@sasktel.net
www.estevanmercury.ca/section/northwest
Circulation: 1,900; *Frequency:* Mon.
Tammi Bullerwell, General Manager
Neil Thom, Editor
editorial@website.com
Debbie Barr, Prepress Manager
prepress@website.com
Denise Allen, Accountant

Wadena: Wadena News
Owned By: Wadena News Ltd.
PO Box 100, 102 - 1st St. NE, Wadena, SK S0A 4J0
Tel: 306-338-2231
wadena.news@sasktel.net
www.wadenanews.ca
Social Media:
twitter.com/wadenanewsed
facebook.com/pages/Wadena-News/164335013609573
Circulation: 2,200; *Frequency:* Wed.
Bruce Squires, Co-Publisher
Alison Squires, Co-Publisher
Kathy Johnson, Editor

Wakaw: Wakaw Recorder
Owned By: Dwaymar Enterprises Ltd.
PO Box 9, 224 - 1st St. South, Wakaw, SK S0K 4P0
Tel: 306-233-4325
Circulation: 1,800; *Frequency:* Wed.
Marjorie Biccum, Publisher

Warman: The Country Press
PO Box 880, 520 Central St. West, Warman, SK S0K 4S0
Tel: 306-934-6191; *Fax:* 306-668-8250
countrypress@sasktel.net
Circulation: 12,300; *Frequency:* Wed.
C. Lynn Handford, Publisher & Editor

Watrous: Watrous Manitou
Owned By: 101026460 Saskatchewan Ltd.
PO Box 100, 309 Main St., Watrous, SK S0K 4T0
Tel: 306-946-3343; *Fax:* 306-946-2026
watrous.manitou@sasktel.net
www.twmnews.com
Social Media:
twitter.com/twmnews
www.facebook.com/thewatrousmanitou
Circulation: 1,400; *Frequency:* Mon.
Daniel Bushman, Publisher & Editor
Kim Bushman, Publisher & Editor
Nicole Lay, Publisher
Robin Lay, Publisher

Weyburn: Weyburn Review
Owned By: Glacier Interactive Media
PO Box 400, 904 East Ave., Weyburn, SK S4H 2K4
Tel: 306-842-7487; *Fax:* 306-842-0282
production@weyburnreview.com
www.weyburnreview.com
Social Media:
twitter.com/WeyburnReview
www.facebook.com/pages/Weyburn-Review/100299633382446
Circulation: 2,800; *Frequency:* Wed.
Darryl Ward, Publisher
Patricia Ward, Editor-in-chief

Weyburn: Weyburn This Week
115 - 2nd St. NE, Weyburn, SK S4H 0T7
Tel: 306-842-3900; *Fax:* 306-842-2515
weyburnthisweek@sasktel.net
www.weyburnthisweek.com
Other information: Advertising, E-mail: advertisingthisweek@sasktel.net
Circulation: 4,600; *Frequency:* Fri.
The free publication covers local news & events in Weyburn & surrounding communities in southeastern Saskatchewan.
Andrea Heath, Publisher & Representative, Sales
Tanya Brown, Editor & Reporter
editorialthisweek@sasktel.net
Leslie Dempsey, Contact, Graphic Design

Whitewood: Whitewood Herald
PO Box 160, 708 South Railway St., Whitewood, SK S0G 5C0
Tel: 306-735-2230; *Fax:* 306-735-2899
herald@whitewoodherald.com
www.whitewoodherald.com
Social Media:
twitter.com/WhitewoodHerald
facebook.com/WhitewoodHerald
Circulation: 800; *Frequency:* Mon.
Chris Ashfield, Publisher
George Brown, Editor

Wolseley: Wolseley Bulletin
PO Box 89, 219 Poplar St., Wolseley, SK S0G 5H0
Tel: 306-698-2271; *Fax:* 306-698-2808
unos@sasktel.net
www.saskfarmnews.com/id6.html
Circulation: 500; *Frequency:* Fri.
The Wolseley Bulletin is distributed in the following communities: Wolseley, Glenavon, Indian Head, Qu'Appelle, Grenfell, Montmartre, Sintaluta, & Regina.

Rick Dahlman, Publisher & Editor
rdahlman@sk.sympatico.ca

***Wynyard:* Wynyard Advance/Gazette**
Owned By: Foam Lake Review Ltd.
PO Box 10, 117 Ave. B East, Wynyard, SK S0A 4T0
Tel: 306-554-2224; *Fax:* 306-554-3226
w.advance@sasktel.net
Circulation: 1,400; *Frequency:* Mon.
Bob Johnson, Publisher
Denise Mozel, Editor

***Yorkton:* The News Review**
Owned By: Glacier Media Inc.
18 - 1st Ave. North, Yorkton, SK S3N 1J4
Tel: 306-783-7355; *Fax:* 306-783-9138
info@yorktonnews.com; office@yorktonnews.com
www.yorktonnews.com
Social Media:
twitter.com/yorktonnews
www.facebook.com/yorkton.newsreview
Circulation: 6,700; *Frequency:* Thurs.
Ken Chyz, Publisher
kenchyz@yorktonnews.com
Shannon Deveau, Editor
editorial@yorktonnews.com

***Yorkton:* Yorkton This Week**
Owned By: Glacier Newspapers Group
PO Box 1300, 20 - 3rd Ave. North, Yorkton, SK S3N 2X3
Tel: 306-782-2465; *Fax:* 306-786-1898
sales@yorktonthisweek.com
www.yorktonthisweek.com
Social Media:
twitter.com/yorktonthisweek
www.facebook.com/pages/Yorkton-This-Week/168910973121215
Circulation: 3,400; *Frequency:* Wed.
Neil Thom, Publisher & General Manager

Yukon Territory

Daily Newspapers in Yukon Territory

***Whitehorse:* The Whitehorse Daily Star**
Owned By: Independent
2149 - 2nd Ave., Whitehorse, YT Y1A 1C5
Tel: 867-668-2060; *Fax:* 867-668-7130
letters@whitehorsestar.com
www.whitehorsestar.com
Social Media:
youtube.com/channel/UCvyLqXij5CDSwiTZc8XZJWg
twitter.com/WhitehorseStar
facebook.com/pages/The-Whitehorse-Star/149024148591580
Circulation: 8,993 total; *Frequency:* Monday-Friday
Jackie Pierce, Publisher
Jim Butler, Editor
editor@whitehorsestar.com

Other Newspapers in Yukon Territory

***Whitehorse:* L'Aurore boréale**
Détenteur: Association Franco-Yukonnaise
Association Franco-Yukonnaise, 302, rue Strickland, Whitehorse, YT Y1A 2K1
Tél: 867-667-2931; *Téléc:* 867-667-2932
www.auroreboreale.ca
Médias sociaux:
twitter.com/l_auroreboreale
www.facebook.com/AFY.Yukon
Tirage: 900; *Fréquence:* Bi-mensuel
Marie-Claude Nault, Coordonnatrice de la publicité
pub@auroreboreale.ca
Pierre-Luc Lafrance, Directeur
dir@auroreboreale.ca

***Whitehorse:* Yukon News**
Owned By: Black Press Ltd.
211 Wood St., Whitehorse, YT Y1A 2E4
Tel: 867-667-6285; *Fax:* 867-668-3755
editor@yukon-news.com
www.yukon-news.com
Social Media:
twitter.com/yukon_news
www.facebook.com/pages/Yukon-News/186396428426
Circulation: 7,150; *Frequency:* Wed., Fri.
Mike Thomas, Publisher
mthomas@yukon-news.com
John Thompson, Editor
johnt@yukon-news.com

Magazine Name Index

D

E

F

N

O

P

Magazines

Business

Aboriginal

Aboriginal Business Magazine
Owned By: Turtle Island News Publications
c/o Turtle Island News, PO Box 329, 2208 Chiefswood Rd., Hagersville, ON N0A 1M0
Tel: 519-445-0868; *Fax:* 519-445-0865
aboriginalbusinessmagazine.com
Social Media:
twitter.com/newsattheturtle
www.facebook.com/TurtleIslandNews
Frequency: Quarterly
Lynda Powless, Publisher & Editor,
lynda@theturtleislandnews.com

Advertising, Marketing, Sales

Adnews Online Daily
Owned By: Bale Communications Inc.
#1463, 1011 Upper Middle Rd. E, Oakville, ON L6H 5Z9
info@adnews.com
www.adnews.com
Social Media:
twitter.com/Adnewscom
Circulation: 65,000
Frequency: Daily
Advertising, marketing, creative, research, sales, technology, PR & media news source
Rob Bale, Publisher
Derek Winkler, Editor

Bio Business Magazine
#202, 30 Beaver Creek Rd. E, Richmond Hill, ON L4B 1J2
Tel: 905-886-5040; *Fax:* 905-886-6615
bio@publicationpartners.com
www.biobusinessmag.com
Circulation: 15,000
Frequency: 4 times a year
Christopher Forbes, Publisher, cforbes@jesmar.com

Blitz Magazine Inc
1360 Bathurst St., Toronto, ON M5R 3H7
Fax: 647-435-0304
Toll-Free: 888-952-5478
editor@blitzmagazine.com
www.blitzmagazine.com
Circulation: 10,000
Frequency: 6 times a year
Media communications magazine, delivered nation-wide
Troy Weston, Editor-in-chief

The Chronicle of Healthcare Marketing
Owned By: Chronicle Companies
c/o Chronicle Companies, #306, 555 Burnhamthorpe Rd., Toronto, ON M9C 2Y3
Tel: 416-916-2476; *Fax:* 416-352-6199
Toll-Free: 866-632-4766
health@chronicle.org
www.chronicle.ca
Other information: Toll-Free Fax: 1-800-865-1632
Circulation: 2,159
Frequency: 9 times a year
Mitchell Shannon, Publisher
R. Allan Ryan, Editorial Director

Direct Marketing Magazine
Previous Name: Canadian Direct Marketing News
Owned By: Lloydmedia, Inc.
137 Main St. North, 3rd Fl., Markham, ON L3P 1Y2
Tel: 905-201-6600; *Fax:* 905-201-6601
Toll-Free: 800-688-1838
www.dmn.ca
Circulation: 6,400
Frequency: Monthly, plus annual directory of suppliers & annual directories The List of Lists...The DM Industry Sourcebook & the Canadian Call Centre Industry Directory
Amy Bostock, Editor, amy@dmn.ca
Mark Henry, Contact, Ad Sales, mark@dmn.ca
Steve Lloyd, President, steve@contactmanagement.ca

Imprint Canada
Owned By: Tristan Communication Ltd.
#16, 190 Marycroft Ave., Woodbridge, ON L4L 5Y2
Tel: 905-856-2600; *Fax:* 905-856-2667
Toll-Free: 877-895-7022
feedback@imprintcanada.com
www.imprintcanada.com/magazine
Other information: Toll-Free Fax: 1-877-895-7023
Social Media:
twitter.com/imprint_canada
www.facebook.com/imprintcanada.shows
Circulation: 6,700
Tony Muccilli, Publisher

Infopresse (IP)
Détenteur: Infopresse
4310, boul Saint-Laurent, Montréal, QC H2W 1Z3
Tél: 514-842-5873; *Téléc:* 514-842-2422
redaction@infopresse.com
www.infopresse.com
Médias sociaux:
twitter.com/infopresse
Tirage: 7 500
Fréquence: 10 fois par an
Bruno Gautier, Président et éditeur
Arnaud Granata, Vice-président, directeur des contenus

Kidscreen
#500, 366 Adelaide St. West, Toronto, ON M5V 1R9
Tel: 416-408-2300; *Fax:* 416-408-0870
Toll-Free: 800-543-4512
www.kidscreen.com
Social Media:
twitter.com/kidscreen
www.facebook.com/pages/Kidscreen/219216124848853
Circulation: 11,500
Frequency: Monthly
Jocelyn Christie, Vice-President & Publisher,
jchristie@brunico.com
Lana Castleman, Editor, lcastleman@brunico.com

Marketing Magazine
Owned By: Rogers Media Inc.
1 Mount Pleasant Rd., Toronto, ON M4Y 2Y5
Toll-Free: 855-748-3677
marketing@halldata.com
www.marketingmag.ca
Social Media:
twitter.com/Marketing_Mag
www.facebook.com/MarketingMagCanada
Circulation: 7,872
Frequency: 18 issues a year
David Thomas, Editor-in-Chief, 416-764-1603,
David.thomas@marketingmag.rogers.com
Jeromy Lloyd, Managing Editor, 416-764-1567,
Jeromy.lloyd@marketingmag.rogers.com

Sign Media
Also Known As: Signs Canada
Owned By: Kenilworth Publishing Inc.
c/o Kenilworth Publishing Inc., #710, 15 Wertheim Crt., Richmond Hill, ON L4B 3H7
Tel: 905-771-7333; *Fax:* 905-771-7336
Toll-Free: 800-409-8688
editor@signmedia.ca
www.signmedia.ca
Social Media:
www.twitter.com/signmediacanada
www.linkedin.com/groups/Sign-Media-Canada-magazine-386611
Circulation: 11,016
Frequency: 7 times a year
Ellen Kral, Publisher
Blair Adams, Editorial Director
Erik Tolles, Sales Manager

Silver Screen
383 Lawrence Ave. West, Toronto, ON M5M 1B9
Tel: 416-488-3393; *Fax:* 416-488-5217
www.msilver.com
Social Media:
www.linkedin.com/groups/Silver-Properties-4979505
twitter.com/MalcolmSil ver
www.facebook.com/malcolm.silver.33
Circulation: 1,800
Occassional newletter containing information about downtown Toronto real estate.
Malcolm Silver, Publisher, malcolm@msilver.com

Strategy
Owned By: Brunico Communications Ltd.
#100, 366 Adelaide St. West, Toronto, ON M5V 1R9
Tel: 416-408-2300; *Fax:* 416-408-0870
Toll-Free: 888-278-6426
customersupportstrategy@brunico.com
strategyonline.ca
Social Media:
twitter.com/strategyonline
www.facebook.com/217618361606458
Circulation: 13,152
Frequency: Monthly
Russell Goldstein, President & CEO, rgoldstein@brunico.com
Emily Wexler, Editor, ewexler@brunico.com

Architecture

Award Magazine
Owned By: Canada Wide Media Limited
4180 Lougheed Hwy., 4th Fl., Burnaby, BC V5C 6A7
Tel: 604-473-0316
dchapman@canadawide.com
www.canadawide.com/canada-wide/our-products/2007/10/23/award-magazine
Circulation: 26,000
Frequency: 6 times a year
Magazine for architects, interior designers & construction industry professionals
Gary Davies, President, gdavies@canadawide.com
Dan Chapman, Publisher, 604-473-0316,
dchapman@canadawide.com

Canadian Architect
Owned By: Annex-Newcom
80 Valleybrook Dr., Toronto, ON M3B 2S9
Tel: 416-510-6806; *Fax:* 416-510-5140
Toll-Free: 800-268-7742
www.canadianarchitect.com
Social Media:
twitter.com/CdnArch
Frequency: Monthly
Tom Arkell, Publisher, 416-510-6806,
tomarkell@canadianarchitect.com

Construction Canada
Owned By: Kenilworth Publishing Inc.
c/o Kenilworth Publishing Inc., #710, 15 Wertheim Ct., Richmond Hill, ON L4B 3H7
Tel: 905-771-7333; *Fax:* 905-771-7333
Toll-Free: 800-409-8688
www.constructioncanada.net
Frequency: Bi-monthly
Blair Adams, Editorial Director
Erik Tolles, Sales Director

Info-Link
#270, 3044 Bloor St. West, Toronto, ON M8X 2Y8
Tel: 416-604-7552; *Fax:* 416-604-2545
www.infolinkcanada.com
Frequency: 4 times a year

Sustainable Architecture & Building Magazine
Also Known As: SAB Mag
Owned By: Janam Publications
81, rue Leduc, Gatineau, QC J8X 3A7
Tel: 819-778-5040; *Fax:* 819-595-8553
www.sabmagazine.com/magazine.html
Social Media:
www.youtube.com/user/SABmagazine?feature=mhum
twitter.com/SABMagazine
www.facebook.com/sabmagcanada
Don Griffith, Publisher, 800-520-6281 ext.304,
dgriffith@sabmagazine.com
Jim Taggart, Editor, 604-874-0195, architext@telus.net

Arts, Art & Antiques

Arabella
Owned By: Arabella Publications Inc.
44 Parr St., St. Andrews, NB E5B 1L7
Tel: 506-814-0119
admin@arabelladesign.com
arabelladesign.com
Social Media:
www.facebook.com/107077652659400
Debra Usher, Editor-in-Chief

Automobile, Cycle, & Automotive Accessories

L'Automobile
Détenteur : Annex-Newcom
#100, 6450, rue Notre-Dame ouest, Montréal, QC H4C 1V4
www.lautomobile.ca

Fréquence: 6 fois par an
Marc Gadbois, Éditeur, 416-510-6776, mgadbois@lautomobile.ca
Élisabeth Poirier-Defoy, Rédactrice principale, 514-409-1970, epoirierdefoy@lautomobile.ca

Bodyshop Magazine
Owned By: Annex-Newcom
80 Valleybrook Rd., Toronto, ON M3B 2S9
Toll-Free: 800-268-7742
www.bodyshopbiz.com
Social Media: twitter.com/BodyshopCanada
Circulation: 11,917
Frequency: 6 times a year
Magazine of automotive information
Andrew Ross, Publisher & Editor, 416-510-6763, aross@jobbernews.com
Jay Armstrong, Sales Manager, Sales, 416-510-6745, jarmstrong@jobbernews.com

Canadian Auto World
Owned By: Premier Publications and Shows
c/o Premier Publications and Shows, #4, 447 Speers Rd., Oakville, ON L6K 3S7
Tel: 905-842-6591; *Fax:* 905-842-4432
Toll-Free: 800-693-7986
www.canadianautoworld.ca
Circulation: 4,529
Frequency: 6 times a year
Vicki Dillane, General Manager, 905-845-8536 x255, vdillane@metroland.com

Canadian Cycling Magazine
Owned By: Gripped Publishing Inc.
75 Harbord St., Toronto, ON M5S 4G1
Tel: 416-927-0774; *Fax:* 416-927-1491
Toll-Free: 800-567-0444
info@cyclingmagazine.ca
cyclingmagazine.ca
Social Media: twitter.com/CDNCyclingMag
www.facebook.com/cyclingmag
Sam Cohen, Publisher, sam@gripped.com

Canadian Technician
451 Attwell Dr., Toronto, ON M9W 5C4
Tel: 416-614-0955; *Fax:* 416-614-2781
www.canadiantechnician.com
Mark Vreugdenhill, Publisher
Allan Janssen, Editor

Collision Quarterly
Automotive Retailer Publishing Company Ltd., #1, 8980 Fraserwood Ct., Burnaby, BC V5J 5H7
Tel: 604-432-7987
publish@ara.bc.ca
www.automotiveretailer.ca/collision-quarterly
Social Media: www.facebook.com/CollisionQuarterly
Frequency: Quarterly
Kara Cunningham, Publisher & Editor

Collision Repair Magazine
c/o Media Matters, 645 Ossington Ave., Toronto, ON M6G 3T6
Tel: 416-628-8344
www.collisionrepairmag.com
Social Media: twitter.com/CollisionMag
Darryl Simmons, Publisher
Mike Davey, Editor

dandyhorse
#813, 22 Close Ave., Toronto, ON M5K 2V4
Tel: 416-822-7910
subscribe@dandyhorsemagazine.com
dandyhorsemagazine.com
Social Media: dandyhorsemagazine.com/blog/
www.twitter.com/dandyhorse
www.facebook.com/pages/Dandyhorse-Magazine/11617638512626
Tammy Thorne, Editor-in-Chief, tammy@dandyhorsemagazine.com

Jobber News
Owned By: Annex-Newcom
80 Valleybrook Dr., Toronto, ON M3B 2S9
Tel: 416-510-6763 *Toll-Free:* 800-268-7742
www.autoserviceworld.com
Social Media: twitter.com/jobbernews
Circulation: 20,000
Frequency: Monthly
Andrew Ross, Publisher & Editor, 416-510-6763, aross@jobbernews.com

Service Station & Garage Management
Owned By: Annex-Newcom
80 Valleybrook Dr., Toronto, ON M3B 2S9
Tel: 416-510-5221
www.ssgm.com
Frequency: Monthly
Kathryn Swan, Managing Director, kathryn@newcom.ca

Taxi News
38 Fairmount Cres., Toronto, ON M4L 2H4
Tel: 416-466-2328; *Fax:* 416-466-4220
www.taxinews.com
Circulation: 10,000
Frequency: Monthly
John Duffy, Publisher
William McOuat, Editor

Aviation & Aerospace

Canadian Aviator Magazine
Previous Name: Aviator Magazine
Owned By: OP Media Group Ltd.
#500, 200 West Esplanade, Vancouver, BC V6Z 2T1
Tel: 604-998-3310 *Toll-Free:* 800-867-0474
canadianaviator@xplornet.com
www.canadianaviatormagazine.com
Social Media: www.facebook.com/CanadianAviatorMedia
Circulation: 16,000
Frequency: 6 times a year
Includes Aviators Blue Pages, a directory of aviation business, products, services and attractions.
Mark Yelic, Publisher
Russ Niles, Editor, canadianaviator@xplornet.com

Canadian Plane Trade
Previous Name: Canada Flight
71 Bank St., 7th Fl., Ottawa, ON K1P 5N2
Tel: 613-236-4901; *Fax:* 613-236-8646
copa@copanational.org
www.copanational.org
Circulation: 15,900
Frequency: Monthly; includes: Canadian Homebuilt Aircraft News, Canadian Ultralight News, Executive Flight News, Seaplane News, Aircraft Maintenance Engineers News, Canadian Plane Trade, Aviation Museum News
Michel Hell, Publisher, Editor, editorial@copanational.org

Experience
Previous Name: Bombardier Magazine
Owned By: Spafax
#101, 1179 King St. West, Toronto, ON M6K 3C5
Tel: 416-350-2425; *Fax:* 416-350-2440
experiencemagazine@spafax.com
bombardierexperiencemagazine.com/magazine. html
Natasha Mekhail, Editor, Luxury Brands, nmekhail@spafax.com

Helicopters
Owned By: Annex Publishing & Printing Inc.
PO Box 530, 105 Donly Dr. South, Simcoe, ON N3Y 4N5
Fax: 519-429-3094
Toll-Free: 888-599-2228
www.helicoptersmagazine.com
Social Media: twitter.com/Helicopters_Mag
Frequency: 5 times a year
Coverage of commercial, corporate, general and military rotary-wing aviation in Canada and around the world.
Matt Nichols, Editor, 416-725-5637, mnicholls@annexweb.com

ICAO Journal
International Civil Aviation Organization, 999, rue University, Montréal, QC H3C 5H7
Tel: 514-954-8219; *Fax:* 514-954-6077
icaohq@icao.int
www.icao.int
Circulation: 13,200
Frequency: 6 times a year
Rick Adams, Editor

Wings
Owned By: Annex Publishing & Printing Inc.
PO Box 530, 105 Donly Dr. South, Simcoe, ON N3Y 4N5
Fax: 519-429-3094
Toll-Free: 888-599-2228
www.wingsmagazine.com
Social Media: twitter.com/wings_magazine
www.facebook.com/WingsMag
Frequency: 6 times a year
Matt Nicholis, Editor, 416-725-5637, mnicholls@annexweb.com

Baking & Bakers' Supplies

Bakers Journal
Owned By: Annex Publishing & Printing Inc.
PO Box 530, 105 Donly Dr. South, Simcoe, ON N3Y 4N5
Fax: 519-429-3094
Toll-Free: 888-599-2228
www.bakersjournal.com
Social Media: twitter.com/BakersJournal
Frequency: 10 times a year
Martin McAnulty, Publisher, mmcanulty@annexweb.com
Laura Aiken, Editor, 416-522-1595, laiken@annexweb.com

Barbers & Beauticians

Canadian Hairdresser Magazine
1300 Bay St., 2nd Fl., Toronto, ON M5R 3K8
Tel: 416-923-1111
info@canhair.com
www.canhair.com
Social Media: twitter.com/canhair
www.facebook.com/pages/Canadian-Hairdresser-Magazine/1504
Circulation: 30,112
Frequency: 10 times a year
Joan Harrison, CEO & Editorial Director

Salon Magazine
Owned By: Salon Communications Inc.
#202, 183 Bathurst St., Toronto, ON M5T 2R7
Tel: 416-869-3131; *Fax:* 416-869-3008
info@salonmagazine.ca
www.salonmagazine.ca
Social Media: twitter.com/Salon_Magazine
www.facebook.com/SalonMag
Frequency: 8 times a year
Anna Lee Boschetto, Editor, annalee@salonmagazine.ca
Laura Dunphy, President/Publisher, laura@salonmagazine.ca

Boating & Yachting

Boating Business
Owned By: Premier Publications and Shows
c/o Premier Publications and Shows, #4, 447 Speers Rd., Oakville, ON L6K 3S7
Tel: 905-842-6591; *Fax:* 905-842-4432
Toll-Free: 800-693-7986
circ@metrolandwest.com
www.boatingbusiness.ca
Circulation: 5,375
Frequency: 6 times a year
Covers issues & challenges of Canada's recreational boating industry
Jonathan Lee, Editor, 905-842-6591 ext.264, Fax: 905-842-4432, jlee@formulamediagroup.com

Poker Runs America Magazine
Owned By: Taylor Publishing Group
#2, 1121 Invicta Dr., Oakville, ON L6H 2R2
Tel: 905-844-8218; *Fax:* 905-844-8219
Toll-Free: 800-354-9145
info@pokerrunsamerica.com
www.pokerrunsamerica.com
Social Media: www.youtube.com/user/steveeditor123
twitter.com/pokerrunamerica
www .facebook.com/PokerRunsAmerica

Books

Access
Owned By: Ontario Library Association
#201, 50 Wellington St. E, Toronto, ON M5E 1C8
Tel: 416-363-3388; *Fax:* 416-941-9581
info@accessola.com
www.accessola.com
Social Media: www.youtube.com/user/ONLibraryAssoc
twitter.com/onlibraryassoc
www.fac ebook.com/accessola

Circulation: 4,500
Frequency: 4 times a year
Shelagh Paterson, Executive Director,
spaterson@accessola.com

Feliciter
c/o Canadian Library Association, #400, 1150 Morrison Dr., Ottawa, ON K2H 8S9
Tel: 613-232-9625; *Fax:* 613-563-9895
publishing@cla.ca
www.cla.ca
Social Media: www.linkedin.com/groups?gid=4137241
twitter.com/cla_web
www.facebook.c om/CanadianLibraryAssociation
Frequency: Bi-monthly
Valoree McKay, Publisher

Broadcasting

Broadcast Dialogue
18 Turtle Path, Lagoon City, ON L0K 1B0
Tel: 705-484-0752
www.broadcastdialogue.com
Circulation: 7,200
Publishers for the Canadian broadcasting industry including consultants, associations, engineers, suppliers, manufacturers & related industry managers
Howard Christensen, Publisher,
howard@broadcastdialogue.com
Ingrid Christensen, Operations, ingrid@broadcastdialogue.com

Broadcaster
Owned By: Annex-Newcom
80 Valleybrook Dr., Toronto, ON M3B 2S9
Tel: 416-510-6865; *Fax:* 416-510-5134
Toll-Free: 800-268-7742
editor@broadcastermagazine.com
www.broadcastermagazine.com
Frequency: 8 times a year
James A. Cook, Senior Publisher, 416-510-6871,
jcook@broadcastermagazine.com

Playback
Owned By: Brunico Communications Ltd.
#500, 366 Adelaide St. West, Toronto, ON M5V 1R9
Tel: 416-408-2300; *Fax:* 416-408-0870
Toll-Free: 888-278-6426
www.playbackmag.com
Social Media:
twitter.com/PlaybackOnline
www.facebook.com/playbackonline
Frequency: 25 times a year
Russell Goldstein, President & CEO, rgoldstein@brunico.com
Mary Maddever, Vice-President & Editorial Director,
mmaddever@brunico.com

Sportscaster Magazine
Previous Name: Cablecaster
Owned By: Annex-Newcom
80 Valleybrook Dr., Toronto, ON M3B 2S9
Tel: 416-442-5600
www.sportscastermagazine.ca
James Cook, Senior Publisher, 416-510-6871,
jcook@mediacastermagazine.com
Lee Rickwood, Editor, lrickwood@mediacastermagazine.com

Building & Construction

Alberta Construction Magazine
816-55 Ave. NE 2nd Fl., Calgary, AB T2E 6Y4
Tel: 403-209-3500; *Fax:* 406-245-8666
Toll-Free: 800-387-2446
circulation@junewarren-nickles.com
www.albertaconstructionmagazine.com
Circulation: 8,500
Frequency: Quarterly
Business magazine for the construction industry

Alberta Construction Magazine
Previous Name: Alberta Construction Service & Supply Directory
Owned By: JuneWarren-Nickle's Energy Group
816 - 55 Ave. NE, 2nd Fl., Calgary, AB T2E 6Y4
Tel: 403-209-3500; *Fax:* 403-245-8666
Toll-Free: 800-387-2446
www.junewarren-nickles.com/page.aspx?id=acm
Circulation: 8,500
Frequency: Quarterly
Agnes Zalewski, Publisher

Annuaire Téléphonique de la Construction du Québec
CP 590, 22, rue St-Charles, Sainte-Thérèse, QC J7E 2A4
Tél: 450-437-1600; *Téléc:* 450-437-0723
Ligne sans frais: 800-437-0547
info@optilog.com
www.construction411.com
Tirage: 7 200
Fréquence: Annuellement
Directory of construction needs
Michel Vaudrin, Éditeur & Rédacteur

BSDA Newsmagazine
Building Supply Dealers Assn. of BC, #2, 19299 - 94th Ave., Surrey, BC V4N 4E6
Tel: 604-513-2205; *Fax:* 604-513-2206
Toll-Free: 888-711-5656
www.bsiabc.ca
Circulation: 1,000
Frequency: 4 times a year
George Tracy

Building Magazine
Owned By: Annex-Newcom
80 Valleybrook Dr., Toronto, ON M3B 2S9
Tel: 416-442-5600; *Fax:* 416-510-5134
Toll-Free: 800-268-7742
www.building.ca
Social Media:
twitter.com/Building_mag
www.facebook.com/239529412803391
Circulation: 10,737
Frequency: 6 times a year
Publishing information on Canada's building products & the companies who distribute & manufacture them
Tom Arkell, Senior Publisher, 416-510-6806,
tomarkell@canadianarchitect.com
Peter Sobchak, Editorial, 416-510-5217, peter@building.ca

Canadian Apartment Magazine
Owned By: MediaEdge Inc.
c/o MediaEdge Inc., 5255 Yonge St., Toronto, ON M2N 6P4
Tel: 416-512-8186 *Toll-Free:* 866-216-0860
www.canadianapartmentmagazine.ca
Social Media: www.linkedin.com/groups?gid=3987507
twitter.com/cdnapartmentmag
www.fa cebook.com/cammediaedge
Circulation: 7,000
Frequency: 6 times a year
Scott Anderson, Editor, scotta@mediaedge.ca
Steve McLinden, Publisher, stevem@mediaedge.ca
Paul Murphy, Publisher, paulm@mediaedge.ca

Canadian Contractor
Owned By: Annex Publishing & Printing Inc.
80 Valleybrook Dr., Toronto, ON M3B 2S9
Tel: 416-442-5600
www.canadiancontractor.ca
Frequency: Monthly
Stephen Dempsey, Publisher, 416-442-5600 x 6780,
sdempsey@bizinfogroup.ca
Stephen Payne, Editor, 416-442-5600 x 6784,
rkoci@bizinfogroup.ca

Canadian Property Management (CPM)
Owned By: MediaEdge Inc.
c/o MediaEdge Inc., 5255 Yonge St., Toronto, ON M2N 6P4
Tel: 416-512-8186 *Toll-Free:* 866-216-0860
www.canadianpropertymanagement.ca
Social Media: www.linkedin.com/groups?home=&gid=3987537
twitter.com/CDNPropMgmt
www. facebook.com/cpmmediaedge
Circulation: 12,504
Frequency: 8 times a year
Sean Foley, Publisher, seanf@mediaedge.ca
Barbara Carss, Editor-in-Chief, barbc@mediaedge.ca

CondoBusiness
Owned By: MediaEdge Inc.
c/o MediaEdge Inc., 5255 Yonge St., Toronto, ON M2N 6P4
Tel: 416-512-8186 *Toll-Free:* 866-216-0860
www.condobusiness.ca
Social Media: www.linkedin.com/groups?gid=3987591
twitter.com/condobusiness
www.face book.com/condomediaedge
Circulation: 2,500
Frequency: 8 times a year
Steve McLinden, Publisher, stevem@mediaedge.ca
Scott Anderson, Editor, scotta@mediaedge.ca

Construire
L'Association de la Construction du Québec, 9200, boul Métropolitain est, Montréal, QC H1K 4L2
Tél: 514-354-0609; *Téléc:* 514-354-8292
Ligne sans frais: 888-868-3424
info@prov.acq.org
www.acqconstruire.com
Tirage: 26,500
Fréquence: 4 fois par an
Claude Girard, Rédacteur en chef

Daily Commercial News
Previous Name: Daily Commercial News & Construction Record
Reed Construction Data, 500 Hood Rd., 4th Fl., Markham, ON L3R 9Z3
Tel: 905-752-5544; *Fax:* 905-752-5450
Toll-Free: 800-959-0502
customercarecanada@cmdgroup.com
www.dailycommercialnews.com
Circulation: 4,900
Frequency: Daily

Equipment Journal
Pace Publishing Limited, #6, 5160 Explorer Dr., Mississauga, ON L4W 4T7
Tel: 905-629-7500; *Fax:* 800-210-5799
Toll-Free: 800-667-8541
info@equipmentjournal.com
www.equipmentjournal.com
Frequency: 17 issues a year, every 3 weeks
John Baker, Publisher

Formes
6718, rue Chambord, Montréal, QC H2G 3C3
Tél: 514-736-7637; *Téléc:* 514-272-3477
info@formes.ca
www.formes.ca
Fréquence: 6 fois par an

Heavy Equipment Guide
Owned By: Baum Publications Ltd.
Baum Publications Ltd., 124 - 2323 Boundary, Vancouver, BC V5M 4V8
Tel: 604-291-9900; *Fax:* 604-291-1906
heg.baumpub.com
Circulation: 21,000
Frequency: 10 times a year
Engelbert J. Baum, Publisher
Lawrence Buser, Editor, lbuser@baumpub.com

Home Builder Magazine
4819 St. Charles Blvd., Pierrefonds, QC H9H 3C7
Tel: 514-620-2200; *Fax:* 514-620-6300
homebuilder@work4.ca
www.homebuildercanada.com
Circulation: 28,000
Frequency: 6 times a year
Nachmi Artzy, Publisher

Journal Constructo
#200, 1500, boul Jules-Poitras, Saint-Laurent, QC H4N 1X7
Tél: 514-856-6600; *Téléc:* 514-339-5233
Ligne sans frais: 866-669-7326
info@groupeconstructo.com
groupeconstructo.com/publications/journal-constructo
Fréquence: 80 fois par an

Le Journal de L'Habitation
Détenteur: TC Transcontinental
Médias-Transcontinental, #900, 1265, boul Charest ouest, Québec, QC G1N 4V4
Tél: 418-686-6400; *Téléc:* 418-686-4841
redaction_quebec@transcontinental.ca
www.journalhabitation.com
Tirage: 28 000
Fréquence: 2 times a month
Yvon Lallier, Éditeur

Journal of Commerce
#101, 4299 Canada Way, Burnaby, BC V5G 1H3
Tel: 604-412-2256 *Toll-Free:* 800-959-0502
editor@journalofcommerce.com
www.joconl.com
Social Media: www.linkedin.com/groups?gid=1867398
twitter.com/JOC_Canada
www.faceboo k.com/pages/Journal-of-Commerce/117845964137
Frequency: 2 times a week

LBMAO Reporter
The Lumber & Building Materials Association of Ontario (LMBAO), 391 Matheson Blvd. East, #A, Mississauga, ON L4Z 2H2
Tel: 905-625-1084; *Fax:* 905-625-3006
Toll-Free: 888-365-2626
www.lbmao.on.ca
Frequency: 6 times a year
David Campbell, Editor-in-Chief

On-Site
Owned By: Annex Publishing & Printing Inc.
80 Valleybrook Dr., Toronto, ON M3B 2S9
Tel: 416-510-6794; *Fax:* 416-510-5140
www.on-sitemag.com
Circulation: 22,000
Frequency: 4 times a year
Serving the commercial construction industry.
Corinne Lynds, Editor, clynds@on-sitemag.com
Peter Leonard, Publisher, pleonard@on-sitemag.com

Ontario Home Builder
Owned By: Ontario Home Builders' Association
#101, 20 Upjohn Rd., Toronto, ON M3B 2V9
Tel: 416-443-1545; *Fax:* 416-443-9982
Toll-Free: 800-387-0109
ohba.ca
Circulation: 30,600
Frequency: 6 times a year
Sheryl Humphreys, Publisher

Ottawa Construction News
Tel: 613-224-3460; *Fax:* 613-224-1076
Toll-Free: 888-432-3555
www.ottawaconstructionnews.com
Circulation: 12,000
Frequency: 12 times a year
Mark Buckshon, Publisher
Terry Tinkess, Editor

Québec Habitation
5930, boul Louis-H.-Lafontaine, Anjou, QC H1M 1S7
Tél: 514-353-9960; *Téléc:* 514-353-4825
Ligne sans frais: 800-468-8160
redaction@quebec-habitation.com
www.apchq.com
Tirage: 39,835
Fréquence: 6 fois par an
Jean Garon, Rédacteur-en-chef

Sanitation Canada
Owned By: MediaEdge Inc.
3 Kennett Dr., Whitby, ON L1P 1L5
Tel: 905-430-7267; *Fax:* 905-430-6418
www.sanitationcanada.com
Frequency: 6 times a year
Tanja Nowotny, Publisher

Business & Finance

Advisor's Edge
Owned By: Rogers Media Inc.
1 Mount Pleasant Rd., Toronto, ON M4Y 2Y5
Tel: 416-764-3859; *Fax:* 416-764-3943
www.advisor.ca
Social Media: www.linkedin.com/company/advisor-ca
twitter.com/advisorca
Circulation: 35,963
Frequency: 10 times a year
Advisor's Edge magazine is an independent Canadian publication focused solely on the information needs of Canadian retail financial advisors (brokers, financial planners, insurance specialists, mutual fund salespeople & bank-based consultants). With a strong emphasis on practice management, the magazine helps advisors stay on top of industry trends, investment insurance products & strategies, as well as marketing & client relationship best practices
Donna Kerry, Publisher, donna.kerry@rci.rogers.com
Philip Porado, Director, Content, philip.porado@rci.rogers.com

Les Affaires
Détenteur: TC Transcontinental
1100, boul René-Lévesque ouest, 24e étage, Montréal, QC H3B 4X9
Tél: 514-392-9000; *Téléc:* 514-392-1586
Ligne sans frais: 800-361-7215
lesaffaires@cdsglobal.ca
www.lesaffaires.com
Médias sociaux: www.youtube.com/user/LesAffairesTV
twitter.com/la_lesaffaires
www.face book.com/100306918236
Tirage: 77 174
Fréquence: 46 fois par an; aussi Affaires 500, PME, Affaires plus (10 fois par an, 93 288)
Il est reconnu pour sa couverture des grandes sociétés canadiennes, des petites et moyennes entreprises québécoises, de l'économie canadienne et des affaires publiques. La moitié de son contenu est consacrée aux finances personnelles et aux placements avec diverses pages spécialisées, des tableaux et des graphiques.
Sylvain Bédard, Éditeur
Géraldine Martin, Éditrice adjointe et rédactrice-en-chef

Affaires Plus Magazine
Détenteur: TC Transcontinental
1100, boul René-Lévesque 24e étage, Montréal, QC H3B 4X9
Tél: 514-392-9000; *Téléc:* 514-392-4726
Ligne sans frais: 800-361-7215
lesaffaires@cdsglobal.ca
www.lesaffaires.com
Médias sociaux: www.youtube.com/user/LesAffairesTV
twitter.com/la_lesaffaires
www.face book.com/100306918236
Tirage: 77 000
Fréquence: 10 fois par an
Créé en 1978, le magazine Affaires PLUS est le magazine d'affaires au plus fort tirage et au plus fort lectorat au Québec. C'est aussi la plus personnelle des publications d'affaires de Médias Transcontinental. Le magazine est bâti autour de trois axes: mon argent, ma carrière, ma vie, qui déterminent à la fois le positionnement et le contenu d'Affaires PLUS
Sylvain Bédard, Éditeur
Géraldine Martin, Éditrice adjointe et rédactrice-en-chef

Alberta Venture
Owned By: Venture Publishing Inc.
10259 - 105 St., Edmonton, AB T5J 1E3
Tel: 780-990-0839; *Fax:* 780-425-4921
Toll-Free: 866-227-4276
admin@albertaventure.com
www.albertaventure.com
Other information: www.instagram.com/albertaventure
Social Media:
www.linkedin.com/groups/Alberta-Venture-3230251
twitter.com/AlbertaVenture
www.facebook.com/albertaventure
Circulation: 40,800
Frequency: Monthly
Alberta Venture keeps readers informed about Alberta's business community, including trends, issues, people and events.
Ruth Kelly, President & CEO

All in the Family Magazine
Owned By: Business Link Media Group
#200, 36 Hiscott St., St Catharines, ON L2R 1C8
Tel: 905-646-9366; *Fax:* 905-646-5486
info@businesslinkmedia.com
www.businesslinkmedia.com
Social Media:
twitter.com/TheBusinessLink
www.facebook.com/BusinessLinkMedia
Focuses on issues facing family businesses.
Adam Shields, Co-Publisher, adam@businesslinkmedia.com
Jim Shields, Co-Publisher, jim@businesslinkmedia.com

Atlantic Business Magazine
Owned By: Communications Ten Limited
PO Box 2356 C, #302, 95 LeMarchant Rd., St. John's, NL A1C 6E7
Tel: 709-726-9300; *Fax:* 709-726-3013
www.atlanticbusinessmagazine.com
Social Media:
www.linkedin.com/company/atlantic-business-magazine
twitter.com/Atlantic Bus
www.facebook.com/atlanticbusinessmagazine
Circulation: 35,000
Frequency: Bi-monthly
An independently owned, bi-monthly glossy publication that covers all areas of business within the four Atlantic provinces.
Hubert Hutton, Publisher, 709-726-9300 ext.226, hhutton@atlanticbusinessmagazine.com
Dawn Chafe, Executive Editor, 709-726-9300 ext.224, dchafe@atlanticbusinessmagazine.com

Avantages
Détenteur: Les Éditions Rogers limitée
1200, ave McGill College, 8e étage, Montréal, QC H3B 4G7
Tél: 514-843-5141; *Téléc:* 514-843-2180
avantages@halldata.com
www.conseiller.ca/avantages
Médias sociaux:
twitter.com/revueavantages
Tirage: 5,056
Fréquence: 8 fois par an
Garth Thomas, Éditeur exécutif, Garth.Thomas@advisor.rogers.com
Simeon Goldstein, Rédacteur-en-chef, Simeon.Goldstein@avantages.rogers.com

Backbone Magazine
187 Rondoval Cres., North Vancouver, BC V7N 2W6
Tel: 604-986-5352; *Fax:* 604-986-5309
info@backbonemag.com
www.backbonemag.com
Social Media:
www.linkedin.com/groups/Backbone-magazine-3999379
twitter.com/BackboneMa g
www.facebook.com/backbone.canada
Circulation: 115,000
Frequency: 6 times a year
Backbone magazine's aim is to provide business people with a tangible tool to enhance the way they do business in Canada's New Economy
Steve Dietrich, Publisher & Editor in Chief, sdietrich@backbonemag.com

BCBusiness
Owned By: Canada Wide Media Limited
#230, 4321 Still Creek Dr., Burnaby, BC
Tel: 604-299-7311; *Fax:* 604-299-9188
www.bcbusiness.ca
Social Media: www.linkedin.com/groups?home=&gid=904687
twitter.com/bcbusiness
www.fa cebook.com/bcbusiness
Focuses on business in British Columbia. Prints annual special editions: B.C.'s Top 100 Companies, Entrepreneur of the Year, & the Best Companies to Work for in B.C.
Matt O'Grady, Editor-in-Chief, mogrady@canadawide.com

BCBusiness Magazine
Owned By: Canada Wide Media Limited
4180 Lougheed Hwy. 4th Fl., Burnaby, BC V5C 6A7
Tel: 604-299-7311; *Fax:* 604-299-9188
bcb@canadawide.com
www.bcbusinessonline.ca
Social Media: www.youtube.com/user/BCBusinessOnline
twitter.com/bcbusiness
www.faceb ook.com/bcbusiness
Circulation: 26,000
Frequency: Monthly
An authoritative voice on the province's business scene, BCBusiness goes beyond the headlines to give readers valuable, relevant insights into today's trends & issues
Peter Legge, Publisher
Matt O'Grady, Editor-in-Chief, mogrady@canadawide.com

Benefits & Pensions Monitor
Owned By: Powershift Communications Inc.
c/o Powershift Communications Inc., #501, 245 Fairview Mall Dr., Toronto, ON M2J 4T1
Tel: 416-494-1066; *Fax:* 416-494-2536
info@powershift.ca
www.bpmmagazine.com
Circulation: 23,017
Frequency: 8 times a year
The magazine also publishees interactive online issues.
John McLaine, Publisher & Editorial Director, jmclaine@powershift.ca
Joe Hornyak, Executive Editor, jhornyak@powershift.ca

Benefits Canada
Owned By: Rogers Media Inc.
1 Mount Pleasant Rd., 12th Fl., Toronto, ON M4Y 2Y5
Toll-Free: 855-748-3677
benefits@halldata.com
www.benefitscanada.com
Other information: Alt. E-mail: BenCanService@rci.rogers.com
Social Media:
twitter.com/BenCanMag
Circulation: 18,200
Frequency: Monthly
Provides information & analysis on pensions, benefits, healthcare and investments to key decision-makers who manage employer-sponsored pension and benefits plans. The publication targets the plan sponsor community, particularly those employers with more than 500 employees
Garth Thomas, Senior Director, Business Publishing, 416-764-3806, garth.thomas@rci.rogers.com
Alyssa Hodder, Editor, 416-764-3823, alyssa.hodder@rci.rogers.com

BIZ Magazine
Previous Name: BIZ Hamilton/Halton Business Report; Hamilton Business Report
Owned By: Town Media Inc.
940 Main St. West, Hamilton, ON L8S 1B1
Tel: 905-522-6117; *Fax:* 905-769-1105
www.bizmagazine.ca
Social Media:
twitter.com/biz_mag
www.facebook.com/122928897735915
Circulation: 24,000
Frequency: 4 times a year
Business publication in the Hamilton/Burlington region, with award-winning features, profiles, real-life photography and controversial opinions
Scott Smith, Publisher, Digital & Print
Marc Skulnick, Editor, marc.skulnick@sunmedia.ca

The Bottom Line
Owned By: LexisNexis Canada Ltd.
#700, 123 Commerce Valley Dr. East, Markham, ON L3T 7W8
Tel: 905-479-2665; *Fax:* 905-479-6460
Toll-Free: 800-668-6481
www.thebottomlinenews.ca
Social Media: www.youtube.com/lexisnexiscanada
twitter.com/lexisnexiscan
www.faceboo k.com/lexisnexiscanada
Circulation: 29,030
Frequency: 16 times a year
The Bottom Line is an independent & specialized business periodical that keeps accredited professional accountants, financial managers, & consultants abreast of news, trends, & technology within the industry
Ann McDonagh, Publisher
Robert Kelly, Managing Editor
Adam Malik, Assistant & Layout Editor, adam.malik@lexisnexis.ca

Business Edge News Magazine
#201, 318 - 26th Ave. SW, Calgary, AB T2S 2T9
Tel: 403-769-9359
info@businessedge.ca
www.businessedge.ca
Social Media:
www.facebook.com/BusinessEdgeNewsMagazine
Circulation: 157,000
Frequency: 18 times annually
Delivered to businesses throughout Western & Central Canada.
Rob Driscoll, Publisher, Rob@BusinessEdge.ca

Business Elite Canada
4 Robert Speck Pwky., 15th Fl., Mississauga, ON L4Z 1S1
Tel: 905-366-7301; *Fax:* 905-248-3329
info@becmag.com
www.businesselitecanada.com
Social Media:
twitter.com/BECMagazine
www.facebook.com/354069204610067
Circulation: 40,000
Business Elite Canada focuses on successful businesses & business leaders.
Sanjeev Amir, Publisher, samir@becmag.com
Cheryl Long, Editor, editor@becmag.com

Business Examiner
Previous Name: Business Examiner - South Island Edition
Owned By: Invest Northwest Publishing Ltd.
25 Cavan St., Nanaimo, BC V9R 2T9
Fax: 250-758-2668
Toll-Free: 866-758-2684
info@businessexaminer.ca
www.businessexaminer.ca
Circulation: 41,900
Frequency: Bi-monthly
Business Examiner publishing four regional editions: Victoria, Vancouver Island, Thompson Okanagan & Peace Cariboo Skeena.
Mark MacDonald, Publisher, mark@businessexaminer.ca
Shawn Bishop, Contact, Sales, Vancouver Island, shawn@businessexaminer.ca
Josh Higgins, Contact, Sales, Thompson Okanagan, josh@businessexaminer.ca
Joanne Iormetti, Contact, Sales, Thompson Okanagan, joanne@businessexaminer.ca
Thom Klos, Contact, Sales, Victoria, thom@businessexaminer.ca

Business in Calgary
#1025, 101 - 6th Ave. SW, Calgary, AB T2P 3P4
Tel: 403-264-3270; *Fax:* 403-264-3276
Toll-Free: 800-465-0322
info@businessincalgary.com
www.businessincalgary.com
Circulation: 33,500
Frequency: Monthly
Articles about the people, trends & events that make Calgary a prominent business centre in the west.
Pat Ottmann, Publisher, pat@businessincalgary.comcom
Tim Ottmann, Publisher, tim@businessincalgary.comcom
John Hardy, Editor, hardy@businessincalgary.com

Business in Focus
Owned By: FMG Publishing Inc.
#210, 1310 Hollis St., Halifax, NS
Tel: 647-479-2163
accounts@fmgpublishing.com
www.businessreviewcanada.ca
Circulation: 363,100
Frequency: Monthly
Provides insight into North American business through interviews with Managers, Founders, Directors & CEOs.
Tim Hocken, Editor, tim.hocken@fmgpublishing.com

The Business Link Hamilton
Owned By: Business Link Media Group
#200, 36 Hiscott St., St Catharines, ON L2R 1C8
Tel: 905-646-9366; *Fax:* 905-646-5486
info@businesslinkmedia.com
www.businesslinkhamilton.com
Social Media:
twitter.com/TheBusinessLink
www.facebook.com/BusinessLinkMedia
Serving the Hamilton-Halton region.
Jim Shields, Publisher, jim@businesslinkmedia.com

The Business Link Niagara
Owned By: Business Link Media Group
#200, 36 Hiscott St., St Catharines, ON L2R 1C8
Tel: 905-646-9366; *Fax:* 905-646-5486
info@businesslinkmedia.com
www.businesslinkhamilton.com
Social Media:
twitter.com/TheBusinessLink
www.facebook.com/BusinessLinkMedia
Jim Shields, Publisher, jim@businesslinkmedia.com

Business London
Previous Name: London Business Magazine
Owned By: Sun Media Corp.
PO Box 7400, 1147 Gainsborough Rd., London, ON N5Y 4X3
Tel: 519-471-2907; *Fax:* 519-473-7859
editorial@businesslondon.ca
www.businesslondon.ca
Circulation: 12,000
Frequency: Monthly
The Magazine provides unparalleled behind-the-scenes coverage, chronicling companies on the move & putting faces to faceless events.
Gord Delamont, Publisher & Editor, gord.delamont@sunmedia.ca

Business Review Canada (BRCA)
www.businessreviewcanada.ca
Social Media:
www.facebook.com/BizReviewCanada
Digital magazine aimed at business executives.
Cutter Slagle, Editor, cutter.slagle@businessreviewcanada.ca

Canada Japan Journal
Previous Name: Canada Japan Business Journal
Also Known As: Japan Advertising Ltd.
c/o Japan Advertising Ltd., #410, 1199 West Pender St., Vancouver, BC V6E 2R1
Tel: 604-688-0303; *Fax:* 604-688-1487
info@canadajournal.com
www.canadajournal.com
Circulation: 15,750
Frequency: Monthly; Japanese
Taka Aoki, Publisher

Canadian Business
Owned By: Rogers Media Inc.
1 Mount Pleasant Rd., 11th Fl., Toronto, ON M4Y 2Y5
Tel: 416-764-2000 *Toll-Free:* 800-465-0700
www.canadianbusiness.com
Social Media:
www.linkedin.com/company/canadian-business-magazine
twitter.com/cdnbiz
www.facebook.com/cdnbiz
Circulation: 80,064
Frequency: Bi-weekly
Canadian Business is Canada's longest-publishing business magazine, providing content for Canadian corporate managers & executives.
Ian Portsmouth, Publisher
James Cowan, Editor-in-Chief

Canadian Business Executive
Previous Name: CA Business Executive
Owned By: TrueLine Publishing, LLC
482 Congress St., Portland, ME
Tel: 207-517-8074; *Fax:* 240-396-5940
info@truelinepublishing.com
www.canadianbusinessexecutive.com
Social Media: www.linkedin.com/groups?gid=8184014
twitter.com/cabusinessexec
www.facebook.com/246177308883523
Trade publication for Canadian business leaders of the following sectors: construction, manufacturing, energy & power, healthcare, technology, food & drink, hospitality & gaming, education, mining & exploration, & agriculture. TrueLine Publishing, LLC has offices in Maine & Maryland.
Haj Carr, President & CEO, TrueLine Publishing, LLC
Jeanee Dudley, Managing Editor

Canadian Business Franchise/L'entreprise
Owned By: Kenilworth Media Inc.
c/o Kenilworth Media Inc., #710, 15 Wertheim Ct., Richmond Hill, ON L4B 3H7
Tel: 905-771-7333; *Fax:* 905-771-7336
Toll-Free: 800-409-8688
editor@franchiseinfo.ca
www.franchiseinfo.ca
Social Media:
www.twitter.com/FranchiseFYI
www.facebook.com/CanadianBusinessFranchiseMagazine
Frequency: Bi-monthly
Features articles on franchise advice from bankers, lawyers & franchise specialists.
Ellen Kral, Group Publisher & CEO, Kenilworth Publishing

Canadian Equipment Finance
Owned By: Lloydmedia, Inc.
137 Main St. North, 3rd Fl., Markham, ON L3P 1Y2
Tel: 905-201-6600; *Fax:* 905-201-6601
Toll-Free: 800-668-1838
www.canadianequipmentfinance.com
Frequency: Bi-monthly
Steve Lloyd, President, steve@canadianequipmentfinance.com
Karen Treml, Editor, karen@canadianequipmentfinance.com

Canadian Gaming Business
Owned By: MediaEdge Inc.
c/o MediaEdge Inc., 5255 Yonge St., Toronto, ON M2N 6P4
Tel: 416-512-8186 *Toll-Free:* 866-216-0860
www.canadiangamingbusiness.com
Chuck Nervick, Publisher, chuckn@mediaedge.ca
Sean Moon, Managing Editor, seanm@mediaedge.ca

Canadian Investment Review
Owned By: Rogers Media Inc.
1 Mount Pleasant Ave., 12th Fl., Toronto, ON M4Y 2Y5
www.investmentreview.com
Circulation: 4,700
Frequency: 4 times a year
Forum for academics, institutional investors & industry practitioners to exchange ideas on the capital markets, investment & economic theory, & the related sociology & demographics.
Alison Webb, Publisher, 416-764-3876, alison.webb@rci.rogers.com
Caroline Cakebread, Editor, 416-624-3505, caroline.cakebread@rogers.com

The Canadian Manager
Canadian Institute of Management, 15 Collier St., Lower Level, Barrie, ON L4M 1G5
Tel: 705-725-8926; *Fax:* 705-725-8196
office@cim.ca
cim.ca/resources/publications/canmanager
Frequency: Quarterly
The Canadian Manager is published 4 times per year by the Canadian Institute of Management (CIM), with a readership over 12,000 (approx.)
Jennifer Tracy, Coordinator, Communications & Membership Services, CIM, jennifer.membership@cim.ca

Canadian Not-For-Profit News
Owned By: Carswell
One Corporate Plaza, 2075 Kennedy Rd., Toronto, ON M1T 3V4
Tel: 416-609-8000; *Fax:* 416-298-5094
www.carswell.com
Frequency: Monthly
Source of current information on the tax implications and practical considerations relating to the most relevant and timely issues surrounding registered charities and other non-profit organizations

The Canadian Taxpayer
Owned By: Carswell
c/o Carswell, One Corporate Plaza, 2075 Kennedy Rd., Toronto, ON M1T 3V4
Tel: 416-609-8000; *Fax:* 416-298-5082
Toll-Free: 800-387-5164
carswell.orders@thomson.com
www.carswell.com
Circulation: 1,000
Frequency: 24 times a year
Provides current news on tax trends, political appointments, tax policies, landmark cases & more. Quarterly consolidated topical indexes are included.
Arthur B.C. Drache, Editor Q.C.

Canadian Treasurer (CT)
Owned By: Lloydmedia, Inc.
137 Main St. North, 3rd Fl., Markham, ON L3P 1Y2
Tel: 905-201-6600; *Fax:* 905-201-6601
Toll-Free: 800-668-1838
www.canadiantreasurer.com
Frequency: Quarterly
Steve Lloyd, President, steve@canadiantreasurer.com
Karen Treml, Editor, karen@canadiantreasurer.com

CGA Magazine
Certified General Accountants Association of Canada, #100, 4200 North Fraser Way, Burnaby, BC V5J 5K7
Toll-Free: 800-663-1529
cgamagazine@cga-canada.org
cgamagazine.ca
Other information: Subscriptions, E-mail: subscription@cga-canada.org
Social Media: www.linkedin.com/groups?gid=2111514
twitter.com/cgacanada
www.facebook .com/cgacanada
Circulation: 75,000
Frequency: Bi-yearly
Contents include articles about professional accountancy & news from the business & regulatory sectors.
Lorriane Pitt, Publisher
Anya Levykh, Managing Editor

Chamber Vision
Owned By: Metro Guide Publishing
Greater Moncton Chamber of Commerce, #200, 1273 Main St., Moncton, NB E1C 0P4
Tel: 506-857-2883
info@gmcc.nb.ca
gmcc.nb.ca/en-us/media/publications/chambervision.aspx
Social Media:
twitter.com/MonctonChamber
www.facebook.com/GreaterMonctonChamberOfCommerce
Circulation: 5000
Frequency: 6 times a year

Commerce & Industry
Owned By: Mercury Publications Ltd.
c/o Mercury Publications Ltd., #16, 1313 Border St., Winnipeg, MB R3H 0X4
Tel: 204-954-2085; *Fax:* 204-954-2057
Toll-Free: 800-337-6372
www.commerceindustry.ca
Circulation: 17,000
Frequency: bi-monthly
A national publication focused on the industrial, manufacturing, resource, transportation & construction sectors. Each issue offers a large variety of sector analysis, in-depth company profiles & reports on key areas of interest to the magazine's target audience.
Edna Saito, National Accounts Manager

Conseiller
Détenteur: Les Éditions Rogers limitée
1200, ave McGill College, 8e étage, Montréal, QC H3B 4G7
Tél: 514-843-5141; *Téléc:* 514-843-2180
www.conseiller.ca
Médias sociaux: www.linkedin.com/groups?gid=2420029
twitter.com/Conseillerca
www.faceb ook.com/conseillerca
Tirage: 9,173
Fréquence: 10 fois par an
Donna Kerry, Éditrice, donna.kerry@advisor.rogers.com

Contact Management
Owned By: Lloydmedia, Inc.
137 Main St. North, 3rd Fl., Markham, ON L3P 1Y2
Tel: 905-201-6600; *Fax:* 905-201-6601
Toll-Free: 800-668-1838
www.contactmanagement.ca
Social Media:
twitter.com/ContactMgmtMag
Circulation: 5,000
Frequency: Quarterly
Steve Lloyd, President, steve@contactmanagement.ca

The Corporate Ethics Monitor
c/o EthicScan, PO Box 54034, Toronto, ON M6A 3B7
Tel: 416-783-6776; *Fax:* 416-783-7386
info@ethicscan.ca
www.ethicscan.ca
Social Media: www.linkedin.com/company/ethicscan
twitter.com/EthicScan
www.facebook. com/EthicScan
Circulation: 400
Frequency: Bi-monthly
The Corporate Ethics Monitor features articles & stories that deal with recognizing & enhancing ethics in the workplace.

Corporate Knights (CK)
Owned By: Corporate Knights Inc.
#207, 147 Spadina Ave., Toronto, ON M5V 2L7
Tel: 416-203-4674 *Toll-Free:* 416-946-1770
inquiries@corporateknights.com
www.corporateknights.com
Social Media:
twitter.com/corporateknight
www.facebook.com/corporateknights
Circulation: 125,000
Frequency: Quarterly
The magazine's focus is corporate responsibility.
Toby Heaps, President & Publisher
Tyler Hamilton, Editor-in-Chief

CPA Magazine
Previous Name: CA Magazine; CMA Management Magazine
277 Wellington St. West, Toronto, ON M5V 3H2
Tel: 416-977-3222; *Fax:* 416-977-8585
Toll-Free: 800-268-3793
www.cpacanada.ca/en/connecting-and-news/cpa-magazine
Circulation: 242,377
Frequency: 10 times a year
CPA Magazine is published by Chartered Professional Accountants Canada (CPA). Articles about careers in chartered accounting are featured while current issues are discussed & explained. The magazine also deals with a wide variety of business topics from the Chartered Accountant's perspective
Nicholas Cheung, Vice-President, Member Services, CPA Canada
Okey Chigbo, Editor

Defined Benefit Monitor
Owned By: Powershift Communications Inc.
c/o Powershift Communications Inc., #501, 245 Fairview Mall Dr., Toronto, ON M2J 4T1
Tel: 416-494-1066; *Fax:* 416-494-2536
www.bpmmagazine.com
Other information: Powershift URL: www.powershift.ca
Frequency: 2 times a year
Sent to a portion of Benefits & Pensions Monitor's circulation list.
John L. McLaine, Publisher & Editorial Director, jmclaine@powershift.ca

Defined Contribution Monitor
Owned By: Powershift Communications Inc.
c/o Powershift Communications Inc., #501, 245 Fairview Mall Dr., Toronto, ON M2J 4T1
Tel: 416-494-1066; *Fax:* 416-494-2536
www.bpmmagazine.com
Other information: Powershift URL: www.powershift.ca
Frequency: 2 times a year
Sent to a portion of Benefits & Pensions Monitor's circulation list.
John L. McLaine, Publisher & Editorial Director, jmclaine@powershift.ca

L'Edition Le Journal des Gens d'Affaires
Détenteur: L'Edition Commerciale
#400, 11905 rue Notre-Dame E, Montréal, QC H1B 2Y4
Tél: 514-257-1000; *Téléc:* 514-257-7505
www.journaledition.com
Tirage: 29 700
Fréquence: Mensuel
Alain Dulong, Président, Éditeur, a.dulong@journaledition.com
Jean-Claude Battle, Rédacteur en Chef, redaction@journaledition.com

Edmonton Commerce News: The Voice of Business in Edmonton
Edmonton Chamber of Commerce, #700, 9990 Jasper Ave. NW, Edmonton, AB T5J 1P7
Tel: 780-426-4620; *Fax:* 780-424-7946
info@edmontonchamber.com
edmontoncommercenews.com
Social Media: www.youtube.com/edmontonchamber
twitter.com/edmontonchamber
www.fac ebook.com/EdmontonChamber
Circulation: 28,000
Frequency: 11 times a year
The official publication of the Edmonton Chamber of Commerce is Commerce News. The publication covers business issues & is of interest to Edmonton's business community, community leaders, & Chamber of Commerce members.
Bobbi-Sue Menard, Editorial Contact, bmenard@edmontonchamber.com
Kathy Kelly, Advertising Contact, kkelley@venturepublishing.ca

Entreprendre
2045, rue de Vouvray, Laval, QC H7M 3J9
Tél: 450-669-8373; *Téléc:* 450-669-9078
www.entreprendre.ca
Tirage: 60 000
Fréquence: 10 fois par an
Le magazine Entreprendre rejoint un auditoire exceptionnel de décideurs du monde des affaires. Outil d'information qui développe des références et éclaire la nature profonde de l'entrepreneurship au Québec
Edmond Bourque, Publisher, ebourque@entreprendre.ca

Exchange Magazine for Business
Owned By: Exchange Business Communication Inc.
c/o Exchange Business Communication Inc., PO Box 248, Waterloo, ON N2J 4A4
Tel: 519-886-0298; *Fax:* 519-886-6409
editor@exchangemagazine.com
www.exchangemagazine.com
Social Media:
twitter.com/ExMorningPost
Circulation: 17,500
Frequency: 9 times a year
Covers business news in the Kitchener-Waterloo area
Jon Rohr, Editor-in-chief, jon.rohr@exchangemagazine.com

Finance et Investissement
Owned By: TC Transcontinental
1100, boul René-Lévesque ouest, 24e étage, Montréal, QC H3B 4X9
Tel: 514-392-9000; *Fax:* 514-392-4726
redaction@finance-investissement.com
www.finance-investissement.com
Circulation: 30,000
Frequency: irregulier
Depuis son lancement en novembre 1999, le journal Finance et Investissement est devenu la source d'information privilégiée des représentants en épargne collective, des conseillers en valeurs mobilières, des conseillers en sécurité financière et des planificateurs financiers
Christian Benoit-Lapointe, Rédacteur en chef

Financial Operations
Owned By: Lloydmedia, Inc.
137 Main St. North, 3rd Fl., Markham, ON L3P 1Y2
Tel: 905-201-6600; *Fax:* 905-201-6601
Toll-Free: 800-668-1838
financialoperations.ca
Frequency: Quarterly
Karen Treml, Editorial Contact, 905-201-6600 Ext.223

Financial Post Business Magazine
Previous Name: National Post Business
Owned By: Postmedia Network Inc.
365 Bloor St. East, 3rd Fl., Toronto, ON M4W 3L4
Tel: 416-386-2828; *Fax:* 416-386-2836
Toll-Free: 800-267-6568
www.financialpost.com/magazine
Social Media:
twitter.com/FinPostMagazine
www.facebook.com/225240580836032
Circulation: 289,000
Frequency: 12 times a year
Terence Corcoran, Editor

FlashFinance
#100, 321, rue de la Commune, Montréal, QC H2Y 2E1
Tel: 514-289-9595; *Fax:* 514-289-9527
www.flashfinance.ca

Circulation: 2 000
Frequency: Weekly
Outil privilégié d'information du monde de l'assurance et de la finance, FlashFinance.ca joint des milliers de dirigeants de compagnies d'assurance, de propriétaires de cabinets, de directeurs de courtage, et de conseillers financiers
Hubert Roy, Rédacteur en chef, hubert.roy@flashfinance.ca

Franchise Canada Directory
Canadian Franchise Association, #116, 5399 Eglinton Ave. West, Toronto, ON M9C 5K6
Tel: 905-625-2896; *Fax:* 905-625-9076
Toll-Free: 800-665-4232
info@cfa.ca
www.cfa.ca
Frequency: Annually
John Schofield, Editor

FranchiseCanada Magazine
c/o Canadian Franchise Association, #116, 5399 Eglinton Ave. West, Toronto, ON M9C 5K6
Tel: 416-695-2896; *Fax:* 416-695-1950
Toll-Free: 800-665-4232
editor@cfa.ca
fc.lookforafranchise.ca
Circulation: 6,000
Frequency: bi-monthly
A bi-monthly magazine published by the Canadian Franchise Association, geared at entrepreneurs interested in acquiring a franchise. Franchise Canada Magazine contains editorial from authorities in the industry as well as tips on how to establish a successful franchise.
Lauren d'Entremont, Editor, CFA Publications

The Golden Highway
Owned By: Business Link Media Group
#200, 36 Hiscott St., St Catharines, ON L2R 1C8
Tel: 905-646-9366; *Fax:* 905-646-5486
info@businesslinkmedia.com
www.businesslinkmedia.com
Social Media:
twitter.com/TheBusinessLink
www.facebook.com/BusinessLinkMedia
Historic stories & photos, as well as profiles of businesses & communities found along the Queen Elizabeth Way.

GST & Commodity Tax
Owned By: Carswell
One Corporate Plaza, 2075 Kennedy Rd., Toronto, ON M1T 3V4
Tel: 416-609-8000; *Fax:* 416-298-5094
www.carswell.com
The exclusive source for what leading experts are saying about the latest developments in GST, federal and provincial sales and commodity taxes, and customs and excise duties

HUB NOW
c/o Truro & District Chamber of Commerce, 605 Prince St., Truro, NS B2N 5B6
Tel: 902-895-6328; *Fax:* 902-897-6641
www.hubnow.ca
Other information: Truro Chamber URL: www.trurocolchesterchamber.com
Social Media:
twitter.com/TruroCoC
www.facebook.com/202576676450847
Circulation: 5,000
Frequency: Monthly
Free local publication dedicated to matters affecting Colchester County. Also provides a platform for the Central Nova Business News, the business news publication of the Truo & Colchester Chamber of Commerce.
Leith Orr, Publisher, Truro & District Chamber of Commerce, 902-422-4990, leith@advocatemediainc.com
Scott MacKinnon, General Manager, Truro & District Chamber of Commerce, 902-485-8014, scott@advocatemediainc.com
Alan Johnson, Exectuive Director, Truro & District Chamber of Commerce

Huronia Business Times
Owned By: Metroland Media Group Ltd.
21 Patterson Rd., Barrie, ON L4N 7W6
Tel: 705-329-2058; *Fax:* 705-329-2059
www.huroniabusinesstimes.com
Other information: Advertising, Phone: 705-728-3090; Fax: 705-728-7716
Circulation: 12,000
Frequency: Monthly
Purchased by Metroland Business Publications in September of 1998, Huronia Business Times, & its sister publication the Mississauga Business Times, was formerly owned by North Island Publishing from 1992-1998. Metroland also publishes five other Business Times newspapers in southern Ontario

Ian Proudfoot, Publisher
Martin Melbourne, Editor, hbteditor@simcoe.com

Investment Executive (IE)
Owned By: TC Transcontinental
#100, 25 Sheppard Ave. West, Toronto, ON M2N 6S7
Tel: 416-733-7600; *Fax:* 416-218-3624
Toll-Free: 888-366-4200
editorial@investmentexecutive.com
www.investmentexecutive.com
Social Media: www.linkedin.com/company/investment-executive
twitter.com/IE_Canada
Circulation: 120,000
Frequency: 16 times a year
Investment Executive is Canada's national newspaper for financial service industry professionals. Topics such as mutual funds, investment research, technology, estate planning, tax, building relationships with clients & developing products & services for the client of the future. Sister publication is Finance et Investissement.
Tracy LeMay, Editor-in-Chief
Ozy Camadu, Sales Director, Sales, 416-218-3677, ocamadu@investmentexecutive.ca

Investor's Digest of Canada
Also Known As: The Digest
Owned By: MPL Communications Inc.
c/o MPL Communications Inc., #700, 133 Richmond St. West, Toronto, ON M5H 3M8
Tel: 416-869-1177 *Toll-Free:* 800-504-8846
customers@mplcomm.com
www.adviceforinvestors.com
Circulation: 42,912
Frequency: 24 times a year
Devoted to uncovering profitable opportunities in every area of investing, using the insights of Canada's leading investment professionals
Michael Popovich, Associate Editor

Ivey Business Journal (IBJ)
Previous Name: Quarterly Review of Commerce; Business Quarterly
c/o Richard Ivey School of Business, University of Western Ontario, London, ON N6A 3K7
Tel: 416-923-9945
www.iveybusinessjournal.com
Social Media: www.linkedin.com/company/ivey-business-school
twitter.com/IveyBusiness
www.facebook.com/iveybusiness
Circulation: 12,013
Frequency: 6 times a year
Covers articles about e-business, managing uncertainty, knowledge management, marketing, strategy & other topics that managers need to know more about to steer their firms to success.
Thomas Watson, Editor, watson@ivey.ca

Kootenay Business Magazine
Owned By: Koocanusa Publications Inc.
#100, 100 - 7th Ave. South, Crawbrook, BC V1C 2J4
Tel: 250-426-7253; *Fax:* 250-426-4125
Toll-Free: 800-663-8555
www.kootenaybiz.com
Social Media: www.flickr.com/photos/kootenaybusiness
twitter.com/kootbusiness
Circulation: 9,400
Frequency: 6 times a year
Kootenay Business magazine is free to businesses within the Kootenay/ Columbia/ Boundary/ Revelstoke area.
Keith Powell, Publisher, publisher@kpimedia.com

Listed Magazine
c/o Canadian Media Connection, 25 Isabella St., Toronto, ON M4Y 1M7
Tel: 416-964-3247; *Fax:* 416-964-0964
listedmag.com
Circulation: 10,000
Frequency: Quarterly
Listed provides content for senior executives & board members of Canadian listed companies.
Marty Tully, Publisher, marty@listedmag.com
Brian Banks, Editorial Director, brian@listedmag.com

MBiz Magazine
c/o Manitoba Chambers of Commerce, 227 Portage Ave., Winnipeg, MB R3B 2A6
Tel: 204-948-0100; *Fax:* 204-948-0110
Toll-Free: 877-444-5222
www.mbchamber.mb.ca
Magazine designed for chambers of commerce, about chambers of commerce.
Bob Cox, Publisher
Pat St. Germain, Editor, pdstgermain@gmail.com

mbot Magazine
Previous Name: Business Bulletin
c/o Mississauga Board of Trade, #701, 77 City Centre Dr., Mississauga, ON L5B 1M5
Tel: 905-273-6151; *Fax:* 905-273-4937
info@mbot.com
www.mbot.com/index.php/communication-a-news/mbot-mag
Other information: E-mail, Advertising: advertising@mbot.com
Social Media: www.youtube.com/user/MBOTMississauga
twitter.com/mbotontario
www.faceb ook.com/MississaugaBoardofTrade
Circulation: 5,000
Frequency: 11 times a year
Business news & updates on MBOT activities.
Bahaar Sachdeva, Managing Editor, bsachdeva@mbot.com

Mingle
Owned By: Apeeling Orange Design Communications
15 Alderney Dr., Dartmouth, NS B2Y 2N2
Tel: 902-446-8231
sites.google.com/site/apeelingorange/mingle-magazine
Social Media:
twitter.com/MingleMagazine
www.facebook.com/groups/36560444626
Circulation: 7,000
Harm Geurs, President, Apeeling Orange Design Communications, harm@apeelingorange.com

The MOMpreneur
#816, C-420 Main St. East, Milton, ON L9T 5G3
themompreneur.com/magazine
Social Media:
www.linkedin.com/company/the-mompreneurs-com
twitter.com/TheMOMpreneurTM
www.facebook.com/TheMOMpreneurTM

MoneySense
Owned By: Rogers Media Inc.
1 Mount Pleasant Rd., 11th Fl., Toronto, ON M4Y 2Y5
Tel: 416-764-1400; *Fax:* 416-764-1376
www.moneysense.ca
Social Media:
www.linkedin.com/company/moneysense-magazine
twitter.com/MoneySenseMag
www.facebook.com/MoneySenseMagazine
Circulation: 146,000
Frequency: 8 times a year
Personal finance magazine.
Ian Portsmouth, Publisher
Duncan Hood, Editor-in-Chief

Motivated
101 Ira Needles Blvd., Waterloo, ON N2J 3Z4
motivatedonline.com
Social Media: www.youtube.com/motivatedmagazine
twitter.com/motivatedonline
Includes inspiring articles from leaders, entrepreneurs, & everyday people with the goal of motivating readers towards success in their business & personal lives.
Lisa Holba, Editor-in-Chief

National Post Business, FP 500
Previous Name: National Post 500; The Financial Post 500
Owned By: Postmedia Network Inc.
365 Bloor St. East, 3rd Fl., Toronto, ON M4W 3L4
Tel: 416-383-2300; *Fax:* 416-383-2305
Toll-Free: 800-267-6568
www.nationalpostbusiness.com
Other information: Business Phone: 416-386-2828; Fax: 416-386-2836
Social Media:
www.facebook.com/225240580836032
Circulation: 289,000
Frequency: Annually, June
Ranking of Canada's largest corporations
Terence Corcoran, Editor

Northern Ontario Business
Owned By: Laurentian Media Group
c/o Laurentian Publishing Co., 158 Elgin St., Sudbury, ON P3E 3N5
Tel: 705-673-5705; *Fax:* 705-673-9542
Toll-Free: 800-757-2766
www.northernontariobusiness.com
Social Media:
www.linkedin.com/companies/northern-ontario-business
twitter.com/NorthOn tarioBiz
www.facebook.com/northerontariobiz
Circulation: 10,000
Frequency: Monthly
Northern Ontario Business is printed every month and is the only publication devoted to the region's business community

Patricia Mills, Founding Publisher, pmills@nob.on.ca
Brandi Braithwaite, Marketing Manager, brandi@nob.on.ca

Nova Scotia Business Journal (NSBJ)
c/o TC Media, #609, 1888 Brunswick St., Halifax, NS B3J 3J8
Tel: 902-425-8255
www.dailybusinessbuzz.ca

Circulation: 70,000
Frequency: Monthly
The publication covers business events & issues that affect Nova Scotia's business environment. Online content is called Daily Business Buzz.
John Brannen, Editor, john.brannen@tc.tc

Ontario Industrial Magazine
#1159, 1011 Upper Middle Rd. East, Oakville, ON L6H 5Z9
Tel: 416-446-1404; *Fax:* 416-446-0502
Toll-Free: 800-624-2776
sales@oim-online.com
www.oim-online.com

Circulation: 20,000
Frequency: Monthly
OIM provides the very latest information about manufacturing technology, material handling products, industrial equipment & services, financial management & general business news
Keith Laverty, Publisher

Ottawa Business Journal (OBJ)
Owned By: Great River Media Inc.
#500, 250 City Centre Ave., Ottawa, ON K1R 6K7
Tel: 613-238-1818
editor@obj.ca
www.obj.ca
Social Media:
twitter.com/obj_news
www.facebook.com/131398571469

Circulation: 16,300
Frequency: Bi-weekly
Ottawa Business Journal is the leading source of local business news and information for Canada's national capital region. Every Monday, the newspaper provides authoritative and in-depth news coverage on the sectors that comprise Ottawa's vibrant business scene, ranging from technology to commercial real estate and corporate finance to hospitality.
Michael Curran, Publisher, mcurran@obj.ca
Peter Kovessy, Editor

Partners, Italy & Canada
Italian Chamber of Commerce of Toronto, #201F, 622 College St., Toronto, ON M6G 1B6
Tel: 416-789-7169; *Fax:* 416-789-7160
info.toronto@italchambers.net
www.italchambers.ca

Circulation: 12,000
Frequency: Quarterly
Partners is the official publication of the Italian Chamber of Commerce of Toronto. Published quarterly, the magazine features editorials and special reports written by international experts and tackles themes such as business ethics, design, multiculturalism, foreign trade, arts and entertainment. Through interviews and company profiles, partners is the voice of the Canadian, Italian and international business community.
Corrado Paina, Editorial Director, paina@italchambers.ca

Payments Business
Owned By: Lloydmedia, Inc.
137 Main St. North, 3rd Fl., Markham, ON L3P 1Y2
Tel: 905-201-6600; *Fax:* 905-201-6601
Toll-Free: 800-668-1838
www.paymentsbusiness.ca

Circulation: 14,000
Frequency: Bi-monthly
Steve Lloyd, President, steve@paymentsbusiness.ca
Karen Treml, Editor, karen@paymentsbusiness.ca

Port of Halifax
Owned By: Metro Guide Publishing
1300 Hollis St., Halifax, NS B3J 1T6
Tel: 902-420-9943; *Fax:* 902-429-9058
mross@metroguide.ca
www.metroguide.ca

Circulation: 20,000
Frequency: Quarterly
Port of Halifax Magazine features information about the Port of Halifax along with stories of interest to the international shipping community
Patty Baxter, Publisher, publishers@metroguide.ca
Trevor Adams, Senior Editor, tadams@metroguide.ca

Private Wealth Canada
Owned By: Powershift Communications Inc.
c/o Powershift Communications Inc., #501, 245 Fairview Mall Dr., Toronto, ON M2J 4T1
Tel: 416-494-1066; *Fax:* 416-494-2536
info@powershift.ca
www.privatewealthcanada.ca

Circulation: 1,200
Provides financial & lifestyle information for senior executives.
Brian McKerchar, Publisher, dbm@powershift.ca
Joe Hornyak, Executive Editor, jhornyak@powershift.ca

Profiles in Business Magazine
Owned By: Business Link Media Group
#200, 36 Hiscott St., St Catharines, ON L2R 1C8
Tel: 905-646-9366; *Fax:* 905-646-5486
info@businesslinkmedia.com
www.businesslinkmedia.com
Social Media:
twitter.com/TheBusinessLink
www.facebook.com/BusinessLinkMedia

Circulation: 15,000
Frequency: Annual
Showcases Niagara businesses & business people.
Adam Shields, Co-Publisher, adam@businesslinkmedia.com
Jim Shields, Co-Publisher, jim@businesslinkmedia.com

Profit
Owned By: Rogers Media Inc.
1 Mount Pleasant Rd., 11th Fl., Toronto, ON M4Y 2Y5
Tel: 416-764-1402; *Fax:* 416-764-1404
www.profitguide.com
Social Media:
twitter.com/profit_magazine
www.facebook.com/PROFITmagazine

Circulation: 84,632
Frequency: 6 times a year
Topics of entrepreneural business & economics. Published as a special section within Canadian Business.
Ian Portsmouth, Publisher

Progress
Previous Name: Atlantic Progress
Owned By: Progress Media Group
#1201, 1660 Hollis St., Halifax, NS B3J 1V7
Tel: 902-494-0999; *Fax:* 902-494-0997
progress@progressmedia.ca
www.progressmedia.ca/progress-magazine
Other information: Alt. E-mails: news@progressmedia.ca; sales@progressmedia.ca
Social Media:
twitter.com/progressmedia
www.facebook.com/ProgressMediaGroup

Circulation: 26,513
Frequency: 10 times a year
Brett Clements, CFO & General Manager, bclements@progressmedia.ca
Corrie Fletcher-Naylor, Managing Editor, cfletcher@progressmedia.ca

Québec Enterprise
269, ch de la Grande Côte, Rosemère, QC H7A 1J2
Tél: 450-420-8408; *Téléc:* 450-970-2205
magazine@quebecentreprise.ca
www.quebecentreprise.ca

Tirage: 20,520
Fréquence: 5 fois par an
Magazine d'affaires couvrant les activités industrielles de toutes les régions du Québec

Québec Franchise
Previous Name: Québec Franchise & Microfranchise
Owned By: Top Franchise MS inc.
PO Box 72132 Atwater, Montréal, QC H3J 2Z6
Tel: 514-383-0034 *Toll-Free:* 888-575-0034
info@Quebec-Franchise.qc.ca
www.quebec-franchise.qc.ca
Social Media:
twitter.com/QC_Franchise
www.facebook.com/quebecfranchise

Circulation: 7,500 copies
Frequency: 4 times a year
Spécialisé dans la franchise et les opportunités d'affaires au Québec et au Canada
Jacques Desforges, Président & Éditeur

Report on Business Magazine (ROB)
c/o The Globe & Mail, 444 Front St. West, Toronto, ON M5V 2S9
Tel: 416-585-5000
newsroom@globeandmail.com
www.theglobeandmail.com/report-on-business/rob-magazine

Frequency: 11 times a year
This business magazine is distributed nationwide with The Globe & Mail to targeted circulation.
Philip Crawley, Publisher & CEO, Globe & Mail
Derek DeCloet, Executive Editor, ddecloet@globeandmail.com

Rotman Management
Owned By: Rotman School of Management
105 St. George St., Toronto, ON M5S 3E6
Tel: 416-946-0103; *Fax:* 416-978-1373
subscriptions@rotman.utoronto.ca
www.rotman.utoronto.ca/rotmanmag
Social Media:
twitter.com/RotmanMgmtMag

Frequency: Three times a year
Karen Christensen, Editor-in-Chief, editor@rotman.utoronto.ca

Senior Executive
Previous Name: Canadian Government Executive
Beacon Publishing Inc., 2150 Fillmore Cres., Ottawa, ON K1J 6A4
Tel: 613-747-1138; *Fax:* 613-747-7319
publisher@seniorexec.ca
www.seniorexec.ca

Circulation: 20,000
Frequency: bi-monthly
Senior Executive magazine features informative articles on topics such as: management techniques; service improvement;business developments; success stories; best practices; IM and IT; innovative use of technology; financial management; personal finance; innovative organizational approaches; modern comptrollership; risk management; policy issues; personnel and retention issues; stress management; transformations; horizontal management;and partnering innovations/successes/challenges between business and government.
John Kiska, Associate Editor
Jonathan Calof, Associate Editor
Chris MacLean, Managing Editor, !cmaclean@seniorexec.ca!
John Kiska, Associate Editor

SOHO Business Report
Previous Name: Home Business Report
Owned By: Dream Launchers Project
439A Marmont St., Coquitlam, BC V3K 4S4
Tel: 604-936-5815; *Fax:* 604-936-5805
Toll-Free: 888-963-5815
www.sohobusinessreport.com

Circulation: 40,000
Frequency: 4 times a year
SOHO Business Report originated in Abbotsford, British Columbia from the home of founding publisher Barbara Mowat. It first started as The B.C. Home Business Report, & was designed to help link home-based businesses across the province, providing entrepreneurs with tips & advice on running their business. Regional editions followed in Alberta & Ontario. In 1994, the Home Business Report became the SOHO Business Report, a national publication.
Chad Thiessen, Publisher, chadt@sohobusinessreport.com
Melanie Jackson, Editor-in-Chief, editor@sohobusinessreport.com

Sounding Board
Owned By: Vancouver Media Group/Vancouver Board of Trade
World Trade Center, #400, 999 Canada Pl., Vancouver, BC V6C 3E1
Tel: 604-681-2111; *Fax:* 604-681-0437
contactus@boardoftrade.com
www.boardoftrade.com/publicationsresources/sounding-board.aspx
Social Media:
twitter.com/BoardofTrade
www.facebook.com/VancouverBoardofTrade

Circulation: 12,500
Frequency: 11 times a year
As the official monthly publication of The Vancouver Board of Trade, the Sounding Board newspaper provides analysis and discussion of regional and national issues facing the business community.
Greg Hoekstra, Manager, Communications, media@boardoftrade.com

The Taxpayer
#265, 438 Victoria Ave. East, Regina, SK S4N 0N7
Tel: 306-352-7199; *Fax:* 306-205-8339
Toll-Free: 800-667-7933
admin@taxpayer.com
www.taxpayer.com
Social Media:
twitter.com/taxpayerdotcom
www.facebook.com/TaxpayerDOTcom

Frequency: Bi-monthly
The Taxpayer is the flagship publication of the Canadian Taxpayers Federation (CTF). It is published six times a year & contains comprehensive updates on CTF happenings & accomplishments around the country. It features articles written by CTF researchers & spokespersons. Guest editorial writers also contribute to this publication.
Dean Smith, Publisher & Webmaster, webmaster@taxpayer.com

Thompson's World Insurance News
PO Box 1027, Waterloo, ON N2J 4S1
Tel: 519-579-2500
mpub@sympatico.ca
www.thompsonsnews.com
Frequency: Weekly
Canada's only independent weekly for p&c insurance professionals, has been the industry's most trusted news source for more than a decade
Mark Publicover, Managing Editor

Thunder Bay Business
Owned By: North Superior Publishing Inc.
#1402, 590 Beverly St., Thunder Bay, ON P7B 6H1
Tel: 807-623-2348; *Fax:* 807-623-7515
nspinc@tbaytel.net
www.thunderbaybusiness.ca
Social Media:
twitter.com/tbay25
www.facebook.com/NorthSuperiorPublishing
Circulation: 5,000
Frequency: Monthly
Northwestern Ontario business publication.
Scott Sumner, President, North Superior Publishing Inc.

Up Here Business
Owned By: Up Here Publishing Ltd.
PO Box 1350, Yellowknife, NT X1A 2N9
Toll-Free: 866-572-1757
upherebusiness.ca
Social Media:
twitter.com/upherebusiness
www.facebook.com/UpHereBusiness
Herb Mathisen, Managing Editor, herb@uphere.ca

Wealth Professional
Owned By: Key Media Inc.
#800, 312 Adelaide St. West, Toronto, ON M5V 1R2
Tel: 416-644-8740; *Fax:* 416-203-9083
subscriptions@kmimedia.ca
www.wealthprofessional.ca
Social Media:
twitter.com/wealth_proca
Frequency: Bi-Monthly
John Mackenzie, General Manager, Sales, 416-644-8740 ext.252, John.mackenzie@kmimedia.ca

Your Workplace (YW)
23 Queen St., Kingston, ON K7K 1A1
Tel: 613-549-1222 *Toll-Free:* 877-668-1945
listedmag.com
Social Media:
twitter.com/yourworkplace
www.facebook.com/YourWorkplace
Circulation: 336,000
Frequency: Bi-monthly
Articles, interviews & profiles for human resources professionals & managers.
Vera Asanin, President & Publisher

Camping & Outdoor Recreation

RV Lifestyle Magazine
Owned By: Taylor Publishing Group
#2, 1121 Invicta Dr., Oakville, ON L6H 2R2
Tel: 905-844-8218; *Fax:* 905-844-5032
info@rvlifemag.com
www.rvlifemag.com; www.rvlifemag-digital.com/rvlifestyle
Social Media: www.flickr.com/groups/rvadventures
Frequency: 7 issues per year
William E. Taylor, Publisher
Peter Tasler, Editor-in-chief, editor@rvlifemag.com

Chemicals & Chemical Process Industries

Canadian Chemical News / L'Actualité chimique canadienne
c/o The Chemical Institute of Canada, #400, 220 Queen St., Ottawa, ON K1P 5V9
Tel: 613-232-6252; *Fax:* 613-232-5862
Toll-Free: 888-542-2242
www.accn.ca
Frequency: 6 times a year
Roberta Staley, Editor

Canadian Process Equipment & Control News
#29, 588 Edward Ave., Richmond Hill, ON L4C 9Y6
Tel: 905-770-8077; *Fax:* 905-770-8075
cpe@cpecn.com
www.cpecn.com
Frequency: 6 times a year
Jerry Cook, Editor, jcook@jcook@cpecn.com

Industrial Process Products & Technology
Owned By: Swan-Erickson Publishing Inc.
#355, 4261 - A14 Highway #7 East, Markham, ON L3R 9W6
Tel: 905-649-8966
www.ippt.ca
Frequency: 6 times a year
Michael Swan, Publisher, mswan@ippt.ca
Glen Scholry, Managing Editor, 403-995-8514, gscholey@ippt.ca

Process West
Owned By: Swan-Erickson Publishing Inc.
#355, 4261 - A14 Highway #7 East, Markham, ON L3R 9W6
Tel: 905-649-8966
www.processwest.ca
Frequency: 6 times a year
Michael Swan, Publisher
Jamie Zachary, Editor, 403-703-9339, jamie.zachary@processwest.ca

Clothing & Accessories

Trends Magazine
Previous Name: Canadian Apparel Magazine
c/o Canadian Apparel Federation, #504, 124 O'Connor St., Ottawa, ON K1P 5M9
Tel: 416-493-3912
kait@trendsmagazine.ca
www.trendsmagazine.ca
Circulation: 7,500
Business to business fashion magazine

Computing & Technology

CIO Canada
Owned By: It World Canada Inc.
#302, 55 Town Centre Ct., Toronto, ON M1P 4X4
Tel: 416-290-0240; *Fax:* 416-290-0238
general@itworldcanada.com
www.itworldcanada.com/publication/cio
Circulation: 8,000
Frequency: 12 times a year
Shane Schick, Editor, sschick@itworldcanada.com

Computer Dealer News
Owned By: IT World Canada Inc.
#302, 55 Town Centre Crt., Scarborough, ON M1P 4X4
Tel: 416-290-0240
info@itbusiness.ca
www.itbusiness.ca/IT/client/en/CDN/Home.asp
Circulation: 18,859
Frequency: 18 times a year
Paolo Del Nibletto, Editor, pdelnibletto@itworldcanada.com

Computing Canada
Owned By: IT World Canada Inc.
#302, 55 Town Centre Ct., Toronto, ON M1P 4X4
Tel: 416-290-0240; *Fax:* 416-290-0238
circulation@itworldcanada.com
www.itworldcanada.com/computing-canada
Frequency: 12 times a year
Fawn Annan, President & Group Publisher
Nestor Arrelano, Editor

ConnectIT
17 Moodie Dr., Richmond Hill, ON L4C 8C9
Tel: 905-763-1200; *Fax:* 905-886-6216
Toll-Free: 800-465-2059
www.integratedmar.com

Direction Informatique
Détenteur: IT World Canada Inc.
#204, 5605 av de Gaspé, Montreal, QC H2T 2A4
Tél: 514-876-9964
redaction@directioninformatique.com
www.directioninformatique.com
Médias sociaux:
www.linkedin.com/groups/Direction-Informatique-2744942
twitter.com/direc tioninfo
www.facebook.com/DirectionInformatique
Dominique Lemoine, Rédacteur en chef, dlemoine@directioninformatique.com
Brad McBride, Directeur des Ventes, bmcbride@itworlcanada.com

eChannelLine Daily News
Previous Name: Computer Reseller News
17 Moodie Dr., Richmond Hill, ON L4C 8C9
Tel: 905-763-1200; *Fax:* 905-886-6216
Toll-Free: 800-465-2059
www.echannelline.com
Circulation: 36,000
Frequency: daily
Steve Wexler, Editor-in-chief, Special Projects

Technologies for Worship Magazine
3891 Holborn Rd., Queensville, ON L0G 1R0
Tel: 905-473-9822; *Fax:* 905-473-9928
info@tfwm.com
www.tfwm.com
Social Media:
twitter.com/tfwm
www.facebook.com/TechnologiesForWorshipMagazine
Circulation: 30,000
Frequency: bi-monthly
Shelagh Rogers, Founder
Kevin Rogers Cobus, Editor

Conventions & Meetings

Meeting Places
c/o BIV Media Group, 303 West 5th Ave., Vancouver, BC V5Y 1J6
Tel: 604-688-2398; *Fax:* 604-688-6058
www.biv.com
Circulation: 13,000
Paul Harris, Publisher
Frank O'Brien, Editor

Meetings + Incentive Travel (M+IT)
Previous Name: Conventions Meetings Canada
Owned By: Annex-Newcom
80 Valleybrook Dr., Toronto, ON M3B 2S9
Tel: 416-442-5600; *Fax:* 416-764-1419
www.meetingscanada.com
Social Media:
twitter.com/meetingscanada
www.facebook.com/MeetingsCanada
Circulation: 130,000
Robin Paisley, General Manager, IncentiveWorks, rpaisley@meetingscanada.com
Lori Smith, Editor, lsmith@meetingscanada.com

Cosmetics

Cosmetics Magazine / Cosmetiques
Owned By: Rogers Media Inc.
1 Mount Pleasant Rd., 8th Fl., Toronto, ON M4Y 2Y5
Tel: 416-764-2000
cosmeticsmag.com
Social Media: instagram.com/cosmeticsmag
twitter.com/cosmeticsmag
www.facebook.com/pages/Cosmetics-Magazine/280002595351473
Circulation: 13,000 (7,000 Cosmetiques)
Frequency: 4 times a year; also Cosmetiques
Melissa Alhstrand, Group Publisher, Fashion & Beauty
Wing Sze Tang, Editor

Credit

The Canadian Co-operator
Previous Name: The Atlantic Co-operator
Owned By: Canadian Publishers Co-operative
123 Halifax St., Moncton, NB E1C 8N5
Tel: 506-858-6617; *Fax:* 506-858-6615
canadianpublisherscooperative@gmail.com
canadiancooperator.coop
Social Media: ca.linkedin.com/in/rayannebrennan
twitter.com/co_operator
www.facebook.com/canadiancooperator
Frequency: Bi-monthly
The Canadian Co-operator provides news & information about the co-operative movement in Canada. Published electronically & in print.
Rayanne Brennan, Manager & Editor, 506-961-3633, editor@theatlanticco-operator.coop

Culture, Current Events

Eighteen Bridges
Owned By: Venture Publishing Inc.
Canadian Literature Centre, 3-5 Humanities Centre, University of Alberta, Edmonton, AB T6G 2E5
ebmag@ualberta.ca
eighteenbridges.com
Social Media:
www.twitter.com/eighteenbridges

Curtis Gillespie, Editor & Publisher

Hush
1610 Pandora St., Vancouver, BC V5L 1L6
editor@hushmagazine.ca
www.hushmagazine.ca
Social Media: www.youtube.com/user/HushMagazine
twitter.com/HUSHvancouver
www.facebook.com/HushVancouver

Barb Sligl, Editor

The Walrus
Owned By: Walrus Foundation
#B15, 411 Richmond St. E, Toronto, ON M5A 3S5
Tel: 416-971-5004 *Toll-Free:* 866-236-0475
info@walrusmagazine.com
walrusmagazine.com
Social Media:
twitter.com/walrusmagazine
www.facebook.com/thewalrusmagazine

Circulation: 60,000
Frequency: 10 times a year
Shelley Ambrose, Executive Director & Publisher, 416-971-5004 x 236, shelley.ambrose@walrusmagazine.com

Dentistry

Canadian Journal of Dental Hygiene
Previous Name: Probe
c/o Canadian Dental Hygienists Assn., 1122 Wellington St. West, Ottawa, ON K1Y 2Y7
Tel: 613-224-5515; *Fax:* 613-224-7283
Toll-Free: 800-267-5235
journal@cdha.ca
www.cdha.ca
Social Media:
twitter.com/theCDHA
www.facebook.com/theCDHA

Frequency: 3 times a year
Megan Sproule-Jones, Managing Editor
Katherine Zmetana, Scientific Editor

Denturism Canada - The Journal of Canadian Denturism / Denturologie Canada
Owned By: Craig Kelman & Associates Ltd.
2020 Portage Ave., 3rd Fl., Winnipeg, MB R3J 0K4
Fax: 204-985-9795
Toll-Free: 866-985-9788
www.denturist.org/magazine.html

Circulation: 1,909
Frequency: 4 times a year
Hussein Amery, Editor-in-Chief, ameryhk@telus.net
Cheryl Parisien, Managing Editor, cheryl@kelman.ca

Journal de l'Ordre des dentistes du Québec
Anciennement: Journal Dentaire du Québec
Ordre des dentistes du Québec, #1640, 800, boul René-Lévesque ouest, Montréal, QC H3B 1X9
Tél: 514-875-8511; *Téléc:* 514-875-9049
journal@odq.qc.ca
www.odq.qc.ca

Tirage: 5600
Fréquence: 6 fois par an
Carole Erdelyon, Rédactrice-en-chef

Manitoba Dentist
Cutting Edge Communications, #2, 1248 Pembina Hwy., Winnipeg, MB
Tel: 204-669-2377; *Fax:* 204-669-2336
jparcells@cecommunications.ca

Circulation: 1,700
Frequency: Annually
Jamie Parcells, Publisher

Ontario Dentist Journal (ODA)
c/o Ontario Dentist Association, 4 New St., Toronto, ON M5R 1P6
Tel: 416-922-3900; *Fax:* 416-922-9005
www.oda.on.ca
Social Media:
www.facebook.com/pages/Canadian-Dental-Health/2034526896 6

Circulation: 9393
Frequency: 10 times a year
Julia Kuipers, Managing Editor

Oral Health
Owned By: Annex-Newcom
80 Valleybrook Dr., Toronto, ON M3B 2S9
Tel: 416-442-5600; *Fax:* 416-510-5140
Toll-Free: 800-668-2374
www.oralhealthjournal.com

Frequency: Monthly
Melissa Summerfield, Senior Publisher, 416-510-6781, msummerfield@oralhealthjournal.com
Catherine Wilson, Editorial Director, cwilson@oralhealthjournal.com

Directories & Almanacs

Canadian Forces Base Kingston Official Directory
Owned By: Sun Media Corporation
18 St. Remy Place, Kingston, ON K7K 6C4
Tel: 613-389-7400; *Fax:* 613-389-7507
www.kingstonpublications.com

Circulation: 3,500
Frequency: Annually, December
Liza Nelson, Publisher, 613-549-8442 ext 132, liza.nelson@sunmedia.ca

Frasers
Previous Name: Frasers Canadian Trade Directory
Owned By: Annex Publishing & Printing Inc.
80 Valleybrook Dr., Toronto, ON M3B 2S9
Tel: 416-510-5220
www.frasers.com

Frequency: Annually, March
Mary Del Ciancio, Editor, mdelciancio@frasers.com

Sources
#201, 812A Bloor St. West, Toronto, ON M6G 1L9
Tel: 416-964-7799; *Fax:* 416-964-8763
sources@sources.ca
www.sources.com

Drugs

L'actualité pharmaceutique
Détenteur: Éditions Rogers Media
1200, ave McGill College, 8e étage, Montréal, QC H3B 4G7
Tél: 514-843-2105; *Téléc:* 514-843-2183
www.professionsante.ca

Tirage: 8,046
Fréquence: 10 fois par an
Caroline Baril, Rédactrice en chef, caroline.baril@rci.rogers.com
Caroline Bélisle, Éditrice, Groupe Santé Québec, 514-843-2569, caroline.belisle@rci.rogers.com

The Canadian Journal of Hospital Pharmacy / Le Journal canadien de la pharmacie hospitalière
The Cdn. Society of Hospital Pharmacists, #3, 30 Concourse Gate., Ottawa, ON K2E 7V7
Tel: 613-736-9733; *Fax:* 613-736-5660
www.cshp.ca

Circulation: 4157
Frequency: 6 times a year

Canadian Pharmacists Journal
1785 Alta Vista Dr., Ottawa, ON K1G 3Y6
Tel: 613-523-7877; *Fax:* 613-523-2332
Toll-Free: 800-917-9489
cpj@pharmacists.ca
www.pharmacists.ca

Frequency: 6 times a year
Ross T. Tsuyuki, Editor-in-chief
Renée Dykeman, Executive Editor

Le Pharmactuel
L'Association des pharmaciens des établissements de santé, #320, 4050, rue Molson, Montréal, QC H1VH3A 1T1
Tél: 514-286-0776; *Téléc:* 514-286-1081
info@apesquebec.org
www.pharmactuel.com
Médias sociaux:
twitter.com/pharmactuel
www.facebook.com/pages/Pharmactuel/3799274153938 55

Tirage: 1 800
Fréquence: 5 fois par an
Julie Méthot, Rédactrice en chef, redaction@pharmactuel.com

Pharmacy Business
Owned By: Stagnito Business Information & Edgell Communications
#1510, 2300 Yonge St., Toronto, ON M4P 1E4
Tel: 416-256-9908; *Fax:* 888-889-9522
Toll-Free: 877-687-7321
pharmacyu.ca
Other information: www.youtube.com/user/pharmacyu
Social Media: www.linkedin.com/company/pharmacy-u
twitter.com/@pharmacyu
www.faceboo k.com/PharmacyU

Serving the retail pharaceutical industry.
Jane Auster, Editor, jauster@stagnitomail.ca

Pharmacy Practice+
Owned By: Rogers Media Inc.
1 Mount Pleasant Rd., Toronto, ON M4Y 2Y5
Tel: 416-764-3920
www.canadianhealthcarenetwork.ca

Circulation: 22,375
Vicki Wood, Editor
Janet Smith, Publisher

Québec Pharmacie
Détenteur: Rogers Media Inc.
#800, 1200, av McGill College, Montréal, QC H3B 4G7
Tél: 514-843-2569
www.professionsante.ca

Caroline Baril, Rédactrice en chef

Education

Agenda (OECTA)
c/o Ontario English Catholic Teachers' Association, #400, 65 St. Clair Ave. East, Toronto, ON M4T 2Y8
Tel: 416-925-2493; *Fax:* 416-925-7764
Toll-Free: 800-268-7230
a.oconnor@oecta.on.ca
www.oecta.on.ca
Social Media:
twitter.com/OECTAProv
www.facebook.com/OECTA

Circulation: 46,000
Frequency: Monthly
Publication for Catholic schools in Ontario
Kevin O'Dwyer, President

The ATA Magazine
The Alberta Teachers' Association, Barnett House, 11010 - 142 St., Edmonton, AB T5N 2R1
Tel: 780-447-9400; *Fax:* 780-455-6481
Toll-Free: 800-232-7208
government@teachers.ab.ca
www.teachers.ab.ca

Circulation: 42,100
Frequency: 4 times a year
Gordon Thomas, Editor
Cory Hare, Associate Editor

Education Forum
c/o Ontario Secondary School Teachers' Federation, 60 Mobile Dr., Toronto, ON M4A 2P3
Tel: 416-751-8300; *Fax:* 416-751-3394
Toll-Free: 800-267-7867
www.osstf.on.ca

Circulation: 60,000
Frequency: 3 times a year
Ronda Allan, Managing Editor
Randy Banderob, Editor

Education Today
Ontario Public School Boards Assn., #1850, 439 University Ave., Toronto, ON M5G 1Y8
Tel: 416-340-2540; *Fax:* 416-340-7571
webmaster@opsba.org
www.opsba.org

Frequency: 3 times a year

ESL in Canada Directory
PO Box 75117, 20 Bloor St. East, Toronto, ON M4W 3T3
Tel: 416-608-4194; *Fax:* 416-513-0026
www.eslincanada.com

Frequency: 2 times a year
Ross McBride, Production Manager

Green Teacher
95 Robert St., Toronto, ON M5S 2K5
Tel: 416-960-1244; *Fax:* 416-925-3474
Toll-Free: 888-804-1486
info@greenteacher.com
www.greenteacher.com
Social Media:
twitter.com/GreenTeacherMag
www.facebook.com/GreenTeacherMagazine

Frequency: Quarterly
Green Teacher magazine offers perspectives on the role of education in creating a sustainable future, practical articles and ready to use activities for various age levels, and reviews of dozens of new educational resources.
Tim Grant, Co-Editor

The Manitoba Teacher
c/o The Manitoba Teachers' Society, McMaster House, 191 Harcourt St., Winnipeg, MB R3J 3H2
Tel: 204-888-7961; *Fax:* 204-831-0877
Toll-Free: 800-262-8803
www.mbteach.org/left-menu-pages/teacher.html

Circulation: 17,500
Frequency: 7 times per year
The Manitoba Teachers' Society is the professional & collective bargaining representative for 15,000 educators in the province. The Manitoba Teacher is the society's newsmagazine.
George Stephenson, Editor, gstephenson@mbteach.org
Mireille Theriault, Contact, Advertising, mtheriault@mbteach.org

Professionally Speaking / Pour parler profession
c/o Ontario College of Teachers, 101 Bloor St. East, Toronto, ON M5S 0A1
Tel: 416-961-8800; *Fax:* 416-961-8822
Toll-Free: 888-534-2222
info@oct.ca
professionallyspeaking.oct.ca
Circulation: 218,570
Frequency: 4 times a year
Richard Lewko, Publisher
William Powell, Editor-in-Chief

Teach Magazine
#321, 1655 Dupont St., Toronto, ON M6P 3T1
info@teachmag.com
www.teachmag.com
Circulation: 22,000
Frequency: 5 times a year
Wili Liberman, Publisher & Editor

University Affairs / Affaires universitaires
c/o Assn. of Universities & Colleges of Canada, #1710, 350 Albert St., Ottawa, ON K1R 1B1
Tel: 613-563-1236; *Fax:* 613-563-9745
ua@univcan.ca
www.universityaffairs.ca
Social Media: www.youtube.com/user/universityaffairsca
twitter.com/ua_magazine
www.f acebook.com/universityaffairs
Circulation: 17,000
Frequency: 10 times a year
Christine Tausig Ford, Publisher
Peggy Berkowitz, Editor

Electrical Equipment & Electronics

Connections + (CNS)
Previous Name: Cabling Networking Systems; Cabling Systems
Owned By: Annex-Newcom
80 Valleybrook Dr., Toronto, ON M3B 2S9
Tel: 416-510-5111; *Fax:* 416-510-5134
Toll-Free: 800-268-7742
www.cnsmagazine.com
Social Media:
twitter.com/connplus2014
www.facebook.com/connectionsplus2014
Circulation: 60,000
Frequency: 6 times a year
Magazine intended for ICT professionals
Maureen Levy, Publisher, mlevy@connectionsplus.ca
Paul Barker, Editor, 416-510-6752, pbarker@connectionsplus.ca

Electrical Business
Owned By: Annex Publishing & Printing Inc.
222 Edward St., Aurora, ON L4G 1W5
Tel: 905-727-0077; *Fax:* 905-727-0017
www.ebmag.com
Social Media:
twitter.com/ebmag
www.facebook.com/pages/Electrical-Business/65191484493974
Circulation: 19,993
Frequency: 12 times a year
John MacPherson, Publisher, jmacpherson@annexweb.com
Anthony Capkun, Editor, acapkun@annexweb.com

Electrical Line
Owned By: Pacific Media Publishing Inc.
Pacific Media Publishing Inc., 1785 Emerson Crt., North Vancouver, BC V7H 2Y6
Tel: 604-924-3661; *Fax:* 604-924-3662
www.electricalline.com
Circulation: 20,000
Frequency: Bi-Monthly
Ken Buhr, Editor/Publisher

Électricité Québec
Anciennement: Le Maître Electricien
5925, boul Decarie, Montréal, QC H3W 3C9
Tél: 514-738-2184; *Téléc:* 514-738-2192
Ligne sans frais: 800-361-9061
info@cmeq.org
www.cmeq.org
Tirage: 9 834
Fréquence: 6 fois par an
Hélène Rioux, Éditrice et rédactrice-en-chef

Electricity Today
Hurst Communications, #215, 1885 Clements Rd., Pickering, ON L1W 3V4
Tel: 905-686-1040; *Fax:* 905-686-1078
Toll-Free: 855-824-6131
www.electricity-today.com
Social Media:
twitter.com/theEForum
www.facebook.com/theelectricityforum
Frequency: 8 times a year
Stu Sinukoff, Publisher

EP&T
Also Known As: Electronic Products & Technology
Owned By: Annex-Newcom
80 Valleybrook Dr., Toronto, ON M3B 2S9
Tel: 416-442-5600; *Fax:* 416-510-5134
info@ept.ca
www.ept.ca
Frequency: 9 times a year; also EP&T's Electrosource Product Reference Guide & Telephone Directory (annually, Jan.)
Peter Loney, Publisher
Stephen Law, Editor, 416-510-5208, slaw@ept.ca

Emergency Services

Canadian Paramedicine
Previous Name: Canadian Emergency News
PO Box 579, Drumheller, AB T0J 0Y0
Fax: 888-264-2854
Toll-Free: 800-567-0911
cp@emsnews.com
www.emsnews.com
Social Media:
twitter.com/CdnParamedicine
www.facebook.com/CanadianParamedicine
Frequency: 6 times a year
Lyle Blumhagen, Publisher/Editor

Engineering

Canadian Consulting Engineer
Owned By: Annex Publishing & Printing Inc.
80 Valleybrook Dr., Toronto, ON M3B 2S9
Tel: 416-510-5119; *Fax:* 416-510-5134
Toll-Free: 800-268-7742
www.canadianconsultingengineer.com
Social Media:
twitter.com/beata_o
Covers all engineering disiplines and all geographical areas.
Maureen Levy, Publisher, 416-510-5111, mlevy@ccemag.com
Bronwen Parsons, Editor, bparsons@ccemag.com

Construction Alberta News
PO Box 48109, St Albert, AB T8N 5B3
Tel: 780-460-8004; *Fax:* 866-860-1639
admin@conaltanews.com
www.conaltanews.com
Frequency: 2 times a year

Engineering Dimensions
#101, 40 Sheppard Ave. West, Toronto, ON M2N 6K9
Tel: 416-224-1100; *Fax:* 416-224-8168
Toll-Free: 800-339-3716
www.peo.on.ca
Other information: Toll Free Fax: 1-800-268-0496
Frequency: Bi-Monthly
Connie Mucklestone, Publisher
Jennifer Coombes, Managing Editor, jcoombes@peo.on.ca

Geomatica
Previous Name: CISM Journal
Canadian Institute of Geomatics, #100D, 900 Dynes Rd., Ottawa, ON K2C 3L6
Tel: 613-224-9851; *Fax:* 613-224-9577
editgeo@magma.ca
www.cig-acsg.ca
Social Media: www.linkedin.com/groups?gid=1095187
Frequency: 4 times a year
Geomatica is dedicated to the dissemination of information on technical advances in the geomatics sciences.
Izaak de Rijcke, Editor, izaak@izaak.ca

The Ontario Technologist
#404, 10 Four Seasons Place, Toronto, ON M9B 6H7
Tel: 416-621-9621; *Fax:* 416-621-8694
www.oacett.org
Social Media:
twitter.com/OACETT
www.facebook.com/OACETT
Circulation: 24,000
Frequency: 6 times a year
Publication of the Ontario Association of Certified Engineering Technicians and Technologists.
Emily Sinkins, Editor

The PEG
APEGGA, Scotia One, #1500, 10060 Jasper Ave. NW, Edmonton, AB T5J 4A2
Tel: 780-426-3990; *Fax:* 780-425-1877
Toll-Free: 800-661-7020
email@apega.ca
www.apega.ca/Members/Publications/toc_PEGG.html
Circulation: 65,000
Frequency: 4 times a year
Official, legislated publication of APEGA.
George Lee, Managing Editor

PLAN
Ordre des ingenieurs du Québec, Gare Windsor, #350, 1100, av des Canadiens-de-Montréal, Montréal, QC H3B 2S2
Tél: 514-845-6141; *Téléc:* 514-845-1833
Ligne sans frais: 800-461-6141
www.oiq.qc.ca
Tirage: 60,000
Fréquence: 9 fois par an
Sandra Etchenda, Coordonnatrice des éditions
Geneviève Terreault, Chef des communications

Plan Canada
Canadian Institute of Planners, #801, 116 Albert St., Ottawa, ON K1P 5G3
Tel: 613-237-7526; *Fax:* 613-237-7045
Toll-Free: 800-207-2138
general@cip-icu.ca
www.cip-icu.ca
Circulation: 4,715
Frequency: Quarterly
Michele Garneau, Publisher
Mark Seasons, Chair, Editorial Board

Publiquip Inc.
Anciennement: Publiquip/Roucam
490, av Gilles Villeneuve, Berthierville, QC J0C 1A0
Tél: 450-836-3666; *Téléc:* 450-836-7401
Ligne sans frais: 800-361-5295
production@publiquip.com
www.publiquip.com
Tirage: 51,000
Fréquence: Mensuel
Françoise Trépanier, Éditrice

Rock to Road Magazine
PO Box 530, 105 Donly Dr. South, Simcoe, ON N3Y 4N5
Fax: 519-429-3094
Toll-Free: 888-599-2228
www.rocktoroad.com
Social Media:
twitter.com/RockToRoad
www.facebook.com/pages/Rock-To-Road/476451425845470
Frequency: 7 times a year
Scott Jamieson, Publisher / Editor, sjamieson@annexweb.com

Supply Post
#105, 26730 - 56th Ave., Langley, BC V4W 3X5
Tel: 604-607-5577; *Fax:* 604-607-0533
Toll-Free: 800-663-4802
info@supplypost.com
www.supplypost.com
Social Media:
twitter.com/supplypost
www.facebook.com/pages/Supply-Post-Newspaper/1736476626 51
Circulation: 13,000+
Frequency: 12 times a year
The publication is of interest to persons involved in the construction equipment, trucking, forestry, mining, oil & gas, & marine industries.
Gary Mazur, Managing Partner, gary.mazur@supplypost.com
Sheryl Kaye, Contact, Editorial Contributions, editorial@supplypost.com
Christine Mazur, Contact, Subscriptions, circulation@postpublishers.com
Gary Mazur, Contact, Sales & IT, gary.mazur@supplypost.com
Debra Watson, Contact, Accounts & Billing, debra.watson@postpublishers.com

Environment & Nature

Ecoforestry
Previous Name: International Journal of Ecoforestry
Ecoforestry Institute Society, PO Box 5070 B, Victoria, BC V8R 6N3
Tel: 250-595-0655; *Fax:* 250- -
journal@ecoforestry.ca
ecoforestry.ca

Frequency: quarterly
Journal looks at issues relating to the forestry industry using a low-impact approach to forest management. Its goal is to increase public awareness of ecoforestry by working with community organizations, offering workshops to the public and providing information.

ehscompliance.ca
Previous Name: Environmental Compliance Report & the Occupational Health & Safety
Owned By: Annex-Newcom
80 Valleybrook Dr., Toronto, ON M3B 2S9
Tel: 416-422-2122; *Fax:* 416-510-5133
Toll-Free: 800-668-2374
customercare@bizinfogroup.ca
www.ehscompliance.ca

Frequency: Monthly
A monthly national newsletter that examines the developments and amendments in Canadian environmental law. It gives its readers commentary on new legislation, proposed environmental bills, changing environmental legislation, and all other issues affecting enviromental law policies in Canada.
Lidia Lubka, Editor/Publisher, llubka@ecolog.com

EnviroLine
PO Box 77042 Chinatown, 4905 - 23 Ave. NW, Calgary, AB T2G 5J8
Tel: 403-263-3272; *Fax:* 403-263-3280
enviroline@shaw.ca
envirolinenews.ca

Circulation: 500
Frequency: 20 times a year
Provides Western Canadian resource industries with reviews of important and up-to-date environmental issues.
Mark Lowey, Publisher & Editor

Recycling Product News
Owned By: Baum Publications Ltd.
Baum Publications Ltd., #124, 2323 Boundary Rd., Vancouver, BC V5M 4V8
Tel: 604-291-9900; *Fax:* 604-291-1906
Toll-Free: 888-286-3630
rpn.baumpub.com

Frequency: 8 times a year
Publication focuses on products, technologies services and industry news in recycling and waste management, ranging from composting to scrap metal.
Ken Singer, Publisher
Keith Barker, Editor, kbarker@baumpub.com

Vecteur Environnement
#750, 255, boul Crémazie Est, Montréal, QC H2M 1L5
Tél: 514-270-7110; *Téléc:* 514-874-1272
Ligne sans frais: 877-440-7110
vecteur@reseau-environnement.com
www.reseau-environnement.com

Fréquence: 5 fois par an
Revue de l'industrie, des sciences et techniques de l'environnement du Québec; publiée par RÉSEAU environnement

Fire Protection

Atlantic Firefighter
Hilden Publishing Ltd., #456, 6 - 295 Queen St. East, Brampton, ON L6W 4S6
Toll-Free: 800-555-2514
info@atlanticfirefighter.ca
www.atlanticfirefighter.ca

Circulation: 6,200
Frequency: Annually
Annual publication of fire safety from firefighters

Canadian Firefighter & EMS Quarterly
Previous Name: EMS Quarterly
Owned By: Annex Publishing & Printing Inc.
PO Box 530, 105 Donly Dr. South, Simcoe, ON N3Y 4N5
Tel: 519-429-3966; *Fax:* 519-429-3094
Toll-Free: 800-265-2827
www.firefightingincanada.com
Social Media:
twitter.com/fireincanada
www.facebook.com/firefightingincanada

Circulation: 7,500
Frequency: 4 times a year
Martin McAnulty, Publisher
Laura King, Editor, 289-259-8077, lking@annexweb.com

Fire Fighting in Canada
Owned By: Annex Publishing & Printing Inc.
PO Box 530, 105 Donly Dr. South, Simcoe, ON N3Y 4N5
Fax: 519-429-3094
Toll-Free: 888-599-2228
www.firefightingincanada.com
Social Media:
twitter.com/FireinCanada
www.facebook.com/firefightingincanada

Frequency: 8 times a year
Educating and informing fire chiefs, senior officers and firefighters in municipal, industrial and military fire departments across the country.
Laura King, Editor, 289-259-8077, lking@annexweb.com
Martin J. McAaulty, Publisher

Fisheries

Aquaculture North America
Previous Name: Northern Aquaculture
Owned By: Capamara Communications
4623 William Head Rd., Victoria, BC V9C 3Y7
Tel: 250-474-3982
www.aquaculturenorthamerica.com
Social Media:
twitter.com/aquaculture_na
www.facebook.com/1433181043650880

Frequency: 6 times a year
Peter Chettleburgh, Editor

Atlantic Fisherman
162 Trider Cres., Dartmouth, NS B3B 1R6
Tel: 902-422-4990; *Fax:* 902-422-4278
editorial@advocatemediainc.com
www.atlanticfisherman.com
Other information: E-mail, classified & circulation:
atlfisherman@advocatemediainc.com

Frequency: Monthly
Atlantic Fisherman serves the commercial fishing industry across the Maritimes & in Newfoundland & Labrador.
Leith Orr, Publisher, leith@advocatemediainc.com
Suzanne Rent, Editor
James Croke, Advertising Executive, james@advocatemediainc.com
Deryck Richardson, Advertising Executive, deryck@advocatemediainc.com

Nova News Now
Owned By: Trancontinental Media Inc.
#6, 28 Aberdeen St., Kentville, NS B3N 3X4
Tel: 902-681-2121; *Fax:* 902-681-0923
novanewsnow@tc.tc
www.novanewsnow.com
Social Media:
twitter.com/NovaNewsNow1

Floor Coverings

Coverings
Owned By: W.I. Media
PO Box 84 Cheltenham, Caledon, ON L7C 3L7
www.coveringscanada.ca

Circulation: 8,000
Frequency: 6 times a year
Kerry Knudsen, Publisher/Editor

Surface
2105, rue de Salaberry, St-Bruno-de-Montarville, QC J3V 4N7
Tél: 450-441-4243; *Téléc:* 450-441-6997
sourycom@gmail.com
www.magazinesurface.ca

Fréquence: 4 fois par an
Marcel Soucy, Rédacteur-en-chef

Florists

Canadian Florist
Previous Name: Canadian Florist, Greenhouse & Nursery
Owned By: Strider Media
PO Box 530, 105 Donly Dr. South, Simcoe, ON N3Y 4N5
Tel: 519-429-3966; *Fax:* 519-429-3094
Toll-Free: 800-265-2827
dmccarthy@annexweb.com
www.canadianfloristmag.com
Social Media:
twitter.com/canadianflorist
www.facebook.com/CanadianFlorist

Circulation: 5,394
Frequency: 8 times a year
Brandi Cowen, Editor, bcowen@annexweb.com
Scott Jamieson, Publisher, sjamieson@annexweb.com

Food & Beverage

L'Actualité Alimentaire
Anciennement: Le Monde Alimentaire
Détenteur: Édikom inc.
615, Notre-Dame, Saint-Lambert, QC J4P 2K8
Tél: 514-990-6967
www.actualitealimentaire.com

Tirage: 5 000
Martin Lemire, Vice-président, développement des affaires, mlemire@edikom.ca

Canadian Pizza Magazine
Owned By: Annex Publishing & Printing Inc.
PO Box 530, 105 Donly Dr. South, Simcoe, ON N3Y 4N5
Tel: 519-429-3966; *Fax:* 519-429-3094
Toll-Free: 800-265-2827
www.canadianpizzamag.com
Social Media:
twitter.com/cdnpizzamag

Circulation: 9,500
Frequency: 8 times a year
Martin McAnulty, Publisher, mmcanulty@annexweb.com
Laura Aiken, Editor, laiken@annexweb.com

Canadian Restaurant News
Owned By: Ishcom Publications Ltd.
#201, 2065 Dundas St. E, Mississauga, ON L4X 2W1
Tel: 905-206-0150; *Fax:* 905-206-9972
Toll-Free: 800-201-8596
canadianrestaurantnews.com
Social Media: www.linkedin.com/company/ishcom-publications
twitter.com/CANRestonews
www.facebook.com/478026652269738

Circulation: 5,500
Frequency: 6 times a year
Publishers of important news in the restaurant & foodservice industries. Also offers regional directories of hospitality industry chains online & in print
Steve Isherwood, Publisher, sisherwood@canadianrestaurantnews.com
Colleen Isherwood, Senior Editor, cisherwood@canadianlodgingnews.com
Kristen Smith, Managing Editor, ksmith@canadianrestaurantnews.com

Food in Canada
Owned By: Glacier Media Inc.
#2, 38 Lesmill Rd., Toronto, ON M3B 2T5
Tel: 416-442-5600; *Fax:* 416-510-6875
Toll-Free: 800-387-0273
www.foodincanada.com
Social Media: www.pinterest.com/foodincanada
twitter.com/FoodInCanada
www.facebook.c
om/pages/Food-in-Canada-magazine/5905553043

Frequency: 9 times a year
Jack Meli, Publisher, 647-823-2300, jmeli@foodincanada.com

Grocery Business
#702E, 460 Queens Quay West, Toronto, ON M5V 2Y4
Tel: 416-817-5278
www.grocerybusinessmedia.ca
Social Media:
twitter.com/GroceryBusiness

Karen Jones, Co-Publisher/Editor, 416-561-4744, KarenJames@grocerybusiness.ca
Kevin Smith, Co-Publisher/Content Director, 416-569-5005, KevinSmith@grocerybusiness.ca

Le Must
Détenteur: Édikom inc.
Édikom inc., 615, av Notre-Dame, Saint-Lambert, QC J4P 2K8
Tél: 514-990-6967 *Ligne sans frais:* 877-875-6878
info@edikom.ca
www.lemust.ca
Médias sociaux:
twitter.com/LEmustWeb
www.facebook.com/LEmustalimentaire
Lyne Gosselin, Présidente

Your Convenience Manager (YCM)
Owned By: Stagnito Business Information & Edgell Communications
#1510, 2300 Yonge St., Toronto, ON M4P 1E4
Tel: 416-256-9908; *Fax:* 888-889-9522
Toll-Free: 877-687-7321
ccentral.ca

Your Foodservice Manager (YFM)
Owned By: Stagnito Business Information & Edgell Communications
#1510, 2300 Yonge St., Toronto, ON M4P 1E4
Tel: 416-256-9908; *Fax:* 888-889-9522
Toll-Free: 877-687-7321
yfmonline.ca
Other information: Alt. URL: www.foodbiz.ca
Social Media:
twitter.com/FoodBizca
www.facebook.com/foodbizca
Circulation: 26,000
Jane Auster, Editor, jauster@stagnitomail.ca

Footwear

Canadian Footwear Journal
Previous Name: Footwear Forum
Owned By: Shoetrades Publications
241 Senneville Rd., Senneville, QC H9X 3X5
Tel: 514-457-8787; *Fax:* 514-457-5832
cfj@shoetrades.com
www.footwearjournal.com
Circulation: 7,000
Frequency: 15 times a year; plus Retail Buyers' Guide (annual), Shoemaking Buyers's Guide (annual)
George McLeish, Publisher, 514-457-8787, Fax: 514-457-5832, grovp@shoetrades.com
Shirley Boake, Associate Publisher, 705-446-1200, Fax: 705-446-1208, sboake@shoetrades.com

Forest & Lumber Industries

Canadian Forest Industries
Owned By: Annex Publishing & Printing Inc.
PO Box 530, 105 Donly Dr. South, Simcoe, ON N3Y 4N5
Fax: 519-429-3094
Toll-Free: 888-599-2228
www.woodbusiness.ca
Social Media:
twitter.com/CFIMag
www.facebook.com/CanadianForestIndustries
Circulation: 14,100
Frequency: Bi-monthly
Andrew Macklin, Editor, 519-429-5181, amacklin@annexweb.com
Andrew Snook, Editor, 905-713-4301, asnook@annexweb.com

Directory of Ontario Home Improvement Retailers & Their Suppliers
Previous Name: Directory of Ontario Lumber & Building Materials Retailers, Buyers' Gu
Lumber & Building Materials Association of Ontario (LBMAO), 391 Matheson Blvd. East, #A, Mississauga, ON L4Z 2H2
Tel: 905-625-1084; *Fax:* 905-625-3006
Toll-Free: 888-365-2626
www.lbmao.on.ca
Social Media:
twitter.com/LBMAO
www.facebook.com/lbmao
Frequency: Annually, October

The Forestry Chronicle
c/o Canadian Institute of Forestry, PO Box 99, 6905 Hwy. 17 West, Mattawa, ON P0H 1V0
Tel: 705-744-1715; *Fax:* 705-744-1716
admin@cif-ifc.org
cif-ifc.org
Circulation: 3000
Frequency: Bi-Monthly
A professional and scientific forestry journal.

Logging & Sawmilling Journal
Also Known As: L&SJ
PO Box 86670, 211 East 1st St., North Vancouver, BC V7L 4L2
Tel: 604-990-9970; *Fax:* 604-990-9971
www.forestnet.com
Social Media:
twitter.com/Forestnet2
www.facebook.com/108109979252130
Frequency: 7 times a year
The journal is free to forestry related businesses. Information is published about forest management, logging, sawmilling, transportation, road & bridge construction, & wood manufacturing.
Paul MacDonald, Editor
Rob Stanhope, Publisher, stanhope@forestnet.com

Madison's Canadian Lumber Directory
PO Box 86670, North Vancouver, BC V7L 4L2
Tel: 604-990-9970; *Fax:* 604-990-9971
forestnet.com/Madisons_directory.php
Frequency: Annually, Spring

Mid-Canada Forestry & Mining
Previous Name: Mid-Canada Woodlands; Central Woodlands
Owned By: Craig Kelman & Associates Ltd.
2020 Portage Ave., 3rd Fl., Winnipeg, MB R3J 0K4
Fax: 204-985-9795
Toll-Free: 866-985-9788
www.mc-fm.ca
Circulation: 4,500
Frequency: 4 times a year
Terry Ross, Editor, terry@kelman.ca

Le Monde forestier
Anciennement: Le Coopérateur forestier
Détenteur: Les Editions forestières
#203, 1175, av Lavigerie, Québec, QC G1V 4P1
Tél: 418-877-4583; *Téléc:* 418-877-6449
www.lemondeforestier.ca
Médias sociaux:
twitter.com/MondeForestier
www.facebook.com/LeMondeForestier
Tirage: 13,500
Fréquence: 10 fois par an
Guy Lavoie, Directeur général, direction@lemondeforestier.ca
Roger Robitaille, Directeur des ventes, roger@lemondeforestier.ca

Opérations forestières et de scierie
Détenteur: Annex Publishing & Printing Inc.
CP 51058, Pincourt, QC J7V 9T3
Tél: 514-425-0025; *Téléc:* 514-425-0068
www.operationsforestieres.ca
Médias sociaux:
twitter.com/op_forestieres
www.facebook.com/operationsforestieres
Fréquence: 4 fois par an
Guillaume Roy, Rédacteur-en-chef, groy@annexweb.com

Yardstick
Also Known As: WRLA YardStick
Owned By: Naylor (Canada) Inc.
c/o Naylor (Canada) Inc., #300, 1630 Ness Ave., Winnipeg, MB R3J 3X1
Tel: 204-975-0434; *Fax:* 204-949-9092
Toll-Free: 800-665-2456
www.wrla.org/media-centre/yardstick-magazine
Frequency: 6 times a year; also WRLA Directory & Buyers' Guide (annually, Jan.)
Bill McDougall, Publisher

Funeral Service

The Canadian Funeral Director Magazine
6546 Bethesda Rd., Tyrone, ON L1C 3K6
Tel: 905-666-8011
info@thefuneralmagazine.com
www.thefuneralmagazine.com
Circulation: 3500
Scott Hillier, Publisher & Editor, scott@thefuneralmagazine.com

Canadian Funeral News
#1025, 101 - 6th Ave. SW, Calgary, AB T2P 3P4
Tel: 403-264-3270; *Fax:* 403-264-3276
Toll-Free: 800-465-0322
info@otcommunications.com
www.otcommunications.com/cfn
Frequency: 12 times a year
The journal provides news, articles, profiles, & columns for funeral service professionals throughout Canada.
Pat Ottmann, Publisher, pat@businessincalgary.com
Tim Ottmann, Associate Publisher
Lisa Johnston, Editor
Jessi Evetts, Director, Art

Network
#1025, 101 - 6th Ave. SW, Calgary, AB T2P 3P4
Tel: 403-264-3270; *Fax:* 403-264-3276
Toll-Free: 800-465-0322
info@otcommunications.com
www.otcommunications.com/network-magazine.html
Frequency: 6 times a year
The magazine covers topics such as cemetery management, cremation, & monument designing & building.
Pat Ottman, Publisher, pat@businessincalgary.com
Tim Ottman, Associate Publisher, tim@businessincalgary.com
Lisa Johnston, Editor
Cher Compton, Director, Art, cher@businessincalgary.com

Gardening & Garden Equipment

Canadian Garden Centre & Nursery
Owned By: Annex Publishing & Printing Inc.
PO Box 530, 105 Donly Dr. South, Simcoe, ON N3Y 4N5
Tel: 519-429-3966; *Fax:* 519-429-3094
Toll-Free: 800-265-2827
www.canadiangardencentre.ca
Circulation: 4,000
Frequency: 5 times a year
Brandi Cowen, Editor, bcowen@annexweb.com
Scott Jamieson, Publisher, sjamieson@annexweb.com

Greenhouse Canada
Owned By: Annex Publishing & Printing Inc.
PO Box 530, 105 Donly Dr. South, Simcoe, ON N3Y 4N5
Fax: 519-429-3094
Toll-Free: 888-599-2228
www.greenhousecanada.com
Social Media:
twitter.com/greenhousecan
www.facebook.com/GreenhouseCanada
Frequency: Monthly
Dave Harrison, Editor

Gifts

CGTA Retail News
Canadian Gift & Tableware Association, 42 Voyager Ct. South, Toronto, ON M9W 5M7
Tel: 416-679-0170; *Fax:* 416-679-1868
Toll-Free: 800-611-6100
retailnews@cgta.org
www.cgta.org
Social Media:
twitter.com/RetailNewsMag
www.facebook.com/RetailNewsMagazine
Circulation: 16,529
Frequency: bi-monthly
Tom Foran, Publisher, tforan@cgta.org
Erica Kirkland, Editor, erica@cgta.org

Glass

Glass Canada
Owned By: Annex Publishing & Printing Inc.
PO Box 530, 105 Donly Dr. South, Simcoe, ON N3Y 4N5
Fax: 519-429-3094
Toll-Free: 888-599-2228
www.glasscanadamag.com
Social Media:
twitter.com/GlassCanadaMag
Frequency: 6 times a year
Patrick Flannery, Editor
Martin McAnulty, Publisher

Government

Government Purchasing Guide
Kenilworth Media Inc., #710, 15 Wertheim Ct., Richmond Hill, ON L4B 3H7
Tel: 905-771-7333; *Fax:* 905-771-7336
Toll-Free: 800-409-8688
www.gpmag.ca
Frequency: 6 times a year

Municipal Redbook
Owned By: Reed Construction Data
c/o Reed Construction Data, #101 - 4299 Canada Way, Burnaby, ON V5G 1H3
Tel: 604-433-8164; *Fax:* 604-433-9549
Toll-Free: 888-878-2121
www.journalofcommerce.com
Circulation: 2,000
Frequency: Annually

Municipal World
42860 Sparta Line, Union, ON N0L 2L0
Tel: 519-633-0031; *Fax:* 519-633-1001
Toll-Free: 888-368-6125
www.municipalworld.com
Social Media:
twitter.com/Municipaljobs
www.facebook.com/MunicipalWorld
Circulation: 46,000
Frequency: Monthly

Optimum Online: The Journal of Public Sector Management
The Summit Group, #100, 263 Holmwood Ave., Ottawa, ON K1S 2P8
Tel: 613-688-0763; *Fax:* 613-688-0767
www.optimumonline.ca
Circulation: 10,000
Gilles Paquet, Editor

Parliamentary Names & Numbers
Sources, #201, 812A Bloor St. West, Toronto, ON M6G 1L9
Tel: 416-964-7799; *Fax:* 416-964-8763
sources@sources.ca
www.sources.com
Circulation: 500
Frequency: 2 times a year
Ulli Diemer, Publisher

Urba
Union des municipalitiés de Québec, #680, 680, rue Sherbrooke ouest, Montréal, QC H3A 2M7
Tél: 514-282-7700; *Téléc:* 514-282-8893
www.umq.qc.ca/publications/magazine-urba
Médias sociaux:
twitter.com/UMQuebec
Tirage: 7800
Fréquence: 5 fois par an
Jules Chamberland-Lajoie, Rédacteur-en-chef

Grocery Trade

L'Alimentation
7063, rue Saint-Denis, Montréal, QC H2S 2S5
Tél: 514-271-6922; *Téléc:* 514-271-1308
dbeaudin@l-alimentation.com
www.l-alimentation.com
Tirage: 16,300
Fréquence: 10 fois par an
Diane Beaudin, Éditrice, dbeaudin@l-alimentation.com

Canadian Grocer
Owned By: Rogers Media Inc.
1 Mount Pleasant Rd., 7th Fl., Toronto, ON M4Y 2Y5
Fax: 416-764-1523
Toll-Free: 800-268-9119
www.canadiangrocer.com
Circulation: 17,000
Frequency: 10 times a year
Libby Begg, Publisher, 416-764-1665, libby.begg@rci.rogers.com
Rob Gerlsbeck, Editor, 416-764-1679, rob.gerlsbeck@canadiangrocer.rogers.com

Western Grocer
Owned By: Mercury Publications Ltd.
#16, 1313 Border St., Winnipeg, MB R3H 0X4
Tel: 204-954-2085; *Fax:* 204-954-2057
Toll-Free: 800-337-6372
www.westerngrocer.com
Circulation: 14,185
Frequency: 6 times a year
Robin Bradley, Associate Publisher/Sales Manager, rbradley@mercurypublications.ca

Hardware Trade

Hardware Merchandising
Owned By: Annex-Newcom
80 Valleybrook Dr., Toronto, ON M3B 2S9
Tel: 416-442-5600; *Fax:* 416-510-5140
Toll-Free: 800-268-7742
www.hardwaremagazine.ca
Social Media:
twitter.com/HardwareMagCa
Frequency: 6 times a year
Serves the home improvement retailing industry.
Robert Koci, Publisher, rkoci@canadiancontractor.ca
Rebecca Reid, Editor, rreid@annexnewcom.ca

Home Improvement Retailing
Owned By: Powershift Communications Inc.
Powershift Communications Inc., #501, 245 Fairview Mall Dr., Toronto, ON M2J 4T1
Tel: 416-494-1066; *Fax:* 416-494-2536
info@powershift.ca
www.hirmagazine.com
Circulation: 14,713
Frequency: 6 times a year
Dante Piccinin, Publisher, homeimprovement@rogers.com

Quart de Rond
Assn. des détaillants de matériaux de construction du Québec, #200, 476, rue Jean-Neveu, Longueuil, QC J4G 1N8
Tél: 450-646-5842; *Téléc:* 450-646-6171
information@aqmat.org
www.aqmat.org
Tirage: 3000
Fréquence: 8 fois par an

Health & Medical

L'Actualité Médicale
Détenteur: Éditions Rogers Media
#800, 1200, av McGill College, Montréal, QC H3B 4G7
Tél: 514-843-5141; *Téléc:* 514-843-2183
www.professionsante.ca
Fréquence: 23 fois par an
Caroline Bélisle, Rédactrice en chef

The Alberta Doctors' Digest
Alberta Medical Association, 12230 - 106 Ave. NW, Edmonton, AB T5N 3Z1
Tel: 780-482-2626; *Fax:* 780-482-5445
Toll-Free: 800-270-9680
amamail@albertadoctors.org
www.albertadoctors.org
Social Media:
twitter.com/Albertadoctors
Frequency: Bi-Monthly
Dr. Dennis W. Jirsch, Editor

British Columbia Medical Journal
#115, 1665 West Broadway, Vancouver, BC V6J 5A4
Tel: 604-638-2815; *Fax:* 604-638-2917
Toll-Free: 800-972-2262
journal@bcma.bc.ca
www.bcmj.org
Social Media:
twitter.com/BCMedicalJrnl
www.facebook.com/BCMedicalJournal
Circulation: 10,500
Frequency: 10 times a year
Provides clinical & review articles written by physicians who debate medicine & medical politics in letters as well as long essays
Dr. D.R. Richardson, Editor MD

Canadian Chiropractor
Owned By: Annex Publishing & Printing Inc.
PO Box 530, 105 Donly Dr. South, Simcoe, ON N3Y 4N5
Tel: 519-429-3966; *Fax:* 519-429-3094
Toll-Free: 800-265-2827
www.canadianchiropractor.ca
Circulation: 5,800
Frequency: 8 times a year
Maria DiDanieli, Editor, mdidanieli@annexweb.com
Martin McAnulty, Publisher, mmcanulty@annexweb.com

Canadian Family Physician
College of Family Physicians of Canada, 2630 Skymark Ave., Mississauga, ON L4W 5A4
Tel: 905-629-0900; *Fax:* 905-629-0893
Toll-Free: 800-387-6197
CFPmedia@cfpc.ca
www.cfp.ca
Social Media:
twitter.com/CanFamPhysician
Frequency: Monthly
Kathryn Taylor, Managing Editor

Canadian Geriatrics Journal
Previous Name: Geriatrics Today: Journal of Canadian Geriatrics Society
The Canadian Geriatrics Society, #6, 20 Crown Steel Dr., Markham, ON L3R 9X9
Tel: 905-415-9161; *Fax:* 905-415-0071
Toll-Free: 866-247-0086
www.canadiangeriatrics.ca/default/index.cfm/journal
Circulation: 15,500
Frequency: 4 times a year
John D. Birkby, Publisher

Canadian Healthcare Technology
#207, 1118 Centre St., Thornhill, ON L4J 7R9
Tel: 905-709-2330; *Fax:* 905-709-2258
info2@canhealth.com
www.canhealth.com
Circulation: 12,715
Frequency: 8 times a year
Jerry Zeidenberg, Publisher

Canadian Journal of Anesthesia / Journal Canadien d'Anesthésie
c/o Canadian Anesthesiologists' Society, #208, 1 Eglinton Ave. East, Toronto, ON M4P 3A1
Tel: 416-480-0602; *Fax:* 416-480-0320
anesthesia@cas.ca
www.cas.ca/English/Canadian-Journal-of-Anesthesia
Social Media:
twitter.com/CASUpdate
Frequency: Monthly
Hilary Grocott, Editor-in-chief
Carolyn Gillis, Editorial Assistant

Canadian Journal of Cardiology
Owned By: Elsevier Inc.
Canadian Cardiovascular Society, #1403, 222 Queen St., Toronto, ON K1P 5V9
Tel: 613-569-3407; *Fax:* 613-569-6574
Toll-Free: 877-569-3407
www.onlinecjc.ca
Circulation: 15,500
Frequency: 14 times a year
The official journal of the Canadian Cardiovascular Society (CCS).
Dr. Stanley Nattel, Editor, stanley.nattel@icm-mhi.org
Jane Grochowski, Publisher, j.grochowski@elsevier.com

The Canadian Journal of Continuing Medical Education
Owned By: STA Communications Inc.
#310, 6500 Trans-Canada Hwy., Pointe-Claire, QC H9R 0A5
Tel: 514-695-7623
www.cjdiagnosis.com
Circulation: 37,000
Frequency: 10 times per year

The Canadian Journal of Diagnosis
Owned By: STA Communications Inc.
#310, 6500 Trans-Canada Hwy., Pointe-Claire, QC H9R 0A5
Tel: 514-695-7623
www.cjdiagnosis.com
Circulation: 37,000
Frequency: Monthly

Canadian Journal of Dietetic Practice & Research / Revue canadienne de la pratique et de la recherche en diété
#604, 480 University Ave., Toronto, ON M5G 1V2
Tel: 416-596-0857; *Fax:* 416-596-0603
editor@dietitians.ca
www.dcjournal.ca
Frequency: Quarterly
Dawna Royall, Editor

Canadian Journal of Emergency Medicine (CJEM/JCMU) / Journal canadien de la médecine d'urgence
Owned By: Decker Publishing
628 Cowan Circle, Pickering, ON L1W 3K7
Tel: 613-523-3343; *Fax:* 613-523-0190
Toll-Free: 800-463-1158
cjem@rogers.com
www.cjem-online.ca
Circulation: 4,000
Frequency: 6 times a year
Dr. Jim Ducharme, Editor-in-Chief

Canadian Journal of Gastroenterology & Hepatology (CJGH) / Journal Canadien de Gastroenterologie
Owned By: Pulsus Group Inc.
2902 South Sheridan Way, Oakville, ON L6J 7L6
Tel: 905-829-4770; *Fax:* 905-829-4799
pulsus@pulsus.com
www.pulsus.com
Frequency: Monthly
Official journal of the Canadian Association of Gastroenterology and the Canadian Association for the Study of the Liver.
Subrata Ghosh, Editor-in-chief

Canadian Journal of Infectious Diseases & Medical Microbiology (CJIDMM)
Owned By: Pulsus Group Inc.
2902 South Sheridan Way, Oakville, ON L6J 7L6
Tel: 905-829-4770; *Fax:* 905-829-4799
pulsus@pulsus.com
www.pulsus.com
Frequency: 6 times a year
Official journal of Medical Microbiology and Infectious Disease Canada (AMMI Canada).

Canadian Journal of Medical Laboratory Science (CJMLS)
Cdn. Society for Medical Laboratory Science, 33 Wellington St. North, Hamilton, ON L8R 1M7
Tel: 905-528-8642; *Fax:* 905-528-4968
Toll-Free: 800-263-8277
info@csmls.org
www.csmls.org
Frequency: Quarterly
Journal available only to members

The Canadian Journal of Occupational Therapy (CJOT) / Revue canadienne d'ergothérapie
Carleton Technology & Training Centre, #3400, 1125 Colonel By Dr., Ottawa, ON K1S 5R1
Tel: 613-523-2268; *Fax:* 613-523-2552
Toll-Free: 800-434-2268
publications@caot.ca
www.caot.ca
Social Media:
twitter.com/CAOT_ACE
www.facebook.com/CAOT.ca
Circulation: 7,000
Frequency: 5 times a year
Marcia Finlayson, Editor

Canadian Journal of Ophthalmology (CJO)
c/o Canadian Ophthalmological Society, #610, 1525 Carling Ave., Ottawa, ON K1Z 8R9
Tel: 613-729-6779; *Fax:* 613-729-7209
www.canadianjournalofophthalmology.ca
Frequency: 7 times a year
Phil Hooper, Editor-in-Chief MD, FRSCSC

Canadian Journal of Public Health (CJPH) / Revue canadienne de santé publique
Canadian Public Health Association, #404, 1525 Carling Ave., Ottawa, ON K1Z 8R9
Tel: 613-725-3769; *Fax:* 613-725-9826
cjph@cpha.ca
www.cpha.ca/en/cjph.aspx
Frequency: Bi-monthly
Louise Potvin, Editor in Chief

Canadian Journal of Rural Medicine (CJRM) / Journal canadien de la médecine rurale
Owned By: Canadian Medical Association
Canadaian Medical Association, PO Box 22015, 45 Overlea Blvd., Toronto, ON M4H 1N9
Tel: 416-961-7775; *Fax:* 416-961-8271
cjrm@cjrm.net
www.cma.ca/cjrm
Circulation: 7,000
Frequency: 4 times a year
Suzanne Kingsmill, Managing Editor, manedcjrm@gmail.com

Canadian Journal of Surgery (CJS/JCC) / Journal canadien de chirurgie
Owned By: Canadian Medical Association
1867 Alta Vista Dr., Ottawa, ON K1G 5W8
Tel: 613-731-8610; *Fax:* 613-565-5471
Toll-Free: 800-663-7336
www.cma.ca/cjs
Frequency: 6 times a year
A peer reviewed journal meeting the medical education needs of Canada's surgical specialists
Wendy Carroll, Managing Editor, wendy.carroll@cma.ca

Canadian Nursing Home
c/o Health Media Inc., PO Box 45566, 2397 King George Blvd., Surrey, BC V4A 9N3
info@nursinghomemagazine.ca
www.nursinghomemagazine.ca
Circulation: 3000
Frequency: 4 times a year
Agnes Forster, Publisher
Frank Fagan, Editor

Canadian Respiratory Journal
Owned By: Pulsus Group Inc.
Pulsus Group Inc., 2902 South Sheridan Way, Oakville, ON L6J 7L6
Tel: 905-829-4770; *Fax:* 905-829-4799
Toll-Free: 866-879-4770
pulsus@pulsus.com
www.pulsus.com
Circulation: 15,600
Frequency: 8 times a year
Official journal of the Canadian Thoracic Society.
Robert B. Kalina, Publisher
Peter Paré, Editor-in-chief

The Chronicle of Cardiovascular & Internal Medicine
Owned By: Chronicle Companies
#306, 555 Burnhamthorpe Rd., Toronto, ON M9C 2Y3
Tel: 416-916-2476; *Fax:* 416-352-6199
Toll-Free: 866-632-4766
health@chronicle.org
chronicle.ca/cardiology_journal.html
Circulation: 5,843
Frequency: 6 times a year
Mitchell Shannon, Publisher
R. Allan Ryan, Editorial Director

The Chronicle of Neurology & Psychiatry
Owned By: Chronicle Companies
#306, 555 Burnhamthorpe Rd., Toronto, ON M9C 2Y3
Tel: 416-916-2476; *Fax:* 416-352-6199
Toll-Free: 866-632-4766
health@chronicle.org
chronicle.ca/neurology&psychiatry_tabloid.html
Circulation: 6,189
Frequency: 9 times a year
Mitchell Shannon, Publisher
R. Allan Ryan, Senior Editor

The Chronicle of Skin & Allergy
Owned By: Chronicle Companies
#306, 555 Burnhamthorpe Rd., Toronto, ON M9C 2Y3
Tel: 416-916-2476; *Fax:* 416-352-6199
Toll-Free: 866-632-4766
health@chronicle.org
chronicle.ca/skin&allergy_tabloid.html
Circulation: 7,045
Frequency: 9 times a year
R. Allan Ryan, Senior Editor
Mitchell Shannon, Publisher

The Chronicle of Urology & Sexual Medicine
Owned By: Chronicle Companies
#306, 555 Burnhamthorpe Rd., Toronto, ON M9C 2Y3
Tel: 416-916-2476; *Fax:* 416-352-6199
Toll-Free: 866-632-4766
health@chronicle.org
chronicle.ca/urology_journal.html
Circulation: 5,020
Frequency: 6 times a year
The Chronicle of Urology & Sexual Medicine is a scientific newspaper providing news and information on practical therapeutics and clinical progress in urology and sexual medicine.
Mitchell Shannon, Publisher
R. Allan Ryan, Senior Editor

Clinical & Investigative Medicine (CIM) / Médecine clinique et expérimentale
CSCI Head Office, 774 Echo Dr., Ottawa, ON K1S 5N8
cimonline.ca
Circulation: 1,000
Frequency: 6 times a year
Dr. Jonathan Angel, Editor, jangel@ohri.ca

Clinical & Refractive Optometry
Previous Name: Practical Optometry
Owned By: Mediconcept Inc.
#250, 2113 St. Regis Blvd, Montréal, QC H9B 2M9
Tel: 514-447-1110
info@mediconcept.ca
www.cscro.com
Circulation: 3000
Frequency: 4 times a year
Official journal of the Canadian Society of Clinical and Refractive Optometry.
Lawrence Goldstein, Publisher, lgoldstein@mediconcept.ca
Mary D. Lemme, Managing Editor, mdilemme@mediconcept.ca

Coup d'oeil
Breton Communications Inc., #202, 495, boul St-Martin ouest, Laval, QC H7M 1Y9
Tél: 450-629-6005; *Téléc:* 450-629-6044
Ligne sans frais: 888-462-2112
info@bretoncom.com
www.bretoncom.com
Tirage: 4,055
Fréquence: mensuel
Martine Breton, President

CrossCurrents: The Journal of Addiction & Mental Health
Centre for Addiction & Mental Health, 33 Russell St., Toronto, ON M5S 2S1
www.camh.ca
Frequency: 4 times a year

Dental Chronicle
Owned By: Chronicle Companies
#306, 555 Burnhamthorpe Rd., Toronto, ON M9C 2Y3
Tel: 416-916-2476; *Fax:* 416-352-6199
Toll-Free: 866-632-4766
health@chronicle.org
chronicle.ca/dentistry_tabloid.html
Circulation: 33,682
Frequency: 6 times a year
Mitchell Shannon, Publisher
R. Allan Ryan, Senior Editor

Dental Practice Management
Previous Name: Dental Guide
Owned By: Annex-Newcom
80 Valleybrook Dr., Toronto, ON M3B 2S9
Tel: 416-510-6785; *Fax:* 416-510-5140
Toll-Free: 800-268-7742
www.oralhealthjournal.com
Other information: Toll Free: U.S. 1-800-387-0273
Circulation: 18,700
Frequency: 4 times a year
Catherine Wilson, Editor, cwilson@oralhealthjournal.com

Doctor's Review
Owned By: Parkhurst Publishing
400 McGill St., 4th Fl., Montréal, QC H2Y 2G1
Tel: 514-397-8833 *Toll-Free:* 800-663-7403
dr_editors@parkpub.com
www.doctorsreview.com
Social Media:
twitter.com/doctorsreview
www.facebook.com/doctorsreview
Frequency: 10 times per year
Monthly travel and lifestyle journal.
David Elkins, Publisher
Annarosa Sabbadini, Editor

doctorNS
Previous Name: Medical Society of Nova Scotia DoctorsNS; Medical Society of Nova Scot
Doctors Nova Scotia, 5 Spectacle Lake Dr., Dartmouth, NS B3B 1X7
Tel: 902-468-1866; *Fax:* 902-468-6578
info@doctorsns.com
www.doctorsns.com
Social Media:
twitter.com/Doctors_NS
Circulation: 3,000
Frequency: 10 times a year
Melissa Murray, Production Manager, 902-481-4923, melissa.murray@doctorsns.com

Drug Rep Chronicle
Owned By: Chronicle Companies
#306, 555 Burnhamthorpe Rd., Toronto, ON M9C 2Y3
Tel: 416-916-2476; *Fax:* 416-352-6199
Toll-Free: 866-632-4766
health@chronicle.org
chronicle.ca/drugrep_tabloid.html

Drugstore Canada
Owned By: Rogers Media Inc.
1 Mount Pleasant Rd., 7 Floor, Toronto, ON M4Y 2Y5
Tel: 416-764-2000; *Fax:* 416-764-3930
www.canadianhealthcarenetwork.ca
Circulation: 16,703
Frequency: 10 times a year

Fédération des Médecins Omnipraticien du Québec (FMOQ)
2, Place Alexis Nihon, #2000, 3500 boul de Maisonneuve ouest, 20e étage, Westmount, QC H3Z 3C1
Tél: 514-878-1911; *Téléc:* 514-878-4455
Ligne sans frais: 800-361-8499
mpsaintgelais@fmoq.org
www.fmoq.org
Médias sociaux: www.youtube.com/lafmoq
twitter.com/OMNIPRATICIENS
www.facebook.com/lafmoq

Tirage: 14,000
Fréquence: Mensuel
Louise Roy, Rédacteur M.D.

Fitness Business Canada
Owned By: Mill Pond Publishing Inc.
30 Mill Pond Dr., Georgetown, ON L7G 4S6
Tel: 905-873-0850; *Fax:* 905-873-8611
Toll-Free: 888-920-6537
www.fitnet.ca
Other information: www.youtube.com/user/FitnessBusinessMag
Social Media:
www.linkedin.com/company/fitness-business-canada
twitter.com/FBCMagazine
www.facebook.com/FitnessBusinessCanada

Circulation: 8,000+
Publication aimed at owners, directors, managers, leaders & staff of health & fitness facilities.
Graham Longwell, President & Editor
Stephen Longwell, General Manager

FMWC Newsletter
Federation of Medical Women of Canada, 780 Echo Dr., Ottawa, ON K1S 5R7
Tel: 613-569-5881; *Fax:* 613-569-4432
Toll-Free: 877-771-3777
fmwcmain@fmwc.ca
www.fmwc.ca

Circulation: 1,000
Frequency: 3 times a year
Crystal Cannon, President

Guide to Canadian Healthcare Facilities
Previous Name: Canadian Hospital Association Buyer's Guide
Also Known As: The Guide
c/o HealthCareCAN, #100, 17 York St., Ottawa, ON K1N 9J6
Tel: 613-241-8005; *Fax:* 613-241-9481
guide@healthcarecan.ca
www.healthcarecan.ca/onlineguide
Social Media:
twitter.com/healthcarecan
www.facebook.com/healthcarecan.soinssantecan

Circulation: 1,300
Frequency: annual
Claire Samuelson, Editor

Health, Wellness & Safety Magazine (HWS)
Owned By: Business Link Media Group
#200, 36 Hiscott St., St Catharines, ON L2R 1C8
Tel: 905-646-9366; *Fax:* 905-646-5486
info@hwsmag.com
www.hwsmag.com
Social Media:
twitter.com/HWSmag
www.facebook.com/110793588938756

Frequency: Bi-monthly
Distributed to health, wellness & safety professionals in the Niagara, Hamilton, Burlington & Oakville regions.
Adam Shields, Co-Publisher, adam@businesslinkmedia.com
Jim Shields, Co-Publisher, jim@businesslinkmedia.com

HEALTHbeat
#319, 9768 - 170 St., Edmonton, AB T5T 5L4
Toll-Free: 800-727-0782
www.mccronehealthbeat.com

Circulation: 40,000
Frequency: 12 times a year
Jan Henry, Publisher

Healthcare Management FORUM / Forum gestion des soins de santé
Canadian College of Health Service Executives, 292 Somerset St. West, Ottawa, ON K2P 0J6
Tel: 613-235-7218; *Fax:* 613-235-5451
Toll-Free: 800-363-9056
www.healthcaremanagementforum.org

Frequency: Quarterly
Ron Lindstrom, Editor-in-Chief

Hospital News, Canada
#401, 610 Applewood Cres., Vaughan, ON L4K 0E3
Tel: 905-532-2600
info@hospitalnews.com
www.hospitalnews.com
Social Media:
www.facebook.com/pages/Hospital-News/106824762695648
Frequency: Monthly
Stefan Dreesen, Publisher
Kristie Jones, Editor

The Journal of Current Clinical Care
info@healthplexus.net
www.healthplexus.net
Social Media:
www.facebook.com/pages/HealthPlexus-and-JCCC/172966859396

Frequency: 6 times a year
Michael Yasny, Publisher
Kristin Casady, Editorial Director

Journal of Medical Imaging and Radiation Sciences / Le Journal Canadien des Techniques en Radiation Médicale
Canadian Assn. of Medical Radiation Technologists, #1000, 85 Albert St., Ottawa, ON K1P 6A4
Tel: 613-234-0012; *Fax:* 613-234-1097
Toll-Free: 800-463-9729
editor@camrt.ca
www.camrt.ca

Frequency: 4 times a year
CAMRT Journal available only to members
Lisa Di Prospero, Editor in Chief

Journal of Obstetrics & Gynaecology Canada (JOGC)
Previous Name: Obstetrics & Gynaecology Canada
Also Known As: SOGC
Owned By: Society of Obstetricians and Gynaecologists of Canada
Women's Health Centre Building, #405A-D, 4500 Oak St., Vancouver, BC V6H 3N1
Tel: 604-875-2424; *Fax:* 604-875-2590
editor@sogc.com
www.jogc.com

Frequency: Monthly
Timothy Rowe, Editor-in-Chief MB, FRCSC
Victoria Allenall, Deputy Editor MD, MSc, FRCSC

Journal of Psychiatry & Neuroscience (JPN) / Revue de psychiatrie & de neuroscience
Owned By: Canadian Medical Association
1867 Alta Vista Dr., Ottawa, ON K1G 5W8
Tel: 613-731-8610; *Fax:* 613-565-7488
Toll-Free: 800-663-7336
jpn@cma.ca
www.cma.ca/jpn

Frequency: 6 times a year
Wendy Carroll, Managing Editor

The Journal of Rheumatology
Journal of Rheumatology Publishing Co. Ltd., #901, 365 Bloor St. East, Toronto, ON M4W 3L4
Tel: 416-967-5155; *Fax:* 416-967-7556
jrheum@jrheum.com
www.jrheum.com
Social Media:
twitter.com/jrheum
www.facebook.com/journalofrheumatology

Frequency: Monthly
Earl D. Silverman, Editor

Journal SOGC
Also Known As: Journal of the Society of Obstetricians & Gynacologists of Canada
c/o Society of Obstetrician & Gynaecology of Canada, 780 Echo Dr., Ottawa, ON K1P 5J3
Tel: 613-730-4192; *Fax:* 613-730-4314
Toll-Free: 800-561-2416
info@sogc.com
www.sogc.org/jogc

Frequency: Monthly
Timothy Rowe, Editor in Chief

Long Term Care
Ontario Long Term Care Association, #500, 425 University Ave., Toronto, ON M5G 1T6
Tel: 647-256-3490
info@oltca.com
www.oltca.com

Circulation: 5800
Frequency: 3 times per year
Robert Thompson, Publisher

Ali Mintenko-Crane, Editor
Roma Ihnatowycz, Editor

Massage Therapy Canada
Owned By: Annex Publishing & Printing Inc.
PO Box 530, 105 Donly Dr. South, Simcoe, ON N3Y 4N5
Tel: 519-429-3966; *Fax:* 519-429-3094
Toll-Free: 800-265-2827
www.massagetherapycanada.com

Circulation: 5,800
Frequency: 4 times a year
Mari-Len De Guzman, Editor, 905-726-4659, mdeguzman@annexweb.com

Médecine/sciences
#800, 500, Sherbrooke ouest, Montréal, QC H3A 3C6
Tél: 514-288-2247; *Téléc:* 514-288-0520

Tirage: 2 007
Fréquence: 10 fois par an
Michel Bergeron, Directeur général

The Medical Post
Owned By: Rogers Media Inc.
1 Mount Pleasant Rd., 7th Fl., Toronto, ON M4Y 2Y5
Tel: 416-764-3920
www.canadianhealthcarenetwork.ca
Social Media:
twitter.com/MedicalPost

Circulation: 47,000
Frequency: 14 times a year
Janet Smith, Publisher
Colin Leslie, Editor

Nutrition - Science en Evolution
Anciennement: Diététique en Action
#1855, 550, rue Sherbrooke ouest, Montréal, QC H3A 1B9
Tél: 514-393-3733; *Téléc:* 514-393-3582
Ligne sans frais: 888-393-8528
opdq@opdq.org
www.opdq.org

Fréquence: 3 fois par ans
Paule Bernier, Présidente

Obesity Surgery
PO Box 1002, 5863 Leslie St., Toronto, ON M2H 1J8
Tel: 416-224-5055; *Fax:* 416-224-5455
journal@obesitysurgery.com
www.springer.com
Social Media:
twitter.com/clinmedjournals

Circulation: 2,300
Frequency: 12 times a year
Victoria Ferrara, Editor, victoria.ferrara@springer.com

Occupational Therapy Now / Actualités ergothérapiques
CTTC Bldg., #3400, 1125 Colonel By Dr., Ottawa, ON K1S 5R1
Tel: 613-523-2268; *Fax:* 613-523-2552
Toll-Free: 800-434-2268
otnow@caot.ca
www.caot.ca/default.asp?pageid=7
Social Media:
twitter.com/CAOT_ACE
www.facebook.com/CAOT.ca

Circulation: 6,500
Frequency: 6 times a year
Fern Swedlove, Editor

Oncology Exchange
Owned By: Parkhurst Publishing
400, rue McGill, 3e étage, Montréal, QC H2Y 2G1
Tel: 514-397-8833; *Fax:* 514-397-0228
www.oncologyex.com

Circulation: 6,000
Frequency: Quarterly
Devon Phillips, Editor, phillips@parkpub.com

Ontario Medical Review (OMR)
Ontario Medical Assn., #900, 150 Bloor St., Toronto, ON M5S 3C1
Tel: 416-599-2580; *Fax:* 416-340-2232
Toll-Free: 800-268-7215
www.oma.org
Social Media:
twitter.com/OntariosDoctors
www.facebook.com/Ontariosdoctors?v=wall

Circulation: 33,000
Frequency: 11 times a year
Jeff Henry, Editor, 416-340-2262, Fax: 416-340-2232, jeff.henry@omr.org

Elizabeth Petruccelli, Managing Editor, 416-340-2264, Fax: 416-340-2232, elizabeth.petruccekku@omr.org
Kim Secord, Circulation Manager, kim.secord@omr.org

Optical Prism
Nusand Publishing Inc., #1113, 250 the East Mall, Toronto, ON M9B 6L3
Tel: 416-233-2487; *Fax:* 416-233-1746
info@opticalprism.ca
www.opticalprism.ca
Social Media: pinterest.com/opticalprism
twitter.com/opticalprism
www.facebook.com/O pticalPrismMagazine
Frequency: 8 times a year
Robert May, Publisher
Sarah McGoldrick, Managing Editor, smcgoldrick@opticalprism.ca

Opti-Guide
Breton Communications Inc., #202, 495, boul St-Martin ouest, Laval, QC H7M 1Y9
Tel: 450-629-6005; *Fax:* 450-629-6044
Toll-Free: 888-462-2112
info@bretoncom.com
www.opti-guide.com
Circulation: 5,481
Frequency: Annually
Martine Breton, President/Publisher, martine@bretoncom.com

L'Optométriste
Association des optométristes du Québec, #217, 1255, boul. Robert-Bourassa, Montréal, QC H3B 3B2
Tél: 514-288-6272; *Téléc:* 514-288-7071
aoq@aoqnet.qc.ca
www.aoqnet.qc.ca/quest-ce-que-laoq/la-revue-loptometris te
Fréquence: 6 fois par an

Paediatrics & Child Health
Owned By: Pulsus Group Inc.
Pulsus Group Inc., 2902 South Sheridan Way, Oakville, ON L6J 7L6
Tel: 905-829-4770; *Fax:* 905-829-4799
Toll-Free: 866-879-9770
pulsus@pulsus.com
www.pulsus.com
Circulation: 14,500
Frequency: 10 times a year
Official journal of the Canadian Paediatric Society.
Robert Kalina, Publisher
Dr. Noni MacDonald, Editor

Pain Research & Management
Previous Name: Pain Research Management
Owned By: Pulsus Group Inc.
Pulsus Group Inc., 2902 South Sheridan Way, Oakville, ON L6J 7L6
Tel: 905-829-4770; *Fax:* 905-829-4799
Toll-Free: 866-879-4770
pulsus@pulsus.com
www.pulsus.com
Circulation: 15,300
Frequency: 4 times a year
Official journal of the Canadian Pain Society.
Robert Kalina, Publisher
Dr. Kenneth D. Craig, Editor

Parkhurst Exchange
Owned By: Parkhurst Publishing
400, rue McGill, 3e étage, Montréal, QC H2Y 2G1
Tel: 514-397-8833; *Fax:* 514-397-0228
Toll-Free: 800-663-7403
parkex@parkpub.com
www.parkhurstexchange.com/
Circulation: 39,453
Frequency: 12 times a year
Monthly GP/FP journal.
Madeleine Pantais, Publisher

Physiotherapy Canada
Owned By: University of Toronto Press
5201 Dufferin St., Toronto, ON M3H 5T8
Tel: 416-667-7777; *Fax:* 416-667-7881
editor@physiotherapy.ca
www.physiotherapy.ca
Frequency: 4 times a year
Dina Brooks, Scientific Editor PhD, dina.brooks@utoronto.ca

The Plastic Surgery / Chirurgie plastique
Previous Name: Canadian Journal of Plastic Surgery
Owned By: Pulsus Group Inc.
2902 South Sheridan Way, Oakville, ON L6J 7L6
Tel: 905-829-4770; *Fax:* 905-829-4799
pulsus@pulsus.com
www.pulsus.com
Frequency: 4 times a year
Official journal of the Canadian Society of Plastic Surgeons, the Canadian Society for Aesthetic (Cosmetic) Plastic Surgery, Groupe pour l'Avancement de la Microchirurgie Canada, and the Canadian Society for Surgery of the Hand (Manus Canada).
Edward Buchel, Editor

Rehab & Community Care Medicine
Previous Name: Rehab & Community Care Management
#803, 255 Duncan Mill Rd., Toronto, ON M3B 3H9
Tel: 416-421-7944; *Fax:* 416-421-8418
Toll-Free: 800-798-6282
www.rehabmagazine.ca
Frequency: Quarterly
Caroline Tapp-McDougall, Publisher & Editor-in-Chief
Helmut Dostal, Managing Editor

Heating, Plumbing, Air Conditioning

Contracting Canada Magazine
114 Donjon Blvd., Port Dover, ON N0A 1N4
Tel: 905-569-2777; *Fax:* 905-569-2444
www.contractingcanada.com
Circulation: 29,000
Frequency: 4 times a year
Contracting Canada's editorial focus is on the latest industry innovations including products, service and troubleshooting techniques, system design and installation profiles, sales and marketing features. Departments include field service and installation tips, technical advice from industry experts, the latest innovations and applications of products, tools and instruments for contractors.
Don B. Beaulieu, Publisher & Editorial Director, 905-569-2777, Fax: 905-569-2444, don@contractingcanada.com

Heating Plumbing Air Conditioning
Owned By: Annex Publishing & Printing Inc.
80 Valleybrook Dr., Toronto, ON M3B 2S9
Tel: 416-442-5600; *Fax:* 416-510-5140
www.hpacmag.com
Social Media:
twitter.com/hpacmag
Frequency: 7 times a year; also Buyers Guide (annually, Aug.)
Peter Leonard, Publisher, 416-510-6847, PLeonard@hpacmag.com
Kerry Turner, Editor, 416-510-5218, KTurner@hpacmag.com

Inter-mécanique du bâtiment (CMMTQ)
8175, boul St-Laurent, Montréal, QC H2P 2M1
Tél: 514-382-2668; *Téléc:* 514-382-1566
Ligne sans frais: 800-465-2668
cmmtq@cmmtq.org
www.cmmtq.org
Tirage: 7000
Fréquence: 10 fois par an
Martin Lessard, Rédacteur-en-chef

Plumbing & HVAC Product News
Previous Name: HVAC Refrigeration; Plumbing, Piping & Heating Magazine
Owned By: Newcon Business Media
451 Attwell Dr., Toronto, ON M9W 5C4
Tel: 416-614-0955; *Fax:* 416-614-8861
www.plumbingandhvac.ca
Frequency: 6 times a year
Simon Blake, Editor, simon@plumbingandhvac.ca
Mark Vreugdenhil, Publisher, mark@plumbingandhvac.ca

Hotels & Restaurants

Bar & Beverage Business Magazine
Owned By: Mercury Publications Ltd.
#16, 1313 Border St., Winnipeg, MB R3H 0X4
Tel: 204-954-2085; *Fax:* 204-954-2057
Toll-Free: 800-337-6372
www.barandbeverage.com
Circulation: 14,500
Frequency: 6 times a year
For managers, owners & staff of nightclubs, bars, cabarets, hotels, restaurants & lounges in Canada
Elaine Dufault, Associate Publisher & National Account Manager, edufault@mercurypublications.ca

BC Restaurant News
Owned By: BC Restaurant & Food Services Association
#2, 2246 Spruce St., Vancouver, BC V6H 2P3
Tel: 604-669-2239; *Fax:* 604-669-6175
Toll-Free: 877-669-2239
info@bcrfa.com
www.bcrfa.com
Social Media:
www.linkedin.com/company/bc-restaurant-&-foodservices
twitter.com/BCRFA
www.facebook.com/BCRFA
Frequency: 8 times a year
Publishes information about British Columbia and its restaurants
Ian Tostenson, President & Chief Executive Officer, itostenson@bcrfa.com

Canadian Lodging News
Owned By: Ishcom Publications Ltd.
#201, 2065 Dundas St. East, Mississauga, ON L4X 2W1
Tel: 905-206-0150; *Fax:* 905-206-9972
Toll-Free: 800-201-8596
canadianlodgingnews.com
Circulation: 9,000
Frequency: 10 times a year
Steven Isherwood, Publisher, sisherwood@can-lodgingnews.com

Chef & Grocer
Previous Name: Le Chef
252, Rte. St-André, Saint-Étienne-de-Lauzon, QC G6J 1E8
Tel: 418-831-5317; *Fax:* 418-831-5172
Toll-Free: 800-363-1727
info@chefandgrocer.com
www.chefandgrocer.com
Social Media:
twitter.com/ChefandGrocer
www.facebook.com/chefandgrocer
Circulation: 26,000
Frequency: Monthly; Bilingual
Maurice LeBlanc, Publisher, mleblanc@chefandgrocer.com
Gabrielle Dubé, Editor-in-chief, redaction@chefandgrocer.com

Foodservice & Hospitality
Previous Name: Canadian Hotel & Restaurant Product News
Owned By: Kostuch Publications Ltd.
#101, 23 Lesmill Rd., Toronto, ON M3B 3P6
Tel: 416-447-0888; *Fax:* 416-447-5333
www.foodserviceandhospitality.com
Circulation: 100,000
Frequency: 11 times a year
Rosanna Caira, Editor & Publisher
Amy Bostock, Managing Editor

Hotelier
Owned By: Kostuch Publications Ltd.
#101, 23 Lesmill Rd., Toronto, ON M3B 3P6
Tel: 416-447-0888; *Fax:* 416-447-5333
www.hoteliermagazine.com
Social Media:
twitter.com/hoteliermag
www.facebook.com/HotelierMagazine
Frequency: 8 times a year
Rosanna Caira, Editor & Publisher
Amy Bostock, Managing Editor

Ontario Restaurant News
Owned By: Ishcom Publications Ltd.
#201, 2065 Dundas St. East, Mississauga, ON L4X 2W1
Tel: 905-206-0150; *Fax:* 905-206-9972
Toll-Free: 800-201-8596
canadianrestaurantnews.com
Frequency: Monthly
Steven Isherwood, Publisher, sisherwood@canadianrestaurantnews.com

Pacific Prairie Restaurants News
Previous Name: Western Hospitality News
Owned By: Ishcom Publications Ltd.
#201, 2065 Dundas St. East, Mississauga, ON M6R 1W8
Tel: 905-206-0150; *Fax:* 905-206-9972
Toll-Free: 800-201-8596
lwu@can-restaurantnews.com
www.can-restaurantnews.com
Circulation: 14,000
Frequency: 6 times a year
Steven Isherwood, Publisher, 905-206-0150,ext.236, sisherwood@canadianrestaurantnews.com
Kristen Smith, Managing Editor, 905-206-0150,ext.238, ksmith@canadianrestaurantnews.com

Western Hotelier
Owned By: Mercury Publications Ltd.
c/o Mercury Publications, 1740 Wellington Ave., Winnipeg, MB R3H 0E8
Tel: 204-979-6071; *Fax:* 204-954-2057
david@mercury.mb.ca
www.westernhotelier.com

Circulation: 5,200
Frequency: 5 times a year
Frank Yeo, Publisher
Kelly Gray, Editor, editorial@mercury.mb.ca
Kristi Balon, Editorial Coordinator, editorial@mercury.mb.ca

Western Restaurant News
Owned By: Mercury Publications Ltd.
#16, 1313 Border St., Winnipeg, MB R3H 0X4
Fax: 204-954-2057
Toll-Free: 800-337-6372
www.westernrestaurantnews.com

Circulation: 15,000
Frequency: Quarterly
Elaine Dufault, Associate Publisher/Sales Manager, edufault@mercurypublications.ca

Housewares

HomeStyle Magazine
Lorell Communication Inc., 146 Cavendish Ct., Oakville, ON L6J 5S2
Tel: 905-338-0799; *Fax:* 905-338-5623
www.homestylemag.ca

Frequency: 6 times per year
Laurie O'Halloran, Publisher & Editor, laurie@homestylemag.ca

Human Resources

Canadian HR Reporter
Owned By: Thomson Reuters Canada Ltd.
1 Corporate Plaza, 2075 Kennedy Rd., Toronto, ON M1T 3V4
Tel: 416-609-3800; *Fax:* 416-298-5031
Toll-Free: 800-387-5164
www.hrreporter.com
Social Media:
twitter.com/hrreporter

Frequency: 22 times a year
John Hobel, Publisher, 416-298-5197, john.hobel@thomsonreuters.com

HR Professional Magazine
Previous Name: Human Resources Professional
c/o HRPA, #200, 150 Bloor St. West, Toronto, ON M5S 2X9
Tel: 416-923-2324; *Fax:* 416-923-7264
Toll-Free: 800-387-1311
info@hrpatoday.ca
www.hrpatoday.ca
Social Media:
linkedin.com/pub/hr-professional-magazine/1a/b96/861
www.facebook.com/HR ProfessionalMag

Frequency: 8 times a year
Jill Harris, Editor

Human Resources Magazine Canada
Also Known As: HRM Canada
Owned By: Key Media Inc.
#800, 312 Adelaide St. West, Toronto, ON M5V 1R2
Tel: 416-644-8740; *Fax:* 416-203-9083
subscriptions@kmimedia.ca
www.hrmonline.ca
Social Media:
www.linkedin.com/groups/HRM-Online-Canada-8336040
twitter.com/HRMCanada
www.facebook.com/HRMOnlineCA

Circulation: 32,000
Vernon Jones, Editor, vernon.jones@kmimedia.ca

Industrial & Industrial Automation

Canadian Electronics
Owned By: Annex Publishing & Printing Inc.
222 Edward St., Aurora, ON L4G 1W6
Tel: 905-727-0077; *Fax:* 905-727-0017
www.canadianelectronics.ca
Social Media:
twitter.com/cdnelectronics

Circulation: 17,448
Frequency: 4 times a year
Klaus Pirker, Publisher, 905-726-4670, kpirker@annexweb.com
Mike Edwards, Editorial Director, 905-713-4389, medwards@annexweb.com

Energy Manager
Owned By: Annex Publishing & Printing Inc.
222 Edward St., Aurora, ON LAG 1W6
Tel: 905-727-0077; *Fax:* 905-727-0017
Toll-Free: 800-265-2827
www.energy-manager.ca
Social Media:
twitter.com/manageurenergy

Circulation: 18,135
Frequency: Monthly
John MacPherson, Group Publisher, 905-713-4335, jmacpherson@annexweb.com
Anthony Capkun, Editor, 905-713-4391, acapkun@annexweb.com

Manufacturing Automation
Previous Name: Manufacturing & Process Automation
Owned By: Annex Publishing & Printing Inc.
222 Edward St., Aurora, ON L4G 1W6
Tel: 905-727-0077; *Fax:* 905-727-0017
www.automationmag.com
Social Media:
twitter.com/automationmag

Circulation: 18,000
Frequency: 7 times a year
Klaus Pirker, Publisher, kpirker@annexweb.com
Alyssa Dalton, Editor, adalton@annexweb.com

MCI
Also Known As: Magazine Circuit Industriel
Détenteur: P.A.P. Communication inc.
P.A.P. Communications Inc., 1627, boul Bastien, Québec, QC G2K 1H1
Tél: 418-623-3383; *Téléc:* 418-623-5033
Ligne sans frais: 800-387-3383
info@magazinemci.com
www.magazinemci.com
Médias sociaux:
twitter.com/MagazineMci
www.facebook.com/pages/Magazine-MCI/212557108776939

Tirage: 23 000
Fréquence: 6 fois par an
Bernard Gauthier, Rédacteur en chef

PLANT
Owned By: Annex Publishing & Printing Inc.
80 Valleybrook Dr., Toronto, ON M3B 2S9
Tel: 416-422-5600; *Fax:* 416-510-5140
info@canadianmanufacturing.com
www.canadianmanufacturing.com/fabrication

Circulation: 30,000
Frequency: Monthly
Joe Terrett, Editor, 416-442-5600 x 3215, JTerrett@plant.ca

Plant Engineering & Maintenance (PEM)
Owned By: Annex Publishing & Printing Inc.
222 Edward St., Aurora, ON L4G 1W6
Tel: 905-727-0077; *Fax:* 905-727-0017
www.pem-mag.com
Social Media:
twitter.com/PEM_Maintenance
www.facebook.com/PlantEngineeringMaint enance

Circulation: 16,800
Frequency: 6 times a year
John MacPherson, Publisher, jmacpherson@annexweb.com
Rehana Begg, Editor, rbegg@annexweb.com

Produits pour l'industrie québécoise
Détenteur: Annex Publishing & Printing Inc.
222, rue Edward, Aurora, ON L4G 1W6
Tél: 905-727-0077; *Téléc:* 905-727-0017
piq@annexweb.com
www.piq-mag.ca
Médias sociaux:
twitter.com/PIQMag

Fréquence: 5 fois par an
Nigel Bishop, Éditeur, nbishop@annexweb.com
Eric Cloutier, Rédacteur-en-chef, ecloutier@annexweb.com

Industrial Safety

Canadian Occupational Safety
Owned By: Thomson Reuters Canada Limited
c/o Thomson Reuters Canada Ltd., 2075 Kennedy Rd., 11th Fl., Toronto, ON M1T 3V4
Tel: 416-609-3800; *Fax:* 416-298-5082
Toll-Free: 800-387-5164
www.cos-mag.com
Social Media:
www.twitter.com/cosmagazine
www.facebook.com/104930002952393

Circulation: 14,000
Frequency: 6 times a year
John Hebel, Publisher
Amanda Silliker, Editor, amanda.silliker@thomsonreuters.com

OHS Canada Magazine (OH&S Canada)
Previous Name: Occupational Health & Safety Canada
Owned By: Annex-Newcom
80 Valleybrook Dr., Toronto, ON M3B 2S9
Tel: 416-510-5189; *Fax:* 416-510-5167
Toll-Free: 800-268-2374
www.ohscanada.com
Social Media:
www.linkedin.com/pub/ohscanada-media/32/28b/912
twitter.com/ohscanada

Frequency: 6 times a year
Peter Boxer, Publisher, 416-510-5102, pboxer@ohscanada.com
Jean Lian, Editor, 416-510-5115, jlian@ohscanada.com

Travail et Santé
#201, 85, rue Saint-Charles ouest, Longueuil, QC J4H 1C5
Tél: 450-651-2855
www.travailetsante.net

Fréquence: Mars, juin, septembre, décembre & Guide-Source
Huguette Beauchamp, Directrice générale

Workplace Safety & Prevention Services (WSPS)
5110 Creekbank Rd., Mississauga, ON L4W 0A1
Tel: 905-614-1400; *Fax:* 905-614-1414
Toll-Free: 800-494-9777
www.iapa.ca
www.iapa.ca

Frequency: Annually
Annual report of workplace safety

Insurance

BC Broker: The Voice of the P&C Insurance Industry in B.C.
Owned By: Insurancewest Media Ltd.
c/o Insurancewest Media Ltd., PO Box 3311 Terminal, 661 Market Hill, Vancouver, BC V6B 3Y3
Tel: 604-874-1001; *Fax:* 604-874-3922
Toll-Free: 800-888-8811
manager@insurancewest.ca
www.insurancewest.ca/bcbroker .shtml

Circulation: 4,500+
Frequency: Bi-monthly
The trade publication is sent to general insurance brokers who are members of the Insurance Brokers Association of British Columbia. BC Broker is also distributed to general insurance companies, independent adjusters, lawyers, & suppliers. A digital edition is also available. Each issue of BC Broker features an educational article on a technical insurance topic & columns from the association's president & chief staff executive.
Bill Earle, Publisher, 604-875-7766
Trudy Lancelyn, Managing Editor, 604-606-8008
Fran Burnside, Publications Manager & Advertising Sales, 604-875-7762

British Columbia Insurance Directory
Owned By: Insurancewest Media Ltd.
c/o Insurancewest Media Ltd., PO Box 3311 Terminal, 661 Market Hill, Vancouver, BC V6B 3Y3
Tel: 604-874-1001; *Fax:* 604-874-3922
Toll-Free: 800-888-8811
manager@insurancewest.ca
www.insurancewest.ca/bcinsura ncedir.shtml

Circulation: 2,563
Frequency: Annually
Contains listings in B.C. of 900 general insurance broker offices, 150 adjusting offices, 80 general insurer offices, & 40 insurance association & government-related offices. In addition, 5000 senior insurance personnel are listed & cross-referenced; 200 trades & suppliers also included. The 340-page coil-bound book is used primarily by general insurance brokers, adjusters & insurers in B.C.
Bill Earle, Publisher, 604-875-7766
Fran Burnside, Publications Manager & Advertising Sales, 604-875-7762

Canadian Insurance Claims Directory
Owned By: University of Toronto Press Inc.
c/o University of Toronto Press, #700, 10 St Mary St., Toronto, ON M4Y 2W8
Tel: 416-978-2239; *Fax:* 416-978-4738
Toll-Free: 800-565-9523
publishing@utpress.untoronto.ca
www.utppublishing.com

Circulation: 1,500
Frequency: Annually, May
This directory is to facilitate the forwarding of insurance claims throughout Canada & the United States. Its subscribers are adjusters, firms specializing in counsel to the insurance industry, insurance companies, & industrial & government offices.

Lynn Fisher, Vice-President, Scholarly Publishing, UTP Publishing, lfisher@utpress.utoronto.ca
Charley LaRose, Publications Coordinator, clarose@utpress.utoronto.ca

Canadian Insurance Top Broker
Owned By: Rogers Media Inc.
1 Mount Pleasant Rd., Toronto, ON M4Y 2Y5
Tel: 416-764-1323
canadianinsurance@rci.rogers.com
www.citopbroker.com
Social Media: twitter.com/CITopBroker
Circulation: 15,441
Frequency: 10 issues per year
Focus on the property & casualty insurance market.
Jeff Pearce, Editorial Contact, 416-764-1323, jeff.pearce@rci.rogers.com

Canadian Underwriter
Owned By: Annex-Newcom
80 Valleybrook Dr., Toronto, ON M3B 2S9
Fax: 416-510-6809
Toll-Free: 800-268-7742
www.canadianunderwriter.ca
Social Media: www.linkedin.com/groups?gid=2940726
twitter.com/CdnUnderwriter
www.fac ebook.com/CanadianUnderwriter
Circulation: 10,061
Frequency: Monthly; also Claims Canada, National Claims Manual, Insurance Marketer, Annual Statistical Issue, Ontario Insurance Directory
Canadian Underwriter is a professional Insurance & Risk Management magazine covering all aspects of Canada's property & casualty Insurance Market.
Steve Wilson, Senior Publisher, 416-510-6800, steve@canadianunderwriter.ca
Angela Stelmakowich, Editor, 416-510-6793, astelmakowich@canadianunderwriter.ca

Forum
Previous Name: CAIFA Forum; Office & Field
c/o Advocis, #209, 390 Queens Quay West, Toronto, ON M5V 3A2
Tel: 416-444-5251; *Fax:* 416-444-8031
Toll-Free: 800-563-5822
forum.mag@sympatico.ca
www.advocis.ca/forum.html
Circulation: 18,100
Frequency: 8 times a year
Peter Wilmshurst, Publisher
Deanne Gage, Editor, dgage@advocis.ca

General Insurance Register
Owned By: Rogers Media Inc.
1 Mount Pleasant Rd., Toronto, ON M4Y 2Y5
Tel: 416-764-1451
deokie.ramnarine@rci.rogers.com
www.rogersmags.com/gir
Circulation: 5,500
Frequency: Annually, January
Lists insurance Adjusters, Appraisers, Legal firms in Canada; Consultants, Engineering, Investigation, Rehabilitation, Replacement, Restoration & other services companies; also lists Brokers, Intermediaries & Managing Agents

The Insurance & Investment Journal / Journal de L'Assurance
Owned By: Les Editions du Journal de l'Assurance
#100, 321 Rue de la Commune West, Montreal, QC H2Y 2E1
Tel: 514-289-9595; *Fax:* 514-289-9527
reception@insurance-journal.ca
www.insurance-journal.ca
Circulation: 64 000
Frequency: 10 times a year
The Insurance Journal targets financial advisors, life insurance producers, financial planners, & general insurance brokers in Canada. The magazine publishes news & examines trends in the development of insurance & financial products, such as group & individual insurance, disability insurance, mutual funds, segregated funds, health care management, & information technology. Published 10 times per year.
Serge Therrien, Publisher, serge.therrien@insurance-journal.ca
Donna Glasgow, Editor-in-Chief, donna.glasgow@insurance-journal.ca

Insurance Business Canada
Owned By: Key Media Inc.
#800, 312 Adelaide St. West, Toronto, ON M5V 1R2
Tel: 416-644-8740; *Fax:* 416-203-9083
insurancebusiness@keymedia.com.au
www.insurancebusiness.ca
Social Media: plus.google.com/+InsurancebusinessCa
twitter.com/InsuranceBizCA
www.facebook.com/IBCanada
John Mackenzie, General Manager, Sales, 416-644-8740 Ext.252, john.mackenzie@kmimedia.ca

Insurance People
Previous Name: Insurancewest
Owned By: Insurancewest Media Ltd.
c/o Insurancewest Media Ltd., PO Box 3311 Terminal, 661 Market Hill, Vancouver, BC V6B 3Y3
Tel: 604-874-1001; *Fax:* 604-874-3922
Toll-Free: 800-888-8811
manager@insurancewest.ca
www.insurancewest.ca/insuranc epeople.shtml
Circulation: 6,000
Frequency: 6 times a year
Launched in 1996, this bi-monthly magazine (formerly a quarterly) circulates to 6000 in Canada's four western provinces - virtually every insurance industry decision-maker in the west. Insurancewest is about insurance people and companies
Bill Earle, Publisher, 604-875-7766
Don McLellan, Managing Editor, 604-436-4900
Cathryn Day, Publications Manager & Advertising Sales, 604-874-1001

Le Journal de l'Assurance
Détenteur: Les Editions du Journal de l'Assurance
#100, 321, rue de la Commune Ouest, Montréal, QC H2Y 2E1
Tél: 514-289-9595; *Téléc:* 514-289-9527
reception@journal-assurance.ca
journal-assurance.ca
Tirage: 64 000
Fréquence: 10 fois par an
Serge Therrien, Président et éditeur, serge.therrien@journal-assurance.ca
Hubert Roy, Rédacteur en chef, hubert.roy@journal-assurance.ca

Ontario Insurance Directory
Owned By: Annex-Newcom
80 Valleybrook Dr., Toronto, ON M3B 2S9
Toll-Free: 800-668-2374
www.canadianunderwriter.ca
Circulation: 3,500
Frequency: Annually, December
Personal address & telephone book dedicated solely to the Ontario insurance industry.
Steve Wilson, Senior Publisher, 416-510-6800, steve@canadianunderwriter.ca

Prairies Insurance Directory
Previous Name: Alberta Insurance Directory
Owned By: Insurancewest Media Ltd.
c/o Insurancewest Media Ltd., PO Box 3311 Terminal, 661 Market Hill, Vancouver, BC V6B 3Y3
Tel: 604-874-1001; *Fax:* 604-874-3922
Toll-Free: 800-888-8811
manager@insurancewest.ca
www.insurancewest.ca/prairies dir.shtml
Frequency: Annually
Contains listings in the Prairie region of more than 1200 general insurance broker offices, 150 adjusting offices, 150 general insurer offices, & 50 insurance association & government-related offices. In addition, 3500 senior insurance personnel are listed & cross-referenced; 130 trades & suppliers also included. The 340-page coil-bound book is used primarily by general insurance brokers, adjusters & insurers in the Prairies.

Interior Design & Decor

AZURE Publishing Inc.
#601, 460 Richmond St. West, Toronto, ON M5V 1Y1
Tel: 416-203-9674
azure@azureonline.com
www.azuremagazine.com
Social Media: www.linkedin.com/company/1482181?trk=tyah
twitter.com/azuremagazine
ww w.facebook.com/AzureMagazine
Circulation: 25,000
Frequency: 8 times a year
Award-winning magazine focussing on contemporary architecture and design
Sergio Sgarmella, Publisher

Canadian Facility Management & Design
c/o MediaEdge, #1000, 5255 Yonge St., Toronto, ON M2N 6P4
Tel: 416-512-8186
cfmd.ca
Circulation: 7,000
Frequency: 7 times a year
Melissa Valentini, Group Publisher

Canadian Interiors (CI)
Owned By: Annex-Newcom
80 Valleybrook Dr., Toronto, ON M3B 2S9
Tel: 416-442-5600; *Fax:* 416-510-5134
Toll-Free: 800-268-7742
www.canadianinteriors.com
Circulation: 13,467
Frequency: 6 times a year
Publishes information on Canada's leading interior design professionals
Michael Totzke, Editor, 416-510-6825, mtotzke@canadianinteriors.com

Ontario Design
Owned By: Homes Publishing Group
178 Main St., Unionville, ON L3R 2G9
Tel: 905-479-4663 *Toll-Free:* 800-363-4663
info@ontariodesigntrade.com
www.ontariodesigntrade.com
Social Media: www.facebook.com/148850138470077
Circulation: 12,000
Frequency: Annually
Michael Rosset, Publisher

Jewellery & Giftware

Canadian Jeweller
#400, 1235 Bay St. West, Toronto, ON M5R 3K4
Tel: 416-203-7900
www.canadianjeweller.com
Social Media: twitter.com/cj_mag
www.facebook.com/Canadian-Jeweller-Magazine-281164748556
Frequency: 7 times a year

Jewellery Business
Owned By: Kenilworth Publishing Inc.
c/o Kenilworth Media Inc., #710, 15 Wertheim Crt., Richmond Hill, ON L4B 3H7
Tel: 905-771-7333; *Fax:* 905-771-7336
Toll-Free: 800-409-8688
editor@jewellerybusiness.com
www.jewellerybusiness.com
Social Media: www.linkedin.com/groups?gid=4069559
twitter.com/jewellerybizmag
Circulation: 8,079
Frequency: 6 times a year

Journalism

L'edition Nouvelles
8030, rue Marie Lefranc, Laval, QC H7Y 2C2
Tel: 450-962-7610; *Fax:* 450-962-7092
Toll-Free: 866-639-7226
www.newscanada.com
Circulation: 1 451
Frequency: mensuel
Ruth Douglas, President & Publisher

Media
Canadian Association of Journalists, PO Box 280, Brantford, ON N3T 5M8
Tel: 613-526-8061; *Fax:* 613-521-3904
www.caj.ca
Circulation: 4,000
Frequency: Quarterly
David McKie, Editor

News Canada / L'Édition Nouvelles
Owned By: News Canada Inc.
#509, 920 Yonge St., Toronto, ON M4W 3C7
Tel: 416-599-9900; *Fax:* 416-599-9700
Toll-Free: 888-855-6397
www.newscanada.com
Frequency: Monthly
Ruth Douglas, President/Publisher

Landscaping

Landscape Alberta - Green for Life
#200, 10331 - 178 St., Edmonton, AB T5S 1R5
Tel: 780-489-1991; *Fax:* 780-444-2152
admin@landscape-alberta.com

Circulation: 700
Frequency: 6 times a year
The magazine targets persons involved in the following businesses in Manitoba, Saskatchewan, & Alberta: retail & wholesale nurseries, greenhouse operators, sod farms, grounds maintenance, landscape contractors, arborists & municipal goverments.
Joel Beatson, Managing Editor

Landscape Ontario
Previous Name: Horticulture Review
Owned By: Landscape Ontario Horticultural Trades Association
7856 - 5th Line South, #RR4, Milton, ON L9T 2X8
Tel: 416-848-7575; *Fax:* 905-875-3942
Toll-Free: 800-265-5656
www.horttrades.com
Circulation: 2,300
Frequency: Monthly
Lee Ann Knudsen, Publisher
Allan Dennis, Editor, adennis@landscapeontario.com

Landscape Trades
Owned By: Landscape Ontario Horticultural Trades Association
7856 - 5th Line South, RR#4, Milton, ON L9T 2X8
Tel: 905-875-1805; *Fax:* 905-875-0183
comments@landscapetrades.com
www.landscapetrades.com
Circulation: 2300
Frequency: 9 times a year
Sarah Willis, Editorial Director, 647-723-5424, sarahw@landscapeontario.com

Landscaping & Groundskeeping
Owned By: Baum Publications Ltd.
Baum Publications Ltd., 124 - 2323 Boundary, Vancouver, BC V5M 4V8
Tel: 604-291-9900; *Fax:* 604-291-1906
lg.baumpub.com
Circulation: 14,229
Frequency: 6 times a year
Engelbert Baum, Publisher
Lee Toop, Editor, ltoop@baumpub.com

Turf & Recreation
275 James St., Delhi, ON N4B 2B2
Tel: 519-582-8873; *Fax:* 519-582-8877
Toll-Free: 800-525-6825
www.turfandrec.com
Frequency: 7 times a year
Bart Crandon, Publisher, turf.bart@on.aibn.com
Brenda Bozso, Administrative & Circulation Manager, turf.brenda@on.aibn.com

Laundry & Dry Cleaning

Fabricare Canada
PO Box 69571, Oakville Central Post Office, Oakville, ON L6J 7R4
Tel: 905-337-0516 *Toll-Free:* 888-287-9785
www.fabricarecanada.com
Frequency: 6 times a year
Fabricare Canada features news about the textile care industry, business ideas, environmental issues, & information about new products. Summaries in French & Korean are included in each issue. The publication is a member off the Canadian Cleaners & Launderers Allied Trades Association.
Marcia Todd, Publisher
Becca Anderson, Editor
Bill Goodbrand, Contact, Advertising Production & Sales, 905-849-1853

Legal

The Advocate
#103, 1529 West 6th Ave., Vancouver, BC V6J 1R1
Tel: 604-737-8757; *Fax:* 604-737-8214
info@the-advocate.ca
www.the-advocate.ca
Circulation: 14,000
Frequency: Bi-monthly
Published by the Vancouver Bar Association, The Advocate is of interest to members of the legal profession, the judiciary, courthouses, & law schools in British Columbia & abroad. The Advocate features legal news & commentary.
Lynda Roberts, Business Manager

Briefly Speaking
Also Known As: Just
c/o Ontario Bar Association, #300, 20 Toronto St., Toronto, ON M5C 2B8
Tel: 416-869-1047; *Fax:* 416-869-1390
Toll-Free: 800-668-8900
ccrocker@oba.org
www.oba.org/en/briefly/main/intro.aspx
Circulation: 13,000
Frequency: 3 times a year
The official, bilingual learned legal journal of the Ontario Bar Association.
Louise Harris, Editor, lharris@oba.org

Canadian Bar Review / La Revue du Barreau canadien
c/o Canadian Bar Foundation, #500, 865 Carling Ave., Ottawa, ON K1S 5S8
Tel: 613-237-2925; *Fax:* 613-237-0185
Toll-Free: 800-267-8860
review@cba.org
www.cba.org
Frequency: 3 times a year
The official, bilingual learned legal journal of the CBA, the Canadian Bar Review is published online three times a year. Fully searchable archives of the Bar Review, dating back to 1923, are available in PDF format. The Review directly meets the educational objective of the CBA. It is frequently cited in the Supreme Court of Canada and boasts an international reputation for quality and excellence.
Prof. Beth Bilson, Editor-in-chief

Le Journal du Barreau
445, boul St-Laurent, Montréal, QC H2Y 3T8
Tél: 514-954-3400; *Téléc:* 514-954-3464
Ligne sans frais: 800-361-8495
journaldubarreau@barreau.qc.ca
www.barreau.qc.ca/fr/publications/journal/
Médias sociaux:
twitter.com/BarreauduQuebec
www.facebook.com/barreauduquebec
Tirage: 32,000
Fréquence: 10 fois par an
Le Journal du Barreau, édité par le Service des communications, est la publication phare du monde juridique québécois. Il traite de l'évolution de l'exercice de la profession d'avocat, de différents domaines du droit, du système judiciaire et des aspects du droit liés aux enjeux de société

Law Times
Owned By: Thomson Reuters Canada Ltd.
One Corporate Plaza, 2075 Kennedy Rd., Toronto, ON M1T 3V4
Tel: 416-298-5141; *Fax:* 416-649-7870
www.lawtimesnews.com
Social Media:
twitter.com/lawtimes
Circulation: 12,550
Frequency: 40 times a year
Ontario's source of legal affairs news and commentary. News Flash: Our weekly coverage offers analysis and insight into the legal profession's key players, news events and court rulings. Focus Sections: Each issue explores in detail a topic of compelling interest to Ontario's legal profession. Our focus sections cover topics as diverse as computer software, private investigators and forensic services
Gail J. Cohen, Editor-in-chief, 416-649-9928
Glen Kouth, Editor, 416-641-9554

The Lawyers Weekly
Owned By: LexisNexis Canada Ltd.
#900, 111 Gordon Baker Rd., Toronto, ON M2H 3R1
Tel: 905-479-2665; *Fax:* 905-479-3758
Toll-Free: 800-668-6481
www.thelawyersweekly.ca
Social Media:
twitter.com/lawyersweeklyca
Circulation: 27,844
Frequency: 48 times a year
Published since 1983, The Lawyers Weekly was the first newspaper for the Canadian legal profession. It serves the national market with bureaus in Ottawa and Toronto and correspondents across the country. Published 48 times a year, The Lawyers Weekly provides lawyers with information essential to maintaining and building a successful practice in today's competitive business environment.
Ann McDonagh, Publisher
Rob Kelly, Editor-in-Chief

McGill Law Journal / Revue de droit de McGill
3644 Peel St., Montréal, QC H3A 1W9
Tel: 514-398-7397; *Fax:* 514-398-7360
journal.law@mcgill.ca
lawjournal.mcgill.ca
Social Media:
linkedin.com/groups/McGill-Law-Journal-Revue-de-4334820
twitter.com/McGi ll_LJ
www.facebook.com/pages/McGill-Law-Journal/18752730793269 6
Frequency: 4 times a year
The McGill Law Journal is an academic legal journal established in 1952 by the students of the McGill University Faculty of Law. More than fifty years later, and still entirely student-run, we remain committed to the advancement of legal scholarship in both the common and civil law. Amongst university law journals, McGill's is especially unique as a result of its bilingual, bijuridical character, and its success as the most frequently quoted university law journal by the Supreme Court of Canada.
William Stephenson, Editor-in-chief

Le Monde Juridique
642, rue Pierre-Tétreault, Montréal, QC H1L 4Y5
Tél: 514-353-3549
agmonde@videotron.ca
www.lemondejuridique.com
Médias sociaux:
twitter.com/Monde_Juridique
www.facebook.com/134956103211634
Fréquence: 4 fois par ans
Magazine des juristes du Québec
André Gagnon, Rédacteur en chef B.A., LLL

National
Canadian Bar Association, #500, 865 Carling Ave., Ottawa, ON K1S 5S8
Tel: 613-237-2925
national@cba.org
www.cba.org/CBA/National/Main
Social Media: www.linkedin.com/company/cbanatmag
twitter.com/CBAnatmag
www.facebook. com/cbanatmag
Frequency: 9 times a year
National is the official magazine of the Canadian Bar Association. It tracks and analyzes the latest trends and developments in the law, provides practice and career information to lawyers, informs members of CBA activities and explores issues of importance to Canadian law practitioners
Beverley Spencer, Editor-in-Chief, beverleys@cba.org

Ontario Legal Directory
Previous Name: Toronto Legal Directory
Also Known As: The Orange Book
University of Toronto Press, #700, 10 St. Mary St., Toronto, ON M4Y 2W8
Tel: 416-978-2239; *Fax:* 416-921-6353
old@utpress.utoronto.ca
www.utpjournals.com/Ontario-Legal-Directory.html
Frequency: Annually, February
Accuracy and completeness of detail have characterized the Ontario Legal Directory since 1925, when the first annual edition of the Toronto Legal Directory was published. With over 30,000 listings of lawyers, law firms, federal and provincial courts and government offices, each complete with names, addresses, telephone and fax numbers, and e-mail and web addresses, the Ontario Legal Directory places all the information you need right at your fingertips. The Blue Pages put governments and courts information right up front, organized in easy-to-find categories with thumb-tab indexing.
Lynn N. Browne, Editor

The Ontario Reports
Owned By: LexisNexis Canada Ltd.
#700, 123 Commerce Valley Dr. East, Markham, ON L3T 7WB
Tel: 905-479-2665; *Fax:* 905-479-3758
Toll-Free: 800-668-6481
info@lexisnexis.ca
Circulation: 51,000
Frequency: Weekly
Published by the Law Society of Upper Canada through LexisNexis Canada, the Ontario Reports, Third Series provides in full text, leading cases decided at all levels of Ontario courts. Published 52 times per year, the soft cover parts also contain official Law Society notices (i.e., Practice Directions), government notices of interest to the legal profession, fee schedules, lawyers announcements and advertising. A personally addressed copy is sent to each of the Law Society's members each Friday.

Osgoode Hall Law Journal
Osgoode Hall Law School of York University, 4700 Keele St., Toronto, ON M3J 1P3
Tel: 416-736-5354; *Fax:* 416-736-5736
journal@osgoode.yorku.ca
www.ohlj.ca
Frequency: Quarterly
The Journal has acquired a reputation for excellence in publishing scholarly articles that represent a wide range of perspectives about law and legal institutions
Stepan Wood, Editor-in-chief, swood@osgoode.yorku.ca
Nicholas Francis, Managing Editor

The Scrivener Magazine
PO Box 44, #1220, 625 Howe St., Vancouver, BC V6C 2T6
Tel: 604-681-4516; *Fax:* 604-681-7258
Toll-Free: 800-663-0343
scrivener@notaries.bc.ca
www.notaries.bc.ca/scrivener
Circulation: 6,000
Frequency: 4 times a year
The Scrivener is published quarterly by The Society of Notaries Public of British Columbia. Celebrates the Notary's role in drafting, communicating, authenticating, and getting the facts straight. Strives to publish articles about points of law and the Notary profession for the education and enjoyment of its members, their Allied Professionals, and the public
Val Wilson, Editor-in-chief

Lighting

Professional Lighting & Production
Owned By: Norris-Whitney Communications Inc.
#7, 23 Hannover Dr., St Catharines, ON L2W 1A3
Tel: 905-641-3471; *Fax:* 905-665-1307
info@nor.com
www.professional-lighting.com
Social Media:
www.twitter.com/plpmag
www.facebook.com/professionallighting
Circulation: 10,200
Frequency: 4 times a year
Jim Norris, Publisher

Machinery Maintenance

Machinery & Equipment MRO
Also Known As: MRO - Maintenancce Repair & Operations
Owned By: Annex Publishing & Printing Inc.
80 Valleybrook Dr., Toronto, ON M3B 2S9
Tel: 416-510-5600; *Fax:* 416-510-5134
Toll-Free: 800-268-7742
www.mromagazine.com
Social Media:
twitter.com/mromagazine
Frequency: 6 times a year
Machinery & Equipment MRO was founded to serve the industrial aftermarket (maintenance, repair and operations).
Jim Petsis, Publisher, jpetsis@mromagazine.com
Bill Roebuck, Editor & Associate Publisher, broebuck@mromagazine.com
Jay Armstrong, Sales Manager, jarmstrong@mromagazine.com

Materials Handling & Distribution

Gestion & Logistique
Détenteur: Les Editions Bomart ltée
Tél: 450-435-3131; *Téléc:* 450-435-3884
www.bomartgroup.com
Tirage: 10 104
Fréquence: 10 fois par an
Pierre Gravel, Président & éditeur
Eric Cloutier, Directeur de la rédaction

Materials Management & Distribution (MM&D)
Owned By: Annex-Newcom
80 Valleybrook Dr., Toronto, ON M3B 2S9
Tel: 416-442-5600; *Fax:* 416-510-5140
Toll-Free: 888-297-7195
www.canadianmanufacturing.com/distribution-and-transportation
Circulation: 17,271
Frequency: 6 times per year
Supply chain magazine covering information management & transportation
Emily Atkins, Editor/Publisher, 416-510-5130, EAtkins@mmdonline.com

Metalworking

Canadian Metalworking
Owned By: Annex Publishing & Printing Inc.
80 Valleybrook Dr., Toronto, ON M3B 2S9
Tel: 416-442-5600; *Fax:* 416-510-5140
www.canadianmetalworking.com
Social Media:
twitter.com/CdnMetalworking
www.facebook.com/CanadianMetalworking
Frequency: 10 times a year
Steve Devonport, Publisher, 416-510-5125, SDevonport@canadianmetalworking.com
Doug Picklyk, Editor, 416-510-5206, DPicklyk@canadianmetalworking.com

Metalworking Production & Purchasing
Owned By: Annex Publishing & Printing Inc.
222 Edward St., Aurora, ON L4G 1W6
Tel: 905-727-0071; *Fax:* 905-727-0017
www.metalworkingcanada.com
Social Media:
twitter.com/metalworkingCA
Frequency: 6 times a year; also The Canadian Machine Tool Dealer
Nigel Bishop, Publisher
Robert Colman, Editor

Military

Canadian Defence Review
PO Box 305, 21 Main St., Markham, ON L3P 3J8
Tel: 905-554-4586
info@canadiandefencereview.com
www.canadiandefencereview.com
Social Media:
twitter.com/CDRmagazine
www.facebook.com/CanadianDefenceReview
Frequency: 6 times a year

Mining

Canadian & American Mines Handbook
Owned By: The Northern Miner Group
#2, 38 Lesmill Rd., Toronto, ON M3B 2T5
Tel: 416-510-6789; *Fax:* 416-447-7658
Toll-Free: 888-502-3456
northernminer2@northernminer.com
www.northernminer.com
Frequency: Annually, November
Anthony Vaccaro, Publisher
Diane Giancola, Editor

Canadian Miner
285 Lynn Ave., North Vancouver, BC V7J 2C3
Tel: 604-980-0794; *Fax:* 604-980-7123
Toll-Free: 800-570-3366
editor@canadianminingnews.com
www.canadianminingnews.com
Circulation: 3,250
Frequency: 4 times a year
Michael J. McGrath, Editor

Canadian Mining Journal
Owned By: The Northern Miner Group
38 Lesmill Rd., Toronto, ON M3B 2T5
Tel: 416-510-6891; *Fax:* 416-447-7658
Toll-Free: 888-502-3456
tmn@northernminer.com
www.canadianminingjournal.com
Circulation: 10,562
Frequency: 11 times a year
Russell Noble, Editor, 416-510-6742, rnoble@canadianminingjournal.com
Robert Seagraves, Publisher, 416-510-6891, rseagraves@canadianminingjournal.com

CIM Magazine
Previous Name: CIM Bulletin
Owned By: Canadian Institute of Mining, Metallurgy & Petroleum
#1250, 3500, boul de Maisonneuve ouest, Westmount, QC H3Z 3C1
Tel: 514-939-2710; *Fax:* 514-939-2714
cim@cim.org
www.cim.org
Circulation: 12,959
Frequency: 8 times a year
Ryan Bergen, Editor-in-Chief, rbergen@cim.org

FP Survey-Mines & Energy
Previous Name: The Financial Post Survey of Mines & Energy Resources
Owned By: Owen Media Partners Inc.
#301, 1599 Hurontario St., Mississauga, ON L5G 4S1
Tel: 905-290-1818; *Fax:* 905-290-1760
Toll-Free: 844-990-6111
owenmediainfo@owen-media.com
www.owen-media.com/surveys/products/mines.c fm
Frequency: Annually, August

Mineral Exploration
Owned By: Canada Wide Media Limited
#230, 4321 Still Creek Dr., Burnaby, BC V5C 6S7
Tel: 604-299-7311; *Fax:* 604-299-9188
www.canadawide.com
Frequency: 4 times a year
Jonathan Buchanan, Editor

The Northern Miner
Owned By: The Northern Miner Group
#2, 38 Lesmill Rd., Toronto, ON M3B 2T5
Tel: 416-510-6789; *Fax:* 416-510-5138
northernminer2@northernminer.com
www.northernminer.com
Social Media: www.linkedin.com/company/2609090
twitter.com/northernminer
www.face book.com/NorthernMiner
Frequency: Weekly
Anthony Vaccaro, Publisher, 416-442-2098, avaccaro@northernminer.com

The Prospector: Investment & Exploration News
#104, 333 East 1st St., North Vancouver, BC V7L 4W9
Tel: 604-639-5495; *Fax:* 604-990-1093
sales@theprospectornews.com
www.theprospectornews.com
Other information: Editorial, E-mail: editor@theprospectornews.com
Frequency: 6 times a year
Published by Foxtrot Communications Ltd., The Prospector includes industry analysis, company profiles, boardroom reports, & enviromental information.

Motor Trucks & Buses

L'Écho du Transport
Détenteur: Les Editions Bomart ltée
48, ch des Centaures, Ste-Anne des lacs, QC J0R 1B0
Tél: 450-224-7000; *Téléc:* 450-224-7711
www.lechodutransport.com
Fréquence: 10 fois par an
Pierre Gravel, Président éditeur, pgravel@bomartgroup.com
Guy Hébert, Directeur de la rédaction, ghebert@bomartgroup.com

The Manitoba Trucking Guide for Shippers
Previous Name: Manitoba Ship-by-Truck Directory
Owned By: Craig Kelman & Associates Ltd.
Tel: 204-985-9791
info@trucking.mb.ca
www.trucking.mb.ca/product-truck-directory.htm
Circulation: 1,000
Frequency: Annually

Over the Road
18 Parkglen Dr., Ottawa, ON K2G 3G9
Tel: 613-224-9947; *Fax:* 613-224-8825
otr@otr.on.ca
www.overtheroad.ca
Circulation: 21,000
Frequency: 12 times a year
Peter Charboneau, Publisher, peter@otr.on.ca

Today's Trucking
c/o New Communications Group Inc., 451 Attwell Dr., Toronto, ON M9W 5C4
Tel: 416-614-2200; *Fax:* 416-614-8861
www.todaystrucking.com
Social Media: www.youtube.com/user/TodaysTrucking1
twitter.com/todaystrucking
www.fa cebook.com/TodaysTrucking
Frequency: 10 times a year
Rolf Lockwood, Editorial Director, rolf@todaystrucking.com
Peter Carter, Editor

Truck News, Truck West & Motortruck
Owned By: Annex-Newcom
80 Valleybrook Dr., Toronto, ON M3B 2S9
Tel: 416-510-6881; *Fax:* 416-510-5134
www.trucknews.com
Social Media:
twitter.com/TruckNewsMag
www.facebook.com/trucknews

Frequency: 6 times a year
Lou Smyrlis, Editorial Director, 416-510-6881, lou@TransportationMedia.ca
James Menzies, Executive Editor, jmenzies@trucknews.com

La Voix du vrac
#235, 670, rue Bouvier, Québec, QC G2J 1A7
Tél: 418-623-7923; *Téléc:* 418-623-0448
revue@ancai.com
www.ancai.com

Fréquence: 6 fois par an
Gaétan Légaré, Éditeur

Western Canada Highway News
Owned By: Craig Kelman & Associates Ltd.
2020 Portage Ave., 3rd Fl., Winnipeg, MB R3J 0K4
Tel: 204-985-9780; *Fax:* 204-985-9795
Toll-Free: 866-985-9785
www.highwaynews.ca
Other information: Toll-Free Fax: 1-866-985-9799
Frequency: 4 times a year
Official publication of the Alberta Motor Transport Association (AMTA), Saskatchewan Trucking Association (STA), & Manitoba Trucking Association (MTA).
Craig Kelman, Publisher
Terry Ross, Editor, terry@kelman.ca

Music

Canadian Music Trade
Owned By: Norris-Whitney Communications Inc.
Norris-Whitney Communications, #202, 4056 Dorchester Rd., Niagara Falls, ON L2E 6M9
Tel: 905-374-8878; *Fax:* 888-665-1307
Toll-Free: 877-746-4692
mail@nor.com
www.canadianmusictrade.com
Social Media:
www.twitter.com/cdnmusictrade
www.facebook.com/canadianmusictrade
Frequency: 6 times a year
Serving Canadian music dealers and suppliers.
Jim Norris, Publisher

Music Directory Canada (MDC)
Owned By: Norris-Whitney Communications Inc.
#7, 23 Hannover Dr., St Catharines, ON L2W 1A3
Tel: 905-641-3471 *Toll-Free:* 800-265-8481
mdc@nor.com
musicdirectorycanada.com
Social Media:
www.twitter.com/mdcanada
www.facebook.com/musicdirectorycanada
Circulation: 6,000
Jim Norris, Publisher

Professional Sound
Owned By: Norris-Whitney Communications Inc.
#202, 4056 Dorchester Rd., Niagara Falls, ON L2E 6M9
Tel: 905-374-8878; *Fax:* 888-665-1307
Toll-Free: 877-746-4692
mail@nor.com
www.professional-sound.com
Social Media: www.youtube.com/D2EEA06A387113CE
twitter.com/profsound
www.facebook.co m/professionalsound
Frequency: 6 times a year
Jim Norris, Publisher

Nursing

Alberta RN
College & Association of Registered Nurses of Alberta, 11620 - 168 St., Edmonton, AB T5M 4A6
Tel: 780-451-0043; *Fax:* 780-452-3276
Toll-Free: 800-252-9392
carna@nurses.ab.ca
www.nurses.ab.ca
Social Media:
twitter.com/AlbertaRNs
www.facebook.com/AlbertaRNs

Circulation: 28,000
Frequency: Quarterly
Margaret Ward-Jack, Managing Editor, 780-451-0043
Rachel Champagne, Editor, 780-451-0043

Canadian Journal of Cardiovascular Nursing (CJCN)
c/o Canadian Council of Cardiovascular Nurses, #202, 300 March Rd., Ottawa, ON K2K 2E2
Tel: 613-599-9210; *Fax:* 613-595-1155
pappin.com/journals/cjcn.php

Circulation: 700
Frequency: Quarterly
CJCN, the official publication of the Canadian Council of Cardiovascular Nurses.
Paula Price, Editor

Canadian Nurse
Canadian Nurses Assn., 50 The Driveway, Ottawa, ON K2P 1E2
Tel: 613-237-2133; *Fax:* 613-237-3520
Toll-Free: 800-361-8404
info@canadian-nurse.com
www.canadian-nurse.com
Social Media:
twitter.com/canadanurses
www.facebook.com/CNA.AIIC

Frequency: 8 times a year
Marc Bourgeois, Interim Editor-in-chief

Canadian Oncology Nursing Journal
Also Known As: Revue canadienne de soins infirmiers en oncologie
Owned By: Pappin Communications
The Victoria Centre, #2, 84 Isabella St., Pembroke, ON K8A 5S5
Tel: 613-735-0952; *Fax:* 613-735-7983
info@pappin.com
pappin.com/advertising/conjads.php

Frequency: 4 times a year
Heather Coughlin, Contact

Infirmière canadienne
Canadian Nurses Assn., 50, rue Driveway, Ottawa, ON K2P 1E2
Tél: 613-237-2159; *Téléc:* 613-237-3520
Ligne sans frais: 800-361-8404
info@canadian-nurse.com
www.infirmiere-canadienne.com

Tirage: 3 000
Fréquence: 9 fois par an
Lucille Auffrey, Editor-in-chief

Newsbulletin
Saskatchewan Registered Nurses' Association, 2066 Retallack St., Regina, SK S4S 7X5
Tel: 306-359-4200; *Fax:* 306-359-0257
Toll-Free: 800-667-9945
srnanewsbulletin@srna.org
www.srna.org

Frequency: 6 times a year
Shelley Svedahl, Managing Editor

Perspective Infirmière
Anciennement: L'Infirmière du Québec; Nursing Québec
4200, rue Molson, Montréal, QC H1Y 4V4
Tél: 514-935-2501; *Téléc:* 514-935-3770
Ligne sans frais: 800-363-6048
revue@oiiq.org
www.oiiq.org
Médias sociaux: www.flickr.com/people/ordreinf
twitter.com/OIIQ
www.facebook.com/Ordre.infirmieres.infirmiers.Quebec
Tirage: 80,452
Fréquence: 5 fois par an
Nathalie Boëls, Secrétaire de rédaction
Lyse Savard, Rédactrice en chef

Registered Nurse Journal
#1600, 438 University Ave., Toronto, ON M5G 2K8
Tel: 416-599-1925; *Fax:* 416-599-1926
Toll-Free: 800-268-7199
rnao.ca/resources/rnj

Circulation: 24,000
Frequency: 6 times a year
Marion Zych, Publisher, mzych@rnao.ca

The Registered Practical Nursing Journal
Previous Name: The Care Connection
Bldg. 4, #200, 5025 Orbitor Dr., Mississauga, ON L4W 4Y5
Tel: 905-602-4664; *Fax:* 905-602-4666
Toll-Free: 877-602-4664
journal@rpnao.org
www.rpnao.org
Social Media:
twitter.com/rpnao
www.facebook.com/RPNAO

Frequency: 4 times a year

Dianne Martin, Executive Director

Santé Québec
Anciennement: l'Infirmière auxiliaire
Ordre des infirmières & infirmiers auxiliaires du Québec, 531, rue Sherbrooke est, Montréal, QC H2L 1K2
Tél: 514-282-9511; *Téléc:* 514-282-0631
Ligne sans frais: 800-283-9511
www.oiiaq.org

Fréquence: 3 fois par an
Catherine-Dominique Nantel, Rédactrice-en-chef

Packaging

Canadian Packaging
Owned By: Annex Media & Printing Inc.
80 Valleybrook Dr., Toronto, ON M3B 2S9
Tel: 416-510-5198; *Fax:* 416-510-5140
www.canadianmanufacturing.com/packaging

Circulation: 11,412
Frequency: 11 times a year
Stephen Dean, Senior Publisher, 416-510-5198, SDean@canadianpackaging.com
George Guidoni, Editor, 416-510-5227, GGuidoni@canadianpackaging.com

Petroleum, Oil & Gas

Air Water Land
Owned By: JuneWarren-Nickle's Energy Group
816 - 55 Ave. NE, 2nd Fl., Calgary, AB T2E 6Y4
Tel: 403-209-3500; *Fax:* 403-245-8666
Toll-Free: 800-387-2446
www.junewarren-nickles.com/page.aspx?id=awl
Circulation: 10,000
Frequency: Annually

Alberta Oil & Gas Directory
Owned By: Armadale Publications Inc.
#203, 10544 - 106SE, Edmonton, AB T5H 2X6
Tel: 780-429-1073
armadale@global-serve.net
www.albertaoilandgas.com

Circulation: 10,000
Frequency: Annually

Canadian Oilpatch Technology Guidebook & Directory
Previous Name: Canadian Oilfield Service & Supply Directory
Owned By: JuneWarren-Nickle's Energy Group
816 - 55 Ave. NE, 2nd Fl., Calgary, AB T2E 6Y4
Tel: 403-209-3500; *Fax:* 403-245-8666
Toll-Free: 800-387-2446
www.junewarren-nickles.com/page.aspx?id=tech_guide
Circulation: 10,000
Frequency: Annually; August
Bill Whitelaw, Publisher

Canadian Petroleum Contractor
Owned By: Stagnito Business Information & Edgell Communications
#1510, 2300 Yonge St., Toronto, ON M4P 1E4
Tel: 416-256-9908; *Fax:* 888-889-9522
Toll-Free: 877-687-7321
cpcaonline.com/cpca-magazine
Social Media: www.linkedin.com/groups/1783995
twitter.com/CSNewsOnline
www.facebook. com/45618009418
Magazine of the Canadian Petroleum Contractors Association
Elijah Hoffman, Contact, ehoffman@stagnitomail.ca

Daily Oil Bulletin
816 - 55 Ave. NE, 2nd Fl., Calgary, AB T2E 6Y4
Tel: 403-209-3500; *Fax:* 403-245-8666
Toll-Free: 800-387-2446
editor@dailyoilbulletin.com
www.dailyoilbulletin.com
Social Media:
twitter.com/dobeditor

Earth Resources
Previous Name: Ocean Resources
Owned By: Metro Guide Publishing
1300 Hollis St., Halifax, NS B3J 1T6
Tel: 902-422-4990; *Fax:* 902-422-4728
www.earth-resources.ca

Frequency: 8 times a year
Suzanne Rent, Editor, srent@metroguide.ca

Energy Processing Canada
Owned By: Northern Star Communications Ltd.
900 - 6th Ave. SW, 4th Fl., Calgary, AB T2P 3K2
Tel: 403-263-6881; *Fax:* 403-263-6886
Toll-Free: 800-526-4177
energy@northernstar.ab.ca
www.northernstar.ab.ca
Circulation: 9,866
Frequency: 6 times a year
Serving the hydrocarbons processing related industries.
Scott Jeffrey, Publisher, scott@northernstar.ab.ca

Heavy Oil & Oilsands Guidebook
Owned By: Glacier Media Inc.
816 - 55 Ave. NE, 2nd Fl., Calgary, AB T2E 6Y4
Tel: 403-209-3500; *Fax:* 403-245-8666
www.heavyoilguidebook.com
Circulation: 15,000
Frequency: Annual

The Journal of Canadian Petroleum Technology
Eau Claire Place II, #900, 521 - 3rd Ave. SW, Calgary, AB T2P 3T3
Tel: 403-930-5454; *Fax:* 403-930-5470
specal@spe.org
www.spe.org
Social Media: www.youtube.com/user/2012SPE
twitter.com/SPE_Events
www.facebook.com/s pemembers
Frequency: 12 times a year
John Donnelly, Editor

New Technology Magazine
Owned By: JuneWarren-Nickle's Energy Group
816 - 55 Ave. NE, 2nd Fl., Calgary, AB T2E 6Y4
Tel: 403-209-3500; *Fax:* 403-245-8666
Toll-Free: 800-387-2446
www.junewarren-nickles.com/page.aspx?id=ntm
Circulation: 7,000
Frequency: 10 times a year
Maurice Smith, Editor

Octane
Owned By: Stagnito Business Information & Edgell Communications
#1510, 2300 Yonge St., Toronto, ON M4P 1E4
Tel: 416-256-9908; *Fax:* 888-889-9522
Toll-Free: 877-687-7321
stagnito-edgell.com
Focuses on the car wash and petroleum industry in Canada; bundled with Your Convenience Manager
Kelly Gray, Editor, kgray@stagnitomail.ca

The Oil & Gas Magazine (OGM)
PO Box 668, Blaketown, NL A0B 1C0
Tel: 709-759-3800; *Fax:* 709-582-3408
info@theogm.com
theogm.com
Social Media:
www.linkedin.com/groups/OGM-4035069?gid=4035069
twitter.com/theogmonline
www.facebook.com/TheOGM
Frequency: Bi-monthly
Bill Abbott, Editor

Oil & Gas Network (OGN)
#300, 840 - 6th Ave. SW, Calgary, AB T2P 3E5
Tel: 403-503-0460; *Fax:* 403-206-7753
jrr@oilgas.net
www.oilgas.net
Social Media:
twitter.com/oilgasnetwork
Circulation: 15,900
Frequency: Bi-Monthly
John Robertson, Editor, jrr@oilgas.net

Oil & Gas Product News
Owned By: Baum Publications Ltd.
Baum Publications Ltd., 124 - 2323 Boundary, Vancouver, BC V5M 4V8
Tel: 604-291-9900; *Fax:* 604-291-1906
ogpn.baumpub.com
Circulation: 10,708
Frequency: 6 times a year
Lee Toop, Editor, ltoop@baumpub.com

Oilsands Review
Owned By: JuneWarren-Nickle's Energy Group
816 - 55 Ave. NE, 2nd Fl., Calgary, AB T2E 6Y4
Tel: 403-209-3500; *Fax:* 403-245-8666
Toll-Free: 800-387-2446
www.oilsandsreview.com
Social Media:
twitter.com/oilsandseditor
www.facebook.com/92980312678?ref=ts
Circulation: 10,000
Frequency: Monthly
Oilsands Review is distributed throughout select Chapters/Indigo locations in Calgary and Edmonton.
Deborah Jaremko, Editor

Oilweek
Owned By: JuneWarren-Nickle's Energy Group
816 - 55 Ave. NE, 2nd Fl., Calgary, AB T2E 6Y4
Tel: 403-209-3500; *Fax:* 403-245-8666
Toll-Free: 800-387-2446
www.junewarren-nickles.com/page.aspx?id=owk
Circulation: 10,000
Frequency: Monthly
Darrell Stonehouse, Managing Editor
Bill Whitelaw, Publisher

Profiler
Owned By: JuneWarren-Nickle's Energy Group
816 - 55 Ave. NE, 2nd Fl., Calgary, AB T2E 6Y4
Tel: 403-209-3500; *Fax:* 403-245-8666
Toll-Free: 800-387-2446
www.junewarren-nickles.com/page.aspx?id=profiler
Frequency: 4 times a year

Propane-Canada
Owned By: Northern Star Communications Ltd.
900 - 6th Ave. SW, 4th Fl., Calgary, AB T2P 3K2
Tel: 403-263-6881; *Fax:* 403-263-6886
Toll-Free: 800-526-4177
propane@northernstar.ab.ca
www.northernstar.ab.ca
Circulation: 8,800
Frequency: 6 times a year
Scott Jeffrey, Publisher, scott@northernstar.ab.ca

The Roughneck
Owned By: Northern Star Communications Ltd.
900 - 6th Ave. SW, 4th Fl., Calgary, AB T2P 3K2
Tel: 780-263-6881; *Fax:* 780-423-6886
Toll-Free: 800-526-4177
roughneck@northernstar.ab.ca
www.northernstar.ab.ca
Scott Jeffrey, Publisher, scott@northernstar.ab.ca

The Roughneck Buy & Sell
Owned By: Northern Star Communications Ltd.
900 - 6th Ave. SW, 4th Fl., Calgary, AB T2P 3K2
Tel: 780-263-6881; *Fax:* 780-423-6886
Toll-Free: 800-526-4177
buyandsell@northernstar.ab.ca
www.northernstar.ab.ca
Circulation: 10,000
Frequency: 12 times a year

Photography

PhotoLife
Previous Name: Master Guide
185 St-Paul St., Québec, QC G1K 3W2
Tel: 418-692-2110; *Fax:* 418-692-3392
Toll-Free: 800-905-7468
www.photolife.com
Other information: Toll Free Fax: 1-800-644-2739
Circulation: 6,500
Frequency: Annually
Guy J. Poirier, Publisher
Xavier Bonaccasi, Editor

Plastics

Canadian Plastics
Owned By: Annex Publishing & Printing Inc.
80 Valleybrook Dr., Toronto, ON M3B 2S9
Tel: 416-442-5600; *Fax:* 416-510-5134
Toll-Free: 800-268-7742
www.canplastics.com
Frequency: 7 times a year
Greg Paliouras, Publisher, 416-510-5124, gpaliouras@canplastics.com

Canadian Plastics Directory & Buyer's Guide
Owned By: Annex-Newcom
80 Valleybrook Dr., Toronto, ON M3B 2S9
Tel: 416-442-5600; *Fax:* 416-510-5134
Toll-Free: 800-268-7742
www.canplastics.com
Circulation: 10,959
Frequency: Annually
Judith Nancekivell, Publisher, jnancekivell@canplastics.com
Mark Stephen, Editor, mstephen@canplastics.com

Police

Blue Line Magazine
#254, 12A - 4981 Hwy. 7 E, Markham, ON L3R 1N1
Tel: 905-640-3048; *Fax:* 905-640-7547
blueline@blueline.ca
www.blueline.ca
Circulation: 12,000
Frequency: 10 times a year
Canada's only independent law enforcement magazine
Morley S. Lymburner, Publisher/Editor
Mark Reesor, Senior Editor

Tour of Duty
Previous Name: News & Views
Toronto Police Assn., #200, 2075 Kennedy Rd., Toronto, ON M1T 3V3
Tel: 416-491-4301
www.tpa.ca
Frequency: Monthly
David Hunter, Editor

Power & Power Plants

Nuclear Canada Yearbook
Canadian Nuclear Society, 700 University Ave., 4th Fl., Toronto, ON M5G 1X6
Tel: 416-977-7620; *Fax:* 416-977-8131
csn-snc@on.aibn.com
www.cns-snc.ca
Frequency: Annually
Colin Hunt, Publisher & Editor

Printing & Publishing

Canadian Magazines Canadiene
#700, 425 Adelaide St. West, Toronto, ON M5V 3C1
Tel: 416-504-0274; *Fax:* 416-504-0437
info@magazinescanada.ca
www.magazinescanada.ca/uploads/cmc
Social Media: cmcblog.magazinescanada.ca
Circulation: 3,500
Frequency: Bi-annual
Resource for publishing professionals.
Chantal Tranchemontagne, Editor-in-Chief, cmceditorial@magazinescanada.ca

Estimators' & Buyers' Guide
Owned By: North Island Publishing Ltd.
#8, 1606 Sedlescomb Dr., Mississauga, ON L4X 1M6
Tel: 905-625-7070; *Fax:* 905-625-4856
Toll-Free: 800-331-7408
www.ebguide.ca
Frequency: Annually
Sandy Donald, Publisher

Graphic Arts Magazine
72 Main St., Mount Albert, ON L0G 1M0
Fax: 905-830-9345
Toll-Free: 877-513-3999
joe@graphicartsmagazine.com
www.graphicartsmagazine.com
Social Media:
www.linkedin.com/company/graphic-arts-magazine
twitter.com/graphicarts
www.facebook.com/pages/Graphic-Arts-Magazine/140386003309
Circulation: 11,200
Frequency: 10 times a year
Joe Mulcahy, Publisher
Scott Bury, Editor

Graphic Monthly
Owned By: North Island Publishing Ltd.
#8, 1606 Sedlecomb Dr., Mississauga, ON L4X 1M6
Tel: 905-625-7070; *Fax:* 905-625-4856
Toll-Free: 800-331-7408
www.graphicmonthly.ca
Circulation: 10,000
Frequency: 6 times a year
Alexander Donald, Publisher, s.donald@northisland.ca
Filomena Tamburri, Editor, ftamburri@graphicmonthly.ca

Livre d'ici
#55, 222, Cours Dominion, Montréal, QC H3J 2X1
Tel: 514-933-8033; *Fax:* 514-933-7958
publicite@livre-dici.qc.ca
livredici.org

Circulation: 1,600
Jacques Therriault, Publisher

Maître Imprimeur
636, rue des Vignobles, Rosemère, QC J7A 4P9
Tél: 450-818-5373; *Téléc:* 450-818-5372
info@maitreimprimeur.com
www.maitreimprimeur.com

Tirage: 5 000
Fréquence: 10 fois par an
Dédié au secteur des arts graphiques et de l'imprimerie.
Luc Saumure, Coéditeur
Gerry Bonneau, Coéditeur

Product Engineering & Design

Design Engineering
Owned By: Annex Publishing & Printing Inc.
80 Valleybrook Dr., Toronto, ON M3B 2S9
Tel: 416-442-5600 *Toll-Free:* 866-543-7888
www.design-engineering.com
Social Media: www.youtube.com/user/designengineeringDEX
twitter.com/design_eng_mag

Circulation: 18,253
Frequency: 6 times a year
Alan Macpherson, Publisher,
AMacPherson@design-engineering.com
Mike Mcleod, Editor, MMcLeod@design-engineering.com

Design Product News
Owned By: Annex Publishing & Printing Inc.
222 Edward St., Aurora, ON L4G 1W6
Tel: 905-727-0077; *Fax:* 905-727-0017
www.dpncanada.com
Social Media:
twitter.com/DPN_Engineering
www.facebook.com/DesignProductNews

Frequency: 6 times a year
Nigel Bishop, Publisher, nbishop@annexweb.com
Mike Edwards, Editor, medwards@annexweb.com

Pulp & Paper

Pulp & Paper Canada
Owned By: Annex Publishing & Printing Inc.
80 Valleybrook Dr., Toronto, ON M3B 2S9
Tel: 416-442-5600; *Fax:* 416-510-5140
Toll-Free: 800-268-7742
media@pulpandpapercanada.com
www.pulpandpapercanada.com
Social Media:
twitter.com/pulppapercanada
www.facebook.com/pages/Pulp-Paper-Canada/8807489586627
18

Frequency: Monthly; also Annual Directory (Dec.)
Jim Bussiere, Publisher, jim@pulpandpapercanada.com
Cindy Macdonald, Editor

Purchasing

Canadian Trade Index
Owned By: Owen Media Partners Inc.
#301, 1599 Hurontario St., Mississauga, ON L5G 4S1
Tel: 905-990-6111; *Fax:* 905-990-6118
Toll-Free: 844-990-6111
customerservice@ctidirectory.com
www.ctidirectory.com
Social Media:
twitter.com/CTIdirectory
www.facebook.com/pages/Canadian-Trade-Index/24029425935
59

Frequency: Annually, May

Purchasing B2B
Owned By: Annex-Newcom
80 Valleybrook Dr., Toronto, ON M3B 2S9
Tel: 416-442-5600
www.purchasingb2b.ca

Frequency: 10 times a year
Dorothy Jakovina, Publisher, 416-510-6899,
djakovina@PurchasingB2B.ca

Real Estate

Canadian Mortgage Professional (CMP)
Owned By: Key Media Inc.
#800, 312 Adelaide St. West, Toronto, ON M5V 1R2
Tel: 416-644-8740; *Fax:* 416-203-9083
www.mortgagebrokernews.ca

Circulation: 10,000
Frequency: Monthly
John Mackenzie, General Manager, Sales, 416-644-8740
ext.252, john.mackenzie@kmimedia.ca

Canadian Property Valuation
Previous Name: Canadian Appraiser
c/o Kelman & Associates, 2020 Portage Ave., 3rd Fl., Winnipeg, MB R3J 0K4
Toll-Free: 866-985-9780
info@aicanada.ca
www.aicanada.ca/industry-resources/canadian-property-valuatio
n-magazine
Other information: Toll-Free Fax: 1-866-985-9799
Social Media: www.linkedin.com/groups?gid=2967439
twitter.com/AIC_Canada
www.face book.com/AppraisalInstitute.Canada

Circulation: 6,500
Frequency: 4 times a year
National magazine serving the Canadian appraisal community, distributed to the membership of the Appraisal Institute of Canada as well as partners, libraries & national/international subscribers.
Craig Kelman, Managing Editor

Espace Montréal
#9235, 800, rue de la Gauchetière ouest, Montréal, QC H5A 1K6
Tél: 514-879-1559
espace@espaceqc.com
www.espaceqc.com

Tirage: 10 000
Fréquence: 4 fois par an
Andrew Cross, Publisher & Editor

Espace Québec
#9235, 800, de la Gauchetière ouest, Montréal, QC H5A 1K6
Tél: 418-523-0523 *Ligne sans frais:* 800-232-9846
espace@espaceqc.com
www.espaceqc.com

Tirage: 5 000
Fréquence: 2 fois par an
Andrew Cross, Éditeur/Rédacteur

Real Estate Professional (REP)
Owned By: Key Media Inc.
#800, 312 Adelaide St. West, Toronto, ON M5V 1R2
Tel: 416-644-8740; *Fax:* 416-203-9083
subscriptions@kmimedia.ca
www.repmag.ca
Social Media: plus.google.com/+RepmagCanada
twitter.com/REPMagCA
www.facebook.com/RE PmagCA

Vernon Jones, Senior Editor, 416-644-8740 ext.238,
vernon.jones@kmimedia.ca
John Mackenzie, General Manager, Sales, 416-644-8740
ext.252, john.mackenzie@kmimedia.ca

REM: Real Estate Magazine
Also Known As: Real Estate Marketing
#1178, 2255B Queen St. East, Toronto, ON M4E 1G3
Tel: 416-425-3504; *Fax:* 416-406-0882
www.remonline.com
Social Media:
twitter.com/REM_Online
www.facebook.com/remcanada

Circulation: 50,000
Frequency: 12 times a year
Heino Molls, Publisher, heino@remonline.com
Jim Adair, Managing Editor, jim@remonline.com

The Western Investor
Owned By: Glacier Media Inc.
102 East 4th Ave., Vancouver, BC V5T 1G2
Tel: 604-669-8500; *Fax:* 604-669-2154
Toll-Free: 800-661-6988
subscribe@westerninvestor.com
www.westerninvestor.com
Social Media:
twitter.com/westerninvestor

Circulation: 16,000
Frequency: Monthly
Frank O'Brien, Editor, 604-669-8500

Rental & Leasing Equipment

Canadian Rental Service
Owned By: Annex Publishing & Printing Inc.
PO Box 530, 105 Donly Dr. South, Simcoe, ON N3Y 4N5
Fax: 519-429-3094
Toll-Free: 888-599-2228
www.canadianrentalservice.com
Social Media:
twitter.com/CRSmagazine
www.facebook.com/pages/Canadian-Rental-Service/1
716104629

Frequency: 9 times a year
Patrick Flannery, Editor, 226-931-0545,
pflannery@annexweb.com

Contractors Magazine
Previous Name: Contractors Rental
Owned By: Baum Publications Ltd.
Baum Publications Ltd., 124 - 2323 Boundary, Vancouver, BC V5M 4V8
Tel: 604-291-9900; *Fax:* 604-291-1906
cm.baumpub.com

Circulation: 14,021
Frequency: 6 times a year
Engelbert Baum, Publisher
Lawrence Buser, Editor, lbuser@baumpub.com

Retailing

Canadian Retailer
#800, 1881 Yonge St., Toronto, ON M4S 3C4
Tel: 416-922-6678; *Fax:* 416-922-8011
cdnretailer@retailcouncil.org
www.retailcouncil.org/cdnretailer

Frequency: 6 times a year
The official publication of Retail Council of Canada.
Sean C. Tarry, Editor-in-chief
Diane Brisebois, Publisher

Monday Report on Retailers & Shopping Centre News
Owned By: Rogers Media Inc.
1 Mount Pleasant Rd., 7th Fl., Toronto, ON M4Y 2Y5
Tel: 416-764-1722
mondayreport@halldata.com
www.mondayreport.ca

Frequency: Weekly
Canada's premier information resource for people seeking in-depth, up-to-date data on the retail, food service & shopping centre industries in Canada
Pamela Kirk, General Manager, Pamela.Kirk@rci.rogers.com

Science, Research & Development

Camford Chemical Report
38 Groomsport Cres., Toronto, ON M1T 2K9
Tel: 416-740-5604; *Fax:* 416-291-3406
ccr@camfordinfo.com
www.camfordinformation.com
Social Media:
twitter.com/cheminfo

Frequency: 50 times a year
Bob Douglas, Publisher

Canadian Journal of Botany / Revue canadienne de botanique
Owned By: National Research Council of Canada - NRC Research Press
c/o NRC Research Press, Bldg. M-55, #203, 65 Aurgiga Dr., Ottawa, ON K2E 7W6
Tel: 613-656-9846; *Fax:* 613-656-9838
botany@nrcresearchpress.com
www.nrcresearchpress.com/journal/cjb
Social Media:
www.facebook.com/BotanyJ

Frequency: Monthly
Tamer Elboki, Managing Editor

LAB Business
Previous Name: Laboratory Business
#202, 30 East Beaver Creek Rd., Richmond Hill, ON L4B 1J2
Tel: 905-886-5040; *Fax:* 905-886-6615
www.labbusinessmag.com
Social Media:
twitter.com/biolabmag
www.facebook.com/biolabmag

Frequency: 5 times a year
Christopher Forbes, Publisher, cforbes@jesmar.com

Laboratory Buyers Guide
Owned By: Annex-Newcom
80 Valleybrook Dr., Toronto, ON M3B 2S9
Tel: 416-510-6835; *Fax:* 416-510-5134
Toll-Free: 800-268-7742
www.labcanada.com
Frequency: Annually
Leslie Burt, Publisher, lburt@labcanada.com

Laboratory Product News
Owned By: Annex-Newcom
80 Valleybrook Dr., Toronto, ON M3B 2S9
Tel: 416-510-6835; *Fax:* 416-510-5134
Toll-Free: 800-268-7742
www.labcanada.com
Frequency: 6 times a year
Leslie Burt, Publisher, lburt@labcanada.com

The Microscopical Society of Canada Bulletin
c/o Sherbrooke University, 2500, boul de l'Université, Sherbrooke, QC J1K 2R1
Tel: 819-821-8000; *Fax:* 819-821-7955
www.msc-smc.org
Frequency: 4 times a year
Nadi Braidy, Editor, nadi.braidy@usherbrooke.ca

OSMT Advocate
#402, 234 Eglinton Ave. East, Toronto, ON M4P 1K5
Tel: 416-485-6768; *Fax:* 416-485-7660
Toll-Free: 800-461-6768
osmt@osmt.org
www.osmt.org
Social Media:
twitter.com/osmt2011
www.facebook.com/217098608317170
Frequency: Annual
Blanca McArthur, Executive Director, bmcarthur@osmt.org

Physics in Canada (PIC) / La Physique au Canada
#112, McDonald Bldg., 150 Louis Pasteur Ave., Ottawa, ON K1N 6N5
Tel: 613-562-5614; *Fax:* 613-562-5615
cap@uottawa.ca
www.cap.ca
Frequency: 6 times a year
Béla Joós, Editor

Security

Canadian Security
Owned By: Annex Publishing & Printing Inc.
222 Edward St., Aurora, ON L4G 1W6
Tel: 905-727-0077; *Fax:* 905-727-0017
www.canadiansecuritymag.com
Social Media:
twitter.com/securityed
www.facebook.com/pages/Canadian-Security/75036793 4990911
Frequency: 6 times a year
Neil Sutton, Editor
Peter Young, Publisher

Security Products & Technology News
Also Known As: SP&T News
Owned By: Annex Publishing & Printing Inc.
222 Edward St., Aurora, ON L4G 1W6
Tel: 905-727-0077; *Fax:* 905-727-0017
Toll-Free: 800-265-2827
www.sptnews.ca
Social Media:
twitter.com/SecurityEd
Circulation: 13,000
Frequency: 8 times a year
Source of information for dealers, installers, system integrators, resellers and specifiers working in the Canadian security industry.
Peter Young, Publisher, 905-713-4344, peter@sptnews.ca
Paul Grossinger, Editor, 905-713-4387, pgrossinger@annexweb.com

Shipping & Marine

BC Shipping News
#300, 1275 West 6th Ave., Vancouver, BC V6H 1A6
Tel: 604-893-8800; *Fax:* 604-708-1920
info@bcshippingnews.com
www.bcshippingnews.com
Social Media: www.linkedin.com/company/bc-shipping-news
twitter.com/bcshipping
www.facebook.com/pages/BC-Shipping-News/109917705757414
Frequency: 10 times a year
A subsidiary of McIvor Communications Inc., BC Shipping News provides information about Canada's west coast commercial marine industry. The magazine is of interest to port & terminal operators, shipbuilders & repairers, ship owners & operators, trade association representatives, & government representatives. Both print & digital editions are available.
Jane McIvor, Contact, Subscriptions & Advertising, jane@bcshippingnews.com

Canadian Sailings
Also Known As: Sailings
#304, av 185 Dorval, Dorval, QC H9S 5J9
Tel: 514-556-3042
concentrate@sympatico.ca
www.canadiansailings.ca
Social Media:
twitter.com/CanSailings
www.facebook.com/pages/Canadian-Sailings-Magazin e/2187715
Frequency: Weekly
Joyce Hammock, Publisher & Editor, jhammock@canadiansailings.ca

Social Welfare

Charity Times Magazine
#11, 6221 Hwy. 7, Vaughan, ON L4H 0K8
Tel: 905-851-6800; *Fax:* 905-851-6225
www.charitytimesmagazine.ca
Social Media:
www.facebook.com/81165429690
Frequency: 6 times a year
Joe Plati, Publisher, jplati@charitytimesmagazine.ca
Cameron Wood, Editor, cwood@charitytimesmagazine.ca

Sporting Goods & Recreational Equipment

Golf Business Canada
#105, 955 Green Valley Cres., Ottawa, ON K1C 3V4
Tel: 613-226-3616; *Fax:* 613-226-4148
ngcoa@ngcoa.ca
www.ngcoa.ca
Circulation: 4,000
Frequency: 4 times a year
Nathalie Lavallée, Chief Operating Officer, 613-226-3616 ext 15

Piscines & Spas
Détenteur: Kenilworth Media Inc.
c/o Kenilworth Media Inc., #710, 15 Wertheim Crt., Richmond Hill, ON L4B 3H7
Tél: 905-771-7333; *Téléc:* 905-771-7336
Ligne sans frais: 800-409-8688
editor@poolspamarketing.com
www.poolspamarketing.com/piscines-spas
Médias sociaux:
twitter.com/PoolSpaMktg
Fréquence: Deux fois par année
Piscines & Spas est également la publication officielle du 'Salon Splash', le salon professionnel qui se tient chaque année à l'automne au Québec.

Pool & Spa Marketing
Owned By: Kenilworth Media Inc.
c/o Kenilworth Media Inc., #710, 15 Wertheim Ct., Richmond Hill, ON L4B 3H7
Tel: 905-771-7333; *Fax:* 905-771-7336
www.poolspamarketing.com
Social Media:
twitter.com/PoolSpaMktg
Frequency: 7 times a year
Richard Hubbard, Publisher

Pools, Spas & Patios
Owned By: Kenilworth Media Inc.
c/o Kenilworth Media Inc., #710, 15 Wertheim Crt., Richmond Hill, ON L4B 3H7
Tel: 905-771-7333; *Fax:* 905-771-7336
Toll-Free: 800-409-8688
editor@poolsspaspatios.com
www.poolsspaspatios.com
Social Media:
twitter.com/poolsspaspatios
www.facebook.com/PoolsSpasPatiosmagazine
Frequency: Annually

Sports & Recreation

Canadian Running
Owned By: Gripped Publishing Inc.
75 Harbord St., Toronto, ON M5S 1G4
Tel: 416-927-0774; *Fax:* 416-927-1491
Toll-Free: 800-567-0444
info@runningmagazine.ca
runningmagazine.ca
Social Media:
twitter.com/CanadianRunning
www.facebook.com/CanadianRunningMagazine
Michael Doyle, Editor-in-Chief, michael@runningmagazine.ca

iRun
Owned By: Sportstats Inc.
#18, 155 Colonnade Rd., Ottawa, ON K2E 7K1
Tel: 613-238-1818
ben@iRun.ca
irun.ca
Social Media: www.youtube.com/user/iRunNation
twitter.com/irunnation
www.facebook.com/iRunMagazine
Circulation: 60,000
Frequency: 6 times a year
Mark Sutcliffe, Group Publisher
Ray Zahab, Editor-in-Chief

Poker Player Magazine
Owned By: HeadsUp Entertainment Inc.
#1739, 246 Stewart Green SW, Calgary, AB T3H 3C8
Tel: 403-269-9039; *Fax:* 403-269-9060
www.headsupentertainment.com
Kelly B. Kellner, President/Founder/COO

Sportsnet Magazine
Owned By: Rogers Media Inc.
1 Mount Pleasant Rd., Toronto, ON M4Y 2Y5
www.sportsnet.ca/magazine
Social Media:
twitter.com/Sportsnet
www.facebook.com/sportsnet
Circulation: 100,000
Frequency: 26 times a year
Steve Maich, Publisher
Brandon Kirk, Editor

Triathlon Magazine Canada
Owned By: Gripped Publishing Inc.
PO Box 819 Main, 75 Harbord St., Markham, ON L3P 8L3
Tel: 416-927-8198; *Fax:* 416-927-1491
Toll-Free: 800-567-0444
info@triathlonmagazine.ca
triathlonmagazine.ca
Social Media:
twitter.com/CanadianRunning
www.facebook.com/CanadianRunningMagazi ne
Kevin Mackinnon, Editor-in-Chief, kevin@triathlonmagazine.ca

Telecommunications

Canadian New Media
#1800, 160 Elgin St., Ottawa, ON K2P 2P7
Tel: 613-230-1984; *Fax:* 613-230-3793
www.decima.com
James Lewis, Editor

Wireless Telecom
Owned By: Canadian Wireless Telecommunications Association
#1110, 130 Albert St., Ottawa, ON K1P 5G4
Tel: 613-233-4888; *Fax:* 613-233-2032
info@cwta.ca
www.cwta.ca
Circulation: 7,273
Frequency: 3 times a year

Television, Radio, Video & Home Appliances

Marketnews Magazine
Bomar Publishing Inc., #102, 701 Evans Ave., Toronto, ON M9C 1A3
Tel: 416-667-9945; *Fax:* 416-667-0609
mail@marketnews.ca
www.marketnews.ca
Social Media:
twitter.com/MarketnewsMag
www.facebook.com/pages/Marketnews-Magazine/130 05201701150
Frequency: Monthly
John Thomson, Associate Publisher, jtomson@marketnews.ca
Bob Grierson, Publisher
Christine Persaud, Editor, cpersaud@marketnews.ca

Erik Devantier, Creative Director

Media Names & Numbers
#201, Bloor St. West., Toronto, ON M6G 1L9
Tel: 416-964-7799; *Fax:* 416-964-8763
sources@sources.ca
www.sources.com

Circulation: 500
Frequency: Annually
Ulli Diemer, Publisher

Textiles

The Textile Journal / La Revue du Textile
#3000 Boullé St., Saint-Hyacinthe, QC J2S 1H9
Tel: 450-778-1870; *Fax:* 450-778-3901
info@gcttg.com
www.groupecttgroup.com

Circulation: 2,800
Frequency: Quarterly

The Textile Journal
Owned By: Groupe CCT
3000, rue Boulle, Saint-Hyacinthe, QC J2S 1H9
Tel: 450-778-1870; *Fax:* 450-778-9016
Toll-Free: 877-288-8378
edition@gcttg.com
www.groupecttgroup.com

Frequency: Trimestriel
Jacek Mlynarek, PDG PhD, jmlynarek@gcttg.com
Martin Filteau, Coéditeur, La Revue du Textile, mfilteau@gcttg.com
Olivier Vermeersch, Coéditeur, La Revue du Textile, overmeersch@gcttg.com

Toys

Toys & Games (T&G)
Owned By: Playtonic Communications
Playtonic Communications, PO Box 94084, 3409 Yonge St., Toronto, ON M4N 3R1
Tel: 416-487-1869
editor@toysandgamesmagazine.ca
toysandgamesmagazine.ca
Social Media:
www.facebook.com/pages/Toys-Games-Magazine/12429854431907

Frequency: 6 times a year

Transportation, Shipping & Distribution

Canadian Automotive Fleet
#206, 1001 Champlain Ave., Burlington, ON L7L 5Z4
Tel: 289-288-9994; *Fax:* 289-288-9996
Toll-Free: 877-870-0055
caf@fleetbusiness.com
www.fleetbusiness.com
Social Media: www.youtube.com/CAFMagazine
twitter.com/CanAutoFleet

Circulation: 13,000
Frequency: 7 times a year
Keith McLaughlin, Publisher, kmclaughlin@fleetbusiness.com
Mario Cywinski, Managing Editor, mario@fleetbusiness.com

Canadian Shipper
Owned By: Annex-Newcom
80 Valleybrook Dr., Toronto, ON M3B 2S9
Tel: 416-510-5108; *Fax:* 416-510-5146
www.canadianshipper.com

Frequency: 11 times a year
Nick Krukowski, Publisher, nkrukowski@canadianshipper.com
Lou Smyrlis, Editorial Director, lou@TransportationMedia.ca

Maritime Magazine
Owned By: Les Productions Maritimes
#200, 4493, Sherbrooke ouest, Westmount, QC H3Z 1E7
Tel: 514-937-9009; *Fax:* 514-937-9088
marketing@maritimemag.com
www.maritimemag.com

Circulation: 11,000
Frequency: 4 times a year
Covers Marine Transport Industry
Leo Ryan, Rédacteur en chef, lryan@maritimemag.com

Repertoire Transport & Logistique
Détenteur: Les Editions Bomart ltée
Tél: 450-224-7000; *Téléc:* 450-224-7711
www.bomartgroup.com

Fréquence: 1 fois par an
Denis Parent, Directeur des ventes, dparent@bomartgroup.com

Routes et Transports
A.Q.T.R., #200, 1255, rue University, Montréal, QC H3B 3B2
Tél: 514-523-6444; *Téléc:* 514-523-2666
www.aqtr.qc.ca

Fréquence: 4 fois par an

Travel

Canadian Travel Press
Owned By: Baxter Publishing Co
310 Dupont St., Toronto, ON M5R 1V9
Tel: 416-968-7252; *Fax:* 416-968-2377
ctp@baxter.net
www.travelpress.com

Frequency: 47 times per year
Michael Baginski, Publisher
Edith Baxter, Editor in Chief

Canadian Traveller
#802, 1166 Alberni St., Vancouver, BC V6E 2Z3
Fax: 604-699-9993
Toll-Free: 888-924-7524
administration@canadiantraveller.net
www.canadiantraveller.net
Social Media:
twitter.com/cantravelmag

Frequency: Monthly
Brad Liski, Publisher, bradl@mypassionmedia.com
Vickie Paget, Editor, vickiep@mypassionmedia.com
Jennifer Prendergast, Associate Publisher, jenniferp@mypassionmedia.com

Personnel Guide to Canada's Travel Industry
Owned By: Baxter Publishing Co
310 Dupont St., Toronto, ON M5R 1V9
Tel: 416-968-7252; *Fax:* 416-968-2377
www.personnelguide.ca
Social Media: www.linkedin.com/company/baxter-travel-media
twitter.com/CdnTravelPress
www.facebook.com/BaxterTravelMedia

Frequency: 2 times a year

Revue Voyage en Groupe / Group Travel
Anciennement: Voyage en Groupe
590, ch St-Jean, La Prairie, QC J5R 2L1
Tél: 450-444-5870

Fréquence: 6 fois par an

Tourisme Plus
CP 7, Succ. Ahuntsic, Montréal, QC H3L 3N5
Tél: 514-881-8583; *Téléc:* 514-881-8292
info@tourismeplus.com
www.tourismeplus.com

Tirage: 9 200
Fréquence: 25 fois par an
Michel Villeneuve, Président, Éditeur, michel@planisphere.qc.ca
Marie Chantal Cholette, Éditrice Adjointe, mariechantal@tourismeplus.com

Travel Courier
Owned By: Baxter Publishing Co
310 Dupont St., Toronto, ON M5R 1V9e
Tel: 416-968-7252; *Fax:* 416-968-2377
www.travelpress.com

Frequency: Weekly
Edith Baxter, Editor-in-chief

Travelweek
Previous Name: Travelweek Bulletin; Canadian Travel Monthly
122 Parliament St., Toronto, ON M5A 2Y8
Tel: 416-365-1500; *Fax:* 416-365-1504
travelweek@travelweek.ca
www.travelweek.ca
Social Media: www.linkedin.com/company/travelweek
twitter.com/TravelweekGroup
www.fa cebook.com/travelweek.ca

Frequency: Weekly
Patrick Dineen, Editor

Vending & Vending Equipment

Canadian Vending & Office Coffee Service Magazine
Previous Name: Canadian Vending
Owned By: Annex Publishing & Printing Inc.
PO Box 530, 105 Donly Dr. Aouth, Simcoe, ON N3Y 4N5
Fax: 519-429-3094
Toll-Free: 888-599-2228
www.canadianvending.com
Social Media:
twitter.com/CanadianVending
www.facebook.com/CanadianVending

Circulation: Digital only
Frequency: 10 times a year
Colleen Cross, Associate Editor, ccross@annexweb.com

Veterinary

The Canadian Veterinary Journal / La Revue Vétérinaire Canadienne
c/o Canadian Veterinary Medical Association, 339 Booth St., Ottawa, ON K1R 7K1
Tel: 613-236-1162; *Fax:* 613-236-9681
Toll-Free: 800-567-2862
admin@cvma-acmv.org
www.canadianveterinarians.net/science-knowledge/cvj
Frequency: Monthly
The Canadian Veterinary Journal, published by the Canadian Veterinary Medical Association, is the 'voice of veterinary medicine in Canada'.
Carlton Gyles, Editor-in-chief

Journal Le Vétérinarius
Anciennement: Le Vétérinarius
#200, 800, av Sainte-Anne, Saint-Hyacinthe, QC J2S 5G7
Tél: 450-774-1427; *Téléc:* 450-774-7635
Ligne sans frais: 800-267-1427
omvq@omvq.qc.ca
www.omvq.qc.ca

Fréquence: 6 fois par an

Water & Wastes Treatment

Environmental Science & Engineering Magazine
Environmental Science & Engineering Publications Inc., #30, 220 Industrial Pkwy. South, Aurora, ON L4G 3V6
Tel: 905-727-4666; *Fax:* 905-841-7271
Toll-Free: 888-254-8769
www.esemag.com

Circulation: 19,000
Frequency: 6 times a year
Steve Davey, Publisher & Editor, steve@esemag.com

Ground Water Canada
Previous Name: Canadian Water Well
Owned By: Annex Publishing & Printing Inc.
PO Box 530, 105 Donly Dr. South, Simcoe, ON N3Y 4N5
Fax: 519-429-3094
Toll-Free: 888-599-2228
www.groundwatercanada.com
Social Media:
twitter.com/groundwatermag
www.facebook.com/pages/Ground-Water-Canada/15840959051757

Frequency: 4 times a year
Serves the water well and geothermal industries.
Laura Aiken, Editor, 416-522-1595, laiken@annexweb.com

Hazardous Materials Management Magazine
Also Known As: Haz-Mat
80 Valleybrook Dr., Toronto, ON M3B 2S9
Tel: 416-442-5600; *Fax:* 416-510-5133
www.hazmatmag.com

Frequency: Bi-monthly
Guy Crittenden, Editor, gcrittenden@hazmatmag.com
Brad O'Brien, Publisher, bobrien@hazmatmag.com

Maritime Provinces Water & Wastewater Report (MPWWR)
MPWWA, PO Box 28142, Dartmouth, NS B2W 6E2
Tel: 902-749-2525; *Fax:* 902-742-2311
contact@mpwwa.ca
www.mpwwa.ca
Circulation: 2,567
Frequency: 4 times a year
Patricia MacInnis, Editor, 902-476-8815, patricia.macinnis@tc.tc

Solid Waste & Recycling Magazine
Previous Name: Solid Waste Management
Owned By: Annex-Newcom
80 Valleybrook Dr., Toronto, ON M3B 2S9
Tel: 416-510-6798; *Fax:* 416-510-5133
Toll-Free: 800-268-7742
www.solidwastemag.com

Circulation: 10,000
Frequency: 6 times a year
The company publishes Solid Waste & Recycling Magazine, providing environmental information to industry and government. Topics include: Recycling, Diversion, Composting, The Haulers Page, Landfill Technology, Equipment, Regulation Roundup, and Final Analysis. The publication is available to qualified Canadians for free.
Brad O'Brien, Publisher, bobrien@solidwastemag.com
Guy Crittenden, Editor, gcrittenden@solidwastemag.com

Woodworking

Focusbois
PO Box 1010, Victoriaville, QC G6P 8Y1
Tel: 819-752-4243; *Fax:* 819-382-2970
www.focusbois.com
Frequency: Daily
Highlights news, resources, markets, technologies, innovations, machinery & equipment, trends & reports about wood
Claude Roy, Owner & Editor, 819-382-2608, Fax: 819-382-2970, info@focusbois.com
Roger Roy, 819-752-9492, Fax: 819-382-2970, r_roy@focusbois.com

Woodworking
Owned By: Kleiser Media Inc.
#203, 520 Riverside Dr., Toronto, ON M6S 4B5
Tel: 416-763-3653
info@kleisermedia.com
www.woodworkingcanada.com
Frequency: 6 times a year
Bert Kleiser, Publisher, 416-763-3653, Bert@kleisermedia.com
Stephan Kleiser, Editor, Stephan@kleisermedia.com

Consumer

Advertising, Marketing, Sales

Sparksheet
Toronto, ON
contact@sparksheet.com
sparksheet.com
Social Media: www.youtube.com/user/sparksheettv
www.twitter.com/sparksheet
www.facebook.com/pages/Sparksheet/185418500634
Circulation: 120,000
Frequency: 6 times a year
For media and marketing professionals
Dan Levy, Editor

Airline Inflight

enRoute
Owned By: Spafax Canada
#707, 4200 boul. St-Laurent, Montréal, QC H2W 2R2
Tel: 514-844-2001; *Fax:* 514-844-6001
info@enroutemag.net
enroute.aircanada.com
Social Media: plus.google.com/116782112608552946379
twitter.com/enroutemag
www.faceb ook.com/enrouteonline
Circulation: 3500
Frequency: Monthly
Ilana Weitzman, Editor-in-Chief

Animals

Canine Review
PO Box 53236 Marlborough, Calgary, AB T2A 7L9
Tel: 403-236-0557 *Toll-Free:* 866-236-0557
editor@caninereview.ca
www.caninereview.ca
Circulation: 2,000
Frequency: 10 times a year
Lisa Ricciotti, Editor, 877-811-3699, editor@caninereview.ca
Merla Thomson, Publisher, 403-236-0557, merla@caninereview.ca

Dogs Dogs Dogs
Owned By: Dogs Dogs Dogs Multimedia
#103, 2192 Queen St. East, Toronto, ON M4E 1E6
Tel: 416-693-0918; *Fax:* 416-691-9784
info@dogsdogsdogs.ca; advertising@dogsdogsdogs.ca
www.dogsdogsdogs.ca
Social Media: M4E 1E6
twitter.com/dddogsmedia
www.facebook.com/pages/Dogs-Dogs-Dogs-Multimedia/285412 35
Circulation: 12,000 / issue
Frequency: 5 times a year
Dogs Dogs Dogs contains advice, reviews, & stories for persons interested in dogs. The newspaper is available through subscription & at veterinary clinics, shelters, & pet supply retailers in the Greater Toronto Area.

Modern Dog
#202, 343 Railway St., Vancouver, BC V6A 1A4
Tel: 604-734-3131; *Fax:* 604-734-3031
Toll-Free: 866-734-3131
info@moderndogmagazine.com
www.moderndogmagazine.com
Social Media:
www.twitter.com/ModernDogMag
www.facebook.com/moderndogmagazine?v=wall
Frequency: 4 times a year
Connie Wilson, Editor-in-chief

Ontario SPCA (OSPCA)
16586 Woodbine Ave., RR#3, Newmarket, ON L3Y 4V8
Tel: 905-898-7122; *Fax:* 905-853-8643
info@ospca.on.ca
www.ontariospca.ca
Circulation: 100,000
Frequency: 2 times a year
Katie Leonard, Contact, kleonard@ospca.on.ca

Pets Magazine
Owned By: Simmons Publishing
c/o Simmons Publishing, 32 Foster Cres., Whitby, ON L1R 1W1
Tel: 905-665-9669; *Fax:* 905-665-9249
Toll-Free: 877-738-7624
editor@petsmagazine.ca
www.petsmagazine.ca
Circulation: 36,565
Frequency: 6 times a year

Arts, Art & Antiques

Border Crossings
#500, 70 Arthur St., Winnipeg, MB R3B 1G7
Tel: 204-942-5778; *Fax:* 204-949-0793
Toll-Free: 866-825-7165
bordercrossings@mts.net
bordercrossingsmag.com
Circulation: 5,500
Frequency: 4 times a year
Meeka Walsh, Editor
Robert Enright, Editor-at-large

C Magazine
Previous Name: C international contemporary art magazine
C The Visual Arts Foundation, PO Box 5 B, Toronto, ON M5T 2T2
Tel: 416-539-9495; *Fax:* 416-539-9903
Toll-Free: 800-745-6312
info@cmagazine.com
www.cmagazine.com
Social Media:
twitter.com/cmagazineart
www.facebook.com/cmagazineart
Circulation: 3,000
Frequency: 4 times a year

Canadian Art
#320, 215 Spadina Ave., Toronto, ON M5T 2C7
Tel: 416-368-8854; *Fax:* 416-368-6135
Toll-Free: 800-222-4762
info@canadianart.ca
www.canadianart.ca
Circulation: 23,500
Frequency: 4 times a year
Publishes material that address the interests of visual artists in Ontario
Richard Rhodes, Editor, rhodes@canadianart.ca
Bryne McLaughlin, Managing Editor

Dance International
The Vancouver Ballet Society, Level 6, 677 Davie St., Vancouver, BC V6B 2G6
Tel: 604-681-1525; *Fax:* 604-681-7732
Editor@DanceInternational.org
www.danceinternational.org
Social Media:
twitter.com/DIMagazine
www.facebook.com/pages/Dance-International/12875748380447
Circulation: 4,000
Frequency: 4 times a year
Maureen Riches, Editor

Downhome
Previous Name: Downhomer Magazine
43 James Lane, St. John's, NL A1E 3H3
Tel: 709-726-5113; *Fax:* 709-726-2135
Toll-Free: 888-588-6353
mail@downhomer.com
www.downhomelife.com
Social Media:
twitter.com/downhomelife
www.facebook.com/downhomelife
Circulation: 225,000
Frequency: Monthly
Ron Young, Publisher

ETC Montréal
#250, 1435, rue St-Alexandre, Montréal, QC H3A 2G4
Tél: 514-848-1125; *Téléc:* 514-848-0071
etc.artactuel@videotron.ca
www.etcmontreal.com
Tirage: 2 500
Fréquence: 4 fois par an
Isabelle Lelarge, Rédacteur-en-chef, etc.lelarge@videotron.ca

Galleries West
#301, 690 Princeton Way SW, Calgary, AB T2P 5J9
Tel: 403-234-7097; *Fax:* 403-243-4649
publisher@gallerieswest.ca
www.gallerieswest.ca
Frequency: 3 times a year
Jennifer MacLeod, Editor

The Grand Theatre Program
Owned By: Sun Media Corporation
Kingston Publications, 18 St. Remy Pl., Kingston, ON K7K 6C4
Tel: 613-389-7400; *Fax:* 613-389-7507
www.kingstonpublications.com/grandtheatre.html
Circulation: 23,625
Frequency: 7 times a year
Print copies available at all Grand Theatre Presents performances. Also available in virtual product.

Inter, art actuel
Anciennement: Intervention
Les Éditions intervention, 345, rue du Pont, Québec, QC G1K 6M4
Tél: 418-529-9680; *Téléc:* 418-529-6933
infos@inter-lelieu.org
www.inter-lelieu.org
Médias sociaux: www.youtube.com/user/intervention22
twitter.com/lelieuinter
www.fac ebook.com/lelieu.actualite
Tirage: 1 200
Fréquence: 3 fois par an
Inter, art actuel est une revue culturelle disséminant diverses formes de l'art actuel: performance, art action, installation, poésie, manouvre, multimédia, etc.
Richard Martel, Coordination artistique, programmation@inter-lelieu.org

Muse
Canadian Museums Assn., #400, 280 Metcalfe St., Ottawa, ON K2P 1R7
Tel: 613-567-0099; *Fax:* 613-233-5438
www.museums.ca/Publications/Muse
Circulation: 2,500
Frequency: 6 times a year

Muzik Etc./Drums Etc.
753, rue Ste-Hélène, Longueuil, QC J4K 3R5
Tel: 450-651-4257; *Fax:* 450-670-8683
www.muziketc.ca
Circulation: 30,000
Frequency: bimestriel
Sofi Gamache, Editor in Chief, 450-674-1114
Ralph Angelillo, Editor in Chief, 450-928-1726

Ontario Craft
Previous Name: Craftnews
Designers Walk, 990 Queen St. West, Toronto, ON M6J 1H1
Tel: 416-925-4222; *Fax:* 416-925-4223
info@craft.on.ca
www.craft.on.ca
Circulation: 2,500
Frequency: 2 times a year
Deborah Kirkegaard, Program & Development Officer

Parachute
#501, 4060, boul Saint-Laurent, Montréal, QC H2W 1Y9
Tel: 514-842-9805; *Fax:* 514-842-9319
info@parachute.ca
www.parachute.ca

Circulation: 4,000
Frequency: 4 times a year
The magazine halted production in 2007, but back issues can be ordered online.
Chantal Pontbriand, Directrice, c.pontbriand@parachute.ca

Qui Fait Quoi
CP 64002 Le Gardeur, 4841, rue Jeanne, Montréal, QC H2V 4J6
Tél: 514-842-5333; *Téléc:* 514-495-1069
info@qfq.com
www.qfq.com
Tirage: 7,000
Fréquence: 9 times a year
Steeve Laprise, Rédacteur en chef / éditeur, redaction@qfq.com

ROM
Previous Name: Rotunda
c/o Royal Ontario Museum, 100 Queen's Park, Toronto, ON M5S 2C6
Tel: 416-586-8000
info@rom.on.ca
www.rom.on.ca
Frequency: Quarterly

Slate
155 King St. East, Kingston, ON K7L 2Z9
Tel: 613-542-3717 *Toll-Free:* 800-871-8093
info@slateartguide.com
www.slateartguide.com
Frequency: 8 times a year
Allan Lochhead, Publisher, allan@slateartguide.com

Spirale
6742, rue Saint-Denis, Montréal, QC H2S 2S2
Tél: 514-934-5651; *Téléc:* 514-934-6390
spiralemagazine@yahoo.com
www.spiralemagazine.com
Tirage: 1 500
Pierre L'Hérault, Direction

Take One
#482, 283 Danforth Ave., Toronto, ON M4K 1N2
Tel: 416-944-1096; *Fax:* 416-465-4356
takeone@interlog.com
www.takeonemagazine.ca
Social Media:
twitter.com/NorthernStarsca
www.facebook.com/nstarseditor
Circulation: 5,000
Frequency: 4 times a year
Wyndham Wise, Publisher

Vie des Arts
#603, 5605, av De Gaspé, Montréal, QC H2T 2A4
Tél: 514-282-0205; *Téléc:* 514-282-0235
admin@viedesarts.com
www.viedesarts.com
Médias sociaux: www.youtube.com/user/ViedesArtsMagzine
twitter.com/ViedesArts
Fréquence: 4 fois par an
Bernard Lévy, Directeur général et rédacteur en chef

Westbridge Art Market Report
Owned By: Westbridge Publications Ltd.
1737 Fir St., Vancouver, BC V6J 5J9
Tel: 604-736-1014; *Fax:* 604-734-4944
info@westbridge-fineart.com
www.westbridge-fineart.com
Anthony R. Westbridge, Publisher & Editor

Automobile, Cycle, & Automotive Accessories

Canadian Biker
PO Box 4122, Victoria, BC V8X 3X4
Tel: 250-384-0333; *Fax:* 250-384-1832
www.canadianbiker.com
Social Media:
www.facebook.com/pages/Canadian-Biker-Magazine/2089578891
Frequency: 10 times a year

Canadian Classics & Performance
33534 Western Rd. #RR 2, Mount Pleasant, PE C0B 1J0
Tel: 902-831-2733; *Fax:* 902-831-2385
Toll-Free: 866-976-8666
canadianclassic@xplornet.com
Circulation: 11,000
Frequency: 12 times a year
Dale Lidstone, Publisher

Cycle Canada
Owned By: Les Éditions Jean Robert inc.
300, rue, Georges VI, Terrebonne, QC J6Y 1N9
Tel: 450-965-9494; *Fax:* 450-965-9009
info@editionsjeanrobert.com
www.cyclecanadaweb.com
Frequency: 10 times a year
Neil Graham, Editor

Le Guide de l'Auto / The Car Guide
Owned By: LC Média inc.
LC Média inc., #305, 414, boul Sir-Wilfrid-Laurier, Mont-Saint-Hilaire, QC J3H 3N9
Tel: 450-464-1479; *Fax:* 450-464-8271
Toll-Free: 866-522-5656
abonnement@lcmedia.ca
www.guideautoweb.com
Social Media: www.youtube.com/user/guideauto
twitter.com/guideauto
www.facebook.com/guideauto

Lemon-Aid New Car Buyer's Guide / Roulez sans vous faire rouler
c/o Automobile Protection Association, 292, St-Joseph Blvd. West, Montréal, QC H2V 2N7
Tel: 514-272-5555; *Fax:* 514-273-0797
apamontreal@apa.ca
www.apa.ca
Social Media:
twitter.com/APA_LEMONAID
www.facebook.com/133864379984212
Frequency: Annual
Online magazine that summarizes road test data, customer reviews, mechanic reviews, manufacturer data and government reports to help consumers choose a car.

Le Monde du VTT
215, rue Principale, Saint-Amable, QC J0L 1N0
Tirage: 9 560
Fréquence: 6 times a year
Richard Jetté, Éditeur

Motocycliste
c/o Fédération Motocycliste du Québec, #460, 9675, Papineau, Montréal, QC H2B 3C8
Tél: 514-252-8121; *Téléc:* 514-252-7857
fmq@fmq.qc.ca
www.fmq.qc.ca
Tirage: 15 500
Fréquence: 5 fois par an

MOTOMAG
1730 - 55e av, Lachine, QC H8T 3J5
Tél: 514-631-6550; *Téléc:* 514-631-0591
www.motomag.com
Médias sociaux:
facebook.com/pages/Moto-Magazine-Actualités-essais-motos-
Tirage: 11 234
Fréquence: 6 fois par an
Genevieve Pepin, Chief Editor
Michel Crepault, Publisher

Old Autos
PO Box 250, 348 Main St., Bothwell, ON N0P 1C0
Tel: 519-695-2303; *Fax:* 519-695-3716
Toll-Free: 800-461-3457
info@oldautos.ca
www.oldautos.ca
Circulation: 20,000
Frequency: Bi-monthly

Pedal Magazine
#200, 260 Spadina Ave., Toronto, ON M5T 2E4
Tel: 416-977-2100; *Fax:* 416-977-9200
Toll-Free: 866-977-3325
info@pedalmag.com
www.pedalmag.com
Social Media:
twitter.com/pedalmagazine
www.facebook.com/101939769846530
Cycling magazine with information on races, adventure touring & recreational cycling

Pole Position
553, rue Calixa-Lavallée, Beloeil, QC J3G 4B6
Tel: 450-464-4076; *Fax:* 450-464-7742
info@poleposition.ca
www.poleposition.ca
Social Media:
twitter.com/PolePositionMag
www.facebook.com/polepositionmagazine
Circulation: 16,625
Frequency: 8 times a year
Philippe Brasseur, Rédaction en Chef

PRN Motorsport Magazine (PRN)
Previous Name: Performance Racing News
#100A, 219 Dufferin St., Toronto, ON M6K 3J1
Tel: 416-922-7223; *Fax:* 416-964-1836
Toll-Free: 800-667-7223
info@prnmag.com
www.prnmag.com
Social Media: www.flickr.com/groups/prnmag
twitter.com/prnmag
www.facebook.com/PRNMAG
Frequency: 12 times a year
Tim Rutledge, Group Publisher & CEO, trutledge@ppgpubs.com

Vancouver International Auto Show Program
Owned By: Carling Media
Carling Media, #115, 1641 Lonsdale Ave., North Vancouver, BC V7M 2J5
Tel: 604-612-6237
editorial@carlingmedia.com
www.carlingmedia.com/show_guides.php
Circulation: 50,000
Frequency: 1 issue per year; English and Chinese
Distributed free to visitors of the Vancouver International Auto Show that runs the last week of March into early April.
Glen Ringdal, Publisher

Vélo Mag
Détenteur: Velo Québec Éditions
Maison des Cyclistes, 1251, rue Rachel est, Montréal, QC H2J 2J9
Tél: 514-521-8356; *Téléc:* 514-521-5711
Ligne sans frais: 800-567-8356
www.velomag.com
Médias sociaux:
twitter.com/velomag_
www.facebook.com/pages/Vélo-Mag/341952746621
Fréquence: 6 fois par an
Jacques Sennechael, Rédacteur-en-chef
Pierre Sormay, Éditeur

Aviation & Aerospace

Canadian Aviation Historical Society Journal
PO Box 2700 D, Ottawa, ON K1P 5W7
Tel: 519-742-6965
www.cahs.com
Frequency: Quarterly
Chapters located in Calgary, Manitoba, Montréal, New Brunswick, Ottawa, PEI, Regina, Toronto and Vancouver.
Terry Higgins, CAHS Editor
Gary Williams, President, 306-543-8123
Rachel Lea Heide, Treasurer

Babies & Mothers

Baby & Child Care Encyclopedia
Owned By: Parents Canada Group
65 The East Mall, Toronto, ON M8Z 5W3
Tel: 416-537-2604; *Fax:* 416-538-1794
admin@parentscanada.com
www.parentscanada.com
Circulation: 100,000
Frequency: 2 times a year (May & Nov.)
Donald G. Swinburne, Publisher

The Compleat Mother - The Magazine of Pregnancy, Birth & Breastfeeding
PO Box 38033, Calgary, AB T3K 5G9
Tel: 403-255-0246
thecompleatmother@shaw.ca
www.compleatmother.com/subscriptions_canada.htm
Frequency: 4 times a year
Angela van Son, Distributor

Parents Canada
Owned By: Parents Canada Group
65 The East Mall, Toronto, ON M8Z 5W3
Tel: 416-537-2604; *Fax:* 416-538-1794
amyb@parentscanada.com
www.parentscanada.com
Social Media:
twitter.com/#%21/ParentsCanada
www.facebook.com/ParentsCanada
Janice Biehn, Editor, 416-537-2604,ext.349, janiceb@parentscanada.com

Parents Canada Best Wishes
Owned By: Parents Canada Group
65 The East Mall, Toronto, ON M8Z 5W3
Tel: 416-537-2604; *Fax:* 416-538-1794
www.parentscanada.com

Frequency: 2 times a year (May & Nov.)

Parents Canada Expecting
Owned By: Parents Canada Group
65 The East Mall, Toronto, ON M8Z 5W3
Tel: 416-537-2604; *Fax:* 416-538-1794
Toll-Free: 866-457-3320
admin@parentscanada.com
www.parentscanada.com

Parents Canada Labour & Birth Guide
Owned By: Parents Canada Group
65 The East Mall, Toronto, ON M8Z 5W3
Tel: 416-537-2604; *Fax:* 416-538-1794
Toll-Free: 866-457-3320
admin@parentscanada.com
www.parentscanada.com

Parents Canada Naissance
Détenteur: Parents Canada Group
2260, des Patriotes, Laval, QC H7L 3K8
Tél: 450-622-0091; *Téléc:* 450-622-0099

Poupon
Anciennement: Mère Nouvelle
Détenteur: Les Éditions Rogers limitée
1200, ave McGill College, 8e étage, Montréal, QC H3B 4G7
Tél: 514-843-5141
www.boutdechou.ca
Tirage: 34,500
Fréquence: 2 fois par an
French magazine for new parents.
Holly Bennett, Rédactrice

Today's Parent Pregnancy
Previous Name: Great Expectations
Owned By: Rogers Media Inc.
1 Mount Pleasant Rd., 8th Fl., Toronto, ON M4Y 2Y5
Tel: 416-764-2000
www.todaysparent.com
Circulation: 131,725
Frequency: 3 times a year
Rosemary Munroe, Publisher

Boating & Yachting

Boatguide Canada
Owned By: Premier Publications and Shows
c/o Premier Publications and Shows, #4, 447 Speers Rd., Oakville, ON L6K 3S7
Tel: 905-842-6591 *Toll-Free:* 800-693-7986
circ@metrolandwest.com
www.boatguidecanada.com
Circulation: 60,000
Frequency: 2 times a year
Boating guide with specifications, photographs & Canadian pricing for powerboats
Dave Harvey, Regional General Manager, dharvey@metroland.com
Jonathan Lee, Editor, 800-693-7986 ext.264, jlee@metroland.com

Boating East Cruising & Waterway Lifestyle Guide
c/o Ontario Travel Guides, PO Box 483, Westport, ON K0G 1X0
Fax: 800-317-2549
Toll-Free: 800-324-6052
www.ontariotravelguides.com/boatingeast.htm
Social Media:
twitter.com/RideauWaterway
www.facebook.com/group.php?gid=13041157700880 2
Circulation: 25,000 / annually
Frequency: Annually
The guide covers the major waterways of Eastern Ontario & upstate New York.
Jenny Ryan, Editor, jenny@ontariotravelguides.com

Boats & Places
Previous Name: Today's Boating
#13, 130 Saunders Rd., Barrie, ON L4N 0R2
Tel: 705-725-4669; *Fax:* 705-725-4996
info@boatsandplaces.com
www.boatsandplaces.com
Circulation: 24,692
Frequency: 6 times a year
Publishes information relevant to Canadian boaters
Brian Minton, President & Publisher, 705-725-4669 ext.224, brianm@lifestyleintegrated.com
Amanda Comission, Associate Publisher & Editor, 705-725-4669 ext.223, amandac@lifestyleintegrated.com

Canadian Yachting
Owned By: Kerrwil Publications Limtied
538 Elizabeth St., Midland, ON L4R 2A3
Tel: 705-527-7666
info@canadianyachting.ca
www.canadianyachting.ca
Social Media: www.pinterest.com/canadianyachtin
twitter.com/CdnYachting
Www.facebook .com/canadian.yachting
Frequency: 6 times a year
Greg Nicoll, Publisher, 877-620-9373, gnicoll@kerrwil.com
Andy Adams, Managing Editor, 416-574-7313, aadams@kerrwill.com

L'Escale Nautique
Détenteur: Les Productions Maritimes
535, route de la Montagne, Notre-Dame-du-Portage, QC G0L 1Y0
Tél: 418-863-5055; *Téléc:* 418-850-4674
redaction@escalenautique.qc.ca
www.escalenautique.qc.ca
Médias sociaux:
www.facebook.com/pages/LEscale-Nautique/283699044980203
Tirage: 12 000
Fréquence: 4 fois par an, plus guide nautique
Michel Sacco, Rédacteur-en-chef

Gam on Yachting
#1, 5650 Tomken Rd., Mississauga, ON L4W 4P1
Tel: 416-368-1559; *Fax:* 416-368-2831
gam@gamonyachting.com
www.gamonyachting.com
Frequency: 6 times a year
John Grainger, Publisher & Editor, 905-465-0458, editor@gameyachting.com

Ontario Sailor Magazine
Previous Name: Lake Ontario Sailor Magazine
91 Hemmingway Dr., Courtice, ON L1E 2C2
Tel: 905-434-7409; *Fax:* 905-434-1654
sails@istar.ca
www.ontariosailormagazine.ca
Circulation: 10,000
Frequency: 7 times a year
Sandra McDowell, Publisher
Greg McDowell, Managing Editor

Pacific Yachting
Owned By: OP Media Group Ltd.
#500, 200 West Esplanade, Vancouver, BC V6Z 2T1
Tel: 604-998-3310 *Toll-Free:* 800-867-0474
subscriptions@oppublishing.com
www.pacificyachting.com
Social Media: pinterest.com/pacificyachting
twitter.com/pacificyachting
www.faceb ook.com/pacificyachtingmagazine
Circulation: 16,975
Frequency: Monthly
Mark Yelic, Publisher
Dale Miller, Editor, 604-998-3323, Fax: 604-998-3320, editor@pacificyachting.com

Les Plaisanciers
Détenteur: Taylor Publishing Group
#310, 970, Montée de Liesse, Saint-Laurent, QC H4T 1W7
Tél: 514-856-0788; *Téléc:* 514-856-0790
info@magazinelesplaisanciers.com
lesplaisanciers.com
Fréquence: 5 fois par an
William E. Taylor, Éditeur/Président

Port Hole / Le Hublot
c/o Canadian Power & Sail Squadrons, 26 Golden Gate Ct., Toronto, ON M1P 3A5
Tel: 416-293-2438; *Fax:* 416-293-2445
Toll-Free: 888-277-2628
theporthole@cps-ecp.ca
www.cps-ecp.ca
Frequency: 4 times a year
Joan Eyolfson Cadham, Editor-in-chief

Power Boating Canada
Owned By: Taylor Publishing Group
#2, 1121 Invicta Dr., Oakville, ON L6H 2R2
Tel: 905-844-5032; *Fax:* 905-844-5032
Toll-Free: 800-354-9145
www.powerboating.com
Social Media: www.youtube.com/user/PowerBoatingCanada
twitter.com/Power_Boating
www. facebook.com/231865076875417
Frequency: 7 times a year
William Taylor, Publisher
Bill Jennings, Editoral Director

Québec Yachting
Anciennement: Québec Yachting Voile & Moteur
43, rue de Dinan, Laval, QC H7N 2X8
Tél: 450-663-4141; *Téléc:* 450-668-7511
Ligne sans frais: 866-433-3553
quebecyachting@quebecyachting.ca
www.quebecyachting.ca
Fréquence: 7 fois par an
Daniel Hébert, Co-Editor, dhebert@quebecyachting.ca
Nicole Bonneville, Co-Editor

Windsport Magazine
Owned By: SBC Media
SBC Media Inc., #3266, 2255B Queen St. East, Toronto, ON M4E 1G3
Tel: 416-406-2400
info@windsport.com
www.windsport.com
Social Media:
twitter.com/windsport
www.facebook.com/pages/Windsport-Magazine/148182847219
Frequency: 4 times a year
Pete Dekay, Editor, pdk@sbcmedia.com

Books

Amphora
c/o Alcuin Society, PO Box 3216, Vancouver, BC V6B 3X8
Tel: 604-937-3293
info@alcuinsociety.com
www.alcuinsociety.com
Social Media: blog.alcuinsociety.com
twitter.com/alcuin
www.facebook.com/alcuinsociety
Circulation: 340
Frequency: 3 times a year; spring, summer, fall
Amphora, the Alcuin Society's journal, presents original articles, interviews and departments focusing on the world of the book arts: collecting, typography, typesetting, calligraphy, papermaking, ornamentation, illustration, printing and binding.
Howard Greaves, Chair, amphora@alcuinsociety.com

BC BookWorld
3516 West 13th Ave., Vancouver, BC V6R 2S3
Tel: 604-736-4011; *Fax:* 604-736-4011
bookworld@telus.net
www.bcbookworld.com
Circulation: 100,000
Frequency: Quarterly
Independent publication with 900 distribution outlets
Alan Twigg, Publisher
David Lester, Editor

Brides, Bridal

Kingston Life Weddings
Owned By: Sun Media Corporation
Kingston Publications, 18 St. Remy Pl., Kingston, ON K7K 6C4
Tel: 613-389-7400; *Fax:* 613-389-7507
www.kingstonpublications.com/kingstonlifeweddings.html
Circulation: 5,000
Frequency: Annually, December
Kingston Life Weddings is distributed through the city's largest bridal show, and at wedding-related retailers and services. Also available in virtual product.

Mariage Québec
Détenteur: St Joseph Media
#1301, 1155, rue Université, Montréal, QC H3B 3A7
Tél: 514-284-2552; *Téléc:* 514-284-4492
info@mariagequebec.com
www.mariagequebec.com
Médias sociaux: instagram.com/mariage_quebec
twitter.com/mariage_quebec
www.faceboo k.com/magazinemariagequebec
Fréquence: 2 fois par an
Denyse Clermont, Éditrice, dclermont@mariagequebec.com

Ottawa Wedding
Owned By: Coyle Publishing
67 Neil Ave., Stittsville, ON K2S 1B9
Tel: 613-271-8903; *Fax:* 613-271-8905
www.ottawaweddingmagazine.com
Social Media:
www.twitter.com/ottweddingmag
www.facebook.com/OttawaWeddingMagazine
Circulation: 10,000
Frequency: 2 times a year
George W. Coyle, General Manager, gcoyle@coylepublishing.com
Pat den Boer, Editor, editor@coylepublishing.com

Sposa Magazine
#2202, 55 York St., Toronto, ON M5J 1R7
Tel: 416-364-5899; *Fax:* 416-364-5996
www.sposa.com
Social Media: www.pinterest.com/sposamagazine
twitter.com/sposamagazine
www.faceb ook.com/sposamagazine
Circulation: 50,000
Frequency: 2 times a year
Gulshan Sippy, Editor, editor@sposa.com

Today's Bride
Owned By: Family Communications Inc.
65 The East Mall, Toronto, ON M8Z 5W3
Tel: 416-537-2604; *Fax:* 416-538-1794
info@canadianbride.com
www.canadianbride.com
Social Media:
twitter.com/Todaysbridemag
www.facebook.com/todaysbridemagcanada
Frequency: 2 times a year

WeddingBells
Owned By: St Joseph Media
#320, 111 Queen St. East, Toronto, ON M5C 1S2
Tel: 416-364-3333 *Toll-Free:* 800-387-9877
feedback@weddingbells.ca
www.weddingbells.ca
Social Media: www.youtube.com/user/weddingbellscanada
twitter.com/WeddingbellsMag
ww w.facebook.com/WeddingbellsMag
Frequency: 2 times a year
Offices in Toronto, Vancouver, Calgary, Leduc, Winnipeg, Ottawa and Montréal.
Alison McGill, Editor-in-Chief

Weddings & Honeymoons
65 Helena Ave., Toronto, ON M6G 2H3
Tel: 416-653-4986
info@weddingshoneymoons.com
www.weddingshoneymoons.com
Social Media:
www.facebook.com/Weddingshoneymoonscom
Frequency: 3 times a year
Joyce Barshow, Publisher & Editor-in-chief, joyce@weddingshoneymoons.com

Business & Finance

Business in Vancouver
Owned By: BIV Media Group
303 West 5th Ave., Vancouver, BC V5Y 1J6
Tel: 604-688-2398
www.biv.com
Social Media:
www.linkedin.com/company/business-in-vancouver
twitter.com/bizinvanco uver
www.facebook.com/BIVMG
Circulation: 10,596
Frequency: Weekly, Tue.
Paul Harris, President & Publisher, 604-608-5156, pharris@biv.com
Fiona Anderson, Editor-in-Chief, 604-608-5183, fanderson@biv.com

Canadian MoneySaver
#700, 55 King St. West, Kitchener, ON N2G 4W1
Tel: 519-772-7632
moneyinfo@canadianmoneysaver.ca
www.canadianmoneysaver.ca
Social Media: www.youtube.com/user/canadianmoneysaver
twitter.com/cdnmoneysaver
www. facebook.com/239193689507527
Frequency: 9 times a year
Canadian MoneySaver is an is an independent, membership-funded investment advisory magazine. Canadian MoneySaver publishes monthly with three double issues (July/August, November/December and March/April).
Peter Hodson, Editor, research@5iresearch.ca

MONEY Magazine
Money Canada Limited, #226, 7181 Woodbine Ave., Markham, ON
info@money.ca
www.money.ca
Social Media:
www.linkedin.com/groups/Money-Magazine-3001638
Frequency: Monthly
Finance & lifestyle magazine
James Dean, Editor-in-Chief

The Wire Report
Owned By: The Hill Times Publishing Inc.
69 Sparks St., Ottawa, ON K1P 5A5
Tel: 613-232-5952; *Fax:* 613-232-9055
roneill@hilltimes.com
www.thewirereport.ca
Social Media:
twitter.com/thewirereport
Circulation: 60,000
Frequency: Weekly
Anja Karadeglija, Editor, 613-688-8823, akarad@thewirereport.ca

Camping & Outdoor Recreation

Camping Caravaning
#100, 1560, rue Eiffel, Boucherville, QC J4B 5Y1
Tél: 450-650-3722; *Téléc:* 450-650-3721
Ligne sans frais: 877-650-3722
info@campingcaravaningmag.ca
www.campingcaravaningmag.ca
Médias sociaux:
twitter.com/magazinecamping
www.facebook.com/Camping.Caravaning
Tirage: 46 000
Fréquence: 8 fois par an
Yvan Lafontaine, Président
André Rivest, Éditeur
Louise Gagnon, Directrice de la publication

explore
Owned By: OP Media Group Ltd.
#202, 9644 - 54th Ave., Edmonton, AB T6E 5V1
Toll-Free: 888-478-1183
info@explore-mag.com
www.explore-mag.com
Social Media: www.youtube.com/user/exploremag
twitter.com/explore_mag
www.facebook.c om/exploremag
Circulation: 30,000
Frequency: 6 times a year
Al Zikovitz, Publisher
James Little, Editor

RV Gazette
Explorer RV Club, #6, 328 Mill St., Beaverton, ON L0K 1A0
Fax: 705-426-1403
Toll-Free: 800-999-0819
info@rvgazette.com
www.rvgazette.com
Circulation: 13,304
Frequency: bi-monthly
Marcia Anderson, General Manager

Vie en Plein Air
Détenteur: Taylor Publishing Group
#310, 970, Montée de Liesse, Saint-Laurent, QC H4T 1W7
Tél: 514-856-0788; *Téléc:* 514-856-0790
info@vieenpleinair.com
www.vieenpleinair.com
Fréquence: 4 fois par an

Celtic

Irish Connections Canada
Toronto, ON
Tel: 416-526-0113
irishconnected.com
Social Media:
twitter.com/irishcanadamag
www.facebook.com/irishconnectionscanadamagazine
Frequency: 4 times a year
Kieran Dowling, Publisher, kieron@irishconnected.com

Children's

Bazoof!
Previous Name: Zamoof!
Owned By: Dream Wave Publishing Inc.
1879 West 2nd Ave., Vancouver, BC V6J 1J1
Tel: 250-762-9624; *Fax:* 905-946-1679
Toll-Free: 877-762-9624
mail@bazoof.com
www.bazoof.com
Social Media:
twitter.com/bazoofmag
www.facebook.com/bazoofmag
Frequency: 6 times a year

chickaDEE
Owned By: Owlkids Books
#400, 10 Lower Spadina Ave., Toronto, ON M5V 2Z2
Tel: 416-340-2700; *Fax:* 416-340-9769
Toll-Free: 800-551-6957
chickadee@owlkids.com
www.owlkids.com
Frequency: 10 times a year
Mandy Ng, Editor

Chirp
Owned By: Owlkids Books
#400, 10 Lower Spadina Ave., Toronto, ON M5V 2Z2
Tel: 416-340-2700; *Fax:* 416-340-9769
Toll-Free: 800-551-6957
chirp@owlkids.com
www.owlkids.com/chirp/index.html
Circulation: 75,000
Frequency: 10 times a year
Sarah Trusty, Assistant Editor

Les Débrouillards
Publications BLD inc., 4475, rue Frontenac, Montréal, QC H2H 2S2
Tél: 514-844-2111; *Téléc:* 514-278-3030
scientifix@lesdebrouillards.com
www.lesdebrouillards.com
Tirage: 27,000
Fréquence: 11 fois par an
Magazines sur la science pour les jeunes
Félix Maltais, Éditeur, 514-844-2111, Fax: 514-278-3030, felix.maltais@lesdebrouillards.com
Hélène Veilleux, Adjointe, Édition, 514-844-2111, Fax: 514-278-3030

Les Explorateurs
Publications BLD inc., 4475, rue Frontenac, Montréal, QC H2H 2S2
Tél: 514-844-2111; *Téléc:* 514-278-3030
lesexplorateurs@lesdebrouillards.com
www.lesexplos.com
Tirage: 20,000
Fréquence: 11 fois par an
Félix Maltais, Éditeur
Sarah Perreault, Rédactrice en chef

The Hospital Activity Book for Children
Owned By: Suggitt Publishing Ltd.
Bell Tower, #950, 10104 - 103 Ave., Edmonton, AB T5J 0H8
Fax: 877-463-6185
Toll-Free: 877-413-6163
reception@habfc.com
www.habfc.com
Activity books for children ages 4-12 who are undergoing medical treatment.
Stephen Kathnelson, President, stephen@habfc.com
Melanie Smith, General Manager, St. John's Office, melanie@habfc.com

J'Aime Lire
Détenteur: Bayard Presse Canada Inc.
4475, rue Frontenac, Montréal, QC H2H 2S2
Tél: 514-844-2111; *Téléc:* 514-278-3030
Ligne sans frais: 800-313-3020
redaction@bayardpresse.qc.ca
www.bayardjeunesse.ca
Tirage: 10,000
Fréquence: 10 fois par an
Suzanne Spino, Directrice générale

Kayak: Canada's History Magazine for Kids
Bryce Hall, Main Fl., 515 Portage Ave., Winnipeg, MB R3B 2E9
Tel: 204-988-9300; *Fax:* 204-988-9309
Toll-Free: 866-952-3444
www.canadashistory.ca/Kids/Kayak.aspx
Frequency: 4 times a year
Nancy Payne, Editor

Kids Tribute
Owned By: Tribute Publishing Inc.
71 Barber Greene Rd., Toronto, ON M3C 2A2
Tel: 416-445-0544; *Fax:* 416-445-2894
info@tribute.ca
kids.tribute.ca
Frequency: 4 times a year

The Magazine / Le Magazine Interdit aux Adultes
Previous Name: The Magazine not for Kids
643 Queen St. East, Toronto, ON M4M 1G4
Tel: 416-778-8727; *Fax:* 416-778-8726
Toll-Free: 866-622-0022
vocals@themagazine.ca
www.themagazine.ca
Social Media: www.youtube.com/magisodes
twitter.com/TheMagazineHQ
www.facebook.com/TheMagazineHQ
Circulation: 3,800,000
Frequency: Bi-monthly
Eric Conroy, Publisher

OWL Magazine
Owned By: Owlkids Books
#400, 10 Lower Spadina Ave., Toronto, ON M5V 2Z2
Tel: 416-340-2700; *Fax:* 416-340-9769
Toll-Free: 800-551-6957
owl@owlkids.com
www.owlkids.com
Frequency: 10 times a year
Kim Cooper, Editor

POP!
Owned By: Paton Publishing
3145 Wolfedale Rd., Mississauga, ON L5C 1A9
Tel: 905-273-8145; *Fax:* 905-273-4991
info@patonpublishing.com
www.patonpublishing.com
Circulation: 279,350
Frequency: Quarterly
Jill Foran, Editor, jforan@redpointmedia.ca
Pete Graves, Publisher, pgraves@redpointmedia.ca

City Magazine

Avenue
#105, 1900 - 11th St. SE, Calgary, AB T2G 3G2
Tel: 403-240-9055; *Fax:* 403-240-9059
info@redpointmedia.ca
www.avenuemagazine.ca
Social Media:
twitter.com/AvenueMagazine
www.facebook.com/avenuecalgary
Frequency: Monthly
Showcasing Calgary's architecture, personality, art, culture, fashion, food & outdoor life
Pete Graves, Publisher
Jennifer Hamilton, Executive Editor, jhamilton@redpointmedia.ca
Kathe Lemon, Editor

Bayview Post
30 Lesmill Rd., Toronto, ON M3B 2T6
Tel: 416-250-7979; *Fax:* 416-250-1737
editorial@postcity.com; advertising@postcity.com
www.postcity.com/Bayview-Post
Other information: Classified Advertising, E-mail: classifieds@postcity.com
Social Media:
twitter.com/PostCity
www.facebook.com/PostCityMagazines
Circulation: 25,000
Frequency: Monthly
The magazine features news, articles, & advertising of interest to persons of Toronto's Bayview neighbourhood.
Lorne London, Publisher, lornelondon@postcity.com
Laurie McGillivray, Associate Publisher, lauriemcgillivray@postcity.com
Andrew Mannsbach, Associate Publisher, Sales, andrewmannsbach@postcity.com
Ron Johnson, Editor, ronjohnson@postcity.com
Lisa London-Shiffman, Vice-President, Sales, LisaLondon@postcity.com
Dorothy Chudzinski, Managing Art Director, DorothyChudzinski@postcity.com
Lynne London, Director, Advertising, LynneLondon@postcity.com
Janice Fletcher, Controller, JaniceFletcher@postcity.com

Elk Point Review
Owned By: Great West Newspapers LP
PO Box 309, 5022 49 Ave., Elk Point, AB T0A 1A0
Tel: 780-724-4087; *Fax:* 780-645-2346
www.greatwest.ca
Circulation: 570
Frequency: Weekly
Janani Whitfield, Publisher, 780-645-3342, jwhitfield@stpaul.greatwest.ca

The False Creek News
661A Market Hill, Vancouver, BC V5Z 4B5
Tel: 604-876-6770
mail@thefalsecreeknews.com
www.thefalsecreeknews.com
Other information: News, E-mail: news@thefalsecreeknews.com
Circulation: 25,000
The False Creek News features reports & information about local issues, arts, & entertainment. The magazine is of interest to residents of Vancouver's False Creek, Fairview Slopes, & Granville Island neighbourhoods. Copies of the magazine are distributed to homes, businesses, & community centres.
M. Juma, Publisher
S. Bowell, Editor
N. Ebrahim, Manager, Advertising, adsales@thefalsecreeknews.com
G. Jiwa, Manager, Administration
A. Rattanshi, Accountant
A. Thobhani, Contact, Circulation

The Georgia Straight
1701 West Broadway St., Vancouver, BC V6J 1Y3
Tel: 604-730-7000; *Fax:* 604-730-7010
contact@straight.com
www.straight.com
Social Media: www.linkedin.com/companies/the-georgia-straight
twitter.com/georgiastrai ght
www.facebook.com/georgiastraight
Frequency: Weekly
Dan McLeod, Publisher/Editor
Matt McLeod, General Manager

Le Guide Prestige Montréal
#700, 2160, de la Montagne, Montréal, QC H3G 2T3
Tél: 514-982-9823; *Téléc:* 514-289-9160
info@prestipresse.com
Tirage: 150,000
Publication officielle de l'Association des hôtels du grand Montréal distribuée exclusivement dans les 76 hôtels membres, Le Guide Prestige Montréal répertorie à l'intention des visiteurs tout ce qu'il y a à voir et à faire à Montréal.
Steve Robins, Executive Vice President, steve@prestipresse.com
André Ducharme, Editor-in-chief

Hamilton Magazine
Previous Name: Hamilton This Month
Owned By: Town Media Inc.
Town Media, 940 Main St. West, Burlington, ON L8S 1B1
Tel: 905-522-6117; *Fax:* 905-769-1105
TM.info@sunmedia.ca
www.hamiltonmagazine.com
Social Media:
twitter.com/hamiltonmag
www.facebook.com/HamiltonMag
Frequency: 5 times a year
Donna Gardener, Publisher, donna.gardener@sunmedia.ca
Marc Skulnick, Editor, marc.skulnick@sunmedia.ca

HighGrader
PO Box 20055, Timmins, ON P4N 1A5
Tel: 705-266-4950
highgrader@nt.net
www.highgradermagazine.com
Circulation: 2,500
Brit Griffin, Publisher

Hour Community
260 Queen St., Montréal, QC H3C 2N8
Tel: 514-848-0777; *Fax:* 514-848-9004
Toll-Free: 877-631-8647
info@hour.ca
www.hour.ca
Social Media:
twitter.com/hourmontreal
www.facebook.com/HourMontreal
Frequency: Weekly

International Guide, Victoria
Previous Name: International Guide, Calgary
Owned By: IG Publications Ltd.
2392 Mt St Michael Rd., Saanichton, BC V8M 1T7
Tel: 250-727-1098; *Fax:* 250-652-8646
visitorschoice@shaw.ca
www.visitors-info.com
Social Media: www.youtube.com/user/VCIG11
twitter.com/visitorsinfo
www.facebook.com/ visitorsinfo
Circulation: 18,000
Wayne Kehoe, Publisher
Cherie Rautio, Editor

Island Times Magazine
PO Box 956, 1182 East Island Hwy, Parksville, BC V9P 2G9
Tel: 250-228-0995; *Fax:* 250-586-4405
publisher@islandtimesmagazine.ca
issuu.com/island-times-magazine
Social Media:
www.facebook.com/islandtimesmagazine.ca
Vancouver Island lifestyles magazine.
Jolene Aarbo, Publisher
Julie McManus, Editor

Kingston Life Magazine
Owned By: Sun Media Corporation
Kingston Publications, 18 St. Remy Pl., Kingston, ON K7K 6C4
Tel: 613-389-7400; *Fax:* 613-389-7507
www.kingstonlife.ca
Social Media:
twitter.com/kingston_life
www.facebook.com/KingstonLifemag
Circulation: 15,000
Frequency: 6 times a year
Kingston Life is delivered by controlled circulation through The Kingston Whig-Standard, sent to subscribers and sold at selected newsstands in Kingston, Ottawa, Toronto and Montreal.
Liza Nelson, Publisher, liza.nelson@sunmedia.ca
Danielle VandenBrink, Managing Editor, danielle.vandenbrink@sunmedia.ca

Kingston Relocation Guide
Owned By: Sun Media Corporation
Kingston Publications, 18 St. Remy Pl., Kingston, ON K7K 6C4
Tel: 613-389-7400; *Fax:* 613-389-7507
www.kingstonpublications.com/relocationguide.html
Circulation: 10,000
Frequency: Annually, February
Print copies available through the Greater Chamber of Commerce, real estate brokers, banks, the Downtown Kingston Business Improvement Association, the Visitor Information Centre, the Queen's University Faculty Recruitment Office, Immigration Services Kingston Area (ISKA) and the Kingston Economic Development Corporation. Also available in virtual format.

Lethbridge Living
1518 - 3rd Ave. South, Lethbridge, AB T1J 0K8
Tel: 403-381-1454; *Fax:* 403-330-3075
editor@lethbridgeliving.com
lethbridgeliving.com
Social Media:
twitter.com/Lethliving
www.facebook.com/lethbridge.living
Circulation: 17,000
Frequency: 6 times a year
Focus on the people and diversity of cultures in Lethbridge and Southern Alberta.
Martin Oordt, Editor
Mary Oordt, Managing Editor

Monday Magazine
Owned By: Black Press Group Ltd.
818 Broughton St., Victoria, BC V8W 1E4
Tel: 250-382-6183
editorial@mondaymag.com
www.mondaymag.com
Social Media:
twitter.com/mondaymag
www.facebook.com/MondayMagazine
Frequency: Weekly
The magazine of Victoria, British Columbia presents alternative news & entertainment information. Print & e-editions are available.
Penny Sakamoto, Publisher, publisher@mondaymag.com
Grant McKenzie, Editor, editor@mondaymag.com
Janet Gairdner, Manager, janet@mondaymag.com
Mary Ellen Green, Contact, Arts, arts@mondaymag.com
Danielle Pope, Contact, News, news@mondaymag.com

Niagara Escarpment Views
Owned By: 1826789 Ontario Inc.
50 Ann St., Georgetown, ON L7G 2V2
Tel: 905-877-9665
www.escarpmentviews.ca
Frequency: Quarterly
The magazine is dedicated to Ontario's Niagara Escarpment community.
Gloria Hildebrandt, Editor & Co-Publisher, 905-873-2834
Mike Davis, Co-Publisher & Accounts Manager, 905-877-9665

Niagara Life Magazine (a division of Downtowner Publications Inc.)
Previous Name: The Downtowner
#1, 3300 Merrittville Hwy., Thorold, ON L2V 4Y6
Tel: 905-641-1984; *Fax:* 905-641-0682
niagaralife@on.aibn.com
www.niagaralifemag.com
Circulation: 45,000
Frequency: 8 times a year
Katherine Nadeau, Editor-in-Chief
Gail Todd, Managing Editor

Northword Magazine
PO Box 817, 3864 2nd Ave., Smithers, BC V0J 2N0
Tel: 250-847-4600; *Fax:* 250-847-4668
Toll-Free: 866-632-7688
www.northword.ca
Frequency: 4 times a year

Now
189 Church St., Toronto, ON M5B 1Y7
Tel: 416-364-1300; *Fax:* 416-364-1166
web@nowtoronto.com
www.nowtoronto.com
Social Media: instagram.com/nowtoronto
twitter.com/nowtoronto
www.facebook.com/nowma gazine
Frequency: Weekly; Thursday
Alice Klein, Editor/CEO
Michael Hollett, Editor/Publisher

Off-Centre Magazine
Schwebs Bridge, #RR1, C58, Falkland, BC V0E 1W0
Tel: 250-379-2124; *Fax:* 250-379-2124
off-centre@off-centre.ca
www.bcnetwork.com/urgentcow/hosted/offcentre
Circulation: 17,000
Frequency: Monthly
Leanne Allen, Publisher

Official Visitor Guide to Kingston
Owned By: Sun Media Corporation
Kingston Publications, 18 St. Remy Pl., Kingston, ON K7K 6C4
Tel: 613-389-7400; *Fax:* 613-389-7507
www.kingstonpublications.com/visitorguide.html
Circulation: 150,000
Frequency: Annually
Available at visitor centres throughout Ontario and the Northern USA; Ontario Travel Information Centres; CAA and AAA offices, Canadian Consulate offices in the USA, Europe and Japan; Sports, travel, leisure and conference shows; airports, bus and train stations; The Kingston Visitor Information Centre; through mail, telephone and Internet inquiries.

Okanagan Life
Owned By: Byrne Publishing Group Inc.
814 Lawrence Ave., Kelowna, BC V1Y 6L9
Tel: 250-861-5399; *Fax:* 250-868-3040
info@okanaganlife.com
www.okanaganlife.com
Other information: Subscriptions, E-mail: subscribe@okanaganlife.com
Social Media: plus.google.com/101929944109754892564
twitter.com/OkanaganLifeMag
w ww.facebook.com/150907958296380
Circulation: 16,000
Contents include information about personalities, food, travel, & recreation in British Columbia's Okanagan region.
Paul Byrne, Publisher & Editor, paul@okanaganlife.com
Laurie Carter, Senior Editor
Mishell Raedeke, Creative Director
Wendy Letwinetz, Contact, Administration

Ottawa City Magazine
St. Joseph Media Inc., 43 Eccles St., Ottawa, ON K1R 6S3
Tel: 613-230-0333
feedback@stjosephmedia.com
www.ottawamagazine.com
Social Media:
twitter.com/ottawamag
www.facebook.com/OttawaMag
Circulation: 35,500
Frequency: 7 times a year
Sarah Brown, Editor, sbrown@stjosephmedia.com
Harvey Chartrand, Editor

Ottawa Life Magazine
301 Metcalfe, Lower Level, Ottawa, ON K2P 1S3
Tel: 613-688-5433; *Fax:* 613-688-1994
info@ottawalife.com
www.ottawalife.com
Social Media:
twitter.com/ottawalifers
www.facebook.com/pages/Ottawa-Life-Magazine/112 3843988222
Harvey Chartrand, Editor

The Ottawa XPress
Owned By: Communications Voir Inc.
704 Somerset St. West, Ottawa, ON K1R 6P6
Tel: 613-237-8226; *Fax:* 613-237-8220
Toll-Free: 866-255-5516
info@ottawaexpress.ca
www.ottawaxpress.ca
Social Media:
twitter.com/ottawaxpress
www.facebook.com/ottawaxpress
Circulation: 63,500
Frequency: Weekly, Thu.
Guillaume Moffet, Managing Editor

Pique Newsmagazine
Owned By: Pique Publishing Inc.
#103, 1390 Alpha Lake Rd., Whistler, BC V0N 1B1
Tel: 604-938-0202
www.piquenewsmagazine.com
Social Media:
twitter.com/piquenews
www.facebook.com/PiqueNewsmagazine
Circulation: 16,500
Frequency: Weekly, Fri.
Sarah Strother, Publisher, sarah@piquenewsmagazine.com
Clare Ogilvie, Editor, edit@piquenewsmagazine.com

Planet S
Owned By: Hullabaloo Publishing Ltd.
#409, 135-21st St. East, Saskatoon, SK S7K 0B4
Tel: 306-651-3423; *Fax:* 306-651-3428
reception@planetsmag.com
www.planetsmag.com
Social Media:
twitter.com/PlanetSMagazine
www.facebook.com/pages/Planet-S-Magazi ne/40716663512
Circulation: 60,000
Stephen Whitworth, Editor, editor@planetsmag.com

the prairie dog
#201, 1836 Scarth St., Regina, SK S4P 2G3
Tel: 306-757-8522; *Fax:* 306-352-9686
reception@prairiedogmag.com
www.prairiedogmag.com
Circulation: 16,000
Frequency: Bi-weekly
April Bourgeois, Publisher
Stephen Whitworth, Editor

Profile Kingston
PO Box 91, Kingston, ON K7L 4V6
Tel: 613-546-6723; *Fax:* 613-546-0707
editor@profilekingston.com
www.profilekingston.com
Circulation: 16,000
Frequency: 6 times a year
Bonnie Golomb, Publisher

Spacing
Owned By: Spacing Media
#B-02, 401 Richmond St. West, Toronto, ON M5V 3A8
Tel: 416-644-1017
info@spacing.ca
spacing.ca
Social Media: www.flickr.com/groups/spacingmagpool
twitter.com/spacing
Matthew Blackett, Publisher/Creative Director, matt@spacing.ca
Todd Harrison, Managing Editor, toddharrison@spacing.ca

Thornhill Post
30 Lesmill Rd., Toronto, ON M3B 2T6
Tel: 416-250-7979; *Fax:* 416-250-1737
editorial@postcity.com; advertising@postcity.com
www.postcity.com/Thornhill-Post
Other information: Classified Advertising, E-mail: classifieds@postcity.com
Social Media:
twitter.com/PostCity
www.facebook.com/PostCityMagazines
Circulation: 25,000
Frequency: Monthly
The magazine serves Thornhill, Ontario by featuring news & information about local people, places, events, restaurants, & shopping.
Lorne London, Publisher, lornelondon@postcity.com
Laurie McGillivray, Associate Publisher, lauriemcgillivray@postcity.com
Andrew Mannsbach, Associate Publisher, Sales, andrewmannsbach@postcity.com
Ron Johnson, Editor, ronjohnson@postcity.com
Lisa London-Shiffman, Vice-President, LisaLondon@postcity.com
Dorothy Chudzinski, Managing Art Director, DorothyChudzinski@postcity.com
Lynne London, Director, Advertising, LynneLondon@postcity.com
Janice Fletcher, Controller, JaniceFletcher@postcity.com

Thunder Bay Guest Magazine
Owned By: Dougall Media
87 North Hill St., Thunder Bay, ON P7A 5V6
Tel: 804-346-2600; *Fax:* 807-345-9923
Frequency: 9 times a year

Toronto Life
Urban Group, St. Joseph Media Corp, #320, 111 Queen St. East, Toronto, ON M5C 1S2
Tel: 416-364-3333; *Fax:* 416-861-1169
editorial@torontolife.com
www.torontolife.com
Social Media: pinterest.com/torontolifemag
twitter.com/toronto_life
www.facebook. com/torontolife
Frequency: Monthly
Sarah Fulford, Editor

Vancouver Magazine
Owned By: TC Transcontinental
Transcontinental Publishing, #560, 2608 Granville St., Vancouver, BC V6H 3V3
Tel: 604-877-7732; *Fax:* 604-877-4848
mail@vancouvermagazine.com
www.vanmag.com
Social Media: instagram.com/vanmag_com
twitter.com/vanmag_com
www.facebook.com/vanco uvermagazine
Frequency: 10 times a year
Lori Chalmers, Publisher
John Burns, Editor-in-chief

Victoria Boulevard
Owned By: Boulevard Lifestyles Inc.
Boulevard Lifestyles Inc., 1845B Fort St., Victoria, BC V8R 1J6
Tel: 250-598-8111; *Fax:* 250-598-3183
Info@VictoriaBoulevard.com
www.victoriaboulevard.com
Social Media:
twitter.com/boulevardmag
www.facebook.com/BoulevardMagazine
Circulation: 45,000
Frequency: Bi-monthly
Evelyn Butler, Publisher

Village Post
30 Lesmill Rd., Toronto, ON M3B 2T6
Tel: 416-250-7979; *Fax:* 416-250-1737
editorial@postcity.com; advertising@postcity.com
www.postcity.com/Village-Post
Other information: Classified Advertising, E-mail: classifieds@postcity.com
Social Media:
twitter.com/PostCity
www.facebook.com/PostCityMagazines
Circulation: 25,000
Frequency: Monthly
The Forest Hill & Yorkville neighbourhoods of Toronto are served by The Village Post, which features reports on local news, people, & lifestyles.
Lorne London, Publisher, lornelondon@postcity.com
Laurie McGillivray, Associate Publisher, lauriemcgillivray@postcity.com
Andrew Mannsbach, Associate Publisher, Sales, andrewmannsbach@postcity.com
Ron Johnson, Editor, ronjohnson@postcity.com
Lisa London-Shiffman, Vice-President, LisaLondon@postcity.com
Dorothy Chudzinski, Managing Art Director, DorothyChudzinski@postcity.com
Lynne London, Director, Advertising, LynneLondon@postcity.com
Janice Fletcher, Controller, JaniceFletcher@postcity.com

Visitors' Choice, BC
102 East 4th Ave., Vancouver, BC V5T 1G2
Tel: 604-608-5180; *Fax:* 604-608-5181
Toll-Free: 800-867-5141
info@visitorschoice.com
www.visitorschoice.com
Social Media:
twitter.com/VisitorsChoice
facebook.com/VisitorsChoice
Circulation: 475,000
Frequency: 3 times a year
Publishes vistor's guides for 12 communities in BC.
Paul Harris, Publisher
Noa Glouberman, Editor

Voilà Québec
#201, 735, boul Wilfrid-Hamel, Québec, QC G1M 2R1
Tél: 418-694-1272; *Téléc:* 418-694-1119
info@voilaquebec.com
voilaquebec.com
Fréquence: 4 fois par an
Louis-Georges Jalbert, Président/éditeur,
louis@voilaquebec.com
Manon Gauvreau, Directrice de l'administration,
comptabilite@voilaquebec.com

Voir Gatineau-Ottawa
#200, 396, rue Cooper, Ottawa, ON K2P 2H7
Tél: 613-237-8226; *Téléc:* 613-237-8220
info@gatineau.voir.ca
www.voir.ca
Fréquence: Hebdomadaire
Céline Lebrun, Directeur général
Guillaume Moffet, Rédactrice-en-chef

Voir Montréal
375, rue Ste-Catherine ouest, 7e étage, Montréal, QC H3B 1A5
Tél: 514-848-0805; *Téléc:* 514-848-9004
Ligne sans frais: 877-631-8647
info@mtl.voir.ca
www.voir.ca
Médias sociaux: me.voir.ca
twitter.com/voir
www.facebook.com/journalvoir
Tirage: 102 000
Simon Jodoin, Rédacteur-en-chef

Voir Québec
#100, 763, rue Saint-Joseph Est, Québec, QC G1K 3C6
Tél: 418-522-7777; *Téléc:* 418-522-7779
Ligne sans frais: 877-632-8647
info@qc.voir.ca
www.voir.ca
Médias sociaux: plus.google.com/116972481648922638029
twitter.com/voir
www.facebook .com/journalvoir
Fréquence: Hebdomadaire
Michel Fortin, Directeur général
Simon Jodoin, Rédacteur-en-chef

Where Calgary
Owned By: St Joseph Media
#206, 1201 - 5 St. SW, Calgary, AB T2R 0Y6
Tel: 403-299-1888; *Fax:* 403-299-1899
Toll-Free: 855-216-6387
editor_calgary@where.ca
www.where.ca/the-west/alberta/ calgary
Social Media:
twitter.com/wherecalgary
www.facebook.com/wherecalgarymag
Frequency: Bi-monthly
Brian French, Publisher

Where Edmonton
Owned By: St Joseph Media
#1, 930 - 50 St., Edmonton, AB T6B 2L5
Tel: 780-465-3362
editor@whereedmonton.com
www.where.ca/the-west/alberta/edmonton
Circulation: 33,240
Frequency: 6 times a year
Rob Tanner, Publisher

Where Halifax
Owned By: St Joseph Media
1300 Hollis St., Halifax, NS B3J 1T6
Tel: 902-420-9943; *Fax:* 902-429-9058
publishers@metroguide.ca
www.where.ca/atlantic-canada/nova-scotia/halifa x
Social Media:
twitter.com/Where_Halifax
Circulation: 25,000
Frequency: 10 times a year
Patty Baxter, Publisher

Where Ottawa
Previous Name: Where Ottawa-Hull
Owned By: St Joseph Media
43 Eccles St., 1st Fl., Ottawa, ON K1R 6S3
Tel: 613-230-0333; *Fax:* 613-230-4441
whereottawa@stjosephmedia.com
www.where.ca/ottawa
Social Media:
twitter.com/whereottawa
Frequency: Bi-Monthly
Amy Allen, Editor
Dianne Wing, Publisher

Where Toronto/Muskoka/Parry Sound
Owned By: St Joseph Media
#320, 111 Queen St. East, Toronto, ON M5C 1S2
Tel: 416-364-3333; *Fax:* 416-861-1169
Toll-Free: 800-387-1156
www.where.ca/central-canada/ontario/toronto
Frequency: Monthly
Linda Luong, Editor-in-chief, lluong@where.ca

Where Victoria
Previous Name: Victoria Today
Owned By: St Joseph Media
818 Broughton St., Victoria, BC V8W 1E4
Tel: 250-383-3633; *Fax:* 250-480-3233
editor@wherevictoria.com
www.where.ca/west-coast/british-columbia/victor ia
Frequency: 6 times a year
Jennifer Blyth, Editor

Where Winnipeg
Owned By: St Joseph Media
#400, 112 Market Ave., Winnipeg, MB R3B 0P4
Tel: 204-943-4439; *Fax:* 204-947-5463
www.where.ca/the-prairies/manitoba/winnipeg
Frequency: 6 times a year
Laurie Hughes, Publisher

Whistler, the Magazine
Owned By: Glacier Newspapers Group
#353, 4370 Lorimer Rd., Whistler, BC V0N 1B4
Tel: 604-932-5131
www.whistlerthemagazine.com
Circulation: 40,000
Frequency: Biannually
Leisure magazine targeted toward tourists in the Whistler resort area.
Catherine Power-Chartrand, General Manager,
cpower@whistlerthemagazine.com
Stephanie Matches, Publisher,
smatches@whistlerthemagazine.com

Windsor Life Magazine
#318, 5060 Tecumseh Rd. East, Windsor, ON N8T 1C1
Tel: 519-979-5433; *Fax:* 519-979-9237
www.windsorlife.com
Circulation: 79,373 Windsor & Essex County
Frequency: 8 times a year
Robert E. Robinson, Publisher
Hal Sullivan, Editor

The Yards
Edmonton, AB
Tel: 306-554-2224; *Fax:* 306-554-3226
www.theyardsyeg.ca
Social Media:
twitter.com/theyardsyeg
www.facebook.com/theyardsyeg
Frequency: Quarterly
Collections of urban planning, development, lifestyle and cultural stories of Edmonton's transformation and growth.
Jarrett Campbell, Publisher, jarrett@theyardsyeg.ca
Omar Mouallem, Editor, editor@theyardsyeg.ca

Computing & Technology

Atout Micro
CP 240, Saint-Isidore, QC G0S 2S0
Tél: 418-882-5214 *Ligne sans frais:* 866-826-1089
atout@atoutmicro.ca
www.atoutmicro.ca
Autre information: Sans frais: 1-866-826-1089
Médias sociaux:
twitter.com/AtoutMicro
Tirage: 8000
François Picard, Éditeur & Rédacteur en chef

We Compute
1232 Kingston Rd., Scarborough, ON M1N 1P3
Tel: 416-481-1955; *Fax:* 416-481-2819
Circulation: 150,000
Frequency: 12 times a year
Eric Macmillan, Editor
George Bachir, Publisher

Conventions & Meetings

Conference Kingston Handbook
Owned By: Sun Media Corporation
Kingston Publications, 18 St. Remy Pl., Kingston, ON K7K 6C4
Tel: 613-389-7400; *Fax:* 613-389-7507
www.kingstonpublications.com/conferencekingston.html
Circulation: 3,500
Frequency: Annually, March
Print copies are distributed at trade shows and conferences by Tourism Kingston.

Cosmetics

Glow
Owned By: St Joseph Media
#320, 111 Queen St. East, Toronto, ON M5C 1S2
Tel: 416-364-3333; *Fax:* 416-594-3374
shoppersoptimum@shoppersdrugmart.ca
glow.shoppersdrugmart.ca
Social Media: pinterest.com/glowmag
twitter.com/glowcanada
www.facebook.com/GlowMag
Frequency: 6 times a year
Juliette Baxter, Editor-in-Chief

The Kit
Owned By: Toronto Star Newspapers Limited
#204, 1 Yonge St., Toronto, ON M5E 1E6
Tel: 416-945-8700
info@thekit.ca
www.thekit.ca
Social Media: pinterest.com/thekit/pins/
twitter.com/thekit
www.facebook.com/TheKITm ag
Frequency: Monthly
Giorgina Bigioni, Publisher

Culture, Current Events

Adbusters
1234 - West 7th Ave., Vancouver, BC V6H 1B7
Tel: 604-736-9401; *Fax:* 604-737-6021
Toll-Free: 800-663-1243
info@adbusters.org
www.adbusters.org
Circulation: 60,000
Frequency: 6 times a year
Non-profit & reader-supported magazine expressing concerns over erosion of physical & cultural environments because of comercial forces

Anthropologica
3333 University Way, Prince George, BC N2L 3C5
Tel: 250-960-5643; *Fax:* 250-960-5545
www.anthropologica.ca
Circulation: 625
Frequency: Semi-annual
Journal of Canadian Anthropology Society
Naomi M. McPherson, Editor-in-Chief Ph.D.,
Naomi.mcpherson@ubc.ca
Sylvie Poirier, French Manuscripts Editor, French Manuscripts,
418-656-2831

Broken Pencil
PO Box 203 P, Toronto, ON M5S 2S7
Tel: 416-204-1700
editor@brokenpencil.com
www.brokenpencil.com
Circulation: 3,000
Frequency: 4 times a year
Devoted exclusively to underground culture and the independent arts.
Lindsay Gibb, Editor, editor@brokenpencil.com

HELLO!
Owned By: Rogers Media Inc.
1 Mount Pleasant Rd., 8th Fl., Toronto, ON M4Y 2Y5
Tel: 416-764-2863; *Fax:* 416-764-2866
contact@hellomagazine.ca
www.hellomagazine.ca
Social Media:
twitter.com/HELLOCanada
www.facebook.com/138543579563513
Circulation: 137,025
Frequency: 46 issues per year
Alison Eastwood, Editor-in-Chief

Maisonneuve
PO Box 53527, 1051 boul Decarie, St Laurent, QC H4L 5J9
Tel: 514-482-5089
business@maisonneuve.org
maisonneuve.org
Social Media:
twitter.com/maisonneuvemag
www.facebook.com/maisonneuvemagazine
Frequency: Quarterly
Jennifer Varkonyi, Publisher
Daniel Viola, Editor-in-Chief

The Newfoundland Herald
Owned By: Skylab Media Group
PO Box 2015, Logy Bay Rd., St. John's, NL A1C 5R7
Tel: 709-726-7060; *Fax:* 709-726-6971
letters@nfldherald.com
nfldherald.com
Circulation: 17,000
Frequency: Weekly
Mark Dwyer, Managing Editor, 709-570-5212, mdwyer@nfldherald.com

Saltscapes Publishing Inc.
c/o Saltscapes, #209, 30 Damascus Rd., Bedford, NS B4A 0C1
Tel: 902-464-7258; *Fax:* 902-464-3755
www.saltscapes.com
Circulation: 40,000
Frequency: 6 times a year
Jim Gourlay, Publisher
Heather White, Editor

WEST
Owned By: Premier Publications and Shows
c/o Premier Publications and Shows, #4, 447 Speers Rd., Oakville, ON L6K 3S7
Tel: 905-842-6591 *Toll-Free:* 800-693-7986
premierpublicationsandshows.com
Upsclae magazine targeting high-income neighbourhoods in Burlington, Oakville and Mississauga.

What's Up Muskoka
Previous Name: North Country Business
Owned By: Sun Media Corp.
PO Box 180, #12, 440 Ecclestone Dr., Bracebridge, ON P1L 1T6
Tel: 705-646-1314; *Fax:* 705-645-6424
mm.info@sunmedia.ca
www.northcountrybusinessnews.com
Frequency: Weekly
What's Up Muskoka covers local news, sports, people, coming events & special sections (including content formerly published as North Country Business).
Curtis Armstrong, Publisher
Sandy Lockhart, Editor

Directories & Almanacs

Black Pages Directory
1390 Eglinton Ave. West, Toronto, ON M6C 2E4
Tel: 416-784-3002; *Fax:* 416-784-5719
info@blackpages.ca
www.blackpages.ca
Frequency: Annually
Black Pages Directory Canada is a comprehensive guide to Canada's Black and Caribbean community.

Drugs

Drugs & Addiction Magazine
Owned By: Suggitt Publishing Ltd.
Bell Tower, #950, 10104 - 103 Ave., Edmonton, AB T5J 0H8
Toll-Free: 866-421-5999
reception@dafacts.com
www.dafacts.com
A teaching tool given free to young people in order to educate them about the dangers of drug abuse.
Stephen Kathnelson, President, stephen@dafacts.com
Melanie Smith, General Manager, melanie@dafacts.com

Elana Sures, Author

Education

Family Getaways
Owned By: Our Kids Media
4242 Rockwood Rd., Mississauga, ON L4W 1L8
Tel: 905-272-1843; *Fax:* 905-272-0474
Toll-Free: 877-272-1845
info@ourkids.net
www.ourkids.net
Social Media: www.youtube.com/ourkidsnet
twitter.com/ourkidsnet
www.facebook.com/ourkidsnet
Circulation: 100,000
Frequency: Annual
Agatha Stawicki, Publisher
Agnes Stawicki, Managing Editor

Life Learning Magazine
Life Media, #52, B2-125 Queensway, Toronto, ON MBY 1H6
publisher@lifelearningmagazine.com
www.lifelearningmagazine.com
Social Media:
twitter.com/LifeLearningMag
www.facebook.com/LifeLearningMagazine
Circulation: 10,000
Frequency: Bi-monthly; digital
Rolf Priesnitz, Publisher

Entertainment

The Buzz
160 Richmond St., Charlottetown, PE C1A 1H9
Tel: 902-628-1958
buzzon@eastlink.ca
www.buzzon.com
Social Media: www.youtube.com/BUZZpei
twitter.com/buzzpei
www.facebook.com/thebuzzpe i
Circulation: Sept.-June - 15,000; July-Aug. - 26,000
Frequency: Monthly
Peter Richards, Managing Editor, 902-628-1958

CineAction: Radical Film Criticism & Theory
40 Alexander St., Toronto, ON M4Y 1B5
Tel: 416-964-3534
cineaction@cineaction.ca
cineaction.ca
Frequency: 3 times a year

Cinema Scope
465 Lytton Blvd., Toronto, ON M5N 1S5
Tel: 416-889-5430
info@cinema-scope.com
www.cinema-scope.com
Social Media:
twitter.com/CinemaScopeMag
www.facebook.com/pages/Cinema-Scope-Magazine/205268252835
Frequency: 4 times a year
Mark Peranson, Publisher & Editor
Andrew Tracy, Managing Editor

Cineplex Magazine
Owned By: Cineplex Media
102 Atlantic Ave., Toronto, ON M6K 1X9
Tel: 416-539-8800; *Fax:* 416-539-8511
theresa.mcvean@cineplex.com
media.cineplex.com/TheMagazines.aspx
Circulation: 700,000
Frequency: Monthly
Marni Weisz, Editor, 416-539-8800ext.5225
Mathieu Chantelois, French Editor, 416-539-8800ext.5230

En Primeur
71 Barber Greene Rd., Toronto, ON M3C 2A2
Tél: 416-445-0544; *Téléc:* 416-445-2894
www.enprimeur.ca
Tirage: 105,000
Sandra I. Stewart, Publisher

En Primeur Jeunesse
Détenteur: Tribute Publishing Inc.
c/o Tribute Entertainment Media Group, 71 Barber Greene Rd., Toronto, ON M3C 2A2
Tél: 416-445-0544; *Téléc:* 416-445-2894
webmaster@enprimeur.ca
www.enprimeur.ca
Fréquence: 4 fois par an

Magazine Le Clap
2360, ch Ste-Foy, Sainte-Foy, QC G1V 4H2
Tél: 418-653-2470; *Téléc:* 418-653-6018
info@clap.ca
www.clap.qc.ca
Médias sociaux:
twitter.com/cinema_leclap
www.facebook.com/cinemaleclap
Fréquence: 6 fois par an
Michel Aubé, Éditeur
Robin Plamondon, Éditeur

Playboard
Archway Publishers, #205 - 4871 Shell Rd., Richmond, BC V6X 3Z6
Tel: 778-294-5881; *Fax:* 778-294-5882
info@playboardmag.com
www.playboardmag.com
Circulation: 15,000
Frequency: 10 times a year
Playboard is prominently displayed and distributed free in all of the Vancouver Civic theatres, the Arts Club Theatres, the Richmond Gateway
Alan Slater, Publisher & Editor

Scene Magazine (SCENE)
PO Box 27048, 35 Hammond Cres., London, ON N5X 3X5
Tel: 519-642-4780; *Fax:* 519-642-0737
news@scenemagazine.com
www.scenemagazine.com
Circulation: 77,000
Frequency: 25 times a year
Bret Downe, Publisher & Editor-in-chief, 519-642-4780, bret@scenemagazine.com
Alma Bernardo Downe, Coordinator, alma@scenemagazine.com

Star Système
Détenteur: TVA Publications inc.
1010, rue de Sérigny, 4e étage, Longueuil, QC J4K 5G7
Tél: 514-370-5823; *Téléc:* 514-270-7079
Ligne sans frais: 888-535-8634
www.tvapublications.com
Médias sociaux:
www.facebook.com/StarSysteme
Fréquence: 51 fois par an

Teen Tribute
Owned By: Tribute Publishing Inc.
71 Barber Greene Rd., Toronto, ON M3C 2A2
Tel: 416-445-0544; *Fax:* 416-445-2894
advertising@tribute.ca
www.tribute.ca
Social Media:
twitter.com/tributemag
Circulation: 300,000
Frequency: 4 times a year
Robin Stevenson, Editor
Sandra Stewart, Publisher

Tribute Magazine
Owned By: Tribute Publishing Inc.
71 Barber Greene Rd., Toronto, ON M3C 2A2
Tel: 416-445-0544; *Fax:* 416-445-2894
info@tribute.ca
www.tribute.ca
Social Media:
twitter.com/tributemag
Frequency: 4 times a year
Sandra Stewart, Editor-in-Chief

View Weekly
Previous Name: View Magazine
370 Main St. West, Hamilton, ON L8P 1K3
Tel: 905-527-3343; *Fax:* 905-527-3721
info@viewmag.com
www.viewmag.com
Circulation: 30,000
Frequency: Weekly
Rob Kilpatrick, Editor-in-chief
Sean Rosen, Publisher, seanr@viewmag.com

Visitor Magazine
PO Box 41030, Waterloo, ON N0K 3K0
Tel: 519-886-2831; *Fax:* 519-886-6409
advertise@exchangemagazine.com
www.visitor.on.ca
Circulation: 100,000
John Rohr, Publisher, jon.rohr@exchangemagazine.com

Vue Weekly
Owned By: Postvue Publishing Inc
#200, 11230 - 119th St. NW, Edmonton, AB T5G 2X3
Tel: 780-426-1996; *Fax:* 780-426-2889
www.vueweekly.com
Social Media: www.youtube.com/vueonline
twitter.com/vueweekly
www.facebook.com/vueweekly
Circulation: 24,274
Frequency: Weekly
Eden Munro, Managing Editor/Associate Publisher, eden@vueweekly.com
Ron Garth, Publisher & Editor, ron@vueweekly.com

Environment & Nature

Alternatives Journal: Canadian Environmental Voice
Previous Name: Alternatives Journal: Environmental Thought, Policy & Action
Also Known As: A\J
c/o Alternatives Journal, 200 University Ave. West, Waterloo, ON N2L 3G1
Tel: 519-888-4442; *Fax:* 519-746-0292
Toll-Free: 866-437-2587
info@alternativesjournal.ca
www.alternativesjournal.ca
Social Media: www.youtube.com/user/alternativesjournal
twitter.com/AlternativesJ
www.facebook.com/AlternativesJ
Circulation: 4,500
Frequency: 6 times a year
A theme-based publication dedicated to illustrating the relationships between the environment and social justice, politics and the economy. It looks at the challenges and issues related to the interaction of humanity and the environment, and the responses to those issues.
Eric Rumble, Editorial Manager, Editorial, 519-888-4505, editor@alternativesjournal.ca

The Atlantic Salmon Journal
Atlantic Salmon Federation, PO Box 5200, St Andrews, NB E5B 3S8
Tel: 506-529-4581; *Fax:* 506-529-1070
Toll-Free: 800-565-5666
www.asf.ca/atlantic-salmon-journal.html
Circulation: 11,000
Frequency: 4 times a year
This magazine is the world's oldest publication regarding conservation-minded salmon angling and protection of the species.
Martin Silverstone, Editor, martinsilverstone@videotron.ca

British Columbia Environmental Network
Owned By: Canadian Environmental Network (CEN)
#122, 718-333 Brooksbank Ave., North Vancouver, BC V7J 3V6
Tel: 604-515-1969
www.ecobc.org
The British Columbia Environmental Report is a journal which features news, analysis, events, & reviews about British Columbia environmental topics.
Dave Stevens, Chair, Board of Directors
Chris Blake, Executive Coordinator

Canadian Geographic
PO Box 923 Main, Ottawa, ON L3P 0B8
Tel: 613-745-4629 *Toll-Free:* 800-267-0824
www.canadiangeographic.ca
Social Media: www.youtube.com/user/CanadianGeographic
twitter.com/CanGeoMag
www.face book.com/canadiangeographic
Circulation: 222,000
Frequency: 6 times a year
Publication aims to promote Canada both to Canadians and around the world. It looks at issues relating to the nature and wildlife within Canada, and what can be done to preserve the natural Canadian landscape.
John Thomson, CEO & Publisher
Rick Boychuk, Editor

Canadian Wildlife
Owned By: Canadian Wildlife Federation
350 Michael Cowpland Dr., Kanata, ON K2M 2W1
Tel: 613-599-9594; *Fax:* 613-599-4428
Toll-Free: 800-563-9453
info@cwf-fcf.org
www.cwf-fcf.org
Frequency: bi-monthly
Aimed at both teenagers and adults, this magazine covers issues relating to Canadian and international wildlife, and reports on the work of the Canadian Wildlife Federation.

Environmental Science & Engineering Magazine
#30, 220 Industrial Parkway South, Aurora, ON L4G 3V6
Tel: 905-727-4666; *Fax:* 905-841-7271
www.esemag.com
Circulation: 19,000
Frequency: bi-monthly
This publicationis the largest documentary magazine in Canada and has articles on various environmental issues, including air pollution, water filtration, hazerdous waste, alternative energy, greenhouse gasses, among others; available only to subscribers.
Steve Davey, President, steve@esemag.com

Green Living Magazine
Key Publishers Company Ltd., 66 The Esplanade, Toronto, ON M5E 1A6
Tel: 416-360-0044; *Fax:* 416-642-1711
Toll-Free: 866-934-0044
info@green-living.ca
www.greenlivingmagazine.ca
Social Media:
twitter.com/GreenLivingPage
www.facebook.com/GreenLivingPage
Circulation: 150,000
Frequency: quarterly
Green Living Magazine attempts to promote living a green lifestyle to its readers by providing information about organics, health, the environment and eco-consumer products. They support sustainable and healthy living and publicizing the green message.
Laurie Simmonds, Publisher

Journal of Environmental Engineering & Science
Owned By: National Research Council of Canada
NRC Research Press, 1200 Montreal Rd., Bldg. M-55, Ottawa, ON K1A 0R6
Tel: 613-990-7873; *Fax:* 613-952-7656
Toll-Free: 800-668-1222
pubs@nrcresearchpress.com
www.nrcresearchpress.com/loi/jees
Frequency: bi-monthly
This publication provides a forum for the discussion of environmental engineering & science research. Topics this journal explores include environmental engineering, physical & analytical sciences, life sciences related to environmental issues, health sciences, & oceanography.

La Maison du 21e siècle
2955, rue du Domaine-du-lac-Lucerne, Sainte-Adèle, QC J8B 3K9
Tél: 450-228-1555
info@maisonsaine.ca
maisonsaine.ca
Médias sociaux: www.linkedin.com/pub/andré-fauteux/b/128/912
twitter.com/Maison21e
www .facebook.com/maisonsaine
Fréquence: 4 fois par an
André Fauteux, Éditeur

Natural Life
Previous Name: Earthkeeper Magazine
Life Media, #52, B2-125 The Queensway, Toronto, ON M8Y 1H6
info@LifeMedia.ca
www.life.ca/naturallife
Circulation: 35,000
Frequency: 6 times a year
This independently owned magazine has an international focus on providing intelligent and in-depth practical information on issues such as healthy cooking, organic gardening, sustainable homes, natural parenting, wellness and natural healing, eco-leisure and eco-travel and sustainable business.
Wendy Priesnitz, Editor
Rolf Priesnitz, Publisher

Nature Canada
c/o Nature Canada, #300, 75 Albert St., Ottawa, ON K1P 5E7
Tel: 613-562-3447; *Fax:* 613-562-3371
Toll-Free: 800-267-4088
info@naturecanada.ca
naturecanada.ca
Social Media: www.youtube.com/user/NatureCanada1
www.facebook.com/NatureCanada
Circulation: 26,400
Frequency: 4 times a year
The mission of this magazine is to protect nature, its diversity and the processes that sustain it, and does this by providing information regarding several environmental topics including bird conservation, wilderness protection, endangered species and national parks. The publication supports community-based efforts to protect wildlife; encourages the development of an effective network of parks and protected areas across Canada; and promoting biodiversity in Canada and abroad.

Ontario Nature
Previous Name: Seasons
#612, 214 King St. West, Toronto, ON M5H 3S6
Tel: 416-444-8419; *Fax:* 416-444-9866
Toll-Free: 800-440-2366
info@ontarionature.org
www.ontarionature.org
Social Media: www.youtube.com/user/ONNature
twitter.com/ontarionature
www.facebook.com/OntarioNature?ref=ts
Circulation: 14,500
Frequency: 4 times a year
ON Nature attempts to bring its readers closer to nature by providing information about Ontario's natural areas and wildlife, and by providing insight into current environmental issues. Magazine features articles by nature specialists, colour photography, information regarding wilderness travel and up-to-date news on conservation battles.
Caroline Schultz, Executive Director
Victoria Foote, Editor

Québec Oiseaux
CP 1000 M, 4545, av Pierre-De Coubertin, Montréal, QC H1V 3R2
Tél: 514-252-3190
www.quebecoiseaux.org
Médias sociaux: www.youtube.com/user/QOiseaux
www.twitter.com/quebecoiseaux
www.facebook.com/quebecoiseaux
Tirage: 7 928
Fréquence: 4 fois par an
Michel Préville, Rédacteur-en-chef

Watershed Sentinel
c/o Watershed Sentinel Educational Society, PO Box 1270, Comox, BC V9M 7Z8
Tel: 250-339-6117
editor@watershedsentinel.ca
www.watershedsentinel.ca
Social Media:
twitter.com/@WatershSentinel
www.facebook.com/pages/Watershed-Sentinel/1 06472301541
Circulation: 3,500
Frequency: 6 times a year
This West Coast publication covers both bioregional and global perspectives on topics such as the environment, health and sustainability.
Delores Broten, Publisher & Editor

Women & Environments International Magazine
Previous Name: Women & Environments; WE International
c/o Faculty of Environmental Studies, #234, HNES Building, York University, 4700 Keele St., Toronto, ON M3J 1P3
Tel: 416-736-2100; *Fax:* 416-736-5679
weimag@yorku.ca
www.yorku.ca/weimag
Circulation: 2,000
Frequency: 2 times a year
Publication examines the relationships between women and the environment from a feminist perspective. It provides a forum for academic research and theory, professional practice and community experience and covers topics such as ecology and environmental activism, community development, childcare, and urban and rural agriculture.
Prabha Khosla
Reggie Modlich

Families

BC Parent Magazine
PO Box 72086, Sasamat RPO, Vancouver, BC V6R 4P2
Tel: 604-221-0366
info@bcparent.ca
www.bcparent.ca
Social Media:
twitter.com/bcparentmag
www.facebook.com/110428089026992
Circulation: 50,000
Frequency: 8 times a year
Independent parenting magazine providing information on health care, education, birthing, arts, community events & more from pregnancy to teens

Calgary's Child Magazine
#723, 105-150 Crowfoot Cres. NW, Calgary, AB T3G 3T2
Tel: 403-241-6066; *Fax:* 403-286-9731
calgaryschild@shaw.ca
www.calgaryschild.com
Circulation: 70,000
Frequency: 6 times a year
Ellen Percival, Publisher & Editor

City Parent
Owned By: Premier Publications and Shows
c/o Premier Publications and Shows, #4, 447 Speers Rd., Oakville, ON L6K 3S7
Tel: 905-842-6591
www.cityparent.com
Social Media: pinterest.com/cityparentmag
twitter.com/CityParentMag
www.facebook.com/cityparent
Circulation: 77,785
Frequency: 12 times a year
Jane Muller, Editor-in-chief, jmuller@metroland.com

Divorce Magazine
#1179, 2255B Queen St. East, Toronto, ON M4E 1G3
Tel: 416-368-8853; *Fax:* 416-368-4978
Toll-Free: 888-217-9538
www.divorcemagazine.com
Social Media: www.myspace.com/divorcemagazine
twitter.com/divorcemagazine
www.facebo ok.com/divorcemagazine
Circulation: 170,000
Frequency: 4 times a year
Dan Couvrette, CEO & Publisher, danc@divorcemag.com
Dinh Nguven, Editor, dinh@divorcemarketinggroup.com

Edmonton's Child Magazine
Owned By: Gryphon Publishing
PO Box 369, 9768 - 170 St., Edmonton, AB T5T 5L4
Tel: 780-484-3360; *Fax:* 780-486-1844
Toll-Free: 866-484-3360
info@edmontonschild.com
www.edmontonschild.com
Social Media:
www.twitter.com/edmontonschild
www.facebook.com/edmontonschild
Circulation: 30,000
Frequency: Monthly
Kerri Leland, Editor, editor@edmontonschild.com

Enfants Québec
Détenteur: Les Éditions Rogers limitée
300, rue Arran, Saint-Lambert, QC J4R 1K5
Tél: 514-875-9612
serviceclient@editionsheritage.com
www.enfantsquebec.com
Médias sociaux:
www.facebook.com/enfantsquebec
Tirage: 60,506
Fréquence: 8 fois par an
Eve Christian, Rédactrice
Sylvie Payette, Éditrice

Fit Parent
Toronto, ON
info@fitparentmagazine.com
www.fitparentmagazine.com
Frequency: 6 times a year
Craig Knight, Publisher, craig@fitparentmagazine.com

Island Parent Magazine
c/o Island Parent Group, 830 Pembroke St., #A, Victoria, BC V8T 1H9
Tel: 250-388-6905; *Fax:* 250-388-6920
Toll-Free: 888-372-0862
mail@islandparent.ca
www.islandparent.ca
Social Media:
twitter.com/islandparent
www.facebook.com/IslandParent
Circulation: 20,000
Frequency: Monthly
Paul Abra, Publisher
Mada Johnson, Editor

Our Kids Go to Camp
Owned By: Our Kids Publications Ltd.
4242 Rockwood Rd., Mississauga, ON L4W 1L8
Toll-Free: 877-272-1845
info@ourkids.net
www.ourkids.net
Circulation: 200,000
Frequency: Annually
Agatha Stawicki, Managing Editor

Our Kids Go to School
Owned By: Our Kids Publications Ltd.
4242 Rockwood Rd., Mississauga, ON L4W 1L8
Tel: 905-272-1843; *Fax:* 905-272-0474
Toll-Free: 877-272-1845
info@ourkids.net
www.ourkids.net
Social Media: www.youtube.com/ourkidsnet
www.twitter.com/ourkidsnet
www.facebook.com/ourkidsnet
Circulation: 250,000
Frequency: Annually
Agatha Stawicki, Publisher

Owlkids
Previous Name: Tree Home Family
Owned By: Owlkids Books
#400, 10 Lower Spadina Ave., Toronto, ON M5V 2Z2
Tel: 416-340-2700; *Fax:* 416-340-9769
Toll-Free: 800-551-6957
owlkids@owlkids.com
www.owlkids.com/owl
Circulation: 66,768
Frequency: 6 times a year
Jennifer Canham, Group Publisher

Pomme d'Api Québec
Détenteur: Bayard Presse Canada Inc.
c/o Bayard Jeunesse Canada, 4475, rue Frontenac, Montréal, QC H2H 2S2
Tél: 514-844-2111; *Téléc:* 514-278-0072
Ligne sans frais: 866-600-0061
redaction@bayardpresse.qc.ca
www.bayardjeunesse.ca
Tirage: 13,000
Fréquence: 11 par an
Suzanne Spino, Présidente, 514-844-2111, Fax: 514-278-3030, suzanne.spino@bayardcanada.com
Nancy Lauzon, Directrice des Périodiques, Marketing, 514-844-2111, Fax: 514-278-0072, nancy.louzon@bayardcanada.com

7 Jours
Détenteur: TVA Publications inc.
1010, rue de Sérigny, 4e étage, Longueuil, QC J4K 5G7
Tél: 514-848-7000; *Téléc:* 514-848-7070
Ligne sans frais: 800-367-0667
7jours@tvapublications.com
7jours.ca
Médias sociaux:
twitter.com/7jours
www.facebook.com/magazine7Jours
Tirage: 121 540
Fréquence: Hebdomadaire
Véronique Letter, Vice President

Today's Parent
Owned By: Rogers Media Inc.
1 Mount Pleasant Rd., 8th Fl., Toronto, ON M4Y 2Y5
Tel: 416-764-2883; *Fax:* 416-764-2894
editors@todaysparent.com
www.todaysparent.com
Social Media:
twitter.com/Todaysparent
www.facebook.com/TodaysParent
Circulation: 160,056
Frequency: Monthly
Penny Hicks, Group Publisher
Sasha Emmons, Editor-in-Chief

Fashion

Clin d'oeil
Détenteur: TVA Publications inc.
Tél: 514-848-7164; *Téléc:* 514-270-7079
clindoeil@publicor.ca
clindoeil.ca
Médias sociaux:
twitter.com/Mag_clindoeil
www.facebook.com/group.php?gid=61535490997
Tirage: 60 372
Fréquence: Mensuel
Claire Syril, Éditeur
Mitsou Gélinas, Directeur de la publication

Dolce Magazine
Owned By: DOLCE Publishing Inc.
DOLCE Publishing Inc., #30, 111 Zenway Blvd., Vaughan, ON L4H 3H9
Tel: 905-264-6789; *Fax:* 905-264-3787
Toll-Free: 888-683-6523
www.dolcemag.com
Social Media:
twitter.com/dolcemag
www.facebook.com/pages/Dolce-Vita-Magazine/24838319 308
Circulation: 290,000
Michelle Zerillo-Sosa, Publisher & Editor-in-chief, michelle@dolce.ca

Fashion Magazine
Owned By: St. Joseph Media
St. Joseph Media, #320, 111 Queen St. East, Toronto, ON M5C 1S2
Tel: 416-364-3333; *Fax:* 416-594-3374
Toll-Free: 800-757-3977
www.fashionmagazine.com
Social Media: pinterest.com/fashionmagazine
twitter.com/FashionCanada
www.facebook.c om/fashioncanada
Circulation: 124,927
Frequency: 10 times a year
Bernadette Morra, Editor-in-Chief

Flare
Owned By: Rogers Media Inc.
One Mount Pleasant Rd., 8th Fl., Toronto, ON M4Y 2Y5
Tel: 416-764-2000; *Fax:* 416-764-2866
www.flare.com
Social Media: flarefashion.tumblr.com
twitter.com/FLAREfashion
www.facebook.com/FLAREFashion
Circulation: 124,646
Frequency: Monthly
Cameron Williamson, Editor-in-Chief
Melissa Ahlstrand, Publisher

Globe Style Advisor
444 Front St. West, Toronto, ON M5V 2S9
Tel: 416-585-5111; *Fax:* 416-585-5698
Toll-Free: 800-387-9012
advertising@globeandmail.com
www.globelink.ca/magazines/titles/styleadvi sor/
Social Media:
twitter.com/@globe_media
Circulation: 168,000 home subscribers
Frequency: Bi-monthly
Discusses personal style, home & design, & entertaining.

Good Life Connoisseur
#317, 1489 Marine Dr., West Vancouver, BC V7T 1B8
Tel: 604-925-0313 *Toll-Free:* 888-925-0313
www.goodlifecanada.com
Social Media:
twitter.com/GLConnoisseur
www.facebook.com/GoodLifeConnoisseur
Frequency: 4 times a year
Terry Tremaine, Publisher & Editor

LOULOU
Owned By: Rogers Media Inc.
#800, 1200 McGill College Ave., Montréal, QC H3B 4G7
Tel: 514-843-2189; *Fax:* 514-843-2189
julia.cyboran@loulou.rogers.com
en.louloumagazine.com
Social Media:
twitter.com/louloumagazine
www.facebook.com/LOULOUMagazine
Circulation: 146,001
Frequency: 11 times a year
Marie-José Desmarais, Publisher

LOULOU
Détenteur: Éditions Rogers Media
#1700, 1200, av McGill College, Montréal, QC H3B 4G7
Tél: 514-843-2189; *Téléc:* 514-843-2189
julia.cyboran@loulou.rogers.com
fr.louloumagazine.com
Médias sociaux:
twitter.com/MagazineLOULOU
Tirage: 73,883
Fréquence: 8 times a year
Marie-Joseé Desmarais, Publisher/Editor
Claude LaFramboise, Executive Editor

Nuvo Magazine
3055 Kingsway, Vancouver, BC V5R 5J8
Tel: 604-899-9380; *Fax:* 604-899-1450
Toll-Free: 877-205-6886
www.nuvomagazine.com
Frequency: 4 times a year
Jim Tobler, Editor

Zink
#2, 94, Ste-Therese, Montréal, QC H2Y 3V5
Tel: 514-759-7702
zinknews@zinkmediagroup.com
www.zinkmagazine.com
Social Media: www.youtube.com/user/ZinkMag
twitter.com/ZINKMagazine
www.facebook.com /ZinkMagazine
Frequency: Monthly
Sheriff J. Ishak, Editor-in-Chief/Publisher/CEO

Fifty-Plus Adults

Active Adult
Owned By: Homes Publishing Group
178 Main St., Unionville, ON L3R 2G9
Tel: 905-479-4663 *Toll-Free:* 800-363-4663
nsicilia@homesmag.com
www.activeadultmag.com
Social Media:
twitter.com/HOMESPublishing
www.facebook.com/pages/activeadultmagc om/150770131613956?
Circulation: 100,000
Frequency: 3 times a year
Michael Rosset, Publisher
Patrick Tivy, Editor

Be Fabulous!
11604 - 113 Ave., Edmonton, AB T5G 0J6
Tel: 780-470-0749; *Fax:* 780-470-0751
info@fabulousat50.com
www.fabulousat50.com/MainMenu/BeFabulousMagazine.a spx
Social Media:
www.youtube.com/user/Befabulousat50?feature=mhum
twitter.com/Fabat50
w ww.facebook.com/#%21/pages/FABULOUS50/86887170329
Magazine for baby boomer women over 50.
Dianna Bowes, Editor, editor@fabulousat50.com

Bel Âge
Détenteur: Publications Senior Inc.
4475, rue Frontenac, Montréal, QC H2H 2S2
Tél: 514-278-9325 *Ligne sans frais:* 800-780-0181
lebelage@cdsglobal.ca
www.lebelage.ca
Médias sociaux: www.youtube.com/user/magazineBelAge
www.twitter.com/BelAgeMagazine
www .facebook.com/belagemagazine
Tirage: 145 872
Fréquence: 11 fois par an
Jean-Louis Gauthier, Rédacteur en chef, jean-louis.gauthier@bayardcanada.com

Calgary Senior
Owned By: Great West Newspapers LP
340 Carleton Dr., St Albert, AB T8N 7L3
Tel: 780-470-5602; *Fax:* 780-460-8220
www.seniorsgotravel.com
Circulation: 50,000
Frequency: Bi-monthly
Danielle Higdon, Editor, 780-418-4741, editor@abr.greatwest.ca

Comfort Life
Owned By: Our Kids Publications Ltd.
Tel: 905-272-1843; *Fax:* 905-272-0474
Toll-Free: 877-272-1845
info@comfortlife.ca
www.comfortlife.ca
Social Media: www.youtube.com/comfortlifetv
www.twitter.com/comfortlife
www.faceb ook.com/comfortlife.ca
Circulation: 30,000
Frequency: Annually

Community Resource Directory
Owned By: Egress Enterprises Inc
Tel: 250-765-3886; *Fax:* 250-765-7346
info@communityresourcedirectories.com
communityresourcedirectories.com
Frequency: Annual
Joel A. Rickard, Publisher

Edmonton Senior
Owned By: Great West Newspapers LP
340 Carleton Dr., St Albert, AB T8N 7L3
Tel: 780-470-5602; *Fax:* 780-460-8220
www.seniorsgotravel.com
Circulation: 60,000
Frequency: 12 times a year
Fisal Asiff, Publisher, 780-470-5655, fasiff@abr.greatwest.ca
Danielle Higdon, Editor, 780-418-4741, editor@abr.greatwest.ca

Fifty-Five Plus
c/o Coyle Publishing Inc., 67 Neil Ave., Stittsville, ON K2S 1B9
Tel: 613-271-8903; *Fax:* 613-271-8905
www.fifty-five-plus.com
Social Media:
twitter.com/55mag
www.facebook.com/Fiftyfiveplus
Circulation: 45,000
Frequency: 8 times a year
George Coyle, Publisher
Pat Den Boer, Editor

Focus 50+
#13-215, 4 Alliance Blvd., Barrie, ON L4M 5J1
Tel: 705-735-2144
www.focus50.ca
Circulation: 11,500
Frequency: Monthly
Focus 50+ is published monthly by Focus Plus Inc. and is distributed free of charge to drop-off points throughout Simcoe County.
Taylor Ledden, Editor
Jeanneke Van Hattem, Publisher

FYI: Forever Young Information
Owned By: Premier Publications and Shows
c/o Premier Publications and Shows, #4, 447 Speers Rd., Oakville, ON L6K 3S7
Tel: 905-842-6591 *Toll-Free:* 800-693-7986
premierpublicationsandshows.com
Circulation: 530,000
Frequency: Monthly

Good Times
Owned By: TC Transcontinental
PO Box 11002 Anjou, Anjou, QC H1K 4H2
Toll-Free: 800-465-8443
editor@goodtimes.ca
www.goodtimes.ca
Social Media:
www.goodtimes.ca
Circulation: 157,086
Frequency: 11 times a year
The Canadian magazine for successful retirement.
Murray Lewis, Editor-in-Chief

Kerby News
1133 - 7th Ave. SW, Calgary, AB T2P 1B2
Tel: 403-265-0661; *Fax:* 403-705-3211
kerbynews@kerbycentre.com
www.kerbynews.com
Circulation: 25,000
Frequency: Monthly
Barry Whitehead, Editor

The Montrealer
Also Known As: Forever Young
342 Ballantyne North, Montreal Lake, QC H4X 2C5
Tel: 514-369-7000
editor@themontrealeronline.com
www.themontrealeronline.com
Social Media:
www.facebook.com/themontrealeronline
Circulation: 30,000
Frequency: Monthly
Peter Kerr, Publisher

PORTS Cruising Guides
Owned By: Premier Publications and Shows
c/o Premier Publications and Shows, #4, 447 Speers Rd., Oakville, ON L6K 3S7
Tel: 905-842-6591 *Toll-Free:* 800-693-7986
www.portsbooks.com
Circulation: 530,000
Frequency: Monthly
Craig Ritchie, Director, Editorial, 905-842-6591 x252, craig.ritchie@metroland.com

The Senior Paper
PO Box 1010 Main, Regina, SK S4P 3B2
Tel: 306-525-8988
www.theseniorpaper.com
The publication is of interest to persons over sixty years of age. Submissions of classified advertising, special events, & milestones are welcomed. Print & electronic issues are available.

The Seniors Review
#B2, 11 Bond St., St. Catharines, ON L2R 4Z4
Tel: 905-687-9861; *Fax:* 905-687-6911
Toll-Free: 800-627-3111
www.seniorsreview.com
Circulation: 40,000
David Irwin, Publisher
Carol Anderson, Editor

The Silver Pages
24 Cherryhill Dr., Grimsby, ON L3M 3B5
Tel: 905-309-1525; *Fax:* 905-309-1524
info@thesilverpages.ca
www.thesilverpages.ca
Social Media:
www.linkedin.com/company/the-silver-pages
www.facebook.com/TheSilv erPages
Circulation: 50,000
Frequency: 6 times a year
John Bauslaugh, Publisher
Tim Miller, Editorial Director

Virage
CP 1000 M, 4545, av Pierre-de-Coubertin, Montréal, QC H1V 3R2
Tél: 514-252-3017; *Téléc:* 514-252-3154
info@fadoq.ca
www.fadoq.ca/fr/Publications/Magazine-Virage
Tirage: 215 027
Fréquence: trimestriel
Martine Langlois, Éditrice
Lyne Rémillard, Rédacteur-en-chef

Zoomer Magazine
Previous Name: CARP Magazine
30 Jefferson Ave., Toronto, ON M6K 1Y4
Tel: 416-363-5562; *Fax:* 416-363-7693
comment@zoomermag.com
www.zoomermag.com
Other information: www.zoomers.ca
Social Media:
twitter.com/zoomermag
www.facebook.com/ZoomerMag
Circulation: 20,000
Frequency: Monthly
Susan Boyd, Editor-in-Chief

Fishing & Hunting

Alberta Fishing Guide
AB T4N 1L2
www.albertafishingguide.com
Social Media:
twitter.com/AlbertaFishing
www.facebook.com/AlbertaFishingGuide
Circulation: 27,825
Frequency: Annually, March
Online fishing & hunting guide

Aventure chasse et pêche
332, rue Veilleux, Saint-Simon-les-Mines, QC G0M 1K0
Tél: 418-774-4443; *Téléc:* 418-774-4444
cregimbald@qacp.com
www.qacp.com
Tirage: 50,600
Fréquence: 4 times a year
Claude Regimbald, Marketing Manager
Denis Lapointe, Production Manager

BC Outdoors
Previous Name: BC Fishing Recreation Guide & Atlas
Owned By: OP Media Group Ltd.
#201a, 7261 River Pl., Mission, BC V4S 0A2
Tel: 604-820-3400; *Fax:* 604-820-3477
Toll-Free: 800-898-8811
info@oppublishing.com
www.bcoutdoorsmagazine.com
Social Media: www.youtube.com/user/BCOSportFishingTV
twitter.com/BCOutdoors
www.facebook.com/group.php?gid=4086426581
Circulation: 15,000
Frequency: Annually
Mike Mitchell, Editor, 604-820-6453, mmitchell@bcoutdoorsmagazine.com

The Canadian Fly Fisher
Tel: 613-836-8295
info@jencor.ca
www.canflyfish.com
Chris Marshall, Editor

Island Angler
30 Acacia Ave., Nanaimo, BC V9R 3L4
Tel: 250-753-2227; *Fax:* 250-753-2295
www.islandangler.net
Circulation: 15,000
Andrew Kolasinski, Publisher, kolapub@yahoo.ca

Ontario Out of Doors
PO Box 8500, Peterborough, ON K9J 0B4
Tel: 705-748-0076; *Fax:* 705-748-9577
mail@oodmag.com
www.oodmag.com
Social Media: www.youtube.com/oodmag
twitter.com/oodmag
www.facebook.com/oodmag
Circulation: 92,026
Frequency: 10 times a year
John Kerr, Editor-in-Chief

Outdoor Canada
Owned By: Cottage Life Media
#100, 54 St. Patrick St., Toronto, ON M5T 1V1
Tel: 416-599-2000
editorial@outdoorcanada.ca
www.outdoorcanada.ca
Social Media: www.youtube.com/outdoorcanadamag
twitter.com/OutdoorCanada
www.faceboo k.com/outdoorcanada
Circulation: 82,574
Frequency: 6 times a year
National fishing and hunting magazine.
Patrick Walsh, Editor-in-Chief
Al Zikovitz, Publisher

The Outdoor Edge
Owned By: Outdoor Group Media
c/o Keywest Marketing Ltd., #202, 9644 - 54 Avenue, Edmonton, AB T6E 5V1
Toll-Free: 800-898-8811
info@outdoorgroupmedia.com
www.outdoorgroupmedia.com/outdooredge
Circulation: 54,517
Frequency: 6 times a year
Mark Yelic, Publisher

Sentier Chasse-Pêche
#201 1650, rue Michelin, Laval, QC H7L 4R3
Tél: 450-665-0271; *Téléc:* 450-665-2974
Ligne sans frais: 800-563-6738
abonnement@sentierchassepeche.com
www.sentierchassepeche.com
Tirage: 80 000
Fréquence: 11 fois par an
Louis Turbide, Rédacteur,
louis.turbide@sentierchassepeche.com

Western Sportsman
Owned By: OP Media Group Ltd.
#202, 9644 - 54th Ave., Edmonton, AB T6E 5V1
Tel: 780-643-3961 *Toll-Free:* 800-898-8811
info@outdoorgroupmedia.com
www.westernsportsman.com
Circulation: 25,933
Frequency: 6 times a year
Michaela Ludwig, Editor, 780-643-3961,
editorial@outdoorgroupmedia.com
Mark Yelic, President & Publisher, 780-643-3962,
myelic@outdoorgroupmedia.com

Food & Beverage

Appeal
Canada Wide Media Ltd.
Owned By: Canada Wide Media Limited
4180 Lougheed Hwy, 4th Fl., Burnaby, BC V5C 6A7
Tel: 604-299-7311; *Fax:* 604-299-9188
cwm@canadawide.com
www.canadawide.com
Circulation: 166,000
Frequency: 2 times a year
A quality & healthy lifestyle magazine that provides expert health & nutrition advice
Kim Mah, Editor, kmah@canadawide.com

Coup de Pouce
Détenteur: TVA Publications inc.
1010, rue de Sérigny, Longueuil, QC J4K 5G7
Tél: 514-848-7000 *Ligne sans frais:* 800-528-3836
www.coupdepouce.com
Médias sociaux: www.pinterest.com/coupdepouce
twitter.com/coupdepouce_mag
www.facebook .com/coupdepouce
Fréquence: 5 fois par an
Francine Tremblay, Éditrice
France Lefebvre, Rédacteur

Elite Wine, Food & Travel Magazine
Previous Name: Enoteca Wine & Food Magazine
88 Rosebury Ln., Vaughn, ON L4L 3Z8
Tel: 905-760-1724; *Fax:* 905-760-1718
editor@elitewinefoodtravel.com
www.elitewinefoodtravel.com
Circulation: 10,000
Frequency: 4 times a year
Anna Cavaliere, Editor

Flavours
Owned By: Fulcrum Media Inc.
#201, 508 Lawrence Ave. West, Toronto, ON M6A 1A1
Tel: 416-504-0504; *Fax:* 416-256-3002
Toll-Free: 866-688-0504
info@fulcrum.ca
fulcrum.ca
Social Media: instagram.com/flavoursmag
twitter.com/FlavoursWorld
www.facebook.com/FlavWorld
Frequency: 4 times a year
Jane Auster, Editor, jauster@fulcrum.ca
Sheryl English Roberts, Contact, 604-728-8640,
sroberts@fulcrum.ca

Food & Drink
Liquor Control Board of Ontario, 55 Lake Shore Blvd. East, Toronto, ON M5E 1A4
Tel: 416-365-5900; *Fax:* 416-365-5935
Toll-Free: 800-668-5226
www.lcbo.com/fooddrink
Circulation: 500,000
Frequency: bi-monthly
Judy Dunn, Editor
Wayne Leek, Publisher

Food & Wine Trails
2250 Camrose St., Penticton, BC V2A 8R1
Tel: 250-492-6036
www.winetrails.ca
Social Media:
twitter.com/BCWineTrails
www.facebook.com/264526741670
Circulation: 15,000
Frequency: 4 times a year
Jennifer Schell-Pigott, Editor-in-Chief, winetrails@blackpress.ca

Le Guide Cuisine (LGC)
Détenteur: Communication Duocom
Communication Duocom Inc., 72B, rue Sainte-Anne, Sainte-Anne-de-Bellevue, QC H9X 1L8
Tél: 514-457-0144; *Téléc:* 514-457-0226
Ligne sans frais: 800-558-5508
info@leguidecuisine.com
www.leguidecuisine.com
Médias sociaux: www.youtube.com/user/leguidecuisine
twitter.com/LeGuideCuisine
www.fac ebook.com/LeGuideCuisine
Tirage: 45,000
Fréquence: Cinq fois par ans
Nicolas Vallée, Rédacteur en chef

InterVin Insider
Owned By: Town Media Inc.
1074 Cooke Blvd., Burlington, ON L7T 4A8
Tel: 905-634-8003; *Fax:* 905-634-7661
www.intervin.ca/sitepages/
Social Media:
twitter.com/intervin
www.facebook.com/intervin
Frequency: 7 issues per year
Publication of the InterVinWine Awards.

Quench
Previous Name: Tidings
Owned By: Kylix Media Inc
#500, 5165 Sherbrooke West, Montréal, QC H4A 1T6
Tel: 514-481-5892
quench.me
Social Media:
twitter.com/QuenchByTidings
www.facebook.com/pages/Quench-Magazine/380999065360646?sk
Circulation: 35,000
Frequency: 8 times a year
Aldo Parise, Editor-in-chief

Taste
Owned By: BC Liquor Distribution Branch
2625 Rupert St., Vancouver, BC V5M 3T5
Tel: 604-252-3000
taste.magazine@bcliquorstores.com
www.bcliquorstores.com/taste/home
Magazine for BC Liquor.

Taste
Owned By: Premier Publications and Shows
c/o Premier Publications and Shows, #4, 447 Speers Rd., Oakville, ON L6K 3S7
Tel: 905-842-6591 *Toll-Free:* 800-693-7986
premierpublicationsandshows.com
An exclusive culinary magazine for residents who live west of Toronto.

Toronto Wine & Cheese Show Guide
#4, 447 Speers Rd., Oakville, ON L6K 3S4
Tel: 905-842-6591; *Fax:* 905-842-6843
Toll-Free: 800-693-7986
www.towineandcheese.com
Social Media:
twitter.com/WineCheeseShow
www.facebook.com/WineandCheeseShow
Circulation: 33,500
Frequency: 1 times a year
Janet Gardiner, Publisher

Vines
Owned By: Town Media Inc.
1074 Cooke Blvd., Burlington, ON L7T 4A8
Tel: 905-634-8003; *Fax:* 905-634-7661
tm.info@sunmedia.ca
www.vinesmag.com
Social Media:
twitter.com/VinesMag
www.facebook.com/VinesMag
Frequency: 7 issues per year
Aimed at Canadians interested in wine.
Donna Gardener, Director, donna.gardener@sunmedia.ca

Fraternal, Service Clubs, Associations

KIN Canada (Kinsmen & Kinette Clubs of Canada)
c/o Kin Canada, PO Box 3460, 1920 Rogers Dr., Cambridge, ON N3H 5C6
Tel: 519-653-1920; *Fax:* 519-650-1091
Toll-Free: 800-742-5546
kinhq@kincanada.ca
www.kincanada.ca
Social Media:
twitter.com/kincanada
www.facebook.com/kincanada
Circulation: 10,000
Frequency: 3 print (Feb., June, Oct.); 3 online (April, Aug. & Dec.)
Michelle Rickard, Editor

Mensa Canada Society
Also Known As: MC2
PO Box 1570, Kingston, ON K7L 5C8
Tel: 613-547-0824; *Fax:* 613-531-0626
mensa@eventsmgt.com
www.mensacanada.org
Social Media:
twitter.com/MensaCanada
www.facebook.com/MensaCanada
Circulation: 2,100
Frequency: 6 times a year
Phyrne Parker, President

Rameses Papyrus
The Rameses Shrine Centre, 124 Queen's Plate Drive, Toronto, ON M9W 7K4
Tel: 416-633-6317; *Fax:* 416-633-6345
shrineoffice@rameses.ca
www.rameses-shriners.ca
Circulation: 7,200
Frequency: 6 times a year

The Sentinel
Orange Headquarters, 94 Sheppard Ave. West, Toronto, ON M2N 1M5
Tel: 416-223-1690; *Fax:* 416-223-1324
Toll-Free: 800-565-6248
grandorangelodge.ca
Circulation: 4,000
Frequency: 4 times a year
James Bell, Editor-in-Chief

Gardening & Garden Equipment

Alberta Gardener
Owned By: Pegasus Publications Inc.
130A Cree Cres., Winnipeg, MB R3J 3W1
Tel: 204-940-2700; *Fax:* 204-940-2727
Toll-Free: 888-680-2008
info@pegasuspublications.net
www.albertagardener.net
Social Media:
www.facebook.com/AlbertaGardener
Circulation: 6,628
Frequency: 6 times a year

BC Home & Garden
Owned By: Canada Wide Media Limited
4180 Lougheed Hwy., 4th Fl., Burnaby, BC V5C 6A7
Tel: 604-299-7311; *Fax:* 604-299-9188
Toll-Free: 800-663-0518
www.bcliving.ca/bc-home-and-garden-magazine
Circulation: 35,000
In 2012, GardenWise magazine & BC Home magazine combined to create BC Home & Garden magazine. The publication offers garden & landscape ideas, design trends, & style advice.
Samantha Legge, Publisher, 604-473-0378, slegge@canadawide.com
Rhea Attar, Director, Sales Operations, rattar@canadawide.com

Canadian Gardening
Owned By: TVA Publications inc.
1010 Sérigny St., Longueuil, QC J4K 5G7
Tel: 514-848-7000
www.canadiangardening.com
Social Media: www.youtube.com/user/CanadianGardening
twitter.com/CDNGardening
www.fa cebook.com/canadiangardening
Circulation: 153,000
Frequency: 8 times a year
Aldona Satterthwaite, Editor-in-chief
Jacqueline Howe, Publisher

Canadian Organic Grower
Previous Name: Eco-Farm & Garden
39 McArthur, Level 1-3, Ottawa, ON K1L 8L7
Tel: 613-216-0741; *Fax:* 613-236-0743
Toll-Free: 888-375-7383
office@cog.ca
www.cog.ca/our-services/magazine/cog-magazine
Social Media:
www.twitter.com/CanadianOrganic
www.facebook.com/CanadianOrganic
Circulation: 2,500
Frequency: 4 times a year
Janet Wallace, Editor, janet@cog.ca

Fleurs, Plantes et Jardins
Détenteur: TVA Publications inc.
2850, rue Jean Perrin, Québec, QC G2C 2C8
Tél: 418-840-3639
fpj@tc.tc
www.jardinage.net
Médias sociaux:
twitter.com/fleursplantesja
www.facebook.com/fleursplantesjardins
Tirage: 55 506
Fréquence: 9 fois par an
Francine Tremblay, Éditeur

Garden Making
Owned By: Inspiring Media Inc.
PO Box 808, #204, 111B Garrison Village Dr. #RR 3, Niagara on the Lake, ON L0S 1J0
Tel: 416-932-5075; *Fax:* 866-857-4262
Toll-Free: 877-832-1444
service@gardenmaking.com
gardenmaking.com
Social Media: www.youtube.com/gardenmaking
www.twitter.com/gardenmaking
www.faceb ook.com/gardenmaking
Circulation: 22,960
Frequency: Quarterly
Beckie Fox, Editor-in-Chief, editor@gardenmaking.com

Manitoba Gardener
Owned By: Pegasus Publications Inc.
130A Cree Cres., Winnipeg, MB R3J 3W1
Tel: 204-940-2700; *Fax:* 204-940-2727
Toll-Free: 888-680-2008
info@pegasuspublications.net
www.manitobagardener.net
Social Media:
www.facebook.com/ManitobaGardener
Circulation: 6,628
Frequency: 6 times a year
Dorothy Dobbie, Publisher
Joan Cohen, Editor

Ontario Gardener
Owned By: Pegasus Publications Inc.
130A Cree Crescentn St., Winnipeg, MB R3J 3W1
Tel: 204-940-2700; *Fax:* 204-940-2727
Toll-Free: 888-680-2008
info@pegasuspublications.net
ontariogardener.net
Social Media:
www.facebook.com/OntarioGardener
Frequency: 6 times a year
Shauna Dobbie, Publisher & Editor

General Interest

L'Agora
CP 96, Ayer's Cliff, QC J0B 1C0
Tél: 819-849-6360
editeurs@agora.homovivens.org
agora.qc.ca
Tirage: 10 000
Hélène Laberge, Rédactrice-en-chef
Jacques Dufresne, Éditeur

Alberta Views
#208, 320 - 23 Ave. SW, Calgary, AB T2S 0J2
Tel: 403-243-5334; *Fax:* 403-243-8599
Toll-Free: 877-212-5334
avadmin@albertaviews.ab.ca
www.albertaviews.ab.ca
Social Media:
twitter.com/AlbertaViewsMag
www.facebook.com/95710929413
Circulation: 20,000
Frequency: 8 times a year
Magazine of politics, education, industry, public service & the arts
Jackie Flanagan, Publisher & Editor

Best Health
Owned By: Reader's Digest Magazines (Canada) Ltd.
1100, boul René Lévesque ouest, Montréal, QC H3B 5H5
Toll-Free: 800-465-0780
www.besthealthmag.ca
Social Media: pinterest.com/besthealthmag/
twitter.com/besthealthmag
www.facebook.com/besthealth
Circulation: 100,000
Frequency: 8 times a year
Our Canada features reader-written stories & photographs.
Beth Thompson, Editor-in-Chief

CAA Magazine
Owned By: Totem Communications Group Inc.
Totem Communications Group Inc., 37 Front St. East, Toronto, ON M5E 1B3
Tel: 416-360-7339; *Fax:* 416-640-6164
caamagazine@totembrandstories.com
www.caamagazine.ca
Social Media:
twitter.com/CAAMagazine
Frequency: Quarterly
Tracy Howard, Editor

Canadian Immigrant Magazine
8508 Ash St., Vancouver, BC V6P 3S4
Tel: 604-872-0102
canadianimmigrant.ca
Frequency: monthly

Canadian Newcomer
222 Parkview Hill Cres., Toronto, ON M4B 1R8
Tel: 416-406-4719
feedback@cnmag.ca
www.cnmag.ca
Frequency: Bi-monthly theme issues, daily features
Online magazine discussing employment, housing, lifestyle, health, finance, education & media in Canada
Dale Sproule, Publisher, dale@cnmag.ca

Contact
Université Laval, 2325, rue de L'Université, Québec, QC G1V 0A6
Tél: 418-656-7266; *Téléc:* 418-656-2809
magazine.contact@dc.ulaval.ca
www.contact.ulaval.ca
Tirage: 37 125
Fréquence: 3 fois par an
Louise Desautels, Rédactrice en chef

Continuité
82, Grande-Allée ouest, Québec, QC G1R 2G6
Tél: 418-647-4525; *Téléc:* 418-647-6483
continuite@magazinecontinuite.qc.ca
www.magazinecontinuite.com
Tirage: 5 000
Fréquence: 4 fois par an
Josiane Ouellet, Rédactrice en chef, redaction@magazinecontinuite.qc.ca

Dernière heure
Détenteur: TVA Publications inc.
7, chemin Bates, Outremont, QC H2V 4V7
Tél: 514-848-7000; *Téléc:* 514-848-9854
www.tvapublications.com
Médias sociaux:
www.facebook.com/MagazineDH
Tirage: 30 000
Fréquence: Hebdomadaire

Digital Journal Magazine
PO Box 1046, Toronto, ON M5C 2K4
Tel: 416-410-9675
www.digitaljournal.com
Social Media:
www.facebook.com/digitaljournal
Christopher A. Hogg, Editor-in-chief

être en ligne
Anciennement: R.G.
CP 222 C, 1613, rue Amherst, Montréal, QC H2L 4K1
Tél: 514-521-3873; *Téléc:* 514-523-2214
info@rgmag.com
www.etremag.com
Médias sociaux:
twitter.com/etremag
www.facebook.com/pages/Magazine-Etre/133489396662525
Tirage: 11 500
Antoine Aubert, Rédactor, antoine@etremag.com

Focus Magazine
Previous Name: Focus on Women
PO Box 5310, Victoria, BC V8R 6S4
Tel: 250-388-7231
focuspublish@shaw.ca
www.focusonline.ca
Circulation: 360,000
Frequency: Monthly
Focus is a monthly print magazine that's been serving Victoria for over 24 years.
David Broadland, Publisher
Leslie Campbell, Editor

Fugues
1212, St-Hubert, Montréal, QC H2L 3Y8
Tél: 514-848-1854; *Téléc:* 514-845-7645
redaction@fugues.com
www.fugues.com
Médias sociaux:
twitter.com/Fuguesmagazine
www.facebook.com/fugues
Tirage: 50,000
Fréquence: 14 times a year
Maurice Nadeau, Publisher

Georgian Bay Today
Also Known As: rattlesnake!
The Bird Room, 5 Little Ave., Toronto, ON M9N 1K3
Tel: 647-378-4938
peter@georgianbaytoday.info
www.georgianbaytodaynews.com
Circulation: 2,000
Frequency: 4 times a year
An independent, quarterly, newspaper/magazine. It offers information, features, news, opinion, illustration and advertising to link all who spend weekends hereabouts (call them "recreationists"), residents and tourists around the shore of Georgian Bay and related lakelands.
Peter Wood, Publisher

Going Natural/Au Naturel
PO Box 186 D, Etobicoke, ON M9A 4X2
Tel: 416-410-6822 *Toll-Free:* 888-512-6833
editor@fcn.ca
fcn.ca/about-the-fcn/going-natural-magazine
Circulation: 2,500
Frequency: 4 times a year

Humanist Perspectives
Previous Name: Humanist in Canada
Owned By: Canadian Humanist Publications
c/o Canadian Humanist Publications, PO Box 3769 C, Ottawa, ON K1Y 4J8
CHPboard@humanistperspectives.org
www.humanistperspectives.org

Circulation: 1,500
Frequency: 4 times a year
Madeline Weld, Editor, editor@humanistperspectives.org
Richard Young, Editor, editor@humanistperspectives.org

Kanata Kourier - Standard EMC
Previous Name: Kanata EMC, Kanata Kourier Standard
#4, 80 Colonnade Rd., Nepean, ON K2E 7L2
Tel: 613-224-3330; *Fax:* 613-224-2265

Circulation: 25,212
Frequency: Weekly
Mike Tracy, Publisher
Theresa Fritz, Managing Editor

Lambert
#10, 426, rue Victoria, Saint-Lambert, QC J4P 2H9
Tél: 450-465-0789; *Téléc:* 450-465-8128
lambert@lookommunication.com
www.magazinelambert.com
Médias sociaux:
twitter.com/magazinelambert
www.facebook.com/MagazineLambert

Tirage: 25,000
Fréquence: 6 times a year
Marcel Renaud, marcelr@magazinelambert.com

Legion Magazine
86 Aird Pl., Kanata, ON K2L 0A1
Tel: 613-591-0116; *Fax:* 613-591-0146
info@legionmagazine.com
www.legionmagazine.com/en/
Social Media:
twitter.com/Legion_Magazine
www.facebook.com/169253049780364

Circulation: 313,217
Frequency: 6 times a year

Magazine Prestige
305, boul René-Lévesque ouest, Québec, QC G1S 1S1
Tél: 418-683-5333; *Téléc:* 418-683-2899
info@magazineprestige.com
www.magazineprestige.com
Médias sociaux:
www.facebook.com/MagazinePRESTIGE?ref=stream

Fréquence: 11 fois par an
Marie-Josée Turcotte, Rédacteur-en-chef, redaction@magazineprestige.com

Muskoka Magazine
Owned By: Cottage Country Communications
PO Box 180, #12, 440 Ecclestone Dr., Bracebridge, ON P1L 1T6
Tel: 705-646-1314; *Fax:* 705-645-6424
mm.info@sunmedia.ca
www.muskokamagazine.com
Social Media:
www.facebook.com/muskokamagazine

Circulation: 14,550
Frequency: 10 times a year
Sandy Lockhart, Editor
Donald Smith, Publisher & Editor

Nouvelles CSQ
Anciennement: Nouvelles CEQ
Centrale des syndicats du Québec, 9405, rue Sherbrooke est, Montréal, QC H1L 6P3
Tél: 514-356-8888; *Téléc:* 514-356-9999
Ligne sans frais: 800-465-0897
www.csq.qc.net
Médias sociaux: www.youtube.com/user/csqvideos
twitter.com/csq_centrale
www.facebook.c om/lacsq

Tirage: 103 000
Fréquence: 5 fois par an
Louise Rochefort, Directrice

On the Bay Magazine
Owned By: TC Transcontinental
#201, 186 Hurontario St., Collingwood, ON L9Y 4T4
Tel: 705-444-9192; *Fax:* 705-444-5658
Toll-Free: 888-282-2014
info@onthebaymagazine.com
www.onthebaymagazine.com
Social Media:
www.facebook.com/pages/On-The-Bay-Magazine/249445781903

Frequency: 6 times a year
Janet Lees, Editor, jlees@onthebaymagazine.com
Jeffrey Shearer, Publisher, jshearer@onthebaymagazine.com

Our Canada
1100, boul René Lévesque ouest, Montréal, QC H3B 5H5
Toll-Free: 800-465-0780
www.readersdigest.ca/our-canada

Frequency: 6 times a year
Our Canada features reader-written stories & photographs.

Pacific Rim Magazine
c/o Langara College, 100 West 49th Ave., Vancouver, BC V5Y 2Z6
Tel: 604-323-5432
langaraprm.com

Circulation: 18,000
Darren Bernaerdt, Publisher

Protégez-Vous
CP 190 Place d'Armes, #305, 2120, rue Sherbrooke est, Montréal, QC H2Y 3G7
Tél: 514-873-3000; *Téléc:* 514-223-7160
Ligne sans frais: 866-895-7186
courrier@protegez-vous.ca
www.protegez-vous.ca
Médias sociaux:
twitter.com/ProtegezVous
www.facebook.com/protegezvous.ca

Tirage: 151 145
Fréquence: 12 fois par an
David Clerk, Contact

Reader's Digest / Sélection du Reader's Digest
1100, boul René Lévesque ouest, Montréal, QC H3B 5H5
Tel: 514-940-0751; *Fax:* 514-940-3637
Toll-Free: 800-465-0780
customerservice@readersdigest.ca
www.readersdigest.ca
Social Media:
twitter.com/readersdigestca
www.facebook.com/readersdigestcanada

Circulation: 1,200,000
Frequency: Monthly
Bonnie Kintzer, President & CEO
Paul Tomkins, Exeuctive Vice-President & CFO
Susan Fraysse Russ, Vice-President, Global Communications
Elizabeth Vaccariello, VP, Editor-in-Chief, Reader's Digest, Chief Content Off

Safarir
c/o Les Publications LOL inc., #106, 905, rue des Prairies, Québec, QC G1K 3M5
Tél: 514-380-1202
www.safarir.com
Médias sociaux:
twitter.com/safarirmag
www.facebook.com/safarir

Fréquence: 12 fois par an
Michel Bouchard, Rédacteur en chef, redaction@safarir.com

Sélection du Reader's Digest
Anciennement: Sélection
1100, boul René Lévesque ouest, Montréal, QC H3B 5H5
Tél: 514-940-0751; *Téléc:* 514-940-3637
Ligne sans frais: 888-459-3333
selection.readersdigest.ca
Médias sociaux:
twitter.com/selectionrd
selection.readersdigest.ca

Tirage: 242,970
Fréquence: Monthly
Robert Goyette, Rédacteur-en-chef

University of Toronto Magazine
University of Toronto, J. Robert S. Prichard Alumni House, 21 King's College Circle, Toronto, ON M5S 3J3
Tel: 416-946-3192; *Fax:* 416-978-3958
Toll-Free: 800-463-6048
uoft.magazine@utoronto.ca
www.magazine.utoronto.ca
Social Media:
twitter.com/uoftmagazine
www.facebook.com/pages/U-of-T-Magazine/176022529092653
Circulation: 300,000
Frequency: Quarterly
Scott Anderson, Editor & Manager, scott.anderson@utoronto.ca

Up Here
Previous Name: Up Here: Life at the top of the World
Owned By: Up Here Publishing Ltd.
PO Box 1350, Yellowknife, NT X1A 2N9
Tel: 867-766-6710; *Fax:* 867-873-9876
Toll-Free: 866-572-1757
www.uphere.ca
Social Media: instagram.com/upheremag
twitter.com/upheremag
www.facebook.com/uphere
Circulation: 24,827
Frequency: 8 times a year
Aaron Spitzer, Editor, aaron@uphere.ca

Valleyfield Express
Détenteur: TC Media
69, boul St-Jean-Baptiste, Châteauguay, QC J6J 3H6
Tél: 450-692-9111; *Téléc:* 450-692-9192
redactionvalleyfieldexpress@tc.tc
www.valleyfieldexpress.ca
Tirage: 39 000
Fréquence: Hebdomadaire
Salaberry-de-Valleyfield, Grande-Île, Saint-Thimothée, Notre-Dame-du-Sourire, Ormstown, Sainte-Barbe, Saint-Stanislas-de-Kostka, Saint-Louis-de-Gonzague, Cazaville, Saint-Anicet, Sainte-Agnès-de-Dundee, Huntingdon, Athelstan, Dewittville, Godmanchester, Hinchinbrook, Melocheville, Coteau-du-Lac, Saint-Zotique, Saint-Clet, Rivière-Beaudette, Saint-Polycarpe, Les Cèdres et Les Coteaux.
Julie Voyer, Éditeur

Western Living Magazine
Owned By: TC Transcontinental
#560, 2608 Granville St., Vancouver, BC V6H 3V3
Tel: 604-877-7732; *Fax:* 604-877-4848
Toll-Free: 800-363-3272
wlmail@westernlivingmagazine.com
www.westernlivingmagazine.com
Social Media: pinterest.com/westernliving/
twitter.com/Western_Living
www.facebook.com/WesternLivingMagazine

Circulation: 165,000
Frequency: 10 times a year
Anicka Quin, Editor-in-Chief

Western Standard
#205, 1550 - 5th St. SW, Calgary, AB T2R 1K3
Tel: 403-216-2270
info@westernstandard.ca
www.westernstandard.ca
Frequency: Bi-weekly
Conservative news & commentary from a Western Canadian perspective.

Westworld Alberta
Owned By: Canada Wide Media Limited
Alberta Motor Association, PO Box 8180 South, Edmonton, AB T6H 5X9
Tel: 604-299-7311; *Fax:* 604-299-9188
Toll-Free: 800-642-3810
cwm@canadawide.com
www.canadawide.com
Circulation: 540,000
Frequency: 5 times a year
Peter Legge, Publisher
Kirsten Rodenhizer, Editor, krodenhizer@canadawide.com

Westworld British Columbia
Owned By: Canada Wide Media Limited
British Columbia Automobile Association, PO Box 6680, Vancouver, BC V6B 4L4
Tel: 604-268-5555 *Toll-Free:* 800-663-1956
cwm@canadawide.com
www.canadawide.com
Circulation: 476,301
Frequency: 4 times a year
Peter Legge, Publisher
Anne Rose, Editor

Westworld Saskatchewan
Owned By: Canada Wide Media Limited
CAA Saskatchewan, 200 Albert St. North, Regina, SK S4R 5E2
Tel: 604-299-7311; *Fax:* 604-299-9188
Toll-Free: 877-564-6222
cwm@canadawide.com
www.canadawide.com
Circulation: 120,000
Frequency: 4 times a year
Peter Legge, Publisher
Sheila Hansen, Editor, shansen@canadawide.com

Graphic Arts

Applied Arts
Previous Name: Electronic Link
#705, 18 Wynford Dr., Toronto, ON M3C 3S2
Tel: 416-510-0909 *Toll-Free:* 800-646-0347
editorial@appliedartsmag.com
www.appliedartsmag.com
Social Media:
twitter.com/appliedarts
www.facebook.com/AppliedArtsMag
Circulation: 12,000
Frequency: Monthly
Monthly magazine publishing visual communications in Canada
Roberta Heckhausen, Publisher, rosetta@appliedartsmag.com
Peter Giffen, Editor, editor@appliedartsmag.com

Uppercase
#201B, 908 - 17th Ave. SW, Calgary, AB T2T 0A3
Tel: 403-283-5318
uppercasemagazine.com
Social Media: instagram.com/uppercasemag
twitter.com/uppercasemag
www.facebook.com/768910297
Frequency: 4 times a year
Janine Vangool, Publisher/Editor/Designer, janine@uppercasemagazine.com

Health & Medical

Abilities Magazine
#803, 255 Duncan Mill Rd., Toronto, ON M5T 3A9
Tel: 416-421-7944; *Fax:* 416-421-8418
info@abilities.ca
www.abilities.ca
Social Media:
twitter.com/abilitiescanada
Circulation: 80,000
Lifestyle magazine for those with disabilities
Raymond Cohen, Founder & Chief Executive Officer
Cameron Graham, Chair

Alive
Owned By: Alive Publishing Group
#100, 12751 Vulcan Way, Richmond, BC V6V 3C8
Fax: 800-663-6597
Toll-Free: 800-663-6580
info@alive.com
www.alive.com
Social Media: plus.google.com/115031422972901434935/posts
twitter.com/aliveHealth
ww w.facebook.com/alive.health.wellness
Circulation: 250,000
Frequency: Monthly
Topics include health, wellness, natural health.
Ryan Benn, Publisher

Beingwell Magazine
Owned By: York Region Media Group
580B Steven Crt., Newmarket, ON L3Y 4X1
Tel: 905-853-8888; *Fax:* 905-853-5379
yrcustomerservice@yrmg.com
www.yorkregion.com
Frequency: Quarterly
A joint project of the York Region Media Group and Southlake Regional Health Care Foundation.
Lee Ann Waterman, Editor

Caregiver Solutions
Previous Name: Canada's Family Guide to Home Health Care & Wellness Solutions
Owned By: BCS Communications Ltd.
#803, 255 Duncan Mill Rd., Toronto, ON M3B 3H9
Tel: 416-421-7944; *Fax:* 416-421-8418
Toll-Free: 800-798-6282
www.solutionsmagazine.ca
Social Media:
www.facebook.com/CaregiverSolutions
Circulation: 30,000
Frequency: 4 times a year
Caroline Tapp-McDougall, Publisher, caroline@bcsgroup.com

Common Ground
Owned By: Common Ground Publishing Corp.
3152 West 8th Ave., Vancouver, BC V6K 2C3
Tel: 604-733-2215; *Fax:* 604-733-4415
Toll-Free: 800-365-8897
joseph@commonground.ca
www.commonground.ca
Circulation: 70,000
Frequency: 12 times a year
Joseph Roberts, Publisher & Senior Editor

Diabetes Dialogue
#1400, 522 University Ave., Toronto, ON M5G 2R5
Toll-Free: 800-226-8464
www.diabetes.ca/publications-newsletters/diabetes-dialogue
Circulation: 45,510
Frequency: Quarterly
Official magazine of the Canadian Diabetes Association.
Marg Churchill, Marketing, mchurchill@keithhealthcare.com

Family Health
PO Box 2421, 10006 - 101 St., Edmonton, AB T5J 2S6
Fax: 780-498-5661
fhonline@familyhealthonline.ca
www.familyhealthonline.ca
Circulation: 97,000
Frequency: 4 times a year
Robert Clarke, Publisher

Future Health
c/o Canadians for Health Research, PO Box 126, Westmount, QC H3Z 2T1
Tel: 514-398-7478; *Fax:* 514-398-8361
www.chrcrm.org/en/future-health-featured
Circulation: 2,000
Frequency: 4 times a year
Tim Lougheed, Chair, Canadians for Health Research

Healthcare Information Management & Communications Canada
Owned By: Healthcare Computing & Communications Canada, Inc
11755 - 108 Avenue, Edmonton, AB T5H 1B8
Tel: 780-489-4521; *Fax:* 780-489-3290
healthcare@shaw.ca
www.healthcareimc.com
Circulation: 6,000
Frequency: Quarterly
Steven A. Huesing, Publisher & Editor

HeartBeat
PO Box 1, Site 100, RR#1, Carvel, AB T0E 0H0
Tel: 780-380-2910; *Fax:* 780-892-3401
www.heartbeatangels.com
Circulation: 4,600
Frequency: 4 times a year
Pauline Newman, Publisher

Impact Magazine
2007 - 2nd St. SW, Calgary, AB T2S 1S4
Tel: 403-228-0605; *Fax:* 403-228-0627
info@impactmagazine.ca
www.impactmagazine.ca
Frequency: Bi-monthly
Elaine Kupser, Publisher, elaine@impactmagazine.ca
Chris Welner, Editor, editor@impactmagazine.ca

Mosaic Mind, Body and Spirit Magazine
PO Box 80588 Bellrose, #209, 10715 - 124 St., St. Albert, AB T8N 7C3
Tel: 780-447-3667; *Fax:* 780-939-0588
mosaicmagazine@shaw.ca
www.mosaicmagazine.ca
Social Media:
www.facebook.com/218630024830514
Circulation: 75,000
Frequency: Quarterly
Holistic medicine.
Connie Brisson, Publisher/Editor

Vision Magazine
Breton Communications Inc., #202, 495, boul St-Martin ouest, Laval, QC H7M 1Y9
Tel: 450-629-6005; *Fax:* 450-629-6044
Toll-Free: 888-462-2112
info@bretoncom.com
www.bretoncom.com/vision/2011/01/index.asp
Circulation: 11,435
Frequency: 6 times a year
Martine Breton, Présidente, martine@bretoncom.com

Vitalité Québec Mag
1025 - 1200 Chomedey, Laval, QC H7V 3Z3
Tél: 450-873-4863; *Téléc:* 450-973-7856
www.vitalitequebec-magazine.com
Tirage: 40 000
Fréquence: 10 fois par an
Pierre Martineau, Président, 514-729-9772, pm@videotron.ca

Vitality Magazine
356 Dupont St., Toronto, ON M5R 1V9
Tel: 416-964-0528
editorial@vitalitymagazine.com
www.vitalitymagazine.com
Circulation: 52,000
Frequency: 10 times a year
Julia Woodford, Editor

WHOLifE Journal
PO Box 278, Kamsack, SK S0A 1S0
Tel: 306-542-3616; *Fax:* 306-542-3619
Toll-Free: 800-780-3564
editor@wholife.com
www.wholife.com
Circulation: 17,000
Frequency: 6 times a year
Covers natural health & wellness for body, mind & spirit, plus environmental issues
Melva Armstrong, Publisher

History & Genealogy

Canada's History Magazine
Previous Name: The Beaver: Canada's History Magazine
Bryce Hall, Main Fl., 515 Portage Ave., Winnipeg, MB R3B 2E9
Tel: 204-988-9300; *Fax:* 204-988-9309
Toll-Free: 866-952-3444
editors@canadashistory.ca
www.canadashistory.ca
Social Media: www.youtube.com/canadashistory
twitter.com/canadashistory
www.faceb ook.com/CanadasHistory
Frequency: 6 times a year
Janet Walker, President/CEO, jwalker@canadashistory.ca

Family Chronicle
Owned By: Moorshead Magazines Ltd.
#312, 505 Consumers Rd., Toronto, ON M2J 4V8
Tel: 416-491-3699; *Fax:* 416-491-3996
Toll-Free: 888-326-2476
admin@familychronicle.com
www.familychronicle.com
Social Media:
www.facebook.com/117640134975204
Frequency: 6 times a year
Edward Zapletal, Editor & Publisher, edward@moorshead.com

Heritage Canada Foundation
190 Bronson Ave., Ottawa, ON K1R 6H4
Tel: 613-237-1066; *Fax:* 613-237-5987
Toll-Free: 866-964-1066
heritagecanada@heritagecanada.org
www.heritagecanada.org
Social Media:
twitter.com/HeritageCanada
www.facebook.com/heritagecanadafoundation?.ref=hl
Frequency: 4 times a year
Membership-based, non-profit organization & registered charity for the conservation & rehabilitation of heritage buildings.
Natalie Bull, Executive Director, 613-237-1066, nbull@heritagecanada.org
Carolyn Quinn, Communications Director, Communications, 613-237-1066, cquinn@heritagecanada.org

The Loyalist Gazette
R.R. #1, Indian River, ON K0L 2B0
Tel: 416-591-1783; *Fax:* 416-591-7506
www.uelac.org
Social Media:
twitter.com/#!/uelac
www.facebook.com/UELAC
Circulation: 2,500
Frequency: 2 times a year
Robert McBride, Editor

OHS Bulletin
Owned By: The Ontario Historical Society
John McKenzie House, 34 Parkview Ave., Toronto, ON M2N 3Y2
Tel: 416-226-9011; *Fax:* 416-226-2740
Toll-Free: 866-955-2755
ohs@ontariohistoricalsociety.ca
www.ontariohistoricalsociety.ca
Social Media:
www.twitter.com/OntarioHistory
www.facebook.com/OntarioHistoricalSociety?fref=ts
Circulation: 2,500
Frequency: 5 times a year
Sheila Creighton, Editor
Patricia K. Neal, Executive Director

Hobbies

The Canadian Amateur Magazine
c/o Radio Amateurs of Canada, #217, 720 Belfast Rd., Ottawa, ON K1G 0Z5
Tel: 613-244-4367; *Fax:* 613-244-4369
Toll-Free: 877-273-8304
rachq@rac.ca
wp.rac.ca/p155
Circulation: 7,200
Frequency: 6 times a year

Canadian Coin News
Owned By: Trajan Publishing Corp.
PO Box 28103 Lakeport, 600 Ontario St., St. Catharines, ON L2N 7P8
Tel: 905-646-7744; *Fax:* 905-646-0995
Toll-Free: 800-408-0352
www.canadiancoinnews.com
Social Media:
twitter.com/trajanpublisher
www.facebook.com/CanadianCoinNews
Circulation: 8,500
Frequency: 26 times a year
Bret Evans, Managing Editor & Associate Publisher
Hans Niedermair, News Editor

Canadian Railway Modeller
Owned By: North Kildonan Publications
c/o North Kildonan Publications, PO Box 35087 Henderson, 963 Henderson Hwy., Winnipeg, MB R2K 4J9
Tel: 204-668-0168; *Fax:* 204-669-9821
www.cdnrwymod.com
Circulation: 25,000
Frequency: 6 times a year
Morgan B. Turney, Editor
John Longhurst, Editor

Canadian Stamp News
Owned By: Trajan Publishing Corp.
PO Box 28103 Lakeport, 600 Ontario St., St. Catherines, ON L2N 7P8
Tel: 905-646-7744; *Fax:* 905-646-0995
Toll-Free: 800-408-0352
www.canadianstampnews.ca
Social Media:
twitter.com/trajanpublisher
www.facebook.com/pages/Canadian-Stamp-News/1
4319926903874
Circulation: 5,000
Frequency: 26 times a year

Comics & Games Monthly
Also Known As: C&G Monthly
#332, 1655 Dupont St., Toronto, ON M6P 3T1
media@cgmagazine.ca
cgmonthly.com
Social Media:
www.twitter.com/cgmonthly
www.facebook.com/ComicsGamingmagazine
Frequency: Monthly
Brendan Frye, Editor-in-Chief, bfrye@cgmagazine.ca

Metalcraft
345 Munster Ave., Toronto, ON M8Z 3C6
Tel: 416-232-0330; *Fax:* 416-234-1516
info@metalcraftmag.com
www.metalcraftmag.com
Frequency: 4 times a year
Nestor Gula, Editor

Model Aviation Canada
Also Known As: MAC Mag
Owned By: Morison Communications
2220 - 25th Ave. NW, Calgary, AB T2M 2C1
Tel: 403-510-5689
adsales@modelaviation.ca
www.maac.ca/en/magazine.php
Social Media:
twitter.com/MAACCanada
www.facebook.com/1502378183363886
Circulation: 12,600
Frequency: 6 times a year
Official publication of the Model Aeronautics Association of Canada.
Keith Morison, Publisher & Editor

Philatélie Québec
275, rue Bryant, Sherbrooke, QC J1J 3E6
editions_ddr@videotron.ca
www.philateliequebec.com
Tirage: 1 500
Fréquence: 6 fois par an
Guy Desrosiers, Rédacteur en chef

Quilter's Connection
Previous Name: Connections for Quilters Newsletter
PO Box 41165 Shaughnessy, Port Coquitlam, BC V3C 5Z9
Tel: 604-290-3454; *Fax:* 604-540-2231
info@quiltersconnection.ca
quiltersconnection.ca
Social Media:
www.twitter.com/QltrsConnection
www.facebook.com/QuiltersConnectio nMagazine
Frequency: Quarterly

Railfan Canada
North Kildonan Publications
PO Box 35087 Henderson, 963 Henderson Hwy, Winnipeg, MB R2K 4J9
Tel: 204-668-0168; *Fax:* 204-669-9821
editor@railfancanada.ca
www.railfancanada.ca
Frequency: Monthly
Railroad photography.

Homes

Canadian Living
Owned By: TVA Publications inc.
c/o TVA Publications, 1010 Sérigny St., Longueuil, QC J4K 5G7
Tel: 514-848-7000
letters@canadianliving.com
www.canadianliving.com
Social Media:
twitter.com/canadianliving
www.facebook.com/canadianliving
Circulation: 533,370
Frequency: 12 times a year
Debbie Gibson, Publisher

Chez Soi
Anciennement: Décoration Chez-Soi
Détenteur: TVA Publications inc.
c/o TVA Publications, 1010, rue de Sérigny, 4e étage, Longueuil, QC J4K 5G7
Tél: 514-848-9854
www.casatv.ca/publications/chez-soi-accueil
Médias sociaux: www.pinterest.com/magazinechezsoi
twitter.com/#!/chez_soi
www.facebook .com/magazineCHEZSOI
Tirage: 576 000
Fréquence: 10 fois par an

Condo Life Magazine
178 Main St., Unionville, ON L3R 2G9
Tel: 905-479-4663 *Toll-Free:* 800-363-4663
info@homesmag.com
www.condolifemag.com
Circulation: 140,000
Michael Rosset, Publisher
Toni Pettit, Editor

Cottage Life
Owned By: Cottage Life Media
54 St. Patrick St., Toronto, ON M5T 1V1
Tel: 416-599-2000; *Fax:* 416-599-0800
Toll-Free: 877-874-5253
letters@cottagelife.com
cottagelife.com
Social Media: youtube.com/CottageLifeMagazine
twitter.com/CottageLifeMag
www.face book.com/cottagelife
Circulation: 70,000
Frequency: 6 times a year
Penny Caldwell, Editor

Cottage Life West
Owned By: Cottage Life Media
54 St. Patrick St., Toronto, ON M5T 1V1
Tel: 416-559-9200; *Fax:* 416-599-0800
edit@cottagelife.com
www.cottagemagazine.com
Social Media: pinterest.com/cottagelife/
twitter.com/cottagelife
www.facebook.com/co ttagelife
Circulation: 13,195
Frequency: 6 times a year
Mark Yelic, Publisher
Anita Willis, Editor, 250-384-5077, awillis@cottagelife.com

The Cottager
PO Box 40, Victoria Beach, MB R0E 2C0
Tel: 204-756-8381; *Fax:* 204-756-2662
editor@thecottager.com
www.thecottager.com
Social Media:
www.facebook.com/pages/The-Cottager/137410736323877
Circulation: 10,000
Frequency: 5 times a year
Glenn Halgren
Cathy Halgren, Circulation

Del Condominium Life
4800 Dufferin St., Toronto, ON M3H 5S9
Tel: 416-661-3151
www.delpropertymanagement.com/condo_life.php
Circulation: 32,500
Frequency: 3 times a year
Patricia MacKellar, Editor/Production Manager

Designer Showcase
Owned By: Metro Guide Publishing
1300 Hollis St., Halifax, NS B3J 1T6
Tel: 902-420-9943; *Fax:* 902-429-9058
jgillard@metroguide.ca
www.metroguide.ca
Circulation: 8,000
Patty Baxter, Publisher, 902-420-9943 ext 231, publishers@metroguide.ca
Dana Edgar, Production Coordinator, 902-420-9943 ext 247, dedgar@metroguide.ca

East Coast Living
Owned By: Metro Guide Publishing
1300 Hollis St., Halifax, NS 3J 1T6
Tel: 902-420-9943; *Fax:* 902-429-9058
publishers@metroguide.ca
www.metroguide.ca
Circulation: 34,100
Frequency: 2 times a year
Trevor Adams, Managing Editor, 902-420-9943 ext 229, tadams@metroguide.ca
Janice Hudson, Editor, 902-420-9943 ext 221, jhudson@metroguide.ca
Patty Baxter, Publisher, 902-420-9943 ext 231, publishers@metroguide.ca
Dana Edgar, Production Coordinator, 902-420-9943 ext 231, dedgar@metroguide.ca

Home Digest
1416 Stonehampton Ct., Pickering, ON L1V 7C9
Tel: 905-509-9900 *Toll-Free:* 855-550-5577
home_digest@rogers.com
www.homedigest.ca
Social Media: www.onlinehomedigest.com
twitter.com/Home_Digestmag
www.facebook.com/H omeDigestmag
Circulation: 700,000
Frequency: 4 times a year
Barry Holmes, Publisher
William Roebuck, Editor

Homes & Cottages
Previous Name: Homes & Cottages
#4, 2650 Meadowvale Blvd., Mississauga, ON L5N 6M5
Tel: 905-567-1440; *Fax:* 905-567-1442
www.homesandcottages.com
Circulation: 79,099
Frequency: 6 times a year
Steven Griffin, Publisher, sgriffin@homesandcottages.com
Janice Naisby, Editor-in-chief, jnaisby@homesandcottages.com

Homes Magazine
Owned By: Homes Publishing Group
#404, 37 Sandiford Dr., Stouffville, ON L4A 7X5
Tel: 905-479-4663; *Fax:* 905-479-4482
Toll-Free: 800-363-4663
info@homesmag.com
www.homesmag.com
Social Media:
twitter.com/HOMESPublishing
www.facebook.com/pages/homesmagcom/122876181095771?ref=ts
Circulation: 100,000
Frequency: 9 times a year
Michael Rosset, Publisher
Gale Beeby, Editor

House & Home
Owned By: House & Home Media
#120, 511 King St. West, Toronto, ON M5V 2Z4
Tel: 416-591-1630; *Fax:* 416-591-1630
Toll-Free: 800-559-8868
www.canadianhouseandhome.com
Social Media: www.pinterest.com/houseandhome
twitter.com/HouseandHome
www.facebook.c om/houseandhomemagazine
Circulation: 249,124
Frequency: 10 times a year
Lynda Reeves, Publisher
Suzanne Dimma, Editor

Les idées de ma maison
Détenteur: TVA Publications inc.
1010, rue de Sérigny, 4e étage, Longueuil, QC J4K 5G7
Ligne sans frais: 888-535-8634
abomag@tva.ca
www.casatv.ca/publications/les-idees-de-ma-maison-accueil
Médias sociaux:
twitter.com/Mag_IdeesMaison
www.facebook.com/Lesideesdemamaison
Tirage: 65 493
Fréquence: 10 fois par an

Maison d'Aujourd'hui
3390, boul Crémazie est, Montréal, QC H2A 1A4
Tél: 514-729-0000; *Téléc:* 514-729-2552
courriel@maisonmax.com
www.maisonaujourdhui.com
Tirage: 50 000
Fréquence: semi-annuel
Phillippe Massé, Président

Montreal Home
#367, 4020 St. Ambroise St., Montréal, QC H4C 2C7
Toll-Free: 855-410-4663
info@movatohome.com
www.movatohome.com/montreal-home

Planimage Magazines
Anciennement: Over 500 Home Plans
#105, 1501, rue Ampere, Boucherville, QC J4B 5Z5
Tél: 450-641-7526; *Téléc:* 450-641-6688
Ligne sans frais: 800-752-6744
contact@planimage.com
www.planimage.com
Médias sociaux: www.planimage.com/blog
twitter.com/planimage
www.facebook.com/Planimage
Tirage: 30 000
Fréquence: 6 times a year
Daniel Therrien, Président, daniel.therrien@planimage.com

Proven & Popular Home Plans
Owned By: Giroux Publishing
Tel: 250-493-0942 *Toll-Free:* 800-361-7526
plan@westhomeplanners.com
www.westhomeplanners.com
Social Media: pinterest.com/westhomeplans
twitter.com/WesthomePlans
www.facebook.com/westhomeplannersltd
Circulation: 10,000
Frequency: Annually

Real Estate Victoria
818 Broughton St., Victoria, BC V8W 1E4
Tel: 250-381-9171; *Fax:* 250-381-9172
rev@revweekly.com
www.revweekly.com
Circulation: 72,000
Frequency: Weekly, Friday

Renovation & Decor Magazine
Also Known As: Reno & Decor
Owned By: Homes Publishing Group
178 Main St., Unionville, ON L3R 2G9
Tel: 905-479-4663 *Toll-Free:* 800-363-4663
info@renoanddecor.com
renoanddecor.com
Social Media:
twitter.com/HOMESPublishing
www.facebook.com/pages/renoanddecorcom/153184468041814?re
Circulation: 75,000
Catherine Daley, Publisher, cdaley.homes@gmail.com

Rénovation Bricolage
Détenteur: TVA Publications inc.
1010, rue de Sérigny, Longueuil, QC J4K 5G7
Tél: 514-848-7000 *Ligne sans frais:* 800-528-3836
renobrico@tvapublications.com
www.casatv.ca/publications/renovation-bric olage-accueil
Médias sociaux:
twitter.com/mag_renobrico
www.facebook.com/RenovationBricolage
Tirage: 33 270
Fréquence: 9 fois par an

Renovation Contractor
Owned By: The Caruk Media Group
#404, 37 Sandiford Dr., Souffville, ON L7L 6W6
Tel: 647-367-0073; *Fax:* 289-997-8260
www.renocontractor.ca
Social Media: www.linkedin.com/company/1968664
www.facebook.com/renocontractor.ca
Serves small- and medium-sized home renovators.
Jim Caruk, Editor-in-Chief, jim@renocontractor.ca
Allan Britnell, Managing Editor, allan@renocontractor.ca

Style at Home
Previous Name: Canadian Select Homes
Owned By: TVA Publications inc.
c/o TVA Publications, 1010, rue de Sérigny, Longueuil, QC J4K 5G7
Tel: 514-848-7000 *Toll-Free:* 800-528-3836
letters@styleathome.com
www.styleathome.com
Social Media: www.youtube.com/user/StyleAtHomeMagazine
twitter.com/StyleAtHome
www.f acebook.com/styleathome
Circulation: 235,000
Frequency: Monthly

Toronto Home
Owned By: MOVATO Home
#1801, 1 Yonge St., Toronto, ON M5E 1W7
Toll-Free: 855-335-7745
info@torontohomemag.com
www.torontohomemag.com

Horses, Riding & Breeding

Atlantic Horse & Pony
NS
dvlporduction@eastlink.ca
www.atlantichorseandpony.com
Social Media:
www.facebook.com/AHP.mag
Frequency: Bi-monthly
Bi-monthly publications of breeding, care, feeding, nutrition, stable management, shows & other information on horses

Canadian Arabian Horse News
Previous Name: Canadian Arabian News
#113, 37 Athabascan Ave., Sherwood Park, AB T8A 4H3
Tel: 780-416-4990; *Fax:* 780-416-4860
editor@cahr.ca
canadianarabian.com
Social Media:
twitter.com/canadianarabian
www.facebook.com/CanadianArabian
Circulation: 2,200
Frequency: 4 times a year
Official publication of the Canadian Arabian Horse Registry.
Nicole Toren, Editor, editor@cahr.ca

Canadian Horse Annual
Owned By: Horse Publications Group
PO Box 670, Aurora, ON L4G 4J9
Tel: 905-727-0107; *Fax:* 905-841-1530
Toll-Free: 800-505-7428
info@horse-canada.com
www.horse-canada.com/canadian-ho rse-annual
Frequency: Annually

Canadian Horse Journal - Central & Atlantic Edition
Previous Name: Pacific Horse Journal
PO Box 2190, #201, 2400 Bevan Ave., Sidney, BC V8L 1W1
Tel: 250-655-8883; *Fax:* 250-655-8913
Toll-Free: 800-299-3799
editor@horsejournals.com
www.horsejournals.com
Social Media:
www.linkedin.com/company/horse-community-journals
twitter.com/HORSEJournals
www.facebook.com/CanadianHorseJournal
Circulation: 20,000
Frequency: 12 times a year
ON to Maritimes, plus ON Equestrian Federation News

Canadian Horse Journal - Pacific & Prairie Edition
Horse Community Journals
Previous Name: Pacific Horse Journal
PO Box 2190, #201, 2400 Bevan Ave., Sidney, BC V8L 1W1
Tel: 250-655-8883; *Fax:* 250-655-8913
Toll-Free: 800-299-3799
news@horsejournals.com
www.horsejournals.com
Social Media:
www.linkedin.com/company/horse-community-journals
twitter.com/HORSEJournals
www.facebook.com/CanadianHorseJournal
Circulation: 20,000
Frequency: 12 times a year
BC to MB, plus Horse Council BC Newsletter
Kathy Smith, Publisher/Editor

Canadian Thoroughbred
Owned By: Horse Publications Group
c/o Horse Publications Group, PO Box 670, Aurora, ON L4G 4J9
Tel: 905-727-0107; *Fax:* 905-841-1530
Toll-Free: 800-505-7428
www.horse-canada.com/canadian-thoroughbred
Circulation: 4,500
Frequency: 6 times a year
Dave Briggs, Managing Editor, dbriggs1969@gmail.com
Chris Lomon, Managing Editor, chris.m.lomon@gmail.com

Courrier Hippique
CP 1000 M, 4545, av Pierre-de-Coubertin, Montréal, QC H1V 3R2
Tél: 514-252-3030; *Téléc:* 514-252-3165
courrier@hippique.qc.ca
www.hippique.qc.ca
Médias sociaux:
www.facebook.com/pages/Courrier-Hippique/312091372180708
Tirage: 7 000
Fréquence: 6 times a year
Nathalie Laberge, Rédactrice-en-chef, redaction@hippique.qc.ca

Horse Canada
Previous Name: Canadian Horseman
Owned By: Horse Publications Group
c/o Horse Publications Group, PO Box 670, Aurora, ON L4G 4J9
Tel: 905-727-0107; *Fax:* 905-841-1530
Toll-Free: 800-505-7428
hceditor@horse-canada.com
www.horse-canada.com
Social Media:
twitter.com/HorseCanada
www.facebook.com/HorseCanadaMagazine
Circulation: 17,000
Frequency: 6 times a year
Amy Harris, Managing Editor, hceditor@horse-canada.com

Horse Country
#203, 23 - 845 Dakota St., Winnipeg, MB R2M 5M3
Tel: 204-256-7467; *Fax:* 204-257-2467
contact@horsecountry.ca
www.horsecountry.ca
Social Media:
www.facebook.com/pages/Horse-Country/140013221802?ref=ts
Circulation: 12,000
Frequency: 8 times a year
Linda Hazelwood, Publisher & Editor

Horse Sport
Owned By: Horse Publications Group
PO Box 670, Aurora, ON L4G 4J9
Tel: 905-727-0107; *Fax:* 905-841-1530
Toll-Free: 800-505-7428
info@horse-canada.com
www.horse-canada.com/horse-sport
Social Media:
twitter.com/horsesport_mag
www.facebook.com/HorseSport

Circulation: 10,000
Frequency: 12 times a year
Jennifer Anstey, Publisher, janstey@horse-canada.com
Susan Stafford, Editor, editor@horse-canada.com

Horsepower
Owned By: Horse Publications Group
c/o Horse Publications Group, PO Box 670, Aurora, ON L4G 4J9
Tel: 905-727-0107; *Fax:* 905-841-1530
Toll-Free: 800-505-7428
fearless.editor@gmail.com
www.horse-canada.com/horsepower
Circulation: 16,000
Frequency: 6 times a year
Published as a special pull-out in Horse Canada Magazine.
Jennifer Anstey, Publisher, janstey@horse-canada.com
Susan Stafford, Editor, fearless.editor@gmail.com

Racing Quarterly
Owned By: Horse Publications Group
PO Box 670, Aurora, ON L4G 4J9
Tel: 905-727-0107; *Fax:* 905-841-1530
Toll-Free: 800-505-7428
info@horse-canada.com
www.horse-canada.com/racing-quar terly
Frequency: 4 times a year
Lee Benson, Editor, lbenson@xplornet.com

The Rider
Previous Name: The Canadian Western Rider
PO Box 10072, 27 Legend Crt., Ancaster, ON L9K 1P2
Tel: 905-387-1900 *Toll-Free:* 877-743-3715
barry@therider.com
www.therider.com
Circulation: 7,000
Frequency: Monthly
Barry Finn, Publisher

Trot
c/o Standardbred Canada, 2150 Meadowvale Blvd., Mississauga, ON L5N 6R6
Tel: 905-858-3060
www.standardbredcanada.ca/trot
Frequency: Monthly

Interior Design & Decor

Designedge Canada
Owned By: C.J. Oyster Publishing Inc.
60 Horner Ave., Toronto, ON M8Z 4X3
Tel: 416-588-0809
designedgecanada.com
Social Media:
twitter.com/Designedgemag
www.facebook.com/DesignEdgeCanada
Frequency: 6 times per year
Leslie Smith, Publisher, 416-588-0809 ext.226
Jef Catapang, Editor, 416-588-6688

Homefront
#803, 255 Duncan Mill Rd., Toronto, ON M3B 3H9
Tel: 416-421-7944; *Fax:* 416-421-8418
Toll-Free: 800-798-6282
www.homefrontmagazine.ca
Circulation: 35,000
Frequency: 4 times a year
Helmut Dostal, Publisher
Caroline Tapp-McDougall, Editor-in-Chief

Ideal Home
Owned By: Premier Publications and Shows
c/o Premier Publications and Shows, #4, 447 Speers Rd., Oakville, ON L6K 3S7
Tel: 905-842-6591 *Toll-Free:* 800-693-7986
premierpublicationsandshows.com
Information about new homes, interior design and landscaping ideas.

Kingston Life Interiors
Owned By: Sun Media Corporation
Kingston Publications, 18 St. Remy Pl., Kingston, ON K7K 6C4
Tel: 613-389-7400; *Fax:* 613-389-7507
www.kingstonpublications.com/kingstonlifeinteriors.html
Circulation: 11,000
Frequency: Annually, April
Kingston Life Interiors is delivered by controlled circulation through The Kingston Whig-Standard, sent to subscribers and sold at selected newsstands in Kingston, Ottawa, Toronto and Montreal.

Plaisirs de Vivre/Living in Style
Previous Name: Résidences
#208, 1600, rue Notre-Dame ouest, Montréal, QC H3J 1M1
Tel: 514-982-9823; *Fax:* 514-289-9160
pdv@prestipresse.com
plaisirsdevivre.info
Circulation: 70,198
Frequency: 6 times a year
Peter Weiss, Publisher
André Ducharme, Editor in Chief

Labour, Trade Unions

Our Times
Owned By: Our Times Publishing Inc.
#407, 15 Gervais Dr., Toronto, ON M3C 1Y8
Tel: 416-703-7661; *Fax:* 416-703-9094
Toll-Free: 800-648-6131
office@ourtimes.ca
www.ourtimes.ca
Social Media:
twitter.com/OurTimesMag
www.facebook.com/ourtimesmagazine
Circulation: 8,000
Frequency: 6 times a year
Independent labour magazine.
Lorraine Endicott, Editor

Socialist Worker
PO Box 339 E, Toronto, ON M6H 4E3
Tel: 416-972-6391; *Fax:* 416-972-6319
sworker@sympatico.ca
www.socialist.ca
Social Media:
twitter.com/socialist_ca
www.facebook.com/socialist.ca
Circulation: 2,000
Frequency: 24 times a year
Paul Kellogg, Editor

LGBTQ

Index: Gay & Lesbian Business Directory
Owned By: Pink Triangle Press
#1600, 2 Carlton St., Toronto, ON M5B 1J3
Tel: 416-925-5221; *Fax:* 416-925-4817
index@xtra.ca
Circulation: 34,000
Frequency: Annually
Directories for Vancouver, Toronto and Ottawa.

Perceptions
PO Box 8581, Saskatoon, SK S7K 6K7
Tel: 306-244-1930; *Fax:* 306-665-1280
perceptions@shaw.ca
Circulation: 1,500
Gens Hellquist, Publisher

Literary

The Antigonish Review
PO Box 5000, Antigonish, NS B2G 2W5
Tel: 902-867-3962; *Fax:* 902-867-5563
tar@stfx.ca
www.antigonishreview.com
Social Media:
twitter.com/#!/antigonishrevie
www.facebook.com/332083480162513
Circulation: 900
Frequency: 4 times a year
Gerald Trites, Managing Editor

Arc Poetry Magazine
PO Box 81060, Ottawa, ON K1P 1B1
Tel: 613-729-3550
arc@arcpoetry.ca
www.arcpoetry.ca
Social Media: www.youtube.com/user/ArcPoetry
twitter.com/arcpoetry
www.facebook.com/ 131264640283363
Circulation: 1,200
Frequency: 2 times a year
Monty Reid, Managing Editor

Brick: A Literary Journal
PO Box 600 P, Toronto, ON M5S 2Y4
Tel: 416-593-9684
info@brickmag.com
www.brickmag.com
Social Media:
twitter.com/BrickMAG
www.facebook.com/brickmagazine
Circulation: 2,200
Frequency: 2 times a year
Publishers of non-fiction literary pieces
Nadia Szilvassy, Publisher & Managing Editor

Canadian Notes & Queries
PO Box 92, Emerville, ON N0R 1A0
Tel: 519-968-2206; *Fax:* 519-250-5713
info@notesandqueries.ca
notesandqueries.ca
Circulation: 500
Frequency: 2 times a year
Tim Inkster, Publisher
John Metcalf, Editor

The Capilano Review
c/o The Arts Factory, 281 Industrial Ave., Vancouver, BC V6A 2P2
Tel: 604-984-1712
info@thecapilanoreview.ca
www.thecapilanoreview.ca
Circulation: 900
Frequency: 3 times a year
Andrea Actis, Editor

the Claremont Review
#101, 1581-H Hillside Ave., Victoria, BC V8T 2C1
Tel: 250-658-5221; *Fax:* 250-658-5387
lmoran@telus.net
www.theclaremontreview.ca
Social Media:
www.twitter.com/tCRArtsMag
www.facebook.com/TheClaremontReview
Circulation: 1,000
Frequency: 2 times a year
Jody Carrow, Editor in chief

Contemporary Verse 2
Also Known As: CV2
#502, 100 Arthur St., Winnipeg, MB R3B 1H3
Tel: 204-949-1365; *Fax:* 204-942-1555
editor@contemporaryverse2.ca
www.contemporaryverse2.ca
Circulation: 650
Frequency: 4 times a year
Clarise Foster, Editor

ELQ Magazine
Also Known As: Exile: The Literary Quarterly
144483 Southgate Rd. - General Delivery, Holstein, ON N0G 2A0
Tel: 416-485-4885
exq@exilequarterly.com
www.exilequarterly.com
Frequency: Quarterly
Michael Callaghan, Publisher
Barry Callaghan, Editor-in-chief

The Fiddlehead
Owned By: University of New Brunswick
Campus House, University of New Brunswick, PO Box 4400 A, 11 Garland Ct., Fredericton, NB E3B 5A3
Tel: 506-453-3501
fiddlehd@unb.ca
www.thefiddlehead.ca
Social Media:
www.facebook.com/174825212565312
Circulation: 1,000
Frequency: 4 times a year
Ross Leckie, Editor

Geist
Owned By: The Geist Foundation
#210, 111 West Hastings St., Vancouver, BC V6B 1H4
Tel: 604-681-9161; *Fax:* 604-677-6319
Toll-Free: 888-434-7834
editor@geist.com, letters@geist.com
www.geist.com
Social Media:
twitter.com/geistmagazine
www.facebook.com/geist.mag
Circulation: 8,000
Frequency: 4 times a year
Stephen Osborne, Editor, editor@geist.com

Grain
PO Box 67, Saskatoon, SK S7K 3K1
Tel: 306-244-2828; *Fax:* 306-244-0255
grainmag@sasktel.net
www.grainmagazine.ca
Social Media:
twitter.com/grainlitmag
www.facebook.com/189449391085557

Circulation: 1,700
Frequency: 4 times a year
Journal of eclectic writing
Rilla Friesen, Editor, 306-224-2828, grainmag@sasktel.net
Sarah Taggart, Business Administrator, 306-244-2828, grainmag@sasktel.net

Little Brother
Toronto, ON
info@littlebrothermagazine.com
littlebrothermagazine.com
Social Media:
twitter.com/yourlb
www.facebook.com/littlebrothermagazine
Frequency: 4 issues per year
Collection of essays and short stories.
Emily M. Keeler, Editor

The Malahat Review
University of Victoria, PO Box 1700 CSC, 3800 Finnerty Road (Ring Road), D262, Victoria, BC V8W 2Y2
Tel: 250-721-8524; *Fax:* 250-472-5051
malahat@uvic.ca
www.malahatreview.ca
Social Media:
twitter.com/malahatreview
www.facebook.com/pages/The-Malahat-Review/1547 05264550
Circulation: 1,300
Frequency: 4 times a year
John Barton, Editor, malahat@uvic.ca
Rhonda Batchelor, Assistant Editor, malahat@uvic.ca

Matrix Magazine
1455 de Maisonneuve Blvd. West, Montréal, QC H3G 1M8
Tel: 514-848-2424
info@matrixmagazine.org
www.matrixmagazine.org
Social Media:
twitter.com/matrixmagazine
www.facebook.com/279322025424646
Circulation: 1,500
Frequency: 4 times a year
Jon Paul Fiorentino, Editor

The New Quarterly
c/o St. Jerome's University, 290 Westmount Rd. North, Waterloo, ON N2L 3G3
Tel: 519-884-8111; *Fax:* 519-884-5759
info@tnq.ca
www.tnq.ca
Circulation: 1,000
Frequency: 4 times a year
Covers Canadian writers & writing
Pamela Mulloy, Editor, editor@tnq.ca

Nuit blanche
Also Known As: Le magazine du livre
#403, 1026, rue Saint-Jean, Québec, QC G1R 1R7
Tél: 418-692-1354; *Téléc:* 418-692-1355
nuitblanche@nuitblanche.com
www.nuitblanche.com
Médias sociaux:
twitter.com/nuitblanchemag
www.facebook.com/NuitBlancheMag
Fréquence: 4 fois par an
Alain Lessard, Rédacteur en chef

ON SPEC Magazine
PO Box 4727, Edmonton, AB T6E 5G6
Tel: 780-413-0215; *Fax:* 780-413-1538
onspec@onspec.ca
onspecmag.wordpress.com
Social Media:
www.twitter.com/onspecmagazine
www.facebook.com/groups/2395098260
Circulation: 2,000
Frequency: 4 times a year
Diane Walton, Managing Editor

paperplates
19 Kenwood Ave., Toronto, ON M6C 2R8
Tel: 416-651-2551; *Fax:* 416-651-2910
magazine@paperplates.org
www.paperplates.org
Frequency: 4 issues a year
Bernard Kelly, Publisher & Editor

Prairie Fire
Owned By: Prairie Fire Press, Inc.
c/o Prairie Fire Press, Inc., #423, 100 Arthur St., Winnipeg, MB R3B 1H3
Tel: 204-943-9066; *Fax:* 204-942-1555
prfire@prairiefire.ca
www.prairiefire.ca
Social Media:
twitter.com/PraireFirePress
Circulation: 1,500
Frequency: 4 times a year
Features new Canadian writing.
Andris Taskans, Editor
Heidi Harms, Associate Editor

The Prairie Journal
c/o Prairie Journal Trust, PO Box 68073, 28 Crawford Terrace NW, Calgary, AB T3G 3N8
prairiejournal@yahoo.com
www.prairiejournal.org
Circulation: 750
Frequency: 2 times a year
Anne Burke, Literary Editor

Prism international
c/o Creative Writing Program, UBC, 1866 Main Mall, Buchanan Bldg. #E462, Vancouver, BC V6T 1Z1
Tel: 604-822-2514; *Fax:* 604-822-3616
circulation@prismmagazine.ca
prismmagazine.ca
Social Media:
www.facebook.com/prism.mag.5
Circulation: 1,200
Frequency: 4 times a year
Jen Macdonald, Circulation, circulation@prismmagazine.ca

Rampike Magazine
c/o Dept. of English, University of Windsor, 401 Sunset Ave., Windsor, ON N9B 3P4
Tel: 519-253-3000; *Fax:* 519-971-3676
jirgins@uwindsor.ca
web4.uwindsor.ca/rampike
Circulation: 4,000
Frequency: 2 times a year
Karl E. Jirgins, Editor/Publisher

subTerrain Magazine
PO Box MPO 3008, Vancouver, BC V6B 3X5
Tel: 604-876-8710; *Fax:* 604-879-2667
subter@portal.ca
www.subterrain.ca
Social Media:
twitter.com/subterrain
www.facebook.com/subTerrain
Circulation: 3,500
Frequency: 3 issues a year
Brian Kaufman, Editor

West Coast Line
Owned By: West Coast Review Publishing Society
West Coast Review Publishing Society, Simon Fraser University, 6079 Academic Quadrangle, 8888 University Dr., Burnaby, BC V5A 1S6
Tel: 778-782-4988; *Fax:* 778-782-5737
wcl@sfu.ca
www.westcoastline.ca/blog
Circulation: 800
Frequency: 3 times a year
Michael Barnholden, Managing Editor

White Wall Review
c/o Department of English, Jorgenson Hall, 350 Victoria St., 10th Fl., Toronto, ON M5B 2K3
Tel: 416-977-9924; *Fax:* 416-977-7709
aleeloy@arts.ryerson.ca
whitewallreview.blog.ryerson.ca
Anne Marie Lee-Loy

Men's

Highrise Magazine
info@highrisemag.com
www.highrisemag.com
Frequency: 4 times a year
Cynthia Cully, Editor-in-chief

Sharp Magazine
Owned By: Contempo Media Inc.
#111, 372 Richmond St. West, Toronto, ON M5V 1X6
Tel: 416-591-0093
webadmin@contempomedia.com
sharpmagazine.com
Social Media: www.linkedin.com/company/1729850
www.twitter.com/sharpmagazine
www.fac ebook.com/Sharpformen
Frequency: Bi-Monthly
Greg Hudson, Editor-in-Chief, greg.hudson@contempomedia.com

Military

Esprit de Corps
#204, 1066 Somerset St. West, Ottawa, ON K1Y 4T3
Tel: 613-725-5060; *Fax:* 613-725-1019
Toll-Free: 800-361-2791
espritdecorp@idirect.com
www.espritdecorps.ca
Circulation: 15,000
Scott Taylor, Publisher

Mining

Canadian Mining Magazine
Owned By: Matrix Group Publishing Inc.
#300, 52 Donald St., Winnipeg, MB R3C 1L6
Fax: 866-244-2544
Toll-Free: 866-999-1299
canadianminingmagazine.com
Social Media:
twitter.com/cminingmagazine
www.facebook.com/CanadianMiningMagazine
Frequency: Quarterly
Maurice LaBorde, Publisher, mlaborde@matrixgroupinc.ne
Shannon Savory, Editor-in-Chief, ssavory@matrixgroupinc.net

Music

Canadian Musician
Owned By: Norris-Whitney Communications Inc.
#202, 4056 Dorchester Rd., Niagara Falls, ON L2E 6M9
Tel: 905-374-8878; *Fax:* 888-665-1307
mail@nor.com
www.canadianmusician.com
Social Media: pinterest.com/cdnmusician/
twitter.com/cdnmusician
www.facebook.com/cd nmusician
Circulation: 27,000
Frequency: 6 times a year
Jim Norris, Publisher

Crescendo
Owned By: Toronto Musicians' Association
c/o Toronto Musicians' Association, #500, 15 Gervais Dr., Toronto, ON M3C 1Y8
Tel: 416-421-1020; *Fax:* 416-421-7011
info@tma149.ca
www.torontomusicians.org
Circulation: 4,000
Frequency: 3 times a year
Richard Sandals, Publisher, 416-461-6892

Exclaim!
849A Bloor St. W., Toronto, ON M6G 1M3
Tel: 416-535-9735; *Fax:* 416-535-0566
exclaim@exclaim.ca
www.exclaim.ca
Social Media:
twitter.com/exclaimdotca
www.facebook.com/exclaimdotca
Circulation: 100,000
Frequency: 11 times a year
Coverage of new music across all genres.
Ian Danzig, Publisher, ian@exclaim.ca

Musicworks magazine
Owned By: Musicworks Society of Ontario, Inc.
#358, 401 Richmond St. West, Toronto, ON M5V 3A8
Tel: 416-977-3546
sound@musicworks.ca
www.musicworks.ca
Social Media: www.youtube.com/user/musicworksmagazine1
twitter.com/MusicworksMag
www .facebook.com/MusicworksMagazine
Circulation: 3,000
Frequency: 3 times a year
Musicworks is dedicated to contemporary experimental music. Each issue includes a CD featuring music by artists appearing in the magazine.
Gayle Young, Publisher, gayle@musicworks.ca

Jennie Punter, Editor, editor@musicworks.ca

Opera Canada
#244, 366 Adelaide St. East, Toronto, ON M5A 3X9
Tel: 416-363-0395 *Toll-Free:* 800-222-5097
editorial@operacanada.ca
operacanada.ca
Circulation: 5,575
Frequency: 4 times a year
Wayne Gooding, Editor

La Scena Musicale / The Music Scene
5409, rue Waverly, Montréal, QC H2T 2X8
Tel: 514-948-2520
info@scena.org
www.scena.org
Social Media:
twitter.com/lascena
www.facebook.com/groups/4470026401/
Circulation: 42,000
Wah Keung Chan, Éditeur & Rédacteur-en-chef, wkchan@lascena.org

TRIBE Magazine
358 Danforth Ave., Toronto, ON M4K 3Z2
Tel: 416-778-4115; *Fax:* 416-405-9473
editor@tribe.ca
www.tribemagazine.com
Circulation: 35,000
Frequency: 10 times a year
Alex Dordevic, Publisher/Editor

The WholeNote
#503, 720 Bathurst St., Toronto, ON M5S 2R4
Tel: 416-603-3786; *Fax:* 416-603-4791
info@thewholenote.com
www.thewholenote.com
Social Media:
twitter.com/thewholenote
www.facebook.com/pages/The-WholeNote/1397 34336957
Circulation: 36,000
Allan Pulker, Publisher

News

L'actualité
Détenteur: Les Éditions Rogers Limitée
1200, av McGill College, 8e étage, Montréal, QC H3B 4G7
Tél: 514-845-5141; *Téléc:* 514-843-2180
redaction@lactualite.rogers.com
www.lactualite.com
Médias sociaux:
twitter.com/Lactualite
www.facebook.com/lactualite
Tirage: 160,070
Fréquence: 20 fois par an
Carole Beaulieu, Éditrice et rédactrice en chef

Columbia Journal
PO Box 2633 Main, Vancouver, BC V6B 3W8
Tel: 604-266-6552; *Fax:* 604-267-3342
editor@columbiajournal.ca
www.columbiajournal.ca
Circulation: 20,000
Frequency: 12 times a year
Jim Lipkovits, Editor
Marco Procaccini, Editor

Le Courrier Parlementaire
Owned By: Publications Mass-Media inc.
30, Grande-Allée ouest, Québec, QC G1R 2G6
Tel: 418-640-4211
editeur@courrierparlementaire.com
www.courrierparlementaire.com
Social Media:
twitter.com/CourrierPar
Denis Massicotte, Publisher

Embassy
Owned By: The Hill Times Publishing Inc.
69 Sparks St., Ottawa, ON K1P 5A5
Tel: 613-232-5952; *Fax:* 613-232-9055
news@embassymag.ca
www.embassymag.ca
Social Media:
twitter.com/EMBASSYMagazine
Circulation: 60,000
Frequency: Weekly; Wednesday
Issues of foreign policy.
Anne Marie Creskey, Publisher, acreskey@embassymag.ca

Inroads
3777 Kent Ave., #A, Montréal, QC H3S 1N4
Tel: 514-731-8383; *Fax:* 519-662-3594
inroadsmagazine@ymail.com
www.inroadsjournal.ca
Frequency: 2 times a year
Robert Chodos, Managing Editor, leischod@rogers.com

Maclean's Magazine
Owned By: Rogers Media Inc.
1 Mount Pleasant Rd., 11th Fl., Toronto, ON M4Y 2Y5
Tel: 416-764-1300; *Fax:* 416-764-1332
Toll-Free: 888-622-5326
letters@macleans.ca
www.macleans.ca
Social Media:
twitter.com/MacleansMag
www.facebook.com/MacleansMagazine
Circulation: 330,203
Frequency: Weekly
Sandra Parente, Publisher
Mark Stevenson, Editor-in-chief

Photography

Blackflash
PO Box 7381 Main, 727-#601, Spadina Cres. E 7th Fl., Saskatoon, SK S7K 3G8
Tel: 306-374-5115
bfinfo@blackflash.ca
www.blackflash.ca
Circulation: 1,300
Frequency: 3 times a year
Promoting photo-based new media in Canada, alongside publishing artwork & writing about art
John Shelling, Managing Editor

Ciel Variable
Previous Name: CV Photo; Productions Ciel Variable
5445, av de Gaspé, Montréal, QC H2T 3B2
Tel: 514-390-1193; *Fax:* 514-390-8802
info@cielvariable.ca
www.cielvariable.ca
Social Media:
www.facebook.com/magazinecielvariable
Circulation: 1,850
Frequency: 4 times a year
Jacques Doyen, Rédacteur en chef et directeur, jdoyon@cielvariable.ca

Photo Life
Previous Name: Photo Digest
Owned By: Les Éditions Apex inc.
#102, 171 St. Paul St., Québec, QC G1K 3W2
Fax: 418-692-3392
Toll-Free: 800-905-7468
info@photolife.com
www.photolife.com
Social Media:
twitter.com/PhotoLifeMag
www.facebook.com/photolifemag
Circulation: 55,000
Frequency: 6 times a year
Guy Poirier, Publisher, gpoirier@photolife.com
Valérie Racine, Editorial Director, vracine@photolife.com

Photo Life Buyers' Guide
Previous Name: National Photo Buyers' Guide
Owned By: Les Éditions Apex inc.
185, rue St-Paul, Québec, QC G1K 3W2
Toll-Free: 800-905-7468
info@photolife.com
www.photolife.com/guide
Other information: Toll Free Fax: 1-800-664-2739
Social Media:
twitter.com/PhotoLifeMag
www.facebook.com/photolifemag
Circulation: 65,000
Frequency: Annually
Valerie Racine, Editor, write@photolife.com
Guy Poirier, Publisher, gpoirier@photolife.com

Political

Briarpatch Magazine
2138 McIntyre St., Regina, SK S4P 2R7
Tel: 306-525-2949 *Toll-Free:* 866-431-5777
editor@briarpatchmagazine.com
www.briarpatchmagazine.com
Social Media:
twitter.com/briarpatchmag
www.facebook.com/briarpatchmagazine
Circulation: 2,000
Frequency: Bi-monthly
Award-winning magazine reporting on politics & culture
Andrew Loewen, Editor & Publisher, andrew@briarpatchmagazine.com
Valerie Zink, Edior & Publisher, valerie@briarpatchmagazine.com

Canadian Dimension
#2E, 91 Albert St., Winnipeg, MB R3B 1G5
Tel: 204-957-1519 *Toll-Free:* 800-737-7051
info@canadiandimension.com
www.canadiandimension.com
Social Media:
twitter.com/CDN_Dimension
www.facebook.com/CDNDimension
Circulation: 3,500
Frequency: 6 times a year (including 2 double issues)
Cy Gonick, Publisher & Coordinating Editor

Dialogue Magazine
Previous Name: Westcoast Logger
Gabriel Communications, 6227 Groveland Dr., Nanaimo, BC V9V 1B1
Tel: 250-758-9877; *Fax:* 250-758-9855
dialogue@dialogue.ca
www.dialogue.ca
Circulation: 700
Frequency: Bi-monthly
Volunteer-based, non-profit publishing.
Maurice J. King, President & Publisher
Janet Hicks, Editor

Parliament Now
Owned By: The Hill Times Publishing Inc.
69 Sparks St., Ottawa, ON K1P 5A5
Tel: 613-232-5952; *Fax:* 613-232-9055
news@parliamentnow.ca
www.parliamentnow.ca

Peace Magazine
Previous Name: The Peace Calendar
Owned By: Canadian Disarmament Information Service (CANDIS)
PO Box 248 P, Toronto, ON M5S 2S7
Tel: 437-887-6978
mspencer@web.net
www.peacemagazine.org
Social Media:
twitter.com/peace_mag
www.facebook.com/224393994267274
Circulation: 2,500
Frequency: 4 times a year
Metta Spencer, Editor, mspencer@web.net

This Magazine
c/o Red Maple Foundation, #417, 401 Richmond St. West, Toronto, ON M5V 3A8
Tel: 416-979-9429 *Toll-Free:* 877-999-8447
editor@this.org
this.org
Social Media:
twitter.com/thismagazine
www.facebook.com/thismagazine
Circulation: 8,000
Frequency: 6 times a year
Lauren McKeon, Editor, 416-979-8400
Lisa Whittington-Hill, Publisher, 416-979-9429

Printing & Publishing

Devil's Artisan: A Journal of the Printing Arts
c/o The Porcupine's Quill, PO Box 160, 68 Main St., Erin, ON N0B 1T0
Tel: 519-833-9158; *Fax:* 519-833-9845
elke@porcupinesquill.ca
devilsartisan.ca
Circulation: 800
Frequency: 2 times a year
Tim Inkster, Publisher
Don McLeod, Editor

Quill & Quire
#320, 111 Queen St. East, Toronto, ON M5C 1S2
Tel: 416-364-3333; *Fax:* 416-595-5415
www.quillandquire.com
Social Media:
itunes.apple.com/ca/podcast/quill-quire/id475815029
twitter.com/quilland quire
www.facebook.com/quillandquire
Frequency: 10 times a year
Magazine of the Canadian book trade.
Stuart Woods, Editor, swoods@quillandquire.com

Alison Jones, Publisher/Advertising Sales, ajones@quillandquire.com

Real Estate

Canadian Real Estate Wealth
Owned By: Key Media Inc.
#800, 312 Adelaide St. West, Toronto, ON M5V 1R2
Tel: 416-644-8740; *Fax:* 416-203-9083
subscriptions@kmimedia.ca
www.canadianrealestatemagazine.ca
Social Media: www.canadianrealestatemagazine.ca
twitter.com/CanRealEstMag
www.facebook.com/Canadianrealestatemag

Frequency: Bi-Monthly
Claudine Ting, Contact, Marketing & Communications, 416-644-8740 Ext.243, claudine.ting@kmimedia.ca

Homes & Land Magazine
Owned By: Suggitt Publishing Ltd.
Bell Tower, #950, 10104 - 103 Ave., Edmonton, AB T5J 0H8
Toll-Free: 866-702-2120
hlcc.ca

Real estate listings for provinces across Canada.
Tom Suggitt, President & CEO, tom@suggitt.com

Religious & Denominational

The Anglican
135 Adelaide St. East, Toronto, ON M5C 1L8
Tel: 416-363-6021; *Fax:* 416-363-7678
Toll-Free: 800-668-8932
editor@toronto.anglican.ca
www.toronto.anglican.ca

Frequency: Monthly
Stuart Mann, Editor

Anglican Journal
Previous Name: Dominion Churchman
Owned By: Anglican Journal Committee
80 Hayden St., Toronto, ON M4Y 3G2
Tel: 416-924-9199; *Fax:* 416-925-8811
editor@anglicanjournal.com
www.anglicanjournal.com
Social Media:
twitter.com/anglicanjournal
www.facebook.com/anglicanjournal

Circulation: 150,000
Frequency: 10 times a year
Marites Sison, Interim Managing Editor

BC Christian News
#301, 291 East 2nd Ave., Vancouver, BC V5T 1B8
Tel: 604-558-1982
www.canadianchristianity.com
Social Media:
www.facebook.com/CanChristian

Circulation: 37,000
Frequency: Monthly
Serve the Christian community by promoting communication, cooperation & continuity throughout churches, their organizations & their members

Canada Lutheran
#600, 177 Lombard Ave., Winnipeg, MB R3B 0W5
Tel: 204-984-9171; *Fax:* 204-984-9185
Toll-Free: 888-786-6707
canaluth@elcic.ca
www.elcic.ca/clweb/index.html
Social Media:
www.facebook.com/CanadianLutherans

Circulation: 14,000
Frequency: 8 times a year
The magazine of the Evangelical Lutheran Church in Canada.
Kenn Ward, Editor

Canadian Mennonite
Previous Name: Mennonite Reporter
Owned By: Canadian Mennonite Publishing Service, Inc. (CMPS)
#C5, 490 Dutton Dr., Waterloo, ON N2L 6H7
Tel: 519-884-3810; *Fax:* 519-884-3331
Toll-Free: 800-378-2524
letters@canadianmennonite.org
canadianmennonite.org

Circulation: 17,000
Frequency: 24 times a year
Dick Benner, Editor & Publisher, editor@canadianmennonite.org

Catholic Insight
PO Box 625 Adelaide, Adelaide St. E, Toronto, ON M5C 2J8
Tel: 416-204-9601
reach@catholicinsight.com
www.catholicinsight.com
Social Media:
twitter.com/catholicmag
www.facebook.com/CatholicInsight

Circulation: 3,700
Frequency: 11 times a year
Catholic Insight seeks to enlighten hearts and minds by proclaiming the splendour of truth and the sanctity of life. It endeavours to foster the culture of life by reporting truthfully, critically, contextually, and comparatively with a view to history and guided by a cultural vision inspired by Catholic doctrine and the classical liberal arts. In a climate of moral and cultural relativism it unequivocally upholds the existence of moral absolutes as a source of hope.
David Beresford, Editor in Cheif

The Catholic Register
#401, 1155 Yonge St., Toronto, ON M4T 1W2
Tel: 416-934-3410; *Fax:* 416-934-3409
Toll-Free: 855-441-4077
news@catholicregister.org
www.catholicregister.org
Social Media:
twitter.com/catholicregistr
www.facebook.com/thecatholicregister

Circulation: 33,000
Frequency: 47 times a year
Jim O'Leary, Publisher & Editor

Christian Courier
2 Aiken Dr., St Catharines, ON L2N 1V8
Tel: 905-937-3314 *Toll-Free:* 800-969-4838
admin@christiancourier.ca
www.christiancourier.ca
Social Media:
twitter.com/ChrCourier
www.facebook.com/ChrCourier

Frequency: Bi-weekly
Angela Reitsma Bick, Editor-in-chief, editor@christiancourier.ca

ChristianCurrent
PO Box 725, Winnipeg, MB R3C 2K3
Tel: 204-982-2060; *Fax:* 204-947-5632
www.christiancurrent.com

Brian Koldyk, Publisher
Robert White, Managing Editor

ChristianWeek
PO Box 725, Winnipeg, MB R3C 2K3
Tel: 204-982-2060; *Fax:* 204-947-5632
Toll-Free: 800-263-6695
admin@christianweek.org
www.christianweek.org
Social Media:
twitter.com/christianweek
www.facebook.com/ChristianWeek

Circulation: 5,000
Frequency: Every other Tue., except every 3 weeks in Dec.
Doug Koop, Editorial Director

Clarion
1 Beghin Ave., Winnipeg, MB R2J 3X5
Tel: 204-663-9000; *Fax:* 204-633-9202
admin@premierprinting.ca
www.premierprinting.ca

Circulation: 3,000
Frequency: Bi-weekly
W. Gortemaker, Publisher

Diocesan Times
c/o Diocese of NS & PEI, 5732 College St., Halifax, NS B3H 1X3
diocesantimes@gmail.com
www.nspeidiocese.ca/page/diocesan%20times.aspx
Frequency: Monthly, excpet July & August
The Diocesan Times, serving Anglicans in Nova Scotia and Prince Edward Island.

Edmonton Jewish News
#207, 11460 Jasper Ave., Edmonton, AB T7K 0A1
Tel: 780-421-7966; *Fax:* 780-424-3951
ejnews@telus.net

Circulation: 2,000
David Moser, Publisher

Faith Today
Owned By: The Evangelical Fellowship of Canada
PO Box 5885 W Beaver Creek, Richmond Hill, ON L4B 0B8
Tel: 905-479-5885 *Toll-Free:* 866-302-3362
infor@faithtoday.ca
www.faithtoday.ca
Social Media:
www.facebook.com/FaithToday
www.facebook.com/FaithToday

Circulation: 20,000
Frequency: 6 times a year
Bill Fledderus, Senior Editor
Karen Stiller, Senior Editor

The Gospel Herald
#200, 1892 West Broadway, Vancouver, ON V6J 1Y9
Tel: 604-715-6288; *Fax:* 604-608-9153
subscription@gospelherald.org
www.gospelherald.com
Social Media:
twitter.com/thegospelherald
www.facebook.com/TheGospelHerald

Circulation: 1,320
Frequency: Monthly
Edward Shih, Publisher & CEO
Eunice Or, Editor

Huron Church News
190 Queens Ave., London, ON N6A 6H7
Tel: 519-434-6893; *Fax:* 519-673-4151
Toll-Free: 800-919-1115
huron@huron.anglican.ca
www.diohuron.org

Bishop Bruce Howe, Publisher
David Parson, Editor

Island Catholic News
PO Box 5424 LCD 9, Victoria, BC V8R 6S4
Tel: 250-727-9429
admin@islandcatholicnews.ca
islandcatholicnews.ca

Circulation: 2,000
Frequency: Monthly
Marnie Butler, Senior Editor
Patrick Jamieson, Managing Editor

Jewish Free Press
Owned By: Jewish Free Press Inc.
8411 Elbow Dr. SW, Calgary, AB T2V 1K8
Tel: 403-252-9423; *Fax:* 403-255-5640
jewishfp@telus.net
www.jewishfreepress.ca

Circulation: 2,000
Frequency: Semi-monthly
Richard Bronstein, Publisher

Jewish Tribune
Previous Name: The Covenant
15 Hove St., Toronto, ON M3H 4Y8
Tel: 416-633-6224; *Fax:* 416-630-2159
info@jewishtribune.ca
www.jewishtribune.ca

Circulation: 60,490
Frequency: weekly
Norm Gordner, Editor

Living Light News
#200, 5306 - 89th St., Edmonton, AB T6E 5P9
Fax: 780-468-6872
Toll-Free: 800-932-0555
shine@livinglightnews.org
www.livinglightnews.org

Circulation: 50,000
Frequency: Bi-Monthly
Jeff Caporale, Editor-in-chief

London Jewish Community News
536 Huron St., London, ON N5Y 4J5
Tel: 519-673-3310; *Fax:* 519-673-1161
www.jewishlondon.ca

Frequency: quarterly

Mennonite Brethren Herald
Owned By: Canadian Conference of Mennonite Brethren Churches
1310 Taylor Ave., Winnipeg, MB R3M 3Z6
Tel: 204-654-5760; *Fax:* 204-654-1865
Toll-Free: 888-669-6575
mbherald@mbchurches.ca
www.mbherald.com
Social Media:
twitter.com/MB_Herald
www.facebook.com/MBHerald

Circulation: 17,500
Frequency: Monthly
Laura Kalmar, Editor

The New Brunswick Anglican
115 Church St., Fredericton, NB E3B 4C8
Tel: 506-459-1801
gmcknight@diofton.ca
anglican.nb.ca/nb_ang.html
Social Media:
www.facebook.com/dfton

Circulation: 10,000
Frequency: 10 times a year
Gisele McKnight, Editor

The New Freeman
c/o Diocese of Saint John, One Bayard Dr., Saint John, NB E2L 3L5
Tel: 506-653-6806; *Fax:* 506-653-6818
tnf@nb.aibn.com
www.dioceseofsaintjohn.org

Circulation: 7,480
Frequency: Weekly
Margie Trafton, Editor

Niagara Anglican
Cathedral Place, 252 James St. North, Hamilton, ON L8R 2L3
Tel: 905-527-1316
editor@niagaraanglican.ca
www.niagara.anglican.ca/newspaper

Circulation: 16,175
Frequency: Monthly exc. July & Aug.
The Rev. Hollis Hiscock, Editor, editor@niagaraanglican.ca

Ottawa Jewish Bulletin
21 Nadolny Sachs, Ottawa, ON K2A 1R9
Tel: 613-798-4696; *Fax:* 613-798-4730
bulletin@ottawajewishbulletin.com
www.ottawajewishbulletin.com

Circulation: 2,500
Frequency: 19 times a year

Outlook
Also Known As: Canadian Jewish Outlook
6184 Ash St., Vancouver, BC V5Z 3G9
Tel: 604-324-5101; *Fax:* 604-325-2470
outlook@vcn.bc.ca
www.vcn.bc.ca/outlook

Frequency: 6 times a year
Carl Rosenberg, Editor-in-chief

Presbyterian Record
50 Wynford Dr., Toronto, ON M3C 1J7
Tel: 800-619-7301; *Fax:* 416-441-2825
record@presbyterianrecord.ca
presbyterianrecord.ca

Circulation: 42,000
Frequency: Monthly exc. Aug.
David Harris, Publisher

Revue L'Oratoire / The Oratory
3800, ch Queen Mary, Montréal, QC H3V 1H6
Tél: 514-733-8211; *Téléc:* 514-733-9735
Ligne sans frais: 877-672-8647
pastorale@saint-joseph.org
www.saint-joseph.org/fr/le-sanctuaire/la-revue-loratoire

Tirage: 7,500 anglais; 42,000 français
Fréquence: 3 fois par an
Père Claude Grou, Éditeur

Salvationist
Previous Name: The War Cry
2 Overlea Blvd., Toronto, ON M4H 1P4
Toll-Free: 800-725-2769
salvationist.ca
Social Media:
twitter.com/salvationist
www.facebook.com/salvationistmagazine

Circulation: 20,000
Frequency: Monthly
Maj. Ken Smith, Editor

Seven
c/o ChristianWeek, PO Box 725, #204, 424 Logan Ave., Winnipeg, MB R3A 0R4
Tel: 204-982-2060; *Fax:* 204-947-5632
Toll-Free: 800-263-6695
admin@christianweek.org
www.christianweek.org

Frequency: Bi-Monthly

Shalom! Magazine
#309, 5670 Spring Garden Rd., Halifax, NS B3J 1H6
Tel: 902-422-7491; *Fax:* 902-425-3722
atlanticjewishcouncil@theajc.ns.ca
theajc.ns.ca/category/shalom-magazine

Circulation: 1,400
Frequency: 3 times a year
Edna LeVine, Editor

Studies in Religion / Sciences Religieuses
Owned By: SAGE Publications
sir.sagepub.com

Circulation: 1,400
Frequency: Quarterly
Patricia Dold, English Language Editor, pdold@mun.ca
Alain Bouchard, French Language Editor, alain.bouchard.8@ulaval.ca

Testimony
Also Known As: The Pentecostal Testimony
c/o The Pentecostal Assemblies of Canada, 2450 Milltower Ct., Mississauga, ON L5N 5Z6
Tel: 905-542-7400
testimony@paoc.org
testimony.paoc.org

Circulation: 14,000
Frequency: Monthly
Stephen Kennedy, Editor

The United Church Observer
478 Huron St., Toronto, ON M5R 2R3
Tel: 416-960-8500; *Fax:* 416-960-8477
Toll-Free: 800-936-4566
www.ucobserver.org
Social Media:
twitter.com/UC_Observer
www.facebook.com/127605123918385

Circulation: 80,000
Frequency: 11 times a year
David Wilson, Editor & Publisher

La Voix Sépharade
#216, 5151, Côte Ste-Catherine, Montréal, QC H3W 1M6
Tél: 514-733-4998; *Téléc:* 514-733-3158
info@csuq.org
csuq.org/decouvrez-nous/la-voix-sepharade

Tirage: 6,000
Fréquence: 4 fois par an
Robert Abitbol, Publisher

Western Catholic Reporter
8421 - 101 Ave., Edmonton, AB T6A 0L1
Tel: 780-465-8030; *Fax:* 780-465-8031
wcr@wcr.ab.ca
www.wcr.ab.ca

Circulation: 37,015
Frequency: 44 times a year
Glen Argan, Editor

Science, Research & Development

Découvrir: La revue de la recherche
Anciennement: Interface
Association francophone pour le savoir, 425, rue de la Gauchetière est, Montréal, QC H2L 2M7
Tél: 514-849-0045; *Téléc:* 514-849-5558
www.acfas.ca/publications/decouvrir
Médias sociaux:
twitter.com/_Acfas
www.facebook.com/33532707807

Fréquence: 6 fois par an
Johanne Lebel, Édimestre & rédactrice en chef, johanne.lebel@acfas.ca

Québec Science (QS)
Détenteur: Vélo Québec
1251, rue Rachel est, Montréal, QC H2J 2J9
Tél: 514-521-8356 *Ligne sans frais:* 800-567-8356
courrier@quebecscience.qc.ca
www.quebecscience.qc.ca
Médias sociaux:
twitter.com/quebecscience
www.facebook.com/280257226593

Tirage: 32 000
Fréquence: 10 fois par an
Pierre Sormany, Éditeur

Revue Spectre
9601, rue Colbert, Anjou, QC H1J 1Z9
Tel: 514-948-6422; *Fax:* 514-948-6423
camille.turcotte@apsq.org
www.apsq.org

Circulation: 3,000

Diane Poulin, Editor-in-chief

Social Welfare

Community Action Newspaper
Owned By: Community Action Publishers
Tel: 416-449-6766; *Fax:* 416-444-5850
comact@interlog.com
www.ohpe.ca/epublish/1

Circulation: 12,010
Frequency: 11 times a year
Canada's Community Service Reporter

WhyNot Magazine
Canadian Foundation for Physically Disabled Persons, #265, 6 Garamond Crt., Toronto, ON M3C 1Z5
Tel: 416-760-7351; *Fax:* 416-760-9405
whynot@sympatico.ca
www.cfpdp.com

Frequency: 3 times a year
Dedicated to its three main events: Great Valentine Gala, Rolling Rampage and The Terry Fox Hall of Fame.
Bill McQuat, Editor
Vim Kochhar, Publisher
Larry Allen, Editor

Sports & Recreation

Athletics Ontario
#211, 3 Concorde Gate, Toronto, ON M3C 3N7
Tel: 416-426-7215; *Fax:* 416-426-7358
www.athleticsontario.ca
Social Media:
www.facebook.com/135196239850966

Circulation: 4,000
Frequency: 8 times a year
Publishing athelete-centered magazines for track & field, road running, cross country & race walking
John Craig, Managing Director, johncraig@athleticsontario.ca

Canadian Cyclist
7 Barker St., Paris, ON N3L 2H4
Tel: 519-442-7905
news@canadiancyclist.com
www.canadiancyclist.com
Social Media:
twitter.com/cdncyclist

Circulation: 8,000
Tracy Harkness, Publisher
Robert Jones, Editor

Canadian Rodeo News
272245, RR#2, Airdrie, AB T4A 2L5
Tel: 403-945-7393; *Fax:* 403-945-0936
editor@rodeocanada.com
www.rodeocanada.com/rodeo_news.htm

Circulation: 4,000
Frequency: Monthly
Darell Hartlen, Editor

Coast & Kayak Magazine
Previous Name: Wavelength
Wild Coast Publishing, PO Box 24 A, Nanaimo, BC V9R 5K4
Tel: 250-244-6437; *Fax:* 866-654-1937
Toll-Free: 866-984-6437
kayak@coastandkayak.com
www.wavelengthmagazine.com

Frequency: Quarterly
The publication presents information about kayaking, paddlesports, & coastal recreation. The magazine is available at retail outlets & through paddling clubs, guides, & manufacturers on the west coast of Canada & the United States.
John Kimantas, Editor, editor@coastandkayak.com

The Curling News
PO Box 53103, 10 Royal Orchard Blvd., Thornhill, ON L3T 7R9
Tel: 905-997-3348 *Toll-Free:* 800-605-2875
sweep@sweepmag.com
thecurlingnews.com
Social Media:
twitter.com/curling

Frequency: 6 times a year; Nov.-April

Diver Magazine
Owned By: Nuytco Research
216 East Esplanade St., North Vancouver, BC V7L 1A3
Tel: 604-988-0711; *Fax:* 604-988-0747
Toll-Free: 877-974-4333
mail@divermag.com
www.divermag.com
Social Media:
twitter.com/divermag
www.facebook.com/divermagazine

Circulation: 7,000
Frequency: 8 times a year
Phil Nuytten, Publisher

Flagstick Golf Magazine
Owned By: Bauder Media Group Inc.
8197 Parkway Rd., Ottawa, ON K0A 2P0
Tel: 613-821-0888; *Fax:* 613-821-4888
Toll-Free: 877-503-0888
info@flagstick.com
www.flagstick.com
Social Media: www.youtube.com/flagstickgolf
www.twitter.com/flagstick
www.faceboo k.com/flagstick

Circulation: 20,000
Frequency: 7 times a year
Jeff Bauder, Publisher, jbauder@flagstick.com
Scott MacLeod, Editor, scotmac@flagstick.com

Golf Guide Magazine
16410 - 137 Ave. NW, Edmonton, AB T5V 1R6
Tel: 780-447-2128; *Fax:* 780-447-1933

Frequency: Annually, April
Paul McCracken, Publisher

Golf West
Previous Name: Golf the West
Owned By: Koocanusa Publications Inc.
#100, 100 - 7th Ave. South, Cranbrook, BC V1C 2J4
Tel: 250-426-7253; *Fax:* 250-426-4125
Toll-Free: 800-663-8555
info@kpimedia.com
www.koocanusapublications.com/magazines/golfwest
Social Media: www.flickr.com/photos/golfwest
twitter.com/@golfwestmag

Circulation: 30,000
Frequency: Annually, Spring
Keith Powell, Publisher, keith@kpimedia.com
Kerry Shelborn, Editor, kerry@kpimedia.com

Hockey Magazine
Owned By: Suggitt Publishing Ltd.
10177 - 105 St. NW, Edmonton, AB T5J 1E2
Tel: 780-425-3642; *Fax:* 780-413-6185
reception@hockeymagazine.net
www.hockeymagazine.net

Frequency: 3 times per year
Minor league hockey coverage; separate magazines for Edmonton & Calgary.
Rob Suggit, President & Publisher

Hockey News
Owned By: TVA Publications inc.
#100, 25 Sheppard Ave. West, Toronto, ON M2N 6S7
Tel: 416-733-7600; *Fax:* 416-340-2786
www.thehockeynews.com
Social Media: www.youtube.com/user/THNTV
twitter.com/thehockeynews
www.facebook.c om/thehockeynews

Circulation: 103,350
Frequency: 42 times a year
Brian Costello, Senior Editor

Hockey Now
Owned By: Paton Publishing
PO Box 88024, Vancouver, BC V6A 4A4
Tel: 604-990-1432 *Toll-Free:* 877-990-0520
office@hockeynow.ca
hockeynow.ca
Social Media:
twitter.com/hockeynow
www.facebook.com/hockeynow.communications

Circulation: 160,000
Frequency: Monthly
Highlighting Canadian hockey stories from Junior legues, to local rinks, to the national stage & even to NHL stars
Larry Feist, Publisher, larry@hockeynow.ca
Andrew Chong, Editor, andrewchong@hockeynow.ca
Scott Whitemarsh, Brand Marketing Manager, Marketing, scott@hockeynow.ca

The Leader
#100, 1345 Baseline Rd., Ottawa, ON K2C 0A7
Tel: 613-224-5131; *Fax:* 613-224-5982
smuehlherr@scouts.ca
www.scouts.ca

Circulation: 38,000
Frequency: 10 times a year
Susan Muehlherr, Executive Editor

MARCHE-Randonnée
c/o Fédération Québécoise de la Marche, CP 1000 M, 4545, ave. Pierre-De Coubertin, Montréal, QC H1V 3R2
Tél: 514-252-3157; *Téléc:* 514-252-5137
Ligne sans frais: 866-252-2065
www.fqmarche.qc.ca

Tirage: 8 225
Fréquence: trimestriel
Raymond Dulude, Advertising
Daniel Pouplot, Production Manager
Louise Giroux, Co-ordinatrice

Motoneige Québec
4545, av Pierre-de-Coubertin, Montréal, QC H1V 0B2
Tél: 514-252-3076; *Téléc:* 514-254-2066
info@fcmq.qc.ca
www.fcmq.qc.ca

Tirage: 65 000
Fréquence: 4 fois par an
Yves Ouellet, Rédacteur en chef indépendant

Newfoundland Sportsman
Previous Name: Outdoor Sportsman
PO Box 13754 A, 36 Pippy Pl., St. John's, NL A1B 4G5
Toll-Free: 877-754-3515
customerservice@newfoundlandsportsman.com
newfoundlandsportsman.com
Social Media:
www.facebook.com/newfoundlandsportsman

Circulation: 14,621
Frequency: 6 times a year
Dwight J. Blackwood, Publisher
Gordon Follett, Editor

NHL PowerPlay
Owned By: Paton Publishing
PO Box 88024, Vancouver, BC V6A 4A4
Tel: 604-990-1432 *Toll-Free:* 877-990-0520
www.nhlpowerplay.com

Circulation: 364,000
Frequency: Four times per year
NHL PowerPlay is appearing in tabloid format as a special 20-page section in four editions of Hockey Now.

Northwestern Ontario Golfing News
Owned By: North Superior Publishing Inc.
North Superior Publishing Inc., 1145 Barton St., Thunder Bay, ON P7B 5N3
Tel: 807-623-2348; *Fax:* 807-623-7515

Circulation: 2,000
Frequency: 5 times a year
Scott Sumner, Publisher & Editor

Northwestern Ontario Snowmobile News
Owned By: North Superior Publishing Inc.
North Superior Publishing Inc., Thunder Bay, ON
Tel: 807-623-2348; *Fax:* 807-623-7515
nspinc@tbaytel.net
www.northsuperiorpublishing.com

Circulation: 2,000
Frequency: 7 times a year
Scott A. Summer, Publisher & Editor

Ontario Tennis
c/o Ontario Tennis Association, #200, 1 Shoreham Dr., Toronto, ON M3N 3A7
Tel: 416-514-1100; *Fax:* 416-514-1112
Toll-Free: 800-387-5066
ota@tennisontario.com
www.tennisontario.com
Social Media: www.youtube.com/user/otatv1
twitter.com/#!/tennisontario
www.facebook.com/OntarioTennisAssociation

Circulation: 20,000
Frequency: 3 times a year
Pam Olley, Editor, pamolley@sympatico.ca

Pedal Magazine / SkiTrax Magazine
#200, 260 Spadina Ave., Toronto, ON M5T 2E4
Tel: 416-977-2100; *Fax:* 416-977-9200
Toll-Free: 866-977-3325
info@pedalmag.com
www.pedalmag.com
Social Media:
twitter.com/pedalmagazine
www.facebook.com/pages/Pedal-Magazine/10 1939769846530
Frequency: 6 times a year

Québec Soccer
QC
www.11x90.com

Tirage: 150 000
Fréquence: 11 fois par an
Pascal Cifarelli, Éditeur/fondateur/directeur
Pablo Ferreri, Directeur géneral

Revue Golf AGP International
12305, boul Métropolitain est, Montréal, QC H1B 5R3
Tél: 514-645-2040; *Téléc:* 514-645-5508
mongolf.ca/magazines

Tirage: 50 000
Fréquence: 5 fois par an
Richard Beaudry, Président et éditeur
Daniel Caza, Rédacteur en chef

RidersWest
Previous Name: Ski& Ride West
Owned By: Koocanusa Publications Inc.
#100, 100 - 7th Ave. South, Cranbrook, BC V1C 2J4
Tel: 250-426-7253; *Fax:* 250-426-4125
Toll-Free: 800-663-8555
www.riderswestmag.com
Social Media:
twitter.com/riderswest
www.facebook.com/RidersWest

Circulation: 32,000
Frequency: 5 times a year
Keith Powell, Publisher, keith@kpimedia.com

SBC Skateboard Magazine
#3266, 2255B Queen St. East, Toronto, ON M4E 1G3
Toll-Free: 800-223-6197
info@sbcskateboard.com
www.sbcskateboard.com
Social Media:
twitter.com/sbcskateboard
www.facebook.com/SBCSkateboardMagazine

Circulation: 25,000
Frequency: 5 times a year
Steve Jarrett, Publisher
Ryan Stutt, Managing Editor

SCORE Golf Québec
Détenteur: Canadian Controlled Media Communications
#101, 5397 Eglinton Ave. West, Toronto, ON M9C 5K6
Tél: 416-928-2909; *Téléc:* 416-966-1181
info@scoregolf.com
scoregolf.com

Tirage: 35,000
Fréquence: 4 fois par an
Peter Robinson, Editor, robinson@scoregolf.com
Kim Locke, Publisher

SCOREGolf
Owned By: Canadian Controlled Media Communications
#101, 5397 Eglinton Ave. West, Toronto, ON M9C 5K6
Tel: 416-928-2909; *Fax:* 416-966-1181
Toll-Free: 800-320-6420
info@scoregolf.com
scoregolf.com

Circulation: 142,438
Frequency: 6 times a year
Jason Logan, Editor

Ski Canada
Previous Name: Sunsports
Owned By: Solstice Publishing Inc.
47 Soho Sq., Toronto, ON M5T 2Z2
Tel: 416-595-1252 *Toll-Free:* 888-666-9754
info@skicanadamag.com
skicanadamag.com
Social Media:
twitter.com/skicanadamag
www.facebook.com/SkiCanadaMag

Circulation: 40,733
Frequency: 6 times a year
Iain MacMillan, Editor
Paul Green, Publisher

Ski Presse
Détenteur: Solisco
655, ave Sainte-Anne, Saint-Hyacinthe, QC J2S 5G4
Tél: 450-773-6028
info@skipresse.com
skipresse.com
Médias sociaux:
twitter.com/skipresse_mag
www.facebook.com/pages/SkipressWorld/108500488 806

Tirage: 182,000
Fréquence: 4 times a year
Anne-Marie Saint-Germain, Rédactrice-en-chef, amsaintgermain@skipresse.com

Jules Older, Editor-in-chief, English version

SkiTrax
#200, 260 Spadina Ave., Toronto, ON M5T 2E4
Tel: 416-977-2100; *Fax:* 416-977-9200
Toll-Free: 866-754-8729
info@skitrax.com
www.skitrax.com
Social Media:
twitter.com/skitrax
www.facebook.com/pages/SkiTrax/115966559512?sk=wall
Circulation: 30,000
Frequency: 4 times a year
North America's Nordic Ski Mag
Benjamin Sadavoy, Publisher

Sledworthy Magazine
13 Pippy Place, St. John's, NL A1C 1V7
Tel: 709-690-2609
info@sledworthy.com
www.sledworthy.com
Social Media: www.youtube.com/user/SledworthyMagazine
twitter.com/Sledworthy
www.facebook.com/pages/Sledworthy-Magazine/25301476142394
Circulation: 30,000
Andrew Goldsworthy, Editor-in-Chief, andrew@sledworthy.com

SnoRiders
Owned By: Koocanusa Publications Inc.
#100, 100 - 7th Ave. South, Cranbrook, BC V1C 2J4
Tel: 250-426-7253; *Fax:* 250-426-4125
Toll-Free: 800-663-8555
info@kpimedia.com
snoriderswest.com
Social Media: www.flickr.com/photos/snoriders
twitter.com/snoriders
www.facebook.com /100894413330321
Frequency: 5 times a year; fall (41,000), winter (30,000), mid-winter (32,000), spring (32,000), summer (32,000)
Kerry Shellborn, Editor, editor@kpimedia.com
Keith Powell, Publisher, publisher@kpimedia.com

Snowboard Canada Magazine
SBC Media, #3266, 2255B Queen St. East, Toronto, ON M4E 1G3
Tel: 416-406-2400; *Fax:* 416-406-0656
www.snowboardcanada.com
Social Media:
twitter.com/snowboardcanada
www.facebook.com/SnowboardCanada
Circulation: 73,000
Frequency: 4 times a year
Steve Jarrett, Publisher

Sporting Scene
18 Oswell Dr., Ajax, ON L1Z 0L6
Tel: 416-272-1789
sportingscene@sympatico.ca
www.sportingscene.com
Circulation: 24,000
Frequency: 11 times a year
Jason Martens, Publisher
Pete Martens, Editor

Supertrax International
Owned By: Supertrax Media Inc.
1008 Capricorn Crt., Minden, ON K0M 2K0
Tel: 905-286-2135; *Fax:* 705-286-6308
Toll-Free: 800-905-8729
info@supertraxmag.com
www.supertraxmag.com
Frequency: 4 times a year
Supertrax International is a snowmobile magazine.

Swim News
356 Sumach St., Toronto, ON M4X 1V4
www.swimnews.com
Circulation: 4,300
Frequency: 10 times a year
N.J. Thierry, Publisher

Volleyball Canada Magazine
Previous Name: True North Volleyball Magazine
#202, 5510 Canotek Rd., Gloucester, ON K1J 9J5
Tel: 613-748-5681; *Fax:* 613-748-5727
info@volleyball.ca
www.volleyball.ca
Circulation: 35,000
Frequency: 4 times a year
Greg Smith, Publisher

Wakeboard SBC Magazine
#3266, 2255B Queen St. East, Toronto, ON M4E 1G3
Tel: 416-406-2400; *Fax:* 416-406-0656
info@sbcmedia.com
www.sbcmedia.com
Circulation: 36,000
Frequency: 2 times a year
Steve Jarrett, Publisher

Television, Radio, Video & Home Appliances

Audio Ideas Guide
Toronto, ON
Tel: 905-833-7177; *Fax:* 905-833-7178
mail@audio-ideas.on.ca
www.audio-ideas.com
Frequency: Quarterly
Publishing articles about the audio world
Andrew Marshall, Editor & Publisher, andrew@audio-ideas.com
Aaron Marshall, Contributing Editor & Webmaster, aaron@audio-ideas.com

Horaire Télé
c/o Le Journal de Montréal, 4545, rue Frontenac, Montréal, QC H1H 2R7
Tél: 514-521-4545; *Téléc:* 514-525-4416
Ligne sans frais: 800-361-9415
services@quebecormedia.com
www.journalmtl.com
Médias sociaux:
twitter.com/JdeMontreal
www.facebook.com/jdemontreal
Tirage: 326 440
Fréquence: Hebdomadaire
Lyne Robitaille, Présidente et éditrice

The Inner Ear
Owned By: TIEMedia
Tel: 905-294-5570
info@innerearmag.com
www.innerearmag.com
Social Media:
www.facebook.com/innerearmagazine
Circulation: 16,000
Frequency: 4 times a year
Ernie Fisher, Editor

The Loop
Owned By: TC Transcontinental
www.theloop.ca
Social Media:
twitter.com/theloopca
www.facebook.com/theloopca
Circulation: 281,955
Frequency: Weekly
Beth Maher, Managing Editor

StarWeek
c/o Toronto Star, One Yonge St., Toronto, ON M5E 1E6
Tel: 416-869-4244; *Fax:* 416-869-4103
canderson@thestar.ca
Circulation: 645,181
Frequency: Weekly; Sat.
Part of the Toronto Star's Saturday edition.
Gord Stimmell, Editor

Sun Television
c/o Calgary Sun, 2615 - 12 St. NE, Calgary, AB T2E 7W9
Tel: 403-250-4220; *Fax:* 403-250-4258
cal-circulation@sunmedia.ca
www.calgarysun.com
Circulation: 63,794
Frequency: Weekly
Jose Rodriguez, Editor-in-Chief, jose.rodriguez@sunmedia.ca

Sun Television
c/o Edmonton Sun, #250, 4990 - 92 Ave., Edmonton, AB T6B 3A1
Tel: 780-468-0100
edm-citydesk@sunmedia.ca
www.edmontonsun.com
Circulation: 95,860
Frequency: Weekly
Steve Serviss, Editor-in-Chief, steve.serviss@sunmedia.ca

Télé-Québec
c/o Le Journal de Québec, 450, ave Béchard, Québec, QC G1M 2E9
Tél: 418-683-1573; *Téléc:* 418-683-8886
commentaires@journaldequebec.com
www.journaldequebec.com
Médias sociaux:
twitter.com/JdeQuebec
www.facebook.com/JdeQuebec
Tirage: 126 689
Fréquence: Hebdomadaire
Louise Cordeau, Éditrice et chef de la direction, louise.cordeau@journaldequebec.com

TV Hebdo
Détenteur: TVA Publications inc.
1010, rue de Sérigny, 4e étage, Longueuil, QC J4K 5G7
Tél: 514-848-7000; *Téléc:* 514-848-7070
tvhebdo@tvapublications.com
www.tvhebdo.com
Tirage: 46 000
Fréquence: 2 fois par an
Louis Lalande, Vice-President

TV Times, Edmonton
10006 - 101 St., Edmonton, AB T5J 0S1
Tel: 780-429-5100; *Fax:* 780-429-5500
www.edmontonjournal.com
Circulation: 150,000
Linda Hughes, Publisher
Allan Mayer, Editor-in-chief

TV Week Magazine (TVW)
Owned By: Canada Wide Media Limited
4180 Lougheed Hwy., 4th Fl., Burnaby, BC V5C 6A7
Tel: 604-299-7311; *Fax:* 604-299-9188
Toll-Free: 800-663-0518
cwm@canadawide.com
www.tvweekonline.ca
Social Media: pinterest.com/bcliving
twitter.com/bc_living
www.facebook.com/bcliving
Circulation: 75,000
Frequency: Weekly
Peter Legge, Publisher
Brent Furdyk, Editor, bfurdyk@canadawide.com

Travel

Above & Beyond Magazine
PO Box 683, Mahone Bay, NS B0J 2E0
Tel: 613-599-4190; *Fax:* 613-599-4191
Toll-Free: 877-227-2842
www.arcticjournal.ca
Circulation: 20,000
Frequency: 6 times a year
Tom Koelbel, Publisher & Editor

AWAY
Owned By: St. Joseph Communications
#320, 111 Queen St. East, Toronto, ON M5C 1S2
Tel: 416-364-3333
www.torontopearson.com/en/away/#
Circulation: 200,000
Frequency: Quarterly
Serves outbound passengers at the Toronto Pearson International Airport.

Bear Country
1475 West Walsh St., Thunder Bay, ON P7E 4X6
Tel: 807-474-2636; *Fax:* 807-474-2658
pgresham@bearskinairlines.com
bearskinairlines.com
Circulation: 150,000
Frequency: Quarterly
Features editorials about people, place & events
Patti Gresham, Production Manager & Editor

British Columbia Magazine
Previous Name: Beautiful British Columbia Magazine
1803 Douglas St., 3rd Fl., Victoria, BC V8T 5C3
Tel: 250-356-5860; *Fax:* 250-356-5896
Toll-Free: 800-663-7611
orders@bcmag.ca
www.bcmag.ca
Other information: Toll Free Fax: 1-800-308-4533
Social Media: www.youtube.com/user/BritishColumbiaMag
twitter.com/bcmagazine
www.facebook.com/19647694193
Circulation: 125,000
Frequency: Quarterly
British Columbia's geographic magazine with researched stories of parks, wilderness, wildlife, travel destinations, outdoor adventures, recreation, geography, ecology, conservation, science, phenomena, First Nations' culture, heritage places & history
Jane Nahirny, Editor, editor@bcmag.ca
Ken Seabrook, Art Director, Art

Dreamscapes Travel & Lifestyle Magazine
Previous Name: American Express Dreamscapes
3 Bluffwood Dr., Toronto, ON M2H 3L4
Tel: 416-497-5353; *Fax:* 416-497-0871
Toll-Free: 888-700-4464
dreamscapesmagazine@rogers.com
www.dreamscapes.ca
Circulation: 110,000
Frequency: 8 times a year
Sandra Kitchen, Publisher
Donna Vieira, Editor
Joe Turkel, President & Group Publisher

Espaces
#205, 911, rue Jean-Talon est, Montréal, QC H2R 1V5
Tél: 514-277-3477; *Téléc:* 514-277-3822
Ligne sans frais: 888-277-6718
info@espaces.qc.ca
www.espaces.qc.ca
Tirage: 50 000
Fréquence: bimestriel
Marie Eisenmann, Rédactrice en chef

Géo Plein Air
Détenteur: Velo Québec Éditions
Maison des Cyclistes, 1251, rue Rachel est, Montréal, QC H2J 2J9
Tél: 514-521-8356 *Ligne sans frais:* 800-567-8356
www.geopleinair.com
Médias sociaux:
twitter.com/geopleinair_
www.facebook.com/351822425904
Tirage: 25 358
Fréquence: 7 fois par an
Magazine québécois de la nature et de l'aventure
Pierre Sormany, Éditeur
Nathalie Schneider, Rédactrice en chef

Greater Halifax Visitor Guide
Owned By: Metro Guide Publishing
1300 Hollis St., Halifax, NS B3J 1T6
Tel: 902-420-9943; *Fax:* 902-429-9058
publishers@metroguide.ca
www.metroguidepublishing.ca
Circulation: 240,000
Frequency: Annually
Sheila Blair, Publisher

Horizon Travel Magazine
#210, 2150 Winston Park Dr., Oakville, ON L6H 5V1
Tel: 905-257-1020
horizon@horizontravelmag.com
www.horizontravelmag.com
Social Media:
twitter.com/horizontravmag
www.facebook.com/pages/Horizon-Travel-Magazine/1718715761
Horizon Travel Magazine is a travel & lifestyle magazine.

Key to Kingston
Owned By: Sun Media Corporation
Kingston Publications, 18 St. Remy Place, Kingston, ON K7K 6C4
Tel: 613-389-7400; *Fax:* 613-389-7507
www.kingstonpublications.com/keytokingston.html
Circulation: 175,000
Frequency: 8 times a year
Liza Nelson, Publisher, liza.nelson@sunmedia.ca
Liza Nelson, Publisher, 613-549-8442 ext 132
Jane Deacon, Editor, 613-549-8442 ext 108

The Laurentians Tourist Guide / Les Laurentides Guide Touristique
#14, 142, rue de la Chapelle, Mirabel, QC J7J 2C8
Tel: 450-436-8532
info-tourisme@laurentides.com
www.laurentides.com
Social Media: www.youtube.com/user/TourismeLaurentides
twitter.com/TLaurentides
www. facebook.com/139848066744
Circulation: 73,000, English edition; 202,000, French edition
Frequency: Annually
Diane Leblond, General Manager

99 North Magazine
Owned By: Canada Wide Media Limited
4180 Lougheed Hwy., Burnaby, BC V5C 6A7
www.canadawide.com
Circulation: 100,000
Frequency: 2 times a year
Samantha Legge, General Manager

Outpost: Canada's Travel Magazine
#207, 250 Augusta Ave., Toronto, ON M5T 2L7
Tel: 416-972-6635
info@outpostmagazine.com
www.outpostmagazine.com
Social Media:
twitter.com/OutpostMagazine
www.facebook.com/Outpostmagazine
Circulation: 28,000
Frequency: Bi-monthly
Matthew Robinson, Publisher, matt@outpostmagazine.com
Deborah Sanborn, Editor, deborah@outpostmagazine.com

Rocky Mountain Visitor's Magazine
Previous Name: Kootenay Visitor's Magazine
Owned By: Koocanusa Publications Inc.
#100, 100 - 7th Ave. South, Cranbrook, BC V1C 2J4
Tel: 250-426-7253; *Fax:* 250-426-4125
Toll-Free: 800-663-8555
publisher@kpimedia.com
www.rockymountainvisitors.com
Frequency: Semi-annually
Kerry Shellborn, Assigning Editor, editor@kpimedia.com
Keith G. Powell, Publisher

Saskatchewan Vacation Guide
Tourism Saskatchewan, 189-1621 Albert St., Regina, SK S4P 2S5
Tel: 306-787-9685; *Fax:* 306-787-0715
Toll-Free: 877-237-2273
www.sasktourism.com
Circulation: 195,000
Frequency: annually

Touring
Owned By: Canadian Automobile Association
444 Bouvier St., Québec, QC G2J 1E3
Tel: 416-847-8548
touring@caaquebec.com
www.caaquebec.com/en/touring/
Social Media:
twitter.com/CAA_Quebec
www.facebook.com/caaQc
Circulation: 608,000
Frequency: 4 times a year

The Travel Society Magazine
Also Known As: Travel Scoop
147 Liberty St., Toronto, ON M6K 3G3
Tel: 416-926-0111
member@thetravelsociety.com
www.thetravelsociety.com
Social Media:
twitter.com/TTravelSociety
www.facebook.com/thetravelsociety
Circulation: 7,000
Nigel D. Raincock, Publisher
Ann Wallace, Editor

WestJet Magazine
Previous Name: up!
#100, 1900 - 11 St. SE, Calgary, AB T2G 3G2
Tel: 403-240-9055; *Fax:* 403-240-9059
www.westjetmagazine.com
Social Media:
www.facebook.com/WestJetMagazine

Where Canadian Rockies
Previous Name: Where Rocky Mountains
Owned By: St Joseph Media
#244, 105 Bow Meadows Cres., Canmore, AB T1W 2W8
Tel: 403-678-1898; *Fax:* 403-678-3658
info@rmvpublications.com
www.where.ca/canadianrockies
Social Media:
twitter.com/whererockies
Frequency: 2 times a year (English with some Japanese)
Jack Newton, Publisher

Where Vancouver/Whistler
Owned By: St Joseph Media
#510, 1755 West Broadway, Vancouver, BC V6J 4S5
Tel: 604-736-5586; *Fax:* 604-736-3465
Toll-Free: 866-727-5586
infovancouver@where.ca
www.where.ca/west-coast/british -columbia/vancouver
Social Media:
twitter.com/wherevancouver
www.facebook.com/wherevancouver
Frequency: Monthly
Peggie Terry, Publisher

Women's & Feminist

L'Actuelle
1043, rue Tiffin, Longueuil, QC J4P 3G7
Tél: 450-442-3983; *Téléc:* 450-442-4363
cerfer@videotron.ca
cfq.qc.ca
Médias sociaux:
www.facebook.com/283417910957
Tirage: 50 000
Fréquence: 5 fois par an
Publication officielle des Cercles de Fermières du Québec (CFQ)

Canadian Guider
c/o Girl Guides of Canada, 50 Merton St., Toronto, ON M4S 1A3
Tel: 416-487-5281 *Toll-Free:* 800-565-8111
cdnguider@girlguides.ca
www.girlguides.ca
Circulation: 30,891
Frequency: 3 times a year
Sharon Jackson, Editor

Canadian Woman Studies / Les Cahiers de la Femme
Owned By: Inanna Publications and Education Inc.
210 Founders College, York University, 4700 Keele St., Toronto, ON M3J 1P3
Tel: 416-736-5356; *Fax:* 416-736-5765
cwscf@yorku.ca
www.cwscf.ca
Circulation: 5,000
Frequency: 4 times a year
Luciana Ricciutelli, Editor-in-Chief

Chatelaine
Owned By: Rogers Media Inc.
One Mount Pleasant Rd., 8th Fl., Toronto, ON M4Y 2Y5
Tel: 416-764-2000; *Fax:* 416-764-1888
Toll-Free: 800-268-9119
www.chatelaine.com
Social Media: pinterest.com/chatelainemag
twitter.com/chatelainemag
www.facebook.com /ChatelaineMagazine
Circulation: 536,447
Frequency: Monthly
Lianne George, Editor-in-Chief

Châtelaine
Détenteur: Les Éditions Rogers Limitée
1200, av McGill College, 8e étage, Montréal, QC H3B 4G7
Tél: 514-845-5141; *Téléc:* 514-843-2185
abonner@chatelaine.com
fr.chatelaine.com
Médias sociaux:
twitter.com/chatelaine_qc
www.facebook.com/ChatelaineQc
Tirage: 160,070
Fréquence: Mensuel

Edmonton Woman
Owned By: Great West Newspapers LP
340 Carleton Dr., St Albert, AB T8N 7L3
Tel: 780-418-4741; *Fax:* 780-470-5670
www.edmontonwoman.com
Social Media:
twitter.com/EdmontonWoman
Circulation: 25,000
Frequency: 6 times a year
Fisal Asiff, Publisher, 780-470-5602, fasiff@abr.greatwest.ca
Danielle Higdon, Editor, edm.woman@abr.greatwest.ca

elevate magazine
Owned By: Salon Communications Inc.
#1902, 365 Bloor St. East, Toronto, ON M4W 3L4
Tel: 416-869-3131; *Fax:* 416-869-3008
letters@elevatemagazine.com
www.elevatemagazine.com
Social Media:
www.facebook.com/ElevateMagazine
Daniela Glacco, Publisher, daniela@elevatemagazine.com
Marissa Ponikowski, Editor-in-chief, marissa@elevatemagazine.com

Elle Canada
Owned By: TC Transcontinental
#100, 25 Sheppard Ave. West, Toronto, ON M2N 6S7
Tel: 416-733-7600
www.ellecanada.com
Social Media: www.youtube.com/user/ellecanadacom
twitter.com/ellecanada
www.faceb ook.com/ellecanada
Jacqueline Howe, Publisher

Noreen Flanagan, Sr. Editor

Elle Québec
Détenteur: TC Transcontinental
c/o TVA Publications, 1100, rue de Sérigny, Longueuil, QC J4K 5G7
Tél: 514-848-7000
www.ellequebec.com
Médias sociaux: www.youtube.com/user/ElleQc
twitter.com/ellequebec
www.facebook.com/ellequebec
Tirage: 88 398
Fréquence: Mensuel
Francine Tremblay, Éditrice
Sylvie Poirier, Rédactrice-en-chef

Femmes etc...
Détenteur: TVA Publications inc.
Sandra Cliche, Éditrice

Magazine les Ailes de la mode
#677, rue Ste-Catherine Ouest, Montréal, QC H3A 3S8
Tél: 514-282-4537
Tirage: 29 751
Fréquence: 6 fois par an
Claude Fortin, Éditeur
Julie Brisson, Rédactrice-en-chef
Camille Roberge, Rédactrice

ORAH Magazine
Canadian Hadassah-WIZO, #208, 90 Eglinton Ave. East, Toronto, ON M4P 2Y3
Tel: 416-477-5964; *Fax:* 416-477-5965
Toll-Free: 855-477-5964
info@chw.ca
www.chw.ca
Social Media: www.youtube.com/user/CHWOrganization
twitter.com/CHWdotCA
www.facebook .com/CanadianHadassahWIZO
Circulation: 14,000
Frequency: 2 times a year
Alina Ianson, Editor-in-Chief

Room Magazine
Previous Name: Room of One's Own
PO Box 46160 D, Vancouver, BC V6J 5G5
contactus@roommagazine.com
www.roommagazine.com
Social Media: www.youtube.com/user/RoomMagazineWomen
twitter.com/RoomMagazine
www.facebook.com/roommagazine
Circulation: 1,100
Frequency: 4 times a year
Rachel Thompson, Managing Editor

Women of Influence
#400, 901 King St. West, Toronto, ON M5V 3H5
Tel: 866-684-4809
info@womenofinfluenceinc.ca
www.womenofinfluence.ca/magazine
Social Media:
www.linkedin.com/company/women-of-influence-inc.
twitter.com/womenofinfl nce
www.facebook.com/womenofinfluenceinc
Circulation: 20,000
Frequency: Quarterly
Alicia Skalin, Co-CEO & Head of Events & Progamming, 647-463-8274, askalin@womenofinfluence.ca
Stephania Varalli, Co-CEO & Head of Media, 416-558-5830, svaralli@womenofinfluence.ca

Youth

Cool!
Détenteur: TVA Publications inc.
1010, rue de Sérigny, 4e étage, Longueuil, QC J4K 5G7
Tél: 514-848-7000; *Téléc:* 514-848-9854
www.magazine-cool.ca
Tirage: 62 000
Fréquence: 12 fois par an

Faze Magazine
#2400, 4936 Yonge St., Toronto, ON M2N 6S3
Tel: 416-222-3060
info@faze.ca
www.faze.ca
Social Media:
twitter.com/FazeMagazine
www.facebook.com/FazeMagazine
Frequency: 5 times a year
Lorraine Zander, Editor-in-Chief

girlworks
Owned By: Girlworks media inc.
PO Box 91559, 47 Main St. South, Georgetown, ON L7G 5M9
girlworks.ca
Social Media:
www.facebook.com/pages/girlworks-media-inc/151751732682
Frequency: Bi-monthly
Janet Kim, Contact, jkim@girlworks.ca

Scouting Life
Also Known As: The Leader
c/o Moongate Publishing Inc., #1100, 120 Eglinton Ave. East, Toronto, ON M4P 1E2
Tel: 416-930-1664
leader@scouts.ca
www.scouts.ca/ca/scouting-life
Social Media: www.youtube.com/scoutscanada
twitter.com/scoutscanada
www.facebook.com /scoutscanada
Circulation: 37,000
Frequency: 3 times a year
Ross Francis, Executive Editor

Vervegirl
Owned By: Youth Culture Inc.
85 Kildonna Dr., Toronto, ON M1N 3B9
Tel: 416-595-1313; *Fax:* 888-707-6298
www.vervegirl.com
Circulation: 178,851
Frequency: 8 times a year
Kaaren Whitney-Vernon, Group Publisher & Sales
Joanna Whitney, Editor

Youthink
4180 Lougheed Hwy., 4th Fl., Burnaby, BC V5C 6A7
Tel: 604-299-7311; *Fax:* 604-299-9188
cwm@canadawide.com
www.youthink.ca
Social Media:
twitter.com/youthinkmag
www.facebook.com/youthinkmag?ref=ts
Circulation: 69,987
Frequency: Monthly
Janine Verreault, Editor

Multicultural

Aboriginal

Alberta Native News
#A 10632, 124 St. NW, Edmonton, AB T5N 1S3
Tel: 780-421-7966; *Fax:* 780-424-3951
editor@albertanativenews.com
www.albertanativenews.com
Circulation: 10,000
Frequency: Monthly
Publishes Aboriginal news & viewpoints

Alberta Sweetgrass
The Aboriginal Multi-Media Society, 13245 - 146 St., Edmonton, AB T5L 4S8
Tel: 780-455-2700; *Fax:* 780-455-7639
market@ammsa.com
www.ammsa.com/publications/alberta-sweetgrass
Social Media:
twitter.com/windspeakernews
www.facebook.com/windspeakernews
Circulation: 7,000
Frequency: Monthly
Bert Crowfoot, Publisher
Shari Narine, Editor

First Nations Free Press
363 Sioux Rd., Sherwood Park, AB T8A 4W7
Tel: 780-449-1803; *Fax:* 780-449-1807
Frequency: Monthly
Flo Baker, Publisher

The First Perspective & The Drum
Taiga Communications Inc., PO Box 299, Peguis, MB R0C 3J0
Tel: 204-645-4214
staff@rezxchange.net
www.firstperspective.ca
Circulation: 10,000
Frequency: Monthly
James Wastasecoot, Publisher
Len Kruzenga, Editor

Ha-Shilth-Sa
PO Box 1383, Port Alberni, BC V9Y 7M2
Tel: 250-724-5757; *Fax:* 250-723-0463
www.hashilthsa.com
Circulation: 3,100
Denise Ambrose, Regional Reporter
Annie Watts, Office Manager

Inuvik Drum
PO Box 2820, Yellowknife, NT X1A 2R1
Tel: 867-873-4031; *Fax:* 867-873-8507
nnsl@nnsl.com
www.nnsl.com/inuvik/inuvik.html
Social Media:
twitter.com/nnslonline
www.facebook.com/pages/NNSLcom/118071834921 181
Circulation: 1,634
Jack Sigvaldson, Publisher
Bruce Valpy, Managing Editor, editorial@nnsl.com
Petra Ehrke, National/Territorial Manager, advertising@nnsl.com

Ktuqcqakyam Newsletter
7468 Mission Rd., Cranbrook, BC V1C 7E5
Tel: 250-489-2464
www.ktunaxa.com
Circulation: 700
Frequency: Bi-monthly
Donna Kraus-Hagerman, Contact

Mi'kmaq-Maliseet Nation News (MMNN)
PO Box 1590, 72 Church Rd., Truro, NS B2N 5V3
Tel: 902-895-2039; *Fax:* 902-893-3030
Toll-Free: 877-895-2038
info@mmnn.ca
www.mmnn.ca
Social Media:
www.facebook.com/MikmaqMaliseetNationsNews
Frequency: Monthly
Don Julien, Publisher
Carol Busby, Manager, manager@easternwoodland.ca

The Nation: The News & Cultural Magazine of the James Bay Cree
c/o Beesum Communications Inc., #403, 4529 Clark, Montréal, QC H2T 2T3
Tel: 514-272-3077; *Fax:* 514-278-9914
beesum@beesum-communications.com
www.beesum-communications.com
Circulation: 6,730
Frequency: 26 times a year; English & James Bay Cree
Aaron MacDevitt, Sales Representative

Native Journal
PO Box 57096, 2020 Sherwood Dr., Sherwood Park, AB T8A 5L7
Tel: 780-448-9693; *Fax:* 780-448-9694
Toll-Free: 866-526-8688
elaine@nativejournal.ca
www.nativejournal.ca
Circulation: 70,000
Frequency: Monthly
Elaine Shuflita, Publisher
Lisa Doucet, Publisher, njeditor@shaw.ca

Native Youth News
363 Sioux Rd., Sherwood Park, AB T8A 4W7
Tel: 780-449-1803; *Fax:* 780-449-1807
Toll-Free: 800-830-1803
fnfpltd@teluseplanet.net
Frequency: Monthly
Flo Baker, Publisher

Natotawin
PO Box 10880, Opaskwayak, MB R0B 2J0
Tel: 204-627-7066
gabriel.constant@opaskwayak.ca
www.opaskwayak.ca/natotawin.php
Circulation: 1,000
Frequency: Weekly
Gabriel Constant, Editor

New Breed Magazine
c/o Gabriel Dumont Institute, #2, 604 - 22nd St. West, Saskatoon, SK S7M 5W1
Tel: 306-657-5716; *Fax:* 306-244-0252
www.metismuseum.ca
Circulation: 1,000
Frequency: 3 times a year
Darren Préfontaine
David Morin
Karon Shmon

Nunavut News/North
c/o Northern News Services Ltd., PO Box 2820, Yellowknife, NT X1A 2R1
Tel: 867-873-4031; *Fax:* 867-873-8507
nnsl@nnsl.com
www.nnsl.com

Frequency: Weekly
J.W. (Sig) Sigvaldason, Publisher
Mike Scott, General Manager

Raven's Eye
13245 - 146 St., Edmonton, AB T5L 4S8
Tel: 780-455-2700; *Fax:* 780-455-7639
www.ammsa.com/raven

Circulation: 6,500
Frequency: Monthly
Bert Crowfoot, Publisher

Saskatchewan Sage
13245 - 146 St., Edmonton, AB T5L 4S8
Tel: 780-455-2700; *Fax:* 780-455-7639
Toll-Free: 800-661-5469
market@ammsa.com
www.ammsa.com/publications/saskatchewan-sage
Circulation: 6,000
Frequency: Monthly
Bert Crowfoot, Publisher
Cheryl Petten, Editor

Secwepemc News, The Voice of the Shuswap Nation
Secwepemc Cultural Education Society, 274A, Halston Connector Rd., Kamloops, BC V2H 1J9
Tel: 778-471-5789; *Fax:* 778-471-5792
www.secwepemc.org
Circulation: 5,000
Frequency: Monthly
Kathy Manuel, Managing Editor

Turtle Island News
Owned By: Turtle Island News Publications
PO Box 329, 2208 Chiefswood Rd., Hagersville, ON N0A 1M0
Tel: 519-445-0868; *Fax:* 519-445-0865
news@theturtleislandnews.com
www.theturtleislandnews.com
Social Media:
twitter.com/newsattheturtle
www.facebook.com/TurtleIslandNews
Circulation: 20,000
Frequency: Weekly
National native newspaper. Affiliated with Aboriginal Business Magazine.
Lynda Powless, Publisher & Editor,
lynda@theturtleislandnews.com

Western Native News Ltd.
#330, 10036 Jasper Ave, Edmonton, AB T5J 1J2
Tel: 780-421-7966; *Fax:* 780-424-3951
nativenews@telus.net
Frequency: Monthly
David Moser, Publisher
Deborah Shatz, Editor

Windspeaker
Also Known As: AMMSA
Owned By: The Aboriginal Multi-Media Society
13245 - 146 St., Edmonton, AB T5L 4S8
Tel: 780-455-2700; *Fax:* 780-455-7639
market@ammsa.com
www.ammsa.com/publications/windspeaker
Social Media:
twitter.com/windspeakernews
www.facebook.com/windspeakernews
Circulation: 24,000+
Frequency: Monthly
National Canadian Aboriginal news source.
Noel McNaughton, President
Bert Crowfoot, Chief Executive Officer, Founder & Publisher
Debora Steel, Contributing News Editor, Windspeaker,
dsteel@ammsa.com

African-Canadian & Caribbean Canadian

Caribbean Camera
#212, 55 Nugget Ave., Toronto, ON M1S 3L1
Tel: 416-412-2905; *Fax:* 416-412-2134
www.thecaribbeancamera.com
Circulation: 35,000
Frequency: Weekly; 2 editions: Montreal & Toronto
Raynier Maharaj, Editor

Hawarya
Owned By: African Network Inc.
PO Box 66036, 1116 Wilson Ave., Toronto, ON M3M 1G7
Tel: 416-459-5964; *Fax:* 905-799-2193
hawarya.publications@sympatico.ca
www.hawarya.net
Frequency: Monthly; Ethiopian
African news, especially Ethiopian.
Muluken Muchie, Editor, editor@hawarya.net

The Jamaican Weekly Gleaner
The Gleaner Company (Canada) Inc, 1390 Eglinton Ave. West, Toronto, ON M6C 2E4
Tel: 416-784-3002; *Fax:* 416-784-5719
Toll-Free: 800-233-9540
gleanercan@gleanerna.com
www.jamaica-gleaner.com
Social Media:
twitter.com/jamaicagleaner
www.facebook.com/TheJamaicaGleaner
Frequency: Weekly; also The Jamaican Weekly Star, The Black Pages Directory
Christopher Barnes, Managing Director,
christopher.barnes@gleanerjm.com
Garfield Grandison, Editor-In-Chief,
garfield.grandison@gleanerjm.com

Pride News Magazine
52 Morecambe Gate, Toronto, ON M1W 2N6
Tel: 416-492-2476; *Fax:* 416-492-2477
pridenews@bellnet.ca
www.pridenewsmagazine.com
Circulation: 25,000
Michael Van Cooten, Publisher & Editor

Word: Toronto's Urban Culture Magazine
#123, 4-2880 Queen St. East, Brampton, ON L6S 6H4
Tel: 905-799-1630; *Fax:* 905-799-2788
info@wordmag.com
www.wordmag.com
Circulation: 160,000
Frequency: 9 times a year
Angela Baldassarre, Editor
Phillip Vassell, Publisher

Arabic

Al-Mustakbal
#200, 1305, Mazurette, Montréal, QC H4N 1G8
Tel: 514-334-0909; *Fax:* 514-332-5419
info@almlustakbal.com
www.almustakbal.com
Circulation: 12,000
Serves the Arab community.
Joseph Nakhlé, Editeur
Ibrahim Ghorqyebo, Rédacteur-en-chef

Arab News International
602 Millwood Rd., Toronto, ON M5A 1K8
Tel: 416-362-0307; *Fax:* 416-861-0238
arab.publishers.@ymail.com
www.arabnews.ca
Frequency: Weekly (Wednesday)
Covers stories for the Arab community
Salah Allam, Publisher
Eynass El Masri, Managing Editor

ARC Arabic Journal
368 Queen St. E, Toronto, ON M5A 1T1
Tel: 416-362-0304; *Fax:* 416-861-0238
arab.publishers.@ymail.com
www.arabnews-canada.com/arcarabic
Circulation: 8,500
Features news from Egypt & Canada, as well as publishes short stories & articles
Emad Nafeh, Editor

Canadian Asian News
3459 Trilogy Tr., Mississauga, ON L5M 0K3
Tel: 905-826-6370
asiannews1@gmail.com
www.canadianasiannews.com
Circulation: 150,000
Frequency: Bi-weekly
Latafat Ali Siddiqui, Editor, asiannews1@hotmail.com

El-Mahroussa Magazine
Egyptian Canadian Friendship Association Inc., 879, av Saint-Charles, Chomedey, Laval, QC H7V 3T5
Tél: 450-687-0273; *Téléc:* 450-505-1908
masri.93@hotmail.com
www.el-mahrousaonline.com
Médias sociaux:
www.facebook.com/ElMahrousaMagazine
Tirage: 12,000
Fréquence: 12 issues a year
Nancy Youssef, Chief of Staff, 450-687-0273, Fax: 450-505-1908, masri.93@hotmail.com

El-Masri Newspaper
879, av St-Charles, Chomedey, Laval, QC H7V 3T5
Tél: 450-687-0273; *Téléc:* 450-505-1908
masri.93@hotmail.com
www.el-masrionline.com
Médias sociaux:
www.facebook.com/elmasrionline
Tirage: 12,000
Fréquence: Bi-weekly
Adel Iskander, General Director, 450-687-0273, Fax: 450-505-1908, masri.93@hotmail.com

The Iran Star
#205, 72 Steeles Ave. West, Thornhill, ON L4J 1A1
Tel: 905-763-9770; *Fax:* 905-763-9771
iranstar@iranstar.com
www.iranstar.com
Circulation: 12,500
Bijan Binesh, Editor-in-chief
Shahram Binesh, Editor & Coordinator

Voice of Egypt in Canada
1274, Dupont, Laval, QC H7Y 1T5
Tel: 514-288-0188; *Fax:* 514-288-1944
georgesaad@videotron.ca
www.voiceofegypt.com
Frequency: 4 times a year
George Saad, Editor-in-chief

Armenian

Abaka
Tekeyan Armenian Cultural Association of Montréal, 825 Manoogian St., Saint-Laurent, QC H4N 1Z5
Tel: 514-747-6680; *Fax:* 514-747-6162
abaka@bellnet.ca
tekeyanmontreal.ca/abaka
Social Media:
www.facebook.com/303091173093256
Frequency: Weekly; Tabloid

Horizon
3401, rue Olivar-Asselin, Montréal, QC H4J 1L5
Tel: 514-332-3757; *Fax:* 514-332-4870
www.horizonweekly.ca
Circulation: 2,000
Vahakn Karakashian, Editor

Lradou Newsletter
3401, rue Olivar-Asselin, Montréal, QC H4J 1L5
Tel: 514-333-1616
www.ars-canada.ca
Frequency: Annually

Pourastan
Parish Council of St. Gregory, 615, av Stuart, Outremont, QC H2V 3H2
Tel: 514-279-3066; *Fax:* 514-279-8008
sourpkrikor@qc.aibn.com
Circulation: 700
Frequency: irregulier
Father Boyajan

Bulgarian

Bulgarian Horizons
5312 Dundas St. West, Toronto, ON M9B 1B3
Tel: 416-962-7100; *Fax:* 416-962-7101
www.bulgarianhorizons.com
Circulation: 2,000
Maxim Bozhilov, Editor

Celtic

Celtic Life International
PO Box 8805 A, Halifax, NS B3K 5M4
Tel: 902-835-2358; *Fax:* 902-835-0080
info@CelticLife.ca
www.celticlifeintl.com
Social Media: www.youtube.com/user/celticlifeint
twitter.com/celticlife
www.facebook .com/pages/CelticLifeca/41377434690
Frequency: 4 times a year

Chinese

Chinese Canadian Times
Also Known As: CC Times
PO Box 35526, 2528 Bayview Ave., Toronto, ON M2L 2Y4
Tel: 416-445-7815; *Fax:* 416-447-9791
web@cctimes.ca
www.cctimes.ca

Frequency: Weekly; Chinese
Publication for Chinese Canadians.
Kathy Lin, Contact, kathy@cctimes.ca

The Chinese Journal
Previous Name: Canadian Chinese Times
10553A - 97 St., Edmonton, AB T5H 2L4
Tel: 780-424-0213; *Fax:* 780-428-7117
chinesejournal@telusplanet.net
www.thechinesejournal.com

Circulation: 7,000
Frequency: Weekly
Vicki Lim, Publisher
Grace Chi, Editor

The Chinese Press
Previous Name: Eastern Chinese Press Inc.
1123, rue Clark, 2e étage, Montréal, QC H2Z 1K3
Tel: 514-397-9969; *Fax:* 514-397-9929
www.chinesepress.com

Circulation: 25,000
Frequency: Weekly
Crescent Chau, Publisher/Editor

Herald Monthly
#28, 300 Steelcase Rd. West, Markham, ON L3R 2W2
Tel: 905-944-1777; *Fax:* 905-944-1778
toronto@cchc.org
www.heraldmonthly.ca

Circulation: 76,000
Frequency: Monthly; first Wed. of the month
Herald Monthly is a free broadsheet monthly Chinese newspaper.
Helena Lee, Chief Editor, 905-944-1999 ext.101, Fax: 905-944-1778, toronto@CCHC.org

Ming Pao Daily News
Owned By: Media Chinese International Limited
1355 Huntingwood Dr., Toronto, ON M1S 3J1
Tel: 416-321-0088; *Fax:* 416-321-9663
advert@mingpaotor.com
www.mingpaocanada.com
Social Media: www.youtube.com/mingpaotoronto
twitter.com/mingpaotoronto
www.facebook .com/mingpaotoronto

Frequency: Daily; Cantonese
Hong Kong news serving the Greater Toronto Area.

Modesty Magazine
#115, 18 Crown Steel Dr., Markham, ON L3R 9X8
Tel: 905-513-1232; *Fax:* 905-513-0483
modestygroup@rogers.com
www.modestymagazine.com

Circulation: 10,000
Frequency: Chinese
Ivy Lee, Publisher & Editor

The New Star Times
#206, 150 Consumers Rd., North York, ON M2J 1P9
Tel: 416-491-8401
www.newstarnet.com

Frequency: Weekly; Fridays; Mandarin
Servces Mandarin-speaking immigrants in Toronto.
Jessica C., Manager

Popular Lifestyle & Entertainment Magazine (PLEM)
3248 Cambie St., Vancouver, BC V5Z 2W4
Tel: 604-872-1285; *Fax:* 604-872-0677
info@plem.com
www.plem.com
Social Media:
www.facebook.com/iPLEM

Circulation: 75,953
Frequency: Monthly; Chinese
Patrick Wong, President & Editor-in-chief
Amanda Pi, Managing Editor
Lorna Chan, Account Executive

Les Presses Chinoises
1123, rue Clark, Montréal, QC H2Z 1K3
Tél: 514-397-9969; *Téléc:* 514-397-9929
www.chinesepress.com

Tirage: 25 000
Fréquence: Weekly
Amy Tsang

Rice Paper
PO Box 74174 Hillcrest, Vancouver, BC V5V 5C8
Tel: 604-872-3464
info@ricepapermagazine.ca
ricepapermagazine.ca
Social Media:
twitter.com/ricepapermag
www.facebook.com/ricepaper

Circulation: 3,000
Frequency: 4 times a year
Ray Hsu, Editor-in-chief

World Journal (Toronto)
#9, 7755 Warden Ave., Markham, ON L3R 0N3
Tel: 416-778-0888; *Fax:* 416-778-1037
webmaster@worldjournal.com
tor.worldjournal.com
Other information: Ads: advertising@worldjournal.com

Circulation: 25,000
Frequency: Daily; Chinese
Paul Chang, Editor-in-chief, editorial@worldjournal.com
David Ting, President

World Journal (Vancouver)
2288 Clark Dr., Vancouver, BC V5N 3G8
Tel: 604-876-1338
bcwebmaster@worldjournal.com
www.worldjournal.com/van
Social Media:
www.facebook.com/wjvancouver

Frequency: Daily; Chinese

Dutch

De Nederlandse Courant
Also Known As: Dutch-Canadian Bi-Weekly
1945 Four Seasons Dr., Burlington, ON L7P 2Y3
Tel: 905-333-3615
www.denederlandsecourant.com

Circulation: 2,700
Frequency: Bi-weekly; 25 times a year; Dutch & English
Theo Luykenaar, Publisher, publisher@denederlandsecourant.com
Bas Opdenkelder, Editor, editor@denederlandsecourant.com

Dutch
Owned By: Mokeham Publishing Inc.
PO Box 20203, 457 Ellis St., Penticton, BC V2A 8M1
Tel: 250-492-3002
info@dutchthemag.com
www.dutchthemag.com
Social Media:
twitter.com/dutchthemag
www.facebook.com/dutchthemag

A magazine in English about The Netherlands & the Dutch.
Tom , Editor, editor@dutchthemag.com

Estonian

Estonian Life
Also Known As: Eesti Elu
3 Madison Ave., Toronto, ON M5R 2S2
Tel: 416-733-4550; *Fax:* 416-733-0944
eetalitus@eestielu.ca
www.eestielu.ca
Social Media: www.youtube.com/user/eestielu
twitter.com/EestiElu
www.facebook.com/pa ges/Eesti-Elu/334488169914646

Frequency: Weekly; Estonian

Filipino

Filipiniana News
1531 Queen St. West, Toronto, ON M6R 1A5
Tel: 416-534-7836; *Fax:* 416-535-9491
filipiniananews@rogers.com

Circulation: 10,000
Frequency: Monthly

Filipino Journal
46 Pincarrow Rd., Winnipeg, MB R3Y 1E3
Tel: 204-489-8894; *Fax:* 204-489-1575
info@filipinojournal.com
filipinojournal.com
Social Media: www.flickr.com/photos/Filipino_Journal
www.facebook.com/FilipinoJournalF ans

Circulation: 4,500
Frequency: 24 times a year

The North American Filipino Star
5320-A, rue Queen Mary, Penthouse, Montréal, QC H3X 1T7
Tel: 514-485-7861
market@filipinostar.org
www.filipinostar.org/index.php

Circulation: 15,000
Frequency: Monthly
Zenaida Ferry-Kharroubi, Publisher & Chief Editor

The Philippine Reporter
PO Box 44529, 2682 Eglinton Ave. East, Scarborough, ON M1K 5K2
Tel: 416-461-8694; *Fax:* 416-461-7399
philreporter@gmail.com
www.philreporter.com

Circulation: 10,000
Frequency: Bi-monthly
Servces the Filipino-Canadian community.
Hermie Garcia, Editor

Finnish

Kanadan Sanomat
Owned By: Vapaa Sana Press Ltd.
#308, 191 Eglinton Ave. East, Toronto, ON M4P 1K1
Tel: 416-321-0808
service@vapaasana.com
finnishcanadian.com
Social Media:
twitter.com/finnishcdnCom

Frequency: Weekly

German

Das Journal
Owned By: SOL Printing & Publishing
1282 Dundas St. W, Toronto, ON M6J 1X7
Tel: 416-534-3177; *Fax:* 416-588-6441
info@dasjournal.ca
www.dasjournal.ca

Frequency: Weekly
Vasco Evaristo, Publisher, 416-538-1788
Mark Liechti, Editor, 416-534-3177

Der Bote
Mennonite Church Canada, 600 Shaftesbury Blvd., Winnipeg, MB R3P 0M4
Tel: 204-888-6781; *Fax:* 204-831-5675
Toll-Free: 866-888-6785

Circulation: 3,300
Frequency: Bi-weekly
Ingrid Jamzen, Editor

Deutsche Zeitung
Previous Name: Deutsche Presse B.C.
85 Inglis St., Ayr, ON N0B 1E0
Tel: 519-632-7700; *Fax:* 519-632-8700
Toll-Free: 888-749-0606
deutschezt@golden.net

Circulation: 7,500
Frequency: Weekly; German
Erhard Matthaes, Editor

Die Mennonitische Post
383 Main St., Steinbach, MB R5G 1Z4
Tel: 204-326-6790
mennpost@mts.net
www.mennonitischepost.com
Social Media:
www.facebook.com/pages/Die-Mennonitische-Post/4732462627 1

Circulation: 5,000
Frequency: 23 times a year

Echo Germanica
118 Tyrrel Ave., Toronto, ON M6G 2G5
Tel: 416-652-1332; *Fax:* 416-658-6909
info@echoworld.com
www.echoworld.com

Circulation: 16,000
Sybille Forster-Rentmeister, Publisher/Editor-in-chief

German Canadian Business & Trade Directory
PO Box 106, 2255B Queen St. East, Toronto, ON M4E 1G3
Tel: 416-465-9957; *Fax:* 416-465-8169
www.germancanadian.com

Circulation: 5,000
Eva Wazda, Publisher

Greek

Greek Canadian Tribune / Ellinokanadiko Vima
7835B, av Wiseman, Montréal, QC H3N 2N8
Tel: 514-272-6873; *Fax:* 514-272-3157
info@bhma.net
www.bhma.net

Frequency: Weekly; Greek & English
Christos Manikis, Editor

Greek Press
6 Chester Ave., Toronto, ON M4K 2Z9
Tel: 416-465-3243; *Fax:* 416-604-2480
info@greekpress.ca
www.greekpress.ca
Circulation: 6,000
Frequency: Bi-weekly
Constantine Kranias, Publisher/Editor

Hellenic Hamilton News
Also Known As: Nea Toy Haminton
#2, 8 Morris Ave., Hamilton, ON L8L 1X7
Tel: 905-549-9208; *Fax:* 905-549-7935
hellenicnews@sympatico.ca
Circulation: 2,000
Frequency: Monthly; Greek
Panos Andronidis, Editor

Patrides, A North American Review
PO Box 266 O, 70 Wynford Dr., Toronto, ON M3C 2S2
Tel: 416-921-4229; *Fax:* 416-921-0723
www.patrides.com
Circulation: 160,000
Frequency: Bi-weekly
Thomas S. Saras, Editor-in-Chief
Kathy Saras, Executive Managing Editor

Hungarian

Kanadai-amerikai Magyarság / Canadian American Hungarians
#103, 747 St Clair Ave. West, Toronto, ON M6C 4A4
Tel: 416-656-8361; *Fax:* 416-651-2442
info@kanadaimagyarsag.ca
www.kekujsag.com
Frequency: Weekly: English, Magyar

New Hungarian Voice
PO Box 74527 Kitsilano, Vancouver, BC V6K 4P4
nhv@newhungarianvoice.com
www.newhungarianvoice.com
Frequency: Quarterly; English
Peter Czink, Editor-in-Chief

Icelandic

Logberg -Heimskringla
#100, 283 Portage Ave., Winnipeg, MB R3B 2B5
Tel: 204-284-5686; *Fax:* 204-284-7099
Toll-Free: 866-564-2374
lh@lh-inc.ca
www.lh-inc.ca
Social Media:
twitter.com/LHNewspaper
www.facebook.com/LogbergHeimskringla
Frequency: 24 times a year; English & Icelandic
Joan Eyolfson Cadham, Editor, joan@lh-inc.ca

Italian

Corriere Canadese
#90, 2700 Dufferin St., Toronto, ON M6B 4J3
Tel: 416-782-9222; *Fax:* 416-782-9333
info@corriere.com
www.corriere.com
Social Media: www.linkedin.com/company/corriere-canadese
twitter.com/CorriereCom
www .facebook.com/CorriereCanadese
Circulation: 30,000 M-F
Frequency: Daily
Corriere Canadese is an Italian language publication.
Joe Volpe, Publisher

Corriere Italiano
Owned By: TC Transcontinental
8000, av Blaise Pascal, Montréal, QC H1E 2S7
Tel: 514-643-2300; *Fax:* 514-899-5001
corriereitaliano@tc.tc
www.corriereitaliano.com
Social Media:
twitter.com/CorriereItalian
www.facebook.com/pages/Corriere-Italia no/192672807476049
Frequency: Weekly

Il Cittadino Canadese
#710, 6020, rue Jean Talon est, Montréal, QC H1S 3B1
Tel: 514-253-2332; *Fax:* 514-253-6574
journal@cittadinocanadese.com
www.cittadinocanadese.com
Circulation: 15,000
Frequency: Weekly
Antonina Mormina, Publisher
Vittorio Giordano, Editor

Il Rincontro / La Recontre
6675, av Wilderton, Montréal, QC H3S 2L8
Tel: 514-739-4213; *Fax:* 514-344-8238
www.ilrincontro.com
Social Media:
www.facebook.com/198534390236066
Frequency: Monthly; Italian
Tony Vellone, Editor, tony.vellone@videotron.ca

Lo Specchio/Vaughan
Also Known As: The Weekly Italian Mirror
#101, 166 Woodbridge Ave., Woodbridge, ON L4L 2S7
Tel: 905-856-2823; *Fax:* 905-856-2825
editorial@lospecchio.com
www.lospecchio.com
Social Media:
www.facebook.com/lo.specchio.52
Frequency: Weekly; Fridays

L'Ora Di Ottawa
203 Louisa St., Ottawa, ON K1R 6Y9
Tel: 613-232-5689
info@loradiottawa.ca
www.loradiottawa.ca
Frequency: Weekly
Paolo Siraco, Managing Editor

Japanese

Nikkei Voice
6 Garamond Ct., Toronto, ON M3C 1Z5
Tel: 416-386-0287; *Fax:* 416-386-0136
nikkeivoice.editors@gmail.com
www.nikkeivoice.ca
Frequency: Monthly
Frank Moritsugu, Publisher

Korean

Korea Central Daily
655 Bloor St. West, Toronto, ON M6G 1L1
Tel: 416-533-5533; *Fax:* 416-533-5500
toronto.koreadaily.com
Hyo Kim, Publisher
James Lim, Editor-in-Chief

Latin American

El Mundo Latino News
Godwick Dr., Mississauga, ON L5N 7X4
Tel: 905-306-7929; *Fax:* 905-279-2702
www.elmundolatinonews.ca
Circulation: 10,000
Frequency: Weekly
Ana Griselda Romero, Publisher

El Popular
2413 Dundas St. West, Toronto, ON M6P 1X3
Tel: 416-531-2495; *Fax:* 416-531-7187
diarioelpopular.com
Frequency: Weekly
Eduardo Urueña, Director

Lithuanian

Teviskes Ziburiai/Lights of Homeland
2185 Stavebank Rd., Mississauga, ON L5C 1T3
Tel: 905-275-4672; *Fax:* 905-290-9802
tevzib@rogers.com
tevzib.com
Circulation: 2,800
Frequency: Weekly
P. Gaida, Editor-in-chief
J. Kuras, Chair

Multicultural (General)

Community Digest / Nouvelles Communautaires
British Columbia Edition, #216, 1755 Robson St., Vancouver, BC V6G 3B7
Tel: 604-875-8313
mail@communitydigest.ca
www.communitydigest.ca
Other information: Advertising: adsales@communitydigest.ca
Circulation: 25,000
Frequency: Weekly (in three editions - British Columbia, Alberta, & Ontario)
The multicultural newsmagazine is available in English & French. It promotes bilingualism & cultural trade & harmony.
N. Ebrahim, Publisher

Community Digest / Nouvelles Communautaires
Alberta Edition, #660, 3545 - 32nd Ave. NE, Calgary, AB T1Y 6M6
Tel: 403-271-8275
mail@communitydigest.ca; news@communitydigest.ca
www.communitydigest.ca
Other information: Advertising: adsales@communitydigest.ca
Frequency: Weekly (in three editions - British Columbia, Alberta, & Ontario)
The multicultural magazine encourages cultural harmony. Issues are available in English & French.
N. Ebrahim, Publisher
A. Thobhani, Alberta Bureau Chief

Ethno-Cultural Networker
129 Browning Blvd., Winnipeg, MB R3K 0L1
Tel: 204-774-3569; *Fax:* 204-783-2029
Circulation: 7000
Frequency: Monthly
Vinod Moudgill, Editor

Peel Multicultural Scene
Peel Multicultural Council, 6630 Turner Valley Rd., Mississauga, ON L5N 2P1
Tel: 905-819-1144; *Fax:* 905-542-3950
pmcgeneral@peelmc.com
www.peelmc.ca
Social Media:
youtube.com/peelpmc
www.facebook.com/profile.php?id=15988712827
Circulation: 400

Persian

Shahrvand Publications Ltd.
#304, 505 Highway 7 East, Toronto, ON L3T 7T1
Tel: 905-764-7022; *Fax:* 905-764-5919
news@shahrvand.com
www.shahrvand.com
Circulation: 30,000
Frequency: Tuesday, Friday
Farsi newspaper
Hassan Zerehi, Editor-in-chief

Polish

Czas/Polish Times
207 Cathedral Ave., Winnipeg, MB R2W 0X2
Tel: 204-582-4392; *Fax:* 204-582-4392
czaspol@mts.net
Circulation: 651
Frequency: Weekly
Krystyna Gajda, President

Glos Polski/Polish Voice
71 Judson St., Toronto, ON M8Z 1A4
Tel: 416-201-9601
glospolski@bellnet.ca
www.polishcanadians.ca/biz_EN/glos_polski_EN.html
Circulation: 6,000
Frequency: Weekly
Wieslaw Maglera, Editor-in-chief

Polish Business Directory
777C The Queensway, Toronto, ON M8Z 1N4
Tel: 416-255-9182; *Fax:* 416-255-9893
Toll-Free: 877-742-9455
mail@master.on.ca
www.przewodnikhandlowy.com
Circulation: 50,000
Frequency: annually
Martin Chlapowski
Robert Wagner, rwagner@master.on.ca

Portuguese

Sol Portugues/Portuguese Sun
977 College St., Toronto, ON M6H 1A6
Tel: 416-538-1788; *Fax:* 416-538-7953
sol@solnet.com
www.solnet.com
Circulation: 12,000
Frequency: Weekly
Newspaper; Magazine; Books; Graphic Design; Printing; Website Development; Signing; Translations
Antonio Perinu, President, 416-538-1788
Vasco Evaristo, Creative Director, 416-538-1788

A Voz de Portugal
4231, boul St-Laurent, Montréal, QC H2W 1Z4
Tél: 514-284-1813; *Téléc:* 514-284-6150
Ligne sans frais: 866-684-1813
jornal@avozdeportugal.com
www.avozdeportugal.com
Tirage: 10,000
Fréquence: Weekly
Sylvio Martins, Editor, sylviomartins@avozdeportugal.com

Russian

Nasha Gazeta
#1073, 40-1110 Finch Ave. West, Toronto, ON M3J 3M2
Tel: 647-435-8619
nashacanada@yahoo.ca
www.nashacanada.com
Circulation: 10,000
Frequency: Weekly
G. Kukuy, President
T. Sergeeva, Managing Editor
I. Toutchinski, Editor-in-chief

Serbian

Bratstvo Srpsko
Owned By: Fraternity Publishing
425 Jane St., Toronto, ON M6S 3Z7
Tel: 416-769-7181
Circulation: 2,250
Frequency: Monthly
William Durovic, Editor-in-chief
Tania Nuttall, Editor

Kisobran
#368, 3495 Cambie St., Vancouver, BC V5Z 4R3
Tel: 604-731-9446
redakcija@kisobran.com
www.kisobran.com
Circulation: 4,000
Frequency: monthly
Dragan Andrejevic, Publisher

Slovak, Czech

Novy Domov
Masaryk Memorial Institute Inc., 450 Scarborough Golf Club Rd., Toronto, ON M1G 1H1
Tel: 647-608-1713
vera.toronto@gmail.com
www.novydomov.com
Frequency: Bi-weekly

Satellite 1-416
ABE, PO Box 176 E, Toronto, ON M6H 4E2
Tel: 416-530-4222; *Fax:* 416-530-0069
abe@zpravy.ca
www.satellite1-416.com
Circulation: 1,600
Ales Brezina, Publisher & Editor

South Asian

Desi News
17600 Yonge St., Newmarket, ON L3Y 8J1
Tel: 416-695-4357
desinews@rogers.com
www.e-desinews.com
Circulation: 30,000
Frequency: Monthly
G.A. Easwar, Publisher
Shagorika Easwar, Editor

Eastern News
119 Royal West Dr., Brampton, ON L6X 0V4
Tel: 905-216-2085; *Fax:* 905-216-2065
mkhan@theeasternnews.com
www.easternnews.ca
Circulation: 7,500
Frequency: 24 times a year
Masood Khana
Masood Khan, Editor

India Journal
#11, 2355 Derry Rd. East, Mississauga, ON L5S 1V6
Tel: 905-405-0420; *Fax:* 905-405-0428
www.indiajournal.ca
Circulation: 22,000
Harjinder Singh, Publisher

Indo Caribbean World
312 Brownridge Dr., Thornhill, ON L4J 5X1
Tel: 905-738-5005; *Fax:* 905-738-3927
indocaribbeanworld@gmail.com
www.indocaribbeanworld.com
Circulation: 30,000
Frequency: 2 times per month
Harry Ramkhelawan, Publisher & Editor

Indo-Canadian Voice
Previous Name: Indo-Canadian Awaaz
8338 - 120 St., Surrey, BC V3W 3N4
Tel: 604-502-6100; *Fax:* 604-501-6111
www.voiceonline.com
Circulation: 10,000
Frequency: weekly
Vinnie Combow, Editor
Rajesh Gupta, Publisher

Journal Apna Watan
4021, boul Notre Dame, Laval, QC H7W 1S8
Tel: 514-798-2838
apnawatan2002@yahoo.com
Circulation: 5,000
Frequency: Monthly
Arshad Randhawa, Editor

Sanjh Savera/Dust and Dawn
7405 Kimbel St., Mississauga, ON L4T 3M6
Tel: 905-789-7787; *Fax:* 905-789-7717
info@sanjhsavera.com
www.sanjhsavera.com
Circulation: 15,000
Nirmal Hansa, Publisher

Thamilar Thakaval
PO Box 3 F, Toronto, ON M4Y 2L4
Tel: 416-920-9250; *Fax:* 416-921-6576
Circulation: 5,000
Frequency: Monthly
Thiru S. Thiuchelvam, Editor-in-chief

The Times of Sri Lanka
58 Sundial Cres., Toronto, ON M4A 2J8
Tel: 416-445-5390; *Fax:* 647-342-2967
timeslanka@rogers.com
www.timeslanka.com
Social Media:
www.facebook.com/timeslanka.tsl?ref=tn_tnmn
Circulation: 20,000
Frequency: TradeWinds e-Magazine is published monthly
Upali Obeyesekere, Managing Editor, 416-418-2207, upaliobey@rogers.com

The Weekly Voice
#206, 2985 Drew Rd., Mississauga, ON L4T 0A4
Tel: 907-958-2821; *Fax:* 905-795-9801
info@weeklyvoice.com
www.weeklyvoice.com
Circulation: 50,000
Binoy Thomas, Editor

Spanish

La Voz de Montreal
#112, 6225, Place Northcrest, Montréal, QC H3S 2T5
Tel: 514-253-2739; *Fax:* 514-343-9697
lavoz@sympatico.ca
Circulation: 15,000
Frequency: Monthly
Gilberto Miranda, Director

Swedish

Scandinavian Press
1294 - 7th Ave. West, Vancouver, BC V6H 1B6
Tel: 604-731-6381; *Fax:* 604-731-2292
office@nordicway.com
www.nordicway.com
Frequency: 4 times a year
Anders Neumuller, Publisher & Editor, anders@nordicway.com

Swedish Press
1950 Cypress St., Vancouver, BC V6J 3L8
Toll-Free: 866-882-0088
info@swedishpress.com
www.swedishpress.com
Social Media: www.linkedin.com/company/2925654
twitter.com/SwedishPress
www.facebook .com/swedishpress
Frequency: Monthly; English & Swedish
Tatty Maclay, Editor in Chief

Ukrainian

"Homin Ukrainy" Publishing Co. Ltd.
Also Known As: Ukrainian Echo
9 Plastics Ave., Toronto, ON M8Z 4B6
Tel: 416-516-2443
homin@on.aibn.com
www.homin.ca
Circulation: 1,000
Frequency: Weekly; Ukrainian & English

Moloda Ukraina
12 Minstrel Dr., Toronto, ON M8Y 3G4
Tel: 416-255-8604

Novy Shliakh/New Pathway
New Pathway Publishers Ltd., #210, 145 Evans Ave., Toronto, ON M5Z 5X8
Tel: 416-960-3424; *Fax:* 416-960-1442
npweekly@look.ca
www.infoukes.com/newpathway
Frequency: Weekly; also New Pathway Almanac (annual)

Progress Ukrainian Catholic News
233 Scotia St., Winnipeg, MB R2V 1V7
Tel: 204-338-7801; *Fax:* 204-339-4006
progressnews.ca
Circulation: 4,900
Rev. Mikhail Kouts, Associate Editor
Lydia Firman, Business Manager
Most Rev. Richard Soo, Managing Editor SJ

Ukrainian News
#1, 12227 - 107 Ave., Edmonton, AB T5M 1Y9
Tel: 780-488-3693; *Fax:* 780-488-3859
ukrnews@compusmart.ab.ca
Frequency: Monthly; English & Ukrainian

Visnyk/The Herald
9 St. John's Ave., Winnipeg, MB R2W 1G8
Tel: 204-586-3093; *Fax:* 204-582-5241
Toll-Free: 877-586-3093
visnyk@uocc.ca
www.uocc.ca
Circulation: 10,000
Frequency: Monthly; English & Ukrainian
Rev. Andrew Jarmus, Editor-in-chief

Vietnamese

Lang Van
250 North Service Rd., RR#2, Grimsby, ON L3M 4E8
Tel: 905-607-8010; *Fax:* 905-607-8011
tapchilangvan@yahoo.com
Circulation: 5,000
Nguyen Huu Nghia, Publisher/Editor-in-chief

Thôi Bâo/Time News
1114 College St., Toronto, ON M6H 1B6
Tel: 416-925-8607; *Fax:* 416-925-0695
www.thoibao.com
Circulation: 14,500
Frequency: Weekly
Lee Nguyen, Manager
Dave Nguyen, Publisher

Vietnam Time Magazine Edmonton
Also Known As: Viet Nam Thoi Bao Edmonton
PO Box 284 Main, 202 - 10711 - 107 Ave. NW, Edmonton, AB T5J 2J1
Tel: 780-429-4781; *Fax:* 780-429-4781
thoibao@telus.net
Circulation: 1,500
Thanh Nguyen, Publisher

Farming

Farming Publications

Aberdeen Angus World
PO Box 177, Stavely, AB T0L 1Z0
Tel: 403-549-2234; *Fax:* 403-549-2207
office@angusworld.ca
www.angusworld.ca
Aberdeen Angus World is the official publication of the Canadian Angus Association. The magazine contains information about the improvement of the Angus breed.
Dave Callaway, Editor & Publisher
Jan Lee, Associate Editor, 403-948-6053, jlee@chicoranches.com

The Ad-Viser
Farm Press Ltd., 1320 - 36th St. North, Lethbridge, AB T1H 5H8
Tel: 403-328-5114; *Fax:* 403-328-5443
Toll-Free: 877-328-0048
www.farmpressltd.com
Circulation: 19,905
Frequency: Every other Thu.

AGDealer Magazine
Owned By: Farm Business Communications
1666 Dublin Ave., Winnipeg, MB R3H OH1
Tel: 204-954-1400; *Fax:* 204-954-1422
admin@agdealer.com
www.agdealer.com
Social Media:
twitter.com/AGCanadadotcom
www.facebook.com/pages/AGCanadacom/1716318006 62

Agri Digest
PO Box 512, Sorrento, BC V0E 2W0
agridigest@fairpoint.net
www.agridigest.com
Social Media: www.linkedin.com/company/agridigest-online
twitter.com/agridigest
www.facebook.com/AgriDigestOnline
The journal examines issues in agriculture.

Agrobiomass
Owned By: Annex Publishing & Printing Inc.
PO Box 530, 105 Donly Dr. South, Simcoe, ON N3Y 4N5
Tel: 888-599-2228; *Fax:* 519-429-3094
www.agannex.com/agrobiomass
Social Media:
twitter.com/AgAnnex
All-digital publication covering the emerging agro-biomass sector in all its forms.

Alberta Barley Commission
#200, 3601A - 21 St. NE, Calgary, AB T2E 6T5
Tel: 403-291-9111; *Fax:* 403-291-0190
Toll-Free: 800-265-9111
barleyinfo@albertabarley.com
www.albertabarley.com
Circulation: 35,000
Frequency: 4 times a year
Information on barley producers of Alberta
Lisa Skierka, General Manager, 403-219-6262, lskierka@albertabarley.com
Trevor Bacque, Communications Co-ordinator, Communications, 403-219-6266, tbacque@albertabarley.com

Alberta Beef Magazine
#230, 6025-12th St. SE, Calgary, AB T2H 1K1
Tel: 403-250-1090; *Fax:* 403-291-9546
Toll-Free: 800-387-2333
www.albertabeef.ca
Circulation: 8,000
Frequency: 12 times a year
Publishers of cow & meat information
Garth McClintock, Publisher

Alberta Farmers Express
Previous Name: Alberta Express
Owned By: Farm Business Communications
1666 Dublin Ave., Winnipeg, MB R3H OH1
Tel: 204-954-1400; *Fax:* 204-954-1422
www.albertafarmexpress.ca
Social Media:
twitter.com/AGCanadadotcom
www.facebook.com/pages/AGCanadacom/1716318006 62
Circulation: 29,500
Frequency: 12 times a year
Will Verboven, Editor, will.verboven@fbcpublishing.com
Dave Bedard, Daily News Editor, daveb@fbcpublishing.com

Alberta Seed Guide
Owned By: Issues Ink
5030 - 50 St., Lacombe, AB T4L 1W8
Tel: 403-782-8022; *Fax:* 866-798-1826
Toll-Free: 877-710-3222
marketing@issuesink.com
www.seed.ab.ca
Circulation: 64,000
seed.ab.ca is Alberta's source for seed, offering the latest variety information, complete crop evaluations, comprehensive grower directories, trends, issues, and more.
Lorena Pahl, General Manager, 403-325-0081, lorena.pahl@seed.ab.ca

B.C. Dairy Directory & Farm Handbook
PO Box 724, Summerland, BC V0H 1Z0
Tel: 250-494-7049 *Toll-Free:* 888-324-7347
info@bcdairydirectory.com
www.bcdairydirectory.com
Frequency: Annually
Publishers of dairy and barn directories
Mike McCarty, Publisher
Karin McCarty, Publisher & Production Co-Ordinator, Production, 250-494-7049, info@bcdairydirectory.com
Jeff Ulmer, Production & Electronic Ad Submission, Advertising, production@bcdairydirectory.com

Beef in B.C. Magazine
#4, 10145 Dallas Dr., Kamloops, BC V2C 6T4
Tel: 250-573-3611; *Fax:* 250-573-5155
Toll-Free: 877-688-2333
www.cattlemen.bc.ca
Circulation: 1,500
Frequency: 6 times a year
Holly Jackson, Editor, 250-573-3611, Fax: 250-573-5155, editor@beefinbc.ca
Bob Somers, Advertising Representative, Advertising, 604-732-8394, Fax: 604-732-8390, ads@beefinbc.ca

Better Farming
Owned By: AgMedia Inc.
ON
Tel: 519-763-4044
publisher@betterfarming.com
www.betterfarming.com
Circulation: 43,000
Information for farmers in Ontario
Robert C. Irwin, Managing Editor, 613-678-2232, Fax: 613-678-5993, rirwin@betterfarming.com
Don Stoneman, Senior Staff Editor, 519-654-9106, Fax: 519-654-9357, dstoneman@betterfarming.com
Mary Baxter, Field Editor, 519-858-0074, mbaxter@betterfarming.com

Better Pork Magazine
Owned By: AgMedia Inc.
ON
Tel: 519-763-4044
admin@betterfarming.com
www.betterfarming.com
Circulation: 6,403
Frequency: 6 times a year
Magazine for Ontario's registered pork producers
Robert C. Irwin, Managing Editor, 613-678-2232, Fax: 613-678-5993, rirwin@betterfarming.com

Le Bulletin des Agriculteurs
#320, 1, Place du Commerce, Ile-des-Soeurs, QC H3E 1A2
Tél: 514-766-9554; *Téléc:* 514-766-2665
www.lebulletin.com
Fréquence: Mensuel
Yvon Therien, Éditeur, yvon.therien@lebulletin.com

CAAR Communicator
Previous Name: WFCD Communicator
628 - 70 Arthur St., Winnipeg, MB R3B 1G7
Tel: 204-989-9300; *Fax:* 204-989-9306
Toll-Free: 800-463-9323
info@caar.org
www.caar.org
Social Media:
twitter.com/CdnAgRetail
Circulation: 17,000
Frequency: 5 times a year
Publication of the Canadian Association of Agri-Retailers.
Lynda Nicol, Manager, Communications & Membership, 204-989-9305, lynda@caar.org

Canadian Ayrshire Review
c/o The Ayrshire Breeders' Association of Canada, 4865, boul Laurier ouest, Saint-Hyacinthe, QC J2S 3V4
Tel: 450-778-3535; *Fax:* 450-778-3531
info@ayrshire-canada.com
www.ayrshire-canada.com
Frequency: Bi-monthly
Michel Boudreault, General Manager

Canadian Biomass Magazine
Owned By: Annex Publishing & Printing Inc.
PO Box 530, 105 Donly Dr. South, Simcoe, ON N3Y 4N5
Tel: 519-429-3966; *Fax:* 519-429-3094
Toll-Free: 800-265-2827
www.canadianbiomassmagazine.ca
Social Media:
twitter.com/AgAnnex
Frequency: Bi-monthly
Scott Jamieson, Editorial Director, 519-429-5180, sjamieson@annexweb.com
Andrew Snook, Editor, 905-713-4301, asnook@annexweb.com
Andrew Macklin, Editor, 905-713-4358, amacklin@annexweb.com

Canadian Cattlemen: The Beef Magazine
Owned By: Farm Business Communications
1666 Dublin AVe., Winnipeg, MB R3H OH1
Tel: 204-944-5753; *Fax:* 204-954-1422
www.canadiancattlemen.ca
Frequency: 13 editions, annually
Gren Winslow, Editor, 204-944-5753, gren@fbcpublishing.com

Canadian Guernsey Journal
Canadian Guernsey Assn., 7660 Mill Rd., Guelph, ON N1H 6J2
Tel: 519-836-2141; *Fax:* 519-763-6582
info@guernseycanada.ca
www.guernseycanada.ca
Frequency: Triannual

Canadian Hereford Digest
5160 Skyline Way NE, Calgary, AB T2E 6V1
Tel: 403-275-2662; *Fax:* 403-295-1333
Toll-Free: 888-836-7242
info@herefordigest.com
www.hereford.ca/5_digest.php
Social Media:
twitter.com/CAN_Hereford
Frequency: 7 times a year
Brad Dubeau, Director, Communications

The Canadian Horsetrader
PO Box 219, Dutton, ON N0L 1J0
Tel: 519-762-3993
pams@wwdc.com
www.horsetradermagazine.com
Social Media:
www.linkedin.com/pub/horse-trader-magazine/50/870/165
twitter.com/HorseT raderMag
www.facebook.com/horsetradermag
Circulation: 10,000
Frequency: Monthly

Canadian Jersey Breeder
#9, 350 Speedvale Ave. West, Guelph, ON N1H 7M7
Tel: 519-821-1020; *Fax:* 519-821-2723
info@jerseycanada.com
www.jerseycanada.com/pages/jersey-breeder-magazine.html
Frequency: 5 times a year

Canadian Poultry Magazine
Owned By: Annex Publishing & Printing Inc.
PO Box 530, 105 Donly Dr. South, Simcoe, ON N3Y 4K5
Tel: 519-429-3966; *Fax:* 519-429-3094
Toll-Free: 800-265-2827
www.agannex.com/canadian-poultry
Social Media:
twitter.com/canadianpoultry
Circulation: 5,300
Frequency: 12 times a year
Kristy Nudds, Editor, knudds@annexweb.com
Marilyn White, Sales Manager, mwhite@annexweb.com

Canola Digest
Canola Council of Canada, #400, 167 Lombard Ave., Winnipeg, MB R3B 0T6
Tel: 204-982-2100 *Toll-Free:* 866-834-4378
admin@canolacouncil.org
www.canola-council.org
Circulation: 40,000
Frequency: 4 times a year
Jay Whetter, Communications Manager, whetterj@canolacouncil.org.

Charolais Banner
124 Shannon Rd., Regina, SK S4S 4B1
Tel: 306-546-3940; *Fax:* 306-546-3942
charolaisbanner@sasktel.net
www.charolaisbanner.com
Social Media:
twitter.com/CharolaisBanner
Frequency: 5 times a year
Helge By, Publisher

Le Coopérateur Agricole
CP 500 Youville, Montréal, QC H2P 2W2
Tél: 514-384-6450
cooperateur@lacoop.coop
www.lacoop.coop/cooperateur
Tirage: 18,000
Fréquence: 10 fois par an
Guylaine Gagnon, Directrice et rédactrice-en-chef

Country Guide
Owned By: Farm Business Communications
1666 Dublin Ave., Winnipeg, MB R3H 0H1
Tel: 204-944-5754; *Fax:* 204-954-1422
www.country-guide.ca

Frequency: Monthly
Eastern and Western editions
Tom Button, Editor, tbutton@twinbanks.com

Drainage Contractor
Owned By: Annex Publishing & Printing Inc.
PO Box 530, 105 Donly Dr. South, Simcoe, ON N3Y 4N5
Tel: 519-429-3966; *Fax:* 519-429-3094
Toll-Free: 800-265-2827
www.agannex.com/drainage-contractor

Circulation: 8,871
Frequency: Annually; November
Ed Cosman, Contact, ecosman@annexweb.com

Eastern Ontario Agrinews
PO Box 368, 7 King St., Chesterville, ON K0C 1H0
Tel; 613-448-2321; *Fax:* 613-448-3260
rm@agrinewsinteractive.com
agrinewsinteractive.com

Circulation: 14,000
Frequency: Monthly
Robin R. Morris, Publisher

Farm Focus
Owned By: TC Transcontinental
211 Horseshoe Lake Dr., Halifax, NS B3S 0B9
Tel: 902-749-2525; *Fax:* 902-742-2311
editor@atlanticfarmfocus.ca
www.atlanticfarmfocus.ca

Heather Jones, Editor, editor@atlanticfarmfocus.ca
Jennifer Lalonde, Representative, Advertising Sales, jennifer.lalonde@transcontinental.ca

Farming for Tomorrow
Previous Name: Farm Light & Power
#200, 2161 Scarth St., Regina, SK S4P 2H8
Toll-Free: 866-525-4338
info@farmingfortomorrow.ca
www.farmingfortomorrow.ca
Other information: Toll Free Fax: 1-888-213-9999
Social Media:
www.facebook.com/pages/Farming-for-Tomorrow/407600566033
5

Circulation: 67,400
Frequency: 2 times a year
Tom Bradley, Publisher

Fruit & Vegetable Magazine
Previous Name: Canadian Fruitgrower
Owned By: Annex Publishing & Printing Inc.
PO Box 530, 105 Donly Dr. South, Simcoe, ON N3Y 4N5
Fax: 519-429-3094
Toll-Free: 800-265-2827
www.agannex.com/fruit-vegetable
Social Media:
twitter.com/FruitVeggieMag
www.facebook.com/fruitandvegetablemagazine

Frequency: 8 times a year
Diane Kleer, Publisher
Marg Land, Editor, mland@annexweb.com

Germination
Owned By: Issues Ink
#301, 313 Pacific Ave., Winnipeg, MB R3A 0M2
Tel: 877-710-3222
www.germination.ca
Social Media:
twitter.com/germinationmag
www.facebook.com/GerminationMag

Circulation: 5,700
Germination is the first and only magazine aimed specifically at Canada's seed industry.
Shawn Brook, President

Gestion et Technologie Agricoles
Détenteur: DBC Communications inc.
655, av Sainte-Anne, Saint-Hyacinthe, QC J2S 5G4
Tél: 450-773-6028; *Téléc:* 450-773-3115
publicite@courrierclarion.qc.ca
www.lecourrier.qc.ca

Fréquence: 11 fois par an

Grainews
Owned By: Farm Business Communications
1666 Dublin Ave., Winnipeg, MB R3H 0H1
Tel: 306-861-2678
www.grainews.ca

Frequency: 18 times a year
Leeann Minogue, Editor, 306-861-2678, leeann.minogue@fbcpublishing.com

Holstein Journal
#301, 9040 Leslie St., Richmond Hill, ON L4B 3M4
Tel: 905-886-4222; *Fax:* 905-886-0037
www.holsteinjournal.com

Frequency: Monthly
G. Peter English, Publisher, peter@holsteinjournal.com
Bonnie Cooper, Editor, bonnie@holsteinjournal.com

iDeal Equipment Magazine
Owned By: Farm Business Communications
1666 Dublin Ave., Winnipeg, MB R3H 0H1
Tel: 204-954-1400; *Fax:* 204-954-1422
www.idealequipment.ca
Social Media:
twitter.com/AGCanadadotcom
www.facebook.com/pages/AGCanadacom/1716318006 62

The Island Farmer
PO Box 790, 567 Main St., Montague, PE C0A 1R0
Tel: 902-838-2515; *Fax:* 902-838-4392
Toll-Free: 800-806-5443
www.peicanada.com
Social Media:
twitter.com/graphicnews

Circulation: 5,200
Frequency: Bi-weekly
Paul MacNeill, Publisher
Heather Moore, Editor

The Limousin Leader
Bollum Marketing, PO Box 10, Site 11, RR#1, Airdrie, AB T4B 2A3
Tel: 403-948-4768; *Fax:* 403-948-7531
www.limousinleader.com

Frequency: 4 times a year
Randy Bollum, Editor

Ma Revue de machinerie agricole
Section Rouge Média Inc., 468, boul Roland-Therrien, Longueuil, QC J4H 4E3
Tél: 450-677-2556; *Téléc:* 450-677-4099
info@marevueagricole.com
www.marevueagricole.com

Fréquence: 11 fois par an

Manitoba Co-Operator
Owned By: Farm Business Communications
1666 Dublin Ave., Winnipeg, MB R3H 0H1
Tel: 204-792-4383 *Toll-Free:* 204-954-1422
www.manitobacooperator.ca

Frequency: Weekly; supplements Seed Manitoba (annual); Yield Manitoba (annual)
Laura Rance, Editor, 204-792-4382, laura@fbcpublishing.com

Manitoba Farmers' Voice
Owned By: Craig Kelman & Associates Ltd.
c/o Keystone Agricultural Producers, #203, 1700 Ellice Ave., Winnipeg, MB R3H 0B1
Tel: 204-697-1140; *Fax:* 204-697-1109
communications@kap.mb.ca
www.kap.mb.ca/pub_mfv.htm

Frequency: 4 times a year
Cheryl Parisien, Managing Editor, cheryl@kelman.ca

Manitoba FarmLIFE
#300, 2050 Cume Blvd., Brandon, MB R7A 5Y1
Toll-Free: 888-756-5459
www.farmpressltd.com

Circulation: 28,000
Frequency: 26 times a year
Dale Coulter, Manager

Manure Manager
Owned By: Annex Publishing & Printing Inc.
PO Box 530, 105 Donly Dr. South, Simcoe, ON N3Y 4N5
Tel: 519-429-3966; *Fax:* 519-429-3094
Toll-Free: 800-265-2827
www.agannex.com/manure-manager
Social Media:
twitter.com/ManureManager

Frequency: 8 times a year
Manure handling industry across North America.
Marg Land, Editor, 888-599-2228 ext.269, mland@annexweb.com

The Northern Horizon
901 - 100th Ave., Dawson Creek, BC V1G 1W2
Tel: 250-782-4888; *Fax:* 250-782-6300
www.northernhorizon.ca

Circulation: 20,000
Frequency: Bi-weekly
The agricultural publication serves British Columbia, north central Alberta, & the Alberta Peace Region.
William Julian, Regional Manager, wj@ahnfsj.ca

Northwest Farmer Rancher
PO Box 1029, 892 - 104th St., North Battleford, SK S9A 3E6
Tel: 306-445-7621; *Fax:* 306-445-3223
battlefords.publishing@sasktel.net

Frequency: 7 times a year
The magazine targets agricultural producers in northwestern Saskatchewan.

Ontario Beef
Ontario Cattlemen's Assn., 130 Malcolm Rd., Guelph, ON N1K 1B1
Tel: 519-824-0334; *Fax:* 519-824-9101
info@ontariobeef.com
www.ontariobeef.com

Circulation: 15,000
Frequency: 5 times a year
LeaAnne Wuermli, Editor
Amber McIntyre, Circulation Manager

Ontario Beef Farmer
Owned By: Postmedia Network Inc.
PO Box 7400, London, ON N5Y 4X3
Toll-Free: 877-358-7773
www.ontariofarmer.com

Frequency: Bi-monthly
Paul Mahon, Publisher & Editor, ontariofarmer.editorial@sunmedia.ca

Ontario Dairy Farmer
Owned By: Postmedia Network Inc.
PO Box 7400, London, ON N5Y 4X3
Toll-Free: 877-358-7773
www.ontariofarmer.com

Circulation: 7,445
Frequency: 8 times a year
Paul Mahon, Publisher

Ontario Farmer
Owned By: Postmedia Network Inc.
PO Box 7400, London, ON N5Y 4X3
Toll-Free: 877-358-7773
www.ontariofarmer.com

Frequency: Weekly, Tue.
Paul Mahon, Publisher/Editor-in-Chief

Ontario Hog Farmer
Owned By: Postmedia Network Inc.
PO Box 7400, London, ON N5Y 4X3
Toll-Free: 877-358-7773
www.ontariofarmer.com

Frequency: 8 times a year
Paul Mahon, Publisher/Editor-in-Chief

Ontario Milk Producer
Dairy Farmers of Ontario, 6780 Campobello Rd., Mississauga, ON L5N 2L8
Tel: 905-821-8970; *Fax:* 905-821-3160
questions@milk.org
www.milk.org

Circulation: 9500
Frequency: Monthly
Sharon Laidlaw, Editor

Porc Québec
Anciennement: Porc Québec - Québec Hog Industry Magazine
#120, 555, boul Roland Therrien, Longueuil, QC J4H 4E9
Tél: 450-679-0530; *Téléc:* 450-679-0102
leseleveursdeporcs@upa.qc.ca
www.leporcduquebec.com

Fréquence: 4 fois par an
Martin Archambault, Rédacteur en chef, marchambault@upa.qc.ca

Prairie Farmer
Previous Name: The Agri Times
PO Box 1356, Winkler, MB R6W 4B3
Tel: 204-325-4771; *Fax:* 204-325-5059
Toll-Free: 888-565-8357
www.winklertimes.com

Circulation: 26,000
Frequency: 25 times a year
Rick Reimer, Publisher

Prairie Hog Country
PO Box 5536, Leduc, AB T9E 2A1
Tel: 780-986-0962; *Fax:* 780-980-9640
hogcountry@shaw.ca
www.prairiehogcountry.ca

Circulation: 4,800
Frequency: bi-monthly
Calvin Daniels, Copy Editor
Laurie Brandly, Publisher

Le Producteur de lait québécois
Les Producteurs de lait du Québec, #415, 555, boul Roland Thérrien, Longueuil, QC J4H 4G3
Tél: 450-679-0530; *Téléc:* 450-679-5899
plq@upa.qc.ca
www.lait.org
Fréquence: 10 fois par an
François Bertrand, Rédacteur en chef

Producteur Plus
CP 147, Farnham, QC J2N 2R4
Tél: 450-293-3145; *Téléc:* 450-293-8383
info@producteurplus.com
producteurplus.com
Fréquence: 8 fois par an
Suzie Le Sauteur, Rédactrice-en-chef

Québec Farmers' Advocate
#255, 555, boul Roland-Therrien, Longueuil, QC J4H 4E7
Tel: 450-679-0540; *Fax:* 450-463-5291
qfa_advocate@upa.qc.ca
www.quebecfarmers.org
Circulation: 4,000
Frequency: 11 times per year
Andrew McClelland, Editor

Regional Country News
Previous Name: The Farm Gate
Owned By: Metroland Printing Publishing & Distribution
11 Wellington St. North, St Marys, ON N4X 1B7
Tel: 519-284-2440
www.southwesternontario.ca
Frequency: Monthly
Stew Slater, Editor, 519-284-1155 ext 105

Rural Roots
PO Box 126, Beaverlodge, AB T0H 0C0
editor@ruralrootsmagazine.ca
www.ruralrootsmagazine.ca
Frequency: Quarterly
The magazine features accounts of rural lifestyles & communities in western Canada. Topics include farming, farm family business ventures, horticulture, livestock, wildlife, conservation, history, antiques, hobbies, country homes & adventures. Rural Roots is distributed to subscribers, and it can be found at agribusinesses, farmers' markets, & tourist centres.

The Rural Voice
Owned By: North Huron Publishing Inc.
PO Box 429, Blyth, ON N0M 1H0
Tel: 519-523-4792
info@northhuron.on.ca
www.northhuron.on.ca
Frequency: Monthly

Saskatchewan Farm Life
#200, 1630 Quebec Ave., Saskatoon, SK S7K 1V7
Tel: 306-384-3276; *Fax:* 306-668-6164
Toll-Free: 888-924-6397
www.farmpressltd.com
Circulation: 41,887
Frequency: Bi-weekly
The magazine provides information for farmers & ranchers in Saskatchewan. A classified section is included.

Sheep Canada
1489 Rte. 560, Deerville, NB E7K 1W7
Tel: 506-328-3599; *Fax:* 506-328-8165
Toll-Free: 888-241-5124
gallivan@sheepcanada.com
www.sheepcanada.com
Social Media:
www.facebook.com/pages/Sheep-Canada-magazine/253659158039
Frequency: 4 times a year
Dr. Cathy Gallivan, Editor

Simmental Country
#13, 4101 - 19 St. NE, Calgary, AB T2E 7C4
Tel: 403-250-5255; *Fax:* 403-250-5121
Toll-Free: 866-860-6051
cansim@simmental.com
www.simmental.com
Frequency: Monthly
The official publication of the Canadian Simmental Association with up to-date information and articles that are of interest to both Purebred and Commercial Cattlemen.

La Terre de chez nous
#100, 555, boul Roland Therrien, Longueuil, QC J4H 3Y9
Tél: 450-679-8483; *Téléc:* 450-670-4788
Ligne sans frais: 877-679-7809
laterre.ca
Médias sociaux: youtube.com/terredecheznous
twitter.com/laterreca
www.facebook.com/lat erreca
Tirage: 26,003
Fréquence: Hebdomadaire
Bernard Blanchard, Rédacteur-en-chef

Top Crop Manager
Owned By: Annex Publishing & Printing Inc.
PO Box 530, 105 Donly Dr. South, Simcoe, ON N3Y 4N5
Tel: 519-429-3966; *Fax:* 519-429-3094
Toll-Free: 800-265-2827
www.agannex.com/top-crop-manager
Social Media:
twitter.com/TopCropMag
Frequency: 8 Western/year, 7 Eastern/year, 1 Potatoes/year
Magazine of crop production and technology, a specialty agricultural trade publication.
Sara Avoledo, Eastern Editor, 226-931-5608, savoledo@annexweb.com
Janet Kanters, Western Editor, 403-499-9754, jkanters@annexweb.com

Union Farmer Quarterly
National Farmers Union, 2717 Wentz Ave., Saskatoon, SK S7K 4B6
Tel: 306-652-9465; *Fax:* 306-664-6226
nfu@nfu.ca
www.nfu.ca/publications/unionfarmerquarterly
Social Media:
twitter.com/NFUcanada
Frequency: 4 times a year

Western Dairy Farmer Magazine
Owned By: Postmedia Network Inc.
Ontario Farmer, PO Box 7400, London, ON N5Y 4X3
Fax: 519-473-2256
Toll-Free: 877-358-7773
ontariofarmer.advertising@sunmedia.ca
www.ontariofarmer.com
Circulation: 4347
Frequency: 10 times a year
Paul Mahon, Publisher/Editor-in-Chief

Western Hog Journal
Alberta Pork Industry Services, 4828 - 89 St., Edmonton, AB T6E 5K1
Tel: 780-474-8288; *Fax:* 780-479-5128
Toll-Free: 877-247-7675
info@albertapork.com
www.albertapork.com/NewsReports/WesternHogJournal
Frequency: 4 times a year
Sheri Monk, Editor, 403-627-1828, sherimonk@gmail.com

Western Horse Review
Previous Name: Northern Horse Review
#814, 3545 - 32 Ave. NE, Calgary, AB T1Y 6M6
Tel: 403-250-1128
enquiries@westernhorsereview.com
www.westernhorsereview.com
Social Media:
twitter.com/westernhorserev
www.facebook.com/pages/Western-Horse-Review/178276713247
Circulation: 15,000
Frequency: 11 times a year
Ingrid Schulz, Publisher & Editor, ingrids@efirehose.net
Jenn Webster, Managing Editor, editorial@westernhorsereview.com

The Western Producer
PO Box 2500, 2310 Millar Ave., Saskatoon, SK S7K 2C4
Tel: 306-665-3544; *Fax:* 306-934-2401
Toll-Free: 800-667-6978
subscriptions@producer.com
www.producer.com
Other information: Advertising, E-mail: advertising@producer.com
Social Media:
twitter.com/westernproducer
www.facebook.com/westernproducer
Frequency: Weekly
The agricultural publication is of interest to farmers & ranchers in western Canada. News & information is included about rural life, technology, production, livestock, markets, & finance. News bureaus are located in Ottawa, Brandon, Winnipeg, Saskatoon, Regina, Calgary, & Camrose.
Brian MacLeod, Editor, brian.macleod@producer.com
Brian Cross, Editor, Supplements, brian.cross@producer.com
Terry Fries, Editor, News, terry.fries@producer.com
Michelle Houlden, Director, Art, michelle.houlden@producer.com
D'Arce McMillan, Editor, Markets & Agri-Finance, darce.mcmillan@producer.com
Karen Morrison, Editor, Farm Living, karen.morrison@producer.com
Michael Raine, Editor, Farm Management, michael.raine@producer.com
Catherine Rumanick, Editor, Layout, catherine.rumanick@producer.com
Paul Yanko, Editor, Website, paul.yanko@producer.com
Kelly Berg, Director, Advertising, 306-665-3524, kelly.berg@producer.com
Robert Magnell, Creative Director, 306-665-9629, robert.magnell@producer.com
Jack Phipps, Director, Marketing, 306-665-3520, jack.phipps@producer.com
Shauna Brand, Manager, Classifieds, 306-665-3536, shauna.brand@producer.com
Gwen Thompson, Supervisor, Subscriptions, 306-665-3596, gwen.thompson@producer.com
Brenda McPhail, Librarian, brenda.mcphail@producer.com

Food & Beverage

Flavourful
Owned By: Issues Ink
#301, 313 Pacific Ave., Winnipeg, MB R3A 0M2
Tel: 204-453-1965
Frequency: 2 times a year
Distributed through Canadian embassies and used as a tool by participants in missions to Canada's key agri-food markets such as the U.S., Japan, European Union, Mexico, and China.

Spud Smart
Owned By: Issues Ink
#403, 313 Pacific Ave., Winnipeg, MB R3A 0M2
Tel: 204-453-1965; *Fax:* 204-475-5247
www.spudsmart.com
Social Media:
twitter.com/SpudSmartMag
www.facebook.com/SpudSmart
Spud Smart is the primary publication in the Canadian potato industry.
Julienne Isaacs, Editor, 204-453-1965 x810, jisaacs@issuesink.com

Industrial & Industrial Automation

Resource Engineering & Maintenance (REM)
Owned By: Annex Publishing & Printing Inc.
PO Box 530, 105 Donly Dr. South, Simcoe, ON N3Y 4N5
Tel: 519-429-3966; *Fax:* 519-429-3094
Toll-Free: 800-265-2827
www.rem-mag.com
Rehana Begg, Editor, 905-726-4655, rbegg@annexweb.com

Scholarly

Scholarly Publications

Acadiensis: Journal of the History of the Atlantic Region / Revue d'Histoire de la Région Atlantique
Campus House, University of New Brunswick, PO Box 4400 A, Fredericton, NB E3B 5A3
Tel: 506-453-4978; *Fax:* 506-453-5068
acadiensis@unb.ca
www.lib.unb.ca/Texts/Acadiensis
Circulation: 900
Frequency: 2 times a year
John G. Reid, Editor, 902-420-5760, john.reid@smu.ca
Sasha Mullally, Editor, 506-453-5181
Stephen Dutcher, Managing Editor, nlang@umce.ca

Annals of Air & Space Law (IASL) / Annales de droit aérian et spatial
Institute & Centre of Air & Space Law, McGill University, 3661, rue Peel, Montréal, QC H3A 1X1
Tel: 514-398-5095; *Fax:* 514-398-8197
www.mcgill.ca/iasl/annals
Circulation: 1,000
Frequency: annually
Provides graduate legal education for students worldwide
Paul S. Dempsey, Director, 514-398-8370, paul.dempsey@mcgill.ca

Arctic Journal
c/o Arctic Institute of North America, University of Calgary, 2500 University Dr. NW, Calgary, AB T2N 1N4
Tel: 403-220-7515; *Fax:* 403-282-4609
arctic.ucalgary.ca
Social Media:
twitter.com/ASTISdatabase
www.facebook.com/ArcticInstituteofNorthA merica
Circulation: 1,500
Frequency: 4 times a year
Publishes books on the North, providing information from the natural, social, earth science & humanities
Dr. Karen McCullough, Editor, 403/220-4049
Dr. Benoît Beauchamp, Executive Director, 403/220-7516

ARIEL
Department of English, University of Calgary, Calgary, AB T2N 1N4
Tel: 403-220-4657; *Fax:* 403-289-1123
ariel@ucalgary.ca
www.ariel.ucalgary.ca/ariel/index.php/ariel/index
Social Media:
www.facebook.com/281828241969527
Circulation: 850
Frequency: 4 times a year
A Review of International English Literature
Michael T. Clarke, Co-Editor
Faye Halpern, Co-Editor

Atlantis: A Women's Studies Journal
Evaristus 231, Halifax, NS B3M 2J6
Tel: 902-457-6319; *Fax:* 902-443-1352
atlantis.journal@msvu.ca
www.msvu.ca/atlantis
Circulation: 500
Frequency: 2 times a year
Prime source in women's studies
Krista Montelpare, Manging Editor

Canadian Ethnic Studies / Études Ethniques au Canada
Dept. of Sociology, University of Calgary, #SS909, Calgary, AB T2N 1N4
Tel: 403-282-9298
ces@ucalgary.ca
umanitoba.ca/publications/ces/index.html
Circulation: 1,800
Frequency: 3 times a year
Fully refereed, interdisciplinary journal devoted to the study of ethnicity, immigration, inter-group relations, and the history and cultural life of ethnic groups in Canada.
Dr. Lloyd Wong, Co-editor
Dr. Shibao Guo, Co-editor

Canadian Foreign Policy Journal / La Politique étrangère du Canada
5306 River Building, Norman Paterson School of International Affairs, 1125 Colonel By Dr., Ottawa, ON K1S 5B6
Tel: 613-520-6655; *Fax:* 613-520-2889
international_affairs@carleton.ca
www.tandfonline.com
Frequency: 3 times a year
Online ISSN is 2157-0817
Brian Tomlin, Editor
Kevin Arthur, Managing Editor

Canadian Historical Review
Owned By: University of Toronto Press
University of Toronto Press - Journals Division, 5201 Dufferin St., Toronto, ON M3H 5T8
Tel: 416-667-7810; *Fax:* 416-667-7881
Toll-Free: 800-221-9985
chr@utpress.utoronto.ca
www.utpjournals.press/loi/chr
Circulation: 1,700
Frequency: 4 times a year
Suzanne Morton, Co-Editor
Dimitry Anastakis, Co-Editor

Canadian Journal of Development Studies / Revue canadienne d'études du développement
Owned By: Canadian Association for the Study of International Development
c/o School for International Studies, Simon Fraser University, #7200, 515 West Hastings St., Vancouver, BC V6B 5K3
Tel: 778-782-7148
cjds@sfu.ca
www.casid-acedi.ca/cjds
Circulation: 500
Frequency: 4 times a year, plus 1 special issue
Haroon Akram-Lodhi, Editor

Canadian Journal of Economics / Revue canadienne d'economique
PO Box 35006, 1221, Fleury est, Montréal, QC H2C 3K4
Tel: 646-257-5906
journals@economics.ca
economics.ca/cje/en/index.php
Circulation: 3,200
Frequency: 4 times a year
Francisco Ruge-Murcia, Managing Editor

Canadian Journal of Higher Education (CJHE) / La revue canadienne d'enseignemnet supérieur
Also Known As: CJHE
Owned By: Canadian Society for the Study of Higher Education
c/o Canadian Society for the Study of Higher Education, #204, 260 Dalhousie St., Ottawa, ON K1N 7E4
Tel: 613-241-0018; *Fax:* 613-241-0019
www.csshe-scees.ca/cjhe.htm; www.cjhe-rces.ca
The peer reviewed journal publishes articles about the structure & processes of the Canadian higher education system. Book reviews are also included in the journal.
Lesley Andres, Editor-in-Chief, lesley.andres@ubc.ca

Canadian Journal of History (CJH) / Annales canadiennes d'histoire
Dept. of History, University of Saskatchewan, 9 Campus Dr., Saskatoon, SK S7N 5A5
Tel: 306-966-5794; *Fax:* 306-966-5852
cjh@usask.ca
utpjournalsreview.com/index.php/CJOH/index
Circulation: 725
Frequency: 3 times a year
Rilla Friesen, Managing Editor

Canadian Journal of Information & Library Science
Owned By: University of Toronto Press
5201 Dufferin St., Toronto, ON M3H 5T8
Tel: 416-667-7810; *Fax:* 416-667-7881
Toll-Free: 800-221-9985
journals@utpress.utoronto.ca
muse.jhu.edu/journals/canadian_journal_of_i nformation_and_library_science/
Circulation: 400
Frequency: 4 times a year
Dr. Clément Arsenault, Editor

Canadian Journal of Law & Society (CJLS/RCDS) / La Revue Canadienne Droit et Société
Dept des sciences juridiques, UQAM, PO Box 8888 Centre-Ville, Montréal, QC H3C 3P8
Tel: 514-987-4133; *Fax:* 514-987-4784
www.acds-clsa.org/en/canadian_journal_law_society.cfm
Circulation: 700
Frequency: Biennially
Benjamin L. Berger, Co-editor
Joane Martel, Co-editor
Dawn Moore, Co-editor

Canadian Journal of Linguistics (CJL/RCL) / Revue Canadienne de Linguistique
Owned By: University of Toronto Press
5201 Dufferin St., Toronto, ON M3H 5T8
Tel: 416-667-7810; *Fax:* 416-667-7881
Toll-Free: 800-221-9985
journals@utpress.utoronto.ca
www.utpjournals.com
Circulation: 900
Frequency: 4 times a year
Éric Mathieu, Co-editor
Elizabeth Cowper, Co-editor

Canadian Journal of Mathematics (CJM)
c/o Canadian Mathematical Society, #209, 1725 St. Laurent Blvd., Ottawa, ON K1G 3V4
Tel: 613-733-2662; *Fax:* 613-733-8994
cms.math.ca/cjm
Social Media:
twitter.com/canmathsociety
www.facebook.com/canmathsoc
Circulation: 1,225
Frequency: 6 times a year
Henry Kim, Editor-in-Chief
Robert McCann, Editor-in-Chief

Canadian Journal of Neurological Sciences
c/o Canadian Neurological Sciences Federation, #709, 7015 MacLeod Trail SW, Calgary, AB T2H 2K6
Tel: 403-229-9544; *Fax:* 403-229-1661
www.cjns.org
Circulation: 1,200
Frequency: Bi-monthly
The journal is the official publication of the four member societies of the Canadian Neurological Sciences Federation: Canadian Neurological Society (CNS), Canadian Neurosurgical Society (CNSS), Canadian Association of Child Neurology (CACN), & the Canadian Society of Clinical Neurophysiologists (CSCN). Peer reviewed articles about the neurosciences are published in the Canadian Journal of Neurological Sciences. The journal is circulated to society members, non-members, & institutions in Canada & around the world.
Lisa Arrington, Managing Editor

Canadian Journal of Philosophy (CJP)
Owned By: University of Calgary Press
Tel: 403-220-3514; *Fax:* 403-282-0085
ucpmail@ucalgary.ca
www.canadianjournalofphilosophy.com
Circulation: 875
Frequency: 4 times a year plus supplementary volume
David Hunter, Editorial Board Coordinator

Canadian Journal of Program Evaluation / La Revue canadienne d'évaluation de programme
155 College St., Toronto, ON M5T 3M7
Tel: 416-978-3901; *Fax:* 416-946-0340
cjpe@evaluationcanada.ca
cjpe.journalhosting.ucalgary.ca/cjpe/index.php/ cjpe
Circulation: 1,900
Frequency: Bi-annually
Robert Schwartz, Editor-in-Chief

Canadian Journal of Psychiatry
#701, 141 Laurier Ave. West, Ottawa, ON K1P 5J3
Tel: 613-234-2815; *Fax:* 613-234-9857
Toll-Free: 800-267-1555
publications.cpa-apc.org/browse/sections/0
Frequency: 12 times a year
Dr. Joel Paris, Editor-in-chief

Canadian Journal of Psychoanalysis / Revue canadienne de psychanalyse
Becker Associates, #202, 10 Morrow Ave., Toronto, ON M6R 2J1
Tel: 416-538-1650; *Fax:* 416-489-1713
journals@beckerassociates.ca
academicjournals.ca/index.php/cjp-rcp/
Circulation: 650
Frequency: Bi-annually
Charles Levin, Editor, charleslevin@videotron.ca

Canadian Journal of Women & The Law (CJWL/RFD) / Revue Femmes et Droit
Previous Name: Revue juridique la femme et la droit
Owned By: University of Toronto Press
5210 Dufferin St., Toronto, ON M3H 5T8
Tel: 416-667-7810; *Fax:* 416-667-7881
www.utpjournals.com/cjwl
Frequency: Biannual
Natasha Bakht, English Language Co-Editor
Annie Rochette, French Language Co-Editor/Corédactrice francophone

Canadian Literature
Owned By: University of British Columbia Press
c/o Anthropology & Sociology Building, University of British Columbia, #8, 6303 NW Marine Dr., Vancouver, BC V6T 1Z1
Tel: 604-822-2780
can.lit@ubc.ca
canlit.ca
Social Media:
twitter.com/canadianlit
www.facebook.com/group.php?gid=17013685211
Circulation: 1,200
Frequency: 4 times a year
Laura Moss, Editor

Canadian Mathematical Bulletin
Owned By: University of Toronto Press
#209, 1725 St. Laurent Blvd., Ottawa, ON K1G 3V4
Tel: 613-733-2662; *Fax:* 613-733-8994
office@cms.math.ca
cms.math.ca/cmb
Circulation: 775
Frequency: 4 times a year
Jie Xiao, Co-editor
Xiaoqiang Zhao, Co-editor

Canadian Modern Language Review (CMLR/RCLV) / Le Revue canadienne des langues vivantes
Owned By: University of Toronto Press
5201 Dufferin St., Toronto, ON M3H 5T8
Tel: 416-667-7777; *Fax:* 416-667-7881
cmlr@utpress.utoronto.ca
www.utpjournals.com/Canadian-Modern-Language-Re view.html

Circulation: 1,000
Frequency: 4 times a year
Murray Munro, Co-Editor
Danièle Moore, Co-Editor

Canadian Poetry
Owned By: Canadian Poetry Press
Dept. of English, University of Western Ontario, London, ON N6A 3K7
Tel: 519-673-1164; *Fax:* 519-661-3776
canadianpoetry@uwo.ca
www.canadianpoetry.ca
Circulation: 400
Frequency: 2 times a year; Spring/Summer, Fall/Winter
D.M.R. Bentley, Editor, dbentley@uwo.ca
R.J. Shroyer, Associate Editor, shroyer@uwo.ca

Canadian Public Administration (CPA/APC) / Administration publique du Canada
#401, 1075 Bay St., Toronto, ON M5S 2B1
Tel: 416-924-8787; *Fax:* 416-924-4992
www.ipac.ca; www.iapc.ca
Circulation: 3,600
Frequency: 4 times a year
Evert A. Lindquist, Editor

Canadian Public Policy / Analyse de Politique
PO Box 35006, 1221, Fleury est, Montréal, QC H2C 3K4
Tel: 646-257-5906
cpp.adp@gmail.com
economics.ca/cpp
Circulation: 1,500
Frequency: 4 times a year
Herb Emery, Managing Editor, hemery@ucalgary.ca

Canadian Review of American Studies
Owned By: University of Toronto Press
5201 Dufferin St., Toronto, ON M3H 5T8
Tel: 416-667-7810; *Fax:* 416-667-7881
journals@utpress.utoronto.ca
www.utpjournals.com/Canadian-Review-of-American-Studies.html
Circulation: 400
Frequency: 3 times a year
Priscilla Walton, Editor

Canadian Review of Sociology / Revue canadienne de sociologie
PO Box 98014, 2126 Burnhamthorpe Rd. West, Mississauga, ON L5L 5V4
Tel: 416-660-4378
office@csa-scs.ca
www.csa-scs.ca
Social Media:
www.youtube.com/profile?user=CanadianSociology
twitter.com/csa_sociology
www.facebook.com/pages/Canadian-Sociological-Association
Circulation: 1,428
Frequency: Quarterly
Rima Wilkes, Editor

Canadian Theatre Review (CTR)
Owned By: University of Toronto Press Inc.
University of Toronto Press, 5201 Dufferin St., Toronto, ON M3H 5T8
Tel: 416-667-7810; *Fax:* 416-667-7881
journals@utpress.utoronto.ca
www.canadiantheatrereview.com
Social Media:
www.facebook.com/pages/Canadian-Theatre-Review/6282249105
Frequency: 4 times a year
Laura Levin, Editor-in-Chief, canadiantheatrereview@gmail.com

Cartographica
Owned By: University of Toronto Press
5201 Dufferin St., Toronto, ON M3H 5T8
Tel: 416-667-7777; *Fax:* 416-667-7881
journals@utpress.utoronto.ca
www.utpjournals.com/Cartographica.html
Circulation: 900
Frequency: 4 times a year
Monica Wachowicz, Co-Editor
Emmanuel Stefanakis, Co-Editor

The Dorchester Review
#204, 1066 Somerset St. West, Ottawa, ON K1Y 4T3
info@dorchesterreview.ca
dorchesterreview.ca/The_Dorchester_Review/Home.html
A historical and literary review.

Eighteenth-Century Fiction
Chester New Hall 421, McMaster University, 1280 Main St. West, Hamilton, ON L8S 4L9
Tel: 905-525-9140; *Fax:* 905-777-8316
ecf@mcmaster.ca
ecf.humanities.mcmaster.ca
Social Media:
twitter.com/ECFjournal
www.facebook.com/290191677662167?sk=wall
Circulation: 750
Frequency: Quarterly
Eugenia Zuroski Jenkins, Editor

Energy Studies Review
Owned By: DeGroote School of Business, McMaster University
DSB-A101, DeGroote School of Business, McMaster University, Hamilton, ON L8S 4M4
Tel: 905-525-9140
esr@mcmaster.ca
digitalcommons.mcmaster.ca/esr
Frequency: 2 times a year
Dean Mountain, Editor-in-Chief

Environments: A Journal of Interdisciplinary Studies
Dept of Geography & Environmental Studies, Wilfred Laurier University, 75 University Ave. West, Waterloo, ON N2L 3C5
environmentsjournal.ca
Circulation: 400
Frequency: 3 times a year
Scott Slocombe, Editor, sslocomb@wlu.ca

Event
PO Box 2503, New Westminster, BC V3L 5B2
Tel: 604-527-5293; *Fax:* 604-527-5095
event@douglascollege.ca
www.eventmagazine.ca
Social Media:
twitter.com/EVENTmags
www.facebook.com/eventmagazine
Circulation: 1,250
Frequency: Every 3 months
Poetry and prose magazine.
Shashi Bhat, Editor

INFOR: Information Systems and Operational Research
Owned By: University of Toronto Press
5201 Dufferin St., Toronto, ON M3H 5T8
Tel: 416-667-7777; *Fax:* 416-667-7881
journals@utpress.utoronto.ca
www.utpjournals.com/infor/infor.html
Circulation: 400
Frequency: 4 times a year
Samir Elhedhli, Co-editor, elhedhli@uwaterloo.ca
Elkafi Hassini, Co-editor, hassini@mcmaster.ca

International Journal
Owned By: Canadian International Council
c/o Canadian International Council, #064S, 1 Devonshire Place, Toronto, ON M5S 3K7
Tel: 416-667-7810
ij@opencanada.org
internationaljournal.ca
Social Media: www.tumblr.com/register/follow/internationaljournal
Circulation: 1,300
Frequency: 4 times a year
Scholarly publication on international relations.
David Haglund, Co-Editor
Joseph Jodcel, Co-Editor

Intersections: Canadian Journal of Music / Intersections: revue canadienne de musique
Owned By: Canadian University Music Society
#202, 10 Morrow Ave., Toronto, ON M6R 2J1
Tel: 416-538-1650
office@muscan.org
www.muscan.org/en/publications/intersections
Circulation: 400
Frequency: 2 times a year
Sophie Stévance, Intersections French Editor
Robin Elliott, Intersections English Editor

Jeunesse: Young People, Texts, Cultures / Littérature Canadienne pour la Jeunesse
Ctr for Research in Young People's Texts & Cultures, Univ. of Winnipeg, 515 Portage Ave., Winnipeg, MB R3B 2E9
jeunesse@uwinnipeg.ca
www.jeunessejournal.ca/index.php/yptc/index
Circulation: 900
Frequency: Bi-annually
Jeunesse has an expanded mandate to publish research on and to provide a forum for discussion about, cultural productions for, by, and about young people. Especially interested in the cultural functions and representations of "the child."
Mavis Reimer, Editor

Journal of Bahá'í Studies / La Revue des Études Bahá'íes/La Revista des Estudios Bahá'í
c/o Association for Bahá'í Studies North America, 34 Copernicus St., Ottawa, ON K1N 7K4
Tel: 613-233-1903; *Fax:* 613-233-3644
www.bahai-studies.ca
Social Media:
www.facebook.com/331784303733
Circulation: 2,000
Frequency: Biannual
Anne Furlong, Editor

Journal of Canadian Art History / Annales d'histoire de l'art canadien
c/o EV-3.819, Concordia University, 1455, boul de Maisonneuve ouest, Montréal, QC H3G 1M8
Tel: 514-848-2424; *Fax:* 514-848-4584
jcah@concordia.ca
jcah-ahac.concordia.ca
Social Media:
www.facebook.com/thecujah
Circulation: 550
Frequency: 2 times a year
Peer-reviewed publication devoted to history and thoery of visual arts in Canada
Sandra Paikowsky, Publisher
Martha Langford, Editor-in-Chief

Journal of Canadian Poetry
Owned By: Borealis Press
8 Mohawk Cres., Nepean, ON K2H 7G6
Tel: 613-829-0150; *Fax:* 613-829-7783
Toll-Free: 877-696-2585
drt@borealispress.com
www.borealispress.com
Circulation: 350
Frequency: Annually
David Staines, Editor

Journal of Canadian Studies (JCS/REC) / Revue d'Études Canadiennes
Owned By: University of Toronto Press
University of Toronto Press - Journals Division, 5201 Dufferin St., Toronto, ON M3H 5T8
Tel: 416-667-7810; *Fax:* 416-667-7881
journals@utpress.utoronto.ca
muse.jhu.edu/journals/journal_of_canadian_s tudies
Circulation: 1,300
Frequency: 4 times a year
Marian Bredin, Editor

Journal of Law & Social Policy / Revue des lois et des politiques sociales
Clinic Resource Office, Legal Aid Ontario, #41, 425 Adelaide St. West, Toronto, ON M5V 3C1
Tel: 416-204-5408; *Fax:* 416-204-5422
Toll-Free: 800-668-8258
jlsp@lao.on.ca
www.legalaid.on.ca
Circulation: 230
Frequency: Annually
Janet Mosher, Editor-in-Chief

Journal of Scholarly Publishing
Owned By: University of Toronto Press
University of Toronto Press - Journals Division, 5201 Dufferin St., Toronto, ON M3H 5T8
Tel: 416-667-7810; *Fax:* 416-667-7881
journals@utpress.utoronto.ca
www.utpjournals.com/Journal-of-Scholarly-Pu blishing.html
Circulation: 800
Frequency: Quarterly
Tom Radko, Editor

Journal of Ukrainian Studies
University of Toronto, #302, 256 McCaul St., Toronto, ON M5T 1W5
Tel: 416-978-8669; *Fax:* 416-978-2672
r.senkus@utoronto.ca
www.utoronto.ca/cius/
Circulation: 250
Frequency: Semi-annually (and occasionally as a double or quadruple issue)
Roman Senkus, Editor

Labour, Capital & Society (LCS/TCS) / Travail, capital et société
Also Known As: LC&S
c/o Suzanne Dansereau, Intl. Devel. Studies, Saint Mary's University, Halifax, NS B3H 3C3
journallcs-tcs@smu.ca
ww.lcs-tcs.com
Frequency: Semi-annually
The bilingual, refereed journal focuses on labour issues in Asia, Africa, the Middle East, Latin America, & the Caribbean.
Suzanne Dansereau, Editor

Labour/Le Travail
Owned By: Athabasca University Press
c/o Canadian Committee On Labour History, Athabasca University Press, #1200, 10011 - 109 St., Edmonton, AB T5J 3S8
Tel: 709-737-2144; *Fax:* 709-737-4342
cclh@athabascau.ca
www.cclh.ca
Circulation: 1,000
Frequency: 2 times a year
Kathy Killoh, Managing Editor

Material Culture Review / Revue de la culture matérielle
Previous Name: Material History Review
c/o Cape Breton University, PO Box 5300, 1250 Grand Lake Rd., Sydney, NS B1P 6L2
Tel: 902-563-1990; *Fax:* 902-563-1910
mcr_rcm@cbu.ca
culture.cbu.ca/mcr
Other information: French URL: culture.cbu.ca/rcm
Circulation: 400
Frequency: 2 times a year
Richard MacKinnon, Managing Editor, 902-563-1284, richard_mackinnon@cbu.ca
Laura Bast, Editorial Assistant, laura_bast@cbu.ca

McGill Journal of Education / Revue des sciences de l'éducation de McGill
c/o Faculty of Education, McGill University, 3700, rue McTavish, Montréal, QC H3A 1Y2
Tel: 514-398-4246
mje.education@mcgill.ca
mje.mcgill.ca
Circulation: 500
Frequency: 3 times a year
Teresa Strong-Wilson, Editor-in-Chief

McMaster Journal of Theology & Ministry
Owned By: McMaster Divinity College Press
c/o McMaster Divinity College, McMaster University, 1280 Main St. West, Hamilton, ON L8S 4K1
Tel: 905-525-9140; *Fax:* 905-577-4782
mjtm@mcmaster.ca
www.mcmaster.ca/mjtm
Frequency: annual

Modern Drama
Owned By: University of Toronto Press
c/o Centre for Drama, University of Toronto, #326, 214 College St., 3rd Fl., Toronto, ON M5T 2Z9
Tel: 416-971-1378
modern.drama@utpress.utoronto.ca
www.utpjournals.com/Modern-Drama.html
Circulation: 1,700
Frequency: Quarterly
R. Darren Gobert, Editor

The Monograph
Ontario Association for Geographic & Environmental Education, #202, 10 Morrow Ave., Toronto, ON M6R 2J1
Tel: 416-538-1650; *Fax:* 416-489-1713
journals@interlog.com
www.oagee.org/monograph-journal
Circulation: 800
Frequency: 4 times a year
Gary Birchall, Editor

Mosaic
#208, Tier Building, University of Manitoba, Winnipeg, MB R3T 2N2
Tel: 204-474-9763; *Fax:* 204-474-7584
mosaic@ad.umanitoba.ca
wwwapps.cc.umanitoba.ca/publications/mosaic
Circulation: 900
Frequency: 4 times a year
A Journal for the Interdisciplinary Study of Literature
Dr. Dawne McCance, Editor

Newfoundland & Labrador Studies
Previous Name: Newfoundland Studies
Faculty of Arts Publications, MS 1004, PO Box 4200, St. John's, NL A1C 5S7
Tel: 709-737-2144; *Fax:* 709-737-4342
www.mun.ca/nls
Circulation: 350
Frequency: 2 times a year
James Feehan, Editor, feehan@mun.ca

Ontario History
Owned By: The Ontario Historical Society
c/o Ontario Historical Society, 34 Parkview Ave., Willowdale, ON M2N 3Y2
Tel: 416-226-9011; *Fax:* 416-226-2740
Toll-Free: 866-955-2755
ohs@ontariohistoricalsociety.ca
www.ontariohistoricalsociety.ca
Circulation: 1,200
Frequency: Annually
Dr. Tory Tronrud, Editor, oh@thunderbaymuseum.com

Pacific Affairs
c/o University of British Columbia, #376, 1855 West Mall, Vancouver, BC V6T 1Z2
Tel: 604-822-6508; *Fax:* 604-822-9452
enquiry@pacificaffairs.ubc.ca
www.pacificaffairs.ubc.ca
Social Media:
twitter.com/PacificAffairs
Circulation: 1,600
Frequency: 4 times a year
Publishes scholarly articles of contemporary Asia and Pacific.
Hyung Gu Lynn, Editor
Carolyn Grant, Managing Editor, cgrant@pacificaffairs.ubc.ca

The Philanthropist - Agora Foundation / Le Philanthrope
c/o Scotia Private Client Group, Exchange Tower, PO Box 430 First Can. Pl., 130 King Street W., 20th Fl., Toronto, ON M5X 1K1
Tel: 902-634-0403
managing_editor@thephilanthropist.ca
www.thephilanthropist.ca
Circulation: 450
Frequency: 4 times a year
Leslie Wright, Publication Manager

Policy Options / Options politiques
Inst. for Research on Public Policy, #200, 1470, rue Peel, Montréal, QC H3A 1T1
Tel: 514-985-2461
irpp@irpp.org
www.irpp.org
Social Media: www.youtube.com/user/IRPP1972
twitter.com/irpp
www.facebook.com/pages/ IRPP/157517894283753
Circulation: 2,000
Frequency: 10 times a year
Dan Gardner, Editor

Prairie Forum
Owned By: University of Regina Press
c/o University of Regina Press, 3737 Wascana Pkwy., Regina, SK S4S 0A2
Tel: 306-585-4758; *Fax:* 306-585-4699
prairie.forum@uregina.ca
uofrpress.ca/prairie-forum
Social Media:
twitter.com/cprcpress
Circulation: 300
Frequency: 2 times a year
Dr. JoAnn Jaffe, Editor

Queen's Quarterly
Queen's University, 144 Barrie St., Kingston, ON K7L 3N6
Tel: 613-533-2667; *Fax:* 613-533-6822
queens.quarterly@queensu.ca
www.queensu.ca/quarterly
Circulation: 3,000
Frequency: 4 per annum
Revies and debates important events in the cultural, political & intellectual life of Canada
Dr. Boris Castel, Editor, 613-533-2667, queens.quarterly@queensu.ca
Penny Roantree, Business Manager, 613-533-2667, queens.quarterly@queensu.ca

Relational Child & Youth Care Practice
Previous Name: The Journal of Child & Youth Care
Tel: 250-753-3245; *Fax:* 250-740-6466
rcycp@cycnetpress.cyc-net.org

Circulation: 450
Frequency: Quarterly
Heather Snell, Managing Editor

Renaissance & Reformation / Renaissance et réforme
c/o Iter, #7009, 130 St George St., Toronto, ON M5S 1A5
Tel: 416-978-7074; *Fax:* 416-978-1668
iter.renref@utoronto.ca
www.itergateway.org
Circulation: 700
Frequency: 4 times a year
Pascale Duhamel, Editor

Resources for Feminist Research / Documentation Sur La Recherche Feministe
OISE, University of Toronto, 252 Bloor St. West, Toronto, ON M5S 1V6
Tel: 416-978-2033; *Fax:* 416-926-4725
rfr@utoronto.ca
www.oise.utoronto.ca/rfr
Circulation: 2,000
Frequency: 2 times a year
A journal of feminist scholarship.
Lorena M. Gajardo, Editor

Revue canadienne de linguistique appliquée / Canadian Journal of Applied Linguistics
Institut des langues secondes, Université d'Ottawa, 600 King Edward, Ottawa, ON K1N 6N5
Tél: 613-562-5743; *Téléc:* 613-562-5126
hknoerr@uottawa.ca
www.aclacaal.org
Fréquence: 2 fois par an
Hélène Knoerr, Editor

Revue Le Médecin Vétérinaire du Québec
Ordre des médecins vétérinaires du Québec, #200, 800, av Ste-Anne, Saint-Hyacinthe, QC J2S 5G7
Tél: 450-774-1427; *Téléc:* 450-774-7635
Ligne sans frais: 800-267-1427
omvq@omvq.qc.ca
www.omvq.qc.ca
Fréquence: 4 fois par an

Russell: the Journal of Bertrand Russell Studies
Previous Name: Russell: The Journal of the Bertrand Russell Archives
Mills Library 108, McMaster University, Hamilton, ON L8S 4L6
Tel: 905-525-9140; *Fax:* 905-522-1277
russjour@mcmaster.ca
escarpmentpress.org/russelljournal/index
Circulation: 400
Frequency: 2 times a year
Kenneth Blackwell, Editor

Scientia Canadensis - Journal of the History of Cdn. Science, Technology & Medicine
Canadian Science & Technology Historical Association, PO Box 8502 T, Ottawa, ON K1G 3H9
cstha-ahstc.ca/scientia-canadensis
Circulation: 200
Frequency: Annually
David Pantalony, Editor-in-chief

Scrivener Creative Review
c/o Arts Building, McGill University, 853, rue Sherbrooke ouest, Montréal, QC H3A 2T6
Tel: 514-398-6588; *Fax:* 514-398-8146
scrivener.review@gmail.com
scrivener.ausmcgill.com/scr
Social Media:
www.facebook.com/groups/6726676175
Circulation: 500
Frequency: Annually
Klara du Plessis, Editor

Seminar
Owned By: University of Toronto Press
University of Toronto Press - Journals Division, 5201 Dufferin St., Toronto, ON M3H 5T8
Tel: 416-667-7810; *Fax:* 416-667-7881
journals@utpress.utoronto.ca
www.utpjournals.com/Seminar
Circulation: 770
Frequency: Quarterly
Karin Bauer, Co-editor
Andrew Piper, Co-editor

Social History / Histoire Sociale
Owned By: University of Toronto Press
5201 Dufferin St., Toronto, ON M3H 5T8
Tel: 416-667-7810; *Fax:* 416-667-7881
journals@utpress.utoronto.ca
www.utpjournals.com/Histoire-sociale-Social -History.html
Circulation: 500
Frequency: Semi-annually
Chad Gaffield, Editor
Gordon Darroch, Editor

Studies in Canadian Literature (SCL/ÉLC) / Études en littérature canadienne
PO Box 4400, 11 Garland Ct., Fredericton, NB E3B 5A3
Tel: 506-453-3501; *Fax:* 506-453-5069
scl@unb.ca
journals.hil.unb.ca/index.php/SCL
Circulation: 500
Frequency: 2 times a year
Cynthia Sugars, Co-editor, cynthia.sugars@uottawa.ca
Herb Wyile, Co-editor, herb.wyile@acadiau.ca

Studies in Political Economy: A Socialist Review
Dunton Tower, Carleton University, #2122, 1125 Colonel By Dr., Ottawa, ON K1A 5B6
Tel: 613-520-2600; *Fax:* 613-520-3713
spe@carleton.ca
spe.library.utoronto.ca/index.php/spe/index
Circulation: 600
Frequency: 2 times a year
Sarah Dandurand, Contact, 613-520-2600

Theatre Research in Canada / Recherches théâtrales au Canada
c/o Drama Centre, University of Toronto, 214 College St., 3rd Fl., Toronto, ON M5T 2Z9
Fax: 416-971-1378
tric.rtac@utoronto.ca
journals.lib.unb.ca/index.php/TRIC/index
Circulation: 350
Frequency: Semi-annually
Marlis Schweitzer, Editor

The Tocqueville Review / La Revue Tocqueville
Owned By: University of Toronto Press
University of Toronto Press - Journals Division, 5201 Dufferin St., Toronto, ON M3H 5T8
Tel: 416-667-7781; *Fax:* 416-667-7881
journals@utpress.utoronto.ca
www.utpjournals.com/The-Tocqueville-Review. html
Circulation: 400
Frequency: Bi-annually
Michel Forsé, Co-editor
Françoise Mélonio, Co-editor
Laurence Guellec, Co-editor
Jennifer Merchant, Co-editor

TOPIA: Canadian Journal of Cultural Studies
240 Vanier College, York University, 4700 Keele St., Toronto, ON M3J 1P3
Tel: 416-736-2100; *Fax:* 416-736-5640
topia@yorku.ca
www.yorku.ca/topia
Circulation: 300
Frequency: 2 times a year
Jody Berland, Editor

Transcultural Psychiatry
Previous Name: Transcultural Psychiatric Research Review
Dept. of Psychiatry, McGill University, 1033, av des Pins ouest, Montréal, QC H3A 1A1
Tel: 514-398-7302; *Fax:* 514-375-1459
transcultural.psychiatry@mcgill.ca
www.mcgill.ca/tcpsych/publications/tp rr
Circulation: 500
Frequency: 4 times a year
Laurence J. Kirmayer, Editor M.D.

Ultimate Reality & Meaning
Owned By: University of Toronto Press
5201 Dufferin St., Toronto, ON M3H 5T8
Tel: 416-667-7810; *Fax:* 416-667-7881
journals@utpress.utoronto.ca
www.utpjournals.com/Ultimate-Reality-and-Me aning.html
Circulation: 380
Frequency: Quarterly
Tom Krettek, Editor-in-Chief
J. Patrick Mohr, Executive Editor

University of Toronto Law Journal
Owned By: University of Toronto Press
5201 Dufferin St., Toronto, ON M3H 5T8
Tel: 416-667-7810; *Fax:* 416-667-7881
journals@utpress.utoronto.ca
www.utpjournals.com/University-of-Toronto-L aw-Journal.html
Circulation: 700
Frequency: Quarterly
David Dyzenhaus, Editor

University of Toronto Quarterly
Owned By: University of Toronto Press
University of Toronto Press - Journals Division, 5201 Dufferin St., Toronto, ON M3H 5T8
Tel: 416-667-7810; *Fax:* 416-667-7881
journals@utpress.utoronto.ca
www.utpjournals.com/University-of-Toronto-Q uarterly.html
Circulation: 1,100
Frequency: Quarterly
Victor Li, Co-editor
Colin Hill, Co-editor

Urban History Review (UHR/RHU) / Revue d'histoire urbaine
Owned By: Becker Associates
#202, 10 Morrow Ave., Toronto, ON M6R 2J1
Tel: 416-538-1650; *Fax:* 416-489-1713
info@urbanhistoryreview.ca
urbanhistoryreview.ca/urbanenglish.html
Circulation: 400
Frequency: 2 times a year
Alan Gordon, Co-Editor
Claire Poitras, Co-Editor

Windsor Review
c/o Dept. of English, University of Windsor, Chrysler Hall North, 401 Sunset Ave., Windsor, ON N9B 3P4
Tel: 519-253-3000; *Fax:* 519-971-3676
uwrevu@uwindsor.ca
windsorreview.wordpress.com
Social Media:
twitter.com/windsorreview
Circulation: 500
Frequency: Bi-annually
Alistair MacLeod, Editor, Fiction
Susan Holbrook, Editor, Poetry
Alex McKay, Editor, Visual Arts
Marty Gervais, Managing Editor

Science, Research & Development

Applied Physiology, Nutrition, & Metabolism
Owned By: Canadian Science Publishing
Ottawa, ON
pubs@nrcresearchpress.com
www.nrcresearchpress.com
Social Media:
www.linkedin.com/company/canadian-science-publishing
twitter.com/cdnsciencepub
www.facebook.com/NRCResearchPress
Frequency: Monthly
Monthly journal of physiology, nutrition, & metabolism to the study of human health, physical activity, & fitness reports
Terry Graham, Editor Ph.D.

Biochemistry & Cell Biology
Owned By: Canadian Science Publishing
Ottawa, ON
pubs@nrcresearchpress.com
www.nrcresearchpress.com
Social Media:
www.linkedin.com/company/canadian-science-publishing
twitter.com/cdnsciencepub
www.facebook.com/NRCResearchPress
Frequency: Bi=monthly
Bi-monthly journal of general biochemistry & research into cellular & molecular biology
James R. Davie, Editor

Botany
Owned By: Canadian Science Publishing
Ottawa, ON
pubs@nrcresearchpress.com
www.nrcresearchpress.com
Social Media:
www.linkedin.com/company/canadian-science-publishing
twitter.com/cdnsciencepub
www.facebook.com/NRCResearchPress
Frequency: Monthly
Monthly journal of plant sciences, ecology, mycology & plant microbe interactions, phycology, physiolohy & biochemistry
Dr. Christian Lacroix, Editor

Canadian Geotechnical Journal
Owned By: Canadian Science Publishing
Ottawa, ON
pubs@nrcresearchpress.com
www.nrcresearchpress.com
Social Media:
www.linkedin.com/company/canadian-science-publishing
twitter.com/cdnsciencepub
www.facebook.com/NRCResearchPress
Frequency: Monthly
Monthly journal of new developments in geotechnical & geoenvironmental engineering
Ian Moore, Editor

Canadian Journal of Chemistry
Owned By: Canadian Science Publishing
Ottawa, ON
pubs@nrcresearchpress.com
www.nrcresearchpress.com
Social Media:
www.linkedin.com/company/canadian-science-publishing
twitter.com/cdnsciencepub
www.facebook.com/NRCResearchPress
Frequency: Monthly
Monthly journal on current chemistry research
Yining Huang, Senior Editor
Robert H. Lipson, Senior Editor

Canadian Journal of Civil Engineering
Owned By: Canadian Science Publishing
Ottawa, ON
pubs@nrcresearchpress.com
www.nrcresearchpress.com
Social Media:
www.linkedin.com/company/canadian-science-publishing
twitter.com/cdnsciencepub
www.facebook.com/NRCResearchPress
Frequency: Monthly
Monthly journal of articles on environmental, hydrotechnical, structure, construction & material engineering
Mike Bartlett, Editor Ph.D.
Tarek Sayed, Editor Ph.D.

Canadian Journal of Earth Sciences
Owned By: Canadian Science Publishing
Ottawa, ON
pubs@nrcresearchpress.com
www.nrcresearchpress.com
Social Media:
www.linkedin.com/company/canadian-science-publishing
twitter.com/cdnsciencepub
www.facebook.com/NRCResearchPress
Frequency: Monthly
Monthly journal about current research of climate, environment, geochronology, geoscience, forensic geoscience & geophysics
Ali Polat, Editor Ph.D.

Canadian Journal of Fisheries & Aquatic Sciences
Owned By: Canadian Science Publishing
Ottawa, ON
pubs@nrcresearchpress.com
www.nrcresearchpress.com
Social Media:
www.linkedin.com/company/canadian-science-publishing
twitter.com/cdnsciencepub
www.facebook.com/NRCResearchPress
Frequency: Monthly
Monthly journal of aquatic sciences
Yong Chen, Editor Ph.D.
Rolf D. Vinebrooke, Editor Ph.D.

Canadian Journal of Microbiology
Owned By: Canadian Science Publishing
Ottawa, ON
pubs@nrcresearchpress.com
www.nrcresearchpress.com
Social Media:
www.linkedin.com/company/canadian-science-publishing
twitter.com/cdnsciencepub
www.facebook.com/NRCResearchPress
Frequency: Monthly
Monthly journal of applied microbiology
James J. Germida, Editor

Canadian Journal of Physics
Owned By: Canadian Science Publishing
Ottawa, ON
pubs@nrcresearchpress.com
www.nrcresearchpress.com
Social Media:
www.linkedin.com/company/canadian-science-publishing
twitter.com/cdnsciencepub
www.facebook.com/NRCResearchPress

Frequency: Monthly
Monthly journal of physics research
Michael Steinitz, Editor

Canadian Journal of Physiology & Pharmacology
Owned By: Canadian Science Publishing
Ottawa, ON
pubs@nrcresearchpress.com
www.nrcresearchpress.com
Social Media:
www.linkedin.com/company/canadian-science-publishing
twitter.com/cdnsciencepub
www.facebook.com/NRCResearchPress

Frequency: Monthly
Monthly journal of physiology, nutrition, pharmacology & toxicology reports
Dr. Grant Pierce
Dr. Donald Smyth, Editor

Canadian Journal of Zoology
Owned By: Canadian Science Publishing
Ottawa, ON
pubs@nrcresearchpress.com
www.nrcresearchpress.com
Social Media:
www.linkedin.com/company/canadian-science-publishing
twitter.com/cdnsciencepub
www.facebook.com/NRCResearchPress

Frequency: Monthly
Monthly journal on zoology
M.B. Fenton, Editor Ph.D.
Helga Guderley, Editor Ph.D.

Environmental Reviews
Owned By: Canadian Science Publishing
Ottawa, ON
pubs@nrcresearchpress.com
www.nrcresearchpress.com
Social Media:
www.linkedin.com/company/canadian-science-publishing
twitter.com/cdnsciencepub
www.facebook.com/NRCResearchPress

Frequency: Quarterly
Quarterly journal about environmental science and related topics
John P. Smol, Editor Ph.D.

Genome
Owned By: Canadian Science Publishing
Ottawa, ON
pubs@nrcresearchpress.com
www.nrcresearchpress.com
Social Media:
www.linkedin.com/company/canadian-science-publishing
twitter.com/cdnsciencepub
www.facebook.com/NRCResearchPress

Frequency: Monthly
Monthly journal about genetics
Arthur J. Hilliker, Editor Ph.D.
Graham Scoles, Editor Ph.D.

Journal of Unmanned Vehicle Systems
Owned By: Canadian Science Publishing
Ottawa, ON
pubs@nrcresearchpress.com
www.nrcresearchpress.com
Social Media:
www.linkedin.com/company/canadian-science-publishing
twitter.com/cdnsciencepub
www.facebook.com/NRCResearchPress

Frequency: Quarterly
Quarterly journal about development of unmanned vehicle systems
David M. Bird, Editor

University

Scholarly Publications

BC Studies: The British Columbian Quarterly
University of British Columbia, 6303 NW Marine Dr., Rm. 2, Vancouver, BC V6T 1Z1
Tel: 604-822-3727
info@bcstudies.com
www.bcstudies.com
Social Media:
twitter.com/bcstudies
www.facebook.com/BCStudies

Circulation: 700
Frequency: Quarterly
Quarterly magazine of exploration of British Columbia's cultural, economic & political life
Jessica Walker, Managing Editor

Student Guides

Accès Média
#31, 1124, Marie-Anne est, Montréal, QC H2J 2B7
Tél: 514-524-1182; *Téléc:* 514-524-7771
info@accesmedia.com
www.accesmedia.com

Tirage: 300,000
Les éditeurs de guides étudiants de partout au Québec
Edgar Donelle

Welcome Back Student Magazine
Owned By: Sun Media Corporation
Kingston Publications, 18 St. Remy Place, Kingston, ON K7K 6C4
Tel: 613-389-7400; *Fax:* 613-389-7507
www.kingstonpublications.com/welcomeback.html
Circulation: 17,000
Frequency: Annually
Liza Nelson, Publisher, liza.nelson@sunmedia.ca

University & Student Publications

L'Accent
Détenteur: Cégep de Rimouski
60, rue de l'Évêché ouest, Rimouski, QC G5L 4H6
Tél: 418-723-1880; *Téléc:* 418-724-4961
Ligne sans frais: 800-463-0617
infoscol@cegep-rimouski.qc.ca
www.cegep-rimouski.qc.ca

L'AccrO
Détenteur: Cégep de Saint-Hyacinthe
3000, av Boullé, Saint-Hyacinthe, QC J2S 1H9
Tél: 450-773-6800; *Téléc:* 450-773-9971
info@cegepsth.qc.ca
www.cegepsth.qc.ca
Fréquence: Mensuel

L'Afficheur
Détenteur: Cégep de Limoilou
1300, 8e av, Québec, QC G1J 5L5
Tél: 418-647-6600; *Téléc:* 418-647-6798
lafficheur@climoilou.qc.ca
www.climoilou.qc.ca

Algonquin Times
Owned By: Algonquin College
Algonquin College, 1385 Woodroffe Ave., Rm. N209, Ottawa, ON K2G 1V8
Tel: 613-727-4723; *Fax:* 613-727-7743
times@algonquincollege.com
times.webcitybeat.com

Frequency: Bi-weekly
Algonquin College newspaper.
Kris Lapenskie, Online Editor

The Aquinian
Owned By: St. Thomas University
PO Box 4400 A, Fredericton, NB E3B 5G3
Tel: 506-452-0532; *Fax:* 506-452-0617
admin@theaq.net
www.theaquinian.net
Social Media:
twitter.com/aquinian
www.facebook.com/aquinian

St. Thomas University newspaper.
Liam McGuire, Editor-in-Chief, eic@theaq.net

The Argosy
Owned By: Mount Allison University
Wallace- McCain Student Centre, #386, 62A York St., Sackville, NB E4L 1H3
Tel: 506-364-2300
argosy@mta.ca
argosy.mta.ca
Social Media:
twitter.com/The_Argosy
www.facebook.com/TheArgosy

Frequency: Weekly; Thursdays
Mount Allison University's Independent Student Newspaper Since 1872
Dan Wortman, Managing Editor
Julie Stephenson, Editor

Arthur Visual Archive
Owned By: Trent University
Sadlier House, 751 George St. N, Peterborough, ON K9H 3T2
Tel: 705-745-3535
editors@trentarthur.ca
trentarthur.ca
Social Media: www.youtube.com/virtualarthur
twitter.com/trentarthur
www.facebook.com/ArthurNews

Circulation: 3,000
Frequency: 25 times a school year
Weekly newspaper providing infomative, interesting & accurate information regarding events and issues relevant to Trent students
Sara Ostrowska, Editor, editors@trentarthur.ca
Patrick Reddick, Editor, editors@trentarthur.ca

The Artichoke
Owned By: Winter's College, York University
#004, 4700 Keele St., Toronto, ON M3J 1P3
Tel: 416-736-5128
wintersfreepress@winterscouncil.com
Social Media:
twitter.com/artichokebywfp
www.facebook.com/pages/Artichoke-Magazine/131605956923469
Frequency: Monthly
Student magazine for Winter's College at York University.
Lindsay Presswell, Editor, editor@wintersfreepress.com

The Athenaeum
Owned By: Acadia University
Student Union Bldg., PO Box 6002, #512, 50 Acadia St., Wolfville, NS B4P 2R5
Tel: 902-585-2147
www.acadiau.ca
Social Media:
twitter.com/athonline
Acadia University newspaper.
Vanessa Gallant, Editor-in-Chief, eic@acadiau.ca

Le Bagou
Détenteur: Cégep du Vieux Montréal
255, rue Ontario est, Montréal, QC H2X 1X6
Tél: 514-982-3437; *Téléc:* 514-982-3400
www.cvm.qc.ca

Bandersnatch
Owned By: Cégep John Abbott
PO Box 2000, Sainte-Anne-de-Bellevue, QC H9X 3L9
Tel: 514-457-6610; *Fax:* 514-457-6091
bandersnatchpaper@gmail.com
www.johnabbott.qc.ca/~bandersnatch

Frequency: 14 times a school year
Zack Duma, Editor-In-Chief
Bee Clarke, Assistant Editor-In-Chief

Le Bonjour
Détenteur: Cégep de Sorel-Tracy
3000, boul Tracy, Sorel-Tracy, QC J3R 5B9
Tél: 450-742-6651; *Téléc:* 450-742-1878
info@cegepst.qc.ca
www.cegep-sorel-tracy.qc.ca

Brunswickan
Owned By: University of New Brunswick
PO Box 4400 A, #35, 21 Pacey Dr., Fredericton, NB E3B 5A3
Tel: 506-447-3388
www.thebruns.ca
University of New Brunswick newspaper.
Sandy Chase, Editor-in-Chief, editor@thebruns.ca

Bulletin d'information du Collège Ahuntsic (BICA)
Détenteur: Cégep d'Ahuntsic
9155, rue St-Hubert, Montréal, QC H2M 1Y8
Tél: 514-389-5921 *Ligne sans frais:* 866-389-5921
bica@collegeahuntsic.qc.ca
www.collegeahuntsic.qc.ca/intranet/bica

The Cadre
Owned By: University of Prince Edward Island
W.A. Murphy Student Centre, 550 University Ave., Charlottetown, PE C1A 2N6
Tel: 902-566-0629; *Fax:* 902-566-0979
editor@thecadre.ca
thecadre.ca
Social Media: www.tumblr.com/register/follow/upeicadre
twitter.com/thecadre
Frequency: Weekly, during the academic year
University of Prince Edward Island newspaper.
Garrett Curley, Editor-in-Chief, editor@thecadre.ca

The Campus
Owned By: Université Bishop's
PO Box 5000, 2600 College St., Sherbrooke, QC J1M 1Z7
Tel: 819-822-9600; *Fax:* 819-822-9661
liaison@ubishops.ca
www.ubishops.ca
Social Media: www.youtube.com/user/bishopsuniversity
twitter.com/ubishops
www.facebo ok.com/bishops
Frequency: Bi-weekly; Thursday, during academic year

Caper Times
Previous Name: The 60th Meridian
Owned By: Cape Breton University
c/o Cape Breton University (CBU), PO Box 5300, 1250 Grand Lake Rd., Sydney, NS B1P 6L2
Tel: 902-563-1473
editor@capertimes.ca
capertimes.ca
Cape Breton University newspaper.
Lucy MacDonald, Editor-in-Chief

Capilano Courier
Owned By: Capilano College
2055 Purcell Way, North Vancouver, BC V7J 3H5
Tel: 604-984-4949
editor@capilanocourier.com
capilanocourier.com
Capilano College newspaper.
JJ Brewis, Editor-in-Chief

The Carillon
Owned By: The University of Regina
227 Riddell Centre, 3737 Wascana Pkwy., Regina, SK S4S 0A2
Tel: 306-586-8867
editor@carillonregina.com
www.carillonregina.com
Social Media:
twitter.com/the_carillon
www.facebook.com/carillon.newspaper
Frequency: 11 times a year; Thursdays
The University of Regina newspaper.
Dietrich Neu, Editor-in-Chief, editor@carillonregina.com

The Cascade
Owned By: University of the Fraser Valley (UFV)
33844 King Rd., Abbotsford, BC V2S 7M8
Tel: 604-854-4529
ufvcascade.ca
Social Media:
twitter.com/ufvcascade
University of the Fraser Valley (UFV) newspaper.
Paul Esau, Editor-in-Chief, esau@ufvcascade.ca

The Cord
Owned By: Wilfrid Laurier University
75 University Ave. West, Waterloo, ON N2L 3C5
Tel: 519-884-0710
www.thecord.ca
Social Media:
twitter.com/cordnews
www.facebook.com/pages/The-Cord/113605339652
Frequency: Weekly
Wilfrid Laurier University newspaper.
Justin Fauteux, Editor, 519-884-0710 x3563, jfauteux@thecord.ca

The Crown
Owned By: Redeemer University College
777 Garner Rd. East, Ancaster, ON L9K 1J4
Tel: 905-648-2131
managing.editor@thecrown.ca
www.thecrown.ca
Redeemer University College newspaper.
Ben Reid, Editor-in-Chief

D.E.C. express
Détenteur: Cégep de Baie-Comeau
537, boul Blanche, Baie-Comeau, QC G5C 2B2
Tél: 418-589-5707; *Téléc:* 418-589-9842
Ligne sans frais: 800-463-2030
www.cegep-baie-comeau.qc.ca
Médias sociaux:
twitter.com/cegepbaiecomeau
www.facebook.com/cegepbaiecomeau

Dal News
c/o Dalhousie University, Halifax, NS B3H 4R2
Tel: 902-494-2541; *Fax:* 902-494-3561
ryan.mcnutt@dal.ca
www.dal.ca/news.html
Social Media:
www.facebook.com/DalhousieUniversity
Frequency: Monthly
Ryan McNutt, Editor

Daily Bulletin
Previous Name: UW Gazette
Owned By: University of Waterloo
200 University Ave. West, Waterloo, ON N2L 3G1
Tel: 519-888-4567
bulletin@uwaterloo.ca
www.bulletin.uwaterloo.ca
Social Media:
twitter.com/uwdailybulletin
Frequency: Daily; online
University of Waterloo newspaper.
Brandon Sweet, Editor

Draft
Owned By: Red Deer College
PO Box 5005, 100 College Blvd., Red Deer, AB T4N 5H5
Tel: 403-342-3200; *Fax:* 403-347-8510
brickers@telusplanet.net
www.sardc.ab.ca/publications
Frequency: Semi-monthly
Red Deer College newspaper.
Martin Cruz, President
Rebecca Tootoosis, Vice President Operations, Operations

L'Écho
Détenteur: Collège de Lévis
9, rue Monseigneur Gosselin, Lévis, QC G6V 5K1
Tél: 418-833-1249; *Téléc:* 418-833-7055
fondation@collegedelevis.qc.ca
www.collegedelevis.qc.ca
Fréquence: Semestriel
Pierre Bélanger, Directeur, belpier28@gmail.com

The Echo
Owned By: Vanier College
821, av Ste-Croix, Saint-Laurent, QC H4L 3X9
Tel: 514-744-7500; *Fax:* 514-744-7023
echo@fclass.vaniercollege.qc.ca
fclass.vaniercollege.qc.ca/echo
Vanier College newspaper.
Caroline Zemokhol, Editor-in-Chief

Échorridor
Détenteur: Cégep d'Alma
675, boul Auger ouest, Alma, QC G8B 2B7
Tél: 418-668-2387; *Téléc:* 418-668-6841
college@calma.qc.ca
www.calma.qc.ca
Fréquence: Quinzomadaire

L'Éclipse
Détenteur: Cégep Saint-Jean-sur-Richelieu
CP 1018, 30, boul du Séminaire, Saint-Jean-sur-Richelieu, QC J3B 5J4
Tél: 450-347-5301; *Téléc:* 450-347-3329
communications@cstjean.qc.ca
www.cstjean.qc.ca
Fréquence: Hebdomadaire

Eclosion
Détenteur: Cégep de Sainte-Foy
#M-106, 2410, ch Ste-Foy, Sainte-Foy, QC G1V 1T3
Tél: 418-658-5389; *Téléc:* 418-658-6798
j.leclosion@gmail.com
asso.cegep-ste-foy.qc.ca/les-comites-de-lasso/eclo sion

The Endeavour
Owned By: Lethbridge Community College
#TE3225, 3000 College Dr. South, Lethbridge, AB T1K 1L6
Tel: 403-320-3301; *Fax:* 403-317-3582
endeavour@lethbridgecollege.ab.ca
lethcollege.ca/commarts/endeavour
Social Media:
twitter.com/LCEndeavour
www.facebook.com/174217563573
Lethbridge Community College newspaper.
Anne Raslask, Publisher

L'Entremetteur
Détenteur: Cégep de l'Outaouais
Campus Gabrielle-Roy, Cégep-Outaouais, 333, boul Cité-des-Jeunes, Hull, QC J8Y 6M4
Tél: 819-770-4012; *Téléc:* 819-770-8167
www.cegepoutaouais.qc.ca

The Eyeopener
Owned By: Ryerson University
55 Gould St., Toronto, ON M5B 1E9
Tel: 416-979-5262
editor@theeyeopener.com
theeyeopener.com
Social Media:
twitter.com/theeyeopener
www.facebook.com/pages/The-Eyeopener/32810756867
Frequency: Monthly
The Eyeopener is Ryerson University's independent student newspaper.
Nicole Schmidt, Editor-in-Chief, 416-979-5000

La FlaMèche
Détenteur: Cégep de l'Abitibi-Témiscamingue
425, boul du Collège, Rouyn-Noranda, QC J9X 5E5
Tél: 819-762-0931; *Téléc:* 819-762-2071
Ligne sans frais: 866-234-3728
cegepat.qc.ca
Fréquence: Hebdomadaire

Folia Montana
Owned By: Mount Saint Vincent University
166 Bedford Hwy., Halifax, NS B3M 2J6
Tel: 902-457-6117; *Fax:* 902-457-6498
www.msvu.ca
Social Media:
www.facebook.com/people/Alumnae-Relations/651842399
Circulation: 17,000
Frequency: Bi-Annually
Mount Saint Vincent University alumni newspaper.

Folio
Owned By: University of Alberta
General Services Bldg., 6th Fl., 114 St. - 89 Ave., Edmonton, AB T6G 2H1
Tel: 780-492-2325; *Fax:* 780-492-2997
www.folio.ualberta.ca
University of Alberta newspaper.
Michael Brown, Acting Editor, 780-492-9407, michael.brown@ualberta.ca

Le Front
Détenteur: Université de Moncton
18, ave Antonine-Maillet, Moncton, NB E1A 3E9
Tél: 506-863-2012; *Téléc:* 506-858-4524
lefront@umoncton.ca
maui-lefront.blogspot.ca
Médias sociaux:
www.facebook.com/164290830264753

The Fulcrum
Détenteur: University of Ottawa
631 King Edward Ave., Ottawa, ON K1N 6N5
Tél: 613-562-5261; *Téléc:* 613-562-5259
thefulcrum.ca
Médias sociaux: www.flickr.com/photos/thefulcrum/
twitter.com/The_Fulcrum
www.facebook .com/UofOFulcrum
The Fulcrum is the independent English-language student newspaper at the University of Ottawa.
Savannah Awde, Editor-in-Chief, editor@thefulcrum.ca

Gargoyle
Owned By: University College
15 King's College Circle, F6, Toronto, ON M5S 3H7
Tel: 416-946-0941
ucgargoyle@gmail.com
www.ucgargoyle.ca
Social Media:
twitter.com/ucgargoyle
University College newspaper.
Angjielin Hila, Editor-in-Chief
Carla Mesa Guzzo, Editor-in-Chief

The Gateway
Owned By: University of Alberta
#3-04, Students' Union Bldg., Edmonton, AB T6G 2J7
Tel: 780-492-5168; *Fax:* 780-492-6665
biz@gateway.ualberta.ca
thegatewayonline.ca
Social Media: www.youtube.com/user/thegatewaymultimedia
twitter.com/the_gateway
www. facebook.com/TheGatewayOnline

Frequency: Weekly; Wednesdays, during the academic year; 3 issues in the spring/summer
The Gateway is the official student newspaper at the University of Alberta.
Josh Greschner, Editor-in-Chief, 780-492-5168, eic@gateway.ualberta.ca

The Gauntlet
Owned By: The University of Calgary
MacEwan Student Centre, #319, 2500 University Dr. NW, Calgary, AB T2N 1N4
Tel: 403-220-7750
editor@thegauntlet.ca
www.thegauntlet.ca
Social Media:
twitter.com/gauntletuofc
www.facebook.com/uofcgauntlet
The University of Calgary newspaper.
Erin Shumlich, Editor-in-Chief, 403-220-7752, eic@thegauntlet.ca

The Gazette
Owned By: University of Western Ontario
#263, University Community Centre, London, ON N6A 3K7
Tel: 519-661-3580
editor@westerngazette.ca
www.westerngazette.ca
Social Media:
twitter.com/uwogazette
Circulation: 11,000
Frequency: 4 times a week; Tues.-Fri.
The Gazette is the student newspaper at the University of Western Ontario in London, Ontario, Canada.
Hamza Tariq, Editor-in-Chief

Gazette
Owned By: Dalhousie University
Student Union Building, #312, 6136 University Ave., Halifax, NS B3H 4J2
Tel: 902-494-1280
editor@dalgazette.com
dalgazette.com
Social Media:
twitter.com/dalgazette
www.facebook.com/DalGazette
Dalhousie University newspaper.
Dylan Matthias, Editor-in-Chief

The Georgian Eye
Owned By: Georgian College
One Georgian Dr., Barrie, ON L4M 3X9
Tel: 705-728-1968; *Fax:* 705-722-5123
georgianeye@gmail.com
georgianeye.com
Social Media:
twitter.com/georgianeye
www.facebook.com/pages/Georgian-Eye/189699477762 452
Georgian College newspaper. The new Georgian Eye Blog is an online site for students to write about things that interest them and comment on other students rants or raves.

La Gifle
Détenteur: Cégep de Trois-Rivières
CP 97, 3500, rue De Courval, Trois-Rivières, QC G9A 5E6
Tél: 819-376-1721; *Téléc:* 819-693-8023
communications@cegeptr.qc.ca
www.cegeptr.qc.ca
Médias sociaux: plus.google.com/109162921820608962493
twitter.com/cegeptr
www.faceb ook.com/cegeptr

Golden Ram
Owned By: Nova Scotia Agricultural College
PO Box 550, Truro, NS B2N 5E3
Tel: 902-895-3963; *Fax:* 902-895-1203
goldenram@nsac.ca
www.nsac.ns.ca
Nova Scotia Agricultural College newspaper.
Katherine Mitchell, Editor
Matthew Morrison, Editor

The Gradzette
Owned By: University of Manitoba
University of Manitoba, 105 University Centre, Winnipeg, MB R3T 2N2
Tel: 204-474-6535; *Fax:* 204-474-7651
editor@gradzette.com
issuu.com/thegradzette
Social Media:
twitter.com/gradzette
www.facebook.com/groups/195842203788275
Circulation: 3,500
Frequency: Monthly
The official magazine of University of Manitoba graduate students.
Ryan Harby, Editor, 204-474-6535, Fax: 204-474-7651, editor@gradzette.com

Le Graffiti
Détenteur: Collège Jean-de-Brebeuf Inc.
3200, ch de la côte Ste-Catherine, Montréal, QC H3T 1C1
Tél: 514-342-9342
ageb@brebeuf.qc.ca
www.brebeuf.qc.ca

The Grapevine
Owned By: Huron University College
1349 Western Rd., London, ON N6G 1H3
Tel: 519-755-5592
Social Media:
www.facebook.com/pages/Hurons-Grapevine/166794663334282
Frequency: Monthly
The Grapevine Magazine is a student-based publication that circulates monthly on the following campuses in London, Ontario: Huron University College, University of Western Ontario, and Kings College.
Whitney Slightham, Editor-in-Chief

The Griff
Owned By: MacEwan University
#7-297C, 10700 - 104 Ave., Edmonton, AB T5J 4S2
Tel: 780-497-4429; *Fax:* 780-497-5470
online@thegriff.ca
www.thegriff.ca
Circulation: 2,500
Frequency: 25 issues per academic year; Weekly; Thursday
the griff is MacEwan University's weekly student newspaper.
Angela Johnston, News Editor

Le Griffonnier
Détenteur: Université du Québec à Chicoutimi
555, boul de l'Université, Chicoutimi, QC G7H 2B1
Tél: 418-545-5011; *Téléc:* 418-545-5012
journal_griffonnier@uqac.ca
www.ceuc.ca/le-griffonnier.html
Médias sociaux:
www.facebook.com/ceuc.ca
Le Griffonnier est le journal des étudiants de l'UQAC.
Nancy Desgagné, Rédactrice-en-chef journal

Hebdo Garneau
Détenteur: Cégep François-Xavier-Garneau
1660, boul de l'Entente, Québec, QC G1S 4S3
Tél: 418-688-8310; *Téléc:* 418-688-1539
communications@cegep-fxg.qc.ca
www.cegep-fxg.qc.ca
Fréquence: Hebdomadaire
Sylvie Fortin, Directrice, sfortin@cegep-fxg.qc.ca

L'IdéePhile
Détenteur: Cégep de Chicoutimi
534, rue Jacques-Cartier est, Chicoutimi, QC G7H 1Z6
Tél: 418-549-9520; *Téléc:* 418-549-1315
info@cchic.ca
www.cchic.ca

Impact Campus
Détenteur: Université Laval
1244, Pavillon Maurice-Pollack, Université Laval, Québec, QC G1V 0A6
Tél: 418-656-5079; *Téléc:* 418-656-2398
redaction@impact.ulaval.ca
impactcampus.qc.ca; www.ulaval.ca
Médias sociaux: www.youtube.com/user/ImpactCampus
twitter.com/ImpactCampus
www.facebook.com/impactcampus
Fréquence: Hebdomadaire
Hubert Gaudreau, Rédacteur en chef

L'Inculte
Détenteur: Cégep de Victoriaville
475, rue Notre-Dame est, Victoriaville, QC G6P 4B3
Tél: 819-758-6401; *Téléc:* 819-758-8126
www.cgpvicto.qc.ca

L'INFO-Cégep
Détenteur : Cégep de Granby-Haute-Yamaska
CP 7000, 235, rue Saint-Jacques, Granby, QC J2G 9H7
Tél: 450-372-6614; *Téléc:* 450-372-6565
www.cegepgranby.qc.ca/nouvelles
Fréquence: Quotidien, juin-août

L'Infomane
Détenteur: Cégep de Bois-de-Boulogne
10500, av de Bois-de-Boulogne, Montréal, QC H4N 1L4
Tél: 514-332-3000; *Téléc:* 514-332-5857
infomane@age.bdeb.qc.ca
www.bdeb.qc.ca
Médias sociaux:
twitter.com/infomane
www.facebook.com/infomane
Laurence Bissonnet, Coordonatrice Générale

Inter
Anciennement: Suites
Détenteur: Université du Québec à Montréal
Service des communications, CP 8888 Centre-Ville, #WB-5300, Montréal, QC H3C 3P8
Tél: 514-987-3000
magazine.inter@uqam.ca
www.uqam.ca/inter

The Intercamp
Owned By: Grant MacEwan College
City Centre Campus, #297C, 10700 - 104 Ave., Edmonton, AB T5J 4S2
Tel: 780-497-5412
intercamp.ca
Grant MacEwan College newspaper.
Jenny Feniak, Managing Editor, managing@intercamp.ca

Le Jets
Détenteur: École de technologie supérieure
1100, rue Notre-Dame ouest, Montréal, QC H3C 1K3
Tél: 514-396-8800; *Téléc:* 514-396-8950
directeur@jets.etsmtl.ca
www.etsmtl.ca

The Journal
Owned By: Queen's University
Queen's University, 190 University Ave., Kingston, ON K7L 3P4
Tel: 613-533-2800; *Fax:* 613-533-6728
journal_editors@ams.queensu.ca
queensjournal.ca
Social Media:
twitter.com/queensjournal
www.facebook.com/queensjournal
Frequency: Two issues a week for the first two months and once a week in the last month of each semester, totalling 40 issues.
Queen's University newspaper.
Katherine Fernandez-Blance, Editor-in-Chief

The Journal
Owned By: Saint Mary's University
Student Centre, 923 Robie St., 5th Fl., Halifax, NS B3H 3C3
Tel: 902-266-9731
www.smujournal.ca
Social Media:
twitter.com/TheSMUJournal
www.facebook.com/SMUJournal
Saint Mary's University newspaper.
Samuel Hammond, Editor, 902-266-9731, samuelphammond@gmail.com

Journal l'Action
Détenteur: Cégep de Shawinigan
CP 610, Shawinigan, QC G9N 6V8
Tél: 819-539-6401
journal@collegeshawinigan.qc.ca
www.ageecs.com; www.collegeshawinigan.qc.ca

Journal L'Interêt
Détenteur: Écoles De Hautes Etudes Commerciales Montréal
#RJ718, 3000, ch de la Côte-Sainte-Catherine, Montréal, QC H3T 2A7
Tél: 514-340-6105
redaction.interet@hec.ca
www.journalinteret.com
Médias sociaux:
www.facebook.com/journalinteret

Labyrinthe
Détenteur: Cégep de Matane
616, av St-Rédempteur, Matane, QC G4W 1L1
Tél: 418-562-1240; *Téléc:* 418-566-2115
Ligne sans frais: 800-463-4299
information@cegep-matane.qc.ca
www.cegep-matane.qc.ca

Lambda
Détenteur: Laurentian University of Sudbury
Student Centre, #SCE301, 935 Ramsey Lake Rd., Sudbury, ON P3E 2C6
Tél: 705-673-6548
lambda@laurentian.ca
thelambda.ca
Médias sociaux:
www.facebook.com/TheLambda
Lambda is Laurentian University's campus newspaper.
Jessica Robinson, Editor-in-Chief

The Lance
Owned By: University of Windsor
CAW Student Centre, B-91, 401 Sunset Ave., Windsor, ON N9B 3P4
Tel: 519-253-3000; *Fax:* 519-971-3624
uwindsorlance.ca
Social Media:
twitter.com/uwindsorlance
www.facebook.com/uwindsorlance
Circulation: 10,000
Frequency: Weekly; Wednesday
University of Windsor newspaper.

The Link
Owned By: Université Concordia
Concordia University Hall Building, Rm H-649, 1455, Maisonneuve Blvd. West, Montréal, QC H3G 1M8
Tel: 514-848-2424; *Fax:* 514-848-4540
editor@thelinknewspaper.ca
thelinknewspaper.ca; www.concordia.ca
Social Media:
twitter.com/linknewspaper
www.facebook.com/TheLinkNewspaper
Julia Wolfe, Editor-in-chief

The Link
Owned By: BC Institute of Technology
3700 Willingdon Ave., Burnaby, BC V5G 3H2
Tel: 604-432-8600
publications@bcitsa.ca
www.bcitsa.ca/wordpress/?page_id=12
Social Media:
www.facebook.com/BCITSA
BC Institute of Technology newspaper.
Kevin Willemse, Editor, linkeditor@bcitsa.ca

Lionel
Détenteur: Cégep Lionel-Groulx
100, rue Duquet, Sainte-Thérèse, QC J7E 3G6
Tél: 450-430-3120; *Téléc:* 450-971-7883
info@clg.qc.ca
www.clg.qc.ca

MacMedia (McLaughlin College)
Owned By: York University
#004, 4700 Keele St., Toronto, ON M3J 1P3
Tel: 416-736-5128
macmedia@yorku.ca
macmediamagazine.com/macmedia
Social Media:
www.facebook.com/groups/6334572703
York University newspaper.

The Manitoban
Owned By: University of Manitoba
105 University Centre, Winnipeg, MB R3T 2N2
Tel: 204-474-6535; *Fax:* 204-474-7651
me@themanitoban.com
www.themanitoban.com
Social Media:
www.facebook.com/groups/195842203788275
The Manitoban is the official student newspaper of the University of Manitoba.
Craig Adolphe, Editor-in-Chief, 204-474-8293, editor@themanitoban.com

Mars' Hill
Owned By: Trinity Western Seminary
7600 Glover Rd., Langley, BC V2Y 1Y1
Tel: 604-888-6158; *Fax:* 604-888-5729
marshill@gmail.com.
www.marshillonline.com
Trinity Western Seminary newspaper.

The Martlet
Owned By: University of Victoria
Student Union Building, PO Box 3035, #B011, 3700 Finnerty Rd., Victoria, BC V8W 3P3
Tel: 250-721-8360; *Fax:* 250-472-4556
edit@martlet.ca
www.martlet.ca
Circulation: 4,200
The Martlet is an independent weekly student newspaper at the University of Victoria in Victoria, British Columbia, Canada.
Myles Sauer, Editor-in-Chief

McGill Reporter
Owned By: McGill University
#110, James Administration Bldg., 845, Sherbrooke St. West, Montréal, QC H3A 2T5
Tel: 514-398-1044
publications.mcgill.ca/reporter; www.mcgill.ca
Social Media:
twitter.com/mcgillreporter
Frequency: 4 times a year
McGill University newspaper.

Le Médiavic
Détenteur: Collège Marie-Victorin
7000, rue Marie-Victorin, Montréal, QC H1G 2J6
Tél: 514-325-0150
promotion@marievictorin.qc.ca
www.marievictorin.qc.ca
Fréquence: Hebdomadaire

The Medium
Owned By: University of Toronto at Mississauga
#200, 3359 Mississauga Rd., Mississauga, ON L5L 1C6
Tel: 905-828-5260; *Fax:* 905-569-4301
info@mediumutm.ca
mediumutm.ca
Social Media:
twitter.com/TheMediumUTM
www.facebook.com/groups/293066010726328
The Medium is the print media voice for the students of the University of Toronto Mississauga.
Michael Di Leo, Editor-in-Chief, editor@mediumutm.ca

The Meliorist
Owned By: University of Lethbridge
166 University Dr. West, Lethbridge, AB T1K 3M4
Tel: 403-329-2334; *Fax:* 403-329-2333
themeliorist.ca
University of Lethbridge newspaper.
Kelti Boissonnault, Editor-in-Chief, 403-329-2334, einc@themeliorist.ca

The Mike
Owned By: St. Michael's College
Elmsley Hall, Main Fl., #2, 81 St. Mary St., Toronto, ON M4S 1J4
Tel: 416-926-7272
editoratlarge@readthemike.com
www.readthemike.com
Social Media:
twitter.com/readthemike
www.facebook.com/readthemike
Circulation: 5,000
Frequency: Bi-weekly
St. Michael's College newspaper
Dan Seljak, Editor-in-Chief, editorinchief@readthemike.com

Le Motdit
Détenteur: Cégep Édouard-Montpetit
#F-045, 945, ch de Chambly, Longueuil, QC J4H 3M6
Tél: 450-679-2631; *Téléc:* 450-679-5570
www.collegeem.qc.ca
Médias sociaux:
twitter.com/collegeedouardm
www.facebook.com/CollegeEdouardM

Mouton Noir
Détenteur: Cégep de Drummondville
#1209, 960, rue St-Georges, Drummondville, QC J2C 6A2
Tél: 819-478-4671; *Téléc:* 819-478-8823
journal.mnoir@gmail.com
www.journauxetudiants.com/moutonnoir

The Muse
Owned By: Memorial University of Newfoundland
PO Box 4200, 230 Elizabeth Ave., St. John's, NL A1C 5S7
Tel: 709-737-8000; *Fax:* 709-737-4569
chief@themuse.ca
www.themuse.ca
Memorial University of Newfoundland newspaper.

The Navigator
Owned By: Vancouver Island University
Bldg. 193, #217, 900 - 5th St., Nanaimo, BC V9R 5S5
Tel: 250-753-2225; *Fax:* 250-753-2257
www.thenav.ca
Social Media:
twitter.com/theNav_VIU
www.facebook.com/thenavigatornewspaper
Frequency: Weekly
The Navigator is Vancouver Island University's (formerly Malaspina University-College) student newspaper.
Gareth Boyce, Editor-in-Chief, editor@thenav.ca

Nexus
Owned By: Camosun College
Lansdowne Campus, Richmond House 201, 3100 Foul Bay Rd., Victoria, BC V8P 5J2
Tel: 250-370-3591
nexus@nexusnewspaper.com
www.nexusnewspaper.com
Social Media:
www.facebook.com/nexusnewspaper
www.facebook.com/nexusnewspaper
Camosun College newspaper.
Greg Pratt, Editor-in-Chief

NightViews
Owned By: Ryerson University
350 Victoria St., Toronto, ON M5B 2K3
Tel: 416-979-5000
inquire@ryerson.ca
www.ryerson.ca
Frequency: Monthly
A monthly newspaper for Ryerson's Continuing Education and Part-time Degree students.

The Nugget
Owned By: The Northern Alberta Institute of Technology
11762 - 106 St., Edmonton, AB T5G 2R1
Tel: 780-423-5834
kerry@playhousepublications.ca
www.thenuggetonline.com
Social Media:
twitter.com/theNAITNugget
www.facebook.com/naitstudents
The Northern Alberta Institute of Technology newspaper.
Celeste Dul, Editor-in-Chief, studenteditor@nait.ca

ô Courant
Détenteur: Cégep régional de Lanaudière
2505, boul des Entreprises, Terrebonne, QC J6X 5S5
Tél: 450-470-0933
www.cegep-lanaudiere.qc.ca

The Omega
Owned By: Thompson Rivers University
Old Main Building, PO Box 3010, #OM2691, 900 McGill Rd., Kamloops, BC V2C 0C8
Tel: 250-828-5069
editorofomega@gmail.com
theomega.ca
Social Media:
twitter.com/TRU_Omega
www.facebook.com/pages/The-Omega/217031195028151
Frequency: Weekly; Wednesdays
The Omega is Thompson Rivers University's independent student newspaper.
Mike Davies, Editor-in-Chief

L'Original déchaîné
Détenteur: Laurentian University of Sudbury
#SCE301, 935 Ramsey Lake Rd., Sudbury, ON P3E 2C6
Tél: 705-673-6548
www.laurentian.ca
Médias sociaux:
www.facebook.com/145697498801833
Newspaper which is written for the Francophone Community of Laurentian.

Other Press
Owned By: Douglas College
PO Box 2503, New Westminster, BC V3L 5B2
editor@theotherpress.ca
theotherpress.ca
Social Media:
twitter.com/TheOtherPress
Frequency: weekly during the fall and winter semesters, and monthly during the summer
Douglas College newspaper.
Sharon Miki, Editor-in-Chief

Over the Edge
Owned By: University of Northern British Columbia
3333 University Way, NUSC 6-350, Prince George, BC V2N 4Z9
Tel: 250-960-5633; *Fax:* 250-960-5407
over-the-edge@unbc.ca
web.unbc.ca/edge
University of Northern British Columbia newspaper.
Shelby Petersen, Editor-in-Chief

La P'tite Antenne
Détenteur: Cégep de Rivière-du-Loup
80, rue Frontenac, Rivière-du-Loup, QC G5R 1R1
Tél: 418-862-6903; *Téléc:* 418-862-4959
www.cegep-rdl.qc.ca/ptite-antenne

The Papercut
Owned By: Marianopolis College
4873, ave Westmount, Westmount, QC H3Y 1X9
Tel: 514-931-8792; *Fax:* 514-931-8790
the.marianopolis.papercut@gmail.com
students.marianopolis.edu/papercut
Social Media:
twitter.com/MarianoPapercut
www.facebook.com/the.marianopolis.papercut
Marianopolis College newspaper.

Le Pastiche
Owned By: Cégep de Saint-Laurent
625, av Ste-Croix, Montréal, QC H4L 3X7
Tel: 514-747-6521; *Fax:* 514-748-1249
info@cegep-st-laurent.qc.ca
www.cegep-st-laurent.qc.ca
Social Media: www.linkedin.com/company/1588262
twitter.com/webcsl
www.facebook.com/137132236299536

The Peak
Owned By: Simon Fraser University
#MBC2901, 8888 University Dr., Burnaby, BC V5A 1S6
Tel: 778-782-4560; *Fax:* 778-782-4343
production@the-peak.ca
www.the-peak.ca
Social Media:
twitter.com/peaksfu
www.facebook.com/PeakSFU
Simon Fraser University newspaper.
David Dyck, News Editor, news@the-peak.ca

The Phoenix
Owned By: Okanagan College
3333 University Way, UNC109O, Kelowna, BC V1Y 1V7
Tel: 250-807-9296
www.thephoenixnews.com
Social Media:
twitter.com/ubcophoenix
www.facebook.com/thephoenixnews
Okanagan College newspaper.
Cameron Welch, Editor-in-Chief,
editorinchief@thephoenixnews.com

La Pige
Détenteur: Cégep de Jonquière
#854.2, pavillon Joseph-Angers, Jonquière, QC G7X 7W2
Tél: 418-547-2191
cegep@cjonquiere.qc.ca
www.lapige.qc.ca/atm
Tirage: 5000

La Placote
Détenteur: Cégep de Lévis-Lauzon
205, rue Mgr Bourget, Lévis, QC G6V 6Z9
Tél: 418-833-5110; *Téléc:* 418-833-8502
www.clevislauzon.qc.ca
Josée Larochelle, V.-p. aux affaires pédagogiques

The Plant
Owned By: Dawson College
3040 Sherbrooke St. West, Montréal, QC H3Z 1A4
Tel: 514-931-8731; *Fax:* 514-931-5181
issuu.com/theplant
Social Media:
twitter.com/issuu
www.facebook.com/issuu
Frequency: Weekly

Le Polyscope
Détenteur: École Polytechnique de Montréal
CP 6079 Centre-ville, Montréal, QC H3C 3A7
Tél: 514-340-4711; *Téléc:* 514-340-4986
direction@polyscope.qc.ca
www.polyscope.qc.ca
Tomasz Drake, Rédacteur en chef, article@polyscope.qc.ca

Portico
Owned By: University of Guelph
University Centre, Level 4, University of Guelph, 50 Stone Rd. East, Guelph, ON N1G 2W1
Tel: 519-824-7962
m.dickieson@exec.uoguelph.ca
www.uoguelph.ca/theportico
Frequency: 3 times a year
The Portico is mailed free to Guelph alumni living around the world.
Mary Dickieson, Editor

Quartier Libre
Détenteur: Université de Montréal
CP 6128 Centre-ville, 3200, rue Jean-Brillant, B-1274-6, Montréal, QC H3T 1N8
Tél: 514-343-7630
quartierlibre.ca
Médias sociaux:
twitter.com/quartierlibre
www.facebook.com/QuartierLibre.ca
Marie Roncari, Directrice, directeur@quartierlibre.ca

The Quill
Owned By: Brandon University
270 - 18th St., Brandon, MB R7A 6A9
Tel: 204-727-9667; *Fax:* 204-571-0029
business.thequill@gmail.com
www.thequill.ca
Social Media:
www.facebook.com/pages/The-Quill/124336617614355
Brandon University newspaper.
Matt Berry, Editor-in-Chief, eic.thequill@gmail.com

The Reflector
Owned By: Mount Royal College
Wyckham House, Mount Royal University, 4825 Mount Royal Gate SW, Calgary, AB T3E 6K6
Tel: 403-440-6268; *Fax:* 403-440-6762
thereflector@thereflector.ca
www.thereflector.ca
Social Media: www.youtube.com/user/SirKrushworth
twitter.com/reflectthis
www.face book.com/TheReflector.ca
Circulation: 10,000
Frequency: Bi-weekly; Sept.-April
Mount Royal College newspaper.
Rachael Frey, Publishing Editor & News Editor,
publishingeditor@thereflector.ca

Le Réveil
Détenteur: Collège universitaire de Saint-Boniface
CP 129, 200, av de la Cathédrale, Saint-Boniface, MB R2H 0H7
Tél: 204-237-1818; *Téléc:* 204-237-3240
mesdiasetudiants@cusb.ca
lereveil.cusb.ca
Le Réveil est un journal francophone par et pour les étudiantes et les étudiants du Collège universitaire de Saint-Boniface (CUSB).
Marie-Christine Bruce, Rédactrice en chef

The Ring
Owned By: University of Victoria
Sedgewick Building, C149, PO Box 1700 CSC, 3800 Finnerty Rd. (Ring Rd.), Victoria, BC V8W 2Y2
Tel: 250-721-7636; *Fax:* 250-721-8955
ucom@uvic.ca
ring.uvic.ca
Social Media: www.youtube.com/uvicring
twitter.com/uvicring
Circulation: 4,200
University of Victoria newspaper.
Bruce Kilpatrick, Director, 250-721-7638, abk@uvic.ca

Rosemont Ici
Détenteur: Cégep de Rosemont
6400, 16e av, Montréal, QC H1X 2S9
Tél: 514-376-1620; *Téléc:* 514-376-1440
www.crosemont.qc.ca
Anne-Marie Lacombe, Éditrice

La Rotonde
Détenteur: University of Ottawa
109, rue Osgoode, Ottawa, ON K1N 6S1
www.larotonde.ca
Médias sociaux:
twitter.com/LaRotonde
University of Ottawa newspaper.
Anais Elboujdaïne, Rédactrice en chef, redaction@larotonde.ca

The Runner
Owned By: Kwantlen Unicersity College
Arbutus Bldg., #3710/3720, 12666 72 Ave., Surrey, BC V3W 2M8
Tel: 778-565-3801
production@runnermag.ca
runnermag.ca
Social Media:
twitter.com/Runnermag
www.facebook.com/runnerpaper
Frequency: 20 issues a year
Kwantlen Polytechnic University newspaper.
Tristan Johnston, Coordinating Editor, editor@runnerrag.ca

The Ryerson Free Press
Owned By: Ryerson University
#SCC-301, 55 Gould St., Toronto, ON M5B 1E9
Tel: 416-979-5000; *Fax:* 416-979-5223
editor@ryersonfreepress.ca
www.ryersonfreepress.ca
Social Media:
twitter.com/RyeFreePress
Frequency: Monthly
The Ryerson Free Press is the definitive alternative monthly of the Continuing Education Student's Association of Ryerson University (CESAR).
Clare O'Connor, Editor-in-Chief

Ryerson Review of Journalism
Owned By: Ryerson University
350 Victoria Street, Toronto, ON M5B 2K3
Tel: 416-979-5319; *Fax:* 416-979-5216
chair.journalism@ryerson.ca
rrj.ca
Social Media:
twitter.com/RyersonReview
www.facebook.com/707355524.2912769015
Frequency: 2 times a year
Produced by final-year students at Ryerson University's School of Journalism in Toronto, Canada,
Kat Eschner, Editor, keschner@ryerson.ca

The Ryersonian
Owned By: Ryerson University
350 Victoria Street, Toronto, ON M5B 2K3
sonian@ryerson.ca
www.ryersonian.ca
Social Media:
twitter.com/TheRyersonian
www.facebook.com/TheRyersonian
Students in Ryerson's School of Journalism's fourth-year undergraduate & second-year graduate program produce The Ryersonian.

Sault College Alumni Magazine
Owned By: Sault College of Applied Arts & Technology
PO Box 60, 443 Northern Ave., Sault Ste Marie, ON P6A 5L3
Toll-Free: - - 0
alumni@saultcollege.ca
www.saultcollege.ca
Social Media:
twitter.com/SaultCollAlumni
www.facebook.com/pages/Sault-College-Alumni/1274688806274
Sault College of Applied Arts & Technology newspaper.
Meggan Rudnicki, Officer, 705-759-2554 x 2622

Le Savoir
Anciennement: Le Virus
Détenteur: Université du Québec en Outaouais
CP 1250 Hull, #E-2000, 243, boul Alexandre-Taché, Gatineau, QC J8X 3X7
Tél: 819-595-3900; *Téléc:* 819-595-3830
savoir@uqo.ca
www4.uqo.ca/savoir
Médias sociaux:
twitter.com/uqo
www.facebook.com/Universite.Quebec.Outaouais
Le Savoir est un bulletin électronique.

The Scanner
Owned By: Saskatchewan Polytechnic Students' Association Inc.
#119, 1130 Idylwyld Dr. South, Saskatoon, SK S7K 3R5
Tel: 306-659-4421; *Fax:* 306-933-8220
ssa.scanner@siast.sk.ca
spsa.ca/campus-life/publications/
Social Media: www.youtube.com/user/0SIASTSA
twitter.com/ur_ssa
www.facebook.com/SIASTSSA
Frequency: 2 times a year
The Scanner is the Students' Association's monthly newspaper

publication for Saskatchewan Institute of Applied Science and Technology (SIAST).

Le Sentier
Détenteur: Cégep de St-Félicien
CP 7300, Saint-Félicien, QC G8K 2R8
Tél: 418-679-5412; *Téléc:* 418-679-0238
sentierfelicien.wordpress.com

The Sentinel
Owned By: Selkirk College
301 Frank Bender Way, Castlegar, BC V1N 4L3
www.selkirksentinel.ca
The Official News Source for Students at Selkirk College.

The Sheaf
Owned By: University of Saskatchewan
108 Memorial Union Building, 93 Campus Dr., Saskatoon, SK S7N 5B2
Tel: 306-966-8689; *Fax:* 306-966-8699
editor@thesheaf.com
www.thesheaf.com
Social Media:
www.facebook.com/thesheaf1912
University of Saskatchewan newspaper.
Kevin Menz, Editor-in-Chief

The Silhouette
Owned By: McMaster University
McMaster University Student Centre, B110, 1280 Main St. West, Hamilton, ON L8S 4K1
Tel: 905-525-9140; *Fax:* 905-521-1504
thesil@thesil.ca
www.thesil.ca
Circulation: 10,000
Frequency: Sept-Mar.
McMaster University newspaper.
Sam Colbert, Executive Editor

The Spit
Owned By: Quest University
3200 University Blvd., Squamish, BC V8B 0N8
Tel: 604-898-8000; *Fax:* 604-815-0829
Toll-Free: 888-783-7808
info@questu.ca
Social Media:
www.facebook.com/QuestU
Quest University's student newspaper.

The Sputnik
Owned By: Wilfrid Laurier University - Brantford Campus
Odeon Building, #208, 50 Market St., Brantford, ON N3T 2Z5
Tel: 519-756-8228
www.thesputnik.ca
Social Media:
twitter.com/thesputnikwlusp
www.facebook.com/pages/The-Sputnik/134603623243364
The official independent newspaper of Laurier Brantford
Christina Manocchio, Editor-in-Chief, eic@thesputnik.ca

The Strand
Owned By: Victoria University
63 Charles St. West, Toronto, ON M5S 1K5
Tel: 416-585-4524; *Fax:* 416-585-4584
editor@thestrand.ca
www.thestrand.ca
Circulation: 2,500
Frequency: 14 times a year
Victoria University newspaper.
Fiona Buchanan, Editor-in-Chief
Pauline Holdsworth, Editor-in-Chief

Student Connection
Owned By: Keyano College
8115 Franklin Ave., Fort McMurray, AB T9H 2H7
Tel: 780-791-4800; *Fax:* 780-791-1555
communicationvp.kcsa@keyano.ca
www.keyano.ca
Frequency: Weekly
Keyano College newspaper.

The Surveyor
Owned By: Holland College of Applied Arts and Technology
140 Weymouth St., Charlottetown, PE C1A 4Z1
surveyoronline.wordpress.com
Frequency: 10 times a year
Holland College of Applied Arts and Technology newspaper.

The Toike Oike
Owned By: University of Toronto
B740 Sanford Fleming, 10 King's College Rd., Toronto, ON M5S 3G4
Tel: 416-978-2011
toike@skule.ca
toike.skule.ca
Publication by The University of Toronto Engineering Society (EngSoc).
Andrew Jerabek, Editor-in-Chief

The Ubyssey
Owned By: University of British Columbia
Student Union Building, 24 - 6138 SUB Blvd., Vancouver, BC V6T 1Z1
Tel: 604-822-2301; *Fax:* 604-822-9279
feedback@ubyssey.ca
ubyssey.ca
Social Media: ubyssey.tumblr.com
twitter.com/ubyssey
www.facebook.com/ubyssey
Frequency: every Monday and Thursday during the school year, and every second Tuesday during the summer.
University of British Columbia newspaper.
Jonny Wakefield, Coordinating Editor, coordinating@ubyssey.ca

The Uniter
Owned By: University of Winnipeg
ORM14, University of Winnipeg, 515 Portage Ave., Winnipeg, MB R3B 2E9
Tel: 204-786-9790; *Fax:* 204-783-7080
uniter@uniter.ca
uniter.ca
Social Media:
twitter.com/TheUniter
www.facebook.com/pages/The-Uniter/129195330426257
University of Winnipeg newspaper.
Aaron Epp, Managing Editor, editor@uniter.ca

UQAR-Info
Anciennement : Uquarium
Détenteur: Université du Québec à Rimouski
Service des communications, #E-215, 300, allée des Ursulines, Rimouski, QC G5L 3A1
Tél: 418-723-1986 *Ligne sans frais:* 800-511-3382
www.uqar.ca/uqar-info
Jean-François Bouchard, Responsable, jean-francois_bouchard@uqar.ca

The Voice
Owned By: Athabasca University
#1213, 10011 - 109th St. NW, Athabasca, AB T5J 3S8
Toll-Free: 800-788-9041
voice@voicemagazine.org
www.voicemagazine.org
Athabasca University newspaper.
Tamra Ross, Editor—in-Chief

The Voice
Owned By: Langara College
100 West 49th Ave., Vancouver, BC V5Y 2Z6
Tel: 604-323-5511; *Fax:* 604-323-5555
www.langara.bc.ca
Social Media: www.youtube.com/user/VoiceLangara
twitter.com/langaravoice
www.faceboo k.com/Langara.Journalism
Frequency: Weekly
Langara College newspaper.

Vox-Populi
Détenteur: Cégep André-Laurendeau
1111, rue Lapierre, Lasalle, QC H8N 2J4
Tél: 514-364-3320; *Téléc:* 514-364-7130
courrier@claurendeau.qc.ca
www.claurendeau.qc.ca

The Watch
Owned By: University of King's College
c/o The University of King's College, 6350 Coburg Rd., Halifax, NS B3H 2A1
watcheditors@gmail.com
watchmagazine.ca
Social Media:
twitter.com/KingsWatch
University of King's College newspaper.
Ben Harrison, Editor-in-Chief
Rachel Ward, Editor-in-Chief

The Weal
Previous Name: The Emery Weal
Owned By: SAIT
1301 - 16 Ave. NW, Calgary, AB T2M 0L4
Tel: 403-284-8110; *Fax:* 403-284-7112
www.theweal.com
Social Media:
twitter.com/theweal
SAIT, Canada's premier technical institute by 2010
Heather Setka, Publications Manager, 403-284-8077, heather.setka@edu.sait.ca

Western News
Owned By: University of Western Ontario
Westminster Hall, #360, 1151 Richmond St., London, ON N6A 5B8
Tel: 519-661-2045; *Fax:* 519-661-3921
communications.uwo.ca/westernnews/index.html
Circulation: 10,000
Frequency: 35 times during the academic year
University of Western Ontario newspaper.
Jason Winders, Editor, newseditor@uwo.ca

The Window
Owned By: New College
40 Willcocks St., Toronto, ON M5S 1C6
Tel: 416-978-2460; *Fax:* 416-978-0554
Social Media:
www.facebook.com/NewCollegeWindow
New College's official student publication.
Michelle Cramer, Michelle.Cramer@utoronto.ca

Xaverian Weekly
Owned By: St. Francis Xavier University
PO Box 5000, #111, Bloomfield Centre, Antigonish, NS B2G 2W5
Tel: 902-867-5007
xw.eic@stfx.ca
www.xaverianweekly.ca
Social Media:
twitter.com/xaverianweekly
www.facebook.com/pages/The-Xaverian-Weekly/15456132459788
Frequency: Weekly; Thursdays
St. Francis Xavier University newspaper.

YorkU
York University, West Office Bldg., 4700 Keele St., Toronto, ON M3J 1P3
Tel: 416-736-5058; *Fax:* 416-736-5681
editor@yorku.ca
www.yorku.ca/yorku
Social Media:
twitter.com/YorkUnews/york-u-feeds/members
Frequency: 3 times a year
YorkU is the magazine of York University
Berton Woodward, Publications Director

Le Zèle
Détenteur: Cégep Montmorency
475, boul de l'Avenir, Laval, QC H7N 5H9
Tél: 450-975-6209; *Téléc:* 450-668-8639
journal_zele@hotmail.com
www.cmontmorency.qc.ca
Tirage: 1,500
Fréquence: 5 fois par année

SECTION 14
RELIGION

Broad Faith-Based Associations

Across Boundaries Multifaith Institute
PO Box 437, Stn. A, Toronto ON M5W 1C2
Tel: 416-850-3598; *Fax:* 416-850-3599
info@acrossboundaries.net
www.acrossboundaries.net
Overview: A small national charitable organization
Chief Officer(s):
Wanda Romer Taylor, Chair, Secretary
Member Profile: Members come from any religious faith.
Description: To strengthen civil society and enhance pluralism in Canada and globallyby promoting dialogue and exchange among faith traditions and between secular and religious perspectives.

American Academy of Religion (AAR)
#300, 825 Houston Mill Rd., Atlanta GA 30329-4205 USA
Tel: 404-727-3049; *Fax:* 404-727-7959
info@aarweb.org
www.aarweb.org
Social Media:
www.facebook.com/256288333448
twitter.com/AARWeb
Overview: A medium-sized national charitable organization founded in 1909
Chief Officer(s):
John R. Fitzmier, Executive Director & Treasurer
jfitzmier@aarweb.org
Otto A. Maduro, President
Warren G. Frisina, Secretary
Membership: 10,000+; *Fees:* Schedule available; *Member Profile:* Teachers; Research scholars; *Committees:* Academic Relations; Executive; Finance; Graduate Student; International Connections; Nominations; Program; Publications; Public Understanding of Religion; Regions; Status of Racial & Ethnic Minorities in the Profession; Status of Women in the Profession; Teaching & Learning; Theological Education Steering Committee
Activities: Sustainability Task Force; Status of Lesbian, Gay, Bisexual, & Transgendered Persons in the Profession; Awards for Excellence in the Study of Religion Book Award Juries; History of Religions Jury; Research Grants Jury; *Speaker Service:* Yes
Description: To promote research, teaching & scholarship in the field of religion; to be dedicated to furthering knowledge of religion & religious institutions in all their forms & manifestations; *Member of:* American Council of Learned Societies

Canadian Association for Spiritual Care (CASC) / Association canadienne de soins spirituels (ACSS)
#27, 1267 Dorval Dr., Oakville ON L6M 3Z4
Tel: 289-837-2272; *Fax:* 289-837-4800
Toll-Free: 866-442-2773
www.spiritualcare.ca
Previous Name: Canadian Association for Pastoral Practice & Education
Overview: A medium-sized national organization founded in 1965
Chief Officer(s):
Tony Sedfawi, Executive Director
office@spiritualcare.ca
Kathy Greig, Manager
kathy@spiritualcare.ca
Finances: *Funding Sources:* Membership dues
Fees: $185 associate members, with any amount of CPE or PCE training, & corporate members; $395 certified specialists or teaching supervisors; *Member Profile:* Persons involved in a variety of ministries, in settings such as parishes, prisons & correctional facilities, pastoral counselling centres, health care facilities & industrial facilities
Activities: Offering educational programs for both clergy & lay persons; Providing certification for supervisors & specialists; Creating networking opportunities
Description: A national multifaith organization committed to the professional education, certification & support of people involved in pastoral care & pastoral counselling.

Canadian Society for the Study of Religion (CSSR) / Société canadienne pour l'étude de la religion (SCÉR)
c/o Richard Mann, 2A51 Paterson Hall, Dept. of Religion, Carleton U., 1125 Colonel By Dr., Ottawa ON K1S 5B6
www.cssrscer.ca
Overview: A small national organization founded in 1966
Chief Officer(s):
Rubina Ramji, President
ruby_ramji@cbu.ca
Arlene Macdonald, Membership Secretary
almacdon@utmb.edu
Richard Mann, Treasurer
Richard_mann@carleton.ca
Fees: $50 students; $60 part-time & retired persons; $90 regular; *Member Profile:* Scholars engaged in various academic approaches to the study of religion
Description: To promote research in the study of religion, with particular reference to Canada; To encourage a critical examination of the teaching of the discipline; *Member of:* International Association for the History of Religions (IAHR); Affiliation(s): Canadian Federation for the Humanities & Social Sciences (CFHSS)

Canadian Theological Society (CTS) / Société théologique canadienne
c/o M. Beavis, St. Thomas More College, 1437 College Dr., Saskatoon SK S7N 0W6
secretary@cts-stc.ca
cts-stc.ca
Social Media:
www.facebook.com/canadiantheologicalsociety
Overview: A small national organization founded in 1955
Chief Officer(s):
Allen Jorgenson, President
ajorgenson@wlu.ca
Bob McKeon, Treasurer
rmckeon@shaw.ca
Fees: $86 full members; $61 associate members; $45 student, retired, & unwaged full members; $22 student, retired, & unwaged associate members; *Member Profile:* Theologians, clergy, scholars, & students from universities, seminaries, & churches; Lay people
Activities: *Awareness Events:* Annual Student Essay Contest
Description: To promote theological reflection & writing in Canada; *Member of:* Canadian Corporation for the Study of Religion (CCSR); Affiliation(s): Canadian Congress of the Humanities & Social Sciences

International Fellowship of Christians & Jews of Canada
Corporate Office, #218, 449 The Queensway South, Keswick ON L4P 2C9
Tel: 416-596-9307; *Fax:* 416-981-7293
Toll-Free: 888-988-4325
info@IFCJ.ca
www.ifcj.ca
Social Media:
www.facebook.com/FellowshipFan
Overview: A medium-sized international charitable organization
Chief Officer(s):
Yechiel Eckstein, Founder & Chair
Activities: Accepting donations to support the work of the organization (c/o Donation Centre, PO Box 670, Station K, Toronto, ON M4P 2H1). Supporting Israel & Jewish people in need
Description: To encourage improved understanding between Christian & Jewish people; To promote cooperation between Christian & Jewish communities

International Institute of Integral Human Sciences (IIIHS) / Institut international des sciences humaines intégrales
PO Box 1387, Stn. H, Montréal QC H3G 2N3
Tel: 514-937-8359; *Fax:* 514-937-5380
Toll-Free: 877-937-8359
iiihs@iiihs.org
www.iiihs.org
Social Media:
www.facebook.com/spiritualsciencef
twitter.com/SSF_IIIHS
Overview: A medium-sized international organization founded in 1975
Chief Officer(s):
Marilyn Rossner, President
mrossner@iiihs.org
Fadel Behman, Vice-President
fadelbehman@sympatico.ca
Finances: *Annual Operating Budget:* $100,000-$250,000; *Funding Sources:* Classes; Workshops; International Conferences; Donations
Staff: 3 staff member(s); 25 volunteer(s)
Membership: 10,000; *Committees:* Local; International
Activities: Offering seminars, lectures, & programs; Conducting international outreach projects; *Internships:* Yes; *Speaker Service:* Yes *Library:* Yes
Description: To explore new sciences of consciousness & healing; To identify paradigms for the convergence of science & spirituality in the global village landscape

Multifaith Action Society (MAS)
949 West 49 Ave., Vancouver BC V5Z 2T1
Tel: 604-321-1302
admin@multifaithaction.org
www.multifaithaction.org
Social Media:
www.facebook.com/113668295376729
twitter.com/mfcalendar
Previous Name: Canadian Ecumenical Action
Overview: A small national charitable organization founded in 1972
Chief Officer(s):
Acharya Shrinath Dwivedi, President
Marcus Hynes, Operations Coordinator
Fees: Schedule available
Activities: Lectures & conferences promoting interreligious dialogue; forums on faith; environmental awareness programs within religious communities; faith centre visits; *Speaker Service:* Yes
Description: To promote interfaith & multifaith dialogue & understanding; To provides information & resources on world religions to the community & develops community service programs

Ontario Consultants on Religious Tolerance (OCRT)
#128, 829 Norwest Rd., Kingston ON K7P 2N3
Toll-Free: 888-806-6115
ocrtfeedback@gmail.com
www.religioustolerance.org
Social Media:
www.facebook.com/groups/115060631838983
Overview: A small provincial organization founded in 1995
Chief Officer(s):
B.A. Robinson, Coordinator
Finances: *Annual Operating Budget:* Less than $50,000; *Funding Sources:* Lecture fees; donations; banner ads
Staff: 1 staff member(s); 5 volunteer(s)
Membership: 1-99
Activities: *Speaker Service:* Yes
Description: To promote religious tolerance & expose religious hatred & misinformation

Société québécoise pour l'étude de la religion
Université de Montréal, #490, 3333, Chemin Queen Mary, Montréal QC H3V 1A2
Tél: 514-343-6568; *Téléc:* 514-343-5738
Aperçu: *Dimension:* petite; *Envergure: provinciale; fondée en 1989*
Membre(s) du bureau directeur:
Patrice Brodeur, Président
Montant de la cotisation: 50$ régulier; 25$ étudiant
Description: Promouvoir la recherche, l'enseignement et la diffusion des connaissances dans les disciplines ayant pour objet l'étude de la religion

World Conference on Religion & Peace (Canada) (WCRP)
#490-1, 333 Queen Mary Rd., Montréal QC H3Z 1A2
Tel: 450-478-3904
www.religionsforpeace.org
Also Known As: Religions for Peace (Canada)
Overview: A medium-sized national organization founded in 1975
Chief Officer(s):
Pascale Frémond, President
pascale.fremond@videotron.ca
Membership: 100-499; *Fees:* $100 institutional; $10 student; $25 individual; $15 senior
Activities: Meetings; occasional conferences; newsletter
Description: To establish peace & justice at the local, national & international levels; to encourage members to work together with like-minded organizations on issues of social & economic justice, human rights, ecological harmony, arms limitation & nuclear disarmament; to aim for world peace through interfaith dialogue & applied ethics; Affiliation(s): World Conference on Religion & Peace (International)

World Council of Churches
PO Box 2100, 150, rte de Ferney, Geneva CH-1211 Switzerland
oikoumene.org
Overview: A medium-sized international organization
Chief Officer(s):
Olav Fykse Tveit, General Secretary
Affiliation(s): International Council of World Religions & Cultures

Specific Faith-Based Associations

Adventism

Adventist Development & Relief Agency Canada (ADRA)

20 Robert St. W., Newcastle ON L1B 1C6
Tel: 905-446-2372; *Fax:* 905-723-1903
Toll-Free: 888-274-2372
info@adra.ca
www.adra.ca
Social Media: www.youtube.com/adracanada
www.facebook.com/adracanada
twitter.com/adracanada

Also Known As: ADRA Canada
Overview: A medium-sized international charitable organization founded in 1985
Chief Officer(s):
James Astleford, Executive Director
Finances: *Annual Operating Budget:* $1.5 Million-$3 Million; *Funding Sources:* Resources & donations received from the public & the Canadian government.
Staff: 14 staff member(s); 1500 volunteer(s)
Membership: 7,000
Activities: Non-sectarian, humanitarian relief agency; community development projects in 50 countries
Description: To provide community development & disaster relief without regard to political or religious association, age, or ethnicity; *Member of:* Canadian Council of Christian Charities, Canadian Churches in Action, Canadian Council for International Cooperation, Canadian Christian Relief and Development Association; Affiliation(s): Canadian Council of Christian Charities

Adventive Cross Cultural Initiatives (ACCI)

89 Auriga Dr., Nepean ON K2E 7Z2
Tel: 613-298-1546; *Fax:* 613-225-7455
lauren@adventive.ca
www.adventive.ca
Social Media:
www.facebook.com/AdventiveCCI

Previous Name: New Life League
Overview: A small national charitable organization founded in 1986
Chief Officer(s):
John Haley, Executive Director
johnhaley@adventive.ca
Lauren Roth, Canadian National Director
lauren@adventive.ca
Finances: *Annual Operating Budget:* Less than $50,000; *Funding Sources:* Donations
Staff: 4 staff member(s); 1 volunteer(s)
Activities: *Internships:* Yes
Description: To operate as an international, interdenominational Christian missionary organization; To minister through printing & literature, children's homes, national workers, evangelism, & church planting; *Member of:* Canadian Council of Christian Charities

Canadian Adventist Teachers Network

c/o Seventh-day Adventist Church in Canada, 1148 King St. East, Oshawa ON L1H 1H8
Tel: 905-433-0011; *Fax:* 905-433-0982
education@adventist.ca
catnet.sdacc.org

Also Known As: CAT-net
Overview: A small national organization
Chief Officer(s):
Dennis Marshall, General Vice-President & Director, Education
marshall.dennis@adventist.ca
Description: Dedicated to promoting excellence in Christian education by helping facilitate communication and the exchange of ideas among Adventist educators.; Affiliation(s): Seventh-day Adventist Church in Canada

International Community for the Relief of Suffering & Starvation Canada (ICROSS)

PO Box 3, Stn. Main, Saanichton BC V8M 2C3
Tel: 250-652-4137
icross-canada.com

Overview: A small national charitable organization founded in 1998
Chief Officer(s):
Billy Willbond, CEO & President
billywillbond@shaw.ca
Finances: *Funding Sources:* Donations
Description: A Canadian Humanitarian NGO with a goal to sending life-saving and ease-suffering medical supplies to the poorest of the poor in the Global Village.

Seventh-day Adventist Church in Canada (SDACC) / Église adventiste du septième jour au Canada

1148 King St. East, Oshawa ON L1H 1H8
Tel: 905-433-0011; *Fax:* 905-433-0982
communication@adventist.ca
www.adventist.ca

Overview: A large national charitable organization founded in 1901
Chief Officer(s):
Mark Johnson, President, 905-433-0011 2086
johnson.mark@adventist.ca
Dennis Marshall, Vice-President, 905-433-0011 2073
marshall.dennis@adventist.ca
Daniel Dragan Stojanovic, Secretary/Vice-President, Administration, 905-433-0011 2083
stojanovic.dragan@adventist.ca
John Ramsay, Treasurer/Vice-President, Finance, 905-433-0011 2088
ramsay.john@adventist.ca
Finances: *Annual Operating Budget:* $3 Million-$5 Million; *Funding Sources:* Donations
Staff: 23 staff member(s)
Membership: 375 churches + 66,907 individual members
Activities: Adventist Development & Relief Agency (ADRA); Native Ministries; It Is Written Canada; Christian Record Services; Canadian University College; Kingsway College
Description: To be a significant Christian movement that recognizes the unique role to which Christ has called it & the urgency of the message of salvation & judgment; To lead people to salvation in Jesus; To teach them the biblical faith & discipline of the Christian life; To equip them to serve with their God-given abilities through the leadership of our various administrative & ministry teams; To proclaim Christ; To nurture believers; To serve humanity

Anglican

The Anglican Church of Canada (ACC) / L'Église anglicane du Canada

80 Hayden St., Toronto ON M4Y 3G2
Tel: 416-924-9192; *Fax:* 416-968-7983
information@national.anglican.ca
www.anglican.ca
Social Media: www.youtube.com/generalsynod
www.facebook.com/canadiananglican
twitter.com/generalsynod

Previous Name: Church of England in Canada
Overview: A large national charitable organization founded in 1893
Chief Officer(s):
Fred Hiltz, Primate, Anglican Church of Canada
primate@national.anglican.ca
Michael Thompson, General Secretary
mthompson@national.anglican.ca
Membership: 500,000+ members; 1,700 churches; *Committees:* Communications & Information Resources; Faith, Worship & Ministry; Financial Management; Partners in MIssions & Ecojustice; Philanthropy
Activities: Operates four incorporated bodies: the Anglican Foundation of Canada, Anglican Journal, Primate's World Relief & Development Fund, & Pension Office Corporation; *Library:* Yes by appointment
Description: To proclaim & celebrate the gospel of Jesus Christ in worship & action, as a partner in the world-wide Anglican Communion & the universal church; to value our heritage of faith, reason, liturgy, tradition, bishops & synods, & the rich variety of life in community; to acknowledge that God calls His followers to greater diversity of membership, wider participation in ministry & leadership, better stewardship in God's creation & a strong resolve in challenging attitudes & structures which cause injustice; *Member of:* Canadian Council of Churches

Anglican Foundation of Canada

Anglican Church House, 80 Hayden St., Toronto ON M4V 3G2
Tel: 416-924-9199; *Toll-Free:* 866-924-9192
foundation@anglicanfoundation.org
www.anglicanfoundation.org
Social Media: www.youtube.com/user/AnglicanFoundation

Overview: A small national charitable organization founded in 1957
Chief Officer(s):
Judy Rois, Executive Director, 416-924-9199 234
Emily Wall, Project Manager, 416-924-9199 322
Activities: *Speaker Service:* Yes
Description: To assist parishes, dioceses & programs of Anglican Church of Canada with low interest loans &/or grants; Affiliation(s): World Council of Churches

Church of the Good Shepherd

116 Queen St. North, Kitchener ON N2H 2H7
Tel: 519-743-3845; *Fax:* 519-743-3375
office@shepherdsway.ca
www.shepherdsway.ca

Also Known As: Swedenborgian Church
Overview: A small local organization
Chief Officer(s):
John Maine, Minister
Membership: 140 individual

Integrity Toronto

PO Box 873, Stn. F, Toronto ON M4Y 2N9
Tel: 416-925-9872
toronto@integritycanada.org
www.toronto.integritycanada.org

Overview: A small local organization founded in 1975
Chief Officer(s):
Chris Ambidge, Co-Convener
Finances: *Annual Operating Budget:* Less than $50,000; *Funding Sources:* Donations
Staff: 6 volunteer(s)
Membership: 100 individual; *Fees:* $15 single, $20 couple
Description: International organization of gay & lesbian Anglicans & their friends; to help its members discover & affirm that we can be both Christian & gay/lesbian/bisexual/transgender; Affiliation(s): Integrity Inc. - USA

Integrity Vancouver

PO Box 3016, Stn. Terminal, Vancouver BC V6B 3X5
Tel: 604-432-1230
www.vancouver.integritycanada.org
Social Media:
www.facebook.com/203812556325704

Overview: A small local charitable organization
Finances: *Annual Operating Budget:* Less than $50,000
Staff: 14 volunteer(s)
Membership: 50-100; *Fees:* $15 single, $20 couple; *Member Profile:* Gay, lesbian, bisexual, transgendered Anglicans
Activities: Monthly services on first Sunday, St. Paul's Anglican Church; monthly potluck dinners at members' homes; *Speaker Service:* Yes
Affiliation(s): Integrity Inc. - USA

The Primate's World Relief & Development Fund (PWRDF) / Le fonds du Primat pour le secours et le développement mondial

Anglican Church of Canada, 80 Hayden St., Toronto ON M4Y 3G2
Tel: 416-924-9192; *Fax:* 416-924-3483
Toll-Free: 866-308-7973
pwrdf@pwrdf.org
www.pwrdf.org
Social Media: www.youtube.com/user/PWRDF
www.facebook.com/111501932203731
twitter.com/PWRDF

Overview: A small international charitable organization founded in 1959
Chief Officer(s):
Fred Hiltz, Archbishop & Primate
Adele Finney, Executive Director
afinney@pwrdf.org
Finances: *Annual Operating Budget:* Greater than $5 Million; *Funding Sources:* Anglican Church contributions; Canadian International Development Agency
Staff: 16 staff member(s); 2000 volunteer(s)
Activities: *Library:* Resource Centre - Anglican Church of Canada (Open to Public)
Description: PWRDF connects Anglicans in Canada to communities around the world in dynamic partnerships to advance development, to respond to emergencies, to assist refugees, and to act for positive change; *Member of:* Canadian Council for International Cooperation; Action by Churches Together (ACT); Affiliation(s): Canadian Council of Churches

Threshold Ministries

National Ministry Centre, 105 Mountain View Dr., Saint John NB E2J 5B5
Tel: 506-642-2210; *Fax:* 506-657-8217
Toll-Free: 888-316-8169
hello@thresholdministries.ca
www.thresholdministries.ca
Social Media: vimeo.com/thresholdministries
www.facebook.com/thresholdministries
twitter.com/thresholdmin

Overview: A medium-sized national charitable organization founded in 1929
Chief Officer(s):
John W. Irwin, B.A., LLD, Chair
Shawn C. Branch, Dip.E.S., National Director
shawn.branch@thresholdministries.ca

Charles Harding, Communications
charles.harding@thresholdministries.ca
Shauna Hooper, Administrative Officer
shauna.hooper@thresholdministries.ca
Mike Hughes, Financial Officer
mike.hughes@thresholdministries.ca
Finances: *Annual Operating Budget:* $1.5 Million-$3 Million; *Funding Sources:* Individuals; churches; foundations
Staff: 12 staff member(s); 75 volunteer(s)
Membership: 70; *Fees:* none
Activities: *Internships:* Yes; *Speaker Service:* Yes *Library:* Taylor College (Open to Public)
Description: Theological & biblical studies; *Member of:* Evangelical Fellowship of Canada; Affiliation(s): Anglican Church of Canada

Bahá'í Faith

Association for Bahá'í Studies (ABS) / Association d'études Bahá'ís
34 Copernicus St., Ottawa ON K1N 7K4
Tel: 613-233-1903; *Fax:* 613-233-3644
www.bahai-studies.ca
Social Media:
www.facebook.com/331784303733
Previous Name: Canadian Association for Studies in the Bahá'í Faith
Overview: A medium-sized international charitable organization founded in 1975
Finances: *Annual Operating Budget:* $100,000-$250,000; *Funding Sources:* Grants; Conference & Literature revenue; Membership fees
Staff: 2 staff member(s)
Membership: 2,000; *Fees:* $50 adult; $60 couple; $25 student/senior; $60 institution; $999 individual life
Activities: *Library:* Yes (Open to Public) by appointment
Description: To foster Bahá'í scholarship & to demonstrate the value of this scholarly approach; to promote courses of study on the Bahá'í faith; to foster relationships with various leaders of thought & persons of capacity; to publish scholarly materials examining the Bahá'í faith, especially on its application to the concerns & needs of humanity; to organize annual meetings & develop chapters of the Association around the world

Bahá'í Community of Ottawa
211 McArthur Ave., Ottawa ON K1L 6P6
Tel: 613-742-8250
www.bahai-ottawa.org
Social Media:
twitter.com/OttawaBahais
Overview: A small local organization
Chief Officer(s):
Corinne Box, Director, Government Relations, 613-233-3712
ogr@bcc-cbc.org
Membership: 9 sectors
Description: To support the development of the Bahá'í Faith Community in Ottawa, Ontario.

The Bahá'í Community of Canada / La communauté bahá'íe du Canada
Bahá'í National Centre, 7200 Leslie St., Thornhill ON L3T 6L8
Tel: 905-889-8168; *Fax:* 905-889-8184
secretariat@cdnbnc.org
ca.bahai.org
Social Media: www.flickr.com/photos/103796735@N05
www.facebook.com/Bahai.Community.of.Canada
Overview: A large national charitable organization founded in 1844
Chief Officer(s):
Karen McKye, Secretary-General
Gerald Filson, Director, External Affairs
externalaffairs@cdnbnc.org
Corinne Box, Director, Government Relations, 613-233-3712
ogr@bcc-cbc.org
Finances: *Annual Operating Budget:* Greater than $5 Million; *Funding Sources:* Contributions from members
Staff: 30 staff member(s)
Membership: 30,000+
Activities: Study circles; Devotional gatherings; Junior youth spiritual empowerment program; Children's classes; *Awareness Events:* Unity in Diversity Week, Nov; *Speaker Service:* Yes *Library:* Yes (Open to Public) by appointment
Description: To teach the oneness of humanity, the common divine source of all the great religions, equality of the sexes & harmony of science & religion; headquarters in Haifa, Israel; 5-6 million adherents in 214 countries & territories; Canada's 30,000 Bahá'ís are located in some 1,200 localities, some of which elect local governing councils called Spiritual Assemblies; National Spiritual Assembly of Bahá'ís of Canada incorporated by Act of Parliament in 1949; *Member of:* Bahá'í International Community; Affiliation(s): Bahá'í International Community

Baptists

Association d'églises baptistes évangéliques au québec
9780, rue Sherbrooke est, Montréal QC H1L 6N6
Tél: 514-337-2555; *Téléc:* 514-337-8892
www.aebeq.qc.ca
Aperçu: *Dimension:* moyenne; *Envergure: nationale; fondée en 1971*
Membre(s) du bureau directeur:
Michel M. Habbib, Secrétaire général
Gilles Lapierre, Directeur général
Membre: 65 000
Activités: Camps de jeunes; retraites; congrès; cohortes; *Stagiaires:* Oui; *Service de conférenciers:* Oui
Description: Aider les églises à communiquer l'évangile de Jésus-Christ à tous les Québécois; former des disciples et des leaders; devenir plus solides et se reproduire; *Membre de:* Fellowship of Evangelical Baptist Churches in Canada; Affiliation(s): Camp des Bouleaux, Camp Patmos, Aujourd'hui l'Espoir, Organisme Renaissance Autochtone

Association of Regular Baptist Churches (Canada) (ARBC)
130 Gerrard St. East, Toronto ON M5A 3T4
Tel: 416-925-3261; *Fax:* 416-925-8305
Overview: A small national organization founded in 1957
Membership: 10 churches, 1500 members

Canadian Baptist Ministries
7185 Millcreek Dr., Mississauga ON L5N 5R4
Tel: 905-821-3533; *Fax:* 905-826-3441
communications@cbmin.org
www.cbmin.org
Social Media:
www.facebook.com/cbmin.org
Merged from: Canadian Baptist International Ministries; Canadian Baptist Federation
Overview: A large national organization founded in 1995
Chief Officer(s):
Sam Chaise, Executive Director
Finances: *Annual Operating Budget:* Greater than $5 Million; *Funding Sources:* Member churches; individuals; CIDA
Staff: 112 staff member(s); 540 volunteer(s)
Membership: 250,000 + 1,000 churches; *Member Profile:* Members of churches affiliated with the four conventions/unions; *Committees:* Public Affairs
Activities: Partners in Mission - 75 missionaries serving in Asia, Africa, Latin America, Europe & Canada; The Sharing Way - relief & development ministries in 13 countries, working in areas of agricultural & community development, community health, etc.; Canadian Baptist Volunteers - short-term ministry opportunities; Canada Caucus - consensus building among the churches in Canada; *Library:* Daniel Global Mission Resource Room
Description: To unite, encourage & enable Canadian Baptist Churches in their national & international endeavor to fulfill the commission of our Lord Jesus Christ, in the power of the Holy Spirit, proclaiming the gospel & sharing the love of God to all people; *Member of:* Canadian Council of Christian Charities; Affiliation(s): Canadian Baptists of Western Canada; Canadian Baptists of Ontario & Quebec; Baptist World Alliance; Convention of Atlantic Baptist Churches; Union d'Églises Baptistes Francophones au Canada; Atlantic Baptist Women; Canadian Baptist Women of Ontario & Quebec

Canadian Baptists of Ontario & Quebec (CBOQ)
#100, 304 The East Mall, Toronto ON M9B 6E2
Tel: 416-622-8600; *Fax:* 416-622-2308
cboq@baptist.ca
baptist.ca
Social Media: vimeo.com/cboq
twitter.com/cboq
Previous Name: Baptist Convention of Ontario & Québec
Overview: A large local organization founded in 1889
Chief Officer(s):
Michel Belzile, President
president@baptist.ca
Tim McCoy, Executive Minister
tmccoy@baptist.ca
Finances: *Annual Operating Budget:* $3 Million-$5 Million; *Funding Sources:* Member churches
Staff: 15 staff member(s)
Membership: 375
Activities: *Internships:* Yes *Library:* Yes (Open to Public)
Description: A family of churches building Christ's kingdom; supports & enables member churches to be healthy, mission congregations as they serve God together; *Member of:* Canadian Baptist Ministries; Affiliation(s): Baptist Women of Ontario & Quebec; McMaster Divinity College; Canadian Council of Churches; Evangelical Fellowship of Canada; Canadian Council of Christian Charities; Convention of Atlantic Baptist Churches; Canadian Baptists of Western Canada; French Union of Baptist Churches

Canadian Baptists of Western Canada (CBWC)
#201, 221 10th Ave. SE, Calgary AB T2G 0V9
Tel: 403-228-9559; *Fax:* 403-228-9048
Toll-Free: 800-820-2479
office@cbwc.ca
www.cbwc.ca
Social Media: www.youtube.com/user/CanadianBaptists
www.facebook.com/115787141838284
twitter.com/@TheCBWC
Previous Name: The Baptist Union of Western Canada
Overview: A medium-sized local charitable organization founded in 1908
Chief Officer(s):
Bob Webber, Director, Ministry, 403-228-9559 311
bwebber@cbwc.ca
Finances: *Funding Sources:* Church congregations
Staff: 30 staff member(s)
Membership: 183 congregations representing 100,000 worshippers; *Committees:* Western Canada Missions; Evangelism; Finance; Youth
Activities: *Internships:* Yes
Description: The Canadian Baptists of Western Canada is a Christ-centred community of churches.; Affiliation(s): Baptist World Alliance; Canadian Baptist Ministries; North American Baptist Fellowship; Evangelical Fellowship of Canada; Canadian Council Of Churches

Canadian Convention of Southern Baptists (CCSB) / Convention canadienne des baptistes du Sud
100 Convention Way, Cochrane AB T4C 2G2
Fax: 403-932-4937
Toll-Free: 888-442-2272
office@ccsb.ca
www.ccsb.ca
Overview: A medium-sized national charitable organization founded in 1985
Chief Officer(s):
Gérald J. Taillon, Executive Director
gtaillon@cnbc.ca
Dwight Huffman, President
Finances: *Funding Sources:* Member churches
Staff: 8 staff member(s); 4 volunteer(s)
Membership: 10,189
Activities: *Library:* Resource Centre (Open to Public)
Description: To help churches build the Kingdom of God; a church for every person across Canada & around the world; Affiliation(s): Southern Baptist Convention

Convention of Atlantic Baptist Churches (CABC) / Convention des Églises Baptistes de l'Atlantique
1655 Manawagonish Rd., Saint John NB E2M 3Y2
Tel: 506-635-1922; *Fax:* 506-635-0366
cabc@baptist-atlantic.ca
www.baptist-atlantic.ca
Social Media: plus.google.com/101053298635931681383
linkedin.com/company/2498898
www.facebook.com/atlanticbaptist
twitter.com/atlanticbaptist
Also Known As: Atlantic Baptist Convention
Previous Name: United Baptist Convention of the Maritime Provinces
Overview: A medium-sized local charitable organization founded in 1905
Chief Officer(s):
Peter Reid, Executive Minister
peter.reid@baptist-atlantic.ca
Kevin Vincent, Associate Executive Minister, New Congregations
kevin.vincent@baptist-atlantic.ca
Finances: *Annual Operating Budget:* $1.5 Million-$3 Million
Staff: 18 staff member(s)
Activities: Providing seminars, conferences, stewardship education, & retreats; *Speaker Service:* Yes
Description: To resource pastors, churches, & people; To facilitate a shared mission on behalf of churches; To establish & maintain professional standards & ethics for clergy

Elgin Baptist Association
ON
elginbaptist@gmail.com
elginbaptist.wordpress.com
Overview: A small local organization founded in 1874
Chief Officer(s):
Margaret Bell, Moderator

Membership: 8 churches; *Member Profile:* Baptist churches in Elgin County
Description: To bring together Baptist churches & to promote the interests of the members; *Member of:* Canadian Baptists of Ontario & Quebec; Canadian Baptist Ministries; Baptist World Alliance

Middlesex-Lambton-Huron Association of Baptist Churches
ON
www.mlha.ca
Overview: A small local organization
Chief Officer(s):
Dave Stephens, Moderator
Membership: 19 churches; *Member Profile:* Baptist churches in Southwestern Ontario
Activities: Camp site; Golf tournament; Annual Picnic
Member of: Canadian Baptists of Ontario & Quebec

Niagara/Hamilton Association of Baptist Churches
ON
nhachurches@gmail.com
baptist.ca
Social Media:
www.facebook.com/niagarahamiltionassoc
Overview: A small local organization
Chief Officer(s):
Peter Dempsey, Moderator
podempsey@yahoo.ca
Member Profile: Baptist churches in the Niagara Falls & Hamilton area
Member of: Canadian Baptists of Ontario & Quebec

Ottawa Baptist Association (OBA)
249 Bronson Ave., Ottawa ON K1R 6H6
Tel: 613-235-7617
www.ottawabaptist.org
Overview: A small local organization founded in 1836
Chief Officer(s):
Hugh Willet, Executive Secretary
hwillett@sympatico.ca
Membership: 20 churches; *Member Profile:* Baptist churches in Ottawa
Member of: Canadian Baptists of Ontario & Quebec; Affiliation(s): Canadian Baptist Ministries; Baptist World Alliance

Oxford-Brant Association of Baptist Churches
ON
baptist.ca
Overview: A small local organization founded in 1896
Chief Officer(s):
David Partridge, Moderator
Membership: 17 churches; *Member Profile:* Baptist churches in Oxford & Brant counties; *Committees:* Area ministry; Association Educational
Member of: Canadian Baptists of Ontario & Quebec

Quebec Association of Baptist Churches
6215 Blvd Côte St. Luc Rd., Montréal QC H3X 2H3
Tel: 514-483-4302
associationbaptistcq@gmail.com
www.quebecbaptist.org
Also Known As: Eastern Association
Overview: A small provincial organization founded in 1887
Chief Officer(s):
Brian Berry, Moderator
bberry@videotron.ca
Membership: 19 churches; *Member Profile:* Baptist churches in Quebec
Description: To help churches carry out their services & goals; *Member of:* Canadian Baptists of Ontario & Quebec

Toronto Baptist Ministries
1585 Yonge St., Toronto ON M4T 1Z9
Tel: 416-425-9472; *Fax:* 416-922-1807
office@torontobaptistministries.org
www.torontobaptistministries.org
Overview: A small local organization
Chief Officer(s):
Jim Parker, Moderator
bethanychurch@sympatico.ca
Membership: 85 churches; *Member Profile:* Baptist churches in the Greater Toronto Area
Description: To support their member churches; *Member of:* Canadian Baptists of Ontario & Quebec

Trent Valley Association of Baptist Churches
ON
trentvalleybaptists@gmail.com
tvabaptist.wordpress.com
Overview: A small local organization
Chief Officer(s):
Clarke Dixon, Moderator, 905-372-5058
clarkedixon@me.com
Member Profile: Baptist churches in the Trent Valley Area
Member of: Canadian Baptists of Ontario & Quebec

Brethren

Brethren in Christ (BIC)
2700 Bristol Circle, Oakville ON L6H 6EH
Tel: 905-339-2335; *Fax:* 905-337-2120
office@canadianbic.ca
www.canadianbic.ca
Social Media: vimeo.com/user10271482
www.facebook.com/BICCanada
twitter.com/BICCanada
Overview: A medium-sized international charitable organization founded in 1788
Chief Officer(s):
Doug Sider, Executive Director
doug.sider@canadianbic.ca
Finances: *Annual Operating Budget:* $500,000-$1.5 Million; *Funding Sources:* Congregational giving
Staff: 8 staff member(s)
Membership: 3,450 + 43 congregations in Canada; *Member Profile:* North American membership is about 20,000 with significant churches in other countries including India, Japan, Zambia, Zimbabwe, Nicaragua, Cuba, Venezuela, Columbia, South Africa
Activities: *Speaker Service:* Yes; *Rents Mailing List:* Yes
Member of: Evangelical Fellowship of Canada; Affiliation(s): Mennonite Central Committee; Canadian Holiness Federation

Christian Brethren Churches of Québec (CBCQ) / Églises de frères chrétiens du Québec (EFCQ)
PO Box 1054, #101, 1520, rue King ouest, Sherbrooke QC J1H 5L3
Tel: 819-820-1693
Also Known As: Plymouth Brethren
Overview: A medium-sized provincial charitable organization founded in 1942
Chief Officer(s):
Pierre Munger, General Director
Finances: *Annual Operating Budget:* Less than $50,000; *Funding Sources:* Dues from local churches
Staff: 2 volunteer(s)
Description: To handle affairs for local affiliated churches regarding government & affairs of civil status

The United Brethren Church in Canada
501 Whitelaw Rd., Guelph ON N1K 1E7
Tel: 519-836-0180; *Fax:* 519-821-8385
www.ubcanada.org
Previous Name: Ontario Conference, Church of the United Brethren in Christ
Overview: A small national charitable organization founded in 1856
Chief Officer(s):
Brian K. Magnus, Bishop
b_magnus@ubcanada.org
Finances: *Annual Operating Budget:* $50,000-$100,000; *Funding Sources:* Donations
Staff: 1 staff member(s)
Membership: 12 churches; *Fees:* Schedule available; *Member Profile:* Personal knowledge of God through faith in Christ; desire to live a life conforming to biblical principles
Activities: *Library:* At Emmanuel Bible College Library
Description: To organize groups of people into congregations to worship God; to make effective application of principles of righteousness in the Society; *Member of:* Church of the United Brethren in Christ, International; Affiliation(s): Evangelical Fellowship of Canada

Buddhism

Buddhist Association of Canada - Cham Shan Temple
7254 Bayview Ave., Toronto ON L3T 2R6
Tel: 905-886-1522
chamshantemple.askus@gmail.com
www.chamshantemple.org
Social Media:
www.facebook.com/temple.chamshan
twitter.com/temple_chamshan
Overview: A small national organization founded in 1973
Chief Officer(s):
Dayi Shi, President & Abbot
Activities: Seminars, sutra reading groups, meditation retreats; *Library:* Yes
Description: In addition to the main worship hall & 2 congregation halls, the Buddhist temple also includes a Dharma seminary for the Chinese community to learn Buddhism.

Jodo Shinshu Buddhist Temples of Canada
11786 Fentiman Pl., Richmond BC V7E 6M6
Tel: 604-272-3330; *Fax:* 604-272-6865
jsbtcheadquarters@gmail.com
www.bcc.ca
Social Media: www.youtube.com/user/livingdharmacentre
www.facebook.com/654327614577625
Previous Name: Buddhist Churches of Canada
Overview: A medium-sized national charitable organization founded in 1933
Chief Officer(s):
Tatsuya Aoki, Bishop
Leslie Kawamura, Director, Living Dharma Centre
Finances: *Annual Operating Budget:* $100,000-$250,000
Staff: 9 staff member(s)
Membership: 2,500; *Fees:* $45
Activities: *Speaker Service:* Yes *Library:* Yes by appointment
Description: Propagation of Buddhism; Affiliation(s): Jodo Shinshu Hongwanji, Kyoto

The Palyul Foundation of Canada
c/o Orgyan Osal Cho Dzong Buddhist Temple & Retreat Centre, 1755 Lingham Lake Rd., Madoc ON K0K 2K0
www.palyulcanada.org
Social Media:
www.facebook.com/Palyul.Canada
twitter.com/OrgyanDzong
Overview: A small local charitable organization founded in 1981
Activities: Classes on Buddhism, meditation, ritual practices; retreats; empowerments; celebration of Buddhist holy days & festivals
Description: Dedicated to the preservation & advancement of the teachings of the Nyingma lineage of Vajrayana Buddhism

Catholicism

Alberta Catholic School Trustees Association
#205, 9940 - 106 St., Edmonton AB T5K 2N2
Tel: 780-484-6209; *Fax:* 780-484-6248
admin@acsta.ab.ca
www.acsta.ab.ca
Social Media:
twitter.com/acstanews
Overview: A medium-sized provincial organization
Chief Officer(s):
Dean Sarnecki, Executive Director
Member of: Canadian Catholic School Trustees Association

Assemblée des évêques catholiques du Québec (AEQ) / Assembly of Québec Catholic Bishops
3331, rue Sherbrooke est, Montréal QC H1W 1C5
Tél: 514-274-4323; *Téléc:* 514-274-4383
aeq@eveques.qc.ca
www.eveques.qc.ca
Nom précédent: Assemblée des Évêques du Québec
Aperçu: *Dimension:* moyenne; *Envergure: provinciale; Organisme sans but lucratif; fondée en 1871*
Membre(s) du bureau directeur:
Bertrand Ouellet, Secrétaire général
Finances: *Budget de fonctionnement annuel:* $500,000-$1.5 Million
Personnel: 8 membre(s) du personnel
Membre: 37; *Critères d'admissibilite:* Évêque diocésain; évêque auxiliaire; *Comités:* Éducation; Laicat; Ministères; Missions; Affaires sociales; Théologie; Communications; Prospective; Législation; Administration; Relations interculturelles; Pastorale des Autochtones
Description: Être un lieu d'échange et de concertation où ses membres s'entraident dans la recherche d'actions à entreprendre pour rendre l'Église au Québec toujours plus vivante et engagée dans la société et la culture contemporaines; Affiliation(s): Conférence des évêques catholiques du Canada

Assembly of Catholic Bishops of Ontario / Assemblée des évêques catholiques de l'Ontario
#810, 90 Eglinton Ave. East, Toronto ON M4P 2Y3
Tel: 416-923-1423; *Fax:* 416-923-1509
acbo@acbo.on.ca
www.acbo.on.ca
Overview: A small provincial organization
Chief Officer(s):
Thomas Collins, President, 416-934-0606, Fax: 416-934-3452
Roger Lawler, General Secretary
rlawler@acbo.on.ca
Description: To provide information and instruction about the principles & moral positions of the Church in all aspects of life

Association des intervenantes et des intervenants en soins spirituels du Québec (AIISSQ)
6910, rue St-Denis, Montréal QC H2S 2S0
Tél: 514-259-9229; *Téléc:* 514-259-3741
secretariat@aiissq.org
www.aiissq.org
Nom précédent: Association québécoise de la pastorale de la santé
Aperçu: *Dimension:* petite; *Envergure:* provinciale; *Organisme sans but lucratif; fondée en 2005*
Membre(s) du bureau directeur:
Lorraine Rooke, Présidente
presidence@aiissq.org
Fernand Patry, Vice-président
vice-presidence@aiissq.org
Finances: *Budget de fonctionnement annuel:* $50,000-$100,000
Personnel: 1 membre(s) du personnel
Membre: 200; *Montant de la cotisation:* 275$; 70$ par jour; *Critères d'admissibilite:* Animateur(trice) de pastorale dans un établissement de santé; *Comités:* Pastorale pratique; pastorale en santé mentale
Activités: Congrès annuel; colloques; sessions de formation; *Stagiaires:* Oui; *Listes de destinataires:* Oui
Description: Formation professionnelle des membres et promotion de leurs intérêts spirituels et professionnels; représentation des membres auprès d'instances civiles et religieuses reconnues; *Membre de:* Association canadienne des périodiques catholiques; Affiliation(s): Association canadienne pour la pratique et l'éducation pastorale; Association catholique canadienne de la santé; Carrefour Humanisation - Santé

Association des parents catholiques du Québec (APCQ)
5425 - 5e av, Montréal QC H1Y 2S8
Tél: 514-276-8068; *Téléc:* 514-948-2595
apcq406@bellnet.ca
www.apcqc.net
Aperçu: *Dimension:* grande; *Envergure:* provinciale; *Organisme sans but lucratif; fondée en 1966*
Membre(s) du bureau directeur:
Diane Joyal, Présidente
Finances: *Budget de fonctionnement annuel:* $50,000-$100,000
Personnel: 25 bénévole(s)
Membre: 4 000; *Montant de la cotisation:* 12$; *Critères d'admissibilite:* Familles; *Comités:* Éducation de la foi; comité provincial d'enseignement privé; carrefour famille-Québec
Activités: Secrétariat permanent; Périodique; Colloques; Conférences; Cours; Congrès parents-jeunes; Pétitions; Rédactions de mémoires; *Service de conférenciers:* Oui
Description: Regroupe des parents catholiques pour promouvoir et défendre leurs droits et leurs intérêts selon les valeurs catholiques en matière d'éducation, de famille, et de culture par l'information et la représentation de ses membres auprès de la population et des autorités civiles et religieuses; *Membre de:* Regroupement Inter-Organismes pour une politique familiale au Québec; Affiliation(s): Organisation internationale de l'enseignement catholique (OIEC)

Augustines de la Miséricorde de Jésus
2655 rue Guillaume - Le Pelletier, Québec QC G1C 3X7
Tél: 418-628-8860
secretaire@augustines.org
www.augustines.org
Aperçu: *Dimension:* petite; *Envergure:* locale; *fondée en 1957*
Description: Les trois dimensions de la vie spirituelle des Augustines d'hier et de demain sont: communion fraternelle; louange et intercession; et miséricorde

Benedictine Sisters of Manitoba (OSB)
225 Masters Ave., Winnipeg MB R4A 2A1
Tel: 204-338-4601; *Fax:* 204-339-8775
stbens@mts.net
www.stbens.ca
Also Known As: Sisters of the Order of St. Benedict
Overview: A small provincial charitable organization founded in 1912
Chief Officer(s):
Virginia Evard, Prioress
Finances: *Funding Sources:* Donations
Staff: 35 staff member(s); 30 volunteer(s)
Membership: 33
Activities: Programs in spirituality, personal growth & a variety of retreats; *Library:* St. Benedict's Monastery Library by appointment
Description: To witness Jesus Christ, through community life & prayer, contemplative living, hospitality, service to the people of God & stewardship of all God's gifts; *Member of:* Federation of St. Gertrude

The Brothers of the Good Shepherd / Les Frères du Bon-Pasteur
Development Office, PO Box 1003, 10 Delaware Ave., Hamilton ON L8N 3R1
Tel: 905-528-9109; *Fax:* 905-528-6967
info@goodshepherdcentres.ca
www.goodshepherdcentres.ca
Social Media: www.youtube.com/channel/UCDb1lcEb-uKK3n_9kuBVbPg
www.facebook.com/goodshepherdhamilton
twitter.com/goodshepherdham
Also Known As: Good Shepherd
Previous Name: Little Brothers of the Good Shepherd
Overview: A small local charitable organization founded in 1951
Chief Officer(s):
Richard MacPhee, Executive Director
Finances: *Annual Operating Budget:* $500,000-$1.5 Million
Activities: Housing for battered women & children; residence for homeless youth; men's hostel; food bank & food line; speakers on topics dealing with violence & abuse; *Speaker Service:* Yes

Calgary Catholic Immigration Society (CCIS)
1111 - 11 Ave. SW, 5th Fl., Calgary AB T2R 0G5
Tel: 403-262-2006; *Fax:* 403-262-2033
contact@ccis-calgary.ab.ca
www.ccisab.ca
Social Media: www.youtube.com/user/CCISTV
www.facebook.com/298577383506539
twitter.com/ccis2
Overview: A small international organization
Chief Officer(s):
Fariborz Birjandian, Executive Director
Activities: Pre-employment training & counseling; community outreach for families & seniors; temporary accommodation facility; Integrated Resettlement Program
Description: CCIS is a non-profit organization which provides settlement & integration services to immigrants & refugees in Southern Alberta.

Canadian Catholic Campus Ministry (CCCM)
#307, 47 Queen's Park Cres. East, Toronto ON M5S 2C3
Tel: 416-506-0183; *Fax:* 416-978-7827
www.cccm.ca
Social Media: www.facebook.com/252224265072
Also Known As: Canadian Catholic Students Association
Overview: A small national charitable organization
Chief Officer(s):
Kidd Sue, Chair & Atlantic Representative
sukidd@upei.ca
Martha Fauteux, Vice-Chair & Central Representative
mfauteux@uwaterloo.ca
Nancy Quan, Western Representative
Nancy.quan@stmu.ab.ca
Chrisandra Skipper, Central Representative
cskipper@assumptionu.ca
Robert Corbeil, National Coordinator, 879-743-7197, Fax: 855-488-0807
nc@cccm.ca
Finances: *Funding Sources:* Donations
Member Profile: Persons who support the purpose of the association
Activities: Supporting prayerful, pastoral action; *Awareness Events:* Catholic Students' Week, March
Description: To unite Catholic students on Canadian post-secondary campuses; To nurture Christian student leadership; Affiliation(s): International Movement of Catholic Students - Canada

Canadian Catholic Historical Association - English Section (CCHA) / Société canadienne d'histoire de l'église catholique - Section anglaise
c/o St. Michael's College, 81 St. Mary St., Toronto ON M5S 1J4
Tel: 905-893-9754; *Fax:* 416-934-3444
www.cchahistory.ca
Social Media: twitter.com/cchahistory
Overview: A medium-sized national organization founded in 1933
Chief Officer(s):
G. Edward MacDonald, President-General
gemacdonald@upei.ca
Edward Jackman, Secretary-General
revedjackman@rogers.com
Finances: *Annual Operating Budget:* Less than $50,000; *Funding Sources:* Membership fees; donations
Staff: 11 volunteer(s)
Membership: 100-499; *Fees:* $50 Canadian; US$50 American; $30 student; $60 French-English
Activities: Annual scholarly conference at the Canadian Congress
Description: The Association promotes interest & research in the history of the Canadian Catholic Church, its dioceses, religious communities, institutions, parishes, buildings, sites, & personalities. It is divided into English & French sections.

Canadian Catholic School Trustees' Association (CCSTA) / Association canadienne des commissaires d'écoles catholique
Catholic Education Centre, 570 West Hunt Club Rd., Nepean ON K2G 3R4
Tel: 613-224-4455; *Fax:* 613-224-3187
ccsta@ocsb.ca
www.ccsta.ca
Overview: A medium-sized national organization founded in 1960
Chief Officer(s):
Mike St. Amand, President
mike@ashlycw.com
Marino Gazzola, Vice-President
marino.gazzola@sympatico.ca
Julian Hanlon, Executive Director
julian.hanlon@ocsb.ca
Finances: *Funding Sources:* Sponsorships
Membership: 8 associations representing 80 Catholic school boards; *Member Profile:* Provincial & territorial Catholic school trustees' associations in Canada
Activities: Promoting Catholic education; Providing professional development opportunities for trustees; Collaborating with the Canadian Conference of Catholic Bishops; Liaising with Canadian government agencies & other Catholic education organizations; *Awareness Events:* Catholic Education Week
Description: To protect the right to Catholic education in Canada; To promote excellence in Catholic education across Canada; *Member of:* National Catholic Education Association (US)

Canadian Conference of Catholic Bishops (CCCB) / Conférence des évêques catholiques du Canada (CECC)
2500 Don Reid Dr., Ottawa ON K1H 2J2
Tel: 613-241-9461; *Fax:* 613-241-8117
cecc@cccb.ca
www.cccb.ca
Social Media: www.youtube.com/user/cccbadmin
www.facebook.com/123711474340639
twitter.com/CCCB_CECC
Previous Name: Canadian Catholic Conference
Overview: A small national charitable organization founded in 1943
Chief Officer(s):
Patrick Powers, P.H., General Secretary, 613-241-9461 209
gensec@cccb.ca
Member Profile: Diocesan bishops in Canada; Coadjutor Bishops; Auxiliary Bishops; Titular Bishops of any rite within the Catholic Church
Activities: Providing aid to developing countries & Christian education; Offering a forum for bishops to share experiences & insights
Description: To exercise pastoral functions for Catholics in Canada

Canadian Latvian Catholic Association
34 Edenvale Cres., Toronto ON M9A 4A4
Tel: 416-244-4576; *Fax:* 416-244-1513
Overview: A medium-sized national organization founded in 1949
Finances: *Annual Operating Budget:* Less than $50,000
Staff: 10 volunteer(s)
Membership: 3,000 individual; *Fees:* $10 individual

Carizon Family & Community Services
400 Queen St. South, Kitchener ON N2G 1W7
Tel: 519-743-6333; *Fax:* 519-743-3496
info@carizon.ca
www.carizon.ca
Social Media: linkedin.com/company/carizon-family-and-community-services
www.facebook.com/carizonupdates
twitter.com/@carizon
Previous Name: kidsLINK; Mosaic Counselling & Family Services; Catholic Family Counselling Centre; Catholic Social Services; Catholic Welfare Bureau
Overview: A small local charitable organization founded in 1952
Chief Officer(s):
Stephen Swatridge, CEO
Lesley Barraball, Director, Children's Mental Health Services
Jennifer Berry, Director, Communications
Ted Conlin, Director, Business
Jean Davies, Director, Pathways to Education
Debbie Engel, Director, Community Services
Dale Gellatly, Director, Community Engagement

Finances: *Annual Operating Budget:* $3 Million-$5 Million; *Funding Sources:* United Way; Government of Canada; Province of Ontario; Regional Municipality of Waterloo; Foundations, such as Pathways to Education Canada
Activities: Offering individual, group, & credit counselling; Providing workplace & employee assistance programs; Offering community outreach services
Description: To provide full-service professional counselling services in Kitchener & the surrounding region; *Member of:* Canadian Association of Credit Counselling Services; Ontario Association of Credit Counselling Services; United Way of Kitchener-Waterloo & Area; Family Service Ontario

Carrefour des mouvements d'action catholique
435, rue du Roi, Québec QC G1K 2X1
Tél: 418-525-6187; *Téléc:* 418-525-6081
Nom précédent: Comité diosésain d'action catholique
Aperçu: *Dimension:* petite; *Envergure:* locale
Membre(s) du bureau directeur:
Bernadette Dubuc, Contact
bernadette@mmtc-infor.com
Description: Groupe de coordination des associations d'action catholique dans le diocèse de Québec

Catholic Biblical Association of Canada (CBAC)
5650 Mavis Rd., Mississauga ON L5V 2N6
Tel: 905-568-4393
catholicbiblicalcanada@gmail.com
www.catholicbiblical.com
Previous Name: Canadian Catholic Biblical Association
Overview: A medium-sized national charitable organization founded in 1974
Chief Officer(s):
Jocelyn Monette, Executive Director
Finances: *Annual Operating Budget:* $100,000-$250,000
Fees: $30
Activities: Workshops; Bible in My Life program; children's summer program; pilgrimages; *Rents Mailing List:* Yes *Library:* Resource Centre (Open to Public)
Description: To foster knowledge & love of the Word of God as found in the Scriptures, through provision of a variety of sources, primarily to the Catholic community.; Affiliation(s): Archdiocese of Toronto; World Catholic Biblical Federation

Catholic Biblical Federation (CBF) / Fédération biblique catholique (FBC)
St. Ottilien 86941 Germany
gensec@c-b-f.org
www.c-b-f.org
Social Media: plus.google.com/u/0/109432940173395804882
www.facebook.com/Cathbibfed
twitter.com/@cbf_gensec
Overview: A small international charitable organization founded in 1969
Chief Officer(s):
Jan J. Stefanów, svd, General Secretary
Membership: 300+ in 130 countries
Activities: Workshops; Plenary Assembly
Affiliation(s): Catholic Biblical Association of Canada

Catholic Centre for Immigrants - Ottawa + CIC Foundation / Centre Catholique pour Immigrants - Ottawa + Fondation du CCI
219 Argyle Ave., Ottawa ON K2P 2H4
Tel: 613-232-9634; *Fax:* 613-232-3660
cic@cic.ca
cciottawa.ca
Social Media:
www.facebook.com/TheCommunityCup
Also Known As: CCI Ottawa
Previous Name: Catholic Immigration Centre + CIC Foundation
Overview: A medium-sized national organization founded in 1984
Chief Officer(s):
Carl Nicolson, Executive Director, 613-232-9634 335
carl@cic.ca
Fees: $10; *Member Profile:* All Canadian residents

Catholic Charismatic Renewal Council (CCRC)
2671 Islington Ave. N., Toronto ON M9V 2X6
Tel: 416-466-0776; *Fax:* 905-454-0876
ccrctoronto@bellnet.ca
www.ccrctor.com
Also Known As: Catholic Charismatic Renewal
Overview: A small local organization
Chief Officer(s):
Hilda Martin, Chair
Activities: Providing the Holy Eucharist with healing services, evangelization, Life in The Spirit seminars, devotional workshops, conferences & special rallies;Serving the local church & parish when called upon by bishops & priests; Providing faith instruction; Offering prayer groups

Description: To offer service that facilitates, educates, & promotes, with activities & resources, the growth & development of the Catholic Charismatic Renewal, throughout the Catholic Communities of Metropolitan Toronto, the Regional Municipalities of York, Peel, a portion of Durham, the County of Simcoe, a portion of the County of Dufferin, & the Town of Orangeville; To promote Baptism of the Holy Spirit; To bring people of the church closer together by exercising the gifts of TheHoly Spirit; To be committed to daily prayer & scripture reading, the love & us of the sacraments, & attendance at mass; Affiliation(s): Archdiocese of Toronto

Catholic Charities of The Archdiocese of Toronto
#400, 1155 Yonge St., Toronto ON M4T 1W2
Tel: 416-934-3401; *Fax:* 416-934-3402
info@catholiccharitiestor.org
www.catholiccharitiestor.org
Social Media:
twitter.com/charitiescares
Previous Name: Council of Catholic Charities
Overview: A medium-sized local licensing charitable organization founded in 1913
Chief Officer(s):
Thomas Cardinal Collins, Chair
Kevin McGivney, President
Michael Fullan, Executive Director
Finances: *Annual Operating Budget:* $250,000-$500,000
Staff: 1 staff member(s); 10 volunteer(s)
Activities: *Speaker Service:* Yes
Description: Catholic Charities of the Archdiocese of Toronto is dedicated to ensuring the provision of health & social sciences & to provide leadership & advocacy on behalf of the member agencies & those in need. The people served live & work throughout the Greater Toronto Area, as well as in Simcoe, Durham, Peel, & York.; Affiliation(s): Catholic Family Services of Toronto & 26 member agencies

Catholic Children's Aid Society of Hamilton (CCAS)
735 King St. East, Hamilton ON L8M 1A1
Tel: 905-525-2012; *Fax:* 905-525-5606
www.hamiltonccas.on.ca
Social Media:
www.youtube.com/channel/UCfl8rgJy4r8oMcepjfErppw/feed
www.facebook.com/hamiltonccas
twitter.com/HamiltonCCAS
Overview: A small local charitable organization founded in 1954
Chief Officer(s):
Ersilia DiNardo, Executive Director
Finances: *Annual Operating Budget:* Greater than $5 Million; *Funding Sources:* Ontario Trillium Foundation; Donations
Staff: 191 volunteer(s)
Membership: 100-499
Activities: Providing foster care & adoption services, Investigating possible instances of child abuse & neglect; *Awareness Events:* Serendipity Auction, Nov; *Internships:* Yes; *Speaker Service:* Yes
Description: To provide child welfare & family services to the Hamilton community; To ensure that services are guided by Catholic values; *Member of:* Ontario Association of Children's Aid Societies; Affiliation(s): Council of Catholic Service Organziations

Catholic Children's Aid Society of Toronto (CCAS)
26 Maitland St., Toronto ON M4Y 1C6
Tel: 416-395-1500; *Fax:* 416-395-1581
communications@torontoccas.org
www.ccas.toronto.on.ca
Previous Name: Catholic Children's Aid Society of Metropolitan Toronto
Overview: A medium-sized local charitable organization founded in 1894
Chief Officer(s):
Janice Robinson, Executive Director
Finances: *Funding Sources:* Provincial government; Private donations
Activities: Offering resources for individuals to report child abuse & neglect; Providing counselling services for children, adults, families, & immigrants; *Awareness Events:* Child Abuse Prevention Campaign
Description: To provide social services that protect children, strengthen family life & are reflective of Catholic values; *Member of:* Catholic Charities of the Archdiocese of Toronto; Affiliation(s): Ministry of Children and Youth Services

Catholic Civil Rights League (CCRL)
2305 Bloor Street West, Toronto ON M6S 1P1
Tel: 416-466-8244; *Fax:* 416-466-0091
Toll-Free: 844-722-2275
ccrl@ccrl.ca
www.ccrl.ca
Social Media: www.youtube.com/user/CatholicCivilRights

Overview: A medium-sized national organization founded in 1985
Chief Officer(s):
Christian D. Elia, Executive Director
Finances: *Funding Sources:* Donations
Fees: $25 individuals; $15 students & seniors; $30 families; *Member Profile:* Catholics over the age of eighteen
Activities: Advocating with government & media
Description: To be witness for church teaching in public life; To combat anti-Catholic defamation in the media; To participate in debates on public policy; Affiliation(s): Archdiocese of Toronto

Catholic Cross Cultural Services (CCS)
#401, 55 Town Centre Ct., Toronto ON M1P 4X4
Tel: 416-757-7010; *Fax:* 416-757-7399
www.cathcrosscultural.org
Previous Name: Catholic Immigration Bureau
Overview: A medium-sized international charitable organization
Chief Officer(s):
Carolyn Davis, Executive Director
Finances: *Annual Operating Budget:* $3 Million-$5 Million
Staff: 98 staff member(s); 20 volunteer(s)
Membership: 60; *Fees:* $20 individual; $35 organization
Description: To promote the settlement & integration of immigrants & refugees facing linguistic & cultural barriers through the provision of community based services; Affiliation(s): Access for New Canadians

Catholic Education Foundation of Ontario (CEFO)
80 Sheppard Ave. East, Toronto ON M2N 6E8
Tel: 416-229-5326; *Fax:* 416-229-5345
office@cefontario.ca
cefontario.ca
Social Media:
www.facebook.com/catholiceducationfoundationontario
Overview: A small provincial charitable organization founded in 1976
Chief Officer(s):
Mary Eileen Donovan, President
president@cefontario.ca
Description: To foster & promote the principles of Catholic education; to support parents in their role as primary educators; to assist the Church in its pastoral responsibilities to the schools; to encourage the establishment of Catholic schools; to promote equity of educational funding in Ontario

Catholic Family Service of Ottawa (CFS Ottawa) / Service familial catholique d'Ottawa (SFC Ottawa)
310 Olmstead St., Ottawa ON K1L 7K3
Tel: 613-233-8478; *Fax:* 613-233-9881
info@cfsottawa.ca
www.cfsottawa.ca
Previous Name: Catholic Family Service of Ottawa-Carleton
Overview: A small local charitable organization founded in 1940
Chief Officer(s):
Isabelle Massip, President
Franca DiDiomete, Executive Director
Finances: *Annual Operating Budget:* $1.5 Million-$3 Million; *Funding Sources:* Provincial/municipal government; United Way; private donations
Staff: 34 staff member(s); 15 volunteer(s)
Membership: 50
Activities: *Internships:* Yes *Library:* Yes (Open to Public)
Description: CFS Ottawa offers a range of social services in English & French to all residents of the Ottawa-Carleton area. Services include counselling, support to the victims or witnesses of family violence or sexual abuse, advocacy, community development. It is a registered charity, BN: 118841105RR0001; *Member of:* Family Service Canada

Catholic Family Services of Hamilton (CFS)
#201, 447 Main St. East, Hamilton ON L8N 1K1
Tel: 905-527-3823; *Fax:* 905-546-5779
Toll-Free: 877-527-3823
intake@cfshw.com
www.cfshw.com
Social Media:
www.youtube.com/channel/UCeLsGYd3vHt5PGRkS8JJFjA
linkedin.com/company/catholic-family-services-of-hamilton
www.facebook.com/Catholic.Family.Services.Hamilton
twitter.com/CFSHW
Previous Name: Catholic Family Services of Hamilton-Wentworth
Overview: A small local organization founded in 1944
Chief Officer(s):
Linda Dayler, Executive Director & Secretary
Paula Forbes, Associate Director
Finances: *Funding Sources:* Government of Canada; Province of Ontario; City of Hamilton; United Way of Burlington & Greater Hamilton; Foundations such as ON Trillium Foundation
Activities: Offering programs, such as the Employee Assistance Program, Debt Management Program, K.I.D.S. (Kids in Divorced

/ Separated Situations), Men's Anti-Violence & Abuse Program, & the Senior's Intervention & Support Program; Providing mediation services, in areas such as the workplace, credit, estates, & commerce; Offering consumer credit education to the general public; Offering money management coaching
Description: To provide individual, marriage, family, & credit counselling services in the Hamilton & Burlington communities; *Member of:* Ontario Association of Credit Counselling Service; Affiliation(s): Ontario Community Support Association; ONTCHILD; Family Services Ontario; Canadian Association for Community Care; Continuing Gerontological Education Cooperative; Older Persons' Mental Health & Addictions Network; Ontario Association on Developmental Diabilities; Ontario Case Managers Association; Ontario Gerontology Association; Ontario Partnership on Aging Development Disabilities

Catholic Family Services of Peel Dufferin (CFSPD)
Emerald Centre, #400, 10 Kingsbridge Garden Circle, Mississauga ON L5R 3K6
Tel: 905-450-1608; *Fax:* 905-897-2467
info@cfspd.com
www.cfspd.com
Social Media:
www.facebook.com/208938825992
Previous Name: Peel Dufferin Catholic Services
Overview: A small local charitable organization founded in 1981
Chief Officer(s):
Ana Hill, Manager, Operations, 905-450-1608 404
anahill@cfspd.com
Finances: *Annual Operating Budget:* $500,000-$1.5 Million
Staff: 30 staff member(s); 85 volunteer(s)
Activities: Individual, couple & family therapy; support groups; workshops; *Internships:* Yes; *Speaker Service:* Yes
Description: CFSPD is a multi-service counselling agency that supports families coping with difficulties, notably violence, trauma & abuse. Services are available in many languages to help people deal with such problems as depression, anxiety, grief, marital difficulties, parent-child conflict, developmental transitions & cutural adjustments. Offices in Mississauga & Brampton have walk-in clinics. The Society is a registered charity, BN: 119087823RR0001; *Member of:* Catholic Charities; Archdiocese of Toronto; United Way of Peel Region

Catholic Family Services of Saskatoon (CFS)
#200, 506 25th St. East, Saskatoon SK S7K 4A7
Tel: 306-244-7773; *Fax:* 306-244-8537
staff@cfssaskatoon.sk.ca
www.cfssaskatoon.sk.ca
Overview: A small local charitable organization founded in 1940
Chief Officer(s):
Trish St. Onge, Executive Director
Finances: *Annual Operating Budget:* $500,000-$1.5 Million; *Funding Sources:* Provincial & regional governments; United Way; Diocese of Saskatoon; community grants & donations
Staff: 50 volunteer(s)
Membership: 1-99
Activities: Counselling; family & children's services; teen parent program; family to family ties program; families & schools together program; employee & family assistance prgrams, marriage preparation, work & family wellness presentations; event speakers; workshop presentations & consultations; *Library:* Yes (Open to Public)
Description: To promote quality of life by developing & supporting the inherent strengths of individuals, families & the community; *Member of:* United Way of Saskatoon; Affiliation(s): Family Service Canada; Family Service Saskatchewan

Catholic Family Services of Simcoe County (CFSSC)
20 Anne St. S, Barrie ON L4N 2C6
Tel: 705-726-2503; *Fax:* 705-726-2570
info@cfssc.ca
www.cfssc.ca
Social Media:
www.facebook.com/CFSSC
twitter.com/CounselorSimcoe
Previous Name: Catholic Family Life Centre-Simcoe South; North Simcoe Catholic Family Life Centre
Overview: A small local charitable organization founded in 1979
Chief Officer(s):
Michelle Bergin, Executive Director
mbergin@cfssc.ca
Finances: *Annual Operating Budget:* $250,000-$500,000; *Funding Sources:* Charities; United Way
Staff: 20 staff member(s)
Membership: 1-99
Activities: Family, individual & group counselling; family life education
Description: To offer professional social services to all residents of Simcoe South; services will be directed to the treatment of troubled families & individuals, as well as to strengthening & enriching family life & individual functioning in all their dimensions & contexts

Catholic Family Services of Toronto (CFS Toronto) / Services familiaux catholiques de Toronto
Catholic Pastoral Centre, #200, 1155 Yonge St., Toronto ON M4T 1W2
Tel: 416-921-1163; *Fax:* 416-921-1579
info@cfsofto.org
www.cfsofto.org
Previous Name: Catholic Welfare Bureau
Overview: A medium-sized local charitable organization founded in 1922
Chief Officer(s):
Ken Yip-Chuck, President
Lucia Furgiuele, Secretary/Executive Director
Finances: *Annual Operating Budget:* $1.5 Million-$3 Million
Staff: 35 staff member(s); 18 volunteer(s)
Activities: *Library:* Yes
Description: CFS Toronto is a non-profit counselling agency for individuals, couples, & families. Within the context of Catholic beliefs, it offers a range of specialised programs, as well as a safe environment for women & families who are victims of abuse; *Member of:* Catholic Charities of the Archdiocese of Toronto; Affiliation(s): Family Service Canada; Family Service Ontario

The Catholic Foundation of Manitoba / Fondation catholique du Manitoba
622 Taché Ave., Winnipeg MB R2H 2B4
Tel: 204-233-4268
cfmb@mts.net
catholicfoundation.mb.ca
Overview: A medium-sized provincial organization founded in 1964
Chief Officer(s):
Tom Lussier, President
Description: The vision of the Catholic Foundation is to provide for the needy, better the situation of the underprivileged, promote cultural advancement and scientific research, and promote the cultural life of the Catholic community of Manitoba by encouraging the funding of endowments and by providing prudent management of funds and responsible distribution of the derived revenue

Catholic Health Alliance of Canada / Alliance catholique canadienne de la santé
Annex C, Saint-Vincent Hospital, 60 Cambridge St. North, Ottawa ON K1R 7A5
Tel: 613-562-6262; *Fax:* 613-782-2857
www.chac.ca
Previous Name: Catholic Health Association of Canada; Catholic Hospital Association of Canada
Overview: A large national charitable organization founded in 1939
Chief Officer(s):
Mike Shea, President & CEO, 780-781-4075
shea.chac@gmail.com
James Roche, Senior Director, Mission & Ethics, 613-562-6262 2164
jroche@bruyere.org
Finances: *Annual Operating Budget:* $1.5 Million-$3 Million; *Funding Sources:* Membership dues
Membership: 7 provincial associations + 12 sponsor organizations + 100 hospitals, community health centres, nursing homes & long-term care facilities; *Fees:* Schedule available; *Member Profile:* Sponsor organizations of Catholic health care in Canada.
Description: To strengthen & support the ministry of Catholic health care organizations & providers, through advocacy & governance

Catholic Health Association of British Columbia (CHABC)
9387 Holmes St., Burnaby BC V3N 4C3
Tel: 604-524-3427; *Fax:* 604-524-3428
smhouse@shawlink.ca
chabc.bc.ca
Overview: A medium-sized provincial organization founded in 1940
Chief Officer(s):
Dianne Doyle, President
Membership: 114; *Committees:* Mission Intergration; Pastral Care; Ethics
Description: To witness to the healing ministry and abiding presence of Jesus. Inspired by the Gospel, this Association strives to have a universal concern for health as a condition for full human development; *Member of:* Catholic Health Alliance of Canada; Health Employers Association of British Columbia; Affiliation(s): Euthanasia Prevention Coalition; Canadian Association of Parish Nurse Ministries

Catholic Health Association of Manitoba (CHAM) / Association catholique manitobaine de la santé (ACMS)
SBGH Education Bldg., #N5067, 409 Taché Ave., Winnipeg MB R2H 2A6
Tel: 204-235-3136; *Fax:* 204-235-3811
www.cham.mb.ca
Overview: A medium-sized provincial charitable organization founded in 1943
Chief Officer(s):
Wilmar Chopyk, Executive Director
wchopyk@cham.mb.ca
Daniel Lussier, Chair
Fees: $20 personal members; $100 associate members; *Member Profile:* Organizations; Health care facilities; Individuals
Activities: Promoting collaboration in health care services; Providing education to health care professionals, parish workers, & volunteers; Engaging in advocacy activities for the needs of the vulnerable & disadvantaged; Promoting the dignity & sacredness of each person; *Awareness Events:* CHAC World Day of the Sick
Description: To carry out the healing ministry of the Catholic Church in the delivery of both health & social services in Manitoba; To treat the people of Manitoba with compassion & respect for all; to recognize the spiritual dimension integral to health & healing; *Member of:* Catholic Health Alliance of Canada; Affiliation(s): Bishops of Manitoba; Diocese of Churchill-Hudson Bay, Northwest Territories

Catholic Health Association of New Brunswick (CHANB) / L'Association catholique de la santé du Nouveau-Brunswick
1773 Water St., Miramichi NB E1N 1B2
Tel: 506-778-5302; *Fax:* 506-778-5303
nbcha@nb.aibn.com
www.chanb.com
Overview: A small provincial organization founded in 1986
Chief Officer(s):
Robert Stewart, Executive Director
rstewart@health.nb.ca
Membership: 300
Description: The Catholic Health Association of New Brunswick is a provincial Christian organization promoting health care in the tradition of the Catholic Church. The Association fosters healing in all its aspects: Physical, psychological, social and spiritual; *Member of:* Catholic Health Alliance of Canada

Catholic Health Association of Saskatchewan (CHAS)
1702 - 20 St. West, Saskatoon SK S7M 0Z9
Tel: 306-655-5330; *Fax:* 306-655-5333
cath.health@sasktel.net
www.chassk.ca
Overview: A medium-sized provincial charitable organization founded in 1943
Chief Officer(s):
Sandra Kary, Executive Director
sandra.chassk@sasktel.net
Brian Martin, President
Christopher Boychuk, Vice-President
Peter Martens, Secretary-Treasurer
Fees: $25 person members; $75 associations; *Member Profile:* Institutions, groups, & individuals who are interested in Catholic health care & support the work of the association
Activities: Providing education & resources to members; Offering programs, such as the Parish Home Ministry of Care Program & the Catholic Health Leadership Program; Engaging in advocacy activities with the government; Providing both provincial & national networking opportunities; *Awareness Events:* Mission Week; World Day of the Sick *Library:* Catholic Health Association of Saskatchewan Resource Library
Description: To provide leadership in mission, ethics, spiritual care, & social justice in Saskatchewan; To promote the sanctity of life & the dignity of all; *Member of:* Catholic Health Alliance of Canada

Catholic Health Corporation of Ontario (CHCO)
PO Box 1879, 712 College Ave. West, Guelph ON N1H 7A1
Tel: 519-767-5600; *Fax:* 519-767-5602
chco@chco.ca
www.chco.ca
Overview: A medium-sized provincial organization
Chief Officer(s):
John P. Ruetz, President, 519-767-5600
Sarah Quackenbush, Consultant, Mission & Education, 705-522-1485
csjsarah@ontera.net
Description: Sponsors member institutions & thereby continues and strengthens Catholic health care in Ontario

Catholic Missions in Canada (CMIC) / Missions catholiques au Canada
#201, 1155 Yonge St., Toronto ON M4T 1W2
Tel: 416-934-3424; *Fax:* 416-934-3425
Toll-Free: 866-937-2642
info@cmic.info
www.cmic.info
Social Media: www.youtube.com/missioncanada; catholicmissionsincanada.tumblr.com
www.facebook.com/catholicmissionsincanada
twitter.com/canadamissions

Previous Name: Catholic Church Extension Society of Canada
Overview: A large national charitable organization founded in 1908
Chief Officer(s):
Thomas C. Collins, Apostolic Chancellor & Chair, Executive Committee
Philip J. Kennedy, President
president@cmic.info
James Milway, Secretary
Finances: *Funding Sources:* Donations; Fundraising
Staff: 11 staff member(s); 1 volunteer(s)
Membership: 26 mission dioceses; *Committees:* Executive; Allocations; Finance; Nominating
Activities: Supporting over 600 missionaries who serve in home mission communities throughout Canada; *Speaker Service:* Yes
Description: To keep the Catholic faith in remote & poor communities throughout Canada; *Member of:* Association of Fundraising Professionals (Toronto); CAGGP

Catholic Organization for Life & Family (COLF) (COLF) / Organisme catholique pour la vie et la famille (OCVF)
2500 Don Reid Dr., Ottawa ON K1H 2J2
Tel: 613-241-9461; *Fax:* 613-241-9048
ocvfcolf@cccb.ca
www.cccb.ca/site/eng/contact-us

Overview: A small national organization founded in 1996
Chief Officer(s):
Michèle Boulva, Director, 613-241-9461 141
Peter D. Murphy, Assistant Director, 613-241-9461 162
Jocelyne Pagé, Administrative Assistant, 613-241-9461 161
Finances: *Funding Sources:* Donations
Staff: 1 staff member(s)
Activities: Promoting the teaching of the Catholic Church in circumstances from conception to natural death; Preparing & providing educational resources; Strengthening the role of the family; Participating in public debate about the family & respect for life; Collaborating with the Canadian Conference of Catholic Bishops & the Knights of Columbus
Description: To build a civilization of love; To promote respect for human life & the important role of the family; Affiliation(s): Canadian Conference of Catholic Bishops (CCCB)

The Catholic Principals' Council of Ontario (CPCO)
PO Box 2325, #3030, 2300 Yonge St., Toronto ON M4P 1E4
Tel: 416-483-1556; *Fax:* 416-483-2554
Toll-Free: 888-621-9190
info@cpco.on.ca
www.cpco.on.ca
Social Media: www.youtube.com/cpcotoronto
linkedin.com/company/1206013
twitter.com/CPCO2012

Overview: A small provincial organization
Chief Officer(s):
Paul Lacalamita, Executive Director
placalamita@cpco.on.ca
Randy Bissonnette, President
president@cpco.on.ca
Finances: *Annual Operating Budget:* $1.5 Million-$3 Million
Staff: 6 staff member(s); 6 volunteer(s)
Membership: 2,000 members who are principals & vice-principals in more than 1,300 elementary & secondary separate schools across Ontario; *Committees:* Communications; Member Security; Professional Development; Finance; Issues in Catholic Education
Activities: Advocacy, professional development; legal services; *Speaker Service:* Yes
Description: CPCO is a voluntary, professional association that serves more than 2,100 principals and vice-principals in twenty-nine Catholic school boards across Ontario

Catholic Teachers Guild
80 Sackville St., Toronto ON M5A 3E5
Tel: 416-393-5204; *Fax:* 416-397-6586
catholicteachersguild.ca

Overview: A medium-sized national organization founded in 2000
Chief Officer(s):
Barry White, President
barry.white@tcdsb.org
Finances: *Funding Sources:* Donations
Fees: $20 initial fee; $10 renewal fee; *Member Profile:* Active or retired Catholics involved in education at any level, including pre-school & post-secondary, who support the mission of the Guild; Catholic lay educators & volunteers who work in Catholic schools, public schools, private schools, & other educational institutions
Activities: Holding an Annual Education Mass & Lenten Retreat; Presenting lectures & workshops; Conducting book club meetings
Description: To support & deepen the vocation of Catholic educators; Affiliation(s): Archdiocese of Toronto

Catholic Women's League of Canada (CWL)
702C Scotland Ave., Winnipeg MB R3M 1X5
Tel: 204-927-2310; *Fax:* 888-831-9507
Toll-Free: 888-656-4040
info@cwl.ca
www.cwl.ca
Social Media:
www.facebook.com/374698529280233
twitter.com/@CWLNational

Overview: A large national organization
Chief Officer(s):
William McGrattan, National Spiritual Advisor
Barbara Dowding, National President
Shari Guinta, Secretary-Treasurer
Kim Scammell, Executive Director
executivedirector@cwl.ca
Finances: *Funding Sources:* Donations
Membership: Over 50,000; *Member Profile:* Catholic women over sixteen years of age who wish to serve within their communities
Description: To assist one another liver holier lives, while carrying out our daily occupations; To become an enlightened & dedicated member of the laity; to grow in relationship with Christ & the church; To carry out the work of Christ at home, in the community, & in the world; To serve the people of God; To ensure local leagues within Archdiocesan Parishes report to regional & provincial councils, & follow the constitution & bylaws of the CWL

Catholic Youth Studio - KSM Inc. (KSM)
183 Roncesvalles Ave., 2nd Fl., Toronto ON M6R 2L5
Tel: 416-588-0555; *Fax:* 416-588-9995
radio@catholicradio.ca
www.catholicradio.ca
Social Media:
www.facebook.com/KSMRADIO
twitter.com/KSMRADIO

Also Known As: Catholic Radio Toronto
Overview: A small local charitable organization founded in 1994
Chief Officer(s):
Marcin Serwin, Director
Finances: *Funding Sources:* Donations
Staff: 4 staff member(s); 50 volunteer(s)
Member Profile: Individuals who donate their talents & time at Catholic Youth Studio - KSM Inc., a media corporation for evangelization, in order to promote the Christian faith; Members are both youth & adults who share the Catholic Youth Studio's charism
Activities: Programming for youth, couples, & seniors; Providing faith instruction; *Awareness Events:* International Festival of Religious Song
Description: To reach those who have not yet experienced their "springtime of faith", by means of evangelization through modern forms of mass media; to broadcast a daily radio program, eleven hours per week in Polish, & to publish a magazine, in order to provide services to families; Affiliation(s): Archdiocese of Toronto

Catholicland
21550 Bathurst St., Holland Landing ON L9N 1P6
Tel: 647-834-2046
victor@catholicland.com
www.catholicland.com

Also Known As: Catholicland & Stella Maris Marina
Overview: A small local organization founded in 1989
Chief Officer(s):
Marilyn Carvalho, Contact
Victor Carvalho, Contact
Fees: $300 individual; $600 family for 5 on-site events with overnights & 10 without overnights; *Member Profile:* Roman Catholic individuals & families, faithful to the Magisterium, who wish to live their faith in fun & fellowship with others
Activities: Assisting those in need in Belize & Africa; Funding volunteers to pursue missions in countries where assistance is needed; Providing land & water based recreational programming for married couples, families, & youth; Offering retreat houses for reflection & retreats
Description: To provide & promote a place (80 acres) for retreat, recreation, & reflection, in a Catholic environment, for families, parish groups, & youth; To assist other countries by volunteering services to those in need; Affiliation(s): Archdiocese of Toronto

Congrégation de Sainte-Croix - Les Frères de Sainte-Croix / Congregation of Holy Cross
4901, rue du Piedmont, Montréal QC H3V 1E3
Tél: 514-731-7828; *Téléc:* 514-731-7820
saintecroixcsc@yahoo.ca
www.ste-croix.qc.ca

Aperçu: *Dimension:* petite; *Envergure:* locale
Description: Congrégation religieuse catholique qui oeuvre en éducation, en milieu paroissial et dans divers autres secteurs de la société

Congregation des Soeurs de Saint-Joseph de Saint-Vallier (SSJ)
860, av Louis-Fréchette, Québec QC G1S 3N3
Tél: 418-683-9653; *Téléc:* 418-681-8781

Nom précédent: Soeurs de Saint-Joseph de Saint-Vallier
Aperçu: *Dimension:* petite; *Envergure:* locale; *fondée en 1683*
Membre(s) du bureau directeur:
Jeanne d'Arc Auclair, Supérieure générale
Membre: 165

Congregation of St-Basil (Basilian Fathers) (CSB)
95 St. Joseph St., Toronto ON M5S 3C2
Tel: 416-921-6674; *Fax:* 416-920-3413
contact@basilian.org
www.basilian.org
Social Media: www.youtube.com/user/cavalka124

Also Known As: Basilian Fathers
Overview: A small international organization founded in 1822
Chief Officer(s):
Michael P. Cerretto, Secretary General
Ronald P. Fabbro, Superior General
Finances: *Annual Operating Budget:* Less than $50,000
Staff: 3 volunteer(s)
Membership: 325; *Member Profile:* Priests; Students for the priesthood
Activities: *Library:* Yes by appointment
Description: Roman Catholic congregation of priests whose primary apostolate is education, parishes, & Hispanic ministry in Canada, USA, Mexico, Colombia, & France; *Member of:* RC Church

Council of Catholic School Superintendents of Alberta (CCSSA)
21 Walters Place, Leduc AB T9E 8S7
Tel: 780-913-0194
www.ccssa.ca
Social Media:
www.facebook.com/NCRegister
twitter.com/acstanews

Overview: A small provincial organization
Chief Officer(s):
Jamie McNamara, Executive Director, 780-913-0194
Membership: 35
Description: Provides a forum for discussion regarding the direction & development of Catholic Education in Alberta

Covenant Health (Alberta) (ACHC)
3033 66 St. NW, Edmonton AB T6K 4B2
Tel: 780-735-9000
www.covenanthealth.ca

Previous Name: Catholic Health of Alberta
Overview: A small provincial organization
Chief Officer(s):
Patrick Dumelie, CEO
Membership: 14 Catholic health care facilities

Dignity Canada Dignité
PO Box 2102, Stn. D, Ottawa ON K1P 5W3
Tel: 613-746-7281
info@dignitycanada.org
www.dignitycanada.org
Social Media:
www.facebook.com/groups/253558468022157

Overview: A medium-sized national organization
Chief Officer(s):
Frank Testin, President
president@dignitycanada.org
Norman Prince, Secretary
Finances: *Funding Sources:* Donations
Activities: Encouraging spiritual development, education, & social involvement
Description: To voice the concerns of Roman Catholic sexual minorities; To promote the development of sexual theology, justice, & acceptance of the lesbian & gay community; To reinforce a sense of dignity & to encourage gay men & lesbian women to become more active members in the Church & society

Dignity Toronto Dignité
175 Windermere Ave., Toronto ON M6S 3J8
Tel: 416-925-9872
toronto@dignitycanada.org
dignitycanada.org/toronto.html
Social Media:
www.facebook.com/dignitytoronto
Overview: A small local organization founded in 1974
Chief Officer(s):
Frank Testin, President
president@dignitycanada.org
Finances: *Annual Operating Budget:* Less than $50,000
Membership: 20; *Fees:* $30
Activities: Monthly liturgical meeting to support gay & lesbian Roman Catholics; social gatherings
Description: To support & affirm gay & lesbian Roman Catholics through spiritual development, education, social involvement, equity issues, & social events; *Member of:* Dignity Canada Dignité

Dignity Vancouver Dignité
PO Box 3016, Stn. Terminal, Vancouver BC V6B 3X5
vancouver@dignitycanada.org
dignitycanada.org/vancouver.html
Overview: A small local organization founded in 1977
Chief Officer(s):
Kevin Simpson, Treasurer, 604-874-3428
treasurer@dignitycanada.org
Finances: *Annual Operating Budget:* Less than $50,000
Membership: 12; *Fees:* $35 individual; *Member Profile:* Roman Catholic gays, lesbians, friends
Description: The organization works within the Catholic Church & with other Catholic groups to reform the church's theological stance pertaining to sexual minorities. It supports gay & lesbian Catholics & their friends, encouraging participation in educational, spiritual, & social activities; *Member of:* Dignity Canada Dignité

Dignity Winnipeg Dignité
PO Box 1912, Winnipeg MB R3C 3R2
Tel: 204-779-6446
winnipeg@dignitycanada.org
www.dignitycanada.org
Overview: A small provincial organization founded in 1970
Chief Officer(s):
Thomas Novak, National Chaplain, 204-287-8583
Finances: *Annual Operating Budget:* Less than $50,000
Staff: 3 volunteer(s)
Membership: 20; *Fees:* $25 (optional); *Member Profile:* LGBT community; non-gay men & women, encompassing a broad spectrum of professions, political beliefs, ethnic & linguistic backgrounds & economic levels
Activities: Regular liturgies/discussion groups; annual retreat; social events; brochures; *Speaker Service:* Yes
Description: To bring together gay & lesbian Catholics & their friends; To encourage a process of self-understanding & personal integration with respect to issues, including spirituality & sexuality; *Member of:* Dignity Canada Dignité

Diocèse militaire du Canada
USFC (O), Site Uplands, Édifice 469, Ottawa ON K1A 0K2
Tél: 613-990-7824; *Téléc:* 613-991-1056
carlone.l@forces.gc.ca
www.eveques.qc.ca/dioceses/Militaire.html
Aperçu: *Dimension:* petite; *Envergure:* nationale; *Organisme sans but lucratif; fondée en 1987*
Membre(s) du bureau directeur:
Donald Thériault, Évêque
Activités: *Bibliothèque:* Centre d'entraînement des aumôniers de Borden
Description: Fournir une dimension spirituelle et morale à toutes les activités affectant le moral et le bien-être des membres catholiques des Forces canadiennes, leurs familles et les employés civils du Ministère de la Défense nationale; *Membre de:* La Conférence des évêques catholiques du Canada

Emmanuel Community / Communauté de l'Emmanuel
QC
info@emmanuelcommunity.com
www.emmanuelca.info
Social Media:
www.facebook.com/172877582427
Overview: A small local organization founded in 1992
Chief Officer(s):
Laurent Albisetti, Canada, 418-977-1977
Activities: Helping one another materially, fraternally, & spiritually
Description: To commit to a contemplative & apostolic life at the heart of the Catholic Church; To participate in the fulfillment of the mission of the Church in the modern world; To advance in the life of holiness

Federation of North American Explorers (FNE)
c/o Paul Ritchi, 43 Bluesky Cres., Richmond Hill ON L4C 8J2
Tel: 416-435-6593
info@fneexplorers.com
www.fneexplorers.com
Social Media:
www.facebook.com/128721180527013
twitter.com/PaulRitchi
Also Known As: FN Explorers
Overview: A small local charitable organization founded in 1956
Chief Officer(s):
Paul Ritchi, General Commissioner & Founder
paul.ritchi@gmail.com
Finances: *Funding Sources:* Donations
Member Profile: Youth must be baptized Christians, or being prepared for baptism. Adults must also be baptized Christians, or being prepared for baptism, & volunteers must clear a police background check
Activities: Participating in camping weekends, outdoor survival skills, & community service; Earning badges by successfully completing certain activities
Description: To deliver traditional values to youth, from a Catholic faith perspective; To provide youth a same gender, education for life program experience; *Member of:* International Union of European FSE Guides & Scouts (Union Internationale des Guides et Scouts d'Europe); Affiliation(s): Archdiocese of Toronto

Filipino Canadian Catholic Charismatic Prayer Communities (FCCCPC)
53 Belvedere Cres., Richmond Hill ON L4C 8VA
Tel: 416-903-3453
fcccpc@yahoo.com
www.fcccpc.com
Overview: A small national organization founded in 1992
Chief Officer(s):
Ben Ebcas, Spiritual Director
Don Quilao, Head Servant
cbquilao@rogers.com
Teresita P. Gutierrez, Secretary & Director, 416-456-0381
terigutierrez@yahoo.ca
Caring Labindao, Treasurer
Membership: 10+ charismatic prayer communities; *Member Profile:* Individuals are members of a Catholic prayer community (majority of members are of Filipino heritage)
Activities: Counselling; Providing faith instruction & prayer groups; Offering renewal programs, general assemblies, & fellowship; Presenting spiritual formation seminars
Description: To defend the Word; To advocate righteousness, through witnessing & instructions; To provide refuge to the weak, needy, & persecuted; Affiliation(s): Archdiocese of Toronto

Foundation of Catholic Community Services Inc. (FCCS) / La Fondation des services communautaires catholiques inc.
1857, boul de Maisonneuve ouest, Montréal QC H3H 1J9
Tel: 514-934-1326; *Fax:* 514-934-0453
info@fccsmontreal.org
www.fccsmontreal.org
Social Media:
www.youtube.com/channel/UCSIZdslLG8cmtCqm_Es2ATQ
facebook.com/pages/CCS-Montreal
twitter.com/CCSMontreal
Previous Name: Catholic Community Services Inc.
Overview: A medium-sized local organization founded in 1974
Chief Officer(s):
Andrea Bobkowicz, President
Finances: *Annual Operating Budget:* $1.5 Million-$3 Million
Staff: 33 staff member(s); 1104 volunteer(s)
Membership: 65; *Fees:* $10
Activities: Youth groups; home sharing; administrative & support services; community organization & development; family support programs; personal development & support groups; camping services; Almage Senior Centre; Teapot Senior Centre; Good Shepherd Community Centre; Home Support Program; volunteer coordination; Home Day Care Program; *Speaker Service:* Yes
Description: To provide a broad spectrum of social services on behalf of the English-speaking Catholic community of the Diocese of Montréal

Foundation of Catholic Community Services Inc (FCCS)
#310, 1857, boul de Maisonneuve ouest, Montréal QC H3H 1J9
Tel: 514-934-1326; *Fax:* 514-934-0453
info@fccsmontreal.org
www.fccsmontreal.org
Overview: A small local organization founded in 1932
Chief Officer(s):
Andrea Bobkowicz, President

Membership: 100 individual

Frères de Notre-Dame de la Miséricorde / Brothers of Our Lady of Mercy
1149, ch Tour du Lac nord, Lac-Sergent QC G0A 2J0
fndm@cite.net
www.crc-canada.org/fr/node/412
Aperçu: *Dimension:* petite; *Envergure:* internationale; *Organisme sans but lucratif; fondée en 1839*
Membre(s) du bureau directeur:
Omer Beaulieu, Délégué du Supérieur général
Finances: *Budget de fonctionnement annuel:* Moins de $50,000
Personnel: 1 membre(s) du personnel; 6 bénévole(s)
Membre: 9
Description: Rassembler des personnes en vue d'un travail apostolique auprès des jeunes et particulièrement auprès des personnes éprouvant des difficultés

Gethsemane Ministries
ON
Tel: 905-789-9909
gethsemaneministries@yahoo.ca
www.gethsemaneministries.com
Overview: A small local charitable organization founded in 1997
Chief Officer(s):
Stan Rodrigo, Contact
stan.rodrigo@gmail.com
Finances: *Funding Sources:* Donations
Fees: Free; *Member Profile:* All age groups
Activities: Counselling; Providing faith instruction & spiritual guidance; Participating in sacramental life; Offering prayer groups, with Rosary, praise & worship, intercession, & fellowship; Assisting the ill, elderly, & needy; Helping youth in their Catholic faith formation, including catechism classes for grades 1-8; Providing youth programs, retreats, & summer camps; Offering retreats for married couples, mainly conducted by preachers; Supporting other parish & diocesan activities; Offering adult & youth music ministry
Description: To offer evangelization through proclamation of the "Word," evangelization outreaches, & personal testimonies; To strengthen Catholic faith & family values through sacraments, personal prayer, reflection of scriptures, & fellowship; To renew commitment to the Church; To protect & uphold the sanctity of life, & the teachings of the Catholic Church on life & family; To undertake charitable acts to serve the community

Holy Childhood Association (HCA)
2219 Kennedy Rd., Toronto ON M1T 3G5
Tel: 416-699-7077; *Fax:* 416-699-9019
Toll-Free: 800-897-8865
hca@missionsocieties.ca
www.missionsocieties.ca
Social Media: www.youtube.com/user/WorldMissionTV
www.facebook.com/pontificalmissionsocieties
Also Known As: Children Helping Children
Overview: A medium-sized international charitable organization founded in 1843
Chief Officer(s):
Osei Alex, National Director
Finances: *Funding Sources:* Donations
Staff: 8 staff member(s)
Description: To develop mission awareness through a school program for elementary Catholic school children; to provide aid to children in developing countries; *Member of:* Pontificial Mission Societies

IMCS Pax Romana
7 Impasse Reille, Paris 75014 France
office@imcs-miec.org
www.imcs-miec.org
Également appelé: International Catholic Organization
Nom précédent: International Movement of Catholic Students; International Catholic Movement for Intellectual & Cultural Affairs
Aperçu: *Dimension:* grande; *Envergure:* internationale; *fondée en 1921*
Membre(s) du bureau directeur:
Charles Ochero, International President
president@imcs-miec.org
Activités: Pax Romana has consultative status with the United Nations Economic & Social Council, UNESCO & the European Council, & has accredited representatives to those organisations in New York, Vienna, Paris, Geneve & Strasbourg
Description: Aims, through its various professional & intellectual commitments in society & the Church, to engage in pro-active dialogue between Christian faith & cultures in order to promote the evangelization of cultures & the inculturation of the Gospel for the realization of the Kingdom of God; Affiliation(s): Mouvement d'étudiants chrétiens du Québec; Association of Canadian Catholic Students

Institut Voluntas Dei / Voluntas Dei Institute
7385, boul Parent, Trois-Rivières QC G9A 5E1
Tél: 819-375-7933; *Téléc:* 819-691-1841
ivd.cent@cgocable.ca
www.voluntasdei.org
Média social:
www.youtube.com/voluntasdeis?feature=mhee#p/u/22/
www.facebook.com/voluntasdei
twitter.com/voluntasdei

Également appelé: I.V. Dei
Aperçu: *Dimension:* petite; *Envergure: internationale; Organisme sans but lucratif; fondée en 1958*
Finances: *Budget de fonctionnement annuel:* $100,000-$250,000
Personnel: 3 membre(s) du personnel
Membre: 752; *Critères d'admissibilite:* Clerics & laymen who commit their lives to the service of Jesus Christ; married people as associate members who live out the same ideal & same apostolic project as the celibate members
Activités: *Stagiaires:* Oui
Description: To make known & communicate God's love for all to all people; To be present in every milieu; apostolic objective is "to create peace & brotherhood in Jesus Christ"; *Membre de:* Roman Catholic Church

International Catholic Deaf Association (ICDA)
mhysell@op.dspt.edu
www.icdacanadasection.wordpress.com
Social Media:
www.facebook.com/ICDACanadianSection

Also Known As: ICDA-Canada
Overview: A small national organization founded in 1949
Chief Officer(s):
Wanda Berrette, President
wberrette@rogers.com
Giuliana Grobelski, Vice-President
julianamusso3@hotmail.com
John Shores, Treasurer
jshores@shaw.ca
Finances: *Annual Operating Budget:* Less than $50,000
Staff: 40 volunteer(s)
Membership: 150 + 5,000 non-members; 16 Canadian chapters; *Fees:* $10 single; $15 couple; *Member Profile:* Practicing Catholics; deaf diaconates; lay ministries
Activities: National conference/workshop; Canadian Catholic Pastoral Workers for the Deaf meetings; fundraising; retreats; signed Mass; assists the Pastoral Workers, seminarians to learn sign languages; spreads the knowledge of the deaf culture among the hearing parishioners
Description: To promote religion, religious education, fellowship & leadership among deaf people of all ages; to promote in Canada & the ICDA various programs in foreign countries with a view to enhancing the life of deaf people

Jeunes canadiens pour une civilisation chrétienne
880 av Louis Fréchette, Québec QC G1S 3N3
Tél: 418-683-5222

Aperçu: *Dimension:* petite; *Envergure: locale; fondée en 1977*
Membre(s) du bureau directeur:
Frank R. Murphy, President
Finances: *Budget de fonctionnement annuel:* Moins de $50,000
Description: Travailler avec la jeunesse pour préserver les principes catholiques et éducatifs

Latin American Mission Program (LAMP)
81 Prince St., Charlottetown PE C1A 4R3
Tel: 902-368-7337; *Fax:* 902-368-7180
www.dioceseofcharlottetown.com
Social Media:
www.facebook.com/dioceseofcharlottetown
twitter.com/chtowndiocese

Overview: A small international organization founded in 1967
Finances: *Annual Operating Budget:* $50,000-$100,000; *Funding Sources:* Share Lent collections taken up annually in all parishes
Membership: 20
Activities: Educational events; orientation & support for missionaries
Description: To send out & receive back missionaries; to learn from the dispossessed & oppressed & to stand with them in building a society of justice; to develop & encourage a Faith response based on the life & struggle of dispossessed peoples; to participate in "return mission" by working with groups committed to social justice in Canada & developing education programs in PEI which analyze the causes of exploitation of the poor & which expose the reality of their lives; Affiliation(s): Diocese of Charlottetown; Les missionnaires du Sacre-Coeur; Scarboro Foreign Mission Society

LAUDEM, L'Association des musiciens liturgiques du Canada
1085, rue de la Cathédrale, Montréal QC H3B 2V3
info@laudem.org
www.laudem.org
Média social:
www.facebook.com/laudemcanada

Nom précédent: L'Association des organistes liturgiques du Canada
Aperçu: *Dimension:* petite; *Envergure: nationale; fondée en 1992*
Membre(s) du bureau directeur:
Paul Cadrin, Président et directeur, Revue
paulcadrin@hotmail.com
Jean-Pierre Couturier, Vice-Président
Alexandra Fol, Secrétaire-trésorière
Membre: 45
Description: De réunir les organistes liturgiques pour la promotion et le développement de leur ministère dans l'Église catholique romaine; *Membre de:* Fédération francophone des amis de l'orgue

Messagères de Notre-Dame de l'Assomption (MNDA)
#4, 45, rue de la Sapinière-dorion, Québec QC G1L 1A3
Tél: 418-626-7492

Aperçu: *Dimension:* petite; *Envergure: locale; Organisme sans but lucratif; fondée en 1964*
Finances: *Budget de fonctionnement annuel:* $50,000-$100,000
Membre: 100-499

Missionary Sisters of The Precious Blood of North America
St Bernard's Convent, 685 Finch Ave. West, Toronto ON M2R 1P2
Tel: 416-630-3298; *Fax:* 416-630-9114
www.preciousbloodsisters.com
Social Media:
www.facebook.com/156106151112902

Overview: A small international organization founded in 1885
Finances: *Funding Sources:* donations
Staff: 60 staff member(s)
Description: Involved in early childhood education & teaching at the elementary, secondary, & college levels. Also work in health care services as nurses, doctors, administrators, physical & occupational therapists, hospital chaplains, caregivers for the elderly, with AIDs patients & in nutrition education. Serves in social work, parish ministry, domestic work, gardening, religious education, work with the mentally & physically handicapped, retreat work, art, & in ministry to the Hispanic & First Nations people.

Newman Centre Catholic Chaplaincy and Parish
89 St. George St., Toronto ON M5S 2E8
Tel: 416-979-2468; *Fax:* 416-596-6920
secretary@newmantoronto.com
www.newmantoronto.com
Social Media:
www.facebook.com/newmanchaplaincy
twitter.com/newmanuoft

Also Known As: The Newman Centre
Previous Name: Newman Foundation of Toronto
Overview: A small local charitable organization
Chief Officer(s):
James Milway, President
Peter Turrone, Executive Director
frpeterturrone@newmantoronto.com
Description: To maintain & support Roman Catholic chaplaincy on University of Toronto campus

Ontario Catholic Supervisory Officers' Association (OCSOA)
730 Courtneypark Dr. West, Mississauga ON L5W 1L9
Tel: 905-564-8206; *Fax:* 905-564-8210
office@ocsoa.ca
www.ocsoa.ca
Social Media: www.youtube.com/watch?v=T3PYrlpouqU
www.facebook.com/CatholicEducationInOntario
twitter.com/catholicedu

Overview: A medium-sized provincial organization founded in 1967
Chief Officer(s):
Theresa Harris, Executive Director
theresaharris@ocsoa.ca
Marie Osborne, Executive Assistant
marieosborne@ocsoa.ca
Membership: 150 individual; 18 associate
Description: To represent supervisory officers employed in Catholic school boards

Ontario English Catholic Teachers' Association (CLC) (OECTA)
#400, 65 St. Clair Ave. East, Toronto ON M4T 2Y8
Tel: 416-925-2493; *Fax:* 416-925-7764
Toll-Free: 800-268-7230
contact@oecta.on.ca
www.oecta.on.ca
Social Media:
www.facebook.com/OECTA
twitter.com/OECTAProv

Overview: A large provincial organization founded in 1944
Chief Officer(s):
Ann Hawkins, President
Marshall Jarvis, General Secretary
m.jarvis@oecta.on.ca
David Church, Deputy General Secretary
d.church@oecta.on.ca
Membership: 45,000; *Fees:* $950; *Committees:* Audit; Awards; Beginning Teachers; Catholic Education; Collective Bargaining; Communications & Public Relations; Educational Aid; Elementary Schools; Finance; Health & Safety; Human Rights; Legislation; Occasional Teachers; Personnel; Political Advisory; Program & Structures; Professional Development Steering; Secondary Schools; Status of Women; Teacher Education Network
Activities: *Library:* Resource Library
Description: To advance Catholic education; To provide professional services, support, protection, & leadership; *Member of:* Canadian Teachers' Federation; Canadian Labour Congress; Ontario Federation of Labour; Affiliation(s): Ontario Teachers' Federation

Orthodox Church in America Archdiocese of Canada (OCA ADOC)
31 Lebreton St. North, Ottawa ON K1R 7H1
Tel: 613-233-7780; *Fax:* 613-233-1931
office@archdiocese.ca
www.archdiocese.ca

Also Known As: Orthodox Church in Canada
Previous Name: Russian Orthodox Greek Catholic Church (Metropolia)
Overview: A medium-sized international organization founded in 1902
Chief Officer(s):
Irénée Rochon, Archbishop, Ottawa & the Archdiocese of Canada, 450-834-2870
bishopirenee@archdiocese.ca
Anatoliy Melnyk, Chancellor, 514-522-2801
montreal.sobor@gmail.com
Membership: 10,000+
Description: A component of the Orthodox Church in America, an autocephalous (self-governing) church with territorial jurisdiction in Canada, the USA & Mexico; its doctrine & worship are those of the world-wide One Holy Catholic & Apostolic Church; *Member of:* Canadian Council of Churches; Churches of Manitoba; Orthodox Clergy Association of Québec

Religious of The Sacred Heart / Religieuses du Sacré-Coeur
#811, 325 Dalhousie St., Ottawa ON K1N 7G2
Tel: 613-241-4050; *Fax:* 613-241-3142
sshcph@on.aibn.com
rscj.org

Also Known As: Society of the Sacred Heart
Overview: A small local charitable organization founded in 1800
Chief Officer(s):
Barbara Dawson, Provincial Superior
Membership: 1-99
Activities: *Library:* Provincial Archives (Open to Public) by appointment
Description: To make known the love of Jesus in the world, through educaton & social justice activities

St. John's Cathedral Polish Catholic Church
186 Cowan Ave., Toronto ON M6K 2N6
Tel: 416-532-8249; *Fax:* 416-532-4653

Previous Name: Polish National Catholic Church of Canada
Overview: A small national organization
Finances: *Annual Operating Budget:* $100,000-$250,000
Membership: 300
Member of: The Canadian Council of Churches

Secrétariat nationale du MFC - Mouvement des femmes Chrétiennes (MFC)
Att: Mme Louisette Gingras, 625 - 1300, chemin Sainte-Foy, Québec QC G1S 0A6
Tél: 581-742-7176
sec.mfcnational@videotron.ca
www.mfcnational.net

Nom précédent: Fédération nationale du MFC - Mouvement des Femmes Chrétiennes

Aperçu: *Dimension:* grande; *Envergure: nationale; Organisme sans but lucratif; fondée en 1962*
Membre(s) du bureau directeur:
Pierrette Vachon, Présidente
Finances: *Budget de fonctionnement annuel:* Moins de $50,000
Personnel: 1 membre(s) du personnel; 700 bénévole(s)
Membre: 3 000; *Montant de la cotisation:* 15$; *Critères d'admissibilite:* Femmes de tout âge, condition et culture
Activités: Rencontre mensuelle sur le programme d'action; formation
Description: Un mouvement d'action catholique générale, il forme des femmes efficaces et dynamiques sur le plan familial, paroissial, social, et chrétien afin de transformer le milieu de vie par des projects concrets et en utilisant la méthode de l'action catholique; *Membre de:* Regroupement des Organismes Volontaires d'Éducation Populaire

ShareLife
1155 Yonge St., Toronto ON M4T 1W2
Tel: 416-934-3411; *Fax:* 416-934-3412
Toll-Free: 800-263-2595
slife@archtoronto.org
www.sharelife.org
Social Media:
www.facebook.com/ShareLifeCan
twitter.com/ShareLifeCan
Overview: A large international charitable organization founded in 1976
Chief Officer(s):
Arthur Peters, Executive Director, 416-934-3411 559
arthurpeters@archtoronto.org
David Clubine, Communications Officer, 416-934-3411 348
dclubine@archtoronto.org
Finances: *Annual Operating Budget:* $500,000-$1.5 Million
Membership: 34 organizations
Activities: Golf tournament; *Awareness Events:* Kickoffs; *Speaker Service:* Yes
Description: ShareLife is the Catholic Community's response to helping the whole community through Catholic agencies by effectively raising & allocating funds; *Member of:* International Catholic Stewardship Council; Affiliation(s): Canadian Centre for Philanthropy

Sisters Adorers of the Precious Blood / Soeurs Adoratrices du Précieux Sang
301 Ramsay Rd., London ON N6G 1N7
Tel: 519-473-2499; *Fax:* 519-473-6590
www.pbsisters.on.ca
Overview: A small local charitable organization founded in 1861
Chief Officer(s):
Eileen Mary Walsh, General Superior
Carol Forhan, rpb, Formation Director
srcforhan@pbsisters.on.ca

Sisters of Charity of Halifax (SC)
215 Seton Rd., Halifax NS B3M 0C9
Tel: 902-406-8077; *Fax:* 902-457-3506
communications@schalifax.ca
www.schalifax.ca
Overview: A small local organization founded in 1849
Chief Officer(s):
Carrie Flemming, Advancement Associate
advancement@schalifax.ca
Ruth Jeppesen, Director, Communications
Membership: 400
Description: To develop a sensitivity to the oppressed through presence, prayer & ministry to others

Sisters of Saint Joseph of Pembroke (CSJ)
1127 Pembroke St. West, Pembroke ON K8A 5R3
Tel: 613-732-3694; *Fax:* 613-732-3319
infoPembroke@csjcanada.org
www.csjcanada.org
Overview: A small local organization founded in 1921
Membership: 1-99
Description: The Sisters of St. Joseph of Pembroke are a group of fifty Roman Catholic women religious based in eastern Ontario

Sisters of Saint Joseph of Peterborough (CSJ)
PO Box 566, Stn. Mount St. Joseph, 1555 Monaghan Rd., Peterborough ON K9J 6Z6
Tel: 705-745-1307; *Fax:* 705-745-1377
infoPeterborough@csjcanada.org
www.csjpeterborough.com
Social Media:
www.facebook.com/112521912120451
twitter.com/CSJCdn
Overview: A small local charitable organization founded in 1890
Membership: 80
Description: To respond to the poor & most needy, particularly where the need is not already met

Sisters of Saint Joseph of Sault Ste Marie
2025 Main St. West, North Bay ON P1B 2X6
Tel: 705-474-3800; *Fax:* 705-495-3028
stephanie.romiti@gmail.com
www.csjssm.ca
Overview: A small local organization
Chief Officer(s):
Shirley Anderson, General Superior
sanderson@csjssm.ca
Description: Lives & works that all people may be united with God & with one another

Sisters of the Child Jesus (SEJ) / Soeurs de l'Enfant-Jésus
318 Laval St., Coquitlam BC V3K 4W4
Tel: 604-939-7545; *Fax:* 604-939-7549
dbillesberger@shaw.ca
sistersofthechildjesus.ca
Also Known As: Sisters of Instruction of the Child Jesus
Overview: A small local charitable organization founded in 1667
Chief Officer(s):
Gilberte Painchaud, Provincial Superior
Description: To be a presence of love to the Father & to others for the definite purpose of awakening & deepening the faith; to enable people to grow in the uniqueness of their person as created by God & to liberate themselves from all that prevents their being truly human; to bring hope & direction to contemporaries; to be at the service of the least favoured, the marginalized & those who have no voice in society

Sisters of the Sacred Heart of Ragusa / Suore del Sacro Cuore di Ragusa
1 Edward St., Welland ON L3C 5H2
Tel: 905-732-4542
sacredhe@hotmail.com
www.sacredheartsisters.ca
Overview: A small local charitable organization founded in 1889
Membership: 500-999
Activities: Day care, schools, orphanages & retirement homes for the elderly; Parish work; Home visits; Missions; Nursing
Description: To live an apostolic life in the church & society through the works of beneficence among the poor & needy; To instruct & educate youth; To collaborate in parish pastoral work, especially through the teaching of catechism

Société canadienne d'histoire de l'Église Catholique - Section française (SCHEC) / Canadian Catholic Historical Association - French Section
SCHEC, Université du Québec à Trois-Rivières, 3351, boul des Forges, Trois-Rivières QC G9A 5H7
Tél: 819-376-5011; *Téléc:* 819-376-5179
schec.cieq.ca
Aperçu: *Dimension:* moyenne; *Envergure: nationale; fondée en 1933*
Membre(s) du bureau directeur:
Lucia Ferretti, Président
Finances: *Budget de fonctionnement annuel:* Moins de $50,000
Personnel: 4 bénévole(s)
Membre: 150 individu; 100 institutionnel; *Montant de la cotisation:* 20$ étudiants; 40$ individu; 50$ institutionnel; *Critères d'admissibilite:* La Société compte des membres dans toutes les parties du Canada de même qu'en Europe et aux États-Unis; les membres peuvent être des individus, ou des institutions publiques ou privées, tels des dépôts d'archives, bibliothèques, diocèses, communautés religieuses
Description: Grouper les personnes intéressées à l'histoire de l'Église catholique au Canada; stimuler l'intérêt pour cette histoire dans le grand public; tenir des congrès annuels dans diverses régions du Canada afin de susciter un dialogue entre chercheurs participants et de promouvoir les travaux d'histoire régionale

Société catholique de la Bible (SOCABI) / Catholic Bible Society
2000, rue Sherbrooke Ouest, Montréal QC H3H 1G4
Tél: 514-925-4300
www.interbible.org/socabi
Aperçu: *Dimension:* moyenne; *Envergure: nationale; Organisme sans but lucratif; fondée en 1940*
Membre(s) du bureau directeur:
Dumais Marcel, Président
Finances: *Budget de fonctionnement annuel:* $100,000-$250,000
Personnel: 6 membre(s) du personnel; 3 bénévole(s)
Membre: 130; *Montant de la cotisation:* 45$ tous les trois ans; *Critères d'admissibilite:* Implication dans le pastorale biblique; *Comités:* Administration; Financement
Activités: Service de librairie; conférences sur cassettes; cours par correspondance; cours d'initiation et formation; voyage en Israël; retraites; publication d'articles; *Bibliothèque:* Oui (Bibliothèque publique) rendez-vous
Description: Rendre la bible accessible au plus grand nombre de personnes possible, en facilitant la lecture et la compréhension; *Membre de:* Association canadienne des périodiques catholiques; Affiliation(s): World Catholic Federation for the Biblical Apostolate

The Society for the Propagation of the Faith (SPF)
2219 Kennedy Rd., Toronto ON M1T 3G5
Tel: 416-699-7077; *Fax:* 416-699-9019
Toll-Free: 800-897-8865
missions@missionsocieties.ca
www.missionsocieties.ca
Overview: A small national charitable organization founded in 1889
Chief Officer(s):
Alex Osei, C.S.Sp., National Director
Finances: *Annual Operating Budget:* $500,000-$1.5 Million; *Funding Sources:* Donations
Staff: 8 staff member(s)
Activities: Funds the training of local clergy & religious missions; *Speaker Service:* Yes
Description: To educate local clergy & religious men & women in developing countries

The Society of St. Peter the Apostle (SPA)
2219 Kennedy Rd., Toronto ON M1T 3G5
Tel: 416-699-7077; *Fax:* 416-699-9019
Toll-Free: 800-897-8865
missions@missionsocieties.ca
www.missionsocieties.ca
Overview: A small national charitable organization founded in 1889
Chief Officer(s):
Alex Osei, C.S.Sp., National Director
Finances: *Annual Operating Budget:* $500,000-$1.5 Million; *Funding Sources:* Donations
Staff: 8 staff member(s)
Activities: Funds the training of local clergy & religious missions; *Speaker Service:* Yes
Description: To educate local clergy & religious men & women in developing countries

Soeurs Auxiliatrices
1637, rue St-Christophe, Montréal QC H2L 3W7
Tél: 514-522-4452; *Téléc:* 514-524-1448
auxiqc@point-net.com
Aperçu: *Dimension:* petite; *Envergure: provinciale; fondée en 1856*
Membre(s) du bureau directeur:
Maria-Paule Lebél
Suzanne Loiselle
Andrée Brosseau

Les Soeurs de Sainte-Anne
1950, rue Provost, Lachine QC H8S 1P7
Tél: 514-637-3783; *Téléc:* 514-637-5400
accueil@ssacong.org
www.ssacong.org
Aperçu: *Dimension:* petite; *Envergure: internationale; Organisme sans but lucratif; fondée en 1850*
Membre(s) du bureau directeur:
Marie Ellen King, Supérieure générale
Madeleine Lanoue, Secrétaire générale
Finances: *Budget de fonctionnement annuel:* $100,000-$250,000
Description: Impliquée dans l'éducation, les soins de santé, l'animation pastorale et sociale en divers milieux

Soeurs de Sainte-Marie de Namur / Sisters of Saint Mary of Namur
68, av Fairmont, Ottawa ON K1Y 1X5
Tél: 613-725-1510
www.ssmn.ca
Aperçu: *Dimension:* petite; *Envergure: internationale; Organisme sans but lucratif; fondée en 1819*
Membre(s) du bureau directeur:
Françoise Sabourin, Supérieure provinciale
jeannettessmn@yahoo.fr
Suzanne Martineau, Secrétaire-trésorière
sr.suzannem@ssmn.ca
Finances: *Budget de fonctionnement annuel:* $250,000-$500,000
Membre: 1-99

Soeurs missionnaires Notre-Dame des Anges / Missionary Sisters of Our Lady of the Angels
323, rue Queen, Sherbrooke QC J1M 1K8
Tél: 819-569-9248; *Téléc:* 819-569-9180
mindalen@videotron.ca
www.misnda.org
Aperçu: *Dimension:* petite; *Envergure: internationale; Organisme sans but lucratif; fondée en 1922*

Membre(s) du bureau directeur:
Fernande Leblanc, Contact
Membre: 142
Description: The congregation is exclusively at the service of the missionary Church. Its specific mission is the formation of religious sisters, catechists and committed lay people. In addition, they respond to the needs of the local churches by working in the medical, social and educational fields when it is possible

Sovereign Military Hospitaller Order of St-John of Jerusalem of Rhodes & of Malta - Canadian Association / Ordre souverain militaire hospitalier de St-Jean de Jérusalem, de Rhodes et de Malte - Association canadienne
#302, 1247 Kilborn Pl., Ottawa ON K1H 6K9
Tel: 613-731-8897; *Fax:* 613-731-1312
smomca@bellnet.ca
www.orderofmaltacanada.org
Previous Name: Association of Canadian Knights of the Sovereign Military Order of Malta
Overview: A medium-sized national charitable organization founded in 1953
Chief Officer(s):
Albert André Morin, President
Finances: *Annual Operating Budget:* $100,000-$250,000; *Funding Sources:* Donations
Staff: 1 staff member(s); 259 volunteer(s)
Membership: Over 12,500
Description: To act as a Roman Catholic religious, chivalric & charitable organization; To provide assistance for: Good Shepherd Refuge, St. Francis, Second Mile Club, Providence Centre in Toronto, Czech Republic, Safe Motherhood Project, Nigeria, & ambulance brigades, Montréal, Cap-de-la-Madeleine, Ste. Anne de Beaupré; Affiliation(s): Sovereign Military Order of Malta

Spiritans, the Congregation of the Holy Ghost
34 Collingsgrove Rd., Toronto ON M1E 3S4
Tel: 416-691-9319; *Fax:* 416-691-8760
secretary@spiritans.com
www.spiritans.com
Social Media: www.youtube.com/user/SpiritansTransCanada
Also Known As: Spiritans of TransCanada
Overview: A medium-sized national organization
Chief Officer(s):
Paul McAuley, Provincial Bursar
bursar@spiritans.com
Membership: 3,000+
Description: Roman Catholic religious congregation specializing in education & mission

Tamil Catholic Community of Toronto (TCCT)
10 Parfield Dr., North York ON M1V 1H5
Tel: 416-499-0554
Overview: A small local charitable organization founded in 1987
Finances: *Annual Operating Budget:* Less than $50,000
Activities: Pilgrimages; Christian holiday celebrations; seminars
Description: To promote the Christian faith while preserving culture & heritage for future generations; Affiliation(s): Archdiocese of Toronto

Union mondiale des organisations féminines catholiques (UMOFC) / World Union of Catholic Women's Organizations (WUCWO)
76, rue de Saints-Pères, Paris F-75007 France
wucwoparis@wanadoo.fr
www.wucwo.org
Aperçu: *Dimension:* grande; *Envergure:* internationale; *fondée en 1910*
Membre(s) du bureau directeur:
Maria Giovanna Ruggieri, Présidente générale
wucwopregen@gmail.com
Liliane Stevenson, Secrétaire générale
wucwosecgen@gmail.com
Membre: Over 50,000; *Critères d'admissibilite:* Organisation féminine catholique ayant 3 ans d'existance; *Comités:* Commissions Permanentes - Droits Humains; Développement et Coopération; Femmes et Église; Famille; Oecuménisme; Comités permanents - Finances; Statutes et Procédures; Communication, Information et Publications; International
Activités: Groupe de travail sur la violence contre les femmes, santé et prises de décisions; éducation; droits humains
Description: Promouvoir l'apport des femmes catholiques à la communauté ecclésiale et humaine; étudier et encourager la participation des femmes dans la mission d'évangélisation de l'Église; promouvoir une action qui rend les femmes capables de mieux remplir leur rôle dans l'Église et dans la société; *Membre de:* Conférence des Organisations Internationales Catholiques (OIC); Affiliation(s): Catholic Women's League of Canada; Ukrainian Catholic Women's League of Canada; Association féminine d'éducation d'action sociale; Mouvement des femmes chrétiennes - Inter-Montréal

Christianity

Accelerated Christian Education Canada
PO Box 1360, Portage la Prairie MB R1N 3N9
Tel: 204-428-5332; *Fax:* 204-428-5386
Toll-Free: 800-976-7226
info@acecanada.net
www.acecanada.net
Also Known As: School of Tomorrow Canada
Previous Name: Canadian National Accelerated Christian Education Association
Overview: A small national organization founded in 1974
Chief Officer(s):
Alfred MacLaren, Manager, 204-428-5332 211
amaclaren@acecanada.net
Finances: *Annual Operating Budget:* Less than $50,000; *Funding Sources:* Provincial dues
Staff: 24 volunteer(s)
Membership: 100-499
Description: To continue to assure Canadians of the freedom to choose alternative Christian education; Affiliation(s): Federation of Independent Schools in Canada

Action des Chrétiens pour l'abolition de la torture (ACAT) / Action by Christians for the Abolition of Torture
#C-246, 2715, ch de la Côte-Sainte-Catherine, Montréal QC H3T 1B6
Tél: 514-890-6169; *Téléc:* 514-890-6484
info@acatcanada.org
www.acatcanada.org
Également appelé: ACAT Canada
Aperçu: *Dimension:* moyenne; *Envergure:* nationale; *Organisme sans but lucratif; fondée en 1984*
Membre(s) du bureau directeur:
Raoul Lincourt, Président
François Poulin, Coordonnateur
Finances: *Budget de fonctionnement annuel:* $50,000-$100,000; *Fonds:* Organisations philanthropiques et particuliers.
Personnel: 2 membre(s) du personnel; 20 bénévole(s)
Membre: 150; *Montant de la cotisation:* 35 $; *Comités:* Commission des interventions; Financement; Relations publiques; Ressourcement
Activités: Campagne annuelle; Bulletins; Appels à l'action; *Stagiaires:* Oui; *Service de conférenciers:* Oui; *Listes de destinataires:* Oui *Bibliothèque:* Oui rendez-vous
Description: Dans un but d'engagement évangélique, encourager les différentes communautés Chrétiennes du Canada à porter ensemble, par la prière, les souffrances des victimes de la torture; dans un but éducatif, sensibiliser particulièrement les Chrétiens au scandale de la torture (par l'information et la formation aux droits de la personne); dans un but de soulager la misère des victimes de la torture, apporter une aide concrète par l'envoi de lettres et pétitions aux responsables de torture et des lettres d'encouragement aux victimes; Affiliation(s): Fédération internationale de l'action des Chrétiens pour l'abolition de la torture (FIACAT)

African Enterprise (Canada) (AE)
4509 West 11th Ave., Vancouver BC V6R 2M5
Tel: 604-228-0930
admin@africanenterprise.ca
www.africanenterprise.com/en/canada
Social Media: www.youtube.com/user/AfricanEnterprise62
www.facebook.com/AEMissions
twitter.com/AEinternational
Also Known As: AE Canada
Overview: A small national charitable organization founded in 1965
Chief Officer(s):
David Richardson, Executive Director & CEO
Activities: *Internships:* Yes; *Speaker Service:* Yes
Description: To service & expand an active partnership among Canadian Christians to raise prayer, financial, material & human resources to enable AE to achieve its mission: to evangelise the cities of Africa through word & deed in partnership with the church; Affiliation(s): AE International

Alberta Restorative Justice Association (ARJA)
#430, 9810 - 111 St., Edmonton AB T5K 1K1
Tel: 780-451-4013
info@arjassoc.ca
www.arjassoc.ca
Social Media:
www.facebook.com/RJAlberta
twitter.com/RJAlberta
Overview: A small provincial organization
Chief Officer(s):
Deborah Nowakowski, Chair
Description: A collective voice to strengthen Restorative Justice in Alberta communities by establishing and providing information, education, and awareness towards best practices in Restorative Justice.

The Antiochan Orthodox Christian Archdiocese of North America
Antiochian Orthodox Christian Archdiocese, PO Box 5238, Englewood NJ 07631-5238 USA
Tel: 201-871-1355; *Fax:* 201-871-7954
archdiocese@antiochian.org
www.antiochian.org
Overview: A small national organization founded in 1875
Chief Officer(s):
Joseph Al-Zehlaoui, Archbishop
Sandra Abdelmessih, Registrar
registrar@antiochian.org
Membership: 275 parishes, 19 in Canada
Description: The Antiochan Orthodox Community in Canada is under the jurisdiction of the Patriarch of Antioch & all the East, with headquarters in Damascus, Syria. There are five churches in Canada & eight missions. The headquarters for all churches in North America is the Antiochan Orthodox Christian archdiocese, in Englewood, New Jersey, under Archbishop Philip Salica; Affiliation(s): Canadian (Can-Am) Region

Armenian Holy Apostolic Church - Canadian Diocese (AHAC)
615, av Stuart, Outremont QC H2V 3H2
Tel: 514-276-9479; *Fax:* 514-276-9960
contact@armenianchurch.ca
www.armenianchurch.ca
Social Media: www.youtube.com/user/CanArmChurch
www.facebook.com/239802236057531
Overview: A medium-sized national charitable organization founded in 1984
Chief Officer(s):
Abgar Hovakimian, Primate
Finances: *Annual Operating Budget:* $250,000-$500,000; *Funding Sources:* Donations; parish dues
Staff: 6 staff member(s)
Membership: Over 50,000; *Member Profile:* Baptized in the Armenian faith; *Committees:* Endowment Fund
Activities: Humanitarian Aid to Armenia; *Library:* Yes (Open to Public) by appointment
Description: To preserve & promote Christian & national heritage; humanitarian aid to Armenia; Affiliation(s): Canadian Council of Churches

Association internationale des études patristiques (AIEP) / International Association for Patristic Studies (IAPS)
c/o University of Ottawa, Desmarais Bldg., 55 Laurier Ave. East, Ottawa ON K1N 6N5
www.aiep-iaps.org
Aperçu: *Dimension:* moyenne; *Envergure:* internationale; *fondée en 1965*
Membre(s) du bureau directeur:
Theodore S. de Bruyen, Président
tdebruyn@uottawa.ca
Finances: *Budget de fonctionnement annuel:* Moins de $50,000
Membre: 740; *Montant de la cotisation:* US$17; *Critères d'admissibilite:* Interessé aux pères de l'Eglise; *Comités:* Executive
Activités: *Listes de destinataires:* Oui
Description: Chercheurs et professeurs qui s'intéressent à l'antiquité chrétienne au général

Association of Christian Churches in Manitoba (ACCM) / Association des églises chrétiennes du Manitoba
151 de la Cathedrale Ave., Winnipeg MB R2H 0H6
Tel: 204-237-9851
Previous Name: Ecumenical Committee of Manitoba
Overview: A medium-sized provincial organization founded in 1990
Finances: *Annual Operating Budget:* Less than $50,000
Description: To bring Christian churches into living encounter with one another; to provide a network of news & events which can help member churches act together in all matters except those in which deep differences compel us to act separately; to act as common Christian voice & media contact on issues of spiritual & social concern in the Province

The Bible League of Canada / Société canadienne pour la distribution de la Bible
PO Box 368, 399 Main Street West, Grimsby ON L3M 4H8
Tel: 905-319-9500; *Fax:* 905-319-0484
Toll-Free: 800-363-9673
www.bibleleague.ca
Social Media:
www.facebook.com/140398061327
twitter.com/BibleLeagueCan
Previous Name: World Home Bible League
Overview: A large international charitable organization founded in 1949
Chief Officer(s):
Paul Richardson, President
Finances: *Annual Operating Budget:* $3 Million-$5 Million; *Funding Sources:* Donations
Staff: 15 staff member(s)
Activities: *Speaker Service:* Yes *Library:* Yes
Description: To introduce people to Jesus Christ; to spread God's Word worldwide; *Member of:* Canadian Council of Christian Charities; International Association of Bible Leagues; Affiliation(s): The Bible League

Bibles & Literature in French Canada (BLF)
256, Marc-Aurele-Fortin, Lachute QC J8H 3W7
Tél: 450-562-7859; *Téléc:* 450-562-7859
info@blfcanada.org
www.blfcanada.org
Également appelé: BLF Canada
Aperçu: *Dimension:* petite; *Envergure:* nationale
Membre(s) du bureau directeur:
Toe-Blake Roy, Director
toeblake@blfcanada.org
Description: BLF Canada distribue une littérature de qualité afin de permettre de présenter, à ces millions de Canadiens, celui qui seul peut leur apporter la vraie vie.

Bibles for Missions Foundation (BFM)
Head Office, 45515 Knight Rd., Chilliwack BC V2R 5L2
Tel: 604-858-4980; *Fax:* 604-858-4334
Toll-Free: 855-204-4980
admin@bfmthriftstores.ca
www.bfmthriftstores.ca
Social Media:
www.facebook.com/279261462189925
twitter.com/bfmfred
Overview: A large international charitable organization founded in 1989
Chief Officer(s):
Casey Langbroek, Executive Director
Finances: *Funding Sources:* Donations
Description: To operates thrift stores across Canada to generate funds for Bible League Canada; *Member of:* The Bible League of Canada (TBLC)

British Israel World Federation (Canada) Inc. (BIWF)
313 Sherbourne St., Toronto ON M5A 2S3
Tel: 416-921-5996; *Fax:* 416-921-9511
info@british-israel-world-fed.ca
www.british-israel-world-fed.ca
Overview: A small international charitable organization founded in 1929
Membership: 1,200; *Fees:* $10
Activities: Meetings; *Speaker Service:* Yes
Description: To proclaim the Gospel of the Kingdom of God as contained in the Holy Bible

Canadian & American Reformed Churches
c/o Rev. E. Kampen, Academic Committee, 55 'C'-Line, RR#2, Orangeville ON L9W 2Y9
Tel: 905-807-6717
comments@canrc.org
canrc.org
Also Known As: Canadian Reformed Churches
Overview: A large national organization
Membership: 50+ organizations
Description: Federation of churches that are rooted in the Great Reformation of the sixteenth century. They aim is to exalt the Triune God by faithfully proclaiming the gospel of Jesus Christ.

Canadian Bible Society (CBS) / Société biblique canadienne
National Support Office, 10 Carnforth Rd., Toronto ON M4A 2S4
Tel: 416-757-4171; *Fax:* 416-757-3376
Toll-Free: 800-465-2425
info@biblesociety.ca
www.biblesociety.ca
Social Media: pinterest.com/canadianbible
www.facebook.com/CanadianBibleSociety
twitter.com/CanadianBible
Overview: A large national charitable organization founded in 1904
Chief Officer(s):
Nesa Gulasekharam, COO & Director, Finance
ngulasekharam@biblesociety.ca
John McLaverty, Director, Development
jmclaverty@biblesociety.ca
Guillaume Duvieusart, Director, National Francophone Services
gduvieusart@societebiblique.ca
Finances: *Funding Sources:* Donations; Sale of gifts; Fundraising
Activities: Offering various programs to share God's Word, such as Operation Bible for the Canadian military, & welcoming newcomers to Canada with God's message
Description: To translate, publish, & distribute Bibles, New Testaments & other Scriptures throughout Canada & Bermuda; *Member of:* United Bible Societies

Canadian Church Press (CCP)
8 MacDonald Ave., Hamilton ON L8P 4N5
Tel: 905-521-2240
cdnchurchpress@hotmail.com
www.canadianchurchpress.com
Social Media:
www.facebook.com/CanadianChurchPress
Overview: A small national organization founded in 1957
Chief Officer(s):
Ian Adnams, President
Saskia Rowley, Vice-President
Jim O'Leary, Treasurer
Finances: *Funding Sources:* Sponsorships
Membership: 56; *Fees:* Annual costs varies according to circulation numbers, from under 4,999 ($60) to over 100,000 ($215); *Member Profile:* Christian publications in Canada
Activities: Offering fellowship for members; Supporting members; Conducting professional development workshops in annual convention
Description: To promote high standards of religious journalism; to encourage a positive Christian influence on contemporary society

Canadian Council of Christian Charities (CCCC)
#1, 43 Howard Ave., Elmira ON N3B 2C9
Tel: 519-669-5137; *Fax:* 519-669-3291
www.cccc.org
Social Media:
linkedin.com/company/canadian-council-of-christian-charities
www.facebook.com/CCCCharities
twitter.com/cccccharities
Overview: A medium-sized national licensing charitable organization founded in 1972
Chief Officer(s):
John Pellowe, Chief Executive Officer
Finances: *Annual Operating Budget:* $500,000-$1.5 Million
Staff: 17 staff member(s); 56 volunteer(s)
Membership: 3,300; *Fees:* $30-$765+
Activities: Education; training on legal, financial & leadership issues
Description: To encourage the Canadian Christian community to a biblical stewardship of all He has entrusted to us by integrating practical concepts of administration, development & accountability with the spiritual concerns of ministry

Canadian Foodgrains Bank Association Inc. (CFGB) / Association de la banque canadienne de grains inc.
PO Box 767, #400, 393 Portage Ave., Winnipeg MB R3C 2L4
Tel: 204-944-1993; *Fax:* 204-943-2597
Toll-Free: 800-665-0377
cfgb@foodgrainsbank.ca
foodgrainsbank.ca
Social Media: www.youtube.com/user/foodgrainsbank
www.facebook.com/CanadianFoodgrainsBank
twitter.com/FoodgrainsJames
Also Known As: Foodgrains Bank
Overview: A large international charitable organization founded in 1983
Chief Officer(s):
Donald Peters, Chair
Jim Cornelius, Executive Director
jcornelius@foodgrainsbank.ca
Finances: *Funding Sources:* Donations; Fundraising
Membership: 15; *Member Profile:* Canadian churches & church-related agencies
Activities: Improving community development; Protecting & building sustainable economic livelihoods; Encouraging peace-building; Strengthening Canadian & international policy & action towards hunger issues; Increasing public awareness & engagement; Collecting grain & cash donations
Description: To provide a Christian response to hunger; to share resources with & support hungry populations outside Canada to achieve food security; to reduce hunger in developing countries

Canadian Society of Biblical Studies (CSBS) / Société canadienne des études bibliques (SCEB)
c/o Prof. Robert A. Derrenbacker, Jr., Regent College, 5800 University Blvd., Vancouver BC V6T 2E4
www.ccsr.ca
Overview: A small national organization founded in 1933
Chief Officer(s):
Robert A. Derrenbacker, Jr., Treasurer & Membership Secretary
rderrenbacker@laurentian.ca
Fees: $35 students & retired & unemployed persons; $72 full membership; *Member Profile:* Individuals interested in all aspects of the academic study of the Bible
Description: To stimulate the critical investigation of the classical biblical literature & related literature

Canadian Society of Church History (CSCH) / Société canadienne d'histoire de l'Église
c/o Robynne R. Healey, Dept. of History, Trinity Western University, 7600 Glover Rd., Langley BC V2Y 1Y1
csch-sche.ca
Overview: A small national organization founded in 1960
Chief Officer(s):
Scott McLaren, President
Lucille Marr, Vice-President & Program Chair
Robynne Rogers Healey, Administrative Secretary
robynne.healey@twu.ca
John H. Young, Treasurer
john.young@queensu.ca
Fees: $15 students; $30 retired academics; $33 individuals; *Member Profile:* Historians of Christianity in Canada & the United States
Description: To encourage research in the history of Christianity, especially the history of Christianity in Canada; *Member of:* Canadian Corporation for Studies in Religion; Congress of Social Sciences & Humanities

Canadian Society of Patristic Studies (CSPS) / Association canadienne des études patristiques
c/o Dr. S. Muir, Religious Studies, Concordia University College of AB, 7128 Ada Blvd., Edmonton AB T5B 4E4
www.ccsr.ca/csps
Overview: A small national organization founded in 1975
Fees: $48 students & retired members (with subscription); $65 regular members (including subscription); *Committees:* Program; Nominating
Description: To encourage the academic study of the Church Fathers; *Member of:* Canadian Federation for the Humanities & Social Sciences / Fèderation canadienne des sciences humaines

Christian Blind Mission International (CBMI)
PO Box 800, 3844 Stoufville Rd., Stouffville ON L4A 7Z9
Tel: 905-640-6464; *Fax:* 905-640-4332
Toll-Free: 800-567-2264
cbm@cbmcanada.org
www.cbmcanada.org
Social Media: www.youtube.com/user/cbmcanada;
pinterest.com/cbmcanada
www.facebook.com/101857609865125
twitter.com/cbmCanada
Overview: A medium-sized international charitable organization founded in 1978
Chief Officer(s):
Jonathan Liteplo, Chair
Ed Epp, Executive Director
Finances: *Annual Operating Budget:* Greater than $5 Million
Staff: 28 staff member(s); 45 volunteer(s)
Activities: Talking Book Library; Craft Store; works with nearly 600 mission agencies, local churches, Christian relief organizations & self-help groups overseas; *Rents Mailing List:* Yes *Library:* Talking Book Library (Open to Public)
Description: With core values based on Christian faith, CBMI serves the blind & disabled in the developing world, irrespective of nationality, race, sex, or religion; prevents & treats blindness & other disabilities through medical care, rehabilitation training & integration programs; helps people to help themselves; *Member of:* Canadian Council of Christian Charities

Christian Catholic Church Canada (CCRCC) / Église catholique-chrétien Canada
PO Box 2043, Stn. Hull, Gatineau QC J8X 3Z2
Tel: 613-738-2942; *Fax:* 613-738-7835
info@ccrcc.ca
www.ccrcc.ca
Previous Name: Canadian Chapter of the International Council of Community Churches
Overview: A large international charitable organization founded in 1858
Chief Officer(s):

Serge A. Thériault, Évêque et président
sergeatheriault@hotmail.com
Finances: *Annual Operating Budget:* Less than $50,000; *Funding Sources:* Clergy; churches; benefactors
Staff: 15 staff member(s); 25 volunteer(s)
Membership: 1,000-4,999; *Fees:* $200 church; $50 clergy; *Committees:* Order of the Crown of Thorns
Activities: Church ministry; Seminary program; Counselling & mediation services; *Library:* Archives (Open to Public) by appointment
Description: Advancing the kingdom of God through worship, pastoral work, & fellowship. Parishes in Ottawa-Gatineau, North Bay, Montreal; Affiliation(s): International Council of Community Churches (ICCC), ICCC Canada, World Council of Churches

Christian Children's Fund of Canada (CCFC)
1200 Denison St., Markham ON L3R 8G6
Tel: 905-754-1001; *Fax:* 905-754-1002
Toll-Free: 800-263-5437
donor-relations@ccfcanada.ca
www.ccfcanada.ca
Social Media: www.youtube.com/YCCCC
www.facebook.com/CCFC
twitter.com/ccfc

Overview: A large international organization founded in 1960
Chief Officer(s):
Mark Lukowski, Chief Executive Officer
Felicitas Adrian, Vice-President, Fund Development & Communications
Jim Carrie, Vice-President, Global Operations
Jeff Hogan, Vice-President, Finance & Corporate Services
Finances: *Funding Sources:* Donations
Staff: 200 volunteer(s)
Membership: 30,000+; *Fees:* $39/month suggested donation
Activities: Working to help those affected by HIV/AIDS; Providng water & sanitation; Offering education; *Internships:* Yes; *Speaker Service:* Yes
Description: To focus upon community development ministry, starting with basic assistance & leading to programs stressing self-help & eventual independence; To work with colleagues & partners in developing countries; To reach out to children & families of all faiths; *Member of:* Canadian Council of Christian Charities; Better Business Bureau; ChildFund Alliance; Imagine Canada; Affiliation(s): Canadian Marketing Association; Association of Fundraising Professionals

Christian Church (Disciples of Christ) in Canada (DISCAN) / Église chrétienne (Disciples du Christ) au Canada
ON
www.canadadisciples.org

Previous Name: All-Canada Committee of the Christian Church (Disciples of Christ)
Overview: A small national charitable organization founded in 1922
Chief Officer(s):
Richard E. (Rick) Hamilton, Interim Regional Minister
Finances: *Annual Operating Budget:* $100,000-$250,000; *Funding Sources:* Donations
Staff: 2 staff member(s)
Membership: 4,000 + 30 churches; *Committees:* Archives; Biennial Convention; Christian Nurture, Service, Witness; Church Development; College; Ministry
Activities: *Internships:* Yes; *Speaker Service:* Yes *Library:* Resource Centre
Member of: The Canadian Council of Churches; Affiliation(s): The Christian Church (Disciples of Christ) in USA

Christian Health Association of Alberta (CHAA)
PO Box 4173, 132 Warwick Rd., Edmonton AB T6E 4P8
Tel: 780-488-8074; *Fax:* 780-475-7968
chaaa@compusmart.ab.ca
www.chaaa.ab.ca

Also Known As: Catholic Health Association of Alberta & Affiliates
Previous Name: Catholic Health Care Conference of Alberta
Overview: A medium-sized provincial charitable organization founded in 1943
Chief Officer(s):
Glyn J. Smith, Administrator
Finances: *Annual Operating Budget:* $50,000-$100,000
Staff: 1 staff member(s); 13 volunteer(s)
Membership: 22 health facilities + 29 associate + 48 personal + 10 life; *Fees:* $25 individual; $75 associate
Description: Represents the shared vision & values of those seeking to make visible Jesus the Healer; provides support & leadership to members & the community through education, advocacy & collaboration; *Member of:* Catholic Health Association of Canada

Christian Labour Association of Canada (CLAC) / Association chrétienne du travail du Canada
2335 Argentia Rd., Mississauga ON L5N 5N3
Tel: 905-812-2855; *Fax:* 905-812-5556
Toll-Free: 800-268-5281
headoffice@clac.ca
www.clac.ca
Social Media: www.youtube.com/user/CLACunion
www.facebook.com/clacunion
twitter.com/clacunion

Overview: A medium-sized national organization founded in 1952
Chief Officer(s):
Dick Heinen, Executive Director
dheinen@clac.ca
Hank Beekhuis, Ontario Provincial Director
Dennis Perrin, Prairies Director
David Prentice, BC Director
Wayne Prins, Alberta Director
Membership: 55,000
Activities: Training programs; *Speaker Service:* Yes *Library:* Yes by appointment
Description: To promote labour relations based on the social principles of justice, respect & dignity; To stand up for fair wages, reasonable work hours, good benefits, a dependable retirement savings plan, job security, professional development & opportunities for advancement; *Member of:* World Organization of Workers

Christian Medical & Dental Society of Canada (CMDS)
9A - 1000 Windmill Rd, Dartmouth NS B3B 1L7
Tel: 902-406-2955; *Toll-Free:* 888-256-8653
office@cmdscanada.org
www.cmdscanada.org
Social Media:
www.youtube.com/channel/UCOB5Hpx1ERDs2anDNy6fYuA
www.facebook.com/CMDSCanada
twitter.com/CMDSCanada

Overview: A medium-sized national organization founded in 1971
Chief Officer(s):
Larry Worthen, Executive Director
lworthen@cmdscanada.org
Stephanie Potter, Manager, Communications
sjpotter@cmdscanada.org
Finances: *Funding Sources:* Dues; Donations
Fees: $365 Full-time Medical & Dental Practitioners; $180 Part-time Practitioners; $55 Residents; $25 Medical or Dental Students or Missionaries; *Member Profile:* Christian physicians, dentists, & students who wish to integrate faith with professional practice
Activities: Offers workshops & conferences; supports a toll-free helpline for medical & dental trainees; publishes a Members Directory & other literature; offers mission opportunities
Description: To uphold a Christian view of medicine & dentistry; to understand & minister to the spiritual needs of colleagues; to create educational materials about public policy & health; to develop programs that promote a Christian view of medical ethics; & to support local group activities, plan conferences, & locate mentorship & other opportunities; *Member of:* International Christian Medical & Dental Association

Christian Reformed Church in North America (CRCNA)
PO Box 5070, Stn. LCD 1, 3475 Mainway, Burlington ON L7R 3Y8
Tel: 905-336-2920; *Fax:* 905-336-8344
Toll-Free: 800-730-3490
crcna@crcna.ca
www.crcna.org
Social Media:
www.facebook.com/crcna
twitter.com/crcna

Overview: A large international organization founded in 1857
Chief Officer(s):
Ben Vandezande, Interim Director
executive-director@crcna.org
Finances: *Annual Operating Budget:* Greater than $5 Million; *Funding Sources:* Gifts & donations
Staff: 225 staff member(s)
Membership: In US & Canada: 245,217 members in more than 1,000 congregations; *Committees:* Abuse Prevention; Back to God Hour; Calvin College; Calvin Theological Seminary; CRC Publications; Home Missions; World Missions; World Relief; Chaplaincy Ministries; CRC Loan Fund; Disability Concerns; Fund for Smaller Churches; Pastor-Church Relations; Pensions & Insurance; Race Relations; Historical; Interchurch Relations; Sermons for Reading Services
Activities: *Awareness Events:* Sea to Sea Celebration Rally; *Speaker Service:* Yes
Description: The denominational office in Canada coordinates the work of the Church in Canada, overseeing the Committee for Contact with the Government (social justice issues), urban Aboriginal Ministry Centres (Edmonton, Regina, Winnipeg), & ecumenical involvement in KAIROS task forces (KAIROS: Canadian Ecumenical Justice Initiatives); Affiliation(s): National Association of Evangelicals; Reformed Ecumenical Council; World Alliance of Reformed Churches; Canadian Council of Churches; Evangelical Fellowship of Canada

Christian Science / La Première Église du Christ, Scientiste
The First Church of Christ, Scientist, 210 Massachusetts Ave., Boston MA 02115 USA
Tel: 617-450-2000; *Toll-Free:* 800-775-2775
info@churchofchristscientist.org
christianscience.com
Social Media: plus.google.com/104001952392468849471
twitter.com/cschurches

Also Known As: The Mother Church
Overview: A large international organization founded in 1879
Chief Officer(s):
Channing Walker, President
Russ Gerber, Manager, Committee on Publication
Finances: *Annual Operating Budget:* Greater than $5 Million; *Funding Sources:* Donations
Staff: 850 staff member(s)
Membership: 2,200 churches in over 70 countries; *Fees:* Per capita tax of not less than 1$; *Member Profile:* The Church is open to those who are "believer(s) [of] the doctrines of [the] Christian Science textbook: Science & Health with Key to the Scriptures, by Rev. Mary Baker Eddy."
Activities: Sunday worship services, Wednesday testimonial meetings; Sunday School for children; worldwide speakers bureau; retail book stores; Christian Science Reading Rooms; Christian Science programs & Weekly Bible Lessons are broadcast on public media; *Internships:* Yes; *Speaker Service:* Yes *Library:* Mary Baker Eddy Library for the Betterment of Humanity (Open to Public) by appointment
Description: Christian Scientists believe in one God, the Bible & in Christ Jesus as the Messiah. They believe that the application of the laws of God are practical & provable, hence scientific.

Christian Stewardship Services (CSS)
#214A, 500 Alden Rd., Markham ON L3R 5H5
Fax: 905-947-9263
Toll-Free: 800-267-8890
admin@csservices.ca
www.csservices.ca

Overview: A medium-sized national charitable organization founded in 1976
Chief Officer(s):
Maynard Wiersma, Executive Director
maynardw@csservices.ca
Mary Benn, Administrator, Finance
finance@csservices.ca
Henry Eygenraam, Coordinator, Special Projects & Succession Plans
eygenraam@csservices.ca
Finances: *Funding Sources:* Christian charities, including churches & schools; Social service organizations
Activities: Providing advice about will & estate planning; Offering the Growing & Giving program, featuring presentations & workshops
Description: To connect families, faith, & finances for efficient estate & gift planning; To promote Biblical stewardship; *Member of:* Canadian Council of Christian Charities; Affiliation(s): Diaconal Ministries of the Christian Reformed Church

Christos Metropolitan Community Church
Trinity St. Paul's Centre, 427 Bloor St. West, Toronto ON M5S 1X7
Tel: 416-925-7924; *Fax:* 416-922-8587

Also Known As: Christos MCC
Overview: A small local charitable organization founded in 1984
Chief Officer(s):
Deana Dudley, Pastor
Judi Bonner, Secretary
Finances: *Annual Operating Budget:* Less than $50,000
Staff: 1 staff member(s); 8 volunteer(s)
Membership: 30
Activities: Weekly worship services; spirituality-based study groups; social events
Description: Ministry by and for the LGBT community of Toronto; *Member of:* Universal Fellowship of Metropolitan Community Churches

Church Council on Justice & Corrections (CCJC) / Conseil des églises pour la justice et la criminologie (CÉJC)

#303, 200 Isabella St., Ottawa ON K1S 1V7
Tel: 613-563-1688; *Fax:* 613-237-6129
ccjc@ccjc.ca
www.ccjc.ca
Social Media:
www.youtube.com/channel/UCbL3WH8MfWbUp-31s9gPjoQ
linkedin.com/company/the-church-council-on-justice-and-corrections
www.facebook.com/180318678672186
twitter.com/CCJCCanada

Overview: A medium-sized national charitable organization founded in 1972
Chief Officer(s):
Schuyler Playford, Manager, Operations & Project Development, 613-563-1688 105
splayford@ccjc.ca
Kathryn Bliss, Manager, Education & Community Engagement, 613-563-1688 101
kbliss@ccjc.ca
Finances: *Annual Operating Budget:* $250,000-$500,000
Staff: 3 staff member(s)
Membership: 46 directors + 292 supporting; *Fees:* $40 individuals; $200 organizations
Activities: *Internships:* Yes; *Speaker Service:* Yes *Library:* Yes
Description: To strengthen churches' ministry in fields of crime prevention, justice & corrections; to initiate, encourage & support programs which sensitize congregations & educate volunteer groups to participate in development of community responses to crime, justice & corrections; to promote a healing justice; to examine & respond to policy concerns with assistance of churches; to call on churches to address issues; to provide resources to churches & other related organizations; *Member of:* National Associations Active in Criminal Justice; Affiliation(s): The Network - Interaction for Conflict Resolution

The Church Lads' Brigade (CLB)

PO Box 28126, 82 Harvey Rd., St. John's NL A1B 4J8
Tel: 709-722-1737; *Fax:* 709-722-1734
info@theclb.ca
www.theclb.ca
Social Media:
twitter.com/TheCLB_NL

Overview: A medium-sized national organization founded in 1892
Chief Officer(s):
Bernard Davis, Executive Director
Finances: *Annual Operating Budget:* $50,000-$100,000; *Funding Sources:* Donations; building rentals; fundraising
Staff: 1 staff member(s); 200 volunteer(s)
Membership: 800; *Fees:* $20; *Member Profile:* Boys & girls of all religious affiliations
Activities: Youth activities; recreational, educational & social; *Internships:* Yes *Library:* CLB Archives (Open to Public) by appointment
Description: The advancement of Christ's kingdom among youth, the promotion of Christian charity, reverence, discipline, self-respect, respect for others & all that lends towards true Christian character; Affiliation(s): The Church Lads' & Church Girls' Brigade (UK)

Citizens for Public Justice (CPJ)

#501, 309 Cooper St., Ottawa ON K2P 0G5
Fax: 613-232-1275
Toll-Free: 800-667-8046
cpj@cpj.ca
www.cpj.ca
Social Media:
www.facebook.com/citizensforpublicjustice
twitter.com/publicjustice

Overview: A medium-sized national organization
Chief Officer(s):
Joe Gunn, Executive Director
Sarah Shepherd, Coordinator, Communications
sarah@cpj.ca
Membership: 1500; *Fees:* $50 individual; $25 low income; $10 student
Activities: *Internships:* Yes
Description: To promote public justice in Canada by shaping key public policy debates through research and analysis, publishing and public dialogue. CPJ encourages citizens, leaders in society and governments to support policies and practices which reflect God's call for love, justice and stewardship.

Congregational Christian Churches in Canada (CCCC)

442 Grey St., #H, Brantford ON N3S 7N3
Tel: 519-751-0606; *Fax:* 519-751-0852
Toll-Free: 866-868-8702
ccccnationaloffice@bellnet.ca
www.cccc.ca

Overview: A small national charitable organization founded in 1821
Chief Officer(s):
David Schrader, National Pastor
nationalpastor@bellnet.ca
Bill MacDougall, Chair
b-pmacdougall@ns.sympatico.ca
Kim Adeniran, Administrative Assistant
ccccnationaloffice@bellnet.ca
Finances: *Annual Operating Budget:* $100,000-$250,000
Staff: 2 staff member(s)
Membership: 8,000 + 100 churches across Canada; *Fees:* $50; *Member Profile:* Churches or individuals in accord with CCCC's Statement of Faith and Founding Principles as set out in their By-Law and Supplementary Letters Patent.
Activities: *Internships:* Yes
Description: To celebrate & serve Jesus Christ in the 21st century through shared concern for others.

CrossTrainers Canada

PO Box 1426, Bradford ON L3Z 2B7
Tel: 416-697-0147
ct@ctministries.ca
www.ctministries.ca
Social Media: www.instagram.com/ctcanada
www.facebook.com/crosstrainerscanada
twitter.com/CT_Canada

Overview: A small local organization founded in 2001
Chief Officer(s):
Jodi Greenstreet, Executive Director
Patti LaRose, Director, Operations
Jenna Wickens, Director, Youth
Finances: *Funding Sources:* Corporate sponsors
Staff: 5 staff member(s)
Activities: Connections Centre with True Vibe program, Playzone, cafe & special events; The Hub Youth Centre with A Hand Up Clothing Room; Mercy House, a women's shelter
Description: The association is a Christian ministry organization with members from several local churches serving the Bradford community. It is a registered charity, BN: 889735023RR0001.

Direction Chrétienne Inc.

#520, 1450, rue City Councillors, Montréal QC H3A 2E6
Tel: 514-878-3035; *Fax:* 514-878-8048
info@direction.ca
www.direction.ca

Also Known As: Christian Direction
Overview: A small provincial charitable organization founded in 1964
Chief Officer(s):
Glenn Smith, Executive Director
Finances: *Annual Operating Budget:* $500,000-$1.5 Million
Staff: 13 staff member(s); 3 volunteer(s)
Membership: 1-99
Description: Rendre visite aux communautés chrétiennes locales et particulièrement celles des grands centres urbains afin de se faire connaître et partager son mandat

Edmonton & District Council of Churches (EDCC)

c/o Garneau United Church, #123, 11148 - 84 Ave., Edmonton AB T6G 0V8
Tel: 780-439-2501; *Fax:* 780-439-3067
admin@EDCCunity.org
www.edccunity.org

Overview: A small local organization founded in 1942
Chief Officer(s):
Julien Hammond, President, 780-469-1010 2271, Fax: 780-465-3003
jhammond@caedm.ca
Finances: *Annual Operating Budget:* Less than $50,000
Staff: 1 staff member(s); 7 volunteer(s)
Membership: 22; *Fees:* $60 denominational member; $30 individual member; *Member Profile:* Christian denominations; *Committees:* Ecumenical Coordinators; Week of Prayer for Christian Unity Service Planning Committee; Way of the Cross Planning Committee; No Room in the Inn Planning Committee
Activities: Organization of events; distribution of information; participation in interdenominational projects; *Awareness Events:* Week of Prayer for Christian Unity, Jan.; Good Friday Way of the Cross; No Room in the Inn Fundraising for Low Income Housing, Dec.
Description: To express through fellowship, consultation, cooperation, & service, the essential unity of the Christian church; To maintain open relationships & foster dialogue with other faith groups & inter-faith organizations; To provide support & monitoring for chaplaincy programs; Affiliation(s): Canadian Council of Churches

Focolare Movement - Work of Mary / Mouvement des Focolari

PO Box 69523, 5845 Yonge St., Toronto ON M2M 4K3
Tel: 416-250-6606
toronto@focolare.ca
www.focolare.ca
Social Media: vimeo.com/focolareorg
www.facebook.com/pages/focolareorg/190678934277979
twitter.com/Focolare_org

Overview: A small local charitable organization founded in 1943
Chief Officer(s):
Brigitte Sass, Contact, Women's Branch
Jacques Maillet, Contact, Men's Branch
Finances: *Funding Sources:* Donations
Member Profile: Individuals of all ages, walks of life, & vocations; Churches of religions & convictions that differ from Catholicism
Activities: Providing gatherings for families, youth, children, & various branches
Description: To fulfill Jesus' last will & testament: "That all may be one"; To strive for the Focolare spirituality to have an impact on family life, youth, & all areas of ecclesial & secular life; To promote the ideals of unity & universal brotherhood; Affiliation(s): Archdiocese of Toronto

Focus on the Family Canada

19946 - 80A Ave., Langley BC V2Y 0J8
Tel: 604-455-7900; *Fax:* 604-455-7999
Toll-Free: 800-661-9800
letters@fotf.ca
www.focusonthefamily.ca
Social Media:
www.facebook.com/fotfcanada
twitter.com/fotfcanada

Overview: A large national charitable organization founded in 1982
Chief Officer(s):
Terence Rolston, President
Finances: *Funding Sources:* Donations
Staff: 250 volunteer(s)
Activities: *Library:* Yes
Description: To strengthen & encourage the Canadian family through education & resources; *Member of:* Canadian Council of Christian Charities

General Church of the New Jerusalem in Canada (GCIC)

c/o Olivet Church of the New Jerusalem, 279 Burnhamthorpe Rd., Toronto ON M9B 1Z6
Tel: 416-239-3054; *Fax:* 416-239-4935
assistant@olivetnewchurch.org
www.newchurch.ca

Overview: A small national organization founded in 1971
Chief Officer(s):
James Cooper, Pastor
pastor@olivetnewchurch.org
Brian Smith, Assistant Pastor
brian.smith@olivetnewchurch.org
Description: An incorporated national organization of individual church members, groups & congregations devoted to the Christian life & teaching expounded in the works of Emanuel Swedenborg.

Global Outreach Mission Inc.

PO Box 1210, St Catharines ON L2R 7A7
Tel: 905-684-1401; *Fax:* 905-684-3069
Toll-Free: 866-483-5787
glmiss@on.aibn.com
www.missiongo.org
Social Media: www.youtube.com/user/missiongo
www.facebook.com/168935979827368
twitter.com/GlobalOutreachM

Previous Name: European Evangelistic Crusade, Inc.
Overview: A small international organization founded in 1943
Chief Officer(s):
Constable Greg, Vice-President, Candidates/Personnel
gconstable@missiongo.org
Affiliation(s): Interdenominational Foreign Mission Association

Gospel Tract & Bible Society

PO Box 180, Ste. Anne MB R5H 1R1
Tel: 204-355-4975
info@gospeltract.ca
www.gospeltract.ca

Overview: A small national organization
Description: Publishes Christian religious tracts; affiliated with Church of God in Christ, Mennonite.

Grace Communion International Canada
#101, 5668 - 192 St., Surrey BC V3S 2V7
Tel: 604-575-2705; *Fax:* 604-575-2758
info@gcicanada.ca
www.gcicanada.ca/welcome.php
Previous Name: Worldwide Church of God Canada
Overview: A small national organization
Chief Officer(s):
Gary Moore, National Director
gmoore@telus.net
Description: To proclaim the gospel of Jesus Christ around the world & to help members grow spiritually

Holy Face Association / Association de la Sainte Face
PO Box 310, Stn. B, Montréal QC H3B 3J7
Tel: 514-747-0357; *Fax:* 514-747-9147
holyface@holyface.com
www.holyface.com
Overview: A small national charitable organization founded in 1976
Finances: *Annual Operating Budget:* $250,000-$500,000; *Funding Sources:* Donations
Staff: 20 volunteer(s)
Membership: 15,000-49,999
Activities: *Speaker Service:* Yes *Library:* Yes by appointment
Description: The goal of this apostolate is reparation to God (Father, Son & Holy Spirit) through contemplative devotion to the Holy Face of Jesus

Independent Assemblies of God International - Canada
PO Box 653, Chatham ON N7M 5K8
Tel: 519-352-1743; *Fax:* 519-351-6070
pmcphail@ciaccess.com
www.iaogcan.com
Also Known As: IAOGI Canada
Overview: A small national charitable organization founded in 1918
Chief Officer(s):
Paul McPhail, General Secretary
pmcphail@ciaccess.com
Finances: *Annual Operating Budget:* $100,000-$250,000; *Funding Sources:* Membership fees; offerings
Staff: 2 staff member(s); 12 volunteer(s)
Membership: 500 churches/ministries; *Fees:* $100; *Member Profile:* Must be called by God to preach His Word
Activities: *Awareness Events:* National Convention, May; *Speaker Service:* Yes
Member of: Independent Assemblies of God International

Indian Métis Christian Fellowship (IMCF)
3131 Dewdney Ave., Regina SK S4T 0Y5
Tel: 306-359-1096
imcf.info@sasktel.net
www.imcf.ca
Overview: A small local organization founded in 1978
Chief Officer(s):
Ben Vandezande, Interim Director
Finances: *Annual Operating Budget:* $100,000-$250,000
Membership: 30 individual
Activities: Drop-in ministry; daily prayer circle; soup & bannock lunch; computer club
Description: IMCF is an urban aboriginal ministry supported by the Christian Reformed Church in North America - Canada. Its mission is to develop a worshipping, working community through serving the spiritual & social needs of aboriginal people in Regina.; Affiliation(s): Canadian Ministry Board; Indian Family Center, Winnipeg; Native Healing Centre, Edmonton

Institut Séculier Pie X (ISPX) / Pius X Secular Institute
CP 87731, Succ. Succ. Charlesbourg, 1645, boul Louis-XIV, Québec QC G1G 5W6
Tél: 418-626-5882; *Téléc:* 418-624-2277
info@ispx.org
www.ispx.org
Aperçu: *Dimension:* petite; *Envergure:* internationale; *Organisme sans but lucratif; fondée en 1939*
Membre(s) du bureau directeur:
Christian Beaulieu, Directeur général
Finances: *Budget de fonctionnement annuel:* $100,000-$250,000
Membre: 17 consacrés + 250 associés
Activités: Apostolat catholique; évangélisation; présence au monde; *Service de conférenciers:* Oui
Description: Évangéliser les milieux populaires par la présence et par des activités apostoliques; *Membre de:* Conférence canadienne des instituts séculiers; Conférence mondiale des instituts séculiers

Intercede International
201 Stanton St., Fort Erie ON L2A 3N8
Tel: 905-871-1773; *Fax:* 905-871-5165
Toll-Free: 800-871-0882
friends@intercedenow.ca
www.intercedenow.ca
Previous Name: Christian Aid Mission
Overview: A medium-sized international charitable organization founded in 1953
Chief Officer(s):
James S. Eagles, President
Finances: *Annual Operating Budget:* $500,000-$1.5 Million; *Funding Sources:* Private donations
Staff: 10 staff member(s); 50 volunteer(s)
Membership: 10; *Committees:* Audit Review
Activities: Sponsorship programs; relief aid; equipment & materials provisions; Missions cafe held in major cities; *Speaker Service:* Yes *Library:* Yes (Open to Public) by appointment
Description: To aid, encourage, & strengthen indigenous New Testament Christianity, particularly where Christians are impoverished, few, or persecuted; to encourage Christian witness & ministry to the international community in North America; *Member of:* Canadian Council of Christian Charities; Affiliation(s): Evangelical Fellowship of Canada

Inter-Varsity Christian Fellowship (IVCF)
1 International Blvd., Toronto ON M9W 6H3
Tel: 416-443-1170; *Fax:* 416-443-1499
Toll-Free: 800-668-9766
info@ivcf.ca
www.ivcf.ca
Overview: A medium-sized national charitable organization founded in 1929
Chief Officer(s):
Geri Rodman, President
Finances: *Funding Sources:* Donations
Activities: Offering Pioneer Camps across Canada; Providing ministry at university & college campuses; Offering travel opportunities through Inter-Varsity's World Services' Global Partnerships; Participating in the Urbana Student Mission Convention
Description: To help young people live a transformed life in Jesus Christ

Jews for Jesus
10 Huntingdale Blvd., Toronto ON M1W 2S5
Tel: 416-444-7020; *Fax:* 805-267-4141
toronto@jewsforjesus.ca
www.jewsforjesus.ca
Social Media:
www.facebook.com/jewsforjesuscanada
twitter.com/jewsforjesuscan
Overview: A small local charitable organization founded in 1981
Chief Officer(s):
Andrew Barron, Canadian Director/Missionary
andrew.barron@jewsforjesus.ca
Description: Jews for Jesus Canada is a Jewish evangelistic agency dedicated to bringing the Gospel into places where a significantly Jewish testimony is needed; *Member of:* Canadian Council of Christian Charities; Evangelical Fellowship of Canada; Interdenominational Foreign Mission Association

Lifewater Canada
#194, 307 Euclid Ave., Thunder Bay ON P7E 6G6
Tel: 807-622-4848; *Fax:* 807-577-9798
Toll-Free: 888-543-3426
www.lifewater.ca
Overview: A small international organization
Chief Officer(s):
Alanna Drost, Contact
Member Profile: Hydrogeologists, well drillers, educators, engineers, environmental scientists, businessmen & many other people with diverse skills & training
Description: Christian organization dedicated to ensuring that people everywhere have access to adequate supplies of safe water; to train & equip nationals with drill rigs & hand pumps so they can solve their own water problems; to place as many technical documents on-line as possible so they can benefit people everywhere, regardless of affiliation

M2/W2 Association - Restorative Christian Ministries (M2/W2)
#208, 2825 Clearbrook Rd., Abbotsford BC V2T 6S3
Tel: 604-859-3215; *Fax:* 604-859-1216
Toll-Free: 800-298-1777
info@m2w2.com
www.m2w2.com
Social Media:
linkedin.com/groups/5100601
www.facebook.com/M2W2Association?ref=hl
twitter.com/M2W2Association
Also Known As: Man-to-Man/Woman-to-Woman
Overview: A small provincial charitable organization founded in 1966
Chief Officer(s):
Raymond Robyn, Executive Director
Finances: *Annual Operating Budget:* $250,000-$500,000; *Funding Sources:* 65% community fundraising; 35% federal & provincial government contracts
Staff: 11 staff member(s); 400 volunteer(s)
Membership: 190; *Fees:* $10; *Member Profile:* Wide range of people whose common interest is the focus of M2/W2; *Committees:* Finance/Promotion; Program/New Initiatives; Personnel
Activities: Organizing annual promotion dinners; *Speaker Service:* Yes
Description: To mutually transform lives - one relationship at a time; To see individuals & communities in British Columbia safer, transformed, reconciled, & restored through justice, accountability, partnerships, mutual support, mediation, education & prevention; To provide one-to-one volunteers for men & women in British Columbia prisons, combined with pre- & post-release support & resources; To counsel prisoners, ex-prisoners, & their families; To prevent crime through one-to-one support for parents of young children at risk; *Member of:* Canadian Council of Christian Charities

Micah House
205 Holton Ave. South, Hamilton ON L8M 2L8
Tel: 905-296-4387
info@micahhouse.ca
www.micahhouse.ca
Social Media:
www.facebook.com/MicahHouseHamilton
twitter.com/micah_house
Overview: A small local organization founded in 2006
Chief Officer(s):
Scott Jones, Executive Director
scott@micahhouse.ca
Finances: *Funding Sources:* Donations
Staff: 6 staff member(s)
Member Profile: Christians from a variety of churches & organizations in Hamilton, Ontario
Activities: *Awareness Events:* Walkathon
Description: To demonstrate God's love to newly arrived refugees in Hamilton, Ontario

Les Missions des Soeurs Missionnaires du Christ-Roi
4730, boul Lévesque ouest, Chomedey QC H7W 2R4
Tél: 450-687-2100
missionsmcr@hotmail.com
www.missa.org/dc_m_smcr.php
Également appelé: Missions MCR
Aperçu: *Dimension:* moyenne; *Envergure:* internationale; *Organisme sans but lucratif; fondée en 1979*
Finances: *Budget de fonctionnement annuel:* $100,000-$250,000; *Fonds:* Fondations; Subventions
Personnel: 1 membre(s) du personnel
Membre: 213 institutionnel
Activités: *Bibliothèque:* Oui (Bibliothèque publique)
Description: Organiser, administrer, maintenir une oeuvre dont les fins sont la religion, la charité; promouvoir l'éducation et le bien-être, particulièrement en ce qui a trait aux différents buts qu'il s'est fixé; aide internationale

New Apostolic Church Canada
319 Bridgeport Rd. East, Waterloo ON N2J 2K9
Tel: 519-884-2862; *Toll-Free:* 866-622-7828
info@naccanada.org
www.naccanada.org
Overview: A medium-sized international organization
Chief Officer(s):
E. Wagner, President
T. Witt, Treasurer
Membership: 10 million internationally
Description: The New Apostolic Church takes a balanced approach to bible-based faith, recognizing three sacraments: Holy Baptism, Holy Sealing & Holy Communion; *Member of:* New Apostolic Church (International)

Les Oblates Missionnaires de Marie Immaculée (OMMI) / Oblate Missionaries of Mary Immaculate
7625, boul Parent, Trois-Rivières QC G9A 5E1
Tél: 819-375-7317
ommi@ommi-is.org
www.ommi-is.org
Aperçu: *Dimension:* petite; *Envergure:* internationale; *fondée en 1952*

OMF International - Canada (OMF)
5155 Spectrum Way, Bldg. 21, Mississauga ON L4W 5A1
Tel: 905-568-9971; *Fax:* 905-568-9974
Toll-Free: 888-657-8010
omfcanada@omf.ca
www.omf.ca
Also Known As: Overseas Missionary Fellowship
Previous Name: China Inland Mission
Overview: A medium-sized international organization founded in 1865
Chief Officer(s):
Ron Adams, Director, Administration & Finance
Jon Fuller, National Director
Membership: 1,300 missionaries worldwide; *Member Profile:* Four years post-secondary education
Member of: Interdenominational Foreign Mission Association; Affiliation(s): Evangelical Fellowship of Canada

Ontario Alliance of Christian Schools (OACS)
790 Shaver Rd., Ancaster ON L9G 3K9
Tel: 905-648-2100; *Fax:* 905-648-2110
oacs@oacs.org
www.oacs.org
Social Media:
twitter.com/oacsnews
Overview: A medium-sized provincial organization founded in 1952
Chief Officer(s):
Julius de Jager, MAT, Executive Director, 905-648-2100 15
julesdj@oacs.org
Finances: *Annual Operating Budget:* $500,000-$1.5 Million; *Funding Sources:* Membership dues
Staff: 12 staff member(s); 200 volunteer(s)
Membership: 1-99; *Fees:* Schedule available; *Committees:* Finance; Education; PR; Planning; Government Relations; Personnel
Activities: *Speaker Service:* Yes; *Rents Mailing List:* Yes
Description: To promote independent schools in Ontario; to promote Christian education in Canada; to provide educational services for member schools; to lobby government for educational choice. Canada's largest & oldest independent school organization, representing 79 schools with approximately 14,000 students.; Affiliation(s): Christian Schools International; Christian Schools Canada

Ontario Christian Music Assembly
90 Topcliff Ave., Downsview ON M3N 1L8
Tel: 416-636-9779; *Fax:* 905-775-2230
landmkooy@rogers.com
Overview: A small provincial organization founded in 1961
Membership: 130 individual
Activities: Spring & Christmas concerts series; annual Christian festival concert

Pacific Life Bible College
15030 - 66A Ave., Surrey BC V3S 2A5
Tel: 604-597-9082; *Fax:* 604-597-9090
Toll-Free: 877-597-7522
info@christcollege.ca
www.christcollege.ca
Social Media: vimeo.com/channels/plbc
www.facebook.com/pacificlifebiblecollege
twitter.com/plbc
Merged from: Pacific Life Bible College; Christ College
Overview: A small national charitable organization founded in 1997
Chief Officer(s):
Dennis Hixson, President, 604-597-9082 254
dhixson@pacificlife.edu
Member Profile: Applicants to the college must be born-again Christians actively involved in a church for a minimum of a full year prior to application.
Activities: *Library:* Wolf Memorial Library
Member of: International Church of the Foursquare Gospel

Pioneer Clubs Canada Inc.
Toll-Free: 800-465-5437
www.pioneerclubs.org
Social Media:
www.facebook.com/pioneerclubs
Also Known As: Pioneer Girls/Pioneer Boys
Overview: A large national licensing charitable organization founded in 1974
Finances: *Annual Operating Budget:* $250,000-$500,000
Staff: 9 staff member(s)
Membership: 216 institutional; 16,000 individual; *Fees:* $12 child
Activities: *Speaker Service:* Yes
Description: To serve God by assisting churches & other ministries in helping children & youth make Christ Lord in every aspect of life; Affiliation(s): Canadian Council of Christian Charities

Prison Fellowship Canada / Fraternite des prisons du Canada
#144, 5945 Airport Road, Mississauga ON L4V 1R9
Tel: 905-673-5867; *Fax:* 905-673-6955
Toll-Free: 844-618-5867
info@prisonfellowship.ca
www.prisonfellowship.ca
Social Media:
twitter.com/ServingLifePFC
Overview: A small national organization founded in 1980
Chief Officer(s):
Stacey Campbell, Executive Director/CEO
Michael Van Dusen, Chair, Advocacy Committee
Description: To challenge, equip, & serve the body of Christ in its ministry to prisoners, ex-prisoners, their families, & victims; To promote the advancement of restorative justice; *Member of:* Prison Fellowship International

Project Peacemakers
745 Westminster Ave., Winnipeg MB R3G 1A5
Tel: 204-775-8178; *Fax:* 204-784-1339
info@projectpeacemakers.org
www.projectpeacemakers.org
Social Media: www.youtube.com/user/peacemakers
www.facebook.com/108617822532248
twitter.com/ProjectPeacmkrs
Overview: A small international charitable organization founded in 1983
Finances: *Annual Operating Budget:* Less than $50,000; *Funding Sources:* Member donations; church grants
Staff: 2 staff member(s); 30 volunteer(s)
Membership: 200; *Fees:* $25 one year; $40 two years; $8 low income
Activities: Concerts; film festivals; protests; witness-for-peace delegations; forums; *Speaker Service:* Yes *Library:* Yes (Open to Public)
Description: Project Peacemakers is a group of people working for peace from a faith perspective. Its activities are varied, from peace delegations in war zones to educational forums on such issues as child soldiers & violent video games; *Member of:* Project Ploughshares; Affiliation(s): Canadian Centre for Arms Control & Disarmament; Manitoba Environmental Network; Mennonite Central Committee; Peace Alliance Winnipeg; Manitoba Japanese-Canadian Citizens Association

REHOBOTH Christian Ministries
3920 - 49th Ave., Stony Plain AB T7Z 2J7
Tel: 780-963-4044; *Fax:* 780-963-3075
provincial_admin@rehoboth.ab.ca
rehoboth.ab.ca
Also Known As: Christian Association for the Mentally Handicapped of Alberta
Overview: A medium-sized provincial charitable organization founded in 1976
Chief Officer(s):
Ron Bos, Executive Director
ron.bos@rehoboth.ab.ca
Finances: *Annual Operating Budget:* Greater than $5 Million; *Funding Sources:* Provincial government; membership fees; donations; church offerings
Staff: 535 staff member(s); 950 volunteer(s)
Membership: 4,600; *Fees:* $10; *Member Profile:* Everybody accepting their mission statement; *Committees:* Regional Advisory
Activities: Residential, vocational & recreational support for individuals who live with disabilities; summer camp program; fundraising golf tournament; *Internships:* Yes
Description: To convey God's love to persons with disabilities through support, advocacy & public education, & by providing opportunities for personal growth & meaningful participation in society; *Member of:* Alberta Council of Disability Services; Canadian Centre for Philanthropy; Affiliation(s): Christian Stewardship Services

The Salvation Army in Canada
Territorial Headquarters, Canada & Bermuda, 2 Overlea Blvd., Toronto ON M4H 1P4
Toll-Free: 800-725-2769
www.salvationarmy.ca
Social Media: www.youtube.com/user/salvationarmy
linkedin.com/company/the-salvation-army-in-canada?trk=prof-0-ovw-p
www.facebook.com/salvationarmy
twitter.com/salvationarmy
Overview: A large international charitable organization founded in 1882
Chief Officer(s):
Susan McMillan, Territorial Commander
Finances: *Annual Operating Budget:* $3 Million-$5 Million
Staff: 152 staff member(s)
Membership: 311 Corps (congregations); 330+ social-service institutes across Canada
Activities: *Speaker Service:* Yes
Description: To preach the Gospel of Jesus Christ; To supply basic human needs; To provide personal counselling & undertake the spiritual & moral regeneration & physical rehabilitation of all persons in need who come within its sphere of influence regardless of race, colour, creed, sex or age; *Member of:* Evangelical Fellowship of Canada

Samaritan House Ministries Inc.
820 Pacific Ave., Brandon MB R7A 0J1
Tel: 204-726-0758
info@samaritanhouse.net
samaritanhouse.net
Social Media:
www.facebook.com/210774752373958
twitter.com/SHM_Brandon
Overview: A small local charitable organization founded in 1987
Chief Officer(s):
Thea Dennis, Executive Director
Activities: *Internships:* Yes; *Speaker Service:* Yes
Description: To provide support & services to at-risk populations - the homeless, those living in poverty, people with literacy challenges or persons leaving abusive relationships

Samaritan's Purse Canada (SPC)
20 Hopewell Way NE, Calgary AB T3J 5H5
Tel: 403-250-6565; *Fax:* 403-250-6567
Toll-Free: 800-663-6500
info@samaritan.ca
www.samaritanspurse.ca
Social Media: www.youtube.com/user/samaritanspursecan;
pinterest.com/spcanada
www.facebook.com/samaritanspurse.ca
twitter.com/spcanada
Also Known As: Operation Christmas Child
Overview: A large international charitable organization founded in 1973
Chief Officer(s):
Franklin Graham, President & CEO
Fred Weiss, Executive Director
Finances: *Annual Operating Budget:* Greater than $5 Million; *Funding Sources:* Donations
Staff: 100 staff member(s); 1500 volunteer(s)
Activities: Operation Christmas Child packages; Turn on the Tap access to safe water program; *Internships:* Yes; *Speaker Service:* Yes
Description: To meet both physical & spiritual needs of people who are victims of war, poverty, natural disasters, disease & famine. Focus is on emergency relief & development programs, medical projects. International offices in Canada, Australia, Germany, Ireland, the Netherlands, the U.S. & the U.K; *Member of:* Canadian Council of Christian Charities; Affiliation(s): Samaritan's Purse USA

The Secular Institute of Missionaries of the Kingship of Christ (SIM)
andre.comtois28@gmail.com
www.simkc.org
Previous Name: Missionaires de la Royauté du Christ
Overview: A small local organization founded in 1919
Membership: 2,200

Society of Christian Schools in British Columbia (SCSBC)
Fosmark Centre, Trinity Western University, 7600 Glover Rd., Langley BC V2Y 1Y1
Tel: 604-888-6366; *Fax:* 604-888-2791
contact@scsbc.ca
www.scsbc.ca
Previous Name: Southwest British Columbia League of Christian Schools
Overview: A small provincial organization founded in 1976
Chief Officer(s):
Ed Noot, Executive Director
ed.noot@scsbc.ca
Darren Spyksma, Director, Learning
darren.spyksma@scsbc.ca
Greg Gerber, Director, Learning
greg.gerber@scsbc.ca
Karen Bush, Designer, Creative Services
karen.bush@scsbc.ca
Membership: 1-99; *Member Profile:* Christian school campuses & societies in British Columbia
Activities: Monitoring government policies & regulations regarding Christian schoools, & advising schools about government relations; Promoting Christian education throughout British Columbia; Offering workshops; Publishing resource handbooks; Assisting new Christian schools & expanding schools; Supporting digital learning; *Library:* Society of Christian Schools in British Columbia Resource Library
Description: To serve Christian schools in British Columbia; To seek support in the provision of Christian education; To develop

policies & curriculum outlines & units; Affiliation(s): Christian Schools International (CSI); Christian Schools Canada (CSC); Christian Teachers Association of British Columbia; Christian Principals Association of British Columbia

Strathcona Christian Academy Society
1011 Clover Bar Rd., Sherwood Park AB T8A 4V7
Tel: 780-467-4752
karen.beaudet@spac.ca
www.scasociety.ca

Overview: A small local organization founded in 1980
Chief Officer(s):
Jim Huth, Chair
Finances: *Annual Operating Budget:* $3 Million-$5 Million; *Funding Sources:* Regional Government
Staff: 47 staff member(s); 120 volunteer(s)
Description: To challenge students, through Christ-centred education, to know Jesus Christ as Savior & Lord in order to pursue a life of godly character, personal & academic excellence & service to others; *Member of:* Elk Island Public Schools

Union of Spiritual Communities of Christ
1876 Brilliant Rd., Castlegar BC V1N 4K2
Tel: 250-365-3613; *Fax:* 250-365-5477
info@iskra.ca
iskra.ca

Overview: A small national organization
Chief Officer(s):
Stephanie Swetlishoff, Editor
Barry Verigin, Editor
Description: The Union of Spiritual Communities of Christ (USCC) is a registered Canadian charitable society dedicated to the sustainability and enrichment of the Doukhobor Life-Concept based on the Law of God and the Teachings of Jesus Christ

VISION TV
64 Jefferson Ave., Toronto ON M6K 1Y4
Tel: 416-368-3194; *Fax:* 416-368-9774
TTY: 416-216-6311
www.visiontv.ca
Social Media: www.facebook.com/visiontelevision
twitter.com/visiontv

Overview: A medium-sized national charitable organization founded in 1988
Chief Officer(s):
Znaimer Moses, Executive Producer
Finances: *Funding Sources:* Sale of airtime; Advertising; Cable fees
Staff: 3 volunteer(s)
Description: To reflect & illuminate the full spectrum of faith & religious beliefs which make up Canada's diverse society; To build bridges of knowledge & understanding between faiths & cultures; To provide paid access to all eligible religious & faith communities & broadcast ministries; To broadcast non-sectarian programs based on values, ethics, & spirituality concerning a wide variety of issues & themes; *Member of:* Canadian Association of Broadcasters; North American Interfaith Network; Affiliation(s): North American Broadcasters Association

Women's Inter-Church Council of Canada (WICC) / Conseil oecuménique des chrétiennes du Canada
47 Queen's Park Cres. East, Toronto ON M5S 2C3
Tel: 416-929-5184; *Fax:* 416-929-4064
wicc@wicc.org
www.wicc.org
Social Media: www.facebook.com/WICCanada

Overview: A medium-sized national organization founded in 1918
Chief Officer(s):
Patricia Burton-Williams, Executive Director
burton-williams@wicc.org
Finances: *Funding Sources:* World Day of Prayer offerings
Member Profile: Representatives from the Anglican Church of Canada, the Canadian Baptist Ministries, the Christian Church (Disciples of Christ), the Evangelical Lutheran Church in Canada, the Mennonite Central Committee, the Presbyterian Church in Canada, the Religious Society of Friends, the Roman Catholic Church, the Salvation Army, & the United Church of Canada; Membership is by appointment & election; *Committees:* Program; Communications; Membership & Nominating; Finance
Activities: Establishing the Ecumenical Network for Women's Justice; Preparing policy statements on issues such as racial justice & health care; Granting funds for a variety of projects that benefit women & children in Canada & around the world; Coordinating the Fellowship of the Least Coin program in Canada; Providing education, such as theology workshops
Description: To focus on national & international issues affecting women, growth in ecumenism, action for social justice, & the sharing of spirituality & prayer

World Renew (CRWRC)
PO Box 5070, Stn. LCD 1, 3475 Mainway, Burlington ON L7R 3Y8
Tel: 905-336-2920; *Toll-Free:* 800-730-3490
info@worldrenew.net
www.worldrenew.net
Social Media: www.youtube.com/c/SeeWorldRenew;
www.pinterest.com/worldrenew
www.facebook.com/worldrenew
twitter.com/worldrenew_net

Previous Name: Christian Reformed World Relief Committee
Overview: A large international charitable organization founded in 1962
Chief Officer(s):
Ida Mutoigo, Director, 905-336-2920 4303
imutoigo@worldrenew.net
Peter Bulthuis, Director, Church Relations, 905-336-2920 4237
pbulthuis@worldrenew.net
Kristen VanderBerg, Director, Communications & Media Relations, 905-336-2920 4306
kvanderberg@worldrenew.net
Finances: *Funding Sources:* Christian Reformed Churches; CIDA; Other denominations
Staff: 31 staff member(s)
Membership: 15,000-49,999
Activities: *Awareness Events:* World Hunger Week, November; *Internships:* Yes; *Speaker Service:* Yes *Library:* CRWRC Development Education Library (Open to Public)
Description: To engage God's people in redeeming resources & developing gifts in collaborative activities of love, mercy, justice, & compassion; *Member of:* Canadian Foodgrains Bank; Canadian Council of Christian Charities; Canadian Council for International Cooperation.; Affiliation(s): Christian Reformed Church in North America

World-Wide Bible Study Association
PO Box 98590, 873 Jane St., Toronto ON M6N 4C0
richard.kruse@sympatico.ca
www.ibcschool.ca

Also Known As: International Bible Correspondence School
Overview: A small local organization founded in 1968
Chief Officer(s):
Richard Kruse, Director

Wycliffe Bible Translators of Canada, Inc. (WBTC)
4316 - 10th St. NE, Calgary AB T2E 6K3
Tel: 403-250-5411; *Fax:* 403-250-2623
Toll-Free: 800-463-1143
info@wycliffe.ca
www.wycliffe.ca
Social Media: www.youtube.com/wycliffecanada;
www.godtube.com/wycliffecanada
linkedin.com/WycliffeBibleTranslatorsCanada
www.facebook.com/WycliffeCanada
twitter.com/wycliffe_canada

Also Known As: Wycliffe Canada
Overview: A large national charitable organization founded in 1968
Chief Officer(s):
Jannice Moore, Chair
Roy Eyre, President
roy.eyre@wycliffe.ca
Finances: *Annual Operating Budget:* Greater than $5 Million; *Funding Sources:* Charitable donations; CIDA funding for literacy projects
Staff: 400 staff member(s); 75 volunteer(s)
Membership: 400 individual
Activities: Overseas Bible translation & literacy programs; *Internships:* Yes; *Speaker Service:* Yes *Library:* Resource Centre (Open to Public)
Description: To serve minority language groups worldwide by fostering an understanding of God's Word through Bible translation, while encouraging literacy, education & stronger communities; *Member of:* Wycliffe Global Alliance; Affiliation(s): Wycliffe Bible Translators International; Summer Institute of Linguistics; Canada Institute of Linguistics; Wycliffe Associates Canada

Yonge Street Mission (YSM)
306 Gerrard St. East, Toronto ON M5A 2G7
Tel: 416-929-9614; *Fax:* 416-929-7204
Toll-Free: 800-416-5111
info@ysm.ca
www.ysm.ca
Social Media: www.facebook.com/YongeStreetMission
twitter.com/YSM_TO

Overview: A medium-sized local charitable organization founded in 1896
Chief Officer(s):
Angela Draskovic, President & CEO
Shirlene Courtis, Chief Development Officer
Rick Tobias, Mission Community Advocate
Brent Mitchell, Mission Program Officer
Paul Davidson, Mission Administrative Officer
Finances: *Annual Operating Budget:* Greater than $5 Million; *Funding Sources:* Donations; churches; individuals; businesses; foundations; grants
Staff: 120 staff member(s); 4000 volunteer(s)
Activities: Recreation; education; social & family events; relief; housing; *Internships:* Yes; *Speaker Service:* Yes
Description: To bring God's peace, love, & justice to people living with economic, social, & spiritual poverty in Toronto

Youth for Christ Canada
#308, 8047 - 199 St., Langley BC V2Y 0E2
Tel: 604-637-3400; *Fax:* 604-243-6992
Toll-Free: 800-899-9322
info@yfccanada.com
www.yfccanada.com

Overview: A medium-sized national organization
Chief Officer(s):
Dave Brereton, National Director
Shirley Loewen, Office Manager
Membership: 31 chapters + 300 Ministry Centres
Activities: Responsible, effective & culturally sensitive evangelism of youth, communicating & caring in ways that are relevant to this generation
Description: To impact every young person in Canada with the person, work & teachings of Jesus Christ & discipling them into the Church

Yukon Church Heritage Society (YCHS)
PO Box 31461, Whitehorse YT Y1A 6K8
Tel: 867-668-2555; *Fax:* 867-667-6258
logchurch@klondiker.com
yukonmuseums.ca/museum/oldlog/oldlog.html

Also Known As: Old Log Church Museum
Overview: A small provincial charitable organization founded in 1982
Chief Officer(s):
Taryn Parker, Director/Curator
Linda Thistle, President
Finances: *Annual Operating Budget:* $50,000-$100,000
Staff: 1 staff member(s); 8 volunteer(s)
Membership: 25; *Fees:* $15 student/senior; $20 adult; $30 family
Activities: Operates Old Log Church Museum; *Library:* Yes (Open to Public) by appointment
Description: To promote & preserve church history in the Yukon; *Member of:* Yukon Historical & Museums Association; Affiliation(s): Canadian Museums Association

Creationism

Creation Science Association of British Columbia
PO Box 39577, Stn. RPO White Rock, Surrey BC V4A 0A9
Tel: 604-535-0019
info@creationbc.org
www.creationbc.org

Overview: A small provincial charitable organization founded in 1968
Chief Officer(s):
George Pearce, President
Finances: *Annual Operating Budget:* Less than $50,000
Staff: 25 volunteer(s)
Membership: 125 individual; *Fees:* $15 individual
Activities: *Speaker Service:* Yes *Library:* DVD Lending Library by appointment
Description: To compile scientific as well as Biblical evidence that supports creation & contradicts evolution; To communicate this information to schools, churches & the general public

Creation Science of Saskatchewan Inc. (CSSI)
PO Box 26, Kenaston SK S0G 2N0
Tel: 306-252-2842; *Fax:* 306-252-2842
www.creation-science.sk.ca

Overview: A small provincial charitable organization founded in 1978
Chief Officer(s):
Keith Miller, President
Finances: *Annual Operating Budget:* Less than $50,000; *Funding Sources:* Donations
Staff: 13 volunteer(s)
Membership: 15 institutional + 140 individual; *Fees:* $10
Activities: Meetings; speakers; book tables; tours; summer camp; *Speaker Service:* Yes *Library:* Yes by appointment
Description: To share scientific & scriptural evidence for special creation & the Creator

Ecumenism

The Canadian Churches' Forum for Global Ministries / Le forum des églises canadiennes pour les ministères globaux
47 Queen's Park Cres. East, Toronto ON M5S 2C3
Tel: 416-924-9351; *Fax:* 416-978-7821
www.ccforum.ca
Social Media:
www.facebook.com/CanadianChurchesForum
Previous Name: Ecumenical Forum of Canada
Overview: A medium-sized international charitable organization founded in 1921
Chief Officer(s):
Jonathan Schmidt, Co-director
Alice Schuda, Co-director
Finances: *Annual Operating Budget:* $100,000-$250,000; *Funding Sources:* Churches; Religious orders; Individuals
Staff: 2 staff member(s); 30 volunteer(s)
Membership: 1-99
Activities: Mission Personnel Programs, Jan., July & Sept.; Annual Katherine Hockin Award & Dinner; International Visitor; *Library:* Yes by appointment
Description: To provide ecumenical orientation & re-entry programs for mission personnel; To stimulate ecumenical dialogue on issues of mission, global concerns & social justice; To prepare individuals to serve faithfully in mission in an ever-changing world; *Member of:* International Association for Mission Studies; Forum on International Personnel; Affiliation(s): Canadian Council of Churches

The Canadian Council of Churches (CCC) / Le Conseil canadien des Églises
47 Queen's Park Cres. East, 3rd Fl., Toronto ON M5S 2C3
Tel: 416-972-9494; *Fax:* 416-927-0405
info@councilofchurches.ca
www.councilofchurches.ca
Social Media:
www.facebook.com/CCC.CCE
twitter.com/ccc_cce
Overview: A large national charitable organization founded in 1944
Chief Officer(s):
Karen A. Hamilton, General Secretary, 416-972-9494 22, Fax: 416-927-0405
hamilton@councilofchurches.ca
Finances: *Funding Sources:* Member churches
Staff: 6 staff member(s); 2 volunteer(s)
Activities: Sponsoring of Project Ploughshares; Maintaining dialogue with all faith groups
Description: To represent the following churches of Anglican, Eastern Catholic, & Roman Catholic, Eastern Orthodox & Oriental Orthodox, Evangelical & Protestant traditions: The Anglican Church of Canada; Archdiocese of Canada of the Orthodox Church in America; Armenian Holy Apostolic Church, Canadian Diocese; Atlantic Baptist Fellowship; Canadian Baptists of Ontario & Québec; Canadian Baptists of Western Canada; Canadian Conference of Catholic Bishops; Canadian Yearly Meeting of the Religious Society of Friends (Quakers); Christian Church (Disciples of Christ)in Canada; Christian Reformed Church in North America - Canada; The Coptic Orthodox Church of Canada; Ethiopian Orthodox Tewahedo Church of Canada; Evangelical Lutheran Church in Canada; Greek Orthodox Metropolis of Toronto (Canada); The Mar Thoma Syrian Church; Mennonite Church Canada; Polish National Catholic Church;Presbyterian Church in Canada; Regional Synod of Canada - Reformed Church in America; The Salvation Army; Ukrainian Catholic Church; Ukrainian Orthodox Church of Canada; The United Church of Canada; Affiliation(s): British Methodist Episcopal Church of Canada; Citizens for Public Justice; Friendship Ministries Canada; The Knowles-Woodsworth Centre for Theology & Public Policy; The Leprosy Mission Canada

The Churches' Council on Theological Education in Canada: an Ecumenical Foundation (CCTE) / Le Conseil des Églises pour l'éducation théologique au Canada: une fondation oecuménique
47 Queen's Park Cres., Toronto ON M5S 2C3
Tel: 416-928-3223; *Fax:* 416-928-3563
director@ccte.ca
www.ccte.ca
Overview: A small national organization founded in 1962
Chief Officer(s):
Rafael Vallejo, Executive Director
Robert Smith, President
Finances: *Annual Operating Budget:* $100,000-$250,000
Staff: 2 staff member(s); 24 volunteer(s)
Membership: 24 individual
Description: To provide for the coordination of consultation, research, & administration of grants awarded by the Council, in order to promote the development of theological education for ministry; Affiliation(s): Association of Theological Schools

KAIROS: Canadian Ecumenical Justice Initiatives / Initiatives canadiennes oecuméniques pour la justice
#200, 310 Dupont St., Toronto ON M5R 1V9
Tel: 416-463-5312; *Fax:* 416-463-5569
Toll-Free: 877-403-8933
info@kairoscanada.org
www.kairoscanada.org
Social Media: www.youtube.com/user/KAIROSCanada
www.facebook.com/19277141685
twitter.com/kairoscanada
Previous Name: Ecumenical Coalition for Economic Justice; GATT-Fly
Overview: A small national organization founded in 2001
Chief Officer(s):
Jennifer Henry, Executive Director, 416-463-5312 236
jhenry@kairoscanada.org
Ed Bianchi, Manager, Programs, 613-235-9956 221
ebianchi@kairoscanada.org
Finances: *Annual Operating Budget:* $1.5 Million-$3 Million; *Funding Sources:* Member denominations; Religious communities; Individual & group donations; Grants
Staff: 18 staff member(s); 300 volunteer(s)
Membership: 11; *Member Profile:* Canadian Churches; Religious organizations
Activities: *Speaker Service:* Yes
Description: To undertake a program of research & action with churches & popular groups emphasizing coalition-building & social transformation; five churches have participated in the Coalition since its inception: the Anglican Church of Canada, the Canadian Conference of Catholic Bishops, the Evangelical Lutheran Church in Canada, the Presbyterian Church in Canada, the United Church of Canada; *Member of:* Canadian Network on Corporate Accountability; Affiliation(s): Canadian Council of Churches

Student Christian Movement of Canada (SCM) / Mouvement d'étudiant(e)s chrétien(ne)s
#200, 310 Dupont Street, Toronto ON M5R 1V9
Tel: 416-463-7622
info@scmcanada.org
scmcanada.org
Social Media:
www.facebook.com/scmcanada
twitter.com/scmcanada
Overview: A medium-sized national charitable organization founded in 1921
Chief Officer(s):
Rick Garland, General Secretary
Finances: *Annual Operating Budget:* $50,000-$100,000
Staff: 2 staff member(s)
Membership: 500; *Member Profile:* Groups at Canadian universities
Description: National, ecumenical student organization; to encourage members in theological/social reflection & in actions for social change. Offices in Toronto & Winnipeg; *Member of:* World Student Christian Federation

World Association for Christian Communication (WACC) / Association mondiale pour la communication
308 Main St., Toronto ON M4C 4X7
Tel: 416-691-1999; *Fax:* 416-691-1997
info@waccglobal.org
www.waccglobal.org
Social Media: vimeo.com/waccglobal
linkedin.com/company/world-association-for-christian-communication
https://www.facebook.com/WACCglobal
twitter.com/waccglobal
Overview: A small international charitable organization founded in 1968
Chief Officer(s):
Karin Achtelstetter, General Secretary, KA@waccglobal.org
Samuel W. Meshack, President
Finances: *Annual Operating Budget:* $3 Million-$5 Million; *Funding Sources:* Church-related sources; Non-governmental & governmental development agencies; Donations
Staff: 12 staff member(s); 2 volunteer(s)
Membership: 1600 worldwide; *Fees:* US$120 corporate; US$40 personal; US$10 student; *Member Profile:* Individuals, churches, church-related agencies, media producers, educational institutions, secular communication organizations, & persons who share WACC's mission
Activities: Facilitating communication-related projects; Providing seminars, workshops, & publications; Offering outreach programs worldwide; *Speaker Service:* Yes *Library:* Yes by appointment
Description: To promote communication as a basic human right through advocacy & communication; To promote open & diverse media; To strengthen communication networks to advance peace & justice; *Member of:* ACT Alliance, Canadian Church Press, ECOSOC

Episcopalism

Atlantic Episcopal Assembly (AEA) / Assemblée des évêques de l'Atlantique
3 Oakley Ave., Halifax NS B3M 3G6
Tel: 902-443-9325
Overview: A small local organization founded in 1967
Chief Officer(s):
Gérald LeBlanc, Secretary-Treasurer
geraldleblanc@eastlink.ca
François Thibodeau, President
Terrence Prendergast
Finances: *Annual Operating Budget:* Less than $50,000
Membership: 12; *Committees:* Executive; Social Affairs
Description: Proposer l'évangile de Jésus Christ dans les diverses situations de la vie ainsi que ses implications pratiques de notre temps; echange d'information pour les évêques

The Christian Episcopal Church of Canada (CECC)
9280 #2 Rd., Richmond BC V7E 2C8
Tel: 604-275-7422
xnec1662@gmail.com
www.xnec.ca
Also Known As: Traditional Anglican Church in Canada
Overview: A small national charitable organization founded in 1991
Chief Officer(s):
Robert D. Redmile
Finances: *Annual Operating Budget:* $100,000-$250,000; *Funding Sources:* Donations
Staff: 12 staff member(s); 40 volunteer(s)
Membership: 450; *Fees:* Free-will offerings; *Member Profile:* Baptised & confirmed Anglican Christians; *Committees:* Parochial Church Council, Assembly & Consistory; Diocesan Synod & Diocesan Council
Activities: Traditional Anglican faith & worship according to the Book of Common Prayer
Member of: Anglican Communion; Affiliation(s): Christian Episcopal Church in the USA

The Reformed Episcopal Church of Canada - Diocese of Central & Eastern Canada (REC)
PO Box 2532, 320 Armstrong St. N., New Liskeard ON P0J 1P0
Tel: 705-647-4565
trinityfed@hotmail.com
recus.org
Overview: A medium-sized provincial charitable organization founded in 1886
Finances: *Annual Operating Budget:* Less than $50,000; *Funding Sources:* Donations
Staff: 4 volunteer(s)
Membership: 210 + 6 churches; *Committees:* Standing; Constitution & Canons; Church Extension
Activities: Synodical Council, 3rd week of Sept; *Library:* Yes (Open to Public) by appointment

The Reformed Episcopal Church of Canada - Diocese of Western Canada & Alaska (RECWCAN)
Victoria BC
rec-canada.com
Overview: A small national licensing charitable organization founded in 1874
Chief Officer(s):
Charles W. Dorrington, Bishop Ordinary
recwcan@islandnet.com
Finances: *Annual Operating Budget:* Less than $50,000; *Funding Sources:* Offerings; bequests; church assessments
Staff: 2 staff member(s)
Membership: 300; *Fees:* Church offerings
Activities: Douglas House Retirement Home Ministry; Victoria Prayer Counselling; Healing Rooms; *Internships:* Yes; *Speaker Service:* Yes *Library:* Diocesan Office Library by appointment
Description: To reach out to those outside the existing congregation; establish new churches; assist congregations within the Diocese; receive congregations wishing to affiliate with the Reformed Episcopal Church; ordain candidates into the ministry; Affiliation(s): Common Cause Network

Evangelism

Africa Inland Mission International (Canada) (AIM) / Mission à l'intérieur de l'Afrique (Canada)
1641 Victoria Park Ave., Toronto ON M1R 1P8
Tel: 416-751-6077; *Fax:* 416-751-3467
Toll-Free: 877-407-6077
www.aimint.org/can
Social Media:
www.facebook.com/aimcanada
Also Known As: AIM Canada
Overview: A medium-sized international charitable organization founded in 1895
Finances: *Annual Operating Budget:* $1.5 Million-$3 Million; *Funding Sources:* Donations from churches & individuals
Staff: 8 staff member(s); 3 volunteer(s)
Membership: 135; *Committees:* Finance; Personnel; Projects
Description: Evangelization of people within Eastern & Central Africa & Islands around India Ocean; Planting & establishing churches; Training leadership for those churches; Providing medical, educational, & agricultural services; *Member of:* Africa Inland Mission International, Bristol, England; Interdenominational Foreign Mission Association

Associated Gospel Churches (AGC) / Association des églises évangéliques (AEE)
1500 Kerns Rd., Burlington ON L7P 3A7
Tel: 905-634-8184; *Fax:* 905-634-6283
admin@agcofcanada.com
www.agcofcanada.com
Social Media: www.youtube.com/user/donnaagc
www.facebook.com/associatedgospelchurches
Overview: A medium-sized national charitable organization founded in 1925
Chief Officer(s):
Bill Fietje, President
bill@agcofcanada.com
Susan Page, Coordinator, Church Relations
sue@agcofcanada.com
Finances: *Annual Operating Budget:* $250,000-$500,000
Staff: 5 staff member(s)
Membership: 21,400 members; 140+ churches; *Fees:* 4% of revenue minus missions support; *Committees:* Doctrine & Credentials; Church Planting; Church Health & Leadership
Description: To glorify God by partnering together in obedience to the Great Commandment & the Great Commission; to become a movement of healthy, reproducing churches; Affiliation(s): World Relief; World Team; UFM International; Evangelical Fellowship of Canada

Baptist Foundation, Alberta, Saskatchewan & the Territories, Inc. (B-FAST)
PO Box 168, 11525 23 Ave., Edmonton AB T6J 4T3
Tel: 780-451-4878; *Fax:* 780-436-4871
febcast@shaw.ca
www.fellowshipprairies.ca
Overview: A small local organization founded in 1982
Chief Officer(s):
Laurie Kennedy, Regional Director
Membership: 15 individual
Description: Funding capital projects for Fellowship of Evangelical Baptist Churches in Alberta, Saskatchewan & the Territories

Baptist General Conference of Canada (BGCC)
#201, 8315 Davies Rd. NW, Edmonton AB T6E 4N3
Tel: 780-438-9127; *Fax:* 780-435-2478
Toll-Free: 844-438-9127
office@bgc.ca
www.bgc.ca
Overview: A large national charitable organization founded in 1981
Chief Officer(s):
Ed Stuckey, Interim Executive Director
Diane Wiebe, Administrator, Global Ministries
Finances: *Funding Sources:* Churches; individuals; BGC Stewardship Foundation
Staff: 5 staff member(s); 12 volunteer(s)
Membership: 7,000+ individuals + 106 churches; *Member Profile:* Agreement with our Affirmation of Faith, Distinctives & ministry goals
Activities: Global Ministries; new church development; leadership training; youth programs; women's ministries; international development consulting; *Library:* BGC Canada Archives by appointment
Description: To unite churches in a fellowship that is scriptual in doctrine, evangelical in character & irenic (peaceful) in spirit, & seeking to fulfil the Great Commission of Christ (Mt.28: 19-20) in Canada & abroad; *Member of:* Evangelical Fellowship of Canada

The Bible Holiness Movement
PO Box 223, Stn. A, Vancouver BC V6C 2M3
www.bible-holiness-movement.com
Previous Name: Religious Freedom Council of Christian Minorities
Overview: A small local organization founded in 1979
Finances: *Annual Operating Budget:* Less than $50,000
Staff: 4 volunteer(s)
Activities: *Speaker Service:* Yes *Library:* Yes by appointment
Description: To act as a sponsored organization of the Bible Holiness Movement. The Bible Holiness Movement is an aggressive Christian evangelistic and missionary movement.

Billy Graham Evangelistic Association of Canada (BGEAC)
20 Hopewell Ave. NE, Calgary AB T3J 5H5
Tel: 403-219-2300; *Fax:* 403-250-6567
Toll-Free: 800-293-3717
info@bgea.ca
www.billygraham.ca
Social Media: www.youtube.com/user/BillyGrahamCanada
www.facebook.com/BillyGrahamEvangelisticAssociationOfCanada
twitter.com/BGEAnews
Also Known As: BGEA of Canada
Overview: A medium-sized national charitable organization founded in 1968
Chief Officer(s):
Fred Weiss, Executive Director
fweiss@samaritan.ca
Finances: *Annual Operating Budget:* Greater than $5 Million; *Funding Sources:* Donations
Staff: 30 staff member(s)
Activities: Television & radio broadcasts; schools of evangelism; evangelistic crusades; teaching seminars
Description: To expose those who are searching to the message of Christ; To help edify the Christian body in Canada; Affiliation(s): Bill Graham Evangelistic Association USA

Canada's National Bible Hour (CNBH)
c/o Global Outreach Mission, PO Box 1210, St Catharines ON L2R 7A7
Tel: 905-684-1401; *Fax:* 905-684-3069
www.missiongo-radio.org/cnbh
Social Media: www.youtube.com/user/missiongo
www.facebook.com/168935979827368
Overview: A small national organization founded in 1925
Chief Officer(s):
Brian Albrecht, President, GOM
Description: The Hour is a bible-teaching ministry, & Canada's oldest religious broadcast, heard from coast to coast. It is sponsored by Global Outreach Mission (GOM), an organization dedicated to evangelism & missions; *Member of:* Global Outreach Mission

Child Evangelism Fellowship of Canada
PO Box 165, Stn. Main, 337 Henderson Hwy., Winnipeg MB R3C 2G9
Tel: 204-943-2774; *Fax:* 204-943-9967
Toll-Free: 866-943-2774
info@cefcanada.org
www.cefcanada.org
Also Known As: CEF Canada
Overview: A medium-sized national charitable organization founded in 1937
Chief Officer(s):
Jerry Hanson, National Director
jhanson@cefcanada.org
Brenda Hanson, Director, Education
bhanson@cefcanada.org
Finances: *Annual Operating Budget:* $500,000-$1.5 Million; *Funding Sources:* Individual, corporate & church donations
Staff: 45 staff member(s); 200 volunteer(s)
Membership: 1-99
Activities: Children's Ministries Institute; offers courses/programs, materials & training for Christian education among children
Description: CEF Canada is a bible-centred organization of born-again believers whose purpose is to evangelize & disciple children with the gospel of Jesus Christ; *Member of:* Canadian Council of Christian Charities; Affiliation(s): Child Evangelism Fellowship Inc.; CEF of Nations

The Christian & Missionary Alliance in Canada (C&MA) / L'Alliance chrétienne et missionnaire au Canada
#100, 30 Carrier Dr., Toronto ON M9W 5T7
Tel: 416-674-7878; *Fax:* 416-674-0808
info@cmacan.org
www.cmacan.org/home
Social Media: www.youtube.com/user/cmacan
www.facebook.com/CMAllianceinCanada
twitter.com/CMAinCanada
Also Known As: The Alliance Church
Overview: A large national charitable organization founded in 1981
Chief Officer(s):
David Hearn, President
Finances: *Annual Operating Budget:* Greater than $5 Million; *Funding Sources:* Donations
Staff: 1642 staff member(s)
Membership: 430 churches + 48,922 baptized + 132,323 inclusive members + 205 Canadian International Workers
Description: To proclaim the truth of God's Word & to disciple people of all nations, particularly where Christ has not been named, emphasizing the Lordship of Jesus Christ & the person & work of the Holy Spirit, & looking for the coming of the Lord; to establish & nurture churches related in fellowship with C&MA around the world, dedicated to evangelism & missions; to establish local churches throughout Canada; to teach & train believers for the work of the ministry of Christ; to provide fellowship for individual believers of kindred spirit with one another without affecting their denominational relations; to encourage the cooperation of such evangelical groups of churches or Christians as may be disposed to send their missionaries through C&MA & contribute their missionary offerings through the general treasury; *Member of:* Canadian Council of Christian Charities; Alliance World Fellowship; Affiliation(s): Alliance Life Magazine; Al Hayat Ministries; Evangelical Fellowship of Canada

Emmanuel Relief & Rehabilitation International (Canada) (EIC)
PO Box 4050, 3967 Stouffville Rd., Stouffville ON L4A 8B6
Tel: 905-640-2111; *Fax:* 905-640-2186
Toll-Free: 866-269-6312
info@eicanada.org
www.eicanada.org
Social Media:
linkedin.com/company/emmanuel-international-canada
www.facebook.com/239293974881
Also Known As: Emmanuel International
Overview: A large national charitable organization founded in 1983
Chief Officer(s):
Richard McGowan, Executive Director, Canada
Finances: *Annual Operating Budget:* $1.5 Million-$3 Million; *Funding Sources:* Government; donations
Staff: 14 staff member(s); 3 volunteer(s)
Membership: 1-99; *Member Profile:* Seven National Affiliates: Australia, Brazil, Canada, Malawi, The Philippines, The United Kingdom & The United States
Activities: Development, relief, rehabilitation & spiritual outreach programs; *Internships:* Yes
Description: To encourage, strengthen, & assist churches worldwide to meet the spiritual & physical needs of the poor in accordance with the Holy Scriptures through programs of relief, rehabilitation, community development, evangelism, & church planting; *Member of:* Canadian Council of Christian Charities

Evangelical Covenant Church of Canada (ECCC)
PO Box 23117, RPO McGillvray, Winnipeg MB R3R 5S3
Tel: 204-269-3437; *Fax:* 204-269-3584
office@covchurch.ca
www.canadacovenantchurch.org
Overview: A medium-sized national charitable organization founded in 1904
Chief Officer(s):
Jeff Anderson, ECCC Conference Superintendent
ccc1@mts.net
Finances: *Funding Sources:* Donations
Member Profile: Evangelical Covenant Churches in Canada
Member of: World Relief Canada; The Evangelical Fellowship of Canada; The Canadian Council of Christian Charities

Evangelical Fellowship of Canada (EFC) / Alliance évangélique du Canada
PO Box 5885, Stn. Beaver Creek, #103, 9821 Leslie St., Richmond Hill ON L4B 0B8
Tel: 905-479-4742; *Toll-Free:* 866-302-3362
efc@evangelicalfellowship.ca
www.evangelicalfellowship.ca
Social Media: www.youtube.com/user/theEFCca
www.facebook.com/theefc
twitter.com/theefc
Overview: A medium-sized national charitable organization founded in 1964
Chief Officer(s):
Bill Fietje, Chair
Bruce J. Clemenger, President
Finances: *Annual Operating Budget:* $1.5 Million-$3 Million; *Funding Sources:* General & corporate donations; member & subscriber fees
Staff: 20 staff member(s); 90 volunteer(s)
Membership: 42 evangelical denominations + 64 organizations + 37 educational institutions + 1,000 churches
Activities: Task forces: Evangelism; Women in Ministry; Aboriginal; Global Mission; Commissions: Education; Religious Liberty; Social Action; *Internships:* Yes; *Speaker Service:* Yes
Description: EFC is the national association of evangelical Christians in Canada. Its aims are to be a public advocate of the gospel of Jesus Christ; to provide an evangelical identity which unites Canadian Christians of diverse backgrounds; to express biblical views on current issues; to assist individuals & groups in proclaiming the gospel & advancing Christian values; *Member of:* World Evangelical Fellowship

The Evangelical Order of Certified Pastoral Counsellors of America (EOCPCA)
3350 Fairview St., Burlington ON L7N 3L5
Tel: 905-639-0137; *Fax:* 905-333-8901
eocpc@cogeco.ca
www.eocpc.com
Previous Name: Order of Certified Pastoral Counsellors of America
Overview: A medium-sized national organization founded in 1982
Chief Officer(s):
Stephen Hambly, Contact
Finances: *Annual Operating Budget:* $500,000-$1.5 Million
Staff: 3 staff member(s)
Membership: 1,200 individual; *Fees:* $100-400
Description: To promote a Christian-oriented order; to certify & accredit pastoral counsellors by federal charter; *Member of:* Canadian Christian Counsellors Association; Canadian Christian Clinical Counsellors College; Affiliation(s): California State Christian University

Evangelical Tract Distributors (EDT)
PO Box 146, Edmonton AB T5J 2G9
Tel: 780-477-1538; *Fax:* 780-477-3795
www.evangelicaltract.com
Overview: A small national organization founded in 1935
Chief Officer(s):
John Harder, President/Managing Director
Description: EDT is a non-profit organization that prints & distributes Christian gospel tracts free of charge. It is a registered charity, BN: 130522659RR0001.

Fellowship of Evangelical Baptist Churches in Canada
PO Box 457, 351 Elizabeth St., Guelph ON N1H 6K9
Tel: 519-821-4830; *Fax:* 519-821-9829
www.fellowship.ca
Also Known As: The Fellowship
Overview: A large national organization
Chief Officer(s):
Steven Jones, President, 519-821-4830 231
sjones@fellowship.ca
Finances: *Annual Operating Budget:* Greater than $5 Million
Staff: 16 staff member(s)
Membership: 500+ churches
Activities: *Library:* Archives
Description: To glorify God & to proclaim the good news of Jesus Christ, evangelizing our generation & producing healthy, growing churches in Canada & around the world; *Member of:* The Evangelical Fellowship of Canada; Affiliation(s): Association d'églises baptistes évangéliques au québec

Fondation Père-Ménard
1195, rue Sauvé est, Montréal QC H2C 1Z8
Tél: 514-274-7645; *Téléc:* 514-274-7647
Ligne sans frais: 800-665-7645
info@fondationperemenard.org
www.fondationperemenard.org
Média social:
www.facebook.com/145827832121166
Aperçu: *Dimension:* petite; *Envergure:* internationale; *Organisme sans but lucratif; fondée en 1970*
Membre(s) du bureau directeur:
Miriam Castro Herrera, Directrice générale
mcastro@fondationperemenard.org
Finances: *Budget de fonctionnement annuel:* $1.5 Million-$3 Million
Personnel: 3 membre(s) du personnel; 10 bénévole(s)
Membre: 15 000+
Description: Améliorer de façon durable la qualité de vie des populations défavorisées des pays en développement, principalement en Amérique du sud, en encourageant et soutenant l'établissement et la gestion de projets communautaires en santé, éducation, eau et alimentation ainsi que la formation de leaders spirituels locaux

Foursquare Gospel Church of Canada
#307, 2099 Lougheed Hwy., Port Coquitlam BC V3B 1A8
Tel: 604-941-8414; *Fax:* 604-941-8415
Toll-Free: 866-941-8414
info@foursquare.ca
www.foursquare.ca
Overview: A medium-sized national charitable organization founded in 1981
Chief Officer(s):
Steve Falkiner, President
Finances: *Annual Operating Budget:* $250,000-$500,000
Staff: 3 staff member(s)
Membership: 67 churches
Member of: Evangelical Fellowship of Canada

Full Gospel Business Men's Fellowship in Canada (FGBMFI)
2891 Martin Rd., Blezard Valley ON P0M 1E0
Tel: 416-449-7272; *Fax:* 416-449-9743
Toll-Free: 877-296-1715
www.fgbmfi.ca
Social Media:
www.facebook.com/groups/5807578145
Overview: A medium-sized national charitable organization founded in 1964
Chief Officer(s):
Ron Hutzal, President
Finances: *Annual Operating Budget:* $100,000-$250,000
Staff: 2 staff member(s); 2 volunteer(s)
Membership: 1,000-4,999; *Fees:* $60 individual
Activities: National convention; *Internships:* Yes; *Speaker Service:* Yes
Description: To reach men at all levels of our modern society, calling them to God, & releasing them into their respective gifts & talents through the Holy Spirit; *Member of:* Full Gospel Business Men's Fellowship International

Gideons International in Canada / Les Gédéons - L'Association Internationale des Gédéons au Canada
PO Box 3619, 501 Imperial Rd. North, Guelph ON N1H 7A2
Tel: 519-823-1140; *Fax:* 519-767-1913
Toll-Free: 888-482-4253
info@gideons.ca
www.gideons.ca
Social Media: www.youtube.com/user/GideonsCanadaMedia
linkedin.com/company/the-gideons-international-in-canada
www.facebook.com/gideonscanada
twitter.com/GideonsCanada
Overview: A medium-sized international charitable organization founded in 1911
Chief Officer(s):
Paul Mercer, Executive Director
Finances: *Annual Operating Budget:* Greater than $5 Million; *Funding Sources:* Membership fees; voluntary donations; funds from other registered charities
Membership: 4,500; *Fees:* $100; *Member Profile:* Christian business & professional people
Activities: Sharing faith; Placing Bibles & New Testaments to the public; Distributing New Testaments to selected groups
Description: The interdenominational lay association communicates/gives away freecopies of God's Word in Canada & around the world.

Good News Broadcasting Association of Canada
PO Box 246, Stn. A, Abbotsford BC V2T 6Z6
Toll-Free: 800-663-2425
bttb@backtothebible.ca
www.backtothebible.ca
Social Media:
www.facebook.com/BTTBCanada
twitter.com/BTTBC
Also Known As: Back to the Bible Canada
Overview: A small local charitable organization
Chief Officer(s):
Byron Reaume, CFO & Director of Stewardship
Bob Beasley, CEO
Member of: Canadian Council of Christian Charities; Evangelican Fellowship of Canada

Lighthouse Mission
669 Main St., Winnipeg MB R3B 1E3
Tel: 204-943-9669; *Fax:* 204-949-9479
info@lighthousemission.ca
www.lighthousemission.ca
Overview: A small local organization founded in 1911
Chief Officer(s):
Joel Cormie, Operations Manager
Activities: Operates a soup kitchen; distributes clothing to the needy
Description: Provides food and services to the needy in Winnipeg.

Living Bible Explorers (LBE)
600 Burnell St., Winnipeg MB R3G 2B7
Tel: 204-786-8667; *Fax:* 204-775-7525
Toll-Free: 866-786-8667
lbe@mymts.net
livingbibleexplorers.com
Social Media:
www.facebook.com/livingbibleexplorers
Overview: A small local charitable organization founded in 1969
Chief Officer(s):
George Hill, General Manager
george_t_hill@hotmail.com
MaryAnn Funk, Girls Program Coordinator
Michelle MacGibbon, Teen Girls Coordinator
Mark Henkleman, Teen Boys Coordinator
Ben Krocker, Childrens Program Coordinator
Diana Cuthbertson, Volunteer Coordinator
Randal Moroski, Ministry Worker
Finances: *Annual Operating Budget:* $250,000-$500,000; *Funding Sources:* Individual and cooperate donations; Provincial government; individual churches; foundations
Staff: 10 staff member(s); 200 volunteer(s)
Membership: 700 individual; *Member Profile:* Manitobans who have a tangible interest by working, volunteering or giving to the work; *Committees:* New Bible Camp; Board of Directors
Activities: Boys & Girls Clubs; summer camps; weekend camps; weekly kids church; teens church; food distribution; weekly home visitation; annual banquet, Mar. Currently constructing a New Bible Camp for children in Hadoshville, Manitoba.; *Awareness Events:* Mission Fest - Feb; Annual Fundraising Banquet - Mar; Garage Sale - May; *Internships:* Yes; *Speaker Service:* Yes *Library:* Resource Library (Open to Public)
Description: To develop relationships with children & teens from inner city homes in an effort to evangelize them & to promote discipleship with a view to integrating them into the life & care of Bible-believing churches; *Member of:* Canadian Council of Christian Charities

SIM Canada
10 Huntingdale Blvd., Toronto ON M1W 2S5
Tel: 416-497-2424; *Fax:* 416-497-2444
Toll-Free: 800-294-6918
info@sim.ca
www.sim.ca
Social Media: www.youtube.com/simcanadavideo
www.facebook.com/SIMCANADA1
twitter.com/SIMCANADA1
Also Known As: Serving In Mission
Previous Name: Society for International Ministries
Overview: A small international organization founded in 1893
Chief Officer(s):
John Denbok, Executive Director
Finances: *Annual Operating Budget:* $3 Million-$5 Million
Staff: 30 staff member(s)
Membership: 300
Activities: *Speaker Service:* Yes
Description: To evangelize the unreached & minister to human need

Solbrekken Evangelistic Association of Canada
PO Box 44220, Stn. Garside, Edmonton AB T5V 1N6
Tel: 780-460-8444
mswm@shaw.ca
www.mswm.org
Also Known As: Max Solbrekken World Mission
Overview: A small national charitable organization founded in 1961
Chief Officer(s):
Max Solbrekken, President
Donna Solbrekken, Secretary
Description: To promote the gospel; Affiliation(s): Europa for Kristus, Oslo, Norway

TEAM of Canada Inc. (TEAM)
#372, 16 Midlake Blvd. SE, Calgary AB T2X 2X7
Toll-Free: 800-295-4160
info@teamcanada.org
www.teamcanada.org
Social Media: instagram.com/teammissions
www.facebook.com/125163240888381
twitter.com/team
Also Known As: The Evangelical Alliance Mission of Canada Inc.
Overview: A medium-sized international charitable organization founded in 1969
Chief Officer(s):
Ralph Friebel, Chair
Scott Henson, International Director
Finances: *Annual Operating Budget:* $1.5 Million-$3 Million
Staff: 6 staff member(s)
Membership: 1-99
Activities: *Internships:* Yes; *Speaker Service:* Yes *Library:* Resource Centre
Description: To help churches send missionaries to establish reproducing churches among the nations, to the Glory of God; *Member of:* Canadian Council of Christian Charities

Friends

Canadian Friends Service Committee (CFSC) / Secours Quaker Canadien
60 Lowther Ave., Toronto ON M5R 1C7
Tel: 416-920-5213; *Fax:* 416-920-5214
cfsc@quakerservice.ca
quakerservice.ca
Social Media:
facebook.com/112772730148
twitter.com/CFSCQuakers
Also Known As: Religious Society of Friends (Quakers)
Overview: A medium-sized national charitable organization founded in 1931
Chief Officer(s):
Jane Orion Smith, General Secretary
janeorion@quakerservice.ca
Matthew Legge, Administration & Communications
matt@quakerservice.ca
Finances: *Annual Operating Budget:* $500,000-$1.5 Million; *Funding Sources:* Individuals; meetings
Staff: 7 staff member(s); 40 volunteer(s)
Activities: Peace & social justice work; *Internships:* Yes; *Speaker Service:* Yes *Library:* Friends House Library (Open to Public)
Description: To unify & expand the concerns of Friends (Quakers); *Member of:* The Canadian Council of Churches; Kairos: Canadian Ecumenical Justice Initiatives; Project Ploughshares; Canadian Council for Refugees; War Resistors Support Campaign

Friends Historical Association (FHA)
Quaker Collection, Haverford College, 370 Lancaster Ave., Haverford PA 19041-1392 USA
Tel: 610-896-1161; *Fax:* 610-896-1102
fha@haverford.edu
www.haverford.edu/library/fha
Overview: A medium-sized international charitable organization founded in 1873
Chief Officer(s):
Kenneth Carroll, President Emeritus
Finances: *Annual Operating Budget:* Less than $50,000; *Funding Sources:* Membership dues; subscriptions; donations
Staff: 1 staff member(s); 21 volunteer(s)
Membership: 800; *Fees:* $15; *Member Profile:* Friends & interested historians
Activities: Pilgrimages to historic Friends Meetings; lectures; *Rents Mailing List:* Yes
Description: To promote the study, preservation & publication of material relating to the history of the Religious Society of Friends; Affiliation(s): Conference of Quaker Historians & Archivists

Friends Historical Society - London (FHS)
c/o Friends House, 173 Euston Rd., London NW1 2BJ United Kingdom
Social Media:
www.facebook.com/QuakersinBritain
twitter.com/BritishQuakers
Overview: A small international organization founded in 1903
Finances: *Funding Sources:* Membership fees
Membership: 400
Description: To encourage the study of Quaker history; *Member of:* Association of Denominational Historical Societies & Cognate Libraries

Hare Krishna

Toronto's Hare Krishna Centre (ISKCON) / Subuddhi Deri Dasi
243 Avenue Rd., Toronto ON M5R 2J6
Tel: 416-922-5415; *Fax:* 416-922-1021
info@torontokrishna.com
iskcontoronto.blogspot.ca
Social Media:
twitter.com/TempleCouncil
Also Known As: ISKCON Toronto
Previous Name: International Society for Krishna Consciousness (Toronto Branch)
Overview: A medium-sized local charitable organization founded in 1966
Finances: *Annual Operating Budget:* $3 Million-$5 Million; *Funding Sources:* Donations from congregations & festivals
Staff: 10 staff member(s); 20 volunteer(s)
Membership: 700 institutional; 2,000 individual; *Fees:* $1,100
Activities: Distribution of free food; taking care of seniors & youth; *Internships:* Yes *Library:* Yes (Open to Public)
Description: To preach Krishna Consciousness around the world, following in the footsteps of the founder & spiritual master, His Divine Grace A.C. Bhaktivedanta Swami Prabhupada.

Hinduism

Hindu Society of Alberta
14225 - 133 Ave., Edmonton AB T5L 4W3
Tel: 780-451-5130
hindu.society@hotmail.com
www.hindusociety.ab.ca
Social Media:
www.facebook.com/hindusociety.ab.ca
twitter.com/Hindu_Society
Overview: A small provincial charitable organization founded in 1967
Chief Officer(s):
Hansa Thaleshvar, President, 587-269-3440
hthalesh@gmail.com
Activities: Classes in yoga & meditation; language classes; lectures & seminars on history & religion; religious celebrations; music & dance performances; hall rentals; *Library:* library
Description: The Society is a cultural, social & religious institute catering to the needs of those influenced by Hinduism.

Yasodhara Ashram Society
PO Box 9, Kootenay Bay BC V0B 1X0
Tel: 250-227-9224; *Fax:* 250-227-9494
Toll-Free: 800-661-8711
info@yasodhara.org
www.yasodhara.org
Overview: A small international charitable organization founded in 1963
Finances: *Annual Operating Budget:* $500,000-$1.5 Million
Staff: 15 volunteer(s)
Membership: 125; *Fees:* $25
Activities: *Internships:* Yes; *Speaker Service:* Yes *Library:* Yes by appointment
Description: To maintain a centre for adults engaged in a life of spiritual intent; to provide instruction in & opportunities for religious & spiritual practice

Islam/Muslim

Ahmadiyya Muslim Centre
525 Kylemore Ave., Winnipeg MB R3L 1B5
Tel: 204-475-2642; *Fax:* 204-452-2455
www.ahmadiyya.ca
Overview: A small local organization founded in 1979
Membership: 1-99
Activities: *Library:* Yes

Ahmadiyya Muslim Jamaat Canada
10610 Jane St., Maple ON L6A 3A2
Tel: 905-303-4000; *Fax:* 905-832-3220
info@ahmadiyya.ca
www.ahmadiyya.ca
Also Known As: Ahmadiyya Muslim Community Canada
Overview: A medium-sized national charitable organization
Chief Officer(s):
Lal Khan Malik, President
Abdul Aziz Khalifa, Vice-President
Aslam Daud, Secretary
Khalid Naeem, Treasurer
Rana Manzoor Ahmed, Librarian, 905-832-2669 2245
Finances: *Annual Operating Budget:* Greater than $5 Million
Staff: 30 staff member(s); 1,00 volunteer(s)
Activities: Offering religious education; muslim TV (www.mta.tv); *Internships:* Yes; *Speaker Service:* Yes *Library:* Ahmadiyya Muslim Jamaat Canada Library (Open to Public) by appointment
Description: To promote interfaith understanding; Affiliation(s): The Ahmadiyya Muslim Medical Association of Canada (AMMAC)

ANNISAA Organization of Canada (ANNISAA)
111 - 7 St. Dennis Dr., Toronto ON M3C 1E4
Tel: 647-761-0745
info@annisaa.org
annisaa.org
Social Media:
www.facebook.com/179651935453963
twitter.com/ANNISAAORG
Overview: A medium-sized national organization founded in 2012
Member Profile: Practising Muslim women
Description: ANNISAA aims to promote the best interest of all Muslim women and their families within the Canadian society, providing a voice for Muslim women. ANNISAA promotes an interest in education, research, sports and recreation, social development, Islamic spiritual advancement and moral values, as well as sponsoring literary, art and other educational and cultural events, festivals, and conventions for the promotion of Islam and Muslims.

Association des Projets charitables Islamiques (AICP) / Association of Islamic Charitable Projects
6691, av du Parc, Montréal QC H2V 4J1
Tel: 514-274-6194; *Fax:* 514-274-0011
www.aicp.ca
Social Media: www.youtube.com/user/aicpmultimediamtl
www.facebook.com/AicpCanada
twitter.com/AICP_CANADA
Overview: A small local organization
Activities: Yearly pilgrimage trip; Madih group; marriage contracts; funerary services
Description: Dénonce tout acte de terrorisme et promouvoit le support envers la communauté musulmane

Canadian Council of Muslim Women (CCMW) / Conseil canadien des femmes musulmanes
PO Box 154, Gananoque ON K7G 2T7
Tel: 613-382-2847
info@ccmw.com
www.ccmw.com
Social Media:
www.youtube.com/channel/UCOF-BIKxWy8jjPOL12GGY0A
linkedin.com/company/ccmw
www.facebook.com/CCMWNational
twitter.com/ccmwcanada
Overview: A medium-sized national organization founded in 1982
Chief Officer(s):
Razia Jaffer, President
Alia Hogben, Executive Director
aliahogben@gmail.com
Finances: *Annual Operating Budget:* Less than $50,000; *Funding Sources:* Fundraising; Public funds
Staff: 3 staff member(s); 50+ volunteer(s)
Membership: 100+; *Member Profile:* Practising Muslim women
Activities: Implementing projects and toolkits
Description: To assist Muslim women in participating effectively in Canadian society;To promote mutual understanding with women of other faiths; To strengthen the bonds of sisterhood among Muslim communities & individuals

International Development & Relief Foundation (IDRF)
908 The East Mall, 1st Fl., Toronto ON M9B 6K2
Tel: 416-497-0818; *Fax:* 416-497-0686
Toll-Free: 866-497-4373
office@idrf.ca
www.idrf.ca
Social Media: www.youtube.com/IDRFCANADA
linkedin.com/pub/idrf-canada
www.facebook.com/IDRFCANADA
twitter.com/IDRF
Overview: A small international organization founded in 1984
Chief Officer(s):
Zeib Jeeva, Chair
Jessica Ferne, Director, Programs
Maheen A. Rashdi, Manager, Communications, Events, Media & Volunteers
Finances: *Annual Operating Budget:* $500,000-$1.5 Million
Staff: 9 staff member(s)
Member Profile: People who regularly donate $100 or more yearly
Activities: Providing relief, rehabilitation & development aid to communities in need, both overseas & in Canada; *Speaker Service:* Yes

Description: To empower the disadvantaged peoples of the world, through emergency relief & participatory development programs based on the Islamic principles of human dignity, self-reliance, & social justice; Affiliation(s): Canadian Council for International Cooperation

Islamic Association of Nova Scotia (IANS)
PO Box 103-136, 287 Lacewood Dr., Dartmouth NS B3M 3Y7
Tel: 902-469-9490
info@islamnovascotia.ca
www.islamnovascotia.ca
Previous Name: Islamic Association of the Maritimes
Overview: A small local organization founded in 1966
Chief Officer(s):
Iftikhar Baig, President, 902-471-8998
Sami Mirza, Vice President
Fees: $50 single; $100 family; $25 student

Islamic Association of Saskatchewan (Saskatoon)
222 Copland Cres., Saskatoon SK S7H 2Z5
Tel: 306-665-6424
info@islamiccenter.sk.ca
www.islamiccenter.sk.ca
Overview: A small provincial organization founded in 1968
Chief Officer(s):
Omaer Jamil, President
president@islamiccenter.sk.ca
Areeb Faruqi, Secretary
Fees: $40 family; $25 single; *Committees:* The Muslim Communications and Outreach Committee (MCOC); The Takaful Fund Committee (TFC); The Strategic Planning Committee (SPC); The Constitution Review Committee (CRC)
Activities: Operates Islamic Centre; represents Muslims; provides activities; responsible for Muslim Cemetery
Affiliation(s): Multi-Faith Group; Saskatchewan Organization for Heritage Language; Saskatchewan Intercultural Association; Saskatchewan Forum for "Racialized" Canadians; Saskatchewan Council for International Cooperation

Islamic Care Centre (ICC)
312 Lisgar St., Ottawa ON K2P 0E2
Tel: 613-232-0210; *Fax:* 613-232-0210
info@islamcare.ca
www.islamcare.ca
Also Known As: Daw'ah Centre
Overview: A small national charitable organization founded in 1999
Chief Officer(s):
Omar Mahfoudhi, Executive Director
Finances: *Annual Operating Budget:* $50,000-$100,000
Staff: 2 staff member(s); 10 volunteer(s)
Membership: 35; *Fees:* $50
Activities: *Speaker Service:* Yes *Library:* Islamic Information (Open to Public)
Description: Islam Care Centre provides the Canadian (Ottawa) Muslim community with resources to meet religious and social needs with the objective of establishing a better relationship with the larger Canadian society; *Member of:* Muslim Community Council of Ottawa; Affiliation(s): Islam Care Centre

Islamic Foundation of Toronto (IFT)
441 Nugget Ave., Toronto ON M1S 5E1
Tel: 416-321-0909; *Fax:* 416-321-1995
info@islamicfoundation.ca
www.islamicfoundation.ca
Social Media: www.youtube.com/user/islamicfoundationca
www.facebook.com/iftlive
twitter.com/iftlive
Also Known As: Nugget Mosque
Overview: A small local charitable organization founded in 1969
Chief Officer(s):
Shakil Akhter, Administrator, 416-321-0909 233
Shabbir Gangat, Coordinator, Funerals, 416-876-3000
Finances: *Annual Operating Budget:* $3 Million-$5 Million
Staff: 72 staff member(s)
Membership: 1,000-4,999; *Committees:* Dawah; Library; School Board; Social Services
Activities: Full time Islamic school, JK to Grade 10; part-time evening Islamic school; Arabic language centre for adults; Friday & Sunday schools

Islamic Information Foundation (IIF)
8 Laurel Lane, Halifax NS B3M 2P6
Tel: 902-445-2494; *Fax:* 902-445-2494
iif@geocities.com
www.institutealislam.com/dr-jamal-badawi
Overview: A small national charitable organization founded in 1981
Chief Officer(s):
Jamal Badawi, Founder & Chair
Jamal.Badawi@StMarys.ca

Finances: *Annual Operating Budget:* $100,000-$250,000; *Funding Sources:* Sale of religious material; donations
Staff: 4 volunteer(s)
Membership: 40 individuals
Activities: *Speaker Service:* Yes
Description: To promote better understanding of Islam among Muslims & Christians through information provided in print, audio & video forms & through lecture, seminars & interfaith dialogues

Islamic Propagation Centre of Ontario (IPC)
Jame Masjid Mississauga, 5761 Coopers Ave., Mississauga ON L4Z 1R9
Tel: 905-507-3323
Secretary@jamemasjid.org
www.jamemasjid.org
Also Known As: Jama Masjid Mississauga
Previous Name: Islamic Propagation Centre International (Canada)
Overview: A small local charitable organization founded in 1984
Chief Officer(s):
Nafis Bhayat, Director, Religious Services, 416-844-9373
Imamjamemasjid.org
Finances: *Annual Operating Budget:* $50,000-$100,000
Staff: 2 staff member(s); 100 volunteer(s)
Membership: 100 student; 1,000 individual; *Fees:* $200 individual; *Committees:* Fundraising; Eid & Ramadhan; Executive
Activities: Congregation; marriages; family counselling; summer & evening school for kids; *Speaker Service:* Yes *Library:* IPC Office Library (Open to Public) by appointment
Description: The Centre offers a selection of resource material for those interested in learning about Islam. Topics covered include comparative religion, history, culture, lifestyle, politics, law & women in Islam. It is a registered charity, BN: 886810191RR0001.

Manitoba Islamic Association (MIA)
2445 Waverley St., Winnipeg MB R3Y 1S3
Tel: 204-256-1347
www.miaonline.org
Social Media:
www.facebook.com/ManitobaIslamicAssociation
Overview: A small provincial organization founded in 1976
Chief Officer(s):
Ismael Mukhtar, President
Khaled Al-Nahar, Office Manager
Fees: $30; *Member Profile:* Muslim persons in Manitoba who abide by the association's rules & regulations; *Committees:* Takaful Fund
Activities: Accepting applications for financial assistance, through the Takaful Fund; Providing funeral services to the Muslim community, through partnership with Cropo Funeral Services; Offering services for marriage; Conducting Sunday Qur'an classes for children & the MIA Al Nur Weekend Islamic School; Sponsoring the Al-Hamd Learning Center, which offers an Arabic & Islamic educational program for preschoolers; *Library:* Al-Hikmah (Wisdom) Library (Open to Public) by appointment
Description: Large collection of English and Arabic books on major Islamic sciences & theology

Muslim Association of Canada (MAC)
2270 Speakman Dr., Mississauga ON L5K 1B4
Tel: 905-822-2626; *Fax:* 905-822-2727
mac@macnet.ca
www.macnet.ca
Overview: A medium-sized national organization
Chief Officer(s):
Abu Nazir, CPA, CMA, Chair
Activities: Schools & community centres; educational & other projects; youth projects; outreach
Description: Seeks to promote a balanced, constructive & integrated Islamic presence in Canada; operates in 13 Canadian cities

Muslim Association of New Brunswick (MANB)
1100 Rothesay Rd., Saint John NB E2H 2H8
Tel: 506-633-1675
info@manb.ca
www.manb.ca
Overview: A medium-sized provincial organization
Chief Officer(s):
Husni Abou El Niaj, President
Activities: *Library:* Yes
Description: The Muslim Association of New Brunswick (MANB) is a Saint John-based, nonprofit organization found to present, serve, & educate the Muslim community in the Saint John Area. MANB aims to strengthen access to Islamic education, facilitate community outreach & interaction with other religious organizations & community groups, consolidate the social fabric of the community, & sustain Islamic work by encouraging & building endowments.

Muslim Community of Québec (MCQ) / Communauté musulmane du Québec (CMQ)
7445, av Chester, Montréal QC H4V 1M4
Tel: 514-484-2967; *Fax:* 514-484-3802
mrdeen25@hotmail.com
www.muslimcommunityofquebec.com
Also Known As: Mosque of Montréal
Overview: A small local organization founded in 1979
Chief Officer(s):
Muhammed Romizuddin, Contact
Finances: *Annual Operating Budget:* $500,000-$1.5 Million
Membership: 500
Activities: *Speaker Service:* Yes
Description: To facilitate Muslim religious life

Muslim Council of Montreal (MCM)
PO Box 180, Stn. St-Laurent, Montréal QC H4L 4Z8
Tel: 514-748-8427
info@muslimcouncil.org
www.muslimcouncil.org
Overview: A small local organization
Finances: *Annual Operating Budget:* Less than $50,000
Staff: 5 volunteer(s)
Membership: 40 Muslim institutions
Description: Seeks effective cooperation among Islamic organizations & Muslims of all nationalities or schools of thought; seeks better understanding of Islam; assists media by open discussion; takes part in multicultural activities

Muslim Education & Welfare Foundation of Canada (MEWFC)
Southbourne Centre, 2580 McGill St., Vancouver BC V5K 1H1
Tel: 604-255-9941
al.iman.education.metrotown@gmail.com
Also Known As: Al Iman Education
Overview: A medium-sized national charitable organization founded in 1987
Activities: *Library:* Jannat Bibi Library
Description: To provide for the educational, religious & welfare needs of the Muslim community

Muslim World League - Canada
2550 Argentia Rd., Mississauga ON L5N 5R1
Tel: 905-542-1050; *Fax:* 905-542-1054
mwl@mwlcanada.org
themwl.org/GLOBAL/node/1205
Overview: A small national organization founded in 1985
Chief Officer(s):
Mohamad Zuhair El-Khateeb, Director
Member Profile: Muslims
Activities: *Rents Mailing List:* Yes *Library:* Yes (Open to Public)
Description: The League is a non-profit, non-governmental organization that serves the religious needs of Muslims in Canada. It promotes Islam & Islamic teachings among Canadian Muslims & helps non-Muslims grasp an accurate understanding of the religion. It also serves as a resource centre, publishing booklets & flyers on current issues.; Affiliation(s): Muslim World League, Makkah, Saudia Arabia

National Council of Canadian Muslims (NCCM)
PO Box 13219, Ottawa ON K2K 1X4
Tel: 613-254-9704; *Fax:* 613-254-9810
Toll-Free: 866-524-0004
info@nccm.ca
www.nccm.ca
Social Media: www.youtube.com/NCCMtv
www.facebook.com/NCCMuslims
twitter.com/NCCM
Previous Name: Council on American-Islamic Relations Canada
Overview: A small international organization founded in 2000
Chief Officer(s):
Kashif A. Ahmed, Chair
Ihsaan Gardee, Executive Director, 613-853-4111
Activities: Seminars & workshops; publication of guides, handbooks & media resource kits
Description: National Council of Canadian Muslims is a nonprofit organization promoting the civic engagement of Canadian Muslims, the protection of their human rights, & the education of non-Muslims so they may hold an accurate understanding of Islam. It is active in the areas of media relations, anti-discrimination & political advocacy.

Ottawa Muslim Association (OMA)
251 Northwestern Ave., Ottawa ON K1Y 0M1
Tel: 613-722-8763
oma@ottawamosque.ca
www.ottawamosque.ca
Overview: A small local charitable organization
Chief Officer(s):
Naeem Malik, President

Activities: Social services; seminars & conferences; *Library:* Yes (Open to Public)
Description: To foster unity among various Muslims; to promote better understanding of Muslims & Islam among Canadians of other faiths; to maintain cultural identity

Scarborough Muslim Association (SMA)
2665 Lawrence Ave. East, Toronto ON M1P 2S2
Tel: 416-750-2253; *Fax:* 416-750-1616
info@smacanada.ca
www.smacanada.ca
Social Media:
twitter.com/SMA_AbuBakrSid
Overview: A small local charitable organization founded in 1984

Windsor Islamic Association (WIA)
c/o Windsor Mosque, 1320 Northwood Dr., Windsor ON N9E 1A4
Tel: 519-966-2355
wia@windsormosque.com
www.wiao.org
Social Media:
www.facebook.com/windsormosque
Overview: A small local organization founded in 1964
Chief Officer(s):
Muhammad Khalid Raana, President
president@windsormosque.ca
Abdallah Shamisa, Vice-President
Majed Mahmoud, Secretary
Activities: Prayer services; funeral services; marriages; Qura'an memorization; Arabic language lessons; teachings about Islam; live broadcast
Description: Serves a population of over 25,000 Muslims in the Windsor locality; Affiliation(s): World Muslim League

Jehovah's Witness

Watch Tower Bible & Tract Society of Canada
PO Box 4100, Georgetown ON L7G 4Y4
Tel: 905-873-4100; *Fax:* 905-873-4554
www.watchtower.org
Also Known As: Jehovah's Witnesses
Overview: A medium-sized national organization
Chief Officer(s):
Kenneth Little, President
Description: To serve Jehovah's Witnesses in Canada

Jesuits

Canadian Jesuits International (CJI)
70 Saint Mary St., Toronto ON M5S 1J3
Tel: 416-465-1824; *Toll-Free:* 800-448-2148
cji@jesuits.ca
www.canadianjesuitsinternational.ca
Social Media:
www.facebook.com/canadianjesuitsinternational
twitter.com/CJIyouth4others
Also Known As: Canadian Jesuit Missions
Overview: A medium-sized national charitable organization founded in 1955
Chief Officer(s):
Jenny Cafiso, Director
Activities: Support projects in Africa, India, Nepal, Jamaica, & Ukraine
Description: Committed to the service of faith & the promotion of justice for the poor of the world; especially dedicated to the educational needs of women, children, elderly & indigenous people at home & abroad

Jesuit Development Office (JDO)
c/o Jesuit in English Canada, Provincial Office, 43 Queen's Park Cres. East, Toronto ON M5S 2C3
Tel: 416-962-4500; *Fax:* 416-962-4501
jdo@jesuits.ca
www.jesuits.ca
Overview: A medium-sized international charitable organization founded in 1940
Chief Officer(s):
Erica Zlomislic, Communications Officer
communications@jesuits.ca
Membership: under 200
Description: To raise & provide the funds necessary for the support of Jesuit brothers & priests in formation, in ministry & in their senior years; *Member of:* Jesuit Fathers & Brothers of Upper Canada

Judaism

Canadian Council for Reform Judaism (CCRJ)
#301, 3845 Bathurst St., Toronto ON M3H 3N2
Tel: 416-630-0375; *Fax:* 416-630-5089
ccrj@ccrj.ca
www.ccrj.ca
Social Media: www.youtube.com/urjweb
linkedin.com/groups?gid=1300517
www.facebook.com/reformjudaism
twitter.com/urj
Previous Name: Canadian Council of Reform Rabbis
Overview: A medium-sized national organization
Chief Officer(s):
Paul Leszner, President
CCRJPresident@ccrj.ca
Morris Cooper, Vice-President
CCRJVicePresident@ccrj.ca
Ron Lubarsky, Secretary/Treasuer
ron.lubarsky@rogers.com
Description: The CCRJ is the Canadian region of the Union for Reform Judaism Congregations, & serves as the umbrella organization for Reform Judaism in Canada, representing about 30,000 affiliated members in 27 Reform Congregations; *Member of:* Union for Reform Judaism

Chosen People Ministries (Canada) (CPM)
PO Box 58103, Stn. Dufferin-Lawrence, Toronto ON M6A 3C8
Tel: 416-250-0177; *Fax:* 416-250-9235
Toll-Free: 888-442-5535
info@chosenpeople.ca
www.chosenpeople.ca
Also Known As: Beth Sar Shalom Mission
Overview: A medium-sized national charitable organization founded in 1894
Chief Officer(s):
Jorge Sedaca, National Director
Finances: *Annual Operating Budget:* $500,000-$1.5 Million; *Funding Sources:* Donations
Staff: 14 staff member(s)
Activities: *Speaker Service:* Yes
Description: To share the Good News of Jesus the Messiah and help others do the same

Congregation Beth Israel - British Columbia
989 West 28th Ave., Vancouver BC V5Z 0E8
Tel: 604-731-4161; *Fax:* 604-731-4989
info@bethisrael.ca
www.bethisrael.ca
Social Media:
www.youtube.com/channel/UCV32q1muJX33op5rSZA7FTQ
Overview: A small local organization founded in 1932
Chief Officer(s):
Gary Miller, President
Jonathan Infeld, Klei Kodesh
rabbiinfeld@bethisrael.ca
Shannon Etkin, Executive Director
shannon@bethisrael.ca
Activities: Youth programs; Hebrew school; facility rental; Rabbi Wilfred & Phyllis Solomon Museum; *Library:* Moe Cohen Library (Open to Public)
Description: The congregation is dedicated to the strengthening of all aspects of Jewish life, including worship & Torah study, religious, educational & social activities for all ages, & the observance of life cycle events; *Member of:* United Synagogue of Conservative Judaism

Kosher Check
#401, 1037 West Broadway, Vancouver BC V6H 1E3
Tel: 604-731-1803; *Fax:* 604-731-1804
info@koshercheck.org
www.koshercheck.org
Social Media: www.youtube.com/watch?v=ujujK_r3xAc
linkedin.com/company/3110427
www.facebook.com/Koshercheck
twitter.com/koshercheck
Previous Name: BC Kosher; Orthodox Rabbinical Council of British Columbia
Overview: A medium-sized international charitable organization founded in 1983
Chief Officer(s):
Avraham Feigelstock, Av Beis Din, 604-731-1803 101
Richard Wood, Director, Business & Marketing, 604-731-1803 103
Finances: *Annual Operating Budget:* $100,000-$250,000
Staff: 5 staff member(s); 6 volunteer(s)
Membership: 100-499
Activities: Providing information about Kashruth (kosher food - kashruth symbol BCK); *Speaker Service:* Yes

National Council of Jewish Women of Canada (NCJWC)
#118, 1588 Main St., Winnipeg MB R2V 1Y3
Tel: 416-633-5100; *Fax:* 416-633-1956
Toll-Free: 866-625-9274
www.ncjwc.org
Overview: A medium-sized national charitable organization founded in 1897
Finances: *Funding Sources:* Donations
Fees: $36
Description: To further human welfare in the Jewish & general communities; To help fulfill unmet needs & to serve the individual & the community; Affiliation(s): International Council of Jewish Women; UNESCO Sub committee on the Status of Women; Coalition of Jewish Women against Domestic Violence & the Coalition for Agunot Rights

Pride of Israel
59 Lissom Cres., Toronto ON M2R 2P2
Tel: 416-226-0111; *Fax:* 416-226-0128
office@prideofisraelshul.org
www.prideofisraelshul.org
Overview: A small local organization founded in 1905
Chief Officer(s):
Steven Bloom, Chair
chairman@prideofisraelshul.org
Sean Gorman, Rabbi
rabbi@prideofisraelshul.org
Bonnie Moatti, Coordinator, Membership
membership@prideofisraelshul.org
Finances: *Funding Sources:* Donations
Activities: Offering a Kosher Food Bank; Providing Jewish educational programming

Shaare Zion Congregation
5575 Côte St. Luc Rd., Montréal QC H3X 2C9
Tel: 514-481-7727; *Fax:* 514-481-1219
info@shaarezion.org
www.shaarezion.org
Social Media: www.youtube.com/user/shaarezionmtl/featured
linkedin.com/company/shaare-zion-congregation
www.facebook.com/shaarezion
twitter.com/ShaareZion_MTL
Overview: A small local charitable organization founded in 1924
Chief Officer(s):
David Moscovitch, Executive Director, 514-481-7727 227
david.moscovitch@shaarezion.org
Lionel E. Moses, Rabbi, 514-481-7727 228
rabbi@shaarezion.org
Affiliation(s): United Synagogue of Conservative Judaism

Toronto Association of Synagogue & Temple Administrators
c/o Beth Tikvah Synagogue, 3080 Bayview Ave., Toronto ON M5N 5L3
Tel: 416-221-3433
Overview: A small local organization
Chief Officer(s):
Doris Alter, President
doris@bethtikvahtoronto.org
Finances: *Annual Operating Budget:* Less than $50,000
Membership: 12; *Fees:* $50; *Member Profile:* Executive directors of synagogues & temples

Vaad Harabonim (Orthodox Rabbinical Council)
3600 Bathurst St., Toronto ON M6A 2C9
Tel: 416-787-1631; *Fax:* 416-785-5378
Also Known As: Rabbinical Council of Ontario
Overview: A small provincial organization founded in 1982
Finances: *Annual Operating Budget:* Less than $50,000
Membership: 40
Description: To serve & guide the Jewish community

Lutheranism

Canadian Lutheran World Relief (CLWR)
#600, 177 Lombard Ave., Winnipeg MB R3B 0W5
Tel: 204-694-5602; *Fax:* 204-694-5460
Toll-Free: 800-661-2597
clwr@clwr.mb.ca
www.clwr.org
Social Media: www.youtube.com/user/CLWRvideo;
instagram.com/canlwr
www.facebook.com/CanadianLutheranWorldRelief
twitter.com/canlwr
Overview: A large national charitable organization founded in 1946
Chief Officer(s):
Robert Granke, Executive Director, 204-631-0113
rgranke@clwr.mb.ca
Tom Brook, Director, Community Relations Team, 204-631-0115
tbrook@clwr.mb.ca

Patricia Maruschak, Director, Program Team, 204-631-0116
patricia@clwr.mb.ca
Diana Koldyk, Director, Finance & Administration Team, 204-631-0507
diana@clwr.mb.ca
Finances: *Funding Sources:* Evangelical Lutheran Church of Canada; Lutheran Church-Canada; Canadian Lutherans; Government
Staff: 23 staff member(s)
Activities: *Speaker Service:* Yes
Description: To provide development programming in Africa, Asia, Latin America, & the Middle East; To provide emergency relief in case of disaster; To enable sponsorships for refugee resettlement in Canada; To focus on development, peace building, alternative approaches to trade, education, & community building; *Member of:* Canadian Foodgrains Bank; The Lutheran World Federation; ACT Alliance; Canadian Churches in Action; Canadian Council for International Cooperation; Manitoba Council for International Cooperation; Saskatchewan Council for International Cooperation

Estonian Evangelical Lutheran Church Consistory (EELC)
383 Jarvis St., Toronto ON M5B 2C7
Tel: 416-925-5465; *Fax:* 416-925-5688
e.e.l.k@eelk.ee
www.eelk.ee/eng_EELCabroad.html
Social Media:
www.facebook.com/EestiKirik
Overview: A medium-sized national organization founded in 1950
Membership: 15,700 + 63 congregations
Description: EELC is an independent, self-governing church which functions on democratic grounds, calls together congregations, ordains pastors, holds services & carries out religious ceremonies according to the Service Book, the Statutes & the established order. The Consistory is the government of the EELC.; Affiliation(s): Lutheran World Federation; World Council of Churches

Evangelical Lutheran Church in Canada (ELCIC)
#600, 177 Lombard Ave., Winnipeg MB R3B 0W5
Tel: 204-984-9173; *Fax:* 204-984-9185
Toll-Free: 888-786-6707
www.elcic.ca
Social Media:
www.facebook.com/CanadianLutherans
twitter.com/elcicinfo
Overview: A medium-sized national charitable organization founded in 1986
Chief Officer(s):
Susan Johnson, National Bishop, 204-984-9157
Trina Gallop, Director, Communications & Stewardship, 204-984-9172
Gloria McNabb, Director, Finance & Administration, 204-984-9178
Finances: *Annual Operating Budget:* $1.5 Million-$3 Million; *Funding Sources:* Donations
Staff: 20 staff member(s)
Membership: 145,376 individuals; approx. 600 congregations; *Member Profile:* Current members in a congregation
Description: The Church shares the gospel of Jesus Christ with people in Canada & around the world through the proclamation of the Word, celebration of the sacraments, & through service in Christ's name. It functions through three major entities: nationally as the ELCIC, regionally as synods, & locally as congregations; *Member of:* Canadian Council of Churches; Lutheran Council in Canada; Lutheran World Federation; World Council of Churches; Affiliation(s): Anglican Church of Canada

Lutheran Association of Missionaries & Pilots (LAMP)
4966 - 92 Ave. NW, Edmonton AB T6B 2V4
Tel: 780-466-8507; *Fax:* 780-466-6733
Toll-Free: 800-307-4036
office@lampministry.org
www.lampministry.org
Social Media: www.youtube.com/user/LAMPMinistry/videos
www.facebook.com/233505351133
Overview: A small international organization founded in 1970
Chief Officer(s):
Ron Ludke, Executive Director
Finances: *Annual Operating Budget:* $500,000-$1.5 Million
Staff: 300 volunteer(s)
Activities: *Speaker Service:* Yes *Library:* Yes (Open to Public)
Description: To share Jesus Christ with the people of remote areas of Canada; Affiliation(s): Lutheran Church Canada; Evangelical Lutheran Church in Canada

Lutheran Bible Translators of Canada Inc. (LBTC)
137 Queen St. South, Kitchener ON N2G 1W2
Tel: 519-742-3361; *Toll-Free:* 866-518-7071
info@lbtc.ca
www.lbtc.ca
Overview: A small international charitable organization founded in 1974
Chief Officer(s):
James Keller, Executive Director
JKeller@lbtc.ca
Finances: *Annual Operating Budget:* $250,000-$500,000
Staff: 5 staff member(s)
Membership: 1-99
Activities: *Speaker Service:* Yes
Description: To bring people to faith in Jesus Christ through Bible translations & literacy work; Affiliation(s): Canadian Council of Christian Charities

Lutheran Church - Canada (LCC) / Église Luthérienne du Canada
3074 Portage Ave., Winnipeg MB R3K 0Y2
Tel: 204-895-3433; *Fax:* 204-832-3018
Toll-Free: 800-588-4226
info@lutheranchurch.ca
www.lutheranchurch.ca
Social Media:
www.facebook.com/117026825048861
twitter.com/CanLutheran
Overview: A medium-sized national organization founded in 1988
Chief Officer(s):
Robert Bugbee, President
president@lutheranchurch.ca
Dwayne Cleave, Treasurer
treasurer@lutheranchurch.ca
Finances: *Funding Sources:* Donations
Membership: 75,000+ members in 319 congregations
Activities: Supporting LCC missionaries in other countries; Working with Canadian Lutheran World Relief; Responding to social needs in local communities, such as establishing food banks & offering English as a Second Language classes; Education children through Sunday schools, Vacation Bible Schools, & confirmation classes; Offering various resources, such as congregation resources, statistical data, & theological documents; Organizing Synod conventions; *Awareness Events:* National Lutheran Open House; National Youth Gathering
Description: To share the Gospel of Jesus Christ; To proclaim the Lutheran belief & faith in word & deed; Affiliation(s): Canadian Lutheran World Relief; Lutheran Women's Missionary League - Canada; Lutheran Laymen's League; Concordia Lutheran Mission Society

Mennonite

Calgary Mennonite Centre for Newcomers Society
#1010, 999 - 36 St. NE, Calgary AB T2A 7X6
Tel: 403-569-3325
info@centrefornewcomers.ca
www.centrefornewcomers.ca
Social Media:
linkedin.com/company/centre-for-newcomers-society-of-calgary
www.facebook.com/centrefornewcomers
twitter.com/YYCNewcomers
Overview: A small local organization founded in 1988
Chief Officer(s):
Anila Lee Yuen, MBA, Chief Executive Officer
a.leeyuen@centrefornewcomers.ca
Member Profile: Members beyond the Mennonite constituency is enoucraged.
Activities: Calgary Career Show for immigrant youth; preschool activities for immigrant children; employment preparation courses; anti-bullying workshop; EthniCity Catering Program; ESL classes
Description: The Society is a not-for-profit, registered charity that operates the Centre for Newcomers, assisting refugees & immigrants arriving in Calgary to meet their settlement needs.; Affiliation(s): Canadian Red Cross

Canadian Conference of Mennonite Brethren Churches (CCMBC)
1310 Taylor Ave., Winnipeg MB R3M 3Z6
Tel: 204-669-6575; *Fax:* 204-654-1865
Toll-Free: 888-669-6575
karen.hume@mbchurches.ca
www.mennonitebrethren.ca
Social Media:
linkedin.com/company/canadian-conference-of-mennonite-brethren-churches
www.facebook.com/mbconf
twitter.com/CdnMBConf
Overview: A medium-sized national organization founded in 1945
Chief Officer(s):
Willy Reimer, Executive Director, 855-256-3211
willy.reimer@mbchurches.ca
Finances: *Funding Sources:* Donations
Staff: 19 staff member(s)
Membership: 31,264; 256 Mennonite Brethren congregations; *Committees:* Mennonite Central Committee; Mennonite Disaster Service; Manitoba Missions/Service
Activities: *Library:* Centre for MB Studies (Open to Public)
Description: To glorify God, to nurture & equip members to live the Christian life & to mobilize them for ministry

Communitas Supportive Care Society
#103, 2776 Bourquin Cres. West, Abbotsford BC V2S 6A4
Tel: 604-850-6608; *Fax:* 604-850-2634
Toll-Free: 800-622-5455
office@communitascare.com
www.communitascare.com
Social Media:
linkedin.com/company/communitas-supportive-care-society
www.facebook.com/CommunitasCare
twitter.com/CommunitasCare
Previous Name: Mennonite Central Committee Supportive Care Services Society
Overview: A small local organization
Chief Officer(s):
Karyn Santiago, Chief Executive Officer
Gary Falk, Chair
Jacquie Lepp, CPA, Treasurer
Finances: *Annual Operating Budget:* Greater than $5 Million
Activities: *Awareness Events:* Curl for Care, Jan.
Description: Provide various resources to persons living & dealing with mental, physical &/or emotional disabilities; *Member of:* Association for Community Living; Community Social Services Employers Association; Psychosocial Rehabilitation Canada; BC Association for Child Development & Intervention; Denominational Health Association; Fraser Valley Brain Injury Association; Affiliation(s): Jean Vanier; Henri Nouwen; Copeland Centre for Wellness & Recovery; International Initiative for Mental Health; Living Room; Mental Health Commission of Canada; STEP Enterprises; Mennonite Central Committee (British Columbia & Canada); Mennonite Disaster Service; Ten Thousand Villages

Evangelical Mennonite Conference (EMC)
440 Main St., Steinbach MB R5G 1Z5
Tel: 204-326-6401; *Fax:* 204-326-1613
www.emconf.ca
Social Media:
www.facebook.com/emconference
Overview: A medium-sized national charitable organization founded in 1812
Chief Officer(s):
Tim Dyck, General Secretary
Finances: *Annual Operating Budget:* $1.5 Million-$3 Million; *Funding Sources:* Donations
Membership: 7,300
Activities: *Library:* Evangelical Mennonite Conference Archives
Description: To encourage local churches to work together on missions in Canada & around the world

MB Mission (MBMSI) / Mennonite Brethren Mission & Service International
International & Western Canada (BC), #300, 32040 Downes Rd., Abbotsford BC V4X 1X5
Tel: 604-859-6267; *Fax:* 604-859-6422
Toll-Free: 866-964-7627
mbmission@mbmission.org
www.mbmission.org
Social Media: www.youtube.com/MBMissionVideos
www.facebook.com/211465999015576
twitter.com/MBMission_EC
Also Known As: Board of Missions & Services of the Mennonite Brethren Churches of North America
Previous Name: MBMS International
Overview: A medium-sized local charitable organization founded in 1900
Chief Officer(s):
Randy Friesen, General Director
randyf@mbmission.org
Finances: *Funding Sources:* Voluntary contributions; grants
Activities: Cross-cultural mission agency of Mennonite Brethren churches in Canada & the US; *Internships:* Yes; *Speaker Service:* Yes
Description: To make disciples & plant churches globally through church planting & evangelism, discipleship & leadership training & social ministry; *Member of:* Evangelical Fellowship of Mission Agencies

Mennonite Central Committee Canada (MCCC)
134 Plaza Dr., Winnipeg MB
Tel: 204-261-6381; *Fax:* 204-269-9875
Toll-Free: 888-622-6337
canada@mennonitecc.ca
mcccanada.ca
Social Media:
www.facebook.com/289561555567
twitter.com/MCCCan
Overview: A large national charitable organization founded in 1920
Chief Officer(s):
Don Peters, Executive Director
Description: To operate as a relief & development service agency; To promote relief, development, & peace; *Member of:* Mennonite Central Committee

Mennonite Church Canada (MC Canada)
600 Shaftesbury Blvd., Winnipeg MB R3P 0M4
Tel: 204-888-6781; *Fax:* 204-831-5675
Toll-Free: 866-888-6785
office@mennonitechurch.ca
www.mennonitechurch.ca
Also Known As: Conference of Mennonites in Canada
Overview: A medium-sized national charitable organization founded in 1903
Chief Officer(s):
Willard Metzger, General Secretary
Finances: *Funding Sources:* Donations
Staff: 40 staff member(s)
Membership: 31,000 baptized believers in 225 congregations & 5 area conferences
Activities: *Library:* Resource Centre
Description: To form a people of God; To become a global church; To grow leaders

Mennonite Economic Development Associates Canada
#I-106, 155 Frobisher Dr., Waterloo ON N2V 2E1
Tel: 519-725-1633; *Fax:* 519-725-9083
Toll-Free: 800-665-7026
meda@meda.org
www.meda.org
Also Known As: MEDA Canada
Overview: A medium-sized international charitable organization founded in 1953
Chief Officer(s):
Allan Sauder, President
Finances: *Annual Operating Budget:* $1.5 Million-$3 Million
Membership: 3,000 Canada & US
Activities: *Library:* Yes by appointment
Description: To be committed to the nurture & expression of Christian faith in a business setting; To enable members to integrate biblical values & business principles in their daily lives; To address the needs of the disadvantaged through programs of economic development

Mennonite Foundation of Canada (MFC)
#12, 1325 Markham Rd., Winnipeg MB R3T 4J6
Toll-Free: 800-772-3257
contact@mennofoundation.ca
www.mennofoundation.ca
Social Media:
linkedin.com/company/221020
www.facebook.com/MennoFoundationCA
twitter.com/MennoFoundation
Overview: A medium-sized national charitable organization founded in 1974
Chief Officer(s):
Darren Pries-Klassen, Executive Director, 519-745-7821 209
dpklassen@mennofoundation.ca
Rick Braun-Janzen, Director, Finance, 204-488-1985 108
rbjanzen@mennofoundation.ca
Milly Siderius, Director, Stewardship Services, 519-745-7821 204
msiderius@mennofoundation.ca
Finances: *Annual Operating Budget:* $500,000-$1.5 Million
Staff: 22 staff member(s)
Membership: 24; *Member Profile:* Representatives of 7 conferences
Activities: *Speaker Service:* Yes *Library:* Yes (Open to Public)
Description: To accumulate, manage & distribute financial resources exclusively for charitable purposes, as a means, for example, of supporting the Mennonite Community; Affiliation(s): Mennonite Church Canada; Evangelical Mennonite Mission Conference; Mennonite Church Eastern Canada; Northwest Mennonite Conference; Evangelical Mennonite Conference; Chortitzer Mennonite Conference; Evangelical Missionary Church of Canada

Northwest Mennonite Conference
PO Box 1316, 2025 - 20 Ave., Didsbury AB T0M 0W0
Tel: 403-337-3283
www.nwmc.ca
Overview: A medium-sized local organization
Chief Officer(s):
Carol Gelleny, Contact
Membership: 14 congregations; *Committees:* Congregational Ministries; Congregational Leadership; Missions & Service; Stewardship
Member of: Mennonite Church North America

Methodist

The Atlantic District of The Wesleyan Church
1830 Mountain Rd., Moncton NB E1G 1A9
Tel: 506-383-8326; *Fax:* 506-383-8333
office@atlanticdistrict.com
www.atlanticdistrict.com
Previous Name: The Wesleyan Church of Canada - Atlantic District
Overview: A medium-sized local organization founded in 1966
Chief Officer(s):
HC Wilson, District Superintendent
wilsonhc@twccanada.ca

The Bible Holiness Movement / Mouvement de sainteté biblique
PO Box 223, Stn. A, Vancouver BC V6C 2M3
Tel: 250-492-3376
www.bible-holiness-movement.com
Previous Name: The Bible Holiness Mission
Overview: A medium-sized international charitable organization founded in 1949
Chief Officer(s):
Wesley H. Wakefield, Bishop-General
Finances: *Annual Operating Budget:* $100,000-$250,000; *Funding Sources:* Unsolicited gifts from Christian believers
Staff: 16 staff member(s); 6 volunteer(s)
Membership: 93,658 worldwide in 89 countries; 954 Canadian; *Fees:* None
Activities: *Internships:* Yes; *Speaker Service:* Yes *Library:* Yes by appointment
Description: To emphasize the original Methodist faith of salvation & scriptural holiness, with principles of discipline, non-conformity, & non-resistance, & to administer overseas indigenous missionary centres in West Africa, the Philippines, East Africa, & the West Indies; South Korea, India; *Member of:* Christian Holiness Partnership; National Black Evangelical Association; Anti-Slavery International; Affiliation(s): Religious Freedom of Council of Christian Minorities; Christians Concerned for Racial Equality

The British Methodist Episcopal Church of Canada (BME)
c/o BME Christ Church St. James, 460 Shaw St., Toronto ON M6G 3L3
Tel: 416-534-3831; *Fax:* 416-534-3367
info@bmechristchurch.org
www.bmechristchurch.org
Overview: A medium-sized national organization
Membership: 130 churches
Affiliation(s): African Methodist Episcopal Church

Free Methodist Church in Canada (FMCIC) / Église méthodiste libre du Canada
4315 Village Centre Ct., Mississauga ON L4Z 1S2
Tel: 905-848-2600; *Fax:* 905-848-2603
ministrycentre@fmc-canada.org
www.fmc-canada.org
Social Media:
www.facebook.com/137599632927885
twitter.com/FMCIC
Overview: A medium-sized national organization founded in 1880
Chief Officer(s):
Daniel Sheffield, Director, Global & Intercultural Ministries
Jared Siebert, Director, Growth Ministries
Mark Molczanski, Director, Administrative Services
Keith A. Elford
Kim Henderson, Director, Personnel
Finances: *Annual Operating Budget:* $1.5 Million-$3 Million
Staff: 11 staff member(s)
Membership: 12,000+ attendees at 144 churches
Activities: *Internships:* Yes; *Speaker Service:* Yes
Description: To make known to people everywhere God's call to wholeness through forgiveness & holiness in Jesus Christ & to invite into membership & to equip for ministry all who respond in faith; to see healthy churches within the reach of all people in Canada & beyond; *Member of:* Free Methodist World Conference; Affiliation(s): Evangelical Fellowship of Canada; Canadian Council of Christian Charities; World Relief Canada

The Wesleyan Church of Canada - Central Canada District
3545 Centennial Road, Lyn ON K0E 1M0
Tel: 613-877-2087
Central.Canada.District.Office@gmail.com
www.ccdwesleyan.ca
Also Known As: The Wesleyan Methodist Church of Canada
Overview: A medium-sized national charitable organization founded in 1897
Chief Officer(s):
Peter Rigby, District Superintendent
Finances: *Annual Operating Budget:* $500,000-$1.5 Million; *Funding Sources:* District churches
Staff: 3 staff member(s)
Membership: 1,736; *Member Profile:* Covenant members & community members
Activities: *Internships:* Yes
Description: To create a context that produces healthy churches; Affiliation(s): Tyndale Seminary; World Hope International; World Relief Canada; Bethany Bible College; Outreach Canada; Evangelical Fellowship of Canada

Mormonism

Church of Jesus Christ of Latter-day Saints
c/o Toronto Ontario Temple, 10060 Bramalea Rd., Brampton ON L6R 1A1
Tel: 905-799-1122; *Fax:* 905-799-1140
www.lds.org
Social Media: www.pinterest.com/ldschurch/
www.facebook.com/LDS
twitter.com/ldschurch
Overview: A medium-sized national organization founded in 1830
Membership: 190,265 members + 479 congregations in Canada
Activities: *Speaker Service:* Yes *Library:* Family History Library by appointment

Community of Christ - Canada East Mission
390 Speedvale Ave. East, Guelph ON N1E 1N5
Tel: 519-822-4150; *Fax:* 519-822-1236
Toll-Free: 888-411-7537
cheryl@communityofchrist.ca
www.communityofchrist.ca/index.php/cem
Also Known As: Saints' Church
Previous Name: Reorganized Church of Jesus Christ of Latter Day Saints (Canada)
Overview: A medium-sized local charitable organization founded in 1830
Chief Officer(s):
Tim Stanlick, Canada East Mission President
tim@communityofchrist.ca
Jim Poirier, Canadian Bishop & Financial Officer
jim@communityofchrist.ca
Description: To promote communities of joy, hope, love, & peace

Community of Christ - Canada West Mission (CWM)
PO Box 345, Stn. #224, 6655 178th St. North West, Edmonton AB T5T 4J5
Tel: 877-411-2632
www.communityofchrist.ca/index.php/cwm
Overview: A medium-sized local organization
Chief Officer(s):
Stephen Thompson, President & Financial Officer, Mission Centre, 877-411-2632 1
steve@communityofchrist.ca
Membership: 15 congregations and missions
Description: To promote communities of joy, hope, love, & peace

New Thought

Association of Unity Churches Canada
2631 Kingsway Dr., Kitchener ON N2C 1A7
Tel: 519-894-0810
info@unitycanada.org
www.unitycanada.org
Social Media:
www.facebook.com/592422397477914
Also Known As: Unity Canada
Overview: A small national charitable organization founded in 1978
Chief Officer(s):
Dagmar Mikkila, President
president@unitycanada.org
Pat Bell, Judicatory Representative
ucjr@unitycanada.org
Finances: *Annual Operating Budget:* $50,000-$100,000
Membership: 20 churches

Activities: *Internships:* Yes; *Speaker Service:* Yes
Description: Unity is a Christian association asserting that reunion with God in mind brings certain fulfillment in life. It is a registered charity, BN: 118794544RR0001.; Affiliation(s): Association of Unity Churches USA

Orthodox

The Coptic Orthodox Church (Canada)
St. Mark's Coptic Orthodox Church, 41 Glendinning Ave., Toronto ON M1W 3E2
Tel: 416-494-4449; *Fax:* 416-494-4196
mail@coptorthodox.ca
stmarkstoronto.ca
Overview: A small national organization
Chief Officer(s):
M.A. Marcos, Priest
FrMarcos@coptorthodox.ca
Member of: The Canadian Council of Churches; Coptic Orthodox Patriarchate.

Greek Orthodox Metropolis of Toronto (Canada)
86 Overlea Blvd., Toronto ON M4H 1C6
Tel: 416-429-5757; *Fax:* 416-429-4588
metropolis@gometropolis.org
www.gometropolis.org
Social Media: www.youtube.com/user/GOMetropolisToronto
twitter.com/GO_Metropolis
Previous Name: Greek Orthodox Church (Canada)
Overview: A large national organization
Membership: Over 50,000
Activities: *Library:* Yes
Description: There are 76 Greek Orthodox Communities in Canada under the jurisdiction of the Greek Orthodox Metropolis of Toronto (Canada); *Member of:* The Canadian Council of Churches

Romanian Orthodox Deanery of Canada
PO Box 4023, Stn. Main, Regina SK S4P 3R9
www.roea.org
Overview: A small national organization
Chief Officer(s):
Cosmin Vint, Parish Preist, Fort Qu'appelle, 306-332-1554
John Bujea, Ph.D., Contact, Fort Qu'appelle, 306-584-8943
eljohn2@accesscomm.ca
Description: The Romanian Orthodox Episcopate of America is grouped geographically into 7 deaneries & the Deanery of Canada is one of them, with 30 parishes across the country. It is non-profit, registered charity, BN: 888289642RR0001; *Member of:* Romanian Orthodox Episcopate of America; Orthodox Church in America

Russian Orthodox Church in Canada
10812 - 108 St., Edmonton AB T5H 3A6
Tel: 780-420-9945
www.orthodox-canada.com
Overview: A medium-sized national organization
Chief Officer(s):
Iov Job, Bishop of Kashira
bishjob@telus.net
Membership: 22 parishes

Serbian Orthodox Church in the United States of America & Canada - Diocese of Canada
7470 McNiven Rd., RR#3, Campbellville ON L0P 1B0
Tel: 905-878-0043; *Fax:* 905-878-1909
vladika@istocnik.com
www.istocnik.com
Overview: A medium-sized national charitable organization founded in 1983
Chief Officer(s):
Georgije, Bishop, 905-878-3438, Fax: 905-878-1909
vladika@istocnik.com
Stavrophor Vasilije Tomic, Episcopal Deputy, 416-450-4555
o.bajo@rogers.com
Finances: *Annual Operating Budget:* $500,000-$1.5 Million; *Funding Sources:* Donations; parish taxes; dispensations
Staff: 23 staff member(s)
Membership: 150,000; *Committees:* Diocesan Executive Board; Diocesan Assembly
Activities: *Library:* Holy Transfiguration (Open to Public) by appointment
Description: To serve the Serbian Orthodox community & teach the Orthodox faith & culture

Ukrainian Orthodox Church of Canada
Ecumenical Patriarchate, 9 St. John's Ave., Winnipeg MB R2W 1G8
Tel: 204-586-3093; *Fax:* 204-582-5241
Toll-Free: 877-586-3093
consistory@uocc.ca
www.uocc.ca
Overview: A large national organization founded in 1918
Chief Officer(s):
Metropolitan Yurij, Primate
metropolitan@uocc.ca
Victor Lakusta, Chancellor & Chair, Presidium
chancellor@uocc.ca
Membership: 120,000
Activities: *Speaker Service:* Yes *Library:* Yes (Open to Public) by appointment

World Fellowship of Orthodox Youth
Syndesmos General Secretariat, 91 rue Olivier de Serres, Paris 75015 France
syndesmos@syndesmos.org
www.syndesmos.org
Also Known As: Syndesmos
Overview: A small international organization founded in 1953
Chief Officer(s):
Jean Rehbinder, President
Georges El Hage, Vice-President
Finances: *Annual Operating Budget:* $50,000-$100,000; *Funding Sources:* Orthodox churches; Orthodox church organisations; council of Eurpoe; European Christina Diakonia age
Staff: 2 staff member(s); 4 volunteer(s)
Membership: 121 organizations in 42 countries; *Fees:* $500 affiliated; *Member Profile:* Christian Orthodox youth organizations & theological schools; *Committees:* Publications
Activities: Orthodox youth camps, festivals, encounters, seminars, consultations, conferences, training courses, workshops; *Internships:* Yes *Library:* Yes (Open to Public)
Description: To serve as a bond of unity among Orthodox youth movements, organisations & theological schools around the world, promoting a consciousness of the catholicity of the Orthodox faith; to foster relations, coordination & mutal aid among them; to promote among young people a full understanding of the Orthodox faith & the mission of the Church in the contemporary world & an active participation of youth in ecclesial life; to promote a way of life founded in eucharistic communion, in the Gospel & in patristic teaching, for witness & service to the world; to assist & promote Orthodox effocrts for visible Christian unity & for positive relations with people of other faiths; to encourage reflection & action on issues affecting the lives of Orthodox Christians & the local churches; to be an instrument for furthering cooperation & deeper communion between the Orthodox Church & the Oriental Orthodox Churches

Pentecostalism

The Apostolic Church in Canada
220 Adelaide St. North, London ON N6B 3H4
Tel: 519-438-7036
cheryl@apostolic.ca
www.apostolic.ca
Social Media:
www.facebook.com/117271988314359
twitter.com/ACCnat
Overview: A small national organization founded in 1934
Chief Officer(s):
D. Karl Thomas, National Leader
Finances: *Annual Operating Budget:* $500,000-$1.5 Million
Staff: 15 staff member(s)
Membership: 500-999
Activities: *Internships:* Yes
Description: A Trinitarian, Pentecostal denomination with a strong commitment to mission.

Apostolic Church of Pentecost of Canada Inc. (ACOP) / Église apostolique de Pentecôte du Canada inc.
International Office, #119, 2340 Pegasus Way NE, Calgary AB T2E 8M5
Tel: 403-273-5777; *Fax:* 403-273-8102
www.acop.ca
Social Media: google.com/+AcopCa
www.facebook.com/ACOPcanada
twitter.com/ACOPcanada
Overview: A small national licensing charitable organization founded in 1921
Chief Officer(s):
Wes Mills, President & National Director
Finances: *Annual Operating Budget:* $1.5 Million-$3 Million; *Funding Sources:* Donations
Staff: 30 staff member(s)
Membership: 155 affiliated churches + 436 members; *Fees:* Varies
Activities: *Internships:* Yes; *Speaker Service:* Yes *Library:* Yes by appointment
Description: To provide fellowship, encouragement & accountability in the proclamation of the Gospel of Jesus Christ by the Power of the Holy Spirit; Affiliation(s): Evangelical Fellowship of Canada

Church of God of Prophecy in Canada
Eastern Canada Head Office, 5145 Tomken Rd., Mississauga ON L4W 1P1
Tel: 905-625-1278; *Fax:* 905-625-1316
info@cogop.ca
www.cogop.ca
Overview: A medium-sized national charitable organization
Chief Officer(s):
Woodroe Thompson, Bishop
revt@cogoop.ca
Finances: *Annual Operating Budget:* $100,000-$250,000
Staff: 3 staff member(s)
Membership: 28 churches
Activities: *Internships:* Yes; *Speaker Service:* Yes
Description: The Church of God of Prophecy has its roots in the Holiness/Pentecostal tradition and has felt a special burden to call attention to the principle of unity in the body of Christ, while faithfully proclaiming the gospel of Jesus Christ before a watching world.

General Conference of the Canadian Assemblies of God / Conférence générale des assemblées de dieu canadiennes
PO Box 37315, Stn. Marquette, 6724 Fabre St., Montréal QC H2E 3B5
Tel: 514-279-1100; *Fax:* 514-279-1131
info@caogonline.org
www.caogonline.org
Previous Name: Italian Pentecostal Church of Canada
Overview: A small national charitable organization founded in 1912
Chief Officer(s):
Dino Cianflone, General Treasurer
Daniel Ippolito, Overseer Emeritus
David Di Staulo, General Superintendent
Raymond Narula, General Secretary
Giulio Gabeli, Overseer
Finances: *Annual Operating Budget:* $100,000-$250,000
Staff: 2 staff member(s); 3 volunteer(s)
Membership: 6,000 + 21 affiliated churches
Activities: Hosting an annual conference; *Internships:* Yes
Description: To provide distinctive ministry to the Italian community, extending to all Canadians, regardless of language, nationality, or race; To proclaim the gospel of Jesus Christ in the power of the Holy Spirit throughout Canada & the world, based on the biblical standard of ministry in the New Testament; *Member of:* The Evangelical Fellowship of Canada; Canadian Council of Christian Charities

Pentecostal Assemblies of Canada (PAOC) / Assemblées de la Pentecôte du Canada
2450 Milltower Ct., Mississauga ON L5N 5Z6
Tel: 905-542-7400; *Fax:* 905-542-7313
info@paoc.org
www.paoc.org
Social Media: www.youtube.com/paoctube
www.facebook.com/ThePAOC
twitter.com/thepaoc
Overview: A large national charitable organization founded in 1919
Chief Officer(s):
David Wells, General Superintendent
David Hazzard, Asst. Superintendent, Fellowship Services
Murray Cornelius, Asst. Superintendent, International Missions
Finances: *Annual Operating Budget:* Greater than $5 Million; *Funding Sources:* Local churches; individuals
Staff: 50 staff member(s)
Membership: 1,100 churches, 3,500 pastors representing 236,000 parishoners; *Committees:* General Executive; Administrative; International Missions; Audit; Credentials
Activities: Task Force; Work Force; Volunteers in Mission; Short-Term Missions; Volunteers in Special Assignment; ERDO (Emergency Relief & Development Overseas); Child Care Plus; *Library:* The PAOC Archives (Open to Public) by appointment
Description: PAOC makes disciples everywhere by the proclamation & practice of the gospel of Christ in the power of the Holy Spirit with the goal to establish local congregations & to train spiritual leaders.; Affiliation(s): World Pentecost; Pentecostal/Charismatic Churches of North America; Pentecostal World Fellowship; World Assemblies of God Fellowship; Focus on the Family; Canadian Foodgrains Bank; Pentecostal European Mission; Seeds International; VisionLEDD; Canadian Council of Christian Charities; Every Home for Christ; Evangelical Missiological Society; Evangelical Fellowship of Canada; Canadian Children's Ministries Network; Canadian Bible Society; Family Life Ministries; Society of Pentecostal Studies

The Pentecostal Assemblies of Newfoundland & Labrador (PAONL)
PO Box 8895, Stn. A, 57 Thorburn Rd., St. John's NL A1B 3T2
Tel: 709-753-6314; *Fax:* 709-753-4945
info@paonl.ca
www.paonl.ca
Social Media:
www.facebook.com/252330011920
twitter.com/paonl
Overview: A medium-sized provincial charitable organization founded in 1911
Chief Officer(s):
Terry W. Snow, General Superintendent
Finances: *Annual Operating Budget:* $1.5 Million-$3 Million
Staff: 13 staff member(s)
Membership: 40,000
Activities: *Internships:* Yes; *Speaker Service:* Yes *Library:* Yes by appointment
Description: To promote evangelism, world missions, famine relief, & education; Affiliation(s): Pentecostal Fellowship of North America

Presbyterianism

L'Église Réformée du Québec (ERQ) / The Reformed Church of Québec. (RCQ)
1355 boul René-Lévesque Ouest (coin Crescent), Montréal QC H3G 1T3
Tél: 514-767-3165
info@erq.qc.ca
erq.qc.ca
Média social:
www.facebook.com/jeunesse.erq
Nom précédent: Église Réformée St-Jean
Aperçu: *Dimension:* moyenne; *Envergure:* provinciale
Membre(s) du bureau directeur:
Jean Zoellner, Pastor
Affiliation(s): Christian Reformed Church; Presbyterian Church of North America

Presbyterian Church in Canada (PCC) / Église presbytérienne au Canada
50 Wynford Dr., Toronto ON M3C 1J7
Tel: 416-441-1111; *Fax:* 416-441-2825
Toll-Free: 800-619-7301
presbyterian.ca
Social Media: youtube.com/presvideo
www.facebook.com/pcconnect
twitter.com/pcconnect
Overview: A large national organization founded in 1875
Chief Officer(s):
Stephen Kendall, Principal Clerk, General Assembly Office
skendall@presbyterian.ca
Tony Plomp, Deputy Clerk, General Assembly Office
tony_plomp@telus.net
Frances Hogg, Secretary, General Assembly Office
fhogg@presbyterian.ca
Donald Muir, Associate Secretary & Deputy Clerk, General Assembly Office
dmuir@presbyterian.ca
Stephen Roche, CFO & Treasurer, Support Services
sroche@presbyterian.ca
Richard Fee, General Secretary, Life & Mission Agency
rfee@presbyterian.ca
Dorcas J. Gordon, Principal, Knox College, Toronto
jd.gordon@utoronto.ca
John Vissers, Principal, Presbyterian College
jvissers@presbyteriancollege.ca
Finances: *Funding Sources:* Congregations
Membership: 125,509; *Member Profile:* Presbyteries; congregations; communicants on roll; ministers; *Committees:* Assembly Council; Committee to Advise with the Moderator
Activities: *Library:* Knox College & Presbyterian College Libraries (Open to Public)
Member of: The Canadian Council of Churches; World Alliance of Reformed Churches; World Council of Churches; Action By Churches Together; Ecumenical Advocacy Alliance

Protestantism

Grand Orange Lodge of Canada
94 Sheppard Ave. West, Toronto ON M2N 1M5
Tel: 416-223-1690; *Fax:* 416-223-1324
Toll-Free: 800-565-6248
www.grandorangelodge.ca
Also Known As: Loyal Orange Association
Previous Name: The Grand Orange Lodge of British America
Overview: A large national organization founded in 1830
Chief Officer(s):
John Chalmers, Grand Secretary
Jodachal@yahoo.ca
Roy Dawe, Grand Master & Sovereign
Finances: *Annual Operating Budget:* Less than $50,000; *Funding Sources:* Membership dues
Staff: 8 staff member(s)
Membership: 100,000; *Member Profile:* Protestant faith
Activities: *Awareness Events:* Annual Golf Tournament
Description: To encourage its members to actively participate in the Protestant church of their choice; to actively support the Canadian system of government; to anticipate legislation & its impact on the civil & religious liberties of all Canadians; to provide social activities which will enrich the lives of its members; to participate in benevolent activities which will enrich our communities & our country; *Member of:* Imperial Orange Council of the World

Operation Mobilization Canada (OM)
84 West St., Port Colborne ON L3K 4C8
Toll-Free: 877-487-7777
info.ca@om.org
www.omcanada.org
Social Media:
www.facebook.com/omcanada
twitter.com/om_canada
Overview: A small international charitable organization founded in 1966
Chief Officer(s):
Harvey Thiessen, Executive Director
Finances: *Annual Operating Budget:* $1.5 Million-$3 Million
Staff: 25 staff member(s)
Activities: *Speaker Service:* Yes *Library:* Yes
Description: Missionary training movement operating in 80 countries with 6,000 people in program every year; mobilizes & trains young Protestant believers for mission fields; *Member of:* Evangelical Fellowship of Canada; Canadian Council of Christian Charities

Scientology

Church of Scientology of Toronto
77 Peter St., Toronto ON M5V 2G4
Tel: 416-925-2145
toronto@scientology.net
www.scientology.ca
Overview: A medium-sized local organization
Member of: Church of Scientology

Seicho-No-Ie

Seicho-No-Ie Toronto Centre
662 Victoria Park Ave., Toronto ON M4C 5H4
Tel: 416-690-8686; *Fax:* 416-690-3917
www.seicho-no-ie.org
Also Known As: Home of Infinite Growth
Previous Name: Seicho-No-Ie Canada Truth of Life Centre
Overview: A small national organization founded in 1963
Description: Provides a place of worship for those who believe in the Seicho-No-Ie Humanity Enlightenment Movement, which says that all religions emanate from one universal god; *Member of:* Seicho-No-Ie (Canada)

Sikhism

Maritime Sikh Society (MSS)
10 Parkhill Rd., Halifax NS B3P 1R3
Tel: 902-477-0008
www.maritimesikhsociety.com
Overview: A small local organization founded in 1968
Chief Officer(s):
S. Major Singh Jassal, President, 902-405-1237
jatinderbhupa@hotmail.com
Finances: *Annual Operating Budget:* Less than $50,000
Membership: 46; *Fees:* $12
Activities: *Library:* Yes by appointment
Member of: Multicultural Association of Nova Scotia

Ontario Sikh & Gurudwara Council (OSGC)
PO Box 38636, 545 Steeles Ave. West, Brampton ON L6Y 4W5
OntarioSikh.GurdwaraCouncil@gmail.com
osgc.ca
Overview: A small provincial organization
Chief Officer(s):
Ranjit S. Dulay, Chair, 647-290-4704
ranjitsinghdulay@hotmail.com
Membership: 62; *Fees:* $51 individual; $251 Gurdwaras
Description: To provide leadership to the Sikh community & to arrange social gatherings for its members

The Sikh Foundation
#4900, 40 King St. West, Toronto ON M5H 4A2
Tel: 416-777-6697; *Fax:* 416-484-9656
Overview: A small national organization
Description: Distributes literature regarding the Sikh religion to anyone who is interested.

World Sikh Organization of Canada (WSO)
1183 Cecil Ave., Ottawa ON K1H 7Z6
www.worldsikh.org
Social Media:
www.facebook.com/WSOCanada
twitter.com/WorldSikhOrg
Overview: A medium-sized international organization founded in 1984
Chief Officer(s):
Amritpal Singh Shergill, President
Kulmit Singh Sangha, Senior Vice-President
Rupinder Kaur Dhaliwal, Director, Administration
Jagdeep Singh Mann, Director, Finance
Membership: 15,000-49,999; *Fees:* $1,000 institutional; $10 student/associate; $100 individual
Activities: *Library:* Yes (Open to Public) by appointment
Description: To foster understanding & goodwill amongst all nations, creeds & races; To promote & protect the rights of humanity as articulated in UN declarations & covenants; Affiliation(s): World Sikh Organization (International)

Sufism

The Jerrahi Sufi Order of Canada
Canadian Sufi Cultural Centre, 270 Birmingham St., Toronto ON M8V 2E4
jerrahi@jerrahi.ca
www.jerrahi.ca
Overview: A medium-sized local organization
Activities: *Library:* Yes
Description: The Jerrahi Sufi Order of Canada holds weekly gatherings where attendees come to gain knowledge about Islam by participating in discourses & discussions, observing the art of Sufi music & poetry, & celebrating the praises of God through prayer & Zikrullah (Sufi remembrance ceremony).

Taoism

Fung Loy Kok Institute of Taoism (FLK)
134 D'Arcy St., Toronto ON M5T 1K3
Tel: 416-656-2110; *Fax:* 416-654-3937
fungloykok@taoist.org
www.taoist.org
Overview: A small international organization
Activities: Tai Chi arts; Taoist meditation
Description: Observes the unified teachings of the three religions of Confucianism, Buddhism & Taoism.; Affiliation(s): Taoist Tai Chi Society of Canada

Taoist Tai Chi Society of Canada
Central Region, 134 Darcy St., Toronto ON M5T 1K3
Tel: 416-656-2110; *Fax:* 416-654-3937
fungloykok@taoist.org
www.taoist.org
Social Media:
www.facebook.com/flkttc
twitter.com/taoisttaichisoc
Overview: A medium-sized national organization founded in 1970
Finances: *Funding Sources:* Membership fees
Staff: 20 staff member(s)
Membership: 15,000; *Fees:* $20; *Member Profile:* Open to everyone
Activities: *Awareness Events:* National Taoist Tai Chi Awareness Day, first Sat. after Labour Day
Description: To make Taoist Tai Chi available to all &, through its teaching & practice, promote health improvement, cultural exchange & helping others; *Member of:* International Taoist Tai Chi Society

Unitarianism

Canadian Unitarian Council (CUC) / Conseil unitarien du Canada
#400, 215 Spadina Ave., Toronto ON M5T 2C7
Tel: 416-489-4121; *Toll-Free:* 888-568-5723
info@cuc.ca
www.cuc.ca
Social Media:
www.youtube.com/channel/UCJ25lMWQwrxSnry11bdBS-g
linkedin.com/company/canadian-unitarian-council
www.facebook.com/CanadianUnitarianCouncil
twitter.com/uucanada
Also Known As: Unitarian Church

Overview: A medium-sized national charitable organization founded in 1961
Chief Officer(s):
Vyda Ng, Executive Director
vyda@cuc.ca
Finances: *Annual Operating Budget:* $250,000-$500,000; *Funding Sources:* Donations; Membership dues
Staff: 9 staff member(s); 20 volunteer(s)
Membership: 50 institutional; *Fees:* Schedule available; *Committees:* Lay & Chaplaincy; Social Responsibility; Congregational Development
Activities: *Library:* CUC Library by appointment
Description: To enhance, nurture & promote Unitarian & Universalist religion in Canada; to provide support for religious exploration, spiritual growth & social responsibility; Affiliation(s): International Association for Religious Freedom; International Council of Unitarians & Universalists; Untarian Universalist Minsters of Canada

Canadian Unitarians for Social Justice (CUJS)
Stn. 40011, Ottawa ON K1V 0W8
membership@cusj.org
cusj.org
Overview: A medium-sized national organization founded in 1996
Chief Officer(s):
Frances Deverell, President
president@cusj.org
Finances: *Annual Operating Budget:* Less than $50,000
Membership: 350 individual
Description: A national, liberal religious organization, founded to actively promote Unitarian values through social action.; Affiliation(s): Canadian Unitarian Council

First Unitarian Congregation of Toronto
175 St. Clair Ave. West, Toronto ON M4V 1P7
Tel: 416-924-9654; *Fax:* 416-924-9655
administrator@firstunitariantoronto.org
www.firstunitariantoronto.org
Social Media: www.facebook.com/223855447667879
Overview: A small national charitable organization founded in 1845
Chief Officer(s):
Shawn Newton, Minister, 416-924-9654 222, Fax: 416-924-9655
ShawnNewton@FirstUnitarianToronto.org
Finances: *Annual Operating Budget:* $250,000-$500,000
Staff: 9 staff member(s); 25 volunteer(s)
Membership: 306 individuals
Activities: Monthly newcomers' orientation, weekly service, library, bookstore, social justice & community outreach, small group activities; *Internships:* Yes *Library:* Yes by appointment
Description: To serve the religious needs of those who embrace Unitarian Universalist principles, who respect the free exercise of private judgment in all matters of belief & who live in the Metropolitan Toronto area; *Member of:* Canadian Unitarian Council

USC Canada
#705, 56 Sparks St., Ottawa ON K1P 5B1
Tel: 613-234-6827; *Fax:* 613-234-6842
Toll-Free: 800-565-6872
info@usc-canada.org
www.usc-canada.org
Social Media: www.youtube.com/user/USCCanada
www.facebook.com/78368904729
twitter.com/usccanada
Also Known As: Unitarian Service Committee of Canada
Overview: A medium-sized international charitable organization founded in 1945
Chief Officer(s):
Lauren Viot, Director, International Programs
Sheila Petzold, Director, Communications
Martin Settle, Director, Finance & Human Resources
Susan Walsh, Executive Director
Finances: *Annual Operating Budget:* Greater than $5 Million; *Funding Sources:* Support from the general public; bequests; foundations & corporations; investment income; government
Staff: 22 staff member(s)
Membership: 1,000; *Member Profile:* Membership is offered to individuals supporting USC through volunteer or financial means; *Committees:* Finance; Executive; Programs
Activities: Communications/Media Program; Development Education Program to raise awareness about development issues & their impact on our lives in Canada; Fundraising & Volunteer Program; Overseas Program to work in partnership with people in the developing world to build self-reliant communities; *Speaker Service:* Yes; *Rents Mailing List:* Yes *Library:* Yes by appointment
Description: Committed to enhancing human development through an international partnership of people linked in the challenge to reduce poverty; *Member of:* Canadian Council for International Cooperation

United Church of Christ

Affirm United / S'affirmer Ensemble
PO Box 57057, Stn. Somerset, Ottawa ON K1R 1A1
affirmunited@affirmunited.ca
www.affirmunited.ca
Overview: A medium-sized national organization founded in 1982
Chief Officer(s):
Linda Hutchinson, Coordinator, Affirming Ministry
Brian Mitchell-Walker, Coordinator, Affirming Ministry
Finances: *Annual Operating Budget:* Less than $50,000
Staff: 20 volunteer(s)
Membership: 200 ministries; *Fees:* $40 individual/household; $100 institutional
Activities: *Speaker Service:* Yes
Description: To affirm gay, lesbian, bisexual & transgender people & their friends, within The United Church of Canada; to provide a network of supports among affirming ministries & regional groups; to act as a point of contact for individuals; to speak to the church in a united fashion encouraging it to act prophetically & pastorally both within & beyond the church structure.; Affiliation(s): United Church of Canada

Alberta CGIT Association
c/o Barbara Spence, 5720 Lodge Cres. SW, Calgary AB T3E 5Y7
Tel: 780-532-2947
cgit@telus.net
www.albertacgit.ca
Also Known As: Canadian Girls in Training - Alberta
Overview: A small provincial organization
Chief Officer(s):
Valerie Jenner, President

Boys & Girls Clubs of Canada - Québec Region
c/o Boys & Girls Clubs of Canada National Office, #400, 2005 Sheppard Ave. East, Toronto ON M5J 5B4
Tél: 905-477-7272; *Téléc:* 416-640-5331
Aperçu: *Dimension:* moyenne; *Envergure:* provinciale
Membre(s) du bureau directeur:
Marlene Deboisbriand, Vice-President, Member Services
mdeboisbriand@bgccan.com
Membre: 7,000; *Critères d'admissibilite:* Children/youth
Membre de: Boys & Girls Clubs of Canada

Boys & Girls Clubs of Canada - Western Region
AB
Tel: 780-415-1734
Overview: A medium-sized provincial organization
Chief Officer(s):
Karen McCullagh, Regional Director, 403-936-0899
KMcCullagh@bgccan.com
Pearl Kapitzke, Regional Services Coordinator
pkapitzke@bgccan.com
Membership: 47,000
Member of: Boys & Girls Clubs of Canada

Boys & Girls Clubs of Manitoba
Central Region, #204, 7100 Woodbine Ave., Markham ON L3R 5J2
Tel: 416-535-9675; *Fax:* 905-477-2056
www.bgccan.com/clubresults.asp?l=e&location=mb
Overview: A medium-sized provincial organization
Activities: Counselling; conflict resolution training; street safety
Description: The Clubs offer educational, recreational & skills development programs & services to children from pre-school to young adulthood. Activities are scheduled after school, evenings & weekends, providinge a safe, supportive place where children & youth can build positive relationships, & develop confidence & skills; *Member of:* Boys & Girls Clubs of Canada

Manitoba CGIT Association Inc.
PO Box 52073, Winnipeg MB R2M 5P9
Tel: 204-254-2378
cgit@cgitmanitoba.ca
www.cgitmanitoba.ca
Social Media: www.instagram.com/cgit_manitoba
www.facebook.com/groups/5409037069
twitter.com/CGITManitoba
Also Known As: Canadian Girls in Training - Manitoba
Previous Name: National CGIT Association - Manitoba & Northwestern Ontario
Overview: A small provincial organization

Maritime Regional CGIT Committee
c/o Chris MacDonald, PO Box 383, Pictou NS B0K 1H0
Tel: 902-485-4011
g.cmacdonald@eastlink.ca
Also Known As: Canadian Girls in Training - Maritimes
Previous Name: National CGIT Association - Maritime Regional Committee
Overview: A small provincial organization
Chief Officer(s):
Chris MacDonald, Contact

Ontario CGIT Association
PO Box 371, Norwich ON N0J 1P0
Tel: 519-863-3060; *Fax:* 519-863-3060
ontario@cgit.ca
www.cgit.ca
Also Known As: Canadian Girls in Training - Ontario
Previous Name: National CGIT Association - Ontario
Overview: A small provincial charitable organization founded in 1915
Finances: *Annual Operating Budget:* Less than $50,000
Staff: 1 staff member(s); 150 volunteer(s)
Membership: 350; *Member Profile:* Teen girls & adult women; *Committees:* Leadership Training; Camps; Publicity & Promotion
Activities: Leadership training weekend; camp council leadership training for senior girls; Red Maple Leaf Program Affiliation(s): The United Church of Canada; The Presbyterian Church in Canada

Provincial CGIT Board of BC
c/o Janice Grinnell, 13780 Hill Rd., Ladysmith BC V9G 1G7
Tel: 250-245-4016
grinncon@nanaimo.ark.com
www.cgit.ca
Also Known As: Canadian Girls in Training - BC
Previous Name: National CGIT Association - BC Provincial Board
Overview: A small provincial organization

Saskatchewan CGIT Committee
c/o 1525, 7th Ave. N, Regina SK S4R 0H7
saskcgit@accesscomm.ca
www.cgitsaskatchewan.ca
Social Media: twitter.com/sk_CGIT
Also Known As: Canadian Girls in Training - Saskatchewan
Previous Name: National CGIT Association - Saskatchewan Committee
Overview: A small provincial organization
Chief Officer(s):
Alice Monks, Co-Chair

United Church of Canada (UCC) / L'Église Unie du Canada
#300, 3250 Bloor St. West, Toronto ON M8X 2Y4
Tel: 416-231-5931; *Fax:* 416-231-3103
Toll-Free: 800-268-3781
info@united-church.ca
www.united-church.ca
Social Media: www.youtube.com/unitedchurchofcanada
linkedin.com/company/unitedchurchcda
www.facebook.com/UnitedChurchCda
twitter.com/UnitedChurchCda
Overview: A large national charitable organization founded in 1925
Chief Officer(s):
Gary Paterson, Moderator
moderator@united-church.ca
Nora Sanders, General Secretary
nsanders@united-church.ca
Finances: *Annual Operating Budget:* Greater than $5 Million; *Funding Sources:* Voluntary givings; Sales; Bequests; Investment income; Foundation
Staff: 5000 staff member(s)
Membership: 650,000; *Member Profile:* Baptism & profession of faith in Jesus Christ as Saviour & Lord
Activities: *Speaker Service:* Yes *Library:* Yes
Description: To foster the spirit of unity in the hope that this sentiment of unity may in due time, so far as Canada is concerned, take shape in a Church which may fittingly be described as national; *Member of:* Canadian Council of Churches; World Council of Churches; Canadian Council for International Cooperation; World Methodist Council; Affiliation(s): United Church of Canada Foundation

United Church of Canada Foundation / Église Unie du Canada
#300, 3250 Bloor St. West, Toronto ON M8X 2Y4
Toll-Free: 866-340-8223
fdn@united-church.ca
www.unitedchurchfoundation.ca
Overview: A large national charitable organization founded in 2002
Chief Officer(s):
David Armour, President, 416-231-5931 2022

Sarah Charters, Manager, Donor & Investor Relations,
416-231-5931 3410
Finances: *Annual Operating Budget:* $3 Million-$5 Million
Staff: 3 staff member(s)
Activities: Managing 40 endowments; grants & scholarships
Description: To help sustain the United Church of Canada; Affiliation(s): United Church of Canada

Wicca

Pagan Federation International - Canada (PFI)
PO Box 986, Tavistock ON N0B 2R0
Nuhyn@paganfederation.org
www.paganfederation.org
Overview: A small national organization founded in 1998

Wiccan Church of Canada
The Occult Shop, 1373 Bathurst St., Toronto ON M5R 3J1
info@wcc.on.ca
www.wcc.on.ca
Overview: A small national organization founded in 1979
Chief Officer(s):
Richard James, Priest
richard@wcc.on.ca
Description: To assist practicing Wiccans in achieving a spiritual balance that brings them into true harmony with the Gods.

Zoroastrianism

Association Zoroastrianne de Québec (AZQ) / Zoroastrian Associaton of Québec (ZAQ)
PO Box 35, Stn. Beaconsfield, Beaconsfield QC H9W 5T6
Tel: 514-426-9929
quebeczoroastrians@gmail.com
zaq.org
Social Media:
www.youtube.com/channel/UCH_sL1HiIIPUnPgg9kt1yew
www.facebook.com/www.zaq.org?ref=hl
twitter.com/ZAQGROUP
Overview: A small provincial charitable organization founded in 1984
Chief Officer(s):
Dolly Dastoor, President
dollydastoor@sympatico.ca
Affiliation(s): Federation of North American Zoroastrian Associations

Ontario Zoroastrian Community Foundation (OZCF)
Zoroastrian Religious and Cultural Centre (OZCF Centre), 1187 Burnhamthorpe Road East, Oakville ON L6H 7B3
Tel: 905-271-0366
www.ozcf.com
Overview: A small provincial charitable organization
Chief Officer(s):
Percy Dastur, President
percydastur@gmail.com
Fees: $100 family; $30 seniors; $65 single; $25 student; *Member Profile:* Zoroastrians living in Ontario; *Committees:* Communication/IT, Social & Entertainment, Facility Management, Finance, Lectures & Learning, Membership, Newsletter, Religious, Seniors, Sports, Youth
Activities: Religious education program for children; Zoroastrian Scouts; Seniors program; Cultural Kanoun for Farsi speakers; Lecture group; Library; Youth group; Committees for newly landed immigrants & others in need; *Library:* Yes

Zoroastrian Society of Ontario (ZSO)
3590 Bayview Ave., Toronto ON M2M 3S6
Tel: 416-225-7771
secretary@zso.org
www.zso.org
Overview: A small provincial charitable organization founded in 1971
Chief Officer(s):
Sam M. Vesuna, President
Kevin Mancherjee, Exec. Vice-President
Fram Sethna, Treasurer
Mehroo Chothia, Secretary
Finances: *Annual Operating Budget:* $100,000-$250,000; *Funding Sources:* Membership fees; donations; investment income
Staff: 1 staff member(s); 200 volunteer(s)
Membership: 1,000; *Fees:* $70 family; $40 individual; $20 seniors & students; *Member Profile:* Zoroastrians living in Ontario; *Committees:* 15 sub-committees reporting to elected executive committee of 9
Activities: Religious, cultural, youth, religious classes, seniors activities; sponsors 100th Scout Group; *Library:* ZSO Library by appointment
Description: Meeting the religious & cultural needs of the Zoroastrian community of Ontario; Affiliation(s): Federation of North American Zoroastrian Associations

SECTION 15
SPORTS

Associations & Organizations

Aquatic Sports

ACUC International
PO Box 1179, #3, 101 Nelson St. East, Port Dover ON N0A 1N0
Tel: 519-583-9798; *Fax:* 519-583-3247
acuchq@acuc.ca
www.acuc.es
Social Media:
www.facebook.com/acucinternational
Also Known As: American & Canadian Underwater Certification Inc.
Overview: A medium-sized international licensing organization founded in 1968
Description: To supply quality training for sport scuba divers & instructors; To teach the highest standards in safety, sport, & marine conservation
Affiliation(s): World Diving Federation; Undersea Hyperbaric Medical Society
Chief Officer(s): Juan Rodriguez, President & Chief Executive Officer
jra@acuc.es
Nancy Cronkwright, Vice-President & Officer Manager, 519-750-5767, Fax: 519-750-5769
acuchq@acuc.ca
Patricia Molina, Vice-President & Manager, Clinet Service
comercial@acuc.es
Activities: *Internships:* Yes; *Speaker Service:* Yes

Aquatic Federation of Canada (AFC) / Fédération aquatique du Canada
c/o Martin Richard, Director, Communications, Swimming Canada, #B140, 2445 St-Laurent Blvd., Ottawa ON K1G 6C3
Tel: 613-260-1348
www.aquaticfederation.ca
Overview: A medium-sized national organization founded in 1968
Description: To promote olympic aquatic sports in Canada
Affiliation(s): Synchro Canada; Canadian Amateur Diving Association Inc.; Water Polo Canada; Swimming Canada
Chief Officer(s): Bill Hogan, President

Canadian Underwater Games Association (CUGA)
c/o Melanie Johnson, Secretary, #2002, 535 Nicola St., Vancouver BC V6G 3G3
info@cuga.org
www.cuga.org
Social Media:
www.facebook.com/cuga.org
Overview: A small national organization founded in 1984
Description: To oversee underwater sports in Canada.
Affiliation(s): World Underwater Federation
Chief Officer(s): Adam Jocksch, President
Activities: Underwater hockey & underwater rugby

Prince Edward Island Underwater Council
PE
Overview: A small provincial organization
Description: The PEI Underwater Council's mission is to help support & promote the sport of scuba diving in Prince Edward Island through safety, advocacy, cultural & environmental awareness, self-governance & education.

Water Polo Canada (WPC)
1084 Kenaston St., #1A, Ottawa ON K1B 3P5
Tel: 613-748-5682; *Fax:* 613-748-5777
office@waterpolo.ca
www.waterpolo.ca
Social Media:
www.youtube.com/waterpolocanada
www.facebook.com/193992167322377
twitter.com/waterpolocanada
Also Known As: Canadian Water Polo Association
Overview: A medium-sized national organization founded in 1976
Description: To promote growth in sport of water polo in Canada; to administer Canada's high performance programs (Olympics, Pan Am Games, etc.) in water polo
Affiliation(s): Aquatic Federation of Canada
Chief Officer(s): Martin Goulet, Executive Director, 613-748-5682 322
mgoulet@waterpolo.ca
Finances: *Funding Sources:* Government; sponsors; members
Staff: 15 staff member(s)
Member Profile: Water polo participant or team
Activities: *Internships:* Yes

Archery

Alberta Bowhunters Association (ABA)
202 Copperfield Grove SE, Calgary AB T2Z 4L7
www.bowhunters.ca
Previous Name: Alberta Bowhunters & Archers Association
Overview: A medium-sized provincial organization
Description: To promote bowhunting in Alberta; *Member of:* Federation of Canadian Archers
Chief Officer(s): Brent Watson, President
brent@albertabowhunters.com
Membership: *Fees:* $35 Adult; $25 Youth; $70 Family; $500 Life

Alberta Target Archers Association (ATAA)
AB
Tel: 780-717-2597
membership@ataa-org.ca
www.ataa-org.ca
Overview: A small provincial organization
Description: To promote all forms of archery in Alberta.
Chief Officer(s): Rene Schaub, President, 780-689-8488
president@ataa-org.ca
Jan Tollenaar, Coordinator, Membership
Membership: *Fees:* Schedule available

Archers & Bowhunters Association of Manitoba (ABAM)
145 Pacific Ave., Winnipeg MB R3B 2Z6
Tel: 204-925-5697; *Fax:* 204-925-5792
www.abam.ca
Social Media:
www.facebook.com/164613433679984
Overview: A small provincial organization
Description: To oversee the sports of archery & bowhunting in Manitoba.; *Member of:* Sport Manitoba
Chief Officer(s): Ryan Van Berkel, Executive Director
execdirector@abam.ca
Activities: Archery development program; olympic program

Archers Association of Nova Scotia (AANS)
c/o Sport Nova Scotia, 5516 Spring Garden Rd., 4th Fl., Halifax NS B3J 1G6
www.aans.ca
Overview: A medium-sized provincial organization founded in 1967
Description: To govern archery in Nova Scotia; *Member of:* Archery Canada Tir à l'Arc
Chief Officer(s): William Currie, President, 902-852-4393
wcurrie@dal.ca
Finances: *Annual Operating Budget:* Less than $50,000
Membership: 22 clubs; 450 individuals; *Fees:* $35 individuals; $60 family; includes membership with the Federation of Canadian Archers (FCA)

Archery Association of New Brunswick (AANB)
141 Isington St., Moncton NB E1A 1Y7
Tel: 506-855-6169
archerynb.ca
Overview: A small provincial organization founded in 1969
Description: To promote & encourage archery in New Brunswick; *Member of:* Archery Canada Tir à l'Arc
Chief Officer(s): Julie Murphy, President
akt@nbnet.nb.ca
Maurice Levesque, Executive Director
mlevesqu@nbnet.nb.ca
Membership: 19 clubs; *Committees:* Executive

Archery Canada Tir à l'Arc
#108, 2255 St. Laurent Blvd., Ottawa ON K1G 4K3
Tel: 613-260-2113; *Fax:* 613-260-2114
information@archerycanada.ca
www.archerycanada.ca
Social Media:
www.facebook.com/ArcheryCanada
twitter.com/ArcheryCanada
Previous Name: Federation of Canadian Archers Inc.
Overview: A medium-sized national charitable organization founded in 1927
Description: To promote & develop the sport of archery in a safe & ethical manner; To act as the official representative for archery to the federal government, & national & international sport organizations
Affiliation(s): World Archery Federation
Chief Officer(s): Scott Ogilvie, Executive Director
Finances: *Funding Sources:* Government support
Member Profile: Archers
Activities: Promoting archery participation across Canada; Supporting high performance excellence in archery; Presenting awards; Providing a vehicle for communication across Canada; Registering competitions; Maintaining Canadian records; Selecting archers to represent Canada at international events; Coordinating research; Training coaches & officials across Canada; Obtaining support for paralympic programs; *Library:* Yes

British Columbia Archery Association (BCAA)
c/o Samantha Wright, 4683 Ten Mile Lake Rd., Quesnel BC V2J 6X1
Tel: 250-992-5586
www.archeryassociation.bc.ca
Overview: A small provincial organization
Description: To be the governing body for the sport of archery in British Columbia.; *Member of:* Archery Canada Tir à l'Arc; Sport BC
Affiliation(s): World Archery Federation
Chief Officer(s): Ron Ostermeier, President, 250-468-3205
rono@justthatsimple.com
Samantha Wright, Secretary
samantha.wright@westfraser.com
Linda Price, Treasurer, 604-826-4906
price.falk@shaw.ca
Finances: *Funding Sources:* Ministry of Community, Sport & Cultural Development; Sport BC

Fédération de tir à l'arc du Québec (FTAQ)
CP 1000, Succ. M, 4545, av Pierre-de Coubertin, Montréal QC H1V 3R2
Tél: 514-252-3054; *Téléc:* 514-252-3165
taq@tiralarcquebec.com
www.tiralarcquebec.com
Média social:
www.facebook.com/tiralarcquebec
Aperçu: *Dimension:* petite; *Envergure:* provinciale
Membre de: Archery Canada Tir à l'Arc
Membre(s) du bureau directeur: Glenn Gudgeon, Président
president@tiralarcquebec.com
Membre: 3 000

Ontario Association of Archers Inc. (OAA)
PO Box 45, Caledon ON L7K 3L3
www.oaa-archery.on.ca
Previous Name: Ontario Archery Association
Overview: A medium-sized provincial organization founded in 1927
Member of: Archery Canada Tir à l'Arc
Chief Officer(s): Michael Martin, President
president@oaa-archery.on.ca
Kelly Chambers, Secretary-Treasurer
secretary@oaa-archery.on.ca
Lynda Savage, Office Administrator
administration@oaa-archery.on.ca
Membership: 800; *Fees:* $70 adult; $55 youth; $140 family; schedule for corporate & club memberships

Saskatchewan Archery Association (SAA)
c/o Gil Segovia, President, 335 Brooklyn Cres., Warman SK S0K 0A1
Tel: 306-370-0640
www.saskarchery.com
Social Media:
www.facebook.com/SaskatchewanArcheryAssociation
Overview: A small provincial organization
Description: To foster, to perpetuate & direct the practice of Archery in a spirit of good fellowship & sportsmanship.; *Member of:* Archery Canada Tir à l'Arc
Chief Officer(s): Gil Segovia, President
gil@segovia-sask.com
Finances: *Annual Operating Budget:* $50,000-$100,000
Staff: 20 volunteer(s)
Membership: 850; *Fees:* $45 adult; $25 youth (17 & under)

Tir-à-l'arc Moncton Archers Inc.
Moncton NB
Tel: 506-382-3522
Previous Name: Moncton Archers & Bowhunters Association
Overview: A small local organization founded in 1968
Description: To enjoy the sport of archery & bowhunting; To promote saftey in each sport
Affiliation(s): New Brunswick Archery Association; Canadian Archery Association
Chief Officer(s): John Langelaan, Director
johnlangelaan@hotmail.com

World Archery Federation
Maison du Sport International, Avenue de Rhodanie 54, Lausanne 1007 Switzerland
info@archery.org
www.worldarchery.org
Social Media:
www.youtube.com/archerytv; instagram.com/worldarchery
www.facebook.com/WorldArcheryPage
twitter.com/worldarchery
Previous Name: International Archery Federation

Overview: A small international organization founded in 1931
Description: To promote & encourage archery throughout the world in conformity with the Olympic principles; to frame & interpret FITA rules & regulations; to arrange for the organization of World Championships; to confirm & maintain world record scores & Olympic Games record scores; to maintain complete lists of scores from FITA Championships & Olympic Games; *Member of:* International Olympic Committee
Affiliation(s): Federation of Canadian Archers Inc.
Chief Officer(s): Ugur Erdener, President
Tom Dielen, Secretary General & Executive Director
Finances: *Annual Operating Budget:* $500,000-$1.5 Million
Staff: 8 staff member(s); 70 volunteer(s)
Membership: 141 countries; *Member Profile:* National federations; *Committees:* Athletes; Elections Procedure; Coaches; Manuals; Information from Judges & Coaches; Constitution & Rules; Field Archery; Judges; Medical & Sport Sciences; Para-Archery; Target Archery; Technical

Athletics

Alberta Cheerleading Association (ACA)
PO Box 31006, Edmonton AB T5Z 3P3
Tel: 780-417-0050; *Fax:* 780-417-0093
Toll-Free: 888-756-9220
info@albertacheerleading.ca
www.albertacheerleading.ca
Social Media:
www.facebook.com/115045571883130
Overview: A small provincial organization
Description: To be the provincial regulator of cheerleading in Alberta.; *Member of:* Cheer Canada
Chief Officer(s): Jennifer Guiney, President
jennifer@albertacheerleading.ca
Denise Fisher, Executive Director
executivedirector@albertacheerleading.ca

Alberta Schools' Athletic Association (ASAA)
Percy Page Centre, 11759 Groat Rd., Edmonton AB T5M 3K6
Tel: 780-427-8182; *Fax:* 780-415-1833
info@asaa.ca
www.asaa.ca
Social Media:
twitter.com/ASAA
Overview: A medium-sized provincial organization founded in 1956
Description: To provide leadership in the promotion of high school sport; to regulate sports competition & promote the belief that education includes development of the whole person; *Member of:* School Sport Canada
Affiliation(s): National Federation of State High School Associations
Chief Officer(s): John F. Paton, Executive Director
john@asaa.ca
Garret Doll, President
gdoll@gsacrd.ab.ca
Finances: *Funding Sources:* Lotteries; membership dues; fundraising; corporate sponsors
Staff: 5 staff member(s)
Membership: 371 schools + 8,000 student athletes

Amateur Athletic Union (AAU)
PO Box 22049, Lake Buena Vista FL 32830 USA
Tel: 407-934-7200; *Fax:* 407-934-7242
Toll-Free: 800-228-4872
www.aausports.org
Social Media:
www.youtube.com/therealaauvideo
www.facebook.com/realaau
twitter.com/therealaau
Overview: A large national organization founded in 1888
Description: To offer a lifelong progression of amateur sports programs for persons of all ages, races & creeds, thereby enhancing the physical, mental & moral development of amateur athletes; to promote good sportsmanship, good citizenship & safety
Chief Officer(s): Henry Forrest, President
Finances: *Funding Sources:* Membership dues
Staff: 1000 volunteer(s)
Membership: 650,000; *Fees:* Schedule available
Activities: Conducts programs & works with other sports organizations to benefit amateur athletes; conducts recognition programs for outstanding amateur athletes; publishes an extensive line of handbooks & brochures on individual sports; *Internships:* Yes; *Rents Mailing List:* Yes; *Library:* Yes (Open to Public)

Athletes International
#2702, 3550 Jeanne Mauce, Montréal QC H2X 3P7
Tel: 514-982-9989; *Fax:* 514-982-0111
Toll-Free: 800-344-1810
info@athletes-int.com
www.athletes-int.com
Social Media:
twitter.com/athletesint
Overview: A small national organization
Description: To promote a sense of community & sharing in Canadian sport; To offer discounted products & services, to members of the Canadian sport community, through partners
Chief Officer(s): Peter Schleicher, President
pschleicher@athletes-int.com
Member Profile: Canadian sport community
Activities: Offering benefits in areas such as airfare, travel insurance, & hotel reservations

AthletesCAN
PO Box 60039, Stn. Findlay Creek, Ottawa ON K1T 0K9
Tel: 613-526-4025; *Fax:* 613-526-9735
Toll-Free: 888-832-4222
info@athletescan.com
www.athletescan.com
Social Media:
instagram.com/athletescan
www.facebook.com/AthletesCAN
twitter.com/AthletesCAN
Also Known As: The Association of Canada's National Team Athletes
Previous Name: The Athletes Association of Canada
Overview: A medium-sized national organization founded in 1992
Description: To work with others in leadership, advocacy & education to ensure a fair, responsive & supportive sport system for athletes
Chief Officer(s): Ashley LaBrie, Interim Executive Director, 613-526-4025 224
alabrie@athletescan.com
Renee Ridout, Chief Content Curator
rridout@athletescan.com
Rob Little, Development Officer
rlittle@athletescan.com
Membership: 3,000+

Athletics Alberta
Percy Page Centre, 11759 Groat Rd., Edmonton AB T5M 3K6
Tel: 780-427-8792; *Fax:* 780-427-8899
info@athleticsalberta.com
www.athleticsalberta.com
Social Media:
www.youtube.com/user/AthleticsAB
www.linkedin.com/groups/Athletics-Alberta-1997317
www.facebook.com/AthleticsAlberta
twitter.com/athleticsAB
Previous Name: Alberta Track & Field Association
Overview: A medium-sized provincial organization founded in 1969
Description: To encourage participation & development of excellence in athletics (track & field, cross-country, & road-running); *Member of:* Athletics Canada
Chief Officer(s): Linda Blade, President
Peter Ogilvie, Executive Director
peterogilvie@athleticsalberta.com
Sheryl Mack, Office Manager
sherylmack@athleticsalberta.com
Finances: *Funding Sources:* Lottery dollars; fundraising; membership fees
Staff: 3 staff member(s)

Athletics Manitoba
#416, 145 Pacific Ave., Winnipeg MB R3B 2Z6
Tel: 204-925-5745
www.athleticsmanitoba.com
Overview: A medium-sized provincial organization founded in 1978
Description: The governing and sanctioning organization for Track and field, Road Running and Cross Country in the province of Manitoba.; *Member of:* Athletics Canada; Sport Manitoba
Chief Officer(s): Grant Mitchell, President
Chris Belof, Manager, Competition & Program
chris.belof@athleticsmanitoba.com

Athletics New Brunswick (ANB) / Athlétisme du Nouveau-Brunswick
66 Belle Foret St., Dieppe NB E1A 8X9
Tel: 506-855-5003; *Fax:* 506-855-5011
anb@anb.ca
www.anb.ca
Social Media:
www.facebook.com/AthNB
twitter.com/AthNB
Overview: A medium-sized provincial organization founded in 1968
Description: To act as the provincial sports organization for the sports of track & field & cross-country running; *Member of:* Athletics Canada
Chief Officer(s): Bill MacMackin, President
Bill.MacMackin@anb.ca
Germain Landry, Vice-President
Germain.Landry@anb.ca
Gabriel (Gabe) LeBlanc, Director, Technical
anb@anb.ca
Camilla MacDougall, Registrar
Camilla.MacDougall@anb.ca
Membership: *Fees:* Schedule available
Activities: *Speaker Service:* Yes; *Rents Mailing List:* Yes

Athletics Nova Scotia
5516 Spring Garden Rd, 4th Fl., Halifax NS B3J 1G6
Tel: 902-425-5450; *Fax:* 902-425-5606
www.athleticsnovascotia.ca
Overview: A small provincial organization
Description: The Association is a non-profit, amateur sport governing body that develops, coordinates & promotes track & field, road running & cross-country running in Nova Scotia.; *Member of:* Athletics Canada
Chief Officer(s): Anitra Stevens, Executive Director
Joanthan Doucette, Manager, Coaching & Officiating
Membership: *Fees:* $60 club athlete; $75 independent athelete; $30 independent coach; $20 Run Jump Throw athlete; *Member Profile:* Track & field clubs

Athletics Ontario
#211, 3 Concorde Gate, Toronto ON M3C 3N7
Tel: 416-426-7215; *Fax:* 416-426-7358
www.athleticsontario.ca
Social Media:
www.facebook.com/135196239850966
twitter.com/athleticsont
Previous Name: Ontario Track & Field Association
Overview: A medium-sized provincial organization founded in 1974
Description: To promote & encourage participation via competitions from the grass roots level through to the very highest level of proficiency; To assist coaches, officials & executives in fulfilling their goals through courses, conferences & clinics; to provide regular communication lines with members; To continually review & update technical programs; To assist in the research & investigation of potential new facilities; To engender more public awareness, interest, & acceptance of the sport of track & field; *Member of:* Athletics Canada
Chief Officer(s): John Craig, Managing Director
Roman Olszewski, Director, Technical Services
roman.otfa@cogeco.ca
Anthony Biggar, Manager, Communications & Public Relations
anthonybiggar@athleticsontario.ca

Athletics PEI
PO Box 302, 40 Enman Cres., Charlottetown PE C1A 7K7
www.athleticspei.ca
Overview: A small provincial organization
Member of: Athletics Canada

Athletics Yukon
4061 - 4th Ave., Whitehorse YT Y1A 1H1
athleticsyukon@gmail.com
www.athleticsyukon.ca
Social Media:
www.facebook.com/pages/Athletics-Yukon/149557131815078
Overview: A small provincial organization
Description: To promote & encourage athletics as a life-long pursuit; *Member of:* Athletics Canada; Sport Yukon
Affiliation(s): Boreal Adventure Running Association; Mount Lorne Mis-Adventure Race; Run Dawson
Chief Officer(s): Ben Yu Schott, President
Membership: *Fees:* $15 youth & senior; $30 regular; $60 family
Activities: Administering the sports of: Road Racing; Cross Country Running; Track & Field; Snowshoeing; & Race Walking

B2ten
QC
b2ten.ca
Social Media:
twitter.com/B2ten

Overview: A small national charitable organization founded in 2005
Description: To help Canadian athletes achieve success in the sporting world, particularly in an international context.
Finances: *Funding Sources:* Donations

BC Athlete Voice (BCAV)
#227, 3820 Cessna Dr., Richmond BC V7B 0A2
Tel: 604-345-1615
info@bcathletevoice.ca
www.bcathletevoice.ca
Social Media:
www.youtube.com/user/BCAthleteVoice;
flickr.com/photos/72052636@N04
www.facebook.com/BCAthleteVoice
twitter.com/BCAthleteVoice
Overview: A medium-sized provincial organization
Description: To offer athletes in British Columbia leadership, education & advocacy programming.
Chief Officer(s): Callum Ng, Executive Director
callum@bcathletevoice.ca
Activities: Funding & sponsoring athletes

BC Cheerleading Association (BCCA)
BC
www.bccheerleading.ca
Overview: A small provincial organization
Description: To maintain athleticism & safety in cheerleading in British Columbia.; *Member of:* Cheer Canada
Chief Officer(s): Krista Gerlich-Fitzgerald, Chair

British Columbia Athletics
#2001, 3713 Kensington Ave., B. Oslo Landing, Burnaby BC V5B 0A7
Tel: 604-333-3550; *Fax:* 604-333-3551
bcathletics@bcathletics.org
www.bcathletics.org
Social Media:
www.facebook.com/BCAthletics1
twitter.com/bc_athletics
Also Known As: BC Amateur Athletics Association
Previous Name: BC Track & Field Association
Overview: A medium-sized provincial licensing organization
Description: To promote, encourage & develop excellence by creating opportunities in athletics (track & field, road-running & cross-country running); *Member of:* Athletics Canada; Sport BC
Chief Officer(s): Brian McCalder, President & CEO
brian.mccalder@bcathletics.org
Membership: *Fees:* Schedule available; *Committees:* Track & Field; Road Running; Cross Country; Masters; Junior Development; Masters
Activities: *Internships:* Yes; *Speaker Service:* Yes; *Rents Mailing List:* Yes; *Library:* Yes (Open to Public)

Canada DanceSport (CDS)
www.dancesport.ca
Previous Name: Canadian Amateur DanceSport Association
Overview: A medium-sized national organization founded in 1978
Member of: World DanceSport Federation
Chief Officer(s): Sandy Brittain, President

Canadian Trail & Mountain Running Association (CTMRA)
BC
www.mountainrunning.ca
Social Media:
www.facebook.com/groups/2229398616
twitter.com/CTMRA
Overview: A small national organization
Description: To oversee the sport of mountain running in Canada.
Chief Officer(s): Adrian Lambert, Contact
adrian.lambert@mountainrunning.ca
Activities: Championship series

Canadian Wheelchair Basketball Association (CWBA) / Association canadienne de basketball en fauteuil roulant (ACBFR)
#8, 6 Antares Dr., Phase 1, Ottawa ON K2E 8A9
Tel: 613-260-1296; *Fax:* 613-260-1456
Toll-Free: 877-843-2922
info@wheelchairbasketball.ca
www.wheelchairbasketball.ca
Social Media:
www.youtube.com/user/WheelchairBball
www.facebook.com/wheelchairbasketball
twitter.com/WCBballCanada
Also Known As: Wheelchair Basketball Canada
Overview: A medium-sized national charitable organization founded in 1994
Description: To act as the governing body for wheelchair basketball in Canada; *Member of:* Canadian Paralympic Committee; International Wheelchair Basketball Federation
Affiliation(s): Canada Basketball
Chief Officer(s): Wendy Gittens, Executive Director
wgittens@wheelchairbasketball.ca
Paul Zachau, Director, High Performance
pzachau@wheelchairbasketball.ca
Jody Kingsbury, Manager, Communications
jkingsbury@wheelchairbasketball.ca
Catherine Ireland, Coordinator, Programs
Courtney Pollock, Coordinator, Communications
cpollock@wheelchairbasketball.ca
Ryan Lauzon, Coordinator, High Performance
rlauzon@wheelchairbasketball.ca
Membership: 2,500

Cheer Canada
c/o Alberta Cheerleading Association, PO Box 31006, Edmonton AB T5Z 3P3
Tel: 780-417-0050; *Fax:* 780-417-0093
Toll-Free: 888-756-9220
info@cheercanada.net
www.cheerleadingcanadainc.com
Social Media:
www.facebook.com/17176451622097б
twitter.com/cheercanada
Overview: A medium-sized national organization founded in 2011
Description: To provide the following to provincial cheerleading organizations: ease of travel between provinces & territories; national coaches' & judges' training & certification programs; insurance for athletes & coaches; & funding for teams.
Affiliation(s): International All Star Federation Worlds; US All Star Federation
Membership: 9 associations; *Member Profile:* Provincial cheerleading associations

Cheer Nova Scotia
NS
www.cheerns.com
Aperçu: *Dimension:* petite; *Envergure:* provinciale
Description: To promote cheerleading in Nova Scotia.; *Membre de:* Cheer Canada
Membre(s) du bureau directeur: Megan Spencer, President
president@nscheer.com
Monique Johnson, Treasurer
communicator@nscheer.com

DanceSport Alberta (DSAB)
AB
president@dancesportalberta.org
www.dancesportalberta.org
Overview: A medium-sized provincial organization founded in 1989
Chief Officer(s): Theresa Jenkins, President

DanceSport Atlantic (DAA)
3273 Beaver Bank Rd., Lower Sackville NS B4C 2S6
Tel: 902-865-9914
dancesport.chebucto.org
Overview: A medium-sized provincial organization
Chief Officer(s): John McDermott, Contact

DanceSport Québec (DSQ)
4545 ave Pierre-De Coubertin, Montréal QC H1V 0B2
Tél: 514-418-8264; *Ligne sans frais:* 800-474-5746
info@dansesportquebec.com
dansesportquebec.com
Aperçu: *Dimension:* moyenne; *Envergure:* provinciale

Fédération de cheerleading du Québec (FCQ)
4545, av Pierre-de Coubertin, Montréal QC H1V 0B2
Tél: 514-252-3145; *Téléc:* 514-252-3146
Ligne sans frais: 866-694-3145
info@cheerleadingquebec.com
www.cheerleadingquebec.com
Média social:
www.facebook.com/252273871484094
Aperçu: *Dimension:* petite; *Envergure:* provinciale
Membre de: Cheer Canada
Membre(s) du bureau directeur: Jocelyn Deslaurier, Président
president@cheerleadingquebec.com
Catherine Marois Blanchet, Directrice générale, 514-252-3000 3465
cmblanchet@cheerleadingquebec.com

Fédération québécoise d'athlétisme (FQA)
4545, av Pierre-de Coubertin, Montréal QC H1V 0B2
Tél: 514-252-3041; *Téléc:* 514-252-3042
fqa@athletisme.qc.ca
www.athletisme.qc.ca
Média social:
www.youtube.com/athletismequebec
www.facebook.com/athletismequebec
twitter.com/Athl_FQA
Nom précédent: Fédération d'athlétisme du Québec
Aperçu: *Dimension:* moyenne; *Envergure:* provinciale; Organisme sans but lucratif; fondée en 1968
Description: Promouvoir l'athlétisme au Québec; *Membre de:* Athletics Canada
Membre(s) du bureau directeur: Sylvain Proulx, Président
Laurent Godbout, Directeur général
lgodbout@athletisme.qc.ca
Montant de la cotisation: Barème; *Critères d'admissibilite:* Coureurs sur route; athlètes; entraîneurs; officiels; membres associés; *Comités:* Technique provinciale; Officiels, règlements et organisations; Jeunes
Activités: *Service de conférenciers:* Oui

Greater Montreal Athletic Association (GMAA) / Association régionale du sport scolaire
#101, 5925, av Monkland, Montréal QC H4A 1G7
Tel: 514-482-8555; *Fax:* 514-487-0121
gmaa@gmaa.ca
www.gmaa.ca
Social Media:
www.facebook.com/RSEQ-Greater-Montreal-GMAA-419767904880749
Overview: A small local charitable organization founded in 1975
Description: Devoted to the promotion of athletics in the English schools of the greater Montreal region.; *Member of:* Réseau du sport étudiant du Québec
Chief Officer(s): Amanda Maks, Executive Director
amanda@gmaa.ca
Finances: *Annual Operating Budget:* $250,000-$500,000
Staff: 3 staff member(s)
Membership: 152; *Fees:* User fees by activity; *Member Profile:* Principals of elementary & secondary schools
Activities: Organize & run sports activities & leagues for English schools on the Island of Montréal

Interior Running Association
BC
Tel: 250-374-1652
www.interiorrunningassociation.com
Social Media:
www.facebook.com/InteriorRunningAssociation
twitter.com/interiorrunning
Overview: A small national organization
Description: To promote fitness & running in the Southern Interior of British Columbia.
Chief Officer(s): Cindy Rhodes, Co-President
John Wilson, Co-President
Activities: Road & trail races

Manitoba Association of Cheerleading (MAC)
MB
Tel: 204-888-0317
info@cheermanitoba.ca
www.cheermanitoba.ca
Social Media:
instagram.com/mac_cheer_mb
www.facebook.com/ManitobaAssociationofCheerleading
twitter.com/MAC_Cheer_MB
Overview: A small provincial organization founded in 1986
Description: To be the official regulating body for cheerleading in Manitoba.; *Member of:* Cheer Canada
Chief Officer(s): Patricia McNeill, President

Manitoba Cheer Federation Inc. (MCF)
PO Box 42010, 1881 Portage Ave., Winnipeg MB R3J 0J0
info@mbcheer.ca
www.mbcheer.ca
Social Media:
www.facebook.com/145664425448394
twitter.com/MCF_Cheer
Overview: A small provincial organization founded in 2010
Description: To regulate, promote & develop cheerleading in Manitoba.; *Member of:* Cheer Canada
Chief Officer(s): Marian Henry, President
Kait Allen, Director, Judging
Amanda Barnes, Director, Communications
Mallory Mitchell, Director, Event

Manitoba High Schools Athletic Association (MHSAA)
145 Pacific Ave., Winnipeg MB R3B 2Z6
Tel: 204-925-5640; *Fax:* 204-925-5624
info@mhsaa.ca
www.mhsaa.ca
Social Media:
www.facebook.com/MBHighSchoolsAthleticsAssociation
twitter.com/MHSAA_
Overview: A medium-sized provincial charitable organization founded in 1962
Description: To promote the value of sports in Manitoba secondary schools; To provide athletic & educational opportunities so that students reach their full potential; *Member of:* School Sport Canada
Chief Officer(s): Morris Glimcher, Executive Director, 204-925-5641
morris@mhsaa.ca
Finances: *Funding Sources:* Sport Manitoba grants; Membership fees; Corporate support; Revenues from admissions to provincial championships; Fundraising
Staff: 3 staff member(s)
Membership: 192 schools + 37,000 athletes; *Fees:* Schedule available, based upon school size; *Member Profile:* Secondary schools in Manitoba
Activities: Encouraging participation in high school sports; Assisting in running equitable & fair sporting events for high schools; Presenting awards & scholarships for athletes, coaches, & volunteeers; Promoting volunteer involvement; Seeking support for the association; Providing educational materials for coaches & teachers

Manitoba Runners' Association (MRA)
PO Box 34148, Winnipeg MB R3T 5T5
Tel: 204-477-5185
office@mraweb.ca
www.mraweb.ca
Social Media:
www.facebook.com/188241213063
Overview: A small provincial organization
Description: To encourage road running in Manitoba.
Chief Officer(s): Kathy Wiens, Executive Director
Membership: *Fees:* Schedule available
Activities: Fun runs; races

National Association of Collegiate Directors of Athletics (NACDA)
24651 Detroit Rd., Westlake OH 44145 USA
Tel: 440-892-4000; *Fax:* 440-892-4007
www.nacda.com
Social Media:
www.facebook.com/nacda
twitter.com/nacda
Overview: A small international organization founded in 1965
Description: To serve as the professional association for those in the field of intercollegiate athletics administration; To serves as a vehicle for networking, the exchange of information, & advocacy on behalf of the profession
Chief Officer(s): Bob Vecchione, Executive Director
bvecchione@nacda.com
Membership: 6,100 individuals; 1,600 institutions; *Fees:* Schedule available; *Member Profile:* Collegiate athletics administrators in the United States, Canada, & Mexico
Activities: Providing educational opportunities

Newfoundland & Labrador Athletics Association (NLAA)
PO Box 3202, Paradise NL A1L 3W4
Tel: 709-576-1303; *Fax:* 709-576-7493
athletics@nlaa.ca
www.nlaa.ca
Social Media:
www.facebook.com/NLAthletics
twitter.com/nlathletics
Previous Name: Newfoundland & Labrador Track & Field Association
Overview: A small provincial organization
Member of: Athletics Canada
Affiliation(s): Athletics North-East; Mariners Athletics Club; Nautilus Running Club; New World Running Club; Pearlgate T&F Club; Trappers Running Club; Trinity-Conception Athletics Club; Westerland Track Club
Chief Officer(s): Bob Walsh, President
bob@atlantichome.net
Alison Walsh, Treasurer
alisonwalsh3@hotmail.com
George Stanoev, Technical Director
Membership: *Fees:* Schedule available; *Member Profile:* Competitive membership (road running, cross country running, & track & field); Non-competitive membership (coaches & officials); *Committees:* Road Race; Coaches; Officials
Activities: Offering courses & clinics for athletes, officials, & coaches; Supervising events; Ensuring that rules are followed & criteria maintained throughout Newfoundland & Labrador

Newfoundland & Labrador Cheerleading Athletics (NLCA)
PO Box 39059, Stn. Topsail Road, St. John's NL A1E 5Y7
nlcheerleading.ca
Social Media:
www.facebook.com/groups/10418436853
twitter.com/NLCAnews
Overview: A small provincial organization
Description: To be the governing body of cheerleading in Newfoundland & Labrador.; *Member of:* Cheer Canada
Chief Officer(s): Ashley Wright, President
Membership: 600

Nova Scotia School Athletic Federation (NSSAF)
5516 Spring Garden Rd., Halifax NS B3J 1G6
Tel: 902-425-8662; *Fax:* 902-425-5606
nssaf.ednet.ns.ca
Overview: A small provincial organization
Description: Motto: "Education Through Sport" which thus emphasises the value of sport in relation to the multitude of benefits that participation gives to their students.; *Member of:* School Sport Canada
Chief Officer(s): Darrell LeBlanc, Chair, Board of Governors
Darrell Dempster, Executive Director
Dianne Weston, Secretary
Membership: 40,000 student athletes; *Member Profile:* Student atheletes and their affiliates including coaches, administrators, and officiates.

Ontario Cheerleading Federation (OCF)
21 Oceanpearl Cres., Whitby ON L1N 0C5
registrar@ocfcheer.com
www.ocfcheer.com
Social Media:
twitter.com/OntarioCheer
Overview: A small provincial organization
Description: To provide training & certification courses for coaches across Ontario.; *Member of:* Cheer Canada

Ontario DanceSport (ODS)
ON
Tel: 905-831-2426
publicity@ontariodancesport.com
www.ontariodancesport.com
Overview: A medium-sized provincial organization
Chief Officer(s): Gord Brittain, President

Ontario Federation of School Athletic Associations (OFSAA) / Fédération des associations du sport scolaire de l'Ontario
#204, 3 Concorde Gate, Toronto ON M3C 3N7
Tel: 416-426-7391; *Fax:* 416-426-7317
www.ofsaa.on.ca
Social Media:
www.instagram.com/OFSAAGRAM
www.facebook.com/OFSAA
twitter.com/OFSAA
Overview: A medium-sized provincial charitable organization founded in 1948
Description: To enhance school sport in Ontario; To handle issues that affect students, coaches, schools, & communities; To work with volunteer teacher-coaches to offer provincial championships & festivals for student-athletes across Ontario; *Member of:* School Sport Canada
Chief Officer(s): Donna Howard, Executive Director, 416-426-7438
donna@ofsaa.on.ca
Devin Gray, Coordinator, Communications, 416-426-7437
devin@ofsaa.on.ca
Finances: *Funding Sources:* Sponsorships
Staff: 9 staff member(s)
Membership: 18 associations; *Member Profile:* Regional school athletic associations throughout Ontario, such as the Central Ontario Secondary Schools Association, Northern Ontario Secondary Schools Association, Southern Ontario Secondary Schools Association, & the Toronto District College Athletic Association; *Committees:* Alpine Skiing; Badminton; Baseball; Basketball; Cross Country; Curling; Field Hockey; Field Lacrosse; Football; Golf; Gymnastics; Hockey; Nordic Skiing; Rugby; Snowboard Racing; Soccer; Swimming; Tennis; Track & Field; Volleyball; Wrestling; Championship Review Ad Hoc; Classifications Ad Hoc; Coaching Ad Hoc; Constitutional Review Ad Hoc; Future Directions Ad Hoc; Gender Equity Ad Hoc; Sanctions Ad Hoc; Transfers Ad Hoc
Activities: Organizing programs, such as student leadership & coach development programs; Sanctioning tournaments; Preparing & distributing resources; Providing professional development opportunities; *Awareness Events:* Canadian School Sport Week

Réseau du sport étudiant du Québec Abitibi-Témiscamingue (RSEQAT)
QC
Ligne sans frais: 866-626-2047
at.rseq.ca
Également appelé: RSEQ Abitibi-Témiscamingue
Nom précédent: Association régionale du sport étudiant de l'Abitibi-Témiscamingue
Aperçu: *Dimension:* petite; *Envergure:* locale; Organisme sans but lucratif; fondée en 1969
Description: Regrouper sur le plan du sport étudiant les représentants des différentes institutions d'enseignement de la région de l'Abitibi-Témiscamingue; stimuler l'intérêt et favoriser le développement du sport étudiant dans cette région; *Membre de:* Réseau du sport étudiant du Québec
Membre(s) du bureau directeur: Alain Dubois, Président
Finances: *Fonds:* Gouvernement provincial
Membre: 1-99

Réseau du sport étudiant du Québec Cantons-de-l'Est
5182, boul Bourque, Sherbrooke QC J1N 1H4
Tel: 819-864-0792
oaudet@ce.rseq.ca
ce.rseq.ca
Also Known As: RSEQ Cantons-de-l'Est
Overview: A small local organization
Member of: Réseau du sport étudiant du Québec
Chief Officer(s): Paul Deshaies, Président

Réseau du sport étudiant du Québec Chaudière-Appalaches (RSEQ-QCA)
762, rue Jacques-Berthiaume, Québec QC G1V 3T1
Tél: 418-657-7678; *Téléc:* 418-657-1367
sportetudiant.qc.ca
Média social:
www.instagram.com/rseqqca
www.facebook.com/RSEQQCA
twitter.com/RSEQ_QCA
Également appelé: RSEQ Chaudière-Appalaches
Nom précédent: Association régionale du sport étudiant de Québec et Chaudière-Appalaches
Aperçu: *Dimension:* petite; *Envergure:* locale
Description: Organisme à but non-lucratif qui regroupe l'ensemble des institutions d'enseignement des régions de Québec et de Chaudière-Appalaches; *Membre de:* Réseau du sport étudiant du Québec
Membre(s) du bureau directeur: Julie Dionne, Directrice générale, 418-657-7678 202
jdionne@qca.rseq.ca

Réseau du sport étudiant du Québec Côte-Nord
#146, 40, rue Comeau, Sept-Iles QC G4R 4N3
Tél: 418-964-2888; *Téléc:* 418-968-4033
cote-nord.rseq.ca
Également appelé: RSEQ Côte-Nord
Nom précédent: Association régionale du sport étudiant de la Côte-Nord
Aperçu: *Dimension:* petite; *Envergure:* locale
Description: Regrouper sur le plan du sport étudiant, les différentes commissions scolaires, institutions privées et institutions collégiales de la Côte-Nord; stimuler l'intérêt et favoriser le développement du sport étudiant; définir les politiques générales du sport étudiant; promouvoir l'établissement des programmes; coordonner et sanctionner les différentes compétitions du sport étudiant; organiser des stages de perfectionnement; établir les règlements que doivent régir les différentes compétitions du sport étudiant; homologuer les records établis lors des compétitions du sport étudiant; *Membre de:* Réseau du sport étudiant du Québec
Membre(s) du bureau directeur: Brigitte Leblanc, Présidente
Cindy Hounsell, Directrice Générale
chounsell@cote-nord.rseq.ca

Réseau du sport étudiant du Québec Lac Saint-Louis
2900, rue Lake, Dollard-des-Ormeaux QC H9B 2P1
Tél: 514-855-4230; *Téléc:* 514-685-4643
www.arselsl.qc.ca
Média social:
www.facebook.com/rseqlsl
twitter.com/RSEQ_LSL
Également appelé: RSEQ Lac Saint-Louis
Nom précédent: Association régionale du sport étudiant Lac Saint-Louis
Aperçu: *Dimension:* petite; *Envergure:* locale
Description: Réseau du sport étudiant du Québec Lac Saint-Louis est un organisme sans but lucratif qui regroupe l'ensemble des institutions d'enseignement affiliées de la région

Lac Saint-Louis; *Membre de:* Réseau du sport étudiant du Québec
Membre(s) du bureau directeur: Karine Mayrand, Directrice générale, 514-855-4230 6524
kmayrand@lsl.rseq.ca

Réseau du sport étudiant du Québec Laurentides-Lanaudière
401, boul du Domaine, Sainte-Thérèse QC J7E 4S4
Tél: 450-419-8786; *Téléc:* 450-419-8892
ll.rseq.ca
Également appelé: RSEQ Laurentides-Lanaudière
Nom précédent: Association régionale du sport étudiant Laurentides-Lanaudière
Aperçu: *Dimension:* petite; *Envergure:* locale; Organisme sans but lucratif
Description: Favoriser la réalisation de l'ensemble des actions éducatives par l'activité physique et particulièrement le sport en vue de contribuer au développement intégral des étudiants des niveaux primaire, secondaire et collégial dans la région Laurentides-Lanaudière; *Membre de:* Réseau du sport étudiant du Québec
Membre(s) du bureau directeur: Jacinthe Lussier, Directrice générale
jacinthe.lussier@cssmi.qc.ca

Réseau du sport étudiant du Québec Montérégie
c/o École secondaire Gérard-Filion, 1330, boul Curé-Poirier ouest, Longueuil QC J4K 2G8
Tel: 450-463-4055; *Fax:* 450-463-4229
info@monteregie.rseq.ca
monteregie.rseq.ca
Social Media:
www.youtube.com/channel/UCUPxwmcQY63heCqnGv8WqaQ
www.facebook.com/RseqMonteregie
twitter.com/RSEQMRG
Also Known As: RSEQ Montérégie
Overview: A small local organization
Member of: Réseau du sport étudiant du Québec
Chief Officer(s): Sylvie Cornellier, Directrice Générale, 450-463-4055 102
scornellier@monteregie.rseq.ca

Réseau du sport étudiant du Québec Outaouais
Complexe Branchaud-Brière, #201, 499, boul Labrosse, Gatineau QC J8P 4R1
Tél: 819-643-6663; *Téléc:* 819-643-6665
www.arseo.qc.ca/ARSEO.php
Média social:
www.facebook.com/RseqOutaouais
Également appelé: RSEQ Outaouais
Aperçu: *Dimension:* petite; *Envergure:* locale
Membre de: Réseau du sport étudiant du Québec
Membre(s) du bureau directeur: Hélène Boucher, Directrice générale, 819-643-6663 205
helene.boucher@arseo.qc.ca

Réseau du sport étudiant du Québec, secteur Mauricie
260, rue Dessureault, Trois-Rivières QC G8T 9T9
Tél: 819-693-5805; *Téléc:* 819-693-1189
mauricie.rseq.ca
Média social:
www.facebook.com/rseqmauricie
twitter.com/rseq_mauricie
Également appelé: RSEQ Mauricie
Nom précédent: Association régionale du sport étudiant de la Mauricie
Aperçu: *Dimension:* petite; *Envergure:* locale
Description: Réseau du sport étudiant du Québec, secteur Mauricie, est un organisme sans but lucratif qui regroupe les institutions d'enseignement situées sur le territoire de la Mauricie et sur la rive sud du fleuve Saint-Laurent, jusqu'à l'autoroute 20; *Membre de:* Réseau du sport étudiant du Québec
Membre(s) du bureau directeur: Micheline Guillemette, Directrice générale, 819-693-5805 6543
mguillemette@mauricie.rseq.ca

Sarnia Minor Athletic Association (SMAA)
Chaytor Building - Germain Park, PO Box 524, Sarnia ON N7T 7J4
Tel: 519-332-1896; *Fax:* 519-332-1569
smaa@ebtech.net
www.sarniaminorathletic.com
Overview: A small local organization founded in 1947
Description: To instill the knowledge that accompanies minor sports participation in the athletes
Chief Officer(s): Murray Rempel, President

Saskatchewan Athletics
2020 College Dr., Saskatoon SK S7N 2W4
Tel: 306-664-6744; *Fax:* 306-664-6761
athletics@sasktel.net
www.saskathletics.ca
Social Media:
twitter.com/SaskAthletics
Overview: A small provincial organization
Description: Promotes the sport of athletics by facilitating the development & maintenance of effective programs which assists athletes, coaches, officials, & volunteers in a fair & positive environment; *Member of:* Athletics Canada
Chief Officer(s): Alan Sharp, President
asharp@mail.gssd.ca
Bob Reindl, Executive Director
Janine Platana, Administrative Assistant
Finances: *Funding Sources:* Saskatchewan Lotteries; Athletics Canada; Sask Sport Inc.; Corporate sponsorships
Staff: 3 staff member(s)

Saskatchewan Cheerleading Association (SCA)
PO Box 31090, Regina SK S4R 8R6
Tel: 306-343-7221; *Fax:* 306-343-7229
sca.ca
Social Media:
www.facebook.com/SaskCheer
twitter.com/SaskCheer
Overview: A small provincial organization
Description: To promote & develop cheerleading in Saskatchewan.; *Member of:* Cheer Canada
Chief Officer(s): Thomas Rath, President
president@sca.ca
Alissa Stewart, Executive Director
executivedirector@sca.ca

Sports Laval
#221, 3235, St-Martin est, Laval QC H7E 5G8
Tél: 450-664-1917
info@sportslaval.qc.ca
sportslaval.qc.ca
Média social:
www.facebook.com/jdq.laval
twitter.com/SportsLaval
Également appelé: RSEQ Laval
Merged from: **Association régionale du sport étudiant de Laval; La Commission Sports Laval**
Aperçu: *Dimension:* petite; *Envergure:* locale; fondée en 2003
Description: Mettre en ouvre des actions permettant aux différents sports de prendre place dans les communautés urbaines et scolaires lavalloises; *Membre de:* Réseau du sport étudiant du Québec
Affiliation(s): Réseau du sport étudiant du Québec
Membre(s) du bureau directeur: Martin Savoie, Directeur général, 450-664-1917 204
martin@sportslaval.qc.ca

Trail & Ultra Running Association Of The Yukon (TURAY)
4061 - 4th Ave., Whitehorse YT Y1A 1H1
Tel: 867-668-4236; *Fax:* 867-667-4237
sportyukon.com
Overview: A small provincial organization
Chief Officer(s): Nancy Thomson, President
nancy.thomson@cbc.ca

Automobile Racing

Motorsport Club of Ottawa (MCO) / Club des sports moteur d'Ottawa
PO Box 65006, Stn. Merivale, Ottawa ON K2G 5Y3
www.mco.org
Social Media:
www.youtube.com/c/McoOrgRacersGatherHere
www.facebook.com/mcofb
twitter.com/TheOfficialMCO
Previous Name: Ottawa Light Car Club
Overview: A small local organization founded in 1949
Description: To foster a spirit of unity & comradership among car owners; to encourage courtesy both to other drivers & to pedestrians; To provide information which may be of aid & interest to car owners; to organize & to encourage the organization of legitimate sporting events
Affiliation(s): ASN Canada FIA; CASC-OR; Rallysport Ontario
Chief Officer(s): John Hodge, President
vicepresident@mco.org
Finances: *Annual Operating Budget:* $50,000-$100,000
Staff: 10 volunteer(s)
Membership: 380; *Fees:* $60 single; $75 family; *Member Profile:* Road racing participants; enthusiasts; all involved at grassroots level; *Committees:* Race; Rally; Solo; Social
Activities: Winter & Summer Solo II; winter driving school; go-karting; rallying; road racing; summer high-performance driving school; Canaska Cup; group tours

Toronto Autosport Club (TAC)
18759 Kennedy Rd., Sharon ON L0G 1V0
treasurer@torontoautosportclub.ca
www.torontoautosportclub.ca
Overview: A small local organization founded in 1956
Member of: Canadian Association of Rally Sport; Canadian Association Sport Clubs - Ontario Region; Rally Sport Ontario
Chief Officer(s): Rob McAuley, President
president@torontoautosportclub.ca
Finances: *Annual Operating Budget:* Less than $50,000; *Funding Sources:* Membership fees; contract sports events
Staff: 80 volunteer(s)
Membership: 80; *Fees:* $50; *Member Profile:* People who compete in car racing & rallying
Activities: Autosports; rallying-auto; racing-ice & autoslalom; *Speaker Service:* Yes

Badminton

Badminton Alberta
c/o Alberta Badminton Centre, 60 Patterson Blvd. SW, Calgary AB T3H 2E1
Tel: 403-297-2722; *Fax:* 403-297-2706
Toll-Free: 888-397-2722
members@badmintonalberta.ca
www.badmintonalberta.ca
Social Media:
www.facebook.com/170234779702176
Previous Name: Alberta Badminton Association
Overview: A medium-sized provincial organization founded in 1928
Description: To promote the sport of badminton in Alberta; *Member of:* Badminton Canada; International Badminton Federation
Chief Officer(s): Jeff Bell, Executive Director, 403-297-2108
jbell@badmintonalberta.ca
Finances: *Funding Sources:* Alberta Sport Recreation Parks & Wildlife Foundation
Staff: 4 staff member(s)
Membership: 7000 members; 350 affliated clubs; *Fees:* Schedule available; *Member Profile:* Athletes, clubs, coaches, & officials; *Committees:* Executive

Badminton BC
#110, 12761 - 16 Ave., Surrey BC V4A 1N2
Tel: 604-385-3595
info@badmintonbc.com
www.badmintonbc.com
Social Media:
instagram.com/badminton_bc
www.facebook.com/badmintonBC
twitter.com/b2dmintonbc
Overview: A medium-sized provincial organization founded in 1925
Description: To provide leadership to develop & promote badminton in BC by increasing the membership base, facilitating a higher standard of participation through competitive & development opportunities for players, coaches, officials & volunteers; *Member of:* Sport BC; International Badminton Federation
Chief Officer(s): Penny Gardner, Executive Director, 604-333-3599
executivedirector@badmintonbc.com
Finances: *Funding Sources:* Government grants; Fundraising; Sponsorships
Staff: 5 staff member(s)
Membership: *Fees:* $15; *Member Profile:* Recreational & competitive players, coaches, & officials; *Committees:* Executive; Nominations; Governance Review; Risk Management; Finance & Audit; Regional/Sport Development; Membership; Performance; Competitions; Officials; Coaches; Judicial
Activities: Organizing tournaments, athlete training, & coaching; *Speaker Service:* Yes; *Library:* Badminton Resource Library (Open to Public)

Badminton Canada
#401, 700 Industrial Ave., Ottawa ON K1G 0Y9
Tel: 613-569-2424; *Fax:* 613-748-5724
badminton@badminton.ca
www.badminton.ca
Social Media:
www.facebook.com/BadmintonCanada
twitter.com/BdmintonCanada
Previous Name: Canadian Badminton Association
Overview: A medium-sized national organization

Description: To provide centralized support, &/or leadership in furthering member association objectives, act as custodian of the laws of badminton & to foster outstanding player development; to act for its members in helping to assure national & international class competition for Canada's outstanding badminton players, & to establish Canada as a leading participant in international badminton
Affiliation(s): International Badminton Federation
Chief Officer(s): Joe Morissette, Executive Director
morissette@badminton.ca

Badminton New Nouveau Brunswick (BNNB)
NB
www.bnnb.ca
Social Media:
www.facebook.com/bnnb.ca
Previous Name: Badminton New Brunswick
Overview: A small provincial organization
Description: To organize junior & senior badminton tournaments; *Member of:* Badminton Canada
Chief Officer(s): Eric Fortin, President
Member Profile: Players, coaches, & officials residing in New Brunswick who are members of organized badminton clubs or teams within the province & who may participate in any National or Provincial event

Badminton Newfoundland & Labrador Inc. (BNL)
PO Box 8082, St. John's NL A1B 3M9
Tel: 902-830-8529
badmintonnl@badmintonnl.ca
www.badmintonnl.ca
Social Media:
www.youtube.com/user/NLBadminton
www.facebook.com/285446971492858
Overview: A small provincial organization founded in 1969
Description: To act as the governing body for badminton in Newfoundland & Labrador; *Member of:* Sport Newfoundland & Labrador
Chief Officer(s): John Gillam, President/Provincial Coach
Finances: *Annual Operating Budget:* $50,000-$100,000
Staff: 1 staff member(s)
Membership: 1-99; *Member Profile:* School & community badminton clubs for recreational & competitive players at junior or senior levels
Activities: Organizing sanctioned tournaments & events

Badminton Ontario (BON)
#209, 3 Concorde Gate, Toronto ON M3C 3N7
Tel: 416-426-7195; *Fax:* 416-426-7346
info@badmintonontario.ca
www.badmintonontario.ca
Social Media:
www.youtube.com/cweculture
www.facebook.com/badmintonontario
twitter.com/badmntonontario
Previous Name: Ontario Badminton Association
Overview: A medium-sized provincial organization founded in 1925
Description: To provide an organized, structured environment for the activity of badminton; To promote & develop badminton in Ontario
Affiliation(s): Badminton World Federation
Chief Officer(s): Ian Moss, President
ian.moss@badmintonontario.ca
Finances: *Annual Operating Budget:* $50,000-$100,000; *Funding Sources:* Ministry of Citizenship, Culture & Recreation
Staff: 1 staff member(s); 60 volunteer(s)
Membership: 1,000; *Fees:* Schedule available; *Member Profile:* Badminton players; clubs; coaches; officials
Activities: *Awareness Events:* Provincial Championships

Badminton Québec
4940, rue Hochelaga est, Montréal QC H1V 1E7
Tél: 514-252-3066; *Téléc:* 514-252-3175
info@badmintonquebec.com
www.badmintonquebec.com
Média social:
www.youtube.com/channel/UCs6AGWlz_zO_Qyu__RkqmQw
www.facebook.com/BadmintonQuebec
twitter.com/@BadmintonQc
Également appelé: Fédération québécoise de badminton inc.
Aperçu: *Dimension:* grande; *Envergure:* provinciale; fondée en 1929
Description: Promouvoir et développer le sport sur tout le territoire québécois en regroupant tous ses membres, les personnes et associations intéressées au rayonnement de notre discipline; *Membre de:* Fédération internationale de badminton
Membre(s) du bureau directeur: Chantal Brouillard, Directrice générale
chantal.brouillard@badmintonquebec.com
Christian Guibourt, Directeur technique
christian.guibourt@badmintonquebec.com
Activités: *Stagiaires:* Oui

Badminton World Federation (BWF)
Amoda Bldg., #17.05, 22 Jalan Imbi, L. 17, Kuala Lumpur 55100 Malaysia
bwf@bwfbadminton.org
www.bwfbadminton.org
Social Media:
www.facebook.com/bwfbadminton
twitter.com/bwfmedia
Previous Name: International Badminton Federation (IBF)
Overview: A medium-sized international organization founded in 1934
Description: To control the game of badminton, from an international aspect, in all countries; to uphold the Laws of Badminton as at present adopted
Chief Officer(s): Poul-Erik Høyer, President
pe.hoyer@bwfbadminton.org
Finances: *Funding Sources:* Subscriptions & sponsorships
Membership: 180 nationally organized bodies; *Committees:* Continental Confederations; IOC & International Relations; Administration; Events; Development & Sport for All; Marketing; Finance; Para-Badminton

Manitoba Badminton Association (MBA)
#323, 145 Pacific Ave., Winnipeg MB R3B 2Z6
Fax: 204-925-5703
www.badminton.mb.ca
Social Media:
www.youtube.com/channel/UC4hcjlz19RcwuqP6KDiBBdg
twitter.com/badmintonmb
Overview: A small local organization
Description: To provide the leadership that promotes the growth of badminton throughout Manitoba as a lifelong sport
Chief Officer(s): Ryan Giesbrecht, Executive Director, 204-925-5621
ryan@badminton.mb.ca
Member Profile: Athletes, coaches, officials & badminton clubs

Northwest Territories Badminton Association
PO Box 11089, Yellowknife NT X1A 3X7
Tel: 867-669-8378; *Fax:* 867-669-8327
Toll-Free: 800-661-0797
www.nwtbadminton.ca
Overview: A small provincial organization
Description: To promote badminton throughout the Northwest Territories
Member Profile: Athletes, clubs, coaches, & officials

Nova Scotia Badminton Association
5516 Spring Garden Rd., Halifax NS B3J 1G6
Tel: 902-425-5450; *Fax:* 902-425-5606
badmintonns.ca
Social Media:
www.youtube.com/channel/UCsiGWD6N394oRJRhLIwzq3w
www.facebook.com/BadmintonNovaScotia
twitter.com/bdmintonNS
Also Known As: Badminton Nova Scotia
Overview: A small provincial organization
Description: To promote the development of badminton for all Nova Scotians, at all levels; To provide leadership, organization, and fair governance for the sport
Chief Officer(s): Jennifer Petrie, Executive Director
executive_director@badmintonns.ca
Membership: *Fees:* $20 recreational/coach & umpire; $40 competitive; $150 club

Prince Edward Island Badminton Association
c/o Sport PEI, PO Box 302, 40 Enman Cres., Charlottetown PE C1N 7K7
Tel: 902-368-4262; *Fax:* 902-368-4548
badm.pei@gmail.com
badmintonpei.weebly.com
Also Known As: Badminton PEI
Overview: A small provincial organization founded in 1987
Description: To promote & develop badminton in Prince Edward Island
Chief Officer(s): Nancy MacKinnon, President
Activities: Organizing tournaments

Saskatchewan Badminton Association (SBA)
55 Dunsmore Dr., Regina SK S4R 7G1
Tel: 306-780-9368
saskbadminton@sasktel.net
www.saskbadminton.ca
Social Media:
www.facebook.com/SaskatchewanBadminton
Overview: A small provincial organization
Description: To develop & promote badminton in Saskatchewan
Chief Officer(s): Frank Gaudet, Executive Director

Yukon Badminton Association
4061 - 4th Ave., Whitehorse YT Y1A 1H1
Tel: 867-393-4343
Overview: A small provincial organization
Chief Officer(s): Michael Muller, President, 867-393-4343
muller@northwestel.net

Ball Hockey

British Columbia Ball Hockey Association (BCBHA)
9107 Norum Rd., Delta BC V4C 3H9
Tel: 604-998-1410
info@bcbha.com
www.bcbha.com
Social Media:
www.facebook.com/BCBallHockey
twitter.com/_BCBallHockey
Overview: A small provincial organization founded in 1980
Description: To govern the sport of ball hockey in British Columbia; To establish bylaws & regulations, in order to ensure a safe & fun activity; To uphold the rules& regulations of ball hockey
Affiliation(s): Canadian Ball Hockey Association
Chief Officer(s): Mike Schweighardt, President, 604-998-1400 201
president@bcbha.com
Darsh Grewall, Technical Director, 604-998-1400 206
technical@bcbha.com
Finances: *Funding Sources:* Sponsorships
Membership: *Fees:* Schedule available; *Member Profile:* Ball hockey leagues in British Columbia which follow the rules & regulations of the British Columbia Ball Hockey Association & the Canadian Ball Hockey Association
Activities: Promoting ball hockey in British Columbia; Assisting in the establishment of ball hockey leagues in the province; Disseminating rulebooks; Organizing provincial championships; Providing certification programs for officials; Resolving disputes

Canadian Ball Hockey Association (CBHA) / Association canadienne de hockey-balle
9107 Norum Rd., Delta BC V4C 3H9
Tel: 604-638-1480; *Fax:* 604-998-1410
info@cbha.com
www.cbha.com
Social Media:
www.facebook.com/BallHockeyCanada
twitter.com/CanBallHockey
Overview: A medium-sized national organization founded in 1977
Description: To promote the sport of ball hockey; To arrange championships
Chief Officer(s): George Gortsos, Executive Director
Member Profile: Leagues, teams, players, associations

Manitoba Ball Hockey Association (MBHA)
#306, 145 Pacific Ave., Winnipeg MB R3B 2Z6
Tel: 204-808-8770
mbha1@hotmail.com
www.winnipegballhockey.com
Overview: A small provincial organization founded in 1978
Description: To promote & encourage the development of competitive & recreational ball hockey in Manitoba; *Member of:* Sport Manitoba
Membership: 2,500+

New Brunswick Ball Hockey Association
NB
site2865.goalline.ca/index.php?league_id=53684
Overview: A small provincial organization
Member of: Canadian Ball Hockey Association
Member Profile: Ball hockey leagues throughout New Brunswick; *Committees:* Disciplinary
Activities: Establishing rules for ball hockey in New Brunswick; Maintaining high standards of officiating; Offering the Rookie Officiating Program

Newfoundland & Labrador Ball Hockey Association (NLBHA)
NL
www.nlbha.com
Social Media:
www.facebook.com/NewfoundlandAndLabradorBallHockeyAssociation
twitter.com/NLBallHockey
Overview: A small provincial organization
Description: To promote the sport of ball hockey in Newfoundland & Labrador; To maintain rules & regulations of the sport; *Member of:* Canadian Ball Hockey Association; Sport Newfoundland & Labrador
Activities: Organizing championships

Nova Scotia Ball Hockey Association (NSBHA)
Tel: 902-463-2833
nsbha@hotmail.com
nsbha.weebly.com
Overview: A small provincial organization
Description: To promote ball hockey in Nova Scotia & to host provincial tournaments
Affiliation(s): Canadian Ball Hockey Association; Sport Nova Scotia
Finances: *Annual Operating Budget:* Less than $50,000
Staff: 20 volunteer(s)
Membership: 650 individual

Ontario Ball Hockey Association (OBHA)
#5, 56 Pennsylvania Ave., Concord ON L4K 3V9
Tel: 905-738-3320; *Fax:* 905-738-3321
www.ontarioballhockey.ca
Social Media:
www.facebook.com/643077945729508
twitter.com/OntarioBallHock
Overview: A medium-sized provincial organization founded in 1974
Description: To promote & increase participation in the sport of ball hockey in Ontario; to improve opportunities for competition at all levels of participation; to create & implement leadership opportunities for officials, coaches & administrators; to establish standards of play & for quality of equipment to ensure good sport & safety for all participants
Affiliation(s): Canadian Ball Hockey Association; International Street & Ball Hockey Association; Sport Canada; Canadian Hockey Association
Chief Officer(s): Jamie Robillard, Coaching & Technical Director
Finances: *Funding Sources:* Self-generated revenue
Staff: 2 staff member(s); 12 volunteer(s)
Membership: 18,000; *Fees:* Schedule available
Activities: *Awareness Events:* Provincial Championships; Regional & National Champions

Québec Ball Hockey Association (QBHA) / Association de Hockey-Balle du Québec (AHBQ)
2890 boul Dagenais West, Laval QC H7P 1T1
Tel: 450-963-9346; *Fax:* 450-622-4466
info@ahbq.com
www.qbha.com
Social Media:
www.facebook.com/AHBQ.QBHA
twitter.com/AHBQ_QBHA
Overview: A small provincial organization
Description: To promote & organize ball hockey in Québec & across the country; *Member of:* Canadian Ball Hockey Association; International Street & Ball Hockey Federation; Hockey Canada

Wild Rose Ball Hockey Association
Edmonton AB
wrbha@telus.net
www.wrballhockey.com
Overview: A small provincial organization
Member of: Canadian Ball Hockey Association
Chief Officer(s): Connie Liosis, Executive Director

Baseball

Alberta Amateur Baseball Council (AABC)
2425 North Parkside Dr., Lethbridge AB T1J 4W3
Tel: 403-320-2025; *Fax:* 403-320-2053
www.albertabaseball.org
Social Media:
twitter.com/AABC_HPC
Overview: A large provincial organization founded in 1998
Description: To be the governing body of baseball associations throughout Alberta.
Chief Officer(s): Ron Van Keulen, President
Kim Brigitzer, Manager, Administration & Communications
k.brigitzer@albertabaseball.org
Aaron Lavorato, Coordinator, High Performance
a.lavorato@albertabaseball.org
Membership: 5 leagues + 31,000 individuals

Aurora King Baseball Association (AKBA)
PO Box 34040, Stn. Hollandview, 446 Hollandview Trail, Aurora ON L4G 0G3
info@akba.ca
www.akba.ca
Social Media:
www.linkedin.com/company/aurora-king-baseball-association
www.facebook.com/AuroraKingBaseball
twitter.com/aurorakingbball
Merged from: Aurora Minor Baseball Association; King Township Baseball Association
Overview: A medium-sized local organization
Chief Officer(s): Matt Giesen, President
president@akba.ca

Baseball Alberta (BA)
Percy Page Centre, 11759 Groat Rd., Edmonton AB T5M 3K6
Tel: 780-427-8943; *Fax:* 780-427-9032
registrar@baseballalberta.com
www.baseballalberta.com
Social Media:
www.facebook.com/pages/Baseball-Alberta/130042917037092
twitter.com/BaseballAlberta
Also Known As: Alberta Baseball Association
Overview: A large provincial organization founded in 1967
Description: To promote & develop Baseball in Alberta; to provide life & leadership skills for all genders through Baseball; to encourage fun & fair play; *Member of:* Western Canada Baseball Association; Edmonton International Baseball Foundation
Affiliation(s): Alberta Amateur Baseball Council
Chief Officer(s): Don Paulencu, President
dpaulencu@deloitte.ca
Darren Dekinder, Registrar & Office Manager, 780-427-9014
registrar@baseballalberta.com
Finances: *Funding Sources:* Membership dues; government; corporate
Staff: 3 staff member(s)
Membership: *Fees:* Schedule available
Activities: Programs include: Rally Cap; Winterball; Reaching Baseball Ideals; Long Term Athlete Development; Canadian Sport for Life; National Coaching Certification Program; programs for girls & women

Baseball BC
#310, 15225 - 104th Ave., Surrey BC V3R 6Y8
Tel: 604-586-3310; *Fax:* 604-586-3311
info1@baseball.bc.ca
www.baseball.bc.ca
Social Media:
www.facebook.com/pages/Baseball-BC/233202485008
twitter.com/Baseball_BC
Previous Name: BC Amateur Baseball Association
Overview: A medium-sized provincial organization
Description: To support the development of baseball & the aspirations of its members; To offer oppoortunities & setting procedures, standards, & policies
Chief Officer(s): David Laing, Executive Director, 604-586-3312
davidlaing@baseball.bc.ca
Finances: *Funding Sources:* Government of B.C., Legacies Now, Rawlings Sporting Goods, Prostock Athletic Supply, Toronto Blue Jays, All Sport Insurance, Gatorade, Sport B.C.
Membership: 4,500

Baseball Canada / Fédération canadienne de baseball amateur
#A7, 2212 Gladwin Cres., Ottawa ON K1B 5N1
Tel: 613-748-5606; *Fax:* 613-748-5767
info@baseball.ca
www.baseball.ca
Social Media:
instagram.com/baseballcanada;
youtube.com/baseballcanadamedia
www.facebook.com/baseballcanada
twitter.com/baseballcanada
Also Known As: Canadian Federation of Amateur Baseball
Overview: A large national charitable organization founded in 1964
Description: To promote the development of baseball across Canada through support of provincial organizations & design of programs, including athletes, coaches, events, umpires & partner groups; *Member of:* International Baseball Association; Confederation of PanAmerican Baseball
Affiliation(s): Canadian Olympic Association
Chief Officer(s): Jason Dickson, President
Don Paulencu, Vice-President
Jody Frowley, Treasurer
Jim Baba, Director General
jbaba@baseball.ca
Finances: *Funding Sources:* Federal government; membership fees; sponsors; sales; program revenues
Staff: 9 staff member(s)
Activities: Hosts seven national championships; selects three national teams for international competition; National Skill Competition; Coach & Umpire Certification; Baseball Canada Cup; Honda Hit-Run-Throw; *Internships:* Yes; *Library:* Yes by appointment

Baseball New Brunswick (BNB) / Baseball Nouveau-Brunswick
#13, 900 Hanwell Rd., Fredericton NB E3B 6A2
Tel: 506-451-1329; *Fax:* 506-451-1325
director@baseballnb.ca
www.baseballnb.ca
Social Media:
www.facebook.com/pages/Baseball-NB/87671406193
twitter.com/NB_Selects
Overview: A medium-sized provincial organization founded in 1989
Description: To promote & govern baseball in New Brunswick.
Affiliation(s): Sport New Brunswick; Baseball Atlantic
Chief Officer(s): David Watling, President
bnbwatling@rogers.com
David Dion, Executive Director
Finances: *Funding Sources:* Provincial government
Staff: 1 staff member(s)
Membership: 5841; *Member Profile:* Baseball players, coaches, officials, volunteers & administrators.; *Committees:* Financial; High Performance; Hall of Fame; Personnel; Linguistics

Baseball Nova Scotia (BNS)
5516 Spring Garden Rd., 4th Fl., Halifax NS B3J 1G6
Tel: 902-425-5454; *Fax:* 902-425-5606
baseball@sportnovascotia.ca
www.baseballnovascotia.com
Social Media:
instagram.com/baseballnovascotia
www.facebook.com/baseballnovascotia
twitter.com/baseball_ns
Overview: A medium-sized provincial organization
Description: To represent baseball teams & leagues under the jurisdiction of BaseballCanada.; *Member of:* Canadian Federation of Amateur Baseball
Chief Officer(s): Brandon Guenette, Executive Director
Trevor Wamback, Technical Director
twamback@sportnovascotia.ca
Brennan Curry, Coordinator, Programs
bcurry@sportnovascotia.ca
Membership: *Fees:* Schedule available

Baseball Ontario
#3, 131 Sheldon Dr., Cambridge ON N1R 6S2
Tel: 519-740-3900; *Fax:* 519-740-6311
baseball@baseballontario.com
www.baseballontario.com
Social Media:
instagram.com/baseball_ontario
www.facebook.com/BaseballOntario
twitter.com/BaseballOntario
Overview: A medium-sized provincial organization founded in 1918
Member of: CSAE
Affiliation(s): Little League Ontario
Chief Officer(s): Mary-Ann Smith, Administrative Director
maryann@baseballontario.com
Finances: *Annual Operating Budget:* $500,000-$1.5 Million
Staff: 2 staff member(s)
Membership: 18 organizations
Activities: Coaching; Umpiring; Elite Player Development; Insurance; Tournaments; Communications; *Awareness Events:* Spring Break Camp; AGM

Baseball PEI
40 Enman Cres., Charlottetown PE C1E 1E6
Tel: 902-368-4203; *Fax:* 902-368-4548
www.baseballpei.ca
Social Media:
www.facebook.com/BaseballPEI
twitter.com/BaseballPEI1
Previous Name: Prince Edward Island Amateur Baseball Association
Overview: A medium-sized provincial organization founded in 1967
Description: To promote & develop minor & amateur baseball in PEI
Chief Officer(s): Don LeClair, President
Randy Byrne, Executive Director
Finances: *Annual Operating Budget:* Less than $50,000
Membership: *Fees:* Schedule available
Activities: Tournments including Bantam, Pee Wee, and Midget levels.

Charlottetown Area Baseball Association (CABA)
c/o Baseball PEI, 40 Enman Cres., Charlottetown PE C1E 1E6
Tel: 902-368-4203; *Fax:* 902-368-4548
baseball@sportpei.pe.ca
www.baseballpei.ca/page/show/1703665-charlottetown-all-seasons
Overview: A medium-sized local organization
Member of: Baseball PEI

Edmonton International Baseball Foundation (EIBF)
12314 - 76 St. NW, Edmonton AB T5B 2E4
Tel: 780-474-0795
webmaster@baseballeibf.ca
baseballeibf.ca
Overview: A small international organization founded in 1979
Description: To help develop amateur baseball through financial assistance; to host international amateur baseball events
Affiliation(s): Baseball Canada; International Baseball Federation
Chief Officer(s): Ron Hayter, Chair
Activities: Championships & world cups; four scholarships awarded annually

Fédération du baseball amateur du Québec
CP 1000, Succ. M, 4545, av Pierre-de Coubertin, Montréal QC H1V 0B2
Tél: 514-252-3075; *Téléc:* 514-252-3134
Ligne sans frais: 800-361-2054
info@baseballquebec.qc.ca
www.baseballquebec.com
Média social:
www.facebook.com/baseballquebec
twitter.com/baseballquebec
Également appelé: Baseball Québec
Aperçu: *Dimension:* moyenne; *Envergure:* provinciale
Description: Donner un cadre général d'ordre et de discipline à tous les intervenants du baseball québécois; Reconnaître le droit pour tous les joueurs d'évoluer au baseball selon des normes et critères précis; Donner un cadre pour l'application d'une réglementation uniforme dans tout le Québec; Fournir les moyens à chacun de s'amuser, de participer et de se perfectionner afin de donner un idéal à ceux qui aspirent à une carrière
Membre(s) du bureau directeur: Maxime Lamarche, Directeur général
mlamarche@baseballquebec.qc.ca

Hamilton Baseball Umpires' Association (HBUA)
Hamilton ON
Tel: 905-538-6071
hamiltonbaseballumpires@gmail.com
hbua.ca
Social Media:
www.facebook.com/190866890945303
Overview: A small local organization
Chief Officer(s): Bill Tunney, President & Assignor
b.tunney@cogeco.ca

Kawartha Baseball Umpires Association (KBUA)
ON
Overview: A small local organization

Little League Canada / Petite ligue Canada
235 Dale Ave., Ottawa ON K1G 0H6
Tel: 613-731-3301; *Fax:* 613-731-2829
canada@littleleague.org
www.littleleague.ca
Social Media:
www.youtube.com/DugoutTheMascot
www.facebook.com/pages/Little-League-Baseball-Canada/137589529592785
twitter.com/LittleLgeCanada
Overview: A large national charitable organization founded in 1951
Description: To provide baseball & softball programs to every boy or girl wishing to participate; *Member of:* Little League Baseball International
Chief Officer(s): Roy Bergerman, President & Chair
rbergerman@littleleague.ca
Joe Shea, Regional Director
Wendy Thomson, Assistant Regional Director
Finances: *Funding Sources:* Membership dues; corporate
Staff: 2 staff member(s)
Membership: 35,000

Manitoba Baseball Association
145 Pacific Ave., Winnipeg MB R3B 2Z6
Tel: 204-925-5763; *Fax:* 204-925-5928
baseball.info@sportmanitoba.ca
www.baseballmanitoba.ca
Social Media:
www.facebook.com/171229052909245
twitter.com/BaseballMB
Also Known As: Baseball Manitoba
Overview: A small provincial organization founded in 1968
Description: To foster the participation, development & competition of amateur baseball in Manitoba
Chief Officer(s): Morgan de Peña, Executive Director
baseball.morgan@sportmanitoba.ca
Membership: 15,000; *Committees:* Management

Newfoundland Baseball
1296A Kenmount Rd., Paradise NL
Tel: 709-576-3401
www.leaguelineup.com/welcome.asp?url=nlbaseball
Social Media:
twitter.com/BaseballNL
Also Known As: Baseball NL
Previous Name: Newfoundland Amateur Baseball Association
Overview: A small provincial organization founded in 1947
Description: Supports amatuer baseball in Newfoundland.; *Member of:* Baseball Canada
Chief Officer(s): Kevin Legge, President
Ryan Garland, Executive Director
Finances: *Annual Operating Budget:* $50,000-$100,000; *Funding Sources:* Membership dues; fundraising; corporate; government
Staff: 10 volunteer(s)
Membership: 20; *Fees:* Schedule available; *Committees:* Hall of Fame
Activities: Amateur baseball development; *Rents Mailing List:* Yes

Ontario Umpires Association
ON
Tel: 905-791-0280
ontario_umpires@sympatico.ca
www.ontarioumpires.com
Overview: A small provincial organization
Description: To provide officials for the games of baseball, softball, volleyball, flag football, hockey, basketball & soccer.
Affiliation(s): Ontario Sports Administration; Ontario Academy of Sports Officials; Sports Events International
Chief Officer(s): Jim Cottrell, President

Prince Edward Island Baseball Umpires Association (PEIBUA)
PE
Tel: 902-367-0564
peibua@gmail.com
www.peibua.com
Overview: A small provincial organization
Description: To represent certified amateur baseball umpires in the province of PEI.
Chief Officer(s): Kent Walker, Supervisor of Officials
kentwalker019@gmail.com
Activities:; *Library:* Yes (Open to Public)

Saskatchewan Baseball Association (SBA)
1870 Lorne St., Regina SK S4P 2L7
Tel: 306-780-9237; *Fax:* 306-352-3669
www.saskbaseball.ca
Social Media:
www.facebook.com/10150095674130384
twitter.com/baseballsask
Overview: A medium-sized provincial organization founded in 1959
Description: To provide quality baseball programs to interested participants at whatever level they may choose; *Member of:* Baseball Canada; International Baseball Association; Sask Sport; Western Canada Baseball Association
Chief Officer(s): Mike Ramage, Executive Director
Finances: *Annual Operating Budget:* $250,000-$500,000; *Funding Sources:* Lottery proceeds
Staff: 3 staff member(s)
Membership: 14,000; *Fees:* Schedule available

Windsor & District Baseball Umpires Association (WDBUA)
Windsor ON
www.windsorumpires.ca
Social Media:
twitter.com/WDBUA
Also Known As: Windsor Umpires
Overview: A small local organization
Description: To train, instruct & evaluate members.
Affiliation(s): Baseball Ontario; Baseball Canada; Sun Parlour Baseball Association
Chief Officer(s): Matthew Tyler, President
president@windsorumpires.ca

Basketball

Basketball Alberta
Percy Page Centre, 11759 Groat Rd., 2nd Fl., Edmonton AB T5M 3K6
Tel: 780-427-9044; *Fax:* 780-427-9124
www.basketballalberta.ca
Social Media:
www.facebook.com/BasketballAlberta
twitter.com/BasketballAB
Overview: A medium-sized provincial organization founded in 1975
Description: To be premier facilitators of participation, development, and excellence in basketball. To champion the sport of basketball as a game for life by inspiring unity facilitating development and delivering superior value.
Chief Officer(s): Bob Mitchell, President
bmitchell@basketballalberta.ab.ca
Paul Sir, Executive Director
psir@basketballalberta.ab.ca
Finances: *Funding Sources:* Provincial government; self-generated
Staff: 6 staff member(s)
Membership: *Fees:* $11 per athlete

Basketball BC
#210, 7888 - 200th St., Langley BC V2Y 3J4
Tel: 604-888-8088; *Fax:* 604-888-8323
info@basketball.bc.ca
www.basketball.bc.ca
Social Media:
www.facebook.com/basketballbc
twitter.com/BasketballBC
Overview: A medium-sized provincial organization
Description: To be British Columbia's leading resource for basketball; To build the game of basketball; *Member of:* Sport BC
Chief Officer(s): Lawrie Johns, Executive Director, 604-455-2812
ljohns@basketball.bc.ca
Finances: *Funding Sources:* Government grant; fundraising; membership dues
Staff: 7 staff member(s)
Membership: *Fees:* $15

Basketball Manitoba
145 Pacific Ave., Winnipeg MB R3B 2Z6
Tel: 204-925-5775; *Fax:* 204-925-5929
info@basketball.mb.ca
www.basketball.mb.ca
Social Media:
www.youtube.com/user/baskmanbaskman
www.linkedin.com/company/basketball-manitoba
www.facebook.com/basketballmanitoba
twitter.com/basketballmb
Overview: A medium-sized provincial organization founded in 1976
Description: To operate as the provincial sport governing body for basketball in Manitoba; To ensure all Manitobians have access to the programs run by the association & that the game of basketball is enjoyed by as many people as possible
Chief Officer(s): Adam Wedlake, Executive Director
awedlake@basketball.mb.ca

Basketball New Brunswick (BNB) / Basketball Nouveau-Brunswick
#13, 900 Hanwell Rd., Fredericton NB E2E 6A2
Tel: 506-472-4667; *Fax:* 506-451-1325
info@basketball.nb.ca
www.basketball.nb.ca
Overview: A large provincial organization founded in 1973
Description: To promote, develop & encourage sport & recreation aspects of basketball in New Brunswick; To assist in establishment of basketball clubs throughout New Brunswick; To liaise with government & private agencies interested in promoting & supporting basketball
Affiliation(s): New Brunswick Association of Approved Basketball Officials; New Brunswick Interscholastic Athletic Association
Chief Officer(s): Mike Lavigne, President
Carolyn Peppin, Executive Director
carolyn.peppin@basketball.nb.ca
Kim Flemming, Office Administrator
kim.flemming@basketball.nb.ca
Finances: *Funding Sources:* Membership dues; Provincial government; Programs
Staff: 3 staff member(s)
Member Profile: All players competing in provincial championships; minor association members
Activities: Offering National Coaching Certification, an Elite Development Program, & junior officials development; *Library:* Training Film Library

Basketball Nova Scotia
5516 Spring Garden Rd., 3rd Fl., Halifax NS B3J 1G6
Tel: 902-425-5450; *Fax:* 902-425-5606
bnsadmin@basketball.ns.ca
basketballnovascotia.com
Social Media:
www.instagram.com/basketballnovascotia
www.facebook.com/BasketballNovaScotia
twitter.com/BasketballNS

Overview: A small provincial organization
Description: To promote & encourage the game of basketball throughout the province; *Member of:* Sport Canada
Affiliation(s): Sport Nova Scotia
Chief Officer(s): David Wagg, Executive Director
bnsexecutivedirector@sportnovascotia.ca
Finances: *Annual Operating Budget:* $250,000-$500,000; *Funding Sources:* Government grants; Membership fees; Special events
Staff: 3 staff member(s); 12 volunteer(s)
Membership: 4,000; *Fees:* Schedule available
Activities: Offering the National Coaching Certificate Program; Facilitating player development programs & camps; Organizing tournaments

Basketball NWT
PO Box 44, Yellowknife NT X1A 2N1
www.bnwt.ca
Social Media:
www.facebook.com/bnwt.ca
Overview: A medium-sized provincial organization
Description: The Association encourages participation in basketball, develops athletes, & provides opportunities for cultural & social interchange among all involved in the sport
Affiliation(s): Steve Nash Youth Basketball; Sport North; Arctic Winter Games
Chief Officer(s): Damien Healy, President & Executive Director

Basketball PEI
#101, 40 Enman Cres., Charlottetown PE C1E 1E6
Tel: 902-368-4986; *Fax:* 902-368-4548
Toll-Free: 800-247-6712
www.basketballpei.ca
Social Media:
twitter.com/basketballpei
Overview: A medium-sized provincial organization
Description: To develop basketball in the province of Prince Edward Island in a fun environment
Chief Officer(s): Katie Hamilton, Executive Director
katie@basketballpei.ca
Activities: Developing the skills needed to play basketball successfully

Basketball Saskatchewan (BSI)
2205 Victoria Ave., Regina SK S4P 0S4
Fax: 306-525-4009
basketball@basketballsask.com
www.basketballsask.com
Social Media:
www.facebook.com/basketballsask
twitter.com/basketballsask
Previous Name: Saskatchewan Basketball
Overview: A medium-sized provincial licensing charitable organization founded in 1988
Description: To support & improve basketball opportunities in Saskatchewan
Affiliation(s): Sask Sport
Chief Officer(s): Greg Lucas, Executive Director, 306-780-9264
glucas@basketballsask.com
Dave Werry, Coordinator, High Performance, 306-780-9249
dwerry@basketballsask.com
Finances: *Funding Sources:* Sask Sport; Fundraising
Staff: 2 staff member(s)
Membership: 12,000; *Fees:* $35 active; $12 associate; $3.50 affiliate; *Member Profile:* Ages 9 to 60
Activities: *Speaker Service:* Yes; *Library:* Yes (Open to Public)

Basketball Yukon
YT
www.basketballyukon.ca
Overview: A medium-sized provincial organization
Description: To assist in player & coaching development in the North; to lead the territory's basketball community through programs & services benefitting all levels of play
Affiliation(s): Sport Yukon, Canada Basketball
Chief Officer(s): Tim Brady, President

Canada Basketball
#11, 1 Westside Dr., Toronto ON M9C 1B2
Tel: 416-614-8037; *Fax:* 416-614-9570
info@basketball.ca
www.basketball.ca
Social Media:
www.youtube.com/user/CanadaBasketball08
www.facebook.com/CanadaBasketball
twitter.com/CanBball
Also Known As: Canadian Basketball Association
Overview: A large national charitable organization founded in 1972
Description: Basketball Canada is the national sport governing body for amateur basketball in Canada; to develop the sport of basketball domestically & to contribute to the development of basketball internationally; *Member of:* International Basketball Federation
Affiliation(s): 10 provincial + 2 territorial associations; Canadian Interuniversity Athletic Union; Canadian Colleges Athletic Association; Canadian School Sports Federation; Toronto Raptors; Canadian Wheelchair Basketball Association; Canadian Association of Basketball Officials; National Association of Basketball Coaches of Canada; Women's Basketball Coaches Association
Chief Officer(s): Wayne Parrish, President & CEO
Michele O'Keefe, Executive Director
mokeefe@basketball.ca
Activities: National Teams; coaching programs; championships; direct mail; licensing; youth basketball programs; *Internships:* Yes

Fédération de basketball du Québec (FBBQ) / Québec Basketball Federation
4545, av Pierre-de Coubertin, Montréal QC H1V 0B2
Tél: 514-252-3057; *Téléc:* 514-252-3357
Ligne sans frais: 866-557-3057
www.basketball.qc.ca
Média social:
www.youtube.com/user/BasketballQc
www.facebook.com/BasketballQc
twitter.com/BasketballQc
Également appelé: Basketball Québec
Aperçu: *Dimension:* grande; *Envergure:* provinciale; Organisme sans but lucratif; fondée en 1970
Description: Développement et promotion de la discipline; Formation de joueurs, entraîneurs et arbitres; organisation de compétitions provinciales; Programme Poursuite de l'Excellence (Équipes et Espoirs du Québec)
Membre(s) du bureau directeur: Olga Hrycak, Présidente
Daniel Grimard, Directeur général
dgrimard@basketball.qc.ca
Mélissa Dion, Coordonnatrice, Communications et marketing
mdion@basketball.qc.ca
Membre: 35,000 personnes
Activités: *Stagiaires:* Oui; *Service de conférenciers:* Oui

Newfoundland & Labrador Basketball Association
1296A Kenmount Rd., Paradise NL A1L 1N3
Tel: 709-576-0247; *Fax:* 709-576-8787
nlba@sportnf.com
www.nlba.nf.ca
Social Media:
www.facebook.com/nlbasketball
twitter.com/nlbasketball
Previous Name: Basketball Newfoundland
Overview: A medium-sized provincial charitable organization founded in 1988
Description: To develop & promote the sport of basketball across Newfoundland; to assist in the establishment of basketball clubs throughout Newfoundland & Labrador.
Chief Officer(s): Bill Murphy, Executive Director
nlba@sportnf.com
David Constantine, President
Finances: *Annual Operating Budget:* $250,000-$500,000
Staff: 3 staff member(s)
Membership: *Fees:* Schedule available; *Member Profile:* Clubs, coaches, volunteers, teams, players; *Committees:* Executive; Minor; Coaching; Awards; Half of Fame; Policy; Hall of Fame Cup; Nominating
Activities: *Internships:* Yes; *Rents Mailing List:* Yes

Ontario Basketball
Abilities Centre, #2A, 55 Gordon St., Whitby ON L1N 0J2
Tel: 416-477-8075; *Fax:* 416-477-8120
basketball.on.ca
Social Media:
www.youtube.com/user/OntarioBasketballOBA
twitter.com/OBANews
Overview: A medium-sized provincial organization founded in 1977
Description: To promote & develop basketball on an amateur basis in the province of Ontario.
Affiliation(s): Provincial Sports Organizations Council; Canada Basketball; Toronto Raptors Basketball Club; NBA Canada; Coaches Association of Ontario; Canadian Sports Centre; and other provincial basketball organizations
Chief Officer(s): Jason Jansson, Executive Director, 416-477-8075 202
jjanson@basketball.on.ca
Lindsay Walsh, Director, Basketball Development, 416-477-8075 203
lwalsh@basketball.on.ca
Finances: *Annual Operating Budget:* $1.5 Million-$3 Million; *Funding Sources:* Sponsorship; fundraising; grants
Staff: 6 staff member(s)
Membership: 9,000; *Fees:* Schedule available; *Member Profile:* Players & coaches
Activities: *Internships:* Yes; *Speaker Service:* Yes; *Library:* Yes (Open to Public) by appointment

Provincial Black Basketball Association (PBBA)
PO Box 2702, Halifax NS B3J 3P7
Tel: 902-452-0682
pbba.blackbasketball@gmail.com
www.blackbasketball.ca
Overview: A medium-sized provincial organization founded in 1972
Description: To promote basketball within the African Canadian community in Nova Scotia & across the country.
Chief Officer(s): Carl Gannon, President
gannoncs@eastlink.ca

Baton Twirling

Alberta Baton Twirling Association (ABTA)
Percy Page Centre, 11759 Groat Rd., Edmonton AB T5M 3K6
Tel: 780-415-1440; *Fax:* 780-415-0170
abta@telusplanet.net
www.albertabaton.com
Social Media:
www.facebook.com/106834729351227
Overview: A small provincial organization founded in 1971
Description: To be the voice of baton twirling in the province; To promote the values & development of the sport; To unite the province in interest of baton twirling; To provide exposure; To manage the business of baton, inform members, provide opportunity & demonstration/competition; *Member of:* Canadian Baton Twirling Federation
Affiliation(s): Alberta Sport, Recreation, Parks, Wildlife Foundation
Chief Officer(s): Bonnie Brinker, Chair
Shari Foster, Executive Director
Activities:; *Library:* Yes (Open to Public)

Baton New Brunswick (BNB)
20 Adams St., Tide Head NB E3N 4T3
Tel: 506-759-7113
www.batonnb.ca
Overview: A small provincial organization
Description: To govern baton twirling in New Brunswick; *Member of:* Canadian Baton Twirling Federation
Chief Officer(s): Nadine LeBelle-Déjario, President

Baton Twirling Association of British Columbia (BTABC)
22411 Westminster Hwy., Richmond BC V6V 1B6
Tel: 604-722-1595
btabc@shaw.ca
batontwirlingbc.com
Overview: A small provincial organization
Description: To promote the sport of baton twirling in British Columbia.; *Member of:* Canadian Baton Twirling Federation
Chief Officer(s): Denise DeWolff, Chair
Shannon Webster, Membership Officer
greataunty@operamail.com
Activities: Competitions; training

Canadian Baton Twirling Federation (CBTF) / Fédération baton canadienne
c/o Jeff Johnson, 35 Ridge Dr., Toronto ON M4T 1B6
Fax: 416-484-1672
www.cbtf.ca
Social Media:
www.facebook.com/CBTFCA
twitter.com/cbtfca
Overview: A medium-sized national charitable organization founded in 1979
Member of: World Baton Twirling Federation
Chief Officer(s): Jeff Johnson, President
Lisa Wilde, Secretary
Michelle Bretherick, Treasurer

Canadian National Baton Twirling Association (CNBTA)
c/o Lisa Ross, Treasurer, 7208 Concession 1, RR#2, Puslinch ON N0B 2J0
info@cnbta.org
www.cnbta.org
Overview: A small national organization
Description: To promote the sport of baton twirling in Canada; to offer twirling events & seminars

Affiliation(s): National Baton Twirling Association - USA; Global Alliance of National Baton Twirling & Majorette Associations
Chief Officer(s): Kevan Latrace, President
cnbta.prez@gmail.com
Darlene King, National Technical Director/Co-Founder
darleneking@shaw.ca

Manitoba Baton Twirling Sportive Association (MBTSA)
MB
www.manitobabaton.com
Overview: A small provincial organization
Description: To oversee the sport of baton twirling in Manitoba.; *Member of:* Canadian Baton Twirling Federation

Ontario Baton Twirling Association (OBTA)
c/o Susan Palmer, Registrar, #263, 55 Collinsgrove Rd., Toronto ON M1E 4Z2
www.obta.ca
Overview: A small provincial organization
Description: To be the largest governing body of the sport of baton twirling in Ontario.; *Member of:* Canadian Baton Twirling Federation
Chief Officer(s): LeeAnn Wilson, President
president@obta.ca
Susan Palmer, Membership Registrar
membership@obta.ca

Saskatchewan Baton Twirling Association (SBTA)
510 Cynthia St., Saskatoon SK S7L 7K4
Tel: 306-975-0847; *Fax:* 306-242-8007
skbaton@shaw.ca
www.saskbaton.com
Also Known As: Sask Baton
Overview: A small provincial organization
Description: To coordinate the sport of baton twirling in Saskatchewan.; *Member of:* Canadian Baton Twirling Federation
Chief Officer(s): Alison Pickrell, Chair
Brenda O'Connor, Sport Coordinator
Finances: *Funding Sources:* Sask Sport Inc.; SaskTel

Biathlon

Association des clubs de Biathlon du Québec (ACBQ)
172, rue Louis-Bureau, Sherbrooke QC J1E 3Z7
Tel: 819-820-4330
www.acbq.qc.ca
Social Media:
www.facebook.com/acbq.qc.ca
Overview: A small provincial organization founded in 2005
Member of: Biathlon Canada
Chief Officer(s): Érika Charron, Président, 819-348-0523
dan10eri@abacom.com
Sandrine Charron, Directrice, Haute performance
charrons@globetrotter.net

Biathlon Alberta
Bob Niven Training Centre, #102, 88 Canada Olympic Rd. SW, Calgary AB T3B 5R5
Tel: 403-202-6548
info@biathlon.ca
www.biathlon.ca
Social Media:
www.facebook.com/588814881135031
twitter.com/biathlonab
Overview: A small provincial organization founded in 1980
Description: To promote, develop & maintain biathlon in Alberta; *Member of:* Biathlon Canada; Alberta Ski & Snowboard Association
Chief Officer(s): Darcy Gullacher, General Manager
Karin Kaarsoo, President
Finances: *Annual Operating Budget:* $100,000-$250,000
Staff: 2 staff member(s); 300 volunteer(s)
Membership: 12 clubs + 357 individual; *Fees:* Schedule available

Biathlon BC
BC
Tel: 604-230-0481
biathlonbc.ca
Social Media:
instagram.com/biathlonbc
www.facebook.com/Biathlon-BC-181268575258202
twitter.com/BiathlonBC
Overview: A small provincial organization
Description: To promote Biathlon throughout British Columbia as a recreational & competitive sport.; *Member of:* Biathlon Canada
Chief Officer(s): Tony Tsang, President
president@biathlonbc.ca

Membership: *Fees:* Schedule available

Biathlon Canada
#100, 1995 Olympic Way, Canmore AB T1W 2T6
Tel: 403-678-4002; *Fax:* 403-678-3644
info@biathloncanada.ca
www.biathloncanada.ca
Social Media:
www.linkedin.com/company/biathlon-canada
www.facebook.com/BiathlonCanada
twitter.com/biathloncanada
Overview: A medium-sized national charitable organization founded in 1976
Description: To act as the governing body for the sport of biathlon in Canada
Affiliation(s): International Biathlon Union; Canadian Olympic Committee
Chief Officer(s): Andy Holmwood, General Manager
aholmwood@biathloncanada.ca
Finances: *Funding Sources:* Sport Canada; Canadian Olympic Committee (COC); International Biathlon Union (IBU); Coaching Association of Canada (CAC)
Staff: 8 staff member(s)
Membership: *Fees:* Schedule available; *Committees:* Human Resources & Compensation; Finance & Audit; Revenue Generation & Marketing; Officials; Canadian International Biathlon Union

Biathlon Manitoba
Sport for Life Centre, 145 Pacific Ave., Winnipeg MB R3B 2Z6
Tel: 204-925-5687
biathlon@sportmanitoba.ca
biathlonmanitoba.ca
Social Media:
www.facebook.com/biathlonmanitoba
twitter.com/BiathlonMB
Overview: A small provincial organization
Description: To promote the sport of biathlon in Manitoba.; *Member of:* Biathlon Canada
Chief Officer(s): Brian Walters, Executive Director

Biathlon Newfoundland & Labrador
Mount Pearl NL
info@biathlonnl.ca
www.biathlonnl.ca
Social Media:
www.facebook.com/biathlonnl
twitter.com/biathlonnl
Overview: A small provincial organization
Description: To govern the sport of biathlon in Newfoundland & Labrador, both competitively & recreationally.; *Member of:* Biathlon Canada
Chief Officer(s): Gary Dawson, Contact
Membership: 3 clubs; *Fees:* Schedule available

Biathlon Nouveau-New Brunswick
11051 Hwy. 430, Trout Brook NB E9E 1R5
Tel: 506-627-6437
biathlon@biathlonnb.ca
www.biathlonnb.ca
Also Known As: Biathlon NB
Overview: A small provincial organization
Description: To govern the sport of biathlon in New Brunswick.; *Member of:* Biathlon Canada
Chief Officer(s): Ray Kokkonen, President
kokkonen@nbnet.nb.ca
Lisa Belliveau, Secretary, 506-854-0524
ddsally@yahoo.com
Paula Septon, Treasurer, 506-622-8047
Membership: *Fees:* Schedule available; *Committees:* Marketing & Fundraising; Coaching Development; Membership; Officials

Biathlon Nova Scotia
c/o Sport Nova Scotia, 5516 Spring Garden Rd., Halifax NS B3J 1G6
Tel: 902-425-5454; *Fax:* 902-425-5606
admin@biathlonns.ca
www.biathlonns.ca
Social Media:
www.facebook.com/biathlonns
Overview: A small provincial organization
Description: To govern the sport of biathlon in Nova Scotia.; *Member of:* Biathlon Canada
Chief Officer(s): Bruce Jarvis, President
Membership: *Fees:* Schedule available; *Committees:* Marketing; Fundraising; Technical; Officials

Biathlon Ontario
61 Kayla Cres., Collingwood ON L9Y 5K8
www.biathlonontario.ca
Also Known As: BiON
Overview: A small provincial organization

Description: To govern the sport of biathlon in the Northwest Territories; to encourage physical activity & community through sport; *Member of:* Biathlon Canada
Chief Officer(s): Mike Scholte, President
mikescholte@rogers.com
Greg Dalton, Vice-President, Member & Club Relations
gdalton@tribsys.com
Daniel Guay, Secretary
dsguay@lakesuperiorbiathlon.com
Membership: 7 clubs

Biathlon PEI
2759 Glasgow Rd., Hunter River PE C0A 1N0
Tel: 902-964-3294
biathlonpei@gmail.com
www.biathlonpei.com
Overview: A small provincial organization founded in 2005
Description: To govern the sport of biathlon in Prince Edward Island.; *Member of:* Biathlon Canada; Sport PEI Inc.
Chief Officer(s): Bob Bentley, President
Steve Woodman, Secretary, 902-566-8003
steven.woodman@vac-acc.gc.ca
Activities: Programs for athletes of all levels

Biathlon Saskatchewan
1860 Lorne St., Regina SK S4P 2L7
Tel: 306-780-9236; *Fax:* 306-780-9462
sask.ski@sasktel.net
biathlon.sasktelwebhosting.com
Overview: A small provincial organization founded in 2005
Description: To govern the sport of biathlon in Saskatchewan.; *Member of:* Biathlon Canada
Chief Officer(s): Alana Ottenbreit, Contact
Membership: 6 clubs

Biathlon Yukon
PO Box 31673, Whitehorse YT Y1A 6L3
Tel: 867-633-5717
biathlonyukon@gmail.com
www.biathlonyukon.org
Overview: A small provincial organization
Description: To enhance opportunities for all Yukon persons in their pursuit of excellence & in their enjoyment of participation in biathlon; *Member of:* Biathlon Canada; Sport Yukon
Chief Officer(s): Bill Curtis, President

Northwest Territories Biathlon Association
NT
Tel: 867-874-2681
www.nwtbiathlon.com
Social Media:
www.facebook.com/172304639531053
Also Known As: NWT Biathlon Association
Overview: A small provincial organization
Description: To govern the sport of biathlon in the Northwest Territories; to encourage physical activity & community through sport; *Member of:* Biathlon Canada
Chief Officer(s): Pat Bobinski, President
pat@nwtbiathlon.com
Ted Kimmins, Vice-President
ted@nwtbiathlon.com
Belinda Whitford, Secretary-Treasurer
belinda@nwtbiathlon.com

Bicycling

Alberta Bicycle Association (ABA)
11759 Groat Rd., Edmonton AB T5M 3K6
Tel: 780-427-6352; *Fax:* 780-427-6438
Toll-Free: 877-646-2453
www.albertabicycle.ab.ca
Overview: A small provincial licensing organization
Description: To promote all aspects of cycling in Alberta
Affiliation(s): Canadian Cycling Association; Union Cycliste International
Chief Officer(s): Heather Lothian, Executive Director
heather@albertabicycle.ab.ca
Membership: *Fees:* Schedule available; *Member Profile:* Cyclists; *Committees:* BMX; Racing; Recreation & Transportation
Activities: *Internships:* Yes

Bicycle Newfoundland & Labrador
PO Box 13241, Stn. A, NL A1B 4A5
admin@bnl.nf.ca
www.bnl.nf.ca
Social Media:
www.facebook.com/BicycleNL
twitter.com/BicycleNL
Overview: A small provincial organization
Membership: *Fees:* Schedule available

Bicycle Nova Scotia (BNS)
5516 Spring Garden Rd., 4th Fl., Halifax NS B3J 1G6
Tel: 902-425-5454; *Fax:* 902-425-5606
staff@bicycle.ns.ca
www.bicycle.ns.ca
Social Media:
www.facebook.com/bicyclenovascotia
twitter.com/bicyclens
Overview: A small provincial organization
Description: To act as the government body for cycling in Nova Scotia & to advocate for on & off road cycling; *Member of:* Canadian Cycling Association
Chief Officer(s): Susanna Fuller, Co-President, Recreation & Transportation
susanna.fuller@bicycle.ns.ca
Lola Doucet, Co-President, Competition
lola.doucet@bicycle.ns.ca
Membership: *Fees:* $15 supporting; $25 general; $125 club
Activities: All aspects of cycling in Nova Scotia

Canadian Independent Bicycle Retailers Association (CIBRA) / Association canadienne des détaillants de vélos isdépendants (ACDVI)
PO Box 1653, Niagara on the Lake ON L0S 1J0
Fax: 866-898-3320
Toll-Free: 866-528-2822
info@btac.org
www.btac.org
Social Media:
www.facebook.com/BikeCIBRA
twitter.com/cibrabike
Previous Name: Bicycle Trade Association of Canada
Overview: A small national organization founded in 2014
Description: To serve the needs of Canada's independent bike retailers & contribute to the development of the bicycle retail industry as a whole
Chief Officer(s): Kevin Senior, President
Finances: *Annual Operating Budget:* $500,000-$1.5 Million; *Funding Sources:* Membership fees; Trade show revenue; Publications revenue
Membership: *Fees:* $197.75 retailer; schedule for suppliers, based upon revenue; *Member Profile:* Independent bicycle retailers, suppliers, distributors, & manufacturers across Canada
Activities: *Rents Mailing List:* Yes

Contagious Mountain Bike Club (CMBC)
4061 - 4th Ave., Whitehorse YT Y1A 1H1
Tel: 867-668-4990
info@cmbcyukon.ca
sportyukon.com/member/cycling-association-of-yukon
Overview: A small provincial organization
Description: To promote off-road cycling in the Yukon.
Chief Officer(s): Sue Richards, President
susanlearichards@gmail.com

Cycling Association of the Yukon
4061 - 4th Ave., Whitehorse YT Y1A 1H1
info@yukoncycling.com
yukoncycling.com
Overview: A small provincial organization
Member of: Cycling Canada Cyclisme; Sport Yukon
Chief Officer(s): Marc LaPointe, President

Cycling British Columbia (CBC)
#201, 210 West Broadway, Vancouver BC V5Y 3W2
Tel: 604-737-3034; *Fax:* 604-737-3141
membership@cyclingbc.net
cyclingbc.net
Social Media:
www.youtube.com/user/cyclingbc
www.facebook.com/122018951154516
twitter.com/raceinbc
Also Known As: Cycling BC
Previous Name: Bicycling Association of BC
Overview: A medium-sized provincial organization founded in 1974
Description: To enable, enhance, & encourage cycling in British Columbia; *Member of:* Cycling Canada Cyclisme
Chief Officer(s): Richard Wooles, Executive Director
richard@cyclingbc.net
Diana Hardie, Director, Finance & Administration
diana@cyclingbc.net
Tara Mowat, Coordinator, High Performance
tara@cyclingbc.net
Membership: *Fees:* Schedule available; *Committees:* Governance Review; Female Program Development
Activities: *Rents Mailing List:* Yes; *Library:* Yes (Open to Public)

Cycling Canada Cyclisme
#203, 2197 Riverside Dr., Ottawa ON K1H 7X3
Tel: 613-248-1353; *Fax:* 613-248-9311
general@cyclingcanada.ca
www.cyclingcanada.ca
Social Media:
www.youtube.com/user/CanadianCycling
www.facebook.com/CyclingCanada
twitter.com/CyclingCanada
Previous Name: Canadian Cycling Association
Overview: A medium-sized national organization founded in 1882
Description: To organize & promote cycling in Canada, including BMX, road racing, track, & mountain biking, for sport & fitness.
Chief Officer(s): Greg Mathieu, CEO & Secretary General
greg.mathieu@cyclingcanada.ca
Jacques Landry, Head Coach & Director, High Performance
jacques.landry@cyclingcanada.ca
Mathieu Boucher, Director, Performance Development
mathieu.boucher@cyclingcanada.ca
Brett Stewart, Director, Finance & Administration
brett.stewart@cyclingcanada.ca
Matthew Jeffries, Director, Marketing & Communications
matthew.jeffries@cyclingcanada.ca

Cycling PEI (CPEI)
Sport PEI, PO Box 302, 40 Enman Cresent, Charlottetown PE C1A 7K7
Tel: 902-368-4985; *Fax:* 902-368-4548
www.cpei.ca
Social Media:
twitter.com/cyclingpei
Overview: A small provincial organization
Description: To develop cycling in PEI; *Member of:* Cycling Canada Cyclisme
Chief Officer(s): David Sims, President
sims@cpei.ca
Mike Connolly, Executive Director
mconnolly@sportpei.pe.ca
Membership: *Fees:* $20 youth general; $30 senior general; $30 youth citizen; $40 senior citizen; $50 youth UCI racing license; $90 senior UCI racing license
Activities: *Awareness Events:* Red Mud Mountain Mayhem, Aug.

Edmonton Bicycle & Touring Club (EBTC)
PO Box 52017, Stn. Garneau, Edmonton AB T6G 2T5
Tel: 780-424-2453
www.bikeclub.ca
Social Media:
www.facebook.com/groups/21002145481
twitter.com/EBTCbikeclub
Overview: A small local organization founded in 1978
Affiliation(s): Alberta Bicycle Association
Chief Officer(s): Charles World, President
president@bikeclub.ca
Finances: *Annual Operating Budget:* $50,000-$100,000
Staff: 7 volunteer(s)
Membership: 301; *Fees:* $33 single; $18 for additional family member (18 years & older); *Member Profile:* Single, married, families, all ages & walks of life
Activities: Day & overnight cycling trips; cross-country skiing; social events; *Awareness Events:* Tour de l'Alberta; *Library:* Yes (Open to Public)

Fédération québécoise des sports cyclistes (FQSC) / Québec Cycling Sports Federation
4545, av Pierre-de Coubertin, Montréal QC H1V 3R2
Tél: 514-252-3071; *Téléc:* 514-252-3165
info@fqsc.net
www.fqsc.net
Média social:
www.facebook.com/176077399110320
twitter.com/FQSC
Nom précédent: Fédération cycliste du Québec
Aperçu: *Dimension:* moyenne; *Envergure:* provinciale; Organisme sans but lucratif; fondée en 1971
Description: Régie et promotion des sports cyclistes au Québec; *Membre de:* Cycling Canada Cyclisme
Affiliation(s): Union cycliste internationale; Sports-Québec; Regroupement loisir Québec
Membre(s) du bureau directeur: Louis Barbeau, Directeur général, 514-252-3071 3523
lbarbeau@fqsc.net
Finances: *Budget de fonctionnement annuel:* $500,000-$1.5 Million
Personnel: 5 membre(s) du personnel; 57 bénévole(s)
Membre: 5 000 individus; 150 clubs; *Montant de la cotisation:* Schedule available
Activités: Temple de la Renommée du Cyclisme Québécois; mérite cycliste québécois; *Bibliothèque:* Oui (Bibliothèque publique)

Manitoba Cycling Association (MCA)
145 Pacific Ave., Winnipeg MB R3B 2Z6
Tel: 204-925-5686
mbcycling.ca
Social Media:
www.facebook.com/182495551800883
twitter.com/ManitobaCycling
Overview: A small provincial organization
Description: To be the provincial organizing body for the sport of cycling in Manitoba.; *Member of:* Cycling Canada Cyclisme
Chief Officer(s): Andy Romanovych, President
tpeabody@shaw.ca
Twila Pitcher, Executive Director
cycling.ed@sportmanitoba.ca
Membership: *Fees:* $59

Ontario Cycling Association (OCA) / Association cycliste ontarienne
#2, 2015 Pan Am Blvd., Milton ON L9T 8Y9
Tel: 416-855-1717
www.ontariocycling.org
Social Media:
www.linkedin.com/company/ontario-cycling-association
www.facebook.com/129640691224
twitter.com/ontariocycling
Overview: A medium-sized provincial licensing organization founded in 1882
Description: To act as the provincial governing body for road, track & cyclocross, mountain biking, & BMX racing in Ontario; To develop & deliver quality programs & services for the sport of cycling in Ontario; *Member of:* Cycling Canada Cyclisme
Chief Officer(s): Jim Crosscombe, Chief Executive Officer, 416-855-1717 1008
Michael Suraci, Manager, High Performance, 416-855-1717 1002
Jen Eaton, Coordinator, Sport, 416-855-1717 1009
Finances: *Funding Sources:* Membership fees; Sponsorships
Membership: *Fees:* Schedule available; *Member Profile:* OCA affiliated club members; Riders who wish to compete only in Ontario; Riders who wish to compete out of the province or at national & international events held within Ontario; Non-racers; Certified Can-Bike & OMBI instructors
Activities: Promoting the benefits of cycling, as well as cycling programs & services in Ontario; Advocating for cyclists in Ontario; Sharing resources & expertise; Promoting safe cycling, through the CanBike safe cycling program; Coordinating mountain bike, road, & track race competitions

Saskatchewan Cycling Association
2205 Victoria Ave., Regina SK S4P 0S4
Tel: 306-780-9299; *Fax:* 306-525-4009
cycling@accesscomm.ca
www.saskcycling.ca
Social Media:
www.facebook.com/327882317318669
Overview: A small provincial organization
Description: To promote & enhance the Saskatchewan cycling experience while recognizing its benefits to the individual & society.; *Member of:* Cycling Canada Cyclisme
Chief Officer(s): Bob Cochran, Interim President
Finances: *Funding Sources:* Saskatchewan Lotteries
Staff: 2 staff member(s)
Activities: *Speaker Service:* Yes; *Rents Mailing List:* Yes

Toronto Bicycling Network
PO Box 279, #200, 131 Bloor St. West, Toronto ON M5S 1R8
Tel: 416-760-4191
info@tbn.ca
www.tbn.ca
Social Media:
twitter.com/TOBikeNetwork
Overview: A small local organization founded in 1983
Chief Officer(s): Ian Rankin, President
president@tbn.ca
Sandra Wong, Technical Director
sandra.wong@tbn.ca
Ed Weiss, Director, Communications
publicity@tbn.ca
Membership: 850; *Fees:* $70 family; $50 individual; $25 student
Activities: Leisure Wheeler Rides; Easy Roller Rides; Tourist & Short Tourist Rides; Sportif Rides; Country Cruise Rides; Snails & Spice Ride; cross-country skiing; in-line skating; ice skating & hiking

Vélo New Brunswick
536 McAllister Rd., Riverview NB E1B 4G1
www.velo.nb.ca
Social Media:
www.facebook.com/VeloNB
Overview: A small provincial organization founded in 1993
Description: To promote all aspects of the activity of bicycling, competitive & recreational, both on & off the road; *Member of:* Cycling Canada Cyclisme
Affiliation(s): Sport New Brunswick
Chief Officer(s): Kelly Murray, President
Kelly.Murray@velo.nb.ca
Michelle Chase, Vice-President
Michelle.Chase@velo.nb.ca
Sheila Colbourne, Executive Director
Sheila.Colbourne@velo.nb.ca

Vélo Québec
Maison des cyclistes, 1251, rue Rachel Est, Montréal QC H2J 2J9
Tél: 514-521-8356; *Téléc:* 514-521-5711
Ligne sans frais: 800-567-8356
www.velo.qc.ca
Média social:
instagram.com/veloquebec
www.facebook.com/VeloQuebec
twitter.com/VeloQuebec
Aperçu: *Dimension:* moyenne; *Envergure:* provinciale; fondée en 1967
Description: µ promouvoir l'utilisation du vélo à travers le Québec
Membre(s) du bureau directeur: Suzanne Lareau, Directrice générale
Montant de la cotisation: 41$
Activités: *Stagiaires:* Oui; *Service de conférenciers:* Oui

VeloNorth Cycling Club
68 Klondike Rd., Whitehorse YT Y1A 3M1
Tel: 867-668-3531
www.velonorth.ca
Overview: A small provincial organization
Description: Their mission is to encourage safe bicyle riding for sport, recreation & fitness.
Affiliation(s): Contagious Mountain Bike Club
Chief Officer(s): Mike McCann, Chair
Bill Curtis, Treasurer
wcurtis@northwestel.net

Blindness

Blind Sailing Association of Canada (BSAC)
17 Boustead Ave., Toronto ON M6R 1Y7
Tel: 416-489-2433
info@blindsailing.ca
www.blindsailing.ca
Social Media:
www.facebook.com/385889524843037
twitter.com/blindcansail
Overview: A small national organization founded in 2002
Description: To provide opportunities for the blind to learn to sail, thus boosting skills, confidence & self-esteem; *Member of:* Ontario Sailing Association; Sail Canada
Membership: *Fees:* $40

Blind Sports Nova Scotia
NS
info@blindsportsnovascotia.ca
www.blindsportsnovascotia.ca
Social Media:
twitter.com/blindsportsns
Overview: A small provincial organization
Description: Blind Sports Nova Scotia is an organization that presents sport & recreational activities for visually impaired athletes in Nova Scotia.; *Member of:* Canadian Blind Sport Association; Sport Nova Scotia
Chief Officer(s): Peter Parsons, Chair
Charlie MacDonald, Secretary
Member Profile: Adults, age 19+ (but 14+ are welcome, too)

British Columbia Blind Sports & Recreation Association (BCBSRA)
#170, 5055 Joyce St., Vancouver BC V5R 6B2
Tel: 604-325-8638; *Fax:* 604-325-1638
Toll-Free: 877-604-8638
info@bcblindsports.bc.ca
www.bcblindsports.bc.ca
Social Media:
www.facebook.com/BCBlindSports
twitter.com/bc_blind
Also Known As: BC Blind Sports
Overview: A medium-sized provincial charitable organization founded in 1975
Description: To provide sports, physical recreation & fitness activities & programs for persons of all ages who are blind/visually impaired; to alleviate isolating & inhibiting effects of blindness/visual impairment; to improve physical capabilities & self-image of blind/visually impaired individuals by providing opportunities for them to learn; to encourage, promote & maintain interest in & cooperation with all such amateur sports & recreation organizations.
Chief Officer(s): Brian Cowie, President
Tami Grenon, Vice-President
Finances: *Funding Sources:* Private donations; provincial government
Membership: *Fees:* $15 athlete; $5 supporting; *Member Profile:* Legally blind athletes; sighted guides; coaches; parents whose children are blind
Activities: Operates in nine regions: Kootenays, Thompson/Okanagan, Fraser Valley, Cariboo/North East, Vancouver/Squamish; Vancouver Island/South, Vancouver Island/North, North West, Fraser River/Delta; fundraisers; trade shows; workshops; *Speaker Service:* Yes

Canadian Blind Sports Association Inc. (CBSA) / Association canadienne des sports pour aveugles inc.
#325, 5055 Joyce St., Vancouver BC V5R 6B2
Tel: 604-419-0480; *Fax:* 604-419-0481
Toll-Free: 866-604-0480
info@canadianblindsports.ca
www.canadianblindsports.ca
Social Media:
www.facebook.com/canadianblindsports
Overview: A medium-sized national charitable organization founded in 1976
Description: To facilitate opportunities for Canadians who are legally blind to participate in amateur sport at the national/international level, & to thereby enhance a healthy lifestyle & individual well-being.
Affiliation(s): International Blind Sports Association; Canadian Paralympic Committee; Active Living Alliance
Chief Officer(s): Jane D. Blaine, Chief Executive Officer
jane@canadianblindsports.ca
Finances: *Annual Operating Budget:* $250,000-$500,000; *Funding Sources:* Donations; government; membership dues
Staff: 2 staff member(s)
Activities: *Rents Mailing List:* Yes

Manitoba Blind Sports Association (MBSA)
145 Pacific Ave., Winnipeg MB R3B 2Z6
Tel: 204-925-5694; *Fax:* 204-925-5792
blindsport@shawbiz.ca
www.blindsport.mb.ca
Previous Name: Manitoba Sport & Recreation Association for the Blind
Overview: A medium-sized provincial organization founded in 1976
Description: To provide blind & visually impaired Manitobans with the opportunity to participate in sport at all levels of skill & ability
Finances: *Annual Operating Budget:* Less than $50,000
Staff: 20 volunteer(s)
Membership: 45; *Fees:* $100 ($10 for membership, $40 program fee, $50 refundable fundraising fee)
Activities: *Awareness Events:* Run for Light; *Speaker Service:* Yes; *Library:* Yes by appointment

Ontario Blind Sports Association (OBSA)
#104, 3 Concorde Gate, Toronto ON M3C 3N6
Tel: 416-426-7191; *Fax:* 416-426-7361
blindsports.on.ca
Social Media:
www.facebook.com/OntarioBlindSports
Overview: A small provincial charitable organization founded in 1984
Description: To organize sporting events & activities for blind & visually impaired athletes in Ontario
Chief Officer(s): Kyle Pelly, Executive Director, 416-426-7244
Greg Theriault, Manager, Programs
greg@blindsports.on.ca
Finances: *Annual Operating Budget:* $100,000-$250,000; *Funding Sources:* Membership fees; government
Staff: 2 staff member(s); 20 volunteer(s)
Membership: 200; *Fees:* $25; *Member Profile:* Sport association
Activities: *Speaker Service:* Yes

Boating

Canadian International Dragon Boat Festival Society (CIDBFS)
Creekside Community Centre, 1 Athletes Way, Vancouver BC V5Y 0B1
Tel: 604-688-2382; *Fax:* 866-571-9004
info@dragonboatbc.ca
dragonboatbc.ca
Social Media:
www.facebook.com/thedragonboatbc
twitter.com/dragonboatbc
Also Known As: Rio Tinto Alcan Dragon Boat Festival
Previous Name: Dragon Boat Festival Society
Overview: A small national organization founded in 1989
Description: To foster learning & exploration of Canada's diverse multicultural heritage through performing, visual & culinary arts, & dragon boat-racing; *Member of:* Vancouver Cultural Alliance
Chief Officer(s): Ann Phelps, Executive Director
Finances: *Funding Sources:* Government; corporate; donations; fund-raising
Staff: 12 staff member(s); 1000 volunteer(s)
Activities: Annual 3 day multicultural festival; year long education program on multiculturalism; *Speaker Service:* Yes

Canadian Power & Sail Squadrons (Canadian Headquarters) (CPS) / Escadrilles canadiennes de plaisance (ECP)
26 Golden Gate Ct., Toronto ON M1P 3A5
Tel: 416-293-2438; *Fax:* 416-293-2445
Toll-Free: 888-277-2628
hqg@cps-ecp.ca
www.cps-ecp.ca
Social Media:
www.youtube.com/CPSECP
www.facebook.com/CPSboat
twitter.com/cpsboat
Overview: A medium-sized national charitable organization founded in 1938
Description: To increase awareness & knowledge of safe boating by educating & training members & the general public, by fostering fellowship among members, & establishing partnerships & alliances with organizations & agencies interested in boating; *Member of:* Canadian Safe Boating Council
Chief Officer(s): Walter Kowalchuk, Executive Director, 416-293-2438 0160
wkowalchuk@cps-ecp.ca
John Gullick, Manager, Government & Special Programs, 416-293-2438 0155
jgullick@cps-ecp.ca
Finances: *Annual Operating Budget:* $1.5 Million-$3 Million
Staff: 13 staff member(s); 5000 volunteer(s)
Membership: 34,000; *Fees:* $30; *Member Profile:* Must pass specified examination & pay dues on annual basis; *Committees:* Public Relations; Training Department
Activities:; *Library:* Yes (Open to Public)

Club nautique de Chibougamau inc.
CP 395, Chibougamau QC G8P 2X8
Tél: 418-748-6180
Aperçu: *Dimension:* petite; *Envergure:* locale

Dragon Boat Canada (DBC) / Bateau-Dragon Canada (BDC)
#331, 2255B Queen St. East, Toronto ON M4E 1G3
Tel: 613-482-1377
dragonboat.ca
Social Media:
www.facebook.com/DBC.BDC
twitter.com/DragonBoatCda
Overview: A medium-sized national organization
Description: To be the official governing of dragon boat racing in Canada.; *Member of:* International Dragon Boat Federation
Chief Officer(s): Chloe Greenhalgh, Executive Director
director@dragonboat.ca
Membership: *Fees:* Schedule available

Bobsledding & Luge

Alberta Bobsleigh Association (ABA)
Bob Niven Training Centre, #205, 88 Canada Olympic Rd. SW, Calgary AB T3B 5R5
Tel: 403-297-2721; *Fax:* 403-286-7213
slide@albertabobsleigh.com
www.albertabobsleigh.com
Social Media:
www.facebook.com/albertabobsleigh

Overview: A small provincial charitable organization founded in 1983
Description: To develop a broad interest in bobsleigh in Alberta; to provide opportunities for all Albertans to participate in bobsleigh; to provide opportunities for Albertans to progress to national & international levels; *Member of:* Bobsleigh Canada
Chief Officer(s): Sarah Monk, Technical Director
Dennis Marineau, Head Coach
Finances: *Annual Operating Budget:* $100,000-$250,000
Staff: 1 staff member(s); 70 volunteer(s)
Membership: 560; *Fees:* Schedule available
Activities: Summer training programs; *Library:* Yes (Open to Public)

Alberta Luge Association (ALA)
#201, BNTC, 88 Canada Olympic Rd. SW, Calgary AB T3B 5R5
Tel: 403-202-6570
admin@albertaluge.com
www.albertaluge.com
Overview: A small provincial organization founded in 1983
Description: To ensure the continued successful growth of the sport of luge in Alberta through the development of its athletes, coaches & volunteers at the recreational & elite levels
Affiliation(s): Canadian Luge Association
Finances: *Annual Operating Budget:* $100,000-$250,000
Staff: 2 staff member(s); 150 volunteer(s)
Membership: 700; *Fees:* Schedule available

Bobsleigh Canada Skeleton
c/o Canada Olympic Park, #329, 151 Canada Olympic Rd. SW, Calgary AB T3B 6B7
Tel: 403-247-5950; *Fax:* 403-202-6561
info@bobsleigh.ca
www.bobsleigh.ca
Social Media:
www.facebook.com/BobsleighCanadaSkeleton
twitter.com/BobsleighCAN
Overview: A medium-sized national charitable organization founded in 1990
Description: To strive to create Olympic & world champions; *Member of:* Canadian Olympic Association
Affiliation(s): Fédération internationale de bobsleigh et de tobogganing
Chief Officer(s): Don Wilson, CEO
Finances: *Funding Sources:* Government & corporate sponsorship
Staff: 8 staff member(s)
Activities: Operating national teams in men's & women's bobsleigh & skeleton; Hosting national & international events

Canadian Luge Association / Association canadienne de luge
#323, 151 Canada Olympic Rd. SW, Calgary AB T3B 6B7
Tel: 403-202-6581
www.luge.ca
Social Media:
www.facebook.com/138340422883168
twitter.com/LugeCanada
Previous Name: Canadian Amateur Bobsleigh & Luge Association
Overview: A medium-sized national organization founded in 1990
Description: To provide leadership & pursue success in promotion & development of all aspects of luge.
Chief Officer(s): Tim Farstad, Executive Director
tfarstad@luge.ca
Finances: *Funding Sources:* donations; Fast Track Capital
Staff: 4 staff member(s)
Member Profile: Provincial associations fully recognized by national association
Activities: *Internships:* Yes

Fédération Internationale de Luge de Course (FIL) / International Luge Federation
Rathausplatz 9, Berchtesgaden 83471 Germany
office@fil-luge.org
www.fil-luge.org
Aperçu: *Dimension:* petite; *Envergure:* internationale; fondée en 1957
Description: Promotion et participation aux compétitions de la luge dans le monde; organise des championnats du monde, des coupes du monde, des championnats régionaux; organise des cours et séminaires pour des arbitres et des entraîneurs
Affiliation(s): Canadian Luge Association
Membre(s) du bureau directeur: Josef Fendt, Président
Svein Romstad, Secrétaire général
Christoph Schweiger, Directeur général
Finances: *Budget de fonctionnement annuel:* $250,000-$500,000
Personnel: 5 membre(s) du personnel
Membre: 49
Activités: *Bibliothèque:* Oui

Ontario Bobsleigh Skeleton Association (OBSA)
22 Lynwood Ave., Ottawa ON K1Y 2B3
Tel: 613-864-0702
www.ontariobobsleighskeleton.ca
Social Media:
www.facebook.com/OntarioBobsleighSkeleton
Overview: A medium-sized provincial organization founded in 1960
Description: To promote bobsleigh & skeleton in Ontario
Affiliation(s): Bobsleigh Canada Skeleton; International Bobsleigh & Skeleton Federation
Chief Officer(s): Esther Dalle, Director, High Performance
edalle@hotmail.com

Ontario Luge Association (OLA)
3073 Victoria Heights Cres., Ottawa ON K1T 3M7
Tel: 613-262-5513
ontarioluge@gmail.com
ontarioluge.ca
Social Media:
www.facebook.com/OntarioLugeAssociation
twitter.com/OntarioLuge
Overview: A medium-sized provincial organization
Description: To promote luge in Ontario
Affiliation(s): Canadian Luge Association
Membership: *Fees:* $5 indiviual; $10 under 16

Bodybuilding

Alberta Bodybuilding Association (ABBA)
Edmonton Centre, PO Box 47248, Edmonton AB T5J 4N1
Tel: 780-709-5309
www.abba.ab.ca
Social Media:
www.facebook.com/Albertabodybuildingassociation
twitter.com/AlbertaBBAssoc
Overview: A small provincial organization
Description: To govern the sport of amateur bodybuilding, fitness & figure in Alberta.; *Member of:* Canadian Bodybuilding Federation; International Federation of Bodybuilding
Chief Officer(s): Asha Belisle, President
president@abba.ab.ca
Tara Jensen, Secretary-Treasurer
secretary@abba.ab.ca

Association des Physiques Québécois (APQ)
529, rue Delorme, Granby QC J2J 2C9
Tél: 450-991-1174; *Téléc:* 450-991-1184
www.apquebec.com
Aperçu: *Dimension:* petite; *Envergure:* provinciale
Membre de: Canadian Bodybuilding Federation; International Federation of Bodybuilding
Membre(s) du bureau directeur: Yves Desbiens, Director technique
photoyd@videotron.ca
Joe Spinello, Directeur des juges
spinellojoe@hotmail.com

British Columbia Amateur Bodybuilding Association (BCABBA)
PO Box 84020, 2844 Bainbridge Ave., Burnaby BC V5A 4T9
bcabbainfo@hotmail.com
www.bcabba.org
Overview: A small provincial organization
Description: To govern the sport of amateur bodybuilding, fitness & figure in British Columbia.; *Member of:* Canadian Bodybuilding Federation; International Federation of Bodybuilding
Chief Officer(s): Sandra Wickham, President
Tamara Knight, Coordinator, Membership
tzonefitness@telus.net
Membership: *Fees:* $75 competitive

Canadian Bodybuilding Federation (CBBF) / Fédération canadienne de culturisme
www.cbbf.ca
Social Media:
www.facebook.com/CanadianBodybuildingFederationCBBF
Overview: A small national organization
Description: To act as the governing body for amateur bodybuilding, fitness, & body fitness (figure) competition
Affiliation(s): British Columbia Amateur Bodybuilding Association; Alberta Bodybuilding Association; Saskatchewan Amateur Bodybuilders Association (SABBA); Manitoba Amateur Bodybuilding Association; Ontario Physique Association (OPA); Association des Physiques Québécois; New Brunswick Physique & Figure Association; Nova Scotia Amateur Bodybuilders Association; Newfoundland & Labrador Amateur Bodybuilding Association
Chief Officer(s): Georgina Dunnington, Chair

Activities: Qualifying competitors for the three IFBB World Championships; Posting championship results

Manitoba Amateur Bodybuilding Association (MABBA)
23 Forestgate Ave., Winnipeg MB R3P 2L2
mabba@shaw.ca
www.bodybuilding.ca
Overview: A small provincial organization
Description: To govern the sport of amateur bodybuilding, fitness & figure in Manitoba.; *Member of:* Canadian Bodybuilding Federation; International Federation of Bodybuilding; Sport Manitoba
Chief Officer(s): Tom Heffner, President
mabbapres@mymts.net
Chris McKee, Executive Director
mabba@shaw.ca

New Brunswick Physique & Figure Association (NBPFA)
NB
www.nbpfa.com
Social Media:
www.facebook.com/191517260859626
Overview: A small provincial organization
Description: To govern the sport of amateur bodybuilding, fitness & figure in New Brunswick.; *Member of:* Canadian Bodybuilding Federation; International Federation of Bodybuilding
Chief Officer(s): Garry Bartlett, President, 506-459-0135
grbartlett@yahoo.com
Duncan Lombard, Vice-President & Chief Judge
dlombard@nbnet.nb.ca

Newfoundland & Labrador Amateur Bodybuilding Association (NLABBA)
12 Walsh's Rd., Logy Bay NL A1K 3G8
www.nlabba.ca
Overview: A small provincial organization
Description: To govern the sport of amateur bodybuilding, fitness & figure in Newfoundland & Labrador.; *Member of:* Canadian Bodybuilding Federation; International Federation of Bodybuilding
Chief Officer(s): Mike Newhook, President
nlabba.exec@gmail.com
Zack Howard, Vice-President
vpnlabba@gmail.com
Pam Slaney, Secretary
pslaney387@gmail.com
Ken French, Treasurer
kenfrenc@gmail.com

Nova Scotia Amateur Bodybuilding Association (NSABBA)
14 White Sands Ct., Hubley NS B3Z 1A5
nsabba@nsabba.com
www.nsabba.com
Overview: A small provincial organization founded in 1980
Description: To govern the sport of amateur bodybuilding, fitness & figure in Nova Scotia.; *Member of:* Canadian Bodybuilding Federation; International Federation of Bodybuilding
Chief Officer(s): Georgina Dunnington, President
Christina Belding, Vice-President
Steve Belding, Treasurer-Secretary

Ontario Physique Association (OPA)
ON
info@physiqueassociation.ca
www.bao.on.ca
Social Media:
www.facebook.com/ontario.physique
twitter.com/AroundtheOPA
Overview: A small provincial organization
Description: To govern the sport of amateur bodybuilding, fitness & figure in Ontario.; *Member of:* Canadian Bodybuilding Federation; International Federation of Bodybuilding
Chief Officer(s): Ron Hache, President
president@physiqueassociation.ca
Al Cook, Vice-President
vicepresident@physiqueassociation.ca
Membership: *Fees:* $100

Saskatchewan Bodybuilding Association (SABBA)
#308, 615 Lynd Cres., Saskatoon SK S7T 0G8
Fax: 306-382-3948
www.sabba.net
Social Media:
twitter.com/Sk_Bodybuilding
Overview: A small provincial organization
Description: To govern the sport of amateur bodybuilding, fitness & figure in Saskatchewan.; *Member of:* Canadian

Bodybuilding Federation; International Federation of Bodybuilding
Chief Officer(s): Colin Keess, President, 306-382-2997
ckeezer@hotmail.com
Vince Wawryk, Vice-President, 306-978-2614
vinneez@sasktel.net
Leigh Keess, Secretary-Treasurer, 306-382-2997
fitrnmom2@yahoo.ca

Bowling

Alberta 5 Pin Bowlers' Association (A5-PBA)
Bowling Headquarters, 432 - 14 St. South, Lethbridge AB T1J 2X7
Tel: 403-320-2695; *Fax:* 403-320-2676
Toll-Free: 800-762-3075
generalenquires@centralalberta5pin.com
www.alberta5pin.com
Social Media:
www.facebook.com/a5pba
Overview: A medium-sized provincial charitable organization founded in 1979
Chief Officer(s): Annette Bruneau, President
Julie Kind, Secretary
Don MacIver, Treasurer
Brian Sudbury, Director, Technical

Bowling Federation of Alberta
11759 Groat Rd., Edmonton AB T5M 3K6
Tel: 780-422-8251
bowlfedab.ca
Overview: A small provincial organization
Description: To promote competitive & noncompetitive bowling in Alberta.
Chief Officer(s): Annette Bruneau, President
Grady Long, Executie Director
gradyed@bowlfedab.ca
Membership: 5 associations

Bowling Federation of Canada / Fédération des quilles du Canada
250 Shields Ct., #10A, Markham ON L3R 9W7
Tel: 905-479-1560
info@canadabowls.ca
www.canadabowls.ca
Overview: A medium-sized national organization
Description: To promote & foster the sport of bowling in Canada; To promote among the recognized national organizations in Canada, sportmanship, good fellowhsip, & the continued interest in the future development of bowling throughout Canada
Affiliation(s): Bowling Proprietors Association of Canada; Canadian 5-pin Bowlers Association; Canadian Tenpin Federation.
Chief Officer(s): Bob Randall, President, 604-533-2695
brandall@shaw.ca
Sheila Carr, Administrator, 613-744-5090
c5pba@c5pba.ca

Bowling Federation of Saskatchewan
#101, 1805 - 8th Ave., Regina SK S4R 1E8
Tel: 306-780-9412; *Fax:* 306-780-9455
bowling@sasktel.net
saskbowl.com
Social Media:
twitter.com/SaskBowl
Overview: A medium-sized provincial organization founded in 1984
Description: Working together through cooperation & harmonization to access & allocate funding for our members programs & services in order to enhance the sport of bowling; *Member of:* Sask Sport; Bowling Federation of Canada
Chief Officer(s): Rhonda Sereda, Executive Director
Finances: *Funding Sources:* Sask Lotteries; sponsorship; fundraising

Bowling Proprietors' Association of BC
#209, 332 Columbia St., New Westminster BC V3L 1A6
Tel: 604-522-2990; *Fax:* 604-522-2055
bowl4fun@bowlbc.com
www.bowlbc.com
Social Media:
www.facebook.com/BowlBc
Also Known As: Bowl BC
Overview: A small provincial organization founded in 1954
Description: To provide opportunities for people to bowl at their individual level
Chief Officer(s): Gord Wiffen, President
Activities: Adult, youth & seniors tournaments

Bowling Proprietors' Association of Canada (BPAC)
#10A, 250 Shields Ct., Markham ON L3R 9W7
Tel: 905-479-1560; *Fax:* 905-479-8613
info@bowlcanada.ca
www.bowlcanada.ca
Social Media:
www.youtube.com/c/bowlcanada
www.facebook.com/Bowl-Canada-703790949700789
twitter.com/bowlcanada
Also Known As: Bowl Canada
Overview: A small national organization
Description: The aim of this association is to improve general conditions in the bowling industry, to promote to the general public the benefits of bowling, to create a better relationship between the many bowling establishments across Canada and to encourage any and all practices which are in the best interests of the game.
Chief Officer(s): Paul Oliveira, Executive Director
paul@bowlcanada.ca
Membership: 500 bowling centres
Activities: Youth Bowling Canada (YBC); Sunshine Bowlers; Club 55+.

Bowling Proprietors' Association of Ontario (BPAO)
#202, 500 Alden Rd., Markham ON L3R 5H5
Tel: 905-940-8200; *Fax:* 905-940-8201
info@bowlontario.ca
www.bowlontario.ca
Also Known As: Bowl Ontario
Overview: A medium-sized provincial organization founded in 1953
Description: To improve conditions in bowling industry; To protect members from unreasonable legislation; To bring attention to the pleasures of bowling
Affiliation(s): Bowling Proprietors' Association of Canada
Membership: 124 bowling centres; *Member Profile:* Bowling centre ownership

British Columbia Tenpin Bowling Association
North Vancouver BC
www.bctenpin.com
Social Media:
www.instagram.com/bctenpin
www.facebook.com/groups/199885590219513
twitter.com/bctenpin
Overview: A small provincial organization
Description: To oversee the sport of tenpin bowling in British Columbia.; *Member of:* Canadian Tenpin Federation, Inc.
Chief Officer(s): Mark Westerberg, President
Bruce Taylor, Vice-President
MaryAnne Madsen, Secretary
Miriam Reid, Treasurer

Canadian 5 Pin Bowlers' Association (C5PBA) / Association canadienne des cinq quilles (AC5Q)
#206, 720 Belfast Rd., Ottawa ON K1G 0Z5
Tel: 613-744-5090; *Fax:* 613-744-2217
www.c5pba.ca
Social Media:
www.facebook.com/117638274967514
Previous Name: Canadian Bowling Congress
Overview: A medium-sized national licensing charitable organization founded in 1978
Description: The sports organization of male & female 5 pin bowlers provides programs & services to its members for their participation in organized 5-pin bowling. It also regulates bowling systems to standardize the sport.
Affiliation(s): Bowling Federation of Canada
Chief Officer(s): Dave Post, President
Sheila Carr, Executive Director
sheila.c5pba@gmail.com
Finances: *Funding Sources:* Membership fees; government; sponsors
Membership: 150,000; *Fees:* $7; *Member Profile:* Male & female 5 pin bowlers
Activities: Awards Program; *Library:* Yes (Open to Public)

Canadian Tenpin Federation, Inc. (CTF) / Fédération canadienne des dix-quilles, inc.
916 - 3 Ave. North, Lethbridge AB T1H 0H3
Tel: 403-381-2830; *Fax:* 855-654-2346
ctf@gotenpinbowling.ca
www.gotenpinbowling.ca
Social Media:
www.facebook.com/CanadianTenpinFederationInc
Overview: A large national organization founded in 1964
Description: To promote & foster the sport of tenpin bowling in Canada by maintaining active membership in the world's appropriate affiliated tenpin organizations, providing competitive opportunities for all skill levels, culminating in the selection of a National Team; To encourage the development of skills through a national coaching certification program
Affiliation(s): Fédération internationale des quilleurs
Chief Officer(s): Cathy Von Richter, President
bvonr@sasktel.net
Stan May, Executive Director
stanmay@gotenpinbowling.ca
Membership: 80,000 + 74 clubs; *Committees:* Membership/Association Services; Awards; Coaching Development; High Performance Unit; Regulatory; Youth
Activities: *Awareness Events:* National Team Trials, every even year, May long weekend

Fédération de pétanque du Québec
4545, av Pierre-de Coubertin, Montréal QC H1V 0B2
Tél: 514-252-3077
petanque@petanque.qc.ca
www.petanque.qc.ca
Média social:
www.facebook.com/189251017803912
Aperçu: *Dimension:* moyenne; *Envergure:* provinciale
Description: Développement du sport de pétanque
Membre(s) du bureau directeur: Janick Provencher, Présidente
Membre: 4 000; 14 organismes régionaux

Manitoba 5 Pin Bowlers' Association (M5PBA)
#432, 145 Pacific Ave., Winnipeg MB R3B 2Z6
Tel: 204-925-5766; *Fax:* 204-925-5792
Toll-Free: 800-282-8069
www.m5pba.com
Overview: A small provincial organization
Member of: Manitoba Five Pin Bowling Federation, Inc.
Chief Officer(s): Marilyn McMullan, President
mgmc.hdqtrs@shaw.ca

Manitoba Five Pin Bowling Federation, Inc. (MFPBF)
145 Pacific Ave., Winnipeg MB R3B 2Z6
Tel: 204-925-5766; *Fax:* 204-925-5767
www.mfpbf.com
Overview: A small provincial organization
Description: To provide services & resources to its members which enable them to increase membership & promote bowling as a lifetime sport through effective programs at all levels of participation; *Member of:* Canadian 5 Pin Bowlers' Association; Sport Manitoba
Affiliation(s): Manitoba 5 Pin Bowlers' Association; Master Bowlers Association of Manitoba; Youth Bowling Canada - Manitoba Divisio
Chief Officer(s): Deanne Zilinsky, Executive Director

Manitoba Tenpin Federation
#407, 145 Pacific Ave., Winnipeg MB R3B 2Z6
Tel: 204-925-5705
www.mbtenpinfed.com
Overview: A small provincial organization
Description: To oversee the sport of tenpin bowling in Manitoba.; *Member of:* Canadian Tenpin Federation, Inc.

Master Bowlers' Association of Alberta
1 Oxbow St., Red Deer AB T4N 5C3
Tel: 403-309-6916
mbaofalberta@gmail.com
mbaofa.ca
Also Known As: MBA of A
Overview: A small provincial organization
Member of: Master Bowlers' Association of Canada
Chief Officer(s): Brian Rossetti, President

Master Bowlers' Association of British Columbia
712 Colinet St., Coquitlam BC V3J 4X8
www.mbaofbc.com
Overview: A small provincial organization
Member of: Master Bowlers' Association of Canada
Chief Officer(s): Joan Ritchie, President
jwritchie@gmail.com
Jim Bushell, Technical Director
jbushell@shaw.ca

Master Bowlers' Association of Canada
c/o Master Bowlers' Association of Alberta, 1 Oxbow St., Red Deer AB T4N 5C3
www.mastersbowling.ca
Social Media:
www.facebook.com/MBAofCanada
Overview: A medium-sized national organization founded in 1970
Description: To connect master bowlers across Canada
Member Profile: NCCP certified coaches & athletes competing as Teaching Masters, Tournament Masters & Senior Masters
Activities: Annual National Championships

Master Bowlers' Association of Manitoba (MBAM)
MB
Overview: A small provincial organization
Member of: Manitoba Five Pin Bowling Federation, Inc.; Master Bowlers' Association of Canada

Master Bowlers' Association of Ontario (MBAO)
PO Box 22, 41 Temperance St., Bowmanville ON L1C 3A0
mbao.ca
Social Media:
www.facebook.com/185964874757498
Overview: A small provincial organization
Member of: Master Bowlers' Association of Canada
Chief Officer(s): Brenda Walters, President

New Brunswick Candlepin Bowlers Association
7 Lilac Cres., Fredericton NB E3A 2G7
Tel: 516-472-7592
Overview: A medium-sized provincial organization
Description: To promote candlepin bowling, a sport unique to the Maritimes & New England; *Member of:* Sport NB
Chief Officer(s): Don Leger, President
Finances: *Funding Sources:* Provincial government

Northwest Territories 5 Pin Bowlers' Association (NWT5PBA)
PO Box 2643, Yellowknife NT X1A 2P9
www.bowlnwt.ca
Overview: A small provincial organization
Description: To promote 5 pin bowling in the Northwest Territories

Ontario 5 Pin Bowlers' Association (O5PBA)
#302, 3 Concorde Gate, Toronto ON M3C 3N7
Tel: 416-426-7167; *Fax:* 416-426-7364
o5pba@o5pba.ca
www.o5pba.ca
Overview: A medium-sized provincial organization founded in 1963
Description: To act as the governing body for 5 pin bowling in Ontario; *Member of:* Canadian 5 Pin Bowlers' Association
Chief Officer(s): John Cresswell, President
Rhonda Gifford, Coordinator, Program
Jackie Henriques, Coordinator, Finances
Al Hong, Coordinator, Events
Membership: 10,000

Ontario Tenpin Bowling Association
3064 Tecumseh Dr., Burlington ON L7N 3M4
am@otba.ca
www.otba.ca
Social Media:
www.facebook.com/groups/800626176718495
Overview: A small provincial organization
Description: To oversee the sport of tenpin bowling in Ontario.; *Member of:* Canadian Tenpin Federation, Inc.
Chief Officer(s): Charlotte Konkle, President
president@otba.ca
Della Trude, 1st Vice-President
1stVicePresident@otba.ca
Wayne Dubs, 2nd Vice-President
2ndVicePresident@otba.ca
Membership: 16 associations

Prince Edward Island Five Pin Bowlers Association Inc.
c/o Sport PEI, PO Box 302, Charlottetown PE C1A 7K7
Tel: 902-368-4110; *Fax:* 902-368-4548
Toll-Free: 800-247-6712
sports@sportpei.pe.ca
www.sportpei.pe.ca
Overview: A medium-sized provincial organization founded in 1981

Saskatchewan 5 Pin Bowlers' Association (S5PBA)
#100, 1805 - 8th Ave., Regina SK S4R 1E8
Tel: 306-780-9412; *Fax:* 306-780-9455
bowling@sasktel.net
www.saskbowl.com/s5pba
Overview: A small provincial organization founded in 1980
Description: To develop trust & harmony among member organizations; to assist in the development & promotion of the sport of bowling through the provision of stable funding; *Member of:* Canadian 5 Pin Bowlers' Association; Bowling Federation of Saskatchewan
Chief Officer(s): Rhonda Kurbis, Executive Director
Finances: *Annual Operating Budget:* $100,000-$250,000
Staff: 1 staff member(s); 1000 volunteer(s)
Membership: 6,500; *Fees:* Schedule available

Youth Bowling Canada (YBC)
c/o Bowl Canada, #10A, 250 Shields Ct., Markham ON L3R 9W7
Tel: 905-479-1560; *Fax:* 905-479-8613
info@bowlcanada.ca
www.youthbowling.ca
Social Media:
instagram.com/bowlcanada
www.facebook.com/youthbowlingcanada
twitter.com/ybcbowling
Previous Name: National Youth Bowling Council
Overview: A small national organization founded in 1963
Description: YBC is a program operating under the auspices of the Bowling Proprietors' Association of Canada (Bowl Canada), a not-for-profit organization comprised of 500 member centres across the country. The YBC league is divided in 5-pin & 10-pin, & further broken down in 3 age groups: bantam, junior & senior.
Membership: *Fees:* Schedule available

Boxing

Boxing Alberta
Percy Page Centre, 11759 Groat Rd., Edmonton AB T5M 3K6
Tel: 780-427-6515; *Fax:* 780-427-1205
www.boxingalberta.com
Previous Name: Alberta Amateur Boxing Association
Overview: A small provincial organization
Member of: Canadian Amateur Boxing Association
Chief Officer(s): Roland Labbe, President
cvcwest@telus.net
Dennis Belair, Executive Director
dbelair@telus.net
Membership: 46 clubs

Boxing BC Association
PO Box 23065, Stn. RPO 11, Prince George BC V2N 6Z2
Tel: 250-964-7750; *Fax:* 250-964-7787
information@boxing.bc.ca
www.boxing.bc.ca
Social Media:
www.facebook.com/489238011141309
Previous Name: British Columbia Amateur Boxing Association
Overview: A small provincial organization founded in 1985
Description: To provide all citizens of British Columbia access to & participation in the opportunities, programs & activities; *Member of:* Canadian Amateur Boxing Association
Finances: *Annual Operating Budget:* $100,000-$250,000
Staff: 1 staff member(s); 150 volunteer(s)
Membership: 1,100 in 42 clubs; *Fees:* Schedule available; *Member Profile:* Competitors, coaches, officials, associated volunteers
Activities: Club shows, tournament highlights & provincial championships & Golden Gloves tournaments; *Awareness Events:* Golden Gloves, March; *Internships:* Yes

Boxing Manitoba
#421, 145 Pacific Ave., Winnipeg MB R3B 2Z6
Tel: 204-925-5658; *Fax:* 204-925-5792
info@boxingmanitoba.com
www.boxingmanitoba.com
Social Media:
www.facebook.com/BoxingManitoba
twitter.com/boxingmanitoba
Previous Name: Manitoba Amateur Boxing Association
Overview: A small provincial organization
Description: To govern the sport of boxing in Manitoba.; *Member of:* Canadian Amateur Boxing Association
Chief Officer(s): Alan Hogg, President
president@boxingmanitoba.com
Roland Vandal, Vice-President & Technical Director
technical@boxingmanitoba.com

Boxing New Brunswick Boxe
413 Millidge Ave., Saint John NB E2K 2N3
Tel: 506-652-8251
nbref@yahoo.ca
boxingnb.com
Also Known As: Boxing NB Boxe
Overview: A small provincial organization
Description: To govern the sport of boxing in New Brunswick.; *Member of:* Canadian Amateur Boxing Association
Chief Officer(s): Ed Blanchard, President

Boxing Nova Scotia
NS
www.boxingnovascotia.com
Social Media:
www.facebook.com/BoxingNovaScotia
twitter.com/boxnovascotia
Overview: A small provincial organization
Description: To govern the sport of boxing in Nova Scotia.; *Member of:* Canadian Amateur Boxing Association
Affiliation(s): Sport Nova Scotia; Nova Scotia Health Promotion & Protection
Membership: *Fees:* Schedule available

Boxing Ontario
#202, 3 Concorde Gate, Toronto ON M3C 3N7
Tel: 416-426-7250; *Fax:* 416-426-7367
info@boxingontario.com
www.boxingontario.com
Social Media:
www.facebook.com/boxingontario
twitter.com/BoxingOntario
Overview: A small provincial licensing organization founded in 1972
Description: This is the only governing body for amateur boxing in Ontario. It aims to organize, promote, develop interest & participation in the sport in the province.; *Member of:* Canadian Amateur Boxing Association
Affiliation(s): Association International de Boxe Amateur (AIBA); Ontario Ministry of Health Promotion
Chief Officer(s): Matt Kennedy, Executive Director
mkennedy@boxingontario.com
Finances: *Annual Operating Budget:* $250,000-$500,000; *Funding Sources:* Membership, Fundraising, Ministry of Tourism and Recreation
Staff: 3 staff member(s)
Membership: 80 clubs; *Fees:* Schedule available
Activities: Governing amateur boxing; sanctioning amateur events

Boxing Saskatchewan
1860 Lorne St., Regina SK S4P 2L7
Tel: 306-780-9305
boxingsask@sasktel.net
www.boxingsask.com
Also Known As: Saskatchewan Amateur Boxing Association
Overview: A small provincial organization
Description: This is a non-profit society that enforces rules & regulations governing amateur boxing in the province. It also promotes the formation of new clubs.; *Member of:* Canadian Amateur Boxing Association
Affiliation(s): Canadian Amateur Boxing Association
Chief Officer(s): Graham Craig, Executive Director
Finances: *Funding Sources:* Sask Sport
Membership: 23 clubs

Calgary Combative Sports Commission
c/o Compliance Services, Animal & Bylaw Services, City of Calgary, PO Box 2100, Stn. M #128, Calgary AB T2P 2M5
Tel: 403-648-6323; *Fax:* 403-221-3528
combativesportscommission@calgary.ca
www.calgary.ca
Previous Name: Calgary Boxing & Wrestling Commission
Overview: A small local licensing organization founded in 2007
Description: The commission acts as a regulation body for professional combative sports within the City of Calgary.; *Member of:* Canadian Professional Boxing Federation
Chief Officer(s): Shirley Stunzi, Chair, 403-710-6148
Shirley.Stunzi@calgary.ca
Kent Pallister, Administrator
Membership: 1-99

Canadian Amateur Boxing Association (CABA) / Association canadienne de boxe amateur (ACBA)
c/o Canadian Olympic Committee, 500, boul René-Lévesque Ouest, Montréal QC H2Z 2A5
Tel: 514-861-3713; *Fax:* 514-819-9228
Toll-Free: 800-861-1319
info@boxingcanada.org
www.boxingcanada.org
Social Media:
www.facebook.com/BoxingCa
twitter.com/boxing_canada
Also Known As: Boxing Canada
Overview: A medium-sized national organization founded in 1969
Description: To develop & maintain uniform rules & regulations to govern amateur boxing competitions in Canada; To develop coaches & officials; To organize national team programs, including development, training, & competition
Affiliation(s): International Amateur Boxing Association
Chief Officer(s): Roy Halpin, Executive Director
rhalpin@boxingcanada.org
Daniel Trépanier, Director, High Performance
dtrepanier@boxingcanada.org
Dionne Andree-Anne, Coordinator, Programs/Projects
adionne@boxingcanada.org
Activities: Providing news & results about the sport

Canadian Professional Boxing Council (CPBC)
www.canadianboxingcouncil.com
Overview: A large national organization founded in 1976
Description: To act as the sanctioning body for professional boxing in Canada; To aid in the development of professional boxing & crown new deserving champions
Chief Officer(s): Don Collette, President
Anne Clarke, Secretary
Activities: Crowning new champions; Working with promoters; Adhering to the uniform rules of boxing in all aspects of competition

Edmonton Combative Sports Commission (ECSC)
c/o Community Standards/Community Services, CN Tower, PO Box 2359, 10004 - 104 Ave., 12th Fl., Edmonton AB T5J 2R7
Tel: 780-495-0382; *Fax:* 780-429-6976
ecsc.ca
Previous Name: Edmonton Boxing & Wrestling Commission
Overview: A small local licensing organization founded in 1938
Description: The ECSC regulates, governs & controls boxing, wrestling & full-contact karate bouts & contests within Edmonton; enforces the CPBF safety code.; *Member of:* Canadian Professional Boxing Federation
Affiliation(s): Association of Boxing Commissions
Chief Officer(s): Pat Reid, Executive Director
pat.reid@edmonton.ca
Finances: *Annual Operating Budget:* $50,000-$100,000; *Funding Sources:* Permit fees
Staff: 24 volunteer(s)
Membership: 8; *Member Profile:* By City Council appointment

Fédération Québécoise de Boxe Olympique (FQBO)
4545, av Pierre-de Coubertin, Montréal QC H1V 0B2
Tél: 514-252-3047; *Téléc:* 514-254-2144
Ligne sans frais: 866-241-3779
info@fqbo.qc.ca
www.fqbo.qc.ca
Média social:
www.youtube.com/channel/UCwrq3BlBvgb28mB6GIVsJaA
www.facebook.com/groups/5136898117
Également appelé: Boxe Québec
Aperçu: *Dimension:* moyenne; *Envergure:* provinciale
Membre de: Canadian Amateur Boxing Association
Membre: 2 000

Manitoba Combative Sports Commission (MCSC)
#628, 213 Notre Dame Ave., Winnipeg MB R3B 1N3
Tel: 204-945-1788; *Fax:* 204-948-3649
www.mbcombativesports.com
Social Media:
twitter.com/MBCombatSports
Previous Name: Manitoba Boxing Commission
Overview: A small provincial licensing organization founded in 1993
Description: To regulate professional boxing, kickboxing and mixed martial arts throughout the province; *Member of:* Canadian Professional Boxing Federation
Chief Officer(s): Joel Fingard, Executive Director
Activities: Licensing participants, promoters, & athletes; Supervising events

Nova Scotia Boxing Authority (NSBA)
NS
Overview: A small provincial organization founded in 1975
Description: The Nova Scotia Boxing Authority regulates professional boxing & other combat sports in the province, as well as establishes & enforces rules for the conduct of boxing, & the training of officials in accordance with national standards. The NSBA answers to the minister of health promotion & protection.; *Member of:* Canadian Boxing Federation

Prince Edward Island Amateur Boxing Association
PE
Overview: A medium-sized provincial organization
Member of: Canadian Amateur Boxing Association

Yukon Amateur Boxing Association
YT
Overview: A small provincial organization
Description: To govern the sport of boxing in the Yukon Territory.; *Member of:* Canadian Amateur Boxing Association

Broomball

Alberta Broomball Association (ABA)
11759 Groat Rd., Edmonton AB T5M 3K6
www.albertabroomball.ca
Overview: A small provincial organization
Member of: Ballon sur glace Broomball Canada
Chief Officer(s): Greg Mastervick, President
gregma@telusplanet.net
Wayne Neigel, Secretary-Treasurer
neigel@shaw.ca

Ballon sur glace Broomball Canada
145 Pacific Ave., Winnipeg MB R3B 2Z6
Tel: 204-925-5656; *Fax:* 204-925-5792
cbfbroomball@shaw.ca
www.broomball.ca
Previous Name: Broomball Canada Federation
Overview: A medium-sized national charitable organization founded in 1976
Chief Officer(s): George Brown, President, 613-253-7787
president@broomball.ca
Membership: 30,000 provincial; *Fees:* $1,000 annual affiliation fee/association
Activities:; *Library:* Yes by appointment

British Columbia Broomball Society (BCBS)
BC
Overview: A small provincial organization
Member of: Ballon sur glace Broomball Canada

Broomball Newfoundland & Labrador
NL
Overview: A small provincial organization
Member of: Ballon sur glace Broomball Canada

Federation of Broomball Associations of Ontario
c/o Gerry Wever, President, 515 Gascon St., Russell ON K4R 1C6
Tel: 613-445-0904; *Fax:* 613-445-9844
www.ontariobroomball.ca
Previous Name: Broomball Federation of Ontario
Overview: A medium-sized provincial organization
Description: To serve broomball players, coaches, & leagues in Ontario; *Member of:* Ballon sur glace Broomball Canada
Chief Officer(s): Gerry Wever, President
gerry.wever@ontariobroomball.ca
Marilyn Squibb, Contact, Registration
marilyn.squibb@ontariobroomball.ca
Archie Wilson, Contact, Technical
archie.wilson@palmerstongrain.com
Finances: *Annual Operating Budget:* $50,000-$100,000
Staff: 20 volunteer(s)
Membership: 4,000; *Fees:* Schedule available; *Committees:* Officials; Coaching; Executive
Activities: Hosting high school tournaments, qualifier tournaments, junior provincials, & senior provincials; Conducting coaching clinics

Fédération québécoise de ballon sur glace
4545, av Pierre-de Coubertin, Montréal QC H1V 3R2
Tél: 514-252-3078
fqbg.comm@gmail.com
www.fqbg.net
Média social:
www.facebook.com/157977357723290
Aperçu: *Dimension:* moyenne; *Envergure:* provinciale
Description: La Fédération Québecoise de Ballon sur Glace a pour but de promouvoir le sport du ballon sur glace dans la province de Québec; *Membre de:* Fédération canadienne de ballon sur glace
Membre(s) du bureau directeur: Normand Perreault, Président
normandperreault8@gmail.com

Manitoba Amateur Broomball Association (MABA)
145 Pacific Ave., Winnipeg MB R3B 2Z6
Tel: 204-925-5668; *Fax:* 204-925-9792
Toll-Free: 866-792-7666
broomballmb@shaw.ca
www.manitobabroomball.com
Overview: A medium-sized provincial organization founded in 1982
Description: To promote the sport of broomball in Manitoba; to offer opportunities to members in competing in provincial & national championships; *Member of:* Ballon sur glace Broomball Canada; Sport Manitoba
Chief Officer(s): Cathy Derewianchuk, Executive Director
Membership: 500
Activities: School clinics; competitions; tournaments; provincials

Maritime Broomball Association
NB
Merged from: New Brunswick Broomball Association; Nova Scotia Broomball Association
Overview: A small provincial organization
Member of: Ballon sur glace Broomball Canada

Northwest Territories Broomball Association
529 Range Lake Rd., Yellowknife NT X1A 3Y1
www.nwtbroomball.com
Overview: A small provincial organization
Member of: Ballon sur glace Broomball Canada
Chief Officer(s): Val Pond, President
netmindr@theedge.ca
Membership: 250; *Fees:* Schedule available

Saskatchewan Broomball Association (SBA)
2205 Victoria Ave., Regina SK S4P 0S4
Tel: 306-780-9215; *Fax:* 306-525-4009
saskbroomball@sasktel.net
www.saskbroomball.ca
Social Media:
www.facebook.com/307730589864
Overview: A medium-sized provincial organization
Description: To promote multi-level programs to members & non-member groups in both competitive & recreational settings; to promote broomball within the province of Saskatchewan; *Member of:* Ballon sur glace Broomball Canada
Chief Officer(s): Stacey Silzer, Executive Director
Membership: *Fees:* Schedule available

Yukon Broomball Association (YBA)
4061 - 4th Ave., Whitehorse YT Y1A 1H1
www.yukonbroomball.net
Previous Name: Yukon Broomball League
Overview: A medium-sized provincial organization
Description: To promote & facilitate Broomball in the Yukon Territory.; *Member of:* Ballon sur glace Broomball Canada; Sport Yukon
Chief Officer(s): Sheena Laluk, President
Membership: 1-99

Canoeing & Rafting

Alberta Sprint Racing Canoe Association
11759 Groat Rd., Edmonton AB T5M 3K6
Tel: 780-203-3987
www.asrca.com
Previous Name: Alberta Flatwater Canoe Association
Overview: A small provincial organization
Member of: CanoeKayak Canada
Chief Officer(s): Jeffrey Baker, President
president@asrca.com

Association québécoise de canoë-kayak de vitesse (AQCKV)
4545, av Pierre-de Coubertin, Montréal QC H1V 0B2
Tél: 514-252-3086
canoekayakquebec.com
Média social:
www.facebook.com/100275890167157
Également appelé: Canoë Kayak Québec
Aperçu: *Dimension:* moyenne; *Envergure:* provinciale; Organisme sans but lucratif; fondée en 1979
Description: Promouvoir les activités de canoë-kayak de vitesse au Québec; *Membre de:* CanoeKayak Canada
Membre(s) du bureau directeur: Christine Granger, Directrice générale
cgranger@canoekayakquebec.com
Franck Gomez, Directeur technique
fgomez@canoekayakquebec.com
Finances: *Budget de fonctionnement annuel:* $50,000-$100,000
Membre: 2 000
Activités: *Stagiaires:* Oui *Bibliothèque:* Oui rendez-vous

Atlantic Division, CanoeKayak Canada (ADCKC)
PO Box 295, 34 Boathouse Lane, Dartmouth NS B2Y 3Y3
Tel: 902-425-5450; *Fax:* 902-425-5606
www.adckc.ca
Social Media:
instagram.com/adckc/
www.facebook.com/196999566862
twitter.com/ADCKC
Previous Name: CanoeKayak Canada - Atlantic Division
Overview: A small local organization
Member of: CanoeKayak Canada; Sport Nova Scotia
Chief Officer(s): Robin Thomson, General Manager
robin@adckc.ca
Jeff Houser, Regional Coach
regionalcoach@adckc.ca

Canoe Kayak New Brunswick (CKNB)
c/o Rob Neish, 1350 Regent St., Fredericton NB E3B 3Z4
Tel: 506-622-5050
communications@canoekayaknb.org
canoekayaknewbrunswick10.wildapricot.org
Social Media:
www.facebook.com/CanoeKayakNewBrunswick
twitter.com/canoekayaknb
Also Known As: Canoe Kayak NB
Overview: A small provincial organization
Description: Canoe-Kayak New Brunswick is a non-profit volunteer organization dedicated to the promotion of safe recreational paddling in the province of New Brunswick.; *Member of:* Paddle Canada
Chief Officer(s): Rob Neish, President
president@canoekayaknb.org

Canoe Kayak Nova Scotia (CKNS)
5516 Spring Garden Rd., Halifax NS B3J 1G6
Tel: 902-425-5454; *Fax:* 902-425-5606
admin@ckns.ca
www.ckns.ca
Social Media:
www.facebook.com/canoekayakns
twitter.com/canoekayakns
Previous Name: Canoe Nova Scotia
Overview: A medium-sized provincial organization founded in 1973
Member of: Paddle Canada
Chief Officer(s): Karl Vollmer, President
president@ckns.ca

Canoe Kayak Ontario
c/o OCSRA, 2078 Lemay Cres., Ottawa ON K1G 2X4
Tel: 613-618-1715
canoeontario.org
Overview: A medium-sized provincial organization
Description: Canoe Kayak Ontario is a collective voice for canoeing and kayaking in Ontario, which promotes the interests and supports the activities of its Affiliates.
Affiliation(s): Ontario Canoe Sprint Racing Affiliation; Ontario Marathon Canoe Racing Association; Whitewater Ontario
Activities: Collective voice for canoeing in Ontario

CanoeKayak BC
Fortius Athlete Development Centre, 3713 Kensington Ave., Burnaby BC V5B 0A7
Tel: 778-689-9007
info@canoekayakbc.ca
www.canoekayakbc.ca
Social Media:
www.facebook.com/canoekayakbc
twitter.com/CanoeKayakBC
Overview: A medium-sized provincial organization
Member of: CanoeKayak Canada
Chief Officer(s): Mary Jane Abbot, Executive Director
mj@canoekayakbc.ca

CanoeKayak Canada (CKC)
#700, 2197 Riverside Dr., Ottawa ON K1H 7X3
Tel: 613-260-1818; *Fax:* 613-260-5137
admin@canoekayak.ca
www.canoekayak.ca
Social Media:
www.facebook.com/CanoeKayakCAN
twitter.com/CanoeKayakCAN
Previous Name: Canadian Canoe Association
Overview: A large national organization founded in 1900
Description: To increase the number of Canadians participating in canoeing & kayaking; To enable participants to realize excellence by providing sound athlete development programs & membership support systems; *Member of:* International Canoe Federation; Pan American Canoe Federation
Chief Officer(s): Casey Wade, Chief Executive Officer, 613-260-1818 2203
cwade@canoekayak.ca
Sally Clare, Director, Finance, 613-721-0504
sclare@canoekayak.ca
John Edwards, Director, Domestic Development, 613-260-1818 2201
jhedwards@canoekayak.ca
Peter Niedre, Director, Coach & Athlete Development, 613-260-1818 2206
pniedre@canoekayak.ca
Scott Logan, Director, Sprint High Performance, 902-499-9984
slogan@canoekayak.ca
Finances: *Annual Operating Budget:* $3 Million-$5 Million; *Funding Sources:* Sport Canada; Corporate Partners; Donations; Event Fees
Staff: 10 staff member(s); 300 volunteer(s)
Membership: 25,000+; *Member Profile:* Individuals, commercial or other groups; *Committees:* Board of Directors; Sprint; Whitewater; Marathon; High Performance; Domestic Development; Officials; Organizational Alignment; By-Law; Planning; Coaches; Awards; History & Archives

CanoeKayak Canada Western Ontario Division (WOD)
c/o Alan Potts, 22 Bowes Garden Ct., Toronto ON M1C 4L8
www.westernontariodivision.com
Social Media:
www.facebook.com/436833409678565
twitter.com/CKC_WOD
Overview: A small provincial organization
Chief Officer(s): Alan Potts, Treasurer
avpotts@rogers.com

Fédération québécoise du canot et du kayak (FQCK)
CP 1000, Succ. M, 4545, av Pierre-de Coubertin, Montréal QC H1V 3R2
Tél: 514-252-3001; *Téléc:* 514-252-3091
info@canot-kayak.qc.ca
www.canot-kayak.qc.ca
Média social:
www.facebook.com/254842564559812
Nom précédent: Fédération québécoise du canot camping inc
Aperçu: *Dimension:* moyenne; *Envergure:* provinciale; Organisme sans but lucratif; fondée en 1976
Description: Regrouper les organismes et individus intéressés à la pratique du canotage récréatif et du canot-camping et de promouvoir la pratique de ces activités en utilisant le canot ouvert de type amérindien autrement appelé Canot Canadien
Membre(s) du bureau directeur: Philippe Pelland, Directeur général
ppelland@canot-kayak.qc.ca
Jean A. Plamondon, Président
Bernard Hugonnier, Directeur, Technique
bhugonnier@canot-kayak.qc.ca
Émilie Bisson, Agent, Information et aux communications
ebisson@canot-kayak.qc.ca
Membre: 4 000; *Montant de la cotisation:* 40$; *Comités:* Cartographie; Formation
Activités: *Stagiaires:* Oui; *Service de conférenciers:* Oui

Ikaluktutiak Paddling Association
NU
Overview: A small provincial organization
Member of: Paddle Canada

Manitoba Paddling Association Inc. (MPA)
145 Pacific Ave., Winnipeg MB R3B 2Z6
Tel: 204-925-5681; *Fax:* 204-925-5792
mpa@sportmanitoba.ca
www.mpa.mb.ca
Social Media:
www.facebook.com/ManitobaPaddlingAssociation
twitter.com/MBPaddling
Overview: A medium-sized provincial organization founded in 1982
Description: To act as the governing body for all competitive paddling sports in Manitoba, including kayak, canoe, & dragon boat; To develop high performance athletes to compete for Manitoba nationally & to qualify for the national team; To develop coaches to coach from the grassroots to the high performance levels; To service paddlers from beginners to elite athletes; To ensure the existence of paddling clubs in Manitoba; *Member of:* CanoeKayak Canada; Sport Manitoba
Finances: *Funding Sources:* Sport Manitoba
Member Profile: Paddling clubs & athletes from Manitoba
Activities: Hosting paddling events; Promoting paddling

Ontario Canoe Kayak Sprint Racing Affiliation (OCSRA)
c/o Joanne Bryant, 118 Batson Dr., Aurora ON L4G 3T2
Tel: 905-841-5489
www.ocsra.ca
Overview: A small provincial organization founded in 1985
Description: To represent the sport of Olympic Sprint Canoe Kayak racing in Ontario.; *Member of:* CanoeKayak Canada
Chief Officer(s): Joanne Bryant, Chair
joanne.i.bryant@gmail.com

Ontario Marathon Canoe & Kayak Racing Association (OMCKRA)
ON
info@omckra.com
www.omcra.ca
Social Media:
www.facebook.com/OntarioMarathonPaddling
Overview: A small provincial organization
Description: To represent, promote & develop the sport of marathon canoe & kayak racing in Ontario.; *Member of:* CanoeKayak Canada

Paddle Alberta
PO Box 71039, Stn. Silverspings, Calgary AB T3B 5K2
Tel: 403-247-0083; *Fax:* 866-477-8791
Toll-Free: 877-388-2722
info@paddlealberta.org
www.paddlealberta.org
Social Media:
www.facebook.com/PaddleAlbertaSociety
twitter.com/PaddleAlberta
Overview: A small provincial organization
Description: To promote safety & sustainability in recreational canoeing & kayaking in Alberta.; *Member of:* Paddle Canada
Chief Officer(s): Karla Handy, Coordinator, Program Services

Paddle Manitoba
PO Box 2663, Winnipeg MB R3C 4B3
info@paddle.mb.ca
www.paddle.mb.ca
Social Media:
www.facebook.com/373524412660987
twitter.com/paddlemanitoba
Previous Name: Manitoba Recreational Canoeing Association
Overview: A small provincial charitable organization founded in 1988
Description: To promote safe canoeing & kayaking in the province.; *Member of:* Paddle Canada
Affiliation(s): Manitoba Paddling Association
Chief Officer(s): Chris Randall, President
president@paddle.mb.ca
Finances: *Funding Sources:* Membership fees; tuition fees; fundraising
Membership: *Fees:* $30 individual; $40 family/affiliate; $50 instructor
Activities: Canoe & kayak instruction (flatwater & moving water); information presentations; resource pamphlets; *Speaker Service:* Yes; *Library:* Resource Centre (Open to Public)

Paddle Newfoundland & Labrador
PO Box 2, Stn. C, St. John's NL A1C 5H4
paddle.nl@gmail.com
paddlenl.ca
Previous Name: Newfoundland Paddling Club
Overview: A small provincial organization
Member of: CanoeKayak Canada
Chief Officer(s): Alan Goodridge, President

Paddle Newfounfdland & Labrador
PO Box 23072, Stn. Churchill Sq., St. John's NL A1B 4J9
Tel: 709-364-1601; *Fax:* 709-368-8357
www.paddlenl.ca
Previous Name: Canoe Newfoundland & Labrador
Overview: A small provincial organization
Description: A local club that welcomes members from all parts of the province. It is a non-profit group of canoeing enthusiasts who get together regularly to enjoy the sport of canoeing and socialize with other canoeing lovers.; *Member of:* Paddle Canada
Chief Officer(s): Hazen Scarth, President
Membership: *Fees:* Individual $20; Associate $50; Family $25

Prince Edward Island Canoe Kayak Association
RR#4, Alliston, Montague PE C0A 1R0
Tel: 902-962-3883; *Fax:* 902-962-3883
Social Media:
www.facebook.com/235534456533194
Overview: A small provincial organization
Member of: CanoeKayak Canada
Chief Officer(s): Justin Richard Batten, President
justin.heidi@windsinc.com

Recreational Canoeing Association BC (RCABC)
1755 East 7th Ave., Vancouver BC V5N 1S1
Tel: 250-592-4170
sec@bccanoe.com
www.bccanoe.com
Overview: A small provincial organization founded in 1984
Member of: Paddle Canada
Chief Officer(s): Kari-Ann Thor, President, 604-253-5410
Tony Shaw, Secretary, 250-468-7955
Finances: *Annual Operating Budget:* Less than $50,000; *Funding Sources:* Membership dues; government
Staff: 16 volunteer(s)
Membership: 350; *Fees:* $20; $45 instructor; *Committees:* Course Standards; Conservation & Access
Activities: Canoe instruction & standards

Whitewater Ontario
411 Carnegie Beach Rd., Port Perry ON L9L 1B6
Tel: 905-985-4585; *Fax:* 905-985-5256
Toll-Free: 888-322-2849
info@whitewaterontario.ca
www.whitewaterontario.ca
Social Media:
www.facebook.com/whitewaterontario
Overview: A small provincial organization
Description: Whitewater Ontario is the sport governing body in the province, & represents provincial interests within the national body CanoeKayak Canada.; *Member of:* CanoeKayak Canada
Chief Officer(s): Jim Tayler, President
Membership: *Fees:* $30 adult; $15 junior; $30 family; $75 commercial

Yukon Canoe & Kayak Club
YT
current@yckc.ca
www.yckc.ca
Overview: A small provincial organization founded in 1961
Chief Officer(s): John Quinsey, President
Membership: *Fees:* $20 adult; $10 child; $40 family
Activities: White water rafting; kayak polo

Yukon River Marathon Paddlers Association
4061 - 4th Ave., Whitehorse YT Y1A 1H1
Tel: 867-333-5628; *Fax:* 888-959-3846
info@yukonriverquest.com
www.yukonriverquest.com
Social Media:
www.facebook.com/186123281403836
Also Known As: Yukon River Quest
Overview: A small provincial organization
Description: To govern the Yukon River Quest canoe & kayak race.
Chief Officer(s): Harry Kern, President
Membership: *Fees:* $20 regular; $100 lifetime
Activities: *Awareness Events:* Yukon River Quest, June

Cerebral Palsy

Alberta Cerebral Palsy Sport Association (ACPSA)
Percy Page Centre, 11759 Groat Rd., Edmonton AB T5M 3K6
Tel: 780-422-2904; *Fax:* 780-422-2663
contact@acpsa.ca
www.acpsa.ca
Social Media:
instagram.com/powerchair_sports
www.facebook.com/165504436855126
twitter.com/AlbertaCPSports
Also Known As: Sportability Alberta
Overview: A small provincial charitable organization founded in 1984
Description: To promote recreational & competitive sporting opportunities for persons with cerebral palsy, brain injury & related conditions; *Member of:* Canadian Cerebral Palsy Sports Association
Finances: *Annual Operating Budget:* Less than $50,000
Staff: 2 staff member(s); 40 volunteer(s)
Membership: 220; *Fees:* $15 individual; $25 family; travelling athletes add $65 to membership fees; *Member Profile:* Individuals with cerebral palsy, brain injury & other related conditions
Activities: Track & field; boccia; cycling; swimming; pre-school children's program; *Speaker Service:* Yes

Canadian Cerebral Palsy Sports Association (CCPSA) / Association canadienne de sport pour paralytiques cérébraux (ACPSA)
#104, 720 Belfast Rd., Ottawa ON K1G 0Z5
Tel: 613-748-1430
info@ccpsa.ca
www.ccpsa.ca
Social Media:
www.facebook.com/112866075626
Overview: A medium-sized national charitable organization founded in 1985
Description: To act as umbrella group for all provincial cerebral palsy sport organizations; To design programs that are designed for athletes with cerebral palsy & non-progressive head injuries
Affiliation(s): Cerebral Palsy International Sports & Recreation Association; International Paralympic Committee
Chief Officer(s): Jennifer Larson, Interim Executive Director, 613-748-1430 2
jlarson@ccpsa.ca
Finances: *Annual Operating Budget:* $500,000-$1.5 Million; *Funding Sources:* Government of Canada, Dept. of Heritage; Sport Canada; donations; fundraising
Staff: 3 staff member(s); 11 volunteer(s)
Membership: 2,500; *Fees:* $25-200; *Committees:* Coaching; Boccia; Classification; Athletics
Activities: Programs include cycling, soccer, athletics & boccia, swimming, bowls, powerlifting

Manitoba Cerebral Palsy Sports Association (MCPSA)
MB
Overview: A small provincial organization
Description: To assist in the development of sport for the disabled in Manitoba by providing an opportunity for a wider participation for persons with cerebral palsy & other neuromuscular disorders; *Member of:* Canadian Cerebral Palsy Sports Association
Membership: 60
Activities: Track; Field; Swimming; Boccia

SportAbility BC (CPSABC)
780 Marine Dr. SW, Vancouver BC V6P 5YZ
Tel: 604-324-1411
sportinfo@sportabilitybc.ca
www.sportabilitybc.ca
Social Media:
www.youtube.com/SportAbilityBC
www.facebook.com/sport.ability.3
twitter.com/SportAbilityBC
Previous Name: Cerebral Palsy Sports Association of British Columbia
Overview: A medium-sized provincial charitable organization founded in 1976
Description: To provide sports & recreational opportunities for people with cerebral palsy, head injury, stroke & similar disabilities at the local, regional, provincial & national level; To provide access to appropriate programming for members including segregated & integrated opportunities
Affiliation(s): Sport BC
Chief Officer(s): Ross MacDonald, Executive Director
rossm@sportabilitybc.ca
Finances: *Annual Operating Budget:* $250,000-$500,000; *Funding Sources:* Fundraising; Sport BC; Gaming; Donations
Staff: 5 staff member(s)
Membership: *Fees:* $25 senior/individual/family; *Member Profile:* Physically disabled athletes, coaches, officials, volunteers
Activities:; *Library:* Yes by appointment

Children

KidSport Alberta
Percy Page Centre, 11759 Groat Rd., Edmonton AB T5M 3K6
www.kidsport.ab.ca
Social Media:
www.facebook.com/KidSportAlberta
twitter.com/KidSportAlberta
Overview: A small provincial organization
Description: To provide financial assistance to children in Alberta, aged 18 & under, who are interested in playing sports; help with registration fees & equipment; *Member of:* KidSport Canada
Chief Officer(s): Erin Bilawchuk, Executive Director, 780-644-1815
ebilawchuk@kidsport.ab.ca
Member Profile: Local chapters
Activities: Providing grants from $100-$500

KidSport British Columbia
#230, 3820 Cessna Dr., Richmond BC V7B 0A2
Tel: 604-333-3434; *Fax:* 604-333-3401
www.kidsportcanada.ca
Social Media:
twitter.com/kidsport
Overview: A small provincial organization
Description: To provide financial assistance to children in British Columbia, aged 18 & under, who are interested in playing sports; help with registration fees & equipment; *Member of:* KidSport Canada; Sport BC
Chief Officer(s): Thea Culley, Manager
thea.culley@sportbc.com
Member Profile: Local chapters
Activities: Providing grants from $100-$500

KidSport Canada
Sport for Life Centre, #423, 145 Pacific Ave., Winnipeg MB R3B 2Z6
Tel: 204-925-5914; *Fax:* 204-925-5916
www.kidsportcanada.ca
Social Media:
www.facebook.com/kidsportcanada
twitter.com/KidSportCA
Overview: A medium-sized national organization founded in 2005
Description: To provide financial assistance to children aged 18 & under who are interested in playing sports; help with registration fees & equipment
Chief Officer(s): Bryan Ezako, Manager
bezako@kidsportcanada.ca
Membership: 11 provincial/territorial chapters + 177 community chapters
Activities: Providing grants from $100-$500

KidSport Manitoba
145 Pacific Ave., Winnipeg MB R3B 2Z6
Tel: 204-925-5600; *Fax:* 204-925-5916
Toll-Free: 866-774-2220
kidsport@sportmanitoba.ca
www.kidsportcanada.ca
Social Media:
www.facebook.com/sportmb
twitter.com/SportManitoba
Overview: A small provincial organization
Description: To provide financial assistance to children in Manitoba, aged 18 & under, who are interested in playing sports; help with registration fees & equipment; *Member of:* KidSport Canada; Sport Manitoba
Member Profile: Local chapters
Activities: Providing grants from $100-$500

KidSport New Brunswick
#13, 900 Hanwell Rd., Fredericton NB E3B 6A2
Tel: 506-451-1320; *Fax:* 506-451-1325
www.kidsportcanada.ca
Social Media:
twitter.com/KidSportNB
Overview: A small provincial organization
Description: To provide financial assistance to children in New Brunswick, aged 18 & under, who are interested in playing sports; help with registration fees & equipment; *Member of:* KidSport Canada; Sport New Brunswick
Member Profile: Local chapters
Activities: Providing grants from $100-$500

KidSport Newfoundland & Labrador
1296A Kenmount Rd., Paradise NL A1L 1N3
Tel: 709-579-5977; *Fax:* 709-576-7493
www.kidsport.nl.ca
Overview: A small provincial organization
Description: To provide financial assistance to children in Newfoundland & Labrador, aged 18 & under, who are interested in playing sports; help with registration fees & equipment; *Member of:* KidSport Canada; Sport Newfoundland & Labrador
Chief Officer(s): Alicia Curran, Coordinator, Events & Marketing, Sport NL
acurran@sportnl.ca
Member Profile: Local chapters
Activities: Providing grants from $100-$500

KidSport Northwest Territories
Don Cooper Bldg., 4908 - 49th St., 3rd Fl., Yellowknife NT X1A 3X7
Tel: 867-669-8332; *Fax:* 867-669-8327
www.kidsportcanada.ca
Overview: A small provincial organization
Description: To provide financial assistance to children in the Northwest Territories, aged 18 & under, who are interested in playing sports; help with registration fees & equipment; *Member of:* KidSport Canada; Sport North Federation
Member Profile: Local chapters
Activities: Providing grants from $100-$500

KidSport Nova Scotia
5516 Spring Garden Rd., 4th Fl., Halifax NS B3J 1G6
Tel: 902-425-5450; *Fax:* 902-425-5606
kidsport@sportnovascotia.ca
www.sportnovascotia.ca/KidSport
Overview: A small provincial organization
Description: To provide financial assistance to children in Nova Scotia, aged 18 & under, who are interested in playing sports; help with registration fees & equipment; *Member of:* KidSport Canada; Sport Nova Scotia
Chief Officer(s): Colin Gillis, Coordinator
Member Profile: Local chapters
Activities: Providing grants from $100-$500

KidSport Ontario
#2041, 875 Morningside Ave., Toronto ON M1C 0C7
Tel: 416-283-0940
www.kidsportcanada.ca/ontario
Social Media:
www.facebook.com/KidSportOntario
twitter.com/KidSportOntario
Overview: A small provincial organization
Description: To provide financial assistance to children in Ontario, aged 18 & under, who are interested in playing sports;

help with registration fees & equipment; *Member of:* KidSport Canada
Member Profile: Local chapters
Activities: Providing grants from $100-$500

KidSport PEI
40 Enman Cres., Charlottetown PE C1E 1E6
Tel: 902-368-4110; *Fax:* 902-368-4548
www.kidsportcanada.ca/prince-edward-island
Social Media:
www.facebook.com/176050449103403
Overview: A small provincial organization
Description: To provide financial assistance to children in Prince Edward Island, aged 18 & under, who are interested in playing sports; help with registration fees & equipment; *Member of:* KidSport Canada; Sport PEI Inc.
Chief Officer(s): Terry Bernard, Contact
tbernard@sportpei.pe.ca
Member Profile: Local chapters
Activities: Providing grants from $100-$500

KidSport Saskatchewan
1870 Lorne St., Regina SK S4P 2L7
Tel: 306-780-9345; *Fax:* 306-781-6021
Toll-Free: 800-319-4263
kidsport@sasksport.sk.ca
www.kidsportcanada.ca/saskatchewan
Overview: A small provincial organization
Description: To provide financial assistance to children in Saskatchewan, aged 18 & under, who are interested in playing sports; help with registration fees & equipment; *Member of:* KidSport Canada; Sask Sport Inc.
Chief Officer(s): Nathan Cole, Provincial Coordinator
Member Profile: Local chapters
Activities: Providing grants from $100-$500

Sport Jeunesse / KidSport Québec
CP 1000, Succ. M, 4545, av Pierre-de Coubertin, Montréal QC H1V 3R2
Tél: 514-252-3114; *Téléc:* 514-254-9621
www.jeuxduquebec.com/Mes_premiers_Jeux-fr-13.php
Également appelé: Mes Premiers Jeux
Aperçu: *Dimension:* petite; *Envergure:* provinciale
Membre de: KidSport Canada; Sports Québec

Coaching

Coaches Association of Ontario (CAO)
#108, 3 Concorde Gate, Toronto ON M3C 3N7
Tel: 416-426-7086; *Fax:* 416-426-7331
www.coachesontario.org
Social Media:
www.youtube.com/user/CoachesOntario
www.linkedin.com/company/coaches-association-of-ontario
www.facebook.com/coachesontario
twitter.com/coaches_ont
Overview: A medium-sized provincial organization founded in 2002
Description: To represent coaches in Ontario
Affiliation(s): National Coaching Certification Program (NCCP)
Chief Officer(s): Susan Kitchen, Executive Director, 416-426-7088
susan@coachesontario.ca
Finances: *Funding Sources:* Federal & provincial government; Ontario Trillium Foundation
Staff: 8 staff member(s); 5 volunteer(s)
Membership: 25,000; *Fees:* Schedule available
Activities: Conducting sport workshops; Providing support & education for sport coaches in all levels

Coaches Association of PEI (CAPEI)
40 Enman Cres., Charlottetown PE C1E 1E6
Tel: 902-368-4110; *Fax:* 902-368-4548
Toll-Free: 800-247-6712
sports@sportpei.pe.ca
www.sportpei.pe.ca
Social Media:
www.facebook.com/pages/Sport-PEI/176050449103403
twitter.com/SportPEI
Overview: A small provincial organization founded in 1992
Description: To educate, develop & promote coaching & coaches for the benefit of athletes, sport & the community in general; To encourage fair play, integrity & the pursuit of excellence; *Member of:* Coaching Association of Canada
Chief Officer(s): Gemma Koughan, Executive Director
gkoughan@sportpei.pe.ca
Finances: *Funding Sources:* Membership fees; fundraising
Staff: 8 staff member(s)
Membership: 50 organizations

Coaching Association of Canada (CAC) / Association canadienne des entraîneurs
#201, 1155 Lola St., Ottawa ON K1K 4C1
Tel: 613-235-5000; *Fax:* 613-235-9500
www.coach.ca
Social Media:
www.youtube.com/CDNcoach2010
www.facebook.com/coach.ca
twitter.com/CAC_ACE
Overview: A large national charitable organization founded in 1971
Description: To improve implementation & delivery of National Coaching Certification Program; To establish coaching as viable career within the Canadian sports system; To increase the number of qualified full-time & part-time remunerated coaches at various levels within the sport system
Affiliation(s): Professional Arm: Canadian Professional Coaches Association
Chief Officer(s): Gabor Csepregi, Chair
Lorraine Lafrenière, Chief Executive Officer, 613-235-5000 2363
llafreniere@coach.ca
Keira Torkko, Chief Operating Officer, 613-235-5000 2365
ktorkko@coach.ca
Valerie Aji, Director, Finance & Administration, 613-235-5000 2358
vaji@coach.ca
Natalie Rumscheidt, Director, Marketing & Communications, 613-235-5000 2051
nrumscheidt@coach.ca
Finances: *Funding Sources:* Sport Canada; Corporations; Foundations
Activities: Offering the following programs: National Coaching Certification Program (NCCP); Sport Nutrition; Petro-Canada Sport Leadership sportif; Investors Group Community Coaching Conferences; *Speaker Service:* Yes

Coaching Manitoba
145 Pacific Ave., Winnipeg MB R2B 2Z6
Tel: 204-925-5692; *Fax:* 204-925-5624
Toll-Free: 888-887-7307
coaching@sportmanitoba.ca
www.coachingmanitoba.ca
Overview: A small provincial organization
Description: To train coaches in Manitoba; *Member of:* Sport Manitoba
Chief Officer(s): Susan Lamboo, Coaching Manager, 204-925-5669
susan.lamboo@sportmanitoba.ca

Commonwealth Games

Commonwealth Games Canada (CGC) / Jeux du Commonwealth Canada
#201, 2255 St. Laurent Blvd., Ottawa ON K1G 4K3
Tel: 613-244-6868; *Fax:* 613-244-6826
info@commonwealthgames.ca
www.commonwealthgames.ca
Social Media:
www.youtube.com/user/cgcTVjcc
www.facebook.com/265526150138420
twitter.com/cgc_jcc
Previous Name: The Commonwealth Games Association of Canada Inc.
Overview: A small international organization founded in 1977
Affiliation(s): Commonwealth Games Federation - London, England
Chief Officer(s): Brian MacPherson, Chief Executive Officer, 613-244-6868 226
brian@commonwealthgames.ca
Kelly Laframboise, Manager, Administration & Operations, 613-244-6868 222
kelly@commonwealthgames.ca
Finances: *Annual Operating Budget:* $100,000-$250,000
Staff: 2 staff member(s); 60 volunteer(s)
Membership: 60 individual
Activities: *Internships:* Yes; *Library:* Yes (Open to Public)

Cricket

British Columbia Mainland Cricket League (BCMCL)
PO Box 100, 12886 - 96th Ave., Surrey BC V3V 6A8
Fax: 604-909-2669
info@bcmcl.ca
www.bcmcl.org
Social Media:
www.youtube.com/thebcmcl
www.facebook.com/bcmcl.ca
twitter.com/bcmcl
Previous Name: British Columbia Cricket Association
Overview: A small provincial organization
Member of: Cricket Canada
Chief Officer(s): Nazir Desai, President, 778-318-6630
ndesai7@hotmail.com
Mohammed Talha Patel, Secretary, 604-445-9752
surreystars@hotmail.com

Canada Cricket Umpires Association Inc. (CCUA)
c/o Basdeo Dookhie, President, 38 Windbreak Cres., Whitby ON L1P 1P9
Tel: 905-430-3844
www.ccua.ca
Overview: A small national organization
Description: To promote & advance cricket umpires throughout Canada.; *Member of:* West Indies Cricket Umpires Association
Chief Officer(s): Basdeo Dookhie, President
b.dookhie@hotmail.com

Cricket Alberta (ACA)
#222, 7 Westwinds CR NE, Calgary AB T3J 5H2
cricket@cricketalberta.ca
www.cricketalberta.ca
Social Media:
www.facebook.com/155440747942009
twitter.com/CricketAlberta
Previous Name: Alberta Cricket Association
Overview: A small provincial organization founded in 1975
Member of: Cricket Canada
Chief Officer(s): Manzoor Choudhary, President, 403-605-4843
manzoor@cricketalberta.ca
Finances: *Annual Operating Budget:* $50,000-$100,000; *Funding Sources:* Government; casino; membership fees
Staff: 30 volunteer(s)
Membership: 500; *Fees:* $500 team; *Member Profile:* 10 to 55 years of age; *Committees:* Executive; By-Laws; Juniors
Activities: Competitions; school cricket; coaching; training camps

Cricket Canada
#301, 3 Concorde Gate, Toronto ON M3C 3N7
Tel: 416-426-7209
info@cricketcanada.org
www.gocricketgocanada.com
Social Media:
www.facebook.com/GoCricketCanada
twitter.com/canadiancricket
Also Known As: Canadian Cricket Association
Overview: A large national organization founded in 1892
Description: To foster growth & development of cricket in Canada
Affiliation(s): International Cricket Council; Kanga Ball Canada
Chief Officer(s): Vimal Hardat, President & Chair
Finances: *Funding Sources:* Ministry of Heritage; International Cricket Council Volunteer Donations
Staff: 130 volunteer(s)
Membership: 30 senior/lifetime + 400 teams + 15,500 players; *Fees:* $85 per team
Activities: *Internships:* Yes; *Speaker Service:* Yes

Cricket Council of Ontario (CCO)
25 Pacific Wind Cres., Brampton ON L6R 2B1
Tel: 905-230-9392
www.cricketcouncilofontario.ca
Social Media:
www.facebook.com/CricketOntario
twitter.com/cricketontario
Previous Name: Ontario Cricket Association Inc.
Overview: A medium-sized provincial organization founded in 2009
Description: To be the provincial governing body of the sport of cricket in Ontario.; *Member of:* Cricket Canada
Chief Officer(s): Praim Persaud, President, 416-621-2020
praimp@yahoo.com
Tan Qureshi, Manager, Public Relations
tqureshi@cricketcouncilofontario.ca
Membership: 9 associations/leagues
Activities: *Rents Mailing List:* Yes

Cricket New Brunswick (CNB)
Fredericton NB
info@cricketnb.org
cricketnb.org
Social Media:
www.facebook.com/CNB.Fredericton
Also Known As: Cricket NB
Previous Name: New Brunswick Cricket Association
Overview: A small provincial organization
Description: To facilitate the development & growth of the sport of cricket; To establish cricket as a competitite sport in New

Brunswick; To promote participation in schools; *Member of:* Cricket Canada
Chief Officer(s): Aditya Aggarwal, President
aditya.aggarwal@cricketnb.org
Devansh Bhavishi, Secretary
dbhavishi@cricketnb.org
Membership: 1-99; *Fees:* $75 full
Activities: Awareness lessons; Cricket camps

La Fédération Québécoise du Cricket Inc. / The Quebec Cricket Federation Inc. (QCF)
7037, boul Acadie, Montréal QC H3N 2V5
Tél: 514-279-6628
www.quebeccricket.com
Aperçu: *Dimension:* petite; *Envergure:* provinciale
Membre de: Cricket Canada
Membre(s) du bureau directeur: Charles Pais, President, 514-824-0370
charles_pais@hotmail.com
Dalip Kirpaul, Secretary
qcf1@hotmail.com

Manitoba Cricket Association (MCA)
145 Pacific Ave., Winnipeg MB R3B 2Z6
Tel: 204-925-5672; *Fax:* 204-925-5703
www.cricket.mb.ca
Overview: A small provincial organization founded in 1937
Description: To make cricket available to all Manitobans.; *Member of:* Cricket Canada
Chief Officer(s): Garvin Budhoo, President
garvin.budhoo@shaw.ca
Rawle Manoosingh, Executive Secretary
Finances: *Annual Operating Budget:* $50,000-$100,000; *Funding Sources:* Manitoba government; Lotteries Foundation
Staff: 1 staff member(s); 10 volunteer(s)
Membership: 362; *Fees:* $900 per team
Activities:; *Library:* Yes

Newfoundland & Labrador Cricket Association
NL
cricketnewfoundland@gmail.com
www.canadacricket.com/nlcricket
Social Media:
www.facebook.com/185095814896295
Also Known As: Cricket NL
Overview: A small provincial organization founded in 2010
Description: To be the provincial governing body of cricket in Newfoundland & Labrador.; *Member of:* Cricket Canada
Chief Officer(s): Senthill Selvamani, President
presidentnlca@gmail.com
David Liverman, Secretary
liverman@mun.ca

Nova Scotia Cricket Association (NSCA)
PO Box 31, Lunenburg NS B0J 2C0
Tel: 902-640-2448
info@novascotiacricket.com
www.novascotiacricket.com
Social Media:
www.facebook.com/296868372047
twitter.com/nscricket
Overview: A small provincial organization founded in 1965
Description: To be the provincial governing body of cricket in Nova Scotia.; *Member of:* Cricket Canada; Sport Nova Scotia
Chief Officer(s): Tushar Sehgal, President
Yash Gugle, Secretary
Amit Joshi, Provincial Director

PEI Cricket Association (PEI-CA)
PE
cricketPEI@gmail.com
www.cricketpei.com
Social Media:
www.facebook.com/375538377835
twitter.com/CricketPEI
Overview: A small provincial organization founded in 2010
Description: To promote the development of cricket in Prince Edward Island.; *Member of:* Cricket Canada
Chief Officer(s): Sarath Chandrasekere, President
Cyril Roy, Secretary
Membership: 100; *Fees:* $20

Saskatchewan Cricket Association (SCA)
Regina SK
www.saskcricket.com
Social Media:
www.facebook.com/SaskatchewanCricketAssociation
twitter.com/saskcricket
Overview: A small provincial organization founded in 1977
Description: To be the provincial governing body of cricket in Saskatchewan.; *Member of:* Cricket Canada
Affiliation(s): Regina Cricket Association; Saskatoon Cricket Association
Chief Officer(s): Azhar (Sam) Khan, President
Raza Naqvi, Secretary
Membership: 2 associations

Scarborough Cricket Association (SCA)
ON
www.scarboroughcricket.ca
Overview: A small local organization founded in 1981
Description: To oversee the game of cricket in Scarborough, Ontario.; *Member of:* West Indies Cricket Umpires Association
Chief Officer(s): Sahaban Khan, President, 647-997-2483
Sahbaankhan1990@hotmail.com

Toronto Cricket Umpires' & Scorers' Association (TCU&SA)
Toronto ON
www.tcuandsa.org
Overview: A small local organization
Description: To train Canadian cricket umpires & scorers.
Chief Officer(s): Saurabh Naik, President
presidenttcusa@gmail.com
Rohan Shah, Vice-President
rohans@rogers.com
Tushar Thakar, Secretary
secretarytcusa@gmail.com

Croquet

Croquet Canada
24 Deloraine Ave., Toronto ON M5M 2A7
croquet@sympatico.ca
www.croquet.ca
Overview: A large national organization
Description: To promote & develop croquet in Canada
Chief Officer(s): Paul Emmett, President, 416-225-7535
pemmett@sympatico.ca
Membership: *Fees:* $20; *Committees:* Handicap; Selection; CroqCan

Fédération des clubs de croquet du Québec (FCCQ)
CP 1000, Succ. M, 4545, av Pierre-de Coubertin, Montréal QC H1V 3R2
Tél: 514-252-3032
croquet@fqjr.qc.ca
croquet.quebecjeux.org
Aperçu: *Dimension:* petite; *Envergure:* provinciale; fondée en 1973
Membre(s) du bureau directeur: Jacques Noël, Président, 819-379-8035
Membre: 635; *Montant de la cotisation:* 10$ individu

Curling

Alberta Curling Federation (ACF)
Percy Page Centre, 11759 Groat Rd., 3rd Floor, Edmonton AB T5M 3K6
Tel: 780-643-0809; *Fax:* 780-427-8103
www.albertacurling.ab.ca
Overview: A medium-sized provincial organization
Description: To promote curling throughout Alberta
Chief Officer(s): J.W. (Jim) Pringle, Executive Director
jim@albertacurling.ab.ca

Canadian Curling Association (CCA) / Association canadienne de curling
1660 Vimont Ct., Orléans ON K4A 4J4
Tel: 613-834-2076; *Fax:* 613-834-0716
Toll-Free: 800-550-2875
boc@curling.ca
www.curling.ca
Social Media:
www.youtube.com/ccacurling
www.facebook.com/curlingcanada
twitter.com/curlingcanada
Also Known As: Curling Canada
Overview: A large national organization founded in 1990
Description: To attract, retain & advance participants to grow the sport of curling
Affiliation(s): World Curling Federation
Chief Officer(s): Patricia Ray, Chief Operating Officer, 613-834-2076 154
pray@curling.ca
Al Cameron, Director, Communications & Media Relations, 403-463-5500
acameron@curling.ca
Activities: Organizing championships; Facilitating tournaments, camps, & development programs

Curl BC
#2001A, 3713 Kensington Ave., Burnaby BC V5B 0A7
Tel: 604-333-3616; *Fax:* 604-333-3615
Toll-Free: 800-667-2875
www.curlbc.ca
Social Media:
www.youtube.com/user/CurlBC
www.facebook.com/318254030482
twitter.com/curlbc
Merged from: Pacific Coast Curling Association; BC Ladies' Curling Association; BC Interior Curling Association
Overview: A medium-sized provincial organization founded in 2004
Description: To deliver all curling programs & services in British Columbia
Affiliation(s): BC Interior Masters Curling Association; Pacific Coast Masters Curling Association
Chief Officer(s): Scott Braley, Executive Director & CEO, 604-333-6321
sbraley@curlbc.ca
Terry Vandale, Chair, 250-865-4353
tvandale@telus.net

Curling Québec
4545, av Pierre-de-Coubertin, Montréal QC H1V 0B2
Tél: 514-252-3088; *Téléc:* 514-252-3342
Ligne sans frais: 888-292-2875
info@curling-quebec.qc.ca
www.curling-quebec.qc.ca
Mèdia social:
www.facebook.com/pages/Curling-Québec/122740094410707
twitter.com/curlingquebec
Également appelé: Fédération québécoise de curling
Aperçu: *Dimension:* moyenne; *Envergure:* provinciale; Organisme sans but lucratif; fondée en 1976
Description: Offrir aux amateurs de curling, et à tous ceux désirant le devenir, la possibilité de jouer au curling à l'intérieur d'une structure organisée appuyée par divers services; *Membre de:* Fédération mondiale de curling
Membre(s) du bureau directeur: Marco Berthelot, Directeur général
mferraro@curling-quebec.qc.ca
Membre: 10 000; *Comités:* Excellence; Championnats; Junior

CurlManitoba Inc.
#309, 145 Pacific Ave., Winnipeg MB R3B 2Z6
Tel: 204-925-5723; *Fax:* 204-925-5720
mca@curlmanitoba.org
www.curlmanitoba.org
Social Media:
www.facebook.com/323935420031
twitter.com/curlmanitoba
Merged from: Manitoba Ladies Curling Association
Overview: A medium-sized provincial organization founded in 2000
Description: To promote the sport of curling in Manitoba.
Affiliation(s): Canadian Curling Association
Chief Officer(s): Craig Baker, Executive Director
cbaker@curlmanitoba.org
Rob Van Kommer, President
president@curlmanitoba.org
Membership: *Fees:* Schedule available; *Committees:* Finance; Board Development; Executive
Activities: Learn to curl clinics; coaching courses; ice technician courses; business of curling courses; club ice & rock consultation; game promotion; competition organization; establishment & governance of competition rules & regulations

Grand Masters Curling Association Ontario
c/o Art Lobel, 106 Kirk Dr., Thornhill ON L3T 3L2
Tel: 905-881-0547
grandmasterscurling.com
Overview: A medium-sized provincial organization founded in 2007
Affiliation(s): Ontario Curling Association
Chief Officer(s): Art Lobel, President
asobel@sympatico.ca
Membership: 28 teams; *Member Profile:* Curlers 70 & older; *Committees:* Executive

International Curling Information Network Group (ICING)
73 Appleford Rd., Hamilton ON L9C 6B5
Tel: 905-389-7781
www.icing.org
Overview: A small international organization founded in 1995
Description: To provide information about the sport of curling worldwide
Chief Officer(s): Peter M. Smith, Contact
psmith@icing.org

New Brunswick Curling Association (NBCA) / Association de Curling du Nouveau-Brunswick (ACNB)
c/o Marg Maranda, 65 Newcastle Centre Rd., Newcastle Centre NB E4B 2L2
Tel: 506-327-3445; *Fax:* 506-388-5708
Toll-Free: 800-592-2875
nbca@nb.sympatico.ca
www.nbcurling.com
Also Known As: Curling NB
Previous Name: New Brunswick Branch of the Royal Caledonian Curling Club of Scotland
Overview: A medium-sized provincial organization founded in 1971
Description: To promote curling in New Brunswick; To establish & govern rules for curling competitions in New Brunswick; *Member of:* Canadian Curling Association / Association canadienne de curling
Affiliation(s): Curl Atlantic
Chief Officer(s): Marg Maranda, Executive Director
Damien Lahiton, President
damilahi@gmail.com
Finances: *Funding Sources:* Canadian Curling Association; Curling Development Fund; Sponsorships
Member Profile: Members of affiliated curling clubs in New Brunswick
Activities: Organizing curling competitions; Offering learn-to-curl clinics, courses for coaching & instruction, & ice making; Supporting "Business of Curling Clinics"; Lending training equipment & resources

Newfoundland & Labrador Curling Association
c/o Gary Oke, PO Box 2352, RR#1, Humber Valley Resort NL A2H 0E1
Tel: 709-686-6388
presidentnlca13@gmail.com
www.curlingnl.ca
Overview: A small provincial organization
Member of: Canadian Curling Association
Chief Officer(s): Gary Oke, President
Susan Curtis, Vice-President
scurtis@nl.rogers.com
Baxter House, Secretary, 709-695-9826
baxterhouse@gov.nl.ca
Carl Loughlin, Treasurer, 709-634-4201
carl.loughlin@nf.sympatico.ca
Jean Blackie, Coordinator, Technical
jeanblackie@gmail.com
Steve Routledge, Coordinator, Tournament
tournamentsnlca@gmail.com
Finances: *Funding Sources:* Membership fees; Sponsorships
Activities: Organizing clinics; Coordinating torunaments

Northern Alberta Curling Association (NACA)
#110, 9440 - 49 St., Edmonton AB T6B 2M9
Tel: 780-440-4270; *Fax:* 780-463-4519
northernalbertacurling@shaw.ca
northernalbertacurling.com
Social Media:
www.facebook.com/108398119223374
Overview: A small local organization founded in 1918
Description: To develop and promote the sport of curling.
Chief Officer(s): Matt Yeo, President
Vicki Baird, Execurive Director

Northern Ontario Curling Association
PO Box 940, #4, 214 Main St. West, Atikokan ON P0T 1C0
Tel: 807-597-8730; *Fax:* 888-622-8884
Toll-Free: 888-597-8730
info@curlnoca.ca
www.curlnoca.ca
Social Media:
www.facebook.com/curlnoca
twitter.com/curlnoca
Merged from: Temiskaming & Northern Ontario Curling Association; Northern Ontario Ladies Curling Association
Overview: A small local organization
Description: To promote curling throughout northern Ontario.
Chief Officer(s): Leslie Kerr, Executive Director
lesliekerr@curlnoca.ca

Northwest Territories Curling Association
PO Box 11089, Yellowknife NT X1A 3X7
Tel: 867-669-8339; *Fax:* 867-669-8327
Toll-Free: 800-661-0797
www.nwtcurling.com
Social Media:
www.facebook.com/pages/NWT-Curling/316251248400802
twitter.com/nwt_curling
Overview: A small provincial organization founded in 1990
Description: To promote curling in the Northwest Territories.

Nova Scotia Curling Association (NSCA)
5516 Spring Garden Rd., 4th Fl., Halifax NS B3J 1G6
Tel: 902-421-2875; *Fax:* 902-425-5606
nsca@sportnovascotia.ca
www.nscurl.com
Previous Name: Nova Scotia Ladies Curling Association
Overview: A medium-sized provincial organization
Affiliation(s): Canadian Curling Association
Chief Officer(s): Kevin Patterson, Technical Director
Membership: 6,000; *Member Profile:* Men's, women's & juniors curlers; *Committees:* Operations; Finance; Competitions; Junior Curling; Athlete Development; Ombudsman; Disciplinary; Nominations; Awards; Curl Atlantic Reps

Nunavut Curling Association (NCA)
PO Box 413, Rankin Inlet NU X0C 0G0
Tel: 867-645-2534
Overview: A small provincial organization

Ontario Curling Association (OCA)
Office Mall 2, #2B, 1400 Bayly St., Pickering ON L1W 3R2
Tel: 905-831-1757; *Fax:* 905-831-1083
Toll-Free: 877-668-2875
www.ontcurl.com
Overview: A large provincial organization founded in 1875
Description: To promote & facilitate the growth & development of curling; *Member of:* Canadian Curling Association
Affiliation(s): Ontario Curling Council; Northern Ontario Curling Association; Ontario Special Olympics
Chief Officer(s): Ian McGillis, President, 613-657-4597
ianmcgillis@hotmail.com
Steve Chenier, Executive Director
steve@ontcurl.com
Finances: *Funding Sources:* Membership dues; competition fees; sponsorships
Staff: 7 staff member(s)
Membership: 55,000 people in 200 clubs; *Committees:* Executive; Credentials; Rules; Nominating
Activities: Competitions; seminars; workshops; Marketing & Development Programme

Ottawa Valley Curling Association (OVCA)
27 Veermeer Way, Ottawa ON K2K 2L9
webmaster@ovca.com
ottawavalleycurling.ca
Social Media:
www.facebook.com/ovcacurling
Overview: A small local organization founded in 1959
Description: To foster curling in the Ottawa & St. Lawrence Valleys & Outaouais
Affiliation(s): Ladies Curling Association; Curling Quebec
Chief Officer(s): Elaine Brimicombe, President
elaine@ovca.com
Peter Smith, Coordinator, Events
ovca.eventscoordinator@hotmail.com
Finances: *Annual Operating Budget:* Less than $50,000
Membership: 45 clubs; *Committees:* OVCA Ottawa Men's Bonspiel; OVCA Mixed Bonspiel; The Royal LePage OVCA Women's Fall Classic; JSI OVCA Junior SuperSpiel
Activities: Overseeing intermediate competitions between Eastern Ontario & Quebec; Offering instruction to new curlers

Peace Curling Association (PCA)
PO Box 265, Grande Prairie AB T8V 3A4
Tel: 780-532-4782; *Fax:* 780-538-2485
peacecurl@telusplanet.net
www.peacecurl.org
Overview: A small local organization
Member of: Alberta Curling Federation; Canadian Curling Association
Finances: *Annual Operating Budget:* Less than $50,000; *Funding Sources:* Casino
Staff: 1 staff member(s)

Prince Edward Island Curling Association (PEICA)
40 Enman Cres., Charlottetown PE C1E 1E6
Tel: 902-368-4208; *Fax:* 902-368-4548
info@peicurling.com
www.peicurling.com
Social Media:
www.facebook.com/peicurling
twitter.com/peicurling
Overview: A medium-sized provincial organization
Description: To advance & promote curling as a competitive & recreational sport in Prince Edward Island
Affiliation(s): Sports PEI, Curl Atlantic
Chief Officer(s): Amy Duncan, Executive Director
aduncan@sportpei.pe.ca

Saskatchewan Curling Association (SCA)
613 Park St., Regina SK S4N 5N1
Tel: 306-780-9202; *Fax:* 306-780-9404
Toll-Free: 877-722-2875
curling@curlsask.ca
curlsask.ca
Social Media:
www.facebook.com/Curlsask
twitter.com/curlsask
Also Known As: CurlSask
Overview: A small provincial organization
Description: To govern and promote the sport of curling in Saskatchewan.
Chief Officer(s): Ashley Howard, Executive Director, 306-780-9403
ashleyhoward@curlsask.ca

Southern Alberta Curling Association (SACA)
#720, 3 St. NW, Calgary AB T2N 1N9
Tel: 403-246-9300; *Fax:* 403-246-9349
curling@saca.ca
www.saca.ca
Overview: A small local organization
Description: To encourage active participation for residents of all ages in our communities by helping member curling clubs offer a wide variety of programs. To assist in providing opportunities to participate in curling.
Chief Officer(s): Brent Syme, General Manager
brent@saca.ca
Stasia Perkins, Director, Clubs & Competitions
stasia@saca.ca

Toronto Curling Association (TCA)
#6A-1409, 170 The Donway West, Toronto ON M3C 2E8
Tel: 416-657-2425
general@torontocurling.com
www.torontocurling.com
Social Media:
www.facebook.com/torontocurling
twitter.com/torontocurling
Overview: A small local organization founded in 1964
Description: To promote curling in the Greater Toronto Area
Chief Officer(s): Hugh Murphy, President
president@torontocurling.com
Membership: 24 clubs

World Curling Federation (WCF)
74 Tay St., Perth PH2 8NP Scotland
info@worldcurling.org
www.worldcurling.org
Social Media:
www.youtube.com/user/WorldCurlingTV
www.linkedin.com/company/world-curling-federation
www.facebook.com/WorldCurlingFederation
twitter.com/worldcurling
Previous Name: International Curling Federation
Overview: A medium-sized international organization founded in 1966
Description: To represent curling internationally & to facilitate the growth of the sport through a network of member nations; *Member of:* General Association of International Sports Federations (GAISF)
Chief Officer(s): Kate Caithness, President
Bent Ånund Ramsfjell, Vice-President
Colin Grahamslaw, Secretary General
Membership: 53 member associations; *Member Profile:* National associations
Activities: World & World Junior & World Senior Curling Championships, Men & Women; World Wheelchair Curling Championship, Mixed teams

Yukon Curling Association (YCA)
4061 - 4th Ave., Whitehorse YT Y1A 1H1
Tel: 867-668-7121; *Fax:* 867-667-4237
www.yukoncurling.ca
Overview: A small provincial organization founded in 1974
Affiliation(s): Watson Lake Curling Club; Mayo Curling Club
Chief Officer(s): Laura Eby, Executive Director
executivedirector@yukoncurling.ca
Membership: 1,000; *Member Profile:* Seniors; masters; adults; juniors; youth; little rockers

Dance

World Dance Council Ltd. (WDC)
63-67 Kingston Rd., New Malden, Surrey KT3 3PB England
gensec@wdcdance.com
www.wdcdance.com
Previous Name: International Council of Ballroom Dancing
Overview: A small international organization founded in 1950

Affiliation(s): International Dance Organization
Chief Officer(s): Hannes Emrich, Company & General Secretary
gensec@wdcdance.com
Membership: 50; *Committees:* Dance Sport; Social Dance

Darts

Association de Dards du Québec inc. (ADQDA) / Québec Dart Association Inc.
#3, 3177, rue Notre Dame, Lachine QC H8S 2H4
Tél: 514-637-2858
www.adqda.com
Média social:
www.facebook.com/groups/ADQDA

Aperçu: *Dimension:* moyenne; *Envergure:* provinciale; Organisme sans but lucratif; fondée en 1978
Description: L'A.D.Q. est la seule et unique Association de dards qui représente la Fédération de dards du Canada et aussi la seule qui est reconnue par la Fédération de Dards mondiale (World Darts Federation); *Membre de:* National Darts Federation of Canada
Membre(s) du bureau directeur: Maggie LeBlanc, Présidente
maggieleblanc417@hotmail.com
Membre: 700; *Montant de la cotisation:* $25

Darts Alberta
PO Box 163, #14, 9977 - 178 St. NW, Edmonton AB T5T 6J6
Tel: 780-908-0475
www.dartsalberta.com

Overview: A small provincial organization
Description: To provide recreational & competitive opportunities for darts players of all levels in Alberta.; *Member of:* National Darts Federation of Canada
Chief Officer(s): Bill Hatter, President, 403-548-2939, Fax: 403-504-4029
president@dartsalberta.com
Sandi Orr, Administrator
administrator@dartsalberta.com
Activities: Sport programs; educational opportunities for coaches & officials; recognition programs

Darts BC Association (DBCA)
BC
executive@dartsbc.ca
www.dartsbc.ca
Social Media:
www.facebook.com/BcDarts

Overview: A small provincial organization
Description: To be the provincial governing body for the sport of darts in British Columbia.; *Member of:* National Darts Federation of Canada
Chief Officer(s): Ray Bode, President
president@dartsbc.ca
Suzie Letude, Provincial Director
provincialdirector@dartsbc.ca
Membership: 8 leagues/associations

Darts Ontario
ON
Tel: 905-426-7493; *Fax:* 905-426-8270
provincialdirector@dartsontario.com
www.dartsontario.com

Overview: A small provincial organization
Description: To promote the sport of darts on the provincial, national & world levels.; *Member of:* National Darts Federation of Canada
Chief Officer(s): Susan Hine, President & Provincial Director
president@dartsontario.com
Katie Murphy, Secretary, 905-534-1426, Fax: 905-534-1464
secretary@dartsontario.com
Membership: *Fees:* $18 affiliate; $20 youth; $23 adult

Ligue de dards Ungava
331, 2e Rue, Chibougamau QC G8P 1M4
Tél: 418-748-8060

Aperçu: *Dimension:* petite; *Envergure:* locale
Membre(s) du bureau directeur: Claude Patoine, Président

Manitoba Darts Association Inc. (MDAI)
c/o MDAI Membership Director, 720 Consol Ave., Winnipeg MB R2K 1T2
info@manitobadarts.com
www.manitobadarts.com
Social Media:
www.facebook.com/ManitobaDartsAssociationInc

Overview: A small provincial organization
Member of: National Darts Federation of Canada
Chief Officer(s): Ron Looker, President, 204-997-7579
ronlooker@hotmail.com
Kim Clawson, Provincial Director
kimmyclawson@live.com

Membership: *Fees:* $30

National Darts Federation of Canada (NDFC) / Fédération nationale de dards du Canada
Tel: 902-401-9650
secretary@ndfc.ca
www.ndfc.ca

Overview: A medium-sized national organization founded in 1977
Description: To promote & organize darts events & promote the betterment of the game
Affiliation(s): World Darts Federation
Chief Officer(s): Bill Hatter, President
president@ndfc.ca
Finances: *Annual Operating Budget:* $50,000-$100,000
Staff: 7 staff member(s)
Membership: 5,000-14,999
Activities: Provincial/national championships; international events

New Brunswick Dart Association (NBDA)
c/o William White, 526 Rte. 845, Kingston NB E3N 1P5
Tel: 506-832-7293
www.nbdarts.bravehost.com

Overview: A small provincial organization
Description: To promote the sport of darts in New Brunswick.; *Member of:* National Darts Federation of Canada
Chief Officer(s): William White, President
Cathy Ross, Secretary-Treasurer, 506-433-3057
cathyross460@hotmail.com

Newfoundland & Labrador Darts Association
NL
nldarts.webs.com
Social Media:
www.facebook.com/NewfoundlandAndLabradorDartsAssociation

Overview: A medium-sized provincial organization founded in 1977
Member of: National Darts Federation of Canada
Chief Officer(s): Cavelle Taylor, President, 709-582-2952
cavtaylor@yahoo.ca

Northern Ontario Darts Association (NODA)
#163, 159 Louis St., Sudbury ON P3B 2H4
Tel: 807-625-9373; *Fax:* 807-625-9391
nodarts.ca
Social Media:
twitter.com/dartsno

Overview: A small provincial organization
Description: To promote the sport of darts on the provincial, national & world levels.; *Member of:* National Darts Federation of Canada
Chief Officer(s): Christine Stark, President
czachary@tbaytel.net
Chris Arsenault, Secretary, 705-626-1030
180king@personainternet.com

Prince Edward Island Sharpshooters Association
PE
www.sharpshooterspei.com

Also Known As: The Sharpshooters
Overview: A small provincial organization
Description: To promote the game of darts in Prince Edward Island.; *Member of:* National Darts Federation of Canada
Chief Officer(s): Malcolm Buchanan, President
drywall56@hotmail.com
Terri Affleck, Provincial Director
taffleck11@hotmail.com

Saskatchewan Darts Association (SDA)
c/o Pat Copeman, 17 Eden Ave., Regina SK S7R 5M2
Tel: 306-949-5180
www.saskdarts.com

Overview: A small provincial organization
Description: To promote the sport of darts for players of all ages & abilities in Saskatchewan.; *Member of:* National Darts Federation of Canada
Chief Officer(s): Pat Copeman, President
pac.mom@accesscomm.ca
Frank Zimmer, Secretary, 306-545-5192
frank.zimmer@sasktel.net

Deafness

Alberta Deaf Sports Association (ADSA)
11404 - 142 St., Edmonton AB T5M 1V1
info@albertadeafsports.ca
www.albertadeafsports.ca
Social Media:
www.facebook.com/AlbertaDeafSports

Also Known As: Federation of Silent Sports of Alberta
Overview: A medium-sized provincial charitable organization founded in 1974
Description: To coordinate sport & recreation activities for the deaf in Alberta; To promote competition at the local, provincial, regional, & national levels; To select Alberta athletes to compete in national championships for the World Games of the Deaf; *Member of:* Canadian Deaf Sports Association
Chief Officer(s): Sally Korol, Contact
Brenda Hillcox, President
Membership: *Fees:* $25 regular; $15 senior citizens; free for students; *Member Profile:* Deaf & hard of hearing persons

Association sportive des sourds du Québec inc. (ASSQ)
4545, av Pierre-de Coubertin, Montréal QC H1V 0B2
Tél: 514-252-3049
www.assq.org
Média social:
www.youtube.com/user/1ASSQ
www.facebook.com/ASSQ1
twitter.com/@ASSQ_Nouvelles

Nom précédent: Association amateur des sports des sourds du Québec; Fédération sportive des sourds du Québec inc.
Aperçu: *Dimension:* moyenne; *Envergure:* provinciale; fondée en 1968
Description: Promouvoir le sport, les loisirs et l'activité physique chez les personnes sourdes et malentendantes du Québec; *Membre de:* Canadian Deaf Sports Association
Membre(s) du bureau directeur: Suzanne Laforest, Directrice générale
slaforest@assq.org
Audrey Beauchamp, Coordinatrice, Projets et des communications
abeauchamp@assq.org
Caroline Hould, Chargée des programmes
chould@assq.org

British Columbia Deaf Sports Federation (BCDSF)
#4, 320 Columbia St., New Westminster BC V3L 1A6
Fax: 604-526-5010
TTY: 604-526-5010
info@bcdeafsports.bc.ca
www.bcdeafsports.bc.ca
Social Media:
www.facebook.com/139556792849947
twitter.com/bcdeafsports

Overview: A medium-sized provincial charitable organization founded in 1975
Description: To provide & support the development of competitive sporting events in BC among deaf & hard of hearing athletes; to encourage training for deaf coaches; to provide financial assistance to deaf athletes to participate in local, provincial & national competitions; *Member of:* Canadian Deaf Sports Association
Affiliation(s): BC Sport & Fitness Council for the Disabled
Chief Officer(s): Marilyn Loehr, Director, Membership
mloehr@bcdeafsports.bc.ca
Finances: *Annual Operating Budget:* $100,000-$250,000; *Funding Sources:* Grants; gaming; membership fees; donations
Staff: 1 staff member(s)
Membership: 300

Canadian Deaf Ice Hockey Federation (CDIHF)
ON
www.cdihf.deafhockey.com
Social Media:
www.facebook.com/canada.deafhockey?fref=ts&ref=br_tf
twitter.com/CDNdeafhockey

Previous Name: Canadian Hearing Impaired Hockey Association
Overview: A small national charitable organization founded in 1983
Description: To offer ice hockey programs for deaf & hard of hearing participants; To administer a hockey team to represent Canada internationally; *Member of:* Canadian Deaf Sports Association
Affiliation(s): Canadian Hockey Association; Ontario Deaf Sports Association, Inc.
Chief Officer(s): Mark Dunn, President
mark.dunn@deafhockey.com
Finances: *Funding Sources:* Donations; Sponsorships
Activities: Hosting training camps & hockey schools; Organizing the CDIHC Hockey Championships; Participating in the World Deaf Ice Hockey Championship

Canadian Deaf Sports Association (CDSA) / Association des sports des sourds du Canada (ASSC)
#202A, 10217 Pie IX Blvd., Montréal QC H1H 3Z5
Tel: 514-321-8686; *Fax:* 514-321-8349
TTY: 514-321-2937
info@assc-cdsa.com
www.assc-cdsa.com
Social Media:
www.facebook.com/assc.cdsa
twitter.com/ASSC_CDSA
Overview: A medium-sized national licensing charitable organization founded in 1964
Description: To promote & facilitate the practice of fitness, amateur sports & recreation among deaf people of all ages in Canada from the local recreational level to Olympics calibre.; *Member of:* Canadian Deaf & Hard of Hearing Forum; Canadian Paralympic Committee; Canadian Sports Coalition.
Affiliation(s): International Committee of Sports for the Deaf
Chief Officer(s): Craig Noonan, Chief Executive Officer
Ghysline "Gigi" Fiset, Manager, Operational Services & Events
Mark Kusiak, President

International Committee of Sports for the Deaf (ICSD) / Comité international des Sports des Sourds (CISS)
PO Box 3441, Frederick MD 21701-3441 USA
Fax: 499-255-0436
office@ciss.org
www.deaflympics.com
Social Media:
www.facebook.com/Deaflympics
twitter.com/deaflympics
Also Known As: International Deaflympics
Overview: A medium-sized international charitable organization founded in 1924
Member of: International Olympic Committee; General Assembly of International Sports Federations
Affiliation(s): Canadian Deaf Sports Association
Chief Officer(s): Rukhledev Valery, President
president@ciss.org
Membership: 109 countries; *Member Profile:* National Deaf Sports Federations
Activities: Deaflympics; Deaf World Championships; *Internships:* Yes

Nova Scotia Deaf Sports Association (NSDSA)
5516 Spring Garden Rd., 4th Fl., Halifax NS B3J 1G6
Overview: A small provincial organization
Description: To govern fitness, amateur sports & recreation for deaf people in Nova Scotia.; *Member of:* Canadian Deaf Sports Association
Chief Officer(s): Matt Ayyash, President

Ontario Deaf Sports Association (ODSA)
ON
Overview: A small provincial organization founded in 1964
Member of: Canadian Deaf Sports Association

Saskatchewan Deaf Sports Association (SDSA)
PO Box 932, Fort Qu'appelle SK S0G 1S0
Overview: A small provincial charitable organization
Description: To foster sporting opportunities to members of the deaf & hard-of-hearing communities; To select & train deaf & hard-of-hearing athletes for international competitions; *Member of:* Canadian Deaf Sports Association
Affiliation(s): Regina Deaf Athletic Club; Saskatoon Deaf Athletic Club; Saskatchewan Sport Inc.
Chief Officer(s): Kevin Goodfeather, President
nivek26@hotmail.com
Finances: *Annual Operating Budget:* Less than $50,000; *Funding Sources:* Provincial subsidy; Sask. Lotteries; tickets sales; special events
Staff: 10 volunteer(s)
Membership: 300-400; *Fees:* $25 adult; $5 adult (no championships); $75 organization

Diving

Alberta Diving
AB
www.albertadiving.ca
Overview: A small provincial organization
Description: To act as the governing body in Alberta for the Olympic sport of amateur diving; to strive for personal & organizational excellence in all areas of diving
Finances: *Funding Sources:* Fundraising; Sponsorships
Activities: Promoting sportsmanship & respect for rules; Encouraging community involvement; Promoting both the physical & mental well being of members

Alberta Underwater Council (AUC)
Percy Page Building, 11759 Groat Rd., 2nd Fl., Edmonton AB T5M 3K6
Tel: 780-427-9125; *Fax:* 780-427-8139
Toll-Free: 888-307-8566
info@albertaunderwatercouncil.com
www.albertaunderwatercouncil.com
Overview: A medium-sized local organization founded in 1962
Description: To represent responsible participation in & awareness of underwater activities
Affiliation(s): Canadian Underwater Games Association
Chief Officer(s): Cathie McCuaig, Executive Director, 780-427-9125, Fax: 780-427-8139
Finances: *Funding Sources:* Alberta Gaming; Alberta Sport Recreation Parks & Wildlife Foundation
Membership: 600 individual; *Fees:* Schedule available
Activities: *Awareness Events:* Divescapes

Association Internationale pour le Développement de l'Apnée Canada
Edmonton AB
Tel: 780-399-4998
www.aidacanada.org
Social Media:
www.facebook.com/AidaCanada
twitter.com/aidacanada
Also Known As: AIDA Canada
Overview: A large national organization founded in 2009
Description: To develop the sport of freediving in Canada as both a pastime & an athletic pursuit
Affiliation(s): AIDA International
Chief Officer(s): Dean Spahic, President
Finances: *Funding Sources:* Membership dues; Donations
Membership: *Fees:* $25; *Member Profile:* Freedivers
Activities: Supporting freediving clubs across Canada; Offering information & resources for members; Organizing competitions

British Columbia Diving
#114, 15272 Croydon Dr., Surrey BC V3S 0Z5
Tel: 604-531-5576; *Fax:* 604-542-0387
www.bcdiving.ca
Also Known As: British Columbia Diving Association
Previous Name: Dive B.C.
Overview: A small provincial charitable organization founded in 1986
Description: To develop and promote diving throughout British Columbia by encouraging participation, quality and personal success among members; *Member of:* Diving Plongeon Canada
Chief Officer(s): Jayne McDonald, Executive Director
jayne@bcdiving.ca
Beverley Boys, Technical Director
boys.bev@gmail.com
Finances: *Funding Sources:* Province of British Columbia through the Ministry of Community, Sport and Cultural Development
Staff: 3 staff member(s)
Membership: *Fees:* Schedule available; *Member Profile:* Divers, associations, coaches, officials

Canadian Association of Freediving & Apnea (CAFA)
19640 - 34A Ave., Lengley BC V3A 7W6
www.freedivecanada.com
Overview: A small national organization
Description: To further the sport of freediving in Canada & abroad.
Chief Officer(s): Andrew Hogan, President
president@freedivecanada.com
Membership: *Fees:* $25 full; $50 associate

Dive Ontario
216 Gilwood Park Dr., Penetanguishene ON L9M 1Z6
Tel: 705-355-3483; *Fax:* 705-355-4663
contactus@diveontario.com
www.diveontario.com
Social Media:
www.facebook.com/DiveOntario
Overview: A small provincial organization
Description: To provide programs & services to its members
Affiliation(s): Community & recreation centres around the province; Dive Plongeon Canada
Chief Officer(s): Bernie Olanski, President
bernie@lexcor.ca
Membership: 11 clubs; *Member Profile:* Diving clubs in Ontario; *Committees:* HP Implementation; Sport Development; Media & Marketing

Diving Plongeon Canada (DPC) / Association canadienne du plongeon amateur Inc.
#312, 700 Industrial Ave., Ottawa ON K1G 0Y9
Tel: 613-736-5238; *Fax:* 613-736-0409
cada@diving.ca
www.diving.ca
Social Media:
www.facebook.com/DivingPCanada
twitter.com/DivingPlongeon
Also Known As: Canadian Amateur Diving Association Inc.
Overview: A medium-sized national charitable organization founded in 1967
Description: To promote the growth & awareness of diving in Canada; To contribute to the development of globally accepted standards of diving; To support the rules & regulations of international competition; *Member of:* FINA
Affiliation(s): Aquatics Federation of Canada; Swimming Natation Canada; Synchronized Swimming; Water Polo Canada
Chief Officer(s): Penny Joyce, Chief Operating Officer
penny@diving.ca
Mitch Geller, Chief Technical Officer
mitch@diving.ca
Scott Cranham, Director, Talent Management
scott@diving.ca
Jeff Feeney, Manager, Events & Communications
jeff@diving.ca
Finances: *Funding Sources:* Government; Self Funding; Donations; Sponsorships
Staff: 10 staff member(s)
Membership: 67 local diving clubs + 4,000 high performance athletes; *Member Profile:* Diving associations; Local diving clubs; High performance athletes; *Committees:* Athlete; Technical; Officials; Rules & Regulations
Activities: Providing programs & services for participants to achieve excellence & self-fulfillment; Obtaining media coverage & increasing spectators at events; Developing elite athletes; Communicating with members; Hosting an annual general meeting; Presenting DPC awards

Fédération du plongeon amateur du Québec (FPAQ)
4545, av Pierre-de Coubertin, Montréal QC H1V 0b2
Tél: 514-252-3096; *Téléc:* 514-252-3094
info@plongeon.qc.ca
www.plongeon.qc.ca
Média social:
twitter.com/PlongeonQuebec
Également appelé: Plongeon Québec
Aperçu: *Dimension:* moyenne; *Envergure:* provinciale; fondée en 1971
Description: Régir le plongeon sur l'ensemble du territoire québécois; promouvoir le plongeon et sa pratique; tenir et organiser des stages de formation et des compétitions de plongeon; regrouper les associations de plongeon; *Membre de:* Diving Plongeon Canada; Sports-Québec; AQUM; Club de la médaille d'or; Institut national du sport-Montréal
Membre(s) du bureau directeur: Claudie Dumais, Directrice exécutive
cdumais@plongeon.qc.ca
Finances: *Budget de fonctionnement annuel:* $250,000-$500,000
Personnel: 3 membre(s) du personnel; 100+ bénévole(s)
Membre: 3,000; *Montant de la cotisation:* Barème; *Comités:* Entraîneurs; Officiels; L'élite
Activités: *Stagiaires:* Oui; *Service de conférenciers:* Oui

Fédération québécoise des activités subaquatiques (FQAS)
4545, av Pierre-de Coubertin, Montréal QC H1V 0B2
Tél: 514-252-3009; *Téléc:* 514-254-1363
Ligne sans frais: 866-391-8835
info@fqas.qc.ca
www.fqas.qc.ca
Média social:
www.facebook.com/FederationQuebecoisedesActivitesSubaquatiques
Aperçu: *Dimension:* moyenne; *Envergure:* provinciale; Organisme sans but lucratif; fondée en 1970
Description: Regrouper les adeptes de la plongée et des activités subaquatiques; promouvoir la sécurite dans la pratique des activités subaquatiques; informer et renseigner ses membres et la population sur les bienfaits de la pratique; promouvoir ces activités comme moyen de formation et comme loisir
Affiliation(s): Confédération mondiale des activités subaquatiques
Membre(s) du bureau directeur: Alain Gauthier, Directeur général
direction@fqas.qc.ca
Finances: *Budget de fonctionnement annuel:* $250,000-$500,000; *Fonds:* Gouvernement provincial
Personnel: 2 membre(s) du personnel; 150 bénévole(s)

Membre: 100 institutionnel + 2 200 individu; *Montant de la cotisation:* $34.50 individu; $56 famille
Activités: *Stagiaires:* Oui; *Service de conférenciers:* Oui
Bibliothèque: Librairie FQAS rendez-vous

Manitoba Diving Association
#430, 145 Pacific Ave., Winnipeg MB R3B 2Z6
Tel: 204-925-5654; *Fax:* 204-925-5792
www.manitobadiving.ca
Social Media:
www.facebook.com/mbdiving
twitter.com/manitobadiving
Overview: A small provincial organization
Description: Provides strong ethical and values driven foundation for diving throughout Manitoba and Canada, and supports athletic development, personal growth and community awareness through excellence in leadership; *Member of:* Diving Plongeon Canada
Chief Officer(s): Ken Stevens, Executive Director
diving@sportmanitoba.ca

Manitoba Underwater Council (MUC)
PO Box 711, Winnipeg MB R3C 2K3
Tel: 204-632-8508
info@manunderwater.com
www.manunderwater.com
Overview: A medium-sized provincial charitable organization founded in 1962
Description: To coordinate, preserve, support & promote sport diving clubs & associations; to promote safety in diving; to exchange & disseminate information concerning the sport of skin & scuba diving & to foster conservation; *Member of:* Sport Manitoba
Chief Officer(s): Ronals Hempel, President
president@manunderwater.com
Finances: *Annual Operating Budget:* Less than $50,000; *Funding Sources:* Provincial Government & membership fees
Staff: 10 staff member(s); 10 volunteer(s)
Membership: 27 institutional + 150 individual; *Fees:* $20; *Member Profile:* Certified scuba divers, divers in training
Activities: Spear fishing competition, pumpkin dive, super dive, underwater football competition

Ontario Underwater Council (OUC)
#109, 1 Concorde Gate, Toronto ON M3C 3C6
Tel: 416-426-7033; *Fax:* 416-426-7280
ouc@underwatercouncil.com
www.underwatercouncil.com
Social Media:
www.facebook.com/groups/39720054237
Overview: A small provincial organization
Description: To represent all divers in Ontario; to promote the sport of scuba diving
Chief Officer(s): Ronald J. Bogart, President
ouc.president@underwatercouncil.com
Sasha Ilich, Director, Communications
communications@underwatercouncil.com
Membership: 2,600+; *Fees:* $20-$37 individual; $145 commercial; schedule for clubs

Saskatchewan Diving
1870 Lorne St., Regina SK S4P 2L7
Tel: 306-780-9405; *Fax:* 306-781-6021
info@divesask.ca
www.saskdiving.ca
Social Media:
www.facebook.com/DIVESASK
twitter.com/divesask
Also Known As: Sask Diving Inc.
Overview: A small provincial organization
Description: To develop & promote safe diving; To ensure that diving clubs operate with safety & integrity; To provide opportunities for self fulfillment & the pursuit of excellence; *Member of:* Diving Plongeon Canada
Chief Officer(s): Karen Swanson, Executive Director
kswanson@divesask.ca
Finances: *Funding Sources:* Sask Lotteries
Staff: 3 staff member(s)
Member Profile: Diving clubs; Individuals, such as coaches, athletes, officials, parents, & executive members
Activities: Ensuring coaches are trained through the National Coaching Certification Program

The Saskatchewan Underwater Council Inc.
PO Box 7651, Saskatoon SK S7K 4R4
Tel: 306-374-8341; *Fax:* 306-374-8341
executive@saskuc.com
www.saskuc.com
Overview: A small provincial organization
Description: To represent those interested in underwater activities in Saskatchewan.
Chief Officer(s): Cliff Lange, Contact

Membership: *Fees:* $30 single; $35 family

Underwater Council of British Columbia (UCBC)
BC
underwatercouncil.bc@gmail.com
www.underwatercouncilbc.org
Social Media:
www.youtube.com/user/TheUCBC
Overview: A small provincial organization
Description: To represent recreational divers in British Columbia.
Chief Officer(s): Paul Sim, President

Yukon Underwater Diving Association (YUDA)
YT
www.yukonweb.com/community/yuda
Overview: A small provincial organization
Description: The Yukon Underwater Diving Association (YUDA) is a non-profit organization created by sport divers to promote the sport of underwater diving in the Yukon, Northern British Columbia & South East Alaska.
Chief Officer(s): Allyn Lyon, President
alyon@yukon.net
Doug Davidge, Contact
ddavidge@yknet.yk.ca

Dynamophilie

Alberta Powerlifting Union (APU)
c/o James Bartlett, 4805 Vandyke Rd. NW, Calgary AB T3A 0J6
Tel: 403-471-4754
www.powerliftingab.com
Social Media:
www.youtube.com/user/AlbertaPL
Overview: A small provincial organization founded in 1983
Description: To promote powerlifting in Alberta
Affiliation(s): Canadian Powerlifting Union; International Powerlifting Federation
Chief Officer(s): Shane Martin, Interim President
mr.shane.c.martin@gmail.com
James Bartlett, Chair, Registration
bartlettJ@bennettjones.com
Membership: *Fees:* $60 open; $50 junior; $40 special

Fédération Québécoise de Dynamophilie (FQD)
679, av du Parc, Sherbrooke QC J1N 3N5
Tél: 819-864-4810
www.fqd-quebec.com
Média social:
www.facebook.com/dynamophilie
Aperçu: *Dimension:* petite; *Envergure:* provinciale
Description: Promouvoir, contrôler et développer la dynamophilie auprès de la population du Québec.
Affiliation(s): Canadian Powerlifting Union; International Powerlifting Federation
Membre(s) du bureau directeur: Louis Lévesque, Président
louis.lvesque2@sympatico.ca
Montant de la cotisation: 55$; 45$ les moins de 18 ans

Equestrian Sports & Activities

Alberta Equestrian Federation (AEF)
#100, 251 Midpark Blvd. SE, Calgary AB T2X 1S3
Tel: 403-253-4411; *Fax:* 403-252-5260
Toll-Free: 877-463-6233
info@albertaequestrian.com
www.albertaequestrian.com
Social Media:
www.linkedin.com/company/alberta-equestrian-federation
www.facebook.com/AlbertaEquestrian
twitter.com/ab_equestrian
Overview: A small provincial organization founded in 1978
Member of: Equine Canada
Chief Officer(s): Les Oakes, President
lesoakes@gmail.com
Sonia Dantu, Executive Director
execdir@albertaequestrian.com
Finances: *Annual Operating Budget:* $100,000-$250,000; *Funding Sources:* Alberta Sport, Recreation, Parks & Wildlife Foundation
Staff: 6 staff member(s)
Membership: 12,000+; *Fees:* $50 individual; $110 family; $75 club; $120 business; *Committees:* Executive; Rec. & Trails; Competitions; Officials; Trail Ride
Activities: Administers equestrian NCCP Level I & II for Western, English & Driving Coaching; coordinating, sanctioning & administering body for equestrian sport & recreation in Alberta; provides assistance & expertise in areas such as competitions, coaching, officials, games & sporting events, recreation & travel insurance, awards, human & equine medication control; *Awareness Events:* Annual Trail Ride

Atlantic Canada Trail Riding Association (ACTRA)
c/o Pat Rideout, 3540 Rte. 890, Hillgrove NB E4Z 5W6
www.ac-tra.ca
Overview: A small local organization founded in 1980
Description: To promote safe horsemanship & friendly competition in the long distance trail competition; *Member of:* Canadian Long Distance Riding Association
Membership: *Fees:* $17.50

British Columbia Competitive Trail Riders Association (BCCTRA)
c/o Christine Pacukiewicz, 14 Amber Pl., Victoria BC V9A 7A2
Tel: 250-881-8153
bcctra@shaw.ca
www.bcctra.ca
Overview: A small provincial organization founded in 1983
Description: To promote & improve the rapidly growing sport of competitive trail riding in BC; *Member of:* Canadian Long Distance Riding Association
Chief Officer(s): Tammy Mercer, President, 250-335-3390
ridingforfreedomranch@shaw.ca
Christine Pacukiewicz, Secretary
Membership: *Fees:* $60 family; $30 senior; $25 senior (65+); $25 junior; $300 lifetime; $20 supporter; *Member Profile:* Senior & junior riders
Activities: Two yearly meetings

Canadian Dressage Owners & Riders Association
c/o Donald J. Barnes, #13, 1475 Upper Gage Ave., Hamilton ON L8T 1E6
Tel: 905-387-2031
dressagegames@aol.com
www.cadora.ca
Social Media:
instagram.com/CadoraInc
www.facebook.com/CadoraInc
twitter.com/CadoraInc
Also Known As: CADORA Inc.
Overview: A medium-sized national organization founded in 1969
Description: To promote interest in dressage riding as a sport throughout Canada; To develop the sport consistent with the principles of the international governing body of the equestrian Olympic disciplines; To ensure progressions leading to competitive International levels; *Member of:* Equine Canada; Ontario Equestrian Federation
Affiliation(s): Dressage Canada
Chief Officer(s): Donald J. Barnes, President & Editor, Omnibus
David Rosensweig, Coordinator, National Clinic
dhr@live.ca
Finances: *Funding Sources:* Fundraising; Donations; Membership fees
Member Profile: Dressage riders from across Canada
Activities: Providing educational workshops & clinics; Coordinating competitions & matches; Presenting awards; Arranging demonstrations of dressage riding in all areas of Canada

Canadian Sport Horse Association (CSHA)
PO Box 970, 7904 Franktown Rd., Richmond ON K0A 2Z0
Tel: 613-686-6161; *Fax:* 613-686-6170
csha@canadian-sport-horse.org
www.c-s-h-a.org
Social Media:
www.facebook.com/138540009572125
twitter.com/cdnsporthorse
Overview: A small national organization founded in 1933
Description: To ensure the production & promotion of a sound, solid horse, with a good disposition, capable of competing successfully in the Olympic Disciplines at all levels of competition.; *Member of:* World Breeding Federation
Chief Officer(s): Soo Olafsen, President
hefka13@gmail.com
Joanna Fast, Vice-President
wrenwoodfarm@gmail.com
Membership: 718; *Fees:* $35 associate/youth; $85 individual; $850 life
Activities: Sport horse inspections; shows

Distance Riders of Manitoba Association (DRMA)
MB
Tel: 204-330-1773
www.distanceridersofmanitoba.ca
Overview: A small provincial organization founded in 1993
Description: DRMA promotes endurance riding in the province of Manitoba & brings together equestrians interested in the sport.; *Member of:* Manitoba Horse Council; Canadian Long

Distance Riding Association
Affiliation(s): American Endurance Ride Conference
Chief Officer(s): Jessica Manness, Secretary
northranch@hotmail.com
Maura Leahy, Treasurer & Membership Contact
Maura.Leahy@live.ca
Membership: 30; *Fees:* $25 single; $40 family; *Member Profile:* Manitoba equestrians
Activities: Supervised rides; competitions

Drive Canada
#100, 208 Legget Dr., Ottawa ON K2K 1Y6
Tel: 613-287-1515; *Fax:* 613-248-3484
Toll-Free: 866-282-8395
info.drivecanada@shaw.ca
drivecanada.ca
Previous Name: Canadian Driving Society
Overview: A small national organization founded in 1983
Description: To represent competitive & non-competitive drivers; *Member of:* Equine Canada
Affiliation(s): American Driving Society
Chief Officer(s): Simon Rosenman, Chair, Canadian Driving Committee
cdc.drivecanada@shaw.ca
Kathleen Winfield, Chair, Regional Council
regionalcouncil.drivecanada@shaw.ca
Wendy Gayfer, Program Coordinator, FEI Non-Olympic Disciplines
wgayfer@equinecanada.ca
Member Profile: Recreational & competitive drivers, coaches & officials; *Committees:* Athlete Development; Coaching Development; Combined Driving; Communications; Competitions; Draft Driving; Finance; High Performance; Licensed Officials; Pleasure Driving; Recreational Driving; Rules
Activities: Promotes sport of carriage driving; trains & evaluates coaches & officials; *Library:* Yes

Endurance Riders Association of British Columbia (ERABC)
5068 - 47A Ave., Delta BC V4K 1T8
Tel: 604-940-6958
tobytrot@telus.net
www.erabc.com
Overview: A small provincial organization founded in 1989
Description: ERABC fosters interest in the equestrian sport of endurance riding & promotes training & competition opportunities for beginning & advanced riders. It also assists in the development & preservation of courses or terrain suitable for endurance competitions.
Affiliation(s): Endurance Canada
Chief Officer(s): Murray Mackenzie, President
macheli@telus.net
Finances: *Annual Operating Budget:* Less than $50,000
Membership: 1-99; *Fees:* $30 adult; $60 family; $20 youth
Activities: *Awareness Events:* Ride Over the Rainbow

Endurance Riders of Alberta (ERA)
AB
Tel: 780-797-5404
enduranceridersofalberta.com
Social Media:
www.facebook.com/269711222453
Overview: A small provincial organization founded in 1981
Description: To promote education & good horsemanship through endurance riding; *Member of:* Alberta Equestrian Federation; Canadian Long Distance Riding Association
Affiliation(s): Canadian Long Distance Riding Association
Chief Officer(s): Owen Fulcher, President
erapresident@live.ca
Membership: *Fees:* $30 individual; $60 family; $25 junior
Activities: Host clinics; sanctions endurance events in Alberta

Equestrian Association for the Disabled
8360 Leeming Rd., RR#3, Mount Hope ON L0R 1W0
Tel: 905-679-8323; *Fax:* 905-679-1705
info@tead.on.ca
www.tead.on.ca
Social Media:
www.facebook.com/TEADStables
Also Known As: TEAD
Overview: A small local charitable organization founded in 1978
Description: To enhance the life of children & adults with physical, mental, & emotional handicaps, through equestrian therapy
Chief Officer(s): Hilary Webb, Manager, Programs, 905-679-8323 224
hilary@tead.on.ca
Helen Clayton, Manager, Farm, 905-679-8323 230
helen@tead.on.ca
Finances: *Funding Sources:* Donations; Grants; Fundraising
Membership: *Fees:* Schedule available
Activities: Offering riding therapy, rehabilitation, & recreation to children & adults with disabilities

Equine Association of Yukon (EAY)
PO Box 30011, Whitehorse YT Y1A 5M2
equineyukon@gmail.com
equineyukon.weebly.com
Overview: A small provincial organization
Description: To be the governing body for equine sports in the Yukon.
Membership: *Fees:* $20 junior; $30 senior; $70 family

Equine Canada (EC) / Canada Hippique
#100, 308 Legget Dr., Ottawa ON K2K 1Y6
Tel: 613-287-1515; *Fax:* 613-248-3484
Toll-Free: 866-282-8395
inquiries@equinecanada.ca
www.equinecanada.ca
Social Media:
www.facebook.com/385910086067
twitter.com/Equine_Canada
Previous Name: Canadian Equestrian Federation
Overview: A large national licensing charitable organization founded in 1977
Description: To promote & develop a unified Canadian Equine Community, an economically viable horse industry, & access to the use of horses for leisure, sport & commerce
Affiliation(s): Provincial Partners: Horse Council of B.C., Alberta Equestrian Federation, Saskatchewan Horse Federation, Manitoba Horse Council, Ontario Equestrian Federation, Fédération Équestre du Quebec, New Brunswick Equestrian Association, PEI Horse Council, Nova Scotia Equestrian Federation, Newfoundland Equestrian Association, Canadian Pony Club
Chief Officer(s): Al Patterson, President
Eva Havaris, Chief Executive Officer
Michael Arbour, Chief Financial Officer, 613-287-1515 108
marbour@equinecanada.ca
Finances: *Funding Sources:* Government of Canada; Donations; Memberships
Membership: 56 corporate + 1,165 associate + 4,897 senior + 183 lifetime + 1,736 junior + 436 junior associate; *Fees:* $250 corporate-syndicate; $35 associate; $78 senior; $700 lifetime; $58 junior; $25 junior associate; *Member Profile:* License Profile: Senior Competitive License Holder - owner, lessee, agent, trainer, or EC certified coach; Junior Competitive License Holder - under 18 with the same qualifications; Lifetime - senior license holder level with the same qualifications; Corporate-syndicate - corporations, business enterprises & syndicates which own a horse or horses; Associate - wishes to compete in EC Provincial Circuit shows, or a member of a breed association competing at EC member shows in that breed's classes only; *Committees:* Audit; Governance; Human Resource; Ethics; Finance; Health & Welfare; Nominations; Joint Steering; Recognition & Awards; LTED Competitions Review
Activities: Coaching program; Rider preparation program; *Awareness Events:* Horse Week; *Rents Mailing List:* Yes; *Library:* Yes

Eventing Canada [!]
59 Hillside Dr., Toronto ON M4K 2M1
Tel: 416-429-1415
www.eventingcanada.com
Social Media:
www.facebook.com/EventingCanada
twitter.com/Eventing_Canada
Overview: A small national organization founded in 1996
Description: To independently promote the sport of eventing
Chief Officer(s): Sue Grocott, Contact
sgrocott@eventingcanada.com

Fédération équestre du Québec inc. (FEQ)
4545, av Pierre-de Coubertin, Montréal QC H1V 0B2
Tél: 514-252-3053; *Téléc:* 514-252-3068
Ligne sans frais: 866-575-0515
infocheval@feq.qc.ca
www.feq.qc.ca
Média social:
www.youtube.com/EquestreQuebec
www.facebook.com/386728291214
Aperçu: *Dimension:* moyenne; *Envergure:* provinciale; Organisme sans but lucratif; fondée en 1970
Description: Promotion et développement de l'activité équestre au Québec; *Membre de:* Canadian Equestrian Federation
Membre(s) du bureau directeur: Richard Mongeau, Directeur général
rmongeau@feq.qc.ca
Membre: 12,000; *Montant de la cotisation:* 46$ junior; 56$ senior

Horse Council British Columbia (HCBC)
27336 Fraser Hwy., Aldergrove BC V4W 3N5
Tel: 604-856-4304; *Fax:* 604-856-4302
Toll-Free: 800-345-8055
reception@hcbc.ca
www.hcbc.ca
Social Media:
www.youtube.com/user/HorseCouncilBC/
www.facebook.com/pages/Horse-Council-BC/116275438383133
twitter.com/horsecouncilbc
Overview: A medium-sized provincial organization founded in 1980
Description: To represent members & work on behalf of their equine interests in British Columbia; To preserve equestrian use of public lands; To foster & promote participation in equine activities; To ensure the well-being of horses; *Member of:* Equine Canada
Chief Officer(s): Lisa Laycock, Executive Director
administration@hcbc.ca
Orville Smith, President, 250-964-2269
orsmith@telus.net
Carol Cody, Secretary, 604-855-6890
crazycreek@telus.net
Carolyn Farris, Treasurer, 250-546-6083
farrisfarms@xplornet.com
Finances: *Funding Sources:* Membership dues; Province of British Columbia
Membership: 21,000+; *Member Profile:* Clubs; Individuals & families; Businesses; Affiliates
Activities: Collaborating with individuals, professionals, industry, businesses, & governments to improve education, safety, & communication; Representing the industry in areas of sport, recreation, agriculture, & industry; Providing education; Granting funds & supporting clubs; Presenting awards; *Awareness Events:* Horse Week, June

Horse Trials New Brunswick
c/o Suzanne Stevenson, 16 Gallaway Dr., Lakeside NB E5N 0K9
Fax: 506-696-4403
info@htnb.org
www.htnb.org
Overview: A small provincial organization
Affiliation(s): Horse Trials Canada
Chief Officer(s): Lori Leach, President
Finances: *Annual Operating Budget:* Less than $50,000; *Funding Sources:* Provincial government; membership fees
Membership: 35; *Fees:* $10

Horse Trials Nova Scotia (HTNS)
c/o Pam Macintosh, 53 Normandy Ave., Truro NS B2N 3J6
Tel: 902-893-2042
www.htns.org
Social Media:
www.facebook.com/groups/290523457701524
Overview: A small provincial organization
Description: To foster & encourage safe & fun enjoyment of the sport of Horse Trials (eventing) through regular training & education of riders, coaches, horses & officials; *Member of:* Canadian Equestrian Federation
Affiliation(s): Horse Trials Canada; Nova Scotia Equestrian Federation
Chief Officer(s): Pam Macintosh, President
pmacintosh@bellaliant.net
Finances: *Annual Operating Budget:* Less than $50,000
Staff: 7 staff member(s)
Membership: 1-99; *Fees:* $25 senior; $20 junior; $45 family; $10 associate; *Committees:* Athlete Development; Coaching; Competitions; Officials & Technical Delegate; Crosss Country Course Advisors Panel; Eventing Rules
Activities: Clinics (lessons); course design seminars; competitions; booth & brochures; seminars

Island Horse Council (IHC)
c/o Sport PEI, 40 Enman Cres., Charlottetown PE C1E 1E6
www.islandhorsecouncil.ca
Social Media:
www.facebook.com/islandhorsecouncil
twitter.com/pei_IHC
Overview: A small provincial organization
Description: The objectives of Island Horse Council are: to promote, conduct and manage a Council for the benefit of Prince Edward Island equestrians; to provide a unified voice for the horse industry on Prince Edward Island; to establish a liaison with any authorities, including federal, provincial, and municipal governments, and provincial or national Horse Councils or Equestrian Federations; and to encourage the development of all aspects of horsemanship, health, education, training,

competition, breeding, facilities and humane practices.; *Member of:* Equine Canada; Sport PEI
Chief Officer(s): Gary Evans, Chair
gevans@upei.ca
Frank Szentmiklossy, Treasurer
frank.szentmiklossy@systronix.net
Finances: *Funding Sources:* Sponsorships; PEI Provincial Government, Community & Cultural Affairs
Membership: 600+ individuals & 12 clubs; *Fees:* $35; *Committees:* Insurance/Membership; Provincial Coaching; Strathgartney; Trails & Recreation
Activities: Offering seminars, on topics such as first aid; Liaising with governments & other authorities; Encouraging the certification of coaches

Manitoba Horse Council Inc.
145 Pacific Ave., Winnipeg MB R3B 2Z6
Tel: 204-925-5719; *Fax:* 204-925-5703
mhc.admin@sportmanitoba.ca
www.manitobahorsecouncil.ca
Social Media:
www.facebook.com/pages/Manitoba-Horse-Council/587153197974798
Overview: A medium-sized provincial organization founded in 1974
Description: To represent clubs & individuals involved with equestrian; *Member of:* Equine Canada; Canadian Equestrian Federation
Chief Officer(s): Geri Sweet, President
Bruce Rose, Executive Director
mhc.exec@sportmanitoba.ca
Finances: *Funding Sources:* Manitoba Lotteries Foundation; membership dues
Staff: 3 staff member(s)
Membership: *Fees:* $60.50 senior; $49.50 junior; $121 family; friends of Horses $27.50; *Committees:* Athlete Development; Bingo; Breeds & Industry; Coaching; Competitions; Equestrian Centre; Officials; Recreation; Special Events; Marketing
Activities: *Rents Mailing List:* Yes; *Library:* Yes (Open to Public)

Manitoba Trail Riding Club Inc. (MTRC)
838 Alfred Ave., Winnipeg MB R2X 0T6
www.mbtrailridingclub.ca
Overview: A small provincial organization founded in 1979
Description: To meet the needs of a growing number of horse people who wanted a type of riding other than in the show ring which could demonstrate good horsemanship and promote sound, sensible trail horses; *Member of:* Manitoba Horse Council
Affiliation(s): Canadian Long Distance Riding Association
Chief Officer(s): Iris Oleksuk, President
irisolek@yahoo.com
Mary Anne Kirk, Treasurer, 204-955-7388
yaknow3@hotmail.com
Membership: *Fees:* $25 individual; $40 family

New Brunswick Equestrian Association (NBEA)
#13, 900 Hanwell Rd., Fredericton NB E3B 6A3
Tel: 506-454-2353; *Fax:* 506-454-2363
horses@nbnet.nb.ca
www.nbea.ca
Social Media:
www.facebook.com/equinenb
twitter.com/equinenb
Overview: A small provincial organization
Description: To promote equestrian & provide education in New Brunswick.; *Member of:* Equine Canada
Affiliation(s): New Brunswick SPCA; Maritime Saddle & Tack Ltd.; Government of New Brunswick; P'tit Trot; Greenhawk; Sport New Brunswick
Chief Officer(s): Deanna Phelan, President
deannaphelan@gmail.com
Bonnie Robertson, Secretary
equinenb@gmail.com
Membership: *Fees:* $43 junior; $50 senior; $85 family
Activities: Recreation; Sport; Dressage; Hunter/jumper; Distance riding; Eventing; Racing; Driving; Coaching

Newfoundland Equestrian Association (NEA)
PO Box 372, Stn. C, St. John's NL A1C 5J9
equestriannl.ca
Social Media:
www.facebook.com/groups/1529209380693900
Overview: A small provincial organization
Member of: Equine Canada
Chief Officer(s): Jessica Anstey, President
president@equestriannl.ca
Dominique Lavers, Secretary
secretary@equestriannl.ca
Membership: *Fees:* $35 individual junior (18 years & under); $35 individual senior (19 years & over); $60 family ($10 for additional juniors); $65 club/corporate; *Member Profile:* Equestrians in Newfoundland; Equestrian associations or clubs
Activities: Offering the Learn to Ride program; Providing coaching programs; *Library:* NEA Library

Nova Scotia Equestrian Federation (NSEF)
5516 Spring Garden Rd., 4th Fl., Halifax NS B3J 1G6
Tel: 902-425-5450; *Fax:* 902-425-5606
nsefmembership@sportnovascotia.ca
www.horsenovascotia.ca
Social Media:
twitter.com/NSEquestrian
Overview: A small provincial organization
Member of: Equine Canada
Chief Officer(s): Heather Myrer, Executive Director
nsef@sportnovascotia.ca
Gidget Oxner, Technical Director
nseftd@sportnovascotia.ca
Membership: 2,100; *Fees:* $40

Ontario Competitive Trail Riding Association Inc. (OCTRA)
c/o Doug Price, 457102 Conc. 3A, RR#4, Chatsworth ON N0H 1G0
Tel: 519-377-0652
www.octra.on.ca
Overview: A small provincial organization founded in 1967
Description: To encourage the growth & popularity of competitive trail, endurance riding & Ride'n'Tie; to establish a set of rules & quality for managing & judging same; to encourage & maintain a high standard of horsemanship & sportsmanship amongst competitors; to encourage the selection, care, training & conditioning of horses for long distance riding; to provide guidance & help to clubs & groups in establishing & running competitive rides; to ensure that all rides are run humanely so as to avoid cruelty & suffering to competing animals; to formulate promotional & educational programs; to foster goodwill & understanding between horse owners, land owners & conservation authorities with a view to opening up more land for riding trails; *Member of:* Canadian Long Distance Riding Association
Affiliation(s): Horse Ontario; Ontario Equestrian Federation
Chief Officer(s): Doug Price, President
khofire@gmail.com
Nancy Beacon, Vice-President
rabbitrun1@me.com
Jackie Redmond, Secretary
jackieredmond@sympatico.ca
Michelle Bignell, Treasurer
arabians@cayusecreekranch.com
Membership: *Fees:* $60 family; $45 individual; $35 associate non-voting; $25 junior; *Committees:* Awards; Competitive; Education; Endurance; Fundraising; Mileage Programs; Newsletter; Publicity & Promotions; Ride 'n' Tie; Ride Management/Sanctioning; Set Speed; Veterinary; Website; Worker Credit; Youth
Activities: *Speaker Service:* Yes; *Rents Mailing List:* Yes; *Library:* Archives by appointment

Ontario Equestrian Federation (OEF)
#201, 1 West Pearce St., Richmond Hill ON L4B 3K3
Tel: 905-709-6545; *Fax:* 905-709-1867
Toll-Free: 877-441-7112
horse@horse.on.ca
www.horse.on.ca
Social Media:
instagram.com/oef_horse
www.facebook.com/OEF.Horse
Overview: A medium-sized provincial organization founded in 1977
Description: Committed to equine welfare & to providing leadership & support to the individuals, associations & industries in Ontario's horse community; *Member of:* Equine Canada
Affiliation(s): Equine Guelph; Ontario Trails Council; Ontario Federation of Agriculture; Ontario Minitry of Tourism, Culture & Sport
Chief Officer(s): Mark Nelson, President, 613-227-9784
mark@oakhurstfarm.com
Iryna Konstantynova, Director, Finance, 905-709-6545 16
i.konstantynova@horse.on.ca
Pam Coburn, Manager, Coaching & Stables Program, 905-709-6545 26
p.coburn@horse.on.ca
Lesley McCoy, Coordinator, Operations, 905-709-6545 13
l.mccoy@horse.on.ca
Finances: *Annual Operating Budget:* $250,000-$500,000; *Funding Sources:* Membership dues; government grant; merchandise sales
Staff: 14 staff member(s); 100 volunteer(s)
Membership: 22,000 individuals; *Fees:* Schedule available; *Member Profile:* Individuals, associations & corporations with interests in equine sport & industry; *Committees:* Associations; Competitions; Horse Facilities; Industry; Recreation
Activities: Education; equine welfare; member services; competitions administration; coaching certification; industry promotion; *Awareness Events:* Horse Day, June; Royal Agricultural Winter Fair, Nov.; Can-Am Equine Emporium, March; *Rents Mailing List:* Yes; *Library:* Yes (Open to Public)

Ontario Horse Trials Association (OHTA)
#201, 1 West Pearce St., Richmond Hill ON L4B 3K3
Tel: 905-709-6545; *Toll-Free:* 877-441-7112
ohtainfo@gmail.com
www.horsetrials.on.ca
Social Media:
www.facebook.com/Ontariohorsetrials
Previous Name: Ontario Horse Trials Canada
Overview: A small provincial charitable organization founded in 1965
Description: OHTA is a volunteer, not-for-profit organization whose main functions are to support, develop & promote events in Ontario.; *Member of:* Canadian Equestrian Federation
Chief Officer(s): Katie Holman, President
katieh22@live.com
Lisa Thompson, Secretary
lisat26@sympatico.ca
Finances: *Annual Operating Budget:* Less than $50,000
Staff: 1 staff member(s)
Membership: 1,257; *Fees:* $35 senior; $25 junior; $126 family; $30 associate; $100 corporate; *Committees:* Championship Selection; Competitions; Young Riders; Event Evaluations; Event Schedule; Funding Programs; Officials; Omnibus; Omnibus Ad Sales; Organizer Meeting; Volunteer Incentive Program; Communications; Memberships; Points/Leaderboard; AGM/Banquet/Royal Winter Fair; Strategic Planning; Coach Outreach Program; Rules; Safety; Budget/Financial Statements
Activities: Overall program development, implementation & monitoring programs regarding the sport

Ontario Trail Riders Association (OTRA)
PO Box 3038, Elmvale ON L0L 1P0
www.otra.ca
Overview: A small provincial organization founded in 1970
Description: To identify, develop, & preserve multi-use trails throughout Ontario
Affiliation(s): Ontario Trails Council; Ontario Equestrian Federation
Chief Officer(s): Helmut Hitscherich, President
helmuthit@gmail.com
Membership: 100-499; *Fees:* $30 single; $50 family; *Committees:* Trail Development; Government Relations; Public Relations; Trail Rides; Education

Professional Association of Therapeutic Horsemanship International (PATH)
PO Box 33150, Denver CO 80233 USA
Tel: 303-452-1212; *Fax:* 303-252-4610
Toll-Free: 800-369-7433
www.pathintl.org
Previous Name: North American Riding for the Handicapped Association
Overview: A medium-sized international charitable organization founded in 1969
Description: Promotes the benefit of the horse riding for individuals with physical, emotional & learning disabilities
Chief Officer(s): Kathy Alm, Chief Executive Officer
kalm@pathintl.org
Membership: 1,000-4,999; *Fees:* $355-$2000

Saskatchewan Horse Federation (SHF)
2205 Victoria Ave., Regina SK S4P 0S4
Tel: 306-780-9449; *Fax:* 306-525-4041
shfadmin@sasktel.net
www.saskhorse.ca
Social Media:
www.facebook.com/SaskHorse
Overview: A medium-sized provincial organization founded in 1976
Description: To work with other equestrian organizations in order to bring educational & recreational programs to the public.; *Member of:* Equine Canada
Affiliation(s): Sask Sport; Western College Veterinary Medicine; SK Agriculture & Food (SAF)
Chief Officer(s): Pam Duckworth, Senior Administrator
pamduckworth@saskhorse.ca
Finances: *Funding Sources:* Self-help; Saskatchewan Lotteries
Staff: 2 staff member(s)
Membership: *Fees:* $50 adults; $35 junior; $120 family; $85-$225 clubs; *Member Profile:* Individuals; family; corporate; clubs; sustaining
Activities: Coaching certification; competition circuit; clinics; grants; rider certification; officials development; horse industry; member insurance; Horsin' Around raffle; Agribition; Youth Equestrian Games; Sask Horse Week

Trail Riding Alberta Conference (TRAC)
PO Box 44, RR#4, Site 5, Lacombe AB T4L 2N4
Tel: 403-782-7363
office@trailriding.ca
www.trailriding.ca
Social Media:
www.facebook.com/299797026778773
Overview: A small provincial organization
Description: To promote long-distance horse riding
Affiliation(s): Canadian Long Distance Riding Association
Chief Officer(s): Ken Vanderwekken, President
Finances: *Funding Sources:* Fundraising; membership fees; ride fees
Membership: 166
Activities: Three divisions: novice, intermediate & open; three categories within each: junior, lightweight & heavyweight.; *Speaker Service:* Yes; *Library:* Long Distance Info (Open to Public)

Yukon Horse & Rider Association (YHRA)
PO Box 31482, Whitehorse YT Y1A 6K8
yukonhorseandriderassociation@gmail.com
yukonhorseandrider.wordpress.com
Social Media:
www.facebook.com/186825158005753
Overview: A medium-sized provincial organization
Description: The YHRA is dedicated to the sport of horseback riding in the Yukon Territory, Canada. The Association aims to encourage good horsemanship & help promote interest in the light horse industry.
Membership: 100+; *Fees:* $40 senior; $30 junior; $65 family; *Committees:* Events; Development

Fencing

Alberta Fencing Association (AFA)
Percy Page Centre, 11759 Groat Rd., Edmonton AB T5M 3K6
Tel: 780-427-9474
info@fencing.ab.ca
www.fencing.ab.ca
Overview: A small provincial organization founded in 1976
Description: To promote the sport of fencing in Alberta; *Member of:* Canadian Fencing Federation
Chief Officer(s): Sean Rathwell, Executive Director
ed@fencing.ab.ca
Finances: *Annual Operating Budget:* $250,000-$500,000
Staff: 1 staff member(s); 16 volunteer(s)
Membership: 800+; *Fees:* $30 associate; $65 competitive

British Columbia Fencing Association (BCFA)
#15, 12900 Jack Bell Dr., Richmond BC V6V 2V8
www.fencing.bc.ca
Social Media:
twitter.com/FENCINGBC
Also Known As: Fencing BC
Overview: A small provincial organization
Description: To promote fencing in BC; To set policies & procedures which govern programs & events
Chief Officer(s): John French, President
president.bcfa@gmail.com
Membership: 15; *Fees:* $40 individual; $65 club

Canadian Fencing Federation (CFF) / Fédération canadienne d'escrime
10 Masterson Dr., St Catharines ON L2T 3P1
Tel: 647-476-2401; *Fax:* 647-476-2402
cff@fencing.ca
www.fencing.ca
Social Media:
www.facebook.com/168914029806258
twitter.com/fencingcanada
Also Known As: Fencing Canada
Overview: A medium-sized national charitable organization founded in 1971
Description: To promote & develop the sport of fencing in Canada
Affiliation(s): Fédération internationale d'escrime
Chief Officer(s): Caroline Sharp, Executive Director
ed@fencing.ca
Finances: *Funding Sources:* Membership fees; Government; Olympic Association
Staff: 3 staff member(s)

Fédération d'escrime du Québec
4545, av Pierre-de Coubertin, Montréal QC H1V 0B2
Tél: 514-252-3045; *Téléc:* 514-254-3451
info@escrimequebec.qc.ca
www.escrimequebec.qc.ca
Média social:
www.facebook.com/280110325350969
Aperçu: *Dimension:* moyenne; *Envergure:* provinciale
Membre(s) du bureau directeur: Marc Lavoie, Directeur
mlavoie@uottawa.ca

Fencing - Escrime New Brunswick (FENB)
47 Sloat St., Hanwell NB E3C 1M4
fencingnb@gmail.com
www.fencingnb.ca
Previous Name: New Brunswick Fencing Association
Overview: A small provincial organization
Description: To promote & develop the sport of fencing in New Brunswick; *Member of:* Canadian Fencing Federation; Sport New Brunswick
Chief Officer(s): Melodie Piercey, Contact
Membership: *Fees:* $20 associate; $25 first-time member; $60 fencing member

Fencing Association of Nova Scotia (FANS) / Association d'escrime de la Nouvelle-Écosse
c/o Sport Nova Scotia, 5516 Spring Garden Rd., 4th Fl., Halifax NS B3J 3G6
Fax: 902-425-5606
info@nsfencing.ca
www.nsfencing.ca
Social Media:
www.facebook.com/246284375433922
twitter.com/FencingNS
Overview: A small provincial organization
Description: To develop & promote the sport of fencing in Nova Scotia; *Member of:* Canadian Fencing Federation
Chief Officer(s): DeAnna Paul, President
drpaul@hotmail.ca
Member Profile: National fencing competitors; Provincial fencing competitors; Recreational fencers; Persons who wish to promote fencing
Activities: Providing information about tournaments

Manitoba Fencing Association (MFA)
#308, 145 Pacific Ave., Winnipeg MB R3B 2Z6
Tel: 204-925-5696; *Fax:* 204-925-5703
fencing@sportmanitoba.ca
www.fencing.mb.ca
Social Media:
www.facebook.com/199898656787720
Overview: A small provincial organization founded in 1978
Description: To promote & develop the sport of fencing in Manitoba
Chief Officer(s): David Cohen, Executive Director
Finances: *Funding Sources:* Fundraising
Staff: 2 staff member(s)
Member Profile: Fencing clubs in Manitoba
Activities: Organizing training programs for high level athletes; Offering coaching training opportunities & clinics; Providing certification opportunities for officials; Conducting school & community outreach programs

Newfoundland & Labrador Fencing Association (N&LFA)
#168, Unit 50 Hamlyn Road Plaza, St. John's NL A1E 5X7
Tel: 709-368-8830
nlfencing@gmail.com
sites.google.com/site/nlfencing
Overview: A small provincial organization
Description: To promote & develop the sport of fencing in Newfoundland
Chief Officer(s): Justin So, President
Membership: 70

Ontario Fencing Association (OFA) / Association d'escrime de l'Ontario
c/o Laurence Bishop, Executive Director, 177 Old River Rd., RR #2, Mallorytown ON K0E 1R0
Tel: 519-496-0613
fencingontario.ca
Overview: A medium-sized provincial organization
Description: To promote & develop the sport of fencing in Ontario
Chief Officer(s): Laurence Bishop, Executive Director
lbishop@fencingontario.ca
Membership: *Fees:* $5 associate; $20 recreation; $80 competitive; $35 coaches & officials

Prince Edward Island Fencing Association (PEIFA)
c/o Sport PEI, PO Box 302, 40 Enman Cres., Charlottetown PE C1A 7K7
Tel: 902-368-4110; *Fax:* 902-386-4548
Toll-Free: 800-247-6712
sports@sportpei.pe.ca
people.upei.ca/fencing/main.htm
Overview: A small provincial organization
Description: To promote & develop the sport of fencing in PEI; *Member of:* Sport PEI
Chief Officer(s): Phil Stewart, Contact, 902-566-1073
pstewart@pei.sympatico.ca
Membership: *Fees:* $25 student; $200 regular

Saskatchewan Fencing Association (SFA)
c/o Marcia Coulic Salahub, Office Manager, 510 Cynthia St., Saskatoon SK S7L 7K7
Tel: 306-975-0823
saskfencing@shaw.ca
saskfencing.com
Social Media:
www.facebook.com/SaskFencingAssoc
twitter.com/SKFencingAssoc
Overview: A small provincial charitable organization
Description: To promote & develop the sport of fencing in Saskatchewan
Affiliation(s): Saskatchewan Sport
Chief Officer(s): Marcia Coulic-Salahub, Office Manager
Finances: *Annual Operating Budget:* $100,000-$250,000; *Funding Sources:* Saskatchewan Sport; Fundraising
Staff: 14 staff member(s); 20 volunteer(s)
Membership: 300; *Fees:* Schedule available
Activities: Organizing competitions & training camps

Field Hockey

Field Hockey Alberta (FHA)
#1, 2135 Westmount Rd. NW, Calgary AB T2N 3N3
Tel: 403-670-0014; *Fax:* 403-670-0018
Toll-Free: 888-670-0018
info@fieldhockey.ab.ca
www.fieldhockey.ab.ca
Social Media:
www.facebook.com/105274359520461
Merged from: Alberta Field Hockey Association
Overview: A small provincial charitable organization founded in 1974
Description: To develop field hockey for all in Alberta; To provide & facilitate provincial field hockey teams; *Member of:* Field Hockey Canada
Chief Officer(s): Burgundy Biletski, Executive Director
burgundy@fieldhockey.ab.ca
Membership: 800; *Fees:* Schedule available; *Committees:* High Performance; Umpiring; South/North Alberta
Activities: School programs, clinics, festivals, equipment rentals; *Speaker Service:* Yes; *Library:* Yes (Open to Public) by appointment

Field Hockey Canada (FHC) / Hockey sur gazon Canada
311 West 1st St., North Vancouver BC V7M 1B5
www.fieldhockey.ca
Social Media:
www.youtube.com/user/hockeysurgazoncanada
www.facebook.com/FHCanada
twitter.com/FieldHockeyCan
Previous Name: Canadian Field Hockey Association
Overview: A medium-sized national charitable organization founded in 1991
Description: To promote the development & growth of field hockey in Canada; To provide coaching, training, & competitive opportunities to prepare Canada's national teams; *Member of:* International Hockey Federation (FIH); Pan American Hockey Federation (PAHF)
Chief Officer(s): Jeff Sauvé, Chief Executive Officer
jsauve@fieldhockey.ca
Shaheed Devji, Manager, Creative & Communication
sdevji@fieldhockey.ca
Finances: *Funding Sources:* Sponsorships; Donations
Membership: 7 provincial associations; *Fees:* $20; *Member Profile:* Members of Field Hockey Canada member clubs
Activities: Hosting world class field hockey events in Canada; Seeking partnerships with corporations; Offering technical programs

Field Hockey Manitoba (FHM)
MB
info@fieldhockeymb.org
www.fieldhockeymb.org
Social Media:
www.facebook.com/fieldhockey.manitoba
Overview: A small provincial organization
Description: The Association fosters growth & development of field hockey & indoor hockey in Manitoba.; *Member of:* Field Hockey Canada
Membership: 100; *Fees:* Schedule available

Field Hockey Nova Scotia
5516 Spring Garden Rd., 4th Fl., Halifax NS B3J 1G6
Tel: 902-425-5450
info@fieldhockey.ns.ca
www.fieldhockey.ns.ca
Overview: A small provincial organization founded in 1971
Description: The Association promotes the sport of field hockey for both men & women in the province of Nova Scotia.; *Member of:* Field Hockey Canada
Chief Officer(s): Sharon Rajaraman, President
president@fieldhockey.ns.ca
Patrick Thompson, Administrative Coordinator

Field Hockey Ontario (FHO)
PO Box 80030, Stn. Appleby, Burlington ON L7L 6B1
Tel: 905-492-1680
info@fieldhockeyontario.com
www.fieldhockeyontario.com
Social Media:
www.facebook.com/FieldHockeyOntario
twitter.com/FieldHockeyOnt
Merged from: Ontario Field Hockey Association; Women's Field Hockey Association
Overview: A medium-sized provincial organization founded in 1985
Description: To promote the sport of field hockey for both men & women in the province of Ontario.; *Member of:* Field Hockey Canada
Chief Officer(s): Ramandeep Brar, President
ramandeep.brar@fieldhockeyontario.com
Joseph Fernando, Coordinator, High Performance/Athlete & Coach Development
joseph.fernando@fieldhockeyontario.com
Bimal Jhass, Coordinator, Technical
bimal.jhass@fieldhockeyontario.com
Finances: *Annual Operating Budget:* $100,000-$250,000; *Funding Sources:* Sponsorship; government grants; membership fees
Staff: 3 staff member(s); 180 volunteer(s)
Membership: 6,000; *Fees:* Schedule available
Activities: *Internships:* Yes

PEI Field Hockey Association
40 Enman Cres., Charlottetown PE C1A 1E6
Tél: 902-368-4110; *Téléc:* 902-368-4548
Ligne sans frais: 800-247-6712
sports@sportpei.pe.ca
Aperçu: *Dimension:* moyenne; *Envergure:* provinciale
Membre(s) du bureau directeur: Barb Carmichael, President, 902-566-4056
bcarmichael@eastlink.ca

Saskatchewan Field Hockey Association
1860 Lorne St., Regina SK S4P 2L7
Tel: 306-780-9256; *Fax:* 306-781-6021
sfha@sasktel.net
Overview: A small provincial organization
Description: To promote the sport of field hockey in Saskatchewan.; *Member of:* Field Hockey Canada

Fishing & Angling

Barrow Bay & District Sports Fishing Association (BB&DSFA)
PO Box 987, Lions Head ON N0H 1W0
Fax: 519-793-3363
barrowbayfishing@hotmail.com
www.bltg.com/bbdsfa
Overview: A small local organization founded in 1993
Member of: Ontario Federation of Anglers & Hunters
Affiliation(s): Ontario Federation of Anglers & Hunters
Finances: *Annual Operating Budget:* $50,000-$100,000; *Funding Sources:* Membership dues; fundraising; government grants
Membership: 92; *Member Profile:* Anglers, residents & associates who reside or who have seasonal residences in the vicinity of Barrow Bay & Lion's Head, Ontario, Canada

Edmonton Trout Fishing Club
Edmonton AB
info@edmontontrout.ca
www.edmontontrout.ca
Social Media:
www.facebook.com/EdmontonTroutFishingClub
Overview: A small local charitable organization founded in 1953
Description: To foster, instruct & promote the art of fly tying, fly casting, & the betterment of trout fishing among its members; *Member of:* Alberta Fish & Game Association
Finances: *Funding Sources:* Membership fees; auction
Membership: *Fees:* $40
Activities: Shares stream enhancement projects with Trout Unlimited

Guysborough County Inshore Fishermen's Association (GCIFA)
PO Box 98, 990 Union St., Canso NS B0H 1H0
Tel: 902-366-2266; *Fax:* 902-366-2679
gcifa@gcifa.ns.ca
www.gcifa.ns.ca
Social Media:
www.facebook.com/GuysboroughCountyInshoreFishermensAssociation
Overview: A small local organization
Description: To provide community based management of the fishing resource & to ensure a sustainable resource fishery & habitat, healthy fish stocks & act as an information liaison between inshore fishermen & the Dept. of Fisheries, as well as provide effective representation within the industry & other associations.
Chief Officer(s): Eugene O'Leary, President
Virginia Boudreau, Manager
Katherine Newell, Lab Technician/Researcher
knewell@gcifa.ns.ca
Membership: 134

New Brunswick Sportfishing Association (NBSFA)
c/o Bert Beek, 758 Rte. 670, Ripples NB E4B 1E9
Tel: 506-385-2335
www.nbsportfishing.ca
Social Media:
www.facebook.com/550441211657133
Overview: A small provincial organization
Description: To elevate the sport of bass fishing in New Brunswick
Finances: *Funding Sources:* Membership fees; Sponsorships
Membership: *Fees:* $50; *Member Profile:* Persons, 19 years of age or older, who are eligible to purchase a fishing license in New Brunswick; Persons, under age 19, who are recommended by a member; Organizations which provide finanial support to the association
Activities: Hosting tournaments; Promoting catch & release programs; Liaising with the government for new regulations for tournament bass fishing; Improving fish handling methods; Helping to fund studies on smallmouth bass in New Brunswick

Ontario Sportfishing Guides' Association (OSGA)
4504 Trent Trail, Washago ON L0K 2B0
Tel: 705-689-3332; *Fax:* 705-689-1085
info@ontariofishcharters.ca
www.ontariofishcharters.ca
Previous Name: Ontario Charterboat Association
Overview: A small provincial organization founded in 1980
Description: To monitor & participate in any regulation reform regarding sportfishing in the province; to lobby as a unified voice on behalf of its members, & serve as a network where members can promote & learn from each other.
Chief Officer(s): George Watkins, Secretary
Finances: *Funding Sources:* Membership fees
Membership: *Fees:* $100; *Member Profile:* Professional fishing charter boat operators & guides

Football

Alberta Amateur Football Association (AAFA)
Percy Page Centre, 11759 Groat Rd., Edmonton AB T5M 3K6
Tel: 780-427-8108; *Fax:* 780-422-2663
admin@footballalberta.ab.ca
www.footballalberta.ab.ca
Social Media:
www.facebook.com/pages/Football-Alberta/503709906338891
twitter.com/FootballAlberta
Also Known As: Football Alberta
Overview: A medium-sized provincial organization founded in 1973
Description: To provide a consistent representative voice for football of all levels throughout the province of Alberta; *Member of:* Football Canada
Chief Officer(s): Jay Hetherington, President
jhetherington@rdpsd.ab.ca
Brian Fryer, Executive Director
bfryer@telus.net
Membership: *Fees:* Schedule available

Canadian Football Hall of Fame & Museum
58 Jackson St. West, Hamilton ON L8P 1L4
Tel: 905-528-7566; *Fax:* 905-528-9781
info@cfhof.ca
www.cfhof.ca
Social Media:
www.youtube.com/user/CFHOFandM
www.facebook.com/CFHOFandM
twitter.com/cfhof
Overview: A small national charitable organization founded in 1963
Description: The Hall & Museum commemorate & promote the names & careers of those who have contributed to the development of Canadian football. Artifacts & other memorabilia that relate to the history of the sport are collected, preserved, documented, & exhibited. Education programs offered to students, grades K-8. The Hall & Museum are a non-profit, registered charity, BN: 106845993RR0001.
Chief Officer(s): Dave Marler, Chair
Mark DeNobile, Executive Director
mark@cfhof.ca
Christopher Alfred, Curator
chris@cfhof.ca
Finances: *Annual Operating Budget:* $100,000-$250,000
Staff: 2 staff member(s); 70 volunteer(s)
Activities: Induction weekend; Grey Cup week; school outreach program; gift shop; collections; *Library:* Yes by appointment

Canadian Football League (CFL) / Ligue canadienne de football (LCF)
50 Wellington St. East, 3rd Fl., Toronto ON M5E 1C8
Tel: 416-322-9650; *Fax:* 416-322-9651
www.cfl.ca
Social Media:
www.youtube.com/CFL
www.facebook.com/CFL
twitter.com/CFL
Overview: A large national licensing organization founded in 1958
Affiliation(s): Canadian Football League Players' Association (CFLPA); Canadian Football League Alumni Association (CFLAA); Football Canada; Canadian Interuniversity Sport (CIS); Canadian Football Hall of Fame; Canadian Football Officials Association
Chief Officer(s): Mark Cohon, Commissioner
Michael Copeland, President & COO
David Cuddy, Vice-President, Finance & Business Operations
Matt Maychak, Vice-President, Communications & Public Affairs
Christina Litz, Senior Vice-President, Content & Marketing
Glen Johnson, Senior Vice-President, Football
Kevin McDonald, Vice-President, Football Operations
Membership: 9 CFL teams
Activities: *Awareness Events:* Grey Cup Championship Game; *Rents Mailing List:* Yes

Canadian Football League Alumni Association (CFLAA)
ON
Tel: 905-639-6359; *Toll-Free:* 877-890-7272
www.cflaa.ca
Social Media:
www.youtube.com/user/CFLAlumniAssociation
www.facebook.com/cflaa
twitter.com/CFL_Alumni
Overview: A large national organization
Description: To foster a lifelong connection between the Canadian Football League & its alumni; to provide support to the alumni community
Chief Officer(s): Hector Pothier, President
Leo Ezerins, Executive Director
leo@cflalumni.org
Finances: *Funding Sources:* Donations

Canadian Football Officials Association (CFOA) / Association Canadienne des Officiels de Football (ACOF)
www.cfoa-acof.ca
Overview: A medium-sized national organization founded in 1969
Chief Officer(s): Ron Paluzzi, Secretary-Treasurer
rpaluzzi@3macs.com

Canadian Junior Football League (CJFL)
www.cjfl.net
Social Media:
www.facebook.com/166507583399023
twitter.com/cjflnews
Overview: A large national organization founded in 1908

Description: To foster community involvement & a positive environment; to teach discipline, perseverance & cooperation; *Member of:* Football Canada
Chief Officer(s): Jim Pankovich, Commissioner
Frank Naso, Deputy Commissioner
Paul Shortt, Executive Director
Ryan Watters, Director, Communications & Digital Media
ryan@onairenterprises.com
Membership: 20 teams; *Member Profile:* Young men aged 17-22
Activities: Canadian Bowl (National championship)

Canadian University Football Coaches Association (CUFCA)

Overview: A small national organization founded in 1977
Description: To improve the coaching of Canadian Interuniversity Athletic Union (CIAU) football teams; to improve the technical aspects of play in CIAU football
Affiliation(s): Canadian Interuniversity Athletic Union
Membership: 60 individuals + 24 teams; *Fees:* $40

Football BC

#434, 6540 Hastings St., Burnaby BC V5B 4Z5
Tel: 604-677-1025
communications@playfootball.bc.ca
www.playfootball.bc.ca
Social Media:
www.facebook.com/footballbc
twitter.com/Football_BC
Also Known As: British Columbia Amateur Football Association
Overview: A medium-sized provincial organization
Description: To operate as the governing body for amateur football in British Columbia. Office location: #222, 6939 Hastings St., Burnaby, BC, V5B 1S9
Chief Officer(s): Patrick Waslen, Executive Director
Membership: 6 associations; *Member Profile:* Football leagues, coaches & officials
Activities: Clnics; Camp; Education sessions

Football Canada

#100, 2255 St. Laurent Blvd., Ottawa ON K1G 4K3
Tel: 613-564-0003; *Fax:* 613-564-6309
info@footballcanada.com
footballcanada.com
Social Media:
www.youtube.com/user/cfltv
www.facebook.com/FootballCanada
twitter.com/FootballCanada
Also Known As: Canadian Amateur Football Association
Previous Name: Canadian Rugby Union
Overview: A medium-sized national charitable organization founded in 1882
Description: Through its members, to initate, regulate, & manage the programs, services & activities that promote participation & excellence in Canadian Amateur Football.
Chief Officer(s): Kim Wudrick, President
Shannon Donovan, Executive Director
sdonovan@footballcanada.com
Aaron Geisler, Manager, Development
ageisler@footballcanada.com
Patrick DeLottinville, Coordinator, Communications
pdelottinville@footballcanada.com
Jean-François Lefebvre, Coordinator, Program Development
jflefebvret@footballcanada.com
Finances: *Annual Operating Budget:* $250,000-$500,000; *Funding Sources:* Membership fees; government; corporate sponsors
Membership: 110,000
Activities: Football Canada Cup; Touch Bowl

Football Nova Scotia Association

5516 Spring Garden Rd., Halifax NS B3J 1G6
Tel: 902-425-5450; *Fax:* 902-425-5606
footballns@ns.aliantzinc.ca
www.footballnovascotia.ca
Social Media:
www.facebook.com/footballnovascotia
twitter.com/footballns
Overview: A small provincial organization founded in 1974
Description: To promote amateur football in Nova Scotia, at both the competitive & recreational levels, to assist members with their programs, & to develop the sport in new areas of the province
Affiliation(s): Canadian Amateur Football Association
Chief Officer(s): Richard MacLean, President
football@eastlink.ca
Rob Manson, Vice-President
rmanson@oceansecurities.com
Finances: *Funding Sources:* Provincial Government
Staff: 1 staff member(s); 14 volunteer(s)
Membership: 1,000 individual
Activities: *Rents Mailing List:* Yes

Football PEI

40 Enman Cres., Charlottetown PE C1E 1E6
Tel: 902-368-4262; *Fax:* 902-368-4548
www.peifootball.ca
Social Media:
twitter.com/footballpei
Overview: A large provincial organization
Description: To operate as the provincial sport governing body for amateur football in Prince Edward Island; To promote & further the development of the sport in its three forms - flag, tackle, & touch
Chief Officer(s): Glen Flood, Executive Director
gflood@sportpei.pe.ca
Shaun Matheson, President
matheson_shaun@yahoo.com

Football Québec (FFAQ) / Fédération de football amateur de Québec

4545, av Pierre-de Coubertin, Montréal QC H1V 0B2
Tél: 514-252-3059; *Téléc:* 514-252-5216
footballquebec.com
Mèdia social:
www.facebook.com/footballquebec
twitter.com/footballquebec
Aperçu: *Dimension:* moyenne; *Envergure:* provinciale; fondée en 1882
Description: Régir le développement du football au Québec, avec règlement de securité, formation des entraîneurs et des officiels, et les championnats provinciaux; *Membre de:* Sport Québec
Affiliation(s): National Football Federation of Canada
Membre(s) du bureau directeur: Jean-Charles Meffe, Directeur général, 514-252-3059 3514
Finances: *Budget de fonctionnement annuel:* $250,000-$500,000; *Fonds:* Gouvernement provincial
Personnel: 3 membre(s) du personnel; 3000 bénévole(s)
Membre: 15 000

Ontario Football Alliance

7384 Wellington Rd. 30, #B, Guelph ON N1H 6J2
Tel: 519-780-0200; *Fax:* 519-780-0705
Toll-Free: 888-313-9419
www.ontariofootball.ca
Social Media:
www.youtube.com/channel/UCNtsuz7nHyHJOCJfciYPZ3A
www.facebook.com/ontariofootball
twitter.com/Ontariofootball
Previous Name: Football Ontario
Overview: A medium-sized provincial organization founded in 1971
Description: To develop football in Ontario by providing programs to improve the game through participation & mandates developed by its membership; *Member of:* Football Canada
Chief Officer(s): Tina Turner, Executive Director
director@ontariofootball.ca
Don Edwards, President
president@ontariofootball.ca
Membership: *Fees:* $25 tackle; $10 coach; $100 association; $500 league
Activities: *Rents Mailing List:* Yes; *Library:* Yes (Open to Public) by appointment

Thunder Bay Minor Football Association (TBMFA)

535 Chapples Dr., Thunder Bay ON P7C 2V7
Tel: 807-251-5052
www.tbmfa.com
Social Media:
www.facebook.com/tbmfa.knights
twitter.com/TBMFAKNIGHTS
Overview: A small local organization founded in 2013
Description: To run a football program for boys & girls ages 7-13 in Thunder Bay
Chief Officer(s): Rob Thompson, President
Sarah Kuzik, Secretary
spkuzik@shaw.ca

Touch Football Ontario (TFO)

21 Bird Cres., Ajax ON L1S 5G3
Tel: 416-399-8792
info@tfont.com
www.tfont.com
Overview: A medium-sized provincial organization
Description: To organize touch football games among amateur teams in Ontario; to represent the sport within the province
Chief Officer(s): Russ Henderson, President
president@tfont.com
Member Profile: Touch football teams

Foundations

Canadian Athletes Now Fund / Fonds des Athlétes Canadiens (FDAC)

106 Berkeley St., Toronto ON M5A 2W7
Tel: 416-487-4442; *Toll-Free:* 866-937-2012
info@canadianathletesnow.ca
www.canadianathletesnow.ca
Social Media:
www.youtube.com/user/CanadianAthletesNow
www.facebook.com/CANFund
Also Known As: See You In CAN Fund; CAN Fund
Overview: A medium-sized national charitable organization
Description: To provide financial assistance to amateur athletes in Canada. It is a registered charity: 856858642RR0003.
Chief Officer(s): Jane Roos, Founder & Executive Director
Finances: *Funding Sources:* Fundraising

Dr. James Naismith Basketball Foundation / La fondation de basketball Dr James Naismith

2729 Draper Ave., Ottawa ON K2H 7A1
Tel: 613-256-3610
www.naismithbasketball.ca
Also Known As: Naismith Foundation; Naismith Museum & Hall of Fame
Overview: A medium-sized national charitable organization founded in 1989
Description: To establish & operate the Naismith International Basketball Centre which will reflect the remarkable heritage & development of Naismith's game in Canada & around the world.
Affiliation(s): Basketball Canada
Finances: *Funding Sources:* Fundraising; merchandise sales; special events
Activities: To preserve, conserve & promote the life & times of Dr. James Naismith & his gift to mankind - basketball, through the museum & related programs; *Library:* Naismith Basketball Resource Collection by appointment

Golf Canada Foundation

#1, 1333 Dorval Dr., Oakville ON L6M 4X7
Tel: 905-849-9700; *Fax:* 905-845-7040
Toll-Free: 800-263-0009
www.golfcanadafoundation.com
Also Known As: RCGA Foundation
Previous Name: Canadian Golf Foundation
Overview: A medium-sized national charitable organization founded in 1979
Description: To raise & grant funds for the betterment of golf in Canada
Chief Officer(s): Spencer Snell, Operations Manager, Golf Canada Foundation
ssnell@golfcanada.ca
Finances: *Funding Sources:* Private & corporate donations
Staff: 2 staff member(s)
Activities: *Internships:* Yes

Newfoundland & Labrador Powerlifting Association

c/o Jason Fancey, 101 Branscombe St., St. John's NL A1A 5R2
Tel: 709-579-1623
www.nlpowerlifting.ca
Overview: A small provincial organization
Member of: Canadian Powerlifting Union
Chief Officer(s): Jason Fancey, President
jasonfancey@gmail.com
Membership: *Fees:* $50 regular; $30 special olympian

Saint John Jeux Canada Games Foundation Inc. / La Fondation Jeux Canada Games Saint John, Inc.

206 King St. West, Saint John NB E2M 1S6
Tel: 506-634-1985
cdagamesapps@acmca.com
www.sjcanadagamesfoundation.ca
Overview: A small national charitable organization founded in 1986
Description: To promote amateur athletics not only in New Brunswick, but across Canada, by providing funding for athletes, amateur athletic organizations, governing bodies, universities & others involved in the training & development of amateur athletes.
Chief Officer(s): Jeff White, Chair

Fundraising

WinSport Canada
88 Canada Olympic Rd. SW, Calgary AB T3B 5R5
Tel: 403-247-5452
info@coda.ca
www.winsportcanada.ca
Social Media:
www.youtube.com/channel/UCXyy8HyMGaBiVmAY-ZZVLsQ
www.facebook.com/CanadaOlympicPark
twitter.com/winsportcanada
Previous Name: Calgary Olympic Development Association
Overview: A small local organization founded in 1956
Description: WinSport Canada is a not-for-profit association that develops & sustains the sporting facilities of Canada Olympic Park. It supports national sports organizations & subsidizes unique facilities used by top athletes & the public.; *Member of:* Calgary Society of Associations Executives
Affiliation(s): Canadian Olympic Committee; Canadian Paralympic Committee
Chief Officer(s): Robert (Bob) Hamilton, Chair
Barry Heck, President & CEO
Activities: Fundraising for Canada Wins, a winter sports institute

Golf

Alberta Golf Association (AGA)
#22, 11410 - 27 St. SE, Calgary AB T2Z 3R6
Tel: 403-236-4616; *Fax:* 403-236-2915
Toll-Free: 888-414-4849
info@albertagolf.org
www.albertagolf.org
Social Media:
www.instagram.com/alberta_golf
www.facebook.com/144026188016
twitter.com/Alberta_Golf
Overview: A medium-sized provincial organization founded in 1912
Description: To promote the positive impacts of golf on both individuals & communities across Alberta; To improve the quality of life for Albertans through sport
Chief Officer(s): Matt Rollins, Executive Director, 403-613-3034
matt@albertagolf.org
Jack Lane, Chief Operating Officer, 403-698-4631
jack@albertagolf.org
Finances: *Funding Sources:* Membership fees; Fundraising; Sponsorships
Staff: 7 staff member(s)
Membership: 57,000 individual + 225 clubs; *Fees:* Schedule available; *Member Profile:* Organized golf clubs in Alberta & member golfers
Activities: *Speaker Service:* Yes; *Library:* Yes (Open to Public) by appointment

Association des golfeurs professionnels du Québec (AGP)
435, boul Saint-Luc, Saint-Jean-sur-Richelieu QC J2W 1E7
Tél: 450-349-5525; *Téléc:* 450-349-6640
agpinfo@agp.qc.ca
www.agp.qc.ca
Média social:
/www.youtube.com/user/AGPduQuebec
www.facebook.com/384893361542645
twitter.com/AGPduQuebec
Aperçu: *Dimension:* petite; *Envergure:* provinciale; fondée en 1927
Description: Vouée à la promotion et à l'évolution du golf
Membre(s) du bureau directeur: Jean Châtelain, Président
Jean Trudeau, Directeur général
jtrudeau@agp.qc.ca
Membre: 500; *Comités:* Finance-vérification; Formation/éducation; Discipline et administrateur; Gouvernance; Ressources humaines; Assistance aux membres; Discipline

Association des surintendants de golf du Québec (ASGQ) / Québec Golf Superintendents Association (QSGA)
1370, rue Notre-Dame ouest, Montréal QC H3C 1K8
Tél: 514-285-4874; *Téléc:* 514-282-4292
info@asgq.org
www.asgq.org
Aperçu: *Dimension:* petite; *Envergure:* provinciale; Organisme sans but lucratif; fondée en 1964
Description: Dédiée à la promotion des intérêts des surintendants; offre à ses membres des avantages, informations et défense des intérêts des surintendants
Membre(s) du bureau directeur: John Scott, Président
john.scott@summerlea.com
Finances: *Budget de fonctionnement annuel:* $50,000-$100,000
Personnel: 1 membre(s) du personnel; 12 bénévole(s)
Membre: 400; *Critères d'admissibilite:* Surintendant; adjoint; aspirant
Activités: Tournois de golf; salon exposition; *Service de conférenciers:* Oui

British Columbia Golf Association (BCGA)
#2110, 13700 Mayfield Pl., Richmond BC V6V 2E4
Tel: 604-279-2580; *Fax:* 604-207-9535
Toll-Free: 888-833-2242
info@britishcolumbiagolf.org
www.britishcolumbiagolf.org
Social Media:
www.facebook.com/BritishColumbiaGolf
twitter.com/bc_golfer
Also Known As: British Columbia Golf
Overview: A large provincial licensing organization founded in 1922
Description: To promote interest in golf in BC; To protect the mutual interests of member clubs & their members; To establish & enforce uniformity in the rules of the game; To establish, control, & conduct amateur championships, matches & competitions; To interest & develop junior golfers; To select all teams to represent BC in national & international matches
Affiliation(s): Canadian Golf Foundation; Professional Golf Association of BC; Canadian Ladies Golf Association of BC; Golf Course Superintendents Association of BC; International Association of Golf Administrators; National Golf Foundation; Pacific Coast Golf Association; Pacific Northwest Golf Association
Chief Officer(s): Kris Jonasson, Executive Director
kris@britishcolumbiagolf.org
Deborah Pyne, Managing Director, Player Development
debbie@britishcolumbiagolf.org
Andy Fung, Director, Finance & Administration
andy@britishcolumbiagolf.org
Kathy Gook, Director, School Golf
kathy@britishcolumbiagolf.org
Shirley Simmons-Doyle, Manager, Membership
shirley@britishcolumbiagolf.org
Finances: *Funding Sources:* Government; Sponsorship; Membership
Staff: 10 staff member(s)
Membership: *Fees:* $46
Activities: *Rents Mailing List:* Yes; *Library:* Yes (Open to Public)

British Columbia Golf Superintendents Association (BCGSA)
PO Box 807, Lake Cowichan BC V0R 2G0
Tel: 250-749-6703; *Fax:* 250-749-6702
admin@bcgsa.com
www.bcgsa.com
Overview: A small provincial organization founded in 1995
Description: To promote the professional recognition of golf course superintendents; To uphold the association's code of ethics
Chief Officer(s): Ginny Tromp, Executive Administrator
Dean Piller, President, 250-658-4445
dpiller@telus.net
Mike Ferdinandi, Secretary/Treasurer
mike.ferdinandi@vancouver.ca
Membership: 300+; *Member Profile:* Turfgrass professionals involved in golf course maintenance & the science of turf management
Activities: Participating in turfgrass research; Exchanging knowledge related to golf course care; Sponsoring educational opportunities to benefit members

Canadian Caribbean Amateur Golfers Association (CCAGA)
#718, 7305 Woodbine Ave, Markham ON L3R 3V7
Fax: 905-420-8421
info@ccaga.ca
www.ccaga.ca
Overview: A small local organization founded in 1980
Description: A Not-For-Profit Association offering beginners and amateur golfers the opportunity to play and compete among each other
Membership: *Fees:* $125 single; $200 family; $100 associate (non-playing)

Canadian Golf Superintendents Association (CGSA) / Association canadienne des surintendants de golf
#201, 5399 Eglinton Ave. West, Toronto ON M9C 5K6
Tel: 416-626-8873; *Toll-Free:* 800-387-1056
cgsa@golfsupers.com
www.golfsupers.com
Social Media:
www.facebook.com/151227228150
twitter.com/GolfSupers
Overview: A medium-sized national organization founded in 1966
Description: To promote excellence in golf course management & environmental responsibility; To uphold the Canadian Golf Superintendents Association Principles Of Professional Practice & Code of Ethics & Conduct; *Member of:* Canadian Turfgrass Research Foundation
Chief Officer(s): Kathryn Wood, Director, Professional Development & Meetings, 905-602-8873 222
kwood@golfsupers.com
Lori Micucci, Manager, Member Services, 905-602-8873 226
lmicucci@golfsupers.com
Finances: *Funding Sources:* Sponsorships
Membership: 1,500; *Fees:* Schedule available; *Member Profile:* Golf course superintendents & turfgrass specialists in Canada; *Committees:* Environment; Communications, Marketing, & Public Relations; Professional Development & Research; Conference & Events; Member Services; Equipment Technicians Advisory
Activities: Providing continuing professional development opportunities for members; Sponsoring research projects; Establishing the Master Superintendent Designation Program; Offering networking opportunities; *Awareness Events:* Canadian International Turfgrass Conference and Trade Show, annual; *Library:* CGSA Office Library

Canadian Junior Golf Association (CJGA)
#6, 170 West Beaver Creek Rd., Richmond Hill ON L4B 1L6
Tel: 905-731-6388; *Fax:* 905-731-6058
Toll-Free: 877-508-1069
info@cjga.com
www.cjga.com
Social Media:
www.facebook.com/cjga.ca
twitter.com/CJGA
Overview: A medium-sized national organization founded in 1993
Description: To provide competition & instruction to junior golfers in Canada
Chief Officer(s): Earl M. Fritz, Executive Director
earl.fritz@cjga.com
Activities: Golf tours & competitions; kids programs

Canadian Society of Club Managers (CSCM) / La Société canadienne des directeurs de club
2943B Bloor St. West, Toronto ON M8X 1B3
Tel: 416-979-0640; *Fax:* 416-979-1144
Toll-Free: 877-376-2726
national@cscm.org
www.cscm.org
Overview: A small national organization
Description: To provide managers with the tools necessary to manage their clubs
Chief Officer(s): Elizabeth Di Chiara, Executive Director
elizabeth@cscm.org
Finances: *Annual Operating Budget:* $250,000-$500,000
Staff: 5 staff member(s); 25 volunteer(s)
Membership: 560; *Fees:* Based on region; *Member Profile:* Managers of private or semi-private clubs in Canada; *Committees:* Executive; Editorial Advisory; Education; Technology; Certification

Club de golf Chibougamau-Chapais inc.
CP 81, 130, rue des Forces-Armées, Chibougamau QC G8P 3A1
Tél: 418-748-4709; *Téléc:* 418-748-2471
golfchibougamau@hotmail.com
Nom précédent: Club de golf de Chibougamau inc.
Aperçu: *Dimension:* petite; *Envergure:* locale

Fédération de golf du Québec / Québec Golf Federation
4545, av Pierre-de Coubertin, Montréal QC H1V 0B2
Tél: 514-252-3345; *Téléc:* 514-252-3346
golfquebec@golfquebec.org
www.golfquebec.org
Média social:
www.youtube.com/user/GolfQuebecMedias
www.facebook.com/golfquebec
twitter.com/golf_quebec
Également appelé: Golf Québec
Nom précédent: Association de golf du Québec
Aperçu: *Dimension:* moyenne; *Envergure:* provinciale; Organisme sans but lucratif; fondée en 1920
Description: Assurer le leadership; Favoriser la croissance et le développement du golf amateur dans toute la province tout en préservant l'intégrité et les traditions du jeu
Membre(s) du bureau directeur: Jean-Pierre Beaulieu, Directeur général, 514-252-3345 3732
jpbeaulieu@golfquebec.org
Membre: 61 000; *Montant de la cotisation:* 29$ adultes; 15$ juniors

Golf Association of Ontario (GAO)

PO Box 970, Uxbridge ON L9P 1N3
Tel: 905-852-1101; *Fax:* 905-852-8893
administration@gao.ca
www.gao.ca
Social Media:
instagram.com/gaogolf
www.facebook.com/GAOGolf
twitter.com/GAOGolf
Merged from: Ontario Golf Association; Ontario Ladies Golf Association
Overview: A large provincial organization founded in 2001
Description: To develop & promote golf in the province
Chief Officer(s): Jim King, President
Steve Carroll, Executive Director
scarroll@gao.ca
Dave Colling, Director, Rules & Competitions
dcolling@gao.ca
Mike Kelly, Managing Director, Sport Development
mkelly@gao.ca
Craig Loughryre, Director, Handicapping & Course Rating
cloughry@gao.ca
Kyle McFarlane, Director, Marketing & Communications
kmcfarlane@gao.ca
Kate Sheldon, Director, Administration
ksheldon@gao.ca
Finances: *Funding Sources:* Membership dues; Tournament entry fees
Staff: 19 staff member(s)
Membership: 115,000 individuals, 420 member clubs; *Fees:* $27.50 Adult; $18 Junior; *Member Profile:* Golfers who are members of private, semi-private or public golf courses; *Committees:* Governance & Nominating; Finance & Risk Management; Hall of Fame; Handicap & Course Rating; Sport; Membership; Marketing & Sponsorship; Scholarship; District Coordinators; Human Resources & Compensation
Activities: Offering tournaments, junior camps, & programming; *Internships:* Yes

Golf Canada (RCGA) / Association royale de golf du Canada

#1, 1333 Dorval Dr., Oakville ON L6M 4X7
Tel: 905-849-9700; *Fax:* 905-845-7040
Toll-Free: 800-263-0009
info@golfcanada.ca
www.golfcanada.ca
Social Media:
www.youtube.com/user/TheGolfCanada
www.facebook.com/TheGolfCanada
twitter.com/TheGolfCanada
Previous Name: Royal Canadian Golf Association
Overview: A large national organization founded in 1895
Description: To work with the provincial golf associations & member clubs to foster the growth & development of golf
Affiliation(s): Canadian Golf Superintendent Association; PGA of Canada; Canadian Society of Club Managers; National Golf Course Owners Association Canada; Canadian Golf Industry Association
Chief Officer(s): Paul McLean, President
Scott Simmons, Chief Executive Officer, 905-849-9700
ssimmon@golfcanada.ca
Bill Paul, Chief Officer, Championships, 905-849-9700 203
bpaul@golfcanada.ca
Jeff Thompson, Chief Officer, Sport, 905-849-9700 436
jthompson@golfcanada.ca
Garrett Ball, Director, Finance, 905-849-9700 226
gball@golfcanada.ca
Adam Helmer, Director, Rules, Competitions & Amateur Status, 905-849-9700 244
ahelmer@golfcanada.ca
Finances: *Funding Sources:* Membership dues; Sponsorships
Membership: 322,000+ at 1,500 clubs; *Fees:* Schedule available; *Member Profile:* Member of a member golf club
Activities: *Awareness Events:* RBC Canadian Open; Canadian Pacific Women's Open; *Speaker Service:* Yes; *Library:* RCGA Library by appointment

Golf Manitoba Inc.

#420, 145 Pacific Ave., Winnipeg MB R3B 2Z6
Tel: 204-925-5730; *Fax:* 204-925-5731
golfmb@golfmanitoba.mb.ca
golfmanitoba.mb.ca
Social Media:
www.facebook.com/217256961725416
twitter.com/golf_manitoba
Previous Name: Manitoba Golf Association Inc.
Overview: A small provincial organization founded in 1915
Description: The Association determines policies & standards relating to the development & promotion of golf in the province.
Chief Officer(s): Tammy Gibson, President & Representative, Provincial Council

Golf Newfoundland & Labrador (GNL)

6 Lester St., St. John's NL A1E 2P6
Tel: 709-364-3534
golf@hnl.ca
www.golfnewfoundland.ca
Social Media:
www.facebook.com/pages/Golf-NL/178044602356289
Previous Name: Newfoundland & Labrador Golf Association
Overview: A medium-sized provincial organization
Chief Officer(s): Greg Hillier, Executive Director
Membership: 20 clubs
Activities: Providing information about golf courses in Newfoundland & Labrador; Promoting golf in the province

National Golf Course Owners Association Canada (NGCOA) / L'Association nationale des propriétaires de terrains de golf du Canada (ANPTG)

#810, 515 Legget Dr., Ottawa ON K2K 3G4
Tel: 613-226-3616; *Fax:* 613-226-4148
Toll-Free: 866-626-4262
ngcoa@ngcoa.ca
www.ngcoa.ca
Social Media:
www.facebook.com/nationalgolfcourseownersassociationcanada
twitter.com/ngcoacanada
Overview: A large national organization
Description: Provides business support to Canadian golf course operators & related stakeholders, networking opportunities, purchasing programs, & education
Chief Officer(s): Jeff Calderwood, Chief Executive Officer, 613-226-3616 20
jcalderwood@ngcoa.ca
Nathalie Lavallée, Chief Operating Officer, 613-226-3616 15
nlavallee@ngcoa.ca
Membership: *Fees:* Schedule available; *Member Profile:* Golf course owner/operators
Activities: Golfmax Purchasing Program, Golfmax Online Tradeshow, Golf Research Centre; *Awareness Events:* Take a Kid to the Course Week, July; GolfBusiness Canada Conference & Trade Show; NGCOA Canada Golf Invitationals

New Brunswick Golf Association (NBGA) / Association de golf du nouveau brunswick

PO Box 1555, Stn. A, Fredericton NB E3B 5G2
Tel: 506-451-1324; *Fax:* 888-307-2963
Toll-Free: 877-833-4662
info@golfnb.ca
www.golfnb.ca
Overview: A medium-sized provincial organization founded in 1934
Description: To determine policies & standards relating to the development & promotion of amateur golf in New Brunswick
Chief Officer(s): Tyson Flinn, Executive Director
tflinn@golfnb.ca
Member Profile: Amateur golfers at member clubs; *Committees:* Executive
Activities: Provincial amateur tournaments; programs & services for members clubs

Nova Scotia Golf Association (NSGA)

#216, 30 Damascus Rd., Bedford NS B4A 0C1
Tel: 902-468-8844; *Fax:* 902-484-5327
www.nsga.ns.ca
Social Media:
www.facebook.com/pages/The-Nova-Scotia-Golf-Association/64019542477
twitter.com/novascotiagolf
Overview: A medium-sized provincial organization founded in 1931
Description: To promote, foster & develop golf at all levels in Nova Scotia; to provide a liaison between member clubs & the Royal Canadian Golf Association; to consult & assist with member clubs on turf maintenance, handicap procedures, slope ratings, rule interpretations & junior development; to organize tournaments, in cooperation with member clubs, that determine provincial champions.; *Member of:* Canadian Golf Foundation; International Association of Golf Administrators; Sport Nova Scotia
Chief Officer(s): David Campbell, Executive Director
david@nsga.ns.ca
Jan Gaudette, Executive Assistant
jan@nsga.ns.ca
Finances: *Funding Sources:* Membership dues; sponsors
Member Profile: Must be a member club

Ontario Golf Superintendents' Association (OGSA)

328 Victoria Rd. South, Guelph ON N1L 0H2
Tel: 519-767-3341; *Fax:* 519-766-1704
Toll-Free: 877-824-6472
admin@ogsa.ca
www.ogsa.ca
Overview: A small provincial organization
Chief Officer(s): Sally E. Ross, Executive Manager, 519-767-3341 202
manager@ogsa.ca

Prince Edward Island Golf Association (PEIGA)

PO Box 51, Charlottetown PE C1A 7K2
Tel: 902-393-3293
peiga@peiga.ca
www.peiga.ca
Social Media:
www.facebook.com/PEIGolfAssociation
twitter.com/PEIGolfAssoc
Overview: A small provincial organization founded in 1971
Description: To be the governing body of amateur golf in the province
Chief Officer(s): Brenda McIlwaine, President
Ron MacNeill, Executive Director

Professional Golfers' Association of British Columbia (PGA of BC)

#3280, 21331 Gordon Way, Richmond BC V6W 1J9
Tel: 604-303-6766; *Fax:* 604-303-6765
Toll-Free: 800-667-4653
info@pgabc.org
www.pgabc.org
Social Media:
www.youtube.com/user/pgaofbc
www.facebook.com/pgabc
twitter.com/pgaofbc
Previous Name: British Columbia Professional Golfers Association
Overview: A medium-sized provincial organization
Description: To promote the game of golf and enhance all players' enjoyment of the sport.; *Member of:* Professional Golf Association
Chief Officer(s): Donald Miyazaki, Executive Director
donald@pgabc.org
Brian McDonald, President
Finances: *Funding Sources:* Corporate sponsorship
Staff: 5 staff member(s)
Membership: 650+; *Member Profile:* Individuals employed in the golf industry; *Committees:* Membership & Employment; Captain's; Education & Events; Long Range Planning & Grow the Game; Buying Show; Awards
Activities: PGA tournaments

Professional Golfers' Association of Canada / Association des golfeurs professionnels du Canada

13450 Dublin Line, RR#1, Acton ON L7J 2W7
Tel: 519-853-5450; *Fax:* 519-853-5449
Toll-Free: 800-782-5764
info@pgaofcanada.com
www.pgaofcanada.com
Social Media:
www.youtube.com/user/thepgaofcanada
www.facebook.com/PGAofCanada
twitter.com/pgaofcanada
Also Known As: PGA of Canada
Previous Name: Canadian Professional Golfers' Association
Overview: A medium-sized national organization founded in 1911
Description: The Canadian Professional Golfer's Association is a member based non-profit organization representing golf professionals across Canada.
Chief Officer(s): Gary Bernard, Chief Executive Officer, 519-853-5450 221
gary@pgaofcanada.com
Heather Bodden, Manager & Member Liaison, Operations, 519-853-5450 260
heather@pgaofcanada.com
Finances: *Annual Operating Budget:* $500,000-$1.5 Million
Staff: 10 staff member(s)
Membership: 3,500
Activities: *Rents Mailing List:* Yes; *Library:* Yes (Open to Public)

Saskatchewan Golf Association Inc.

510 Cynthia St., Saskatoon SK S7L 7K7
Tel: 306-975-0850; *Fax:* 306-975-0840
info@golfsaskatchewan.org
www.saskgolf.ca
Social Media:
www.facebook.com/GolfSaskatchewan
twitter.com/GolfSK
Also Known As: Golf Saskatchewan
Merged from: Saskatchewan Golf Association; Canadian Ladies Golf Association of Saskatchewan
Overview: A large provincial organization founded in 1999

Description: To promote & maintain amateur golf in Saskatchewan by providing access to information & clinics on golf skills development, rules, handicapping, & etiquette
Chief Officer(s): Richard Smith, President
Brian Lee, Executive Director, 306-975-0841
Darren Dupont, Manager, Tournaments & Player Services, 306-975-0834
Candace Dunham, Manager, Programs & Member Services, 306-975-0850
Membership: *Fees:* $42 adult public players club; $31.50 junior public players club; $28.35 adult club member; $22.05 junior club member
Activities: Providing provincial championships, scholarships, player clinics, & rules workshops, & handicap clinics; *Internships:* Yes

Yukon Golf Association
4061 - 4th Ave., Whitehorse YT Y1A 1H1
Tel: 867-633-3364; *Fax:* 867-393-3051
sportyukon.com/member/yukon-golf-association
Overview: A small provincial organization
Description: The Yukon Golf Association is an organization that enhances opportunities for all Yukonners in their pursuit of excellence & in their enjoyment of participation.
Chief Officer(s): Gordon Zealand, President
zealandg@northwestel.net

Gymnastics

Alberta Gymnastics Federation (AGF)
#207, 5800 - 2 St. SW, Calgary AB T2H 0H2
Tel: 403-259-5500; *Fax:* 403-259-5588
Toll-Free: 800-665-1010
www.abgym.ab.ca
Social Media:
www.youtube.com/albertagymnastics;
flickr.com/photos/albertagymnastics
www.facebook.com/AlbertaGymnastics
twitter.com/agf_comm
Overview: A medium-sized provincial organization founded in 1971
Description: To operate as the governing body of gymnastics in Alberta; To provide administrative support in the development & delivery of programs & competitions in recreational gymnastics, national coaching certification programs, women's artistic gymnastics, trampoline & tumbling, men's artistic gymnastics, & special events
Chief Officer(s): Scott Hayes, President & CEO
shayes@abgym.ab.ca
Membership: 75 member clubs; *Committees:* Women's Program; Women's Program Judging; Trampoline & Tumbling Technical; Men's Technical; Recreational Development

British Columbia Rhythmic Sportive Gymnastics Federation (BCRSGF)
#268, 828 West 8th Ave., Vancouver BC V5Z 1E2
Tel: 604-333-3485; *Fax:* 604-909-1749
bcrsgf@rhythmicsbc.com
www.rhythmicsbc.com
Social Media:
www.youtube.com/user/bcrsgf
www.facebook.com/Rhythmicsbc
Also Known As: BC Rhythmic Gymnastics Federation
Overview: A small provincial organization
Description: To be the governing body of the sport of rhythmic gymnastics in British Columbia, including special olympics, Aethetic Group Gymnastics & men's rhythmic gymnastics.
Chief Officer(s): Sashka Gitcheva, Program Coordinator

Fédération de gymnastique du Québec (FGQ) / Québec Gymnastics Federation
4545, av Pierre-de Coubertin, Montréal QC H1V 0B2
Tél: 514-252-3043; *Téléc:* 514-252-3169
info@gymnastique.qc.ca
www.gymnastique.qc.ca
Média social:
www.facebook.com/fedgymnastique.duqc
twitter.com/FGQ01
Aperçu: *Dimension:* grande; *Envergure:* provinciale; fondée en 1971
Description: Promouvoir et assurer le développement de la gymnastique à travers tout le Québec; favoriser l'éclosion des talents en vue d'une participation aux plans national et international; unir et coordonner les efforts de toutes les personnes intéressées dans le sport de la gym; *Membre de:* Canadian Gymnastics Federation
Membre(s) du bureau directeur: Serge Sabourin, Président
Helen Brossard, Vice-présidente
Critères d'admissibilite: Athléthes, entraîneurs, membres
Activités: *Evénements de sensibilisation:* Semaine de la prévention; *Stagiaires:* Oui *Bibliothèque:* Oui (Bibliothèque publique)

Gymnastics B.C. (GBC)
#268, 828 West 8 Ave., Vancouver BC V5Z 1E2
Tel: 604-333-3496; *Fax:* 604-333-3499
Toll-Free: 800-556-2242
info@gymnastics.bc.ca
www.gymnastics.bc.ca
Social Media:
www.youtube.com/user/gymnasticsbc1
www.linkedin.com/groups/Gymnastics-BC-3800514
www.facebook.com/GymnasticsBC
twitter.com/GymnasticsBC
Also Known As: British Columbia Gymnastics Association
Overview: A large provincial organization founded in 1969
Description: To provide, promote & guide positive lifelong gymnastics experiences by: directing the development & delivery of quality, comprehensive provincial programs; promoting the benefits of gymnastics as a foundation for human movement, sport, health, wellness & enjoyment; coordinating, suppporting & promoting programs in the pursuit of national & international excellence in consultation with Gymnastics Canada Gymnastique; *Member of:* Gymnastics Canada Gymnastique
Chief Officer(s): Brian Forrester, CEO
bforrester@gymbc.org
Twyla Ryan, President
evolveconsulting@telus.net
Finances: *Annual Operating Budget:* $1.5 Million-$3 Million; *Funding Sources:* Membership dues; sponsorship; programs
Staff: 13 staff member(s)
Membership: 46,000; *Committees:* Men's Technical; Women's Technical; Trampoline & Tumbling; Gymnastics for All; Provincial Advisory
Activities: Provincial championships, Fall congress, Gymnaestrada; *Library:* Resource Library (Open to Public)

Gymnastics Canada Gymnastique (GCG)
#120, 1900 Promenade City Park Dr., Ottawa ON K1J 1A3
Tel: 613-748-5637; *Fax:* 613-748-5691
info@gymcan.org
www.gymcan.org
Social Media:
www.youtube.com/user/gymnasticscanada
www.facebook.com/gymcan
twitter.com/GymnasticsCan
Previous Name: Canadian Gymnastics Federation
Overview: A large national charitable organization founded in 1969
Description: To lead, promote, facilitate & guide gymnastics in Canada as a sport for the pursuit of excellence & world prominence, & as an activity for lifelong participation; To act as the national umbrella organization for provincial & territorial associations which are members; To publish & enforce a standard set of rules & regulations to serve as guidelines for all members; To represent Canadian gymnastics as a member of national & international agencies & federations; To coordinate application of regulations in Canada; To promote, develop & direct high performance gymnastics programs; To promote, facilitate & guide development of national gymnastics programs; To promote, guide & encourage general gymnastics activities; to promote gymnastics as a healthy & safe sport/activity
Affiliation(s): Fédération internationale de gymnastique
Chief Officer(s): Richard Crepin, Chair
Peter Nicol, Acting President & CEO
pnicol@gymcan.org
Cathy Haines, Chief Technical Officer
chaines@gymcan.org
Stephan Duchesne, Director, High Performance
sduchesne@gymcan.org
Marieve Millaire, Director, Event
mmillaire@gymcan.org
Finances: *Funding Sources:* Sport Canada; Membership; Marketing; Fundraising
Staff: 20 staff member(s)
Membership: 250,000 individuals; *Committees:* Audit; Nominating; Human Resources; Awards; By-Law & Policy Review; Women's Artistic Gymnastics; Men's Artistic Gymnastics; Trampoline Gymnastics Program; Rhythmic Gymnastics Program; National Development/Education Program
Activities: National & international programs & competitions; *Awareness Events:* National Gymnastics Week; *Internships:* Yes; *Library:* Yes

Gymnastics Newfoundland & Labrador Inc.
1269A Kenmount Rd., Paradise NL A1L 1N3
Tel: 709-576-0146; *Fax:* 709-576-7493
gymnastics@sportnl.ca
www.gymnastics.nl.ca
Social Media:
www.facebook.com/gymnasticsnl
twitter.com/gymnastics_nl
Overview: A small provincial organization
Description: GNL promotes & supports the development of gymnastics throughout the province.; *Member of:* Canadian Gymnastics Federation
Chief Officer(s): Carol White, Executive Director
Membership: 8 clubs

Gymnastics Nova Scotia (GNS)
5516 Spring Garden Rd., 4th Fl., Halifax NS B3J 1G6
Tel: 902-425-5450; *Fax:* 902-425-5606
gns@sportnovascotia.ca
www.gymns.ca
Social Media:
www.facebook.com/GymnasticsNovaScotia
twitter.com/gymnasticsns
Previous Name: Nova Scotia Gymnastics Association
Overview: A small provincial organization
Description: To operate as the governing body of gymnastics in Nova Scotia; To promote gymnastics, from the recreational level to the high performance level; To encourage participation, fitness, & well-being; To promote safe & positive gymnastics environments
Chief Officer(s): Nick Lenehan, President
Angela Gallant, Executive Director
David Brown, Technical Director
gnscoach@sportnovascotia.ca
Membership: *Fees:* Schedule available; *Member Profile:* Active & associatte gymnastics clubs throughout Nova Scotia; Judges; Recreational & competitive coaches; Pre-school, recreational, & competitive gymnasts & trampolinists; *Committees:* Men's Program; Trampoline Program; Women's Program; Education & Recreation; Fair Play & Equity; Competition
Activities: Training & certifying coaches, officials, & judges; Organizing & sanctioning gymnastics competitions; Providing resources about gymnastics; Offering the introductory Tumblebugs progam for children from 3.5 to 5 years of age

Gymnastics PEI
Sport PEI, 40 Enman Cres., Charlottetown PE C1E 1E6
Tel: 902-368-6570; *Fax:* 902-368-4548
Toll-Free: 800-247-6712
www.gymnasticspei.ca
Overview: A small provincial organization
Chief Officer(s): Valerie Vuillemot, Executive Director
vvuillemot@sportpei.pe.ca

Gymnastics Saskatchewan
1870 Lorne St., Regina SK S4P 2L7
Tel: 306-780-9229; *Fax:* 306-780-9475
info@gymsask.com
www.gymsask.com
Social Media:
www.facebook.com/gymsask
twitter.com/gymsask
Previous Name: Saskatchewan Gymnastics Association
Overview: A medium-sized provincial organization
Member of: Sask Sport Inc.; Canadian Gymnastics Federation
Chief Officer(s): Klara Miller, Chief Executive Officer
kmiller@gymsask.com
Cheryl Russell, Manager, Operations
crussell@gymsask.com
Finances: *Annual Operating Budget:* $250,000-$500,000; *Funding Sources:* Grants; self-generated revenues
Staff: 5 staff member(s)
Membership: 9,000
Activities: *Awareness Events:* Gymnastics Awareness Week

Manitoba Gymnastics Association (MGA)
145 Pacific Ave., Winnipeg MB R3B 2Z6
Tel: 204-925-5781; *Fax:* 204-925-5932
mga@sportmanitoba.ca
www.gymnastics.mb.ca
Social Media:
www.facebook.com/pages/Manitoba-Gymnastics/427931587283744
twitter.com/GymnasticsMB
Overview: A small provincial organization founded in 1968
Description: To develop, promote & guide gymnastics as a lifetime activity in Manitoba; *Member of:* Canadian Gymnastics Federation
Chief Officer(s): Kathy Stoesz, Executive Director
mga.kathy@sportmanitoba.ca

New Brunswick Gymnastics Association (NBGA) / Association gymnastique du Nouveau-Brunswick (AGNB)
1991 Route 112, Upper Cloverdale NB E1J 1Z1
Tel: 506-215-0085
nbga@gym.nb.ca
gym.nb.ca
Social Media:
www.youtube.com/user/GymnasticsNB
www.facebook.com/NBGym
twitter.com/gymnasticsnb
Overview: A small provincial organization founded in 1967
Description: To promote gymnastics in New Brunswick; *Member of:* Gymnastics Canada Gymnastique
Chief Officer(s): Nathalie Colpitts-Waddell, Executive Director
director@gym.nb.ca
Diane Kirk, President
president@gym.nb.ca
Membership: 2500; *Committees:* Executive; Technical

Ontario Gymnastic Federation (OGF)
#214, 3 Concorde Gate, Toronto ON M3C 3N7
Tel: 416-426-7100; *Fax:* 416-426-7377
Toll-Free: 866-565-0650
info@ogf.com
www.ogf.com
Also Known As: Gymnastics Ontario
Overview: A small provincial organization founded in 1968
Description: To lead the sport of gymnastics throughout Ontario; To provide services & programs which encourage lifelong involvement in gymnastics
Affiliation(s): Gymnastics Canada
Chief Officer(s): Dave Sandford, Chief Executive Officer, 416-426-7095
ceo@gymnasticsontario.ca
Linda Clifford, President
Angel Crossman, Director, Policies & Procedures
Michelle Pothier, Coordinator, Recreation
recreation@gymnasticsontario.ca
Yuliana Korolyova, Coordinator, Education, 416-426-7096
education@gymnasticsontario.ca
Kristina Galloway, Coordinator, Membership Services, 416-426-7096
membership@gymnasticsontario.ca
Siobhan Covington, Manager, Finance, 416-426-7094
scovington@gymnasticsontario.ca
Finances: *Funding Sources:* Fundraising
Activities: Providing professional development & training activities; Offering resources such as technical manuals, workbooks, & videos; Providing a development award program; *Awareness Events:* I Love Gymnastic Week; *Library:* Gymnastics Ontario Resource Centre

Polarettes Gymnastics Club
4061 - 4th Ave., Whitehorse YT Y1A 1H1
Tel: 867-668-4794
info@polarettes.org
www.polarettes.org
Overview: A small provincial organization
Description: To promote recreational & competitive gymnastics programs to Yukon residtents. Physical address: 16 Duke St., Whitehorse, YT Y1A 4M2.
Chief Officer(s): Kimberly Jones, Head Coach
Activities: Toddler Movement program (18 months); competitive programs start from 6-8 years old

Rhythmic Gymnastics Alberta (RGA)
c/o Percy Page Centre, 11759 Groat Rd., Edmonton AB T5M 3K6
Tel: 780-427-8152; *Fax:* 780-427-8153
Toll-Free: 800-881-2504
rga@rgalberta.com
www.rgalberta.com
Previous Name: Alberta Rhythmic Sportive Gymnastics Federation
Overview: A medium-sized provincial organization founded in 1979
Description: To foster & encourage participation & the development of excellence in rhythmic gymnastics; *Member of:* Gymnastics Canada Gymnastique
Finances: *Annual Operating Budget:* $100,000-$250,000
Staff: 2 staff member(s); 100 volunteer(s)
Membership: 800; *Fees:* Schedule available; *Member Profile:* Children 5-18; Active adults/coaches 16-80
Activities: Provincial Gymnastrada; National & international competitions & events; *Speaker Service:* Yes

Yukon Gymnastics Association
4061 - 4th Ave., Whitehorse YT Y1A 1H1
Tel: 867-456-7896; *Fax:* 867-668-6922
yukongymnastic.com
Overview: A small provincial organization
Member of: Canadian Gymnastics Federation
Chief Officer(s): Shannon Albisser, President
shannonalbisser@yahoo.ca

Halls of Fame

Alberta Sports Hall of Fame & Museum (ASHFM)
#102 - 4200 Hwy 2, Red Deer AB T4N 1E3
Tel: 403-341-8614; *Fax:* 403-341-8619
info@ashfm.ca
www.ashfm.ca
Social Media:
www.youtube.com/user/ABSportsHallOfFame/videos
www.facebook.com/ashfm.ca
twitter.com/ashfm1
Overview: A medium-sized provincial charitable organization founded in 1957
Description: To honour Albertans who have distinguished themselves in sport & to operate a facility to house artifacts that are significant in Alberta's sports history; *Member of:* Museums Alberta; Canadian Museums Association; Canadian Association for Sport Heritage; International Sport Heritage Association
Chief Officer(s): Dennis Allan, Chair
Donna Hateley, Managing Director
Finances: *Annual Operating Budget:* $250,000-$500,000
Staff: 5 staff member(s); 40 volunteer(s)
Membership: 950
Activities: Induction into Sports Hall of Fame; Museum; fundraising; *Awareness Events:* Induction Banquet; Annual Golf Tournament; *Library:* Alberta Sport History Library (Open to Public)

British Columbia Sports Hall of Fame & Museum
Gate A, BC Place Stadium, 777 Pacific Blvd. South, Vancouver BC V6B 4Y8
Tel: 604-687-5520; *Fax:* 604-687-5510
sportsinfo@bcsportshalloffame.com
www.bcsportshalloffame.com
Social Media:
www.facebook.com/bcsportshall
twitter.com/BCSportsHall
Overview: A medium-sized provincial charitable organization founded in 1966
Description: To collect, preserve & display sports artifacts from BC's sporting history; to provide an exciting & educational environment for sports history; *Member of:* Canadian Museums Association; BC Museums Association
Affiliation(s): International Association of Sports Museums & Halls of Fame
Chief Officer(s): Allison Mailer, Executive Director
allison.mailer@bcsportshalloffame.com
Jason Beck, Curator
jason.beck@bcsportshalloffame.com
Finances: *Funding Sources:* Corporate & private
Staff: 5 staff member(s); 50 volunteer(s)
Membership: 1-99
Activities: Champions Banquet & Tournament of Champions; *Awareness Events:* Banquet of Champions, Induction Ceremonies; *Internships:* Yes; *Library:* Yes by appointment

Canada's Sports Hall of Fame / Temple de la renommée des sports du Canada
169 Canada Olympic Rd. SW, Calgary AB T3B 6B7
Tel: 403-776-1040
info@cshof.ca
www.sportshall.ca
Social Media:
www.facebook.com/CANsportshall
twitter.com/CANsportshall
Overview: A medium-sized national organization founded in 1955
Description: To inspire Canadian identity & national pride by telling the compelling stories of those outstanding achievements that make up Canada's sports history.
Chief Officer(s): Mario Siciliano, President & CEO
msiciliano@cshof.ca
Janice Smith, Director, Exhibits & Programming
jsmith@cshof.ca
Membership: 100-499

Canadian Golf Hall of Fame & Museum (CGHF) / Musée et Temple canadien de la renommée du golf
Glen Abbey Golf Club, 1333 Dorval Dr., Oakville ON L6M 4X7
Tel: 905-849-9700
cghf@golfcanada.ca
www.rcga.org
Also Known As: Canadian Golf Museum
Overview: A small national charitable organization founded in 1971
Description: Celebrates the outstanding individuals of Canadian golf: amateur and professional players, and others who have played a key role in the evolution of the game of golf in Canada. Open year round, with a shortened schedule during the winter months.; *Member of:* Ontario Museum Association; Canadian Museum Association; Ontario Archives Association; Canadian Association for Sport Heritage; International Sports Heritage Association
Chief Officer(s): Karen Hewson, Managing Director, Heritage Services, 905-849-9700 213
khewson@golfcanada.ca
Meggan Gardner, Curator, 905-849-9700 412
mgardner@golfcanada.ca
Finances: *Funding Sources:* Golf Canada
Activities:; *Library:* Canadian Golf Hall of Fame & Museum Library (Open to Public)

Canadian Lacrosse Hall of Fame
PO Box 308, 65 - 6th Ave., New Westminster BC V3L 4Y6
Tel: 604-527-4640; *Fax:* 604-527-4641
info@canadianlacrossehalloffame.com
www.canadianlacrossehalloffame.org
Overview: A small national organization founded in 1967
Description: To present the history of lacrosse in Canada & to induct worthy receipients into the Hall of Fame
Chief Officer(s): Allan Blair, Curator
Activities:; *Library:* Canadian Lacrosse Hall of Fame Archives by appointment

Canadian Olympic Hall of Fame / Temple de la renommée olympique du Canada
c/o COC, #1400, 85 Albert St., Ottawa ON K1P 6A4
Tel: 613-244-2020; *Fax:* 613-244-0169
olympic.ca/canadian-olympic-hall-of-fame
Overview: A small national organization founded in 1948
Description: To honor those who have served the cause of the Olympic Movement with distinction; those athletes, coaches, officials, administrators & volunteers whose dedication, sportsmanship & achievements have made an exemplary contribution to the Canadian Olympic Movement; *Member of:* Canadian Olympic Committee
Membership: 351

Manitoba Sports Hall of Fame & Museum (MSHF&M)
145 Pacific Ave., Winnipeg MB R3B 2Z6
Tel: 204-925-5735; *Fax:* 204-925-5916
halloffame@sportmanitoba.ca
www.halloffame.mb.ca
Social Media:
www.youtube.com/user/sportmanitoba
www.facebook.com/sportmb
twitter.com/SportManitoba
Overview: A small provincial charitable organization founded in 1980
Description: The mandate of the Manitoba Sports Hall of Fame is to recognize and honour those people who have made their mark in Manitoba's rich sports history through their activities and achievements. The core business of the Hall of Fame is to honour people by telling their story through articles and exhibits, or right here on this website.; *Member of:* Association of Manitoba Museums (AMM), the Association of Manitoba Archives (AMA), the Canadian Association for Sport Heritage (CASH) and the Canadian Heritage Information Network (CHIN).
Affiliation(s): Association of Manitoba Museums; Association of Manitoba Archives; Canadian Association for Sport Heritage; Canadian Heritage Information Network
Chief Officer(s): Rick Brownlee, Sport Heritage Manager
Finances: *Funding Sources:* Fundraising; lotteries; provincial government
Activities: Casino Fun Nite; Stanley Cup Nite; Induction Dinner

New Brunswick Sports Hall of Fame (NBSHF) / Temple de la renommée sportive du N.-B.
503 Queen St., Fredericton NB E3B 5H1
Tel: 506-453-3747
nbsportshalloffame@gnb.ca
www.nbsportshalloffame.com
Social Media:
www.facebook.com/150319378347024
twitter.com/NBSHF
Overview: A small provincial charitable organization founded in 1970
Description: N.B. Sports Hall of Fame recognizes & honours achievement in competitive sport & its development; with honour comes distinction & a rich sport legacy for the youth of the future; such achievement & legacy are kept alive for inductees, the sport community & generations of New Brunswickers through celebration, public exhibition & preservation of our sport heritage; *Member of:* Canadian Association for Sport Heritage; Canadian Museums Association
Affiliation(s): International Sports Heritage Association
Chief Officer(s): Jamie Wolverton, Executive Director, 506-453-8930
jamie.wolverton@gnb.ca

Finances: *Funding Sources:* Provincial government; fundraising; sponsorships; donations
Activities: Annual dinner & Induction Ceremony; exhibits; receptions; lectures; tours; *Library:* Sports Heritage Resource Centre (Open to Public) by appointment

Northwestern Ontario Sports Hall of Fame & Museum
219 May St. South, Thunder Bay ON P7E 1B5
Tel: 807-622-2852; *Fax:* 807-622-2736
nwosport@tbaytel.net
www.nwosportshalloffame.com
Social Media:
www.youtube.com/user/nwosport
Also Known As: NWO Sports Hall of Fame
Overview: A small local charitable organization founded in 1978
Description: To preserve & honour the sports heritage of northwestern Ontario; *Member of:* Canadian Association for Sport Heritage; International Association of Sports Museums & Halls of Fame; Ontario Museum Association; Archives Association of Ontario; Canadian Museums Association; Thunder Bay Chamber of Commerce
Chief Officer(s): Kathryn Dwyer, Curator
Diane Imrie, Executive Director
Finances: *Annual Operating Budget:* $100,000-$250,000
Staff: 3 staff member(s); 25 volunteer(s)
Membership: 400; *Fees:* $25 individual; $40 family; $60 business/organization
Activities: A variety of structured programs are available for different grade levels; Annual Induction Dinner & Ceremony, last Sat. in Sept.; *Library:* Yes

Novia Scotia Sports Hall of Fame (NSSHF)
#446, 1800 Argyle St., Halifax NS B3J 3N8
Tel: 902-421-1266; *Fax:* 902-425-1148
sporthalloffame@eastlink.ca
www.novascotiasporthalloffame.com
Social Media:
www.linkedin.com/company/nova-scotia-sport-hall-of-fame
www.facebook.com/116064731766960
twitter.com/NSSHF
Previous Name: Nova Scotia Sport Heritage Centre
Overview: A small provincial organization founded in 1964
Chief Officer(s): Don Mills, Chair
Bill Robinson, CEO
bill@nsshf.com
Activities: *Awareness Events:* Golf Tournament, June; Bingo @ the Halifax Forum

Ottawa Sports Hall of Fame Inc. (OSHOF) / Temple de la renommée des sports d'Ottawa
Heritage Bldg., Ottawa City Hall, 110 Laurier St. East, Ottawa ON K0A 1B0
ottawasportshalloffame@gmail.com
www.ottawasportshalloffame.com
Social Media:
www.facebook.com/195672987173454
twitter.com/OttawaSportsHoF
Overview: A small local organization founded in 1968
Description: To preserve the history & development of sports in Ottawa
Chief Officer(s): Dave Best, Chair
Finances: *Funding Sources:* Sponsorships
Membership: 200+ inductees
Activities: Recognizing individuals & teams who, through their achievements in or contributions to sport, have brought fame to Ottawa; *Awareness Events:* Inducation Ceremony, May

Prince Edward Island Sports Hall of Fame & Museum Inc.
40 Enman Cres., Charlottetown PE C1E 1E6
Tel: 902-368-4547
publicrelations@sportpei.pe.ca
www.peisportshalloffame.ca
Social Media:
www.facebook.com/210800825622110
Previous Name: Prince Edward Island Sports Hall of Fame
Overview: A small provincial charitable organization founded in 1968
Chief Officer(s): Nick Murray, Executive Director
Finances: *Funding Sources:* Fees; events; admissions; fundraising events; government grants; sponsorships
Membership: 150+ inductees
Activities:; *Library:* Yes

Saskatchewan Sports Hall of Fame & Museum (SSFHM)
2205 Victoria Ave., Regina SK S4P 0S4
Tel: 306-780-9232; *Fax:* 306-780-9427
sshfm@sasktel.net
www.sasksportshalloffame.com
Social Media:
www.youtube.com/channel/UC2j_-agyX9f2-xa5laFueXQ
www.facebook.com/SaskSportsHF
twitter.com/SaskSportsHF
Overview: A small provincial charitable organization founded in 1966
Description: To recognize sport excellence, preserve sport history & educate the public on the contribution of sport to Saskatchewan's cultural fabric; *Member of:* Canadian Museums Association; Museums Association of Saskatchewan; Canadian Association for Sports Heritage; International Association of Sport Museums & Halls of Fame
Chief Officer(s): Sheila Kelly, Executive Director
skelly@sshfm.com
Brock Gerrard, Curator
bgerrard@sshfm.com
Finances: *Annual Operating Budget:* $250,000-$500,000; *Funding Sources:* Lotteries & self-help
Staff: 4 staff member(s); 95 volunteer(s)
Membership: 1,450
Activities: Museum galleries, archives, research facilities; Induction dinner; Annual Hall of Fame Game (Football); *Speaker Service:* Yes; *Library:* Yes by appointment

Handball

Alberta Handball Association (AHA)
AB
www.albertahandball.com
Social Media:
www.facebook.com/Albertateamhandball
Overview: A small provincial organization
Description: To promote & develop the sport of handball in Alberta
Activities: Operates three clubs: Calgary, Edmonton & Sherwood Park

Alberta Team Handball Federation (ATHF)
Percy Page Centre, 11749 Groat Rd., Edmonton AB T5M 3K6
Tel: 780-415-2666; *Fax:* 780-422-2663
Handballalberta@gmail.com
www.teamhandball.ab.ca
Social Media:
www.youtube.com/user/HandballAlberta1;
vimeo.com/channels/123390
www.facebook.com/pages/Alberta-Team-Handball-Federation/111368133359
twitter.com/handballalberta
Overview: A medium-sized provincial organization founded in 1960
Description: To govern the promotion of team handball throughout Alberta, by encouraging the development of athletes, coaches, referees, & administrators of all ages & abilities; *Member of:* Canadian Team Handball Federation
Chief Officer(s): Dan Stetic, CEO
Surroosh Ghofrani, Chief Financial Officer
Finances: *Funding Sources:* Membership & course fees; fundraising; donations; Alberta Sport, Recreation, Parks & Wildlife Foundation
Activities: Organizing provincial championships, regional leagues, coaching courses; programs for 8 years of age to adults, sport outreach clinics, & the City of Champions Tournament

Balle au mur Québec (BAMQ) / Québec Handball Association
CP 1000, Succ. M, 4545, av Pierre-de Coubertin, Montréal QC H1V 3R2
Tél: 514-252-3062; *Téléc:* 514-252-3103
info@sports-4murs.qc.ca
www.balleaumur.qc.ca
Média social:
www.facebook.com/BalleAuMurQuebecBamq
Aperçu: *Dimension:* moyenne; *Envergure:* provinciale; fondée en 1971
Affiliation(s): Association canadienne de Balle au mur
Membre(s) du bureau directeur: Michel Séguin, Directeur général
Finances: *Budget de fonctionnement annuel:* $50,000-$100,000; *Fonds:* Gouvernement provincial
Personnel: 2 membre(s) du personnel; 10 bénévole(s)
Membre: 10 institutionnel; 1 000 individu

British Columbia Team Handball Federation (BCTHF)
Vancouver BC
bchandball@gmail.com
bchandball.wix.com/bchandball
Social Media:
www.facebook.com/BCHandball
twitter.com/van_handball
Overview: A small provincial organization founded in 2003
Description: To act as the governing body for handball in BC; *Member of:* Canadian Team Handball Federation
Chief Officer(s): David Lee, Executive Director
Membership: *Fees:* Schedule available

Canadian Handball Association (CHA) / Fédération de balle au mur du Canada
Toronto ON
www.canadianhandball.com
Overview: A medium-sized national organization
Description: To promote handball in Canada
Chief Officer(s): Chris Simmons, President
Membership: 3,000

Canadian Team Handball Federation (CTHF) / Fédération canadienne de handball olympique (FCHO)
453, rue Jacob-Nicol, Sherbrooke QC J1J 4E5
Tel: 819-563-7937; *Fax:* 819-563-5352
handballcanada.ca
Overview: A medium-sized national charitable organization founded in 1966
Affiliation(s): International Handball Federation; Pan American Team Handball Federation; Commonwealth Handball Federation
Chief Officer(s): Raquel Marinho, President
raquelpedercini@hotmail.com
François LeBeau, Chief Operating Officer
f.leleau@videotron.ca
Finances: *Annual Operating Budget:* $500,000-$1.5 Million; *Funding Sources:* Sport Canada; COO; CAC
Staff: 1 staff member(s); 1 volunteer(s)
Membership: 15,000; *Fees:* $5; *Committees:* Management; Officials; Coaches; National Teams
Activities: Canadian Championship; Canada Cup; Pan-American Championships & Games; *Speaker Service:* Yes

Fédération québécoise de handball olympique (FQHO)
CP 1000, Succ. M, 4545, av Pierre-de-Coubertin, Montréal QC H1V 3R2
Tél: 514-252-3067; *Téléc:* 514-252-3176
handball@handball.qc.ca
www.handball.qc.ca
Aperçu: *Dimension:* petite; *Envergure:* locale
Description: Handball Québec est le seul organisme reconnu par le Secrétariat au Loisir et au Sport du Gouvernement du Québec pour régir le handball au Québec.; *Membre de:* Canadian Team Handball Federation
Membre(s) du bureau directeur: Michelle Lortie, Directrice
mlortie@handball.qc.ca

Handball Association of Newfoundland & Labrador
NL
www.nlhandballontherock.com
Social Media:
www.facebook.com/nlhandballontherock
Overview: A small provincial organization
Member of: Canadian Team Handball Federation
Chief Officer(s): Wayne Amminson, President

Handball Association of Newfoundland & Labrador
St. John's NL
www.nlhandballontherock.com
Social Media:
www.facebook.com/nlhandballontherock
Also Known As: NL Handball Association; Handball on the Rock
Overview: A small provincial organization
Description: To promote & develop the sport of handball in Newfoundland & Labrador, with emphasis on junior programs
Chief Officer(s): Wayne Amminson, President

Handball Association of Nova Scotia (HANS)
NS
nshandball.com
Social Media:
twitter.com/nshandball
Overview: A small provincial organization
Description: To promote & develop the sport of handball in Nova Scotia
Chief Officer(s): Daniel Marcil, President & CEO
dan@nshandball.com
Activities: Tournaments; junior program

Manitoba Team Handball Federation
MB
Overview: A small provincial organization
Description: Promotes team handball, by establishing & developing participative & competitive programs for Manitobans throughout Manitoba; *Member of:* Canadian Team Handball Federation

Manitoba Team Handball Federation
MB
www.manitobahandballassociation.com
Social Media: www.facebook.com/1421693301388004
twitter.com/TeamHandballMB
Previous Name: Manitoba Handball Association Inc.
Overview: A small provincial organization
Description: To promote & develop the sport of handball in Manitoba

New Brunswick Team Handball Federation
NB
info.handballnb@gmail.com
www.handballnb.org
Média social: www.facebook.com/pages/Handball-NB/195293907261100
Également appelé: Handball NB
Aperçu: *Dimension:* petite; *Envergure:* locale; Organisme sans but lucratif
Membre de: Canadian Team Handball Federation
Membre(s) du bureau directeur: Jason A. Ferguson, President

Ontario Handball Association (OHA)
ON
www.ontariohandball.ca
Overview: A small provincial organization
Description: To promote & develop the sport of handball in Ontario
Chief Officer(s): Jenine Wilson, President
president@ontariohandball.ca
Activities: Tournaments; junior programs

Saskatchewan Handball Association (SHA)
SK
Tel: 306-584-8035
dkazymyra@cableregina.com
nonprofits.accesscomm.ca/sha
Overview: A small provincial organization
Description: To promote & develop the sport of handball in Saskatchewan

Team Handball Ontario (THO)
Toronto ON
info@handballontario.com
www.handballontario.com
Social Media: www.facebook.com/TeamHandballOntario
Overview: A medium-sized provincial organization
Description: To represent team handball in Ontario
Chief Officer(s): Nick Cuddemi, President
Membership: *Fees:* $200 full; $125 half season; $10 per drop in session; $25 social

Hang Gliding

British Columbia Hang Gliding & Paragliding Association (BCHPA)
BC
www.bchpa.ca
Previous Name: Hang Gliding Association of British Columbia
Overview: A small provincial organization
Description: To protect, maintain & improve flying sites throughout the province.
Chief Officer(s): Margit Nance, President
margitnance@show.ca

Great Lakes Gliding Club (GLGC)
7272 - 6 Line, RR#3, Tottenham ON L0G 1W0
Tel: 416-466-7016
postmaster@greatlakesgliding.com
www.greatlakesgliding.com
Social Media: www.facebook.com/flyglgc
Overview: A small local organization founded in 1998
Description: The club offers license training as well as flying competitions
Membership: 35; *Fees:* $250 associate; $375 students; $550 full; *Member Profile:* Students; Licenced pilots

Hang Gliding & Paragliding Association of Atlantic Canada (HPAAC)
hpaac.ca
Social Media: www.facebook.com/HPAAC
Previous Name: Hang Gliding Association of Newfoundland
Overview: A small local organization founded in 1979
Description: To develop & promote the sports of hang gliding & paragliding in Atlantic Canada
Affiliation(s): Hang Gliding & Paragliding Association of Canada
Membership: 1-99; *Fees:* $140
Activities: Paragliding & hang gliding at coastal cities in Nova Scotia, Prince Edward Island, New Brunswick & Newfoundland & Labrador; *Awareness Events:* Atlantic Annual Paragliding/Hang Gliding Festival, May

Hang Gliding & Paragliding Association of Canada (HPAC) / Association canadienne de vol libre (ACVL)
#404, 1718 Venables St., Vancouver BC V5L 2H4
Fax: 604-731-4407
Toll-Free: 877-370-2078
admin@hpac.ca
www.hpac.ca
Social Media: www.facebook.com/groups/HPAC.ACVL
Overview: A medium-sized national organization founded in 1977
Description: To promote unpowered foot-launched flight in hang gliders & paragliders.; *Member of:* Aero Club of Canada; Fédération aéronautique internationale
Chief Officer(s): Margit Nance, Executive Director
Finances: *Annual Operating Budget:* $50,000-$100,000; *Funding Sources:* Membership fees
Staff: 1 staff member(s)
Membership: 890; *Fees:* Schedule available; *Committees:* Safety

Manitoba Hang Gliding Association (MHGA)
c/o Sport Manitoba, 145 Pacific Ave., Winnipeg MB R3B 2Z6
mhga.ca
Overview: A small provincial organization founded in 1980
Description: To promote safety, excellence & public awareness of the sport of hang gliding.; *Member of:* Hang Gliding & Paragliding Association of Canada

Southwestern Ontario Gliding Association (SOGA)
#6981, 7179 - 3 Line, Arthur ON N0G 1A0
soga.ca
Previous Name: K-W Hang Gliding Club; Hang-On-Tario
Overview: A medium-sized provincial organization founded in 1979
Description: To organize hang gliding space & time for its members
Chief Officer(s): John Pop, Contact
jpop@golden.net
Membership: *Fees:* $25 associate; $250 full/tow

Health

Physical & Health Education Canada / Éducation physique et santé Canada
#301, 2197 Riverside Dr., Ottawa ON K1H 7X3
Tel: 613-523-1348; *Fax:* 613-523-1206
Toll-Free: 800-663-8708
info@phecanada.ca
www.phecanada.ca
Social Media: www.facebook.com/PHECanada
twitter.com/PHECanada
Also Known As: PHE Canada
Previous Name: Canadian Physical Education Association; Canadian Association for Health, Physical Education, Recreation, & Dance
Overview: A large national charitable organization founded in 1933
Description: To promote quality school health programs & the healthy development of Canadian children & youth
Chief Officer(s): Fran Harris, President
Chris Jones, Executive Director & CEO, 613-523-1348 224
Chris@phecanada.ca
Jodie Lyn-Harrison, Chief Administrative Officer, 613-523-1348 223
Jodie@phecanada.ca
Stephanie Talsma, Program Manager, 613-523-1348 236
Stephanie@phecanada.ca
Member Profile: Principals, teachers, public health professionals, & recreation leaders from across Canada; *Committees:* Quality Daily Physical Education; Health Promoting Schools; Quality School Intramural Recreation; Dance Education
Activities: Advocating for quality, school-based physical & health education; Offering professional learning experiences; Creating networking opportunities

Hiking

Federation of Mountain Clubs of British Columbia (FMCBC)
Mountain Equipment Co-op Store, PO Box 18673, 130 West Broadway, 2nd Fl., Vancouver BC V5T 4E7
Tel: 604-873-6096; *Fax:* 604-873-6086
fmcbc@mountainclubs.org
www.mountainclubs.org
Social Media: www.facebook.com/129423370477517
twitter.com/mountainclubs
Overview: A small provincial charitable organization founded in 1980
Description: To promote hiking & mountaineering; *Member of:* Donations; Membership dues
Chief Officer(s): Scott Webster, President
Jodi Appleton, Manager, Program and Administration
admin.manager@mountainclubs.org
Membership: 3500; *Fees:* Individual $25

Hockey

British Columbia Amateur Hockey Association (BCAHA) / Association de hockey amateur de la Colombie-Britannique
6671 Oldfield Rd., Saanichton BC V8M 2A1
Tel: 250-652-2978; *Fax:* 250-652-4536
info@bchockey.net
www.bchockey.net
Social Media: www.instagram.com/bchockeysource;
www.youtube.com/user/BCHockeySource
www.facebook.com/BCHockeySource
twitter.com/BCHockey_Source
Also Known As: BC Hockey
Overview: A medium-sized provincial organization founded in 1919
Description: To foster, improve & perpetuate amateur hockey in BC; *Member of:* Hockey Canada
Chief Officer(s): Bill Ennos, Director, Programs
bennos@bchockey.net
Finances: *Annual Operating Budget:* $500,000-$1.5 Million
Staff: 7 staff member(s); 2000 volunteer(s)
Membership: 60,000 individual + 4,500 referees; *Fees:* Schedule available; *Member Profile:* Amateur hockey teams/leagues/associations; referees' organizations

Calgary Sledge Hockey Association
Calgary AB
info@calgarysledgehockey.ca
calgarysledgehockey.ca
Social Media: www.facebook.com/CalgarySledgeHockey
Overview: A small local charitable organization
Affiliation(s): Hockey Alberta; Hockey Canada
Chief Officer(s): Dave TAylor, Director of Marketing, 403-891-9295
Membership: 3 teams

Canadian Adult Recreational Hockey Association (CARHA)
#610, 1420 Blair Pl., Ottawa ON K1J 9L8
Tel: 613-244-1989; *Fax:* 613-244-0451
Toll-Free: 800-267-1854
hockey@carhahockey.ca
www.carhahockey.ca
Social Media: www.facebook.com/carhahockey
twitter.com/CARHAHockey
Also Known As: CARHA Hockey
Previous Name: Canadian Oldtimers' Hockey Association
Overview: A medium-sized national charitable organization founded in 1975
Description: To develop & provide a wide range of innovative hockey benefits & solutions to customers; To build & retain relationships among the adult recreational hockey community across Canada
Chief Officer(s): Michael S. Peski, President
mpeski@carhahockey.ca
Lori Lopez, Director, Business Operations
llopez@carhahockey.ca
Karen Hodgson, Manager, Member Services
kHodgson@carhahockey.ca
Laurie Snider, Coordinator, Member Services & Special Projects
lsnider@carhahockey.ca

Finances: *Funding Sources:* Membership; Sponsorship
Membership: *Fees:* $23; *Member Profile:* Men & women, 19 years of age or older
Activities: *Internships:* Yes

Canadian Hockey League
#201, 305 Milner Ave., Toronto ON M1B 3V4
Tel: 416-332-9711; *Fax:* 416-332-1477
www.chl.ca
Social Media:
twitter.com/CHLHockey

Overview: A large national organization
Description: To act as the umbrella organization for the three major junior hockey leagues in Canada: Ontario Hockey League, Western Hockey League & Quebec Major Junior Hockey League
Activities: Mastercard Memorial Cup; Home Hardward Top Prospects Game; Subway Super Series; CHL Import Draft; *Rents Mailing List:* Yes

Cape Breton County Minor Hockey Association (CBCMHA)
PO Box 6003, 1174 Kings Rd., Sydney River NS B1S 3V9
Tel: 902-562-1767; *Fax:* 902-562-1833
cbcmha@ns.aliantzinc.ca
www.cbcmha.ca

Overview: A medium-sized local organization
Description: The Cape Breton County Minor Hockey Association is dedicated to the advancement of minor hockey & promoting the development & personal growth of all participants through progressive leadership, by ensuring meaningful & equal opportunities, & providing enjoyable experiences in a safe & respectful environment.; *Member of:* Hockey Canada; Hockey Nova Scotia
Chief Officer(s): Shannon Fuller, Registrar
Membership: *Fees:* Schedule available

Fédération internationale de hockey (FIH) / International Hockey Federation
Rue du Valentin 61, Lausanne CH-1004 Switzerland
info@fih.ch
www.fih.ch
Média social:
www.youtube.com/user/fihockey
www.facebook.com/fihockey
twitter.com/FIH_Hockey

Aperçu: *Dimension:* moyenne; *Envergure:* internationale; fondée en 1924
Description: The federation works in co-operation with both the national and continental organisations to ensure consistency and unity in hockey around the world. The FIH not only regulates the sport, but is also responsible for its development and promotion so as to guarantee a secure future for hockey
Affiliation(s): Field Hockey Canada
Membre(s) du bureau directeur: Leandro Negre, President
Membre: 5 federations; *Comités:* Appointments; Athletes; Competitions; Risk & Compliance; Rules; Umpiring; Equipment Advisory Panel; High Performance & Coaching Advisory Panel; Judicial Commission; Medical Advisory Panel

Floorball Québec
2105 Guerin St., Laval QC H7E 1R7
Tel: 514-567-8449
info@floorballqc.ca
www.floorballqc.ca
Social Media:
www.youtube.com/user/iffchannel
www.facebook.com/floorballqc
twitter.com/floorballqc

Overview: A small provincial organization founded in 2014
Description: To promote floorball in Quebec; *Member of:* Floorball Canada

Hockey Alberta / Hockey l'Alberta
PO Box 5005, #2606, 100 College Blvd., Red Deer AB T4N 5H5
Tel: 403-342-6777; *Fax:* 403-346-4277
info@hockeyalberta.ca
www.hockeyalberta.ca
Social Media:
www.facebook.com/HockeyAlberta
twitter.com/HockeyAlberta

Overview: A large provincial organization founded in 1907
Description: To act as the governing body for organized hockey in Alberta; To create positive opportunities & experiences for players through service & leadership; *Member of:* Hockey Canada
Chief Officer(s): Rob Litwinski, Executive Director
rlitwinski@hockeyalberta.ca
Justin Fesyk, Senior Manager, Hockey Development
jfesyk@hockeyalberta.ca
Mike Klass, Senior Manager, Business Operations
mklass@hockeyalberta.ca
Membership: 450 organizations + 90,000+ individual members
Activities: Hosting regional & provincial tournaments & competitions; Providing access to certified coaching clinics; Holding an appeal board to which any member, team, or player can appeal disciplinary measures; Issuing permits for tournaments & exhibition games to ensure that teams meet eligibility requirements; Providing rule books, training manuals, & bulletins for teams & officials; *Internships:* Yes; *Speaker Service:* Yes; *Rents Mailing List:* Yes; *Library:* Yes

Hockey Canada
801 King Edward Ave., #N204, Ottawa ON K1N 6N5
Tel: 613-562-5677; *Fax:* 613-562-5676
www.hockeycanada.ca
Social Media:
www.youtube.com/hockeycanadavideos;
www.instagram.com/hockeycanada
www.linkedin.com/company/hockey-canada
www.facebook.com/HockeyCanada
twitter.com/hockeycanada

Also Known As: Canadian Hockey Association
Merged from: Canadian Amateur Hockey Association; Hockey Canada
Overview: A large national organization founded in 1914
Description: To advance amateur hockey for all individuals through progressive leadership, ensuring meaningful opportunities & enjoyable experiences in a safe, sustainable environment
Affiliation(s): International Ice Hockey Federation
Chief Officer(s): Tony Renney, President
Francis Dupont, Contact, Communications & Media Relations
fdupont@hockeycanada.ca
Finances: *Funding Sources:* Government; Sponsorship; Sales; Fundraising

Hockey Canada Foundation
#N204, 801 King Edward Ave., Ottawa ON K1N 6N5
Tel: 613-562-5677; *Fax:* 613-562-5676
foundation@hockeycanada.ca
www.hockeycanada.ca

Overview: A large national charitable organization
Description: To establish & grow endowment & general purpose funds for Hockey Canada
Chief Officer(s): Chris Bright, Executive Director
cbright@hockeycanada.ca
Finances: *Funding Sources:* Donations; fundraising
Activities: Focus areas: Skill Development & Qualified Coaching; Accessibility & Diversity; Health & Wellness; Athlete & Alumni Support; Facilities; *Awareness Events:* Golf Gala

Hockey Development Centre for Ontario (HDCO)
#215, 19 Waterman Ave., Toronto ON M4B 1Y2
Tel: 416-426-7252; *Fax:* 416-426-7348
Toll-Free: 888-843-4326
hockey@hdco.on.ca
www.hdco.on.ca
Social Media:
twitter.com/theHDCO

Overview: A medium-sized provincial organization founded in 1984
Description: To provide educational, developmental & financial opportunities for amateur hockey participants in Ontario
Chief Officer(s): Wayne Dillon, Executive Director
wdillon@hdco.on ca
Finances: *Annual Operating Budget:* $500,000-$1.5 Million; *Funding Sources:* Provincial government; sponsorships
Staff: 3 staff member(s)
Membership: 10 institutional; 2 associate
Activities: Hockey Trainers Certification Program; *Rents Mailing List:* Yes; *Library:* Hockey Resources (Open to Public)

Hockey Eastern Ontario (HEO)
813 Shefford Rd., Ottawa ON K1J 8H9
Tel: 613-224-7686; *Fax:* 613-224-6079
info@hockeyeasternontario.ca
www.hockeyeasternontario.ca
Social Media:
www.youtube.com/channel/UCIc6D9wLXpCkGsA2ETjpkhg
www.facebook.com/HockeyEasternOntario
twitter.com/HEOhockey

Overview: A medium-sized provincial organization founded in 1920
Description: To act as the governing body of amateur hockey in Eastern Ontario; To foster, improve, & encourage amateur hockey through leadership
Chief Officer(s): Debbie Rambeau, Executive Director, 613-224-7686 201
drambeau@hockeyeasternontario.ca

Hockey Manitoba
145 Pacific Ave., Winnipeg MB R3B 2Z6
Tel: 204-925-5755; *Fax:* 204-925-5761
info@hockeymanitoba.ca
www.hockeymanitoba.ca
Social Media:
www.youtube.com/hockeymanitoba;
www.instagram.com/hockeymanitoba
www.facebook.com/hockeymanitoba
twitter.com/hockeymanitoba

Also Known As: Manitoba Amateur Hockey Association
Overview: A medium-sized provincial organization founded in 1914
Description: To foster, develop, & promote amateur hockey throughout Manitoba; To encourage fair play; To secure the enforcement of rules as adopted by by the assosication; To conduct games between member clubs to determine provincial champions
Chief Officer(s): Peter Woods, Executive Director, 204-925-5757
peter@hockeymanitoba.ca
Bernie Reichardt, Director, Hockey Development, 204-925-5759
bernie@hockeymanitoba.ca
Membership: 30,000; *Committees:* Officials Development; Athlete Development
Activities: Administering clinics & skills camps; Collaborating in development programs for players, coaches & officials

Hockey New Brunswick (HNB) / Hockey Nouveau-Brunswick
PO Box 456, 861 Woodstock Rd., Fredericton NB E3B 4Z9
Tel: 506-453-0089; *Fax:* 506-453-0868
www.hnb.ca
Social Media:
www.facebook.com/148777865135246
twitter.com/HockeyNB

Previous Name: New Brunswick Amateur Hockey Association
Overview: A medium-sized provincial organization founded in 1968
Description: To act as the governing body for hockey in New Brunswick
Chief Officer(s): Nic Jansen, Executive Director, 506-453-0866
njansen@hnb.ca

Hockey Newfoundland & Labrador (NLHA) / Association de hockey de Terre-Neuve et Labrador
PO Box 176, 32 Queensway, Grand Falls-Windsor NL A2A 2J4
Tel: 709-489-5512; *Fax:* 709-489-2273
office@hockeynl.ca
www.hockeynl.ca
Social Media:
twitter.com/Hkynl

Overview: A medium-sized provincial organization founded in 1935
Description: To act as the governing body for hockey in Newfoundland & Labrador; To foster & encourage positive player experiences through development & leadership; *Member of:* Hockey Canada
Chief Officer(s): Craig Tulk, Executive Director
ctulk@hockeynl.ca

Hockey North
c/o Kyle Kugler, Executive Director, Hockey North, 237 Borden Dr., Yellowknife NT X1A 3R2
Tel: 867-446-8890
www.hockeynorth.ca

Overview: A small provincial organization
Description: To govern & register all amateur hockey programs in the Northwest Territories & Nunavut Territory
Chief Officer(s): Kyle Kugler, Executive Director
kylek@hockeynorth.ca

Hockey Northwestern Ontario (HNO)
#301, 214 Red River Rd., Thunder Bay ON P7B 1A6
Tel: 807-623-1542; *Fax:* 807-623-0037
info@hockeyhno.com
www.hockeyhno.com
Social Media:
www.facebook.com/HNOHockey
twitter.com/HNOHockey

Previous Name: Thunder Bay Amateur Hockey Association
Overview: A small provincial organization
Description: To encourage & improve the sport of amateur hockey throughout Northwestern Ontario; *Member of:* Hockey Canada
Chief Officer(s): Trevor Hosanna, Executive Director, 807-623-1542 2
thosanna@hockeyhno.com

Hockey Nova Scotia
#17, 7 Mellor Ave., Dartmouth NS B3B 0E8
Tel: 902-454-9400; *Fax:* 902-454-3883
www.hockeynovascotia.ca
Social Media:
www.youtube.com/channel/UC8gbE0o_HAAQ6bj2c8S6kdg
www.facebook.com/hockeynovascotia
twitter.com/HockeyNS
Previous Name: Nova Scotia Hockey Association
Overview: A medium-sized provincial organization founded in 1974
Description: To act as the governing body for hockey in Nova Scotia; To encourage positive player experiences through development, resources, & leadership; *Member of:* Hockey Canada
Chief Officer(s): Darren Cossar, Executive Director
dcossar@hockeynovascotia.ca
Membership: 20,000

Hockey PEI
PO Box 302, #209, 40 Enman Cres., Charlottetown PE C1E 1E6
Tel: 902-368-4334; *Fax:* 902-368-4337
info@hockeypei.com
hockeypei.com
Social Media:
twitter.com/hockeypei
Previous Name: Prince Edward Island Hockey Association
Overview: A medium-sized provincial organization founded in 1974
Description: To act as the governing body for hockey in Prince Edward Island; *Member of:* Hockey Canada
Chief Officer(s): Rob Newson, Executive Director
rob@hockeypei.com
Finances: *Annual Operating Budget:* $250,000-$500,000
Staff: 3 staff member(s); 100 volunteer(s)
Membership: 6,000

Hockey Québec (FQHG)
#210, 7450, boul. les Galeries d'Anjou, Montréal QC H1M 3M3
Tél: 514-252-3079; *Téléc:* 514-252-3158
communication@hockey.qc.ca
www.hockey.qc.ca
Média social:
www.youtube.com/channel/UCjHSK9n17ccFJca_wbfJakQ
www.facebook.com/HockeyQuebec
twitter.com/HockeyQuebec
Nom précédent: Fédération québécoise de hockey sur glace
Aperçu: *Dimension:* grande; *Envergure:* provinciale; fondée en 1976
Description: Assurer l'encadrement du hockey sur glace; favoriser la promotion et le développement de la personne qui pratique le hockey; *Membre de:* Hockey Canada
Membre(s) du bureau directeur: Sylvain B. Lalonde, Directeur général
sblalonde@hockey.qc.ca
Activités: La Méthode d'apprentissage de hockey sur glace; excellence; développement régional; entraîneurs et officiels; formation des administrateurs bénévoles; hockey féminin; franc jeu; sports-études; *Service de conférenciers:* Oui; *Listes de destinataires:* Oui

Hockey Yukon
4061 - 4th Ave., Whitehorse YT Y1A 1H1
Tel: 867-393-4501
yaha@sportyukon.com
hockeyyukon.ca
Previous Name: Yukon Amateur Hockey Association
Overview: A small provincial organization
Description: The Yukon Amateur Hockey Association is the sports governing body for amateur hockey in the Yukon.; *Member of:* British Columbia Amateur Hockey Association; Sport Yukon

International Ice Hockey Federation (IIHF)
Brandschenkestrasse 50, Zurich CH-8027 Switzerland
office@iihf.com
www.iihf.com
Social Media:
www.facebook.com/294239820899
twitter.com/IIHFHockey
Overview: A large international organization founded in 1908
Description: To govern, develop & promote ice & in-line hockey throughout the world; To develop & control international ice & in-line hockey; To promote friendly relations among the member national associations; To operate in an organized manner for the good order of the sport; *Member of:* Association of International Olympic Winter Sports Federations
Affiliation(s): Hockey Canada
Chief Officer(s): René Fasel, President
Horst Lichtner, General Secretary
Membership: 73 national associations; *Member Profile:* National ice hockey associations & in-line hockey associations; *Committees:* Athletes; Competition &Inline; Co-ordination; Development & Coaching; Disciplinary; Event; Facilities; Historical; Legal; Medical; Officiating; Player Safety Consulting Group; Social & Environment; Strategic Consulting Group; Women's; Asian Strategic Planning Group
Activities: *Internships:* Yes; *Speaker Service:* Yes; *Library:* Hockey Hall of Fame, Toronto Canada (Open to Public)

Lethbridge Oldtimers Sports Association (LOSA)
PO Box 84, Lethbridge AB T1J 3Y3
www.losa.ca
Overview: A small local organization
Description: To organize recreational hockey games for adults
Chief Officer(s): Brian Wright, President
Membership: *Fees:* $50

Minor Hockey Alliance of Ontario
71 Albert St., Stratford ON N5A 3K2
Tel: 519-273-7209; *Fax:* 519-273-2114
www.alliancehockey.com
Social Media:
www.facebook.com/114981545258512
twitter.com/ALLIANCE_Hockey
Also Known As: Alliance Hockey
Overview: A small provincial organization founded in 1993
Description: To organize, coordinate & develop hockey programs for all ages; *Member of:* Canadian Hockey Association; Ontario Hockey Federation
Chief Officer(s): Tony Martindale, Executive Director
Membership: 29,734; *Committees:* Development; Constitution; House League & Select; Minor Development; Group Structure; Insurance & Risk Management; Discipline & Suspension; Championship; Overseas; AGM

National Hockey League Alumni Association (NHLA)
400 Kipling Ave., Toronto ON M8V 3L1
Tel: 416-798-2586; *Fax:* 416-798-2582
info@nhlalumni.net
nhlalumni.net
Social Media:
la.linkedin.com/groups?gid=1039337
www.facebook.com/nhlalumni
twitter.com/NHLAlumni
Also Known As: NHL Alumni Association
Overview: A medium-sized national charitable organization founded in 1999
Description: Provides programs and assistance for all retired NHL players, including career transition with the BreakAway Program.
Affiliation(s): National Hockey League (NHL); National Hockey League Players' Association
Chief Officer(s): Mark Napier, Executive Director
mark@nhlalumni.net
Mike Pelyk, Chair
Membership: 28 chapters + 2,500 members
Activities: *Speaker Service:* Yes; *Rents Mailing List:* Yes

National Hockey League Players' Association (NHLPA)
#1700, 20 Bay St., Toronto ON M5J 2N8
www.nhlpa.com
Social Media:
www.youtube.com/user/NHLPA
www.facebook.com/nhlpa
twitter.com/nhlpa
Overview: A medium-sized national organization founded in 1967
Description: The union for professional hockey players in the National Hockey League (NHL).
Affiliation(s): National Hockey League (NHL); National Hockey League Players' Association
Chief Officer(s): Don Fehr, Executive Director

Northern Ontario Hockey Association (NOHA)
110 Lakeshore Dr., North Bay ON P1A 2A8
Tel: 705-474-8851; *Fax:* 705-474-6019
noha@noha.on.ca
www.noha.on.ca
Social Media:
www.facebook.com/NorthernOntarioHockeyAssociation
twitter.com/nohahockey
Overview: A small local organization founded in 1919
Description: To foster the sport of amateur hockey in northern Ontario
Affiliation(s): Ontario Hockey Federation
Chief Officer(s): Jason Marchand, Executive Director
jmarchand@noha.on.ca
Finances: *Funding Sources:* Sponsorships; Membership fees
Staff: 13 staff member(s)
Member Profile: Amateur hockey clubs in northern Ontario
Activities: Hosting tournaments; Presenting awards; Organizing specialty clinics

Nova Scotia Minor Hockey Council
c/o Hockey Nova Scotia, #17, 7 Mellor Ave., Dartmouth NS B3B 0E8
Tel: 902-454-9400; *Fax:* 902-454-3883
Overview: A medium-sized provincial organization founded in 1974
Description: To provide a standard set of playing rules for minor hockey in Nova Scotia
Affiliation(s): Nova Scotia Hockey Association
Chief Officer(s): Arnie Farrell, Chair, 902-863-0221
arniefarrell@ns.sympatico.ca

Ontario Hockey Federation (OHF)
#9, 400 Sheldon Dr., Cambridge ON N1T 2H9
Tel: 226-533-9070; *Fax:* 519-620-7476
info@ohf.on.ca
www.ohf.on.ca
Social Media:
www.facebook.com/OHFHockey
twitter.com/ohfhockey
Overview: A medium-sized provincial organization founded in 1989
Description: To foster & promote the sport of amateur hockey in Ontario; To provide opportunities for all players to participate in the sport; To coordinate & conduct competitions & tournaments for branch, regional, & national championships; *Member of:* Hockey Development Centre for Ontario (HDCO)
Affiliation(s): Minor Hockey Alliance of Ontario; Greater Toronto Hockey League; Northern Ontario Hockey Association; Ontario Minor Hockey Association; Ontario Hockey Association; Ontario Hockey League; Ontario Women's Hockey Association
Chief Officer(s): Phillip McKee, Executive Director, 226-533-9075
pmckee@ohf.on.ca
Membership: 228,251 registered players; 33,500 coaches; 7,300 officials; *Committees:* Constitution; Finance; Rules; Risk Management; Registration; Minor Council; Junior Council; Hockey Development Council; Senior / Adult Recreational Council; Female Hockey (operates under the auspices of the Ontario Women's Hockey Association)
Activities: *Internships:* Yes

Ontario Minor Hockey Association (OMHA)
#3, 25 Brodie Dr., Richmond Hill ON L4B 3K7
Tel: 905-780-6642; *Fax:* 905-780-0344
omha@omha.net
www.omha.net
Social Media:
instagram.com/ontariominorhockey
www.facebook.com/HometownHockey
twitter.com/HometownHockey
Overview: A medium-sized provincial organization founded in 1935
Description: To provide community-based minor hockey programming for men, women, & children; To monitor the safety of the game, from equipment to rules
Affiliation(s): Ontario Hockey Federation
Chief Officer(s): Richard Ropchan, Executive Director, 905-780-2150
Martha Dickie, Manager, Membership Services, 905-780-2159
Ian Taylor, Director, Hockey Development, 905-780-2172
Finances: *Funding Sources:* Membership fees; Sponsorships
Activities: Providing development programs; Conducting seminars, coaches clinics, skills camps, & festivals; Initiating safety measures, such as the concussion awareness program, a mouthguard policy, & helmets for all on-ice personnel

Ontario Sledge Hockey Association (OSHA)
ON
www.alpineontario.ca
Social Media:
www.facebook.com/467967866581968
twitter.com/OSHASledge
Overview: A medium-sized provincial organization
Description: To oversee three regular season sledge hockey leagues; *Member of:* Ontario Hockey Federation; Hockey Canada
Chief Officer(s): Dave Kisel, President, 905-560-8287
dkisel@bell.net
Membership: 20 clubs + 400 players; *Committees:* Rules

Ontario Women's Hockey Association (OWHA) / Association de hockey féminin de l'Ontario
225 Watline Ave., Mississauga ON L4Z 1P3
Tel: 905-282-9980; *Fax:* 905-282-9982
info@owha.on.ca
www.owha.on.ca
Social Media:
twitter.com/OWHAhockey
Overview: A medium-sized provincial organization founded in 1975

Description: To provide & develop opportunities for girls & women to play female hockey in all aspects of female hockey; To foster & encourage leadership programs in all areas related to the development of female hockey in Ontario; To promote hockey as a game played primarily for enjoyment while also fostering sportsmanship; *Member of:* Hockey Canada
Chief Officer(s): Fran Rider, President & Chief Executive Officer, 416-573-5447
fran@owha.on.ca
Pat Nicholls, Director, Operations, 416-571-9198
pat@owha.on.ca

Original Hockey Hall of Fame & Museum
Invista Centre, 1350 Gardiners Rd., 2nd Fl., Kingston ON K7L 4V6
Tel: 613-507-1943
info@originalhockeyhalloffame.com
www.originalhockeyhalloffame.com
Social Media:
www.facebook.com/207141552735961
twitter.com/ihhof43
Previous Name: International Hockey Hall of Fame & Museum; International Ice Hockey Federation Museum Inc.
Overview: A small local organization founded in 1943
Description: The first sports hall of fame in Canada, the Hall features exhibits on the original six NHL teams, Kingston native Don Cherry & historic hockey artifacts
Chief Officer(s): Mark Potter, President
mpotter1@cogeco.ca
Larry Paquette, Vice-President
ihhof@kos.net
Finances: *Funding Sources:* Provincial government grants; special events; museum
Activities: *Awareness Events:* Historic Hockey Series, 1st Sat. in Feb.

Ottawa District Minor Hockey Association (ODMHA)
#300, 1247 Kilborn Pl., Ottawa ON K1H 6K9
Tel: 613-224-3589; *Fax:* 613-224-4625
odmha@odmha.on.ca
www.odmha.on.ca
Overview: A medium-sized local organization founded in 1972
Description: To promote minor hockey throughout the region; *Member of:* Hockey Canada
Chief Officer(s): Denis Dumais, President
denisdumais@sympatico.ca
Activities: *Speaker Service:* Yes; *Library:* Resource Centre (Open to Public)

Pan American Hockey Federation (PAHF)
c/o Ian Baggott, Field Hockey Canada, 311 West 1st St., North Vancouver BC V7M 1B5
info@panamhockey.org
www.panamhockey.org
Social Media:
www.youtube.com/user/PAHFvideo;
instagram.com/panamhockey
www.facebook.com/174792322573292
twitter.com/PanAmHockey
Overview: A large international organization founded in 1955
Description: To be the governing continental federation for all field hockey in the Pan American region; *Member of:* International Hockey Federation
Chief Officer(s): Alberto Budeisky, President
president@panamhockey.org
Derek Sandison, Honorary Treasurer
derek.sandison@rogers.com
Julio F. Neves, Managing Director
Julio.Neves@panamhockey.org
Finances: *Annual Operating Budget:* $100,000-$250,000; *Funding Sources:* Grants; Membership dues; Tournament fees; International Hockey Federation; Sponsorship
Membership: 26 national associations; *Member Profile:* National association recognized by national olympic committees & the International Hockey Federation; *Committees:* Appointments; Competitions; Development & Coaching; Media & Communications; Medical; Umpiring
Activities: Organizing international hockey tournaments; organizing instructional courses

Prince Edward Island Hockey Referees Association
c/o Hockey PEI, 40 Enman Cres., Charlottetown PE C1A 7K7
Tel: 902-367-8373
Overview: A medium-sized provincial organization
Member of: Hockey PEI; Hockey Canada

Saskatchewan Hockey Association (SHA) / Association de hockey de la Saskatchewan
#2, 575 Park St., Regina SK S4N 5B2
Tel: 306-789-5101
www.sha.sk.ca
Social Media:
www.facebook.com/324377598563
twitter.com/sask_hockey
Overview: A medium-sized provincial organization founded in 1912
Description: To administer the operation of amateur hockey in the Province of Saskatchewan; To foster & promote amateur hockey within the province & to assist in the promotion of amateur hockey outside the province; To promote, supervise & administer all competitions for amateur hockey within the jurisdiction of the SAHA; *Member of:* Hockey Canada
Chief Officer(s): Kelly McClintock, General Manager
kellym@sha.sk.ca
Finances: *Annual Operating Budget:* $1.5 Million-$3 Million
Staff: 10 staff member(s)
Membership: 46,000

Sledge Hockey of Canada (SHOC)
c/o Hockey Canada, #N204, 801 King Edward Ave., Ottawa ON K1N 6N5
Tel: 613-562-5677; *Fax:* 613-562-5676
www.hockeycanada.ca
Social Media:
www.youtube.com/hcsledge
www.facebook.com/HCSledge
twitter.com/HC_Sledge
Overview: A small national organization
Description: To promote & govern the sport of sledge hockey in Canada

Summerside & Area Minor Hockey Association (SAMHA)
PO Box 1454, Summerside PE C1N 4K4
info@summersideminorhockey.com
summersideminorhockey.com
Overview: A medium-sized local organization

Superior International Junior Hockey League (SIJHL)
529 Dublin Ave., Thunder Bay ON P7B 5A1
Tel: 807-626-2316
sijhlmedia@gmail.com
www.sijhlhockey.com
Social Media:
www.facebook.com/SIJHL
twitter.com/SIJHL
Overview: A small local organization
Member of: Canadian Junior Hockey League
Chief Officer(s): Ron Whitehead, President/Commissioner
Membership: 6 teams

Thunder Bay Minor Hockey Association (TBMHA)
#101, 212 East Miles St., Thunder Bay ON
Tel: 807-346-4510; *Fax:* 807-346-4511
www.tbmha.com
Overview: A small local organization
Chief Officer(s): Larry Busniuk, President

Township of Clarence Minor Hockey Association (TCMHA)
PO Box 212, Clarence Creek AB K0A 1N0
clarencehockey.ca
Overview: A small local organization
Description: To govern & promote minor hockey in Clarence
Chief Officer(s): Linda Thompson, President
castorpresident@gmail.com

Western Hockey League (WHL)
Father David Bauer Arena, 2424 University Dr. NW, Calgary AB T2N 3Y9
Tel: 403-693-3030; *Fax:* 403-693-3031
info@whl.ca
www.whl.ca
Social Media:
www.facebook.com/WHLHockey
twitter.com/theWHL
Overview: A medium-sized local organization founded in 1966
Description: To remain the world's premiere major junior hockey league by continuing to provide the best player development & educational opportunities while enhancing the entertainment value of the game for our fan base; *Member of:* Canadian Hockey League
Chief Officer(s): Ron Robison, Commissioner
Membership: Comprised of 22 hockey teams in Western Canada & the northwest United States

Whitehorse Minor Hockey Association (WMHA)
4061 - 4th Ave., Whitehorse YT Y1A 1H1
Tel: 867-393-4698; *Fax:* 867-667-4237
office@whitehorseminor.ca
www.whitehorseminorhockey.ca
Overview: A medium-sized provincial organization
Description: Promotes and coordinates minor hockey leagues in Whitehorse.; *Member of:* Sport Yukon
Affiliation(s): Yukon Amateur Hockey Association
Chief Officer(s): Justin Halowaty, President
justin@ttlp.com
Richelle Bierlmeier, Vice-President, Operations
richelle99@gmail.com

Whitehorse Women's Hockey Association (WWHA)
c/o Sport Yukon, 4061 - 4th Ave., Whitehorse YT Y1A 1H1
wwhayukon@gmail.com
whitehorsewomenshockey.com
Social Media:
www.facebook.com/whitehorsewomenshockeyassn
Overview: A small local organization founded in 1993
Description: To administer women's hockey in Whitehorse.

Horse Racing

Alberta Horse Trials Association (AHTA)
c/o Aislyn Havell, Membership Secretary, #23, 38440 Range Rd. 284, Red Deer County AB T4S 2E2
albertahorsetrials@gmail.com
www.albertahorsetrials.com
Overview: A small provincial organization
Description: To promote & develop 3-day eventing in Alberta & Canada & assist in producing Olympic athletes
Affiliation(s): Canadian Equestrian Federation
Chief Officer(s): Kristine Haut, President
ahtapresident@gmail.com
Finances: *Annual Operating Budget:* Less than $50,000; *Funding Sources:* National Government, Provincial Government
Staff: 13 volunteer(s)
Membership: 170 student; 240 individual; 20 associate; *Fees:* $30 associate; $50 junior; $60 senior; $120 family; *Committees:* Membership; Competitions; Special Events; Communications; Athlete Development; Clinics; Marketing

Association Trot & Amble du Québec (ATAQ) / Québec Trotting & Pacing Society
#216, 5375, rue Paré, Montréal QC H4P 1P7
Tél: 514-731-9484; *Ligne sans frais:* 800-731-9484
courses@qc.aira.com
www.trotetamble.ca
Aperçu: *Dimension:* moyenne; *Envergure:* provinciale
Description: Coopérer avec les promoteurs afin de s'assurer de la bonne conduite des programmes de courses aux différents hippodromes du Québec; améliorer les lois et règlements en vue de favoriser le sport des courses sous harnais; représenter et aider tous les members; encourager et promouvoir les courses d'élevage québécois et les courses régulières; collaborer avec les différents organismes afin d'établir un juste équilibre pour le bien-être de l'industrie
Membre(s) du bureau directeur: Marc Camirand, Président
Gilles Fortier, Secrétaire général, 514-731-9484
Montant de la cotisation: Barème
Activités: Service d'assurances; activités sociales; promotion

Jockey Club of Canada / Jockey Club du Canada
PO Box 66, Stn. B, Toronto ON M9W 5K9
Tel: 416-675-7756; *Fax:* 416-675-6378
jockeyclub@bellnet.ca
www.jockeyclubcanada.com
Social Media:
twitter.com/jockeyclubofCAN
Overview: A small national licensing organization founded in 1973
Description: Promote good quality racing throughout Canada; *Member of:* Thoroughbred Racing Industry participants in Canada
Affiliation(s): The Jockey Club (New York)
Chief Officer(s): James Lawson, Chief Steward
Stacie Roberts, Executive Director
Member Profile: Liaises with foreign Jockey Clubs; promotes Thoroughbred ownership; and represents Canada at international racing conferences.
Activities:; *Library:* Yes (Open to Public) by appointment

Jockeys Benefit Association of Canada (JBAC)
c/o Thoroughbred Race Office, 555 Rexdale Blvd., Toronto ON M9W 5L2
Overview: A small national organization
Description: The Jockey's Benefit Association of Canada (JBAC) has been in operation for over 40 years as a non profit corporation which operates to assist & represent jockeys as a

group across Canada. Operated under a number of directors across the country, the JBAC is the official spokesperson of jockeys in Canada.
Membership: 150

Ontario Horse Racing Industry Association (OHRIA)
PO Box 456, Stn. B, Toronto ON M9W 5L4
Tel: 416-679-0741; *Fax:* 416-679-9114
ohria@ohria.com
www.ohria.com
Social Media:
twitter.com/value4money_ca
Overview: A small provincial organization founded in 1994
Description: Promote the horse racing industry as a vital part of Ontario's lifestyle, heritage & agricultural economy
Chief Officer(s): Sue Leslies, President and Chair
Membership: 21 associations; *Member Profile:* Industry organization/associations

Horses

Canadian Pony Club (CPC)
PO Box 127, Baldur MB R0K 0B0
Fax: 204-535-2289
Toll-Free: 888-286-7669
www.canadianponyclub.org
Social Media:
www.youtube.com/channel/UCduYBFvUP5UBL8xapYrfsFQ/play lists
www.facebook.com/CanadianPonyClub
Overview: A medium-sized national organization founded in 1934
Description: To encourage & instruct young people to ride & care for their horses, while promoting loyalty, character & sportsmanship.; *Member of:* Equine Canada
Affiliation(s): Ontario Equestrian Federation
Chief Officer(s): Kim Leffley, National Chair
kleffley@gmail.com
Maria Berry, National Secretary
meb@mts.net
Finances: *Funding Sources:* Fees
Membership: 3,500, in 150 branches; *Member Profile:* Young people between the ages of 6-21 who wish to learn all about horses; *Committees:* Management; Communications; Dressage; PPG; Rally; Testing; Tetrathlon; Finance; Human Resources; Education; Quiz; Show Jummping; Disciplines; Rally; Prince Philip Games
Activities: Instruction in dressage, show jumping, Tetrathlon

Horseshoe Pitching

Alberta Horseshoe Pitchers Association (AHPA)
AB
Tel: 403-946-4109
abhorseshoepitchers.com
Overview: A small provincial organization founded in 1977
Description: To promote the sport of horseshoe pitching in Alberta.; *Member of:* Horseshoe Canada
Chief Officer(s): Bruce Grandel, President
brucegrandel@hotmail.com

B.C. Horseshoe Association
c/o Sam Tomasevic, 7987 Graham Ave., Burnaby BC V3N 1V8
Tel: 604-525-2186
administrator@bchorseshoe.com
www.bchorseshoe.com
Overview: A small provincial organization
Description: To promote the sport of horseshoe pitching in British Columbia.; *Member of:* Horseshoe Canada
Chief Officer(s): Sam Tomasevic, President
samtom@telus.net
Membership: 346

Fédération des clubs de fers du Québec
4545, av Pierre-de Coubertin, Montréal QC H1V 0B2
Tél: 514-252-3032
fers@fqjr.qc.ca
fers.quebecjeux.org
Média social:
www.facebook.com/1433138876961682
Aperçu: *Dimension:* moyenne; *Envergure:* provinciale; fondée en 1961
Description: La FCFQ veut promouvoir la pratique du lancer de fers. Elle favorise les rencontres et les tournois qui contribuent au développement de la discipline. Elle distribue de l'information, donne des cours et des démonstrations; *Membre de:* Horseshoe Canada
Membre(s) du bureau directeur: Kenny Weightman, Président
Montant de la cotisation: 12$ individuel; 50$ club/ligue/ville

Horseshoe Canada
NS
Tel: 902-852-3231
www.horseshoecanada.ca
Social Media:
www.facebook.com/Horseshoe-Canada-Association-361777939646
Overview: A medium-sized national organization founded in 1979
Description: To promote & foster the sport of horseshoe pitching in Canada.
Chief Officer(s): Jason Rideout, President
jrideout.tp@gmail.com
Membership: 10 member associations with 3,500 individual members
Activities: *Awareness Events:* Canadian Horseshoe Pitching Championship

Horseshoe New Brunswick
c/o Jason Rideout, President, 14 Nicholas Dr., Old Ridge NB E3L 4Y6
Tel: 506-467-9100
www.horseshoenb.com
Social Media:
www.facebook.com/HorseshoeNB
twitter.com/SSHPC
Overview: A small provincial organization
Description: To promote the sport of horseshoe pitching in New Brunswick.; *Member of:* Horseshoe Canada
Chief Officer(s): Jason Rideout, President
jrideout.tp@gmail.com

Horseshoe Ontario
c/o Terrie Singbeil, 103 John St. East, Waterloo ON N2J 1G2
www.horseshoeontario.com
Overview: A small provincial organization
Description: To promote the sport of horseshoe pitching in Ontario.; *Member of:* Horseshoe Canada
Chief Officer(s): Terrie Slingbeil, Contact
tsingbeil@rogers.com
Membership: 450; *Fees:* $25 regular; $1 junior

Horseshoe Saskatchewan Inc.
PO Box 29029, Saskatoon SK S7N 4Y2
horseshoesask@sasktel.net
www.horseshoesask.ca
Overview: A small provincial organization founded in 1973
Description: Clubs in this horseshoe-pitching association represent areas in Saskatchewan, Alberta & Manitoba.; *Member of:* Horseshoe Canada
Chief Officer(s): Tammy Christensen, President, 306-565-1409
Denise Squires, Executive Coordinator, 306-374-8233
Finances: *Annual Operating Budget:* Less than $50,000; *Funding Sources:* Raffles; merchandise sales; Saskatchewan Lotteries
Staff: 2 staff member(s); 30 volunteer(s)
Membership: 13 clubs
Activities: Annual Western Classics Tournament

Nova Scotia Horseshoe Players Association
NS
Tel: 902-852-3231; *Fax:* 902-852-2311
Overview: A small provincial organization
Description: To promote the sport of horseshoes in Canada; *Member of:* Horseshoe Canada
Chief Officer(s): Cecil Mitchell, Contact
cmitchell@rainbownetrigging.com

Nova Scotia Horseshoe Players Association (NSHPA)
NS
Overview: A small provincial licensing organization founded in 1973
Description: To promote the enjoyment & health benefits of the sport of horseshoe pitching throughout Nova Scotia; *Member of:* Sport Nova Scotia; Horseshoe Canada
Affiliation(s): Maritime Horseshoe Players Association
Finances: *Annual Operating Budget:* Less than $50,000; *Funding Sources:* Membership dues; fundraising; government grants
Staff: 40 volunteer(s)
Membership: 35; *Committees:* Club Forming; Membership; Palladian Construction; Promotion
Activities: 8 sanctioned tournaments; TV Series; conducts Special Olympics for horseshoes; *Rents Mailing List:* Yes

Kayaking

Canoe Kayak Saskatchewan (CKS)
510 Cynthia St., Saskatoon SK S4P 2L7
Tel: 306-975-7002; *Fax:* 306-242-8007
canoekayaksask.ca
Previous Name: Saskatchewan Canoe Association
Overview: A small provincial charitable organization founded in 1987
Description: To operate as the provincial sport governing body for canoe & kayak in Saskatchewan; *Member of:* CanoeKayak Canada
Chief Officer(s): Kia Schollar, Executive Director
ed@canoekayaksask.ca
Finances: *Funding Sources:* Saskatchewan Lotteries
Membership: *Fees:* $15; *Member Profile:* Competitive athletes; Novice athletes; Recreational paddlers; Coaches; Officials; Supporters
Activities: Encouraging participation; Developing excellence; Overseeing activities related to whitewater, recreation paddling, sprint racing (flatwater), & marathon

Fédération québécoise de canoë-kayak d'eau vives
4545, av Pierre-de Coubertin, Montréal QC H1V 0B2
Tél: 438-333-1913
www.federationkayak.qc.ca
Média social:
www.facebook.com/fqckev
Aperçu: *Dimension:* petite; *Envergure:* provinciale; fondée en 1971
Description: Promouvoir le sport et la pratique d'activités en eau vive au Québec; *Membre de:* CanoeKayak Canada

Ontario Recreational Canoeing & Kayaking Association (ORCKA)
#209, 3 Concorde Gate, Toronto ON M3C 3N7
Tel: 416-426-7016; *Fax:* 416-426-7363
info@orcka.ca
www.orcka.ca
Social Media:
www.facebook.com/228950560506530
Previous Name: Canoe Ontario; Ontario Recreational Canoeing Association
Overview: A medium-sized provincial organization founded in 1975
Description: To promote development of safe, competent & knowledgeable recreational paddlers
Chief Officer(s): Bruce Hawkins, President, 613-623-9950
bhawkins@orcka.on.ca
Finances: *Annual Operating Budget:* $100,000-$250,000; *Funding Sources:* Trillium Grant
Staff: 2 staff member(s)
Membership: *Fees:* $42.20 - $141.25; *Member Profile:* Canoe, kayak instructors & recreational paddlers in Ontario; *Committees:* Safety; Promotion; Environment; Instructor Service; Membership
Activities: Canoeing in Ontario

Paddle Canada (PC) / Pagaie Canada
PO Box 126, Stn. Main, Kingston ON K7L 4V6
Tel: 613-547-3196; *Fax:* 613-547-4880
Toll-Free: 888-252-6292
info@paddlecanada.com
www.paddlingcanada.com
Social Media:
www.youtube.com/user/PaddleCanada
www.facebook.com/pages/Paddle-Canada/111266462242503
twitter.com/paddlecanada
Previous Name: Canadian Recreational Canoeing Association
Overview: A large national licensing charitable organization founded in 1971
Description: To promote all forms of recreational paddling to Canadians of diverse abilities, culture or age; to advocate for a healthy natural environment; To develop an appreciation for the canoe & the kayak in our Canadian heritage
Affiliation(s): Active Living Alliance for Canadians with a Disability; Girl Guides of Canada
Chief Officer(s): Graham Ketcheson, Executive Director
Finances: *Funding Sources:* Membership fees; Donations; Program delivery; Sponsorships
Staff: 80 volunteer(s)
Membership: 1,700; *Fees:* $42 individual; *Committees:* Canoeing Program Development; River Kayaking Program Development; Sea Kayaking Program Development; SUP Board Program Development; Finance; Instruction & Safety; Communications (Marketing & Promotions); Member Services; Environment
Activities: Reviewing park management plans, hydroelectric developments & timber management plans; Promoting waterway conservation through the Waterwalker Film Festival; Providing

educational programs; Increasing environmental awareness; *Awareness Events:* National Paddling Week, June 6-15

Wilderness Canoe Association (WCA)
PO Box 91068, 2901 Bayview Ave., Toronto ON M2K 2Y6
Tel: 416-223-4646
info@wildernesscanoe.ca
www.wildernesscanoe.ca
Overview: A small local organization founded in 1973
Description: Organization of individuals interested in wilderness travel, mainly by canoe, kayak, and backpacking and, in winter, by skis and snowshoes; *Member of:* Federation of Ontario Naturalists
Chief Officer(s): David Young, Chair
chair@wildernesscanoe.ca
Finances: *Annual Operating Budget:* Less than $50,000
Membership: 750; *Fees:* $35 single; $45 family
Activities: Winter pool training sessions; Paddle the Don River; year-round outings; *Awareness Events:* Wine & Cheese, Nov.; Paddlers' Club Night, Feb.

Labour Unions

Canadian Football League Players' Association (CFLPA) / Association des joueurs de la ligue de football canadienne
175 Barton St. East, Stoney Creek ON L8E 2K3
Tel: 905-664-0852; *Fax:* 905-664-9653
Toll-Free: 800-616-6865
admin@cflpa.com
www.cflpa.com
Social Media:
www.youtube.com/user/cflpa
www.facebook.com/CFLPA
twitter.com/cflpa
Overview: A small national organization founded in 1965
Description: The Canadian Football League Players' Association was established in 1965 & has since that time represented the professional football players in the Canadian Football League with the objective of establishing fair & reasonable working conditions for the players.
Chief Officer(s): Jeff Keeping, President
Marwan Hage, 1st Vice-President
Brian Ramsay, Executive Director
Membership: approx. 400 + 8 locals

Major League Baseball Players' Association (Ind.) / Association des joueurs de la Ligue majeure de baseball (ind.)
12 East 49th St., 24th Fl., New York NY 10017 USA
Tel: 212-826-0808; *Fax:* 212-752-4378
feedback@mlbpa.org
www.mlb.com/pa
Social Media:
twitter.com/MLB_PLAYERS
Overview: A medium-sized international organization
Description: To represent and protect the interests of professional baseball players in the United States.
Chief Officer(s): Tony Clark, Executive Director
Martha Child, CAO
Marietta DiCamillo, Chief Financial Officer
Membership: 80 + 2 locals (in Canada)
Activities: Baseball Card Clubhouse; Baseball Tomorrow Fund; Rookie Career Development; *Awareness Events:* Players Choice Awards

Professional Hockey Players' Association (PHPA)
3964 Portage Rd., Niagara Falls ON L2J 2K9
Tel: 289-296-5561; *Fax:* 289-296-4567
www.phpa.com
Social Media:
instagram.com/thephpa
www.facebook.com/173409159401617
twitter.com/thephpa
Overview: A small national organization founded in 1967
Membership: 1,600+; *Member Profile:* All professional hockey players in the AHL & ECHL; *Committees:* Alumni Association; Workers' Compensation; Panel of Attorneys; Registered Agents Program; Career Enhancement Program; Membership Assistance Program

Lacrosse

Alberta Lacrosse Association (ALA)
11759 Groat Rd., Edmonton AB T5M 3K6
Tel: 780-422-0030; *Fax:* 780-451-6414
Toll-Free: 866-696-7694
www.albertalacrosse.com
Social Media:
www.facebook.com/257864104242295
twitter.com/AlbertaLacrosse
Overview: A small provincial organization
Description: To oversee the sport of lacrosse in the province of Alberta.; *Member of:* Canadian Lacrosse Association
Chief Officer(s): Greg Lintz, President
greg@tarrabain.com
Lisa Grant, Executive Director
lisa@albertalacrosse.com

BC Lacrosse Association (BCLA)
#101, 7382 Winston St., Burnaby BC V5A 2G9
Tel: 604-421-9755; *Fax:* 604-421-9775
info@bclacrosse.com
www.bclacrosse.com
Social Media:
www.youtube.com/user/BCLacrosseA
www.facebook.com/481524661862119
twitter.com/BCLacrosse
Overview: A medium-sized provincial organization
Description: Promotes and regulates the sport of lacrosse in British Columbia; *Member of:* Canadian Lacrosse Association
Chief Officer(s): Rochelle Winterton, Executive Director
rochelle@bclacrosse.com
Dave Showers, Technical Director
dave@bclacrosse.com

Canadian Lacrosse Association (CLA) / Association canadienne de crosse (ACC)
Gladstone Sports & Health Centre, #310, 18 Louisa St., Ottawa ON K1R 6Y6
Tel: 613-260-2028; *Fax:* 613-260-2029
info1@lacrosse.ca
www.lacrosse.ca
Social Media:
www.facebook.com/CanadianLacrosseAssociation
twitter.com/LacrosseCanada
Overview: A medium-sized national licensing charitable organization founded in 1867
Description: To promote, develop & preserve the sport of Lacrosse & its heritage as Canada's national summer sport.
Affiliation(s): International Lacrosse Federation; International Federation of Women's Lacrosse Associations; Fédération internationale d'Inter-crosse; Canadian Lacrosse Foundation; Sport Canada; Coaching Association of Canada
Chief Officer(s): Joanne Thomson, Executive Director
joanne@lacrosse.ca
Britany Gordon, Coordinator, Events & Communications
britany@lacrosse.ca
Finances: *Annual Operating Budget:* $250,000-$500,000; *Funding Sources:* Sport Canada; membership fees; sponsors; donations; sales
Staff: 3 staff member(s)
Membership: 11 provincial organizations; *Fees:* $350 - $1,050; *Member Profile:* Provincial associations/leagues; *Committees:* Equipment Review; Transfer Review; Appeals; Discipline; Aboriginal Development
Activities: *Awareness Events:* Lacrosse Week, 3rd week of May; *Internships:* Yes; *Speaker Service:* Yes; *Rents Mailing List:* Yes

Fédération de crosse du Québec (FCQ)
CP 1000, Succ. M, 4545, av Pierre-de Coubertin, Montréal QC H1V 3R2
crosse@crosse.qc.ca
www.crossequebec.com
Aperçu: *Dimension:* moyenne; *Envergure:* provinciale; fondée en 1971
Description: Offrir des services et des programmes axés vers le développement du sport de la crosse sur un plan régional et international; *Membre de:* Fédération Internationale d'Inter-Crosse; Canadian Lacrosse Association
Affiliation(s): Sports Québec; Regroupement Loisir Québec
Membre(s) du bureau directeur: Pierre Filion, Directeur
pierrefilion@bell.net
Finances: *Budget de fonctionnement annuel:* $100,000-$250,000
Personnel: 2 membre(s) du personnel; 45 bénévole(s)
Activités: Stages de formation, conférences, ligues d'inter-crosse, compétitions; *Stagiaires:* Oui; *Service de conférenciers:* Oui

Lacrosse New Brunswick
850 Old Black River Rd., Saint John NB E2J 4T3
Tel: 506-632-9188
www.laxnb.ca
Social Media:
www.facebook.com/128267803907009
Also Known As: Lacrosse NB
Overview: A small provincial organization
Description: To oversee the sport of lacrosse in the province of New Brunswick.; *Member of:* Canadian Lacrosse Association
Chief Officer(s): Dave Higdon, President
davehigdon@rogers.com
Dave Arsenault, Technical Director, 506-648-1098
majorlac@nbnet.nb.ca
Libby O'Brien, Director, Administration, 506-849-9081
obriend@nb.sympatico.ca

Lacrosse Nova Scotia
5516 Spring Garden Rd., 4th Fl., Halifax NS B3J 1G6
Tel: 902-425-5450; *Fax:* 902-425-5606
lacrosse@sportnovascotia.ca
lacrossens.ca
Social Media:
www.facebook.com/421011914655642
Overview: A small provincial organization founded in 1971
Member of: Canadian Lacrosse Association; Sport Nova Scotia
Chief Officer(s): Greg Knight, Executive Director
Chet Koneczny, Technical Director
lacrossetechdirector@sportnovascotia.ca
Finances: *Funding Sources:* Provincial government

Lethbridge Lacrosse Association
PO Box 874, Lethbridge AB T1J 3Z8
Tel: 403-715-3291
www.lethbridgelacrosse.com
Social Media:
www.facebook.com/lethbridge.lacrosse
twitter.com/lethlax
Overview: A small local organization
Description: To promote lacrosse in southern Alberta
Chief Officer(s): Mark Stewart, Program Director
progdirector@lethbridgelacrosse.com

Manitoba Lacrosse Association
145 Pacific Ave., Winnipeg MB R3B 2Z6
Tel: 204-925-5684; *Fax:* 204-925-5792
lacrosse@sportmanitoba.ca
manitobalacrosse.mb.ca
Social Media:
twitter.com/MBLacrosse
Overview: A small provincial organization
Description: To oversee the sport of lacrosse in the province of New Brunswick.; *Member of:* Canadian Lacrosse Association
Chief Officer(s): Paul Magnan, President
pmagnan@sunrisesd.ca
Don Jacks, Executive Director

Newfoundland & Labrador Lacrosse Association (NLLA)
PO Box 26037, 250 Lemarchant Rd., St. John's NL A1E 0A5
general@nllacrosse.ca
nllacrosse.ca
Overview: A small provincial organization founded in 2009
Description: To manage & operate the sport of lacrosse in Newfoundland & Labrador.; *Member of:* Canadian Lacrosse Association
Chief Officer(s): Mike Lilly, President
president@nllacrosse.ca
Jim Swyer, Executive Director
director@nllacrosse.ca

Ontario Lacrosse Association
#306, 3 Concorde Gate, Toronto ON M3C 3N7
Tel: 416-426-7066; *Fax:* 416-426-7382
www.ontariolacrosse.com
Social Media:
twitter.com/OntarioLacrosse
Overview: A small provincial organization founded in 1897
Member of: Canadian Lacrosse Association
Chief Officer(s): Stan Cockerton, Executive Director
stan@ontariolacrosse.com

Saskatchewan Lacrosse Association
2205 Victoria Ave., Regina SK S4P 0S4
Tel: 306-780-9216; *Fax:* 306-525-4009
Toll-Free: 844-780-9216
lacrosse@sasktel.net
www.sasklacrosse.net
Social Media:
www.facebook.com/SaskLacrosse
Also Known As: Sask Lacrosse
Overview: A medium-sized provincial organization

Description: To promote & deliver lacrosse programs to the residents of Saskatchewan; *Member of:* Canadian Lacrosse Association; Sask Sport Inc.
Chief Officer(s): Shawn Williams, President
Bridget Pottle, Executive Director
ed@sasklacrosse.net
Chris Lesanko, Coordinator, Programs
programs@sasklacrosse.net
Finances: *Annual Operating Budget:* $250,000-$500,000
Staff: 1 staff member(s); 10 volunteer(s)
Membership: 3,000; *Fees:* Schedule available

Lawn Bowling

Bowls British Columbia
c/o Jackie West, 2168 Stirling Cres., Courtenay BC V9N 9X1
info@bowlsbc.com
bowlsbc.com
Social Media:
twitter.com/bowlsbc
Also Known As: Bowls BC
Overview: A medium-sized provincial organization founded in 1925
Description: To foster & promote the game of Lawn Bowls; To make the game available to all in accordance within the Canadian Human Rights Code within the Province of British Columbia
Affiliation(s): World Bowls Board; World Indoor Bowls Board
Chief Officer(s): Jim Aitken, President, 604-904-8834
bowlsbc.prez@yahoo.ca
Harry Carruthers, Vice-President, 604-985-2241
hcarruthers@telus.net
Diane Fulton, Secretary
pacu@shaw.ca
Carolle Allen, Treasurer
cjallen@live.ca
Activities:; *Library:* BBC Library at Pacific Indoor Bowls Club (Open to Public)

Bowls Canada Boulingrin (BCB)
#206, 33 Roydon Pl., Nepean ON K2E 1A3
Tel: 613-244-0021; *Fax:* 613-244-0041
Toll-Free: 800-567-2695
office@bowlscanada.com
www.bowlscanada.com
Social Media:
www.facebook.com/BCBOfficial
twitter.com/BCBBowls
Previous Name: Lawn Bowls Canada Boulingrin
Overview: A medium-sized national charitable organization founded in 1902
Description: To promote, foster & safeguard the sport of indoor & outdoor lawn bowling in all its forms in Canada, through events & programs; *Member of:* World Bowls Board; International Women's Bowls Board; World Indoor Bowls Council
Affiliation(s): Commonwealth Games Association of Canada
Chief Officer(s): Anna Mees, Executive Director, 613-244-0021 101
amees@bowlscanada.com
Finances: *Annual Operating Budget:* $250,000-$500,000; *Funding Sources:* Membership dues; marketing; advertising; merchandising; donations
Staff: 4 staff member(s); 100 volunteer(s)
Membership: 15,000; 252 clubs; *Fees:* $11; *Committees:* Team Canada; National Officials
Activities: Canadian championships; Canadian Senior Triples; Canadian Junior Championships; Under 25 World Junior Cup Qualifier; Canadian Mixed Pairs Championships; Canadian Indoor Singles.

Bowls Manitoba
145 Pacific Ave., Winnipeg MB R3B 2Z6
Tel: 204-925-5694; *Fax:* 204-925-5792
bowls@shawbiz.ca
www.bowls.mb.ca
Social Media:
www.facebook.com/BowlsMBInc
twitter.com/BowlsManitoba
Previous Name: Manitoba Lawn Bowling Association
Overview: A medium-sized provincial organization
Description: To promote lawnbowling in the province of Manitoba; To host various lawnbowling events; *Member of:* Sport Manitoba
Affiliation(s): Bowls Canada Boulingrin; World Bowls Ltd
Chief Officer(s): Cathy Derewianchuk, Executive Director, 204-925-5694

Bowls Saskatchewan Inc.
#102, 1860 Lorne St., Regina SK S4P 2L7
Tel: 306-780-9426
bowlsask@sasktel.net
www.bowls.sk.ca
Social Media:
www.facebook.com/Bowls-Saskatchewan-732190793489071
Also Known As: Saskatchewan Lawn Bowling Association
Overview: A medium-sized provincial organization founded in 1991
Description: To promote & expand the sport of bowls, which contains programs that accommodate/challenge all those interested, with the result that bowls becomes a high profile sport
Chief Officer(s): Denise Eberle, Executive Director
Duncan Holness, President
daholness@hotmail.com
Finances: *Annual Operating Budget:* $50,000-$100,000; *Funding Sources:* Saskatchewan lotteries
Staff: 1 staff member(s)
Membership: 503 in 9 clubs; *Fees:* Schedule available; *Committees:* Executive; Officiating; Coaching; Sport for All
Activities: Learn to Bowl; Junior; Clinics; summer & fall tournaments; Regina Mixed Pairs Open Tournament

Lawn Bowls Association of Alberta
11759 Groat Rd., Edmonton AB T5M 3K6
Tel: 780-427-8119
office@bowls.ab.ca
www.bowls.ab.ca
Overview: A small provincial organization founded in 1989
Affiliation(s): Commonwealth; Highlands; Royal Lawn Bowling Club; Edmonton Indoor Lawn Bowling Club; Bow Valley; Calgary Lawn; Rotary Park; Stanley Park; Ted Petrunia Lawn Bowling Green; Medicine Hat Lawn Bowling Green
Chief Officer(s): Anthony Peter Spencer, President
Dave Cox, Vice-President
Laura Lochanski, Vice-President

Ontario Lawn Bowls Association
c/o Edith Pedden, 471 Silvery Lane, Marberly ON K0H 2B0
olba@olba.ca
www.olba.ca
Social Media:
www.facebook.com/groups/138144062931120
Overview: A medium-sized provincial organization
Chief Officer(s): Mike Landry, President
olba@olba.ca
Elaine Stevenson, Contact, Membership
membership@olba.ca
Finances: *Funding Sources:* Membership fees; Sponsorships
Membership: *Fees:* Schedule available; *Member Profile:* Ontario lawn bowls clubs; *Committees:* Annual General Meetings; Achievement Awards; Annual; Bowls Canada Delegates; By-Laws; Championships, Indoors/Short-Mat & Championship Awards; Coaching; Database; Distribution, Sales, New Bowler Kits; E-Banter; Finance; Funding/Grants; Greens; Juniors; Marketing/Go Lawn Bowl; Memorial Fund; Nominating; Officiating; Planning & Development; Player Development; Promotion & Sponsorship; Safety & Risk Management; Visually Impaired/Physically Disabled Bowlers; Website
Activities: Providing programs, information & resources to member clubs; Campaigning for member recruitment; Assisting clubs that want to host provincial or national championships; Presenting awards, plaques, & certificates

Prince Edward Island Lawn Bowling Association
Sport PEI, PO Box 302, Charlottetown PE C1A 7K7
Tel: 902-368-4110; *Fax:* 902-368-4548
Toll-Free: 800-247-6712
sports@sportpei.pe.ca
Overview: A small provincial organization
Description: To provide guidance to bowlers and all people interested in the sport. They wish to assit in the growth and development of Lawn Bowling on PEI Island, they wish to promote and encourage fair play in the sport at club level and at National lvel, they wish to develop leadership and to provide oppourtunities for development in the field of coaching, umpiring, and administration. They also provide interesting tournaments and events throughout the playing season.

Québec Lawn Bowling Federation / Fédération de Boulingrin du Québec
QC
www.bowlsquebec.com
Overview: A medium-sized provincial organization

Martial Arts

Aikido Yukon Association
c/o Sport Yukon, 4061 - 4th Ave., Whitehorse YT Y1A 1H1
Tel: 867-667-4690; *Fax:* 867-667-4237
info@aikidoyukon.ca
www.aikidoyukon.ca
Social Media:
www.facebook.com/aikidoyukon
Overview: A small provincial organization
Description: To teach the martial art of Aikido in the Yukon.
Chief Officer(s): Gaël Marchanfd, President

Alberta Taekwondo Association (ATA)
7619 - 104 St., Edmonton AB T6E 4C3
Tel: 780-432-0721
www.taekwondoalberta.com
Social Media:
twitter.com/TKD_Alberta
Overview: A small provincial organization
Affiliation(s): Taekwondo Canada; World Taekwondo Federation
Chief Officer(s): Ken Froese, Chair
kenf@calgarytkd.com
Kevin Olsen, Secretary General
mu-shimtkd@hotmail.com

Association de taekwondo du Québec
4545, av Pierre-de Coubertin, Montréal QC H1V 3R2
Tél: 514-252-3198; *Téléc:* 514-254-7075
Ligne sans frais: 800-762-9565
info@taekwondo-quebec.ca
www.taekwondo-quebec.ca
Mèdia social:
www.facebook.com/115348592723
Également appelé: Taekwondo Québec
Aperçu: *Dimension:* moyenne; *Envergure:* provinciale
Description: Favoriser le développement du taekwondo québécois
Membre(s) du bureau directeur: Jean Faucher, Président
jfaucher@taekwondo-quebec.ca
Martin Desjardins, Vice-président
mdesjardins@taekwondo-quebec.ca
Abdel Ilah Es Sabbar, Directeur exécutif
essabbar@taekwondo-quebec.ca

BC Taekwondo Association
#101, 32885 Ventura Ave., Abbotsford BC V2S 6A3
www.bctaekwondo.org
Overview: A small provincial organization founded in 1994
Description: To govern the sport of Tae Kwon Do in British Columbia.
Chief Officer(s): Michael Smith, President
Darryl Mitchell, Treasurer/Secretary
dmitchell@axisls.com

Canadian Chito-Ryu Karate-Do Association
89 Curlew Ave., Toronto ON M3A 2P8
Tel: 416-444-5310
info@canadianchitoryu.ca
www.canadianchitoryu.ca
Social Media:
www.youtube.com/channel/UCBzr2eWZs8oJHXOBKgY0fYg
Overview: A small national organization founded in 1991
Description: Committed to understanding and propagating the karate-do of its founder O'Sensei Dr. Tsuyoshi Chitose.
Chief Officer(s): David Smith, President
Derek J. Ryan, Vice-President

Canadian Jiu-jitsu Council
PO Box 543, Madoc ON K0K 2K0
Tel: 613-473-4366
www.jiujitsucouncil.ca
Overview: A medium-sized national organization founded in 1968
Description: A non-profit educational Martial Arts organization under the Canadian Province of Ontario Charter. The CJC is administered by a volunteer group of senior Black Belts whose objective is to guide and assist the growth of Jiujitsu in a friendly, healthy environment and to help more people get more benefits, knowledge and pleasure from the Martial Art and Science of Jiujitsu.
Chief Officer(s): Robert Walthers, President
rwalther@kos.net
Membership: *Fees:* $40 club; $40 black belts; $25 senior students; $10 junior students

Canadian Kendo Federation (CKF) / Fédération canadienne de kendo
c/o Christian D'Orangeville, 65 St. Paul St. West, Montréal QC H2Y 35S
www.kendo-canada.com
Social Media:
www.facebook.com/KendoCanada
twitter.com/KendoCanada

Also Known As: Kendo Federation
Overview: A small national organization
Description: To support Kendo, Iaido, & Jodo in Canada
Chief Officer(s): Christian D'Orangeville, President
cdorangeville@kendo-canada.com
Finances: *Funding Sources:* Membership fees; Donations; Sale of CKF souvenirs
Membership: *Fees:* $15 junior (age 15 & under); $35 regular; $75 club; *Committees:* Kendo Grading; Iaido Grading; Jodo Grading; Finance; Internal Review; Budget & Event; Team Canada; Secretary's; CKF History

Club de karaté Shotokan Chibougamau
576, Bordeleau, Chibougamau QC G8P 1A6
Tél: 418-748-4048
ville.chibougamau.qc.ca

Aperçu: *Dimension:* petite; *Envergure:* locale; fondée en 1972
Membre(s) du bureau directeur: Claude Bédard, Instructeur chef, 418-770-6933
cbedard@karatechibougamau.com

International Judo Federation (IJF)
Avenue Frédéric-César-de La Harpe 49, Lausanne 1007 Switzerland
www.intjudo.eu
Social Media:
www.youtube.com/judo
www.facebook.com/ijudo
twitter.com/IntJudoFed

Overview: A large international charitable organization
Chief Officer(s): Marius Vizer, President
president@ijf.org
Andrei Bondor, Commission Director
andrei.bondor@sintezis.ro
Liz Roach, Commission Adviser, 416-580-1885
info@masterathlete.com
Membership: 200 Federations + 5 Continental Unions
Activities: World Championships; World Judo Tour; World Ranking List

Judo Alberta
Percy Page Centre, 11759 Groat Rd., Edmonton AB T5M 3K6
Tel: 780-427-8379; *Fax:* 780-447-1915
Toll-Free: 866-919-5836
judo@judoalberta.com
www.judoalberta.com
Social Media:
www.flickr.com/photos/judoalberta
www.facebook.com/judoalberta
twitter.com/JudoAlberta

Also Known As: Alberta Kodokan Black Belt Association - AKBBA
Overview: A small provincial organization founded in 1960
Description: To promote the principles & teachings of the sport of kodokan judo to all levels in all parts of Alberta; To have qualified facilities & equipment in places throughout Alberta; To promote judo as a lifelong interest; to develop competitive opportunities throughout Alberta; To promote greater public awareness of the sport; To increase the number of participants in the sport; To develop & maintain qualified judo officials & coaches throughout Alberta; To develop high performance athletes; To develop recreational opportunities throughout Alberta; *Member of:* Judo Canada
Affiliation(s): International Judo Federation
Chief Officer(s): Kelly Thornton, President
kellyt4d@telus.net
Nate MacLellan, Executive Director
Finances: *Annual Operating Budget:* $100,000-$250,000
Staff: 2 staff member(s); 200 volunteer(s)
Membership: 1,200; *Fees:* Schedule available; *Committees:* Grading; Technical; Referee; Coaching; Women's Ctee
Activities:; *Library:* Video Library (Open to Public)

Judo BC
#523, 4438 West 10th Ave., Vancouver BC V6R 4R8
Tel: 604-333-3513; *Fax:* 604-333-3514
www.judobc.ca
Social Media:
www.facebook.com/JudoBritishColumbia
twitter.com/OfficialJudoBC

Overview: A medium-sized provincial organization founded in 1952
Description: To promote & support the development of all aspects of Judo in the province; To inform & report on all aspects of Judo & planned activities in BC & elsewhere; To promote Judo & public awareness of the sport; To increase the number of participants in the sport; To keep close liaison with Judo clubs in BC in order to share all things of common interest to members; *Member of:* Judo Canada; Sport BC; Pan-American Confederation of Judo; International Judo Federation; Kodokan Judo Institute
Chief Officer(s): Sandy Kent, President
Katie Thomson, Executive Director
executivedirector@judobc.ca
Finances: *Annual Operating Budget:* $100,000-$250,000; *Funding Sources:* Provincial government; self-generated revenue; gaming
Staff: 1 staff member(s)
Membership: 2,200; *Fees:* Schedule available; *Committees:* Technical; Grading & Kata Board; Referee; NCCP; Membership
Activities: Offering coaching clinics; Organizing tournaments; Providing athlete & referee training; *Awareness Events:* Judo Awareness Week, 3rd week of Sept.; *Library:* Yes by appointment

Judo Canada
c/o Judo Canada, #201, 1155 Lola St., Ottawa ON KIK 4C1
Toll-Free: 877-738-5836
info@judocanada.org
www.judocanada.org
Social Media:
www.facebook.com/judocanada
twitter.com/judocanada

Also Known As: Canadian Kodokan Black Belt Association
Overview: A large national charitable organization founded in 1956
Description: To promote the principles & teachings of the sport of Kodokan Judo; To work towards the advancement of Judo throughout Canada; *Member of:* Pan American Judo Union
Affiliation(s): International Judo Federation
Chief Officer(s): Andrien Landry, Executive Director
a.landry@judocanada.org
Andrzej Sadej, Director, Sports
a.sadej@judocanada.org
Stewart Tanaka, Coordinator, Events
s.tanaka@judocanada.org
Francine Latreille, Office Manager
f.latreille@judocanada.org
Finances: *Funding Sources:* Sport Canada; Membership dues; Sponsorships
Staff: 9 staff member(s)
Member Profile: Black belt & provincial members; *Committees:* High Performance; NCCP/LTAD; Women's Programs; Grading; Kata; Referee; Aboriginal & Territorial Affairs; Tournament; Legal; Awards; Finance & Audit
Activities: Providing Rendez-Vous Canada & the Canadian Championships; *Library:* Yes by appointment

Judo Manitoba
c/o Sport Manitoba, #311, 145 Pacific Ave., Winnipeg MB R3B 2Z6
Tel: 204-925-5691; *Fax:* 204-925-5703
judo@sportmanitoba.ca
www.judomanitoba.mb.ca

Also Known As: Manitoba Judo Black Belt Association Inc.
Overview: A small provincial organization founded in 1963
Description: To propagate & perpetuate the sport of Judo; To improve the calibre of athletes, referees & coaches; *Member of:* Judo Canada; Sport Manitoba; International Judo Federation; Canadian Olympic Committee
Chief Officer(s): Oscar Li, Executive Director
David Minuk, President
Finances: *Annual Operating Budget:* $100,000-$250,000
Staff: 2 staff member(s)
Membership: 86 Black Belts + 594 others; *Fees:* Schedule available; *Committees:* Fundraising; Officials; Grading; Bingo; NCCP; Grassroots; Awards
Activities:; *Library:* Yes

Judo New Brunswick / Judo Nouveau Brunswick
#13, 900 Hanwell St., Fredericton NB E3B 6A3
Tel: 506-451-1322; *Fax:* 506-451-1325
judonb@nb.aibn.com
www.judonb.org
Social Media:
www.facebook.com/judonewbrunswick
twitter.com/judo_nb

Also Known As: Judo NB
Overview: A small local organization
Description: To promote judo in New Brunswick; *Member of:* Judo Canada
Chief Officer(s): Curtis Lauzon, Executive Director, 506-261-0867
Membership: 500; *Committees:* Grading

Judo Nova Scotia
NS
Tel: 902-425-5450
admin@judons.ca
www.judons.ca
Social Media:
www.facebook.com/judons
twitter.com/judonovascotia

Overview: A small provincial organization
Description: To promote the principles of judo &, in collaboration with members & interested parties, to work towards the advancement of judo, at all levels & areas of Nova Scotia; *Member of:* Judo Canada
Chief Officer(s): Chris Hattie, President
chattie@judons.ca
Scott Tanner, Provincial Coach
stanner@judons.ca

Judo Nunavut
PO Box 2135, Iqaluit NU X0A 0H0
Tel: 867-979-4540
judo.nunavut@gmail.com
Social Media:
www.facebook.com/NunavutJudo

Overview: A small provincial organization
Member of: Judo Canada

Judo Ontario
#2040, 875 Morningside Ave., Toronto ON M1C 0C7
Tel: 416-447-5836; *Fax:* 416-449-5836
Toll-Free: 866-553-5836
info@judoontario.ca
www.judoontario.ca
Social Media:
www.facebook.com/JudoOntario

Overview: A small provincial organization founded in 1959
Description: To govern the sport of Judo in Ontario; *Member of:* Judo Canada; International Judo Federation
Chief Officer(s): Aartje Sheffield, President, 905-251-0202
aartjes@judoontario.ca
Pedro Guedes, Technical Coach & Director
pedrog@judoontario.ca
Steve Sheffield, Administrator
Finances: *Annual Operating Budget:* $250,000-$500,000
Staff: 2 staff member(s); 100 volunteer(s)
Membership: 1,000-4,999; *Fees:* Schedule available; *Committees:* HPC; Grading Board; Referee; LTAD; NCCP; Aboriginal; Differently Abled; Quest for Gold; Website; Membership

Judo Prince Edward Island
PO Box 302, 40 Enman Cres., Charlottetown PE C1A 7K7
Tel: 902-368-4262
www.judopei.ca
Social Media:
www.facebook.com/JUDOPEI
twitter.com/judopei

Overview: A small provincial organization
Description: To promote and govern the sport of Judo in Prince Edward Island; *Member of:* Sport PEI Inc.; Judo Canada
Chief Officer(s): Michael Sheppard, President
president@judopei.ca
Trish Shaw, Secretary
secretary@judopei.ca

Judo Saskatchewan
c/o Sandy Taylor, Treasurer, PO Box 1464, Warman SK S0K 4S0
Tel: 306-668-6879
www.judosask.ca

Also Known As: Saskatchewan Kodokan Black Belt Association
Overview: A small provincial licensing organization founded in 1950
Description: To govern the sport of Judo in Saskatchewan; *Member of:* Judo Canada; Pan-American Judo Federation
Affiliation(s): International Judo Federation
Chief Officer(s): T.V. Taylor, President, 306-668-6879
tvtaylor@sasktel.net
Sandy Taylor, Treasurer
taylor.s@sasktel.net
Finances: *Annual Operating Budget:* $100,000-$250,000
Staff: 1 staff member(s); 10 volunteer(s)
Membership: 300+; *Fees:* Schedule available

Judo Yukon
4061 - 4th Ave., Whitehorse YT Y1A 1H1
Tel: 867-668-4236; *Fax:* 867-667-4237
judoyukon@gmail.com
www.judoyukon.ca

Overview: A small provincial charitable organization founded in 1995

Description: To govern the sport of Judo in the Yukon; *Member of:* Judo Canada; Sport Yukon; True Sport; Sport Officials Canada
Chief Officer(s): Richard Zebruck, President
Bianca Ockedahl, Head Coach
judoyukon.hc@gmail.com
Finances: *Annual Operating Budget:* Less than $50,000
Membership: 100+; *Member Profile:* Juniors & seniors; ages 8 & up; *Committees:* NCCP; Officials
Activities: Organizing competitions & demonstrations; *Awareness Events:* Judo Yukon Open Tournament, April; *Library:* Resource Library (Open to Public)

Judo-Québec inc

4545, av Pierre-de Coubertin, Montréal QC H1V 0B2
Tél: 514-252-3040; *Téléc:* 514-254-5184
info@judo-quebec.qc.ca
www.judo-quebec.qc.ca
Média social:
www.youtube.com/user/judoquebec
www.facebook.com/JudoQuebec
Également appelé: Association québécoise de judo-kodokan
Aperçu: *Dimension:* moyenne; *Envergure:* provinciale; Organisme sans but lucratif; fondée en 1966
Description: Assurer la promotion et le développement du judo au Québec; éduquer, développer et servir nos membres; *Membre de:* Judo Canada; Sport Québec
Affiliation(s): Fédération internationale de Judo; Union panaméricaine du Judo
Membre(s) du bureau directeur: Daniel De Angelis, Président
Jean-François Marceau, Directeur général, 514-252-3040 27
jfmarceau@judo-quebec.qc.ca
Patrick Vesin, Coordonnateur technique, 514-252-3040 24
pvesin@judo-quebec.qc.ca
Finances: *Budget de fonctionnement annuel:* $500,000-$1.5 Million; *Fonds:* Secrétariat au loisirs et aux sports
Personnel: 6 membre(s) du personnel; 200 bénévole(s)
Membre: 10 000; *Montant de la cotisation:* Barème; *Critères d'admissibilite:* Personne de 7 à 77 ans; *Comités:* Arbitrage; excellence; développement; grade; éthique; ju-jutsu
Activités: Competition; stage; colloque; gala; formation; *Stagiaires:* Oui; *Service de conférenciers:* Oui *Bibliothèque:* Oui

Karate Alberta Association (KAA)

c/o Stewart Price, 56 Auburn Crest Park, Calgary AB T3M 0Z3
Tel: 403-389-5072
www.karateab.org
Overview: A small provincial organization
Description: To be the provincial governing organization for karate in Alberta.; *Member of:* Karate Canada
Finances: *Funding Sources:* Government of Alberta

Karate BC (KBC)

Fortius Athlete Development Centre, Sydney Landing, #2002A, 3713 Kensington Ave., Burnaby BC V5B 0A7
Tel: 604-333-3610; *Fax:* 604-333-3612
Toll-Free: 855-806-8126
www.karatebc.org
Social Media:
www.youtube.com/channel/UC4hYqyDIEqjjKeD-sgXxdBA
www.facebook.com/OfficalKarateBC
twitter.com/KarateBC
Overview: A small provincial charitable organization founded in 1974
Description: To promote the traditions & integrity of karate-do; to improve opportunities to excel in a competitive environment; to be the governing body of the sport of karate in British Columbia.; *Member of:* Karate Canada; BC Recreation & Parks Association; BC Coaches Association; Sport BC
Chief Officer(s): Norma Foster, President
guseikai@hotmail.com
Jonathan Wornell, Executive Director
jwornell@karatebc.org
Conan Cooper, Coordinator, Coaching Development
coachdev@karatebc.org
Finances: *Annual Operating Budget:* $250,000-$500,000; *Funding Sources:* Provincial government; gaming; fundraising
Staff: 2 staff member(s)
Membership: 4,000; *Fees:* Schedule available; *Member Profile:* Instructor must hold bona-fide Dan certificate, be certified at level I NCCP & pass a criminal records check; *Committees:* Executive; Officials; Technical; Tournament; Marketing; Newsletter; High Performance
Activities: Tournaments; coaching clinics; officials seminars; athlete assistance program; coaching grants; first aid clinics; BC Winter Games; mall demos; annual recognition banquet for outstanding athletes & volunteers; *Internships:* Yes; *Speaker Service:* Yes; *Library:* Yes by appointment

Karate Canada

4545, av Pierre-de Coubertin, Montréal QC H1V 0B2
Tel: 514-252-3209; *Fax:* 514-252-3211
info@karatecanada.org
www.karatecanada.org
Social Media:
www.facebook.com/459465044133223
Previous Name: National Karate Association of Canada
Overview: A medium-sized national organization founded in 1963
Description: To be the national governing body for the sport of karate in Canada.; *Member of:* Sport Canada; Canadian Olympic Committee; World Karate Federation
Chief Officer(s): Olivier Pineau, Executive Director
olivier@karatecanada.org
Membership: 10 provincial & territorial associations; 13,000 individuals; *Committees:* Finance; Communications & Marketing; Governance & Policy; Domestic Development; Events; High Performance; Officials; NCCP / LTAD; Technical; AWAD

Karate Manitoba

145 Pacific Ave., Winnipeg MB R3B 2Z6
Tel: 204-925-5605; *Fax:* 204-925-5916
info@karatemanitoba.ca
www.karatemanitoba.ca
Social Media:
www.youtube.com/user/KarateManitoba
www.facebook.com/KarateManitobaWKF
twitter.com/KarateManitoba
Also Known As: Manitoba Karate Association
Overview: A small provincial organization founded in 1974
Description: To promote & develop karate in the province of Manitoba at all levels (grassroots to elite athlete) & as recreation.; *Member of:* Karate Canada; World Karate Federation; Sport Manitoba
Chief Officer(s): Debra Kofsky, President
president@karatemanitoba.ca
Sharon Andrews, Secretary
km.officials@live.ca
Membership: 600; *Committees:* NCCP; Officials; Athlete Development; Finance; Grassroots

Karate New Brunswick

NB
karatenb.com
Previous Name: New Brunswick Karate Association
Overview: A small provincial organization
Member of: Karate Canada
Chief Officer(s): Don Mazerolle, President
djmaz@bellaliant.net
Finances: *Funding Sources:* Provincial government
Staff: 1 staff member(s); 15 volunteer(s)
Membership: 600 individual
Activities: *Rents Mailing List:* Yes

Karate Newfoundland & Labrador

388 Pine Line, Torbay NL A1K 1A2
karatenl@gmail.com
www.karatenl.ca
Overview: A small provincial organization
Description: To be the provincial governing organization for karate in Newfoundland & Labrador.; *Member of:* Karate Canada
Chief Officer(s): Derek J. Ryan, President

Karate Nova Scotia

5516 Spring Garden Rd., 4th Fl., Halifax NS B3J 3G6
info@novascotiakarate.com
www.novascotiakarate.com
Overview: A small provincial organization
Description: To be the official governing body for the sport of karate in Nova Scotia.; *Member of:* Karate Canada

Karate Ontario (KAO)

#160, 2 County Court Blvd., Brampton ON L6W 4V1
Tel: 647-706-4835
info@karate-ontario.com
karate-ontario.com
Social Media:
www.youtube.com/channel/UCnjL8YhmflRwiK1FZQBAIUA
www.facebook.com/309961174058
Overview: A medium-sized provincial organization
Description: To promote & perpetuate karate as a martial art & lifetime activity; to promote karate for physical fitness, mental fitness, & as a way of life; to develop provincial standards & programs; to encourage all participants in safely achieving their maximum at the recreational or competitive level; to provide safe competitive opportunities for karate-ka wishing to participate in the sport aspect of karate; to govern the amateur sport of karate & the conduct of all karate-ka under its jurisdiction; *Member of:* Karate Canada
Affiliation(s): World Karate Federation; Sport Alliance of Ontario; Coaches Association of Ontario
Chief Officer(s): Pravilal Pravibhavan, President
ppravibhavan@karate-ontario.com
Activities: *Awareness Events:* Sport Science Karate Symposium, June

Karaté Québec

CP 1000, Succ. M, 4545, av Pierre-de Coubertin, Montréal QC H1V 3R2
Tél: 514-252-3161; *Téléc:* 514-252-3036
Ligne sans frais: 877-527-2835
info@karatequebec.com
www.karatequebec.com
Média social:
www.facebook.com/karatequebec
Aperçu: *Dimension:* moyenne; *Envergure:* provinciale; fondée en 1995
Description: Karaté Québec est une organisation structurée et démocratique qui vise à promouvoir, à organiser et à administrer la pratique du karaté au Québec de manière à ce que cet art martial ne perde jamais son sens premier : favoriser une progression saine et équilibrée des karatékas dans une société en mouvance perpétuelle; *Membre de:* Karate Canada

National Taekwon-Do Federation (NTF)

c/o Whitecroft Hall, #314, 52313 Range Rd. 232, Sherwood Park AB T8B 1B5
Tel: 780-468-3418
www.ntf.ca
Social Media:
www.facebook.com/CanadaNTF
Overview: A medium-sized national organization
Description: To develop the art of Tae-Kwon-Do; To encourage overall fitness, stress reduction, well-being, & self-defense
Chief Officer(s): Wilfred Ho, President & Founder
wilfho@ntf.ca
Membership: *Fees:* $70/month adults & children; $140/month family

Newfoundland & Labrador Judo Association

#112, Hamlyn Rd. Plaza, Unit 50, St. John's NL A1E 5X7
nljawebmaster1@gmail.com
www.judonl.ca
Also Known As: Judo Newfoundland & Labrador
Overview: A small provincial organization
Description: To govern & promote the sport of Judo in Newfoundland & Labrador; *Member of:* Judo Canada
Chief Officer(s): Chris Wellon, President, 709-424-4084
cwellon@nf.sympatico.ca

Ontario Jiu-Jitsu Association (OJA)

#7, 40 Bell Farm Rd., Barrie ON L4M 5L3
Tel: 705-725-9186; *Fax:* 705-725-8562
Toll-Free: 800-352-1338
www.ontariojiujitsu.com
Social Media:
www.facebook.com/jiujitsuontario
Overview: A medium-sized provincial organization founded in 1963
Description: To promote Jiu Jitsu among amateurs in Ontario
Chief Officer(s): Doug Knispel, President
dknispel@rci.rogers.com
Membership: *Fees:* $150 club; $20 club; $35 black belt; $25 adult; $190 private training centre; *Committees:* Finance; Membership & Promotion; Safety & Insurance; Technical; Tournament; Volunteer; Canadian Jiu Jitsu Grading Board

Ontario Taekwondo Association

#500, 4560 Hwy 7 East, Markham ON L3R 1M5
Tel: 416-245-8582; *Fax:* 416-245-8582
otatkdinfo@gmail.com
www.taekwondo.on.ca
Overview: A medium-sized provincial organization
Chief Officer(s): Hwa Sun Myung, President
otapresident@gmail.com
Hwan Yong Seong, Secretary General
masterseong@gmail.com

Prince Edward Island Karate Association (PEIKA)

c/o Dawn Brown, 131 Blue Heron Lane, Cornwall PE C0A 1H0
www.karatepei.ca
Also Known As: Prince Edward Island Karate Association
Overview: A small provincial organization founded in 1971
Description: To teach, train & coach karate & allied physical arts; to teach physical culture generally; to promote the principles & teaching of the sport of karate & to work toward the advancement of the sport in conjunction with all other groups throughout Canada; to arrange matches, contests & competitions of every nature relating to karate & to offer or grant & contribute towards judges, awards & distinctions; to provide

conditional assistance on the approval of the Executive of the Association; *Member of:* Karate Canada; Sport PEI
Chief Officer(s): Dawn Brown, President
dawn.brown@pei.sympatico.ca
Finances: *Annual Operating Budget:* Less than $50,000

Sask Taekwondo
106 Franklin Ave., Yorkton SK S3N 2G4
Tel: 306-782-1272
taekwondosk@sasktel.net
www.saskwtf.ca
Also Known As: Sask. WTF
Overview: A small provincial organization founded in 1981
Description: To govern the sport of Tae Kwon Do in Saskatchewan.; *Member of:* World Taekwondo Federation
Chief Officer(s): Audrey Ashcroft, Executive Director, 306-621-9696

Saskatchewan Karate Association (SKA)
510 Cynthia St., Saskatoon SK S7L 7K7
Tel: 306-374-7333; *Fax:* 306-374-7334
sk.karate@shaw.ca
www.saskarate.com
Overview: A small provincial organization founded in 1977
Description: To promote & develop karate as a sport throughout the province of Saskatchewan.; *Member of:* Karate Canada
Chief Officer(s): Owen Hartman, President
Linda Crosson, Executive Director

Saskatchewan Martial Arts Association (SMAA)
1210 Lorne St., Regina SK S4R 2J8
Tel: 306-565-2266
smaa@sasktel.net
www.saskmaa.com
Overview: A small provincial organization
Description: To be a provincial sport governing body for a variety of martial arts styles practiced in Saskatchewan.; *Member of:* Sask Sport Inc.

Taekwondo Canada
#313A, 3 Concorde Gate, Toronto ON M3C 3N7
Tel: 416-426-7322; *Fax:* 416-426-7334
taekwondo-canada.com
Social Media:
www.facebook.com/Taekwondo.Canada
twitter.com/TKD_Canada
Overview: A medium-sized national organization
Description: To develop, promote & govern the sport of Taekwondo in Canada.
Chief Officer(s): Kate Nosworthy, Chair
knosworthy@taekwondo-canada.com
Rebecca Khoury, Chief Executive Officer
ceo@taekwondo-canada.com
Activities: National Championships

Taekwondo Manitoba
145 Pacific Ave., Winnipeg MB R3B 2Z6
Fax: 204-925-5703
secretary@taekwondomanitoba.ca
www.taekwondomanitoba.ca
Previous Name: Manitoba Tae Kwon-Do Association
Overview: A small provincial organization
Description: To promote & govern the sport of Taekwondo in Manitoba.

World Amateur Muay Thai Association of Canada (WAMTAC)
164 Macatee Pl., Cambridge ON N1R 6Z8
Tel: 519-584-5426
info@wamtac.org
www.wamtac.org
Overview: A medium-sized national organization
Description: To govern amateur muay thai in Canada
Affiliation(s): World Muay Thai Council; Olympic Committee of Asia; General Association of International Sports Federations
Chief Officer(s): Khan Phady, President
Membership: *Fees:* $500 club; $50 coach/athlete/official

WTF Taekwondo Federation of British Columbia
c/o Grand Master Dae Lim, #3, 511 Cottonwood Ave., Coquitlam BC V3J 2R4
Tel: 604-939-8232
wtfbccanada@gmail.com
taekwondobc.com
Also Known As: BC Taekwondo Federation
Overview: A small provincial organization
Description: To be the governing body of taekwondo in British Columbia; sanctioned to send athletes to the Olympic Games, World Taekwondo Championships, World Junior Taekwondo Championships, World Cup Taekwondo Games, Pan-American Games, Canadian National Championships & Canadian Junior National Championships.; *Member of:* WTF Taekwondo Canada; Sport BC
Affiliation(s): International Olympic Committee
Chief Officer(s): Dae Lim, President
Tony Kook, Secretary General, 604-986-5558
northshoretkd@shaw.ca

WushuCanada
2370 Midland Ave., #B25, Toronto ON M1S 5C6
Tel: 416-321-5913
info@wushucanada.com
wushucanada.com
Social Media:
www.facebook.com/pages/WushuCanada/211084358925927
twitter.com/WushuCanada
Previous Name: Confederation of Canadian Wushu Organizations
Overview: A small national organization
Description: To promote & develop the Olympic sport of Wushu in Canada

WushuOntario
2370 Midland Ave., #B25-22, Toronto ON M1S 5C6
Tel: 416-321-5913
www.wushuontario.ca
Previous Name: United Wushu Association of Ontario
Overview: A small provincial organization founded in 1997
Description: To govern & promote Wushu in Ontario

Massage Therapy

Canadian Sport Massage Therapists Association (CSMTA) / Association canadienne des massothérapeutes du sport
1030 Burnside Rd. West, Victoria BC V8Z 1N3
Tel: 250-590-9861; *Fax:* 250-388-7835
natoffice@csmta.ca
www.csmta.ca
Overview: A medium-sized national licensing organization founded in 1987
Description: To provide leadership in the field of sport massage therapy & education in Canada through the establishment of professional standards & qualifications of its members, as a certifying body
Affiliation(s): Canadian Olympic Committee; Expert Provider Group
Chief Officer(s): Trish Schiedel, President
Roberta Graham, National Office Coordinator
Jessica Sears, Vice President
Monty Churchman, Secretary
Finances: *Annual Operating Budget:* Less than $50,000; *Funding Sources:* Membership fee; workshop
Staff: 1 staff member(s); 5 volunteer(s)
Membership: 70; *Member Profile:* 2,200-hr massage school or member of provincial association affiliated with CSMTA; *Committees:* Membership; Education; Certification; Examination
Activities: Enhances the health care needs of Canadian athletes through its National Sport Massage Certification Program (NSMCP) & the effective application of sport massage during all phases of their training, performance & competition; promotes a professional climate for the growth of sport massage therapy in Canada

Mediation

Sport Dispute Resolution Centre of Canada (SDRCC)
#950, 1080 Beaver Hall Hill, Montréal QC H2Z 1S8
Tel: 514-866-1245; *Fax:* 514-866-1246
Toll-Free: 866-733-7767
www.crdsc-sdrcc.ca
Social Media:
www.linkedin.com/company/sport-dispute-resolution-centre-of-canada
www.facebook.com/pages/SDRCC-CRDSC/424545007600467
Also Known As: ADRsportRED
Overview: A small national organization founded in 2004
Description: To provide to the sport community a national alternative dispute resolution service for sport disputes
Chief Officer(s): Allan J. Sattin, Chair
Marie-Claude Asselin, Executive Director
mcasselin@crdsc-sdrcc.ca

Motorcycles

Canadian Motorcycle Association (CMA) / Association motocycliste canadienne
605 James St. North, 4th Fl., Hamilton ON L8L 1J9
Tel: 905-522-5705; *Fax:* 905-522-5716
registration@canmocycle.ca
www.canmocycle.ca
Social Media:
www.facebook.com/motorcyclingcanada
Overview: A medium-sized national licensing organization founded in 1946
Description: To encourage & develop motorcycling for the benefit & enjoyment of its members
Affiliation(s): Fédération internationale motocycliste; Canadian Olympic Association; FIM North America Union
Chief Officer(s): Joseph Godsall, President
Marilyn Bastedo, Chief Executive Officer
mbastedo.cma@bellnet.ca
Finances: *Annual Operating Budget:* $500,000-$1.5 Million; *Funding Sources:* Membership fees; event fees
Staff: 4 staff member(s); 150 volunteer(s)
Membership: 100 club + 150 lifetime + 9,000 individual; *Fees:* $30; $15 family (per individual); *Member Profile:* Interest in motorcycling; *Committees:* Strategic Planning; Technical; Environmental; Awards; Nominations; Trials Advisory; Development of Alternative Energy Competition

Mountaineering

Alpine Club of Canada (ACC) / Club alpin du Canada (CAC)
PO Box 8040, Stn. Main, 201 Indian Flats Rd., Canmore AB T1W 2T8
Tel: 403-678-3200; *Fax:* 403-678-3224
info@alpineclubofcanada.ca
www.alpineclubofcanada.ca
Social Media:
www.facebook.com/alpineclubofcanada
twitter.com/alpineclubcan
Overview: A large national charitable organization founded in 1906
Description: To encourage & promote mountaineering & mountain crafts; To educate Canadians in the appreciation of mountain heritage; To explore alpine & glacial regions primarily in Canada; To preserve the natural beauty of mountains & their fauna & flora; to promote mountain art & literature; To disseminate scientific & educational knowledge concerning mountains & mountaineering through meetings & publications; To conduct summer & ski mountaineering camps
Affiliation(s): International Union of Alpinist Associations
Chief Officer(s): Lawrence White, Executive Director
lwhite@alpineclubofcanada.ca
Chelsea Selinger, Director, Programs
cselinger@alpineclubofcanada.ca
Kish Stephenson, Manager, Finance
kstephenson@alpineclubofcanada.ca
Finances: *Funding Sources:* Donations; Grants; Corporate
Staff: 11 staff member(s)
Membership: *Fees:* $38 individual; $58 family; $26 youth
Activities: Providing financial support necessary to advocate protection & preservation of mountain & climbing environments; Enhancing constitutional objective of ACC to work towards preservation of alpine environment & flora & fauna in their natural habitat; *Library:* Yes (Open to Public)

Association of Canadian Mountain Guides (ACMG) / Association des guides de montagne canadiens
PO Box 8341, Canmore AB T1W 2V1
Tel: 403-678-2885; *Fax:* 403-609-0070
acmg@acmg.ca
www.acmg.ca
Social Media:
www.facebook.com/ACMG.ca
twitter.com/ACMGca
Overview: A small national organization founded in 1963
Description: To represent mountain guides in dealing with both public & private official bodies; to maintain standards of guiding & acts as a public relations body to promote the sport in a safe & educational manner.; *Member of:* International Federation of Mountain Guides Associations
Chief Officer(s): Marc Ledwidge, President, 403-762-4129
pres@acmg.ca
Peter Tucker, Executive Director, 403-949-3587
ed@acmg.ca
Finances: *Funding Sources:* Membership fees
Membership: 904; *Fees:* Schedule available; *Member Profile:* Personal membership is open exclusively to trained/certified professional guides & instructors.
Activities: Training & Certification Program

British Columbia Mountaineering Club
PO Box 20042, Vancouver BC V5Z 0C1
Tel: 604-268-9502
info@bcmc.ca
www.bcmc.ca
Overview: A small provincial organization founded in 1907
Description: BCMC is a group of active individuals who organize mountaineering & skiing trips throughout the year. The primary mode of locomotion is pedestrian to allow appreciation of the mountains with least environmental impact. The Club is also active in conservation, trail & hut construction, trail maintenance, mountain safety & education.
Affiliation(s): Federation of Mountain Clubs of BC
Chief Officer(s): David Scanlon, President
Membership: 500 individual; *Fees:* $45 individual; $68 couple; $23 youth/senior; $800 lifetime; *Committees:* Conservation
Activities: Hiking; climbing; mountaineering; backcountry skiing; snowshoeing; hiking, backpacking; *Library:* Yes by appointment

Native Peoples

Yukon Aboriginal Sport Circle (YASC)
2166 - 2nd Ave., Whitehorse YT Y1A 4P1
Tel: 867-668-2840; *Fax:* 867-668-6577
aboriginalsport@yasc.ca
www.yasc.ca
Social Media:
www.facebook.com/343599029002109
twitter.com/yukonasc
Merged from: Yukon Aboriginal Sport Development Office Interim Steering Committee & YIGSC
Overview: A medium-sized provincial organization founded in 1990
Description: The Yukon Aboriginal Sport Circle is a non-profit society dedicated to the advancement of Aboriginal recreation and sport in the Yukon through a variety of programs to increase participation and skill levels and to increase awareness.; *Member of:* Sport Yukon
Chief Officer(s): Gael Marchand, Executive Director
ed@yasc.ca
Justin Ferbey, President
Member Profile: The Yukon Aboriginal Sport Circle is a non-profit society dedicated to the advancement of Aboriginal recreation and sport in the Yukon.

Yukon Indian Hockey Association (YIHA)
PO Box 31769, Whitehorse YT Y1A 6L3
Tel: 867-456-7294; *Fax:* 867-456-7290
yihahockey@gmail.com
www.yiha.ca
Overview: A medium-sized provincial organization founded in 1984
Description: To establish a hockey league in the Yukon to enable Native athletes to compete with other Canadian Provinces & Territories in the sport.
Chief Officer(s): Jeanie Dendys, President

Netball

British Columbia Netball Association
BC
Tel: 604-293-1820
mwebb1@shaw.ca
bcnetball.ca
Social Media:
www.facebook.com/BCNetballAssoc
twitter.com/BCNetball
Also Known As: BC Netball
Overview: A small provincial organization
Description: To oversee the sport of netball in British Columbia.; *Member of:* Netball Canada
Affiliation(s): International Federation of Netball Associations
Chief Officer(s): Ann Willcocks, President

Fédération de Netball du Québec / Québec Amateur Netball Federation (QANF)
CP 1000, Succ. M, 4545, av Pierre-de Coubertin, Montréal QC H1V 3R2
Tél: 514-486-2769
www.netballquebec.ca
Média social:
www.facebook.com/QuebecNetball
Également appelé: Netball Québec
Aperçu: *Dimension:* moyenne; *Envergure:* provinciale; fondée en 1974
Description: Promouvoir et développer le netball féminin au Québec; *Membre de:* Netball Canada
Affiliation(s): International Federation of Netball Associations
Membre(s) du bureau directeur: Avice Roberts-Joseph, Présidente
Sheryl Stephens, Secrétaire
Membre: 750; *Comités:* Technique
Activités: Tournois; Ligues; Cliniques pour entraîneurs et arbitres

Netball Alberta
PO Box 270, 7620 Elbow Dr. SW, Calgary AB T2V 1K2
Tel: 403-238-8041; *Fax:* 888-213-9218
contact@netballalberta.com
www.netballalberta.com
Social Media:
www.facebook.com/groups/2223869141
Previous Name: Alberta Netball Association
Overview: A small provincial charitable organization founded in 1992
Description: To promote & encourage the sport of netball in Alberta; to facilitate exchange of information & ideas; to promote education & development; to sponsor clinics & classes; to collect & distribute information; to raise funds for the Association; to organize & conduct competitions; *Member of:* Netball Canada
Affiliation(s): International Federation of Netball Associations
Chief Officer(s): Julie Arnold, President
president@netballalberta.com
Finances: *Annual Operating Budget:* Less than $50,000; *Funding Sources:* Fundraising
Staff: 10 volunteer(s)
Membership: 350

Netball Canada
AB
netballcanada@gmail.com
netballcanada.ca
Social Media:
www.facebook.com/netballcanada
twitter.com/NetballCanada
Overview: A small national organization founded in 1976
Description: To be the national governing body for netball throughout Canada
Affiliation(s): International Federation of Netball Associations
Membership: 4 provincial associations

Netball Ontario
ON
info@netballontario.com
www.netballontario.com
Social Media:
www.facebook.com/NetballOntario
Previous Name: Ontario Amateur Netball Association
Overview: A small provincial organization founded in 1974
Description: To promote & develop the sport of netball in Ontario.; *Member of:* Netball Canada
Affiliation(s): International Federation of Netball Associations

Olympic Games

Canadian Olympic Committee (COC) / Comité olympique canadien
Corporate Office, #900, 21 St. Clair Ave. East, Toronto ON M4T 1L9
Tel: 416-962-0262; *Fax:* 416-967-4902
digital@olympic.ca
www.olympic.ca
Social Media:
www.youtube.com/teamcanada; instagram.com/teamcanada
www.facebook.com/teamcanada
twitter.com/teamcanada
Overview: A small national charitable organization founded in 1952
Description: To be responsible for all aspects of Canada's involvement in the Olympic movement, including Canada's participation in the Olympic & Pan American Games & a wide variety of programs that promote the Olympic Movement in Canada through cultural & educational means.
Chief Officer(s): Christopher Overholt, CEO & Secretary General
Finances: *Annual Operating Budget:* Greater than $5 Million; *Funding Sources:* National & international sponsors
Staff: 26 staff member(s); 400 volunteer(s)
Membership: 400
Activities: *Speaker Service:* Yes

Orienteering

Alberta Orienteering Association (AOA)
PO Box 1576, Cochrane AB T4C 1B5
Tel: 403-981-4444
www.orienteeringalberta.ca
Overview: A small provincial organization founded in 1974
Description: To promote, encourage, co-ordinate and administer orienteering as sport and recreation in Alberta which includes providing orienteering opportunities for all levels of ability.; *Member of:* Canadian Orienteering Federation
Chief Officer(s): Kim Kasperski, President
Kitty Jones, Treasurer
Pascale Levesque, Executive Director
pascale@orienteeringalberta.ca
Membership: *Fees:* $30 individual; $45 group
Activities: Sport orienteering; amateur sport; navigation; map reading; *Library:* Yes (Open to Public)

Canadian Orienteering Federation (COF) / Fédération canadienne de course d'orientation
1239 Colgrove Ave. NE, Calgary AB T2C 5C3
Tel: 403-283-0807; *Fax:* 403-451-1681
info@orienteering.ca
www.orienteering.ca
Social Media:
www.youtube.com/orienteeringcanada
www.facebook.com/orienteeringcanada
twitter.com/orienteeringcan
Also Known As: Orienteering Canada
Overview: A large national organization founded in 1967
Description: To provide leadership & resources to individuals involved in orienteering in Canada
Affiliation(s): International Orienteering Federation
Chief Officer(s): Anne Teutsch, President
Bruce Rennie, Vice-President
Dave Graupner, Secretary
Tracy Bradley, Executive Director
Member Profile: Coaches, officials, volunteers, athletes, & youth leaders involved in orienteering; *Committees:* Coaching Program; High Performance; Officials Program; Sass Peepre Junior Development; Technical; Nominations; Finance & Audit; HR; Governance; Celebration, Awards & Recognition; Long Term Athlete Development; New Participant Recruitment; Mountain Bike Orienteering; Ski Orienteering
Activities: *Rents Mailing List:* Yes

Manitoba Orienteering Association Inc. (MOA)
145 Pacific Ave., Winnipeg MB R3B 2Z6
Tel: 204-925-5706; *Fax:* 204-925-5792
info@orienteering.mb.ca
www.orienteering.mb.ca
Overview: A medium-sized provincial organization
Description: Promotes and supports orienteering in Manitoba.; *Member of:* Canadian Orienteering Federation
Affiliation(s): Sports Manitoba
Membership: *Fees:* $5 adult; $3 junior

Orienteering Association of British Columbia (OABC)
1428 Edinburgh St., New Westminster BC V3M 2W4
www.orienteeringbc.ca
Overview: A small provincial organization
Member of: Sport BC; Orienteering Canada
Affiliation(s): Canadian Orienteering Federation (COF); Coaching Association of Canada
Chief Officer(s): John Rance, President
rance1@shaw.ca
Activities: Offering technical coaching courses in orienteering; *Awareness Events:* National Orienteering Week

Orienteering Association of Nova Scotia (OANS)
5516 Spring Garden Rd., 4th Fl., Halifax NS B3J 1G6
Tel: 902-446-2295
info@orienteeringns.ca
www.orienteeringns.ca
Overview: A small provincial organization founded in 1971
Description: To operate as the governing body for orienteering in Nova Scotia; To train & certify orienteering coaches, officials, & mapmakers; *Member of:* Canadian Orienteering Federation; Sport Nova Scotia
Chief Officer(s): Ashley Harding, President
ashleyaharding@hotmail.com
Ian Clark, Vice-President
clark@eastlink.ca
Dale Ellis, Treasurer
dale.ellis@ns.sympatico.ca
Activities: Coordinating local club activities; Publishing event results; Promoting orienteering; Providing programs in map, compass, & wilderness navigation skills, introductory skills, & junior development; Preparing orienteering maps

Orienteering New Brunswick (ONB)
c/o Robert Hughes, 69 Kingsclear Dr., Upper Kingsclear NB E3E 1R6
www.orienteering.nb.ca
Social Media: www.facebook.com/OrienteeringNB
Overview: A small provincial organization founded in 1975
Description: To promote, develop & encourage the sport & recreation of orienteering in New Brunswick; *Member of:* Canadian Orienteering Federation
Affiliation(s): International Orienteering Federation
Chief Officer(s): Robert Hughes, Secretary
rustics@nb.sympatico.ca
Finances: *Annual Operating Budget:* Less than $50,000
Membership: *Fees:* $15 adult; $10 junior (under 20 years old); $50 family/group; *Member Profile:* Family groups; individuals; cadets & scouts
Activities: Competitive & recreational orienteering

Orienteering Ontario Inc.
ON
info@orienteeringontario.ca
www.orienteeringontario.ca
Also Known As: Ontario Orienteering Association, Inc.
Overview: A small provincial licensing organization founded in 1975
Description: To encourage, promote & give leadership in all aspects of the sport of orienteering & associated activities at local, provincial & national levels; *Member of:* Canadian Orienteering Federation
Chief Officer(s): Chris Laughren, President
Membership: *Fees:* Schedule available

Orienteering Québec (OQ) / Fédération québécoise de course d'orientation
QC
orientering_quebec@orienteeringquebec.ca
www.orienteeringquebec.ca
Overview: A small provincial charitable organization founded in 1967
Member of: Canadian Orienteering Federation (COF); International Orienteering Federation (IOF)
Affiliation(s): Ramblers Orientering Club; Lou Garou Orienteering Club; Ottawa Orienteering Club
Chief Officer(s): Isabelle Robert, President
liriel@sympatico.ca
Paul Dubois, Vice-President
dubpaul@gmail.com
Bill Meldrum, Treasurer
bill.meldrum@videotron.ca
Finances: *Funding Sources:* Members
Activities: Organizing events; Posting event results; Coordinating club activities; mapping

Yukon Orienteering Association (YOA)
4061 - 4th Ave., Whitehorse YT Y1A 1H1
Tel: 867-335-2287
info@yukonorienteering.ca
www.yukonorienteering.ca
Overview: A small provincial organization
Description: To provide both friendly & quality competitive orienteering opportunities in Yukon, & encourage the development & growth of the sport of orienteering where possible; *Member of:* Canadian Orienteering Federation
Chief Officer(s): Afan Jones, President
Bob Sagar, Vice-President
Membership: *Fees:* $5; *Member Profile:* Male & female, 0-70 yrs old, enjoys outdoors
Activities: Kids Running Wild; Yukon Orienteering Team; Yukon Championships; clinics

Pan American Games

Pan American Sports Organization (PASO)
Valentin Gomez Farias #51, San Rafael 06470 Mexico
Tel: 52 55 57054657; *Fax:* 52 55 57052275
www.paso-odepa.org
Overview: A large international organization founded in 1948
Mission: Its principal objectives are the celebration and conduct of the Pan American Games and the development and protection of Sports, as well as the Olympic Movement in the Americas through its member National Olympic Committees.
Chief Officer(s): Julio Cesar Maglione, President
Membership: *Committees:* Technical; Pan American Olympic Solidarity; Marketing & Financial Sources; Image; Sports Venues; Olympic Academies; Legislative; Women & Presentation of Awards
Activities: Pan American Games

Parachuting

Alberta Sport Parachuting Association (ASPA)
c/o Tina Connolly, #301, 7708 - 106 Ave., Edmonton AB T6A 1H5
Tel: 780-996-5266
admin@aspa.ca
www.aspa.ca
Social Media: www.facebook.com/groups/5261851254/
Overview: A small provincial organization
Description: To promote & facilitate the development of the sport of skydiving in Alberta; *Member of:* Canadian Sport Parachuting Association
Chief Officer(s): Dan Stith, President
Finances: *Annual Operating Budget:* $50,000-$100,000
Staff: 2 staff member(s)
Membership: 1,400; *Fees:* $20
Activities: *Awareness Events:* Provincial Championships, early July; *Speaker Service:* Yes

Canadian Sport Parachuting Association (CSPA) / Association canadienne du parachutisme sportif (ACPS)
#204, 1468 Laurier St., Rockland ON K4K 1C7
Tel: 613-419-0908; *Fax:* 613-916-6008
office@cspa.ca
www.cspa.ca
Overview: A medium-sized national charitable organization founded in 1956
Member of: Aero Club of Canada
Chief Officer(s): Michelle Matte-Stotyn, Executive Director, 613-419-0908 2
michelle.matte-stotyn@cspa.ca
Membership: 2,000 + 48 member groups; *Committees:* Coaching Working; Technical Safety; Competition & National Teams; Web / Information Technology
Activities:; *Library:* Yes (Open to Public)

Manitoba Sport Parachute Association (MSPA)
145 Pacific Ave., Winnipeg MB R3B 2Z6
membership@mspa.mb.ca
www.mspa.mb.ca
Overview: A small provincial organization founded in 1978
Description: To promote awareness & participation in skydiving in Manitoba; *Member of:* Canadian Sport Parachuting Association
Chief Officer(s): Kaneena Vanstone, President
president@mspa.mb.ca
Finances: *Funding Sources:* Manitoba Sports Federation; Manitoba Lotteries; Sport Directorate
Membership: *Fees:* $25

Sport Parachute Association of Saskatchewan
SK
www.skydive.sk.ca
Overview: A small provincial organization
Member of: Canadian Sport Parachuting Association
Chief Officer(s): Craig Skihar, President
stimpysplace@gmail.com
Jayson Pister, Vice-President
jay.pister@gmail.com

Pentathlon

Ontario Modern Pentathalon Association
c/o Shaun LaGrange, 513428 - 2 Line Amaranth, RR#4, Orangeville ON L9W 2Z1
Tel: 519-940-3721
www.ompa.ca
Overview: A medium-sized provincial organization
Description: To promote modern pentathalon
Chief Officer(s): Shaun LaGrange, President
salagrange@sympatico.ca
Membership: *Fees:* $65 competitive; $20 supporting; $15 coach

Pentathlon Alberta
AB
info@pentathlonalberta.com
www.pentathlonalberta.com
Previous Name: Alberta Modern Pentathlon Association
Overview: A small provincial organization
Description: To develop world-class athletes while promoting & developing the sport in Alberta.; *Member of:* Canadian Modern Pentathlon Association
Chief Officer(s): Connie Olsen, President, 403-703-4951
Membership: 4 local clubs/groups

Pentathlon Canada
c/o Shaun LaGrange, 513428 - 2nd Line, Amaranth ON L9W 0S4
Tel: 519-940-3721; *Fax:* 450-458-1746
www.pentathloncanada.ca
Social Media: www.facebook.com/PentathlonCanada
Previous Name: Canadian Modern Pentathlon Association
Overview: A medium-sized national charitable organization
Description: To promote Modern Pentathlon in Canada
Affiliation(s): Union internationale de pentathlon moderne et biathlon
Chief Officer(s): Shaun LaGrange, President
president@pentathloncanada.ca
Bob Noble, Vice-President
Membership: 2,000

Physical Education & Training

Fédération des éducateurs et éducatrices physiques enseignants du Québec (FEEPEQ)
2500, boul de l'Université, Sherbrooke QC J1K 2R1
Tél: 819-821-8000; *Téléc:* 819-821-7970
info@feepeq.com
www.feepeq.com
Média social: www.facebook.com/180360724546
twitter.com/feepeq
Nom précédent: Confédération des Éducateurs physiques du Québec
Aperçu: *Dimension:* moyenne; *Envergure:* provinciale; Organisme sans but lucratif; fondée en 1960
Description: Répresenter plus du tiers des éducateurs/trices physiques oeuvrant activement partout au Québec
Affiliation(s): Sports Québec; Fédération québécoise du sport étudiant
Membre(s) du bureau directeur: Patrick Parent, Président
Nathalie Morneau, Directrice, Opérations
Finances: *Budget de fonctionnement annuel:* $100,000-$250,000
Personnel: 4 membre(s) du personnel; 40 bénévole(s)
Membre: 1 700; *Montant de la cotisation:* Barème; *Critères d'admissibilité:* Éducateur physique enseignant selon les régions d'appartenance; *Comités:* Exécutif; finances; partenariats; publications; pédagogie; professionnalisation; congrès; dossiers Internet
Activités: Formation; information; sensibilisation; congrès; Mouvement Pupilles de l'Enseignement Public; *Service de conférenciers:* Oui; *Listes de destinataires:* Oui *Bibliothèque:* Oui rendez-vous

Manitoba Physical Education Teachers Association (MPETA)
c/o Sport for Life Centre, #319, 145 Pacific Ave., Winnipeg MB R3B 2Z6
Tel: 204-926-8357; *Fax:* 204-925-5703
mpeta@sportmanitoba.ca
mpeta.ca
Social Media: twitter.com/MPETA_news
Overview: A small provincial organization
Description: MPETA is an educational and professional organization which is dedicated to serve physical education in Manitoba Schools.
Affiliation(s): Manitoba Teacher's Society
Chief Officer(s): Ray Agostino, President
Membership: *Fees:* $25 full; $15 student/retired/associate

Ontario Physical & Health Education Association (OPHEA)
#608, 1 Concorde Gate, Toronto ON M3C 3N6
Tel: 416-426-7120; *Fax:* 416-426-7373
Toll-Free: 888-446-7432
www.ophea.org
Social Media: www.youtube.com/opheacanada
www.facebook.com/OpheaCanada
twitter.com/opheacanada
Overview: A medium-sized provincial organization
Description: To support communities & schools to encourage healthy active living
Chief Officer(s): Lori Lukinuk, President
Chris Markham, Executive Director & CEO, 416-426-7126
Activities: Promoting physical activity, & health & physical literacy; Providing program supports to schools & communities; Forming partnerships; Engaging in advocacy activities

Réseau du sport étudiant du Québec Est-du-Québec
#J-201, 60 rue de L'Evêché ouest, Rimouski QC G5L 4H6
Tél: 418-723-1880; *Téléc:* 418-722-0457
rseq-eq.com
Mèdia social:
www.facebook.com/RSEQEstDuQuebecviesaine
Également appelé: RSEQ Est-du-Québec
Nom précédent: Association régionale du sport étudiant de l'Est du Québec
Aperçu: *Dimension:* petite; *Envergure:* locale; fondée en 1989
Description: Favoriser la réalisation de l'ensemble des actions éducatives par l'activité physique et particulièrement le sport en vue de contribuer au développement intégral des étudiants des niveaux primaire, secondaire et collégial dans la région Est du Québec.; *Membre de:* Réseau du sport étudiant du Québec
Membre(s) du bureau directeur: Marc Boudreau, Directeur, 418-722-0457 2539
marcboud@cegep-rimouski.qc.ca
Finances: *Budget de fonctionnement annuel:* $250,000-$500,000; *Fonds:* Unité régionale de loisir et de sport de Québec
Personnel: 2 membre(s) du personnel; 25 bénévole(s)
Membre: 28; *Critères d'admissibilite:* Institutions scolaires
Activités: *Stagiaires:* Oui

Réseau du sport étudiant du Québec Montréal
6875, rue Jarry est, Montréal QC H1P 1W7
Tél: 514-645-6923; *Téléc:* 514-354-8632
secretariat@montreal.rseq.ca
www.rseqmontreal.com
Mèdia social:
www.youtube.com/user/RSEQMontreal
www.facebook.com/RSEQMontreal
Également appelé: RSEQ Montréal
Nom précédent: Association régionale du sport étudiant de Montréal
Aperçu: *Dimension:* petite; *Envergure:* locale; Organisme sans but lucratif; fondée en 1989
Description: Regrouper les associations régionales de sport scolaire, de sport collégial et de sport universitaire de l'Ile de Montréal et les représenter; développer et soutenir des réseaux de compétition régionaux en concertation avec les autres partenaires; offrir des stages de formation et de perfectionnement de cadres en étroite collaboration avec une fédération de sport donnée; participer à la programmation développée par leur instance provinciale; déléguer des officiers auprès des instance provinciales du sport en milieu d'éducation; développer une approche du sport en milieu d'éducation pour chacun des niveaux d'enseignement et développer des programmes en conséquence; promouvoir la pratique de l'activité physique et du sport en milieu d'éducation; coopérer dans le respect des valeurs éducatives avec les organismes intéressés au développement de l'activité physique et du sport; *Membre de:* Réseau du sport étudiant du Québec
Membre(s) du bureau directeur: Jacques Desrochers, Directeur général, 514-645-6923 2
jdesrochers@montreal.rseq.ca
Finances: *Fonds:* Gouvernement provincial
Personnel: 5 membre(s) du personnel
Critères d'admissibilite: Personnel du monde de l'éducation
Activités: Ligues; championnats; stages de perfectionnement pour entraOneurs, officiels et arbitres; *Stagiaires:* Oui

Saskatchewan Physical Education Association (SPEA)
PO Box 193, Harris SK S0L 1K0
Tel: 306-656-4423; *Fax:* 306-656-4405
spea@xplornet.com
www.speaonline.ca
Social Media:
www.facebook.com/speaonline
twitter.com/SPEA4
Overview: A small provincial organization founded in 1951
Description: The Saskatchewan Physical Education Association is a provincial nonprofit incorporated organization that provides quality leadership, advocacy and resources for professionals in physical education and wellness in order to positively influence the lifestyles of Saskatchewan's children and youth.; *Member of:* PHE Canada, SPRA, STF, SHSAA, U of S, U of R,SHEA, In Motion
Affiliation(s): Physical Health Education Canada; Saskatchewan Parks & Recreation Association; Saskatchewan Teachers Federal PHE Canada; Saskatchewan Teachers' Federation
Chief Officer(s): Holly Stevens, Executive Director
Cole Wilson, President
Finances: *Annual Operating Budget:* $100,000-$250,000; *Funding Sources:* Membership fees; Sask Lotteries Trust; Sponsorships
Staff: 1 staff member(s); 15 volunteer(s)
Membership: 485; *Fees:* $25 regular; $10 student; $15 retired teacher; *Member Profile:* Individuals with a professional interest in the teaching of physical education; *Committees:* Social Media, Journal Editor/Website, New Resources/Wellness, Curriculum, Advocacy/Mentorship, Membership Services, Regional Directors
Activities:; *Library:* Yes (Open to Public)

Physical Fitness

The Canadian Association of Fitness Professionals / Association canadienne des professionnels en conditionnement physique
#110, 225 Select Ave., Toronto ON M1X 0B5
Tel: 416-493-3515; *Fax:* 416-493-1756
Toll-Free: 800-667-5622
info@canfitpro.com
www.canfitpro.com
Social Media:
www.youtube.com/user/canfitpro/featured
www.linkedin.com/groups?gid=1773770&trk=hb_side_g
www.facebook.com/canfitpro
twitter.com/canfitpro
Also Known As: Can-Fit-Pro
Overview: A medium-sized national licensing organization founded in 1993
Description: Can-Fit-Pro takes today's fitness professionals' challenges & creates tomorrow's solutions through ongoing relative knowledge & personal enrichment; *Member of:* National Fitness Leadership Advisory Committee
Chief Officer(s): Maureen Hagan, Executive Director
Kathy Ash, Contact, Administration
Finances: *Annual Operating Budget:* $1.5 Million-$3 Million; *Funding Sources:* Sponsorship; private; membership dues; courses
Staff: 10 staff member(s); 400 volunteer(s)
Membership: 30,000; *Member Profile:* Interest in fitness industry
Activities: Certification & standards for fitness instructors & personal trainers, who work at private & public fitness facilities; continuing education; events & six conferences a year

Canadian Fitness & Lifestyle Research Institute (CFLRI) / Institut canadien de la recherche sur la condition physique et le mode de vie
#201, 185 Somerset St. West, Ottawa ON K2P 0J2
Tel: 613-233-5528; *Fax:* 613-233-5536
www.cflri.ca
Previous Name: Canada Fitness Survey (1985)
Overview: A medium-sized national charitable organization founded in 1980
Description: To conduct research, monitor trends, & make recommendations to increase physical activity & improve health in Canada
Chief Officer(s): Nancy Dubois, Chair
Christine Cameron, Acting President
Mathilde Costa, Senior Manager, Finance, Administration, & Human Resources
Cora Lynn Craig, Senior Researcher
Finances: *Funding Sources:* Fitness / Active Living Program Unit of Health Canada; Contracts; Grants; Publication sales; Donations
Activities: Providing education about leading active & healthy lives; Developing a aprovider-based intervention known as PACE Canada; Conducting surveys, such as The Canadian Physical Activity Levels Among Youth (CAN PLAY)

Canadian Society for Exercise Physiology (CSEP) / Société canadienne de physiologie de l'exercice (SCPE)
#370, 18 Louisa St., Ottawa ON K1R 6Y6
Tel: 613-234-3755; *Fax:* 613-234-3565
Toll-Free: 877-651-3755
info@csep.ca
www.csep.ca
Social Media:
www.linkedin.com/company/csep-scpe
www.facebook.com/520719817945510
twitter.com/CSEPdotCA
Previous Name: Canadian Association of Sport Sciences
Overview: A medium-sized national organization founded in 1967
Description: To promote the generation, synthesis, transfer, & application of knowledge & research related to exercise physiology, encompassing physical activity, fitness, health, nutrition, epidemiology & human performance; To act as the voice for exercise physiology in Canada
Chief Officer(s): Phil Chilibeck, President/Chair
Membership: 5,400; *Fees:* $20 first-time sponsored students; $50 students; $175 active & affiliate members; *Member Profile:* Active members with the graduate degree, PhD, MD, or MSc; Affiliate members with a BSc, BA, BPE, BKin, or no degree; Organizations; Students currently enrolled full-time in university studies; Retired active members; *Committees:* Annual General Meeting Program; Applied Physiology, Nutrition, & Metabolism (APNM) Editorial; Finance; Graduate Student; CSEP Health & Fitness Program National Advisory; Knowledge Transfer; Physical Activity Measurement & Guidelines (PAMG) Steering; Expert Advisory (Scientific Advisors); CSEP Health & Fitness Program Executive; CSEP Certified Exercise Physiologist Technical; CSEP Certified Personal Trainer Technical; Strategic Health & Fitness Program Initiatives; CSEP Health & Fitness Program Marketing; Research Subcommittees (Existing & New Guidelines)
Activities: Offering the National Health & Fitness Program; Engaging in advocacy activities; Advertising job postings; Facilitating national communication through committees & networks; Providing networking opportunities

The Recreation Association / L'Association récréative
2451 Riverside Dr., Ottawa ON K1H 7X7
Tel: 613-733-5100; *Fax:* 613-736-6238
racentre@racentre.com
www.racentre.com
Social Media:
twitter.com/RACentreOttawa
Also Known As: RA Centre
Overview: A large national organization founded in 1941
Description: To provide quality leisure & lifestyle activities to the membership
Chief Officer(s): Diana Monnet, President
Gord Aitken, Acting CEO/General Manager
gaitken@racentre.com
Jane Proudfoot, Director, Recreation, Sports & Fitness Services, 613-736-6227
jproudfoot@racentre.com
Finances: *Annual Operating Budget:* Greater than $5 Million; *Funding Sources:* Membership dues; program revenue; special projects revenue
Staff: 70 staff member(s); 500 volunteer(s)
Membership: 27,000; *Fees:* $33-$57
Activities: 100+ programs & services in health, fitness, recreation & leisure

Physical Therapy

Sport Physiotherapy Canada (SPC)
#75, 2192 Queen St. East, Toronto ON M4E 1E6
Tel: 647-722-3461
info@sportphysio.ca
www.sportphysio.ca
Social Media:
www.youtube.com/user/physiotherapycan
www.facebook.com/sportphysiocanada
twitter.com/sportphysiocan
Previous Name: Sport Physiotherapy Division of the Canadian Physiotherapy Association
Overview: A small national organization founded in 1972
Description: To promote professional development of members; To ensure high-quality health care for Canada's athletes; *Member of:* Canadian Physiotherapy Association; Sport Medicine Council of Canada
Chief Officer(s): Ashley Lewis, Executive Director
alewis@sportphysio.ca
Ereka Roach, Coordinator, Member Services
program@sportphysio.ca
Membership: 1,200; *Member Profile:* Members can be physiotherapists, students, graduate / practising physiotherapists, or SPD-certified sport physiotherapists

Polo

Canadian Polo Association (CPA)
#100, 180 Renfrew Dr., Markham ON L3R 9Z2
Tel: 647-208-7656; *Fax:* 905-477-6897
info@polocanada.ca
www.polocanada.ca
Social Media:
www.facebook.com/polocanada
Also Known As: Polo Canada
Overview: A small national charitable organization founded in 1985
Description: To develop & maintain standards of excellence for the sport of polo in Canada; To promote polo across the nation
Finances: *Funding Sources:* Membership fees; Donations
Membership: 12 clubs; *Fees:* $30 juniors; $60 adults; *Member Profile:* Individual junior & adult polo players, & clubs from across Canada
Activities: Supporting polo players & clubs across Canada; Providing resources; Raising awareness of polo & attracting new

players to the game; Supporting training programs, educational workshops, & clinics for coaches, umpires, & players; Encouraging international competition; Offering junior polo programs; Facilitating communication between member clubs

Powerlifting

British Columbia Powerlifting Association (BCPA)

#222, 12085 - 228 St., Maple Ridge BC V2X 6M2
bc-powerlifting.com
Social Media:
www.facebook.com/291376977556248
Overview: A small provincial organization founded in 2011
Description: To promote powerlifting throughout British Columbia; *Member of:* Canadian Powerlifting Union; International Powerlifting Federation
Chief Officer(s): Joe Oliveira, President, 604-734-2932
olivejoe1969@gmail.com
Membership: *Fees:* $60 first time; $85 general; $60 special olympics; $25 associaite

Canadian Powerlifting Federation (CPF)

www.canadianpowerliftingfederation.com
Social Media:
www.facebook.com/Canadian-Powerlifting-Federation-CPF-1173 59724995464
Previous Name: Canadian Powerlifting Organization
Overview: A small national organization
Description: Promoting powerlifting in Canada; *Member of:* World Powerlifting Congress; World Powerlifting Organization
Member Profile: Individuals & organizations, from across Canada, who are interested in powerlifting
Activities: Providing results from CPF meets & its affiliates

Canadian Powerlifting Union (CPU)

c/o Mike Armstrong, 4709 Fordham Cres. SE, Calgary AB T2A 2A5
Tel: 403-402-4142
www.powerlifting.ca
Social Media:
www.facebook.com/CDNpowerliftingunion
Previous Name: Canadian Powerlifting Federation
Overview: A medium-sized national organization founded in 1982
Description: To oversee & regulate all IPF style powerlifting in Canada
Affiliation(s): International Powerlifting Federation
Chief Officer(s): Mark Giffin, President
mark@powerlifting.ca
Ryan Fowler, Chair, Coaching
rfowler@powerlifting.ca
Mike Armstrong, Secretary
mike@powerlifting.ca
Barry Antoniow, Treasurer
bantoniow@powerlifting.ca

Manitoba Powerlifting Association (MPA)

MB
manitobapowerlifting.ca
Overview: A small provincial organization founded in 1967
Member of: Manitoba Sports Federation; Manitoba Sports Directorate; Canadian Powerlifting Union; International Powerlifting Federation

Nova Scotia Powerlifting Association

240 Cusack Dr., Sydney NS B1P 6A1
Tel: 902-567-0893
Overview: A small provincial licensing organization
Description: To provide opportunities for lifters to learn the sport of powerlifting through seminars, gyms & clubs; to participate in meets locally, nationally & internationally; *Member of:* International Powerlifting Union
Chief Officer(s): John Fraser, President
johnfraser56@hotmail.com
Member Profile: Novice; Junior; Master; Open; Special Olympian divisions; provincial, national & world calibre lifters
Activities: Lifters attend competitions on provincial, national & international levels & receive medallions or trophies according to placement; seminars given upon request

Ontario Powerlifting Association (OPA)

c/o Karen Maxwell, Registrar, 555 O'Brien Rd., Renfrew ON K7V 3Z3
info@ontariopowerlifting.org
www.ontariopowerlifting.org
Social Media:
instagram.com/ontariopowerliftingassociation
www.facebook.com/OntarioPowerliftingAssociation
Overview: A small provincial organization
Chief Officer(s): Glyn Moore, President
mgmoore13@outlook.com

Membership: *Fees:* $85 regular; $65 student/special athlete; $30 associate

PEI Powerlifting Association (PEIPLA)

PE
www.peipowerlifting.ca
Overview: A small provincial organization founded in 1996
Member of: Canadian Powerlifting Union
Affiliation(s): Canadian Powerlifting Union; International Powerlifting Federation
Chief Officer(s): John MacDonald, President
john@peipowerlifting.ca
Membership: *Fees:* $70 regular; $40 high school; *Committees:* Fundraising; Competition & Promotion; Selection & Grant

Saskatchewan Powerlifting Association (SPA)

PO Box 42, North Weyburn SK S0C 1X0
Tel: 306-842-4299; *Fax:* 306-842-2682
saskpowerlifting@gmail.com
www.saskpowerlifting.ca
Social Media:
www.facebook.com/saskpowerlifting
Overview: A small provincial organization
Description: To promote fitness & provide opportunities to weightlifting athletes.
Chief Officer(s): Ryan Fowler, President
Membership: 100+; *Fees:* $60 regular; $35 new/special; $10 referee; $2 associate

Racquetball

Alberta Racquetball Association (ARA)

47 Walden Cres., St Albert AB T8N 3N5
Tel: 780-918-5332
albertaracquetball@shaw.ca
www.albertaracquetball.com
Social Media:
www.youtube.com/channel/UCdxaKwImilNEEnGN5dDpNig
www.facebook.com/Alberta-Racquetball-Association-813120186 23
Overview: A small provincial organization founded in 1971
Description: To develop the sport of racquetball in Alberta.; *Member of:* Racquetball Canada
Chief Officer(s): Barbara May, Executive Director
Membership: *Fees:* $10

Association québécoise de racquetball (AQR) / Quebec Racquetball Association

4545, av Pierre-de Coubertin, Montréal QC H1V 0B2
Tél: 514-252-3062
info@sports-4murs.qc.ca
www.racquetball.qc.ca
Média social:
www.facebook.com/427582940621028
Aperçu: *Dimension:* petite; *Envergure:* provinciale
Description: Promouvoir le développement du racquetball au Québec en offrant différentes opportunités aux adeptes, tout en encourageant la participation sportive à travers un ensemble de services et de programmes; *Membre de:* Racquetball Canada; Sports-Québec; Regroupement Loisir Québec
Membre(s) du bureau directeur: Rino Langelier, Président
rinolang@hotmail.com
Finances: *Budget de fonctionnement annuel:* $50,000-$100,000; *Fonds:* Éducation, Loisir et Sport Québec
Personnel: 4 membre(s) du personnel
Membre: 10 000; *Montant de la cotisation:* Barème
Activités: Tournois, championnats; formation d'arbitres et d'entraîneurs; *Stagiaires:* Oui

British Columbia Racquetball Association (BCRA)

BC
info@racquetballbc.ca
www.racquetballbc.ca
Social Media:
twitter.com/bcracquetball
Overview: A medium-sized provincial charitable organization founded in 1970
Member of: Racquetball Canada
Chief Officer(s): Travis Einarson, President, Coaching
traviseinarson@gmail.com
Cal Smith, Vice-President, Officiating
cdsmithh@shaw.ca
Finances: *Funding Sources:* Fundraising; SportsFunder Lottery; Sponsorships
Membership: *Fees:* $15
Activities: Supporting tournaments; Providing rules, skills, & junior development clinics; Hosting school programs

New Brunswick Racquetball Association (NBRA)

NB
nbracquetball@gmail.com
www.nbracquetball.ca
Social Media:
twitter.com/nbrball
Overview: A small provincial organization founded in 1977
Description: To promote the sport of racquetball throughout New Brunswick; *Member of:* Racquetball Canada
Chief Officer(s): Michael McCabe, Vice-President, Membership
Activities: Providing racquetball classes; Offering racquetball coaching

Newfoundland Racquetball Association

NL
Overview: A small provincial organization
Member of: Racquetball Canada; Sport Newfoundland & Labrador

Racquetball Canada

145 Pacific Ave., Winnipeg MB R3B 2Z6
Tel: 613-692-5394
www.racquetball.ca
Social Media:
twitter.com/RBallCanada
Previous Name: Canadian Racquetball Association
Overview: A medium-sized national charitable organization founded in 1972
Description: To promote racquetball as a sport & physical activity; To provide leadership by developing & coordinating services & programs designed to meet the needs of the racquetball community; *Member of:* International Racquetball Federation
Affiliation(s): Canadian Sport Council; Canadian Olympic Association; Coaching Association of Canada
Chief Officer(s): Jack McBride, President
mcbridejm@shaw.ca
Cheryl Adlard, Executive Director
ed.rbcanada@sportmanitoba.ca
Daniel MacDonald, Administrator, Athlete Development
daniel.macdonald@umoncton.ca
Geri Powell, Administrator, High Performance / Sport Development
gpowellthpdirector@gmail.com
Finances: *Funding Sources:* Government; Membership dues; Sponsorships
Staff: 50 volunteer(s)
Membership: 5 life + 700 individual + 350 club + 8 provincial associations (incl. 18,000 members); *Fees:* $1,500 life; $25 individual; $50 club; *Member Profile:* Individual resident in Canada or Canadian citizen involved in the sport of racquetball at any level of structured activity; *Committees:* National Team; Coaching; Sport Science; Tournament; Ranking; Officiating; Junior Development; Membership; Ways & Means; Wheelchair; Women
Activities: *Awareness Events:* National Championship Week, May; *Speaker Service:* Yes; *Rents Mailing List:* Yes

Racquetball Manitoba Inc.

145 Pacific Ave., Winnipeg MB R3B 2Z7
Tel: 204-925-5666; *Fax:* 204-925-5703
racquetballmb.ca
Overview: A small provincial organization founded in 1974
Description: To promote racquetball as a sport & a physical activity throughout the Province of Manitoba; To provide leadership by developing & coordinating services & programs designed to meet the needs of the racquetball community; *Member of:* Racquetball Canada; Sport Manitoba
Membership: 600; *Fees:* $25 adult; $10 juniors/students

Racquetball Ontario (RO)

51 Springgarden Cres., Stoney Creek ON L8J 2S5
www.racquetballontario.ca
Social Media:
twitter.com/Rball_Ontario
Overview: A medium-sized provincial organization
Member of: Racquetball Canada
Chief Officer(s): Greg Doricki, President
Peter Fisher, Director, Development
Tanya Hodgin, Director, Memberships
Sue Swaine, Director, Coaching
Membership: *Fees:* $25 individual; $50 family; $100 event coordinator

Racquetball PEI

c/o Sport PEI, 40 Enman Cres., Charlottetown PE C1E 1E6
Overview: A small provincial organization
Member of: Racquetball Canada

Saskatchewan Racquetball Association (SRA)
SK
racquetballsask.com
Social Media:
www.facebook.com/SaskatchewanRacquetballAssociation
twitter.com/saskracquetball
Overview: A small provincial organization
Description: To To promote the sport of racquetball throughout Saskatchewan.
Chief Officer(s): Karla Drury, President
k.drury@sasktel.net
Tim Landeryou, Executive Director
ed.rballsask@gmail.com

Recreation

British Columbia Fishing Resorts & Outfitters Association (BCFROA)
PO Box 3301, #106, 1383 McGill Rd., Kamloops BC V2C 6B9
Tel: 250-374-6836; *Fax:* 250-374-6640
Toll-Free: 866-374-6836
bcfroa@bcfroa.ca
www.bcfroa.ca
Social Media:
www.youtube.com/user/BCFROA; pinterest.com/bcfroa
www.facebook.com/wheretofishinbc
twitter.com/Fish_BC
Overview: A small provincial organization founded in 1974
Description: Works with the public & private sector to protect areas currently in use; to preserve the wildlife experience in BC for the enjoyment of future generations; a lobby group whose members are dedicated to providing a quality outdoor experience; *Member of:* Outdoor Recreation Council of British Columbia
Chief Officer(s): Matt Jennings, Executive Director
Finances: *Annual Operating Budget:* $100,000-$250,000; *Funding Sources:* Membership dues; funding programs; promotions; sponsorships
Membership: 130+; *Fees:* $105-$519.75; *Member Profile:* Resort owner or angling & hunting guide
Activities: Marketing; lobbying; advocacy

Canadian Volkssport Federation (CVF) / Fédération canadienne volkssport (FCV)
PO Box 2668, Stn. D, Ottawa ON K1P 5W7
Tel: 613-234-7333
cvffcv@rogers.com
www.walks.ca
Overview: A medium-sized national organization founded in 1987
Description: To promote non-competitive participation in walking & other recreational activities for fun, fitness & friendship; *Member of:* International Federation of Popular Sports
Chief Officer(s): Beverley Cattrall, President
bevpor@telus.net
Finances: *Annual Operating Budget:* Less than $50,000; *Funding Sources:* Sanctioning fees
Staff: 1 staff member(s); 150 volunteer(s)
Membership: 51 clubs; *Fees:* $150 individual; $50 affiliate; *Member Profile:* Mostly ages 35-70; *Committees:* Board of Directors; Executive
Activities: Walking; swimming; skating; skiing - all non-competitively; *Speaker Service:* Yes

Fitness New Brunswick (NBCFAL) / Conditionnement physique Noueau-Brunswick (CCPVANB)
Lady Beaverbrook Gym, University of New Brunswick, PO Box 4400, #A112A, 2 Peter Kelly Dr., Fredericton NB E3B 5A3
Tel: 506-453-1094; *Fax:* 506-453-1099
Toll-Free: 888-790-1411
membershipservices@fitnessnb.ca
www.fitnessnb.ca
Social Media:
www.facebook.com/Fitness.New.Brunswick
twitter.com/FitnessNB
Previous Name: New Brunswick Council for Fitness & Active Living (NBCFAL); New Brunswick Fitness Council
Overview: A small provincial organization founded in 1988
Description: To certify fitness professionals in New Brunswick; to promote professionalism in the fitness industry; To offer standardization & consistency in training programs; To uphold professional ethics through the Code of Conduct for fitness service providers; *Member of:* Coalition for Active Living (CCAL)
Affiliation(s): Atlantic Canadian Society for Exercise Physiology (CSEP) Health & Fitness Program (H&FP); National Fitness Leadership Alliance (NFLA)
Chief Officer(s): Marilynn Georgas, Executive Director
executivedirector@fitnessnb.ca
Erin Maranda, Coordinator, Projects
projectscoordinator@fitnessnb.ca
Membership: *Fees:* $62.15; *Committees:* Professional Development; Marketing & Communications; Human Resources; Translation; Conference
Activities: Providing fitness education in New Brunswick; Raising public awareness of safe & effective practices for fitness professionals

Golden Age Society
4061A - 4th Ave., Whitehorse YT Y1A 1H1
Tel: 867-668-5538
goldenagesociety@gmail.com
yukon-seniors-and-elders.org/goldenage/goldenage.home.htm
Overview: A small provincial organization founded in 1976
Description: To promote & give opportunity for social, recreational activities for seniors in the Yukon
Membership: *Fees:* $20

Halifax Sport & Social Club (HSSC)
PO Box 8821, Halifax NS B3K 5M5
Tel: 902-431-8326
info@halifaxsport.ca
www.halifaxsport.ca
Social Media:
www.facebook.com/HalifaxSSC
twitter.com/HalifaxSSC
Overview: A medium-sized local organization
Description: To offer co-ed recreational sport leagues, tournaments & social events for adults.
Chief Officer(s): Lael Morgan, Executive Director, 902-431-8326 113

ParaSport & Recreation PEI
Royalty Center House Of Sport, PO Box 841, Charlottetown PE C1A 7L9
Tel: 902-368-4540; *Fax:* 902-368-4548
info@parasportpei.ca
www.parasportpei.ca
Previous Name: Paralympics PEI Inc.
Overview: A small provincial charitable organization founded in 1974
Description: To ensure the ample provision of sport & recreation opportunities for persons who are physically challenged; *Member of:* Canadian Blind Sport Association; Canadian Association for Disabled Skiing; Canadian Wheelchair Sports Association
Affiliation(s): The JoyRiders Therapeutic Riding Association of PEI Inc.; The Canadian Council of the Blind - Prince County and Queensland Chapters; The Abegweit Club of Summerside; G.E.A.R. (Getting Everyone Accessibly Riding)
Chief Officer(s): Tracy Stevenson, Executive Director, 902-368-4540
tracy@parasportpei.ca
Finances: *Funding Sources:* Province of PEI; City of Charlottetown; business sector; community & service clubs; fundraising
Staff: 2 staff member(s)
Activities: Demonstrations; presentations; sport/recreation events; *Speaker Service:* Yes; *Library:* Yes (Open to Public)

Rhythmic Sportive Gymnastics

Rhythmic Gymnastics Manitoba Inc. (RGM)
145 Pacific Ave., Winnipeg MB R3B 2Z6
Tel: 201-925-5738
rhythmic@sportmanitoba.ca
www.rgmanitoba.com
Previous Name: Manitoba Rhythmic Sportive Gymnastics Association
Overview: A medium-sized provincial organization founded in 1985
Description: To support & promote rhythmic gymnastic programs
Affiliation(s): Sport Manitoba; Rhythmic Gymnastics Canada; Gymnastics Canada; International Gymnastics Federation; Canadian Sport Centre - Manitoba; Coaching Manitoba; Gymnastics Manitoba
Membership: 8 clubs in the Winnipeg & Eastman regions
Activities: Hosting performing & competitive events; Posting event results; Providing programs to the rhythmic gymnastics community in Manitoba, such as the long term athlete development program & training for gymnastics coaches, & judges; Promoting standards for programs

Ringette

Association de Ringuette de Longueuil
2258, rue Papineau, Longueuil QC J4K 3M1
Tél: 450-442-0808
www.ringuettelongueuil.com
Aperçu: *Dimension:* petite; *Envergure:* provinciale
Membre de: Ringuette-Québec
Membre(s) du bureau directeur: Marie-Lyne Fortin Thibault, Président
marielynefortin87@outlook.com
Montant de la cotisation: Barème

Association de ringuette de Lotbinière
c/o Marie-Noël Duclos, 412, rue Belanger, Saint-Narcisse-de-Beaurivage QC G0S 1W0
Tél: 418-475-4125
Aperçu: *Dimension:* petite; *Envergure:* provinciale
Description: Site Internet: kreezee.com/sport/association/association-de-ringuette-de-lotbiniere/7671; *Membre de:* Ringuette-Québec
Membre(s) du bureau directeur: Marie-Noel Duclos, Présidente
robertetmarie@axion.ca
Membre: 7 équipes; *Montant de la cotisation:* Barème

Association de Ringuette de Sainte-Marie
QC
www.ringuettestemarie.com
Média social:
www.facebook.com/181771528541007
Aperçu: *Dimension:* petite; *Envergure:* provinciale; fondée en 1983
Membre de: Ringuette-Québec
Membre(s) du bureau directeur: Tony Fecteau, Président, 418-387-8847
presidence@ringuettestemarie.com

Association de Ringuette de Ste-Julie
QC
Aperçu: *Dimension:* petite; *Envergure:* provinciale
Membre de: Ringuette-Québec

Association de Ringuette de Sept-Iles
QC
www.ringuettesept-iles.org
Média social:
fr.facebook.com/228073003907401
Aperçu: *Dimension:* petite; *Envergure:* provinciale
Membre de: Ringuette-Québec
Membre(s) du bureau directeur: Frédéric Lesage, Président, 418-968-2036
fred.lesage@icloud.com
Membre: 7 équipes

Association de Ringuette de Thetford
555 St-Alphonse nord, Thetford Mines QC G6G 3X1
Tél: 418-338-3729
www.ringuettethetford.com
Aperçu: *Dimension:* petite; *Envergure:* provinciale
Membre de: Ringuette-Québec
Membre(s) du bureau directeur: Dany Harvey, Président
dharvey27@hotmail.ca
Membre: 5 équipes

Association de Ringuette de Vallée-du-Richelieu
CP 85113, 345, boul Sir-Wilfrid-Laurier, Mont-Saint-Hilaire QC J3H 5W1
vdrringuette@hotmail.com
www.ringuettevdr.com
Média social:
www.youtube.com/user/VDRringuette
www.facebook.com/145272202165165
twitter.com/ringuettevdr
Aperçu: *Dimension:* petite; *Envergure:* provinciale
Membre de: Ringuette-Québec
Membre(s) du bureau directeur: Patrick Beauchemin, Président

Association de Ringuette des Moulins
840, rue Brien, Mascouche QC J7K 2X3
Tél: 450-961-9295
admin@ringuettedesmoulins.com
www.ringuettedesmoulins.com
Aperçu: *Dimension:* petite; *Envergure:* provinciale
Membre de: Ringuette-Québec
Membre(s) du bureau directeur: Daniel Gagné, Président
president@ringuettedesmoulins.com

Association de Ringuette Lévis
CP 1807, Saint-Rédempteur QC G6K 1N6
communications.arl@gmail.com
www.ringuettearl.com
Média social:
www.facebook.com/ringuettelevis/
Nom précédent: Association de Ringuette Chutes Chaudière
Aperçu: *Dimension:* petite; *Envergure:* provinciale
Membre de: Ringuette-Québec
Membre(s) du bureau directeur: Tanya Moore, Présidente
Membre: 14 équipes

Association de Ringuette Repentigny
QC
www.ringuetterepentigny.com
Média social:
www.facebook.com/Ringuette-Repentigny-1773415112879301
Aperçu: *Dimension:* petite; *Envergure:* provinciale
Membre de: Ringuette-Québec
Membre(s) du bureau directeur: Gordon Britton, Président
gordon.britton@ringuetterepentigny.com
Membre: 10 équipes

Association de ringuette Roussillon
CP 164, Saint-Constant QC J5A 2G2
communications@ringuetteroussillon.ca
www.ringuetteroussillon.ca
Média social:
www.youtube.com/playlist?list=PLjva740E_gw1xyVGbSm6XtpLc R-HOjbYD
www.facebook.com/ARRoussillon
twitter.com/ARRoussillon
Aperçu: *Dimension:* petite; *Envergure:* provinciale
Membre de: Ringuette-Québec

Association régionale de ringuette Laval
3235, boul, St-Martin est, Laval QC H7E 5G8
Tél: 450-664-1917
ringuettelaval.org
Aperçu: *Dimension:* petite; *Envergure:* provinciale
Membre de: Ringuette-Québec
Membre(s) du bureau directeur: Eric Allard, Président

Association Régionale de Ringuette Richelieu Yamaska
QC
www.ringuette-quebec.qc.ca/regionale_richelieu-yamaska.php
Aperçu: *Dimension:* petite; *Envergure:* provinciale
Membre de: Ringuette-Québec

Association Sportive de Ringuette Brossard
CP 210, 8000, boul Leduc, Brossard QC J4Y 0E9
communications@ringuetteroussillon.ca
www.ringuettebrossard.com
Média social:
www.facebook.com/AssociationSportiveDeRinguetteDeBrossard
twitter.com/ARRoussillon
Également appelé: Ringuette Brossard
Aperçu: *Dimension:* petite; *Envergure:* provinciale
Membre de: Ringuette-Québec
Membre(s) du bureau directeur: Sylvain Lebel, President
slebel1@sympatico.ca

Berwick & District Ringette Association
NS
ringette.wordpress.com
Overview: A small local organization
Member of: Ringette Nova Scotia
Chief Officer(s): Marlene Connell, President
ron.connell@ns.sympatico.ca

British Columbia Ringette Association (BCRA) / Association de ringuette de Colombie-Britannique
#420, 789 West Pender St., Vancouver BC V6C 1H2
Tel: 604-629-4583
info@bcringette.org
www.bcringette.org
Social Media:
www.youtube.com/user/ringettebc
www.facebook.com/pages/BC-Ringette-Association/388774601776
twitter.com/bcringette
Overview: A small provincial organization founded in 1976
Description: To promote ringette & allow for opportunities for people in British Columbia to play ringette.
Chief Officer(s): Colin Ensworth, Manager, Sports Operations
manager@bcringette.org
Rob Tait, Chair
chair@bcringette.org

Cole Harbour Ringette Association (CHRA)
NS
Overview: A small local organization
Member of: Ringette Nova Scotia
Membership: 1-99; *Fees:* schedule

Dartmouth Ringette Association
NS
harbourcitylakers@gmail.com
dartmouthringette.com
Overview: A small local organization
Description: To operate the Harbour City Lakers League.; *Member of:* Ringette Nova Scotia
Chief Officer(s): Susan Graham, President
Membership: 11 teams

Eastern Shore Ringette Association (ESRA)
NS
esringette.goalline.ca
Overview: A small local organization
Member of: Ringette Nova Scotia
Chief Officer(s): Mary Stienburg, President
presidentESRA@gmail.com
Membership: 3 teams; *Member Profile:* Teams with players 4-10; Teams with players 18+

Fédération sportive de ringuette du Québec
4545, av Pierre-de Coubertin, Montréal QC H1V 3R2
Tél: 514-252-3085; *Téléc:* 514-254-1069
ringuette@ringuette-quebec.qc.ca
www.ringuette-quebec.qc.ca
Média social:
www.youtube.com/channel/UChlZmg35-zhVgQBkgru8k7g
www.facebook.com/RinguetteQuebec-139856822762458
twitter.com/ringuetteqc
Aperçu: *Dimension:* petite; *Envergure:* provinciale; fondée en 1973
Description: Promouvoir le sport de la ringuette au Québec
Membre(s) du bureau directeur: Louise Morin, Contact

Halifax Hurricanes Ringette Association
NS
hhringette.ca
Merged from: Halifax Chebucto Ringette Association; Halifax - St. Margaret's Ringette Association
Overview: A small local organization
Member of: Ringette Nova Scotia
Chief Officer(s): Chad Mombourquette, President
president@hhringette.ca
Mark Whidden, Director, Coaching
dc@hhringette.ca
Membership: 1-99; *Fees:* Schedule available

International Ringette Federation - Canada
#201, 5510 Canotek Rd., Ottawa ON K1J 9J4
Tel: 613-748-5655; *Fax:* 613-748-5860
ringette@ringette.ca
www.ringette.ca
Social Media:
www.youtube.com/ringettecanada
www.facebook.com/pages/Ringette-Canada-Ringuette-Canada/231647530090
twitter.com/redringette
Overview: A small national organization
Description: To promote the game of Ringette around the world.
Chief Officer(s): Natasha Johnston, Executive Director
natasha@ringette.ca
Jane Casson, President
president@ringette.ca
Activities: *Awareness Events:* Canadian Ringette Championships - Apr.

Manitoba Ringette Association (MRA) / Association de ringuette du Manitoba
145 Pacific Ave., Winnipeg MB R3B 2Z6
Tel: 204-925-5710; *Fax:* 204-925-5925
ringette.admin@sportmanitoba.ca
www.manitobaringette.ca
Social Media:
twitter.com/MBRingette
Overview: A medium-sized provincial organization founded in 1970
Description: To develop, encourage and promote Ringette for the enjoyment of all Manitobans through the provision of programs, services and resources that inform, educate and teach skills.; *Member of:* International Ringette Federation
Affiliation(s): Sport Manitoba
Chief Officer(s): Laralie Higginson, Executive Director
edringette@sportmanitoba.ca
Melanie Reimer, Coordinator, Program
ringette@sportmanitoba.ca
Finances: *Funding Sources:* Sponsorship; grants & registration fees
Staff: 4 staff member(s)
Activities: Tournaments; provincial competitions; national competitions; world competitions; *Library:* Yes (Open to Public)

Nova Central Ringette Association
NS
novacentralringette.ca
Social Media:
www.facebook.com/NovaCentralRingetteAssociation
Overview: A small local organization
Member of: Ringette Nova Scotia
Affiliation(s): Bedord Ringette Association; Berwick Ringette Association; Sackville Ringette Association
Chief Officer(s): Greg Giffin, President
Membership: 15 teams

Ontario Ringette Association (ORA) / Association de ringuette de l'Ontario
#207, 3 Concorde Gate, Toronto ON M3C 3N7
Tel: 416-426-7204; *Fax:* 416-426-7359
admin@ontario-ringette.com
www.ontario-ringette.com
Social Media:
www.youtube.com/channel/UCWGddPSY6p6_X8wQqe1csPw
twitter.com/OntRingette
Overview: A medium-sized provincial organization founded in 1963
Description: To promote fun, fitness, & friendship in a safe play environment; To be dedicated to quality performance & fair play opportunity for all ages; *Member of:* Ringette Canada
Chief Officer(s): Keith Kaiser, President
president@ontario-ringette.com
Michael Beaton, Executive Director, 416-426-7205
ed@ontario-ringette.com
Karla Romphf, Director, Technical, 416-426-7206
tech@ontario-ringette.com
Rose Snagg, Coordinator, Administration, 416-426-7204
admin@ontario-ringette.com

Régionale Ringuette Rive-Sud
QC
www.ringuetterivesud.com
Média social:
instagram.com/regionale_rsud
www.facebook.com/RegionaleRinguetteRiveSud
twitter.com/RinguetteRRS
Aperçu: *Dimension:* petite; *Envergure:* provinciale
Membre de: Ringuette-Québec
Membre(s) du bureau directeur: Clémence Duchesneau, Présidente
clemdu@hotmail.com

Ringette Alberta
Percy Page Centre, 11759 Groat Rd., 2nd Fl., Edmonton AB T5M 3K6
Tel: 780-451-1750; *Fax:* 780-415-1749
www.ringettealberta.com
Social Media:
www.youtube.com/channel/UCx0Yyv-Iwy-mZJPFUPf8xZQ
www.facebook.com/ringettealberta
twitter.com/ringettealberta
Overview: A medium-sized provincial organization
Description: To provide ringette services to its members; *Member of:* Ringette Canada
Chief Officer(s): David Myers, Executive Director
david@ringettealberta.com

Ringette Association of Saskatchewan (RAS) / Association de ringuette de Saskatchewan
1860 Lorne St., Regina SK S4P 2L7
Tel: 306-780-9432; *Fax:* 306-780-9460
www.ringettesask.com
Social Media:
twitter.com/RingetteSask
Overview: A medium-sized provincial organization founded in 1976
Description: To develop, promote, communicate, & administer programs, policies & procedures which will enhance the development & participation of coaches, players, officals, volunteers, & administrators from all levels throughout Saskatchewan; *Member of:* Sask Sport
Chief Officer(s): Jodi Lorenz, President
Crystal Gellner, Executive Director
executivedirector@ringettesask.com
Keith Doering, Director, Technical
technicaldirector@ringettesask.com
Finances: *Funding Sources:* Saskatchewan Lotteries; Corporate sponsorships; Membership fees
Staff: 2 staff member(s)
Activities: Coaching & officiating clinics; Providing player development camps; Organizing provincial championships

Ringette Canada (RC) / Ringuette Canada
#201, 5510 Canotek Rd., Ottawa ON K1J 9J4
Tel: 613-748-5655; *Fax:* 613-748-5860
ringette@ringette.ca
www.ringette.ca
Social Media:
www.youtube.com/ringettecanada
twitter.com/ringettecanada
Overview: A large national organization founded in 1975
Description: To formulate, publish & administer national policies beneficial to the sport; To enforce laws & regulations governing ringette; To encourage ringette participants to strive for excellence in teamwork, team spirit & team discipline; *Member of:* International Ringette Federation
Chief Officer(s): Jane Casson, President
president@ringette.ca
Natasha Johnston, Executive Director
natasha@ringette.ca
Frances Losier, Director, High Performance & Events, 613-748-5655 221
frances@ringette.ca
Nathalie Muller, Director, Technical, 613-748-5655 224
nathalie@ringette.ca
Alayne Martel, Contact, Media & Public Relations, 902-839-2532
alayne@ringette.ca
Finances: *Annual Operating Budget:* $1.5 Million-$3 Million; *Funding Sources:* Membership fees; Federal government; Corporate sponsorships
Staff: 7 staff member(s)
Member Profile: Provincial or territorial ringette associations; *Committees:* Coach Development; Officials Development; High Performance; National Ringette League
Activities: Organizing the Canadian Ringette Championships; *Library:* Resource Centre (Open to Public)

Ringette New Brunswick (RNB) / Ringuette Nouveau-Brunswick
487 rte La Vallée, Memramcook NB E4K 3C7
Tel: 506-851-5641
www.ringette-nb.com
Social Media:
twitter.com/RingetteNB
Also Known As: New Brunswick Ringette Association
Overview: A small provincial organization
Description: To ensure the well-being & development of ringette athletes in New Brunswick
Chief Officer(s): Chantal Poirier, Manager, Program
cpoirierRNB@hotmail.com
Activities: Consulting with the Province of New Brunswick Wellness, Culture, & Sport; Providing direction in areas such as athlete development, officiating, coaching, & technical issues; Organizing coaching & officiating clinics; Establishing standards for bench staff

Ringette Nova Scotia
5516 Spring Garden Rd., 4th Fl., Halifax NS B3J 1G6
Tel: 902-425-5450; *Fax:* 902-425-5606
ringette@sportnovascotia.ca
www.ringette.ns.ca
Social Media:
www.facebook.com/ringettenovascotia
twitter.com/RingetteNS
Overview: A small provincial organization founded in 1973
Description: To promote, develop & administer the sport of ringette within Nova Scotia; *Member of:* International Ringette Federation
Chief Officer(s): Lainie Wintrup, Executive Director
Finances: *Annual Operating Budget:* Less than $50,000; *Funding Sources:* Provincial Sport & Recreation Commission
Staff: 20 volunteer(s)
Membership: 800; *Fees:* Schedule available; *Committees:* Canada Winter Games; Fundraising; Provincial Teams; Strategic Plan
Activities: *Awareness Events:* Ringette Week, Feb.; *Library:* Resource Library by appointment

Ringette PEI (RPEI)
40 Enman Cres., Charlottetown PE C1A 7K7
Tel: 902-368-6570
ringettepei.ca
Social Media:
www.facebook.com/ringettepei
twitter.com/RingettePEI
Also Known As: Prince Edward Island Ringette Association
Overview: A small provincial organization founded in 1982
Description: To promote ringette throughout PEI
Chief Officer(s): Valerie Vuillemot, Executive Director
vvuillemot@sportpei.pe.ca
Michael James, President
mjames@islandtelecom.com
Steve Campbell, Vice-President
steve@curranandbriggs.com
Breanne MacInnis, Treasurer
bemacinnis@gmail.com
Activities: Offering officiating clinics, coaching courses & related resources; Providing tournament & championship information

Ringuette 96 Montréal-Nord-Est
QC
Tél: 514-644-0153
ringuette96mn@hotmail.com
www.ringuette96mtlnord.com
Média social:
www.facebook.com/1426672734232724
Aperçu: *Dimension:* petite; *Envergure:* provinciale
Membre de: Ringuette-Québec
Membre(s) du bureau directeur: Sylvie Horth, Président
Montant de la cotisation: Barème

Ringuette Boucherville
490, ch du Lac, Boucherville QC J4B 6X3
info@ringuetteboucherville.com
www.ringuetteboucherville.com
Média social:
www.youtube.com/channel/UCrhUtjVgaP9vNRmEeFxmVLA
www.facebook.com/1460659494210802
Aperçu: *Dimension:* petite; *Envergure:* provinciale
Membre de: Ringuette-Québec
Membre(s) du bureau directeur: Sylvain St-Cyr, Président
Critères d'admissibilite: Filles de 4 ans et plus

Ringuette Bourrassa-Laval-Lanaudière
QC
www.ringuettebll.com
Aperçu: *Dimension:* petite; *Envergure:* provinciale
Membre de: Ringuette-Québec

Ringuette de la Capitale
#316, 1311, rue des Loisirs, Québec QC
Tél: 418-877-3000
ca@ringuettedelacapitale.com
www.ringuettedelacapitale.com
Média social:
www.facebook.com/ringuettedelacapitale
Aperçu: *Dimension:* petite; *Envergure:* provinciale
Membre de: Ringuette-Québec
Membre(s) du bureau directeur: Steve Caron, Présidente, 418-655-8759
steven.caron@carons.ca
Membre: 4 équipes

Ringuette St-Hubert
CP 29542, 5950, boul Cousineau, Saint-Hubert QC J3Y 9A9
ringuette@ringuette-st-hubert.com
www.ringuette-st-hubert.com
Aperçu: *Dimension:* petite; *Envergure:* provinciale
Membre de: Ringuette-Québec
Membre(s) du bureau directeur: David Létouneau, Président
Davidletourneau.cma@gmail.com

Ringuette St-Hyacinthe
CP 40502, QC J2R 1K8
info@ringuettesth.com
www.ringuettesth.com
Média social:
www.facebook.com/ringuettesthyacinthe
Aperçu: *Dimension:* petite; *Envergure:* provinciale
Membre de: Ringuette-Québec
Montant de la cotisation: Barème

Ringuette-Québec
4545, av Pierre-de Coubertin, Montréal QC H1V 0B2
Tél: 514-252-3085; *Téléc:* 514-254-1069
ringuette@ringuette-quebec.qc.ca
www.ringuette-quebec.qc.ca
Média social:
www.youtube.com/channel/UChlZmg35-zhVgQBkgru8k7g
www.facebook.com/139856822762458
twitter.com/ringuetteqc
Aperçu: *Dimension:* petite; *Envergure:* provinciale
Membre de: Ringuette-Canada
Membre(s) du bureau directeur: Jocelyne Fortin, Président
jocfortin@videotron.ca

Road Running

Prince Edward Island Roadrunners Club
c/o Sport PEI, 40 Enman Cres., Charlottetown PE C1E 1E6
peiroadrunners.pbworks.com
Overview: A small provincial organization founded in 1977
Description: The PEI RoadRunners Club is an organization whose objective is to promote & encourage running as a sport & healthful exercise. The Club welcomes all runners, regardless of ability & attempts to meet the needs of competitive & recreational runners.
Chief Officer(s): Janet Norman-Bain, President
Membership: *Fees:* $20 individual; $30 family

Rowing

Alberta Rowing Association (ARA)
11759 Groat Rd., Edmonton AB T5M 3K6
Tel: 780-427-8154
office@albertarowing.ca
www.albertarowing.ca
Social Media:
www.facebook.com/pages/Alberta-Rowing-Association/131265308366
twitter.com/AlbertaRowing
Overview: A medium-sized provincial organization
Description: To act as the organizing body, which promotes all aspects of rowing in Alberta. The ARA is a not for profit association run by volunteers, relying on membership fees, fundraising, and government support for operating funds.; *Member of:* Rowing Canada Aviron
Chief Officer(s): Carol Hermansen, President
Membership: 7 clubs

Association québécoise d'aviron (AQA)
CP 1000, Succ. M, 4545, av Pierre-de Coubertin, Montréal QC H1V 3R2
Tél: 514-252-3191
info@avironquebec.ca
www.avironquebec.ca
Aperçu: *Dimension:* moyenne; *Envergure:* nationale; fondée en 1981
Membre de: Rowing Canada Aviron
Membre(s) du bureau directeur: Daniel Aucoin, Président

Boxing Newfoundland & Labrador
NL
www.boxingnewfoundlandandlabrador.ca
Overview: A small provincial organization
Description: To govern the sport of boxing in Newfoundland & Labrador.; *Member of:* Canadian Amateur Boxing Association; Sport NL
Chief Officer(s): Mike Summers, President
mgsone@hotmail.com

Manitoba Rowing Association
Sport for Life Centre, 145 Pacific Ave., Winnipeg MB R3B 2Z6
Tel: 204-925-5653
rowing@sportmanitoba.ca
rowingmanitoba.ca
Overview: A medium-sized provincial organization
Description: To govern the sport of rowing in Manitoba.; *Member of:* Rowing Canada Aviron
Chief Officer(s): Andrea Katz, Executive Director

Ontario Rowing Association (ORA)
#206, 19 Waterman Ave., Toronto ON M4B 1Y2
Tel: 416-759-8405
rowontarioadmin@rowontario.ca
www.rowontario.ca
Social Media:
www.facebook.com/pages/ROWONTARIO/84916401948
twitter.com/ROWONTARIO
Overview: A medium-sized provincial organization founded in 1970
Description: To promote the sport of rowing at all levels in Ontario; to provide assistance to member clubs in the encouragement of competitive & recreational rowing; to maintain the principles of amateurism; to develop provincial rowing teams to represent Ontario at the Canada Games; to host an annual provincial rowing championship; *Member of:* Rowing Canada Aviron
Affiliation(s): Ontario Sport Council
Chief Officer(s): Derek Ventor, Executive Director
derek@rowontario.ca
Finances: *Funding Sources:* Membership dues; services; government grants; donations
Membership: 6,000 individuals; *Fees:* $1 non-rower; $3 highschool; $10 sport rower; $44 competitive rower; $275 club; *Member Profile:* Organized amateur rowing clubs in Ontario; *Committees:* Adaptive; Umpire

Row Nova Scotia
#400, 5516 Spring Garden Rd., Halifax NS B3J 1G6
Tel: 902-425-5450
rowing@rowns.ca
www.rowns.ca
Social Media:
www.facebook.com/RowNovaScotia
twitter.com/RowNovaScotia
Overview: A medium-sized provincial organization
Description: To govern the sport of rowing in Nova Scotia.; *Member of:* Rowing Canada Aviron
Chief Officer(s): Peter Webster, President

Rowing British Columbia
#155, 3820 Cessna Dr., Richmond BC V7B 0A2
Tel: 604-273-4769; *Fax:* 888-398-5818
Toll-Free: 877-330-3638
admin@rowingbc.ca
www.rowingbc.ca
Social Media:
www.facebook.com/rowingbc
twitter.com/rowing_bc
Also Known As: Rowing BC
Overview: A medium-sized provincial organization founded in 1987
Description: To govern the sport of rowing in British Columbia.; *Member of:* Rowing Canada Aviron
Chief Officer(s): Jennifer Fitzpatrick, Executive Director
exdirector@rowingbc.ca
Member Profile: Community, secondary & post-secondary educational rowing clubs

Rowing Canada Aviron (RCA) / Association canadienne d'aviron amateur
#321, 4371 Interurban Rd., Victoria BC V9E 2C5
Fax: 250-220-2503
Toll-Free: 877-722-4769
rca@rowingcanada.org
www.rowingcanada.org
Social Media:
www.youtube.com/user/RowingCan
www.facebook.com/81982893039
twitter.com/rowingcanada
Also Known As: Canadian Amateur Rowing Association
Previous Name: The Canadian Association of Amateur Oarsmen
Overview: A large national organization founded in 1880
Description: To encourage the formation of rowing clubs & provincial associations; To encourage the organization of national regattas; To define & to maintain the principles of amateurism in all competitions; To organize, develop, & select national rowing teams to represent Canada internationally
Affiliation(s): Fédération Internationale des Sociétés d'Aviron; Canadian Olympic Association
Chief Officer(s): Michael Walker, President
Donna Atkinson, Chief Executive Officer
datkinson@rowingcanada.org
Finances: *Funding Sources:* Sport Canada; Sponsors
Staff: 12 staff member(s)
Membership: *Fees:* $650 rowing association; $500 associate organization & special association; $350 rowing club; *Committees:* Governance Review; Executive

Rowing New Brunswick Aviron
PO Box 30047, Stn. Prospect Plaza, Fredericton NB E3B 0H8
info@rowingnb.ca
www.rowingnb.ca
Also Known As: Rowing NB Aviron
Overview: A medium-sized provincial organization
Description: To govern the sport of rowing in New Brunswick.; *Member of:* Rowing Canada Aviron

Rowing Newfoundland
NL
freeteams.net/rowingnl
Previous Name: Newfoundland Rowing Association
Overview: A small provincial organization
Description: To govern the sport of rowing in Newfoundland.; *Member of:* Rowing Canada Aviron

Rowing PEI
c/o Daphne Dumont, Macnutt & Dumont Law Office, PO Box 965, 57 Water St., Charlottetown PE C1A 7M4
rowingpei@gmail.com
rowingpei.ca
Overview: A medium-sized provincial organization founded in 2010
Description: To govern the sport of rowing in Prince Edward Island.; *Member of:* Rowing Canada Aviron
Chief Officer(s): Mike Gibson, President
Membership: *Fees:* $320

Saskatchewan Rowing Association (SRA)
510 Cynthia St., Saskatoon SK S7L 7K7
Tel: 306-975-0842; *Fax:* 306-242-8007
saskrowing@sasktel.net
www.saskrowing.ca
Overview: A medium-sized provincial organization founded in 1977
Description: To promote & develop the sport of rowing for all individuals in addition to the development of competitive excellence; *Member of:* Sask Sport; Rowing Canada Aviron
Affiliation(s): Rowing Aviron Canada, Saskatchewan Sports Hall of Fame & Museum, Saskatchewan Coaches Association
Chief Officer(s): John Haver, Provincial Head Coach North
haver_john@hotmail.com
Raymond Blake, President
Raymond.blake@uregina.ca
Finances: *Funding Sources:* Sponsors; Merchandise
Activities: *Internships:* Yes; *Library:* Yes (Open to Public)

Rugby

Alberta Rugby Football Union
Percy Page Centre, 11759 Groat Rd., Edmonton AB T5M 3K6
Tel: 780-415-1773; *Fax:* 780-422-5558
info@rugbyalberta.com
www.rugbyalberta.com
Social Media:
twitter.com/AlbertaRugby
Overview: A medium-sized provincial organization founded in 1961
Description: To develop & promote an interest in rugby in Alberta; *Member of:* Rugby Canada
Chief Officer(s): Sandy Nesbitt, President
Simon Chi, Vice-President
Debby Ashmore, Executive Director, 780-638-4547
Rick Melia, Director, Finance & Administration
Finances: *Funding Sources:* Alberta Sport, Recreation, Parks and Wildlife Foundation
Staff: 3 staff member(s)
Activities:; *Library:* Yes (Open to Public)

British Columbia Rugby Union
#203, 210 West Broadway, Vancouver BC V5Y 3W2
Tel: 604-737-3065; *Fax:* 604-737-3916
www.bcrugby.com
Social Media:
www.youtube.com/bcrugbyunion
www.facebook.com/bcrugbyunion
twitter.com/bcrugbyunion
Also Known As: BC Rugby
Overview: A medium-sized provincial organization founded in 1889
Description: To promote, sustain & manage the game of rugby in BC in a manner that will ensure wide participation & the continuous development in a safe & responsible manner; *Member of:* Rugby Canada
Chief Officer(s): Annabel Kehoe, Chief Executive Officer, 604-499-7494
Louise Wheeler, Manager, Member Services
Membership: 14,000; *Fees:* Schedule available; *Committees:* Competition; Discipline; Youth; Medical Science; Appeal
Activities:; *Library:* Yes (Open to Public)

Fédération de rugby du Québec (FRQ) / Quebec Rugby Union
CP 1000, Succ. M, 4545, av Pierre-de Coubertin, Montréal QC H1V 3R2
Tél: 514-252-3189; *Téléc:* 514-252-3159
info@rugbyquebec.qc.ca
www.rugbyquebec.qc.ca
Média social:
www.facebook.com/98779487768
twitter.com/RugbyQuebec
Aperçu: *Dimension:* moyenne; *Envergure:* provinciale
Description: Promouvoir le sport et la santé physique en général, et sans limiter ce qui précède le sport du rugby; organiser des tournois de Rugby dans la province de Québec; regrouper les associations régionales et les clubs de Rugby du Québec; *Membre de:* Rugby Canada
Membre(s) du bureau directeur: Martin Cormier, Directeur général
Membre: 2 610

New Brunswick Rugby Union (NBRU)
#13, 900 Hanwell Rd., Fredericton NB E3B 6A2
Tel: 506-261-2176
www.nbru.ca
Overview: A medium-sized provincial organization
Description: To govern rugby in New Brunswick & organize games between teams; *Member of:* Rugby Canada
Chief Officer(s): Sherry Doiron, President
sherrydoiron@gmail.com
Finances: *Funding Sources:* Membership fees; donations; fund raising

Newfoundland & Labrador Rugby Union
PO Box 9, Mount Pearl NL A1N 2C1
www.rockrugby.ca
Also Known As: The Rock Rugby
Overview: A small provincial organization
Member of: Rugby Canada
Chief Officer(s): John Cowan, President
jcowan@mun.ca

Nova Scotia Rugby Football Union
5516 Spring Garden Rd., 4th Fl., Halifax NS B3J 1G6
Tel: 902-425-5450; *Fax:* 902-425-5606
rugby@sportnovascotia.ca
www.rugbyns.ns.ca
Also Known As: Rugby Nova Scotia
Overview: A small provincial organization founded in 1965
Description: To promote, control, encourage & develop the game of rugby union football throughout Nova Scotia; *Member of:* Rugby Canada
Affiliation(s): International Rugby Board
Chief Officer(s): Geno Carew, President

Prince Edward Island Rugby Union (PEIRU)
10 Kenwood Circle, Charlottetown PE C1E 1Z8
peirugbyunion@gmail.com
peirugbyunion.com
Social Media:
twitter.com/PEIRugbyUnion
Also Known As: PEI Rugby Union
Overview: A medium-sized provincial organization
Description: To promote rugby in Prince Edward Island; *Member of:* Rugby Canada
Chief Officer(s): Alex Field, President
Finances: *Funding Sources:* Membership fees; Gate receipts; Government; Sponsorship

Rugby Canada
#110, 30 East Beaver Creek Rd., Richmond Hill ON L4B 1J2
Tel: 905-707-8998
info@rugbycanada.ca
www.rugbycanada.ca
Social Media:
www.facebook.com/RugbyCanada
twitter.com/rugbycanada
Previous Name: Canadian Rugby Union
Overview: A medium-sized national organization founded in 1974
Description: To be the national governing body for the sport of rugby in Canada.
Chief Officer(s): Pat Aldous, Chair
paldous@rugbycanada.ca
Graham Brown, Chief Executive Officer, 905-707-8998 225
gbrown@rugbycanada.ca
Myles Spencer, Chief Operating Officer, 905-707-8998 238
mspencer@rugbycanada.ca
Member Profile: Official rugby teams in Canada
Activities: Player development; youth clinics

Rugby Manitoba
145 Pacific Ave., Winnipeg MB R3B 2Z6
Tel: 204-925-5664
www.rugbymanitoba.com
Overview: A medium-sized provincial organization
Description: To govern rugby in Manitoba; *Member of:* Rugby Canada
Chief Officer(s): Brad Hirst, Executive Director
executivedirector@rugbymanitoba.com

Rugby Ontario
#201, 111 Railside Rd., Toronto ON M3A 1B2
Tel: 647-560-4790; *Fax:* 647-560-4790
info@rugbyontario.com
www.rugbyontario.com
Social Media:
www.facebook.com/RugbyOntario
twitter.com/rugbyontario
Overview: A medium-sized provincial organization founded in 1949

Affiliation(s): Canadian Rugby Union
Chief Officer(s): Andrew Backer, Chief Executive Officer, 647-560-4790 101
abacker@rugbyontario.com
Greg Haley-Williams, Manager, Development, 647-560-4790 104
gwilliams@rugbyontario.com
Brock Smith, Coordinator, Communications, 647-560-4790 106
bsmith@rugbyontario.com
Finances: *Annual Operating Budget:* $1.5 Million-$3 Million
Staff: 8 staff member(s)
Membership: 10827; *Member Profile:* Athletes, coaches, officials, administrators; *Committees:* Coaching; Executive

Saskatchewan Rugby Union (SRU)
#213, 1870 Lorne St., Regina SK
Tel: 306-780-9353
www.saskrugby.com
Social Media:
www.facebook.com/SaskRugby
Overview: A small provincial charitable organization
Description: To encourage, promote, organize, administer & otherwise regulate the sport of Rugby Union Football in the province of Saskatchewan in accordance with the laws of the game in a safe & proper manner; *Member of:* Rugby Canada; Sask Sport
Chief Officer(s): Grant Cranfield, President
Finances: *Annual Operating Budget:* $100,000-$250,000
Staff: 1 staff member(s); 200 volunteer(s)
Membership: 2,500; *Fees:* Schedule available

Sailing

Alberta Sailing Association (ASA)
PO Box 52058, Stn. Edmonton Trail, Calgary AB T2E 8K9
info@albertasailing.com
www.albertasailing.com
Overview: A small provincial organization founded in 1973
Description: Alberta Sailing Association in partnership with its member clubs, sailing schools & Sail Canada addresses the needs of sailors; encourages improved access to water & sailing facilities; sail training & safety programs & opportunities to compete at the club, provincial & international levels; *Member of:* Sail Canada
Chief Officer(s): Ron Hewitt, President
president@albertasailing.com
Fie Hulsker, Executive Director, 403-827-5578
Finances: *Annual Operating Budget:* $50,000-$100,000
Staff: 1 staff member(s)
Membership: 1,500; *Fees:* $20

BC Sailing Association
#195, 3820 Cessna Dr., Richmond BC V7B 0A2
Tel: 604-333-3628; *Fax:* 604-333-3626
crew@bcsailing.bc.ca
www.bcsailing.bc.ca
Social Media:
www.facebook.com/bcsailing
Also Known As: BC Sailing
Overview: A medium-sized provincial organization
Description: The provincial sport authority for sailing; *Member of:* Sail Canada; Sport BC
Affiliation(s): International Sailing Federation
Chief Officer(s): Tine Moberg-Parker, Executive Director
tmpsailing@shaw.ca
Finances: *Funding Sources:* Provincial government; membership fees; programs
Staff: 2 staff member(s)
Membership: 5,000; *Fees:* Schedule available

Canadian Albacore Association (CAA)
PO Box 98093, 970 Queen St. East, Toronto ON M4M 1J8
www.albacore.ca
Social Media:
www.facebook.com/pages/Canadian-Albacore-Association/160940480620584
twitter.com/AlbacoreSailCan
Overview: A small national organization founded in 1961
Description: To promote & support the development of the Albacore fleet
Chief Officer(s): Mary Neumann, Commodore
John Cawthorne, Treasurer
Membership: *Fees:* $60 full member; $27 associate member; $21 youth member; *Member Profile:* Canadian owners & sailors of Albacore dinghies
Activities: Sharing news & information about Canadian Albacore sailing; Sponsoring events & regattas

Fédération de voile du Québec
4545, av Pierre-de-Coubertin, Montréal QC H1V 0B2
Tél: 514-252-3097; *Téléc:* 514-252-3044
www.voile.qc.ca
Média social:
www.facebook.com/voilequebec
Aperçu: *Dimension:* petite; *Envergure:* provinciale; fondée en 1970
Description: Encourager et promouvoir la pratique de la voile, sous toutes ses formes au Québec
Membre(s) du bureau directeur: Natalie Matthon, Directrice générale

New Brunswick Sailing Association (NBSA)
c/o Sharon Mills, Executive Director, 105 Bird Ave., Fredericton NB E2A 2H8
Tel: 506-472-2117
www.nbsailing.nb.ca
Overview: A small provincial organization
Description: The New Brunswick Sailing Association is the provincial governing body for boating & the sport of sailing. It is the Canadian Yachting Association's representative in New Brunswick.; *Member of:* Sail Canada
Chief Officer(s): Sharon Mills, Executive Director
smills@nbsailing.nb.ca

Ontario Sailing / Association de voile de l'Ontario
#17, 70 Unsworth Dr., Hamilton ON L8W 3K4
Tel: 905-572-7245; *Fax:* 905-572-6056
Toll-Free: 888-672-7245
info@ontariosailing.ca
www.ontariosailing.ca
Social Media:
www.facebook.com/OntarioSailing
twitter.com/ontariosailing
Also Known As: Sail Ontario
Previous Name: Ontario Sailing Association
Overview: A medium-sized provincial organization founded in 1970
Description: To foster interest in sailing & to promote & encourage proficiency in the sport, particularly among young people in the province of Ontario; to promote sailboat racing events & to encourage the development of skills in sailboat handling & seamanship; *Member of:* Sail Canada
Affiliation(s): International Sailing Federation; Canadian Safe Boating Council
Chief Officer(s): Glenn Lethbridge, Executive Director, 905-572-7245 224
execdir@ontariosailing.ca
Finances: *Annual Operating Budget:* $500,000-$1.5 Million; *Funding Sources:* Membership fees; provincial government; corporate sponsorship; grants
Staff: 6 staff member(s); 25 volunteer(s)
Membership: 180 clubs/schools/associations; 10,000 families; 100,000 boaters

PEI Sailing Association (PEISA)
c/o Ellen MacPhail, PO Box 6708, York Point PE C0A 1H0
save@waveskills.ca
www.peisailing.com
Also Known As: Sail Prince Edward Island
Overview: A medium-sized provincial organization
Description: The PEI Sailing Association is a volunteer organization that promotes sailing in the province of Prince Edward Island, Canada. As the provincial chapter of the Canadian Sailing Association the PEI Sailing Association provides support and training to anybody interested in learning to sail or expanding their sailing.; *Member of:* Sail Canada
Chief Officer(s): Ellen McPhail, Executive Director

Sail Canada / Voile Canada
Portsmith Olympic Harbour, 53 Yonge St., Kingston ON K7M 6G4
Tel: 613-545-3044; *Fax:* 613-545-3045
Toll-Free: 877-416-4720
sailcanada@sailing.ca
www.sailing.ca
Social Media:
www.facebook.com/196992790349209
twitter.com/SailCanada
Previous Name: Canadian Yachting Association
Overview: A medium-sized national charitable organization founded in 1931
Description: To promote the sport of sailing in Canada
Affiliation(s): International Sailing Federation; International Sailing Schools Association
Chief Officer(s): Paddy Boyd, Executive Director
paddy@sailing.ca
Ken Dool, Head Coach & Director, High Performance
ken@sailing.ca
Finances: *Annual Operating Budget:* $1.5 Million-$3 Million
Staff: 12 staff member(s)
Membership: 10 provincial associations; 255 clubs; 175 sailing schools; 30 class associations; 80,000 active members; over 1 million Canadian sailors; *Member Profile:* Member of member yacht club or person with interest in sailing; *Committees:* Provincial; Nominating; Standing Board; Governance; Human Resources; Audit; Finance; Racing Appeals; Olympic Policy; Athlete Appeals; Operational; Athlete Development; Business Development; Training & Certification
Activities:; *Library:* Yes

Sail Manitoba
#409, 145 Pacific Ave., Winnipeg MB R3B 2Z6
Tel: 204-925-5650
sailing@sportmanitoba.ca
sailmanitoba.com
Social Media:
www.facebook.com/200107080070072
twitter.com/SailManitoba
Previous Name: Manitoba Sailing Association Inc.
Overview: A small provincial organization founded in 1965
Description: To be the sport's provincial regulator; *Member of:* Sail Canada
Chief Officer(s): Max Desmarais, President
Membership: 1,000; *Committees:* Finance; Operations; Recreation; Training; Racing; Team

Sail Nova Scotia
5516 Spring Garden Rd., 4th Fl., Halifax NS B3J 1G6
Tel: 902-425-5450
office@sailnovascotia.ca
www.sailnovascotia.ca
Social Media:
www.facebook.com/sailnovascotia
Previous Name: Nova Scotia Yachting Association
Overview: A small provincial organization
Description: To regulate the sport of sailing in Nova Scotia; *Member of:* Sail Canada; Sport Nova Scotia
Affiliation(s): Canadian Sport Centre
Chief Officer(s): Frank Denis, Executive Director & Media Contact

SailNL
PO Box 23102, Stn. Churchill Sq., St. John's NL A1B 4J9
sailing.nl@gmail.com
www.sailnl.ca
Social Media:
www.facebook.com/sailnl.ca
Also Known As: Newfoundland & Labrador Sailing Association
Overview: A small provincial organization founded in 1966
Description: To regulate the sport of sailing in Newfoundland & Labrador; *Member of:* Sail Canada; Sport NL
Chief Officer(s): Ryan Kelly, President
ryan.kelly033@gmail.com

S.A.L.T.S. Sail & Life Training Society (SALTS)
451 Herald St., Victoria BC V8W 3N8
Tel: 250-383-6811; *Fax:* 250-383-7781
Toll-Free: 888-383-6811
info@salts.ca
www.salts.ca
Social Media:
www.facebook.com/saltsvictoria
twitter.com/saltsvictoria
Overview: A small provincial charitable organization founded in 1974
Description: Christian organization that believes through the medium of sail training both spiritual & physical development is encouraged in each individual; *Member of:* Canadian Council of Christian Charities
Chief Officer(s): Loren Hagerty, Executive Director
Finances: *Annual Operating Budget:* $500,000-$1.5 Million; *Funding Sources:* Trainee fees; donations; membership fees; fundraising
Staff: 7 staff member(s); 40 volunteer(s)
Membership: 450 single & family; *Fees:* $50 single; $100 family; $200 corporate

Saskatchewan Sailing Clubs Association (SSCA)
SK
sasksail@sasktel.net
www.sasksail.com
Overview: A small provincial organization
Description: To regulate the sport of sailing in Saskatchewan; *Member of:* Sail Canada
Chief Officer(s): L.P. Gagnon, President
lpgagnon@hotmail.fr
Mark Lammens, Technical Director & Coach, 306-975-0833

Wind Athletes Canada
PO Box 29047, Stn. Portsmouth, Kingston ON K7M 8W6
www.windathletes.ca
Social Media:
www.facebook.com/windathletes
twitter.com/windathletes
Overview: A medium-sized national organization
Description: To promote the sport of sailing in Canada; to provide funding to the Canadian Sailing Team
Chief Officer(s): John Curtis, President
Finances: *Funding Sources:* Fundraising
Activities: Training programs

Schools

New Brunswick Interscholastic Athletic Association (NBIAA)
PO Box 6000, 125 Hilton Rd., Fredericton NB E3B 5H1
Tel: 506-457-4843; *Fax:* 506-453-5311
nbiaa@gnb.ca
www.nbiaa-asinb.org
Overview: A medium-sized provincial organization
Member of: School Sport Canada
Chief Officer(s): Yvan Arseneault, President, 506-684-7610
Allyson Ouellette, Executive Director
Membership: 75 schools; *Fees:* $300 per school; *Committees:* Executive

NWT School Athletic Federation (NWTSAF)
PO Box 266, Fort Smith NT X0E 0P0
www.nwtsaf.com
Overview: A medium-sized provincial organization
Member of: School Sport Canada
Affiliation(s): Canadian School Sport Federation; Sport North
Chief Officer(s): Fraser Oliver, President, 867-873-4888
fraser_oliver@mail.ycs.nt.ca
Kelly Webster, Vice-President, 867-874-6538
kwebster66@bdec.learnnet.nt.ca
Richard Daitch, Executive Director, 867-872-2334
rwdaitch@yahoo.com
Activities: Regional tournaments

Prince Edward Island School Athletic Association (PEISAA)
#101, 250 Water St., Summerside PE C1N 1B6
Tel: 902-438-4846; *Fax:* 902-438-4884
www.peisaa.pe.ca
Overview: A medium-sized provincial organization
Description: Supporting sports including but not exclusive to, badminton, softball, wrestling, golf, cross country, curling, and volleyball, in PEI.; *Member of:* School Sport Canada
Chief Officer(s): Trevor Bridges, Chair
Rick MacKinnon, Coordinator
Gerald MacCormack, Secretary-Treasurer

Saskatchewan High Schools Athletic Association (SHSAA)
#1, 575 Park St., Regina SK S4N 5B2
Tel: 306-721-2151; *Fax:* 306-721-2659
shsaa@shsaa.ca
www.shsaa.ca
Social Media:
www.facebook.com/264860913591330
twitter.com/shsaasport
Overview: A medium-sized provincial organization founded in 1948
Description: To use interschool athletics as a means for fostering positive opportunities for students; *Member of:* School Sport Canada
Chief Officer(s): Roger Morgan, President
morgan.roger@prairiesouth.ca
Kevin Vollet, Executive Director
k.vollet@shsaa.ca

School Sport Canada (SSC) / Sport Scolaire Canada
c/o Alberta Schools' Athletic Association, 11759 Groat Rd., Edmonton AB T5M 3K6
Tel: 780-860-4200
schoolsportcanada@gmail.com
www.schoolsport.ca
Overview: A large national organization
Description: To be the national body for school sport in Canada
Chief Officer(s): John Paton, President
john@asaa.ca
Membership: 12 member associations

School Sports Newfoundland & Labrador (SSNL)
PO Box 8700, 1296A Kenmount Rd., St. John's NL A1B 4J6
Tel: 709-729-2795; *Fax:* 709-729-2705
www.schoolsportsnl.ca
Previous Name: Newfoundland & Labrador High School Athletic Federation
Overview: A medium-sized provincial charitable organization founded in 1969
Description: To organize, promote & govern all high school sports within the province; to assist student athletes in reaching their full physical, educational & social potential through participation & sportsmanship in interscholastic sports; *Member of:* School Sport Canada; National Federation of High Schools
Chief Officer(s): Karen Richard, Executive Director
karen@sportnl.ca
Mike Ball, President
mikeball@nlesd.ca
Finances: *Annual Operating Budget:* $500,000-$1.5 Million; *Funding Sources:* Provincial government; Federal government; corporate sponsors; membership dues
Staff: 3 staff member(s); 700 volunteer(s)
Membership: 150 schools; *Fees:* Schedule available
Activities: School sports tournaments; *Internships:* Yes

Yukon Schools' Athletic Association (YSAA)
YT
www.yesnet.yk.ca/ysaa
Overview: A medium-sized provincial organization founded in 1996
Description: To encourage participation of students in inter school athletics, emphasize interschool athletics as an integral part of the total educational process & plan, promote, supervise & administer a program of inter-school athletics in all approved competitions.; *Member of:* School Sport Canada
Chief Officer(s): Marc Senécal, President
marc.senecal@yesnet.yk.ca
James Shaw, Vice-President
james.shaw@yesnet.k.ca
Ron Billingsley, Secretary/Treasurer
ron.billingsley@yesnet.yk.ca

Senior Citizens

Alberta Senior Citizens Sport & Recreation Association (ASCSRA)
#400, 7015 Macleod Trail., Calgary AB T2H 2K6
Tel: 403-803-9852; *Fax:* 403-800-5599
info@alberta55plus.ca
www.alberta55plus.ca
Also Known As: Alberta 55 Plus
Overview: A medium-sized provincial organization founded in 1980
Description: To promote sport & recreation development for seniors (55+) across Alberta; to act as a provincial voice to ensure input by age categories for seniors in Alberta Winter & Summer Games; to promote future Alberta Seniors' Games
Affiliation(s): Alberta Sport, Recreation, Parks & Wildlife Foundation
Chief Officer(s): Vern Hafso, President, 780-336-2270, Fax: 780-336-3525
tollarav@mscnet.ca
Finances: *Annual Operating Budget:* $100,000-$250,000; *Funding Sources:* Government & private sector sponsorship
Staff: 2 staff member(s); 100 volunteer(s)
Membership: 4,000; *Fees:* $15/1yr, $25/2yrs individual; $50 association; $25-$50 club
Activities: Workshops & instructional clinics; *Speaker Service:* Yes

Elder Active Recreation Association (ERA)
4061 - 4th Ave., Whitehorse YT Y1A 1H1
Tel: 867-456-8252
office@elderactive.ca
www.elderactive.ca
Overview: A medium-sized provincial organization
Description: To enhance the quality of life of Yukon seniors & elders by supporting them in living healthy lives with independence & dignity; to support seniors & elders in helping other seniors & elders to live full, active & healthy lives, & to develop active communities throughout the Yukon where seniors & elders can make positive lifestyle choices, exchange wisdom & connect with others in friendship, recreation & creativity. Physical office address: #302, 309 Strickland St., Whitehorse, YT Y1A 2J9.
Chief Officer(s): Glen Doumont, Office Coordinator
Jennifer Massie, Program Coordinator
programs@elderactive.ca
Membership: *Fees:* $10; *Member Profile:* Yukoners 55 years of age and over

Ontario Senior Games Association (OSGA)
#310, 3 Concorde Gate, Toronto ON M3C 3N7
Tel: 416-426-7031; *Fax:* 416-426-7226
Toll-Free: 800-320-6423
info@ontarioseniorgames.ca
www.ontarioseniorgames.ca
Social Media:
www.facebook.com/Ontario55plus
Overview: A medium-sized provincial organization
Description: To provide physical & social activities to senior citizens
Chief Officer(s): Gail Prior, President
president@ontarioseniorgames.ca
Geoffrey Johnson, Program Coordinator
geoff@ontarioseniorgames.ca

Shooting Sports

Alberta Federation of Shooting Sports (AFSS)
Percy Page Centre, 11759 Groat Rd., Edmonton AB T5M 3K6
Tel: 780-415-1775; *Fax:* 780-422-2663
afss@abshooters.org
www.abshooters.org
Overview: A small provincial organization
Description: The AFSS provides funding & support to 11 shooting organizations throughout the province.
Affiliation(s): Alberta Handgun Association; Alberta Smallbore Rifle Association; Alberta Provincial Rifle Association; International Practical Shooting Confederation Alberta; Alberta Sporting Clays Association; Alberta Skeet Shooting Association; Alberta International Skeetshooting Association; Alberta International Style Trapshooting Association; Alberta Metallic Silhouette Association; Alberta Black Powder Association; Alberta Frontier Shootists Society
Chief Officer(s): Kyla Clark, Office Manager
Membership: 11 associations; *Member Profile:* Shooting associations in Alberta

Alberta Metallic Silhouette Association
2306 - 22nd St. South, Lethbridge AB T1K 2K2
Tel: 403-327-7552
www.absilhouetteassoc.ca
Overview: A small provincial charitable organization founded in 1977
Description: The association seeks to promote & advance the sport of metallic silhouette shooting. It is the governing body for Rifle Metallic Silhouette Target Shooting in Alberta and as such, it sanctions matches for the following disciplines: small bore rifle, high power rifle, small bore hunting rifle, high power hunting rifle, as well as black powder cartridge rifle.
Affiliation(s): Shooting Federation of Canada; Alberta Federation of Shooting Sports
Chief Officer(s): Ralph Oler, President
president@silhouette-alberta.org
Kathy Oler, Sec.-Treas.
secretary@silhouette-alberta.org
Finances: *Annual Operating Budget:* Less than $50,000; *Funding Sources:* Provincial government
Staff: 20 volunteer(s)
Membership: 106 individual; *Fees:* $20 individual; $25 family; $60 club

Atlantic Marksmen Association
PO Box 181, Stn. Dartmouth Main, Dartmouth NS B2Y 3Y3
www.atlanticmarksmen.ca
Overview: A small local organization founded in 1954
Member of: Shooting Federation of Canada
Chief Officer(s): Sean Hansen, President
Membership: 200; *Fees:* $200 senior, plus induction fee of $100; $30 juniors (18 & under)
Activities: Owns & operates two range facilities

British Columbia Rifle Association (BCRA)
PO Box 2418, Stn. Sardis Main, Chilliwack BC V2R 1A7
contact@bcrifle.org
www.bcrifle.org
Overview: A medium-sized provincial organization founded in 1874
Description: To create a public sentiment for the encouragement of marksmanship in all its trades among citizens of British Columbia, both as a sport & as a definite contribution to the defence of Canada; *Member of:* Dominion of Canada Rifle Association
Membership: *Fees:* Schedule available
Activities: BC Marksmanship Championships in 7 different shooting sports

British Columbia Target Sports Association
PO Box 496, Kamloops BC V2C 5L2
targetsports@bctsa.bc.ca
www.bctsa.bc.ca

Previous Name: BC Smallbore Rifle Association
Overview: A small provincial organization
Description: To promote target rifle sports in British Columbia; *Member of:* Shooting Federation of Canada
Finances: *Funding Sources:* Membership dues; donations; sports grants; entry fees
Membership: *Fees:* $25 family/senior; $10 junior; $10 associate; $25 club
Activities: Provincial/national championships

Buckskinners Muzzleloading Association, Limited
PO Box 4127, Stn. Champlain Place, 2493 Route 490, Dieppe NB E1A 6E8
Tel: 506-576-1959; *Fax:* 506-859-1249
buckskinnersweb@yahoo.com
buckskinnersweb.weebly.com
Overview: A small local organization founded in 1978
Description: To promote good & safe blackpowder shooting, marksmanship & sportsmanship; to encourage & promote buckskinning knowledge & skills
Affiliation(s): New Brunswick Wildlife Federation
Chief Officer(s): Shirley Stuart, Contact
Finances: *Annual Operating Budget:* Less than $50,000
Staff: 36 volunteer(s)
Membership: 36; *Fees:* $20 single; $35 family; *Member Profile:* Buckskinners, Civil War & pre-1840 re-enactors
Activities: Winter Rendezvous, Feb.; Summer Rendezvous, June

Calgary & District Target Shooters Association (CDTSA)
#142, 612 - 500 Country Hills Blvd., Calgary AB T3K 5K3
Tel: 403-275-3257
www.cdtsa.ca
Overview: A small local organization founded in 1981
Affiliation(s): Alberta Federation of Shooting Sports; Alberta Fish & Game Association; Alberta Black Powder Association; Alberta Metallic Silhouette Association
Finances: *Annual Operating Budget:* Less than $50,000
Staff: 12 volunteer(s)
Membership: *Fees:* Schedule available

Canadian Shooting Sports Association (CSSA)
116 Galaxy Blvd., Etobicoke ON M9W 4Y6
Tel: 416-679-9959; *Fax:* 416-679-9910
Toll-Free: 888-873-4339
info@cdnshootingsports.org
cssa-cila.org
Merged from: Ontario Handgun Association; Ontario Smallbore Federation
Overview: A medium-sized national organization
Description: To provide the knowledge, guidance & services to ensure the continuation promotion of the shooting sports & related activities & to represent their interests to the government, the regulatory bodies, the media & the public
Affiliation(s): Ontario Council of Shooters; Shooting Federation of Canada
Finances: *Funding Sources:* Membership fees
Membership: 15,000; *Fees:* $45; $80 family; $27 junior; $250 corporate; *Member Profile:* Member of a recognized shooting club
Activities: To provide liability insurance & training courses

Canadian Trapshooting Association (CTA)
Saskatoon SK
www.shootcanada.ca
Overview: A medium-sized national organization founded in 1950
Description: To promote clay target shooting as a recreational sport among shooters of every age, both sexes, & at every level of ability, the ultimate objective being to compete in the world championships held each year in Ohio; *Member of:* Amateur Trapshooting Association
Chief Officer(s): Dwight Smith, President
Finances: *Annual Operating Budget:* Less than $50,000; *Funding Sources:* Fees collected at the national championships
Staff: 150 volunteer(s)
Membership: 1,800

Dominion of Canada Rifle Association (DCRA) / L'Association de tir dominion du canada
45 Shirley Blvd., Ottawa ON K2K 2W6
Tel: 613-829-8281; *Fax:* 613-829-0099
office@dcra.ca
www.dcra.ca
Overview: A small national charitable organization founded in 1868
Chief Officer(s): Jim Thompson, Executive Director
Stan E. Frost, Executive Vice-President
T.F. deFaye, President
Finances: *Annual Operating Budget:* $100,000-$250,000
Staff: 3 staff member(s); 60 volunteer(s)
Membership: 1,000; *Member Profile:* 10 provincial rifle associations; Yukon Rifle Association; National Capital Region Rifle Association
Activities: Annual Canadian Fullbore Rifle Championships

Fédération québécoise de tir (FQT) / Québec Shooting Federation
6897, rue Jarry est, Montréal QC H1P 1W7
Tél: 514-252-3056; *Téléc:* 514-252-3060
Ligne sans frais: 888-514-7847
fqt@fqtir.qc.ca
www.fqtir.qc.ca
Aperçu: *Dimension:* petite; *Envergure:* provinciale; Organisme sans but lucratif; fondée en 1978
Description: La FQT est un organisme à but non lucratif voué à la promotion du tir sportif sur tout le territoire de la province du Québec et qui est reconnue et subventionnée par l'intermédiaire du Secrétariat au loisir et au sport (Gouvernement du Québec); *Membre de:* Fédération de tir du Canada; Shooting Federation of Canada
Affiliation(s): Regroupment Loisir Québec; Sports Québec
Membre(s) du bureau directeur: Gilles Bédard, Directeur exécutif, 514-252-3056 3611
gbedard@fqtir.qc.ca
Gérald Tousignant, Président
Finances: *Budget de fonctionnement annuel:* $250,000-$500,000; *Fonds:* Gouvernement du Québec
Personnel: 3 membre(s) du personnel; 400 bénévole(s)
Membre: 6,000; *Comités:* Carabine; pistolet; plateaux; chasse; moderne; poudre noire; pratique pour policiers et civils
Activités: Assemblée général annuelle; *Stagiaires:* Oui

Manitoba Provincial Handgun Association (MPHA)
PO Box 314, Stn. Corydon Ave., Winnipeg MB R3M 3S7
www.handgunmb.ca
Overview: A small provincial organization
Description: To provide opportunities & programming for handgun athletes, coaches & officials; to help participants learn, practice & develop skills in the sport of handgun shooting.; *Member of:* Sport Manitoba
Chief Officer(s): Randy Myrdal, President
Membership: *Fees:* $10 individual; $25 club

Manitoba Provincial Rifle Association Inc. (MPRA)
795 Valour Rd., Winnipeg MB R3G 3B3
Tel: 204-783-0768
www.manitobarifle.ca
Overview: A medium-sized provincial organization founded in 1872
Description: To promote & encourage safe firearm handling & competitive target shooting in Manitoba; *Member of:* Shooting Federation of Canada; Dominion of Canada Rifle Association
Affiliation(s): Sports Manitoba
Membership: *Fees:* $40 full member; $25 associate member/under 25; $65 family; $350 lifetime; *Member Profile:* Individuals & clubs interested in rifle target shooting
Activities: Shooting practices & competitions

Nova Scotia Rifle Association (NSRA)
PO Box 482, Dartmouth NS B2Y 3Y8
Tel: 902-456-7468
nsrifle@ns.sympatico.ca
www.nsrifle.org
Overview: A small provincial organization founded in 1861
Description: To promote & organize recreational shooting; *Member of:* Dominion of Canada Rifle Association
Affiliation(s): Shooting Federation of Canada
Chief Officer(s): Andy S. Webber, President
asw@tangenttheta.com
Dave G. Beaulieu, Secretary
Finances: *Annual Operating Budget:* Less than $50,000
Staff: 12 volunteer(s)
Membership: 300; *Fees:* $295 senior; $20 junior (under 19); *Member Profile:* Residents of the province with a valid firearm license

Ontario Muzzle Loading Association (OMLA)
433 Queen St., Chatham ON N7M 5K5
Tel: 519-352-0924; *Fax:* 519-352-4380
Overview: A small provincial organization founded in 1973
Activities: Posting results from provincial matches & the Soper event

Ontario Provincial Trapshooting Association (OPTA)
ON
info@ontariotrap.com
www.ontariotrap.com
Social Media:
www.facebook.com/groups/OntarioTrap
Overview: A small provincial organization
Chief Officer(s): Neville Henderson, President
Pam Muma, Secretary-Treasurer
Finances: *Annual Operating Budget:* Less than $50,000
Membership: 500-999

Ontario Rifle Association (ORA)
c/o ORA Membership Secretary, PO Box 22019, Stn. Elmwood Square, St Thomas ON H5R 6A1
oraatt@yahoo.ca
www.ontariorifleassociation.org
Overview: A medium-sized provincial organization founded in 1868
Affiliation(s): Dominion of Canada Rifle Association
Chief Officer(s): Fazal Mohideen, Secretary
orafazal@bell.net
Membership: *Fees:* $157 Probationary Basic; $182 Probationary ORA Membership with Associate DCRA; $257 Probationary ORA Membership with Full DCRA

Ontario Skeet Shooting Association (OSSA)
PO Box 96, Hampton ON L0B 1J0
Tel: 905-263-8174; *Fax:* 905-263-4870
info@ontarioskeet.com
www.ontarioskeet.com
Overview: A small provincial organization
Description: To educate persons in the safe & efficient handling of shotguns; to encourage competition in shotgun target shooting; to promote the sport of skeet shooting in the province of Ontario; *Member of:* Shooting Federation of Canada; National Skeet Shooting Association
Chief Officer(s): Jennie Marsh, Secretary-Treasurer
Brad McRae, President
Finances: *Annual Operating Budget:* Less than $50,000
Staff: 8 volunteer(s)
Membership: 165

Province of Québec Rifle Association (PQRA) / Association de tir de la province de Québec (ATPQ)
973, rue Turcotte Est, Thetford Mines QC G1J 5K3
info@pqra.org
www.pqra.org
Social Media:
twitter.com/atpq
Overview: A small provincial organization founded in 1869
Description: To promote marksmanship training & competition especially at long range; To provide extensive cadet program; To organize & run cadet provincial championships; *Member of:* Dominion of Canada Rifle Association; Shooting Federation of Canada
Chief Officer(s): Robert Fortier, President
Finances: *Funding Sources:* Membership fees
Activities: Long Range Target Shooting; Black Powder Long Range; Service Rifle Matches; Cadet Shooting Programs

Saskatchewan Black Powder Association (SBPA)
PO Box 643, Saskatoon SK S7K 3L7
www.sbpa.ca
Overview: A small provincial organization founded in 1980
Description: To provide a common voice for all Black Powder Shooters in the province; To encourage development of the old skills & trades related to Black Powder; & to co-ordinate activities of the Black Powder Shooters in the province; *Member of:* Shooting Federation of Canada
Finances: *Funding Sources:* Membership dues; Donations
Membership: *Fees:* $6 individual; $10 family; $25 associate member
Activities:; *Library:* Yes (Open to Public)

Saskatchewan Provincial Rifle Association Inc. (SPRA)
PO Box 40, Mazenod SK S0H 2Y0
Tel: 306-354-7493
www.saskrifle.ca
Overview: A small provincial organization founded in 1885
Description: The governing body for fullbore target rifle shooting in Saskatchewan & promotes the pursuit of excellence in marksmanship & the safe & responsible handling of firearms
Chief Officer(s): Keith Skjerdal, Match Director, 306-652-2065
Finances: *Funding Sources:* Membership dues; SaskSport Inc.
Membership: *Fees:* Schedule available

Shooting Federation of Canada (SFC) / Fédération de tir du Canada (FTC)
45 Shirley Blvd., Nepean ON K2K 2W6
Tel: 613-727-7483; *Fax:* 613-727-7487
info@sfc-ftc.ca
www.sfc-ftc.ca
Overview: A medium-sized national charitable organization founded in 1932
Description: To represent firearms users in matters of legislation, shooting sports promotion, & program activities;

Member of: International Shooting Sport Federation
Affiliation(s): Canadian Shooting Sports Association
Chief Officer(s): Pat Boulay, President
president@sfc-ftc.ca
Finances: *Funding Sources:* Sales; Donations; Government
Membership: 108 organizations; *Committees:* Coaching; National Officials Development; Commonwealth Games; Awards & Merits; High Performance
Activities: *Awareness Events:* National Smallbore Rifle Championships; National Trapshooting Championships; National Skeet Shooting Championships; *Library:* Yes

Shooting Federation of Nova Scotia (SFNS)
PO Box 28023, Dartmouth NS B2W 6E2
www.sfns.info
Overview: A small provincial organization founded in 1972
Member of: Sport Nova Scotia
Affiliation(s): Shooting Federation of Canada
Finances: *Annual Operating Budget:* Less than $50,000
Staff: 12 volunteer(s)
Membership: 1600

Yellowknife Shooting Club (YKSC)
PO Box 2931, Yellowknife NT X1A 2R2
yellowknifeshootingclub.ca
Overview: A small local organization founded in 1961
Description: Safe shooting of all types for firearms for sport & recreational purposes
Affiliation(s): NWT Federation of Shooting Sports; Shooting Federation of Canada; NRA
Chief Officer(s): Scott Cairns, President, 867-669-9220
Bud Rhyndress, Vice-President, 867-873-6209
Membership: *Fees:* $170 individual; $280 family; $10 youth; *Member Profile:* Firearms owners & users
Activities: Caribou Carnival; Wolverine Days; fun shoot; media shoot; turkey shoot; Sight-In Days

Yukon Shooting Federation
4061 - 4th Ave., Whitehorse YT Y1A 1H1
Tel: 867-667-6728
sportyukon.com/member/yukon-shooting-federation
Overview: A small provincial organization
Description: To promote & facilitate air rifle & air pistol shooting in the Yukon Territory.; *Member of:* Sport Yukon
Chief Officer(s): Lyle Thompson, President
Activities: Junior Shooters Program

Skating

Alberta Amateur Speed Skating Association (AASSA)
2500 University Dr. NW, Calgary AB T2N 1N4
Tel: 403-220-7911; *Fax:* 403-220-9226
info@aassa.ca
www.albertaspeedskating.ca
Social Media:
instagram.com/albertaspeedskating
www.facebook.com/albertaspeedskating
twitter.com/AB_SpeedSkating
Also Known As: Alberta Speed Skating
Overview: A small provincial organization
Member of: Speed Skating Canada
Chief Officer(s): Nicole Cooney, President
Wendy Walker, Program Coordinator
Mike Marshall, Technical Director

British Columbia Speed Skating Association
PO Box 2023, Stn. A, Abbotsford BC V2T 3T8
Tel: 604-746-4349; *Fax:* 604-746-4549
www.speed-skating.bc.ca
Social Media:
www.instagram.com/BCSpeedSkating
www.facebook.com/BCSpeedSkating
twitter.com/BCSpeedSkating
Overview: A small provincial organization
Description: To foster the growth & development of Speed Skating in B.C.; *Member of:* Speed Skating Canada
Chief Officer(s): Ted Houghton, Executive Director, 604-309-8178
ted.houghton@shaw.ca

Club de patinage artistique Les lames givrées inc.
CP 453, Chibougamau QC G8P 2X9
Tél: 418-748-2671
leslamesgivrees@hotmail.com
Aperçu: *Dimension:* petite; *Envergure:* locale
Membre(s) du bureau directeur: Joline Bélanger, Présidente, 418-748-2339

Fédération de patinage artistique du Québec (FPAQ)
4545, av Pierre-de Coubertin, Montréal QC H1V 0B2
Tél: 514-252-3073; *Téléc:* 514-252-3170
patinage@patinage.qc.ca
www.patinage.qc.ca
Média social:
www.facebook.com/patinageqc
Aperçu: *Dimension:* grande; *Envergure:* provinciale; fondée en 1969
Description: Rendre accessible à tous, les programmes de Patinage Canada, que ce soit par amour, par plaisir ou pour atteindre l'excellence; a l'unisson, nous contribuons ainsi à l'avancement de notre sport.
Membre(s) du bureau directeur: Sylvie Simard, Présidente
ssimard@patinage.qc.ca
Any-Claude Dion, Directrice générale, 514-252-3073 3550
Membre: 40 000; 18 associations régionales; 242 organismes locaux

Fédération de Patinage de Vitesse du Québec
930, av Roland Beaudin, Sainte-Foy QC G1V 4H8
Tél: 418-651-1973; *Téléc:* 418-651-1977
Ligne sans frais: 877-651-1973
www.fpvq.org
Média social:
www.facebook.com/FPVQ.org
twitter.com/PatinVitesseQc
Aperçu: *Dimension:* petite; *Envergure:* provinciale
Description: Depuis un peu plus d'un mois déjà, les athlètes du Centre national courte piste sont en entraînement hors glace sous la surveillance des entraîneurs et avec la grande collaboration du groupe Actiforme.; *Membre de:* Speed Skating Canada

International Skating Union (ISU) / Union Internationale de Patinage
Avenue Juste-Olivier 17, Lausanne 1006 Switzerland
info@isu.ch
www.isu.org
Social Media:
www.youtube.com/user/SkatingISU/featured
www.facebook.com/isuofficial
Overview: A small international organization founded in 1892
Description: To regulate, control & promote the sports of figure & speed skating & their organized development on the basis of friendship & mutual understanding between sportsmen & women & to broaden interest in figure & speed skating sports by increasing their popularity, improving their quality & increasing the number of participants throughout the world
Chief Officer(s): Fredi Schmid, Director General
Finances: *Annual Operating Budget:* Greater than $5 Million
Staff: 11 staff member(s); 60 volunteer(s)
Membership: 73; *Fees:* 300 Swiss francs; *Member Profile:* National skating associations
Activities: Administration of figure skating & speed skating sports throughout the world

Manitoba Speed Skating Association
145 Pacific Ave., Winnipeg MB R3B 2Z6
Tel: 204-925-5657; *Fax:* 204-925-5792
Toll-Free: 888-628-9921
office@mbspeedskating.ca
www.mbspeedskating.org
Social Media:
instagram.com/mbspeedskating
twitter.com/mbspeedskating
Overview: A small provincial organization
Description: The MSSA is dedicated to the development, growth & effective administration of the sport of speed skating in Manitoba through the provision of leadership, support & promotion of its members & clubs.; *Member of:* Speed Skating Canada
Chief Officer(s): Brad Chambers, President
Activities: Short-track, long-track speed skating

Newfoundland & Labrador Speed Skating Association (NLSSA)
NL
Overview: A small provincial organization
Member of: Speed Skating Canada

Northwest Territories Amateur Speed Skating Association (NWTASSA)
c/o Sport North, 4908 - 49 St., Yellowknife NT X1A 2P9
Tel: 867-669-8326; *Fax:* 867-669-8327
Toll-Free: 800-661-0797
nwtspeedskating@gmail.com
sportnorth.com/tso/speed-skating/about-us
Overview: A small provincial organization
Description: To promote the sport of speed skating in the NWT; *Member of:* Sport North Federation; Speed Skating Canada
Chief Officer(s): Julie Jeffery, Director
Finances: *Annual Operating Budget:* Less than $50,000
Staff: 40 volunteer(s)
Membership: 140

Nunavut Speed Skating Association
c/o John Maurice, President, PO Box 761, 563 Suputi St., Iqaluit NU X0A 0H0
Tel: 867-979-1226; *Fax:* 867-975-3384
www.nunavutspeedskating.ca
Overview: A small provincial organization
Member of: Speed Skating Canada
Chief Officer(s): John Maurice, President
jtmaurice@northwestel.net
Don Galloway, Secretary & Director, Coaching
don.galloway@aandc-aadnc.gc.ca

Ontario Speed Skating Association (OSSA)
PO Box 1179, Lakefield ON K0L 2H0
Tel: 705-652-9490; *Fax:* 705-652-1227
ossa@ontariospeedskating.ca
ontariospeedskating.ca
Social Media:
www.flickr.com/photos/ontariospeedskating
www.facebook.com/OntarioSpeedSkating
twitter.com/OSSA
Previous Name: Ice Skating Association of Ontario
Overview: A medium-sized provincial organization founded in 1981
Description: To promote & develop the sport of speed skating in Ontario.; *Member of:* Speed Skating Canada
Chief Officer(s): Jacqueline Deschenes, Executive Director
executivedirector@ontariospeedskating.ca
Sarah Leslie, Manager, Sport Programs, 613-422-5210
sportmanager@ontariospeedskating.ca
Finances: *Funding Sources:* Membership fee
Activities: *Speaker Service:* Yes

Saskatchewan Amateur Speed Skating Association (SASSA)
2205 Victoria Ave., Regina SK S4P 0S4
Tel: 306-780-9400; *Fax:* 306-525-4009
sassa@sasktel.net
www.saskspeedskating.ca
Social Media:
www.facebook.com/SaskatchewanSpeedSkating
Previous Name: Saskatchewan Speed Skating Association
Overview: A medium-sized provincial organization
Description: Working together to develop & promote the sport of speed skating at all levels as a fun, competitive, healthy, family activity; *Member of:* Speed Skating Canada
Affiliation(s): Sask Sport Inc.
Chief Officer(s): Jordan St. Onge, Executive Director
Finances: *Annual Operating Budget:* $100,000-$250,000; *Funding Sources:* Provincial government
Staff: 2 staff member(s); 650 volunteer(s)
Membership: 10 institutional; 200 student; 600 individual

Skate Canada / Patinage Canada
865 Shefford Rd., Ottawa ON K1J 1H9
Tel: 613-747-1007; *Fax:* 613-748-5718
Toll-Free: 888-747-2372
skatecanada@skatecanada.ca
www.skatecanada.ca
Social Media:
www.youtube.com/channel/UCsc7hNfnY3b65mZqXkVKNZw
www.facebook.com/skatecanada
twitter.com/SkateCanada
Also Known As: Canadian Figure Skating Association
Overview: A large national licensing charitable organization founded in 1914
Description: To enable all Canadians to participate in skating throughout their lifetime for fun, fitness, & achievement; *Member of:* International Skating Union
Chief Officer(s): Leanna Caron, President
Dan Thompson, Chief Executive Officer
Norm Proft, Director, Member Services
Barb MacDonald, Director, Corporate Communications
Michael Slipchuk, Director, High Performance
Finances: *Funding Sources:* User fees; Television events; Marketing; Membership fees
Staff: 50 staff member(s)
Membership: *Fees:* $32 associate; $100 coaching; *Committees:* CEO Operational Review; Governance; External Relations; Membership Policy; Finance & Risk Management; Athlete Fund & Alumni; Officials Development; Coaching Development; Sections Coordinating; Hall of Fame & Heritage; High Performance Development; Officials Assignment & Promotion; Skating Programs Development; Strategic Planning Steering
Activities: *Speaker Service:* Yes

Skate Ontario
ON
www.skateontario.org
Social Media:
www.facebook.com/SkateOntario
twitter.com/SkateOntario
Also Known As: Ontario Figure Skating Association
Overview: A small provincial organization founded in 1982
Description: To enable every citizen of the province to participate in skating through out his/her lifetime for fun &/or achievement
Chief Officer(s): Tracey McCague-McElrea, Executive Director
tracey@skateontario.org
Wendy St. Denis, President
wendy.stdenis@skateontario.org
Membership: 75,000; *Member Profile:* Competitive & recreational skaters as well as coaches & officials; *Committees:* Events; Programs; Technical

Speed Skate New Brunswick
NB
speedskatenb@gmail.com
speedskatenb.ca
Social Media:
twitter.com/SpeedSkateNB
Previous Name: New Brunswick Speed Skating Association
Overview: A small provincial organization
Description: The association provides members with access to coaching & chances to compete. It serves as a hub for information on the sport & for members to network.; *Member of:* Speed Skating Canada
Chief Officer(s): Joe Oliver, Chair

Speed Skate Nova Scotia
5516 Spring Garden Rd., Halifax NS B3J 1G6
Tel: 902-425-5450
info@speedskatens.ca
www.speedskatens.ca
Social Media:
twitter.com/SpeedSk8NS
Previous Name: Nova Scotia Speed Skating Association
Overview: A small provincial organization
Member of: Speed Skating Canada
Chief Officer(s): Brent Thompson, President

Speed Skate PEI
PO Box 383, Charlottetown PE C1A 7K7
info@speedskatepei.ca
www.speedskatepei.com
Social Media:
www.youtube.com/channel/UCwDjLpo01Om1QBMoZn5EQLw
www.facebook.com/SpeedSkatePEI
twitter.com/SpeedSkatePEI
Previous Name: Prince Edward Island Speed Skating Association
Overview: A small provincial organization
Description: Supporting the sport of speedskating in PEI.; *Member of:* Speed Skating Canada
Chief Officer(s): Jeff Wood, President
president@speedskatepei.ca
Shirliana Bruce, Secretary
secretary@speedskatepei.ca

Speed Skating Canada (SSC) / Patinage de vitesse Canada
#17F, 850 Industrial Ave., Ottawa ON K1G 4K2
Tel: 613-260-3669; *Fax:* 613-260-3660
Toll-Free: 877-572-4772
ssc@speedskating.ca
www.speedskating.ca
Social Media:
www.youtube.com/user/SpeedSkatingCanada;
instagram.com/ssc_pvc
www.facebook.com/SSC.PVC
twitter.com/SSC_PVC
Overview: A medium-sized national organization founded in 1887
Description: To develop & promote long & short track speed skating in Canada; To prepare athletes, coaches, officials, & volunteers to make contributions to speed skating & to Canada's image abroad through development & international programs
Affiliation(s): International Skating Union
Chief Officer(s): Ian Moss, Chief Executive Officer
imoss@speedskating.ca
Janice Dawson, Director, Sport Development
jdawson@speedskating.ca
Patrick Godbout, Manager, Communications & Media Relations, 514-213-9897
pgodbout@speedskating.ca
Mariamanda Espinoza, Officer, Finance & Administration
mespinoza@speedskating.ca
Finances: *Funding Sources:* Government; Sport Canada; Canadian Olympic Association; Sponsorships; Membership
Staff: 50 volunteer(s)
Membership: 10,000; *Member Profile:* Participants in competitive or recreational speed skating; *Committees:* High Performance - Short Track & Long Track; Competitions Development; Club & Membership Development; Coaching Development; Officials Development
Activities: *Internships:* Yes; *Speaker Service:* Yes

Yukon Amateur Speed Skating Association
4061 - 4th Ave., Whitehorse YT Y1A 1H1
Tel: 867-660-5347
www.shorttrack06.com
Also Known As: Whitehorse Rapids Speed Skating Club
Overview: A small provincial organization

Skiing

Alberta Alpine Ski Association (AASA)
Bill Warren Training Centre, #100, 1995 Olympic Way, Canmore AB T1W 2T6
Tel: 403-609-4730; *Fax:* 403-678-3644
memberservices@albertaalpine.ca
www.albertaalpine.ca
Social Media:
www.facebook.com/122652134004
Also Known As: Alberta Alpine
Overview: A small provincial organization
Description: To govern & promote alpine skiing in Alberta.
Chief Officer(s): Adam Hull, President, 403-609-4731
adam@albertaalpine.ca

Alberta Freestyle Ski Association (AFSA)
88 Canada Olympic Rd., Calgary AB T3B 5R5
Tel: 403-297-2718; *Fax:* 403-202-2522
info@abfreestyle.com
www.abfreestyle.com
Social Media:
www.facebook.com/AlbertaFreestyleSkiingAssociation
twitter.com/ABFreestyleSki
Overview: A small provincial charitable organization founded in 1990
Description: To develop & coordinate the sport of freestyle skiing in Alberta; *Member of:* Canadian Freestyle Ski Association
Chief Officer(s): Dan Bowman, Chair
DBowman@shaw.ca
Paulo Kapronczai, Vice-Chair
deekorber@shaw.ca
Dan Jefferies, Treasurer
djefferies@bdo.ca
Maureen Calder, Executive Director
Finances: *Funding Sources:* Sponsorships
Activities: Promoting freestyle skiing at all levels in Alberta; Supporting the high performance Alberta Mogul Team & the Alberta Park & Pipe Team; Offering judges' clinics

Alberta Ski Jumping & Nordic Combined (ASJNC)
88 Canada Olympic Rd., Calgary AB T3B 5R5
Tel: 403-247-5960
skijumpingalberta.com
Social Media:
www.facebook.com/ASJNC
Also Known As: Ski Jumping Alberta
Overview: A small provincial organization founded in 1991
Description: To oversee ski jumping & nordic combined programs in Alberta.

Alpine Canada Alpin
Canada Olympic Park, #302, 151 Canada Olympic Rd. SW, Calgary AB T3B 6B7
Tel: 403-777-3200; *Fax:* 403-777-3213
info@alpinecanada.org
alpinecanada.org
Social Media:
www.youtube.com/user/AlpineCanadaAlpin;
instagram.com/alpinecanada
www.facebook.com/AlpineCanada
twitter.com/Alpine_Canada
Overview: A medium-sized national organization
Description: The ACA is the governing body for ski racing in Canada. Founded in 1920 & accounting for close to 200,000 supporting members, ACA represents coaches, officials, supporters & athletes, including elite racers of the Canadian Alpine Ski Team & the Canadian Disabled Alpine Ski Team.
Chief Officer(s): Mark Rubinstein, President & CEO, 403-777-4246
mrubinstein@alpinecanada.org
Nicholas Bass, Chief Operating Officer, 403-777-3218
nbass@alpinecanada.org
Linsey Ferguson, Vice-President, Partnerships, 416-967-9339
lferguson@alpinecanada.org

Alpine Ontario Alpin (AOA)
#10, 191 Hurontario St., Collingwood ON L9Y 2M1
Tel: 705-444-5111; *Fax:* 705-444-5116
admin@alpineontario.ca
www.alpineontario.ca
Overview: A medium-sized provincial organization
Description: To provide skiing opportunities for competitive & recreational athletes
Chief Officer(s): Scott Barrett, Acting Executive Director
sbarrett@alpineontario.ca
Membership: 30,000+ in 44 clubs; *Fees:* Schedule available

Alpine Saskatchewan
1860 Lorne St., Regina SK S4P 2L7
Tel: 306-780-9236; *Fax:* 306-780-9462
office@saskalpine.com
saskalpine.webs.com
Also Known As: Sask Alpine
Overview: A small provincial organization
Description: To be the provincial governing body for noncompetitive & competitive alpine skiing in Saskatchewan.
Chief Officer(s): Karen Musgrave, President
president@saskalpine.com
Alana Ottenbreit, Office Manager

Association des stations de ski du Québec (ASSQ)
1347, rue Nationale, Terrebonne QC J6W 6H8
Tél: 450-765-2012; *Téléc:* 450-765-2025
media@assq.qc.ca
www.quebecskisurf.com
Média social:
www.facebook.com/skiqc
twitter.com/assq_maneige
Aperçu: *Dimension:* moyenne; *Envergure:* provinciale; Organisme sans but lucratif; fondée en 1979
Description: Représenter et défendre les intérêts des membres; favoriser la pratique du ski alpin; améliorer la qualité du produit ainsi que la performance des stations
Membre(s) du bureau directeur: Yves Juneau, Président-directeur général
ski@assq.qc.ca
Membre: 75 stations de ski
Activités: *Listes de destinataires:* Oui

BC Freestyle Ski Association
#636, 280 Nelson St., Vancouver BC V6B 2E2
Tel: 604-398-8830
info@bcfreestyle.com
bcfreestyle.com
Social Media:
www.facebook.com/BCFreestyleSkiAssociation
twitter.com/bcfreestyle
Overview: A small provincial organization
Description: To develop, promote & coordinate the sport of freestyle skiing in British Columbia.; *Member of:* Canadian Freestyle Ski Association
Chief Officer(s): Adrian Taggart, President

British Columbia Alpine Ski Association
#403, 1788 West Broadway, Vancouver BC V6J 1Y1
Tel: 604-678-3070; *Fax:* 604-678-8073
office@bcalpine.com
www.bcalpine.com
Overview: A small local organization
Description: To promote the sport of alpine skiing in British Columbia
Chief Officer(s): Bruce Goldsmid, CEO
bruceg@bcalpine.com
Membership: 35 ski clubs; *Fees:* Schedule available

Canadian Association of Nordic Ski Instructors (CANSI) / Association canadienne des moniteurs de ski nordique
c/o Secrétariat, 164, rue Adrien-Robert, Gatineau QC J8Y 3S2
Tel: 819-360-6700; *Fax:* 819-778-0017
office@cansi.ca
www.cansi.ca
Social Media:
www.facebook.com/162657427089855
Overview: A small national organization founded in 1976

Description: To promote & advance cross-country & Telemark skiing in Canada, establishing standards, & offering levels of certification in technique & training
Chief Officer(s): Gaétan Lord, President
Françoise Chatenoud, Office Coordinator
Membership: *Fees:* Schedule available; *Member Profile:* Completed Level I Cross Country or Telemark course
Activities: Providing resources to instuctors; liaising nationally & internationally with the Nordic disciplines; coordinating national level courses

Canadian Freestyle Ski Association / Association canadienne de ski acrobatique
808 Pacific St., Vancouver BC V6Z 1C2
Tel: 604-714-2233; *Fax:* 604-714-2232
Toll-Free: 877-714-2232
info@freestyleski.com
www.freestyleski.ca
Social Media:
instagram.com/canfreestyleski
www.linkedin.com/company/8580796
www.facebook.com/CanFreestyleSki
twitter.com/canfreestyleski
Overview: A medium-sized national organization
Description: The national governing body of the sport of freestyle skiing with a mandate to develop the sport within Canada; to represent our country internationally; to promote the safe development of the sport; to promote excellence in national & international competitions
Affiliation(s): Canadian Ski & Snowboard Association
Chief Officer(s): Bruce Robinson, Chief Executive Officer
brucerobinson@freestyleski.com
Finances: *Annual Operating Budget:* $500,000-$1.5 Million
Membership: 2,000; *Fees:* $10
Activities: *Rents Mailing List:* Yes

Canadian Masters Cross-Country Ski Association (CMCSA) / Association canadienne des maîtres en ski de fond
2 MacNeil Cres., Stephenville NL A2N 3E3
Tel: 709-643-3259
www.canadian-masters-xc-ski.ca
Overview: A medium-sized national organization founded in 1980
Description: To promote Masters cross-country skiing across Canada, establish rules & regulations for activities, & representing members at meetings at the WMA.
Affiliation(s): World Masters Cross-Country Ski Association; Cross-Country Canada
Chief Officer(s): Bruce Legrow, National Director
bruce.legrow@nf.sympatico.ca
Finances: *Funding Sources:* Membership fees
Membership: *Fees:* $20; $35 in Québec; *Member Profile:* 30 years of age & over
Activities: Cross country ski races in Canada & abroad; Masters World Cup; Canadian Masters National Championships

Canadian Ski Council (CSC) / Conseil canadien du ski
#14, 76000 Hwy. 27, Woodbridge ON L4H 0P8
Tel: 905-856-4754
info@skicanada.org
www.skicanada.org
Social Media:
www.pinterest.com/gosnow
www.facebook.com/GoSkiingGoSnowboarding
twitter.com/cdnskicouncil
Overview: A medium-sized national organization founded in 1977
Description: To encourage participation in recreational skiing & snowboarding.; *Member of:* Canadian Society of Association Executives; Tourism Industry Association of Canada.
Affiliation(s): Canadian Association for Disabled Skiing; Canadian Ski Instructors' Alliance; Canadian Ski Patrol; Canadian Association of Snowboard Instructors; Association des stations de ski du Québec; Atlantic Ski Area Association; Canadian Snowsports Association; Canada West Ski Areas Association; Ontario Snow Resorts Associations
Chief Officer(s): Claude Péloquin, Chair
Patrick Arkeveld, President & CEO
Finances: *Funding Sources:* Sponsorship; associate membership; service fees; research
Membership: 11 organizations; *Committees:* Marketing & Research; Toronto Snow Show
Activities: Skier Development Programs; product development; research; *Speaker Service:* Yes; *Rents Mailing List:* Yes

Canadian Ski Instructors' Alliance (CSIA) / Alliance des moniteurs de ski du Canada
#220, 4900, rue Jean Talon ouest, Montréal QC H4P 1W9
Tel: 514-748-2648; *Fax:* 514-748-2476
Toll-Free: 800-811-6428
national@snowpro.com
www.snowpro.com
Social Media:
www.youtube.com/user/CSIAAMSC
www.facebook.com/CSIAAMSC
Overview: A large national organization founded in 1938
Description: To promote professionalism & high standards for the profession of ski instruction; To certify ski instructors across Canada; *Member of:* Canadian Ski Council
Affiliation(s): International Ski Instructors Association
Chief Officer(s): Dan Ralph, Managing Director
dralph@snowpro.com
Lisa Cambise, Director, Shared Services
lisa@snowpro.com
Martin Jean, Director, Education & Membership Services
martinj@snowpro.com
Benoit Fournier, Coordinator, National Programs
benoit@snowpro.com
Finances: *Funding Sources:* Membership dues
Staff: 14 staff member(s)
Activities: Providing education & leadership that contributes to a vibrant mountain experience for the skiing public; *Internships:* Yes

Canadian Ski Instructors' Alliance (CSIA) / Fédération des entraîneurs de ski du Canada
#220, 4900 rue Jean Talon ouest, Montréal QC H4P 1W9
Tel: 514-748-2648; *Fax:* 514-748-2476
Toll-Free: 800-811-6428
national@snowpro.com
www.snowpro.com/en
Social Media:
www.youtube.com/user/CSIAAMSC
Previous Name: Canadian Ski Coaches Federation
Overview: A medium-sized national organization founded in 1938
Description: To help produce the best skiers in the world for Canada
Chief Officer(s): Dan Blankstein, Chair
dan@snowpro.com
Dan Ralph, Managing Director
dralph@snowpro.com

Canadian Ski Marathon (CSM) / Marathon canadien de ski (MCS)
266, rue Viger, Papineauville QC J0V 1R0
Tel: 819-483-0456; *Fax:* 819-483-0450
Toll-Free: 877-770-6556
ski@csm-mcs.com
www.csm-mcs.com
Social Media:
www.youtube.com/user/csmmcs
www.facebook.com/csmmcs
twitter.com/csmmcs
Overview: A medium-sized national charitable organization founded in 1967
Description: The Canadian Ski Marathon is an historic cross-county ski tour for people of all ages in celebration of Canadian winter. Their mission is to organize an annual & fully supported weekend in the wilderness, the Canadian Ski Marathon provides a uniquely Canadian cross-country skiing event with a broad appeal.
Affiliation(s): Tourisme Outaouais; Tourisme Laurentides
Chief Officer(s): Paul "Boomer" Throop, President
pthroop@magma.ca
Frédéric Ménard, Director, Events
Finances: *Annual Operating Budget:* $250,000-$500,000; *Funding Sources:* Sponsors; participants
Staff: 3 staff member(s); 500 volunteer(s)
Membership: 2,000; *Fees:* Schedule available
Activities: Cross-Country Ski Tour; *Internships:* Yes

Canadian Ski Patrol (CSP) / Patrouille canadienne de ski (PCS)
4531 Southclark Pl., Ottawa ON K1T 3V2
Tel: 613-822-2245; *Fax:* 613-822-1088
Toll-Free: 900-565-2777
info@skipatrol.ca
www.csps.ca
Social Media:
www.facebook.com/CSP.PCS
twitter.com/CdnSkiPatrol
Overview: A medium-sized national charitable organization founded in 1940
Description: To provide first aid & safety programs throughout Canada; *Member of:* Fédération Internationale des Patrouilles de Ski (FIPS) / International Federation of Ski Patrollers
Chief Officer(s): Colin Saravanamuttoo, President & CEO, 613-822-2245 224
csaravan@skipatrol.ca
Renée Thivierge, Office Manager, 613-822-2245 231
manager@skipatrol.ca
Finances: *Funding Sources:* Sponsorships; Donations
Membership: 5,450; *Member Profile:* Volunteer patrollers, over the age of eighteen, who have undergone training sessions in first aid & rescue; *Committees:* Communications; Fund Development; Education; Finance & Administration; Operations
Activities: Patrolling over 200 resorts across Canada on alpine, Nordic, & tele-mark skis, as well as on snow boards; Providing year-round safety & rescue services by volunteering at non-skiing events during the summer; Presenting awards; Providing first aid training; *Awareness Events:* National First Aid Competition

Canadian Snowsports Association (CSA) / L'Association canadienne des sports d'hiver (ACSH)
#202, 1451 West Broadway, Vancouver BC V6H 1H6
Tel: 604-734-6800; *Fax:* 604-669-7954
info@canadiansnowsports.com
www.canadiansnowsports.com
Previous Name: Canadian Ski & Snowboard Association; Canadian Ski Association
Overview: A large national organization founded in 1920
Description: To develop elite amateur athletes; To pursue excellence at national & international level competition
Chief Officer(s): Chris Robinson, President
David Pym, Managing Director
dpym@isrm.com
Lillian Alderton, Administrator
lillianalderton@hotmail.com
Membership: 700+ ski clubs + 97,000 members

Centre de plein air du Mont Chalco
CP 173, 264, rte 167, Chibougamau QC G8P 2K6
Tél: 418-748-7162; *Téléc:* 418-748-4685
info@montchalco.ca
www.montchalco.ca
Aperçu: *Dimension:* petite; *Envergure:* locale

Cross Country Alberta (CCA)
Percy Page Centre, 11759 Groat Rd., Edmonton AB T5M 3K6
Tel: 780-415-1738; *Fax:* 780-427-0524
manager@xcountryab.net
www.xcountryab.net
Social Media:
www.facebook.com/CrossCountryAlberta
twitter.com/xcountryab
Overview: A medium-sized provincial organization
Description: To lead, develop, & promote the sport of cross-country skiing througout Alberta; *Member of:* Cross Country Canada
Chief Officer(s): Jo Wolach, Chair
jo@xsitra.com
Michael Neary, Manager, Sport
Laura Filipow, Coordinator, Programs
cca@xcountryab.net
Membership: 3,890; *Fees:* $11 child; $13 youth; $18 adult; $100 club
Activities: Quality service; leadership & skier development; management & education

Cross Country British Columbia (CCBC)
#106, 3003 - 30th St., Vernon BC V1T 9J5
Tel: 250-545-9600; *Fax:* 250-545-9614
office@crosscountrybc.ca
www.crosscountrybc.ca
Social Media:
instagram.com/crosscountrybc
www.facebook.com/Cross-Country-BC-829014633823512
Also Known As: Cross Country BC
Overview: A small provincial organization
Description: The association is the governing body for the sport of cross country skiing in BC.; *Member of:* Cross Country Canada
Chief Officer(s): Wannes Luppens, Executive Director
wannes@crosscountrybc.ca
Dennis Wu, Coordinator, Administration & Communications
Membership: 14,000

Cross Country Canada (CCC) / Ski de fond Canada (SFC)
Bill Warren Training Centre, #100, 1995 Olympic Way, Canmore AB T1W 2T6
Tel: 403-678-6791; *Fax:* 403-678-3885
Toll-Free: 877-609-3215
info@cccski.com
www.cccski.com
Social Media:
www.youtube.com/user/xccanada
www.facebook.com/138553616175807
twitter.com/cccski
Overview: A medium-sized national charitable organization
Description: To develop & deliver programs designed to achieve international excellence in cross-country skiing; to provide national programs for continuous development of cross-country skiing from introductory experience to international excellence, for participants of all ages & abilities, fostering the principles of ethical conduct & fair play; *Member of:* True Sport
Affiliation(s): Canadian Ski & Snowboard Association
Chief Officer(s): Jamie Coatsworth, Chair, 416-486-0825
jamie.coatsworth@gmail.com
Davin MacIntosh, Chief Executive Officer, 403-678-6791 38
dmacintosh@cccski.com
Mike Edwards, Director, High Performance Para-Nordic, 403-678-6791 35
medwards@cccski.com
Thomas Holland, Director, High Performance, 403-678-6791 37
tholland@cccski.com
Finances: *Annual Operating Budget:* $500,000-$1.5 Million
Staff: 25 staff member(s)
Membership: 55,000; *Committees:* Women's; Events; High Performance; Coach & Athlete Development; Fundraising; Communications
Activities: *Internships:* Yes

Cross Country New Brunswick / Ski de fond Nouveau-Brunswick
c/o Manon Losier, 1482, ch Saulnier ouest, Benoit NB E1X 2A8
Tel: 506-395-0020
xcskinb@bellaliant.net
www.xcski-nb.ca
Social Media:
www.facebook.com/nbskiteam
Overview: A medium-sized provincial organization
Description: To promote cross country skiing among the general population of New Brunswick; To provide a sense of leadership; To offer a variety of programs & services; *Member of:* Cross Country Canada
Chief Officer(s): Dave Moore, Chair
moored@bellaliant.net
Arthur Austin, Treasurer
arthur.austin@gmail.com

Cross Country Newfoundland & Labrador
c/o Gerry Rideout, 301 Curtis Cres., Labrador City NL A2V 2B8
Tel: 709-944-5842
www.crosscountrynl.com
Overview: A medium-sized provincial organization
Chief Officer(s): Gerry Rideout, President
rideoutg@crrstv.net

Cross Country Nova Scotia (CCSNS)
5516 Spring Garden Rd., 4th Fl., Halifax NS B3J 1G6
Tel: 902-425-5454; *Fax:* 902-425-5606
ccns@sportnovascotia.ca
crosscountryns.ca
Social Media:
www.facebook.com/114825378670589
Previous Name: Nordic Ski Nova Scotia
Overview: A medium-sized provincial organization founded in 1968
Description: To promote & encourage the sport/recreation of cross-country skiing; To provide & maintain rules & regulations in the province; To encourage & foster general public support of the activities & programs of CCSNS; To provide a resource centre for the membership & the general public; To select & train members of the provincial team to represent the province; *Member of:* Cross Country Canada
Membership: 200; *Fees:* Schedule available

Cross Country Ontario (CCO)
c/o Liz Inkila, 738 River St., Thunder Bay ON P7A 3S8
Tel: 807-768-4617
admin@xco.org
www.xco.org
Social Media:
twitter.com/xcoorg
Overview: A medium-sized provincial organization
Description: To govern the sport of cross country skiing in Ontario.; *Member of:* Cross Country Canada
Chief Officer(s): Liz Inkila, Director, Administration

Cross Country PEI
PO Box 532, PE C0A 2B0
srobrien@eastlink.ca
www.cccski.com/Contacts/Division-Offices.aspx
Overview: A small provincial organization
Description: The association is the governing body for the sport of cross country skiing in PEI.; *Member of:* Cross Country Canada
Chief Officer(s): Steve O'Brien, Contact
srobrien@eastlink.ca

Cross Country Saskatchewan (CCS)
1860 Lorne St., Regina SK S4P 2L7
Tel: 306-780-9240; *Fax:* 306-780-9462
ccs@sasktel.net
crosscountrysask.ca
Social Media:
www.facebook.com/431140886944432
twitter.com/XCSask
Overview: A small provincial organization
Description: CCS is a non-profit, volunteer-directed organization of skiing clubs. It develops & supports competitive & recreational cross country skiing programs throughout Saskatchewan.; *Member of:* Sask Ski Association; Sask Sport; Cross Country Canada
Chief Officer(s): Dan Brisbin, President
danbrisbin@sasktel.net
Alana Ottenbreit, Executive Director
Finances: *Annual Operating Budget:* $100,000-$250,000
Staff: 1 staff member(s)
Membership: 26 clubs; *Fees:* Schedule available; *Member Profile:* Skiing clubs with at least 10 members

Cross Country Ski Association of Manitoba (CCSAM)
Sport for Life Centre, 145 Pacific Ave., Winnipeg MB R3B 2Z6
Tel: 204-925-5639
info@ccsam.ca
www.ccsam.ca
Social Media:
www.youtube.com/xcountryskimb
www.facebook.com/ccski
twitter.com/xcountryskimb
Overview: A small provincial organization
Description: CCSAM is a volunteer-based organization that provides leadership and direction towards broad participation in the sport of cross country skiing.; *Member of:* Cross Country Canada
Affiliation(s): Sport Manitoba
Chief Officer(s): Richard Huybers, Chairperson
richard.huybers@grainscanada.gc.ca
Karin McSherry, Executive Director
Member Profile: Any member of a cross country ski club in MB may join.

Cross Country Yukon (CCY)
4061 - 4th Ave., Whitehorse YT Y1A 1H1
Tel: 867-334-9220
www.crosscountryyukon.com
Previous Name: Yukon Ski Division
Overview: A medium-sized provincial organization founded in 1985
Description: To develop cross country skiing in the Yukon; *Member of:* Cross Country Canada
Chief Officer(s): Alain Masson, Sport Coordinator & Head Coach
xcyukon@gmail.com
Finances: *Annual Operating Budget:* $100,000-$250,000; *Funding Sources:* Yukon territorial government; Yukon Lotteries; fundraising
Staff: 2 staff member(s); 200 volunteer(s)
Membership: 900 + 17 clubs; *Fees:* Schedule available; *Committees:* Events & Technical; High Performance; Leadership Development; Youth Development
Activities: Clinic courses include: coaching; ski trail design; trail grooming; avalanche awareness; jackrabbit leader course; backcountry; ski patrol

Fédération québécoise de la montagne et de l'escalade (FQME)
4545, av Pierre-de Coubertin, Montréal QC H1V 0B2
Tél: 514-252-3004; *Téléc:* 514-252-3201
Ligne sans frais: 866-204-3763
operations@fqme.qc.ca
www.fqme.qc.ca
Média social:
twitter.com/Escalade_FQME
www.facebook.com/FQMEescalade
Aperçu: *Dimension:* petite; *Envergure:* provinciale; Organisme sans but lucratif; fondée en 1969
Description: Regrouper les adeptes de l'escalade et de l'alpinisme au Québec; promouvoir l'escalade (rocher et glace) et le ski de l'alpinisme et de randonnée en montagne; promouvoir une pratique sécuritaire de ces activités; protéger et rendre accessibles les différents sites d'escalade et de grande randonnée à skis au Québec; *Membre de:* Canadian Avalanche Association; Outdoor Recreation Coalition of America (ORCA)
Affiliation(s): Union internationale des associations d'alpinisme
Membre(s) du bureau directeur: André St-Jacques, Directeur des opérations, 514-252-3000 3406
Finances: *Budget de fonctionnement annuel:* $100,000-$250,000
Membre: 2 000; *Montant de la cotisation:* Barème; *Comités:* Formation; Site; Expédition
Activités: Amateur d'activités montagnes; *Stagiaires:* Oui
Bibliothèque: Centre de documentation rendez-vous

Freestyle Ski Nova Scotia (FSNS)
5516 Spring Garden Rd., 4th Fl., Halifax NS B3J 1G6
Tel: 902-425-5450; *Fax:* 902-425-5606
alpinens@sportnovascotia.ca
freestylenovascotia.ca
Social Media:
www.facebook.com/Freestyle-Ski-Nova-Scotia-15104795658964 82
twitter.com/FreestyleNS
Overview: A small provincial organization
Description: To govern the sport of freestyle skiing in Nova Scotia.; *Member of:* Canadian Freestyle Ski Association; Alpine Ski Nova Scotia
Chief Officer(s): Lorraine Burch, Executive Director

Freestyle Skiing Ontario (FSO)
134 Osler St., Toronto ON M6N 2Y8
Tel: 416-238-7604; *Toll-Free:* 877-578-6581
info@ontariofreestyle.com
www.ontariofreestyle.com
Social Media:
instagram.com/freestyleskiingontario
www.facebook.com/156749758280
twitter.com/FreestyleSkiOnt
Overview: A small provincial organization
Description: To direct the sport of freestyle skiing in Ontario.; *Member of:* Canadian Freestyle Ski Association
Chief Officer(s): Jeff Ord, Executive Director, 416-238-7604 700
jefford@ontariofreestyle.com

Manitoba Freestyle Ski Association
145 Pacific Ave., Winnipeg MB R3B 2Z6
Tel: 204-795-9754
info@mbfreestyle.com
www.mbfreestyle.com
Overview: A small provincial organization
Description: To promote the sport of freestyle skiing in Manitoba.; *Member of:* Canadian Freestyle Ski Association
Chief Officer(s): Steve Carpenter, President
president@mbfreestyle.com

Nakiska Alpine Ski Association (NASA)
PO Box 68080, Stn. Crowfoot, Calgary AB T3G 3N8
Tel: 403-613-5935
www.skinasa.org
Social Media:
www.facebook.com/122652134004
Overview: A small local organization founded in 2009
Description: To train athletes in alpine ski racing.
Chief Officer(s): Scott Zahn, Director, Program & Technical
szahn@skinasa.org
Membership: 6 clubs + 300 individual

National Winter Sports Association (NWSA)
c/o Cross Country Canada, Bill Warren Training Centre, #100, 1995 Olympic Way, Canmore AB T1W 2T6
Tel: 403-678-6791; *Fax:* 403-678-3885
Toll-Free: 877-609-3215
info@cccski.com
www.cccski.com
Social Media:
www.youtube.com/user/xccanada
www.facebook.com/CrossCountryCanada
twitter.com/cccski
Overview: A small national organization founded in 2007
Description: To provide financial assistance to cross country ski coaches, athletes & racing programs across Canada; grants administered through Cross Country Canada; *Member of:* Cross Country Canada
Chief Officer(s): Pierre Lafontaine, Executive Director, Cross Country Canada, 403-678-6791 38
plafontaine@cccski.com

Nordic Combined Ski Canada (NCSC)
#388, 305 - 4625 Varsity Dr. NW, Calgary AB T3A 0Z9
Tel: 403-863-7951
skijumpingcanada.com
Overview: A small national organization
Description: To be the national governing body for the sport of ski jumping in Canada, alongside Ski Jumping Canada.
Affiliation(s): Ski Jumping Canada
Chief Officer(s): Andy Mah, Chair
Savill Wes, Director
wsavill@gmail.com

Northwest Territories Ski Division
PO Box 1916, Yellowknife NT X1A 2P4
Tel: 867-445-5855
nwtski@gmail.com
www.nwtski.com
Previous Name: Cross Country Northwest Territories
Overview: A small provincial organization
Member of: Cross Country Canada

Ontario Track 3 Ski Association for the Disabled
PO Box 67, Stn. D, Toronto ON M9A 4X1
Tel: 416-233-3872; *Fax:* 416-233-7862
Toll-Free: 877-308-7225
track3@track3.org
www.track3.org
Social Media:
www.facebook.com/OntarioTrack3
twitter.com/OntarioTrack3
Also Known As: Track 3
Overview: A small provincial charitable organization founded in 1972
Description: To discover ability through the magic of snow sports.
Chief Officer(s): Steve Jones, President
Darrell Jarvic, Secretary
Tracy Johnston, Treasurer
Activities: *Speaker Service:* Yes

Patrouille de ski St-Jean
651, 6e rue ouest, Chibougamau QC G8P 2T8
Tél: 418-748-7162
Aperçu: *Dimension:* petite; *Envergure:* locale
Membre(s) du bureau directeur: Fabien Belleau, Président, 418-770-8447
Sébastien d'Amboise, Vice-Président, 418-809-6059

Prince Edward Island Alpine Ski Association
PO Box 2026, Charlottetown PE C1A 7N7
Tel: 902-368-4110; *Fax:* 902-368-4548
Toll-Free: 800-247-6712
sports@sportpei.pe.ca
www.sportpei.pe.ca
Overview: A medium-sized provincial organization

Saskatchewan Freestyle Ski Incorporated
SK
saskfreestyle.ca
Also Known As: Sask Freestyle Ski Incorporated
Overview: A small provincial organization
Description: To run programs developed by the Canadian Freestyle Ski Association.; *Member of:* Canadian Freestyle Ski Association
Chief Officer(s): Kim Ryan, President
kimeryan64@gmail.com

Ski de fond Québec
4545, av Pierre-de Coubertin, Montréal QC H1V 0B2
Tel: 450-745-1888
info@skidefondquebec.ca
www.skidefondquebec.ca
Overview: A small provincial organization
Member of: Cross Country Canada

Ski Hawks Ottawa
c/o Bruce Meredith, 522 Hillcrest Ave., Ottawa ON K2A 2M9
Tel: 613-725-2472
www.cads-ncd.ca/skihawks/Skihawks_home.html
Overview: A small local charitable organization founded in 1978
Description: To promote skiing to the visually impaired community; *Member of:* Canadian Association of Disabled Skiing - National Capital Division (CADS-NCD)
Chief Officer(s): Bruce Meredith, Treasurer
brucemeredith@rogers.com
Carolyn Mitrow, President, 613-222-7718
cmitrow@gmail.com
Member Profile: Visually impaired skiers & snowboarders, aged 8 to 88, in all ability levels

Ski Jumping Canada (SJC) / Canada Saut à Ski
#418, 305 - 4625 Varsity Dr. NW, Calgary AB T3A 0Z9
www.skijumpingcanada.com
Social Media:
www.facebook.com/SkiJumpingCanada
Overview: A small national organization
Description: To be the national governing body for the sport of ski jumping in Canada, alongside Nordic Combined Ski Canada.
Chief Officer(s): Tom Reid, Chair
tomreid@skijumpingcanada.com

Ski Québec alpin (SQA)
4545, av Pierre-de Coubertin, Montréal QC H1V 3R2
Tél: 514-252-3089; *Téléc:* 514-252-5282
www.skiquebec.qc.ca
Média social:
www.youtube.com/channel/UCVQGzGbkN8J3tuPQD5WXIOw
www.facebook.com/skiqcalpin
twitter.com/SkiQuebecAlpin
Également appelé: Cross Country Québec
Aperçu: *Dimension:* moyenne; *Envergure:* provinciale; fondée en 1967
Description: D'organiser et de gérer le ski alpin et concours;
Membre de: Cross Country Canada
Membre(s) du bureau directeur: Daniel Paul Lavallée, Directeur général, 514-252-3089 3564
daniel@skiquebec.qc.ca
Éric Préfontaine, Directeur athlétique, 514-252-3089 3621
eprefontaine@skiquebec.qc.ca
Sylvie Grenier, Responsable, Services comptables, 514-252-3089 3565
comptabilité@skiquebec.qc.ca
Anthony Lamour, Responsable, Communications et du service aux partenaires, 514-252-3090
alamour@skiquebec.qc.ca

Union internationale des associations d'alpinisme (UIAA) / International Climbing & Mountaineering Federation
PO Box 23, Monbijoustrasse 61, Bern CH-3000 Switzerland
office@uiaa.ch
www.theuiaa.org
Social Media:
www.youtube.com/uiaabern
www.facebook.com/theuiaa
twitter.com/UIAAmountains
Overview: A medium-sized international organization founded in 1932
Description: To study & solve all problems in connection with mountaineering in general & particularly those of an international nature; To contribute to the development & promotion of mountaineering on an international level
Affiliation(s): Alpine Club of Canada; Fédération québecoise de la montagne
Chief Officer(s): Vrijlandt Frits, President
Membership: 80 institutional from 50 countries; *Member Profile:* National alpine associations from all over the world; *Committees:* Management; Mountaineering; Sports; Access; Anti-Doping; Ice Climbing; Medical; Mountain Protection; Safety; Youth

Whitehorse Cross Country Ski Club
#200, 1 Sumanik Dr., Whitehorse YT Y1A 6J6
Tel: 867-668-4477
info.xcskiwhitehorse@gmail.com
www.xcskiwhitehorse.ca
Overview: A small provincial organization
Description: To maintain high-quality ski trails & facilities, maintain a safe environment, ensure the long-term viability of the club & secure land tenure for the Yukon's trail system.
Chief Officer(s): Miriam Lukszova, Club Manager
Jan Polivka, Operations Manager
grooming.xcskiwhitehorse@gmail.com
Membership: *Fees:* Schedule available

Yukon Freestyle Ski Association
4061 - 4th Ave., Whitehorse YT Y1A 1H1
Tel: 867-393-3369
www.yfsa.ca
Social Media:
www.facebook.com/239011292821887
Overview: A small provincial organization
Description: To promote & facilitate freestyle skiing in the Yukon Territory.; *Member of:* Canadian Freestyle Ski Association; Sport Yukon

Skipping

Canadian Rope Skipping Federation (CRSF)
c/o Bonnie Popov, Registrar, 906 County Rd. 46, RR#3, Essex ON N8M 2X7
info@ropeskippingcanada.com
www.ropeskippingcanada.com
Social Media:
twitter.com/RopeSkippingCA
Also Known As: Rope Skipping Canada (RSC)
Previous Name: Canadian Skipping Association
Overview: A small national organization
Description: To promote rope skipping as a fitness & recreational activity, as well as a competitive sport.
Chief Officer(s): Bonnie Popov, Registrar
Membership: *Fees:* $20 full; $10 administrative; $7 recreational

Snowboarding

Alberta Snowboarding Association (ASA)
Bob Niven Training Centre, Bldg. 140, #202, 88 Canada Olympic Rd. SW, Calgary AB T3B 5R5
Tel: 403-247-5609
admin@albertasnowboarding.com
www.albertasnowboarding.com
Social Media:
instagram.com/albertasnowboard
www.facebook.com/albertaSnowboardingAssociation
twitter.com/AB_Snowboard
Overview: A small provincial organization
Description: To be the provincial governing body of competitive snowboarding in Alberta.; *Member of:* Canadian Snowboard Federation
Chief Officer(s): Kevin Higgins, President
Aletta de Rooij, Office Manager

Association of Ontario Snowboarders (AOS)
#203, 4 - 115 First St., Collingwood ON L9Y 4W3
Tel: 705-446-1488
aosadmin@ontariosnowboarders.ca
www.ontariosnowboarders.ca
Also Known As: Snowboard Ontario (SO)
Overview: A small provincial organization founded in 1998
Description: To be the governing body for the sport of competitive snowboarding in Ontario.; *Member of:* Canadian Snowboard Federation
Chief Officer(s): Mary Frances Carter, President
maryfrances@ontariosnowboarders.ca
Janet Richter, Manager, Administration

Association Québec Snowboard (AQS) / Québec Snowboard Association
4545, av Pierre-de Coubertin, Montréal QC H1V 0B2
Tél: 581-995-0615
quebecsnowboard.ca
Média social:
www.facebook.com/AssociationQuebecSnowboard
twitter.com/aqsnowboard
Aperçu: *Dimension:* petite; *Envergure:* provinciale
Membre de: Canadian Snowboard Federation
Membre(s) du bureau directeur: Patrick Lussier, Président

BC Snowboard Association
PO Box 2040, Kelowna BC V1X 4K5
Tel: 250-491-7626
admin@bcsnowboard.com
bcsnowboard.com
Social Media:
www.facebook.com/BCSnowboardAssociation
Overview: A small provincial organization
Description: To support snowboard athletes, coaches & officials in the province of British Columbia.; *Member of:* Canadian Snowboard Federation
Chief Officer(s): Cathy Astofooroff, Executive Director
cathy@bcsnowboard.com

Canadian Association of Snowboard Instructors (CASI) / Association canadienne des moniteurs de surf des neiges (ACMS)
60 Canning Cres., Cambridge ON N1T 1X2
Tel: 519-624-6593; *Fax:* 519-624-6594
Toll-Free: 877-976-2274
headoffice@casi-acms.com
www.casi-acms.com
Social Media:
www.youtube.com/casiacms
www.facebook.com/CASIACMS
twitter.com/casiacms
Overview: A medium-sized national licensing organization founded in 1994

Description: To promote the sport of snowboarding, snowboard instruction & coaching & the professions of snowboard teaching & coaching in Canada by training & certifying snowboard instructors & coaches; to ensure that a standard of safe & efficient snowboard instruction is maintained.; *Member of:* Canadian Ski Council
Affiliation(s): Canadian Ski Instructors Alliance; Canadian Snowboard Federation
Chief Officer(s): Dan Genge, Executive Director
dgenge@casi-acms.com
Membership: *Fees:* $91.33 regular; $48.36 associate; $26.34 student; $142.85 affiliate; *Committees:* Technical & Educational
Activities: Instructor & coaching certification courses; *Internships:* Yes; *Speaker Service:* Yes

Canadian Snowboard Federation
#301, 333 Terminal Ave., Vancouver BC V6A 4C1
Tel: 604-568-1135; *Fax:* 604-568-1639
info@canadasnowboard.ca
www.canadasnowboard.ca
Social Media:
www.youtube.com/user/CanadaSnowboardVideo
www.facebook.com/canadasnowboard
twitter.com/CanadaSnowboard
Also Known As: Canada~Snowboard
Overview: A medium-sized national organization
Description: To be the national governing body of competitive snowboarding in Canada.
Chief Officer(s): Patrick Jarvis, Executive Director
patrick.jarvis@canadasnowboard.ca
Robert Joncas, Director, High Performance
lebob@canadasnowboard.ca
Brendan Matthews, Manager, Business Operations
Brendan@canadasnowboard.ca
Activities: Freestyle; alpine; snowboardcross; para-snowboard

HeliCat Canada
PO Box 968, Revelstoke BC V0E 2S1
Tel: 250-837-5770
info@helicatcanada.com
www.helicatcanada.com
Social Media:
www.youtube.com/channel/UCmMNdyDIRkF3Udowcl5R-2A
Previous Name: BC Helicopter & Snowcat Skiing Operators Association
Overview: A small provincial organization founded in 1975
Member of: Council of Tourism Associations BC; Wilderness Tourism Association
Chief Officer(s): Rob Rohn, President
Ian Tomm, Executive Director
ed@helicatcanada.com

New Brunswick Snowboard Association
45, av Des Ormes, Edmundston NB E3V 4J8
Tel: 506-739-9843
Overview: A small provincial organization
Description: To be the provincial governing body of competitive snowboarding in New Brunswick.; *Member of:* Canadian Snowboard Federation
Chief Officer(s): Raymond Turgeon, Contact
rturgeon@nbnet.nb.ca

Newfoundland & Labrador Snowboard Association
PO Box 259, Steady Brook NL A2H 2N2
Tel: 709-634-4664
newfoundland@canadasnowboard.ca
nlsnowboard.com
Also Known As: NL Snowboard
Overview: A small provincial organization
Description: To be the provincial governing body of competitive snowboarding in Newfoundland & Labrador.; *Member of:* Canadian Snowboard Federation
Chief Officer(s): Emily Pittman, Contact

NWT Boardsport Association
PO Box 11089, Yellowknife NT X1A 3X7
Tel: 867-669-8326; *Fax:* 867-669-8327
Toll-Free: 800-661-0797
www.nwtboardsport.ca
Overview: A small provincial organization
Description: To be the governing body of competitive boardsports in the Northwest Territories.; *Member of:* Canadian Snowboard Federation; Sport North Federation
Chief Officer(s): Louise Dundas-Mathews, President
Justin Mager, Coach & Technical Director

Prince Edward Island Snowboard Association
Charlottetown PE
Also Known As: Snowboard PEI
Overview: A small provincial organization
Description: To be the provincial governing body of competitive snowboarding in Prince Edward Island.; *Member of:* Canadian Snowboard Federation
Chief Officer(s): Zak Likely, Contact
zak.likely@gmail.com

Saskatchewan Snowboard Association (SSA)
PO Box 844, Outlook SK S0L 2N0
Tel: 306-867-8489
contact@sasksnowboard.ca
sasksnowboard.ca
Social Media:
www.facebook.com/238209089572128
twitter.com/sasksnowboard
Overview: A small provincial organization
Description: To be the provincial governing body of competitive snowboarding in Saskatchewan.; *Member of:* Canadian Snowboard Federation
Chief Officer(s): Brent Larwood, President
brent@sasksnowboard.ca
Dave Woods, Coordinator, Sport Development
dave@sasksnowboard.ca

Snowboard Association of Manitoba
4180 Henderson Hwy., East St Paul MB R2E 1B4
Overview: A small provincial organization
Description: To be the provincial governing body of competitive snowboarding in Manitoba.; *Member of:* Canadian Snowboard Federation
Chief Officer(s): Glenn Luff, Contact
gkluff@mymts.net

Snowboard Nova Scotia
#311, 5516 Spring Garden Rd., Halifax NS B3J 1G6
Tel: 902-425-5450; *Fax:* 902-425-5606
www.snowboardnovascotia.ca
Social Media:
www.facebook.com/SnowboardNovaScotia
Previous Name: Nova Scotia Snowboard Association
Overview: A small provincial organization
Description: To be the provincial governing body of competitive snowboarding in Nova Scotia.; *Member of:* Canadian Snowboard Federation; Sport Nova Scotia
Chief Officer(s): Karen Chassé, President
benmarc@ns.sympatico.ca
Kristin d'Eon, Technical Director
kdeon@accesswave.ca
Andrew Hayes, Administrative Coordinator
ahayes@sportnovascotia.ca

Snowboard Yukon
YT
info@snowboardyukon.com
www.snowboardyukon.com
Overview: A medium-sized provincial organization
Description: To organize & sanction events, train athletes & coaches, form & administer teams for out of territory competitions, & represent Yukon riders in the Canadian Snowboard Federation.; *Member of:* Canadian Snowboard Federation

Snowmobiles

Alberta Snowmobile Association (ASA)
11759 Groat Rd., Edmonton AB T5M 3K6
Tel: 780-427-2695; *Fax:* 780-415-1779
www.altasnowmobile.ab.ca
Social Media:
www.facebook.com/103977149653938
twitter.com/Altasnowmobile
Overview: A medium-sized provincial organization founded in 1971
Description: To promote safe recreational snowmobiling in the province of Alberta
Affiliation(s): Canadian Council of Snowmobile Organizations
Chief Officer(s): Lyle Birnie, President
ljbirnie@telus.net
Denise England, Vice-President
plasticandpowder@hotmail.com
Membership: *Fees:* $60-$70

British Columbia Snowmobile Federation (BCSF)
PO Box 277, 18 - 1st St., Keremeos BC V0X 1N0
Tel: 250-499-5117; *Fax:* 250-499-2103
Toll-Free: 877-537-8716
office@bcsf.org
www.bcsf.org
Social Media:
instagram.com/bcsnowmobilefederation
www.facebook.com/BCSnowmobileFederation
twitter.com/BCSnowmobile
Overview: A medium-sized provincial organization founded in 1965
Description: To encourage & promote the sport of operating snowmobiles in BC by enhancing cooperation & communication between & among snowmobile clubs, recreation industry & racing divisions, the provincial government, other motorized recreational organizations & groups supportive of snowmobiling; *Member of:* Outdoor Recreation Council of British Columbia; Wilderness Tourism Association; BC Avalanche Association
Affiliation(s): International Snowmobile Council; Canadian Council of Snowmobile Organizations
Chief Officer(s): Richard Cronier, President
president@bcsf.org
Donegal Wilson, Executive Director
Finances: *Annual Operating Budget:* $50,000-$100,000; *Funding Sources:* Membership fees
Staff: 1 staff member(s); 70 volunteer(s)
Membership: 6,000 individual + 70 clubs; *Fees:* Schedule available; *Committees:* Trails; Charities; Safety; Environment; Government Relations; Snow Show
Activities: Tread Lightly Program; Safety Training Program; SnoVision 2000 Program; Exemplary Service Recognition Program; *Awareness Events:* Snowarama (charity ride); *Speaker Service:* Yes; *Rents Mailing List:* Yes

Canadian Council of Snowmobile Organizations (CCSO) / Conseil canadien des organismes de motoneige (CCOM)
PO Box 21059, Thunder Bay ON P7A 8A7
Tel: 807-345-5299
ccso.ccom@tbaytel.net
www.ccso-ccom.ca
Social Media:
www.facebook.com/126035004176384
twitter.com/@ccsosnow
Overview: A large national organization founded in 1974
Description: To provide leadership & support to organized snowmobiling in Canada
Chief Officer(s): Steven McLelan, President
Dennis Burns, Executive Director
Activities: Promoting the welfare & betterment of snowmobile recreational activities; Cooperating with provincial & federal officials, other organizations, & the public on issues affecting snowbiles; Coordinating legislative activities; Promoting a code of ethics for snowmobiling; Completing the Trans-Canadian Snowmobile Trail; *Awareness Events:* National Safety Week, January; Take a Friend Snowmobiling Week, February

Club d'auto-neige Chibougamau inc.
CP 43, Chibougamau QC G8P 2K5
Tél: 418-748-3065
www.motoneigechibougamau.ca
Aperçu: *Dimension:* petite; *Envergure:* locale

Fédération des clubs de motoneigistes du Québec (FCMQ)
CP 1000, Succ. M, 4545, av Pierre-de Coubertin, Montréal QC H1V 3R2
Tél: 514-252-3076; *Téléc:* 514-254-2066
Ligne sans frais: 844-253-4343
info@fcmq.qc.ca
www.fcmq.qc.ca
Média social:
www.facebook.com/FCMQ40
twitter.com/Fed_MotoneigeQc
Aperçu: *Dimension:* moyenne; *Envergure:* provinciale; Organisme sans but lucratif; fondée en 1974
Description: La Fédération des clubs de motoneigistes du Québec est un organisme à but non lucratif, voué au développement et à la promotion de la pratique de la motoneige dans tout le Québec
Membre(s) du bureau directeur: Serge Ritcher, Président
Finances: *Budget de fonctionnement annuel:* $3 Million-$5 Million
Personnel: 10 membre(s) du personnel; 3000 bénévole(s)
Membre: 228; *Montant de la cotisation:* 250$/club

Great Slave Snowmobile Association
4209 - 49A Ave., Yellowknife NT X1A 1B3
Tel: 867-766-4353
Also Known As: GSSA Trail Riders
Overview: A small provincial organization founded in 1988
Description: The Association is a non-profit organization that is dedicated to promoting safe, responsible snowmobiling in Yellowknife.
Affiliation(s): Canadian Council of Snowmobile Organizations; International Snowmobile Council
Chief Officer(s): Bill Braden, President
Finances: *Annual Operating Budget:* Less than $50,000
Staff: 6 volunteer(s)
Membership: 300 individual; *Fees:* $35 single; $50 family

Activities: Community fund-raising; clearing trails; adding signage along trail system

Klondike Snowmobile Association (KSA)
4061 - 4th Ave., Whitehorse YT Y1A 1H1
Tel: 867-667-7680
klonsnow@yknet.ca
www.ksa.yk.ca
Social Media:
www.facebook.com/253094448062816
Overview: A small local organization
Member of: Canadian Council of Snowmobile Organizations
Affiliation(s): Trans Canada Trail - Yukon
Chief Officer(s): Mark Daniels, President
mnd@northwestel.net
Membership: 500; *Fees:* $20 single; $30 family; $100 corporate

Ojibway Power Toboggan Association (OPTA)
PO Box 1466, Sioux Lookout ON P8T 1B9
Tel: 807-737-1976; *Fax:* 807-737-1722
www.opta.ca
Overview: A medium-sized provincial organization
Mission: To keep snowmobile trails in the Sioux Lookout area in good condition and promote safe snowmobiling
Member of: North West Ontario Snowmobile Trails Association; Ontario Federation of Snowmobile Clubs; Sunset Country; Patricia Region Tourist Bureau
Chief Officer(s): Gail Sayers, President
president@opta.ca
Membership: *Committees:* Trails; Membership; Grooming; Safety; Building; Equipment; Signage; Risk Management; STOP
Activities: Training courses; *Awareness Events:* Poker Derby; Snowmobile Raffle; Snowarama

Ontario Federation of Snowmobile Clubs (OFSC)
ON
www.ofsc.on.ca
Social Media:
www.facebook.com/gosnowmobilingontario
twitter.com/GoSnowmobiling
Overview: A medium-sized provincial organization founded in 1966
Description: To support member snowmobile clubs & volunteers; To establish & maintain quality snowmobile trails; To further the enjoyment of organized snowmobiling; *Member of:* Canadian Council of Snowmobile Organizations
Finances: *Funding Sources:* Sale of trail permits; Donations; Sponsorships
Staff: 6 volunteer(s)
Membership: 231 clubs in 17 districts, consisting of 200,000 families; *Member Profile:* Ontario local snowmobile clubs
Activities: Setting policies & procedures; Providing advice to member clubs; Handling trail plans & issues; Promoting concern for the environment & safety; Campaigning to attract new participants

Saskatchewan Snowmobile Association (SSA)
PO Box 533, 221 Centre St., Regina Beach SK S0G 4C0
Tel: 306-729-3500; *Toll-Free:* 800-499-7533
sasksnow@sasktel.net
www.sasksnow.com
Social Media:
www.youtube.com/channel/UC5gfjL3DgXAI3Z7te4leEuA
www.facebook.com/sask.snow
twitter.com/sasksnow
Previous Name: Saskatchewan Snow Vehicles Association
Overview: A medium-sized provincial organization founded in 1971
Description: To promote the benefits of snowmobiling & increase access & participation; To provide leadership & support to members; To establish & maintain safe, high quality trails; To provide support to club development; *Member of:* International Snowmobile Council; Canadian Council of Snowmobile Organizations
Finances: *Funding Sources:* Membership dues; Saskatchewan Lotteries
Staff: 20 volunteer(s)
Membership: 5,000; *Fees:* Schedule available; *Committees:* Membership; Raffles; Rallies; Grants; Equipment; Safety; Trails

Snowmobilers Association of Nova Scotia (SANS)
5516 Spring Garden Rd., 4th Fl., Halifax NS B3J 3G6
Tel: 902-425-5450; *Fax:* 902-425-5606
www.snowmobilersns.com
Overview: A small provincial organization founded in 1976
Description: To provide leadership & support to member snowmobile clubs so that they may enjoy quality recreational snowmobiling opportunities on a province-wide network of safe & well-developed snowmobile trails
Chief Officer(s): Mike Eddy, General Manager, 902-425-5450 360
Martha Dunlop, Manager, Finance & Administration, 902-425-5450 324
Membership: 21 member clubs; *Member Profile:* Snowmobile clubs

Snowmobilers of Manitoba Inc.
2121 Henderson Hwy., Winnipeg MB R2G 1P8
Tel: 204-940-7533; *Fax:* 204-940-7531
info@snoman.mb.ca
www.snoman.mb.ca
Social Media:
www.facebook.com/SnomanInc
Also Known As: Snoman
Overview: A small provincial organization founded in 1975
Description: To provide strong leadership & support to member clubs; to develop & maintain safe & environmentally responsible snowmobile trails; to further the enjoyment of organized snowmobiling throughout Manitoba
Affiliation(s): Canadian Council of Snowmobile Organizations
Chief Officer(s): Yvonne Rideout, Executive Director
execdirector@snoman.mb.ca
Finances: *Annual Operating Budget:* $500,000-$1.5 Million
Staff: 2 staff member(s); 2500 volunteer(s)
Membership: 2,500; *Fees:* $150

Thunder Bay Adventure Trails
PO Box 29190, Thunder Bay ON P7B 6P9
Toll-Free: 800-526-7522
tbat_den@hotmail.com
Overview: A medium-sized local organization founded in 1990
Description: To groom & maintain 700 kilometres of snowmobile trails, from Thunder Bay to Shabaqua; *Member of:* North Superior Snowmobile Association (NOSSA)
Chief Officer(s): Marcel Gauthier, Club Executive
Lloyd Chaykowski, Club Executive
Harold Harkonen, Club Executive
Bradley Pollock, Club Executive
Membership: *Fees:* $200-before Dec.1; $250-after Dec.1; $100-3-day permit; $140-7-day permit; $125-classic permit

Soaring

Alberni Valley Soaring Association
8064 Richards Trail, Duncan BC V9L 6B2
Toll-Free: 866-590-7627
info@avsa.ca
www.avsa.ca
Social Media:
www.facebook.com/AlberniValleySoaringAssociation
Overview: A small local organization
Description: To offer opportunities to fly to its members & guests; *Member of:* Soaring Association of Canada
Affiliation(s): Vancouver Island Soaring Centre; Vancouver Soaring Association
Membership: *Fees:* Schedule available

Alberta Soaring Council
PO Box 13, Black Diamond AB T0L 0H0
Tel: 403-813-6658
asc@stade.ca
www.soaring.ab.ca
Social Media:
www.facebook.com/AlbertaSoaringCouncil
Overview: A medium-sized provincial organization founded in 1966
Description: To promote soaring sports provincially in all aspects; To plan & support local & provincial events & national competitions; *Member of:* Aero Club of Canada
Chief Officer(s): Phil Stade, Executive Director
asc@stade.ca
Membership: 5 member associations
Activities:; *Library:* Yes

Association de vol à voile Champlain
10, 745 de Martigny, Montréal QC H2B 2N1
Tél: 450-771-0500
info@avvc.qc.ca
www.avvc.qc.ca
Aperçu: *Dimension:* petite; *Envergure:* locale; Organisme sans but lucratif
Description: Former des pilotes de planeur et les amener au niveau du vol voyage; répondre aux attentes de ses membres actifs; *Membre de:* Soaring Association of Canada
Montant de la cotisation: 620$

Base Borden Soaring (BBSG)
PO Box 286, Borden ON L0M 1C0
Tel: 705-424-1200
ourplace@csolve.net
users.csolve.net/~ourplace/contents.htm
Overview: A small local organization founded in 1974
Member of: Soaring Association of Canada
Chief Officer(s): Ray Leiska
Membership: *Fees:* $50

Bonnechere Soaring Club
ON
Tel: 613-584-4636
Overview: A small local organization
Member of: Soaring Association of Canada

Central Alberta Gliding Club
Netook Airport, Olds AB
www.cagcsoaring.ca
Overview: A small local organization founded in 1989
Description: To train pilots for glider licences; To create opportunities for glider pilots to fly club-owned aircraft; *Member of:* Alberta Soaring Council; Innisfail Flying Club; Soaring Association of Canada
Chief Officer(s): Leo Deschamps, President
president@cagcsoaring.ca
Finances: *Funding Sources:* Membership dues

Club de vol à voile de Québec
CP 9276, Sainte-Foy QC G1V 4B1
Tél: 418-337-4905
www.cvvq.net
Média social:
www.facebook.com/CVVQPlaneur
twitter.com/Planeur_Quebec
Aperçu: *Dimension:* petite; *Envergure:* locale; fondée en 1954
Description: Les principaux objectifs de notre association sont de fournir une plate-forme d'opération sécuritaire pour la pratique de notre sport et d'offrir une formation de qualité à de nouveaux adeptes qui se joignent à nous.
Membre(s) du bureau directeur: Pierre Beaulieu, Président
Montant de la cotisation: Barème; *Comités:* Aménagement; Planification de la flotte; Recrutement

Cu Nim Gliding Club
PO Box 17, #11, RR#1, Okotoks AB T1S 1A1
Tel: 403-938-2796
www.cunim.org
Overview: A small local organization
Member of: Soaring Association of Canada
Affiliation(s): Alberta Soaring Council
Chief Officer(s): Pablo Wainstein, President
Finances: *Annual Operating Budget:* $50,000-$100,000
Staff: 6 volunteer(s)
Membership: 60; *Fees:* $450

Edmonton Soaring Club (ESC)
Chipman AB
Tel: 780-363-3860
info@edmontonsoaringclub.com
www.edmontonsoaringclub.com
Overview: A small local organization founded in 1957
Description: To promote soaring & provide enthusiasts with the means to practice soaring; *Member of:* Soaring Association of Canada
Affiliation(s): Alberta Soaring Council; other soaring clubs
Membership: *Fees:* Schedule available
Activities: Flying gliders; teaching how to fly; expeditions; social events

Erin Soaring Society
ON
Overview: A small local organization

Gatineau Gliding Club (GGC)
PO Box 8145, Stn. T, Ottawa ON K1G 3H6
Tel: 613-673-5386
ggc@gatineauglidingclub.ca
www.gatineauglidingclub.ca
Overview: A small local organization
Member of: Soaring Association of Canada
Membership: 100

Grande Prairie Soaring Society
PO Box 64, Hythe AB T0H 2C0
www.gpsoaringsociety.ca
Overview: A small local organization
Member of: Soaring Association of Canada
Chief Officer(s): Dwayne Doll, President
dddoll.canada@gmail.com
Lloyd Sherk, Secretary-Treasurer
lsherk@telusplanet.net

London Soaring Club
315816 - 31st Line, Embro ON N0J 1J0
Tel: 519-661-7844
info@londonsoaringclub.ca
www.londonsoaringclub.ca
Social Media:
www.facebook.com/124146337603689
twitter.com/Londonsoaring
Overview: A small local organization
Member of: Soaring Association of Canada

Manitoba Soaring Council
200 Main St., Winnipeg MB R3C 4M2
www.wgc.mb.ca/msc/Manitoba_Soaring_Council_Home_Page.htm
Overview: A small provincial organization founded in 1970
Description: To foster the art of soaring as an environmentally friendly safe & competitive life sport accessible to all Manitobans
Membership: 1,000-4,999

Montréal Soaring Council (MSC) / Club de Vol à Voile MSC
PO Box 147, Montréal QC H4L 4V4
Tel: 613-632-5438
info@montrealsoaring.ca
montrealsoaring.com
Social Media:
www.facebook.com/montrealsoaring
twitter.com/MontrealSoaring
Overview: A small local organization founded in 1946
Description: To promote the sport of soaring & gliding, including the provision of gliding training; *Member of:* Soaring Association of Canada
Chief Officer(s): Kurt Sermeus, Vice-President, 514-919-7374
Finances: *Annual Operating Budget:* $100,000-$250,000
Staff: 11 staff member(s); 30 volunteer(s)
Membership: 100; *Fees:* Schedule available; *Member Profile:* Open to individuals interested in soaring

Prince Albert Gliding & Soaring Club (PAG&SC)
219 Scissons Ct., Saskatoon SK S7S 1B7
Tel: 306-789-1535; *Fax:* 306-792-2532
soar@soar.sk.ca
www.soar.sk.ca/pagsc
Overview: A small local organization founded in 1986
Description: To foster the sport of soaring
Affiliation(s): Soaring Association of Saskatchewan; Soaring Association of Canada
Chief Officer(s): Keith Andrews, President, 306-249-1859
k.andrews@sk.sympatico.ca
Rob Lohmaier, Treasurer, 306-764-7381
Finances: *Funding Sources:* Annual membership dues; Launch fees; Glider rental fees
Membership: 15; *Fees:* $85 youth; $170 regular
Activities: Promoting the sport of soaring; Providing flying activities; Offering flight instruction

Regina Gliding & Soaring Club
PO Box 4093, Regina SK S4P 3W5
Tel: 306-536-4119
fly@soar.regina.sk.ca
www.soar.regina.sk.ca
Overview: A small local organization
Member of: Soaring Association of Canada; soaring Association of Saskatchewan
Membership: *Fees:* $55-$390

Rideau Valley Soaring
PO Box 1164, Manotick ON K4M 1A9
Tel: 613-366-8208
club.pres@rvss.ca
rvss.ca
Social Media:
www.facebook.com/200156480081876
twitter.com/rvssca
Overview: A small local organization
Member of: Soaring Association of Canada
Affiliation(s): Gatineau Gliding Club; Montreal Soaring Club
Chief Officer(s): George Domaradzki, President & Chief Flight Instructor
club.pres@rvss.ca
Membership: *Fees:* $715 adult ($506 for additional spouse); $375 junior; $345 youth; $546 tow pilot/self launch

Saskatoon Soaring Club
510 Cynthia St., Saskatoon SK S7L 7K7
saskatoonsoaringclub@gmail.com
www.soar.sk.ca/ssc
Overview: A small local organization
Description: To promote the sport of gliding and soaring in Saskatoon.; *Member of:* Soaring Association of Canada

Soaring Association of Canada (SAC) / Association canadienne de vol à voile (ACVV)
c/o COPA National Office, #903, 75 Albert St., Ottawa ON K1P 5E7
Tel: 613-236-4901; *Fax:* 613-236-8646
sacoffice@sac.ca
www.sac.ca
Social Media:
twitter.com/canglide
Overview: A medium-sized national organization founded in 1945
Description: To promote, enhance & protect the sport of soaring in Canada; To provide information & services to the soaring community: licensing, medical requirements for glider pilots, aircraft certification, technical issues, courses & training, insurance plan, & services to clubs
Affiliation(s): Aero Club of Canada; International Gliding Commission of the Fédération Aéronautique Internationale
Chief Officer(s): Sylvain Bourque, President & Director, Eastern Zone
bourques@videotron.ca
Finances: *Funding Sources:* Membership fees; Sales; Donations
Staff: 40 volunteer(s)
Membership: 1,500 club affiliates; *Fees:* Schedule available; *Committees:* Air Cadets; Airspace; Archives/Historian; Contest Letters; FAI Awards; FAI Records; Fit Training & Safety; Free Flight; Insurance; Medical; Technical; Trophy Claims; World Contest; Flight Records
Activities:; *Library:* Yes (Open to Public) by appointment

SOSA Gliding Club
PO Box 81, Rockton ON L0R 1X0
Tel: 519-740-9328
sosa@sosaglidingclub.com
www.sosaglidingclub.com
Social Media:
www.facebook.com/groups/2228522913
twitter.com/sosaglidingclub
Overview: A small local organization
Member of: Soaring Association of Canada

Toronto Soaring Club
ON
www.toronto-soaring.ca
Social Media:
www.facebook.com/TheTorontoSoaringClub
Overview: A small local organization
Member of: Soaring Association of Canada
Chief Officer(s): David Cole, President
dmcole1212@gmail.com

Vancouver Soaring Association
PO Box 3251, Vancouver BC V6B 3X9
Tel: 604-869-7211
vancouversoaring@gmail.com
vancouversoaring.com
Social Media:
www.flickr.com/photos/128138428@N03
www.facebook.com/148597568530530
twitter.com/vancouversoaring
Overview: A small local organization
Member of: Soaring Association of Canada

Winnipeg Gliding Club (WGC)
PO Box 1255, Winnipeg MB R3C 2Y4
Tel: 204-735-2868
info@wgc.mb.ca
www.wgc.mb.ca
Overview: A small local organization
Description: The Winnipeg Gliding Club is a non-profit organization dedicated to the promotion of gliding and soaring; *Member of:* Soaring Association of Canada
Membership: 70; *Fees:* $25-$450

York Soaring Association
Airfield, 7296, 5th Line, RR#1, Belwood ON NOB 1J0
Tel: 519-848-3621
www.yorksoaring.com
Social Media:
www.facebook.com/yorksa
Overview: A small local organization founded in 1961
Member of: Soaring Association of Canada
Chief Officer(s): Jim Fryett, President
Finances: *Annual Operating Budget:* $250,000-$500,000
Staff: 10 volunteer(s)
Membership: 100-499
Activities: Soaring & gliding facilities; advanced training of glider pilots

Soccer

Airdrie & District Soccer Association
Genesis Pl., 800 East Lake Blvd., Airdrie AB T4A 0H6
Tel: 403-948-6260; *Fax:* 403-948-6290
admin@airdriesoccer.com
airdriesoccer.com
Social Media:
www.facebook.com/airdriesoccerassociation
Overview: A small local organization
Member of: Alberta Soccer Association
Chief Officer(s): Steve Thomas, Technical Director
td@airdriesoccer.com
Juliet Smith, Office Manager/Registrar
manager@airdriesoccer.com
Membership: *Fees:* Schedule available

Alberta Soccer Association (ASA)
9023 - 111 Ave., Edmonton AB T5B 0C3
Tel: 780-474-2200; *Fax:* 780-474-6300
Toll-Free: 866-250-2200
office@albertasoccer.com
www.albertasoccer.com
Social Media:
www.youtube.com/SoccerAlberta
twitter.com/AlbertaSoccer
Overview: A large provincial organization founded in 1909
Description: To govern & promote the sport of soccer in Alberta; *Member of:* Canadian Soccer Association
Chief Officer(s): Ole Jacobsen, President
jacobsen5@shaw.ca
Richard Adams, Executive Director, 780-378-8108 230
execdir@albertasoccer.com
Anthony Traficante, Operations Officer, 780-378-8101 221
operations@albertasoccer.com
Carmen Charron, Coordinator, Program, 780-378-8104 225
programs@albertasoccer.com
Membership: 90,000; *Committees:* Constitution & By-Laws; Technical; Competitions; Referee Development; Appeals & Discipline; Development of Women in Soccer

Australian Football League Ontario (AFLO)
The Exchange Tower, PO Box 99, #3680, 130 King St. West, Toronto ON M5X 1B1
Tel: 416-304-0032
exec@aflontario.com
www.aflontario.com
Social Media:
www.youtube.com/channel/UC0FrzrNpBBtFdZAVYjKxbTA
www.facebook.com/AFLOntario
twitter.com/AFLOntario
Also Known As: AFL Ontario
Overview: A medium-sized provincial organization founded in 1989
Description: To organize amateur Australian football competitions in Ontario & Québec.; *Member of:* AFL Canada
Chief Officer(s): Martin Walter, President
Membership: 11 clubs

Battle River Soccer Association
PO Box 5558, Leduc AB T9E 2A1
Tel: 780-717-1962
admin@battleriversoccer.com
www.battleriversoccer.com
Overview: A small local organization founded in 1983
Description: Physical office address: Quality Inn, #116, 501 - 11th Ave., Nisku, AB T9E 7N5; *Member of:* Alberta Soccer Association; Federation Internationale de Football Association; Canada Soccer Association
Affiliation(s): Breton Soccer Association; Calmar Soccer Association; Devon Soccer Association; Leduc Soccer Association; Millet Soccer Association; New Sarepta Soccer Association; Pigeon Lake Soccer Association; Thorsby Soccer Association; Warburg Soccer Association; Wetaskiwin Soccer Association
Chief Officer(s): Craig Cooper, President
ck_cooper@yahoo.ca
Sara Letourneau, Office Administrator
Membership: 3,000 players in 10 associations; *Committees:* Human Resources; Bylaw Reviewl Financial Policy; IT

BC Soccer Referees Association
8130 Selkirk St., Vancouver BC V6P 4H7
bcreferees@gmail.com
www.bcsra.com
Social Media:
www.facebook.com/BcSoccerRefereesAssociation
Overview: A small provincial organization

Description: To support referees in the province of British Columbia.
Chief Officer(s): Chris Wattam, President
chris.wattam@shaw.ca
Membership: *Fees:* $10 (18 & under); $25 (19 & over)

British Columbia Soccer Association
#250, 3410 Lougheed Hwy., Vancouver BC V5M 2A4
Tel: 604-299-6401; *Fax:* 604-299-9610
info@bcsoccer.net
www.bcsoccer.net
Social Media:
twitter.com/1bcsoccer
Overview: A medium-sized provincial organization founded in 1907
Description: To promote & develop the sport of soccer in British Columbia; *Member of:* Canadian Soccer Association
Chief Officer(s): Jason Elligott, Executive Director
jasonelligott@bcsoccer.net

Calgary Minor Soccer Association (CSMA)
#7, 6991 - 48 St. SE, Calgary AB T2C 5A4
Tel: 403-279-8686; *Fax:* 403-236-3669
info@calgaryminorsoccer.com
calgaryminorsoccer.com
Social Media:
instagram.com/calgaryminorsoccer
www.facebook.com/calgaryminorsoccer
twitter.com/cmsasoccer
Overview: A small local organization
Member of: Alberta Soccer Association
Chief Officer(s): Daryl Leinweber, Executive Director, 403-279-8686 1007
execdirector@calgaryminorsoccer.com
Cory Letendre, Manager, 403-279-8686 1002
operations@calgaryminorsoccer.com
Melissa Collinson, League Director, 403-279-8686 1003
leagues@calgaryminorsoccer.com

Calgary Soccer Federation
Calgary Soccer Centre, 7000 - 48 St. SE, Calgary AB T2C 4E1
Tel: 403-279-8453; *Fax:* 403-279-8796
www.calgarysoccerfederation.com
Social Media:
www.facebook.com/calgarysoccerfederation
twitter.com/calgarysoccer1
Overview: A small local organization
Member of: Alberta Soccer Association

Calgary United Soccer Association
#183, 2880 Glenmore Trail SE, Calgary AB T2C 2E7
Tel: 403-270-0363; *Fax:* 403-270-0573
info@cusa.ab.ca
www.cusa.ab.ca
Social Media:
www.facebook.com/CalgaryUnitedSoccerAssociation
twitter.com/cusa_events
Overview: A small local organization
Member of: Alberta Soccer Association
Chief Officer(s): Pearl Doupe, Executive Director, 403-648-0861
pearl@cusa.ab.ca

Calgary Women's Soccer Association (CWSA)
#110, 4441 - 76 Ave. SE, Calgary AB T2C 2G8
Tel: 403-720-6692; *Fax:* 403-720-6693
office@mycwsa.ca
www.womensoccer.ab.ca
Social Media:
www.facebook.com/124525960988252
Overview: A small local organization
Member of: Alberta Soccer Association
Chief Officer(s): Jacquie Herltein, Executive Director
execdir@mycwsa.ca

Canadian Soccer Association (CSA) / Association canadienne de soccer
Place Soccer Canada, 237 Metcalfe St., Ottawa ON K2P 1R2
Tel: 613-237-7678; *Fax:* 613-237-1516
info@soccercan.ca
www.canadasoccer.com
Social Media:
www.youtube.com/CanadaSoccerTV
www.facebook.com/canadasoccer
twitter.com/CanadaSoccerEN
Overview: A large national organization founded in 1912
Description: To promote the growth & development of soccer for all Canadians at all levels; to provide leadership & good governance for the sport
Affiliation(s): Féderation Internationale de Football Association, FIFA; Football Confederation; Canadian Olympic Association
Chief Officer(s): Victor Montagliani, President
Peter Montopoli, General Secretary
Earl Cochrane, Deputy General Secretary
Sean Hefferman, CFO
Ray Clark, Director, Coaching & Player Development
rclark@canadasoccer.com
Cathy Breda, Manager, Administration
cbreda@soccercan.ca
Michèle Dion, Acting Director, Communications
mdion@soccercan.ca
Membership: 850,000 registered players

Central Alberta Soccer Association (CASA)
4108A - 60 St., Camrose AB T4V 3G7
Fax: 780-672-4224
casa9@telus.net
www.central-alta-soccer.ca
Overview: A small local organization
Member of: Alberta Soccer Association
Chief Officer(s): David McCarthy, Techncial Director
davidmccarthy.coach@gmail.com

Edmonton District Soccer Association (EDSA)
17415 - 106A Ave., Edmonton AB T5S 1M7
Tel: 780-413-0140; *Fax:* 780-481-4619
www.edsa.org
Social Media:
www.facebook.com/99060275311
twitter.com/EdmontonSoccer
Overview: A small local organization
Chief Officer(s): Mike Thome, Executive Director, 780-413-0140 8

Edmonton Interdistrict Youth Soccer Association (EIYSA)
#307, 8925 - 51 Ave., Edmonton AB T5E 5J3
Tel: 780-462-3537; *Fax:* 780-444-4321
admin@eiysa.com
www.eiysa.com
Overview: A small local organization
Member of: Alberta Soccer Association
Chief Officer(s): Barrie White, President & COO
exdir@eiysa.com
Membership: 11 teams

Edmonton Minor Soccer Association (EMSA)
Edmonton South Soccer Centre, 6520 Roper Rd., Edmonton AB T6B 3K8
Tel: 780-413-3672; *Fax:* 780-490-1652
edmontonsoccer.com
Social Media:
instagram.com/emsamain
www.facebook.com/254791561239153
twitter.com/EMSAmain
Overview: A small local organization
Member of: Alberta Soccer Association
Membership: 89 teams

Fédération de soccer du Québec (FDSDQ)
#210, 955, av Bois-de-Boulogne, Laval QC H7N 4G1
Tél: 450-975-3355
courriel@federation-soccer.qc.ca
www.federation-soccer.qc.ca
Média social:
www.youtube.com/user/FederationSoccerQC
www.facebook.com/SoccerQuebec
twitter.com/SoccerQuebec
Également appelé: Soccer Québec
Nom précédent: Fédération québécoise de soccer football
Aperçu: *Dimension:* grande; *Envergure:* provinciale; fondée en 1911
Membre de: Canadian Soccer Association
Finances: *Fonds:* Société de Promotion du Soccer
Membre: 82 000; *Comités:* Exécutif; Compétitions; Provincial Arbitrage; Technique

Fort McMurray Youth Soccer Association (FMYSA)
PO Box 10, 8115 Franklin Ave., Fort McMurray AB T9H 2H7
Tel: 780-791-7090; *Fax:* 780-791-1446
fmysa@shaw.ca
www.fmyouthsoccer.com
Overview: A small local organization
Member of: Alberta Soccer Association
Chief Officer(s): Ian Diaz, Technical Director
fmysatechnicaldirector@gmail.com
Bill Carr, President
president.fmysa@shaw.ca

Halifax County United Soccer Club
#7, 102 Chain Lake Dr., Halifax NS B3S 1A7
Tel: 902-876-8784; *Fax:* 902-446-3620
info@hcusoccer.ca
www.hcusoccer.ca
Overview: A medium-sized local organization founded in 1998
Description: To foster a love of soccer & help individuals of all ages achieve their full potential.
Membership: 1,600 players; *Fees:* Schedule available

Lakeland District Soccer Association (LDSA)
PO Box 4801, Bonnyville AB T9N 0H2
Tel: 780-201-4346
lakelandsoccer.ca
Overview: A small local organization
Member of: Alberta Soccer Association
Chief Officer(s): Kristy L'Hirondelle, Executive Director
execdir@lakelandsoccer.ca
Membership: 1-99

Lethbridge Soccer Association
2501 - 28 St. South, Lethbridge AB T1K 7L6
Tel: 403-320-5425; *Fax:* 403-327-5847
lethbridgesoccer.com
Social Media:
www.facebook.com/LethbridgeSoccerAssociation
twitter.com/LethSoccer
Overview: A small local organization
Member of: Alberta Soccer Association
Chief Officer(s): Steven Dudas, General Manager
steve@lethbridgesoccer.com

Medicine Hat Soccer Association
#101, 533 - 2nd St. East, Medicine Hat AB T1A 0C5
Tel: 403-529-6931; *Fax:* 403-526-6590
mhsa@telusplanet.net
www.medicinehatsoccer.com
Social Media:
www.facebook.com/medicinehatsoccer
twitter.com/mhsasoccer
Overview: A small local organization founded in 1971
Member of: Alberta Soccer Association
Chief Officer(s): Jeff Vangen, President
Heather Bach, Director, Communications
Membership: 2,700

Newfoundland & Labrador Soccer Association
39 Churchill Ave., St. John's NL A1A 0H7
Tel: 709-576-0601; *Fax:* 709-576-0588
info@nlsa.ca
www.nlsa.ca
Previous Name: Newfoundland Soccer Association
Overview: A large provincial organization
Description: To provide opportunities for the general public to engage in the game of soccer while having fun & competition; *Member of:* Canadian Soccer Association
Chief Officer(s): Doug Redmond, President
Dragan Mirkovic, Director, Technical, 709-576-2262
dragan@nlsa.ca
Mike Power, Director & Staff Coach, Player Development, 709-576-7310
mike@nlsa.ca
Rob Comerford, Manager, Business, 709-576-0601
rob@nlsa.ca

Northwest Peace Soccer Association (NWPSA)
11727 - 88A St., Grande Prairie AB T8X 1L8
Tel: 780-832-1627
nwpsoccer@gmail.com
www.northwestpeacesoccer.ca
Overview: A small local organization
Member of: Alberta Soccer Association

Northwest Territories Soccer Association (NWTSA)
PO Box 11089, Yellowknife NT X1A 3X7
Tel: 867-669-8396; *Fax:* 867-669-8327
Toll-Free: 800-661-0797
www.nwtkicks.ca
Social Media:
www.facebook.com/NWTSoccerAssociation
twitter.com/NwtSoccer
Overview: A medium-sized provincial organization
Description: The NWT Soccer Association is a volunteer-run organization & the governing body for all soccer activities in the NWT; focus is on the grassroots development of the game, as well as the promotion of high performance. Physical delivery address: c/o Sport North Federation, 4908 - 49th St., 1st Fl., Yellowknife, NT X1A 2N4; *Member of:* Canadian Soccer Association
Affiliation(s): Sport North Federation
Chief Officer(s): Ollie Williams, President
Lyric Sandhals, Executive Director

Finances: *Funding Sources:* Operates on Sport Lottery funding
Activities: Summer camps; leagues & tournaments; developmental clinics

Ontario Soccer Association (OSA)
7601 Martin Grove Rd., Vaughan ON L4L 9E4
Tel: 905-264-9390; *Fax:* 905-264-9445
www.soccer.on.ca
Social Media:
www.youtube.com/OSAVideoMaster
www.facebook.com/TheOntarioSoccerAssociation
twitter.com/OSA_Tweeter
Overview: A medium-sized provincial organization founded in 1901
Description: To provide leadership & support for the advancement of soccer; To provide programs & services; *Member of:* Canadian Soccer Association
Chief Officer(s): Ron Smale, President
Lisa Beatty, Executive Director
lbeatty@soccer.on.ca
Membership: 500,000 players; 70,000 coaches; 10,000 referees; *Committees:* Discipline & Appeals; Competitions; Information Management System Oversight; League Management; Referee Development; Technical Advisory; Women in Soccer; Rules Review; Audit; Executive; Finance; Governance; Human Resources; Nominations; Risk Management; Strategic Planning

Prince Edward Island Soccer Association (PEISA)
40 Enman Cres., Charlottetown PE C1E 1E6
Tel: 902-368-6251; *Fax:* 902-569-7693
admin@peisoccer.com
www.peisoccer.com
Social Media:
www.facebook.com/197098723677560
twitter.com/peisoccerassoc
Overview: A medium-sized provincial organization founded in 1979
Description: To promote & regulate soccer in PEI; to provide competitive opportunities for members.; *Member of:* Canadian Soccer Association; Sport PEI
Chief Officer(s): Peter Wolters, Executive Director
Jonathan Vos, Technical Director
jvos@peisoccer.com
Finances: *Annual Operating Budget:* $250,000-$500,000
Staff: 1 staff member(s)
Membership: 6,000 individual + 14 clubs; *Fees:* Schedule available

Red Deer City Soccer Association
6905 Edgar Industrial Dr., Red Deer AB T4P 3R2
Tel: 403-346-4259; *Fax:* 403-340-1044
office@rdcsa.com
www.rdcsa.com
Social Media:
www.facebook.com/RedDeerCitySoccerAssociation
twitter.com/RDCSA
Overview: A small local organization
Member of: Alberta Soccer Association
Chief Officer(s): Joan Van Wolde, Administrator
Ado Sarcevic, Manager, Soccer Operations
asarcevic@rdcsa.com

St. Albert Soccer Association (SASA)
61 Riel Dr., St. Albert AB T8N 3Z3
Tel: 780-458-8973; *Fax:* 780-458-8994
www.stalbertsoccer.com
Overview: A small local organization
Member of: Alberta Soccer Association
Chief Officer(s): Chris Spaidal, Executive Director, 780-458-8973 127
chris@stalbertsoccer.com

Saskatchewan Soccer Association Inc. (SSA)
SaskSport Administration Bldg., 1870 Lorne St., Regina SK S4P 2L7
Tel: 306-780-9225; *Fax:* 306-780-9480
www.sasksoccer.com
Social Media:
www.youtube.com/SaskatchewanSoccer
www.facebook.com/SaskatchewanSoccer
twitter.com/SaskSoccerAssoc
Overview: A medium-sized provincial organization founded in 1906
Member of: Canadian Soccer Association
Chief Officer(s): Doug Pederson, Executive Director, 306-780-9225 4
d.pederson@sasksoccer.com
Membership: 33,000
Activities: *Internships:* Yes

Sherwood Park District Soccer Association
Millenium Pl., #131.2, 2000 Premier Way, Sherwood Park AB T8H 2G4
Tel: 780-449-1343; *Fax:* 780-464-5821
www.spdsa.net
Social Media:
www.facebook.com/416487478408692
twitter.com/SPDSASoccer
Overview: A small local organization founded in 1976
Member of: Alberta Soccer Association; Federation Internationale de Football Association; Canada Soccer Association
Affiliation(s): Breton Soccer Association; Calmar Soccer Association; Devon Soccer Association; Leduc Soccer Association; Millet Soccer Association; New Sarepta Soccer Association; Pigeon Lake Soccer Association; Thorsby Soccer Association; Warburg Soccer Association; Wetaskiwin Soccer Association
Chief Officer(s): Debbie Ballam, General Manager
d.ballam@spdsa.net
Membership: 3,000 players in 10 associations; *Committees:* Human Resources; Bylaw Reviewl Finance Policy; IT

Soccer New Brunswick
#2, 125 Russ Howard Dr., Moncton NB E1C 0L7
Tel: 506-830-4762; *Fax:* 506-382-5621
admin@soccernb.org
www.soccernb.org
Social Media:
www.facebook.com/SoccerNb
twitter.com/SoccerNB
Also Known As: Soccer NB
Overview: A medium-sized provincial organization founded in 1965
Description: To foster & promote the development & growth of the sport of soccer in New Brunswick & to assure equitable accessibility through quality programs; *Member of:* Canadian Soccer Association
Chief Officer(s): Younes Bouida, Executive Director & Director, Technical Development, 506-830-4762 2
younes@soccernb.org
Finances: *Annual Operating Budget:* $500,000-$1.5 Million; *Funding Sources:* Government; membership
Staff: 2 staff member(s); 9 volunteer(s)
Membership: 16,500

Soccer Nova Scotia (SNS)
210 Thomas Raddall Dr., Halifax NS B3S 1K3
Tel: 902-445-0265; *Fax:* 902-445-0258
admin@soccerns.ns.ca
www.soccerns.ns.ca
Social Media:
www.youtube.com/user/SoccerNovaScotia
www.facebook.com/pages/Soccer-Nova-Scotia/290512917639108
twitter.com/SoccerNS
Overview: A medium-sized provincial organization founded in 1913
Description: To promote the sport of soccer in Nova Scotia; To provide information & resources to aid player training, coaching education, & referee programs; *Member of:* Canadian Soccer Association
Chief Officer(s): George Athanasiou, Chief Executive Officer
ceo@soccerns.ns.ca
Carman King, Officer, Referee Development
ref.services@soccerns.ns.ca
Membership: 27,000+ players; 2,500+ coaches; 700+ referees

Sunny South District Soccer Association
RR#8, Site 34, Comp 0, Lethbridge AB T1J 4P4
Tel: 403-894-2277
www.sunnysouthsoccer.com
Overview: A small local organization
Member of: Alberta Soccer Association
Chief Officer(s): Paul Anwender, Executive Director
paul.anwender@gmail.com

Tri-County Soccer Association
c/o Fran Glenn, President, 9904 - 109 St., Fort Saskatchewan AB T8L 2K2
tricounty.district@yahoo.ca
www.tricountysoccer.net
Overview: A small local organization
Member of: Alberta Soccer Association
Chief Officer(s): Fran Glenn, President
tricouny.president@yahoo.ca

Whitehorse Minor Soccer Association (WMS)
4061 - 4th Ave., Whitehorse YT Y1A 1H1
Tel: 867-667-2445
yukonsoccer@sportyukon.com
www.yukonsoccer.yk.ca/whitehorseminorsoccer.html
Overview: A medium-sized provincial organization founded in 1977
Member of: Sport Yukon
Chief Officer(s): Cali Battersby, Sport Administrator

Women's Soccer Association of Lethbridge (WSAL)
4401 University Dr., Lethbridge AB T1K 3M4
Tel: 403-329-2232
www.losa.ca
Social Media:
twitter.com/wsal_soccer
Overview: A small local organization founded in 2001
Chief Officer(s): Ilsa Wong, President

Yukon Soccer Association
4061 - 4th Ave., Whitehorse YT Y1A 1H1
Tel: 867-633-4625; *Fax:* 867-667-4237
yukonsoccer@sportyukon.com
www.yukonsoccer.yk.ca
Overview: A small provincial organization
Description: The Yukon Soccer Association is the sport governing body for the sport of soccer in the Yukon Territory. It is a volunteer based organization that coordinates & administers various programs devoted to the promotion & development of soccer.; *Member of:* Canadian Soccer Association
Chief Officer(s): Cali Battersby, Sport Administrator
John MacPhail, Technical Director
jmac@sportyukon.com

Softball

Alberta Amateur Softball Association (AASA)
9860 - 33 Ave., Edmonton AB T6N 1C6
Tel: 780-461-7735; *Fax:* 780-461-7757
info@softballalberta.ca
www.softballalberta.ca
Social Media:
www.facebook.com/238456432957672
Also Known As: Softball Alberta
Overview: A large provincial organization founded in 1971
Description: To foster & promote the playing of amateur softball; to regulate play in all classifications of the game as may be deemed in its best interests; *Member of:* Canadian Amateur Softball Association
Affiliation(s): Western Canada Softball Association
Chief Officer(s): Michele Patry, Executive Director
michele@softballalberta.ca
Finances: *Funding Sources:* Alberta Sport, Recreation & Parks; Wildlife Foundation
Staff: 4 staff member(s)
Activities: *Internships:* Yes; *Speaker Service:* Yes; *Library:* Yes (Open to Public)

British Columbia Amateur Softball Association (BCASA)
#201, 8889 Walnut Grove Dr., Langley BC V1M 2N7
Tel: 604-371-0302; *Fax:* 604-371-0344
info@softball.bc.ca
www.softball.bc.ca
Social Media:
www.facebook.com/softball.bc
Also Known As: Softball BC
Overview: A medium-sized provincial organization
Description: To promote, govern & build the sport of Softball in British Columbia; *Member of:* Canadian Amateur Softball Association
Chief Officer(s): Rick Benson, Chief Operating Officer
rbenson@softball.bc.ca
Jeana Boyd, Coordinator, Programs
programcoordinator@softball.bc.ca
Membership: *Fees:* Schedule available; *Member Profile:* Softball players, coaches, umpires

Canadian Amateur Softball Association
#212, 223 Colonnade Rd., Ottawa ON K2E 7K3
Tel: 613-523-3386; *Fax:* 613-523-5761
info@softball.ca
www.softball.ca
Social Media:
plus.google.com/108685588748854542444
www.facebook.com/SoftballCanadaNSO
twitter.com/softballcanada
Also Known As: Softball Canada
Overview: A medium-sized national organization founded in 1965
Description: To develop & promote softball in Canada
Chief Officer(s): Kevin Quinn, President, 902-368-3024
kevin.quinn1@pei.sympatico.ca
Hugh Mitchener, CEO, 613-523-3386 3106
hmitchener@softball.ca
Membership: 13 provincial/territorial associations

NWT Softball
PO Box 11089, Yellowknife NT X1A 3X7
Tel: 867-669-8339; *Fax:* 867-669-8327
Toll-Free: 800-661-0797
www.nwtsoftball.ca
Overview: A small provincial organization
Description: To be responsible for fastpitch, minor ball & slo-pitch softball in the Northwest Territories.; *Member of:* Canadian Amateur Softball Association
Chief Officer(s): James McCarthy, President
kingsting55@hotmail.com
Kyle Kruger, Executive Director
edcurlingsoftball@sportnorth.com

Ontario Amateur Softball Association (OASA)
c/o Registrar, RR#1, 44 Hilltop Blvd., Gormley ON L0H 1G0
Tel: 905-727-5139
www.oasa.ca
Overview: A medium-sized provincial organization founded in 1923
Description: To coordinate the game of softball for players of all ages throughout Ontario; *Member of:* Canadian Amateur Softball Association; Softball Ontario
Chief Officer(s): Roy Patenaude, President, 705-549-2485
rpatenaude@hotmail.ca
Mary Myers, Registrar
mjnm@sympatico.ca
Finances: *Funding Sources:* Sponsors; Partners; Government grants; Player/team fees

Ontario Rural Softball Association (ORSA)
c/o Secretary-Treasurer, 716029 - 18th Line, RR#1, Innerkip ON N0J 1M0
Tel: 519-469-3593
www.ontarioruralsoftball.ca
Overview: A small provincial organization founded in 1931
Description: To promote softball in rural districts, communities & small villages; *Member of:* Canadian Amateur Softball Association; Softball Ontario
Chief Officer(s): Earl Hall, President, 519-882-1599
Carl Littlejohns, Secretary-Treasurer
clittlejohnsorsa@live.ca
Finances: *Funding Sources:* Sponsors; Partners; Government grants; Player/team fees

Provincial Women's Softball Association of Ontario (PWSAO)
c/o Registrar, 50 Capri St., Thorold ON L2V 4S8
Tel: 905-227-7574; *Fax:* 905-227-3574
info@ontariopwsa.com
www.ontariopwsa.ca
Social Media:
www.facebook.com/OntarioPWSA
twitter.com/OntarioPWSA
Overview: A medium-sized provincial organization founded in 1931
Description: To support & advance women softball players in Ontario; *Member of:* Canadian Amateur Softball Association; Softball Ontario
Chief Officer(s): Debbie Malisani, Chair & President, 905-564-3533
littlehands1@rogers.com
Debbie DeMoel, Registrar
jondeb50@cogeco.ca
Finances: *Funding Sources:* Sponsors; Partners; Government grants; Player/team fees

Slo-Pitch Ontario Association (SPO)
#7, 8 Hiscott St., St Catharines ON L2R 1C6
Tel: 905-646-7773; *Fax:* 905-646-8431
spoa@slopitch.org
www.slopitch.org
Social Media:
www.youtube.com/user/slopitchontario
www.facebook.com/172816356093689
twitter.com/slopitchontario
Overview: A medium-sized provincial organization founded in 1982
Description: To institute & regulate slo-pitch softball in Ontario; *Member of:* Canadian Amateur Softball Association; Softball Ontario
Chief Officer(s): Tom Buchan, CEO
tbuchan@slopitch.org
Ron Hawthorne, President, 613-831-8393
rhawthorne@slopitch.info
Finances: *Funding Sources:* Sponsors; Partners; Government grants; Team fees
Membership: *Fees:* Schedule available; *Member Profile:* Slo-pitch teams & leagues in Ontario

Softball Manitoba
#321, 145 Pacific Ave., Winnipeg MB R3B 2Z6
Tel: 204-925-5673; *Fax:* 204-925-5703
softball@softball.mb.ca
www.softball.mb.ca
Also Known As: Softball Manitoba
Overview: A small provincial organization founded in 1965
Description: To promote & develop softball at all levels by providing leadership, programs & services; *Member of:* Canadian Amateur Softball Association
Chief Officer(s): Bill Finch, President
Membership: 15,000+ players & coaches; *Committees:* Finance; Facilities; Development; Umpire Development; Competition

Softball NB Inc. (SNB) / Softball Nouveau-Brunswick Inc.
4242 Water St., Miramichi NB E1N 4L2
Tel: 506-773-5343; *Fax:* 506-773-5630
www.softballnb.ca
Social Media:
www.facebook.com/210596526327
twitter.com/softballnb
Also Known As: Softball New Brunswick
Overview: A medium-sized provincial organization founded in 1925
Description: To foster, develop, promote & regulate the playing of amateur softball in New Brunswick; *Member of:* Canadian Amateur Softball Association
Finances: *Annual Operating Budget:* $50,000-$100,000
Staff: 1 staff member(s); 17 volunteer(s)
Membership: 350 teams; 225 officials
Activities: *Awareness Events:* Hall of Fame, 1st Sat. in June

Softball Newfoundland & Labrador
PO Box 21165, #115, 183 Kenmount Rd., St. John's NL A1A 5B2
Tel: 709-576-7231; *Fax:* 709-576-7049
softball@sportnl.ca
www.softballnl.ca
Overview: A small provincial organization
Member of: Canadian Amateur Softball Association
Chief Officer(s): Paul F. Smith, President

Softball Nova Scotia
5516 Spring Garden Rd., 4th Fl., Halifax NS B3J 1G6
Tel: 902-425-5454; *Fax:* 902-425-5606
softballns@sportnovascotia.ca
www.softballns.ca
Overview: A small provincial organization
Description: To oversee the sport of softball in Nova Scotia.; *Member of:* Canadian Amateur Softball Association
Chief Officer(s): Dave Houghton, President & CEO

Softball Ontario
3 Concorde Gate, Toronto ON M3C 3N7
Tel: 416-426-7150; *Fax:* 416-426-7368
info@softballontario.ca
www.softballontario.ca
Social Media:
www.facebook.com/SoftballOntario
twitter.com/SoftballOntario
Overview: A medium-sized provincial organization founded in 1971
Description: To promote & develop the sport of softball for its athletes, officials & volunteers by providing programs & services at all levels of competitions; *Member of:* Canadian Amateur Softball Association
Affiliation(s): Provincial Women's Softball Association (PWSA); Ontario Amateur Softball Association (OASA); Ontario Rural Softball Association (ORSA); Slo-Pitch Ontario Association (SPOA)
Chief Officer(s): Wendy Cathcart, Executive Director
wcathcart@softballontario.ca
Membership: 5 associations; *Committees:* Finance; Coaching; Participation; Scorekeeping; Fast Pitch & Slo-Pitch Umpire

Softball PEI (SPEI)
PO Box 1044, Charlottetown PE C1A 7M4
Tel: 902-569-4747; *Fax:* 902-569-3366
Toll-Free: 800-661-0797
softballpei.com
Social Media:
www.facebook.com/SoftballPEI33
twitter.com/SoftballPEI
Overview: A small provincial organization
Description: To promote & develop the sport of softball for all participating athletes in Prince Edward Island.; *Member of:* Canadian Amateur Softball Association
Chief Officer(s): Alan Petrie, President, 902-393-0274
albob@pei.sympatico.ca

Activities: Umpire Program; Coaching & Athlete Development Program; Scorekeeping Program; Participation Program; Communication/Promotion; Resources

Softball Québec
4545, av Pierre-de Coubertin, Montréal QC H1V 3R2
Tél: 514-252-3061; *Téléc:* 514-252-3134
softballqc@gmail.com
www.softballquebec.com
Média social:
www.facebook.com/softballquebec
twitter.com/SoftballQuebec
Aperçu: *Dimension:* moyenne; *Envergure:* provinciale; Organisme sans but lucratif; fondée en 1970
Description: Promouvoir la pratique du softball sur le territoire du Québec; offrir aux athlètes, aux entraîneurs, aux officiels et aux administrateurs québécois un support technique et des services de qualité; *Membre de:* Canadian Amateur Softball Association
Membre(s) du bureau directeur: Chantal Gagnon, Directrice générale
cgagnon@loisirquebec.qc.ca
Michel Nero, Président
mikeump@hotmail.com
Membre: 30,000
Activités: Programmes de formation pour officiels et entraîneurs; ligues; compétitions; *Stagiaires:* Oui

Softball Saskatchewan
2205 Victoria Ave., Regina SK S4P 0S4
Tel: 306-780-9235; *Fax:* 306-780-9483
info@softball.sk.ca
www.softball.sk.ca
Overview: A small provincial organization
Description: To make softball the number one choice for participation by athletes, coaches, parents and umpires.; *Member of:* Canadian Amateur Softball Association
Chief Officer(s): Guy Jacobson, Executive Director
guy@softball.sk.ca
Jacqueline Eiwanger, Technical Director
jac@softball.sk.ca

Softball Yukon
c/o Sport Yukon, 4061 - 4th Ave., Whitehorse YT Y1A 1H1
Tel: 867-667-4487
softball@sportyukon.com
www.softballyukon.com
Overview: A small provincial organization
Member of: Canadian Amateur Softball Association
Chief Officer(s): George Arcand, Executive Director
garcand@northwestel.net

Special Olympics

Jeux Olympiques Spéciaux du Québec Inc. (OSQ) / Québec Special Olympics
5311, boul. de Maisonneuve ouest, 2e étage, Montréal QC H4A 1Z5
Tél: 514-843-8778; *Téléc:* 514-843-8223
Ligne sans frais: 877-743-8778
www.olympiquesspeciaux.qc.ca
Média social:
www.facebook.com/olympiquesspeciauxquebec
twitter.com/athletesOSQ
Aperçu: *Dimension:* petite; *Envergure:* provinciale; fondée en 1981
Description: Les Olympiques spéciaux, actifs dans plus de 170 pays, ont pour mission d'enrichir, par le sport, la vie des personnes présentant une déficience intellectuelle. Plus de 3.7 millions d'athlètes spéciaux, de tous âges, sont inscrits dans le monde dont plus de 31,000 au Canada et 4,850 aux programmes récréatifs scolaire ou compétitifs offerts dans toutes les régions du Québec. Les 14 sports officiels sont pratiqués à l'intérieur d'un réseau de compétitions annuelles, comptant plus de 80 événements conçus pour tous les niveaux d'habiletés.; *Membre de:* Special Olympics Canada
Membre(s) du bureau directeur: Daniel Granger, Président

Special Olympics BC (SOBC)
#210, 3701 East Hastings St., Burnaby BC V5C 2H6
Tel: 604-737-3078; *Fax:* 604-737-3080
Toll-Free: 888-854-2276
info@specialolympics.bc.ca
www.specialolympics.bc.ca
Social Media:
www.facebook.com/specialolympicsbc
twitter.com/sobcsociety
Previous Name: British Columbia Special Olympics
Overview: A medium-sized provincial charitable organization founded in 1980

Description: The Association provides individuals with intellectual disability the opportunity to enhance their lives & celebrate personal achievement through positive sport experiences.; *Member of:* Special Olympics Canada
Affiliation(s): Special Olympics International
Chief Officer(s): Dan Howe, President & CEO, 604-737-3079
dhowe@specialolympics.bc.ca
Finances: *Funding Sources:* Donations; fundraising events; sponsors
Staff: 17 staff member(s); 3300 volunteer(s)
Membership: 4,300
Activities: Operates in 54 communities in British Columbia; *Speaker Service:* Yes

Special Olympics Canada (SOC) / Olympiques spéciaux Canada

#600, 21 St. Clair Ave. East, Toronto ON M4T 1L9
Tel: 416-927-9050; *Fax:* 416-927-8475
Toll-Free: 888-888-0608
www.specialolympics.ca
Social Media:
www.youtube.com/specialocanada
www.facebook.com/SpecialOCanada
twitter.com/SpecialOCanada
Previous Name: Canadian Special Olympics Inc.
Overview: A large national organization founded in 1969
Description: To provide sport training & competition for people with an intellectual disability, at local, regional, provincial, national & international levels, year round
Affiliation(s): Special Olympics International; The Order of United Commercial Travelers of America; The Sandbox Project
Chief Officer(s): Sharon Bollenbach, Chief Executive Officer, 416-927-9050 4389
sbollenbach@specialolympics.ca
Finances: *Funding Sources:* Foundations; Corporate sponsors; Individual donations
Staff: 1630 volunteer(s)
Membership: 34,000 athletes; *Member Profile:* To improve the lives of Canadians with an intellectual disability through sport
Activities: Offering national & international games; Providing coaching development

Special Olympics Manitoba (SOM)

#304, 145 Pacific Ave., Winnipeg MB R3B 2Z6
Tel: 204-925-5628; *Fax:* 204-925-5635
Toll-Free: 888-333-9179
som@specialolympics.mb.ca
www.specialolympics.mb.ca
Social Media:
www.facebook.com/117937068263657
twitter.com/SpecOManitoba
Previous Name: Manitoba Special Olympics
Overview: A small provincial charitable organization founded in 1980
Description: To enrich the lives of Manitobans with an intellectual disability, through active participation in sport; *Member of:* Special Olympics Inc.
Chief Officer(s): Simon Mundey, President & CEO
Finances: *Funding Sources:* Sport Manitoba; Various events
Staff: 13 staff member(s)
Membership: *Fees:* $25 athlete; *Committees:* Human Resources; Marketing & Communications; Sport Program; Fundraising & Development
Activities: *Speaker Service:* Yes

Special Olympics New Brunswick

#103, 411 St. Mary's St., Fredericton NB E3B 8H4
Tel: 506-455-0404; *Fax:* 506-455-0410
infosonb@specialolympics.ca
www.specialolympicsnb.ca
Social Media:
www.facebook.com/specialolympicsnb
twitter.com/specialonb
Previous Name: New Brunswick Special Olympics
Overview: A small provincial charitable organization founded in 1979
Description: To offer athletic programs to people with intellectual disabilites in New Brunswick
Chief Officer(s): Josh Astle, Executive Director
Member Profile: Athletes between 2 & 88 with an intellectual disability

Special Olympics Newfoundland & Labrador

87 Elizabeth Ave., St. John's NL A1B 1R6
Tel: 709-738-1923; *Fax:* 709-738-0119
Toll-Free: 877-738-1913
sonl@sonl.ca
www.sonl.ca
Social Media:
www.facebook.com/TeamSONL
twitter.com/SpecialONL
Previous Name: Newfoundland-Labrador Special Olympics
Overview: A small provincial charitable organization founded in 1986
Description: To provide sport, fitness & recreation programs for individuals with an intellectual disability
Chief Officer(s): Trish Williams, Executive Director
trishw@sonl.ca
Finances: *Annual Operating Budget:* $100,000-$250,000
Staff: 2 staff member(s); 250 volunteer(s)
Activities: *Awareness Events:* Provincial Winter & Summer Games

Special Olympics Northwest Territories (SONWT)

PO Box 1691, Yellowknife NT X1A 2N1
Tel: 867-446-2873
www.sonwt.ca
Previous Name: Northwest Territories Special Olympics
Overview: A small provincial organization founded in 1989
Description: Special Olympics N.W.T. is the territorial sport governing body responsible for the delivery of sport for people with intellectual disabilities in the Northwest Territories.; *Member of:* Sport North; Special Olympics Canada
Chief Officer(s): Lynn Elkin, Executive Director
lynn@sonwt.ca
Finances: *Funding Sources:* Law Enforcement Torch Run, public donations, grants, corporate sponsors and special fundraising events.

Special Olympics Nova Scotia (SONS)

#201, 5516 Spring Garden Rd., Halifax NS B3J 1G6
Tel: 902-429-2266; *Fax:* 902-425-5606
Toll-Free: 866-299-2019
www.sons.ca
Social Media:
www.facebook.com/SpecialONS
twitter.com/SpecialONS
Previous Name: Nova Scotia Special Olympics
Overview: A small provincial charitable organization founded in 1978
Description: Special Olympics is a non-profit organization dedicated to providing year-round sports training and athletic competition in a variety of Olympic-type sports for children and adults with an intellectual disability.
Chief Officer(s): Mike Greek, President/CEO
greekmr@sportnovascotia.ca
Membership: 1700 athletes

Special Olympics Ontario (SOO)

#200, 65 Overlea Blvd., Toronto ON M4H 1P1
Tel: 416-447-8326; *Fax:* 416-447-6336
Toll-Free: 888-333-5515
www.specialolympicsontario.com
Social Media:
www.youtube.com/specialolympicson
www.facebook.com/specialolympicsontario
twitter.com/soontario
Previous Name: Ontario Special Olympics
Overview: A medium-sized provincial charitable organization founded in 1979
Description: To provide sports training & competition for people with an intellectual disability through community-based programs; *Member of:* Special Olympics Canada
Chief Officer(s): Glenn MacDonell, President & Chief Executive Officer, 416-447-8326 225
glennm@specialolympicsontario.com
Linda Ashe, Vice-President, 416-447-8326 220
lindaa@specialolympicsontario.com
Willie E, Manager, Accounting Services, 416-447-8326 223
williee@specialolympicsontario.com
Lynn Miller, Manager, Marketing Services, 416-447-8326 226
lynnm@specialolympicsontario.com
James Noronha, Manager, Program Services, 416-447-8326 240
jamesn@specialolympicsontario.com
Finances: *Annual Operating Budget:* Greater than $5 Million; *Funding Sources:* Individual & corporate donations; Provincial government
Staff: 22 staff member(s); 9000 volunteer(s)
Membership: 19,000 athletes; *Member Profile:* Athletes 2 years of age or older with an intellectual disability; *Committees:* Finance; Marketing & Fundraising; Program Services
Activities: Offering 18 official sports; Providing network & support opportunities for families; Facilitating outreach & education programs to Special Olympics athletes and students across Ontario; *Internships:* Yes; *Speaker Service:* Yes

Special Olympics Prince Edward Island (SOPEI)

PO Box 822, #240, 40 Enman Cres., Charlottetown PE C1A 7L9
Tel: 902-368-8919; *Toll-Free:* 800-287-1196
sopei@sopei.com
www.sopei.com
Social Media:
www.youtube.com/channel/UCqsAGVtPqglJeQRN_GeNOtw
www.facebook.com/Specialopei
twitter.com/Specialopei
Previous Name: PEI Special Olympics
Overview: A small provincial charitable organization founded in 1987
Description: To provide sport, recreation & fitness for the intellectually disabled in PEI; To provide competitive opportunities for its members
Chief Officer(s): Charity Sheehan, Executive Director
csheehan@sopei.com
Finances: *Annual Operating Budget:* $100,000-$250,000
Staff: 2 staff member(s); 75 volunteer(s)
Membership: 235; *Member Profile:* Athletes with an intellectual disability; *Committees:* Program; Board of Directors

Special Olympics Saskatchewan

353 Broad St., Regina SK S4R 1X2
Tel: 306-780-9247; *Fax:* 306-780-9441
Toll-Free: 888-307-6226
sos@specialolympics.sk.ca
www.specialolympics.sk.ca
Social Media:
www.youtube.com/user/SpecialOSk
www.facebook.com/SOSaskatchewan
twitter.com/SpecialOSask
Previous Name: Saskatchewan Special Olympics Society
Overview: A small provincial organization
Chief Officer(s): Faye Matt, Chief Executive Officer, 306-780-9277
fmatt@specialolympics.sk.ca

Special Olympics Yukon (SOY) / Les Jeux Olympiques Spéciaux du Yukon

#102, 221 Hanson St., Whitehorse YT Y1A 1H1
Tel: 867-668-6511; *Fax:* 867-667-4237
info@specialolympicsyukon.ca
www.specialolympicsyukon.ca
Social Media:
www.facebook.com/pages/Special-Olympics-Yukon/191453284318177
twitter.com/SpecialOYukon
Previous Name: Yukon Special Olympics
Overview: A medium-sized provincial charitable organization founded in 1981
Description: To provide a full continuum of sport apportunities for Yukoners with a mental disability
Affiliation(s): Special Olympics International
Chief Officer(s): Serge Michaud, Executive Director
smichaud@specialolympicsyukon.ca
Thomas Gibbs, President
Membership: 100+; *Fees:* Schedule available; *Member Profile:* Individuals with a mental disability
Activities: *Awareness Events:* Sports Celebrities Dinner Auction; Golf Gala; Law Enforcement Torch Run

Sport Medicine

Alberta Athletic Therapists Association

PO Box 61115, Kensington RPO, Calgary AB T2N 4S6
Tel: 403-220-8957
www.aata.ca
Social Media:
www.facebook.com/452665388145479?ref=ts&fref=ts
twitter.com/AATA_therapy
Overview: A small provincial organization
Member of: Canadian Athletic Therapists Association
Chief Officer(s): Breda Lau, President
president@aata.ca
Danielle Larsen, Secretary
secretary@aata.ca

Athletic Therapy Association of British Columbia (ATABC)

#200, 4170 Still Creek Dr., Burnaby BC V5C 6C6
Tel: 604-918-5077
info@athletictherapybc.ca
www.athletictherapybc.ca
Social Media:
www.facebook.com/264629906893091
twitter.com/ATABC
Previous Name: Athletic Therapists' Association of British Columbia
Overview: A small provincial organization founded in 1994

Description: ATABC is a non-profit organization that represents athletic therapists in the province. It ensures that all of its members are in good standing with the Canadian Athletic Therapists Association. It promotes injury prevention, immediate care & rehabilition of musculoskeletal injuries.; *Member of:* Canadian Athletic Therapists Association
Chief Officer(s): Sandy Zinkowski, President
Membership: 1-99; *Member Profile:* Certified athletic therapists & certification candidates
Activities: Sports medical coverage throughout BC; *Speaker Service:* Yes

Atlantic Provinces Athletic Therapists Association (APATA) / Association des Therapeuets de Sport des Provinces Altantique (ATSPA)
c/o Memorial University, PO Box 4200, 2300 Elizabeth Ave., St. John's NL A1C 5S7
Tel: 709-737-3442
info@apata.ca
www.apata.ca
Overview: A small local organization
Member of: Canadian Athletic Therapists Association
Chief Officer(s): Colin King, President
colin.king@acadiau.ca

Canadian Academy of Sport Medicine (CASM) / Académie canadienne de médecine du sport (ACMS)
#1400, 180 Elgin St., Ottawa ON K2P 2K3
Tel: 613-748-5851; *Fax:* 613-912-0128
Toll-Free: 877-585-2394
admin@casem-acmse.org
www.casm-acms.org
Social Media:
www.facebook.com/119018054888639
twitter.com/CASEMACMSE
Overview: A medium-sized national charitable organization founded in 1970
Description: To promote excellence in the practice of medicine, as it applies to physical activity; To advance the art & science of sport medicine
Affiliation(s): World Federation of Sport Medicine
Chief Officer(s): Dawn Haworth, Executive Director
Finances: *Funding Sources:* Membership fees; Donations
Member Profile: All medical doctors; Residents & fellows; Medical students with an interest in sport medicine; *Committees:* Athletes with a Disabilty; Annual Symposium; Clinical Journal of Sport Medicine; Credentials (Diploma); Communications, Marketing & Membership; Fellowship; Official Languages; Paediatric Sport & Exercise Medicine; Timely Topics; Publications; Research; Selection; Sport Safety; Team Physician; Team Physician Development; Women's Issues in Sport Medicine; Interest Groups
Activities: Conducting research; Offering continuing medical education; Providing current information; Creating networking opportunities

Canadian Athletic Therapists Association (CATA) / Association canadienne des thérapeutes du sport
#300, 400 - 5th Ave. SW, Calgary AB T2P 0L6
Tel: 403-509-2282; *Fax:* 403-509-2280
info@athletictherapy.org
www.athletictherapy.org
Social Media:
www.facebook.com/211459688972240
twitter.com/CATA_Canada
Overview: A medium-sized national licensing organization founded in 1968
Description: CATA is dedicated to delivery of quality care through injury prevention, emergency services & rehabilitative techniques.
Chief Officer(s): Sandy Jespersen, Executive Director, 416-549-1682
executivedirector@athletictherapy.org
Richard DeMont, President
demont.conu@gmail.com
Membership: 1,000-4,999; *Fees:* $204.95; *Member Profile:* Certified Athletic Therapists; Certification candidates; *Committees:* Canadian Board of Certification for Athletic Therapy; Education; Marketing, Sponsorship & Insurance Billing; Program Accredition; Member Services; High-Performance Providers; International Relations; Financial Advisory; Ethics; Ombudsperson; President's Committee
Activities: Monitoring of professional standards; Hosting conferences

Corporation des thérapeutes du sport du Québec (CTSQ)
#SP165, 7141, rue Sherbrooke ouest, Montréal QC H4B 1R6
Tél: 514-848-2424
admin@ctsq.qc.ca
www.ctsq.qc.ca
Mèdia social:
www.facebook.com/therapeutesdusport
twitter.com/therapiedusport
Aperçu: *Dimension:* petite; *Envergure:* provinciale; Organisme sans but lucratif; Organisme de réglementation
Membre de: Canadian Athletic Therapists Association
Membre(s) du bureau directeur: Fayez Abdulrahman, President
president@ctsq.qc.ca
Eric Grenier-Denis, Executive Director
Finances: *Budget de fonctionnement annuel:* Moins de $50,000
Membre: 100-499
Activités: Développement professionnel ainsi que réglementation et attribution de licences professionnelles

Manitoba Athletic Therapists Association Inc. (MATA)
145 Pacific Ave., Winnipeg MB R3B 2Z6
Tel: 204-925-5930; *Fax:* 204-925-5624
mata@sportmanitoba.ca
www.mata.mb.ca
Social Media:
www.facebook.com/162809277115285
twitter.com/MATATherapist
Overview: A small provincial organization founded in 1983
Description: Committed to the prevention and care of activity-related injuries, at all levels of sport and recreation, ranging from the grass roots level to the elite athlete, throughout Manitoba.; *Member of:* Canadian Athletic Therapists Association; Sports Medicine Council of Manitoba; Sport Manitoba
Chief Officer(s): Mike Hutton, President
mhutton@mbteach.org
Finances: *Annual Operating Budget:* $50,000-$100,000
Staff: 2 staff member(s)
Membership: 200; *Fees:* Schedule available
Activities: Athletic First Aid Programs; medical coverage for sport & recreation; *Library:* Yes (Open to Public)

Ontario Athletic Therapists Association (OATA)
#302, 140 Allstate Pkwy., Markham ON L3R 5Y8
Tel: 905-946-8080; *Fax:* 905-946-1517
oatamembers@cggroup.com
www.ontarioathletictherapists.org
Social Media:
www.youtube.com/watch?v=FnbJdWyZD6Y&feature=plcp
www.linkedin.com/groups?gid=4044330&trk=myg_ugrp_ovr
www.facebook.com/187942491304864
twitter.com/ontherapists
Overview: A small provincial organization
Member of: Canadian Athletic Therapists Association
Chief Officer(s): Andrew Laskoski, President
drew.laskoski@bellnet.ca
Membership: 400; *Fees:* $50-$200; *Member Profile:* Must be enrolled or graduate of an accredited institution - Sheridan College, Oakville Athletic Therapy Program or York University, Sport Therapy Program

Saskatchewan Athletic Therapists Association (SATA)
309B Durham Dr., Regina SK S4S 4Z4
Tel: 306-291-6069
info@saskathletictherapy.ca
www.saskathletictherapy.ca
Social Media:
twitter.com/therapySK
Overview: A small provincial organization
Description: To certify, regulate, & discipline athletic therapists in Saskatchewan in order to protect the public; *Member of:* Canadian Athletic Therapists Association; Athletic Therapists in Canada
Chief Officer(s): Nicole Renneberg, President
president@saskathletictherapy.ca
Member Profile: Athletic therapists in Saskatchewan; *Committees:* Ethics; Insurance Billing

Sport Medicine & Science Council of Manitoba Inc.
145 Pacific Ave., Winnipeg MB R3B 2Z6
Tel: 204-925-5750; *Fax:* 204-925-5624
sport.med@sportmanitoba.ca
sportmed.mb.ca
Social Media:
twitter.com/smsc_mb
Overview: A small provincial organization
Description: To meet the needs of Manitoba's sport, recreation and fitness communities through an organized cooperative forum of medical, paramedical and sport science provider groups
Chief Officer(s): Russ Horbal, Presidnet
Activities:; *Library:* Sport Medicine & Science Council of Manitoba Resource Library (Open to Public)

Sport Medicine Council of Alberta (SMCA)
Percy Page Centre, 11759 Groat Rd., Main Fl., Edmonton AB T5M 3K6
Tel: 780-415-0812; *Fax:* 780-422-3093
www.sportmedab.ca
Social Media:
twitter.com/SportMedAB
Overview: A medium-sized provincial licensing organization founded in 1983
Description: To develop, promote & coordinate programs & services optimizing safe & healthful participation in sport & leisure activities for all Albertans; *Member of:* Sport Medicine
Chief Officer(s): Steve Johnson, President
Barb Adamson, Executive Director
badamson@sportmedab.ca
Membership: *Fees:* $50 subscriber; $265 corporate; *Member Profile:* Athletic therapists & teachers; sport physiotherapists; sport medicine physicians; sport scientists (including exercise physiologists, sport nutrition specialists, sport psychologists); teams; clubs
Activities: Athletic first aid courses; taping & strapping; sport nutrition courses; medical supply sales; kit rentals; speakers bureau; resource library; *Internships:* Yes; *Speaker Service:* Yes; *Library:* Yes (Open to Public)

SportMedBC
#2350, 3713 Kensington Ave., Burnaby BC B5B 0A7
Tel: 604-294-3050; *Fax:* 604-294-3020
Toll-Free: 888-755-3375
info@sportmedbc.com
www.sportmedbc.com
Social Media:
www.youtube.com/user/SportMedBC
www.facebook.com/sportmedbc
twitter.com/SportMedBC
Previous Name: Sport Medicine Council of British Columbia
Overview: A small provincial organization founded in 1982
Chief Officer(s): Robert Joncas, Executive Director, 604-294-3050 102
executivedirector@sportmedbc.com
Finances: *Annual Operating Budget:* $100,000-$250,000; *Funding Sources:* Service fees; grants
Staff: 6 staff member(s)
Membership: 275; *Fees:* $52.50 individual
Activities: Injury Prevention; Athlete Development; Drug-free Sport

Sport Sciences

Canadian Society for Psychomotor Learning & Sport Psychology (CSPLSP) / Société canadienne d'apprentissage psychomoteur et de psychologie du sport (SCAPPS)
#360, 125 University Private, Ottawa ON K1N 6N5
www.scapps.org
Overview: A small national organization founded in 1977
Description: To promote the study of motor development, motor learning, motor control, & sport psychology
Chief Officer(s): Chris Shields, President
Erin Cressman, Secretary, Communications
Activities: Facilitating the exchange of scientific information related to psychomotor learning & sport psychology

Sports

Aboriginal Sport & Wellness Council of Ontario (ASWCO)
2425 Matheson Blvd. East, 7th Fl., Mississauga ON L4W 5K4
Tel: 416-479-0928; *Fax:* 905-412-0325
aswco@shaw.ca
www.aswco.ca
Social Media:
www.instagram.com/aswco
www.facebook.com/aswco
twitter.com/aswco
Overview: A medium-sized provincial organization founded in 2011
Description: To organize sporting events for Aboriginal athletes throughout Ontario; To promote active & healthy Aboriginal individuals & communities in Ontario
Chief Officer(s): Marc Laliberté, President
marclaliberte@shaw.ca

Activities: Offering sporting programs & leadership development opportunities

Alberta Floorball Association
Edmonton AB
Tel: 780-999-5333
info@floorballalberta.com
www.floorballalberta.com
Social Media:
www.facebook.com/FloorballAlberta
twitter.com/Floorball_AB
Also Known As: Floorball Alberta
Overview: A small provincial organization founded in 2010
Description: To be the provincial governing body for the sport of floorball in Ontario.; *Member of:* Floorball Canada
Chief Officer(s): Shawn Murray, President
shawn@floorballalberta.com
Membership: 6 regional associations

Arctic Winter Games International Committee (AWGIC)
www.awg.ca
Overview: A medium-sized local organization founded in 1968
Description: To provide common ground for developing Northern athletes; to promote cultural & social exchanges among Northern regions of the continent
Chief Officer(s): Jens Brinch, President
Ian Legaree, Technical Director
Finances: *Annual Operating Budget:* $100,000-$250,000
Staff: 9 volunteer(s)
Membership: 1-99
Activities: To invite & review bids from communities wanting to host the Games; to select sports for each set of Games & prepare the technical package of rules, categories, events, team composition, medals to be awarded, competition format; to oversee the preparations of a Host Society for the Games; *Library:* Arctic Winter Games Archives by appointment

Atlantic University Sport Association (AUS)
#403, 5657 Spring Garden Rd., Halifax NS B3J 3R4
Tel: 902-425-4235; *Fax:* 902-425-7825
www.atlanticuniversitysport.com
Social Media:
www.youtube.com/ATLuniversitysport
www.facebook.com/AtlanticUniversitySport
twitter.com/AUS_SUA
Also Known As: Atlantic University Sport
Previous Name: Atlantic Universities Athletic Association
Overview: A medium-sized local organization founded in 1974
Description: To advance student athletes & university sport; *Member of:* Canadian Interuniversity Sport Association
Chief Officer(s): Philip M. Currie, Executive Director
pcurrie@atlanticuniversitysport.com
Finances: *Funding Sources:* Memberships; Partners
Staff: 4 staff member(s)
Membership: 11 institutional, 2,000 individuals; *Fees:* Schedule available; *Member Profile:* Institutions of higher learning

BC Floorball Federation (BCFF)
3183 Edgemont Blvd., North Vancouver BC V7R 2N8
Tel: 778-385-7825
info@bcfloorball.com
www.bcfloorball.com
Social Media:
www.facebook.com/BCFloorball
twitter.com/bcfloorball
Overview: A small provincial organization
Description: To be the provincial governing body for the sport of floorball in British Columbia.; *Member of:* Floorball Canada
Chief Officer(s): Blair Zimmerman, President

BC Games Society
#200, 990 Fort St., Victoria BC V8V 3K2
Tel: 250-387-1375; *Fax:* 250-387-4489
www.bcgames.org
Social Media:
www.instagram.com/bcgames1
www.facebook.com/BCGamesSociety
twitter.com/BCGames1
Previous Name: British Columbia Games Society
Overview: A small provincial organization
Description: To provide event management leadership in the creation of development opportunities for individuals, sport organizations & host communities
Chief Officer(s): Kelly Mann, President & CEO
kellym@bcgames.org

BC School Sports (BCSS)
Sydney Landing, #2003A, 3713 Kensington Ave., Burnaby BC V5B 0A7
Tel: 604-477-1488; *Fax:* 604-477-1484
info@bcschoolsports.ca
www.bcschoolsports.ca
Social Media:
www.youtube.com/channel/UCbaiTGzwF92qYAk7ICIkS6Q
www.facebook.com/224539464369947
twitter.com/bcschoolsports
Previous Name: BC Federation of School Athletic Associations
Overview: A medium-sized provincial charitable organization founded in 1968
Description: To encourage student participation in extra-curricular athletics, assist schools in the development & delivery of their programs & provide governance for interschool competition; *Member of:* School Sport Canada; Sport BC
Affiliation(s): USA National Federation of State High Schools
Chief Officer(s): Sydney Landing, Executive Director
Shannon Key, Manager, Sport
skey@bcschoolsports.ca
Finances: *Annual Operating Budget:* $500,000-$1.5 Million; *Funding Sources:* Membership fees; government; sponsors; advertising
Staff: 3 staff member(s); 6 volunteer(s)
Membership: 400; *Fees:* Schedule available; *Member Profile:* Accredited secondary school in British Columbia; *Committees:* Administrators; Coaching Development; Competitive Standards; Disciplinary; Eligibility; Scholarship & Awards
Activities: Provincial championships; advocacy; regulatory services; fundraising services; coaching conference; leadership camp; *Awareness Events:* Milk Run; Spirit Week; National School Sports Week, Oct.

Canada Bandy
Winnipeg MB
Overview: A small national organization
Description: To govern the sport of bandy in Canada

Canada Games Council (CGC) / Conseil des jeux du Canada
#701, 2197 Riverside Dr., Ottawa ON K1H 7X3
Tel: 613-526-2320; *Fax:* 613-526-4068
canada.games@canadagames.ca
www.canadagames.ca
Social Media:
www.youtube.com/cgc1967;
instagram.com/canadagamescouncil
www.facebook.com/CanadaGames
twitter.com/CanadaGames
Overview: A medium-sized national organization founded in 1967
Description: The Canada Games Council is a well-established, national organization that fosters on-going partnerships with organizations at the municipal, provincial and national levels. It allocates resources in support of the following mission and strategic directions.
Chief Officer(s): Sue Hylland, Chief Executive Officer
shylland@canadagames.ca
Patrick Kenny, Director, Marketing & Communications
pkenny@canadagames.ca
Finances: *Annual Operating Budget:* $250,000-$500,000; *Funding Sources:* Federal Government (operation costs); Federal Government, Provincial Government & host city (capital).
Staff: 9 staff member(s); 5000 volunteer(s)
Activities: *Internships:* Yes

Canada West Universities Athletic Association
PO Box 78090, Stn. Northside, Port Coquitlam BC V3B 7H5
Tel: 604-475-1213; *Fax:* 604-475-1997
sportsinfo@canadawest.org
www.canadawest.org
Overview: A small local organization
Description: To organize inter-collegiate sporting events between members
Chief Officer(s): Diane St. Denis, Executive Director
dstdenis@canadawest.org
Membership: 17 universities; *Member Profile:* Western Canadian universities

Canadian Centre for Ethics in Sport (CCES) / Centre canadien pour l'éthique dans le sport
#350, 955 Green Valley Cres., Ottawa ON K2C 3V4
Tel: 613-521-3340; *Fax:* 613-521-3134
Toll-Free: 800-672-7775
info@cces.ca
www.cces.ca
Social Media:
www.youtube.com/ccesonline
www.facebook.com/CanadianCentreforEthicsinSport
twitter.com/EthicsInSport
Overview: A medium-sized national organization founded in 1991
Description: Foster ethical sport for all Canadians
Affiliation(s): True Sport Foundation
Chief Officer(s): David Zussman, Chair
Paul Melia, President & CEO
pmelia@cces.ca

Canadian Sport Tourism Alliance (CSTA)
#600, 116 Lisgar St., Ottawa ON K2P 0C2
Tel: 613-688-5843; *Fax:* 613-238-3878
info@canadiansporttourism.com
www.canadiansporttourism.com
Overview: A small national organization founded in 2000
Description: To market Canada internationally as a preferred sport tourism destination
Chief Officer(s): Greg Stremlaw, Chair
gstremlaw@curling.ca
Rick Traer, CEO
rtraer@canadiansporttourism.com
Membership: 200; *Committees:* Membership; Marketing & Communications; Research; Training & Education; Government Relations

Disc BC
BC
discbc.com
Also Known As: BC Disc Sports
Previous Name: BC Disc Sports Society
Overview: A small provincial organization
Description: To be the provincial governing body of disc sports in British Columbia.
Affiliation(s): BC Ultimate
Chief Officer(s): Craig Sheather, President
Membership: 187; *Fees:* $5 through a recognized club; $10 individual
Activities: Disc golf; double disc court; freestyle; goaltimate; guts; ultimate

Floorball Canada (FC)
347 Brunswick Ave., Toronto ON M5R 2Z1
Tel: 416-970-2529
info@floorballcanada.org
www.floorballcanada.org
Social Media:
www.facebook.com/CanadaFloorball
twitter.com/CanadaFloorball
Overview: A small national organization
Description: To be the official governing body of the sport of floorball in Canada.; *Member of:* International Floorball Federation
Affiliation(s): International Olympic Committee
Chief Officer(s): Randy Sa'd, President

Floorball Nova Scotia
NS
playfloorball.weebly.com
Social Media:
www.linkedin.com/pub/floorball-nova-scotia/5a/831/b28
www.facebook.com/256739071063733
Overview: A small provincial organization
Description: To be the provincial governing body for the sport of floorball in Nova Scotia.; *Member of:* Floorball Canada
Membership: 5 provincial leagues

Floorball Ontario (FO)
ON
info@floorballontario.com
www.floorballontario.com
Overview: A small provincial organization
Description: To be the provincial governing body for the sport of floorball in Ontario.; *Member of:* Floorball Canada
Chief Officer(s): Kultar Singh, President
David Thomas, Director, Corporate Relations

Fort Saskatchewan Minor Sports Association (FSMSA)
Jubilee Recreation Center, PO Box 3071, Fort Saskatchewan AB T8L 2T1
Tel: 780-998-1835
fsmsa@telus.net
www.fsmsa.net
Overview: A small local organization
Description: To govern minor sports in Fort Saskatchewan
Chief Officer(s): Vaughan McGrath, President, 780-992-1735
vmcgrath@telusplanet.net

FunTeam Alberta
11759 Groat Rd., Edmonton AB T5M 3K6
Tel: 780-490-0242; *Fax:* 780-485-0262
www.funteamalberta.com
Social Media:
www.facebook.com/145733822158095

Overview: A small provincial organization founded in 1990
Description: To provide the opportunity for children, youth, & adults in Alberta to engage in sporting activities at low cost; to foster leadership skills
Chief Officer(s): Randy Gregg, President
Finances: *Funding Sources:* Government of Alberta
Activities: FunTeam (12 & under); RecTeam (13+); Family Try-Athlon; Mini Try-Athlon; FunTeam Young Leaders

International Federation of Broomball Associations (IFBA)
4, rue du Chambertin, Montréal QC H9H 5E5
secretary@internationalbroomball.org
www.internationalbroomball.org
Social Media:
www.facebook.com/internationalbroomball
Overview: A large international organization
Description: To represent international Broomball associations; To foster an appreciation for the sport & encourage inclusivity & participation
Chief Officer(s): Marc Desparois, Vice-President, Operations
Activities: Organizing international tournaments

International Masters Games Association (IMGA)
Maison du Sport International, Avenue de Rhodanie 54, Lausanne 1007 Switzerland
info@imga.ch
www.imga.ch
Social Media:
www.youtube.com/user/TheIMGA
www.facebook.com/134323223278024
twitter.com/IMGALausanne
Overview: A large international organization founded in 1995
Description: To govern the World Masters Games
Chief Officer(s): Kai Holm, President, Board of Governors
Jens V. Holm, Chief Executive Officer
Member Profile: International Sports Federations participating in the World Masters Games
Activities: World Masters Games; European Masters Games

Kitchener Sports Association (KSA)
50 Ottawa St. South, Kitchener ON N2G 3S7
Tel: 519-208-9302
www.kitchenersports.ca
Social Media:
www.facebook.com/pages/Kitchener-Sports-Association/492371234132957
twitter.com/KitchenerSA
Overview: A small local organization founded in 1944
Description: To govern sports & sporting facilities in Kitchener
Chief Officer(s): Bill Pegg, President
ksapresident@kitchenersports.ca

Lower Mainland Independent Secondary School Athletic Association (LMISSAA)
BC
athletics@yorkhouse.ca
www.lmissaa.com
Overview: A small local organization
Member of: BC School Sports
Chief Officer(s): Carm Renzullo, President

Manitoba Organization of Disc Sports (MODS)
145 Pacific Ave., Winnipeg MB R3B 2Z6
Tel: 204-925-5665; *Fax:* 204-925-5916
mods.mb.ca
Social Media:
twitter.com/modsmbca
Overview: A small provincial organization founded in 1988
Description: To organize & govern disc sports in Manitoba, including ultimate, disc golf & Goaltimate.; *Member of:* Sport Manitoba
Chief Officer(s): Corey Draper, Executive Director
director@mods.mb.ca
Josh Drury, Program Coordinator
programcoordinator@mods.mb.ca

Napanee Sports Association
16 McPherson Dr., Napanee ON K7R 3L1
Tel: 613-354-4423; *Fax:* 613-354-2212
info@napaneesportsassociation.com
www.losa.ca
Overview: A small local organization founded in 2006
Description: To provide funding to local sports teams
Chief Officer(s): Chuck Airhart, Chair

Ontario Disc Sports Association (ODSA)
3 Concorde Gate, Toronto ON M3C 3N7
Fax: 855-847-6948
Toll-Free: 855-847-6942
www.ondisc.org
Social Media:
www.facebook.com/196714475958
twitter.com/ondisc
Overview: A small provincial organization
Description: To be the provincial governing body for disc sports in Ontario.
Chief Officer(s): Ryan Briggs, Executive Director
Activities: Beach ultimate; discathon; disc golf; double disc court; field events; freestyle; Goaltimate; guts; Catch & Fetch; ultimate

Ontario Shuffleboard Association (OSA)
PO Box 1690, Guelph ON N1H 6Z9
ontarioshuffleboard.com
Overview: A medium-sized provincial organization founded in 1964
Member of: Canadian Shuffleboard Congress
Chief Officer(s): Rico Beaulieu, President
rick@ritewayaluminum.com

Ottawa Carleton Ultimate Association (OCUA)
#1, 875 Banks St., Ottawa ON K1S 3W4
Tel: 613-860-6282
info@ocua.ca
www.ocua.ca
Social Media:
www.facebook.com/ocua.ca
twitter.com/ocua
Overview: A medium-sized local organization founded in 1993
Description: To promote ultimate & disc sports in the Ottawa-Carleton region
Chief Officer(s): Christiane Marceau, Executive Director
ed@ocua.ca
Christopher Castonguay, Program Officer
christopher@ocua.ca
Nevan Sullivan, Program Officer, Youth & Junior
nevan@ocua.ca
Activities: Organizing & conducting the operations of leagues & tournaments; Operating a multi-field sports facility designed for ultimate

Pacific Institute for Sport Excellence (PISE)
4371 Interurban Rd., Victoria BC V9E 2C5
Tel: 250-220-2512
piseworld.com
Social Media:
www.youtube.com/user/piseworld
www.facebook.com/PacificInstituteforSportExcellence
twitter.com/PISEworld
Overview: A small provincial organization
Description: To be a leader in high performance sport development; community programs; sport & exercise education; & applied research & innovation.
Chief Officer(s): Robert Bettauer, CEO
rbettauer@piseworld.com
Andrea Carey, Director, Operations & Community Engagement, 250-220-2511
rbettauer@piseworld.com

Parksville Golden Oldies Sports Association (PGOSA)
PO Box 957, Parksville BC V9P 2G9
mail@pgosa.org
www.pgosa.org
Overview: A small local organization founded in 1993
Description: To provide physical activities to citizens of Parksville over 55.
Chief Officer(s): Bruan Ball, President, 250-240-0007
parksville.pgosa.executive@gmail.com
Membership: *Fees:* $15; *Member Profile:* People over 55

Réseau du sport étudiant du Québec (RSEQ)
4545, av Pierre-de Coubertin, Montréal QC H1V 0B2
Tél: 514-252-3300; *Téléc:* 514-254-3292
info@rseq.ca
rseq.ca
Média social:
www.facebook.com/RSEQ1
twitter.com/RSEQ1
Nom précédent: Fédération québécoise du sport étudiant
Aperçu: *Dimension:* moyenne; *Envergure:* provinciale; Organisme sans but lucratif; fondée en 1988
Description: Favoriser les actions éducatives dans le domaine de l'activité physique et sportive que se donne le milieu de l'éducation dans le but de contribuer, et cela dans les trois ordres d'enseignement, au développement intégral des élèves, des étudiantes et des étudiants du Québec; *Membre de:* Sport Scolaire Canada; Canadian Colleges Athletic Association
Membre(s) du bureau directeur: Gustave Roel, Président-directeur général, 514-252-3300 3600
groel@rseq.ca
Finances: *Budget de fonctionnement annuel:* Plus de $5 Million
Personnel: 28 membre(s) du personnel
Critères d'admissibilité: Établissements scolaires, collégiaux et universitaires
Activités: *Stagiaires:* Oui

Réseau du sport étudiant du Québec Saguenay-Lac St-Jean
CEGEP de Chicoutimi, 534, rue Jacques Cartier Est, Chicoutimi QC G7H 1Z6
Tél: 418-543-3532; *Téléc:* 418-693-0503
saglac.rseq.ca
Également appelé: RSEQ Saguenay-Lac St-Jean
Nom précédent: Association régionale du sport étudiant du Saguenay-Lac St-Jean
Aperçu: *Dimension:* petite; *Envergure:* locale; Organisme sans but lucratif; fondée en 1974
Description: Favoriser la réalisation de l'ensemble des actions éducatives dans le domaine de l'activité physique et particulièrement du sport en vue de contribuer au développement intégral des élèves et étudiants de niveaux primaire, secondaire, collégial et universitaire dans la région du Saguenay-Lac St-Jean; *Membre de:* Réseau du sport étudiant du Québec
Membre(s) du bureau directeur: Éric Benoît, Directeur général, 418-543-3532 1214
ebenoit@saglac.rseq.ca
Finances: *Fonds:* Gouvernement provincial
Membre: 16; *Critères d'admissibilité:* Écoles privées; commissions scolaires; CÉGEPS; universités
Activités: Manifestations sportives régionales et provinciales; perfectionnement; *Stagiaires:* Oui; *Service de conférenciers:* Oui

Sask Sport Inc.
1870 Lorne St., Regina SK S4P 2L7
Tel: 306-780-9300; *Fax:* 306-781-6021
sasksport@sasksport.sk.ca
www.sasksport.sk.ca
Overview: A medium-sized provincial organization founded in 1972
Description: To ensure the total development of amateur sport through the provincial sport governing bodies; to promote extensive participation towards excellence
Chief Officer(s): Kevin Gilroy, Chief Executive Officer
Finances: *Annual Operating Budget:* $500,000-$1.5 Million; *Funding Sources:* Lotteries
Staff: 50 staff member(s); 13 volunteer(s)
Membership: 70 active & affiliate; *Fees:* Schedule available
Activities:; *Library:* Resource Centre for Sport, Culture & Recreation

Société des Jeux de l'Acadie inc. (SJA)
#210, 702, rue Principale, Petit-Rocher NB E8J 1V1
Tél: 506-783-4207; *Téléc:* 506-783-4209
sja1@nbnet.nb.ca
www.jeuxdelacadie.org
Média social:
www.youtube.com/user/AcajouxJeuxdelAcadie
www.facebook.com/societedesjeuxdelacadie
twitter.com/acajoux
Aperçu: *Dimension:* petite; *Envergure:* locale; Organisme sans but lucratif; fondée en 1981
Description: Voir au maintien et au développement du Mouvement des Jeux de l'Acadie dans ses régions constituantes par l'entremise de rencontres sportives grâce à des ressources humaines, financières et des infrastructures adéquates; *Membre de:* Fondation des Jeux de l'Acadie inc.; Conseil économique du N.-B.; Sports N.-B.
Membre(s) du bureau directeur: Mylène Ouellet-LeBlanc, Directrice générale
sjadg@nb.aibn.com
Finances: *Budget de fonctionnement annuel:* $250,000-$500,000
Personnel: 4 membre(s) du personnel; 3500 bénévole(s)
Membre: 8; *Comités:* Développement sportif; Développement régional; Financement et Marketing
Activités: Programme Académie jeunesse; relations publiques, représentations et communications

Sport BC
#230, 3820 Cessna Dr., Richmond BC V7B 0A2
Tel: 604-333-3400; *Fax:* 604-333-3401
info@sportbc.com
sportbc.com
Social Media:
www.facebook.com/SportBC
twitter.com/SportBC

Overview: A medium-sized provincial organization founded in 1966
Description: To provide leadership, direction, & support to member organizations in their delivery of sport opportunities to all British Columbians; *Member of:* Sport West
Chief Officer(s): Pete Quevillon, Director, KidSport BC
Rob Newman, President & CEO
rob.newman@sportbc.com
Finances: *Annual Operating Budget:* $1.5 Million-$3 Million; *Funding Sources:* Provincial Funding; Membership Fees; Corporate Support, Event & Fundraising; Fee for Services; All Sport Insurance; SBC Insurance Operations
Staff: 7 staff member(s)
Membership: 80 Associations; *Fees:* Schedule available; *Member Profile:* Non-profit society sport organization with province-wide representation; *Committees:* Finance & Audit
Activities: Participation & Excellence; KidSport Fund; Leadership; Sport Promotion; Advocacy; Organizations Development; *Internships:* Yes; *Speaker Service:* Yes

Sport Manitoba

Sport for Life Centre, 145 Pacific Ave., Winnipeg MB R3B 2Z6
Tel: 204-925-5600; *Fax:* 204-925-5916
info@sportmanitoba.ca
www.sportmanitoba.ca
Social Media:
www.youtube.com/user/sportmanitoba
www.facebook.com/sportmb
twitter.com/SportManitoba
Previous Name: Manitoba Sports Federation Inc.
Overview: A large provincial organization founded in 1996
Description: To create the best sport community in Canada through provision of resources to recognized sport organizations, enabling them to encourage participation in sport at all levels of skill & ability & to develop athletes of national & international calibre
Chief Officer(s): Jeff Palamar, Chair
Jeff Hnatiuk, President & CEO
jeff.hnatiuk@sportmanitoba.ca
Tara Skibo, Communications/Public Relations Officer
tara.skibo@sportmanitoba.ca
Finances: *Funding Sources:* Provincial government
Staff: 45 staff member(s)
Activities: Operating & overseeing the Sport for Life Centre; Coaching Manitoba; Sport Medicine Centre; Manitoba Sports Hall of Fame; KidSport Manitoba; Power Smart Manitoba Games; & Team Manitoba; *Awareness Events:* Polar Bear Dare; *Speaker Service:* Yes; *Library:* Yes by appointment

Sport New Brunswick / Sport Nouveau-Brunswick

#13, 900 Hanwell Rd., Fredericton NB E3B 6A2
Tel: 506-451-1320; *Fax:* 506-451-1325
director@sportnb.com
www.sportnb.com
Social Media:
twitter.com/SportNB
Also Known As: Sport NB
Overview: A medium-sized provincial charitable organization founded in 1968
Description: To promote the development of amateur sport in New Brunswick through services, programs, advocacy; *Member of:* Canadian Council of Provincial Territorial Sport Federations
Chief Officer(s): Darcy McKillop, Chief Executive Officer, 506-451-1327
director@sportnb.com
Sally Hutt, Coordinator, Programs
programs@sportnb.com
Finances: *Annual Operating Budget:* $250,000-$500,000; *Funding Sources:* Provincial government; membership fees; corporate sponsorship
Staff: 3 staff member(s)
Membership: 68 organizations with 120,000 participants; *Fees:* Schedule available
Activities: *Awareness Events:* McInnes Cooper Dragon Boat Festival; *Internships:* Yes; *Speaker Service:* Yes; *Library:* Yes by appointment

Sport Newfoundland & Labrador

PO Box 8700, 1296A Kenmount Rd., St. John's NL A1B 4J6
Tel: 709-576-4932; *Fax:* 709-576-7493
sportnl@sportnl.ca
www.sportnl.ca
Social Media:
www.facebook.com/sportnl
twitter.com/sportnl
Also Known As: Sport NL
Previous Name: Newfoundland & Labrador Amateur Sports Federation
Overview: A medium-sized provincial organization founded in 1972
Description: To promote & advance amateur sport throughout Newfoundland & Labrador; to represent collective interests & goals of members; to provide various programs & services; to liaise & lobby with government, communities, media & other representative organizations; to provide direction & leadership on issues which affect members
Chief Officer(s): Troy Croft, Executive Director
troy@sportnl.ca
Membership: 45 provincial sport organizations; 70,000 individual

Sport North Federation

Don Cooper Building, PO Box 11089, 4908 - 49 St., Yellowknife NT X1A 3X7
Tel: 867-669-8326; *Fax:* 867-669-8327
Toll-Free: 800-661-0797
www.sportnorth.com
Social Media:
www.youtube.com/user/SportNorthFederation
www.facebook.com/pages/Sport-North/279234862113396
twitter.com/SportNorth
Previous Name: Northwest Territories Sport Federation
Overview: A small provincial organization founded in 1976
Description: To represent NWT sports organizations; *Member of:* Athletics Canada
Chief Officer(s): Maureen Miller, President
mmiller@sportnorth.com
Doug Rentmeister, Executive Director
drent@sportnorth.com

Sport Nova Scotia (SNS)

5516 Spring Garden Rd., 4th Fl., Halifax NS B3J 1G6
Tel: 902-425-5450; *Fax:* 902-425-5606
sportns@sportnovascotia.ca
www.sportnovascotia.ca
Social Media:
www.facebook.com/sportnovascotia
twitter.com/SportNovaScotia
Overview: A medium-sized provincial organization founded in 1974
Description: To promote the development of amateur sport in Nova Scotia through services, programs, advocacy & technical consultation
Chief Officer(s): Jamie Ferguson, Chief Executive Officer, 902-425-5450 315
jferguson@sportnovascotia.ca
Finances: *Annual Operating Budget:* $1.5 Million-$3 Million; *Funding Sources:* Membership; sponsors; government
Staff: 17 staff member(s); 15 volunteer(s)
Membership: 86 groups + 150,000 individuals; *Fees:* Schedule available

Sport PEI Inc.

PO Box 302, 40 Enman Cres., Charlottetown PE C1E 1E6
Tel: 902-368-4110; *Fax:* 902-368-4548
Toll-Free: 800-247-6712
sports@sportpei.pe.ca
www.sportpei.pe.ca
Social Media:
www.facebook.com/176050449103403
twitter.com/sportpei
Overview: A small provincial organization founded in 1973
Description: To assist in the development & promotion of amateur sport in the province of Prince Edward Island; To offer services & programs to meet the needs of the membership
Chief Officer(s): Tracey Clements, President
Gemma Koughan, Executive Director
gkoughan@sportpei.pe.ca
Finances: *Annual Operating Budget:* $100,000-$250,000; *Funding Sources:* Government; Private sector sponsorhips
Staff: 8 staff member(s); 15 volunteer(s)
Membership: 6 corporate + 39 active + 15 affiliate + 11 honorary; *Fees:* Schedule available; *Member Profile:* Provincial sport organizations; *Committees:* Finance; Administration; Fundraising; Marketing; Sport Development
Activities: Advising member associations; Acting in consultative capacity with member associations; Offering fundraising opportunities for amateur sport in PEI; *Internships:* Yes; *Library:* Yes (Open to Public)

Sport Yukon

4061 - 4 Ave., Whitehorse YT Y1A 1H1
Tel: 867-668-4236; *Fax:* 867-667-4237
news@sportyukon.com
www.sportyukon.com
Social Media:
www.youtube.com/channel/UCX5XUbz5y6XN3je1bDXU5ig
www.facebook.com/sportyukon
twitter.com/sportyukon
Overview: A small provincial organization
Description: To promote the development of amateur sport in the Yukon through services, programs, advocacy
Chief Officer(s): Tracey Bilsky, Executive Director
tbilsky@sportyukon.com

Membership: 68 clubs; *Fees:* $210

Sports-Québec

4545, av Pierre-de Coubertin, Montréal QC H1V 3R2
Tél: 514-252-3114; *Téléc:* 514-254-9621
sports@sportsquebec.com
www.sportsquebec.com
Média social:
www.facebook.com/sportsquebec
twitter.com/sportsquebec
Aperçu: *Dimension:* moyenne; *Envergure:* provinciale; Organisme sans but lucratif; fondée en 1988
Description: Assurer la synergie de ses membres et de ses partenaires du système sportif québécois et du système sportif canadien pour favoriser le développement et l'épanouissement de l'athlète et la promotion de la pratique sportive; *Membre de:* Canadian Council of Provincial & Territorial Sport Federation
Membre(s) du bureau directeur: Alain Deschamps, Directeur général, 514-252-3114 3621
adeschamps@sportsquebec.com
Isabelle Ducharme, Directrice, Programmes, 514-252-3114 3624
iducharme@sportsquebec.com
Michelle Gendron, Coordonnatrice, Communications stratégiques, 514-252-3114 3622
mgendron@sportsquebec.com
Membre: 900,000 personnes; *Critères d'admissibilite:* Ordinaires; Régionaux; Affinitaires
Activités: *Stagiaires:* Oui *Bibliothèque:* Centre de documentation (Bibliothèque publique)

Toronto Ukraina Sports Association

#75, 6 Point Rd., Toronto ON M8Z 2X3
Tel: 416-535-0681
postmaster@ukrainasports.com
www.ukrainasports.com
Overview: A small local organization founded in 1948
Description: To promote an interest in sports among its members
Chief Officer(s): Constantino Czoli, Contact
choli66@hotmail.com

True Sport Foundation / Fondation sport pur

#350, 955 Green Valley Cres., Ottawa ON K2C 3V4
Tel: 613-521-9533; *Fax:* 613-521-3134
info@truesport.ca
www.truesportfoundation.ca
Previous Name: Spirit of Sport Foundation
Overview: A small national charitable organization founded in 1993
Description: To ensure that sport makes a positive contribution to Canadian society, to our athletes & to the physical & moral development of Canada's youth; to bring together leading organizations to promote, celebrate & recognize sporting excellence; *Member of:* Canadian Centre for Ethics in Sport; Athletics Canada
Chief Officer(s): Karri Dawson, Executive Director, 613-521-9533 3213
kdawson@truesport.ca
Finances: *Annual Operating Budget:* $250,000-$500,000
Staff: 3 staff member(s); 14 volunteer(s)
Membership: 1-99

Ultimate Canada

4382 Shelbourne St., Vancouver BC V8N 3G3
Toll-Free: 888-691-1080
info@canadianultimate.com
www.canadianultimate.com
Social Media:
www.facebook.com/UltimateCanada
twitter.com/Ultimate_Canada
Previous Name: Canadian Ultimate Players Association
Overview: A medium-sized national charitable organization founded in 1993
Description: To be the governing body for the sport of ultimate in Canada.
Chief Officer(s): Danny Saunders, Executive Director
ed@canadianultimate.com
Finances: *Annual Operating Budget:* $50,000-$100,000; *Funding Sources:* Membership dues
Staff: 4 staff member(s); 50 volunteer(s)
Membership: 800; *Fees:* $30 junior; $55 regular
Activities: *Awareness Events:* Canadian National Championships; Canadian National University Championships

ViaSport
#1351, 409 Granville St., Vancouver BC V6C 1T2
Tel: 778-654-7542; *Toll-Free:* 800-335-7549
info@viasport.ca
www.viasport.ca
Social Media:
www.youtube.com/user/viaSportBC
www.facebook.com/viaSportBC
twitter.com/ViaSportBC
Overview: A medium-sized provincial organization
Description: To provide the opportunity for participation in sports for all British Columbians, at every age & level of skill.
Chief Officer(s): Sheila Bouman, Chief Executive Officer
sheilab@viasport.ca
Michelle Tice, Director, Communications & Engagement
michellet@viasport.ca
Scott Stefani, Manager, Grants
scotts@viasport.ca
Activities: Funding & grants

World Armwrestling Federation (WAF)
Sofia Park Trading Zone, Bldg. 16V, Fl.1, Office 1-2, Sofia 1166 Bulgaria
www.waf-armwrestling.com
Overview: A medium-sized international organization founded in 1977

York Region Athletic Association (YRAA)
#1038, 44 Main St. South, Unionville ON L3R 2E4
Tel: 905-470-1551; *Fax:* 905-470-9092
www.yraa.com
Social Media:
twitter.com/yraa_news
Overview: A small local organization
Description: To offer athletics in York Region high schools
Chief Officer(s): Scot Angus, President
scot.angus@yrdsb.edu.on.ca

Sports Cars

Sunbeam Sportscar Owners Club of Canada (SSOCC)
Overview: A small national organization founded in 1978
Finances: *Annual Operating Budget:* Less than $50,000; *Funding Sources:* Membership fees; advertising; regalia sales
Membership: 130; *Member Profile:* Owner or enthusiast of British "Rootes Group" production automobile of any year
Activities:; *Library:* Yes by appointment

Sports for the Disabled

Active Living Alliance for Canadians with a Disability (ALACD) / Alliance de vie active pour les canadiens/canadiennes ayant un handicap
#104, 720 Belfast Rd., Ottawa ON K1G 0Z5
Tel: 613-244-0052; *Fax:* 613-244-4857
Toll-Free: 800-771-0663
TTY: 888-771-0663
ala@ala.ca
www.ala.ca
Social Media:
www.linkedin.com/company/the-active-living-alliance-for-canadians-with
Overview: A medium-sized national organization
Description: To promote inclusion & active living lifestyles of Canadians with disabilities by facilitating communication & collaboration among organizations, agencies & individuals
Affiliation(s): Canadian Amputee Sports Association; Canadian Association for Disabled Skiing; Canadian Association for Health, Physical Education, Recreation & Dance; Canadian Blind Sports Association; Canadian Cerebral Palsy Sports Association; Canadian Deaf Sports Association; Canadian Intramural Recreation Association; Canadian National Institute for the Blind; Canadian Paralympic Committee; Canadian Paraplegic Association; Canadian Parks/Recreation Association; Canadian Red Cross Society; Canadian Special Olympics; Learning Disabilities Association of Canada; National Network for Mental Health
Chief Officer(s): Jane Arkell, Executive Director
Chris Bourne, Manager, Community Development
Finances: *Annual Operating Budget:* $100,000-$250,000; *Funding Sources:* Fitness program
Staff: 3 staff member(s); 25 volunteer(s)
Membership: 4,000

Alberta Amputee Sports & Recreation Association (AASRA)
PO Box 708, Stn. M, Calgary AB T2P 2J3
Tel: 403-201-0507; *Fax:* 403-256-7611
Toll-Free: 888-501-0507
info@aasra.ab.ca
www.aasra.ab.ca
Social Media:
www.facebook.com/495810413773520
Overview: A small provincial charitable organization founded in 1977
Description: To support & provide opportunities for amputees in recreational & sporting activities, in events for both the disabled & able-bodied; To provide moral support to new amputees & family
Chief Officer(s): Shane Westin, President
Gwen Davies, Executive Director
Finances: *Funding Sources:* Donations; corporate & government support
Membership: *Fees:* $20 Annual; $150 Lifetime; *Member Profile:* People who have lost a limb(s) at a major joint; *Committees:* Volunteer
Activities: Annual Pro/Amp Golf Tournament; cycling clinic, golf clinic; support group meetings; *Speaker Service:* Yes; *Library:* Yes

Alberta Northern Lights Wheelchair Basketball Society
Go Center, University of Alberta, #2-209, 11610 - 65 Ave., Edmonton AB T6G 2E1
programs@albertanorthernlights.com
www.albertanorthernlights.com
Social Media:
www.facebook.com/172864392765380
Overview: A medium-sized provincial charitable organization founded in 1976
Description: To develop health, fitness, & sport for men, women, & children with physical disabilities
Chief Officer(s): Neil Feser, Manager, Program

Alberta Sports & Recreation Association for the Blind (ASRAB)
#007, 15 Colonel Baker Pl. NE, Calgary AB T2E 4Z3
Tel: 403-262-5332; *Fax:* 403-265-7221
Toll-Free: 888-882-7722
info@asrab.ab.ca
www.asrab.ab.ca
Overview: A small provincial charitable organization founded in 1975
Description: To provide recreation & sports opportunities for Albertans who are blind & partially sighted; *Member of:* CBSA
Chief Officer(s): Linda MacPhail, Executive Director
execdirector@asrab.ab.ca
Membership: *Fees:* $15 individual; $30 family
Activities: Swimming; Lawn Bowling; Powerlifting; Goalball Athletics; Tandem Cycling; *Awareness Events:* Sight Night, Nov.; *Speaker Service:* Yes

Association des sports pour aveugles de Montréal (ASAM)
4545, av Pierre-de Coubertin, Montréal QC H1V 0B2
Tél: 514-252-3178
infoasaq@sportsaveugles.qc.ca
www.sportsaveugles.qc.ca/asam
Média social:
www.facebook.com/ASAMONTREAL
Aperçu: *Dimension:* petite; *Envergure:* locale; Organisme sans but lucratif; fondée en 1983
Description: Promouvoir l'accessibilité et la pratique des sports et loisirs aux personnes handicapées visuelles; organiser et structurer les différentes activités sportives; recruter et former des bénévoles accompagnateurs
Affiliation(s): Association sportive des aveugles du Québec
Membre(s) du bureau directeur: Nathalie Chartrand, Directrice générale
nchartrand@sportsaveugles.qc.ca
Finances: *Budget de fonctionnement annuel:* $50,000-$100,000
Personnel: 1 membre(s) du personnel; 75 bénévole(s)
Membre: 175 individu; 2 associées; *Critères d'admissibilité:* Personne ayant un handicap visuel
Activités: Goalball; conditionnement physique; aqua forme; tandem; ski alpin et ski de fond; tai-chi; activités ponctuelles: équitation, escalade, canot, randonnée pédestre; *Événements de sensibilisation:* Tournoi de golf, sept.

Association québécoise de sports pour paralytiques cérébraux (AQSPC)
4545, av Pierre-de Coubertin, Montréal QC H1V 0B2
Tél: 514-252-3143; *Téléc:* 514-254-1069
www.sportpc.qc.ca
Média social:
www.facebook.com/189413534433667
Aperçu: *Dimension:* petite; *Envergure:* provinciale
Membre de: Canadian Cerebral Palsy Sports Association
Membre(s) du bureau directeur: José Malo, Directrice générale, 514-252-3143 3742
jmalo@sportpc.qc.ca

Association sportive des aveugles du Québec inc. (ASAQ)
4545, av Pierre-de Coubertin, Montréal QC H1V 3R2
Tél: 514-252-3178
infoasaq@sportsaveugles.qc.ca
www.sportsaveugles.qc.ca
Aperçu: *Dimension:* petite; *Envergure:* provinciale; fondée en 1979
Description: Promouvoir la pratique du sport amateur auprès des personnes handicapées de la vue et de favoriser ainsi leur intégration
Membre(s) du bureau directeur: Nathalie Chartrand, Directrice générale
Membre: 135; *Montant de la cotisation:* 15$
Activités: *Service de conférenciers:* Oui

BC Adaptive Snowsports (BCAS)
780 Marine Dr. SW, Vancouver BC V6P 5Y7
Tel: 604-333-3630
info@bcadaptive.com
www.bcadaptive.com
Social Media:
www.linkedin.com/company/the-disabled-skiers-association-of-bc
www.facebook.com/bcadaptive
twitter.com/BC_adaptive
Previous Name: Disabled Skiers Association of BC
Overview: A medium-sized provincial charitable organization founded in 1973
Description: To promote adaptive skiing, snowboarding, & mountain accessbility as a form of rehabilitation for participants with physical disabilities; To contribute to an inclusive & healthy lifestyle for residents of British Columbia; *Member of:* BC Disability Sports; Canadian Association for Disabled Skiing
Chief Officer(s): Wayne Leslie, Executive Director, 604-333-3631
wayne@bcadaptive.com
Finances: *Annual Operating Budget:* $100,000-$250,000; *Funding Sources:* Donations, Corporate sponsors; Government
Staff: 7 staff member(s); 700 volunteer(s)
Membership: 1,326; *Fees:* $46 participant; $41 volunteer/instructor
Activities: Offering adaptive snow sports throughout BC; *Awareness Events:* Scotiabank Charity Challenge; Black Diamond Gala; Sun Peaks Grand Golf Tournament; *Speaker Service:* Yes

Blind Bowls Association of Canada (BBAC)
SK
bbacanada.org
Overview: A small national organization
Description: To govern the sport of bowls in Canada; to promote the interests of visually impaired lawn bowlers in Canada & around the world.
Chief Officer(s): Vivian Berkeley, President
vberkeley@sympatico.ca
Shirley Ahern, Secretary
shirice@sympatico.ca

British Columbia Wheelchair Sports Association (BCWSA)
780 Southwest Marine Dr., Vancouver BC V6P 5Y7
Tel: 604-333-3520; *Fax:* 604-333-3450
Toll-Free: 877-737-3090
info@bcwheelchairsports.com
www.bcwheelchairsports.com
Social Media:
www.youtube.com/user/BCWheelchairSports
www.facebook.com/BCWSA
twitter.com/BCWSA
Overview: A medium-sized provincial charitable organization
Description: To promote & develop wheelchair sport opportunities for British Columbians who identify with physical disabilities; *Member of:* Canadian Wheelchair Sports Association
Chief Officer(s): Gail Hamamoto, Executive Director, 604-333-3520 201
gail@bcwheelchairsports.com
Member Profile: Individuals who identify with a disability & able bodied individuals

Activities: *Awareness Events:* Rick Hansen Wheels in Motion Event, June; *Speaker Service:* Yes

Canadian Amputee Golf Association (CAGA)

PO Box 6091, Stn. A, Calgary AB T2H 2L4
canamps@caga.ca
www.caga.ca
Overview: A small national organization founded in 2000
Description: To provide support for amputees both before & after amputation; To raise awareness to the general population on the effects of amputation; To offer rehabilitation, through teaching amputees golf; To run amputee golf tournaments
Chief Officer(s): Gwen Davies, President
Membership: *Fees:* $25; $150 lifetime

Canadian Amputee Sports Association (CASA) / Association canadienne des sports pour amputés

Toronto ON
www.canadianamputeesports.ca
Overview: A medium-sized national charitable organization founded in 1977
Description: To promote & organize amateur sport competitions in Canada for persons who are without a limb or part of a limb; To promote research in prosthetic devices for sport activities; To select a Canadian national team for participation in international sports events for amputees
Affiliation(s): Canadian Paralympic Committee; Hockey Canada
Finances: *Funding Sources:* Membership dues
Staff: 10 volunteer(s)
Member Profile: Amputees & other athletes

Canadian Association for Disabled Skiing (CADS) / Association canadienne pour les skieurs handicapés (ACSH)

791 Strathcona Dr. SW, Calgary AB T3H 1N8
Tel: 587-315-5870; *Fax:* 866-531-9644
disabledskiing.ca
Overview: A medium-sized national charitable organization founded in 1976
Description: To assist individuals with a disability to participate in recreational & competitive snow skiing & snowboarding
Chief Officer(s): Maureen O'Hara-Leman, Executive Director
executive.director@disabledskiing.ca
Finances: *Funding Sources:* Sponsorships; Donations
Staff: 1900 volunteer(s)
Membership: 1,130 disabled members; *Fees:* $25
Activities: Ensuring that programs are delivered at an appropriate level of expertise, through the work of a technical committee; Providing information about adaptive equipment; *Awareness Events:* CADS Ski Improvement & Race Development Festival, March

Canadian Association for Disabled Skiing - Alberta (CADS Alberta)

11759 Groat Rd., Edmonton AB T5M 3K6
Tel: 780-427-8104; *Fax:* 780-422-2663
info@cadsalberta.ca
www.cadsalberta.ca
Social Media:
www.facebook.com/CADSAB
twitter.com/CADSAlberta
Overview: A small provincial charitable organization founded in 1961
Description: CADS Alberta is a volunteer-based organization assisting individuals with a disability to lead fuller lives through active participation in recreational & competitive snow skiing & snowboarding. It is a registered charity, BN: 133967406RR0001.; *Member of:* Canadian Association for Disabled Skiing
Affiliation(s): Canadian Ski Instructors' Alliance (CSIA), Canadian Association of Snowboard Instructors (CASI)
Chief Officer(s): Edward Shaw, President
president@cadsalberta.ca
Sharon Veeneman, Executive Coordinator
Finances: *Annual Operating Budget:* $50,000-$100,000
Staff: 500 volunteer(s)
Membership: 800+; *Fees:* $40

Canadian Association for Disabled Skiing - National Capital Division (CADS-NCD)

1216 Bordeau Grove, Ottawa ON K1C 2M7
Tel: 819-827-4378
cads-ncd.ca
Overview: A medium-sized provincial charitable organization
Member of: Canadian Association for Disabled Skiing
Chief Officer(s): Bernie Simpson, President
berniesimpson@sympatico.ca

Canadian Association for Disabled Skiing - New Brunswick

35 Bloomfield Station Rd., Bloomfield Station NB E5N 4M5
Tel: 506-832-1104
Social Media:
www.facebook.com/CADSNB
Overview: A medium-sized provincial charitable organization
Member of: Canadian Association for Disabled Skiing
Chief Officer(s): Jim Bowland, Contact
jimbowland.cadsnb@nb.sympatico.ca

Canadian Association for Disabled Skiing - Newfoundland & Labrador Division

6 Albany Pl., St. John's NL A1E 1Y2
Tel: 709-753-3625; *Fax:* 709-777-4884
disabledskiing.ca/?page_id=123
Also Known As: CADS Newfoundland/Labrador
Overview: A small provincial organization
Member of: Canadian Association for Disabled Skiing
Chief Officer(s): Marg Tibbo, Representative
margaret.tibbo@easternhealth.ca

Canadian Association for Disabled Skiing - Nova Scotia

c/o Alpine Ski Nova Scotia, 5516 Spring Garden Rd., 4th Fl., Halifax NS B3J 1G6
Tel: 902-425-5450; *Fax:* 902-425-5606
alpinens@sportnovascotia.ca
disabledskiing.ca/provincial-programs/nova-scotia
Also Known As: CADS Nova Scotia
Overview: A medium-sized provincial organization
Member of: Alpine Canada Alpin; Canadian Association for Disabled Skiing
Chief Officer(s): Lorraine Burch, Executive Director
Finances: *Annual Operating Budget:* $250,000-$500,000
Staff: 1 staff member(s); 5 volunteer(s)
Membership: 1-99

Canadian Association for Disabled Skiing - Ontario

c/o Hennum, 1481 Jalna Ave., Mississauga ON L5J 1S6
www.disabledskiingontario.com
Social Media:
twitter.com/cads_ontario
Also Known As: CADS Ontario
Overview: A medium-sized provincial organization
Member of: Canadian Association for Disabled Skiing
Chief Officer(s): Carl Hennum, President
carl@disabledskiingontario.com

Canadian Deaf Curling Association (CDCA) / Association de Curling des Sourdes du Canada

Edmonton AB
Fax: 780-437-1808
TTY: 780-437-1808
www.deafcurlcanada.org
Also Known As: Deaf Curl Canada
Overview: A small national organization
Description: To provide deaf & hard of hearing curlers with opportunities across Canada.; *Member of:* Canadian Deaf Sports Association; Canadian Curling Association
Affiliation(s): British Columbia Deaf Sports Federation; Alberta Deaf Curling Association; Saskatchewan Deaf Sports Association; Manitoba Deaf Curling Association; Ontario Deaf Curling Assocation; Association de Curling des Sourds du Quebec; Nova Scotia Deaf Curling Association
Chief Officer(s): Bradford Bentley, President, 250-539-3264
president-cdca@shaw.ca
Allard Thomas, Vice-President, 306-565-8420
vice-pres-cdca@att.biz
Susanne Beriault, Secretary
cdca-secretary@gmail.com
David Pickard, Treasurer
dpickard@telus.net
Dean Sutton, Chief Technical Director
curlingtd@shaw.ca

Canadian Deaf Golf Association (CDGA) / Association Canadienne de Golf des Sourds

c/o Roger Beernink, Treasurer, 3575 Settlement Trail, London ON N6P 0A8
www.deafgolf.ca
Overview: A small national organization
Description: To aid in the development of leadership & golfing skills among deaf golfers across Canada.; *Member of:* Canadian Deaf Sports Association
Chief Officer(s): Dana McCarthy, President
dhmccarthy@teksavvy.com
Peter Mitchell, Vice-President
pmitchell25@rogers.com
Rob Cundy, Secretary
robcundy@telus.net
Roger Beernink, Treasurer
rbeernink@sympatico.ca
Aurele Bourgeois, Director
abourgeois10@cogeco.ca
Membership: *Fees:* $10

Canadian Electric Wheelchair Hockey Association (CEWHA)

#920, 200 Yorkland Blvd., Toronto ON M2J 5C1
Tel: 416-757-8544; *Fax:* 416-490-9334
info@cewha.ca
www.cewha.ca
Social Media:
www.youtube.com/cewhanational
www.facebook.com/cewha
twitter.com/canadianewha
Overview: A small national charitable organization founded in 1980
Description: To provide a hockey program for persons with disabilities who have limited upper body strength & mobility
Chief Officer(s): Bob Cassidy, Executive Director
Finances: *Funding Sources:* Donations; Sponsorships; Fundraising
Membership: 200 players + 80 volunteers; *Member Profile:* All persons with disabilities who would benefit from an electric wheelchair in competitive sport & daily living
Activities: Offering recreation & social programs; Organizing national tournaments

Canadian Paralympic Committee (CPC) / Comité paralympique canadien

#310, 225 Metcalfe St., Ottawa ON K2P 1p9
Tel: 613-569-4333; *Fax:* 613-569-2777
www.paralympic.ca
Social Media:
www.youtube.com/user/CDNParalympics
www.facebook.com/CDNParalympics
twitter.com/CDNParalympics
Previous Name: Canadian Federation of Sport Organizations for the Disabled
Overview: A medium-sized national charitable organization founded in 1982
Description: The CPC is responsible for creating an optimal environment for high-performance Canadian Paralympic Athletes to compete and win in the Paralympic and Parapan American Games, and by promoting their success, inspire all Canadians with a disability to get involved in sport.
Affiliation(s): International Paralympic Committee
Chief Officer(s): Karen O'Neill, CEO, 613-569-4333 223
koneill@paralympic.ca
Gaétan Tardif, President
Finances: *Funding Sources:* Government; private & public sector
Staff: 22 staff member(s)
Membership: 25 national organizations; *Member Profile:* Any National Sport Organization for Athletes with a Disability or National Sport Organization representing a sport on the Paralympic program, provided that such organization is properly constituted in Canada and is the recognized Canadian member of the appropriate international federation. Each active member shall be entitled to one (1) vote each at each meeting of members.; *Committees:* High Performance Committee; Paralympic Development Committee; Coach Council; Athlete School; Classification Taskforce
Activities: *Internships:* Yes; *Speaker Service:* Yes; *Library:* Yes by appointment

Canadian Wheelchair Sports Association (CWSA) / Association canadienne des sports en fauteuil roulant (ACSFR)

#108, 2255 St. Laurent Blvd., Ottawa ON K1G 4K3
Tel: 613-523-0004; *Fax:* 613-523-0149
info@cwsa.ca
www.cwsa.ca
Social Media:
www.youtube.com/wheelsportscanada
www.facebook.com/wheelchairrugbycanada
twitter.com/wcrugbycanada
Overview: A large national charitable organization founded in 1967
Description: To promote excellence & develop opportunities for Canadians in wheelchair sport

Affiliation(s): International Stoke Mandeville Wheelchair Sports Federation
Chief Officer(s): Donald Royer, President
Cathy Cadieux, Executive Director
ccadieux@cwsa.ca
Duncan Campbell, Director, National Development, 604-333-3539, Fax: 604-333-3450
duncancampbell@cwsa.ca
Andy Van Neutegem, Director, High Performance, Fax: 250-220-2501
andyvan@cwsa.ca
Don Lane, Manager, Program, 613-523-0004, Fax: 613-523-0149
dlane@cwsa.ca
Arley McNeney, Coordinator, Communications, Fax: 604-333-3450
arley@cwsa.ca
Finances: *Funding Sources:* Federal government; Independent corporations; General public; Man in Motion Foundation
Staff: 7 staff member(s)
Member Profile: Wheelchair athletes
Activities: Offering high performance sport programs for rugby; Engaging in advocacy activities

Commission de Ski pour Personnes Handicapées du Québec (CSPHQ)
QC
Aperçu: *Dimension:* petite; *Envergure:* provinciale
Description: Promouvoir et pratiquer le ski alpin; *Membre de:* Ski Québec; Canadian Association for Disabled Skiing
Critères d'admissibilite: Adolescent et adulte ayant une déficience physique
Activités: Cours de ski alpin adapté (luge, bi-ski)

Disabled Sailing Association of BC (DSA)
#318, 425 Carrall St., Vancouver BC V6B 6E3
Tel: 604-688-6464; *Fax:* 604-688-6463
info@disabilityfoundation.org
www.disabilityfoundation.org
Social Media:
www.facebook.com/DisabilityFoundation
twitter.com/disabilityfdn
Overview: A small provincial charitable organization founded in 1985
Description: To help people with disabilities live independent lives
Affiliation(s): BC Sport & Fitness Council for the Disabled
Chief Officer(s): Matthew Wild, Communications Coordinator
matthew@disabilityfoundation.org
Membership: 6 non profit societies
Activities: Adopt-a-boat program; sailing experiences

George Bray Sports Association (GBSA)
9606 Tower Rd., RR#3, St Thomas ON N5P 3S7
Tel: 519-633-9411
www.georgebraysports.ca
Social Media:
www.facebook.com/pages/George-Bray-Sports-Association/563729230361725
Overview: A small local organization founded in 1968
Description: To organize hockey games for children with learning disabilities
Chief Officer(s): Murray Howard, President
murrayhoward@execulink.com

Manitoba Deaf Sports Association Inc. (MDSA)
18 Aylmer St., Winnipeg MB R2R 2G8
deafeagle@hotmail.com
Overview: A small provincial organization
Description: To govern fitness, amateur sports & recreation for deaf people in Manitoba.; *Member of:* Canadian Deaf Sports Association
Chief Officer(s): Cliff Beaulieu, President

Manitoba Wheelchair Sports Association
145 Pacific Ave., Winnipeg MB R3B 2Z6
Tel: 204-925-5790; *Fax:* 204-925-5792
mwsa@sportmanitoba.ca
www.mwsa.ca
Social Media:
www.facebook.com/manitobawheelchairsports
Overview: A small provincial organization founded in 1962
Description: Committed to leadership in the promotion of well being and a healthy lifestyle through the development of sport and fitness related opportunities for physically disabled Manitobans.; *Member of:* Canadian Wheelchair Sports Association
Chief Officer(s): Angela Lloyd, Executive Director
Membership: *Fees:* $5

Newfoundland & Labrador Deaf Sports Association (NLDSA)
98 Penney Cres., St. John's NL A1A 5L8
Overview: A small provincial organization
Description: To govern fitness, amateur sports & recreation for deaf people in Newfoundland & Labrador.; *Member of:* Canadian Deaf Sports Association
Chief Officer(s): Bryan Johnson, President
bryan.johnson@nf.sympatico.ca

Ontario Amputee & Les Autres Sports Association (OALASA)
c/o Rodney Reimer, 15 Tanner Dr., London ON N5W 6B4
oalasa.webs.com
Previous Name: Ontario Amputee Sports Association
Overview: A small provincial organization founded in 1976
Member of: Sport for Disabled Ontario; Canadian Amputee Sports Association
Chief Officer(s): Rodney Reimer, President, 519-659-7452
rodreimer@rogers.com
Finances: *Annual Operating Budget:* Less than $50,000; *Funding Sources:* Bingos
Staff: 15 volunteer(s)
Membership: 100 individual; *Fees:* $20 regular; $15 associate; *Member Profile:* Anyone interested in amputee & les autres sports
Activities: Golf clinics & tournaments; speakers; lawn bowls tournament; boccia tournament; *Speaker Service:* Yes

Ontario Cerebral Palsy Sports Association (OCPSA)
PO Box 60082, Ottawa ON K1T 0K9
Tel: 613-723-1806; *Fax:* 613-723-6742
Toll-Free: 866-286-2772
ocpsa.com
Overview: A small provincial organization
Description: To provide, promote & coordinate competitive opportunities for persons with with cerebral palsy & other neuromuscular disorders in Ontario.; *Member of:* Canadian Cerebral Palsy Sports Association
Affiliation(s): Canadian Sport Institute - Ontario; Coaches Association of Ontario; ParaSport Ontario
Chief Officer(s): Don Sinclair, President
Membership: *Fees:* $20
Activities: Athletics; Boccia; other sports

Ontario Wheelchair Sports Association (OWSA)
#104, 3 Concordia Gate, Toronto ON M3C 3N7
Tel: 416-426-7189
info@ontwheelchairsports.org
ontwheelchairsports.org
Overview: A medium-sized provincial organization founded in 1972
Description: To provide sporting & recreational opportunities for athletes who compete in wheelchairs; *Member of:* Canadian Wheelchair Sports Association
Affiliation(s): Canadian Wheelchair Sports Association
Chief Officer(s): Ken Thom, President
kenthom@rogers.com
Bonnie Hartley, Interim Executive Director
Finances: *Funding Sources:* Provincial Government
Staff: 3 staff member(s)

Paralympic Sports Association (Alberta) (PSA)
10024 - 79 Ave., Edmonton AB T6E 1R5
Tel: 780-439-8687; *Fax:* 780-432-0486
info@parasports.net
www.parasports.net
Overview: A medium-sized provincial charitable organization founded in 1965
Description: To provide sports & recreation programs for people with a physical disability
Affiliation(s): Wheelchair Sports Alberta
Chief Officer(s): Kim McDonald, Executive Director
kim@parasports.net
Suzanne Harrison, Coordinator, Programs
suzanne@parasports.net
Membership: *Fees:* $20 individual; $40 family; *Member Profile:* Persons with physical disabilities
Activities: *Speaker Service:* Yes

ParaSport Ontario
#104, 3 Concorde Gate, Toronto ON M3C 3N7
Tel: 416-426-7187; *Fax:* 416-426-7361
Toll-Free: 800-265-1539
info@parasportontario.ca
www.parasportontario.ca
Social Media:
www.instagram.com/parasportontario
twitter.com/parasport_ont
Previous Name: Sport for Disabled - Ontario; Paralympics Ontario
Overview: A medium-sized provincial charitable organization founded in 1981
Description: To provide leadership, resources, & opportunities to ensure a strong community for persons with a disability in the Ontario sport & recreation community
Affiliation(s): Ontario Amputee & Les Autres Sports Association; Ontario Blind Sports Association; Ontario Cerebral Palsy Sports Association; Ontario Wheelchair Sports Association
Chief Officer(s): Alan Trivett, Executive Director, 416-426-7186
alan@parasportontario.ca
Membership: 1800+
Activities: *Speaker Service:* Yes

Parasports Québec
4545, av Pierre-de Coubertin, Montréal QC H1V 0B2
Tél: 514-252-3108; *Téléc:* 514-254-9793
info@parasportsquebec.com
www.parasportsquebec.com
Média social:
www.facebook.com/367668269915613
Nom précédent: Association québécoise des sports en fauteuil roulants
Aperçu: *Dimension:* moyenne; *Envergure:* provinciale; Organisme sans but lucratif; fondée en 1983
Description: Favoriser un accès à la pratique sportive en fauteuil roulant à tous les niveaux de performance pour le bénéfice des personnes ayant une limitation physique; *Membre de:* Canadian Wheelchair Sports Association
Membre(s) du bureau directeur: Donald Royer, Président
Finances: *Budget de fonctionnement annuel:* $250,000-$500,000
Personnel: 5 membre(s) du personnel; 25 bénévole(s)
Membre: 350; *Montant de la cotisation:* Barème
Activités: *Service de conférenciers:* Oui

Saskatchewan Blind Sports Association Inc. (SBSA)
510 Cynthia St., Saskatoon SK S7L 7K7
Tel: 306-975-0888; *Toll-Free:* 877-772-7798
sbsa.sk@shaw.ca
www.saskblindsports.ca
Overview: A small provincial organization founded in 1978
Description: To assist persons who are blind or with visual impairment to achieve excellence in sport, satisfaction in recreation, independence, self-reliance & full community participation
Chief Officer(s): Glenn Hunks, Executive Director
Finances: *Annual Operating Budget:* $100,000-$250,000
Staff: 1 staff member(s); 250 volunteer(s)
Membership: 100-499; *Fees:* $10
Activities: *Awareness Events:* Run for Light

Saskatchewan Ski Association - Skiing for Disabled (SASKI)
1860 Lorne St., Saskatoon SK S4P 2L7
Tel: 306-780-9236; *Fax:* 306-781-6021
www.saski.ca
Also Known As: SASKI - Skiing for Disabled
Overview: A medium-sized provincial organization founded in 1982
Description: To promote all aspects of winter skiing in Saskatchewan, including alpine, biathlon, cross country & skiing for disabled, & to provide assistance to clubs & individual athletes, instruction & training, adaptive equipment, & a resource library; *Member of:* Canadian Association for Disabled Skiing
Chief Officer(s): Pat Prokopchuk, Contact
prokr@sasktel.net
Finances: *Funding Sources:* Provincial lotteries; occasional grants; bingos
Membership: 1,000-4,999
Activities: Alpine/cross country/biathlon/freestyle skiing; skiing for disabled; snowboarding

Saskatchewan Wheelchair Sports Association (SWSA)
510 Cynthia St., Saskatoon SK S7L 7K7
Tel: 306-975-0824
info@swsa.ca
www.swsa.ca
Social Media:
www.youtube.com/user/SKWheelchairSports
www.facebook.com/182080694193
twitter.com/skwcsports
Overview: A small provincial organization founded in 1977
Description: Dedicated to developing & supporting opportunities for children, teens & adults with disabilities to participate in the Association's sport, recreation & leisure time activities to the best of their abilities.; *Member of:* Canadian Wheelchair Sports Association
Membership: *Fees:* $20 individual; $40 family

Special Olympics Alberta (SOA)
Percy Page Centre, 11759 Groat Rd., Edmonton AB T5M 3K6
Tel: 780-415-0719; *Fax:* 780-415-1306
Toll-Free: 800-444-2883
info@specialolympics.ab.ca
www.specialolympics.ab.ca
Social Media:
www.facebook.com/specialolympicsalberta
twitter.com/SpecialOAlberta
Previous Name: Alberta Special Olympics Inc.
Overview: A medium-sized provincial charitable organization founded in 1980
Description: To enrich the lives of Albertans with an intellectual disability, through sport
Chief Officer(s): John Byrne, President & CEO
jbyrne@specialolympics.ab.ca
Finances: *Annual Operating Budget:* $500,000-$1.5 Million; *Funding Sources:* Donations; Grants; Fundraising events; Sponsorship
Staff: 12 staff member(s); 1500 volunteer(s)
Membership: 3,000 athletes; 32 affiliates throughout Alberta; *Member Profile:* Athletes with intellectual disabilities; *Committees:* Strategic Development; Volunteer Management; New Community Development; New Sport Programs; Sport Development; Provincial Games; Team AB
Activities: Offering 15 official sports for athletes; Providing training; *Awareness Events:* Law Enforcement Torch Run; Sports Celebrities Festival; *Speaker Service:* Yes

Wheelchair Sports Alberta
11759 Groat Rd., Edmonton AB T5M 3K6
Tel: 780-427-8699; *Toll-Free:* 888-453-6770
wsa1@telus.net
www.abwheelchairsport.ca
Social Media:
www.facebook.com/WheelchairSportsAlberta
twitter.com/WSA_Alberta
Overview: A small provincial organization
Description: To develop wheelchair sports throughout Alberta; *Member of:* Canadian Wheelchair Sports Association
Chief Officer(s): Sharleen Edwards, Executive Director
Membership: *Fees:* $10 board/coach/official; $25 athlete; $30 family; *Member Profile:* Any athlete, club, official, coach or board member

Wheelchair Sports Association of Newfoundland & Labrador (WSANL)
NL
Overview: A small provincial organization
Member of: Canadian Wheelchair Sports Association

Wolverines Wheelchair Sports Association
10 Knowledge Way, Grande Prairie AB T8W 2V9
Tel: 780-402-3331; *Fax:* 780-402-3318
info@gpwolverines.com
www.gpwolverines.com
Overview: A small local organization founded in 1990
Description: To provide people with disabilities the opportunity to engage in physcial & recreational activities.
Membership: *Fees:* Schedule available

Squash

NWT Squash
NT
www.nwtsquash.com
Social Media:
twitter.com/NWTSquash
Overview: A small provincial organization
Description: To develop & provide squash programs to athletes of all ages in the Northwest Territories.; *Member of:* Squash Canada
Chief Officer(s): Bruce Jones, President
Garrett Hinchey, Secretary

Saskatchewan Squash
214 Wickenden Cres., Saskatoon SK S7N 3X7
Tel: 306-280-4320
sasksquash@gmail.com
www.sasksquash.com
Overview: A medium-sized provincial organization
Member of: Squash Canada
Chief Officer(s): Brad Birnie, Executive Director

Squash Alberta
3415 - 3rd Ave. NW, Calgary AB T2N 0M4
Tel: 403-270-7344; *Fax:* 403-270-8445
Toll-Free: 877-646-6566
membership@squashalberta.com
www.squashalberta.com
Previous Name: Alberta Squash Racquets Association
Overview: A medium-sized provincial charitable organization founded in 1967
Description: To promote & facilitate the development of the sport of squash in Alberta; *Member of:* Squash Canada
Chief Officer(s): Grant Currie, President
currieg@shaw.ca
Tim Landeryou, Executive Director
tim@squashalberta.com
Finances: *Annual Operating Budget:* $100,000-$250,000; *Funding Sources:* Membership dues; programs; government grants
Staff: 2 staff member(s); 100 volunteer(s)
Membership: 1,600; *Fees:* $50 adult; $50 junior; $130 family

Squash British Columbia
Vancouver Racquets Club, 4867 Ontario St., Vancouver BC V5V 3H4
Tel: 604-737-3084; *Fax:* 604-736-3527
info@squashbc.com
www.squashbc.com
Social Media:
www.instagram.com/squashbc
www.facebook.com/squashbc
twitter.com/squashbc
Overview: A medium-sized provincial organization
Description: To promote the growth of squash by providing orderly development opportunities for athletes, & encouraging participation through a variety of programs & activities organized by Squash BC & its partners; *Member of:* Sport BC; Squash Canada
Chief Officer(s): Jordan Abney, Executive Director
jordan@squashbc.com
Membership: *Fees:* $44 individual; $20 young adult (19-24); $15 junior (under 18)
Activities:; *Library:* Yes

Squash Canada
20 Jamie Ave., Nepean ON K2E 6T6
Tel: 613-228-7724; *Fax:* 613-228-7232
info@squash.ca
www.squash.ca
Social Media:
www.facebook.com/squashcanada
twitter.com/squashcanada
Previous Name: Canadian Squash Racquets Association
Overview: A large national charitable organization founded in 1913
Description: To develop athletes, coaches & officials in the sport of squash; to set standards for squash in Canada; to promote growth & development in the sport across the country; *Member of:* World Squash Federation
Chief Officer(s): Lolly Gillen, President
Dan Wolfenden, Executive Director, 613-228-7724 201
dan.wolfenden@squash.ca
Jamie Hickox, Director, Performance
performance@squash.ca
Britany Gordon, Manager, Programs, 613-228-7724 202
britany.gordon@squash.ca
Finances: *Funding Sources:* Government; Donations; Sponsorship
Member Profile: Provincial/territorial clubs & members; *Committees:* High Performance; Squash Canada Officiating; Governance Review; Finance & Audit; Junior Development; Doubles; Masters; Patrons Fund; Community Endowment Fund; Nominations; Competitions; Coaching; Canada Games; Doubles Competition; Doubles Officiating

Squash Manitoba
145 Pacific Ave., Winnipeg MB R3B 2Z6
Tel: 204-925-5661; *Fax:* 204-925-5792
squash@sportmanitoba.ca
www.squashmb.org
Social Media:
twitter.com/squashmanitoba
Overview: A medium-sized provincial organization
Description: To promote the game of squash in Manitoba; To establish & enforce rules & programs for all levels of play; *Member of:* Squash Canada
Affiliation(s): Brandon squash & athletic centre; Dauphin Squash Club; University of Winnipeg; Winnipeg Squash Racquet Club; Winnipeg Winter Club
Chief Officer(s): Lynn Colliou, Executive Director
Membership: *Fees:* $20

Squash Newfoundland & Labrador Inc.
PO Box 21254, St. John's NL A1A 5B2
hongngee@gmail.com
www.hongngee.com/squashnl
Also Known As: Squash NL
Overview: A small provincial organization
Description: To coordinate & promote the sport of squash in Newfoundland & Labrador.; *Member of:* Squash Canada

Squash Nova Scotia
PO Box 3010, Stn. Park Lane Centre, #401, 5516 Spring Garden Rd., Halifax NS B3J 3G6
Tel: 902-425-5450; *Fax:* 902-425-5606
www.squashns.ca
Overview: A medium-sized provincial organization
Description: Fosters & promotes a squash community for players of all abilities from across the province to improve the profile of the sport & its enjoyment by its members.; *Member of:* Squash Canada
Chief Officer(s): Alfred Seaman, President
alfieseaman@gmail.com
Finances: *Annual Operating Budget:* Less than $50,000
Membership: 100-499; *Fees:* $20 student; $25 adult

Squash Ontario
c/o Glendon College, Proctor Field House, #226, 2275 Bayview Ave., Toronto ON M4N 1J8
Fax: 416-426-7393
admin@squashontario.com
www.squashontario.com
Social Media:
www.facebook.com/SquashOntario
twitter.com/SquashOntario
Overview: A medium-sized provincial organization founded in 1976
Description: To act as the governing body for the sport of squash in Ontario; To develop & promote the sport of squash across Ontario; To provide an environment in which the sport of squash can thrive; To meet the needs of present & potential players
Chief Officer(s): Janice Lardner, President
board@squashontario.com
Jamie Nicholls, Executive Director, 416-426-7202
jmnicholls@squashontario.com
Lauren Sachvie, Coordinator, Programs, 416-426-7201
programs@squashontario.com
Activities: Developing squash players, from beginners to elite athletes, as well as teams, coaches, & officials; Establishing & maintaining technical standards

Squash PEI
PE
Overview: A small provincial organization
Description: To promote squash in PEI; to provide competitive opportunities for members; *Member of:* Squash Canada; Sport PEI Inc.

Squash Québec
4545, av Pierre-de Coubertin, Montréal QC H1V 0B2
Tél: 514-252-3062
info@sports-4murs.qc.ca
www.squash.qc.ca
Média social:
www.facebook.com/SquashQuebec
Aperçu: *Dimension:* petite; *Envergure:* provinciale
Description: Promouvoir le développement du Squash au Québec en offrant différentes opportunités aux adeptes, tout en encourageant la participation sportive à travers un ensemble de services et de programmes; *Membre de:* Squash Canada
Membre(s) du bureau directeur: Michel Séguin, Directeur général
Finances: *Budget de fonctionnement annuel:* $50,000-$100,000
Personnel: 2 membre(s) du personnel; 20 bénévole(s)
Membre: 5,000-14,999
Activités: *Stagiaires:* Oui

Squash Yukon
YT
squashyukon.yk.ca
Overview: A small provincial organization
Member of: Squash Canada

Swimming

Alberta Summer Swimming Association (ASSA)
c/o Swim Alberta, 11759 Groat Rd., Edmonton AB T5M 3K6
Tel: 780-454-7462; *Fax:* 780-415-1788
assaadmin@gmail.com
www.assa.ca
Overview: A medium-sized provincial organization
Description: To provide a summer swimming program for swimmers of all ages in Alberta.
Chief Officer(s): Don Smith, President
presidentassa@gmail.com
Membership: 59 clubs + 3,323 individuals

BC Summer Swimming Association (BCSSA)
#205, 2323 Boundary Rd., Vancouver BC V5M 4V8
Tel: 604-473-9447; *Fax:* 604-473-9660
office@bcsummerswimming.com
www.bcsummerswimming.com
Social Media:
www.facebook.com/bcsummerswimming
twitter.com/BCSSAstaff
Overview: A medium-sized provincial organization founded in 1958
Description: To provide summer swimming opportunities to children across British Colubia through member clubs.
Membership: 60 clubs + 5,000 athletes
Activities: Speed swimming; diving; water polo; synchronized swimming

Club de natation Natchib inc.
CP 213, Chibougamau QC G8P 2K7
Tél: 418-748-8038
Aperçu: *Dimension:* petite; *Envergure:* locale
Membre(s) du bureau directeur: Stéphanie McKenzie, Président

Fédération de natation du Québec (FNQ)
CP 1000, Succ. M, 4545, av Pierre-de Coubertin, Montréal QC H1V 0B2
Tél: 514-252-3200; *Téléc:* 514-252-3232
fnq@fnq.qc.ca
www.fnq.qc.ca
Média social:
www.facebook.com/163831313666941
twitter.com/fednatationqc
Aperçu: *Dimension:* moyenne; *Envergure:* provinciale
Membre de: Swimming Canada
Affiliation(s): Éducation, Loisir et Sport Québec; AQUAM Équipes; Groupe Hospitalité Westmont (Quality et Comfort Inn); Location Sauvageau; Trophies Dubois; Westjet; Financière Manuvie; McAuslan
Membre(s) du bureau directeur: Isabelle Ducharme, Directrice générale
iducharme@fnq.qc.ca

Solo Swims of Ontario Inc. (SSO)
c/o Greg Taylor, 32 Coxwell Cres., Brantford ON N3P 1Z1
www.soloswims.com
Overview: A small provincial organization founded in 1975
Description: To promote safety in marathon swimming in Ontario
Chief Officer(s): Greg Taylor, President
gwc.taylor@sympatico.ca
Finances: *Funding Sources:* Provincial government

Swim Alberta
Percy Page Centre, 11759 Groat Rd., Edmonton AB T5M 3K6
Tel: 780-415-1780; *Fax:* 780-415-1788
office@swimalberta.ca
www.swimalberta.ca
Social Media:
www.facebook.com/swim.alberta
twitter.com/SwimAlberta
Overview: A medium-sized provincial organization founded in 1963
Description: To maintain a progressive athletic / club development program & a high performance program; *Member of:* Swimming Natation Canada
Chief Officer(s): Dean Schultz, Interim President
president@swimalberta.ca
Cheryl Humphrey, Executive Director
chumphrey@swimalberta.ca
Finances: *Funding Sources:* Membership fees; Sponsorships; Lottery
Staff: 4 staff member(s)
Activities: *Speaker Service:* Yes; *Library:* Yes (Open to Public)

Swim BC
PO Box 1749, Garibaldi Highlands BC V0N 1T0
Tel: 604-898-9100; *Fax:* 604-898-9200
www.swim.bc.ca
Social Media:
facebook.com/SwimBC
twitter.com/swimbcstaff
Overview: A small provincial organization founded in 1974
Description: To provide the opportunity, leadership & means for members to achieve excellence in all areas of the sport of swimming; *Member of:* Swimming Canada
Chief Officer(s): Jerome Beauchamp, President
Mark Schuett, Executive Director
markschuett@swimbc.ca
Finances: *Annual Operating Budget:* $500,000-$1.5 Million; *Funding Sources:* Self-generated; provincial government
Staff: 4 staff member(s); 16 volunteer(s)
Membership: 8,000
Activities:; *Library:* Yes

Swim Nova Scotia (SNS)
5516 Spring Garden Rd., Halifax NS B3J 1G6
Tel: 902-425-5454; *Fax:* 902-425-5606
swimming@sportnovascotia.ca
www.swimnovascotia.com
Overview: A small provincial charitable organization
Member of: Swimming Canada
Affiliation(s): AthletesCAN
Chief Officer(s): Sue Jackson, President
suejack01@yahoo.com
Bette El-Hawary, Executive Director
Finances: *Annual Operating Budget:* $50,000-$100,000
Staff: 1 staff member(s); 20 volunteer(s)
Membership: 2,800
Activities: Swim competitions & fundraising events

Swim Ontario
#206, 3 Concorde Gate, Toronto ON M3C 3N7
Tel: 416-426-7220; *Fax:* 416-426-7356
info@swimontario.com
www.swimontario.com
Social Media:
www.facebook.com/117335688316744
twitter.com/SwimOntario
Overview: A medium-sized provincial organization founded in 1922
Member of: Swimming Canada
Chief Officer(s): Eric Martin, President
ericmartin@rogers.com
John Vadeika, Executive Director
john@swimontario.com
Membership: 10,000+ in 140+ clubs; *Committees:* Strategic Planning; Administration; Finance; Risk Management; Programme Policy
Activities: Learn-to-Swim; training for competitions & fitness

Swim Saskatchewan
2205 Victoria Ave., Regina SK S4P 0S4
Tel: 306-780-9291; *Fax:* 306-525-4009
office@swimsask.ca
www.swimsask.ca
Social Media:
www.facebook.com/325400947571418
Overview: A medium-sized provincial organization
Description: To promote excellence through sport development, competition, education, training and strong member organizations.; *Member of:* Swimming Canada
Chief Officer(s): Susan Miazga, President
barrymiazga@sasktel.net
Marj Walton, Executive Director, 306-780-9238
marjwalton@swimsask.ca

Swim Yukon
4061 - 4th Ave., Whitehorse YT Y1A 1H1
swimyukon@gmail.com
sportyukon.com/member/swim-yukon
Overview: A medium-sized provincial organization
Description: Swim Yukon is the Sport Governing Body for competitive swimming in the Yukon.; *Member of:* Sport Yukon
Affiliation(s): Swimming Canada
Chief Officer(s): Michael McArthur, President
Activities: Swim meets

Swimming Canada / Natation Canada
#B140, 2445 St. Laurent Blvd., Ottawa ON K1G 6C3
Tel: 613-260-1348; *Fax:* 613-260-0804
natloffice@swimming.ca
www.swimming.ca
Social Media:
www.youtube.com/swimmingcanada;
instagram.com/swimmingcanada
www.facebook.com/56320144853
twitter.com/SwimmingCanada
Overview: A large national organization founded in 1909
Description: To direct & develop competitive swimming in Canada; To represent Canada in international organizations & events
Affiliation(s): Aquatic Federation of Canada
Chief Officer(s): Ahmed El-Awadi, Chief Executive Officer, 613-260-1348 2007
aelawadi@swimming.ca
Larry Clough, Chief Financial Officer, 613-260-1348 2008
lclough@swimming.ca
Ken Radford, Director, Domestic Operations, 250-220-2537
kradford@swimming.ca
James Hood, Senior Manager, High Performance Para-Swimming Programs, 613-222-8061
jhood@swimming.ca
Iain McDonald, Senior Manager, High Performance Operations, 613-260-1348 2010
imcdonald@swimming.ca
Nathan White, Manager, Communications, 613-260-1348 2002
NWhite@swimming.ca
Finances: *Funding Sources:* Membership fees; Corporate sponsorships; Sport Canada; Canadian Olympic Association
Staff: 21 volunteer(s)
Membership: Over 50,000
Activities: *Rents Mailing List:* Yes

Swimming New Brunswick / Natation Nouveau-Brunswick
#13, 900 Hanwell Rd., Fredericton NB E3B 6A3
Tel: 506-451-1323; *Fax:* 506-451-1325
swimnb@nb.aibn.com
www.swimnb.ca
Social Media:
www.facebook.com/1401518450068316
twitter.com/SwimmingNB
Overview: A medium-sized provincial organization
Member of: Swimming Canada
Chief Officer(s): David Frise, President
dfrise@gmail.com
Pat Ketterling, Executive Director
Membership: 668; *Fees:* $12-70; *Committees:* Nomination & Succession; Policy & Governance; Risk Management; Strategic Plan; Finance; Technical; Officials; Communication & Promotion; President's Council

Swimming Newfoundland & Labrador
1296A Kenmount Rd., Paradise NL A1L 1N3
Tel: 709-576-7946; *Fax:* 709-576-7493
swimnl@sportnl.ca
www.swimnl.nfld.net
Social Media:
www.youtube.com/user/SwimmingNL
www.facebook.com/swimmingNL
twitter.com/SwimmingNL
Overview: A medium-sized provincial organization founded in 1974
Member of: Swimming Canada
Chief Officer(s): Joan Butler, President
joanb@mun.ca
Corina Hartley, Executive Director
swimnl@sportnl.ca

Swimming Prince Edward Island
40 Enman Cres., Charlottetown PE C1E 1E6
Tel: 902-569-0583; *Toll-Free:* 800-247-6712
swimpei@sportpei.pe.ca
www.swimpei.com
Also Known As: Swim PEI
Previous Name: Swimming PEI
Overview: A small provincial charitable organization
Member of: Swimming Canada
Chief Officer(s): Marguerite Middleton, Chief, Island Officials
memiddleton@gov.pe.ca
Finances: *Annual Operating Budget:* Less than $50,000
Staff: 1 staff member(s); 30 volunteer(s)
Membership: 200; *Fees:* $40; *Member Profile:* Ages 6-70; *Committees:* Finance; Coaching; Officials; Awards
Activities: Competitive swimming; swimming development; *Speaker Service:* Yes

Swim-Natation Manitoba (SNM)
#209, 145 Pacific Ave., Winnipeg MB R3B 2Z6
Tel: 204-925-5778; *Fax:* 204-925-5624
swim@sportmanitoba.ca
www.swimmanitoba.mb.ca
Social Media:
twitter.com/Swim_Manitoba
Previous Name: Swim Manitoba
Overview: A medium-sized provincial organization founded in 1913

Description: To produce fast swimmers & to make the experience a healthy, fun, exiting & rewarding adventure; *Member of:* Swimming Canada; Sport Manitoba
Chief Officer(s): Steve Armstrong, President
Mark Fellner, Executive Director
swim.ed@sportmanitoba.ca
Finances: *Annual Operating Budget:* $250,000-$500,000
Staff: 3 staff member(s); 1500 volunteer(s)
Membership: 18 clubs + 1500 swimmers + 300 coaches + 1300 officials & volunteers; *Committees:* Advancement; Competition Hosting; Executive; Finance & Operations; Governance; Sport

Synchro Alberta
The Percy Page Centre, 11759 Groat Rd., Edmonton AB T5M 3K6
Tel: 780-415-1789; *Fax:* 780-415-0056
www.synchroalberta.com
Social Media:
www.facebook.com/SynchroAlberta
Overview: A medium-sized provincial organization
Member of: Synchro Canada
Chief Officer(s): Jennifer Luzia, Executive Director
jluzia@synchroalberta.com
Membership: 1200
Activities: Competitive & recreational meets

Synchro BC
#2002C, 3713 Kensington Ave., Burnaby BC V5B 0A7
Tel: 604-333-3640
www.synchro.bc.ca
Social Media:
www.youtube.com/channel/UCSpuYX-rsu9m6VJs6nKx-fA/feed
www.facebook.com/Synchro-BC-213448205667190/?ref=hl
twitter.com/SynchroBC
Overview: A medium-sized provincial licensing organization
Description: To foster & promote a fully integrated Synchronized Swimming Sport System throughout BC, which will offer opportunities for excellence at all levels of participation from Recreational to International; *Member of:* Synchro Canada
Chief Officer(s): Annie Smith, Executive Director
ed@synchro.bc.ca
Kara Kalin Zader, Technical Director
td@synchro.bc.ca
Finances: *Funding Sources:* Government; donations
Membership: 1,200; *Fees:* Schedule available
Activities: *Speaker Service:* Yes; *Rents Mailing List:* Yes

Synchro Canada
#401, 700 Industrial Ave., Ottawa ON K1G 0Y9
Tel: 613-748-5674; *Fax:* 613-748-5724
synchroinfo@synchro.ca
www.synchro.ca
Social Media:
www.youtube.com/synchrocanada
www.facebook.com/synchrocanada
twitter.com/synchrocanada
Previous Name: Canadian Amateur Synchronized Swimming Association
Overview: A medium-sized national charitable organization founded in 1968
Description: To develop & operate the sport of synchronized swimming in Canada, through a variety of programs designed to develop athletes, coaches & officials
Chief Officer(s): Jackie Buckingham, Chief Executive Officer, 613-748-5674 222
jackie@synchro.ca
Isabelle Lecompte, Manager, High Performance
isabelle@synchro.ca
Membership: 5,000-14,999

Synchro Manitoba
145 Pacific Ave., Winnipeg MB R3B 2Z6
Tel: 204-925-5693; *Fax:* 204-925-5703
execdirector@synchromb.ca
www.synchromb.ca
Previous Name: Canadian Amateur Synchronized Swimming Association (Manitoba Section)
Overview: A small provincial organization founded in 1958
Description: To promote, teach, foster, encourage, & improve, synchronized swimming in Manitoba; to regulate synchro swim in Manitoba in accordance with the constitution by-laws & rules; *Member of:* Synchro Canada
Affiliation(s): Manitoba Sports Federation
Chief Officer(s): Allison Gervais, Executive Director
execdirector@synchromb.ca
Activities:; *Library:* Resource Centre

Synchro New Brunswick
436 Young St., Saint John NB E2M 2V2
Tel: 506-672-2399; *Fax:* 506-672-6020
www.synchronb.ca
Overview: A medium-sized provincial organization
Member of: Synchro Canada

Synchro Newfoundland & Labrador
c/o Sport Newfoundland & Labrador, 1296-A Kenmount Rd., Paradise NL A1L 1N3
synchronl@hotmail.com
www.synchronl.com
Social Media:
www.facebook.com/synchronl
twitter.com/synchronl
Overview: A small provincial organization
Member of: Synchro Canada
Chief Officer(s): Jennifer Folkes, President, 709-368-1996

Synchro Nova Scotia
5516 Spring Garden Rd., 4th Fl., Halifax NS B3J 1G6
Tel: 902-426-5454; *Fax:* 902-425-5606
synchro@sportnovascotia.ca
www.sportnovascotia.ca
Social Media:
www.facebook.com/pages/Synchro-Nova-Scotia/177261688979414
Overview: A medium-sized provincial organization
Description: To promote synchronized swimming throughout the province; *Member of:* Synchro Canada
Chief Officer(s): Pam Kidney, Executive Director

Synchro PEI
c/o Sport PEI, 40 Enman Cres., Charlottetown PE C1E 1E6
synchropei.goalline.ca
Also Known As: PEI Synchronized Swimming Association
Overview: A small provincial organization
Member of: Synchro Canada
Chief Officer(s): Jodi Williams, President

Synchro Saskatchewan
#209, 1860 Lorne St., Regina SK S4P 2L7
Tel: 306-780-9227; *Fax:* 306-780-9445
synchro.sk@sasktel.net
www.synchrosask.com
Overview: A small provincial organization
Description: To promote & develop synchronized swimming in Saskatchewan; *Member of:* Synchro Canada; SaskSport
Chief Officer(s): Tanya Pohl, President
president@synchrosask.com
Kathleen Reynolds, Executive Director
ed@synchrosask.com
Finances: *Annual Operating Budget:* $100,000-$250,000; *Funding Sources:* Saskatchewan Lottery Trust Fund
Staff: 3 staff member(s); 30 volunteer(s)
Membership: 1,200; *Fees:* Schedule available; *Committees:* Finance; Marketing; Technical; Competitions; Officials; Marketing; Grassroot Programming

Synchro Swim Ontario
128 Galaxy Blvd., Toronto ON M9W 4Y6
Tel: 416-679-9522; *Fax:* 416-679-9535
synchroontario.com
Social Media:
www.facebook.com/SynchroSwimOntario
twitter.com/SynchroONTARIO
Overview: A medium-sized provincial licensing organization
Description: To oversee synchronized swimming in Ontario, including varsity competiton, competitive clubes & community recreation programs; to develop, promote, support & regulate synchronized swimming through the immplementation of an integrated sports system that is accessible to all Ontarians by providing opportunites for enjoyment & the pursuit of individual goals; *Member of:* Synchro Canada
Chief Officer(s): Mary Dwyer, Executive Director, 416-679-9522 222
mdwyer@synchroontario.com
Member Profile: Athlete development at recreational through to elite levels; officials development; coach development; competition structures; *Committees:* Executive; Finance; High Performance; High Performance Hiring & Selection; Novice; Ontario Officials Management Team; Provincial Jury of Appeal; Technical Training & Development; Volunteer Management

Synchro Yukon Association
4061 - 4th Ave., Whitehorse YT Y1A 1H1
Tel: 867-668-7441
synchro_yukon@hotmail.com
sportyukon.com/member/synchro-yukon-association
Overview: A medium-sized provincial organization
Description: To promote the sport of Synchronized Swimming in the Yukon.; *Member of:* Synchro Canada; Sport Yukon
Chief Officer(s): Lindsay Roberts, President

Synchro-Québec
4545, av Pierre-de Coubertin, Montréal QC H1V 0B2
Tél: 514-252-3087; *Ligne sans frais:* 866-537-3164
fnsq@synchroquebec.qc.ca
www.synchroquebec.com
Média social:
www.facebook.com/synchro.quebec
twitter.com/synchroquebec
Nom précédent: Fédération de nage synchronisée
Aperçu: *Dimension:* moyenne; *Envergure:* provinciale; Organisme sans but lucratif
Description: Planifier et supporter le développement de la nage synchronisée au Québec; administrer l'ensemble des compétitions qui se déroule au Québec; veiller au perfectionnement de ses entraîneurs, officiels et bénévoles; *Membre de:* Synchro Canada
Membre(s) du bureau directeur: Diane Lachapelle, Directrice générale
dlachapelle@synchroquebec.qc.ca
Activités: *Stagiaires:* Oui

Whitehorse Glacier Bears Swim Club
c/o Sport Yukon, 4061 - 4th Ave., Whitehorse YT Y1A 1H1
Fax: 867-667-4237
whseglacierbears@yahoo.ca
www.whitehorseglacierbears.ca
Social Media:
www.facebook.com/569737653073155
Overview: A small local organization
Description: To promote competitive swimming.

Table Soccer

Canadian Table Soccer Federation
Previous Name: Canadian Table Soccer Association
Overview: A small national organization
Description: To oversee & monitor the growth of foosball in Canada.

Foosball Québec
QC
Tél: 418-906-0977
foosballquebec@gmail.com
www.foosballquebec.com
Média social:
www.facebook.com/foosballquebec
Aperçu: *Dimension:* petite; *Envergure:* provinciale
Membre(s) du bureau directeur: Lévesque Olivier, Président

Ontario Table Soccer Association
ON
Toll-Free: 866-247-7702
www.ontariotablesoccer.com
Overview: A small provincial organization founded in 2002
Description: To promote the sport of table soccer through hosting, sanctioning, & coordinating tournaments, events & clinics for players based in Ontario & to assist them in competing in national & international sanctioned events
Chief Officer(s): Mario Recupero, Executive Director, 905-812-9994
director@ontariotablesoccer.com

Table Tennis

Alberta Table Tennis Association (ATTA)
Percy Page Centre, 11759 Groat Rd., Edmonton AB T5M 3K6
Tel: 780-427-8588
atta@abtabletennis.com
www.abtabletennis.com
Overview: A small provincial organization founded in 1970
Description: To foster & promote the play of table tennis in a sportsmanlike manner; to award, sanction &, when necessary, supervise or manage all championship matches & tournaments; to interpret & enforce the laws & rules of table tennis; to provide & keep a permanent & official record of all championships established under its jurisdiction; generally to govern the sport in Alberta; *Member of:* Table Tennis Canada
Affiliation(s): International Table Tennis Federation
Chief Officer(s): Lei Jiang, Program Coordinator
Finances: *Annual Operating Budget:* $100,000-$250,000; *Funding Sources:* Fundraising; Alberta Sport, Park & Wildlife Foundation; Alberta Gaming
Staff: 2 staff member(s); 100 volunteer(s)
Membership: 1,200; *Fees:* Schedule available; *Committees:* Communication; Tournaments; Ratings; Officials; Membership/Marketing; Regional/Junior Developments; Schools
Activities: Coaching & officials development; club assistance; sport outreach; summer camps; high performance athletic training; provincial tournament hosting; preparation & sending of athletes to events; *Rents Mailing List:* Yes

British Columbia Table Tennis Association (BCTTA)
#208, 5760 Minoru Blvd., Richmond BC V6X 2A9
Tel: 604-270-3393
bctta@lightspeed.ca
www.bctta.ca
Overview: A small provincial organization
Member of: Table Tennis Canada; Sport BC
Affiliation(s): International Table Tennis Federation
Chief Officer(s): Amelia Ho, President
Membership: 200+; *Fees:* $30 voting members; $20 non-voting members

Fédération de tennis de table du Québec (FTTQ)
4545, av Pierre-de Coubertin, Montréal QC H1V 0B2
Tél: 514-252-3064; *Téléc:* 514-251-8038
www.tennisdetable.ca
Média social:
www.youtube.com/user/TennisdetableQC
www.facebook.com/tennisdetableQC
twitter.com/tennisdetableQC
Aperçu: *Dimension:* moyenne; *Envergure:* provinciale
Membre de: Table Tennis Canada
Membre(s) du bureau directeur: Yves Surprenant, Président

Manitoba Table Tennis Association (MTTA)
145 Pacific Ave., Winnipeg MB R3B 2Z6
Tel: 204-925-5690; *Fax:* 204-925-5916
table.tennis@sportmanitoba.ca
www.mtta.ca
Overview: A small provincial organization founded in 1959
Description: To develop & promote the sport of table tennis at all levels within Manitoba; *Member of:* Table Tennis Canada; Sport Manitoba
Affiliation(s): International Table Tennis Federation
Chief Officer(s): Ron Edwards, Executive Director
Finances: *Annual Operating Budget:* $100,000-$250,000; *Funding Sources:* Sport Manitoba; Manitoba Lotteries; program revenue
Staff: 2 staff member(s); 25 volunteer(s)
Membership: 504; *Fees:* $25 active (adult); $15 active (junior); $10 associate (adult); $5 associate (junior); $35 associate (club); *Committees:* Tournaments; Leagues; Athlete Development; Grass Roots & Regional Developments; Coaching Development; Officials Development; Facilities & Equipment; Special Events; Finance & Administration; Bylaws & Policy Review; Privacy Officer; Fundraising & Bingos; Publicity & Promotion; Membership, Stats & Ranking; Banquets & Awards; Disciplinary; Nominations
Activities:; *Library:* MTTA Resource Library (Open to Public)

Newfoundland & Labrador Table Tennis Association (NLTTA)
NL
Tel: 709-834-8402
www.freewebs.com/nltta
Overview: A small provincial organization
Description: To promote the sport of Table Tennis in Newfoundland & Labrador.; *Member of:* Table Tennis Canada
Affiliation(s): International Table Tennis Federation
Chief Officer(s): Brian Ash, President
qeash@yahoo.ca
Rick Fisher, Treasurer, 709-834-0015
topsail369@gmail.com
Denise Simms, Manager, 709-673-2537
jd.taylor@nf.sympatico.ca

Nova Scotia Table Tennis Association (NSTTA)
5526 Spring Garden Rd., Halifax NS B3J 3G6
Tel: 902-425-5450
info@nstta.ca
nstta.ca
Overview: A small provincial organization
Member of: Table Tennis Canada
Affiliation(s): International Table Tennis Federation
Chief Officer(s): Dave Greenough, President
dwg@eastlink.ca

Ontario Table Tennis Association (OTTA)
#110, 9140 Leslie St., Richmond Hill ON L4B 0A9
otta@ontariotabletennis.com
ontariotabletennis.com
Social Media:
www.flickr.com/photos/135121071@N06/
www.facebook.com/TableTennisOntario
Overview: A small provincial organization founded in 1934
Member of: Table Tennis Canada
Affiliation(s): International Table Tennis Federation
Chief Officer(s): Attila Mosonyi, President
attila.mosonyi@gmail.com
Membership: 500+; *Fees:* Schedule available

Prince Edward Island Table Tennis Association (PEITTA)
c/o Sport PEI Inc., 40 Enman Cres., Charlottetown PE C1E 1E6
www.freewebs.com/peitta
Overview: A small provincial organization founded in 1965
Description: To promote table tennis in PEI; to provide competitive opportunities for its members; *Member of:* Table Tennis Canada; Sport PEI Inc.
Affiliation(s): International Table Tennis Federation
Finances: *Annual Operating Budget:* Less than $50,000; *Funding Sources:* Provincial government; fundraising
Staff: 10 volunteer(s)
Membership: 55-75; *Fees:* Schedule available; *Member Profile:* Table tennis players; *Committees:* Fundraising; Coaching
Activities: Hosts provincial championships, local tournaments & recreational games; *Internships:* Yes

Saskatchewan Table Tennis Association Inc. (STTA)
510 Cynthia St., Saskatoon SK S7L 7K7
Tel: 306-975-0835; *Fax:* 306-952-0835
sktta@shaw.ca
www.sktta.ca
Social Media:
www.facebook.com/ttsask
twitter.com/SKTableTennis
Overview: A small provincial organization
Description: To promote & govern the sport of table tennis in Saskatchewan.; *Member of:* Table Tennis Canada; Sask Sport
Affiliation(s): International Table Tennis Federation
Chief Officer(s): Jeffrey Woo, Executive Director
Membership: 2,200; *Fees:* $185 club; $5.25 individual
Activities: *Rents Mailing List:* Yes

Table Tennis Canada / Tennis de Table Canada
18 Louisa St., Ottawa ON K1R 6Y6
Tel: 613-733-6272; *Fax:* 613-733-7279
ttcan@ttcan.ca
ttcan.ca
Previous Name: Canadian Table Tennis Association
Overview: A medium-sized national organization founded in 1937
Description: To increase the popularity of the sport of table tennis through programs & activities; to increase participation in table tennis at all levels; *Member of:* International Table Tennis Federation
Affiliation(s): Sports Council of Canada; International Table Tennis Federation
Chief Officer(s): Tony Kiesenhofer, Chief Executive Officer
tonyk@ttcan.ca
Brian Ash, Director, Marketing
brian@ttcan.ca
Finances: *Annual Operating Budget:* $500,000-$1.5 Million; *Funding Sources:* Sponsorship; membership; government
Staff: 6 staff member(s)
Membership: 20,000; *Committees:* Technical; Administrative
Activities: STIGA Canada Cup; Canadian Championships; Canadian Junior Championships; *Rents Mailing List:* Yes

Table Tennis Yukon
4061 - 4th Ave., Whitehorse YT Y1A 1H1
Tel: 867-668-3358
sportyukon.com/member/table-tennis-yukon
Overview: A small provincial organization
Description: To promote the sport of Table Tennis in the Yukon.; *Member of:* Table Tennis Canada; Sport Yukon
Affiliation(s): International Table Tennis Federation
Chief Officer(s): David Stockdale, President
stockdale@yknet.ca

Teaching

Physical Education in British Columbia (PE-BC)
c/o British Columbia Teachers' Federation, #100, 550 West 6th Ave., Vancouver BC V5Z 4P2
Tel: 604-871-2283; *Fax:* 604-871-2286
www.bctf.ca/pebc
Social Media:
www.facebook.com/PhysicalEducationBC
Previous Name: British Columbia Physical Education Provincial Specialist Association
Overview: A medium-sized provincial organization
Description: To provide leadership, advocacy, & resources for teachers of physical education; *Member of:* British Columbia Teachers' Federation
Chief Officer(s): Lisa Manzini, President

Tennis

Alberta Tennis Association (ATA)
11759 Groat Rd., Edmonton AB T5M 3K6
Tel: 780-415-1661; *Fax:* 780-415-1693
info@tennisalberta.com
www.tennisalberta.com
Social Media:
www.facebook.com/tennisalberta
twitter.com/tennisalberta
Also Known As: Tennis Alberta
Overview: A medium-sized provincial charitable organization founded in 1973
Description: To facilitate participation, development, & visibility of tennis throughout Alberta; *Member of:* International Tennis Federation; Tennis Canada
Chief Officer(s): Jill Richard, Executive Director, 780-644-0440
jill.richard@tennisalberta.com
Brendan Smith, Coordinator, Tournament & Programs
Finances: *Funding Sources:* ASRPW Foundation; Tennis Canada; Sponsors; Self-generated revenue
Staff: 3 staff member(s)
Activities: Coaching; Officiating; *Library:* Tennis Resource Centre

Club 'Les Pongistes d'Ungava'
129, 4e av, Chibougamau QC G8P 3C4
Aperçu: *Dimension:* petite; *Envergure:* locale
Membre(s) du bureau directeur: David Pichette, Président

International Tennis Federation (ITF)
Bank Lane, Roehampton, London SW15 5XZ United Kingdom
www.itftennis.com
Social Media:
www.youtube.com/OfficialITFTennis
www.facebook.com/InternationalTennisFederation
twitter.com/ITF_Tennis
Overview: A medium-sized international organization founded in 1913
Affiliation(s): Tennis Canada
Chief Officer(s): Francesco Ricci Bitti, President
Juan Margets, Executive Vice-President
Membership: 205 nations; *Fees:* Schedule available
Activities: Grand Slam tennis events; Davis Cup; Grand Slam Cup

Northwest Territories Tennis Association
PO Box 671, Yellowknife NT X1A 2N5
Tel: 867-444-8330
www.tennisnwt.com
Also Known As: Tennis NWT
Previous Name: Tennis Northwest Territories
Overview: A small provincial organization
Description: To grow & promote the sport of tennis in the Northwest Territories; *Member of:* Tennis Canada
Chief Officer(s): Jon Brennan, President
Julie Bennett, General Manager

Nova Scotia Tennis Association
5516 Spring Garden Rd., 4th Fl., Halifax NS B3J 1G6
Tel: 902-425-5454
tennisns@sportnovascotia.ca
www.tennisnovascotia.ca
Social Media:
www.facebook.com/109415259125199
twitter.com/TennisNovaScoti
Overview: A medium-sized provincial organization
Description: To promote & create opportunities for people to play tennis in Nova Scotia; *Member of:* Tennis Canada
Chief Officer(s): Craig Bethune, President
Roger Keating, Executive Director
Marijke Nel, Technical Director
mnel@sportnovascotia.ca
Member Profile: Individuals & clubs

Ontario Tennis Association (OTA)
#200, 1 Shoreham Dr., Toronto ON M3N 3A7
Tel: 416-514-1100; *Fax:* 416-514-1112
Toll-Free: 800-387-5066
ota@tennisontario.com
www.tennisontario.com
Social Media:
www.instagram.com/ontariotennisassociation
www.facebook.com/OntarioTennisAssociation
twitter.com/TennisOntario
Previous Name: Ontario Lawn Tennis Association
Overview: A medium-sized provincial organization founded in 1918
Description: To act as the provincial governing body for tennis in Ontario; To promote participation in tennis in Ontario; To create tennis opportunities for players of every level, from

grassroots to national calibre athlete; To encourage the quest for excellence for all players; *Member of:* Tennis Canada
Chief Officer(s): Scott Fraser, President
James N. Boyce, Executive Director
jboyce@tennisontario.com
Andrew Chappell, Manager, Events
achappell@tennisontario.com
Peter Malcomson, Manager, Marketing
pmalcomson@tennisontario.com
Jay Neill, Manager, Membership
jneill@tennisontario.com
Finances: *Funding Sources:* Membership fees; Sponsorships; The Ontario Trillium Foundation
Membership: 220 clubs (55,000 youth & adult tennis players) + 2,200 individuals; *Member Profile:* Tennis clubs across Ontario, including private & commercial clubs, recreation departments, municipal parks, community clubs, & resorts
Activities: Offering professional development activities, such as clinics & tennis instructor courses; Coordinating the OTA Tennis Fair for clubs; Sanctioning tournaments; Providing guidance to clubs in the area of club management

Prince Edward Island Tennis Association
PO Box 302, 40 Enman Cres., Charlottetown PE C1A 7K7
Tel: 902-368-4985; *Fax:* 902-368-4548
tennisprinceedwardisland@gmail.com
www.tennispei.ca
Social Media:
www.facebook.com/286640596313
twitter.com/TennisPEI
Also Known As: Tennis PEI
Overview: A medium-sized provincial organization
Description: To promote the sport of tennis on PEI; *Member of:* Tennis Canada
Chief Officer(s): Daniel Arseneault, President
daniel.arseneault@gmail.com
Finances: *Funding Sources:* Government; Sponsors; Participants
Staff: 2 staff member(s); 20 volunteer(s)
Membership: 600; *Fees:* Schedule available
Activities: Offering clinics, tournaments, & other programs

Tennis BC (TBC)
#204, 210 West Broadway, Vancouver BC V5Y 3W2
Tel: 604-737-3086; *Fax:* 604-737-3124
tbc@tennisbc.org
www.tennisbc.org
Social Media:
www.youtube.com/user/TennisBC1
www.facebook.com/tennisbc
twitter.com/TennisBC
Previous Name: British Columbia Tennis Association
Overview: A medium-sized provincial organization founded in 1978
Member of: Tennis Performance Association (TPA); Tennis Canada
Chief Officer(s): Roger Skillings, President
Mark Roberts, Chief Executive Officer, 604-737-3086 9
mroberts@tennisbc.org
Finances: *Funding Sources:* Government Sponsors; Tennis Canada; Sports Grants; Events; Member Clubs
Staff: 12 staff member(s)
Membership: *Fees:* $46 adult; $27 junior
Activities: *Library:* Yes (Open to Public)

Tennis Canada
Aviva Centre, #100, 1 Shoreham Dr., Toronto ON M3N 3A6
Tel: 416-665-9777; *Fax:* 416-665-9017
Toll-Free: 877-283-6647
info@tenniscanada.com
www.tenniscanada.com
Social Media:
www.instagram.com/tennis_canada
www.facebook.com/TennisCanada
twitter.com/TennisCanada
Previous Name: Canadian Tennis Association
Overview: A large national organization founded in 1890
Description: To stimulate participation & excellence in the sport at the local, provincial, national, & international levels; To provide encouragement, support, & leadership to organizations & individuals who seek to enhance the enjoyment, quality & image of Canadian tennis; *Member of:* International Tennis Federation; Canadian Olympic Association; Canadian Paralympic Committee; International Wheelchair Tennis Association
Chief Officer(s): John LeBoutillier, Chair
Kelly D. Murumets, President & CEO
Hatem McDadi, Senior Vice-President, Tennis Development
Finances: *Funding Sources:* Government
Member Profile: Provincial tennis associations
Activities: Holding a number of championships; programs for all ages & abilities; *Awareness Events:* Rogers Cup tournament; Davis Cup; Fed Cup; *Internships:* Yes

Tennis Manitoba
#419, 145 Pacific Ave., Winnipeg MB R3B 2Z6
Tel: 204-925-5660; *Fax:* 204-925-5703
info@tennismanitoba.com
www.tennismanitoba.com
Social Media:
www.youtube.com/channel/UCXBmclr50I7GpGTP9u6UE3w
www.facebook.com/TennisManitoba
twitter.com/tennismanitoba
Also Known As: Manitoba Tennis Association
Overview: A medium-sized provincial organization founded in 1880
Description: To stimulate participation & advancement in tennis by all Manitobans; *Member of:* Sport Manitoba; Tennis Canada
Chief Officer(s): Mark Arndt, Executive Director
mark@tennismanitoba.com
Finances: *Funding Sources:* Provincial government; Manitoba Lotteries; Private sponsors
Membership: *Fees:* Schedule available

Tennis New Brunswick
PO Box 604, Fredericton NB E3B 5A6
Tel: 506-444-0885
tnb@tennisnb.net
www.tennisnb.net
Social Media:
www.facebook.com/TennisNewBrunswick
twitter.com/10sNB
Overview: A medium-sized provincial organization
Description: To be the body governing the sport of tennis in New Brunswick; *Member of:* Sport NB; Tennis Canada
Chief Officer(s): Dana Brown, President
Mark Thibault, Executive Director
Membership: *Fees:* Schedule available

Tennis Newfoundland & Labrador
Greenbelt Tennis Club, 114 Newtown Rd., St. John's NL A1B 3A7
Tel: 709-722-3840
newfoundland.tenniscanada.com
Social Media:
www.facebook.com/TennisNFLD
twitter.com/tennisnfld
Previous Name: Newfoundland & Labrador Tennis Association
Overview: A medium-sized provincial organization
Description: To grow & promote the sport of tennis throughout Newfoundland & Labrador; To increase participation at levels consistent with the personal goals & aspirations of competitors in all age groups; *Member of:* Tennis Canada
Chief Officer(s): Nancy Taylor, President
Alan Mackin, Executive Director

Tennis Québec (TQ)
285, rue Gary-Carter, Montréal QC H2R 2W1
Tél: 514-270-6060; *Téléc:* 514-270-2700
courrier@tennis.qc.ca
www.tennis.qc.ca
Média social:
www.youtube.com/user/tennisquebec
www.facebook.com/tennisquebec270
Nom précédent: Fédération québécoise de tennis
Aperçu: *Dimension:* moyenne; *Envergure:* provinciale; Organisme sans but lucratif; fondée en 1899
Description: Promotion et développement du tennis au Québec auprès de toutes les catégories d'âge et de tous les calibres; *Membre de:* Tennis Canada
Membre(s) du bureau directeur: Réjean Genois, Président
Jean François Manibal, Directeur général, 514-270-6060 606
dg1@tennis.qc.ca
Finances: *Budget de fonctionnement annuel:* $500,000-$1.5 Million
Personnel: 8 membre(s) du personnel; 30 bénévole(s)
Membre: 35 000; *Comités:* Comité des entraîneurs; Commission des officiels; Commission d'enseignement
Activités: Tournée sports experts; *Stagiaires:* Oui; *Service de conférenciers:* Oui *Bibliothèque:* Centre d'information (Bibliothèque publique) rendez-vous

Tennis Saskatchewan
2205 Victoria Ave., Regina SK S4P 0S4
Tel: 306-780-9410; *Fax:* 306-525-4009
www.tennissask.com
Previous Name: Saskatchewan Tennis Association
Overview: A medium-sized provincial organization founded in 1976
Description: To advance tennis throughout Saskatchewan by stimulating participation & excellence in the sport; To provide players throughout Saskatchewan with systematic opportunities to participate in tennis & to achieve a level of competence consistent with their abilities & aspirations, with particular emphasis on youth; To stage tennis events; To produce teams & athletes capable of winning national championships; *Member of:* Tennis Canada
Affiliation(s): Sask Sport Incorporated
Chief Officer(s): Rory Park, Executive Director
Finances: *Funding Sources:* Saskatchewan Lotteries; Tennis Canada

Tennis Yukon Association
Whitehorse YT
Tel: 867-393-2621
tennisyukon@gmail.com
www.courtsidecanada.ca/communities/Yukon
Overview: A small provincial organization
Description: To promote the sport of Tennis in the Yukon.
Chief Officer(s): Stacy Lewis, President, 867-393-2621

Therapeutic Riding

Antigonish Therapeutic Riding Association
42 Lower North Grant Rd., Antigonish NS B2G 2L1
Tel: 902-863-6221
Overview: A small local charitable organization founded in 1987
Description: To provide a therapeutic and recreational horseback riding program for physically, mentally, and emotionally handicapped people, and to promote public awareness of such a program
Chief Officer(s): Amanada Workman, President
Activities: Two six-week sessions per year; weekly horseback riding lessons for handicapped children & adults

British Columbia Therapeutic Riding Association (BCTRA)
3885B - 96th St., Delta BC V4K 3N3
Tel: 604-590-0897
ponypalstra@yahoo.ca
www.vcn.bc.ca/bctra
Overview: A small provincial charitable organization founded in 1986
Description: To adhance the quality of life of people with disabilities; *Member of:* Canadian Therapeutic Riding Association; Horse Council of British Columbia
Affiliation(s): Horse Council BC; Sports & Fitness Council for the Disabled
Chief Officer(s): Candice Miller, President
Finances: *Funding Sources:* Membership dues; donations
Membership: *Fees:* $30 group/centre; $10 individual; *Member Profile:* Therapeutic riding centres/individuals
Activities: *Speaker Service:* Yes

Canadian Therapeutic Riding Association / Association canadienne d'équitation thérapeutique
5420 Hwy. 6 North, RR#5, Guelph ON N1H 6J2
Tel: 519-767-0700
ctra@golden.net
www.cantra.ca
Social Media:
twitter.com/CanTRA_ACET
Also Known As: CanTRA
Overview: A large national charitable organization founded in 1980
Description: To foster therapeutic riding for persons with disabilities by establishing riding standards in collaboration with the medical profession; To accredit programs, certify instructors & promote research; To promote equestian sport & competition for persons with disabilities; *Member of:* Riding for Disabled International; Canadian Paralympic Committee; Canadian Equestrian Federation
Finances: *Funding Sources:* Donations; Membership fees; Fund-raising
Membership: *Fees:* $40
Activities: Offering the Certification Program for Therapeutic Riding Instructors (CTRI); *Speaker Service:* Yes

Cavalier Riding Club Ltd. (CRC)
705 Pine Glen Rd., Pine Glen NB E1J 1S1
Tel: 506-386-7652
cavalierridingclub.weebly.com
Also Known As: Greater Moncton Riding for the Disabled; CRC Therapeutic Horseback Riding for the Disabled
Overview: A small local organization
Description: To use hippotherapy in order to treat certain physical and emotional conditions of individuals with a disability; *Member of:* Canadian Therapeutic Riding Association

Central Ontario Developmental Riding Program (CODRP)
Pride Stables, 584 Pioneer Tower Rd., Kitchener ON N2P 2H9
Tel: 519-653-4686; *Fax:* 519-653-5565
info@pridestables.com
www.pridestables.com
Social Media:
www.facebook.com/PrideStables

Also Known As: Pride Stables
Overview: A small local charitable organization founded in 1973
Description: To provide a safe, high-quality riding program for persons with disabilities; to foster personal growth & improvement through the use of horses as a medium for development & therapy with the assistance of volunteers; *Member of:* Ontario Equestrian Federation; Association of Riding Establishments of Ontario
Affiliation(s): Ontario Therapeutic Riding Association (ONTRA)
Chief Officer(s): Heather Mackneson, Executive Director
Finances: *Funding Sources:* Service clubs; company & individual donations; municipal grants; special events
Staff: 8 staff member(s); 250 volunteer(s)
Membership: 350+ riders; *Member Profile:* Physical, mental & behavioral challenges
Activities: Integrated summer camp; therapeutic horseback riding; *Speaker Service:* Yes; *Library:* Yes by appointment

Community Association for Riding for the Disabled (CARD)
4777 Dufferin St., Toronto ON M3H 5T3
Tel: 416-667-8600; *Fax:* 416-739-7520
info@card.ca
www.card.ca
Overview: A medium-sized local charitable organization founded in 1969
Description: To improve the lives of children & adults with disabilities through quality therapeutic riding programs; *Member of:* Canadian Therapeutic Riding Association
Affiliation(s): Ontario Therapeutic Riding Association
Chief Officer(s): Penny Smith, Executive Director
Penny@card.ca
Finances: *Funding Sources:* Government; fundraising; special events; corporate donations; private donations
Staff: 9 staff member(s); 350 volunteer(s)
Membership: 600; *Fees:* $25
Activities: Summer program; Ride-a-thon; dinner; auction

Comox Valley Therapeutic Riding Society (CVTRS)
PO Box 3666, Courtenay BC V9N 7P1
Tel: 250-338-1968; *Fax:* 250-338-4137
cvtrs@telus.net
www.cvtrs.com
Also Known As: Therapeutic Riding
Overview: A small local charitable organization founded in 1986
Description: To provide a therapeutic riding program for physically, mentally & emotionally disabled, hearing & visually impaired children & adults; *Member of:* Canadian Therapeutic Riding Association
Affiliation(s): North American Handicapped Riding Association
Chief Officer(s): Margaret Hind, Program Director
Finances: *Funding Sources:* United Way; donations; fundraising
Staff: 13 staff member(s); 175 volunteer(s)
Membership: 130; *Fees:* $20 individual; $30 group/family
Activities: Therapy with the use of a horse

Cowichan Therapeutic Riding Association (CRTA)
c/o Providence Farm, 1843 Tzouhalem Rd., Duncan BC V9L 5L6
Tel: 250-746-1028; *Fax:* 250-746-1033
info@ctra.ca
www.ctra.ca
Social Media:
instagram.com/cowichantherapeuticriding
www.facebook.com/cowichantherapeuticridingassociation
Overview: A small local charitable organization founded in 1985
Description: To use horses to help persons with various disabilities in the Cowichan area of British Columbia achieve physical & mental health, behavioral, communication, cognitive, & social goals; To provide therapeutic or sporting activities in a safe environment with qualified instruction in order to improve the quality of life for persons with disabilities
Activities: Receiving referrals from doctors, psychologists, physiotherapists, schools, & other health care organizations; Offering individualized riding programs; Providing a training program & workplace for persons with barriers to employment; Educating the public to see the contributions of persons with disabilities

Errington Therapeutic Riding Association (ETRA)
Pyramid Stables, PO Box 462, 7581 Harby Rd., Lantzville, Parksville BC V9P 2G6
etrainfo@shaw.ca
www.etra.ca
Overview: A small local organization founded in 1989
Description: ETRA is an independent, non-profit association that gives people with disabilities the chance to ride a horse, to improve their physical and/or mental well-being, & enhance their sense of achievement & self-worth.; *Member of:* CanTRA; B.C. Therapeutic Riding Association
Affiliation(s): BC Therapeutic Riding Association; Canadian Therapeutic Riding Association
Chief Officer(s): Barry Galenzoski, President
barry.galenzoski@etra.ca
Finances: *Annual Operating Budget:* Less than $50,000; *Funding Sources:* Provincial government; rider fees; donations; community organizations
Staff: 40 volunteer(s)
Membership: 112; *Fees:* $5; *Committees:* Volunteer Coordinator; Program Coordinator; Pledge Ride; Horse & Stable Care; Newsletter; Publicity
Activities: *Speaker Service:* Yes

Halifax Area Leisure & Therapeutic Riding Association
The Stables, 1690 Bell Rd., Halifax NS B3H 2Z3
Tel: 902-423-6723
hjbl@ns.sympatico.ca
www.bengallancers.com/haltr.html
Social Media:
www.facebook.com/pages/Halifax-Junior-Bengal-Lancers/14695 17326609058
twitter.com/hfxbengalancers
Previous Name: Lancer Rehab Riders
Overview: A small local charitable organization
Description: HALTR is a volunteer-run group that provides horse-riding & driving programs for people with special needs. It is a registered charity, BN: 890783947RR0001.; *Member of:* Equine Canada; Canadian Therapeutic Riding Association
Affiliation(s): Sport Canada
Chief Officer(s): Jill Barker, Manager, 902-423-6723
hjblmanager@bellaliant.com
Member Profile: Mostly children & young adults with disabilities

Lanark County Therapeutic Riding Program (LCTRP)
30 Bennett St., Carleton Place ON K7C 4J9
Tel: 613-257-7121; *Fax:* 613-257-2675
info@therapeuticriding.ca
www.therapeuticriding.ca
Overview: A small local charitable organization founded in 1986
Description: To provide individuals a holistic approach to therapy, rehabilitation & recreation; the opportunity to experience freedom & movement astride a horse; *Member of:* Canadian Therapeutic Riding Association; Ontario Therapeutic Riding Association; Lanark Health & Community Services
Chief Officer(s): Maria Hofbauer, Head Instructor
Finances: *Annual Operating Budget:* $50,000-$100,000; *Funding Sources:* Local fundraising events; fees for service
Staff: 1 staff member(s); 45 volunteer(s)
Membership: 105 riders; *Committees:* Advisory; Fundraising
Activities: Provides individuals a holistic approach to therapy, rehabilitation & recreation & the opportunity to experience freedom when riding a horse; *Internships:* Yes

Lethbridge Therapeutic Riding Association (LTRA)
RR#8-24-6, Lethbridge AB T1J 4P4
Tel: 403-328-2165; *Fax:* 403-317-0235
info@ltra.ca
www.ltra.ca
Also Known As: Rainbow Riding Centre
Overview: A small local charitable organization founded in 1977
Description: To provide the opportunity for improved physical & emotional well-being for people of all ages & abilities who participate in therapeutic, recreational, educational & competitive riding programs at Rainbow Riding Centre; *Member of:* Canadian Therapeutic Riding Association
Chief Officer(s): Rick Austin, Executive Director
raustin@ltra.ca
Finances: *Annual Operating Budget:* $100,000-$250,000
Staff: 2 staff member(s); 200 volunteer(s)
Membership: 260; *Fees:* Schedule available; *Committees:* Facility; Program; Fundraising; Public relations; Foundation
Activities: 5-6 riding sessions per year; summer Ride On camp; Easter clinic

Little Bits Therapeutic Riding Association
PO Box 29016, Stn. Pleasantview, Edmonton AB T6H 5Z6
Tel: 780-476-1233; *Fax:* 780-476-7252
info@littlebits.ca
www.littlebits.ca
Social Media:
www.facebook.com/LittleBitsVolunteers
Overview: A small local charitable organization founded in 1978
Description: To provide recreational riding programs that have therapeutic benefits for disabled children & adults in Edmonton & surrounding area. Physical address: Whitemud Equine Learning Centre Association, 12504 Fox Dr. NW, Edmonton, AB T6G 2L6; *Member of:* Central Canadian Therapeutic Riding Association; North American Riding for the Handicapped Association
Chief Officer(s): Linda Rault, Riding Administrator
Membership: 200; *Committees:* Finance; Fundraising; Public Relations; Riding Program; Camp Horseshoe

Manitoba Riding for the Disabled Association Inc. (MRDA)
145 Pacific Ave., Winnipeg MB R3B 2Z6
Tel: 204-925-5905; *Fax:* 204-925-5792
exedir@mrda.cc
www.mrda.cc
Social Media:
www.facebook.com/105010909544565
Overview: A small provincial charitable organization founded in 1977
Description: To provide a therapeutic horseback riding program for children with disabilities.; *Member of:* Canadian Therapeutic Riding Association
Chief Officer(s): Peter Manastyrsky, Executive Director
Finances: *Funding Sources:* corporate sponsors
Staff: 100 volunteer(s)

Mirabel Morgan Special Riding Centre
1201 - 2nd Line South, Bailieboro ON K0L 1B0
Tel: 705-939-6485
mirabelmf@gmail.com
Overview: A small local organization
Description: Year round program for anyone who wishes to ride who has medical, physical, or emotional needs; for those who enjoy the outdoors & animals, want to improve flexibility, balance, joint, muscle & nerve stimulation; designed to meet unique needs, limitations & abilities of the rider; *Member of:* Canadian Therapeutic Riding Association

Mount View Special Riding Association (MVSRA)
PO Box 1637, Didsbury AB T0M 0W0
Tel: 403-335-9146; *Fax:* 403-556-6480
www.mountviewriding.com
Previous Name: Mountview Handicapped Riding Association
Overview: A small local charitable organization founded in 1983
Description: To provide recreational & therapeutic riding to specially abled adults & children with mental &/or physical disabilities; *Member of:* Canadian Therapeutic Riding Association
Chief Officer(s): Karla Brautigam, President
Karla@asc-mva.ab.ca
Finances: *Annual Operating Budget:* Less than $50,000
Staff: 40 volunteer(s)
Membership: 75; *Fees:* $5

Ontario Therapeutic Riding Association (OnTRA) / Association ontarienne d'équitation thérapeutique
47 Fairlane Rd., London ON N6K 3E3
info@ontra.ca
www.ontra.ca
Overview: A small provincial charitable organization founded in 1983
Description: The Ontario Therapeutic Riding Association (OnTRA) promotes horseback riding as a form of therapy and sport for children and adults living with physical, cognitive, emotional, and/or behavioural challenges. OnTRA provides volunteers and therapeutic riding professionals with on-going information and training to ensure riders with disabilities receive the best possible therapy.; *Member of:* Canadian Therapeutic Riding Association; Ontario Equestrian Federation
Chief Officer(s): Megan Watson, Acting President
Virginia Pohler, Treasurer
Finances: *Annual Operating Budget:* Less than $50,000
Staff: 2500 volunteer(s)
Membership: 250; *Fees:* $20 individual; $30 family; $12 junior; $300 lifetime; *Committees:* Fundraising; Education; Competition; Public Relations; Physiotherapy
Activities: Competitions; promotion; educational clinic; grants; Used Equipment Program; *Speaker Service:* Yes

Pacific Riding for Developing Abilities (PRDA)
1088 - 208 St., Langley BC V2Z 1T4
Tel: 604-530-8717; *Fax:* 604-530-8617
www.prda.ca
Social Media:
www.facebook.com/PRDALangley
Previous Name: Pacific Riding for Disabled Association
Overview: A small local charitable organization founded in 1973
Description: To enhance the quality of life for people with a range of disabilities, providing therapeutic equestrian activities & educational opportunities.; *Member of:* Canadian Therapeutic Riding Association; Langley Chamber of Commerce; North American Riding for the Handicapped Association
Affiliation(s): Ishtar Transition Housing Society; Burnaby Association for Community Inclusion
Chief Officer(s): Michelle Ingall, Executive Director
Finances: *Funding Sources:* Donations; fundraising; United Way of the Lower Mainland
Staff: 8 staff member(s)
Activities: Day camp; summer camp; horse shows; *Speaker Service:* Yes; *Rents Mailing List:* Yes; *Library:* Yes (Open to Public)

PARD Therapeutic Riding (PARD)
PO Box 1654, Peterborough ON K9J 5S4
Tel: 705-742-6441
info@pard.ca
www.pard.ca
Social Media:
www.facebook.com/137292022962475
Previous Name: Peterborough Association for Riding for the Disabled
Overview: A small local charitable organization
Description: Provides the benefits of riding to people with disabilities.; *Member of:* Canadian Therapeutic Riding Association; Ontario Therapeutic Riding Association
Chief Officer(s): Angie Muir, Co-Chair
Activities: Horseback riding instruction as a form of therapeutic & social recreation for physically, emotionally, developmentally challenged individuals

Peace Area Riding for the Disabled (PARDS)
8202 - 84 St., Grande Prairie AB T8X 0L6
Tel: 780-538-3211; *Fax:* 780-538-3683
www.pards.ca
Overview: A small local charitable organization founded in 1984
Description: To enhance the lives of individuals with disabilities through "equine assisted therapy"; To promoten physical, emotional, intellectual & social growth for individuals with disabilities through therapeutic riding services; To build a community that embraces differences & supports growth & success for all of its members; *Member of:* Canadian Therapeutic Riding Association
Chief Officer(s): Raymond Binks, Chair
Jennifer Douglas, Executive Director
Activities: Summer camp

Quinte Therapeutic Riding Association (QUINTRA)
173 McGee Rd., RR#2, Stirling ON K0K 3E0
Tel: 613-395-4472
www.quintra.org
Overview: A small local charitable organization founded in 1985
Description: To offer therapeutic horseback-riding sessions to disabled children & young adults to maximize the disabled person's physical & mental capabilities; To improve disabled young people's self-confidence & the ability to cope with everyday living; *Member of:* Canadian Therapeutic Riding Association; Ontario Therapeutic Riding Association
Affiliation(s): United Way of Quinte
Chief Officer(s): Barb Davis, Contact
barbara.davis@sympatico.ca
Finances: *Funding Sources:* Donations; Bingos; United Way Quinte
Activities: *Speaker Service:* Yes

Regina Therapeutic Riding Association (RTRA)
PO Box 474, Regina SK S4P 3A2
Tel: 306-530-0794
ReginaTRA@sasktel.net
rtra.ca
Social Media:
www.facebook.com/reginatherapeuticridingassociation
Overview: A small provincial charitable organization founded in 1992
Description: To provide medically supervised horseback riding lessons for individuals with special needs.
Chief Officer(s): John Van Knoll, Chair

SARI Therapeutic Riding
12659 Medway Rd., RR#1, Arva ON N0M 1C0
Tel: 519-666-1123; *Fax:* 519-666-1971
office@sari.ca
www.sari.ca
Social Media:
www.facebook.com/pages/SARI-Therapeutic-Riding/144808638863962
Also Known As: Special Ability Riding Institute
Previous Name: SARI Riding for Disabled
Overview: A medium-sized local charitable organization founded in 1978
Description: To provide opportunities for people with special needs to move towards greater independence & freedom, through their connection with horses, by providing therapeutic riding & driving programs which meet individual needs; To balance safety & challenge to maximize opportunities for growth; To support contributions of participants, parents, volunteers & staff; *Member of:* Canadian Therapeutic Riding Association
Affiliation(s): Ontario Therapeutic Riding Association
Chief Officer(s): Diane Blackall, Executive Director
Finances: *Funding Sources:* Individual & service club donations; fundraising events
Staff: 200 volunteer(s)
Membership: 150; *Committees:* Fund Development; Human Resources; Program; Marketing & Communications
Activities: Summer equestrian program

Sunrise Therapeutic Riding & Learning Centre
6920 Concession 1, RR#2, Puslinch ON N0B 2J0
Tel: 519-837-0558; *Fax:* 519-837-1233
info@sunrise-therapeutic.ca
www.sunrise-therapeutic.ca
Social Media:
www.facebook.com/224072694372280
Also Known As: Sunrise
Previous Name: Sunrise Equestrian & Recreation Centre for the Disabled
Overview: A small local charitable organization founded in 1982
Description: To develop the full potential of children & adults with disabilites & lead them closer to independence through therapy, recreation, horse riding, life skills & farm related activity programme; *Member of:* Canadian Therapeutic Riding Association; Ontario Therapeutic Riding Association
Affiliation(s): Ontario's Promise
Chief Officer(s): Rob Vandebelt, Chief Executive Officer, 519-837-0558 32
rob@sunrise-therapeutic.ca
Nikki Duffield, Program Director & Head Instructor, 519-837-0558 29
nikkid@sunrise-therapeutic.ca
Lynne O'Brien, Manager, Operations & Volunteer, 519-837-0558 31
lynne@sunrise-therapeutic.ca
Finances: *Annual Operating Budget:* $250,000-$500,000; *Funding Sources:* Service clubs; Foundations; Industry; Corporate; Private; Golf tournament; Ride-a-thon
Staff: 18 staff member(s); 175 volunteer(s)
Membership: 250; *Fees:* $30; *Committees:* Finance; Fundraising; Public Relations/Marketing; Medical Advisory; Farm Management
Activities: Therapeutic riding; life skills program; Employment preparation courses for young adults with special needs; Therapeutic Riding Instructor Training School; integrated day camps; equestrian clinics; schooling shows; "Little Breeches" Club (4-7 years); education program for school groups (JK-3); monthly board & instructor meetings; Fall Open House; demonstrations at Royal Winter Fair; invitational horse shows; *Internships:* Yes; *Library:* Resource Centre for Instructor School (Open to Public) by appointment

Therapeutic Ride Algoma
2627 Second Line West, Sault Ste Marie ON P6A 6K4
Tel: 705-759-9282
therapeuticridealgoma@hotmail.ca
www.ridealgoma.com
Overview: A small local organization
Member of: Canadian Therapeutic Riding Association
Chief Officer(s): Bob Trainor, President

Victoria Therapeutic Riding Association (VTRA)
PO Box 412, Brentwood Bay BC V8M 1R3
Tel: 778-426-0506
vtra.ca
Social Media:
www.facebook.com/VictoriaTherapeuticRidingAssociation
Previous Name: Victoria Riding for Disabled Association
Overview: A small local charitable organization founded in 1982
Description: To provide a therapeutic riding program for children & adults with disabilities to promote their physical, psychological, & social well-being; *Member of:* Canadian Therapeutic Riding Association
Affiliation(s): B.C. Therapeutic Riding Association; Horse Council of British Columbia; Volunteer Victoria; Canadian Therapeutic Riding Association's; Association of Fundraising Professionals
Chief Officer(s): Carol Hubberstey, President
Sue Colgate, Executive Director
Finances: *Funding Sources:* Service club; fund-raising events; foundations
Staff: 4 staff member(s); 100 volunteer(s)
Membership: *Fees:* $20 individual; $200 life; $10 riders

Windsor-Essex Therapeutic Riding Association (WETRA) / Association d'équitation thérapeutique Windsor-Essex
3323 North Maklen Rd., RR#2, Essex ON N8M 2X6
Tel: 519-726-7682; *Fax:* 519-726-4403
info@wetra.ca
www.wetra.ca
Social Media:
www.facebook.com/525824287490852
twitter.com/WETRA_
Overview: A small local charitable organization founded in 1969
Description: To improve the quality of life of physically, emotionally, mentally challenged persons through equine related therapy; *Member of:* Canadian Therapeutic Riding Association
Affiliation(s): Ontario Therapeutic Riding Association
Chief Officer(s): Becky Mills, Managing Director

Finances: *Annual Operating Budget:* $100,000-$250,000; *Funding Sources:* United Way; Donations; Bingo
Staff: 12 staff member(s); 80 volunteer(s)
Membership: 200 riders
Activities: Offering therapeutic riding & horse shows; Hosting an open house, benefit horse show, & golf tournament; *Awareness Events:* Ride-a-Thon, March

Track & Field Sports

Achilles Canada
123 Snowden Ave., Toronto ON M4N 2A8
Tel: 416-485-6451; *Fax:* 416-485-0823
www.achillescanada.ca
Previous Name: Achilles Track Club Canada
Overview: A medium-sized national charitable organization founded in 1999
Description: To encourage & assist all persons with disabilities to enjoy running for health in a social environment
Chief Officer(s): Brian McLean, Contact
bmclean@achillescanada.ca
Membership: *Fees:* $25 donation encouraged
Activities: Provides support, training, & technical expertise to runners at all levels; Achilles welcomes people with all disabilities: visual disability, cerebral palsy, paraplegia, arthritis, epilepsy, multiple sclerosis, amputation, cystic fibrosis, stroke, cancer, traumatic head injury, & many others; runners participate with crutches, in wheelchairs, on prostheses, & without aids; *Awareness Events:* Achilles St. Patrick's Day 5K Run/Walk, March

Athletics Canada / Athlétisme Canada
#B1-110, 2445 St-Laurent Blvd., Ottawa ON K1G 6C3
Tel: 613-260-5580; *Fax:* 613-260-0341
athcan@athletics.ca
www.athletics.ca
Social Media:
www.youtube.com/AthleticsCanada
www.facebook.com/Canadatrackandfield
twitter.com/athleticscanada
Previous Name: Canadian Track & Field Association
Overview: A large national organization
Description: To promote & encourage participation via competitions from the grass roots level through to the very highest level of proficiency; To assist coaches, officials & executives in fulfilling their goals through courses, conferences & clinics; To provide regular communication lines with members; To continually review & update technical programs; To assist in the research & investigation of potential new facilities; To engender more public awareness, interest & acceptance of the sport of track & field; *Member of:* International Association of Athletics Federations
Affiliation(s): International Amateur Athletic Federation
Chief Officer(s): Gordon Orlikow, Chair
gordon.orlikow@kornferry.com
Rob Guy, CEO
rguy@athletics.ca
Sally Clare, Director, Finance
sclare@athletics.ca
Mathieu Gentès, Director, Public Relations & Corporate Services
mgentes@athletics.ca
Kristine Deacon, Coordinator, National Team Programs
kdeacon@athletics.ca
Activities: Offering national team events

Canadian Masters Athletic Association (CMAA)
Tel: 416-380-2503
canadianmasters.ca
Previous Name: Canadian Masters Track & Field Association
Overview: A medium-sized national organization founded in 1972
Chief Officer(s): Paul Osland, President
paul.osland@hotmail.com
Sherry Watts, Contact, Membership
pacertraining@yahoo.ca
Finances: *Funding Sources:* Membership fees
Membership: 1,527; *Member Profile:* Men & women 30 and up

Ontario Masters Athletics (OMA)
1185 Eglinton Ave. East, Toronto ON M3C 3C6
Tel: 416-426-4427; *Fax:* 416-426-7358
douglasj.smith@sympatico.ca
www.ontariomasters.ca
Social Media:
www.youtube.com/OntarioMasters
twitter.com/OntarioMasters
Previous Name: Ontario Masters Track & Field Association
Overview: A small provincial organization founded in 1973

Member of: Canadian Masters Athletic Association
Affiliation(s): Athletics Ontario; Athletics Canada
Chief Officer(s): Doug Smith, President
douglasj.smith@sympatico.ca
Karla Del Grande, Vice-President
karla.delgrande@bell.net
Membership: *Fees:* $40 individual; $60 family

Triathlon

Alberta Triathlon Association (ATA)
Percy Page Centre, 11759 Groat Rd., Edmonton AB T5M 3K6
Tel: 780-427-8616; *Fax:* 780-427-8628
Toll-Free: 866-888-7448
info@triathlon.ab.ca
www.triathlon.ab.ca
Social Media:
www.facebook.com/160835077267482
twitter.com/TriAlberta
Overview: A small provincial organization founded in 1984
Description: ATA is the official, non-profit governing body for, & has a mandate to develop, the sports of triathlon, duathlon, aquathlon & other related multi-endurance sports in Alberta.; *Member of:* Triathlon Canada
Chief Officer(s): Calli Stromner, General Manager
general.manager@triathlon.ab.ca
Sebastian Porten, Manager, Programs
coordinator@triathlon.ab.ca
Finances: *Annual Operating Budget:* $100,000-$250,000
Staff: 1 staff member(s); 16 volunteer(s)
Membership: 1,000+; *Fees:* $15 youth (19 & under); $50 adult/coach
Activities: *Speaker Service:* Yes

Ontario Association of Triathletes (OAT)
#2, 2015 Pan Am Blvd., Milton ON L9T 879
Tel: 416-426-7025
info@triathlonontario.com
www.triathlonontario.com
Social Media:
www.facebook.com/TriathlonOntario
twitter.com/TriOntario
Also Known As: Triathlon Ontario
Overview: A small provincial organization
Description: To encourage participation in multi-sport events & to ensure safety & fair competition; to assist, support & promote Ontario athletes; *Member of:* Triathlon Canada
Chief Officer(s): Phil Dale, Executive Director
ed@triathlonontario.com
Emma Leeder, Manager, Program
technical@triathlonontario.com
Greg Kealey, Coach, Provincial Development
coach@triathlonontario.com
Finances: *Funding Sources:* Fees; sponsorship; government
Membership: 1,000-4,999; *Fees:* Schedule available

Saskatchewan Triathlon Association Corporation (STAC)
PO Box 21008, Saskatoon SK S7H 5N9
Tel: 306-292-8270; *Fax:* 306-477-0495
info@triathlonsaskatchewan.org
www.triathlonsaskatchewan.org
Social Media:
www.facebook.com/287275596696
twitter.com/SaskTriathlon
Overview: A small provincial organization
Description: To be the provincial governing body of triathlon in Saskatchewan.; *Member of:* Triathlon Canada
Chief Officer(s): Mark Gibson, President
Fred Dyck, Executive Director

Triathlon British Columbia
PO Box 34098, Stn. D, Vancouver BC V6J 4M1
Tel: 604-736-3176; *Fax:* 604-736-3180
info@tribc.org
www.tribc.org
Social Media:
www.facebook.com/TriathlonBC
Also Known As: Triathlon BC
Overview: A small provincial organization
Description: To be the provincial governing body of triathlon, duathlon, aquathon & winter triathlon in British Columbia.; *Member of:* Triathlon Canada
Chief Officer(s): Les Pereira, President
Allan Prazsky, Executive Director

Triathlon Canada
#121, 1925 Blanshard St., Victoria BC V8T 4J2
Tel: 250-412-1795; *Fax:* 250-412-1794
info@triathloncanada.com
www.triathloncanada.com
Social Media:
www.facebook.com/148631098541373
twitter.com/TriathlonCanada
Previous Name: National Federation for the Sports of Triathlon, Duathlon & Aquathlon in Canada
Overview: A small national organization
Description: To function as the National Federation for triathlon & duathlon in Canada, & to represent Canada internationally; to promote the triathlon & duathlon, both competitive & non-competitive in Canada; to encourage support of Triathlon Canada programmes by the public generally; to provide guidance, information & assistance to the provincial triathlon associations, zones & clubs in respect to these objects & in the development of programmes for competitive & non-competitive triathletes & duathletes; to affiliate all provincial associations to Triathlon Canada who are the Provincial Sports Governing Bodies, or who are in the process of becoming the Provincial Sports Governing Bodies in their province; to organize training courses for triathletes, duathletes, coaches & administrators to national & international standards; to promote other multi-disciplined endurance events & excluding the traditional decathlon, pentathlon, heptathlon, modern pentathlon & biathlon, which are part of existing National Federations
Chief Officer(s): Tim Wilson, Chief Executive Officer
tim.wilson@triathloncanada.com
Chris Dornan, Manager, Communications, 403-620-8731
hpprchris@shaw.ca

Triathlon Manitoba
c/o Sport for Life Centre, 145 Pacific Ave., Winnipeg MB R3B 2Z6
Tel: 204-925-5636; *Fax:* 204-925-5703
www.triathlon.mb.ca
Social Media:
www.facebook.com/TriathlonManitoba
twitter.com/MBTri
Overview: A small provincial organization
Description: To be the provincial governing body of triathlon in Manitoba.; *Member of:* Triathlon Canada; Sport Manitoba
Chief Officer(s): Kevin Freedman, Executive Director
kevin.freedman@triathlon.mb.ca

Triathlon New Brunswick
PO Box 22053, Stn. Landsdowne, Saint John NB E2K 4T7
Tel: 506-848-1144
www.trinb.ca
Social Media:
www.facebook.com/17550162914547
twitter.com/TriathlonNB
Also Known As: Triathlon NB
Overview: A small provincial organization
Description: To be the provincial governing body of triathlon in New Brunswick.; *Member of:* Triathlon Canada
Chief Officer(s): Paul Lavoie, President
lavoiep19@gmail.com
Jim Johnson, Executive Director
jimejohnson@gmail.com

Triathlon Newfoundland & Labrador
PO Box 872, Stn. C, St. John's NL A1C 5L7
admin@trinl.com
www.trinl.com
Social Media:
www.facebook.com/triathlon.nl
twitter.com/trinl
Also Known As: TriNL
Overview: A small provincial organization
Description: To be the governing body for the sport of triathalon in Newfoundland & Labrador; *Member of:* Triathlon Canada
Affiliation(s): International Triathlon Union
Chief Officer(s): Rob Coleman, President
president@trinl.com
Membership: *Fees:* $10 youth/one event; $20 adult

Triathlon Nova Scotia
c/o Sport Nova Scotia, 5516 Spring Garden Rd., 4th Fl., Halifax NS B3J 1G6
Tel: 902-425-5450; *Fax:* 902-425-5606
triathlon@sportnovascotia.ca
www.trins.ca
Social Media:
www.facebook.com/17550162914547
twitter.com/TriathlonNB
Overview: A small provincial organization
Description: To be the provincial governing body of triathlon in Nova Scotia.; *Member of:* Triathlon Canada; Sport Nova Scotia

Triathlon PEI
40 Enman Cres., Charlottetown PE C1A 7K7
triathlonpei@gmail.com
www.tripei.com
Social Media:
twitter.com/triathlonpei
Overview: A small provincial organization founded in 2012
Description: To be the provincial governing body of triathlon in Prince Edward Island.; *Member of:* Triathlon Canada
Chief Officer(s): Jamie Nickerson, President

Triathlon Québec
4545, av Pierre-de Coubertin, Montréal QC H1V 3R2
Tél: 514-252-3121
www.triathlonquebec.org
Média social:
www.facebook.com/132997480092478
twitter.com/triathlonquebec
Aperçu: *Dimension:* petite; *Envergure:* provinciale; fondée en 1985
Membre de: Triathlon Canada
Affiliation(s): Triathlon Canada
Membre(s) du bureau directeur: Marie-Eve Sullivan, Directrice générale, 514-252-3121 4
msullivan@triathlonquebec.org
Finances: *Budget de fonctionnement annuel:* $250,000-$500,000
Personnel: 3 membre(s) du personnel; 20 bénévole(s)
Membre: 1 100
Activités: *Stagiaires:* Oui

Universities & Colleges

Alberta Colleges Athletic Conference (ACAC)
Percy Page Centre, 11759 Groat Rd., Edmonton AB T5M 3K6
www.acac.ab.ca
Social Media:
www.facebook.com/AlbertaCollegesAthleticConference
twitter.com/ACAC_Sport
Previous Name: Western Inter-College Conference (WICC)
Overview: A small provincial charitable organization founded in 1964
Description: To act as the governing body for intercollegiate athletics in Alberta; To develop student athletes; *Member of:* Canadian Colleges Athletic Association
Chief Officer(s): Mark Kosak, Chief Executive Officer, 403-875-7329, Fax: 780-427-9289
markk@acac.ab.ca
Anthony Wong, Manager, Operations, 780-644-1143
anthonyw@acac.ab.ca
Finances: *Funding Sources:* Membership; Government of Alberta, through the Alberta Sport, Recreation, Parks, & Wildlife Foundation
Membership: 17 schools; *Member Profile:* Colleges & universities in Saskatchewan & Alberta
Activities: Administering intercollegiate athletics

Canadian Collegiate Athletic Association (CCAA) / Association canadienne du sport collégial (ACSC)
2 St. Lawrence Dr., Cornwall ON K6H 4Z1
Tel: 613-937-1508; *Fax:* 613-937-1530
sandra@ccaa.ca
www.ccaa.ca
Social Media:
www.youtube.com/ccaasportsacsc;
instagram.com/ccaasportsacsc
www.facebook.com/CCAAsportsACSC
twitter.com/CCAAsportsACSC
Overview: A medium-sized national organization founded in 1974
Description: To operate as the national governing body for men's & women's college sport in Canada
Affiliation(s): Atlantic Colleges Athletic Association; Fédération québécoise du sport étudiant; Ontario Colleges Athletic Association; Alberta Colleges Athletic Conference; British Columbia Colleges Athletic Association
Chief Officer(s): Sandra Murray-MacDonell, Executive Director
sandra@ccaa.ca
Membership: 108 institutional

Canadian Council of University Physical Education & Kinesiology Administrators (CCUPEKA) / Conseil canadien des administrateurs universitaires en éducation physique et kinésiologie (CCAUEPK)
c/o Dr. J. Starkes, Department of Kinesiology, McMaster University, Hamilton ON L8S 4K1
www.ccupeka.ca
Overview: A small national organization founded in 1971

Description: To serve as an accrediting body for physical education & kinesiology programs at universities in Canada; To offer a voice for academics, through lobbying initiatives
Chief Officer(s): Angela Belcastro, President
Member Profile: Administrators of physical education & kinesiology programs at Canadian universities
Activities: Offering a forum for discussion among members

Canadian Interuniversity Sport (CIS) / Sport interuniversitaire canadien (SIC)

#N205, 801 King Edward, Ottawa ON K1N 6N5
Tel: 613-562-5670; *Fax:* 613-562-5669
feedback@universitysport.ca
www.cis-sic.ca
Social Media:
www.youtube.com/universitysport; www.instagram.com/CIS_SIC
www.facebook.com/cissports
twitter.com/CIS_SIC

Previous Name: Canadian Interuniversity Athletic Union
Overview: A medium-sized national organization
Description: To act as the national governing body for men's & women's university sport in Canada
Affiliation(s): Atlantic University Sport; Québec Student Sport Federation; Ontario University Athletics; Canada West Universities Athletic Association
Chief Officer(s): Drew Love, Interim Chief Operating Officer, 613-568-5670 26
dlove@universitysport.ca
Debbie Villeneuve, Director, Finance & Administration, 613-568-5670 24
villeneuve@universitysport.ca
Membership: 55 institutional (these are also members of four regional associations)

Ontario University Athletics (OUA) / Sports universitaires de l'Ontario

#2, 3305 Harvester Rd., Burlington ON L7N 3N2
Tel: 905-635-5510; *Fax:* 905-635-5820
info@oua.ca
www.oua.ca
Social Media:
www.youtube.com/ouachampionsforlife;
www.instagram.com/ouasport
www.facebook.com/OntarioUniversityAthletics
twitter.com/ouasport

Previous Name: Ontario Universities Athletics
Overview: A small provincial organization founded in 1898
Description: To provide leadership, stewardship & policy direction for university sport; To govern interuniversity sport competition in Ontario on behalf of member institutions; *Member of:* Canadian Interuniversity Sport
Chief Officer(s): Gord Grace, Chief Executive Officer, 905-635-7470
gord.grace@oua.ca
Finances: *Annual Operating Budget:* $250,000-$500,000
Staff: 8 staff member(s)
Membership: 19 schools; 9,000 student athletes
Activities: *Awareness Events:* Women of Influence Luncheon, Nov.; *Internships:* Yes

Volleyball

Fédération de volleyball du Québec (FVBQ)

4545, av Pierre-de-Coubertin, Montréal QC H1V 0B2
Tél: 514-252-3065; *Téléc:* 514-252-3176
info-fvbq@volleyball.qc.ca
www.volleyball.qc.ca
Média social:
www.youtube.com/volleyballquebec
www.facebook.com/VolleyballQC
twitter.com/volleyballqc

Également appelé: Volleyball Québec
Aperçu: *Dimension:* moyenne; *Envergure:* provinciale; Organisme sans but lucratif; fondée en 1968
Description: Régir le volleyball à l'intérieur et à l'extérieur du Québec; promouvoir le volleyball; former les intervenants impliqués dans l'encadrement du participant; offrir des services aux membres
Affiliation(s): Sports Québec; Regroupement loisirs Québec
Membre(s) du bureau directeur: Félix Dion, Président
Finances: *Budget de fonctionnement annuel:* $500,000-$1.5 Million; *Fonds:* Gouvernement provincial
Personnel: 5 membre(s) du personnel; 100 bénévole(s)
Membre: 20,000; *Critères d'admissibilite:* Entraîneurs, athlètes, arbitres, adeptes, bénévoles; *Comités:* Entraîneurs; Arbitres; Élite; Techniques
Activités: Volleybal compétitif et récréatif; édition, publication et vente de documents techniques et pédagogiques; programme de formation des entraîneurs; vente de vidéos; *Stagiaires:* Oui; *Service de conférenciers:* Oui *Bibliothèque:* Oui rendez-vous

International Volleyball Association / Fédération Internationale de Volleyball (FIVB)

Château Les Tourelles, Edouard-Sandoz 2-4, Lausanne 1006 Switzerland
info@fivb.org
www.fivb.ch
Social Media:
www.youtube.com/videofivb; instagram.com/fivbvolleyball
www.facebook.com/FIVB.InternationalVolleyballFederation
twitter.com/fivbvolleyball

Overview: A small international organization founded in 1947
Affiliation(s): Canadian Volleyball Association
Chief Officer(s): Ary S. Graça Filho, President
president.office.sec@fivb.org
Fabio Azevedo, General Director
Membership: 211

Manitoba Volleyball Association (MVA)

#412, 145 Pacific Ave., Winnipeg MB R3B 2Z6
Tel: 204-925-5783; *Fax:* 204-925-5786
www.volleyballmanitoba.ca
Social Media:
twitter.com/VBManitoba

Overview: A small provincial organization founded in 1977
Description: To govern the sport of volleyball in Manitoba; To promote the development & growth of volleyball in the province
Chief Officer(s): John Blacher, Executive Director
volleyball.ed@sportmanitoba.ca
Finances: *Funding Sources:* Fundraising
Staff: 4 staff member(s)
Member Profile: Elite & recreational athletes, coaches, officials; *Committees:* Grassroots Development; Competitions; Finance & Audit; Marketing; Awards & Recognition; Conduct & Ethics; Nominations; Governance; High Performance Development; Hall of Fame
Activities: Offering coaching clinics; Training & certifying officials; Providing competitive programs; Conducting Youth Talent Identification Camps; *Library:* Manitoba Volleyball Association Resource Library

Newfoundland & Labrador Volleyball Association (NLVA)

1296A Kenmount Rd., Paradise NL A1L 1N3
Tel: 709-576-0817; *Fax:* 709-576-7493
www.nlva.net

Overview: A small provincial organization founded in 1986
Description: To promote volleyball in Newfoundland & Labrador; To provide competitive opportunities for its members
Chief Officer(s): Russell Jackson, Executive Director
nlvaruss@sportnl.ca
Luke Harris, Director, Technical
nlvaluke@sportnl.ca

Northwest Territories Volleyball Association (NWTVA)

4909 - 49 St., 3rd Fl., Yellowknife NT X1A 3X7
Tel: 867-669-8396; *Fax:* 867-669-8327
www.nwtvolleyball.ca
Social Media:
www.facebook.com/NWTVolleyballAssociation
twitter.com/NWTVA

Overview: A medium-sized provincial organization
Description: To promote volleyball in the Northwest Territories; To provide competitive opportunities for members
Chief Officer(s): Lyric Sandhals, Executive Director
lsandhals@sportnorth.com

Ontario Volleyball Association (OVA)

#304, 3 Concorde Gate, Toronto ON M3C 3N7
Tel: 416-426-7316; *Fax:* 416-426-7109
Toll-Free: 800-372-1568
info@ontariovolleyball.org
www.ontariovolleyball.org
Social Media:
www.youtube.com/user/ontariovolley;
www.instagram.com/ova_updates
www.facebook.com/OntarioVolleyball
twitter.com/ova_updates

Overview: A large provincial organization founded in 1929
Description: To lead in the promotion & development of volleyball in Ontario
Chief Officer(s): Jo-Anne Ljubicic, Executive Director, 416-426-7414
jljubicic@ontariovolleyball.org
Membership: *Fees:* Schedule available; *Committees:* Train to Compete; Beach; Executive
Activities: *Internships:* Yes

Saskatchewan Volleyball Association

1750 McAra St., Regina SK S4N 6L4
Tel: 306-780-9250; *Fax:* 306-780-9288
Toll-Free: 800-321-1685
meta@saskvolleyball.ca
www.saskvolleyball.ca
Social Media:
www.instagram.com/saskvolleyball
www.facebook.com/saskvolleyball
twitter.com/saskvolleyball

Overview: A small provincial organization
Description: To develop interest, participation & excellence in volleyball through the promotion & provision of quality services for all
Chief Officer(s): Aaron Demyen, Executive Director, aaron@saskvolleyball.ca, 306-780-9801
Finances: *Annual Operating Budget:* $500,000-$1.5 Million; *Funding Sources:* Corporate sponsors
Staff: 9 staff member(s); 2200 volunteer(s)

Volleyball Alberta

Percy Page Centre, 11759 Groat Rd., Edmonton AB T5M 3K6
Tel: 780-415-1703; *Fax:* 780-415-1700
info@volleyballalberta.ca
www.volleyballalberta.ca
Social Media:
www.youtube.com/channel/UCofbTw7zPP30PVt8pzDrPAw
www.facebook.com/VolleyballAlberta
twitter.com/volleyballab

Overview: A medium-sized provincial charitable organization founded in 1974
Description: To promote volleyball in Alberta; To provide competitive opportunities for members
Affiliation(s): Federation of Outdoor Volleyball Associations
Chief Officer(s): Terry Gagnon, Executive Director, 587-273-1513
tgagnon@volleyballalberta.ca
Activities: *Internships:* Yes; *Rents Mailing List:* Yes

Volleyball BC

Harry Jerome Sports Centre, 7564 Barnet Hwy., Burnaby BC V5A 1E7
Tel: 604-291-2007; *Fax:* 604-291-2602
www.volleyballbc.org
Social Media:
instagram.com/volleyballbc
www.facebook.com/pages/Volleyball-BC/236547563024786
twitter.com/VolleyballBC

Also Known As: British Columbia Volleyball Association
Overview: A medium-sized provincial organization founded in 1965
Description: To promote volleyball in British Columbia; To provide competitive opportunities for members
Chief Officer(s): Chris Densmore, Executive Director, 604-291-2007 223
execdirector@volleyballbc.org
Chris Berglund, Director, Technical & High Performance, 604-291-2007 222
cberglund@volleyballbc.org
Dave Brewin, Manager, Marketing & Communications, 604-291-2007 226
communications@volleyballbc.org

Volleyball Canada (VC)

National Office, #1A, 1084 Kenaston St., Ottawa ON K1B 3P5
Tel: 613-748-5681; *Fax:* 613-748-5727
info@volleyball.ca
www.volleyball.ca
Social Media:
instagram.com/volleyballcanada
www.facebook.com/VolleyballCanada
twitter.com/VBallCanada

Also Known As: Canadian Volleyball Association
Overview: A large national charitable organization founded in 1953
Description: To lead the growth of & excellence in the sport of volleyball for all Canadians
Affiliation(s): International Volleyball Federation; Canadian Olympic Association; Coaching Association of Canada
Chief Officer(s): Debra Armstrong, President
Mark Eckert, Executive Director, 613-748-5681 225
meckert@volleyball.ca
Jackie Skender, Director, Communications, 613-748-5681 226
jskender@volleyball.ca
Lucie Leclerc-Rose, Office Manager, 613-748-5681 236
lucie@volleyball.ca
Linden Leung, Director, Finance & Operations, 613-748-5681 223
linden@volleyball.ca
Finances: *Funding Sources:* Membership dues; Fundraising; Merchandise & publications sale; Government; Sponsorships

Staff: 28 staff member(s)
Member Profile: Athletes, officials; *Committees:* Domestic Development; National Championships; Sitting Volleyball; High Performance Management; National Referee; Alumni & Awards; National Registration Systems Project Management; National Registration System Operation Group; Nominations & Elections; Finance & Audit; Legal; Ethics; External Relations
Activities: Offering National Championships for Indoor & Beach Volleyball & National Team Challenge Cup (for Provincial Teams); Providing coaching certification & education programs; Producing publications & videos; Coordinating international & national officials programs; Hosting international events; Marketing & promoting volleyball to the corporate community & the media; *Internships:* Yes; *Rents Mailing List:* Yes

Volleyball New Brunswick
#13, 900 Hanwell Rd., Fredericton NB E3B 6A3
Tel: 506-451-1346; *Fax:* 506-451-1325
vnb@nb.aibn.com
www.vnb.nb.ca
Social Media:
www.instagram.com/volleyballnb
www.facebook.com/volleyballnb
twitter.com/volleyballnb
Also Known As: VNB
Overview: A medium-sized provincial organization
Description: To promote volleyball in New Brunswick; To provide competitive opportunities for members
Chief Officer(s): Ryley Boldon, Executive Director
Rachelle Duguay, Coordinator, Programs, 506-878-3064
vnbcoordinator@nb.aibn.com
Membership: *Fees:* Schedule available; *Committees:* Executive; Officials; Beach; Senior; Age Class; Female High Performance; Male High Performance; Coaching

Volleyball Nova Scotia
5516 Spring Garden Rd., 4th Fl., Halifax NS B3J 1G6
Tel: 902-425-5606
vns@sportnovascotia.ca
www.volleyballnovascotia.ca
Social Media:
www.facebook.com/Volleyballnovascotia
twitter.com/volleyballNS
Overview: A medium-sized provincial organization founded in 1965
Description: To promote volleyball in Nova Scotia; To provide competitive opportunities for members
Chief Officer(s): Jason Trepanier, Executive Director, 902-425-5450 322
vns@sportnovascotia.ca
Shane St-Louis, Director, Technical, 902-425-5450 514
volleyballtd@sportnovascotia.ca

Volleyball Nunavut
PO Box 208, Iqaluit NU X0A 0H0
Tel: 250-718-8411; *Fax:* 250-984-7600
volleyballnunavut.ca
Social Media:
www.facebook.com/VolleyballNunavut
Overview: A medium-sized provincial organization founded in 1999
Description: To promote volleyball in Nunavut & provide programs throughout the territory; *Member of:* Sport & Recreation Nunavut
Chief Officer(s): Scott Schutz, Executive Director
scott@volleyballnunavut.ca
Finances: *Funding Sources:* Sport & Recreation Nunavut

Volleyball Prince Edward Island
PO Box 302, Charlottetown PE C1A 7K7
Tel: 902-569-0583; *Fax:* 902-368-4548
Toll-Free: 800-247-6712
www.volleyballpei.com
Social Media:
www.facebook.com/volleyballpei
Overview: A small provincial organization
Description: To promote volleyball in PEI; To provide competitive opportunities for members
Affiliation(s): Sport PEI
Chief Officer(s): Cheryl Crozier, Executive Director, 902-569-0583
cgcrozier@sportpei.pe.ca
Finances: *Funding Sources:* Government grants; Membership fees; Fund-raising
Member Profile: Coaches & players
Activities: *Rents Mailing List:* Yes

Volleyball Yukon
Sport Yukon Building, 4061 - 4th Ave., Whitehorse YT Y1A 1H1
Fax: 867-667-4237
volleyballyukon@gmail.com
www.volleyballyukon.com
Social Media:
www.facebook.com/pages/Volleyball-Yukon/283652915006482
Overview: A small provincial organization
Description: To promote volleyball in the Yukon; To provide competitive opportunities for its members
Chief Officer(s): D'Arcy Hill, Executive Director, 867-333-2424
darcy.j.hill@gmail.com

Water Polo

Alberta Water Polo Association (AWPA)
PO Box 54, 2225 Macleod Trail SE, Calgary AB T2G 5B6
Tel: 403-281-7797; *Fax:* 403-281-7798
office@albertawaterpolo.ca
www.albertawaterpolo.ca
Social Media:
www.facebook.com/pages/Alberta-Water-Polo-Association/143394719017308
Overview: A medium-sized provincial organization founded in 1974
Description: To provide a safe & positive environment for the ongoing development & growth of water polo in Alberta for the recreational to the elite athlete; *Member of:* Water Polo Canada
Chief Officer(s): Cori Paul, President
cpaul@gss.org
Dayna Christmas, Executive Director
office@albertawaterpolo.ca
Nicolas Youngblud, Treasurer
Blud_1@hotmail.com

British Columbia Water Polo Association
#227, 3820 Cessna Dr., Richmond BC V7B 0A2
Tel: 604-333-3480; *Fax:* 604-333-3450
office@bcwaterpolo.ca
www.bcwaterpolo.ca
Social Media:
www.instagram.com/bcwaterpolo
www.facebook.com/BCWPA
twitter.com/bcwaterpolo
Also Known As: BC Water Polo
Overview: A medium-sized provincial organization founded in 1975
Description: To develop water polo in BC; to train provincial team & national team athletes; *Member of:* Water Polo Canada
Finances: *Funding Sources:* Direct access funding; sponsorshp; government grant; membership fees
Staff: 1 staff member(s); 300 volunteer(s)
Membership: 1,000; *Fees:* Schedule available; *Committees:* Technical Advisory
Activities:; *Library:* Yes (Open to Public)

Fédération de Water-Polo du Québec (FWPQ) / Water Polo Québec
4545, av Pierre-de Coubertin, Montréal QC H1V 0B2
Tél: 514-252-3098
www.waterpolo-quebec.qc.ca
Média social:
www.facebook.com/federationwaterpoloquebec
Aperçu: *Dimension:* petite; *Envergure:* provinciale; Organisme sans but lucratif
Description: Regrouper en association représentative, toute personne qui s'adonne à l'activité du water-polo; sensibiliser la population du Québec à cette activité de loisirs; favoriser le développement sous toutes ses formes; *Membre de:* Sports Québec; Regroupement Loisirs Québec; Water Polo Canada
Membre(s) du bureau directeur: Ariane Clavet-Gaumont, Directrice générale
Finances: *Fonds:* Ministère de l'Éducation.
Activités: Coordonne les programmes des équipes féminines et masculines du Québec; sanctionne les différents tournois provinciaux; organise des stages, cliniques et autres événements

Manitoba Water Polo Association Inc.
#307, 145 Pacific Ave., Winnipeg MB R3B 2Z6
Tel: 204-925-5777; *Fax:* 204-925-5730
mwpa@shaw.ca
www.mbwaterpolo.com
Overview: A small provincial organization
Description: To promote & govern the sport of water polo in Manitoba; *Member of:* Water Polo Canada
Affiliation(s): Sport Manitoba
Chief Officer(s): Bruce Rose, Executive Director
Cindra Leclerc, President

Ontario Water Polo Association Incorporated (OWP) / L'Association de water polo d'Ontario
#206, 3 Concorde Gate, Toronto ON M3C 3N7
Tel: 416-426-7028; *Fax:* 416-426-7356
www.ontariowaterpolo.ca
Also Known As: Ontario Water Polo
Overview: A medium-sized provincial organization founded in 1967
Member of: Water Polo Canada
Chief Officer(s): Kathy Torrens, Secretary
kathy.torrens@ontariowaterpolo.ca
Finances: *Annual Operating Budget:* $100,000-$250,000
Staff: 2 staff member(s); 100 volunteer(s)
Membership: 1,200 individual; *Fees:* Schedule available
Activities: *Speaker Service:* Yes

Water Polo New Brunswick (WPNB)
NB
waterpolonb.ca
Overview: A medium-sized provincial organization
Member of: Water Polo Canada
Chief Officer(s): JC Besner, President
president@waterpolonb.ca

Water Polo Newfoundland (WPNL)
NL
waterpolonl.ca
Overview: A medium-sized provincial organization
Member of: Water Polo Canada

Water Polo Nova Scotia
c/o Sport Nova Scotia, #311, 5516 Spring Garden Rd., Halifax NS B3J 1G6
Tel: 902-425-5450; *Fax:* 902-425-5606
info@waterpolonovascotia.ca
waterpolons.ca
Previous Name: Provincial Water Polo Association
Overview: A small provincial organization founded in 2006
Description: To promote the sport of water polo in Nova Scotia; *Member of:* Water Polo Canada
Chief Officer(s): Joey Postma, Chair

Water Polo Saskatchewan Inc. (WPS)
1860 Lorne St., Regina SK S4P 2L7
Tel: 306-780-9260; *Fax:* 306-780-9467
admin@wpsask.ca
www.wpsask.ca
Social Media:
www.facebook.com/waterpolosask
Previous Name: Saskatchewan Water Polo Association
Overview: A small provincial organization
Member of: Water Polo Canada
Finances: *Funding Sources:* Saskatchewan Lotteries; self-help projects

Water Skiing

Fédération ski nautique et planche Québec
CP 1000, Succ. M, 4545, av Pierre-de Coubertin, Montréal QC H1V 3R2
Tél: 514-252-3092; *Téléc:* 514-252-3186
info@skinautiqueetplanchequebec.qc.ca
www.skinautiqueetplanchequebec.qc.ca
Aperçu: *Dimension:* petite; *Envergure:* provinciale
Membre(s) du bureau directeur: Louis Simard, Président
Membre: 600; *Montant de la cotisation:* 45$ individuelle; 70$ familiale

Ontario Water Ski Association (OWSA)
#209, 3 Concorde Gate, Toronto ON M3C 3N7
Tel: 416-426-7092; *Fax:* 416-426-7378
office@wswo.ca
www.wswo.ca
Social Media:
www.facebook.com/waterskiwakeboardontario
twitter.com/wswo
Also Known As: Water Ski Wakeboard Ontario
Overview: A medium-sized provincial organization founded in 1976
Description: To promote & develop the sport of water skiing through safety & instructional tournaments, courses & demonstrations; *Member of:* Water Ski & Wakeboard Canada
Chief Officer(s): Paul Roberts, President
pwroberts@sympatico.ca
Finances: *Funding Sources:* Private; provincial grant
Staff: 1 staff member(s)
Membership: *Fees:* $10 associate; $40 active; $100 family; $80 camp; $100 club/school; *Member Profile:* Individual & families involved in recreational &/or competitive water skiing, also water ski schools, camps & clubs

Activities: Watersport/waterski/wakeboard events & tournaments in Ontario; *Library:* Yes by appointment

Water Ski - Wakeboard Manitoba (WSWM)
#415, 145 Pacific Ave., Winnipeg MB R3B 2Z6
Tel: 204-925-5700; *Fax:* 204-925-5792
info@wswm.ca
www.wswm.ca
Social Media:
www.flickr.com/photos/wswm/sets/
Overview: A small provincial organization founded in 1956
Description: To meet the needs of all those interested in the sport of water skiing by providing the resources necessary to help them achieve their goals & to encourage fun, friendship, fitness & fair play for skiers at all ability levels; *Member of:* Water Ski & Wakeboard Canada
Chief Officer(s): Alanna Boudreau, Executive Director
Mark Mueller, President
Finances: *Funding Sources:* Provincial grants
Membership: *Fees:* $35 regular; $75 family; $5 associate
Activities: Slalom, tricks and jump water skiing; barefoot water skiing; wakeboarding; adaptive skiing

Water Ski & Wakeboard Alberta (WSWA)
Percy Page Centre, 11759 Groat Rd., Edmonton AB T5M 3K6
Tel: 780-415-0088; *Fax:* 780-422-2663
Toll-Free: 866-258-2754
info@wswa.ca
www.wswa.ca
Social Media:
www.facebook.com/WaterSkiWakeboardAlberta
twitter.com/WaterskiWakeAB
Previous Name: Water Ski Alberta
Overview: A small provincial organization founded in 1967
Description: To promote participation & excellence in the sport of water skiing & wakeboarding in Alberta; *Member of:* Alberta Sport Council; Water Ski & Wakeboard Canada
Affiliation(s): International Water Ski Federation
Chief Officer(s): Peter Peebles, President
peterpeebles@gmail.com
Melanie Oliver, Executive Director
melanie@wswa.ca
Finances: *Funding Sources:* Alberta government; fundraising (casinos) membership fees; program fees
Membership: 1,000; *Fees:* $40

Water Ski & Wakeboard British Columbia (WSWBC)
PO Box 56011, 1511 Admiral's Rd., Victoria BC V9A 2P8
Toll-Free: 888-696-6677
info@wswbc.org
www.wswbc.org
Social Media:
twitter.com/WSWBC
Previous Name: BC Water Ski Association
Overview: A medium-sized provincial charitable organization founded in 1969
Description: To promote organized towed water sports in British Columbia; *Member of:* Water Ski & Wakeboard Canada
Chief Officer(s): Kim McKnight, Executive Director
Shawn Shorsky, President, 250-479-7828
Finances: *Funding Sources:* Government; advertising sales; fundraisings
Membership: 1,250; *Fees:* $40 active single; $80 family
Activities: Provincial championships; Protour; *Internships:* Yes

Water Ski & Wakeboard Canada (WSWC) / Ski nautique et planche Canada
#22, 1554 Carling Ave., Ottawa ON K1Z 7M4
Tel: 613-526-0685; *Fax:* 613-701-0385
Toll-Free: 888-526-0685
info@wswc.ca
wswc.ca
Social Media:
www.youtube.com/user/TheWSWCanada;
instagram.com/wswcanada
www.facebook.com/wswcanada
twitter.com/wswc_canada
Previous Name: Canadian Water Ski Association
Overview: A medium-sized national charitable organization
Description: To promote & organize competitive Canadian towed water sports
Chief Officer(s): Glenn Bowie, Chair
Jasmine Northcott, Chief Executive Officer
jasmine@wswc.ca
Finances: *Annual Operating Budget:* $500,000-$1.5 Million
Staff: 4 staff member(s)
Membership: 4,500; *Committees:* Water Ski; Wakeboard; Barefoot; Adaptive Towed Water Sports; Athlete Development; Coaching; Safety; Waterways; Hall of Fame

Water Ski & Wakeboard Saskatchewan (WSWS)
SK
Tel: 306-931-2901
info@wswsask.com
wswsask.com
Social Media:
www.facebook.com/wswsask
twitter.com/wswsask
Previous Name: Saskatchewan Water Ski Association
Overview: A small provincial organization
Description: To promote & develop towed water sports in Saskatchewan; *Member of:* Water Ski & Wakeboard Canada; Sask Sport Inc.
Membership: *Fees:* $25 recreational; $30 competitive; $45 recreational family; $50 competitive family
Activities: All activity & advocacy related to towed water sports; tournaments

Water Ski Wakeboard Nova Scotia
PO Box 97, Greenfield, Queen's County NS B0T 1E0
www.nswsa.com
Social Media:
www.facebook.com/waterskiwakeboardns
Previous Name: Nova Scotia Water Ski Association
Overview: A small provincial organization
Member of: Water Ski & Wakeboard Canada
Chief Officer(s): Blair O'Neill, President
Membership: 135; *Fees:* $25 single; $50 family

Waterski & Wakeboard New Brunswick (NBWSWBA)
NB
info@nbwswba.com
www.nbwswba.com
Also Known As: NB Waterski
Overview: A small provincial organization
Description: To promote organized pulled watersports in the province of New Brunswick.; *Member of:* Water Ski & Wakeboard Canada
Membership: *Fees:* $20 individual; $40 family

Weightlifting

British Columbia Weightlifting Association (BCWA)
5249 Laurel Dr., Delta BC V4K 4S4
info@bcweightlifting.ca
www.bcweightlifting.ca
Social Media:
www.facebook.com/bcweightlifting
twitter.com/bcweightlifting
Also Known As: BC Weightlifting Association
Overview: A small provincial organization founded in 1969
Description: To promote the sport of Olympic weightlifting in British Columbia
Affiliation(s): Canadian Weightlifting Federation
Finances: *Funding Sources:* Membership fees; Donations; Sponsorships
Membership: *Fees:* $25 youth athlete (12 & under); $40 student/junior (13-18); $55 standard; $110 family; $8 associate/volunteer; $50 club; *Member Profile:* Coaches; Officials: Youth (age 12 & under), student, senior, & master (age 35 & over) athletes; Volunteers
Activities: Providing information about champtionships

Ontario Weightlifting Association (OWA)
PO Box 14012, Stn. Glebe, Ottawa ON K1S 3T2
owamembership@gmail.com
www.onweightlifting.ca
Social Media:
www.youtube.com/user/ontarioweightlifting
www.facebook.com/OntarioWeightlifting
twitter.com/ONWeightlifting
Overview: A medium-sized provincial organization founded in 1968
Description: To govern weightlifting in Ontario; *Member of:* Ontario Hockey Federation; Hockey Canada
Affiliation(s): Canadian Weightlifting Federation; Sport Alliance of Ontario; Sport4Ontario
Chief Officer(s): Moira Lassen, President
owapresident1@gmail.com
Membership: 36 clubs; *Fees:* $80 competitive; $50 introductory; $35 participation/coach/official; $2 volunteer

Yukon Weightlifting Association
YT
yukonweightlift.weebly.com
Overview: A small provincial organization
Description: To promote & facilitate competitive weightlifting in the Yukon Territory.; *Member of:* Sport Yukon
Chief Officer(s): Kim Haehnel, President
frozenveggies@hotmail.com
Jeane Lassen, Development Coordinator
jeanelassen@gmail.com

Women in Sports

Abbotsford Female Hockey Association (AFHA)
#476, 33771 George Ferguson Way, Abbotsford BC V2S 2M5
afharegistrar@gmail.com
www.abbotsfordfemalehockey.com
Social Media:
www.facebook.com/AbbotsfordFemaleHockeyAssociation
twitter.com/AbbyIceGirls
Overview: A small local organization
Description: The Abbotsford Female Hockey Association seeks to provide an opportunity for females of all ages & all skill levels to play hockey in Abbotsford in an all-female league.; *Member of:* BC Hockey

Canadian Association for the Advancement of Women & Sport & Physical Activity (CAAWS) / Association canadienne pour l'avancement des femmes du sport et de l'activité physique (ACAFS)
801 King Edward Ave., #N202, Ottawa ON K1N 6N5
Tel: 613-562-5667; *Fax:* 613-562-5668
caaws@caaws.ca
www.caaws.ca
Social Media:
www.facebook.com/CAAWS
twitter.com/caaws
Overview: A medium-sized national organization founded in 1981
Description: To promote an equitable sport & physical activity system, in which girls & women are participants & leaders; To foster equitable support & diverse opportunities, in sport & physical activity for females across Canada
Chief Officer(s): Karin Lofstrom, Executive Director
klofstrom@caaws.ca
Sydney Millar, Manager, National Program
snmillar@caaws.ca
Haley Wolfenden, Manager, Communications, Marketing & Events
hwolfenden@caaws.ca
Finances: *Funding Sources:* Donations
Activities: Fostering positive experiences for women in sport & physical activitythroughout Canada; Providing education on issues related to female participation in sport & physical activity; Creating community awareness about the value of an equitable sport & physical activity system; Collaborating with related organizations to foster an equitable system; Presenting awards, grants, & scholarships

Field Hockey BC (FHBC) / Hockey sur gazon C-B
#202, 210 West Broadway, Vancouver BC V5Y 3W2
Tel: 604-737-3046; *Fax:* 604-737-6488
info@fieldhockeybc.com
www.fieldhockeybc.com
Social Media:
www.youtube.com/user/fieldhockeybc
www.facebook.com/fieldhockeybc
twitter.com/fieldhockeybc
Merged from: British Columbia Field Hockey Association; British Columbia Women's Field Hockey Federation
Overview: A medium-sized provincial organization founded in 1992
Description: To foster, promote & encourage the development & organization of field hockey in BC at all levels; *Member of:* Field Hockey Canada
Chief Officer(s): Mark Saunders, Executive Director, 604-737-3045
mark@fieldhockeybc.com
Finances: *Annual Operating Budget:* $500,000-$1.5 Million; *Funding Sources:* Provincial government; membership fees
Staff: 5 staff member(s)
Membership: 7,275; *Fees:* Schedule available; *Committees:* High Performance; Finance

Ladies' Golf Union (LGU)
The Scores, St. Andrews, Fife KY16 9AT United Kingdom
www.lgu.org
Social Media:
youtube.com/ladiesgolfunion1893; pinterest.com/ladiesgolfunion
www.facebook.com/ladiesgolfunion
twitter.com/LadiesGolfUnion
Overview: A small international organization founded in 1893
Description: To uphold the rules of golf; to advance & safeguard the interests of ladies' golf & to decide all doubtful & disputed points in connection therewith; to maintain LGU Scratch

Score System; to employ the funds of the LGU in such a manner as shall be deemed best for the interests of ladies' golf, with power to borrow or raise money for the same purpose; to promote, maintain & regulate international events, championships & competitions held under the LGU regulations & to promote the interests of Great Britain & Ireland in ladies' international golf; to promulgate, maintain, enforce & publish such regulations as may be considered necessary
Affiliation(s): Canadian Ladies' Golf Association
Chief Officer(s): Diane Bailey, President
Susan Simpson, Head, Golf Operations
Membership: 2,750 clubs; *Committees:* Finance & General Purposes; International Selection; Rules & Regulations; Scratch Score; Training
Activities:; *Library:* Yes by appointment

ProMOTION Plus
#301, 470 Granville St., Vancouver BC V6C 1V5
Tel: 604-333-3475; *Fax:* 604-629-2651
info@promotionplus.org
www.promotionplus.org
Overview: A small provincial organization founded in 1990
Description: To promote equity & opportunity for British Columbian women in sport.
Affiliation(s): Sport BC
Chief Officer(s): Bryna Kopelow, Chair
Stephanie Marshall-White, Coordinator
Communications & Events
Finances: *Funding Sources:* BC Ministry of Community; Sport & Cultural Development; 2010 Legacies Now; BC Gaming Commission; Government of Canada
Membership: *Fees:* $20 students; $35 adults; $75 organizations

Wrestling

Alberta Amateur Wrestling Association (AAWA)
Percy Page Centre, 11759 Groat Rd., Edmonton AB T5M 3K6
Tel: 780-415-0140; *Fax:* 780-427-0524
aawa@ocii.com
www.albertaamateurwrestling.ca
Social Media:
www.facebook.com/AlbertaWrestling
twitter.com/AlbertaWrestlin
Overview: A small provincial organization founded in 1974
Description: The AAWA is the governing body for amateur wrestling & grappling in Alberta.; *Member of:* Canadian Amateur Wrestling Association
Chief Officer(s): Tammie Bradley, Executive Director
Michael Drought, Technical Director, 780-643-0799
aawatechnical@gmail.com
Finances: *Annual Operating Budget:* $100,000-$250,000; *Funding Sources:* Government grants; fundraising
Staff: 2 staff member(s)
Membership: 2,000; *Fees:* Schedule available; *Member Profile:* Male & female ages 13+
Activities: Training camps; officials & coaches clinics; school clinics; major games; coordinate provincial program

British Columbia Wrestling Association (BCWA)
3333 Ardingley Ave., Burnaby BC V5B 4A5
Tel: 604-737-3092; *Fax:* 604-737-6043
info@bcwrestling.com
www.bcwrestling.com
Social Media:
www.facebook.com/bcwrestling
twitter.com/wrestlingBC
Also Known As: Wrestling BC
Previous Name: British Columbia Amateur Wrestling Association
Overview: A small provincial organization founded in 1979
Description: To promote & enhance the well-being of young people through their participation in wrestling; *Member of:* Sport BC
Affiliation(s): BC School Sports
Chief Officer(s): Phil Cizmic, President, 250-923-0735
philip.cizmic@sd72.bc.ca
Membership: 2,200; *Member Profile:* Wrestlers, coaches, and officials
Activities: Camps; clinics; tournaments

Canadian Amateur Wrestling Association (CAWA) / Association canadienne de lutte amateur
#7, 5370 Canotek Rd., Gloucester ON K1J 9E6
Tel: 613-748-5686; *Fax:* 613-748-5756
info@wrestling.ca
www.wrestling.ca
Social Media:
www.linkedin.com/company/wrestling-canada-lutte
www.facebook.com/WrestlingCanada
twitter.com/wrestlingcanada
Also Known As: Wrestling Canada Lutte
Overview: A medium-sized national organization founded in 1970
Description: To operate as the national sport governing body for Olympic style wrestling in Canada; To implement a long term athlete development model; To develop coaches, officials, & administrators; To achieve podium finishes for Canadian wrestlers at World Championships & Olympic Games
Chief Officer(s): Don Ryan, President
Tamara Medwidsky, Executive Director
tamara@wrestling.ca
Alex Davidson, Manager, High Performance
adavidson@wrestling.ca
Kyle Hunter, Manager, Domestic Development
kylehunter@wrestling.ca
Eric Smith, Coordinator, Finance & Administration
ericsmith@wrestling.ca
Finances: *Funding Sources:* Sponsorships
Activities: Encouraging participation in Olympic wrestling in Canada; Liaising with provincial sport governing bodies; Selecting & preparing Canada's teams which compete at the world championships & multi-sport events, such as the Olympic Games; Overseeing three national championships & one international cup on an annual basis

Canadian Arm Wrestling Federation (CAWF)
c/o Tracey Arnold, Secretary-Treasurer, 1635 - 8th Ave., Saskatoon SK S7K 2X8
www.cawf.ca
Overview: A medium-sized national organization
Description: To oversee & promote the sport of arm wrestling in Canada.; *Member of:* World Armwrestling Federation
Chief Officer(s): Rick Pinkney, President
Ryan Espey, Vice-President
espey76@gmail.com
Tracey Arnold, Secretary-Treasurer
tarnold001@hotmail.com
Anthony Dall'Antonia, Director, Communications
vancouverarm@hotmail.com
Membership: 3,500; *Fees:* $20

Fédération de lutte olympique du Québec / Québec Wrestling Association
4545, av Pierre de Couberlin, Montréal QC H1V 3R2
Tél: 514-252-3044
www.quebecolympicwrestling.ca
Aperçu: *Dimension:* moyenne; *Envergure:* provinciale

Lutte NB Wrestling (LNBW)
NB
www.luttenbwrestling.com
Overview: A small provincial organization
Description: Lutte New Brunswick Wrestling (LNBW) is a non-profit, equal opportunity organization, dedicated to the development, administration and promotion of amateur wrestling throughout the Province.
Chief Officer(s): Mary Singh, Executive Director
exec@luttenbwrestling.com
Chris Falconer, President

Manitoba Amateur Wrestling Association (MAWA)
c/o Sport Manitoba, 145 Pacific Ave., Winnipeg MB R3B 2Z6
mawawrestling@mts.net
www.mawawrestling.ca
Overview: A small provincial organization founded in 2007
Description: The Manitoba Amateur Wrestling Association (MAWA) is the recognised provincial sport organization (PSO) for the sport of wrestling in Manitoba. MAWA is dedicated to the continuing development of wrestling across the province and to maintain a safe, fun environment for all its members. MAWA is an organization that promotes teamwork, leadership and healthy lifestyles through wrestling in Manitoba for all ages.
Chief Officer(s): Sally McNabb, President
Membership: *Fees:* Schedule available; *Member Profile:* Individual wrestlers & clubs; *Committees:* Tournament; Athlete Development; Marketing

Manitoba Arm Wrestling Association (MAWA)
MB
Tel: 204-509-9896
info@manitobaarmwrestling.com
www.manitobaarmwrestling.com
Overview: A small provincial organization
Description: To oversee & promote the sport of arm wrestling in Manitoba.; *Member of:* Canadian Arm Wrestling Federation
Chief Officer(s): Darrell Steffenson, Contact

Newfoundland & Labrador Amateur Wrestling Association (NLAWA)
NL
nlawa.wordpress.com
Overview: A small provincial organization
Description: The NLAWA is a small organization comprised of coaches, officials, parents and athletes who are dedicated to advancing the sport of wrestling in Newfoundland and Labrador
Chief Officer(s): Randy Ralph, President
randolphralph@esdnl.ca

Nova Scotia Arm Wrestling Association (NSAWA)
c/o Rick Pinkney, President, 192 Beaver Bank Rd., Lower Sackville NS B4E 1J7
Tel: 902-489-9008
info@novascotiaarmwrestling.com
novascotiaarmwrestling.com
Overview: A small provincial organization
Description: To oversee & promote the sport of arm wrestling in Nova Scotia.; *Member of:* Canadian Arm Wrestling Federation
Chief Officer(s): Rick Pinkney, President
Shawn Ross, Vice-President, 902-765-4656
shawnross1111@gmail.com
Chris Scott, Treasurer, 902-865-6525
chrisscottauto@hotmail.com
Mark MacPhail, Director, 902-822-1180
markmacphail3@hotmail.com

Ontario Amateur Wrestling Association (OAWA)
#213, 3 Concorde Gate, Toronto ON M3C 3N7
Tel: 416-426-7274
admin@oawa.ca
www.oawa.ca
Social Media:
twitter.com/OAWA_Wrestling
Also Known As: Ontario Wrestling
Overview: A medium-sized provincial organization founded in 1980
Description: To provide essential services & programs dedicated to developing amateur wrestling at all age levels within Ontario
Affiliation(s): International Amateur Wrestling Association; Canadian Amateur Wrestling Association
Chief Officer(s): Tim MaGarrey, Provincial Director
Finances: *Annual Operating Budget:* $100,000-$250,000; *Funding Sources:* Government; private donors; sponsors; fundraising; user fees
Membership: 1,800; *Fees:* $85 coach; $65 official/athlete (older than 9 years); $55 athletes (7-8 years); $45 supporter
Activities: Competitons; demonstrations

Saskatchewan Amateur Wrestling Association (SAWA)
510 Cynthia St., Saskatoon SK S7L 7K7
Tel: 306-975-0822; *Fax:* 306-242-8007
sk.wrestling@shaw.ca
www.saskwrestling.com
Social Media:
www.facebook.com/groups/253817611302960
twitter.com/SaskWrestling
Overview: A small provincial organization founded in 1972
Description: To govern & promote the sport of wrestling in Saskatchewan
Chief Officer(s): Anna-Beth Zulkoskey, Executive Director
Finances: *Annual Operating Budget:* $250,000-$500,000; *Funding Sources:* Sasksport; lotteries
Staff: 1 staff member(s); 12 volunteer(s)
Membership: 700; *Fees:* $65 coach/official/patron/junior, senior, juvenile, cadet athlete; $45 bantam, pee wee, novice, freshie athlete; $15 non-competitive; *Committees:* High Performance; Development; Administration; Finance
Activities: Athlete assistance grants

Wrestling Nova Scotia
NS
www.wrestlingnovascotia.ca
Overview: A small provincial organization

Wrestling PEI
c/o Sport PEI, PO Box 302, 40 Enman Crescent, Charlottetown PE C1A 7K7
Tel: 902-368-4262; *Fax:* 902-368-4548
sports@sportpei.pe.ca
www.wrestlingpei.ca
Overview: A small provincial organization
Description: To promote wrestling in PEI; to provide competitive opportunities for members; *Member of:* Wrestling Canada
Chief Officer(s): Glen Flood, Executive Director
gflood@sportpei.pe.ca
Activities: Canada Games; Provincials; Atlantics; Nationals

Professional Leagues & Teams

Baseball, Professional Leagues/Teams: Major

Major League Baseball/MLB
245 Park Avenue
31st Floor
NEW YORK, NY 10167

212-931-7800
Fax: 212-949-5654
www.mlb.com

Rob Manfred, Commissioner of Baseball
Bob Bowman, President, Business & Media
Dan Halem, Chief Legal Officer
Jonathan Mariner, Chief Investment Officer
Bob Starkey, CFO & Senior Advisor
Joe Torre, Chief Baseball Officer
Allan H Selig, Commissioner of Baseball Emeritus

Nature of Service:
Administrates professional baseball. Established and enforces rules regarding franchise operation. Supervises national radio and television contracts. Handles publicity and marketing of baseball and legal matters pertaining to baseball as an industry. Operates the World Series and All-Star games.

Membership Requirements:
Teams operating in the American or National Leagues.

Year Founded:
1903

Sponsors:
Arm & Hammer, Aquafina, Bank of America, Budweiser, Cheez-It, Chevrolet, Draft Kings, EMC, Esurance, Frito Lay, Gatorade, Gillette, Head & Shoulders, The Hartford, Keebler, Kellog's Rice Krispies, MasterCard International, Maytag, Nike, Kellog's NutriGrain, Oxi-Clean, Pepsi-Cola, Scotts, SiriusXM, T-Mobile

Teams:

Toronto Blue Jays
Rogers Centre
One Blue Jays Way
Suite 3200
TORONTO, ON M5V 1J1
416-341-1000
888-654-6529
toronto.bluejays.mlb.com
Mark Shapiro, President & CEO
Rick Brace, President, Rogers Media
Phil Lind, Vice-Chair, Rogers Communication, Inc.
Ross Atkins, General Manager
Andrew Miller, Executive Vice President
Mario Coutinho, Vice President, Stadium Operations and Security
Jason Diplock, Vice President, Ticket Sales and Service
Ed Rogers, Chairman
John Gibbons, Manager
Matthew Shuber, Vice President, Business Affairs & Legal Counsel
Jay Stenhouse, Vice President, Communications
Howard Starkman, Consultant
George Poulis, Head Trainer
Perry Minasian, Director, Professional Scouting
Heather Connolly, Manager, Major League Administration

Stadium:
Rogers Centre, a recently renovated stadium that includes the TD Comfort Clubhouse (Club 200 VIP), Acura Executive Lounge and the 400 Summit Suite. Seating capacity 46,095.

Baseball, Professional Leagues/Teams: Minor

Can-Am League
1415 Highway 54 West
Suite 210
DURHAM, NC 27707

919-401-8150
Fax: 919-401-8152
www.canamleague.com

Miles Wolff, Commissioner
Dan Moushon, President/COO
Jim Grillo, Director of Umpires

Description:
The Can-Am league, also known as the Canadian American Association of Professional Baseball, operates in cities where the Major and Minor leagues do not operate.

Teams:

Ottawa Champions
Rcgt Park
300 Conventry Road
OTTAWA, ON K1K 4P5
613-746-2255
www.ottawachampions.com
Miles Wolff, Owner
David Gourlay, President & Minority Owner
Ben Hodge, General Manager
Davyd Balloch, Assistant General Manager
Craig Richenback, Marketing & Communications Director

Quebec Capitales
Stade Municipal De Quebec
100, Rue Du Cardinal Maurice-Roy
QUEBEC, QUEBEC G1K 8Z1
418-521-2255
Fax: 418-521-2266
info@capitalesdequebec.com
www.capitalesdequebec.com
Jean Tremblay, Owner
Michel Laplante, President & CEO
Julie Lefrancois, Administrative Director
Maxime Aubry, Director of Communications
Émilie Gilbert, Administrative Assistant

Trois-Rivieres Aigles
First Floor Industrial Building
1760 Avenue Gilles Villeneuve
TROIS-RIVIERES, QUEBEC G9A 5L9
819-379-0404
Fax: 819-379-5087
info@lesaiglestr.com
www.lesaiglestr.com
Marc-Andre Bergeron, President
Rene Martin, General Manager
Simon Laliberte, Director, Communications and Marketing
Richard Lahaie, Deputy General Director

Northwest Baseball League
140 North Higgins Avenue
Suite 211
MISSOULA, MT 59802

406-541-9301
Fax: 406-543-9463
mellisnwl@aol.com
ww.milb.com/index.jsp?sid=l126

Mike Ellis, League President
Mike McMurray, League Vice President
Jerry Walker, League Secretary
Judy Ellis, Administrative Assistant

Teams:

Vancouver Canadians
Scotiabank Field
4601 Ontario Street
VANCOUVER, BC V5V3H4
604-872-5232
Fax: 604-872-1714
staff@canadianbaseball.com
Jake Kerr, Principal Owner, Managing General Partner
Andy Dunn, President
J.C. Fraser, General Manager
John Schneider, Manager

Stadium:
Scotiabank Field. Seating capacity, 6,013.

Basketball, Leagues/Teams

National Basketball Association/NBA
645 Fifth Avenue
NEW YORK, NY 10022

212-407-8000
Fax: 212-832-3861
info@nba.com
www.nba.com

Adam Silver, Commissioner
Kathleen Behrens, President, Social Responsibility
Amy Brooks, EVP, Team Marketing & Business Operations
Robert Criqui, President, Administration
Jason Cahilly, Chief Strategic and Financial Officer

Description:
The premier professional basketball league in North America. Many of the world's best players play in the NBA, and the overall standard of the competition is considerably higher than any other professional competition. The NBA was founded in New York City on June 6, 1946 as the Basketball Association of America (BAA). It adopted the name National Basketball Association in the fall of 1949 after adding several teams from the rival National Basketball League.

Teams:

Toronto Raptors
The Air Canada Centre
#400, 40 Bay St.
TORONTO, ON M5J 2X2
416-815-5600
Fax: 416-359-9332
www.nba.com/raptors
Masai Ujiri, President & General Manager
Jeff Weitman, EVP, Basketball Operations
Bobby Webster, VP, Basketball Management & Strategy
Dwayne Casey, Head Coach

History:
Founded in 1995 in Toronto. Division titles, 4.

Arena:
Air Canada Centre. Seating capacity, 19,800.

Football, Professional Leagues/Teams

Canadian Football League/CFL
50 Wellington Street East
3rd Floor
TORONTO, ON M5E 1C8

416-322-9650
Fax: 416-322-9651
www.cfl.ca

Jeff Orridge, Commissioner
Doug Allison, Vice President, Finance & Business Operations
Kevin McDonald, Vice President, Football Operations
Matt Maychak, Vice President, Communications & Public Affairs
Christina Litz, Senior Vice-President, Content & Marketing
Glen Johnson, Senior Vice-President, Football

History:
The Canadian Football League was founded in 1958, in Montreal, Quebec, after the Canadian Football Council (CFC) left the Candaian Rugby Union (CRU). Since 2010 the league has expanded stadiums and added the forthcoming Ottawa Redblacks to its rosters.

Teams:
9

Founded:
1958

Teams:

BC Lions
BC Place
10605 City Parkway
SURREY, BC V3T 4C8
604-930-5466
Fax: 604-583-7882
communityrelations@bclions.com
www.bclions.com
David Braley, Owner & CFL Governor
Dennis Skulsky, President & CEO
Wally Buono, General Manager & Vice President, Football Ops.
George Chayka, Vice President, Business
Mike Benevides, Head Coach
Jamie Cartmell, Director, Communications
Kevin Hanson, Director, Corporate Partnerships
Stefan Kalenchuk, Director, Marketing
Roy Shivers, Director, Player Personnel
Jamie Taras, Director, Community Relations

Home Field:
BC Place. Seating capacity 54,320.

Calgary Stampeders
McMahon Stadium
1817 Crowchild Trail Nw
CALGARY, AB T2M 4R6
403-289-0205
800-6673267
Fax: 403-282-6741
stampeder@stampeders.com
www.stampeders.com
Ken King, Chairman
Stephanie Collins, Director, Marketing
Gordon Norrie, President
John Hufnagel, General Manager & Head Coach
Stan Schwartz, Executive Vice President
Tanya Mettimano, Director, Ticketing & Customer Relations

Home Field:
McMahon Stadium. Seating capacity 35,650.

Edmonton Eskimos
Commonwealth Stadium
11000 Stadium Road
EDMONTON, AB T5B 2R7
780-448-1525
Fax: 780-448-2531
eescouting@esks.com
www.esks.com
Bruce Bentley, Chair
Len Rhodes, President & CEO
Ed Hervey, General Manager
Chris Jones, Head Coach
Ryan Wagner, Director, Football Operations
Home Field:
Commonwealth Stadium. Seating capacity 60,000.

Hamilton Tiger-Cats
Tim Hortons Field
1 Jarvis Street
HAMILTON, ON L8R 3J2
905-547-2287
Fax: 905-547-8423
customerservice@ticats.ca
www.ticats.ca
Robert Young, Caretaker/Owner
Scott Mitchell, Chief Executive Officer
Glenn Gibson, President & Chief Operating Officer
Laura McLeod, Director, Ticket Sales
Steve Lowe, Senior Director, Marketing & Game Operations
Kent Austin, Head Coach/General Manager/Director, Football Ops.
Jim Edmands, Vice President, Sales & Marketing
Home Field:
Tim Hortons Field. Seating capacity 22,500.

Montreal Alouettes
4545 Pierre-De-Coubertin
PO Box 65, Station M
Percival Molson Memorial Stadium
MONTREAL, QC H1V 3L6
514-253-0008
Fax: 514-253-8821
info@montrealalouettes.com
www.montrealalouettes.com
Larry Smith, President & CEO
Robert Wetenhall, Owner
Tim Higgins, Head Coach
Jim Popp, General Manager, Director of Football Operations
Laurie Bennett, Vice President, Business Operations
Marcel Desjardins, Assistant General Manager
Olivier Poulin, Director, Communications
Home Field:
Percival Molson Memorial Stadium. Seating capacity 25,012.

Ottawa Redblacks
TD Place Stadium
2016 Ogilvie Rd.
OTTAWA, ON K1J 7N9
613-232-6767
www.ottawareblacks.com
Jeff Hunt, President/Owner
Bernie Ash, Chief Executive Officer
Mike Goude, Chief Financial & Operational Officer
John Mathers, Vice President Ticket Sales
Marcel Desjardins, General Manager
Rick Campbell, Head Coach

Saskatchewan Roughriders
Mosaic Stadium At Taylor Field
1910 Piffles Taylor Way
PO Box 1966
REGINA, SK S4P 3E1
306-569-2323
888-474-3377
Fax: 306-566-4280
ryanw@saskriders.com
www.saskriders.com
Jim Hopson, President & CEO
Craig Reynolds, President/CEO
Steve Mazurak, Vice President, Sales & Partnerships
Greg Sauter, Vice President, Business Development & Marketing
Brendan Taman, General Manager/Director of FB OPS
Jeremy O'Day, Assistant General Manager
Roger Brandvold, Chairman
Correy Chamblin, Head Coach
Home Field:
Mosaic Stadium at Taylor Field. Seating capacity 32,848.

Toronto Argonauts
#501, 212 King St. West
TORONTO, ON M5H 1K5
416-341-2700
Fax: 416-341-2714
info@argunauts.on.ca
www.argonauts.ca
David Braley, Owner
Chris Rudge, Executive Chair & CEO/President
Lou Ragagnin, President, Chief Operating Officer
David Bedford, Senior Vice President, Business Operations
Mike Hagen, Player Personnel
Beth Waldman, Vice President, Marketing & Communications
Jim Barker, General Manager
Scott Milanovich, Head Coach
Carlos Ferreira, Director, Marketing
Jason Colero, Manager, Community Relations
Home Field:
BMO Field. Seating capacity: 26,500

Winnipeg Blue Bombers
Investors Group Field
315 Chancellor Matheson Rd.
WINNIPEG, MB R3T 1Z2
204-784-2583
Fax: 204-783-5222
bbombers@bluebombers.com
www.bluebombers.com
Kyle Walters, General Manager
Jim Bell, President & Chief Operating Officer
Jerrry Maslowsky, Vice President, Marketing
Dave Siddal, Director, Football Operations
Wade Miller, President, Chief Executive Officer
Michael O'Shea, Head Coach
Home Field:
Investors Group Field. Seating capacity 33,420-40,000.

Independent Women's Football League / IWFL

PO Box 1844
ROUND ROCK, TX 78680
512-215-4238
Fax: 866-482-1342
info@iwflsports.com
www.iwflsports.com
Laurie Frederick, President/CEO
Kezia Disney, Chief Operating Officer
Kim Hampson, VP of Administration
Description:
A full tackle women's football league focused on creating a fun, safe and positive atmosphere for the players and fans. It was founded in 2000 and currently has over 51 teams in North America. The IWFL enables its members to function independently while providing a stable organization to draw from and combine resources for the promotion of women's football.
Year Founded:
2000
Teams:
Georgia Stingers, North Texas Knockouts, Monterey Black Mambas, Seattle Majestics, California Quake, Madison Cougars, and Austin Yellow Jackets.

Hockey, Professional Leagues/Teams

National Hockey League/NHL

1185 Avenue of the Americas
15th Floor
NEW YORK, NY 10036
212-789-2000
Fax: 212-789-2020
www.nhl.com
Gary Bettman, Commissioner
William Daly, Deputy Commissioner
Craig Harnett, Senior Executive Vice President, Treasurer & CFO
Ed Horne, Senior Executive VP & President, NHL Enterprises
Brian Jennings, Executive Vice President, Marketing
Steven Walkom, Senior Vice President & Director, Officiating
Jim Haskins, Vice President, Consumer Product Licensing
Year Founded:
1917
Description:
League of professional hockey teams
Membership Requirements:
Approval by NHL Board of Governors
Publications:
NHL Rule Book, annual; NHL Schedule, annual; NHL MEDIA DIRECTORY, annual; NHL Official Guide and Record Book, annual
Additional Offices:
75 International Blvd, Ste 300, Toronto, ON, Canada M9W 6L9. 416 798-0809; FAX: 416 798-0819. Montreal Office: 1800 McGill College Ave, Ste 2600, Montreal, QC, Canada H3A 3J6. 514 288-9220; FAX: 514 284-0300

Teams:

Calgary Flames
PO Box 1540
Station M
CALGARY, AB T2P 3B9
403-777-2177
888-5-FLAMES
Fax: 403-777-2171
customerservice@calgaryflames.com
www.flames.nhl.com
N. Murray Edwards, Owner
Alvin G. Libin, Owner
Allan P. Markin, Owner
Jeffrey J. McCaig, Owner
Clayton H. Riddell, Owner
Jaques Cloutier, Associate Coach
Ken King, President And Chief Executive Officer
kking@calgaryflames.com
Brad Treliving, General Manager
Bob Hartley, Head Coach
Ken Zaba, Vice President, Finance & Administration
Jim Bagshaw, Vice Pres., Advertising, Sponsorship & Marketing
Rollie Cyr, Vice President, Sales
Peter Hanlon, Senior Vice President, Communications
Trent Anderson, Director, Building Operations
Jim Peplinski,
Libby Raines, Vice President, Building Operations
Brian Burke, President of Hockey Operations
Pat Halls, Senior Director, Sponsorship Sales
John Bean, Chief Operating Officer
Kevin Gross, Director, Corporate Sponsorship
Jillian Frechette, Director, Marketing and Promotions
Cameron Olson, Chief Financial Officer
Year Founded:
1972
Description:
The Calgary Flames are a National Hockey League team based in Calgary, Alberta
Home Arena:
Scotiabank Saddledome. Seating capacity 19,289.

Edmonton Oilers
11230 110th Street
2nd Fl
EDMONTON, AB T5H 3H7
780-414-4000
Fax: 780-409-5890
www.oilers.nhl.com
Bob Nicholson, Chief Executive Officer
Peter Chiarelli, President, Hockey Operations/General Manager
Darryl Boessenkool, Chief Financial Officer/Vice President, Finance
Stew MacDonald, Chief Revenue Officer
Scott Howson, Senior Vice President, Hockey Operations
Daryl A. Katz, Owner & Governor
Todd McLellan, Head Coach
Bill Scott, Assistant General Manager
Rick Carriere, Senior Director, Player Development
Year Founded:
1972
Description:
The Edmonton Oilers are a National Hockey League team based in Edmonton, Alberta
Home Arena:
Rogers Place. Seating capacity 18,641.

Montreal Canadiens
1909 Av Des Canadiens-De-Montreal
MONTREAL, QC H3C 5L2
514-932-2582
www.canadiens.nhl.com
Geoff Molson, President/Owner/Chief Executive Officer
Fred Steer, EVP/Chief Financial Officer
Alain Gauthier, Executive Vice President/GM, Facilities Operations
Jacques Aube, Executive Vice President & Chief Operating Officer
Michel Therrien, Head Coach
Dan Lacroix, Assistant Coach
Stephane Waite, Goaltending Coach
Kevin Gilmore, Executive Vice President & COO
Donald Beauchamp, SVP, Communications & Community Relations
France Margaret Belanger, Senior Vice President & Chief Legal Officer

Year Founded:
1909
Description:
Based in Montreal, Quebec, the Montreal Canadiens is one of the oldest teams in the National Hockey League.
Home Arena:
Centre Bell. Seating capacity 21,273.

Ottawa Senators
Canadian Tire Centre
1000 Palladium Drive
OTTAWA, ON K2V 1A5
613-599-0250
ticketing@ottawasenators.com
www.senators.nhl.com
Eugene Melnyk, Owner/Governor/Chairman
Cyril Leeder, President/Alternate Governor
Ken Taylor, EVP/CFO
Peter O'Leary, Chief Marketing Officer/ VP, Ticketing
Jim Steel, VP, Broadcast
Bryan Murray, President, Hockey Operations/GM/Alt. Governor
Randy Lee, Assistant GM/Director of Player Development
Dave Cameron, Head Coach
Jason Smith, Assistant Coach
Year Founded:
1990
Description:
The Ottawa Senators are a National Hockey League team based in Ottawa, Ontario
Home Arena:
Canadian Tire Centre

Toronto Maple Leafs
50 Bay Street
Suite 500
TORONTO, ON M5J 2L2
416-703-5323
Fax: 416-359-9205
FanServices@MLSE.com
www.mapleleafs.nhl.com
Brendan Shanahan, President & Alternate Governor
Larry Tanenbaum, Chair, Maple Leafs Sports & Entertainment (MLSE)
Ian Clarke, Chief Financial Officer
Dave Morrison, Director, Pro Scouting
Kyle Dubas, Assistant General Manager
Scott McNaughton, Senior Manager, Media Relations
Reid Mitchell, Director, Hockey & Scouting Administration
Mike Babcock, Head Coach
Mark Hunter, Director, Player Personnel
Steve Keogh, Director, Media Relations
Year Founded:
1917
Description:
The Toronto Maple Leafs are a National Hockey League team based in Toronto, Ontario.
Home Arena:
Air Canada Centre. Seating capacity 19,800.

Vancouver Canucks
800 Griffiths Way
VANCOUVER, BC V6B 6G1
604-899-7400
Fax: 604-899-7401/7490
fanservices@canucks.com
www.canucks.nhl.com
Francesco Aquilini, Chairman/Gov
Trevor Linden, President, Hockey Operations & Alternate Governor
John Weisbrod, Assistant General Manager
TC Carling, VP Hockey Administration
Victor de Bonis, Chief Operating Officer & Alternate Governor
Todd Kobus, CFO & Vice President, Finance
Trent Carroll, Executive Vice President, Sales & Marketing
Jim Benning, General Manager
Willie Desjardins, Head Coach
Ben Brown, Director, Media Relations & Team Operations
Year Founded:
1970
Description:
The Vancouver Canucks are a National Hockey League team based in Vancouver, British Columbia
Home Arena:
Rogers Arena. Seating capacity 18,910.

Winnipeg Jets
345 Graham Avenue
WINNIPEG, MB R3C 5S5
204-987-7825
www.jets.nhl.com
Jim Ludlow, President, True North Development
Mark Chipman, Executive Chairman
Kevin Cheveldayoff, EVP/ General Manager
Norva Riddell, Senior Vice President Sales & Marketing
Craig Heisinger, SVP/Director Of Hockey Operations/Assistant GM
Paul Maurice, Head Coach
John Olfert, Executive Vice President & CFO
Kevin Donnelly, Senior Vice President, Venues & Entertainment
Robert Thorsten, Vice President, Venue & Patron Services
Year Founded:
2011
Description:
The Winnipeg Jets are a National Hockey League team based in Winnipeg, Manitoba. The franchise was formerly known as the Atlanta Thrashers until their purchase in 2011.
Home Arena
MTS Centre. Seating capacity 15,004.

Hockey, Professional, Minor Leagues

American Hockey League/AHL
One Monarch Place
Suite 2400
SPRINGFIELD, MA 01144
413-781-2030
Fax: 413-733-4767
info@theahl.com
www.theahl.com

David Andrews, President & CEO
info@theahl.com
Chris Nikolis, EVP Marketing & Business Development
cnikolis@theahl.com
Michael Murray, VP Hockey Operations
info@theahl.com
Jason Chaimovitch, VP Communications
info@theahl.com
Year Founded:
1936
Description:
Professional ice hockey league that serves as the primary developmental circuit for the National Hockey League.
Membership Requirements:
Purchase of a franchise
Publications:
Official guide and record book; Rule book; Schedule; Year End Statistical Package

Teams:

Manitoba Moose
345 Graham Avenue
WINNIPEG, MB R3C 5S6
204-987-7825
www.moosehockey.com
Craig Heisinger, General Manager
Brad Andrews, Director, Hockey Operations
Dan Hursh, Vice President, Operations
Keith McCambridge, Head Coach
Mark Morrison, Assistant Coach
Rick St Croix, Developmental Goaltending Coach
Home Ice:
MTS Centre. Seating capacity, 15,294.

St. John's Icecaps
PO Box 1880, Station C
ST JOHN'S, NL A1C 5R4
709-576-2277
www.stjohnsicecaps.com
Danny Williams, President/CEO
Glenn Stanford, Governor/Chief Operating Officer
glenn.stanford@stjohnsicecaps.com
Rob Mullowney, Vice President, Operations
rob.mullowney@stjohnsicecaps.com
Jason King, Director, Hockey Operations
jason.king@stjohnsicecaps.com
David Salter, Director, Communications
david.salter@stjohnsicecaps.com
Heather McKay, Director, Finance
heather.mckay@stjohnsicecaps.com
Home Arena:
Mile One Centre. Seating capacity 6,287.

Toronto Marlies
45 Manitoba Dr.
TORONTO, ON M6K 3C3
416-815-5982
Fax: 416-815-6050
FanServices@MLSE.com
www.marlies.ca
Kyle Dubas, General Manager & Alternate Governor
Brad Lynn, Director, Team Operations & Alternate Governor
Taylor Jenkins, Manager, Marketing
Stefano Toniutti, Coordinator, Media Relations
Justin Ratushniak, Event Coordinator, Fan Services
Sherry Jean, Community Manager
Peter Church, General Manager, Ricoh Coliseum
Home Arena:
Ricoh Coliseum. Seating capacity 7,851.

East Coast Hockey League/ECHL
116 Village Boulevard
Suite 230
PRINCETON, NJ 08540
609-452-0770
Fax: 609-452-7147
echl@echl.com
www.echl.com

Brian McKenna, Commissioner
Ryan Crelin, Senior Vice President Of Business Operations
rcrelin@echl.com
Joe Ernst, Vice President Of Hockey Operations
jernst@echl.com
Rich Bello, Director, Team Business Development
rbello@echl.com
Todd Corliss, Director, Finance
tcorliss@echl.com
Joe Babik, Director, Communications
jbabik@echl.com
Todd Merton, Director, Marketing & Licensing
tmerton@echl.com
Jeff Zavatsky, Director, Hockey Operations
jzavatsky@echl.com
Valerie Persinger, Manager, Business Operations
vpersinger@echl.com

Teams:

Brampton Beast
7575 Kennedy Road South
BRAMPTON, ON L6W 4T2
905-564-1684
Fax: 905-564-4881
info@bramptonbeast.com
www.bramptonbeast.com
Gregg Rosen, Majority Owner
Cary Kaplan, President/General Manager
Michael Miele, Vice President of Sales & Marketing
Ken Vezina, Vice President of Business Operations
Abhinav Nongmeikapam, Vice President of Digital Media
Colin Chaulk, Vice President of Hockey Operations/Head Coach
Evan Colborne, Director, Ticket Operations
Peter Goulet, Assistant Coach
Home Ice:
Powerade Centre

Ontario Hockey League/OHL
305 Milner Ave.
Suite 200
SCARBOROUGH, ON M1B 3V4
416-299-8700
Fax: 416-299-8787
www.ontariohockeyleague.com

David E. Branch, Commissioner
dbranch@chl.ca
Ted Baker, Vice President
tbaker@chl.ca
Joe Birch, Sr. Director, Hockey Development & Special Events
jbirch@chl.ca
Adam Dennis, Director, Recruitment
adennis@chl.ca
Ray Hollowell, Director, Finance
rhollowell@chl.ca
Year Founded:
1896

Teams:

Barrie Colts
555 Bayview Drive
BARRIE, ON L4N 8Y2
705-722-6587
Fax: 705-721-9709
operations@barriecolts.com
www.barriecolts.com
Howie Campbell, President & Owner
hcampbell@barriecolts.com
Jim Payetta, Co-Owner/VP, Business Development & Marketing
jpayetta@barriecolts.com
Andrew Cunningham, Media Relations Director
acunningham@barriecolts.com
Melissa Hamilton, Sales & Marketing
mhamilton@barriecolts.com
Jason Ford, General Manager & Head Scout
Dale Hawerchuk, Head Coach
Todd Miller, Assistant Coach
Mike Rosati, Goaltending Coach/Assistant Coach
Andrew Sachkiw, Head Athletic Therapist/Equipment Manager
Home Arena:
Barrie Molson Centre. Seating capacity 4,195.

Guelph Storm
55 Wyndham Street North
GUELPH, ON N1H 7T8
519-837-9690
Fax: 519-837-9692
info@guelphstorm.com
www.guelphstorm.com
Rick Gaetz, Governor
Rick Hoyle, President
Mike Kelly, Vice President & General Manager
Matt Newby, Director, Business Operations
Lindsay Newby, Media Relations & Special Event Coordinator
Bill Stewart, Head Coach
Todd Harvey, Assistant Coach
Matt Smith, Goaltending Coach
Home Arena:
Sleeman Centre. Seating capacity 5,100.

Hamilton Bulldogs
101 York Boulevard
HAMILTON, ON L8R 3L4
905-529-8500
Fax: 905-777-2360
www.hamiltonbulldogs.com
Michael Andlauer, Owner
Steve Staios, President
Peggy Chapman, Senior Director, Operations
Daniella Thomson, Director, Finance
Kris Young, Director, Marketing
George Burnett, Head Coach & General Manager
Troy Smith, Associate Coach & Assistant General Manager
Ron Wilson, Assistant Coach
Mike Parson, Goalie Coach
Home Arena:
FirstOntario Centre. Seating capacity 17,383.

Kingston Frontenacs
1 the Tragically Hip Way
KINGSTON, ON K7K 0B4
613-542-4042
Fax: 613-542-2834
info@kingstonfrontenacs.com
www.kingstonfrontenacs.com
Doug Springer, President & Governor
Justin Chenier, Executive Director, Business Operations
justin@kingstonfrontenacs.com
Darren Keily, Director, Hockey Operations
darren@kingstonfrontenacs.com
Doug Gilmour, General Manager
Paul McFarland, Head Coach
paul@kingstonfrontenacs.com
John Goodwin, Assistant Coach
john@kingstonfrontenacs.com
David Franco, Goaltending Coach
Home Ice:
Rogers K-Rock Centre. Seating capacity 5,700.

Kitchener Rangers
Kitchener Rangers Hockey Club
400 East Avenue
KITCHENER, ON N2H 1Z6
519-576-3700
Fax: 519-576-7571
info@kitchenerrangers.com
www.kitchenerrangers.com
Steve Bienkowski, Chief Operating Officer & Governor
sbienkowski@kitchenerrangers.com
Norm Leblond, President
Brad Sparkes, Director, Marketing & Sales
Murray Hiebert, General Manager
mhiebert@kitchenerrangers.com
Mike Van Ryn, Head Coach
Mike McKenzie, Assistant General Manager & Assistant Coach
Home Arena:
Kitchener Memorial Auditorium. Seating capacity 7,234.

London Knights
Budweiser Gardens
99 Dundas Street
LONDON, ON N6A 6K1
519-681-0800
Fax: 519-668-7291
info@londonknights.com
www.londonknights.com
Trevor Whiffen, Governor
Dale Hunter, Owner/President/Head Coach
Mark Hunter, Owner/Vice President
Basil McRae, Owner/Alternate Governor/General Manager
Geoffrey Hare, Director, Marketing
ghare@londonknights.com
Cindy Mitro, Director, Ticketing
tickets@londonknights.com
Rob Simpson, Assistant General Manager/Assistant Coach
Dylan Hunter, Assistant Coach
Dave Rook, Goaltending Coach
Home Arena:
Budweiser Gardens. Seating capacity 9,100.

Mississauga Steelheads
5500 Rose Cherry Place
MISSISSAUGA, ON L4Z 4B6
905-502-7788
Fax: 905-502-0169
info@mississaugasteelheads.com
www.mississaugasteelheads.com
Elliott Kerr, President
jekerr@landmarksport.com
Scott Rogers, Vice President/Director, Business Operations
srogers@mississaugasteelheads.com
James Boyd, General Manager/Head Coach
Alana Davidson, Manager, Public Relations & Community Initiatives
adavidson@mississaugasteelheads.com
Kory Cooper, Goaltender Coach
Binne Brouwer, Head Athletic Therapist
Home Ice:
Hershey Centre. Seating capacity 5,800.

Niagara Icedogs
One Icedogs Way
ST. CATHARINES, ON L2R 0B3
905-687-3641
Fax: 905-682-9129
info@niagaraicedogs.net
www.niagaraicedogs.net
Bill Burke, Governor/Director, Corporate Sales
b.burke@niagaraicedogs.net
Denise Burke, President
d.burke@niagaraicedogs.net
Marty Williamson, General Manager & Head Coach
m.williamson@niagaraicedogs.net
Jamie Amell, Office & Retail Manager
Beth Milligan, Corporate Sponsorship
b.milligan@niagaraicedogs.net
Joey Burke, Assistant General Manager
j.burke@niagaraicedogs.net
Ryan Ludzik, Goaltending Coach
r.ludzik@niagaraicedogs.net
Home Ice:
Meridian Centre. Seating capacity 5,300.

North Bay Battalion
100 Chippewa Street West
NORTH BAY, ON P1B 6G2
705-495-8603 EXT 2700
Fax: 705-475-1673
info@battalionhockey.com
www.battalionhockey.com
Mike Griffin, President & Alternate Governor
mgriffin@battalionhockey.com
Stan Butler, Director, Hockey Operations & Head Coach
Scott Walpole, Manager, Marketing & Communications
swalpole@battalionhockey.com
Matt Rabideau, Assistant General Manager & Director, Player Dev.
mrabideau@battalionhockey.com
John Dean, Assistant Coach
Ryan Oulahen, Assistant Coach
Home Arena:
North Bay Memorial Gardens. Seating capacity 4,025.

Oshawa Generals
99 Athol Street East
OSHAWA, ON L1H IJ8
905-433-0900
Fax: 905-433-0868
www.oshawagenerals.com
Rocco Tullio, President & Governor
John McMahon, Vice President
Roger Hunt, Vice President & General Manager
rhunt@oshawagenerals.com
Andrew Edwards, Director, Business Operations
aedwards@oshawagenerals.com
Jason Hickman, Director, Ticket Sales & Services
jhickman@oshawagenerals.com
Bob Jones, Head Coach
bjones@oshawagenerals.com
Eric Wellwood, Assistant Coach
ewellwood@oshawagenerals.com
Zac Bierk, Goaltending Consultant
Home Ice:
General Motors Centre. Seating capacity 6,107.

Ottawa 67's
TD Place
1015 Bank Street
OTTAWA, ON K1S 3W7
613-232-6767
Fax: 613-690-0468
info@ottawa67s.com
www.ottawa67s.com
Jeff Hunt, Owner/President, Sports Operations
jhunt@oseg.ca
Bernie Ashe, Chief Executive Officer
Randy Burgress, Vice-President, Communications & Fan Experience
rburgess@oseg.ca
Jeff Brown, Head Coach & General Manager
jbrown@ottawa67s.com
Chris Hamilton, Head Equipment Manager
chamilton@ottawa67s.com
Mike Eastwood, Associate Coach
meastwood@ottawa67s.com
Paul Schonfelder, Goalie Coach
pschonfelder@ottawa67s.com
Dan Marynowski, Head Trainer
Home Ice:
TD Place Arena. Seating capacity 10,000.

Owen Sound Attack
1900 Third Avenue East
OWEN SOUND, ON N4K 2M6
519-371-7452
1-866-528-8225
Fax: 519-371-7990
attack@bmts.com
www.attackhockey.com
Peter MacDermid, Governor
Paul MacDermid, Alternate Governor to the OHL
Fay Harshman, Secretary-Treasurer
Frank Coulter, Owner
Bob Severs, President
Dale DeGray, General Manager
ddegray@attackhockey.com
Ryan McGill, Head Coach
Brad Tiley, Assistant Coach
Greg Redquest, Goaltender Coach
Andy Brown, Athletic Therapist
Home Ice:
J.D. McArthur Arena, Harry Lumley Bayshore Community Centre. Seating capacity 3,500.

Peterborough Petes
151 Landsdowne Street West
PETERBOROUGH, ON K9J 1Y4
705-743-3681
Fax: 705-743-5497
petes@gopetesgo.com
www.gopetesgo.com
Bob Neville, Governor
Jim Devlin, President
jdevlin@gopetesgo.com
Mike Oke, General Manager
Jody Hull, Head Coach
Andrew Verner, Assistant Coach
Jake Grimes, Assistant Coach
Brian Miller, Head Trainer
bmiller@gopetesgo.com
Home Ice:
Peterborough Memorial Centre. Seating capacity 4,329.

Sarnia Sting
1455 London Road
SARNIA, ON N7S 6K7
519-542-4494
Fax: 519-542-2388
info@sarniasting.com
www.sarniasting.com
Derian Hatcher, Governor/Owner/Head Coach
Bill Abercrombie, President
Gord Currie, Chief Financial Officer
Dach Hiller, Director, Marketing & Communications
dhiller@sarniasting.com
Nick Sinclair, General Manager
Chris Lazary, Assistant Coach
Home Ice:
RBC Centre. Seating capacity 5,500.

Sault Ste. Marie Greyhounds
269 Queen Street East
SAULT STE. MARIE, ON P6A 1Y9
705-253-5976
Fax: 705-945-9458
info@soogreyhounds.com
www.soogreyhounds.com
Lou Lukenda, Chairman of the Board & President
George Shunock, Governor
Gerry Liscumb, Jr., Director, Public Relations & Hockey Administration
(705)574-0087
gerry@soogreyhounds.com
Kyle Raftis, General Manager
Drew Bannister, Head Coach
Joe Cirella, Associate Coach
Donald MacLean, Assistant Coach
Home Ice:
Essar Centre. Seating capacity 5,000.

Sudbury Wolves
240 Elgin Street
SUDBURY, ON P3E 3N6
705-675-3941
Fax: 705-675-3944
info@sudburywolves.com
www.sudburywolves.com
Mark W. Burgess, Chairman & CEO
Blaine Smith, President
Barclay Branch, General Manager
David Matsos, Head Coach
Ken MacKenzie, Assistant General Manager
Drake Berehowsky, Associate Coach
Home Ice:
Sudbury Community Arena. Seating capacity 5,100.

Windsor Spitfires
8787 McHugh Street
WINDSOR, ON N8S 0A1
519-254-5000
Fax: 519-254-9257
frontoffice@windsorspitfires.com
www.windsorspitfires2.com
Bob Boughner, President
Warren Rychel, Vice President & General Manager
Bill Bowler, Vice President, Hockey Operations
Steve Horne, Director, Business Development
Rocky Thompson, Head Coach
Trevor Letowski, Associate Coach
Jerrod Smith, Assistant Coach
Paul Billing, Goaltending Coach
Joey Garland, Athletic Therapist
Home Ice:
WFCU Centre. Seating capacity 6,500.

Quebec Major Junior Hockey League/QMJHL
1205 Ampere Street
Office #101
BOUCHERVILLE, QC J4B 7M6
450-650-0500
Fax: 450-650-0510
hockey@lhjmq.qc.ca
www.theqmjhl.ca
Gilles Courteau, Commissioner
Pierre Daoust, Vice President, Administration
pdaoust@lhjmq.qc.ca
Karl Jahnke, Director, Marketing & Corporate Bus. Developm
kjahnke@lhjmq.qc.ca
Pierre Leduc, Director, Hockey Operations
pleduc@lhjmq.qc.ca
Troy Dumville, Director, Recruitment
tdumville@lhjmq.qc.ca
Photi Sotiropoulos, Director, Communications
psotiropoulos@lhjmq.qc.ca
Richard Trottier, Director, Officiating
rtrottier@lhjmq.qc.ca
Description:
Member of Canadian Hockey League.

Teams:

Acadie-Bathurst Titan
850 St. Anne Street
BATHURST, NB E2A 6X2
506-549-3300
Fax: 506-549-3311
info@letitan.com
www.en.letitan.com
Sylvian Couturier, General Manager
Mario Pouliot, Head Coach
Kris MacDonald, Assistant Head Coach
Isabelle Morrier, Director of Operations
(506)549-3303
isabelle.morrier@letitan.com
Gilles Cormier, Sales Representative
(506)549-3344
gilles.cormier@letitan.com
Home Ice:
K.C. Irving Regional Centre. Seating capacity 3,162.

Baie-Comeau Drakkar
70 Avenue Michel-Hemon
BAIE-COMEAU, QC G4Z 2A5
418-296-2522
Fax: 418-296-0011
drakkar@globetrotter.net
www.le-drakkar.com
Serge Proulx, Dir. Administration, Communications & Marketing
sergeprouix@le-drakkar.com
Steve Ahern, General Manager
Marco Pietroniro, Head Coach
Chris Bartolone, Assistant Coach
Denis Francoeur, Assistant General Manager
Home Ice:
Henry Leonard Center. Seating capacity 3,042.

Blainville-Boisbriand Armada
3600 Boul Grand-Allee
CP 9
BOISBRIAND, QC J7H 1M9
450-276-2328
1-855-276-2328
Fax: 450-276-2327
info@armadahockey.ca
www.armadahockey.ca
Mario Marois, Vice President
mmarois@armadahockey.ca
Joel Bouchard, President and General Manager
Alexandra Simard, Communications Coordinator
asimard@armadahockey.ca
Marcel Patenaude, Assistant General Manager
Jean-Francois Fortin, Assistant Coach and Player Development
Alexandre Jacques, Coach Technical Skills
Home Ice:
Centre d'Excellence Sports Rousseau. Seating capacity 3,100.

Cape Breton Screaming Eagles
481 George Street
PO Box 8
SYDNEY, NS B1P 6G9
902-567-6378
Fax: 902-567-6303
admin@capebretoneagles.com
www.capebretoneagles.com
Andre Cote, President
Peter MacDonald, General Manager, Business Operations
(902)539-7115
peter.macdonald@capebretoneagles.com
Henri Izard, Assistant Coach
Chris Tournidis, Marketing Manager
(902)539-6271
chris.tournidis@capebretoneagles.com
Bill Sidney, Director of Sales Corporate Partnerships
(902)539-6127
Pauline Chisholm, Director of Finance
(902)539-6508
pauline.chisholm@capebretoneagles.com
Gary MacLean, Education Coordinator
(902)567-0651
gary.maclean@capebretoneagles.com
Home Ice:
Centre 200. Seating capacity 5,000.

Charlottetown Islanders
46 Kensington Road.
CHARLOTTETOWN, PE C1A 5H7
902-892-7349
Fax: 902-892-7350
admin@charlottetownislanders.com
www.charlottetownislanders.com
Grant Sonier, General Manager
grant.sonier@charlottetownislanders.com
Paul Drew, Goaltender Coach
Luke Beck, Assistant Coach
Connor Cameron, Assistant Coach
Craig Foster, President, Operations
(902)892-7352
craig.foster@charlottetownislanders.com
Jason Maclean, Director, Sales & Marketing
(902)892-7354
jason.maclean@charlottetownislanders.com
Johnathan Doiron, Chief Financial Officer
(902)892-2059
johnathan.doiron@charlottetownislanders.com
Home Arena:
Eastlink Centre. Seating capacity 3,717.

Chicoutimi Sagueneens
643 Rue Begin
CHICOUTIMI, QC G7H 4N7
418-549-9489
administration@sagueneens.com
www.sagueneens.com
Renald Nepton, Director of Operations
Eric Lamoureux, Vice President of Marketing
Yanick Jean, General Manager
Louis Robitaille, Assistant Coach
Denis Guathier, Assistant Coach
Frederick Malette, Goaltending Coach
Yanick Jean, Head Coach
Home Ice:
George-Vezina Centre. Seating capacity 4,724.

Drummondville Voltigeurs
300 Cockburn Street
DRUMMONDVILLE, QC J2C 4L6
819-477-9400
Fax: 819-477-0561
info@voltigeurs.ca
www.voltigeurs.ca
Louis Brousseau, Governor
Eric Verrier, President
David Boies, Director, Operations
dboies@voltigeurs.ca
Stephan Leblanc, Vice President, Hockey Operations
Dominic Ricard, General Manager
Denis Gauthier, Assistant Coach
Genevieve Ally, Games and Marketing Coordinator
Home Ice:
Centre Marcel Dionne. Seating capacity 3,038.

Gatineau Olympiques
125 Rue Carillion
HULL, QC J8X 3X7
819-777-0661
hockey@olympiquesdegatineau.ca
www.olympiquesdegatineau.ca
Alain Sear, President/Owner
asear@olympiquesdegatineau.ca

Melissa Fortin, Marketing Coordinator
gtetu@olypiquesdegatineau.ca
Josee Tasse, Advertising Development Director
Benoit Groulx, General Manager & Head Coach
Eric Landry, Assistant Coach
Home Ice:
Robert Gatineau Arena. Seating capacity 3,196.

Halifax Mooseheads
5284 Duke Street
HALIFAX, NS B3J 3L2
902-429-3267
Fax: 902-423-6413
mooseheads@halifaxmooseheads.ca
www.halifaxmooseheads.ca
Bobby Smith, Majority Owner & President
Brian Urquhart, Vice President, Business Operations
(902)496-5654
brian@halifaxmooseheads.ca
Travis Kennedy, Vice President, Corporate Relations
(902)496-5995
travis@halifaxmooseheads.com
Cam Russell, General Manager
cam@halifaxmooseheads.ca
Dominique Ducharme, Head Coach
dominique@halifaxmooseheads.ca
Jim Midgley, Assistant Coach
jim@halifaxmooseheads.ca
Jon Greenwood, Assistant Coach
jon@halifaxmooseheads.ca
Eric Raymond, Goaltender Coach
ericraymondmtl@yahoo.ca
Diane Ouimet, Athletic Therapist
diane@halifaxmooseheads.ca
Home Ice:
Scotiabank Centre. Seating capacity 10,595.

Moncton Wildcats
377 Killam Drive
Gate 2
MONCTON, NB E1C 3T1
506-382-5555
Fax: 506-858-2222
info@moncton-wildcats.com
www.moncton-wildcats.com
Jean Brousseau, Governor
Ryan Jenner, Vice President, Business Operations
jenner.ryan@moncton-wildcats.com
Roger Shannon, Director, Hockey Operations
(506)382-5555
shannon.roger@moncton-wildcats.com
Darren Rumble, Head Coach
Home Ice:
Moncton Coliseum. Seating capacity 6,554.

Quebec Remparts
Colisee Pepsi
250w Boulevard Wilfrid-Hamel
QUEBEC, QC G1L 5A7
418-525-1212
888-299-9595
Fax: 418-525-2242
info@remparts.ca
www.remparts.ca
Jacques Tanguay, President
Julien Gagnon, Governor
Louis Painchaud, General Manager
Jean-Sebastien Montminy, Director, Marketing
Daniel Renaud, Assistant Coach
Maxime Ouellet, Goaltending Coach
Philippe Boucher, Head Coach
Gabriel Hardy, Physical Trainer
Home Ice:
Colisee Pepsi. Seating capacity 15,176.

Rimouski Oceanic
111 2nd Street West
PO Box 816
RIMOUSKI, QC G5L 7C9
418-723-4444
Fax: 418-725-0944
hockey@oceanic.qc.ca
www.oceanic.qc.ca
Camille Leblanc, Governor
Kevin Cloutier, Director, Hockey Operations
Serge Beausoleil, General Manager & Head Coach
Eric Boucher, President & Executive Director
Eric Dubois, Assistant Coach
Charles Juneau, Assistant Coach
Jean-Philippe Berube, Director, Sales & Marketing
Home Ice:
Colisee de Rimouski. Seating capacity 5,062.

Rouyn-Noranda Huskies
218 Avenue Murdoch
ROUYN-NORANDA, QC J9X 1E6
819-797-3022
Fax: 819-797-4311
admin@huskies.qc.ca
www.huskies.qc.ca
Denis Pilon, Governor
Jacques Blais, President
Gilles Bouchard, Head Coach/General Manager
Simon Nadeau, Assistant Coach
Ian Clermont, Administrative Director
(819)797-3022
iclermont@huskies.qc.ca
Home Ice:
Arena Iamgold. Seating capacity 2,150.

Saint John Sea Dogs
99 Station Street
Suite 200
SAINT JOHN, NB E2L 4X4
506-657-3647
Fax: 506-696-0611
info@saintjohnseadogs.com
www.saintjohnseadogs.com
Wayne Long, President
waynelong@saintjohnseadogs.com
Scott McCain, Chief Executive Officer
Rick Walsh, Controller
(506)632-8155
rickwalsh@saintjohnseadogs.com
Darrell Young, General Manager
Danny Flynn, Head Coach
Mike Cotton, Manager, Marketing & Business Analytics
(506)632-8159
mike.cotton@saintjohnseadogs.com
Jeff Cowan, Assistant Coach
Jim Fleming, Goaltending Coach
info@saintjohnseadogs.com
Home Ice:
Harbour Station. Seating capacity 6,300.

Shawinigan Cataractes
1, Rue Jacques-Plante
SHAWINIGAN, QC G9N 1P6
819-537-6327
Fax: 819-537-3538
cats@cataractes.qc.ca
www.en.cataractes.qc.ca
Martin Mondou, General Manager
Martin Bernard, Head Coach
Mario Carriere, Assistant Coach
Steve Larouche, Assistant Coach
Justin Darchen, Governor
Roger Lavergne, President
Home Ice:
Centre Bionest de Shawinigan. Seating capacity 5,195.

Sherbrooke Phoenix
360 Cegep Street
2nd Floor
SHERBROOKE, QUEBEC J1E 2J9
819-560-8842
info@hockeyphoenix.ca
www.hockeyphoenix.ca
Patrick Charbonneau, General Manager
Ronald Thibault, Governor
Denis Bourque, President
Judes Vallee, Head Coach
Stephane Julien, Director, Player Development
Benoit Desrosiers, Assistant Coach
Sylvie Fortier, Executive Director
Jean-Francois Labbe, Assistant Coach
Home Ice:
Palais des Sports. Seating capacity 3,646.

Val D'Or Foreurs
810 6th Avenue
VAL-D'OR, QC J9P 1B4
819-824-0093
Fax: 819-824-7602
admin@foreurs.qc.ca
www.foreurs.qc.ca
Daniel Masse, President
Guylaine Daigle, Vice President, Finance & Corporate Affairs
Daniel Gamache, Governor
Dany Marchand, Vice President, Marketing
Marc Larouche, Vice President, Hockey
Daniel Bujold, Vice President, Education
Alexandre Rouleau, General Manager
Genevieve Rouleau, Director of Communications & Marketing
Mario Durocher, Head Coach

Yannick Dube, Assistant Coach
Donovan Delarosbil, Athletic Therapist
Home Ice:
Centre Air Creebec. Seating capacity 3,504.

Victoriaville Tigers
400 Jutras Boulevard East
VICTORIAVILLE, QC G6P 7W7
819-752-6353
Fax: 819-758-2846
info@tigresvictoriaville.com
www.tigresvictoriaville.com
Johnny Izzi, President/Vice President, Hockey
Patrick Poudrier, Vice President, Marketing
Alexandre Fortin, Vice President, Finances
Jean Marcotte, Governor
Yanick Jean, General Manager
Yves Bonneau, Director of Marketing
Bruce Richardson, Head Coach
Kevin Bergin, Assistant Coach
Maxime Desruisseaux, Assistant Coach
Home Ice:
Desjardins Coliseum. Seating capacity 3,420.

Western Hockey League

Father David Bauer Arena
2424 University Drive Northwest
CALGARY, AB T2N 3Y9
403-693-3030
Fax: 403-693-3031
info@whl.ca
www.whl.ca

Ron Robison, Commissioner
Richard Doerksen, Vice President, Hockey
Yvonne Bergmann, Vice President, Business
Stacy Baker, Director, Finance
Alyson Chambers, Director, Marketing
Kevin Muench, Director, Officiating
Corey St. Laurent, Sr. Manager, Communications
Description:
Member of the Canadian Hockey League.

Teams:

Brandon Wheat Kings
2-1175 18th Street
BRANDON, MB R7A 7C5
204-726-3535
www.wheatkings.com
Kelly McCrimmon, Owner/General Manager/Head Coach
Matt McNish, Director, Marketing & Ticket Sales
Rick Dillabough, Director, Business Operations & Sponsorships
Chris Falko, Director, Game Day Operations/Community Relations
Darren Ritchie, Assistant Coach
David Anning, Assistant Coach
Home Ice:
Westman Communications Group Place at Keystone Centre. Seating capacity 5,102.

Calgary Hitmen
PO Box 1540
Station M
CALGARY, AB T2P 3B9
403-777-4646
info@hitmenhockey.com,
customerservice@calgaryflames.com
www.hitmenhockey.com
N. Murray Edwards, Chairman/Director/Co-Owner
Ken King, Governor/President/CEO
Kelly Kisio, President, Hockey Operations & Alternate Governor
Mike Moore, General Manager & VP of Business Operations
Mark French, Head Coach
Joel Otto, Assistant Coach
Home Ice:
Scotiabank Saddledome. Seating capacity 19,289.

Edmonton Oil Kings
Telus Field
10233 - 96 Avenue
EDMONTON, AB T5K 0A5
780-414-4000
Fax: 780-409-5890
www.oilkings.ca
Kevin Radomski, Director, Business Operations
Jody Young, Director, Service & Ticket Operations
Randy Hansch, General Manager
Steve Hamilton, Head Coach
Ryan Marsh, Assistant Coach
Brian Cheeseman, Head Athletic Therapist

Home Arena:
Rogers Place. Seating capacity: 18,641.

Kamloops Blazers
300 Mark Recchi Way
KAMLOOPS, BC V2C 1W3
250-828-1144
Fax: 250-828-7822
info@blazerhockey.com
www.blazerhockey.com
Tom Gaglardi, President & Governor
Stu MacGregor, Alt. Governor/Vice President/General Manager
Angie Mercuri, Executive Director, Business Operations
amercuri@blazerhockey.com
Dave Chyzowski, Director, Sales & Marketing
dchyzowski@blazerhockey.com
Matt Recchi, Director, Player Personnel
Don Hay, Head Coach
Terry Bangen, Assistant Coach
Chris Murray, Assistant Coach
Mike Needham, Assistant Coach
Home Ice:
Sandman Centre. Seating capacity 5,464.

Kelowna Rockets
101, 1223 Water Street
KELOWNA, BC V1Y 9V1
250-860-7825
Fax: 250-860-7880
info@kelownarockets.com
www.kelownarockets.com
Bruce Hamilton, Owner/President/General Manager
bruceh@kelownarockets.com
Gavin Hamilton, Vice President Of Business Development
gavinh@kelownarockets.com
Lorne Frey, Director, Player Personnel & Head Scout
lornef@kelownarockets.com
Anne-Marie Hamilton, Director, Marketing & Game Operations
annyh@kelownarockets.com
Kevin Parnell, Director, Media Relations
kevin@kelownarockets.com
Brad Ralph, Head Coach
Kris Mallette, Assistant Coach
Home Ice:
Prospera Place. Seating capacity 6,886.

Kootenay Ice
#2 - 1777 2nd Street North
CRANBROOK, BC V1C 7G9
250-417-0322
Fax: 250-417-0323
info@kootenayice.net
www.kootenayice.net
Jeff Chynoweth, President/General Manager
chinny@kootenayice.net
Chris Wahl, Director, Sales & Public Relations
cwahl@kootenayice.net
Luke Pierce, Head Coach
Nella Rounsville, Education Advisor
edu.kootenay@gmail.com
Mike Bergren, Goaltending Coach
Cory Cameron, Athletic Consultant
Home Ice:
Western Financial Place. Seating capacity 4,654.

Lethbridge Hurricanes
2,2510 Scenic Drive South
LETHBRIDGE, AB T1K 7V7
403-328-1986
Fax: 403-329-1622
admin@lethbridgehurricanes.com
www.lethbridgehurricanes.com
Doug Paisley, President & Governor
Reid Williams, Vice President
Blair Sanderson, Treasurer
Tyler Brack, Secretary
Peter Anholt, General Manager
Brent Kisio, Head Coach
Mike Craig, Assistant Coach
Josh MacNevin, Assistant Coach
Home Ice:
ENMAX Centre. Seating capacity 5,479.

Medicine Hat Tigers
2802 Box Springs Way Northwest
MEDICINE HAT, AB T1C 0H3
403-526-2666
Fax: 403-526-3072
admin@tigershockey.com
www.tigershockey.com
Darrell Maser, President/Governor
Brent Maser, Vice President
Dave Andjelic, Director, Marketing & PR
Darren Kruger, Director, Player Development
Shaun Clouston, Head Coach/General Manager
Joe Frazer, Assistant Coach
Bill McLellan, Scouting Consultant
Mikki Lanuk, Athletic Therapist
Home Ice:
Canalta Centre. Seating capacity 5,500.

Moose Jaw Warriors
110 1st Avenue Northwest
MOOSE JAW, SK S6H 3L9
306-694-5711
Fax: 306-692-7833
warriors@mjwarriors.com
www.mjwarriors.com
Chad Taylor, President & Governor
Larry Sentes, Vice President & Alternate Governor
Dave Kiefer, Finance
Dean Lang, Secretary
Allan Millar, General Manager
Tim Hunter, Head Coach
Mark O'Leary, Assistant Coach
Jamie Hodson, Goaltender Coach
Brooke Kosolofski, Athletic Therapist
Home Ice:
Mosaic Place. Seating capacity 4,465.

Prince Albert Raiders
690 - 32nd Street East
PRINCE ALBERT, SK S6V 2W8
306-764-5348
Fax: 306-764-5454
info@raiderhockey.com
www.raiderhockey.com
Dale McFee, President
Gord Broda, Governor & Vice President
Curtis Hunt, General Manager
Marc Habscheid, Head Coach
Dave Manson, Associate Coach
Kelly Guard, Assistant Coach
Duane Bartley, Athletic Therapist & Equipment Manager
Home Ice:
Art Hauser Centre. Seating capacity 2,591.

Prince George Cougars
#102, 2187 Ospika Boulevard South
PRINCE GEORGE, BC V2N 6Z1
250-561-0783
Fax: 250-561-0743
info@pgcougars.com
www.pgcougars.com
Greg Pocock, President/Governor/Owner
John Pateman, Alternate Governor
Braydon Ouellet, Manager, Game Operations & Promotions
Todd Harkins, General Manager
Mark Holick, Head Coach
markh@pgcougars.com
Roman Vopat, Assistant Coach
Craig Hyslop, Athletic Therapist
Home Ice:
CN Centre. Seating capacity 5,967.

Red Deer Rebels
4847c 19th Street
RED DEER, AB T4R 2N7
403-341-6000
Fax: 403-341-6009
info@redderrrebels.com
www.reddeerrebels.com
Brent Sutter, Owner/General Manager/Head Coach
Merrick Sutter, Senior Vice President & Alternate Governor
Dean Williams, Vice President Of Marketing & Sales
Brett Kelly, Director, Ticket Sales
Nelson Lacourse, Director, Finance
Jeff Truitt, Associate Coach
Steve O'Rourke, Assistant Coach
Dave Horning, Head Trainer
Home Ice:
ENMAX Centrium. Seating capacity 6,706.

Regina Pats
PO Box 104
REGINA, SK S4P 2Z5
306-522-7287
Fax: 306-569-1021
pats@reginapats.com
www.reginapats.com
Anthony Marquart, Governor
Todd Lumbard, President
Mark Rathwell, Vice President of Communications
Joel Pickering, Director, Game Day Operations
John Paddock, General Manager & Head Coach
Dave Struch, Assistant Coach & Assistant General Manager
Brad Herauf, Assistant Coach
Rob Muntain, Goaltending Coach
Greg Mayer, Athletic Therapist
Home Ice:
Brandt Centre. Seating capacity 6,136.

Saskatoon Blades
#201, 3515 Thatcher Avenue
SASKATOON, SK S7R 1C4
306-975-8844
Fax: 306-934-1097
info@saskatoonblades.com
www.saskatoonblades.com
Mike Priestner, Owner & Governor
Colin Priestner, Managing Partner
Steve Hogle, President
Bob Woods, General Manager & Head Coach
Chad Scharff, Equipment Manager
Steve Hildebrand, Assistant General Manager
Dean Brockman, Assistant Coach
Jerome Engele, Assistant Coach
Tim Cheveldae, Goaltending Coach
James MacDonald, Athletic Therapist
Home Ice:
SaskTel Centre. Seating capacity 15,100.

Swift Current Broncos
PO Box 2345
2001 Chaplin Street East
SWIFT CURRENT, SK S9H 4X6
306-773-1509
Fax: 306-773-5406
s.c.broncos@sasktel.net
www.scbroncos.com
Liam Choo Foo, Chairman Of The Board
Al Stewart, Governor
Mark Lamb, General Manager & Head Coach
Ryan Switzer, Director, Communications & Digital Media
Jamie Porter, Director, Player Personnel & Assistant GM
Jamie Heward, Director, Player Development & Assistant Coach
Dianne Sletten, Assistant General Manager, Business Operations
Ryan Smith, Assistant Coach
Jamie LeBlanc, Head Athletic Trainer
Home Ice:
Credit Union iPlex. Seating capacity 3,239.

Vancouver Giants
100 North Renfrew Street
VANCOUVER, BC V5K 3N7
604-444-2687
Fax: 604-254-2687
info@vancouvergiants.com
www.vancouvergiants.com
Ron Toigo, Owner/President/Governor
Scott Bonner, Executive Vice President/General Manager
Dale Saip, Vice President Of Business Development
Tony Hall, Vice President Of Finance & Administration
Peter Toigo, Vice President Of Operations
Brendan Batchelor, Director, Media Relations
Matt Erhart, Assistant Coach
Tyler Kuntz, Assistant Coach
Ian Gallagher, Strength & Conditioning Coach
Nick Murray, Head Athletic Therapist
Home Ice:
Pacific Coliseum. Seating capacity 16,281.

Victoria Royals
1925 Blanshard Street
VICTORIA, BC V8T 4J2
250-220-2600
info@victoriaroyals.com
www.victoriaroyals.com
Graham Lee, Owner/Governor
Dave Dakers, Director
Dave Marritt, Chief Financial Officer
Cameron Hope, President & General Manager
Darren Parker, Senior Vice President Of Sales & Marketing
(250)889-0993

darren.parker@victoriaroyals.com
Devin Mazur, Director, Ticketing
(250)220-2610
devin.mazur@victoriaroyals.com
Dave Des Roches, Business Development
(250)220-7890
ddr@sofmc.com
Dave Lowry, Head Coach
Enio Sacilotto, Assistant Coach
Home Ice:
Save-On-Foods Memorial Centre. Seating capacity 7,006.

Lacrosse, Leagues/Teams

National Lacrosse League
53 West 36th Street
Suite 406
NEW YORK, NY 10018
212-764-1390
Fax: 917-510-9890
comments@nll.com
www.nll.com

George Daniel, Commissioner
Jeff Baker, Media Relations Coordinator
Brian Lemon, VP of Lacrosse Operations
Doug Fritts, Vice President, Broadcast Services & Communic
Justin Rubino, Director, Business & Administrative Operation
Description:
Founded 1997. Professional Indoor Lacrosse League.

Teams:

Calgary Roughnecks
PO Box 1540, Station M
CALGARY, AB T2P 3B9
403-777-2177
Fax: 403-777-3695
info@calgaryroughnecks.com
www.calgaryroughnecks.com
Ken King, President & CEO
John Bean, Governor and COO
Mike Board, General Manager and Director of Business Operation
Curt Malawsky, Head Coach & Assistant General Manager
Bruce Codd, Assistant Coach
Bob McMahon, Assistant Coach
Home Arena:
Scotiabank Saddledome. Seating capacity 19,289.

Saskatchewan Rush
123 2nd Avenue South
Suite 9
SASKATOON, SK S7K 7E6
306-978-7874
www.saskrush.com
Derek Keenan, Head Coach & General Manager
Bruce Urban, Owner & Governor
Jeff McComb, Assistant Coach
Jimmy Quinlan, Assistant Coach
Andrea Haughian, VP Marketing & Partnerships
Myrna Januario, Director, Operations & Controller
Home Arena:
SaskTel Centre. Seating capacity 15,195.

Toronto Rock
1132 Invicta Drive
OAKVILLE, ON L6H 6G1
416-596-3075
855-665-7625
Fax: 905-339-3473
info@torontorock.com
www.torontorock.com
Jamie Dawick, President
John Lovell, Head Coach
Blaine Manning, Assistant Coach
Dan Ladouceur, Assistant Coach
Matt Sawyer, Assistant Coach
Terri Giberson, Director, Business Operations
Mike Hancock, Director, Communications & Lacrosse Operations.
Home Arena:
Air Canada Centre. Seating capacity 18,819.

Vancouver Stealth
7888 200th Street
Suite 273
LANGLEY, BC V2Y 3J4
604-882-8800
Fax: 604-882-8877
info@stealthlax.com
www.stealthlax.com
Denise Watkins, Owner
Doug Locker, President & General Manager
David Takata, Chief Financial Officer
Dan Perreault, Head Coach
Clay Richardson, Assistant General Manager
Michelle Buziak, Coordinator, Community Relations
Home Arena:
Langley Events Centre. Seating capacity 5,500.

Soccer, Leagues/Teams

Canadian Soccer League/CSL
5160 Explorer Drive
MISSISSAUGA, ON L4W 4T7
905-564-2297
888-216-9913
Fax: 905- 671-6450
info@canadiansoccerleague.com
www.canadiansoccerleague.com

Vincent Ursini, Chairman
(905)564-2297
vincentursini@canadiansoccerleague.com
Pino Jazbec, League Administrator
(905)564-2297
pjazbec@canadiansoccerleague.ca
Stan Adamson, Director of Media and PR
(905)564-2297
stanadamson@canadiansoccerleague.ca
Tony Camacho, Director of Officials
(905)564-2297

Teams:

Brampton City United FC
215 Carlingview Dr.
ETOBICOKE, ON M9W 5X8
416-798-9844
Fax: 416-798-1455
mike@bramptoncityunitedfc.ca
www.bramptoncityunitedfc.ca
Silvio Cariati, General Manager
Juan Barreto, Head Coach & Technical Director
Michael Dimatteo, Director, Operations
Home Field:
Victoria Park Stadium.

London City
133 Southdale Rd. West
LONDON, ON N6J 2J2
519-701-1202
Fax: 519-438-4625
info@londoncity.ca
www.londoncity.ca
Andrew Crowe, Owner
Manuel Hernandez, General Manager
Jasmin Halkik, Head Coach
Home Field:
Cove Road Stadium.

Mississauga Eagles FC
3135 Unity Drive
MISSISSAUGA, ON, CANADA L5L 4L4
905-820-9740
Fax: 905-820-5412
president@mississaugaeaglesfc.com
erinmillssoccer.com/mefc
Susan Rossiter, President
president@mississaugaeaglesfc.com
Josef Komlodi, Head Coach
headcoach@mississaugaeaglesfc.com
Paul Dhillion, Assistant Coach
Richard Machado, Assistant Coach
Home Field:
Hershey Centre.

Montreal Impact Academy
4750 Rue Sherbrooke Est
MONTREAL, QC H1V 3S8
514-328-3668
Fax: 514-328-1287
info@impactmontreal.com
www.impactmontreal.com/en
Joey Saputo, President
Nicolas Coupleux, Chief Administration Officer, Academy
Marco Schallibaum, Head Coach
Philippe Eullaffroy, Director, Academy
Rino Folino, Director, Business Development
Veronique Fortin, Director, Public Relations & Asst. to President
Patrick Vallee, Director, Communications
Home Field:
Stade Saputo.

Niagara United
7704 Chorozy Street
NIAGARA FALLS, ON L2H 2N9
905-984-9118
info@niagaraunitedscooer.ca
www.niagaraunitedsc.com
James McGillivray, Head Coach
james.mcgillivray@hotmail.ca
Tony Visca, Manager
Mike Pratley, Assistant Coach
Home Field:
Kalar Sports Park.

North York Astros
#6, 37 Kodiak Cres.
TORONTO, ON M3J 3E5
647-499-5445
Fax: 647-932-1957
info@northyorkastros.ca
www.northyorkastros.ca
Bruno Ierullo, General Manager
Jorge Collazo, Sports Director
Sergio Espindola, Manager, International Business
Gerardo Lezcano, Coach
Kerwin Skeete, Coach
Home Field:
Esther Shiner Stadium.

SC Toronto
779 Crawford Street
Station E
TORONTO, ON M6H 4E3
416-588-9355
Fax: 416-588-7545
info@sctoronto.ca
www.sctoronto.ca
Victor Raleza, President
Patrice Gheisar, Head Coach
Luis Barros, Vice President
Joe Silva, General Manager
Kevin Alvarez, Director, Sponsorship & Fundraising
Home Field:
Allan A. Lamport Stadium.

SC Waterloo
422a Dunvegan Drive
WATERLOO, ON N2K 2C7
519-465-4050
info@scwaterloo.com
scwaterloo.ca
Tony Kocis, President
Vojislav Brisevac, Manager
(519)465-4050
info@scwaterloo.ca
Lazo Dzepina, Head Coach
Radmila Djekic, Manager, Busniess Development
Zoran Kukic, Recruitments & Team Development Officer
Home Field:
Warrior Field.

Serbian White Eagles FC
#15, 30 Titan Road
TORONTO, ON M8Z 5Y2
416-252-4752
Fax: 416-252-4668
info@serbianwhiteeagles.ca
serbianwhiteeagles.ca
Dragan Bakoc, President
dragan@serbianwhiteeagles.ca
Misko Zdravkovic, Treasurer
Milan Djuric, Secretary
Uros Stamatovic, Head Coach
Home Field:
Centennial Park Stadium.

St. Catharines Wolves
125 Vansickle Road
ST. CATHARINES, ON L2R 6P7
905-933-5749
Fax: 905-680-6030
romasoccer.info@gmail.com
www.romasoccer.com
Nick Fabiano, President
nickfabiano@hotmail.com
Domenic Scozzafava, 1st Vice President

d jscoz@yahoo.com
Carlo Arghittu, Head Coach
Martin Beswick, Director, Minor Soccer
Armand Di Fruscio, Director, Senior Soccer
Home Field:
Club Roma Stadium.

Major League Soccer
420 Fifth Avenue
7th Floor
NEW YORK, NY 10018

212-450-1200
Fax: 212-450-1300
feedback@mlssoccer.com
www.mlssoccer.com

Don Garber, Commissioner
Mark Abbott, President & Deputy Commissioner
Sean Prendergast, Chief Financial Officer

Teams:

Montreal Impact
4750 Rue Sherbrooke Est
MONTREAL, QC H1V 3S8
514-328-3668
Fax: 514-328-1287
info@impactmontreal.com
www.impactmontreal.com/en
Joey Saputo, President
Richard Legendre, EVP, Soccer Operations
Mauro Biello, Head Coach
Home Field:
Stade Saputo. Seating capacity 20,801.

Toronto FC
Bmo Field
170 Princes' Boulevard
TORONTO, ON M6K 3C3
416-360-4625
www.torontofc.ca
Bill Manning, President
Tim Bezbatchenko, General Manager
Greg Vanney, Head Coach
Home Field:
BMO Field. Seating capacity 22,453.

Vancouver Whitecaps FC
375 Water Street
Suite 550
VANCOUVER, BC V6B 5C6
604-669-9283
Fax: 604-684-5173
info@whitecapsfc.com
www.whitecapsfc.com
Bob Lenarduzzi, President
John Furlong, Executive Chair
Rachel Lewis, Chief Operating Officer
Martin Rennie, Head Coach
Paul Ritchie, Assistant Coach
Home Field:
BC Place. Seating capacity 21,000.

North American Soccer League
112 W 34th Street
Suite 2110
NEW YORK, NY 10120

646-832-3565
Fax: 646-832-3581
info@nasl.com
www.nasl.com

Bill Peterson, Commissioner
Rishi Sehgal, Director, Business Development & Legal Affairs
Neal Malone, Director, Public Relations
Brian Melekian, Director, Operations

Teams:

FC Edmonton
9725-62 Avenue
EDMONTON, AB T6E 0E4
780-700-2600
Fax: 780-439-7557
info@fcedmonton.com
www.fcedmonton.com
Claudia Bognar, Business Operations
Colin Miller, Head Coach

Ottawa Fury FC
1015 Bank Street
OTTAWA, ON K1S 3W7
www.ottawafuryfc.com
John Pugh, President
jpugh@ottawafuryfc.com
Melanie Ireton, Director, Operations
mireton@ottawafuryfc.com
Paul Dalglish, Head Coach

Premier Development League
1715 N Westshore Boulevard
Suite 825
TAMPA, FL 33607

813-963-3909
Fax: 813-963-3807
www.uslpdl.com

Description:
A development league in the fourth tier of the U.S. soccer league system.
Founded:
1995
Member Clubs:
65 (57 U.S., 6 Canada, 2 Expansion)

Teams:

Calgary Foothills FC
www.foothillsfc.ca

Forest City London
515 Richmond Street
LONDON, ON N6A 4V3
519-200-7120
Fax: 519-645-0781
info@fclondon.ca
www.fclondon.ca
Ian Campbell, President & Chief Executive Officer
Domenic Mescia, Director of Soccer
Martin Painter, Head Coach

K-W United FC
kwunitedfc.ca
Barry MacLean, President
bmaclean@kwunitedfc.com
Niki Budalic, Director of Operations
nbudalic@kwunitedfc.com
Chris Pozniak, Head Coach

Thunder Bay Chill
Chapples Soccer Park
530 Chapples Park Drive
THUNDER BAY, ON P7E 3H1
807-623-5911
www.thunderbaychill.com

Toronto FC Academy
35 Carl Hall Road
NORTH YORK, ON M3K 2B6
academy@torontofc.ca
www.torontofc.ca/academy
Stuart Neely, Head Coach

WSA Winnipeg
www.wsawinnipeg.ca
Eduardo Badescu, President

U.S. Soccer League W
1715 North Westshore Boulevard
Suite 825
TAMPA, FL 33607

813-963-3909
Fax: 813-963-3807
http://www.wleague.uslsoccer.com/

Tim Holt, President
Amanda Duffy, League Commissioner

Teams:

Thunder Bay Chill
191 Hazelwood Dr.
THUNDER BAY, ON P7G 1Y5
807-623-5911
Fax: 807-623-0433
tbchill@tbaytel.net
www.thunderbaychill.com
John Marrello, General Manager
Tony Colistro, PDL Head Coach & Technical Director
Saverio Lento, Academy Head Coach & Youth Director
Mike Tallari, Director, Marketing & Sales
Home Field:
Chapples Park Stadium. Seating capacity 2,000.

WSA Winnipeg
1411 Dudley Cres.
WINNIPEG, MB R3M 1P2
www.wsawinnipeg.com
Eduardo Badescu, President
Constantin Ignat, Vice President
William Rosales, Vice President
Lee Haber, Director, Business Operations
Home Field:
John Scouras Field/Winnipeg Soccer Complex. Seating capacity 2,000.

United Soccer League
1715 N Westshore Boulevard
Suite 825
TAMPA, FL 33607

813-963-3909
Fax: 813-963-3807
www.uslsoccer.com

Rob Hoskins, Chairman
Alec Papadakis, Chief Executive Officer
Jake Edwards, President

Teams:

FC Montreal
Stade Saputo
4750 Rue Sherbrooke Est
MONTREAL, QC H1V 3S8
514-328-3668
Fax: 514-328-1287
www.impactmontreal.com/en/fcmontreal
Joey Saputo, Owner
Philippe Eullaffroy, Head Coach

Toronto FC II
Ontario Soccer Centre
7601 Martin Grove Road
WOODBRIDGE, ON L4L 9E4
905-264-9390
www.torontofc.ca/tfcII
Bill Manning, President
Tim Bezbatchenko, General Manager
Jason Bent, Head Coach

Vancouver Whitecaps FC 2
Thunderbird Stadium
6288 Stadium Road
VANCOUVER, BC V6T 1Z3
604-822-1523
Alan Koch, Head Coach

Facilities

Arenas & Stadiums

Air Canada Centre
40 Bay Street
Suite 400
TORONTO, ON M5J 2L2

416-815-5500
Fax: 416-359-9332
www.theaircanadacentre.com

Michael Friisdahl, President & CEO, Maple Leaf Sports & Entertainment
Tom Anselmi, Chief Operating Officer
Robert Hunter, Chief Facilities & Live Entertainment Officer
Shannon Hosford, Vice President, Marketing & Communications
Wayne Zronik, Vice President, Live Entertainment
Owners:
Maple Leaf Sports & Entertainment Ltd.
Year Opened:
1999
Tenant(s):
NBA - Toronto Raptors, NHL - Toronto Maple Leafs, NLL - Toronto Rock.
Seating Capacity:
Basketball - 19,800. Hockey - 18,800. Lacrosse - 18,819. Concerts - 19,800. Theater - 5,200.

BC Place Stadium
777 Pacific Boulevard
VANCOUVER, BC V6B 4Y8

604-669-2300
Fax: 604-661-3412
stadium@bcpavco.com
www.bcplace.com

Paul McArdle, General Manager
(604)661-7242
pmcardle@bcpavco.com
Zeeshan Khan, Director of Operations
(604)661-3423
zeeshan.khan@centerplate.com
Shuhei Tada, Sales Manager
(604)661-7239
stada@bcpavco.com
Owners:
Province of British Columbia.
Operators:
BC Pavilion Corporation (PavCo).

Year Opened:
1983
Seating Capacity:
54,500
Tenant(s):
BC Lions (CFL), Vancouver Whitecaps FC (MLS)

Bell Centre
1909 Avenue Des Canadiens-De-Montreal
MONTREAL, QC H3C 5L2

514-932-2582
800-663-6786
Fax: 514-989-2871
www.centrebell.ca

Owners:
Molson Family.
Year Opened:
1996
Seating Capacity:
21,288
Tenant(s):
Montreal Canadiens (NHL).

BMO Field
170 Princes' Blvd.
Toronto, ON M6K 3C3

416-263-5700
Fax: 416-815-6050
Fanservices@mlse.com
bmofield.com

Owners:
City of Toronto
Operator: Maple Leaf Sports & Entertainment
Year Founded: 2007
Seating Capacity: Football: 26,500. Rugby/Soccer: 30,228
Tenants(s): Toronto Argonauts (CFL). Toronto FC (MLS).

Budweiser Gardens
99 Dundas Street
LONDON, ON N6A 6K1

519-681-0800
866-455-2849
Fax: 519-668-7291
info@londonknights.com
www.budweisergardens.com

Geoffrey Hare, Director of Marketing
ghare@londonknights.com
Sean Adams, Marketing Manager
sadams@londonknights.com
Ryan Starr, Public Relations & Communications Manager
ryan.starr@londonknights.com
Owners:
London Civic Centre Corporation.
Operator:
Global Spectrum.
Year Founded:
2002
Seating Capacity:
10,200
Tenant(s):
London Knights (OHL), London Lightning (NBL).

Canadian Tire Centre
1000 Palladium Drive
OTTAWA, ON K2V 1A5

613-599-0100
www.canadiantirecentre.com

Year Opened:
1996
Seating Capacity:
20,041
Tenant(s):
NHL - Ottawa Senators

Commonwealth Stadium (Edmonton)
11000 Stadium Road
PO Box 2359
EDMONTON, AB T5J 2R7

780-442-5311
Fax: 780-944-7545
311@edmonton.ca
www.edmonton.ca

Evelyn Ehrman, Director
Owners:
City of Edmonton
Year Opened:
1978
Seating Capacity:
60,000
Tenant(s):
CFL - Edmonton Eskimos.

Exhibition Place
100 Princes' Boulevard
Suite 1
TORONTO, ON M6K 3C3

416-263-3600
Fax: 416-263-3029
info@explace.on.ca
www.explace.on.ca

Mark Grimes, Chair
Owners:
City of Toronto.
Year Opened:
1879.

Expocite
250 Boul Wilfrid-Hamel
QUEBEC, QC G1L 5A7

418-691-7110
888-866-3976
Fax: 418-691-7249
info@expocite.com
www.expocite.com

Vincent Dufresne, President
Owners:
Quebec City.
Operators:
ExpoCite.
Year Founded:
1898

Harbour Station
99 Station Street
SAINT JOHN, NB E2L 4X4

506-632-6103
Fax: 506-632-6121
www.harbourstation.ca

Michael Caddell, General Manager
Ewan Cameron, Operations Director
Ken Moore, Director, Marketing
Brenda Lee, Box Office Manager
Kirby Williams, Director, Finance
Year Opened:
1993, renovated 2005.
Seating Capacity:
7,205
Tenant(s):
Saint John Sea Dogs (QMJHL), Saint John Mill Rats

Mosaic Stadium At Taylor Field
1910 Piffles Taylor Way
REGINA, SK S4P 3E1

306-569-2323
football.ballparks.com/CFL/Saskatchewan

Opened:
1936
Team:
Saskatchewan Roughriders
Seating Capacity:
33,427

MTS Centre
345 Graham Avenue
WINNIPEG, MB R3C 5S6

204-987-7825
888-626-6673
Fax: 204-926-5555
www.mtscentre.ca

Mark Chipman, Chairman
Jim Ludlow, President & CEO
Owners:
True North Sports & Entertainment
Year Opened:
2004
Seating Capacity:
Hockey - 15,294; End-Stage Concert - 16,170; Center-Stage Concert - 16,345; Rodeo/Motocross - 13,198; Basketball - 15,570
Tenant(s):
Winnipeg Jets (NHL)

Northlands Park
7410 Borden Park Road Nw
EDMONTON, AB T5B 4W9

780-471-7365
Fax: 780-471-7134
info@northlands.com
northlandspark.ca

Olympic Stadium
4141 Pierre-De Coubertin Avenue
MONTREAL, QC H1V 3N7

514-252-4141
877-997-0919
Fax: 514-252-0372
rio@rio.gouv.qc.ca
parcolympique.qc.ca

Maya Raic, Chair
Michel Labrecque, President
Founded:
1976
Seating Capacity:
56,040

Pacific Coliseum
2901 E Hasting Street
VANCOUVER, BC V5K 5J1

604-253-2311
www.pne.ca

Opened:
1968
Team:
Vancouver Giants (WHL)
Seating Capacity:
15,713

Percival Molson Memorial Stadium
475 Pine Ave. West
MONTREAL, QC H2W 1S4

514-398-7000
Fax: 514-398-4901
info.athletics@mcgill.ca
www.mcgillathletics.ca

G. Andrew Love, Building Director
Phil Quintal, Deputy Building Director
Eyal Baruch, Contact, Facilities
Owners:
McGill University
Year Opened:
1919
Seating Capacity:
25,012.
Tenant(s):
CFL - Montreal Alouettes. McGill Redmen

Raymond Chabot Grant Thornton Park
300 Coventry Road
OTTAWA, ON K1K 4P5

613-749-2020
www.canamleague.com/teams/ottawa.php

Ben Hodge, General Manager
Hal Lanier, Field Manager
Founded:
1993
Team:
Ottawa Champions (Can-Am League)
Seating Capacity:
10,332

RBC Centre
1455 London Road
SARNIA, ON N7S 1P6

519-541-1000
877-364-8232
Fax: 519-541-0303
guestservices@rbccentresarnia.com
www.ssec.on.ca

Ryan Chamney, Assistant General Manager
Edgar Hunt, Contact, Finance
Amanda Rossell, Contact, Guest Services
Owners:
City of Sarnia.
Year Opened:
1998
Seating Capacity:
Hockey - 5,000. Concerts - 6,000.
Tenant(s):
OHL - Sarnia Sting.

Ricoh Coliseum
100 Princes' Boulevard
TORONTO, ON M6K 3C3

416-263-3900
Fax: 416-263-3901
www.mlsemarketing.com/Speak.jsp?cid=155&scid=19
www.ricohcoliseum.com

Peter Church, General Manager
Jodie Becker, Manager, Event Services
Curtis Dray, Manager, Building Operations
Owners:
City of Toronto.

Operators:
Maple Leafs Sports & Entertainment Ltd.
Seating Capacity:
Hockey - 8,140. Concerts - 9,250. Wrestling - 10,279.
Tenant(s):
AHL - Toronto Marlies.

Rogers Arena
800 Griffiths Way
VANCOUVER, BC V6B 6G1

604-899-7444
Fax: 604-899-7490
fanservices@canucks.com
www.rogersarena.ca

Michael Doyle, Executive Vice President & General Manager, Arena
Indira Fisher, Director, Event Services
Owners:
Canucks Sports & Entertainment.
Year Opened:
1995
Seating Capacity:
Hockey - 18,910. Basketball - 19,700. Concerts - 19,000.
Tenant(s):
NHL - Vancouver Canucks

Rogers Centre
One Blue Jays Way
TORONTO, ON M5V 1J1

416-341-3000
Fax: 416-341-1103
guestservices@rogerscentre.com
www.rogerscentre.com

Mark Shapiro, President & Chief Executive Officer
Kelley Keyes, Vice President, Building Services
Wayne Sills, Director, Facility Services
Owners:
Rogers Communications, Inc
Operators:
Rogers Stadium Limited Partnership.
Year Opened:
1989
Seating Capacity:
Baseball - 49,282. Canadian football - 31,074-52,230. American football - 54,000. Soccer - 47,568. Basketball - 22,911-28,708. Concerts - 10,000-55,000.
Tenant(s):
MLB - Toronto Blue Jays

Rogers Place
10220 - 104 Ave. NW
EDMONTON, AB TYJ 4Y8

780-414-4625
info@rogersplace.com
www.rogersplace.com

Owners:
City of Edmonton
Operators:
Oilers Entertainment Group
Year Opened:
2016
Seating Capacity:
Hockey - 18,641. Concerts - 20,734
Tenant(s):
NHL: Edmonton Oilers. WHL: Edmonton Oil Kings

Scotiabank Saddledome
555 Saddledome Rise SE
CALGARY, AB T2G 2W1

403-777-4646
Fax: 403-777-3695
customerservice@calgaryflames.com
www.scotiabanksaddledome.com

Libby Raines, Vice-President, Building Operations
Garry McKenzie, Marketing VP
George Greenwood, Operations Manager
John Vidalin, Advertising/Promotions Director
Owners:
City of Calgary.
Operators:
Saddledome Foundation/Calgary Flames LP.
Year Opened:
1983
Seating Capacity:
19,289
Tenant(s):
NHL - Calgary Flames. NLL - Calgary Roughnecks. WHL - Calgary Hitmen.

Shaw Park
One Portage Avenue East
WINNIPEG, MB R3B 3N3

204-982-2273
Fax: 204-982-2274
goldeyes@goldeyes.com
www.goldeyes.com

Andrew Collier, General Manager
andrew@goldeyes.com
Don Ferguson, Facility Manager
Dan Chase, Director of Sales & Marketing
dan@goldeyes.com
Kevin Arnst, Box Office Manager
kevin@goldeyes.com
Bonnie Benson, Administrative Assistant
Sport:
Baseball
Team:
Winnipeg Goldeyes
Year Founded:
1999
Capacity:
7,481

Stade Municipal De Quebec
100 Rue Du Cardinal Maurice-Roy
QUEBEC, QC G1K 8Z1

418-521-2255
877-521-2244
Fax: 418-521-2266
info@capitalesdequebec.com
www.capitalesdequebec.com

Jean Tremblay, Owner
Michel Laplante, President
Owners:
City of Quebec
Year Opened:
1938, renovated 1999
Seating Capacity:
4,800
Tenant(s):
Can-Am - Quebec Capitales

Stade Saputo
4750 Rue Sherbrooke Est
MONTREAL, QC H1V 3S8

514-328-3668
Fax: 514-328-1287
saputo@saputo.com
www.stadesaputo.com

Joey Saputo, President, Montreal Impact & Stade Saputo
Richard Legendre, Executive VP, Montreal Impact & Stade Saputo
Eric Girouard, Director, Stadium Operations
Owners:
Saputo, Inc.
Operators:
Montreal Impact
Year Opened:
2008, expanded 2012.
Seating Capacity:
20,801
Tenant(s):
MLS - Montral Impact. CSL - Montreal Impact Academy.

TD Place
1015 Bank Street
OTTAWA, ON K1S 3W7

613-580-2429
www.lansdownepark.ca

Bernie Ashe, CEO, Ottawa Sports & Entertainment Group (OSEG)
Mark Goudie, Contact, Finance, HR & IT, OSEG
Bronwen Heins, Vice President, OSEG
Owners:
City of Ottawa.
Year Opened:
1908
Seating Capacity:
TBD (under renovation).
Tenant(s):
NASL - Ottawa Fury. CFL - Ottawa Redblacks.

Telus Field
10233 96th Ave. Nw
EDMONTON, AB T5K 0A5

780-423-2255
http://www.edmontonsport.com/facilities/telus_field

Owners:
City of Edmonton
Year Opened:
1995
Seating Capacity:
10,000.
Tenant(s):
WMBL - Edmonton Prospects.

Race Tracks - Auto

Sanair International Raceway
669 Petit Rang St Francois
CP222
SAINT-PIE, QC J0H 1W0

450-772-6400
Fax: 450-772-2236
www.sanairr.ca

Description:
Auto race track.

Shannonville Motorsport Park
7047 Old Highway #2
PO Box 259
SHANNONVILLE, ON K0K 3A0

613-969-1906
800-959-8955
Fax: 613-966-6890
info@shannonville.com
www.shannonville.com

Jean Gauthier, Promoter
Description:
Auto Race Track.
Long Track:
4.03km.
Pro Track:
2.47km
Fabi Circuit:
2.23km.

Race Tracks - Equestrian Downs & Parks

Calgary Exhibition & Stampede
1410 Olympic Way SE
CALGARY, AB T2P-2KB

403-261-0101
800-661-1260
Fax: 403-265-7197
reception3@calgarystampede.com
www.calgarystampede.com

Bill Gray, President

Clinton Raceway
147 Beech Street
CLINTON, ON N0M 1LO

519-482-5270
Fax: 519-482-1489
ifleming@clintonraceway.com
www.clintonraceway.com

Jessica Carnochan, Marketing Director
Ian Fleming, General Manager
Description:
Horse race track.

Stampede Park
1410 Olympic Way Se
CALGARY, AB T2G 2W1

403-261-0214
Fax: 403-265-7197
kmarrington@calgarystampede.com
www.calgarystampede.com

Patti Hunt, Promotions & Advertising Manager
(403)261-0253
phunt@calgarystampede.com

Sudbury Downs Holdings
400 Bonin Rd
Chlemsford
ON POM 1LO

705-855-9001
Fax: 705-855-5434
sudburydowns@gmail.com
www.sudburydowns.com

Patrick H. MacIsaac, President
Ken M. Le Drew, General Manager
Steve Burke, Ass.General Manager
Brent Powell, Director of Racing
Jim Hume, Director of Food & Beverage
Rob Nevins, Supritendent
Year Founded:
1974
Nature of Sports Service:
Harness horse race track.

Windsor Raceway
5555 Ojibway Parkway
PO Box 998
WINDSOR, ON N9A 6P6

519-969-8311 EXT 347
Fax: 519-969-0780
youbet@windsorraceway.com
www.windsorraceway.com

Richard Jacob, VP Operations
Patrick Soulliere, President
Description:
Horse race track.

Woodstock Raceway
5555 Ojibway Parkway
PO Box 998
WINDSOR, ON N9A 6P6

519-969-8311
Fax: 519-969-0780
youbet@windsorraceway.com
www.windsorraceway.com

Paul Masters, General Manager
Patrick Soulliere, President

SECTION 16
TRANSPORTATION

Associations

Aerospace Industries Association of Canada (AIAC) / Association des industries aérospatiales du Canada
#703, 255 Albert St., Ottawa ON K1P 6A9
Tel: 613-232-4297; *Fax:* 613-232-1142
info@aiac.ca
www.aiac.ca
Previous Name: Air Industries Association of Canada
Overview: A large national organization founded in 1962
Description: To promote & facilitate the continued success & growth of this strategic industry; To establish & maintain a public policy environment that enables sustained aerospace industry growth; To strengthen the international competitiveness of all aerospace firms in Canada; To strengthen Canadian aerospace SME capabilities & position them as "suppliers of choice"; To represent & involve the full range of aerospace companies that operate in Canada
Chief Officer(s): Jim Quick, President & CEO, 613-232-4297
Barry Kohler, Chair
Membership: 400; *Committees:* International Exhibition; Technology Council; Defence Procurement Council; Suppliers Development; Space; Civil Aviation; Public Affairs
Activities: *Library:* Yes

Air Canada Pilots Association (ACPA) / L'Association des pilotes d'Air Canada
#205, 6299 Airport Rd., Mississauga ON L4V 1N3
Tel: 905-678-9008; *Fax:* 905-678-9016
Toll-Free: 800-634-0944
info@acpa.ca
www.acpa.ca
Overview: A medium-sized national organization founded in 1995
Affiliation(s): Association of Star Alliance Pilots
Chief Officer(s): Paul Strachan, President
Jon Webster, Secretary-Treasurer, 905-678-9008 240
jwebster@acpa.ca
Paul Strachan, Chair, Master Executive Council
Membership: 3,100

Air Line Pilots Association, International - Canada (ALPA)
#1715, 360 Albert St., Ottawa ON K1R 7X7
Tel: 613-569-5668
www.alpa.org
Social Media:
www.youtube.com/user/WeAreALPA;
www.instagram.com/we_are_alpa
linkedin.com/companies/air-line-pilots-association
www.facebook.com/WeAreALPA
twitter.com/WeAreALPA
Previous Name: Canadian Air Line Pilots Association
Overview: A large national organization founded in 1931
Description: To promote & represent the interests of the airline pilot profession; To safeguard the rights of individual members; To promote & maintain the highest standards of flight safety; To function as a trade union & professional association
Affiliation(s): International Federation of Air Line Pilots' Associations; Canadian Labour Congress
Chief Officer(s): Tim Canoll, President
Joe DePete, First Vice-President
Rick Dominguez, Executive Administrator
Finances: *Funding Sources:* Membership dues
Staff: 10 staff member(s); 360 volunteer(s)
Membership: 2,200 + 19 locals in Canada; *Member Profile:* Active airline pilots employed by airlines in Canada; *Committees:* Air Safety; Aeromedical; Insurance; Membership

Air Transport Association of Canada (ATAC) / Association du transport aérien du Canada
#700, 255 Albert St., Ottawa ON K1P 6A9
Tel: 613-233-7727; *Fax:* 613-230-8648
atac@atac.ca
www.atac.ca
Overview: A medium-sized national organization founded in 1934
Description: To advance the issues that affect members from the commercial aviation & flight training industries as well as avaiation industry suppliers
Chief Officer(s): John McKenna, President & Chief Executive Officer
jmckenna@atac.ca
Fred Gaspar, Vice-President, Policy & Strategic Planning, 613-233-7727 314
fgaspar@atac.ca
Bill Boucher, Vice-President, Flight Operations
bboucher@atac.ca
Wayne Gouveia, Vice-President, Commercial General Aviation
wgouveia@atac.ca
Cedric Paillard, Vice-President, Communications & Marketing
cpaillard@atac.ca
Mike Skrobica, Vice-President, Industry Monetary Affairs
mikes@atac.ca
Brian Whitehead, Vice-President, Technical Operations
bwhitehead@atac.ca
Membership: 200; *Member Profile:* Operators; Associates; Affiliates; *Committees:* Cabin Operations; Environmental Affairs; Flight Operations; Maintenance, Repair and Overheaul; Safety Advisory; Technical Operations; Accessible Transportation; Air Cargo Carrier; Facilitation; Industry and Monetary Affairs; Legal; Security; Tax; Dangerous Goods; Flight Training and Fixed Wing
Activities: Engaging in lobbying activities; *Speaker Service:* Yes

Airport Management Council of Ontario
#5, 50 Terminal St., North Bay ON P1B 8G2
Tel: 705-474-1080; *Fax:* 705-474-4073
Toll-Free: 877-636-2626
amco@amco.on.ca
www.amco.on.ca
Overview: A small provincial organization founded in 1985
Description: To monitor the airport industry, lobby, provide networking opportunities & training to airports & businesses that work to enhance airport operations.
Chief Officer(s): Bryan Avery, Executive Director, 877-636-2626
bryan.avery@amco.on.ca
Membership: 58 airports + 56 businesses; *Fees:* Schedule available
Activities: Workshops, presentations, conventions; *Speaker Service:* Yes; *Library:* Resource Centre

Alberta Construction Trucking Association (ACTA)
#400, 1040 - 7 Ave. SW, Calgary AB T2P 3G9
Tel: 403-244-4487; *Fax:* 403-244-2340
info@myacta.ca
www.myacta.ca
Previous Name: Alberta Gravel Truckers Association
Overview: A medium-sized provincial organization founded in 1983
Description: To develop & promote the business of transporting construction & construction-related material
Chief Officer(s): Jennifer Singer, President
Membership: *Fees:* $210-$525 Regular; $525 Affliate

Alberta Motor Transport Association (AMTA)
#1, 285005 Wrangler Way, Rocky View AB T1X 0K3
Fax: 403-243-4610
Toll-Free: 800-267-1003
amtamsc@amta.ca
www.amta.ca
Social Media:
linkedin.com/company/alberta-motor-transport-association
www.facebook.com/AlbertaMotorTransportAssociation
twitter.com/AMTA_ca
Merged from: Alberta Trucking Industry Safety Association; Alberta Trucking Association
Overview: A medium-sized provincial organization
Description: To take a leadership role in fostering a healthy, vibrant industry; *Member of:* Canadian Council of Motor Transport Administrators
Chief Officer(s): Richard Warnock, President & CEO, 403-214-3439
richardw1@amta.ca
Lorraine Card, Executive Director, 403-214-3429
lorrainec1@amta.ca
Membership: 12,000; *Member Profile:* All sectors of the highway transportation industry; *Committees:* Injury Reduction & Training; Compliance & Regulatory Affairs; Member Services

Alberta Pioneer Railway Association (APRA)
24215 - 34 St., Edmonton AB T5Y 6B4
Tel: 780-472-6229; *Fax:* 780-968-0167
www.albertarailwaymuseum.com
Also Known As: Alberta Railway Museum
Overview: A small provincial charitable organization founded in 1968
Description: To collect, preserve, restore, exhibit & interpret artifacts which represent the history & social impact of the railways in Western Canada, with emphasis on Canadian National Railways & Northern Alberta Railways & their predecessors in northern & central Alberta; *Member of:* Alberta Museums Association; Museums Canada
Affiliation(s): Heritage Canada
Chief Officer(s): Herb Dixon, President
Finances: *Funding Sources:* Grants; donations
Membership: *Fees:* $34 regular; $45 family; $20 senior/associate; *Member Profile:* Railway enthusiasts; retired railway workers
Activities: Operates Alberta Railway Museum; *Library:* John Rechner Memorial Library (Open to Public) by appointment

Amalgamated Transit Union (AFL-CIO/CLC) / Syndicat uni du transport (FAT-COI/CTC)
5025 Wisconsin Ave. NW, Washington DC 20016 USA
Tel: 202-537-1645; *Fax:* 202-244-7824
Toll-Free: 888-240-1196
www.atu.org
Social Media:
www.youtube.com/user/stpatuorg
www.facebook.com/ATUInternational
twitter.com/ATUComm
Overview: A medium-sized international organization
Description: The Amalgamated Transit Union fights for the interests of its members and promotes mass transit.
Chief Officer(s): Lawrence J Hanley, President
Oscar Owens, Sec.-Treas.
Membership: *Member Profile:* Transit workers

Association des usagers du transport adapté de Longueuil (AUTAL)
#211, 150, rue Grant, Longueuil QC J4H 3H6
Tél: 450-646-2224
Aperçu: *Dimension:* petite; *Envergure:* locale; fondée en 1981
Description: Défendre les droits des personnes handicapées qui utilisent le système de transport aménagé à Longueuil

Association du camionnage du Québec inc. (ACQ) / Québec Trucking Association Inc.
#200, 6450, rue Notre Dame ouest, Montréal QC H4C 1V4
Tél: 514-932-0377; *Téléc:* 514-932-1358
info@carrefour-acq.org
www.carrefour-acq.org
Média social:
linkedin.com/company/association-du-camionnage-du-québec
twitter.com/asscamionnageqc
Aperçu: *Dimension:* moyenne; *Envergure:* provinciale; Organisme sans but lucratif; fondée en 1951
Description: Favoriser l'amélioration des normes de sécurité, d'efficacité et d'éthique dans l'industrie du camionnage; maintenir un contact avec l'autorité gouvernementale, les usagers des services de camionnage et le public en général; soutenir le perfectionnement professionnel; soutenir les entreprises dans la défense de leurs intérêts
Affiliation(s): Union Internationale des Transports Routiers - Genève; American Trucking Association - Washington, DC
Membre(s) du bureau directeur: Marc Cadieux, Président-directeur général, 513-932-0377 204
mcadieux@carrefour-acq.org
Finances: *Budget de fonctionnement annuel:* $500,000-$1.5 Million
Personnel: 13 membre(s) du personnel
Membre: 500 entreprises; *Critères d'admissibilité:* Transporteurs et locateurs publics & privés
Activités: *Stagiaires:* Oui

Association du transport urbain du Québec (ATUQ) / Quebec Urban Transit Association
#8090, 800, rue de la Gauchetière, Montréal QC H5A 1J6
Tél: 514-280-4640; *Téléc:* 514-280-7053
info@atuq.com
www.atuq.com
Média social:
linkedin.com/company/association-du-transport-urbain-du-quebe c-atuq
Aperçu: *Dimension:* moyenne; *Envergure:* provinciale; fondée en 1983
Description: Organisme de concertation et de représentation politique qui a pour mandat d'assurer la promotion du transport en commun et la défense des intérêts de ses membres auprès des partenaires de l'industrie et des différentes instances gouvernementales
Membre(s) du bureau directeur: Patrice Martin, Président
France Vézina, Directrice générale
Valérie Leclerc, Responsable de communications, 514-280-8167
valerie.leclerc@atuq.com
Membre: 9; *Critères d'admissibilité:* Sociétés de transport en commun du Québec
Activités: *Bibliothèque:* Oui (Bibliothèque publique)

Association nationale des camionneurs artisans inc. (ANCAI)
#235, 670, rue Bouvier, Québec QC G2J 1A7
Tél: 418-623-7923; *Téléc:* 418-623-0448
infos@ancai.com
www.ancai.com
Aperçu: *Dimension:* moyenne; *Envergure:* provinciale; fondée en 1966
Description: Défendre les intérêts des transporteurs en vrac (gravier et forêts) auprès des gouvernements, organismes patronaux et entreprises privées
Membre(s) du bureau directeur: Guy Laplante, Président
g.laplante@ancai.com

Gaétan Légaré, Directeur général
g.legare@ancai.com
Membre: 5,000; *Montant de la cotisation:* $205; *Critères d'admissibilité:* Camionneur propriétaire de son véhicule; *Comités:* Négociations
Activités: Congrès annuel; Tirage camion

Association of Canadian Port Authorities (ACPA)
#1006, 75 Albert St., Ottawa ON K1P 5E7
Tel: 613-232-2036; *Fax:* 613-232-9554
www.acpa-ports.net
Social Media: twitter.com/ACPA_AAPC
Previous Name: Canadian Port & Harbour Association
Overview: A medium-sized national organization founded in 1958
Description: To encourage, mentor & stimulate the development of excellence within Canadian ports
Affiliation(s): American Association of Port Authorities
Chief Officer(s): Wendy Zatylny, Executive Director
wzatylny@acpa-ports.net
Finances: *Funding Sources:* Membership fees; seminars
Staff: 2 staff member(s)
Membership: 18 corporate + 37 supporters; *Fees:* $750 associate/supporters; $100 individual; *Committees:* Finance & Administration; National Operations; Executive; Audit; Governance; Enviroment; Law
Activities: Annual conferences where papers are given by experts in the field of port operations & where members inspect the host port's dock & industrial facilities; port-related research; special seminars; *Speaker Service:* Yes

Association québécoise du transport aérien (AQTA)
Aéroport international Jean-Lesage, 600, 6e av de l'Aéroport, Québec QC G2G 2T5
Tél: 418-871-4635; *Téléc:* 418-871-8189
aqta@aqta.ca
www.aqta.ca
Aperçu: *Dimension:* moyenne; *Envergure:* provinciale; Organisme sans but lucratif; fondée en 1975
Description: Voué à la défense et la promotion des intérêts de tous les secteurs du transport aérien
Membre(s) du bureau directeur: Éric Lippé, Président-directeur général
Membre: 135; *Montant de la cotisation:* Barème; *Critères d'admissibilite:* Transporteurs aériens et fournisseurs de produits et services liés à l'aviation

Association québécoise du transport et des routes inc. (AQTR)
Bureau de Montréal, #200, 1255, boul Robert-Bourassa, Montréal QC H3B 3B2
Tél: 514-523-6444; *Téléc:* 514-523-2666
www.aqtr.qc.ca
Média social: www.facebook.com/AQTransports
twitter.com/AQTransports
Aperçu: *Dimension:* grande; *Envergure:* provinciale; fondée en 1965
Description: Assumer un leadership technique; définir des règles en matière de sécurité et d'environnement; Favoriser l'échange international des expertises; promouvoir la recherche et le développement des expertises et des produits en transport; promouvoir la formation dans le domaine des transports; Assumer la représentativité de l'AQTR par la participation aux principaux forums sur les transports; Contribuer à servir la société par l'éducation et l'information du grand public
Membre(s) du bureau directeur: Marc Des Rivières, Président
Dominique Lacoste, Présidente-directrice générale
Finances: *Budget de fonctionnement annuel:* $500,000-$1.5 Million
Personnel: 7 membre(s) du personnel; 100 bénévole(s)
Membre: 950; *Montant de la cotisation:* Barème; *Critères d'admissibilité:* Secteur privé - Ingénieur conseils; Entrepreneurs; Fournisseurs et manufacturiers; Laboratoires; Transporteurs; Architectes et urbanistes; Étudiants; Spécialistes en environnement; Secteur public et parapublic - Ministères; Municipalités; Maisons d'enseignement; Sociétés de transport; Autres sociétés, départements et services publics; *Comités:* Directions techniques - Infrastructures de transport; Transport des personnes; Circulation; Sécurité dans les transports; Transport aérien; Recherche et développement; Comités - Transport des marchandises; Environnement; Revue; Congrès; Activités municipales
Activités: Regrouper les personnes impliquées dans les techniques du transport; Encourager les échanges multidisciplinaires et favoriser la collaboration entre différents secteurs; Recommander toute mesure permettant de développer des techniques du transport; *Listes de destinataires:* Oui

Association sectorielle - Fabrication d'équipement de transport et de machines (ASFETM) / Sectorial Association - Transportation Equipment & Machinery Manufacturing (SATEMM)
#202, 3565, rue Jarry est, Montréal QC H1Z 4K6
Tél: 514-729-6961; *Téléc:* 514-729-8628
Ligne sans frais: 888-527-3386
info@asfetm.com
www.asfetm.com
Aperçu: *Dimension:* grande; *Envergure:* provinciale; Organisme sans but lucratif; fondée en 1983
Description: Aider les employeurs et les travailleurs à prévenir les accidents du travail et les maladies professionnelles, en faisant pour eux de la recherche, en leur dispensant de l'information, de la formation et de l'assistance technique qui visent essentiellement à rendre impossibles les accidents et les maladies au travail, et en privilégiant, à cette fin, l'élimination de cette possibilité à sa source même selon un processus de participation paritaire; *Membre de:* National Safety Council (USA); Association du camionnage du Québec
Membre(s) du bureau directeur: Arnold Dugas, Directeur général
adugas@asfetm.com
Suzanne Ready, Chargée de l'information
sready@asfetm.com
Finances: *Budget de fonctionnement annuel:* $500,000-$1.5 Million
Personnel: 20 membre(s) du personnel
Membre: 8 groupes corporatifs - 3 patronaux + 5 syndicaux; *Critères d'admissibilite:* Etre une association patronale ou syndicale du secteur
Activités: Programme d'action annuel (30 projets); journées de sessions et de formation; colloques; *Service de conférenciers:* Oui

Atlantic Provinces Trucking Association (APTA)
#800, 105 Englehart St., Dieppe NB E1A 8K2
Tel: 506-855-2782; *Fax:* 506-853-7424
Toll-Free: 866-866-1679
www.apta.ca
Social Media: linkedin.com/groups/Atlantic-Provinces-Trucking-Association-48 1142
twitter.com/APTA_Trucking
Overview: A medium-sized local organization founded in 1950
Description: To promote an efficient, safe & environmentally sound trucking industry in Atlantic Canada
Chief Officer(s): Jean Marc Picard, Executive Director
jmpicard@apta.ca
Danielle Hébert, Coordinator, Marketing
dhebert@apta.ca
Membership: 325+; *Fees:* Schedule available; *Member Profile:* Open to anyone having an interest in the trucking industry in Atlantic Canada, including common carriers, owner-operators & private fleets; *Committees:* Associated Trades Council; Safety Council; Charity; Human Resource & Education; Marine; Legislative; Future Leaders
Activities: Improving infrastructure; Establishing training programs; Holding an annual meeting; *Rents Mailing List:* Yes

Bike to Work BC (BTWBC)
PO Box 74591, Stn. Kitsilano, Vancouver BC V6K 4P4
www.biketowork.ca
Overview: A small provincial organization founded in 2008
Description: To help communities in BC deliver successful Bike to Work & Bike to School events; To encourage as many people as possible to experience the benefits of commuting by bicycle
Chief Officer(s): Penny Noble, Executive Director, 604-805-5637
pnoble@biketowork.ca
Finances: *Funding Sources:* Donations; Government
Staff: 2 staff member(s)
Activities: Organizing events by securing & sharing resources; *Awareness Events:* Bike to Work Week, May; Bike to School Week, May

British Columbia Aviation Council (BCAC)
PO Box 31040, RPO Thunderbird, Langley BC V1M 0A9
Tel: 604-278-9330; *Fax:* 604-278-8210
info@bcaviationcouncil.org
www.bcaviationcouncil.org
Social Media: www.flickr.com/photos/63124160@N08/
twitter.com/bcac1938
Also Known As: BC Aviation Council
Overview: A small provincial organization founded in 1936
Description: A self-sustaining organization with the mission to "promote the safe and orderly development of aviation and aviation services to the province of British Columbia."
Chief Officer(s): Mike Matthews, Chair
mmatthews@bcaviationcouncil.org
Donna Farquar, Executive Administrator
Finances: *Funding Sources:* Membership fees

British Columbia Ferry & Marine Workers' Union (CLC) (BCFMWU) / Syndicat des travailleurs marins et de bacs de la Colombie-Britannique (CTC)
1511 Stewart Ave., Nanaimo BC V9S 4E3
Tel: 250-716-3454; *Fax:* 250-716-3455
Toll-Free: 800-663-7009
mailroom@bcfmwu.com
www.bcfmwu.com
Social Media: twitter.com/BCFMWU
Also Known As: Ferry Workers' Union
Overview: A medium-sized provincial organization founded in 1977
Description: To unite in the Union all workers eligible for membership; to seek the best possible wage standards & improvements in the conditions of employment for these workers & to represent members in protecting & maintaining their rights; to act as the representative of the membership; to establish free child day care for all individuals; to engage in educational, legislative, political, civic, social, welfare, community & other activities to safeguard & promote economic & social benefits & justice for all workers, unionized & non-unionized.; *Member of:* National Union of Public and General Employees
Affiliation(s): BC Federation of Labour; National Union of Public & General Employees (NUPGE)
Chief Officer(s): Kevin Lee, Sec.-Treas.
kevinlee@bcfmwu.com
Chris Abbott, President
chrisabbott@bcfmwu.com
Finances: *Annual Operating Budget:* $1.5 Million-$3 Million; *Funding Sources:* Union dues
Staff: 9 staff member(s)
Membership: 4,400; *Fees:* $60 initiation fee; 1.5% of gross monthly income; *Committees:* Asbestos; Apprenticeship; Communications; Convention; Education; Finance; Hours of Work; Human Rights; Occupational Health and Safety; Solidarity; Young Workers

British Columbia Railway Historical Association (BCRHA)
1148 Balmoral Rd., Victoria BC V8T 1B1
bcrha@shaw.ca
www.trainweb.org/bcrha
Overview: A small provincial charitable organization founded in 1961
Description: To preserve railway exhibits, manuscripts & film of BC railways; *Member of:* Heritage Society of BC
Finances: *Funding Sources:* Donations; book sales; membership dues
Membership: *Fees:* $15 full; *Member Profile:* Interest in BC railway history
Activities: Research & publication of books on BC railway history; *Library:* Yes (Open to Public)

British Columbia Supercargoes' Association
#206, 3711 Delbrook Ave., North Vancouver BC V7N 3Z4
Tel: 604-878-1258; *Fax:* 604-904-6545
president@supercargoes.bc.ca
www.supercargoes.bc.ca
Overview: A medium-sized provincial organization founded in 1952
Description: To provide expert marine cargo planning & onsite management & supervision of shiploading & discharge of all types of cargoes & vessels on the west coast of North America
Chief Officer(s): Terry Stuart, President
Finances: *Funding Sources:* Membership dues
Membership: 9; *Member Profile:* Marine professionals in the shipping industry

British Columbia Trucking Association (BCTA)
#100, 20111 - 93A Ave., Langley BC V1M 4A9
Tel: 604-888-5319; *Fax:* 604-888-2941
bcta@bctrucking.com
www.bctrucking.com
Social Media: www.facebook.com/TruckingBC
twitter.com/BCTruckingAssoc
Previous Name: BC Motor Transport Association
Overview: A large provincial organization founded in 1913
Description: To act as the recognised voice of the commercial road transportation industry in British Columbia, by consulting & communicating with the industry, government, & the public; To promote a prosperous, safe, efficient & responsible road transportation industry; To provide programs & services to members
Chief Officer(s): Louise Yako, President & Chief Executive Officer
Finances: *Funding Sources:* Membership dues

Membership: 1,000 corporate; *Fees:* Schedule available; *Member Profile:* Trucking company operating in BC; Supplier to trucking industry; *Committees:* Convention; Insurance; International; Labour; Freight Claims & Hazardous Goods; Safety; Truxpo; Vehicle Standards
Activities: *Speaker Service:* Yes; *Rents Mailing List:* Yes; *Library:* Yes by appointment

Bytown Railway Society (BRS)
PO Box 47076, Ottawa ON K1B 5P9
Tel: 613-745-1201; *Fax:* 613-745-1201
info@bytownrailwaysociety.ca
www.bytownrailwaysociety.ca
Overview: A medium-sized national charitable organization founded in 1969
Description: To promote an interest in railways & railway history, with particular emphasis on Canadian railways.
Finances: *Funding Sources:* Publications sale; memberships
Activities: Restoration/preservation of owned railway equipment; *Library:* Yes (Open to Public) by appointment

Canadian Aeronautics & Space Institute (CASI) / Institut aéronautique et spatial du Canada
#104, 350 Terry Fox Dr., Ottawa ON K2K 2W5
Tel: 613-591-8787; *Fax:* 613-591-7291
casi@casi.ca
www.casi.ca
Previous Name: Canadian Aeronautical Institute (CAI)
Merged from: Institute of Aircraft Technicians; Ottawa Aeronautical Society; US Institute of Aeronautical Science
Overview: A medium-sized national licensing organization founded in 1954
Description: To advance the art, science, engineering, & applications of aeronautics & associated technologies in Canada; To promote Canadian competence & international competitiveness
Affiliation(s): Canadian Air Cushion Technology Society; Canadian Navigation Society; Canadian Remote Sensing Society
Chief Officer(s): Geoff Languedoc, Executive Director
April Duffy, Coordinator, Publications, Information & Membership Services
Membership: 1,600; *Fees:* $36.75 juniors; $63 seniors; $94.50 associates & individuals
Activities: Facilitating communications among the Canadian aeronautics & space community; Developing members' skills;

Canadian Airports Council (CAC) / Conseil des aéroports du Canada
#600, 116 Lisgar St., Ottawa ON K2P 0C2
Tel: 613-560-9302; *Fax:* 613-560-6599
www.cacairports.ca
Overview: A medium-sized national organization founded in 1991
Description: To act as the voice for Canadian airports on a great range of important issues; *Member of:* Airports Council International - North America (ACI-NA)
Affiliation(s): Air Transport Association of Canada (ATAC); Canadian International Freight Forwarders Association (CIFFA); Canadian Chamber of Commerce; Canadian Tourism Commission; Tourism Industry Association of Canada (TIAC)
Chief Officer(s): Daniel-Robert Gooch, President, 613-560-9302 16
daniel.gooch@cacairports.ca
Nicole Larocque, Administrative Assistant, 613-560-9302 14
nicole.larocque@cacairports.ca
Finances: *Funding Sources:* Sponsorships
Membership: 48; *Member Profile:* Canadian airports (CAC members are also members of Airports Council International - North America)
Activities: Preparing submissions to governmental bodies & agencies

Canadian Association of Movers (CAM) / Association canadienne des déménageurs (ACD)
PO Box 30039, Stn. New Westminster, Thornhill ON L4J 0C6
Tel: 905-848-6579; *Fax:* 905-756-1115
Toll-Free: 866-860-0065
admin@mover.net
www.mover.net
Overview: A small national organization
Description: To further the interests of the owner-managed moving & storage companies by providing for its members leadership, motivation, research, education, programs of mutual benefit, consultation & technical advice
Affiliation(s): American Moving & Storage Association; British Association of Removers; International Association of Movers
Chief Officer(s): Ted LeLacheur, Chair
ted@westernmoving.com
John Levi, President
jlevi@mover.net
Membership: 400
Activities: Government & political affairs; membership development; volunteer participation & recognition; van lines; public affairs & publications; research & development; education & training; professional ethics & standards; organizational competency

Canadian Association of Railway Suppliers / Association canadienne des fournisseurs de chemins de fer
#901, 99 Bank St., Ottawa ON K1P 6B9
Tel: 613-237-3888; *Fax:* 613-237-4888
info@railwaysuppliers.ca
www.railwaysuppliers.ca
Previous Name: Canadian Railway & Transit Manufacturers Association
Overview: A medium-sized national organization
Description: To provide their members with more opportunities allowing their businesses to prosper
Chief Officer(s): Sylvia Newell, Executive Director
sylvie_newell@railwaysuppliers.ca
Membership: 400+ companies; *Fees:* Schedule available; *Member Profile:* Companies that supply products & services to Canadian railways

Canadian Automobile Association (CAA) / Association canadienne des automobilistes
National Office, #500, 1545 Carling Ave., Ottawa ON K1Z 8P9
Tel: 613-247-0117; *Fax:* 613-247-0118
www.caa.ca
Social Media:
www.youtube.com/TheCAAChannel
twitter.com/CAA
Overview: A large national organization founded in 1913
Description: To promote, develop & implement programs & information related to the rights, responsibilities, & needs of the motorist as a consumer
Affiliation(s): Alliance internationale de tourisme; Fédération internationale de l'automobile; Federacion interamericana de touring y automovil-clubes; Commonwealth Motoring Conference; American Automobile Association
Finances: *Funding Sources:* Membership dues
Membership: 9 clubs serving 6,000,000
Activities: Roadside assistance; driver training; insurance; travel packages; Savings & Rewards program; *Speaker Service:* Yes; *Library:* Yes

Canadian Aviation Historical Society (CAHS)
PO Box 2700, Stn. D, Ottawa ON K1P 5W7
www.cahs.ca
Overview: A small national charitable organization founded in 1962
Description: To collect & disseminate information about Canada's aviation heritage; to foster public interest in the field.
Chief Officer(s): Gary Williams, National President, 306-543-8123
Rachel Heide, Treasurer, 613-443-9975
Jim Bell, Secretary, 204-293-5402
Finances: *Funding Sources:* Donations
Membership: *Fees:* $50 Canadian members; $60 USA; $70 overseas; *Member Profile:* Individuals with an interest in the history of aviation
Activities: Supporting research in Canadian aeronautical history

Canadian Business Aviation Association (CBAA) / Association canadienne de l'aviation d'affaires (ACAA)
#155, 955 Green Valley Cres., Ottawa ON K2C 3V4
Tel: 613-236-5611; *Fax:* 613-236-2361
www.cbaa-acaa.ca
Previous Name: Canadian Business Aircraft Association Inc.
Overview: A medium-sized national organization founded in 1962
Description: To act as a collective voice for the business aviation community in Canada, assisting its members in all aviation related matters, & promoting the Canadian business community globally.
Affiliation(s): National Business Aviation Association; International Business Aviation Council; European Business Aircraft Association
Chief Officer(s): Frank Burke, Chair
Rudy Toering, President & CEO
rtoering@cbaa.ca
Finances: *Funding Sources:* Membership dues; convention/tradeshow
Staff: 7 staff member(s)
Membership: 600; *Fees:* Schedule available; *Member Profile:* Business: owns or operates a Canadian privately or state registered aircraft as an aid to conduct its business; Commercial: owns or operates Canadian commercially registered aircraft; Associate: businesses primarily concerned with aviation activities, including the manufacture of aircraft; Affiliate: owns or operates aircraft exclusively registered in a nation other than Canada
Activities: Leadership; excellence; collaboration; ethics

Canadian Council for Aviation & Aerospace (CCAA) / Conseil canadien de l'aviation et de l'aérospatiale
#155, 955 Green Valley Cres., Ottawa ON K2C 3V4
Tel: 613-727-8272; *Fax:* 613-727-7018
Toll-Free: 800-448-9715
secretariat@camc.ca
www.camc.ca
Previous Name: Canadian Aviation Maintenance Council
Overview: A medium-sized national licensing organization founded in 1992
Description: To develop occupational training standards & facilitate the implementation of a human resources strategy for the Canadian Aviation Maintenance Industry.
Chief Officer(s): Robert Donald, Executive Director
Finances: *Annual Operating Budget:* $250,000-$500,000; *Funding Sources:* Aviation maintenance industry; Human Resources Development Canada; federal government
Membership: 1,000-4,999; *Committees:* CCAA Accreditation Board; CCAA Certification Board; CCAA National Standing Trade Advisory; Youth Internship Advisory
Activities: Certification; accreditation; training; youth programs; *Internships:* Yes

Canadian Council of Motor Transport Administrators (CCMTA) / Conseil canadien des administrateurs en transport motorisé (CCATM)
2323 St. Laurent Blvd., Ottawa ON K1G 4J8
Tel: 613-736-1003; *Fax:* 613-736-1395
ccmta-secretariat@ccmta.ca
www.ccmta.ca
Overview: A medium-sized national charitable organization founded in 1940
Description: To coordinate operational matters dealing with the administration, regulation, & control of motor vehicle transportation & highway safety
Chief Officer(s): Ward Keith, President
Methusalah Kunuk, Vice-President
Finances: *Funding Sources:* Member assessments; Special projects; Membership fees
Membership: 100-499; *Fees:* $433.50 associate; *Member Profile:* Members include representatives of provincial, territorial, & federal governments, & associate members from transportation related organizations.; *Committees:* Drivers & Vehicles; Compliance & Regulatory Affairs; Road Safety Research & Policies
Activities: Developing strategies & programs; Managing a communications network, called the Interprovincial Record Exchange system; *Rents Mailing List:* Yes

Canadian Federation of AME Associations (CFAMEA)
c/o AME Association of Ontario, PO Box 160, Stn. Toronto AMF, Mississauga ON L5P 1B1
Tel: 905-673-5681; *Fax:* 905-673-6328
www.cfamea.com
Also Known As: Aircraft Maintenance Engineers Association
Overview: A medium-sized national organization
Description: To represent regional AME associations & to prmote the aircraft maintenance profession
Chief Officer(s): Ole Nielsen, President, 519-870-5786
onielsen@rogers.com
Finances: *Funding Sources:* Membership dues
Membership: 5 regional associations; *Member Profile:* Canadian AME Associations
Activities: Liaison with government concerning aircraft maintenance & AME licensing

Canadian Ferry Operators Association (CFOA) / Association canadienne des opérateurs de traversiers
c/o Mr. Serge Buy, 70 George St., 3rd Fl., Ottawa ON K1N 5V9
Tel: 613-686-3838; *Fax:* 613-482-3604
www.cfoa.ca
Overview: A small national organization founded in 1987
Description: To establish & maintain a standard of professional & technical excellence in the operation of Canadian ferries; To promote & protect the interests of members of the association
Chief Officer(s): Serge Buy, Executive Director
sbuy@cfoa.ca
David Miller, President, 604-467-7298, Fax: 604-463-5693
dave_miller@translink.bc.ca
Finances: *Funding Sources:* Sponsorships
Membership: 37; *Member Profile:* Major ferry owners & operators in Canada
Activities: Providing opportunities for discussion of matters of interest to members; Promoting the safety, reliability, & efficiency

of Canadian ferry operators; Providing representation at regulatory forums such as CMAC

Canadian Heartland Training Railway

226 Christie Park View SW, Calgary AB T3H 2Z4
Tel: 403-601-8731; *Fax:* 403-601-8704
www.chtr.ca

Overview: A small national organization
Description: To support the practical training needs of the railway industry in Canada & around the world; *Member of:* Railway Association of Canada; Railway Suppliers Association of Canada
Chief Officer(s): Joe Bracken, President
joebracken@chtr.ca

Canadian Institute of Traffic & Transportation (CITT) / Institut canadien du trafic et du transport

#400, 10 King St. East, Toronto ON M5C 1C3
Tel: 416-363-5696; *Fax:* 416-363-5698
info@citt.ca
www.citt.ca
Social Media:
https://linkedin.com/company/citt
twitter.com/CITTLogistics

Overview: A medium-sized national organization founded in 1958
Description: To promote high standards of professionalism among transportation logisticians
Chief Officer(s): Catherine Viglas, President, 416-363-5696 27
cviglas@citt.ca
Chrissy Aitchison, Senior Manager, Marketing & Strategic Initiatives, 416-363-5696 28
caitchison@citt.ca
Jennifer Traer, Senior Manager, Member Support & Events, 416-363-5695 32
jtraer@citt.ca
Maria Murjani, Manager, Programs, 416-363-5696 24
mmurjani@citt.ca
Membership: 2,000+
Activities: Offering CLLP certification program

Canadian Institute of Transportation Engineers (CITE)

PO Box 81009, Harbour Square PO, 89 Queens Quay West, Toronto ON M5J 2V3
Tel: 202-785-0060; *Fax:* 202-785-0609
www.cite7.org

Overview: A large international organization
Description: To facilitate the application of technology & scientific principles for modes of ground transportation
Chief Officer(s): Peter Truch, President
president@cite7.org
Membership: 2,000+; *Member Profile:* Transportation engineers, planners, technologists and students across Canada.
Activities: Promoting professional development; Supporting education; Encouraging research; Increasing public awareness; Exchanging professional information

Canadian International Freight Forwarders Association, Inc. (CIFFA) / Association des transitaires internationaux canadiens, inc. (ATIC)

#480, 170 Attwell Dr., Toronto ON M9W 5Z5
Tel: 416-234-5100; *Fax:* 416-234-5152
Toll-Free: 866-282-4332
secretariat@ciffa.com
www.ciffa.com

Overview: A large international organization founded in 1948
Description: To represent & support members of the Canadian international freight forwarding industry in providing the highest level of quality & professional services to their clients; *Member of:* Federation internationale des associations de transitaires et assimiles
Affiliation(s): International Federation of Freight Forwarders Associations
Chief Officer(s): Jeff Cullen, President
jeff.cullen@dhl.com
Ruth Snowden, Executive Director, 416-234-5100 226
Finances: *Annual Operating Budget:* $500,000-$1.5 Million; *Funding Sources:* Membership dues; education fees
Staff: 5 staff member(s); 20 volunteer(s)
Membership: 188 regular + 94 associate; *Fees:* Schedule available; *Committees:* Airfreight; By Laws; Customs; Education; Ethics & Standards; FIATA; Finance; Judicial; Membership; Seafreight; Security
Activities: CIFFA Professional Training Program; education courses; dangerous goods courses, topical workshops

Canadian Marine Pilots' Association (CMPA) / Association des pilotes maritimes du Canada (APMC)

#1302, 155 Queen St., Ottawa ON K1P 6L1
Tel: 613-232-7777; *Fax:* 613-232-7667
cmpa@tnpa.ca
www.marinepilots.ca

Overview: A small national organization founded in 1966
Description: To represent Canadian marine pilots; To raise awareness of marine pilots' role to protect public safety; To ensure a healthy Canadian marine sector; *Member of:* International Maritime Pilots' Association; Canadian Merchant Service Guild
Chief Officer(s): Simon Pelletier, President
Bernard Boissonneault, Vice-President
Laurentian Region
Mike Burgess, Vice-President
Great Lakes Region
Fred Denning, Vice-President
Pacific Region
Andrew Rae, Vice-President
Atlantic Region
Membership: 400; *Member Profile:* Marine pilots in Canada
Activities: Upholding a Code of Conduct for Canadian pilots; Contributing to matters of safety & regulatory issues; Collaborating with marine stakeholders to maintain a vibrant marine sector

Canadian National Railways Police Association (Ind.) (CNRPA) / Association des policiers des chemins de fer nationaux du Canada (ind.)

c/o CN Headquarters, 935 de La Gauchetière St. West, Montréal QC H3B 2M9
Toll-Free: 800-465-9239

Also Known As: CNR Police Association
Overview: A small national organization founded in 1923
Chief Officer(s): Gerry St. George, National President

Canadian Northern Society (CNS)

PO Box 1174, Camrose AB T4V 1X2
Tel: 780-672-3099
canadiannorthern@telus.net
www.canadiannorthern.ca
Social Media:
www.facebook.com/pages/Canadian-Northern-Society/211046248914713

Overview: A small local charitable organization founded in 1987
Description: To preserve prairie heritage
Chief Officer(s): Lorrie Tiegs, President
Norm Prestage, Vice-President
Shawn I. Smith, Treasurer
Dean Tiegs, Secretary
secretary@canadiannorthern.ca
Finances: *Funding Sources:* Donations; Fundraising; Grants
Membership: *Fees:* $20 full members; $10 associate; *Committees:* Camrose Railway Station Park & Morgan Railway Garden; Meeting Creek Grain Elevator & Railway Station Heritage Site; Big Valley Railway Station & Roundhouse Interpretive Park; Canora Chronicle; Audit
Activities: Preserving railway station sites at Camrose, Big Valley & Meeting Creek, Alberta, as well as the grain elevator at Meeting Creek;

Canadian Owners & Pilots Association (COPA)

71 Bank St., 7th Fl., Ottawa ON K1P 5N2
Tel: 613-236-4901; *Fax:* 613-236-8646
copa@copanational.org
www.copanational.org

Overview: A medium-sized national charitable organization founded in 1954
Description: The recognized voice of general aviation in Canada
Chief Officer(s): Kevin Psutka, President
kpsutka@copanational.org
Finances: *Annual Operating Budget:* $500,000-$1.5 Million; *Funding Sources:* Membership dues; advertising
Staff: 9 staff member(s); 20 volunteer(s)
Membership: 17,000; *Fees:* $50 individual; $250 corporate; *Member Profile:* Pilots & aircraft owners; corporate members; *Committees:* Air Navigation Services National Advisory Group; Canadian Aviation Regulation Advisory Committee
Activities: COPA Flight Chapters located across Canada; *Library:* Yes (Open to Public)

Canadian Parking Association (CPA)

#350, 2255 St. Laurent Blvd., Ottawa ON K1G 4K3
Tel: 613-727-0700; *Fax:* 613-727-3183
info@canadianparking.ca
www.canadianparking.ca
Social Media:
linkedin.com/company/2241893?trk=tyah
www.facebook.com/173429676044219?sk=wall
twitter.com/canadianparking

Also Known As: Association canadienne du stationnement
Overview: A medium-sized national organization founded in 1983
Description: The Association is the national organization that represents the parking industry & provides a dynamic forum for learning & sharing to enhance member's ability to serve the public & improve the economic vitality of communities.
Chief Officer(s): Carole Whitehorne, Executive Director, 613-727-0700 10
carole@canadianparking.ca
Membership: 320; *Fees:* $475 full

Canadian Railroad Historical Association (CRHA) / Association canadienne d'histoire ferroviaire

110 St-Pierre St., Saint-Constant QC J5A 1G7
Tel: 450-632-2410; *Fax:* 450-638-1563
info@exporail.org
www.exporail.org
Social Media:
www.facebook.com/Exporail
twitter.com/Exporail

Overview: A medium-sized national charitable organization founded in 1932
Description: To collect, preserve & disseminate information/items relating to the history of railways in Canada
Chief Officer(s): C. Stephen Cheasley, President
Finances: *Annual Operating Budget:* $1.5 Million-$3 Million
Membership: *Fees:* $50 regular; $110 friend of the museum; *Committees:* Executive; Collection; Membership; Audit
Activities: *Library:* Yes (Open to Public) by appointment

Canadian Seaplane Pilots Association (CSPA)

#1001, 75 Albert St., Ottawa ON K1P 5E7
Tel: 613-236-4901; *Fax:* 613-236-8646

Overview: A medium-sized national organization
Description: To maintain communications among seaplane pilots; to represent them at all levels of government; to help develop regulations conducive to safe & pleasurable flying; to prepare & disseminate educational material; to advance among its members information & knowledge of seaplane flying.
Affiliation(s): Seaplane Pilots Association International
Chief Officer(s): Chris Bullerdick, Director
Finances: *Annual Operating Budget:* $50,000-$100,000
Staff: 2 staff member(s); 10 volunteer(s)
Membership: 400; *Fees:* US$28
Activities: Fly-ins; safety seminars

Canadian Shipowners Association (CSA) / Association des armateurs canadiens (AAC)

#705, 350 Sparks St., Ottawa ON K1R 7S8
Tel: 613-232-3539; *Fax:* 613-232-6211
shipowners.ca
Social Media:
twitter.com/canshipowners

Previous Name: Dominion Marine Association
Overview: A medium-sized national organization founded in 1903
Description: To promote an economic & competitive Canadian marine transportation industry; to support a national policy conducive to the development & maintenance of the Canadian flag merchant fleet in the inland, coastal & Arctic waters of Canada & foster the growth of a Canadian flag deep sea merchant fleet.; *Member of:* International Chamber of Shipping; International Shipping Federation; Chamber of Maritime Commerce; Canada Maritime Law Association
Chief Officer(s): Robert Lewis-Manning, President
Silvie Dagenais, Secretary-Treasurer
dagenais@shipowners.ca
Membership: 6 corporate; *Committees:* Marine Environment; Marine Operations
Activities: Monitors Canadian & US government legislative/regulatory actions, initiatives by various international marine organizations, political trends, public policy relating to navigation, safety & the Canadian shipping environment; executes strategic communications & public relations campaigns to effectively represent the interests of member companies

Canadian Transport Lawyers Association (CTLA)

24 Duncan St., 3rd Fl., Toronto ON M5V 2B8
Tel: 416-601-1340; *Fax:* 416-601-1190
marc@isaacsco.ca
www.ctla.ca

Overview: A small national organization

Description: To provide a professional and social forum for lawyers engaged or otherwise interested in transportation law, regulatory policy, procedure and related legal interests.
Chief Officer(s): Kim E. Stoll, President
Louis A. Amato-Gauci, Vice-President & Secretary
lamato-gauci@airdberlis.com
Douglas I. Evanchuk, Treasurer
devanchuk@mross.com
Roger Watts, Director, Communications
Membership: *Fees:* $100 - $195; *Member Profile:* Lawyers engaged in transportation law, regulatory policy, procedure, & related legal interests

Canadian Transportation Equipment Association (CTEA) / Association d'équipement de transport du canada (AETC)
#3B, 16 Barrie Blvd., St Thomas ON N5P 4B9
Tel: 519-631-0414; *Fax:* 519-631-1333
transportation@ctea.ca
www.ctea.ca
Social Media:
ca.linkedin.com/groups?gid=6508608
Overview: A medium-sized national organization founded in 1963
Description: To promote excellence in commercial vehicle manufacturing; to develop standard practices
Chief Officer(s): Don Moore, Executive Director
don.moore@atminc.on.ca
Kevin Last, President
Membership: 544; *Fees:* $825; *Member Profile:* Commercial vehicle & component manufacturers; Dealers & distributors; Service providers
Activities: Lobbying; Providing access to technical & regulatory information; Offering networking opportunities; Encouraging research; *Speaker Service:* Yes

Canadian Transportation Research Forum (CTRF) / Groupe de recherches sur les transports au Canada
PO Box 23033, Woodstock ON N4T 1R9
Tel: 519-421-9701; *Fax:* 519-421-9319
www.ctrf.ca
Social Media:
twitter.com/ForCtrf
Overview: A medium-sized national charitable organization founded in 1967
Description: To promote the development of research in transportation & related fields; to publish research papers through media & through national & regional forum meetings.
Chief Officer(s): Marc-André Roy, President
mroy@cpcstrans.com
Carole Ann Woudsma, Secretary
cawoudsma@ctrf.ca
Jean Patenaude, Executive Vice-President
jean.patenaude@cn.ca
Mark Hemmes, Vice-President External
mhemmes@quorumcorp.net
Gerry Kolaitis, VP Finance/Treasurer
Gerry_Kolaitis@viarail.ca
Hanna Maoh, Vice-President Program/Publications
maohhf@uwindsor.ca
William Anderson, Vice-President Meetings
bander@uwindsor.ca
Garland Chow, VP Organization/Development
garland.chow@sauder.ubc.ca
Membership: *Fees:* $135 individual; $79 senior; $32 student; *Member Profile:* Open to anyone interested in any aspect of transportation; membership is individual rather than corporate; present membership is drawn from carriers, shippers, consultants & suppliers in the commercial sector, the policy, regulatory, planning & research environments at all levels of government, students & professors at universitites & community colleges

Canadian Trucking Alliance (CTA) / L'Alliance canadienne du camionnage (ACC)
555 Dixon Rd., Toronto ON M9W 1H8
Tel: 613-236-9426; *Fax:* 866-823-4076
publicaffairs@cantruck.ca
www.cantruck.ca
Social Media:
twitter.com/OnTruck
Overview: A medium-sized national organization founded in 1937
Description: To promote business excellence in trucking; to participate in the development of public policy which supports the economic growth, safety & prosperity of the industry; to provide services, including research, development, products & information to meet the needs of the industry
Membership: *Member Profile:* Motor carriers & associated trades
Activities: *Speaker Service:* Yes

Canadian Trucking Human Resources Council (CTHRC) / Conseil canadien des ressources humaines en camionnage
#203, 720 Belfast Rd., Ottawa ON K1G 0Z5
Tel: 613-244-4800; *Fax:* 613-244-4535
info@cthrc.com
www.cthrc.com
Overview: A medium-sized national organization
Description: To respond to the human resource needs of the trucking industry
Affiliation(s): CCA Truck Driver Training Ltd.; Capilano Truck Driver Training Institute; JVI Provincial Transportation & Safety Academy; Mountain Transport Institute Ltd.; Red Deer College; SK Driver Training Ltd.; Wheels On Ltd. / Training & Driver Training
Activities: Conducting research; Training; Offering advice; Liaising with industry members

Canadian Urban Transit Association (CUTA) / Association canadienne du transport urbain (ACTU)
#1401, 55 York St., Toronto ON M5J 1R7
Tel: 416-365-9800; *Fax:* 416-365-1295
www.cutaactu.ca
Social Media:
linkedin.com/company/canadian-urban-transit-association
www.facebook.com/CanadianTransit/?ref=hl
twitter.com/canadiantransit?lang=en
Overview: A large national organization founded in 1904
Description: To represent the public transit community throughout Canada; To strengthen the industry
Chief Officer(s): Patrick Leclerc, President & Chief Executive Officer, 613-788-7982
leclerc@cutaactu.ca
Becky Benaissa, Director, Finance & Administration, 416-365-9800 108
benaissa@cutaactu.ca
Alex Maheu, Director, Public Affairs, 613-788-7985
maheu@cutaactu.ca
Lauren Rudko, Team Lead, Statistics & Research, 416-365-9800 113
rudko@cutaactu.ca
Kevin Brown, Acting Manager, Training & Professional, 416-365-9800 121
brown@cutaactu.ca
Johanne Palermo, Content Strategist, Publications, 416-365-9800 120
palermo@cutaactu.ca
Membership: 488; *Member Profile:* Transit systems; Manufacturers & suppliers of transit equipment; Federal, provincial, & municipal government agencies; Consultants; Affiliated individuals & companies; *Committees:* Business Members; Communications & Public Affairs; Human Resources; Technical Services; Transit Board Members
Activities: Conducting research & preparing statistics; Providing technical & operational information; Liaising with government; Partnering with other transportation associations & community development stakeholders; Engaging in advocacy activities; Raising public awareness of transit's contributions to communities; *Library:* Canadian Urban Transit Association Library (Open to Public)

Carefree Society
2832 Queensway St., Prince George BC V2L 4M5
Tel: 250-562-1394; *Fax:* 250-562-1393
carefree_society@telus.net
www.transitbc.com/regions/prg/accessible/handydart.cfm
Also Known As: handyDART
Overview: A small local charitable organization founded in 1971
Description: To provide transportation services for the disabled
Affiliation(s): BC Transit
Finances: *Annual Operating Budget:* $250,000-$500,000; *Funding Sources:* Provincial government; regional government
Staff: 12 staff member(s); 10 volunteer(s)
Membership: 15; *Fees:* $6; *Committees:* Accessible Transportation Awareness

Central British Columbia Railway & Forest Industry Museum Society
850 River Rd., Prince George BC V2L 5S8
Tel: 250-563-7351; *Fax:* 250-563-3697
trains@pgrfm.bc.ca
www.pgrfm.bc.ca
Social Media:
www.facebook.com/railwayandforestrymuseum
twitter.com/pgrailmuseum
Also Known As: Railway & Forestry Museum
Overview: A small local charitable organization founded in 1983
Description: Administers Prince George Railway & Forest Industry Museum; *Member of:* Canadian Railway Historical Association; Canadian Museum Association; British Columbia Museum Association; American Railway Museum Association

Chief Officer(s): Laura Williams, General Manager
Finances: *Annual Operating Budget:* $50,000-$100,000
Staff: 6 staff member(s); 15 volunteer(s)
Membership: 75; *Fees:* $15-$40
Activities: *Awareness Events:* Steam Day; Forester Day; Family Carnival; *Library:* Canfor Library by appointment

Centre for Transportation Engineering & Planning (C-TEP)
c/o Stantec, Transportation, #200, 325 - 25 St. SE, Calgary AB T2A 7H8
Tel: 403-607-4482; *Fax:* 403-716-8129
www.c-tep.com
Overview: A medium-sized national organization
Description: To provide professional development & research related to Canadian transportation engineering & planning; to provide a forum for collaboration between institutions & various levels of government; to act as a resource centre for the transportation engineers & planners
Chief Officer(s): Gerard Kennedy, President
Neil Little, Executive Director
nlittle@c-tep.com
Membership: 42 organizations; *Fees:* Schedule available

Chamber of Marine Commerce (CMC) / Chambre du commerce maritime (CCM)
#700, 350 Sparks St., Ottawa ON K1R 7S8
Tel: 613-233-8779; *Fax:* 613-233-3743
email@cmc-ccm.com
www.marinedelivers.com
Social Media:
www.flickr.com/photos/marinecommerce/sets/
twitter.com/MarineDelivers
Previous Name: Great Lakes Waterways Development Association
Overview: A large national organization founded in 1959
Description: To bring together all sectors of the economy that rely on a cost efficient & safe marine transportation system
Chief Officer(s): Stephen Brooks, President
sbrooks@cmc-ccm.com
Raymond W. Johnston, Special Advisor
rjohnston@cmc-ccm.com
Julia Fields, Manager, Communications
jfields@cmc-ccm.com
Finances: *Funding Sources:* Membership dues
Membership: 150+ institutional; *Member Profile:* Major Canadian & American shippers, ports & marine service providers, domestic & international shipowners

Chartered Institute of Logistics & Transport (CILT)
Earlstrees Court, Earlstrees Rd., Corbyn NN17 4AX UK
www.ciltinternational.org
Social Media:
linkedin.com/groups?about=&gid=780717
Previous Name: Chartered Institute of Transport
Overview: A medium-sized international charitable organization founded in 1919
Description: To promote, encourage & coordinate the study & advancement of the science & art of transportation in all its branches
Affiliation(s): Integrated in UK with Institute of Logistics UK section now titled Institute of Logistics & Transport
Chief Officer(s): Dorothy Chan, President
Finances: *Annual Operating Budget:* Greater than $5 Million; *Funding Sources:* Membership dues
Staff: 21 staff member(s)
Membership: 33,000 worldwide; *Fees:* Schedule available; *Member Profile:* Professionals in transport & logistics; *Committees:* Membership; Education
Activities: Providing education programs, lecture meetings, & training; Presenting transport reports; *Speaker Service:* Yes; *Library:* Chartered Institute of Logistics & Transport Library (Open to Public)

The Chartered Institute of Logistics & Transport in North America (CILT) / Institut agréé de la logistique et des transports Amérique du Nord
#205, 1435 Sandford Fleming Ave., Ottawa ON K1G 3H3
Tel: 613-738-3003; *Fax:* 613-738-3033
requestinfo@ciltna.com
www.ciltna.com
Also Known As: CILT in North America
Previous Name: Chartered Institute of Transport Canadian Division
Overview: A medium-sized international organization founded in 1919
Description: To promote, encourage, coordinate study & advancement of science & art of transportation.; *Member of:* Chartered Institute of Transport
Chief Officer(s): Bob Armstrong, President, 416-418-3990
armstrong@ciltna.com

David Collenette, Chair
david.collenette@hillandknowlton.ca
Finances: *Funding Sources:* Membership fees, conferences, workshop revenue
Staff: 1 staff member(s); 15 volunteer(s)
Membership: 250; *Fees:* Schedule available; *Member Profile:* Individuals with experience, interest & education in the transportation field.; *Committees:* Regional

Chatham Railroad Museum Society
PO Box 434, 2 McLean St., Chatham ON N7M 5K5
Tel: 519-352-3097
crms@mnsi.net
www.chathamrailroadmuseum.ca
Social Media:
www.facebook.com/pages/Chatham-Railroad-Museum-CRMS/195849387130379
Overview: A small local charitable organization founded in 1989
Description: To present history from a retired CN baggage car
Membership: 1-99

Club de trafic de Québec
CP 2501, Succ. Normandie, Saint-Nicolas QC G7A 4X5
info@clubtraficqc.com
www.clubtraficqc.org
Aperçu: *Dimension:* moyenne; *Envergure:* provinciale; Organisme sans but lucratif; fondée en 1960
Description: Regrouper les représentants oeuvrant dans le domaine du transport de la grande région de Québec
Membre(s) du bureau directeur: Benoit Latour, Président
b.latour@pmtroy.com
Finances: *Budget de fonctionnement annuel:* $100,000-$250,000
Membre: 137; *Montant de la cotisation:* 85$

Company of Master Mariners of Canada
c/o Captain G.O. Baugh Memorial Fund, 13375 - 14A Ave., Surrey BC V4A 7P9
www.mastermariners.ca
Overview: A medium-sized national organization founded in 1967
Description: To maintain the standard of ability & professional conduct of the officers, & also develop education, training & qualifications for young cadets
Affiliation(s): Master Mariner organizations in the UK, USA, South Africa, Australia & NZ
Chief Officer(s): John McCann, National Master
jmccann@sjport.com
Ivan Lantz, Secretary
lantzivan@gmail.com
Yezdee Kooka, Membership Chair
ykooka@sympatico.ca
Finances: *Funding Sources:* Membership dues
Membership: *Fees:* $80 senior/associate/companion; $50 full; *Member Profile:* Master Mariners
Activities: *Speaker Service:* Yes

Construction Owners Association of Alberta (COAA)
Sun Life Place, #800, 10123 - 99 St. NW, Edmonton AB T5J 3H1
Tel: 780-420-1145; *Fax:* 780-425-4623
coaa-mail@coaa.ab.ca
www.coaa.ab.ca
Overview: A medium-sized provincial organization
Description: COAA provides leadership to enable the Alberta heavy industrial construction and industrial maintenance industries to be successful in a drive for safe, effective, timely and productive project execution.
Chief Officer(s): Ernie Tromposch, President
Membership: *Member Profile:* Principal Members who are users of construction services in their day-to-day operations.; *Committees:* Safety; Productivity; Workforce Development; Contracts

Dewdney-Alouette Railway Society (DARS)
22520 - 116 Ave., Maple Ridge BC V2X 0S4
Tel: 604-463-5311; *Fax:* 604-463-5317
mrmuseum@telus.net
www.mapleridgemuseum.org
Overview: A small local organization
Description: The Society preserves the railway history of Maple Ridge, promotes the craft of model railroading, & offers advice to the public who are engaged in the building & operating of model railroads.
Affiliation(s): National Model Railway Association; Pacific Northwest Region 7th Division Society; BC Heritage Society; Maple Ridge Historical Society; Maple Ridge Museum
Chief Officer(s): Dick Sutcliff, Contact
ras1@uniserve.com
Activities: Port Haney diorama;

Edmonton Radial Railway Society (ERRS)
PO Box 76057, Stn. Southgate, Edmonton AB T6H 5Y7
Tel: 780-437-7721; *Fax:* 780-437-3095
info@edmonton-radial-railway.ab.ca
www.edmonton-radial-railway.ab.ca
Social Media:
www.facebook.com/edmontonstreetcar
twitter.com/yegstreetcar
Overview: A small national charitable organization founded in 1980
Description: The Society collects, preserves & restores vintage streetcars, primarily those from 1908-1951.; *Member of:* Canadian Museum Association
Affiliation(s): Association of Tourist Railroads and Railway Museums; Alberta Museums Association; Virtual Museum of Canada
Chief Officer(s): Hans Ryffel, President
Finances: *Annual Operating Budget:* $100,000-$250,000; *Funding Sources:* Municipal, provincial & federal governments; donations
Staff: 60 volunteer(s)
Membership: 130; *Fees:* $20
Activities: Operating 2 historic street railway lines within Edmonton from May to Oct.; streetcar museum; streetcar chartering service; restoration, maintenance and operation of historic streetcars; *Library:* Yes

Electric Mobility Canada (EMC) / Mobilité Électrique Canada
#309, 9-6975 Meadowvale Town Centre Circle, Mississauga ON L5N 2V7
Tel: 905-301-5950; *Fax:* 905-826-0157
www.emc-mec.ca
Social Media:
www.youtube.com/user/ElectricMobilityCA
linkedin.com/pub/al-cormier/15/985/559
www.facebook.com/240477292643669?ref=ts
twitter.com/EMC_MEC
Overview: A small national organization
Description: Electric Mobility Canada is a national membership-based not-for-profit organization dedicated exclusively to the promotion of electric mobility as a readily available and important solution to Canada's emerging energy and environmental issues.
Chief Officer(s): Chris Hill, President & CEO
chris.hill@emc-mec.ca
Membership: 125; *Committees:* Government Relations; Working Group on PEV Readiness; Electric Bus

Electric Vehicle Council of Ottawa (EVCO)
PO Box 4044, Stn. E, Ottawa ON K1S 5B1
info@evco.ca
www.evco.ca
Social Media:
www.youtube.com/EVCOdotCA
Overview: A small local organization founded in 1980
Description: To promote the use of electric vehicles as a viable transportation alternative
Chief Officer(s): Darryl McMahon, President
president@evco.ca
Barry Hoover, Vice-President
bhoover@evco.ca
David French, Treasurer
dfrench@evco.ca
Activities: Offering technical literature; Organizing displays, demonstrations, talks, & competitions; Hosting monthly meetings; Participating in advocacy projects; *Library:* Electric Vehicle Council of Ottawa Print & Video Library

Electric Vehicle Society of Canada (EVS)
c/o #40, 55 Kelfield St., Toronto ON M9W 5A3
Tel: 416-788-7438
info@evsociety.ca
www.evsociety.ca
Social Media:
linkedin.com/company/electric-vehicle-society-of-canada
www.facebook.com/EVSociety
Overview: A medium-sized national organization founded in 1991
Description: To investigate & promote clean transportation technologies
Chief Officer(s): Emile Stevens, President
president@evsociety.ca
Membership: *Fees:* $20 students, spouses, & seniors; $30 adults; $50 families; $100 corporations; *Member Profile:* Engineers; Environmentalists; Enthusiasts for electric energy for propulsion
Activities: Providing a forum for member discussions; Examining modes of electric transportation

Fédération des transporteurs par autobus
#250, 5700, boul des Galeries, Québec QC G2K 0H5
Tél: 418-476-8181; *Téléc:* 418-476-8177
Ligne sans frais: 844-476-8181
www.federationautobus.com
Merged from: Association des propriétaires d'autobus du Québec; Association du transport écolier du Québec
Aperçu: *Dimension:* moyenne; *Envergure:* provinciale; fondée en 2014
Description: La Fédération des transporteurs par autobus a pour mission de favoriser la mobilité efficace et sécuritaire des personnes et ainsi contribuer à l'image, la valorisation et la stabilité du transport collectif de personnes.
Membre(s) du bureau directeur: Luc Lafrance, Directeur général, 418-476-8181 214
llafrance@federationautobus.com
Membre: 700; *Critères d'admissibilite:* Transportateurs par autocars; Vendeurs de produits touristiques pour les groupes; *Comités:* Audit; Assurance; Sécurité; Urbain et interurbain; Transport scolaire; Nolisé-touristique; Transport spécialisé (adapté, aéroportuaire, médical, abonnement et collectif rural)

Freight Carriers Association of Canada (FCA)
#3-4, 427 Garrison Rd., Fort Erie ON L2A 6E6
Fax: 905-994-0117
Toll-Free: 800-559-7421
info@fca-natc.org
www.fca-natc.org
Previous Name: Canadian Transport Tariff Bureau Association
Overview: A medium-sized national organization
Description: To provide quality information, products & services to users, providers & third parties involved in motor carrier transportation
Affiliation(s): North American Transportation Council
Chief Officer(s): David J. Sirgey, President, 800-559-7421 214
dsirgey@natc.com
Julie Gauthier, Administrative Assistant, 800-559-7421 218
julieg@natc.com
Finances: *Annual Operating Budget:* $1.5 Million-$3 Million; *Funding Sources:* Membership fees; Sales of publications & software
Staff: 5 staff member(s)
Membership: *Member Profile:* For-hire motor carriers
Activities: Holding carrier meetings & seminars; Disseminating information; *Speaker Service:* Yes

Freight Management Association of Canada (FMA) / Association canadienne de gestion du fret (AGF)
#405, 580 Terry Fox Dr., Ottawa ON K2L 4C2
Tel: 613-599-3283; *Fax:* 613-599-1295
info@fma-agf.ca
www.cita-acti.ca
Social Media:
linkedin.com/company/canadian-industrial-transportation-association-cita
twitter.com/CITA_ACTI
Previous Name: Canadian Industrial Transportation Association
Overview: A medium-sized national organization founded in 1916
Description: To promote a competitive & cost effective North American transportation system serving Canada and its NAFTA allies.
Chief Officer(s): Bob Ballantyne, President
ballantyne@fma-agf.ca
Kelsey Lemieux, Manger, Marketing
lemieux@fma-agf.ca
Cindy Hick, Vice-President
hick@fma-agf.ca
Finances: *Funding Sources:* Membership dues
Membership: 86; *Fees:* Schedule available; *Member Profile:* Companies involved in the shipping industry
Activities: Advocacy; education; *Speaker Service:* Yes; *Library:* Yes (Open to Public)

HASTe Hub for Active School Travel
928 East 17th Ave., Vancouver BC V5V 1C2
Tel: 603-347-7704
info@hastebc.org
www.hastebc.org
Social Media:
www.facebook.com/150876098306478
twitter.com/HASTeBC
Overview: A small provincial organization founded in 2007
Description: To connect children, schools & communities through walking & cycling; To help schools work towards reducing their emissions; To increase safe & active travel in BC communities
Chief Officer(s): Carol Sartor, Facilitator, Active & Safe Routes to School
carol@hastebc.org

Katelyn McDougall, Facilitator, School Travel Planning
katelyn@hastebc.org
Finances: *Funding Sources:* Government
Staff: 5 staff member(s)
Activities: Facilitates communication between schools, parents, students, planners, & engineers to encourage active travel to and from school; Supporting School Travel Planning (STP); Offering workshops, consulting, & education; *Internships:* Yes

Heavy Equipment & Aggregate Truckers Association of Manitoba (HEAT)
2215 Henderson Hwy., East St Paul MB R2E 0B8
Tel: 204-654-9426; *Fax:* 204-224-4907
heatmb.ca
Overview: A small provincial organization
Description: To raise awareness about the the heavy equipment idustry & to set standards for the companies & people who are involved in the business
Chief Officer(s): Ken McKeen, President
Membership: 185

Hope Air / Vols d'espoir
#207, 124 Merton St., Toronto ON M4S 2Z2
Tel: 416-222-6335; *Fax:* 416-222-6930
Toll-Free: 877-346-4673
mail@hopeair.ca
www.hopeair.ca
Social Media:
www.facebook.com/pages/Hope-Air
twitter.com/Hope_Air
Previous Name: Mission Air Transportation Network
Overview: A small national charitable organization founded in 1986
Description: To provide free air transportation to Canadians in financial need who must travel between their own communities & recognized facilities for medical care
Chief Officer(s): Doug Keller-Hobson, Executive Director
Wayne Twaits, Chair
Robert Reeves, Vice-Chair
Finances: *Annual Operating Budget:* $250,000-$500,000; *Funding Sources:* Corporate; private donations; government
Staff: 6 staff member(s); 30 volunteer(s)
Membership: 1-99; *Fees:* N/A; *Committees:* Air Coordination; Funding; Finance; Office Administrations; Planning; Public Relations

Huntsville & Lake of Bays Railway Society
88 Brunel Rd., Huntsville ON P1H 1R1
Tel: 705-789-7576; *Fax:* 705-789-6169
www.portageflyer.org
Also Known As: The Portage Railway
Overview: A small local charitable organization founded in 1984
Description: Maintains & displays original artifacts of the old Huntsville & Lake of Bays Railway, plus vintage railway equipment of the turn of the century
Affiliation(s): Muskoka Heritage Place
Chief Officer(s): David Topps, President
president@portageflyer.org
Finances: *Funding Sources:* Fundraising; Rotary Club; local industry; donations
Membership: *Fees:* $35 regular; $45 foreign
Activities: A fully functional operating railway

Industrial Truck Association (ITA)
#460, 1750 K St. NW, Washington DC 20006 USA
Tel: 202-296-9880; *Fax:* 202-296-9884
www.indtrk.org
Social Media:
www.facebook.com/Indtrk
Overview: A medium-sized international organization
Description: Represents the manufacturers of lift trucks & their suppliers who do business in Canada, the United States or Mexico
Chief Officer(s): William Montwieler, Executive Director
Finances: *Annual Operating Budget:* $1.5 Million-$3 Million
Staff: 5 staff member(s)
Membership: 100; *Fees:* Schedule available; *Member Profile:* Manufacturers of forklifts & suppliers
Activities: *Awareness Events:* National Forklift Safety Day, June 14

Institute of Transportation Engineers (ITE)
#600, 1627 Eye St. NW, Washington DC 20006 USA
Tel: 202-785-0060; *Fax:* 202-785-0609
ite_staff@ite.org
www.ite.org
Social Media:
www.youtube.com/user/ITEHQ
linkedin.com/groups?gid=166463
www.facebook.com/74169838900
twitter.com/ITEHQ
Overview: A large international organization founded in 1930
Description: To facilitate the application of technology & scientific principles for modes of ground transportation
Chief Officer(s): Shawn J Leight, PE; PTOE; PTP, International President
Membership: 13,000; *Fees:* Schedule available; *Member Profile:* Transportation professionals with the responsibilities for meeting mobility & safety needs, such as transportation educators, researchers, consultants, planners, & engineers
Activities: Promoting professional development; Supporting education; Encouraging research; Increasing public awareness; Exchanging professional information

Intermodal Association of North America (IANA)
#1100, 11785 Beltsville Dr., Calverton MD 20705 USA
Tel: 301-982-3400; *Fax:* 301-982-4815
info@intermodal.org
www.intermodal.org
Overview: A medium-sized international organization founded in 1991
Description: To represent the combined interests of intermodal freight transportation companies & their suppliers
Chief Officer(s): Joanne F. (Joni) Casey, President/CEO, 301-982-3400 349
Membership: 700; *Fees:* Schedule available; *Committees:* Maintenance & Repair; Operations

International Air Transport Association (IATA) / Association du transport aérien international
PO Box 113, 800, Place Victoria, Montréal QC H4Z 1M1
Tel: 514-874-0202; *Fax:* 514-874-1753
www.iata.org
Social Media:
www.youtube.com/iatatv
linkedin.com/groups?mostPopular=&gid=3315879
twitter.com/iata
Overview: A small international organization founded in 1945
Description: To promote safe, regular & economical air transport for the benefit of the peoples of the world; to foster air commerce; to study the problems connected with air transport; to provide a means for collaboration among the air transport enterprises engaged directly or indirectly in international air transport service; to cooperate with the International Civil Aviation Organization & other international organizations; to furnish for governments a forum for developing industry working standards &, as appropriate, coordinating international fares & rates; to simplify the travelling process for the general public
Affiliation(s): International Civil Aviation Organization
Chief Officer(s): Tony Tyler, Director General

International Association of Ports & Harbours (IAPH)
7F South Tower, New Pier Takeshiba, 1-16-1 Kaigan, Minato-Ku, Tokyo 105-0022 Japan
info@iaphworldports.org
www.iaphworldports.org
Social Media:
www.facebook.com/iaphworldports
Overview: A large international organization founded in 1955
Description: To promote the development of the international port & maritime industry by fostering cooperation among members in order to build a more cohesive partnership among the world's ports & harbors, thereby promoting peace in the world & the welfare of mankind; to ensure that the industry's interests & views are represented before international organizations involved n the regulation of international trade & transportation & incorporated in the regulatory initiatives of these organizations; & to collect, analyse, exchange & distribute information on developing trends in international trade, transportation, ports & the regulations of these industries
Affiliation(s): International Maritime Organization; United Nations Conference on Trade & Development; United Nations Economic & Social Council; Permanent International Association of Navigation Congresses; International Cargo Handling Coordination Association; International Maritime Pilots Association; International Association of Independent Tanker Owners; Baltic & International Martime Council
Chief Officer(s): Susumu Naruse, Secretary General
Finances: *Annual Operating Budget:* $1.5 Million-$3 Million; *Funding Sources:* Membership fees
Staff: 7 staff member(s)
Membership: 360; *Fees:* Schedule available; *Member Profile:* 90 maritime countries are represented; *Committees:* Executive; Communication & Community Relations; Port Finance & Economics; Port Safety & Security; Port Environment; Legal; Port Planning & Development; Port Operations & Logistics; Trade Facilitation & Port Community System; Conference; Finance; Constitution & By-Laws; Membership; Long Range Planning/Review
Activities: *Library:* Yes (Open to Public)

International Industry Working Group (IIWG)
International Air Transport Association, PO Box 416, Route de l'Aéroport 33 1215, 15 Airport, Geneva Switzerland
www.iata.org/whatwedo/workgroups/Pages/iiwg.aspx
Overview: A small international organization founded in 1970
Description: To promote & develop an open exchange of information to minimize interface problems through well-informed design, development & operation of both aircraft & airports; to study jointly solutions to major problems which impede the development of the air transport system
Chief Officer(s): Koos Noordeloos, Chair
Colin Spear, Secretariat
spearc@iata.org
Membership: 50; *Member Profile:* Aircraft & aeroengine manufacturers; airlines & airport authorities

International Maritime Organization (IMO) / Organisation maritime internationale
4 Albert Embankment, London SE1 7SR United Kingdom
info@imo.org
www.imo.org
Social Media:
www.youtube.com/user/IMOHQ; www.flickr.com/photos/imo-un
www.facebook.com/IMOHQ
twitter.com/imohq
Overview: A large international organization founded in 1948
Description: To encourage the adoption of high standards in matters concerning maritime safety, security, efficiency of navigation & control of marine pollution from ships
Chief Officer(s): Koji Sekimizu, Secretary General
Finances: *Annual Operating Budget:* Greater than $5 Million; *Funding Sources:* Government
Staff: 300 staff member(s)
Membership: 170 member states + 3 associate; *Fees:* Schedule available, based upon shipping fleet tonnage; *Committees:* Maritime Safety; Marine Environment Protection; Legal; Technical Cooperation; Facilitation
Activities: *Awareness Events:* Day of the Seafarer, June; *Library:* Yes by appointment

Locomotive & Railway Historical Society of Western Canada
87 Chelsea St. NW, Calgary AB T2K 1P1
Tel: 403-282-3485
Overview: A small local charitable organization founded in 1985
Description: To promote the preservation of railway equipment integral to the history of Western Canada; to act in a consultative capacity on heritage rail projects; *Member of:* Canadian Council for Railway Heritage
Chief Officer(s): James E. Lanigan, President
Finances: *Annual Operating Budget:* Less than $50,000
Staff: 9 volunteer(s)
Membership: 9
Activities: Preservation & restoration of important historic Canadian railway equipment; *Speaker Service:* Yes

The Logistics Institute
#501, 20 Maud St., Toronto ON M5V 2M5
Tel: 416-363-3005; *Fax:* 416-363-5598
loginfo@loginstitute.ca
www.loginstitute.ca
Social Media:
linkedin.com/groups?home=&gid=1581887
www.facebook.com/129220600590938
twitter.com/CdnProfLogInst
Overview: A medium-sized national organization founded in 1990
Chief Officer(s): Victor S. Deyglio, Founding President, 416-363-3005 1200
vdeyglio@loginstitute.ca
Ben Avery, Coordinator, Technology & Administrative Support, 416-363-3005 1500
bavery@loginstitute.ca
Jasmine Gill, Coordinator, Program & Membership, 416-363-3005 1700
jgill@loginstitute.ca

Manitoba Trucking Association (MTA)
25 Bunting St., Winnipeg MB R2X 2P5
Tel: 204-632-6600; *Fax:* 204-694-7134
info@trucking.mb.ca
www.trucking.mb.ca
Social Media:
linkedin.com/manitobatruckingassociation
www.facebook.com/manitobatruckingassociation
twitter.com/truckingmb
Overview: A medium-sized provincial organization founded in 1932
Description: To develop & maintain a safe and healthy business environment for its members
Affiliation(s): Canadian Trucking Alliance; Canadian Council of Motor Transport Administrators; Canadian Trucking Human

Resource Council; Winnipeg Chamber of Commerce; Manitoba Chamber of Commerce; Infrastructure Council of Manitoba; Employers' Task Force on Workers' Compensation; Manitoba Employers' Council
Chief Officer(s): Terry Shaw, Executive Director
Finances: *Funding Sources:* Membership dues & fundraising through services
Staff: 6 staff member(s)
Membership: 250 organizations; *Member Profile:* PSV Carriers; City Transportation; Private Fleet; Household Goods Carriers; Associated Trades; Vehicle Maintenance; *Committees:* Safety; Professional Truck Driving Championships; Scholarship Fund; Human Resources; Workers Compensation
Activities: *Speaker Service:* Yes; *Library:* Yes (Open to Public) by appointment

Motorcycle & Moped Industry Council (MMIC) / Le Conseil de l'industrie de la motocyclette et du cyclomoteur (CIMC)
#201, 3000 Steeles Ave. East, Markham ON L3R 4T9
Tel: 416-491-4449; *Fax:* 416-493-1985
Toll-Free: 877-470-6642
info@mmic.ca
www.mmic.ca
Overview: A small national organization founded in 1971
Description: To represent the manufacturers & distributors of street legal motorcycles and related products and services in Canada.
Chief Officer(s): Jo-Anne Farquhar, Director, Communications & Public Affairs
jfarquhar@mmic.ca
Luc Fournier, Director, Policy & Government Relations
lfournier@mmic.ca
Tim Stover, Director, Operations
tstover@mmic.ca
Membership: 12; *Fees:* Schedule available; *Member Profile:* Companies involved in the manufacturing or distribution of motorcycles, mopeds or scooters

National Association of Railroad Passengers (NARP)
#300, 505 Capitol Court NE, Washington DC 20002-7706 USA
Tel: 202-408-8362; *Fax:* 202-408-8287
narp@narprail.org
www.narprail.org
Social Media:
plus.google.com/110252908993287069826
www.facebook.com/narprail
twitter.com/narprail
Overview: A medium-sized national charitable organization founded in 1967
Description: To encourage & promote a more balanced US transporation system including promotion of federal & state policies beneficial to all forms of rail service, urban rail transit, rural public transporation & intermodal terminals
Affiliation(s): Transport 2000 Ltd.
Chief Officer(s): Ross Capon, President
Finances: *Funding Sources:* Membership dues
Staff: 6 staff member(s)
Membership: *Fees:* Schedule available
Activities: *Rents Mailing List:* Yes; *Library:* Yes (Open to Public)

National Transportation Brokers Association (NTBA)
PO Box 31047, RPO Westney Heights, Ajax ON L1T 3V2
www.ntba-brokers.com
Overview: A medium-sized national organization
Description: Promotes & continually improves business relationships among shippers, carriers, government & freight brokers
Chief Officer(s): Larry Cox, Chair, 905-671-3100, Fax: 905-671-4600
larry@polaristransport.com
Finances: *Funding Sources:* Member fees
Membership: *Fees:* $300; *Member Profile:* Freight brokerage services providers

The Ninety-Nines Inc./International Organization of Women Pilots
4300 Amelia Earhart Rd., #A, Oklahoma City OK 73159 USA
Tel: 405-685-7969; *Fax:* 405-685-7985
Toll-Free: 800-994-1929
PR@ninety-nines.org
www.ninety-nines.org
Social Media:
www.facebook.com/100905045593
Also Known As: 99's
Overview: A small international charitable organization founded in 1929
Description: To promote world fellowship through flight; to provide networking & scholarship opportunities for women & aviation education in the community; to preserve the unique history of women in aviation
Chief Officer(s): Kathy Fox, Governor, East Canada Section
Angelee Skywork, Governor, West Canada Section
Martha Phillips, President
president@ninety-nines.org
Membership: *Fees:* US$65 for US; US$57 Canadian; US$44 other countries; US$35 US/Canadian associate; US$30 international associate; *Member Profile:* Women pilots
Activities: *Speaker Service:* Yes; *Library:* 99s Museum of Women Pilots

North America Railway Hall of Fame (NARHF)
750 Tabot St., St Thomas ON N5P 4H4
Tel: 519-633-2535; *Fax:* 519-633-3087
info@narhf.org
www.narhf.org
Overview: A small national charitable organization founded in 1996
Description: To establish a tribute to those who have made significant contributions relating to the railway industry in North America; To honour railway organizations, related innovations & technical accomplishments; To preserve & display a collection of library materials & railway heritage artifacts related to the Hall of Fame inductees; To educate the public about the impact of railway transportation on history & the development of communities, nations & international relations
Chief Officer(s): Matt Janes, President

Northern Air Transport Association (NATA)
PO Box 20102, Yellowknife NT X1A 3X8
Tel: 867-446-6282; *Fax:* 866-977-6282
admin@nata-yzf.ca
www.nata-yzf.ca
Overview: A small local organization founded in 1977
Description: To promote safe & effective Northern air transportation
Chief Officer(s): Stephen Nourse, Executive Director, 613-219-9305, Fax: 613-489-0143
exec@nata-yzf.ca
Stephen Nourse, President
snourse@firstair.ca
Teri Arychuk, Secretary-Treasurer
teri@airtindi.com
Membership: *Member Profile:* Northern air carriers
Activities: Advocating for Northern air transport; Establishing partnerships with governments & within the transportation industry; *Speaker Service:* Yes

Ontario Good Roads Association (OGRA)
#22, 1525 Cornwall Rd., Oakville ON L6J 0B2
Tel: 289-291-6472; *Fax:* 289-291-6477
info@ogra.org
www.ogra.org
Social Media:
ca.linkedin.com/pub/ontario-good-roads-association/43/b08/829
twitter.com/Ont_Good_Roads
Overview: A medium-sized provincial organization founded in 1894
Description: To represent the transportation & public works-related interests of Ontario's municipalities & First Nation communities; To deliver programs & services that meet the needs of members; To support municipalities in the provision of effective & efficient transportation systems throughout Ontario
Chief Officer(s): Joseph W. Tiernay, Executive Director
Brian Anderson, Manager, MEmber & Technical Services
Scott Butler, Manager, Policy & Research
Heather Crewe, Manager, Education & Training
Rayna Gillis, Manager, Finance & Administration
Colette Caruso, Coordinator, Communications & Marketing
Roni Kean, Coordinator, Curriculum
Cherry-Lyn Sales, Coordinator, Training Services
Fahad Shuja, Coordinator, Member Services & OPS
James Smith, Coordinator, Member Services & Infrastructure
Finances: *Funding Sources:* Membership fees; Sponsorships
Membership: 400+ municipalities; *Member Profile:* Ontario municipalities; First Nations communities; Corporations; Life & honourary members; *Committees:* Executive; Policy; Member Services; Nominating; Combined Conference; Companions Program
Activities: Advocating for the collective interests of municipal transportation & works departments; Analyzing policies; Reviewing legislation; Consulting with stakeholders & partners; Offering education & training opportunities

Ontario Milk Transport Association (OMTA)
#301, 660 Speedvale Ave. West, Guelph ON N1K 1E5
www.milk.org/Corporate/View.aspx?Content=Students/Transportation
Overview: A medium-sized provincial organization founded in 1967
Chief Officer(s): John Johnston, General Manager, 519-766-1133
Membership: 60 companies; *Member Profile:* Transporters of milk, such as producer-owned co-operatives, which collect raw milk from Ontario farms & take it to processing plants in Ontario, Quebec, & Manitoba

Ontario Public Transit Association (OPTA)
#400, 1235 Bay St., Toronto ON M5R 3K4
Tel: 416-229-6222; *Fax:* 416-969-8916
www.ontariopublictransit.ca
Previous Name: Ontario Community Transit Association
Overview: A medium-sized provincial organization founded in 1997
Description: To strengthen & improve public transit services in Ontario; To ensure excellence & sustainability in public transit
Chief Officer(s): Dave Sherlock, Chair
Alex Milojevic, Vice-Chair
Norman Cheesman, Chief Executive Officer
Mike Spicer, Secretary
Pat Delmore, Treasurer
Membership: *Fees:* Annual fees for transportation service providers sales based on operating budget or net sales; $560 for affiliates; *Member Profile:* Representatives of public transit systems; Health & social service agency transportation providers; Government representatives; Suppliers to the industry; Consultants
Activities: Engaging in advocacy activities; Sharing information; *Awareness Events:* OTE, annual conference & trade show

Ontario Traffic Council (OTC)
#2068, 170 The Donway West, Toronto ON M3C 2C3
Tel: 647-346-4050; *Fax:* 647-346-4060
info@otc.org
www.otc.org
Social Media:
twitter.com/ontariotraffic
Overview: A medium-sized provincial organization founded in 1950
Description: To improve traffic conditions & traffic safety in municipalities of Ontario
Chief Officer(s): Marco D'Angelo, Executive Director
Jeffrey Smart, President
Nelson Cadete, Vice-President
Kimberly Rossi, Treasurer
Heide Schlegl, Director Engineering
John Crass, Director of Training & Education
Scott Godwin, Operations Manager

Ontario Trucking Association (OTA)
555 Dixon Rd., Toronto ON M9W 1H8
Tel: 416-249-7401; *Fax:* 866-713-4188
www.ontruck.org
Social Media:
www.youtube.com/user/ontruck
linkedin.com/groups/4783727/profile
www.facebook.com/202193323261162
twitter.com/ontruck
Overview: A large provincial organization founded in 1926
Description: To represent companies & industry suppliers; To provide political advocacy, education, & information services to North American freight transport companies
Finances: *Funding Sources:* Membership fees
Membership: 1,700 member companies; *Committees:* Axle Weight; Credit; Education; Executive; Social/Labour; Tech./Ops; Convention; Dues; Membership; Insurance; Finance; Environmental Issues
Activities: Offering training courses & seminars; *Awareness Events:* Annual Spring Golf Tournament, May; *Speaker Service:* Yes; *Library:* Yes

Ontario Trucking Association Education Foundation
555 Dixon Rd., Toronto ON M9W 1H8
Tel: 416-249-7401; *Fax:* 866-713-4188
info@otaef.com
www.otaef.com
Overview: A small provincial charitable organization founded in 1958
Description: To further education for post-secondary students in Ontario who have links to the Ontario trucking industry
Chief Officer(s): Betsy Sharples, Executive Director
Finances: *Funding Sources:* Donations
Activities: Providing scholarships for Ontario post-secondary students with a parent empolyed by an Ontario trucking company or trucking service

Operation Lifesaver (OL) / Opération Gareautrain
#1401, 99 Bank St., Ottawa ON K1P 6B9
Tel: 613-564-8100; *Fax:* 613-567-6726
admin@operationlifesaver.ca
www.operationlifesaver.ca
Social Media:
www.youtube.com/user/OperationLifesaverCA
www.facebook.com/oplifesaver
twitter.com/oplifesaver
Overview: A small national organization founded in 1981
Description: To create an awareness by the general public of the potential hazards of rail/highway crossings; to improve drivers' & pedestrians' behaviour at these intersections; to inform the public of the dangers associated with trespassing on railway property; & to reduce the number of accidents resulting in fatalities, injuries & monetary losses
Chief Officer(s): Dan Di Tota, National Director
Finances: *Annual Operating Budget:* $250,000-$500,000; *Funding Sources:* Transport Canada; Railway Association of Canada
Staff: 2 staff member(s); 150 volunteer(s)
Activities: *Awareness Events:* OL Rail Safety Week, April

Pharmaceutical & Personal Care Logistics Association (PPCLA) / Association de logistique des soins personnels et pharmaceutiques
PO Box 40568, Stn. Six Points Plaza, Toronto ON M9B 6K8
Tel: 416-232-6817; *Fax:* 416-232-6818
Toll-Free: 866-293-1238
ppcla@ppcla.org
www.ppcla.org
Previous Name: Pharmaceutical & Toilet Preparations Traffic Association
Overview: A medium-sized national organization founded in 1958
Description: To develop & promote the interchange of ideas & information concerning traffic & transportation matters of the pharmaceutical & toilet preparations industry; To foster fair dealings & cordial relationships among members & between representatives of the various modes of transportation employed by members
Chief Officer(s): Doris Hamel, President
dhamel@shire.com
Finances: *Annual Operating Budget:* Less than $50,000
Staff: 1 volunteer(s)
Membership: 47 institutional; *Fees:* $350; *Member Profile:* Logistics managers in the pharmaceutical & personal care industries

Prince Edward Island Trucking Sector Council (PEITSC)
#211, 420 University Ave., Charlottetown PE C1A 7Z5
Tel: 902-566-5563; *Fax:* 902-566-4506
info@peitsc.ca
www.peitsc.ca
Social Media:
www.youtube.com/user/peitruckingsc
www.facebook.com/peitsc
twitter.com/peitsc
Overview: A medium-sized provincial organization
Description: To addressing human resources issues and opportunities in the Trucking Industry on Prince Edward Island and provide a vehicle for effective industry participation in identifying and addressing issues related to workforce attraction and retention, career awareness, skills upgrading and training.; *Member of:* Prince Edward Island Literacy Alliance Inc.
Chief Officer(s): Scott Annear, Chair
Brian Oulton, Executive Director

Private Motor Truck Council of Canada (PMTC) / Association canadienne du camionnage d'entreprise (ACCE)
#115, 1660 North Service Rd. East, Oakville ON L6H 7G3
Tel: 905-827-0587; *Fax:* 905-827-8212
Toll-Free: 877-501-7682
info@pmtc.ca
www.pmtc.ca
Overview: A medium-sized national organization founded in 1977
Description: Recognized as the leader of the private trucking community in Canada; represents the varied interests of private fleet operators with integrity & sound business practices.; *Member of:* North American Private Truck Council
Affiliation(s): National Private Truck Council
Chief Officer(s): Bruce J. Richards, President
trucks@pmtc.ca
Richard Lalonde, Québec Director
richard_lalonde@praxair.com
Finances: *Annual Operating Budget:* $250,000-$500,000; *Funding Sources:* Seminars; social events; membership fees
Staff: 4 staff member(s)
Membership: 400; *Member Profile:* Private truck fleets or suppliers to same; private truck fleets operated by companies whose principal business is other than transportation, but use their own truck fleets to further their business
Activities: Seminars; annual conference; benchmarking and best practices survey;National Vehicle Graphics Design Competition

Railway Association of Canada (RAC) / L'Association des chemins de fer du Canada (ACFC)
#901, 99 Bank St., Ottawa ON K1P 6B9
Tel: 613-567-8591; *Fax:* 613-567-6726
rac@railcan.ca
www.railcan.ca
Social Media:
www.youtube.com/user/racmain
twitter.com/RailCanada
Overview: A large national organization founded in 1917
Description: To promote the commercial viability & the safe & efficient operation of the Canadian railway industry; to act on behalf of, or work jointly with, member companies to promote public policy & regulation that provides equitable treatment between shipping modes; to provide factual information on the railway industry for the public, government & industry, & to provide the views of the industry on public policy issues. PUBLICATIONS: Interchange; Canadian Railway Medical Rules Handbook; Canada's Railway Lead North America.
Affiliation(s): Association of American Railroads
Chief Officer(s): Michael Bourque, President & CEO, 613-564-8090
Gérald Gauthier, Vice-President, Public & Corporate Affairs, 613-564-8106
geraldg@railcan.ca
Finances: *Annual Operating Budget:* Greater than $5 Million; *Funding Sources:* Members fees
Staff: 23 staff member(s)
Membership: 55 railways & 40 associates; *Fees:* $2,000 minimum; *Member Profile:* Railway companies operating in Canada; *Committees:* Policy; Accounting; Finance; Human Resources; Safety & Operations Management; Taxation
Activities: Operation Lifesaver;

Recreational Aircraft Association (RAA) / Réseau aéronefs amateur
22 - 4881 Fountain St. North, Breslau ON N0B 1M0
Tel: 519-648-3030; *Toll-Free:* 800-387-1028
raa@raa.ca
www.raa.ca
Previous Name: Experimental Aircraft Association of Canada
Overview: A medium-sized national organization founded in 1983
Description: To be a national leader in the development & advancement of recreational aviation; to promote recreational flying & building of amateur built aircraft, restorations of classic & antique aircraft
Affiliation(s): Recreational Aviation Foundation
Chief Officer(s): Gary Wolf, President, 519-648-3030
garywolf@rogers.com
Wayne Hadath, Treasurer
whadath@rogers.com
Finances: *Annual Operating Budget:* $100,000-$250,000; *Funding Sources:* Membership dues
Staff: 1 staff member(s); 150 volunteer(s)
Membership: 2,000; *Fees:* $40; *Committees:* 12 regional
Activities: Fly-ins across Canada; *Speaker Service:* Yes

Saskatchewan Trucking Association (STA)
1335 Wallace St., Regina SK S4N 3Z5
Tel: 306-569-9696; *Fax:* 306-569-1008
Toll-Free: 800-563-7623
www.sasktrucking.com
Social Media:
linkedin.com/company/saskatchewan-trucking-association
www.facebook.com/154582251242283
twitter.com/sasktrucking
Overview: A medium-sized provincial licensing organization founded in 1937
Description: To represent the freight transportation industry in Saskatchewan
Chief Officer(s): Al Rosseker, Executive Director
arosseker@sasktrucking.com
Finances: *Funding Sources:* Membership fees; Sponsorship of programs
Staff: 3 staff member(s)
Membership: *Fees:* Schedule available

Shipping Federation of Canada / Fédération maritime du Canada
#326, 300, rue St-Sacrement, Montréal QC H2Y 1X4
Tel: 514-849-2325; *Fax:* 514-849-8774
Toll-Free: 877-534-7367
info@shipfed.ca
www.shipfed.ca
Overview: A medium-sized national organization founded in 1903
Description: The association that represents and promotes the interests of the owners, operators and agents of ships involved in Canada's world trade.
Chief Officer(s): Michael H. Broad, President
Anne Legars, Vice President
David Cardin, Chairman
Jean-François Belzile, Director of Marine Operations
James Moram, Director Marine Administration
Caroline Gravel, Director Environmental Affairs
Mario Minotti, Director Finance/Administration
Karen Kancens, Director of Customs and Immigration
Finances: *Funding Sources:* International shipping
Staff: 8 staff member(s)
Membership: 83; *Member Profile:* Direct involvement in steamship business; *Committees:* Customs; Dangerous Goods; EDI; Immigration; Pilotage; Railways; Tanker Safety
Activities: To protect members in all matters affecting the operation of shipping from & to Eastern Canada, the St. Lawrence River, the Great Lakes & Arctic ports; areas of concern include pilotage, pollution, navigation aids, port operations, port charges, & federal government legislation & regulation;

Shipyard General Workers' Federation of British Columbia (CLC) / Fédération des ouvriers des chantiers navals de la Colombie-Britannique (CTC)
#130, 111 Victoria Dr., Vancouver BC V5L 4C4
Tel: 604-254-8204; *Fax:* 604-254-7447
office@bcshipyardworkers.com
www.bcshipyardworkers.com
Overview: A medium-sized provincial organization
Affiliation(s): Machinists, Fitters & Helpers Industrial Union #3, Marine Workers & Boilerworkers' Industrial Union #1, Shipwrights, Joiners & Caulkers' Industrial Union #9
Chief Officer(s): George MacPherson, President
Quentin Del Vecchio, General Secretary
Membership: 1,100 + 3 locals

Société des traversiers du Québec (STQ)
Bureau de la traverse, 10, rue des Traversiers, Québec QC G1K 8L8
Tél: 418-643-8420; *Téléc:* 418-643-5178
Ligne sans frais: 877-787-7483
stq-quebec@traversiers.gouv.qc.ca
www.traversiers.gouv.qc.ca
Aperçu: *Dimension:* petite; *Envergure:* provinciale; fondée en 1971
Description: Contribuer à la mobilité des personnes et des marchandises en assurant des services de transport maritime de qualité, sécuritaires et fiables, favorisant ainsi l'essor social, économique et touristique du Québec
Membre(s) du bureau directeur: Jocelyn Fortier, Présidente/directrice générale
Finances: *Budget de fonctionnement annuel:* Plus de $5 Million
Membre: 100-499

Sydney & Louisburg Railway Historical Society / Le Musée de chemin de fer de Sydney à Louisburg
PO Box 225, Louisbourg NS B0A 1M0
Tel: 902-733-2720
Also Known As: S&L Museum
Overview: A small local organization founded in 1973
Description: To commemorate the history of the S&L Railway by preserving & displaying the artifacts & documents which survive; to commemorate the people who worked for the S&L Railway; to explain the local & commercial history of the area which relates to the S&L Railway; to explain & commemorate the general themes of railway & transportation history & technology; *Member of:* Federation of the Nova Scotian Heritage; Heritage Canada
Activities: Annual reunion, Sept.; *Library:* Resource Centre (Open to Public) by appointment

Teamsters Canada Rail Conference (TCRC) / Conference ferroviaire de Teamsters Canada (CFTC)
#1710, 130 Albert St., Ottawa ON K1P 5G4
Tel: 613-235-1828; *Fax:* 613-235-1069
info@teamstersrail.ca
www.teamstersrail.ca
Previous Name: Brotherhood of Locomotive Engineers
Overview: A medium-sized national organization
Chief Officer(s): Rex Beatty, President

Membership: 16,000 in 21 divisions; *Fees:* $15
Activities: *Library:* Yes (Open to Public)

Toronto Transportation Society (TTS)
PO Box 5187, Stn. A, Toronto ON M5W 1N5
www.torontotransportationsociety.org
Overview: A small local organization founded in 1973
Chief Officer(s): Kevin Nichol, President
Richard Hooles, Vice-President
Robert Giles, Secretary
Robert Lubinski, Treasurer
Finances: *Funding Sources:* Membership fees
Membership: *Fees:* $25 CDN Canadians; $30 USD USA residents; $45 CDN international; *Member Profile:* Transportation enthusiasts with an interest in buses, streetcars, railways, & subways
Activities: Hosting monthly meetings; Organizing a Memorabilia Night, featuring an auction of transit collections; Arranging charters using unique transit vehicles

Transport Action Canada
Bronson Centre, PO Box 858, Stn. B, #303, 211 Bronson Ave., Ottawa ON K1P 5P9
Tel: 613-594-3290; *Fax:* 613-594-3271
info@transport-action.ca
www.transport-action.ca
Previous Name: Transport 2000 Canada
Overview: A medium-sized national charitable organization founded in 1976
Description: National federation of environmental & consumer groups concerned about the importance of transportation on our environment & quality of life; to inform Canadians of the need for a coherent national transport policy which recognizes that conservation of resources must be a priority & that access to good public transportation is a right of all Canadians; to work for the improvement & greater use of bus & rail transportation in the interests of public safety, social equity & the protection of the environment; to press for the coordination of all transport services for the benefit of users; to demand more attention to the needs of pedestrians, cyclists & public transport users; to maximize the use of the energy-efficient rail & marine modes for the shipment of freight.
Affiliation(s): Transport 2000 International
Chief Officer(s): David Jeanes, President
Justin Bur, VP East
Peter Lacey, VP West
Tony Turrittin, Secretary
Klaus Beltzner, Treasurer
Bert Titcomb, Manager
Finances: *Annual Operating Budget:* $50,000-$100,000; *Funding Sources:* Donations
Staff: 15 volunteer(s)
Membership: 1,500; *Fees:* $35 regular; $30 senior; $50 family; $75 affiliate non-profit; $170corporate
Activities: Research, public education & advocacy, representation of the consumer interests before federal, provincial, municipal public hearings & regulatory bodies, direction of consumer complaints to public carriers; *Speaker Service:* Yes; *Library:* Yes (Open to Public)

Transportation Association of Canada (TAC) / Association des transports du Canada (ATC)
2323 St. Laurent Blvd., Ottawa ON K1G 4J8
Tel: 613-736-1350; *Fax:* 613-736-1395
secretariat@tac-atc.ca
www.tac-atc.ca
Social Media:
linkedin.com/company/transportation-association-of-canada
www.facebook.com/tac2014atc
twitter.com/TAC_TranspAssn
Previous Name: Canadian Good Roads Association; Roads & Transportation Association of Canada
Overview: A large national organization founded in 1914
Description: To promote the provision of safe, efficient, effective & environmentally sustainable transportation services in support of Canada's social & economic goals; To act as a neutral forum for the discussion of transportation issues & matters; to act as a technical focus in the highway transportation area
Chief Officer(s): Sarah Wells, Executive Director, 613-736-1350 229
swells@tac-atc.ca
Meena Peruvemba, Director, Finance & Administration, 613-736-1350 254
mperuvemba@tac-atc.ca
Sandra Majkic, Director, Technical Programs, 613-736-1350 228
smajkic@tac-atc.ca
Erica Andersen, Director, Communications & Member Services, 613-736-1350 235
eandersen@tac-atc.ca
Finances: *Annual Operating Budget:* $3 Million-$5 Million; *Funding Sources:* Membership dues
Staff: 20 staff member(s); 800 volunteer(s)
Membership: 500+ corporate; *Fees:* Schedule available based on institution; *Member Profile:* Federal, provincial, & territorial departments of transportation; municipalities; private sector firms; academic institutions & associations; *Committees:* Chief Engineer; Education & Human Resources Development; Environment; Urban Transportation; Climate Change; Small Municipalities; World Road Association; Operations
Activities: *Library:* Transportation Information Service by appointment

Truck Training Schools Association of Ontario Inc. (TTSAO)
Fax: 519-858-0920
Toll-Free: 866-475-9436
training@ttsao.com
www.ttsao.com
Overview: A small provincial licensing organization founded in 1992
Description: To provide the trucking industry with the highest quality driver training programs for entry level individuals that earn & maintain public confidence, adhering to sound & ethical business practices
Affiliation(s): Ontario Trucking Association; Ministry of Education, Ministry of Transportation
Chief Officer(s): Yvette Lagrois, President
Finances: *Annual Operating Budget:* $100,000-$250,000
Staff: 7 staff member(s)
Membership: 75; *Fees:* Schedule available
Activities: *Internships:* Yes

Truckers Association of Nova Scotia (TANS)
#3, 779 Prince St., Truro NS B2N 1G7
Tel: 902-895-7447; *Fax:* 902-897-0487
Toll-Free: 800-232-6631
contact@tans.ca
www.tans.ca
Overview: A medium-sized provincial organization founded in 1968
Description: Promotes all matters aiding the development and improvement of the trucking industry and the allied trades in Nova Scotia, including social, recreational, benevolent, educational and charitable activities. In addition, the Truckers Association of Nova Scotia makes presentations to government and other regulatory bodies in relation to the economic welfare of the trucking industry and is the main proponent in gaining access to the provincial haul rates and beneficial changes to the contract specifications used by the contractors; *Member of:* The Transportation Sector of Voluntary Planning
Affiliation(s): Atlantic Provinces Trucking Association of Nova Scotia
Chief Officer(s): Taunia MacAdam, Executive Director

Ultralight Pilots Association of Canada (UPAC) / Association canadienne des pilotes d'avions ultra-légers
907289 Township Rd. 12, RR#4, Bright ON N0J 1B0
Tel: 519-684-7628
info@upac.ca
www.upac.ca
Overview: A small national organization
Description: To promote ultralight aviation in Canada
Chief Officer(s): K. Lubitz, President
Finances: *Annual Operating Budget:* Less than $50,000; *Funding Sources:* Membership fees
Staff: 10 volunteer(s)
Membership: 500+; *Fees:* $40 individual; $60 family; *Member Profile:* Interest in ultralight aviaton
Activities: Video library for members; *Library:* Video Library (Open to Public)

Union of Canadian Transportation Employees (UCTE) / Union canadienne des employés des transports (UCET)
#702, 233 Gilmour St., Ottawa ON K2P 0P2
Tel: 613-238-4003; *Fax:* 613-236-0379
www.ucte.com
Overview: A medium-sized national organization
Description: The Union represents members working in the public & private sectors of the Canadian transportation industry (ports, airports, NAV Canada, pilotage authorities, transportation companies, canals, the Dept. of Transport, lighthouses, ships and Canadian Coast Guard bases)
Chief Officer(s): Gardenia Li, Finance & Administration Officer
Membership: 7,500 + 90 locals

United Transportation Union (AFL-CIO/CLC) - Canada
71 Bank St., 7th Fl., Ottawa ON K1P 5N2
Tel: 613-747-7979; *Fax:* 613-747-2815
Overview: A medium-sized national organization
Member of: United Transportation Union (AFL-CIO/CLC), Cleveland USA

University of Toronto Institute for Aerospace Studies
Faculty of Applied Science & Engineering, 4925 Dufferin St., Toronto ON M3H 5T6
Tel: 416-667-7700; *Fax:* 416-667-7799
www.utias.utoronto.ca
Overview: A medium-sized national organization founded in 1949
Description: UTIAS is a graduate studies and research institute, forming part of the faculty of Applied Science and Engineering at the University of Toronto.
Affiliation(s): Canadian Aeronautics & Space Institute; Institute for Space & Terrestrial Science; Canadian Space Agency; Intelligent Sensing for Innovative Structures Canada
Chief Officer(s): D.W. Zingg, Director
dwz@oddjob.utias.utoronto.ca
H.T. Liu, Associate Director
liu@utias.utoronto.ca
O.L. Gülder, Associate Director
ogulder@utias.utoronto.ca
Membership: 68
Activities: *Library:* Yes

The Van Horne Institute for International Transportation & Regulatory Affairs
2500 University Dr. NW, Calgary AB T2N 1N4
Tel: 403-220-8455; *Fax:* 403-282-4663
vanhorne@ucalgary.ca
www.vanhorne.info
Overview: A small international organization founded in 1991
Description: To contribute to public policy development & education in the areas of transportation & regulated industries. PUBLICATIONS: On-Trac.
Affiliation(s): University of Calgary; University of Alberta; Southern Alberta Institute of Technology
Chief Officer(s): Peter C. Wallis, President & CEO, 403-220-3967
pcwallis@ucalgary.ca
Bryndis Whitson, Manager, Strategic Development & Member Relations, 403-220-2114
bwhitson@ucalgary.ca
Gerald Maier, Chairman
Finances: *Annual Operating Budget:* Less than $50,000; *Funding Sources:* Private sector
Staff: 4 staff member(s)
Membership: 60; *Member Profile:* Government; industry; education; *Committees:* Centre for Transportation; Centre for Regulatory Affairs; Centre for Innovation & Communication
Activities: Transporation research & education; programs to assist in improving the efficiency & equity of transportation & regulated industries; *Speaker Service:* Yes; *Rents Mailing List:* Yes; *Library:* Yes (Open to Public)

Via Prévention
#301, 6455, boul Jean-Talon Est, Montréal QC H1S 3E8
Tél: 514-955-0454; *Téléc:* 514-955-0449
Ligne sans frais: 800-361-8906
info@viaprevention.com
www.viaprevention.com
Aperçu: *Dimension:* moyenne; *Envergure:* provinciale; fondée en 1982
Description: Pour protéger les personnes qui travaillent dans les transports, de l'Entreposage et de l'environnement en leur donnant une formation en santé et sécurité routière
Membre(s) du bureau directeur: Alain Lajoie, Directeur général

Vintage Locomotive Society Inc.
PO Box 33021, RPO Polo Park, Winnipeg MB R3G 3N4
Tel: 204-832-5259; *Fax:* 866-751-2348
info@pdcrailway.com
www.pdcrailway.com
Also Known As: Prairie Dog Central Steam Train
Overview: A small local charitable organization founded in 1968
Description: To collect, restore for operation & maintain steam locomotives & rolling stock of early part of twentieth-century; to provide source of historical information relating to origin & past operation of acquired equipment & buildings
Chief Officer(s): Paul Newsome, General Manager
Finances: *Annual Operating Budget:* $250,000-$500,000
Staff: 170 volunteer(s)
Membership: 170 individuals; *Fees:* $25 full; $15 junior; $40 family; *Committees:* Restoration-Locomotive; Restoration-Coaches; Painting; Sign Work; Public Relations; Advertising; Photography; Operations & Maintenance
Activities: *Speaker Service:* Yes

West Coast Railway Association (WCRA)
PO Box 2790, Stn. Term., Vancouver BC V6B 3X2
Tel: 604-681-4403; *Fax:* 604-876-4104
Toll-Free: 800-722-1233
info@wcra.org
www.wcra.org
Overview: A small local charitable organization founded in 1961
Description: Collects, preserves, restores, operates & exhibits artifacts relating to the history of railways, especially those of BC; the West Coast Railway Heritage Park in Squamish BC develops educational exhibits on railway heritage for all age groups; the tour program encourages the public to travel today's railways to see Canada; *Member of:* Association of Rail Museums; Tourist Railroad Association
Chief Officer(s): Gerry Burgess, Executive Director
board@wcra.org
Finances: *Annual Operating Budget:* $500,000-$1.5 Million; *Funding Sources:* Tours; government grants; donations; fundraising; foundation
Staff: 12 staff member(s); 150 volunteer(s)
Membership: 1500; *Fees:* Schedule available; *Member Profile:* Interest in railways past & present; *Committees:* Museum; Tours; Collections; Motive Power; Children; Education
Activities: Develops & operates West Coast Railway Heritage Park in Squamish B.C. - collection of over 60 locomotives, freight & passenger cars; operates tour progrm; other community event; Day out with Thoma, June; *Speaker Service:* Yes; *Library:* Archives (Open to Public) by appointment

Western Transportation Advisory Council (WESTAC)
#401, 899 Pender St. West, Vancouver BC V6C 3B2
Tel: 604-687-8691; *Fax:* 604-687-8751
infoservices@westac.com
www.westac.com
Social Media:
linkedin.com/company/2275285?trk=tyah
www.facebook.com/181099878620851
twitter.com/WESTAC
Overview: A small local organization founded in 1973
Description: To advance Western Canadian economy through the improvement of the region's transportation system.
Chief Officer(s): Lisa Baratta, Director, Strategy
Ruth Sol, President
Marcella Szel, Chairman (Executive Committee)
Lois Jackson, Chairman of the Board
Finances: *Annual Operating Budget:* $500,000-$1.5 Million; *Funding Sources:* Membership fees; project fees; professional services fees
Staff: 4 staff member(s)
Membership: 52 corporate; *Fees:* Revenue-related scale; *Member Profile:* Carriers; shippers; ports & terminals; labour unions; government
Activities: *Library:* Yes by appointment

Companies

Airline Companies

Aer Lingus
#130, 300 Jericho Quadrangle, Jericho, NY 11753
Tel: 516-622-4222; *Fax:* 516-622-4281
www.flyaerlingus.com

Aerolineas Argentinas
#1500, 701 West Georgia St., Vancouver, BC V7Y 1C6
Tel: 604-937-2507; *Fax:* 604-937-2502
Toll-Free: 800-688-0008
arcanada@destinosenterprises.com
www.aerolineas.com.ar

Air Canada
Air Canada Centre, 7373, boul Côte-Vertu Ouest, Montréal, QC H4S 1Z3
Tél: 514-422-5000; *Ligne sans frais:* 888-247-2262
shareholders.actionnaires@aircanada.ca
www.aircanada.ca
Ticker Symbol: AC / TSX
Profile: Scheduled air transportation; Travel agencies; Arrangement of transportation of freight & cargo
Calin Rovinescu, President & CEO
Michael Rousseau, Executive Vice-President & CFO
Klaus Goersch, Executive Vice-President & COO

Air Creebec
18 Nottaway St., Waskaganish, QC J0M 1R0
Tél: 819-825-8375; *Ligne sans frais:* 800-567-6567
www.aircreebec.ca
Profile: Air Creebec is 100% owned by the Cree Nation of Quebec. It flys passengers within Eeyou Istchee.
Matthew Happyjack, President

Air France
#1510, 2000 rue Mansfield, Montreal, QC H3A 3A3
Tel: 514-847-1106; *Toll-Free:* 800-667-2747
www.airfrance.ca

Air India Ltd.
#218, 5955 Airport Rd., Mississauga, ON L4V 1R9
Tel: 905-405-2160; *Fax:* 905-405-2169
Toll-Free: 800-625-6424
yyz@airindiacanada.ca
www.airindia.com
Rohit Nandan, Chairman & Managing Director, Air India
S. Venkat, Director, Finance
Pankaj Srivastava, Director, Commercial

Air Nootka
PO Box 19, 800 Mill Rd., Gold River, BC V0P 1G0
Tel: 250-283-2255; *Fax:* 250-283-2256
Toll-Free: 877-795-2255
info@airnootka.com
www.airnootka.com
Profile: Air Nootka is a floatplane operation based out of Gold River, British Columbia. It provides service to all of Vancouver Island, including Victoria, Nanaimo, Comox, Campbell River & Kyuquot, as well as Vancouver.
Ron Sine, Owner

Air North Airlines
150 Condor Rd., Whitehorse, YK Y1A 6E6
Tel: 867-668-2228; *Fax:* 867-393-4601
Toll-Free: 800-661-0407
customerservice@flyairnorth.com
www.flyairnorth.com
Profile: Service connects to Vancouver, Calgary & Edmonton; charter & cargo services are also offered

Air Saint-Pierre
PO Box 4225, 18, rue Albert Briand, 97500
Toll-Free: 877-277-7765
contact@airsaintpierre.com
www.airsaintpierre.com

Air Transat
Parent: Transat A.T. Inc.
Tour Transat, #600, 300 Léo-Pariseau St., Montréal, QC H2X 4C2
Tel: 514-987-1616; *Toll-Free:* 800-387-2672
customerrelations@transat.com
www.transat.com
Profile: Air Transat is a wholly owned subsidiary of Transat A.T. Inc. They specialize in both scheduled & charter flights from Canada to vacation destinations. In the winter months, the majority of flights are between Canada to vacation desintations. In the winter months, the majority of flights are between Canada & the Caribbean/USA & in the summer between Canada & many European countries. Year-round schedule services operate between Europe & Canada. The Air Transat fleet of 15 aircraft serves over 90 destinations in 25 countries.
Jean-Marc Eustache, President & CEO

Alitalia
Pearson International Airport, PO Box 188, Mississauga, ON L5P 1B1
Tel: 905-364-4166; *Fax:* 905-673-6089
Toll-Free: 800-361-8336
www.alitalia.ca

American Airlines Inc. / AA
Fort Worth Airport, PO Box 619616, Dallas, TX
Tel: 817-931-3423; *Toll-Free:* 800-433-7300
www.aa.com

Austrian Airlines
c/o Pearson Internatinoal Airport, Mississauga, ON L5P 1A2
Toll-Free: 800-563-5954
www.austrian.com

British Airways
c/o British Airways Customer Relations, USA, PO Box 300686, Jamaica, NY
Toll-Free: 800-247-9297
www.britishairways.com

CanJet Airlines
Parent: IMP Group Ltd.
PO Box 980, Enfield, NS B2T 1R6
Fax: 902-873-6580
Toll-Free: 800-809-7777
www.canjet.com

Central Mountain Air Ltd. / CMA
Formerly: Central Mountain International
PO Box 998, 6431 Airport Rd., Smithers, BC V0J 2N0
Tel: 250-877-5000; *Fax:* 250-874-3744
Toll-Free: 888-865-8585
info@flycma.com
www.flycma.com
Profile: Centreal Mountain Air was established in 1987 & offers scheduled & charter flights to over 18 communities in British Columbia & Alberta.
Douglas McCrea, President

CHC Helicopter Corporation
4740 Agar Dr., Richmond, BC V7B 1A3
Tel: 604-276-7500
commercial@chc.ca
www.chc.ca
Ticker Symbol: FLY / TSX
Profile: Nonscheduled & scheduled air transportation; Airports, flying fields & airport terminal services; Vocational schools
Karl S. Fessenden, President & CEO
Lee Eckert, CFO & Sr. Vice-President, Finance

Cougar Helicopters Inc.
Parent: VIH Aviation Group
St. John's International Airport, PO Box 21300, St. John's, NL A1A 5G6
Tel: 709-758-4800; *Fax:* 709-758-4850
info@cougar.ca
www.cougar.ca
Profile: The company's main service is flying oil rig workers to & from their offshore locations, with search & rescue as a secondary service provided to offshore operators.
Hank Williams, General Manager

Cubana
c/o Canada (GSA CGO) Exp-Air Cargo, #206, 675 King St. West, Toronto, ON M5V 1M9
Tel: 416-967-2822; *Fax:* 416-967-2824
Toll-Free: 866-428-2262
ventastoronto@cubanaairlines.ca
www.cubana.cu

Czech Airlines
#830, 5915 Airport Rd., Mississauga, ON L4V 1T1
Fax: 416-972-0185
Toll-Free: 855-359-2932
www.czechairlines.com
Shekhar Ramamoorthy, Contact
sramamoorthy@aviaworldna.com

Discovery Air Innovations / DAI
#201, 1675 Trans Canada Hwy., Montréal, QC H9P 1J1
Tél: 514-694-5565; *Téléc:* 514-694-3580
Ligne sans frais: 866-694-5565
www.discoveryair-ds.com
Ticker Symbol: DA.A; DA.B. / TSX
Profile: DAI is a specialty aviation company that provides air transport, maintenance, & logistics services for its clients in government & business. It was founded in 2004 & currently has 150 aircraft operated & maintained by 850 employees.

El Al Israel Airlines
#803, 1000 Finch Ave. West, Toronto, ON M3J 2V5
Tel: 416-967-4222; *Fax:* 416-967-1643
ca.reservations@elal.co.il
www.elal.co.il

Fast Air Ltd.
80 Hangar Line Rd., Winnipeg, MB R3J 3Y7
Tel: 204-982-7240; *Fax:* 204-783-2483
Toll-Free: 888-372-3780
info@flyfastair.com
www.flyfastair.com
Profile: Fast Air operates from a private business-class terminal at the Winnipeg James Armstrong Richardson International Airport, & provides aircraft charter, air ambulance & aircraft management services.
Dylan Fast, President

Finnair G.S.A Canada
PO Box 15, Finnair
Toll-Free: 800-950-5000
www.finnair.com

First Air
20 Cope Dr., Kanata, ON K2M 2V8
Tel: 613-254-6200; *Fax:* 613-254-6398
Toll-Free: 800-267-1247
contact@firstair.ca
www.firstair.ca
Profile: Specializes in travel to Northern Canada. First Air offers scheduled service to 29 destinations in Nunavut, Northwest

Territories, Manitoba, Alberta, Yukon, Quebec, and Ontario. The Inuit owned airline has over 1,000 employees.
Brock Friesen, President & CEO
Vic Charlebois, Vice-President, Flight Operations
Rashwan Domloge, Vice-President, Maintenance
Bert van der Stege, Vice-President, Commercial
Alexandra Pontbriand, Vice-President, Finance

Harbour Air Ltd.
4760 Inglis Dr., Richmond, BC V7B 1W4
Tel: 604-274-1277; *Toll-Free:* 800-665-0212
www.harbour-air.com
Profile: Harbour Air operates Harbour Air Seaplanes, West Coast Air & Whistler Air, all companies providing sea plane service connecting Vancouver, Victoria, Nanaimo, South Vancouver, Sechelt, Comox & the Gulf Islands. Adventure tours & charter services are also offered.
Greg McDougall, Chief Executive Officer

Helijet International Inc.
c/o Vancouver International Airport, 5911 Airport Rd. South, Richmond, BC V7B 1B5
Tel: 604-273-4688
www.helijet.com
Profile: Helijet are the first scheduled helicopter service in Canada & since their inception in 1986, they now have a fleet of 10 helicopters & airplanes with a staff of over 100 employees. They also have cargo services which ship time sensitive envelops & packages with speed & reliability.
Daniel Sitnam, President & CEO
dsitnam@helijet.com

Icelandair
1900 Crown Colony Dr., Quincy, MA 02169
Toll-Free: 800-223-5500
www.icelandair.com
Birkir Hólm Guonason, CEO
Hlynur Elisson, Senior Vice-President, Finance & Administration
Jen Bjarnason, Senior Vice-President, Operations
Helgi Már Björgvinsson, Senior Vice-President, Marketing & Sales

Japan Airlines
c/o Vancouver International Airport, #C3152.0B, Richmond, BC V7B 1X8
Toll-Free: 800-525-3663
www.japanair.com
Yoshiharu Ueki, President

Jazz Aviation LP
Formerly: Air Canada Jazz
Parent: Chorus Aviation Inc.
3 Spectacle Lake Dr., Dartmouth, NS B3B 1W8
Tel: 902-873-5000; *Fax:* 902-873-2098
www.flyjazz.ca
Profile: The core of Jazz's business is the Air Canada Express brand, which operates under a commercial agreement with Air Canada. The airline operates approximately 800 daily flights to 74 locations across North America.
Joseph (Joe) D. Randell, President & CEO
Colin Copp, Chief Administrative Officer

Keewatin Air LP
50 Morberg Way, Winnipeg, MB R3H 0A4
Tel: 204-888-0100; *Fax:* 204-888-3300
Toll-Free: 877-879-8477
www.kivalliqair.com
Profile: Keewatin Air's primary function is medical air travel, although they also offer charter & scheduled airline services to Nunavut & northern Manitoba.
Wayne McLeod, President & CEO
wmcleod@keewatinair.ca
Brian Hodge, Director, Finance
bhodge@keewatinair.ca

KF Cargo
Parent: KF Aerospace
5655 Airport Way, Kelowna, BC V1V 1S1
Tel: 250-491-5500
www.kfaero.ca/cargo-operations
Profile: KF Cargo is a dedicated carrier for Canada Post & Purolator Courier.
Len Carrado, Cargo Operations Manager

KLM Royal Dutch Airlines
Formerly: Northwest/KLM Royal Dutch Airlines
235 King St. East, Kitchener, ON N2G 4N5
Toll-Free: 800-375-8723
www.klm.com

Korean Air
1813 Wilshire Blvd., Los Angeles, CA 90057
Toll-Free: 800-438-5000
www.koreanair.com

LAN Airlines
Formerly: LanChile
#256, 5945 Airport Rd., Missisauga, ON L4V 1R9
Toll-Free: 866-435-9526
www.lan.com

LOT Polish Airlines
Pearson International Airport, Terminal 1, 3111 Convair Dr., Mississauga, ON L5P 1B2
Tel: 416-236-4242
www.lot.com
Sebastian Mikosz, President & CEO

Lufthansa German Airlines
PO Box 1588 Stn. Main, Peterborough, ON K9J 7H7
Toll-Free: 800-563-5954
www.lufthansa.com

Northern Thunderbird Air Inc.
#101, 4245 Hangar Rd., Prince George, BC V2N 4M6
Tel: 250-963-9611; *Fax:* 250-963-8422
Toll-Free: 800-963-9611
www.ntair.ca

Olympic Air
www.olympicair.com

Pacific Coastal Airlines
c/o Vancouver International Airport, #204, 4440 Cowely Cres., Richmond, BC V7B 1B8
Tel: 604-273-8666; *Fax:* 604-273-6864
reserve@pacificcoastal.com
www.pacificcoastal.com
Profile: Pacific Coastal Airlines operates 13 bases & a fleet of 21 aircraft.
Daryl Smith, CEO & Founder

PIA Pakistan International Airlines
#620, 56 Aberfoyle Cres., Toronto, ON M8X 2W4
Tel: 416-972-6480; *Fax:* 416-926-0507
ytouupk@piac.aero
www.piac.com.pk
Nasser N.S. Jaffer, Chairman
Shahnawaz Rehman, Managing Director

Royal Jordanian
Pierre Elliot Trudeau Airport, #441, 975, boul Roméo-Vachon Nord, Dorval, QC H4Y 1H1
Tél: 514-288-1647; *Téléc:* 514-631-9859
www.rj.com
Abdelmajid Elhoussami, Contact, Canada
Abdelmajid.Elhoussami@rj.com

Skyservice Airlines Inc.
6120 Midfield Rd., Mississauga, ON L4W 2P7
Tel: 905-677-3000; *Fax:* 905-677-2747
Toll-Free: 888-759-3269
toronto@skyservice.com
www.skyservice.com

Swiss International Air Lines
#800, 1555 Peel St., Montréal, ON H3A 3L8
Toll-Free: 877-359-7947
www.swiss.com
Olivier Schlegel, General Manager

Trans North Helicopters
PO Box 8, 115 Range Rd., Whitehorse, YK Y1A 5X9
Tel: 867-668-2177; *Fax:* 867-668-3420
email@tntaheli.com
www.tntaheli.com
Arden Meyer, General Manager
Clint Walker, Operations Manager
Charlie Hoeller, Director of Maintenance
Stephen Soubliere, Chief Pilot
Diane Pachiorka, Manager, Administration & Accouting

Transat A.T. Inc.
Place du Parc, #600, 300, rue Léo-Pariseau, Montréal, QC H2X 4C2
Tél: 514-987-1616; *Ligne sans frais:* 800-387-2672
www.transat.com
Ticker Symbol: TRZ.B / TSX
Profile: Offices of holding companies; Air transportation, scheduled; Travel agencies; Airports, flying fields, & airport terminal services; Tour operators
Jean-Marc Eustache, Chair, President & CEO
Denis Pétrin, Vice-President & CFO, Finance & Administration
Michel Bellefeuille, Vice-President & CIO

United Airlines
Formerly: Continental Airlines
233 South Wacker Dr., Chicago, IL
www.united.com
Profile: Subsidary company: Continental Mirconesia, Inc.
Jeffrey Smisek, President & CEO
Gregory Hart, Executive Vice-President & COO
Thomas O'Toole, Senior Vice-President & Chief Marketing Officer
Gerald Laderman, Acting CFO & Senior Vice-President, Finance
Howard Attarian, Senior Vice-President, Flight Operations
Linda Jojo, Executive Vice-President & Chief Information Officer
Irene Foxhall, Executive Vice-President, Communications & Government Affairs
Dave Hilfman, Senior Vice-President, Worldwide Sales

VIH Aviation Group
1962 Canso Rd., North Saanich, BC V8L 5V5
Tel: 250-656-3987; *Fax:* 250-655-6839
Toll-Free: 866-844-4354
vih@vih.com
www.vih.com
Profile: VIH is a helicopter management company, with operations in the following divisions: Cougar Helicopters; VIH Helicopters; VIH Aerospace; YYJ FBO Services; & VIH Execujet. VIH Helicopters Ltd. can be contacted at the Group head office address.
Ken Norie, President/CEO
Charlie Mooney, Senior Vice-President, Finance & Chief Financial Officer

VIH Execujet Inc.
Parent: VIH Aviation Group
Victoria International Airport, #101, 1962 Canso Rd., North Saanich, BC V8L 5V5
Toll-Free: 800-277-5421
charter@vih.com
www.vihexecujet.com
Profile: VIH Execujet operates executive-class jet charter services out of Victoria International Airport.
Jeff Wolfe, Operations Manager/Chief Pilot

WestJet Airlines Ltd.
22 Aerial Pl. NE, Calgary, AB T2E 3J1
Tel: 403-444-2600; *Fax:* 403-444-2604
Toll-Free: 888-937-8538
www.westjet.com
Ticker Symbol: WJA / TSX
Profile: Scheduled air transportation throughout North America.
Gregg Saretsky, President & CEO

Airport Authorities

Aéroport de Québec Inc. / ADQ
505, rue Principale, 2e étage, Québec, QC G2G 0J4
Tel: 418-640-3300; *Toll-Free:* 877-769-2700
www.aeroportdequebec.com
Profile: Aéroport de Québec Inc. is responsible for the operation of Jean Lesage International Airport in Québec City, which serves around 1.3 million passengers annually.
Gaëtan Gagné, LLIF. C. Dir. ASCPresident & CEO

Aéroports de Montréal / ADM
#1000, 800, place Leigh-Capreol, Montréal, QC H4Y 0A5
Tel: 514-394-7377; *Toll-Free:* 800-465-1213
www.admtl.com
Profile: Aéroports de Montréal is responsible for managing & operating the Montréal-Trudeau & Montréal-Mirabel international airports. Montréal-Trudeau serves around 13.8 million passengers annually, while Montréal-Mirabel is currently used only for cargo shipments, having lost its last passenger service in 2004.
James C. Cherry, President & CEO

The Calgary Airport Authority
2000 Airport Rd. NE, Calgary, AB T2E 6W5
Tel: 403-735-1200; *Fax:* 403-735-1281
Toll-Free: 877-254-7427
www.calgaryairport.com
Profile: The Calgary Airport Authority operates Calgary International Airport, which serves around 14.3 million passengers annually. Flights are offered to major cities in Canada, the USA, Mexico, the Caribbean, Europe & East Asia.
Garth F. Atkinson, President & CEO

Charlottetown Airport Authority / CAA
#132, 250 Maple Hills Ave., Charlottetown, PE C1C 1N2
Tel: 902-566-7997; *Fax:* 902-566-7929
www.flypei.com
Profile: The Charlottetown Airport Authority operates & is financially responsible for the Charlottetown Airport, which

provides flights to Montreal, Halifax, Toronto, New York, & seasonal flights to Cuba & the Dominican Republic.
Doug Newson, Chief Executive Officer

Edmonton Airports
Aéroports d'Edmonton
Formerly: Edmonton Regional Airports Authority
Edmonton International Airport, #1, 1000 Airport Rd., Edmonton, AB T9E 0V3
Tel: 780-890-8900; *Fax:* 780-890-8329
Toll-Free: 800-268-7134
info@flyeia.com
www.flyeia.com
Profile: Edmonton Airports operates Edmonton International Airport, which offers flights to 50 destinations worldwide & serves around 6.5 million passengers annually.
Tom Ruth, President & CEO

Fredericton International Airport Authority Inc. / FIAA
Formerly: Greater Fredericton Airport Authority Inc.
#22, 2570 Route 102 Hwy., Lincoln, NB E3B 9G1
Tel: 506-460-0920; *Fax:* 506-460-0938
www.frederictonairport.ca
Profile: The Fredericton International Airport Authority operates Fredericton International Airport, which provides flights to Halifax, Montréal, Ottawa, Toronto, & seasonal flights to Cuba & the Dominican Republic.
Johanne Gallant, President & CEO

Gander International Airport Authority Inc. / GIAA
PO Box 400, 1000 James Boul., Gander, NL A1V 1W8
Tel: 709-256-6668; *Fax:* 709-256-6725
www.ganderairport.com
Profile: The Gander International Airport Authority operates Gander International Airport, which provides flights to Toronto, Goose Bay, Sept-Iles, St. John's, Wabush, Halifax & Iqaluit. Charter flights are also available to the Dominican Republic.
Reg Wright, President & CEO

Greater London International Airport Authority / GLIAA
1750 Crumlin Rd., London, ON N5V 3B6
Tel: 519-452-4015; *Fax:* 519-453-6219
info@londonairport.on.ca
flylondon.ca
Profile: The Greater London International Airport Authority operates London International Airport, which provides flights to Ottawa, Toronto, Montréal, Chicago, Calgary, Winnipeg, & seasonal flights to Orlando, Mexico & Cuba.
Mike Seabrook, President & CEO

Greater Moncton International Airport Authority Inc. / GMIAA
Direction de l'Aéroport international du Grand Moncton Inc.
#12, 777 Aviation Ave., Dieppe, NB E1A 7Z5
Tel: 506-856-5444; *Fax:* 506-856-5431
admin@cyqm.ca
www.cyqm.ca
Profile: The Greater Moncton International Airport Authority operates Greater Moncton International Airport, which provides flights to Halifax, Montréal, Toronto, Ottawa, Hamilton, & seasonal flights to Florida, Mexico, Cuba, the Dominican Republic & Jamaica.
Bernard LeBlanc, President & CEO
bleblanc@cyqm.ca

Greater Toronto Airports Authority / GTAA
Autorité aéroportuaire du Grand Toronto
Toronto Pearson International Airport, PO Box 6031, 3111 Convair Dr., Mississauga, ON L5P 1B2
Tel: 416-776-3000
www.torontopearson.com/gtaa.aspx
Profile: The Greater Toronto Airports Authority operates Toronto Pearson International Airport, which provides flights to over 155 locations worldwide via 65 airlines, & serves around 38.6 million passengers annually, making it the busiest airport in Canada.
Howard Eng, President & CEO

Halifax International Airport Authority / HIAA
Halifax Stanfield International Airport, 1 Bell Blvd., Enfield, NS B2T 1K2
Tel: 902-873-4422; *Fax:* 902-873-4750
info@hiaa.ca
www.hiaa.ca
Profile: The Halifax International Airport Authority operates Halifax Stanfield International Airport provides flights to a number of national & international destinations.
Joyce Carter, President & CEO

Ottawa International Airport Authority
Administration de l'aéroport international d'Ottawa
#2500, 1000 Airport Pkwy. Private, Ottawa, ON K1V 9B4
Tel: 613-248-2000
ottawa-airport.ca
Profile: The Ottawa International Airport Authority operates Ottawa Macdonald-Cartier International Airport offers flights to a number of national & international destinations.
Mark Laroche, President & CEO

Prince George Airport Authority Inc. / PGAA
#10, 4141 Airport Rd., Prince George, BC V2N 4M6
Tel: 250-963-2400
www.pgairport.ca
Profile: The Prince George Airport Authority operates Prince George Airport, which provides flights to locations in BC (such as Vancouver, Fort Nelson, Kamloops, Fort St. John, Terrace, Kelowna, Smithers & Williston Lake), as well as seasonal service to Mexico.
John Gibson, President & CEO
jgibson@pgairport.ca

Regina Airport Authority Inc. / RAA
#1, 5201 Regina Ave., Regina, SK S4W 1B3
Tel: 306-761-7555
comments@yqr.ca
www.yqr.ca
Profile: The Regina Airport Authority operates Regina International Airport, which provides flights to Toronto, Calgary, Edmonton, Vancouver, Winnipeg, Montréal, Ottawa, Saskatoon, Minneapolis/St. Paul, Chicago, & seasonal flights to Las Vegas, Phoenix, Mexico, Jamaica, the Dominican Republic & Cuba.
Dick Graham, President & CEO
rgraham@yqr.ca

Saint John Airport Inc.
Aéroport de Saint John Inc.
4180 Loch Lomond Rd., Saint John, NB E2N 1L7
Tel: 506-638-5555
fly@sjairport.ca
www.saintjohnairport.com
Profile: Saint John Airport provides flights to Halifax, Montreal, Toronto, & seasonal flights to the Dominican Republic, Mexico, Cayo Santa Maria, & Cuba.
David Allen, President & CEO
dallen@sjairport.ca

St. John's International Airport Authority Inc. / SJIAA
Airport Terminal Bldg., PO Box 1, 100 World Pkwy., St. John's, NL A1A 5T2
Tel: 709-758-8500; *Fax:* 709-758-8521
Toll-Free: 866-758-8581
www.stjohnsairport.com
Profile: The St. John's International Airport Authority operates St. John's International Airport, which provides flights to major destinations in Canada, as well as seasonal service to London, UK, & locations such as the Dominican Republic, Cuba & Mexico. Charter service to the Alberta Oil Sands is also available.
Keith Collins, President & CEO

Saskatoon Airport Authority / SAA
#1, 2625 Airport Dr., Saskatoon, SK S7L 7L1
Tel: 306-975-8900
yxe.ca
Profile: The Saskatoon Airport Authority operates Saskatoon John G. Diefenbaker International Airport, which serves around 1.4 million passengers annually. Flights are offered to major Canadian destinations, with an emphasis on western Canada & locations in the USA.
Stephen Maybury, President & CEO

Thunder Bay International Airports Authority Inc. / TBIAA
#340, 100 Princess St., Thunder Bay, ON P7E 6S2
Tel: 807-473-2600; *Fax:* 807-475-9627
info@tbairport.on.ca
www.tbairport.on.ca
Profile: The Thunder Bay International Airports Authority operates Thunder Bay International Airport, which provides flights to major Canadian cities & Chicago, as well as seasonal service to Cuba & Mexico.
Ed Schmidtke, President & CEO

Vancouver International Airport Authority
PO Box 23750 Stn. Airport, Richmond, BC V7B 1Y7
Tel: 604-207-7077
www.yvr.ca
Profile: The Vancouver International Airport Authority operates Vancouver International Airport, which serves around 19.36 million passengers annually, making it the second busist airport in Canada (behind Toronto Pearson International Airport). Flights are available to major destinations in Canada & around the world.
Craig Richmond, President & CEO

Victoria Airport Authority / VAA
#201, 1640 Electra Blvd., Sidney, BC V8L 5V4
Tel: 250-953-7500; *Fax:* 250-953-7509
www.victoriaairport.com
Profile: The Victoria Airport Authority operates Victoria International Airport, which serves around 1.5 million passengers annually. Flights are provided to major cities in Canada, as well as cities such as Seattle & San Francisco in the continental USA, & seasonal flights to Mexico & Hawaii.
Geoff Dickson, President & CEO
geoff.dickson@victoriaairport.com

Winnipeg Airports Authority Inc. / WAA
#249, 2000 Wellington Ave., Winnipeg, MB R3H 1C2
Tel: 204-987-9400; *Fax:* 204-987-2732
reception@waa.ca
www.waa.ca
Profile: The Winnipeg Airports Authority operates Winnipeg James Armstrong Richardson International Airport. Flights are offered to major cities Canada, the USA, the Caribbean & Mexico, as well as to many remote communities in Northern Manitoba, Northwestern Ontario & Nunavut.
Barry Rempel, President & CEO

Maritime Shipping

Admiral Marine Inc.
6127 Steeles Ave. West, Toronto, ON M9L 2V1
Tel: 416-792-8955; *Fax:* 888-635-0247
admiral@admiralmarine.ca
www.admiralmarine.ca
Profile: Canstar Ocean Line through Admiral Marine operate a regular break-bulk/conventional service from North America to Europe with transshipment via Antwerp to Eastern Europe, the Middle East and Africa. Canstar is a full service transportation consulting company that specializes in the shipment of over-dimensional, ro.ro, break-bulk, heavy lift, and project cargoes.

Algoma Central Corporation
#600, 63 Church St., St Catharines, ON L2R 3C4
Tel: 905-687-7888; *Fax:* 905-687-7840
Inquiry@algonet.com
www.algonet.com
Ticker Symbol: ALC / TSX
Profile: Algoma Central Corporation operates vessels throughout the Great Lakes-St. Lawrence Waterway from the Gulf of St. Lawrence, through all 5 Great Lakes. The corporation owns 19 Canadian-flagged dry-bulk vessels. The operational & commercial activities of the Canadian-flag dry-bulk team are managed by Seaway Marine Transport, a partnership with Upper Great Lakes Shipping Inc., an unrelated company. The Corporation also has an interest in one tug & one barge.
Ken Bloch Soerensen, FCAPresident & CEO
Peter D. Winkley, CACFO & Vice-President, Finance
Dennis J.A. McPhee, Vice-President, Sales & Traffic
Wesley Newton, Secretary & General Counsel

American President Lines Ltd.
APL Canada, #828, 10 Four Seasons Pl., Toronto, ON M9B 6H7
Tel: 416-620-7790; *Fax:* 416-620-7723
www.apl.com
Profile: APL provides customers around the world with container transportation services through a network combining high-quality intermodal operations with state-of-the-art information technology.
Kenneth Glen, President

Anglo-Eastern Group
Formerly: Anglo-Eastern Ship Management Ltd.
#235, 6600, rte Trans-Canada, Pointe Claire, QC H9R 4S2
Tél: 514-697-3091; *Téléc:* 514-697-3048
aesm.mtl@angloeasterngroup.com
www.angloeasterngroup.com
Profile: Currently the Anglo-Eastern Group looks after a varied fleet and crew base trading and operates worldwide.
Peter Cremers, Chief Executive Officer

Atlantic Towing Limited / ATL
Parent: J.D. Irving, Limited
300 Union St., 2nd Fl., Saint John, NB E2L 4M3
Tel: 506-648-2750; *Fax:* 506-648-2752
www.atlantictowing.com
Profile: ATL provides marine towing services including harbour, coastal, & offshore.

Mary Keith, Vice-President, Communications, J.D. Irving, Limited
506-632-5122, keith.mary@jdirving.com

Canada Steamship Lines Inc.
Parent: The CSL Group
759 Victoria Square, 6th Fl., Montreal, QC H2Y 2K3
Tel: 514-982-3800; *Fax:* 514-982-3901
www.cslships.com
Profile: Canada Steamship Lines' fleet includes self-unloaders & gearless bulk carriers.
Louis Martel, President
Claude Dumais, Vice President, Technical Operations
Kirk Jones, Director, Sustainability, Government & Industry Affairs

CMA CGM (Canada) Inc.
Parent: CMA CGM S.A.
#850, 5915 Airport Rd., Mississauga, ON L4V 1T1
Tel: 905-362-2272; *Fax:* 905-362-2273
cda.genmbox@cma-cgm.com
www.cma-cgm.com/local/canada
Profile: CMA CGM provides container shipping & multimodal services.
Nelum Attanayake, General Manager, CMA CGM Logistics, Canada

The CSL Group
759 Victoria Square, 6th Fl., Montreal, QC H2Y 2K3
Tel: 514-982-3800; *Fax:* 514-982-3801
www.cslships.com
Profile: Specializes in bulk transportation & self-loading technology
Rod Jones, President & CEO
Louis Martel, Executive Vice-President

F.K. Warren Ltd.
PO Box 1117, Halifax, NS B3J 3X1
Tel: 902-423-8136; *Fax:* 902-429-1326
www.fkwarren.ca
Profile: F.K. Warren provides a range of Marine Agency Services at all ports throughout Atlantic Canada.
Gordon Smith, President
gsmith@fkwarren.ca
Richard Danells, Vice-President
rdanells@fkwarren.ca

Fednav Group
Formerly: Fednav Limited
#3500, 1000, rue de la Gauchetière ouest, Montréal, QC H3B 4W5
Tel: 514-878-6500; *Toll-Free:* 800-678-4842
info@fednav.com
www.fednav.com
Profile: Deep sea foreign transportation of freight; Freight transportation on the Great Lakes-St.Lawrence Seaway; Marine cargo handling
Mark Pathy, President & co-CEO

Groupe Desgagnés Inc.
21, rue Marché-Champlain, Québec, QC G1K 8Z8
Tél: 418-692-1000; *Téléc:* 418-692-6044
info@desgagnes.com
www.groupedesgagnes.com
Profile: La flotte du Groupe Desgagnés comprend 14 navires et 1 barge, 6 navires pour le transport de marchandises en vrac générale et sec, 7 camions-citernes et une barge pour le transport de vracs liquides et 1 passager et fret aux navires desservant la rive Moyen et Bas du Nord.
Louis-Marie Beaulieu, Chef de la direction

Hapag-Lloyd (Canada) Inc.
Parent: Hapag-Lloyd AG
#1200, 3400, boul de Maisonneuve ouest, Montréal, QC H3Z 3E7
Téléc: 866-784-4282
Ligne sans frais: 877-893-4421
www.hapag-lloyd.com
Profile: Hapag-Lloyd is an international shipping company headquartered in Hamburg, Germany.
Wolfgang Schoch, Senior Vice-President
wolfgang.schoch@hlag.com

Holmes Maritime Inc.
1345 Hollis St., Halifax, NS B3J 1T8
Tel: 902-422-0400; *Fax:* 902-422-9439
info@holmesmaritime.com
www.holmesmaritime.com
Profile: Holmes Maritime Inc. is a privately owned Canadian headquartered in Halifax, Nova Scotia, providing port agency & logistics services to international ship owners & operators throughout eastern Canada & along the Great Lakes.
Louis Holmes, President

Kent Line Limited
Parent: J.D. Irving, Limited
PO Box 66, 300 Union St., Saint John, NB E2L 3X1
Tel: 506-632-1660; *Fax:* 506-634-4278
www.kentline.com
Profile: Kent Line provides maritime shipping services including bulk, project cargo, & agency. The company mainly serves the forest products, steel, fertilizer, grain, & construction industries.
Dave Keating, Supervisor, Operations
506-644-2576, keating.dave@kentline.com
Gordon Ferris, Director, Business Development
506-648-3119, ferris.gordon@kentline.com
Kevin Lagos, Manager, Kent Line Limited - Agency
506-648-2718, lagos.kevin@kentline.com

Logistec Corporation
#1500, 360 Saint-Jacques St., Montréal, QC H2Y 1P5
Tel: 514-844-9381
corp@logistec.com
www.logistec.com
Ticker Symbol: LGT.B / TSX
Profile: Deep sea foreign transportation of freight; Freight transportation on the Great Lakes & the St. Lawrence Seaway; Marine cargo handling; Various water transportation services; Refuse systems
Madeleine Paquin, President & CEO
Jean-Claude Dugas, Vice-President, Finance
Nicole Paquin, Vice-President, Information Systems

Marine Atlantic Inc.
Baine Johnston Centre, #302, 10 Fort William Pl., St. John's, NL A1C 1K4
Toll-Free: 800-897-2797
customer_relations@marine-atlantic.ca
www.marine-atlantic.ca
Profile: Deep sea domestic transportation of freight; Ferries; Various water transportation of passengers

Montship Inc.
#1000, 360, rue Saint-Jacques, Montreal, QC H2Y 1R2
Tél: 514-286-4646; *Téléc:* 514-286-4650
www.montship.ca
Profile: Montship Maritime Inc.'s objective is to ensure the outgoing competitiveness of Maritime operations, & to continue to provide service for Principals.
Bob Greer, General Manager
514-908-0001, rgreer@montship.ca
Dennis Merner, Port Superintendent
dmerner@montship.ca

Oceanex Inc.
#2550, 630 René-Lévesque Blvd. West, Montreal, QC H3B 1S6
Tel: 514-875-9244; *Fax:* 514-877-0200
www.oceanex.com
Profile: Oceanex provides cost-effective pick-up, handling & delivery of any cargo, including full-load & LTL.

Rigel Shipping Canada
PO Box 5151, Shediac, NB E4P 8T9
Tel: 506-533-9000; *Fax:* 506-533-9010
www.rigelcanada.com
Profile: The company provides safe, efficient, environmentally friendly & cost-effective marine transportation.
Brian Ritchie, President

Truck Freight International / TFI
Parent: Paterson GlobalFoods
333 Main St., 22nd Fl., Winnipeg, MB R3C 4E2
Tel: 204-956-3450; *Fax:* 204-942-4758
Toll-Free: 888-421-4433
info@truck-freight.com
www.truck-freight.com
Profile: Freight transportation of grains across western Canada & the United States.

Upper Lakes Group Inc.
#403, 250 Merton St., Toronto, ON M4S 1B1
Tel: 416-920-7610
www.upperlakes.com
Profile: Upper Lakes Group specializes in moving, handling, & storing wet & dry bulk commodoties & containerized cargoes in Canada & around the world.

Railroad Companies

Agence métropolitaine de transport / AMT
700, rue De La Gauchetière Ouest, Montréal, QC H2Y 2W2
Tél: 514-287-8726; *Ligne sans frais:* 888-702-8726
www.amt.qc.ca
Profile: 5 lignes de train de banlieue; 51 gares; 1 autobus express métropolitains; 61 stationnements incitatifs; 16 terminus métropolitains; 85.2 km de voies réservées
Nicolas Girard, Président-directeur général

Alberta Prairie Railway
PO Box 1600, Stettler, AB T0C 2L0
Tel: 403-742-2811; *Fax:* 403-742-2844
Toll-Free: 800-282-3994
info@absteamtrain.com
www.absteamtrain.com

Algoma Central Railway Inc. / ACR
Parent: Canadian National Railway Company
PO Box 130, 129 Bay St., Sault Ste Marie, ON P6A 6Y2
Tel: 705-946-7300; *Fax:* 705-541-2989
Toll-Free: 800-242-9287
www.agawacanyontourtrain.com
Profile: Algoma Central Railway offers the following services: the Agawa Canyon Tour Train, the Snow Train, Tour of the Line, Canyon View Camp Car, snowmobile excursions, Ecotours, lodging & special packages.

Big Sky Rail Corp.
Parent: Mobil Grain Ltd.
PO Box 3192, Regina, SK S4P 3G7
Tel: 306-992-5920; *Fax:* 306-992-5920
inquiries@bigskyrail.com
bigskyrail.com
Profile: This 400-km-long shortline railway is owned & operated by Mobil Grain, & consists of three subdivisions: Conquest, Elrose & Matador. The company's locomotives are also used by sister company Last Mountain Railway.

BNSF Railway Company
Formerly: Burlington Northern Sante Fe Railway
2650 Lou Menk Dr., Fort Worth, TX 76161-0056
Toll-Free: 800-795-2673
www.bnsf.com
Profile: 24,000 miles of track (30 miles in Canada); over 80,000 freight cars; 6,400 locomotives
Carl Ice, President & CEO

British Columbia Railway Company / BCRC
#600, 221 West Esplanade Ave., North Vancouver, BC V7M 3J3
Tel: 604-678-4735; *Fax:* 604-678-4736
www.bcrco.com
Profile: Offices of holding companies; Real estate operators of nonresidential buildings; Real estate agents & managers; Railroads, line-haul operating; Marine cargo handling
Gordon Westlake, President & CEO
604-678-4742
Kevin Steinberg, CFO & Vice-President, Finance
604-678-4747

Canadian National Railway Company / CN
935, rue de la Gauchetière ouest, Montréal, QC H3B 2M9
Ligne sans frais: 888-888-5909
www.cn.ca
Ticker Symbol: CNR / TSX
Profile: Railroads & line-haul operating; Railroad switching & terminal establishments. Founded in 1919.
Luc Jobin, President & CEO
Serge Leduc, Vice-President & CIO

Canadian Pacific Railway Limited
7550 Ogden Dale Rd. SE, Calgary, AB T2C 4X9
Tel: 403-319-7000; *Toll-Free:* 888-333-6370
www.cpr.ca
Ticker Symbol: CP / TSX, NYSE
Profile: Transcontinental carrier; Rail network operates in Canada & the USA. Founded in 1881.
Andrew Reardon, Chair
E. Hunter Harrison, Chief Executive Officer
Keith Creel, President & Chief Operating Officer
Timothy Marsh, Senior Vice-President, Sales & Marketing
Mark Erceg, Executive Vice-President & Chief Financial Officer

Cando Contracting Ltd.
#400, 740 Rosser Ave., Brandon, MB R7A 0K9
Tel: 204-725-2627; *Fax:* 204-725-4100
Toll-Free: 866-989-5310
info@candoltd.com
www.candoltd.com
Profile: Cando operates three shortlines in Canada: Barrie-Collingwood Railway, Central Manitoba Railway Inc. & Orangeville-Brampton Railway. The company also provides the following services: industrial rail, rail car storage, mechanical, transload, engineering & track & railway material sales.
Gord Peters, President
gord.peters@candoltd.com

Brent Mills, Chief Executive Officer
brent.mills@candoltd.com

Cape Breton & Central Nova Scotia Railway
PO Box 2240, 121 King St., Stellarton, NS B0K 1S0
Tel: 902-752-3357
www.gwrr.com

Shannon Toner, General Manager
902-752-3357 ext: 229

Cape Breton & Central Nova Scotia Railway / CBNS
Parent: Genesee & Wyoming Inc.
PO Box 2240, 121 King St., Stellarton, NS B0K 1S0
Tel: 902-752-3357; *Fax:* 888-641-2243
Toll-Free: 888-641-2175
cbns-cs@gwrr.com
www.gwrr.com
Profile: 245 miles of track stretching from Truro to Sydney; interchanges with CN & SCR; moves paper, coal, lumber, petrolum products & chemicals
Shannon Toner, General Manager
902-752-3357 ext: 229

Carlton Trail Railway Company / CTR
Parent: OmniTRAX, Inc.
1545 - 5th Ave. East, Prince Albert, SK S6V 7Z5
Tel: 306-763-9474; *Fax:* 306-763-9471
www.omnitrax.com
Profile: The company operates on 103 miles of former CN track & specializes in transporting lumber from the Prince Albert area.
Matt Jurgens, General Manager

Cartier Railway Company
Parent: Arcelor Mittal
#201, 24, boulevard des îles, Port-Cartier, QC G5B 2H3
Tél: 418-766-2000; *Téléc:* 418-768-2512
www.arcelormittal.com

Central Manitoba Railway / CEMR
Parent: Cando Contracting Ltd.
2675 Day St., Box 27 Grp 514, RR#5, Winnipeg, MB R2C 2Z2
Tel: 204-235-1175
info@candoltd.com
www.cemrr.com
Profile: The company owns & maintains 118 miles of track, & offers services such as transloading, track maintenance, locomotive repair, rail car repair & equipment leasing, storage & sales.
John Pennock, General Manager
john.pennock@candoltd.com

Chemin de fer St-Laurent et Atlantique / SL&A
St. Lawrence & Atlantic Railroad
Parent: Genesee & Wyoming Inc.
#201, 225 First Flight Dr., Auburn, ME 04210
Tel: 207-782-5680; *Fax:* 207-782-5857
www.gwrr.com
Profile: 260 miles of track between Maine & Québec; interchanges with CN & sister railroad Saint Lawrence & Atlantic Railroad; facilities served include warehouse distribution, intermodal & bulk transloading
Denys Del Cardo, General Manager
819-826-5640

Chemins de fer Québec-Gatineau Inc.
Quebec Gatineau Railway Inc.
Parent: Genesee & Wyoming Inc.
#600, 9001, boul de l'Acadie, Montréal, QC H4N 3H5
Tél: 514-948-6999
www.gwrr.com
Louis-Rene Pelletier, General Manager
450-420-7966, Fax: 450-435-0154

Compagnie du chemin de fer Lanaudière inc. / CFL
PO Box 2999, 5300, ch St-Gabriel, Saint-Félix-de-Valois, QC J0K 2M0
Tél: 450-889-5944; *Ligne sans frais:* 800-361-5598
www.cflanaudiere.com

CSX Transportation Inc.
500 Water St., 15th Fl., Jacksonville, FL 33202
Tel: 904-359-3200
www.csx.com
Profile: Operates trains that serve cities in Ontario & Quebec
Michael J. Ward, Chair, President & CEO

Essex Terminal Railway Co. / ETR
Parent: Essex Morterm Holdings
1601 Lincoln Rd., Windsor, ON N8Y 2J3
Tel: 519-973-8222; *Fax:* 519-973-7234
info@etr.ca
www.etr.ca
Profile: Freight only; 24 miles of main track; connections with CN, CP, CSX & NS; 5 locomotives; 5 cars
Terry J. Berthiaume, President & CEO
tjb@etr.ca

Fife Lake Railway Ltd. / FLR
Parent: Great Western Railway Ltd.
c/o Great Western Railway, PO Box 669, 254 Centre St., Shaunavon, SK S0N 2M0
Tel: 306-729-3073
Profile: Owned by 7 municipalities & Great Western Railway, Fife Lake operates on 62 miles of track in Assiniboia.
Vern Palmer, Contact

Genesee & Wyoming Inc. / G&W
20 West Ave., Darien, CT 06820
Tel: 203-202-8900; *Fax:* 203-656-1092
corpcomm@gwrr.com
www.gwrr.com
Profile: Genesee & Wyoming owns shortline & freight railroads in the USA, Canada, Australia, the Netherlands & Belgium. Canadian operations include: Cape Breton & Central Nova Scotia Railway; Goderich-Exeter Railway; Huron Central Railway; Ottawa Valley Railway; Southern Ontario Railway; St. Lawrence & Atlantic Railroad/St-Laurent & Atlantique Railroad; & Western Labrador Rail Services.
John C. Hellmann, President & CEO
Timothy J. Gallagher, Chief Financial Officer
David A. Brown, Chief Operating Officer

Goderich-Exeter Railway Company Ltd. / GEXR
Parent: Genesee & Wyoming Inc.
101 Shakespeare St., 2nd Fl., Stratford, ON N5A 3W5
Tel: 519-271-4441; *Fax:* 888-641-2243
Toll-Free: 888-641-2175
gexr-cs@gwrr.com
www.gwrr.com
Profile: 181 miles of track in Ontario; interchanges with CN & CP; moves salt, fertilizer, wheat, grains, soy meal, rice & automotive parts
Wesley Logan, General Manager
519-271-4441 ext: 1

Great Sandhills Railway / GSR
106 - 3rd St. West, Leader, SK S0N 1H0
Tel: 306-628-4774; *Fax:* 306-628-4772
Toll-Free: 866-938-4774
generaloffice@gsrail.ca
www.gsrail.ca
Profile: Great Sandhills Railway was established in 2009 & operates a shortline railway on a former CP subdivision.
Perry Pellerin, Chief Executive Officer
perrypellerin@gnptransportation.com

Great Western Railway Ltd. / GWR
PO Box 669, 254 Centre St., Shaunavon, SK S0N 2M0
Tel: 306-297-2777; *Fax:* 306-297-2508
www.greatwesternrail.com
Profile: Great Western Railway offers the following services: grain & related product transportation; transportation of oil products; & railcar storage. GWR also co-owns Fife Lake Railway, & services Red Coat Road & Rail.
Andrew Glastetter, General Manager
andrew.glastetter@greatwesternrail.com

Greater Winnipeg Water District Railway
c/o Water & Waste Department, City of Winnipeg, #109, 1199 Pacific Ave., Winnipeg, MB R3E 3S8
www.winnipeg.ca/waterandwaste/dept/railway.stm
Profile: The railway is owned by the City of Winnipeg & is used to transport workers & supplies to the city's aqueduct, & the water intake facility at Shoal Lake.

Hudson Bay Railway Company / HBRY
Parent: OmniTRAX, Inc.
PO Box 2129, 728 Bignell Ave., The Pas, MB R9A 1L8
Tel: 204-627-2007; *Fax:* 204-623-3095
www.omnitrax.com
Profile: The company owns & operates 627 miles of former CN track & runs from Manitoba to the Hudson Bay.
Chuck Walsh, General Manager

Huron Central Railway / HCR
Parent: Genesee & Wyoming Inc.
30 Oakland Ave., Sault Ste Marie, ON P6A 2T3
Tel: 705-254-4504; *Fax:* 705-254-5056
csc-bb@gwrr.com
www.gwrr.com
Profile: 173 miles of track; interchanges with CN & CP; moves pulp & paper, forest products, chemicals, petroluem products, steel & scrap
Alison Horbatuk, General Manager
ahorbatuk@gwrr.com

Keewatin Railway Company Ltd. / KRC
#710, 294 Portage Ave., Winnipeg, MB R3C 0B9
Tel: 204-942-2944; *Toll-Free:* 800-761-7110
www.krcrail.ca
Profile: Keewatin Railway is the second First Nations railway to be created with financial assistance from the Government of Canada. It operates on 185-mile stretch of track formerly belonging to Hudson Railway Company.
Anthony Mayham, Chief Executive Officer

Last Mountain Railway / LMR
Parent: Mobil Grain Ltd.
PO Box 3192, Regina, SK S4P 3G7
Tel: 306-992-5915; *Fax:* 306-992-5915
inquiries@lastmountainrailway.com
lastmountainrailway.com
Profile: Last Mountain Railway operates on a shortline track formerly owned by CN, that runs between Regina & Davidson. The company's locomotives are also used by sister company Big Sky Rail.

Long Creek Railroad
PO Box 40, Oungre, SK S0C 1Z0
Tel: 306-471-7791
Profile: Long Creek Railroad is community-owned & was established in 2012 with the help of an interest-free loan from the government of Saskatchewan. The railway operates on 66 miles of former CP track.

New Brunswick Southern Railway Company Limited / NBSR
Parent: J.D. Irving, Limited
PO Box 3189, 11 Gifford Rd., Saint John, NB E2M 4X8
Tel: 506-632-6314; *Fax:* 506-632-5818
Toll-Free: 877-838-6277
nbm.sales@nbmrailways.com
www.nbsouthern.com
Profile: NBSR is a short railway line specializing in truck/rail reloading for goods such as logs & lumber, wood chips, wood pulp, chemicals, & dry bulk.

Norfolk Southern Corp.
Three Commercial Place, Norfolk, VA 23510-9241
Toll-Free: 855-667-3655
www.nscorp.com
Ticker Symbol: NSC / NYSE
Profile: Operating Subsidiary: Norfolk Southern Railway Co.; 21,500 track miles (245 miles in Canada); 3,000 locomotives
Charles Moorman, Chairman & CEO
James A. Squires, President

OmniTRAX, Inc.
252 Clayton St., 4th Fl., Denver, CO 80206
Tel: 303-398-4500; *Fax:* 303-398-4540
info@omnitrax.com
www.omnitrax.com
Profile: OmniTRAX operates 17 regional & shortline railroads in 11 states & 3 provinces. The company has interests in railroads, terminals, ports & industrial real estate.
Kevin L. Shuba, Chief Executive Officer
Sergio A. Sabatini, COO

Ontario Northland Transportation Commission
555 Oak St. East, North Bay, ON P1B 8L3
Tel: 705-472-4500; *Fax:* 705-476-5598
Toll-Free: 800-363-7512
info@ontarionorthland.ca
www.ontarionorthland.ca
Profile: Owned by Province of Ontario; 26 locomotives; 700 cars
Corina Moore, President & CEO

Ontario Southland Railway Inc.
896 Cresthaven Cres., London, ON N6K 4W1
Tel: 519-471-9606; *Fax:* 519-471-7334
info@osrinc.ca
www.osrinc.ca

Orangeville Brampton Railway / OBRY
49 Town Line, Orangeville, ON L9W 1V1
Tel: 519-940-4204

Ottawa Valley Railway / OVR
Parent: Genesee & Wyoming Inc.
445 Oak St. East, North Bay, ON P1B 1A3
Tel: 705-472-6200; *Toll-Free:* 800-565-5715
ovr-cs@gwrr.com
www.gwrr.com
Profile: 150 miles of track between Ontario & Québec; interchanges with CP, ONTC & Ontario Northland; moves forest products & chemicals
Daryl Duquette, General Manager
705-472-6200 ext: 223

Port Stanley Terminal Rail / PSTR
309 Bridge St., Port Stanley, ON N5L 1C5
Tel: 519-782-3730; *Fax:* 519-782-4385
Toll-Free: 877-244-4478
info@pstr.on.ca
www.pstr.on.ca

Profile: An historic railway featuring four diesel electric locomotives from the 1940s & 50s, & nine passenger cars; the railway is maintained by volunteers.

Québec North Shore & Labrador Railway Company
Chemin de fer QNS&L
1 Retty St., Sept-Iles, QC G4R 3C7
Tél: 418-968-7603
www.qnsl.ca

Red Coat Road & Rail Ltd. / RCRR
c/o Great Western Railway, PO Box 669, 254 Centre St., Shaunavon, SK S0N 2M0
Tel: 306-459-2544; *Fax:* 306-459-2468
RCRR-shortline@xplornet.com
www.redcoatroadandrail.ca

Profile: Red Coat Road & Rail is a community-owned shortline railway, & contracts Great Western Railway & Southern Prairie Railway as operators.
Ed Howse, President

Rocky Mountaineer Rail
#101, 369 Terminal Ave., Vancouver, BC V6A 4C4
Tel: 604-606-7200
reservations@rockymountaineer.com
www.rockymountaineer.com

Profile: Rocky Mountaineer offers vacation packages & train excursions through the Canadian Rockies.
Randy Powell, President & CEO

Saint Lawrence & Atlantic Railroad / SLR
Parent: Genesee & Wyoming Inc.
#201, 225 First Flight Dr., Auburn, ME 04210
www.gwrr.com

Profile: 157 miles of track; interchanges with CN, New Hampshire & Vermont Railroad, New Hampshire Central Railroad, Pan Am Railways & sister railroad St-Laurent & Atlantique Railroad; moves aggregates, brick & cement, chemicals, food & feed, forest products, intermodal loads, & steel & scrap
Denys Del Cardo, General Manager
819-826-5640, denys.delcardo@gwrr.com

South Simcoe Railway
c/o South Simcoe Railway Heritage Corp., PO Box 186, Tottenham, ON L0G 1W0
Tel: 905-936-5815
info@southsimcoerailway.ca
www.southsimcoerailway.ca

Profile: The South Simcoe Railway is the oldest operating steam-powered railway in Ontario, & offers excursions through the Beeton Creek valley.
Eric Smith, President, Operations Manager & Master Mechanic
smith@southsimcoerailway.ca

Southern Ontario Railway / SOR
Parent: Genesee & Wyoming Inc.
241 Stuart St. West, Hamilton, ON L8R 3H2
Tel: 519-271-4441; *Fax:* 888-641-2243
Toll-Free: 888-641-2175
sorr-cs@gwrr.com
www.gwrr.com

Profile: 69 miles of track; interchanges with CN & CP; moves steel, agricultural products, fuel & chemicals
Wesley Logan, General Manager
519-271-4441 ext: 1

Southern Prairie Railway
Railway Ave., Ogema, SK S0C 1Y0
Tel: 306-459-1200; *Fax:* 306-459-1201
Toll-Free: 855-459-1200
www.southernprairierailway.com

Profile: The railway provides historical excursions to passengers, allowing visitors to visit the Town of Ogema & the Deep South Pioneer Museum.

Southern Rails Cooperative Ltd. / SRCL
PO Box 297, Avonlea, SK S0H 0C0
Tel: 306-868-4435

Profile: Southern Rails Cooperative was the first shortline railway in Saskatchewan, & is owned & operated by local farmers. Two railways are operated, at a total of 71 km of trackage; both railways are on former CP subdivisions.

Southern Railway of British Columbia Limited
2102 River Dr., New Westminster, BC V3M 6S3
Tel: 604-521-1966; *Fax:* 604-526-0914
www.sryraillink.com

Profile: The company provides freight services only, on around 125 miles of track; 29 locomotives; 700 cars; service on Vancouver Island via Southern Railway of Vancouver Island (SVI).
Frank Butzelaar, President
604-527-6352, Fax: 604-526-0914

Stewart Southern Railway Inc.
PO Box 70, Fillmore, SK S0G 1N0
Tel: 306-722-7712

Profile: The shortline railway operates 82 miles of track & serves Fill-More Seeds Inc., which has facilities located along the track.

Thunder Rail Ltd.
PO Box 328, Arborfield, SK S0E 0A0
Tel: 306-769-8383
www.arborfieldsk.ca/thunder_rail.htm

Profile: The shortline railway is owned & operated by the community of Arborfield, who purchased the track from Carlton Trail Railway (OmniTRAX) in 2005.
Wayne Friske, President

Torch River Rail Inc.
PO Box 368, Choiceland, SK S0J 0M0
Tel: 306-276-9434

Profile: The shortline railway has 45 km of track & runs on the former White Fox CP subdivision.

Toronto Terminals Railway Company Ltd.
#1400B, 50 Bay St., Toronto, ON M5J 3A5
Tel: 416-864-3440
info@ttrly.com
www.ttrly.com
George Huggins, Interim Director of Operations

Train touristique de Charlevoix Inc.
Parent: Le Massif de Charlevoix
50, rue de la ferme, Baie-Saint-Paul, QC G3Z 0G2
Tél: 418-240-4124
info_LeTrain@lemassif.com
www.lemassif.com/fr/train
Nancy Belley, Directrice générale

Trillium Railway Co. Inc. / TRRY
PO Box 21, 42 Centre St., Welland, ON L3B 5N9
Tel: 905-735-5529; *Fax:* 905-735-7559
www.trilliumrailway.com

Profile: Trillium operates the Port Colborne Harbour Railway
Karen Ettinger, President
Karen.Ettinger@trilliumrailway.com

Tshiuetin Rail Transportation Inc.
148, boul des Montagnais, Uashat, QC G4R 5R2
Tél: 418-960-0982; *Téléc:* 418-960-0984
billetterie@tshiuetin.ca
www.tshiuetin.net

Profile: The railway is owned by the First Nations of Uashat Mak Mani-Utenam, Matimekush-Lac John & Kawawachikamach, & operates between Labrador & Québec.
Orlando Cordova, General Manager & COO

VIA Rail Canada Inc.
PO Box 8116 Stn. A, Montréal, QC H3C 3N3
Téléc: 514-871-6104
Ligne sans frais: 888-842-7245
customer_relations@viarail.ca
www.viarail.ca

Profile: Railroads, line-haul operating; Local & suburban transit
Yves Desjardins-Sicili, President & CEO
Patricia Jasmin, Chief Financial Officer

Waterloo Central Railway
Southern Ontario Locomotive Restoration Society, PO Box 546, 50 Isabella St., St Jacobs, ON N0B 2N0
Tel: 519-664-0900; *Fax:* 519-664-0896
waterloocentralrailway.com

Profile: Owned & operated by the Southern Ontario Locomotive Restoration Society, the railway offers steam engine tours from Waterloo to St. Jacobs.
Peter McGough, General Manager & Superintendent, Operations

Western Labrador Rail Services / WLRS
Parent: Genesee & Wyoming Inc.
#1, 210 Humber Ave., Labrador City, NL A2V 2W8
Tel: 709-944-6564; *Fax:* 709-944-6297
www.gwrr.com

Profile: Provides rail service to mining companies in Labrador & the North Shore of Québec
Sheila Cluney, Manager, Operations
709-944-6564

Wheatland Railway Inc.
PO Box 32, Hoey, SK S0J 1E0
Tel: 306-422-5401

Profile: The shortline railway has 74 km of track leased from CN, & utilizes CN staff & locomotives.

White Pass & Yukon Route / WP&YR
#4, 1109 Front St., Whitehorse, YT Y1A 5G4
Tel: 867-633-5710; *Fax:* 867-456-7082
wpyr@northwestel.net
wpyr.com

Profile: Provides a scenic 20 mile journey through the Yukon & Alaska
John Finlayson, President

Windsor & Hantsport Railway Co.
PO Box 578, 2 Water St., Windsor, NS B0N 2T0
Tel: 902-798-0798; *Fax:* 902-798-0816
www.whrail.ca

Profile: The company operates 56 miles of track between Windsor Junction & New Minas, Nova Scotia.
James H. Taylor, General Manager
jtaylor@whrail.ca

York-Durham Heritage Railway / YDHR
PO Box 462, Stouffville, ON L4A 7Z7
Tel: 905-852-3696
ydhr@ydhr.ca
www.ydhr.ca

Profile: The historic railway is owned & operated by the York-Durham Heritage Railway Association & provides excursions between Stouffville, Goodwood & Uxbridge.

Port Authorities

Halifax Port Authority / HPA
Formerly: Halifax Port Corporation
PO Box 336, 1215 Marginal Rd., Halifax, NS B3J 2P6
Tel: 902-426-8222; *Fax:* 902-426-7335
www.portofhalifax.ca

Profile: The HPA sees an annual cargo tonnage of around 9.5 million metric revenue tons. Cargo types include: Bulk Cargo (Oil, Fuel, Gypsum), Breakbulk Cargo (Iron/Steel, Machinery, Rubber), Roll-on, Roll-off Cargo (Cars & Trucks) & Containerized Cargo.
Karen Oldfield, President & CEO
Paul MacIsaac, Senior Vice-President

Hamilton Port Authority
605 James St. North, 6th Fl., Hamilton, ON L8L 1K1
Tel: 905-525-4330; *Toll-Free:* 800-263-2131
www.hamiltonport.ca

Profile: The Port of Hamilton handles more than 10 million tons of cargo per year, including bulk, breakbulk, project cargo & liquid bulk.
Bruce Wood, President & CEO
Janet Knight, Chief Financial Officer

Nanaimo Port Authority / NPA
PO Box 131, Nanaimo, BC V9R 5K4
Tel: 250-753-4146; *Fax:* 250-753-4899
info@npa.ca
www.npa.ca

Profile: The NPA administers the federal harbour from the Nanaimo Assembly Wharf to the Petro-Canada dock on Newcastle Channel & extending to Newcastle & Protection Islands.
Bernie Dumas, President & CEO
bdumas@npa.ca
Ian Marr, Vice-President
imarr@npa.ca

Port Alberni Port Authority
2750 Harbour Rd., Port Alberni, BC V9Y 7X2
Tel: 250-723-5312; *Fax:* 250-723-1114
www.portalberniportauthority.ca

Profile: Port Alberni Port Authority is a continuation of the Port Alberni Harbour Commission, & has jurisdiction over the Alberni Inlet from the Somass River to Tzartus Island.
Zoran Knezevic, President & CEO
zknezevic@alberniport.ca
Rod Hiltz, Coordinator, Terminal Operations
rhiltz@alberniport.ca

Port Metro Vancouver
Formerly: Fraser River Port Authority
The Pointe, #100, 999 Canada Place, Vancouver, BC V6C 3T4
Tel: 604-665-9000; *Fax:* 866-284-4271
www.portmetrovancouver.com
Profile: The Graser River, North Fraser, & Vancouver Port Authorities united to become Vancouver Fraser Port Authority on January 1, 2008; the Vancouver Fraser Port Authority has since become the Port Metro Vancouver.
Robin Silvester, President & CEO
Allan Baydala, Chief Financial Officer

Port of Belledune
112 Shannon Dr., Belledune, NB E8G 2W2
Tel: 506-522-1200; *Fax:* 506-522-0803
info@portofbelledune.ca
www.portofbelledune.ca
Profile: The Port is located in Northern New Brunswick, & handles bulk, break bulk, containers, trailer, liquid, & roll-on/roll-off. Space & storage is available for lease.
Denis Caron, President & CEO
Wynford Goodman, Director, Operations
goodman@portofbelledune.ca

Portuaire de Montréal
Montreal Port Authority
Édifice du port de Montréal, #1, 2100, av Pierre-Dupuy, Montréal, QC H3C 3R5
Tél: 514-283-7011; *Téléc:* 514-283-0829
info@port-montreal.com
www.port-montreal.com
Profile: Le mandat de l'Administration portuaire de Montréal est de faciliter le commerce intérieur et international et contribuer ainsi à la réalisation des objectifs socio-économiques locales, régionales et nationales
Sylvie Vachon, Présidente-directrice générale

Prince Rupert Port Authority
#200, 215 Cow Bay Rd., Prince Rupert, BC V8J 1A2
Tel: 250-627-8899; *Fax:* 250-627-8980
www.rupertport.com
Profile: The Port of Prince Rupert is the closest North American port to Asia, & includes five terminals & undeveloped industrial land.
Don Krusel, President & CEO
Gary Paulson, Harbour Master & Vice-President, Operations

Quebec Port Authority
PO Box 80 Stn. Haute-Ville, 150, rue Dalhousie, Québec, QC G1R 4M8
Tél: 418-648-3640; *Téléc:* 418-648-4160
marketing@portquebec.ca
www.portquebec.ca
Profile: The mission of the Québec Port Authority is to promote & develop maritime trade, to serve the economic interests of the Quebec area & of Canada & to ensure that it is profitable while respecting both its community & the environment.
Mario Girard, Président-directeur général

Saguenay Port Authority
6600, rue Quai-Marcel-Dionne, La Baie, QC G7B 3N9
Tél: 418-697-0250; *Téléc:* 418-697-0243
info@portsaguenay.ca
www.portsaguenay.ca
Profile: The Port of Saguenay is the only public port in the Saguenay-Lac-St-Jean area, & features two terminals & a cruise-ship wharf.
Carl Laberge, Directeur général
418-697-0250 ext. 204

Saint John Port Authority
111 Water St., Saint John, NB E2L 0B1
Tel: 506-636-4869; *Fax:* 506-636-4443
www.sjport.com
Profile: The port of Saint John handles more than 31 million metric tons of cargo per year, including dry & liquid bulk, break bulk, container, & cruise.
Jim Quinn, President & CEO
Capt. Chris Hall, Harbour Master & Vice-President, Operations & Infrastructure

Sept-Iles Port Authority
1 Quai Mgr-Blanche, Sept-Iles, QC G4R 5P3
Tel: 418-968-1231; *Fax:* 418-962-4445
www.portsi.com
Profile: The port primarily handles ore through its 13 docks. 23 million tons of cargo passes through the port every year.
Pierre D. Gagnon, President & CEO
pgagnon@portsi.com

Toronto Port Authority / TPA
60 Harbour St., Toronto, ON M5J 1B7
Tel: 416-863-2000; *Fax:* 416-863-0495
www.portstoronto.com
Profile: Maintains a paved facility of over 50 acres centrally located, adjacent to downtown Toronto. The yard provides access to railroads, as well as all major highways. The facility is fully bonded has 24-hour security.
Geoffrey A. Wilson, CEO
Alan J. Paul, Senior Vice-President & Chief Financial Officer

Windsor Port Authority
3190 Sandwich St., Windsor, ON N9C 1A6
Tel: 519-258-5741; *Fax:* 519-258-5905
www.portwindsor.com
Profile: The mission of the Windsor Port Authority is to manage, develop, & promote the Port of Windsor for the benefit of its stakeholders & ensure the general security of the port while striving for a high degree of safety & environmental responsibility.
David Cree, President & CEO

Public Transit Systems

100 Mile House & Area Transit System
Formerly: 100 Mile House Transit System (Paratransit)
Parent: BC Transit Corporation
c/o LDN Transportation, 6119 Reita Cres., 100 Mile House, BC V0K 2E0
Tel: 250-395-2834
bctransit.com/100-mile-house
Profile: The 100 Mile House Transit System has many routes which offer service to major residenial areas of 100 Mile House, 103 Mile & 108 Ranch. It also has several accessible services, including rural transit service, handyDART & priority seating. The system is operated by LDN Transportation.

Agassiz-Harrison Transit System
Parent: BC Transit Corporation
c/o FirstCanada ULC, 44275 Yale Rd. West, Chilliwack, BC V2R 4H2
Tel: 604-795-3838; *Fax:* 604-795-5110
bctransit.com/agassiz-harrison
Profile: The Agassiz-Harrison Transit System connects Chilliwack with Harrison Hot Springs. The system is operated by FirstCanada ULC.

Agence métropolitaine de transport / AMT
700, rue De La Gauchetière Ouest, 26e ét, Montréal, QC H3B 5M2
Tél: 514-287-8726; *Téléc:* 866-765-8886
Ligne sans frais: 888-702-8726
www.amt.qc.ca
Nicolas Girard, Président-directeur général

Ashcroft - Clinton Transit System
Parent: BC Transit Corporation
c/o Yellowhead Community Services, 612 Park Dr., Clearwater, BC V0E 1N1
Toll-Free: 855-359-3935
bctransit.com/ashcroft-clinton
Profile: The transit system runs a fixed-route service three days a week, & serves the communities of Ashcroft & Clinton. On-request service is also available.

Barrie Transit
24 Maple Ave., Barrie, ON L4N 7W4
Tel: 705-739-4209
transit@barrie.ca
Profile: The City of Barrie offers both conventional bus service with Barrie Transit and specialized transit services for people with mobility restrictions with Barrie Accessible Community Transportation Service (BACTS)

BC Transit Corporation
520 Gorge Rd. East, Victoria, BC V8W 2P3
Tel: 250-385-2551; *Fax:* 250-995-5639
transitinfo@bctransit.com
www.bctransit.com
Profile: BC Transit coordinates public transportation throughout British Columbia, excluding the Greater Vancouver Regional District, as mandated by the British Columbia Transit Act. Over 130 communities are served, with 81 transit systems in operation, including conventional, custom & paratransit.
Manuel Achadinha, President & CEO
Brian Anderson, COO & Vice-President, Operations

Bella Coola Valley Transit System
Parent: BC Transit Corporation
c/o Bella Coola Valley Bus Co. Ltd., PO Box 783, 925 Mackenzie Hwy., Bella Coola, BC V0T 1C0
Tel: 250-799-0079
bus@belco.bc.ca
bctransit.com/bella-coola-valley
Profile: The system is a paratransit service providing door-to-door & curb-to-curb services. The service is operated by Bella Coola Valley Bus Co. Ltd.

Belleville Transit
165 Pinnacle St., Belleville, ON K8N 3A5
Tel: 613-967-4938
www.city.belleville.on.ca
Profile: Belleville Transit operates 7 days a week with 9 routes servicing the city's urban area. The fleet consists of 15 coaches travelling approximately 2,550 kilometers per day & carries 3,000 riders daily.

Boundary Transit System
Parent: BC Transit Corporation
c/o Regional District of Kootenay Boundary, #202, 843 Rossland Ave., Trail, BC V1R 4S8
Tel: 250-443-2179
bctransit.com/boundary
Profile: The Boundary Transit System has many routes within Grand Forks, with trips to & from Greenwood on Fridays. It also has several accessible services, including handyDART & priority seating. The system is operated by the Interior Health Authority.

Brampton Transit
185 Clark Blvd., Brampton, ON L6T 4G6
Tel: 905-874-2750
transit@brampton.ca
www.brampton.ca/en/residents/transit
Profile: Brampton Transit operates 45 routes, including 4 rapid transit routes, with a fleet of 359 buses.

Brandon Transportation Services
800 Rosser Ave., Brandon, MB R7A 6N5
Tel: 204-729-2300
brandontransit.ca
Profile: Brandon City Transit offers many services to the community, including Handi-Transit, an environmentally friendly way of traveling, and specialized schedules.
Tim Sanderson, Director, Transportation Services

Brantford Transit
64 Darling St., Brantford, ON N3T 6G6
Tel: 519-753-3847; *Fax:* 519-750-0491
transit@brantford.ca
www.brantford.ca/transit
Profile: Operated by the Transportation Services Department of the Corporation of the City of Brantford. It serves around 1.3 million riders annually.

British Columbia Ferry Services Inc. / BCF
Formerly: British Columbia Ferries Corporation
1010 Canada Pl., Vancouver, BC
Toll-Free: 888-223-3779
customerservice@bcferries.com
www.bcferries.com
Profile: BC Ferries provides passenger & vehicle ferry services for coastal & island communities in British Columbia. The company currently operates 35 ferries on 47 routes.
Mike Corrigan, President & CEO

British Columbia Rapid Transit Company Ltd. / BCRTC
Parent: South Coast British Columbia Transportation Authority (TransLink)
6800 - 14th Ave., Burnaby, BC V3N 4S7
Tel: 604-520-3641; *Fax:* 604-521-2818
www.translink.ca
Profile: The BC Rapid Transit Company maintains two of three SkyTrains in Vancouver on behalf of TransLink, as well as the West Coast Express train service.
Cathy McLay, Acting CEO

Burlington Transit
3332 Harvester Rd., Burlington, ON L7N 3M8
Tel: 905-639-0550; *Fax:* 905-335-7878
Toll-Free: 877-213-3609
cms.burlington.ca/Page4370.aspx
Profile: Burlington Transit connects to Hamilton Street Railway & Oakville Transit, as well as a number of GO Transit stations. Burlington's fleet consists of 59 buses. A door-to-door service for people with disabilities, called the Handi-Van, is also offered.

Calgary Transit
125 - 7 Ave. SW, Calgary, AB T2G 5R2
Tel: 403-262-1000
www.calgarytransit.com
Profile: Calgary Transit serves a ridership of 110 million with the help of 1203 vehicles on 155 routes
Doug Morgan, Director

Campbell River Transit System
Parent: BC Transit Corporation
1050 - 9th Ave., Campbell River, BC V9W 4C2
Tel: 250-287-7433; *Fax:* 250-287-7488
www.transitbc.com/regions/cam
Profile: The Campbell River Transit System has several services available to the community, including three types of Accessible Service, including Low Floor Busses, handyDART & the Taxi Saver Program. It has routes to most major destinations in Campbell River, & to Willow Point & Oyster Bay. The system is operated by Watson & Ash Transportation Company Ltd.

Cape Breton Transit
320 Esplanade, Sydney, NS B1P 7B9
Tel: 902-539-8124
epw@cbrm.ns.ca
www.cbrm.ns.ca
Profile: Transit Cape Breton offers the community travel within Industrial Cape Breton.

Central Fraser Valley Transit System
Parent: BC Transit Corporation
1225 Riverside Rd., Abbotsford, BC V2S 7P1
Tel: 604-854-3232; *Fax:* 604-854-3598
www.transitbc.com/regions/cfv
Profile: The Central Fraser Valley Transit System has several services available to the community, including routes to most major destinations in the City of Abbotsford & the District of Mission, as well as accessible services such as low floor busses, handyDART & a taxi saver program. The system is operated by FirstCanada ULC.

Chatham-Kent Transit
Formerly: Chatham Transit
PO Box 640, 315 King St. West, Chatham, ON N7M 5K8
Tel: 519-360-1998; *Fax:* 519-436-3240
cktransit@chatham-kent.ca
www.chatham-kent.ca/transportation
Profile: Operated by the Engineering & Transportation division of Chatham-Kent. Services include conventional & accessible transit within Chatham, as well as inter-urban transit between communities in the Chatham-Kent area. Accessible transit is also available to the communities of Wallaceburg, Erie Shores & Four Counties.

Chilliwack Transit System
Parent: BC Transit Corporation
First Canada, 44275 Yale Rd. West, Chilliwack, BC V2R 4H2
Tel: 604-795-3838; *Fax:* 604-796-8516
www.bctransit.com/regions/chw
Profile: The Chilliwack Transit System has several routes available to the community, which go to most major destinations in the City of Chilliwack, & to Rosedale, Popkum, Agassiz & Harrison Hot Springs, including service to Minter Gardens, Bridal Falls & Dusty's Dino Town. It also has accessible services including low floor busses, handyDART, a specialized handyDART flex route & a taxi saver program. The system is operated by FirstCanada ULC.

Clearwater & Area Transit System
Parent: BC Transit Corporation
c/o Yellowhead Community Services, 612 Park Dr., Clearwater, BC V0E 1N0
Tel: 250-674-3935
bctransit.com/clearwater
Profile: The Clearwater & Area transit system services an area that covers Vavenby, Birch Island, Clearwater & Blackpool. On the last Thursday of every month the bus goes to Kamloops & back to Clearwater. It has several accessible services including door-to-door services, handyDART & priority seating. The system is operated by Yellowhead Community Services.

Coach Atlantic Group
703 Malenfant Blvd., Dieppe, NB E1A 5T8
Tel: 506-857-8517; *Fax:* 506-857-8319
Toll-Free: 888-599-4287
coachatlanticgroup.com
Profile: Coach Atlantic is a bus charter company that can transport large groups across Prince Edward Island, Nova Scotia & New Brunswick.
Mike Cassidy, President

Coast Mountain Bus Company Ltd. / CMBC
Parent: South Coast British Columbia Transportation Authority (TransLink)
#700, 287 Nelson's Ct., New Westminster, BC V3L 0E7
Tel: 778-375-6400
www.coastmountainbus.com
Profile: Coast Mountain Bus Company operates conventional buses, smaller community shuttles, SeaBus & a fleet of trolley buses in Greater Vancouver, in the largest single transit service area in Canada.
Haydn Acheson, President & General Manager

Cobourg Transit
c/o Town of Cobourg, 55 King St. West, Cobourg, ON K9A 2M2
Tel: 905-372-4555
transit@cobourg.ca
cobourg.ca/transit-information.html
Profile: Cobourg Transit is operated by the Engineering Department, & is a fully accessible community transit system that combines fixed-route & door-to-door service (known as the Wheels program).

Codiac Transit Commission
140 Millennium Blvd., Moncton, NB E1E 2G8
Tel: 506-857-2008; *Fax:* 506-859-2680
info@codiactranspo.ca
www.codiactranspo.ca
Profile: Transit system for Moncton with express routes, charters and airport routes.

Columbia Valley Transit System
Parent: BC Transit Corporation
PO Box 1019, Golden, BC V0A 1H0
Toll-Free: 877-343-2461
bctransit.com/columbia-valley
Profile: The Columbia Valley Transit System has three routes serving Canal Flats, Fairmont, Invermere, Radium & Edgewater. On-Request & handyDART services are available. The system is operated by Olympus Stage Lines Ltd.

Comox Valley Transit System
Parent: BC Transit Corporation
1635 Knight Rd., Comox, BC V9M 4A2
Tel: 250-339-5453; *Fax:* 250-339-2797
www.bctransit.com/regions/com
Profile: Comox Valley Transit has several routes available to the community, which go to Cumberland, Royston/Buckley Bay, Courtenay, Comox, & BC Ferries & the airport. It has accessible services including low floor busses, handyDART & a taxi saver program. The system is operated by Watson & Ash Transportation Co. Ltd.

Cornwall Transit
863 - 2nd St. West, Cornwall, ON K6J 1H5
Tel: 613-930-2636
www.cornwall.ca/en/transit/cornwalltransit.asp
Profile: The City-operated transit system transports approximately 818,000 passengers annually. A parallel service called Handi-Transit is available for people with disabilities.
Len Tapp, Manager

Cowichan Valley Regional Transit System
Parent: BC Transit Corporation
c/o First Canada ULC, #3, 5280 Polkey Rd., Duncan, BC V9L 6W3
Tel: 250-746-9899
www.transitbc.com/regions/cow
Profile: The Cowichan Valley Regional Transit System has several routes to the Duncan/North Cowichan area, including Quamichan, Mt Prevost & Maple Bay; the Cowichan Lake area, including Youbou & Honeymoon Bay; & the South End communities including Mill Bay, Shawnigan Lake, Cobble Hill & Cowichan Bay. It also has accessible services including low floor busses, handyDART & priority seating. Services are operated by FirstCanada ULC, Volunteer Cowichan & Cowichan Lake Community Services Society.

Cranbrook Transit System
Parent: BC Transit Corporation
c/o Sun City Coachlines, 1229 Cranbrook St. North, Cranbrook, BC V1C 3S6
Tel: 250-417-4636; *Fax:* 250-426-5101
www.bctransit.com/regions/cra
Profile: Cranbrook Transit System has several routes available to the community, & many services, such as low-floor busses & handyDART, for those who are in need of them. The system is operated by Sun City Coachlines.

Creston Valley Transit System
Parent: BC Transit Corporation
c/o Arrow & Slocan Lakes Community Services, PO Box 100, 205 - 6th Ave. North, Nakusp, BC V0G 1R0
Tel: 250-428-7750; *Fax:* 250-265-3378
bctransit.com/creston-valley
Profile: The Creston Valley Transit System has routes that go to most of the major destinations in the area. It also has several accessible services including door-to-door service & priority seating. The system is operated by Arrow & Slocan Community Services.

Dawson Creek Transit System
Parent: BC Transit Corporation
10404 - 87th Ave., Fort St John, BC V1J 5K7
Tel: 250-782-4636; *Fax:* 250-787-9322
www.transitbc.com/regions/daw
Profile: Dawson Creek Transit system has several routes available to the community, which go to most of the major destinations in Dawson Creek. It has several low floor busses & priority seating. The system is operated by Diversified Transportation Ltd.

Durham Region Transit
605 Rossland Rd. East, Whitby, ON L1N 6A3
Toll-Free: 866-247-0055
DRThelps@durham.ca
www.durhamregiontransit.com
Profile: Durham Region Transit (DRT) is an integrated transit system serving all communities in Durham Region. The service area is divided into West, East, Centre and North service sectors. Door to door transit for disabled passengers is provided by Specialized Services
Vincent Patterson, General Manager

Edmonton Transit System
PO Box 2610 Stn. Main, Edmonton, AB T5J 3R5
Tel: 780-442-5311
311@edmonton.ca
Profile: Today, Edmonton Transit's fleet encompasses over 1116 vehicles. The system covers 425 routes, including a Light Rail Transit (LRT) system. ETS also offers transportation to persons with disabilities, called the Disabled Adult Transit Service (DATS)

Elk Valley Transit System
Parent: BC Transit Corporation
c/o Sun City Coachlines, 1229 Cranbrook St. North, Cranbrook, BC V1C 3S6
Toll-Free: 855-417-4636
bctransit.com/elk-valley
Profile: The Elk Valley Transit System offers one route serving Sparwood, Elkford & Fernie. The system is operated by Sun City Coachlines.

Fort St. John Transit System
Parent: BC Transit Corporation
c/o Diversified Transportation Ltd., 10404 - 87 Ave., Fort St John, BC V1J 5K7
Tel: 250-787-7433; *Fax:* 250-787-9322
www.transitbc.com/regions/fsj
Profile: The Fort St. John Transit system has many routes available to the community, reaching most of the major destinations in the city. It has low floor busses for easy accessibility, handyDART & priority seating. The system is operated by Diversified Transportation Ltd.

Fredericton Transit
PO Box 130, 397 Queen St., Fredericton, NB E3B 4Y7
Tel: 506-460-2200; *Fax:* 506-460-2042
transit@fredericton.ca
fredericton.ca/en/transportation/transportation.asp
Profile: The City of Fredericton Transit Division operates 28 buses on nine routes, Monday to Saturday, 6:15 am until 11:00 pm. Chartered buses are available to various school, tour & conference groups in & around Fredericton, & a parallel service, Dial-A-Bus, for persons with a disability.

GO Transit
Parent: Metrolinx
#600, 20 Bay St., Toronto, ON M5J 2W3
Tel: 416-869-3200; *Fax:* 416-869-3525
Toll-Free: 888-438-6646
www.gotransit.com
Profile: GO Transit provides transit service for the Greater Toronto & Hamilton Area via trains & buses. The company's train service features 7 lines, 63 stations, 65 locomotives & 450 route kilometres; their bus service features 15 stations, 461 buses & 2,853 route kilometres.
Greg Percy, President
416-202-5544, greg.percy@gotransit.com

GP Transit
City Hall, PO Box 4000, 9505 - 112 St., Grande Prairie, AB T8V 6V3
Tel: 780-538-0337; *Fax:* 780-538-4667
gptransit@cityofgp.com

Grand River Transit / GRT
250 Strasburg Rd., Kitchener, ON N2E 3M6
Tel: 519-585-7555
www.grt.ca
Profile: Grand River Transit serves the communities of Cambridge, Kitchener & Waterloo. An accessible service called MobilityPLUS is available for people with disabilities.

Greater Sudbury Transit
c/o City of Sudbury, PO Box 5000 Stn. A, Sudbury, ON P3A 593
Tel: 705-675-3333
www.greatersudbury.ca/transit
Profile: Operates a fleet of 60 buses
Robert Gauthier, Manager, Transit Operations

Guelph Transit
City Hall, 1 Carden St., Guelph, ON N1H 3A1
Tel: 519-822-1811; *Fax:* 519-822-1322
transit@guelph.ca
guelph.ca/living/getting-around/bus
Profile: Guelph Transit has low-floor conventional buses in its fleet & guarantees accessible service on the majority of its transit routes, & a door-to-door Mobility Service for those in need.

The Hamilton Street Railway Company
36 Hunter St. East, Hamilton, ON L8N 3W8
Tel: 905-527-4441
Profile: Operates over 30 bus routes serving Hamilton, Stoney Creek, Dundas, Ancaster and Burlington. Buses run seven days a week on most routes, from around 5:30 a.m. to 1:00 a.m. the next morning
David Dixon, Director

Hazeltons' Regional Transit System
Parent: BC Transit Corporation
c/o Coastal Bus Lines Ltd., 780 Lahakas Blvd., Kitimat, BC V8C 1T9
Tel: 250-847-2134; *Toll-Free:* 877-842-2131
bctransit.com/hazeltons
Profile: The Hazeltons' Regional Transit System has routes to most communities within the Hazeltons', as well as major destinations like Wrinch Memorial Hospital, Northwest Community College, First Nations Education Centre & the historic Village of 'Ksan. It also has routes to Moricetown & Smithers on Tuesday & Thursdays. It has accessible services which include door to door service & priority seating. The system is operated by First Canada ULC.

Kamloops Transit System
Parent: BC Transit Corporation
c/o FirstCanada ULC, 1460 Ord Rd., Kamloops, BC V2B 7V4
Tel: 250-376-1216; *Fax:* 250-376-7398
www.transitbc.com/regions/kam
Profile: The Kamloops Transit System has several routes available to the public which go to all regions of Greater Kamloops. It also has several services available, including low floor busses, handyDART, a Taxi Saver Program & priority seating. The system is operated by FirstCanada ULC.

Kelowna Regional Transit System
Parent: BC Transit Corporation
c/o FirstCanada ULC, 1494 Hardy St., Kelowna, BC V1Y 8H2
Tel: 250-860-8121; *Fax:* 250-861-7872
www.transitbc.com/regions/kel
Profile: The Kelowna Transit System has several routes available to the public, which go to all regions of Greater Kelowna. It also offers accessible services, including low floor busses, handyDART, a Taxi Saver program & priority seating. Buses are operated by FirstCanada ULC.

Kimberley Transit System
Parent: BC Transit Corporation
260 - 4 Ave., Kimberley, BC V1A 2R6
Tel: 250-427-7400
bctransit.com/kimberley
Profile: The Kimberley Transit System has routes between Kimberley & Cranbrook from Tuesday to Friday. It also has several accessible services, including door to door service & priority seating. The system is operated by the Kimberley Transportation Committee.

Kings Transit Authority
29 Crescent Dr., New Minas, NS B4N 3G7
Tel: 902-678-7310; *Fax:* 902-678-2545
Toll-Free: 888-546-4442
info@kingstransit.ns.ca
www.kingstransit.ns.ca
Profile: King Transit Authority is a public tranist system that operates in the Annapolis Country between the towns of Bridgetown, Annapolis Royal and Greenwood. Their service also extends to Cornwallis Park and Upper Clements Park, as well as Digby County to Weymouth.
Stephen Foster, General Manager

Kitimat Transit System
Parent: BC Transit Corporation
c/o FirstCanada ULC, 780 Lahakas Blvd. South, Kitimat, BC V8C 1T9
Tel: 250-632-4444
www.transitbc.com/regions/kit
Profile: The Kitimat Transit System has many routes that go to most of the major destinations in Kitimat. It also has several accessible services, including low floor busses, handyDART, & priority seating. Buses are operated by FirstCanada ULC.

Lethbridge Transit
619 - 4 Ave. North, Lethbridge, AB T1H 0K4
Tel: 403-320-3885; *Fax:* 403-380-3876
transit@lethbridge.ca
Profile: Lethbridge Transit's mission is to provide a safe and efficient public transportation system that allows community access to economic, social, educational or leisure opportunities.
Audra McKinley, Manager, Transit

London Transit Commission
450 Highbury Ave. North, London, ON N5W 5L2
Tel: 519-451-1347
ltc@londontransit.ca
www.ltconline.ca
Profile: L.T.C. services 44 routes, all of which are accessible. Annual ridership reaches 22.8 million people.
Kelly S. Paleczny, General Manager

Medicine Hat Transit
333 - 6 Ave. SE, Medicine Hat, AB T1A 2S6
Tel: 403-529-8214; *Fax:* 403-527-5844
mhtransit@medicinehat.ca
www.medicinehat.ca
Profile: Apart from general public transportation, Medicine Hat's transit system also offers charter & special needs services.

Merritt & Area Transit System
Parent: BC Transit Corporation
c/o Nicola Valley Transportation Society, PO Box 934, Merritt, BC V1K 1B8
Tel: 250-378-4080
bctransit.com/merritt
Profile: The Merritt & Area Transit System provides four routes serving North End, Collettville, Diamond Vale & Lower Nicola. The system is operated by Nicola Valley Transportation Society.

Metro Transit
PO Box 1749, Halifax, NS B3J 3A5
www.halifax.ca/transit
Profile: Metro Transit has many services available to the community, including Accessible Low-Floor Buses, Charter Services & FRED (Free Rides Everwhere in Dowtown Halifax).

Metrobus Transit
25 Messenger Dr., St. John's, NL A1B 0H6
Tel: 709-570-2020; *Fax:* 709-722-0018
informationservices@metrobus.com
www.metrobus.com
Profile: St. John's Metrobus System has recently been revitalized and is now offering more frequent services, more direct routes, reduced travel times and more express routes.

Metrolinx
97 Front St. West, Toronto, ON M5J 1E6
Tel: 416-874-5900; *Fax:* 416-869-1755
www.metrolinx.com
Profile: Metrolinx is an agency of the Government of Ontario & is mandated to coordinate & integrate all forms of transportation in the Greater Toronto & Hamilton Area. The agency merged with GO Transit in 2009. The Union Pearson Express project was completed in 2015, & the PRESTO fare card was introduced in 2011.
Bruce McCuaig, President & CEO
416-202-5908, CEO@metrolinx.com

MiWay
Formerly: Mississauga Transit
3484 Semenyk Ct., Mississauga, ON L5C 4R1
Tel: 905-615-4636
www.mississauga.ca/portal/miway
Profile: City-operated since 1974 with a fleet of over 460 buses

Moose Jaw Transit System
City Hall, 228 Main St. North, Moose Jaw, SK S6H 3J8
Tel: 306-694-4400; *Fax:* 306-694-4480
Profile: The City of Moose Jaw Transit System offers bus service to all areas of the community. Routes are designed to provide the most efficient service possible to the citizens of Moose Jaw. Charter Service is also available, as is a Special Needs Service.

Mount Waddington Transit System
Parent: BC Transit Corporation
c/o North Island Community Services, PO Box 1028, #1705, 5A Campbell Way, Port McNeill, BC V0N 2R0
Tel: 250-956-3151
bctransit.com/mount-waddington
Profile: The Mount Waddington Transit System offers seven routes around the Mount Waddington area. Accessible services are offered, including the handyDART service. The system is operated by the North Island Community Services Society & the Volunteer Transportation Network.

Niagara Transit Commission
8208 Heartland Forest Rd., Niagara Falls, ON L2H 0L7
Tel: 905-356-1179; *Fax:* 905-356-5576
www.niagarafalls.ca
Profile: Niagara Transit has supplied public transportation for the City of Niagara Falls since 1960. Presently supplies the city with 15 bus routes
Dave Stuart, General Manager

North Bay Transit
190 Wyld St., North Bay, ON P1B 1Z2
Tel: 705-474-0419
transit@cityofnorthbay.ca
Remi Renaud, Transit Manager
705-474-0400 ext: 2165, Remi.Renaud@cityofnorthbay.ca

Oakville Transit
1225 Trafalgar Rd., Oakville, ON L6H 0H3
Tel: 905-815-2020; *Fax:* 905-338-4703
transit@oakville.ca
www.oakvilletransit.com
Profile: Oakville Transit has been providing bus service to Oakville since 1972

OC Transpo
1500 St. Laurent Blvd., Ottawa, ON K1G 0Z8
Tel: 613-842-3600; *Fax:* 613-842-3633
www.octranspo1.com
Profile: OC Transpo provides public transit services in the Ottawa region, including the Transitway & O-Train.
John Manconi, General Manager, Transit Services

Osoyoos Transit System
6210 - 97th St., Osoyoos, BC V0H 1V2
Tel: 250-495-8054
www.transitbc.com/regions/oso
Profile: Osoyoos Transit System operates Monday through Thursday, with Monday catering to destinations between Osoyoos and Kelowna Airport, including Oliver, Okanagan Falls, Penticton, Summerland, Peachland, Westbank and Kelowna, and Tuesday through Thursday servicing all destinations between Osoyoos and Summerland, including Oliver, Okanagan Falls and Penticton. It also has accessible services including handyDART and priority seating.

Pemberton Transit System
Parent: BC Transit Corporation
8011 Hwy. 99, Whistler, BC V0N 1B8
Tel: 604-932-4020
bctransit.com/pemberton-valley
Profile: The Pemberton Transit System offers two commuter routes & one local route. Service between Pemberton & Whistler is operated by Whistler Transit Ltd. Local service is operated by Pemberton Taxi.

Penticton & Okanagan-Similkameen Transit System
Parent: BC Transit Corporation
301 Warren Ave. East, Penticton, BC V2A 3M1
Tel: 250-492-4042
bctransit.com/penticton
Profile: The Penticton Transit System & Okanagan-Similkameen Transit System have many routes available both in the community & in rural areas. They also have several accessible services, including low floor busses,

handyDART, a taxi saver program & priority seating. The systems are operated by Penticton Transit Service Ltd.

Peterborough Transit
190 Simcoe St., Peterborough, ON K9H 2H7
Tel: 705-745-0525
transitoperations@peterborough.ca
www.peterborough.ca
Profile: Services the City of Peterborough, Ontario with regular and Handi-Van transit services. All regular Peterborough Transit routes have fully accessible buses
Kevin Jones, Manager

Port Alberni/Clayoquot Transit System
Parent: BC Transit Corporation
c/o Diversified Transportation Ltd., 3701 - 4th Ave., Port Alberni, BC V9Y 4H7
Tel: 250-724-1311; *Fax:* 250-724-1377
bctransit.com/port-alberni
Profile: The Port Alberni/Clayoquot Transit System has several routes that go to most of the major destinations in the area, as well as many accessible services, including low floor busses, handyDART & priority seating.

Powell River Regional Transit System
Parent: BC Transit Corporation
c/o Powell River Municipal Transportation, 6910 Duncan St., Powell River, BC V8A 1W2
Tel: 604-485-4287; *Fax:* 604-485-4219
bctransit.com/powell-river
Profile: The Powell River Transit System has many routes available to the community, which go to most of the major destinations in the area. It also has several accessible services, including a rural transit service, low floor busses, handyDART & priority seating. The systems are operated by Powell River Municipal Transportation & Powell River Taxi 2001.

Prince George Transit System
Parent: BC Transit Corporation
1041 Great St., Prince George, BC V2N 2K8
Tel: 250-563-0011; *Fax:* 250-564-4901
bctransit.com/prince-george
Profile: The Prince George Transit System has many routes that go to most of the major regions in the area. It also has several accessible services available to the community, including community travel training, low floor busses, handyDART, a taxi saver program & priority seating. The systems are operated by Prince George Transit Ltd. & the Carefree Society.

Prince Rupert/Port Edward Transit
Parent: BC Transit Corporation
c/o FirstCanada ULC, 225 - 2 Ave. West, Prince Rupert, BC V8J 1G4
Tel: 250-624-3343
www.bctransit.com/regions/prr
Profile: The Prince Rupert/Port Edward Transit system has several routes available to the community that go to most of the major destinations in the area, as well as many accessible services, including low floor busses, handyDART, a taxi saver program & door to door service. Both services are operated by First Canada ULC.

Princeton Regional Transit System
Parent: BC Transit Corporation
c/o Princeton & District Community Services, PO Box 1960, 47 Harold Ave., Princeton, BC V0X 1W0
Tel: 250-295-6666; *Toll-Free:* 800-291-0911
bctransit.com/princeton
Profile: The Princeton & Area Transit System runs Monday through Friday, with door-to-door trips within Princeto & to & from Penticton, Hedley, Keremeos & Coalmont. The system is operated by Princeton & District Community Services.

Quesnel Transit System
Parent: BC Transit Corporation
c/o Five Five Transport, 98A Pinecrest Rd., Quesnel, BC V2J 5W6
Tel: 250-992-1109; *Fax:* 250-992-1146
bctransit.com/quesnel
Profile: Quesnel Transit has several routes that go to most of the major destinations in the area, as well as many accessible services, including handyDART and priority seating. The system is operated by Five Five Transport.

RDN Transit System
Formerly: Nanaimo Regional Transit System
c/o Transit Manager, Regional District of Nanaimo, 6300 Hammond Bay Rd., Nanaimo, BC V9T 6N2
Tel: 250-390-4531
bctransit.com/nanaimo
Profile: RDN Regional Transit System provides both regular transit & handyDART custom transit service. Regional Transit is operated by the Regional District of Nanaimo in partnership with BC Transit.

Red Deer Transit
PO Box 5008, Red Deer, AB T4N 3T4
Tel: 403-342-8225; *Fax:* 403-314-5837
transit@reddeer.ca
Profile: Red Deer Transit has several services available to the community, including Low Floor Buses, Overload Busses, Charter Bus Services, and a Citizen's Action Bus.

Regina Transit
PO Box 1790, Regina, SK S4P 3C8
Tel: 306-777-7726; *Fax:* 306-949-7211
Profile: The City of Regina Transit System has several services available to the community, including a charter service, a safebus, night stops, and paratransit.

Réseau de transport de la capitale (RTC-Québec)
720, rue des Rocailles, Québec, QC G2J 1A5
Tél: 418-627-2511; *Téléc:* 418-641-6716
www.rtcquebec.ca
Alain Mercier, Directeur Général

Le Réseau de transport de Longueuil
1150, boul Marie-Victorin, Longueuil, QC J4G 2M4
Tél: 450-442-8600
www.rtl-longueuil.qc.ca
Guy Benedetti, Directeur général

Revelstoke Transit System
Parent: BC Transit Corporation
c/o Lyndon Enterprises Ltd., 796 Lundell Rd., Revelstoke, BC V0E 2S0
Tel: 250-837-3888
bctransit.com/revelstoke
Profile: The Revelstoke Transit System offers fixed-route & handyDART services. Funding for the service is split between the City of Revelstoke & BC Transit, while Revelstoke City Council is responsible for fares, routes & service levels. The system is operated by Lyndon Enterprises Ltd.

Saint John Transit Commission
55 McDonald St., Saint John, NB E2J 0C7
Tel: 506-658-4700; *Fax:* 506-658-4704
sjtransitcustomerservice@saintjohn.ca
www.saintjohntransit.com
Profile: The Saint John Transit Commission was established in 1979 to provide scheduled transit service to the city. It is the largest public transit system in New Brunswick in terms of both mileage and passengers. Its ridership averages 2.5 million passengers per year.

St. Albert Transit
235 Carnegie Dr., St Albert, AB T8N 5A7
Tel: 780-418-6060; *Fax:* 780-459-4050
transit@stalbert.ca
www.stalbert.ca/transit
Profile: St Albert Transit (StAT) local routes serve all neighbourhoods within the City of St. Albert, connecting with StAT commuter services to Edmonton destinations at either (or both) the Village Transit Station or St. Albert Centre Exchange. Edmonton destinations include downtown, the University of Alberta, MacEwan, NAIT, Government Centre and West Edmonton Mall.

St Catherines Transit Commission
2012 - 1st St. South, St Catharines, ON L2S 3V9
Tel: 905-687-5555
www.yourbus.com

Salt Spring Island Transit System
Parent: BC Transit Corporation
#5, 105 Rainbow Rd., Salt Spring, BC V8K 2V5
Tel: 250-537-6758
bctransit.com/salt-spring-island
Profile: The Salt Spring Island Transit System offers six routes around the island. Buses are wheelchair accessible & handyDART service is available. The system is operated by Ganges Faerie Minishuttle.

Sarnia Transit
1169 Michener Rd., Sarnia, ON N7S 4W3
Tel: 519-336-3271; *Fax:* 519-336-3361
transit@sarnia.ca
www.sarnia.ca
Profile: Operates and maintains a fleet of 25 buses on the conventional transit system and 6 specialized vehicles on their Care-a-Van service (provided to people with disabilities)
Jim Stevens, Director

Saskatchewan Transportation Company
1717 Saskatchewan Dr., Regina, SK S4P 2E2
Tel: 306-787-3347
www.stcbus.com
Profile: Saskatchewan Transit has been providing passenger and freight transportation services for over 60 years, and provides passenger transportation and parcel express services throughout Saskatchewan operating main terminals in Regina, Saskatoon and Prince Albert with an additional 206 rural agencies in the Province.
Shawn Grice, President & CEO

Saskatoon Transit Services
226 - 23rd Ave. East, Saskatoon, SK S7K 0J4
Tel: 306-975-3100
Profile: Saskatoon Transit's mission is to provide cost-effective, safe and affordable public transit services using clean and enviornmentally friendly equipment that enables all residents to access work, education, health care, shopping, social and recreational opportunities.

Sault Ste. Marie Transit
111 Huron St., Sault Ste Marie, ON P6A 5P9
Tel: 705-759-5438; *Fax:* 705-759-5834
transit@cityssm.on.ca
Profile: The Sault Ste. Marie Transit has a fleet of 28 regular Transit vehicles, 9 Para Transit buses, and 1 Community Bus
Don Scott, Transit Manager
d.scott@cityssm.on.ca

SeaBus
Parent: South Coast British Columbia Transportation Authority (TransLink)
#700, 287 Nelson's Ct., New Westminster, BC V3L 0E7
Tel: 778-375-6400
www.translink.ca
Profile: The SeaBus passenger ferries linking North Vancouver & downtown Vancouver, crossing the Burrard Inlet, are operated by Coast Mountain Bus Company, & owned by TransLink.
Haydn Acheson, President & General Manager, Coast Mountain Bus Company

Shuswap Regional Transit System
Parent: BC Transit Corporation
875B Lakeshore Dr. SW, Salmon Arm, BC V1E 1E4
Tel: 250-832-0191
bctransit.com/shuswap
Profile: The Shuswap Regional Transit System offers routes serving Salmon Arm, Canoe, Sorrento, Blind Bay, Eagle Bay, Silver Creek, Deep Creek & Enderby. Accessible services such as handyDART are offered.

Skeena Regional Transit System
Parent: BC Transit Corporation
c/o FirstCanada ULC, 4904 Hwy. 16, West Terrace, BC V8G 1L8
Tel: 250-632-4444; *Toll-Free:* 877-632-4443
bctransit.com/skeena
Profile: The Skeena Regional Transit System operates eight routes serving Kitimat & Skeena. Accessible services such as handyDART are available. Buses are operated by FirstCanada ULC.

Smithers & District Transit System
Parent: BC Transit Corporation
c/o Smithers Community Services, PO Box 3759, 3815 Railway Ave., #B, Smithers, BC V0J 2N0
Tel: 250-847-9515
bctransit.com/smithers
Profile: The Smithers & District Transit System offers one fixed route serving major destinations & residential areas. Accessible services such as the handyDART are available. The system is operated by the Smithers Community Services Association.

Société de transport de l'Outaouais
111, rue Jean-Proulx, Gatineau, QC J8Z 1T4
Tél: 819-770-3242; *Ligne sans frais:* 800-855-0511
www.sto.ca
Line Thiffeault, Directrice générale

Société de transport de Laval
2250, av Francis-Hughes, Laval, QC H7S 2C3
Tél: 450-688-6520; *Téléc:* 450-662-5457
www.stl.laval.qc.ca
Guy Picard, Directeur général

Société de transport de Montréal
800, rue de la Gauchetière ouest, Montréal, QC H5A 1J6
Tél: 514-786-4636
www.stm.info
Luc Tremblay, Directeur général

Société de transport de Sherbrooke
895, rue Cabana, Sherbrooke, QC J1K 2M3
Tél: 819-564-2687
www.sts.qc.ca

South Coast British Columbia Transportation Authority
Formerly: Greater Vancouver Transportation Authority
#400, 287 Nelson's Ct., New Westminster, BC V3L 0E7
Tel: 778-375-7500; *Fax:* 778-375-7510
www.translink.ca
Profile: TransLink, the South Coast British Columbia Transportation Authority, is involved with transportation planning, administration of service contracts with subsidiary companies & contractors, the management of capital projects, financial management & planning, public affairs & supporting business functions. Operating companies include: Coast Mountain Bus Company, West Coast Express & British Columbia Rapid Transit Company.
Kevin Desmond, Chief Executive Officer

South Okanagan Transit System
Parent: BC Transit Corporation
6210 - 97th St., Osoyoos, BC V0H 1V4
Tel: 250-495-8054
bctransit.com/south-okanagan
Profile: The South Okanagan Transit System offers three routes around the Osoyoos area. Accessible services such as the handyDART service are available. The system is operated by the South Okanagan Transit Society.

Squamish Transit System
Parent: BC Transit Corporation
c/o Diversified Transportation Ltd., 38928A Production Way, Whistler, BC V8B 0K4
Tel: 604-892-5559
bctransit.com/squamish
Profile: The Squamish Transit System has many routes that go to Valleycliffe, Brackendale, Highlands, Downtown, Woodfibre Ferry, Garibaldi Highlands & most major destinations in Squamish. It also has accessible services including low floor busses, handyDART & priority seating. The system is operated by Diversified Transportation Ltd.

Stratford City Transit
PO Box 874, 60 Corcoran St., Stratford, ON N5A 6W3
Tel: 519-271-0250
Michael Mousley, Manager, Transit

Strathcona Transit
2001 Sherwood Dr., Sherwood Park, AB T8A 3W7
Tel: 780-464-7433
transit@strathcona.ca
Profile: Strathcona's Transit's mission is to provide an effective, efficient and customer-focused transit service that aligns with the County's three pillars of sustainability: environmental, economic and social.

Summerland Transit System
Parent: BC Transit Corporation
c/o Penticton & Dist. Community Resources Society, 330 Ellis St., Penticton, BC V2A 4L7
Tel: 250-492-5814
bctransit.com/summerland
Profile: The Summerland Transit System operates a single fixed route between Summerland & Penticton. Accessible services such as the handyDART & Taxi Saver programs are available. The system is operated by the Penticton & District Community Resources Society.

Sunshine Coast Transit System
Parent: BC Transit Corporation
1975 Field Rd., Sechelt, BC V0N 3A1
Tel: 604-885-6893; *Fax:* 604-885-7909
bctransit.com/sunshine-coast
Profile: The Sunshine Coast Transit System has many routes that go to the most built-up residential neighbourhoods between the Langdale, Gibsons & Sechelt. In addition, there is service to Halfmoon Bay & limited service on Saturday, Sunday & holidays to Secret Cove in the summertime. Buses are operated by the Regional District.

Terrace Regional Transit System
Parent: BC Transit Corporation
c/o FirstCanada ULC, 4904 Hwy. 16 West, Terrace, BC V8G 1L8
Tel: 250-635-2666
bctransit.com/terrace
Profile: The Terrace Regional Transit System has many routes through the City of Terrace & the Regional District of Kitimat-Stikine. It also has several accessible services including low floor busses, handyDART & priority seating. The system is operated by First Canada ULC.

Thunder Bay Transit
570 Fort William Rd., Thunder Bay, ON P7B 2Z8
Tel: 807-684-3744; *Fax:* 807-345-5744
transit@thunderbay.ca
www.thunderbay.ca/Living/Getting_Around/Thunder_Bay
Profile: Thunder Bay Transit operates with a fleet of 49 buses on 14 routes, & is completely accessible.
Brad Loroff, Manager

Timmins Transit
220 Algonquin Blvd. East, Timmins, ON P4N 1B3
Tel: 705-360-2654; *Fax:* 705-360-2698
transit@timmins.ca
www.timminstransit.ca
Profile: Timmins Transit is a service operated by the City of Timmins. They operate a fleet of over 25 buses, low floor buses, and accessible mini-buses
Catherine Verreault, Manager, Transit

The Toronto Transit Commission / TTC
1900 Yonge St., Toronto, ON M4S 1Z2
Tel: 416-393-4000
www.ttc.ca
Profile: Operates & maintains Toronto's urban transit system, including buses, subways & streetcars. Subsidiaries include Toronto Coach Terminal Inc., Toronto Transit Infrastructure Ltd. & TTC Insurance Company Ltd.
Josh Colle, Chair
Andy Byford, Chief Executive Officer
Vincent Rodo, Chief Financial & Administration Officer
Gary Shortt, Chief Operating Officer

Transit Windsor
3700 North Service Rd. East, Windsor, ON N8W 5X2
Tel: 519-944-4111; *Fax:* 519-944-5121
tw@city.windsor.on.ca
www.citywindsor.ca/transitwindsor
Profile: Fleet consists of 112 transit coaches, including 102 accessbile buses.

Vernon Regional Transit System
Parent: BC Transit Corporation
c/o North Okanagan & Vernon Regional Transit, 2400 - 43 St., Vernon, BC V1T 6W8
Tel: 250-545-7221
bctransit.com/vernon
Profile: The Vernon Regional Transit System has many routes available to the community which go to to most major destinations in the City of Vernon, to the District of Coldstream, & Spallumcheen, Armstrong, Endergy, Lavington, Whitevale & Lumby. It has accessible services including community travel training, a taxi saver program, low floor busses & handyDART. The system is operated by First Canada ULC.

Victoria Regional Transit System
Formerly: Victoria Regional Transit Commission
Parent: BC Transit Corporation
c/o BC Transit, 520 Gorge Rd. East, Victoria, BC V8W 2P3
Tel: 250-382-6161
transitinfo@bctransit.com
www.bctransit.com/regions/vic
Profile: The Victoria Regional Transit System began operation on 22 February 1890 with a fleet of four streetcars. The system now serves approximately 312,000 persons & operates in a 400-square-kilometre area. Fares, routes & service levels are overseen by the Victoria Regional Transit Commission.
Susan Brice, Chair, Victoria Regional Transit Commission

Welland Transit
c/o Civic Square, 60 East Main St., Welland, ON L3B 3X4
Tel: 905-735-1700
transit@welland.ca
www.welland.ca/transit
Alfred Stockwell, Manager, Transit

West Coast Express Ltd. / WCE
Parent: South Coast British Columbia Transportation Authority (TransLink)
#295, 601 West Cordova St., Vancouver, BC V6B 1G1
Tel: 604-488-8906; *Fax:* 604-689-3896
Toll-Free: 800-570-7245
www.translink.ca
Profile: The West Coast Express connects Vancouver to Mission via eight stations.
Mike Richard, Acting President & General Manager

West Kootenay Transit
Formerly: Kootenay Boundary Transit System
Parent: BC Transit Corporation
#101, 310 Ward St., Nelson, BC V1L 5S4
Toll-Free: 855-993-3100
bctransit.com/west-kootenay
Profile: West Kootenay Transit has routes available to the communities of Nelson & District, Trail & area, Nakusp & District, Castlegar & District, Slocan Valley & Kaslo & District. It also has many accessible services, including low floor busses, HandyDART, & priority seating. It operates in three zones: Kootenay. Slocan & Columbia. The system is operated by Trail Transit Services, Arrow & Slocan Lakes Community Services & the City of Nelson.

Whistler Transit System
Formerly: WAVE Whistler & Valley Express
Parent: BC Transit Corporation
8011 Hwy. 99, Whistler, BC V0N 1B8
Tel: 604-932-4020
operations@whistlertransit.pwt.ca
bctransit.com/whistler
Profile: The Whistler transit system runs through Emerald Estates, Alpine Meadows, Spruce Grove, White Gold, Nesters, Tapleys Farm, Blueberry Hill, Whistler Village, the Upper Village, Alta Vista, Nordic Whistler Creek, Tamarisk, Function Junction & Pemberton. The service runs 365 days a year. Buses are operated by Whistler Transit Ltd.

Whitehorse Transit
139 Tlingit St., Whitehorse, YT Y1A 1C2
Tel: 867-668-8396
transit@whitehorse.ca
Profile: Whitehorse Transit runs six days a week, with no service on Sundays or holidays. There is also a Handy Bus which provides door-to-door service for those who are unable to use regular transit.
Cheri Malo, Transit Manager

Williams Lake Transit System
Parent: BC Transit Corporation
c/o Laker's Go-Bus Society, 88 - 1st Ave. North, Williams Lake, BC V2G 1Y6
Tel: 250-398-7812
bctransit.com/williams-lake
Profile: The Williams Lake Transit System operates four routes around the community, with accessible services such as handyDART available. The system is operated by the Laker's Go-Bus Society.

Winnipeg Transit
421 Osborne St., Winnipeg, MB R3L 2A2
Tel: 204-986-5717; *Toll-Free:* 877-311-4974
311@winnipeg.com
winnipegtransit.com
Profile: Winnipeg Transit has 94 routes throughout the city, including main line routes, express routes and suburban feeders, as well as a 'Handi-Transit' system.

Wood Buffalo Transit
9816 Hardin St., Fort McMurray, AB T9K 4K3
Tel: 780-743-7931; *Fax:* 780-788-4391
transit@woodbuffalo.ab.ca
Profile: The Fort McMurray Public Transit System provides efficient bus service on a fixed route, fixed schedule basis. Offering eight regular routes and service five days a week, it carries 4,000 riders daily and links all of Fort McMurray's subdivisions through direct or feeder connections. The service is reduced on weekends and not available on some statutory holidays.

York Region Transit
50 High Tech Rd., 5th Fl., Richmond Hill, ON L4B 4N7
Tel: 905-762-2100; *Toll-Free:* 866-668-3978
transitinfo@york.ca
www.yorkregiontransit.com
Profile: YRT offers more than 120 routes including conventional services, GO Shuttles, Express services, community buses & high school, college & university services & links with Brampton Transit, Durham Transit, MiWay & the TTC; VIVA bus rapid transit service is integrated with YRT to provide a 1-fare transit system across York Region.

Trucking Companies

Accord Transportation Ltd.
#801, 17665 - 66A Ave., Surrey, BC V3S 2A7
Tel: 604-575-7500; *Fax:* 604-575-7510
www.accordtransportation.com
Profile: Accord provides LTL, TL, cartage, logistics & regional services.

Albatrans Canada Inc.
#402, 21 St. Clair Ave. East, Toronto, ON M4T 1L9
Tel: 416-923-6060; *Fax:* 416-923-6051
infotor@albatrans.com
www.albatrans.com
Profile: Albatrans provides sea & air freight, customs brokerage, storage & IT services in major countries all over the world, specializing in wine & spirits.
Maja Vukosavljevic, Chief Executive Officer, Albatrans Canada Inc.

Alchemist Specialty Carriers Inc.
9697 - 190 St., Port Kells, BC V4N 3M8
Tel: 604-882-1518; *Fax:* 604-882-1399
Toll-Free: 888-255-6311
asc@alchemistspecialty.com
www.alchemisttransport.com
Profile: Alchemist provides specialty hauling services to customers in the commercial, government & industrial sectors in Canada & the USA. Services include waste removal, hazardous material & biological waste transportation & 24/7 emergency service.
Will MacLean, General Manager
will@alchemistspecialty.com

Allied Automotive (Canada) Company
8950 Keele St., Vaughan, ON L4K 2N2
Tel: 905-669-2930; *Toll-Free:* 888-477-6997
www.alliedautomotive.com/canadian-network
Profile: Allied provides automotive hauling across North America.
Harry Porquet, Manager, Concord Terminal
harry.porquet@alliedautomotive.com

Ameri-Can Logistics
32146 King Rd., Abbotsford, BC V2T 5Z5
Tel: 604-851-5000; *Fax:* 604-851-5300
Toll-Free: 888-884-6225
www.ameri-canlogistics.com
Profile: Ameri-Can provides transportation logistics services, including expedited, cross-border, overnight & next-day & dangerous goods/hazmat.

AMJ Campbell Inc.
#830, 100 Milverton Dr., Mississauga, ON L5R 4H1
Tel: 905-795-3785; *Fax:* 905-670-3787
Toll-Free: 888-265-6683
contact@amjcampbell.com
www.amjcampbell.com
Ticker Symbol: AMJ
Profile: AMJ Campbell provides residential, commercial & corporate moving services.
Bruce Bowser, President & CEO
Brian Farquhar, Executive Vice-President, Operations

Aquatrans Distributors Inc.
#204, 19099 - 25th Ave., Surrey, BC V3S 3V2
Tel: 604-541-8784; *Fax:* 604-541-8785
Toll-Free: 800-666-8832
aquatrans@aquatrans.ca
www.aquatrans.ca
Profile: Aquatrans provides refrigerated, container & bulk commodity services.

Argus Carriers Ltd.
3839 Myrtle St., Burnaby, BC V5C 4G1
Tel: 604-433-1556; *Fax:* 604-433-3547
Toll-Free: 800-663-1890
office@arguscarriers.com
www.arguscarriers.com
Profile: Argus offers same-day as well as next-day local pickup & delivery. Regional LTL is also offered. The company serves Greater Vancouver, Fraser Valley, Vancouver Island, Thompson/Okanagan & the Northwest USA.

Armbro Transport Inc.
6050 Dixie Rd., Mississauga, ON L5T 1A6
Tel: 416-213-7298; *Fax:* 905-670-2692
Toll-Free: 800-268-0940
www.armbrotransport.com
Profile: Armbro offers regular & specialized local TL & LTL services, including dangerous goods. The company provides same-day services, as well as overnight services within 500 miles of Toronto.
Jim Davidson, President
jdavidson@armbrotransport.com

Armour Transportation Systems
689 Edinburgh Dr., Moncton, NB E1E 2L4
Tel: 506-857-0205; *Fax:* 506-859-9339
Toll-Free: 800-561-7987
armour@armour.ca
www.armour.ca
Profile: Armour provides regional LTL, North American TL, express courier, warehousing & distribution, specialized & port-to-door services. Long-haul subsidiaries include PoleStar, Triple B & Hillman's.
Wesley Armour, President & CEO

Arnold Bros. Transport Ltd.
739 Lagimodiere Blvd., Winnipeg, MB R2J 0T8
Tel: 204-257-6666; *Toll-Free:* 800-665-9018
customerservice@arnoldbros.com
www.arnoldbros.com
Profile: Arnold Bros. specializes in full truckload services, with dry van & temperature-controlled transportation methods, in Canada & various locations in the USA. The company is ISO 9001:2008 registered.

Arrow Transportation Systems Inc.
PO Box 38, #1300, 999 West Hastings St., Vancouver, BC V6C 2W2
Tel: 604-324-1333; *Fax:* 604-323-7427
arrowtransportation.ca
Profile: Arrow provides transportation & logistics services in Canada & the USA. Subsidiaries include Alberta Trucking & Arrow Reload Systems Inc.
Jack W. Charles Jr., CEO
jcharles@arrow.ca

Atlas Courier Ltd.
#112, 4238 Lozells Ave., Burnaby, BC V5A 0C4
Tel: 604-875-1111; *Fax:* 604-879-2311
Toll-Free: 888-595-6633
info@atlascourier.com
www.atlascourier.com
Profile: Atlas is a courier company, delivering packages in the Greater Vancouver Area.

ATS Andlauer Transportation Services Ltd. Partnership
100 Vaughan Valley Blvd., Vaughan, ON L4H 3C5
Tel: 416-744-4900; *Fax:* 416-744-4935
h-general1@ats.ca
www.atshealthcare.ca
Profile: ATS provides temperature-controlled transporation to the healthcare industry.
Bob Brogan, Chief Operating Officer

AYR Motor Express Inc.
46 Poplar St., Woodstock, ON E7M 4G2
Fax: 506-325-2008
Toll-Free: 800-668-0099
www.ayrmotor.com
Profile: AYR offers truckload, freight shipping, freight cross dock, freight brokerage & driver training services.
Joe Keenan, President
joe.keenan@ayrmotor.com

B&R Eckel's Transport Ltd.
PO Box 6249, 5514B - 50 Ave., Bonnyville, AB T9N 2G8
Tel: 780-826-3889; *Fax:* 780-826-4301
Toll-Free: 800-661-3290
admin@breckels.com
www.breckels.com
Profile: B&R Eckel's provides transportation services mainly to the oilfield industry, but also serves areas across Canada & the USA. Services include LTL, overdimensional, jack & roll, rig & tank moving, lifting & tubular storage.
Victor Ringuette, President

Besner
Parent: TransForce Inc.
1950, 3e rue, Saint-Romuald, QC G6W 5M6
Tél: 418-834-9891; *Ligne sans frais:* 800-463-4460
info@besner.com
www.transport-besner.com
François LeBlanc, Directeur, Ventes
fleblanc@besner.com

Bison Transport
1001 Sherwin Rd., Winnipeg, MB R3H 0T8
Tel: 204-833-0000; *Fax:* 204-833-0112
Toll-Free: 800-462-4766
online@bisontransport.com
www.bisontransport.com
Profile: Bison offers dry van, refrigerated, intermodal, warehousing & distribution, asset-based logistics & long-combination vehicle services.
Don Streuber, President & CEO

Brady Oilfield Services LP
Parent: Mullen Group Ltd.
PO Box 271, Midale, SK S0C 1S0
Tel: 306-458-2644
www.brady.sk.ca
Profile: Brady provides hauling services to & from drill sites, as well as operating vacuum & pressure trucks & providing storage for sand & gravel.
Scott Juravle, Director, Operations

Brookville Carriers Flatbed LP
Parent: Contrans Flatbed Group LP
79 Parkway Dr., Truro, NS B2N 5A9
Toll-Free: 800-565-1676
www.contransflatbedgroup.com/brookville-carriers
Profile: Brookeville specializes in transporting tandem, tridem & over-dimensional loads.
Harm Singh, General Manager
hsingh@brookville.ca

Bruce R. Smith Limited
RR#2, Simcoe, ON N3Y 4K1
Tel: 519-426-0904
www.brsmith.com
Profile: Bruce R. Smith specializes in refrigerated & heavy haul freight. The company also provides truckload, heated truckload, fleet maintenance & truckload logistics services.

Bulk Carriers (PEI) Ltd.
779 Bannockburn Rd., Cornwall, PE C0A 1H0
Tel: 902-675-2600
www.bulkcarrierspei.com
Profile: Bulk Carriers offers refrigerated & dry trucking services, as well as logistics.
Jack Kelly, President & CEO
jack@bulkcarrierspei.com

Calyx Transportation Group Inc.
107 Alfred Kuehne Blvd., Brampton, ON L6T 4K3
Tel: 905-494-4747; *Fax:* 905-494-4748
www.calyxinc.com
Profile: Calyx provides transportation & logistics services through its operating companies: National Fast Freight, Indis, Euroworld Transport, Muir's Cartage Limited, Totalline Transport & Hyphen.
Marcus Pryce-Jones, Chief Executive Officer
905-494-4739, mpryce-jones@calyxinc.com
Bill Gurd, Executive Vice-President
905-494-4746, billg@calyxinc.com

Canada Cartage System
1115 Cardiff Blvd., Mississauga, ON L5S 1L8
Tel: 905-564-2115; *Fax:* 905-795-4253
Toll-Free: 800-268-2228
info@canadacartage.com
www.canadacartage.com
Profile: Canada Cartage provides dedicated trucking, freight management & warehouse & distribution services.
Jeff Lindsay, President & CEO

Canadian American Transportation Inc.
4, rue du Transport, Coteau-du-Lac, QC J0P 1B0
Tél: 450-763-6363; *Téléc:* 450-763-2400
Ligne sans frais: 800-363-5313
cat@cat.ca
www.cat.ca
Profile: C.A.T. offers truckload, logistics & warehousing services.
Daniel Goyette, President
dgoyette@cat.ca

Canadian Freightways
Parent: TransForce Inc.
234040A Wrangler Rd., RR#5, Rocky View, AB T1X 0K2
Tel: 403-287-1090; *Fax:* 403-287-4343
Toll-Free: 888-868-7923
cf.cfmvmt.com
Profile: Canadian Freightways provides services to 25,000 points across Canada & the USA through a network of regional carriers including sister companies Epic Express & Click Express, & partners Averitt Express, New England Motor Freight, Midwest Motor Express & the Connection Company. Each partner in the North American network provides overnight & second day service within their region.
Ken Enns, President

Can-Am West Carriers Inc.
Parent: Vedder Transportation Group of Companies
400 Riverside Rd., Abbotsford, BC V2S 4P4
Toll-Free: 866-857-1375
info@canamwest.com
www.canamtransportation.com
Profile: Can-Am West provides the following transportation services: van, flat deck, step deck, Super B Train, asset-based logistics, multi-commodity & international freight.

Canpar Courier
Parent: TransForce Inc.
#102, 201 Westcreek Blvd., Brampton, ON L6T 0G8
Toll-Free: 800-387-9335
customerservice@canpar.com
www.canpar.com
Profile: Canpar offers day-to-day shipping services in Canada & to the USA.
Laurie Stoneburgh, Vice-President, Sales & Customer Service

Can-Truck Inc.
25 Hale Rd., Brampton, ON L6W 3J9
Tel: 905-595-0408; *Fax:* 905-595-0438
www.can-truck.com
Profile: Concentrates mainly on truckload freight including consolation and distribution throughout North America
Jagtar Raman, President
jraman@can-truck.com

Caravn Logistics Inc.
2284 Wyecroft Rd., Oakville, ON L6L 6M1
Tel: 905-338-5885; *Fax:* 905-338-8450
Toll-Free: 888-828-1727
info@caravanlogistics.ca
caravanlogistics.com
Profile: Caravan provides TL, just-in-time & LTL services across North America.

Cascade Carriers LP
Parent: Mullen Group Ltd.
6111 Ogdendale Rd. SE, Calgary, AB T2C 2A4
Tel: 403-236-7110; *Fax:* 403-236-7103
Toll-Free: 800-661-3109
www.cascadecarriers.com
Profile: Cascade transports dry bulk goods for customers in the construction, building, oil & gas & food industries.
Kevin James, Senior Vice President

Cavalier Transportation Services Inc.
PO Box 10, 14091 Humber Station Rd., Bolton, ON L7E 5T1
Tel: 905-857-6981; *Fax:* 905-857-1932
Toll-Free: 800-263-2394
info@cavalier.ca
www.cavalier.ca
Profile: Cavalier provides the following services: overnight LTL, freight brokerage, warehousing & distribution, specialized transportation (such as flatbed, intermodal, refrigerated & hazardous materials).

Celadon Canada
Parent: Celadon Trucking Services Inc.
280 Shoemaker St., Kitchener, ON N2E 3E1
Tel: 519-748-9773; *Toll-Free:* 800-332-0515
www.driveceladoncanada.com
Profile: Celadon provides dry van truckload, logistics, temperature-controlled & intermodal services, among others.
Paul Will, CEO, Celadon Trucking Services Inc.

Challenger Motor Freight Inc.
300 Maple Grove Rd., Cambridge, ON N3E 1B7
Tel: 519-653-6226; *Fax:* 519-653-9810
Toll-Free: 800-265-6358
Websiteinquiry_Info@challenger.com
www.challenger.com
Profile: Challenger transports goods between Canada & anywhere in North America. The company offers a full range of transportation, warehousing & logistics services.
Dan Einwechter, Chair & CEO

Chief Hauling Contractors ULC
Parent: Gibson Energy
5654 - 55 St. SE, Calgary, AB T2C 3G9
Tel: 403-215-4312; *Fax:* 403-203-0240
Toll-Free: 800-242-3187
info@chiefhauling.com
www.chiefhauling.com
Profile: Chief operates three main divisions: liquid bulk, high & low-density bulk.

CK Logistics
Parent: TransForce Inc.
6750, ch Saint-François, Montréal, QC H4S 1B7
Tél: 514-856-7580; *Téléc:* 514-332-1694
Ligne sans frais: 877-856-7580
www.cklogistics.ca

Concord Transportation
Parent: TransForce Inc.
96 Disco Rd., Toronto, ON M9W 0A3
Tel: 416-679-7400; *Fax:* 416-679-7422
Toll-Free: 800-387-4292
concordtransportation.com
Profile: Concord specializes in the transport of time-sensitive LTL & truckload freight throughout North America.

Consolidated Fastfrate Inc.
9701 Hwy. 50, Woodbridge, ON L4H 2G4
Fax: 905-893-1575
Toll-Free: 800-268-1564
www.fastfrate.com
Profile: Fastfrate provides LTL, dedicated, transload, warehousing & logistics services, as well as a range of specialty services.
Larry Rodo, President & CEO

Continental Cartage Inc. / CCI
Parent: Landtran Systems Inc.
412 - 26215 Township Rd. 531A, Acheson, AB T7X 5A4
Tel: 780-452-9414; *Fax:* 780-447-2292
Toll-Free: 877-452-9414
edmonton@continentalcartage.com
www.continentalcartage.com
Profile: Continental Cartage provides the following services: flat deck hauling, over-dimensional & heavy hauling, contract hauling, tractor services, hot shot & pilot car services.

Contrans Flatbed Group LP
Parent: Contrans Group Inc.
80 - 3rd Line, Hagersville, ON N0A 1H0
Toll-Free: 877-790-1226
www.contransflatbedgroup.com
Profile: Contrans Flatbed provides flatbed carrier services through the following divisions: Tri-Line Carriers, Brookville Carriers & Transportation Solutions Group. The company is able to transport legal weights all across North America, & heavy loads in Ontario, Quebec, the Maritimes, Michigan, Ohio, Indiana & New York, among other places. Over-dimensional loads can also be accommodated.
Steven Brookshaw, Vice-President
sbrookshaw@contrans.ca

Contrans Group Inc.
Formerly: Contrans Income Fund; Contrans Corp.
PO Box 1669, 1179 Ridgeway Rd., Woodstock, ON N4S 0A9
Tel: 519-421-4600
info@contrans.ca
www.contrans.ca
Ticker Symbol: CSS
Profile: Contrans provides freight transportation services through its range of subsidiaries.
Gregory W. Rumble, President & COO
James S. Clark, CFO & Vice-President, Finance

Cooney Transport Ltd.
PO Box 186, Trenton, ON K8V 5R2
Tel: 613-962-6666; *Fax:* 613-966-0896
info@cooney.ca
www.cooney.ca
Profile: Cooney provides general freight transportation, including van, flatbed & tanker services.

Cornerstone Logistics LP
Parent: Contrans Group Inc.
#204, 2180 Buckingham Rd., Oakville, ON L6H 6H1
Tel: 905-339-1456; *Fax:* 905-339-3226
Toll-Free: 877-388-2888
info@cornerstonelogistics.com
www.cornerstonelogistics.com
Profile: Cornerstone provides the following services: LTL, TL, port-to-door, cargo, flatbed & specialized equipment, cross-border, logistics & trucking across North America.

Couture
Parent: TransForce Inc.
99, route 271 sud, Saint-Éphrem-de-Beauce, QC G0M 1R0
Tél: 418-484-2104; *Téléc:* 418-484-5440
Ligne sans frais: 800-463-1671
info@tcfl.com
www.tcfl.com
Serge Poulin, Directeur général
serge.poulin@tcfl.com

La Crete Transport(79)Ltd.
Parent: Canadian Freightways (CF Group of Companies)
PO Box 248, La Crete, AB T0H 2H0
Tel: 780-928-3989; *Fax:* 780-928-3680
latrans@telusplanet.net
latrans.ca
Profile: La Crete Transport offers overnight shipping from Edmonton to most of northern Alberta.
Jake Fehr, General Manager
jfehr@latrans.ca

Day & Ross Freight
Parent: Day & Ross Transportation Group
398 Main St., Hartland, NB E7P 1C6
Toll-Free: 800-561-0013
custservice@dayandrossinc.ca
www.dayross.ca
Profile: Day & Ross Freight provides Canadian & USA LTL & TL, as well as temperature-controlled & speciality services.
Brian Murray, President

Day & Ross Transportation Group
Parent: McCain Foods Limited
398 Main St., Hartland, NB E7P 1C6
Toll-Free: 800-561-0013
custservice@dayandrossinc.ca
www.dayross.ca
Profile: Day & Ross offers LTL & TL services within Canada & to the USA, as well as temperature-controlled transportation & a range of specialized services, including warehousing, heavy haul moves & small package service. Subsidiaries include Day & Ross General Freight, Sameday Worldwide, Day & Ross Dedicated Logistics & Day & Ross Supply Chain Solutions.
Brian Murray, President

DB Schenker
Parent: Deutsche Bahn AG
5935 Airport Rd., 10th Fl., Mississauga, ON L4V 1W5
Tel: 905-676-0676; *Fax:* 905-677-0587
Toll-Free: 800-461-3686
sales.canada@dbschenker.com
www.dbschenker.ca
Profile: DB Schenker is a logistics & transportation company offering air freight, ocean freight & ground transport services. The company also customs brokerage & consulting services.
Eric Dewey, President & CEO
Michael Schulz, Chief Financial Officer

Deck-Way
Parent: Hi-Way 9 Group of Companies
4120 - 78 Street Cres., Red Deer, AB T4P 3E3
Tel: 403-342-4266; *Toll-Free:* 877-444-9299
www.hi-way9.com/division_deckway_services.php
Profile: Deck-Way offers LTL flat-deck services throughout Alberta & southwest Saskatchewan.
Samantha Loranger, Team Leader

Durocher International
Parent: TransForce Inc.
1214, route 255, Saint-Félix-de-Kingsey, QC J0B 2T0
Téléc: 819-848-3003
Ligne sans frais: 800-267-2042
direction@durocherinternational.com
www.durocherinternational.com

E&L Logistics
Parent: TransForce Inc.
#202, 6185, boul Taschereau, Brossard, QC J4Z 1A6
Tél: 450-462-0941; *Téléc:* 450-462-0669
Ligne sans frais: 800-567-3068
info@ellogistics.ca
www.ellogistics.ca
Albert Léger, Président

Eassons Transport Limited
1505 Harrington Rd., Kentville, NS B4N 3V7
Tel: 902-679-1153; *Fax:* 902-679-1162
www.eassons.com
Profile: Eassons Transport provides freight shipping services, with offices in Nova Scotia, Newfoundland & Ontario.
Paul Easson, President
902-679-7131

E-Can Oilfield Services LP
Parent: Mullen Group Ltd.
PO Box 510, Elk Point, SK T0A 1A0
Tel: 780-724-4018; *Fax:* 780-724-2166
Toll-Free: 866-684-4728
ecan@e-can-oilfield.com
www.e-can-oilfield.com
Profile: E-Can provides fluid hauling & general oilfield production services.
Clifford Smith, Vice-President & General Manager

ECL Carriers LP
Parent: Contrans Group Inc.
7236 Colonel Talbot Rd., London, ON N6L 1H8
Tel: 519-652-3900; *Fax:* 519-652-9726
Toll-Free: 800-265-0934
www.elgincartage.com
Profile: ECL Carriers specializes in the transportation of waste across North America, as well as reclamation, storage & trans-shipment & logistics services.

Ray Fillion, Director, Business Development

Edge Transportation Services Ltd.
Parent: Siemens Transportation Group Inc.
3550 Idylwyld Dr. North, Saskatoon, SK S7L 6G3
Tel: 306-242-0442; *Fax:* 306-975-9396
Toll-Free: 800-667-7333
customerservice@edgetransport.com
www.edgetransport.com
Profile: Edge Transportation offers specialized flat deck equipment for over-dimensional loads.

Elite Fleet
Parent: Eassons Transport Limited
106 Caledonia Rd., Moncton, NB E1H 3C6
Tel: 506-863-0100; *Fax:* 506-858-0450
elite@elitefleet.ca
www.elitefleet.ca

Essen Transport Ltd.
PO Box 2229, 300 Airport Dr., Winkler, MB R6W 4B9
Tel: 204-325-5200; *Fax:* 204-325-5252
www.essentransport.com
Profile: Founded in 1987, the transportation company operates a fleet of 50 trucks that delivery throughout Canada & the United States.
Nathan Elias, Manager
nathan@essentransport.com

Euroworld Transport
Parent: Calyx Transportation Group Inc.
107 Alfred Kuehne Blvd., Brampton, ON L6T 4K3
Tel: 905-494-4813; *Fax:* 905-494-4814
Toll-Free: 866-899-3451
sales@euroworld.ca
www.euroworld.ca
Profile: Euroworld Transport's main specialty is the transportation of liquor for control boards, breweries, wineries & distilleries in Canada, the USA & Mexico. The company also transports furniture/wood products, agricultural products, steel, food (includiug fresh, frozen & canned), garments, machinery, electronics & both non-hazardous & hazardous chemicals & liquids.

Formula Powell LP
Parent: Mullen Group Ltd.
PO Box 1328, Grande Prairie, BC T8V 4Z1
Tel: 780-814-6045; *Fax:* 780-539-5822
www.formulapowell.com
Profile: Formula Powell specializes in equipment hauling, mud & fluids hauling, mud warehousing & fluid storage & road mats for the oilfield industry.

Garry Mercer Trucking Inc.
1140 Midway Blvd., Mississauga, ON L5T 2C1
Toll-Free: 800-668-2980
www.gmercer.com
Profile: Garry Mercer Trucking specializes in LTL & FTL freight between Ontario & the USA.
Gerry Mercer, President

GHL Transport
Parent: TransForce Inc.
#102, 7887, rue Grenache, Anjou, QC H1J 1C4
Tél: 514-351-4501; *Ligne sans frais:* 800-589-3236
info@ghltransport.com
www.camionnageghl.com
Patrick Sarrazin, Directeur Général

Ghost Transportation Services
715E - 46th St. West, Saskatoon, SK S7L 6A1
Tel: 306-249-3515; *Fax:* 306-249-3335
customerservice@ghosttrans.com
www.ghosttrans.com
Profile: Ghost Transportation Services provides air, road, rail & ocean transportation services, as well as warehousing, distribution & storage.
Clay Dowling, CEO

Gibson Energy Inc.
#1700, 440 - 2nd Ave. SW, Calgary, AB T2P 5E9
Tel: 403-206-4000; *Fax:* 403-206-4001
www.gibsons.com
Ticker Symbol: GEI / TSX
Profile: Gibsons provides a range of services for the energy industry, including transportation, marketing, terminals & pipeline, custom treating terminals & distribution & processing. The company's trucking division mostly transports crude oil, asphalt, diluent, frac oils, chemicals, natural gas liquids & liquefied petroleum gases. They also handle sulphur, petroleum coke, gypsum & iron calcine through their wholly owned affiliate company, Chief Hauling Contractors ULC.
A. Stewart Hanlon, President & CEO
Donald A. Fowlis, Chief Financial Officer

Gibson Transport Ltd.
PO Box 100, 206 Church St. South, Alliston, ON L9R 1T9
Tel: 705-435-4342; *Fax:* 705-435-3869
Toll-Free: 800-461-4374
www.warrengibson.com
Profile: Warren Gibson provides LTL & TL services between Ontario, Québec & 48 states. They also specialize in cross docking, maintenance & warehousing services. The company is certified ISO 9001:2000 & 9001:2008.

Glen Tay Transportation LP
Parent: Contrans Group Inc.
42 Lanark Rd., Perth, ON K7H 3K5
Toll-Free: 800-450-9483
www.contrans.ca/glentay.html
Profile: Glen Tay specializes in transporting dry & liquid bulk goods.
Dan Roberts, General Manager

GN Transport Ltd.
163 Bowes Rd., Concord, ON L4K 1H3
Tel: 905-760-2888; *Fax:* 905-760-2040
www.gntransport.com
Profile: GN Transport owns 50 semi-tractors & 10 straight trucks. The company also provides warehousing & other transportation services.

Go Transport Ltd.
9975 - 199B St., Langley, BC V1M 3G4
Tel: 604-525-0800; *Toll-Free:* 888-363-6699
dispatch@gotransport.ca
gotransport.ca
Profile: Go Transport provides delivery services for customers needing tractor tailor transportation.
Mark Maarsman, President

Golden International
Parent: TransForce Inc.
801, boul Industriel, Bois-des-Filion, QC J6Z 4T3
Tél: 450-628-8000; *Téléc:* 450-628-1003
Ligne sans frais: 800-363-2828
www.goldenintl.ca
Martin Godbout, Directeur général
m.godbout@goldenintl.ca

Green for Life Corp. / GFL
125 Villarboit Cres., #B, Vaughan, ON L4K 4K2
Tel: 289-695-2550; *Fax:* 289-695-2551
info@gflenv.com
gflenv.com
Profile: GFL provides waste, organic waste & recycling services.
Patrick Dovigi, President & CEO

Grimshaw Trucking LP
Parent: Mullen Group Ltd.
PO Box 960, 11510 - 151 St., Edmonton, AB T5J 2L8
Fax: 780-455-7818
Toll-Free: 888-414-2850
GRM-CustServ@gtlp.ca
www.grimshaw-trucking.com
Profile: Grimshaw provides general merchandise carrying (LTL & TL) services to communities in Alberta, Northwest Territories & British Columbia.
Gary Leddy, Vice-President & General Manager
780-414-2847

Group Express Inc.
170 Main St. North, Alexandria, ON K0C 1A0
Tel: 613-525-1275; *Fax:* 613-525-1278
traffic@groupexpress.ca
www.groupexpress.ca
Profile: Groupex offers LTL, TL & dedicated transportation services.
Jeff ManKinnon, Traffic Manager

Groupe Boutin Inc.
128, ch du Tremblay, Boucherville, QC J4B 6Z6
Tel: 450-449-7373; *Fax:* 450-449-4436
Toll-Free: 800-267-4509
www.boutinexpress.com
Profile: Groupe Boutin offers roll-away, B-Train, closed van & flat bed services, as well as warehousing & distribution.
Bernard Boutin, President

Groupe Guilbault Ltd.
435, rue Faraday, Québec, QC G1N 4G6
Tél: 418-681-4111; *Téléc:* 418-681-9198
Ligne sans frais: 800-463-2655
www.groupeguilbault.com

Groupe Robert Inc.
20, boul Marie-Victorin, Boucherville, QC J4B 1V5
Tel: 514-521-1011; *Toll-Free:* 800-361-8281
information@robert.ca
www.robert.ca
Profile: Groupe Robert operates in two lines of business: transportation & storage & distribution. Under transportation, the company provides LTL, TL, intermodal, transborder & specialized services. Robert's storage division includes 20 warehouses in the areas of Montréal, Toronto & Québec City, with over 2.5 million total sq. ft. of space.
Michael Robert, President

H&R Transport Ltd.
3601 - 2nd Ave. North, Lethbridge, AB T1H 5K7
Tel: 403-328-2345; *Fax:* 403-328-2877
www.hrtrans.com
Profile: H&R Transport provides a range of satellite-tracked transportation services, including intermodal & logistics.
Paul Cook, Chief Executive Officer

Harold Newell & Son Trucking Ltd.
998 Oak Park Rd., Barrington, NS B0W 1E0
Tel: 902-637-2243; *Fax:* 902-637-1563

Harv Wilkening Transport Ltd. / HWT
Parent: Siemens Transportation Group Inc.
4205 - 76th Ave., Edmonton, AB T6B 2H7
Tel: 780-466-9155; *Fax:* 780-469-5646
Toll-Free: 800-611-7228
customerservice@hwtransport.com
www.hwtransport.com
Profile: HWT offers truckload services with satellite tracking, as well as warehousing & distribution.

Heavy Crude Hauling LP / HCH
Parent: Mullen Group Ltd.
6601 - 62 St., LLoydminster, AB T9V 3A9
Tel: 780-875-5358; *Fax:* 780-875-5825
Toll-Free: 877-875-5358
info@heavycrudehauling.com
www.heavycrudehauling.com
Profile: HCH provides fluid transportation for the oilfield industry.
Gordon Snider, Vice-President & General Manager

Highland Transport
Parent: TransForce Inc.
2815 - 14th Ave., Markham, ON L3R 0H9
Fax: 905-477-0940
Toll-Free: 800-263-3356
www.highlandtransport.com
Profile: Highland provides truckload & intermodal services.
Terry Gardiner, Vice-President, Operations
tgardiner@highlandtransport.com
John Hutton, General Manager, Intermodal
jhutton@highlandtransport.com

Hillman's Transfer Limited
Parent: Armour Transportation Systems
Sydport Industrial Park, 410 Gateway Ave., Sydney, NS B2A 4V1
Tel: 902-564-8113; *Fax:* 902-539-9498
Toll-Free: 800-565-9437
www.hillmanstransfer.com
Profile: Hillman's transports perishable & non-perishable goods to the Maritimes, Central Canada & Eastern USA.

Hi-Tech Express Inc.
Parent: Siemens Transportation Group Inc.
Bldg. A, #1, 1743 West County Rd. C, Roseville, MN 55113
Tel: 763-537-1690; *Fax:* 763-537-1692
Toll-Free: 800-328-8351
customerservice@hitechexpress.net
www.hitechexpress.net
Profile: Hi-Tech Express offers TL & LTL services to & from Canada, as well as within the USA.

Hi-Way 9 Express Ltd.
Parent: Hi-Way 9 Group of Companies
711 Elgin Close, Drumheller, AB T0J 0Y0
Tel: 403-823-4242; *Fax:* 403-823-7424
Toll-Free: 800-622-5800
rates@hi-way9.com
www.hi-way9.com/division_hiway9_services.php
Profile: Hi-Way 9 Express provides overnight, same-day & time-critical LTL services to central & southern Alberta.

Hi-Way 9 Group of Companies
Parent: Mullen Group Ltd.
711 Elgin Close, Drumheller, AB T0J 0Y0
Tel: 403-823-4242; *Fax:* 403-823-7424
Toll-Free: 800-622-5800
rates@hi-way9.com
www.hi-way9.com
Profile: Hi-Way 9 provides LTL, custom freight, flat deck & dry goods services through their four subsidiaries: Hi-Way 9 Express Ltd., Streamline Logistics, Deck-Way & Load-Way.
Reg Trentham, Vice-President & General Manager

Hyndman Transport (1972) Limited
1001 Belmore Line, Wroxeter, ON N0G 2X0
Tel: 519-335-3575; *Fax:* 519-335-3633
Toll-Free: 800-265-3071
www.hyndman.ca
Profile: Hyndman specializes in time-sensitive, transit-sensitive & high-value goods, such as consumer goods for large retailers, office furniture, food products, automotive after-market supplies (North America) & livestock (Canada).
Mike Campbell, President
mcampbell@hyndman.ca

Hyphen Transportation Management Inc.
Parent: Calyx Transportation Group Inc.
107 Alfred Kuehne Blvd., Brampton, ON L6T 4K3
Tel: 905-494-4770; *Toll-Free:* 877-549-7436
info@hyphentmi.com
www.hyphenateit.com
Profile: Hyphen provides dry van, reefer, flatbed & intermodal transportation across Canada & to the USA.
Greg Stamkos, Executive Vice-President

ICS Courier
Parent: TransForce Inc.
300 Talbot St. West, Aylmer, ON N5H 1K2
Toll-Free: 888-427-8729
cservice@icscourier.ca
www.icscourier.ca
Profile: ICS is a business-to-business courier that specializes in transporting packages & documents for next-day delivery.

International Truck & Engine Corporation Canada
Parent: Navistar Canada Inc.
PO Box 5337, Burlington, ON L7R 5A4
Tel: 905-332-2500
www.internationaltrucks.com
Profile: Dealers of trucks, buses, vans: engines, parts, services & financing
James J. Schumacher, President

International Truckload Services Inc. / ITS
#1450, 107 Belleville Dr., Belleville, ON K8N 5J1
Tel: 613-961-5144; *Fax:* 613-961-1255
Toll-Free: 800-267-1888
info@itstruck.ca
itstruck.ca
Profile: ITS provides dry van, long haul, flatbed & dedicated transportation services.
Max Haggarty, Chair & CEO
rmh@itsinc.on.ca
Rob Haggarty, President & COO
rhaggarty@itsinc.on.ca

Jackson Transportation Systems / JTS
PO Box 2293, 475 Memorial Ave., Orillia, ON L3V 6S2
Tel: 705-326-8888; *Fax:* 705-325-7345
Toll-Free: 800-661-7711
sales@jacksontransportation.com
www.jacksontransportation.com
Profile: Jackson Transportation provides expedited shipping services to the Greater Toronto Area.

JDI Logistics
Parent: J.D. Irving, Limited
300 Union St., Saint John, NB E2L 4M3
Tel: 506-633-6767; *Fax:* 506-648-3082
Toll-Free: 888-675-4888
customerservice@jdilogistics.com
www.jdilogistics.com
Profile: JDI Logistics is a third-party logistics company specializing in pulp & paper, & the food & beverage industry.

Kindersley Transport Ltd.
Parent: Siemens Transportation Group Inc.
2501 Faithfull AVe., Saskatoon, SK S7K 4K6
Tel: 306-668-2777; *Fax:* 306-668-2773
Toll-Free: 800-667-8508
customerservice@kindersleytransport.com
www.kindersleytransport.com
Profile: Kindersley provides TL & LTL services in Canada & the USA.
Erwen Siemens, President & General Manager

Kingsway Transport
Parent: TransForce Inc.
Bldg. 2, 5425 Dixie Rd., Mississauga, ON L4W 1E6
Toll-Free: 800-856-5559
www.kingswaytransport.com
Profile: Kingsway provides overnight LTL service & cross-border shipping throughout North America.

Kleysen Group LP
Parent: Mullen Group Ltd.
2800 McGillivray Blvd., Winnipeg, MB R3Y 1N3
kleysen@kleysen.com
www.kleysen.com
Profile: Kleysen provides bulk, deck, intermodal & multi-commodity distribution to customers throughout Canada & the USA.

Kobelt Transportation
Parent: TransForce Inc.
276, rue Queen, Sherbrooke, QC J1M 1K6
Tél: 819-566-0116; *Téléc:* 819-566-1917
www.kobelttransportation.com

Kooi Trucking Inc.
1906 Blue Line Rd., Waterford, ON N0E 1Y0
Tel: 519-443-0668; *Fax:* 519-443-5074
www.kooitrucking.com
Profile: Kooi Trucking Inc. is an experienced freight company, specializing in the transportatoin needs of North American importers and exporters since 1993.

Kriska Holdings Ltd.
PO Box 879, 850 Sophia St., Prescott, ON K0E 1T0
Tel: 613-925-5903; *Fax:* 613-925-1246
Toll-Free: 800-461-8000
info@kriska.com
www.kriska.com
Profile: Kriska primarily serves the area between Windsor & the greater Montréal area, but also provides North American coverage. Services include dry & temperature-controlled transportation & specialized warehousing.
Mark Seymour, President

Laidlaw Carriers Bulk LP
Parent: Contrans Group Inc.
PO Box 1651, 240 Universal Rd., Woodstock, ON N4S 0A9
Tel: 519-539-0471; *Fax:* 519-537-5321
www.laidlaw.ca/bulk_carriers
Profile: Laidlaw Carriers Bulk division offers bulk material transportation, as well as storage in their London, ON, warehouse.
Scott Talbot, Vice-President & General Manager
stalbot@laidlaw.ca

Laidlaw Carriers PCS GP
Parent: Contrans Group Inc.
3111, rue Bernard Pilon, Saint-Mathieu-de-Beloeil, QC J3G 4S5
Téléc: 450-536-3013
Ligne sans frais: 800-363-9412
www.laidlaw.ca/pcs
Profile: Laidlaw Carriers PCS division provides traditional flatbed services to Quebec, Ontario, the Atlantic provinces & the USA. PCS also operates a logistics division.
Pierre Labarre, General Manager
plabarre@laidlaw.ca

Laidlaw Carriers Tank LP
Parent: Contrans Group Inc.
PO Box 1571, 605 Athlone Ave., Woodstock, ON N4S 0A7
Fax: 519-539-0177
Toll-Free: 800-465-8265
www.laidlawcarrierstank.ca
Profile: Laidlaw Carriers Tank division provides dry or liquid bulk transportation.
Dave Golton, Vice-President & General Manager

Laidlaw Carriers Van LP
Parent: Contrans Group Inc.
21 Kerr Cres., Puslinch, ON N0B 2J0
Fax: 519-766-9800
Toll-Free: 800-263-8267
www.laidlaw.ca/van_carriers
Profile: Laidlaw Carriers Van division offers full truckload service, mostly between Ontario, Quebec, the Maritimes & the continental USA, for products such as paper, metals, food grade products, building materials, general merchandise & hazardous materials.
Laban Herr, Vice-President, Van Operations
lherr@laidlaw.ca

Landtran Systems Inc.
9011 - 50th St., Edmonton, AB T6B 2Y2
Tel: 780-468-4300; *Fax:* 780-468-6970
info@landtran.com
www.landtran.com
Profile: Through its subsidiaries, Landtran offers the following services: LTL, TL deck, TL van, cross-border, ice roads, dedicated delivery, warehousing, heavy haul/over-dimensional, transportation management, refrigerated transportation, & local cartage/tractor service. Subsidiaries include: Continental Cartage, Landtran Logistics, Monarch Transport, Pacific Coast Express, Tli Cho Landtran & Valley Roadways.

Lighthouse Transport Services Ltd.
PO Box 38010, #2, 150 Wright Ave., Dartmouth, NS B3B 1X2
Tel: 902-468-3696; *Fax:* 902-468-5267
Toll-Free: 800-770-5457
www.lighthousetransport.com
Profile: Offers FTL and LTL transport, container transport, warehousing and crating, oversized cargo moves, pilot car services, flatbed moves, deconsolidations, in bond warehousing, exclusive deliveries, in bond transport.
Ernest O'Toole, President

Load-Way
Parent: Hi-Way 9 Group of Companies
711 Elgin Close, Drumheller, AB T0J 0Y0
Tel: 403-823-4242; *Toll-Free:* 800-622-5800
www.hi-way9.com/division_loadway_services.php
Profile: Load-Way is a service provided by Hi-Way 9 that seeks to stack loads more safely than other systems, thereby reducing damage during delivery.
Virginia Rathgeber, Team Leader

Loomis Express
Parent: TransForce Inc.
200 Westcreek Blvd., Brampton, ON L6T 5S6
Tel: 905-460-2530; *Toll-Free:* 855-256-6647
www.loomis-express.com
Profile: Loomis delivers packages domestically & internationally, including to 220 countries & 120,000 global destinations.
Richard Hashie, President
Rick.hashie@loomis-express.com

Majestic Oilfield Services Inc.
Parent: Mullen Group Ltd.
9201 - 148 Ave., Grande Prairie, AB T8V 7W1
Tel: 780-513-2655; *Fax:* 780-532-8729
www.pandatank.com
Profile: Majestic specializes in fluid distribution & transportation, as well as operating other oilfield service units & trucks, such as hot oiler, vacuum, pressure, filtration & end-dump. Fluid storage & inventory management services are also offered.

Manitoulin Group of Companies
PO Box 390, 154 Hwy. 540B, Gore Bay, ON P0P 1H0
Fax: 705-282-1788
Toll-Free: 800-461-1168
www.manitoulingroup.com
Profile: Manitoulin provides a range of transportation services, including ground transport, logistics, customs brokerage, warehousing & distribution & global forwarding, through their five divisions.
Gord Smith, President & CEO

Maritime-Ontario Freight Lines Limited / M-O
1 Maritime-Ontario Blvd., Brampton, ON L6S 6G4
Tel: 905-792-6100; *Toll-Free:* 888-748-4388
www.m-o.com
Profile: M-O provides transportation & logistics services through its six divisions: FreightWORKS, COLDChain, LogisticWORKS, BULKServices, PaperXPRESS & ParcelWORKS/DedicatedWORKS.
Doug Munro, President
905-792-6134, dmunro@m-o.com
John Lepore, Executive Vice-President
905-792-6159, jlepore@m-o.com

Marol Express Inc.
2100, 95e rue, Saint-Georges, QC G5Y 8J3
Tél: 418-227-7379; *Téléc:* 418-222-5539
Ligne sans frais: 800-807-7379
info@crs-express.com
www.marolexpress.com
Profile: Marol Express fournit des services de transport et de stockage de semi-remorques.
Carol Gilbert, Fondatrice
Marc Rodrigue, Fondateur

McArthur Express Inc.
Parent: TransForce Inc.
170 Werlich Dr., Cambridge, ON N1T 1N6
Tel: 519-740-7080; *Fax:* 519-740-1612
Toll-Free: 800-668-9691
www.mcarthurexpress.com

Profile: McArthur provides specialty trucking services (such as for furniture, store fixtures & valuable products), as well as LTL & TL, warehousing & emergency & expedited services.
David Wyville, Vice-President & General Manager

McKevitt Trucking Ltd.
1200 Carrick St., Thunder Bay, ON P7B 5P9
Tel: 807-623-0054; *Fax:* 807-622-8616
www.mckevitt-trucking.com

Profile: McKevitt provides LTL & TL services from southern Ontario, as well as warehousing & cross docking services. Transport methods include refrigerated, heated, dry vans & flat deck trailers.

McMurray Serv-U Expediting Ltd.
Parent: TransForce Inc.
#2, 350 MacAlpine Cres, Fort McMurray, AB T9H 4A8
Tel: 780-791-3530; *Fax:* 780-790-0860
admin@mcmurrayservu.com
www.mcmurrayservu.com

Profile: McMurray provides transportation services to the resource industry in the Fort McMurray area.
Elvis Penton, General Manager

Meyers Transport Inc.
53 Grills Rd., Belleville, ON K8N 4Z5
Fax: 613-966-2824
Toll-Free: 800-565-3708
www.shipmts.com

Profile: Meyers serves Toronto, Montréal, Ottawa & the surrounding area. The company provides the following services: LTL, truckload, logistics, warehousing & storage trailers.
Jacquie Meyers, President
JMeyers@shipMTS.com

Midland Transport Limited
Parent: J.D. Irving, Limited
100 Midland Dr., Dieppe, NB E1A 7G9
Toll-Free: 888-643-5263
customerservice@midlandtransport.com
www.midlandtransport.com

Profile: Midland specializes in less-than-truckload & truckload services in eastern Canada & the United States. Divisions include: UniLine, Prime Time, Econo Line, Courier, Coast Line, Dedicated Solutions, Green Line & Refrigerated Distribution Services.
Scott Newby, Vice-President, Sales, Marketing & Customer Service

Mill Creek Motor Freight LP
Parent: Mullen Group Ltd.
PO Box 1120, Cambridge, ON N1R 5Y2
Tel: 519-623-6632; *Fax:* 519-740-0081
Toll-Free: 800-265-7868
www.millcreek.on.ca

Profile: Mill Creek provides van, flatbed, warehousing, logistics, intermodal & customs services.
Renate Hargreaves, General Manager
rhargreaves@millcreek.on.ca
Nathan McNamee, Director, Operations
nmcnamee@millcreek.on.ca

Monarch Transport (1975) Ltd.
Parent: Landtran Systems Inc.
3464 - 78th Ave., Edmonton, AB T6B 2X9
Tel: 780-440-6528; *Fax:* 780-463-3552
Toll-Free: 800-661-9937
www.monarchtransport.com

Profile: Monarch provides transportation logistics to points in Canada, the USA & Mexico.

Morneau Sego
Parent: Transport Morneau inc.
902, rue Phillipe Paradis, Québec, QC G1N 4E4
Tel: 418-527-5687; *Fax:* 418-527-8163
www.morneausego.com

Profile: Sego provides LTL & TL, flat bed, dry van & tanker services for products such as hazardous material, oversized shipments, concrete, timber, military, steel, non-perishable food & others. Storage space & containers are also offered.

Motrux Inc.
731 Belgrave Way, Delta, BC V3M 5R8
Tel: 604-527-1000; *Fax:* 604-527-1002
Toll-Free: 800-663-3436
info@motrux.com
www.motrux.com

Profile: Over the years Motrux has evolved from a designated carrier, serving only a few specific customers in Western Canada, to one that now serves many customers across a variety of industries - throughout North America.

Muir's Cartage Limited
Parent: Calyx Transportation Group Inc.
107 Alfred Kuehne Blvd., Brampton, ON L6T 4K3
Tel: 905-494-4774; *Fax:* 905-494-4776
Toll-Free: 800-646-2013
www.gomuirs.com

Profile: Muir's provides LTL, TL, dedicated transportation, as well as specialized "core carrier" services for big box retailers. Warehousing & distribution is also available.
Ted Brown, Executive Vice-President
ted.brown@muirscartage.com

Mullen Group Ltd.
Formerly: Mullen Transportation Inc.
#121A, 31 Southridge Dr., Okotoks, AB T1S 2N3
Tel: 403-995-5200; *Fax:* 403-995-5298
Toll-Free: 866-995-7711
IR@mullen-group.com
www.mullen-group.com
Ticker Symbol: MTL / TSX

Profile: Offices of holding companies; Long-distance trucking; Local trucking with storage; Various oil & gas fields services
Murray K. Mullen, President & CEO
Richard Maloney, Senior Vice-President
P. Stephen Clark, Chief Financial Officer

Mullen Oilfield Services LP
Parent: Mullen Group Ltd.
#600, 333 - 11 Ave. SW, Calgary, AB T2R 1L9
Fax: 403-213-4710
Toll-Free: 877-213-4700
www.mullenoilfield.com

Profile: Mullen Oilfield specializes in moving, transferring & relocating drilling rigs throughout Western Canada.
Rick Henning, Vice-President
403-213-4715

Mullen Trucking LP
Parent: Mullen Group Ltd.
#100, 80079 Maple Leaf Rd., Aldersyde, AB T0L 0A0
Tel: 403-652-8888; *Fax:* 403-652-1368
Toll-Free: 800-661-1469
info@mullentrucking.com
www.mullentrucking.com

Profile: Mullen Trucking provides LTL, TL & hot shot services throughout North America. Mullen operates its own satellite system to track deliveries.
Ed Scherbinski, President

Musket/Melburn Transportation Ltd.
2215 Royal Windsor Dr., Mississauga, ON L5J 1K5
Tel: 905-823-7800; *Fax:* 905-823-7555
support@musket.ca
www.musket.ca

Profile: Musket/Melburn provides intermodal shipping between Ontario, Québec & the USA. The company is ISO 9002 registered.

National Fast Freight / NFF
Parent: Calyx Transportation Group Inc.
107 Alfred Kuehne Blvd., Brampton, ON L6T 4K3
Tel: 905-494-4808; *Fax:* 905-494-4809
Toll-Free: 800-563-2223
cs@calyxinc.com
www.nationalfastfreight.com

Profile: National Fast Freight primarily specializes in intermodal LTL service within Canada.
Terry Jessup, Executive Vice-President

Normandin Transit Inc.
151, boul Industriel, Napierville, QC J0J 1L0
Tél: 450-245-0445; *Téléc:* 450-245-0441
Ligne sans frais: 800-667-8780
info@normandintransit.com
www.normandintransit.com

Northern Industrial Carriers Ltd. / NIC
7823 - 34 St., Edmonton, AB T6B 2V5
Tel: 780-465-0341; *Fax:* 780-469-4206
www.nictrucking.com

Profile: NIC provides transportation services to the petroleum, mining & manufacturing industries. Operating divisions include: Van, Dry & Liquid Bulk, Oilfield, Deck, Heavy Haul & Project Management.

Overland West Freight Lines Ltd.
Formerly: Overland Freight Lines; West Arm Truck Lines
#300, 10362 King George Hwy., Surrey, BC V3T 2W5
Tel: 604-580-4600; *Fax:* 604-580-4601
Toll-Free: 800-698-2111
admin@overlandwest.ca
www.overlandwest.ca

Profile: The company provides LTL-freight-courier service in British Columbia, Alberta, & the Western USA, & primarily serves the retail, commercial, mineral, forestry & municipal construction sectors.
Al Mason, General Manager

P&W Intermodal
Parent: TransForce Inc.
560 Maple Grove Dr., Oakville, ON L6J 7Y7
Tel: 905-815-9412; *Fax:* 905-815-1516
www.mtmx.ca

Mark Joczys, General Manager
mark@mtmx.ca

Pacific Coast Express Ltd.
Parent: Landtran Systems Inc.
10299 Grace Rd., Surrey, BC V3V 3VY
Tel: 604-582-3230; *Fax:* 604-588-7906
service@pcx.ca
www.pcx.ca

Profile: The primary service offered by the company is expedited LTL/TL, dry van motor freight service between all points in Western Canada & markets in Arizona, California, Oregon Washington & Mexico. The company also provides selected service to points in Idaho & Utah from British Columbia & Alberta, as well as transportation to & from Vancouver Island.

Patriot Freight Services Inc.
Parent: TransForce Inc.
6750, ch Saint-Francois, Montréal, QC H4S 1B7
Tél: 514-631-2900; *Téléc:* 514-631-4600
Ligne sans frais: 866-338-2900
info@patriotfreight.com
www.patriotfreight.com

Paul's Hauling Ltd.
250 Oak Point Hwy., Winnipeg, MB R2R 1V1
Tel: 204-633-4330; *Fax:* 204-694-4335
info@paulshauling.com
www.paulshauling.com

Profile: Paul's is a transporter of bulk goods primarily for the agricultural & petroleum industries.
Rod Corbett, Vice-President

Payne Transportation LP
Parent: Mullen Group Ltd.
PO Box 67, Group 200, RR#2, Winnipeg, MB R3C 2E6
Tel: 204-953-1400; *Fax:* 204-694-5810
Toll-Free: 866-467-2963
www.paynetransportation.com

Profile: Payne Transportation provides open deck, expedited LTL, dry van, logistics & specialized heavy haul services.
Tom Payne, President

Pe Ben Oilfield Services LP
Parent: Mullen Group Ltd.
605 - 17 Ave., Nisku, AB T9E 7T2
Tel: 780-955-2618; *Fax:* 780-955-7286
Toll-Free: 855-955-7473
info@peben.com
www.peben.com

Profile: Pe Ben specializes in transporting Oil Country Tubular Goods (OCTG), such as drill pipe, casing & tubing, for the oilfield industry. The company mainly focuses on Western Canada, but is capable of operating anywhere in North America.
Darryl Esch, Senior Vice-President & General Manager
VP@Peben.com

Pedersen Transport Ltd.
Parent: TransForce Inc.
234040B Wrangler Rd. SE, Rockview, AB T1X 0K2
Tel: 403-625-3656; *Fax:* 403-625-2430
info@pedersentransport.com
www.pedersentransport.com

Profile: Pedersen provides overnight & same-day LTL & LT services.
Wayne Pedersen, President

Penner International Inc.
20 PTH 12 North, Steinbach, MB R5G 1B7
Toll-Free: 866-729-7134
www.penner.ca
Profile: Penner provides TL dry van (both international & domestic) & distribution services. Shipments are tracked via satellite.
Allan Penner, President

PMK Logistics Inc.
Parent: Siemens Transportation Group Inc.
7542 Progress Way, Delta, BC V4G 1E9
Tel: 604-940-9828; *Fax:* 604-940-9838
customerservice@pmklogistics.com
www.pmklogistics.com
Profile: PMK offers a range of logistics services, as well as direct access to transportation resources offered by other Siemens divisions.

Polar Express Transportation Ltd.
#4, 10097 - 201 St., Langley, BC V1M 3G4
Tel: 604-888-3729; *Fax:* 604-888-3759
Toll-Free: 800-938-3525
www.polarexpresstrans.com
Profile: Polar Express offers LTL, full load, pickup/delivery & warehousing servies.
Jamie Plowman, President & General Manager

Portage Transport Inc.
1450 Lorne Ave. East, Portage la Prarie, MB R1N 3C3
Tel: 204-239-6451; *Fax:* 204-857-9104
portagetransport.com
Profile: Portage Transport provides short & long distance freight services to customers in Manitoba.
Bernie Driedger, President & CEO
Bernie.driedger@portagetransport.com
Liz Driedger, Vice-President & CFO
liz.driedger@portagetransport.com

Premay Equipment LP
Parent: Mullen Group Ltd.
11310 - 215 St., Edmonton, AB T5S 2B5
Tel: 780-447-5555; *Fax:* 780-447-3744
Toll-Free: 800-661-9315
inquiries@premayequipment.com
www.premay.com
Profile: Premay provides specialized transportation & rigging services to clients in the oilfield industry, including conventional transport, hydraulic heavy haul & railcar on- & off-loading. Other services include jack & roll, gantry work, engineering & logistics & mine services.

Premay Pipeline Hauling LP
Parent: Mullen Group Ltd.
22703 - 112 Ave., Edmonton, AB T5S 2M4
Tel: 780-447-3014; *Fax:* 780-447-3040
Toll-Free: 800-471-7976
info@premaypipeline.com
www.premaypipeline.com
Profile: Premay Pipeline operates a fleet of equipment including tractors, trailers, cranes & side booms that allow them to coordinate & transport pipeline for the oilfield industry.
Paul Schultz, Vice-President

Premium Transportation Inc.
PO Box 553, Huron Park, ON N0M 1Y0
Tel: 519-228-7779; *Fax:* 519-228-7799
Toll-Free: 888-875-0030
www.premiumtransportation.ca
Profile: Premium Transportation specializes in moving temperature controlled dry freight. They provide services to & from the U.S. & Western Canada.
Mike Hogan, President

Purolator Inc.
Formerly: Purolator Courier Ltd.
5995 Avebury Rd., Mississauga, ON L5R 3T8
Toll-Free: 888-744-7123
www.purolator.com
Profile: Purolator provides a range of courier & freight services to Canadian & international destinations.
Patrick Nangle, President & CEO
Deb Craven, Senior Vice-President & CFO

Quik X
Parent: TransForce Inc.
6767 Davand Dr., Mississauga, ON L5T 2T2
Tel: 905-565-8811; *Fax:* 905-565-8643
Toll-Free: 800-461-8023
www.quikx.com
Profile: Quik X provides LTL, truckload, intermodal, logistics & warehousing services through its five divisions: Quik X Transportation, Quik X Logistics, Roadfast, Quiktrax Intermodal & Axiom Warehousing.
Jeff King, President

Quill Transport Ltd.
Parent: Siemens Transportation Group Inc.
2501 Faithfull Ave., Saskatoon, SK S7K 4K6
Tel: 306-668-2777; *Fax:* 306-668-2773
Toll-Free: 800-667-8508
customerservice@quilltransport.com
www.quilltransport.com
Profile: Quill offers TL & LTL pickup & delivery services.

Rebel Transporting
Parent: TransForce Inc.
1910 - 91 Ave., Edmonton, AB T6P 1K9
Tel: 780-464-5171; *Fax:* 780-449-3522
edmonton@rebeltransport.ca
www.rebeltransport.ca
Profile: Rebel provides transportation services to the oil & gas & construction industries in Canada & the USA.
Ron Lystang, General Manager
rlystang@rebeltransport.ca

Rollex Transport Ltd.
Parent: Groupe Robert Inc.
9910, boul Lionel Boulet, Varennes, QC J3X 1P7
Tél: 450-652-4282; *Téléc:* 450-652-3038
Ligne sans frais: 888-283-5539
info@transportrollex.com
www.rollex.ca

Rolls Right Industry
2864 Norland Ave., Burnaby, BC V5B 3A6
Tel: 604-298-0080; *Fax:* 604-298-1366
info@rollsright.ca
www.rollsright.ca
Profile: Rolls Right Industries offers LTL, TL, container hauling & warehouse moving services.

The Rosedale Group
6845 Invader Cres., Mississauga, ON L5T 2B7
Tel: 905-670-0057; *Fax:* 905-670-7271
Toll-Free: 877-588-0057
hello@rosedalegroup.com
www.rosedale.ca
Profile: Rosedale offers LTL & TL service in Canada & between Canada & the USA; USA domestic TL & flatbed service; in-house logistics; & warehousing. The company's equipment is satellite-tracked.
Rolly Uloth, President

Rosenau Transport Ltd.
#200, 2950 Parsons Rd. NW, Edmonton, AB T6N 1B1
Tel: 780-431-2877; *Fax:* 780-431-0599
Toll-Free: 800-371-6895
info@rosenau.org
www.rosenau.org
Profile: Rosenau provides LTL, full load, bulk, hot shot/express, consolidated, overnight, deck, container, heated van & scheduled delivery services.

RST Industries
Parent: J.D. Irving, Limited
485 McAllister Dr., Saint John, NB E2L 4H8
Tel: 506-634-8800; *Toll-Free:* 800-463-8551
sales@rsttransport.com
www.rsttransport.com
Profile: RST specializes in the transportation of petroleum, propane, chemicals, food grade products & dry bulk, & offers flatbed services as well. The Commodities Division, based in Toronto, provides customers with logistics services.

Sameday Worldwide
Parent: Day & Ross Transportation Group
6975 Menkes Dr., Mississauga, ON L5S 1Y2
Toll-Free: 877-726-3329
sameday.dayrossgroup.com
Profile: Sameday Worldwide provides specialized shipping services in domestic & transborder categories. Within those, the company provides morning, afternoon, two-day & expedited ground services.

Service Ganeca Inc.
Parent: TransForce Inc.
1155, ch Brunelle, Carignan, QC J3L 0L1
Ligne sans frais: 800-561-7444
info@ganeca.ca
www.ganeca.ca
Yvan LaPointe, Administrateur
yvan.lapointe@amtransport.net

SGT 2000 Inc.
354, ch Yamaska, Saint-Germain, QC J0C 1K0
Tel: 819-395-4213; *Fax:* 819-395-2010
Toll-Free: 800-363-4216
www.sgt2000.com
Profile: SGT offers dry box, flatbed, container, warehousing, logistics & trailer-leasing services.
Denis Coderre, President

Shadow Lines Transportation Group
9975 - 199B St., Langley, BC V1M 2X5
Tel: 604-888-2928; *Toll-Free:* 800-663-1421
www.shadowlines.com
Profile: Shadow Lines offers the following services through its subsidiary companies: container, flat deck, linehaul, logistics, bulk solutions, waste mangement, portable toilets & security fencing. They operate in Canada, from British Columbia to Ontario, & throughout the continental USA.

Siemens Transportation Group Inc.
2311 Wentz Ave., Saskatoon, SK S7K 3V6
Tel: 306-934-1911; *Toll-Free:* 800-667-8557
www.siemenstransport.com
Profile: Siemens operates 10 trucking divisions whose services include international TL, LTL, international flat deck, ground courier & warehousing.
Doug Siemens, President
doug.siemens@siemenstransport.com
Scott Johnston, Vice-President & COO
scott.johnston@siemenstransport.com

Simard Transport Ltd.
1212 - 32nd Ave., Montréal, QC H8T 3K7
Tél: 514-636-9411; *Téléc:* 514-633-8078
Ligne sans frais: 888-282-9321
www.simard.ca
Profile: Simard provides local, regional & national transportation services including van, LTL, container, intermodal & logistics.
Peter Abraham, President
pabraham@simard.ca

SLH Transport Inc.
1585 Centennial Dr., Kingston, ON K7P 0K4
Tel: 613-384-9515; *Fax:* 613-384-5925
Toll-Free: 888-854-7548
customerservice@slh.ca
www.slh.ca
Profile: SLH provides the following services: truckload (Canada & cross-border), freight management throughout North America & fleet outsourcing services.
Paul Cooper, President

Smook Contractors Ltd.
Parent: Mullen Group Ltd.
101 Hayes Rd., Thompson, MB R8N 1M3
Tel: 204-677-1560; *Fax:* 204-778-7836
www.smook.ca
Profile: Smook provides winter road, oversized & heavy hauling, as well as other contracting services such as brilling & blasting, earth & rock excavation, environmental clean-up & soil remediation, mine construction & site restoration & more.
Peter Paulic, Vice-President & General Manager

Streamline Logistics
Parent: Hi-Way 9 Group of Companies
#200, 229 - 33 St. NE, Calgary, AB T2A 4Y6
Tel: 403-250-1563
www.hi-way9.com/division_streamline_services.php
Profile: Streamline provides logistics services from warehousing to distribution.
Rick Johnson, Team Leader

Sunbury Transport
Parent: J.D. Irving, Limited
Saint John, NB
Tel: 506-634-8800; *Fax:* 888-559-9799
Toll-Free: 800-786-2879
customerservice@sunbury.ca
www.sunbury.ca
Profile: Sunbury provides transportation by van & flatbed, specializes in dry bulk goods, & also provides logistics & brokerage services.

Sure Track Courier Ltd.
321 Courtland Ave., Concord, ON L4K 5B5
Tel: 905-832-8324; *Fax:* 905-832-1238
Toll-Free: 800-269-1151
www.suretrackcourier.com
Profile: Sure Track offers courier, trucking, freight & warehousing services.
Paul Bahous, President
Paul@suretrackcourier.com

System 55 Transport Inc.
2466 Beryl Rd., Oakville, ON L6J 7X4
Tel: 905-842-6800; *Fax:* 905-842-6632
Toll-Free: 800-268-5070
www.system55.com
Profile: System 55 offers dry van, flat bed & logistics services.
Zoran Popovic, President & CEO

Tenold Transportation LP
Parent: Mullen Group Ltd.
19470 - 94th Ave., Surrey, BC V4N 4E5
Tel: 604-888-7822; *Fax:* 604-888-0394
Toll-Free: 800-663-0094
www.tenold.com
Profile: Tenold provides intermodal, open deck, van, warehousing & distributing services.
Keith DeBlaere, General Manager

TForce Integrated Solutions
Parent: TransForce Inc.
96 Disco Rd., Toronto, ON M9W 0A3
Tel: 416-679-7979; *Fax:* 416-679-7845
Toll-Free: 800-265-6085
contact_sales@tforce-solutions.com
www.tforce-solutions.com
Profile: TForce provides small parcel, LTL, truckload & air freight services.
Rick Hashie, President
contact_executive@tforce-solutions.com

Thomson Terminals Limited
100 Iron St., Toronto, ON M9W 5L9
Tel: 416-240-0897; *Fax:* 416-240-0624
www.thomsongroup.com
Profile: Thomson provides services in four main categories: Warehousing, Freight & Transportation, Design Build & Consulting. Under the Freight & Transportation division the company offers FTL (Canada & USA), LTL (Canada), expedited services, as well as fleet management, plant & warehouse moves & job site delivery.
Jim Thomson, President & CEO

Tiger Courier Inc.
Parent: Siemens Transportation Group Inc.
2501 Faithful Ave., Saskatoon, SK S7K 4K6
Tel: 306-242-1256; *Fax:* 306-244-0070
Toll-Free: 888-844-3724
info@tigercourier.com
www.tigercourier.com
Profile: Tiger Courier offers transportation services for time-sensitive shipments. The company has offices in eight major cities across Canada.

Tli Cho Landtran Transport Ltd.
Parent: Landtran Systems Inc.
PO Box 577, 358 Old Airport Rd., Yellowknife, YT X1A 2N4
Tel: 867-873-4044; *Fax:* 867-873-2780
www.tlicholandtran.com
Profile: The company offers transportation services between the Northwest Territories & the rest of North America, including ice road services.

TMT Freight System
14 Cadetta Rd., Brampton, ON L6T 3Z8
Tel: 905-794-9845; *Fax:* 905-794-9846
Toll-Free: 888-817-4410
info@tmtfreight.com
www.tmtfreight.com
Profile: TMT Freight System was established in 1993 & provides intermodal & warehousing services.
Bobby Mahal, President
bobby@tmtfreight.com
Jasbir Sanghera, Vice-President

Total Transfer Services Ltd.
Parent: TransForce
2840 - 76 Ave. NW, Edmonton, AB T6P 1J4
Tel: 780-468-5171; *Fax:* 780-440-9853
Toll-Free: 888-242-9377
info@totaltransferservices.com
www.totaltransferservices.com
Profile: Total Transfer provides LTL service to Alberta, British Columbia, Saskatchewan, Manitoba & Northwest Territories.

Totalline Transport
Parent: Calyx Transportation Group Inc.
107 Alfred Kuehne Blvd., Brampton, ON L6T 4K3
Tel: 905-494-4747; *Fax:* 905-494-4748
Toll-Free: 800-565-3556
contactus@totallinetransport.com
www.totalline.com
Profile: Totalline provides LTL & TL general freight & custom delivery services with Canada-wide coverage. The company also provides warehousing & a Premier Express service for expedited shipping.

Trans4 Logistics
Parent: TransForce Inc.
#101, 5425 Dixie Rd., Mississauga, ON L4W 1E6
Tel: 905-212-9001; *Fax:* 905-212-1495
Toll-Free: 800-268-0475
info@trans4.com
www.trans4.com
Profile: Trans 4 is a full service logistics company specializing in the transportation of food items, products requiring special permits, hazardous & non-hazardous chemicals & communication components. Both road & rail transportation are offered & service is provided in four main categories: home & office delivery, truckload, intermodal, highway brokerage & warehousing.
Brenda Everitt, Vice-President & General Manager

TransForce Inc.
Formerly: TransForce Income Fund
#500, 8801 Trans-Canada Hwy., Saint-Laurent, QC H4S 1Z6
Tél: 514-331-4000; *Téléc:* 514-337-4200
www.transforcecompany.com
Ticker Symbol: TFI / TSX
Profile: Long-distance trucking; Local trucking without storage
Alain Bedard, FCPA, FCAChair, President & CEO

Transport Bourassa Inc.
800, rue Dijon, Saint-Jean-sur-Richelieu, ON J3B 8G3
Tél: 450-346-5313; *Téléc:* 450-346-5150
Ligne sans frais: 800-363-9254
www.bourassa.ca
Profile: Transport Bourassa provides LTL & TL services in Quebec, Ontario & the USA, including the transportation of hazardous materials.

Transport Grégoire
Parent: TransForce Inc.
850, rue Labonté, Drummondville, QC J2C 5Y4
Ligne sans frais: 800-461-8813
info@transportgregoire.com
www.transportgregoire.com

Transport Morneau inc.
40, rue Principale, Saint-Arsène, QC G0L 2K0
Tel: 418-862-2727; *Fax:* 418-862-7063
www.groupemorneau.com
Profile: Morneau provides general LTL & TL services through its Transport division; temperature-controlled transportaton through Eskimo Express; import/export services through Groupe Réflexion; & transportation management services through Solution Morneau.
André Morneau, President

Transport St-Lambert
Parent: TransForce Inc.
1950, 3e rue, Saint-Romuald, QC G6W 5M6
Tél: 418-839-6655; *Téléc:* 418-839-9424
Ligne sans frais: 888-338-3381
info@st-lambert-transport.com
www.st-lambert-transport.com

TransX Group of Companies
2595 Inkster Blvd., Winnipeg, MB R3C 2E6
Tel: 204-632-6694; *Fax:* 204-694-2958
Toll-Free: 800-665-7392
www.transx.com
Profile: Through a fleet of 1,500 trucks, 4,000 trailers & 1,000 intermodal containers, TransX provides LTL, TL, flat deck, intermodal, logistics, customs brokerage & specialized services. The company operates 12 terminals throughout North America.

Trappers Transport Ltd.
PO Box 23, Group 514, RR#5, Winnipeg, MB R2C 2Z2
Tel: 204-697-7647; *Fax:* 204-224-6258
Toll-Free: 800-561-9696
www.trapperstransport.com
Profile: Trappers Transport specializes in transporting refrigerated LTL or full loads throughout North America. The company's maintenance shop services & repairs all makes & models of trucks, trailers, heavy equipment & reefer units.
Dan Omeniuk, President & CEO

Travelers Transport Services
Services de transport Travelers
195 Heart Lake Rd. South, Brampton, ON L6W 3N6
Tel: 905-457-8789; *Fax:* 905-457-8084
Toll-Free: 800-265-8789
www.travelers.ca
Profile: Travelers provides expedited, regular van, heated, warehousing, logistic equipment & third-party logistics services.

Triangle Freight Services Ltd.
Parent: Siemens Transportation Group Inc.
3550 Idylwyld Dr. North, Saskatoon, SK S7L 6G3
Tel: 306-373-7744; *Toll-Free:* 800-667-8402
customerservice@trianglefreight.com
www.trianglefreight.com
Profile: Triangle Freight provides flat deck transportation services to the oilfield, farm & industrial equipment sectors.

Tri-Line Carriers LP
Parent: Contrans Flatbed Group LP
235185 Ryan Rd., Rocky View, AB T1X 0K1
Toll-Free: 800-661-9191
www.contransflatbedgroup.com/tri-line-carriers
Profile: Tri-Line provides transportation services to the oilfield equipment, steel, machinery & building products industries, among others.
Steven Brookshaw, Vice-President
sbrookshaw@contrans.ca

Trimac Transportation Services LP
Formerly: Trimac Corporation
3215 - 12 St. NE, Calgary, AB T2E 7S9
Tel: 403-298-5100; *Fax:* 403-298-5258
canadacustomercare@trimac.com
www.trimac.com
Ticker Symbol: TMA.UN
Profile: The company provides services in highway transportation & North American hauling of bulk commodities.
Ed Malysa, President & COO

Tripar Transportation LP
Parent: Contrans Group Inc.
#100, 2180 Buckingham Rd., Oakville, ON L6H 6H1
Toll-Free: 800-387-7210
www.contrans.ca/tripar.html
Profile: Tripar offers LTL services between Canada & the Eastern USA.
Don Burditt, General & Sales Manager

TST Overland Express
Parent: TransForce Inc.
5200 Maingate Dr., Mississauga, ON L4W 1G5
Tel: 905-625-7500; *Fax:* 905-224-7062
www.tstoverland.com
Profile: TST specializes in time-sensitive LTL transportation across North America, plus Alaska, Hawaii & Puerto Rico.
Rob O'Reilly, President

UPS Canada
Parent: United Parcel Service Inc.
1022 Champlain Ave., Burlington, ON L7L 0C2
Toll-Free: 800-742-5877
www.ups.com/ca
Profile: UPS provides shipping & freight services to every address in Canada, either through their own company or through independent contractors. The parent company is one of the largest shipping companies in the world, with operations in more than 200 countries.
Mike Tierney, President, UPS Canada

VA Inc.
600, rue Louis-Pasteur, Boucherville, QC J4B 7Z1
Tél: 450-641-0082; *Ligne sans frais:* 800-363-8175
asc.csr@vatransport.com
www.vatransport.com
Profile: VA provides LTL, TL & container transportation services.

Valley Roadways Ltd.
Parent: Landtran Systems Inc.
1115 Chief Louis Way, Kamloops, BC V2H 1J8
Tel: 250-374-3467; *Toll-Free:* 888-374-3440
info@valleyroadways.com
www.valleyroadways.com
Profile: The company offers flat deck transportation services, as well as equipment hauling, camp setup & relocation, warehousing & reload services. They also operate a full maintenance shop serving tractors, trailers & other commercial vehicles.

Vedder Transport Ltd.
Parent: Vedder Transportation Group of Companies
400 Riverside Rd., Abbotsford, BC V2S 4P4
Toll-Free: 800-661-8883
info@veddertransport.com
www.veddertransportation.com
Profile: Vedder provides transportation services in the following categories: liquid & dry edible, liquid rail car transloading, food grade tank wash, international freight & warehousing.

Vedder Transportation Group of Companies
400 Riverside Rd., Abbotsford, BC V2S 4P4
Toll-Free: 866-859-1375
info@vtlg.com
www.vtlg.com
Profile: The Vedder Group provides transportation, repair & sales services through its operating companies: Vedder Transport Ltd., Can-Am West Carriers Inc., Vedder Multi Commodity Transload, Big Rig Collision & Paint Ltd., & Larry's Used Truck & Trailer Sales Ltd.
Fred Zweep, President
Larry Wiebe, Chief Executive Officer

Verspeeten Cartage Ltd.
PO Box 247, Ingersoll, ON N5C 3K5
Tel: 519-425-7881; *Fax:* 519-425-4962
www.verspeeten.com
Profile: The company is ISO 9001:2000 registered.
Ron Verspeeten, President & CEO
ron@verspeeten.com

Vitran Express Canada Inc.
Formerly: Vitran Corporation Inc.
1201 Creditstone Rd., Concord, ON L4K 0C2
Tel: 416-798-4965; *Fax:* 416-798-4753
Toll-Free: 800-263-9588
ltl.cda.webmaster@vitran.com
www.vitran.com
Ticker Symbol: VTN
Profile: Vitran specializes in long-distance trucking, arrangement of transportation of freight & cargo, general warehousing & storage & refuse systems.

VTL Group
#208, 1221 - 32 Ave., Montréal, QC H8T 3H2
Tel: 514-631-6669; *Fax:* 514-631-2694
Toll-Free: 800-561-8194
dispatch@vtltransport.com
www.vtltransport.com
Profile: VTL operates three divisions: VTL V-Trans (logistics), VTL Transport (general transportation) & Nautica (international freight & forwarding). A 100 per cent company-owned trucking fleet operates under VTL Transport.

Westfreight Systems, Inc.
Parent: TransForce Inc.
7530 - 84 St. SE, Calgary, AB T2C 4W3
Tel: 403-279-8388; *Fax:* 403-279-8390
Toll-Free: 800-881-1266
www.westfreight.com
Profile: Westfreight provides full load, van, LTL & heavy hauling services between Canada & the USA.

Winalta Transport Ltd.
Parent: TF Energy Solutions
53026 Range Rd. 262, Spruce Grove, AB T7X 5A1
Tel: 780-447-3521; *Fax:* 780-447-4558
Toll-Free: 888-447-3521
Profile: Winalta serves the construction, plant & oilfield industries.

Withers LP
Parent: Mullen Group Ltd.
PO Box 1480, 3602 - 93 St., Grande Prairie, AB T8V 4Z2
Tel: 780-539-5347; *Fax:* 780-539-5299
Toll-Free: 800-700-7965
info@witherslp.com
www.witherstrucking.com
Profile: Withers hauls & stores tubular products used by the oilfield industry, as well as hauling service rigs, tanks & other support equipment.

Wolverine Freight System
2500 Airport Rd., Windsor, ON N8W 5E7
Tel: 519-966-8970; *Fax:* 519-966-2800
Toll-Free: 800-265-5051
inquiries@wolverinefreight.ca
www.wolverinefreight.ca
Profile: Wolverine offers overnight TL services between Ontario & Michigan, Wisconsin, Illinois, Ohio, Pennsylvania, Kentucky & New York. Warehousing & logistics services are also offered. The company is ISO 9001:2000 registered.

XTL Transport Inc.
75 Rexdale Blvd., Toronto, ON M9W 1P1
Tel: 416-742-0610; *Toll-Free:* 800-361-5576
www.xtl.com
Profile: XTL provides transportation, logistics & distribution services, as well as temperature-controlled transportation through its XTL TempSolution division.
Genevieve Gagnon, President
genevieve.gagnon@xtl.com
Serge Gagnon, CEO & Founder
serge.gagnon@xtl.com

Zeena Transport
245 Kimberly Rd., Winkler, MB R6M 1A8
Tel: 204-362-2778
info@zeenatransport.com
www.zeenatransport.com
Profile: Zeena Transport offers refrigerated & dry van services.

Transportation Manufacturers & Services

2Source Manufacturing Inc.
5261 Bradco Blvd., Mississauga, ON L4W 2A6
Tel: 905-361-9998; *Fax:* 905-282-9924
Toll-Free: 866-361-9997
info@2Source.com
www.2source.com
Profile: 2Source specializes in producing landing gear bushings & similar parts for specific aircraft platforms.
Robert Glegg, CEO

3 Points Aviation
91 Watts Ave., Charlottetown, PE C1E 2B7
Tel: 902-628-8846; *Fax:* 902-628-8838
www.3pointsaviation.com
Profile: 3 Points supplies aircraft parts & support, including airframe parts, engines, propellers, & landing gear.
John Druken, Owner
709-834-6034, Fax: 709-834-6058, johnd@3pointsaviation.com
Leo Druken, CFO
709-628-8846 ext: 6042, Fax: 709-628-8838,
leo@3pointsaviation.com

3M Canada Company
300 Tartan Dr., London, ON N5V 4M9
Tel: 800-325-2376; *Fax:* 800-479-4453
www.3m.com/aerospace
Ticker Symbol: MMM / NYSE
Profile: This division of 3M Canada Company specializes in manufacturing, maintenance, & repair of aircraft, airframes, & engines for both commercial & space flight.

ABB Inc.
8585 route Transcanadienne, Montréal, QC H4S 1Z6
Tél: 514-856-6222; *Téléc:* 514-856-6297
Ligne sans frais: 800-905-0222
www.abb.ca
Ticker Symbol: ABB / NYSE; ABBBN / SIX
Profile: The company specializes in the manufacture of analytical technologies, targeting the industrial processes, defense, & space markets.
Daniel Assandri, President & CEO, ABB Canada

ACS-NAI, Ltd.
Formerly: Aero Consulting Services; Northern Aero Industries
Parent: EMTEQ, Inc.
25 Dunlop Ave., Winnipeg, MB R2X 2V2
Tel: 204-783-5402; *Fax:* 204-783-5436
www.acs-nai.com
Profile: The company provides engineering, manufacturing & certification services to the global aviation industry. They have offices in Manitoba & Québec.
Udaya Silva, Vice-President & General Manager, Canada

Action Aero Inc.
34 Belmont St., Charlottetown, PE C1A 5H1
Tel: 902-370-3311; *Fax:* 902-370-3313
info@actionaero.com
www.actionaero.com
Profile: The company provides overhaul & repair services for fuel, oil, & air related engine accessories.
Dave Trainor, President
dave@actionaero.com
Chad Crockett, Manager, Customer Service
ccrockett@actionaero.com
Larry Wilson, Manager, Quality
lwilson@actionaero.com

Adacel Inc.
PO Box 48, #300, 895, rue de la Gauchetière ouest, Montréal, QC H3B 4G1
Tel: 514-636-6365; *Fax:* 514-636-2326
www.adacel.com
Ticker Symbol: ADA / ASX
Profile: The company creates software & simulation products for the training of air traffic controllers, pilots, & airport vehicle operators.
Seth Brown, CEO
Gary Pearson, COO

ADGA Group
Groupe ADGA
110 Argyle Ave., Ottawa, ON K2P 1B4
Tel: 613-237-3022; *Fax:* 613-237-3024
info@adga.ca
www.adga.ca
Profile: The Group serves the defense & aerospace sectors through its three companies: ADGA Group Consultants Inc., AEPOS Technologies Corporation, & APS Aviation Inc. Its specialities are: weapons systems management; airframe systems; avionics; armaments; automatic test equipment; maintenance support; instrument & electrical systems; technical documentation; & C4ISR.

Advanced Integration Technology Canada / AIT
Parent: Advanced Integration Technology, Inc.
26977 - 56th Ave., Langley, BC V4W 3Y2
Tel: 604-856-8939; *Fax:* 604-856-8993
www.aint.com
Profile: AIT is an industrial automation & tooling company providing turnkey factory integration & the design, manufacture, & installation of machines & systems for the automated assembly of aerospace structures. Their Aldergrove, BC, facility specializes in fabrication, machining, assembly & metrology.
Frank Colarossi, Contact
frank.colarossi@aint.com

Advanced Precision
70 Thornhill Dr., Dartmouth, NS B3B 1S3
Tel: 902-468-5653; *Fax:* 902-468-5737
advancedprecision.ca
Profile: The company provides precision component machining, fabrication & assembly services to the aerospace, military & industrial sectors.
Jason Farris, Manager, Estimation
jfarris@advancedprecision.ca

Aéro Montréal
#8000, 380, rue Saint-Antoine ouest, Montréal, QC H2Y 3X7
Tel: 514-987-9330; *Fax:* 514-987-1948
info@aeromontreal.ca
www.aeromontreal.ca
Profile: A think tank designed to bring members of Quebec's aerospace industry together to meet common goals & promote shared interests.
Suzanne M. Benoît, President & CEO
suzanne.benoit@aeromontreal.ca

Aero Recip Canada Ltd.
Parent: Gregorash Aviation
540 Marjorie St., Winnipeg, MB R3H 0S9
Tel: 204-788-4765; *Fax:* 204-786-2775
Toll-Free: 800-561-5544
info@aerorecip.com
www.aerorecip.com
Profile: Aero Recip exchanges, overhauls, & repairs piston engines & specializes in Pratt & Whitney radial engines.
Dave Wakeman, Contact, Sales
dwakeman@aerorecip.com

AeroInfo Systems
Parent: Boeing
#200, 13575 Commerce Pkwy., Richmond, BC V6V 2L1
Tel: 604-232-4200; *Fax:* 604-232-4201
www.aeroinfo.com
Profile: AeroInfo is a business & technology consulting firm serving commercial aviation, defence, marine, & natural resource & energy sectors.
Bob Cantwell, President/CEO
Stig Westerlund, CFO

Aero-safe Technologies Inc.
PO Box 335, 1767 Pettit Rd., Fort Erie, ON L2A 5N1
Tel: 905-871-1663; *Fax:* 905-871-7093
sales@aerosafe.ca
www.aerosafe.ca
Profile: The company specializes in high precision CNC manufacturing & assembly for the aerospace & defence industries.

Aerospace BizDev
5057 - 2A Ave., Delta, BC V4M 3M6
Tel: 604-839-5504
www.aerospacebizdev.com
Profile: A consulting company specializing in business development in the aerospace industry.
Linda Wolstencroft, President
linda@aerospacebizdev.com

Aerospace Welding Inc. / AWI
Parent: Groupe DCM
890, boul Michèle-Bohec, Blainville, QC J7C 5E2
Tel: 450-435-9210; *Fax:* 450-435-7851
info@groupedcm.com
www.aerospacewelding.com
Profile: The company specializes in fabricating & repairing metallic aircraft & engine parts of all sizes.

Aerosystems International Inc. / ASI
3538, rue Ashby, Montréal, QC H4R 2C1
Tel: 514-336-9426; *Fax:* 514-336-4383
info@asiiweb.com
www.asiiweb.com
Profile: The company was founded in 1971, & provides services to the aviation industry including wire harness assemblies, ground support equipment, component integration, & logistical support.
Fergie Legge, President & CEO
legge@asiiweb.com

AeroTek Manufacturing Ltd.
1449 Hopkins St., Whitby, ON L1N 2C2
Tel: 905-666-3400; *Fax:* 905-666-3413
customerservice@aerotekmfg.com
www.aerotekmfg.com
Profile: AeroTek provides processing services such as electroplating, anodizing, chemical conversions, painting, non-destructive testing & sub-assembly, among others.
Jonathan Schofield, President

Aflare Systems Inc.
37 Edgemont Dr., Brampton, ON L6V 1K9
Tel: 289-298-2978
info@aflaresystems.com
www.aflaresystems.com
Profile: The company was founded in 2005, & specializes in engineering power systems, sensor suites, software applications, & wireless communication for the automotive, telecommunications, aerospace, & medical industries.
Roman Ronge, President & Principal Engineer

AgustaWestland
Parent: Finmeccanica S.p.A.
10 Somerset St. West, Ottawa, ON K2P 0H4
Tel: 613-782-2241
ca.agustawestland.com
Profile: AugustaWestland is the manufacturer of the Cormorant helecopter used by the Canadian Forces for search & rescue operations. The company also manufactures a range of rotocraft for civil & military use.
Jeremy Tracy, Head, Canada Region
jeremy.p.tracy@gmail.com

Airbus Helicopters Canada
PO Box 250, 1100 Gilmore Rd., Fort Erie, ON L2A 5M9
Tel: 905-871-7772; *Fax:* 905-871-3320
Toll-Free: 800-267-4999
www.airbushelicopters.ca
Profile: The company sells aircraft, manufactures composites, & provides engineering solutions, repairs, & overhaul. Canadian customers include the RCMP & the Canadian Coast Guard.
Romain Trapp, President & CEO
romain.trapp@airbus.com
Laura Senecal, Director, Communications & Corporate Affairs
905-871-7772

AleniaAermacchi
Parent: Finmeccanica S.p.A.
#1150, 45 O'Connor St., Ottawa, ON K1P 1A4
www.aleniana.com
Profile: The company manufactures the C-27J Spartan search & rescue twin turboprop aircraft, which has been in production since 2001 & is currently used by nine national air forces.

Alloy Concepts Inc. Precision CNC Machining
59 Guildford Ave., Dartmouth, NS B3B 0H5
Tel: 902-468-1144; *Fax:* 902-468-7632
www.alloyconceptscnc.com
Profile: The company specializes in prototyping, production manufacturing, & programming for sectors including avionics, automotive manufacturing, military, renewable energy, & ocean science, among others.
David Schnare, Owner/Operator
dschnare@alloyconceptscnc.com
Perry MacIsaac, Contact, Sales & Customer Relations
pmacisaac@alloyconceptscnc.com

Alphacasting Inc.
391, av Ste-Croix, Montréal, QC H4N 2L3
Tel: 514-748-7511; *Fax:* 514-748-0237
Toll-Free: 800-567-7511
www.alphacasting.com
Profile: The company manufactures castings from ferrous, non-ferrous, titanium & exotic alloys for industries such as aerospace, military & telecommunications.
Frederik-Pierre Centazzo, Vice-President, Sales & Operations
fcentazzo@alphacasting.com
Steve Kennerknecht, Vice-President, Engineering

Altitude Aerospace Inc.
#200, 2705, boul Pitfield, Montréal, QC H4S 1T2
Tél: 514-335-6922; *Téléc:* 514-335-3356
info@altitudeaero.com
www.altitudeaero.com
Profile: The company aids in the development of new aircraft, as well as providing support for existing fleets, through its work in conceptual design, structural analysis, & certification.
Nancy Venneman, President
Fadi Al-Ahmed, Executive Vice-President & Chief Engineer

Apex Industries Inc.
100 Millennium Blvd., Moncton, NB E1C 8M6
Tel: 506-857-7544; *Fax:* 506-857-7563
www.apexindustries.com
Profile: The company's Aerospace Division is responsible for manufacturing & integrating structural assemblies, sub-assemblies, kitting, & components for the aerospace industry (commercial & defence).
Keith Donaldson, Director, Sales & Business Development
kmdonaldson@apexindustries.com

Argus Industries
20 Murray Park Rd., Winnipeg, MB R3J 3T9
Tel: 204-837-4660; *Fax:* 204-896-4250
info@argus.ca
www.argusindustries.ca
Profile: Argus custom manufactures rubber molded products & die cut gasket seals. They have facilities in Manitoba & Ontario.

Arnprior Aerospace Inc.
107 Baskin Dr. East, Arnprior, ON K7S 3M1
Tel: 613-623-4267
sales@arnprioraerospace.com
www.arnprioraerospace.com
Profile: Originally part of Boeing, the company became independent in 2005 & now operates facilities in Canada, the US & Mexico. Arnprior Aerospace supplies products & services (including design, fabrication, machining, processing, assembly, kitting, & product integration) to the aerospace & defence industries.

ASCO Aerospace Canada Ltd.
Parent: ASCO Industries
8510 River Rd., Delta, BC V4G 1B5
Tel: 604-946-4900; *Fax:* 604-946-4671
www.asco.be
Profile: The company's specialty is the design & manufacture of very large aluminum structures, as well as titanium & steel components for aircraft.
Kevin Russell, Vice-President & General Manager
krussell@ascoaerospace.ca

Avcorp Industries Inc.
10025 River Way, Delta, BC V4G 1M7
Tel: 604-582-6677
www.avcorp.com
Ticker Symbol: AVP / TSX
Profile: Avcorp is a designer & builder of major airframe structures & components, including stabilizers, cargo liners, floor panels, engine nacelles, packboards & wing components.
Peter George, Chief Executive Officer
Ed Merlo, Vice-President, Finance

Aversan Inc.
#500, 30 Eglinton Ave. West, Mississauga, ON L5R 3E7
Tel: 416-289-1554; *Fax:* 416-289-1554
aversan.com
Profile: Aversan specializes in designing, testing, & integrating embedded systems, system integration labs, & test equipment for the aerospace & defence industries. The company has offices in North America, South East Asia, & India.
Ted Sherlock, B.Sc.CEO
Daniel Pirog, Chief Technology Officer

Aviya Technologies Inc.
2495 Meadowpine Blvd., Mississauga, ON L5N 6C3
Tel: 905-812-9995; *Fax:* 905-812-0933
info@aviyatech.com
www.aviyatech.com
Profile: The company specializes in engineering systems, mechanics, hardware, & software for aerospace & defence applications, as well as providing program management & testing of electronic hardware components.
John Koumoundouros, President

BASF Canada
Parent: BASF SE; BASF Corporation
100 Milverton Dr., 5th Fl., Mississauga, ON L5R 4H1
Tel: 289-360-1300; *Fax:* 289-360-6000
Toll-Free: 866-485-2273
aerospace.basf.com
Profile: BASF's Aerospace Division specializes in cabin interiors, fuel & lubricants, flame retardants & fire protection, & more.
Mark Mielke, Senior Manager, Aerospace

Bell Helicopter Textron Canada Ltd.
Parent: Bell Helicopter Textron Inc.
12 800, rue de l'Avenir, Mirabel, QC J7J 1R4
Tel: 450-437-3400
www.bellhelicopter.com
Profile: Bell Helicopter produces rotary-wing aircraft for the civilian & military sectors, including the Griffin Helicopter fleet flown by the Canadian Forces.

Bluedrop
#300, 36 Solutions Dr., Halifax, NS B3S 1N2
Toll-Free: 800-563-3638
info@bluedrop.com
www.bluedropts.com
Profile: Bluedrop Training & Simulation provides advanced training services for the military & commercial markets.
Jean-Claude Siew, Vice-President, Technology & Simulation
Eva Martinex, Senior Director, Business Development (Aerospace)
Wayne Shaddock, Senior Director, Business Development (Naval)

Bluedrop Performance Learning
18 Prescott St., St. John's, NL A1C 3S4
Tel: 709-739-9000; *Toll-Free:* 800-563-3638
info@bluedrop.com
www.bluedrop.com
Ticker Symbol: BPL / TSX-V
Profile: Bluedrop provides advanced training technologies to individuals, corporations, the military & the public sector. The company operates two Groups: CoursePark Learning Services & Defence & Aerospace.
Emad Rizkalla, Founder & CEO
John Moores, COO
Bernard Beckett, CFO

Boeing Canada Operations
Parent: Boeing
World Exchange Plaza, #1220, 45 O'Connor St., Ottawa, ON K1P 1A4
Tel: 613-745-8111
www.boeing.ca
Ticker Symbol: BA / NYSE
Profile: Boeing manufactures commercial jetliners & military aircraft, as well as rotorcraft, electonic & defence systems, milliles, satellites, launch vehicles, & information & communication systems.
Kim Westenskow, General Manager

Bombardier Inc.
800, boul René-Lévesque ouest, Montréal, QC H3B 1Y8
Tél: 514-861-9481; *Téléc:* 514-861-2420
www.bombardier.com
Ticker Symbol: BBD.B / TSX
Profile: Manufacturers of railroad equipment, aircraft, aircraft engines & engine parts, aircraft parts & auxiliary equipment, various transportation equipment; Personal credit institutions; Real estate land subdividers & developers
Alain Bellemare, President & CEO
Jean Séguin, President, Aerostructures & Engineering Services
Lutz Bertling, President & COO, Transportation

Bradean's Tool & Die Limited
#1B, 46 Anson Ave., Amherst, NS B4H 4R2
Tel: 902-661-0669; *Fax:* 902-661-1748
bradeans@bradeans.com
www.bradeans.com
Profile: The company, manufactures aerospace & related parts, as well as conducting research & development, prototyping & other experimental projects.
Dean Smith, Co-Founder
Brad Sprague, Co-Founder

Brican Flight Systems Inc.
54 Van Kirk Dr., Brampton, ON L7A 1C7
Tel: 905-846-5175; *Fax:* 905-846-5946
info@brican.com
bricanflightsystems.com
Profile: BFS supplies the aerospace & defence industry with mission-ready unmanned aerial vehicles.
Brian McLuckie, President

Cadorath Aerospace Inc.
2070 Logan Ave., Winnipeg, MB R2R 0H9
Tel: 204-633-9420; *Fax:* 204-633-7101
Toll-Free: 800-470-7069
info@cadorath.com
www.cadorath.com
Profile: Cadorath Aerospace provides customers with aeronautical repair, modification, & overhaul services.
Gerry Cadorath, President/CEO
Norm Comeault, CFO
Dave Haines, Senior Vice-President

CAE Inc.
8585, ch de Côte-de-Liesse, Montréal, QC H4T 1G6
Tél: 514-341-6780; *Téléc:* 514-341-7699
Ligne sans frais: 800-564-6253
www.cae.com
Ticker Symbol: CAE / TSX, NYSE
Profile: The company specializes in modelling, simulation, & training for civil & defence aviation sectors.
Marc Parent, President/CEO
Hélène Gagnon, Vice-President, Public Affairs & Global Communications
Media.Relations@cae.com

Canadian Centre for Unmanned Vehicle Systems / CCUVS
#4, 49 Viscount Ave. SW, Medicine Hat, AB T1A 5G4
Tel: 403-488-7208
info@ccuvs.com
www.ccuvs.com
Profile: The company is a federally registered not-for-profit entity that provides the following services to the unmanned systems sector: systems training, providing facilities for tests & launches, consulting & promotion of civil & commercial use of unmanned systems.
Roger Haessel, Chief Executive Officer
Sterling Cripps, COO

Canadian Composites Manufacturing R&D Inc. / CCMRD
c/o Composites Innovation Centre Manitoba Inc., 158 Commerce Dr., Winnipeg, MB R3P 0Z6
Tel: 204-262-3400; *Fax:* 204-262-3409
www.ccmrd.ca
Profile: The CCMRD is a national consortium of industry leaders, whose goal is to develop & promote advanced composite manufacturing technologies & techniques in order to increase Canada's global competitiveness in this field.
Gene Manchur, Executive Director

Canadian Light Source Inc. / CLS
Centre canadien de rayonnement synchrotron
44 Innovation Blvd., Saskatoon, SK S7N 2V3
Tel: 306-657-3500; *Fax:* 306-657-3535
cls@lightsource.ca
www.lightsource.ca
Profile: The Canadian Light Source centre is one of the most powerful synchrotron facilities in the world, generating intense beams of light that allow researchers to view the microstructures of materials. This technology is useful in the fields of aviation & aerospace.
Rob Lamb, CEO

Canadian Propeller Ltd.
462 Brooklyn St., Winnipeg, MB R3J 1M7
Tel: 204-832-8679; *Fax:* 204-888-4696
Toll-Free: 800-773-6853
info@canadianpropeller.com
www.canadianpropeller.com
Profile: The company is an authorized service & repair station for Hartzell & McCauley propellers, among others.
Maurice Wills, President & General Manager

CanRep Inc.
Parent: CanRep Group
12900, rue Brault, Mirabel, QC J7J 1P3
Tel: 450-434-9898; *Fax:* 450-434-6996
sales@canrep.com
www.canrep.com
Profile: CanRep provides distribution services for aircraft interior components & equipment, engine components & airborne security & surveillance systems.
Marc Gregory, Executive Vice-President
David A. Gregory, President

Carillon Information Security Inc.
356, rue Joseph-Carrier, Vaudreuil-Dorion, QC J7V 5V5
Tel: 514-485-0789
info@carillon.ca
www.carillon.ca
Profile: The company provides identity management consulting services to clients in the air transport & aerospace industries.
Patrick Patterson, President & CEO

CarteNav Solutions Inc.
#708, 1809 Barrington St., Halifax, NS B3J 3K8
Tel: 902-446-4988; *Fax:* 902-446-4987
Toll-Free: 877-723-8729
www.cartenav.com
Profile: CarteNav produces situational awareness software for maritime, land, & air environments, targeting the defence, security & industry markets.
Paul Evans, CEO

Cascade Aerospace Inc.
1337 Townline Rd., Abbotsford, BC V2T 6E1
Tel: 604-850-7372; *Fax:* 604-857-2655
info@cascadeaerospace.com
www.cascadeaerospace.com
Profile: Cascade provides clients in the military, government, & commercial aerospace sectors with management, engineering, & support services. The company also designs & manufactures various aircraft systems & kits.
Benjamin Boehm, Executive Vice-President & COO

Celestica Inc.
844 Don Mills Rd., Toronto, ON M3C 1V7
Tel: 416-448-5800; *Toll-Free:* 888-899-9998
contactus@celestica.com
www.celestica.com
Ticker Symbol: CLS / TSX, NYSE
Profile: Celestica provides the aerospace & defence industries with design, engineering, manufacturing, logistics, after-market, & supply chain network services. Its specialties are complex printed circuit assembly, system assembly, system integration, & box build assembly.
Craig Muhlhauser, President & CEO

CFN Consultants
#1502, 222 Queen St., Ottawa, ON K1P 5V9
Tel: 613-232-1576; *Fax:* 613-238-5519
info@cfncon.com
www.cfnconsultants.com
Profile: CFN specializes in defence & security issues, & has worked with the Canadian Forces, departments of the Canadian Government, & NATO, as well as off-shore companies in the defence, IM/IT & aerospace sectors.
Pierre Lagueux, Managing Senior Partner
plagueux@cfncon.com

Ciara Technologies Inc.
9300, rte Transcanadienne, Montréal, QC H4S 1K5
Tél: 514-798-8880; *Téléc:* 514-798-8889
Ligne sans frais: 877-242-7272
www.ciaratech.com
Profile: Ciara provides technology & software solutions & services from companies ranging from small businesses to educational, & government & defence.
Robert Ahdoot, President

CLS Lexi-tech
10 Dawson St., Dieppe, MB E1A 6C8
Tel: 506-859-5200; *Fax:* 506-859-5205
info@lexitech.ca
www.cls-lexitech.ca
Profile: CLS lexi-tech provides writing, editing, translation, proof-reading, TACT & final formatting services for technical publications & corporate documents.
Robin Ayoub, Vice-President, Business Development & Sales
416-409-8202, rayoub@lexitech.ca
Eric Parisien, Contact, Government Sales & Marketing
613-314-1694, eparisien@lexitech.ca

CMTIGroup Inc.
9404, rue du Saguenay, Montréal, QC H1R 3Z8
Tel: 514-328-2166
info@cmtigroup.com
www.cmtigroup.com
Profile: The company offers specialty engineering services to clients in the aerospace, defence, space & transportation sectors, including black box developers, subsystem integrators & government agencies.

COM DEV International Ltd.
155 Sheldon Dr., Cambridge, ON N1R 7H6
Tel: 519-622-2300; *Fax:* 519-622-1691
www.comdev.ca
Ticker Symbol: CDV / TSX
Profile: COM DEV is a major designer & manufacturer of space satellite hardware & other space & defence-related products, including microwave electronics & optics systems & subsystems.
Michael Pley, CEO

Composites Atlantic Limited / CAL
Parent: EADS Sogerma
PO Box 1150, 71 Hall St., Lunenburg, NS B0J 2C0
Tel: 902-634-8448; *Fax:* 902-634-8398
www.compositesatlantic.com
Profile: The company provides structural analysis & manufacturing services to the aeronautics, defence & space sectors.
Claude Baril, Managing Director
902-634-4475, claude.baril@stelia-aerospace.com

Convergent Manufacturing Technologies Inc.
#403, 6190 Agronomy Rd., Vancouver, BC V6T 1Z3
Tel: 604-822-9682; *Fax:* 604-822-9659
info@convergent.ca
www.convergent.ca
Profile: Convergent produces composite process modelling software & services, useful in the aerospace industry for the modelling of production hardware. The company was originally part of the University of British Columbia's Composites Group, & although they became separately incorporated in 1998, they continue to hold strong ties to UBC.
Anoush Poursartip, Director, Research & Development

CRIAQ
#1515, 740, rue Notre-Dame ouest, Montréal, QC H3C 3X6
Tél: 514-313-7561; *Téléc:* 514-398-0902
info@criaq.aero
www.criaq.aero
Profile: Le Consortium de recherche et d'innovation en aérospatiale au Québec (CRIAQ) vise à améliorer la base de connaissances de l'industrie aérospatiale de la province par l'éducation et la formation des étudiants. Leur objectif est d'accroître la compétitivité du Québec sur le marché international de l'aéronautique. C'est une organisation à but non lucratif soutenue par le gouvernement du Québec.
Denis Faubert, Président et directeur général

Cyclone Manufacturing Inc.
7300 Rapistan Ct., Mississauga, ON L5N 5S1
Tel: 905-567-5601; *Fax:* 905-567-6911
info@cyclonemfg.com
www.cyclonemfg.com
Profile: Cyclone specializes in manufacturing & assembling medium & large structures for the aerospace industry.
Andrew Sochaj, President
andrew.sochaj@cyclonemfg.com
Robert Sochaj, Executive Vice-President
robert.sochaj@cyclonemfg.com

DECA Aviation Engineering Ltd.
#200, 7050 Telford Way, Mississauga, ON L5S 1V7
Tel: 905-405-1371; *Fax:* 905-405-1371
inquiry@deca-aviation.com
www.deca-aviation.com
Profile: DECA provides engineering, certification, aircraft modification, program management, & integrated kit supply services to the domestic & international aviation community.

Deep Vision Inc.
Quaker Landing Bldg., #125, 33 Ochterloney St., Dartmouth, NS B2Y 4P5
Tel: 902-461-1615
www.deepvision.ca
Profile: Deep Vision specializes in developing what they call Intelligent Machine Perception Technology, which allows machines to sense & recognize objects, as well as read & comprehend text. This technology is useful in sectors such as aerospace & defence, intelligent transportation, robotics, surveillance & autonomous systems, among others.

Defense & Aviation Wiring Inc.
695 Sovereign Rd., London, ON N5V 4K8
Tel: 519-451-0888; *Fax:* 519-451-2052
Toll-Free: 866-828-8057
quotes@davwire.com
www.davwire.com
Profile: DAVWIRE specializes in wire harnesses, electrical panels, & electro-mechanical assemblies for the aviation, defence, medical, & rail markets.
Mark MacKenzie, President & CEO
519-451-0888 ext: 232
Duncan McTavish, Chief Operating Officer
519-451-0888 ext: 223

Delastek Inc.
#14, 2699, 5e av, Grand-Mère, QC G9T 5K7
Tél: 819-533-5788; *Téléc:* 819-533-3494
www.delastek.com
Profile: La société fabrique des pièces composites et intérieurs d'avions, ainsi que de soutenir les différentes phases de développement du produit. Elle est spécialisée dans les

systèmes électriques et électroniques pour les autres types de véhicules, ainsi que les pare-chocs et l'intégration des produits.
Claude Lessard, Président

DRS Pivotal Power
Parent: DRS Power Solutions
150 Bluewater Rd., Bedford, NS B4B 1G9
Tel: 902-835-7268; *Fax:* 902-835-6026
www.pivotalpower.com

Profile: DRS Pivotal Power, as part of DRS Power Solutions, supplies power generation products to the army, naval, aerospace, vehicle export power, alternative energy, marine, government & emergency services sectors, among others.
Nancy Preeper, Manager, Business Development
902-832-7357, n.preeper@pivotalpower.com

Earnscliffe Strategy Group
Formerly: Policy Insights Inc.
#200, 46 Elgin St., Ottawa, ON K1P 5K6
Tel: 613-563-4455; *Fax:* 613-236-6173
Toll-Free: 844-564-4455
www.earnscliffe.ca

Profile: Founded in 1989, Earnscliffe Strategy Group is a government relations firm specializing in the fields of high technology, aerospace, defence & communications.
Ken Mackay, Principal

EAS Exhibition Services Inc.
827 Primrose Ct., Pickering, ON L1X 2S7
Tel: 905-837-5095; *Fax:* 905-837-1544
eas-exhibitions.com

Profile: The company specializes in exhibit management at international trade shows & conferences & has long-standing ties with the Aerospace Industries Association of Canada & the Canadian aerospace industry in general.

Esterline CMC Electronics Inc.
Parent: Esterline Corporation
600 Dr. Frederik Philips Blvd., Montréal, QC H4M 2S9
Tél: 514-748-3148; *Téléc:* 514-748-3100
www.esterline.com/avionicssystems
Ticker Symbol: ESL / NYSE

Profile: The company designs & manufactures electonics for the military & commercial aviation sectors.

Explorer Solutions
#205, 1494, rue Montarville, St-Bruno-de-Montarville, QC J3V 3T5
Tel: 450-441-9055; *Fax:* 514-375-1388
info@explorersolutions.ca
www.explorersolutions.ca

Profile: The company provides business intelligence, government relations, & senior management coaching to companies in the aerospace industry, as well as economic development agencies & municipalities.
Christian Perreault, Senior Partner & CEO
christian@explorersolutions.ca

Field Aviation
Parent: AMAVCO
#125, 4300 - 26 St. NE, Calgary, AB T1Y 7H7
Tel: 403-516-8200; *Fax:* 403-516-8317
generalinfo@fieldav.com
www.fieldav.com

Profile: Field Aviation provides design, engineering, integration, certification & aircraft delivery services to clients involved in search & rescue, surveillance & border protection.

Fleetway Inc.
Parent: J.D. Irving, Limited
#200, 155 Chain Lake Dr., Halifax, NS B3S 1B3
Tel: 902-494-5700; *Fax:* 902-494-5792
www.fleetway.ca

Profile: Fleetway provides engineering services to the military & government, shipbuilding, oil & gas, & commercial sectors.
Pierre Poulain, Director, Business Development
902-494-2280, Poulain.Pierre@fleetway.ca

Flexibülb Inc.
PO Box 635, 9000, boul Parent, Trois-Rivières, QC G9A 5E1
Tel: 819-374-9250; *Fax:* 819-374-5143
www.flexibulb.com

Profile: The company specializes in designing, developing, manufacturing, & integrating aircraft interior systems, components & ground support equipment for clients in the aerospace, military, & paramilitary sectors.

Flightcraft Maintenance Services / FMS
2450 Saskatchewan Ave., Winnipeg, MB R3J 3Y9
Tel: 204-783-2754; *Fax:* 204-783-2848
fltcraft@mymts.net
www.flightcraftmaintenance.com

Profile: The company provides the following services: repairs & modifications; avionics installations, retrofits & repairs, maintenance & overhauls & line maintenance services. They also technical & mechanical assistance.
Jim Peroff, President

General Dynamics Canada
1941 Robertson Rd., Ottawa, ON K2H 5B7
Tel: 613-596-7000
info@gd-ms.ca
www.gdcanada.com

Profile: The company provides information, surveillance, & reconnaissance services for air & sea platforms, & networking & computing solutions for land platforms.

General Electric Canada Inc.
Parent: General Electric
#1205, 60 Queen St., Ottawa, ON K1P 5Y7
Tel: 613-235-3421; *Fax:* 613-235-2481
www.ge.com/ca

Profile: GE-Aviation serves the Canadian military & commercial aviation markets through its two plants in Bromont, QC, & Orillia, ON. GE manufactures, markets, & supports aircraft engines, as well as gas turbines for the Canadian Navy.
Jeff Immelt, CEO, GE Canada

Green Aviation Research & Development Network / GARDN
#1515, 740 rue Notre-Dame ouest, Montréal, QC H3C 3X6
Tél: 514-398-9772
info@gardn.org
www.gardn.org

Profile: GARDN was created in 2009 with the goal of bringing together partners in industry, government, & education to reduce the aerospace industry's environmental footprint.
Sylvain Cofsky, Executive Director
514-398-9772 ext: 295, sylvain.cofsky@gardn.org

Greyhound Canada Transportation Corp.
#700, 1111 International Blvd., Burlington, ON L7L 6W1
Toll-Free: 800-661-8747
canada.info@greyhound.ca
www.greyhound.ca

Profile: Intercity & rural bus transportation; travel agencies; courier services
Stuart Kendrick, Sr. Vice President, Canada

Héroux-Devtek inc
Tour est, #658, 1111, rue Saint-Charles ouest, Longueuil, QC J4K 5G4
Tel: 450-679-3330
www.herouxdevtek.com
Ticker Symbol: HRX / TSX

Profile: Manufacturers of aircraft parts & auxiliary equipment; Wholesalers of transportation equipment & supplies; Airport, flying fields & airport terminal services
Gilles Labbé, President & CEO
Stéphane Arsenault, CFO

Honeywell Canada
Parent: Honeywell International Inc.
3333 Unity Dr., Mississauga, ON L5L 3S6
Tel: 905-608-6021; *Fax:* 905-608-6057
aerospace.honeywell.com
Ticker Symbol: HON / NYSE

Profile: Honeywell Canada's Aerospace Division deals in the following business lines: electric power, electronic control systems, in-flight communication systems, in-flight data networking solutions, repair & overhaul services & aftermarket services. The company operates sites in Ontario & Prince Edward Island.

The Ian Martin Group
465 Morden Rd., 2nd Fl., Oakville, ON L6K 3W6
Tél: 905-815-1600; *Téléc:* 905-845-2100
Ligne sans frais: 800-567-9675
www.ianmartin.com

Profile: A consulting firm specializing in engineering, telecommunications, & information technology, with past projects involving the development & manufacturing of landing gear, flight controls, & aircraft programs.
Tim Masson, Chief Stewart & CEO
Loree Bennett, Vice-President

IDBLUE
Parent: Cathexis Innovations Inc.
#302, 44 Torbay Rd., St. John's, NL A1A 2G4
Tel: 709-754-7343; *Fax:* 709-754-7349
Toll-Free: 866-304-7343
info@idblue.com
idblue.com

Profile: The company produces mobile Bluetooth radio frequency identification (RFID) readers (HF & UHF) for smartphones & tablets. These readers are applicable in the aerospace, healthcare, oil & gas, retail & utilities markets.

IMP Group International, INC
2651 Joseph Howe Dr., Halifax, NS B3L 4T1
Tel: 902-453-2400; *Toll-Free:* 877-244-0878
www.impgroup.com

Profile: IMP Group consists of the following divisions: aerospace & defence, airline, aviation, healthcare, hotels, information services & properties & development. Please see the company's website for specific divisional contact information.
Kenneth C. Rowe, Executive Chair
Stephen Plummer, Group President/CEO
David A. Gossen, President, IMP Aerospace & Defence
Kirk A. Rowe, President, Innotech-Execaire Aviation Group
Stephen K. Rowe, President, CanJet Airlines

Integral Machining Ltd. / IML
#8, 1252 Speers Rd., Oakville, ON L6L 5N9
Tel: 905-847-1565; *Fax:* 905-847-9518
www.imach.ca

Profile: IML specializes in micromachining, which is loosely defined as being the machining of any features less than two millimeters in size. The company's main clients are in the aerospace, medical & photonics industries.
Peter Reypa, President

International Custom Products Inc. / ICP
49 Howden Rd., Toronto, ON M1R 3C7
Tel: 416-285-4311; *Fax:* 416-285-7329
Toll-Free: 800-268-4482
info@icpinc.com
www.icpinc.com

Profile: The company manufactures parachute components for ordnance delivery & unmanned vehicle systems, as well as meeting unique packaging requirements for defence-related initiatives.

International Water Guard Industries Inc.
Parent: IWG Technologies, Inc.
#1, 3771 North Fraser Way, Burnaby, BC V5J 5G5
Tel: 604-255-5555; *Fax:* 604-255-5685
Toll-Free: 800-667-0331
support@water.aero
www.water.aero
Ticker Symbol: IWG / TSX.V

Profile: IWG provides aircraft water treatment systems & components to corporate, VIP, & military operators.
Bruce Gowan, Chair
Bruce MacCoubrey, President

Irving Shipbuilding Inc. / ISI
Parent: J.D. Irving, Limited
3099 Barrington St., Halifax, NS B3K 5M7
Tel: 902-423-9271
www.irvingshipbuilding.com

Profile: Irving provides services including shipbuilding & repair, drill rig construction & conversion, offshore fabrication, industrial manufacturing, engineering, supply chain management & technical services.

ISE Metal Inc.
Formerly: ISE Stamping Inc.
20, rte de Windsor, Sherbrooke, QC J1C 0E5
Tel: 819-846-1044; *Fax:* 819-846-4268
www.ise.qc.ca

Profile: The company specializes in the laser cutting, bending, stamping, assembly, welding, zinc plating, & enameling of sheet metal for markets including recreational vehicles, automotive, & aerospace.

J.D. Irving, Limited / JDI
PO Box 5777, 300 Union St., Saint John, NB E2L 4M3
Tel: 506-632-7777; *Fax:* 506-648-2205
info@jdirving.com
www.jdirving.com

Profile: J.D. Irving provides services through the following business units: fForestry & Forest Products; Transportation; Shipbuilding & Industrial Marine; Retail; Industrial Equipment, Construction Services & Building Materials; & Consumer Products. The company was founded in 1882, & now has operations in Eastern Canada & the United States.

KF Aerospace / KF
Formerly: Kelowna Flightcraft
5655 Airport Way, Kelowna, BC V1V 1S1
Tel: 250-491-5500
www.kfaero.ca

Profile: The company's main operations are conducted in Kelowna, BC, & Hamilton, ON, & include maintenance, flight operations, & military flight training. Kelowna Flightcraft Air Charter Ltd., a subsidiary, is a dedicated carrier for Canada Post, & an air cargo carrier for Purolator Courier.

Tracy Medve, President
Barry Lapointe, Chair & CEO

KPMG LLP
#2000, 160 Elgin St., Ottawa, ON K2P 2P8
Tel: 613-212-3613; *Fax:* 613-212-2896
www.kpmg.com
Profile: KPMG's Aerospace & Defence (A&D) practice, which is part of the firm's global Diversified Industrials practice, offers Audit, Tax, & Advisory services to clients in the A&D industry. The firm also offers a service called KPMG Enterprise for private A&D companies, which involves growth management, tax planning, & financial business.
Grant McDonald, National Sector Leader, Aerospace & Defence
gmcdonald@kpmg.ca

L-3 Communications
Parent: L-3 Communications Holdings, Inc.
#804, 255 Albert St., Ottawa, ON K1P 6A9
Tel: 613-569-5257
www.l-3com.com
Ticker Symbol: LLL / NYSE
Profile: L-3 Communications is a global company specializing in aerospace & defence. In Canada, L-3 operates the following divisions: L-3 Electronic System Services (L-3 ESS); L-3 MAS; L-3 Targa Systems; & L-3 WESCAM. Through these divisions, the company offers the following services: logistics & support; maintenance of avionics & components; manufacturing advanced systems; aircraft management; solid state memory systems; & surveillance & targeting systems.
Michael T. Strianese, Chairman, President & CEO

Lear Canada Ltd.
530 Manitou Dr., Kitchener, ON N2G 4C2
Tel: 519-895-1600; *Fax:* 519-895-1608
www.lear.com
Ticker Symbol: LEA / NYSE
Profile: Designs, tests & produces automotive interiors
Matthew J. Simoncini, President, CEO & Director
Jeffrey H. Vanneste, CFO & Sr. Vice-President

Linamar Corporation
287 Speedvale Ave. West, Guelph, ON N1H 1C5
Tel: 519-836-7550; *Fax:* 519-824-8479
www.linamar.com
Ticker Symbol: LNR / TSX
Profile: Manufacturers of motor vehicle parts & accessories, fabricated plate work, carburetors, pistons, piston rings, valves, farm machinery equipment, aircraft parts & auxiliary equipment, pumps & pumping equipment; Wholesalers of farm & garden machinery & equipment
Linda Hasenfratz, CEO
Jim Jarrell, President & COO
Dale Schneider, CFO
Mark Stoddart, Chief Technology Development Officer & Vice-President, Sales & Marketing

Lockheed Martin Canada Inc.
Parent: Lockheed Martin Corporation
#870, 45 O'Connor St., Ottawa, ON K1P 1A4
Tel: 613-688-0698; *Fax:* 613-688-0702
www.lockheedmartin.ca
Ticker Symbol: LMT / NYSE
Profile: Lockheed Martin Canada supplies electronic defence & surveillance systems for naval, airborne, land, & civil operations.
Rosemary Chapdelaine, Vice-President & General Manager

Luxfer Canada Ltd.
4410 - 46 Ave. SE, Calgary, AB T2B 3N7
Tel: 403-720-0262; *Fax:* 403-720-0263
Toll-Free: 888-396-3835
alternativefuel@luxfer.net
www.luxfercylinders.com
Ticker Symbol: DNK
Profile: Manufacturers of cylinders, fuel cell storage systems

Lynch Dynamics Inc.
1799 Argentia Rd., Mississauga, ON L5N 3A2
Tel: 905-363-2400; *Fax:* 905-363-1191
Toll-Free: 888-626-4365
lynch.ca
Profile: The company designs & manufactures hydraulic motion control systems for the aerospace, military & medical sectors.
Ernie Lynch, President & CEO

MacDonald, Dettwiler & Associates Ltd. / MDA
13800 Commerce Pkwy., Richmond, BC V6V 2J3
Tel: 604-278-3411; *Fax:* 604-231-2750
www.mdacorporation.com
Ticker Symbol: MDA.TO / TSX
Profile: MDA, a Canadian company, supports commercial, civil & military clients in the global surveillance, intelligence, communication, & advanced technology marketplaces. It builds & operates unmanned aerial vehicles & provides clients with aircraft, sensors, training, maintenance, in-service support, system certification, data handling & exploitation systems.

MacKenzie Atlantic Tool & Die Machining
PO Box 121, #3, 6 Rowling Dr., Musquodoboit Harbour, NS B0J 2L0
Tel: 902-889-3047; *Fax:* 902-889-3673
info@mackenzieatlantic.com
www.mackenzieatlantic.com
Profile: MacKenzie Atlantic is a full-service tool-making & machining company serving the aerospace, marine, military, & oil & gas sectors.
Matthew MacKenzie, Owner & President
902-889-3633

Magellan Aerospace Corporation
3160 Derry Rd. East, Mississauga, ON L4T 1A9
Tel: 905-677-1889; *Fax:* 905-677-5658
corporate@magellan.aero
www.magellanaerospace.com
Ticker Symbol: MAL / TSX
Profile: Manufacturers of aircraft parts & auxiliary equipment, aircraft engines & engine parts
Phillip Underwood, President & CEO
John B. Dekker, CFO & Corporate Secretary

Magna International Inc.
337 Magna Dr., Aurora, ON L4G 7K1
Tel: 905-726-2462
www.magna.com
Ticker Symbol: MG / TSX; MGA / NYSE
Profile: Manufacturers of motor vehicle parts & accessories, automotive stampings, various fabricated metal products, motor vehicles & passenger car bodies, vehicular lighting equipment, various fabricated textile products, public building & related furniture; Wholesalers of motor vehicle supplies & new parts; Racing, including track operation; Various amusement & recreation services
Donald J. Walker, CEO
Vincent J. Galifi, CFO & Exec. Vice-President

Marand Engineering Ltd.
105 Watts Ave., Charlottetown, PE C1E 2B7
Tel: 902-368-8954; *Fax:* 902-368-7041
Profile: The company manufactures precision sheet metal, machined components, assemblies, & automated test equipment & control systems for the light rail & aerospace & defence markets.
Mario Van Wiechen, Contact
mario.vanwiechen@marandeng.com

MarineNav Ltd.
Panmure Island Wharf, 1466 Panmure Island, Montague, PE C0A 1R0
Tel: 902-838-7011
info@marinenav.ca
www.marinenav.ca
Profile: MarineNav designs & manufactures offshore navigation, multimedia & vessel monitoring systems.

Marinvent Corporation
#23, 50, ch de la Rabastalière est, Saint-Bruno, QC J3V 2A5
Tel: 450-441-6464; *Fax:* 450-441-2411
info@marinvent.com
www.marinvent.com
Profile: Marinvent specializes in aerospace research & development. The company was founded in 1983 & now has operations in Canada, the USA & Russia. It is also a founding partner in Canada's Flight Test Centre of Excellence (FTCE).

Marsh Metrology
Parent: Marsh Group
#2, 1016C Sutton Dr., Burlington, ON L7L 6B8
Tel: 905-331-9783; *Fax:* 905-331-5991
info@marshmetrology.com
www.marshmetrology.com
Profile: The company provides accredited calibration services, including repair & re-manufacture of printed circuit boards, & distribution for test & measurement equipment.

MDS Coating Technologies Corporation / MCT
PO Box 312, 60 Aerospace Blvd., Slemon Park, PE C0B 2A0
Tel: 902-888-3900; *Fax:* 902-888-3901
pr@mdscoating.com
www.mdscoating.com
Profile: MDS is a developer & manufacturer of coatings for gas turbine engines used in the commercial & aerospace & defence industries, with offices in PEI, Québec & Washington, DC.

Meggitt Training Systems Canada Inc. / MTSC
Parent: Meggitt PLC
#3, 1735 Brier Park Rd. NW, Medicine Hat, AB T1C 1V5
Tel: 403-528-8782; *Fax:* 403-529-2629
www.meggittcanada.com
Profile: MTSC offers weapon simulation training packages & programs to military, law enforcement & security personnel. The company operates two Canadian facilities: the Targets & Unmanned Vehicle Group in Medicine Hat, AB & the Weapons Training Simulation Group in Montréal, QC.

Meloche Group Inc.
491, boul des Érables, Salaberry-de-Valleyfield, QC J6T 6G3
Tél: 450-371-4646; *Téléc:* 450-371-4957
info@melocheinc.com
www.melocheinc.com
Hugue Meloche, Président et chef de la direction
hmeloche@melocheinc.com

Metal Action Machining Ltd.
Parent: Analytic Systems Ware 1993 Ltd.
#206, 12448 - 82nd Ave., Surrey, BC V3W 3E9
Tel: 604-543-7378; *Fax:* 604-592-7372
www.metalaction.ca
Profile: The company specializes in precision machining of aluminum alloys, alloy steels, titanium, & stainless steel. Other operations include punching, press break forming, anodizing, painting, plating, engraving & screen printing, using both in-house & outside services. The company also specializes in aerospace tooling. They mainly serve the aerospace, military, marine, cleantech & commercial markets.
Jim Hargrove, Manager, Sales
778-724-4653, jimh@metalactionmachining.ca

Mevotech Inc.
240 Bridgeland Ave., Toronto, ON M6A 1Z4
Tel: 416-783-7800; *Fax:* 416-783-0904
info@mevotech.com
www.mevotech.com
Profile: Mevotech manufactures parts for automobiles, including suspension, steering & driveline.
Ezer Mevorach, Chief Executive Officer
emevorach@mevotech.com

MicroPilot
PO Box 720, 72067 Rd. 8E, Sturgeon Rd., Stony Mountain, MB R0C 3A0
Tel: 204-818-0598; *Fax:* 204-818-0594
info@micropilot.com
www.micropilot.com
Profile: The company manufactures small autopilot systems for unmanned aerial vehicles & micro aerial vehicles.
Howard Loewen, President

MilAero Electronics Atlantic Inc.
81 Mount Hope Ave., Dartmouth, NS B2Y 4M9
Tel: 902-469-6232
info@mil-aero.com
www.mil-aero.com
Profile: MilAero specializes in cables, wire harnesses & electro-mechanical enclosures for the defence, aerospace & industrial sectors.

National Research Council of Canada / NRC
Bldg. M-3, 1200 Montréal Rd., Ottawa, ON K1A 0R6
Tel: 613-990-0765; *Fax:* 613-952-9907
www.nrc-cnrc.gc.ca/eng/rd/aerospace/index.html
Profile: NRC Aerospace is Canada's national aerospace laboratory, which conducts research & technology development on aerospace topics such as safety, weight, cost & the environment.
Matthew Tobin, Portfolio Business Advisor
matthew.tobin@nrc-cnrc.gc.ca

NAV Canada
PO Box 3411 Stn. T, Ottawa, ON K1P 5L6
Tel: 613-563-5588; *Fax:* 613-563-3426
Toll-Free: 800-876-4693
service@navcanada.ca
www.navcanada.ca
Profile: Provides, maintains & enhances an air navigation service
John W. Crichton, President/CEO
Marc Courtois, Chair
Brian K. Aitken, CFO & Vice-President, Finance
Sidney Koslow, Vice-President/Chief Technology Officer

Neptec Design Group Ltd.
#202, 302 Legget Dr., Kanata, ON K2K 1Y5
Tel: 613-599-7602; *Fax:* 613-599-7604
www.neptec.com
Profile: The company manufactures & operates spaceflight sensors, payloads, instruments, & equipment. It has been a

NASA contractor since 1995, & has supported over 40 Shuttle missions. It operates facilities in Canada, the US & the UK.
Paul Nephin, CEO

Newmercial Technologies International / NTI
#717, 680, rue Sherbrooke ouest, Montréal, QC H3A 2M7
Tél: 514-398-2671
sales@newmerical.com
www.newmerical.com
Profile: The company specializes in engineering research & development related to in-flight icing certifications for aircraft.
Wagdi Habashi, President

NeXsys Group Inc.
#115, 5800 Ambler Dr., Mississauga, ON L4W 4J4
Tel: 905-593-1504
info@nexsysgroup.ca
www.nexsysgroup.ca
Profile: NeXsys helps companies increase productivity & profit through direct consulting & a software suite comprised of NeXflow, NeXwave, & NeXview. The company's clients are in the aerospace, automotive, pharmaceutical, logistics, & manufacturing industries.
Douglas R. Sutherland, President & CEO

NGRAIN (Canada) Corporation
#200, 740 Nicola St., Vancouver, BC V6G 2C1
Toll-Free: 866-420-1781
www.ngrain.com
Profile: NGRAIN serves the defence, civil aviation, nuclear, oil & gas, & medical industries with interactive 3D simulation software for maintenance training & support.
David Sutin, CEO
Jennifer Smyth-Whelly, Vice-President

Noranco Inc.
710 Rowntree Dairy Rd., Woodbridge, ON L4L 5T7
Tel: 905-264-2050; *Fax:* 905-264-1471
www.noranco.com
Profile: The company manufactures landing gear & aircraft structure & engine components & assemblies for the commercial, business & military aerospace sectors.
David Camilleri, President & CEO

Northern Centre for Advanced Technology Inc. / NORCAT
1545 Maley Dr., Sudbury, ON P3A 4R7
Tel: 705-521-8324; *Fax:* 705-521-1040
www.norcat.org
Profile: NORCAT is a non-profit corporation, & its Innovation & Development department specializes in research pertaining to space drilling.
Don Duval, CEO

Northstar Aerospace
Formerly: Derlan Industries Ltd.
Milton Plant, 180 Market Dr., Milton, ON L9T 3H5
Tel: 905-875-4000; *Fax:* 905-875-4087
infomilton@nsaero.com
www.nsaero.com
Ticker Symbol: NAS
Profile: Manufacturers of motor vehicle parts & accessories, aircraft parts & auxiliary equipment, speed changers, industrial high-speed drives, gears, aircraft engines & engine parts; Airports, flying fields & airport terminal services
David McConnaughey, President & CEO
Robert L. Burkhardt, Chief Financial Officer

Paradigm Shift Technologies Inc.
60 Signet Dr., Toronto, ON M9L 2Y4
Tel: 416-748-1779; *Fax:* 416-748-5889
info@paradigmshift.com
www.paradigmshift.com
Profile: The company seeks to improve the reliability of weapon systems & other platforms (commercial & military) through their coating & engineering services.
Gennady Yumshtyk, Founder, President & CEO

Pathix ASP
Parent: Vector Aerospace Corporation
PO Box 13306 Stn. A, 21 Hallett Cres., St. John's, NL A1B 4B7
Fax: 709-724-8545
Toll-Free: 866-724-8500
inquiries@pathix.com
www.pathix.com
Profile: Pathix is an information technology company specializing in networking & platform implementation, as well as being the producer of the Navixa aviation software, meant to aid operating & repair & overhaul companies.

Patlon Aircraft & Industries Limited
8130 - 5th Line, Halton Hills, ON L7G 0B8
Tel: 905-864-8706; *Fax:* 905-864-8728
patlon@patlon.com
www.patlon.com
Profile: Patlon provides its clients in the aerospace, military, transportation, & electronics industries with application development & selling. Its products include aircraft interiors, cables, electrical systems, environmental systems, fuel systems, ground power units, hydraulic systems, painting, sensors, & valves, among other things. It also provides services such as repair, calibration, assembly & training.
Patrick Mann, President

Pratt & Whitney Canada Corp.
1000, boul Marie-Victorin, Longueuil, QC J4G 1A1
Tel: 450-677-9411
www.pwc.ca
Profile: Manufacturers of aircraft engines & engine parts; Wholesalers of transportation equipment & supplies
John Saabas, President
Maria Della Posta, Senior Vice-President, Sales & Marketing
Akhil Bhandari, Chief Information Officer

Prevost Car Inc.
35, boul Gagnon, Sainte-Claire, QC G0R 2V0
Tel: 418-883-3391; *Fax:* 418-883-4157
prevostcar@volvo.com
www.prevostcar.com
Profile: Manufacturers of intercity coaches & coach shells for motorhomes & specialty conversion
Gaetan Bolduc, President/CEO

Provincial Aerospace Ltd.
St. John's International Airport, PO Box 29030, St. John's, NL A1A 5B5
Tel: 709-576-1800; *Fax:* 709-576-1709
inquiries@provair.com
www.provincialaerospace.com
Profile: Provincial Aerospace specializes in maritime surveillance, systems integration, aircraft modification, training, integrated logistics support & mission operations. The company, & parent the PAL Group of Companies, was sold to Winnipeg-based Exchange Income Corporation (EIC) in 2014.

Public Storage Canadian Properties
5403 Eglinton Ave. West, Toronto, ON M9C 5K6
Toll-Free: 877-777-8672
info@publicstoragecanada.com
www.publicstoragecanada.com
Ticker Symbol: PUB
Profile: General warehousing & storage
Troy McLellan, Senior Vice-President & CEO

Rolls-Royce Canada Ltd.
9500, ch de la Côte-de-Liesse, Montréal, QC H8T 1A2
Tel: 514-636-0964
RRNAWebmaster@rolls-royce.com
www.rolls-royce.com
Profile: Airports, flying fields & airport terminal services; Manufacturers of steam, gas, hydraulic turbines & turbine generator units
Marion Blakey, President & CEO, North America
David Smith, CFO

Samuel, Son & Co., Limited
2360 Dixie Rd., Mississauga, ON L4Y 1Z7
Tel: 905-279-5460; *Fax:* 905-279-9658
Toll-Free: 800-267-2683
sales@samuel.com
www.samuel.com
Profile: The Samuel Aerospace Metals division was formed in 2010, & provides materials including surface machining & plastic coating & services such as plate sawing, water jet profiling, tube & extrusion cutting, shearing & kitting.

Sanmina-SCI Corporation
500 Palladium Dr., Ottawa, ON K2V 1C2
Tel: 613-886-6000; *Fax:* 613-886-6001
www.sanmina-sci.com
Profile: The company manufactures micro-electronics, radar sub-systems, microwave radios, & optical communication systems for the aerospace, defence, industrial, medical, & renewable energy markets.
Jure Sola, CEO

Sermatech Power Solutions LP
Parent: Praxair Surface Technologies
10300 Ryan Ave., Montréal, QC H9P 2T7
Tél: 514-631-2240; *Téléc:* 514-636-6196
www.praxairsurfacetechnologies.com
Profile: Sermatech provides coating services to the Canadian aerospace industry.
Freddie Sarhan, Vice-President, Americas Coating Services

Solace Power Inc.
#201, 1118 Topsail Rd., Mount Pearl, NL A1N 5E7
Tel: 709-745-6099; *Fax:* 888-887-5441
sales@solace.ca
www.solace.ca
Profile: The company specializes in wireless power technology applicable to the aerospace & defence, consumer electronics & firefighting electronics markets.

Sonaca Montréal
Parent: Sonaca Group
13075, rue Brault, Mirabel, QC J7J 1P3
Tél: 450-434-6114
www.sonacamontreal.com
Profile: The company specializes in manufacturing large aluminum structures for the aerospace industry, particularly wing & empennage structures.
Sylvain Bédard, CEO

Sonovision Canada Inc.
Parent: Sonovision Group Inc.
#400, 85 Albert St., Ottawa, ON K1P 6A4
Tel: 613-234-4849; *Fax:* 613-234-2631
sonovisioncanada.com
Profile: Sonovision Canada manages, authors, & translates technical publications for aerospace & defence manufacturers with an in-house team of writers, editors, illustrators, compositors, translators & quality assurance staff.
Vincent Laithier, Director, Sales & Business Development
514-344-5008 ext: 33, vincent.laithier@sonovisiongroup.com

Southwest United Canada
Parent: Southwest United Industries, Inc.
#9, 8201 Keele St., Concord, ON L4K 1Z4
Tel: 905-738-9225; *Fax:* 905-738-5970
www.swunitedcanada.com
Profile: The company specializes in metal finishing & provides services such as stress relief, non-destructive testing, shot peening, anodizing, passivation, plating, HVOF thermal spraying, precision grinding, super finishing, & painting. They are accredited to work on aerospace projects & have two Canadian facilities located in Brampton & Concord, ON.

TDM Technical Services
3924 Chesswood Dr., Toronto, ON M3J 2W6
Tel: 416-777-0007; *Fax:* 416-777-1117
tdm@tdm.ca
www.tdm.ca
Profile: TDM's Aerospace Division provides stress analysis, structural design, certification & systems engineering services to clients in the aerospace industry.
Iain Dainter, Senior Account Manager
iain@tdm.ca

Testori Americas Corp. Canada
Parent: Testori Group
45 Cannon Dr., Summerside, PE C0B 2A0
Tel: 902-888-3200; *Fax:* 902-436-4456
www.testoriamericas.com
Profile: Testori specializes in the engineering & production of interiors for railcars, ships & aircraft.

Thales Canada Inc.
2800, av Marie-Curie, Montréal, QC H4S 2C2
Tel: 514-832-0900
www.thalesgroup.com/canada
Profile: Thales Canada provides technology & equipment for the defence & security, aerospace & transportation markets. The company has offices in Québec, Ontario & British Columbia.
Mark Halinaty, President & CEO

Tronos
PO Box 7, Slemon Park, PE C0B 2A0
Tel: 902-436-5318; *Fax:* 902-436-5319
www.tronosjet.com
Profile: Tronos is an aviation services provider specializing in aircraft leasing, maintenance & asset management. The company also has operations in the UK serving Europe, the Middle East, Asia & Africa.

TrueNorth Avionics, Inc.
1682 Woodward Dr., Ottawa, ON K2C 3R8
Tel: 613-224-3301; *Fax:* 613-224-0954
Toll-Free: 877-610-0110
info@truenorthavionics.com
www.truenorthavionics.com
Profile: The company provides satellite communication technology to allow executives to communicate via Wi-Fi, voice, fax, e-mail, & mobile divices while on board private business aircraft.
Mark van Berkel, President/CEO

Tube-Fab Ltd.
105 Industrial Cres., Summerside, PE C1N 5P8
Tel: 902-436-3229; *Fax:* 902-436-3219
www.tube-fab.com
Profile: Together with its sister company TFL Technologies Inc., Tube-Fab manufactures & assembles precision tubular & machined components, & complete assemblies for fluid delivery & structural assemblies. They serve clients in the aerospace, defence, marine, medical, drug & food processing, robotics, energy, & oil & gas industries.
Wesley Eric Foley, President & COO
416-569-8621, efoley@tube-fab.com
James Dennie, Director, Quality
jdennie@tube-fab.com

Uniglobe Travel International L.P.
#900, 1199 West Pender St., Vancouver, BC V6E 2R1
Tel: 604-718-2600
info@uniglobetravel.com
www.uniglobetravel.com
Profile: Travel franchise specializing in corporate travel services for small to medium accounts as well as individual travelers.
U. Gary Charlwood, Chair & CEO
Tracy Bartram, CFO & Exec. Vice-President

UTC Aerospace Systems
Formerly: Hamilton Sundstrand; Goodrich Corporation
Parent: United Technologies Corporation
1400 South Service Rd. West, Oakville, ON L6L 5Y7
Tel: 905-827-7777; *Fax:* 905-825-1583
utcaerospacesystems.com
Profile: UTC Aerospace Systems was created in 2012 by merging Hamilton Sundstrand & Goodrich. UTC Aerospace Systems is comprised of two main divisions: Aircraft Systems; & Power, Controls, & Sensing Systems. Within these are the following subdivisions: Actuation Systems; Aerostructures; Air Management Systems; Electric Systems; Engine Components; Engine & Control Systems; Fire Protection Systems; Interiors; ISR Systems; Landing Gear; Propeller Systems; Sensors & Integrated Systems; Space Systems; & Wheels & Brakes.
David Gitlin, President

VAC Developments Limited
2270 Bristol Circle, Oakville, ON L6H 5S3
Tel: 905-855-6855; *Fax:* 905-855-6856
contact@vacdev.com
www.vacdev.com
Profile: VAC provides the aerospace industry with precision machining, sheet metal & welding services.
Bill Hristovski, President

Vector Aerospace Corporation
#1920, 2 Bloor St. East, Toronto, ON M4W 1A8
Tel: 416-640-2100; *Fax:* 416-925-7214
info@vectoraerospace.com
www.vectoraerospace.ca
Ticker Symbol: RNO / TSX
Profile: Manufacturers of aircraft parts & auxiliary equipment; Electrical & electronic repair shops; Various repair shops & related services
Declan O'Shea, President & CEO
Randal L. Levine, Sr. Vice-President & CFO

Versacold Income Fund
Formerly: Versacold Corporation
2115 Commissioner St., Vancouver, BC V5L 1A6
Tel: 604-255-4656; *Toll-Free:* 800-563-2653
info@versacold.com
www.versacold.com
Ticker Symbol: ICE
Profile: Refrigerated logistics services: storage & transportation
Doug Harrison, President & CEO
Michael Spence, CFO

Versatile Spray Painting Ltd. / VSP
102 Healey Rd., Bolton, ON L7E 5A9
Tel: 905-857-4915; *Fax:* 905-857-4924
Toll-Free: 877-857-4915
www.versatilespray.com
Profile: VSP specializes in industrial finishing for military, aerospace, medical sectors, as well as for business machines, & electronic packaging.

VIH Aerospace
Parent: VIH Aviation Group
1962 Canso Rd., North Saanich, BC V8L 5V5
Fax: 250-655-6861
Toll-Free: 866-844-4354
viha@vih.com
www.vih.com/Services/vihaerospace.html
Profile: VIH Aerospace offers helicopter maintenance products & services to the aerospace industry, including maintenance of communication & navigation equipment.

Viking Air Ltd.
1959 de Havilland Way, Sidney, BC V8L 5V5
Tel: 250-656-7227; *Fax:* 250-656-0673
Toll-Free: 800-663-8444
info@vikingair.com
www.vikingair.com
Profile: Viking manufactures seven aircraft types, & provides support services including spares sales, customer service, technical support, engineering, maintenance, repair, overhaul & conversions.
David Curtis, President & CEO

Virtual Marine Technology / VMT
20 Hallett Cres., St. John's, NL A1B 3N4
Tel: 709-738-6306; *Fax:* 709-738-5996
www.vmtechnology.ca
Profile: The company produces simulators for survival craft, fast response craft & high-speed electronic navigation training.

Wescast Industries Inc.
150 Savannah Oaks Dr., Brantford, ON N3V 1E7
Tel: 519-750-0000; *Fax:* 519-720-1628
north.america@wescast.com
www.wescast.com
Ticker Symbol: WCS / TSX
Profile: Manufacturers of motor vehicle parts & accessories; Wholesalers of motor vehicle supplies & new parts

Wiebel Aerospace (1995) Inc.
Parent: Testori Group
PO Box 70, 175 Greenwood Dr., Summerside, PE C1N 4P6
Tel: 902-888-2568; *Fax:* 902-888-2008
customerservice@wiebel.ca
www.testoriamericas.com
Profile: Wiebel manufactures custom precision machined parts & speciality components & assemblies.

Xiphos Systems Corporation
#500, 3981, boul St-Laurent, Montréal, QC H2W 1Y5
Tel: 514-847-9474
info@xiphos.com
www.xiphos.com
Profile: Xiphos provides customers in the aerospace industry with processors integrated into avionics packages, mainly for the space & unmanned aerial vehicles markets. Customers include the Canadian Space Agency & the United States Air Force.

YYJ FBO Services
Parent: VIH Aviation Group
Victoria International Airport, #101, 1962 Canso Rd., North Saanich, BC V8L 5V5
Tel: 250-655-8833; *Fax:* 250-655-5020
www.yyjfbo.com
Profile: The company is a fixed-base operator (FBO) located at Victoria International Airport, & offering fueling services, passenger, executive & pilot lounges, car & hotel reservations, catering services, flight planning room & other amenities.
Jen Norie, General Manager
jnorie@vih.com
Martin Childs, Manager, Operations
mchilds@yyjfbo.com

Government Agency Guide

AIRPORTS & AVIATION

See Also: Transportation

Canadian Air Transport Security Authority, 99 Bank St., 13th Fl., Ottawa, ON K1P 6B9
Fax: 613-990-1295, 888-294-2202

Transport Canada, Place de Ville, 330 Sparks St., Tower C, Ottawa, ON K1A 0N5
613-990-2309, Fax: 613-954-4731, 866-995-9737

Transportation Appeal Tribunal of Canada, #1201, 333 Laurier Ave. West, 12th Fl., Ottawa, ON K1A 0N5
613-990-6906, Fax: 613-990-9153, info@tatc.gc.ca

Newfoundland & Labrador
Newfoundland & Labrador Department of Transportation & Works, Confederation Bldg., Prince Philip Dr., PO Box 8700, St. John's, NL A1B 4J6
709-729-2300, tw@gov.nl.ca

Northwest Territories
Northwest Territories Department of Transportation, New Government Bldg., 5015 - 49 St., 4th Fl., PO Box 1320, Yellowknife, NT X1A 2L9
867-767-9089, Fax: 867-873-0606

Nunavut
Nunavut Territory Department of Community & Government Services, W.G. Brown Bldg., 4th Fl., PO Box 1000 700, Iqaluit, NU X0A 0H0
867-975-5400, Fax: 867-975-5305

Ontario
Ontario Ministry of Transportation, Ferguson Block, 77 Wellesley St. West, 3rd Fl., Toronto, ON M7A 1Z8
416-327-9200, Fax: 416-327-9185, 800-268-4686

Saskatchewan
Saskatchewan Highways & Infrastructure, Victoria Tower, 1855 Victoria Ave., Regina, SK S4P 3T2
306-787-4800, communications@highways.gov.sk.ca

Yukon Territory
Yukon Highways & Public Works, PO Box 2703, Whitehorse, YT Y1A 2C6
867-393-7193, Fax: 867-393-6218, 800-661-0408, hpw-info@gov.yk.ca

APPRENTICESHIP PROGRAMS

Canadian Council of Directors of Apprenticeship, 140 Promenade du Portage, 5th Fl, Phase IV, Gatineau, QC K1A 0J9
Fax: 819-994-0202, 877-599-6933, redseal-sceaurouge@hrsdc-rhdcc.gc.ca

Alberta
Alberta Advanced Education, Legislature Bldg., #403, 10800 - 97 Ave., Edmonton, AB T5K 2B6
780-422-5400, -310-0000

Apprenticeship & Student Aid Division, Commerce Place, 10155 - 102 St., 6th Fl., Edmonton, AB T5J 4L5

New Brunswick
New Brunswick Department of Post-Secondary Education, Training & Labour, Chestnut Complex, PO Box 6000, Fredericton, NB E3B 5H1
506-453-2597, Fax: 506-453-3618, dpetlinfo@gnb.ca

Northwest Territories
Apprenticeship, Trade & Occupations Certification Board, PO Box 1320, Yellowknife, NT X1A 2L9
867-873-7357, Fax: 867-873-0200

Prince Edward Island
Prince Edward Island Department of Workforce & Advanced Learning, Shaw Bldg., 105 Rochford St., 5th Fl., PO Box 2000, Charlottetown, PE C1A 7N8
902-368-5956, Fax: 902-368-5277

SkillsPEI, Atlantic Technology Centre, #212, 176 Great George St., Charlottetown, PE C1A 4K9
902-368-6290, Fax: 902-368-6340, 877-491-4766

Québec
Conseil consultatif du travail et de la main d'oeuvre, #17.100, 500, boul René-Lévesque ouest, Montréal, QC H2Z 1W7
514-873-2880, Fax: 514-873-1129, cctm@cctm.gouv.qc.ca

Saskatchewan
Saskatchewan Advanced Education, #1120, 2010 - 12 Ave., Regina, SK S4P 0M3
306-787-9478, aeeinquiry@gov.sk.ca

Saskatchewan Apprenticeship & Trade Certification Commission, 2140 Hamilton St., Regina, SK S4P 2E3
306-787-2444, Fax: 306-787-5105, 877-363-0536, apprenticeship@gov.sk.ca

Yukon Territory
Yukon Education, PO Box 2703, Whitehorse, YT Y1A 2C6
867-667-5141, Fax: 867-393-6339, contact.education@gov.yk.ca

RAIL TRANSPORTATION

See Also: Transportation

Transportation Safety Board of Canada, 200, Promenade du Portage, 4th Fl., Gatineau, QC K1A 1K8
819-994-3741, Fax: 819-997-2239, 800-387-3557, communications@bst-tsb.gc.ca

VIA Rail Canada Inc., CP 8116 A,Montréal, QC H3C 3N3
514-871-6000, Fax: 514-871-6104, 888-842-7245, customer_relations@viarail.ca

Alberta
Alberta Transportation, Communications Branch, Twin Atria Building, 4999 - 98 Jasper Ave., 2nd Fl., Edmonton, AB T6B 2X3
780-427-2731, Fax: 780-466-3166, -310-0000, Trans.Contact.Us.m@gov.ab.ca

Manitoba
Manitoba Infrastructure, Legislative Building, #203, 450 Broadway Ave., Winnipeg, MB R3C 0V8
204-945-3723, Fax: 204-945-7610

New Brunswick
New Brunswick Department of Transportation & Infrastructure, Kings Place, PO Box 6000, Fredericton, NB E3B 5H1
506-453-3939, Fax: 506-453-7987,
Transportation.Web@gnb.ca

Newfoundland & Labrador
Newfoundland & Labrador Department of Transportation & Works, Confederation Bldg., Prince Philip Dr., PO Box 8700, St. John's, NL A1B 4J6
709-729-2300, tw@gov.nl.ca

Nova Scotia
Nova Scotia Department of Transportation & Infrastructure Renewal, Johnston Bldg., 1672 Granville St., 2nd Fl., PO Box 186, Halifax, NS B3J 2N2
902-424-2297, Fax: 902-424-0532, 888-432-3233,
tpwpaff@novascotia.ca

Ontario
Metrolinx, 97 Front St. West, Toronto, ON M5J 1E6
416-874-5900, Fax: 416-869-1755
Ontario Northland Transportation Commission, 555 Oak St. East, North Bay, ON P1B 8L3
705-472-4500, Fax: 705-476-5598, 800-363-7512,
info@ontarionorthland.ca

Québec
Société du port ferroviaire Baie-Comeau-Haute-Rive, 18, rte Maritime, Baie-Comeau, QC G4Z 2L6
418-296-6785, Fax: 418-296-2377,
societeduport@globetrotter.net

Saskatchewan
Saskatchewan Grain Car Corporation, #1210, 1855 Victoria Ave., Regina, SK S4P 3T2
306-787-1137, Fax: 306-798-0931
Saskatchewan Highways & Infrastructure, Victoria Tower, 1855 Victoria Ave., Regina, SK S4P 3T2
306-787-4800, communications@highways.gov.sk.ca

TRANSPORTATION

Atlantic Pilotage Authority, Cogswell Tower, #910, 2000 Barrington St., Halifax, NS B3J 3K1
902-426-2550, Fax: 902-426-4004, 877-272-3477,
dispatch@atlanticpilotage.com
Automotive & Surface Transportation Facilities, Ottawa Uplands Research Facilities, 2320 Lester Rd., Ottawa, ON K1V 1S2
613-998-9639
Canadian Air Transport Security Authority, 99 Bank St., 13th Fl., Ottawa, ON K1P 6B9
Fax: 613-990-1295, 888-294-2202
Canadian Coast Guard, Centennial Towers, #6S018, 200 Kent St., Ottawa, ON K1A 0E6
613-993-0999, Fax: 613-990-1866, info@dfo-mpo.gc.ca
Canadian Transportation Agency, Les Terrasses de la Chaudière, 15 Eddy St., Gatineau, QC J8X 4B3
Fax: 819-997-6727, 888-222-2592, info@otc-cta.gc.ca
Federal Bridge Corporation Limited, #1210, 55 Metcalfe St., Ottawa, ON K1P 6L5
613-998-8427, Fax: 613-993-6945, info@federalbridge.ca
Great Lakes Pilotage Authority, 202 Pitt St., 2nd fl., PO Box 95, Cornwall, ON K6H 5R9
613-933-2991, Fax: 613-932-3793
Laurentian Pilotage Authority, Head Office, #1401, 999, boul Maisonneuve ouest, Montréal, QC H3A 3L4
514-283-6320, Fax: 514-496-2409, administration@apl.gc.ca
Marine Atlantic Inc., Corporate Office, Baine Johnston Centre, #302, 10 Fort William Pl., St. John's, NL A1C 1K4
800-897-2797, customer_relations@marine-atlantic.ca
Old Port of Montréal Corporation Inc., 333, rue de la Commune ouest, Montréal, QC H2Y 2E2
514-283-5256, 800-971-7678
Pacific Pilotage Authority Canada, #1000, 1130 West Pender St., Vancouver, BC V6E 4A4
604-666-6771, Fax: 604-666-1647, info@ppa.gc.ca
St. Lawrence Seaway Management Corporation, 202 Pitt St., Cornwall, ON K6J 3P7
613-932-5170, Fax: 613-932-7286, marketing@seaway.ca
Transport Canada, Place de Ville, 330 Sparks St., Tower C, Ottawa, ON K1A 0N5
613-990-2309, Fax: 613-954-4731, 866-995-9737
Transportation Appeal Tribunal of Canada, #1201, 333 Laurier Ave. West, 12th Fl., Ottawa, ON K1A 0N5
613-990-6906, Fax: 613-990-9153, info@tatc.gc.ca
Transportation Safety Board of Canada, 200, Promenade du Portage, 4th Fl., Gatineau, QC K1A 1K8
819-994-3741, Fax: 819-997-2239, 800-387-3557,
communications@bst-tsb.gc.ca
VIA Rail Canada Inc., CP 8116 A,Montréal, QC H3C 3N3
514-871-6000, Fax: 514-871-6104, 888-842-7245,
customer_relations@viarail.ca

Alberta
Alberta Automobile Insurance Rate Board, Canadian Western Bank Place, #2440, 10303 Jasper Ave., Edmonton, AB T5J 3N6
780-427-5428, Fax: 780-638-4254, -310-0000,
airb@gov.ab.ca
Alberta Infrastructure, Infrastructure Building, 6950 - 113 St., Edmonton, AB T6H 5V7
780-415-0507, Fax: 780-427-2187, -310-0000,
Infra.Contact.Us.m@gov.ab.ca
Alberta Transportation, Communications Branch, Twin Atria Building, 4999 - 98 Jasper Ave., 2nd Fl., Edmonton, AB T6B 2X3
780-427-2731, Fax: 780-466-3166, -310-0000,
Trans.Contact.Us.m@gov.ab.ca
Corporate Strategies & Services Division, Infrastructure Bldg., 6950 - 113 St., 2nd Fl., Edmonton, AB T6H 5V7
Safety, Policy & Engineering Division, Twin Atria Building, 4999 - 98 Ave., Main Fl., Edmonton, AB T6B 2X3
780-427-8901, Fax: 780-415-0782, 800-666-5036
Transportation Safety Board, North Office, Twin Atria Building, 4999 - 98 Ave., Main Fl., Edmonton, AB T6B 2X3
780-427-7178, Fax: 780-422-9739, -310-0000

British Columbia
British Columbia Ferry Commission, PO Box 9279 Prov Govt, Victoria, BC V8W 9J7
250-952-0112, info@bcferrycommission.com
British Columbia Ferry Services Inc., c/o BC Ferry Authority, #500, 1321 Blanshard St., Victoria, BC V8W 0B7
250-381-1401, 888-223-3779,
customerservice@bcferries.com
British Columbia Ministry of Transportation & Infrastructure, PO Box 9850 Prov Govt, Victoria, BC V8W 9T5
250-387-3198, Fax: 250-356-7706,
tran.webmaster@gov.bc.ca
British Columbia Transit, 520 Gorge Rd. East, Victoria, BC V8W 2P3
250-385-2551
Passenger Transportation Board, #202, 940 Blanshard St., PO Box 9850 Prov Govt, Victoria, BC V8W 9T5
250-953-3777, Fax: 250-953-3788, ptboard@gov.bc.ca
Transportation Policy & Programs Department, PO Box 9850 Prov Govt, Victoria, BC V8W 9T5
250-387-5062, Fax: 250-387-6431

Manitoba
Highway Traffic Board/Motor Transport Board, #200, 301 Weston St., Winnipeg, MB R3E 3H4
204-945-8912, Fax: 204-783-6529
License Suspension Appeal Board/Medical Review Committee, #200, 301 Weston St., Winnipeg, MB R3E 3H4
204-945-7350, Fax: 204-948-2682
Manitoba Infrastructure, Legislative Building, #203, 450 Broadway Ave., Winnipeg, MB R3C 0V8
204-945-3723, Fax: 204-945-7610
Taxicab Board, #200, 301 Weston St., Winnipeg, MB R3E 3H4
204-945-8919, Fax: 204-948-2315,
taxicabboardoffice@gov.mb.ca

New Brunswick
New Brunswick Department of Transportation & Infrastructure, Kings Place, PO Box 6000, Fredericton, NB E3B 5H1
506-453-3939, Fax: 506-453-7987,
Transportation.Web@gnb.ca
Vehicle Management Agency, Vehicle Management Centre, PO Box 6000, Fredericton, NB E3B 5H1
506-453-3939, Fax: 506-453-3628,
Transportation.Web@gnb.ca

Newfoundland & Labrador
Newfoundland & Labrador Department of Transportation & Works, Confederation Bldg., Prince Philip Dr., PO Box 8700, St. John's, NL A1B 4J6
709-729-2300, tw@gov.nl.ca

Northwest Territories
Northwest Territories Department of Transportation, New Government Bldg., 5015 - 49 St., 4th Fl., PO Box 1320, Yellowknife, NT X1A 2L9
867-767-9089, Fax: 867-873-0606

Nova Scotia
Nova Scotia Department of Transportation & Infrastructure Renewal, Johnston Bldg., 1672 Granville St., 2nd Fl., PO Box 186, Halifax, NS B3J 2N2
902-424-2297, Fax: 902-424-0532, 888-432-3233,
tpwpaff@novascotia.ca

Nunavut
Nunavut Territory Department of Community & Government Services, W.G. Brown Bldg., 4th Fl., PO Box 1000 700, Iqaluit, NU X0A 0H0
867-975-5400, Fax: 867-975-5305
Nunavut Territory Department of Economic Development & Transportation, Inuksugait Plaza, Bldg. 1104A, PO Box 1000 1500, Iqaluit, NU X0A 0H0
867-975-7800, Fax: 867-975-7870, 888-975-5999,
edt@gov.nu.ca

Ontario
Licence Appeal Tribunal, #530, 20 Dundas St. West, Toronto, ON M5G 2C2
416-314-4260, Fax: 416-314-4270, 800-255-2214
Metrolinx, 97 Front St. West, Toronto, ON M5J 1E6
416-874-5900, Fax: 416-869-1755
Ontario Highway Transport Board, 151 Bloor St. West, 10th Fl., Toronto, ON M5S 2T5
416-326-6732, Fax: 416-326-6738, ohtb@mto.gov.on.ca
Ontario Ministry of Infrastructure, Hearst Block, 900 Bay St., 8th Fl., Toronto, ON M7A 2E1
416-325-6666, 800-268-7095
Ontario Ministry of Transportation, Ferguson Block, 77 Wellesley St. West, 3rd Fl., Toronto, ON M7A 1Z8
416-327-9200, Fax: 416-327-9185, 800-268-4686
Ontario Northland Transportation Commission, 555 Oak St. East, North Bay, ON P1B 8L3
705-472-4500, Fax: 705-476-5598, 800-363-7512,
info@ontarionorthland.ca
Owen Sound Transportation Company Ltd., 717875, Hwy. 6, Owen Sound, ON N4K 5N7
519-376-8740, 800-265-3163
Road User Safety Division, Bldg A, #191, 1201 Wilson Ave., Downsview, ON M3M 1J8
416-235-2999, Fax: 416-235-4153

Prince Edward Island
Prince Edward Island Department of Transportation, Infrastructure & Energy, Jones Bldg., 11 Kent St., 3rd Fl., PO Box 2000, Charlottetown, PE C1A 7N8
902-368-5100, Fax: 902-368-5395

Québec
Agence métropolitaine de transport, 700, rue de la Gauchetière ouest, 26e étage, Montréal, QC H3B 5M2
514-287-2464
Commission des transports du Québec, 200, ch Sainte-Foy, 7e étage, Québec, QC G1R 5V5
514-873-6424, Fax: 418-644-8034, 888-461-2433,
courier@ctq.gouv.qc.ca
Ministère des Transports, de la Mobilité durable et de l'Électrification des transports, 700, boul René-Lévesque est, 29e étage, Québec, QC G1R 5H1
418-643-6980, Fax: 418-643-2033, 888-355-0511,
communications@mtq.gouv.qc.ca
Société de l'assurance automobile du Québec, 333, boul Jean-Lesage, CP 19600 Terminus, Québec, QC G1K 8J6
418-643-7620, Fax: 418-644-0339, 800-361-7620
Société des traversiers du Québec, 250, rue Saint-Paul, Québec, QC G1K 9K9
418-643-2019, Fax: 418-643-7308, 877-787-7483,
stq@traversiers.gouv.qc.ca
Société du parc industriel et portuaire de Bécancour, 1000, boul Arthur-Sicard, Bécancour, QC G9H 2Z8
819-294-6656, Fax: 819-294-9020, spipb@spipb.com
Société du port ferroviaire Baie-Comeau-Haute-Rive, 18, rte Maritime, Baie-Comeau, QC G4Z 2L6
418-296-6785, Fax: 418-296-2377,
societeduport@globetrotter.net

Saskatchewan
Global Transportation Hub Authority, #350, 1777 Victoria Ave., Regina, SK S4P 4K5
306-787-4842, Fax: 306-798-4600
Highway Traffic Board, 1621A mcDonald St., Regina, SK S4N 5R2
306-775-8336, Fax: 306-775-6618,
contactus@highwaytrafficboard.sk.ca
Saskatchewan Highways & Infrastructure, Victoria Tower, 1855 Victoria Ave., Regina, SK S4P 3T2
306-787-4800, communications@highways.gov.sk.ca
Saskatchewan Transportation Company, 1717 Saskatchewan Dr., Regina, SK S4P 2E2
306-787-3347, Fax: 306-787-1633, info@stcbus.com

Yukon Territory
Driver Control Board, #102, 211 Hawkins St., PO Box 2703, Whitehorse, YT Y1A 2C6
867-667-5623, Fax: 867-667-5799, dcb@gov.yk.ca
Yukon Community Services, PO Box 2703, Whitehorse, YT Y1A 2C6
867-667-5811, Fax: 867-393-6295, 800-661-0408,
inquiry@gov.yk.ca
Yukon Highways & Public Works, PO Box 2703, Whitehorse, YT Y1A 2C6
867-393-7193, Fax: 867-393-6218, 800-661-0408,
hpw-info@gov.yk.ca

SECTION 17
UTILITIES

Associations

Alberta Water & Wastewater Operators Association (AWWOA)
10806 - 119 St., Edmonton AB T5H 3P2
Tel: 780-454-7745; *Fax:* 780-454-7748
Toll-Free: 877-454-7745
www.awwoa.ab.ca
Social Media:
youtube.com/channel/UCBPP0dUISDng-gTnNX_bK5g/feed
www.facebook.com/157981630910194
twitter.com/awwoa
Overview: A small provincial organization founded in 1976
Description: To contribute to the training & upgrading of persons employed in the water & wastewater field in Alberta; To encourage the best possible operation of water & wastewater facilities
Affiliation(s): Western Canada Water & Wastewater Association
Chief Officer(s): Bert Miller, Chair
Activities: Providing manuals to operators

American Council for an Energy-Efficient Economy (ACEEE)
#600, 529 14th St. NW, Washington DC 20045-1000 USA
Tel: 202-507-4000; *Fax:* 202-429-2248
www.aceee.org
Social Media:
www.facebook.com/67449893973
twitter.com/ACEEEdc
Overview: A medium-sized national organization founded in 1980
Description: To advance energy-conserving technology & policies; to assist utilities & regulators to implement cost-effective conservation programs; to support the adoption of comprehensive new policies for increasing energy efficiency; to show how energy efficiency improvements can protect the environment; to analyse & promote technologies & policies for increasing vehicle fuel efficiency & reducing vehicle use; to help developing & Eastern European countries undertake energy efficiency programs
Chief Officer(s): Steven Nadel, Executive Director, 202-507-4011
snadel@aceee.org
Activities: *Library:* Yes

American Public Works Association (APWA)
#700, 2345 Grand Blvd., Kansas City MO 64108-2625 USA
Tel: 816-472-6100; *Fax:* 816-472-1610
Toll-Free: 800-848-2792
apwa@apwa.net
www.apwa.net
Social Media:
www.youtube.com/apwatv
www.facebook.com/AmericanPublicWorksAssociation
twitter.com/apwatweets
Overview: A medium-sized international organization founded in 1938
Description: To provide high quality public works goods & services
Chief Officer(s): Peter King, Executive Director
pking@apwa.net
Julie Burrell, Director, Human Resources / Office Services, 816-595-5280
jburrell@apwa.net
Finances: *Annual Operating Budget:* Greater than $5 Million; *Funding Sources:* Membership dues; Federal grants; Products
Staff: 50 staff member(s); 250 volunteer(s)
Membership: 26,000; *Fees:* Schedule available; *Member Profile:* Public agencies, private sector companies, & individuals engaged in public works services; *Committees:* Transportation; Solid Waste; Water Resources; Engineering & Technology; Management & Leadership; Emergency Management; Fleet Services; Facilities & Grounds; Utility & Public Right of Way

Association de l'industrie électrique du Québec (AIEQ)
#1470, 1155, rue Metcalfe, Montréal QC H3B 2V6
Tél: 514-281-0615; *Téléc:* 514-281-7965
info@aieq.net
www.aieq.net
Média social:
www.youtube.com/user/aiequebec
linkedin.com/groups/4314122/profile
www.facebook.com/AIEQuebec
twitter.com/_AIEQ
Nom précédent: Club d'électricité du Québec inc.
Aperçu: *Dimension:* moyenne; *Envergure:* provinciale; Organisme sans but lucratif; fondée en 1916
Description: Etre porte parole de l'industrie 'électrique au Québec; favoriser la circulation de toute information et intérêt pour les membres et l'industrie électrique en général; contribuer au développement de nos membres et à la promotion de leurs intérêts par des initiatives de concertation et de représentation; encourager l'utilisation rationnelle des ressources dans une perspective de développement
Affiliation(s): ABB; AECOM; ALSTOM; DESSAU; SNC-LAVALIN; VOITH; BPR: Brookfield; Mitsubishi Electric Power Products, Inc.; Qualitas
Membre(s) du bureau directeur: Daniel Laplante, Président et directeur général, 514-281-0615 122
dlaplante@aieq.net
Finances: *Budget de fonctionnement annuel:* $500,000-$1.5 Million
Personnel: 7 membre(s) du personnel
Membre: 121; *Montant de la cotisation:* Barème, selon le nombre d'employés au Québec; *Critères d'admissibilite:* Membres industriels; *Comités:* Consultatif; Finances; Services aux membres; Promotion; Débats projects
Activités: Déjeuners; conférences; activités sociales; *Service de conférenciers:* Oui

Association of Major Power Consumers in Ontario (AMPCO)
Thomson Bldg., #1510, 65 Queen St. West, Toronto ON M5H 2M5
Tel: 416-260-0280; *Fax:* 416-260-0442
www.ampco.org
Social Media:
linkedin.com/profile/view?id=11277536
twitter.com/powerconsumer
Overview: A large provincial organization founded in 1975
Description: To represent Ontario's electricity-intensive companies; To ensure reliability of power supply to support the economy of Ontario; To advocate a fair & equitable pricing system for electricity; To present views on energy matters to such groups as the Ontario Energy Board, the Ontario Government, Ontario Hydro, the news media, & the general public; To provide decision makers with recommendations on resolving issues
Chief Officer(s): Adam White, President
awhite@ampco.org
Fareeda Heeralal, Contact
Finances: *Funding Sources:* Membership fees
Membership: 44; *Fees:* Based on electrical energy usage; *Member Profile:* Companies that are major manufacturers, employers, & power consumers (represents key industries - mining, pulp & paper, automobile manufacturing, petro-chemicals, metals, consumer products, steel, etc.)

Association of Manitoba Hydro Staff & Supervisory Employees (AMHSSE)
MB
Overview: A small provincial organization
Membership: 415

Association of Power Producers of Ontario (APPrO)
#1602, 25 Adelaide St. East, Toronto ON M5C 3A1
Tel: 416-322-6549; *Fax:* 416-481-5785
appro@appro.org
www.appro.org
Social Media:
www.youtube.com/channel/UCAwW194Kmge1AcvSuAV2ihg
linkedin.com/company/association-of-power-producers-of-ontario-appro
twitter.com/APPrOntario
Previous Name: Independent Power Producers Society of Ontario (IPPSO)
Overview: A medium-sized provincial organization founded in 1986
Description: To act as the voice of electricity generators in Ontario; To support a reliable & secure electricity supply in Ontario
Chief Officer(s): Jake Brooks, Executive Director
jake.brooks@appro.org
David Butters, President
david.butters@appro.org
Membership: 100+; *Member Profile:* Companies involved in the generation of electricity in Ontario, including suppliers of services & consulting services
Activities: Advocating for generators; Offering resources to assist business, government, utilities, & researchers; Organizing educational programs

L'association québécoise des fournisseurs de services pétroliers et gaziers du Québec (AFSPC) / Oil & Gas Services Association of Québec (OGSAQ)
QC
Tél: 418-391-1155
info@afspg.com
www.afspg.com
Aperçu: *Dimension:* petite; *Envergure:* provinciale; fondée en 2011
Description: L'AFSPG a été créé dans le but de pouvoir développer le gaz de schiste au Québec et surtout, de pouvoir améliorer le présent mais, avant tout, l'avenir de chaque Québécois. Dans les prochaines années, l'AFSPG souhaite être en mesure de créer plus de deux cents puits par année au Québec, où l'on retrouve des sources de gaz schiste. Pour ce faire, ils utiliseront les plus grandes mesures de sécurité lors de l'extraction des gaz, limitant les chances de contaminations des sols environnants.
Membre: 60

Atlantic Canada Water & Wastewater Association (ACWWA)
PO Box 28141, Dartmouth NS B2W 6E2
Tel: 902-434-6002; *Fax:* 902-435-7796
contact@acwwa.ca
www.acwwa.ca
Social Media:
twitter.com/ACWWA
Overview: A medium-sized local organization
Description: To improve drinking water in Atlantic Canada; *Member of:* American Water Works Association (AWWA); Water Environment Federation (WEF)
Chief Officer(s): Clara Shea, Executive Director
Kendall Mason, Director, Communication
Membership: 430+; *Fees:* Schedule available; *Member Profile:* Water professionals in Atlantic Canada, from areas such as service provision, contracting, utility management, operations, system design, consulting, & academia; *Committees:* Scholarship; Conference; Operator Involvement; Education; Government Affairs; Magazine; Young Professionals; Membership; Volunteer; Media; Website; Technical Papers; Water For People; Cross Connection Control; Government Relations
Activities: Providing training & information about the water & wastewater industry to members; Enhancing government relations; Offering networking opportunities

Biogas Association
#900, 275 Slater St., Ottawa ON K1P 5H9
Tel: 613-822-1004
jgreen@biogasassociation.ca
www.biogasassociation.ca
Social Media:
linkedin.com/groups/3854330/profile
www.facebook.com/168782246502009
twitter.com/BiogasOntario
Previous Name: Agrienergy Producers' Association of Ontario
Overview: A medium-sized provincial organization founded in 2008
Description: The Biogas Association is the collective voice of the biogas industry.
Membership: *Fees:* $500 small business; $1500 large business
Activities: Advancing policy and regulatory developments; supporting research; outreach events

British Columbia Sustainable Energy Association (BCSEA)
PO Box 44104, Stn. Gorge Plaza, 2947 Tillicum Rd., Victoria BC V9A 7K1
Tel: 604-332-0025
info@bcsea.org
www.bcsea.org
Social Media:
www.youtube.com/BCSEA
ca.linkedin.com/company/bc-sustainable-energy-association
www.facebook.com/BCSEA
twitter.com/bcsea
Overview: A medium-sized provincial organization founded in 2004
Description: To empower British Columbians to build a clean, renewable energy future
Affiliation(s): Canadian Renewable Energy Association; Canadian Solar Industries Association; Canadian Wind Energy Association; Climate Action Network Canada; KyotoPLUS; Livable Region Coalition; NorthWest Energy Coalition; Oil Free Coast Alliance; Organizing for Change: Priorities for Environmental Leadership
Chief Officer(s): Ali Grovue, Interim Executive Director
aligrovue@bcsea.org
Finances: *Funding Sources:* Donations
Membership: *Fees:* Schedule available; *Member Profile:* Individuals & organizations
Activities: Providing education through programs & webinars

British Columbia Water & Waste Association (BCWWA)
#620, 1090 West Pender St., Vancouver BC V6E 2N7
Tel: 604-433-4389; *Fax:* 604-433-9859
Toll-Free: 877-433-4389
contact@bcwwa.org
www.bcwwa.org
Social Media:
linkedin.com/company/2646273
www.facebook.com/BCWWA
twitter.com/bcwwa

Overview: A medium-sized provincial organization founded in 1964
Description: To safeguard public health & the environment through the sharing of skills, knowledge, experience & education; To provide a voice for the water & waste community in British Columbia & the Yukon; *Member of:* American Water Works Association (AWWA); Water Environment Federation (WEF); Canadian Water & Wastewater Association (CWWA)
Chief Officer(s): Tanja McQueen, Chief Executive Officer, 604-433-7824
tmcqueen@bcwwa.org
Carlie Thauvette, Senior Manager, Member Services, 604-630-0011
cthauvette@bcwwa.org
Jennifer Thorne, Manager, Finance, 604-433-6941
jthorne@bcwwa.org
Edel Burke, Coordinator, Communications, 604-630-5348
eburke@bcwwa.org
Finances: *Funding Sources:* Membership fees; Courses; Seminars; Annual conference
Membership: *Fees:* $25 students; $35 operators; $60 full members; *Member Profile:* British Columbia & Yukon professionals & students in the water & wastewater fields; *Committees:* Annual Conference; Cross Connection Control; Education Advisory Council; Young Professionals; Yukon; Drinking Water; Infrastructure Management; Risk & Resilience; SCADA & IT; Wastewater & Residuals Management; Water Sustainability; Wastewater Collection; Watershed Management
Activities: Promoting dialogue & information dissemination on environmental matters; Offering operator education & training opportunities (online training now available); Providing networking opportunities such as our Annual Conference; Certifying backflow assembly testers in British Columbia & Yukon through our Cross Connection Control program; Creating awareness of the value of water through Drinking Water Week, which occurs annually in May.; *Awareness Events:* Drinking Water Week, May; *Library:* British Columbia Water & Waste Association Library

Building Energy Management Manitoba (BEMM)
#309, 23 - 845 Dakota St., Winnipeg MB R2M 5M3
Tel: 204-452-2098
info@bemm.ca
www.bemm.ca

Overview: A medium-sized provincial organization
Description: To promote energy efficiency & management in the various building sectors
Chief Officer(s): Monica Samuda Poitras, Chair, 204-261-0718
monica@samudaenergy.com
Robert Bisson, Treasurer, 204-945-8452
robert.bisson@gov.mb.ca
Kent Glenday, Contact, Membership, 204-669-3346, Fax: 204-669-3350
kent.glenday@philips.com
Membership: *Fees:* $125; *Member Profile:* Engineers, architects, property managers, contractors & energy management professionals; government, school boards, hospitals & utility representatives

CAMPUT, Canada's Energy & Utility Regulators (CAMPUT)
#646, 200 North Service Rd. West, Oakville ON L6M 2Y1
Tel: 905-827-5139; *Fax:* 905-827-3260
info@camput.org
www.camput.org

Previous Name: Canadian Association of Members of Public Utility Tribunals / Association canadienne des membres des tribunaux d'utilité publique
Overview: A small national organization founded in 1976
Description: To improve public utility regulation in Canada
Affiliation(s): National Association of Regulatory Utility Commissioners (NARUC)
Chief Officer(s): Terry Rochefort, Executive Director, 905-827-5139
rochefort@camput.org
Membership: 14 member boards and commissions, & 7 associate member boards and commissions; *Member Profile:* Any Canadian tribunal, board, commission, or agency that is responsible for the economic regulation of utilities; Any Canadian energy tribunal, board, commission, or agency that makes binding decisions through adjudicative or quasi-judicial processes; *Committees:* Regulatory Affairs; Education
Activities: Educating & training commissioners & staff of public utility tribunals; Communicating with members; Liaising with parallel regulatory organizations

Canada - Newfoundland & Labrador Offshore Petroleum Board (C-NLOPB)
TD Place, 140 Water St., 5th Fl., St. John's NL A1C 6H6
Tel: 709-778-1400; *Fax:* 709-778-1473
information@cnlopb.nl.ca
www.cnlopb.nl.ca
Social Media:
twitter.com/CNLOPB

Description: To apply the provisions of the *Atlantic Accord* & the *Atlantic Accord Implementation Acts*; To regulate the oil & gas industry for the Newfoundland & Labrador Offshore Area
Chief Officer(s): Scott Tessier, Chair & CEO
Ed Williams, Vice-Chair
John P. Andrews, Director, Legal, Regulatory & Public Affairs
Mike Baker, Director, Administration & Industrial Benefits
Dave Burley, Director, Environmental Affairs
Craig Rowe, Director, Exploration
Daniel B. Chicoyne, Director & Chief Safety Officer, Safety
Sean Kelly, Manager, Public Relations, 709-778-1418, Fax: 709-689-0713
skelly@cnlopb.nl.ca
Jeff O'Keefe, Director & Chief Conservation Officer, Resource Management
Jeffrey M. Bugden, Director, Operations
Activities: Facilitating the exploration for & development of hydrocarbon resources

Canada - Nova Scotia Offshore Petroleum Board (CNSOPB)
TD Centre, 1791 Barrington St., 8th Fl., Halifax NS B3J 3K9
Tel: 902-422-5588; *Fax:* 902-422-1799
info@cnsopb.ns.ca
www.cnsopb.ns.ca
Social Media:
twitter.com/CNSOPB

Description: To regulate petroleum activities in the Nova Scotia Offshore Area
Chief Officer(s): Stuart Pinks, P.Eng., Chief Executive Officer, 902-496-3206
spinks@cnsopb.ns.ca
Carl Makrides, Director, Resources, 902-496-0747
cmakrides@cnsopb.ns.ca
Christine Bonnell-Eisnor, Director, Regulatory Affairs & Finance, 902-496-0734
cbonnell@cnsopb.ns.ca
Shanti Dogra, General Counsel, 902-496-0736
sdogra@cnsopb.ns.ca
Troy MacDonald, Director, Information Services, 902-496-0734
tmacdonald@cnsopb.ns.ca
Kathleen Funke, Advisor, Communications, 902-496-0750
Activities: Issuing licences for offshore exploration & development; Collecting & distributing data

Canadian Association of Drilling Engineers (CADE)
PO Box 957, Stn. M, Calgary AB T2P 2K4
Toll-Free: 877-801-1820
info@cadecanada.com
www.cadecanada.com
Social Media:
linkedin.com/groups?home=&gid=3309291
twitter.com/cade_can

Overview: A medium-sized national organization founded in 1974
Description: To provide a forum for the exchange of technical drilling knowledge & expertise
Affiliation(s): Canadian Association of Oilwell Drilling Contractors
Chief Officer(s): Dan Schlosser, President, 403-988-2335
dschlosser@ncsfrac.com
Ryan Richardson, Vice-President, 587-223-7016
rrichardson@secure-energy.ca
Finances: *Funding Sources:* Membership dues
Membership: 500+; *Fees:* $10 student; $47.50 retiree; $95 full member; *Member Profile:* Open to those who work in the petroleum industry

Canadian Association of Petroleum Land Administration (CAPLA)
First St. Plaza, #620, 138 - 4th Ave. SE, Calgary AB T2G 4Z6
Tel: 403-452-6497; *Fax:* 403-452-6627
office@caplacanada.org
www.caplacanada.org
Social Media:
www.facebook.com/caplacanada
twitter.com/caplacanada

Overview: A small local organization founded in 1993
Chief Officer(s): Tracey Stock, President
tstock@tdstock.com
Matt Worthy, General Manager, 403-452-6591
matt@caplacanada.org
Membership: 2,800; *Fees:* $75 student; $175 active; $75 retired; *Committees:* Awards; Certification; Conference; Education Delivery & Facilitation; Education Development; Events; Executive; Knowledge Bank; Leadership Forum; Member Services; Mentorship; NEXUS Editorial; Social Media; Surface Stakeholder Engagement

Canadian Association of Petroleum Landmen (CAPL)
#350, 500 - 5 Ave. SW, Calgary AB T2P 3L5
Tel: 403-237-6635; *Fax:* 403-263-1620
reception@landman.ca
www.landman.ca

Overview: A medium-sized national organization founded in 1948
Description: To enhance all facets of the land profession
Chief Officer(s): Michelle Radomski, President
Nikki Sitch, Vice-President
Kent Gibson, Director, Member Services
Brad Reynolds, Director, Communications
Connie De Ciancio, Director, Education
Gary Richardson, Director, Public Relations
Finances: *Annual Operating Budget:* $1.5 Million-$3 Million
Membership: 1,500+
Activities: Liaising with government departments & other resource based associations; Communicating with members; Providing professional development opportunities; Offering networking events

Canadian Association of Petroleum Producers (CAPP) / Association canadienne des producteurs pétroliers
#2100, 350 - 7 Ave. SW, Calgary AB T2P 3N9
Tel: 403-267-1100; *Fax:* 403-261-4622
communication@capp.ca
www.capp.ca
Social Media:
www.youtube.com/cappvideos
linkedin.com/groupRegistration?gid=2632445
www.facebook.com/OilGasCanada
twitter.com/oilgascanada

Merged from: Canadian Petroleum Association; Independent Petroleum Association of Canada
Overview: A large national organization founded in 1992
Description: To represent companies that produce Canada's natural gas & crude oil; To enhance the economic sustainability of the Canadian upstream petroleum industry; To ensure work is conducted in a safe & environmentally & socially responsible manner; To work with government to develop regulatory requirements
Chief Officer(s): Tim McMillan, President
Janet Annesley, Vice-President, Communications
janet.annesley@capp.ca
Bob Bleaney, Vice-President, External Relations
bob.bleaney@capp.ca
David Pryce, Vice-President, Operations
pryce@capp.ca
Nick Schultz, Vice-President, Pipeline Regulation and General Counsel
schultz@capp.ca
Greg Stringham, Vice-President, Oil Sands & Markets
stringham@capp.ca
Membership: 100+ producer members + 150 associate members; *Member Profile:* Producer members range from two person operations to internationally recognized corporations employing thousands; Associate members provide services, such as drilling, baniking, & computing, for Canada's oil & gas industry; *Committees:* Industry Equalization Steering Committee
Activities: Reviewing, analyzing, & recommending industry policy positions; Participating in regulatory change dialogues; Representing the industry on multi-sector international, federal, & provincial consultation bodies; Communicating with governments, regulators, stakeholders, & the public; Offering seminars & workshops; Providing industry trends, statistics, & research information; Informing members of industry standards & guidelines; Monitoring pipeline expansions; Improving coordinated land use planning processes

Canadian Association on Water Quality (CAWQ) / Association canadienne sur la qualité de l'eau (ACQE)
PO Box 5050, Burlington ON L7R 4A6
Tel: 289-780-0378
www.cawq.ca

Also Known As: Canadian National Committee of the International Association on Water Quality

Previous Name: Canadian Association on Water Pollution Research & Control
Overview: A medium-sized national charitable organization founded in 1967
Description: To promote research on scientific, technological, legal & administrative aspects of water pollution research & control; To further the exchange of information & the practical application of such research for public benefit; *Member of:* International Association on Water Quality
Chief Officer(s): Chris Marvin, President, 905-319-6919, Fax: 905-336-6430
chris.marvin@ec.gc.ca
Yves Comeau, Secretary, 514-340-4711 3728, Fax: 514-340-5918
yves.comeau@polymtl.ca
Hubert Cabana, Treasurer, 819-821-8000 65457, Fax: 819-821-7974
hubert.cabana@usherbrooke.ca
Finances: *Funding Sources:* Membership fees; Subscriptions; Grants
Membership: 10 corporate + 210 individual; *Fees:* Schedule available; *Member Profile:* Joint or individual - engaged in water quality & pollution research & control; Corporate - organizations engaged in water quality & pollution research & control; Sustaining - individuals & organizations interested in support & results of water quality & pollution research & control; Joint or student - students engaged in full-time study on water quality & pollution research & control

Canadian Centre for Energy Information / Centre info-énergie
#201, 322 - 11th Ave. SW, Calgary AB T2R 0C5
Tel: 403-263-7722; *Fax:* 403-237-6286
Toll-Free: 877-606-4636
www.centreforenergy.com
Social Media:
twitter.com/centreforenergy
Also Known As: Centre for Energy
Overview: A medium-sized national organization founded in 2002
Description: To provide information about the Canadian energy system & energy-related issues
Chief Officer(s): Pierre Alvarez, Chair
Thomas Cotter, Secretary
David Luff, Treasurer
Activities: Raising awareness & understanding about the Canadian energy system; Providing learning resources for teachers & students; *Speaker Service:* Yes

Canadian Clean Power Coalition (CCPC)
c/o David Butler, 64 Chapala Heath, Calgary AB T2X 3P9
Tel: 403-606-0973; *Fax:* 403-256-0424
www.canadiancleanpowercoalition.com
Overview: A medium-sized national organization
Description: To secure a future for coal-fired electricity generation, along with a mix of fuels such as solar, wind, hydro, & nuclear; To research & develop clean coal technology
Chief Officer(s): David Butler, Executive Director
dave.butler@cleanerpower.ca
Membership: *Member Profile:* Canadian coal & coal-fired electricity producers
Activities: Addressing environmental issues with governments & stakeholders

Canadian Electricity Association (CEA) / Association canadienne de l'électricité (ACE)
#1500, 275 Slater St., Ottawa ON K1P 5H9
Tel: 613-230-9263; *Fax:* 613-230-9326
info@electricity.ca
www.electricity.ca
Social Media:
powerforthefuture.ca/blog
linkedin.com/company/canadian-electricity-association
twitter.com/CDNElectricity
Overview: A medium-sized national organization founded in 1891
Description: To ensure a safe, secure, reliable, sustainable & competitively priced supply of electricity. CEA is the voice of the Canadian electricity industry, promoting electricity as a key social, economic and environmental enabler that is essential to Canada's prosperity.
Chief Officer(s): Jim Burpee, President & CEO, 613-230-9263
burpee@electricity.ca
Francis Bradley, Vice-President, Policy Development, 613-230-5027
bradley@electricity.ca
Sandra Schwartz, Vice-President, Policy Advocacy, 613-230-9876
schwartz@electricity.ca
Tracy Walden, Director, Communications, 613-627-4333
Angela Baker-MacLeod, Corporate Secretary, 613-230-7384
macleod@electricity.ca
Richard Lussier, Controller, 613-688-2065
Membership: 31 Corporate Utility Members; 53 Corporate Partner Members; *Member Profile:* Members generate, transmit, & distribute electrical energy to residential, commercial, institutional, & industrial customers throughout Canada; *Committees:* Human Resources; Occupational Health and Safety; Technology
Activities: Analyzing national & international business issues; Providing a national forum for the electricity business; Advocating industry views; Helping companies in evolving markets; Communicating findings about concerns such as mercury emissions & electric & magnetic fields

Canadian Energy Efficiency Alliance (CEEA) / L'Association de l'efficacité énergétique du Canada
#500, 150 Laurier Ave. West, Ottawa ON K1P 5J4
Tel: 905-614-1642; *Toll-Free:* 866-614-1641
info@energyefficiency.org
www.energyefficiency.org
Social Media:
linkedin.com/groups?gid=4036109
www.facebook.com/111344902257508
twitter.com/CdnEnergyEffic
Overview: A medium-sized national organization founded in 1995
Description: To become the leading energy efficiency advocate in Canada; To work in partnership with industry, environmental & consumer leaders to promote energy efficiency programs & policies that will move Canada toward a more sustainable future
Affiliation(s): Canadian Energy Efficiency Centre
Chief Officer(s): Elizabeth McDonald, President & CEO
elizabethmcdonald@energyefficiency.org
Sylvie Powell, Vice-President, Member Services & Operations
sylviepowell@energyefficiency.org
Finances: *Annual Operating Budget:* $250,000-$500,000; *Funding Sources:* Membership dues & projects
Membership: 40; *Fees:* $1,500 corporate; $15,000 leader
Activities: Establishing a National Energy Efficiency Centre to be North America's energy technology showcase; promoting/advocating energy efficiency; breakfast policy updates; annual meeting

Canadian Energy Law Foundation (CELF)
c/o Robert Grant, Purdy's Wharf Tower One, 1959 Upper Water St., Halifax NS B3J 3N2
Tel: 902-420-3328; *Fax:* 902-420-1417
www.energylawfoundation.ca
Previous Name: Canadian Petroleum Law Foundation
Overview: A small national organization founded in 1963
Description: To study oil & gas laws
Chief Officer(s): Carolyn Wright, President
caw@bdplaw.com
Robert Grant, Coordinator, Membership
rgrant@stewartmckelvey.com
Membership: *Fees:* $500 Class A; $100 Class B; *Member Profile:* Legal practitioners from law firms, companies, governmental entities, administrative bodies, professional societies, and institutions of learning, as well as sole practitioners.

Canadian Energy Pipeline Association (CEPA) / Association canadienne de pipelines d'énergie
#200, 505 - 3rd St. SW, Calgary AB T2P 3E6
Tel: 403-221-8777; *Fax:* 403-221-8760
aboutpipelines@cepa.com
www.cepa.com
Social Media:
www.youtube.com/aboutpipelines;
www.slideshare.net/aboutpipelines
www.facebook.com/aboutpipelines
twitter.com/aboutpipelines
Overview: A medium-sized national organization founded in 1993
Description: To represent Canada's transmission pipeline companies; To ensure a strong transmission pipeline industry
Chief Officer(s): Chris Bloomer, President & Chief Executive Officer
Jim Donihee, Chief Operating Officer
Patrick Smyth, Director, Safety & Engineering
Alexandra Frison, Director, Communications
Sonya Savage, Director, Policy & Regulatory Affairs
Evan Wilson, Manager, Regulatory & Financial
Membership: *Member Profile:* Canada's pipeline companies that transport natural gas & crude oil throughout North America; *Committees:* Damage Prevention Regulations; Emergency Security Management; Environment; Health & Safety; Land Issues Task Force; Pipeline Integrity; Aboriginal Affairs; Climate Change; Corporate Tax; Commodity Tax; Pipeline Abandonment Obligations; Pipeline Economics; Property Tax; Regulatory Accounting; Regulatory Policy
Activities: Liaising with government regarding industry practices

Canadian Energy Research Institute (CERI)
#150, 3512 - 33 St. NW, Calgary AB T2L 2A6
Tel: 403-282-1231; *Fax:* 403-284-4181
info@ceri.ca
www.ceri.ca
Social Media:
twitter.com/ceri_canada
Overview: A medium-sized national organization founded in 1975
Description: To provide the public, industry, & the government with information concerning all aspects of energy
Chief Officer(s): Allan Fogwill, President & CEO
David McWhinney, Director, Finance & Operations
Dinara Millington, Vice-President, Research
Jon Rozhon, Senior Researcher
Deanne Landry, Manager, Marketing & Communications
Membership: 150
Activities: *Speaker Service:* Yes; *Library:* I.N. McKinnon Memorial Library

Canadian Energy Workers' Association (CEWA)
9908 - 106 St., Edmonton AB T5K 1C4
Tel: 780-420-7887; *Fax:* 780-420-7881
cewa@cewa.ca
www.cewa.ca
Previous Name: Canadian Utilities & Northland Utilities Employees' Association; Alberta Power Employees' Association
Overview: A small national organization founded in 1969
Description: To represent the interests of members, by serving as a bargaining agent for matters related to working relations with employers
Chief Officer(s): Christine Robinson, Interim Manager, Business, 780-977-3418
crobinson@cewa.ca
Activities: Engaging in problem solving between members & management; Creating programs for members in the areas of safety, security, & skills development; Seeking opportunities to organize & represent workers; Offering an annual bursary program

Canadian Fluid Power Association (CFPA) / Association canadienne d'énergie fluide
#310, 2175 Sheppard Ave. East, Toronto ON M2J 1W8
Tel: 416-499-1416; *Fax:* 416-491-1670
info@cfpa.ca
www.cfpa.ca
Social Media:
linkedin.com/groups?gid=4704028
twitter.com/CANADIANFPA
Overview: A medium-sized national organization founded in 1974
Description: To build public awareness of fluid power technology; To provide a forum for the exchange of information & opinion; To represent the Canadian fluid power industry to government, educational institutions & other organizations; To ensure that members' concerns are known to those in government; To ensure that students are able to be properly prepared for careers in the fluid power industry; To ensure that members are kept abreast of the latest developments in the fluid power industry; *Member of:* National Fluid Power Association
Chief Officer(s): Trish Torrance, Manager
torrance@cfpa.ca
John Lamb, Emerson, Chairman
Finances: *Funding Sources:* Membership fees; Sponsorships
Staff: 10 volunteer(s)
Membership: 80 corporate; *Fees:* $588.50 large corporation; $401.25 small corporation; $160.50 individual; *Member Profile:* Open to manufacturers, distributors, assemblers, educators, consultants & designers of fluid power components, systems & services; *Committees:* Communications; Membership; Market Insights; Education; Industrial Relations; Regional Events
Activities: Representing the fluid power industry on the Canadian advisory committee with regard to the drafting of international standards; Representing the fluid power industry in the formulation of applicable national standards; *Speaker Service:* Yes

Canadian Fuels Association / Association canadienne des carburants
#1000, 275 Slater St., Ottawa ON K1P 5H9
Tel: 613-232-3709; *Fax:* 613-236-4280
canadianfuels.ca
Social Media:
www.linkedin.com/company/canadianfuels—carburantsca
www.facebook.com/CanadianFuels
Previous Name: Canadian Petroleum Products Institute
Overview: A large national organization founded in 1989

Description: To represent its membership to governments on issues related to business, the environment, & health & safety in the petroleum products sector; To ensures its own adherence to the Competition Act, & provide a competition compliance program & training sessions to all staff & members
Chief Officer(s): Peter Boag, President
Membership: 10; *Member Profile:* Companies engaged in petroleum refining, marketing & distribution
Activities: Training & education; news releases, reports & technical documents; Driver Certification Program for petroleum transport drivers

Canadian Gas Association (CGA) / Association canadienne du gaz
#809, 350 Sparks St., Ottawa ON K1R 7S8
Tel: 613-748-0057; *Fax:* 613-748-9078
info@cga.ca
www.cga.ca
Social Media:
linkedin.com/company/canadian-gas-association
twitter.com/GoSmartEnergy
Overview: A large national organization founded in 1907
Description: To act as the voice of the natural gas distribution industry in Canada
Chief Officer(s): Timothy M. Egan, President & CEO, 613-748-0057 300
Paula Dunlop, Director, Public Affairs & Strategy, 613-748-0057 341
Bryan Gormely, Director, Policy, Economics, & Information, 613-748-0057 315
Jim Tweedie, Director, Operations, Safety, & Integrity Management, 613-748-0057 311
Valerie Prokop, Manager, Finance & Corporate Services, 613-748-0057 309
Membership: *Member Profile:* Equipment manufacturers; Distribution companies; Transmission companies; Service providers
Activities: Advancing policy positions with federal & provincial decision makers; Developing educational information

Canadian GeoExchange Coalition (CGC) / Coalition canadienne de l'énergie géothermique
#100, 442, rue St-Gabriel, Montréal QC H2L 1H9
Tel: 514-807-7559; *Fax:* 514-807-8221
www.geo-exchange.ca
Overview: A medium-sized national organization
Description: To develop industry standards; To expand the market for geoexchange technology in Canada; *Member of:* Energy Dialogue Group
Chief Officer(s): Denis Tanguay, President & CEO, 514-807-7559 24
denis.tanguay@geo-exchange.ca
Pierre Jolicoeur, Comptroller, 514-807-7559 22
pierre.jolicoeur@geo-exchange.ca
Membership: 126; *Fees:* Schedule available; *Member Profile:* Organizations involved with residential & commercial heating & air conditioning; *Committees:* Training; Technology
Activities: Providing information, training, & certification; Increasing public awareness; Working with stakeholders to foster the growth of the Canadian geoexchange industry; Liaising with provincial ministries of energy in Canada

Canadian Hydropower Association (CHA) / Association canadienne de l'hydroélectricité
#1402 - 150 Metcalfe St., Ottawa ON K2P 1P1
Tel: 613-751-6655; *Fax:* 613-751-4465
info@canadahydro.ca
canadahydro.ca
Social Media:
twitter.com/CanadaHydro
Overview: A small national organization founded in 1998
Description: To provide leadership for the responsible growth & prosperity of the Canadian hydropower industry
Chief Officer(s): Jacob Irving, President, 613-751-6655 3
jacob@canadahydro.ca
Membership: 50; *Member Profile:* Hydroelecic generation; hydroelectric industry; Associated associations & organizations

Canadian Institute for Energy Training (CIET) / Institut canadien de formation de l'énergie
#5600, 100 King St. West, Toronto ON M5X 1C9
Tel: 647-255-3107; *Toll-Free:* 800-461-7618
info@cietcanada.com
www.cietcanada.com
Overview: A medium-sized national organization founded in 1994
Description: To focus on the advancement of energy efficiency in industrial, commercial, & public sector organizations; To provide effective training solutions for the incorporation of energy management into organizational management priorities
Chief Officer(s): Douglas Tripp, President
Finances: *Funding Sources:* Fees for service
Activities: Offers the following training courses: Certified Energy Manager (CEM); Certified Measurement & Verification Professional (CMVP); Certified Energy Auditor (CEA); Certified Building Commissioning Professional (CBCP); Certified Professional in Energy Performance Contracting (CIET); Building Operator Certification (BOC); Certified in the Use of RETScreen; International Energy Efficiency Financing Protocol (IEEFP); ISO 50001 Standard Implementation; and more;

Canadian Institute of Energy (CIE)
#26, 181 Ravine Dr., Port Moody BC V3H 4T3
Tel: 604-949-1346; *Fax:* 604-469-3717
cienergybc@gmail.com
cienergybc.blogspot.ca
Overview: A medium-sized national organization founded in 1979
Description: To provide a Canadian perspective on energy technology, business & policy, nationally & internationally, for those affected professionally or personally by energy issues; To encourage energy research, education & dissemination of topical information; To provide an unbiased forum for discussion & debate
Chief Officer(s): Penny Cochrane, Chair
Melissa McArthur, Administrator
John Oliver, Treasurer
Finances: *Funding Sources:* Membership fees
Staff: 6 volunteer(s)
Membership: 500; *Fees:* $60; *Member Profile:* Professionally involved in all aspects of energy, whether in exploring for sources, conducting energy research, converting or using energy, or in energy planning
Activities: *Speaker Service:* Yes; *Rents Mailing List:* Yes

Canadian Institute of Mining, Metallurgy & Petroleum (CIM) / Institut canadien des mines, de la métallurgie et du pétrole
CIM National Office, #1250, 3500, boul de Maisonneuve ouest, Westmount QC H3Z 3C1
Tel: 514-939-2710; *Fax:* 514-939-2714
cim@cim.org
www.cim.org
Previous Name: Canadian Institute of Mining & Metallurgy
Overview: A large national organization founded in 1898
Description: To act as a source of leadership for its members, by offering conferences & courses, liaising with government departments, commissioning special volumes & reports, & publishing technical papers
Chief Officer(s): Garth Kirkham, President
gdkirkham@shaw.ca
Jean Vavrek, Executive Director, 514-939-2710 1301, Fax: 513-939-2714
jvavrek@cim.org
Lise Bujold, Director, Conferences & Exhibitions
lbujold@cim.org
Angela Hamlyn, Director, Communication, Publications & Media
ahamlyn@cim.org
Danielle Langlois, Director, Administration & Information Technology
dlanglois@cim.org
Deborah Sauvé, Manager, Canadian Mining Metallurgical Foundation
dsauve@cim.org
Membership: 12,000+; *Member Profile:* Professionals in the Canadian minerals, metals, materials, & energy sectors, from industry, government, & academia; *Committees:* Central Publications; Audit; Bulletin; By-Laws; CIM Valuation of Mineral Properties; Education; Estimation Guidelines; Human Resources; International Advisory Liaison; Membership; President Elect Nominating; Public Affairs; Special Volumes
Activities: Providing technical forums & professional networking opportunities; Offering continuing education; Recognizing excellent programs; *Speaker Service:* Yes; *Library:* Canadian Institute of Mining, Metallurgy & Petroleum Library

Canadian Oil Heat Association (COHA)
c/o COHA Ontario Chapter, PO Box 388, Stn. Main, Lindsay ON K9V 4S3
Tel: 905-604-8884; *Fax:* 866-946-0316
Toll-Free: 855-336-8943
info@coha-ontario.ca
www.cleanerheat.ca
Social Media:
www.facebook.com/ilovecleanerheat
twitter.com/CanadianOilHeat
Overview: A small national organization founded in 1983
Description: A voluntary membership organization, COHA serves as the industry's voice to provincial & federal regulators & government decision makers on matters of policy, safety, & certification. COHA works with government & other stakeholders to foster a sustainable business environment for its members. Chapters may be contacted at the following E-mail addresses: newbrunswick@coha.ca; newfoundland@coha.ca; novascotia@coha.ca; pei@coha.ca.; *Member of:* Canadian Association Executives
Chief Officer(s): Stephen Koch, Executive Director, Ontario Chapter
stephen.koch@coha.ca
Membership: 400; *Fees:* $300 - $18,000; *Member Profile:* Oil companies; HVAC manufacturers & suppliers; service contractors
Activities: Promoting the benefits of residential fuel oil to the consumer public

Canadian Propane Association (CPA) / Association canadienne du propane (ACP)
#616, 130 Albert St., Ottawa ON K1P 5G4
Tel: 613-683-2270; *Fax:* 613-683-2279
info@propane.ca
www.propane.ca
Social Media:
linkedin.com/groups/Canadian-Propane-Association-4355062
twitter.com/Propanedotca
Merged from: Propane Gas Association of Canada Inc.; Ontario Propane Association
Overview: A medium-sized national licensing organization founded in 2011
Description: To act as the national voice of the Canadian propane industry; To supports its members in the development of a safe, environmentally responsible Canadian propane industry
Affiliation(s): Propane Training Institute (PTI), a division of the CPA; Liquefied Petroleum Gas Emergency Response Corporation, a wholly owned subsidiary of the CPA
Chief Officer(s): Guy Marchand, Chair
Andrea Labelle, Executive Director, 613-683-2270 277
Allison Mallette, Manager, Research & Communications, 416-220-2244
Peter Maddox, Regional Manager, Ontario, 416-903-8518
Finances: *Annual Operating Budget:* $1.5 Million-$3 Million; *Funding Sources:* Membership dues
Staff: 15 staff member(s)
Membership: 400+; *Fees:* Schedule available; *Member Profile:* Producers; Wholesalers; Retailers; Transporters; Manufacturers of appliances, cylinders, & equipment; Associates; *Committees:* Governance; Policy & Advocacy; Regulatory Affairs; Audit & Finance
Activities: Providing industry related training & emergency response; Promoting the interests of the industry; Engaging in regulatory relations; *Internships:* Yes

Canadian Public Works Association (CPWA) / Association canadienne des travaux publics
c/o Kealy Dedman, President, 1 Carden St., Guelph ON N1H 3A1
Tel: 202-408-9541; *Fax:* 202-408-9542
Toll-Free: 800-848-2792
cpwa@cpwa.net
www.cpwa.net
Overview: A medium-sized national organization founded in 1986
Description: To improve the quality of public works services for Canadian citizens; To share information about public works issues that are unique to Canada
Chief Officer(s): Kealy Dedman, P.Eng, President
Peter King, Executive Director
pking@apwa.net
Gail Clark, Manager, Outreach
gclark@apwa.net
Alan Young, Consultant, Government Relations
young@tactix.ca
Laura Bynum, Contact, Media Relations
lbynum@apwa.net
Membership: *Member Profile:* Public works employees in Canada who are members of the American Public Works Association; Any person or organization in Canada with an interest in infrastructure & public works issues
Activities: Engaging in advocacy projects; Producing position statements; Facilitating the exchange of information for public works employees

Canadian Renewable Energy Alliance (CanREA)
www.canrea.ca
Previous Name: Canadian Renewable Energy Association
Overview: A large national organization founded in 2006
Description: To promote a global transition to energy conservation & efficiency, & the use of renewable energy. A founding member of the North American Alliance for Renewable Energy, CanREA & its members advocate to all levels of government & work with like-minded organizations worldwide to recommend new policy directions & practical strategies; *Member of:* North American Alliance for Renewable Energy
Affiliation(s): BC Sustainable Energy Association; David Suzuki

Foundation; Ecology Action Centre; Environmental Coalition of Prince Edward Island; The Falls Brook Centre; Green Communities Canada; Greenpeace Canada; Nova Scotia Cooperative Council; Ontario Sustainable Energy Association; Canadian Institute for Sustainable Living; Pembina Institute; Sierra Club Canada; Saskatchewan Environmental Society; Toronto Renewable Energy Coop; Windfall Ecology Centre
Membership: 16; *Member Profile:* Registered & incorporated not-for-profit organizations which actively promote renewable energy policy & implementation & are in good standing under applicable laws
Activities: Conferences

Canadian Society of Petroleum Geologists (CSPG)

#110, 333 - 5th Ave. SW, Calgary AB T2P 1G7
Tel: 403-264-5610; *Fax:* 403-264-5898
cspg@cspg.org
www.cspg.org
Social Media:
linkedin.com/groups/Canadian-Society-Petroleum-Geologists-4153517
www.facebook.com/CSPGOnline
Previous Name: Alberta Society of Petroleum Geologists
Overview: A medium-sized national organization founded in 1929
Description: To advance the science of geology, especially as it relates to petroleum, natural gas & other fossil fuels; to promote the technology of exploration for finding & producing these resources; to foster the spirit of scientific research; to develop a sense of pride & community among Canadian Petroleum Geologists; to provide the means to ensure that the Canadian Petroleum Geologist is the best trained, best supported & most skillful practitioner in the world
Chief Officer(s): Lis Bjeld, Executive Director, 403-513-1235
lis.bjeld@cspg.org
Finances: *Annual Operating Budget:* $250,000-$500,000; *Funding Sources:* Membership dues; publications; programs; trust fund
Staff: 3 staff member(s); 300 volunteer(s)
Membership: 3,500; *Fees:* $65; $20 students; $500 corporate
Activities: Education trust fund; member programs;

Canadian Solar Industries Association

#605, 150 Isabella St., Ottawa ON K1S 1V7
Tel: 613-736-9077; *Fax:* 613-736-8938
Toll-Free: 866-522-6742
info@cansia.ca
www.cansia.ca
Social Media:
linkedin.com/company/canadian-solar-industries-association-cansia-
www.facebook.com/cansia
twitter.com/CanadianSIA
Also Known As: CanSIA
Overview: A medium-sized national organization founded in 1992
Description: To develop a strong Canadian solar energy industry; To act as the voice for the solar energy industry in Canada; *Member of:* CanCORE
Chief Officer(s): John A. Gorman, President & CEO
jgorman@cansia.ca
Finances: *Annual Operating Budget:* $500,000-$1.5 Million; *Funding Sources:* Membership fees
Staff: 8 staff member(s)
Membership: 250; *Fees:* Schedule available; *Member Profile:* Solar energy companies across Canada; *Committees:* Policy & Market Development; Utilities & Regulatory Affairs; Communications
Activities: Offering education & networking events for members; Liaising with federal & provincial governments; *Speaker Service:* Yes

Canadian Telecommunications Consultants Association (CTCA)

PO Box 361, St. Davids ON L0S 1P0
Tel: 289-477-1465; *Toll-Free:* 866-584-2822
membership@ctca.ca
www.ctca.ca
Overview: A small national organization founded in 1985
Description: CTCA advocates high standards of professionalism & expertise in the provision of telecommunications solutions. Towards this vision, the association encourages the dissemination & exchange of information among telecommunications consultants & organizations.
Chief Officer(s): Scott Murphy, President
Mary Pawlus, Contact
Finances: *Funding Sources:* Membership dues; conference registrations
Membership: 1-99; *Fees:* Schedule available; *Member Profile:* Independent telecommunications consultants
Activities: Providing networking, collaboration, & educational opportunities for members; Promoting integrity, competence, & professionalism among members according to its Code of Ethics & Professional Conduct; *Speaker Service:* Yes

Canadian Water & Wastewater Association (CWWA) / Association canadienne des eaux potables et usées (ACEPU)

#11, 1010 Polytek St., Ottawa ON K1J 9H9
Tel: 613-747-0524; *Fax:* 613-747-0523
admin@cwwa.ca
www.cwwa.ca
Social Media:
linkedin.com/company/canadian-water-and-wastewater-association
www.facebook.com/117350581695487
twitter.com/CWWACEPU
Overview: A medium-sized national organization founded in 1986
Description: To represent the common interests of Canadian municipal water & wastewater systems to federal & interprovincial bodies; *Member of:* Canadian National Committee for the International Water Association
Chief Officer(s): Mike Darbyshire, President
Robert Haller, Executive Director
rhaller@cwwa.ca
Anita Wilson, Coordinator, Conference, Event & Sponsorship
awilson@cwwa.ca
Membership: *Member Profile:* Utility members are owners or operators of municipal infrastructure or services; Associate members are the private sector & academics; Subscription members are federal, provincial, or territorial government departments or agencies; *Committees:* Wastewater & Stormwater; Water & Energy Efficiency; Drinking Water Quality; Security & Emergency Management; Biosolid; Climate Change
Activities: Monitoring policies, legislation, & standards; Liaising with federal & interprovincial organizations; Hosting workshops; Facilitating networking opportunities; Increasing & improving public awareness; Cooperating with regional water & wastewater associations

Canadian Water Quality Association (CWQA)

#504, 295 The West Mall, Toronto ON M9C 4Z4
Tel: 416-695-3068; *Fax:* 416-695-2945
Toll-Free: 866-383-7617
info@cwqa.com
www.cwqa.com
Social Media:
linkedin.com/groups/Canadian-Water-Quality-Association-3948494
Overview: A medium-sized national organization founded in 1967
Description: To promote the individual right to quality water; To educate water quality professionals; To promote the growth of the water quality improvement industry; To serve as a unified voice in government & public relations; To provide a role in consumer education
Chief Officer(s): Kevin Wong, CAE, Executive Director
k.wong@cwqa.com
Membership: 106 dealers/distributors + 16 manufacturers/suppliers + 10 associates; *Fees:* Schedule available

Canadian Water Resources Association (CWRA) / Association canadienne des ressources hydriques (ACRH)

1401 - 14th St. North, Lethbridge AB T1H 2W6
Tel: 403-317-0017
services@aic.ca
www.cwra.org
Social Media:
linkedin.com/groups/CWRA-2294668
twitter.com/CWRA_Flows
Overview: A large national charitable organization founded in 1947
Description: To encourage recognition of the high priority & value of water
Affiliation(s): Canadian Water & Wastewater Association; International Water Resources Association; American Water Resources Association; British Hydological Society; American Institute of Hydrology
Chief Officer(s): Dave Murray, President
F.A. (Rick) Ross, Executive Director
Finances: *Annual Operating Budget:* $100,000-$250,000; *Funding Sources:* Membership dues; Donations
Staff: 3 staff member(s); 50 volunteer(s)
Membership: 1000; *Fees:* Schedule available; *Member Profile:* Individuals & organizations interested in the management of Canada's water resources, including private & public sector water resource managers, administrators, scientists, academics, students, & users; *Committees:* Finance; Publications; Fundraising; Scholarship; Communications; Website
Activities: Increasing awareness & understanding of Canada's water resources; Providing a forum for the exchange of information; Participating with appropriate agencies in international water management activities; *Internships:* Yes; *Speaker Service:* Yes

Canadian Wind Energy Association Inc. (CanWEA) / Association canadienne d'énergie éolienne

#710, 1600 Carling Ave., Ottawa ON K1Z 1G3
Tel: 613-234-8716; *Fax:* 613-234-5642
Toll-Free: 800-922-6932
info@canwea.ca
www.canwea.ca
Social Media:
www.youtube.com/canwea
linkedin.com/company/canadian-wind-energy-association
www.facebook.com/163408037028327
twitter.com/canwindenergy
Overview: A small national organization founded in 1984
Description: To promote the social, economic, & environmental benefits of wind energy in Canada; To encourage the appropriate development & application of wind energy; To create suitable environmental policy
Chief Officer(s): Robert Hornung, President
Jean-François Nolet, Vice-President, Policy & Communications
Tim Levy, Director, Technical & Utility Affairs
Tim Weis, Director, Policy
Finances: *Funding Sources:* Membership fees; Conference & workshop fees
Membership: 420; *Fees:* $100 individual; $550 associate; $2,750-$60,000 corporate; *Member Profile:* Organizations & individuals who are involved in the development & application of wind energy technology, products, & services in Canada
Activities: Providing information about wind energy; Offering networking opportunities for all stakeholders; Facilitating research; Forming strategic alliances; *Library:* Canadian Wind Energy Association Library by appointment

Clean Energy BC

#354, 409 Granville St., Vancouver BC V6C 1T2
Tel: 604-568-4778; *Fax:* 604-568-4724
Toll-Free: 855-568-4778
www.cleanenergybc.org
Social Media:
linkedin.com/groups/Clean-Energy-Association-BC-4767428
www.facebook.com/781621211850050?xprOpenPopup=1
twitter.com/CleanEnergyBC
Previous Name: Independent Power Association of BC
Overview: A small provincial organization founded in 1992
Description: To ensure that British Columbia's independent power producer industry is a contributor to the electricity market in the province
Chief Officer(s): Paul Kariya, Executive Director
paul.kariya@cleanenergybc.org
Donald MacLachlan, Contact, Media & Communications
claritymediapr@gmail.com
Lisa Bateman, Coordinator, Events
lisa.bateman@cleanenergybc.org
Kristen McIntyre, Contact, Membership Services, Registration, & Administration
kristen.mcintyre@cleanenergybc.org
Activities: Engaging in policy implementation

Coalition for Competitive Telecommunications

#880, 45 O'Connor St., Ottawa ON K1P 1A4
Tel: 613-566-7053; *Fax:* 613-566-2026
Overview: A small national organization founded in 2003
Description: To be the authoritative voice for Canadian business & institutional users of telecom equipment & services on critical legislative, regulatory & policy issues affecting business operations
Chief Officer(s): Ian C. Russell, Chair

Community Energy Association (CEA)

#1400, 333 Seymour St., Vancouver BC V6B 5A6
Tel: 604-628-7076; *Fax:* 778-786-1613
info@communityenergy.bc.ca
www.communityenergy.bc.ca
Overview: A medium-sized provincial charitable organization founded in 1993
Description: To support local governments in British Columbia in energy conservation & climate change activities
Chief Officer(s): Dale Littlejohn, Executive Director, 604-628-7076
dlittlejohn@communityenergy.bc.ca
Patricia Bell, Senior Community Energy Planner, 604-936-0470
pbell@communityenergy.bc.ca
Megan Lohmann, Senior Energy Planner, 250-423-7212
Finances: *Funding Sources:* Membership revenues; Fundraising

Activities: Communicating with elected officials, municipal & regional district staff, & First Nations in British Columbia; Offering advisory services to local governments regarding energy innovations; Promoting energy efficiency & renewable energy for infrastructure; Encouraging local governments to consider energy in land planning & development; Conducting research on energy related topics; *Speaker Service:* Yes

Electricity Distributors Association (EDA)

#1100, 3700 Steeles Ave. West, Vaughan ON L4L 8K8
Tel: 905-265-5300; *Fax:* 905-265-5301
Toll-Free: 800-668-9979
email@eda-on.ca
www.eda-on.ca
Social Media:
www.facebook.com/EDAMembersAssistSandy
twitter.com/EDA_ONT

Previous Name: Municipal Electric Association
Overview: A large provincial organization founded in 1986
Description: To be the voice of Ontario's electricity distributors, the publicly & privately owned companies that deliver electricity to Ontario homes, businesses & public institutions. Focus is on advocacy & representation to government, analysis of legislation & market regulations, communication & networking among members & industry colleagues
Chief Officer(s): Charlie Macaluso, President & CEO, 905-265-5363
John Loucks, Vice President, Association & Member Affairs, 905-265-5317
Teresa Sarkesian, Vice President, Policy & Government Affairs, 905-265-5313
Finances: *Annual Operating Budget:* Greater than $5 Million; *Funding Sources:* Membership dues
Staff: 18 staff member(s); 100 volunteer(s)
Membership: 256; *Fees:* $750 commercial member; *Member Profile:* Public & privately owned electricity distributors

Electricity Human Resources Canada (EHRC)

#405, 2197 Riverside Dr., Ottawa ON K1H 7X3
Tel: 613-235-5540; *Fax:* 613-235-6922
info@electricityhr.ca
electricityhr.ca
Social Media:
www.facebook.com/278647015504485?sk=wall
twitter.com/electricityHR

Previous Name: Electricity Sector Council
Overview: A medium-sized national organization
Description: Collective national partnership of business, labour & education working to develop a highly skilled workforce for the industry now & in the future
Chief Officer(s): Michelle Branigan, Chief Executive Officer
Membership: *Fees:* $1,000-$6,000

Electro-Federation Canada Inc. (EFC)

#300, 180 Attwell Dr., Toronto ON M9W 6A9
Tel: 905-602-8877; *Fax:* 905-602-5686
Toll-Free: 866-602-8877
www.electrofed.com
Social Media:
linkedin.com/groups?gid=3236862&trk=hb_side_g
twitter.com/EFC_Tweets

Overview: A medium-sized national organization founded in 1995
Description: To represent members provincially, federally, & internationally on issues affecting the electro-technical business
Chief Officer(s): Jim Taggart, President/CEO, 647-260-3093
jtaggart@electrofed.com
Ken Frankum, Chair
Philip Lefrancq, Vice-President, Finance & Administration, 647-260-3086
plefrancq@electrofed.com
Wayne Edwards, Vice-President, Sustainability & Electrical Safety, 647-258-7483
wedwards@electrofed.com
Membership: 300 companies; *Member Profile:* Companies that manufacture, distribute, & service electrical, electronics, & telecommunications products; *Committees:* Canadian Appliance Manufacturers Association; Consumer Electronics Marketers of Canada; Electrical Equipment Manufacturers Association of Canada; Supply & Manufacturers' Reps Councils; Installation Maintenance & Repair Sector Council & Trade Association; Electro-Federation Canada Alumni Association
Activities: Collecting & disseminating market data; Providing networking opportunities; Hosting annual conferences; Researching; Offering educational programs; Communicating with members; Promoting the industry; Conducting surveys;

Energy Council of Canada / Conseil canadien de l'énergie

#608, 350 Sparks St., Ottawa ON K1R 7S8
Tel: 613-232-8239; *Fax:* 613-232-1079
www.energy.ca
Social Media:
twitter.com/EnergyCouncilCA

Previous Name: World Energy Council - Canadian Member Committee
Overview: A medium-sized national organization founded in 1924
Description: To foster a greater understanding of energy issues; To enhance the effectiveness of the Canadian energy strategy; *Member of:* World Energy Council
Chief Officer(s): Graham Campbell, President, 613-232-8239 601
graham.campbell@energy.ca
Brigitte Svarich, Director, Operations, 613-232-8239 602
brigitte.svarich@energy.ca
Jessie Pierre, Coordinator, Events & Activities, 613-232-8239 603
jessie.pierre@energy.ca
Membership: 75+; *Member Profile:* Representatives from all facets of Canada's energy sector
Activities: Providing networking opportunities; Sponsoring forums & conferences; Disseminating current energy reports & information; Contributing to the development of the Canadian energy policy

Energy Probe Research Foundation (EPRF)

225 Brunswick Ave., Toronto ON M5S 2M6
Tel: 416-964-9223; *Fax:* 416-964-8239
webadmin@eprf.ca
epresearchfoundation.wordpress.com
Social Media:
www.facebook.com/277852842290873

Overview: A large national charitable organization founded in 1980
Description: To educate Canadians about the benefits of conservation & renewable energy; to help Canada secure long-term energy self-sufficiency in the shortest possible time with the fewest disruptive effects & with the greatest societal, environmental & economic benefits; to provide business, government & the public with information on energy & energy-related issues; to help Canada contribute to global harmony & prosperity; recipient of the 1990 Lieutenant Governor's Conservation Award, the first time that an environmental organization has been so honoured; divisions include Energy Probe, Probe International, Environment Probe, Margaret Laurence Fund, Consumer Policy Institute, Environmental Bureau of Investigations, Urban Renaissance Institute
Affiliation(s): Energy Probe; Probe International; Environment Probe; Consumer Policy Institute; Urban Renaissance Institute; Environmental Bureau of Investigation; Three Gorges Probe; Canadian Environmental News Network
Chief Officer(s): Patricia Adams, President
Elizabeth Brubaker, Executive Director, Environment Probe
Finances: *Annual Operating Budget:* $1.5 Million-$3 Million; *Funding Sources:* Donations
Staff: 15 staff member(s); 10 volunteer(s)
Membership: 50,000 supporters
Activities: Policy research & education; *Internships:* Yes; *Speaker Service:* Yes; *Library:* Yes (Open to Public)

Enform: The Safety Association for the Upstream Oil & Gas Industry

Head Office, 5055 - 11th St. NE, Calgary AB T2E 8N4
Tel: 403-516-8000; *Fax:* 403-516-8166
Toll-Free: 800-667-5557
customerservice@enform.ca
www.enform.ca

Previous Name: Petroleum Industry Training Service
Overview: A large national licensing charitable organization founded in 2005
Description: To improve the Canadian upstream oil & gas industry's safety performance; To prevent work-related injuries in the upstream oil & gas industry in Canada
Affiliation(s): Canadian Association of Geophysical Contractors (CAGC); Canadian Association of Oilwell Drilling Contractors (CAODC); Canadian Association of Petroleum Producers (CAPP); Canadian Energy Pipeline Association (CEPA); Petroleum Services Association of Canada (PSAC); Small Explorers & Producers Association of Canada (SEPAC); Petroleum Human Resources Council of Canada; Western Canadian Spill Services
Chief Officer(s): Duane Mather, Chair
Cameron MacGillivray, President & CEO
Jeff Rose, Chief Operating Officer
Paula Campkin, Vice-President & Chief Safety Officer, Industry Development
Rick Shatosky, Vice-President, Accounting & Planning
Activities: Providing training courses; Offering saftey information; Promoting shared safety practices in the Canadian oil & gas industry; Providing the Small Employers Certificate of Recognition (SECOR), the Certificate of Recognition (COR), & the Petroleum Competency Program

Explorers & Producers Association of Canada (EPAC)

#1060, 717 - 7th Ave. SW, Calgary AB T2P 0Z3
Tel: 403-269-3454; *Fax:* 403-269-3636
info@explorersandproducers.ca
www.explorersandproducers.ca

Previous Name: Small Explorers & Producers Association of Canada
Overview: A small national organization founded in 1986
Description: To represent & promote the interests of small producers & explorers, not only to government & regulatory bodies, but to other sectors of the conventional oil & gas industry; To educate the public at large about the importance of emerging companies in resource development in Western Canada, & investment opportunities available in the growing segment of the oilpatch; To propose long-term, effective fiscal & operating strategies for the ongoing health & vitality of this important sector of the Canadian economy
Chief Officer(s): Ken McCagherty, Chair
Gary Leach, President
Membership: 387 corporate; *Fees:* $525-$9,000

FogQuest

448 Monarch Pl., Kamloops BC V2E 2B2
Tel: 250-374-1745; *Fax:* 250-374-1746
info@fogquest.org
www.fogquest.org

Overview: A small international charitable organization founded in 1987
Description: To plan & implement water projects for rural communities located in developing countries
Chief Officer(s): Robert Schemenauer, Executive Director
Melissa Rosato, Associate Executive Director
Finances: *Funding Sources:* Grants; donations; membership fees
Membership: *Fees:* $40

Fondation Hydro-Québec pour l'environnement / Hydro-Québec Foundation for the Environment

75, rue Notre-Dame ouest, 2e étage, Montréal QC H2Z 1A4
Tél: 514-289-5384; *Téléc:* 514-289-2840
fondation_environnement@hydro.qc.ca
www.hydroquebec.com/fondation_environnement

Aperçu: *Dimension:* petite; *Envergure:* provinciale
Description: Promouvoir la conservation, la restauration et la mise en valeur de la faune, de la flore et des habitats naturels; soutenir les besoins locaux en matière de prise en charge de l'environnement; contribuer à l'utilisation responsable et durable des ressources naturelles
Membre(s) du bureau directeur: Stella Leney, Présidente

Gas Processing Association Canada (GPAC)

#400, 1040 - 7th Ave. SW, Calgary AB T2P 3G9
Tel: 403-244-4487; *Fax:* 403-244-2340
info@gpacanada.com
www.gpacanada.com
Social Media:
linkedin.com/groups/Gas-Processing-Association-Canada-4334615
twitter.com/GPACanada

Previous Name: Canadian Gas Processors Association
Overview: A medium-sized national organization founded in 1960
Description: To promote interaction & exchange of ideas & technology that will add value to those who are involved with or affected by the hydrocarbon processing industry
Affiliation(s): Gas Processors Association (USA)
Chief Officer(s): Josh Carter, President
josh.carter@zedi.ca
Cheryl Lafond, Director, Safety
crlafond@shaw.ca
Rob Nadalutti, Director, Academic
rob.nadalutti@megenergy.com
Brenda Hong, Coordinator, Events
brendah@associationsplus.ca
Finances: *Funding Sources:* Membership dues
Staff: 17 volunteer(s)
Membership: 750 individuals; *Fees:* $75 Regular, $9 Retired; $20 student; *Member Profile:* Open to those employed in companies processing gaseous & liquid hydrocarbons; *Committees:* Safety; Research; Environment; Membership; Publications; Northern
Activities: *Library:* Yes

Independent Power Producers Society of Alberta (IPPSA)

#2600, 144 - 4th Ave. SW, Calgary AB T2P 3N4

Fax: 403-256-8342
www.ippsa.com

Overview: A small provincial organization founded in 1993
Description: To represent Alberta's major power producers; To encourage dialogue among power producers in Alberta
Chief Officer(s): Evan Bahry, Executive Director, 403-282-8811, Fax: 403-256-8342
Evan.Bahry@ippsa.com
Joe Novecosky, Contact, Membership & Events, 403-256-1587, Fax: 403-256-8342
joeno@telusplanet.net
Membership: 100+; *Fees:* $10,000 power member; $5,000 junior power member; $1,000 corporate member; $250 associate member; *Member Profile:* Operators of Alberta's power supply
Activities: Engaging with Alberta's government & its agencies in policy development; Reviewing legislation, regulations, & market rules; Promoting competition in Alberta's electrical market; Providing news about the industry; Sponsoring a bursary for a student at the University of Calgary's Schulich School of Engineering (Electricity Department);

Independent Telecommunications Providers Association (ITPA)

29 Peevers Cres., Newmarket ON L3Y 7T5

Tel: 519-595-3975; *Fax:* 519-595-3976
www.ota.on.ca

Previous Name: Ontario Telecommunications Association
Overview: A small provincial organization
Description: Assists its members to successfully provide state-of-the-art telecommunications services to the benefit of their customers.
Chief Officer(s): Jonathan L. Holmes, Executive Director
Finances: *Funding Sources:* Membership dues
Staff: 1 staff member(s)
Membership: 20; *Fees:* $395.50 associate; *Member Profile:* Independent Local Exchange Carriers in British Columbia and Ontario.
Activities: Liaising with government departments & agencies & industry associates, such as Bell Canada; Setting policies & compliance guidelines; Offering a forum to share expertise

Industrial Gas Users Association Inc. (IGUA) / Association des consommateurs industriels de gaz (ACIG)

#502, 350 Sparks St., Ottawa ON K1R 7S8

Tel: 613-236-8021; *Fax:* 613-230-9531
info@igua.ca
www.igua.ca

Overview: A medium-sized national organization founded in 1973
Description: To provide a coordinated & effective voice for industrial firms depending on natural gas as fuel or feedstock; to represent industrial users of natural gas before regulatory boards & governments
Chief Officer(s): Shahrzad Rahbar, President
srahbar@igua.ca
Martin Phipps, Chair
Finances: *Annual Operating Budget:* $500,000-$1.5 Million; *Funding Sources:* Membership dues
Staff: 3 staff member(s)
Membership: 39 corporate; *Fees:* Based on gas consumption, $1,200-$36,099; *Member Profile:* Open to end users of natural gas

Infrastructure Health & Safety Association (IHSA)

Centre for Health & Safety Innovation, #400, 5110 Creekbank Rd., Mississauga ON L4W 0A1

Tel: 905-625-0100; *Fax:* 905-625-8998
Toll-Free: 800-263-5024
info@ihsa.ca
www.ihsa.ca
Social Media:
ca.linkedin.com/pub/ihsa-news/41/986/aa3
twitter.com/IHSAnews

Merged from: CSAO; E&USA; THSAO
Overview: A medium-sized provincial organization founded in 2010
Description: To serve the utilities, electrical, natural gas, aggregates, ready-mix, construction, & transportation industries in Ontario; To develop prevention solutions for work environments
Chief Officer(s): Al Beattie, Chief Executive Officer & President
Activities: Providing training that meets regulatory requirements & compliance standards

Institute of Power Engineers (IPE)

PO Box 878, Burlington ON L7R 3Y7

Tel: 905-333-3348; *Fax:* 905-333-9328
ipenat@nipe.ca
www.nipe.ca

Overview: A medium-sized national organization founded in 1940
Description: To promote business relations, social activities & mutual understanding among power engineers
Chief Officer(s): Jude Rankin, National President
Bruce King, 1st National Vice President
Don Purser, National Secretary
Finances: *Annual Operating Budget:* $50,000-$100,000
Staff: 1400 volunteer(s)
Membership: 1,420; *Fees:* $105; *Member Profile:* Persons holding certificates of qualification as recognized by the Institute; persons enrolled in recognized power engineering courses; persons engaged in any pursuit identified or allied with power engineering

International Academy of Energy, Minerals, & Materials (AEMM)

PO Box 62047, Stn. Convent Glen, Orleans ON K1C 7H8

Tel: 613-830-1760
info@iaemm.com
iaemm.com

Overview: A medium-sized international organization
Description: To provide information about technological advancements in the fields of energy, minerals, & materials to academia & industry

International Association for Hydrogen Energy (IAHE)

#303, 5794 40th St. SW, Miami FL 33155 USA

info@iahe.org
www.iahe.org

Overview: A medium-sized international organization
Description: To provide information about the role of hydrogen energy
Chief Officer(s): T. Nejat Veziroglu, President
veziroglu@iahe.org
David Sanborn Scott, Vice-President, North America
davidsanbornscott@gmail.com
Membership: *Member Profile:* Professional persons in fields related to hydrogen energy; Laypersons with an interest in hydrogen energy; IAHE Fellows; Emeritus members; Students

International Atomic Energy Agency (IAEA) / Agence internationale de l'énergie atomique

Vienna International Centre, PO Box 100, Wagramer Strasse 5, Vienna A-1400 Austria

official.mail@iaea.org
www.iaea.org
Social Media:
www.youtube.com/user/IAEAvideo
www.facebook.com/iaeaorg
twitter.com/iaeaorg

Overview: A large international organization founded in 1957
Description: An independent intergovernmental organization within the UN system; to accelerate & enlarge the contribution of atomic energy to peace, health & prosperity throughout the world; to ensure that assistance provided is not used to further any military purpose
Affiliation(s): United Nations
Chief Officer(s): Yukiya Amano, Director General
Janice Dunn Lee, Deputy Director General, Management
Finances: *Annual Operating Budget:* Greater than $5 Million; *Funding Sources:* Member states contributions
Staff: 2300 staff member(s)
Membership: 158 sovereign states; *Fees:* Percentage of share of regular budget is fixed by UN General Assembly; *Member Profile:* Intergovernmental organization; *Committees:* Board of Governors composed of 35 member states
Activities: Verification in framework of Nuclear Non-Proliferation Treaty (NPT) that over 1,000 nuclear facilities in over 60 non-nuclear weapon states are used for peaceful purposes only; *Library:* Yes by appointment

International Atomic Energy Agency: Canadian Regional Office

PO Box 20, #1702, 365 Bloor St. East, Toronto ON M4W 3L4

Tel: 416-928-9149; *Fax:* 416-928-0046
official.mail@iaea.org
www.iaea.org
Social Media:
www.facebook.com/iaeaorg

Overview: A large international organization founded in 1957
Description: Serves as the global focal point for nuclear cooperation
Activities: Develops nuclear safety standards

International Electrotechnical Commission - Canadian National Committee (IEC-CNC) / Commission Électrotechnique Internationale - Comité National du Canada (CEI-CNC)

c/o Standards Council of Canada, #600, 55 Metcalfe St., Ottawa ON K1P 6L5

Tel: 613-238-3222; *Fax:* 613-569-7808
scc.ca

Overview: A medium-sized international organization founded in 1912
Description: The Standards Council of Canada (SCC) sponsors the Canadian National Committee of the International Electrotechnical Commission, an SCC advisory committee which is the Canadian member body at IEC. It promotes international cooperation on all questions of electrotechnical standardization & related matters, such as the assessment of conformity to standards, in the fields of electricity, electronics & related technologies.; *Member of:* Standards Council of Canada
Chief Officer(s): Jacques Régis, President
Lynne M. Gibbens, Secretary
Finances: *Funding Sources:* Parliamentary appropriation; corporate sponsors; individuals
Staff: 2 staff member(s); 1000 volunteer(s)
Membership: 16; *Committees:* Approx. 100, paralleling the IEC committee structure

International Energy Foundation (IEF)

Clear Mountain Estates, PO Box 64, Site 8, RR#1, Okotoks AB T1S 1A1

Tel: 403-938-6210; *Fax:* 403-938-6210
www.ief-energy.org

Overview: A medium-sized international charitable organization founded in 1989
Description: To facilitate the transfer of research & technology in all areas of energy with special emphasis on developing countries; interested in better ways to produce, transmit & conserve energy; to sponsor & conduct research studies, surveys & state-of-the-art studies; to undertake consulting projects & organize training programs for the interchange of knowledge & expertise amongst the international community; to provide scholarships for the education of students in fields of interest consistent with the objectives of the Foundation; to administer awards for the purpose of recognition & encouragement of outstanding achievement in areas of study consistent with objectives of the Foundation; to recommend standards to existing national & international associations & promote adoption of such approved standards for energy consumption, production & conservation; *Member of:* International Standards Organization
Chief Officer(s): Peter J. Catania, Chair
Finances: *Annual Operating Budget:* $100,000-$250,000; *Funding Sources:* Contributions, donations, subventions, aids & grants made by donors & benefactors; fees for membership
Staff: 50 volunteer(s)
Membership: fellows in 49 countries, committee members in 175 countries; *Member Profile:* Open to all professionals, educational institutes, industries, governmental or quasi-governmental bodies operating in the field of energy; *Committees:* Constitution & Bylaws; External Administrative Centres; External & Internal Meetings; Finance; Goals & Objectives; Membership; Publications & Public Relations
Activities: Conferences, symposiums, workshops; *Speaker Service:* Yes

International Institute for Energy Conservation (IIEC)

#100, 10005 Leamoore Lane, Vienna VA 22181 USA

Tel: 703-281-7263; *Fax:* 703-938-5153
iiecdc@iiec.org
www.iiec.org
Social Media:
www.linkedin.com/company/international-institute-for-energy-conservation

Overview: A medium-sized international organization founded in 1984
Description: To bring the power of sustainable energy solutions to developing countries & economies in transition
Chief Officer(s): Robert L. Pratt, Chair
Felix Gooneratne, Chief Executive Officer

International Solar Energy Society (ISES)

International Headquarters, Villa Tannheim, Wiesentalstrasse 50, Freiburg 79115 Germany

hq@ises.org
www.ises.org
Social Media:
www.youtube.com/channel/UC3JPtjqpPBqw0q5hE9neM_Q
linkedin.com/company/international-solar-energy-society
www.facebook.com/InternationalSolarEnergySociety
twitter.com/ISES_Solar

Overview: A medium-sized international charitable organization founded in 1954

Description: A United Nations accredited NGO, with members in 50+ countries worldwide; goals include the promotion of renewable energy, with solar energy being a focus, sustainable development, and research; *Member of:* International Renewable Energy Alliance
Chief Officer(s): David Renné, President
Membership: 4,000; *Fees:* Schedule available; *Member Profile:* Persons engaged in the research development & utilisation of solar energy & persons who have an interest in advancing the purposes of the society
Activities: All aspects of solar energy, including characteristics, effects & methods of use; international congresses on solar energy

International Solid Waste Association (ISWA)
Auerspergstrasse 15, Top 41, Vienna 1080 Austria
iswa@iswa.org
www.iswa.org
Social Media:
linkedin.com/company/iswa-international-solid-waste-association
www.facebook.com/123367611068687
Overview: A medium-sized international organization founded in 1931
Description: To promote efficiency in environmental practice
Chief Officer(s): David Newman, President
newman@iswa.org
Hermann Koller, Managing Director
Gerfried Habenicht, Manager, Communications
Alfred Holzschuster, Manager, Finance & Member Services
Kim Winternitz, Manager, Events & Projects
Finances: *Funding Sources:* Sponsorships
Membership: *Member Profile:* Non-profit waste management associations representing the waste management industry in a particular country; Organizations or companies associated with or working in the field of waste management
Activities: Promoting professionalism; Supporting developing countries

International Telecommunications Society (ITS)
Bohdan (Don) Romaniuk, ITS Secretariat, 416 Wilverside Way SE, Calgary AB T2J 1Z7
secretariat@itsworld.org
www.itsworld.org
Overview: A small international organization
Description: To address issues in telecommunications & related industries, such as public policy, user requirements, & industry changes
Chief Officer(s): Erik Bohlin, Chair
erik.bohlin@chalmers.se
Bronwyn Howell, Secretary
Bronwyn.Howell@vuw.ac.nz
Leland W. Schmidt, Treasurer
lschmidt@metrocast.net
Membership: 400; *Fees:* $125 USD individual; $6000 USD corporate; $3000 USD international; $!500 USD society; $500 USD government/not-for-profit; *Member Profile:* Professionals from the communications, technology, & information sectors; *Committees:* Strategic Planning; Conference & Seminars; Publications; Membership & Nominations; Finance; Marketing & Promotions; Web Development
Activities: Organizing courses, seminars, & workshops; Disseminating research results & news to members & the public

Manitoba Water & Wastewater Association (MWWA)
PO Box 1600, #215, 9 Saskatchewan Ave. West, Portage la Prairie MB R1N 3P1
Tel: 204-239-6868; *Fax:* 204-239-6872
Toll-Free: 866-396-2549
mwwa@mymts.net
www.mwwa.net
Social Media:
www.facebook.com/167933616574016
Overview: A small provincial organization founded in 1975
Description: To provide operator members with educational opportunities for operating & maintaining water & wastewater treatment facilities & water distribution & wastewater collection systems; To promote operator certification & facility classification; *Member of:* Western Canada Water & Wastewater Association
Chief Officer(s): Karly Friesen, Chair
kfriesen@city-plap.com
Iva Last, Executive Director
Activities: Exchnaging information & experiences

Marine Renewables Canada
PO Box 34066, 1690 Hollis St., 10th Fl., Halifax NS B3J 3S1
www.marinerenewables.ca
Social Media:
linkedin.com/groups/Marine-Renewables-Canada-2689413
www.facebook.com/marinerenewablescanada
twitter.com/Canadian_MRE
Previous Name: Ocean Renewable Energy Group
Overview: A medium-sized national charitable organization founded in 2004
Description: Marine Renewables Canada aligns industry, academia & government to ensure that Canada is a leader in providing ocean energy solutions to a world market.
Chief Officer(s): Elisa Obermann, Exective Director, 902-817-4317
elisa@marinerenewables.ca
Membership: *Fees:* $50 student; $300 individual; $750 organization; $1,000 government dept.; $3,000-$10,000 Marine Energy Leader/Champion
Activities: Conferences

The Maritimes Energy Association
Cambridge Tower 1, #305, 202 Brownlow Ave., Dartmouth NS B3B 1T5
Tel: 902-425-4774; *Fax:* 902-422-2332
info@maritimesenergy.com
www.maritimesenergy.com
Social Media:
twitter.com/MEnergyAssoc
Previous Name: Offshore / Onshore Technologies Association of Nova Scotia (OTANS)
Overview: A small provincial organization founded in 1982
Description: To represent companies that offer goods & services to the maritime energy industry; To identify, promote, & support opportunities in the energy industry on Canada's east coast for member businesses
Chief Officer(s): Sue Ritter, Chair
Barbara Pike, Chief Executive Officer
barbara@maritimesenergy.com
Sara Colburne, Director, Stakeholder Engagement
sara@maritimesenergy.com
Lori Peddle, Manager, Business & Operations
lori@maritimesenergy.com
Paula Broaders, Coordinator, Member Relations
Paula@MaritimesEnergy.com
Membership: 300+; *Fees:* $30 student membership; $498 companies with 1-10 employees; $760.50 businesses with 11-50 employees; $998 for companies with 51 or more employees; *Member Profile:* Businesses throughout Atlantic Canada that supply goods & services to the energy sector, including the gas, oil, wind, tidal, & solar industries; *Committees:* Audit; Executive; Membership; Oil & Gas; Core Energy Conference Organizing; Government Relations; Nominations; Renewable Energy
Activities: Collaborating with provincial & federal governments & regulatory authories; Facilitating trade missions to investigate export opportunities; Advocating for the interests of the energy industry; Conducting policy research; Offering industry history & news; Organizing sessions with guest speakers who address current topics of interest in the energy industry; Providing networking opportunities

Municipal Engineers Association (MEA)
#22, 1525 Cornwall Rd., Oakville ON L6J 0B2
Tel: 289-291-6472; *Fax:* 289-291-6477
www.municipalengineers.on.ca
Overview: A medium-sized provincial organization founded in 1974
Description: To provide focus & unity for licensed engineers employed by municipalities in Ontario; To address issues of common concern to members; To facilitate the dissemination of information
Chief Officer(s): Reg Russwurm, President
rrusswurm@thebluemountains.ca
Alan Korell, Executive Director
alan.korell@municipalengineers.on.ca
Membership: *Member Profile:* Public sector professional engineers in full time employment of municipalities, who perform functions in the field of municipal engineering; *Committees:* Administrative & Seconded; Municipal Transportation Advisory; MEA/CEO Liaison; Development Engineering; MEA/MNR/CO Liaison; MEA Training; MEA/MOE Liaison; Ontario Works Network; Tri-Committee Board
Activities: Organizing training events; Advocating for sound municipal engineering; Championing positions on municipal engineering issues; Recognizing achievements of municipal engineers

Municipal Equipment & Operations Association (Ontario) Inc.
38 Summit Ave., Kitchener ON N2M 4W2
Tel: 519-741-2600; *Fax:* 519-741-2750
admin@meoa.org
www.meoa.org
Also Known As: MEOA
Overview: A small provincial organization founded in 1965
Description: To promote high standards & cost effectiveness in public services across Ontario
Chief Officer(s): Mike Beattie, President
Finances: *Funding Sources:* Annual membership dues
Membership: 250; *Member Profile:* Supervisory employees & management support staff from any government body; Suppliers of equipment & services used by municipal corporate organizations; Honorary members who have been beneficial to the association; Affiliate members who have an interest in the association
Activities: Offering education & training; Organizing field trips; Facilitating the exchange of information; Providing networking opportunities

National Energy Conservation Association Inc. (NECA) / Association nationale pour la conservation de l'énergie
#400, 283 Bannatyne Ave., Winnipeg MB R3B 3B2
Tel: 204-956-5888; *Fax:* 204-956-5819
Toll-Free: 800-263-5974
neca@neca.ca
Previous Name: National Insulation & Energy Conservation Contractors Association
Overview: A medium-sized national organization founded in 1983
Description: To promote energy efficiency in the building sector; To work towards a sustainable future

National Ground Water Association (NGWA)
601 Dempsey Rd., Westerville OH 43081 USA
Tel: 614-898-7791; *Fax:* 614-898-7786
Toll-Free: 800-551-7379
ngwa@ngwa.org
www.ngwa.org
Social Media:
www.youtube.com/user/NGWATUBE
linkedin.com/groups?home=&gid=4204578
www.facebook.com/NGWAFB
twitter.com/ngwatweets
Overview: A medium-sized international organization founded in 1948
Description: To advance the expertise of all ground water professionals & furthering ground water awareness & protection through education & outreach; *Member of:* Advisory Committee on Water Information; American National Standards Institute; Coalition for National Science Funding; Geological Society of America; Global Water Partnership; Groundwater Foundation; International Union of Geological Sciences; Source Water Collaborative; U.S. Water Alliance
Chief Officer(s): Kevin McCray, Chief Executive Officer
kmmcray@ngwa.org
Finances: *Annual Operating Budget:* Greater than $5 Million
Membership: *Fees:* Schedule available; *Member Profile:* Ground water scientists & engineers; water well drillers; pump installers; suppliers & manufacturers; *Committees:* Geothermal Heat Pump Technical; Government Affairs; Membership Standing; Professional Development; Public Awareness; Publishing and Information Products; Standard Development Oversight; Water Systems Technical
Activities: *Speaker Service:* Yes; *Library:* National Ground Water Information Centre

National Waste & Recycling Association (NWRA)
#300, 4301 Connecticut Ave. NW, Washington DC 20008 USA
Tel: 202-244-4700; *Fax:* 202-966-4824
Toll-Free: 800-424-2869
info@wasterecycling.org
wasterecycling.org
Social Media:
www.youtube.com/user/envasns
linkedin.com/company/national-waste-&-recycling-association
www.facebook.com/wasterecycling
twitter.com/wasterecycling
Overview: A medium-sized international organization founded in 1962
Description: To promote the environmentally responsible, efficient, profitable, & ethical management of waste
Chief Officer(s): Sharon H. Kneiss, President & Chief Executive Officer, 202-364-3730
skneiss@wasterecycling.org
David Biderman, General Counsel & Vice President, Government Affairs & Chapter Operations, 202-364-3743
davidb@wasterecycling.org
Jonathan Sper, Director, Membership Marketing & Business Development, 202-364-3707
jsper@wasterecycling.org
Sheila R Alkire, Director, Education, 202-364-3786
salkire@wasterecycling.org
Craig Branson, Manager, Communications, 202-364-3773
cbranson@wasterecycling.org
Anne Germain, Director, Waste & Recycling Technology, 202-364-3724
agermain@wasterecycling.org

Catherine Maimon, Manager, Meetings, 202-364-3715
cmaimon@wasterecycling.org
Membership: *Member Profile:* For-profit companies in North America that provide solid, hazardous, & medical waste collection, recycling, & disposal services; Companies that provide professional & consulting services to the waste services industry
Activities: Offering educational & training opportunities; Engaging in research; Facilitating networking;

Natural Gas Employees' Association (NGEA)
#316, 9426 - 51 Ave., Edmonton AB T6E 5A6
Tel: 780-483-9330; *Fax:* 780-469-2504
Toll-Free: 877-912-9330
ngea@telus.net
www.ngea.ca
Overview: A small national organization
Description: To represent the employees of ATCO Gas & Pipelines Limited-Gas Division & ATCO Gas & Pipelines Limited-Pipelines Division
Chief Officer(s): Jim Steele, President, 403-894-0958
Danny Burrell, Business Agent, 780-499-2946
danny.ngea@telus.net

Noia
Atlantic Pl., #602, 215 Water St., St. John's NL A1C 6C9
Tel: 709-758-6610; *Fax:* 709-758-6611
noia@noia.ca
www.noia.ca
Also Known As: Newfoundland & Labrador Oil & Gas Industries Association
Overview: A medium-sized provincial organization founded in 1977
Description: To assist, promote & facilitate the participation of members in ocean industries, with particular emphasis on oil & gas, to enhance their growth & development; to promote the growth of ocean industry; to act as a focal point for representations to government bodies & agencies; to act as a source of information & education for members
Chief Officer(s): Robert Cadigan, President & CEO
Finances: *Annual Operating Budget:* $500,000-$1.5 Million; *Funding Sources:* Membership fees; conferences, seminars & special events
Staff: 10 staff member(s); 100 volunteer(s)
Membership: 600; *Fees:* Schedule available; *Member Profile:* Those who develop, manufacture & market products & services in the oil & gas industry, both offshore & onshore; *Committees:* Board of Directors; Conference; Executive; Arctic Greenland Committee; Exploration; Diversity; Petroleum Industry Human Resources Committee (PIHRC)
Activities: Promotes development of East Coast Canada's hydrocarbon resources & facilitates its membership's participation in oil & gas industries; *Library:* Yes by appointment

Offshore Energy Research Association of Nova Scotia (OERA)
Bank of Montreal Building, #602, 5151 George St., Halifax NS B3J 1M5
Tel: 902-406-7010; *Fax:* 902-406-7019
Toll-Free: 888-257-8688
www.oera.ca
Merged from: Offshore Energy Environmental Research (OEER); Offshore Energy Technical Research (OETR)
Overview: A medium-sized provincial organization founded in 2012
Description: To foster offshore energy & environmental research & development; To develop offshore petroleum exploration & development for Nova Scotia
Chief Officer(s): Stephen Dempsey, Executive Director, 902-406-7011, Fax: 902-406-7019
Wanda Barrett, Manager, Operations, 902-406-7010, Fax: 902-406-7019
Jennifer Pinks, Manager, Research, 902-406-7013, Fax: 902-406-7019

Ontario Energy Association (OEA)
#202, 121 Richmond St. West, Toronto ON M5H 2K1
Tel: 416-961-2339; *Fax:* 416-961-1173
oea@energyontario.ca
www.energyontario.ca
Social Media:
linkedin.com/company/ontario-energy-association
twitter.com/ontarioenergy
Overview: A small provincial organization
Description: To represent the energy industry of Ontario
Chief Officer(s): Elise Herzig, President & Chief Executive Officer
Tina Arvanitis, Vice-President, Government Relations & Communications, 647-920-3269
tarvanitis@energyontario.ca
Finances: *Funding Sources:* Sponsorships
Membership: 150+ corporate members; *Member Profile:* Members of Ontario's energy industry, such as power producers, manufacturers, contractors, service providers, energy retailers, marketers, energy distributors, & energy consultants; *Committees:* Energy Markets Joint Sector; Environment Joint Sector; Government Relations Joint Sector; Green Energy & Conservation Joint Sector; Marketers & Retailers Sector; Utility Sector
Activities: Providing education & resources about the energy sector; Engaging in advocacy activities for members; Conducting research into energy matters; *Speaker Service:* Yes

Ontario Municipal Water Association (OMWA)
c/o Doug Parker, 43 Chelsea Cres., Belleville ON K8N 4Z5
Tel: 613-966-1100; *Fax:* 613-966-3024
Toll-Free: 888-231-1115
www.omwa.org
Overview: A medium-sized provincial organization
Description: To act as the voice of municipal water supply in Ontario; To ensure the safety, quality, reliability, & sustainability of drinking water in Ontario
Affiliation(s): Ontario Water Works Association (a section of the American Water Works Association)
Chief Officer(s): Andrew J. Henry, President, 519-930-3505 3505
ahenry@london.ca
Ed Houghton, Executive Director, 705-445-1800, Fax: 705-445-0791
ehoughton@collus.com
Membership: 200+ public drinking water authorities in Ontario; *Fees:* Schedule available, based upon population; *Member Profile:* Ontario's public water supply authorities; *Committees:* Resolutions; Communications & Website; Annual Conference; Awards/Service Recognition/Bursary; Nominations; Government Affairs; Finance
Activities: Reviewing policy, & legislative, & regulatory issues; Liaising with government, agencies, & associations to maintain safe & sustainable water sources; Lobbying to improve conditions; Promoting high standards of treatment, infrastructure, & operations; Offering technical training for operating authorities, operators, & owners of drinking water systems; Encouraging dissemination of information for public education; Joint conferences with the Ontario Water Works Association (OWWA)

Ontario Petroleum Institute Inc. (OPI)
#104, 555 Southdale Rd. East, London ON N6E 1A2
Tel: 519-680-1620; *Fax:* 519-680-1621
opi@ontariopetroleuminstitute.com
ontariopetroleuminstitute.com
Social Media:
www.facebook.com/700315586681356
twitter.com/opi1963
Overview: A medium-sized provincial organization founded in 1963
Description: To promote responsible exploration & development by Ontario's oil, gas, hydrocarbon storage, & solution-mining industries
Chief Officer(s): Hugh Moran, Executive Director
hughmoran@ontariopetroleuminstitute.com
Finances: *Funding Sources:* Sponsorships
Membership: *Member Profile:* Geologists in Ontario; Geophysicists; Explorationists; Producers; Contractors; Petroleum engineers; Companies involved in the oil & gas, hydrocarbon storage, & solution mining industries
Activities: Liaising with government agencies; Disseminating information to members; Increasing public awareness of the importance of the industry in Ontario; *Library:* Ontario Oil, Gas, & Salt Resources Library

Ontario Public Works Association (OPWA)
#22, 1525 Cornwall Rd., Oakville ON L6J 0B2
Tel: 647-726-0167; *Fax:* 289-291-6477
info@opwa.ca
opwa.ca
Social Media:
www.youtube.com/user/apwatv?feature=watch
www.facebook.com/149305988463789
Overview: A medium-sized provincial organization
Description: The Ontario Public Works Association (OPWA) promotes professional excellence and public awareness through education, advocacy and the exchange of knowledge regarding public works in Ontario.; *Member of:* American Public Works Association
Chief Officer(s): Terry Hardy, Executive Director, 647-726-0167, Fax: 289-291-6477
Membership: 630; *Committees:* Adovacy; Young Professionals; Awards; Historical; IT Symposium; APWA Congress Networking; Nominating; Membership; National Public Works Week; Communications; Annual Conference & Awards Luncheon; Education; Special Functions

Ontario Sewer & Watermain Construction Association (OSWCA)
#300, 5045 Orbitor Dr., Unit 12, Mississauga ON L4W 4Y4
Tel: 905-629-7766; *Fax:* 905-629-0587
info@oswca.org
www.oswca.org
Overview: A small provincial organization
Description: To represent sewer & watermain construction contractors throughout Ontario; To increase business opportunities for members
Chief Officer(s): Giovanni Cautillo, Executive Director, 905-629-8658
giovanni.cautillo@oswca.org
Patrick McManus, Manager, Stakeholder Relations and Services, 905-629-8819
patrick.mcmanus@oswca.org
Daniela Di Ilio, Office Coordinator, 905-629-8638
daniela.diilio@oswca.org
Membership: 700+ companies; *Committees:* Young Executives; Government Relations; Members Services; Marketing Initiatives; Education Program; Administration
Activities: Liaising with the Government of Ontario & its agencies; Increasing public awareness about the maintenance of water & wastewater systems in Ontario; Providing apprenticeship training & upgrading training; Informing members of industry developments

Ontario Sustainable Energy Association (OSEA)
#400, 3284 Yonge St., Toronto ON M4N 3M7
Tel: 416-977-4441; *Fax:* 416-644-0116
admin@ontario-sea.org
www.ontario-sea.org
Social Media:
www.youtube.com/ontariosea2009
linkedin.com/company/ontario-sustainable-energy-association
www.facebook.com/ontariosea
twitter.com/ontariosea
Overview: A small provincial organization founded in 2002
Description: To represent & serve municipalities, First Nations, institutions, businesses, cooperatives, farms, & households; To support the work of local sustainable energy organizations
Chief Officer(s): Nicole Risse, Interim Executive Director
nicole@ontario-sea.org
Finances: *Funding Sources:* Sponsorships; Donations
Staff: 6 staff member(s)
Membership: *Fees:* Schedule available
Activities: Engaging in advocacy activities, capacity building, & non-partisan policy work; Providing public outreach services;

Ontario Water Works Association (OWWA)
#100, 922 The East Mall Dr., Toronto ON M9B 6K1
Tel: 416-231-1555; *Fax:* 416-231-1556
Toll-Free: 866-975-0575
waterinfo@owwa.ca
www.owwa.com
Social Media:
linkedin.com/company/ontario-water-works-association
twitter.com/OWWA1
Overview: A medium-sized provincial organization
Description: To protect public health through the delivery of safe, sufficient, & sustainable drinking water in Ontario; *Member of:* American Water Works Association
Affiliation(s): Ontario Municipal Water Association; Ontario Water Works Equipment Association
Chief Officer(s): Saad Jasim, President
jasims@windsor.ijc.org
Lee Anne E. Jones, Vice-President
ljones@toronto.ca
Bill Balfour, Executive Director, 905-642-5283
bbalfour@owwa.ca
Lesia Lachmaniuk, Manager, Marketing & Membership, 416-231-1555, Fax: 416-231-1556
llachmaniuk@owwa.ca
Glenn Powell, Director, Communications, 905-827-4508, Fax: 905-827-6483
gpowell@owwa.ca
Ray Miller, Secretary-Treasurer
rmiller@clowcanada.com
Membership: 1,100+; *Member Profile:* Drinking water professionals in Ontario, such as hydrogeologists, scientists, engineers, chemists, & managers & technicians employed by Ontario's municipal water systems; *Committees:* Climate Change; C-PAC; Conference Management; Continuing Education; Cross Connection Control; Distribution; Government Affairs; Groundwater; Joint OWWA / OMWA; Management; Membership; OWWA / WEAO Joint Asset Management; Publications; Small Systems; Source Water Protection; Training, Certification, & Safety; Treatment; University Forum; Water Efficiency; Water for People - Canada; Young Professionals; Youth Education

Activities: Improving technology, science & management; Influencing government policy; Providing education for members; *Library:* Ontario Water Works Association Library

Ontario Waterpower Association (OWA)
#264, 380 Armour Rd., Peterborough ON K9H 7L7
Toll-Free: 866-743-1500
info@owa.ca
www.owa.ca
Social Media:
www.facebook.com/108513999167943
twitter.com/ONWaterpower

Overview: A medium-sized provincial organization founded in 2001
Description: Promotes the achievement of sustainable development, provides a source for quality information about waterpower & grows & enhances the competitiveness of the Ontario waterpower industry.
Chief Officer(s): Paul Norris, President, 866-743-1500 22

Petroleum Human Resources Council of Canada (PHRCC)
5055 - 11 St. NE, Calgary AB T2E 8N4
Tel: 403-516-8100; *Fax:* 403-516-8171
info@petrohrsc.ca
www.petrohrsc.ca
Social Media:
twitter.com/PetroHRCouncil

Overview: A medium-sized national organization
Description: Collaborative forum that addresses human resources issues within the petroleum industry
Membership: 11; *Member Profile:* Oil and gas national and regional industry organizations

Petroleum Research Newfoundland & Labrador
Baine Johnston Centre, #802, 10 Fort William Pl., St. John's NL A1C 1K4
Tel: 709-738-7916; *Fax:* 709-738-7922
www.pr-ac.ca

Previous Name: Petroleum Research Atlantic Canada (PRAC)
Overview: A small local organization founded in 1999
Description: To fund & facilitate research & development on behalf of the offshore oil & gas industry of Newfoundland & Labrador
Chief Officer(s): Lisa A. Hutchens, Chief Executive Officer, 709-738-7921
lisa.hutchens@petroleumresearch.ca
David Finn, Chief Operating Officer, 709-738-7917
dave.finn@petroleumresearch.ca
Susan Hunt, Manager, Research Project Development, 709-738-7904
susan.hunt@petroleumresearch.ca
Matilda Maddigan, Manager, Office, 709-738-7916
matilda.maddigan@petroleumresearch.ca
Metzi Prince, Manager, Project Delivery, 709-738-7919
metzi.prince@petroleumresearch.ca
Membership: *Member Profile:* Representatives from the oil & gas industry

Petroleum Services Association of Canada (PSAC)
#1150, 800 - 6 Ave. SW, Calgary AB T2P 3G3
Tel: 403-264-4195; *Fax:* 403-263-7174
Toll-Free: 800-818-7722
info@psac.ca
www.psac.ca
Social Media:
linkedin.com/groups/PSAC-Working-Energy-4706150

Overview: A large national organization founded in 1981
Description: To represent the supply, manufacturing, & service sectors of the upstream petroleum industry
Chief Officer(s): Wally Dumont, Chair
Mark Salkeld, MBA, President & CEO
msalkeld@psac.ca
Elizabeth Aquin, CAE, Senior Vice-President
eaquin@psac.ca
Patrick J. Delaney, MBA, CRSP, Vice-President, Health & Safety
pdelaney@psac.ca
Eileen Kahler, Vice-President, Communications & Member Relations
ekahler@psac.ca
Heather Doyle, Manager, Corporate Meetings & Events
hdoyle@psac.ca
Membership: 230 companies; *Fees:* Schedule available; *Member Profile:* Petroleum services industry companies; *Committees:* Corporate Finance; Education Fund; Health & Safety; Human Resources; Special Events; Transportation Issues; Manufacturing; Oilwell Perforators' Safety Training & Advisory; Snubbing Services; Well Testing
Activities: Engaging in lobbying activities; Providing educational opportunities

Petroleum Tank Management Association of Alberta (PTMAA)
#980, 10303 Jasper Ave., Edmonton AB T5J 3N6
Tel: 780-425-8265; *Fax:* 780-425-4722
Toll-Free: 866-222-8265
ptmaa@ptmaa.ab.ca
www.ptmaa.ab.ca

Overview: A medium-sized provincial licensing charitable organization founded in 1994
Description: To offer programs to enhance the management of petroleum storage tank systems in Alberta
Chief Officer(s): Mark Tse, Chair
Activities: Monitoring new storage tank installations; Inspecting existing storage tank installations; Investigating accidents & incidents

Petroleum Technology Alliance Canada (PTAC)
Chevron Plaza, #400, 500 - 5th Ave. SW, Calgary AB T2P 3L5
Tel: 403-218-7700; *Fax:* 403-920-0054
info@ptac.org
www.ptac.org

Overview: A medium-sized national organization
Description: To facilitate innovation, technology transfer & research & development in the upstream oil & gas industry
Chief Officer(s): Soheil Asgarpour, President, 403-218-7701
sasgarpour@ptac.org
Tannis Such, Director, Environmental Research Initiatives, 403-218-7703
tsuch@ptac.org
Activities: *Library:* PTAC Knowledge Centre (Open to Public)

Petrolia Discovery
PO Box 1480, 4381 Discovery Line, Petrolia ON N0N 1R0
Tel: 519-381-5979; *Fax:* 519-882-4209
petdisc@xcelco.on.ca
www.petroliadiscovery.com

Overview: A small national charitable organization founded in 1980
Description: To provide information about Petrolia's oil heritage
Activities: Maintaining historical displays; Organizing programs for schools

Pipe Line Contractors Association of Canada (PLCAC)
#201, 1075 North Service Rd. West, Oakville ON L6M 2G2
Tel: 905-847-9383; *Fax:* 905-847-7824
plcac@pipeline.ca
www.pipeline.ca

Overview: A small national organization founded in 1954
Description: To represent contractors in labour relations
Chief Officer(s): Mark H. Scherer, President
Neil G. Lane, Executive Director
Membership: 40 regular members; 87 associate members; 19 honorary members; *Member Profile:* Employers engaged in contacting for the construction, installation, & maintenance of piplines; Corporations or individuals engages in manufacturing, supplying, & transporting material for the construction & maintenance of piplines; *Committees:* Convention Planning; Education & Training; Executive; Membership & Promotion; National Labour Relations; Negotiating - Distribution; Negotiating - Mainline; Negotiating - Maintenance; Pipeline Standards; Safety
Activities: Establishing training courses; Reviewing legislation

Planetary Association for Clean Energy, Inc. (PACE) / Société planétaire pour l'assainissement de l'énergie
#1001, 100 Bronson Ave., Ottawa ON K1R 6G8
Tel: 613-236-6265; *Fax:* 613-235-5876
paceincnet@gmail.com
pacenet.homestead.com

Overview: A medium-sized international charitable organization founded in 1975
Description: To steward & facilitate the implementation of clean energy systems worldwide
Chief Officer(s): Andrew Michrowski, President
Finances: *Annual Operating Budget:* $100,000-$250,000; *Funding Sources:* Membership fees; donations
Staff: 2 staff member(s); 10 volunteer(s)
Membership: 3,600 in 60 countries; *Fees:* $50
Activities: Electromagnetic bioaffect, analyses & abatement; monitors unclean developments; peer review of new technologies; books, databases & technical reports; *Internships:* Yes; *Speaker Service:* Yes; *Library:* Yes by appointment

Power Workers' Union (PWU)
244 Eglinton Ave. East, Toronto ON M4P 1K2
Fax: 416-481-7115
pwu@pwu.ca
www.pwu.ca

Overview: A large provincial organization founded in 1944
Affiliation(s): Canadian Union of Public Employees; Canadian Labour Congress; Ontario Federation of Labour; Labourers International Union of North America; Canadian Union of Skilled Workers
Chief Officer(s): Don MacKinnon, President
dmackinnon@pwu.ca
Brad Carnduff, Vice-President, Sector 2
bcarnduff@pwu.ca
Mel Hyatt, Vice-President, Sector 3
hyattm@pwu.ca
Bob Walker, Vice-President, Sector 1
bwalker@pwu.ca
Membership: 15,000-49,999; *Member Profile:* Individuals who work in the power production industry in Ontario.

Professional Petroleum Data Management Association (PPDM)
PO Box 22155, Stn. Bankers Hall, #860, 736 - 8th Ave. SW, Calgary AB T2P 4J5
Tel: 403-660-7817; *Fax:* 403-660-0540
info@ppdm.org
www.ppdm.org
Social Media:
linkedin.com/groups?home=&gid=146440
www.facebook.com/108325212519325?ref=ts
twitter.com/PPDMAssociation

Previous Name: Public Petroleum Data Model Association
Overview: A small national organization founded in 1991
Description: To develop data management standards for the collection & exchange of data in the petroleum industry; To promote information standards
Chief Officer(s): Trevor Hicks, Chair
trevor.hicks@noah-consulting.com
Janet Hicks, Secretary
jhicks@lgc.com
Peter MacDougall, Treasurer
peter.macdougall@ihs.com
Trudy Curtis, CEO
curtist@ppdm.org
Activities: Increasing awareness of the value of data management; Providing training

Public Works Association of British Columbia (PWABC)
#102, 211 Columbia St., Vancouver BC V6A 2R5
Toll-Free: 877-356-0699
info@pwabc.ca
www.pwabc.ca
Social Media:
www.linkedin.com/groups/5156461/profile
www.facebook.com/pages/Public-Works-Association-of-BC/2489 64305172358
twitter.com/PWABCExecDir

Overview: A medium-sized provincial organization
Description: PWABC is a non-profit society registered in B.C. that exists to serve its members by providing opportunities for mutual support, education and professional development. It does this through workshops, newsletters, teleconferences and an annual technical conference.; *Member of:* American Public Works Association
Chief Officer(s): Deryk Lee, President, 250-361-0467
Membership: *Fees:* $164 individual; $403.00 for Heritage, $1683 for Prestige, $7991 for Crown corporations

The Road & Infrastructure Program Canada (TRIP Canada)
#1900, 275 Slater St., Ottawa ON K1P 5H9
Tel: 613-236-9455; *Fax:* 613-236-9526
cca@cca-acc.com
careersincivilconstruction.ca
Social Media:
www.youtube.com/user/CareersInCivil
twitter.com/CareersInCivil

Overview: A small national organization
Description: To articulate the need for increased investment in Canada's municipal infrastructure & national highway system; *Member of:* Canadian Construction Association
Chief Officer(s): Bill Ferreira, Executive Director
Finances: *Annual Operating Budget:* $50,000-$100,000
Staff: 1 staff member(s); 35 volunteer(s)
Membership: 11 associations
Activities: *Speaker Service:* Yes

Saskatchewan Water & Wastewater Association (SWWA)
PO Box 7831, Saskatoon SK S7K 4R5
Tel: 306-761-1278; *Toll-Free:* 888-668-1278
office@swwa.ca
www.swwa.ca
Social Media:
www.facebook.com/SaskatchewanWaterAndWastewaterAssocia tion

Overview: A medium-sized provincial organization
Description: Dedicated to the professional operation and maintenance of water & wastewater facilities
Chief Officer(s): Tim Cox, President
t.cox@swiftcurrent.ca
Membership: *Fees:* $60.50; *Member Profile:* People involved in the operation, maintenance & troubleshooting of water & wastewater systems
Activities: Hosting workshops & training sessions; Providing access to job opportunities; Publishing a newsletter; Providing certification through the Operator Certification Board

The Society of Energy Professionals
2239 Yonge St., Toronto ON M4S 2B5
Tel: 416-979-2709; *Fax:* 416-979-5794
Toll-Free: 866-288-1788
society@thesociety.ca
www.thesociety.ca
Overview: A medium-sized provincial organization founded in 1948
Description: To represent employees of Ontario's electricity industry; To ensure the best working conditions for members; *Member of:* Canadian Council of Professionals; Professional Employees' Network
Affiliation(s): International Federation of Professional & Technical Engineers; Canadian Labour Congress / Congrès du travail du Canada; American Federation of Labour / Congress of Industrial Organizations, (AFL/CIO); UNI Global Union
Chief Officer(s): Scott Travers, President, 416-979-2709 5002
traverss@thesociety.ca
Michelle Johnston, Executive Vice-President, Policy, 416-979-2709 5001
johnstonm@thesociety.ca
Dennis Minello, Executive Vice-President, Member Services, 416-979-2709 3027
minellod@thesociety.ca
Rob Stanley, Executive Vice-President, Finance, 416-979-2709 3019
stanleyr@thesociety.ca
Finances: *Funding Sources:* Membership dues
Membership: *Member Profile:* Professional members of the elctricity industry in Ontario, such as scientists, engineers, financial specialists, & supervisors

Society of Petroleum Engineers (SPE)
PO Box 833836, 222 Palisades Creek Dr., Richardson TX 75083-3868 USA
Tel: 972-952-9393; *Fax:* 972-952-9435
Toll-Free: 800-456-6863
spedal@spe.org
www.spe.org
Social Media:
www.youtube.com/user/2012SPE?feature=mhee
linkedin.com/groups?about=&gid=57660
www.facebook.com/spemembers
twitter.com/SPE_Events
Overview: A large international organization founded in 1957
Description: To collect, disseminate & exchange technical knowledge concerning the exploration, development & production of oil & gas resources & related technologies for the public benefit; provide opportunities for professionals to enhance their technical & professional competence
Chief Officer(s): Mark A. Rubin, Executive Director
execdir@spe.org
Egbert Imomoh, President
president@spe.org
Finances: *Annual Operating Budget:* $3 Million-$5 Million
Staff: 87 staff member(s)
Membership: 79,000+ (active operations in some 50 countries); *Fees:* $10-$90; *Member Profile:* Managers, engineers, operating personnel & scientists engaged in the exploration, drilling & production sectors of the global oil & gas industry; *Committees:* Student Development; Global Training; Distinguished Lecturer; Membership; Forum Series Coordinating; DAA For PE Faculty; Education & Accreditation; Oil & Gas Reserves; Editorial Review; Twenty Five Year Club; TIG Coordinating; Research & Development; Young Professional Coordinating; SPE Energy Information; Sustainability; Robert Earll McConnell; Online Communities Advisory; Awards
Activities: *Speaker Service:* Yes; *Library:* Yes

Solid Waste Association of North America (SWANA)
#700, 1100 Wayne Ave., Silver Spring MD 20910 USA
Fax: 301-589-7068
Toll-Free: 800-467-9262
info@swana.org
www.swana.org
Social Media:
linkedin.com/groups?home=&gid=45037
www.facebook.com/MySWANA
twitter.com/SWANA
Previous Name: Government Refuse Collection & Disposal Association
Overview: A medium-sized international organization founded in 1961
Description: To serve individuals & communities responsible for the operation & management of solid waste management systems; To advance professional standards in the field through training programs, technical assistance, & education; *Member of:* International Solid Waste Association; Federation of Canadian Municipalities
Chief Officer(s): David Biderman, Executive Director & CEO, 301-585-2898
Finances: *Annual Operating Budget:* $3 Million-$5 Million; *Funding Sources:* Membership dues; publications
Staff: 22 staff member(s)
Membership: 8,000; *Fees:* US$68 student; US$78 retired; US$212 public sector; US$281 small business; US$398 private sector; *Committees:* Technical; Recycling & Special Waste Management; Communication, Education & Marketing; Collection & Transfer; Landfill; Landfill Gas; Planning & Management; Waste-to-Energy
Activities: Technical divisions: collection & transfer, waste-to-energy, landfill gas management, landfill management, planning & management, special waste management; waste reduction, recycling & composting, communication, education & marketing; publications; trade shows & conferences; *Internships:* Yes; *Library:* Yes (Open to Public)

Syndicat professionnel des ingénieurs d'Hydro-Québec (ind.) (SPIHQ) / Hydro-Québec Professional Engineers Union (Ind.)
#1400, 1255 rue University, Montréal QC H3B 3X1
Tél: 514-845-4239; *Téléc:* 514-845-0082
Ligne sans frais: 800-567-1260
spihq@spihq.qc.ca
www.spihq.qc.ca
Aperçu: *Dimension:* moyenne; *Envergure:* provinciale; fondée en 1964
Description: Le Syndicat travaille pour la défense & le développement des intérêts économiques, sociaux, & professionnels des membres
Membre(s) du bureau directeur: Jacqueline Pilote, Chef administration, 514-845-4239 112
chefadmin@spihq.qc.ca
Carole Leroux, Présidente, 514-845-4239 103
president@spihq.qc.ca
Finances: *Budget de fonctionnement annuel:* $500,000-$1.5 Million
Personnel: 3 membre(s) du personnel
Membre: 1 700

TechnoCentre éolien / Wind Energy TechnoCentre
70, rue Bolduc, Gaspé QC G4X 1G2
Tél: 418-368-6162; *Téléc:* 418-368-4315
info@eolien.qc.ca
www.eolien.qc.ca
Aperçu: *Dimension:* petite; *Envergure:* provinciale; fondée en 2000
Description: Le TechnoCentre éolien a pour mission de contribuer au développement d'une filière industrielle éolienne québécoise, compétitive à l'échelle nord-américaine et internationale, tout en mettant en valeur la Gaspésie-Iles-de-la-Madeleine au cour de ce créneau émergeant de l'économie du Québec.
Membre(s) du bureau directeur: Frédéric Côté, Directeur général
fcote@eolien.qc.ca

Telecommunications Employees Association of Manitoba (TEAM)
#200, 1 Wesley Ave., Winnipeg MB R3C 4C6
Tel: 204-984-9470; *Fax:* 204-231-2809
Toll-Free: 877-984-9470
team@teamunion.mb.ca
www.teamunion.mb.ca
Social Media:
www.facebook.com/teamunion161
twitter.com/teamunion161
Overview: A medium-sized provincial organization founded in 1972
Description: To promote the interests of members; To advance the economic & social welfare of members
Chief Officer(s): Misty Hughes-Newman, President
m.hughes-newman@teamunion.mb.ca
Bob Linsdell, Executive Director, 204-984-9471
bob.linsdell@teamunion.mb.ca
Wesley Emerson, Officer, Labour Relations, 204-984-9473
wesley.emerson@teamunion.mb.ca
Darlene Buan, Secretary
d.buan@teamunion.mb.ca
Activities: Presenting TEAM scholarships;

Telecommunications Workers' Union (CLC) (TWU) / Syndicat des travailleurs en télécommunications (CTC) (STT)
Head Office, 5261 Lane St., Burnaby BC V5H 4A6
Tel: 604-437-8601; *Fax:* 604-435-7760
twu@twu-stt.ca
www.twu-stt.ca
Overview: A medium-sized national organization founded in 1980
Description: To represent communications workers & workers in related fields
Affiliation(s): Canadian Labour Congress; National Alliance of Communications Workers
Chief Officer(s): Lee Riggs, President
Lee.Riggs@twu-stt.ca
Betty Carrasco, Vice-President
Betty.Carrasco@twu-stt.ca
Colin Brehaut, Secretary-Treasurer
colin.brehaut@twu-stt.ca
Activities: Negotiating collective agreements; Promoting fair wages; Protecting & improving benefits & working conditions

Toronto Renewable Energy Co-operative (TREC)
#240, 401 Richmond St. West, Toronto ON M5V 3A8
Tel: 416-977-5093; *Fax:* 416-306-6476
info@trec.on.ca
www.trec.on.ca
Social Media:
www.facebook.com/TRECCoop
twitter.com/TRECCoop
Overview: A small local organization founded in 1998
Description: A non-profit organization of citizens dedicated to renewable energy & energy conservation; *Member of:* Canadian Renewable Energy Alliance
Affiliation(s): Toronto District School Board; Ontario Trillium Foundation; Ontario Power Authority Conservation Fund; Toronto Atmospheric Fund; Community Power Fund; Ontario Sustainable Energy Ass'n
Chief Officer(s): Judy Lipp, Executive Director, 416-977-5093 2340
jlipp@trec.on.ca
Finances: *Funding Sources:* Donations
Activities: Community energy projects; interactive, hands-on education; Green City Bike Tours; Green Collar Career program; Our Power solar initiative; solar home tours; round table discussions; Bruce County wind energy co-operative project

United Utility Workers' Association (UUWA)
1207 - 20 Ave. NW, Calgary AB T2M 1G2
Tel: 403-284-4521; *Fax:* 403-282-1598
info@uuwac.org
www.uuwac.org
Previous Name: Calgary Power Employees Association; TransAlta Employees' Association
Overview: A medium-sized national organization founded in 1943
Description: To represent employees in the energy secotr
Chief Officer(s): Chuck Pozzo, Chief Executive Officer
Grace Thostenson, Manager, Business
Membership: 1,400; *Member Profile:* Employees in the energy sector, such as meter readers, power line technicians, designers, & administrators
Activities: Offering training courses

Utility Contractors Association of Ontario, Inc. (UCA)
PO Box 762, Oakville ON L6K 0A9
Tel: 905-847-7305; *Fax:* 905-412-0339
www.uca.on.ca
Overview: A medium-sized provincial organization founded in 1968
Description: To negotiate & administer collective agreements with operating engineers & labourers in Ontario's utility sector
Chief Officer(s): Rene Beaudry, President
Barry Brown, Executive Director
bbrown@uca.on.ca
Glen Hansen, Treasurer
Membership: 10 contractor members + 34 associate (supplier) members
Activities: Organizing networking events; Recognizing exellence in safety through the presentation of awards

World Energy Council (WEC) / Conseil Mondial de l'Energie (CME)
62-64 Cornhill St., London EC3V 3NH United Kingdom
www.worldenergy.org
Social Media:
linkedin.com/company/world-energy-council
twitter.com/WECouncil
Overview: A small international organization founded in 1923

Description: To promote the sustainable supply & use of energy for the greatest benefit of all
Chief Officer(s): Marie-José Nadeau, Chair
Finances: *Annual Operating Budget:* $3 Million-$5 Million
Staff: 14 staff member(s)
Membership: 92 member countries; *Fees:* Schedule available; *Member Profile:* Commercial; government; non-government
Activities: Energy; energy conservation; *Library:* Information Services by appointment

World Petroleum Congress (WPC) / Congrès mondiaux du pétrole
#1, 1 Duchess St., 4th Fl., London W1W 6AN United Kingdom
info@world-petroleum.org
www.world-petroleum.org

Overview: A medium-sized international organization founded in 1933
Description: To help the oil industry in the development of petroleum resources & the use of petroleum products for the benefit of mankind; to promote petroleum science & technology; to encourage the application of scientific advances & the transfer of technology
Affiliation(s): IEA; OPEN; United Nations
Chief Officer(s): Pierce Riemer, Director General
pierce@world-petroleum.org
Randy Gossen, President
Finances: *Funding Sources:* Membership dues; royalties; levy on registration
Staff: 4 staff member(s)
Membership: 57 countries; *Fees:* Schedule available; *Member Profile:* Major oil producing & consuming nations of the world; each country has a National Committee made up of representatives of the oil industry, academic & research institutions, & government departments; *Committees:* Permanent Council; Executive Board; Scientific Program; Congress Arrangements; Environmental Affairs; Development

Government Agency Guide

CONSERVATION & ECOLOGY

Canadian Heritage, 15 Eddy St., Gatineau, QC K1A 0M5
819-997-0055, 866-811-0055,
PCH.info-info.PCH@canada.ca

Commission for Environmental Cooperation, Secretariat, #200, 393, rue St-Jacques ouest, Montréal, QC H2Y 1N9
514-350-4300, Fax: 514-350-4314, info@cec.org

Environment & Climate Change Canada, 10 Wellington St., Gatineau, QC K1A 0H3
819-997-2800, Fax: 819-994-1412, 800-668-6767,
enviroinfo@ec.gc.ca

Natural Resources Canada, 580 Booth St., Ottawa, ON K1A 0E4
343-292-6096, Fax: 613-992-7211

North American Bird Conservation Initiative, Canadian Wildlife Service, 351, boul St-Joseph, 3e étage, Gatineau, QC K1A 0H3
819-994-0512, Fax: 819-994-4445, nabci@ec.gc.ca

North American Waterfowl Management Plan, NAWCC (Canada) Secretariat, Place Vincent Massey, 351 St. Joseph Blvd., 7th Fl., Gatineau, QC K1A 0H3
819-934-6034, Fax: 819-934-6017, nawmp@ec.gc.ca

Parks Canada, National Office, 30 Victoria St., Gatineau, QC J8X 0B3
819-420-9486, 888-773-8888, information@pc.gc.ca

Polar Knowledge Canada, 2464 Sheffield Rd., Ottawa, ON K1B 4E5
613-943-8605, info@polar.gc.ca

Alberta

Alberta Environment & Parks, Information Centre, Great West Life Bldg., 9920 - 108 St., Main Fl., Edmonton, AB T5K 2M4
780-427-2700, Fax: 780-427-4407, -310-3773,
ESRD.Info-Centre@gov.ab.ca

Alberta Environmental Appeals Board, Peace Hills Trust Tower, #306, 10011 - 109 St., Edmonton, AB T5J 3S8
780-427-6207, Fax: 780-427-4693

Alberta Used Oil Management Association, Empire Building, #1008, 10080 Jasper Ave., Edmonton, AB T5J 1V9
780-414-1510, Fax: 780-414-1519, 866-414-1510,
auoma@usedoilrecycling.ca

Beverage Container Management Board, #100, 8616 - 51 Ave., Edmonton, AB T6E 6E6
780-424-3193, Fax: 780-428-4620, 888-424-7671,
info@bcmb.ab.ca

Forestry Division, Petroleum Plaza ST, 9915 - 108 St. 10th Fl., Edmonton, AB T5K 2G8

Land Use Secretariat, Centre West Building, 10035 - 108 St., Edmonton, AB T5J 3E1
780-644-7972, Fax: 780-644-1034, luf@gov.ab.ca

Natural Resources Conservation Board, Sterling Place, 9940 - 106 St., 4th Fl., Edmonton, AB T5K 2N2
780-422-1977, Fax: 780-427-0607, 866-383-6722,
info@nrcb.ca

Special Areas Board, Special Areas Board Administration, 212 - 2nd Ave. West, PO Box 820, Hanna, AB T0J 1P0
403-854-5600, Fax: 403-854-5527

British Columbia

British Columbia Assessment Authority, #400, 3450 Uptown Blvd., Victoria, BC V8Z 0B9
604-739-8588, Fax: 855-995-6209, 866-825-8322

British Columbia Ministry of Environment, PO Box 9339 Prov Govt, Victoria, BC V8W 9M1
250-387-9870, Fax: 250-387-6003, env.mail@gov.bc.ca

Environmental Appeal Board, 747 Fort St., 4th Fl., PO Box 9425 Prov Govt, Victoria, BC V8W 3E9
250-387-3464, Fax: 250-356-9923, eabinfo@gov.bc.ca

Forest Appeals Commission, 747 Fort St., 4th Fl., PO Box 9425 Prov Govt, Victoria, BC V8W 9V1
250-387-3464, Fax: 250-356-9923, facinfo@gov.bc.ca

Forest Practices Board, PO Box 9905 Prov Govt, Victoria, BC V8W 9R1
250-213-4700, Fax: 250-213-4725, 800-994-5899,
fpboard@gov.bc.ca

North Area, 1011 - 4 Ave., 5th Fl., Prince George, BC V2L 3H9
250-565-6100

Manitoba

Clean Environment Commission, #305, 155 Carlton St., Winnipeg, MB R3C 3H8
204-945-0594, Fax: 204-945-0090, 800-597-3556,
cec@gov.mb.ca

Ecological Reserves Advisory Committee, c/o Manitoba Conservation, Parks & Natural Areas Branch, 200 Saulteaux Cres., PO Box 53, Winnipeg, MB R3J 3W3
204-945-4148, Fax: 204-945-0012

Manitoba Sustainable Development, 200 Saulteaux Cres., PO Box 22, Winnipeg, MB R3J 3W3
204-945-6784, 800-214-6497, mgi@gov.mb.ca

New Brunswick

New Brunswick Department of Environment & Local Government, Marysville Place, PO Box 6000, Fredericton, NB E3B 5H1
506-453-2690, Fax: 506-457-4994, elg/egl-info@gnb.ca

Newfoundland & Labrador

Newfoundland & Labrador Department of Environment & Conservation, Confederation Bldg., West Block, 4th Fl., PO Box 8700, St. John's, NL A1B 4J6
709-729-2664, Fax: 709-729-6639, 800-563-6181,
envcinquires@gov.nl.ca

Northwest Territories

Northwest Territories Department of Environment & Natural Resources, #600, 5102 - 50 Ave., Yellowknife, NT X1A 3S8
867-767-9231

Nova Scotia

Nova Scotia Department of Natural Resources, Founder's Square, 1701 Hollis St., 3rd Fl., PO Box 698, Halifax, NS B3J 2T9
902-424-5935, Fax: 902-424-7735, 800-565-2224

Ontario

Integrated Environmental Policy Division, 77 Wellesley St. West, 11th Fl., Toronto, ON M7A 2T5
416-314-6338, Fax: 416-314-6346

Niagara Escarpment Commission, 232 Guelph St., Georgetown, ON L7G 4B1
905-877-5191, Fax: 905-873-7452

Ontario Ministry of Environment & Climate Change, Public Information Centre, Macdonald Block, 900 Bay St., 2nd Fl., Toronto, ON M7A 1N3
416-325-4000, Fax: 416-314-6713, 800-565-4923

Ontario Ministry of Natural Resources & Forestry, 300 Water St., PO Box 7000, Peterborough, ON K9J 8M5
800-667-1940

Prince Edward Island

Prince Edward Island Department of Economic Development & Tourism, PO Box 2000, Charlottetown, PE C1A 7N8
902-368-5540, Fax: 902-368-5277, tpswitch@gov.pe.ca

Prince Edward Island Department of Justice & Public Safety, Shaw Bldg. South, 95 Rochford St., 4th Fl., PO Box 2000, Charlottetown, PE C1A 7N8
902-368-6410, Fax: 902-368-6488

Québec

Comité consultatif de l'environnement Kativik, CP 930, Kuujjuaq, QC J0M 1C0
819-964-2961, Fax: 819-964-0694, keac-ccek@krg.ca

Fondation de la faune du Québec, Place Iberville II, #420, 1175, av Lavigerie, Québec, QC G1V 4P1
418-644-7926, Fax: 418-643-7655, 877-639-0742,
ffq@fondationdelafaune.qc.ca

Ministère du Développement durable, de l'Environnement et de la Lutte contre les changements climatiques, Édifice Marie-Guyart, 675, boul René-Lévesque est, 29e étage, Québec, QC G1R 5V7
418-521-3830, Fax: 418-646-5974, 800-561-1616,
info@mddefp.gouv.qc.ca

Société de développement de la Baie James, #10, 462, 3e rue, Chibougamau, QC G8P 1N7
418-748-7777, Fax: 418-748-6868, chi@sdbj.gouv.qc.ca

Société québécoise de récupération et de recyclage, #411, 300, rue Saint-Paul, Québec, QC G1K 7R1
418-643-0394, Fax: 418-643-6507, 866-523-8290,
info@recyc-Québec.gouv.qc.ca

Saskatchewan

Saskatchewan Assessment Management Agency, #200, 2201 - 11th Ave., Regina, SK S4P 0J8
306-924-8000, Fax: 306-924-8070, 800-667-7262,
info.request@sama.sk.ca

Saskatchewan Conservation Data Centre, Fish & Wildlife Branch, Ministry of Environment, 3211 Albert St., Regina, SK S4S 5W6
306-787-7196, Fax: 306-787-9544

Saskatchewan Environment, 3211 Albert St., 2nd Fl., Regina, SK S4S 5W6
306-787-2584, Fax: 306-787-9544, 800-567-4224,
Centre.Inquiry@gov.sk.ca

Saskatchewan Water Security Agency, #400, 111 Fairford St. East, Moose Jaw, SK S6H 7X9
306-694-3900, Fax: 306-694-3105, comm@wsask.ca

Wascana Centre Authority, 2900 Wascana Dr., PO Box 7111, Regina, SK S4P 3S7
306-522-3661, Fax: 306-565-2742, wca@wascana.ca

Yukon Territory

Alsek Renewable Resource Council, 180 Alaska Hwy., PO Box 2077, Haines Junction, YT Y0B 1L0
867-634-2524, Fax: 867-634-2527, admin@alsekrrc.ca

Carmacks Renewable Resource Council, PO Box 122, Carmacks, YT Y0B 1C0
867-863-6838, Fax: 867-863-6429,
carmacksrrc@northwestel.net

Dawson District Renewable Resource Council, PO Box 1380, Dawson City, YT Y0B 1G0
867-993-6976, Fax: 867-993-6093,
dawsonrrc@northwestel.net

Mayo District Renewable Resources Council, PO Box 249, Mayo, YT Y0B 1M0
867-996-2942, Fax: 867-996-2948, mayorrc@northwestel.net

North Yukon Renewable Resources Council, PO Box 80, Old Crow, YT Y0B 1N0
867-966-3034, Fax: 867-966-3036, nyrrc@northwestel.net

Selkirk Renewable Resources Council, PO Box 32, Pelly Crossing, YT Y0B 1P0
867-537-3937, Fax: 867-537-3939,
selkirkrrc@northwestel.net

Teslin Renewable Resource Council, PO Box 186, Teslin, YT Y0A 1B0
867-390-2323, Fax: 867-390-2919, teslinrrc@northwestel.net

Yukon Environment, 10 Burns Rd., PO Box 2703 V-3A, Whitehorse, YT Y1A 2C6
867-667-5652, Fax: 867-393-7197,
environment.yukon@gov.yk.ca

Yukon Land Use Planning Council, #201, 307 Jarvis St., Whitehorse, YT Y1A 2H3
867-667-7397, Fax: 867-667-4624, ylupc@planyukon.ca

ENERGY

Canadian Nuclear Safety Commission, 280 Slater St., PO Box 1046 B,Ottawa, ON K1P 5S9
613-995-5894, Fax: 613-995-5086, 800-668-5284,
cnsc.information.ccsn@canada.ca

Indian Oil & Gas Canada, #100, 9911 Chiila Blvd., Tsuu T'ina (Sarcee), AB T2W 6H6
403-292-5625, Fax: 403-292-5618,
ContactIOGC@inac-ainc.gc.ca

National Energy Board, 517 - 10 Ave. SW, Calgary, AB T2R 0A8
403-292-4800, Fax: 403-292-5503, 800-899-1265

Office of Energy Efficiency, CEF, Building 3, Observatory Cres., 930 Carling Ave., Ottawa, ON K1A 0Y3

Waste Biotreatability Facility, c/o Montréal (av Royalmount) Research Facilities, 6100, av Royalmount, Montréal, QC H4P 2R2

Alberta

Alberta Energy, North Petroleum Plaza, 9945 - 108 St., Edmonton, AB T5K 2G6
780-427-8050, Fax: 780-422-9522, -310-0000

Alberta Energy Regulator, #1000, 250 - 5 St. SW, Calgary, AB T2P 0R4
403-297-8311, Fax: 403-297-7336, 855-297-8311, inquiries@aer.ca
Alberta Innovates - Energy & Environmental Solutions, AMEC Place, #2540, 801 - 6th Ave. SW, Calgary, AB T2P 3W2
403-297-7089, Fax: 403-297-3638, ees@albertainnovates.ca
Alberta Utilities Commission, Fifth Avenue Place, 425 - 1st St. SW, 4th Fl., Calgary, AB T2P 3L8
403-592-8845, Fax: 403-592-4406, -310-0000, info@auc.ab.ca
Surface Rights Board, 1229 - 91 St. SW, Edmonton, AB T6X 1E9
780-427-2444, Fax: 780-427-5798, -310-0000, srb.lcb@gov.ab.ca

British Columbia
British Columbia Hydro, 6911 Southpoint Dr., Burnaby, BC V3N 4X8
604-224-9376, 800-224-9376
British Columbia Ministry of Energy & Mines (& Responsible for Core Review), PO Box 9060 Prov Govt, Victoria, BC V8W 9E3
British Columbia Utilities Commission, 900 Howe St., 6th Fl., PO Box 250, Vancouver, BC V6Z 2N3
604-660-4700, Fax: 604-660-1102, 800-663-1385, commission.secretary@bcuc.com
Columbia Power Corporation, #200, 445 - 13th Ave., Castlegar, BC V1N 1G1
250-304-6060, Fax: 250-304-6083, cpc.info@columbiapower.org
Oil & Gas Commission, #100, 10003 - 110 Ave., Fort St. John, BC V1J 6M7
250-794-5200, Fax: 250-794-5375
Powerex Corp., #1300, 666 Burrard St., Vancouver, BC V6C 2X8
604-891-5000, Fax: 604-891-6060, 800-220-4907
Powertech Labs Inc., 12388 - 88 Ave., Surrey, BC V8W 7R7
604-590-7500, Fax: 604-590-6611

Manitoba
Manitoba Hydro, 360 Portage Ave., PO Box 815 Main,Winnipeg, MB R3C 2P4
204-480-5900, Fax: 204-360-6155, 888-624-9376, publicaffairs@hydro.mb.ca
Manitoba Mineral Resources, The Paris Building, 259 Portage Ave., 9th Fl., Winnipeg, MB R3B 3P4
204-945-6569, 800-223-5215, minesinfo@gov.mb.ca
Power Engineers Advisory Board, Norquay Bldg., #500, 401 York Ave., Winnipeg, MB R3C 0P8
204-945-3373, Fax: 204-948-2309

New Brunswick
New Brunswick Department of Energy & Resource Development, Hugh John Flemming Forestry Centre, 1350 Regent St., Fredericton, NB E3C 2G6
506-453-3826, Fax: 506-444-4367, dnr_mrnweb@gnb.ca

Newfoundland & Labrador
Canada-Newfoundland & Labrador Offshore Petroleum Board, TD Place, 140 Water St., 5th Fl., St. John's, NL A1C 6H6
709-778-1400, Fax: 709-778-1473, information@cnlopb.ca
Churchill Falls (Labrador) Corporation Limited, Hydro Place, 500 Columbus Dr., PO Box 12500, St. John's, NL A1B 4K7
709-737-1859, Fax: 709-737-1816
Nalcor Energy, 500 Columbus Dr., St. John's, NL A1E 2B2
709-737-1400, Fax: 709-737-1800, info@nalcorenergy.com
Newfoundland & Labrador Board of Commissioners of Public Utilities, Prince Charles Bldg., #E-210, 120 Torbay Rd., PO Box 21040, St. John's, NL A1A 5B2
709-726-8600, Fax: 709-726-9604, 866-782-0006, ito@pub.nf.ca
Newfoundland & Labrador Hydro, Hydro Place, 500 Columbus Dr., PO Box 12400, St. John's, NL A1B 4K7
709-737-1400, Fax: 709-737-1800, 888-737-1296, hydro@nlh.nl.ca
Office of Climate Change & Energy Efficiency, PO Box 8700, St. John's, NL A1B 4J6
709-729-1210, Fax: 709-729-1119, climatechange@gov.nl.ca
Twin Falls Power Corporation, PO Box 12500, St. John's, NL A1B 3T5

Northwest Territories
Northwest Territories Department of Environment & Natural Resources, #600, 5102 - 50 Ave., Yellowknife, NT X1A 3S8
867-767-9231
Northwest Territories Power Corporation, 4 Capital Dr., Hay River, NT X0E 1G2
867-874-5200, info@ntpc.com

Nova Scotia
Canada-Nova Scotia Offshore Petroleum Board, TD Centre, 1791 Barrington St., 8th Fl., Halifax, NS B3J 3K9
902-422-5588, Fax: 902-422-1799, info@cnsopb.ns.ca
Nova Scotia Department of Energy, Joseph Howe Bldg., 1690 Hollis St., PO Box 2664, Halifax, NS B3J 3J9
902-424-4575, Fax: 902-424-0528, enerinfo@novascotia.ca
Nova Scotia Utility & Review Board, Summit Place, 1601 Lower Water St., 3rd Fl., PO Box 1692 M,Halifax, NS B3J 3S3
902-424-4448, Fax: 902-424-3919, 855-442-4448, board@novascotia.ca

Ontario
Hydro One Inc., North Tower, 483 Bay St., 15th Fl., Toronto, ON M5G 2P5
416-345-5000, Fax: 905-944-3251, 877-955-1155, customercommunications@hydroone.com
Independent Electricity System Operator, #1600, 120 Adelaide St. West, Toronto, ON M5H 1T1
905-403-6900, Fax: 905-403-6921, 888-448-7777, customer.relations@ieso.ca
Ontario Energy Board, #2700, 2300 Yonge St., PO Box 2319, Toronto, ON M4P 1E4
416-481-1967, Fax: 416-440-7656, 888-632-6273
Ontario Ministry of Energy, Hearst Block, 900 Bay St., 4th Fl., Toronto, ON M7A 2E1
Fax: 416-325-8440, 888-668-4636
Ontario Ministry of Environment & Climate Change, Public Information Centre, Macdonald Block, 900 Bay St., 2nd Fl., Toronto, ON M7A 1N3
416-325-4000, Fax: 416-314-6713, 800-565-4923
Ontario Power Generation, 700 University Ave., Toronto, ON M5G 1X6
416-592-2555, 877-592-2555, webmaster@opg.com

Prince Edward Island
Prince Edward Island Department of Justice & Public Safety, Shaw Bldg. South, 95 Rochford St., 4th Fl., PO Box 2000, Charlottetown, PE C1A 7N8
902-368-6410, Fax: 902-368-6488
Prince Edward Island Energy Corporation, Sullivan Bldg., 16 Fitzroy St., PO Box 2000, Charlottetown, PE C1A 7N8

Québec
Agence de l'efficacité énergétique, #B406, 5700, 4e av ouest, Québec, QC G1H 6R1
418-627-6379, Fax: 418-643-5828, 877-727-6655, efficaciteenergetique@mern.gouv.qc.ca
Coopérative régionale d'électricité de Saint-Jean-Baptiste-de-Rouville, 3113, rue Principale, Saint-Jean-Baptiste, QC J0L 1B0
450-467-5583, Fax: 450-467-0092, 800-267-5583, info@coopsjb.com
Hydro-Québec, 75, boul René-Lévesque ouest, 19e étage, Montréal, QC H2Z 1A4
514-289-2211
Régie de l'énergie, Tour de la Bourse, #2.55, 800, Place Victoria, Montréal, QC H4Z 1A2
514-873-2452, Fax: 514-873-2070, 888-873-2452, secretariat@regie-energie.qc.ca
Société d'énergie de la Baie-James, #1200, 800, de Maisonneuve est, Montréal, QC H2L 4L8
514-286-2020

Saskatchewan
Energy & Resources, 2101 Scarth St., Regina, SK S4P SH9
306-787-2528
NorthPoint Energy Solutions Inc., 2025 Victoria Ave., Regina, SK S4P 0S1
306-566-2103, Fax: 306-566-3364, info@northpointenergy.com
Saskatchewan Power Corporation (SaskPower), 2025 Victoria Ave., Regina, SK S4P 0S1
306-566-2121, 888-757-6937
SaskEnergy Incorporated, 1777 Victoria Ave., Regina, SK S4P 4K5
306-777-9225, 800-567-8899

Yukon Territory
Yukon Energy, Mines & Resources, PO Box 2703, Whitehorse, YT Y1A 2C6
867-667-3130, Fax: 867-456-3965, 800-661-0408, emr@gov.yk.ca

HYDRO, ELECTRIC POWER

National Energy Board, 517 - 10 Ave. SW, Calgary, AB T2R 0A8
403-292-4800, Fax: 403-292-5503, 800-899-1265

Alberta
Alberta Energy Regulator, #1000, 250 - 5 St. SW, Calgary, AB T2P 0R4
403-297-8311, Fax: 403-297-7336, 855-297-8311, inquiries@aer.ca
Alberta Utilities Commission, Fifth Avenue Place, 425 - 1st St. SW, 4th Fl., Calgary, AB T2P 3L8
403-592-8845, Fax: 403-592-4406, -310-0000, info@auc.ab.ca

British Columbia
British Columbia Hydro, 6911 Southpoint Dr., Burnaby, BC V3N 4X8
604-224-9376, 800-224-9376
Columbia Power Corporation, #200, 445 - 13th Ave., Castlegar, BC V1N 1G1
250-304-6060, Fax: 250-304-6083, cpc.info@columbiapower.org
Powertech Labs Inc., 12388 - 88 Ave., Surrey, BC V8W 7R7
604-590-7500, Fax: 604-590-6611

Manitoba
Manitoba Hydro, 360 Portage Ave., PO Box 815 Main,Winnipeg, MB R3C 2P4
204-480-5900, Fax: 204-360-6155, 888-624-9376, publicaffairs@hydro.mb.ca

Newfoundland & Labrador
Churchill Falls (Labrador) Corporation Limited, Hydro Place, 500 Columbus Dr., PO Box 12500, St. John's, NL A1B 4K7
709-737-1859, Fax: 709-737-1816
Nalcor Energy, 500 Columbus Dr., St. John's, NL A1E 2B2
709-737-1400, Fax: 709-737-1800, info@nalcorenergy.com
Newfoundland & Labrador Hydro, Hydro Place, 500 Columbus Dr., PO Box 12400, St. John's, NL A1B 4K7
709-737-1400, Fax: 709-737-1800, 888-737-1296, hydro@nlh.nl.ca
Twin Falls Power Corporation, PO Box 12500, St. John's, NL A1B 3T5

Northwest Territories
Northwest Territories Power Corporation, 4 Capital Dr., Hay River, NT X0E 1G2
867-874-5200, info@ntpc.com

Nova Scotia
Nova Scotia Utility & Review Board, Summit Place, 1601 Lower Water St., 3rd Fl., PO Box 1692 M,Halifax, NS B3J 3S3
902-424-4448, Fax: 902-424-3919, 855-442-4448, board@novascotia.ca

Ontario
Hydro One Inc., North Tower, 483 Bay St., 15th Fl., Toronto, ON M5G 2P5
416-345-5000, Fax: 905-944-3251, 877-955-1155, customercommunications@hydroone.com
Independent Electricity System Operator, #1600, 120 Adelaide St. West, Toronto, ON M5H 1T1
905-403-6900, Fax: 905-403-6921, 888-448-7777, customer.relations@ieso.ca
Ontario Power Generation, 700 University Ave., Toronto, ON M5G 1X6
416-592-2555, 877-592-2555, webmaster@opg.com

Québec
Coopérative régionale d'électricité de Saint-Jean-Baptiste-de-Rouville, 3113, rue Principale, Saint-Jean-Baptiste, QC J0L 1B0
450-467-5583, Fax: 450-467-0092, 800-267-5583, info@coopsjb.com
Hydro-Québec, 75, boul René-Lévesque ouest, 19e étage, Montréal, QC H2Z 1A4
514-289-2211
Société d'énergie de la Baie-James, #1200, 800, de Maisonneuve est, Montréal, QC H2L 4L8
514-286-2020

Saskatchewan
Saskatchewan Power Corporation (SaskPower), 2025 Victoria Ave., Regina, SK S4P 0S1
306-566-2121, 888-757-6937

OIL & NATURAL GAS RESOURCES

See Also: Energy
Indian Oil & Gas Canada, #100, 9911 Chiila Blvd., Tsuu T'ina (Sarcee), AB T2W 6H6
403-292-5625, Fax: 403-292-5618, ContactIOGC@inac-ainc.gc.ca
National Energy Board, 517 - 10 Ave. SW, Calgary, AB T2R 0A8
403-292-4800, Fax: 403-292-5503, 800-899-1265
Northern Pipeline Agency Canada, #470, 588 Booth St., Ottawa, ON K1A 0Y7
613-995-1150, info@npa.gc.ca

Alberta
Alberta Energy, North Petroleum Plaza, 9945 - 108 St., Edmonton, AB T5K 2G6
780-427-8050, Fax: 780-422-9522, -310-0000
Alberta Energy Regulator, #1000, 250 - 5 St. SW, Calgary, AB T2P 0R4
403-297-8311, Fax: 403-297-7336, 855-297-8311, inquiries@aer.ca

Surface Rights Board, 1229 - 91 St. SW, Edmonton, AB T6X 1E9
780-427-2444, Fax: 780-427-5798, -310-0000, srb.lcb@gov.ab.ca

British Columbia

British Columbia Ministry of Natural Gas Development (& Responsible for Housing), PO Box 9052 Prov Govt, Victoria, BC V8W 9E2
250-953-0900, Fax: 250-953-0927

British Columbia Utilities Commission, 900 Howe St., 6th Fl., PO Box 250, Vancouver, BC V6Z 2N3
604-660-4700, Fax: 604-660-1102, 800-663-1385, commission.secretary@bcuc.com

Oil & Gas Commission, #100, 10003 - 110 Ave., Fort St. John, BC V1J 6M7
250-794-5200, Fax: 250-794-5375

Surface Rights Board of British Columbia, #10, 10551 Shellbridge Way, Richmond, BC V6X 2W9
604-775-1740, Fax: 604-775-1742, 888-775-1740, office@surfacerightsboard.bc.ca

Manitoba

Surface Rights Board, #360, 1395 Ellice Ave., Winnipeg, MB R3G 3P2
204-945-0731, Fax: 204-948-2578, 800-282-8069

New Brunswick

New Brunswick Department of Energy & Resource Development, Hugh John Flemming Forestry Centre, 1350 Regent St., Fredericton, NB E3C 2G6
506-453-3826, Fax: 506-444-4367, dnr_mrnweb@gnb.ca

Newfoundland & Labrador

Canada-Newfoundland & Labrador Offshore Petroleum Board, TD Place, 140 Water St., 5th Fl., St. John's, NL A1C 6H6
709-778-1400, Fax: 709-778-1473, information@cnlopb.ca

Nova Scotia

Canada-Nova Scotia Offshore Petroleum Board, TD Centre, 1791 Barrington St., 8th Fl., Halifax, NS B3J 3K9
902-422-5588, Fax: 902-422-1799, info@cnsopb.ns.ca

Nova Scotia Utility & Review Board, Summit Place, 1601 Lower Water St., 3rd Fl., PO Box 1692 M,Halifax, NS B3J 3S3
902-424-4448, Fax: 902-424-3919, 855-442-4448, board@novascotia.ca

Nunavut

Nunavut Territory Department of Environment, PO Box 1000 1300, Iqaluit, NU X0A 0H0
867-975-7700, Fax: 867-975-7742, environment@gov.nu.ca

Ontario

Ontario Ministry of Natural Resources & Forestry, 300 Water St., PO Box 7000, Peterborough, ON K9J 8M5
800-667-1940

Saskatchewan

NorthPoint Energy Solutions Inc., 2025 Victoria Ave., Regina, SK S4P 0S1
306-566-2103, Fax: 306-566-3364, info@northpointenergy.com

SaskEnergy Incorporated, 1777 Victoria Ave., Regina, SK S4P 4K5
306-777-9225, 800-567-8899

Yukon Territory

Oil & Gas Mineral Resources Division, PO Box 2703, Whitehorse, YT Y1A 2C6
867-667-5087, Fax: 867-393-6262, oilandgas@gov.yk.ca

PUBLIC UTILITIES

Alberta

Alberta Energy Regulator, #1000, 250 - 5 St. SW, Calgary, AB T2P 0R4
403-297-8311, Fax: 403-297-7336, 855-297-8311, inquiries@aer.ca

Alberta Utilities Commission, Fifth Avenue Place, 425 - 1st St. SW, 4th Fl., Calgary, AB T2P 3L8
403-592-8845, Fax: 403-592-4406, -310-0000, info@auc.ab.ca

British Columbia

British Columbia Hydro, 6911 Southpoint Dr., Burnaby, BC V3N 4X8
604-224-9376, 800-224-9376

British Columbia Utilities Commission, 900 Howe St., 6th Fl., PO Box 250, Vancouver, BC V6Z 2N3
604-660-4700, Fax: 604-660-1102, 800-663-1385, commission.secretary@bcuc.com

Columbia Power Corporation, #200, 445 - 13th Ave., Castlegar, BC V1N 1G1
250-304-6060, Fax: 250-304-6083, cpc.info@columbiapower.org

Manitoba

Manitoba Hydro, 360 Portage Ave., PO Box 815 Main,Winnipeg, MB R3C 2P4
204-480-5900, Fax: 204-360-6155, 888-624-9376, publicaffairs@hydro.mb.ca

Newfoundland & Labrador

Churchill Falls (Labrador) Corporation Limited, Hydro Place, 500 Columbus Dr., PO Box 12500, St. John's, NL A1B 4K7
709-737-1859, Fax: 709-737-1816

Nalcor Energy, 500 Columbus Dr., St. John's, NL A1E 2B2
709-737-1400, Fax: 709-737-1800, info@nalcorenergy.com

Newfoundland & Labrador Board of Commissioners of Public Utilities, Prince Charles Bldg., #E-210, 120 Torbay Rd., PO Box 21040, St. John's, NL A1A 5B2
709-726-8600, Fax: 709-726-9604, 866-782-0006, ito@pub.nf.ca

Newfoundland & Labrador Hydro, Hydro Place, 500 Columbus Dr., PO Box 12400, St. John's, NL A1B 4K7
709-737-1400, Fax: 709-737-1800, 888-737-1296, hydro@nlh.nl.ca

Northwest Territories

Inuvialuit Water Board, Professional Bldg., #302, 125 Mackenzie Rd., PO Box 2531, Yellowknife, NT X0E 0T0
867-678-2942, Fax: 867-678-2943, info@inuvwb.ca

Northwest Territories Power Corporation, 4 Capital Dr., Hay River, NT X0E 1G2
867-874-5200, info@ntpc.com

Nova Scotia

Nova Scotia Utility & Review Board, Summit Place, 1601 Lower Water St., 3rd Fl., PO Box 1692 M,Halifax, NS B3J 3S3
902-424-4448, Fax: 902-424-3919, 855-442-4448, board@novascotia.ca

Ontario

Hydro One Inc., North Tower, 483 Bay St., 15th Fl., Toronto, ON M5G 2P5
416-345-5000, Fax: 905-944-3251, 877-955-1155, customercommunications@hydroone.com

Independent Electricity System Operator, #1600, 120 Adelaide St. West, Toronto, ON M5H 1T1
905-403-6900, Fax: 905-403-6921, 888-448-7777, customer.relations@ieso.ca

Ontario Power Generation, 700 University Ave., Toronto, ON M5G 1X6
416-592-2555, 877-592-2555, webmaster@opg.com

Prince Edward Island

Prince Edward Island Regulatory & Appeals Commission, National Bank Tower, #501, 134 Kent St., PO Box 577, Charlottetown, PE C1A 7L1
902-892-3501, Fax: 902-566-4076, 800-501-6268, info@irac.pe.ca

Québec

Coopérative régionale d'électricité de Saint-Jean-Baptiste-de-Rouville, 3113, rue Principale, Saint-Jean-Baptiste, QC J0L 1B0
450-467-5583, Fax: 450-467-0092, 800-267-5583, info@coopsjb.com

Hydro-Québec, 75, boul René-Lévesque ouest, 19e étage, Montréal, QC H2Z 1A4
514-289-2211

Régie de l'énergie, Tour de la Bourse, #2.55, 800, Place Victoria, Montréal, QC H4Z 1A2
514-873-2452, Fax: 514-873-2070, 888-873-2452, secretariat@regie-energie.qc.ca

Saskatchewan

Saskatchewan Power Corporation (SaskPower), 2025 Victoria Ave., Regina, SK S4P 0S1
306-566-2121, 888-757-6937

Saskatchewan Water Corporation (SaskWater), #200, 111 Fairford St. East, Moose Jaw, SK S6H 1C8
Fax: 306-694-3207, 888-230-1111, comm@saskwater.com

SaskEnergy Incorporated, 1777 Victoria Ave., Regina, SK S4P 4K5
306-777-9225, 800-567-8899

Yukon Territory

Yukon Utilities Board, #19, 1114 - 1st Ave., PO Box 31728, Whitehorse, YT Y1A 6L3
867-667-5058, Fax: 867-667-5059, yub@utilitiesboard.yk.ca

ENTRY NAME INDEX

A

B

C

D

E

F

G

H

I

J

K

L

M

N

O

P

Q

R

S

T

U

V

W

X

Y

Z

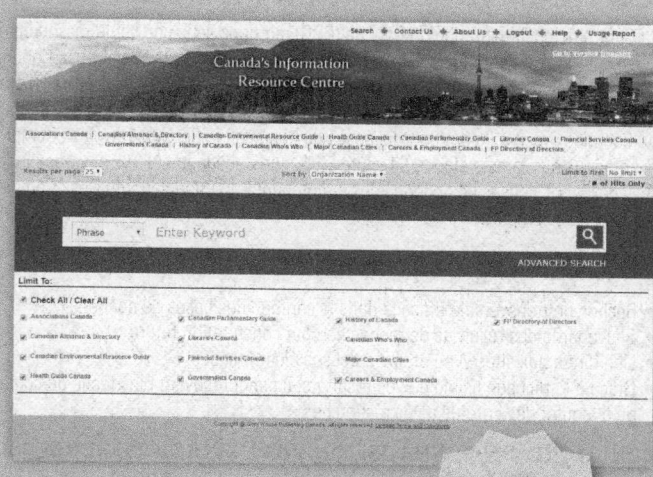

CENTRE DE DOCUMENTATION DU CANADA (CDC)

Consultez en tout temps toutes ces excellentes ressources en ligne grâce au Centre de documentation du Canada (CDC) à http://circ.greyhouse.ca

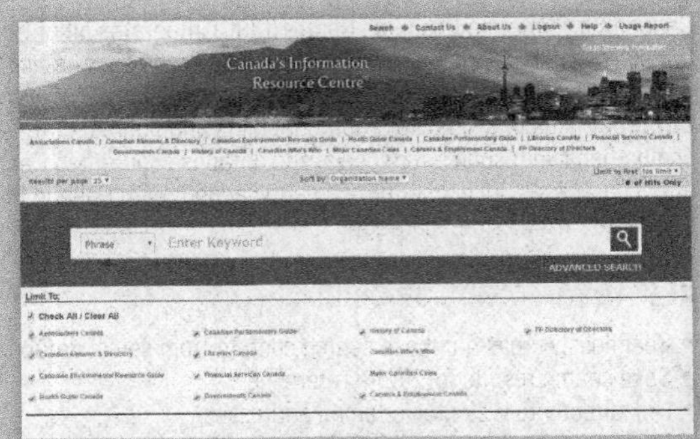

Le Centre de documentation du Canada (CDC) regroupe sous une seule ressource en ligne conviviale tout le contenu des ouvrages de référence primés de Grey House Canada. Répertoriant plus de **100 000 entreprises canadiennes**, **et plus de 140 600 personnes-ressources**, faits et chiffres, il s'agit de la ressource la plus complète en matière de bases de données spécialisées au Canada! Grâce à l'ajout de trois bases de données, le Canada Info Desk Complete est plus avantageux que jamais alors qu'il coûte 50 % que l'abonnement aux ouvrages individuels. Accédez aux 13 bases de données dès maintenant – le Canadian Info Desk Complete vous offre un ensemble complet!

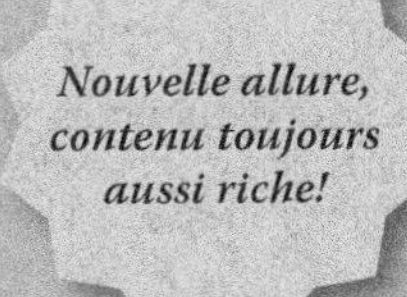

PRINCIPAUX AVANTAGES DU CDC

- Recherche transversale efficace dans le contenu des bases de données
- Sauvegarde des résultats de recherche pour consultation future
- Lien direct aux sites Web et aux adresses électroniques
- Grâce à l'affichage lisible de vos résultats, il est dorénavant plus facile de compiler les résultats ou d'ajouter des critères à vos recherches

CONCEPTION PERSONNALISÉE DE VOS LISTES DE PERSONNES-RESSOURCES!

Le CDC vous permet de définir et d'extraire vos propres listes, et ce, en quelques secondes. Découvrez des clients potentiels, effectuez des recherches par mot-clé, trouvez les participants à une conférence à venir : l'information dont vous avez besoin, au bout de vos doigts.

CHOISISSEZ ENTRE RECHERCHES MOT-CLÉ ET AVANCÉE!

Grâce au CDC, vous pouvez choisir entre une recherche Mot-clé ou Avancée pour localiser l'information avec précision. Vous avez la possibilité d'effectuer des recherches en texte simple ou booléennes puissantes – les recherches sont conçues à l'intention des chercheurs débutants et avancés.

LES PROFILS DU CDC COMPRENNENT :

- Numéros de téléphone, adresses électroniques, numéros de télécopieur et adresses complètes pour toutes les succursales d'un organisme
- Comptes de médias sociaux, comme Twitter et Facebook
- Personnes-ressources clés en fonction des appellations d'emploi
- Budgets, frais d'adhésion, tailles du personnel et plus!

Effectuez des recherches dans le CDC à l'aide de champs uniques ou communs, personnalisés selon vos besoins!

SEULS LES RÉPERTOIRES DE GREY HOUSE VOUS OFFRENT UN CONTENU PARTICULIER QUE VOUS NE TROUVEREZ NULLE PART AILLEURS!

- **Le répertoire des associations du Canada :** sources de financement, activités, publications, congrès, membres, prix, profil de membre
- **Guide parlementaire canadien :** carrières privées et politiques des membres élus, liste complète des comtés et des représentants
- **Guide des ressources environnementales canadiennes :** produits/services/domaines d'expertise, langues de travail, marchés nationaux, type de propriétaire, sources de revenus
- **Services financiers :** type de propriétaire, nombre d'employés, année de la fondation, immobilisations, revenus, symbole au téléscripteur
- **Bibliothèques Canada :** personnel, collections particulières, services, année de la fondation, symbole de bibliothèque national, système régional
- **Gouvernements du Canada :** population municipale
- **Canadian Who's Who :** ville d'origine, publication, formation (diplômes et alma mater), carrière/emploi et employeur
- **Principales villes canadiennes :** données démographiques, ethnicité, immigration, langue, éducation, logement, revenu, main-d'œuvre et transport
- **Guide canadien de la santé :** maladies chroniques et mentales, ressources generales, annexes et statistiques.
- **Carrières et emplois Canada :** associations professionnelles, sites Web d'emplois, employeurs, répertoires par industrie, recruteurs, bourses, conseils sectoriels et emplois d'été
- **Répertoire des administrateurs :** prénom, nom de famille, poste de cadre et d'administrateur, parcours scolaire et professionnel et adresse électronique des cadres supérieurs canadiens; liste des sociétés les plus importantes au Canada et l'information complète des compagnies

Le nouveau CDC facilite la recherche au sein de toutes nos ressources au Canada et procure plus rapidement des résultats plus poussés – des associations au gouvernement en passant par les principales entreprises et les zoos, sans oublier tout un éventail d'organisations! Que vous ayez besoin d'information très détaillée au sujet de votre personne-ressource ou d'une simple adresse électronique, vous pouvez personnaliser votre requête afin qu'elle réponde à vos besoins. Contactez-nous sans tarder pour obtenir un **essai gratuit** ou visitez http://circ.greyhouse.ca

Pour obtenir plus d'information, veuillez contacter Grey House Publishing Canada

par tél. : 1 866 433-4739 ou 416 644-6479 par téléc. : 416 644-1904 | info@greyhouse.ca | www.greyhouse.ca

Health Guide Canada

An Informative Handbook on Health Services in Canada

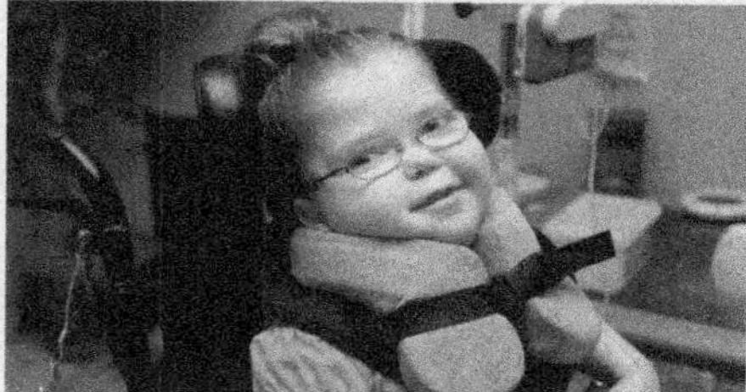

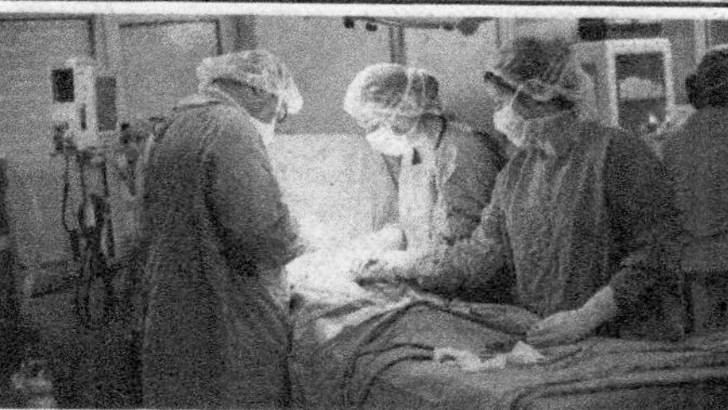

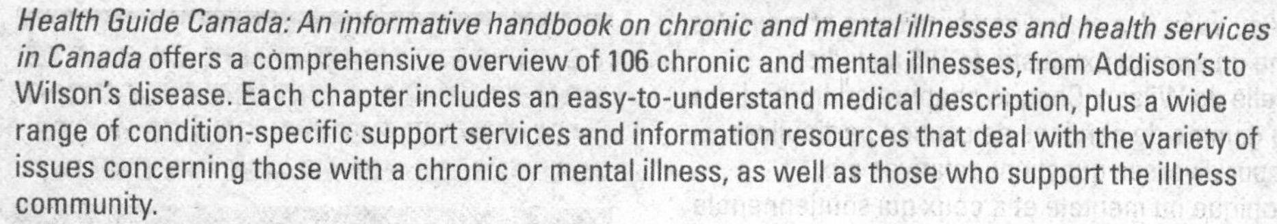

Health Guide Canada: An informative handbook on chronic and mental illnesses and health services in Canada offers a comprehensive overview of 106 chronic and mental illnesses, from Addison's to Wilson's disease. Each chapter includes an easy-to-understand medical description, plus a wide range of condition-specific support services and information resources that deal with the variety of issues concerning those with a chronic or mental illness, as well as those who support the illness community.

Health Guide Canada contains thousands of ways to deal with the many aspects of chronic or mental health disorder. It includes associations, government agencies, libraries and resource centres, educational facilities, hospitals and publications. In addition to chapters dealing with specific chronic or mental conditions, there is a chapter relevant to the health industry in general, as well as others dealing with charitable foundations, death and bereavement groups, homeopathic medicine, indigenous issues and sports for the disabled.

Specific sections include:

- Educational Material
- Section I: Chronic & Mental Illnesses
- Section II: General Resources
- Section III: Appendices
- Section IV: Statistics

Each listing will provide a description, address (including website, email address and social media links, if possible) and executives' names and titles, as well as a number of details specific to that type of organization.

In addition to patients and families, hospital and medical centre personnel can find the support they need in their work or study. *Health Guide Canada* is full of resources crucial for people with chronic illness as they transition from diagnosis to home, home to work, and work to community life.

PRINT OR ONLINE—QUICK AND EASY ACCESS TO ALL THE INFORMATION YOU NEED!

Available in softcover print or electronically via the web, *Health Guide Canada* provides instant access to the people you need and the facts you want every time. Whereas the print edition is verified and updated annually, ongoing changes are added to the web version on a regular basis. The web version allows you to narrow your search by using index fields such as name or type of organization, subject, location, contact name or title and postal code.

HEALTH GUIDE CANADA HELPS YOU FIND WHAT YOU NEED WITH THESE VALUABLE SOURCING TOOLS!

Entry Name Index—An alphabetical list of all entries, providing a quick and easy way to access any listing in this edition.

Tabs—Main sections are tabbed for easy look-up. Headers on each page make it easy to locate the data you need.

Create your own contact lists! Online subscribers have the option to instantly generate their own contact lists and export them into spreadsheets for further use—a great alternative to high cost list broker services.

Guide canadien de la santé

Un manuel informatif au sujet des services en santé au Canada

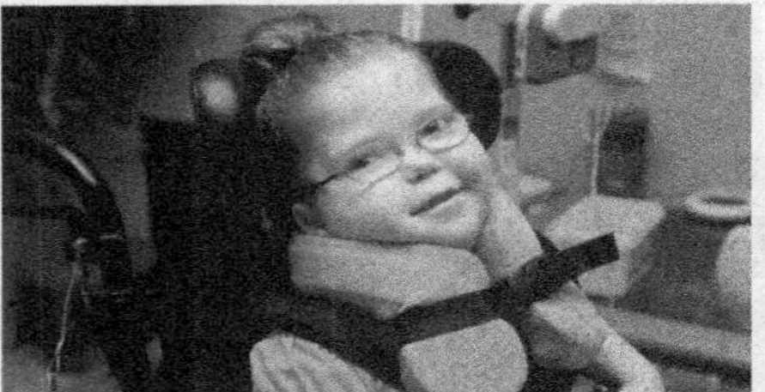

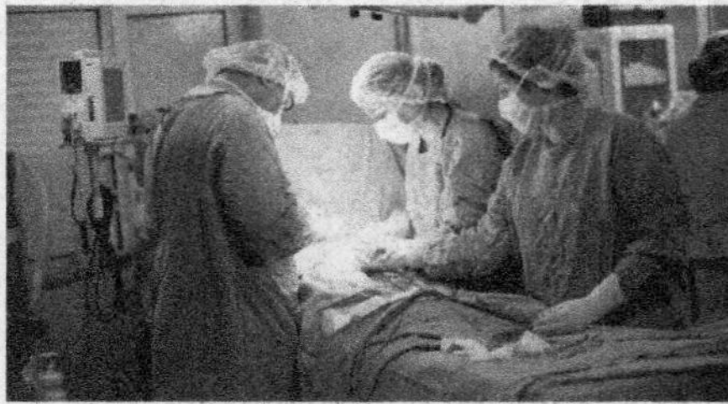

Le *Guide canadien de la santé : un manuel informatif au sujet des maladies chroniques et mentales de même que des services en santé au Canada* donne un aperçu exhaustif de 106 maladies chroniques et mentales, de la maladie d'Addison à celle de Wilson. Chaque chapitre comprend une description médicale facile à comprendre, une vaste gamme de services de soutien particuliers à l'état et des ressources documentaires qui portent sur diverses questions relatives aux personnes qui sont aux prises avec une maladie chronique ou mentale et à ceux qui soutiennent la communauté liée à cette maladie.

Le *Guide canadien de la santé* contient des milliers de moyens pour composer avec divers aspects d'une maladie chronique ou d'un problème de santé mentale. Il comprend des associations, des organismes gouvernementaux, des bibliothèques et des centres de documentation, des services d'éducation, des hôpitaux et des publications. En plus des chapitres qui portent sur des états chroniques ou mentaux, un chapitre traite de l'industrie de la santé en général; d'autres abordent les fondations qui réalisent des rêves, les groupes de soutien axés sur le décès et le deuil, la médecine homéopathique, les questions autochtones et les sports pour les personnes handicapées. Les sections incluent

- Matériel didactique
- Section I : Les maladies chroniques ou mentales
- Section II : Les ressources génériques
- Section III : Les annexes
- Section IV : Les statistiques

Chaque entrée comprend une description, une adresse (y compris le site Web, le courriel et les liens des médias sociaux, lorsque possible), les noms et titres des directeurs de même que plusieurs détails particuliers à ce type d'organisme.

Les membres du personnel des hôpitaux et des centres médicaux peuvent trouver, au même titre que parents et familles, le soutien dont ils ont besoin dans le cadre de leur travail ou de leurs études. Le *Guide canadien de la santé* est rempli de ressources capitales pour les personnes qui souffrent d'une maladie chronique alors qu'elles passent du diagnostic au retour à la maison, de la maison au travail et du travail à la vie au sein de la communauté.

OFFERT EN FORMAT PAPIER OU EN LIGNE—UN ACCÈS RAPIDE ET FACILE À TOUS LES RENSEIGNEMENTS DONT VOUS AVEZ BESOIN!

Offert sous couverture souple ou en format électronique grâce au web, le *Guide canadien de la santé* donne invariablement un accès instantané aux personnes et aux faits dont vous avez besoin. Si la version imprimée est vérifiée et mise à jour annuellement, des changements continus sont apportés mensuellement à la base de données en ligne. Servez-vous de la version en ligne afin de circonscrire vos recherches grâce à des champs spéciaux de l'index comme le nom de l'organisation ou son type, le sujet, l'emplacement, le nom de la personne-ressource ou son titre et le code postal.

LE GUIDE CANADIEN DE LA SANTÉ VOUS AIDERA À TROUVER CE DONT VOUS AVEZ BESOIN GRÂCE À CES OUTILS DE REPÉRAGE PRÉCIEUX!

Répertoire nominatif—une list alphabétique offrant un moyen rapide et facile d'accéder à toute liste de cette edition.

Onglets—les sections principals possèdent un onglet pour une consultation facile. Les notes en tête de chaque page vous aident à trouver les données voulues.

Créez vos propres listes! Les abonnés au service en ligne peuvent générer instantanément leurs propres listes de contacts et les exporter en format feuille de calcul pour une utilisation approfondie – une solution de rechange géniale aux services dispendieux d'un commissionnaire en publipostage.

Canadian Environmental Resource Guide

The Only Complete Guide to the Business of Environmental Management

he *Canadian Environmental Resource Guide* provides data on every aspect of the environmental ndustry in unprecedented detail. It offers one-stop searching for details on government offices nd programs, information sources, product and service firms and trade fairs that pertain to the usiness of environmental management. All information is fully indexed and cross-referenced for asy use. The directory features current information and key contacts in Canada's environmental ndustry including:

NVIRONMENTAL UP-DATE

Information on prominent environmentalists, environmental abbreviations and a summary of recent environmental events

Updated articles, rankings, statistics and charts on all aspects of the environmental industry

Trade shows, conferences and seminars for the current year and beyond

NVIRONMENTAL PRODUCTS & SERVICES

Comprehensive listings for companies and firms producing and selling products and services in the environmental sector, including markets served, working language and percentage of revenue sources: public and private

Detailed indexes by subject, geography and ISO

NVIRONMENTAL GOVERNMENT LISTINGS

Information on important intergovernmental offices and councils, and listings of environmental trade representatives abroad

In-depth listings of environmental information at the municipal level, including population and number of households, water and waste treatment, landfill statistics and special by-laws and bans, as well as key environmental contacts for each municipality

vailable in softcover print and electronically via the web, the *Canadian Environmental Resource uide* provides instant access to the people you need and the facts you want every time. The anadian Environmental Resource Guide* is verified and updated annually. Ongoing changes are dded to the web version on a regular basis.

CANADIAN ENVIRONMENTAL RESOURCE GUIDE OFFERS EVEN MORE CONTENT ONLINE!

Environmental Information Resources—An all-inclusive list of environmental law firms, special libraries and resource centres, educational programs, research centres and foundations and grants

Associations—Thousands of environmental associations, with information on membership, environmental activities, key contacts and more

Government Listings—Every federal and provincial department and agency influencing environmental initiatives and purchasing policies

The web version allows you to narrow your search by using index fields such as name or type of organization, subject, location, contact name or title and postal code.

Create your own contact lists! Online subscribers have the option to instantly generate their own contact lists and export them into spreadsheets for further use—a great alternative to high cost list broker services.

For more information please contact Grey House Publishing Canada

Tel.: (866) 433-4739 or (416) 644-6479 Fax: (416) 644-1904 | info@greyhouse.ca | www.greyhouse.ca

GREY HOUSE
PUBLISHING
CANADA

Services financiers au Canada

Une couverture sans pareille de l'industrie des services financiers canadiens

Grâce à plus de 30 000 organisations et renseignements commerciaux rares, *Services financiers du Canada* est la source la plus à jour de noms et de coordonnées de professionnels, de membres de la haute direction, de gestionnaires de portefeuille, de conseillers financiers, de fonctionnaires et de représentants élus de l'industrie.

Services financiers du Canada intègre les plus récentes modifications à l'industrie afin de vous offrir les détails les plus à jour au sujet de chaque entreprise, notamment le nom, le titre, l'organisation, les numéros de téléphone et de télécopieur, le courriel et l'adresse du site Web. Servez-vous de la base de données en ligne et raffinez votre recherche selon le symbole, le revenu, l'année de création, les immobilisations, le type de propriété ou le nombre d'employés.

DES INDEX PUISSANTS VOUS AIDENT À TROUVER LES RENSEIGNEMENTS FINANCIERS ESSENTIELS DONT VOUS AVEZ BESOIN.

C'est avec l'utilisateur en tête que Services financiers au Canada a été conçu; il contient des listes catégorisées et quatre index faciles d'utilisation :

Alphabétique—les organisations financières apparaissent en ordre alphabétique, selon le nom de l'entreprise.

Géographique—les institutions financières et leurs succursales sont détaillées par ville.

Nom de directeur—tous les agents, directeurs et cadres supérieurs sont classés en ordre alphabétique, selon leur nom de famille.

Classe d'assurance—toutes les entreprises selon leur type d'assurance.

Passez moins de temps à préparer des listes, à faire des recherches ou à chercher des contacts et des courriels. Que vous soyez intéressé à contacter un avocat en droit des affaires au sujet de projets conjoints internationaux et nationaux, que vous ayez besoin de générer une liste des banques étrangères au Canada ou que vous souhaitiez communiquer avec la Bourse de Toronto, *Services financiers au Canada* vous permet de trouver toutes les données dont vous avez besoin.

OFFERT EN FORMAT PAPIER OU EN LIGNE – UN ACCÈS RAPIDE ET FACILE À TOUS LES RENSEIGNEMENTS DONT VOUS AVEZ BESOIN!

Offert sous couverture rigide ou en format électronique grâce au Web, Services financiers du Canada donne invariablement un accès instantané aux personnes et aux faits dont vous avez besoin. Si la version imprimée est vérifiée et mise à jour annuellement, des changements continus sont apportés mensuellement à la base de données en ligne. Servez-vous de la version en ligne afin de circonscrire vos recherches grâce à des champs spéciaux de l'index comme le nom de l'organisation ou son type, le sujet, l'emplacement, le nom de la personne-ressource ou son titre et le code postal.

Créez vos propres listes! Les abonnés au service en ligne peuvent générer instantanément leurs propres listes de contacts et les exporter en format feuille de calcul pour une utilisation approfondie – une solution de rechange géniale aux services dispendieux d'un commissionnaire en publipostage.

ACCÉDEZ AUX LISTES ACTUELLES...

Banques et institutions de dépôt
- Banques nationales et d'épargne
- Banques étrangères et leurs succursales
- Bureaux des représentants de banques étrangères
- Sociétés de fiducie
- Coopératives d'épargne et de crédit

Établissements financiers
- Entreprises de notation des obligations
- Agences de placement
- Compagnies de carte de crédit
- Sociétés de financement et de prêt
- Syndics de faillite

Sociétés de gestion de placements, y compris les valeurs et marchandises
- Entreprises de planification financière et de gestion des investissements
- Maisons de courtage de valeurs Courtiers en épargne collective
- Entreprises de gestion de la pension/de trésorerie
- Bourses
- Sociétés de portefeuille

Compagnies d'assurance, fédérales et provinciales
- Compagnies de réassurance
- Sociétés fraternelles
- Sociétés de secours mutuel
- Échanges selon la formule de réciprocité — comptabilité et droit
- Comptables
- Cabinets d'actuaires-conseils
- Cabinets d'avocats (spécialisés en finance)
- Principales entreprises canadiennes
- Principaux contacts financiers pour les sociétés de capitaux publiques, privées et de la Couronne
- Gouvernement
- Personnes-ressources aux paliers fédéral, provinciaux et territoriaux

Annexe de publications
- Principales publications qui desservent l'industrie des services financiers

Pour obtenir plus d'information, veuillez contacter Grey House Publishing Canada

par tél. : 1 866 433-4739 ou 416 644-6479 par téléc. : 416 644-1904 | info@greyhouse.ca | www.greyhouse.ca

Principales villes canadiennes

Comparaison et classement

Principales villes canadiennes offre à l'utilisateur de nombreuses manières de classer et de comparer 50 villes principales du Canada. Toute l'information statistique se trouve au bout de vos doigts : vous pouvez obtenir des détails sur les villes, chacune comptant 100 000 habitants ou plus. Dans le Centre de documentation du Canada (CDC), vous pouvez classer instantanément les villes selon vos préférences et créer vos propres tableaux analytiques à l'aide des données fournies. Ces tableaux de classement répondent à des centaines de questions, notamment : quelles villes comptent la population la plus jeune? À quel endroit la croissance économique est-elle la plus forte? Quelles villes présentent les meilleures statistiques en matière de main-d'œuvre?

Un profil de ville offre des renseignements supplémentaires afin de vous donner une idée de son emplacement, de son histoire, de ses activités récréatives et culturelles. Suivent des classements qui démontrent l'unicité de la ville dans un spectre de villes qui se trouvent partout au Canada. Vous trouverez également des remarques intéressantes au sujet de la ville et de son classement parmi les 50 principales villes, par exemple selon celle où il fait le mieux vivre, où se trouvent les plus riches et où il fait le plus froid. Ces rapports sont disponibles uniquement auprès de Grey House Publishing Canada et dans le cadre de votre abonnement à ce nouveau produit emballant!

PRINCIPALES VILLES CANADIENNES COMPREND CES TABLEAUX STATISTIQUES :

Données démographiques

- Croissance de la population
- Caractéristiques relatives à l'âge
- Ratio homme/femme
- État matrimonial

Logement

- Type et taille du logement
- Âge et valeur du logement

Main-d'œuvre

- Population active
- Emploi
- Industrie
- Lieu de travail

Ethnicité, immigration et langue

- Langue maternelle
- Connaissance des langues officielles
- Langue parlée à la maison
- Populations minoritaires
- Formation
- Niveau scolaire

Revenu

- Revenu médian
- Revenu médian après impôts
- Revenu médian par type de famille
- Revenu médian après impôts par type de famille

Transport

- Moyen de transport vers le travail

OFFERT EN VERSION ÉLECTRONIQUE!

Principales villes canadiennes est offert en version électronique sur le Web. Vous accédez donc instantanément aux faits dont vous avez besoin pour chaque ville, de même que des éléments intéressants qui illustrent la comparaison entre les villes.

Servez-vous de la version en ligne pour effectuer des recherches parmi les statistiques et créer vos propres tableaux, ou consulter les tableaux déjà prêts en format PDF. Elle peut vous aider dans le cadre de recherches pour des travaux universitaires, pour le développement d'infrastructures ou consultez-la par simple curiosité – autant de données réunies en une source modifiable.

Pour obtenir plus d'information, veuillez contacter Grey House Publishing Canada

par tél. : 1 866 433-4739 ou 416 644-6479 par téléc. : 416 644-1904 | info@greyhouse.ca | www.greyhouse.ca

Mailing List Services

As a boutique provider of mailing lists, Grey House Publishing Canada specializes in the areas below to ensure a high level of accuracy. Our clients return to us time and time again because of the reliability of our information and great customer service. We'll work with you to develop a campaign that provides results. No other list services will work as closely as we do to meet your unique needs.

Associations—the most extensive list of Canadian associations available, featuring all professional, trade and business organizations together with not-for-profit groups.

Arts & Culture—the definitive source of key prospects in various Canadian arts and cultural outlets.

Education—the most comprehensive list of educational institutions and organizations in Canada.

Health Care / Hospitals—includes all major medical facilities with chief executives.

Lawyers—key prospects for a number of direct mail offers.

Media—the definitive source of key prospects in various Canadian media outlets, offering the top business managers and/or publishers.

Environmental—a complete profile of the Canadian Environmental scene, constantly revised for the annual Canadian Environmental Resource Guide.

Financial Services—a list of key contacts from the full range of Canada's financial services industry.

Government Key Contacts—a list of key Government contacts, maintained by the Canadian Almanac & Directory, Canada's standard institutional reference for 170 years.

Libraries—the most unique and complete list of government, special and public libraries available.

Major Canadian Companies—listings of Canada's largest private, public and Crown corporations with major key contacts of the top business decision-makers.

AVAILABILITY

Lists are available on CD, labels and via e-mail. They are provided on a one-time use basis or for a one-year lease. For a quotation on tailor-made lists to suit your needs, inquire using the contact information listed below.

For more information please contact Grey House Publishing Canada

Tel.: (866) 433-4739 or (416) 644-6479 Fax: (416) 644-1904 | info@greyhouse.ca | www.greyhouse.ca

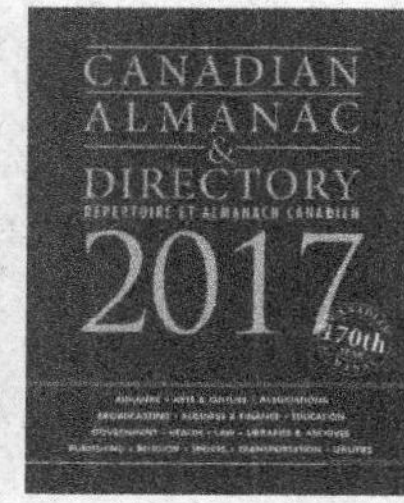

Canadian Almanac & Directory

Grey House Publishing Canada
555 Richmond Street West, Suite 512
Toronto, Ontario M5V 3B1

Fax completed forms to: (416) 644-1904

FREE LISTING & UPDATE
Be sure your organization appears in Canadian Almanac & Directory!

Canadian Almanac & Directory is a comprehensive, carefully updated directory of national information on major institutions, governments, associations, education, health, honours & awards, statistics & almanac data, published every year since 1847.

This listing is **FREE**. To ensure a complete and accurate listing in the upcoming edition, simply fill in the questionnaire and return it by **fax or by mail**. Include any relevant information such as phone, fax or toll free numbers, website and email addresses, and official translations (if applicable).

If you have any questions, please call Stuart Paterson at (416) 644-6478 or 1-866-433-4739 You can return this form either by **FAX**: (416) 644-1904, by **mail** to the address above, or **email** info@greyhouse.ca.

Is your organization already listed in this publication? Yes, we're updating existing information______ No, we're new______

Completed by: ____________________Phone:____________________Email:____________________

ORGANIZATION

Name: ____________________

Street Address: ____________________

Phone: ____________________

Toll Free: ____________________

Fax: ____________________

Email: ____________________

Website: ____________________

Translated Name: ____________________

Also known as: ____________________

Acronym: ____________________

Founded: ____________________

CHIEF OFFICERS/STAFF

President - ____________________

Secretary - ____________________

Treasurer - ____________________

Vice-President - ____________________

Other Staff: please see following page

Number of staff: ____________; Volunteers: ____________

OTHER STAFF: (attach list if necessary)

Name: ____________________ Title: ____________________
Telephone: ____________________ Email: ____________________

Name: ____________________ Title: ____________________
Telephone: ____________________ Email: ____________________

Name: ____________________ Title: ____________________
Telephone: ____________________ Email: ____________________

MEMBERSHIP

Member of: ____________________

Number of members: ____________

Membership profile: ____________________

Membership fee: ____________________

ADDITIONAL INFORMATION

SUBJECT FOCUS:

i. ______________________ ii. ______________________

iii. ______________________ iv. ______________________

SCOPE OF ACTIVITY:

- ❑ International
- ❑ National
- ❑ Provincial/Territorial
- ❑ Local
- ❑ Regional

ORGANIZATION TYPE:

- ❑ Professional
- ❑ Trade/Industry/Business
- ❑ Other (special/common interest)

Please indicate if you are a: ❑ Licensing Body ❑ Registered Charity

MISSION STATEMENT/GOALS/MANDATE:

____

____

____

ANNUAL OPERATING BUDGET:

❑ Less than $50,000	❑ $50,000 - $99,999	❑ $100,000 - $249,999
❑ $250,000 - $499,999	❑ $500,000 - $1,499,999	❑ $1,500,000 - $2,999,999
❑ $3,000,000 - $4,999,999	❑ Over $5,000,000	

DO YOU:			
	Rent your Mailing Lists?	❑ Yes	❑ No
	Have a Speakers Service?	❑ Yes	❑ No
	Have an Internship Program?	❑ Yes	❑ No

SERIAL PUBLICATIONS:

Type: (eg. newsletter, journal, magazine) ______________________ Title: ______________________

Frequency: ______________________ Price: ______________________ Editor:: ______________________

ISBN: ______________________ ISSN: ______________________ Accept advertising? ❑ Yes ❑ No

Description of contents:

____

____

____

LIBRARY/RESOURCE CENTRE:

Does your organization have a library, resource centre or documentation centre? ❑ Yes ❑ No

Library/Resource/Documentation Centre Name: ______________________

Open to the Public: ❑ Yes ❑ No ❑ By Appointment Only

Library Contact Person: ______________________ Title: ______________________

Telephone: ______________________ Fax: ______________________ Email: ______________________

CONFERENCE/CONVENTIONS:

Please submit any literature pertaining to future conferences as it becomes available.

	2017	2018	2019	2020
Name of Meeting:				
Location: (City/Province/Country)				
Facility:				
Date:				
Number of Attendees:				

OTHER:

Awards: Please attach a list

Awareness Events (Please include the date): ______________________

Activities: ______________________

Committees: ______________________

Sources of funding: ______________________

WE THANK YOU FOR TAKING THE TIME TO PROVIDE YOUR VALUABLE INFORMATION.

Ottawa Public
Library
Bibliothèque
publique d'Ottawa